ENCYCLOPÆDIA BRITANNICA

VOLUME

18

First Published in 1768

by A Society of Gentlemen in Scotland

ENCYCLOPÆDIA BRITANNICA, INC.

William Benton, Publisher

CHICAGO · LONDON · TORONTO · GENEVA · SYDNEY · TOKYO · MANILA

FOUNDED A.D. 1768

ENCYCLOPÆDIA BRITANNICA

Volume 18

PLASTICS *TO* RAZIN

PLASTICS, in the modern meaning of the word, are synthetic materials that are capable of being formed into usable products by heating, milling, molding, and similar processes. The term is derived from the Greek *plastikos,* "to form." By some interpretations of the word, rubber and other natural products are said to be plastic, but the modern definition, especially in relation to industry, excludes rubber and also such other natural products as wood, leather, and metals. In simplest terms, plastics can be described as resins in their molded form (although not all plastics are resins and not all resins can be or necessarily are molded; they can be cast or converted to coatings, self-supporting films, or fibres). Plastics are one of the physical manifestations of resins, as indicated in the title of one of the first books in this field, *Synthetic Resins and Their Plastics,* by Carleton Ellis (1923). (*See* RESINS.)

The term plastic is, therefore, essentially a commercial classification to which no strictly scientific definition can be applied. The Society of the Plastics Industry has defined plastics as "any one of a large and varied group of materials consisting wholly or in part of combinations of carbon with oxygen, hydrogen, nitrogen, and other organic or inorganic elements which, while solid in the finished state, at some stage in its manufacture is made liquid, and thus capable of being formed into various shapes, most usually through the application, either singly or together, of heat and pressure."

The use of plastics began slowly in the last half of the 19th century following the introduction of Celluloid and other cellulose plastics. The invention of Bakelite brought about a marked increase in the use of plastics early in the 20th century. Shortages of natural materials caused by World Wars I and II led to the development of new plastic substitutes. By the 1960s plastics were available in forms that were superior, in certain uses, at least, to leather, paper, glass, metal, wood, rubber, and other natural materials. Plastics were used for a wide variety of purposes; for example, in the manufacture of automobile parts and bodies, toys, television cabinets, clothing, housewares, wall and floor coverings, beverage cases, military body armour, cigarette packages, and furniture.

The leading plastics, on the basis of tonnages produced in the 1960s, were the polyolefin resins, vinyl resins, styrene-type plas-

tics, phenolic and other coal tar acid resins, alkyds, urea and melamine resins, coumarone-indene and petroleum polymer resins, polyester resins, cellulose plastics, polyamide resins, epoxy resins, and polyurethanes.

By custom, the fibre industry is considered to be outside the plastics industry, although the same raw materials—polyamides (nylon), cellulose, and cellulose acetate—are used by the two industries. The manufacture of films, such as photographic film and cellophane, is not considered part of the plastics industry. Even though polymers may be converted to leatherlike products, it is current policy to refer to these as synthetic poromeric materials and not as plastics.

The major headings of this article are as follows:

I. History of Development and Fabrication
    1. Early Observations of Resinification
    2. Causes of Resinification
    3. Production of New Plastics
    4. Fabrication Technology
II. Plastic Materials
    A. Cellulose Plastics
        1. Nitrocellulose
        2. Cellulose Acetate
        3. Cellulose Acetobutyrate and Other Esters
        4. Cellulose Ethers
    B. Other Natural Products
        1. Casein Plastics
        2. Shellac
    C. Synthetic Resin Plastics
        1. Thermosetting Resins
        2. Thermoplastic Resins
        3. Foamed Plastics

I. HISTORY OF DEVELOPMENT AND FABRICATION

The modern plastics industry represents an integration of many different and unrelated bodies of knowledge. One part is derived from investigations into the chemistry, physics, and biology of such high-molecular-weight natural products as natural resins, rubber, gutta-percha, cotton, cellulose, ramie, pectins, chitin, starch, glycogen, wool, silk, and hair. Initially, optical methods were used in the investigation of these products; later ultramicroscopy was employed. Somewhat later colloidal chemical methods were developed and used in the study of the gross morphology of these substances. X-rays indicated that some natural products, such as cellulose, gutta-percha, and silk, were crystalline; others were amorphous; and still others were both crystalline and amorphous, depending on the state. Natural rubber in the unstretched state was amorphous when examined by X-ray diffraction methods, but it became crystalline when stretched. The ultracentrifuge made it possible to measure viscosity and sedimentation of these products under extremely high centrifugal forces. The idea grew that the natural products must of necessity be of a very high molecular weight.

1. Early Observations of Resinification.—Early chemists observed that in the preparation and synthesis of new compounds, materials would often resinify, through unknown and uncontrollable reactions, either during the course of the preparation or spontaneously after the product was formed and isolated. J. J. Berzelius in 1833 introduced the term "polymer," which eventually came to mean a giant molecule with the same percentage composition as some smaller starting substance (called the monomer). The term high polymer is now restricted to high-molecular-weight compounds composed of simple molecules, while the term polymerization (*q.v.*) relates to the process by which large molecules are synthesized from smaller ones.

In the same year (1833), nitrocellulose was prepared; H. V. Regnault in 1838 noted that vinyl chloride polymerized in sunlight, and in the following year E. Simon polymerized styrene; J. Redtenbacher prepared acrylic acid in 1843; W. Caspary and B. Tollens in 1873 synthesized the methyl, ethyl, and allyl esters; and G. W. A. Kahlbaum prepared the polymer of methyl acrylate in 1880. Isoprene was prepared by G. Williams in 1860, and it was polymerized by G. Bouchardat in 1879. R. Anshutz prepared polymers of itaconic acid esters in 1881, and in 1865 E. Frankland and B. F. Duppa discovered a method of making ethyl methacrylate from hydroxyisobutyric esters. Many condensation-type resins were also discovered during this interval, and many polyesters were also prepared, particularly those derived from glycerol and dibasic acids. The transformation of ethylene oxide from monomer to polymer was studied by M. A. von Lourenço, who showed that the boiling point and the viscosity increased progressively with the molecular weight of the polymer. I. Ostromislensky maintained that there was a stepwise synthesis of rubberlike substances. Similarly, it was observed that when glycine was condensed, a series of products was obtained in which there was a regular change in the physical properties. Emil Fischer performed his classical work in synthesizing numerous polypeptides out of simple amino acids, and although he showed that his synthetic product possessed many of the properties of the hydrolytic products of naturally occurring proteins, it was generally considered that the natural products (such as proteins, cellulose, and rubber) possessed unique properties that were not shared by laboratory products.

Part of the dilemma presented by the different behaviour of natural and synthetic products was resolved by Hermann Staudinger (*q.v.*) in 1926. He demonstrated the interrelationship between the structure as determined physically by X-rays and the size and structure of the polymer as determined chemically from analysis, as well as the size of the molecule determined by the nature and number of end groups existing in the high-molecular-weight compound. These various ideas were consolidated in Staudinger's *Die hochmolekularen organischen Verbindungen-Kautschuk und Cellulose* (1932), in which he shows the similarities between polystyrene, a synthetic substance, and rubber, and between the polyoxymethylenes and naturally occurring cellulose. He demonstrated that the products of the laboratory have many properties in common with natural products and that the synthetic materials can be used as prototypes in evaluating the natural materials.

2. Causes of Resinification.—The causes of resinification of organic compounds remained obscure for a long time, since the chemical reactions that led to it were unknown. It was recognized very early that unsaturated compounds yielded resins, and when the phenol-formaldehyde resins were first introduced the unsaturation hypothesis was advanced. The resin formation of phenol-formaldehyde resins was attributed to the polymerization

of methylene quinones. Somewhat later the concept of "resinophoric" groupings was introduced by W. Herzog and I. Kreidl, and although the theory was shown to be untenable, it focused attention on the relationship of structure and it led to studies that revealed there were essentially two chemical reactions responsible for resinification: one involving a condensation reaction, where the polymer differs from the starting material by the elements eliminated in the condensation; and a second involving a polymerization reaction, where the polymer and starting material have the same chemical composition.

About the same time that Staudinger was conducting his investigations in Europe, studies were being made in the United States on various condensation-type resins, and the foundation was laid for the so-called functionality concepts that enabled a clear distinction to be made between the chemistry of the thermoplastic resins and the behaviour of the thermosetting type of product. W. H. Carothers, using condensation reactions, made fibrelike materials, *e.g.*, nylon, that possessed many of the crystalline properties previously associated only with natural products.

To make a chemical compound condense to a material of high molecular weight, each molecule of that compound must contain two or more functional groups that can react with one another. When a compound contains molecules possessing only one functional group, these molecules on interaction will yield a product that can be, at best, twice as large as the molecules of the starting material. When a compound possesses molecules containing more than two functional groups, then each molecule can be joined to two other molecules. Preferably these functional groups should be at the ends of the molecule or at least so situated sterically that cyclization (ring formation) or intramolecular reaction cannot occur. These important steric, or spatial, configuration factors were first thoroughly evaluated by Carothers. When all these requirements are met, it is possible for the functional groups to react with one another intermolecularly, leading to a reaction product containing long chains. These long chains are molecules of high molecular weight. When the product contains molecules having more than two functional groups, the reaction product formed by condensation leads to the formation of complex structures. Such complex molecules are responsible for the industrially valuable physical properties of plastics.

The functional groups referred to above are simply any chemical groups that can react with others. For example, two organic acid molecules can react to form an anhydride (1, below). If the original starting molecule contains two acid groups, and these groups are so situated sterically that ring formation can occur, then ring formation takes place without the formation of a high-molecular-weight compound; for example, succinic acid dehydrates to an anhydride (2). If, on the other hand, the acid groups are situated sufficiently far apart to preclude cyclization (as in sebacic acid), polymeric, high-molecular-weight, linear anhydrides are formed (3).

$$2R - COOH \rightarrow R - CO - O - CO - R + H_2O \qquad (1)$$

$$\begin{array}{c} CH_2 - CO - OH \\ | \\ CH_2 - CO - OH \end{array} \rightarrow \begin{array}{c} CH_2 - CO \\ | \qquad\qquad O + H_2O \\ CH_2 - CO \end{array} \qquad (2)$$

$$HOOC - (CH_2)_8 - COOH \rightarrow H_2O +$$
$$HOOC - (CH_2)_8 - CO - O - CO - (CH_2)_8 - COOH \qquad (3)$$

Likewise, an alcohol and acid can react to form an ester. If a simple organic molecule contains an acidic group on one end and an alcoholic group on the other, the initial condensation product still possesses a hydroxyl group and a carboxyl group, which can react similarly to the starting materials (4).

$$HO - R - COOH + HO - R - COOH \longrightarrow H_2O +$$
$$HO - R - CO - O - R - COOH \qquad (4)$$

Such a condensation can proceed to yield a high-molecular-weight polymer. Unreacted groups at the ends of such large molecules are called "end groups."

A similar situation exists with respect to polymerization products. Under certain conditions, cyclization to a low-molecular-weight compound can occur (5); or if the conditions are properly selected, a polymer of high molecular weight may result (6).

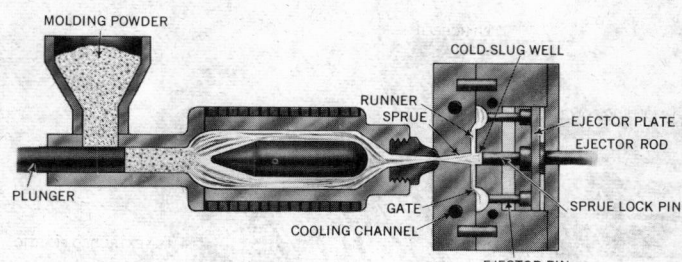

MOLDING POWDER, COLD-SLUG WELL, RUNNER SPRUE, EJECTOR PLATE, EJECTOR ROD, PLUNGER, GATE, COOLING CHANNEL, SPRUE LOCK PIN, EJECTOR PIN

$$\text{(5)}$$

$$CH_2=CH-CH=CH_2 \longrightarrow (-CH_2-CH=CH-CH_2-)_x \quad (6)$$

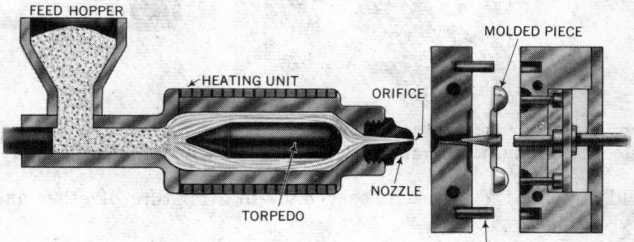

FEED HOPPER, MOLDED PIECE, HEATING UNIT, ORIFICE, NOZZLE, TORPEDO, GUIDE PIN

ADAPTED FROM H. SIMONDS, "A CONCISE GUIDE TO PLASTICS," 1957

FIG. 1.—SCHEMATIC DIAGRAM OF AN INJECTION MOLDING OPERATION WITH THE MOLD CLOSED (ABOVE) AND OPEN (BELOW)

3. Production of New Plastics.—Later studies gave some insight into the size and structure of the large molecules in plastic materials. Minor changes during the preparation, and the addition of small amounts of other chemicals, may markedly change both the proportion and the distribution of the molecular species, leading to formation of a new product of differing physical properties. Moreover, the same materials, under different chemical processing, may yield resins and polymers of widely different physical characteristics. By means of these two procedures innumerable types of resinous compositions can be produced. Since the chemical industry is the source of raw materials for plastic products, it follows that as soon as a new chemical is developed it is immediately tested by plastic manufacturers to determine whether it may serve as a partial or a total replacement for the material then employed. New materials are quickly introduced into the plastics industry, allowing the preparation of new products with different structures and different characteristics.

4. Fabrication Technology.—The development of molding technology parallels the study of resinification, since it was only by fabricating the synthetic laboratory products that these materials could be turned into articles of commerce. The art of molding developed following Charles Goodyear's discovery of the vulcanization of rubber in 1839. This involved the use of a simple hand-operated hydraulic press of a sort that came to be used in all types of molding operations in which the mold must be sufficiently light to warrant manual handling. With the development of phenolic resins, larger objects could be molded, and this necessitated the improvement of compression molding to increase the output of any single mold. Automatic presses were developed and pins were incorporated into the mold itself to permit automatic ejection of molded pieces. Where metallic inserts had to be introduced into the specimen during molding, semiautomatic presses were constructed. To reduce error and to speed production, automatic presses were fashioned that could measure the charge, preheat the charge, load it into the cavity, close the mold, mold the object, open the mold, and eject the final piece. Still greater efficiencies are achieved by electronic preheating of the plastic before introducing it into the mold.

Injection Molding.—Conventional compression molding is both awkward and expensive when applied to thermoplastic materials. Where compression molding is used on thermosetting materials, the mold can be kept at a constant temperature. During the molding and curing operations, the plasticity decreases because of chemical reaction, with the result that the product becomes sufficiently rigid, even while hot, to be ejected from the mold. Thermoplastic resins, on the other hand, do not undergo any chemical change, and the fabricated piece cannot be taken out until the mold has been cooled to a point at which the piece becomes rigid.

The idea arose that if it were possible to inject the hot plastic into a cool mold, following the procedure used in the die-casting of metals, it would obviate the periodic heating and cooling of the mold. The first experiments directed toward injection molding were made by John and Isaiah Hyatt, who were also instrumental in first commercializing nitrocellulose (*see* below), but they abandoned the work. Later the technique was revived, this time in Germany. The first presses had an injection capacity of about 0.5 to 1.5 oz. per cycle and were useful only for the manufacture of small objects such as buttons, combs, and costume jewelry. Once the value of these presses was demonstrated and a suitable plastic composition developed, larger and larger presses

were designed until it became possible to inject 32 oz. of plastic into a mold in a single cycle.

Transfer Molding.—The advent of injection equipment speeded up the production of thermoplastic resins. To increase the mold capacity of the thermosetting resins a type of injection molding known as transfer molding was developed, whereby the molten plastic was transferred from the heated zone into the mold. Since thermosetting resins remain plastic for only a very short time, they cannot be preheated in the manner employed for thermoplastic resins; the heating chamber must be loaded for each cycle and the heated charge forced into a hot mold. Transfer molding

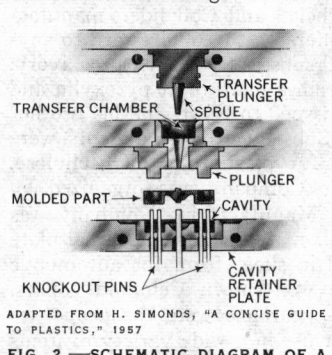

TRANSFER CHAMBER, TRANSFER PLUNGER, SPRUE, PLUNGER, MOLDED PART, CAVITY, KNOCKOUT PINS, CAVITY RETAINER PLATE

ADAPTED FROM H. SIMONDS, "A CONCISE GUIDE TO PLASTICS," 1957

FIG. 2.—SCHEMATIC DIAGRAM OF A TRANSFER MOLDING OPERATION

not only decreases the time of molding of certain objects but also allows the introduction of inserts, which sometimes cannot be introduced into conventional compression moldings; the plastic enters the mold in a highly fluid state and will not displace or break fragile inserts such as glass and fine metal parts. The separation of resin and filler is minimized by this type of molding, and the resulting molded objects are stronger, of more uniform density, and freer of gas pockets.

Extrusion Molding.—A third type of molding is by the so-called extrusion method, which was used for many years in the rubber industry before it was applied to thermoplastic resins. The resin is fed from a hopper, thence to a screw conveyor where it is heated and from which it emerges through a die in a continuous strip in the form of the die opening. To minimize distortion, the heated plastic is frequently supported on a moving belt. By this means rods and tubing of various sizes and shapes can be produced efficiently.

II. PLASTIC MATERIALS

A. CELLULOSE PLASTICS

1. Nitrocellulose.—In 1833 Henri Braconnot, a professor of chemistry at Nancy, prepared a "xyloidine" by treating starch, sawdust, and cotton with nitric acid. He found that this material was soluble in wood vinegar and attempted to make coatings, films, and shaped articles of it. In these early experiments lay the beginnings of both the plastics and the lacquer-coating industries. Somewhat later, in 1846, C. F. Schönbein nitrated cotton by using a mixture of nitric and sulfuric acids. He also found that he

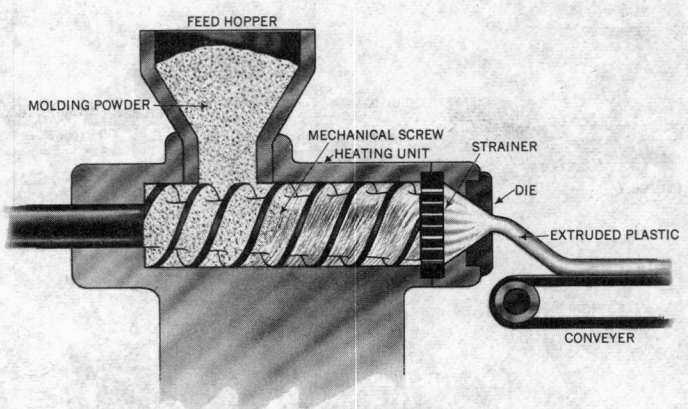

FEED HOPPER

MOLDING POWDER

MECHANICAL SCREW
HEATING UNIT
STRAINER

DIE

EXTRUDED PLASTIC

CONVEYER

ADAPTED FROM H. SIMONDS, "A CONCISE GUIDE TO PLASTICS," 1957

FIG. 3.—SCHEMATIC DIAGRAM OF AN EXTRUSION MOLDING OPERATION

could dissolve the nitrocellulose (*q.v.*) in a mixture of ether and ethyl alcohol.

Investigations into various methods of conducting nitration indicated that several types of nitrated cotton might be made. The nitrocellulose possessing the highest degree of nitration, in which the nitrogen content was more than 13%, was referred to as guncotton; when the nitrogen content was 12.6 to 12.8%, the material was referred to as pyrocollodion; and when the nitrogen content was 11.5 to 12% the materials were known as pyroxylin, collodion, or photocotton. The nitration reaction is very complicated, involving a heterogeneous system of cellulose, nitric and sulfuric acids, and water. Each constituent may play several physical and chemical roles, the reagents swelling as well as reacting with the cellulose. (*See also* GUNCOTTON; COLLODION.)

Some attempts had been made to prepare coating compositions out of collodion, but the first successful plastic was made in 1868 by a young U.S. printer, John W. Hyatt, by dissolving nitrocellulose under pressure. In 1863 Phelan and Collander, manufacturers of ivory billiard balls, had offered a $10,000 reward to anyone who developed an adequate substitute for natural ivory. Procedures for making the balls from a mixture of pyroxylin and camphor were disclosed in patents issued to Hyatt and his brother Isaiah between 1870 and 1872. Subsequently, 75 patents were taken out on various procedures for plasticizing nitrocellulose. In 1870 the Albany Dental Plate Company was organized by Hyatt, and in 1871 the Celluloid Manufacturing Company was formed. The immediate use of this material was for dental plate blanks; later the plastic was used in sheet form for automobile side curtains, as well as for the well-known Celluloid collars. Toughness, flexibility, and good appearance were the properties that made the material suitable for use in a wide variety of items such as combs, brush handles, spectacle frames, and various novelty and decorative items. (*See also* CELLULOID.)

In 1884 Count Hilaire de Chardonnet, a pupil of Louis Pasteur, deposited with the French Academy of Sciences a document entitled "Artificial Textile Material Resembling Silk." The paper, opened in 1887, described a method of transforming guncotton into fibrous, silklike material. At the Paris Exposition in 1899 Chardonnet was awarded the grand prize for his discovery. The fibre was highly flammable, but it focused attention on the possibility of manufacturing synthetic filaments from a vegetable source.

The discovery by John H. Stevens that amyl acetate could be used as a solvent for nitrocellulose was made in 1882. This solvent proved to be far superior to anything used previously and enabled uniform films to be made without haze. The first successful attempt to secure transparent flexible film for photographic purposes was made by H. Goodwin of Newark, N.J., during the years 1887–98. A somewhat similar process was developed independently by H. Reichenbach in 1889. Further work resulted in processes that allowed the nitrocellulose to be fabricated in continuous fashion, enabling the production of suitable base for both still and motion-picture photography. Another important use for nitrocellulose in sheet form was in safety glass, in which sheet nitrocellulose was laminated between glass sheets to form a glass-plastic sandwich. The nitrocellulose film discoloured rapidly, however, and was eventually superseded by other, more light-stable plastics; but it served as an invaluable guide and established the importance of safety glass in the automotive industry.

Prior to World War I, Russia supplied the largest volume of fusel oil. This oil, remaining after the distillation of grain alcohol, was the raw material used in the synthesis of amyl acetate. Following the loss of this source of supply during the Russian Revolution and with the loss of additional supplies caused by the enactment of the U.S. prohibition laws, the amount of this potential lacquer solvent became exceedingly small. New solvents for nitrocellulose were being developed rapidly, however. During 1920–23 the normal butyl alcohol process was perfected by Chaim Weizmann, and about the same time anhydrous ethyl acetate made its appearance. Moreover, plasticizers other than camphor were being developed. Tricresyl phosphate was prepared in 1920 and triacetin in 1921.

Since the theoretical nitrogen content for mono-, di-, and trinitrated forms of cellulose is 6.77, 11.3, and 14.16%, respectively, it can readily be seen from the nature of the manufactured products that the most valuable nitrocellulose plastic compositions contain from two to three nitrate groups per glucose residue in the cellulose molecule. Explosives are made from those materials having from 12.2 to 13.8% of nitrogen; lacquers and films from 11.5 to 12.2%; and plastics from 10.5 to 11.5%. The properties of the nitrocellulose thus secured are dependent not only on the degree of nitration but also on the uniformity of nitration of the cellulose molecule. Moreover, the length of the chain of the nitrocellulose molecule is very important since the longer the chain—that is, the larger the value of x in the equation below—the more viscous the solution of nitrocellulose in organic liquids. The reaction leading to cellulose trinitrate may be expressed by

$$[C_6H_7O_2(OH)_3]_x + 3xHNO_3 \longrightarrow [C_6H_7O_2(ONO_2)_3]_x + 3xH_2O \qquad (7)$$

For coating applications high-viscosity lacquers are a disadvantage, since excessively large amounts of solvent would be required to produce the necessary thin films.

Several factors contributed to a twentyfold expansion of the use of nitrocellulose in the decade following World War I: (1) the availability of desirable solvents at relatively low cost; (2) the large quantities of nitrocellulose on hand following termination of the war; (3) the development of a method for preparing lacquers possessing a high-solids content with relatively low viscosity; and (4) the tremendous demand for quick-drying finishes by the rapidly expanding automotive industry. Through the use of nitrocellulose with alkyds, it was possible to decrease the time of finishing an automobile body from weeks to hours.

For plastic manufacture, the pyroxylin is mixed with alcohol and camphor and kneaded into a doughlike mass. Colouring matter is added, either in the form of dyes for transparent colours or as pigments for opaque colours. The coloured masses are rolled to discharge some of the volatile solvent, sheeted, and pressed into blocks. After seasoning, the blocks are sliced; then either they are further fabricated, or the process is repeated for various mottled and variegated effects. The sheets may be molded and when sufficiently soft may be fashioned by "blow molding" into hollow objects. Rods and tubes are fabricated by extrusion.

Despite its obvious disadvantages of flammability, discoloration on aging, and limited resistance to heat and to strong organic solvents such as alcohols, ketones, and esters, the nitrocellulose plastic is colourful, tough, flexible, of good appearance, and resistant to wear, water, and humidity. It is easy to fabricate into many diverse forms and finds wide acceptance for billiard balls, piano keys, mirror and spectacle frames, combs, brush handles, machine keys, radio dials, and novelty and decorative items.

2. Cellulose Acetate.—The deficiency inherent in nitrocellulose for plastic use brought up the possibility of adapting other esters of cellulose, particularly the esters of organic acids. Paul Schützenberger acetylated cellulose in 1865, and A. Franchimont in 1879 found that the esterification reaction could be catalyzed by sulfuric acid. In 1894 C. F. Cross and E. J. Bevan, working in England, patented a process for preparing a chloroform-soluble type of cellulose acetate. The most important commercial development was made by G. W. Miles in 1903–05 with the discovery that if the highly acetylated cellulose was subjected to hydrolysis, it became transformed to a less highly acetylated compound that was soluble in cheap organic solvents such as acetone. In 1911 Henri Dreyfus perfected a manufacturing process for the preparation of the acetylated compound and its hydrolysis. The same basic process is employed in the manufacture of the cellulose acetate as that employed in the manufacture of a nitrate, except that the anhydride used as the esterification reagent results in acetic acid rather than water as the by-product.

$$[C_6H_7O_2(OH)_3]_x + 3x(CH_3CO)_2O \longrightarrow$$
$$[C_6H_7O_2(OCOCH_3)_3]_x + 3xCH_3COOH \qquad (8)$$

The cellulose acetate, with an acetate content of about 62.5%, is then hydrolyzed, precipitated, washed, and dried. Depending on whether the acetate is to be used as a film, molding powder, or safety glass, different quantities, amounts, and types of plasticizers are employed, allowing one type of polymer to fill many diverse applications.

The first use of this material was in the so-called "safety film" for photographic use. Acetone-soluble cellulose acetate found extensive use in World War I as the dope for coating aircraft wings because it was much less flammable than nitrocellulose. After the war the excess plant capacity was used to produce cellulose acetate as an acetate rayon. However, another very important development, the new procedure for molding thermoplastic resins mentioned above, was occurring simultaneously. It was found that the acetate was particularly amenable to injection molding, and the cellulose-acetate plastic was given a new impetus by this rapid and efficient means of fabrication. The acetate was preferred since the nitrate could not be subjected to the temperature required in injection molding. Cellulose acetate became widely used in the automotive industry because of its mechanical strength, toughness, wear-resistance, transparency, and ease of moldability. Its high resistance to impact made it a desirable material for protective goggles, tool handles, oil gauges, and the like. In fibre form, cellulose acetate became one of the more effective filters for removing phenolic bodies from tobacco smoke.

3. Cellulose Acetobutyrate and Other Esters.—Since one of the more serious limitations of cellulose acetate lies in its poor resistance to moisture and weathering, attempts were made to use longer, less water-soluble organic acids in esterification. The use of mixed acids was not overlooked, and it was found that a mixture of butyric and acetic acids (as anhydrides) yielded mixed esters that were very similar in properties to the acetate but were more resistant to moisture and weathering and had superior adhesion qualities. When molded by injection, cellulose acetobutyrate required somewhat less pressure than acetate and yielded better welded joints.

Other cellulose esters were prepared commercially. During World War II processes for the manufacture of propionic acid and its anhydride were developed, and cellulose esters made from this acid appeared on the market. Since propionic acid contains three carbon atoms, it is intermediate between acetic and butyric acids. It follows that the cellulose propionate possesses many excellent properties similar to those exhibited by the acetobutyrate as well as many characteristics of its own, particularly a shorter molding cycle and easier machining qualities. Cellulose benzoate was manufactured in Germany, but the material did not find a market in the U.S.

4. Cellulose Ethers.—Since cellulose is a polyhydric alcohol, it can undergo etherification reactions as well as the esterification reactions mentioned above. Ether linkages cannot be saponified, so it is not surprising to find that the cellulose ethers are among the more stable of the cellulose derivatives. The idea of ethylating cellulose was first conceived by W. von Suida in 1905 with the primary object of changing the affinity of cellulose for dyestuffs. Cellulose ethers were studied simultaneously by Leon Lilienfeld

in Austria, Otto Leuchs in Germany, and Henri Dreyfus in France. It was found that the cellulose ethers, and in particular ethyl cellulose, were soluble in organic liquids and possessed potentialities in plastic as well as in lacquer and in rayon applications.

Ethyl cellulose was first produced commercially in Germany and it was not until 1935 that large-scale production was undertaken in the U.S. The chief uses of ethyl cellulose are in coatings, in adhesives, and as plastics possessing a high degree of toughness over a wide temperature range.

Many other cellulose ethers are known. The methyl cellulose, glycol cellulose, and cellulose glycolic acid prepared respectively from methyl sulfate (or chloride), from ethylene oxide (or chlorohydrin), and from sodium monochloroacetate are dispersible in water and have found use as sizing and finishing agents in the textile industry. (*See* also CELLULOSE: *Uses of Cellulose and Derivatives*.)

B. OTHER NATURAL PRODUCTS

1. Casein Plastics.—Casein (the protein derived from milk) was condensed with formaldehyde by A. Spitteler and W. Krische in 1897 to form a tough, insoluble mass that could be fabricated readily. Production of this plastic was begun shortly after 1900 in Germany and France and in 1914 in England under the name of Galalith (milkstone). Manufacture was undertaken in the U.S. in 1919. At the time the casein plastic came into prominence it possessed an immediate advantage over competitive products in that it was much less flammable than nitrocellulose and could be fabricated into objects of lighter colour than was possible with the phenolic resins. When an attempt was made to introduce the casein plastic into the United States, its limitations became apparent, especially under the country's extremes of humidity. The product was wholly unsuited for electrical fixtures and other applications requiring some degree of dimensional tolerance. The limitation of the composition, along with the advent of synthetic resins that could be handled more rapidly yet did not possess the limitations inherent in the protein plastic, gradually restricted the use of casein plastic until the only large outlet for the product was in the manufacture of buttons from alum-hardened casein. (*See* also CASEIN: *Uses*.)

2. Shellac.—This natural resin finds some use in the manufacture of molding compositions. In many respects shellac is an ideal plastic binder for certain types of electrical equipment and for communication instruments. The resin is often used by itself as well as in combination with such fillers as flaked mica and asbestos.

C. SYNTHETIC RESIN PLASTICS

Synthetic resins can be grouped in many different ways, but one generally accepted classification divides them into thermoplastic and thermosetting types. The thermoplastic resins are characterized by their ability to remain plastic after numerous heating treatments, while the thermosetting, or thermocuring, resins, when once heated, are converted to a cured or infusible form that cannot be fused again without serious chemical degradation. From the molecular structural standpoint, the thermoplastic resins are characterized by molecules that are essentially linear or threadlike in form, while the thermosetting resins consist of molecules that are considered to be linked three-dimensionally into a network arrangement. Resins may also be classified according to the chemical means employed to effect reaction. Certain resins formed without the elimination of volatile components are generally referred to as the polymerization type. Where volatile ingredients such as water and alcohol are formed during the resin preparation, this type of product can be considered a condensation resin. When the chemical and physical types are superimposed, it is possible to have the grouping:

1. Thermoplastic condensation resins
2. Thermoplastic polymerization resins
3. Thermosetting condensation resins
4. Thermosetting polymerization resins

The equations leading to the formation of these various types may be written schematically as follows:

$$2n\text{H-R-OH} \longrightarrow \text{H-}[\text{R} - \text{R}]_n\text{-OH} + (2n\text{-}1)\text{H}_2\text{O}$$

Linear polymer formed by condensation reaction

$$n\text{CH}_2 = \overset{\displaystyle R}{\underset{\displaystyle R_1}{\text{C}}} \longrightarrow -\text{CH}_2 - \overset{\displaystyle R}{\underset{\displaystyle R_1}{\text{C}}}\text{-} \left[-\text{CH}_2 - \overset{\displaystyle R}{\underset{\displaystyle R_1}{\text{C}}}\text{-} \right]_{n-2} -\text{CH}_2 - \overset{\displaystyle R}{\underset{\displaystyle R_1}{\text{C}}}\text{-}$$

Linear polymer formed by loss of unsaturation

$$2n \begin{array}{l} \text{H-R} - \text{OH} \\ \text{H-R}_1 - \text{OH} \end{array} \longrightarrow \begin{array}{l} \text{H-} \left[\begin{array}{l} \text{R} - \text{R} \\ \text{R}_1 - \text{R}_1 \end{array} \right]_n \begin{array}{l} \text{-OH} \\ \text{-OH} \end{array} \end{array} + (4n\text{-}2)\text{H}_2\text{O}$$

Network polymer formed by condensation reaction

$$n\text{R} \begin{array}{l} \text{CH} = \text{CH}_2 \\ \\ \text{CH} = \text{CH}_2 \end{array} \longrightarrow \left[\begin{array}{l} -\text{CH} - \text{CH}_2 - \\ \quad\quad \text{R} \\ -\text{CH} - \text{CH}_2 - \end{array} \right]_n$$

Network polymer formed by loss of unsaturation

Generally the thermosetting resins will tolerate substantial quantities of inert fillers such as cellulose flock, wood flour, asbestos, and the like, whereas the thermoplastic resins are fabricated clear; or, when fillers or opacifiers are used, the quantity employed is much less than with the thermosetting types of resin. Different methods of fabrication are utilized with thermoplastic and thermosetting resins since chemical changes occur during the molding of the latter, whereas physical changes predominate in the molding and extruding of thermoplastic resins. (*See* RESINS.)

1. Thermosetting Resins.—*Phenol-Formaldehyde Resins.*— When Leo H. Baekeland patented a phenol-formaldehyde resin in 1909, nitrocellulose plastics were being used extensively in the U.S. Yet this new material found a ready market because, unlike the nitrocellulose product, the phenolformaldehyde resin could be made insoluble and infusible. Moreover, the thermosetting phenolic condensation product would tolerate considerable amounts of inert ingredients and thus could be modified through the incorporation of various fillers.

In making phenolic molding powders, phenol and formaldehyde are heated in the presence of suitable catalysts, generally acids, and the condensation is conducted to the stage where the water separates. The viscous phenolic condensation product, on cooling to room temperature, becomes hard and brittle. The resin at this stage can be dissolved in various organic liquids; such solutions are employed for laminating and impregnating purposes. The structure can be represented schematically as follows:

Intermediate condensation product

Cross-linked

To make the molding compound, the resin is ground and mixed with the appropriate filler, lubricants, and dyes. To render the combination as homogeneous as possible, the mixture is milled and then ground. For general use, wood flour is the preferred filler, but where heat resistance, impact strength, or electrical characteristics are involved, other fillers such as cotton flock, asbestos, and chopped fabric are used. The resin, because of its excellent insulating characteristics, is used in manufacturing radio parts such as sockets, binding parts, knobs, and dials, and in the electrical system of automobiles.

For laminated structures, the resin in alcoholic solution is used to impregnate either paper or fabric. After impregnation the sheets are dried, consolidated, and subsequently heated under pressure to form a rigid, tough assembly of high strength and good electrical properties that can be machined and fabricated. Power transformers, timing gears, cams, clutches, fan belts, and many other materials can be made from such structures. When fabric is substituted for paper, the laminated compositions can be machined to form gears and bearings.

Phenol-Furfural Resins.—Furfural, an aldehyde, is derived from waste farm products such as the hulls of oats, rice, cottonseed, and from corn husks. This aldehyde will condense with phenol to produce a resin similar to that secured from phenol and formaldehyde. The plastic properties of the two compositions differ, however, in that the furfural product possesses a long period of flow at low temperatures; this property enables it to be used in certain types of intricate moldings.

Urea-Formaldehyde Resins.—The resins derived from urea and formaldehyde have been considered truly synthetic materials inasmuch as all the basic materials are derived from gases. These gases are ammonia, carbon dioxide, carbon monoxide, and hydrogen. Reaction of ammonia and carbon dioxide under pressure yields urea, whereas the reduction of carbon monoxide results in the formation of formaldehyde. Condensation of urea with commercial formalin (aqueous solution of formaldehyde) yields the water-soluble intermediate condensation products known as mono- and dimethylolurea, which on further reaction form water-soluble, resinous condensation products. The intermediate water-soluble resins are starting materials for the production of resin, adhesives, surface coatings, and molding powders.

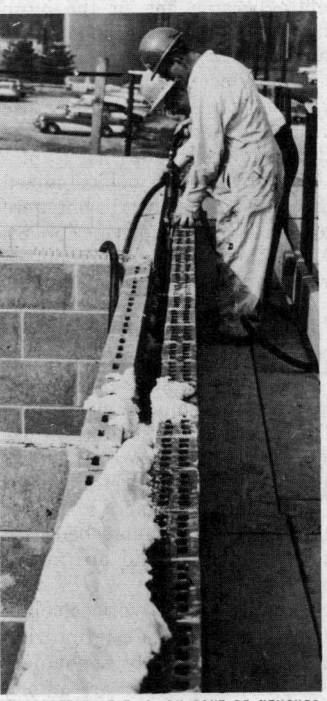

FILLING MASONRY WALL CAVITIES WITH URETHANE FOAM FOR INSULATION AND MOISTURE RESISTANCE

The combination of the urea-formaldehyde resin with various fillers was investigated by many chemists, but the combination of cellulose and resin has been generally associated with the developmental work of Carleton Ellis in the U.S. A parallel development occurred in England, however, where, because of lack of timber, Norwegian pulp was imported and used. The introduction of fillers destroyed the transparency of the product, but the resin-filler combination, when suitably compounded with flow promoters, plasticizers, lubricants, accelerators, and catalysts, could then be molded in steel dies under heat and pressure to insoluble and infusible products possessing a wide utility. Manufacture of one of these materials began in the U.S. in 1929. The plastic can be produced in any colour, from translucent and colourless to ivory and pure white, through pastels and brilliant hues to jet black. In thin sections the natural uncoloured combination of urea and cellulose transmits light in a highly diffused state, and, by altering the thickness and pigmentation, reflection and transmission can be modified at will. The molded product is used in the manufacture of buttons, wall plates, instrument dials, display boxes, dress accessories, and housings of all types.

$$NH_2 - CO - NH_2 \longrightarrow NH_2 - CO - NH - CH_2 - OH$$
$$HO - CH_2 - NH - CO - NH - CH_2 - OH$$
$$\downarrow - H_2O$$
$$CO - NH - CH_2OH$$

Preparation of urea-formaldehyde resin

The resin in solution possesses many other applications. Resin solutions are used in the preparation of cements that can be hardened hot or, through the proper addition of catalysts, may be set cold. When the water-soluble resin is suitably dispersed in organic solvents, it forms the basis of a very important class of resin finishes and enamels for metal coating. As an impregnant for wood veneer, the water-soluble condensation products serve both as a binder and a protective coating. Since the resin is colourless, the cured resin materially enhances the beauty of the wood. The solutions are also used to treat textiles in order to control their shrinkage and render them crease or crush resistant.

In the manufacture of laminated stock, sheets of absorbent paper are impregnated, dried, and assembled to appropriate thickness and then heated between platens to yield a sheet stock that is used in lighting reflectors, signs, wall panels, table tops, and decorative murals.

Melamine-Formaldehyde Resins.—Prior to 1939 melamine was available only in limited amounts at $40 a pound. Although the compound was rare, it had been known for more than 100 years and had been first prepared in 1834 by Justus von Liebig. After new industrial processes became available in 1939, melamine was made in ton quantities, and like urea it is secured from the air. Combining nitrogen from the air with calcium carbide yields calcium cyanamide, which can be hydrolyzed to cyanamide, which in turn can be dimerized to dicyandiamide. Under high temperature and pressure, dicyandiamide is transformed to melamine, an extremely stable substance containing only carbon, hydrogen, and nitrogen. These reactions can be represented by the following chemical equations:

$$CaC_2 + N_2 \longrightarrow CaCN_2 + C$$
$$CaCN_2 + 2H_2O \longrightarrow Ca(OH)_2 + NH_2 - CN$$
$$2NH_2 - CN \longrightarrow NH_2 - C(=NH) - NH - CN$$

Preparation of melamine from calcium cyanamide

When condensed with formaldehyde, melamine forms products that in superficial respects resemble the condensation products of urea, but, where only mono- and dimethylolureas have been prepared, a much wider number of the initial melamine-formaldehyde condensation products are known. Di-, tri-, and hexamethylol melamines have been prepared.

Melamine formaldehyde   Trimethylol melamine

Network condensation of melamine with formaldehyde

The melamine resin can tolerate fillers, such as asbestos and other minerals, that cannot be used with the urea condensation product. Because of their excellent heat and arc resistance, good dielectric strength, and low water pickup, mineral-filled melamines suitably modified with other resins were used in ignition systems.

Cellulose-filled melamine plastics have been used in many of the applications already discussed for the urea resins, but since the melamine resin is more resistant to high temperatures, to boiling water, and to more alkaline solutions, and since it does not retain food odours, it is particularly useful in tableware. The melamine resin possesses extreme hardness; this, together with its good colour and abrasion resistance, makes it an invaluable material for surfacing laminated assemblies. Translucent moldings may be made, for example, in button manufacture.

Anhydrous Thermosetting Resins.—The thermosetting resins used for laminating and molding depend on the loss of water to become insoluble. To reduce the water content to the smallest possible amount, the resin is carried to an advanced stage of condensation in which considerable heat and pressure must be utilized to cause the resin to flow sufficiently to fill the mold. During World War II, new types of products appeared that did not require the loss of water to bring about insolubility and infusibility of the resin. These compositions have been referred to as anhydrous thermosetting resins and solventless varnishes, while the process has been called low-pressure, or contact, molding. They belong to the thermosetting polymerization type of resins. Irrespective of the name, all of these resins have one characteristic in common: the polymerizable molecules possess a plurality of unsaturated groups and undergo reaction to insolubility quickly and exothermically without the evolution of low-molecular-condensation residues. The unsaturation can be introduced into the initial molecule by the incorporation of either unsaturated acid residue, or unsaturated alcohol residues, or both. The polymerization is generally catalyzed by peroxides. The physical state of the anhydrous thermosetting resins can be varied within wide limits; some are thin fluids, others viscous liquids, whereas still others are solid or greaselike in consistency. Since only low pressure is required in fabrication, comparatively inexpensive molds can be utilized. In many instances the fluid-molding technique may be employed for making complex shapes; this procedure depends on delivering pressure uniformly over a large area through the use of rubber bags, and by such means large structural parts of airplanes and boats have been built. The most spectacular development in this field is the fibre-glass-reinforced automobile body. In certain respects the high strength and the low weight of the plastic combined with its ability to recover practically undamaged from impacts and its higher resistance to corrosive atmospheres and moisture penetration have been assets. In large-scale production, however, the assembly could not compete with steel construction. Some efforts have been directed to the use of these reinforced resins as reinforcing agents in the manufacture of plastic pipe and in the manufacture of equipment for use in the chemical process industries. Here again the outstanding advantage arises from corrosion resistance. When such rigid sheets of plastics are laminated into a cellular or honeycomb core, the highly rigid and lightweight combinations produced possess good strength and insulating characteristics. Large volumes of this resin are utilized in the manufacture of boats, in construction, and in transportation equipment.

The anhydrous thermosetting products are frequently referred to as polyester resins since ester groups are present in the molecule. Another product designated as a polyester is the polyethylene glycol terephthalate. Again, ester linkages are present in the molecular pattern, but the physical properties of the polymer are very different. Being of much higher molecular weight and crystalline in structure the product can be oriented into fibres and into sheet stock of exceptional clarity and strength. Polycarbonates likewise fall into the class of polyesters. Polyarylcarbonates, formed by the condensation of bisphenol A (4, 4'-isopropylidenediphenol) through reaction with phosgene (carbonyl chloride), yield high-molecular-weight thermoplastic compositions having exceptionally good dimensional stability and mechanical properties. The high impact strength of this polycarbonate resin is employed wherever exceptional toughness is necessary. The electrical properties are such that it finds application in electrical connectors, coil forms, and terminal blocks.

Epoxy Resins.—As the name implies these resins have as their chief functional group the epoxide linkage. When first produced commercially, these resins were prepared by condensing bisphenol A (as a salt) with epichlorohydrin. Later the reaction was extended to a series of products derived from resorcinol. These resins may be cured through the use of polyamines, as well as with acid anhydrides, to yield infusible resins without the loss of volatile components. Initially, these resins were used in surface coatings but later found wide application in lamination with glass fibres, as well as in casting, potting, capsulation, and in embedments. When used as molding compounds with various fillers very low pressures must be used, and the molds must be tight to prevent excessive flashing.

2. Thermoplastic Resins.—*Vinyl Resins.*—As noted above, acetic anhydride is required in the manufacture of cellulose acetate. Following World War I various methods were investigated for converting the acid to the anhydride since it was anticipated that large quantities of this cellulose plastic would be required in the manufacture of fibre, film, and safety glass. Among the methods investigated was the reaction of acetic acid with acetylene to form ethylidene diacetate, which in turn could be decomposed to acetic anhydride. In conducting the reaction between acetylene and acetic acid, investigators obtained substantial quantities of an organic liquid that had a boiling point too low to be the desired product. This liquid was monomeric vinyl acetate. Although the investigation was directed primarily to the preparation of an acetylating agent, vinyl acetate was in time destined to be the basis of the manufacture of most of the plastic used in safety glass.

Polyvinyl Acetate Resins.—The transformation of vinyl acetate (CH_2=CH—O—CO—CH_3) to a safety-glass interlayer did not occur all at once, however. Manufacture of the early product was difficult because little was known concerning the chemistry of transformation of a vinyl monomer to its polymer. Moreover, the early development was hazardous from a commercial standpoint since there were no uses for such a resinous product. It was first investigated as a shellac sub-

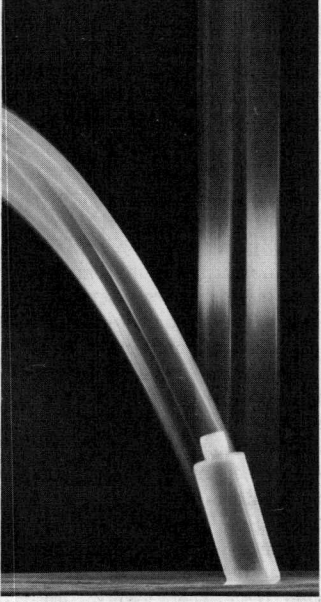

NEW PRODUCT MADE OF THERMO-PLASTIC RESIN UNDERGOING TESTS FOR RESILIENCE AND TOUGHNESS
High-speed photograph shows path of water-filled bottle when dropped 20 ft. and its degree of elastic recovery

stitute, but its remarkable adhesive properties, when hot, made it invaluable for uniting many diverse materials such as cloth, paper, leather, wood, and glass. Compounded with fillers, glycerin, sugar, and flavouring, polyvinyl acetate makes a chicle substitute in the manufacture of chewing gum. Hydrolysis of polyvinyl acetate causes cleavage of the ester grouping, resulting in the formation of polyvinyl alcohol,

$$-(CH_2-CH-)_x \longrightarrow (-CH_2-CH-)_x$$
$$O-CO-CH_3 \qquad\qquad OH$$

a resinous polymeric alcohol that forms viscous solutions in water and finds some utility as a thickening agent for emulsions and in the preparation of plastics that, although sensitive to water, are highly resistant to oils. Polyvinyl alcohol can be spun into a fibre, and, although the fibre is soluble in water, special uses can be made of this solubility in the weaving of sheer laces; fibres of polyvinyl alcohol and any other fibre can be woven and the synthetic water-soluble fibre dissolved, leaving a sheer fabric. The major shortcoming appears to be in lack of heat resistance. On the other hand, the dry tenacity of the product is outstanding.

Many chemical transformations of polyvinyl alcohol are possible. It can be condensed with other low-molecular compounds, particularly aldehydes, to form new resinous materials. Condensation with formaldehyde, acetaldehyde, and butyraldehyde results, respectively, in polyvinyl formal, polyvinyl acetal, and polyvinyl butyral. The polyvinyl formal finds use as a coating resin for electrical insulation; the acetal possesses potentialities as a photographic film base and as an injection-molding material; but it is the butyral that is the most useful, and as much as 100,000,000 sq.ft. have been produced annually for safety-glass manufacture. The resin when suitably plasticized yields a tough, high-impact film that maintains its properties at low temperature, and when laminated between glass it produces a composite assembly that displays little tendency to splinter on impact.

Polyvinyl Chloride Resins.—Vinyl chloride is a gas at room temperature and can readily be prepared from either ethylene or acetylene. Addition of hydrogen chloride directly to acetylene yields the monomer, or ethylene can be chlorinated and dehydrohalogenated to vinyl chloride. The polymerization was extensively studied by I. Ostromislensky, who sought in 1916 to dehalogenate the polymer to a rubberlike substance. Polyvinyl chloride was transformed to a rubber substitute about 20 years after these basic investigations but by an entirely different procedure.

Polymeric vinyl chloride, —(CH_2—$CHCl$)$_x$—, is practically infusible and for a long time proved to be a rather intractable substance. In efforts to plasticize the product it was milled and compounded with polyvinyl acetate, mentioned above, but with no great success until it was found that by mixing the ingredients prior to polymerization and then chemically combining the two materials into a polymeric structure, it was possible to achieve in this conjoint polymer, or copolymer, a new type of product that was easier to handle and one that could be further flexibilized through the addition of high-boiling liquids and plasticizers. By varying the ratio of acetate to chloride, resins of varying plasticity and stiffness can be secured.

Intensive investigations were made into the nature of plasticizing methods and techniques of direct plasticizing of vinyl chloride without the necessity of copolymerization. It was generally conceded, however, that the copolymer is more amenable to plasticization by a larger number of widely diverse liquids than is the unmodified polymer. Both types, however, have found extensive use as sheet stock, as wire insulating compounds, and as substitutes and replacements for rubber. Since these polymers possess considerable amounts of chlorine, they will not support combustion and they therefore possess distinct advantages in wiring where nonflammability is of importance. The halogen, however, is labile, and, when the resin is exposed to heat or to ultraviolet light, loss of hydrogen halide occurs, resulting in discoloration. By dry spinning the vinyl chloride-acetate copolymer, it is possible to produce filaments that can be woven into chemically resistant fabric. In Germany fibres were fabricated directly from polyvinyl chloride.

Polyvinylidene Chloride Resins.—By doubling the amount of chlorine in vinyl chloride, a new chemical entity, vinylidene chloride, is obtained. Because of the symmetrical arrangement of the chlorine atoms in polyvinylidene chloride, $-(CH_2-CCl_2)_x-$, the polymer is crystalline, and advantage can be taken of this crystalline characteristic to form oriented filaments and tubing. Such oriented forms have molecules arranged in an ordered manner with the result that in the direction of orientation the product is very strong. When extruded, quenched, and drawn, the polyvinylidene chloride makes an excellent substitute for reed and rattan and a corrosion-resistant substitute for insect screening; in the form of tubing, the resin can be used to pipe many corrosive chemicals.

Acrylic Resins.—The term acrylic resin covers not only the acrylic esters but also the polymerizable derivatives of both acrylic and methacrylic acids as well as the acid chlorides, nitriles, amides, and substituted amides. Acrylic derivatives generally involve cyanide in their synthesis, but investigations indicate that, at least in the case of the acrylic acid derivative, there may be an alternative procedure involving carbon monoxide (in the form of a metallic carbonyl) and acetylene. Considerable investigation was also undertaken in an attempt to prepare acrylic esters from natural lactic acid derived from milk, but it remained to be demonstrated whether the natural lactic acid could compete with the synthetic product. The names of Otto Röhm and Rowland Hill were associated with the preparation and polymerization of acrylic and methacrylic esters, respectively.

From the standpoint of plastic molding, methacrylic esters are preferred, since they are harder and more rigid than the corresponding acrylic esters. By changing the type of alcohol used in esterification of the original monomeric ester, it is possible to modify the hardness of the resulting polymer. Polymethyl acrylate is tough and rubbery; polyethyl acrylate is softer and more rubbery; polybutyl acrylate is sticky. Continuing up the homologous series of alcohol esters, the polymers become softer and more plastic until at polyoctyl acrylate it is found that the polymer is almost liquid in consistency.

Polymethyl methacrylate,

$$(- CH_2 - \underset{\underset{COOCH_3}{|}}{\overset{\overset{CH_3}{|}}{C}} -)_x$$

is the hardest ester in the methacrylate series, and, as in acrylates, introduction of long-chain alcohols into the ester lowers the softening point of the plastic. Some idea of the relative hardness is seen in the fact that polyamyl methacrylate is about as hard as polymethyl acrylate. While polymethyl methacrylate is the preferred resin for injection molding and plastic applications, it was found that cyclohexyl methacrylate is superior for lens casting, since this liquid undergoes less shrinkage during polymerization than does the methyl ester. Cyclohexyl methacrylate polymer, together with styrene resin, was used in combination in the preparation of plastic achromatic lenses.

Without doubt the largest single outlet for the methyl methacrylate resin has been in sheet form for windows in aircraft, particularly military aircraft. The resin was cast in glass molds, and the finished sheet could then be "post-formed" to a wide variety of shapes necessary for blisters, noses, cockpits, windshields, and canopies. The high clarity of these plastics, as well as the ability to transmit or "pipe" light, also favoured their use in surgical instruments, highway reflectors, and edge-lighted advertising displays. Transparent sheeting in oriented form also is used in motorcycle windshields, instrument windows, glazing, patio shelters, partitions, and mobile home windows. Large moldings of methyl methacrylate resins are used in transilluminated signs.

Whereas styrene was copolymerized with butadiene to form a general-purpose rubber, acrylonitrile ($CH_2=CH-CN$), the nitrile of acrylic acid, was copolymerized with butadiene to yield a special oil-resistant rubber extensively used where rubber had to be in contact with gasoline and other hydrocarbon liquids. Acrylonitrile forms conjoint polymers with many other vinyl compounds such as acrylic esters and styrene, but from all indications it promised to play its most important role as a polymer in the form of a synthetic fibre.

Polyamides.—By the condensation of diamines and dibasic acid, linear condensation products may be formed, and by varying the nature of the acid and the amine it is possible to produce products that are hard and tough or soft and rubbery. These linear condensation products are referred to as polyamides

$$[- NH - R - NH - CO - R' - CO -]_n$$

Polyamides are most generally known in the form of fine and coarse filaments in such articles as hosiery, parachutes, bristles, and brushes. As has been pointed out, however, high-molecular-weight organic resinous compounds of certain types can be converted into fibres. The polyamides were first offered commercially in the form of filaments but were later directed to the molding trade, particularly toward the injection-molding field where their toughness and ability to flow around complicated inserts are prime considerations. Polyamides, particularly those derived from primary amines, are characterized by a high degree of crystallinity, whether in the form of filaments or as moldings. Under stress, orientation of molecules begins to occur and this orientation continues until the specimen is drawn to about four times its initial size; although this property is of outstanding importance in filaments, it has more limited utility in molded articles. The resin exhibits a sharp melting point and on melting is more liquid and plastic than conventional resinous materials. The fluidity is both an advantage and a disadvantage: the high fluidity necessitates the use of specialized equipment, but on molding there is no need to use excessive pressure in injection molding, since the liquid resin transmits its pressure onto the molded specimen hydrostatically.

Inasmuch as adipic acid and hexamethylene diamine are the ingredients most often used in nylon synthesis and since both of these ingredients contain six carbon atoms, this product has been referred to as nylon 6–6. Another variety of nylon can be made from amino caproic acid; this polymer is referred to as nylon 6. However, a preparation of nylon 6 can be effected much more easily through the use of caprolactam. Extensive facilities are available both in Europe and in the United States for the manufacture of this polymer from caprolactam. (*See also* FIBRE.)

Caprolactam is a 7-membered heterocyclic ring. A 5-membered ring has been polymerized to a high-molecular-weight substance, polypyrrolidone, or, in the alternative designation, nylon 4.

A product somewhat similar to the polyamides, manufactured in Germany during World War II, utilized isocyanates, particularly the diisocyanates. Reaction of these unsaturated compounds with glycols yielded polyurethanes

$$[- NH - R - NH - CO - O - R' - O]_n,$$

which could be fabricated into bristles. A wide variety of other urethane products has been derived from isocyanates. When reacted with the appropriate alkyds, foamed resins are produced that have wide utility in the manufacture of laminates, upholstery, and in insulation. Reacted with another variety of alkyds, these same isocyanates yield synthetic rubbers having unusual abrasion resistance. Other uses for these isocyanate products are being discovered.

Polymers from Cycloxabutanes.—From pentaerythritol can be prepared a cyclic monomeric chlorinated ether that can be polymerized to a high-molecular-weight plastic containing a fair proportion of halogen. Because of the position of the chlorine in the polymer molecule, it is difficult to remove and consequently the product possesses unusual stability. Inasmuch as the groups are symmetrically positioned in the polymer, the product is crystalline and capable of being drawn.

Polystyrene Resins.—That styrene, or vinylbenzene, would polymerize has been known for a long time. The designation vinylbenzene ($CH_2=CH-C_6H_5$) immediately relates it to the other polymerizable vinyl compounds, such as vinyl chloride, fluoride, and acetate. The designation styrene arose from the fact that this liquid was first prepared by heating the natural resin storax. The first patents on the possible uses of styrene were taken out by F. E.

Matthews in 1911. Monomeric styrene is present in the light oils of coal-tar manufacture, and, although extensive investigations were undertaken to remove styrene from this source, the processes proved too costly and could not compete economically with the synthetic methods. In order to secure a satisfactory plastic out of styrene, it is necessary that a highly purified product be subject to polymerization. Where the monomeric styrene is of inferior quality, the resulting resin is too brittle, and on aging the surface of the plastic becomes covered with fine hair lines similar in appearance to those appearing in an unfilled urea-formaldehyde resin. By using a reaction discovered by P. E. M. Berthelot in 1869, it was found that by dehydrogenating ethylbenzene catalytically at elevated temperatures and fractionating the resulting mixture, it is possible to secure a product that on polymerization under appropriate conditions yields a polymer possessing valuable chemical and physical properties. Chemically, the resin is highly resistant to both weak and strong acids, although oxidizing types of acids may lead to some discoloration. Alkalies and the lower alcohols do not attack the polymer, and the water absorption of the resin is extremely small. The resin can be dissolved in coal tar and in chlorinated solvents. In electrical characteristics, the plastic possesses an extremely low power (or loss) factor, and, when the resin is properly prepared, this power factor remains substantially unchanged over a wide range of frequency. The low power factor combined with low water absorption makes polystyrene an ideal material for various electrical and electronic applications. The presence of a multiplicity of aromatic rings in the polymer renders the product responsive to temperature, with the result that the resin can be handled expediently by the injection-molding technique. Among the noteworthy applications of this plastic is the fabrication of battery boxes, ranging in size from those employed in a small automobile to the type that is ordinarily used in portable radio sets. It has found utility in manufacture of condensers, tube sockets, coil forms, and switch plates. As a copolymer with divinylbenzene, the resin was employed for certain radar applications that involved operating temperatures higher than could be tolerated with polystyrene. The monomer was also cast directly for certain optical parts such as prisms and lenses.

Since polystyrene possesses a high dispersion value, it could be combined with polycyclohexylmethacrylate to make corrected plastic achromatic lenses.

One of the limitations of polystyrene for many applications is its inability to tolerate excessive heat; and although the modification with divinylbenzene increases its resistance to heat distortion, it does so at the expense of moldability. In order to increase the heat resistance of polystyrene and maintain moldability, the monomer has been copolymerized with various nitrogen-containing compounds such as acrylonitrile, fumaric nitrile, and vinylcarbazole. The increase in softening point is attained at the sacrifice of colour.

Later developments included the so-called ABS polymers, in which acrylonitrile, butadiene, and styrene are reacted simultaneously. The acrylonitrile-styrene copolymers are likewise prepared in substantial volume. In addition, styrene-methacrylate copolymers were projected into fields where unmodified methacrylate polymers dominated, such as in signs and automotive parts.

Extensive investigation was carried out in the direction of introducing various groups into the styrene nucleus in an attempt to reduce heat distortion directly. One of the methods that proved successful involves the introduction of multiple halogens into the aromatic nucleus. Another method of securing styrenelike plastics having softening points above that of boiling water involves the use of ring-substituted methyl groups in the monomer. By introducing methyl groups into the benzene nucleus of the monomer, the properties of the resulting resin, on polymerization, can be modified. Two syntheses based on alternative isomers have been employed commercially. One procedure, based on the conventional dehydrogenation of the appropriate methyl ethyl benzene, yields a *meta-para* mixture; the other process involves the decomposition of diaryl ethanes, permitting the formation of *ortho*-methyl styrenes. The presence of a methyl group, *ortho* to the vinyl, imparts important heat-resistant characteristics to the fin-

ished polymer; the composition comprising 67% of *para* and 33% of *ortho* yields derivatives, which, on injection molding, remain stable in boiling water.

Acetal Resins.—Through the direct polymerization of highly purified formaldehyde it is possible to secure an unbranched polyoxymethylene comprising more than 1,000 formaldehyde residues in the chain. A polymer thus constituted has, because of its symmetry, high crystallinity and a high melting point. High strength, rigidity, good resilience, and toughness, together with low water absorption, make this plastic extremely versatile in the fabrication of mechanical parts, appliances, and automotive items. Because of the crystallinity this acetal resin is unusual among thermoplastic substances in being resistant to a wide variety of organic liquids. At room temperature no common liquid dissolves the resin. This characteristic permits the plastic to be used without danger of staining by either food or industrial materials. The same statement cannot, however, be made with respect to its reaction with strong acids or bases.

Stereo Polymers.—In the early 1950s Karl Ziegler (*q.v.*) of the Max Planck Institute for Coal Research at Mülheim, Ger., studied the polymerization of ethylene using organic compounds of aluminum as catalysts. Under certain reaction conditions it was possible to polymerize ethylene even at atmospheric pressure. Subsequently, the Italian firm named Montecatini secured licenses under the Ziegler patents, and Giulio Natta (*q.v.*) at the Polytechnic Institute of Milan extended the use of these and related catalysts to the polymerization of *alpha* olefins. Eventually, these systems, known as the Ziegler-Natta catalysts, comprised a wide variety of halides of transition elements for use in polymerization. Somewhat similar investigations were carried out simultaneously by various firms in the United States. Consequently, there developed a wide spectrum of substances that may be used to polymerize not only ethylene but also other hydrocarbons, such as propylene, butadiene, styrene, and a variety of stereospecific polymeric substances.

Certain types of structures in chain molecules permit an alternate steric arrangement. Isomerism involving the double bond, such as the cis-trans isomerism, was known to exist in natural products, and it has been known for a long time that the physical properties of balata and rubber differ because of different arrangements of the double bonds in the otherwise similar molecules. Similarly, in condensation polymers, cis and trans isomers could be produced by condensing maleic and fumaric esters with appropriate polyhydric alcohols.

Another type of stereo isomerism results when different atoms or groups are attached tetrahedrally to a carbon atom. If the two parts of the main chain attached to any carbon atom are structurally nonequivalent, the isotactic structure comprises those polymers in which the basic repeating unit appears to have all of the substituents on the same side of the main chain. Syndiotactic polymers comprise those systems where the substituents alternate on both sides of the main chain.

$$\begin{array}{cccccccc}
H & H & H & H & H & H & H & H \\
-C-C-C-C-C-C-C-C- \\
H & R & H & R & H & R & H & R
\end{array}$$

Isotactic

$$\begin{array}{cccccccc}
H & R & H & H & H & R & H & H \\
-C-C-C-C-C-C-C-C- \\
H & H & H & R & H & H & H & R
\end{array}$$

Syndiotactic

The use of these novel catalysts secures through positioning a symmetry that results in products possessing much higher melting points. These catalysts also have been utilized with diolefins yielding, under polymerization conditions, a different type of symmetry in the diene polymer. With isoprene it is possible, utilizing the Ziegler-Natta catalysts, to arrange a very large proportion of the double bonds in a cis position, yielding a synthetic rubber that closely simulates the physical and chemical properties of that obtained from the rubber tree *Hevea brasiliensis*.

Polypropylene.—The development of crystalline high-molecular-weight polypropylene came out of the catalytic studies designed for the low-pressure polymerization of ethylenes as noted above. These heterogeneous metal alkyl substances are capable of directing the polymerization of substituted olefins to yield an ordered polymer.

The development of commercial processes involving the formation of crystalline polypropylene was expensive. Where there is a high portion of isotacticity a more ordered crystalline polymer is obtained, characterized by greater hardness, toughness, and higher melting points. Polypropylene is one of the lightest of the plastics; its low density, together with good physical properties, means high strength-to-weight ratios in finished parts.

Polyvinylcarbazole Resins.—Reaction of acetylene with carbazole yields vinylcarbazole

$$\begin{bmatrix} CH_2 = CH \\ | \\ N - C_{12}H_8 \end{bmatrix}$$

which can be converted to a plastic possessing high heat resistance and excellent electrical properties; but the brittleness of the product limits its uses to specialized industrial applications.

Polyethylene Resins.—Although ethylene is the simplest unsaturated compound, it proved to be one of the most difficult to convert into a high-molecular-weight polymer, with extremely high pressures and moderately high temperatures required to effect conversion. As might be predicted from its structure, polyethylene, $-(CH_2-CH_2)_x-$ is completely nonpolar and possesses a low power factor and a low dielectric constant. Being highly symmetrical, it is also crystalline. In common with other crystalline polymers, thin sheets of the resin exhibit high resistance to penetration by water vapour.

At ordinary temperatures the resin is highly resistant to attack by organic and inorganic reagents. At moderate temperatures the resin can be dissolved in certain organic liquids and such solutions can be applied as a coating, but satisfactory results are obtained only by keeping the coated object in a heated condition until the solvent has evaporated. Polyethylene, however, can be applied more easily by direct extrusion of the molten plastic. It proved suitable for insulating high-frequency and high-voltage circuits.

A type of polyethylene that takes on characteristics of a more rigid plastic is frequently referred to as "linear" polyethylene. That such linear products were possible was known for a long time. These products had been prepared by the decomposition of diazomethane, but to prepare such materials directly from ethylene was recognized as a major achievement. Such linear products possess a higher softening point that permits sterilization, a procedure that was impossible with the earlier type.

By combining covalent and ionic bonds in a thermoplastic, a family of polymers known as ionomer resins has been produced. These substances are based on the observation that by introducing ionic forces in a semicrystalline polymer, such as polyethylene, visible crystallinity is decreased, while the modulus of elasticity and resistance to oil and solvents are markedly increased. The covalent bonds, being intramolecular, unite the atoms of the polymer chain, while the ionic bonds are intermolecular and act between chains. These ionic interchain lengths toughen the polymer without destroying its ability to be fabricated as a plastic.

Polyisobutylene Resins.—Isobutylene is a hydrocarbon boiling at about $-5°$ C, and when dimerized it can be converted by reduction to 2-methylheptane. By conducting the polymerization at very low temperatures, using boron fluoride as a catalyst, a high-molecular-weight product

$$\begin{bmatrix} & CH_3 \\ & | \\ - CH_2 - C - \\ & | \\ & CH_3 \end{bmatrix}_x$$

is formed. This polymer is rubberlike, but, inasmuch as the material is saturated, it cannot be vulcanized. By conducting the polymerization of isobutylene along with a diene such as butadiene, isoprene, or dimethyl butadiene, unsaturated residues are introduced into the polymer. These residues can act as nuclei for vulcanization with sulfur.

Polyvinylpyrrolidone (PVP).—The polymer secured from N-vinyl-2-pyrrolidone is a water-soluble product, possessing many unusual characteristics and having a wide variety of pharmaceutical applications including that of blood plasma extender. The product is used in the United States chiefly in hair-spray lacquers and in detergents. The polymer has a high affinity for many dyestuffs and in many laundering applications will prevent the bleeding of migrant colours from one garment to another. When hair is placed in contact with aqueous solutions of polyvinylpyrrolidone a certain amount of polymer enters into the hair shaft. Subsequent rinsing will not remove all of the polymer, leaving the hair with an improved appearance both from the standpoint of clarity and of natural colour. A number of preparations employ PVP as a retardant vehicle for drugs since it permits the drug to remain in the body for a longer period.

Polyvinyl Methyl Ether (PVM).—Another high polymer possessing water-soluble characteristics and simultaneously dispersible in a number of organic liquids is the polymer secured from vinyl ether. Like PVP it is a derivative of the high-pressure synthesis of acetylene. The direct addition of methanol to acetylene under pressure using appropriate catalysts yields a monomer. When alcohols other than methyl are used with acetylene similar vinylization occurs yielding vinyl alkyl ethers. If the alcohol is long enough, such as stearyl alcohol, no excessive pressure is required to carry out the reaction. These vinyl ethers will polymerize among themselves or with other vinyl materials. One product used extensively as a water-soluble colloid is the copolymer of vinyl methyl ether with maleic anhydride, which has been designated as PVM/MA. Inasmuch as acidic groups are still present in the polymer, a number of esters with widely varying physical characteristics may be prepared.

Polyacrylamide.—Still another polymer possessing water solubility in its resinous plastic form is polyacrylamide. The amide linkage is capable of reaction with formaldehyde, yielding an intermediate that can undergo further condensation reactions.

Perhalogenated Plastics.—Several references can be found in the patent literature for the preparation of polymeric materials that possess only carbon and halogen in their molecular structure. One of the perhalogenated products, polytrifluorochloroethylene, $-(CF_2-CFCl)_x-$, is described in a patent issued to F. Schloffer and O. Scherer (1934), while another patent, that of R. J. Plunkett in 1941, refers to tetrafluoroethylene polymer $-(CF_2-CF)_x-$. The latter product was produced commercially in limited quantities and found its chief use in the preparation of corrosion-resistant gaskets. Polymeric tetrafluoroethylene is a remarkably stable substance and is insensitive to all organic and inorganic liquids. As would be expected from its symmetrical structure, the polymer is crystalline and the resin on heating undergoes a phase transition at about $327°$ C, where the moldings become transparent and the tensile strength decreases markedly. Other perhalogenated plastics utilize perfluoropropylene as a reactive monomer.

3. Foamed Plastics.—Under appropriate conditions almost any thermosetting or thermoplastic resin can be converted into a foam. While foam rubber anteceded foamed plastics, there is now available a number of products, such as foamed vinyl, expandable polystyrene, cellular polyethylene, foamed phenolics, foamed silicones, cellular cellulose acetate, and urethane foams. A distinction is made between the closed-cell foam and the open-cell variety. The open-cell foams are produced by incorporating an inert gas with the resin under pressure and then releasing the mixture to the atmosphere and curing the resulting foam. Closed-cell foams are produced by incorporating a blowing agent that decomposes at the fusion point, releasing gas during the gelling and fusion.

The urethane foams are formed by reaction of hydroxyl-rich materials and polyisocyanates, usually tolylene diisocyanate. While initially the main hydroxylating agent was a polyester, polyethers have come into extensive use. It is claimed that the polyethers give a more flexible urethane that is more desirable in cushioning. Through the proper choice of proportions and ingredients the foamed urethane may be flexible or rigid and have applications in furniture, transport, toys, packaging, thermal installations, aircraft, and as sponges. Rigid polyurethane foams are being used to make plastic boats and to fabricate beams and panels for buildings.

See also references under "Plastics" in the Index.

BIBLIOGRAPHY.—C. E. H. Bawn, *The Chemistry of High Polymers* (1948) ; R. H. Boundy, R. F. Boyer, and S. M. Stoesser (eds.), *Styrene: Its Polymers, Copolymers, and Derivatives* (1952) ; T. S. Carswell, *Phenoplasts, Their Structure, Properties and Chemical Technology* (1947) ; G. F. D'Alelio, *Fundamental Principles of Polymerization* (1952), *Experimental Plastics and Synthetic Resins* (1946) ; C. Ellis, *The Chemistry of Synthetic Resins,* 2 vol. (1935) ; Faraday Society, *Phenomena of Polymerisation and Condensation* (1936) ; P. J. Flory, *Principles of Polymer Chemistry* (1953) ; E. Müller, "Makromolekulare Stoffe," *Methoden der organischen Chemie,* vol. XIV/1 (1961), vol. XIV/2 (1963) ; R. Houwink, *Chemie und Technologie der Kunststoffe* (1939), *Technology of Synthetic Polymers* (1947), *Fundamentals of Synthetic Polymer Technology* (1949), *Elastomers and Plastomers,* vol. 1 (1950), vol. 2 (1949), vol. 3 (1948) ; G. Kranzlein and R. Lepsius, *Kunststoff-Wegweiser* (1939) ; K. H. Meyer, *Natural and Synthetic High Polymers* (1942) ; R. S. Morrell *et al.* (eds.), *Synthetic Resins and Allied Plastics* (1937) ; J. Scheiber and K. Sändig, *Artificial Resins,* Eng. trans. by E. Fyleman (1931) ; C. E. Schildknecht, *Vinyl and Related Polymers* (1952) ; H. R. Simonds and C. Ellis, *Handbook of Plastics* (1943) ; H. Staudinger, *Die hochmolekularen organischen Verbindungen-Kautschuk und Cellulose* (1932) ; E. C. Worden, *Technology of Cellulose Esters* (1921) ; R. L. Wakeman, *The Chemistry of Commercial Plastics* (1947) ; D. F. Gould, *Phenolic Resins* (1959) ; C. R. Martens, *Alkyd Resins* (1961) ; T. C. Patton, *Alkyd Resin Technology* (1962) ; Mayo W. Smith, *Vinyl Resins* (1958) ; M. B. Horn, *Acrylic Resins* (1960) ; H. L. Lee and K. Neville, *Epoxy Resins* (1957) ; I. Skeist, *Epoxy Resins* (1958) ; R. B. Akin, *Acetal Resins* (1962) ; J. F. Blais, *Amino Resins* (1959) ; E. G. Fisher, *Extrusion of Plastics* (1958) ; P. Morgan (ed.), *Glass Reinforced Plastics,* 3rd ed. (1961) ; A. F. Bick, *Plastics: Projects and Procedures with Polyesters* (1962) ; D. J. Duffin and C. Nerzig, *Laminated Plastics* (1958) ; J. Delmonte, *Metal-Filled Plastics* (1961) ; J. R. Lawrence, *Polyester Resins* (1960) ; C. E. Schildknecht, *Vinyl and Related Polymers* (1952) ; W. Brenner, D. Lum, and M. W. Riley, *High-Temperature Plastics* (1962) ; D. E. Floyd, *Polyamide Resins* (1958) ; R. S. Morrell and H. M. Langton, (eds.), *Synthetic Resins and Allied Plastics,* 3rd ed. (1951) ; H. R. Simonds, *Source Book of the New Plastics,* vol. 1 (1959), vol. 2 (1961) ; Society of the Plastics Industry, *SPI Plastics Engineering Handbook,* 3rd ed. (1960) ; V. Stannett, *Cellulose Acetate Plastics* (1950) ; J. H. Saunders and K. C. Frisch, *Polyurethanes: Chemistry and Technology* (1962). (E. L. KA.)

PLASTIC SURGERY derives its name from the Greek *plastikos,* which means "mold or form." Plastic surgery is concerned with the "molding" or shaping of tissues for the restoration or improvement of function and appearance.

To effect such alterations, the plastic surgeon uses a variety of techniques for the rearrangement of local tissues or the transfer of tissues from one part of the body to another. Although plastic surgery in its early development was limited to the correction of facial deformities, it has come to include a great variety of problems involving many areas of the body. These can be grouped into four general categories: (1) congenital anomalies, (2) tumours, (3) traumatic lesions, and (4) physical irregularities.

History.—As a special surgical discipline, plastic surgery is fairly young, having had its first major development in World War I. Many of the techniques employed in the late 1960s, however, had their origins in antiquity. Contrary to popular belief, the Ebers and Smith papyri of ancient Egypt contain no descriptions of plastic surgical operations. Susruta, the greatest figure of Hindu medicine, who probably lived in the 6th century B.C., described the reconstruction of the nose by the use of tissue from the cheek, however, as well as the repair of defects of the ears. Amputation of the nose was a common punitive practice in ancient times, and it is believed that members of the potter (tilemaker) caste reconstructed noses in India as early as 1000 B.C.

Celsus (1st century A.D.) in his *De re medicina* described advancement flaps and operations on the nose, ear, and lips. Galen (*c.* A.D. 130–*c.* 200) described dislocation of the jaw and coloboma (congenital fissure) of the lip, ear, and nose. Repair of cleft lips was performed in China in the Ch'in dynasty (221–207 B.C.), and in the T'ang dynasty (A.D. 618–906), Fang Kan gained renown as a "lip restorer." The Nestorians and Arabs probably transmitted knowledge of plastic surgery from the East to Western civilization. Susruta, at any rate, is mentioned often by Rhazes, Avicenna, and other early Arabian physicians.

In the 15th century, the Brancas, father and son, gained renown in Sicily for reconstructing the nose by means of a flap taken from the arm, but they left no writings. Heinrich von Pfolspeundt performed similar procedures, but his description, written in 1460, *Buch der Bundth-Ertznei,* was not published until 1858. The Vianeo family in Calabria, Italy, may have learned the same operation from the Brancas. Andreas Vesalius and Ambroise Paré both mentioned the technique, but apparently did not fully understand it. The first textbook of plastic surgery, *De Curtorum chirurgia per insitionem* ("On the Surgical Restoration of Defects by Grafting"), was by Gaspare Tagliacozzi of Bologna in 1597. A great masterpiece of the Renaissance, it contained 298 pages and 22 illustrations, and described beautifully the reconstruction of the nose and lip by means of a flap taken from the arm. This technique is still often called the "Italian method."

In the next two centuries plastic surgery languished, and only rare mention of operations was made in books. F. Chopart described the repair of the lower lip by means of a cervical flap in 1791. The *Gentleman's Magazine,* published in Calcutta in 1794, contains the next report of plastic surgery, the reconstruction of a nose by means of a flap brought down from the forehead. This technique had evidently been used for centuries by the tilemaker caste, and is now referred to as the "Indian method" of rhinoplasty. Joseph C. Carpue of London reported two similar cases in 1816.

The next great treatise on plastic surgery was *Rhinoplastik* (1818), by Karl Ferdinand von Gräfe of Berlin. He used the arm flap, and was also the first to surgically reconstruct eyelids (1809). J. F. Dieffenbach (1792–1847) described many plastic surgical procedures on the lids, nose, ear, lips, cheek, urethra, and bladder. In France, J. M. Delpech, P. J. Roux, and F. Lisfranc made other contributions to plastic surgical literature. In Paris, Guillaume Dupuytren (1777–1835) operated on the jaw, classified burns according to their depth, and described the pathology of the deformity of the hand which bears his name.

J. P. Mettauer of Virginia is credited with the first repair of the soft palate (1827), and John Mason Warren of Boston, Mass., first repaired the hard palate in 1843. Bernard von Langenbeck (1810–1887) of Berlin described a technique of palatal repair still widely used. T. D. Mütter and J. Pancoast, both of Philadelphia, reported on the use of skin grafts in the early 1840s.

The term for plastic surgery was introduced by Edward Zeis in his *Handbuch der plastischen Chirurgie* (1838), and F. A. von Ammon and Baumgarten followed soon afterward with *Die Plastische Chirurgie nach ihren bisherigen Leistungen Kritisch dargestellt* (1842). R. Liston was the first English surgeon to devote considerable discussion to plastic surgery in his textbooks of 1831 and 1837. In France, A. A. L. M. Velpeau (1839), J. F. Malgaigne (1849), P. J. Roux (1854), and A. A. Verneuil (1877) followed suit. P. Sabattini of Bologna wrote a history of plastic surgery in 1838, and Julius von Szymanowski of Kiev wrote a superb section on plastic surgery in his *Manual of Operative Surgery* (1869). The first description of a cross-leg flap was by F. Hamilton of Buffalo, N.Y., in 1854. Gurdon Buck of New York City was the leading figure in plastic surgery in the Civil War and published his *Contributions to Reparative Surgery* in 1876.

The history of the free grafting of skin dates to G. Baronio's successful transplants in sheep (1804). J. J. Leroux (1817) quotes an account by R. J. H. Dutrochet of the reconstruction of the nose in India at a much earlier date by means of a free graft of skin and fat from the buttock. C. Bünger (1823) apparently did the first modern free skin graft, and J. M. Warren successfully grafted skin from the arm to the nose in 1840. J. L. Reverdin described thin (epidermal) grafts in 1869, and L. X. E. L. Ollier (1872) and Carl Thiersch (1874) enlarged upon this technique, using larger and thicker grafts. J. R. Wolfe of Glasgow used free full-thickness grafts of skin to repair the edge of the eyelid (1876). Full-thickness grafts are often called by his name today. F. Krause (1893) used similar grafts. John Staige Davis of Baltimore, the first surgeon to devote his full time to plastic surgery, introduced "pinch grafts" in 1914. They are now rarely used. Jacques Joseph (1865–1934) of Berlin is widely regarded as the father of cosmetic rhinoplasty. Robert Abbe (1851–1928) of New York City made many contributions to reconstructive surgery early in the 20th century.

In World War I great strides were made in the treatment of wounds of the face and jaws under the leadership of Harold D. Gillies (later Sir Harold) of England, and J. S. Davis, R. H. Ivy, and others in the United States. Plastic surgery developed rapidly in response to the need for repairing great numbers of men with wounds of the face and the soft tissues of the body. The development of the tubed pedicle flap by Gillies, and independently by N. F. Filatov of Russia, was a major step forward, since it made possible the safe transplantation of large pieces of tissue from one part of the body to another. Davis' *Plastic Surgery* was published in 1919, and Gillies' *Plastic Surgery of the Face* appeared in 1920. Between World Wars I and II extensive further development of techniques occurred, facilitated in part by the introduction of large skin-grafting knives by Vilray P. Blair of St. Louis, G. Humby of England, and Ferris Smith of Grand Rapids, and of the dermatome by E. C. Padgett and G. Hood (1939), which made possible the cutting of large (4 × 8 in.) skin grafts of measured thickness. The Reese dermatome is a useful refinement of the latter instrument. The Brown, Stryker, and Padgett electric dermatomes facilitate the rapid cutting of large pieces of skin.

During World War II a number of plastic surgical centres were established to care for the very large number of men whose wounds required reconstructive procedures. Among the outstanding advances during this period were the early closure of wounds, the extended use of local flaps, improved measures for treating burns, and the fostering of cooperation among plastic surgeons, neurosurgeons, orthopedists, dentists, psychiatrists, and ancillary medical and paramedical personnel, so that truly comprehensive care could be given to the wounded.

Journals for dissemination of new knowledge in the field include *Plastic and Reconstructive Surgery* (U.S., 1946–) and the *British Journal of Plastic Surgery* (Edinburgh, 1948–). The first plastic surgery society was the American Association of Plastic Surgeons (1921), followed by the American Society of Plastic and Reconstructive Surgeons (1931), the British Association of Plastic Surgeons (1946), the Educational Foundation of the American Society of Plastic and Reconstructive Surgeons (1948), and the Plastic Surgery Research Council (1955), all of which meet annually. The International Confederation for Plastic and Reconstructive Surgery (1955) meets quadrennially.

Types of Problems.—The plastic surgeon is called upon to treat a variety of deformities and defects, only a few of which can be mentioned within the scope of this article.

Congenital Anomalies ("Birth Defects").—The commonest extracranial anomalies of the head and neck are cleft lip and cleft palate, which may occur independently or together. The degree of severity of the clefts varies tremendously, and clefts may be associated as well with malformations of other parts of the body. A cleft lip is usually repaired within the first few days or weeks of life in order to facilitate sucking and to improve the appearance of the face. Repair of the cleft palate is usually done at the age of 12 to 18 months, although some surgeons prefer to wait until the child is older. An intact palate is necessary to prevent food from going into the nose, and to assist with speech. While one operation on the palate may suffice, additional procedures may be required to provide a better anatomical mechanism for normal speech. Other common malformations of the head and neck repaired by plastic surgeons are: deformities of the ear such as microtia (abnormal smallness); branchial arch and cleft anomalies; thyroglossal duct cysts; giant nevi (birthmarks, moles, tumours); hemangiomas (tumours of blood vessels) and lymphangiomas (tumours of lymph vessels); nasal, skull, and eyelid defects; micrognathia and prognathism (undersized and protruding jaws). Deformities of the hand, such as syndactyly (fused fingers), accessory fingers, congenital bands, and complete or partial absence of parts, can be corrected. Genitourinary problems such as hypospadias (deformity of the penis) and exstrophy of the bladder, and neuroskeletal defects such as spina bifida (malformation of the spine) and meningocoele (protrusions from the skull or spine)

are repaired by the plastic surgeon, either alone or in cooperation with other specialists.

Tumours.—This group, especially tumours arising in the skin and in the head and neck, includes benign tumours of the skin such as nevi, papillomas, cysts, lipomas, etc., and malignant tumours of the skin, most of which are basal cell carcinomas, squamous cell carcinomas, and malignant melanomas. Tumours of the head and neck include benign and malignant tumours of the salivary glands, eyelids, nose, lips, thyroid, larynx, and the oral cavity (tongue, floor of mouth, jaws, palate, and pharynx). The plastic surgeon, by virtue of his broad training, is able to perform not only the removal of the tumour but also the repair of the defect that results therefrom.

A special problem is the keloid, which consists of overdeveloped scar tissue. While most common in pigmented races, keloids occur also in Caucasians, usually as the result of surgery, injury, infection, or delayed healing of a wound. Considerable success in treatment has been achieved with surgery and locally administered adrenal cortical steroids.

Traumatic Lesions.—Particularly common are burns, and injuries involving the head and neck, hands, and the soft tissues in general. Included are facial lacerations and resulting scars; fractures of the facial bones and jaws; gunshot wounds of the face and soft tissues; dog bites; and injuries to the skin, bones, tendons, and nerves of the hand. Burns present special problems of fluid balance, wound coverage, nutrition, and the prevention and treatment of deformities produced by the scars resulting from burns. Thermal, electrical, and chemical burns are treated, as well as the latent damage to the skin and underlying tissues produced by X rays, radium, and other forms of ionizing radiation.

Physical irregularities include the conditions corrected by what is often called "cosmetic surgery." Examples are unattractive noses, protruding ears, redundant skin of the face, neck, and eyelids, tattoos, and excessively large or small breasts. These conditions do not usually represent a threat to the patient's physical health, but their psychological implications may have a serious effect on the individual's social adjustment. In modern society, unsightly facial features, especially in women, may interfere with the acquisition of a mate, acceptance into a group, or selection for a job. The presentation of a youthful appearance may be necessary for continuing success in acting, sales and public-relations work, and other fields involving personal contacts. Many patients can be afforded considerable improvement by plastic surgery. At times a small objective alteration can produce great subjective improvement.

In dealing with all his patients, the plastic surgeon must be aware of the limitations of surgery, and must be sure that the patient understands what can and cannot be accomplished. Consultation with other specialists, particularly the internist and the psychiatrist, is sometimes essential.

Techniques.—The basic objective in plastic surgery is to eliminate the pathologic condition and to restore the appearance and function of the involved area to as near normal as possible. Meticulous suturing together of the wound edges may be all that is required. In order to conceal the surgical scar, an effort is made to place it in, or at least parallel with, the lines or folds of the skin. When a scar lies counter to the folds, it can often be adjusted by means of a Z-plasty or W-plasty. The Z-plasty is an extremely useful technique by which the direction of a scar can be changed, length gained (at the expense of some width), tension relieved, and the recurrence of a contracture prevented. When a defect is too large to be closed by simple approximation of the wound edges, tissue must be brought in from an adjacent or distant site. The plastic surgeon must select from a variety of techniques the procedure or procedures that can be best utilized for the solution of each individual problem.

Tissue may be transplanted by a free graft or a pedicle flap.

A free graft is a piece of tissue completely cut loose from one area and transplanted to another area. An autograft is tissue transplanted from one area of an individual to another area of the same individual. A homograft (allograft) is tissue transplanted from one individual in a species to a different individual in the same species. An isograft is a graft between two individuals with the same genetic makeup, such as identical twins or two experimental animals of the same inbred strain. A heterograft is a transplant between two individuals of different species. The term zoögraft denotes the transplantation of tissue from a lower animal to a human being.

Tissues commonly transplanted as free grafts are skin, cartilage, bone, fat, and fascia. Barring complications, an autograft or an isograft can be expected to "take" and live permanently in its new location. A homograft or a heterograft survives only temporarily, however, and is eventually rejected by its host (see TRANSPLANTS, TISSUE AND ORGAN). In the case of skin, a free graft "takes" by means of fibrous connections and blood-vessel communications that develop between the graft and the recipient bed. Although blood flow is established between the graft and the host within a day or two, seven to ten days are required for the attachment to become secure.

Skin may be transplanted as a full- or a "split-" (partial-) thickness graft. A full-thickness graft consists of the entire epidermis and dermis. A split-thickness graft contains the entire epidermis, but only part of the dermis, and is removed from its original location (the donor site) by means of a freehand knife or a dermatome, which can be adjusted to cut a graft of any desired thickness. The thicker the graft, the less it tends to contract and the better it retains its colour and texture, but the greater the hazard to its "take." Whole-thickness grafts are particularly useful on the face to repair relatively small defects. Split-thickness grafts are more useful when larger areas need to be covered. For any free graft to "take," it must be placed on a recipient bed containing adequate blood vessels to nourish it.

Autografts are always preferred because they survive permanently. In the case of extensive loss of skin, however, such as occurs in severe burns, homografts or heterografts may be employed as "physiologic dressings" to provide temporary coverage of the wounds until the patient is able to withstand resurfacing with autografts.

A *pedicle flap* is a piece of tissue, usually skin and the attached subcutaneous fat, left partially attached to its original location during its transfer. Its attachment, or pedicle, contains the blood vessels that maintain the vitality of the tissues until such time as new vascular communications are established between the flap and the recipient bed. In most areas of the body, such new vascular connections are not adequate until two to three weeks have elapsed.

In many instances, the flap can be transferred in one stage. If there is inadequate flow of blood through the pedicle, however, the flap is simply resutured in its original position until the vessels have enlarged sufficiently to sustain the flap during transplantation. This stage of transfer is often called a "delay." Because pedicle flaps carry their blood supply with them, they are used to transplant thicker and bulkier tissue than can be transferred as a free graft. They are required when (1) the recipient site has a poor vascular bed; (2) bone, tendon, or cartilage must be covered, *e.g.*, in the hand; (3) a cavity must be closed, *e.g.*, reconstruction of the full thickness of the cheek; and (4) a thick pad of skin and fat must be provided, *e.g.*, repair of a pressure sore, or "decubitus ulcer."

Three of the more commonly used "local" flaps are: (a) advancement, where the tissue is freed, and advanced directly without angulation of its pedicle; (b) rotation, where the flap is swung through an arc into its new position; and (c) bipedicle, where two parallel incisions are made and the flap between the incisions is shifted laterally. When local tissue is inadequate for the construction of a flap, tissue can be transferred in stages from a distant site.

The two most commonly used "distant" flaps are: direct, or "jump," where the flap is sutured directly to its recipient site (*e.g.*, a flap from the chest to repair a defect of the hand) or is transferred via an intermediate "carrier," *e.g.*, abdomen to wrist to face; and tubed pedicle, the type popularized by Gillies, which is a closed fat-filled tube of skin, attached to the body only at the ends. It is transferred in stages by detaching one end and insetting it into the recipient area. The tubed pedicle has great versatility, al-

though its transplantation via several stages may be very time consuming. Wherever possible, the direct flap has come to be preferred to the tube. After the distant flap has developed adequate vascular communications with the recipient bed, the original pedicle can be divided.

Implants.—Over the years many foreign substances have been used subcutaneously for the restoration of contour. Most of these have failed to stand the test of time, because of absorption, chronic irritation and drainage, or spontaneous extrusion. Medical-grade silicone, an extremely inert substance, is usually well accepted by the body, and has found considerable favour for situations where a foreign implant has been required. Autogenous grafts of cartilage, bone, or dermis and fat are generally preferred, however, and foreign implants are used only where natural tissues are inadequate to produce the desired result.

Research.—Plastic surgeons have made significant contributions to the solution of many basic problems in surgery. Some of the subjects that have received particular attention are: wound healing; transplantation of tissues and organs; embryology and teratogenesis; physiology of skin, cartilage, and bone; fluid balance and nutrition, particularly in burns; surgical bacteriology; microsurgical techniques for the repair of minute nerves and blood vessels; cellular biology, especially with relation to cancer; and anatomy and musculoskeletal dynamics in the hand.

The Specialty of Plastic Surgery.—Although many of the techniques of plastic surgery are employed by specialists in other surgical fields, surgeons who devote their full time to this type of surgery in the United States usually obtain certification by the American Board of Plastic Surgery. To be eligible for examinations by this board, the candidate must have graduated from an approved medical school, served a year's internship, served at least three years of residency training in general surgery, and at least two years of additional residency in plastic surgery. He must have spent at least two years in the practice of plastic surgery after completion of his formal training. By the late 1960s, about 900 plastic surgeons had received certification by the board.

BIBLIOGRAPHY.—M. T. Gnudi and J. P. Webster, *The Life and Times of Gaspare Tagliocozzi* (1950); J. S. Davis, *Plastic Surgery* (1919); H. D. Gillies, *Plastic Surgery of the Face* (1920); H. D. Gillies and D. R. Millard, Jr., *The Principles and Art of Plastic Surgery* (1957); R. B. Stark, *Plastic Surgery* (1962); H. Conway and R. B. Stark, *Plastic Surgery at the New York Hospital 100 Years Ago* (1953); W. C. Grabb and J. W. Smith (eds.), *Plastic Surgery: a Concise Guide to Clinical Practice* (1968); I. A. McGregor, *Fundamental Techniques of Plastic Surgery*, 4th ed. (1968); J. M. Converse (ed.), *Reconstructive Plastic Surgery*, 5 vol. (1964); E. C. Padgett, *Skin Grafting* (1942); J. B. Brown and F. McDowell, *Skin Grafting* (1958); H. Conway, N. E. Hugo, and J. F. Tulenko, *The Surgery of Tumors of the Skin*, 2nd ed. (1966); R. H. Ivy, *A Link with the Past* (1962).   (B. H. GR.)

PLATA, RÍO DE LA (PLATE RIVER), has two meanings: in the most limited sense, it is a broad estuary, approximately 171 mi. (275 km.) long, located between Argentina and Uruguay and flowing southeast into the South Atlantic; in a more comprehensive sense, it is the mouth of an enormous drainage basin which includes the Paraguay, Paraná and Uruguay rivers and numerous smaller rivers and streams. This basin drains the southern portion of South America, as the Orinoco and Amazon drain the northern. The area covered, 1,679,535 sq.mi. (4,350,000 sq.km.), includes the whole of Paraguay, southeastern Bolivia, most of Uruguay and large portions of Brazil and Argentina, thereby ranking this river system fourth in the world by size. The rate of discharge, however, estimated at 2,800,000 cu.ft. per second, makes this system second only to the Amazon in volume.

The Estuary.—At its upper extremity, where this estuary receives the waters from the great river systems of the Paraná and the Uruguay, the width is 19 mi. The Argentine island of Martín García is located near this extremity and provides a control point for navigation. The estuary gradually widens to 63 mi. (101 km.) at Montevideo and then fans out to 140 mi. (225 km.) at its mouth. Despite the enormous amount of water discharged into the ocean, the Río de la Plata is relatively shallow. The depth of the main channel above Montevideo is 36 ft. The average depth outside the main channel is 10 to 20 ft. Seasonal rates of flow, winds and tide have a considerable effect on the depth. Constant dredging is necessary to keep a 20 mi. side channel, 31 ft. deep, open to the port of Buenos Aires, and to clear other parts of the main channel. Consequently, ships, after entering the Río de la Plata, are restricted to prescribed courses. The bottom is composed of sand and silt. The expanse of low plain or pampas on the southern or Argentine side permits violent winds, known as *pamperos,* to build up and whip the waters of the estuary into violent storms at certain times of the year.

Upper Paraná and Affluents.—The Paraná, meaning "mother of the sea" in the Guarani language, is the larger and more important of the two river systems which flow into the Río de la Plata estuary. About 1,400 mi. of its estimated 2,796 mi. (4,500 km.) length is above its juncture with the Paraguay river and is known as the Upper Paraná (Alto Paraná). The Paraná is formed by the union of the Paranaíba and Grande rivers at 20° S., these two rivers having traced the western and southern borders of the state of Minas Gerais, Brazil, in their previous course. The Paranaíba originates a few miles from the headwaters of the São Francisco river, but flows in the opposite direction, at first west and then southwest. By the time it joins the Grande it has already received eight sizable tributaries. The Grande originates in the Serra da Mantiqueira, almost within sight of Rio de Janeiro, Braz., and descends in many falls and rapids for about 845 mi. (1,360 km.) to its juncture with the Paranaíba.

A number of Brazilian rivers from the states of Mato Grosso, São Paulo and Paraná empty into the Paraná as it flows generally southwest. Most of these tributaries, such as the Sucuriú, Verde, Pardo, Ivinheima, Amambaí and Iquatemí on the west and the Tietê, rising within the vicinity of the city of São Paulo, the Peixe, Ivaí, Piquiri on the east, are navigable only for short stretches by canoes or small launches and are broken by frequent waterfalls and rapids. The largest of the eastern tributaries is the Paranapanema, which descends 559 mi. (900 km.) from the Serra do Paranapiacaba overlooking the Atlantic ocean.

Small river boats can navigate the upper reaches of the Paraná river in Brazil for 400 mi. between the falls of the Urubupungá and the falls of Guairá (or Sete Quedas). At this latter point, the river has torn a 2-mi. gorge through the red sandstone of the Serra de Maracaju (Serra do Mbaracayú). The result is a stupendous although not well-known sight. The river, which widens to a 3-mi. lagoon, suddenly becomes constricted between canyon walls only 300 ft. apart. As a result the water boils in deafening crescendo, which can be heard for 20 mi., through several channels and some 18 cataracts in a total descent of approximately 300 ft. There the Paraná becomes an international boundary and serves to divide Brazil and Paraguay for a distance of 130 mi. until joined by the Iguaçu (Iguassú) river.

Iguaçu.—This river, the most spectacular of the Paraná's affluents, also rises in the Brazilian coastal range, the Serra do Mar, and flows nearly directly west for 430 mi. For its last 75 mi. it divides the Argentine province of Misiones from Brazil. About 15 mi. before it joins the Paraná, the river plunges over an escarpment, which is 2½ mi. in width. The resultant cataracts are among the most famous falls in the world, often compared with the Niagara or the Victoria on the Zambezi. Although most of the escarpment is broken into two descents of approximately 100 ft. each, one mass of water roars 269 ft. down the Garganta del Diablo or Devil's Throat. As many as 275 separate waterfalls have been counted in the dry season, while at flood stage the volume exceeds that of Niagara. (*See* IGUAÇU.)

From the mouth of the Iguaçu to the juncture with the Paraguay, 420 mi. farther on, the Paraná serves as the boundary between Paraguay and Argentina. There are no important tributaries which join the river in this stretch. Near the capital of the province of Misiones, Posadas, 27° 22′ S., the Paraná turns westward. The relatively narrow river, 1,500 ft. in width, has cut several channels between high rocky banks, creating large islands in its course, such as Yaciretá, Apipé Grande and Apipé Chica, and Talavera. The current in these channels is strong and the passage is made difficult by rapids such as those of the Apipé. Shortly after these rapids, however, the Paraná escapes from its red sandstone bed, and its flow becomes more leisurely as the river widens.

The banks of the river are lower and the bottom is sandy.

Paraguay.—This main affluent of the Paraná is 1,584 mi. (2,549 km.) long. It rises in the Brazilian state of Mato Grosso, near the town of Diamantino, 14° 24′ S., not far from the headwaters of the Tapajós and the Xingu, tributaries of the Amazon. It flows first southwest and then south into the morass of Xarayes, which expands into still vaster swamps as the river grows in size. Few streams feed the Paraguay from the west with the exception of the Jauru. There are, however, a number of large shallow lakes to the west of the Paraguay which receive overflow from the morass of Xarayes. Several important affluents swell the Paraguay from the east and drain a vast area of Mato Grosso. These Brazilian rivers, north to south, are the Cuiabá and São Lorenzo, the Taquari, Miranda and Apa, the last serving as a boundary between Mato Grosso and northern Paraguay. In this northern area, the Paraguay is a shallow, sluggish river. During the rainy season, it spreads out for hundreds of miles from each bank, turning the vast swampland between 17° and 20° S. into great lakes. In this Corumbá territory of Brazil, as much as 30,000 sq.mi. (77,700 sq.km.) have been inundated.

South of the mouth of the Apa river, the Paraguay flows through Paraguayan territory. On the west, the vast Chaco jungle and morass is only imperfectly drained by the Pilcomayo and Bermejo rivers and by innumerable smaller streams. Much of the east bank of the Paraguay, in particular the lowland between Concepción and Asunción, is also subject to seasonal flooding. About 250 mi. south of Asunción, the Paraguay merges its slow-moving mass (140 ft. above sea level) with the Paraná river.

Pilcomayo, Bermejo and Salado.—These three rivers, north to south, rise in the Andes and flow southeast in parallel courses. The Pilcomayo, "river of the birds" in Guarani language, descends from its source north of Potosí, Bolivia, 8,000 ft. in 350 mi. to the Chaco plains. The course of the river then loses itself in the Chaco morass and finally wanders in three separate branches to its juncture with the Paraguay opposite Asunción. The main channel, such as it is, marks the boundary between Argentina and Paraguay.

The Bermejo rises on the Bolivian-Argentine frontier. After a rapid plunge to the Chaco lowlands, the river flows in a sinuous course around islands and sandbars which make any estimate of depth meaningless. The current is stronger than that of the Pilcomayo. Much silt is carried in suspension thus originating its name to describe the reddish colour. It has been estimated that this river alone carries off 6,400,000 cu.yd. of soil from the Chaco each year.

The Salado is formed by several rivers which drain the Argentine province of Salta and emerge on the Chaco lowlands. Like the Pilcomayo and Bermejo, the Salado follows no prescribed channel but wanders in a braided pattern across the countryside, particularly at floodtime. The Indian use of such alluvial croplands has been imitated by settlers growing maize, wheat, flax and cotton, although permanent or continuous use of the land is, at best, difficult when irrigated only by such annual floods.

Lower Paraná.—After its juncture with the Paraguay, the Paraná flows slightly southwest until it reaches the city of Santa Fe and is joined by the Salado river. Then it curves in a gradual arc until at Rosario it is flowing southeast to join the Río de la Plata. The Lower Paraná is entirely within Argentine territory, passing through some of the richest agricultural land in the world. On the east lie the pastoral provinces of Corrientes and Entre Ríos, while on the west is the breadbasket of Santa Fe and northern Buenos Aires.

The Paraná becomes a truly imposing river after it joins forces with the Paraguay. Even at low water, its 800-mi. course to the Río de la Plata is from 2 to 4 mi. wide. Unlike the clear waters of its Brazilian sources, however, it is now tremendously burdened with silt. The Paraguay brings soil from Mato Grosso, while the Pilcomayo, Bermejo and Salado, eating away at the Andes, add tons of alluvium. The western bank of the lower Paraná is a high bluff of red clay rising 25–75 ft. above the river level and is constantly undermined by the current.

The amounts of silt lend themselves to a building as well as a tearing away process. Unlike the high rocky islands of the Upper Paraná, the Lower Paraná is dotted with large, low, often forested islands. During flood season, however, the Paraná may widen to 10 mi. and, in places, even 30 mi., burying islands and overflowing into marginal swamps. The periodic floods as well as the seasonal rise and fall of the water level naturally wreak havoc with islands and channels. Below Rosario, the islands and the main channel are more stable, because the total rise, even of flood waters, is distributed over a wider area and consequently is not as great. The mouth of the Paraná river or the head of the Río de la Plata estuary, until a recent geological period, must have been located much farther inland, perhaps as far as 32° S., near the present town of Diamante in Entre Ríos. Subsequently, silt has built up island structures from the sandy bottom. The clustering of these islands forms a huge delta, 40 mi. wide and 100 mi. long, at the mouth of the Paraná.

The lower Paraná finds its way through the Paraná delta in 11 outlets and several canals. The two principal channels which are used by ocean vessels are the Paraná Bravo with a depth of 36 ft. and the Paraná Guazú with a depth of 20 ft. The depths of the other channels and connecting canals used by coasting craft vary greatly but are announced periodically. Constant dredging is naturally required to keep these channels open for navigation.

Uruguay and Its Affluents.—This is the second major system, 932 mi. (1,500 km.) in length, which flows into the Río de la Plata. Like the Upper Paraná and the Paraguay, the Uruguay originates in Brazil, formed by several small streams which rise on the western slopes of the Serra do Mar, at 27° 09′ S. From the south it is joined by the Pelotas, the two rivers serving to divide the states of Rio Grande do Sul and Santa Catarina. After flowing west, the Uruguay turns southwest at its juncture with the Peperi Guaçu, the first sizable affluent to join it from the north. For most of its course, the fast flowing Peperi Guaçu marks the boundary between the Argentine province of Misiones and Brazil. Now the Uruguay serves to divide Brazil and Argentina. A few miles beyond the juncture with the Peperi Guaçu, the river is constricted between rocky walls in the Salto Grande de Misiones, a 2 mi. stretch of rapids with a total descent of 26 ft. in 8 mi. At the cataracts, the river narrows suddenly from 1,500 ft. to an extreme of 70 ft.

Several small rivers join the Uruguay from the west and are navigable in their lower reaches by canoes and small boats. The principal of these, from north to south, are the Aguaypey, Mirinay, Mocoretá, which divides Entre Ríos and Corrientes, and Gualeguaychú. The important affluents of the Uruguay, however, come from the east. The Ijuí, Ibicuí and the Quaraí (Guareim) are short rivers but of considerable volume; the last forms part of the boundary between Brazil and Uruguay. At the mouth of the Quaraí, the Uruguay becomes the boundary line between Argentina and Uruguay, and the river flows almost directly south. The Negro river, 434 mi. (699 km.) long and the Uruguay's largest tributary, joins the latter only 60 mi. from the estuary of the Río de la Plata. The Negro rises on the Brazilian border in Rio Grande do Sul and flows westward through the middle of the Republic of Uruguay. Sizable river craft can reach Mercedes, 32 mi. from its mouth. Like the Upper Paraná, the Uruguay is generally clear and carries little silt except in the seasonal floods. After its juncture with the Negro, the Uruguay broadens sharply to a width of 4 to 6 mi., and becomes a virtual extension of the Río de la Plata estuary.

Navigation and Economic Importance.—The economic usefulness of these river systems is not commensurate with the area which they drain. A principal problem is that of navigation. A large portion of the rivers cannot be used at all or only by very shallow draught vessels. Elsewhere navigation can only be maintained by constant dredging and renovation of port facilities. The other economic uses to which these rivers might lend themselves, such as irrigation or hydroelectric power, are equally difficult to achieve. The swamps of Xarayes and the Chaco make agriculture a virtual impossibility in these areas, while under present conditions the potential electric power represented by the falls of Guairá or Iguaçu is too remote from any centres to be harnessed.

Buenos Aires is one of the principal seaports of the world and the main port of Argentina. Vessels approach it from the main estuary channel by one of two side channels which are clearly marked and dredged to depths of 31 ft. Ocean vessels can travel up the Paraná river as far as Santa Fe or Paraná. The channel depth from the mouth of the Paraná to Rosario is dredged to 21 ft., from Rosario to Paraná to 19 ft. Ocean trade can also reach Concepción del Uruguay directly by the Uruguay river where the dredged depth of the channel is 19 ft.

Commerce farther upstream on these river systems operates under conditions which fluctuate considerably. Passage of vessels depends to a large extent on seasonal variations in depth. A 6-ft. depth is assured from Paraná to Corrientes and usually to Posada, although vessels of deeper draught can often pass. Long fleets of barges carry the bulk of the river freight. The current, narrowness, and curves above Corrientes on the Upper Paraná, however, rule out such barge transport. Several rapids on the Upper Paraná can only be passed with the use of winches to pull the vessels. Narrowness of the river, whirlpools and the increased speed of the current to 5 m.p.h. make navigation more dangerous as the mouth of the Iguaçu is approached. The absolute head of navigation is located at Pôrto Mendes below the Guairá falls in Brazil. A railroad, 38 mi. long, circumvents the falls to the town of Guairá, and opens up another 400 mi. of navigable river farther up the Paraná. Beyond, stretches of the Paraná and of tributaries are navigable only by launches and canoes.

On the Paraguay river, vessels drawing 7 ft. and displacing 2,000 tons are able to reach Corumbá in Brazil at all seasons. The most traveled stretch of this river is the 250 mi. from Corrientes to Asunción which is accessible to vessels of 10 ft. draught. Although Corumbá is considered as the head of navigation on the Paraguay, the Bolivian town of Puerto Suárez, 10 mi. away, was built to provide this landlocked nation with a port. Vessels can reach it from Corumbá during the flood season, March to Sept., but its canton population of 3,279 (1962 est.) indicates that it is hardly a major commercial centre.

Some ocean vessels with a draught of 15 ft. can go 25 mi. beyond Concepción del Uruguay on the Uruguay river to Fábrica Colón. A 9 ft. depth is assured as far as Concordia and 6 ft. as far as Salto. Ships of deeper draught reach these river ports in flood time. Above Salto, there are few ports and no measurement of depths is taken. A considerable commerce and movement, however, is carried on by small launches, rafts and canoes.

Navigation of the Pilcomayo, Bermejo and Salado is negligible, because of shifting channels, sandbars and shallowness. Vessels of 3 ft. draught can ascend the Pilcomayo for the first 120 mi. to Fontana, although in a straight line this means only 45 mi. Barges and motorboats on the Bermejo reach Presidencia Rosa, 160 mi. from the mouth, on a regular schedule, although the depth in the shallows is reduced to 2 ft. in the dry season. During high water, November to April, small vessels can ascend the Bermejo 400 mi. from its mouth. Only very shallow draught vessels can use stretches of the Salado.

The value of these river systems as a commercial artery is, therefore, concentrated on the lower reaches. A large volume of ocean shipping reaches Rosario and Concepción del Uruguay, although the major seaports are Buenos Aires and Montevideo. The great bulk of river transport is concentrated within the limits of Asunción on the Paraguay, Corrientes on the Paraná, and Salto on the Uruguay. The Argentine Flota Fluvial del Estado, the Lloyd Brasileiro and the Compañía Uruguaya de Navegación, however, provide regular passenger and freight service to all navigable parts of these river systems. Rafts, canoes and motorboats provide irregular although important service on the tributaries and upper reaches of these rivers.

A lack of population, remoteness of markets and difficulty of transport are partial reasons for the failure to develop other uses from these river systems. Seasonal rainfall with consequent flooding of large areas may provide a very crude basis for agriculture along the Salado, but it prevents agriculture in vast areas of the Chaco and Mato Grosso. The same remoteness has prevented any effective harnessing of the rivers' power. One exception is the headwaters of the Tieté which, pumped across an intervening range, provide water for a hydroelectric plant near São Paulo.

History.—The Río de la Plata was discovered by Juan Díaz de Solís, chief navigator of Spain, in 1516, as a result of efforts to find a route to the Pacific. The estuary was temporarily named in his memory after his death on its shores at the hands of un-friendly Charrua Indians. Magellan touched at the estuary in 1520 during his circumnavigation of the globe. In 1526, Sebastian Cabot ascended the rivers as far as the present city of Asunción and obtained silver trinkets in barter with the Guaraní Indians. Spanish dreams gave the estuary its permanent name, Río de la Plata, in the hope that it might indeed become a river of silver. The major Spanish expedition which settled near the present location of Buenos Aires in 1536 under Pedro de Mendoza proved a fiasco. After much misfortune the survivors moved up-stream to the surroundings of the more docile Guaraní Indians at Asunción. Buenos Aires was not refounded until 1580, and throughout the Spanish colonial era, the Río de la Plata remained a backwash of the empire. The estuary was virtually closed to legal commerce until the end of the 18th century. Spain only renewed its interest in the area when Portuguese and English ambitions threatened to expand into the Río de la Plata in the 1760s.

Navigation of the river systems became a problem when the national states of Argentina, Uruguay, Paraguay, Brazil and Bolivia emerged on its courses. Territorial conflicts and restrictions on navigation caused several wars, culminating in the titanic struggle by Francisco Solano López's Paraguay against Brazil, Uruguay and Argentina from 1864 to 1870. In the 20th century, similar conflicts sharpened by rumoured oil wealth resulted in the Chaco war between Paraguay and Bolivia.

The development of agricultural wealth, particularly in Argentina, resulted in greater appreciation of the commercial value of these river systems after the mid-19th century. Wheat, beef, wool and hides entered the river and world trade in increasing quantities from Argentina and Uruguay, while from Brazil and Paraguay came forest and tropical products and *yerba mate* or Paraguayan tea. Port construction and dredging made Buenos Aires more valuable as a seaport, and by 1902 similar improvements had been completed at Rosario. Marking of channels, soundings, dredging and other aids to navigation became a responsibility of all the riparian states. *See also* SOUTH AMERICA; BRAZIL; ARGENTINA; PARAGUAY; URUGUAY.   (Js. R. S.)

PLATAEA, an ancient city of Boeotia, Greece, was situated on a triangular ledge 1,000 ft. above sea level, on the north side of Mt. Cithaeron below the modern village of Plataiai; there are remains of ancient walls, and a temple of Hera has been excavated. Strong springs near the city flow into the valley of the Asopus River, which marked the ancient boundary with the territory of Thebes. The city was important in time of war because it was able to threaten the main road from Thebes through Megaris to the Isthmus of Corinth which passed east of Plataea over Mt. Cithaeron.   (N. G. L. H.; X.)

PLATEAU INDIANS constituted a major culture of aboriginal North America. The culture area corresponded roughly to the plateau between the Rocky Mountains on the east and the Cascade Mountains (U.S.) and the Coast Range (Canada) on the west. The northern boundary was approximately the great bend of the Fraser River in northern British Columbia (*q.v.*); the southern limit on the west was near the present California-Oregon boundary and on the east it was the Blue Mountains. The essential cultural uniformity in the Plateau existed despite the geographic contrasts of vast rolling treeless areas, dense forests, and perpetually snow-covered mountains.

Kinship (*q.v.*) was bilateral throughout the Plateau; polygyny (*q.v.*) was permitted but rare; such voluntary associations as clubs were absent. However, linguistic differences were great, many mutually unintelligible languages being spoken. The major linguistic stocks (from north to south) with representative tribes were: Athapaskan (*q.v.*; Sekani, Carrier, Chilcotin); Interior Salish (*see* SALISHAN; Shuswap, Lillooet, Thompson, Lake, Wenatchi, South Okanagon, Sanpoil, Kalispel, Flathead, Coeur d'Alene, Spokan, Columbia); Sahaptin (*q.v.*; Kittitas, Yakima, Klikitat, Wanapam, Umatilla, Cayuse, Nez Percé); and Upper Chinook (*q.v.*; Wishram, Wasco). *See also* KUTENAI.

Highly diversified tribal economies depended on fish, game, and wild plants. Agriculture was not known, and, except for dogs, there were no domestic animals. The taking of salmon was a prime pursuit except at elevations where waterfalls barred migrating fish. The area is drained primarily by two great systems, the Fraser and the Columbia (world's greatest salmon-producing river). Even tribes on the interior deserts had a regular salmon supply. These and other fish (fresh, or dried for winter) sometimes supplied almost half the tribal subsistence. Deer, elk, and antelope were the principal game; camas, bitterroot, and kause (cous) the main plant foods.

The main dwellings were a semisubterranean lodge used only for winter, and a gabled mat-covered house. The lodge was generally round with a low conical roof of radiating poles covered with mats and earth. The house, a framework of light poles covered with sewn mats of tule or cattail reeds, had a steep roof that sloped to the ground, the ridge being open to release smoke. These light, airy, waterproof and windproof structures were sometimes nearly 100 ft. long. With villages commonly on waterways, dugouts and bark canoes were widely used.

Full body dress of finely dressed skins, with supplementary woven or sewed bast fabrics, was characteristic for both sexes. Decoration of beads and embroidery was often elaborate, but facial and body painting was used sparingly.

While the material accomplishments of Plateau Indians were modest, their ideological and political achievements are impressive. Concepts of democracy, equality, and pacifism dominated thought and action. In aboriginal times war was virtually unknown; slavery was rare or absent. Religion was paramount and the unique American Indian guardian spirit concept reached its highest degree of development in this area. Shamans of both sexes were important and respected religious, social, and intellectual leaders (*see* SHAMANISM).

In what is now the northeastern part of the state of Washington the primary political unit was the village; the tribe was largely an aggregation with a sense of cultural unity that led to recognition of common leadership. Among the Sahaptin a strong tribal system of government put heavy emphasis on chieftainship; chiefly families married intertribally. The Wanapam (Oregon) developed the concept of capital villages and evolved a representative government with a precise hierarchy of village and tribal chiefs. The remarkable Columbia Confederacy (central Washington) embraced the Columbia, Entiat, Wenatchi, and Chelan tribes, with Chief Moses, the most gifted Indian leader of the Northwest, as its notable head. A similar confederation later united the Yakima, Kittitas, Wanapam, Klikitat, and Palouse (Palus) tribes, with Chief Kamaiakan as their greatest leader. Chief Joseph, leader of the Nez Percé in their war with the U.S., was another noted Plateau chief.

See also CANADA: *Native Peoples;* CAYUSE; COEUR D'ALENE; FLATHEAD; NEZ PERCÉ.

BIBLIOGRAPHY.—J. A. Teit, *The Salishan Tribes of the Western Plateaus* (1930); V. F. Ray, *The Sanpoil and Nespelem* (1933), *Cultural Relations in the Plateau of Northwestern America* (1939).   (V. F. R.)

PLATEN-HALLERMÜNDE, AUGUST, GRAF VON (1796–1835), German poet and dramatist who opposed romanticism and in his own work aimed at classical purity of style, was born Oct. 24, 1796, at Ansbach. He entered the Bavarian life guards in 1814, and took part in the campaign in France in 1815. After a tour in Switzerland and the Bavarian Alps, he entered the University of Würzburg in 1818 as a student of philosophy and philology.

In 1819 he moved to Erlangen, where he studied under the philosopher of romanticism, F. W. von Schelling, and made the acquaintance of Jean Paul, Jacob Grimm, the oriental scholar and poet Friedrich Rückert, Goethe and Ludwig Uhland. He became a first-rate scholar and as a result of his oriental studies he published a little volume of poems, *Ghaselen* (1821), in which he imitated the style of Rückert. This was followed by *Lyrische*

Blätter (1821), *Spiegel der Hafis* (1822), *Vermischte Schriften* (1822) and *Neue Ghaselen* (1823).

Though Platen was at first influenced as a dramatist by the romantics and particularly by Spanish models, the plays he wrote while at Erlangen (*Der gläserne Pantoffel, Der Schatz des Rhampsinit, Berengar, Treue um Treue, Der Turm mit sieben Pforten*) show a clearness of plot and expression foreign to the romantic style. His antagonism to romanticism became more pronounced, and he attacked its extravagances, particularly the *Schicksaldrama,* or fate drama, in the witty "Aristophanic" comedies *Die verhängnisvolle Gabel* (1826) and *Der romantische Oedipus* (1829). *Der romantische Oedipus* earned him the enmity of Karl Immermann, whose work was ridiculed in it, and of Heinrich Heine, a close friend of Immermann, but he had many admirers, who delighted in the classical purity of his plays and their polished form and diction. After 1826 he lived in Italy, and his last play, *Die Liga von Cambrai* (1833), and the epic fairy tale *Die Abbassiden* (1834), were written at Naples. He died at Syracuse, Dec. 5, 1835. Platen's odes and sonnets, and his *Polenlieder* (1831) expressing sympathy for the Poles in their rising against the tsar's rule, are among the best classical poems of their time.

Platen's *Gesammelte Werke* were published in one volume in 1839. There is a critical edition in 12 vol. by M. Koch and E. Petzet (1910). His *Tagebücher* (1813–35) were edited by G. von Laubmann and L. von Scheffler, 2 vol. (1896–1900); his correspondence by L. von Scheffler and P. Bornstein, 4 vol. (1911–31).

See R. Schlösser, *August Graf von Platen,* 2 vol. (1910–13); F. Redenbacher, *Platen-Bibliographie* (1926).   (A. Gs.)

PLATERESQUE, the earliest of Spanish Renaissance styles, so called either because the Renaissance found its first popular Spanish expression in silverware (*platero,* "silversmith") or because its rich and delicate ornament resembled silversmith work. *See* RENAISSANCE ART AND ARCHITECTURE.

PLATFORM TENNIS is a combination of tennis and squash invented in 1928 by Fessenden Blanchard and James Cogswell at Scarsdale, N.Y. It is played on specially constructed 60 × 30 ft. wooden platforms surrounded by back and side stops of tightly strung wire netting 12 ft. high. The actual court measures 44 × 20 ft., and the net is 2 ft. 10 in. at centre. The paddles, or bats, used instead of rackets, are oval plywood, metal bound and perforated, and have short handles. Balls are made of sponge rubber. The rules are the same as for tennis, except that balls may be taken off the back or side stops, after first striking inside the proper court, and only one serve is allowed.   (F. S. BD.)

PLATINUM is a chemical element which is a very heavy precious silver-white metal. It is the best known and most widely used of the six platinum metals. (*See* PLATINUM METALS and the articles on individual elements, IRIDIUM, OSMIUM, PALLADIUM, RHODIUM and RUTHENIUM.) The chemical symbol for platinum is Pt, atomic number 78 and atomic weight 195.09. The usefulness of this metal is due to its resistance to corrosion or chemical attack and to its high melting point of 1,769° C. For example, when brought to a white heat in air, it retains its bright surface. It is scarcely attacked by simple acids but does dissolve readily in aqua regia (HCl;HNO_3). With such a high melting point platinum is not easily fused or cast. In the fabrication of the metal a sponge is commonly made by decomposition of its compounds. The sponge can be hammered and welded at a white heat into massive sheets and various objects. The massive metal has the very high specific gravity of 21.46. However, it is soft and ductile, and thereby unsuited for many purposes. Small amounts of iridium are commonly added to give a harder, stronger alloy which retains the advantages of the platinum. The boiling point of platinum is estimated to be 4,500° C., but the loss of weight of the solid by volatilization above 1,000° C. is very gradual but detectable.

Platinum did not receive general recognition in ancient times. Large deposits as heavy river sands were uncovered in the 16th-century Spanish conquest of South America. The Spaniards called the new metal *Platina del Pinto* after the Río Pinto, from which its present name was taken. Samples of the element received the general attention of European scientists in the latter 18th century. Platinum occurs in native alloys which frequently contain smaller amounts of other platinum metals. It is recovered as a by-product in a number of metallurgical operations for the production of copper, nickel, lead and other metals.

Uses.—Platinum and its alloys are indispensable in the chemical laboratory for crucibles and dishes in which materials can be heated to high temperatures. However, some caution must be used, for it is attacked and alloyed by carbon, phosphorus, silicon and some low-melting metals such as lead, arsenic and antimony. It also alloys readily with other platinum metals and with copper, gold and silver. Caustic alkalies at high temperature must be avoided, although alkali carbonates may be fused in platinum ware.

Platinum is used in the preparation of electrical contacts and sparking points because it resists the high temperature and chemical attack of electric arcs. The manufacture of jewelry and dental alloys consumes large amounts of the metal. The prototype international standard metre of length and standard kilogram of mass together with several national copies have been made from the alloy, 90% platinum and 10% iridium. Fine laboratory weights are frequently electroplated with platinum. Platinum electrodes are used in the important electrolytic preparation of hydrogen peroxide, strongly oxidizing salts and acids which corrode other metals. Electrodes of platinum also serve for quantitative electroplating operations in chemical analyses.

The electrical resistance and its temperature coefficient for platinum are relatively high for a metal, and the resistance of coils of exceptionally pure platinum wire therefore gives a precise measure of temperature. The international temperature scale from − 190° C. to 660° C. is defined in terms of such a platinum resistance thermometer. At higher temperatures, from 660° C. to 1,063° C. (the melting point of gold), the international temperature scale is defined by the electromotive force of a thermocouple with a wire of pure platinum against another of the alloy, 90% platinum and 10% rhodium. The coefficient of thermal expansion of platinum is low for a metal and near to those of soft glasses, so that thin electrical leads of the metal can be conveniently sealed through glass walls.

Platinum metal surfaces are exceptionally good catalysts for many chemical reactions, especially for reactions which involve the gases hydrogen or oxygen. For this purpose thin deposits of the metal may be formed on an inert supporting material, or fine gauze may be utilized. Also, very finely divided platinum black can be prepared by the reduction of solutions of its compounds or may be deposited by electrolysis on platinum sheet. Large quantities of platinum, which were used to catalyze the oxidation of sulfur dioxide in the manufacture of sulfuric acid, have been mostly replaced by vanadium oxide and other materials; but platinum gauzes serve as catalyst when ammonia is burned in air to yield nitric oxide in the manufacture of nitric acid. Vapours of hydrocarbons or alcohols in air ignite spontaneously, sometimes explosively, on these surfaces. The platinum catalysts can be used in the laboratory for hydrogenation or reduction of organic compounds. The catalytic properties of a platinum-black electrode allows the reversible oxidation of hydrogen gas, and the resultant hydrogen electrode serves as the standard reference electrode for potentials in electrochemistry. Bright platinum wires in ionic solutions function as reversible electrodes for a number of oxidation-reduction systems.

Platinum Compounds.—Platinum forms important series of compounds with the oxidation states of + 2 and + 4. Many of these compounds contain co-ordination complexes in which chloride, ammonia or other groups are bonded covalently to a central platinum atom. There are bonds from a platinum atom to six groups arranged symmetrically around it toward the corners of an octahedron for the + 4 state. For compounds of + 2 platinum, four bonds are commonly directed toward the corners of a square, a geometrical arrangement which can occur in chemical systems only under special circumstances of electronic configuration. Complexes of both oxidation states are kinetically inert in that groups are replaced slowly. The preparation of numerous isomers (complex compounds with the same composition, for example, Peyrone's chloride, cis-[Pt(NH₃)₂Cl₂], Reiset's second chloride, trans-[Pt(NH₃)₂Cl₂], and Magnus' green salt, [Pt(NH₃)₄]-[PtCl₄]), provided an important stimulus to the evolution of theories concerning structural arrangements of atoms (stereochemistry). All the compounds of platinum are readily decomposed or reduced to the metal. Many of their aqueous solutions decompose with an appreciable rate below boiling temperature.

When platinum dissolves in aqua regia, hexachloroplatinic (IV) acid, H_2PtCl_6, is formed. The slightly soluble yellow potassium and ammonium hexachloroplatinate (IV) are readily precipitated and are useful in analysis. Pure sponge metal is usually prepared by ignition of $(NH_4)_2PtCl_6$. Heated with sodium hydroxide, hexachloroplatinic (IV) acid gives soluble $Na_2Pt(OH)_6$ which yields yellow hydrous hydroxide when neutralized with weak acid. The hydroxide can be dehydrated to give black PtO_2. Electrolysis of the alkaline solutions gives a hydrous oxide corresponding to a higher oxidation state. Hydrates of hexachloroplatinic (IV) acid can be crystallized; and if the crystals are heated to 300° C. in an atmosphere of chlorine, a reddish-brown $PtCl_4$ is formed.

$PtCl_4$, heated to above 360° C., yields a green-brown platinum (II) chloride, $PtCl_2$, which is insoluble in water but dissolves very slowly in HCl solutions to give the red solution of tetrachloroplatinic (II) acid, H_2PtCl_4. This acid is readily prepared by the reduction of H_2PtCl_6 with sulfur dioxide. When alkali is added to a solution of a tetrachloroplatinate (II), a hydrous black platinum (II) hydroxide is precipitated. It can be dehydrated to gray PtO with some decomposition to metal. Hydrogen sulfide precipitates a black sulfide, PtS.

See also references under "Platinum" in the Index.

(D. S. Mⁿ.)

PLATINUM METALS are a group of six chemical elements, including platinum, which are generally found together in nature with varying proportions in the metallic form. The elements are listed in the accompanying table together with their important atomic and physical properties.

(See also IRIDIUM; OSMIUM; PALLADIUM; PLATINUM; RHODIUM; RUTHENIUM.)

The group is naturally divided into light and heavy triads of three elements each. For each light element there is a heavy element whose atomic number is greater by 32. The two elements in each such pair belong to the same family of the periodic table of elements so that three families are represented. As is normally the case, elements of the same family have strikingly similar chemical and physical properties. Although some similarities are noted among the entire group, there are wide differences in the chemical behaviour between different families. The six platinum metals are included together with iron, cobalt and nickel as Group VIII of the periodic table of elements.

Each of the individual elements is a silver-white metal. Although none melt below a white heat, there is still a wide range in the melting points. With such high melting points they are difficult to fuse or cast. Their boiling points can only be estimated roughly from extrapolations of vapour pressure measurements. The specific gravities of the light triad fall in the narrow range of 12.0–12.5; the heavy triad are exceptionally dense.

Osmium and iridium are the densest terrestrial materials known. The most accurate evaluations of density are based upon the spacings of the atoms as determined by X-ray diffraction. From the best values of these spacings available, osmium appears to be slightly the more dense; however, the difference in density is scarcely larger than the experimental uncertainty. Platinum and palladium are soft, duc-

tile and easily worked; the other members are hard and difficult to work in the cold. However, iridium and rhodium can be worked at a white heat. An important common property of the group is the instability of their chemical compounds, which are readily decomposed or reduced to yield the free elements in the form of a metal sponge or powder. Chemists accordingly classify all members of the group as noble metals.

History and Occurrence.—None of the platinum metals received widespread recognition in ancient times, although artifacts containing platinum have been uncovered occasionally by archaeologists. Large deposits of platinum were first recognized in South America during the 16th-century Spanish conquest. The Spanish government originally held a low regard for the metal because its high density permitted the preparation of counterfeits for gold which were difficult to detect. The new metal came to the general attention of European scientists in the late 18th century. Within the two-year period 1803–04 the discoveries of four new elements from crude platinum were announced in England—palladium and rhodium by William H. Wollaston and osmium and iridium by Smithson Tennant. Although other elements were thought to be contained in crude platinum at times, Carl Claus in Russia demonstrated the existence of the remaining rare metal of the platinum group in 1844. He chose for it the name ruthenium, which G. W. Osann had suggested earlier.

Since compounds of all the platinum elements are readily decomposed to give dense metals, it is not surprising that the six elements have been concentrated together as native alloys by geological processes. The earliest deposits to be worked were heavy river sands which had been concentrated by gravity. Primary deposits of the metals dispersed in basic and ultrabasic igneous rocks have since been productive. They are normally accompanied by other elements such as gold, and compounds of iron and nickel. Platinum metals are sometimes included in sulfide deposits and are recovered as by-products in the metallurgical operations for copper, nickel and other metals. The earliest workings of platinum were in Colombia and Brazil. In 1819 platinum was discovered in the Ural mountains, and since about 1825 Russia has been a dominant producer of the metals. For a period, 1828–41, coins were minted from a platinum-iridium alloy in Russia. Limited occurrences have been found in many areas of the world. Ores from the Republic of South Africa and the nickel ores of the Sudbury, Ont., area have given especially high continued yields. Because sources of the elements are limited, the metals command high prices which have fluctuated widely.

In atomic energy reactors isotopes of the light triad are formed together with more than 30 other elements as products of the nuclear fission of uranium, plutonium or thorium. It is necessary to effect their removal from the fissionable materials and sometimes from other fission products under difficult conditions imposed by the radiation hazards for large-scale applications of atomic energy.

Uses.—Platinum is the most readily available and widely used of the metals in the group. Its utility depends mostly upon its

Atomic and Physical Properties of the Platinum Metals

Metal	Ruthenium	Rhodium	Palladium	Osmium	Iridium	Platinum
Symbol	Ru	Rh	Pd	Os	Ir	Pt
Atomic number	44	45	46	76	77	78
Atomic weight	101.07	102.905	106.4	190.2	192.2	195.09
Mass number of stable isotopes	96 98 99 100 101 102 104	103	102 104 105 106 108 110	184 186 187 188 189 190 192	191 193	190* 192 194 195 196 198
Outer electron configuration	$4d^7 5s^1$	$4d^8 5s^1$	$4d^{10}$	$5d^6 6s^2$	$5d^9$	$5d^9 6s^1$
Ionization energy (electron volts)	7.5	7.7	8.33	8.7	9.2	8.96
Structure	hexagonal close-packed	cubic close-packed	cubic close-packed	hexagonal close-packed	cubic close-packed	cubic close-packed
Density (g./cm.³ at 20° C.)	12.38	12.42	12.03	22.59	22.55	21.46
Metallic radius (C.N. 12) (angstroms)	1.34	1.34	1.37	1.35	1.36	1.39
Melting point (° C.)	2,250	1,960	1,552	3,227	2,454	1,769
Boiling point (° C.)	>2,700	>2,500	2,500	>5,300	>4,100	>4,500
Specific heat (cal./g.deg. C.)	0.0551	0.0589	0.05838	0.0310	0.0307	0.03168

*Possibly radioactive.

high melting point and its resistance to chemical attack by the atmosphere and by many chemical agents. The metals are used in the electrical industry for resistors, contacts and sparking points. In the chemical industry and laboratory they are used for dishes, crucibles, electrodes, nozzles and other objects which must resist corrosion. Also large quantities are consumed for dental alloys and decorative purposes in jewelry. The surfaces of these metals are extremely active catalysts for a number of chemical reactions. Therefore they are widely used in the laboratory and in industry to accelerate chemical reactions despite their high cost. However, unless wastage is very small, cheaper materials, which may be less effective catalysts, are frequently used.

Chemical Properties.—Platinum can be heated to a white heat in air without losing its bright surface. It is not attacked by simple acids but does dissolve readily in aqua regia. None of the metals in the massive form is appreciably oxidized by the atmosphere at room temperature. However, when heated in air osmium is converted to the tetraoxide, OsO_4, a volatile poisonous compound (boiling point $131°$ C.) with an unpleasant odour; and ruthenium oxidizes to give RuO_2. The other elements oxidize only superficially in the air. Palladium slowly dissolves in concentrated nitric or sulfuric acid, and osmium forms OsO_4 with fuming nitric acid. Even aqua regia scarcely attacks ruthenium, rhodium or iridium. A fused mixture of sodium hydroxide and sodium nitrate is an effective agent which will oxidize all of the elements.

A few examples suffice to show the wide differences in chemical properties among the group. Osmium and ruthenium are alone among all known elements in forming a few well-characterized compounds with the $+8$ oxidation state, for example RuO_4, OsO_4, and $KOsO_3N$. The volatility of the tetraoxides permits convenient, efficient and rapid separation of these two elements.

All the platinum metals can form compounds with more than one oxidation state. For ruthenium there is evidence for compounds in every oxidation state from $+1$ through $+8$. However, both ruthenium and osmium are normally encountered in the states $+3$, $+4$, $+6$ or $+8$. In contrast, rhodium is limited with a few exceptions to the $+3$ oxidation state, whereas iridium forms important compounds for the $+3$ and $+4$ states. Palladium and platinum compounds are largely confined to the $+2$ and $+4$ states, the latter being very unstable for palladium.

All the platinum elements are characterized by a tendency to form co-ordination complexes in which chloride, ammonia, water or other groups are bonded covalently to the central metal ion. Replacements of one group by another, especially in the complexes of the heavy triad, are frequently slow.

Separation.—Processes for the recovery of the metals from the ores remain somewhat as trade secrets of individual firms and depend partly upon the composition and nature of metallurgical concentrates which must be handled. Commonly, at one step a mixture of the metals is dissolved in aqua regia. However, the mineral osmiridium, an alloy rich in osmium and iridium, is not dissolved by aqua regia. If it is heated with zinc it yields an alloy which is acid-soluble. The osmium distills away from the aqua regia solution as OsO_4 upon boiling. NH_4Cl added to an HCl solution of the remaining elements precipitates $(NH_4)_2PtCl_6$ and $(NH_4)_2IrCl_6$. These two compounds can be separated by repeated fractional crystallizations of the less soluble platinum compound. After platinum and iridium are removed, a precipitate of $Pd(NH_3)_2Cl_2$ can be formed by the addition of aqueous ammonia followed by HCl. If the remaining material in solution is reduced to metal and treated with fused potassium hydrogen sulfate, the rhodium is recovered as a soluble complex sulfate, $K_3Rh(SO_4)_3$. A ruthenium concentrate which remains can best be dissolved by a potassium hydroxide-potassium nitrate fusion and purified by a distillation procedure. (D. S. Mn.)

PLATO (428/427–348/347 B.C.), Greek philosopher whose influence on thought has been continuous for more than 2,400 years, was the son of Ariston and Perictione. His family was, on both sides, one of the most distinguished of Athens. Ariston is said to have traced his descent through Codrus to the god Poseidon; on the mother's side, the family, that was related to Solon, goes back to

Dropides, archon of the year 644 B.C. Perictione apparently married as her second husband her uncle Pyrilampes (*Parmenides* 126 *b*), a prominent supporter of Pericles, and Plato was probably chiefly brought up in his house: Critias and Charmides, leading men among the extremists of the oligarchic terror of 404, were respectively cousin and brother of Perictione; both were old friends of Socrates, and through them Plato must have known the philosopher from boyhood.

His own early ambitions as he tells us in the *Epistle* vii, 324 *b*– 326 *b*, were political. The reactionaries urged him to enter public life under their auspices—at the age of 24—but he wisely held back until their policy should declare itself. He was soon repelled by their violences, particularly by their attempt to implicate Socrates in the illegal execution of their victim Leon. He hoped better things from the restored democracy, but its condemnation of Socrates finally convinced him that there was no place for a man of conscience in active politics. Hermodorus, an immediate disciple, is the authority for the statement that, on the execution of Socrates in 399 B.C., Plato and other Socratic men

took temporary refuge with Euclid at Megara. The later biographies represent the next few years as spent in extensive travels in Greece, in Egypt and in Italy. Plato's own statement is only that he visited Italy and Sicily at the age of 40 and was disgusted by the gross sensuality of life there, but found a kindred spirit in Dion, brother-in-law of Dionysius I of Syracuse.

BY COURTESY OF THE STAATLICHE MUSEEN, BERLIN

PLATO: ANCIENT GREEK CARVING, CONSIDERED AN AUTHENTIC PORTRAIT. IN THE STAATLICHE MUSEEN, BERLIN

The Academy and Sicily.— About or soon after 387, Plato founded the Academy as an institute for the systematic pursuit of philosophical and scientific research. He presided over it for the rest of his life, making it the recognized authority alike in mathematics and in jurisprudence. From the allusions of Aristotle we gather that Plato lectured without manuscript, and we know that "problems" were propounded for solution by the joint researches of students. On the political side there are traces of tension between the Academy and the rival school of Isocrates.

The one outstanding event in Plato's later life is his intervention in Syracusan politics. On the death of Dionysius I in 367, Dion conceived the idea of bringing Plato to Syracuse as tutor to his successor, whose education had been neglected. Plato himself was not sanguine of results, but as both Dion and the philosopher-statesman Archytas of Tarentum thought the prospect promising, he felt bound in honour to risk the adventure. The project was by training Dionysius II in severe science to fit him for the position of a constitutional king who might hold Carthaginian encroachment in Sicily at bay. The scheme was crushed by his natural jealousy of the stronger Dion, whom he drove into virtual banishment. Plato paid a second and longer visit to Syracuse in 361–360, in the hope of still effecting an accommodation, but failed, not without some personal danger. When Dion captured Syracuse by a *coup de main* in 357, Plato wrote him a short letter of congratulation and warning against his own lack of tact and graciousness. After the murder of Dion in 354 the philosopher drew up his important *Epistles* vii and viii, reviewing and justifying the policy of Dion and himself and making proposals, unsuccessfully, for a conciliation of Sicilian parties. He is said to have died "at a marriage feast" or while "writing" and to have been buried in the Academy.

The above account presupposes the authenticity of Plato's *Epistles* and in any case the reliability of their factual information, but it should be noted that on neither of these do all scholars agree.

To us Plato naturally is important primarily as one of the greatest of philosophical writers, but to himself the foundation and organization of the Academy must have appeared his chief work. In *Epistle* vii, 341 *b–e,* 344 *c,* he utters on his own account the same comparatively unfavourable verdict on written works, in contrast with the contact of living minds, as a vehicle of "philosophy," which he ascribes to Socrates in the *Phaedrus*. It can hardly be doubted that he regarded his dialogues as intended in the main to interest an educated outside world in the more serious and arduous labours of his "school."

All the most important mathematical work of the 4th century was done by friends or pupils of Plato. Theaetetus, the founder of solid geometry, was a member of the Academy, as were also the first students of the conic sections. Eudoxus of Cnidus, author of the doctrine of proportion expounded in Euclid's *Elements,* inventor of the method of finding the areas and volumes of curvilinear figures by exhaustion and propounder of the astronomical scheme of concentric spheres adopted and altered by Aristotle, removed his school from Cyzicus to Athens for the purpose of co-operation with Plato; during one of Plato's absences he seems to have acted as the head of the Academy. Archytas, the inventor of mechanical science, was a friend and correspondent. The Academy is thus the link between the mathematics of the 5th-century Pythagoreans and the mathematics of the geometers and arithmeticians of Alexandria.

Nor were other sciences neglected. Speusippus, Plato's nephew and successor, was a voluminous writer on natural history; Aristotle's biological works have been shown to belong largely to the early period in his career immediately after Plato's death, before the breach between the younger philosopher and the Academy. The comic poets found matter for mirth in the attention of the school to botanical classification. The Academy was particularly active in jurisprudence and practical legislation. "Plato sent Aristonymus to the Arcadians, Phormion to Elis, Menedemus to Pyrrha. Eudoxus and Aristotle wrote laws for Cnidus and Stageirus. Alexander asked Xenocrates for advice about kingship; the man who was sent to Alexander by the Asiatic Greeks and did most to incite him to his war on the barbarians was Delius of Ephesus, an associate of Plato." (Plutarch, *Adversus Coloten,* 1126 *c–d*). The creation of the Academy as a permanent society for the prosecution of both exact and humane sciences was, some assert, the first establishment of a university. (*See* ACADEMY, GREEK.)

Formative Influences.—The most important formative influence to which the young Plato's mind was exposed was that of Socrates. But it does not appear that Plato, whose first ambitions were political, belonged to the innermost circle of the old man's intimates, or regarded himself as a "disciple." In *Epistle* vii he is careful to speak of Socrates not as a "master" but as an older "friend" (*hetairos*) for whose character he has a profound respect; and he has recorded his own absence (through indisposition) from the death scene of the *Phaedo*. It would seem that his own vocation to philosophy dawned on him only afterward, as he reflected on the moral to be learned from the treatment of Socrates by the democratic leaders. Aristotle incidentally ascribes to him an early familiarity with the Heraclitean Cratylus, a younger man than Socrates and apparently an admirer of the philosopher. This may be only Aristotle's inference from the existence of the dialogue *Cratylus*.

It is more important to remember Plato's connection with Pyrilampes and Critias. Pyrilampes was a Periclean politician, and Critias was known as a democrat until his moral balance was upset by the collapse of the Periclean system in 404. Early upbringing in a family of Periclean politics having connection with Solon may explain why Plato's own estimate of democracy in the *Politicus* and *Laws* is much less unfavourable than that which he ascribes to Socrates in the *Gorgias* and *Republic*.

Beyond this, we can say only that Plato in early life must have been exposed to the same influences as his contemporaries. His early experiences covered the disastrous years of the Deceleian War, the shattering of the Athenian empire and the fierce civil strife of oligarchs and democrats in the year of anarchy 404–

403. He was too young to have known anything by experience of the imperial democracy of Pericles and Cleon, or of the tide of the sophistic movement. It is certainly not from memory that he depicts Protagoras, or even Alcibiades, as they were in their great days.

THE DIALOGUES

The fixing of the canon and text of Plato has often been attributed to two scholars, Dercylides and Thrasylus, either shortly before or shortly after the Christian era (but *see* ACADEMY, GREEK). Thrasylus is uncertainly identified with Thrasylus of Mende and generally assumed to have been astrologer to and friend of Tiberius. By reckoning the *Epistles* as one item, the list was made to consist of 36 works, arranged in nine tetralogies, or groups of four. (Aristophanes of Byzantium had already attempted an arrangement in trilogies, or groups of three, which, however, he did not carry through.)

No genuine work of Plato has been lost, but there is a general agreement of modern scholars to reject a number of small items from the text. Their verdict may be said to have gone strongly against the following: *Alcibiades I, Alcibiades II* (suspected by some even in ancient times), *Theages, Erastae, Clitophon, Hipparchus, Minos*. Most or all of these are probably early Academic work, and possibly not all later in date than Plato's death. Most, though not all, contemporary scholars also regard the *Epinomis*—in the present writer's opinion wrongly—as an appendix to the *Laws* added *de suo* by the mathematician Philippus of Opus, who is recorded by Diogenes Laërtius (iii, 37) to have transcribed the work for circulation. The *Hippias Major* and the *Menexenus* are still regarded as doubtful by some, though Aristotle used both in a way which seems to prove that he regarded them as Platonic (he expressly quotes the *Menexenus*). Plato's will, preserved by the same Diogenes (iii, 41–43), is pretty certainly authentic. Some of the 32 epigrams ascribed to him in the *Anthology* may conceivably be genuine.

Order of Composition.—Plato's literary career extended over the greater part of a long life. The *Apology* must have been written while the memory of Socrates' appearance before his judges was still fresh; the *Laws* is confessedly the work of an old man with a long experience of life behind him, and the state of its text fully bears out the tradition, preserved by Proclus, that its aged author never lived to give it final revision. Half a century or more must have elapsed between Plato's last and his earliest composition.

This of itself would prove that F. Schleiermacher, with whom modern critical study of Plato begins, went astray in assuming that Plato started his career with a ready-made complete "system" to be disclosed. We must expect to find in his writings evidence of the development of his mind. But if we are to read the development aright we must have some trustworthy way of determining the order of the dialogues. Plato himself has given us only the scantiest indications of the order. He has linked the *Sophistes* and the *Politicus* externally with the *Theaetetus* as continuations of the conversation reported in that dialogue; he has also, as most students recognize, linked up the *Timaeus* in the same way with the *Republic*. Aristotle adds one other piece of information: that the *Laws* were written after the *Republic*.

Further investigation of the problem opens in 1867 with L. Campbell's edition of the *Sophistes* and the *Politicus,* and the work thus begun was continued by others, notably W. Dittenberger, M. Schanz, C. Ritter, H. Arnim and W. Lutoslawski.

By consideration of independent stylistic criteria, it has been definitely established that the dialogues *Sophistes, Politicus, Philebus, Timaeus* (with its fragmentary sequel *Critias*) and *Laws* form a distinct linguistic group, which must belong to the later years of Plato's life, as we might have presumed from the consideration that Socrates, the central figure of other dialogues, becomes, in those of this group (with a solitary exception for the *Philebus,* the one member of the group which is wholly preoccupied with ethics), a secondary personage, and disappears altogether from the *Laws*. The whole group must therefore be later than the *Sophistes,* which professes to be a sequel to the *Theaetetus*. Now the *Theae-*

tetus can be dated with some accuracy, since it commemorates the recent death of the eminent mathematician after whom it is named from disease and injury contracted in a campaign before Corinth, which, as elaborately proved by Eva Sachs (*De Theaeteto Atheniensi*, 1914), must be that of 369 B.C. The dialogue may thus be safely ascribed to 368–367, the eve of Plato's departure for Syracuse, and the marked change of style visible in the *Sophistes* is best explained by the supposition that there was a break in Plato's literary activity during the years 367–360 when he was specially occupied with Sicilian affairs. So much may be regarded as fairly certain.

It is not so easy to reach conclusions about the order of composition of the earlier group of dialogues. It is generally recognized, on linguistic and other grounds, that the series ends with the *Theaetetus* and the closely related *Parmenides*. Ritter, Lutoslawski and others tried to determine the internal order of the group on linguistic evidence, but there are obvious reasons for doubting whether the methods which proved successful in establishing the distinction between the two great groups of earlier and of later dialogues can be applied with the same degree of confidence to works belonging to the same general period of their author's life and composed probably at no great distance of time from one another.

In point of fact, there is no complete agreement between the arrangements proposed by different "stylometrists," and their advocates have usually eked out the strictly philological argument by more or less dubious assumptions about the development of Plato's thought, though it is very questionable whether any real development can be traced before the *Theaetetus* and the *Parmenides*. Perhaps all that can be said with certainty is that the great outstanding dialogues, *Symposium, Phaedo, Republic* (and perhaps also *Protagoras*), in which Plato's dramatic power is at its highest, mark the culmination of this first period of literary activity. The comparative decline of dramatic power, accompanied by compensating maturity of critical acumen, is the most striking contrast between the dialogues of the second and those of the first period. A good account of the work done by the "stylometrists" is to be found in H. Raeder, *Platons philosophische Entwickelung* (1905), another in an article by C. Ritter in *Bursians Jahresbericht*, vol. 187, i (1921).

The Persons of the Dialogues.—The great initial difficulty which besets the modern student of Platonic philosophy is that created by the dramatic form of Plato's writings. Since Plato never introduces himself into his own dialogues, he is not formally committed to anything which is taught in them. The speakers who are formally bound by the utterances of the dialogues are their protagonists, Socrates, Parmenides, the Pythagorean Timaeus, and all these are real historical persons. The question thus arises, with what right do we assume that Plato means us to accept as his own the doctrines put into the mouths of these characters? Is his purpose dogmatic and didactic, or may it be that it is mainly dramatic? Are we more at liberty to hold Plato responsible for what is said by his dramatis personae than we should be to treat a poet like Robert Browning in the same fashion?

It is tempting to evade this formidable issue in one of two ways. One is that of Grote, who held that Plato allows himself freely to develop in a dialogue any view which interests him for the moment, without pledging himself to its truth or considering its compatibility with other positions assumed elsewhere in his writings. Thus, according to this theory, Plato can make Socrates tolerate hedonistic utilitarianism in the *Protagoras* and denounce it in the *Gorgias,* or can assert the so-called ideal theory through the mouth of Socrates in the *Phaedo* and refute it in the character of Parmenides in the dialogue of that name, with equal gusto and without pledging himself to any view. His championships are purely dramatic, or, at most, reflect his passing mood at the moment of composition.

The more common assumption of the 19th century was that some of Plato's characters, notably Socrates and Timaeus, are "mouthpieces" through whom he inculcates tenets of his own, without concern for dramatic or historical propriety. Thus it was

and often still is held that the most famous philosophical doctrines of the *Phaedo* and *Republic,* the "ideal theory," the doctrine of "recollection" and of the tripartite soul, were originated by Plato after the death of Socrates (to whom these speculations were supposed to be entirely unknown) and consciously fathered on the older philosopher by a mystification too glaring to deceive any one seriously. Careful study of the dialogues should satisfy us that neither of these two extreme views is tenable.

The Thought of the Earlier and Later Dialogues.—There is undeniably a real difference between the thought of the dialogues which are later than the *Theaetetus* and those which are earlier, and this difference will have to be accounted for. But there are no serious discrepancies of doctrine between the individual dialogues of the same period.

Now Plato seems to announce his own personal conviction of certain doctrines of the second group of dialogues by a striking dramatic device. In the *Sophistes* and *Politicus* the leading part is taken by an Eleatic and in the *Laws* by an Athenian who are the only anonymous, indeed almost certainly the only imaginary, personages in the whole of Plato's writings (except the two minor personages of the *Laws,* a Spartan and a Cretan, who have really nothing to do except to say "Yes," "No," in the appropriate places). It can hardly be doubted that the reason why these two characters have been left anonymous is precisely that the writer may be free to use them as "mouthpieces" for his own teaching. Plato thus takes on himself the responsibility for the logic and epistemology of the *Sophistes* and of the *Politicus* and for the ethics and educational and political theory of the *Politicus* and of the *Laws* in a specially marked way, and by doing so compels us to face the question how far he means the utterances of Socrates in his earlier dialogues to be taken as expressions of a philosophy of his own.

Forms.—It may be regarded as an established result of the inquiries of Henry Jackson and others that there is a definite philosophical doctrine running through the earlier dialogues which has as its main features the theory of "Forms" (the ideal theory; *see* FORM), the theory that knowledge is "recollection" and the theory of the "tripartite soul." In the dialogues of the second period these tenets, as we have learned to know them from the earlier dialogues, appear only in the mouth of Timaeus, a 5th-century Pythagorean older than Socrates; and the most important of them all, the theory of "Forms" is actually made the object of what looks like a refutation in the *Parmenides.*

The problem is to find an explanation of this puzzling fact. Are we to distinguish two philosophies, both originated by Plato after the death of Socrates, an earlier and a later? Or are we to suppose that in the main the object of the first group of Plato's dialogues is to preserve the memory of Socrates and that the philosophy expounded is in the main what it professes to be, the thought of Socrates, coloured, no doubt, unconsciously but not consciously distorted, in its passage through the mind of Plato? On the second view we should have to say that, strictly speaking, Plato had no distinctive Platonic philosophy until a late period in his life, much as we can say that, though Kant was all through his life a prolific writer on philosophy, there was no distinctive Kantian philosophy before the *Critique of Pure Reason.* Most Platonic scholars reject this interpretation of the facts, known as the Taylor-Burnet hypothesis, but there are weighty considerations which plead strongly for it. The following will assume its probability.

Socrates and Plato.—It is significant that the only dialogue not earlier than the *Theaetetus* in which Socrates takes a leading part is the *Philebus,* the one member of the second group which deals exclusively with those ethical problems on which the thought of the historical Socrates had been specially concentrated. This is most naturally explained by supposing that Plato, from regard to fact, was unwilling to make Socrates the exponent of doctrines which he knew to be his own property, though it is hard to understand his misgivings if he had already for years been employing him in that very capacity. (If, as is most probable, *Epistle* ii is authentic, the question would be definitely settled by the sentence of the latter [314 *c*] "there is not, and never will be, a work of

Plato; the works which now go by that name belong to Socrates embellished and rejuvenated.")

It is notable, too, that Aristotle apparently knew nothing of an earlier and a later version of Platonism. He attributes a definite doctrine to Plato which is quite unlike anything to be found in the first great group of dialogues, and seems to be known to him from oral communications in the Academy, though something similar to it can, by looking hard, be read between the lines in the *Philebus*. It was also the view of Neoplatonic scholars such as Proclus that the ideal theory expounded in the great earlier dialogues really originated with Socrates and that something of the same kind was also held by contemporary Pythagoreans in Italy (Proclus, *Commentarii in Parmenidem*, edited by V. Cousin [1864], 659, 729), and the fact that Proclus does not find it necessary to argue the point seems to show that this had been the standing tradition of the Academy.

Similarly Galen, early in the 3rd century A.D., cites the definite statement of the learned Stoic Poseidonius that the doctrine of the "tripartite soul," often said in modern times to be another invention of Plato's, is as old as Pythagoras (*De Placitis Hippocratis et Platonis*, 425, 478 Kühn).

Moreover, as J. Burnet argued, it is hard to believe that any writer would introduce a far-reaching novel speculation of his own to the world in the curious fashion which Plato is supposed to have adopted in the *Phaedo*, where Socrates is made to describe the ideal theory as something quite familiar which he has for years constantly canvassed with his intimates (nearly all, if not all, of whom, were certainly living when the *Phaedo* was circulated). It is not necessary here to determine the historical question. We may be content to turn to the Platonic dialogues, carefully distinguishing the successors of the *Theaetetus* from its predecessors, and attempt a summary of their contents. The general doctrine of the first period will be described without any more or less arbitrary attempt to say how much of it may be actually Socratic. We may then consider how far this doctrine is modified in later dialogues, or in the version of Platonism presupposed by Aristotle's criticisms.

No attempt will be made here to describe the personality or temperament of Plato which is, in fact, as elusive as that of Shakespeare and for the same reason. He is often credited with a strongly "mystical" and "erotic" temperament. He does ascribe such a temperament to Socrates, but it is puerile to treat his picture of Socrates as evidence about himself, though the mistake is constantly committed.

It should therefore be noted that the "mysticism" is confined to dialogues of the first period, in which Socrates is its exponent, and that the "erotic" language in which Plato's Socrates speaks of his devotion to his young friends was also used by the Socrates of Aeschines to describe his relations with Alcibiades (fragment 4, edited by H. Krauss, 1911). There is no evidence that Plato personally ever fired the imagination of gifted boys as Socrates did. Apart from the *Epistles*, the most valuable light we possess on Plato's personality is afforded by Aristotle's description of him as a man "whom it is blasphemy in the base even to praise."

THE EARLIER DIALOGUES

In the *Republic*, the greatest of all the dialogues which precede the *Theaetetus*, there may be said to be three main strands of argument deftly combined into a consummate artistic whole, the ethical and political, the aesthetic and mystical and the metaphysical. Other major dialogues belonging to this period give special prominence to some one of these three lines of thought; the *Phaedo* to the metaphysical theme, the *Protagoras* and the *Gorgias* to the ethical and political, the *Symposium* and the *Phaedrus* to the aesthetic and mystical, though in none does Plato make an artificially rigid separation of any one of the great ideal interests of human life from the rest.

The shorter dialogues deal with more special problems, usually of an ethical character, and mostly conform to a common type. A problem in moral science, often that of the right definition of a virtue, is propounded, a number of tentative solutions are considered and are all found to be vitiated by difficulties which we cannot dispel; we are thus left, at the end of the conversation, aware of our discreditable ignorance of the very things it is most imperative for man to know. We have formally learned nothing but have been made alive to the worthlessness of what we had hitherto been content to take for knowledge and the need of seeking further enlightenment.

The effect of these dialogues of search is thus to put us in tune with the spirit of Socrates, who had said that the one respect in which he was wiser than other men was just his keen appreciation of his own ignorance of the most important matters. We learn the meaning of his ruling principle that the supreme business of life is to "tend" the soul (to make it as good as possible) and his conviction that "goodness of soul" means first and foremost, *knowledge* of good and evil. The three dialogues directly concerned with the trial of Socrates have manifestly a further purpose. They are intended to explain to a puzzled public why Socrates thought it stuff of the conscience neither to withdraw from danger before trial, nor to make a conciliatory defense, nor, finally, to avail himself of the opportunity of flight after conviction. Even well-wishers such as Xenophon, as we know, were puzzled by what had seemed his wilfully defiant attitude; it was therefore a debt of honour to his memory to put the matter in the true light. In the remarks which follow, we will consider these shorter dialogues in an order adopted simply for purposes of convenience.

Hippias I and II.—In these dialogues Socrates has as respondent the well-known polymath Hippias of Elis, whose self-complacency is sharply satirized. In the *Hippias Major* the question propounded is "What is the fine" (*kalon*)? "Fine" is a predicate by which we are constantly expressing both aesthetic and moral approval; do we really know what we mean by it? We discover that we do not, though incidentally we also learn that "fine" or "beautiful" is certainly not a synonym for either "useful" or "pleasant." *Hippias Minor* deals directly with the famous Socratic paradox that "wrong-doing is involuntary." It is commonly held that it is much worse to tell a willful untruth than to blunder into an unintentional false statement. Yet the analogy of the arts and professions seems to show that the man who errs intentionally, if there is such a person, is a better man than he who errs unintentionally. (The suggested thought, of course, is that there is no such person. The man who knows what is good will always aim at this and at nothing else —the familiar doctrine of Socrates.)

Ion, Menexenus.—Both these are occasional works. Socrates had said that he found the poets, who as a class are commonly reckoned "wise," quite unable to explain to him how they came to say their best things, or what they meant by them. (*Apology* 22 a–c.) The *Ion* develops this thought into the theory that neither the poet, nor his interpreter the rhapsode, produces his effects "by science," that is, as a result of conscious artistry; the effect in both cases is due to a nonrational inspiration, or, as we now say, native genius. (The importance of this is that it rules out appeal to the poets as specially competent authorities on the conduct of life.)

The *Menexenus*, which professes to repeat a funeral oration learned from the famous Aspasia, is apparently meant as a satire on patriotic distortion of history. Apparently the discourses satirized are those of Pericles in Thucydides, Lysias (*Oratio* ii) and Isocrates (the *Panegyricus*). The singular anachronism by which Socrates (and Aspasia) are represented as commenting on the events of the Corinthian War down to the year 387 must be intentional, whatever its object.

Charmides, Laches, Lysis.—These are typical dialogues of search. The question of the *Charmides*, which contains a particularly delightful picture of the way of Socrates with a promising lad, is what is meant by *sophrosyne*, the virtue which is shown alike in graceful and easy command of one's appetites and passions, in dutiful behaviour to parents, elders, official "superiors," in balance and sanity amid the ups and downs of fortune. We seem to be in a fair way to identify this virtue with "knowledge of self"—the self-knowledge Socrates had valued so highly—when we are confronted with an ambiguity. Self-knowledge might be taken to mean a knowledge which has knowledge itself for its object, in fact for epistemology. But it is hard to be sure that there is any such science as the knowledge of knowledge and harder still to see how such knowledge could possibly be directive of conduct.

In the *Laches* we are concerned with valour, the soldier's virtue. Here again we are on the point of defining the virtue as knowledge of what is and what is not really to be dreaded. But this is tantamount to saying the true knowledge of evil and good, and the resultant definition "valour is knowledge of good," would identify valour with the whole goodness of man. That is, the definition is only possible if we can meet the popular objections to the Socratic thesis of the unity of virtue.

The *Lysis* examines in the same tentative way, friendship, the relation in which self-forgetting devotion most conspicuously displays itself. The crux of the problem is that after many false starts, we seem to have reached a promising result in the view that each friend is really "a part of" the other in "soul or temper or body," and yet it is hard to reconcile this position with the facts which seem to show that "unlikeness" is a potent source of attraction. Aristotle has taken up and discussed the issues raised in the dialogue in his own treatment of the same subject (*Nicomachean Ethics*, viii–ix).

Cratylus.—The question here, one much agitated in the age of Socrates, is whether names are significant by nature or convention. Is there some special appropriateness of the sounds of names to the objects called by them, or is there no bond between the thing and its name but that of the "usage of the community"? The absurdity of attempts to get metaphysics out of etymologies is humorously exposed by showing that the method can be used at pleasure to prove either that the "giver of names" agreed with Heraclitus that motion is the sole reality or that he held, with Parmenides, that motion is an illusion. Yet there are real analogies between "vocal gestures" and the things signified by them, which are pointed out with a good deal of insight. The main purpose of Plato, however, is to dwell on the point that language is an instrument of thought; the test of its rightness is not mere social usage, but its genuine capacity to express true thought accurately.

Euthydemus.—The dialogue is, in large part, broad satire on "eristics" who misapply the logic of Zeno for the purpose of entangling anyone who commits himself to any assertion in fallacies because of the ambiguity of language. (Aristotle has drawn freely upon it in his essay on fallacies, the *De Sophisticis Elenchis*.) Its more serious purpose is to contrast this futile contradiction mongering with the "protreptic" of Socrates. The lad Clinias is simply bewildered by the questions of the two professors of "eristic"; those of Socrates have the purpose of convincing him that the happiness we all desire is not guaranteed by the *possession* of the things the world accounts good, but depends on our making the right *use* of them. If we would attain happiness we must "tend" our "souls," and that means that we must acquire the "royal" science which ensures that we shall make the right use of all the gifts of mind, body and fortune, in other words, the knowledge of true and absolute good.

Gorgias.—The *Gorgias* is a greater as well as a much longer work than any of those hitherto considered. Beginning ostensibly as an inquiry into the nature and worth of rhetoric, the art of advocacy professed by Gorgias, it develops into a plea of sustained eloquence and logical power for absolute right, as against expediency, as the sovereign rule of life private and public, and ends with an imaginative picture, on Orphic lines, of the eternal destinies of the righteous and of the unrighteous soul. Literature has no more impressive presentation of the claim of conscience to unqualified obedience and the impossibility of divorcing the politically from the morally right.

Gorgias holds that "rhetoric" is an "art," the application of knowledge to practice, and the queen of all "arts," since it gives its possessor the object of man's highest ambition, power to enforce his will on society. The statesman, who is the man of men, is just a consummate advocate speaking from a brief. If he is clever enough he will, though a layman, carry the day with an audience of laymen, even against the expert specialist. To his audience he will seem, though he is not, the superior of the real expert. Socrates declares that "rhetoric" is not an "art," a matter of native principles, but a mere "empiric knack" of humouring the prejudices and pleasing the tastes of an audience. It is a subspecies of parasitism.

There are two genuine arts conducive to the health of the body, those of the trainer and of the physician; each has its parasitic counterfeit, the one in the profession of the beautifier, the other in that of the confectioner. So there are two arts conducive to health of soul, those of the legislator, who lays down the rule of morally sane life, and of the judge, who corrects moral disorders. The sophist counterfeits the first, as the rhetorician the second, by taking the pleasant instead of the good as his standard. The rhetorician is thus not the wise physician of the body politic but its toady.

This severe judgment is disputed by Polus, the ardent admirer of Gorgias, on the ground that the successful rhetorician is virtually the autocrat of the community: every man's life and property are at his mercy. To be such an autocrat is the summit of human happiness; even if, like Archelaus of Macedonia, the aspirant only reaches the position by a series of shocking crimes, he is the most enviable of mankind, because he is above law and can do whatever he likes.

Socrates rejects this view. The autocrat always does "as he pleases," and for that reason never does "what he wishes"; as all mankind, he wishes for true happiness or good, but no act which is immoral ("unjust") ever leads to happiness. To suffer a wrong is an evil, but to inflict one is much worse. And if a man has committed a wrong, it is much worse for him to go unpunished than to be cured of his moral malady by the sharp but wholesome medicine of punishment. If rhetoric is of real service to men, it should be most of all serviceable to an offender. If he knew his own interest, he would employ all his powers of persuasion to move the authorities to inflict the penalties for which the state of his soul calls. Polus is unable to meet this stringent reasoning, because he had at least conceded to current morality that it is more disgraceful, though not more evil, to inflict wrong than to suffer it.

This is denied by Callicles of Acharnae, an otherwise unknown politician, who proceeds recklessly to develop the doctrine of the "will to power." It may be a convention of the herd that unscrupulous aggression is discreditable and wrong, but "nature's convention" (a phrase which appears here for the first time in literature) is that the strong are justified in using their strength as they please, while the weak "go to the wall." Callicles and Socrates thus appear as champions of two contrasted moralities of private and public life. Callicles stands for self-assertion in ethics and aggressive imperialism in politics. Socrates opposes both. In his judgment the creators of the imperialistic Athenian democracy were no true statesmen, because they were content to give Athens a navy and a commerce without creating a morally sound national character. They may have been capable domestic servants of the democracy for whose tastes they catered; they were not its physicians. The one true statesman of the past was the just Aristides; in the present, Socrates himself is the one man who shows a statesmanlike mind, though it is perfectly true that he might at any moment have to pay with his life for refusing to call that good which pleases the public fancy. It is not true, as Callicles supposes it to be, that the secret of happiness is to have strong and vehement passions and be able to gratify them to the full. That would be a condition like that of the fabled sinners who are punished in Hades by being set to spend eternity in filling leaking pitchers. The truly happy life is that of measure in which the gratification of desire is strictly regulated by regard for justice and *sophrosyne*. If we may believe the Orphic doctrine of judgment to come, the votary of passion and injustice has a heavy reckoning to await hereafter.

Meno.—The *Meno* is nominally concerned with the question of what virtue is and whether it can be taught, but it is further interesting for two reasons. It states clearly the doctrine, which we have not met so far, that knowledge is "recollection"; it also introduces as a character the democratic politician Anytus, the main author of the prosecution of Socrates. It seems plain that Plato wishes to indicate his opinion that it was Socrates' severe criticism of the great figures of the history of Athenian democracy which led to the prosecution.

Can virtue be taught or learned (as must be the case, if the professional sophists can really do what they profess)? That depends on what virtue is. We are on the way to define it as "ability to secure good things by honest means," when we reflect that honesty itself is a "good thing," and the definition consequently is circular. This reminds us of the current dilemma that all such inquiries are futile because it is idle to inquire into what you already know, useless to inquire into what you do not know (since you could not recognize the unknown, even if you found it). This difficulty would vanish if it were true that the soul is immortal and has long ago learned all truth, so that it needs now only to be reminded by sense-experiences of truths which it once knew and has forgotten. This (Orphic) doctrine seems to be supported by the experience that a lad who has never studied geometry can be brought to recognize mathematical truths by merely showing him a diagram and asking him appropriate questions about it. He produces the right answer "out of himself." (The point thus is the presence of an a priori element in mathematical truth.)

In any case, we may say that if "virtue" is knowledge, it can be taught; if it is not knowledge, it cannot. But is it knowledge? If it is, one would suppose that there must be professional teachers of it. But Anytus assures us vehemently that the sophists, who claim to be such professionals, are mischievous impostors; and we can be sure that the ordinary decent citizen cannot "teach virtue," as Anytus maintains, since the "best men" of the democracy, Themistocles and the rest, have been unable to teach it to their own sons.

Perhaps, then, we must say that the "best men" of Athens have no genuine knowledge of good; their successes have been due not to knowledge, but to mere correct opinions. Still, for practical purposes a correct opinion will serve as well as knowledge. The trouble is that you cannot depend on its permanency unless you fasten it down by thinking out the reason why of it. Then it becomes knowledge. If a man should arise who could actually teach statesmanship to others, he would be one who really *knew* what good is; the virtue of such a scientific statesman would be to that of other men as substance is to shadow.

Protagoras.—This finely dramatic dialogue gives us the most complete presentation to be found in Plato of the main principles of the Socratic morality and is the direct source of Aristotle's statements about the teaching of Socrates in the *Nicomachean Ethics*.

Socrates meets, in the house of Callias, the eminent sophist Protagoras, who is attractively drawn and represented as a great admirer of the younger man's ability. Protagoras explains that his profession is the "teaching of goodness," and that by "goodness" he means the art of making a success of one's own life, of one's household and of one's city. (Thus he teaches the conduct of life, private and public, and has done so for years with success.) Socrates urges that there are two considerations which make it look doubtful whether this art can be taught. The Athenians have a high reputation for intelligence, but it is notorious that their assembly requires no evidence of expert knowledge in a speaker who discusses the morality of a proposed course of action.

Also the eminent democratic statesmen have never taught their own "goodness" to their sons. Public opinion and the practice of the eminent few alike suggest that the conduct of life is not teachable. Protagoras, to be sure, thinks that the absence of special teachers only proves that every citizen of a civilized city can, in his degree, act as teacher, exactly as he can teach his children his native language or his trade. Goodness depends on the sense of right and conscience, and the whole of life in a civilized society is a process of education in these. His exposition at once raises the problem of the unity of virtue. Are the various commonly recognized virtues really different, so that a man may be strong in one but weak in another? Protagoras is at first inclined to say that they are, but on reconsideration is ready to identify all of them but one with wisdom or sound judgment.

An exception must be made for courage, a virtue which is popularly regarded as having something conspicuously nonrational about it. The dialogue culminates in an argument by which Socrates attempts to show that there is no need to make this exception. The general public, the party which insists so much on the nonrational character of courage, would be ready to accept the identification of the good and the pleasant and to grant that the goodness of courage means that by facing pain and danger one escapes worse pain or danger. On their own theory, then, courage and the rest of virtue can be reduced to prudent computation of pleasures and of pains. The humour of the situation is that Socrates and Protagoras have thus changed places. Socrates, who had raised a difficulty about the teachability of virtue, is left satisfied that virtue must be knowledge; Protagoras, who claimed to be able to teach it, ends by declaring that, whatever virtue may be, it cannot be knowledge.

It is important to observe that the dialogue does not teach hedonism. The equation *good = pleasant* is advanced only as one which would be accepted by the mass of men, and should forbid them to find a paradox in the identification of virtue with knowledge; it is expressly repudiated by Protagoras as unworthy of a man of high character.

All that Socrates asserts is that virtue is knowledge and wrongdoing consequently involuntary. There is no disagreement in moral principle between the *Protagoras* and the *Phaedo* or the *Gorgias*. If the mass of men are ready to accept the hedonist formula, that is because they are votaries of the body-loving life; this is why we are told in the *Phaedo* that "popular" virtue is illusory. The true explanation of Socrates' doubts is that, though he holds that true virtue, being knowledge, is teachable, he does not believe that what Protagoras is trying to teach is true virtue. Success depends on personal tact and tact cannot be learned from an instructor.

Euthyphro, Apology, Crito.—The main purpose of these three works, which deal with the bearing of Socrates before, during and after his trial, is to obviate possible serious misunderstandings of his position and motives; the theme of all three may be said to be the true meaning and importance of care or tending of the soul.

The problem of the *Euthyphro* is what is religion. The respondent Euthyphron is certainly meant to be a kind of Orphic sectary, not, as has been fancied, a representative of ordinary Athenian belief and practice. Socrates had associated with such men and was known to hold unusual beliefs about the soul; hence it was important to make it plain that he was something different from a fanatic. The dialogue, interesting also from its well-developed logical terminology, enables Socrates to repudiate immoral mythology and to reject the conception of "religious duty" as fulfilment of purely arbitrary commands. Its central thought, which, however, is not formally asserted as a conclusion, is that the service of God which in religion means co-operation with God and under God is the production of a noble work, the nature of which is not further defined, though it is sufficiently clear that the "work" meant is the "tending of the soul."

Consideration of the *Apology* and *Crito* in detail belongs rather to the study of Socrates than to that of Plato. Of the *Apology* we must be content to say here that the real defense of Socrates is contained in the pages which explain that the mainspring of his life has been his conviction that he has a mission from God to spend his life in "philosophy," the endeavour to "make his own soul as good as possible," and to incite mankind to do the same; to this mission it is his duty to be strictly faithful, even if faithfulness means condemnation as a traitor by the democracy. The *Apology* thus depicts Socrates as carrying out in his own practice the ethical program of the *Gorgias*. The actual accusation is treated with contempt and satirical humour. (See SOCRATES.)

The point of the *Crito,* though simple, is often missed. Was Socrates wantonly throwing away a valuable life by refusing to escape from prison? Why did he make this refusal? Because, though the conviction was materially iniquitous, it was the verdict of a legitimate court, which could not be disregarded without real disloyalty. Socrates has been wronged not by the law, but by politicians who have abused the law. If he disregarded the conviction, he would be directly doing a wrong against the whole social system.

Foundation of Plato's Doctrine.—In the works so far considered we have the foundation of a moral and political doctrine based on Socratic principles, from which Plato never departed. The main underlying thought is that the great concern of man, a concern not limited to this earthly life, is the development of a rational moral personality (the tending of the soul). Our felicity depends wholly on our success in this task (to use J. Butler's language, on "our conduct," not on "our condition"). And this success, again, depends on rational insight into the true scale of good. It is not because they do not desire it that men fail to attain felicity: on the contrary, no man ever really desires anything else. The reason why men forfeit felicity is that they mistake apparent good for real, the conditionally for the absolutely good. If a man ever knew with assurance what absolute good is, he would in practice never pursue anything else. It is in this sense that "all virtue is knowledge" and that "all wrong-doing is involuntary" (*i.e.*, consists in the pursuit of what is falsely supposed to be good).

"Popular morality" is confused in theory and unreliable in practice because it does not rest on any assured insight into absolute good; "philosophic morality," just because it does rest on such certain insight, is a morality of absolute and unconditional obedience to conscience, such as Socrates had shown. Since the task of the statesman is simply the task of tending the soul extended to the national soul as its object, the philosophical moralist is also the only true statesman. True statesmanship means the promotion of national character as the one thing which matters, and is therefore simply the application, on the grand scale, of the principles of absolute morality; what falls short of this is opportunism masquerading as statesmanship.

These convictions clearly imply a far-reaching metaphysic as their foundation and justification. The principles of this metaphysic, though they are frequently hinted at in passages of dialogues already reviewed, are put before us more explicitly in those which we have now to consider; in connection with them we shall also observe an explicit theory of knowledge and scientific method.

Phaedo.—The *Phaedo* is often treated as though its object were to provide a demonstration of the immortality of the soul. It does not really profess to do this. The object is to justify faith in immortality as a rational faith by showing that it follows naturally from a fundamental metaphysical doctrine (the ideal theory or doctrine of forms), which seems to afford a rational clue to the structure of the universe, though it is expressly said at the end of the whole discussion that this doctrine itself still requires further examination. At the same time, it is made fully clear that the writer accepts this metaphysical doctrine, with the reservation just mentioned, and is passionately sincere in the faith in "personal immortality" which he brings into connection with it. To be strictly accurate, indeed, we ought to say that the faith to be defended goes beyond belief in immortality. What is being maintained is the divinity of the soul; its survival of death is a consequence of this inherent divinity.

The argument is briefly as follows: A true philosopher may naturally look forward to death without dismay. For death is the separation of soul from body, and the philosopher's whole life has been spent in trying to liberate the soul from dependence on her body. In life, the body is always interfering with the soul's activity. Its appetites and passion interrupt our pursuit of wisdom and goodness; its infirmities are perpetually hindering our thinking. Even in our scientific work, we only attain exact and certain truth in proportion as we detach ourselves from reliance on sense-perception and learn to depend on pure thinking.

Death, then, only completes a liberation which the philosopher has been "rehearsing" all through life—if, that is, the soul continues to exist after death, as there are reasons for thinking. For:

1. There is a belief that the soul has a succession of many lives and that, when it is born into this world, it has come back from another; and there are two considerations to be urged on behalf of this belief. In the first place, the processes of nature in general are cyclical: the hot becomes cold, the cold hot; the waking go to sleep, the sleeping wake. It is reasonable to suppose that this applies to the case of dying and coming to life, so that the dead return to life, just as the living die. If this were not so, if the process of dying were not reversible, life would ultimately vanish from the universe. Secondly, we may appeal to the doctrine that what we call "learning" is really "recollection," being reminded of something. This certainly seems to be the case, for in all our science we are perpetually being put in mind of precise ideal standards, mathematical or moral, with which sense or experience never presents us. We must therefore have become acquainted with them before we were confined to our bodies, and therefore must have existed before our birth. These two considerations together would prove what we want to prove, the soul's survival of death, though our dread of the dark makes us demand a more convincing argument.

2. We may consider the antithesis between the divine and eternal and the temporal and mutable which runs through the universe. The body is certainly temporal and mutable. The soul is relatively immutable, like the fixed ideal standards or norms which she contemplates in her scientific thinking. Her thought is concerned with eternal objects and she herself has the likeness of that which she contemplates. If, then, some constituents of the body are nearly indestructible how much more should one expect the divine element in us, the soul, to resist destruction, as the traditions about rebirth assert that it does.

There are two grave "scientific" difficulties still to face. It may be argued: (1) that the soul is an epiphenomenon, the tune (*harmonia*) given out by the body, and if so, its superior divinity will not protect it from vanishing when the instrument which makes the music is broken; (2) that though the soul actually makes its own body, and perhaps can make a long succession of bodies, it cannot do so without expending energy, so that a time will come when it can no longer make a fresh body, and then it will itself disappear. But we must not be driven into misology, antipathy to science, by this apparent clash between science and a faith to which we are attached.

The answer to (1) is that there are good souls and bad ones, and the good soul is more in tune than the bad one. But that which can be more or less in tune is clearly not itself a tune. And if the soul were the tune resulting from the functioning of the body, its character at any moment would be a resultant of the condition of the body. How then could we have the experience, characteristic of the moral life, of the conflict between the soul with its aspirations and the body with its carnalities? The answer to (2) can only be given as part of a whole theory of the causes of "coming into being and passing out of being." Socrates had been led, early in life, to frame a tentative theory of the matter in consequence of his dissatisfaction with the chaotic state of physical speculation and in particular with the failure of Anaxagoras to make any satisfactory use of his apparently teleological principle that "mind is the cause of all order and structure." He fell back on the method of "hypothesis."

What distinguishes this method from all others is that it begins by making an undemonstrated postulate (*hypothesis*). It then proceeds from this point to consider the truth or falsehood of the consequences which follow logically, from the initial postulate; the question of the truth of the postulate is, for the present, left unasked. Socrates' own fundamental unproved postulate has always been that usually, but loosely, called the theory of ideas. The postulate is that there really is a single determinate and immutable something answering to every significant general term and apprehended only by pure thought. The sensible things of which we predicate general terms temporarily partake in or communicate with the idea or form (*idea, eidos*). When we say that a thing becomes beautiful, what we mean is that the form "beauty" begins to be present to that thing, the thing begins to partake of the form. When we say that a thing ceases to be beautiful, we mean that this relation of presence, participation, communication is dissolved. This is the true account of the cause of "coming into and passing out of being," and if we accept it, we may proceed to our final argument for immortality.

3. There are forms which are mutually incompatible, such as warmth and cold. Heat is never cool, and cold is never warm. But there are also certain sensible things of which it is an essential character to partake of a given form. Such things will never admit an incompatible form. Thus it is an essential character of snow to partake of cold. It will never, therefore, partake of the form heat. Similarly it is an essential character of a soul to be alive, to partake of the form life. It refuses to partake of the form death. At the approach of death, the soul must either retire or be annihilated (the metaphors are military). What we have said of its divinity forbids us to think that it is annihilated; we must therefore assume that it retires to some other region. The proof of immortality is thus hypothetical; it is shown to be involved as a consequence by the doctrine of forms. This doctrine has been stated as a fundamental unproved postulate and it is admitted that it demands fuller consideration.

But our inquiry has at least satisfied us that the hope of immortality is a reasonable one. (To distrust it would be to call the foundation of our whole philosophy into question.) The discourse ends with an imaginative cosmological myth depicting the future of the just and the unjust, respectively.

In this statement of the theory of forms we may note the following points: (1) The doctrine is a piece of realist metaphysics in so far as it is assumed that a universally predicated general term denotes or stands for an individual reality, apprehensible by thought, though not by sense; (2) there are a plurality of such forms, standing in various logical relations with one another (whether they constitute a system with a definite structure the *Phaedo* does not tell us); (3) they are at once the objects known in all genuine science and the formal causes of all the temporal processes of the sensible world; (4) the sensible things which have the same names as forms are said to owe their character to their participation of the forms, or, equivalently, to the presence or communication of the forms to them, though the precise character of this relation of participation is admitted to need further explanation (so far as the language of the *Phaedo* goes, a sensible thing would seem to be thought of as a temporary complex or meeting place of universal characters and as nothing more).

Symposium, Phaedrus.—It is by no means clear that these two dialogues are closely connected in point of date (some scholars place the latter after the *Timaeus*), but they may be considered together as both presenting the forms in a special light, as objects of mystical contemplation and excitant of mystical emotion.

The argument of the *Symposium* cannot be reproduced here as a whole. The immediate object of the dialogue, which professes to record the discourses made in eulogy of Eros by a group of eminent speakers at a banquet in honour of the tragic poet Agathon, in the year 416–415, is to find the highest manifestation of the love which controls the world in the mystic aspiration after union with the eternal and supercosmic beauty; to depict Socrates as the type of the aspirant who has reached the goal of union; and to set in sharp opposition to him the figure of Alcibiades, who has sold his spiritual birthright for the pleasures and ambitions of the world. The centre of philosophical interest lies in the discourse of Socrates, which he professes to have learned a quarter of a century ago from the priestess Diotima of Mantinea.

The main argument may be summarized thus: Eros, desirous love, in all its forms, is a reaching out of the soul to a good to which it aspires but has not yet in possession. The desirous soul is not yet in fruition of good. It is on the way to fruition, just as the "philosopher" is not yet in possession of wisdom but is reaching out after it. The object which awakens this desirous love in all its forms is beauty, and beauty is eternal. In its crudest form, love for a beautiful person is really a passion to beget offspring by that person and so to attain, by the perpetuation of one's stock, the *succedaneum* for immortality which is all the body can achieve. A more spiritual form of the same craving for eternity is the aspiration to win immortal fame by combining with a kindred soul to give birth to sound institutions and rules of life. Still more spiritual is the endeavour, in association with

chosen minds, to enrich philosophy and science with noble discourses and thoughts.

But the goal still lies far ahead. When a man has followed the pilgrimage so far, he suddenly descries a supreme beauty that is the cause and source of all the beauties discerned by him so far. The true achievement of immortality is finally effected only by union with this. The philosopher's path thus culminates in a supreme beatific vision. It is clear that the object of this vision, the beauty sole and eternal of the dialogue, means what the *Republic* calls "the good" or "form of good" which by its presence actually causes the goodness of everything else to which the name of good can be given. The forms are thus thought of as a hierarchy with a supreme form at their head, though no attempt is made at a rational theory of the way in which the supreme form unites the rest into the system.

The immediate subject of the *Phaedrus* is the principles of rhetoric or, as we should say, prose composition. The *Gorgias* had told us that rhetoric as commonly practised is not a matter of rational principles at all, but a mere empirical trick of adapting one's tone to the prejudices of an audience. The *Phaedrus* aims at showing how a really scientific rhetoric might be built on the double foundation of logical method and scientific study of human passions. Plato contrives, however, by making a real or supposed "erotic" composition of Lysias the starting point of his criticisms, to unite with this topic a discussion of the psychology of love, and this, as in the *Symposium*, leads him to speak of the forms as the objects of transcendental emotion. The soul is immortal, because it has within itself a native source of spontaneous movement. (This is the argument for immortality to which Plato trusts in the *Laws*. It is not specially mentioned in the *Phaedo*, but this can hardly mean that Plato had not yet discovered it, since it is, in fact, taken from Alcmaeon of Crotona, a medical man of the beginning of the 5th century.) In its disembodied state it shared the life of the gods and could enjoy the direct contemplation of unbodied reality—that is, of the forms. It has suffered an antenatal fall into an embodied condition in which it is blind to everything which does not come in at the avenues of sense.

Now our senses only suggest few and faint images of such forms as justice and temperance, but they can suggest beauty in a much more impressive and startling way. To fall in love is to come under the influence of such sudden and arresting suggestions of beauty; the unreason and madness of the lover mean that he is being awakened to realities which other men ignore. The wings of his soul are beginning to grow again, and his experience, rightly used, will be the first step in the soul's return to its high estate. This section of the *Phaedrus* is the *locus classicus* in Plato for the forms as objects of mystical contemplation.

Republic.—The philosophy presupposed in all these dialogues receives its fullest exposition in the *Republic*. Here the immediate problem is strictly ethical. What is justice? Can it be shown that justice is always a boon, injustice a curse, to its possessor, apart from all consideration of consequences in this life or another? That is, is there a rational principle at the root of moral distinctions, and does the principle carry with itself its own intrinsic and indefeasible authority?

Plato's answer is that there is such a principle; each of us, in virtue of his special endowments and aptitudes, has a specific work or vocation; there is some special contribution which he, and no other, can make most effectively to the life of a rational society. Morality, justice, is to discharge that vocation to the height and with a single mind. To live thus is to be in spiritual health; to live otherwise is to be spiritually diseased. The obligation is thus intrinsic and absolute. This position has to be made good against the incoherencies of a morality of uncriticized traditional maxims, as well as against the immoralism of advanced thought (represented by Thrasymachus in book i, expounded more intelligently by Glaucon in book ii).

This leads us to consider what would be the general type of life in a society where the principle of justice had power as well as manifest authority, and how it might acquire that power. Hence the need for a sketch (books ii–iii) of the institutions of the reformed society, and particularly of its moral and religious education. We have next to satisfy ourselves that the principles which regulate the public life of the morally healthy society are also recognizably the principles of the great virtues of private life. For this purpose, we need a psychology of voluntary action which is provided (book iv) by the doctrine of the tripartite soul. This is not, indeed, a scientific psychology, but proves adequate to describe the moral life of the ordinary good citizen of such a society as we have conceived. The foundation of all this moral excellence is thus laid in absolute loyalty to a sound moral tradition enforced by education.

To ensure that the tradition shall be thoroughly sound, we must stipulate that the authorities who create it do not themselves depend on tradition for their convictions about good and evil; they must not opine, but know, by personal insight. The statesmen at the head of the community must be "philosophers" as well as kings (book vi).

But the vision of "the good" will only dawn on them if they have been prepared for it by an intellectual discipline in hard thinking which leads them through the curriculum of the exact sciences to the critical study of the metaphysical principles involved in science (book vii). The central books of the *Republic* thus present us with an outline of metaphysics and a philosophy of the sciences. We now turn back to consider the various stages of degeneration through which national and personal character pass when the true moral ideal is allowed to fall more and more completely out of view. As we pass them in review, we are increasingly confirmed in our conviction that, in respect of happiness, the life of regard for right is immeasurably superior to that of sating one's cupidities or gratifying one's personal ambitions (books viii and ix), and this conclusion is finally clinched (book x) by reaffirmation of the immortality of the soul. Since the soul is immortal, the issue which hangs upon our choice to live well or ill is one of infinite moment.

The ethical scheme of the *Republic*, like that of the *Gorgias* and *Phaedo*, is dominated by the conception of the "three lives," ascribed by Heraclides Ponticus to Pythagoras. The "lives" are those of the philosopher, of the man of action and of the votary of enjoyment. The end of the first is wisdom, of the second, distinction, of the third, the gratification of appetite. Distinction is a worthier end than mere satisfaction of appetite; the supremely worthy end is wisdom. In a well-lived life, then, the attainment of wisdom will be the paramount end, and ambition and appetite will be allowed only such gratification as is compatible with loyalty to the pursuit of that paramount end. The psychological foundation of this doctrine is the theory of the tripartite soul, expounded fully in book iv. Analysis of familiar experience reveals three elements or active principles within us: (1) considered rational judgment of good; (2) a multitude of clamant appetites for particular gratifications, which may be in violent conflict with our own considered judgment of good; (3) a factor of spirited higher ideal emotion, which manifests itself as resentment against both the infringement of our just rights by others and the rebellion of our own appetites against our judgment.

The same distinctions reappear in the structure of society. A society naturally falls into three divisions: the statesmen, who direct the public life; the general civilian population, who carry on the business of providing for material needs; and the executive force (army and police), whose function is, in a rightly ordered society, to give effect to the counsels of the statesmen by repressing attacks from without and rebellion from within.

These three orders are thus respectively, the judgment, the appetitive element and the spirited element in the national soul. On this basis, we can proceed to work out an ethical and political theory. In ethics we can define the great types of goodness, the quadrilateral, later known as the cardinal virtues. Wisdom is the excellence of the thinking part, clear and assured knowledge of the good; courage, the fighting man's virtue, is the excellence of the spirited part, unswerving loyalty, unshaken by pain, by danger, by the seductions of pleasure, to the rule of life laid down by judgment; temperance, the special excellence of the appetitive part, is the contented acquiescence of the nonrational elements in the soul in the plan of life prescribed by judgment;

justice is just the state in which each of the elements is vigorously executing its own function and confining itself within the limits of that function. In the rightly ordered society, the national wisdom has the statesmen as its organ, the national courage the executive force; the national temperance consists in the agreement as to who, being by nature superior, should rule over whom; and the national justice is shown in the loyal contentment of each class in the community with its prescribed place and its duties.

Such a society is a true aristocracy, or rule of the best. Timocracy, the military state, in the better sense of that phrase, arises when the mere man of action, only competent to fill the part of a good soldier, takes the place which rightly belongs to the thinker as directing statesman. Oligarchy (*e.g.*, the dominance of merchant princes, plutocracy) is a further deviation from the ideal, which arises when political power is bestowed on property as such. A still worse system is democracy, in which no attempt is made to connect political power with any special qualifications. Worst of all is tyranny, exercise of irresponsible power by the positively disqualified, the man of criminal will. The psychological scheme on which this construction is based is not given by Plato as a piece of strict science. We are carefully warned that exact truth is not to be reached by such an analysis of prima facie facts of social life (435 *d*) and reminded later on that this apparent triplicity of the soul may prove to be only a temporary consequence of its conjunction with the body (611 *c*). The tripartite psychology, it is meant, enables us to give an account of the moral life, as it actually appears in a good citizen, which will fairly describe the facts. It is good popular psychology, useful for the moralist, but it is no more.

Hence it is improbable that the analysis originated with Plato himself. More probably it was, as the Stoic Poseidonius asserted, a piece of earlier Pythagorean doctrine, as is also suggested by the constant recurrence, throughout the section of the *Republic* in which the analysis is offered, of analogies from the specially Pythagorean science of harmonics; and by the fact that the same doctrine is taught by the Pythagorean speaker in the *Timaeus*. Plato has, however, worked the theory into his ethics so completely that through him it has actually become a part of the psychology of Thomism, where it has to be squared, not quite satisfactorily, with the radically divergent psychological scheme of Aristotle.

In point of fact, the tripartite schema proves inadequate in the *Republic* itself when we advance in book vi to the consideration of the moral life of the philosopher-king, whose virtue is founded on a personal knowledge of good. A higher level of moral goodness is demanded of him than of other citizens even of the ideal state; his courage, for example, is declared to be no mere loyalty to right opinions inculcated by early education, but a high serenity arising from the knowledge of the relative insignificance of a brief individual life in the great universe which lies open to his contemplation. This has an important bearing on the teaching of the *Republic* about the unity of virtue.

In the ideal state itself, virtue does not appear as a complete unity. The leading types of moral excellence receive their several definitions. It is recognized that a special demand may be made on a particular section of the society in respect of a particular virtue of which it is, so to say, the public organ, as the fighting force is of the valour of the whole society. This is because, even in the ideal state, the moral convictions of citizens, other than the men of superlative intelligence and character who become kings, are not supposed to arise from personal insight. They rest on opinions implanted by education and are thus taken on trust. The good civilian or soldier, after all, is not living by a knowledge which is his own. But the rulers, by whose knowledge the rest of the community lives, must not, of course, themselves take their convictions on trust. They must know with a personal knowledge. The foundation of their virtue must be insight into a system of absolute values embodied in the very structure of the universe. In virtue of this deeper foundation the virtues in them are, so to say, transubstantiated and can no longer be distinguished from one another. They will fuse in knowledge of the good, as, in the Christian saints, they are fused in knowledge and love of God. It is in this form that the Socratic doctrine, "all virtue is one thing, knowledge" reappears in the *Republic* as the foundation of a society in which mankind has at last "escaped from its wretchedness," because knowledge rules.

In the *Republic*, as in the *Phaedo*, the forms appear in the double character of objects of all genuine science and formal causes of the world of events and processes. It is expressly denied that there can be knowledge, in the proper sense of the word, of the temporal and mutable. In the scheme laid down for the intellectual training of the philosophic rulers, ten years, from the age of 20 to that of 30, are assigned for systematic study of the exact sciences in the order: arithmetic, plane geometry, solid geometry, astronomy and harmonics. Special stress is laid on the points that the object of these studies is not practical applications but the familiarizing of the mind with relations between terms which can only be apprehended by thought, and that diagrams and models are to be treated merely as incidental aids to imagination. Five years are then further to be given to the still severer study which Plato calls dialectic, a study which avails itself of no sensible aids to imagination. It proceeds "by means of forms, through forms, to forms" (511 *b*). It is, in fact, what we should call a critical metaphysic of the sciences. It examines the *hypotheses* or unproved postulates, of the various sciences, and its object is to destroy their character as unproved ultimate postulates (533 *c*) by discovering some still more ultimate really self-evident principle (511 *b*) from which they follow as consequences.

There can be no doubt that this most ultimate principle which is more than a postulate means the good or form of good which is said to be the source at once of the reality and the knowability of all that is real and knowable, though it is itself neither knowledge nor being, but transcendent of both (509 *b*). On the methodological side the *Republic* thus completes the teaching of the *Phaedo* by providing the answer to the question then left open, when a postulate may be regarded as finally established. It may be so regarded when it is seen to follow itself from the good, which is the principle at once of existence and of value.

Socrates is made to confess (506 *d-e*) that he can give no positive account of this supreme metaphysical principle; he can only indicate its nature by an analogy. It is to the whole system of forms what the sun is to the system of visible things, the source at once of their existence and of the light by which they are apprehended. The good is thus thought of, to use scholastic terminology, as a transcendent reality which can be apprehended but never fully comprehended. The comparison with the sun and the free employment of the metaphor of vision indicate that the thought of the *Republic* is here the same as that of the *Symposium*: the good is no other than the supreme beauty which was there said to dawn suddenly upon the pilgrim of love as he draws near to the goal of the journey. R. L. Nettleship rightly says that it holds the place taken in later philosophies by God, when God is thought of as the "Light of the world." But it would be deforming Plato's thought to call the good of the *Republic* God. The *Republic* is permeated by religious faith, but theism as a principle of metaphysical explanation only makes its appearance in Plato's latest dialogues, and there as the solution of a problem which can hardly be said to have been adequately faced in the dialogues so far considered.

How the good gives systematic structure to the plurality of forms, the *Republic* does not tell us.

Development of the Doctrine of Forms.—So far we have been presented with a body of thought which has remained recognizably the same without serious modification throughout its various expositions. When we come to the two works which there is reason to regard as directly preluding to the dialogues of Plato's old age, the *Parmenides* and *Theaetetus*, we are struck by a remarkable difference of tone. With Plato, as with Kant, the middle years of life were clearly a period of fruitful critical reconstruction. There is an obvious motive for each reconstruction suggested by the *Phaedo* and *Republic* themselves.

The theory there expounded does not allow enough reality to the sensible world. It is quite false to say that even the *Phaedo* teaches an absolute dualism of two disconnected worlds, a realm of genuine being which never appears and a realm of sensible appearances which are merely unreal. What is true is that both *Phaedo* and *Republic* leave us with an unsolved problem. They tell us that a sensible thing is a complex or meeting place of a plurality of forms. What else, or what more, it is they do not tell us. And yet it is clear that a thing is not simply a bundle of universal predicates.

Or, to put the point rather differently, according to the *Phaedo* a thing becomes for a while beautiful because beauty "becomes present to it." But why does beauty become present to this particular thing at just this particular moment? Clearly the relation between a thing and a form which has been called participation needs further elucidation. Again the simple epistemological formula that knowledge is confined to forms and their relations, while we can only have shifting opinions about temporal facts does less than justice to our scientific knowledge of the natural world; truths of fact have not yet come by their rights. Finally, if the forms constitute a rationally ordered system, there must be definite principles of interrelation between forms themselves as well as between forms and sensible things and these principles demand investigation. (If the good is what the *Republic* says it is, not only will things "participate" in forms; forms also will "participate" in it.) Here are internal motives for active re-examination of the whole system.

It is clear that there was also an external motive. The *Parmenides*, the *Theaetetus* and the *Sophistes* all reveal a special interest in the Eleatic philosophy, and the first and third show an anxiety on Plato's part to maintain that, in spite of important divergences, he, and not the professed Eleatics, is the true spiritual heir of Parmenides. This is easily explained when we remember that Plato was personally a friend of the chief representative of Eleaticism among the Socratic circle, Euclid of Megara, while Polyxenus of Megara, an associate of Euclid, was a hostile critic of the doctrine of participation. The doctrine of Euclid, like that of Parmenides was that sensible appearances are illusions with no reality at all. Against criticism from this quarter, it would be necessary for Plato to show that the *Phaedo* itself does not allow too much reality to the sensible; the attempt to prove this point would inevitably show that it had conceded too little. Continued reflection on the same problem of the worth of propositions about sensible fact leads straight to the discussion of the meaning of the copula, and the significance of denial, which is the subject of the *Sophistes*.

Parmenides.—Formally the dialogue conducts to an impasse. In its first half the youthful Socrates expounds the doctrine of the participation of things in forms to the Eleatic philosophers Parmenides and Zeno as the solution of the problem of the one and the many. Parmenides raises what appear to be insoluble objections to the conception of participation, though he admits that dialectic would be impossible if the existence of forms were denied; he hints that the helplessness of Socrates under his criticism arises from insufficient training in logic.

In the second and longer half, Parmenides gives an example of the logical training he recommends. He takes for examination his own thesis, the one is, and constructs an elaborate set of antinomies after the fashion of Zeno, apparently proving that whether this thesis be affirmed or denied, in either case we are compelled either to affirm simultaneously or to deny simultaneously a series of contradictory predicates, alike of the one and of the many. The conclusion is patently ironical, and we are left to divine the author's purpose, if we can.

The objections to participation, which is formulated precisely as in the *Phaedo*, are directed not against the existence of forms, but against the possibility that sensible things should participate in them. From the point of view of this criticism Socrates' error is that he attributes some sort of secondary reality to the sensible. The main arguments are two. First, the doctrine does not really reconcile unity with plurality, since it leads to a perpetual regress. It says that the many things which have a common predicate participate in or imitate a single form. But the form itself also admits of the common predicate, and there must therefore be a second form, participated in or imitated alike by the sensible things and the first form, and so on endlessly. We could not escape by the suggestion that the form exists only in our minds, since that would mean that a form is a thought, and it would follow that things are made of thoughts. But if so, either everything thinks, or there are thoughts which do not think, and both alternatives are absurd. Secondly, a graver difficulty is that if there are two realms, a realm of forms and a realm of sensible things, the relations between forms must belong to the realm of forms, those between sensible things to the realm of things. We ourselves belong to the second, and therefore all our knowledge belongs to it too; we know nothing of the true realities, the forms: if anyone knows them, it is God, but God's knowledge, being knowledge of realities, will not extend to our world, the sensible. The purpose of the objections is thus to suggest that the manifold of sense has not even a derivative reality; it is mere illusion.

This is precisely the position of the Eleatics and their Megarian continuators. The inference is that Plato is reproducing Megarian criticisms of the doctrine ascribed by himself to Socrates, an inference confirmed by the notice preserved by Alexander of Aphrodisias (on *Metaphysics* 990 *b* 15) of the "third man" argument of the Megarian Polyxenus against participation. Plato does not indicate his own opinion of the cogency of the reasoning, which is, in fact, fallacious, as was pointed out by Proclus. (For a detailed discussion, *see* A. E. Taylor, "Parmenides, Zeno and Socrates," in *Proceedings of the Aristotelian Society,* vol. xvi, pp. 234 ff.)

The purpose of the antinomies which follow has been differently understood. It seems possible that they may be deliberate parody, the object being to show that the methods of the Megarian logicians are even more damaging to their own fundamental metaphysical tenet than they are to the doctrine of participation. Megarian logic is a double-edged weapon, and Plato, if he chooses, can apply it even more dexterously than its inventors.

Theaetetus.—Except for a magnificent interlude in praise of the contemplative life, the dialogue is a straightforward discussion of the question how knowledge should be defined. It naturally ends negatively. None of the proposed definitions will stand examination (the reason is that we are really trying to define truth and truth is an ultimate). But the incidental results of the discussion are of the first importance. We learn (1) that knowledge cannot be identified with sensation nor with any formless simple apprehension; (2) that pure relativism is as impossible in epistemology as in metaphysics. We have the beginning of a doctrine of the categories which is further developed in the *Sophistes*.

The increasing value which Plato is coming to put upon natural knowledge is marked by the use of the word *doxa* (which in earlier dialogues had commonly meant mere uncertain opinion) in the new sense of "judgment" which it retains in Plato's subsequent work. The most striking negative feature of the *Theaetetus* is that it discusses knowledge at length without making any reference to the forms or to the mythology of recollection. It remains to this day the best of introductions to the problem of knowledge. The main argument may be briefly summarized as follows:

1. It seems plausible at first to say that knowledge (*episteme*) is sensation (*aisthesis*). This sounds like the proposition of Protagoras, "what seems to me is so to me; what seems to you is so to you." We might base such a thoroughgoing doctrine of the relativity of all knowledge on a still more ultimate metaphysical theory, if we said—it is implied that Protagoras himself said nothing of the kind—that, within us and without us, the only reality is motion. Organ and environment are both motions; when these motions impinge on one another, they give rise to the twin product, felt sensation–sensible quality.

Both the sensation and the quality sensed will therefore be affected by any difference in the pair of slower motions which cause them (the organ and its environment), and each percipient, therefore, is confined to his strictly private world, which exists only for him. There is no common perceived world, and therefore no standard of truth or reality other than the individual percipient. A teacher does not aim, any more than a physician, at convincing his pupil of the falsity of his judgments, but at giving him useful or healthy convictions in place of harmful or diseased convictions.

The full discussion of such a theory would demand a thorough study both of the Heraclitean philosophy, which says that there is nothing but motion, and the Eleatic philosophy which says that motion is an illusion. But for our immediate purpose, a more summary argument is sufficient. It is certain that even the relativists, who hold that each man is the one infallible measure of his present perceptions, do not hold that he is the only and inerrant measure of his future sensations.. A physician can often judge better than his patient whether the patient is going to have, say, the sensations of an ague. A man's own opinion whether a certain course will be expedient or good for him is often far from being the soundest. We must distinguish carefully between what the soul perceives through bodily organs—the data of sense—and what she apprehends by herself without organs. The latter class includes number, sameness, difference, likeness, unlikeness, being, good, bad, right, wrong; *i.e.*, the great universal categories of fact and value. These are apprehended not by sense, but by thinking, and as they are the formal element in all knowledge, knowledge must be found not in our sensations, but in the judgment (*syllogismos*) of the mind upon them.

2. Is knowledge, then, true judgment? The statement implies that we know what we mean by false judgment, error. But is this the case? Error must not be confused with mere false recognition, misinterpretation of present sensation, since there are purely intellectual errors, and we find ourselves unable to explain the nature of this kind of error. And, in fact, it is clear that persuasive rhetoric may produce in the hearer judgments which are true, but have no claim to be called knowledge.

3. Finally, is knowledge "true judgment accompanied by discourse, true judgment for which we can give grounds"? This would distinguish knowledge from simple apprehension and would harmonize with the theory of those who hold that knowledge is always of complexes, never of their simple constituents. But this doctrine has difficulties of its own, and, in any case, if we say that knowledge is true judgment + discourse, the discourse meant must be a statement of the logical *differentia* of the object of which I have knowledge. The proposed definition therefore amounts to saying that knowledge is true judgment about an object + *knowledge* of the *differentia* of that object and so is circular.

LATER DIALOGUES

Sophistes and Politicus.—Formally these two important dialogues are closely connected. They are made to appear as a sequel to the *Theaetetus*, and a further connection is afforded between them by the fact that both are ostensibly concerned with a problem of definition, which is treated by the characteristic Platonic method of repeatedly subdividing a *genus* until we obtain the *definiendum* as a subspecies. The real purpose of the *Sophistes* is logical or metaphysical; it aims at explaining the true nature of negative predication and so as to dispose of the Eleatic thesis that the temporal and sensible realm, containing, as it does, a negative moment, must be mere unreal illusion. The object of the *Politicus* is to consider the respective merits of two contrasted forms of government, personal rule and constitutionalism, and to recommend the second, particularly in the form of limited monarchy, as most suitable to the actual condition of mankind. The *Sophistes* lays the foundations of all subsequent logic, the *Politicus* those of all constitutionalism.

A more temporary purpose in both dialogues is to illustrate the value of careful classification as a basis for scientific definition. In both dialogues Socrates is almost silent; his place as chief speaker is taken by an unnamed and very unorthodox Eleatic, who seems to be a purely fictitious character. Plato is, in fact, claiming that he, and not the formal logicians of Megara, is the continuator of Parmenides, much as Aristotle in his polemic against Xenocrates claims to be the true successor of Plato.

In the *Sophistes* the main discussion is led up to through a definition of the "sophist" as an "illusionist," a person who, by abuse of logic, produces the illusion, or false appearance, that nature and human life are alike riddled by insoluble contradictions. (This shows that the persons aimed at under the name sophist are the Megarian controversialists who make an illegitimate use of the dialectic of Zeno and Socrates). Now the sophist himself would retort that this definition is senseless, for there can be no such thing as a false statement or a false impression. For the false means "what is not," and "what is not" is nothing at all and can neither be uttered nor thought. To refute him we need to correct the fundamental thesis of so venerable a thinker as Parmenides. Either we must admit that there can be no false statements, or we must be prepared to maintain that "what is not, in some sense also is," and "what is, in some sense is not" (*i.e.,* we must explain what is the meaning of a significant negative proposition). In our theory of being we have to meet at once Parmenides and two different types of pluralist opponents of Parmenides, (1) the corporealists who say that the real, "what is," is just visible and tangible body and (2) certain friends of forms who maintain that the real is a multitude of incorporeal forms, denying that sense-perception gives us any apprehension of it. The corporealist is sufficiently refuted by the consideration that he himself cannot deny the reality of force (*dynamis*) and that force is not a body. The incorporealist friends of forms cannot be met in this way. They regard force, or activity itself, as belonging to the unreal realm of becoming. We meet them by urging that knowing is itself an activity and that we cannot deny intelligence and knowledge to the supreme reality. This means that it has a "soul" and is alive. But if life is real, movement and repose from movement must be real too.[1]

This leaves us free to attack the Parmenidean monism itself. That is refuted by drawing the distinction between absolute and relative nonbeing. A significant denial, *A is not B,* does not mean that *A* is nothing, but that *A* is other than *B.* Every one of the great categorical features of reality is other than every other, and the true business of dialectic is to study the various possible combinations of these universal categories. The dialogue mentions five of them, being, identity, difference, motion and rest. (Though it is not said that this is a complete list of categories, it was treated as such by the Neoplatonists.)

The important result is thus that we have learned to think of forms themselves as an interrelated system, with relations of compatibility and incompatibility among themselves. Negation is a moment in the system of intelligible reality, and therefore its presence in the sensible realm does not stamp that realm as illusion. This is the ontological position which interests Plato; the recognition of the function of the logical copula is a consequence.

The *Politicus* has as its main result the conclusion that government by the personal direction of a benevolent dictator is not suitable to the conditions of human life, where the direction is necessarily that of a fallible man, not of a god. In an actual human society, the surrogate for personal direction by a god is the impersonal supremacy of inviolable law. Where there is such a recognized sovereign law, monarchy is the most satisfactory type of constitution, democracy the least satisfactory, but where there is no fundamental law, this situation is inverted. A sovereign democracy is preferable to an irresponsible autocrat. The dialogue is rich in thoughts which have passed into the substance of Aristotle's ethics and politics. Aristotle took directly from it the conception of politics as the architectonic practical science to which all others are subordinate; the formula of the right mean comes from it together with the *Philebus.*

Philebus.—The subject of the dialogue is a strictly ethical one, and this, no doubt, explains why it is the only dialogue after the *Theaetetus* in which Socrates is the principal speaker. The issue propounded is the question whether the good is pleasurable feeling or whether it is thought, the exercise of intelligence.

Comparison with the notices of Aristotle in the *Nicomachean Ethics* shows that this was the subject of a sharp division in the

Academy, the hedonist party being led by the mathematician and astronomer Eudoxus, the antihedonists by Speusippus. Under the guidance of Socrates the question is narrowed down to a consideration of the good for man in particular, and a mediating conclusion is reached. The best life for man contains both elements but intelligence is the predominant partner.

All forms of knowledge find a place in it, but only those pleasures which are compatible with wisdom and virtue; *i.e.,* those which are "unmixed" (not preceded by a sense of want or craving) and those of the "mixed" pleasures (the satisfactions of appetite) which are innocent and moderate. The *Philebus* contains Plato's ripest moral psychology; it is the immediate source of the famous doctrine of the mean.

Philosophically the most important feature of the dialogue is a classification adopted with a view to determining the formal character of the two claimants to recognition as the good. All components of the actual belong to one of four classes, (1) the infinite or unbounded (*apeiron*), (2) the limit (*peras*), (3) the mixture or combination of infinite and limit, (4) the cause of the mixture. (Infinite and limit are just the two fundamental opposites of Pythagoreanism.) All the good things of life belong to the third class, that is, they are produced by the introduction of definite limit or ratio into an indeterminate continuum. (This is precisely the doctrine of the mean.) The establishment of such a ratio is a genesis into being, a process resulting in a stable being, and it is indicated that the cause or agent in such a process is always intelligence, human or divine.

There has been much discussion of the question in which of these classes the forms should be placed. The only tenable alternatives would be to put them into the class of limit or into that of the mixture (a view suggested both by the teaching of the *Sophistes* and by Aristotle's express statement that Plato distinguished two constituents within the form and advocated ably by H. Jackson). The truth seems to be that the particular classification in the *Philebus* is devised for a special purpose and that it is not intended to apply to anything but the things and processes of the sensible realm. In that case, though there is a close correspondence between what the *Philebus* teaches about stable being in the sensible realm and what, as we know from Aristotle, Plato taught about the forms, it will be a mistake to look for any actual exposition of the metaphysic of the forms in the *Philebus.*

Timaeus.—The *Timaeus* is an exposition of cosmology, physics and biology put into the mouth of the astronomer Timaeus of Locri. Though Plato avoids expressly describing the speaker as a Pythagorean, his doctrine is revealed by attentive analysis as an attempt to combine the mathematics and astronomy of the Pythagoreans with the biology of Empedocles, the real founder of Sicilian medicine. The discussion is introduced by the famous narrative of the gallantry of the prehistoric Athenians who defeated the kings of the imaginary Atlantis in their ambitious attempt to become masters of the world. The story was to have been told more in detail in the unfinished *Critias.*

Timaeus opens his discussion by drawing a distinction between eternal being and temporal becoming and by insisting on the point that it is only of the former that we can have exact and final knowledge. All accounts of the temporal can be only tentative and liable to repeated revision. Cosmology, then, at best, is not exact science. The visible world, being mutable and temporal, is a copy of a model which is eternal, and the copy is the work of God. The reason why there is a copy at all is the unceasingly active and generous goodness of God. (In the sequel Timaeus speaks of the forms which God had before Him as His model in much the same language as the *Phaedo,* except that he uses the Pythagorean word imitation, not participation, to describe the relation of sensible things to forms.)

The world, then, had a beginning. (The Academic tradition from the first was that this is not to be understood literally; Aristotle insists on taking it literally.) God first formed its soul out of three constituents, identity, difference, being. Its body was made later from the four Empedoclean elements. The world soul was placed in the circles of the sidereal equator and ecliptic, the latter being split into seven lesser circles, those of the planets,

---

[1] It is still a much agitated question who are the logical atomists described in the *Sophistes* as the friends of forms. The view that they are adherents of the philosophy of the *Phaedo* and *Republic* is defended by some. They are still often supposed to be Megarians, but this seems inconsistent with the way in which they are carefully distinguished from the followers of Parmenides as belonging to the other side at 245 *e.* Proclus (*Commentarii in Parmenidem,* 659) says positively, as though it were the only view known to him, that they are Italian Pythagoreans, and this is probably correct, since the Eleatic of the dialogue refers to them as persons with whom he is familiar. It is important to remark that the identification of being with force is given merely as a consequence which would follow from, and contradict, the corporealist hypothesis. The implication of the passage is rather that the identification is false than that it is true.

and the two were animated with movements in opposite senses. Subsequently were formed the various subordinate gods and the souls of human beings, that is the immortal and rational element in the human soul, which come straight from the hands of God Himself.

The formation of the human body and of the two lower mortal components of the human soul was effected through the intermediacy of the "created gods" (*i.e.*, the stars). The most important question of detail arising from this part of the dialogue is that debated between A. Boeckh and G. Grote. Does Timaeus ascribe a motion to the earth? The restoration of the correct text at 40 *c* ("going up and down on the path about the axis of the universe") proves definitely that he does, but it is not a diurnal revolution, as Grote supposed; it must be a rectilinear displacement of an unknown period.

The contact is made between Pythagorean geometry and the Empedoclean biology which will be needed for the physiology and medicine of the dialogue by a mathematical construction of the elements. Starting with two primitive triangles, the isosceles right-angled, and the right-angled scalene in which the hypotenuse is double the shortest side, Timaeus constructs four of the regular solids, cube, tetrahedron, octahedron, icosahedron, and these are assumed to be the shapes of the corpuscles of earth, fire, air, water. These four in their turn are the immediate constituents of all organic and inorganic compounds.

The important features of the dialogue are not the particular tentative scientific hypotheses but its leading methodological principles. We should note the introduction of God as the intelligent efficient cause of all order and structure in the world of becoming, which preludes to the natural theology of the *Laws*, and the emphatic recognition of the essentially tentative and therefore progressive character of natural science. It is also noticeable that though Plato's scientific ideal is a mathematical corpuscular physics—his influence in creating this ideal has been much more important than that of the ancient atomists—he constructs his physical world without matter as a metaphysical substrate. The place of matter is taken in his analysis, as Aristotle complained, by *chora,* space, as in the *Principia* of Descartes, a point of view to which physical speculation seems to be returning. He analyzes the passage of nature into three factors: being (a form), space and happening (genesis) much as A. N. Whitehead analyzes it into objects, events and the ingredients of object into event.

It is a fundamental point that the presence of space as a factor makes it necessary to recognize over and above God or mind a subordinate element of *ananke,* "necessity," in events. Since necessity is also called the errant cause, *planomene aitia* (with an allusion to the name of the planets or tramp-stars) the word clearly does not mean conformity to law. It is rather a name for the fact that there is always in the actual an irreducible remainder of brute datum, "conjunctions" in Hume's phrase, which we cannot rationalize completely into intelligible connections. Thus *ananke* is not a rebel or evil principle in the constitution of things; its function is everywhere to be instrumental to the intelligent and beneficent purpose of mind or God. There are many facts which we have to be content to accept simply as facts without seeing their reason why. We do not know and may never know, why it is "best" that they should be as they are (*e.g.,* why it is "best" that we should live on a moving earth) but we may be sure that, since it is the fact, it is in some way best that it should be so. This seems to be what is meant by the statement that God or mind (*nous*) persuades *ananke.* It is the expression of a rational faith in Providence and the supremacy of the moral order. The details of the cosmology, physiology and psychophysics of the dialogue are of great importance for the history of science, but metaphysically of secondary interest.

Laws and Epinomis.—The *Laws*, Plato's longest, is also his most intensely practical work and contains his ripest utterances on ethics, education and jurisprudence, as well as his one entirely nonmythical exposition of theology. The immediate object is to meet a practical need by providing a model of constitution making and legislation for members of the Academy who may be called on to assist his advisers in the actual founding or refounding of cities.

Plato's attempt to do work of this kind himself at Syracuse had borne no immediate fruit but had given the Academy a recognized standing as a school of scientific politics and jurisprudence. The work of constitution making and legislation was going on in many quarters at the end of his life, and his experience might be made fruitful in sage counsels to younger men. The practical character of the subject explains some novelties in the outward form of the work. As the dialogue is assumed to be dealing with the actual present, Socrates has disappeared and his place is taken by an unnamed Athenian who is, to all intents, Plato himself.

The scene is laid in Crete; the imagined situation is that the Cretans are about to found a settlement on the site of a long deserted city. The chief commissioner for the project is walking out to inspect the proposed site with a Spartan friend, when they meet the Athenian and being favourably impressed by his conversation invite him to join them as an expert adviser.

The problem thus differs from that of the *Republic;* the question is not the construction of an ideal state, but the framing of a constitution and code which might be successfully adopted by a society of average Greeks in the middle of the 4th century. Hence the demands made on average human nature, though exacting, are not pitched too high; the communism of the *Republic* is dropped. And for the same reason it is assumed all through that the regulations are carefully adapted to the particular economic and geographical conditions, though it is said that these conditions will not really suit any actual Cretan locality. If so, we must suppose that Plato, under a transparent disguise, is contemplating the actual conditions in quarters from which the Academy was more likely to receive appeals for help.

The special purpose of the work also explains why purely speculative philosophy and science are excluded from its purview. The metaphysical interest is introduced only so far as to provide a basis for a moral theology; the one matter of first-rate scientific importance touched on is the diurnal motion of the earth, and this is only hinted in connection with the practical problem of the construction of the calendar. In compensation, the *Laws* is exceptionally rich in political and juristic wisdom and appears, indirectly, through its influence on the law of the Hellenistic age, to have left its mark on the great system of Roman jurisprudence.

It is impossible to do more than to call attention to a few of the striking features of this great work. The ethical ideal is still that familiar from earlier dialogues. It is interesting that the demand is expressly made that all unnatural vices shall be completely suppressed and that the rule of sexual life is to be monogamous marriage with strict chastity, outside the limits of marriage, for both sexes. In politics, Plato declares himself definitely in favour of a mixed constitution; a good government demands a balance between two principles, *eleutheria,* "popular control," and *monarchia,* "personal authority." Persia is an illustration of the mischief of unqualified autocracy, Athens of the evils which come from elimination of the authoritarian principle, and considerable care is taken in the suggested system of magistracies to secure both genuine popular representation and the proper regard for personal qualifications. The basis of society is to be agriculture, not commerce; the citizens are to be peasant proprietors—communism is regretfully abandoned as impracticable in a society of ordinary human beings. But the patrimony of each household is to be strictly inalienable, and differences in personal property are to be kept within strict bounds by what amounts to a supertax of 100% on incomes beyond the statutory limits. Education, as in the *Republic*, is regarded as the most important of all the functions of government; it is placed under the control of a minister who is the premier. As far as possible, the distinction between the sexes is, as in the *Republic,* to be treated as irrelevant to the educational program.

The most striking features of the scheme are the careful attention paid to the problems of the physical training of children in their earliest infancy and to the right utilization of the child's instinct for play and the demand, made now for the first time, that in adolescence, the young shall be taught in institutions where expert instruction in all the various subjects is co-ordinated. It is from this proposal that the grammar school, or secondary school, has taken its origin. Though we hear no more of philosopher-kings the demand is still made that the members of the "nocturnal council," the supreme council of the state, which is always in permanent session, and exercises a general control over administration, shall be thoroughly trained, not only in the exact sciences but in the supreme science, which "sees the one in the many and the many in the one"; that is, they are to be dialecticians.

The work is full of suggestions for the practical application of science, such, for example, as that of the necessity of strictly standardizing all weights and measures, or that of basing the calendar on a solar year (of 365 days). The object of the apparently arbitrary selection of the number of patrimonies and the scheme of subdivision of the whole society into smaller groups appears to be the practical one of making it easy to determine exactly what quotum each subdivision may justly be called on to contribute to the revenue or the defenses.

At least two fundamental improvements are made on the Attic jurisprudence which Plato has adopted as the foundation of his own code. One great blot on the heliastic system is removed by the regulations which ensure that trials for serious offenses shall take place before a court which contains highly qualified magistrates, and shall proceed with due deliberation and that there shall be provision for appeals from the primary tribunal to a court of cassation. It is even more important, perhaps, that *Laws* ix by drawing a clear distinction between *blabe,* "detriment," and *adikia,* "infringement," of rights, lays the foundation for the discrimination between civil and criminal actions at law.

An incidental passage in the *Laws* (822 *a-b*) and another in the *Epinomis* (987 *b*) definitely show that Theophrastus was right in crediting Plato with belief in the earth's motion. In the *Laws* it is said that the real orbit of each planet is a single closed curve; in the *Epinomis* the view that the circle of the stars communicates its motion to those of the planets is called that of men "who know but little of the subject." The allusion is to the famous theory of the celestial motions put forward by Plato's friend and associate, the great mathematician Eudoxus.

According to this, the first great geocentric theory in scientific astronomy, the movements of each planet can be analyzed into a combination of circular revolutions, the unmoved earth being taken as the common centre of all. What Plato asserts is that each planet has only one proper revolution; the remaining revolutions are apparent, not real. The implication is that these apparent revolutions of the planet must be real motions of the earth from which we make our observations. The earth is thus a planet, though not a satellite of the sun. The language of the *Epinomis*—which may be safely regarded as at least true to Plato's thought—definitely makes the sun, itself, one of the planets. We have, therefore, to think of the earth as also a planet revolving with the rest round an unseen centre. We may infer from the words of Theophrastus that Plato, like some of the Pythagoreans, held that there is a luminary, the "central fire," at this centre. The period of the earth's revolution would certainly be taken to be the natural day, so that the motion ascribed to the earth is equivalent to the diurnal rotation, though from Plato's point of view it is not a rotation on an axis, but a revolution round a centre. It follows that the alternation of day and night is no longer accounted for by a rotation of the heaven of the fixed stars. This outermost circle is still credited in the *Epinomis* with a revolution in the sense east to west, but its period is not specified. We need not suppose either that Plato could have specified the period or that he used it to explain any special appearances. It has nothing to do with precession of the equinoxes, being in the wrong sense for that purpose.

What is to Plato's credit is that he has the insight to see that, with all its attractions, the scheme of Eudoxus starts from a wrong presupposition, a stationary earth.

In *Laws* x Plato, for a practical purpose, creates natural theology. There are three false beliefs which are fatal to moral character, atheism, denial of the moral government of the world, the belief that divine judgment can be bought off by offerings. Plato

holds that he can disprove them all. The refutation of atheism turns on the identification of the soul with the "movement which can move itself," already used in the *Phaedrus*. All motion is either communicated from without or self-initiated, and the ultimate source of all communicated motion must be self-initiated motion. The only thing which can move itself is a soul. It follows that all motion throughout the universe is ultimately initiated by souls. It is then inferred from the regular character of the great cosmic motions and their systematic unity that the souls which originate them form a hierarchy with a best soul, God, at their head. Disorderly and irregular motions are equally due to souls, but to bad and disordered souls, and from the fact that there are disorderly motions, it is inferred that the best soul cannot be the only soul.

There is no suggestion that there is a worst soul, a devil or evil world-soul; all that is said is that there must be one soul which is not the best, and may be more. This is Plato's way of excluding pantheism, as incompatible with the reality of evil. The argument thus establishes at once the immortality of the soul and the existence of God. The other two heresies can now be disposed of. It is inconsistent with the goodness of the best soul to be indifferent to our conduct, and still more so to be venal. The moral government of the world is, in fact, assured by the establishment of the single principle that every soul gravitates into the society of its desires and consequently does and has done to it what it befits such a soul to do and have done to it. Plato thus becomes the originator of the view that there are certain theological truths which can be strictly demonstrated by reason.

It is these demonstrable truths which are subsequently named by M. Terentius Varro natural or philosophical theology in contradistinction to the poetical theology, the myths related by the poets, and the civil theology, the ritual cultus instituted by politicians. From Varro the distinction of three theologies passed to St. Augustine and thus in the end became the foundation of the scholastic distinction between natural theology, those truths about God which can be ascertained independently of any specific revelation, and revealed theology, the further truths which are only made accessible by the Christian revelation. Since Plato's object in demonstrating his three propositions is an ethical one, he goes on to enact that the denial of any of them shall be a grave crime to be visited by the state with penalties ranging from a minimum of five years' solitary confinement, and with death on a second conviction. Plato is thus the inventor, so far as European society is concerned, of the proposal to make an official creed for the state and to treat dissent from it as criminal, an innovation foreign to the spirit of the Hellenic cities, in which religion was a matter not of beliefs but of cultures. Plato's last word, then, on the problem how the sensible comes to partake of form is that it does so through the agency of divine goodness and wisdom. God molds the sensible upon the pattern of the intelligible. The obvious question, how God, who is a soul not a form, is related to the good which is the supreme form, never receives discussion or solution. To answer that question was to be the main business of Plotinus.

PLATONISM AFTER PLATO

Aristotle's Account of Platonism.—Since Plato refused to write any formal exposition of his own metaphysic, our knowledge of its final shape has to be derived from the statements of Aristotle, which are confirmed by scanty remains of the earliest Platonists preserved in the Neoplatonist commentaries on Aristotle. These statements can, unfortunately, only be interpreted conjecturally. According to Aristotle (*Metaphysics* i, 987 *b* 18–25) Plato's doctrine of forms was, in its general character, not different from Pythagoreanism, the forms being actually called numbers. The two points on which Aristotle regards Plato as disagreeing with the Pythagoreans are (1) that whereas the Pythagoreans said that numbers have as their constituents the unlimited and the limit, Plato taught that the forms have as constituents the one and the great and small; and (2) that whereas the Pythagoreans had said that things are numbers, Plato intercalated between his forms (or numbers) and sensible things an intermediate class of mathematicals. It is curious, that in connection with the former difference Aristotle dwells mainly on the substitution of the "duality of the great and small" for the "unlimited," not on the much more significant point that the one, which the Pythagoreans regarded as the simplest complex of unlimited and limit, is treated by Plato as itself the element of limit. He further adds that the "great and small" is, in his own technical terminology, the matter, the one, the formal constituent, in a number.

If we could be sure how much of the polemic against number-forms in *Metaphysics* xiii–xiv is aimed directly at Plato, we might add considerably to this bald statement of his doctrine, but unluckily it is certain that much of the polemic is concerned with the teaching of Speusippus and Xenocrates. It is not safe, therefore, to ascribe to Plato statements other than those with which Aristotle explicitly credits him. We have then to interpret, if we can, two main statements: (1) the statement that the forms are numbers; (2) the statement that the constituents of a number are the great and small and the one.

Light is thrown on the first statement if we recall the corpuscular physics of the *Timaeus* and the mixture of the *Philebus*. In the *Timaeus*, in particular, the behaviour of bodies is explained by the geometrical structure of their corpuscles, and the corpuscles themselves are analyzed into complexes built up out of two types of elementary triangle, which are the simplest elements of the narrative of Timaeus. Now a triangle, being determined in everything but absolute magnitude by the numbers which express the ratio of its sides, may be regarded as a triplet of numbers. If we remember then, that the triangles determine the character of bodies and are, themselves, determined by numbers, we may see why the ultimate forms on which the character of nature depends should be said to be numbers, and also what is meant by the mathematicals intermediate between the forms and sensible things. According to Aristotle, these mathematicals differ from forms because they are many, whereas the form is one, from sensible things in being unchanging. This is exactly how the geometer's figure differs at once from the type it embodies and from a visible thing. There is, for example, only one type of triangle whose sides have the ratios 3:4:5, but there may be as many pure instances of the type as there are triplets of numbers exhibiting these ratios; and again, the geometrical triangles which are such pure instances of the type, unlike sensible three-sided figures, embody the type exactly and unchangingly. A mathematical physicist may thus readily be led to what seems to be Plato's view that the relations of numbers are the key to the whole mystery of nature, as is actually said in the *Epinomis* (990 *e*).

We can now, perhaps, see the motive for the further departure from Pythagoreanism. It is clear that the Pythagorean parallelism between geometry and arithmetic rested upon the thought that the point is to spatial magnitude what the number 1 is to number. Numbers were thought of as collections of units, and volumes, in like fashion, as collections of points; that is, the point was conceived as a minimum volume. As the criticisms of Zeno showed, this conception was fatal to the specially Pythagorean science of geometry itself, since it makes it impossible to assert the continuity of spatial magnitude. (This, no doubt, is why Plato, as Aristotle tells us, rejected the notion of a point as a fiction.)

There is also a difficulty about the notion of a number as a collection of units, which must have been forced on Plato's attention by the interest in irrationals which is shown by repeated allusions in the dialogues, as well as by the later anecdotes which represent him as busied with the problem of doubling the cube or finding two mean proportionals. Irrational square and cube roots cannot possibly be reached by any process of forming collections of units, and yet it is a problem in mathematics to determine them, and their determination is required for physics (*Epinomis* 990 *c*–991 *b*).

This is sufficient to explain why it is necessary to regard the numbers which are the physicist's determinants as themselves determinations of a continuum (a great and small), by a limit and

why, at the same time the one can no longer be regarded as a blend of unlimited and limit but must be, itself, the factor of limit. (If it were the first result of the blending, it would reappear in all the further blends; all numbers would be collections of one and there would be no place for the irrationals.) There is no doubt that Plato's thought proceeded on these general lines. Aristotle tells us that he said that numbers are not really addible (*Metaphysics* xiii, 1083 *a* 34), that is, that the integer series is not really made by successive additions of 1; and the *Epinomis* is emphatic on the point that, contrary to the accepted opinion, surds are just as much numbers as integers. The underlying thought is that numbers are to be thought of as generated in a way which will permit the inclusion of rationals and irrationals in the same series. In point of fact there are logical difficulties which make it impossible to solve the problem precisely on these lines. It is true that mathematics requires a sound logical theory of irrational numbers and, again, that an integer is not a collection of units; it is not true that rational integers and real numbers form a single series.

The Platonic number theory was inspired by thoughts which have since borne fruit abundantly but was itself premature. We learn partly from Aristotle, partly from notices preserved by his commentators, that in the derivation of the integer series, the even numbers were supposed to be generated by the dyad which doubles whatever it lays hold of, the odd numbers in some way by the one which limits or equalizes, but the interpretation of these statements is, at best, conjectural. In the statement about the dyad there seems to be some confusion between the number 2 and the indeterminate dyad, another name for the continuum also called the great and small, and it is not clear whether this confusion was inherent in the theory itself, or has been caused by Aristotle's misapprehension.

Nor, again, is it at all certain exactly what is meant by the operation of equalizing ascribed to the one. It would be improper here to propound conjectures which our space will not allow us to discuss. A collection and examination of the available evidence is given by L. Robin in his *Théorie platonicienne des idées et des nombres d'après Aristote* (1908), and an admirable exposition of the significance of the problem of the irrational for Plato's philosophy by G. Milhaud in *Les Philosophes-géomètres de la Grèce, Platon et ses prédécesseurs*, new ed. (1934). For a conjectural interpretation *see* A. E. Taylor, "Forms and Numbers," in *Mind*, new series, vol. xxxv and xxxvi (1926, 1927).

The Academy After Plato.—Plato's Academy continued to exist as a corporate body down to A.D. 529 when the emperor Justinian, in his zeal for Christian orthodoxy, closed the schools of Athens and appropriated their emoluments (*see* ACADEMY, GREEK). Plato's greatest scholar, Aristotle, had finally gone his own way and organized a school of his own in the Lyceum, claiming that he was preserving the essential spirit of Platonism while rejecting the difficult doctrine of the forms. The place of official head of the Academy was filled first by Speusippus, Plato's nephew (*c.* 347–339 B.C.), then by Xenocrates (*c.* 339–314 B.C.). Under Arcesilaus (*c.* 276–241 B.C.) the Academy began its long-continued polemic against the sensationalist dogmatism of the Stoics, which accounts both for the tradition of later antiquity which dates the rise of a New (some said Middle) and purely skeptical Academy from Arcesilaus and for the 18th-century associations of the phrase "academic philosophy."

In the 1st century B.C. the most interesting episode in the history of the school is the quarrel between its president Philo of Larissa and his scholar Antiochus of Ascalon, of which Cicero's *Academica* is the literary record. Antiochus, who had embraced Stoic tenets, alleged that Plato had really held views indistinguishable from those of Zeno of Citium and that Arcesilaus had corrupted the doctrine of the Academy in a skeptical sense. Philo denied this. The gradual *rapprochement* between Stoicism and the Academy is illustrated from the other side by the work of Stoic scholars such as Panaetius of Rhodes and Poseidonius of Apamea, who commented on Platonic dialogues and modified the doctrines of their school in a Platonic sense.

The history of the Academy after Philo is obscure, but since the late 1st century A.D. we meet with a popular literary Platonism of which the writings of Plutarch are the best example. This popular Platonism insists on the value of religion, in opposition to Epicureanism, and on the freedom of the will and the reality of human initiative, in opposition to the Stoic determinism; a further characteristic feature, wholly incompatible with the genuine doctrine of Plato, is the notion that matter is inherently evil and the source of moral evil.

Genuine Platonism was revived in the 3rd century A.D., in Rome, and independently of the Academy, by Plotinus. His Neoplatonism (*q.v.*) represents a real effort to do justice to the whole thought of Plato. Two aspects of Plato's thought, however, in the changed conditions inevitably fell into the background, the mathematical physics and the politics. The 3rd century A.D. had no understanding for the former, and the Roman empire under a succession of military chiefs no place for the latter. The doctrine of Plotinus is Platonism seen through the personal temperament of a saintly mystic, and with the *Symposium* and the teaching of the *Republic* about the form of good always in the foreground. Plotinus lived in an atmosphere too pure for sectarian polemic, but in the hands of his successors, Neoplatonism was developed in conscious opposition to Christianity. Porphyry, his disciple and biographer, was the most formidable of the anti-Christian controversialists; in the next century, "Platonists" were among the allies and counsellors of the emperor Julian in his attempts to invent an Hellenic counterpart to Christianity.

Early in the 5th century, Neoplatonism flourished for a short time in Alexandria (which disgraced itself by the murder of Hypatia in 415) and captured the Athenian Academy itself, where its last great representative was the acute Proclus (A.D. 410–485). The latest members of the Academy, under Justinian, occupied themselves chiefly with learned commentaries on Aristotle, of which those of Simplicius are the most valuable. The doctrine of the school itself ends in Damascius with mystical agnosticism.

Influence on Christian Thought.—Traces of Plato are probably to be detected in the Alexandrian *Wisdom of Solomon;* the thought of the Alexandrian Jewish philosopher and theologian Philo, in the 1st century A.D., is at least as much Platonic as Stoic. There are, perhaps, no certain marks of Platonic influence in the New Testament, but the earliest apologists (Justin, Athenagoras) appealed to the witness of Plato against the puerilities and indecencies of mythology. In the 3rd century Clement of Alexandria and after him Origen made Platonism the metaphysical foundation of what was intended to be a definitely Christian philosophy. The church could not, in the end, conciliate Platonist eschatology with the dogmas of the resurrection of the flesh and the final judgment, but in a less extreme form the platonizing tendency was continued in the next century by the Cappadocians, notably St. Gregory of Nyssa, and passed from them to St. Ambrose of Milan. The main sources of the Platonism which dominated the philosophy of western Christian theologians through the earlier middle ages, were, however, Augustine, the greatest thinker among the western fathers, who had been profoundly influenced by Plotinus read in a Latin version, before his conversion to Christianity; and Boëthius, whose wholly Platonist vindication of the ways of Providence in his *De Consolatione Philosophiae* was the favourite serious book of the middle ages.

A further powerful influence was exerted by the writings of the so-called Dionysius the Areopagite (*q.v.*), which laid down the main lines of medieval mystical theology and angelology. These works are, in fact, an imperfectly Christianized version of the speculations of Proclus and cannot date before the end of the 5th century A.D. at the earliest, but they enjoyed an immense authority based on their attribution to an immediate convert of St. Paul. After their translation into Latin in the 9th century by Johannes Scotus Erigena, they became popular in the west.

Apart from this theological influence, Plato dominated the thought of the earlier Renaissance which dates from the time of Charlemagne in another way. Since the west possessed the philosophical writings of Cicero, with the Neoplatonic comment of Macrobius on the *Somnium Scipionis,* as well as the Latin translation of the first two thirds of the *Timaeus* by Chalcidius, with his

commentary on the text, and versions, also, at least of the *Phaedo* and of the *Meno,* whereas nothing was known of the works of Aristotle except Latin versions of some of the logical treatises, the middle age, between Charlemagne and the beginning of the 13th century, when the recovery of Aristotle's physics and metaphysics from Moors, Persians and Jews began, was much better informed about Plato than about Aristotle; in particular, in the various encyclopaedias of this period, it is the *Timaeus* which forms the regular background.

The 13th century saw a change. Aristotle came to displace Plato as the philosopher, partly in consequence of the immediately perceived value of his strictly scientific works as a storehouse of well-digested natural facts, partly from the brilliant success of the enterprise carried through by St. Thomas Aquinas, the reconstruction of philosophical theology on an Aristotelian basis. Plato is, however, by no means supplanted in the Thomist system; the impress of Augustine on western thought has been far too deep for that. Augustine's "exemplarism," that is, the doctrine of forms in the version, ultimately derived from Philo of Alexandria, which makes the forms creative thoughts of God, is an integral part of the Thomist metaphysics, though it is now denied that the exemplars are themselves cognizable by the human intellect, which has to collect its forms, as best it can, from the data of sense.

Directly or through Augustine, the influence of Plato, not only on strictly philosophic thought but on popular ethics and religion, has repeatedly come to the front in ages of general spiritual requickening and shows no signs of being on the wane.

Two revivals in particular are famous. The first is that of the 16th century, marked by the Latin translation of Marsilio Ficino and the foundation of Lorenzo de' Medici's fantastic Florentine Academy. What was revived then was not so much the spirit of Plato as that of the least sober of the Neoplatonists; the influence of the revival was felt more in literature than in philosophy or morals, but in literature its importance may be measured by the mere mention of such names as Michelangelo, Sir Philip Sidney and Edmund Spenser.

In the 17th century, Plato, seen chiefly through the medium of Plotinus, supplied the inspiration of a group of noble thinkers who were vindicating a more inward morality and religion against the unspiritual secularism and Erastianism of Hobbes: namely the so-called Cambridge Platonists (*q.v.*), Benjamin Whichcote, Henry More, Ralph Cudworth and John Smith. In the 20th century, on the one hand A. N. Whitehead tried to work out a philosophy of the sciences which confessedly connected itself with the ideas of the *Timaeus;* and on the other the rise of totalitarian governments produced a number of publications confronting Plato with the theories (Communist, Fascist, etc.) inherent in their policies. Neo-Kantianism, existentialism, and analytical philosophy produced their own interpretations of Plato. *See* also references under "Plato" in the Index.

BIBLIOGRAPHY.—The works of Plato are arranged in nine tetralogies as follows: (1) *Euthyphro, Apology, Crito, Phaedo;* (2) *Cratylus, Theaetetus, Sophistes, Politicus;* (3) *Parmenides, Philebus, Symposium, Phaedrus;* (4) *Alcibiades I, Alcibiades II, Hipparchus, Erastae;* (5) *Theages, Charmides, Laches, Lysis;* (6) *Euthydemus, Protagoras, Gorgias, Meno;* (7) *Hippias I (major), Hippias II (minor), Ion, Menexenus;* (8) *Clitophon, Republic, Timaeus, Critias;* and (9) *Minos, Laws, Epinomis, Epistles.* Of the manuscript codices, none of which are earlier than the 9th century A.D., the most important are the Bodleianus-Clarkianus (containing the first six tetralogies), the Parisinus 1807 A (containing the eighth and the ninth) and the Venetus (containing the first seven and part of the eighth). Since the end of the 19th century papyrus fragments have been found; on these, *see* H. Leisegang, "Platon" (1950), in Pauly-Wissowa, *Real-Encyclopädie der Classischen Altertumswissenschaft.* On the text and the canon *see:* H. Alline, *Histoire du texte de Platon* (1915); L. A. Post, *The Vatican Plato and Its Relations* (1935); G. Jachmann, "Der Platontext" in *Nachrichten der Akademie der Wissenschaften in Göttingen, Phil.-hist. Klasse 1941* (1942); E. Bickel, "Das Platonische Schriftenkorpus . . ." and "Geschichte und Recensio des Platontextes," in *Rheinisches Museum,* 92 (1943).

Modern editions of Plato refer to the pagination of that by (J. Serranus and) H. Stephanus, 3 vol. (1578), used in the foregoing text of this article. The standard edition is that by J. Burnet, 5 vol. (1900–06, repr. 1952–54). It contains the 36 works of the nine tetralogies and the *spuria* (*Definitions, On Justice, On Virtue, Demodo-*

cus, Sisyphus, Halcyon, Eryxias, Axiochus). Earlier editions deserving mention: G. Stallbaum, 12 vol. (1827–42) with Latin commentary, and K. F. Hermann, 6 vol. (1851–53), rev. by M. Wohlrab (repr. 1921–36), containing Plato's works and the *spuria*, but also the Pseudo-Timaeus Locrus *On the World Soul*, two writings by Albinus, the biography by Olympiodorus, the scholia, and index of names, etc. Collected editions: in Greek and English by W. R. M. Lamb *et al.* (1914–29), in Greek and French by A. Croiset *et al.*, with index (1920–64). The English translation by B. Jowett, 4th ed., rev. by D. J. Allan and H. E. Dale (1953), omits *Alcibiades II, Hipparchus, Erastae, Theages, Clitophon, Minos, Epinomis, Epistles*. With the exception of the last two they are also omitted in E. Hamilton and H. Cairns (eds.), *The Collected Dialogues of Plato* (1961). Among translations into other languages are those into German by H. Müller, most comprehensive, 8 vol. (1850–66); by O. Apelt, 25 vol. (1912–22, many vol. in rev. ed.), with bibliographies and index; into French by L. Robin and J. Moreau, 2 vol. (1940–55); into Italian by E. Turolla, 3 vol., 1953.

For individual works mentioned in the text, the following editions, annotated translations and commentaries may be recommended: *Hippias I*, ed. by D. Tarrant (1928); *Hippias II*, ed. by G. Calogero (1948); *Ion*, ed. by W. J. Verdenius (1959); *Menexenus*, ed. by J. A. Shawyer (1906); *Charmides, Laches, Lysis*, ed. by G. Ammendola (1930, 1933, 1936); *Cratylus*, ed. by G. Manzoni (1936); *Euthydemus*, ed. by E. H. Gifford (1905); *Gorgias*, ed. by E. R. Dodds (1959); *Meno*, ed. by R. S. Bluck (1961); *Protagoras*, ed. by F. Dirlmeier and H. Scharold (1959); *Euthyphro*, ed. by G. C. Field and W. D. Woodhead (1953); *Apology and Crito* (1924) and *Phaedo* (1911) ed. by J. Burnet; *Apology*, ed. by J. Riddell (1867); *Phaedo*, trans. by R. S. Bluck (1955), and by R. Hackforth (1955), ed. and trans. by F. Dirlmeier (1949); *Symposium*, ed. by R. G. Bury, 2nd ed. (1932); *Phaedrus*, trans. by R. Hackforth (1952), and by J. B. Skemp (1952); *Republic*, ed. by J. Adam and D. A. Rees (1963), trans. by F. M. Cornford in *Plato and Parmenides* (1939); *Theaetetus* and *Sophistes*, trans. by F. M. Cornford in *Plato's Theory of Knowledge* (1935); *Theaetetus*, ed. by L. Campbell, 2nd ed. (1883); *Politicus*, trans. by J. B. Skemp, *Statesman* (1952), by A. E. Taylor (1961); *Philebus*, ed. by G. Stallbaum (1826), by R. B. Bury (1897), and trans. by R. Hackforth, *Plato's Examination of Pleasure* (1945); *Timaeus*, commentary by A. E. Taylor (1928), trans. by F. M. Cornford, *Plato's Cosmology* (1937), by A. E. Taylor (1929); *Laws*, commentary by C. Ritter (1896), ed. with commentary by E. B. England (1921), trans. by A. E. Taylor (1960); *Epinomis*, ed. by F. Novotný (1960); trans. by J. Harward (1928); with *Philebus*, trans. by A. E. Taylor (1956); *Epistles*, ed. by F. Novotný (1930), by G. Pasquali (1938) and by A. Maddalena (1948), and trans. by G. R. Morrow (1962); *Scholia Platonica*, ed. W. C. Greene *et al.* (1939).

Comprehensive presentations are to be found in J. Burnet, *Greek Philosophy* (1914); E. Zeller, *Die Philosophie der Griechen*, vol. ii, part 2, 5th ed. (1922); T. Gomperz, *Griechische Denker*, vol. ii, 4th ed. (1925); F. Ueberweg, *Die Philosophie des Altertums*, 12th ed. by K. Praechter (1926, repr. 1956); J. Geffcken, *Griechische Literaturgeschichte*, vol. ii (1934); J. Chevalier, *Histoire de la pensée*, vol. i (1955); K. Jaspers, *Die grossen Philosophen*, vol. i (1957). Separate studies are J. Burnet, *Platonism* (1928); I. M. Crombie, *An Examination of Plato's Doctrines*, 2 vol. (1962–63); R. Demos, *The Philosophy of Plato* (1939); G. C. Field, *Plato and His Contemporaries*, 2nd ed. (1948); P. Friedländer, *Platon* (vol. i, ii, 3rd ed., 1964; vol. iii, 2nd ed., 1960); G. M. A. Grube, *Plato's Thought* (new ed. 1958); E. Hoffmann, *Platon* (1950); A. Koyré, *Introduction à la lecture de Platon* (1945); G. Meáutis, *Platon vivant* (1950); L. Robin, *Platon* (1935); P. M. Schuhl, *L'oeuvre de Platon* (1954); P. Shorey, *What Plato Said* (1933); L. Stefanini, *Platone*, 2nd ed. (1949); A. E. Taylor, *Plato*, 6th ed. (1949); U. von Wilamowitz-Moellendorff, *Platon*, vol. i, 5th ed. (1959), vol. ii, 3rd ed. (1962); W. Broecker, *Platons gespräche*, 2nd ed. (1967). On Plato's relations to his predecessors, the Orient, posterity, and some special aspects of his philosophy *see* P. M. Schuhl, *Essai sur la formation de la pensée grecque*, 2nd ed. (1949); V. de Magalhães-Vilhena, *Socrate et la légende platonicienne* (1952); E. Frank, *Plato und die sogenannten Pythagoreer* (1923); J. Bidez, *... Eos; ou, Platon et l'Orient* (1945); W. J. W. Koster, *Le Mythe de Platon, de Zarathoustra et des Chaldéens* (1951); P. Shorey, *Platonism, Ancient and Modern* (1938); R. Klibansky, *The Continuity of the Platonic Tradition During the Middle Ages*, 2nd ed. (1950); P. Frutiger, *Les Mythes de Platon* (1930); R. Schaerer, *La question platonicienne* (1938); A. J. Festugière, *Contemplation et vie contemplative selon Platon*, 2nd ed. (1950); M. Heidegger, *Platons Lehre von der Wahrheit* (1947); J. Stenzel, *Studien zur Entwicklung der platonischen Dialektik ...*, 3rd ed. (1961); R. Robinson, *Plato's Earlier Dialectic*, 2nd ed. (1953); N. Hartmann, *Zur Lehre vom Eidos bei Platon und Aristoteles* (1944); P. Natorp, *Platons Ideenlehre*, 2nd ed. (1921); W. F. R. Hardie, *A Study in Plato* (1936); J. Moreau, *Réalisme et idéalisme chez Platon* (1951); W. D. (Sir David) Ross, *Plato's Theory of Ideas* (1951); J. Stenzel, *Zahl und Gestalt bei Platon und Aristoteles*, 3rd ed. (1959); G. Capone Braga, *Il mondo delle Idee* (1928); A. Wedberg, *Plato's Philosophy of Mathematics* (1955); P. E. More, *The Religion of Plato*, 3rd ed. (1928); F. Solmsen, *Plato's Theology* (1942); O. Reverdin, *La religion dans la cité platonicienne* (1945); V. Goldschmidt, *La religion de Platon* (1949); N. R. Murphy, *The Interpretation of Plato's Republic* (1951); P. Lachièze-Rey, *Les idées morales, sociales et politiques de Platon*, 2nd ed. (1951); H. G. Gadamer, *Platos dialektische Ethik* (1931); J. Gould, *The Development of Plato's Ethics* (1955); E. Barker, *Greek Political Theory: Plato. ...*, 4th ed. (1951); W. Jaeger, *Paideia*, vol. ii, 3rd ed. (1947); P. M. Schuhl, *Platon et l'art de son temps*, 2nd ed. (1952); H. J. Krämer, *Arete bei Platon und Aristoteles*, 2nd ed. (1967); K. Gaiser, *Platons ungeschriebene Lehre* (1963). Collections of papers on various topics: *Recherches sur la tradition platonicienne* (1957); R. E. Allen (ed.), *Studies in Plato's Metaphysics* (1965); R. Bambrough (ed.), *New Essays on Plato and Aristotle* (1965); T. L. Thorson (ed.), *Plato: Totalitarian or Democrat?* (1963). For additional literature *see* W. Totok, *Handbuch der Geschichte der Philosophie* (1964). *See also Bibliographies* of ACADEMY, GREEK; NEOPLATONISM.

(A. E. TA.; PP. M.)

PLATO (fl. *c.* 400 B.C.), Greek poet, was a writer of Old Comedy. His earliest play was probably produced in 427 B.C., his last in 387. Of his 28 comedies most were on political themes. He attacked Hyperbolus in his *Perialges* ("The Sufferer"; 420?), Dieitrephes in the *Heortai* ("The Festivals"; 414?) and Peisander and Cleophon in the so-named plays. Mythological burlesques are represented by such plays as the *Adonis*, the *Daidalos*, the *Phaon*, etc., and social (= Middle) comedy by the *Sophistai*.

BIBLIOGRAPHY.—T. Kock, *Comicorum Atticorum fragmenta* (1880–88); G. Norwood, *Greek Comedy* (1931); J. M. Edmonds, *Fragments of Attic Comedy* (1957); H. J. Rose, *Greek Literature* (1936).

(M. PR.)

PLATONIC LOVE, a locution used in two senses, with allusion in both cases to Plato's account of love in his *Symposium* (*see* PLATO: *The Earlier Dialogues*).

1. In common speech, platonic love means a supremely affectionate relationship between human beings in which sexual intercourse is neither desired nor practised. In this sense, it most often refers to a heterosexual relationship. By extension, it may be used to cover that stage of chivalrous or courtly love in which sexual intercourse is indefinitely postponed.

2. From the Renaissance to the end of the 19th century platonic love was used as an occasional euphemism for homosexual love, in view of the comparatively tolerant attitude to such love discernible in Plato as well as in other Greek authors.

PLATOON, the principal subdivision of a military company (*q.v.*), battery, or troop. Customarily commanded by a lieutenant, it consists of from 25 to 50 men organized into two or more sections or squads led by noncommissioned officers.

In the 17th century the term referred to a small body of musketeers who fired together in a volley, alternately with another platoon, and it has always retained some sense of systematic alternate employment. Hence "platoon fire" meant a regulated fire of alternating platoon volleys, and "platoon" sometimes referred to the volley itself. In the 18th century battalions were often organized for tactical purposes into 16 platoons of about 24 men each, plus 2 or 4 platoons of grenadiers or light infantry.

The term "platoon" has been used in U.S. military manuals since 1779 and throughout the 19th century meant half a company. The platoon was reintroduced into the British Army in 1913.

The "platoon system" in municipal police and U.S. football organizations signifies the use of two or more shifts or teams of comparable strength that alternate on duty. (F. P. T.)

PLATT, THOMAS COLLIER (1833–1910), U.S. senator and for a time the political boss of New York State, was born in Owego, N.Y., July 15, 1833. Educated in Owego and at Yale College, he entered banking and later became secretary and then president of the United States Express Company. After serving as chairman of the Tioga County Republican Committee in the 1860s, Platt was elected in 1873 to the U.S. House of Representatives, where he served until 1877. He had meanwhile become a political ally of Sen. Roscoe Conkling and in January 1881 was himself elected to the U.S. Senate. Because of a quarrel with Pres. James Garfield over patronage, both Platt and Conkling resigned from the Senate in May 1881.

After Conkling's retirement from politics, Platt gained control of the Republican Party in New York State. He remained prominent in the Republican Party for a number of years and attended every national convention of the party from 1876 to 1904. He helped obtain the declaration for the gold standard at the 1896 convention.

He reluctantly gave his support to the campaign of Theodore Roosevelt for governor of New York and later for vice-president of the United States. Platt served in the U.S. Senate again from 1897 to 1909, but his political power waned steadily after 1903. He died in New York City, March 6, 1910. (RI. W. C.)

PLATT AMENDMENT, an amendment to the U.S. army appropriation bill of March 1901, offered by Sen. Orville H. Platt of Connecticut and adopted by congress, which defined the conditions on which the United States was willing to end the military occupation of Cuba that had followed the Spanish-American War of 1898. Elihu Root, secretary of war, had previously formulated the terms on which the United States would withdraw and leave the government of Cuba to the Cubans. It was the Root formulation that Platt offered in the senate, with the proviso that the conditions must be embodied in the new Cuban constitution and also in a permanent treaty with the United States. The Cuban Constitutional convention reluctantly accepted the amendment. In so doing, it agreed that Cuba would validate the acts, and carry out the sanitary program, of the U.S. military government; that it would not impair Cuban independence by treaty with, or cession of territory to, any "foreign" power, or contract any debt beyond the capacity of the ordinary revenues to pay. It conceded to the United States the right to a naval base in Cuban territory and waters (later fixed at Guantánamo bay) and gave the United States the right to intervene in Cuba for the preservation of orderly government or of Cuban independence—a right the United States exercised repeatedly during the next 30 years. The Cubans never liked the Platt amendment, for they regarded it as an infringement of their sovereignty. In 1934 the United States negotiated a new treaty with Cuba that abrogated all provisions of the Platt amendment except the right to the naval base at Guantánamo bay.

BIBLIOGRAPHY.—P. C. Jessup, *Elihu Root,* 2 vol. (1938); Dexter Perkins, *The Monroe Doctrine, 1867–1907* (1937); J. W. Pratt, *America's Colonial Experiment* (1950). (J. W. PR.)

PLATTE, a river system of the western United States, tributary to the Missouri river. The Platte river, 310 mi. long, is formed at North Platte, Neb., where the North Platte, 618 mi. long, and the South Platte, 424 mi. long, flow together. The North Platte river rises in the Medicine Bow and Park ranges and the Rabbit Ears mountains of north-central Colorado. It flows north into Wyoming and bends east-southeast at Casper, Wyo., flowing into western Nebraska. In eastern Wyoming the North Platte valley is one to ten miles wide and from 100 to 300 ft. below the surrounding uplands. On the Wyoming-Nebraska boundary the North Platte flows through the Goshen Hole where the valley has widened to 50 mi. in places and the bordering bluffs are 400 ft. high. Torrington, Wyo., and Scottsbluff, Neb., mark the western and eastern extremities of the Goshen Hole. On the North Platte there are three large reservoirs used for irrigation and power: Pathfinder reservoir near Alcova, Wyo., completed in April 1909, with storage capacity of 1,010,900 ac.ft.; Seminoe reservoir near Leo, Wyo., completed in March 1939, capacity 1,012,000 ac.ft. and Alcova reservoir at Alcova completed in Jan. 1938, capacity 190,500 ac.ft.

The South Platte river rises in Park county on the Mosquito range of central Colorado and flows southeast across South Park. West of Divide, Colo., the river turns sharply northeast, flows through the Front range via the Platte River canyon and emerges on the flat land of the Colorado piedmont southeast of Denver. Continuing its northeast course, it flows through Denver to Greeley, Colo., where it bends eastward to North Platte. From Greeley east the valley of the South Platte is from two to ten miles wide. The river bed is filled with sandbars and the stream channel is often braided. Cheesman, Eleven Mile Canyon, and Antero reservoirs on the upper South Platte are storage units for Denver's water supply.

From North Platte the Platte river flows southeast into a big bend at Kearney, Neb., turns northeast and empties into the Missouri at Plattsmouth, Neb. During the spring runoff the Platte river is a mile wide in many places and almost dry the remainder of the year. Important tributaries of the North Platte are the Sweetwater and Laramie rivers and Medicine Bow creek. South Platte tributaries are Clear creek and Boulder creek and the Big Thompson, St. Vrain and Cache La Poudre rivers. The Loup river is the largest tributary of the Platte. The vast quantities of water diverted for irrigation agriculture and for municipal use are the most significant aspects of the Platte river system.

(M. J. L.)

PLATTER, THOMAS (1499–1582), Swiss writer and humanist, best known for his autobiography, was born at Grächen, Valais, on Feb. 10, 1499, and died at Basel on Jan. 26, 1582. After years of hardship, spent as a goatherd in the Alps and as a "fag" to a traveling scholar in Germany, he was initiated at Zürich into Huldreich Zwingli's teachings and the newly discovered world of Greek, Latin and Hebrew culture by Oswald Myconius, the first biographer of the Swiss reformer. Moving to Basel, Platter first earned his living as a ropemaker but contributed to the renown of this great centre of humanistic learning by teaching Hebrew, working as partner to the printer, Andrew Cratander, and after 1541 reforming Basel grammar school. His autobiography, completed in 1576, is an interesting and important document of the period and tells the story of his lifelong struggle against heavy odds in self-education. The work of his son, FELIX (1536–1614), physician at Basel, anticipated modern psychopathology.

BIBLIOGRAPHY.—Platter's *Selbstbiographie* (with the *Tagebuch* of his son Felix), ed. by H. Boos, 2nd ed. (1918), Eng. trans. by E. A. McCaul Finn, 2nd ed. (1847); *Briefe an seinen Sohn Felix,* ed. by A. A. Burckhardt (1890). See also Fritz Ernst, "Die beiden Platter," in *Neue Schweizer Rundschau* (1927) and, without bibliography, in *Essais,* vol. 1 (1946). (A. Bx.)

PLATTSBURGH, a city of Clinton county, N.Y., U.S., on the west shore of Lake Champlain. Plattsburgh is surrounded by beautiful scenery: the broad island-studded lake in front, the Green mountains beyond, and on the southern horizon the distant Adirondacks. Part of Plattsburgh air force base, serving the Strategic Air Command, is on the site of an army post established in 1815. An experimental businessmen's military training camp at this post in 1915 served as a prototype for reserve officer training facilities during World War I. After World War II the first university for U.S. veterans was established there and later disbanded. Located in the city is the State University College at Plattsburgh, which originated in 1889 as a normal and training school and which became a unit of the State University of New York in 1949. Plattsburgh is a recreational area and marketing and manufacturing centre of pulp, paper and allied products. The city was founded by Zephaniah Platt (1740–1807), who brought a colony from Long Island. Recognized as a town April 4, 1785, it was incorporated as a city in 1902. The opening naval engagement of the American Revolution (a victory for the British) took place at Valcour Island 5 mi. S.E. of Plattsburgh on Oct. 11, 1776. In the War of 1812 the city was the headquarters of the U.S. army on the northern frontier. In Sept. 1814 the village was besieged in what was planned to be a joint attack by sea and by land; on Sept. 11 Commodore Thomas Macdonough and the U.S. forces defeated the invading British fleet and the British army, deprived of naval support, retreated. *See* WAR OF 1812.

For comparative population figures *see* table in NEW YORK: *Population.* (G. L. F.)

PLATYHELMINTHES (PLATODARIA), a phylum of invertebrate animals, the flatworms, soft-bodied creatures that are bilaterally symmetrical and usually somewhat flattened in shape. The group includes both free-living (*see* FLATWORM) and parasitic (*see* FLUKE; TAPEWORM) species.

PLATYPUS (*Ornithorhynchus anatinus*), one of the most primitive of living mammals, composing with the echidnas (*q.v.*) or spiny anteaters the order Monotremata. Often referred to as the duck-billed platypus or duckbill because of its elongate, flattened, leathery bill-like muzzle, this species is confined to eastern Australia and Tasmania. Being a mammal, the platypus possesses hair and provides milk for its young. Like all monotremes, however, it differs from other mammals in laying eggs and lacking true nipples. The milk of lactating females exudes from the mammary glands and is lapped up by the young from the mother's abdominal fur. The adult male may be about two feet long, the

BY COURTESY OF AUSTRALIAN NEWS AND INFORMATION BUREAU

PLATYPUS (ORNITHORHYNCHUS ANATINUS), AN EGG-LAYING MAMMAL

female being smaller. A dense, gray-brown fur covers the body and the flattened beaverlike tail. Teeth are lacking in the adult. Both front and hind feet are webbed. The male possesses on the inside of each ankle a sharp, horny spur connected to a poison sac. These spurs are wielded with a slashing or stabbing motion. The wound, infiltrated with venom, is fatal in some small animals but merely painful in larger ones, including man.

The platypus is semiaquatic, living along the banks of rivers. Two types of burrows are constructed. One is used by both sexes outside of the breeding season and by bachelors during the latter period. The other is made by the female and contains a nest chamber in which she deposits and incubates her two white, soft-shelled, roundish eggs.

The food of the platypus consists principally of aquatic insects, worms, small crustaceans and mollusks. *See* also MONOTREME; MAMMAL.   (R. T. O.)

PLAUEN, a town of East Germany in the *Bezirk* (district) of Karl-Marx-Stadt, German Democratic Republic. It lies 90 km. (56 mi.) SW of Karl-Marx-Stadt (Chemnitz) by road. Pop. (1962 est.) 78,983. Situated on the slopes of the Weisse Elster valley, Plauen is the principal town in the scenically beautiful Vogtland. It was severely damaged by air raids in World War II. The old town hall (enlarged in 1508) is adjoined by the modern town hall; the 12th-century Johanneskirche was restored in the 19th century; the old castle is now a lawcourt. There is a textile craft school. Plauen is a junction on the Berlin–Leipzig–Hof–Munich railway. The town's best-known industry is lace making, but linen, cotton, and embroidered goods, curtains, printing presses, trucks, and machinery are among its many manufactures. In the Middle Ages Vogtland was directly administered by the Vogts or bailiffs, the term surviving in the name of the region. First mentioned in 1122, Plauen became the centre of a flourishing textile craft.

PLAUTUS (fl. late 3rd and probably early 2nd century B.C.) was the great comic dramatist of ancient Rome. Twenty-one plays (*Amphitruo, Asinaria, Aulularia, Bacchides, Captivi, Casina, Cistellaria, Curculio, Epidicus, Menaechmi, Mercator, Miles Gloriosus, Mostellaria, Persa, Poenulus, Pseudolus, Rudens, Stichus, Trinummus, Truculentus* and the fragmentary *Vidularia*) ascribed to Plautus have survived in the manuscripts (*i.e.*, the 4th-century Ambrosian palimpsest, known as "A," and various manuscripts of the 10th century and later, known as the "Palatine" family). According to Festus and Jerome he was born at Sarsina, in Umbria: his death occurred in 184 B.C. according to Cicero; in 200, according to Jerome. The two *didascaliae* (notes in the form of a preface) preserved in "A" are usually regarded as firm evidence that the *Stichus* was produced in 200 and the *Pseudolus* in 191; but *see* H. B. Mattingly, "The Plautine 'Didascaliae,'" *Athenaeum* (nuova serie), xxxv, pp. 78–88 (1957).

According to Cicero, Plautus in his old age took great pleasure in his *Pseudolus* and *Truculentus.* This may be invention, indicating merely that these were popular plays in Cicero's day; but on it is founded the usual view that Plautus was born about 250 B.C. The only extant record as to his life is that of Aulus Gellius (based on Varro), the historical character of which is questioned by Friedrich Leo in his *Plautinische Forschungen* (2nd ed.; 1912). It is probably invention or mistaken inference, but the record may be near the truth in stating that from an early age Plautus was connected with the theatre (perhaps as an actor). The prologue to the *Asinaria* gives the author's name as *Maccus;* the prologue to the *Mercator* gives it (in the genitive) as *mactici* (*Macci Titi?*); at the end of the *Casina* in "A" it is given (in the genitive) as *T. Macci Plauti.* The poet Accius, however, seems to have distinguished between Plautus and Titus Maccus. It will be remembered that *Maccus* was the clown in the *Atellanae fabulae* (*q.v.*) and that *Plautus* is said by Festus to mean *planis pedibus* (*cf. planipes,* "mime"). The other prologues which give the name give it as "Plautus."

There is no certain evidence as to the dates of the plays. *Cistellaria* (201 ff.) refers to approaching victory over the Carthaginians. The supposed reference in *Miles Gloriosus* (211 ff.) to the imprisonment of the poet Naevius is perhaps itself the source of that story. Evidently Plautus' plays were popular and were revived after his death (*see* the post-Plautine prologue to the *Casina*). The works of other dramatists came to be attributed to him; by Varro's day the number of his plays had risen to 130. Varro made out a list of 21 (evidently those now known) which he said were universally agreed to be genuine (perhaps on grounds of style); others he himself accepted on grounds of style but did not include in the 21; still others he rejected. He can scarcely have been right in excluding the *Commorientes* (attested as Plautine by Terence and Accius) and, perhaps, the *Colax,* mentioned by Terence as either partly or doubtfully Plautine.

Attempts to arrange the plays in chronological order, on the evidence of topical allusions, metrical development, etc., must be regarded as speculative. What one scholar thinks a topical allusion by Plautus another will ascribe to the Greek original and yet another to a post-Plautine hand. Metrical variety is indeed characteristic of Plautus; but the prominence of the so-called "lyrical" metres might just as plausibly be attributed to the poet's youth as to his age. (*See,* however, W. B. Sedgwick, "The Origin and Development of Roman Comic Metres," *Classica et Mediaevalia,* 10, pp. 171–181, 1949.)

Indebtedness and Originality.—The plays of Plautus are based on Greek originals of the New Comedy, of which original examples are to be found in the fragments of Menander (including the *Dyscolus,* discovered in 1956). But Plautus was not a mere translator. This was shown by K. M. Westaway (*The Original Element in Plautus,* 1917) and Eduard Fraenkel (*Plautinisches im Plautus,* 1922); later, Italian scholars pointed to the vitality and verve which pervade all his work. On the other hand, there are passages in which he does not hesitate to take over allusions which can hardly have been intelligible to a Roman audience; *e.g.*, the reference in the *Rudens* to Stratonicus, a musician of the time of Alexander the Great. Terence refers twice to Plautus' "carelessness" as a translator, says that he omitted a scene from Diphilus' *Synapothnescontes* in his *Commorientes* and implies that he himself is following Plautus' example in his own practice of borrowing from a second original. Of large-scale remodeling there is no evidence; Aulus Gellius speaks rather of difference for the worse in style. Are the prologues mainly Greek, or Plautine, or post-Plautine? The romanization of the plays by way of allusions to towns in Italy, to the streets, gates and markets of Rome, to Roman magistrates and their duties and to Roman laws and the business of Roman law courts, banks, comitia and senate, etc., still leaves the structure Greek. Frank inconsistency is shown by his use, side by side, of the contemptuous expressions *barbarus* (applied to the Romans) and *pergraecari,* "to play the Greek" (applied to the Greeks). Frequently, as in passages in the *Aulularia,* the *Poenulus* and the *Pseudolus,* he seems to take delight in casting dramatic illusion to the winds.

But as an adapter for the Roman stage Plautus is nothing less than masterly. His command of Latin is such that his plays read like original works. Some of his characters stand out so vividly from his canvas that they have ever since served as representatives of certain types of humanity; *e.g.,* Euclio in the *Aulularia,* the model of Molière's miser. Alliteration, assonance, deft use of metre for dramatic effect, plays upon words and happy coinages of new terms give his plays a charm of their own. "To read Plautus is to be once for all disabused of the impression that Latin is a dry and uninteresting language," wrote Franz Skutsch in *Die Cultur der Gegenwart* (1905). It is a mistake to regard the Latin of Plautus as "vulgar" Latin. It is essentially a literary idiom, based upon the language of Roman society in his day.

Characters and Plots.—The characters in his plays are the stock characters of New Comedy (though there may well be a suspicion that he has heightened the farcical element, perhaps under the influence of native Italian farce). The finer insight into human nature and the delicate touch in character drawing which Terence presents in his reproductions of Menander may be missing, but there is wonderful life and vigour and considerable variety in Plautus' characters. Their language is often downright and sometimes obscene, but, as has been said, "the coarseness of Plautus' plays is not as great as is sometimes supposed" (John N. Hough, "Miscellanea Plautina," *Transactions of the American Philological Association,"* 71, p. 186, 1940). The careful reader will take note of occasional touches of serious thought, examples of which are to be found in the *Pseudolus* (683 ff.); the *Stichus* (124); the *Rudens* (1235–1248), etc. The *Captivi* is the story of the heroic self-sacrifice of a slave; the *Amphitruo* is a mythological burlesque; the *Rudens* tells of shipwreck and treasure trove. But most of his plays depend for their main interest on intrigue. In the *Menaechmi* and *Amphitruo* and as a subordinate element in the *Bacchides* the theme of mistaken identity is to be found.

Metres.—In the metrical structure of his plays Plautus (no doubt following the earlier Latin dramatists) made an important change from the Greek model. The New Comedy had confined itself for the most part to the metre of dialogue (the six-foot iambic trimeter), occasionally relieved in moments of excitement by the trochaic tetrameter catalectic (seven and a half feet), which latter was accompanied by the pipe. Plautus greatly developed this trochaic metre in its Latin form (trochaic septenarius); it is actually more common than the iambic senarius (six-foot line), the only metre not accompanied by the pipe. But he used many other metres as well, all accompanied by the pipe; in fact the senarius or metre of unaccompanied speech (*diuerbium*) is only about half as common as the metre (whatever its form) of *canticum,* or declamation supported by the pipe. The *cantica* are not mere inserts or accessories, like the songs introduced in the Shakespearean drama; they comprise two-thirds of the text. The effect was probably not that of full song but rather that of the recitative "patter" of W. S. Gilbert, in which the words and rhythm are important and the music simply supports the rhythm. In *Stichus* (758 ff.) the piper (*tibicen*) is given a drink, and while he is drinking the metre changes for seven lines to iambic senarius. The *tibicen* was on the stage throughout the play; in *Pseudolus* (573a) he is asked to supply a solo.

The origin of the *cantica* has been much debated. Leo put forward the view that Plautus derived their metrical structure from contemporary Hellenistic music-hall songs; Fraenkel suggested that some earlier Latin dramatist had endeavoured to enliven comedy by introducing the metrical variety which he found in Greek tragedy; A. M. G. Little and others have sought the origin in Italian popular comedy (see *Harvard Studies in Classical Philology,* 49, p. 226, 1938). The individual metres employed were not indeed invented by Plautus; they are adapted from Greek and are common to Roman tragedy and Roman comedy, however, Plautus handled them with peculiar literary and dramatic skill.

Reputation.—Plautus held the stage until the end of the republic. Aelius Stilo, Cicero's teacher, praised his Latinity. Cicero, though in the *Orator* he found fault with the iambics of the Latin comedians generally as *abiecti* ("slovenly"), admired

Plautus' type of wit as *elegans, urbanum, ingeniosum, facetum.* Varro ranked him above all other Latin comic dramatists for dialogue. Horace in the *Ars Poetica* is a more severe critic: he is impatient with the taste of an earlier age which had admired Plautus' command of rhythm and jest, and in *Epistles* ii he accuses Plautus of carelessness in character drawing and indifference to everything except box-office success. The mime seems to have driven Plautus off the stage during the empire (though a ticket has been found at Pompeii giving admission to a performance of the *Casina,* and Arnobius says that the *Amphitruo* was performed in the reign of Diocletian). But he was still read; Aulus Gellius praises his style; Sidonius Apollinaris ranked him above the Greeks in wit; Jerome, after a night of weeping over his own sins, would console himself by reading Plautus; Eusebius praised him. In the middle ages he seems to have been best known as the supposed author of the *Querolus* (5th century A.D.?). Only the first eight of his plays were known to Petrarch and other scholars at the beginning of the Renaissance; but in 1429 Nicolaus Cusanus brought to Rome a manuscript containing the 12 later plays; this event gave a strong impulse to the study of Plautus, who took rank as one of the great dramatists of antiquity.

Influence on Modern Literature.—Carl von Reinhardstoettner in his *Spätere Bearbeitungen plautinischer Lustspiele* (1886) deals at length with the influence of Plautus on modern literatures. In the 15th century Italian scholars were producing Plautus' plays, new Latin plays and new Italian comedies (the *commedia erudita*) based on Plautus and Terence. In 1484 the *Aulularia* was presented on the Quirinal. An important play on the theme of the *Menaechmi* was *Gl'Ingannati,* by the members of the Sienese Academy; this was translated into Spanish as *Los Enganados* by Lope de Rueda. In the 16th century Plautine influence was strong in Germany, Holland and France. In England the *Menaechmi* was performed by the boys of St. Paul's school in 1527. Nicholas Udall's *Ralph Roister Doister,* the first English comedy, was written about 1552; it is based on the *Miles Gloriosus.* Shakespeare's *Comedy of Errors* (about 1591), based upon the *Menaechmi,* with additional material from the *Amphitruo,* is thought to reflect the poet's Latin studies at school; his Falstaff and Parolles and Ben Jonson's Captain Bobadil owe much to the Plautine braggart warrior; the *Taming of the Shrew* has been influenced by the *Mostellaria.* In *Hamlet* II, ii, 377–382, Polonius says "The best actors in the world . . . Seneca cannot be too heavy nor Plautus too light." Ben Jonson's *The Case is Alterd* (1609) is adapted from the *Captivi* and the *Aulularia.* Thomas Heywood adapted the *Amphitruo* in his *Silver Age* (1613), the *Rudens* in his *Captives* (1624) and the *Mostellaria* in his *English Traveller* (1633). John Dryden's *Amphitryon* (1690) is based partly on the Latin *Amphitruo* but chiefly on Molière's adaptation. Henry Fielding's *Miser* (acted 1732) rests on Molière's *L'Avare* rather than on the *Aulularia.* In 1929 Jean Giraudoux scored a resounding success with his *Amphitryon 38,* based on the *Amphitruo.*

BIBLIOGRAPHY.—*Standard texts:* G. Goetz and F. Schoell (1893–95); F. Leo, 2 vol. (1895–96; 2nd ed., 1958); W. M. Lindsay, 2nd ed. (1910); A. Ernout, with French trans. (1932–40). Paul Nixon's Loeb text, with Eng. trans. (1916–38), is based on Leo's text. *Editions with notes:* Captivi by W. M. Lindsay (1900); *Epidicus* by G. E. Duckworth (1940); *Mercator,* 2 vol. (1932) and *Truculentus,* 2 vol. (1953) by P. J. Enk; *Mostellaria,* 2nd ed. (1907) and *Rudens* (ed. min., 1901) by E. A. Sonnenschein; *Rudens* by F. Marx (1928); other plays in Macmillan's "Classical Series" and the "Pitt Press Series," or the annotated Teubner series by Brix-Niemeyer and others. *Lexicon:* Gonzalez Lodge, *Lexicon Plautinum,* 2 vol. (1924 and 1933). *Syntax:* W. M. Lindsay, *Syntax of Plautus* (1936). *Metre and Prosody:* W. M. Lindsay, *Early Latin Verse* (1922); E. A. Sonnenschein, *What is Rhythm?,* ch. vi (1925); W. Beare, *Latin Verse and European Song* (1957). *General:* G. E. Duckworth, *The Nature of Roman Comedy* (1952); W. Beare, *The Roman Stage,* 2nd ed. (1955); E. Paratore, *Storia del teatro latino* (1957). (WM. BE.)

PLAY, ANIMAL. At the beginning of any discussion of play in animals it is necessary to emphasize that understanding of the subject is extremely limited and coloured by anthropomorphisms, comparisons with human behaviour. The factual evidence consists exclusively of descriptions of a wide variety of responses that have been lumped arbitrarily together in the category of play. The explanations and interpretations are speculative, deductively derived and untested. Some of the theories purporting to elucidate the causes and results of play are emotionally appealing but scientifically unsound; others appear plausible and may be valid, but none has been subjected to stringent objective verification.

Characteristics of Play.—The general characteristics of playful behaviour in animals as set forth by most students of the subject can be stated briefly: (1) It is almost universally agreed that in animals, as in men, playful responses carry an emotional element of pleasure. (2) Play is characteristic of the immature animal rather than of the adult; mature individuals sometimes play, but apparently less frequently than juvenile members of their species. (3) The majority of students concur in the belief that play differs from nonplayful activities in having no immediate, utilitarian result affecting the continued existence of the individual. (4) The type of play is characteristic of the species; furthermore, the nature and amount of play exhibited by members of a particular species vary according to evolutionary position. (5) Play is more common, occurs during a greater portion of the life span and appears in more diversified form in the higher animals than in the lower.

These generalizations refer to the commonly accepted characteristics of play. They are descriptive rather than analytical; and they cannot be used as explanations or interpretations.

Types of Behaviour Regarded as Play.—*General Bodily Activity.*—Young children take delight in racing about a room at top speed, stamping violently upon the floor, shouting loudly in utter abandon. Many young animals display similar behaviour. Colts, calves, kids, puppies and kittens expend vast amounts of energy in vigorous locomotor activity to no apparent biologically useful end. They gallop, run, bound and gambol to the point of apparent exhaustion. Many observers regard this behaviour as a form of play. It is assumed to constitute an outlet for surplus energy, to bring pleasure to the performer and to lack any practical purpose.

Youthful Practice of Adult Activities.—The African lion cub lies in hiding and creeps forth, belly close to the ground, to stalk and leap upon an unsuspecting brother or sister. Two puppies wrestle and roll in mock combat, sinking tiny teeth into thick fur and uttering infantile growls. Twin lambs face each other with heads lowered and forefeet pawing the earth; charging forward, they meet head-on and tumble awkwardly on the grass. The common element in such activities lies in their resemblance to similar behaviour patterns that the animal will display in somewhat different form later in life.

There are, however, several significant differences between the behaviour of the young and the adult individual. These responses, when they appear during infancy, do not terminate in the same result they will achieve in the adult stage. The kitten's chase of a ball or a blowing leaf mirrors the cat's pursuit of a mouse; but in one instance food is obtained and in the other it is not. The puppy's battle with his brother reflects the adult dog's combat with other grown animals; but in the infant's struggle no damage is inflicted. The young animal's performance is often imperfect and incomplete; whereas that of the adult is relatively polished and well integrated. From such observations it was deduced by Karl Groos and others that this type of play serves to prepare the animal for a more efficient adult life. It is thought that incomplete and imperfect instincts are modified, strengthened or suppressed during the practice period of youthful play. C. Lloyd Morgan suggested that the play period of infancy permits the practice of vital responses under conditions in which error and incompleteness are not fatal. The perfection of essential reactions is thus held to take place before the animal is subjected to the exigencies of an independent existence, wherein the forces of natural selection are constantly operating to weed out inefficiency and the penalty for error may be sudden death.

It seems probable that this theory may hold good for the play of certain higher mammals. The chimpanzee, for example, passes through a lengthy period of infancy and childhood during which a number of highly important reactions are exercised and possibly organized into biologically effective form. There is, however, no proof that the generalization may correctly be extended to include all examples of this type of behaviour. The kitten's play with small, moving objects may indeed improve its abilities as a mouser, but there is no factual evidence to prove or disprove the assumption. In some cases youthful practice is demonstrably unnecessary. It is certain, for example, that the common sex play of some animals, such as the immature rat, has no demonstrable effect upon the efficiency of adult mating performance. The existence of a preparatory function of play can be established only by direct test of each activity in each species.

Exploration and Experimentation.—Young animals often peck, scratch, claw, pull and bite at objects in their environment, and such activities are sometimes classified as experimental play. The puppy's destructive attentions to a book or pillow are interpreted as play that serves to acquaint the animal with the properties and potentialities of the object thus investigated. Similarly, certain reactions of the young animal to its companions can be listed under the heading of exploratory or experimental play. An eventually practical outcome of such behaviour is held to lie in its tendencies to promote the development of new modes of conduct and to inhibit biologically dangerous reactions. Although this assumed function of exploratory play is based chiefly upon *a priori* reasoning, there are some instances in which it can be shown to exist. Wolfgang Köhler reported that captive chimpanzees given stout sticks or poles soon devised a crude form of vaulting or jumping, using the pole as a sort of crutch. Originally this response was apparently indulged in as a form of amusement and was not used as a means of achieving any secondary objective. Although further test and observation would be necessary to establish the point, it seems probable that the pole vaulting response was a form of play and the outgrowth of experimentation with the stick. Later, however, when the chimpanzees were confronted with the problem of obtaining a banana suspended above their reach, they quickly turned the vaulting technique to good use, employing it as a means of getting the fruit.

Social Play.—Young British warblers are described as engaging in "tilting matches," during which each bird commands a perch and attempts to dislodge other birds from theirs. African lion cubs play "king of the mountain." When one assumes possession of a high spot of ground or climbs on top some low object, all others try to force him off and take his place. "Follow the leader" games occur in the repertory of several mammalian species. Otters have been observed sliding down muddy banks into the water, one after the other in quick succession, and then climbing out to repeat the performance time and again.

Young monkeys in the jungle often swing single file through the branches, each copying roughly the actions of the animal ahead of him.

The group play of chimpanzees is highly diversified, and often resembles certain human activities. Köhler's description of "dancing" is illustrative. Several chimpanzees start to march in single file around a box or post. Gradually their pace quickens, and they trot, often with emphasis upon one foot, so that a primitive kind of rhythm emerges; and as they trot and stamp the animals wag their heads in time with the rhythm. Other kinds of social play occur in this species; and O. L. Tinklepaugh suggested that this type of behaviour early in life enhances the individual's adaptability and co-operativeness, both of which are essential characteristics of the chimpanzee.

Play Between Species.—Although young animals of one species may investigate those of a foreign species, they do not often play together. Exceptions to this generalization sometimes occur when two domesticated animals are reared together.

Thus a dog and a goat may engage in mock battles if they have been associated long enough to establish friendly relations, so to speak.

The outstanding type of interspecies play is that which occurs between man and his pets. If any of the criteria of play that have been accorded common use are to be accepted, it must be agreed that the dog frequently plays with his master. The dog may enter into mock chases or battles with a man much as he would with another dog. On the other hand, he will with equal willingness participate in a learned game such as fetching the ball or performing tricks without any material reward. It is significant that the animal may initiate the play and in many different ways signalize his desire to stimulate playful relations with the human partner.

Explanations of Play.—Several theories have been formulated in an attempt to elucidate the causes of playful behaviour. None is completely satisfactory although several are partially serviceable.

Surplus Energy Theory.—This holds that play is a safety valve, providing an outlet for unused vigour. This interpretation has little to recommend it. Energy is not stored up in the organism like water in a reservoir. Animals are either completely rested and ready to react quickly to stimuli from the environment, or they are tired and sluggish in their responses. All types of behaviour occur more promptly and persist longer in the rested individual.

The energy expended in play differs in no way from that used in nonplayful pursuits.

Joie-de-Vivre Theory.—A second attempt to explain play is found in the *joie-de-vivre* theory, which interprets play as the expression of a general exuberance, an overflowing enthusiasm for life itself. A serious objection to explanations of this type is that they add nothing to basic understanding of natural phenomena; they explain nothing. They involve merely the substitution of one word or phrase for another, with the meaning or significance of the new term being no more precise nor illuminating than the old.

Instinctive Theory.—The instinctive theory of play in animals was championed by Karl Groos, who interpreted all play as responses based upon inherited tendencies or predispositions. However, to label an act as "instinctive" is not to explain it; and although the form that play takes in various animal species is unquestionably influenced by hereditary constitution, the serious student of behaviour is still faced with the responsibility for determining the stimuli that evoke playful responses, identifying the physiological and psychological processes that mediate the behaviour, and describing in objective terms the eventual effects and results.

Future Theories.—Although no completely satisfactory explanation for the occurrence of play in animals is available, it is possible to predict with reasonable certainty the form which such a theory must assume.

1. In the first place it is obvious that no single hypothesis can be formulated to explain all forms of play in every animal species. The types of activity that have been labeled "play" are so variable in form and complexity that a different interpretation is indicated for each major category.

2. It must be recognized that playful behaviour differs from nonplayful pursuits in subtle and often elusive fashion. There is no sharp border line between play and work for animals or for man. The two types of activity merge insensibly one into the other, and some complex responses may be partly play and partly work. Therefore, any acceptable definition of play must be based upon a list of predominating characteristics that combine to set it off from nonplayful behaviour, and cannot be derived from adherence to a single, rigid criterion such as nonutilitarianism or imperfect, juvenile performance. It is, for example, permissible to state that playful reactions as a class tend to lack the immediate, biologically practical results that normally accompany nonplayful responses, but it is not permissible to set up as an inflexible rule the dictum that no activity is play if it achieves a useful end.

3. Play must be explained in purely objective terms. A small start in this direction was made by workers such as J. B. Cooper, who suggested that the playful execution of certain behaviour patterns is characterized by the absence of the consummatory phase and by the rapid shift from one element of the pattern to another. Cooper noted that the play of lions is more prevalent on cool days, and tends to occur most frequently following a major change in the environmental situation (such as release of the animals from an indoor cage, the introduction of new lions into the pride, or the sudden appearance of the keeper). Much more extended analysis along lines such as these will provide the basis for an interpretation of play that is biologically significant and subject to direct test and verification.

The play of human beings is no more clearly understood than is that of lower forms, and the careful study of animal play offers potentially important results in the increased understanding of similar behaviour in man. *See also* ANIMAL BEHAVIOUR; PSYCHOLOGY, COMPARATIVE.

BIBLIOGRAPHY.—J. B. Cooper, *An Exploratory Study on African Lions,* Comparative Psychology Monographs (1942); W. Köhler, *The Mentality of Apes* (1931); C. L. Morgan, *Animal Behaviour* (1900); Karl Groos, *Play of Animals* (1898). (F. A. BH.)

PLAYER PIANO, a piano equipped with a mechanical device conceived at first for playing music automatically—*i.e.,* by means of pedals and hand levers—and later for reproducing the playing of a pianist. In its original form as the Pianola, patented in 1897 by a U.S. engineer, E. S. Votey, it was a mechanism placed in front of the keyboard and operated by the player's hands and feet. The notes of the music were in the form of perforations on a paper roll which passed over a tracker bar. Foot-operated pedals and hand levers controlled the release of air by pneumatic devices which set in motion hammers that struck the notes on the keyboard. Control of dynamics and accentuation was principally obtained by the pedals, while the levers were used to bring the melodic line into relief. Later this mechanism was built into the body of the piano. The roll and tracker bar were fitted in front of the hammers and the hand levers on a ledge in front of the keyboard. The foot pedals were lowered over the piano pedals. A considerable range of expression in both dynamics and tempo was available to the operator, who could thus perform music without having acquired a keyboard technique.

In the early 20th century several companies manufactured player-piano rolls that reproduced with considerable accuracy performances by distinguished figures, among them Alfred Cortot and Debussy. These performances were played on the "reproducing piano" and some of them were later transferred to phonograph records. The player piano also attracted composers, who were able to write for the keyboard without considering the limitations of the human hand. Stravinsky's *Étude* for pianola (1917) and Hindemith's *Toccata* for mechanical piano (1926) are among such works, and the resources of the player piano were widely explored by the U.S. composer Conlon Nancarrow (b. 1912). The vogue of the pneumatic player piano reached its height in the early 1920s, with some resurgence of popularity in the U.S. in the 1950s and 1960s. Its decline was attributed to the diffusion not only of piano music but of all forms of instrumental and vocal music by phonograph, radio, and television.

PLAYFAIR, LYON PLAYFAIR, 1ST BARON (1818–1898), British scientist and reformer, was born at Chunar, Bengal, on May 21, 1818. He was educated at five universities, including St. Andrews and London, and took his doctorate at Giessen, Ger., under J. von Liebig, whose *Chemistry of Agriculture* he translated. He was professor of chemistry at the Royal Institution, Manchester, 1843–45, and at Edinburgh University, 1858–69. Meanwhile he sat on numerous committees of inquiry, including the royal commission on the health of towns whose report (1846) laid the foundations of modern sanitation. He played an important role in organizing industrial exhibits for the exhibition of 1851 at the Crystal Palace in London. As secretary of the department of science (1853–58), Playfair advocated—without success—the use of chemical weapons in the Crimean War. He was a Liberal member of Parliament for the universities of Edinburgh and St. Andrews, 1868–85, and for South Leeds, 1885–92. In 1873–74 he was postmaster general and then presided over a commission that regulated clerkships in the civil service. From the spring of 1880 he served for three years as chairman of committees in the House of Commons, encountering and overcoming much obstruction. He was knighted in 1883; held minor office in Gladstone's home rule government of 1886; and was made a baron in 1892. He died in London on May 29, 1898.

See Sir T. Wemyss Reid, *Memoirs and Correspondence of Lord Play-fair* (1899).   (M. R. D. F.)

PLAYFORD, JOHN (1623–*c.* 1686), English bookseller and music publisher whose best-known work, the collection of traditional tunes, *The English Dancing-Master* (1650, but dated 1651), is an important source for English traditional music. Born in Norwich in 1623, by 1648 he had established his business in London where he became a clerk of the Temple Church and moved to the Inner Temple. His numerous publications, which include songs, catches, and instrumental music for cittern, lyra viol, and harpsichord, reflect the taste of English amateur musicians of the latter half of the 17th century.

The friend as well as publisher of most of the English composers of his time, Playford was himself a competent musician, as may be seen from the songs and psalm settings by him that appear in his collections. His *A Brief Introduction to the Skill of Musick*, a handbook on music theory and practice, went into many editions between 1654 and 1730. In 1694 it was revised by Henry Purcell, who completely rewrote the section on composition, originally by Thomas Campion with additions by Christopher Simpson. Playford died in London, probably about November 1686. Of the several elegies on his death, one, "Gentle Shepherds, You That Know," by Nahum Tate, was set to music by Henry Purcell.

The English Dancing-Master, a collection of tunes for country dances, set for the fiddle, went into numerous editions between 1650 and 1728. Other Playford publications include: John Hilton's *Catch that Catch can* (1652); *Select Ayres and Dialogues* (1652–69); *Court Ayres* (1655); and *Musick's Handmaid* (1663).

Playford's son HENRY PLAYFORD (1657–*c.* 1709) continued the family business, which from 1696 he conducted in his own name. As well as bringing out new editions of his father's publications, he issued a small number of new works, notably John Blow's "Ode on the Death of Mr. Henry Purcell" (1696) and two posthumous collections of music by Purcell, *Orpheus Britannicus* (1698–1702) and *A Choice Collection of Lessons for the Harpsichord or Spinnet* (1696). Henry Playford also engaged in organizing concerts in London and Oxford and in picture dealing; by 1707 he had retired from music publishing. He died in London, probably in 1709.

PLAYGROUNDS: *see* PARK AND PLAYGROUND.

PLEADING, that branch of the law which governs the successive formal papers in which litigants in the opening stages of a lawsuit set forth the facts upon which they claim legal relief or challenge the claims of their opponents to such relief. *See* PRACTICE AND PROCEDURE.   (C. E. CL.)

PLEBISCITE, a vote of all the electors in a country or given area on some specific question, such as approval of a transfer of sovereignty or of a ruler's assumption of authority. The most familiar example of the use of the plebiscite in French history was in 1852, when the *coup d'état* of 1851 was confirmed and the title of emperor was given to Napoleon III. Unlike a referendum (*q.v.*), a plebiscite is not a normal method or procedure of voting.

As a means of settling the destination of populations and territories, the plebiscite was first used in the French Revolution to legitimize the wholesale annexations of territory made by the conquering French republic, and subsequently by Napoleon I. It was revived by Napoleon III and applied (successfully for him) in the case of Nice and Savoy, and (successfully for Victor Emmanuel) in the duchies of north Italy during the years 1859–60. The peace conference of 1919 proposed the taking of 17 plebiscites to settle difficult national questions, of which 8 were actually held. One of these, the Turkish plebiscite in Transcaucasia, was a farce. Others, which decided the fate of Allenstein and Marienwerder, of the Burgenland, the attribution of the northern and southern zones of Schleswig, the partition of Upper Silesia, the fate of Klagenfurt and the economic destiny of Luxembourg had substantial and important results.

By a plebiscite of Jan. 14, 1935, the Saar, which had been administered by the League of Nations since 1920, voted to return to Germany. Another plebiscite in 1947 favoured France but on Oct. 23, 1955, a third plebiscite rejected a Europeanization proposal and led to a Franco-German agreement on July 4, 1956, to reunite the Saar with Germany on Jan. 1, 1957.

BIBLIOGRAPHY.—H. W. V. Temperley (ed.), *A History of the Peace Conference of Paris,* references in subject index to vol. vi, 703 (1920–24); Sarah Wambaugh, *A Monograph on Plebiscites* (1920), *Plebiscites Since the World War,* 2 vol. (1933); F. Llewellyn Jones, *Plebiscites,* Grotius Society Transactions (1927); C. R. M. F. Cruttwell, *A History of Peaceful Change in the Modern World* (1937).

PLECOPTERA, the order of insects known as stone flies. The immature stages are aquatic, living in streams and rocky lake margins. The female lays several thousand eggs, discharging them in masses into the water. The nymphs are active and elongate, have long antennae and a pair of long "tails." Some forms have gills, but most do not. They feed on microorganisms, decaying organic matter or other insects. Nymphs may be found in clumps of rotted leaves, masses of debris or beneath submerged logs and stones. When mature, the nymph crawls out of the water and attaches itself firmly by its claws to a rock or tree trunk. The nymphal skin then bursts along the back and the adult emerges.

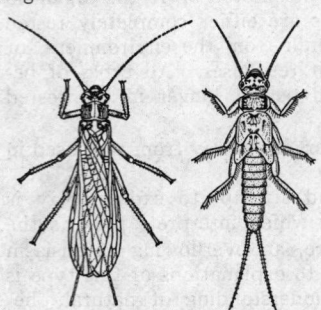

BY COURTESY OF THE ILLINOIS STATE NATURAL HISTORY SURVEY

STONE FLY (ISOPERLA CLIO)
(Left) adult, length about 0.8 in.; (right) nymph, length about 0.6 in.

The adults are soft-bodied and range in length from $\frac{1}{8}$ to $1\frac{1}{2}$ in., plus the tails (minute in some forms). They have long, many-segmented antennae, and usually two pairs of membranous wings folded flat over the back. In a few species the wings are mere stubs. Most species are black or dark brown, but some are bright yellow or leaf green and others may be marked with orange or red. Stone flies fly rather slowly, but run actively. They are found on stones, foliage or tree trunks along the edge of a stream, or hiding in crevices of bridges or bark. Most species emerge from the water in spring, but there is a fairly large group of winter species, and a few in summer and autumn. Most adults do not feed, but some species eat algae, pollen and bud exudates. All forms are important as fish food and in general stream ecology.

The order Plecoptera contains about 1,200 species classified in nine families, distributed throughout the world. There are about 450 species in North America, 34 in the British Isles. Australia and New Zealand contain many primitive forms.

Fossil stone flies appear first in the Permian period, but are reasonably common only in the middle Tertiary amber of the Baltic region of Europe.

See also INSECT.

BIBLIOGRAPHY.—J. G. Needham and P. W. Claassen, *The Plecoptera of North America,* Entomological Society of America (1925); T. H. Frison, "Stoneflies, or Plecoptera of Illinois," *Illinois Natural History Survey Bulletin,* 20:281–471 (1935); W. E. Ricker, *Systematic Studies in Plecoptera,* "Indiana University Publications, Science Series," 18 (1952); H. B. N. Hynes, *A Key of the Adults and Nymphs of British Stone-flies (Plecoptera),* Freshwater Biological Association, Scientific Publication, 17 (1958).   (W. E. R.)

PLEDGE OF ALLEGIANCE TO THE U.S. FLAG. This pledge was first published in the juvenile periodical *The Youth's Companion* on Sept. 8, 1892, in the following form: "I pledge allegiance to my Flag and the Republic for which it stands; one nation indivisible, with liberty and Justice for all." The words "the Flag of the United States of America" were substituted for "my Flag" in 1924, and the pledge was officially recognized by the U.S. in 1942. In 1954 "under God" was added, making it read: "I pledge allegiance to the flag of the United States of America and to the Republic for which it stands, one Nation under God, indivisible, with liberty and justice for all." A controversy arose concerning the authorship of the pledge of 1892. Claims were made on behalf of both James B. Upham, one of the editors of *The Youth's Companion,* and Francis Bellamy, an assistant editor. In 1939 a committee of the U.S. Flag Association ruled in favour of Bellamy, however, and a detailed report issued by the Library of Congress on July 18, 1957, concluded that "the Bellamy claim to authorship rests upon the more solid ground."

PLEHVE (Pleve), **VYACHESLAV KONSTANTINO-VICH** (1846–1904), Russian statesman, a firm upholder of the autocratic principle, bureaucratic government, and class privilege, was born on April 20 (new style; 8, old style), 1846, in Kaluga province, the son of a russified schoolteacher of German descent. He served in the department of justice from 1867, and in 1881, shortly after the assassination of the emperor Alexander II, was appointed director of the police department in the ministry of the interior. His efficiency in suppressing the terrorist movement earned him promotion to the post of deputy minister of the interior in 1884. He became head of the imperial chancellery in 1894 and acting minister and state-secretary for the grand duchy of Finland in 1899 (appointment confirmed 1900).

Plehve's appointment as minister of the interior, which S. Yu. Witte had previously blocked, came in April 1902, at a time when unrest was growing among all sections of the population. His approach to political and social problems was that of a skilled police investigator: he endeavoured to set the different elements in the opposition against one another, neutralizing some and bending others to do his will. To silence the liberals he made conciliatory gestures accompanied by measures of intimidation. To deflect the industrial workers' discontent against their employers rather than the government he promoted "patriotic" labour unions managed by police agents. He fomented national antagonisms by an energetic policy of russification, applied with particular harshness against the Armenians and the Finns. He encouraged anti-Semitic propaganda, which in April 1903 led to a *pogrom* at Kishinev. When these methods failed, he entertained the idea that "a victorious little war" might help to consolidate the absolutist regime, and lent his support to the adventurist policy in Korea which provoked the conflict with Japan. On July 28 (N.S.), 1904, Plehve was assassinated in a St. Petersburg street by E. S. Sazonov, of the Socialist-Revolutionary party. It might be said that he fell victim to his own methods, for it later transpired that the coup was planned by E. F. Azef (1869–1918), a double agent working simultaneously for the revolutionaries and the police.   (J. L. H. K.)

PLÉIADE, LA, the name given to a group of seven writers of the 16th century whose leader was Pierre de Ronsard and whose spokesman was Joachim du Bellay (*qq.v.*). The other members of the group were Jean Dorat, J. A. de Baïf, Rémy Belleau, Pontus de Tyard, and Étienne Jodelle (*qq.v.*). The name (derived from the seven stars of the Pleiades) was taken from that given by the Alexandrian critics to seven tragic poets of the reign of Ptolemy II Philadelphus (285–246 B.C.). The aim of the *Pléiade* was to enrich the French language and literature by discreetly imitating and borrowing from the classics and the Italian poets of the Petrarchan school. *See* French Literature: *16th Century.*

PLEIADES, an asterism, or star cluster; in mythology the seven daughters of Atlas and Pleione, and sisters of the Hyades (*q.v.*). Because of their grief at the death of their sisters or at the sufferings of their father, they were changed into stars. In another account, the Pleiades and their mother met the amorous hunter Orion (*q.v.*) in Boeotia; for five years he pursued them through the woods, until Zeus translated them all—Pleione and her daughters, Orion and his dog—to the sky. This is one of the few myths really astronomical in origin, for it is based on the relative positions of the constellations in the sky. The names of the sisters are Alcyone, Asterope, Electra, Celaeno, Maia, Merope and Taygeta; one is always dim or invisible, because she is Electra mourning for Troy, or Merope, who is ashamed of having wedded a mortal, Sisyphus. All the Pleiades became the ancestresses of divine or heroic families. The early winter rising and spring setting of the Pleiades (Lat. *Vergiliae*) are important dates to the farmer. (For an American Indian legend, *see* Devils Tower National Monument.)

See H. J. Rose, *Handbook of Greek Mythology*, 5th ed. rev. (1953).

The stars are situated in the constellation Taurus (*q.v.*). They are referred to in the Old Testament (Job ix, 9; xxxviii, 31). The brightest star is Alcyone (η Tauri), of the third magnitude. This group is physically connected, being distinguished from the background stars by community of proper motion. Photographs show a faint nebulosity filling the whole region; there is little doubt that this is rarefied matter made luminous by stimulation of the radiation of the hot stars comprised in it. The distance of the Pleiades from the solar system is estimated at 100 parsecs (300 light-years), but is not very certainly known.

Alcyone and the other bright stars are of the hottest type of spectrum (Type B) and give out several hundred times as much light as the sun.

PLEISTOCENE EPOCH. This is the sixth of the seven epochs that constitute the Cenozoic era (*q.v.*) of geological history (if, as is indicated on the accompanying geologic time chart, the Recent is taken as the seventh and the Pleistocene is not separated as the Quaternary era). By recommendation of the commission, 18th International Geological congress, the nonglacial Pleistocene (Greek *pleistos,* most, and *kainos,* recent) is defined on the basis of its fauna and separated from the preceding Pliocene by this means. Broadly speaking, however, it is thought to coincide with a period when glacial and interglacial conditions alternated over a large part of the earth's surface and because of this it is often known as the Glacial epoch or the Great Ice Age. During the glacial ages, widespread continental ice sheets repeatedly covered large areas in the northern hemisphere and alpine glaciers were more numerous and extensive in both the northern and southern hemispheres. During the interglacial ages, the climate seems to have been as warm or warmer than the present. The glaciated areas were reclothed with vegetation and repopulated with animal life and soils were formed. This epoch, the major part of the Quaternary period, is believed to have lasted several hundreds of thousands of years. It is generally regarded as having been terminated by the change of climate which caused the melting away of the latest of the great ice sheets, but at the same time it is also recognized that the Recent epoch of warm climate is not dissimilar to the interglacial ages, though shorter, and therefore the conditions of the Pleistocene glacial epoch have continued uninterruptedly to the present day.

This article is divided into sections and subsections dealing with various aspects of the epoch. The general geology of the period is considered under Quaternary. In addition to the cross references to related articles given under the several headings in this article *see* also Archaeology: *Prehistory;* Glacier; Man, Evolution of; Paleobotany; Paleontology.

Following are the main divisions of this article:

I. THE CONCEPT OF THE GREAT ICE AGE

The concept of the Great Ice Age, when the climate produced glaciers far more extensive than they are at present, was initially set forth by German forestry professor A. Bernhardi in 1832 and emphasized by Louis Agassiz (*q.v.*) in 1837. Agassiz' concept was the outgrowth of examining evidence that certain glaciers in the Alps had formerly extended far down their valleys. He confirmed his views after a field study in Scotland in 1840, and extended them still further after he went to the United States in 1846, where he spent the rest of his life. His public lectures in Boston in 1846 took the people by storm. The naturalists of that day had credited the extensive glacial deposits and the widespread evidence of glacial erosion in the lowlands to the work of a cataclysmal flood—the Noachian deluge in popular belief—or of a temporary submergence

Geologic Time Chart

System and Period	Series and Epoch	Distinctive Records of Life	Began (Millions of Years Ago)
CENOZOIC ERA			
Quaternary . . .	Recent (last 11,000 years)		
	Pleistocene	Early man	2+
	Pliocene	Large carnivores . . .	10
Tertiary . . .	Miocene	Whales, apes, grazing forms	27
	Oligocene	Large browsing mammals .	38
	Eocene	Rise of flowering plants .	55
	Paleocene	First placental mammals .	65–70
MESOZOIC ERA			
Cretaceous		Extinction of dinosaurs .	130
Jurassic		Dinosaurs' zenith, primitive birds, first small mammals	180
Triassic		Appearance of dinosaurs .	225
PALEOZOIC ERA			
Permian		Reptiles developed, conifers abundant	260
Carboniferous			
Upper (Pennsylvanian) . . .		First reptiles, coal forests .	300
Lower (Mississippian) . .		Sharks abundant . . .	340
Devonian		Amphibians appeared, fishes abundant	405
Silurian		Earliest land plants and animals	435
Ordovician		First primitive fishes .	480
Cambrian		Marine invertebrates .	550–570
PRECAMBRIAN TIME			
		Few fossils . . .	more than 3,490

of the lands beneath the sea, with or without icebergs to help carry the large quantity of stones and boulders visible in the deposits.

Not until three decades after Agassiz' first pronouncements were the majority of scientific men on either side of the Atlantic convinced that glaciers rather than water had been responsible for these features. During that time Agassiz' name became fixed in the annals of Harvard university and his contributions to the popularization of science, especially of geology, in North America widely acknowledged.

II. EXTENT OF GLACIATION

1. Areas of Continental Glaciation.—The convincing evidence of the former, much greater extent of glaciers is so generally accepted that it need not be presented here. The areas within the northern hemisphere that were formerly ice-covered are shown in the accompanying maps (the glaciers in the southern hemisphere were less extensive). The mountainous western part of North America was occupied by a vast complex of glaciers which throughout most of the Canadian sector formed a nearly continuous covering of ice. The vast area from the Atlantic to the Rocky mountains, Canada and the northern part of the United States (as far south as New York city, Cincinnati, O., Carbondale, Ill., St. Louis, Mo., Kansas City, Mo., and Pierre, S.D.) were buried beneath an ice sheet (the Laurentide ice sheet) that had its source in Canada and also reached north to the Arctic ocean. The Laurentide ice sheet overtopped the White mountains in New Hampshire and so was at least 5,000 ft. thick in that region. This is the greatest minimum thickness that is shown by direct evidence, but it is considered probable that this ice sheet was 5,000 to 10,000 ft. thick throughout the greater part of its extent.

Greenland and Iceland were almost entirely ice-covered. Nearly half of Europe—from the North Cape off the north coast of Norway south to Kiev on the banks of the Dnieper—was covered by a single sheet of ice (the Scandinavian ice sheet) which is believed to have attained a maximum thickness of 10,000 ft. Much of Siberia was overspread by mountain glaciers and by a great ice sheet (the Siberian ice sheet) on its northwestern plain. The Alps, the Caucasus and the Pyrenees in Europe and most of the high mountains on other continents carried glaciers of varying dimensions. The antarctic continent was even more nearly completely ice-covered than now, and the glaciers of the southern Andes spread westward to tidewater in Chile and eastward onto the pampas of Argentina. The highest mountains of Hawaii, Japan and New Guinea were marked by glaciers.

At present about 10.4% of the land area of the globe is covered by glacier ice, but 98% of this ice is in the distant higher latitudes of Antarctica and Greenland. In contrast, when glaciers were at their maximum during the Ice Age, they extended into temperate

latitudes now the sites of highly organized civilizations and abundant agricultural and manufacturing production.

2. Source-Areas of Glacial Radiation.—During the early part of the last glacial age, the Wisconsin, the great Laurentide ice sheet over Canada had two primary areas of glacial radiation, one known as the Labradorean area located over the highlands of Labrador and eastern Quebec, and the other known as the Keewatin area located on the plains of Manitoba and adjacent territory of Ontario and Hudson bay. Later there was another area of almost equal importance, the Patrician, which developed south of Hudson bay and sent ice lobes southward through the Lake Michigan basin to form the moraines around the southern end of that basin and westward and southwestward through the Lake Superior basin into northern Wisconsin and northeastern Minnesota. The Keewatin ice lobe was crowded westward by it but even so the Keewatin ice received sufficient snowfall and possessed the energy to advance nearly as far south as Des Moines, Ia. Over the Cordilleras of western Canada the excessive snowfall, though much greater than today's, failed to form a continuous ice cap because of the rapid movement of the valley glaciers, especially on the west side, and the calving of icebergs into the sea.

The Scandinavian ice sheet had its origin on the high divide between Norway and Sweden. The Siberian ice sheet possibly began as small glaciers on three separate highlands: the Putorana mountains, the Byrranga ridge on the Taimyr peninsula and the Severnaya Zemlya archipelago.

A consideration of these ice fields makes it appear that they were all in response to a changing glacial atmospheric organization measurably different from the present; some ice fields began on plains, some on highlands, all necessarily being in the paths of maritime air masses charged with moisture. These ice fields varied in relative importance from age to age. During the Nebraskan age the Keewatin was the dominant field. During the following Kansan both fields were important. During the Illinoian, the third glacial age, the Labradorean area of radiation was preponderant and the Keewatin played a minor role.

This history emphasizes the fact that the nature of the atmospheric organization is unpredictable. The facts lie in the stratigraphic record. (*See also The Glacial Climates, below.*)

III. REVOLUTIONARY EFFECTS OF GLACIATION

1. Effect of the Continental Glaciers.—The northern part of North America and of Eurasia as well suffered profound changes from continental glaciation. The features of the latest glacier are indeed climactic. In North America the Great Lakes—the greatest fresh-water bodies on earth—are due more to glacial scour on a grand scale of former lowlands than to glacial deposition and later crustal deformation that followed the unloading of the earth's crust by the melting of the continental ice sheet. The moraines of glacial drift that lie beyond the basins are in large part the debris resulting from the glacial scour. The lake floors have irregular contours due to both glacial scour and deposition. However, the present outlines of the Great Lakes were assumed when crustal deformation tipped the land southward and helped to fix the present outlets. Northern Lake Michigan is more than 100 ft. shallower than when the glacier scoured it, and the northern part of Lake Huron and Georgian bay is something like 600 ft. shallower.

The lakes, muskegs, embossed and striated rock and other features of the irregular topography of Canada, the 10,000 lakes of Minnesota and large portions of the terrain of North Dakota, South Dakota, Wisconsin and Michigan are mainly such as only the processes of a continental glacier can bring about. New England and areas adjacent to it show the beautiful flowing lines of glaciated hills once buried deeply beneath the great ice sheet that terminated in the Atlantic. The lake basins among the hills, the anomalous sources of streams, the setting of the lakes and the strewing of the countryside with boulders and stony deposits are also features that result from glaciation. Maine has its eskers (rounded ridges of sand and gravel) crossing hill and dale, marking for mile after mile the courses of subglacial streams.

To the south and southwest of Lake Michigan, westerly and

southward from Lake Erie, southwest from Saginaw bay, and in northern Iowa and the eastern Dakotas, the spreading continental glacier made a plains country and left upon its retreat a successive series of moraines that fashioned the country into a rhythmic succession of ridge-and-plain topography remarkably suited to agriculture and transportation. This central interior lowland, however, is not all glacial. The glaciers left within it a Driftless area of about 10,000 sq.mi., a topographic "island" of rugged hills and valleys branching treelike, dendritic in pattern and made only by running-water erosion, a relict of preglacial times left between the Keewatin and Patrician ice fields and unmodified by them. Regardless of the direction of his travel, the motorist can see in contrast these pristine erosional forms of the Driftless area and the bordering, newer and higher glacial landscape which has beneath it the older stream-eroded topography.

Most of the ancient master streams that preceded the glacial invasion did not survive. The ancient Teays-Mahomet river which once had its source in the distant western fringe of Virginia and which flowed northwesterly and westerly, eventually crossing the present course of the Ohio river and traversing central Indiana and central Illinois to Havana where it joined the ancient Mississippi, indeed formed one of the master valleys of the great interior of the continent. The Nebraskan and Kansan glaciers which crossed it transversely finished it off. This ancient valley was discovered by a study of thousands of records of well drilling. The present course of the Ohio river along the south-western boundary of Ohio is a consequence of this geological accident to the Teays-Mahomet valley, as is the upper portion of the Wabash river. One hundred fifty miles of the course of the present Mississippi river above the mouth of Illinois river is also

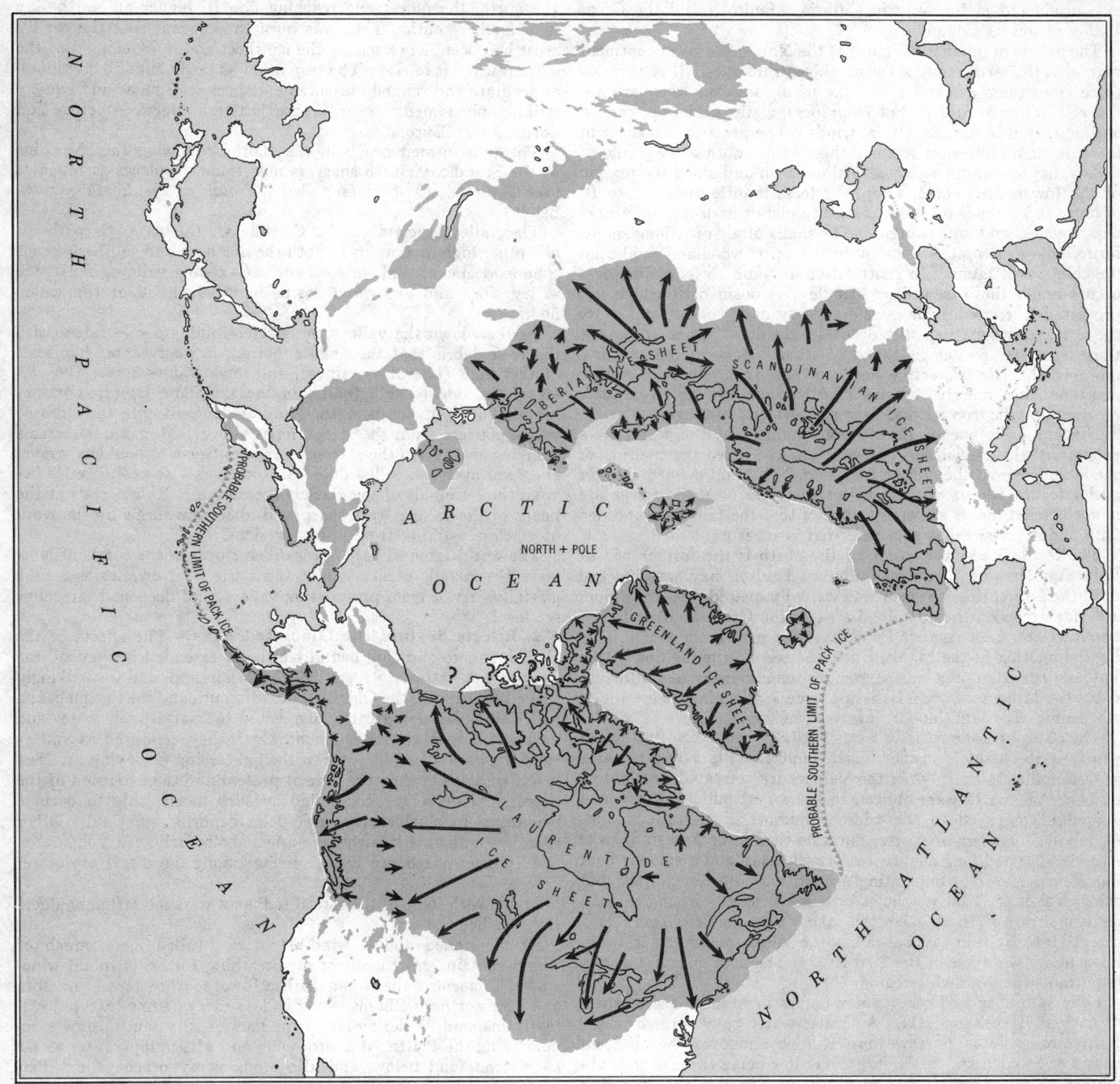

NORTHERN PART OF THE NORTHERN HEMISPHERE SHOWING AREAS GLACIATED DURING THE PLEISTOCENE EPOCH

Arrows show principal directions of flow (much generalized) of former glaciers, where information is available. Base from Hydrographic and Map service, Can. Polar Equidistant projection. Glacial data from many sources, notably Glacial Map of North America published by the Geological Society of America; Great Soviet atlas; E. Antevs, Gerasimov and Markov

an accident of continental glaciation, as is the Missouri river for 500 mi. in North and South Dakota.

These phenomena of the glacial age in North America are in a real sense duplicated in continental Europe—the glacial topography, lake regions, terminal and recessional moraines, buried valleys and other features—but there is no counterpart of the Great Lakes. A vast river flowed across northern Germany, along the southern part of the North sea floor and through the English channel because the normal drainage to the north was blocked by the Scandinavian ice sheet. (The English channel and much of the North sea floor were then dry land.) Capacious abandoned valleys excavated by the previous drainage are present in the north German plain. Where the land surface sloped toward the ice sheet, there were formed large temporary lakes, one shore of which was against the glacier ice. Lakes of great extent, now drained, also originated in this way in Ontario, Manitoba and the Great Plains region of Canada.

The people of many other parts of the North American continent marvel at the fertile soils of the north central states. It is common to refer to them as glacial. In the main, however, they are not derived from glacial drift but from loess, a silt picked up, carried and deposited by terrific glacial winds. The greatest thickness of loess in the middle west is along the east or southeasterly side of wide valleys containing silty glacial outwash and along the margin of the Iowan drift sheet, where the loess mantle averages 50 ft. or more and extends over the adjacent uplands in decreasing thickness, fineness and lime content. The shells of air-breathing snails, forms whose habitat is commonly the open woodland, make up the chief fossil fauna. In central Illinois some 10 ft. of the loess occurs under the Tazewell or Middle Wisconsin drift which has protected it from leaching. Here peaty and woody remains of the original vegetation still occur in the loess, some in layers, thus recording pauses in the deposition. Beyond the terminal moraine and the protective cover of the Tazewell there are no plant remains, merely thin layers of orange-coloured iron oxide representing the iron residue from the former plant layers.

Niagara falls, one of the natural wonders of the world, is a product of the glacial age. It was initiated when the melting of the ice uncovered the cliff at Lewiston, N.Y., and opened a lower outlet for the waters of Lake Erie. That this occurred fairly late in geological times is shown by the fact that the falls have receded only about seven miles at a rate that is measurable.

The fertile Red river valley of the north is the former bed of Lake Agassiz whose natural outlet to Hudson bay was blocked until the Laurentide ice sheet was virtually melted. Its maximum area far exceeded the combined area of the Great Lakes. It had two histories, Lake Agassiz I and Lake Agassiz II, the first following the melting of the Mankato ice, the second the melting of the Valders ice. Its outlet was of great volume, flowing like a torrent down the Minnesota and Mississippi rivers, widening their valleys, steepening the bluffs and truncating the headlands.

The basin of Lake Agassiz I was entirely overridden by the advance of the Valders glacier which built the Big Stone moraine at Ortonville, Minn. When the Valders ice retreated, the waters of Lake Agassiz II were obliged to cut a new outlet, narrow and gorgelike compared to the wide Minnesota river valley below Ortonville. Though of shorter duration than Lake Agassiz I, Lake Agassiz II lasted long enough to form beaches and a smooth floor out of a moderately undulating ground moraine topography, but the gravel of the beaches shows little wave wear. Upon the complete melting of the glacier the lake, from its very south end, drained into Hudson bay, beheading the Minnesota river and forming a new river system, the Red river. The area today is a very important wheat-growing region.

Lake Winnipeg and other water bodies in Manitoba are relicts of ancient Lake Agassiz II. A similar water body formed in the Baltic sea basin of northwestern Europe and over the adjacent coasts of Sweden and Finland, its overflow being through the submerged channel between Denmark and Sweden. A lake of similar origin is reported in the headwater region of Irtysh river, western Siberia. Obstructed by the Siberian ice sheet the lake overflowed southward into the ancient Aral sea, at that time probably a part of the Caspian sea-Black sea-Mediterranean water body.

The various outlets of the glacial Great Lakes, which were also held back by the ice sheet, hold interest too because of their great size. Among these overflow routes may be mentioned: (1) from Chicago to the Illinois river valley and thence to the Mississippi river; (2) from Fort Wayne, Ind., via the Maumee and Wabash river valleys to the Ohio river; (3) from Lake Erie via the Mohawk river valley to the Hudson river; (4) from North Bay, Ont., via the Ottawa river valley to the St. Lawrence river. The old lake shores are variously marked by distinct cliffs, beaches and bars, many of which later served the early Indian as travel routes and still later were adopted in part for highways.

In the course of early geological investigations the students of glacial geology were amazed to find that some of the later beaches, which have a northward trend, rise higher and higher to the north, the oldest one reaching 600 ft. higher at North Bay than farther south. Thus was born the concept that the earth's crust had been depressed by the ice sheet and that removal of the ice permitted it to rise. The response was tardy but still continues, as accurate and refined measurements prove. Similar and equally striking phenomena occur in northeastern North America and northwestern Europe.

The first-formed beach in the Baltic, following the shrinkage of the Scandinavian ice sheet, is now found in places as much as 700 ft. above sea level (*see* also *Warping of the Earth's Crust*, below).

The valley glaciers of the Cordilleras, the Alps, Carpathians and other high mountains in both the northern and southern hemispheres deepened and widened the pre-existing valleys, cliffed the valley sides and excavated basins in the bedrock of the valley floors.

Farther down the valleys the glaciers built up side ridges with the rock debris that they had acquired, in many cases hundreds of feet high (lateral moraines), and made ridges across the valleys from side to side (end moraines). Some lateral moraines consist partly of debris washed and avalanched onto the sides of valley glaciers from the steep slopes above. Melt-water streams coursing away from the glaciers spread outwash of boulders, gravel and sand over the valley floors, in some cases scores of miles beyond the terminals of the glaciers themselves. Ridge crests at the heads of the valleys were sharpened to serrate forms by the work of glaciers working from opposing sides.

The world-famous, deep, steep-sided fjords of the coasts of Norway, Greenland, Alaska, Chile and parts of New Zealand were glacially carved from pre-existing valleys, and deepened far below sea level.

2. Effects Beyond the Glaciated Area.—The effects of the glacial climate and continental ice sheets extended far beyond the limits of glaciation. Rivers like the Mississippi and its strikingly spaced tributaries, the Ohio and the Missouri, and the Susquehanna and Columbia were greatly augmented by glacial melt water and overloaded with glacial sediment which they deposited as valley-train outwash all of the way to their receiving embayments. Sea levels were lower than they are at present and the extension of the Mississippi delta was controlled by such levels, only to become platforms upon which the later delta deposits were laid. Other river systems of the earth were affected similarly, the Volga, Don and Dnieper of eastern Europe being among those that are better known.

Mixed with some of the glacial sediment were ice-rafted boulders that reached the sea.

As mentioned above, wind-blown silt, called loess, much of which contains gastropods of air-breathing forms, is found widespread adjacent to the Iowan drift in Iowa, southeastern Minnesota and over northern Illinois, along valleys carrying fine-textured valley trains, and bordering lacustrine flats of silty sands. Loess occurs along the Platte, Missouri, Ohio and Mississippi rivers as far as Natchez and below, and also along many other valleys that carried valley trains. Promiscuously distributed loess deposits are also found in dry areas.

In the dry regions in low and middle latitudes on all continents there is impressive evidence both of former lakes where none now

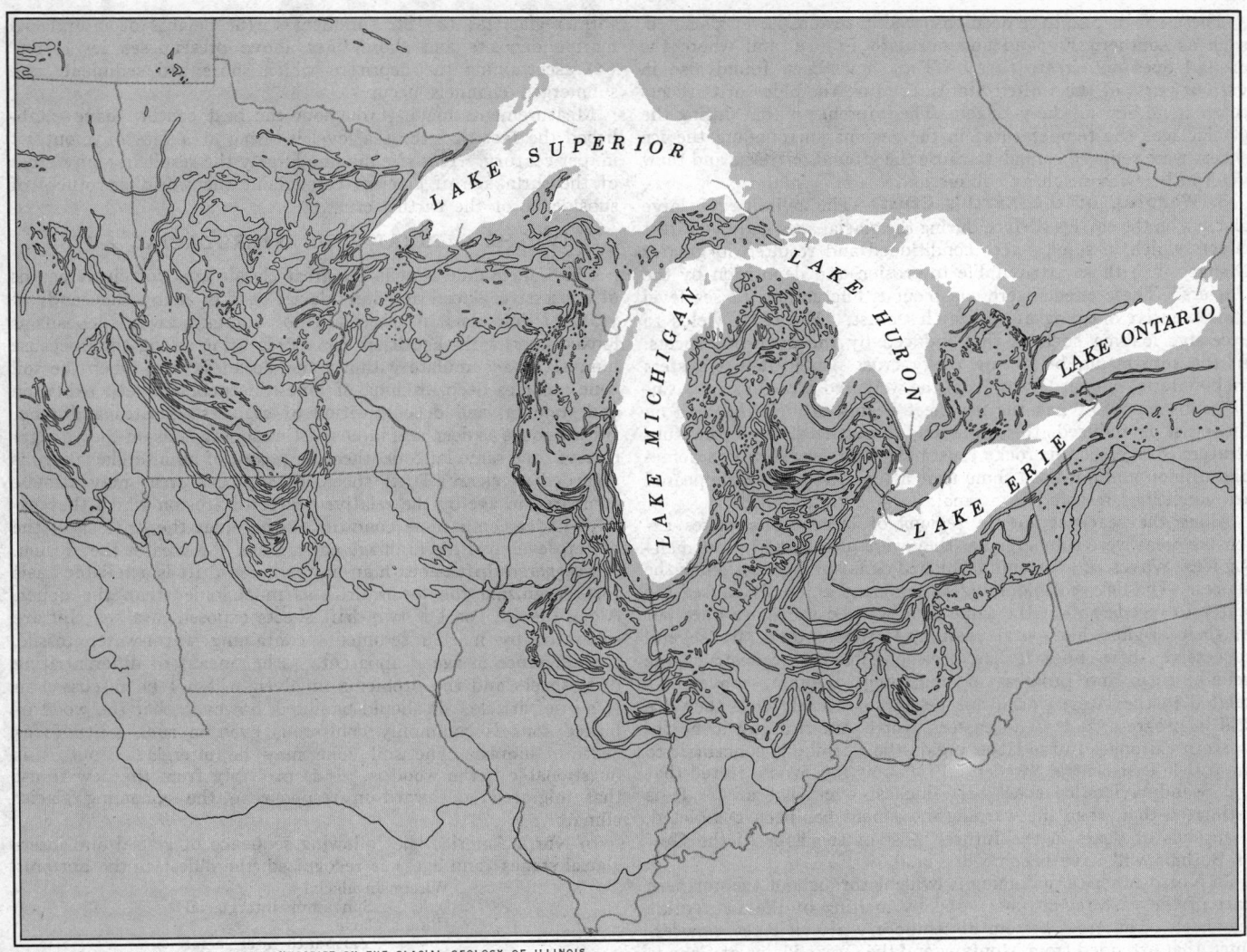

OUTLINES OF GLACIAL MORAINES AROUND THE DISTAL ENDS OF THE GREAT LAKES SHOWING THE LOBATE ORGANIZATION OF THE LAST ICE SHEET

exist and of the former much larger size of existing lakes. These phenomena show that in these regions there were repeated times of greater precipitation and smaller evaporation than now occur. In at least two cases (Lake Bonneville in Utah and Mono lake in California) a close time relationship was established between the shore lines of the expanded lakes and glacial moraines. It is firmly believed that the times of greater precipitation and less evaporation coincided with the glacial ages, and that the times of low water or even desiccation coincided with the interglacial periods.

The most widely studied of these dry regions is in the western United States, where no fewer than 68 former lakes have been identified by their abandoned shore lines and sediments. The largest of these lakes was Lake Bonneville which filled a number of coalescent intermontane basins in Utah, Nevada and Idaho and had a maximum area of more than 20,000 sq.mi. and a maximum depth of more than 1,000 ft. Since the last glacial age this enormous fresh-water body has been shrunken by evaporation to Great Salt lake, Provo lake and Sevier lake. Second only to Bonneville in size was Lake Lahontan, which had a maximum area of 8,422 sq.mi. in Nevada, Oregon and California. Pyramid lake, Winnemucca lake, the Carson lakes and Walker lake are its reduced successors. Some of the 68 basins, studied in detail, have yielded evidence of two and even three high-water stages separated by stages of partial or complete desiccation.

In Eurasia a similar record has been recognized. The Caspian sea and the Aral sea east of it had at least three expansions separated by drier times. Both basins filled and overflowed. Similar though less fully determined records have been reported from the larger undrained basins of central Asia. According to Max Blanckenhorn the Dead sea of biblical fame filled, at least once.

In northern, eastern and southern Africa the record of former lakes is closely similar. This repeated expansion and desiccation form the basis for the Pleistocene sequence on that continent.

The low temperatures responsible for the formation of glaciers in higher latitudes are believed to have been the basic cause of the lake expansions. Decreased evaporation directly resulted. As the ice sheets formed, they became the sites of high atmospheric pressure, which in turn pushed the principal middle-latitude belts of moving cyclones south of where they presently lie. These cyclones brought added precipitation to broad regions in lower latitudes that in nonglacial times were semiarid. As a consequence of increased precipitation and diminished evaporation, lakes either came into existence or were enlarged.

Because they were in part the result of increased rainfall, the high-lake stages are termed pluvial stages. The lakes appear to have reached their maxima at about the times when the ice sheets were at their maxima. Thus the glacial ages and the pluvial ages are thought to have been coincident and closely related in origin.

A conspicuous effect of the glacial climates in regions that lay a short distance beyond the ice sheets is the effect of frost heaving and solifluction. Solifluction is the slow creeping of soil, even on gentle slopes, as a result of freezing and thawing. It takes place today in arctic and antarctic regions and on high mountain summits in lower latitudes. The effects of solifluction in producing contortion of stratification and the patterned arrangements of stones resulting from frost-heaving of the soil are distinctive.

These effects also have been observed in regions never glaciated, such as southern England and northern France, and where the ground does not freeze today. They have been found also in various parts of the United States, even on the older drift sheets that extend beyond the younger. The inference is that during the glacial ages the temperatures in the regions surrounding the ice sheets were reduced enough to cause the ground to freeze and thaw vigorously, with resulting solifluction.

3. Warping of the Earth's Crust.—The building of large glaciers on the earth's surface during the glacial ages had two direct effects which in some places conditioned and resulted in greater changes than those attributable to erosion and deposition by the glaciers. These effects were conspicuous fluctuations of sea level and extensive warping of the earth's crust. The crust yields to excessive loading such as that induced by the great ice sheets. In the substratum below the rocky crust plastic flow transfers rock material outward away from the weighted area causing basin-like subsidence. When the ice sheet begins to melt the load on the crust is reduced, the direction of plastic flow in the substratum is reversed, the rocky crust bulges up very slowly in dome-like fashion and not until some time after the ice has disappeared are conditions restored to normal.

Along the seacoast and in regions of large glacial lakes extensive areas were submerged as they were uncovered by the melting ice. Waves and currents fashioned cliffs and beaches along the shores. The delayed updoming of the crust gradually caused the water to recede and at the same time warped the shore lines out of their original horizontal positions. Where there are several successive shore lines it has been possible to reconstruct the general form and progress of updoming. Doming movements related to the latest glacial age began so recently that they are still in progress, at least in eastern North America and in northwestern Europe. In the latter region the warping is concentric to an area in east-central Sweden. From this fact it is inferred that the Scandinavian ice sheet was thickest over that area. It is estimated that when the warping movement has been completed, thousands of years in the future, most of the floor of the Gulf of Bothnia will have become dry land.

In North America updoming is evident throughout the northern part of the vast region uncovered by melting of the Laurentide ice sheet. The great system of temporary glacial lakes, now extinct, that extended from Montana and the Great Plains of Canada on the west to northern New York and northern Ontario on the east left an array of shore lines whose measurements have yielded much information about the progress of updoming of the crust as the ice sheet disappeared. The thickest part of this ice sheet—at least during its later history—is inferred to have stood over the Hudson bay region because the warped shore lines are generally concentric to that region. Farther east along the St. Lawrence, in the maritime provinces of Canada and in Newfoundland, well-developed marine strand lines record submergence beneath the sea as the ice melted, followed by slow upwarping toward the northwest. This movement is still continuing throughout much of the region. It is predicted that the future completion of the doming movement will cause Hudson bay virtually to disappear.

4. Fluctuations of Sea Level.—The other direct effect of glaciation is the fall and rise of sea level throughout the world. As was correctly deduced by Charles Maclaren in 1842, the building of large glaciers when none existed before requires that vast quantities of atmospheric moisture be precipitated in the form of snow. As this moisture must come from the sea, the result is lowering of the sea level. Under warming climates the existing glaciers melt and large volumes of melt water are returned to the sea, thereby raising its level. The alternation of glacial and interglacial ages therefore has resulted in fluctuation of the sea level through a range of hundreds of feet, including levels both somewhat higher and much lower than today. It is generally thought that the sea level has stood, during glacial ages, perhaps 400 ft. lower than now, and during interglacial ages several scores of feet higher than now. These figures are arrived at by two methods: (1) calculation from estimated volumes of present and former glaciers; (2) measurement of the heights of interglacial marine deposits and shore lines above present sea level; and (3) ascertaining the depth to which shoreward sediments and submerged channels occur.

Measurements made throughout the past century have established the fact that the sea level is rising at a rate of about 2.5 in. per century. This rise may be largely the result in many areas of the shrinkage of glaciers throughout the world, in others of subsidence of the earth's crust.

IV. THE GLACIAL AND INTERGLACIAL AGES

The U.S. middle west is the great classic area for clear records of successive glacial and interglacial ages of many thousands of years of duration. A mere layer of humus between deposits is looked upon with skepticism for representing a long time because humus can accumulate within a few decades. But when the soil zone includes deep leaching of limestone pebbles, deep oxidation and staining, and decomposition of granites, diorites and other silicate rocks as deep and intense as in modern soils on the younger drifts in the same latitude, then the record of an interglacial age is regarded as clear. Drift sheets of adjacent areas may also be compared in age by the relative degree of erosion which they exhibit under comparable conditions—the older the drift sheet the better developed the drainage pattern and the greater the erosion. A weathered drift beneath an unweathered drift is a reliable basis for recognizing the lower drift as much older than the upper. Along the sea coast if two drift sheets exposed in a sea cliff are separated by marine sediments containing warm-water fossils, the difference in age is apparent. Other means of differentiating drift sheets and the problems involved will not be discussed in this brief article. It should be noted, however, that the wood of buried soils is commonly coniferous even in such latitudes as central Illinois. The soil zone may be interglacial but it is questionable if the wood is. It is probably from the new forest that migrated southward in response to the oncoming glacial climate.

In North America the following sequence of glacial and interglacial stages (and ages) is recognized, the oldest at the bottom:

Wisconsin glacial
Sangamon interglacial
Illinois glacial
Yarmouth interglacial
Kansan glacial
Aftonian interglacial
Nebraskan glacial

All of these names originated in the upper Mississippi valley states where the type areas or sections occur. Certain correlations have been made with the Atlantic coast and with the Cordilleras. The Kansan is the surface drift over a large part of southern, western and eastern Iowa, northern Missouri, northeastern Kansas and eastern Nebraska. It also extends north into Minnesota and South Dakota. The Nebraskan is exposed beneath the Kansan at a great many places, rather commonly with a deep weathered zone preserved. For many years northeastern Iowa as far south as Dubuque was regarded as driftless, but patches of Nebraskan have been found on the upland ridges, making it quite certain that the Nebraskan ice sheet covered all of Iowa. A deposit of old weathered drift which some believe to be Nebraskan occurs on a high rock terrace at the mouth of the Wisconsin river valley. The Illinoian drift covers a large portion of Illinois and parts of southern Indiana and southwestern and eastern Ohio, and in places a fringe extends eastward beyond the Wisconsin. The Kansan seems to extend almost as far south in Illinois, Indiana and Ohio as the Illinoian. Naturally the Wisconsin drift, being the youngest, is the surface drift over a much greater territory than the older drift sheets.

In the western mountains glacial deposits of at least three different ages have been found. The youngest is probably of Wisconsin age; the older ones have not been confidently correlated. Deposits as old as the Kansan, which in the middle states has been greatly eroded with only small ground moraine remnants remaining, are probably the oldest that can be positively identified in the mountains.

For many years the following classification of glacial deposits in the Alps by A. Penck and E. Brückner has been recognized:

Würm glacial
　　Riss-Würm interglacial
Riss glacial
　　Mindel-Riss interglacial
Mindel glacial
　　Günz-Mindel interglacial
Günz glacial

Though some would add to this a suggested older deposit, the Donau, this classification seems to stand. In the area of continental drift in northern Germany and Denmark three stages are recognized. They are:

Weichsel glacial (includes Brandenburg)
　　Eem interglacial (marine)
Saale glacial (Warthe, an upper member)
　　Holstein interglacial (marine)
Elster glacial

As in the case of North American geological literature the European literature is replete with suggested revisions, concerning the merit of which only the test of further investigations will tell. The fact, however, is patent that the effects of the glacial period were world-wide and it comprised a series of glacial and interglacial equivalents. Much research remains to be done to perfect the record. See also QUATERNARY.

1. Subdivisions of the Latest Glacial Age.—Because there is much hidden history of the older glaciations the Wisconsin offers the best opportunity to learn the nature of a glacial stage and from some standpoints the substages of the Wisconsin glacial stage hold greater interest than the older glacial stages. In North America the substages of the Wisconsin deposits are recognized from youngest to oldest as follows:

Valders
Mankato
Cary
Tazewell
Iowan
Farmdale

The Farmdale and the Iowan lobes are somewhat similar in that both ice sheets had their axial directions of movement diagonal to the succeeding stages; they were of short duration; and, like the fall season, they preceded the greater and more intense glaciation of the Tazewell. The Tazewell marks the "winter" of the glacial age. The ice sheet was bulkier, more persistent and extended farther than any other substage of the Wisconsin. It was inferred that the temperature reached its lowest point and snowfall was heaviest. The Cary marks a late resurge of low temperature and heavy precipitation but it did not last long. The Mankato and Valders have the earmarks of late pulsations that were brief and portended another interglacial summer.

Some geologists are inclined to regard the Recent epoch as beginning when the Valders ice began to melt back. Others regard the Cochrane minor advance which terminated at Cochrane, Ont.—less than 200 mi. south of James bay—as the last substage. The former group of geologists thinks of the Cochrane as minor in degree and insignificant in the role of geologic processes that characterized the Recent.

In Europe as in North America, the last glacier did not steadily wane after the maximum advance, but there were climatic pulsations, each less severe and shorter than the preceding, resulting in glacial and intraglacial substages. International correlations of some of the interstadial intraglacial deposits have received much attention.

2. Nonglaciated Regions.—Southeastern California, now a very arid region, had a chain of large lakes, hundreds of feet in depth, of which the dry floor of Searle's lake is a successor. Radiocarbon dates of the upper part of the sediments agree closely with dates of the Wisconsin drift in Illinois. The overlying beds of salts and carbonates, which are 65 ft. to 100 ft. thick, are the result of evaporation in postglacial time. It does not seem too much to anticipate that an alternating series of salts and clays and silts will be found to match the older interglacial and glacial climates.

3. Duration of the Glacial Epoch.—The method of carbon dating back to the beginning of the Wisconsin (Würm) rapidly came into use after 1949. W. F. Libby and J. R. Arnold developed the radiocarbon method by which discretely selected samples of wood, charcoal and certain other organic remains from deposits younger than 20,000 years could be dated. Radiocarbon C^{14}, a radioisotope of carbon with the mass number of 14 produced in the upper atmosphere by the bombardment of nitrogen by cosmic-ray neutrons, reacts with oxygen to form carbon dioxide. In that form it enters into all organic matter and all material exchangeable with atmospheric carbon dioxide, including carbonate in sea water. Upon death of any organism the radiocarbon diminishes by its own radioactive disintegration at a known rate. Therefore, by determining accurately the loss that has taken place from wood, for example, since its burial, the age of the wood, i.e., the time since burial, can be computed. The method of determination has been improved to include specimens somewhat older than 30,000 years. (See RADIOCARBON DATING; GEOCHRONOLOGY.) According to this method wood from the Farmdale loess, the oldest known Wisconsin deposit, is from 25,000 to 29,000 years old. This does not take into account the time required for the development of the Laurentide ice sheet, for its movement into the drainage basin of the upper reaches of the Mississippi and for development of the valley train from which the loess was blown. The date of wood in the Iowan loess is 21,000 to 23,000 years; in Tazewell sediments, 15,000 to 19,000 years; Cary, 13,000 to 14,000 years; Mankato, about 12,200 years; and Valders advance, 11,400 years, all before the present time. E. Antevs, on the basis of varves and other geological evidence, disagrees. He calculates the date for the Mankato substage at about 19,000 years. In the early 1940s G. F. Kay estimated the retreat of the Mankato to have been about 25,000 years ago.

It is seen that radiocarbon dating allows only about one-half of the time permitted by the older estimates. In the second half of the 20th century research was being conducted to determine whether microorganisms of decay and other factors affect dating. Minute shells associated with low temperatures have been recovered from deep sea cores taken from the Caribbean and mid-Atlantic. Some C^{14} measurements have been made of them which show an age range from 10,000 to about 55,000 years. Those that record the lowest temperatures are about 15,000 years old, which is the latter part of the Tazewell. The feeling of conservative glacial geologists is that research should be pursued to acquire further and broader information. In the meantime respect is held for carefully documented stratigraphic work and sampling.

The extensive erosion of the Kansan drift and the prolonged exposure recorded by its zone of weathering are so impressive that it seems quite clear that the Kansan glacial stage was several hundred thousand years ago. The deep weathering of the Nebraskan before that drift sheet was superseded by the Kansan ice sheet, together with the apparent extensive erosion of the Nebraskan in northeastern Iowa, make the Nebraskan antedate the Kansan by an interval many times the duration of the Recent epoch. Hence, the over-all age of the Glacial epoch is at least several hundreds of thousands of years.

Another method of age determination, which has been applied to the older stages, is the "per cent of equilibrium method for uranium, ionium and radium," worked out by W. D. Urry. This method, which relies on the analysis of radioactive disintegration products, has been applied to ocean-bottom sediments in areas where they indicate alternating warm and cold periods, as for example alternating layers of globigerina ooze (see FORAMINIFERA) and red clay in the southeastern Pacific ocean. The dates obtained, according to Jack L. Hough, seem to correlate well with Pleistocene events on the North American continent, including six substages of the Wisconsin glacial stage (11,000, 15,000, 26,000, 37,000, 51,000 and 64,000 years ago), three substages of the Illinoian glacial stage (274,000, 310,000 and 330,000 years ago) and, by extrapolation, with the end of the Kansan glacial stage, about 700,000 years ago. The above data corroborate the former conclusions drawn from geologic study of the drift sheets that the Yarmouth interglacial, between Kansan and Illinoian times, was longer than the Sangamon interglacial between Illinoian and Wisconsin times, and that the interglacial ages were much longer than the glacial ages.

One of the intriguing methods for studying the glacial history of the earth, also based on marine deposition but employing radio-carbon dating instead of the per cent of equilibrium method, is that of taking deep-sea cores some 60 ft. or more long where the rate of sea-floor sedimentation is slow. These cores bring up alternating layers of oozes of microorganisms and red clay. The fossil microorganisms include those that are sensitive to temperature changes (Foraminifera, diatoms) and thus they afford opportunity to study the ocean temperatures of the Pleistocene. These temperatures, based on carbon-isotope ratios and the C^{14} datings of the shells, provide comparison for this information from the ocean depth with the C^{14} datings of wood and other carbon remains from soils and peat beds of known geological positions on the land. This is a frontier of scientific investigation in glacial geology.

V. LIFE OF THE PLEISTOCENE EPOCH

The extent to which the plants and animals of the earth have become adapted to the new environment since the end of the glacial age is an indication of what can transpire in something like 10,000 years. The older glaciations, Illinoian, Kansan and Nebraskan, had similar effects on the life of those of the last ice age. Since the interglacial ages that followed are estimated to have had a duration of something like 100,000, 300,000 and 200,000 years respectively, it is to be inferred that the land surface from which the ice had retreated became completely reclothed with vegetation, and repopulated several times during the glacial period.

Mammalian life changed greatly both through extinctions and through the appearance of new forms. Among the new ones were zebrine horses, cattle, camels, certain elephants, rhinoceroses and a woolly mammoth, a distinctly cold climated form not known to have lived before the first glaciation. Horses and moose were immigrants near or at the close of the Kansan glaciation. The greatest number of the extinctions came in the period roughly from 5,000 to 10,000 years ago, and included all the camels, horses and ground sloths; two genera of musk oxen; peccaries; antelope-like ruminants; all but one species of bison; a giant beaver-like animal; a stag moose; and several kinds of cats, some of which were of lion size. The huge mammoths, larger than living elephants, which had become common throughout the United States also disappeared as did the forest dwellers, the mastodon and the woolly mammoth of tundra and level stretches. Their extinction in North America, as well as Europe, is credited to early man. Man's appearance in North America was rather sudden, probably taking place when there was a land bridge across the Bering strait.

1. North America.—There were forms that lived on the tundra close to the ice front—the woolly mammoth (*Mammuthus primigenius*) and the caribou; in the subarctic forest the mastodon, moose, stag moose, giant beaver (*Castoroides*), deer and bears; farther removed, the other elephants of the mammoth line, tapirs, peccaries and a variety of deer and carnivores; in the central Great Plains elephants, horses, bison, elk, antelope, ground sloths from South America and many small mammals. The late glacial forms that lived in Florida included the mastodon, elephant, camels, a huge bison, peccaries, deer, tapirs, horses, ground sloths, armadillos, several carnivores including a sabre-toothed cat (*Smilodon*), wolves and bears. In central Alaska the frozen ground of alluvial silt contains fossils of bears, wolves, foxes, badgers, wolverines, sabre-toothed cat, jaguar, lynx, woolly mammoth, mastodon, horses, camel, saiga antelope, four bisons, caribou, moose, stag moose, elk, sheep, musk ox, ground sloth and various rodents. It is suggested that this fauna may be interglacial.

Today the Bering strait separates Alaska from Siberia. The fossil record indicates that this was a land connection one or more times during the Pleistocene. The Japanese current probably gave it a mild climate and permitted the growth of long thick grass like that on the Alaska peninsula. The immigrants and emigrants appear to have been entirely cold-temperate or boreal forms.

Not only may crustal warping have produced the bridge, but lowered sea level prevailed during the early and late parts of the different glacial ages when much sea water was still locked up in the ice sheets.

Immigration from South America is recorded in the ground sloths which came to live as far north as central Alaska. The North American horse and deer traversed the Isthmus of Panama to live in South America.

2. Europe.—The Pleistocene mammal fauna went through a series of striking changes in Europe as it did in North America. Basically there was a steady change as certain species like the elephants, rhinoceroses and horses evolved, while at the same time other forms became extinct against the competition of immigrants from the east. Superimposed on this progression, however, was an oscillation due to a north-south shift of animal population as the glaciers waxed and waned, so that faunas which were very similar appeared at two or more different times, separated by a fauna of quite different character.

The very earliest part of the Pleistocene (Villafranchian) produced some strange inhabitants of western Europe—lynx, several species of bear, a macaque monkey and the great sabre-toothed cat, *Machairodus*. The elephants included *Mastodon arvernensis*, but also the first of the true elephants, *Elephas meridionalis*. This fact, and the appearance of the true horses (in the form of *Equus stenonis*), is regarded by many as the criterion of the Pleistocene.

In the later part of the Lower Pleistocene (the Günz-Mindel interglacial stage, the Aftonian in North America, identified in *The Glacial and Interglacial Ages,* above), though the macaque monkey, sabre-toothed cat and *Elephas meridionalis* persisted, the latter was accompanied by a more advanced type, *trogontheri*. Two species of rhinoceros (*mercki* and *etruscus*) were present, a giant extinct beaver (*Trogontherium*) was found, and the red deer and hippopotamus made their appearance.

The Middle Pleistocene started with the Mindel-Riss, or Great Interglacial, with the macaque monkey and Merck's rhinoceros still lingering on. A deer, *Dama clactonianus*, was distinctive. For the first time the straight-tusked elephant (*antiquus*) appeared, with the great ox (the aurochs, *Bos primigenius*) and the bison and the modern species of horse; and most interesting of all, *Homo sapiens*. (Fossil specimens from Steinheim, Ger., and Swanscombe, Kent, Eng., are discussed in MAN, EVOLUTION OF: *Antiquity of Homo Sapiens.*) As the climate changed to the Riss glaciation, a characteristic cold-climate fauna replaced that of the preceding interglacial. For the first time appeared the woolly mammoth (*Mammuthus primigenius*) and woolly rhinoceros (*Tichorhinus antiquitatus*), both extinct, the bison and animals like the reindeer and musk ox which are associated with the arctic tundra.

The Upper Pleistocene started with the Riss-Würm, or Last Interglacial, and the fauna was once more "warm," with the hippopotamus, straight-tusked elephant, brown bear, beaver, lion, leopard, marmot, red deer and the giant elk (*Megaceros giganteus*). As the Würm glaciation developed, so a "cold" fauna very like that of the Riss glacial period once more migrated in—the woolly rhinoceros and mammoth, cave bear, lynx, arctic fox, bison, aurochs, musk ox, horse and arctic lemmings. After the vicissitudes of this last glaciation, the progress to the present-day climate included the extinction of the mammoth and woolly rhinoceros (whose frozen remains have been found in the Russian tundra), the elimination of the beaver and the driving to the far north of the reindeer and the musk ox. *See* F. E. Zeuner, *The Pleistocene Period* (1959).   (F. W. SN.)

3. Early Man.—In the examination of the past for the physical and cultural records of man, the written record gives way to the archaeological record of pottery, drawings and carvings on the walls of caves and pieces of ivory, and artifacts of stone and bone, the basic materials of the science of archaeology. By the late 1960s, available data on the physical anthropology of man—the family of Hominidae—predated the beginning of the Ice Age in Europe. Heidelberg man, a Pleistocene species of the genus *Homo*, lived at approximately the close of the Mindel glacial stage (Kansan in North America). Nonhomo manlike species, Archanthropic, prophetic of man, appeared in Europe during the Günz-Mindel interglacial stage (Aftonian). The last of these are not known to have lived after the Mindel-Riss interglacial stage (Yarmouth). However, the time span from the beginning of the first interglacial to near the end of the Mindel-Riss interglacial is much longer than all subsequent time. Extinct fossil species of the genus *Homo* (paleoanthropic man)—Heidelberg, Neanderthal, Rhodesian and Solo—cover the period from the close of the Mindel glacial to the early part of the Würm glacial (Wisconsin). *Homo sapiens*, the present world-wide species, has lived since the close of the Mindel-Riss interglacial. Cro-Magnon man, the modern erect man, was found in fossilized condition in the Cro-Magnon cave in Dordogne, France. His appearance is dated as in the fourth glacial. (*See* also Man, Evolution of.)

The skeletal parts show that marked evolution took place during the 1,000,000-year stretch of Pleistocene time, particularly in the brain, which increased greatly in size. The artifacts show a general progressive increase in perfection and adaptability, which in turn record an increase in intelligence and skill among the people who made them. These increases, however, apparently took place at different rates in different regions; very different degrees of culture flourished at the same time in different parts of the world. This has been learned in part through dating the various groups of artifacts and skeletal remains, both by means of fossil mammals that have been preserved with them and by identification of the deposits in which some of the remains occur with deposits of known glacial or interglacial age. Radiocarbon C^{14} datings have made significant contributions.

The record in the Americas does not extend as far back in time as that in the old world. No skeletons or artifacts dating from early in the Pleistocene have been found, but discoveries indicate that man may have come to America at about the close of the Sangamon interglacial or the beginning of the Wisconsin glacial.

VI. THE GLACIAL CLIMATES

1. Character.—At the height of the glacial ages at least 28% of the land area of the world was covered by glacial ice. At present more than 10% is so covered, but significantly this is in the higher latitudes. The same was probably true for the interglacial ages. Some differences between the present and one of the interglacial ages are apparent, however, from comparison of fossil faunas with the living forms.

Glacial cirques (theatrelike valley heads fashioned by the action of snow fields at the heads of individual glaciers in mountainous terrain) bear a rough general relation to the snow line or lower limit of perennial snow. Through measurements of the altitudes of cirques in many parts of the world the approximate position of the snow line at the height of the latest glacial age has been determined. Wherever measured, this former snow line is lower than the snow line of today—at the equator as well as in polar latitudes.

In order to determine the glacial-age climate of a coastal point A, a point B on the same coast is located by finding the place where the present snow line has the same altitude as the glacial-age snow line of A. The present climate of B is then taken as representative of the former climate of A. The method is rough, but over a wide region it gives consistent results. Coastal points such as A are seen to have received much greater precipitation than they do at present, and to have had mean annual temperatures of the order of 7° C. to 8° C. lower than now, whereas in interior regions the increase in precipitation and decrease in temperature, compared with present conditions, were less pronounced. In other words, the subpolar climate belts were shifted toward the equator during the glacial ages. This shift may have amounted to as much as 15° of latitude for the boreal, or northern, belt, less for the warmer belts.

The pluvial conditions of the dry regions of middle and low latitudes support this conclusion in that they appear to show equatorward shifting of the middle-latitude belts of rain-bringing cyclonic storms. The evidence of fossil animals in the northern hemisphere likewise indicates southward shifting of the cold northern climatic zone through many degrees of latitude.

On the other hand the evidence of fossil plants and animals indicates that during the interglacial ages the climatic zones were shifted toward the poles, and that at least once these zones, in the northern hemisphere, have been pushed north of the positions they occupy at present. It is generally believed, though it has not been conclusively proved, that these climatic shifts were synchronous throughout the world. In summary, the climatic changes were world-wide and apparently contemporaneous; the climatic belts were shifted alternately, equatorward and poleward; and changes in mean annual temperatures amounted to several degrees centigrade.

2. Causes.—The causes of these remarkable climatic changes have received the attention of geologists, astronomers, physicists and meteorologists for a century. Of the many hypotheses put forward, a few may be mentioned only to be dismissed: (1) Changes in the amount of volcanic or cosmic dust in the earth's atmosphere, thereby varying the thermal insulating effect of the atmosphere. This hypothesis encounters many objections and is wholly inadequate to meet the facts. (2) Displacement of all or part of the earth's crust relative to the earth's axis, thus bringing different regions into the positions of the poles at various times. This hypothesis is negated by the consistent relative positions of the climatic zones throughout long periods of time and by the lack of independent geophysical evidence of crustal displacement. (3) Broad uplifts of continents and localized uplifts of mountain masses, thus reducing temperatures and creating conditions favourable for the formation of glaciers. This hypothesis, which usually also applies to shifts in ocean currents, was proposed before the fact of the interglacial ages was fully established, and fails because it demands frequently repeated crustal uplifts and subsidences of which there is no independent evidence.

The basis of a theory that has received wide adherence was suggested by J. Adhémar in 1832. It was extended by J. Croll in 1875, and much later was elaborated, with variations, by M. Milankovitch, R. Spitaler, W. Köppen and A. Wegener, W. Soergel and others. This theory, sometimes termed "the astronomical theory," is based on the periodic changes that affect the earth's motion in three different respects: (1) eccentricity of the orbit (period 91,800 years); (2) inclination of the axis to the ecliptic plane (period 40,000 years); (3) shifting of the perihelion (period 21,000 years). These changes affect the distribution of solar heat received by the earth's surface, though they do not affect its total amount. The results of these changes can be plotted as a curve showing variations in the amount of heat received during the summer at any selected latitude. Because the three periods differ, such curves are nonperiodic. They show irregularly spaced maxima and minima of heat, which are taken by the advocates of the theory to represent the interglacial and glacial ages respectively. Four pairs or groups of temperature minima (nine in all), held to indicate four principal glacial ages, are represented as having occurred within the past 600,000 years.

Four objections to this theory may be mentioned: (1) it demands that the cold times alternate between the two polar hemispheres, yet there is no geologic evidence that such was the case; (2) it requires that at the equator there be little or no heat fluctuation, yet there is clear evidence in the east African mountains, directly on the equator, that the snow line there fluctuated throughout more than 3,000 ft. between glacial and interglacial ages; (3) the heat-fluctuation curves deduced from the theory show nine minima; these do not agree with the geologic evidence, which records only four glacial ages.

Another group of theories is based on the premise that there is a considerable variation in the absolute quantity of radiant energy emitted by the sun, and holds that terrestrial climatic fluctuations take place in accordance with such variations. E. Huntington's version of this idea laid emphasis on a supposed connection between solar energy and the incidence of cyclonic storms on the earth. Sir G. Simpson's version deduced an elaborate and ingenious scheme in which glacial ages are offset in time with respect to the maxima and minima of solar radiation. It applies best to the antarctic region. A. Penck's version deduces a direct connection between reduced solar radiation, world-wide temperature reduction and glaciation. Although there is no proof whatever that large fluctuations in solar energy have occurred, the assumption that they have occurred appears to meet all the requirements for the causes of the glacial climates. *See* GEOLOGY; *see* also references under "Pleistocene Epoch" in the Index.

BIBLIOGRAPHY.—J. K. Charlesworth, *The Quaternary Era,* 2 vol. (1957), and R. F. Flint, *Glacial and Pleistocene Geology* (1957), include useful bibliographies; Flint's "Historical Perspectives" in *The Quaternary of the United States,* ed. by H. E. Wright, Jr., and David G. Frey (1965), traces the development of Quaternary and Pleistocene geology. Among works of special interest are Louis Agassiz' classic *Études sur les glaciers* (1840; Eng. trans. by A. V. Carozzi, 1967); Albrecht Penck and E. Brückner, *Die Alpen im Eiszeitalter* (1912); Ernst Antevs, *The Last Glaciation* (1928). Also C. E. P. Brooks, *Climate Through the Ages* (1949); R. A. Daly, *The Changing World of the Ice Age* (1934); Morris M. Leighton and H. B. Willman, *Loess Formations of the Mississippi Valley* (1950); Friedrich E. Zeuner, *Dating the Past,* 4th ed. (1958); A. L. Kroeber (ed.), *Anthropology Today* (1953); Paul Woldstedt, *Das Eiszeitalter* (1954); Willard F. Libby, *Radiocarbon Dating,* 2nd ed. (1955); Kalervo Rankama (ed.), *Quaternary,* vol. 1 (1965); H. G. Richards, *Studies on the Marine Pleistocene,* pt. 1 and 2 (1963); Gwen Schultz, *Glaciers and the Ice Age* (1963); M. Schwartzbach, *Climates of the Past* (1963); H. E. Wright and David G. Frey (eds.), *International Studies on the Quaternary* (1965); Morris M. Leighton, *Review of Papers on Continental Glaciation,* INQUA volume on the Quaternary (1966); H. E. Wright and R. M. Morrison (eds.), *Means of Correlation of Quaternary Successions* (1967); E. L. Krinitzky and W. J. Turnbull, *Loess Deposits of Mississippi,* Special GSA Paper Number 94 (1967).   (M. M. L.)

PLEKHANOV, GEORGI VALENTINOVICH (1856–1918),

the founder and for many years leading exponent of Russian Marxism, was born at Gudalovka in Tambov province, on Dec. 11 (new style; Nov. 29, old style), 1856, the son of a landlord. As a student he was attracted to the Narodniki (*q.v.*) or Populists, and he became a member of the clandestine organization Zemlya i Volya (Land and Freedom). In 1879, however, objecting to the increasing emphasis laid on terror as opposed to mass agitation, he formed a splinter group, Cherny Peredel (Black Redistribution). Emigrating to Western Europe in 1880, he plunged into the study of Marxist literature and soon decided that "scientific socialism" alone offered a solution to the problems besetting the Russian revolutionary movement. In September 1883 he founded in Geneva a small circle, Osvobozhdenie Truda (Liberation of Labour) to spread Marxist ideas in Russia.

Plekhanov unequivocally condemned any attempt by a revolutionary minority to seize power on the people's behalf. The revolution, he maintained, must be the work of the masses themselves, in particular of the industrial proletariat. This class, guided by a militant social-democratic party, should lead the struggle of the entire Russian people against the "feudal" absolutist order; the ensuing "bourgeois-democratic" revolution would in turn pave the way for socialism and the dictatorship of the proletariat. A determinist, Plekhanov held that the advent of socialism was assured by the inexorable laws of historical development. In his philosophical writings he adhered rigidly to Marxist dialectical and historical materialism, and his works on aesthetic subjects were inspired by considerations of political utility. In both fields his views command official approval in the U.S.S.R.

In the leadership of the Russian Social-Democratic Workers' Party Plekhanov was eventually eclipsed by Lenin. Not without misgivings, Plekhanov collaborated with Lenin in publishing *Iskra* ("The Spark") and, at the 2nd party congress (1903), supported him against the Mensheviks; but in November 1903 the two men parted company. Plekhanov saw in Bolshevism a revival of Populist "Jacobinism": Lenin, he held, was seeking to turn the party into a pliant instrument with which to seize power and introduce socialism in Russia "from above," regardless of whether the objective historical conditions for it had as yet matured. During the revolutionary crisis of 1905–06 Plekhanov maintained that it was essential for socialists to collaborate with bourgeois liberals against absolutism, but his efforts to propagate this view among the party rank and file met with little success. A similar situation obtained in 1917, when Plekhanov at last returned to Russia. His standpoint, that the class struggle should be temporarily suspended in the interests of national defense, was unpopular with the war-weary masses.

In November 1917 he condemned the Bolshevik Revolution as a betrayal of Marxist principles. A few weeks later, threatened with violence by a band of revolutionary sailors, he had to flee from his home.

He died, disillusioned, at Terijoki in Finland on May 30 (N.S.), 1918.

English translations of Plekhanov's works include *In Defence of Materialism* (1947), *The Role of the Individual in History* (1946), and *Art and Social Life* (1953).

See S. H. Baron, *Plekhanov . . .* (1963).   (J. L. H. K.)

PLEURA, DISEASES OF.

The pleura is a continuous thin sheet which lines the interior of the thoracic cavity (parietal pleura) and is reflected at the root of each lung to cover the entire surface of the lung (visceral pleura).

Pleurisy.—Inflammation of the pleura, which may occur as an accompaniment to almost any major lung disease, is often called pleurisy or pleuritis. The word is sometimes used in a loose and inaccurate manner to indicate any type of thoracic pain. The pain of pleural inflammation is usually sharp in character, well localized and clearly related to breathing.

Pleural Effusion.—Accumulation of excess amounts of fluid between the visceral pleura and the parietal pleura (pleural effusion) frequently results from pleural inflammation or circulatory congestion. The amount of fluid may be very great, even several pints, sufficient to prevent expansion of the lung and, hence, result in respiratory insufficiency. Small amounts are often difficult to detect except by X-ray examination. The fluid is usually clear and straw coloured but may be cloudy and occasionally tinged with blood.

Infection of the pleural space with tuberculosis, secondary to a tuberculous lesion in the lung, is a common cause of pleural effusion. The fluid is usually clear and straw coloured and contains moderate numbers of lymphocytes. It may contain tubercle bacilli, but often biopsy of a small portion of the pleura is necessary to establish the diagnosis. Often, but not always, it is possible to diagnose the associated tuberculosis of the lung by the usual methods. Treatment of tuberculous pleural effusion is usually effective when the specific antituberculosis chemotherapeutic drugs are administered, as for pulmonary tuberculosis. Untreated tuberculous pleural effusions are often followed by manifestations of lung tuberculosis after an interval of several months or several years of good health, during which latent period there may be no X-ray evidence or other indication of the infection.

Acute inflammatory diseases of the lung, including pneumonia (*q.v.*), are sometimes associated with pleural pain, and occasionally with accumulations of pleural fluid. The amount of such fluid is usually small, and it usually disappears promptly when the lung inflammation subsides.

Impaired circulation of blood in the lungs due to ineffectual heart action often leads to a seeping of fluid from the swollen and congested lungs into the pleural space. Treatment of the heart failure may relieve the congestion and permit resorption of the fluid. Often this requires the administration of diuretic drugs, limitation of sodium intake, rest, and administration of digitalis. Occasionally needle aspiration of the pleural fluid may accelerate improvement.

Empyema of the Thorax.—A collection of pus in the pleural space, known as empyema, is the result of severe and prolonged infection. Treatment is difficult and requires removal of the pus, either by repeated needle aspirations or by surgical drainage. Antibacterial drugs are selected which are active against the causative organism, hence bacteriologic examination of the pus is important. Surgical treatment sometimes requires the removal of large portions of the infected pleural membrane (decortication).

Tumours of the Pleura.—Most tumours which originate from the pleura can be classified as mesotheliomas. They may be either malignant or benign, and may be either localized or extended over a large area of pleural surface. Diagnosis is rarely possible without microscopic examination, and that necessitates surgical biopsy in most circumstances.

Cancer of the lung (bronchogenic carcinoma) often extends peripherally to involve the pleura, producing symptoms and findings similar to those of infection. Malignant implants on the pleura of tumours originating elsewhere in the body are rather common in the latter stages of widespread metastatic cancer. Such implants often lead to marked pleural effusion, and the fluid is often bloody. Diagnosis is established by X-ray examinations and sometimes by biopsy. Treatment is difficult, but radiation, using either X-ray or radioactive isotopes, and chemotherapy with tumour-inhibiting drugs may provide some temporary symptomatic relief.

Chylothorax.—Rupture of the thoracic duct, a lymphatic channel which transmits chyle from the abdominal cavity to the large veins of the upper thorax, may lead to accumulation of chyle within the pleural space. This material is recognized by its milky appearance and its high fat content. The two commonest causes of chylothorax are injury and metastatic malignancy.

Hemothorax.—Accumulation of blood in the pleural space may be a serious result of injury, especially when there has been damage to the larger blood vessels of the chest wall. Sometimes the rupture of adhesions between visceral and parietal pleura, occurring in association with pneumothorax, will lead to occult bleeding, which may become serious before it can be recognized. It is possible for a patient to lose very large amounts of blood by this type of internal hemorrhage. Diagnosis often requires needle aspiration as well as X-ray examination, and treatment may or may not require open operation for repair.

Fibrothorax.—Pleural fluid may contain large amounts of fibrin, which may be deposited on the pleural surfaces and eventually organized into scar tissue. Sometimes this is sufficient to envelop all or a portion of the lung in a thick inelastic coating which limits lung expansion and impairs breathing ability. Surgical removal may improve respiratory function in selected cases. Small localized collections of fibrin are frequent and of little or no significance.

For other diseases of the chest, see LUNG, DISEASES OF; PNEUMOTHORAX; RESPIRATORY SYSTEM, DISEASES OF.

(H. C. H.; H. C. Hw.)

PLEVE, VYACHESLAV KONSTANTINOVICH: see PLEHVE, VYACHESLAV KONSTANTINOVICH.

PLEVEN, RENÉ (1901–   ), French statesman, twice premier of the Fourth Republic, was born at Rennes on April 13, 1901. After graduating in law from the University of Paris he became an industrial executive. In 1940, during World War II, he joined Gen. Charles de Gaulle, who gave him civilian responsibility for the colonies from 1941 to November 1944, when he became minister of finance in De Gaulle's first government formed in Paris. Pleven left the government with De Gaulle in January 1946 but did not long remain a Gaullist.

Pleven had been elected a deputy for Côtes-du-Nord in 1945 and was reelected subsequently. He was a leader of the Union Démocratique et Socialiste de la Résistance (UDSR), a left-centre group. He was twice minister of defense (1949–50 and 1952–54), and was premier from July 11, 1950, to Feb. 28, 1951, and again from Aug. 8, 1951, to Jan. 7, 1952. He helped to formulate the plan for the European Defense Community in 1950, but none of the cabinets to which he belonged was willing to stake its life on the ratification of the necessary treaty. He was foreign minister in Pierre Pflimlin's short-lived cabinet in May 1958.

Pleven did not oppose De Gaulle's return to power and left the UDSR in October 1958 when François Mitterrand induced it to oppose the new constitution, to which Pleven gave a qualified assent. In February 1959 he formed the Union pour une Démocratie Moderne. In 1966 he spoke against France's withdrawal from NATO.   (P. W. C.)

PLEVEN (PLEVNA), chief town of the *okrug* (district) of that name in northern Bulgaria, is situated about 5 mi. (8 km.) to the east of the Vit River, a tributary of the Danube, at an altitude of 381 ft. (116 m.). Pop. (1961 est.) 72,171. The town has been known since Thracian times when it was called Storgosia (Stergezia), and it was later occupied by Romans and Turks. It is now a service centre for the surrounding fertile agricultural region, has food-processing industries, and manufactures textiles, machinery, ceramic articles, and cement. Pleven is a route centre and

an important junction on the main Sofia-Varna railway, having a branch line which connects with the small Danube port of Somovit, 25 mi. N. The town has several monuments and museums which commemorate various battles fought in and around Pleven, and also the important Liberation museum.

PLEVEN OKRUG lies between the foothills of the Balkan Mountains (Stara Planina) and the Danube. Its approximate area is 4,132 sq.km. (1,596 sq.mi.). Pop. (1963 est.) 357,100. The main rivers are the Danube, Iskur (Isker), Vit, and Osum, all of which are used for irrigation. The northern area is part of the Danubian Platform region where the rich black soil and summer rainfall allow good grain harvests. Grapes and fruit are grown and cattle are bred. Industries are varied and include timber and food processing. The chief towns of the district, besides Pleven, are Cherven Bryag, Levski, and Nikopol.   (S. H. BR.)

The Battle of Pleven.—Pleven was the scene of a major battle during the Russo-Turkish War of 1877–78. Having crossed the Danube, a Russo-Rumanian army under Gen. Baron N. P. von Krüdener marched on Pleven but, on July 20 (new style; 8, old style), 1877, was stopped there by a Turkish army under Gen. Osman Pasha. After two further attacks (July 30 and Sept. 11–12) had been repulsed by the Turks, the Allies then began a siege; Pleven fell to them on Dec. 10, when the Turks, having failed to break through the cordon, surrendered. See RUSSO-TURKISH WARS.

PLEYEL, IGNAZ (JOSEPH) (1757–1831), Austrian composer and founder of one of the principal French firms of piano makers. The 24th child of a poor village schoolmaster, he was born at Ruppersthal, near Vienna, on June 1, 1757. He studied the piano under J. B. Vanhal and composition under Haydn, whose close friend he became. In 1776 he produced his puppet opera *Die Fee Urgele*, on a libretto derived from Voltaire and Chaucer, at Esterház, and in 1780 his opera *Ifigenia in Aulide* was produced in Naples. In 1783 Pleyel was appointed deputy *maître de chapelle* and in 1789 principal *maître de chapelle* at the cathedral in Strasbourg, where in 1791 he became involved in the troubles of the French Revolution and barely escaped the guillotine. In 1795 he moved to Paris, where he opened a music shop, published the first complete set of Haydn's string quartets, and in 1807 founded the pianoforte factory which still bears his name. Pleyel was a prolific composer with a facile and spirited invention. A few of his numerous symphonies, concertos, serenades, and string quartets were revived toward the middle of the 20th century. He died near Paris, Nov. 14, 1831.

See L. de Fourcaud, *La Salle Pleyel* (1893); I. Klingenbeck, *I. Pleyel und seine Kompositionen für Streichquartett* (1926).

PLIMER, ANDREW (c. 1763–1837), English miniature painter, was the son of a clockmaker at Wellington. With his brother Nathaniel (1757–c. 1822), who also became a miniature painter, he joined a party of gypsies and wandered about with them, eventually reaching London, where in 1781 he was engaged by the miniaturist Maria Cosway as studio boy. Her husband, Richard Cosway, the leading miniature painter of the time, then received him into his own studio. In 1785 he set up for himself in Great Maddox Street. He exhibited many times in the Royal Academy. His miniatures are of great brilliance and are in considerable demand among collectors. They are distinguished by the peculiar wiry treatment of the hair and by the large, expressive eyes that Plimer invariably gave to his female sitters. He died at Brighton in 1837 and was buried at Hove.

See G. C. Williamson, *Andrew and Nathaniel Plimer* (1903).
(G. C. W.; X.)

PLIMSOLL, SAMUEL (1824–1898), British politician and social reformer who dedicated himself to achieving greater safety for seamen and whose name has been given to the mark that indicates the limit to which a ship may be loaded, was born at Bristol on Feb. 10, 1824. Before entering business on his own account as a coal merchant in 1853, he worked as a clerk. He became interested in shipping conditions, and strongly criticized "coffin ships," unseaworthy and overloaded vessels, often heavily insured, in which unscrupulous owners risked the lives of their crews. He entered Parliament as Liberal member for Derby in 1868, and, failing to secure passage of a bill dealing with the safety of shipping, published *Our Seamen* (1873), which attacked the shipowners and made a great impression throughout the country. On Plimsoll's motion, a royal commission was appointed in 1873, and in 1875 a Merchant Shipping Bill was introduced, which Plimsoll, though regarding it as inadequate, resolved to accept. When the bill was dropped he lost his self-control, applied the term "villains" to members of the House, and shook his fist in the Speaker's face. He later apologized, but there was strong support for his view that the bill had been stifled by the pressure of the shipowners.

The government was pressed into passing a bill, which in 1876 was amended into the Merchant Shipping Act. This gave stringent powers of inspection to the board of trade and fixed the loading line for ships. Plimsoll was reelected for Derby in 1880, but decided to give up his seat. Later he was estranged from the Liberal leaders by their neglect of shipping reform. Moreover his views on other questions were frequently at variance with theirs. He became president of the National Amalgamated Sailors' and Firemen's Union in 1887 and three years later raised a further agitation about the horrors of the cattle ships. He died at Folkestone on June 3, 1898.   (A. Bri.)

PLINY THE ELDER (GAIUS PLINIUS SECUNDUS) (A.D. 23 or 24–79), Roman savant and author of the celebrated *Natural History,* was born at Novum Comum (Como), in Transpadane Gaul. On this ground he claimed Catullus, a native of Verona in the same region, as a fellow countryman. His own writings and those of his nephew Pliny the Younger show that the date of his birth was in A.D. 23 or 24, that he must have come to Rome at an early age and that he practised for some time as an advocate. He saw military service in Germany. Under Vespasian, with whom he was on the most intimate terms, he served as procurator in Hispania Tarraconensis and elsewhere. He was in Africa, Gallia Narbonensis and Gallia Belgica and perhaps also in Judaea and Syria.

Finally Vespasian appointed him prefect of the Roman fleet at Misenum, in Campania, which Augustus had made one of the principal Roman naval stations. He was stationed at Misenum when, on Aug. 24, 79, there occurred the great eruption of Vesuvius which overwhelmed Herculaneum and Pompeii and cost Pliny his life. The circumstances are vividly told in a letter of the younger Pliny to the historian Tacitus. Pliny, wishing to assist those persons who were in danger, sailed from Misenum to his friend Pomponianus at Stabiae (Castellamare) on the southern shore of the Bay of Naples. There, in order to allay the fears of his friends, he dined, as his nephew says, "cheerfully, or what was equally splendid, with a pretence of cheerfulness," and then retired to rest. In the middle of the night, when stones and ashes were already falling about the house and the house itself was rocking alarmingly, he was roused and he and his party determined to seek safety in the open, binding pillows about their heads as a protection against falling debris. "Now it was day elsewhere," runs his nephew's account, "but there night darker and denser than any night, alleviated a little by numerous torches and lights of various sorts. It was decided to go out upon the shore and see at close quarters whether the sea now offered any prospect of safety; it still continued wild and adverse. There Pliny lay down upon a cast-off linen cloth, and once and again he asked for cold water, which he drank. Then flames and a smell of sulfur announcing the approach of flames caused the others to take to flight and roused him. Supported by two slaves he got upon his feet, but immediately collapsed, his breathing, I gather, being obstructed by the thickening vapour which closed up his windpipe—naturally weak and narrow and frequently painful. When day returned—the third (in English reckoning the second, *i.e.,* Aug. 26) after the last day (Aug. 24) that he had seen—his body was found intact and uninjured, covered as he had been dressed. The appearance of the body suggested one sleeping rather than dead."

A list of Pliny's books in chronological order is given in a letter by his nephew: (1) *De iaculatione equestri unus* ("On Throwing the Javelin From Horseback, in One Book"), "written while he was serving as commander of a cavalry regiment with equal ability and care." (2) *De vita Pomponi Secundi duo* ("Life of Pomponius Secundus, in Two Books"), "the discharge, as it were, of a debt due to the memory of a friend who had entertained a singular affection for him." Pomponius, described by Tacitus as a man "of refined character and conspicuous ability" was a tragic poet who had also a military career of some distinction. (3) *Bellorum Germaniae viginti* ("German Wars, in Twenty Books"), "in which he brought together all the wars waged between us and Germany. He began the work while he was serving in Germany, being admonished by a dream. The ghost of Drusus (stepson of Augustus and brother of Tiberius) who, having carried his conquest of Germany to the widest extent, died there, stood by him as he slept and commended to him his memory and entreated him to vindicate him from the injustice of oblivion." This work is cited by Tacitus, who probably used it in his *Germania.* (4) *Studiosi tres* ("The Student, in Three Books") "in which he instructs and perfects the orator from the cradle up." (5) *Dubii sermonis octo* ("Dubious Language, in Eight Books") "written in the last years of the reign of Nero when slavery had rendered dangerous every study of a free and elevated character." Fragments of the treatise were edited by J. W. Beck (1894). (6) *A fine Aufidi Bassi triginta unus* ("Continuation of the History of Aufidius Bassus, in Thirty-One Books"). The history of Bassus of which the terminal point is not known, Pliny continued down to his own day. (7) *Historiae Naturalis XXXVII* ("Natural History in Thirty-Seven Books"). This work alone is extant.

Pliny the Younger has given a description of his uncle's studious habits. He would call upon the emperor Vespasian before daybreak and then after performing his official duties return home and devote what time remained to study. After a light meal, if it were summer and he had leisure, he would often lie in the sun while a book was read and notes and extracts were made: he never read a book without making extracts, holding that no book was so bad as not to contain something good. Next he frequently had a cold bath, a snack and a short siesta, after which, "as if it were another day," he studied until dinnertime. During dinner a book was read and notes were made. He rose from the dinner table in summer before nightfall, in winter within the first hour of night. Thus at Rome; but in vacations no time was exempt from study, save bathtime, and even then he had something read to him or dictated something, while he was rubbed and dried. When traveling he was accompanied by a shorthand writer armed with book and notebook and in winter provided with gloves. To procure time for study he was carried even in Rome and his nephew tells how he was once reproved by him for wasting valuable time in walking. When he died Pliny bequeathed to his nephew 160 volumes of extracts (*electorum commentarios*) "written on both sides and in the minutest hand," for which, when he was procurator in Spain and when the number of volumes was rather less, he had declined an offer from Larcius Licinus of 400,000 sesterces (*c.* £3,100).

The *Natural History,* which appeared with a dedication to Titus, son of Vespasian and his successor as emperor, two years before Pliny's death, is, as stated above, in 37 books. Book i has a general preface and contains a table of contents of the other books, to each being appended a list of the authors consulted. These lists contain the names of 146 Latin and 327 foreign authors. Book ii is devoted to a mathematico-physical description of the world and deals with the heavenly bodies—sun, moon, planets, fixed stars; various meteorological phenomena; the succession of the seasons; the earth's shape and surface phenomena—seas, rivers, springs and the like. The subject matter of this book affords Pliny an opportunity, of which he readily avails himself, to expound his own philosophic creed, which is a modified Stoicism. His view of nature is pantheistic. Books iii–vi are devoted to geography and ethnography. This is unscientific and uncritical but extremely valuable for the incidental facts which it presents. There is an interesting mention of maps of Armenia in book vi, 40.

Books vii–xi are occupied with zoology and are the most generally interesting section. The seventh book deals with man and is occupied less with the normal than with the marvelous and portentous, which the scientific creed of the author and his belief in the infinite power of *ingeniosa natura* enabled him to accept or at least not to reject outright. Thus there are tales such as would have charmed the ear of Desdemona—of men whose feet were turned the wrong way; of the Mouthless Men (Astomi) who subsisted upon the mere fragrance of flower and fruit; of the Umbrella-feet (Sciapodes) who used their extensive feet as parasols to protect them from the sun; of monstrous births; of precocity or exceptional development of physical strength or speed, sight or hearing, and mental powers; of men who were unconscionably long in dying. Incidentally, Pliny here declares his disbelief in immortality. Book viii treats of terrestrial animals other than man. Here again, amid much that is interesting in detail, there is an unfortunate absence of scientific arrangement and an excessive proneness to accept the marvelous, of which he was so unconscious that he expresses surprise at the credulity of the Greeks (*mirum est quo procedat Graeca credulitas*). Hence side by side with sound science, which comes mostly from Aristotle and, so far as concerns Africa, from Juba, there is a host of imaginary animals—winged horses, unicorns and like monstrosities. Book ix deals with aquatic animals and scientifically is the soundest of all the zoological books, which is no doubt due to the fact that Pliny's information is mainly derived, at least ultimately, from the *History of Animals* of Aristotle, who treats of aquatic animals with unusual fullness. The marvelous in this book is chiefly represented by Pliny's belief in Nereids and Tritons and the usual stories of the human sympathies of the dolphin. Book x treats of birds, commencing, according to Pliny's practice of beginning with the largest, with the ostrich. Such classifications as he makes of birds are of an empirical kind and based on very superficial observations. The first part of book xi is occupied with insects—the bee being treated with some fullness—and the latter part with what may be called comparative anatomy. Books xii–xix deal, generally speaking, with botany, including forestry and agriculture, the subject of book xviii, which is one of the most interesting in this section. Books xx–xxvii treat of medical botany or the medicines derived from plants. Books xxviii–xxxii deal with other than botanical *materia medica, i.e.,* with medicines derived from the bodies of man and other animals.

The remaining books are occupied with mineralogy and with metals and metallic products, the precious metals, gold and silver, being discussed in book xxxiii; bronze, bronze statuary, iron and lead in book xxxiv; chiefly painting in book xxxv; stone, including its use in building and sculpture, in book xxxvi, gems and precious stones in book xxxvii.

Pliny's *Natural History* is a storehouse of ancient errors, but there are many branches of ancient manners and culture, such as sculpture and painting, concerning which he gives valuable information which can be found in no other extant writer. His style is sometimes dry and abrupt and sometimes slovenly, but at other times strongly rhetorical, pointed or mannered. The influence of his work on later times was great. About three-quarters of the *Collectanea rerum memorabilium* of C. Julius Solinus (3rd century A.D.) were based on it, and on books xx–xxxii was based the *Medicina Plinii,* a compilation of the 4th century.

See also references under "Pliny the Elder" in the Index.

BIBLIOGRAPHY.—*Editions by:* J. Sillig (1851–58); L. von Jan, Teubner series, 6 vol. (1854–65); D. Detlefsen, 6 vol. (1866–82); C. Mayhoff, Teubner series (1892–1909).
Editions with translation, etc., by: A. Ernout *et al.,* with French trans. and notes (1947–); in Loeb series, with Eng. trans. by H. Rackham and W. H. S. Jones (1938–); K. C. Bailey, *The Elder Pliny's Chapters on Chemical Subjects,* with Eng. trans. and notes, 2 parts (1929–1932); E. Sellers (ed.), *The Elder Pliny's Chapters on the History of Art,* with Eng. trans. by K. Jex-Blake (1896).
English translations by: Philemon Holland (1601); J. Bostock and H. T. Riley (1855–57).
General: W. Kroll, *Die Kosmologie des Plinius* (1930); A. Klotz, *Quaestiones Plinianae geographicae* (1906); D. Detlefsen, *Die Anordnung der geographischen Bücher des Plinius und ihre Quellen* (1909); A. Nies, *Die Mineralogie des Plinius* (1884); H. Le Bonniec, *Bibliographie de l'histoire naturelle de Pline l'ancien* (1946); A Önnerfors, *Pliniana: in Plinii maioris naturalem historiam studia grammatica, semantica, critica* (1956); H. N. Wethered, *The Mind of the Ancient World: a Consideration of Pliny's Natural History* (1937); J. W. Duff, *A Literary History of Rome in the Silver Age, From Tiberius to Hadrian,* pp. 347–385 (1927); Pauly-Wissowa, *Real-Encyclopädie der classischen Altertumswissenschaft,* vol. xxi, col. 271–439 (1951).
(A. W. MA.; G. B. A. F.)

PLINY THE YOUNGER (GAIUS PLINIUS CAECILIUS SECUNDUS) (A.D. 61 or 62–*c.* 113), Roman author and administrator, nephew and adopted son of the elder Pliny, who left a collection of private letters of great literary charm which intimately illustrate public and private life in the heyday of the Roman empire. His official correspondence as a provincial governor is a unique set of documents, and his career is characteristic of those concerned with the management of the peaceful areas of the Roman empire.

Born *c.* A.D. 61–62 of a wealthy family at Comum in north Italy, he was educated at Rome and began to practise law when aged 18. He made a reputation in the courts of civil law, and later was in demand in the political court that tried provincial officials on charges of extortion. His most notable success was in A.D. 100, when he secured the condemnation of the proconsular governor of Africa, and of a group of officials from southern Spain. Meanwhile he had reached the highest grades of the administration by securing the titular posts of praetor in 93 and of consul in 100, despite the fact that he was the first member of his family to become a Roman senator. In this he owed much to the influence of friends of his uncle. Pliny had financial ability, and was head successively of the military treasury (*aerarium militare*) and of the senatorial treasury (*aerarium Saturni*) (A.D. 94–100). After administering the drainage board of the city of Rome—*cura alvei Tiberis*—(*c.* A.D. 104–106) he was sent (*c.* A.D. 110) by the emperor Trajan on a special mission to investigate corruption in the municipal administration of Bithynia. He apparently died there in office about two years later. His military experience was limited to a short commission on the staff of the governor of Syria at the beginning of his career, where his duties were financial. The details of his life are known from his letters, and from inscriptions set up in his honour at Comum.

Pliny, like his contemporary Tacitus, was a conventional man who accepted the Roman empire, serving under "good" and "bad" emperors alike, and making in his writings the conventional complaints against the latter. He concealed the preferment which he secured from the hated Domitian, and even claimed, later, that he had been in political danger through his tenuous connection with the faction that had criticized Domitian and had suffered accordingly in a famous state trial in the year of Pliny's praetorship.

The Letters.—*Publication and Chronology.*—He published selections of his private letters in nine books, issued apparently in three or four groups at irregular intervals between 100—109. After essaying the state of the market with the first two volumes, possibly issued separately, since they contain no interconnecting links, he issued a series of five or six, in which the letters are arranged to a certain extent in interconnected series. The ninth volume contained a miscellany of mostly very short letters of uneven interest and uncertain date, which may well represent the residue of publishable material in his files before he left Italy for the governorship of Bithynia. The tenth book is a posthumous publication. The chronology of the letters has been much discussed. The material in the first eight books is chronologically coherent. Books i and ii overlap, covering events from after the death of Domitian in Oct. 97 to the early part of 100. Book iii touches events of the next three years. Thereafter books iv to vii inclusive (with the exception of iv, 9, for a special reason) are confined each to the events of about a 12-month period from 104–105 to 107–108. The last two books cover much the same period as vii, but contain a few letters from earlier periods of the correspondence. This chronology depends not only upon a number of dated or datable historical references, and of obviously continuous groups of letters, but also on a series of subsidiary cross-references and interrelations in the subject matter which have not yet received sufficient attention.

Style and Content.—The letters are neither imaginary epistles in the style of Seneca nor unimproved copies of daily correspondence like those of Cicero. They are carefully written occasional letters. The topics are very diverse. Each letter contains an item of recent social, literary, political or domestic news or sometimes an account of an earlier but contemporary historical event, or else initiates moral discussion of a particular problem. Each has a single subject, and is written with considerable artifice in a style which mixes, in Pliny's terminology, the historical, the poetical and the oratorical manner, to fit the theme. Length depends on theme, but brevity is preferred. Pliny apologizes for the unusual length of certain letters. Whether they were all written as genuine letters is much discussed, but is the wrong question. Several are obvious literary revises of more practical originals, as when he discusses a new building with his agent, but omits its dimensions. Touches of revision can be detected in some of the longest historical letters that most resemble formal essays (*e.g.*, i, 5). The composition of these *litterae curiosius scriptae* ("letters written with special care") was a contemporary fashion which Pliny developed into a miniature art form, to which the closest parallel lies in the similar occasional verses of Martial. Pliny is a prose Martial, without the indecency. The form arose naturally in a wealthy and cultured class of interrelated families lacking rapid communications.

There are letters of advice to young men, often illustrated by anecdotes; short notes of greeting and inquiry to absent friends; descriptions of newly discovered scenes of natural beauty or of natural curiosities. There are compressed accounts of the lives and habits of famous men. Estate business is a frequent theme—crises in farming, famines, sales and floods. Forensic scenes play a large role; the longest letters describe the triumphs of Pliny in the political courts. Roman society is there in all its diversity—an aged and decrepit roué cheating his toadies in his last testament, or an octogenarian relict of the court of Nero maintaining bygone depravities in a more strait-laced age.

Pliny reveals himself as a successful and complacent, kindly man, patronizingly generous toward his juniors and inferiors, and smoothly tolerant of all but the most objectionable of his peers. His character is often unfavourably judged, but the model of the magnanimous man, which he consciously imitates, was honoured in antiquity as the highest pattern of human virtue.

Pliny was a shrewd man, who kept a careful eye on his landed estates, now discussing the pros and cons of a new purchase, now advising a friend how to prevent a municipality from wasting its endowments, now offering his wholesale buyer a price reduction when the grape market broke, with an eye to future deals, now modifying his system of rentals in order to keep the tenantry on his estates. Such letters reveal the abilities for which Trajan chose him to reorganize the municipal finances and local government of Bithynia. The tenth book of letters contains the minutes which he addressed to Trajan on sundry problems, and the emperor's replies. He consulted Trajan 42 times in a period of some 18 months. The topics include municipal expenditure on public works, the qualification of municipal councilors, the treatment of criminals and the prosecution of Christians.

Pliny has been criticized for lack of independent judgment and responsibility by those with little experience of modern bureaucracy, but it must be remembered that his province was lacking in archives and permanent administrative staff. Official documents were known only from copies held by plaintiffs and petitioners. Many problems required an alteration of the basic law of the province, or the amendment of an imperial edict. Others involved the rights of Roman citizens, or the privileges of independent imperial officials. Pliny was also anxious that his decisions should be based on general rules approved by the central government instead of on *ad hoc* decisions. Hence he had good reasons for the submission of most of his inquiries to the emperor at Rome, who only once reproves him for writing needlessly.

On eight occasions Pliny seeks Trajan's approval for large public building operations—theatres, aqueducts, baths, sports stadium, and a canal; it seems that Trajan initiated a rule that required central sanction for new municipal expenditure of this sort. Pliny was also anxious to secure Roman engineers and architects to supervise these works for a reason which Trajan failed to understand—that he did not trust the local experts, who had been responsible for extensive jerry-building. Pliny's humanity was in several instances notably greater than that of the emperor. In the affair of the Christians his examination of prisoners led him to query the assumption that the new cult was associated with vicious practices. Though ready to execute Christians as members of a proscribed sect, he sought confirmation that this was the policy of the central government.

Pliny's letters introduce many of the leading figures of Roman society in the 12 years after the death of Domitian—men of letters, politicians, administrators, generals and rising young men of rank. They make possible the social reconstruction of an age for which there is otherwise no serious historical record. He was an adept at brief character sketches, less satirical, more kindly and possibly more complete than those of Tacitus. His portrait of the learned lawyer Titius Aristo is typical (i, 22, 1–3). He was also a devotee of literature. He has left a detailed picture of the amateur literary world of his time, and of the salons in which it was the custom to recite one's work and to seek critical revision from one's friends.

Pliny published his forensic and literary speeches with loving care, and late in life took to the contemporary fashion for light verse in the style of Martial, at which his samples show that he was no adept. Though fulsome in the praise of contemporary writers, his judgment of the dead Statius was fair: "he was ever writing poems with greater pains than ability." His letters addressed to his fellow advocate Tacitus (*q.v.*), then occupied with his first major work, tell the little that is known about the date and circumstances of the composition of the *Historiae*, to which Pliny contributed his famous account of the eruption of Vesuvius. The biographer Suetonius was among his *protégés*.

A seldom noticed aspect of Pliny's mentality is his semiscientific interest in natural phenomena, which he shared with his uncle, author of the *Naturalis Historia*. Four long letters describe with careful accuracy the peculiar behaviour of subterranean springs, the course of the Vesuvian eruption and the floating islets of the Vadimonian lake (iv, 30; vi, 16, 20; viii, 20). His speculations about their causes are rational. His discussion of dreams and visions has the same quality (vii, 27). His description of external scenery, whether natural or artificial, is remarkably precise, with an exact sense of detail, despite an elaborate literary style.

Style as an Orator.—Pliny's grand oratorical style is known from his panegyric, delivered in the senate when he entered office as consul. This is elaborately antithetical, colourful in ornament, inflated in substance, passionate and violent in tone, and contrasts with the delicacy and balance of the letters. In it he contrasts the merits of the new emperor Trajan with the vices of Domitian, in a most partial manner, but still provides a valuable historical account of Trajan's succession and the first phase of his reign. Pliny's normal forensic manner was probably a great deal quieter and more argumentative, as in viii, 14. He debates the "battle of styles" in several letters.

BIBLIOGRAPHY.—The best modern editions of the letters and of the panegyric of Trajan are those in the "Teubner Series," by M. Schuster, 2nd ed. (1952) and in the "Budé Series," vol. i–iii, by A.-M. Guillemin (1927–43), vol. iv by M. Durry (1947). *See* the Eng. trans. by W. Melmoth, *The Letters of Pliny the Consul* (1746), rev. by W. M. Hutchinson, "Loeb Series," 2 vol. (1915). There are no modern general commentaries except E. G. Hardy, *Plinii epistulae ad Traianum* (1889); M. Durry, *Panégyrique de Trajan* (1938). *See* also (for Pliny's life and chronology) T. Mommsen, *Gesammelte Schriften*, vol. iv (1906), pp. 366 ff.; A. N. Sherwin-White, "Pliny's Praetorship Again," in *Journal of the Royal Society*, pp. 126 ff. (1957); R. Syme, *Tacitus*, ch. vii–viii (1958); (for Pliny and literature) A.-M. Guillemin, *Pline et la vie littéraire de son temps* (1929). (A. N. S.-W.)

PLIOCENE (from Gr. *pleion*, "more," and *kainos*, "recent"), the geological epoch immediately preceding the Glacial (Pleistocene) epoch as indicated on the accompanying geologic time chart. Many modern genera appeared before the epoch was over.

The name Pliocene was introduced by Sir Charles Lyell (1830, published 1833) for the youngest of his three divisions of the Tertiary (*q.v.*) period of time. Lyell initially recognized a "Newer" and an "Older Pliocene." In 1839 he substituted the name "Pleistocene" for "Newer Pliocene," restricting the "Pliocene" to "the formations of Tuscany, and of the Sub-Apennine hills in the north of Italy, as also the English Crag." In 1846 Edward Forbes redefined the Pleistocene, making it equivalent to the time interval of continental glaciation in Europe. This was considered

Geologic Time Chart

System and Period	Series and Epoch	Distinctive Records of Life	Began (Millions of Years Ago)
CENOZOIC ERA			
Quaternary	Recent (last 11,000 years)		
	Pleistocene	Early man	2+
	Pliocene	Large carnivores	10
Tertiary	Miocene	Whales, apes, grazing forms	27
	Oligocene	Large browsing mammals	38
	Eocene	Rise of flowering plants	55
	Paleocene	First placental mammals	65–70
MESOZOIC ERA			
Cretaceous		Extinction of dinosaurs	130
Jurassic		Dinosaurs' zenith, primitive birds, first small mammals	180
Triassic		Appearance of dinosaurs	225
PALEOZOIC ERA			
Permian		Reptiles developed, conifers abundant	260
Carboniferous			
Upper (Pennsylvanian)		First reptiles, coal forests	300
Lower (Mississippian)		Sharks abundant	340
Devonian		Amphibians appeared, fishes abundant	405
Silurian		Earliest land plants and animals	435
Ordovician		First primitive fishes	480
Cambrian		Marine invertebrates	550–570
PRECAMBRIAN TIME			
		Few fossils	more than 3,490

to have begun somewhat later than was originally envisaged by Lyell and resulted in controversy as to the age of strata falling between the Pliocene as defined by Lyell and the Pleistocene as described by Forbes. During the 18th International Geological congress, in 1948, discussion of criteria for definition of the Pliocene-Pleistocene boundary indicated that the beginning of the Glacial epoch occurred earlier than previously recognized. The boundary has been placed at the original Lyell horizon.

Miocene-Pliocene Boundary.—Type sections of the Lyellian epochs do not occur in the same region. Deposits in many areas of the world cannot exactly be correlated with the Lyell units but are intermediate in position. The problem of the Miocene-Pliocene boundary, for example, has become complex. Vertebrate-bearing Sarmatian and Pontian strata of eastern Europe are not represented in the type sections of either epoch. Vertebrate paleontologists consider the advent of *Hipparion,* a primitive horse found in North America, Europe, Asia and Africa, as marking the beginning of the Pliocene. This genus first occurs in Pontian faunas; hence they are recognized as basal Pliocene. Correlative marine faunas are of distinctive Miocene aspect; invertebrate paleontologists assign the containing strata to the Upper Miocene (*q.v.*), which is the classification used in this article.

PHYSICAL HISTORY

The Miocene epoch closed with a widespread marine regression and consequent development of continental deposits. The expanded Black Sea and Caspian basins, cut off from the Tethyan (ancestral Mediterranean) sea, became brackish water bodies that persisted through the Pliocene. The marine life trapped in these basins underwent striking evolutionary changes.

The Pliocene began with a marine transgression and closed with a regression. In the Sub-Apennine area of Italy, considered as the type area of the epoch, the transgressive phase is represented by blue marls with offshore faunas. These pass upward into yellow sands with littoral faunas regarded as regressive deposits. Above are intertonguing marine (Calabrian) and nonmarine (Villafranchian) strata that, prior to 1948, were assigned to the Upper Pliocene. Much of Italy was flooded by Pliocene seas but small gulfs in the mouths of the larger river valleys characterize most of the Mediterranean Pliocene.

Embayments from the North sea covered Belgium and eastern England. Lower strata have a fauna of warm water affinities indicating a seaway opening toward the south. The deposits in England include the Coralline Crag (crag = shell sand) remarkable for the abundance of bryozoans, formerly identified as coral. The overlying Red Crag of Sussex has a cold water fauna suggesting that the southerly connection had closed.

In eastern Europe large fresh-water lakes formed. Most im-

portant were: (1) the Pannonian lake covering the Hungarian plains; (2) the Dacian lake, separated from the Pannonian by the Carpathian mountains, covering the lower Danubian plains; (3) the Aegean lake occupying the area of the Sea of Marmora, most of the Aegean sea, and parts of Greece and Thrace.

Marine Pliocene deposits in eastern North America are confined to peninsular Florida (Caloosahatchee formation) and coastal South Carolina and southern North Carolina (Waccamaw formation). The thickest known marine Pliocene, however, occurs in southern California where more than 13,000 ft. of sediments are found in the Ventura basin. Local embayments occurred from Lower California to Alaska.

Occasional mammalian teeth in the shallow water marine formations aid in correlating the marine and nonmarine strata of California. The Thousand Creek formation of Nevada and the Rattlesnake beds of Oregon are of Pliocene age, as is the upper part of the Ogallala group of the high plains; the lower part is correlated with the Pontian stage. These sandy deposits contain seeds of grasses and herbs, bones and teeth of grazing mammals, and leaves of poplar, willow, hackberry, elm and other trees that grew along stream valleys.

In Texas the first appearance of large ground sloths (*Megalonyx*), migrants from South America, testifies to the re-establishment of the connection between the two continents.

Pliocene deposits are not extensive in South America. In Argentina continental Hermoso beds of the Pampas, and the Tunuyan and Araucanian deposits of the Andean foothills yield mammalian remains. Marine faunas occur in the Mancora and Sechura formations of northwestern Peru.

In Japan, marine deposits are widespread but thin and discontinuous due to deposition in small gulfs. An exception occurs in the Yezo-Karafuto geosyncline bordering the Japan sea in northern Honshu island. Here a thick sequence of Miocene-Pliocene strata has no evidence of stratigraphic break between the two epochs. Elsewhere a major hiatus is evident.

Many Pacific islands show raised reefs and reef limestones that are believed to be of Pliocene age. There are also areas of local embayment, as in the Cagayan valley of northern Luzon and the Iloilo basin of Panay, in the Philippines, where clastic sediments represent marine transgressions. In New Zealand Pliocene sediments occur only along the coast of South Island, but an embayment or strait transected North Island in the Napier Bay-Wanganui area. Noteworthy is the fact that whereas the Lower Pliocene faunas are of colder water facies than those of the Miocene, the Upper Pliocene (Castlecliffian) Mollusca indicate warmer waters. This trend which continued into the Pleistocene is interpreted as resulting from the shifting of oceanic currents caused by Late Pliocene diastrophism in the Pacific basin.

Continental deposits of Pontian age are widely distributed in Asia; true Pliocene deposits, however, occur only in the Nagri and Dhok Pathan formations of the Siwalik series of northern India, and at a few poorly known localities in China.

Volcanism.—The volcanic Massif Central of France was initiated as early as Oligocene time, but the first well-dated flows are of Upper Miocene (Pontian) age. During the Pliocene, however, the great volcanoes of Cantal and Mont-Dore grew to elevations comparable to Mt. Etna. Ash and lava flows, 1,000 m. in thickness entomb Lower Pliocene plants and insects. Activity continuing into Villafranchian time culminated in basalt flows that form the present Massif surface.

Tertiary volcanism in North America occurred mainly during the Miocene epoch, but in many areas eruptions continued throughout Pliocene time.

PLIOCENE LIFE

Marine Life.—Marine mollusks show a predominance of recent species. Notable is the trend toward cooler water conditions than are evidenced by Miocene life. The only major exception is in New Zealand. Marine mammals reached their maximum development in the Miocene seas. Many genera became extinct at the end of that epoch, but nearly all families persisted, in reduced numbers, into the recent. Pliocene additions are the rorqual

(Balaenopteridae) and the right whales (Balaenidae).

Continental Life.—The Pliocene mammalian fauna of the northern hemisphere is of modern aspect with the majority of the families represented still being extant. A limited amount of faunal exchange took place between Eurasia and North America during Pontian time at the end of the Miocene, but there is little to suggest a connection during the Pliocene itself. No representatives of the Bovidae (cattle, bison, antelope, etc.) or of the Cervidae (deer), families of Eurasian origin, were in the North American fauna. Their place was taken by antilocaprids, related to the pronghorn. *Hypohippus*, a long-necked, long-bodied, short-limbed, forest horse, and *Hipparion*, a three-toed horse, reached Europe during the Upper Miocene and are present in Eurasia and North America during the Pliocene; typical North American Pliocene horses including *Pliohippus*, ancestor of *Equus*, did not reach the old world. (*See also* EQUIDAE.)

Characteristic North American Pliocene mammals include camels (*Pliauchenia, Procamelus*); hornless rhinoceroses (*Aphelops, Peraceras*); short-legged, hippopotamuslike rhinoceros, *Teleoceras;* beavers (*Castor, Dipoides*); large cats (*Felis*) and sabretooths (*Machairodus*); proboscideans, including *Tetralophodon*, shovel-tusked *Amebelodon*, and mastodons; and many others.

Eurasian faunas are strikingly like those of modern Africa. Bovids include cattle, bison, sheep and goatlike forms and many genera of antelopes. Deer, including *Cervus,* flourished, along with abundant suids and, in Asia, varied giraffids. Proboscideans include the peculiar *Dinotherium* with recurved lower jaw tusks, *Stegodon,* an ancestral elephant, and *Mastodon.* Among the Primates are the monkeys *Macacus* and *Cercopithecus,* and the apes *Dryopithecus* and *Pliopithecus* in Europe, and a larger number of genera in Asia.

Floras.—Pliocene floras are, generically, almost identical with those of today. Distributional differences reflect differing climatic conditions that obtained during the epoch. Unusual is the flora of England, dominated by a mixture of Japanese and North American forms with some Himalayan and Indo-Malayan types. *See* also PALEOBOTANY; PALEONTOLOGY; also references under "Pliocene" in the Index.

BIBLIOGRAPHY.—C. W. Cooke *et al., Bull. Geol. Soc. America,* vol. 54, p. 1713 (1943); C. W. Durham *et al., Calif. Div. Mines, Bull. 170,* ch. 3, p. 59 (1953); M. Gignoux, *Stratigraphic Geology,* trans. by G. G. Woodford, p. 554 (1955); R. C. Moore *et al., Bull. Amer. Ass. Petrol. Geol.,* vol. 33, p. 1276 (1949); R. A. Stirton, *Rep. 18th Intern. Geol. Congress,* pt. 11, p. 74 (1951); A. S. Romer, *Vertebrate Paleontology* (1945); C. E. Weaver *et al., Bull. Geol. Soc. America,* vol. 55, p. 659 (1944). (H. E. V.)

PLOMER, WILLIAM CHARLES FRANKLYN (1903–   ), South African writer, whose varied and original gifts have been shown in poetry, fiction, memoirs, editing the memoirs of others, and in collaborating with the composer Benjamin Britten (*q.v.*) on the librettos of several major works. Born on Dec. 10, 1903, in the northern Transvaal, but of English parents, he was educated in England, at a private school on the outbreak of war in 1914, and then at Rugby. After the war he returned with his family to South Africa.

His experiences as an apprentice "Memorial Settler" on a remote farm in the eastern part of Cape Province, at the age of 17, deeply coloured his thought and imagination. He returned to England in the late 1920s, to settle in London. His first novel, *Turbott Wolfe,* originally published by Leonard and Virginia Woolf at the Hogarth Press in 1925, held the promise of genius: a high-tension story of the conflicts of South African life as he had come to know them, the violence of the telling of which was matched by the violence of the reaction in the country in which he had been born. It was at this time that he collaborated with Roy Campbell (*q.v.*) and Laurens van der Post in the fiercely radical magazine *Voorslag,* which castigated the dealings of the ultraconservative Boers with the native population. And yet, neither here nor in his later novels and stories, was conflict, whether racial, class, or sexual, his essential intention; rather reason, imaginative understanding, and reconciliation.

His most striking achievement is in poetry (*Collected Poems,* 1960), in which he has developed an unusual vein, often in ballad form, combining grotesque satire with a sense of the precarious hold of 20th-century man on the edge of the abyss of a disintegrating civilization; and in four volumes of short stories, *I Speak of Africa* (1927), *Paper Houses* (1929), *The Child of Queen Victoria* (1933), and *Four Countries* (1949). He traveled widely in South Africa, Japan, and Greece, and most of his fiction, as well as his early poems, has these countries as background.

Plomer first reached a wider public with his dramatic novel of the shabbier side of London life, *The Case Is Altered* (1932), followed by *The Invaders* (1934). His love of the eccentric and flair for macabre comedy are apparent throughout his writing, but are given full play in the book of social reminiscences, *Curious Relations* (1945), which he wrote with his friend Anthony Butts, originally under the pseudonym William D'Arfey, and in his semi-fictional memoir, *Museum Pieces* (1952). Some of his deeper preoccupations, reflections on his uncommon adventures and encounters, emerge in two volumes of family and personal memoirs, *Double Lives* (1943) and *At Home* (1958); yet even in these, in spite of their wit and frank observation, the reader has a sense of something of ultimate significance withheld.

Plomer is also known for his skilful and sympathetic editorship (3 vol., 1938–40) of the diaries (1870–79) of the idiosyncratic Victorian clergyman Francis Kilvert (on whom he wrote the article for the *Encyclopædia Britannica*); and for his association with Benjamin Britten in the librettos for the opera *Gloriana* (1953), and the cantatas *Curlew River* (1964), *The Burning Fiery Furnace* (1966), and *The Prodigal Son* (1968). He served in Naval Intelligence in London during World War II, and has been a senior editor with the publishing firm of Jonathan Cape for many years. In 1963 he was awarded the Queen's Gold Medal for Poetry; and in 1968 was made a Commander of the Order of the British Empire. (Jo. LE.)

PLOTINUS (A.D. 205–270) was the founder and incomparably the greatest philosopher of the Neoplatonist School (*see* NEOPLATONISM). There is a good deal of reliable information about his life, since his pupil and editor Porphyry wrote his master's biography as an introduction to his edition of the works of Plotinus, the *Enneads* (it appears at the beginning of all complete manuscripts of the *Enneads* and is printed in the same place in all editions). But Plotinus himself would never say anything about his family or birthplace, and it is not known for certain to what race or country he belonged, though it is generally assumed, on the strength of a statement of rather doubtful reliability in Eunapius, that he came from Upper Egypt. He was certainly Greek by education and cultural background. He studied philosophy at Alexandria, where he could find no teacher to satisfy him until someone introduced him to the mysterious Ammonius Saccas, with whom he remained for 11 years. He went east in 243 with the emperor Gordian III's expedition, in the hope of studying Persian and Indian philosophy. But Gordian was murdered in Mesopotamia in 244, and Plotinus escaped to Antioch without having made any contact with eastern thinkers. In the same year he went to Rome, where he spent the rest of his life teaching philosophy and, after ten years, began to write. This is the period when he is known best from Porphyry's biography, where he appears not only as a great teacher and spiritual director but also as a man of great charm and of far-reaching and efficient practical kindness. He died in his 66th year, after a long and painful illness (what it was is not certain) which he bore most bravely. His writings were collected and published by Porphyry in the rather artificial arrangement known as the *Enneads;* but Porphyry also kept and published in his biography a record of the chronological order in which they were written, which is followed in some modern editions.

The importance of Plotinus in the history of European thought is very great indeed. For more than two centuries before his time a revived Platonism and a closely allied revival of Pythagoreanism had been developing. But it was Plotinus, a philosophical genius of the first order and at the same time a man of deep contemplative religion and one of the world's greatest mystical writers, who made this new Platonism into one of the great religious philosophies. The success of Neoplatonism was rapid. Soon after Plotinus' death it came to dominate the Greek philosophical world completely. It deeply influenced, too, the new intellectual world of the great Christian thinkers and, later, the Muslim and Jewish philosophers. It is true that the beginnings of Christian Platonism go back beyond Plotinus and that the great Christian Platonists were more original and independent than has sometimes been supposed and so must not be represented as merely passive recipients of the influence of Plotinus and his school. Nevertheless that influence did go very deep with many of the Christian Fathers, notably with St. Augustine in the West and with the great Cappadocians, St. Basil and St. Gregory of Nyssa, in the East; and, later, the enigmatic but extremely influential Pseudo-Dionysius (*see* DIONYSIUS) the Areopagite was much influenced by Neoplatonism. Plotinus, through these and other intermediaries, had a great indirect influence on the thought of the Middle Ages and both a direct (after the publication of Marsilio Ficino's Latin translation in 1492) and an indirect influence on the Renaissance; and his philosophy, still living and actual in the 20th century, seems likely to continue to be so, for his writings have in them an unusual power to inspire a new outlook on the world, to raise men's minds to the eternal and to encourage a moral virility very valuable in precarious times.

Philosophy.—Like other philosophers of the Hellenistic and Roman periods, Plotinus is a religious and moral teacher as well as a professional philosopher engaged in the critical interpretation of a long and complicated school tradition. He is an acute critic and a formidable arguer, with the intellectual honesty of a true philosopher; but philosophy for him is not primarily a matter of abstract speculation, or critical discussion of language or concepts, but a way of life in which, through an exacting intellectual and moral self-discipline and purification, those who are capable of the ascent can return to the source from which they came. His philosophy is an account of how from the eternal creative act, at once spontaneous and necessary, of that transcendent source, the One or the Good, proceeds a world of living reality constituted by repeated double movements of outgoing and return in contemplation; and this account, showing the way for the human self, which can experience and be active on every level of being, to return to the One, is itself an exhortation to follow that way.

Plotinus always insists that the One or the Good is beyond the reach of thought or language; what he says about this supreme principle is only intended to point the mind along the way to it, not to describe or to define it. But though no adequate concept or positive definition of the Good is possible, it is certainly not for Plotinus a mere negation or ultimate void in attaining to which the human personality disintegrates into unconscious nothingness. It is a positive reality of infinite richness and superabundant excellence. Plotinus often speaks of it in extremely negative language—to some extent inherited from his predecessors. But his object in doing so is to stress the inadequacy of all our ways of thinking and speaking to express this supreme reality, or to make clear the implications of saying that the Good is absolutely one and infinite and the source of all defined and limited realities.

The original creative act of the One produces the first great derived reality, *nous*, intellect or spirit; from this again comes soul, which forms, orders, and maintains in being the material universe. It should be remembered that the generation of this ordered universe is timeless; *nous* is eternal, and soul has a timeless life prior to time which it generates by its motion, and the material universe is everlasting. Also we must remember that the "levels of being" are not spatially separate or cut off from each other. They are really distinct, but all intimately present in every part of the universe and in each one of us. To ascend through soul to intellect and from intellect to the One we do not have to travel in space to another world, but must wake to a new kind of awareness.

Intellect for Plotinus is both thought and object of thought; it is a mind which is perfectly one with its object. As object, it is the world of forms or ideas, the totality of real being in the Platonic sense. These forms are produced by intellect's apprehension in multiplicity of the rich unity of its principle, the One; and, being one with intellect, they are not merely static objects but living, thinking subjects, each not only itself but capable

in contemplation of becoming the whole. They are archetypes and causes of the necessarily imperfect realities on lower levels, souls and the forms in body. We, at our highest, are intellects, or souls perfectly conformed to intellect; we become aware of our intellectual nature when, passing beyond not only sense perception but also the discursive reasoning characteristic of the life of soul, we attain to an intuitive contact and immediate possession of eternal realities.

Soul in Plotinus is very much what it is in Plato, the intermediary between the worlds of intellect and sense and the representative of the former in the latter. It is produced by intellect, as intellect is by the One, by a double movement of outgoing and return in contemplation, but the relationship between the two is more intimate and the frontier less clearly defined. For Plotinus, as for Plato, the characteristic of the life of the soul is movement, and this soul movement is the cause of all other movements. Soul, insofar as it leaves its rest in intellect, does not possess being as a whole, one with itself in immediate awareness; it is on the level, as already mentioned, of discursive thought which does not grasp its object immediately but has to seek it by a process of reasoning. The life of the soul in this movement is time, and on it all physical movement depends. Soul in relation to the material universe exists on two levels, a higher and a lower. The higher, in close and unbroken touch with intellect, forms and rules the material universe from above; the lower, which Plotinus often calls nature, acts as an immanent principle of life and growth and in its dreamlike contemplation, the last and lowest of contemplations, produces the immanent forms in body, which are noncontemplative and so sterile. Below these lies the darkness of matter, the absolute limit, the final absence of being at which the expansion of the universe from the One through diminishing degrees of reality and increasing degrees of multiplicity comes to an end. Because of its utter negativity, matter (at least the matter of the lower regions of the sense world) is for Plotinus the principle of evil. But though matter is evil, bodies composed of form and matter are not, and he strongly maintained against the Gnostic dualists of his time the goodness and nobility of the physical universe as the best possible work of soul; in this he was faithful to the teaching of Plato in his later dialogues, as expressed most impressively and influentially in the *Timaeus* (*see* PLATO: *Later Dialogues*).

We, as souls in bodies, can exist on any level of the soul's experience and activity. (Our descent into bodies is for Plotinus, who has some difficulty in reconciling Plato's various statements on this point, both a fall and a necessary compliance with universal law.) We can ascend in spirit to the level of universal soul, become that whole which we already are potentially and, in soul, attain to intellect; or we can isolate ourselves on the lower level, shutting ourselves up in the experiences, desires, and concerns of the lower nature to which we are attached and remaining ignorant of any higher kind of awareness than that of the senses. Philosophical conversion, the beginning of the ascent to the One, consists precisely in turning away from the life of the body, dominating and rising above its desires and "waking to another way of seeing, which everyone has but few use." This, Plotinus insists, is possible while we are still in an earthly body and without neglecting the duties of our embodied state. But the body and bodily life are things which weigh us down and hamper us in our ascent; Plotinus' language when speaking of it in this connection is strongly dualistic and other-worldly. In this he follows Plato in the *Phaedo*, but it is not impossible that he was unconsciously influenced by the Gnosticism that he consciously opposed.

The material universe for Plotinus is a living organic whole. Its organic wholeness is the best possible reflection on the material level of the living unity-in-diversity of the world of forms in intellect. It is held together in every part by a universal sympathy and harmony (a belief in which, deriving both from Stoic philosophy and from some very primitive conceptions, Plotinus shared with contemporary magicians and occultists). In this harmony external evil and suffering take their place as necessary elements in the great pattern, the great dance of the universe.

Evil and suffering can affect our lower selves but cannot touch our true, higher selves and so cannot interfere with the real well-being of the philosopher who chooses to live on that higher level.

From what has been said so far something of the nature of Plotinus' religion should have become clear. It is essentially the effort to actualize in ourselves the great impulse of return to the Good which constitutes reality on all its levels. By a rigorous moral and intellectual self-discipline we awake from the alienation of our lower state and rediscover our true selves. We become intellect and then, when the One manifests to us his continual presence, we rise to the mystical union, carried on the surge of the current of the impulse of return in its strongest and final flow, the pure love of intellect for its source. There is no consciousness of duality in that union; we are not aware of ourselves; but we are not destroyed or dissolved into the One because even in the union we are still intellect, though intellect "out of itself," transcending its normal nature and activity. The mystical union was for Plotinus, in this life at any rate, a rare and transitory experience. He attained to it, Porphyry tells us, four times while Porphyry himself was a member of the school. But it was the goal of all his effort and the source of the continuing power of his teaching. Philosophy for him was the way to union with the Good through moral purification and intellectual enlightenment.

See also PHILOSOPHY, HISTORY OF: *Later Greek Philosophy;* and references under "Plotinus" in the Index.

BIBLIOGRAPHY.—The Greek text of the *Enneads* was first printed by P. Perna (1580), together with the Latin trans. by Marsilio Ficino which had already appeared (1492). The best complete modern edition of the text of Plotinus is that begun by R. Harder and continued by R. Beutler and W. Theiler, with the treatises arranged in Porphyry's chronological order, published with Harder's German trans. (revised) and notes (1956-67). The great critical edition by P. Henry and H. R. Schwyzer was still in progress in the early 1970s (1951 *et seq.*). A minor edition of this, with extensive revisions, was also being published (1964 *et seq.*), and substantially the same text was appearing with an English trans. and notes by A. H. Armstrong (1966 *et seq.*). The edition of E. Bréhier (1924-38), though the text is poor, is valuable for the notes and introductions to the several treatises.

Plotinus has been translated into most modern European languages. In English there is a complete trans. by S. MacKenna and B. S. Page, 4th ed. (1970); also selections trans. with introduction and notes by A. H. Armstrong (1953; paperback edition 1962). For Armstrong's complete English trans. and Harder's German trans. *see* above. There is a good Italian trans. with critical notes by V. Cilento (1947-49).

For a complete bibliography of the extensive literature on Plotinus up to 1949, *see* B. Mariën, *Bibliografia critica degli studi plotiniani* (1949), published with the last volume of Cilento's trans. Since 1949 there has been a great increase in activity in Neoplatonic studies. Only a few works published since that date can be mentioned individually here: H. R. Schwyzer, "Plotinos" in Pauly-Wissowa, *Real-Encyclopädie der classischen Altertumswissenschaft*, vol. xxi (1951); J. Trouillard, *La Procession plotinienne* and *La Purification plotinienne* (1955); *Fondation Hardt,* vol. v, *Les Sources de Plotin* (1960); P. Hadot, *Plotin ou la simplicité du regard* (1963); J. M. Rist, *Plotinus: the Road to Reality* (1967), with select bibliography. (A. H. AG.)

PLOUGH (PLOW): *see* FARM MACHINERY.

PLOVDIV, the second largest town of Bulgaria and the chief town of Plovdiv *okrug* (administrative and economic district). It lies on both banks of the Maritsa River, 99 mi. (160 km.) ESE of Sofia by rail. Pop. (1969 est.) 236,627, of whom about 90% are Bulgars and the remainder mostly Turks, Armenians, Jews, and gypsies. The town is picturesquely situated on and around six syenite hills rising from the western Thracian Plain, with distant views of the Balkan and Rhodope (Rodopi) mountain ranges. In the old quarter, Trimontium (*see* below), built on three of the hills, parts of the Roman walls remain, and there are original old houses with characteristic overhanging upper stories. The main thoroughfare of the modern town is Vassil Kolarov Street. Educational and cultural institutions include schools of medicine and of agriculture, a theatre, an opera house, an ethnographic museum, and an archaeological museum containing a collection of ancient Thracian gold vessels. The town is a railway junction on the Belgrade-Sofia-Istanbul line and has an airport. The chief market of a fertile region, producing tobacco, rice, vegetables, and fruit (including grapes), it has important tobacco, food-processing, and textile industries; also motor repair works, a shoe factory, and a lead and zinc works. An international trade fair is held biennially.

Within the district, 11 mi. (18 km.) SE of Plovdiv is Asenovgrad (Stanimaka), also an industrial centre. Nearby are ruins of a fortress built by Tsar Ivan Asen II (1218-41), and, about 7 mi. (11 km.) distant, the 11th-century monastery of Bachkovo.

Plovdiv was called Pulpudeva in Thracian times. It was renamed Philippopolis in 341 B.C., after conquest by Philip II of Macedonia. Under the Romans (from A.D. 46) it became the capital of the Thracian province, with the name of Trimontium. It was repeatedly sacked by Goths and Huns and changed hands many times during the Middle Ages. In 1364 it was taken by the Turks, who called it Philibé. After the Russo-Turkish War of 1877-78 it became the capital of the utonomous Turkish province of Eastern Rumelia, which united with Bulgaria in 1885.

PLOVDIV OKRUG is one of 28 major administrative and economic districts (including the urban district of Sofia) into which the country was divided in 1964, when the cities of Plovdiv and Varna lost the status of centrally administered urban districts which they had held since 1959 (*see also* BULGARIA: *Administration and Social Conditions*). Area 2,159 sq.mi. (5,591 sq.km.). Pop. (1969 est.) 654,782.

The district stretches across the Thracian Plain from the Rhodopes in the south to the Balkan Mountains, whose highest peak, Botev, is on the northern boundary. In the north, around Vazovgrad, Levskigrad, and Kolofer, roses are cultivated for the distillation of attar. (L. DI.)

PLOVER, the name for many plump-breasted birds of the shorebird family Charadriidae, which also includes surfbirds, turnstones, and lapwings. There are about three dozen species of plovers, 6 to 12 in. long, with long wings, moderately long legs, short necks, and straight bills that are shorter than the head. Many species are plain brown, gray, or sandy above and whitish below. The group of so-called ringed plovers (certain *Charadrius* species) have white foreheads, one or two black bands ("rings") across the breast, and occasional other bold markings. Some plovers, like the golden (*Pluvialis* species) and black-bellied (*Squatarola squatarola*), are finely patterned dark and light above and black below in breeding dress.

Many plovers feed by running along beaches and shorelines, snapping up small aquatic invertebrate animals for food. Others, like the killdeer (*q.v.*), of upland meadows and grasslands, are chiefly insectivorous. Plovers and their relatives are wary birds, quick to give alarm. When flushed, they take swift and direct flight. Many utter melodious whistled calls, which can be used to distinguish the species. Plovers nest in a slight hollow in the ground where two to five (usually four) spotted eggs are laid. Both parents help incubate and care for the downy young, which soon after hatching run about and accompany their parents.

Plovers are found in most parts of the world. Those nesting

(LEFT) ALLAN D. CRUICKSHANK AND (RIGHT) H. C. KYLLINGSTAD FROM NATIONAL AUDUBON SOCIETY

BLACK-BELLIED PLOVER (SQUATAROLA SQUATAROLA) SHOWING (LEFT) FALL AND (RIGHT) SPRING PLUMAGE

in the north are strongly migratory and like to travel and feed in flocks. Most notable as long-range migrants are the golden plovers—the American (*Pluvialis dominica*) and the Eurasian (*P. apricaria*)—which breed in the Arctic and winter in the Southern Hemisphere, often far south of the Equator. The American golden plovers of the eastern range fly over the Atlantic and South America as far south as Patagonia, and most return via the Mississippi Valley; those in the western range travel, presumably nonstop, to groups of islands in the South Pacific. The Eurasian golden plovers winter in South Africa, Tasmania, and New Zealand.

(A. L. Rd.)

PLÜCKER, JULIUS (1801–1868), German mathematician and physicist, best known as an analytic geometer, but also carried out important research in magnetism and spectroscopy. He was born at Elberfeld on June 16, 1801. After studying at the universities of Bonn, Heidelberg, and Berlin he went in 1823 to study in Paris, where he came under the influence of the great school of French geometers whose founder, Gaspard Monge, had only recently died. In 1825 he was received as *Privatdozent* (official but unpaid lecturer) at Bonn, and after three years he was made professor extraordinary. He then held the following posts: professor of mathematics at Friedrich Wilhelm's *Gymnasium*, Berlin (1833–34), professor of mathematics at Halle (1834–36), professor of mathematics (1836–47) and finally professor of physics (1847) at Bonn. He died at Bonn on May 22, 1868.

From his lectures at Bonn sprang his first great work, *Analytisch-geometrische Entwickelungen*, 2 vol. (1828–31), in which he introduced the abridged notation in analytical geometry. (*See* ANALYTIC GEOMETRY.) He applied this notation to the straight line, circle, and conic sections, and he used it in his theory of cubic curves. Also he established the great principle of duality. He discovered the six equations known as "Plücker's equations" connecting the numbers of singularities in algebraical curves. (*See* CURVES.) Plücker communicated his formulas in the first place to *Crelle's Journal*, vol. xii (1834) and gave a further extension and complete account of his theory in his *Theorie der algebraischen Curven* (1839). In his *System der analytischen Geometrie* (1835) he introduced the use of linear functions in place of the ordinary co-ordinates; he also made the fullest use of the principles of collineation and reciprocity. He discussed curves of the third order and gave a complete enumeration of them, including 219 species. In 1846 Plücker published his *System der Geometrie des Raumes in neuer analytischer Behandlungsweise*, but this contains merely a more systematic and polished rendering of his earlier results.

After his appointment as professor of physics at Bonn, Plücker began a series of researches in physics. His first physical memoir, published in J. C. Poggendorff's *Annalen der Physik und Chemie* (1847), deals with the behaviour of crystals in a magnetic field. Then followed a long series of researches, mostly published in the same journal, on the properties of magnetic and diamagnetic bodies, establishing results which are now part and parcel of our magnetic knowledge. This was followed by researches on the discharge tube; he investigated the deflection of the discharge by a magnet and the behaviour of the negative glow in a magnetic field. Plücker, first by himself and afterward in conjunction with J. W. Hittorf, made many important discoveries in the spectroscopy of gases. He anticipated R. Bunsen and G. R. Kirchhoff in announcing that the lines of the spectrum were characteristic of the chemical substance which emitted them and in indicating the value of this discovery in chemical analysis. According to Hittorf he was the first who saw the three lines of the hydrogen spectrum, which a few months after his death were recognized in the spectrum of the solar protuberances, and thus solved one of the mysteries of modern astronomy. Induced by his mathematical friends in England, Plücker in 1865 returned to "line geometry." His first memoir on the subject was published in the *Philosophical Transactions* of the Royal Society in 1865. Plücker worked out the theory of complexes of the first and second order, introducing in his investigation of the latter the famous complex surfaces of which he caused those models to be constructed which are now well known to the student of higher mathematics. He left an

uncompleted work on the subject which was so far advanced that his pupil and assistant, Felix Klein, was able to complete and publish it.

PLUM, a fruit tree belonging to the genus *Prunus* of the rose family (Rosaceae). Like the peach and cherry, also members of the same genus, it is a stone or drupe fruit. Plums are the most widely distributed of the stone fruits. The fruit is also grown over a wide region in Europe from Italy on the south to Norway and Sweden on the north. Yugoslavia is the leading country with a

ROCHE
PLUM BLOSSOMS

tree potential of more than a million tons' production. A liqueur called *Slivovica* made from plums is an important article of commerce in Yugoslavia. Germany is the next largest producer of plums in Europe with a tree potential that in some years has equaled that of the U.S. in production. Turkey and Japan are leading countries in plum production in Asia.

It is not known just when European plums were introduced into North America, but probably pits were brought over by the first colonists. It is reported that plums were planted by the Pilgrims in Massachusetts and importations were made by the French into Canada. These European plums have done remarkably well in the new world, and they constitute the most important group grown commercially for canning and drying.

Plant Characteristics.—The trees of some plum species are vigorous in growth with upright branches reaching a height of 20–30 ft., while others are much smaller; some are small shrubs with drooping branches, and some have great beauty as ornamental plants. The flower buds on most varieties and species are borne on short spurs or along the terminal shoots of the main branches. Each bud may contain from one to five flowers, two or three being most common; and where the buds are close together, they give an appearance of densely packed, showy flower clusters when the trees are in full bloom. Characteristic of the genus *Prunus*, the individual flower is made up of a receptacle forming a hollow cup bearing sepals, petals and stamens on the outer rim surrounding a single pistil attached at the bottom of the cup. After fertilization of the flower, the receptacle and attachments fall off and the style withers and drops off, leaving the enlarged basal portion of the pistil, the ovary, which develops into the fruit.

The fruit of the plum develops from a single ovary. As the fruit grows to maturity, the outer part of the ovary ripens into a fleshy, juicy exterior making up the edible part of the fruit and a hard interior called the stone or pit. The seed is enclosed within the stone. The fruits show a wide range of size, flavour, colour and texture.

Species.—The common European plum, known botanically as *Prunus domestica,* appears to have originated somewhere in southeastern Europe or western Asia, probably in the region around the Caucasus and the Caspian Sea. Although it is called the European plum, some botanists who have summarized the history of these stone fruits are doubtful that *P. domestica* is indigenous to Europe. According to the earliest writings in which this plum is mentioned, the species dates back about 2,000 years.

Another old world plum species, probably of European or Asiatic origin, is the damson plum (*P. insititia*). This species seems to antedate *P. domestica,* as is suggested by the finding of damson plum pits in ancient ruins. The ancient writings connect the early cultivation of these plums with the region around Damascus.

An important species native to China is the plum (*P. salicina*), which was domesticated in Japan and was introduced into the United States about 1870.

Two less important species are the myrobalan plum (*P. cerasifera*), a native of Europe, and the Simon or apricot plum (*P.*

simonii), a native of China. The myrobalan plum has been used a great deal in the United States as a rootstock. Varieties of *P. cerasifera* and *P. simonii* are noted for their ornamental foliage.

Botanists have divided the native American plums into a number of species and subspecies. Many of them have numerous characteristics in common, so that they overlap somewhat in horticultural groups and classifications. *P. americana*, the most important of the native species, has a wide range of adaptation in the United States, extending from Maine to Florida, westward to Utah, and northwestward into Manitoba. The tree is small, not so vigorous as the European, and it has rough, shaggy, grayish bark. The fruit is red, reddish-yellow, or reddish-orange, possesses a pleasant flavour and is of good quality, but it has a thick, tough skin and the flesh clings to the pit. Desoto and Weaver are among the typical cultivated varieties of americanas.

Other American species of minor importance from a commercial standpoint but of interest to the fruit breeder are the native varieties of *P. hortulana*, the chickasaw plum (*P. angustifolia*), and the wildgoose plum (*P. munsoniana*) of the southeastern and south central United States, of which Wildgoose and Robinson are important varieties.

Still other species of plums growing in North America are the Canada plum (*P. nigra*), which is adapted to the north central United States and Canada; the small beach plum (*P. maritima*), which grows along the eastern seacoast; and the western or Pacific plum (*P. subcordata*), which grows east of the Coast range in southern Oregon and northern California.

Varieties and Cultivation.—Cultivated varieties of at least 12 species of plums are to be found in U.S. orchards or growing in the wild, but most of the important commercial varieties are confined to four of the species already mentioned, namely, *domestica, insititia, salicina* and *americana*.

The best known and most important of these groups are varieties of *Prunus domestica,* the European plums and prunes. These are vigorous-growing trees, upright spreading in habit. Unfortunately, they are not well adapted to regions with hot, dry summers or dry, cold winters. They are at home in the northeastern United States and in sheltered sections along the Great Lakes; but they are at their best in the irrigated regions of the intermountain and Pacific coast states, as is evidenced by the extensive production of fresh fruit and dried prunes in this region. The trees do well on medium heavy soils that are well drained. They blossom later than peaches and thus escape spring frosts. The European plums have been under domestication longest, and the fruits are notable for large size and attractive appearance. They vary in colour from the green and golden yellow of the Reine Claude (greengage) and Yellow Egg groups to the red and dark purple of the Lombard and Italian prune.

The damsons (*P. insititia*) of the old world are quite different from the domesticas. The trees are more upright, compact and dwarfish; the leaves and flowers are smaller; and the fruits are small, round and quite tart, so that they are especially suitable for preserves and jams. Varieties of this group are hardy, vigorous and productive, and the trees make good stocks for other species, being adapted to a wide range of conditions and thriving even when they are neglected. The Shropshire and the French are important blue damsons in the United States, while the yellow Mirabelles are popular in France. The demand for varieties of plums of this type is limited, and they are not planted as extensively as those varieties that can be consumed fresh, dried or canned.

The oriental plums (*P. salicina*) are relatively new to North America, but they were widely planted and became second to the domesticas in commercial production. The trees are more spreading in habit than the domesticas or damsons, and in leaf and fruit characters they are very different, resembling the native American plums. The fruits are very attractive and are characterized by a yellow ground colour overlaid by various shades of red. In some varieties the flesh colour is striking red, whereas fruit of the domesticas and damsons is green or yellow. Some newer hybrids of the salicina group show distinct superiority in flavour and in commercial possibilities over the early importations. Varieties of

this group appear to be widely adapted in the United States except in the very coldest climates. While the quality is not equal to that of the best domesticas, and the commercial varieties are not so satisfactory for canning and drying, the fresh fruit is delicious in its blend of flavours. The varieties cross readily with one another and with the native americanas. Among the first so-called Japanese plums grown in the United States, Kelsey, Burbank, Abundance and Satsuma are typical. The trees are hardy and productive, and they tolerate a variety of soils as well as climatic conditions. The blossoms open earlier, however, than those of the domesticas and damsons and are frequently killed by spring frosts in the eastern part of the United States.

The native American plums were doubtless used for food by the Indians long before the white man set foot on the shores of North America. Reports of early explorers mention the finding of plums growing in abundance. According to the descriptions of the early settlers, these plums were inferior to the domesticas of the old world in quality, so that the colonists soon began importing varieties from Europe. As a result, European plums soon became predominant in home fruit gardens as well as commercial orchards in the northeastern United States. Varieties of native species, however, while not grown in commercial orchards, do fill a need in supplying fruit for the home garden in regions where the domesticas are not well adapted, as for example in the southwestern and south central United States. American varieties also have been selected for planting in the northern Great Plains where only cold hardy sorts can survive. Varieties like Assiniboin and Cheney of the *P. nigra* group, and Wyant and Desoto of the americanas, survive in this region.

Hybrids produced by crossing American and oriental varieties have given larger fruited varieties of better quality, also adapted to the colder climates. Waneta and Underwood are two varieties that have been planted in home gardens. Furthermore, American species hybridize with the sand cherry (*P. pumila*), and plant breeders have produced new varieties adapted to cold and dry conditions in the northern Great Plains. Important varieties are Opata, Sapa and Oka.

ROCHE

PLUMS (PRUNUS)

In the United States, as well as in Europe, the plum has long been recognized as one of the most delicious of fruits, and among the stone fruits it ranks next to the peach in commercial production. Many of the varieties of plums cultivated in the United States have been introduced from elsewhere, and when these are added to the native varieties they give plums the largest number and greatest diversity of kinds and species among the stone fruits.

Fortunately varieties can be selected that are adapted to a wide variety of soils and climatic conditions. Plums respond to good soil management practices. As trees come into bearing they do not require much pruning and in the home fruit garden can be grown satisfactorily if insects and diseases are controlled.

Insects and Diseases.—The fruit and tree of the plum are attacked by a number of troublesome insects and diseases that seriously limit production if not controlled by spraying. One of the most serious of the insect pests is the plum curculio, a small beetle that deposits its eggs in the fruit. As the larvae hatch and feed on the fruit, the affected fruits drop prematurely. Sometimes all of the fruits will drop off before harvest. This insect can be controlled by timely spraying with arsenate of lead or by the insecticide malathion.

Brown rot caused by a fungus that gains entrance through breaks in the skin or through punctures caused by the curculio may also be a serious menace. Fortunately this disease can be controlled by the timely application of fungicides of sulfur or copper. A bacterial leaf disease called bacterial spot, or shot hole, is serious in the more southern latitudes of the United States. Some varieties are quite resistant to this disease while others are susceptible. For the successful production of plums in any region a timely spray program must be followed to protect the fruit and foliage against these insect and disease pests.

Prunes.—Prune is a name given to a plum that can be dried into a firm long-keeping product. This term is frequently applied as a group name to plum varieties that have a sufficiently high sugar content and firm flesh, qualities that favour their being preserved by drying. In California most of the plums are dried in the sun, whereas in Oregon and Washington drying is done in specially built dehydrators, with artificial heat. The growing of plums for the production of prunes in the United States is confined largely to the states of California, Oregon, Washington, and Idaho. Prune d'Agen, Italian, Sugar and Imperial Epineuse, all of European origin, are among the principal varieties in the U.S.

See also Fruit Farming.

Bibliography.—W. H. Chandler, *Deciduous Orchards*, 3rd ed., pp. 338–352 (1957); F. P. Cullinan, "Plums," U.S. Department of Agriculture *Yearbook*, pp. 703–723 (1937); U. P. Hedrick, *Plums of New York* (1911); C. F. Kinman, "Plum and Prune Growing in the Pacific States," U.S. Department of Agriculture *Farmers' Bulletin 1372* (1943); W. F. Wight, "Native American Species of Prunus," U.S. Department of Agriculture *Bulletin 179* (1915). (F. P. C.)

PLUMBAGO: *see* Graphite.

PLUMBING is the system of pipes and fixtures installed in a building for the distribution of potable (drinkable) water and the removal of water-borne waste materials. A plumbing system should perform in such a manner that the building's occupants are never endangered by contaminated drinking water or by contact with harmful wastes. Safe plumbing systems can only result from careful planning which takes account of the location of the building, the particular conditions arising from the design of the building and the activity taking place within it, the limitations of the municipal water and sewerage systems, and the plumbing standards enforced by the local, state or national governments. Properly designed, a plumbing system will maintain sanitary conditions over a broad range of both normal and abnormal operating conditions.

The piping system installed within a building is usually distinguished from the water and sewerage systems which serve a building, a group of buildings or a city.

The building plumbing system is usually considered to start at the point where the municipal water and sewerage lines cross the property lines of the building, or at some defined point just outside the building.

History.—One of the problems of every civilization in which the population has been centralized in cities and towns has been the development of adequate water and sewerage systems. In certain parts of Europe the complex aqueducts built by the Romans to supply their cities with potable water can still be seen. However, the early systems built for the disposal of human wastes were not quite so elaborate. Human wastes were often transported from the cities in carts or buckets or else discharged into an open, water-filled system of ditches which led from the city to a lake or stream.

Improvement in plumbing systems was very slow. Virtually no progress was made from the time of the Romans until the 19th century. The relatively primitive sanitation facilities were inadequate for the large, crowded population centres which sprang up during the Industrial Revolution, and outbreaks of typhoid fever and dysentery were often spread by the consumption of water contaminated with human wastes. Eventually these epidemics were curbed by the development of separate, underground water and sewage systems which eliminated open sewage ditches. In addition, plumbing fixtures—among them the lavatory basin, bathtub and water closet or toilet—were designed to handle potable water and water-borne wastes within buildings. However, these early fixtures often allowed sewer gases, bacteria and vermin to enter buildings through the open drain pipes with which they were connected to the sewer, and it was not until the latter

part of the 19th century that the siphon water closet and the sanitary fixture trap were widely introduced, although the first patent for a water-sealed trap had been granted a century earlier.

Plumbing Fixtures and Materials.—The term plumbing fixture embraces not only showers, bathtubs, lavatory basins and water closets but also such devices as washing machines, garbage-disposal units, hot-water heaters, dishwashers and drinking fountains.

The materials used in a plumbing system must be strong, noncorrosive and durable enough to equal or exceed the expected life of the building in which they are installed. In addition, the materials used in fixtures that are exposed to view should be attractive and easy to clean.

Water closets, urinals and lavatories usually are made of stable porcelain or vitreous china, although they sometimes are made of glazed cast iron or steel or of stainless steel.

Ordinary water pipes usually are made of steel, copper, brass, lead, plastic or other nontoxic material, while the most common materials for sewerage pipes are cast iron, steel, copper, and asbestos cement.

Special fixtures—and entire plumbing systems of special design —are required for chemical laboratories and for plants manufacturing and processing chemicals and food products. Piping and fixtures for such applications may be made of glass, stainless steel, glass-lined metal, plastic, ceramics or special alloys. Drains often must be of special design to ensure proper disposal of corrosive or toxic materials. In the design of food-processing plants, the criterion is ease of cleaning equipment and piping.

Water-Supply Systems.—Usually only potable water is distributed in the water-supply system, but occasionally separate systems are installed for the distribution of nonpotable water used in industrial processes, fire-fighting equipment, or irrigation.

For towns and cities, municipally or privately owned water companies treat and purify water collected from wells, lakes, rivers and ponds and distribute it to individual buildings.

In rural areas water is commonly obtained directly from individual wells.

In most cities, water is forced through the distribution system by pumps, although in rare instances, when the source of water is located in mountains or hills above a city, the pressure gen-

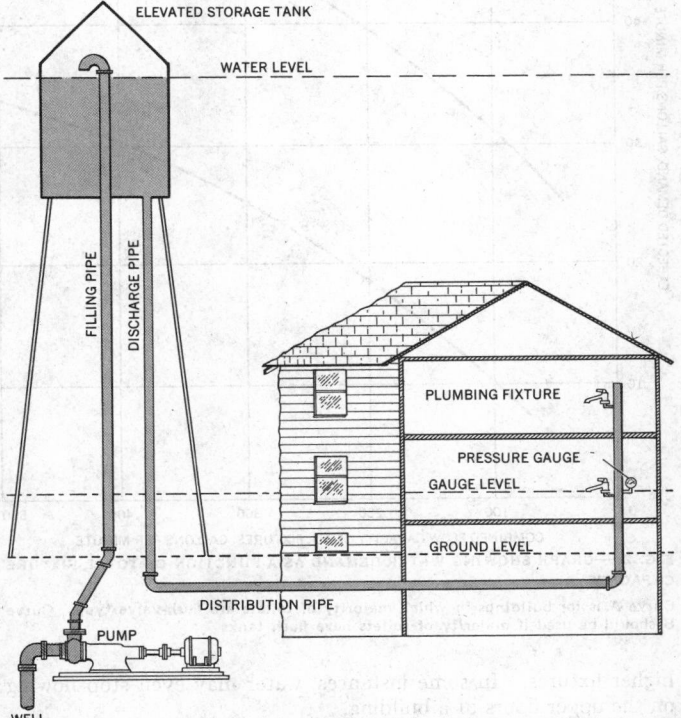

FIG. 1.—SIMPLIFICATION OF A WATER-SUPPLY SYSTEM, SHOWING HOW WATER PRESSURE AND HEIGHT ARE RELATED

erated by gravity is sufficient to distribute water throughout the system.

In other cases, water is pumped from the collection and purification facilities into elevated storage tanks and then allowed to flow throughout the system by gravity.

However, in most municipalities, water is pumped directly through the system; elevated storage tanks may also be provided to serve as pressure stabilization devices and as an auxiliary source in the event of pump failure or of a catastrophe, such as fire, that might require more water than the pumps or the water source are able to supply. (*See* WATER SUPPLY AND PURIFICATION.)

The pressure developed in the water-supply system and the friction generated by the water moving through the pipes are the two factors which limit both the height to which water can be distributed and the maximum flow rate available at any point in the system. For example, if no water is drawn from the system in fig. 1, the pressure at any point in the building is equal to the pressure developed by the water tank less the pressure exerted by the column of water in the building below the point where the pressure is being measured.

If water is drawn from the system, the pressure at any point in the building will drop by an amount equal to the pressure required to overcome friction generated by the water moving in the pipes. As more and more fixtures draw water, the pressure will continue to drop, and eventually all the pressure developed by the water tank will be expended in overcoming friction and in pushing water up into the building against the force of gravity.

Subsequently, if more water is drawn by the fixtures on the lower floors of the building, the pressure used to overcome the increased friction will be balanced by a lowering of pressure on the upper floors, resulting in a decreased flow rate from the

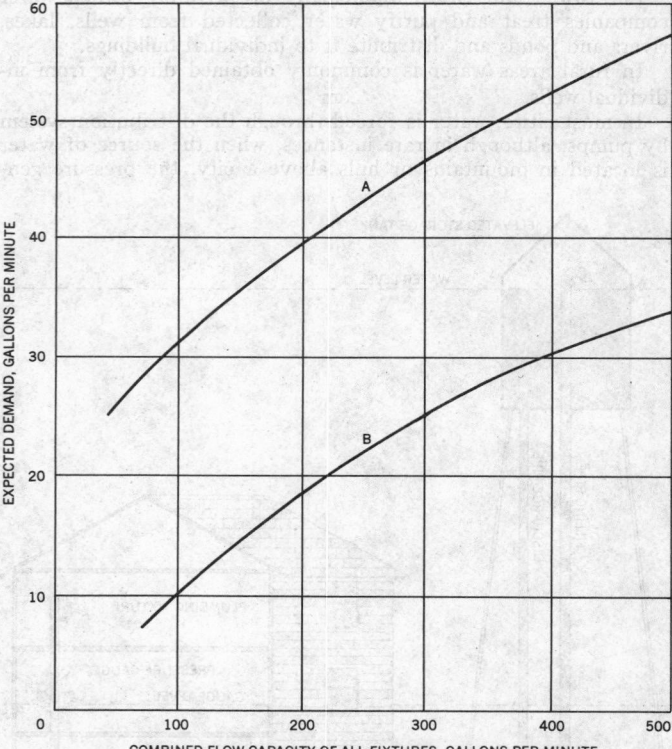

FIG. 2.—GRAPH SHOWING WATER DEMAND AS A FUNCTION OF TOTAL FIXTURE CAPACITY

Curve A is for buildings in which majority of toilets are flush-valve type. Curve B should be used if majority of toilets have flush tanks

higher fixtures. In some instances, water may even stop flowing on the upper floors of a building.

Because friction losses increase approximately as the square of the velocity of the water flowing in the pipes, water pressure

can be increased without decreasing the amount of water drawn from the pipes only by increasing the pipe diameter or providing booster pumps. Larger pipes can carry the same volume of water at lower velocities and, hence, with lower frictional pressure losses.

Pressure losses are also caused by the formation of mineral deposits that decrease the effective diameter of the pipes and increase frictional pressure losses. For this reason, all pipes installed in a building should be large enough to allow for the restrictions caused by normal formation of mineral deposits during the life of the building.

Because it is extremely unlikely that all the fixtures in a building will be used at the same time, the pipe diameter selected by the plumbing designer is based on the frictional pressure losses caused by the maximum probable flow rate, not upon the maximum potential flow rate. Fig. 2 shows the relationship between the probable maximum demand for water and total potential

Pressures and Flow Rates for Common Plumbing Fixtures

Fixture	Recommended Pressure at Fixture (p.s.i.)	Ordinary Maximum Flow Rate (g.p.m.)
Lavatory basin	8	3.0
Bathtub	5	6.0
Shower	12	5.0
Water closet (with flush tank)	15	3.0
Water closet (with flush valve)	10 to 20	15 to 40

flow capacities of the installed fixtures. To calculate the maximum probable flow rate for a new building, the plumbing designer refers to statistical tables which list the observed water demands of fixtures installed in buildings housing equivalent activities.

Recommended operating pressures and customary maximum flow rates for some common plumbing fixtures are shown in the accompanying table.

Booster pumps are sometimes installed in outlying areas of municipal water systems to offset the frictional head losses in long supply lines. Likewise, booster pumps are used in tall buildings when supply pipes of adequate size would be either too expensive or too bulky. The additional pressure supplied by the booster pump offsets the increased frictional losses of the smaller pipe and ensures that enough pressure will be available to maintain the flow of water to the upper floors during peak periods of consumption.

Sewerage System.—The sewerage system of a building consists of two parts: the drainage system and the venting system. The drainage portion comprises pipes leading from the various fixture drains to the central main, which is connected to the municipal or private sewerage system.

The venting system consists of pipes leading from an air inlet (usually located on the roof of the building) to various points within the drainage system; it protects the sanitary traps from siphoning or blowing by equalizing the pressure inside and outside the drainage system. Fig. 3 shows a typical arrangement of plumbing fixtures and drain and vent piping, with the drainage sections shaded.

Sanitary fixture traps provide a water seal between the sewer pipes and the rooms in which plumbing fixtures are installed. The most commonly used sanitary trap is a U bend, or dip, installed in the drainpipe adjacent to the outlet of each fixture. A portion of the waste water discharged by the fixture is retained in the U, forming a seal which separates the fixture from the open drainpipes. Fig. 4 shows how water standing in the trap seals the pipe.

Sometimes the protection offered by sanitary traps is inadequate, and a device known as an indirect waste must be installed on the fixture to prevent sewage from backing up in a clogged drainpipe. Indirect wastes are designed so that liquids discharged from the fixture fall through an air gap into a receiver; this is connected through an ordinary sanitary trap to the sewer. If the section of pipe connected to the fixture drain ends at a level above that which wastes can reach in the receiver, the air gap between the fixture drain and the receiver top will prevent wastes from backing up into the fixture.

Plumbing regulations usually specify that indirect wastes be installed on restaurant coffee urns, automatic washing machines, dishwashers and other apparatus where great caution must be exercised to prevent contamination.

In addition to sanitary traps and indirect wastes, fixture outlets are sometimes equipped with interceptors to separate and retain materials that should not be discharged into the sewerage system. For example, grease interceptors are often installed in restaurants to remove insoluble oils, fats and greases that, in large quantities, may impair the digestive action required for proper sewage treatment. (*See* also REFUSE DISPOSAL; SEWAGE DISPOSAL.)

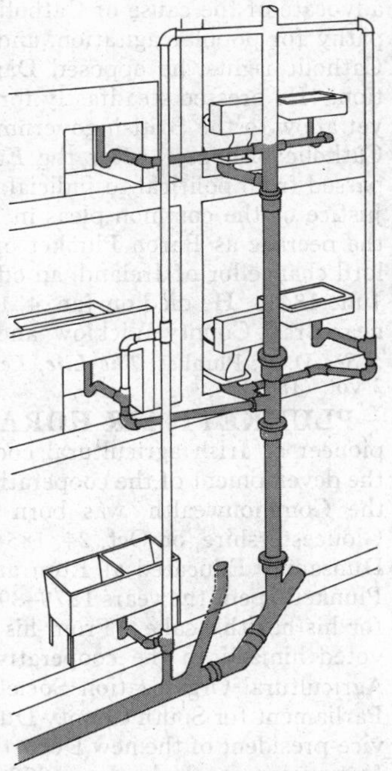

Venting System.—If the drainage system is not vented, or if it is improperly vented, the air in the pipes will be evacuated by the flow of waste materials. For example, when the water discharged from a lavatory basin flows through the drainpipe, it pushes some of the air out of the pipe. If the waste water flows past openings where branch pipes join the system, air may be drawn from these branches by the suction created by the running water. If there were no sanitary traps at the fixture outlets, air drawn from the drainpipes by the flow of waste water would be replaced by air drawn into the pipes through the open drains on the fixtures.

However, the water retained in the sanitary traps blocks such a flow of air into the sewerage system just as it blocks the flow of sewer gases out of the system. Therefore, a partial vacuum may be formed inside an unvented drain, siphoning water from the sanitary trap and breaking the seal between the fixture and the sewer. Conversely, the water in the trap may be blown out through the fixture drain if the pressure within the drainage system should suddenly rise above atmospheric pressure. This could occur in an improperly vented system if air were trapped and forced into side branches by the flow of large quantities of water through the pipes.

In a small dwelling, where all the bathroom and kitchen fixtures can be located adjacent to a large vertical drainpipe, a separate venting system is usually not needed if the top of the vertical drain is open to the atmosphere. However, when this type of venting is used, the drainpipes must be large enough to handle peak waste loads without filling with water; otherwise, air will not be able to reach all parts of the system, and some of the traps may siphon or blow. If some fixtures are far enough from the central drainpipe so that they cannot be vented properly through the drainage system itself, separate air vents must be provided for them.

Water closets are usually provided with individual vents because the volume of water which they discharge makes it difficult to vent them properly through the drainpipes without using excessively large pipes.

FIG. 3.—BUILDING DRAINAGE AND VENTING SYSTEM (DRAINAGE PIPING SHADED)

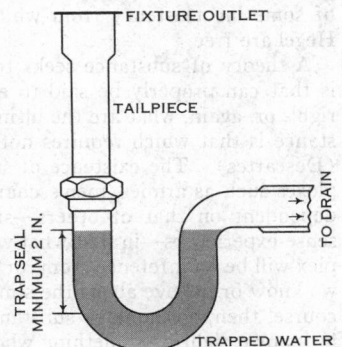

FIXTURE OUTLET

TAILPIECE

TRAP SEAL MINIMUM 2 IN.

TO DRAIN

TRAPPED WATER

FIG. 4.—SANITARY FIXTURE TRAP SHOWING THE WATER COLUMN WHICH SEALS THE FIXTURE FROM SEWER GASES, BACTERIA AND VERMIN THAT ARE COMMONLY FOUND IN DRAINAGE SYSTEMS

Sanitation.—The central problem in the construction and repair of plumbing systems is the maintenance of sanitary conditions. Because both potable water and waste water are in close proximity in plumbing fixtures, such as water closets, lavatories and bathtubs, there is always danger of a cross connection which will allow contaminated water to enter the potable water pipes. Most cross connections are the result of faulty plumbing design and installation; they occur in leaking plumbing fixtures or through back siphonage in water-supply pipes. An example of a cross connection caused by leaking plumbing fixtures is an overhead sewerage pipe which drips sewage into an open laundry tub or sink. This could be eliminated by repairing the leak, but a better way would be to install the drainage pipes so that they never cross above open plumbing fixtures.

Another example of bad design which can lead to hazardous cross connections is a building in which both potable and nonpotable water are distributed in interlocked systems separated only by valves. If one of the interlocking valves fails or is inadvertently opened, the nonpotable water can contaminate the potable water.

Although the pressure in a water-supply system normally remains above atmospheric pressure, abnormal conditions may lower it sufficiently to induce back siphoning. The easiest way to safeguard fixtures against back siphoning is to install the water inlet well above the level of the waste water in the fixture. Most sinks and bathtubs are designed so that the inlet pipe is above the top of the overflow outlet. In these fixtures waste water cannot possibly submerge the inlet pipe and form a cross connection.

However, in some fixtures the space between the inlet pipe and the highest level of the waste water is so small that waste water could be sucked across the air gap and into the supply pipe under certain conditions.

Fixtures which have submerged inlets or improperly sized air gaps should never be installed unless they are safeguarded with vacuum breakers. Whenever the water pressure drops below atmospheric pressure, the vacuum breaker opens and allows air to flow into the water pipes, thus destroying the partial vacuum inside the pipes and eliminating the danger of back siphoning. Because vacuum breakers are mechanical devices subject to wear and corrosion, they should be checked from time to time to make sure that they are operating properly. In the case of the water closet, proper flushing action cannot be achieved unless the water inlet is submerged in the waste-water bowl, and thus plumbing codes specify that both flush-valve and flush-tank water closets should be equipped with vacuum breakers.

BIBLIOGRAPHY.—J. Rawlinson, "Sanitary Engineering: Sanitation," in Charles Singer *et al.* (eds.), *A History of Technology*, vol. 4 (1958); S. B. Bennett, *Manual of Technical Plumbing and Sanitary Science*, 8th ed. (1956); L. Blendermann, *Design of Plumbing and Drainage Systems* (1959); S. Webster, *Plumbing Materials and Techniques* (1959); E. R. Haan, *Home Plumbing Guide* (1957); V. T. Manas (ed.), *National Plumbing Code Handbook* (1957). (F. M. D.)

PLUM RAINS are the persistent precipitation of the "Bai-u" season, the period when plums are ripening, in Japan and immediately adjacent areas. In Japan proper, particularly from Kyushu to northeastern Honshu, these rains, which are also important to the rice economy, extend from approximately early June to about the middle of July.

The rains tend to be of the moderate, prolonged type, rather than the cloudburst type. The sky is overcast for many hours, and the weather is depressing. The phenomenon is much better developed on the east side of Japan than on the west. Tokyo, for example, has an average in June of 1 clear day, 9 partly cloudy and 20 cloudy days; bright sunshine is observed during only about a third of the daylight hours. Tokyo records measurable rainfall on an average of 16 days in June, and the average monthly total is about $6\frac{1}{2}$ in. The accompanying average maximum temperature is about 68° F (20° C); the average minimum is about 62° F (about 17° C).

The beginning of the plum rains is earliest in low latitudes and later northward. In Formosa and the Ryukyus, precipitation begins to increase in the middle of May and continues heavy until early July. In northern Korea, the season begins in late June and lasts through July.

The rains are associated with eastward-moving cyclones, decelerated near Japan by the Pacific high-pressure area. Occasional failure of the rains to appear has resulted in damaging droughts.

(W. A. Bm.)

PLUNKET, OLIVER (1629–1681), Roman Catholic primate of all Ireland and martyr, who was the last man to suffer martyrdom for the Catholic faith in England, was born at Loughcrew, Meath. He was in Rome from 1645 until 1669, being educated and ordained there and serving then as professor of theology at the College of Propaganda Fide and as the representative of the Irish bishops at the Holy See. Appointed archbishop of Armagh and primate of all Ireland in 1669, he arrived in the following year at a time when, after prolonged repression, the Catholic Church was greatly disorganized, with only one aged bishop at liberty. Setting himself to restore order and discipline in accordance with the precepts of the Council of Trent, Plunket kept on good terms with the English and the Protestants until in 1673, under renewed persecution, he was obliged to go into hiding. For the next five years he laboured under conditions of increasing difficulty, brought to a climax by the Titus Oates (*q.v.*) plot of 1678. In the following year he was betrayed, arrested, and imprisoned in Dublin Castle. His trial at Dundalk was made absurd by the ignominious witnesses for the prosecution; he was taken to London, where, after protracted and farcical legal proceedings, he was sentenced to be hanged, disemboweled, and quartered; the sentence was carried out at Tyburn on July 1, 1681, before a large crowd. Plunket was beatified by Benedict XV in 1920. His head is preserved at Drogheda and his body at Downside Abbey, near Bath.

(M. Dk.)

PLUNKET, WILLIAM CONYNGHAM PLUNKET, 1st Baron (1764–1854), Irish lawyer, orator, and statesman, lord chancellor of Ireland from 1830 to 1841, was born at Enniskillen in County Fermanagh on July 1, 1764, the fourth son of Thomas Plunket, a Presbyterian minister. Educated at Trinity College, Dublin, he entered Lincoln's Inn in 1784, and was called to the Irish bar in 1787. He achieved a wide practice in the courts of equity, was made a king's counsel in 1797, and in the following year was elected to the Irish Parliament as member for Charlemont, County Armagh. He was an ardent upholder of the Irish Parliament's new independence (*see* Ireland: *History*), but he abhorred the democratic doctrines of the French Revolution. He admired British constitutional traditions, and held that increased political rights should be given to Roman Catholics and Protestant Dissenters.

Entering the Irish Parliament after the abortive Irish insurrection of 1798, Plunket found that the English prime minister William Pitt was actively completing his plans to achieve a legislative union between England and Ireland which would abolish the Irish Parliament. Henry Grattan, the chief defender of Irish legislative independence, had withdrawn from public life in 1797, and the defense of the Irish Parliament fell largely to Plunket. His vehement speeches made him the chief spokesman of the opposition to Pitt's designs and when Grattan returned to Parliament in January 1800, he deliberately took his seat beside Plunket as its most uncompromising champion. In one of the most famous speeches of those historic debates, Plunket declared that he would oppose the union "to the last gasp of my existence and with the last drop of my blood; and when I feel the hour of my dissolution approaching I will, like the father of Hannibal, take my children to the altar and swear them to eternal hostility against the invaders of their country's freedom."

However, with the passing of the Act of Union in August 1800, his passions cooled and he devoted himself to his legal practice and soon became a leader of the equity bar in Dublin. In 1803 he appeared for the crown in prosecuting Robert Emmet for his futile rising in Dublin. He accepted office under Pitt as Irish solicitor general (1803–05) and attorney general (1805–07). He was elected to the English Parliament as member for Trinity College, Dublin, in 1812 and was soon regarded as one of the finest orators in the House of Commons, where he became a leading

advocate of the cause of Catholic emancipation. He had no sympathy for popular agitation, and though he pleaded for increased Catholic rights, he opposed Daniel O'Connell's Catholic association. He pressed steadfastly for a Catholic relief bill which would yet allow to the British government a veto on the appointment of Catholic bishops. After the Emancipation Act (1829), Plunket passed from political to judicial eminence; he was appointed chief justice of the common pleas in Ireland in 1827 and was raised to the peerage as Baron Plunket of Newton. In 1830 he was made lord chancellor of Ireland, an office he held until his retirement in June 1841. He died on Jan. 4, 1854, at his house, Old Connaught, near Bray, County Wicklow, and was buried in Dublin.

See D. R. Plunket, *The Life, Letters and Speeches of Lord Plunket,* 2 vol. (1867). (D. G.)

PLUNKETT, SIR HORACE (CURZON) (1854–1932), pioneer of Irish agricultural cooperation who strongly influenced the development of the cooperative movement in Great Britain and the Commonwealth, was born at Sherborne House, Sherborne, Gloucestershire, on Oct. 24, 1854, the third son of the 16th Baron Dunsany. Educated at Eton and at University College, Oxford, Plunkett spent the years 1879–89 cattle ranching in Wyoming, U.S., for his health's sake. From his return to Ireland in 1889, he devoted himself to the cooperative movement, founding the Irish Agricultural Organization Society in 1894. Unionist member of Parliament for South County Dublin from 1892 to 1900, he became vice-president of the new Department of Agriculture and Technical Instruction for Ireland in 1899. His subsequent experience convinced him of the need for the independence of a united Ireland within the commonwealth. Plunkett's friendship with Theodore Roosevelt and his continued visits to the United States had considerable influence on country life policy there. In 1919, in London, he endowed a trust, now the Plunkett Foundation for Cooperative Studies, as a commonwealth agricultural research and information centre. He had been made a fellow of the Royal Society in 1902 and knight commander of the Royal Victorian Order in 1903. His writings include *Ireland in the New Century* (1904) and *The Rural Life Problem of the United States* (1910). Plunkett died at Weybridge, Surrey, on March 26, 1932. (M. Di.)

PLURALISM AND MONISM are theories giving respectively the answers "many" and "one" to two quite distinct questions: first, *how many things are there in the world?;* and second, *how many kinds of things are there in the world?* Much confusion is engendered if this distinction is not clearly maintained. Pluralism and monism as theories of substance, answers to the first question, have no necessary connection with pluralism and monism as theories of *kinds* of substance, answers to the second question. Philosophers can be cited to exemplify the four possible combinations of views: Descartes is a pluralist and Hegel a monist in both senses, Spinoza is a monist of substance and a pluralist of kinds, Bertrand Russell a pluralist of substance and a monist of kinds. Such definitions as "monism attempts to explain the entire universe from a single principle" misleadingly suggest, by compounding the two questions, that Spinoza and Russell are guilty of some inconsistency from which the writings of Descartes and Hegel are free.

A theory of substance seeks to establish the nature of what it is that can properly be said to exist independently or in its own right, or, again, what are the ultimate subjects of discourse: "Substance is that which requires nothing but itself in order to exist" (Descartes). The existence of some subjects of discourse—complexes such as armies, men's characters, material objects—will be dependent on that of others—simples such as soldiers, actions, sense-experiences—in that what we know or believe about the complex will be an inference from, or a convenient paraphrase of, what we know or believe about the simple. An ultimate subject of discourse, then, a simple or substance proper, something that exists in its own right, is something whose existence we can discover directly and without having first to discover or assume the existence of something else. The natural answer to the question "how many simple things, existing and discoverable independently, are there in the world?" is "many." Monism of substance—the theory that the world as a whole is the only true thing, held by Parmenides, Spinoza and Hegel—being at odds with our common beliefs, requires substantiation by argument. The point requiring proof is that nothing but the world as a whole is really independent of anything else. This—the doctrine of internal relations—will be stated and examined below.

A theory of kinds, "ultimate" kinds, of substance seeks to establish how many irreducibly different kinds of knowledge or experience we must admit. Two things are of different kinds, in a very wide sense, if there is any feature that one has and the other lacks. And since, unless there were such a feature, they would not be distinct and thus not be two things at all (the identity of indiscernibles), everything is of a different kind from everything else. But we do not in practice use such a generous criterion of difference in kind. Only some features of things are relevant to answering the question "what kind of thing is that?"; e.g., its being a chair or a tree or a house or a star. Other features are relevant to answering questions about what kind of chair, tree, house or star it may be. Others again are not relevant to answering any questions about kinds at all; e.g., being two feet from the wall, being the property of King Faruk. The set of features determining "natural kinds," possible answers to the question "what kind of thing is that?" is wider than the set determining "ultimate kinds." Roughly, the latter set consists of various forms of occupancy of space—location, volume, solidity. Whatever occupies space can be discovered only and always by sensation. Whatever does not occupy space can be discovered only and always by self-consciousness and introspection ("reflection"). The natural answer to the question "how many ultimate kinds of thing, objects of distinct types of knowledge or experience, are there in the world?" is "many." Monism of kinds—the theory that there is only one fundamental type of knowledge or experience, held by Democritus, Berkeley and Russell—being nearly as much at odds with common beliefs as monism of substance, also requires substantiation by argument. The point requiring proof is that there is only one source of knowledge, only one type of experience.

Whether or not parts of the world are independent of one another and whether or not there is more than one source of knowledge are questions whose internal connection, if any, does not at once leap to the eye. Hence the importance of distinguishing the varieties of pluralism and monism to which the attempt to answer them gives rise.

THEORIES OF SUBSTANCE

The Eleatics.—Xenophanes is credited with the remark "All is One," but his main importance is rather as a critic of polytheism than as a philosopher. It is with Parmenides that the first significant statement appears of the view that only the world as a whole ("being") exists in its own right. The world confronts us as a theatre of change; but this becoming, of which the senses inform us, is unreal, an illusory appearance, no proper object of knowledge. Only "being," discovered by reason, is real and truly exists. Being does not change, it never came into existence, it will never pass away, it is timeless. For what could change it, how could it arise from or pass into not-being? It is also, incidentally, spatial, finite and spherical in shape. Since empty space is a contradictory notion, "being" is everywhere. This tinge of materialism, important for its influence on Democritus and the atomists, is hardly consistent with the view that only reason informs us about reality, and it was not taken over by Plato.

Zeno, Parmenides' disciple, reinforced his master's theory with famous arguments against plurality and motion. Of these the most influential and relevant to the present purpose concerns the size of a world of many things, which, Zeno argues, must be both infinitely large and infinitely small and is thus an impossibility: infinitely small, since its ultimate components must be indivisible and thus without size, and no collection, however large, of things without size has any size; infinitely large, since the world, being divisible, has size, and the parts into whichever has size is divided, however far the division is carried, must themselves have size, so that it must consist of an infinite number of parts with size. This is a harder nut to crack than Parmenides' arguments against pluralism and was considered by Hume, Kant and Russell.

Spinoza.—In Part I of Spinoza's *Ethics* the classical argument for monism of substance—the proof that only the world as a whole (*Deus sive Natura*—God or Nature) exists independently—is to be found. It depends ultimately on Spinoza's theory of explanation. To understand anything, to have knowledge of it, is to know its cause or explanation. Now the causes of most of the things with which we are familiar are external to them, the changes of state of other things. To have knowledge of something whose cause is external to it requires us, therefore, to look beyond the thing itself to whatever it is that is needed to explain it. A thing of this kind, then being essentially dependent on something other than itself, does not come up to Spinoza's somewhat exigent requirement for being a substance; viz., "that, the conception of which can be formed independently of another thing." Now either this quest for causes must continue indefinitely or terminate in a thing which somehow explains itself, a *causa sui*, which will be a true substance. All its characteristics being essential or definitive parts of its inner nature, we will be able to deduce all the truths requisite to total "understanding" of it from the conception of the thing by itself.

Spinoza argues that if there is a plurality of things each must be limited by and thus dependent on the others. There can only be one truly independent, self-subsistent, self-explanatory thing, and it must be unlimited, infinite. It follows that the view that God transcends the world that He created is mistaken, a conclusion supported by such unhappy consequences of the creation theory as the problem of evil and the consequent imperfection, in respect of power or goodness, of God. God is therefore immanent in, indeed identical with, created Nature, they are not two things but the same thing viewed in different ways: as creating (*Natura naturans*) and as created (*Natura naturata*). Only the whole, then, is intelligible in itself, for the rather negative reason, it would seem, that it at any rate must be self-explanatory since the existence of anything external to it which could explain it is logically excluded.

Hegel.—It is one of the aims of Hegel to overcome the deficiency last mentioned. He attempts to produce a conception of the world as a whole, the absolute, which will provide a positive ground for thinking it to be self-explanatory and thus to exclude the possibility (compatible with Spinoza's view) that the world as a whole is a brute fact, neither self-explanatory nor to be explained by anything else. This attempt involves the distinction of cause from reason. The cause of something is merely externally connected with it, a mere concomitant happening. The reason for a thing, however, has an internal, logical connection with it, in this case there is real connection not just coincidence. But only thoughts stand in logical relationships to one another. So the absolute is a logically articulated system of thoughts. Hegel, like Spinoza, bases his version of monism on the unintelligibility on its own account of what is finite or limited (for the finite is necessarily limited by something else and so to that extent dependent on it). But his requirement that truly intelligible explanation must be rational or logical, a matter of the logical interrelation of thoughts, is a further development.

Internal Relations.—The monisms of Spinoza and Hegel are both variants of the doctrine of internal relations. Their fundamental thesis may be expressed in two ways: (1) nothing but the world as a whole is independent of everything else; and (2) everything in the world is in its real nature essentially related to everything else. For, it is argued, we do not fully understand anything until we know all of its relations to other things. As against the normal view that things, identified by the set of their defining or essential properties, stand in various external, contingent relations which are not part of their definition or essence, it is held that the true definition of a thing contains all its qualities and relations, everything that can truly be affirmed of it. This sets an ideal of understanding that cannot be attained, since it requires that to understand anything properly one must know everything about it, in effect everything whatever. To "understand" a thing, to know what it is, it is enough to be able to recognize or identify it: by picking out a set of qualities as a thing we obtain a reference point whose relations to other such reference points empirical inquiry must establish. Not only is the theory of internal relations no account of our actual conception of things, it is not an account of any conception of things in which inquiry into the nature of the world remains possible, but rather a dream of the termination of science, of a way of thinking fit for an omniscient being.

THEORIES OF KINDS

The question "how many ultimate kinds of thing are there?" is, it has been seen, an inquiry into the number of sources of knowledge or forms of experience. In practice the philosophical debate on this issue has predominantly concerned itself with the nature of our experience of and knowledge about minds. Do we get to know about thoughts, decisions and feelings (our own and those of others) in the same way as we get to know about material, extended, spatially located things? Prima facie, we seem to have independent access to two quite distinct orders of things: by sensation to an outer world of material things and other persons, by introspection to an inner world of our own mental states. Monism of kinds denies this apparent independence and distinctness. Sensation and introspection are assimilated into experience *simpliciter*, the impassable frontier between inner and outer is dismantled. That there is some distinction, at least prima facie, between the mental and the material is not denied by any but the most ardent materialist. What is objected to is the view that this distinction, this "bifurcation of nature" as A. N. Whitehead calls it, is ultimate, that we are the inhabitants of two distinct worlds, at best contingently connected. For the theory of bifurcation has given rise to two historically obtrusive problems, that of the relation between mind and body and that of our knowledge of other minds (the latter problem, on a wide view, may be seen as a more modern version of the former).

Dualism.—The classical exponent of dualism is Descartes. On his view the created world is composed of two quite distinct kinds of substance, minds and bodies, to be distinguished by their "essential attributes" which are, respectively, thought and extension. In practice Descartes takes these essential attributes as constituting the whole essence of mind and body, so that he comes to hold that the mind is always active and thinking and that matter *is* extension and empty space an impossibility. Locke complements this account of things with an appropriate account of our knowledge of things when he declares that all knowledge is based on sensation and reflection. For Descartes the distinction of the two kinds of thing depends on his theory of self-knowledge. Our own existence, he holds, is self-evident, since, whatever we may doubt, we cannot doubt that we doubt and, therefore, exist. On the other hand our knowledge of the external world is mediate, indirect. Our natural propensity to infer external causes for our sensations is only to be indulged and trusted if we are assured of the existence of God. The essential feature of dualism, then, is its intuitive theory of self-knowledge which contrasts our immediate and infallible knowledge of our own minds with our more devious and fallible acquaintance with everything else.

The first difficulty to arise from this is the familiar mind-body problem. In human perception and action we are confronted with what seem to be clear cases of the interaction of these two quite distinct orders of things, mental and material. Now there are two grounds on which philosophers have refused to acknowledge this apparent interaction: first, the conservation principles of physics seem to exclude the irruption of mental causes into the physical order; second, it was held that effects must resemble their causes. This did not prevent Descartes from inconsistently accepting the interaction of mind and body, with the pineal gland as a medium of divine agency. But since, by the conservation principle, every physical event is already physically accounted for and, by the metaphysical principle, that cause must resemble effect, mental causes of physical events are impossible as well as superfluous, mental events can at best be occasions and not causes of physical ones. This result leads in Descartes' immediate successors to the view that there are two quite independent but divinely adjusted series of events within which, but not between which, causal relations obtain: on the one hand is the system of inner experiences, the felt, private order of states of mind; on

the other is extended nature, a true causal system of material substances with merely geometrical, "primary" qualities. The triumphs of physics tend to degrade the mental world to a shadow play, an epiphenomenon, the view of materialism. The remote and unintelligible character of material substance conceived in purely geometrical terms leads to idealism.

Materialism.—This doctrine regards mental life as a more or less illusory exhalation of physiological processes, on its relation to which experienced mental life depends for such reality as it can be held to possess. Only that which can be mechanically explained is real. Mental life, as experienced, is a by-product, a mere symptom of mechanical transformations at the physiological level. The determination, which this theory evidences, to replace the obvious by the speculative in the interests of tidiness is still to be found among scientists and depends on laying down as universally to be followed in all spheres of inquiry a method notably successful in certain specialized investigations. Even the advances of contemporary neurophysiology do little to transform the speculative metaphysics of physiological materialism into a well-confirmed scientific theory.

Idealism.—Where materialism arises from the triumph of the material conception of cause, idealism is based on the paradox of the material conception of substance. Berkeley attacked the notion of material substance propounded by Descartes and Locke as unintelligible, a nonentity. It could not cause, or, a fortiori, resemble, the ideas of sensation on which all knowledge is based since *ex hypothesi* it could not be independently observed and compared with them. Material things are not distinct substances of a purely geometrical character on this view, for such things are unknowable, but are, rather, orderly and regular systems of sense experiences. Idealists of a Hegelian type argued that reality to be knowable must be mental in character, a system of ideas, which derives its objectivity for the observer not so much from being the beneficent contrivance of God as from being the logically necessary unfolding of the thoughts of an absolute mind (which is not perhaps very different).

Neutral Monism.—Idealists, while rejecting material substance, still distinguish mental substance, mind, from the ideas that it has. In Berkeley this leads to an uncomfortable and arbitrary proposal of a theory of notions to explain knowledge of mental substance, a theory required because we do not have any ideas of mind. But the "mental" character of ideas is based on their essential dependence on these somewhat feebly supported substances. Neutral monism reverses the relation by construing the ideas of sense as fundamental, the immediate objects of knowledge, and things, mental and material, as constructions out of these basic neutral elements. This view, developed by William James from some ideas of J. F. Herbart, became the foundation of Russell's theory of knowledge.

Other Minds.—The second major problem to which dualism gives rise is that of our knowledge of other minds. For, if dualism is correct, while we know about ourselves directly and infallibly we only find out about the mental life of others on the evidence of their behaviour and can never directly verify what we infer from this. Other minds are as unknowable in themselves, apart from their supposed effects, as the material substance attacked by Berkeley. Attempts have been made to identify our knowledge of self and others, to bridge the abyss exposed by criticism of the argument from analogy, by asserting that we have direct, "intuitive" knowledge of the mental states of others or that we have to find out about our own mental states by a more or less prolonged, tentative and piecemeal procedure. "Telepathic" idealism comes to grief on the inescapable logical distinctness of your experience of your anger from my, telepathic, experience of your anger. Its diametrical opposite, G. Ryle's "dispositional" materialism, provides a valuable criticism of the Cartesian intuitive theory of self-knowledge in all departments of mental life. But the attempt to construe having pains, sensations and images as tendencies to behave in certain ways comes up against a mass of very ordinary conviction to the contrary.

See also references under "Pluralism and Monism" in the Index.

(A. M. Q.)

PLURALITY OF CAUSES is the matter of the philosophical question whether one and the same kind of effect can be produced in different cases by different causes. This is distinct from the question whether the cause of an effect is as a rule a complex of several factors or conditions. Even if each cause is allowed to be complex, there still remains the question whether any one of several such complex causes can produce the same kind of effect as another. In other words, can one cause ever act vicariously for another? J. S. Mill in his *System of Logic* gave an affirmative answer, which examples taken from practical experience seem to support. For instance, many different causes can produce death. But many effects that are sufficiently similar for practical purposes are really very different when closely scrutinized. While two bodies may be equally dead, examination will show different effects in the one that died, say, of poisoning and in the one that died naturally. In short, the total effect produced by one kind of cause can always be distinguished, in theory at least, from that produced by any other, but, where the interest is centred in broad kinds of effect and where differences of detail do not matter much, the doctrine of the plurality of causes holds good. *See* also CAUSALITY.

PLUTARCH (*c.* 46–after 119), Greek biographer and miscellaneous writer, who from the 16th century to the early 19th was among the most popular of classical authors. His writings were admired for their wisdom as well as for their information, and they were long used as source books for anecdotes and moral *exempla*; they influenced the origins and development of the essay, the biography, and the writing of history; and from his *Lives* were derived the generally accepted images of the great historical figures of Greece and Rome.

Plutarch was born at Chaeronea in Boeotia, the son of Aristobulus, himself a biographer and Academic philosopher. At the time of Nero's visit to Greece in 66/67 Plutarch was studying mathematics and philosophy at Athens under Ammonius. Later, public duties brought him several times to Rome, where he lectured on philosophy, made many friends and perhaps enjoyed the acquaintance of Trajan and Hadrian; the Suda lexicon's statement that Trajan bestowed consular rank upon him may be true, but Eusebius' story that Hadrian made him governor of Greece is probably apocryphal. A Delphic inscription reveals that he possessed Roman citizenship; his *nomen* Mestrius was no doubt adopted from his friend, the consular L. Mestrius Florus.

Plutarch traveled widely, visiting central Greece, Sparta, Corinth, Patrae (Patras), Sardes, and Alexandria, but he made his normal residence at Chaeronea, where he held the chief magistracy and other municipal posts, and directed a school with a wide curriculum, in which philosophy, especially ethics, occupied the central place. He maintained close links with the Academy at Athens (he possessed Athenian citizenship), and with Delphi, where from *c.* 95 he held a priesthood for life; he may have won Trajan's interest and support for the renewed vogue of the oracle. The size of Plutarch's family is uncertain. In the *Consolatio* to his wife Timoxena on the death of their infant daughter he mentions four sons; of these at least two survived childhood, and he may have had other children.

Plutarch's literary output was immense. The 227 titles listed in the so-called catalogue of Lamprias which is usually printed with his works are not all authentic, but equally they do not include all he wrote. The order of composition cannot be determined.

Lives.—Plutarch's popularity rests primarily on his *Bioi Paralleloi* (*Parallel Lives*) of Greek and Roman soldiers, legislators, orators, and statesmen. These, dedicated to Trajan's friend Sosius Senecio, who is mentioned in the *Demosthenes, Theseus,* and *Dion,* were designed to encourage mutual respect between Greeks and Romans. By exhibiting noble deeds and characters they were also to provide patterns of behaviour to copy.

The first pair, *Epaminondas* and *Scipio,* and perhaps an introduction and formal dedication, are lost. But the plan was clearly to publish in successive books biographies of Greek and Roman heroes in pairs, chosen as far as possible for their similarity of character or career, and each followed by a formal comparison. Internal evidence suggests that the *Lives* were composed in Plutarch's latest years, but the order of composition can be only partially determined; the present order is a later rearrangement based largely on the chronology of the Greek subjects, who are placed first in each pair. In all, 22 pairs survive (one pair being the double group of *Agis and Cleomenes* and the *Gracchi*) and four single biographies, of Artaxerxes, Aratus, Galba, and Otho. The *Aratus* is addressed to one Polycrates, a descendant of the Achaean general.

The *Lives* display impressive learning and research. Many sources are quoted, and, though Plutarch probably had not consulted all these at first hand, his investigations were clearly extensive, and compilation must have occupied many years. For the Roman *Lives* he was handicapped by an imperfect knowledge of Latin, which he had learned late in life; for, as he explains in *Demosthenes,* political tasks and the teaching of philosophy fully engaged him during his stay in Rome and Italy. The form of the *Lives* represents a new achievement, not closely linked with either previous biography or Hellenistic history. The general scheme is to give the birth, youth and character, achievements, and circumstances of death, interspersed with frequent ethical reflections; but the details vary with both the subject and the available sources, which include anecdote mongers and writers of memoirs as well as historians. Plutarch never claims to be writing history, which he distinguishes clearly from biography. He seeks to delight and edify the reader, and does not conceal his own sympathies, which are especially evident in his warm admiration for the words and deeds of Spartan kings and generals; his virulent and unfair attack on Herodotus probably sprang from his feeling that the Ionian had done Athens more and Boeotia less than justice.

Moralia.—Plutarch's surviving writings on ethical, religious, physical, political, and literary topics are collectively known as *Ethica* (*Moralia*), and amount to more than 60 essays. They are mainly cast in the form of dialogues or diatribes. The former vary from a collection of set speeches to informal conversation pieces set among members of Plutarch's family circle; the date and dramatic occasion are rarely indicated. The diatribes, which often show the influence of Menippean satire, are simple and vigorous. The literary value of both is enhanced by the frequent quotation of Greek poems, especially verses of Euripides and other dramatists.

The two educational works "How a young man ought to hear poetry" (which qualifies the old Platonic objection to poetry) and "How to listen," together with the pseudo-Plutarchean treatise "On the education of children," were popular and influential during the Renaissance. In the treatise on moral virtue Plutarch discusses how virtue must subordinate unreason to reason within the soul, a theme developed in many other of the works dealing with popular ethical problems; these adduce examples from the lives of famous men, and contain sound but unoriginal moralizing. Among them are "Vice and Virtue," "How to recognize progress in virtue" (dedicated, like the *Lives,* to Sosius Senecio), "How to distinguish a flatterer from a friend," "On having many friends," and "On Fortune." Another group of a rhetorical and epideictic character includes the historical essays "On the fortune of Alexander," "On the fortune of the Romans," and "Whether the Athenians were more famous in war or in wisdom"; these resemble the traditional topics of declamation, and parallel to them are "Whether water or fire is more useful," "Whether virtue can be taught," and "Whether mental or bodily afflictions are the worse."

Plutarch's interest in animals and their minds emerges in two books "On eating flesh," in "Whether land or sea animals are more intelligent" (a question which receives no clear answer), and *Gryllus* or "Do animals reason?" an entertaining dialogue set on Circe's island in which a pig, one of Odysseus' transformed companions, attacks the Stoic argument denying reason to animals, and convinces Odysseus of the moral superiority of many animals over man. The tenets of the philosophical schools are the subject of several essays, for instance "Platonic questions," "On the creation of the soul in the Timaeus" (expounding Plutarch's views about Plato's teaching on the soul), "Against Colotes" (attacking Epicurean views), and "On the impossibility of living pleasurably according to Epicurus' teaching"; several other essays criticize

Stoic doctrines. Physical and medical problems are discussed in "Precepts on health," "On the face of the moon's disk," and "On primary cold" (which argues that cold is something real, not the mere absence of warmth).

The treatises dealing with political issues are of especial interest. "Political precepts" is an enlightening account of political life in contemporary Greece; in "Whether a man should engage in politics when old" he urges his friend Euphanes to continue in public life at Athens; Stoic ideas appear in the short work "To the unlearned ruler" and the fragmentary argument that "The philosopher should converse especially with princes"; in "The one, the many, and the few in government" the author (who may not be Plutarch) favours monarchy. The virtues of family life are treated in "On brotherly love," "On the love of one's offspring," and "Conjugal precepts"; with the *Consolatio* to his wife goes the fine essay "On exile"; the *Amatorius* is a discussion of love, which favours normal heterosexual relationships.

Plutarch's interest in religious history and antiquarian problems can be seen especially in a group of striking essays, the early "Daemon of Socrates," and three later works concerning Delphi, "On the failure of the oracles," in which the decline of the oracle is linked with the decline in the population, "On the E at Delphi," interpreting the word EI at the temple entrance, and "On the Pythian responses," seeking to reestablish belief in the oracle. Contemporary with these is "On Isis and Osiris," with its mystical tones; the dialogue "On the late vengeance of God," staged in Delphi, argues that the postponement of divine vengeance is to give time for repentance. "Convivial questions" (nine books) and "Greek and Roman questions" assemble a vast collection of antiquarian lore; "On the malignity of Herodotus" displays the local patriotism of a Boeotian; and the "Comparison of Aristophanes and Menander" prefers Menander for moral reasons.

Among the more important works no longer accepted as authentic are the *Consolatio* to Apollonius for his son, the "Lives of the Ten Orators," "On Fate," the "Short sayings of kings and commanders," the "Short sayings of Spartans" and "Proverbs of the Alexandrines."

Assessment.—Plutarch's perennial charm and popularity arise in part from his treatment of specific human problems without raising disquieting solutions. He writes easily and superficially with a wealth of anecdote. His style is predominantly Attic, though influenced by the contemporary Greek which he spoke; he follows rhetorical theory in avoiding hiatus between words, and he is careful in his use of prose rhythms. He is clear, but rather more diffuse than the strict Attic canon would allow. Plutarch's philosophy was eclectic, with borrowings from the Stoics, Pythagoreans and Peripatetics (but not the Epicureans) grouped around a core of Platonism. His main interest was in ethics, but he developed a mystical side, especially in his later years; he remarks that he had been initiated into the mysteries of Dionysus, and both as a Platonist and as an initiate he believed in the immortality of the soul. He believed too in the superiority of Greek culture and in the meritoriousness and providential character of the Roman empire. Personally he preferred a quiet and humane civic life as a citizen of a small Boeotian town, where his writing and teaching did much to illuminate the darkness of provincial life in 1st-century Greece.

Reputation and Influence.—Plutarch's later influence has been profound. In his own time and in later antiquity he was loved and respected; his *Lives* inspired the rhetorician Aristides and the historian Arrian to similar comparisons, and a copy accompanied the emperor Marcus Aurelius when he took the field against the Marcomanni. Gradually Plutarch's reputation faded in the Latin West, but he continued to influence philosophers and scholars in the Greek East, where his works became a school book. Proclus, Porphyry, and the emperor Julian all quote him, and the Greek Church Fathers, Clement of Alexandria and Basil the Great, imitate him without acknowledgment. His works were familiar to all cultivated Byzantines, who set no barrier between the pagan past and the Christian present. It was mainly the *Moralia* which appealed to them; but in the 9th century Photius read the *Lives* with his friends. At the end of the 13th century Planudes set out to transcribe Plutarch's works in an edition which has left its mark on the manuscript tradition.

Plutarch's works were introduced to Italy by Byzantine scholars with the revival of classical learning in the 15th century, and Italian humanists had already translated them into Latin and Italian before 1509, when the Aldine *Moralia*, the first of his works to be printed in the original Greek, appeared at Venice. The first original Greek text of the *Lives* was printed by P. Junta at Florence in 1517, and by the Aldine Press in 1519. The *Lives* were translated into French in 1559 by Jacques Amyot (q.v.), who also translated the *Moralia* (1572). The first complete edition of the Greek texts by H. Stephanus (Estienne; q.v.), in 1572, marked a great improvement in the text.

That Rabelais knew Plutarch well is proved by the frequency with which he quotes from both the *Lives* and the *Moralia*. It was Montaigne, however, who read Plutarch in Amyot's version, who first made his influence widely felt. The style of the *Essais* (1580–88) owed much to the *Moralia*, and from the *Lives* Montaigne adopted Plutarch's method of revealing character by illustrative anecdote and comment, which he applied to self-revelation. Moreover, the *Essais* made known the ideal, derived from Plutarch's presentation of character and openly expressed opinion, of "high antique virtue and the heroically moral man" which became the humanist ideal of the Renaissance period.

The *Lives* were translated into English, from Amyot's version, by Sir Thomas North (q.v.) in 1579. His vigorous idiomatic style made his *Lives of Noble Grecians and Romans* an English classic, and it remained the standard translation for more than a century. Even when superseded by more accurate translations, it continued to be read as an example of Elizabethan prose style. North's Plutarch was Shakespeare's source for his Roman plays, and influenced the development of his conception of the tragic hero. The literary quality of North's version may be judged from the fact that Shakespeare lifted whole passages from it with only minor changes.

The complete *Moralia* was first translated into English from the Greek by Philemon Holland (q.v.) in 1603. Its influence can be seen in the 1612 edition of Bacon's *Essays*, which contain counsels of public morality and private virtue recognizably derived from Plutarch. Bacon was more attracted by Plutarch the moralist than by Plutarch the teller of stories or painter of character, but to the Renaissance mind it was the blend of these elements that gave him his particular appeal. His liking for historical gossip, for the anecdote and the moral tale, his portrayal of characters as patterns of virtue or vice (in the manner of the morality play and the "character"), his emphasis on the turn of fortune's wheel in causing the downfall of the great, all suited the mood of the age, and from him was derived the Renaissance conception of the heroic and of the "rational" moral philosophy of the ancients.

Historians and biographers in the 16th and 17th centuries followed Plutarch in treating character on ethical principles. Izaak Walton knew Plutarch well, and his *Lives* (collected 1670, 1675) imitated him in dwelling on the strength, rather than the weakness, of his subjects' characters.

Plutarch continued to be read throughout the 17th and 18th centuries. John Dryden edited a new translation of the *Lives* first published in 1683–86, and abridged editions of it appeared in 1710, 1713 and 1718. Another translation, by John and William Langhorne, published in 1770, was frequently reprinted. The *Moralia* was retranslated in 1683–90 and also frequently reprinted. In France, Amyot's translations were still being reprinted in the early 19th century, and their influence on the development of French classical tragedy equaled that of North's version on Shakespeare. Admiration for those heroes of Plutarch who overthrew tyrants, and respect for his moral values, inspired the leaders of the French Revolution; Charlotte Corday, who assassinated Jean Paul Marat, spent the day before that event in reading Plutarch.

In Germany, the first collected edition of Plutarch's works was published in 1774–82. The *Moralia* was edited by D. Wyttenbach in 1796–1834, and was first translated in 1783–1800. The *Lives*, first edited in 1873–75, had already been translated in 1799–1806. The German classical poets—Goethe, Schiller, and Jean Paul

(Johann Paul Richter) especially—were influenced by his works, and he was read also by Beethoven and Nietzsche. During the 18th century the veneration in which Plutarch was held as a moralist led to the rumour that he had written a life of Jesus, which was said to have been discovered.

In the 19th century, Plutarch's direct influence began to decline, partly as a result of the reaction against the French Revolution, partly because the rise of the Romantic Movement introduced new values and emphasized the free play of passions rather than their control, partly because the more critical attitude of scholars to historical accuracy drew attention to the bias of his presentation of fact. He was still admired, however, notably by the U.S. poet, philosopher and essayist Ralph Waldo Emerson, and although in the 20th century his direct influence was small, the popular ideas of Greek and Roman history continued to be those derived from his pages.

BIBLIOGRAPHY.—*Editions and Translations* (see also *Influence* above): *Lives:* ed. by C. Lindskog and K. Ziegler in the Teubner series (1914–39) and by B. Perrin with Eng. trans. in the Loeb series, 11 vol. (1914–26); a selection ed. by H. Holden with commentary (1881–98); *Galba* and *Otho,* ed. by E. G. Hardy with commentary (1890); *Aratus,* ed. with commentary by W. H. Porter (1937). *See also Shakespeare's Plutarch,* ed. by W. W. Skeat (1875) and by T. J. B. Spencer (1964). *Moralia:* ed. by G. Bernadakis in the Teubner series, 7 vol. (1888–96); new ed. by C. Hubert *et al.,* vol. 1 ff. (1925 *et seq.*); ed. by D. Wyttenbach (incomplete) with commentary (1795–1830); ed. by F. C. Babbitt *et al.,* with Eng. trans., in the Loeb series, vol. 1 ff. (1927 *et seq.*).

Studies: R. C. Trench, *Plutarch* (1873); R. Hirzel, *Plutarch* (1912); R. M. Jones, *The Platonism of Plutarch* (1916); K. M. Westaway, *The Educational Theory of Plutarch* (1922); A. Weizsäcker, *Untersuchungen über Plutarchs biographische Technik* (1931). For comprehensive survey with full bibliography *see* K. Ziegler, *Plutarchos von Chaironea* (1949), reprinted with corrections in Pauly-Wissowa, *Real-Encyclopädie der classischen Altertumswissenschaft,* vol. 21, col. 636–962 (1951). (F. W. Wa.)

PLUTARCH OF ATHENS (4th–5th century A.D.), Greek philosopher, preceded Syrianus as head of the Platonic School at Athens and was one of the teachers of Proclus. He died at an old age in A.D. 431/432. The commentaries that he wrote on a number of Platonic dialogues and on Aristotle's *De Anima* have not survived and are known only from allusions in later writers. The commentary on the *De Anima* had a particularly high reputation, ranking with that of Alexander of Aphrodisias. So little is known of Plutarch's teaching that it is impossible to form any estimate of its importance or originality. What later writers say does not suggest that it was notably different from that of other Athenian Neoplatonists, though perhaps he was more interested in and influenced by Aristotle's philosophy than some of them. (All Neoplatonists of course studied Aristotle and were to some extent influenced by him; he was in particular their principal authority in logic and natural philosophy.) Plutarch seems to have been particularly interested in Aristotle's psychology: it is said that he not only wrote a commentary on Aristotle's chief psychological work but that in his own teaching on the soul he combined the Platonic doctrine of recollection with the Aristotelian theory of the intellect. (A. H. AG.)

PLUTO (PLUTON): *see* HADES.

PLUTO is the outermost known major planet, ninth in order of distance from the sun. Its mean distance from the sun is 39.5 times that of the earth, but its orbit is so eccentric (e = 0.25) that at perihelion, as will occur in 1989, it will come closer to the sun than Neptune does. The inclination (17°) and the orientation of its orbit (node to perihelion = 114°) are such that the orbits of Neptune and Pluto do not now intersect. Pluto's period of revolution is 248 years. Pluto is so faint, 15th magnitude, that a 20-in. telescope is necessary to see it. Its diameter has been measured as 3,700 mi., halfway between that of Mars and Mercury. This measurement is difficult because of Pluto's faintness and small angular diameter (0″.23). With a diameter of approximately 3,600 mi., Pluto's volume is 0.1 that of the earth and its mass would probably be about 0.1 that of the earth also, since it is not likely that its density exceeds that of the earth. Pluto's reflecting power derived from its apparent brightness and measured diameter is about what might be expected (albedo = 0.17). Its mass as derived from its attraction on Neptune is about that of the

earth, but this value is also uncertain. If Pluto is as large as the earth, as indicated by its calculated mass, its reflectivity must be extremely low. It therefore seems probable that Pluto's diameter is about 0.45 and its mass one-tenth that of the earth.

The brightness of Pluto varies about 10% in a period of 6.39 days, indicating that its surface is not uniformly bright and that the planet rotates on its axis in a period of 6.39 days.

Pluto was discovered in a systematic search for a trans-Neptunian planet predicted by Percival Lowell on the basis of its attraction on Uranus (*Memoirs of the Lowell Observatory,* vol. i, 1915). William Henry Pickering, using discrepancies in the motion of Neptune, also predicted a trans-Neptunian planet in about the same place as that derived by Lowell (*Harvard Annals,* vol. lxxxii, no. 3, 1919). Pluto was discovered on Feb. 18, 1930, by Clyde William Tombaugh at the Lowell Observatory on photographs he had taken on Jan. 23 and 29, 1930 (*Scientific Monthly,* vol. xxxiv, Jan. 1932). He recognized the new planet by its motion, which was much slower than that of the numerous asteroids also recorded on the photographs. In spite of the fact that Pluto was near the position predicted by the computations, its small mass indicates that its discovery was due to the thoroughness of the search rather than to the theoretical calculations. Both Lowell and Pickering predicted that the unknown planet would be much larger and brighter than Pluto is. (S. B. N.)

PLUTONIUM, a chemical element, centrally important in nuclear engineering and in the history of atomic weapons, has the symbol Pu and atomic number 94. Since all of its isotopes are produced synthetically, the atomic weight depends on the particular isotopic composition of any given sample, which in turn depends on the source of the sample. Plutonium occupies a position in the periodic system of the elements as the fifth member of a transition series, the actinide series, which includes the heavy elements with atomic numbers 90 to 103—elements in which an inner electronic shell (the 5f shell) is being filled (*see* PERIODIC LAW; TRANSURANIUM ELEMENTS).

Discovery.—Plutonium was discovered at the University of California at Berkeley by Glenn T. Seaborg, Edwin M. McMillan, Joseph W. Kennedy and Arthur C. Wahl. In late 1940 and early 1941, bombarding uranium with deuterons, they produced the isotope with mass number 238 of the 94-proton element, which they named plutonium, after the planet Pluto. The fissionable isotope of major importance, Pu^{239}, was discovered immediately thereafter in 1941 by Kennedy, Emilio Segrè, Wahl and Seaborg, working in the same laboratory. Only a very small specimen of plutonium was produced for the first experiments conducted with a weighable amount—0.0005 mg. (about $\frac{1}{50,000,000}$ oz.). However, this minute sample was sufficient to reveal that plutonium-239 was susceptible to fission by bombardment with slow neutrons, and therefore that its production in substantial quantities was a matter of extreme importance to national defense. The team of scientists, who sent communications concerning the discovery to the editor of the *Physical Review* in January, March and May 1941, decided to withhold these reports from publication. *The Transuranium Elements* (Yale University Press, 1958) by Seaborg points out that "the announcement to the world of the existence of plutonium was in the form of the nuclear bomb dropped over Nagasaki." The first pure chemical compound of plutonium, in the form of Pu^{239}, free from carrier material and all other foreign matter, was isolated by Burris B. Cunningham and Louis B. Werner at the wartime Metallurgical Laboratory of the University of Chicago (now the Argonne National Laboratory) in August 1942. This provided the first sight of a synthetic element and was the first isolation of a weighable amount of an artificially produced isotope of any element.

Occurrence.—Plutonium occurs in nature in very small concentrations in uranium-bearing ores. Such plutonium was first detected, in Canadian pitchblende, by Seaborg and Morris L. Perlman in 1942. The isotope involved is Pu^{239}, which is formed continuously as a result of the absorption of neutrons by U^{238}. The neutrons are those emitted during the spontaneous fission of uranium and those resulting from the action of alpha particles on the nearby light elements. The concentration of Pu^{239} is deter-

Ore	Pu^{239}/ore*
Pitchblendes:	
Canada (13.5% U)	9.1 x 10^{-13}
Belgian Congo (38% U)	4.8 x 10^{-12}
Colorado (50% U)	3.8 x 10^{-12}
Monazites:	
Brazil (0.24% U)	2.1 x 10^{-14}
North Carolina (1.64% U)	5.9 x 10^{-14}

*Fraction by weight of Pu^{239} in ore.

mined by the equilibrium balance between its rate of formation and its rate of radioactive decay.

Production.—By far the most important source of plutonium is one or another type of nuclear reactor, or chain-reacting pile, in which it is manufactured. An example is a nuclear reactor consisting of natural uranium, or uranium slightly enriched in the fissionable isotope U^{235}, and some neutron-slowing material, or moderator, such as carbon (graphite) or heavy water (deuterium oxide). In such a reactor a self-sustaining nuclear chain reaction results from the fission of the uranium isotope U^{235} with neutrons. A large proportion of the excess neutrons are absorbed by nonfissionable U^{238} to form U^{239}, which decays by two successive beta-particle emissions to fissionable Pu^{239}. In such production methods some of the Pu^{239} captures neutrons to form heavier isotopes (Pu^{240}, Pu^{241}, etc.); hence the isotopic composition of any given sample of plutonium depends on its source (*see* ATOMIC ENERGY: *Nuclear Reactors;* NEUTRON: *Nuclear Energy*). The plutonium is separated by chemical means from the highly radioactive fission products and the uranium and other foreign material. The chemical plants for this purpose are massive structures designed to solve the grave problems inherent in handling extremely high levels of radioactivity due to the fission products, and the operations are carried out entirely by remote control through heavy walls of shielding material. (*See* NUCLEAR ENGINEERING.)

The earliest industrial process for the isolation of plutonium, used at the Hanford Engineer Works in the state of Washington during World War II, was based on bismuth phosphate and lanthanum fluoride as carrier precipitation agents. This process was conceived by Stanley G. Thompson, Seaborg and their collaborators at the Metallurgical Laboratory of the University of Chicago. Neutron-irradiated uranium was dissolved in nitric acid and, after the addition of sulfuric acid, plutonium in oxidation state IV was coprecipitated with bismuth phosphate. The precipitate was dissolved in nitric acid, the plutonium IV was oxidized to plutonium VI, and a by-product precipitate of bismuth phosphate was formed and removed, the plutonium VI remaining in solution. After the reduction of plutonium VI to plutonium IV, the latter was again coprecipitated with bismuth phosphate and the whole decontamination cycle was repeated. At this point the carrier was changed to lanthanum fluoride, and a similar oxidation-reduction cycle was carried out using this carrier, which achieved further decontamination and concentration. The plutonium at this point was sufficiently concentrated so that final purification could be carried out without the use of carrier compounds.

Many of the present-day commercial processes for the separation and decontamination of plutonium are based upon extraction into organic solvents. Solvent extraction is performed in packed columns or pulsed columns, or in a series of mixing-settling chambers in which the aqueous phase and solvent phase pass in countercurrent flow in a multistage process. Throughout the world these processes are very similar in principle, and can be illustrated by one of the U.S. processes, the industrial "Purex" process, which uses tributyl phosphate diluted with a kerosene-type solvent. The uranium slugs are dissolved in nitric acid, plutonium is fixed as plutonium IV, and the acid strength is adjusted so that plutonium IV and uranium VI are extracted away from the fission products. In a second part of the process, the solvent is contacted with a nitric acid solution containing a reducing agent. Uranium VI is left in the tributyl phosphate phase while plutonium III is removed. Both the uranium and the plutonium undergo additional processing before complete purification is achieved.

Uses.—The main use of plutonium—specifically isotope Pu^{239}—is in the production of nuclear (atomic) energy. Nuclear reactors may be built to use Pu^{239} as fuel, and these reactors can also be operated in conjunction with the abundant isotope of uranium, U^{238}. The reactors can generate energy by "burning" the Pu^{239}, while at the same time they produce more Pu^{239} as a result of the absorption of neutrons in U^{238}. Such a system is known as a "breeder." In theory, this process should make it possible eventually to convert all the nonfissionable U^{238} into fissionable Pu^{239}. Hence the rate of nuclear power production could be increased steadily. A fissionable isotope such as Pu^{239} gives rise to an amount of heat energy equivalent to about 10,000,000 kw-hr. per pound when it undergoes the fission reaction completely. For industrial purposes the energy may be used in this heat form, but in most cases it is converted into the more convenient electrical form by means of more or less standard turbine equipment. The efficiency with which heat energy can be turned into electrical power in an industrial nuclear reactor depends on the details of the particular machine, but it seems likely that efficiencies of the order of 30–50% may in time be realized.

Pu^{239} can be used as an explosive ingredient for nuclear (atomic) weapons. Nuclear explosives also have important peaceful applications: in large-scale excavation, in undertakings where high temperatures and pressures are needed (*e.g.*, in mining and in the recovery of oil and gas from low-grade sources) and in research.

Although most of the chemical and metallurgical investigations of plutonium have been conducted with Pu^{239} (half-life 24.4 × 10^3 years), the future will see increasing use of the longer-lived Pu^{242} (half-life 3.79 × 10^5 years) and eventually the much longer-lived Pu^{244} (half-life 7.6 × 10^7 years). These isotopes can be produced by intensive slow neutron irradiation of Pu^{239}; at best, the Pu^{244} yield is very small and requires extremely high neutron flux and extremely long irradiation time. Radioactive tracers—by-products formed by neutron absorption in various chemical elements inserted into a chain-reacting unit—are used in basic science, agriculture, industry and medicine.

The isotope Pu^{238} can be used as a source of electricity through conversion of its heat of radioactive decay by means of thermoelectric or thermionic devices. Such power units are long-lived, since the half-life of Pu^{238} is 86.4 years; and, because they are very compact and light in weight, they are admirably suited for use in space and in certain terrestrial circumstances. Huge amounts of Pu^{238}, perhaps amounting to ton quantities, are being prepared for this purpose, through the neutron irradiation of Np^{237} (*see* NEPTUNIUM) by the reaction Np^{237} (n,γ) Np^{238} $\xrightarrow{\beta-}$ Pu^{238}

Metallic Plutonium.—Plutonium metal has unusual properties. It exists in six allotropic forms below its melting point (639° C) at atmospheric pressure—behaviour unique to this metal. The temperatures at which the phase changes occur have been determined by a dilatometric method and by thermal analysis.

The density of α-plutonium (monoclinic) is quite high, 19.737 g. per cubic centimetre; however, the densities of the other phases are lower: 17.65 for β-plutonium (body-centred monoclinic), 17.19 for γ-plutonium (face-centred orthorhombic), 15.92 for δ-plutonium (face-centred cubic), 15.99 for δ'-plutonium (face-centred tetragonal) and 16.48 for ε-plutonium (body-centred cubic).

Marked changes in electrical resistivity and thermal expansion accompany the phase changes. The electrical resistivity of α-plutonium is higher than that of any other metallic element at room temperature, being 145 μ ohm-cm. Plutonium metal is highly electropositive.

The metal also forms intermetallic compounds with aluminum, beryllium, cobalt, iron, manganese, nickel and silver. These com-

TABLE II.—*Phase Transitions in Plutonium Metal*

Phase Change	Temperature of Transition on Heating (° C)	
	Dilatometer	Thermal Analysis
α—β	122±2	122
β—γ	206±3	203
γ—δ	319±5	317
δ—δ'	451±4	453
δ'—ε	476±5	477
ε—liquid		639.5±2

TABLE III.—*Isotopes of Plutonium*

Isotope*	Half-life	Type† and energy of radiation (Mev)
Pu232	36 min.	EC ($\geq$98%) α ($\leq$2%) 6.58
Pu233	20 min.	EC α (0.1%) 6.30
Pu234	9.0 hr.	EC (94%) α (6%) 6.196, 6.145, 6.025
Pu235	26 min.	EC α (3 x 10⁻³%) 5.85
Pu236	2.85 yr.	α5.763, 5.716, 5.610, 5.448
Pu237	45.6 days	EC α (3 x 10⁻³%) 5.65, 5.36
Pu237m	0.18 sec.	IT 0.145
Pu238	86.4 yr.	α5.49 (72%) 5.45 (28%)
Pu239	24.4 x 10³ yr.	α5.150 (69%) 5.137 (20%) 5.099 (11%)
Pu240	6,580 yr.	α5.16 (76%) 5.12 (24%)
Pu241	13 yr.	β^-~0.02 α (2.3 x 10⁻³%) 4.893, 4.848
Pu242	3.79 x 10⁵ yr.	α4.898
Pu243	4.98 hr.	β^-0.579 (62%) 0.490 (38%)
Pu244	7.6 x 10⁷ yr.	α4.55 est.
Pu245	10.6 hr.	β^-
Pu246	10.85 days	β^-0.33, 0.15

*The symbol m placed after the mass number refers to an isomeric form of isotope.
†EC = electron capture; α = alpha particle; β^- = negative beta particle; IT = isomeric transition.

pounds include $PuAl_2$, $PuAl_3$, $PuAl_4$, $PuBe_{13}$, $PuCo_2$, $PuFe_2$, $PuMn_2$, $PuNi_2$, $PuNi_5$ and Pu_2Ni_{17}.

Chemical Properties in Aqueous Solution.—The chemistry of plutonium is markedly similar to that of uranium and neptunium, the elements immediately preceding it in the periodic table. The differences in the chemical properties of these elements are due primarily to a progressive increase in the energy required to form the ions in their higher oxidation states.

Plutonium exhibits four oxidation states in aqueous solution: 3+, 4+, 5+ and 6+. The ionic species corresponding to these oxidation states vary with the acidity of the solution. In moderately strong (one molar) acid the species are Pu^{3+}, Pu^{4+}, PuO_2^+ and PuO_2^{2+}. The potential scheme of the ions in one-molar perchloric acid is the following:

$$Pu^0 \xrightarrow{+2.03 \text{ v.}} Pu^{3+} \xrightarrow{-0.982 \text{ v.}} Pu^{4+} \xrightarrow{-1.172 \text{ v.}} PuO_2^+ \xrightarrow{-0.9133 \text{ v.}} PuO_2^{2+}$$

$$-1.043 \text{ v.}$$
$$-1.0224 \text{ v.}$$

The potentials are in volts relative to the hydrogen-hydrogen ion couple as zero.

The potentials of the various couples are so nearly the same that the intermediate oxidation states are unstable with respect to self-oxidation and reduction:

$$3Pu^{4+} + 2H_2O = 2Pu^{3+} + PuO_2^{2+} + 4H^+$$

and

$$2PuO_2^+ + 4H^+ = Pu^{4+} + PuO_2^{2+} + 2H_2O$$

These net changes do not indicate the mechanisms of the reactions, which are more complex. The disproportionation of PuO_2^+ is accompanied by a simultaneous oxidation of PuO_2^+ by Pu^{4+} (with the products PuO_2^{2+} and Pu^{3+} formed).

The oxidation-reduction relationships of the plutonium ions in acid solution are among the most intricate in inorganic chemistry.

The values given for the potential scheme in one-molar acid may be altered extensively by a change in hydrogen-ion concentration or as a result of the addition of substances capable of forming complex ions with the plutonium species. Among such substances are sulfate, phosphate, fluoride and oxalate ions, and various organic compounds, especially those known as chelating agents. The tetrapositive and hexapositive ions are complexed appreciably even by nitrate and chloride ions. The stability of the complex formed with a specified anion increases in this order: PuO_2^+, Pu^{3+}, PuO_2^{2+}, Pu^{4+}.

The hydrolysis of the ions follows a similar order: Pu^{4+} begins to hydrolyze even in tenth-molar acid and in hundredth-molar acid

forms partly the hydroxide $Pu(OH)_4$ and partly a colloidal polymer of variable but approximate composition $Pu(OH)_{3.85}X_{0.15}$, where X is an anion present in the solution. Further reduction of the acidity results in the hydrolysis of PuO_2^{2+} near pH 5, of Pu^{3+} at about pH 7, and of PuO_2^+ at about pH 9.

The potentials of the couples involving either of the two lower states with either of the two upper states have an approximately fourth-power hydrogen-ion concentration dependence in moderately acid solution. This dependence, together with the hydrolytic effects just mentioned, causes rapid alteration of the potential values with change in acidity.

The plutonium ions in aqueous solution possess characteristic colours: blue-lavender for Pu^{3+}, yellow-brown for Pu^{4+} and pink-orange for PuO_2^{2+}. Pure solutions of PuO_2^+ have not been prepared, and since the ion shows but little absorption of visible light, its appearance in solution is not definitely known. The colours of the plutonium ions are altered by hydrolysis or complex ion formation. The absorption spectra of plutonium solutions are found to consist of a number of relatively narrow bands. Each oxidation state exhibits a characteristic spectrum that may be used for the quantitative as well as the qualitative analysis for that oxidation state in solution. Absorption bands as sharp as those found in plutonium solutions are observed only in solutions of other actinide elements or of the rare earths. It is inferred that in plutonium, as in the rare earths, the bands originate from transitions occurring in protected inner f electron orbitals.

The aqueous ions of plutonium are strongly paramagnetic, and measurements of the magnetism are in agreement with the assignment of five, four, three and two f electrons, respectively, for the oxidation states from 3+ through 6+.

Pure solutions of the upper and lower oxidation states may be obtained without difficulty, the former by oxidation with oxidizing agents such as bromate, dichromate or ozone, and the latter by treatment with reducing agents such as sulfur dioxide, hydroxylamine or hydrogen in the presence of platinum black. Because of the disproportionation reactions mentioned previously, the intermediate oxidation states are not stable. However, fairly pure solutions of Pu^{4+} may be obtained by dissolving the hydroxide in warm, concentrated perchloric acid, allowing several days at room temperature for reproportionation, and diluting the resulting solution. The disproportionation reaction is rather slow and the concentrations of Pu^{3+} and PuO_2^{2+} remain small for some hours.

The pentapositive state is quite unstable in strongly acid solution, but becomes increasingly stable as the hydrogen-ion concentration is decreased, down to about ten-thousandth molar. Dilute solutions containing a major proportion of plutonium as PuO_2^+ are stable at this acidity.

The precipitation properties of Pu^{3+} are similar to those of the tripositive rare-earth ions, of Pu^{4+} to Ce^{4+}, and of PuO_2^{2+} to the corresponding ions of uranium and neptunium.

Tri- and tetrapositive plutonium ions form salts of low solubility with fluoride, oxalate, ferricyanide and hydroxide ions. The tetrapositive ion is precipitated also by iodate and arsenate, even in strongly acid solution.

Pentapositive plutonium may be precipitated as a potassium salt from strong carbonate solutions, but no other solid compounds of this oxidation state are known.

The plutonyl ion, PuO_2^{2+}, separates as the beautifully crystalline pink salt $NaPuO_2(CH_3COO)_3$, sodium plutonyl acetate, from solutions containing a high concentration of sodium ions and acetate ions. This salt is analogous to sodium uranyl acetate and sodium neptunyl acetate. Under special conditions fluorescence is observed in crystalline tripositive compounds of plutonium.

Nonaqueous Chemistry.—Many of the most important compounds of plutonium are formed by reactions between solid phases or solid and gas phases, rather than in aqueous media. The most interesting and important of these compounds are the oxides, the halides and oxyhalides, and the binary compounds with carbon, nitrogen, silicon or sulfur.

Hydrides.—The plutonium hydrides PuH_2 (fluorite structure) and PuH_3 (hexagonal structure) are prepared by the action of hydrogen on plutonium metal at temperatures between 150° and

200° C. The entire composition range PuH_2–PuH_3 has been studied. The hydrides are of special importance because thermal decomposition produces finely divided metal which is a useful starting point for the preparation of many other compounds.

Oxides.—The plutonium oxygen system does not present the degree of complexity exhibited by the uranium oxygen system (*see* URANIUM), largely because of the stability of the dioxide. Analogous behaviour is shown in the variable composition of the so-called sesquioxide ($PuO_{1.5-1.75}$), a typical mixed oxidation state oxide, similar to those formed by uranium, praseodymium, terbium, titanium, and many other metals. Its composition shows continuous variation with changes in temperature and pressure of oxygen above the oxide. The limits of composition given above are only approximate. Near the lower limit of the oxygen range the structure is hexagonal. A higher proportion of oxygen causes the oxide to assume the cubic C type of modification of the rare-earth sesquioxides. Plutonium sesquioxide may be formed by the thermal decomposition of the dioxide at about 1,500° C in high vacuum.

Plutonium dioxide is the most important oxide of the element. Almost all compounds of plutonium are converted to the dioxide upon ignition in air at about 1,000° C. The ignited oxide is chemically inert at ordinary temperatures and has a well-defined composition; for these reasons it is a satisfactory compound for weighing in the gravimetric determination of plutonium.

The dioxide is frequently used as the starting material in the synthesis of other compounds of plutonium. In these cases prolonged high-temperature ignition of the oxide is avoided, since this leads to progressive chemical inertness.

Plutonium dioxide was the first compound of the element to be isolated and weighed in pure form; in fact, it was the first compound of any synthetic element to be separated in pure form in weighable amounts. It was also the first compound of a synthetic element to be identified by X-ray diffraction methods.

Halides and Oxyhalides.—All of the halides except the tri-iodide, the hexafluoride and the oxyfluoride may be prepared by the hydrohalogenation of the dioxide or of the oxalate of plutonium III at a temperature of about 700° C. With hydrogen fluoride the reaction product is PuF_4, unless hydrogen is added to the gas stream, in which case the trifluoride is produced. With hydrogen iodide the reaction product is PuOI, and the other oxyhalides may be formed by the addition of appropriate quantities of water vapour to the hydrogen halide gas. Plutonium tri-iodide is produced by the reaction of the metal with hydrogen iodide at about 400° C.

TABLE IV.—*Important Halides and Oxyhalides of Plutonium*

Compound	Colour	Crystal Structure	Density (g./cc.)	M.P. (° C)	B.P. (° C)
PuF_3	violet	hexagonal, tysonite type	9.32	1,425	2,190*
PuF_4	light brown	monoclinic	7.0	1,037	—
PuF_6	deep brown gas, red or reddish-brown solid	orthorhombic	—	50.75	—
$PuCl_3$	emerald green	hexagonal, UCl_3 type	5.70	760	1,770*
$PuBr_3$	green	orthorhombic	6.69	681	1,510*
PuI_3	bright green	orthorhombic, $PuBr_3$ type	6.9	777	1,380*
PuOF	metallic	tetragonal	9.76	above 1,635	—
PuOCl	blue green	tetragonal, PbFCl type	8.81	—	—
PuOBr	deep green	tetragonal, PbFCl type	9.07	—	—
PuOI	green	tetragonal, PbFCl type	8.46	—	—

*Estimated value.

Although PuF_5 has not been prepared, compounds such as $CsPuF_6$ and $RbPuF_7$ have.

Plutonium hexafluoride, the volatile plutonium analogue of uranium hexafluoride, can be prepared by the reaction of pure gaseous fluorine with plutonium tetrafluoride at 700° C. It is unstable with respect to dissociation into fluorine and plutonium tetrafluoride and is a powerful fluorinating agent. The rate of decomposition when stored as a vapour is, however, only about 0.1% per day. When it is stored principally as a solid, the radiation decomposition induced by the intense alpha-particle activity destroys about 1.5% of the hexafluoride per day.

Plutonium oxyfluoride has been prepared by heating PuF_3 to 1,635° C in an atmosphere of argon and oxygen.

The trihalides are appreciably volatile at moderately elevated temperatures and all except the trifluoride may be purified by sublimation in quartz tubes in high vacuum at around 800° to 1,000° C.

Except for the trifluoride, the halides are so hygroscopic that they must be handled in an anhydrous atmosphere. The trifluoride shows so little tendency to hydration that the anhydrous salt is obtained directly upon precipitation from aqueous solution.

The crystal chemistry of the halides and oxyhalides of plutonium is closely similar to that of the analogous compounds of the rare earths—a consequence of the fact that these compounds are predominantly ionic and that the cations have nearly the same ionic radii. Sharp absorption bands and, under certain conditions, fluorescence similar to that in the analogous rare-earth compounds also are observed.

Carbides, Nitrides, Silicides and Sulfides.—Plutonium forms several binary compounds which are of interest because of their refractory character and stability at high temperatures. These compounds include carbides and at least one nitride, one silicide and one sulfide of the element. The monocarbide is formed by the reaction of the dioxide in intimate mixture with carbon at about 1,600° C; higher carbides such as Pu_2C_3 and PuC_2 can also be synthesized. The mononitride may be obtained by heating the trichloride in a stream of anhydrous ammonia at 900° C; it is prepared more easily, however, by the reaction of finely divided metal with ammonia at 650° C. Although the lower temperatures are favourable to the production of higher nitrides, none is readily obtained, in contrast with the uranium-nitrogen system in which compositions up to $UN_{1.75}$ are easily realized.

The disilicide is formed when a slight stoichiometric excess of calcium disilicide is heated with plutonium dioxide in vacuum at about 1,550° C. The disilicide is only moderately stable in air and burns slowly to the dioxide when heated to about 700° C.

Plutonium "sesquisulfide" may be prepared by prolonged treatment of the dioxide in a graphite crucible with anhydrous hydrogen sulfide at 1,340°–1,400° C, or by reaction of the trichloride with hydrogen sulfide at 900° C. A monosulfide is also known to exist.

Only the most important compounds of plutonium have been mentioned in this article; very many compounds are known.

See also references under "Plutonium" in the Index.

BIBLIOGRAPHY.—G. T. Seaborg and J. J. Katz (eds.), *Actinide Elements,* National Nuclear Energy Series, Div. IV, vol. 14A (1954); G. T. Seaborg, J. J. Katz, and W. M. Manning (eds.), *The Transuranium Elements,* National Nuclear Energy Series, Div. IV, vol. 14B, 2 pts. (1949); J. J. Katz and G. T. Seaborg, *The Chemistry of the Actinide Elements* (1957); G. T. Seaborg, *The Transuranium Elements* (1958); *Man-Made Transuranium Elements* (1963); W. D. Wilkinson (ed.), *Extractive and Physical Metallurgy of Plutonium and Its Alloys* (1960); A. S. Coffinberry and W. N. Miner (eds.), *The Metal Plutonium* (1961); M. Haissinsky *et al., Nouveau Traité de Chimie Minérale, Uranium et Transuraniens,* XV (1962).   (G. T. Sg.)

PLUTUS, in Greek mythology, the god of abundance or wealth, a personification of *ploutos,* the Greek for "riches." According to Hesiod, he was born in Crete, the son of Demeter (*q.v.*) and Iasion. His birth was represented at the Eleusinian mysteries. A blind god, he receives his sight in the *Plutus,* the last of Aristophanes' comedies, with fantastic results. In art he appears chiefly as a child with a cornucopia. He was sometimes confused with Pluto.

PLYMOUTH, a city, county and parliamentary borough, naval base, and seaport of Devon, Eng., 42 mi. (68 km.) SW of Exeter by road. Pop. (1961) 204,409; (1963 est.) 209,900. It lies between the rivers Plym and Tamar which flow into Plymouth Sound, the city's southern boundary. The Sound, with an area of 4,500 ac. (1,821 ha.), is sheltered by a mile-long breakwater. In the Sound lies Drake's (formerly St. Nicholas) Island. The southern waterfront is called the Hoe. To the north lies Dartmoor. The Cattewater (the estuary of the Plym) covers 290 ac. (117 ha.), with 8,000 ft. (2,438 m.) of quayage; at its mouth is Sutton Harbour with 4,500 ft. (1,372 m.) of quayage. The Hamoaze (the estuary of the Tamar) is an extensive anchorage used principally by the Royal Navy. West of the Hoe lie Millbay Docks with an outer basin of 35 ac. (14 ha.) and an inner basin of 13 ac. (5 ha.). The Cattewater, Sutton Pool (the ancient tidal harbour), and Millbay Docks accommodate merchant ships and yachts. Plymouth Hoe is dominated eastward by the Citadel, built by Charles II to replace the Tudor castle defending the approaches to the Cattewater and Sutton Harbour. Plymouth was created a county borough in 1888, became a city in 1928, and was granted the dignity of a lord mayor in 1935.

Plymouth suffered severe damage from air raids in World War II. More than 1,100 citizens were killed, and among thousands of buildings destroyed or damaged were every major civic building and half the city's schools and churches, including the 15th-century mother church of St. Andrew. A plan for reconstruction was approved during the war, and the first new road in the central area, Royal Parade, was opened by King George VI in 1947. The near completion of the central reconstruction was celebrated when Queen Elizabeth II opened the 14-story civic centre in 1962. The new Plymouth has some of the most modern commercial, shopping, and civic centres in Great Britain. The central area is built around a 1,000-yd. north–south axis (Armada Way) between the new central station and the Hoe. Shopping and business streets extend at right angles to this axis. New approach roads from the east and west link Plymouth with new bridges over the Plym and Tamar. Reconstruction included the building of several satellite communities where light industries were introduced. Among the more important buildings restored are the Church of St. Andrew, the 19th-century guildhall, and the central public library. The city is the headquarters of the Marine Biological Association. It has several museums and an art gallery; an extensive new College of Technology; the Royal Naval Engineering College; two television stations; and several parks, one of which, Central Park, contains a zoo and a sports centre. The oldest district, the Barbican, features a number of 16th- and 17th-century buildings.

Plymouth Airport lies 4 mi. NNE of the city centre; main line railways communicate with all parts of Britain, and the main road between the Midlands and Cornwall passes through the city. Plymouth is an important yachting centre.

The principal industry is that in the naval dockyard of Devonport; others include the manufacture of machine tools, shoes, clothing, precision instruments, office equipment, lubrication equipment, radio and television sets, fertilizers, chemicals, and engineering products. These goods constitute the principal exports; the main imports are timber, fruit, vegetables, grain, and coal.

Plymouth was named Sudtone in Domesday Book, and its original harbour is still called Sutton Harbour. A developing trade and the shipment of armies to France in the 14th century led to rapid growth. In 1439 Plymouth became the first English town to be incorporated by act of Parliament. In the 16th century the attempts of Sir Walter Ralegh (Raleigh) to colonize Virginia were made from Plymouth; it was the home port of Drake, Grenville, and the Hawkins family, and from there the British fleet sailed to attack the Spanish Armada. Storm damage caused the "Mayflower" to call at the Devonian port, and so well were the Pilgrim Fathers received that they wrote afterward how they had been "courteously used by divers friends there dwelling." In 1620 they sailed from Barbican quay (recorded by a stone slab, an arch, and an inscription) to found Plymouth, Mass. In the Civil War Plymouth was intermittently besieged by Royalist forces. In 1690 the royal dockyard was begun on the eastern bank of the Tamar, and the town of Plymouth Dock (in 1824 renamed Devonport) was founded adjacent to it. The third town of Stonehouse developed between Devonport and Plymouth, all amalgamating as Plymouth in 1914. The painters Sir Joshua Reynolds, James Northcote, and Benjamin Haydon were all natives of the area, and the explorer Robert Falcon Scott was born at Devonport. Plymouth has two parliamentary divisions, Devonport and Sutton. The American-born Nancy Viscountess Astor, elected for Sutton in 1919, became the first woman to sit in the House of Commons.   (Wi. B. H.)

PLYMOUTH, the seat of Plymouth County, Mass., U.S., and site of the first permanent settlement by Europeans in New England, is 37 mi. SE of Boston on Plymouth Bay. Thousands of visitors are drawn annually by the historic interest of the town and its attractions as a summer resort. The modern town had a large cordage works, supplied by its own ships. Other important industries are cranberry growing and processing, commercial fishing, and varied manufactures such as sheeting for photoengraving and curtains. Seafaring was the heart of the older business life of the community and active wharves and boatyards remain.

Plymouth was founded by Pilgrims (*see* PILGRIM FATHERS)—Separatists from the Church of England who, in their search for religious toleration, had emigrated first to the Netherlands and then to North America. Sailing in the "Mayflower" (*q.v.*), the settlers reached the coast of New England in November 1620, and an exploring party arrived in the Plymouth area on December 21, now celebrated as Forefathers' Day. The "Mayflower" anchored in the harbour five days later. (For a more detailed account of the colony's beginnings, and for its subsequent history, *see* MASSACHUSETTS: *History.*) The storied Plymouth Rock, first identified in 1741, became a symbol of freedom in 1774 when it was split by dragging it to Liberty Pole Square in prerevolutionary agitation. It rests today on its original waterfront site under a protecting portico of granite. Rising behind the rock is Cole's Hill, where during their first terrible winter the Pilgrims buried half their number, leveling the ground, and sowing it to grain in the spring "lest the Indians know how many were the graves." The first fort and watchtower were on Burial Hill, which contains the graves of William Bradford (*q.v.*) and others of the original Pilgrims, although the oldest stone is dated 1681. "Plimoth Plantation," a nonprofit educational foundation, in 1957 began reconstructing an accurate replica of First Street in 1627 and other buildings of the early village. "Mayflower II," a good-will ship sent as a gift from England in 1957, is on display. Several mid-17th-century houses still stand in the town. Pilgrim Hall, built in 1824, contains relics of the Pilgrims and early colonial times. Many original records of the colony are in the Registry Building. The National Monument to the Forefathers was dedicated in 1889. Pop. (1970) 18,606. For comparative population figures *see* table in MASSACHUSETTS: *Population. See* also references under "Plymouth, Mass.," in the Index.   (Ca. M. C.)

PLYMOUTH BRETHREN, a community of Christians who received the name from Plymouth, Eng., where their first congregation in England was established in 1831, under the leadership of Benjamin Wills Newton, Samuel Prideaux Tregelles, and others. The movement had originated in Dublin some six years earlier, as a spontaneous endeavour by a few young men (chiefly Edward Cronin and Anthony Norris Groves) to enjoy Christian fellowship in disregard of denominational frontiers and thus to recapture the simplicity of the apostolic church. They were early caught up in the keen contemporary interest in biblical prophecy, particularly after they were joined by John Nelson Darby (1800–82). This former clergyman in the Church of Ireland quickly became the dominant personality in the movement, and he founded groups of like-minded people in many parts of the British Isles and on the continent of Europe, especially in French Switzerland, where he spent the greater part of 1838–45.

His return to England in 1845 was followed by a cleavage among the Brethren. The principal occasion was a conflict which developed between Darby and Newton, on grounds partly of doctrine and partly of ecclesiastical polity. Darby's followers formed a closely knit federation of churches and were known as Exclusive Brethren; the others, called Open Brethren, maintained a congregational polity and less rigorous standards of communion. The leading Open Brethren church was Bethesda Chapel, Bristol, where George Müller (famous for his philanthropic work for orphans) was joint pastor. Exclusive Brethren, by carrying through consistently their basic tenets on church fellowship (summed up in Darby's words, "separation from evil is God's principle of unity"), have suffered further worldwide divisions. The first of these took place in 1881, when Darby's ablest disciple, William Kelly, separated with his followers from the main Exclusive body. Today, while some Exclusive parties refuse practically all collaboration with Christians outside their own circle, others take an active part in interdenominational work of an evangelical character, as do the Open Brethren.

Brethren of all parties recognize no order of clergy or ministers as distinct from the laity, although a number of them who are suitably qualified give all their time to evangelistic or pastoral ministry. Their most distinctive meeting is the communion service, where members of the local church, together with Christian friends who care to join them, sit round the Lord's Table with no presiding minister, and their devotions (prayer, hymn singing, Bible reading, and exposition) proceed in no prearranged order. Practically all Open Brethren and some of the Exclusive parties practise believers' baptism; many Exclusives, however, following Darby, baptize the children of members ("household baptism").

All parties maintain the faith of the ecumenical creeds, except that one Exclusive group denies that Christ was the Son of God before his incarnation, while acknowledging his eternal preexistence in the Godhead. For the rest, their doctrines are generally evangelical (more Calvinist than Arminian) and their approach to the Bible conservative. They have inherited from their founders a live eschatological awareness, which frequently finds expression in their hymnology; but no single line of eschatological interpretation is imposed.

Brethren are found throughout the English-speaking world and in most European countries. In the United States, which they reached in the early 1860s, there are eight groups, distinguished for statistical purposes by roman numerals I through VIII, with an inclusive membership of around 33,000. The largest groups are I and II (the latter with about 15,000 members), which are in practice one group.

The Plymouth Brethren have been active in foreign missionary work ever since Groves led a missionary expedition to Baghdad in the early 1830s. Groves later established missionary work in India. Their missionaries are located principally in Central Africa, India and Latin America; they observe the comity of missions. The editors of the periodicals *Echoes of Service* (Bath, Eng.) and *The Fields* (New York) act as channels of communication for the Open Brethren's foreign mission field, commonly called "Christian Missions in Many Lands."

BIBLIOGRAPHY.—W. B. Neatby, *A History of the Plymouth Brethren*, 2nd ed. (1902); D. J. Beattie, *Brethren: the Story of a Great Recovery* (1939); G. H. Lang, *Anthony Norris Groves*, 2nd ed. (1949). J. N. Darby's *Collected Works* were edited by W. Kelly, 32 vol., with supplementary vol. (1867–83).   (F. F. B.)

PLYNLIMON (PUMLUMON meaning five "risings" or "swellings"), a hilly superstructure or monadnock on the surface of the high plateau of central Wales, partly in Cardiganshire and partly in Montgomeryshire, is about 14 mi. inland from Aberystwyth and 10 mi. W of Llanidloes. The highest point, known as Pen Pumlumon Fawr, attains 2,468 ft. (752 m.). The monadnock consists of Lower Paleozoic rocks of a gritty nature which in turn are smeared with a coating of stiff boulder clay. This type of country was most likely forested in early times, certainly up to the 1,000-ft. (305 m.) contour, but it is now grass covered with wide stretches of bracken. These areas provide only a poor pasture for sheep and summer grazing for young beef cattle. Much of the surface is boggy. Heavy rainfall and deep winter snows feed the many streams which radiate from the upland—the Severn, Wye, and Clywedog flowing to the Bristol Channel in a southeastward direction, and the Rheidol and Llyfnant westward to Cardigan Bay. Mining for lead, zinc, and copper, and quarrying are no longer carried on. Anthropologists have noted the survival of a number of very early (Paleolithic) physical characteristics among the present-day inhabitants of this upland area.   (E. G. Bow.)

PLYWOOD, a composite wood panel made of three or more layers glued together with the grain of adjoining plies at right angles to each other. For thin panels veneer is used exclusively, but for thicker panels sawed lumber often is used as the centre ply, or core, in which case it is known as lumber-core plywood.

The veneer may be rotary cut (*i.e.*, peeled from the log), sliced or, less commonly, sawed in thin sheets from a flitch or bolt. Rotary-cut veneer always presents a flat-grain or tangential surface, whereas sliced and sawed veneers may be cut in a radial or any other plane through the log. Veneer used for plywood usually varies in thickness from $\frac{1}{28}$ to $\frac{1}{8}$ in., but both thinner and thicker veneers often are used. Thin veneers have an advantage, especially for the outer or face plies, in that they set up less severe transverse stresses with changes in moisture content, thereby reducing warping and surface checking of panels. The use of thin veneer also makes valuable wood go further. In lumber-core panels the plies next to the faces, or the crossbands, usually are thicker than the face plies and largely control the stability of the panel. Plywood is almost always composed of an odd number of plies so that the grain of corresponding plies from the outside in runs in the same direction, thereby balancing and stabilizing the construction.

Plywood has a number of advantages over solid wood: it can be manufactured into large sheets with limited defects; it is stronger across the grain of the face plies than are boards of the same thickness; because the plies cross each other, shrinking and swelling are almost eliminated; splitting in handling and nailing is greatly reduced; and wood of the lower grades can be used for the interior plies. Since veneer can be dried in a few minutes, dry plywood can be produced from green logs in a day.

Two types of plywood are made: interior plywood, for use only in dry locations, and exterior plywood, for which water-resistant glues are used.

Since successively cut layers of thin veneers are similar in appearance, identical areas from adjacent sheets can be matched so as to make highly ornamental symmetrical patterns.

In sandwich construction thin facings are bonded on a thick core. The facings are made of strong material, such as thin, dense plywood, and the core of a lightweight material, such as balsa wood, cellular cellulose acetate or paper honeycomb. The core serves primarily to separate and stabilize the thin faces, which are the principal load-carrying portions. The complete assembly is exceedingly strong and stiff for its weight.

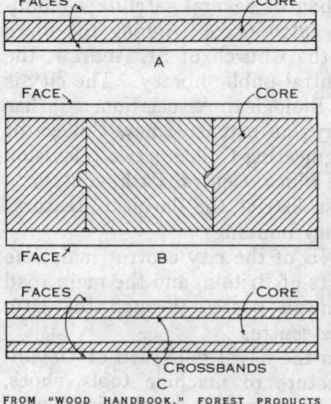

FROM "WOOD HANDBOOK," FOREST PRODUCTS LABORATORY, U.S. DEPARTMENT OF AGRICULTURE

PLYWOOD CONSTRUCTION

(A) Three-ply, all veneer; (B) three-ply, lumber core; (C) five-ply, all veneer. Edge views

Plywood is used whenever a material is required to cover large areas with a light but strong and rigid sheeting; *e.g.*, in cabinet-making (for chests, dressers, wardrobes, tables, etc.), housebuilding (for walls, ceilings, floors, doors, cupboards, cement forms, etc.), coachbuilding (for trucks, vans, trailers, etc.), shipbuilding (for small boat hulls, decks, cabins, etc.), boxmaking (for shipping and storage chests and cases, etc.) and aircraft construction (for fuselages, wings, floors, hydroplane hulls, etc.). *See* also references under "Plywood" in the Index.

BIBLIOGRAPHY.—A. D. Wood and T. G. Linn, *Plywoods, Their Development, Manufacture and Application* (1942); L. H. Meyer, *Plywood: What It Is—What It Does* (1947); T. D. Perry, *Modern Plywood*, 2nd ed. (1948); Forest Products Laboratory, U.S. Department of Agriculture, *Wood Handbook* (1955).   (Ar. K.)

PLZEN (German PILSEN), the fifth largest city of Czechoslovakia, and the administrative and industrial centre of the West Bohemian *kraj* (region), lies about 68 mi. (110 km.) SW of Prague by rail. Pop. (1961) 141,583. Geographically it has a remarkable site, for the great fan of five tributary streams which forms the Berounka River gathers in the Plzen Basin, of which the city is the focal point. The convergence of valleys is emphasized now by the railway network, and the meeting there of seven main roads. There is a coalfield to the northwest but the once profitable seams have been worked out. The brown forest soils of the countryside, long cleared of woodland, are relatively fertile and on the whole well farmed in spite of the recurrent problem of summer drought. The farming specialties are sugar beets and hops, although the famous breweries depend largely on the hop farms round Zatec. The concentration of urban growth in one sizable city, unlike the clusters of secondary towns in the Ohre (Eger) Basin, and the markedly Czech nature of the greater part of the population, distinguish Plzen from much of Bohemia.

Plzen was recorded as a settlement in the 10th century and is said to have received its charter as a town in 1292. Its medieval and Renaissance prosperity is evident from the fine church of St. Bartholomew and the 16th-century town hall. The church has the highest tower in Bohemia (325 ft. [99 m.]). Plzen was one of the strongholds of Roman Catholicism during the Hussite Wars in the 15th century (*see* HUSSITES).

Plzen's industrial importance developed mainly in the mid-19th century, notably with the establishment of the Mestansky pivovar (citizens' brewery) in 1842 and of the Skoda (now V. I. Lenin) armament works in 1859. The reputation of the "Pilsener" beer became international, and the Skoda factories, although better known for arms production, manufactured rolling stock, machinery for breweries and sugar refineries, and later parts for the motor industry. The factories, severely damaged in World War II, were quickly rebuilt and remain the basic group of Czechoslovak heavy industry. The nearby Sumava (Bohemian) Forest favoured the timber and paper industries, and the kaolin clays of Horni Briza in the Plzen Basin supplied the potteries. The school of medicine and the mechanical and electrical engineering colleges were established after World War II. (H. G. S.)

PNEUMATIC CONVEYING

PNEUMATIC CONVEYING is a method of transporting dry bulk (nonpackaged) materials through pipeline systems by the use of negative or positive compressed air power. The negative pressure of air power creates a partial vacuum whereby materials are sucked into and through a pipeline system; hence the term "sucker" given to the earliest pneumatic conveyors. The positive pressure type blows material through a pipeline system by means of expanding compressed air.

The earliest pneumatic conveyor, using the term loosely, was a system used to transport shavings and sawdust from machines of a wood-planing mill to the refuse pile. This system used the planing mill fan, a flat-bladed type, to suck the sawdust and shavings from the machines into a pipeline, pass the material through the fan, and blow it to the refuse pile. At the end of the 19th century the positive rotary blower, having demonstrated its ability to deliver higher vacuums and pressures, was brought into use for pneumatic conveying systems.

The use of pneumatic conveyors was greatly increased at the beginning of the 20th century, when the countries of Europe were importing large quantities of grain. The large, high-capacity grain unloader, or "sucker," removed grain from ships' holds faster than any previous equipment. Later, pneumatic conveyors were developed to transport not only grains but also dry, powdery materials, nonabrasive as well as abrasive. Modern industries using pneumatic conveyors for transporting dry bulk materials include chemical, plastic, cement, pulp and paper, rubber, and kaolin. Pneumatic conveyors offer certain advantages: they can easily transport material around corners and up an incline; they are clean, safe, and accessible; they have low handling loss or shrinkage; and they reduce labour costs. However, they are restricted in types and sizes of materials they can carry, limited to one-way flow, and require higher capital investment and higher power costs than for mechanical handling equipment.

Vacuum System.—The vacuum system is used today for unloading railroad cars, ships, and barges, and in situations with a multiplicity of pickup points and a single discharge point. Such an arrangement is also used in the process industries to transport material from two or more bins or sources of supply to a single terminal point such as a weigh hopper, mixer, or similar facility.

A typical unloading system is shown in fig. 1. The exhauster unit (positive displacement blower) is used to create a partial vacuum in the conveying duct as well as a stream of flowing air to carry the material. The material flows into the portable twin-type nozzle located underneath the covered hopper car; it is then conveyed through a flexible hose and steel-pipe conveying duct to the receiving station where it is filtered from the air stream and retained in cloth bags, allowing the clean air to pass through the exhauster unit to the atmosphere. The material on separation is discharged from the filter through the rotary air lock to the screw conveyors, from which it is distributed to the storage bins.

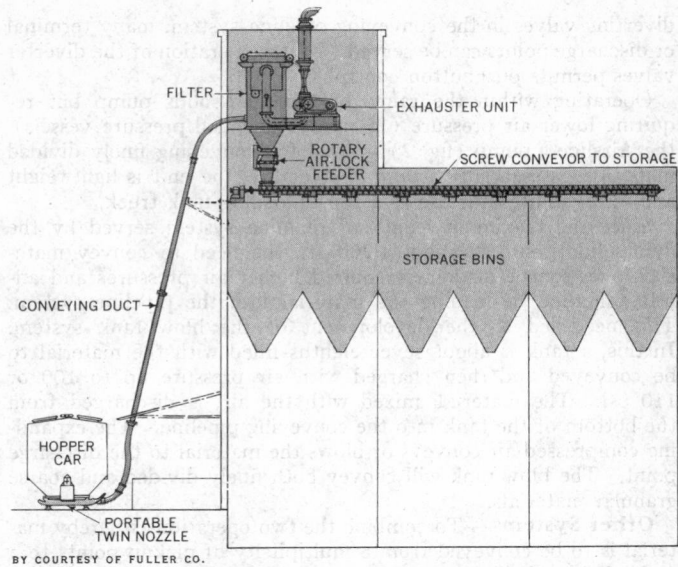

FIG. 1.—TYPICAL PNEUMATIC UNLOADING SYSTEM

Pressure System.—The vacuum type of system is excellent for transporting materials from numerous pickup points to a single discharge point, but many industries required materials to be transported from a single pickup point to a multiplicity of discharge points. This called for reversing the position of the power plant of the pneumatic conveyor from the point beyond the pipeline system to the point where conveying was to begin, and resulting in a pressure system. Starting with low pressures, 2 psi (pounds per square inch) to 12 psi, rotary feeders having star-type wheels enclosed in dust- and pressure-tight housings, with minimum clearances between the wheels and the housings, are used to meter and feed the materials into the conveying pipeline. For higher pressures, fluid-solids pumps and pressure tanks (blow tanks) are utilized to blow large tonnages over distances up to 7,600 ft.

Conveying systems using rotary feeders convey both granular and powdered, nonabrasive or mildly abrasive materials, including grains, soft feeds, flour, starch, and many chemicals. For granular abrasive materials, gate locks of the three-gate type are substituted for the rotary feeders. When finely divided abrasive materials such as portland cement or pulverized phosphate rock are to be conveyed, the fluid-solids pump is used.

The fluid-solids pump will handle only pulverized material, at least 60% of which can pass through a 200-mesh screen, 75% through a 100-mesh screen, and all through a 50-mesh screen. The maximum air pressure at which this pump will operate is 45 psi.

Air supply for the conveying system and the pump is usually furnished by a rotary type of air compressor. Through

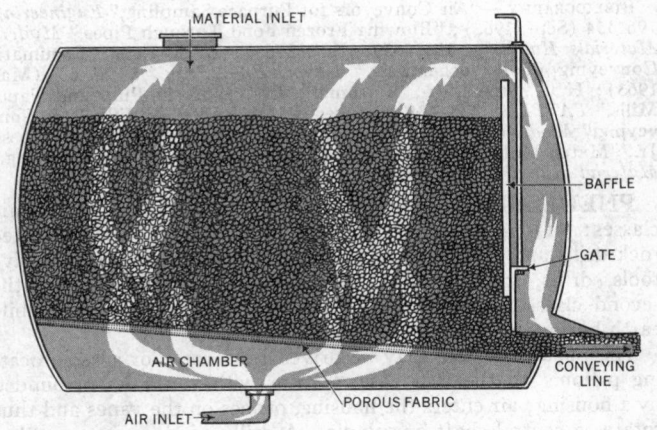

FIG. 2.—AIRSLIDE® PUMP UNIT

diverting valves in the conveying pipeline system, many terminal or discharge points can be served. Motor operation of the diverter valves permits pushbutton control.

Operating within the range of the fluid-solids pump but requiring lower air pressure (15 psi for uncoded pressure vessels), the Airslide® pump (fig. 2) is used for conveying finely divided materials. Essentially a tank in structure, the unit is lightweight and ideally suited for use as a self-unloading tank truck.

Since the maximum length of pipeline system served by the fluid-solids pump is about 1,200 ft., the need to convey materials over longer distances required higher air pressures and another method of feeding the material into the pipeline system. This need led to the development of the blow tank system. In this, a tank is about seven-eighths filled with the material to be conveyed and then charged with air pressure up to 100 or 110 psi. The material, mixed with the air, is discharged from the bottom of the tank into the conveying pipeline. The expanding compressed air conveys or blows the material to the discharge point. The blow tank will convey both finely divided and coarse granular materials.

Other Systems.—To combine the two operations whereby material is to be conveyed from a multiplicity of pickup points to a multiplicity of discharge points, a combination vacuum-pressure type of system is used as illustrated in fig. 3.

The air-activated gravity conveyor, while not a pneumatic conveyor in the true sense of the word, belongs to the family. This

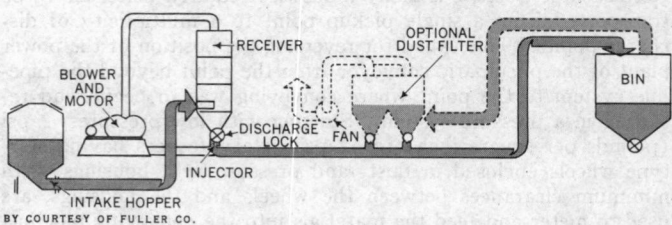

FIG. 3.—COMBINATION VACUUM-PRESSURE SYSTEM

conveyor uses low-pressure air to aerate or fluidize a pulverized material, causing the material to flow by the force of gravity. The angle of repose of the pulverized mound of material at rest is 47° from the horizontal. To convey this material down or through a sloping spout, the angle of the spout must be above 47°, approaching 52°. When the material is placed on a low-permeable porous medium through which air is passed, the aerated material will fluidize so that it acts like water and will flow on a slope of 4°.

An offshoot of pneumatic conveying systems is the pneumatic tube, which has been used to transport small items such as messages or currency in a container built to fit closely in the tube and driven by either a partial vacuum or expanding compressed air. Pneumatic tubes have been used for internal communications in hotels, offices, and stores.

See also MATERIAL HANDLING.

BIBLIOGRAPHY.—"Air Conveyors for Furnace Sampling," *Engineering*, 196:354 (Sept. 1963); "Blowing Frozen Food Through Pipes," *Modern Materials Handling*, 18:58–59 (July 1963); E. J. Reta, "Pneumatic Conveying of Petrochemicals," *Chem. Eng. Prog.*, 59:59–63 (May 1963); H. A. Stoess, Jr., "Pneumatic Conveyors in Pulp and Paper Mills," *TAPPI*, 35:433–438 (October 1952); Robert G. Zilly, "Air Conveying," *Modern Materials Handling* (December 1957); H. A. Stoess, Jr., "Match Material to System for Successful Pneumatic Conveying," *Material Handling Engineering*, 16:4 (April 1961). (H. A. St.)

PNEUMATIC TOOLS can be divided into two main classes: (1) air-operated portable tools; and (2) air-operated rock drills and associated tools. The first class includes abrasive tools, drills, screw drivers, hammers, riveters and hoists; the second class, hand-held rock drills and paving breakers, mobile earth-boring machines, etc.

The pneumatic tool may be driven by a rotor or a reciprocating piston. In the first case, a rotor with vanes is surrounded by a housing; air enters the housing, pushes on the vanes and thus rotates a central shaft or spindle. A drill, grinder or some other part may be fastened to the spindle. In the second case, com-

pressed air enters a cylinder, expands and pushes a piston back and forth. The reciprocating piston may be connected to or may strike some part such as a riveting hammer or a chisel. Pneumatic tools are usually supplied with compressed air at about 90 lb. per square inch above atmospheric pressure. A compressed-air system with a compressor, piping and an air motor is analogous to an electric system with an electric generator, electric wires and an electric motor.

With compressed air as the power source, it is possible to use tools which are relatively light in weight, compact, portable and easy to operate. Air motors introduce no spark hazard in explosive atmospheres, and they also are employed in wet conditions because they present no danger of electric shock. In underwater service, the compressed air prevents water from entering the motor.

Portable Tools.—Air-driven portable tools include such devices as grinders, buffers, sanders, drills and reamers, screw drivers and nut setters, all of which are powered by rotary-vane motors; trench diggers, riveters and various types of hammers, powered by pistons; and such specialty tools as concrete vibrators, cranking motors and railway roadbed tampers.

Air-driven grinders, drills, screw drivers, etc., are of conventional design except that an air motor is substituted for the more familiar electric motor; operating speeds usually can be varied by throttling the air to the motor.

In the pneumatic chipping or scaling hammer there is an air-operated piston that delivers successive blows to a chisel or forming tool at the end of the hammer. In the valve type of tool there is a separate mechanism to control the flow of air to the piston, thus allowing the operator to govern the speed and force of the blows; in the valveless type, the piston itself performs the valving action and the operator can exercise only an on-off control of the tool. The former type is used for chipping and riveting, for which control of the blows is important; the latter is used for such work as removing scale.

Riveting hammers are of two designs: in a compression riveter the compression or squeezing action on the rivet is obtained from an air piston and cylinder connected to a cam, wedge or toggle; a yoke riveter has an air-operated clamp or vise that holds the work in place; the yoke absorbs the hammering action and thus reduces operator fatigue.

Hoists operated by compressed air are used in operations which require accurate and definite control of lifting and lowering speeds. Air hoists are used outdoors and under conditions where corrosive fumes, explosive gases and inflammable fluids are present. Safety devices prevent sudden dropping of the load when the air pressure falls or the brakes fail.

There are various portable pneumatic tools which are usually classed as specialty tools, such as concrete vibrators, countersinking tools, spike drivers, paint mixers, air cranking motors, railway roadbed tampers, valve grinders, reciprocating filing machines, shank grinders and saws.

Rock Drills.—For mining and general rock excavation the usual air-operated tool is the hammer drill or percussion hammer, composed of a piston and a drill made of high-carbon steel. The shank of the drill is not attached directly to the piston but is held loosely in a chuck at the end of the cylinder and is struck by rapid blows from the freely moving piston.

For downward-sloping holes, some means must be provided to remove drill cuttings, dust and sludge; thus, a hollow bit is used, and water or air is passed through it to remove the cuttings and cool the drill bit. In addition, the bit must be rotated to produce a round, uniform hole, and this may be done either manually by the operator, with a wrench attached to the drill, or automatically by a ratchet-and-pawl mechanism that turns the bit slightly after each blow from the piston.

Hand-Held Rock Drills.—The hand-held rock drill, with a self-rotating hammer, is sometimes called a sinker or a jackhammer. Rock drills are frequently classified on the basis of weight—a drill of less than 25 lb. may be used for drilling shallow holes in brick or concrete; a 55-lb. drill may be used for road construction.

Drifter, Stoper and Wagon Drills.—The drifter drill is generally

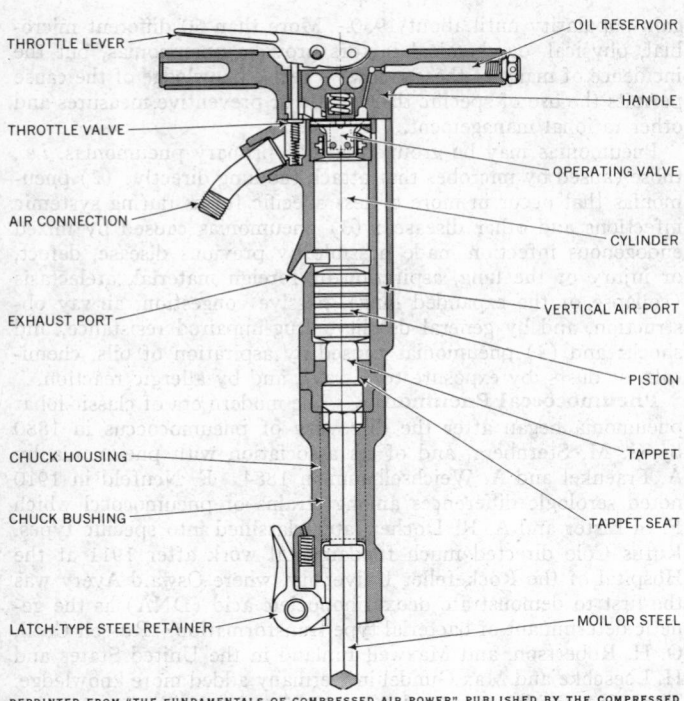

THROTTLE LEVER

THROTTLE VALVE

AIR CONNECTION

EXHAUST PORT

CHUCK HOUSING

CHUCK BUSHING

LATCH-TYPE STEEL RETAINER

OIL RESERVOIR

HANDLE

OPERATING VALVE

CYLINDER

VERTICAL AIR PORT

PISTON

TAPPET

TAPPET SEAT

MOIL OR STEEL

REPRINTED FROM "THE FUNDAMENTALS OF COMPRESSED AIR POWER" PUBLISHED BY THE COMPRESSED AIR AND GAS INSTITUTE

PORTABLE PNEUMATIC PAVING BREAKER

used for horizontal holes in mining operations and tunnel driving. The usual air-cylinder bore diameters are 3 in., 3½ in. and 4 in. The drill is mounted on some type of rig or frame. The usual drifter is mechanically fed into the work. Stoper drills are used primarily on up-hole or overhead drilling. The usual stoper is a hammer drill with a self-rotating drill and an automatic feed by means of an air piston.

Large air-operated earth drills, mounted on motor trucks or trailers, are used for putting down water wells and blast holes for quarry operations. A high-capacity compressor provides air not only to power the drilling tool but also to raise and lower the tools in the hole and remove drill cuttings from the hole. Such machines are used to advantage in areas where surface water supplies are insufficient to provide the drilling fluid needed for standard rotary and cable-tool well drilling machines.

Paving Breakers.—Hand-operated pneumatic paving breakers generally use solid drill steels and are not equipped with automatic rotation. One type of tool is valve actuated; the other is valveless. Heavy machines, weighing about 80 lb., are used to break concrete pavement, foundations and boulders. Medium breakers, weighing 50 to 70 lb., are used to break light concrete floors, macadam and frozen ground. The light tools, weighing less than 50 lb., are used for breaking floors, paving and masonry walls. Heavy- and medium-weight breakers can be adapted for use in driving spikes. (R. C. BR.; X.)

PNEUMATISM. The theory of pneumatism in medicine, based on the premise that life is associated with a subtle vapour called the pneuma, was expounded by the Alexandrian anatomist and physiologist Erasistratus, who flourished about 300 B.C. The concept of pneumatism had been previously suggested by other commentators. Unlike Herophilus, who accepted the old theory of humoral pathology, Erasistratus held that health and disease and, in fact, the nature of life were intimately connected with the pneuma, which had affinities with the air man breathes. Erasistratus drew a distinction between two kinds of pneuma: one was a "vital spirit" formed in the heart from air; the second type was formed in the brain from the first kind. The former was transported by arteries to the parts of the body and the latter, styled the "animal spirit," by the nerves, being the prime cause of movement. Although Erasistratus held that hindrance of the action of the pneuma, or an excess of blood, was the essential cause of certain diseases, he did not follow the contemporary prac-

tice of blood-letting, preferring to attempt to control the blood supply by diet and other less violent measures.

PNEUMOCONIOSIS, also called pneumonoconiosis, a term denoting a variety of industrial diseases of the lung caused by breathing dust particles. Precise definition of the term is a matter of legal consequence, because occupational chest diseases are among the most litigious of medicolegal issues. In several countries many of these conditions are obligatorily compensable. To more than 3,000 naturally occurring minerals presenting respiratory hazard are added yearly an ever-increasing number of synthetic chemical agents. The biological action of less than 1% of these substances is known, yet about 10% of working persons handle such agents. While pneumoconiosis is a generic term, silicosis has for many years been its chief specific manifestation. Because of the increasing range of dangerous respirable agents, however, emphasis is shifting from silicosis to other forms of pneumoconioses. The majority of the significant reactions represent insidiously progressive chronic responses, frequently with a distinct latent period during which the workman is symptom-free. Fulminating cases also occur when exposure has been unduly severe or adjuvant factors play a part. A simplified etiological classification of the main varieties of pneumoconioses is given in the table.

Pneumoconioses

Siliceous	Nonsiliceous
Free silica (SiO₂)	Carbonaceous
Crystalline	Anthracosis* ⎱......coal miners
Silicosis proper	Emphysema* ⎰
Mining*	Graphitosis.........graphite
Ceramics*	Smog lung.........carbon and chemicals
Glass industry*	
Abrasives*	Metallogenic
Sandblasting*	Siderosis.............iron
Foundry*	Baritosis...........barium
Etc.	Stannosis............tin
Aberrant silicosis	Cobaltosis..........cobalt
Tridimytosis*	Argyrosis...........silver
Cristobalitosis*	Aluminosis†........aluminum
Amorphous	Berylliosis*.......beryllium
Natural	Cadmiosis*.........cadmium
Diatomatosis{raw	Manganosis†........manganese
calcined*	Vanadosis†.........vanadium
Synthetic	Thioconiosis........sulfur
Submicron, 20Å–4,000 Å	Plumboconiosis......lead
	Welder's lung†......iron + ozone or nitrogen dioxide
Silicates (SiO₄)	Brass foundry lung..copper + zinc
Mineral	
Asbestosis*	Organic
Talcosis*	Byssinosis*.........cotton
Micatosis	Bagassosis*.........sugar cane
Kaolinosis	Ptilosis............feather
Fuller's earth†	Tabacosis..........tobacco
Artificial	Papricosis..........pepper
Cementosis	Suberosis...........cork
Glass wool†	Hemp lung..........hemp
	Flax lung..........flax
Mixed forms	Wood lung†.........wood
Disease in Bauxite extractors*	Rubber lung*.......rubber
Granite polishers*	Plastics lung†......plastics
Slate workers*	Farmer's lung*......fungi
Boiler scalers*	Silo filler's lung*....nitrogen dioxide
Kiln liners*	Wheat handler's
Basic slag workers	lung†..............?
Hematite miners*	
Magnetite miners*	Miscellaneous
Kolar gold miners	Oleogranuloma......oil mists
Insulation workers*	Fume injury*........nitric acid, etc.
Transite pipe workers*	Gas injury*.........hydrogen fluoride, etc.
	Chemical
	pneumonitis*......inorganic, organic

*Disabling and lethal.   †Disputed entities.

History.—Man-made lung diseases have been known for the past 2,000 years and were discussed by, among others, Hippocrates and Pliny. "Potters' rot" of ceramic workers, "grinders' rot" of steel implement sharpeners, and "coal miners' asthma" evolved as by-products of the Industrial Revolution. But this group of disorders first assumed major importance when, at the turn of the 20th century, thousands of gold miners in South Africa began to die from "miners' phthisis." Since that time, research and the introduction of rigorous environmental hygiene measures have brought about control over these diseases.

In modern industries, dust hazards have been virtually eliminated by advance engineering planning. Employees in well-controlled plants can anticipate trouble-free working periods of 30 to 40 years in spite of processing highly dangerous substances. Pneumoconiosis arises in such industries in exceptional cases only.

The explanation usually is either extreme individual susceptibility, predisposing disease such as tuberculosis, accidental excessive exposures, hazardous technical innovations, or the potentiating effects of exposure to several different substances. The pneumoconioses have in a few instances affected nonworking persons. Police officers, housewives, and school children have contracted berylliosis from the inhalation of smokestack effluvia, dust from soiled working clothes, or fluorescent lamp phosphors. The lung injury caused by city smog results from the action of chemical agents adsorbed onto carbon particles emanating in industrial operations. The catastrophic deaths at Donora, Pa. (1946), the Meuse Valley in Belgium (1949), and in London (1952) illustrate the disastrous potential of industrial waste products immoderately disseminated into the air of cities.

Causes.—Theories of the causation of pneumoconiosis include tissue injury by mechanical trauma, protoplasmic poisoning, metabolic changes in cells through a disturbance of pH, protein denaturing through piezoelectric and surface molecular forces, immune and antibody reactions, polymerization, and the nonspecific action of submicron particles. No single explanation is universally acceptable. The pathogenic propensity of a number of specific agents has been proved by experimental reproduction of characteristic lesions in animals.

Symptoms.—Pneumoconioses range from innocuous through variably disabling to lethal syndromes. Symptoms are determined by the focus of major lung injury, combinations of lesions, severity and rate of exposure, and infective or other complications. Dominant states include bronchitis, bronchiolitis, bronchiectasis, emphysema, pulmonary fibrosis, and pulmonary hypertension. The main complications, which also determine the mode of lethal outcome in most instances, are cor pulmonale (pulmonary heart disease) with congestive cardiac failure, tuberculosis, pneumonia, pulmonary insufficiency, hemorrhage, lung gangrene, and erosion of a blood vessel, a bronchus, or the esophagus. Remote lesions may also occur; e.g., portal artery obstruction, metastatic tuberculosis, and liver, kidney, or suprarenal failure. Respiratory tract cancer is closely associated with exposures to monochromates, asbestos, beryllium, nickel, arsenic, and radioactive particles.

Diagnosis and Treatment.—Precise diagnosis depends largely on radiography, but so eclectic and diversified are the manifestations of the pneumoconioses that interpretation of the X-rays requires great skill and experience. Advanced physiological studies have contributed greatly to understanding of the associated disability. Final diagnosis, however, often must await histopathological and petrographic confirmation.

Once established, the majority of the severe pneumoconioses are irreversible. Some syndromes may become arrested on cessation of exposure but others, such as silicosis and asbestosis, progress inexorably. Therapy is directed at the alleviation of symptoms such as pain or bronchospasm, support of the failing heart, and treatment of complicating infection. Apart from dust suppression, adequate ventilation, and the use of exhaust equipment, the only effective prophylactic agent against silicosis is inhaled aluminum administered in the form of aerosols of aluminum oxide, hydroxide, or hydroxychloride. Good results have been achieved in cases of berylliosis by means of the chelating agent aurin tricarboxylic acid or by cortisone. No specific therapy is available for other pneumoconioses.

See also Dangerous Occupations; Dust; Industrial Medicine; Respiratory System, Diseases of; Silicosis.

(G. W. H. S.)

PNEUMONIA, an inflammation of the lung, was recognized in ancient times. Leopold Auenbrugger in 1761 and René Laënnec in 1819 brought order into its classification and advanced existing knowledge. From then until the bacteriologic era, nosology (the branch of medicine that is concerned with the classification of diseases), depended on anatomic or clinical features. Adjectives such as lobar, lobular, broncho-, interstitial, pleural, double, central, croupous, and catarrhal came into use. Aspiration, contusion, hypostatic, or terminal pneumonias depended upon mechanical factors. Although after 1880 various bacteria and viruses were known to cause pneumonia, modern etiologic classification did not gain popularity until about 1930. More than 50 different microbial, physical, or chemical factors provoke pneumonias, but the incidence of many of these is low. Precise knowledge of the cause permits the use of specific therapeutic or preventive measures and other rational management.

Pneumonias may be grouped as (1) primary pneumonias, *i.e.,* those caused by microbes that attack the lung directly; (2) pneumonias that occur in more or less specific forms during systemic infections and other diseases; (3) pneumonias caused by mixed endogenous infection made possible by previous disease, defect, or injury of the lung, aspiration of foreign material, atelectasis (collapse of the expanded lung), passive congestion, airway obstruction, and by general debility, drug-impaired resistance, and shock; and (4) pneumonias caused by aspiration of oils, chemicals, or dusts, by exposure to X rays, and by allergic reaction.

Pneumococcal Pneumonia.—The modern era of classic lobar pneumonia began after the discovery of pneumococcus in 1880 by G. M. Sternberg, and of its association with pneumonia by A. Fraenkel and A. Weichselbaum in 1884. F. Neufeld in 1910 noted serologic differences among strains of pneumococci which F. S. Lister and A. R. Dochez later classified into specific types. Rufus Cole directed much fundamental work after 1911 at the Hospital of the Rockefeller University, where Oswald Avery was the first to demonstrate deoxyribonucleic acid (DNA) as the genetic determinant of bacterial type transformation. Russell Cecil, O. H. Robertson, and Maxwell Finland in the United States and H. Loeschke and Max Gundel in Germany added more knowledge. The sulfonamide compounds after 1935 and penicillin in 1942 displaced antiserums for treatment.

Etiology.—Of the 75 serotypes and subtypes of pneumococci, types 1 to 8 and 14 account for about 80% of classic lobar pneumonias. Other types, often present normally in the throat, usually cause atypical or bronchopneumonia. Inhaled pneumococci or those resident in a person become invasive when pulmonary resistance is impaired by some preceding condition, especially minor viral infections of the respiratory tract, bodily chilling, thoracic trauma, and debilitation. Resistance lowered by existing chronic conditions and by old age leads to a bronchopneumonia clinically and pathologically unlike the lobar form.

Pathology.—Pneumococci settle and multiply in an area suitable for growth, and cause inflammation conditioned by partial immunity, allergy, and neural influences. Inflammation spreads rapidly and involves part or all of a lobe, first as congestion and then with an accumulation of fibrin, polymorphonuclear leukocytes, and cocci in the alveolar spaces. The exudate soon solidifies, but it softens and is resorbed when recovery occurs. Pneumococci often enter the blood and occasionally localize on the cardiac valves, in the meninges, joints, or peritoneum with serious consequence. Pleural invasion results in empyema.

Epidemiology.—Susceptibility to infection is determined largely by the resistance of the host. The prevalence of pneumonia usually parallels the incidence of minor respiratory tract infections in winter but may occur at any season. Household and institutional epidemics rarely occur. Pneumonia varies in incidence from year to year and somewhat clinically depending on the type of pneumococcus predominant at the time. All races are susceptible. Men are affected oftener than women. The disease is commonest in early adult life. In 1963 pneumonia was the fifth most important cause of death in the United States, with an incidence of 37.5 per 100,000 population in contrast to 202 in 1900 when it headed the list (followed by tuberculosis).

Clinical Features.—Classic (typical) lobar pneumonia often develops during a cold and begins suddenly with a chill, thoracic pain, high fever, cough, and thick brownish sputum. These are present in variable combination and constitute the chief features. Headache, rapid pulse and respiration rates, dyspnea (difficult or laboured breathing), cyanosis, and herpes labialis (cold sores) occur. Illness in untreated patients lasts several days to a week or more. Characteristic early signs in the chest are those of congestion changing to evidence of consolidation of a lobe or lobes and occasionally with pleural friction sounds. Radiography aids in locating and observing the course of the lesion. Signs of fluid appear with pleural effusion or empyema (pus in the pleural cavity). The number of leukocytes and the sedimentation rate of red cells increase and bacteremia often occurs. In decrepit patients the onset is apt to be gradual and the course is irregular and atypical as bronchopneumonia.

Recovery in untreated patients often begins abruptly as a "crisis," with rapid improvement unless other involvement occurs. In fatal cases death results from toxemia, overwhelming infection, circulatory collapse, or extrapulmonary localization—chiefly empyema, meningitis, and endocarditis. Fatalities occur especially in infants, in debilitated or senile patients, in those with other chronic disease, or when antimicrobic (antibiotic) treatment is postponed. Overwhelming infection may be unresponsive to any treatment. The death rate is 30% in untreated patients. Antimicrobic therapy usually is curative within 48 hours and lowers the death rate to about 5% in previously healthy patients. One attack of pneumonia rarely predisposes to another, although some persons, probably due to a hereditary tendency, have repeated attacks caused by the same or by different types of pneumococci or by other bacteria.

Diagnosis is made by clinical, X-ray, and bacteriologic methods. Sputum, blood, or exudate for tests must be obtained before any antimicrobic drug is given.

Treatment.—Penicillin or other antimicrobics, such as lincomycin, cephalothin, tetracycline, or sulfadiazine, must be promptly injected or given orally daily until the temperature becomes normal and for several days afterward. Empyema may need open thoracotomy and drainage. Appropriate symptomatic treatment is essential.

Prevention.—Prophylaxis consists of preventing minor respiratory-tract infections and other conditions that predispose to pneumonia. Pneumococcal polysaccharide vaccine has practical advantage only among small groups of persons who have been exposed to infection.

Hemolytic Streptococcal Pneumonia occasionally complicates influenza, as it did in the pandemic of 1918, or occurs alone sporadically or in small epidemics. Any of the 27 types of group A hemolytic streptococci are causal. The interstitial pulmonic tissue, the bronchi, and the trachea are inflamed as is characteristic of bronchopneumonia. Pleuritis induces massive, thin, bloody exudate containing streptococci.

The disease begins with chills, fever, cough, sore throat, and thoracic pain. Its severity ranges from mild to severe with prostration, ashy pallor or cyanosis, and circulatory failure. The pulmonic signs are those of congestion and later of undeveloped consolidation. The sputum is thin, mucopurulent, bloody, and contains streptococci. Bacteremia (bacteria in the blood) is uncommon. The leukocytes are normal or increased in number.

The mortality rate in untreated patients varies from 10% to 60%; with penicillin therapy, recovery is the rule.

Diagnosis is made chiefly by the epidemiologic characteristics of the disease and by the predominance of hemolytic streptococci in the sputum or by their presence in the blood or exudate. Retrospective diagnosis is made by demonstrating rising titres of specific precipitin or antistreptolysin O in the blood. X rays show the nature and extent of pneumonia and the presence of pleural fluid. Massive pleural effusion should be aspirated repeatedly. Empyema requires closed thoracotomy. Penicillin or alternative drugs must be given in large dosage. During epidemics the prophylactic use of penicillin protects exposed persons.

Staphylococcal Pneumonia, described by Henry T. Chickering in 1919 and by Hobart A. Reimann in 1933, occurs sporadically or in epidemic form during epidemics of viral respiratory-tract disease or during primary septicemia. Many cases occurred during the influenza pandemics of 1918 and 1957. Corticosteroid and radiation therapy given for other diseases also lowers resistance and favours the invasion of aureus and (rarely) albus staphylococci. The cocci usually are those present normally in the patient but they may be acquired from the environment. Infection gives rise to inflammatory areas in the lungs. Later multiple abscesses may form and tend to coalesce, and pneumatoceles occasionally ensue.

Illness usually begins gradually and varies greatly from mild to severe with high remittent fever, chills or chilliness, sweating, cough, purulent sputum, cyanosis, and prostration. The number of leukocytes varies and bacteremia seldom occurs. Abscesses may be resorbed or leave cavities. If they evacuate into the bronchi, the sputum increases in amount and the signs change to those of cavitation. Empyema may occur. The mortality rate is variable; in some cases studied, most patients recovered, in others 70% died.

Diagnosis is based on the epidemiologic aspects, the predominance of staphylococci in the sputum, their presence in exudates or in the blood, the signs and X-ray evidence of patchy pneumonia, and later of abscesses or cavities.

Penicillin must be given in large amounts injected intramuscularly or intravenously. Semisynthetic penicillins, lincomycin, and vancomycin attack staphylococci resistant to penicillin.

Meningococcus and *Mima polymorpha* rarely cause pneumonia.

Gram-Negative Bacillary Pneumonias.—Gram-negative bacilli, as causes of about 3% of pneumonias, gained prominence in the antimicrobic era by supplanting pathogenic cocci eliminated by antimicrobic drugs. Infection occurs chiefly in patients debilitated by chronic disease, old age, alcoholism, trauma, corticosteroid therapy, or radiation therapy. Antimicrobic treatment often is unsuccessful. For these reasons, the mortality rate nears 50% either from the pneumonia or from the underlying trouble. *Klebsiella aerobacter, E. coli, Pseudomonas, Bacteroides, Proteus, Hemophilus, Achromobacter,* and *Serratia marcesens*—bacilli found normally in the respiratory tract or environment—are the invaders. Combinations of microbes often are present in the pneumonic areas as mixed infections.

Most of the entities with a few exceptions have similar clinical and pathologic characteristics. They are nonseasonal and are seldom preceded by minor viral infections. Cough, dyspnea, chills, irregular fever, sweating, stethalgia (pain in the chest), rales, nasopharyngitis, patchy or diffuse lesions of bronchopneumonia, and leukocytosis are common to all. Bacteremia, empyema, and metastatic localization also may occur. Death results from toxemia, exhaustion, and shock. Etiologic diagnosis may be uncertain from sputum examination alone; cultures from the blood, exudates, or lung give conclusive evidence.

Klebsiellar pneumonia differs somewhat with weak lobar consolidation and occasionally viscid, bloody sputum containing the bacilli. Bacteremia, multiple abscesses, and empyema occur. Chronic disease resembles tuberculosis. Lesions caused by *E. coli* and *Ps. aeruginosa* have mononuclear cell infiltrates in pneumonic areas.

Tularemic, tuberculous, brucellar, melioidal, glanders, anthrax, and plague pneumonias are integral parts of the respective systemic infections but the lungs may be involved primarily.

Treatment.—Correction of an underlying condition and symptomatic management are essential. Because most gram-negative bacilli resist most antimicrobic drugs, recovery depends largely on the underlying condition. When tests indicate bacillary sensitivity, the drugs of choice are gentamycin, kanamycin, ampicillin, tetracycline, streptomycin, erythromycin, polymixin, or bacitracin. Many are either ototoxic or nephrotoxic (having toxic effect on the ear or kidneys).

The Viral Pneumonias.—Between 1920 and 1938 European and U.S. radiologists demonstrated pulmonic involvement in occasional patients with colds presumably caused by bacterial super-invasion. Bacteria-free pneumonic lungs found during pandemic influenza in 1918 and the production of pneumonia in animals inoculated with viruses indicated that viruses do cause pneumonia.

In 1938 H. A. Reimann established viral pneumonias as entities representing the severest forms of up to 10% of minor viral respiratory tract infections. One group was caused by influenza viruses, the rest presumably by ones then unknown but later found to be *Mycoplasma pneumoniae.* Thereafter, besides influenza viruses, the adenoviruses, parainfluenza, respiratory syncytial, rhinoviruses, Coxsackie, and ECHO (enteric cytopathogenic human orphan) viruses emerged as causes. Viral pneumonias outnumber those of bacterial origin but usually are overlooked unless X rays are made. Their incidence varies from year to year depending upon the prevalence of the respective minor viral infections.

The symptoms and signs are similar for each entity. Most are inapparent clinically. As a mild cold worsens, malaise, headache, dry paroxysmal cough, pharyngitis, chilliness, sweating, and irregular fever intensify. Because rales and dullness appear late, X rays soon after the onset discover patchy or diffuse pulmonic involvement which may be minimal or surprisingly extensive. Recovery occurs after a week, but illness may become severe, lasting longer with photophobia (abnormal sensitiveness of the eyes to light), dyspnea, cyanosis, and prostration. Complications are rare. The death rate is less than 1%, usually from circulatory failure in decrepit patients. The interstitial pulmonic tissue is invaded by mononuclear cells. The lesion resolves slowly, seldom with sequels.

The pneumonias of measles, vaccinia, and variola are integral parts of the systemic infections and are occasionally complicated by bacterial superinvasion. Cytomegaloviral (giant-cell) pneumonia occurs when resistance is greatly impaired.

Diagnosis is made by epidemiologic aspects, the clinical behaviour, a normal leukocyte count, and sparse sputum minus pathogenic bacteria. Etiologic proof depends upon the identification of the causal viruses and serologic evidence of their activity. Mycoplasmal pneumonia is recognized by the appearance of a hemal cold-agglutinin in 50% of cases after a week or more, by the isolation of the microbe and serologic evidence of its activity. It is important to recognize the similar pneumonias of nonviral mycoplasmosis, psittacosis, ornithosis, rickettsioses, Q fever, toxoplasmosis, pneumocystosis carinii, and of mycoses, which when severe need specific antimicrobic therapy.

Vaccines against most of the infections mentioned are under study. No prophylactic nor therapeutic antiviral agents were available at the beginning of the 1970s. Chemotherapy and prophylaxis are in the experimental stage.

Mycotic Pneumonias.—As in the case of viral diseases, *Histoplasma capsulatum* (predominantly in the Midwestern U.S. and elsewhere in the world) and *Coccidioides immitis* (in the Southwestern U.S.) cause mild respiratory illness occasionally with virallike pneumonia. Pulmonic cavitation may be mistaken for tuberculosis. *Nocardia, Aspergillus, Candida* and others also are causes. Amphotericin B is of therapeutic value but only for severe disease.

Pneumonias in Systemic Diseases.—Pneumonia may dominate the clinical course, or may be a minor feature, or may not occur at all during systemic cytomegalovirosis, measles, and vaccinia, or during systemic infections as already mentioned. Pulmonic involvement also may occur during rheumatic fever, sarcoidosis, polyvasculitis, lupus erythematosus, uremia, helminth infections, and others.

Pneumonias of Mixed Infection.—Injury or defect of the lungs, interference with their self-cleansing process and the iatrogenic reduction of bodily resistance by corticosteroids, radiation, and other factors enables the invasion of microbes normally resident in the air passages. Airway obstruction by foreign bodies or tumours, failing circulation, submersion in or aspiration of fluids, trauma, atelectasis after surgical operation or other cause, senility, chronic illness, shock, coma and many other factors favour infection. Pneumococci, gram-negative bacilli, hemolytic streptococci, staphylococci, viruses, and yeasts are implicated. The treatment is directed primarily to the control or removal of an underlying disorder. Antimicrobic agents are given according to the sensitivity of the invaders, and appropriate supportive measures are applied.

Pneumonias Caused by Noninfective Agents.—The aspiration of bland oils in large amounts, or in small amounts for long periods, causes chronic lipoid pneumonia. Repeated exposure to X rays in some persons gives rise to pneumonitis leading to fibrosis. The inhalation of irritant chemicals (silo filler's disease), oxygen, dusts (farmer's lung, pigeon breeders' disease, byssinosis, bagassosis, berylliosis, pituitary snuff), toxic gases used in warfare or industry, or fumes from certain molten metals may cause pneumonia. Iodism and drugs such as methotrexate, hexamethonium,

nitrofurantoin, hydrallazine, bisulphan, aspirin, and others may cause pneumonialike disease either by direct irritation or by allergy. Allergic pneumonia (Loeffler's syndrome; eosinophilic pneumonia) is a transient reaction after exposure of sensitized tissue to specific antigens. These include drugs, systemic diseases, and many other allergens. Mites and parasites are implicated in the chronic eosinophilic lung. Removal of the offending agent constitutes the prevention and treatment of each of these conditions. Severe allergic reactions are controlled by epinephrine or corticosteroid therapy. *See* also RESPIRATORY SYSTEM, DISEASES OF; DANGEROUS OCCUPATIONS; and references under "Pneumonia" in the Index.

BIBLIOGRAPHY.—R. Heffron, *Pneumonia* (1939); H. A. Reimann, *The Pneumonias* (1938), *Pneumonia*, rev. ed. (1970); J. R. Tillotson and A. M. Lerner, "Pneumonias Caused by Gram Negative Bacilli," *Medicine*, 45:65, 1966.   (H. A. Rn.)

PNEUMOTHORAX. A pneumothorax exists if the two layers of the pleura (*see* COELUM AND SEROUS MEMBRANES) are separated by air and the lung collapses away from the chest wall. This may occur either as the result of trauma to the chest wall (traumatic pneumothorax), after which air penetrates through an opening into the pleural space, or after a spontaneous rupture of the lung (spontaneous pneumothorax), or by injecting air by means of a needle inserted through the chest wall (artificial pneumothorax).

There are three types of pneumothorax: closed, open, and valvular. In the closed pneumothorax the opening through which the air penetrated is closed after the lung collapses, and the air is reabsorbed from the pleural space. In the open pneumothorax the penetration occurs through a wide opening, often a bronchopleural fistula, and does not seal off, but establishes a free two-way connection between the pleural space and the lung (or the exterior). The air pressure in the pneumothorax remains stable at the level of atmospheric pressure. In the valvular pneumothorax the opening is small and acts as a valve, allowing the air to enter the pleural space, but not to leave it, creating an increasing tension (tension pneumothorax). In this type immediate intervention is obligatory.

The traumatic pneumothorax occurs when air is sucked into the pleural space through a penetrating wound in the chest wall (rib fracture, knife stabbing, gunshot wound, etc.). Since the elastic lung tissue contracts toward the mediastinum, principally during expiration, a slightly negative pressure develops in the pleural space, causing this penetration of air.

The spontaneous pneumothorax is caused by the sudden collapse of the lung. Two chief causes are the rupture of a subpleural emphysematous bulla or the rupture of a subpleural tuberculous focus. The precipitating cause is the sudden rise in the intrapleural pressure due to coughing, abnormally deep breathing (*e.g.*, while swimming), heavy weight lifting, etc.

The artificial pneumothorax is now mostly of historic interest. Used first in 1882 by Carlo Forlanini in the treatment of pulmonary tuberculosis, it principally helped to close and allow healing of cavities in the collapsed lung and to occlude small bronchi draining these cavities and spreading the disease. With the advent of chemotherapy and thoracic surgery, there is no indication for the application of an artificial pneumothorax in the modern treatment of tuberculosis.

See M. Pinner, *Pulmonary Tuberculosis in the Adult,* p. 395 (1945); E. H. Rubin, *Diseases of the Chest,* p. 564 (1947).
                                    (R. H. E.; D. K.-W.)

PO (the ancient PADUS), Italy's longest river, rises in the Monte Viso group of the Cottian Alps on Italy's western frontier, and in its uppermost course is a rapid and precipitous stream, descending about 5,500 ft. (1,675 m.) in its first 22 mi. (35 km.). Just west of Saluzzo the Po turns sharply northward, flows through Turin (Torino) and skirts the Monferrato upland, then turns east at Chivasso and continues in a generally easterly course to its delta on the Adriatic. Having received the waters of the Dora Riparia and the Dora Baltea below Turin, the Po has as its principal tributaries the Sesia, Ticino, Adda, Oglio, and Mincio from the north, these contributing most of the river's waters. Among the numerous streams that drain into the Po from the south, the Tanaro (from the Maritime Alps), and the Scrivia and Trebbia (from the Apennines) are important, but many of the others are torrential and carry little water through much of the year.

The length of the Po from its source to its delta, when all meanders are taken into account, is 405 mi. (652 km.). The basin of the river covers 27,062 sq.mi. (70,091 sq.km.). Throughout its middle and lower course, especially downstream from the Sesia confluence, the Po describes many meanders and has left numerous oxbows. The delta is the most complex of any European river, its geologic history showing at least five distinct phases of development. In the 1960s the delta had 14 mouths, usually arranged in five groups, these being (from north to south) the Po di Levante, Po di Maestra, Po della Pila, Po delle Tolle, and Po di Goro e di Gnocca. Of these mouths, the Po della Pila carries the greatest volume of water and is the only navigable one. The river is navigable from its mouth to Pavia. At Pontelagoscuro, 60 mi. from the sea, the average discharge of the Po is 58,800 cu.ft. per sec., with variations from 910 to 340,000 cu.ft. per sec., although in the great flood of 1951 the discharge in the lower river was estimated at 424,000 cu.ft. per sec. The most devastating floods during the Christian era have been those of 589, 1150, 1438, 1882, 1917, 1926, 1951, 1957, and 1966, all in the autumn.

The silt load carried by the river is considerable, and the extension of the delta is estimated at 200 ac. per year. Certain ancient ports south of the delta, such as Ravenna, now find themselves as much as 6 mi. from the sea, as a result of silt from the Po carried down by currents in the Adriatic. The floods of the river and the silt load carried by it have long challenged hydraulic engineers. The Venetian Republic built dikes to control floods and canals to divert silt, and in the area between Ferrara and the Adriatic numerous undertakings have reclaimed thousands of acres during the past three centuries. The most recent of these projects, undertaken in 1953 by the Italian Land Reform, was devoted to soil improvement, reclamation of marshy areas such as the *valli*

AUTHENTICATED NEWS INTERNATIONAL

THE PO RIVER FLOWING THROUGH TURIN

("marshes") of Comacchio, and the creation of small peasant farms in the delta area, or Polesine, an area that nevertheless suffered enormously in the great floods of 1951 and 1966.

The lower valley of the Po was at an early period occupied by people of the Paleolithic and Neolithic stages of civilization, who built houses on piles along the swampy borders of the streams. The river regulation works originated in pre-Roman times. The reclaiming and protecting of the riparian lands went on rapidly under the Romans, and in several places the rectangular divisions of the ground are still distinct. (*See* ESTE.) During the barbarian invasions much of the protective system decayed but the later Middle Ages saw the works resumed, so that the present arrangement existed in the main by the close of the 15th century.

The Ligurian name of the Po was Bodincus or Bodencus; *i.e.*, the bottomless. The name Padus was taken from the Celts or the Veneti. Thus Bodincomagus is found as a town name on the upper course, and Padua as a name of one of the mouths of the river.

See A. Cappellini, *Il Polesine* (1925); J. Popescu *et al.*, "The Po," in *Rivers of the World* (1962). (G. KH.)

POACHING, the stealing of game or fish from land or stretches of water either privately owned or where the shooting, trapping, or fishing rights are specially reserved. Until the 20th century most poaching was subsistence poaching, the taking of

game by impoverished peasants to augment a scanty diet. In medieval Europe feudal landowners, from the king downward, stringently enforced their rights and special laws protected the vast "forests" reserved as royal hunting grounds. Because England was a highly centralized and strongly governed kingdom, a vast amount is known of the working of its forest laws; and for this reason the account of forest and game laws given in the historical sections of this article is based on conditions in England. It may be assumed that landlords in other countries made similar attempts to protect their rights and that poachers equally sought to infringe them. (X.)

Poaching in Medieval Times.—In England, under the Norman kings, large stretches of the countryside were subject to a special law of the forest, intended to preserve the beasts of the chase, the red, fallow, and roe deer, and the wild boar for the king's hunting. The greatest men in the land could hunt in a royal forest only with his permission. The justification for these laws was the need to provide the king with sport, his household with meat, and his government with timber for domestic and defensive building. The royal forests were at their greatest extent under the Norman kings and thenceforward there was continuous conflict between the king, who wished to maintain or extend the area under forest law, and his subjects, who wished to reduce it. The readiness with which the barons, knights, and freemen of a shire combined to secure disafforestation meant that the king could raise considerable sums by selling exemptions from forest law. The extensive forest concessions won by the barons from King John in Magna Carta (*q.v.*) were expanded into a Charter of the Forest in 1217.

Pressure of population gradually eroded the actual area of afforested land. Assarting (ploughing up for crops) reduced the area covered by trees and underwood. Hunting and poaching reduced the animal population. Wild boars were almost exterminated by 1250 and the roe deer ceased to be protected in Edward III's reign because it was said to drive away the other deer. Hares, rabbits, and cats, "beasts of warren," were never protected and the king readily gave landowners permission to hunt them because they disturbed the forest beasts and encroached on their food. Occasionally the king granted a forest to a favoured subject who then had within it all royal rights in regard to hunting and timber and the holding of forest courts. Magnates often enclosed areas of their estates as "parks" for their own hunting, but if these parks were near a royal forest, royal permission was necessary for their enclosure.

Up to 1238 forest law was administered under the ultimate authority of a chief justice of the forest, but in that year England was divided at the River Trent into two regions, each under an officer called a justice or a warden. Under them were wardens, and in each forest generally four verderers, who sat in the attachment courts held every six weeks to deal with those accused of forest offenses. The swanimote court was held in each forest three times a year to regulate the use of the woods within the forest. In the Charter of the Forest (1217), the king promised that "in future no one shall lose life or limb for our venison" (cap. 10), but it remained a serious crime to kill a forest beast. An inquest was held, and the guilty, if found, was imprisoned to await trial. Outside the forest such beasts could be freely hunted provided the king had not granted hunting rights to a subject. But the area of wild country in which the common man could hunt was constantly diminishing. Nevertheless, the forest law was probably more hated by the landowner who could not freely hunt in his own woods than by the humble inhabitants of a forest who enjoyed special rights of collecting deadwood and pasturing their animals. Inherited cunning in the ways of birds, beasts, and fish often helped them to avoid detection in seeking illicit rewards from within the king's forests. (D. M. S.)

The 16th–20th Centuries.—Cumulative destruction of forests, enclosure of wastes, and taking of communal land into private use constituted a long process stretching over several centuries, but as it continued, particularly in the 18th and early 19th centuries, the scope and scale of poaching changed. Private owners of land resented what they thought of as a growing threat to the security of their property and introduced special legislation in the form of game laws. In England, by an act of Charles II (22 & 23 Car. II, cap. 25) it was illegal for anyone to buy and sell game, with the result that prices obtained by well-organized poachers could often stimulate illicit trade. It was also illegal for anyone who was not a squire or a squire's eldest son to kill game even if invited by the owner. During the 18th century the practice of protecting property by gamekeepers increased, although it was claimed that some at least of the gamekeepers were poachers themselves, "taking one brace for the master and two for themselves." Poachers were confronted on the spot by gamekeepers, and in the courts, as the game laws became more severe in the reign of George III, by justices of the peace who were often the owners of the land on which they had been poaching. Farmers were often said to be more sympathetic to poachers than landlords, but the poaching "game" as a whole became far more serious, with landlords and squires insisting on their game rights as a matter of social privilege and with poachers resenting them for this reason.

During the privation years of the late 18th and early 19th centuries, when population was rising sharply, food prices were high, and rural labourers were losing something of their independence, poachers frequently joined together in organized gangs. Fierce battles frequently ensued between gangs and gamekeepers, with shotguns being used at close range and with man-traps and spring guns being placed in brushwood to catch intruders. Transportation was the most severe penalty, one which sympathetic juries were loath to impose, and it is partly because of memories of the severity of this punishment that in Australia bushrangers and cattle thieves became popular heroes. In the United States, where game rights and social privileges were not associated, there was no such hero worship. Although the social exclusiveness of landowners' shooting rights disappeared in England with the Game Act of 1831, it remained in Scotland and Ireland, where poaching was a familiar offense throughout the whole of the 19th century. Nor did a provision in the act of 1831 allowing persons holding game certificates to sell game to persons licensed to deal remove economic incentives to poach for the market. In the long run changes in society and forms of behaviour made poaching offenses a less important element in national crime statistics. Throughout the 19th century attitudes toward poaching remained conditioned by social factors. Landlords emphasized the correlation between poaching and other kinds of social misbehaviour. Opponents of the landed interest identified game laws and corn laws and described both as attempts to protect an antisocial monopoly. Without openly supporting individual poachers, they bitterly attacked "braces of sporting justices." The views and practices of landlords and squires were compared with those of pre-Revolutionary France and the most backward parts of 19th-century feudal Europe. Humanitarians related the incidence of poaching to rural distress and sought to suppress cruel and excessive punishments. On the continent of Europe poaching history was directly related to the history of feudalism; with the abolition of feudalism in France and the diffusion of peasant ownership, poaching became a more specialized activity. (A. Bri.)

Poaching in the Mid-20th Century.—Subsistence poaching largely died out after World War II because living standards rose. Exceptions existed in some parts of eastern Europe where occasional hunger continued to cause peasants from time to time to defy their countries' game laws, and in Africa where illegal killing of horned game for meat remained a problem for conservationists. Elsewhere poaching continued for other reasons. In western Europe and North America the two most powerful remaining incentives to poaching were the commercial profits from large-scale raids by organized gangs and the daredevil aspect of small-scale operations motivated by defiance of the law as well as the desire for sport. Because of the larger concentrations of game there, particularly of winged game, commercial poaching was most highly developed in Britain. The usual method was for car-borne gangs of six or eight men to invade by night the game-holding coverts of properties not less than 100 mi. from their town bases. As many as 500 pheasants in a night were sometimes stolen, thanks

to careful prior reconnaissance, generally by an informer maintained on the spot, perhaps in the guise of a visiting workman. The very high price of salmon early in the open season led to much highly organized river poaching. Generally this was carried out by stunning fish by underwater explosions or by poisoning a river with some asphyxiating agent that kills the fish without harming the flesh. So serious did this poaching become in Scotland that in 1951 the Labour government passed an act drastically increasing the maximum fine for offenses, providing for prison sentences, and authorizing the confiscation of equipment found in the offenders' possession. Pressure continued for the extension of this law to the rest of the United Kingdom. In North America, where the main anxiety was the salmon stock of some rivers near large cities, efficient patrolling by game wardens held market-killing in check. (W. S.)

POBEDONOSTSEV, KONSTANTIN PETROVICH (1827–1907), Russian jurist, civil servant, and political philosopher who exerted a profound reactionary influence on Russian domestic policy from 1880 to 1905, was born in Moscow on Dec.

H. ROGER-VIOLLET

KONSTANTIN PETROVICH POBEDO-NOSTSEV

12 (new style; Nov. 30, old style), 1827. After being educated at home by his father, a professor of Russian literature at Moscow University, Pobedonostsev received training in law in St. Petersburg. He returned to Moscow in 1846 to enter the bureaucracy. A number of articles on the history of Russian law which he published in the late 1850s won him a position as lecturer in Russian law at Moscow University in 1859, and he was soon thereafter named tutor in Russian law and history to the emperor Alexander II's children. His work as a historian of Russian law led him to become an advocate of judicial reform, and from

1861 he participated in preparing the judicial reforms issued in 1864. Gradually, however, he turned against all the reforms of Alexander II, particularly that of the courts. His service as one of the tutors and closest advisers of Alexander III helped make the latter a most reactionary ruler.

Pobedonostsev moved to St. Petersburg in 1865, was nominated to the senate in 1868 and to the council of state in 1872, and became *oberprokuror,* or lay head, of the Holy Governing Synod of the Russian Orthodox Church in 1880. This high position in the government and his great influence over Alexander III and Nicholas II gave Pobedonostsev immense power, which he used in domestic policy, particularly in matters affecting religion, education, and censorship. He was to a large extent responsible for the government's repressive policy toward religious and racial minorities and those who wanted to make Russia more like a Western European state. His influence declined gradually after 1895, but he was so unpopular that he was called the "Grand Inquisitor" and became the symbol of the old regime for all who wanted radical or revolutionary change. He was retired from office during the revolution of 1905.

Pobedonostsev's deep hatred and fear of constitutional and democratic government, freedom of the press, religious freedom, trial by jury, and free lay education was best expressed in a collection of essays, *Moskovski Sbornik* (1896), which has been translated into several Western languages, as also have many of his letters. His three-volume study of Russian civil law, *Kurs grazhdanskago prava* (1868–80), went through several editions and was praised for its careful scholarship. He was a man of great learning, traveled frequently in Western Europe, and spoke many Western languages. He was a close friend of Dostoevski in the 1870s and was highly respected as a scholar and critic before his rise to high state positions. A man of powerful religious fervour, he was especially interested in primary religious education.

Pobedonostsev died in St. Petersburg on March 23 (N.S.; 10, O.S.) 1907.

See F. Steinmann, *K. P. Pobjedonoszew, der Staatsman der Reaktion unter Alexander III* (1933); Robert F. Byrnes, *Pobedonostsev: His Life and Thought* (1968). (R. F. By.)

POCAHONTAS (*c.* 1595–1617), daughter of the North American Indian chief Powhatan and heroine of one of the best-known traditions of early American history. As a young girl she was very helpful to the settlers of the Jamestown colony. In April 1613 she was kidnapped by one of the settlers, Samuel Argall, who hoped to use her to negotiate permanent peace between her tribe and the Virginians. While living in Jamestown she was instructed in Christian doctrine and baptized Rebecca. She married John Rolfe, who introduced the cultivation of tobacco in Virginia. In 1616 the governor of the colony, Sir Thomas Dale, seeing in the adaptable Indian princess an advertisement for the London Company of Virginia, took her and her husband to England, where she was received at court and lionized by London society. On the return voyage she died and was buried at Gravesend. Her one son, Thomas Rolfe, later came to America and settled in Virginia.

Pocahontas' popular fame derives from a story told by Captain John Smith (*q.v.*), one-time leader of the Jamestown settlers. In a letter to the queen at the time of Pocahontas' arrival in London, Smith related that he had been captured by Powhatan's men and was to be put to death; but just as he laid his head on the sacrificial stone and was awaiting death, Pocahontas embraced him and begged her father to spare him. Although this story is consonant with Indian custom and has never been refuted, Smith's habit of self-dramatization and the fact that he failed to include the story in his first account of the Virginia colony (1608) have led some historians to doubt its authenticity. (M. E. Yo.)

BIBLIOGRAPHY.—P. W. Edmunds, *The Pocahontas-John Smith Story* (1956); W. Robertson, *Pocahontas, Alias Matoaka, and Her Descendants* (1887; repr. 1968); G. S. Woodward, *Pocahontas* (1969).

POCATELLO, a city of southeastern Idaho, U.S., the seat of Bannock County, occupies a mountain valley (elevation 4,460 ft. [1,359 m.]) at the mouth of Portneuf Canyon about 15 mi. (24 km.) from the Snake River. Settled in 1882 during railway construction and named for an Indian leader friendly to the whites, Pocatello grew slowly at first because of its location on the Fort Hall Indian Reservation. But its strategic position as a major railway junction brought important Union Pacific shops there in 1887; with the opening of the Fort Hall Reservation to settlement in 1902, Pocatello grew rapidly and became the most prominent railway centre on the Union Pacific between Omaha and Portland. The Academy of Idaho was established in Pocatello in 1901 and began instruction at college level in 1927; the name was changed to Idaho State College in 1947 and to Idaho State University in 1963. Expansion of nearby irrigation helped the city to become a wholesale distributing centre with a variety of manufacturing and agricultural processing plants. An army air base reverted to a municipal airport after World War II, but the community expanded industrially with the acquisition of a large naval ordnance plant in 1942 and of important phosphate reduction works in 1946. The city has a council-manager form of government, in effect since 1951. In 1962 Pocatello was consolidated with Alameda. Pop. (1970) 40,036. For comparative population figures *see* table in IDAHO: *Population.* (M. D. B.)

POCHARD, any diving duck of the tribe Aythyini (*see* DUCK); specifically, a common European duck (*Aythya,* or *Nyroca, ferina*). In the male in full plumage the head is coppery-red, the breast black, and the back and flanks a dull white, closely barred with fine undulating black lines. The tail coverts and quill feathers are black and the lower surface dull white. The female is duller. The pochard breeds throughout much of northern Eurasia, migrating chiefly to southern coasts in winter. Its North American congener is the redhead (*Aythya americana*), a somewhat larger bird. Another American species is the canvasback (*q.v.*).

PO CHÜ-I (A.D. 772–846), one of the outstanding poets of the T'ang period in China, was born at Hsin-cheng in 772. He came of a family of minor officials and rose to high posts in the civil service, entirely owing to his literary talents. In 800 he did well in several examinations at Ch'ang-an (Sian), the capital, and in 806 he obtained a minor post at a small place near Ch'ang-an. In the next year he was summoned to Ch'ang-an and became a member of the Han-lin academy. In 811 his mother died and he fulfilled his mourning at a village to the east of the capital. He returned to court in 812 and took an active part in politics. In 814 he was suddenly relegated to a minor post at Kiukiang (Chiuchiang), on the Yangtze River. What led to this banishment is far from clear. Po himself regarded it as due to the jealousy of senior statesmen over whose heads he had been promoted. In 818 he became governor of Chung-chou, high up the Yangtze. When in 820 a new emperor came to the throne, Po was recalled to the capital, where he resumed his previous task of composing imperial letters and rescripts. In 822 he became governor of the important town of Hangchow and then of Soochow. He was summoned back to the capital in 827 and became head of the imperial library. In 829 he settled permanently at the eastern capital, Lo-yang, and in 831 became mayor of the city. In 833 he retired from this post owing to illness and lived uneventfully at Lo-yang till 839, when he had a paralytic stroke, from which he never fully recovered. He died there in the autumn of 846.

There were in Po's day no organized political parties, but there was a loose cleavage between those who rose owing to family influence and those who made their way to the top solely by literary eminence and success in examinations. Po Chü-i belonged to the latter class and was at loggerheads with some of the most bigoted members of the aristocratic clique. But no hard and fast line divided the two groups and some of his best friends were in the opposite camp. Two outstanding features of his life were his devotion to Buddhism and his friendship with Yüan Chen, one of the most famous friendships in Chinese history. *See* also CHINESE LITERATURE.

See A. Waley, *The Life and Times of Po Chü-i* (1949). (A. D. Wa.)

POCKET MOUSE, the name of a number of small, mouse-like, western North American rodents belonging to the subfamily Perognathinae of the family Heteromyidae and including several genera, all with fur-lined external cheek pouches. The typical pocket mice (*Perognathus*) are small, with rather long tails and hind feet. They live in deserts and on the Great Plains, feeding on seeds. *Heteromys* and *Liomys,* the spiny pocket mice (subfamily Heteromyinae), have bristles mixed in the coat. They are dark gray or blackish in colour. Most species of these two genera are Central American, extending to northern South America. *See* also RODENT. (J. E. Hl.; X.)

POCKET VETO, the term applied when legislation is killed because of the failure to act by the chief executive before the adjournment of the legislature. In the United States, if a bill is sent to the president and he does not sign it within ten days, it automatically becomes law. Should Congress adjourn, however, within the ten-day period and the president has retained the bill unsigned, it is automatically vetoed, and the veto is absolute. The latter action is then known as the pocket veto. *See* also the article VETO.

POCOCKE, EDWARD (1604–1691), English orientalist and biblical scholar, who introduced the study of Arabic at Oxford and collected many valuable ancient manuscripts, was born, the son of a Berkshire clergyman, at Oxford and baptized Nov. 8, 1604. He was educated at Corpus Christi College, Oxford. He served as English chaplain at Aleppo (1630–35) and on his return to England was appointed first professor of Arabic at Oxford, succeeding to the chair of Hebrew in 1648. Pococke discovered in a manuscript at the Bodleian Library at Oxford the missing Syriac versions of the four New Testament epistles (II Peter, II and III John, and Jude) which were not in the old Syriac canon; his edition of these was published at Leiden in 1630. In 1649 he published *Specimen historiae arabum,* a short account of the origin and manners of the Arabs, followed in 1655 by *Porta Mosis,* extracts from the Arabic commentary of Maimonides on the Mishna, with translation and notes. His *magnum opus*—a complete edition of the Arabic history of Bar-Hebraeus, with a Latin translation, was dedicated to the king in 1663. Pococke died on Sept. 10, 1691.

See L. Twells (ed.), *Theological Works of the Learned Dr. Pocock*, 2 vol. (1740), which contains a biography.

PODEBRADY, GEORGE OF (Czech Jiří z Poděbrad) (1420–1471), king of Bohemia from 1458, was born at Podebrady, ENE of Prague, on April 23, 1420, the son of Viktorin of Kunstat and Podebrady, a Czech nobleman who was a leader of "the Orphans," or moderate Taborites, in the Hussite wars (*see* Bohemia; Hussites). George early became prominent in the party organized, chiefly by the Utraquist Hussites, to promote the Bohemian national cause; and when Ptacek of Pirkstejn died (1444) he was recognized as its head. Meanwhile the prospective king of Bohemia, Ladislav (the Habsburg Ladislas Posthumus; *see* Laszlo V of Hungary), was still a minor; and in 1448 George, having raised a force of 9,000 men in northeastern Bohemia, where his ancestral castle stood and where his party was strongest, occupied Prague. He subsequently defeated the Romanist or pro-Habsburg (Austrian) party led by Oldrich of Rozmberk; and in 1451 Ladislav's guardian, the future Holy Roman emperor Frederick III, entrusted George with the administration of Bohemia. In the same year a diet at Prague appointed George regent of Bohemia for Ladislav.

When Ladislav began to rule in his own name (1453), George's position became difficult, since the king sympathized strongly with the Catholics in the continuing religious struggle, though he undertook to respect the ancient rights of Bohemia and the *Compactata* or "compacts" whereby the claims of the Utraquists had been acknowledged. Ladislav, however, died suddenly in 1457. Hostile opinion from an early date accused George of having poisoned him; but the charge is undoubtedly false.

On March 2, 1458, the Bohemian estates unanimously elected George as king, even the Romanists voting for him. His rule, however, was obstructed by the hostility of the new pope, Pius II. George refused the pope's demand that the compacts should be abolished, but tried to placate him by measures against the most extreme enemies of the papacy, including the newly founded community of the Bohemian Brethren. Even so, Pius was planning a crusade against Bohemia when he died (1464). Though Bohemia itself prospered under George, malcontent nobles of the Romanist party formed a confederacy against him at Zelena Hora (Nov. 28, 1465), which the new pope, Paul II, supported. On Dec. 23, 1466, Paul excommunicated George and pronounced him deposed from the kingship, forbidding all Catholics to continue their allegiance to him. The emperor Frederick III and George's former ally Matthias Corvinus of Hungary joined the insurgents, and Matthias, having conquered much of Moravia, was proclaimed king of Bohemia at Brno on May 3, 1469. War went on till George died, in Prague, on March 22, 1471.

PODESTA (Latin *potestas*, "power"), the highest magistrate of medieval Italian communes. The emperor Frederick I Barbarossa appointed imperial *podestàs* in most Italian cities under his control (*see* Italy: *History*); but from the end of the 12th century onward, *podestàs* elected by the communes themselves gradually superseded the collegiate government of the consuls (*see* Commune [Medieval]). Normally a nobleman from another city or, sometimes, from a neighbouring feudal family, the *podestà* was at first usually elected for one year, later often for six months. He summoned the councils, led the communal army, and administered civil and criminal jurisdiction. Though the office was subject to strict statutory limitations, it sometimes served as a starting point for the establishment of a despotic government or *signoria*. After the 13th century, it declined in importance; in 15th-century Florence, its principal functions were judicial.

Podestà was the title of mayors in the Austrian territories of Italy from 1815 to 1918; and of mayors appointed by the Italian government between 1926 and the end of the Fascist regime.

Bibliography.—E. Salzer, *Über die Anfänge der Signorie in Oberitalien* (1900); G. Hanauer, "Das Berufspodestat im dreizehnten Jahrhundert," *Mitteilungen des Instituts für österreichische Geschichtsforschung*, 33 (1902); F. Hertter, *Die Podestàliteratur Italiens im 12. und 13. Jahrhundert* (1910).

PODGORICA: *see* Titograd (Yugos.).

PODIATRY (Chiropody) is the healing art concerned with the human foot. The Ebers medical papyrus (*c.* 1500 B.C.) records foot remedies from earlier centuries. Other references are found in the literature of all succeeding cultures. The word chiropody derives from a 1774 treatise, *Chiropodologia*, by D. Low, of London, where a Dr. Lyons in 1785 applied for a licence limited to practice on the feet. The term podiatry was coined in 1917 by M. J. Lewi of New York.

The first practice act was enacted in New York State in 1895, and by 1938 all the states of the United States, Canada, the United Kingdom, Australia, and New Zealand had licensure provisions. In the United States the National Association of Chiropodists was organized in 1912 and adopted the name American Podiatry Association in 1958. In Great Britain chiropodists function under the national health service. The first college of podiatry was organized in 1912.

Podiatrists diagnose and treat by medical, surgical, and other means diseases and deformities of the human foot; they utilize mechanical devices, special shoes, physiotherapy, pharmaceuticals, and surgery. (A. Ru.)

PODIUM, in architecture, a continuous pedestal, a low wall supporting columns, or the lowest portion of the wall of a building when given a separate architectural treatment. Sometimes the basement story of a classic building may be treated as a podium. The podium is usually designed with a molded base and plinth at the bottom, a central plane surface known as a die, or dado, and a projecting cornice or cap. The majority of Etruscan and Roman temples were raised on podiums, and the entrance steps ascended between wing walls, which were the continuations of the podium at the sides. By extension the term has been applied to other raised platforms, particularly those used by orchestra conductors.

PODOCARPACEAE, a family of conifers consisting of large trees and shrubs, found predominantly in the southern hemisphere. Many are cultivated for ornament and some are important as timber trees in Australia. The seven genera commonly admitted are *Pherosphaera, Microcachrys, Saxegothaea, Dacrydium, Acmopyle, Podocarpus* and *Phyllocladus*. All occur in the Australasian region except *Saxegothaea*, which is South American; *Podocarpus* and *Dacrydium* also extend their range to that continent. The Podocarpaceae are usually dioecious (having separate male and female plants) and have leaves variously awl-shaped, needlelike or broad, with many parallel veins. In the genus *Phyllocladus*, the foliar leaves are replaced by flattened branchlets (phylloclades) resembling leaves. The staminate, or pollen-bearing, cones are borne in a terminal or axillary position on leafy twigs, each scale bearing two pollen sacs. The ovulate, or seed-bearing, cones may have numerous scales but usually are reduced to one or a few scales with a single ovule and several sterile scales below. At maturity the latter become fleshy and sometimes brightly coloured and surmount the fleshy cone axis. There are two cotyledons (seed leaves) in the mature embryo. *See also* Conifers. (R. W. H.)

PODOLIA, an area of western Ukraine south of Volhynia. Extending between the Rivers Dniester and Southern Bug as far as the old Polish frontier of 1772, it is essentially a plateau cut by deep canyons or *yars* of many left-bank tributaries of the Dniester—all flowing from north to south. The name appeared in the 14th century when, after King Casimir III's incorporation of Galicia (1349), Poland began to colonize the steppe lying to the southeast, transforming it gradually into rich arable land. Under Polish rule Podolia was divided between the *wojewodztwa* of Kamieniec Podolski and Braclaw. In 1772 the part west of the Zbrucz (Zbruch) River became Austrian, the rest Russian. The Russian part formed the Podolian *gubernya*. After World War I the Zbrucz was the frontier between the restored Poland and the U.S.S.R., but after World War II all Podolia became part of the U.S.S.R. It was then divided between the *oblasti* of Ternopol (Tarnopol), Khmelnitski, and Vinnitsa. Its population had always a Ukrainian majority. (K. Sm.)

PODOLSK, a town in Moscow Oblast of the Russian Soviet Federated Socialist Republic of the U.S.S.R., 40 km. (25 mi.) due south of Moscow, on the right bank of the Pakhra River, a tributary of the Moskva. Pop. (1970 prelim.) 169,000. The village of Podol, created a town in 1781, owed its development to its position on the main highway running south from Moscow. In the 1860s the main railway to the south was built through Podolsk and on to Tula, and industry developed. Sewing machines, steam boilers, ventilating equipment, and cables are manufactured. There are also nonferrous metallurgical and food-processing industries, and cement is made from local limestones.   (R. A. F.)

PODOSTEMONACEAE, the river weed family of dicotyledonous plants, a remarkable group living only on rocks in rushing streams. The seeds are shed on the rocks during the dry season, and germinate when the rocks become submerged in the rainy season. The vegetative parts consist mainly of a flattened green thallus, usually derived from adventitious roots. There are more than 40 genera and about 140 species, nearly all tropical; a single representative, *Podostemon ceratophyllum* (river weed), occurs in North America, in shallow streams from Quebec southward to Georgia and Arkansas.

For a treatment of the genera, *see* A. Engler, "Podostemonaceae" in A. Engler and K. Prantl, *Natürlichen Pflanzenfamilien,* 2nd ed., 18a: 3–68, fig. 1–61 (1930).

POE, EDGAR ALLAN (1809–1849), U.S. poet, critic, and short-story writer, who cultivated the literature of mystery and the macabre, was born Jan. 19, 1809, in Boston, Mass. He was the son of the English-born actress Elizabeth Arnold Poe and David Poe, Jr., an actor from Baltimore. After his mother died in Richmond, Va., in 1811, the boy was taken into the home of the Richmond merchant John Allan, presumably his godfather, and his childless wife. He was taken to Scotland and England (1815–20), where he was given a classical education that was continued in Richmond. For 11 months in 1826 he attended the University of Virginia, where he studied Greek, Latin, French, Spanish, and Italian; but his gambling losses at the university so incensed his guardian that he refused to let him continue, and Poe returned to Richmond to find his sweetheart, Elmira Royster, engaged. Poe went to Boston where he published a pamphlet of youthful Byronic poems, *Tamerlane and Other Poems* (1827), some of which concern Elmira. Poverty forced him to join the army under the name of Edgar A. Perry, but on the death of his foster mother Allan purchased his release from the army, and helped in getting him an appointment to the U.S. Military Academy at West Point, N.Y. Before going, Poe published a new volume at Baltimore, *Al Aaraaf, Tamerlane and Minor Poems* (1829), show-

BY COURTESY OF BROWN UNIVERSITY, PROVIDENCE

EDGAR ALLAN POE, DAGUERREOTYPE BY S. W. HARTSHORN DATED 1848

ing the influence of the local poet E. C. Pinkney and an awakened interest in Milton and Thomas Moore. He successfully sought expulsion from the academy, where he was absent from all drills and classes for a week. He proceeded to New York City and brought out a volume of *Poems* (1831), containing several masterpieces, some showing the influence of Keats, Shelley, and Coleridge. He then returned to Baltimore, where he began to write stories. The rumour that he was again in the army under another name in 1832 seems credible. In 1833 his "Manuscript found in a Bottle" won $50 from a Baltimore weekly, and by 1835 he was in Richmond as editor of the *Southern Literary Messenger.* There he made a name as a critical reviewer and married his young cousin Virginia Clemm, who was only 13. Poe seems to have been an affectionate husband and son-in-law and wrote the tribute "Sonnet to My Mother" to his aunt, Mrs. Clemm, in 1849.

Poe was dismissed from his job in Richmond, apparently for drinking, and went to New York. His drinking was the bane of his life. To talk well in a large company he needed a slight stimulant, but a glass of sherry might start him on a spree; and although he rarely succumbed, he was often seen in public when he did. Medical testimony is that Poe was not a drug addict, but had had a brain lesion. While in New York he published a long prose narrative, *The Narrative of Arthur Gordon Pym* (1838), combining (as so often in his tales) much factual material with the wildest fancies. It is considered one inspiration of Melville's *Moby Dick.* In 1839 he began editing *Burton's Gentleman's Magazine* in Philadelphia. There a contract for a monthly feature stimulated him to write "William Wilson" and "The Fall of the House of Usher"—stories of supernatural horror. The latter contains a study of a neurotic now known to have been an acquaintance of Poe, not Poe himself.

Later in 1839 his *Tales of the Grotesque and Arabesque* appeared (dated 1840). He resigned from *Burton's* about June 1840 but returned in 1841 to edit its successor, *Graham's Magazine,* in which he printed the first detective story, "The Murders in the Rue Morgue." In 1843 his "The Gold Bug" won a prize of $100 from the *Philadelphia Dollar Newspaper,* which gave him great publicity. In 1844 he returned to New York, wrote the "Balloon Hoax" for the *Sun,* and became subeditor of the *Evening Mirror* under N. P. Willis, thereafter another lifelong friend. In the *Evening Mirror* of Jan. 29, 1845, appeared, from advance sheets of the *American Review,* his most famous poem, "The Raven," which gave him national fame at once. Poe then became editor of the *Broadway Journal,* a short-lived weekly in which he republished most of his short stories, in 1845. During this year the poet Frances Sargent Osgood pursued Poe. Virginia did not object, but "Fanny's" indiscreet writings about her literary love caused great scandal. His *The Raven and Other Poems* and a selection of his *Tales* came out in 1845, and in 1846 Poe moved to a cottage at Fordham (now part of New York City), where he wrote for *Godey's Lady's Book* (May–October 1846) on the "Literati of New York"— gossipy sketches on personalities of the day which led to a libel suit.

His wife, Virginia, died in January 1847. In 1848 Poe went to Providence, R.I., to woo the poet Helen Whitman. There was a brief engagement. Poe had close but platonic entanglements with Annie Richmond and with Sarah Anna Lewis, who helped him financially. He composed poetic tributes to all of them. In 1848 also he published the lecture *Eureka,* a transcendental "explanation" of the universe, which has been hailed as a masterpiece by some critics and as nonsense by others. In 1849 he went south, had a wild spree in Philadelphia but got safely to Richmond, where he again became engaged to Elmira Royster, by then the widowed Mrs. Shelton, and spent a happy summer with only one or two relapses. He enjoyed the companionship of childhood friends and an unromantic friendship with a young poet, Susan Archer Talley.

Poe had some forebodings of death when he left Richmond for Baltimore late in September. There he toasted a lady at her birthday party and began to drink heavily. The indulgence proved fatal, for Poe had a weak heart. He died on Oct. 7, 1849, and was buried in Westminster Presbyterian churchyard in Baltimore.

Appraisal.—Poe's work owes much to the drift of romanticism, of which he was a late heir, toward the occult and satanic. It owes much also to his own feverish dreams, to which he applied a rare faculty of shaping plausible fabrics out of impalpable materials. With an air of objectivity and spontaneity, his productions are closely dependent on his own idiosyncrasy and an elaborate technique. His keen and sound judgment as appraiser of contemporary literature, his idealism and musical gift as a poet, his weirdness and dramatic power as a storyteller, considerably appreciated in his lifetime, secured him a prominent place among universally known men of letters.

The outstanding fact in Poe's character is a strange duality. The wide divergence of contemporary judgments on the man seems to point to the coexistence in him of two persons. With those he loved he was gentle and devoted. Others, who were the butt of his sharp criticism, found him irritable and self-centred and went so far as to accuse him of lack of principle. Was it, in the latter case, a double of the man rising from harrowing nightmares, or from the haggard inner vision of dark crimes, or from appalling graveyard fantasies that loomed in Poe's unstable being?

Much of Poe's best work is concerned with terror and sadness, but in ordinary circumstances the poet was a pleasant companion. He talked brilliantly, chiefly of literature, and read his own poetry and that of others in a voice of surpassing beauty. He admired Shakespeare and Alexander Pope. He had a sense of humour, apologizing to a visitor for not keeping a pet raven. If the mind of Poe is considered, the duality is still more striking. On one side, he was an idealist and a visionary. His yearning for the ideal was both of the heart and of the imagination. His sensitiveness to the beauty and sweetness of women inspired his most touching lyrics ("To Helen," "Annabel Lee," "Eulalie," "To One in Paradise") and the full-toned prose hymns to beauty and love in "Ligeia" and "Eleonora." In "Israfel" his imagination carried him away from the material world into a dreamland. This Pythian mood was especially characteristic of the later years of his life.

More generally, in such verses as "Valley of Unrest," "Lenore," "The Raven," "For Annie," and "Ulalume" and in his prose tales, his familiar mode of evasion from the universe of common experience was through eerie thoughts, impulses, or fears. From these materials he drew the startling effects of his tales of death ("The Fall of the House of Usher," "The Masque of the Red Death," "Valdemar," "Premature Burial," "Oval Portrait," "Shadow"), his tales of wickedness and crime ("Berenice," "Black Cat," "William Wilson," "Imp of the Perverse," "Cask of Amontillado," "Tell-Tale Heart"), his tales of survival after dissolution ("Ligeia," "Morella," "Metzengerstein"), and his tales of fatality ("Assignation," "Man of the Crowd"). Even when he does not hurl his characters into the clutch of mysterious forces or onto the untrodden paths of the beyond, he uses the anguish of imminent death as the means of causing the nerves to quiver ("The Pit and the Pendulum"), and his grotesque inventions deal with corpses and decay in an uncanny play with the aftermath of death.

On the other side, Poe is conspicuous for a close observation of minute details, as in the long narratives and in many of the descriptions that introduce the tales or constitute their settings. Closely connected with this is his power of ratiocination. He prided himself on his logic and carefully handled this real accomplishment so as to impress the public with his possessing still more of it than he had; hence the would-be feats of thought reading, problem unraveling, and cryptography which he attributed to his Legrand and Dupin. This suggested to him the analytical tales, which introduced into literature the detective story, and his tales of pseudoscience.

The same duality is evinced in his art. He was capable of writing angelic or weird poetry, with a supreme sense of rhythm and word appeal, or prose of sumptuous beauty and suggestiveness, with the apparent abandon of compelling inspiration; yet he would write down a problem of morbid psychology or the outlines of an unrelenting plot in a hard and dry style. In Poe's masterpieces the double contents of his temper, of his mind, and of his art are fused into a oneness of tone, structure, and movement, the more effective, perhaps, as it is compounded of various elements that give depth and intensity to the total sheen or dismal glow.

As a critic Poe laid great stress upon correctness of language, metre, and structure. He formulated rules for the short story, in which he sought for the unities of time, place, and action, and added that of mood or effect. He regarded didacticism as not necessary, and so was a leading advocate of art for art's sake. He was not extreme in these views, however. He praised longer works and sometimes thought allegories and morals admirable if not crudely presented. Poe admired originality, often in work very different from his own, and was sometimes an unexpectedly generous critic of decidedly minor writers.

Poe's genius was recognized abroad. No one did more to persuade the world and, in the long run, the United States, of Poe's greatness than Baudelaire and Mallarmé.

See also AMERICAN LITERATURE: *Early 19th Century;* MYSTERY AND DETECTIVE STORIES.

BIBLIOGRAPHY.—The best biographies of Poe are by G. E. Woodberry, *Life of Edgar Allan Poe,* 2 vol. (1909) ; A. H. Quinn, *Edgar Allan Poe* (1941) ; and V. Buranelli, *Edgar Allan Poe* (1961). The first biographer, R. W. Griswold (1850), blackened Poe's character; the most popular, Hervey Allen's *Israfel,* 2 vol. (1926), is partly fictionalized. Mary E. Phillips, *Edgar Allan Poe, the Man,* 2 vol. (1926), uncritically collects much information. Most noteworthy perhaps among the many other books on Poe are Arthur Ransome, *Edgar Allan Poe* (1910) ; and N. B. Fagin, *Histrionic Mr. Poe* (1949).

(C. C.; T. O. M.)

POERIO, ALESSANDRO (1802–1848) and **CARLO** (1803–1867), brothers distinguished for their services to liberalism in the Italian Risorgimento, were the sons of Baron Giuseppe Poerio, a Neapolitan lawyer well known for his own liberal sympathies.

ALESSANDRO was born in Naples on Aug. 27, 1802. Having been taken into exile by his father on the Bourbon restoration in 1815 (*see* NAPLES, KINGDOM OF), he returned to Naples in 1818 and was able in 1821 to enlist as a volunteer in the army; he fought against the Austrians at Rieti. After this defeat he again went with his family into exile and traveled in Germany, where he became the friend of Goethe. He began to write poetry, which was highly esteemed though its bulk was small because of his perfectionism. His writings had great inspirational importance during the Risorgimento. When the family was again allowed to come back to Naples (1833), Alessandro came with them. In 1848 he again volunteered to fight the Austrians (*see* ITALIAN INDEPENDENCE, WARS OF) and died in Venice on Nov. 3 of wounds received at Mestre.

CARLO was born in Naples on Oct. 13, 1803. He shared in the exiles of his family, and when he returned to Naples in 1833 he was an object of constant suspicion, though he was careful to play no part in politics. He was arrested in 1837, 1844, and 1847. In the revolution of 1848 he helped to formulate the demands of the constitutionalists and then became at first director of police and afterward minister of education in the Liberal government. After his resignation in May 1848 he led the constitutional opposition. He was again arrested in July 1849, but was not tried until February 1851, when he was sentenced with his fellow Liberals to 24 years in irons. The illegality of the trials, the atrocious sentences, and the sufferings of the prisoners horrified the visiting English politician W. E. Gladstone (*q.v.*), who denounced the conditions of the Neapolitan prisons in his two *Letters to Lord Aberdeen* (July 1851) and so made Poerio's case notorious throughout Europe. Poerio was not released until January 1859 and then made his way to London. After the outbreak of war between Sardinia-Piedmont and Austria he went to Turin (Torino). A deputy in the Parliament of the new Kingdom of Italy (1861), he later refused a governmental portfolio. He died in Florence on April 28, 1867, of a complaint contracted during his imprisonment.

BIBLIOGRAPHY.—A. V. del Giudice, *I Fratelli Poerio* (1899) ; G. Secrétant, *Alessandro Poerio* (1912) ; M. Cocco, *Alessandro Poerio* (1950).

(J. M. Rs.)

POETIC IMAGERY. The term "poetic imagery" may be considered as including all possible methods of making the kind of statement by which one thing is perceived as resembling, or in terms of, another. These may be compressed into three broad classifications: simile, metaphor, and symbol (*see also* FIGURES OF SPEECH). The simile, introduced by "like" or "as," indicates a specific and unequivocal correspondence; its variant, the so-called Homeric or epic simile, is merely a passage of greater or less length introduced by "as" or "like" and bound into the main narrative by "so" or some equivalent. Metaphor also involves such a correspondence, but here the statement is direct, without the introductory "like" or "as"; the reader is invited to infer the poet's intention by an effort of his own imagination and to set up, as it were, a fusion between the object and the image. The symbol carries the method a stage further, calling for a more intense and subtle imagination and often employing a system of correspondences of great complexity.

From classical times the making of images has been recognized as a central poetic activity. Aristotle pointed out that the capacity for making metaphors was the mark of the superior poet, Shelley that the language of poetry was "vitally metaphorical." Longinus devoted 17 chapters of his treatise *On the Sublime* to a consideration of the "figures" of speech. The methods of using them were elaborated and analyzed by the classical rhetoricians (*see* RHETORIC), and passed into English criticism with the Renaissance. Such analysis belongs to a method of poetic composition that is only of academic interest to modern critics and writers; and its terms have only a limited critical application. Here an attempt must be made to return to first principles.

The object or experience that the poet is contemplating is perceived by him in a relationship to some second object or event, person or thing, to which he directs attention. By this act he may be thought to transfer from this image certain qualities which are then perceived as attributes of the original object; the poet's intention being to decorate, illuminate, emphasize, or renew by such transferences the original character of that which he contemplates. The making or finding of the image is an activity by which the poet is inviting the reader to establish certain relationships, which in turn involve judgments of value. Image and symbol are, in one sense, the outcome of the poet's impulse to perceive unity in diversity, or to draw together a number of apparently unrelated experiences, or to communicate through their submerged or penumbral statements meanings that are beyond the resources of direct language. Images also differ in the depth or profundity or complexity of the meanings implied, as well as in their purpose and origin; and they may derive additional force and vitality from their contextual relation to other images in the poem, from the tradition in which the poet is working, and from the meanings which he may have established in his other work. All may be modified by the usual methods of poetic technique; they may become charged with special significance or interact one upon another.

In making these comparisons the "gap" between the object and the image will vary; if this gap is small, so that the least possible imaginative effort is needed to bridge it, the image may soon become "dead" or ineffectual, as with much "household" or proverbial imagery; for instance, "black as pitch," "sharp as a needle," "dumb as an ox." If the gap is too wide, the imagination may refuse to bridge it, and the comparison fails in its purpose. Good metaphysical imagery, at its best, involves a gap that is wide enough to startle the reader into attention, yet not so wide as to frustrate the imaginative effort. Bad metaphysical imagery, on the other hand, may become ineffective because the comparison is too remote, fantastic, or unduly cerebral in its origins; hence Dr. Johnson's famous stricture on Abraham Cowley: "The most heterogeneous ideas are yoked by violence together." Both good and bad categories are included in the term "conceit," meaning any farfetched comparison; that it is not necessarily used with pejorative intention can be seen from Dr. Johnson's comment on the metaphysical poets: "If their conceits were far-fetched, they were often worth the carriage."

Examples of unsuccessful metaphysical imagery are to be found in Joseph Addison's "Essay on True and False Wit" (*Spectator*, No. 62):

The passion of love in its nature has been thought to resemble fire; for which reason the words fire and flame are made use of to signify love. The witty poets therefore have taken an advantage from the doubtful meaning of the word fire, to make an infinite number of witticisms. Cowley, observing the cold regard of his mistress's eyes, and at the same time their power of producing love in him, considers them as burning-glasses made of ice; and finding himself able to live in the greatest extremes of love, concludes the Torrid Zone to be habitable. When his mistress has read his letter written in juice of lemon by holding it by the fire, he desires her to read it over a second time by love's flames. . . . Sometimes he is drowned in tears, and burnt in love, like a ship set on fire in the middle of the sea.

The foregoing aspects of poetic imagery may be illustrated by quotations of varying degrees of complexity. The simplest type of simile occurs in the lines:

Set me as a seal upon your heart, as a seal upon your arm;
for love is strong as death, jealousy is cruel as the grave.
(Song of Solomon, 8:6)

In the following simile from Bishop Henry King's *Exequy* on the death of his young wife, we are aware of a greater depth:

But hark! My pulse, like a soft drum,
Beats my approach, tells *Thee* I come . . . .
(Bishop Henry King, *The Exequy*, c. 1624)

since the "*soft drum,*" in conjunction with the "*approach,*" suggests both the advance party of the army nearing the billets for the night and the slow, inexorable, and welcome progress to death and reunion. When John Donne uses the metaphor of "*spider love*" in "Twicknam Garden":

But O selfe-traytor, I do bring
The *spider love,* which transubstantiates all,
And can convert Manna to gall . . . .

we can distinguish several differing overtones of meaning: the web or net (and perhaps a hair-image behind that), the destruction of male by female, voraciousness, subtlety, patience, the Elizabethan lore of the poisonous spider, the peculiar force of the theological "transubstantiates" in conjunction with "manna" and "gall," which themselves have a double biblical reference. But there is a wholly different usage or invention of the metaphor in the following passage from "Solomon and the Witch" by W. B. Yeats, in which some of the connotations of "*spider*" mentioned above are joined by the new idea of the spider's "*eye*" with its host of magnifying lenses:

For though love has a spider's eye
To find out some appropriate pain—
Aye, though all passion's in the glance—
For every nerve, and tests the lover
With cruelties of Choice and Chance . . .
(Reprinted with permission of the publisher from
The Collected Poems of W. B. Yeats. Copyright
1924 by The Macmillan Company. Renewed 1952
by Bertha Georgie Yeats.)

Many metaphors are used for the human body, such as "the vessel of clay," "the soul's dark cottage," the dungeon in which the soul is imprisoned. It may also be regarded as something "woven" or "knotted"; thus Donne's

As our blood labours to beget
Spirits, as like souls as it can,
Because such fingers need to knot
This *subtle knot,* which makes us man . . . .
(*The Ecstasy*)

or Cleopatra's

Come, thou mortal wretch
With thy sharp teeth this *knot intrinsicate*
Of life at once untie.
(*Antony and Cleopatra*, Act V, scene 2, ll. 306–308)

Sometimes we have a system of technical references which (depending on the degree to which we are prepared to consider and accept such technicalities) may succeed as an image or fail as a conceit; as in Shakespeare's *King John:*

The tackle of my heart is crack'd and burn'd
And all the shrouds wherewith my life should sail
Are turned to one thread, one little hair . . . .
(Act V, scene 7, ll. 52–54)

where the normal image of the voyage of life is "compounded" with the details of seamanship, Elizabethan physiology (the "heartstrings"), and perhaps the familiar image of the "thin-spun thread" of life.

The metaphor shades into the symbol; and if the same image is used consistently throughout a poem it may be appropriate to call it a symbol. It may be thought of also in terms of correspondences; a person, event, object, or myth is perceived by the poet to embody a number of significances, to which he directs the reader's attention. Religious symbols offer the most familiar examples: *e.g.*, cross, cup, lamb, rose, candle. Birds, beasts and reptiles, the heavenly bodies, sea and desert, forest and river, music and dance, artifacts of many kinds are symbols often used in poetry. If we contrast these symbols with metaphor, we may recognize correspondences involving a far more complicated series of meanings. The poet will justify himself by asserting that these meanings can be communicated in this manner and in no other; they are not susceptible to analysis. In this lies a danger; for in the interpretation of many symbols, and of some metaphors, there is an element which is in part subjective. This gives rise to the accusation of impreciseness often leveled against certain types of symbolism, as well as to variations in exegetical findings among critics (*see* TEXTUAL CRITICISM).

The field of symbolism is one of immense complexity, and here again illustrations must be arbitrary. The tower appears traditionally in many forms; as man's aspiration toward heaven, as a defense or refuge, as an expression of his pride or defiance. We may think of Milton's poet-scholar in the "high lonely tower" of "Il Penseroso" or of Shelley's *Prince Athanase*. The tower may have many ancillary aspects: an upper room lit by night (for the dissemination of wisdom and learning); its battlements may be defensible or in decay; the poet may emphasize aspects of its winding stair. To quote Yeats:

> I declare this tower is my symbol; I declare
> This winding, gyring, spiring treadmill of a stair is my
>   ancestral stair;
> That Goldsmith and the Dean, Berkeley and Burke have
>   travelled there.
>   ("Blood and the Moon," II. Reprinted with permission of the
>   publisher from *The Collected Poems of W. B. Yeats.* Copy-
>   right 1933 by The Macmillan Company. Renewed 1961 by
>   Bertha Georgie Yeats.)

Blake offers symbols of profound significance in apparent simplicity; as in "The Sick Rose," to which his own illustration provides subsidiary but complementary symbols in the caterpillar and the thorns on which humanity is as it were crucified:

> O Rose thou art sick.
> The invisible worm,
> That flies in the night
> In the howling storm:
> Has found out thy bed
> Of crimson joy:
> And his dark secret love
> Does thy life destroy.

It is possible to isolate some of these symbols, in their traditional aspects, and so to indicate some points of departure toward the apprehension of their meaning. The rose is traditionally the symbol of womanhood, the worm (or serpent or dragon) the male principle; the storm suggests any conflict, physical or mental. But (as always with the symbol) its peculiar qualities and significance rest in the totality of the statement of which the symbol is a component part.

For a last example of a different kind of complexity, in which the symbol is fused with mythology, we may consider the swan. All birds are likely (for obvious reasons) to become associated with the human soul or spirit. The swan has many associated qualities: whiteness, purity, strength, fidelity in love, its mysterious music of wingbeat or of cry, its song at death; therefore the human associations become more intense. These qualities are stabilized in myth and folklore; they pass through many imaginations and emerge, for instance, in Yeats' poem "Leda and the Swan" in which the symbol has become enriched not only by tradition but also by contextual images and associations in the rest of the poet's work.

It should be stressed again that the correspondences that appear in the symbol do not make use of the arbitrary or precise equivalents such as are found in allegorical or emblematic writing (*see* ALLEGORY; EMBLEM BOOKS). The symbol is independent in usage and meaning in each work in which it exists (however much it may be rooted in tradition); it appears to renew itself and to radiate fresh significance, when it is handled afresh by genius, in each new context in which it manifests itself.

Certain metaphors and symbols, because they are constant throughout world literature, are often called archetypal. Their continued vitality suggests that they correspond to profound and perennial aspects of the human situation. Among them are many myths, such as the descent into the underworld, the slaying of the dragon, the rescue from the enchanted castle; flowers of all kinds, often symbolizing womanhood or its virtues; tower, tree, cave; the sea voyage; fountain or well; and birds, beasts, and reptiles of many kinds. The investigation of them has brought both anthropology and psychology to the service of literary criticism.

See also FIGURES OF SPEECH; FOLKLORE; MYTH.

BIBLIOGRAPHY.—Samuel Johnson, *Lives of Addison, Cowley* (1779; ed. by G. Birkbeck Hill, 1905, vol. 1 of *Lives of the . . . Poets . . .*); W. Empson, *Seven Types of Ambiguity* (1930) and *The Structure of Complex Words* (1951); J. Middleton Murry, *Countries of the Mind*, 2nd series (1931); M. Bodkin, *Archetypal Patterns in Poetry* (1934) and *Studies of Type-Images in Poetry, Religion, and Philosophy* (1951); A. Tate (ed.), *The Language of Poetry* (1942); C. M. Bowra, *The Heritage of Symbolism* (1943); C. Day-Lewis, *The Poetic Image* (1947); R. Tuve, *Elizabethan and Metaphysical Imagery* (1947); Cleanth Brooks, *Modern Poetry and the Tradition* (1948) and *The Well Wrought Urn* (1943); A. Farrer, *A Rebirth of Images* (1949); A. Warren and R. Wellek, *Theory of Literature* (1949); W. H. Auden, *The Enchafèd Flood* (1950); W. H. Clemen, *The Development of Shakespeare's Imagery* (1951); J. Chiari, *Symbolisme from Poe to Mallarmé* (1957); R. Skelton, *The Poetic Pattern* (1956); Northrop Frye, *Anatomy of Criticism* (1957); F. Kermode, *Romantic Image* (1957).
(T. R. HN.)

POET LAUREATE.

In England, since the 17th century, the title "poet laureate" has been used to refer to a salaried member of the royal household, and it has little to do with the early civic and university degrees of baccalaureate, except as an extension of the tradition. Its uniqueness lies in its continuity, for in no other country has the death of a pensioned poet called for the immediate appointment of a successor, with the same rights, duties, and emolument. The office began with a pension granted to Ben Jonson by James I in 1616, and confirmed and increased by Charles I in 1630 (when the famous annual "butt of canary wine" was added, to be discontinued at the request of Henry James Pye—made laureate in 1790—who preferred the equivalent in money). Jonson's pension specifically recognized his services to the crown as a poet, and envisaged their continuance; but it was 16 months after his death in 1637 before a similar pension for similar services was granted to Sir William Davenant.

It was with Dryden's appointment in 1668 within a week of Davenant's death that the laureateship was recognized as a royal office to be filled automatically when vacant. At the Revolution of 1688 Dryden was dismissed for refusing the oath of allegiance, and this gave the appointment a political flavour which it retained for more than 200 years; as late as 1896 Alfred Austin was appointed as a Conservative, rather than for his poetry.

Dryden's successor, Thomas Shadwell, inaugurated the custom of the new year and birthday odes which hardened into a tradition between 1690 and about 1820, becoming the principal mark of the office. The odes were set to music and performed in the sovereign's presence, providing a long series of the worst poems ever written. On his appointment in 1813 Robert Southey sought unsuccessfully to end this custom, but although it was allowed tacitly to lapse in about 1820 it was only finally abolished by Queen Victoria. Her appointment of Wordsworth in 1843 recognized that the laureateship had become the reward for eminence in poetry rather than the vehicle for providing fulsome verses, and since then the office has carried no specified duties; laureates from Tennyson onward have written poems for royal and national occasions as the spirit has moved them.

Poets who have enjoyed the official title of poet laureate are (with date of appointment): Dryden (1668); Shadwell (1688); Nahum Tate (1692); Nicholas Rowe (1715); Laurence Eusden (1718); Colley Cibber (1730); William Whitehead (1757); Thomas Warton (1785); Henry James Pye (1790); Southey (1813); Wordsworth (1843); Tennyson (1850); Alfred Austin (1896); Robert Bridges (1913); John Masefield (1930); Cecil Day-Lewis (1968). *See* separate articles for many of the above.

See E. K. Broadus, *The Laureateship* (1921); Kenneth Hopkins, *The Poets Laureate* (1954).
(K. Ho.)

POETRY.

It seems probable that poetry originated in the magical spells, the ritualistic incantations, and the highly rhythmical and formalized storytelling of early tribal society. It made use of sympathetic magic in its listing of desired events in order to cause them to occur. It appears to have developed a sophisticated use of symbols and of various "levels" of diction quite early in its history, if evidence from the current oral literature of primitive tribal societies in different parts of the world is to be relied on. While being, in some forms, a "sacred" art or "mystery" associated with the practice of fertility and purification rituals, and with ideas of spiritual possession, it seems also always to have had recreational aspects. Even in its periods of greatest religious and magical significance, it seems to have been regarded as a game to be played with words, an entertainment, pastime, and mode of personal emotional release, as well as a religio-political ceremonial.

As poetry became detached from its religio-political functions, it became free to develop as entertainment, while continuing to include narrative, ritualistic, incantatory, and pseudoreligious elements. The figure of the poet, who had been revered as either priest or divine lunatic, lost its stature; though a poet might still be regarded with awe and given considerable status as a consequence of his work, his importance was seen to lie more in the value of his products than in his possession of spiritual powers. Moreover, poetry became a matter for public discussion and evaluation rather than a "mystery" of which only the elect might speak.

Several kinds of poetry have developed as a consequence of the poet's attempts to regain his lost status. Thus, satirical poetry can be regarded as a product of the poet's attempt to regain his position as an authoritative (because possessed or inspired) regulator of manners, morals, and forms; it is not merely the consequence of particular social conditions at a particular time. The epic, which, as an oral form, came into being to satisfy the human desire to recall past glories and establish genealogies at the same time as being entertained, owes its existence in written literature to the poet's attempt to set himself up as historian, genealogist, and mythmaker to a whole culture. It can even be argued that the poet's ventures into drama, particularly religious drama, are connected to this drive for lost authority, and many other kinds and attributes of poetry may also be related to the attempt of the poet in a literate and sophisticated society to regain the position and power he had in an illiterate and primitive one.

Poetry is not, however, simply residual. Although its relationship to society has altered it has not become insignificant. Up to the end of the 18th century, for example, poetry was still capable of having considerable effect upon public events; since then little poetry has had much social influence, though W. B. Yeats once wondered whether his words had aroused a destructive amount of national zeal in his fellow-Irishmen. In the 20th century poetry has become of importance to the solitary reader rather than to the political establishment, though in totalitarian states the poet's work is viewed with more respect and less tenderness. This "private" aspect of poetry is reflected in the numerous attempts at a definition made since the 17th century. Only a few treat poetry as a social phenomenon; the majority describe it either in terms of its relationship to the emotional perceptions of its makers or, more pretentiously, in terms of its profound insights into eternal truths. George Eliot neatly combined these attitudes in her statement (in her novel *Middlemarch,* 1872) that "To be a poet is to have a soul . . . in which knowledge passes instantaneously into feeling, and feeling flashes back as a new organ of knowledge." This, with its leaning toward the idea of a "fourth way of knowing" as described by the English Platonists, is a typically 19th-century view. Moreover, it elevates the poet to the status of a seer, and thus echoes the attitudes to poetry of both Wordsworth and Coleridge (*qq.v.*). Another 19th-century view is that of Herbert Spencer, who defined poetry (in his essay "On the Origin and Function of Music") as "a form of speech for the better expression of emotional ideas." Louis MacNeice, in the 20th century, has described it as "a precision instrument for recording a man's reactions to life." This statement implies recognition of the psychological accuracy of poetry's modes of procedure, and suggests that the various devices of poetry correspond to certain deep-seated needs and instinctive behaviour patterns possessed by all men. The word "precision" is, indeed, a pointer to the modern emphasis, in poetic theory, on the examination of linguistic procedures and their relationship to the structure of society and the psychology of the individual.

This approach to poetry, which is, obviously, yet another attempt to give it a publicly acceptable "image," may well have its origin in Matthew Arnold's view that "Poetry is at bottom a criticism of life," to which T. S. Eliot retorts "Arnold might just as well have said that Christian worship is at bottom a criticism of the Trinity." In the confrontation between Arnold and Eliot can be seen clearly the main division among those critics who have attempted to define poetry in terms of its purpose. The one view sees poetry as a mode of discovering or expressing universal truth, and the other regards it as a mode of exploring and expressing the individual's reactions to experience in such a way that, while so-called general truths may emerge, they are not inextricably an element of poetry itself. This second view is trenchantly expressed by Christopher Fry, in his statement that "Poetry is the language in which man explores his own amazement." This is still, however, a definition based upon a notion of purpose, and can easily be countered by listing other purposes which appear to have animated poetry from time to time.

Another kind of definition attempts an analysis of the effect of poetry upon the reader; by describing the sensations which invariably accompany a reader's recognition of "poetry" the critic hopes to provide a formula to describe the stimulus which arouses those sensations. One of the most satisfactory formulations is that of Clive Sansom, who includes in his definition a reference to the physical properties of poetry. He states that "Poetry is a rhythmical form of words which expresses an imaginative-emotional-intellectual experience of the writer's, and expresses it in such a way that it creates a similar experience in the mind of his reader or listener." This, if the word rhythmical is not taken as referring only to metrical writing, probably comes fairly close to the target. It does, however, suggest that the reader's experience must necessarily be similar to that of the writer. This seems unlikely. The writer may have created his poem without conscious thought, or almost by accident, or he may have created it by taking enormous pains and as a consequence of largely technical concern. Those definitions of poetry which presume any close similarity between the attitude of the maker while making and that of the reader while reading are based upon an altogether too naïve view of the nature of the creative process. Nevertheless, it is likely that no reader will regard a piece of writing as a poem unless he derives from it an "imaginative-emotional-intellectual" experience which includes a recognition of the verbal dexterity of the writer and a satisfying conviction of the completeness of the experience. The poem must satisfy the reader's need to arrange emotional experience in patterns for the purpose of better understanding and better manipulation, as well as provide him with a more than usual intensity of perception.

This intensity of perception experienced by the reader has often been related to that experienced by the poet while writing. Although many poems are made with an almost complete awareness of the techniques that are being used, it is also true that almost no poem is completed without the poet's being aware of subconscious promptings. A part of every poem, indeed, and all of some, is made by the poet in a condition of "trance," or, as Brewster Ghiselin has expressed it, "with a consciousness partially unfocused." This has been emphasized by many critics: Goethe referred to "That undisturbed, direct manner of working, almost like a sleepwalker," and C. Day-Lewis, concentrating upon another aspect, insisted that "it cannot be said too often that a poet does not fully know what is the poem he is writing until he has written it." This, and other aspects of the creative process are being investigated by psychologists, but no consensus has yet been reached. It seems probable, however, that the "trance" is a maneuvre, intuitively organized, on the part of the poet, to arrange that his associative powers be given freedom to work at full strength without overmuch restraint by the fully conscious intelligence, and to arrange also that certain complex movements be made intuitively because they cannot be achieved consciously. Just as a juggler, once trained, can perform, without thought, feats which he could not possibly manage were he to calculate every trajectory, so the poet, engaged in manipulating rhythm, cadence, syntax, diction, connotative richnesses, and symbolic profundities, is obliged to operate without taking too much thought. It is, however, interesting to note that the "deepest" poetic trances are usually experienced in a poet's youth or by comparatively unpractised poets; the "professional" poet finds, as time goes on, that he can rely more and more upon his conscious powers.

When this is taken into account, it becomes clear that those definitions of poetry which are dependent upon a near-mystical view of the nature of "inspiration" are as ill-based as those which refer to the poet's "intention," or to the reader's sharing the poet's experience. It is easier, indeed, to approach the definition of poetry by analyzing its appearance than either its purpose or its origins. This approach leads to varying conclusions, for at different times and in different societies poetry has been shaped differently and differently regarded. In the history of English and American poetry, for instance, there have been many fashions, each one of which has given rise to different ideas of the poetic task, and established, implicitly or explicitly, different criteria for the judging of poetic success. Thus the early 18th-century emphasis upon "correctness" produced a view of poetry, and a kind of poetry, very different from that influenced by the Coleridgean emphasis upon "organic form" in the 19th century. In the 20th century each of a number of "movements" has suggested different approaches, and has emphasized one aspect of poetry at the expense of others. Thus, Imagism, Symbolism, and Surrealism have all given rise to different definitions of, and practices in, poetry.

Nevertheless, though it is difficult to define poetry, it is comparatively easy to describe its various manners and modes, though one must be careful not to allow pedantry to become a straitjacket, and even more careful to point out that the classification of phenomena is not the establishment of laws.

Poetry can be said to make use of various media, the most usual being verse, though some poems have been deliberately composed in prose, and some "prose" can be described as poetry. Verse may be defined as an obviously rhythmical use of language, manipulating accent, stress, and cadence in such a way as to create recurrent patterns of emphasis. Free verse (q.v.), or vers libre, though it often makes use of the repetition of syntactical forms and of words and phrases, is not governed by any other rule. Metrical verse, on the other hand, has many very restrictive manifestations, although in the 20th century it has become usual to mingle metres and to treat so-called "laws" with easy familiarity, if not with downright contempt. The main English metres are the iambic, trochaic, anapaestic, and dactylic, the last-named usually appearing in a catalectic form. (See also VERSE; METRE, and for the metres of classical poetry, PROSODY, CLASSICAL.)

Poetry has its modes as well as its media. Some of these have their origin in the work of particular groups of people working at a particular period; thus, for instance, the terms Petrarchan, Cavalier, Metaphysical, Augustan, Romantic, Symbolist, Imagist, and Surrealist, used to describe particular poetic modes, are connected with particular episodes or periods in the history of poetry. Nevertheless, these terms do describe modes of operation, basic attitudes, and varied views of the poet's role, and, on this account, are of value in describing the poetry of periods other than that in which they originated.

Poetry has its genres also, both major and minor. The major genres are satire (q.v.), epic (see EPIC POETRY), lyric, and drama (q.v.). Satire includes didactic or critical poetry of a humorous or invective kind. The epic genre includes any long poem, or fragment of a presumed long poem, which deals with heroic themes of historical importance in high-sounding language. The English view of the epic derives largely from Homer and Virgil, although it does not differ in essentials from the view held in other countries with different traditions. The lyric genre includes any poetry intended to be sung, or clearly derived from a song tradition; thus both the ode and the epigram (qq.v.) belong to the lyric genre, and a short satiric poem may belong both to the lyric and satiric genres. Drama as a poetic genre includes masque (q.v.) and litany as well as poetic drama, and such forms as the pastoral eclogue (see PASTORAL) and the dramatic monologue (q.v.) should properly be considered as drama.

The minor poetic genres are numerous. The most important are parody, elegy, hymn, and ballad (qq.v.). These are to be regarded as genres rather than as forms because in each much variety of structure is possible. All but the parody are subspecies of the lyric. Parody is, of course, satiric, and may be also lyric, epic, or dramatic.

Within these general categories poetry also includes various "established" forms. Among the forms in use in English and American literature are some imitated from forms first established in other linguistic cultures: e.g., the sonnet, villanelle, ballade, rondeau, chant royal, canzone, sestina, and triolet (qq.v.) which are all of European origin; and, from non-European literatures the Malayan pantoum (pantun; see MALAY LITERATURE), and the Japanese haiku and tanka (see JAPANESE LITERATURE). Forms used usually for jocular purposes are the limerick and the clerihew (qq.v.).

In attempting to define poetry it is not necessary to explore the minutiae of verse, and only necessary to mention that certain stanza forms have become as established as those forms mentioned above. The most important of these are the Spenserian and neo-Spenserian stanza, and the Burns stanza. In addition to these there are forms which, having no set rules, do follow certain principles established by their previous usage in other languages. Notable among such imitated forms are the Horatian and the Pindaric ode (see ODE; PINDARICS).

Verse is, however, only one of the media of poetry, and much verse is not poetry at all. This has been recognized, but the recognition has never led to a satisfactory distinction between poetic and nonpoetic verse, or between poetic and nonpoetic prose. It seems finally that once those criteria provided by past poetic fashions, and habitual beliefs about what is "usual" in poetry, are found useless, we are thrown back upon simple assertion concerning the nature of the reader's experience. If any one reader says of a piece of writing "this is poetry" we are obliged to admit that it may be so for him, though it need not be so for us. Thus the concept "poetry" is, ultimately, many-faceted, manipulatable, and definable only in terms of established practices which it is the chief endeavour of every poet to oppose, alter, and transform. It is also clear that, from another view, and in the last resort, poetry is a quality, not of the thing written, but of the reader.

See also POETIC IMAGERY; RHYME; LIGHT VERSE. For the history of poetry see articles on the national literatures: GREEK LITERATURE; LATIN LITERATURE; AMERICAN LITERATURE; ENGLISH LITERATURE; FRENCH LITERATURE; etc. See also articles on various forms and metres not mentioned above: ALEXANDRINE VERSE; BLANK VERSE; OTTAVA RIMA; RIME ROYAL; COUPLET; EPITHALAMIUM; FABLIAU; LAI; VIRELAI; articles on particular poetic movements: e.g., SYMBOLISTS, THE; and references to "Poetry" in the Index.

BIBLIOGRAPHY.—Clive Sansom (ed.), The World of Poetry: Poets and Critics on the Art and Functions of Poetry (an anthology of extracts) (1959); Robin Skelton, The Poetic Pattern (1956), Poetry, in the Teach Yourself . . . series (1963); C. Day-Lewis, The Poetic Image (1947); Owen Barfield, Poetic Diction (1928), Saving the Appearances (1957); Rosamond Harding, An Anatomy of Inspiration (1940); Brewster Ghiselin (ed.), The Creative Process: a Symposium (1952); Marjorie Boulton, The Anatomy of Poetry (1953); Babette Deutsch, Poetry Handbook (1957).   (R. S.)

POGGIO (GIAN FRANCESCO POGGIO BRACCIOLINI) (1380–1459), Italian humanist, foremost among scholars of the early Renaissance as a rediscoverer of classical Latin manuscripts, was born at Terranuova in Valdarno on Feb. 11, 1380. From 1399 to 1400 he studied in Florence to be a notary, and was befriended by Coluccio Salutati, who also used him as a copyist of manuscripts. Poggio's invention of the humanist script, based on the Caroline minuscule, is attributed to these years. (See PALEOGRAPHY.) In 1403 he moved to Rome, where he became a secretary to Boniface IX. The rediscovery of the treasures of the ancient world, with which his name will always be associated, began soon after his attendance on the schismatic pope John XXIII at the Council of Constance in 1414. During a visit to Cluny in the spring of 1415 he brought to light two unknown orations of Cicero. At Saint-Gall in June–July 1416, in the company of his friends and fellow scholars, Cencio de' Rustici and Bartolomeo da Montepulciano, he found the first complete text of Quintilian's Institutio oratoria, the first three books and part of book four of Valerius Flaccus' Argonautica, and the commentaries of Asconius Pedianus on some of Cicero's orations. Various expeditions in 1417, alone or with Bartolomeo da Montepulciano, to Fulda, Saint-Gall, and other monasteries, produced P. Festus, De verborum significatu; Lucretius, De rerum natura; Manilius, Astronomicon; Silius Italicus, *De bello punico;* Ammianus Marcellinus, *Res Gestae;* Apicius on cooking; and other lesser works. He also found at Langres in 1417 Cicero's oration *pro Caecina,* and perhaps at Cologne seven other orations of Cicero. It is not known where and when he discovered the *Silvae* of Statius. Poggio made copies of the newfound works, in his elegant script, several of which still survive.

On the election of Martin V in 1417, Poggio failed to regain his post at the Curia, and decided to accept the invitation of Henry Beaufort, bishop of Winchester, to enter his service. He spent four not very happy years (1418–23) in England, where his hopes of continuing his discoveries were disappointed by English libraries; and this lack of facilities combined with the scholasticism prevalent in England led him to direct his studies to the early Fathers. At this time he also took minor orders, which enabled him to enjoy certain benefices, though he was never ordained priest.

He returned to Rome early in 1423 and was reappointed curial secretary soon after. Taking up his researches with renewed vigour, seeking in person, inquiring by letter, interrogating foreign visitors to Rome, he made further discoveries, including Frontinus' *De aquaeductibus* and Firmicus Maternus' *Matheseos libri,* the latter found at Monte Cassino in 1429. He also sought Greek manuscripts from abroad and translated into Latin Xenophon's *Cyropaedia,* the histories of Diodorus Siculus, and Lucian's *Ass.* His classical interests extended to the study of ancient buildings and the collections of inscriptions (of which two autograph copies survive) and of works of sculpture, with which he adorned the garden of his villa near Florence. The attraction of his native Tuscany, and the invitation from Florence to succeed Carlo Aretino as chancellor, finally drew him from his long career in Rome (1453). His last years were spent in exercising this office and in writing his history of Florence, which he completed not long before his death on Oct. 30, 1459.

Besides his talent for rediscovery of ancient manuscripts, Poggio was gifted with a lively eloquence and a capacity for artistic representation of character and conversation that distinguish his moral dialogues from the numerous contemporary works of a similar kind. The most important of these are *De avaritia* (1428–29), *De varietate fortunae* (1431–48), *De nobilitate* (1440), and *Historia tripartita disceptativa convivialis* (1450). A vein of sadness and pessimism runs through some of these works (especially that concerning Fortune), and appears strongly in his *De miseria humanae conditionis* (1455). Though professedly an ardent Ciceronian, Poggio was hardly inhibited in practice by preoccupations of style, and commanded a wide, racy, and sometimes obscene Latinity, frequently used with mordant wit against critics and enemies. His *Facetiae* (1438–52), a collection of humorous, often indecent, tales, contain vigorous satire on monks and clerics and on rival scholars such as Francesco Filelfo, with whom, as also with Lorenzo Valla (*q.v.*), Poggio engaged in the most notorious and vituperative polemics of a polemical age. This same spirit of violent invective and satire informs his dialogue *Contra hypocritas* (1447–48), directed against ecclesiastics of all kinds and against certain individuals in particular. Poggio's ability to handle Latin as a live idiom is best shown in his copious correspondence, which for its form as much as for its content stands out among the *epistolari* of the humanists. His *Historia florentina* in eight books is largely a narrative of the wars of Florence from 1350 to 1445. Lack of comment on internal affairs and of critical awareness of cause and effect make it a work of limited historical value.

BIBLIOGRAPHY.—Some of the dialogues and the *Facetiae* were printed in the 15th century; there were collected editions in 1511 and 1513, and in 1538; and editions of *Historia florentina,* in *Rerum Italicarum Scriptores,* vol. XX (1731), and of *Epistolario,* by T. Tonelli, 3 vol. (1832–61). There are modern editions of *Contra hypocritas,* by G. Vallese, with Italian trans. (1946); and of *De avaritia* in E. Garin, *Prosatori latini del' 400* (1952).

See also W. Shepherd, *The Life of Poggio Bracciolini* (1802; Italian trans. with notes and additions by T. Tonelli, 1825); E. Walser, *Poggius Florentinus, Leben und Werke* (1914); R. Sabbadini, *Le scoperte dei codici latini e greci ne' secoli XIV e XV,* 2 parts (1905–14); B. L. Ullman, *Studies in the Italian Renaissance* (1955) and *The Origin and Development of Humanistic Script* (1960); R. Weiss, *Humanism in England During the 15th Century* (1957); N. Rubinstein, article in *Italia medievale e umanistica,* I (1958). (Ce. G.)

POGONOPHORA, a remarkable phylum of wormlike, sedentary marine animals that lack a digestive tract, possess a body cavity (coelom), and bear one to many fringed tentacles at the anterior end. Commonly called beard worms because of their tentacles, pogonophores are long and slender, ranging in length from 4 to 12 in., with a diameter up to $\frac{1}{10}$ in. in larger species. Pogonophores are widely distributed in seas off continents and large islands.

Representatives of this group, assigned to the genus *Siboglinum* and described by M. Caullery in 1914, were dredged by the Dutch ship "Siboga" off Malaya at the turn of the century. The phylum was established in 1955 by the Soviet zoologist A. V. Ivanov, who intensively studied and described many of the known species.

Natural History.—Pogonophores dwell in long, cylindrical, secreted tubes composed of chitin and protein. They occur from depths of 750 to 32,000 ft.

The method of obtaining and digesting food among the pogonophores, which lack mouth, anus, and gut, is of great interest. In *Lamellisabella* and *Spirobrachia* the extended tentacles are fused in the form of a cylinder throughout most of their length; in *Siboglinum* the single tentacle is coiled to form a tube. The pinnules, extending into the lumen of the cylinder, intermesh to form a filter. Alongside each pinnule base is a ciliary tract. These tracts produce in each intertentacular region a current of water that carries in microorganisms and detritus that are filtered out by the pinnule mesh. Water leaves by an opening at the base of the ventral tentacles. Digestive enzymes are secreted by gland cells located at the pinnule bases. Digestion is thus external, according to Ivanov, and nutritive material is presumably absorbed by the pinnules. It has also been suggested that at least some pogonophores may absorb dissolved substances resulting from bacterial decomposition of animals and detritus.

Structure and Function.—The body is divided into three regions, each provided with separate coelomic sacs. A short anterior section, including the protosome and mesosome, is separated from a long trunk section, or metasome, by an external constriction and an internal muscular diaphragm. The protosome is drawn out dorsally into a medial cephalic lobe that contains the central nerve ganglion. One to many hollow tentacles, whose cavities are continuous with the protocoel, arise from the ventral side of the protosome, at the base of the cephalic lobe; the tentacles are

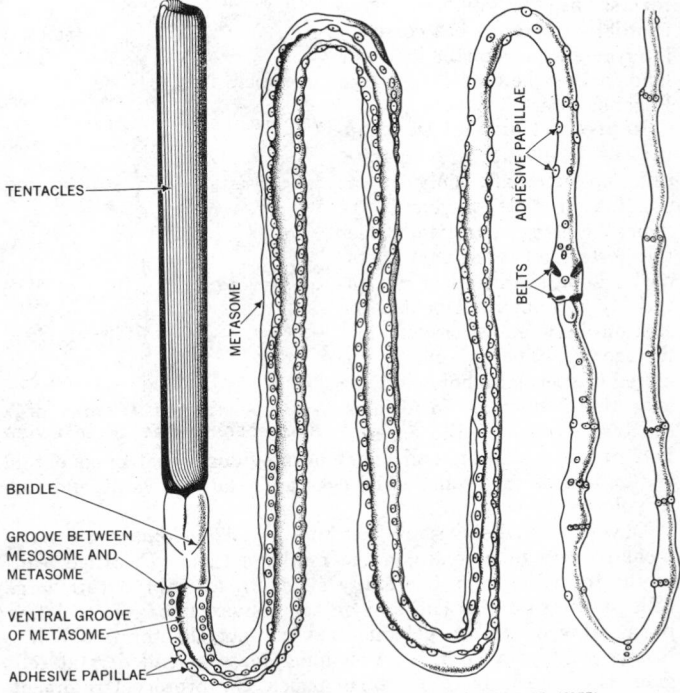

TENTACLES

METASOME

BRIDLE

GROOVE BETWEEN MESOSOME AND METASOME

VENTRAL GROOVE OF METASOME

ADHESIVE PAPILLAE

ADHESIVE PAPILLAE

BELTS

FROM A. V. IVANOV, IN "ZOOLOGISCHE JAHRBUCHER ABT. I SYSTEMATIK," 85 (1957)

FIG. 1.—FEMALE SPECIMEN OF SPIROBRACHIA BEKLEMISCHEVI, **VENTRAL VIEW WITH POSTERIOR ONE-SIXTH OF TRUNK NOT SHOWN**

POGROM

provided with lateral projections, or pinnules. The mesosome, with a pair of coelomic sacs, is usually separated from the protosome by a constriction and is marked externally by the bridle, a pair of cuticular ridges on the dorsal side, extending obliquely backward to meet or fuse in the midventral line; the bridle supports the protruding worm on the edge of its tube.

The metasome, also with paired coelomic sacs, is divided into two sections by a pair of oblique, parallel ridges called belts, which are beset with rows of small platelets armed with minute teeth. The first part of the metasome, lying anterior to the belts (the preannular region of Ivanov), bears a ventral groove bordered by low folds, each bearing a row of papillae. In *Siboglinum* these papillae contain multicellular glands or are topped with chitinlike platelets, and probably help the animal to cling to the inner surface of the tube. Behind the midventral groove the papillae decrease in number and are arranged irregularly. A ciliated band, possibly sensitive to chemical changes, runs on the dorsal side of the preannular region. Behind the belts the papillae, with their platelets, are borne in transverse rows ventrally. In primitive genera these structures are scattered irregularly or are absent entirely.

A previously unknown posterior extremity of the body of *Siboglinum,* named the anchor, was described in 1964 by M. Webb who believes it is the true metasome. It is set off from the rest of the body by a narrow waist, and terminates with a sucker. It breaks off readily and tends to remain in the tube.

The body wall comprises an outer cuticle and an epidermis overlying a thin circular, and a thicker longitudinal, muscle layer. A plexus of nerves lies in the epidermis, with a fibrous stratum developed between the basal ends of the epidermal cells. The brain, located in the cephalic lobe, gives off nerves to the tentacles and a middorsal nerve to the hind end of the body. Giant nerve fibres are found in the dorsal cord of some genera.

The closed circulatory system includes a middorsal and a midventral blood vessel. In addition, two pairs of lateral trunk vessels occur in *Siboglinum.* Ivanov reported that the ventral vessel is provided with a muscular heart in the protosome and that its contractions propel blood forward into the tentacular vessels. In the order Athecanephria a pericardial sac lies apposed to the dorsal side of the heart. The efferent tentacular vessels carry the blood to the dorsal vessel, in which the flow is posterior. The course of the blood is thus the reverse of that in the Hemichordata, if Ivanov has correctly interpreted the cephalic lobe as a landmark of the dorsal surface of Pogonophora.

Reproduction and Development.—The sexes are separate, differing externally only in the position of the gonoducts. In males, an elongate testis occupies the posterior half of each metacoel. Long sperm ducts run anteriorly and open out behind the septum between mesosome and metasome. The sperm are enclosed in spermatophores bearing long, thin filaments. In females, the ovaries occupy the anterior half of the metasome and have short oviducts that open out in the middle of the trunk. The eggs are relatively large and rich in yolk.

Developmental stages are best known in *Siboglinum.* Development of eggs takes place in the mother's tube. Cleavage leads to the formation of a bilaterally symmetrical embryo with large cells at the posterior end and on the convex side. Gastrulation presumably occurs by delamination without the formation of a blastopore. At a later stage an inner mass of endodermal cells gives rise anteriorly to a median pouch, the protocoel rudiment, from which paired outgrowths extend posteriorly as the rudiments of the mesocoels and metacoels. Mouth and anus fail to develop,

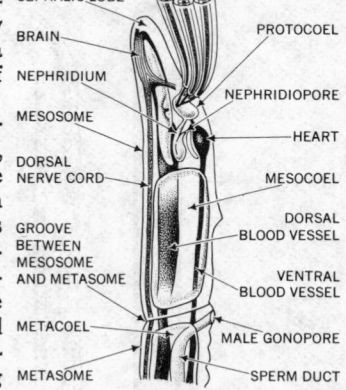

FIG. 2.—INTERNAL ANATOMY OF A MALE POGONOPHORE, LATERAL VIEW

and the endoderm disappears as its yolk is used up. Later, furrows develop to separate metasome from mesosome, and the latter from the protosome.

Relationships and Classification.—Although several authors had pointed out the affinities of the Pogonophora with the echinoderm-hemichordate-chordate assemblage of animals, it was the work of Ivanov that placed this relationship on a sound basis. The manner of development of the coelomic sacs, the division of the body into three regions, and the structure of the nervous system all point to an especially close relationship with the hemichordates. But details of the arrangement of the coelomic sacs and the openings of ducts to the exterior, the origin of the tentacles from the protosome, the absence of a midventral nerve cord, and the absence of a gut support establishing the Pogonophora as an independent phylum.

Ivanov's proposal, in 1955, to name the new phylum Brachiata which would include the class Pogonophora has not been generally received. The more familiar name of Pogonophora is widely used for the phylum. Ivanov recognizes two orders:

Athecanephria.—The protosome and mesosome are delineated externally by a constriction. Nephridiopores open out laterally. One or a number of separate tentacles are present. A pericardial sac is present. There are no transverse ventral rows of adhesive papillae posterior to the belts.

Thecanephria.—The protosome and mesosome may or may not be marked off by an external constriction. Nephridiopores open out medially. Tentacles are few to numerous, separate or fused basally. There is no pericardial sac. Transverse ventral rows of adhesive papillae are present on the metasome posterior to the belts.

BIBLIOGRAPHY.—L. H. Hyman, *The Invertebrates,* vol. 5, pp. 208–227 (1959); A. V. Ivanov, *Pogonophora* (1963); S. M. Manton, "Embryology of Pogonophora and Classifications of Animals," *Nature,* 181:748–751 (1958); M. Webb, "A Redescription of *Siboglinum ekmani Jägersten* (Pogonophora)," *Sarsia,* 15:37–47 (1964).

(WI. D. H.)

POGROM, a Russian word meaning "devastation" or "riot," came into international use as a result of the wide notoriety given to a number of outbursts against the Jews in Russia between 1881 and 1917. The character of these events was such that the word came to have a particular meaning: a mob attack, either approved or condoned by authorities, against the persons and property of a religious, racial, or national minority.

The first extensive pogroms followed the assassination of Tsar Alexander II in 1881. Although the assassin was not a Jew, and only one Jew was associated with him, false rumours aroused Russian mobs in more than 200 cities and towns to attack Jews and destroy their property. In the two decades following, pogroms gradually became less prevalent; but in 1903 they again began to spread and for a three-year period were common throughout the country. Thereafter, from 1906 to the end of the Russian monarchy, mob action against the Jews was intermittent and less widespread.

The pogrom in Kishinev, in April 1903, although more severe than most, was typical in many respects. For two days mobs, inspired by local leaders acting with official support, killed, looted, and destroyed without hindrance from police or soldiers. When troops were finally called out and the mob dispersed, 45 Jews had been killed, nearly 600 had been wounded, and 1,500 Jewish homes had been pillaged. Those responsible for inciting the outrages were not punished.

The Russian central government did not organize pogroms, as was widely believed; but the anti-Semitic policy that it carried out from 1881 to 1917 made them possible. Official persecution and harassment of Jews led the numerous anti-Semites to believe that their violence was legitimate, and their belief was strengthened by the active participation of a few high and many minor officials in fomenting attacks and by the reluctance of the government either to stop pogroms or to punish those responsible for them.

Pogroms have also occurred in other countries, notably in Poland and in Germany during the Hitler regime. *See* ANTI-SEMITISM; JEWS: *Modern Period.*

BIBLIOGRAPHY.—S. M. Dubnov, *The History of the Jews in Russia* and Poland, 3 vol. (1916–20); L. Greenberg, *The Jews in Russia*, 2 vol. (1944–51); M. Vishniak, "Antisemitism in Tsarist Russia: a Study in Government-Fostered Antisemitism," in *Essays on Antisemitism*, ed. by K. S. Pinson (1942). (SI. H.)

POHJOIS-KARJALA (Swedish NORRA KARELEN, North Karelia), a *lääni* (county) of east-central Finland bordering the Karelian Autonomous Soviet Socialist Republic of the U.S.S.R. Pop. (1960) 203,934. It centres on the northeast reaches of Lake Saimaa, there represented by the lake Pielinen. Highest altitudes are reached in the scenically magnificent Koli heights (about 1,000 ft.). Softwood forests are the principal source of income, with small-scale, mixed farming as subsidiary. Joensuu (commune pop. 28,335) is the administrative centre and northern terminal of summer steamboat routes, and contains a fine regional hospital and local museum. Smaller market centres are Lieksa (4,361) and Nurmes (2,165). (W. R. ME.)

POINCARÉ, (JULES) HENRI (1854–1912), French mathematician and philosopher of science, who at the turn of the century was generally acknowledged to be the outstanding mathematician of his age, was born at Nancy on April 29, 1854. He was a first cousin of Raymond Poincaré, president of the French republic during World War I. After attending the École Polytechnique, Henri Poincaré entered the École des Mines. In 1879 he was appointed to a mathematical post at Caen university. In 1881 he moved to Paris university, where he lectured in turn on almost all branches of pure and applied mathematics. He was a prolific writer, producing more than 30 books and 500 original memoirs.

Poincaré's first great achievement was in pure mathematics. He generalized the idea of functional periodicity in his theory of automorphic functions which are invariant under a denumerably infinite group of linear fractional transformations. He showed how these functions can be used to integrate linear differential equations with rational algebraic coefficients and also to uniformize algebraic curves; *i.e.*, to express the co-ordinates of any point of an algebraic curve as uniform functions of a single parameter. The class of automorphic functions which he called Fuchsian, after the German mathematician I. L. Fuchs (1833–1902), he found to be associated with transformations arising in non-Euclidean geometry.

In celestial mechanics he made important contributions to the theory of orbits, particularly in connection with the classical three-body problem. In the course of this work he developed powerful new mathematical techniques, including the theories of asymptotic expansions and integral invariants, and he made fundamental discoveries on the behaviour of the integral curves of differential equations near singularities. His researches on new mathematical methods in astronomy were summed up in his great three-volume treatise *Les Méthodes nouvelles de la Mécanique céleste* (1892, 1893 and 1899). In his theory of periodic orbits he founded the subject of topological dynamics. His memoirs on *analysis situs*, as it was then called, mark the beginning of modern topology.

Poincaré made important contributions to the theory of the figures of equilibrium of rotating fluid masses, and in particular discovered the pear-shaped figures which played so prominent a part in the researches of G. H. Darwin, J. H. Jeans and A. M. Liapunov. But his greatest contribution to mathematical physics was his famous paper on the dynamics of the electron published in 1906. In this paper he obtained, independently of Einstein, many of the results of the special theory of relativity. The principal difference was that Einstein developed the theory from elementary considerations concerning light signaling, whereas Poincaré's treatment was based on the full theory of electromagnetism and so was essentially restricted to phenomena associated with the latter.

Poincaré's writings on the philosophy of science, gathered together in his books *La Science et l'hypothèse* (1903; Eng. trans., 1905), *La Valeur de la Science* (1904) and *Science et Méthode* (1908; Eng. trans., 1914), were no less important than his contributions to mathematics. He was a forerunner of the modern intuitionist school founded by L. E. J. Brouwer and believed that some mathematical ideas precede logic. In one of the most famous of his essays he made an original analysis of the psychology of mathematical discovery and invention. But the greatest of his contributions to philosophy was his emphasis on the role played by convention in scientific method.

In his writings on philosophical topics Poincaré revealed himself as a master of French prose and was read by thousands in all walks of life. He was elected to the Académie Française in 1908 to fill the vacancy caused by the death of the poet R. F. A. P. Sully Prudhomme. Poincaré died in Paris on July 17, 1912.

See J. S. Hadamard, *The Early Scientific Work of Henri Poincaré* (1922), *The Later Scientific Work of Henri Poincaré* (1933); T. Dantzig, *Henri Poincaré, Critic of Crisis* (1954). (G. J. Ww.)

POINCARÉ, RAYMOND (1860–1934), French statesman, ninth president of the Third Republic and five times premier, was born at Bar-le-Duc, the son of an engineer. He early showed intellectual powers and won many academic distinctions; and after a year's military service with the *Chasseurs à pied* he was admitted to practice as a barrister in Paris in 1882. He soon began also to write for newspapers. Elected to the Chamber of Deputies by the Meuse *département* in 1887, he sat on the left centre and first made his name as an expert on law and finance. He served as minister of education (April–November 1893) and as minister of finance (May 1894–January 1895) under Charles Dupuy and as minister of education again (January–October 1895) under Alexandre Ribot. His bill of 1893 reorganized the university system.

ROGER-VIOLLET

RAYMOND POINCARÉ, PHOTOGRAPHED IN 1913, THE YEAR HE WAS ELECTED PRESIDENT OF FRANCE

On leaving office, Poincaré was elected vice-president of the Chamber. For several years subsequently he played an important role on the Finance Committee, at the same time enhancing his reputation as a lawyer. Though he was opposed to the Radicals, he was never a reactionary, and at the climax of the Dreyfus Affair he declared himself convinced of the alleged traitor's innocence (*see* DREYFUS, ALFRED). In 1903 he left the Chamber of Deputies and entered the Senate. His marriage to the widowed Mme Bazire took place in 1904. He accepted the finance portfolio in Ferdinand Sarrien's cabinet in March 1906, but retired when Georges Clemenceau (*q.v.*), whose dictatorial manner he disliked, succeeded Sarrien as premier in October.

Prominent in Parliament, famous as a barrister, and also, from 1909, a member of the French Academy, Poincaré thought that henceforth he could not accept anything less than the premiership, and so declined several other cabinet posts. His time came in January 1912. Joseph Caillaux (*q.v.*), the Radical premier, had conducted a difficult negotiation with Germany without taking much account of the views of his foreign minister, Justin de Selves; and this caused some disquiet in political circles. Poincaré, a member of the Senate's committee of inquiry into the matter, played a part in the scene which led to Caillaux's resignation and was then entrusted by the president of the republic, Armand Fallières, with the formation of a new government (Jan. 12, 1912).

Stimulated by pinpricks from Germany, patriotism was running high in France; and the new premier, whose patriotism had always been unquestionable, was one whom public opinion could greet with widespread satisfaction. Taking charge of foreign affairs at the same time, Poincaré forthwith undertook to give a new and stronger style to French diplomacy. While he looked askance at Germany and Italy, he devoted himself to strengthening France's links with Russia and Great Britain. On a visit to St. Petersburg in August 1912 he assured the Russian government that his country would stand by the Franco-Russian alliance; and in November he and the British foreign secretary, Sir Edward Grey, concluded an agreement whereby their respective governments should consult one another at moments of international crisis and take account of plans jointly established by their naval and military authorities. Throughout the Balkan Wars (1912–13), Paris and London cooperated constantly to prevent hostilities from spreading.

As Fallières was approaching the end of his term of office, Poincaré was urged by his friends to stand for the presidency of the Republic. Though he was opposed by the left under Clemenceau's leadership, he was elected president on Jan. 17, 1913, by 483 votes to 376.

Poincaré's supreme ambition was now attained. But he resented being merely a decorative figure at the head of the state and sometimes spoke of the Élysée Palace as "a prison." However, he gave effective support to the governments of Aristide Briand and of Jean Louis Barthou (qq.v.) in order to secure the voting of the bill that raised the length of compulsory military service from two to three years. The high command judged this move indispensable if France was to compensate Germany's overwhelming superiority in population. When the general election of May 1914 gave the left a majority in the Chamber, Poincaré feared that this Three Years Act might be repealed: for a time he thought of resigning, but finally he decided that his duty was to remain in office, to help France to weather the impending storm.

In July 1914, returning via Scandinavia from an official visit to Russia, Poincaré learned by radio of Austria-Hungary's ultimatum to Serbia and promptly cut short his homeward journey. It was clear that the mechanism of the existing European alliances made war inevitable, and he was welcomed back in Paris with enthusiasm and cheering. Though later he was wrongly represented as having been a warmonger, he in fact sincerely desired peace; but since Germany intended war he saw no other course than to fight it out, with the further hope that the issue might restore to France the territory lost in 1871 (Alsace-Lorraine). In a letter to George V of Great Britain he pleaded for a clear declaration that the Anglo-French entente would, if necessary, prove its strength on the battlefield.

Germany declared war on France on Aug. 3, 1914; and on Aug. 4 Poincaré sent a message to both houses appealing for the *union sacrée* of all Frenchmen against the invader.

Throughout the war Poincaré performed his duty energetically but with discretion, never transgressing the narrow limits of his constitutional powers. He gave fresh proof of his patriotic loyalty in November 1917 by entrusting the premiership to Clemenceau, who had recently made bitter attacks on him. Differences of opinion again estranged him from Clemenceau during the peace negotiations, in which his advice was disregarded; and on Feb. 18, 1920, after the completion of his presidential term of office, he was glad to leave the Élysée.

Reelected to the Senate, Poincaré was for a time chairman of the commission on the reparations (q.v.) due from Germany. He wrote articles for the press on the necessity of compelling Germany to fulfill the obligations imposed by the Treaty of Versailles. Briand meanwhile was inclined to agree with the British on the subject of reparations; but when he resigned office Poincaré on Jan. 12, 1922, succeeded him as premier and foreign minister. Poincaré failed to reach any understanding with the British; and at a conference held in Paris early in January 1923 he rejected the compromise suggested by Andrew Bonar Law. With the British dissenting, the Reparations Commission eventually declared that the Germans had failed to meet their obligations; and Poincaré, in agreement with Belgium and Italy, then decided that France should occupy the Ruhr (q.v.). The "passive resistance" in the area, ordered by the German government, came to an end on Sept. 26, 1923, after the French had retaliated by taking full control of railways and mines there. Though the Ruhr magnates were thenceforward ready for close industrial cooperation with France, Poincaré would not listen to their proposals. He finally accepted the British-U.S. suggestion that a group of experts should deal with the problem of reparations; this resulted in the adoption of the Dawes Plan.

For the first three months of 1924 Poincaré had to face a financial crisis. By inducing Parliament to vote new taxes, he saved the situation, but there was strenuous opposition by the Radicals and the Socialists, united in a *cartel des gauches* or left bloc. His fi-

nance minister, Charles de Lasteyrie, resigned on March 26, and Poincaré reconstituted his cabinet two days later. The general election of May 1924 gave the cartel a majority, and on June 1 Poincaré resigned.

Further deterioration of the French finances, which successive cabinets had been unable to remedy, brought Poincaré to power once more. On July 21, 1926, the exchange rate of the franc fell to 48 to the U.S. dollar (as against 5 in 1914). Next day Poincaré was appointed premier and formed a coalition government, taking the portfolio of finance for himself and giving that of foreign affairs to Briand. Public opinion was immediately appeased, and with the help of a few technical measures Poincaré restored confidence in the franc, which by the end of the year stood at 24 to the dollar. The next difficulty was to prevent this rise of the franc from continuing to a point at which French exports would be adversely affected; but Poincaré succeeded in maintaining a stabilization *de facto* for a year and a half. The general election of April 1928 returned a majority in favour of Poincaré's policy, and in June he obtained the passing of a bill establishing his stabilization *de jure* and basing the French franc on gold again. It was altogether one of the most successful operations of its kind in history.

The withdrawal of the Radical ministers from his cabinet caused Poincaré's resignation on Nov. 7, 1928, but he formed a new government immediately. France was now prosperous, and the premier's prestige was unbounded. In spring 1929 he tried to induce Parliament to ratify the agreements negotiated in Washington and London on Inter-Allied debts, but his efforts had strained him too far, and he fell dangerously ill. He resigned office on July 26, 1929. Never fully recovering health, he occupied himself with the continuation of his memoirs, *Au service de la France*, ten volumes of which appeared between 1926 and 1933. He died in Paris on Oct. 15, 1934.

Supremely clever, deeply learned, fastidiously scrupulous, Poincaré sometimes revealed a sort of narrow-mindedness. But on the whole he was a great man of honour, a very able statesman, and a great Frenchman.

See S. Huddleston, *Poincaré* (1924); J. Chastenet, *Raymond Poincaré* (1948).   (J. C. DE C.)

POINCIANA, a genus of tropical and subtropical shrubs or small trees (usually not more than ten feet high) of the pea family (Leguminosae), grown for their showy orange or yellow and red flowers. The best-known species are the Barbados pride, or dwarf poinciana (*P. pulcherrima*), and the bird-of-paradise bush (*P. gilliesii*), both of which are widely grown in warm regions. *Poinciana* is sometimes included in the genus *Caesalpinia*.

The royal poinciana is a different but closely related ornamental tree (see FLAMBOYANT TREE).

POINSETT, JOEL ROBERTS (1779–1851), U.S. statesman noted primarily for his diplomacy in Latin America, was born on March 2, 1779, in Charleston, S.C. He was educated in England and the United States. In 1810 he became a special agent for the United States in Buenos Aires and Chile, initiating diplomatic relations with those states. Poinsett was elected to the South Carolina legislature in 1816 and two years later won election to the U.S. House of Representatives. He went on a special governmental mission to Mexico in 1822 and 1823, and in 1824 published *Notes on Mexico,* a book describing his experiences. In March 1825 he gave up his seat in Congress to become the first minister to Mexico, a post he held until December 1829.

In 1830 Poinsett became a leader of the Unionist Party in South Carolina, a group that opposed those who sought to carry John C. Calhoun's doctrine of nullification into effect. As a reward for his services in that controversy, Pres. Martin Van Buren appointed him secretary of war, a post he held with distinction for four years. In 1841 he retired to his plantation in South Carolina where he opposed the growing secessionist movement in his state. He died near Statesburg, S.C., on Dec. 12, 1851.

Poinsett's varied intellectual interests included the fine arts, agriculture, and botany. He was honoured by having the flower he brought from Mexico, the poinsettia, named after him. His main contribution to learning was his work in helping to found the National Institute for the Promotion of Science and the Useful Arts in 1840, a precursor of the Smithsonian Institution. Poinsett was one of the most versatile and cosmopolitan Americans of his time. (A. DeC.)

POINSETTIA, a showy tropical shrub of the spurge family (Euphorbiaceae; *q.v.*), native to Mexico and Central America. It is a traditional flower of the Christmas season, known scientifically as *Euphorbia pulcherrima,* the latter term meaning most beautiful. The poinsettia was named after Joel R. Poinsett of Charleston, S.C., who introduced the plant to the United States in 1828 when he was minister to Mexico. The true flowers of the poinsettia are inconspicuous, forming a yellow cluster in the centre of the red, white or pink bracts. In the rarer double poinsettia most of the flowers have been transformed into bracts giving a more showy effect. The poinsettia is abundantly used as a yuletide gift plant in the north, while in Florida and other tropical lands it is a popular flowering shrub.

ROCHE

COMMON POINSETTIA (EUPHORBIA PULCHERRIMA)

When used as a gift plant it should be placed in a room with constant temperature as it cannot tolerate drafts or fluctuating temperatures. It needs plenty of water while blooming. Although it is possible to carry a plant over from one year to the next, it is not advisable unless greenhouse facilities are available. Poinsettias are propagated by cuttings in March.

See also HOUSE PLANTS. (R. T. V. T.)

POINTE-À-PITRE, the principal town of Guadeloupe (*q.v.*) in the French Antilles, is situated on the southwest coast of Grande-Terre, the low-lying island which forms the eastern half of Guadeloupe. The town lies on the east shore of the estuary of the Rivière Salée, a channel that connects two large bays to north and south and separates Grande-Terre from Basse-Terre, the mountainous western half of Guadeloupe. Several islets in the southern bay guard the approach to the harbour of Pointe-à-Pitre, and in the vicinity of the town there are extensive mangrove swamps. The total population (1962) was 27,737.

Pointe-à-Pitre was founded in the mid-17th century, soon after the French settlement of Guadeloupe, but it was eclipsed in importance by Basse-Terre, which still remains the administrative capital. In 1906 a road bridge across the Rivière Salée replaced the existing ferry and, favoured by its central position and harbour facilities, Pointe-à-Pitre became the chief commercial town. Near the centre of the town there are many old houses with stone lower and wooden upper stories; in the mid-20th century there was extensive suburban development, particularly north toward Raizet Airport and the nearby town of Les Abymes. (D. R. H.)

POINTE-NOIRE, the principal port of the Congo Republic, west-central Africa, lies 316 mi. W of Brazzaville, at the terminus of the Congo–Ocean Railway line which was built to avoid the rapids of the lower Congo River. Pop. (1958) 54,573, including about 3,000 Europeans. It was the country's capital from 1950 to 1958. The so-called European town developed in three distinct areas. To the west is the plain, across a marshy dip partly filled up; the plateau, a slight well-drained rise, is the residential quarter; to the south along the road to the airport is an industrial district with timber and engineering works. The inhabitants of the European town are chiefly French, with some Portuguese traders. Alongside old houses in Norman style with gardens are buildings of concrete. The plateau also contains the shopping centre, hospital, mission houses, cathedral, oceanography centre, and schools. Northeast of the plateau, in the swampy valley of the Tchinouka, the African village was created. The Africans come from all parts and include about 140 ethnic groups. The huts are often in the traditional style, of wood, dried mud, or brick with palm-leaf roofs. The need for settled workers led to the building of a new town,

Tie-Tie, where many houses are of more durable materials.

The port, on the Atlantic Ocean, stands on a calm bay, protected by breakwaters and approached through a well-cleared fairway. Begun in 1934, it was opened in 1939. Because of World War II the installations, including an oil store, workshops, and repair yards, were only completed in 1946. There is a factory producing phosphorous cellulose, and plans were made for an industrial combine, using hydroelectric power from the Kouilou, to treat iron from Mekambo and manganese from Franceville. (J. D.)

POINT SET, in mathematics, is a collection of points selected from a given space. Generally speaking, the properties of a point set may be classified as topological or metric. For a description of the former *see* TOPOLOGY, GENERAL. A brief introduction to the metric properties of point sets follows.

The Problem of Measure.—Consider the simple example in which the given space is an ordinary straight line L. If P and Q are distinct points of L, then the point set consisting of P and Q together with all points between them is called an interval, denoted $[P,Q]$. A common foot rule can be applied to L, and the interval $[P,Q]$ can be measured as a certain number of feet. The length of a single point, in accordance with ordinary geometry, is zero. If two intervals have no point in common, it is not customary to speak of the length of the set of points they represent, the word length being usually applied only to connected pieces. In this case the word measure is used; the measure of this point set is the sum of the lengths of the two intervals.

However, to speak of a point set on L does not necessarily imply an interval, a single point, or a set of intervals; it sometimes means a set of points that contains no connected portion; *i.e.,* no interval. Since a point has length zero, the measure of such a set might be expected to be the sum of the lengths of its individual points; *i.e.,* the sum of a set of zeros, and hence zero. However, if we determine upon a measure for two point sets A and B which have no points in common, the sum of their measures should be the measure of the point set comprising A and B taken together. Thus, above, it is stated that the measure of a set of two intervals with no common point is the sum of the lengths of those intervals. Any interval $[P,Q]$ can be shown to be the sum of two sets A and B each of which fails to contain any interval, and if the measure of both A and B is arbitrarily called zero, the sum of their measures would be zero, which is not the length of $[P,Q]$, no matter how small. In other words, a measure of a set of points is wanted that will correspond to the ordinary idea of length.

This has introduced what is known in the theory of sets of points as the problem of measure. Among several methods devised for finding a measure of an arbitrary set of points, the theory of Lebesgue measure is the foundation of the theory of integration (*see* INTEGRATION AND MEASURE: *The Extension Period*).

Lebesgue Measure.—Any set A is said to be covered by a collection G of intervals, when every point of A is in some interval of G. If the set of intervals G is denumerable, then it is said to be a covering of A. (The set is called denumerable if its elements can be tagged with positive integers in such a way that no two elements of the set are tagged with the same integer.) If the sum of the lengths of the intervals of G exists, let this be called the sum-length of the covering. Of all possible coverings of A consider the corresponding sum-lengths, and let N be the largest number that is not greater than any of these sum-lengths. Then N is called the exterior (outer) measure of A and is denoted $m_e A$. Suppose, now, that $[P,Q]$ is some interval of length d, such that all points of A are within $[P,Q]$. Let B be the set of all points of $[P,Q]$ that do not belong to A, and let $m_e B$ denote the exterior measure of B, found just as $m_e A$ was found. If it happens that $m_e A + m_e B = d$, then $m_e A$ is accepted as the measure of A and is what is known as the Lebesgue measure of A. At the same time $m_e B$ is the Lebesgue measure of B, and in accordance with ideas of length it is required that the sum of the two measures give the length of $[P,Q]$. To be sure, the Lebesgue measure of a set of points may not exist, but it does exist for all ordinary point sets. Indeed it is not easy to give an example of a set of points with no Lebesgue measure; all examples that have been given use methods unacceptable to many mathematicians.

For the measure of a set of points in a plane, areas are employed. Thus, the measure of the set of all points in a square is the area of the square. And to get the measure of a general plane point set M, a covering of M is made by means of squares. In three dimensions cubes are employed, and concern is with sum-volumes.

The introduction of the notion of measure led to an enrichment of general analysis that hardly could have been realized otherwise. The effect has been felt not only in mathematics itself, but in the closely allied fields of mechanics and dynamics. *See also* SET THEORY (THEORY OF AGGREGATES); FOURIER SERIES.

BIBLIOGRAPHY.—E. W. Hobson, *The Theory of Functions of a Real Variable and the Theory of Fourier's Series* (1921); E. Kasner and J. Newman, *Mathematics and the Imagination*, pp. 201–207 (1940); J. H. Williamson, *Lebesgue Integration* (1962). (R. L. WI.)

POISON is a substance, natural or synthetic, which causes damage to living tissues and has an injurious or fatal effect on the body, whether it be taken by mouth, inhaled, absorbed through the skin, or gain entry by any other route. The degree of toxicity is inversely proportional to the dose required to bring about a noxious effect, or to kill, but this is not a precise statement, for degrees of toxicity vary from one subject to another and according to the circumstances.

Many poisons act nonspecifically, destroying indiscriminately those tissues upon which they impinge. Thus, corrosives, such as phenol, or caustics, such as sodium hydroxide, bring about direct cell necrosis. On the skin they burn and erode. In the eyes they ulcerate and may penetrate. If inhaled as fine droplets they irritate the linings of the bronchi and the lungs. When swallowed they may inflict such trauma upon the mucous membranes and other structures of the mouth, gullet, stomach, and intestines that the consequences can be fatal. Other poisons are biochemically specific. Thus, arsenic interferes with particular cellular enzymes that are essential to metabolic survival; strychnine alters nervous conduction in the brain and spinal cord; and the organophosphorus compounds, introduced originally as agents of chemical warfare and now used widely as agricultural and horticultural pesticides, derange the function of the peripheral nerves. According to the degree to which these vital processes are distorted, and according to the persistence of the changes so wrought, there is either bodily dysfunction from which recovery is possible or such disorganization that death ensues.

Poisoning does not necessarily have an all-or-none effect. Degrees of poisoning are recognized, and some substances are more toxic than others. Potassium cyanide, of which as little as 0.25 g. may be lethal, is rated as highly toxic. Common salt, on the other hand, usually regarded as benign and as an item of the diet, can nevertheless kill if a large enough single dose is taken. It is of comparatively low toxicity.

Toxicology is the study of poisons and poisoning. As a science it first developed forensically in the investigation of death by poisoning, especially homicide. The preoccupation then was with natural toxins, principally those derived from plants and animals, though mineral sources were acknowledged as well. The ancients, it will be recalled, were well-nigh obsessed with fear of poisoning. Mithradates VI Eupator (d. 63 B.C.), king of Pontus, seeking protection against this eventuality, worked on the principle that by taking successively augmented doses of an increasingly wider range of toxins a person could generate a resistance to them all. From this theory the verb "mithridatize" was derived. Though murder by poison was believed to have reached its heyday in the Italy of the Borgias, its forensic investigation at that time could be virtually discounted. Toxicology as a science is said to have been established as recently as the beginning of the 19th century, with the work of Mathieu Orfila (1787–1853). The subject today embraces human poisoning—accidental as well as suicidal and homicidal—in industry and in the home, resulting from drugs, pesticides, and even food additives. Furthermore, attention is now being paid to contamination of the environment as a whole.

The modern study of poisons and poisoning has thus become a multidisciplinary exercise. Experimental toxicology is carried out principally in the laboratory, usually with animals, and brings together biochemistry, physics, physiology, pharmacology, path-

ology, and statistics in an effort to reveal the fundamental phenomena and mechanisms and to express them quantitatively as well as descriptively. Clinical toxicology relates these findings to the practice of medicine for the diagnosis, treatment, and prevention of poisoning in man. Veterinary toxicology is correspondingly related to animals. Forensic toxicology deals with the association between poisoning and the law, to some extent in civil actions but more notably in criminal cases. This discipline provides common ground between the pathologist and the lawyer, with indispensable assistance from the forensic analyst. Industrial toxicology demands an understanding of factory processes and conditions, dangerous chemicals, and the exposure that may arise from them; analytical techniques to determine the prevailing conditions; and clinical, biochemical, and sometimes psychological examination of personnel to detect, treat, and prevent overexposure where it does occur. This work leads to the formulation and adoption of the principles of factory hygiene and to cooperation between employers and employees in their implementation. A closely allied specialty is agricultural toxicology, now recognized in its own right because of the widespread use in the second half of the 20th century of chemical pesticides.

The developing conception of environmental toxicology gives a new dimension to the study of poisoning, embracing as it does the whole realm of biological activity. From the chemical industry, so prominent a part of the contemporary economy, a host of potentially toxic products and by-products, albeit in very low concentrations, can be dispersed throughout the atmosphere, the soil, the water supplies, and the natural habitat in general. Not only is man in danger, but also all other forms of life. The 1960s witnessed extraordinary refinements in analytical procedures to detect and measure extraneous compounds at remarkably low levels; *e.g.*, parts per thousand-million, or even less. Mere presence, though alerting, is not to be automatically equated with danger. Properly to assess the hazards calls for the services of—besides the analysts who sound the alarm—experimental toxicologists, epidemiologists, nutritionists, physicians, pathologists, practitioners in public health, veterinarians, biologists, agriculturalists, ecologists and experts in wild life, meteorologists, statisticians, and a host of other specialists, all working in concert. Government and other authorities must also take an interest, for corrective action may very well demand communal or statutory control. By the late 1960s little and uncertain progress had been made in this field. (*See* POLLUTION, ENVIRONMENTAL.)

Types of Poisoning.—Poisoning may be acute or chronic. When a single dose of, for example, phosphorus, corrosive sublimate (mercuric chloride), or arsenic trioxide is followed directly by symptoms that imperil the victim, the course is said to be acute. By contrast, a person may consume an arsenical "tonic" for weeks or months without noticing anything amiss, and only gradually do symptoms of indigestion, skin rashes, and changes in the nerves of the arms and legs make their appearance. Similarly, a child with a propensity for chewing old and flaking paint, or a labourer reclaiming lead from old electrical batteries, may suffer no injury at the outset. Only after weeks or months will they have accumulated so much of the metal in their bodies that the signs of chronic lead poisoning emerge. Over the intervening period, accumulation has taken place, because intake has exceeded excretion. The normal subject may harbour a small quantity of a particular substance, *e.g.*, fluoride, iodine, or zinc, throughout life without any distress. Indeed, this trace may be essential to health. A somewhat higher level may confer increased benefit, as is the case with fluoride and its protection against dental decay. Only when a still higher critical level is exceeded do adverse complications ensue. Consequently it is sometimes very difficult to classify a substance as a poison, in isolation; so much depends on circumstances.

Chronic poisoning can, however, occur without the causal substance actually becoming stored in the body. The pain-relieving drug phenacetin, taken daily, even in large doses, is completely metabolized and eliminated. Yet a person who indulges in such self-medication excessively over months or years can sustain severe and irreversible kidney damage.

A peculiar variant of chronic toxicity is chemical carcinogenicity.

Prolonged exposure to certain oils, to benzidine, to beta-naphthylamine, to asbestos, and, perhaps more impressively, to cigarette smoking, can lead, after a falsely reassuring interval, often of many years, to the development of distinctive and characteristic cancers. No dose-response relationship has been worked out for this process; repeated contact seems to be the essential feature, together, possibly, with a particular chemical configuration. (*See* Carcinogenic Chemicals.)

Route of Entry.—The mode of entry of a poison into the body has a marked bearing on the subsequent reactions. Commonly it is by mouth, though it may be via the lungs, through the skin, or by more devious routes; *e.g.*, injection. An atmosphere heavy with carbon dioxide to the extent that the oxygen content is below the minimum needed to support life may prove lethally asphyxiating. Solid carbon dioxide (dry ice), however, is likely to cause skin burns when it is handled without adequate protection. Liquid mercury can be swallowed as a single dose almost with impunity, but the same mercury incorporated into an ointment and applied repeatedly to the skin may be the reason for severe chronic poisoning. The same metal, moreover, inadvertently injected into a vein can provoke calamitous changes in the circulation, by physical means and without any biochemical reactions. Ordinary domestic soap, too, can obviously come into contact with the skin without harm. Swallowed, it does little more than set up nausea and vomiting. Introduced into the pregnant uterus it can have generally drastic consequences for the woman, far in excess of the deliberate abortion for which it was intended. Introduced into the blood vessels it may break up the red cells to an alarming extent.

Assessment of Toxicity.—The dose of a poison needed to kill, or to bring about even a definite undesirable result on the body, differs from one person to another and markedly among the various species of animals. Thus, toxicity assessment is beset by the vagaries of biological variation. Objective tests to determine fatal dosages in man being ethically indefensible, the best method that can be achieved is to arrive at vague estimates from accidents, suicides, and homicides where known amounts have been administered and the outcome is documented. This leads to extensive gaps in knowledge, especially for new chemicals. Therefore, animals are used to determine the lethal dose, which is expressed as an average figure for a group in terms of grams or milligrams per kilogram body weight—the so-called LD_{50}. This is qualified according to the species selected, the sex, the route of administration, and occasionally the age as well. Man will not necessarily display the same susceptibility and, when extrapolating from animal figures, the most sensitive species is usually chosen as a precaution.

The single dose, however, that will kill is always more than that which, administered repeatedly over a course of time, can prove ultimately injurious. For this reason, chronic toxicity tests are also undertaken in animals. Ranging from a few weeks to the length of the life span, these tests seek to establish the maximum daily dose that is found to have no toxicity, either evidenced in the animal during life or disclosed pathologically postmortem. This is referred to as the no-effect level. In order to lay down for man what is a safe dose day after day, the no-effect level from a chronic study in the most sensitive species is divided by some arbitrary figure—the safety factor, commonly 100—and this is regarded as the human acceptable daily intake.

Carcinogenicity testing is still more exacting. If there is no clinical indication from man or, at the most, no more than suspicion, at least two species of animals are dosed with the substance in question throughout their life span. Extra groups may be selected in order that more than one route of administration may be carried out—subcutaneous, by inhalation, or oral. Then the behaviour of the animals is observed and any that die before the conclusion of the test are examined. Finally, the survivors are killed and searching tests are made of all the organs, macroscopically and microscopically, to see whether any cancerous changes are present. Since in any group of animals a few cancers will arise spontaneously, a statistical comparison has to be made between the treated and untreated (*i.e.*, control) groups.

So long as the animal experiments are accurately designed for the stated objective and so long as they are carried out by experienced scientists, the results will afford a reasonable foundation from which to predict relative toxicity to man, though never a guarantee of absolute safety.

Intent of Poisoning.—Historically, poisoning was often homicidal. Before the advance of forensic toxicology, murder by poisoning was an attractive method for disposing of one's enemies, rivals, and other objects of passion without fear of being found out. Although today this is less common, homicidal poisoning is by no means nonexistent in modern society. Indeed, forensic toxicology is largely concerned with such cases.

Suicidal poisoning is, by comparison, reaching near-epidemic proportions in 20th-century Western civilization. The term, however, is no longer accurate. Of those who take poison by their own hands probably only a minority are committed to a fatal outcome. The majority are simply contriving an exhibition, a demonstration, or a crisis to call attention to themselves. They feel overburdened, disregarded, and neglected. By taking a sufficient amount of some noxious substance to make themselves ill they immediately muster intense medical care and attract anxiety, sympathy, and consideration from their friends and relatives. In modern parlance they are making a cry for psychological help.

Accidental poisoning is quite a separate category. It may come about from a genuine mistake in the dose of a drug, from swallowing a poison in error for something else, from a breakdown in factory or industrial hygiene, or from some other mishap. More disturbingly, accidental poisoning is a common feature of childhood. Youngsters, especially those under four or five years of age, experience their surroundings more by their oral than by their visual and tactile senses. To put things into their mouths is instinctive. Since at this immature stage they have little faculty for discrimination, poisoning is a likely outcome. Given access, they will eat toxic plants and fungi, drugs and medicines left within their reach, household requisites, chemicals for the garden, or virtually anything which may come their way. Accidental poisoning is one of the commonest reasons for children being hospitalized, and deaths so attributable are of annually increasing incidence in the second half of the 20th century.

PREVENTION

Legislation.—That prevention is preferable to treatment and cure, and still more so to a fatal outcome, is no less axiomatic in poisoning than it is in other realms of medicine. At first the aim was—understandably enough in the context of earlier centuries—to deter or impede the would-be murderer. Statutory provision has been made in most countries to ensure that noxious substances should not be freely available. A balance has had to be struck between those who have a bona fide need of such substances for their trade or profession, *e.g.*, chemical manufacturers or doctors, and those who have no rightful business with them. This balance has been achieved, in the main, by listing or scheduling under some statutory instrument just those substances which are to be regarded as poisons, notwithstanding the imprecision of the scientific criteria for reaching a decision. In the end, pragmatic judgments very often obtain. Next it is directed that the specified substances shall be stocked, sold, and supplied only through approved and limited agencies and outlets, *e.g.*, registered pharmacies or authorized merchants. Then, certain conditions are laid down about containers, packaging, and labeling, together with rules about storage and records—these being subject to official inspection. Finally, purchasers may be designated, usually according to their profession or occupation: doctors, dentists, pest destroyers, etc. In any event, a check is imposed on every purchaser and every transaction. By these means it is made difficult for malefactors and the ignorant to procure poisons at all; and, if they should contrive to do so, their subsequent apprehension in the event of some misdeed or misadventure is considerably facilitated.

The pattern of this legislation, of course, varies from one country to another. On examination it may well appear to lack singularity of intention and comprehensiveness, having evolved piecemeal over the years in response to passing demands and political exigencies. This is well illustrated in Britain, where the relevant statutes include the Pharmacy and Poisons Act (1933), the Therapeutic Substances Act (1956), the Drugs (Prevention of Misuse) Act (1964), and the Dangerous Drugs Act (1965), together with the consequential statutory instruments made thereunder. Further powers have been taken and some rationalization of the previous medley of legislation has been brought about by the Medicines Act, 1968.

In the United States similar control on a federal scale has been effected by such enactments as the Caustic Poison Act (1927), the federal Food, Drug and Cosmetic Act (1938), the Insecticide, Fungicide and Rodenticide Act (1947), and the Narcotic Control Act (1956), supported and sometimes extended by state legislation with the same objective.

Industrial.—As chemical manufacture expanded rapidly during the 19th century, poisoning became more common among the workers. Gradually the reason became apparent. It was repeated contact with such agents as lead, mercury, arsenic, zinc, aromatic hydrocarbons, and organic solvents—to name only a few. As early as 1864 official action was taken in Britain to safeguard those who worked with lead, and these directions were given statutory backing by the Factories (Prevention of Lead Poisoning) Act (1883). Then the Factories Act (1898) first made it obligatory to report industrial diseases, and that of 1937 stipulated particular forms of poisoning occurring among workers that should be reported to the chief inspector of factories. By this means not only were afflicted individuals assured of proper treatment but, in addition, the conditions of employment could be investigated and suitably modified to prevent any recurrence.

In the United States the principles of industrial hygiene took longer to be applied, notwithstanding the pioneer work of Alice Hamilton. A few states made sporadic efforts toward the end of the 19th century but the first official stimulus was derived from the workmen's compensation laws that were introduced after 1901. These were reinforced by the Social Security Act (1935). Today, through the state public health agencies, considerable activity is directed toward protecting the health of workers generally and against occupational poisoning in particular.

In practically every other developed country, and in many others that are still developing, concerted action is being taken to avoid poisoning in industry. At the same time, international liaison and exchange of information are promoted by the World Health Organization and the International Labour Office.

In one section of industry, poisoning has lately taken on a special significance, notably in relation to pesticides used in agriculture, horticulture, and food storage. Some, though not all, of these chemicals can be dangerous to man. Spurred on by the economic advantages to be gained, farmers and growers may be tempted to handle these substances with more enthusiasm than caution, in consequence of which numerous casualties have occurred in different parts of the world. From self-interest combined with a sense of public responsibility, the manufacturers and vendors of these chemicals generally issue recommendations for safe use. This guidance must be based on the known toxicity and other characteristics of each product as ascertained by specific study and experiment. Unfortunately many of the people called upon to use these chemicals in the field either choose to disregard or are incapable of heeding the warnings. Constant supervision is imperative for their own sakes. In this sphere, moreover, official intervention has been commonly delayed, is inadequate, or is totally lacking. The salutary record of safety evident in Britain may well be ascribed to the working of the agriculture (poisonous substances) regulations.

Medicines.—From the published morbidity and mortality statistics it is obvious that by far the major incidence of poisoning is due to drugs and medicines, whether taken accidentally or deliberately. Until about the 1920s most of the medications at the disposal of the physician were just as safe as they were ineffective. With few exceptions, such as digitalis for heart disorders, emetine for amoebiasis, opium and its derivatives as analgesics, the pharmaceutical stock-in-trade owed its reputation largely to faith and suggestion. Most drugs available in the late 1960s were undeniably potent, therapeutically beneficent, and unquestionably dangerous. Their misuse and abuse can be truly calamitous.

Commonly the margin between dose and overdose is fairly narrow. Mistakes can easily happen, so that what was intended as a curative dose may in fact prove an overwhelming one. Children may accidentally, or adults purposely, take an excess. In addition there may be adverse reactions even when the dose is correct. For instance, the antibiotic chloramphenicol, given to control an infection, may damage the bone marrow and so interfere with the formation of blood cells. Another drug that relieves mental depression may simultaneously derange the liver. Simple aspirin may provoke severe bleeding from the stomach. Then there are the less immediate sequelae. Thalidomide, outstandingly safe though it appeared to be as a hypnotic and sedative, proved to be teratogenetic; i.e., given to women in the early stages of pregnancy it was followed by the birth of devastatingly deformed children. Such a catalog may be continued indefinitely.

There still remains the phenomenon of addiction—at least a form of poisoning, of the mind if not of the body. This is usually associated with morphine, heroin, cocaine, cannabis products, and the amphetamines.

The possibilities of poisoning, in a general sense, from drugs and medicines are therefore enormous. Yet because of the indispensability of drugs to medical practice a balance must be drawn between prescription and proscription. To this end a series of safeguards is adopted.

First the drug is subjected to pharmacological and toxicity testing in large numbers of animals. Its actions and limitations can thus be provisionally assessed. Next it is given in successive doses to volunteers whose responses are carefully checked. Then it undergoes clinical trials in patients. Only after this stage is it released for general clinical use, at first cautiously and then on a wider scale. Monitoring for further reactions continues to be maintained. A body of information is accumulated in this way about each drug from which it is possible to pronounce upon its indications, its contraindications, and its limitations. All of this work devolves primarily upon the pharmaceutical companies responsible for producing new drugs. Their efforts, nonetheless, are customarily supervised and checked by an official body: in Britain the Medicines Commission, and in the United States the federal Food and Drug Administration.

Even after all this scrutiny it may be decided that a particular drug, though valuable, is liable to cause harm if it is distributed for self-medication by the public at large. So its sale and supply must be limited to a doctor's order or prescription. Each country has its own laws to effect this arrangement.

Additionally, educational campaigns are promoted by pharmaceutical companies, professional associations, and medical journals in order to induce doctors to prescribe judiciously and discriminatingly and, further, to convince the public that the misuse of medicines can have tragic consequences. Despite all this activity aimed at prevention, more poisoning is due to medicines than to any other cause.

Environmental.—The sources of contamination of the environment are, as previously mentioned, manifold. From chimneys, furnaces, and other outlets irrespirable gases, toxic vapours, and troublesome droplets or particulate material may be emitted. These may prove inimical not just to the surrounding human population but to other animal and plant life as well. Other effluents may find their way directly to the land or into watercourses. What, moreover, has only lately been realized is that outstandingly persistent chemicals, which resist chemical and biological degradation, make their way through the natural food-chain—from soil and water to plant, from plant to animal, and from plant and animal to man. In this way their presence becomes ubiquitous, if only in trace amounts. Notorious in this respect are some of the organochlorine pesticides—dicophan (DDT), aldrin, and dieldrin.

Positive nuisances, especially if they convey toxicity, must be abated. To do this simply by shutting down the factory, discontinuing the process, or stopping some technical operation is, however, seldom feasible. This may be tantamount to economic suicide. Once again some compromise is sought. Flue and exhaust gases may be dispersed out of reach or treated so as to render them harmless; effluents may be detoxified or channeled away to safety.

Sometimes alternative processes or chemicals may be employed that yield no toxic by-products. Any of these devices may add to the operating expense and there is then a conflict between what is commercially preferable and what is healthy for the community. To expect the parties immediately concerned satisfactorily to resolve such differences is unreasonable. Government or some other authoritative agency must make the decision, objectively and with the welfare of society as the paramount criterion. This is the policy that is officially followed today in practically every country of the world. In Britain the appropriate powers are granted under the Alkali Act and the Public Health Act. Provision is also made for a technical inspectorate, charged with ensuring that the specific regulations are enforced and exercising in addition a constant watch for further sources of pollution that may require to be controlled. For, in this context, biological survival depends on eternal vigilance.

Food Additives are of two types: first, nonnutritive substances deliberately added to food in small quantities to assist in its preparation, preservation, palatability, and appearance; and, second, the residues of pesticides that are utilized in food production (both plant and animal) and which find their way into the diet. Widespread alarm is sounded from time to time about the deleterious effects these additives, both intentional and nonintentional, may exert on the health of consumers. Today, most countries exercise some official or statutory control to guard against such risks, and jointly the Food and Agriculture Organization and the World Health Organization of the UN provide continuous and expert guidance.

The acceptability, or unacceptability, of a food additive or residue is customarily decided in the following manner. Chemical analyses are performed upon the foodstuffs treated according to the prevailing technical or agricultural practices, in order to ascertain the nature of the chemicals remaining and their concentration. These chemicals are tested in animals to discover whether they are toxic and, if so, how they act. Then, with prolonged feeding to large groups, the highest dose is determined that fails to retard growth, influence reproduction, alter behaviour, or bring about any pathological change, either during life or on postmortem inspection, in whatever is found to be the most susceptible species. This is referred to as the "maximum no-effect level." By dividing the no-effect level by the customary safety factor (100), a maximum acceptable daily intake is arrived at for man and this is expressed in milligrams per kilogram body weight. In analyzing the additive and residue levels it is possible to calculate, from the foodstuffs embodying them and their contribution to the diet, the total quantity of extraneous chemical likely to be ingested daily. If this is greater than the maximum acceptable daily intake, adjusted for the total body weight of man, then the additive or residue is excessive and its use cannot be condoned. If, on the other hand, the additive or residue load is within the calculated acceptable intake, it is regarded as permissible. The countries that exercise control in this way—all the major food-consuming and food-importing nations—entrust this work to their governmental food, agriculture, and health departments.

In practice there seems to be an even greater margin of safety. Not all foodstuffs are treated with additives and only a fraction of them harbour pesticide residues. Where comprehensive analyses have been undertaken, not on selected samples but on total diets, as, for example, by the so-called "market basket survey," the quantities of additives and residues detected have always been appreciably lower, and often far lower, than would be expected from the theoretical calculations. So, although the vogue in the late 1960s for deploying chemicals in food production and processing was a potential source of poisoning to the populace, the restrictions and surveillance constantly imposed should set most fears at rest.

TREATMENT

History has unfortunately left a strange and misleading legacy on treatment of acute poisoning. From the earliest times each separate toxin has been endowed, more by conjecture than by scientific inquiry, with its own distinctive characteristics and mode of action. Treatment has accordingly been planned on the philosophy of specific antidotes, as though the law of physics, which states that to every action there is an equal and opposite reaction, could be followed toxicologically. With a few notable exceptions this theory has proved inaccurate and is at last being abandoned medically, even though it still lingers in the minds of the lay public.

To only a small minority of the known poisons has an intrinsic toxicological mechanism been ascribed and for only a few of these have effective biochemical antidotes been prepared. Treatment, in the main, must therefore follow more general lines.

First Aid.—In the first place it should be appreciated that even acute poisoning is seldom of dramatic urgency. Cyanides admittedly can kill within a few minutes and adrenalin injected as an overdose can be rapidly lethal. These, however, are exceptions; more often there is time for maneuver. As soon as the patient is seen, further exposure or access to the poison should be prevented. If he is breathing a toxic gas he should be removed from the offending atmosphere, or the outflow should be turned off. Sometimes, as with a child or mental patient, dangerous drugs can be snatched from the hands. Contaminated clothing should be torn off, and skin or eyes washed promptly and copiously with water. Such action seldom takes more than a minute or two. The urgent priority is the breathing. Anyone with totally arrested breathing is unlikely to survive more than five minutes. Any dentures or other obstruction should be removed from the mouth, the tongue should be drawn forward, and a clear airway should be established. If then spontaneous breathing fails to return, artificial respiration should be applied and carried on for as long as necessary, substituting a mechanical technique for the manual method as soon as the apparatus can be procured.

When the patient appears to be in shock, *i.e.,* when he is pale, faint, and has a rapid, thready pulse, the circulation can often be restored, at least temporarily, by putting him in the head-down position, with the head a little lower than the feet. Should there be convulsions, the movements should be gently but firmly restrained and protection should be afforded against falls and injury. Only after these basic preliminaries should any thought be given to recovering any swallowed poison from the stomach.

Vomiting should never be induced nor gastric lavage performed as a routine. In certain circumstances this may do more harm than good. Definite contraindications are ingested corrosives and caustics, when the "burning" and eroding of the mouth and throat betoken possibly worse damage lower down the gullet and in the stomach. Paraffin (kerosene), petrol (gasoline), white spirit (turpentine substitute), and products containing solvents or vehicles of this kind, *e.g.,* polishes and cleaners, are also better left undisturbed. In themselves they are not very toxic; regurgitated they may find their way into the bronchi and lungs and there set up an intractable bronchopneumonia. If there is a good reason to think that the substance swallowed is not very poisonous, or the dose is small, there is no virtue in essaying prompt recovery and if more than about four hours have elapsed, it is too late. Finally, emesis and the use of a stomach pump should never be attempted as a first-aid measure on an unconscious person.

Where none of these provisos obtains, vomiting may be encouraged. Tickling the back of the throat with a finger may be effective, though one stands the chance of being bitten for one's efforts. In a child, a dose of 10–15 millilitres Syrup of Ipecacuanha may be tried. There are some who advocate a dose of salt and water, dilute copper sulfate, or mustard, but such forms of provocation are not universally accepted. Indeed, opinion is far from unanimous about either the efficacy or the desirability of causing vomiting in the poisoned patient. Yet almost all are agreed that, in this condition, apomorphine should never be injected to produce emesis.

Provision for Treatment.—The general practitioner may well be called first to a case of poisoning. He can diagnose, assess the severity, and carry out emergency resuscitation. For thorough and continuing treatment, however, the patient must be moved to a hospital—preferably one equipped with an intensive care unit, with facilities for controlled respiration, intravenous and dialysis techniques, laboratory support, and, above all, experienced and adequate nursing, including physiotherapy.

Laboratory Toxicology.—In the treatment of acute poisoning, the part played by the laboratory is still a minor one. Treatment can nearly always be satisfactorily directed according to clinical findings and the observed responses. Nevertheless, if more advanced systems are to be developed for eliminating the poison from the body, then laboratory monitoring must surely be accorded a more salient role.

Forensically, the analytical methods for detecting and estimating poisons in tissues and other specimens have reached a high degree of specificity, precision, sensitivity, and accuracy. In academic departments of forensic medicine and, more so, in the state-sponsored forensic science departments attached to the police forces, modern and often extremely sophisticated apparatus and equipment is installed for the analysis—spectrophotometry, fluorimetry, gas-liquid chromatography, mass spectrometry, and atomic absorption. It is probably fair to say that, with poisoning, the assistance that can be afforded by the chemical laboratory is more valuable than in any other branch of crime investigation.

For industrial toxicology the analytical services are commonly furnished both by the independent companies concerned and by the government departments which have an official responsibility for the health of the workers. Where risks are believed to arise, repeated checks are usually made on the working conditions, largely as a measure of factory hygiene. Further, the workers themselves may be examined at stated intervals and chemical tests made on their urine, blood, etc. Research in this area is also carried on by university departments of occupational medicine. The relevant technical information is widely exchanged between members of specialist societies and associations, between governments, and through the International Labour Office and the World Health Organization. Thus, international agreement is reached, for example, on the transport of poisonous chemicals or the maximum concentrations of noxious gases and vapours that can be permitted in the working atmosphere.

It is only in the second half of the 20th century that more than sporadic efforts have been made chemically and analytically to check for contamination in the environment. Some of this work has been initiated by sectional groups, *e.g.*, those devoted to the protection of wildlife. For the sake of community welfare, however, a more comprehensive approach is desirable, such as can be launched or undertaken only at an official or governmental level. Regrettably, the findings of the interested parties are inclined to be tendentiously interpreted. Any conclusions drawn must be related to all the operative factors and must be impartial. (*See* also POLLUTION, ENVIRONMENTAL.)

Poisons Information and Control.—When someone has swallowed a large overdose of sleeping tablets, or has collapsed after inhaling hydrogen cyanide, there is little doubt that poisoning has occurred. But a diagnosis cannot always be made with the same assurance. Numerous plants and other natural products abound the toxicity of which is far from common knowledge. The modern world is beset with chemical products, medicines, drugs, household aids, farm and garden pesticides, and even strange gases and vapours. Not all of them are poisonous but, for any particular item, it is difficult to be sure. The psychoneurotic may gulp down some lavatory cleaner and the small child may sip its mother's perfume. At once it is assumed that both of them are in jeopardy, but who is to be sure and what action should be taken? Having been repeatedly confronted with this problem, the chief pharmacist at Presbyterian–St. Luke's Hospital in Chicago started the first poisons control centre in 1953. The movement begun there has since spread to numerous other countries throughout the world. Across the United States there are now more than 500 such centres, coordinated by the federal Clearing House in Washington, D.C. Canada, too, has a similar network, with headquarters in Ottawa. Corresponding organizations have been set up in Europe, Australasia, and elsewhere.

An index is compiled showing the composition of most of the products being distributed and sold in each country, territory, or region. These comprise drugs, medicines, veterinary preparations, household requisites, toiletries and cosmetics, farm and garden pesticides, industrial chemicals, together with plants, fungi, etc.

An indication is given of the toxicity of each item, the symptoms to which it may give rise, and an outline of treatment. The preparation of this information is a large task, depending on expert assistance and the ready cooperation of all the commercial firms whose wares have to be included. The latter have been commendably forthcoming, despite the trade secrets that have had to be disclosed. The end result has been a compendious toxicological guide to each country's products. Copies are distributed to each centre and filed for rapid retrieval. With a professional staff to man the telephone throughout the 24 hours, answers can be given at once to inquiries about actual incidents of suspected poisoning.

The mode of operation varies according to the country. In North America, the centres are numerous and widely dispersed, their telephone numbers are publicized, and they entertain calls from anyone seeking help, whether lay or medical. In the United Kingdom, by contrast, there are only four centres, including the principal one in London, and queries are accepted only from doctors, to whom, alone, the telephone numbers are divulged.

For financing this service most countries look to public funds. Trade support may also be enlisted. While each country is obliged to create its own index, because of the language and because most products are peculiarly national, an international exchange of ideas is promoted through regional associations.

A poisons information or control service is primarily designed to help with the diagnosis and effective treatment of poisoning. In some areas this basic function is extended to studies in epidemiology and sociology, or to campaigns for prevention, while in other places an information centre may be closely associated with a hospital treatment unit.

Research.—The knowledge of poisoning mechanisms at a cellular level is still very sparse. For example, the means by which barbiturates selectively depress the tissues of the central nervous system remains biochemically a mystery, and the way in which certain antidepressant drugs affect the heart muscle is not yet explained. Similarly, although it is accepted that mercury and arsenic are toxic by virtue of their interference with body enzymes, the precise manner in which this is brought about has not been elucidated. Accordingly, there is considerable scope for toxicological research in molecular biology. Few specialized institutes exist for this purpose, but the Toxicological Research Institute of the British Medical Research Council is a notable exception.

On the clinical side, the prognosis for acutely poisoned patients has been tremendously improved since the 1950s by the application of the local resuscitative measures already outlined.

See also CHEMICAL WARFARE; DRUG ADDICTION; FOOD POISONING, BACTERIOLOGICAL; HEALTH AND SAFETY LAWS; NARCOTICS AND DANGEROUS DRUGS, LAWS RELATING TO; POISONOUS PLANTS; and articles on the various chemicals, plants, etc. *See* also references under "Poison" in the Index.

BIBLIOGRAPHY.—D. Hunter, *The Diseases of Occupations* (1955); J. D. P. Graham, *The Diagnosis and Treatment of Acute Poisoning* (1962); A. S. Curry, *Poison Detection in Human Organs* (1963); R. Goulding and R. R. Watkin, "National Poisons Information Service," *Bulletin of the Ministry of Health and Public Health Service* (monthly), 24, 26 (1963); S. Moeschlin, *Poisoning: Diagnosis and Treatment* (1965); I. Sunshine *et al.*, *Les Centres Anti-Poisons dans le Monde* (1966); T. A. Loomis, *Essentials of Toxicology* (1968); E. Boyland and R. Goulding (eds.), *Modern Trends in Toxicology* (1968).
(R. Gg.)

POISON IVY, the name commonly applied to several, mostly white-fruited, trifoliate species of woody vines or shrubs of the genus *Toxicodendron* of the cashew or sumac family (Anacardiaceae), native to North America. The forms with bushy habit and lobed leaflets are often called poison oak, especially in the western United States. The common poison ivy (*Toxicodendron radicans*), the most widespread species, abundant in eastern North America and less common westward, is a variable species with a bushy or climbing habit and leaves with three leaflets which may be smooth and glossy or hairy, entire, toothed or lobed. Many of these not too constant variations have been designated as separate species or varieties. The commoner of these forms with their ranges are: *T. quercifolium*, with deeply lobed leaflets, Maryland to Texas; *T. radicans rydbergi*, with thicker leaves, Great Plains to Rocky mountains; and *T. diversilobum,* with leaflets mostly scalloped on the margin, Pacific coast. The poison sumac (*T. vernix*), native in swamps from Quebec to Minnesota and south to Texas and Florida, is a tall bush or small tree with pinnately compound leaves with 7 to 13 entire leaflets and drooping, axillary clusters of persisting white fruits. (The common nonpoisonous sumacs of the genus *Rhus* [see SUMAC] have distinctive reddish fruit.)

All species of *Toxicodendron* are poisonous to touch, producing in many persons a severe inflammation of the skin, or dermatitis (*see* below). The toxic principle, urushiol, is produced in the resinous juice of the resin ducts of the leaves, flowers, fruits and bark of stems and roots but not in the pollen grains. Being almost nonvolatile, the urushiol may be carried from the plant on clothing, shoes, tools, soil, by animals, by smoke from burning plants, to persons who never go near the poison ivy plants. Poisoning may occur if clothing is worn a year after contact with poison ivy. (W. C. M.)

Poison Ivy Dermatitis.—The juice of all portions of the poisonous plants discussed above is not irritating or poisonous on first exposure; but after one or more contacts, most persons become sensitized or allergic and will react to the juice with a rash. The sap must get on the skin for the dermatitis to develop. The hands and clothing may transfer sap to other portions of the body not directly exposed. The rash may develop as early as 6 to 12 hours or as late as a week or more after exposure; most commonly it appears within 24 to 48 hours. No one is born with sensitivity; it is generally acquired during childhood and tends to be highest at this time, but over the years it declines despite exposure to the plants. Once sensitivity is lost, a solid immunity remains and the person cannot easily be made sensitive again. The plants are so common and the juices such highly potent sensitizers that over three-fourths of the American population acquires poison ivy dermatitis at some time.

The severity of the rash varies directly with the quantity of sap deposited on the skin and with the person's inherent degree of sensitivity. Sensitivity may be so great that the sap diluted 50,000,000 times will still induce a rash. Even a mildly sensitive person can develop an intense eruption following a high degree of exposure, but the rash heals in a week or less as contrasted with two or three weeks for the highly sensitized.

A moderate degree of immunity can be established, plant extracts given orally (very small doses at first, increased daily over the next few months) being effective. Although complete desensitization is impossible, and skin rash may occur as a side effect, this prophylactic treatment is justified for the highly sensitive because it lessens the intensity and duration of the rash.

Anointing the skin before exposure with "barrier" or detoxifying creams is generally useless, and washing the skin with solvents, soaps or detoxicants is ineffective unless performed within a few minutes after contact. ACTH and cortisonelike drugs, by mouth or injection, promptly control the rash; this is the only known treatment that has a clear-cut beneficial effect. The great majority of popular and folk remedies for local application are without benefit and many are harmful. Bland compresses and soothing lotions do not restrain the rash, but provide comfort and maintain hygiene until the skin recovers spontaneously. *See also* POISONOUS PLANTS. (A. M. K.)

POISONOUS PLANTS are plants that produce adverse physical effects, and sometimes death, when eaten or touched by man or animals. Most plant species are harmless; a few are poisonous under ordinary conditions, others are poisonous under special conditions. Toxic materials are often very strictly localized in the plant. Opium and its related drugs come from the milky latex of the opium poppy (*Papaver somniferum*) but are absent from the seeds, which may be eaten for food. In the water hemlock (*Cicuta maculata*) the root and fruit are poisonous, whereas in corn cockle (*Agrostemma*) the poisonous glycoside is confined to the seeds. The leaf blades of rhubarb (*Rheum rhaponticum*) are highly poisonous but the leaf stalks are nonpoisonous. Some plants are harmless when eaten green and fresh but poisonous when wilted or dried. Others are poisonous when raw but nonpoisonous when cooked. While it is not possible to classify poisonous plants by the toxic ingredient, knowledge of the type of toxic substance is helpful in diagnosing symptoms and treatment.

Types of Toxic Substance.—In general the poisonous character of a plant is due to the presence of one of four groups of organic compounds: an alkaloid, a glycoside, a resin or an organic acid.

Alkaloids.—An alkaloid is a nitrogen-containing organic base; it is colourless, odourless, nearly insoluble in water and very bitter. Except for the fungus ergot (*Claviceps purpurea*), a parasite on rye, and poisonous mushrooms, the sources of all alkaloids are flowering plants. Notable among alkaloids are the opiates and codeines of the opium poppy, the atropine-nicotine groups in the Solanaceae (the nightshade family) and the curines (curare poisons) in tropical members of several families. (*See* ALKALOIDS.)

Glycosides.—A glycoside (glucoside, in part) is a complex carbohydrate which on hydrolysis and in the presence of amino acids or enzymes produces one or more simple sugars and a nonsugar end product called aglycon. These carbohydrates are water-soluble, bitter, often odour producing and may be coloured or colourless. Three primary groups of plant glycosides yielding toxic products on hydrolysis are: (1) cyanogenetic glycosides, in which the poisonous by-product is hydrocyanic acid or prussic acid and found in species of *Sorghum, Prunus* (wild cherries, almonds) and *Linum* (flax); (2) saponin glycosides, produced in species of *Agrostemma* (cockle), *Digitalis* (foxglove), *Actinea* (rubberweed); and (3) solanine glycosides, produced in members of the nightshade family, especially berries of *Solanum*. (*See also* GLYCOSIDES, NATURAL.)

Resins.—The toxic resins or resinoids occur in poisonous members of the heath family (Ericaceae), water hemlock (*Cicuta*) of the carrot family, and in the milkweeds (Asclepiadaceae). For the most part they are an insoluble gummy material of complex organic structure, localized in resin- or latex-containing ducts.

Organic Acids.—Only a few of the organic acids commonly found in plants are toxic in the amount or in the form in which they occur naturally. The family of nettles (Urticaceae) owes its reputation to the irritant properties of formic acid, which is borne in the hairs of the leaves and stems of most of the species. The toxic properties of *Prunus* species (leaves, bark, and seeds), as mentioned earlier, depend on the generation of hydrocyanic acid. Oxalic acid, occurring usually as oxalates, is present in considerable amounts in the leaves of rhubarb, in *Oxalis* and *Rumex* species, and in rhizomes of Jack-in-the-pulpit.

Types of Physiological Action.—Poisonous plants may be grouped according to the physiological actions they produce. These groups and some plant examples include: (1) blood poisons: species of *Prunus*, seeds of castor bean (*Ricinus*) and rosary pea (*Abrus*); (2) nerve poisons: poisonous mushrooms, Jimson weed (*Datura*) and henbane (*Hyoscyamus*); (3) neuromuscular poisons: ergot, foxglove and arrow poisons (curare); (4) muscular poisons: false hellebore (*Veratrum*); and (5) skin irritants or dermatitis-producing plants: poison ivy (*Toxicodendron radicans*), parsnip (*Pastinaca*), mustard (*Brassica*), poisonwood (*Metopium*) and snow-on-the-mountain (*Euphorbia marginata*).

Plants Poisonous on Contact.—Skin poisoning, or dermatitis, is the typical plant contact poisoning. This type of reaction varies from a minor or temporary irritation to an itching rash or a painful inflammation with watery blisters that may last for days or weeks. In most plants that produce this reaction the toxic ingredient is concentrated in a resinous or milky juice. The severity of the symptoms varies with the susceptibility of the individual and with the amount of contact with the toxic agent. Some persons may be immune to poisoning by one species but susceptible to that by another; immunity may be complete or only partial; it may be lost or acquired over the years.

Plants noted for dermatitis-producing qualities include:

Cashew Family (Anacardiaceae).—Poison ivy and poison oak (*Toxicodendron* species), poison sumac and poison dogwood (*Toxicodendron vernix*) and Japanese lacquer tree (*Toxicodendron verniciflua*) are native to temperate regions and may be distinguished from nonpoisonous sumacs by the white (not red) fruits.

In poison ivy and its relatives the leaves are of three leaflets (never five), are usually coarsely toothed, and are glossy on the upper surface when young. Poison sumac leaves have 7 to 15 leaflets, whose margins are never toothed, and the hairless leaf stalk is usually reddish. The poisonwood of southeastern United States and the West Indies (*Metopium toxiferum*) resembles the more northern poison sumac.

Spurge Family (Euphorbiaceae).—The milky sap of the following plants produces varying degrees of dermatitis in susceptible individuals: many species of spurge (*Euphorbia*), including the cultivated ornamental snow-on-the-mountain (*E. marginata*), an annual whose leaves are margined white; and the manchineel tree (*Hippomane mancinella*) of the American tropics.

Nettles.—Some plants produce a nonpoisonous but very irritating stinging rash of short duration, termed an urtication. These plants bear sharp, brittle, glandular hairs that are hollow and filled with an irritating watery material which enters the skin when punctured by the hair. Included among these are the common nettle (*Urtica gracilis, U. urens*), the stinging nettle (*U. dioica*) and the wood nettle (*Laportea canadensis*).

Others.—Miscellaneous kinds of dermatitis-producing plants include the wild parsnip (*Pastinaca sativa*), which has coarse, celery-like foliage and bright yellow flowers; certain primroses (especially *Primula obconica, P. malacoides* and *P. sinensis*); several kinds of ladyslipper orchids (*Cypripedium acaule, C. calceolus, C. reginae* and *C. parviflorum*); several species of milkweed (*Asclepias*) and osage orange (*Maclura pomifera*). Foods made of buckwheat flower (*Fagopyrum esculentum*) produce dermatitis in some individuals.

Plants Poisonous on Ingestion.—Most plants that are poisonous when eaten are not tasty or likely to be eaten, except by children. Unfortunately, the quantity of poison fatal for a child is only a fraction of that fatal for an adult. These plants may be conveniently grouped according to the plant part that carries the toxic substance.

Roots.—Roots of the following may cause serious or fatal poisoning when eaten: (1) Jack-in-the-pulpit (*Arisaema*); the tuberous rhizome is rich in calcium oxalate crystals and produces inflammation of the membranes of the mouth and the throat when eaten raw; boiling in water dissolves the crystals and renders the tubers edible. (2) Death camass (*Zigadenus*); the bulbs are rich in the highly toxic alkaloid zygadenine, and sometimes are eaten by children. (3) Star-of-Bethlehem (*Ornithogalum*); all parts of the plant are poisonous, and the bulbs especially should not be kept where children have access to them. (4) Amaryllis and relatives (*Hippeastrum, Zephyranthes, Crinum* and *Hymenocallis*) produce bulbs containing poisonous alkaloids; they also should not be kept where children may obtain them. (5) Water hemlock (*Cicuta*) and poison hemlock (*Conium maculatum*) contain a highly toxic yellowish resin in the roots; fatal poisoning may result from eating them. These plants belong to the carrot family, produce flat-topped clusters of white flowers and grow in wet lowlands or along streams. (6) Potato (*Solanum tuberosum*) is poisonous when the tuber grows at the surface of the soil and becomes green through exposure to the sun; "greened" potato tubers should never be eaten.

Shoots and Foliage.—Shoots and foliage of the following may cause poisoning: (1) Pokeweed (*Phytolacca americana*); young shoots cooked as a potherb are edible, but the water should be poured off and replaced with fresh to remove the water-soluble toxic material. (2) Poison hemlock (*Conium maculatum*); children have been fatally poisoned by eating small quantities of foliage or stalk. (3) Fool's-parsley (*Aethusa cynapium*), an annual with parsleylike leaves, is sometimes eaten in error for garden parsley, with fatal results; the leaves are never mosslike or curly. (4) Tansy (*Tanacetum vulgare*); a tea made from the foliage is poisonous, and overdoses have been fatal.

Flowers.—Flowers of poisonous plants are rarely eaten deliberately. However, children eating flowers or buds of tiger lily (*Lilium tigrinum*) have been poisoned with near-fatal results. The anthers contain an alkaloid not known in other lily species.

Fruits and Seeds.—Fruits and seeds of poisonous plants are occasionally eaten with fatal or near-fatal results, especially by children. The following, while by no means complete, is a listing of common poisonous fruits to be avoided: (1) Baneberry (*Actaea*, a woodland perennial herb bearing bright red or white berries about half an inch long; the berries are not tasty and are moderately toxic. (2) Belladonna (*Atropa belladonna*), a perennial producing bell-shaped dull-purplish flowers and black berries with violet juice; the toxic alkaloid hyoscyamine is present in all parts of the plant. (3) Bittersweet (*Celastrus*), a woody vine producing orange-red berrylike fruits in autumn, prized for decorative uses; the outer scarlet pulp contains a moderately toxic, sweetish but disagreeable-tasting alkaloid, celastrin. (4) Black nightshade, or garden huckleberry (*Solanum nigrum*), an annual herb with drooping clusters of black, globose berries about three-quarters of an inch in diameter; the unripe berries are poisonous, but the ripe fruit is edible, and cooking or boiling destroys remnants of the poisonous material. (5) Blue cohosh (*Caulophyllum thalictroides*), a low, perennial herb of moist, rich, woodland areas, produces stiffly erect stalks of pea-sized dark-blue "berries" above the foliage; the very bitter berries contain a poisonous alkaloid. (6) Chinaberry (*Melia azedarach*) is a tree of warm temperate regions producing panicles of fragrant purple flowers followed by pale yellow, berrylike drupes about half an inch across; the fleshy pulp of the fruit contains a paralyzing nerve poison. Coyotillo (*Karwinskia humboldtiana*), a rangeland shrub with oval, brownish-black berries about half an inch long; the leaves and fruit pulp are less toxic than the seeds. (7) Daphne (*Daphne*), a low shrub producing fragrant, showy flowers in spring, followed by orange or red berrylike drupes about one-fourth inch long; a small number of the berries may cause fatal poisoning in children. (8) English ivy (*Hedera helix*), an evergreen vine, produces umbels of black or orange poisonous berries sometimes eaten by children. (9) Euonymus, burning bush, wahoo (*Euonymus atropurpureus*), a shrub with reddish capsules whose few seeds are each covered by a bright, orange-red, fleshy aril; the fruits and seeds are moderately poisonous when eaten. (10) European bittersweet, or blue nightshade (*Solanum dulcamara*), is a clambering vine, herbaceous becoming woody, with clusters of small white flowers followed by attractive bright red berries about one-third inch across; both leaves and bark have a strong, disagreeable odour, and the berries, moderately poisonous if eaten in quantity, contain the alkaloidal glucoside solanine. (11) Henbane (*Hyoscyamus niger*), a much-branched, clammy-hairy herb with a fetid odour when crushed, produces yellowish, funnel-shaped flowers with purple veins, followed by a seed pod enclosed in a persistent calyx; children eating seed pods or seeds have been poisoned by the alkaloid hyoscyamine. (12) Holly (*Ilex*) produces attractive red, yellow or black berries that are somewhat (but not highly) poisonous and should not be eaten. (13) Jerusalem cherry (*Solanum pseudo-capsicum*) is grown as an ornamental pot plant and prized for its showy globose orange berries nearly an inch across; the fruits contain toxic quantities of several poisonous materials and should never be eaten. (14) Jimson weed (*Datura stramonium*), an annual weed with showy white or purplish funnel-form flowers, three to six inches long, followed by globose prickly pods about one inch across; the soft, unripe seed pods are poisonous when eaten, and the seeds are increasingly toxic. (15) Manchineel tree (*Hippomane mancinella*), a small subtropical tree of the Euphorbiaceae, produces milky sap, spikes of small greenish flowers, followed by berrylike drupes about $1\frac{1}{4}$ in. across; persons eating the fruits in the belief that they were edible have been fatally poisoned. (16) Matrimony vine (*Lycium halimifolium*), a woody clambering vine of the Solanaceae, somewhat thorny, produces small white funnelform flowers in leaf axils, followed by bright orange-red berries about one-third inch across; the berries are moderately toxic and contain a hyoscyaminelike alkaloid. (17) May apple (*Podophyllum*) is a perennial herb of rich, open woodlands or pastures, producing large, umbrella-shaped leaves, beneath which appear one or two nodding white flowers an inch across, followed by a yellow or reddish berry about $1\frac{1}{2}$ in. long; when fully ripe the berries are edible, but when hard, green and immature, they contain highly

Ohio buckeye (*Aesculus glabra*), which some authorities maintain has seeds and leaves that are poisonous to cattle

May apple (*Podophyllum peltatum*), showing the flower and the unripe berry. The berry is moderately poisonous at this stage but edible when fully ripe; the roots are poisonous

Allamanda (*Allamanda cathartica*), of the dogbane family, many members of which are poisonous

Bittersweet, or false bittersweet (*Celastrus scandens*), a decorative vine. The scarlet pulp of the fruit is moderately toxic

Mistletoe (*Phoradendron flavescens*), whose whitish berries are poisonous

Common sneezeweed (*Helenium autumnale*), a powerful respiratory and contact irritant

BY COURTESY OF (CENTRE LEFT) MISSOURI BOTANICAL GARDEN; PHOTOGRAPHS, (ALL) JOHN H. GERARD

PLATE II

POISONOUS PLANTS

Croton (*Codiaeum*), one of the Euphorbiaceae, many members of which have a poisonous milky juice

Poison ivy (*Toxicodendron radicans*), a skin irritant. The whitish berries and three-parted leaves are distinctive features

Jack-in-the-pulpit (*Arisaema triphyllum*) inflames the membranes of the mouth and throat if eaten raw

Jimson weed (*Datura stramonium*). The seed pods and seeds are a dangerous nerve poison

Cardinal flower (*Lobelia cardinalis*), suspected of being poisonous to livestock

Pokeweed (*Phytolacca americana*). The seeds and roots are poisonous

toxic quantities of a purgative resin, podophyllin. (18) Mistletoe (*Phoradendron, Viscum album*), an evergreen parasitic plant growing on trees, produces decorative whitish berries that are reported to have been fatally poisonous when eaten by children. (19) Pokeweed (*Phytolacca americana*), a coarse tall perennial herb with reddish-purple stems and glossy green leaves, produces dense terminal racemes of small white flowers followed by crimson-juiced, glossy black berries; the berry pulp is believed to be non-poisonous, but the black glossy seeds contain toxic quantities of saponins and alkaloids. (20) Privet (*Ligustrum*), a common shrub often grown for hedges, has small racemes of white flowers followed by bluish-black berries about one-fourth inch across; the berries are reported to be fatally toxic to children.

Mushrooms.—Mushroom poisoning commonly is fatal to man. Many mushrooms contain toxic alkaloids (muscarine, agaricine, phalline) and identification of poisonous types from the non-poisonous should be made only by an expert. The edible mushroom of commerce is *Agaricus campestris*, but some species of the genus are poisonous. The designation of poisonous types as toadstools and the nonpoisonous as mushrooms is common but meaningless. (*See* also MUSHROOM.)

Stock-Poisoning Plants.—These are of many kinds and vary with the different countries and regions. Of particular importance in North America are cocklebur, black nightshade, water hemlock, death camass, milkweed, sneezeweed, Jimson weed and the locoweeds. The symptoms of stock poisoning are varied, rendering diagnosis difficult.

Arrow Poisons.—These, concocted from the juices and resins of a variety of plants, are of importance to aborigines of many areas, particularly of the tropics, for shooting of animals and fish and in warfare. In the 20th century the active ingredients have proved to be important in medicine. All South American Indian arrow poisons are grouped under the name curare and may be classified as neuromuscular toxins. From them the alkaloid curine has been isolated. Derivatives of this arrow poison have proved useful in anesthetics to induce muscle relaxation. The material as used by the Indians is a dark gummy mass. Small quantities carried on the tip of an arrow to the flesh of man or animal induce paralysis of the voluntary muscles followed by stupor and death due to failure of respiratory muscles.

Crude arrow-poisoning material was first introduced to modern civilization in 1595, when Sir Walter Ralegh brought a tiny vial of it to England. From that time onward reports of its preparation, use and efficacy became a mixture of folklore and fact. The aboriginal use of the potion was accurately observed in 1800 and reported in 1807 by Humboldt. Later the German botanist R. H. Schomburgk witnessed its preparation by Indians in British Guiana and reported it in detail in 1844. Preparation of the poison was a closely guarded secret and ritual, handed down from father to son, and today, through the influence of firearms, it is rapidly becoming a lost art in much of South America.

Detailed information on the plants used and procedures for making the poison were learned from the Tecuna Indians of Brazil by B. A. Krukoff, who reported on them in 1937. Bundles of stems of the plants *Strychnos castelnaei* and *Chondodendron polyanthum* were gathered and brought from the forest. The outer bark was peeled or scraped from the stems, packed into a bundle, wrapped in palm leaves and allowed to set over night. It was then suspended over an empty clay pot and opened at the top. About two quarts of cold water was poured very slowly over the bark and collected in the pot. This extract was transferred to a larger pot and brought to boil over a steady fire. Several collections of the cold-water extract were similarly prepared and added to the concoction, which was kept boiling for at least eight hours, when it was reduced to about one-eighth its original volume. On the third day the extract was triple-strained through a palm spathe and again boiled gently for several more hours. To this a decoction of macerated roots of other plants (*e.g.*, species of *Piper*) was added, boiled and strained. During the process an extract of stems and leaves of *Dieffenbachia insignis* and of tubers of *Aristolochia* was added and the whole boiled down to a thick,

gluelike sirup of dark chocolate colour. When cool its potency was tested on some bird or animal. The material was stored in covered pots, gourds or bamboo tubes and kept as dry and cool as possible.

The identity of all the plants used in the preparation of curare remains incomplete, but leaves and stems of the following plants are known to be used: *Chondodendron tomentosum* (Menispermaceae), *Strophanthus* (Apocynaceae), *Strychnos* (Loganiaceae) and *Cocculus* (Menispermaceae).

See POISON; CURARE; and articles on the various poisonous plants; *see* also references under "Poisonous Plants" in the Index.

BIBLIOGRAPHY.—L. H. Pammel, *Manual of Poisonous Plants* (1911); A. Bernhard-Smith, *Poisonous Plants of All Countries* (1923); D. G. Steyn, *The Toxicology of Plants in South Africa* (1934); A. R. McIntyre, *Curare: Its History, Nature, and Clinical Use* (1947); L. V. Blubaugh and C. R. Linegar, "Curare and Modern Medicine," *Econ. Bot.*, 2:73–82 (1948); B. A. Krukoff and A. C. Smith, "Notes on the Botanical Components of Curare," *Bull. Torrey Bot. Cl.*, 64:401–409 (1937); R. N. Chopra and R. L. Badhwar, *Poisonous Plants of India* (1949); W. C. Muenscher, *Poisonous Plants of the United States*, 2nd ed. (1951). (G. H. M. L.)

POISONS, AFFAIR OF THE, one of the most sensational criminal cases of 17th-century France. Brought to light in 1679, three years after the execution of the marquise de Brinvilliers (*q.v.*), it revealed that nobles, prosperous bourgeois and the common people alike had been resorting secretly to women fortune-tellers—at that time very numerous in Paris—for drugs and poisons, for black masses (incantations of black magic) and for other criminal purposes. The inquiry into the affair was entrusted by Louis XIV to the lieutenant of police, Nicolas de La Reynie, whose diligent investigation took three years. A special tribunal for the trial of the accused, known as the *Chambre ardente,* was set up in April 1679: it held 210 sessions at the Arsenal in Paris, issued 319 writs of arrest (218 of which were carried out), conducted 865 interrogations and sentenced 36 persons to death (34 of whom were actually executed), 4 to labour in the galleys and 34 to banishment or fines, while 30 persons were acquitted. The poisoner called La Voisin (Catherine Deshayes, Madame Monvoisin) was burned in the Place de Grève on Feb. 22, 1680.

Persons who were compromised included the comtesse de Soissons (Olympe Mancini, a niece of the late Cardinal Mazarin), whose flight from France was abetted by the king; the duchesse de Bouillon (Marie Anne Mancini, also a niece of Mazarin's); the comtesse de Gramont (Marie Christine de Noailles); the vicomtesse de Polignac (Jacqueline de Grimoard de Beauvoir); the princesse de Tingry (Marie Charlotte de Luxembourg); the maréchale de La Ferté (Madeleine d'Angennes); the maréchal duc de Luxembourg, who was found innocent; the duchesse de Vivonne (Antoinette de Mesmes, sister-in-law of the marquise de Montespan); and the marquise de Montespan (*q.v.*) herself. La Voisin under interrogation had always denied any dealings with Madame de Montespan; but after she was executed her daughter and her accomplices accused Madame de Montespan of having been one of La Voisin's clients since 1667, of having used philtres and "love powders" to win the king's love and to supplant the duchesse de La Vallière, of having taken part in black masses and of having tried to poison her rival Mademoiselle de Fontanges (Marie Angélique Scorraille de Roussilles) and Louis XIV himself. When her name was mentioned the king suspended the public proceedings, but ordered that the inquiry should go on. Thus the chief offenders, who had managed by their statements to transform a criminal trial into an affair of state, escaped the stake or the gallows and ended their lives in various provincial prisons. Madame de Montespan certainly had dealings with La Voisin and had recourse to magic in order to win and keep the king's love, but the charges concerning black masses and attempted poisonings have not been proved against her. Her accusers cannot be taken at their word in the absence of independent evidence.

BIBLIOGRAPHY.—P. Clément, *Madame de Montespan* (1868); F. Ravaisson, *Archives de la Bastille,* vol. iv–vii (1870–74); F. Funck-Brentano, *Le Drame des poisons* (1899; new ed. 1928); J. Lemoine, *Madame de Montespan et la légende des poisons* (1908), *Les Des Oeillets* (1939); P. Emard and S. Fournier, *Les Années criminelles de*

Madame de Montespan (1939); G. Mongrédien, *Madame de Montespan et l'affaire des poisons* (1953).   (G. Mo.)

POISSON, SIMÉON DENIS (1781–1840), French mathematician, known for his work on definite integrals, electromagnetic theory and probability, was born at Pithiviers in the *département* of Loiret on June 21, 1781. He studied medicine but gave it up in favour of mathematics. In 1798 he entered the École Polytechnique at Paris, where he attracted the notice of Lagrange and Laplace. Until his death on April 25, 1840, he was almost entirely occupied in mathematical research and in teaching. He was made deputy professor at the École Polytechnique in 1802, and full professor in succession to Fourier in 1806. In 1808 he became astronomer at the Bureau des Longitudes; and when the Faculté des Sciences was instituted in 1809 he was appointed professor of pure mechanics. His most important work was on the application of mathematics to physics, and in particular to electrostatics and magnetism. In the field of pure mathematics, his most important works were his series of memoirs on definite integrals, and his discussion of Fourier's series, which paved the way for the classical researches of Dirichlet and Riemann on the same subject. His studies on probability and the Poisson distribution law are of great importance.

Besides his many memoirs, Poisson published a number of treatises: *Traité de mécanique*, two volumes (1811 and 1833), which was long a standard work; *Théorie nouvelle de l'action capillaire* (1831); *Théorie mathématique de la chaleur* (1835); *Supplément* to the same (1837); *Recherches sur la probabilité des jugements*, etc. (1837). *See* also references under "Poisson, Siméon Denis" in the Index.   (O. Oe.)

POITIERS, COUNTS OF, one of the great feudal dynasties of medieval France. The counts of Poitiers in Merovingian times were dim and insignificant officials administering Poitou (*q.v.*); the countships gradually became hereditary in the Carolingian period. Ramnulf I, who appears as count of Poitiers under King Pepin II of Aquitaine in 840, fought well against the Northmen or Normans and was killed in battle at Brissarthe in 866. His son Ramnulf II, in possession of the countship from 878, gave proof of his ambitions by annexing Saintonge. After his death (890 or 891) his house suffered a setback, during which Poitiers was ruled by the counts of Angoulême; but his bastard son, Eble Manzer, not only recovered the countship of Poitiers in 902 but also held Limousin and probably Auvergne as well from 927. Eble Manzer's son William I Towhead, count of Poitiers from 940 at the latest, finally styled himself duke of Aquitaine (*q.v.;* as duke he is reckoned as William III); and his son William II and IV Fier-à-Bras or Strong-in-the-Arm consolidated the position (963–*c.* 994), so that the name William, or Guilhem in the language of southern France, became traditional in the house. His son William III and V the Great (d. 1030) extended the dynasty's power, being recognized as suzerain in distant Velay and Périgord. By the second of his three marriages—to Brisca, sister of the Gascon duke Sancho William—he paved the way for a reconstitution of the Aquitania of Roman times. On good terms with England, Castile, and Navarre, he cared little for the French king's overlordship. He founded the abbey of Maillezais, where he was entombed.

William the Great's sons, William IV and VI the Fat (d. 1038), Eudes or Odo (d. 1039), William V and VII Aigret (called Peter before assuming the name of William; d. 1058), lost Loudun, Mirebeau, and Saintes to the counts of Anjou, but Aigret's brother and successor, Guy Geoffrey (William VI and VIII; d. 1086), brilliantly restored the dynasty's fortunes. He had already won Gascony during Aigret's lifetime; and he fought successfully against the Angevins and the counts of Toulouse and campaigned against the Muslims in Spain. He founded the great abbey of Montierneuf, in which he was buried. His son, the aggressive William VII and IX (d. 1126), is chiefly remembered as a troubadour of genius and as the patron of a flourishing literary and artistic civilization; but the troubadour's son William VIII and X the Toulousain (d. 1137) was preoccupied by local disputes with refractory lords and also quarreled with St. Bernard of Clairvaux. Through the successive marriages of this William's daughter Aliénor (*see* ELEANOR of Aquitaine) the countship passed first to

the Capetians of France, then to the Angevins of England, thus losing its individuality sometime before France's recovery of Poitou in the 13th century.   (RE. C.)

POITIERS, a town of west-central France, capital of the former province of Poitou (*q.v.*) and of the modern *département* of Vienne, located 290 km. (180 mi.) SW of Paris. It commands the so-called gate of Poitou, a 44-mi.-wide gap between the Massif Armoricain (Armorican Massif) and the Massif Central, facilitating communication between northern and southern Europe. Poitiers occupies the slopes of a protuberance between the valley of the Clain River and that of its affluent the Boivre, a position which is suitable for defense and which explains much of the town's history. It is the seat of a bishopric. Pop. (1962) 59,799.

The streets are mostly narrow and tortuous, except for the modern Rue Victor Hugo (1869), which runs straight from the *préfecture* in the Place Aristide-Briand eastward to the *hôtel de ville* in the Place Maréchal Leclerc. The ring of boulevards surrounding the town follows the line of the medieval fortifications. Suburbs (*faubourgs*) have sprung up along the outskirts of the town.

In Poitiers is the oldest building of Christian Gaul, the baptistery of Saint-Jean (4th and 7th centuries) just south of the cathedral. There are many beautiful Romanesque churches including the 11th–12th-century Notre-Dame-la-Grande; the church of St. Radegunda (d. 587), wife of the Frankish king Clotaire I, which contains her tomb, an object of pilgrimage; and that of St. Hilary (Saint-Hilaire-le-Grand; fl. *c.* 315–367), a native of Poitiers and its first known bishop, which was built over his tomb in the 11th–12th centuries in an unusual plan, its chief architect being the Anglo-Norman Gautier Coorland. The cathedral of Saint-Pierre, in the local Angevin style associated with Gothic, was begun in the mid-12th century and finished toward 1300. Its great Crucifixion window was the gift of Henry II of England (1133–89) and his queen, Eleanor (Aliénor) of Aquitaine (*c.* 1122–1204). A notable secular building is the *palais de justice* (formerly the palace of the dukes of Aquitaine, who were also counts of Poitou), incorporating Eleanor's so-called King's Hall. Poitiers has a university dating from 1432 and several professional and technical schools, including a *conservatoire* of music and a training institution for the deaf and dumb. There are four museums.

Poitiers had close ties with England, not only through Eleanor of Aquitaine but also through her son by Henry II, Richard I Coeur de Lion, who spent more time there than in London; and through Sir John Chandos, seneschal of Poitou (1360–72). Great numbers of Irish (who had their own college) and even more of Scots attended the university from the 15th to the 17th century; many of them settled in Poitiers.

Poitiers is an important railway junction on the Paris–Bordeaux–Bayonne line which continues over the Spanish frontier via Hendaye. There is a commercial airport at Poitiers-Biard.

The town's chief commercial activity is its trade in the wheat, wines, timber, and cattle from the surrounding plain and heathland. The fair held every Oct. 18 is an international market for grass seed. There has been considerable development of industry at the suburbs of Chasseneuil (electric batteries), Saint-Benoît (chemical products), and Pointe-à-Miteau. A characteristic occupation is the dressing of downy goose skins (called swan skins) for the luxury trade.

History.—First occupied by the Celtic Pictones or Pictavi (hence its name), Poitiers became an important Roman town under the name of Limonum. Having been ruled by the Visigothic kings of Aquitaine, it saw the defeat of the Visigoths by Clovis' Franks at the Battle of Vouillé (507); the halting by Charles Martel of the Islamic invasion of Europe (732); and the famous battle of 1356 (*see* below) during the Hundred Years' War. Some of the offices of royal government were removed to Poitiers between 1418 and 1436; Joan of Arc underwent an interrogation there in 1429. After a revival from the 14th to the 16th century the town sank into a torpor from which it gradually recovered during the 19th century. (*See* also POITIERS, COUNTS OF.)

The Battle of Poitiers, 1356.—This encounter, from its location more accurately called the Battle of Nouaillé-Maupertuis, was the second of the three great English victories of the Hundred Years'

War and took place in September 1356. It began with a foray from Bordeaux toward Bourges by the 7,000-strong Anglo-Gascon Army of Edward the Black Prince, which then withdrew toward Poitiers via Tours and the Clain River Valley. But the larger French Army of King John II the Good cut them off by crossing the Vienne River at the Chauvigny Bridge, having reached this point from Chartres via Blois. The commander of Edward's Gascons, who outnumbered the English, was Jean III de Grailly, captal de Buch. He was also the real leader of the cavalcade. The Black Prince's right-hand man, Sir John Chandos, was the *de facto* English leader and hero of the battle. The Army was accompanied by wagonloads of booty and the whole expedition was well-organized. The French Army, however, consisted of an assemblage of very independent-minded knights and was disunited.

Hostilities began on the morning of Saturday, Sept. 17, when the Anglo-Gascons ambushed a small French detachment at La Chaboterie. They then pushed on to Nouaillé Wood, where they could conceal their dispositions, and used it as their key position throughout the battle. A truce, observed throughout Sunday, Sept. 18, at the instance of the papal legate Hélie Cardinal de Talleyrand-Périgord, was spent by the Anglo-Gascons in preparing the ground and by the French, somewhat injudiciously, in eating, drinking, and sleeping. At dawn on Sept. 19, a small party of English feigned flight down the bad Maupertuis road along the west side of Nouaillé Wood, so drawing the French vanguard into hedges and marshy ground where it became bogged. Meanwhile King John had arrived with the rest of his army at a small clearing within an arm of the Miosson to the west of Maupertuis. The Anglo-Gascons gradually surrounded it and the Gascon captain De Grailly led the final charge which captured the French king and a number of his knights. Booty and a large number of prisoners were sent to Bordeaux. Four years later the Treaty of Brétigny (*see* BRÉTIGNY, TREATY OF) included Poitou, with the whole of Aquitaine, in the territory ceded by John II to Edward III of England.

See AQUITAINE; ELEANOR of Aquitaine; HUNDRED YEARS' WAR.
(Jo. Sa.)

POITOU, a former province of France, bounded west by the Atlantic, north by Brittany, Anjou and Touraine, east by La Marche and Limousin, and south by Angoumois and Aunis, thus roughly corresponding to the modern *départements* of Vienne, Deux-Sèvres, and Vendée (*qq.v.*). The Seuil du Poitou, a zone of sedimentary rocks about 60 mi. (96 km.) wide between two higher countries of older rocks (Limousin and the southern part of the Massif Armoricain), forms the easiest passage between northern and southwestern France.

Poitou derives its name from the Gallic tribe of Pictones or Pictavi, whose *civitas* or community formed part of Roman Aquitania. For centuries the northern part of Aquitaine (*q.v.*), it was a border country and a battlefield (Battle of Vouillé in 507 between Franks and Visigoths; Charles Martel's victory of 732 over the Muslims; the Anglo-French Battle of Poitiers in 1356; and the Battle of Moncontour in 1569 between Catholics and Huguenots) as well as the meeting place of northern and southern cultures. Its golden age (11th–12th centuries) is represented by a great school of Romanesque architecture, sculpture, and painting. The great counts of Poitiers (*q.v.*) were succeeded by the Angevin kings of England in the 12th century, but Philip II Augustus and Louis VIII of France conquered the country early in the 13th. Poitou was ceded to the English by the treaties of Brétigny and Calais (1360), but by 1375 the French had won it back. Poitou suffered in the Wars of Religion; its later history was quieter, apart from the Wars of the Vendée (*q.v.*) in the Revolutionary period.

BIBLIOGRAPHY.—P. Boissonnade, *Histoire de Poitou*, 8th ed. (1941); Jean Chagnolleau *et al.*, *Visages du Poitou*, 2nd ed. (1946); R. Crozet, *Histoire du Poitou* (1949).

POKEBERRY (POKEWEED), the popular name (from the American Indian *pocan*, applied to any plant yielding a red or yellow dye) of *Phytolacca americana*, a strong-smelling perennial herb, native of North America. It has ovate-lanceolate sharp-pointed leaves, racemes of small greenish-white flowers and flat-

tish berries nearly ½ in. in diameter, which contain a crimson juice. The young asparaguslike shoots are sometimes used as a potherb, but the roots are poisonous. The plant is often cultivated in Europe, and has become naturalized in the Mediterranean region.

POKER, a card game played in various forms throughout the world. Its popularity is greatest in the English-speaking countries and after the 1850s it was called "the national card game of the United States." Because Queen Victoria found the principle of the game interesting, poker had a brief vogue in British court circles in the 1870s, but its acceptance in Great Britain and on the continent came chiefly in the decade 1911–20 and was undoubtedly much influenced by the American Expeditionary Forces in World War I.

For nearly 100 years in the United States poker was considered a gambling game for men, unsuited to polite or mixed gatherings, but after the 1920s its popularity extended to both sexes and all levels of society. Surveys made in the second half of the 20th century showed poker to be the favourite U.S. game of men and the third-most-favoured (after rummy and bridge) with women; and in Great Britain it ranked next after contract bridge with both sexes.

In one respect poker is rather a family of games than a single game (see *History*, below). It is played in countless variants and at least 150 are named and described in the literature of the game. All forms of poker, however, share certain essential features: A poker hand comprises five cards. The value of the hand is in inverse proportion to its mathematical frequency; that is, the more unusual the combination of cards, the higher the hand ranks. Each player may bet that he has the best hand, and other players must either "call" or meet his bet or concede. Therefore a player may "bluff" by betting he has the best hand when in fact he does not, and he may win by bluffing if players holding superior hands will not call his bet.

GENERAL PRINCIPLES OF POKER

The following principles apply to nearly all forms of poker:

Players.—There are forms of poker suitable to any number of players from 2 to 14, but in most forms the ideal number is 6, 7 or 8 players.

Cards.—Poker is almost always played with the standard 52-card deck, the cards in each of the four suits (♠, ♥, ♦, ♣) ranking A (high), K, Q, J, 10, 9, 8, 7, 6, 5, 4, 3, 2, A (low only in the straight or straight flush 5–4–3–2–A and in certain variants described below).

Wild Cards or "Freaks."—A wild card stands for any other card its holder wishes to name. There are many methods of introducing wild cards into the game. The most popular are: (1) Joker; a 53-card pack is used, including the joker as a wild card. (2) Bug; the same 53-card pack including the joker is used, but the joker (here called the bug) counts only as a fifth ace or to fill a flush, straight or special hand (described below). (3) Deuces wild or freak pots; all four deuces are wild cards. (4) One-eyes; in the usual British or U.S. pack, the ♦ K, ♠ J and ♥ J are the only cards shown in profile. They are often designated as wild cards.

Rank of Poker Hands.—The traditional, universally accepted ranking of poker hands, from highest to lowest, is:

1. Straight flush: five cards of the same suit and in sequence. The highest straight flush is A-K-Q-J-10 of the same suit, called a royal flush; the lowest straight flush is 5-4-3-2-A of the same suit.
2. Four of a kind, as all four 6s, with any fifth card.
3. Full house or full hand: three of one kind and two of another, as 10-10-10-3-3.
4. Flush: five cards of the same suit.
5. Straight: five cards in sequence, in two or more suits. The highest straight is A-K-Q-J-10, the lowest 5-4-3-2-A.
6. Three of a kind or triplets, with any two other cards, not a pair.
7. Two pairs, as A-A-9-9 and any fifth card.
8. One pair, with three unmatched cards.
9. No pair, each such hand being rated by its highest card or cards, as ace high or ace-king high.

When there is any wild card in the game the highest possible hand is five of a kind, which beats any straight flush.

As between two hands having combinations in the same category, the winner is determined as follows:

Straight flushes, flushes, straights or no pair: the one containing the highest card wins; if these cards are identical in rank, the next-highest decides and so on. Four of a kind or three of a kind (or five of a kind): the one composed of the higher-ranking cards. Full house: the higher three of a kind. Two pairs: the highest pair; if these are identical, the higher of the second pairs; if these are identical, the higher of the unmatched cards. One pair: the higher pair; if the pairs are identical, the highest of the unmatched cards and so on. When there are several wild cards there may be identical fours of a kind or threes of a kind, in which case ties are broken by the highest unmatched cards or secondary pairs (in a full house).

Two or more identical hands tie and divide any winning equally. The suits have no relative rank in poker.

In some games value is accorded to one or more (but seldom all) of the following special hands or to other combinations arbitrarily adopted by the players.

    1. Big tiger or big cat: king high, 8 low, no pair, as K-J-10-9-8.
    2. Little tiger or little cat: 8 high, 3 low, no pair, as 8-7-6-5-3.
    3. Big dog: ace high, 9 low, no pair, as A-Q-J-10-9.
    4. Little dog: 7 high, 2 low, no pair, as 7-5-4-3-2.
    (Tigers and dogs rank in the order listed. Any tiger or dog beats a straight but loses to a flush.)
    5. Skeet: five cards, 9 high, including 9,5,2, no pair, as 9-7-5-3-2; beats a straight, loses to a flush.
    6. Skip straight or Dutch straight, as 2-4-6-8-10: or round-the-corner straight, as 3-2-A-K-Q; beats three of a kind, loses to a straight. (The name pelter or kilter is sometimes applied to the skeet or skip straight.)
    7. Blaze: five face cards, as K-Q-Q-J-J; beats any two pair, loses to three of a kind.
    8. Four-flush: four cards of the same suit; beats one pair, loses to two pairs.

As between two special hands in the same category, ties are broken as between regular poker hands.

Object of the Game.—The object is to win the "pot," which is the aggregate of all bets made by all players in any one deal. The pot may be won either by having the highest-ranking poker hand or by making a bet that no other player calls.

Preliminaries and Rotation.—At the start of the game any player takes a pack of cards and deals them in rotation to his left, one at a time face up, until a knave (jack) appears; the player receiving that card becomes the first dealer. The turn to deal and the turn to bet always pass from player to player to the left. For each deal, any player may shuffle the cards, the dealer having last right. The dealer must offer the shuffled pack to his right-hand opponent for a cut. If that player declines to cut, any other player may cut.

Betting Procedure.—In each deal there are one or more betting intervals. In each betting interval one player, as designated by the rules of the variant being played, has the privilege or obligation of making the first bet. This player and each player in turn after him must place in the pot a number of chips (representing money, for which poker is almost invariably played) to make his total contribution to the pot at least equal the total contribution of any player before him. When a player does this he is said to be in the pot or an active player. If a player declines to do this, he discards his hand and is said to drop or pass and he may no longer compete for the pot.

Before the deal, each player may be required to make a contribution to the pot, called an ante. In each betting interval, the first player to make a bet is said to bet; a player who exactly meets the last previous bet is said to call or stay (in); and a player who bets more than the last previous bettor is said to raise. In some variants a player is permitted to check, which is to stay in without betting, provided no other player has made a bet in that betting interval.

At the end of each betting interval except the last, dealing is resumed; at the end of the last betting interval there is the "showdown," in which each active player shows his full hand and the highest-ranking hand wins the pot. In practice, especially in informal games, players usually announce the values of their hands and show their hands as confirmation only, but on demand of any player the full hand must be shown and any mistaken announce-

ment is not valid: "The cards speak for themselves."

Betting Limits.—In poker legends there were "no-limit" or "sky's-the-limit" games, but in practice some limit is placed on what one may bet in any game. There are three popular methods.

Fixed Limit.—No one may bet or raise by more than the established limit. In draw poker the limit is usually twice as much after the draw as before; for example, two chips before the draw, four chips after. In stud poker the limit is usually twice as much in the final betting interval as in previous betting intervals. (The higher limit applies also when any player's exposed cards include a pair.) These respective forms of the game are described below. In a fixed limit game a limit is usually placed on the number of raises that may be made in any betting interval.

Pot Limit.—A player may bet or raise by no more than the amount in the pot at the time the bet or raise is made. When raising, he may first put in the pot the number of chips required to call the previous bet and then raise by the number of chips in the pot. When pot limit is played, it is customary also to place a maximum limit on any bet or raise, regardless of the size of the pot or to play table stakes.

Table Stakes.—This method most closely approximates the legendary no-limit game. Each player's limit is the number of chips he has on the table at the beginning of the deal. He may not bet more, but for this amount he may call any higher bet and compete for the pot in the showdown. Other players having more chips may continue to bet, but their further bets go into one or more side pots in which the winner is decided as among the players who contributed fully to the side pot. When a player drops out of any side pot he has dropped out of the original pot as well, in effect surrendering his rights in the original pot to the player whose later bet he did not call.

PRINCIPAL FORMS OF POKER

Poker has two main branches: closed (straight or draw) poker, in which each player's full hand remains concealed until the showdown; and open (stud) poker, in which some but not all of a player's cards are dealt or turned face up. Within each of these branches, but especially in closed poker, there are "pass-and-out" games, in which a player must bet or drop in each turn, and "pass-and-back-in" games, in which in certain circumstances a player is permitted to check.

Straight Poker.—Each player is dealt five cards, face down. There is one betting interval, beginning with the player nearest dealer's left, then a showdown. This was the original form of poker and has almost passed out of existence except, paradoxically, in the highest-stake games among professional gamblers.

Draw Poker.—This game has two main branches: (1) blind opening, played almost to the exclusion of other variants in England, Europe and the British Commonwealth except Canada, and favoured in men's clubs in the U.S. and Latin America; and (2) jackpots, the draw poker variant most played in the U.S. and Canada. In draw poker, each player is dealt five cards, face down. There is a betting interval. Then each active player, in turn beginning at dealer's left, may discard one or more of his original cards and receive replacements for them, dealt from the undealt portion of the pack. (A player who declines to draw cards is said to stand pat.) After this process, called the draw, there is a final betting interval, followed by the showdown.

Blind Opening.—There are three contributions to the pot before the deal. The dealer (or in some games, every player) puts in an ante, which does not rank as a bet. The player at dealer's left, formerly called the "age" or "edge," now called the opener, makes an opening bet of one chip or unit, called the blind. The player at his left puts in two or three units, constituting a call of the blind opening bet and a raise of one or two units; this is called the straddle or blind raise. Each player in turn thereafter may call (for the amount bet by the preceding player), raise (by one unit) or drop. The limit before the draw is usually the one unit of the ante. The limit after the draw is twice this amount or more; in some games it is the amount bet by each player before the draw. After the draw the betting begins with the active player nearest the dealer's left, and checking is permitted.

Jackpots.—Before the deal, each player antes one chip of lowest value. The game is pass-and-back-in both before and after the draw. In the first betting interval each player in turn, beginning with the one at dealer's left, may check (called also pass) or open (make the first bet); in most games a player may not open unless he has jacks or better (a pair of jacks or any higher-ranking hand), but the requirements for openers may be set higher or lower. If any player opens, each player in turn after him may call or raise until the betting interval is ended. There follow the draw, a second betting interval beginning with the opener (or if he has dropped, with the active player nearest his left), and a showdown. There are penalties for opening without openers (see *Laws*, below). In a similar game, called passout, no openers are required and the game is played pass-and-out (*see* above) before the draw.

Stud Poker.—Each player receives one card face down, called his hole card, then one card face up. The deal is then interrupted for a betting interval. There follow three rounds of dealing, each consisting of one face-up card to each active player, with a betting interval after each round. There is a showdown in which the hole cards are shown after the fourth and last betting interval. In each betting interval the first bettor is the player with the highest-ranking poker combination in his face-up cards; if two or more players have the same combinations, the "first" one (nearest the dealer's left) bets first. In the first betting interval the high player must bet at least an established minimum; in any later betting interval he may check. Few games have lost popularity so fast as regular five-card stud. In the 1920s and into the 1930s it was played in two-thirds of the high-stake and professional games in the U.S.; after the 1950s it was not played in one-tenth of them.

Seven-Card Stud.—Each player is dealt two hole cards, then a face-up card, followed by a betting interval; then three more face-up cards and one final face-down card, each followed by a betting interval. For the showdown each player selects the best five of his seven cards to be his poker hand. There are six-card and eight-card variants of this game, in each of which a player ultimately selects five of his cards.

High-Low Poker.—The highest-ranking poker hand and the lowest-ranking poker hand divide the pot equally. If there is an odd chip, the high hand gets it. If two or more hands tie for high or low, they divide their half of the pot equally. Nearly any form of poker may be played high-low. In most games the lowest possible hand is 7–5–4–3–2 in two or more suits, but in some games the ace may optionally be treated as the lowest card and 6–4–3–2–A becomes the lowest hand, while a pair of aces is the lowest pair.

High-Low Seven-Card Stud.—The high and low hands divide the pot, but each player may select any five of his cards as his candidate for high hand and any five as his candidate for low hand and so win the entire pot. In some games declarations are required: before the showdown each player must announce whether he is trying for high, for low or for both, and he cannot win unless his entire announcement is fulfilled.

Low Poker or Lowball.—This is draw poker played similarly to jackpots except that a player may open on any hand and the lowest-ranking hand wins the pot. In California, where the game is most popular, straights and flushes never count and the ace is always the lowest-ranking card, so the lowest possible hand is 5–4–3–2–A regardless of suits, called a bicycle or wheel.

Dealer's Choice or Dealer's Option.—In informal poker games, each successive dealer is usually permitted to dictate the variant of poker that will be played. This privilege is most often expressed by the dealer's selecting one of the forms of poker described above. He may also designate certain cards to be wild. Sometimes it is agreed that the dealer can select or invent any variant he wishes, subject to only two restrictions: the dealer cannot require any player to ante more than any other player; if the game requires a minimum to open (as jackpots) and is passed out, the same dealer deals again.

LAWS OF POKER

No code of poker laws has been universally adopted as the laws of bridge have been. Nearly every club or serious game has cer-

tain house rules that may differ in some respects (usually minor) from those of other clubs and groups. The usual practice is to adopt a published code and add the house rules to it. A code prepared by O. Jacoby in 1940 and another (nearly identical in substance) appearing in *The Official Rules of Card Games* since 1945, are the ones most often adopted in the United States. Poker laws, unlike those of other card games, provide only rectification and no penalties for irregularities.

Certain departures from regular procedure are necessarily treated differently in draw poker and stud poker. The following summary follows the Jacoby code.

Laws Applying to All Forms of Poker.—*Misdeal.*—The same dealer deals again with the same pack if: a card is exposed in the cut; two or more cards are exposed in the deal; the pack is found to be imperfect (but after the next deal begins, all previous deals stand); a player is dealing out of turn and attention is drawn to that fact by a player who has not looked at any of his cards. If one card is exposed during the deal the player must take it.

Betting.—Money (chips) put in the pot may not be removed for any reason; except that in a jackpots game when a player has opened illegally each other player may remove his chips bet after the pot was opened and before the disclosure of the false openers. A player has no redress if he misunderstood a previous bet or announcement. In table stakes a player may never bet more than his entire stack.

Action Out of Turn.—An announcement out of turn of intention to drop or bet is binding, but is temporarily canceled pending action by any player rightfully in turn. When the offender's turn comes, he may forfeit the announced amount and drop, if that amount was insufficient to call; he may if necessary add enough to call but not to raise; he is deemed to have raised by any excess of the announced amount over the amount necessary to call. (In some games action out of turn is simply void.)

Incorrect Number of Cards.—A player who has only four valid cards may play on but may not make a flush, straight or any special hand based on five cards. (In many games a four-card hand is dead and cannot win the pot.)

Laws Applying to Draw Poker.—*Incorrect Hand.*—If one player is dealt four cards, another six, and if neither has looked at his hand, the former draws a card from the latter; if either has looked at his hand, the hand is foul (cannot win the pot). If a player has not looked at his hand and has four cards, the dealer gives him another from the top of the pack; if he has six cards, the dealer draws one card and places it on the bottom of the pack.

Card Exposed During the Draw.—If the card was faced in the pack, it is discarded and the draw continues. If the card was exposed in dealing, it is discarded and the player is given a replacement after all other players have drawn.

Wrong Number of Cards Drawn.—A player must take the number of cards he asked for, unless he corrects himself before he looks at any card drawn and before the next player has drawn. If he has discarded, he may discard more to make room for additional cards or he may if necessary play on with four (but no fewer) cards; he may not reclaim any discard. If he has been given too many cards and looks at any of them, his hand is foul. He has no redress whether an error was his or the dealer's.

Insufficient Cards in Pack.—The bottom card of the pack may not be dealt. If there are too few cards remaining to complete the draw, the dealer gathers together all discards of players who have dropped or have already drawn, shuffles them, has them cut and continues the draw. The opener's discards, if identifiable, are exempted.

Laws Applying to Stud Poker.—*Incorrect Hand.*—If a player, for any reason, has an incorrect number of cards his hand is foul.

Exposed Card.—If a hole card is exposed accidentally in the deal, the dealer gives the player his next card face down. A player may not intentionally expose a hole card and receive a subsequent card face down; he may play on with that card exposed. If a card to be dealt is exposed before a betting interval is ended, then that card and one card for each other active player are buried before the deal is resumed.

Insufficient Cards in Pack.—The bottom card of the pack may not be dealt. If there are not enough cards to complete every active player's hand, the dealer flashes (exposes) a card instead of dealing the last round, and the exposed card is considered the last card of every active player's hand.

SKILLFUL PLAY

Poker better rewards skillful play than any other card game. Though it is not so complex a game as bridge and numerous other games, the player has greater control over the result (largely because he is permitted to drop bad hands); consequently a good player is less likely to lose in a game with inferior players.

Since poker has a mathematical basis (the less probable a particular holding, the higher its rank), the science of the game begins with the relative expectancies of the several hands, though this is only background knowledge that seldom has practical application in play.

There are possible 2,598,960 different five-card hands that may be dealt from a 52-card pack, as follows:

Possible Poker Hands In 52-Card Pack

Hand	No. possible	Chance of being dealt
Straight flush..........	40	64,974
Four of a kind........	624	4,165
Full house.............	3,744	694
Flush	5,108	509
Straight	10,200	256
Three of a kind........	54,912	48
Two pairs.............	123,552	21
One pair.............	1,098,240	2.5
No pair..............	1,302,540	2

A person beginning the study of poker on purely theoretical grounds would find such a table indispensable. It would tell him, for example, that if he is dealt a flush there are only a few thousand possible hands that might beat him while there are more than 2,500,000 he can beat, whereupon he would be justified in making or calling a maximal bet.

From a practical standpoint, the player needs chiefly to know what constitutes a good hand, a fair hand and a poor hand in a given form of poker. Experience as well as mathematics indicates the following as the average winning hands in the forms of poker most frequently played.

Game	Average winning hand
Draw poker, nothing wild................Jacks up
Five-card stud..........................Aces or kings
Seven-card stud........................3 eights
Draw poker, joker wild..................3 eights
Draw poker, with bug...................Aces up
Draw poker, deuces wild................3 aces
Draw poker, high-low...................Jacks up high; 10 or 9 low
Lowball 9–6–x–x–x

The fundamental principle of skillful play is that a person should stay in the pot only if: (1) he probably has the best hand or (2) the odds against his drawing the best hand are less than the odds offered by the pot. To illustrate the latter: There are four chips in the pot and the player must put in one chip to stay; therefore the pot offers 4-to-1 odds. The player has a four-flush or "bobtail" straight (open at both ends as 8–7–6–5), to either of which he can draw one card. The odds against filling either of these hands ranges $4\frac{1}{4}$–5 to 1. The pot offers less than the odds against filling, so the player should drop.

The approximate odds against improving the original hand in draw poker are as follows:

Hand	Odds against improving
One pair............................	$2\frac{1}{2}$ to 1
Two pairs...........................	11 to 1
Three of a kind......................	$8\frac{1}{2}$ to 1
Straight, open.......................	5 to 1 (39 to 8)
Straight, inside (as 8–7–5–4).............	11 to 1
Straight flush, open..................	2 to 1
Straight flush, inside.................	3 to 1

In five-card stud poker it is wise to stay in only if one has a pair, a hole card higher than any card showing or a card at least as high as any card showing plus another high card. It is never wise to stay in when another player has showing a pair higher than one's own pair (or if one has no pair). In seven-card stud, it is usually best to stay in only if one has a pair, three cards of the same suit or three cards in sequence. In seven-card high-low stud, the guiding principle is to play for low.

The only hand with which to play for high is three of a kind in the first three cards.

Bluffing and psychological play, though they are of essential importance, depend more on experience and moral ascendancy than on rules of play or maxims.

HISTORY

The principle of poker is very ancient. One of its ancestral games (Sp. *primero*, It. *primiera*, Fr. *la prime*) appears in literature at least as early as 1526. In this game each player had three cards and the counting combinations were three of a kind, a pair and a flux (flush), three cards of the same suit. In later developments certain cards had special value, equivalent to wild cards in modern poker. By about 1700 the betting and bluffing aspects had produced the games brag in England (one of four card games about which Edmond Hoyle wrote) and *pochen* (Ger. "to bluff") in Germany. From the latter the French developed a similar game called *poque*, played in French America in 1803, when the Louisiana purchase made New Orleans and its environs territories of the United States. During the next 20 years English-speaking settlers in the Louisiana territory adopted the game, anglicized its name to poker and established the essential features of the modern game.

The earliest-known reference to poker in American literature occurs (1829) in the memoirs of Joe Cowell, a touring English actor. From his description it is clear that the original American game was played with a pack of cards that included five cards for each player: all the cards were dealt and the players bet on which had the best five-card combination.

So played, poker is virtually indistinguishable from an older Persian game called *As nas*, a four-hand game played with a 20-card pack, five cards dealt to each player. This coincidence has led some students of games to call poker a derivative of *As nas*, but there is no record of any connection between the two.

By 1834, the date of the second known reference to poker, the game had been adapted to the 52-card deck. No description of poker is given in any book of the rules of games before 1858, but in such books published in the 1860s it is not characterized as a new game. The history of the game since then consists entirely of new features introduced to encourage freer betting: the straight, introduced as an additional valuable hand; the draw, so that players might stay in even when they were not originally dealt good hands; stud poker, to increase the number of opportunities for betting; jackpots, originally only applying to a pot to which each player antes, creating an unusually large pot at the start. Most of these innovations came in the decade 1861–70 and probably were engendered in the great amount of poker played by soldiers on both sides in the Civil War.

The spread of poker to other countries probably began in 1871 when Col. Jacob Schenck, the U.S. minister to Great Britain, explained the game to a group of gentlemen including members of the British court. Queen Victoria heard about the game and expressed interest, whereupon Schenck wrote and had privately printed (1872) a set of rules to send to her. This is the earliest-known work devoted exclusively to poker, although the game had previously (1858, 1864, etc.) been treated in compendiums. Poker was already sufficiently identified with the United States so that Schenck described it as "our national game." However, this may have been only because all other card games played in the U.S. were undeniably of European origin.

Whether rapidly or gradually, between 1870 and the end of the 19th century, poker became a matter of general knowledge in the United States, and early in the 20th century it spread to other parts of the world.

See *Oswald Jacoby on Poker* (1947) for the game as played in the

U.S.; Maurice Ellinger, *Poker* (1950) for the game as played in England. (O. Jy.; A. H. Md.)

POKOMAM AND POKONCHÍ, two closely related dialects of the easternmost Highland Maya. Culturally the people who speak them are very similar and in the 16th century they were scarcely distinguishable, even linguistically. Speakers of Pokomam in the 1960s numbered about 100,000, and of Pokonchí nearly 50,000, in the departments of Alta Verapaz, Baja Verapaz, El Progreso, Guatemala, Jutiapa, Chiquimula, Zacapa, and Jalapa in Guatemala (*q.v.*). Until the 19th century Pokomam was spoken in several towns in western El Salvador. In the period *c.* A.D. 850, these peoples produced some of the finest figure-painted ceramics in the Americas. Contemporary hispanicized life shows remnants of the politics and clan and hierarchical society described by B. de Las Casas (*q.v.*) in the 16th century. Christianized simple burial practices contrast with magnificent old tombs (*see* ARCHAEOLOGY: *Mesoamerica*). Ancient tomb-shrines are still adoratories, modern myths and dances perpetuating traditions of earlier days. The count of the 20 day names of the old Maya calendar is still employed in healing and fortunetelling. *See also* CALENDAR: *Middle American Calendars;* MAYA INDIANS.

BIBLIOGRAPHY.—B. de Las Casas, *Apologética historia . . . de estas Indias . .* . (1909); S. W. Miles, *The Sixteenth-Century Pokom-Maya* (1957); Thomas Gage, *The English-American, His Travail by Land and Sea,* etc. (1648; reprinted 1947); R. E. Reina, *Chinautla: a Guatemalan Indian Community* (1960). (S. W. M.)

POLABS (POLABIANIE; from *po,* "along," *Laba,* "Elbe"), the westernmost Slavs of Europe, dwelt between the lower Elbe to the west, the Baltic to the north, the lower Oder to the east, and Lusatia (*q.v.*) to the south. In Charlemagne's time they were organized in two confederations or principalities, the Obodrites (*q.v.*) in the west and the Lutycy or Wilcy in the east. The latter comprised many tribes, of which the Ratarowie (Ger. Redarier) and Stodoranie or Hawolanie (Ger. Heveller) were the most important. The Lutycy, who had allied themselves with the German king Henry II against Boleslaw I of Poland in 1003, were subdued by the Germans in the 12th century: Lothair of Saxony destroyed Radogoszcz (Rethra), the Ratarian capital, in 1121; and the margrave Albert the Bear began a war against the Hawolanie in 1147 and incorporated their lands in Brandenburg when their prince, Pribislav, died childless in 1150. Even so, the Polabian language, related to Kaszub and Polish, survived on the Lüneburg Heath till the beginning of the 19th century. (K. SM.)

POLAND (POLSKA), a country of east-central Europe lying between the Baltic Sea to the north and the Sudetes and Carpathian mountains to the south and bounded, since 1945, on the east and northeast by the U.S.S.R., on the south by Czechoslovakia, and on the west by Germany. Its area is 120,359 sq.mi. (311,730 sq.km.), and population (1960 census) 29,775,508. The capital is Warsaw (Warszawa).

This article contains the following sections and subsections:

I. PHYSICAL GEOGRAPHY

1. Structure and Relief.—The main morphological features have been molded by two great influences: the northward thrust of the Alpine-fold mountains against the Hercynian plateaus (represented there by the Bohemian Massif and the submerged Polish Platform which reaches the surface in the Lysa Gora [Lysica], east of Kielce) and the southward invasions of the Scandinavian ice sheet. Conditioned by these two influences the natural regions tend to form zones running broadly east and west across the country.

In the extreme south, the mountain frontier zone is divided into two sections. The first, composed of the older, peneplained rocks of the Sudetes Mountains, reaches its highest point in Mt. Sniezka (5,259 ft. [1,603 m.]) in the Giant Mountains; the second, formed by the young fold mountains of the Carpathians, assumes a truly alpine appearance in the High Tatra, the highest point of which, Gerlachovka (8,737 ft. [2,663 m.]), lies across the frontier in Slovakia. The submontane zone of southern Poland, consisting of upland-rimmed river basins interconnected by narrow gateways, is again capable of subdivision. Thus Silesia, drained northwestward by the Oder, forms a unity centring upon Wroclaw (Breslau); bounded on the north by the Kocie Hills near Trzebnica, this basin contains extensions of the great carboniferous deposits of northwestern Europe. The sub-Carpathian basins, on the other hand, occupy a tectonic hollow running from the Moravian Gate through the small Oswiecim Basin and the Cracow Gate to the wider Sandomierz Basin drained by the Vistula and San. The Little Polish (Malopolska) Tableland, between the Silesian and sub-Carpathian basins, consists of the Cracow-Czestochowa limestone plateau (reaching 1,653 ft. [504 m.]), which opens southeastward to the Tertiary deposits of the Nida Basin, and the Holy Cross (Swietokrzyskie) Mountains (Lysa Gora, 2,005 ft. [611 m.]). The southeastern edge of the latter, the Sandomierz Tableland, is noted for its fertile loess deposits. Finally, east of the Vistula the upland rim is represented by the Lublin Tableland, with its rich soils derived from chalk marl, and the Roztocze ridge.

The remainder of Poland is dominated by glacial features. The characteristic east-west sectors of the great rivers and their tributaries (e.g., the lines formed by the Bug-Vistula-Notec-Warta and the Warta-Obra-Oder) mark stages in the successive northward retreat of the ice sheet, when drainage was forced toward the west. Central Poland, an undulating country crossed by the great valleys, includes the Great Polish (Wielkopolska) and Kujavian lowlands around Poznan and the Mazovian Podlasian lowlands around the capital city, Warsaw. The soils are based on fluvioglacial and fluvial deposits. Farther north, breached by the Oder and Vistula in their lower courses, lies the Baltic lake zone, Pomorze (Pomerania) to the west and Mazovia to the east of the Vistula. It is a region of classic morainic topography: boulder clay, sands and gravels form hummocky ridges, often reaching more than 650 ft. (198 m.) in height and interspersed with numerous lake-filled, peaty hollows. The morainic hills descend to a low sandy plain skirting the Baltic coast. Along this coast, with its slight tidal range, longshore drift eastward has modified deltaic construction by the Oder and Vistula to produce classic examples of lagoon-and-bar formation as the Vistula Lagoon (Zalew Wislany or Frisches Haff; q.v.) and the Stettin Lagoon (Zalew Szczecinski or Oder Haff). Such deposition had hindered access to the older ports such as Elblag (Elbing).

2. Climate.—Climatically, Poland belongs to the major zone which includes eastern Germany, most of Finland, and western U.S.S.R. It is open to the influence of the prevailing, variable, westerly winds, except when these are replaced during winter by the heavy masses of cold air cushioning the interior of the continent. Summers are warm or very warm, according to distance from the sea and latitude, although temperatures in the south are modified by the increasing altitude. Winters are cold and are particularly unpleasant when pressure conditions allow an influx of strong winds from the Russian plains. Temperatures are below freezing point for at least two winter months in the west and three months in the east. The Oder, for example, is frozen for an average of 80 days, the Vistula 80–100 days, and the Baltic harbours, especially where distant from the open sea, are icebound for a period every year—Swinoujscie for 20 days on the average, Szczecin (Stettin) for 61 days. The open Baltic itself is frequently impeded by drift ice, but navigation usually continues along the sea-lanes connecting the favourably placed docks of Gdynia-Gdansk (Danzig). The following figures are typical mean January and July temperatures: Szczecin, 30.4° and 65° F (−1° and 18° C); Warsaw, 27° and 66° F (−3° and 19° C); Tomaszow Lubelski, 24° and 64° F (−5° and 18° C). Sniezka, with a range between 19° and 47° F (−7° and 8° C), and below freezing point for six months, is typical of conditions in the highest mountain regions; even in the Tatra, however, there are no permanent snows.

Precipitation, in winter mostly falling as snow, is moderate, 20–27.5 in. (508 mm.–698 mm.), except along the southern highland fringe. There is greater precipitation in the summer half year, because of the development of thundery conditions in early summer and of the passage of depressions in autumn. The skies are on the whole cloudy, mean cloudiness averaging somewhat less than seven out of ten pt.; the summers are brighter and less humid, although more rainy, than the winters. Wroclaw is representative, with a mean annual precipitation of 23.3 in. (591 mm.) and cloudiness of 6.8 pt.; precipitation is distributed seasonally, in percentages of the total, beginning with winter, as follows: 16, 24, 38, and 22. Sniezka

has a mean annual precipitation of 45.6 in. (1,159 mm.), typical of the narrow mountain fringe.

3. Geographical Regions.—Six regions can be distinguished, defined broadly along east-west axes, and based on relief and land-use factors. Ranging inland and southward the regions are: the maritime lowlands, the Baltic lake zone, the central lowlands, the region of old mountains and highlands, the sub-Carpathian basins, and the Carpathian Mountains.

The Maritime Lowlands include the Szczecin Plain in the west and the low-lying coastal region, where the landscape is varied by large lakes (Lebske and Gardno) and sand dunes. The Zulawy region of the Vistula delta though vulnerable to floods is highly fertile and the considerably drained areas are important for agriculture and animal breeding. The main economic activity centres on the docks and shipyards of the ports of Szczecin, Gdynia, and Gdansk (Danzig), while the growing tourist industry is centred on Kolobrzeg, Darlowo, and Leba.

The Baltic Lake Zone characterized by glacial lakes and morainic hills embraces the two subregions, the Pomeranian and Masurian lake districts, lying respectively to the west and east of the lower Vistula. Agriculturally the area is highly diverse; contrasts in land use are related to detailed variations in soil and drainage conditions. With few resources other than timber and peat the zone is of little economic significance. It is, however, an area of considerable tourist potential.

The Central Lowlands may be divided into two sections, the Great Polish or Wielkopolska (Poznan area) and Kujavian lowlands in the west and the Mazovian Podlasian lowlands in the east. The great parallel river valleys form the major east-west traffic routes. The region is of considerable agricultural importance, especially for cereal production. The two great urban focuses of Poznan and Warsaw are important centres of engineering and transport.

The Old Mountains and Highlands region farther south is considerably diverse and structurally complex with distinct subregions defined by the intersecting drainage of the upper Odra and upper Vistula. The region contains a variety of nonferrous minerals, e.g., the copper deposits in the Legnica district. Building materials are also an important product, e.g., the cement industry of Oppeln. In the middle section lies the major industrial area of the Upper Silesian coalfield.

The Sub-Carpathian Basins form a triangle narrowing toward the Cracow Gate which separates the western part of the Raciborz-Oswiecim Basin from the Sandomierz Basin. In the east lies an overpopulated traditionally agricultural area which remains comparatively backward economically. The post-1945 development of the Nowa Huta steelworks near Cracow was initiated to promote industrial activity in the region.

The Carpathian Mountains stretch from the Moravian Gate to the border with the Ukraine, U.S.S.R. A foothill zone is succeeded to the south by the Beskidy Uplands and then by the Podhale Basin which lies between the Beskidy and the southernmost massif of the High Tatra. The attractive landscape has made this region economically significant for its tourist industry, with a principal centre at Zakopane. Considerable attention has been given to the role of the Carpathians as the main water catchment area of Poland and a source of hydroelectricity.   (G. W. S.; ED. BR.)

4. Vegetation.—Poland belongs to the Central European floral region. The species which make up its flora include about 2,250 seed plants (Phanerogamae), 900 mosses and liverworts (Bryophyta), 1,200 Lichens, 10,000 Algae, and 12,000 species of Fungi, Myxomycetes, and other groups of the Cryptogamae. The most significant plant associations are forests, which cover 23% of the country. The economically important forests are the deciduous oak-hornbeam, beech, and alder forests; the mixed pine-oak and fir-beech forests; and the coniferous pine and spruce forests. Of the few endemic species two trees are worth mentioning; the Polish larch (*Larix polonica*) and the Ojcow birch (*Betula oycoviensis*).

Some relics of the Ice Age (e.g., *Betula nana*) exist on the peat bogs and in the lake district. The lime and gypsum rocks and the loess areas have a thermophil vegetation of relict xerophils (*Stipa*

BY COURTESY OF THE POLISH CULTURAL INSTITUTE, LONDON

ZAKOPANE. A RESORT CENTRE IN THE TATRA MOUNTAINS NEAR THE POLISH-CZECHOSLOVAKIAN BORDER

pennata, Prunus fruticosa, and others) and Atlantic plant species (*e.g., Erica tetralix*) are present near the Baltic Sea.

In the late 1960s there were 11 national parks with an area of 235,425 ac. (95,277 ha.), and other reserves with a total area of 86,490 ac. (35,000 ha.) were maintained to protect animals, plants, and geological features. (W. Sz.; A. Wy.)

5. Animal Life.—The fauna of Poland belongs to the zone of deciduous and mixed forests of the Palearctic region, and differs little from that of neighbouring countries. Roe deer, red deer, and wild boar predominate and inhabit mainly the deciduous forests. Typical birds of the coniferous forests in the north and the mountains are the nutcracker, capercaillie, and black grouse. Alpine species such as the chamois and marmot are encountered in the Carpathians, and the ground squirrel and hamster found mainly in the south are steppe elements.

The once-abundant fauna of the forests was harried by hunting and driven out by deforestation as early as the Middle Ages. The last aurochs (*q.v.*) was killed in 1627. The European bison (*Bison bonasus*) teemed in the Belovezh Forest until World War I when it was exterminated. A bison herd was later rebuilt from specimens preserved in zoological gardens and by the 1960s there were more than 100 bison in the Polish reserves, about half of them roaming at liberty. Elks and beavers are preserved in northeastern Poland, and bears, lynxes, and wildcats occur in the Carpathian forests. The lake district in the north has a rich avifauna including swans, cormorants, and cranes.

Trout and salmon, the latter becoming increasingly rare, live in the mountain rivers; lowland rivers and lakes are inhabited by eels, pike, perch, tench, and bream. (KA. K.)

II. THE PEOPLE

1. Origins.—The Poles belong to the North Indo-European language group comprising also other Slavs, the Balts, and the Germans. As far back as the first half of the 1st millennium B.C. the Slavs and the Balts formed a nondifferentiated linguistic entity. Hence, the primordial homeland of the Slavs should be localized in the immediate vicinity of the most ancient settlements of Germans and Balts. This has been illustrated by the Polish anthropologist Tadeusz Sulimirski. He projected on the map of Europe the schema of the relationship between Indo-European languages prescribed by the German linguists Johannes Schmidt and Hermann Hirt. This diagram indicates that the area occupied by the Poles in the basins of the Oder and Vistula rivers corresponds to the territory of the presumed primordial homeland of the Slavs. (*See* also SLAVS.)

The Polish nation originated from a union of the following west-Slavonic tribes: Polanians (Polans; *Polanie*), Vistulans (Vislans; *Wislanie*), Silesians (*Slazacy*), East Pomeranians or Cassubians (*Kaszuby*), and Mazovians (*Mazowszanie*). The factor uniting Polish tribes into a historic nation was the state ruled by the Polanian Piast dynasty which appeared in the middle of the 9th century, although the year 963 is the date first confirmed in historical sources. This state gave the name of Poles (*Polak,* plural *Polacy*) to the united tribes. To the present time, however, these tribes have preserved a feeling of belonging to their region, a certain local patriotism linked with their dialect, dress, and customs. This feeling was most vital among the Cassubians who were finally incorporated into the Polish state only in 1466. The Vistulans failed to preserve their traditional name, which was mentioned in historical sources of the 9th century (the so-called Bavarian Geographer and King Alfred). The conquest of the Vistulans (*Visle land* mentioned by King Alfred) in the 9th century by the Great Moravian state, its inclusion in the Czech state in the 10th century, and, finally, its participation in the state of Polanian Piasts and their successors, obviously obliterated from the memory of the people their traditional tribal name. They became Little Polanians (*Malopolanie*) while the original Polanians began to call themselves Great Polanians (*Wielkopolanie*).

The hypothetical limits of the Polish language in the year 1000, as established by Kazimierz Nitsch, indicate the extent of territorial losses sustained as a consequence of the germanization of the Great Polanians and Silesians. The boundary of the Polish language in 1750 shows the losses suffered during the previous centuries not only by the Silesians, the Great Polanians, and particularly the Pomeranians, but even by the Mazovians whose northern frontier region became germanized. (*See* POLISH LANGUAGE.)

From an anthropological point of view Poland is a part of central Europe. The main racial components of its population are the Nordic, Mediterranean, Armenoid, and Lapponoid elements. The last two elements are not distinguished by many anthropologists, who denote them jointly as the Alpine race. In a strip of the eastern border region of the Polish ethnic area small but tangible admixtures of the Paleo-Europoid or Paleo-Asiatic components may be discerned. These are strongly represented in archaic northeastern Europe and are a characteristic element of the Finno-Ugrian peoples; this element is supposed to be a remnant of the Mesolithic European populations.

The characteristic peculiarity of the anthropological structure of the population of Poland is that the region of the last glaciation corresponds to the zone of the strongest predominance of the Nordic element, while farther south the Lapponoid element is more numerous. Rather closely connected with this significant conformity of the anthropological and geological boundaries is the equilibrium line of the admixture of the two less essential components. The Mediterranean admixture prevails in the Nordic, and the Armenoid in the Lapponoid area. The equilibrium line of admixtures is a characteristic boundary separating anthropological central Europe from its northern periphery—an area with a decided prevalence of the Nordic anthropological element.

The equilibrium line of admixture runs from the mouth of the western Neisse (Nysa) toward the lower Warta, from the upper course of which it passes to the Vistula, reaching it in the vicinity of the mouth of the San River. From the Vistula it turns to the Bug River and encircles Polesie from the north. The deviation of the equilibrium line reaching far to the south between the Warta and Vistula is undoubtedly due to migratory movements in a southeastern direction. It is unknown whether this is only a consequence of the rule of the Piasts and their expansion from the 10th century onward, or whether it is the joint effect of that expansion and of the hypothetical expansion of the Baltic-Lekhitian Slavs which can be dated to the 7th century.

It is very probable that toward the end of the 6th century the incursion of the presumably Mongolian tribe of the Avars disrupted the political organizations formed in the sub-Carpathian and sub-Sudeten regions after the invasion of the Huns, and caused not only the transfer of the Serbs, Croats, and Volhynian Dulebians to the west, and later to the south, but also enabled the Baltic-Lekhitian (Polabian) Slavs to subdue the continental Slavonic tribes as far as the Carpathian Mountains, including the Czechs. The hypothesis of an assumed Lekhitian state of such vast extent is supported by the results of linguistic, anthropological, and archaeological investigations as well as by the unequivocal though indirect evidence of the so-called Nestor *Chronicle* of the 11th century. Moreover, one might suppose that the attacks of Charlemagne against the Slavs reaching as far as the estuary and source of the Oder disrupted that state and liberated the continental Slavonic tribes; this enabled the Polanian Piasts to consolidate the continental Lekhitian tribes within the framework of a new, now Polish, state organism.

The historical Polish tribes are still clearly marked by anthropological differences. The Polanians, Kujavians, Pomeranians, and Mazovians preserved an anthropological composition closely related to the primordial Slavs, with a characteristic predominance of the Nordic element. On the other hand, beyond the zone transformed by the pressure of their northern neighbours, the tribes of Silesians and Little Polanians are characterized by a prevalence of the Lapponoid element. Hence it is possible that they became Polish only in consequence of the Lekhitian expansion.

One of the most essential results of ethnographic investigations is the assertion that Poland is transected by one of the most important cultural confines of Eurasia which runs from the Baltic to Tonkin Bay. This is the borderline between the limits of reach of two-shaft cart harnesses with one horse and harnesses with one-shaft carts and two horses. Primarily one-shaft harnesses were connected with cattle traction and have been later adapted to horse traction. The terminology of western Polish carts is of Upper-German origin and was introduced into Poland by way of Moravia. This would be an evidence that this revolution in the domain of transport coincided with the period of the growing influence of the Franconian monarchy at the time of the Samon state or, even later, of the Great Moravian state. It is significant that single (two-shaft) harness is used by the Finns, Balts, and Russians and was probably derived from Turkic and Mongolian nomads, whereas the Ukrainians still use the archaic one-shaft harness and cattle traction. In the territory of Poland the limit of one-horse harness seems to determine the boundary of the area ruled by the Balts that was in later times absorbed by the Polish ethnic expansion.

2. Religion.—The overwhelming majority of Poles (nearly 95%) belong to the Roman Catholic Church. The Polish Protestant Church and the Polish autocephalous Orthodox Church make up about 3% of the total number of citizens, and the number of Jews, which before World War II represented 10% of the population, was reduced by the German extermination policy to no more than 0.3%. The awareness of belonging to the Polish nation linked with Catholicism is a consequence of historical processes through which the Polish people passed during the last thousand years. When Poland was endowed with its own church hierarchy in 1000, and with the Gniezno archbishopric depending directly on Rome, it became an equal member of the European community of Christian lands. Since that time the church hierarchy has played an important role in Polish history. During the period of division of the kingdom into autonomous principalities (12th–14th centuries), when the supreme princely power did not have much authority, or in the period following the 18th-century partitions of Poland, when the nation was deprived of its own statehood, the Polish people were linked together by the church hierarchy. Furthermore, that hierarchy preserved the unity of the nation also where the state neglected to defend it. Although Casimir III the Great renounced in 1335 his claims to Silesia, that province remained until 1818 dependent on the Gniezno archdiocese.

This union of Poles with their church is reflected in the domain of folklore where festivities and rites, at first undoubtedly of pagan origin, became linked with church solemnities and observances. Traces of the most remote past can be found in archaic ritual songs of a pentatonic scale and in ordinances not connected with church ceremonies, as well as in amusements, especially in children's plays and in postharvest celebrations which have the character of folk entertainments.

(J. Cz.)

III. HISTORY

Archaeology indicates that tribes on Polish territory began to be politically organized, around Cracow and Gniezno, between the 6th and the 9th century. Probably about the end of that period the princes of Gniezno, leaders of the Polanie tribe, created the larger state organization that was to become Poland. Poland's written history begins in the year 963 when a German border knight came into contact with Mieszko I (*see* MIESZKO), prince of Poland till 992. The unity of the Polish state, surrounded as it was by other pagan and mostly Slavonic tribes, had been achieved under the descendants of Piast (said to have been either of peasant origin or an official at the court of an older dynasty), who founded the dynasty which gave his people strong and valiant rulers down to 1370. Mieszko's predecessors had succeeded in establishing a highly developed political community which had neither enjoyed the benefits nor suffered the disadvantages of contact with the high civilizations of western and southern Europe. To meet the dangers that arose when the Germans began to penetrate the barrier formed by the western Slavonic tribes, Mieszko conceived that policy of deliberately adopting Western civilization which was the chief object of the rulers of Poland for several centuries. He secured his state from the aggression of his new neighbours by acknowledging himself a tributary of the Holy Roman emperor Otto I, and removed all danger of a hostile crusade by accepting Christianity for himself and for his people in 966 with the help of the Czech princess Dubravka or Dabrowka, whom he had married a year before. Finally he placed all his lands in the hands of the pope, thus inaugurating a close relationship that gave Poland the special protection of the Holy See. He seems to have been successful in gaining Pomorze (Pomerania; *i.e.,* the seaboard), but he lost part of his eastern territory to the Russian prince Vladimir the Saint.

A. THE PIAST KINGDOM

Mieszko's son Boleslaw I the Brave (*see* BOLESLAW I; 992–1025) was one of the great soldiers and statesmen of his time. From the Congress of Gniezno (1000) with his friend the emperor Otto III, where he secured for Poland an independent church, organized in a number of bishoprics under a metropolitan at Gniezno, to his coronation as king (1025), he achieved the transformation of his father's principality into a powerful and independent kingdom. His wars of defense and expansion against Germany and Bohemia ended successfully in 1018; then he turned east and, during an armed intervention, occupied the Russian capital, Kiev. His younger son Mieszko II (1025–34) succeeded him as king, but the decentralizing tendencies of the nobles diminished the power of the kingdom in spite of its partial revival under Mieszko II's son Casimir (Kazimierz) I the Restorer (1039–58) and the strong rule of Casimir's son Boleslaw II the Bold (1058–79). But under Boleslaw III the Wry-Mouthed (1102–38), a nephew of Boleslaw II, Poland made great advances. Boleslaw maintained the independence of his country by a victory at Glogow when the emperor Henry V invaded Silesia in 1109. His reign saw a considerable cultural advance, and an anonymous chronicler recorded the earlier history of Poland. He collaborated with Otto, bishop of Bamberg, in converting the Pomeranians to Christianity after occupying and subduing the greater part of that area.

1. The Period of Division, 1138–1314.—Boleslaw III divided Poland among his sons, so that Poland, like its neighbours Germany and Kievan Russia, ceased to be a united state for two centuries. The capital was established in Cracow, the ruler of which, originally the prince of Silesia, also owned Pomorze and had "seniority" over his brothers, who ruled over Great Poland with Poznan and western Kujavia, Mazovia and eastern Kujavia, and Sandomierz. In each of these principalities there grew up round the Piast prince a powerful upper class consisting of the officials and the clergy headed by the local bishop, a process which modified the *jus ducale,* or ducal right, of the monarchical system. This period of divided loyalties laid the country open to many dangers; while the empire remained strong, a ruler like Frederick I Barbarossa in 1157 could assert his claim to Polish allegiance, and a major disaster like the Mongol or Tatar invasion in 1241 found the chivalry of Little (or southern) Poland unsupported and the heroic efforts of Prince Henry II the Pious of Silesia (1238–41) made in vain. Worst of all were the incessant raids of the barbarian neighbours, notably the Lithuanians and Prussians. To avert these, Prince Konrad of Mazovia called in the Teutonic Order (*q.v.*), a purely German crusading organization that had lost a sphere for its activities in Palestine. Well established on the northern border, the order was helped by the Poles to occupy not only the borderland but the whole of Prussia, which was speedily colonized mainly by German immigrants. By a brilliant piece of diplomacy the grand master Hermann von Salza persuaded the emperor Frederick II to accept his homage as ruler of the newly acquired lands (1226). The divided Polish states found themselves face to face with a powerful German state on their northern border.

In spite of the political weakness of Poland, the great Mongol-Tatar invasion, and the menace from Germany, this age was one of great importance to the development of Poland. In the process of decentralization, each province was able to assert its own individuality, helping its prince and bishop to intensify their efforts to develop the resources of its small territory. The petty princes and great landowners were able to imitate Western Europe by encouraging the immigration of German peasants, townsmen, and artisans, who helped them to raise the level of economic life. The ideal of the prince, especially in Silesia, was *melioratio terrae* (the improvement of his land), to achieve which he was prepared to sacrifice both part of his own sovereign power and vague national ideals. This ideal resulted in the loss to Poland of some areas: Lower Silesia, the district of Lubusz on the lower Oder, and western Pomorze were gradually colonized by Germans. But the economic and cultural advance of the country as a whole strengthened the community which was able to maintain its ethnical frontier in spite of political disaster for six centuries.

In most of Poland the Germans were ultimately absorbed. The princes further reduced their sovereign power by the granting of charters to different groups and individuals. The Jews, whom crusading zeal had expelled from nearly every country, were granted the right to settle in Poland, to maintain their own schools, and to practise their religion. For the Poles they were skilled middlemen who made an important contribution to the economic life of the country but who were never absorbed as the Germans were. The achievements of the period of division can be appreciated through a comparison of the low social and economic situation in the 12th century with the resources available to the revived monarchy after 1305, whereby the rulers were able to reunite the divided principalities and had no need to copy the social and economic life of their neighbours.

2. Wladyslaw I, 1314–33.—The idea of reuniting the Polish principalities in one state first appears in the experiments of the princes of Silesia, especially in those of Henry I the Bearded (1201–38). These princes failed partly because they gradually succumbed to the attraction of German civilization and joined the empire under Czech auspices. Przemysl II of Great Poland actually assumed the royal title in 1295; but the real task of reunion was undertaken, at a time when Poland had come under the rule of Czech kings, by the hard-fighting Wladyslaw Lokietek (the Short; *see* WLADYSLAW) of Kujavia. The idea was supported by the gentry and the ecclesiastical leaders. These men had represented for a long time the links that bound Poles together and led the enlightened magnates who realized that a divided Poland would suffer extinction at the hands of such powerful neighbours as Bohemia, Brandenburg, Hungary, and the Teutonic Order.

Wladyslaw cleverly availed himself of the support of Hungary and of the traditional protection of the Holy See. After occupying Little Poland in 1305 and Great Poland in 1314, he was crowned king of Poland in 1320 as Wladyslaw I. He had many disappointments: the Teutonic Order seized Pomorze in 1308; his country long continued to suffer from the raids of the pagan Lithuanians; and he never reigned over Silesia or Mazovia, which preferred to do homage to John of Bohemia. But he held his own against the

order in the Battle of Plowce (1331), strengthened his position by his diplomatic friendship with Hungary (which was sealed in 1320 by his daughter Elizabeth's marriage to the new Angevin king Charles I), and ended for a time the Lithuanian raids by marrying his son Casimir to Anne (Aldona), daughter of Gediminas in 1325. Wladyslaw died in 1333.

3. Casimir III the Great, 1333–70.—Unlike his father, Casimir succeeded to a kingdom already in being and was a man of peace. A realist and a shrewd diplomat with a zest for the Latin culture that he learned at the court of his sister in Hungary, he was ready to make great sacrifices to secure the independence, unity, and prosperity of his kingdom. Happily for Poland the disunity of Germany, the weakness of Russia, and the death of the last great khan of the Tatars lessened the dangers on the western and eastern frontiers. Poland had to face in the south the powerful kingdom of Bohemia, whose king in 1355 was crowned Holy Roman emperor as Charles IV, and in the north the great military strength of the Teutonic Order. Basing his foreign policy on a close alliance with Hungary, Casimir was content to allow Charles IV, another lover of peace, to hold Silesia, and limited his claim to Pomorze and the border districts held by the order. As compensation for this loss of Polish territory, he found himself able by inheritance and diplomacy to annex in 1349 the principality of Halicz (*see* GALICIA) and to begin that policy of conciliation with the Lithuanian princes which was to bring such important results later on. His own prestige grew abroad, and he made Poland a full member of the European community.

By gaining for Poland a long period of peace and security, Casimir was able to make great changes in the internal relations of the country. He codified the laws of Great and Little Poland and succeeded in persuading these two rival provinces to cooperate, while the local officials of Little Poland became national ministers. The princes of Mazovia were persuaded to acknowledge Casimir as their king. He acquired great wealth, reformed the currency, and introduced Western methods in town and country. He befriended the Jews, improved the position of the peasants, and encouraged the immigration of Germans and Armenians, so that the cities grew in size and prosperity, especially Cracow and Lwow (Lvov). He was a great builder and was said to have "found a country of wood and left a country of stone." The administration was made more efficient, and it was mainly to train young men in law that Casimir founded the University of Cracow in 1364. He encouraged learning and was able, through the Italian influences at the court of Hungary and the French connections of Prague, to raise the level of learning among the Poles to Western European standards. By his foresight, his patience, and genius for creation and adaptation, this great statesman made possible the strong and prosperous position of the Polish kingdom during his lifetime and its great development in the next two centuries.

4. Louis I of Hungary, 1370–82.—Having no sons, Casimir III bequeathed his kingdom to his sister Elizabeth's son the Angevin Louis I of Hungary (1370–82), already one of the leading rulers of central Europe, who continued the cooperation of his two realms in the spirit of his predecessor. Like Casimir, he left no sons, and the future of central Europe depended to some extent on the fate of his two daughters. After an interregnum of two years the Poles accepted his younger daughter Jadwiga as their queen (1384–99) and consummated the efforts of Casimir III to conciliate the pagan rulers of Lithuania by arranging the marriage of Jadwiga to Jagiello, grand prince of Lithuania, who became king of Poland as Wladyslaw II (1386–1434).

5. Social and Constitutional Development, 1138–1384.—The social structure of the Polish state at the time of the dynastic union with Lithuania was very different from what it had been under the early kings. In the period of division there had grown up around each prince a class of ecclesiastical and lay magnates whose function was at first to advise him and later to share with him the government of his principality. In addition to this privileged class, the general mass of the gentry, organized in their clans, each with its coat of arms and slogan, was becoming conscious of its own importance as a social and political element in the country. As the prince gradually lost his monopoly of political and legal power by the grant of charters to various groups, this body, which came to be called the *szlachta*, began to share political privileges with the magnates. The extinction of the Piast dynasty gave them the opportunity by the Pact of Koszyce (Kosice) in 1374 to obtain from Louis a number of privileges, the magna carta of Poland. The chief of these was the right to pay no taxes beyond a certain sum, unless they had expressly consented to them. During the period of division the church, which had established its position at the Congress of Leczyca in 1180, played a leading part, not only in the social and moral life of the community but also as a factor of unity among the numerous principalities. Strengthened by the Gregorian reforms, it obtained judicial and financial autonomy as well as independence from the princes. The inhabitants of the towns had received charters mainly under Magdeburg law to encourage the settlement of both Poles and Germans. Besides Wroclaw and Poznan, the two great cities Cracow and Lwow grew to prosperity on the great Eastern trade route. These towns, though at first largely foreign in race, became integral members of the community, able to aid and to advise the prince and to attain political importance. The peasants, with the rise of the gentry, lost in social standing but gained economically by the tenant system, developed to a great extent mainly during the reign of Casimir III—a situation that only slowly worsened as serfdom grew up a century later. From the small body of educated men who made the court of Boleslaw III superior to that of the early kings (with the famous Otto, later bishop of Bamberg, and the anonymous scholar who wrote the first history of Poland), through the spread of Western social and moral ideas (at first chiefly by the Cistercians) to the writing of a real historical work by Wincenty Kadlubek (d. 1223), the great progress of learning in the Polish community can be followed. The great problem of the Poles was to seek and assimilate Western institutions and ideas while retaining and cherishing their own native civilization. They were forced to learn mainly from the Germans. But the political exploitation of this position by the latter led to the rise of strong anti-German feeling and to the practice of seeking models in Italy, France, or the Low Countries in preference to Germany. The union of Poland and Lithuania was a mortal blow to the position of the Teutonic Order, the greatest German power on the Polish border; and it opened vast new territories for political and economic development by the strengthened gentry and nobility.

B. The Jagiellon Dynasty

1. Jadwiga and Wladyslaw II Jagiello.—The magnates of Cracow, Casimir III's pupils and successors, were able to instruct the girl queen and the pagan king in the arts of government. One of the first acts of the new king was to receive Christianity for himself and his people. The Lithuanians, unlike the Ruthenians of their principality, who were Orthodox, joined the Roman Catholic Church. So the Poles gained by peaceful agreement what the Teutonic Order had sought by violence for a century and failed to win: the conversion of the last great body of pagans in Europe.

The very reason for the existence of the order had gone, and it would have to struggle to preserve its territories, which included Pomorze and the whole of Prussia. But the settlement was delayed for some time, partly because of Jadwiga's religious scruples against fighting a crusading body, and partly because Wladyslaw Jagiello had to solve the difficult problem of Lithuania, where he had a rival in his cousin Vytautas (Witold). The order exploited this situation so adroitly that the king was forced to recognize Vytautas as grand prince of Lithuania. This arrangement was successful for a time, and in 1409 the aggression of the order provoked the two cousins to join their forces against their common enemy. Advancing into Prussia they completely defeated the Knights in the great Battle of Grunwald (*q.v.*) in 1410. Unfortunately, though the victory was followed by the union of Horodlo (1413), which established in Lithuania institutions based on those of Poland, the two cousins did not always agree; and Poland was exposed in the south to the hostility of Sigismund of Bohemia, who had succeeded to the possessions of Louis of Hungary in 1387

and to the German kingdom in 1410.

Jagiello lost his wife Jadwiga in 1399 and remained without male issue by his next two wives; but his fourth, whom he married in 1422, the Lithuanian princess Zofia of Alsenai (Holszanska) gave him what Poland needed: two sons. Throughout his long reign he continued to collaborate amicably with the Polish leaders or, occasionally, to oppose them, knowing well that the union with Lithuania depended on his own person. As a cautious ruler he supported the Czech Hussites, but refrained from interventions abroad. He suffered great anxiety from the ambitions of Vytautas, who was a great warrior and statesman and planned to conquer the Tatars and to annex Moscow. Beloved by the Lithuanian people, Vytautas died in 1430. Wladyslaw Jagiello died in 1434, after a reign of 48 years, at a great age. He was, like most of his family, a prudent, tolerant, and tenacious ruler, and he founded a dynasty that was to be one of the greatest in Europe.

2. Wladyslaw III, 1434–44.—Jagiello was succeeded by his ten-year-old son Wladyslaw III, the chief position in the realm being held by the most eminent of the Cracow magnates, Zbigniew Olesnicki (*q.v.*), bishop of Cracow and one of the previous king's chief advisers, who became first Polish cardinal. Olesnicki had to deal with a number of urgent problems: the spread of Hussitism among the gentry; the threat to European civilization from the Turks on the Danube; the possibility of the recovery of Silesia from the Czechs and of Pomorze from the Teutonic Order; and the dangerous rise of rebellion in Lithuania among the Orthodox Ruthenians. A highly cultured scholar, a great orator and diplomat, he played a leading part in the Council of Basel. The Lithuanian rebels, though supported by the master of Livonia (the Knights of the Sword had been amalgamated with the Teutonic Order in 1237), were decisively defeated in 1435 near Wilkomierz (Ukmerge).

A churchman, Olesnicki was, like Queen Jadwiga, prepared to conciliate the Teutonic Order and to concentrate the national forces against the heretical Czechs (so as to recover Silesia) and against the Turks in the south. He failed in the first project, and his great crusade, which involved securing the throne of Hungary for Wladyslaw III (who thus became Ulászló I of Hungary), was brought to a disastrous end by the defeat at Varna (1444), where Wladyslaw was killed. Until his death was certain, Poland remained without a ruler for three years (1444–47). Then Wladyslaw II Jagiello's second son, Casimir, who had made himself popular in Lithuania, ascended the Polish throne.

(A. B. Bo.; A. Wy.)

3. Casimir IV, 1447–92.—The difficulties which confronted Casimir were great. He recognized not only the vital necessity of the maintenance of the union between the two states but also the fact that the chief source of danger to the union lay in Lithuania. For political reasons, during the earlier years of his reign, Casimir was obliged to reside for the most part in Lithuania, and his interest in that principality was always resented in Poland, where, to the very end of his reign, he was regarded with suspicion. In particular, he could never rely on adequate Polish support in the struggle with the Teutonic Order.

The struggle assumed a new form in 1454, when Casimir accepted the suzerainty offered to him by the Prussian league, which had repudiated the authority of the order and needed a protector. The acquisition of the Prussian lands was vital to the existence of Poland. It meant the command of the principal rivers of Poland, the Vistula and the Niemen, and the acquisition of a seaboard with its corollaries of sea power and commerce. Yet, except in the border province of Great Poland, which was interested commercially, the king received little support, military or financial, and it was only with his victory at Zarnowiec (Sept. 17, 1462) that he obtained any decisive success against the order. The war was ended in 1466 by the second Treaty of Torun (Oct. 19), by which Poland recovered the provinces of Pomorze, Chelmno, and Michalow, with the bishopric of Warmia (Ermland), numerous cities and fortresses, including Malbork (Marienburg), Elblag (Elbing), Gdansk (Danzig), and Torun. The territory of the order was now reduced to Prussia proper, embracing, roughly speaking, the district between the Baltic, the lower Vistula, and the lower Niemen, with Königsberg (modern Kaliningrad) as its capital. For this territory each grand master within nine months of his election was in the future to render homage to the Polish king. The regained part of Pomorze, now called Royal Prussia, became a largely autonomous Polish province, and Poland had again acquired a seaboard.

The whole foreign policy of Casimir IV was influenced by the Prussian question. At the beginning of the war both the empire and the papacy were against him. He therefore allied himself with George of Podebrady, whom the Hussites had placed on the throne of Bohemia. On the death of George (1471), Casimir's eldest son, Vladislav (i.e., in Polish, Wladyslaw), was elected king of Bohemia despite the determined opposition of Matthias I Corvinus (Mátyás Hunyadi), the king of Hungary, who thenceforward deliberately set about traversing all the plans of Casimir. He encouraged the Teutonic Order to rebel against Poland; he entertained at his court anti-Polish embassies from Moscow; he encouraged the Tatars to ravage Lithuania; he thwarted Casimir's policy in Moldavia. His death in 1490 came, therefore, as a distinct relief to Poland, and all danger from the side of Hungary was removed when Vladislav, already king of Bohemia, was elected king of Hungary also as Ulászló II.

It was in the reign of Casimir IV that Poland first came into direct collision with the Turks. The Jagiellons, as a rule, prudently avoided committing themselves to any political system which might irritate the still distant but much-dreaded Turks; but when their dominions extended so far southward as to embrace Moldavia the observance of a strict neutrality became exceedingly difficult. Poland had established a sort of suzerainty over Moldavia as early as the end of the 14th century, but at best it was a loose and vague overlordship which the hospodars repudiated whenever they were strong enough to do so. The Turks themselves were too much occupied elsewhere to pay much attention to the Danubian principalities till the middle of the 15th century, and it was not till 1484 that they became inconvenient neighbours to Poland. In that year a Turkish fleet captured the strongholds of Kilia and Akkerman, commanding, respectively, the mouths of the Danube and Dniester. This aggression seriously threatened the trade of Poland, and induced Casimir IV to accede to a general league against the Porte. In 1485 the Polish king, at the head of 20,000 men, proceeded to Kolomyya on the Pruth, where he received the homage of Prince Stephen of Moldavia; and the hostilities with Bayazid II were suspended by a truce (1489). During the remainder of Casimir's reign the Turks gave no trouble.

Casimir IV strengthened the royal authority by supporting the gentry against the nobles and by obtaining from the Holy See the right of appointing bishops.

4. John Albert and Alexander.

The death of Casimir was followed by the temporary separation of Poland and Lithuania and by a strong but short-lived aristocratic reaction in Poland. Casimir's third son, John Albert, was elected king of Poland, and his fourth son, Alexander, became grand prince of Lithuania.

The short reign of John Albert (1492–1501), a friend of the gentry, was occupied by contention with the Teutonic Order, which evaded paying homage to the king; and by an unsuccessful Polish expedition against Moldavia.

On the death of John Albert, Alexander succeeded him as king (1501–06), and the union of Poland and Lithuania assumed a more definite character, the Senate of each country agreeing that in the future the king of Poland should always be grand prince of Lithuania. The acquiescence of Lithuania was essentially the result of a new danger which had arisen in the East. Until the accession of Ivan III in 1462 Moscow had been a negligible factor in Polish politics. During the earlier part of the 15th century the Lithuanian princes had successfully contested Muscovite influence even in Pskov and Great Novgorod. But since the death of Vytautas the military efficiency of Lithuania had sensibly declined, and the natural attraction of the Orthodox Greek element in Lithuania toward Moscow threatened the integrity of the principality. During the reign of Alexander, who was too poor to maintain any adequate standing army in Lithuania, the Muscovites and Tatars ravaged the whole country at will and were prevented from conquering it altogether only by their inability to capture the chief fortresses. In Poland, meanwhile, Alexander had practically surrendered his authority to an incapable aristocracy till 1505, when the gentry led by the Laski family extorted a constitution based on the principle *Nihil novi* ("No innovations"). The dependent states of Prussia in the north and Moldavia in the south made strenuous efforts to break away.

5. Sigismund I, 1506–48.

When Sigismund I, the energetic but extremely cautious younger brother and successor of Alexander, began his reign, the state was threatened by its neighbours and needed internal reforms. The Teutonic Order refused to pay homage and was preparing war; there was a latent hostility between Moscow and Lithuania; and the Holy Roman emperor Maximilian I was trying to coordinate the actions of both those enemies against Poland. Tatar and Moldavian raids started simultaneously from the southeast, followed soon by a Turkish advance. The state needed, in particular, the means of increasing expenditure and a standing army. Renewed attempts at reforms failed because of the opposition of the gentry and its representatives in the *sejm,* or diet. In 1537, near Lwow, the assembled gentry almost threatened open mutiny. Despite those difficulties the internal structure of the state was gradually strengthened, the economy was developed, fiscal resources increased, and the strongholds of Kamieniec and Bar were fortified.

The Vienna agreement (1515) with the emperor Maximilian contributed to the breakdown of the anti-Polish coalition by allowing for Habsburg influence in Hungary and Bohemia. At the same time Konstanty Ostrogski's victory over the Muscovite armies at Orsha in 1514 enabled the Poles to give closer attention to the problem of Prussia and the Teutonic Order. Sigismund began war in 1519 and won some success against the order; but its grand master Albert (q.v.), a member of the house of Hohenzollern, became a Lutheran and created a secular duchy known as Ducal Prussia (1525). Sigismund did not achieve the incorporation of the order's lands into Poland, but the new duchy, which was the first Protestant state in this part of Europe, became autonomous under allegiance to the Polish crown.

The most important political event in Eastern Europe during the reign of Sigismund was the collapse of the ancient Hungarian monarchy at Mohács in 1526. After the death of King Louis II in the battle, the archduke Ferdinand (later Holy Roman emperor as Ferdinand I) and John Zápolya, voivode of Transylvania, competed for the vacant Hungarian crown, and both were elected almost simultaneously, Ferdinand also securing election to the kingdom of Bohemia. In Poland Zápolya's was the popular cause, and he also found powerful support among the gentry and in the influential and highly gifted Laski family, represented by the Polish primate Jan Laski the Elder and his nephews (see LASKI).

Polish policy toward Hungary, based on noncommitment, was expressed in attempts at mediation between the two competitors, while care was taken not to provoke the Turks, whose settlement in Hungary it was desired to prevent. Sigismund I was closely connected with the Zápolya family through his first wife Barbara Zápolya (d. 1515), and later through the marriage of his daughter Izabella to John Zápolya (1539). On the other hand he reckoned also with the Habsburgs, treating with the emperor Charles V as well as with Ferdinand, to whose daughter Elizabeth he married his son Sigismund Augustus in 1543; but he attempted to check the Habsburgs by his ties with France (1524). His treaty with Turkey (1533), however, gave Poland no protection from predatory raids by the Moldavians or by the Tatars. The Moldavians, defeated by Jan Tarnowski at Obertyn (1531), made peace; but the safeguarding of the frontier from the Tatars was mainly achieved by bribes and by turning them against Muscovy.

The incorporation of Mazovia into the royal territory (1526) was a great success for Sigismund I's internal policy. But the last years of his long reign were affected by his illness and by the constant interference of his second wife, Bona Sforza, in Polish affairs.　　　　　　　　　　　　　　　　(R. N. B.; A. Wy.)

6. Sigismund II Augustus, 1548–72.

Already in the 15th century the University of Cracow had brought forth humanist scholars of European repute and begun to attract distinguished lecturers and numerous students from abroad. Because of Sigismund I's marriage to the Milanese Bona Sforza (1518), the royal court in Cracow became the home of the highest Renaissance art of Italy, and the royal castle on Wawel Hill, rebuilt by Italian architects and their Polish disciples, became one of the finest monuments of Renaissance style north of the Alps. Under Sigismund II the third great spiritual factor of the age, next to humanist scholarship and Renaissance art—the doctrine of the Reformation—entered potently into Poland's intellectual life, uniting with Italian culture on the common ground of literature and helping to produce the first great age of Polish poetry and prose. There followed the clash between the New Learning and the strong tradition of Poland's chivalrous Catholicism; the difficulties with the Scandinavian powers and the rising empire of the Moscow tsars; the dilemma produced between the evolution of the Polish parliamentary system and the Renaissance tendency toward the strengthening of the central government. Even a king of genius could be only partially successful in coping with all these tasks, and the reign of Sigismund II, in many respects one of the most brilliant in Polish annals, left many problems unsolved.

Reformation and Counter-Reformation.—The new king having shown his temper by marrying a lady of the noble house of Radziwill without asking for the opinion of the Senate, the reign began in a storm of demands for constitutional guarantees to secure the parliamentary "gentry democracy" against the powers of the crown and the nobility. The king resolutely allied himself with Austria abroad and with some bishops and nobles at home, against a threatened revolt of the gentry and the intrigues of his mother. In doing so, he had to take the bishops' side in the issue between the Reformation and Catholic orthodoxy, and he affirmed this by an edict against heresy in 1550. But this act only opened up the long-maturing dispute about the creation of a national church after the recent example of Henry VIII of England. The king, a man of enlightened mind, the first Polish monarch who habitually used the vernacular language instead of Latin at public functions, showed in many ways a sympathetic understanding for the tendencies of the new era. The influence of the Bohemian Hussite movement of 100 years before combined with nascent modern nationalism to inspire definite programs for a Reformed Polish Church with Polish ritual, independent of Rome, and with a priesthood subject to government authority. The large Greek Orthodox element among the citizens of the eastern provinces of the monarchy furnished an additional stimulus, which gave strength to such demands as that for the abolition of clerical celibacy in the Lutheran fashion. The bishops resorting to highhanded measures of repression, the *sejm* of Piotrkow in 1552 voted, at the king's own suggestion, the suspension of clerical courts for a year. This was extended afterward and solemnly renewed by another *sejm* in 1555, during which the gentry required Masses in Polish and the communion to be administered in two kinds. A religious interim of about ten years followed, during which Protestantism in Poland flourished.

Presently reformers of every shade of opinion, even those who were tolerated nowhere else, poured into Poland, which speedily became the battleground of all the sects of Europe. Soon the Protestants became numerous enough to form ecclesiastical districts of their own. The first Calvinist meeting in Poland was held at Pinczow in 1550. The Bohemian Brethren, expelled from their own country, ultimately coalesced with the Calvinists at the Synod of Kozminek (August 1555). In the *sejm* itself the Protestants were absolutely supreme and generally elected a Calvinist to be their marshal. The king, however, perceiving a danger to the constitution in the violence of the gentry, not only supported the bishops but quashed reiterated demands for a national synod. The *sejm* of 1558–59 indicates the high-water mark of Polish Protestantism. From this time forward it began to subside, gradually but unmistakably, chiefly because of the division among the reformers themselves. From the chaos of creeds resulted a chaos of ideas on all imaginable subjects, politics included. The anti-Trinitarian heresy proved to be the chief dissolvent, and from 1560 onward the relations between the Lutherans and the Calvinists were fratricidal rather than fraternal; Jan Laski the Younger

vainly strove to unite all Polish Protestants round the Helvetian standard, and a federation of all Poles of the Reformed faith—the "Concord of Sandomierz" (1570), predominantly Calvinist in character—met resolute Lutheran opposition and led to nothing.

While the strong individualism of the Polish national character thus thwarted all endeavours at Protestant consolidation, political factors told in favour of Catholicism; so did presently the wiser policy of Rome. Pope Pius IV, unlike his predecessor, adopted a conciliatory attitude toward the Polish crown in the matter of disputed appointments of bishops. The new bishops were holy and learned men, very unlike the creations of Queen Bona, and capable papal nuncios reorganized the scattered and fainthearted Catholic forces in the land. From one of the ablest of them, Giovanni Commendone, the king, at the *sejm* of 1564, accepted the book of the decrees of the Council of Trent. In 1565 the Jesuits, the vanguard of the Catholic Counter-Reformation, appeared in Poland. At their best, the various forms of Protestantism had never won more than a scanty noble and intellectual elite of the nation; they had never taken root among the peasantry or the petty *bourgeoisie*—except in the cities of Royal Prussia.

Livonia.—In the middle of the 16th century the Livonian Order (formerly the Order of the Knights of the Sword), whose territory embraced Estonia, Livonia, Courland, and the islands of Dagö and Oesel, was tottering. All the Baltic powers were more or less interested in the apportionment of this vast tract of land, whose geographical position made it not only the chief commercial link between East and West but also the emporium whence the English, Dutch, Swedes, Danes, and Germans obtained their grain, timber, and most of the raw products of Lithuania and Moscow. Poland and Moscow as the nearest neighbours of this moribund state, which had so long excluded them from the sea, were vitally concerned in its fate. After an anarchic period of suspense, lasting from 1546 to 1561, during which Sweden secured Estonia while Ivan IV, the Terrible, fearfully ravaged Livonia, Sigismund II, to whom both the master of Livonia and the archbishop of Riga (brother of the duke of Prussia) had appealed more than once for protection, at length intervened decisively. At his camp before Riga in 1561 the last master, who had long been at the head of the Polish Party in Livonia and had embraced Protestantism, and the archbishop of Riga gladly placed themselves beneath Sigismund's protection, and by a subsequent convention signed at Wilno (Vilnius) on Nov. 28, 1561, Livonia was incorporated with Lithuania partly in the same way as Royal Prussia had been incorporated with Poland 95 years previously; and Courland, as a new Protestant duchy, became a fief of the Polish crown, with local autonomy and freedom of worship. (*See* also LIVONIA.)

Union with Lithuania, 1569.—The danger to Lithuania, revealed in the Baltic wars with Ivan the Terrible, as well as the requests on these matters of the Polish *sejm*, must have convinced Sigismund II of the necessity of preventing any cleavage in the future between the two halves of his dominions. A personal union under one monarch had proved inadequate. A further step must be taken—the two independent countries must be transformed into a single state. The principal obstacle was the opposition of the Lithuanian magnates, who feared to lose their dominance in the grand principality if they were merged in the *szlachta* ("gentry") of the kingdom. When things came to a deadlock in 1564, the king tactfully intervened and voluntarily relinquished his hereditary title to Lithuania, thus placing the two countries on a constitutional equality and preparing the way for fresh negotiations. The death in 1565 of Mikolaj Radziwill (the Black), the chief opponent of the union, still further weakened the Lithuanians, but the negotiations, reopened at the *sejm* of Lublin in 1569, at first also led only to rupture. Then Sigismund executed his master stroke. Suddenly, of his own authority, he formally incorporated Podlasia, Volhynia, and the province of Kiev into the kingdom of Poland, whereupon deputies from these provinces took their places on the same benches as their Polish brethren. The hands of the Lithuanians were forced. Even a complete union on equal terms was better than mutilated independence. Accordingly they returned to the *sejm* and the union was unanimously adopted on July 1, 1569. Henceforth the kingdom of

Poland and the grand principality of Lithuania were to be one inseparable and indivisible body politic; all dependencies and colonies, including Prussia and Livonia, were to belong to Poland and Lithuania in common. The retention of the old duality of dignities was the one reminiscence of the original separation; it was not abolished till 1791, four years before the final partition of Poland.

The union definitely shifted Poland's political centre of gravity eastward; it created a common interest in the Russian menace to the long and naturally defenseless eastern frontier and in the millions of Greek Orthodox people living in the eastern borderlands. Warsaw was appointed one of the meeting places of the joint *sejm*, thus preparing the transfer of the capital from Cracow to Warsaw. The union was the last great historical act of the Jagiellon dynasty; it put the coping stone to the structure of a monarchy which, with growing consolidation, seemed to bear in it the promise of empire.

7. Political Development, 1384–1572.—Simultaneously with the transformation into a great power of the petty principalities which composed ancient Poland, another and equally momentous political transformation was proceeding within the country itself.

The origin of the Polish constitution is to be sought in the *wiece*, or councils, of the Polish princes during the period of division. The privileges conferred upon the magnates of whom these councils were composed, especially upon the magnates of Little Poland (who brought the Jagiellons to the throne, directed their policy and grew rich upon their liberality), angered the less-favoured gentry or *szlachta*, who, toward the end of the 14th century, combined for mutual defense in their *sejmiki* or local diets.

The first *sejm* known to legislate for all Poland was that of Piotrkow (1493), summoned by John Albert to grant him subsidies; but its decrees were to have force for only three years. John Albert's second *sejm* (1496), after granting subsidies, the burden of which fell entirely on the towns and peasantry, passed a series of statutes benefiting the nobility at the expense of the other classes—especially the peasants. These were followed by others of the same kind under his successor, Alexander. Nevertheless, so long as the Jagiellon dynasty lasted, the political rights of the cities were jealously protected by the crown against the usurpations of the nobility. The burghers of Cracow, enlightened economists, supplied Sigismund I with his most capable counselors during the first 20 years of his reign (1506–26). Sigismund's predecessor, Alexander, had been compelled to accept the statute *Nihil novi* (1505), which became the basis of the parliamentary rule that new laws could be introduced only by a resolution of the *sejm*. Under Sigismund I some of the royal prerogatives were recovered, but in his later years, after the mutiny of 1537, the influence of the gentry returned. The Polish parliamentary system, vesting supreme powers in the two houses of the *sejm*, was an established fact.

Sigismund II knew that only a strengthening of the central authority could save the state. His endeavours to maneuver his way between the two rival powers of the magnates and the lesser gentry were, on the whole, successful. A patriotic party of gentry democrats arose, veiling its program of democratic reforms under the conservative watchword of the "execution of the laws," dealing further legislative blows against the nobles and the Catholic hierarchy, and demanding fiscal, military, and judicial reforms, complete union with Lithuania, and religious freedom. The king at first sided with the great nobles against the "executionists," but the Livonian War forced him to make an alliance with the latter to put into effect the fiscal reforms and to curtail the power of the magnates by a repeal of former royal grants of land and by the imposition of a tax on all tenants of crown lands for the maintenance of the standing army (1562–63).

Poland's favourable economic situation facilitated not only internal reforms and international activity, but also cultural development, especially the rise of national literature, science, and fine arts. The rising demand in Western Europe, for agricultural produce, particularly of grain, and a rise in its prices, contributed to the wealth of the countryside; and the towns also grew richer and more numerous despite their limited role in political and social life.

C. The Elective Kings

The childless Sigismund II Augustus died suddenly in 1572. Domestic affairs were in bad condition. The union of Lublin, barely three years old, was anything but consolidated, and in Lithuania it continued to be unpopular. Worst of all, there was no recognized authority in the land to curb its jarring centrifugal political elements. Civil war was averted by the confederation of the gentry throughout the entire country and by the decision to hold the election *viritim*, that is, with all the nobles and squires participating in it; and a national convention assembled in Warsaw in April 1573 for the purpose of electing a new king. Five candidates for the throne were already in the field. Lithuania favoured the Russian tsar Ivan IV. In Poland the bishops and most of the Catholic magnates were for an Austrian archduke, while the strongly anti-German *szlachta* were inclined to accept almost any candidate but a German. It was easy, therefore, for the adroit and energetic French ambassador, Jean de Lasseran Massencome de Monluc, bishop of Valence, to procure the election of the French candidate, Henry de Valois, duc d'Anjou. Well provided with funds, he speedily bought over many of the leading magnates, but he was regarded askance by the Protestants. The religious difficulty in Poland, however, had meanwhile been adjusted to the satisfaction of all parties by the Compact of Warsaw (Jan. 28, 1573), which granted absolute religious liberty to all non-Catholic denominations without exception. Finally, on May 11, 1573, the election *sejm* in Warsaw elected Henry king of Poland.

1. Henry de Valois, 1573–74.—The election had been preceded by a reform of the constitution, which resulted in the famous "Henrician articles" converting Poland from a limited monarchy into a republic with an elective chief magistrate. The king was obliged to convoke the *sejm* every two years; and in the periods between sessions he was to be advised by a group of senators. Should the king fail to observe any one of these articles, the nation was *ipso facto* absolved from its allegiance. Whatever its intrinsic demerits, the disastrous fruits of this reform were largely caused by the geographical position of Poland, and it must be remembered that Poland alone with England preserved the tradition of parliamentary government in the increasing absolutist Europe of the time. Besides constitutional restrictions, the new king had to undertake certain personal obligations called *pacta conventa*.

Henry reached Poland on Jan. 25, 1574, and was crowned in Cracow on Feb. 21. His reign lasted 14 months. The tidings of the death of his brother Charles IX of France determined him to exchange a thorny for what he hoped would be a flowery throne, and at midnight on June 18, 1574, he literally fled from Poland to become Henry III of France. The king's escape caused dismay, and trouble broke out while the country was awaiting his return; finally an *interregnum* was proclaimed. In November 1575 the senate elected the emperor Maximilian II to the throne; but the gentry democracy, at the suggestion of its new leader Jan Zamoyski, chose a prince of Transylvania, Stephen Báthory, assigning him as husband to Anne, the last surviving princess of the Jagiellon dynasty, and enforced this election by arms.

2. Stephen Báthory, 1575–86.—With the insight of a born statesman Báthory focused his energy on two vital objectives: the maintenance of Poland's access to the sea by way of Gdansk (Danzig), and the defense of its newly gained further seaboard in the northeast against the rising power of Moscow. Gdansk, on Báthory's election, began to intrigue against him with the emperor Maximilian (until his death in October 1576) and with Russia and Denmark. In spite of a deplorable lack of understanding on the part of the Polish gentry for the issue at stake, Báthory, who had throughout the able and strenuous support of his chancellor Zamoyski, conducted a campaign against Gdansk both by land and sea and finally enforced its complete submission to his rule.

Before peace was made with Gdansk, Ivan the Terrible had raided Livonia once more. Báthory, using infantry rather than cavalry and calling peasants and burghers to arms together with the gentry, achieved in the operations against Russia the great military triumphs of his reign. In three successive expeditions he pushed his way northeastward as far as Pskov, and the tsar was willing enough to obtain the pope's intervention by a promise of making Russia Catholic. As a result of Báthory's victories, Poland pushed Russia entirely away from the Baltic for a long time and regained sway over nearly the whole of Livonia.

Báthory, a skilled politician, knew how to make the most of the important minority groups, the Ukrainian Cossacks and the Jews. The Cossacks were largely runaway serfs, who had organized themselves into a sort of military republic on the vast and scantily inhabited plains of the Ukraine or "borderland," stretching from the southeast of the monarchy toward the Black Sea along the Dnieper River. The Cossack community had been drawn into the Polish military system under Báthory's predecessors by registration and pay and had already been granted exemption from taxation, as well as their own jurisdiction. Báthory, who needed them for his Russian wars, confirmed and enlarged these privileges. His successors used the Cossacks against the Russians, Turks, and Tatars; but soon the Cossacks were to be a factor of trouble for Poland, not without serious errors of policy on the Polish side. (*See* also UKRAINIAN SOVIET SOCIALIST REPUBLIC: *History*.)

The privileges which the Jews had obtained from former kings were augmented; from Báthory's day until 1764 the Polish Jews had a Parliament of their own, meeting twice a year, with powers of taxation. It was also chiefly in the interest of the Jews that Báthory restricted, by special edict, the trading rights of Scottish pedlars who were very numerous in Poland at the time. Among other domestic measures, Báthory reformed the Polish judicial system by the creation of a Supreme Court of Appeal for civil and penal cases, and he founded, in 1579, the University of Wilno as the first institution of higher education in Lithuania.

For internal affairs Báthory knew how to strengthen his position and authority, despite the existing restrictions on royal power. Hungarian tradition and relations with the Habsburgs and with the Holy See induced him to plan a great expedition against the Turks. But this project was carried with Báthory to his grave on his sudden death in 1586.

3. Sigismund III, 1587–1632.—The Vasa period of Polish history, which began with the election of Sigismund, son of John III of Sweden and of Sigismund I's daughter Catherine, was one of last and lost chances. The collapse of the Muscovite tsardom and the submersion of Germany by the Thirty Years' War presented Poland with an unprecedented opportunity of consolidating, once for all, its hard-won position as the dominating power between central and eastern Europe; it might even have wrested the best part of the Baltic littoral from the Scandinavian powers and pushed Russia back. That this was not achieved was partly caused by the opposition of the *szlachta*, who persisted in a defense of "republican liberty" at the very time when the need of a strong central executive was more urgent than ever.

But other grave causes of failure were not wanting. One of them consisted in the very personality of the new foreign-bred king: the tenacity with which he clung to his hereditary rights to the Swedish crown involved Poland in unnecessary wars with Sweden at most inopportune times; and his bigoted devotion to the cause of Catholicism introduced a new spirit of religious fanaticism and persecution into the atmosphere of a country hitherto distinguished for toleration, while the same bigotry served Poland's interests very ill abroad. Poland's greatest statesman of the time, Jan Zamoyski, discovered in the earliest years of the reign that the king, who had married Anna, daughter of the Habsburg Charles of Styria, was willing to surrender the crown of Poland to an Austrian archduke and to return to his native Sweden in order to bring it back to the Catholic fold. Zamoyski, who had himself placed Sigismund on the throne by conquering a rival Austrian candidate, was naturally indignant, and the whole disgraceful affair of the king's secret negotiations with Austria culminated in his having to answer the charges of a special "diet of inquisition" (1592)—the first time that the prestige of the crown in Poland was exposed to such an ordeal.

The Uniate Church.—It was only where the expansion of Catholicism served the interests of the Polish state that Zamoyski saw eye to eye with the king's Catholic zeal. Thus, he became in-

EDMUND KUPIECKI, WARSAW

CASTLE SQUARE IN WARSAW

In the centre is the Column of King Sigismund III Vasa which was first erected in 1644 and re-erected after World War II. At left is St. Anne's Church which dates from 1454. In the upper right is the Palace of Culture and Science which was given to the people of Poland by the U.S.S.R. in 1955

strumental in creating, at the Synod of Brzesc in 1596, the Uniate Church as a halfway house for those of the republic's Greek Orthodox citizens who were willing to recognize the supremacy of Rome but desired to preserve their accustomed Eastern ritual and Slavonic liturgy. The Uniate Church served the purpose of drawing a large section of the population of the eastern border provinces out of the orbit of Moscow and into that of Polish influences; but by the antagonisms which soon began between Uniates and non-Uniates, it became in itself a source of new troubles for Poland. Besides this, the pride of Poland's Roman Catholic prelates, who looked down on the Uniate Church as a "peasant religion," and the forced enlargement of that church together served to increase social and religious opposition and to provoke anti-Polish Ukrainian nationalism. Even in Sigismund's time, Austria, competing with Poland for influence in the eastern Balkans, began to seduce the Ukrainian element (represented in organized form by the military community of the Cossacks) against Poland—a policy which the same Austria was to resume later in changed form and under different conditions when in possession of eastern Galicia.

Swedish, Muscovite, and Turkish Wars.—The dispute over Sigismund's rights to the Swedish crown began, from the earliest years of the reign, to drag its weary course of alternate victories and defeats. Having obtained the Swedish crown (1592), Sigismund III met strong Protestant opposition, which defeated him in 1598, forcing him to abdicate. This eventually was the beginning of the wars between Poland and Sweden. At first the areas that later became Estonia and Latvia were both the scene and the principal object of the strife; in the later stages, Gustavus II Adolphus of Sweden transferred the ground nearer to the heart of Poland which helped the cause of the elector of Brandenburg, who had come into possession of Ducal Prussia and thus laid the foundation of a large Protestant power on the Baltic. The danger to Gdansk and Poland's grain exports roused even the gentry from their apathy; but in spite of some brilliant victories by sea and land, an armistice toward the end of the reign was highly unfavourable to Poland.

Sigismund's persistent Swedish ambitions, his equally persistent Austrian sympathies, but, more than all, his absolutist leanings and cherished plans for a drastic and arbitrary constitutional reform on foreign models and on antiparliamentary lines, occasioned in 1606 an armed revolt of the Polish gentry against their king—the *rokosz* ("insurrection") of Mikolaj Zebrzydowski, who was supported by the discontented Protestants. The *rokosz* was at last suppressed in 1607, but it left as its legacy such ruinous precedents as an enforced recognition of the doctrine of the subjects' right to depose their king (*de non praestanda obedientia*) and, after being undertaken in justified defense of the native parliamentary tradition against wholesale foreign innovations, had the harmful effect of blocking the way toward any and every reform of the parliamentary system.

Soon after the constitutional cataclysm of the *rokosz*, Poland became embroiled in prolonged wars with Moscow. The motive was partly a vague conception of a Polish-Russian union as opposed to the king's Austrian propensities, but partly also the very real desire of some border magnates for more and more land east of the Dnieper. An occasion was furnished by the extinction of the dynasty of Rurik in Russia and the subsequent struggle for the throne, particularly the emergence of one candidate—the ill-fated false Dimitri (*see* DIMITRI, FALSE)—whom certain Polish nobles and finally also the king supported. The appearance of a second false Dimitri after the fall of the first served to prolong the strife.

Throughout the campaigns against Moscow the king found himself at variance with the gentry and with some leading Polish statesmen and soldiers of the time, such as Stanislaw Zolkiewski; Sigismund thought of the problem only in terms of conquest, of the establishment of Catholicism in Russia and of strong monarchical rule over the united kingdoms, while Zolkiewski, even at the height of military successes against Russia, had a union like that of Poland with Lithuania in his mind and advocated tolerance of Russia's creed and social order. The Poles actually held the Kremlin of Moscow for a time (1610–11) and once again laid siege to it (1618); Sigismund's son Wladyslaw was elected tsar, and his opponent did homage to Sigismund as a prisoner. But a national insurrection in Russia and the establishment of the Romanov dynasty checked the Polish advance, and only certain territorial gains (including Smolensk), as well as a good deal of influence of Polish customs and institutions on the Russian nobility, were definite results of the struggle in Sigismund's time. It was to be continued under his successors.

The wars with Moscow temporarily ended in an armistice at the very moment (1618) when the Thirty Years' War broke out in central Europe. In this Poland remained officially neutral, but Sigismund's favourable attitude toward the Habsburgs (whom he sent unofficial reinforcements) entangled Poland in renewed and long wars with Turkey, which the later Jagiellons and their first successors had managed to avoid. A definite success was attained against the Turks at Khotin (Hotin), on the Dniester, in Bessarabia (1621), a year after Zolkiewski's heroic death at Cecora (Tutora in Moldavia). But the Swedish trouble began anew in the same year, and Sigismund's long and unlucky reign ended 11 years later amid turmoil abroad and at home, setbacks to Polish power on all sides without, and seriously increased constitutional disorder within.

4. Wladyslaw IV, 1632–48.—Sigismund's son, born in Poland and brought up as a Pole, enjoyed a popularity which had never been his father's lot. As crown prince, he had been successful in military operations against Moscow and Turkey; on his ascension to the throne he ingratiated himself with the gentry; but essentially he collaborated with a group of nobles at his court. The "wisest of the Polish Vasas," as he has been called, intended to create a basis of public favour and confidence for the constitutional reforms which he planned.

But the international difficulties inherited from his father diverted his energies largely into channels of foreign policy. The very first years of his reign were marked by new victories over Russia near Smolensk (1634) and also by a new and much more advantageous truce with Sweden which, in 1635, withdrew from Royal (or Polish) Prussia. He was less fortunate in a new conflict with Gdansk, and with its supporter Denmark, over the tolls he intended to impose on the trade of the Baltic ports; no interest in these matters was to be awakened in the gentry, and the most powerful magnates—those of the eastern border—thought more of expansion into the fertile Ukrainian regions than of sea power.

Accordingly, the Polish Navy, which had begun to develop in a promising manner under Sigismund II, was allowed to fall into permanent decay, and Wladyslaw's plans for foreign action on a large scale were unrealized. He wavered in his diplomacy between Austrian and French influences, represented by his two successive queens; his tolerant and friendly attitude toward the Orthodox East caused serious trouble with the Vatican; and his project of a great crusade against the Turks, although encouraged by the Venetian republic and acclaimed by the South Slav nations, in the end came to nothing. He did not profit from the Thirty Years' War, obtaining only for several years the possession of a small part of Silesia (the duchy of Opole and Raciborz), whereas his predecessors had thought of regaining all Silesia.

The Cossack Revolt.—The chief obstacle which prevented Wladyslaw's Turkish plans from maturing was the impossibility of winning the help of the decisive factor, the Ukrainian Cossacks, who had become too numerous and powerful to be willing instruments of Polish policy. Catholic intolerance toward this Orthodox population, in the time of Sigismund III, had combined with the policies of Polish landowners to produce in the Cossacks a spirit of religious, racial, and social enmity against the Polish element; the Polish Parliament had not kept the financial terms of its compacts with the Cossacks; repressions inspired by the border magnates had infuriated them. Polish magnates, creating immense land estates, oppressed the peasants and town dwellers, enforcing on them high and unfair levies; and this prepared ground for revolutionary movements. Already in the earlier years of Wladyslaw's reign (as during that of Sigismund III) terrible Cossack revolts had flared up and been unwisely punished by the abolition of ancient privileges. Now, instead of letting themselves be made the tools of Wladyslaw's anti-Turkish plans, the Cossacks made common cause with the Tatars of the Crimea, who were the most immediate objective of the king's crusading plans; and the reign ended amid a wave of Cossack insurrection, engineered by the sultan, assisted by Tatar hordes and led by Bohdan Chmielnicki (*q.v.*), a country gentleman personally wronged by a Polish official. It was only the resistance of the Polish burghers of Lwow that stemmed the Cossack and Tatar tide from flooding the inner provinces of Poland. But the defense of Lwow meant only a respite, and on Wladyslaw's death his brother and successor, the last of the Polish Vasas, found himself faced by a powerful renewal of Chmielnicki's attack on central Poland.

5. John Casimir, 1648–68.—John Casimir, summoned to the throne from Italy, where he had lived as a priest and become a cardinal, was obliged to begin his reign by negotiating with his rebel subject Chmielnicki. But Chmielnicki's conditions of peace were so hard that the negotiations came to nothing. It was only after a second invasion of Poland, in 1649, by a host of Cossacks and Tatars, that the Compact of Zborow was concluded, by which Chmielnicki was officially recognized as chief (hetman) of the Cossack community. A general amnesty was also granted, and it was agreed that all official dignities in the Orthodox palatinates of the Polish kingdom should henceforth be held solely by the Orthodox gentry. For the next 18 months Chmielnicki ruled the Ukraine like a sovereign prince. He made Czehryn (Chehryn), his native place, the Cossack capital, subdivided the country into 16 provinces and entered into direct relations with foreign powers. The Orthodox patriarchs of Alexandria and Constantinople were his friends and protectors, and Russia established relations with him. But fortune, so long Chmielnicki's friend, deserted him, and at Beresteczko (Berestechko; 1651) the hetman, betrayed by the Tatars who had helped him thus far, was utterly routed by John Casimir. All hope of an independent or even autonomous Cossackdom was at an end, yet it was not Poland but Moscow which reaped the fruits of successive victories and defeats.

Chmielnicki, by laying bare the nakedness of the Polish republic, had opened the eyes of Moscow to the fact that its ancient enemy was no longer formidable. Three years after his defeat at Beresteczko, Chmielnicki, unable to cope with the Poles singlehanded, very reluctantly transferred his allegiance to the tsar Alexis Mikhailovich, whose armies, after the Pereyaslav agreement (1654), invaded Poland and began what is known in Russian history as the Thirteen Years' War. The Russians occupied Wilno and a large part of Lithuania.

In the summer of 1655, while Poland was still reeling beneath the shock of the Muscovite invasion, Charles X Gustavus of Sweden, on the flimsiest of pretexts, launched a war to establish a Swedish mastery over the Baltic; and before the year was out his forces had occupied Warsaw, Cracow, and the best half of Poland. John Casimir, betrayed and abandoned by his own subjects (headed by the nobles of the country), fled to Silesia.

In this crisis Poland was saved, first, by an upsurge of patriotic and religious feeling among the peasants, townsmen, and gentry, and, second, by the formation of a league against Sweden with the participation of Austria and reinforcements from the Tatars. The people undertook guerrilla warfare; and the famous defense of the monastery of Czestochowa by its prior Augustyn Kordecki was followed by the king's return, by the organization of a new national army, and by the recovery of almost all the Polish provinces from the Swedes, who after a long fight were pushed back to the sea by Stefan Czarniecki. As well as the alliance with the Holy Roman emperor Leopold I (1657), Poland secured a truce with Moscow, whose armies acted against the Swedes in Livonia. Neither the help of György Rákóczy II, prince of Transylvania, nor that of Frederick William, elector of Brandenburg, brought any relief to the Swedes.

On the sudden death of Charles X, Poland seized the opportunity of adjusting all its outstanding differences with Sweden. By the peace of Oliwa (Oliva; 1660), made under French mediation, John Casimir ceded northern Livonia and renounced all claim to the Swedish crown. The worst setback was that Poland was obliged, by the Treaty of Welawa (Wehlau) in 1657, to renounce sovereignty over Ducal Prussia. The war with Moscow was then prosecuted with renewed energy and changing luck. In 1664 a peace congress was opened, and the prospects of Poland seemed most brilliant; but at the very moment when it needed all its armed strength to sustain its diplomacy, the rebellion of Prince Jerzy Lubomirski involved the country in a dangerous civil war, compelled it to reopen negotiations with the Muscovites and practically to accept the Muscovite terms. By the truce of Andruszow (Andrusovo; 1667) Poland received back from Moscow Vitebsk, Polotsk, and Polish Livonia, but ceded in perpetuity Smolensk, Starodub, and, in the Ukraine, the whole of the eastern bank of the Dnieper. The Cossacks of the Dnieper were henceforth to be divided between the dominion of the tsar and the king of Poland. Kiev, the religious metropolis of southwestern Russia, was to remain in the hands of Moscow for two years.

The "truce" of Andruszow proved to be one of the most permanent peaces in history, and Kiev, though pledged to Russia for only two years, was never again to be recovered. Henceforth the political impact of Russia toward Poland was steadily to increase, without any struggle at all, although influences of Polish culture and manners, exercised chiefly through the Academy of Kiev, still continued to permeate Russia down to the advent of Peter I the Great.

6. The "Liberum Veto" in the 17th Century.

Poland had, in fact, emerged from the cataclysm of 1648–67 a moribund state, though its not unskilful diplomacy had enabled it for a time to save appearances. Its territorial losses, though considerable, were, in the circumstances, not excessive, and it was still a power in the opinion of Europe. But a fatal change had come over the country during the age of the Vasas. The period synchronized with and was partly determined by the new European system of dynastic diplomatic competition and the unscrupulous employment of unlimited secret service funds. This system was based on the rivalry of the houses of Bourbon and Habsburg, and very soon nearly all the monarchs of the continent and their ministers were in the pay of one or other of the antagonists. Poland was no exception to the general rule. To do them justice, the *szlachta* at first not only were free from the taint of official corruption but endeavoured to fight against it. But they themselves unconsciously played into the hands of the enemies of their country by making the so-called *liberum veto* an integral part of the Polish Constitution. The *liberum veto* was based on the assumption of the absolute political equality of every Polish gentleman, with the corollary that every measure introduced into the Polish *sejm* must be adopted unanimously. Consequently, if any single deputy believed that a measure already approved of by the rest of the house might be injurious to his constituency, he had the right to exclaim *Nie pozwalam*, "I disapprove," the measure in question falling at once to the ground. All efforts toward increasing the power of the central government were held to be aimed against traditional freedom and were opposed. Subsequently this vicious principle was extended still further. A deputy, by interposing his individual veto, could at any time dissolve the *sejm*, and all measures previously passed had to be resubmitted to the consideration of the following *sejm*. The *liberum veto* was used for the first time during the *sejm* of 1652. Before the end of the 17th century it was used so recklessly that all business was frequently brought to a standstill. It became the chief instrument of foreign ambassadors or native magnates for dissolving inconvenient sessions, as a deputy could always be bribed to exercise his veto.

7. Michael Wisniowiecki, 1669–74.

With the election of Michael Wisniowiecki in 1669 a new era began. A native Pole, he was freely elected by the unanimous vote of the gentry; but he was chiefly chosen for the merit of his father, a great border magnate who had victoriously kept down the Cossacks, and he proved to be a passive tool in the hands of the Habsburgs. In view of this the French party rallied round Jan Sobieski, a military commander of rising fame. The dissensions between the two camps cost Poland a new defeat at the hands of the united Turks and Cossacks. Sealed by a shameful Treaty of Buczacz (Buchach; 1672), by which all Polish Ukraine came under Turkish suzerainty, this defeat was only wiped out by a brilliant victory of Sobieski's at Khotin (1673), which also, after King Michael's early death, carried him to the throne against an Austrian candidate.

8. John III Sobieski, 1674–96.

Connected with France by marriage and by political sympathies, Sobieski (see JOHN III), although he had half a lifetime of constant wars against the Turks behind him, stood at first, in accordance with French policy, for peaceful relations with Turkey and directed his eyes toward the Baltic, attempting with French help to check the rising Hohenzollern power in that quarter. But his secret dealings with France turned his own subjects against him, while continuous Turkish invasions forced him into war, until an attack of great magnitude, aimed at the very heart of Europe, called forth that unprecedented outburst of Polish heroism—the gallant rescue of Vienna in 1683. That great act was the last noble reflex of the great crusading impulse of the Middle Ages; it was a unique service, rendered in the old chivalrous spirit by one nation to another in an age of Machiavellian diplomacy and growing national selfishness. It won Poland offers of friendship from all the great powers. But its positive gains for Poland proved little. The "perpetual peace" negotiated by Krzysztof Grzymultowski in Moscow in 1686, by which Kiev was recognized as a part of Russia, did not buy any active support in further campaigns against Turkey, nor did the delivered Austria assist Poland in its endeavour to reestablish the Rumanian outpost against the Turks. In internal affairs various cliques of the nobles, some attached to Austria and some to France, obstructed the restoration of the hereditary monarchy.

9. Augustus II, 1697–1733.

On the death of John III no fewer than 18 candidates for the vacant Polish throne presented themselves. The successful competitor was Frederick Augustus I, elector of Saxony, who cheerfully renounced Lutheranism for the coveted crown and won the day because he happened to arrive last of all, with fresh funds, when the agents of his rivals had spent all their money. He was crowned, as Augustus II (*q.v.*), in 1697, and his first act was to expel from the country his French rival, François Louis de Bourbon, prince de Conti, whose defeat was also partly caused by the growing Russian influence, which, from the accession of Peter I the Great, especially after 1700, became a permanent factor in Polish domestic politics.

Good fortune attended the opening years of the new reign. In 1699 the long Turkish War, which had been going on since 1683, was concluded by the Peace of Karlowitz (Karlovci), whereby Podolia, the Ukraine and the fortress of Kamieniec Podolski were retroceded to Poland by the Ottoman Porte. But the permanent weakening of Turkey brought little good, for the power of Russia soon became a greater menace to Poland than Turkey had ever been.

Shortly after the Peace of Karlowitz, Augustus was persuaded by the plausible Livonian exile Johann Reinhold Patkul to form a nefarious league with Frederick IV of Denmark and Peter I of Russia, for the purpose of despoiling the youthful king of Sweden, Charles XII. This he did as elector of Saxony, but it was Poland which paid for the hazardous speculation of its newly elected king. Throughout the Northern War (q.v.), which wasted northern and central Europe for 20 years (1700–21), all the belligerents treated Poland as if it had no political existence. Swedes, Saxons, and Russians not only lived upon the country, but plundered it systematically. The *sejm* was the humble servant of the conqueror of the moment, and the leading magnates chose their own sides without the slightest regard for the interests of their country, the Lithuanians for the most part supporting Charles XII, while the Poles divided their allegiance between Augustus and Stanislaw Leszczynski (see STANISLAW I), whom Charles introduced and maintained upon the throne from 1704 to 1709. At the end of the war Poland was ruined materially as well as politically. Augustus offered Courland, Polish Prussia, and even part of Great Poland to Frederick William I of Prussia, provided that he were allowed a free hand in the disposal of the rest of his kingdom. When Prussia declined this tempting offer for fear of Russia, Augustus went a step further and actually suggested that "the four eagles" (viz., the black ones of Austria, Prussia, and Russia and the white eagle of Poland proper) should divide the other Polish territories among them. He died, however, before he could give effect to this shameless design.

10. Augustus III, 1733–63.—On the death of Augustus II, Stanislaw Leszczynski, who had, in the meantime, become the father-in-law of Louis XV of France, attempted to regain his throne with the aid of a small French force under Louis de Bréhan, comte de Plélo. Some of the best men in Poland, including the Czartoryski family (see CZARTORYSKI), were in Leszczynski's favour, and he was elected king for the second time. But there were many malcontents, principally among the Lithuanians, who solicited the intervention of Russia in favour of Frederick Augustus II of Saxony, son of the late king. A Russian Army appeared before Warsaw and compelled a phantom *sejm* (it consisted of but 15 senators and 500 of the *szlachta*) to proclaim Augustus III. Stanislaw and his partisans were besieged by the Russians in Gdansk, and with its surrender their cause was lost. He retired to become duke of Lorraine and Bar, keeping the title of king of Poland but leaving Augustus III in possession of the kingdom. (See POLISH SUCCESSION, WAR OF THE.)

Augustus III left everything to his minister, Heinrich von Brühl (q.v.), and Brühl entrusted the government of Poland to the Czartoryskis, who had close relations of long standing with the court of Dresden. "The Family," as their opponents sarcastically called them, were to dominate Polish politics for the next half century, promoting their own interests but also trying to introduce constitutional reforms such as the abolition of the *liberum veto* and the formation of a standing army.

Unfortunately, the other great families of Poland were obstinately opposed to any reform or, as they called it, any "violation" of the existing Constitution. The Potockis (see POTOCKI), in particular, whose possessions in southern Poland and the Ukraine covered thousands of square miles, hated the Czartoryskis and successfully obstructed all their efforts. In the Saxon period, every *sejm* was dissolved by the hirelings of some great lord or of some foreign potentate.

After a period of cooperation with the Saxon court, the Czartoryskis broke with their old friend Brühl and turned to Russia. Their intermediary was their nephew Stanislaw August Poniatowski, whom they sent, as Saxon minister, to the Russian court in the suite of the English minister Sir Charles Hanbury Williams in 1755. The handsome and insinuating Poniatowski speedily won the heart of the grand duchess Catherine, but he won nothing else and returned to Poland in 1759 somewhat discredited. Never-

theless, the Czartoryskis looked to Russia again for support on Augustus III's death and rejected with derision the pacific overtures of their political opponents.

The reigns of Augustus II and Augustus III saw the economic, political, and cultural decline of Poland. The Polish economy, based on farming, serfdom, and grain export, was in serious difficulties because of decreasing opportunities on Western European markets. The situation was aggravated by the devastations of war and by a general agricultural crisis lasting from the middle of the 17th century to the middle of the 18th. The peasants and the towns were ruined; and the small gentry suffered likewise to a great extent, losing its estates to the magnates, whose wealth and political influence rose considerably. The Jesuit schools were chiefly concerned with spreading religious devotion, and the standard of general culture was much hampered by wars and by economic regression. The first symptoms of economic revival, together with attempts at reforming the school system, appeared toward the middle of the 18th century, announcing the coming of the Enlightenment.

11. Stanislaw II Poniatowski and the Partitions, 1764–95.—The simplicity of the Czartoryskis was even more mischievous than their haughtiness. They took advantage of the *interregnum* to carry out a *coup d'état* restricting the *liberum veto*, creating ministerial commissions, and initiating other reforms. Their naïve expectations were very speedily disappointed. Catherine II and Frederick II had already determined (Treaty of St. Petersburg, 1764) that the existing state of things in Poland must be maintained, and as early as 1763 Catherine had recommended the election of Stanislaw August Poniatowski as "the individual most convenient for our common interests."

Shortly afterward Poniatowski was elected king with the help of Russian troops (see STANISLAW II), and crowned. But late in November 1763 Prince Nikolai V. Repnin (q.v.) was sent as Russian minister to Warsaw with instructions which led to further discord in Polish affairs. The first weapon employed was the question of the dissidents. At that time the population of Poland was, in round numbers, 11,420,000 of whom about 1,000,000 were dissidents or dissenters. Half of these were the Protestants of the towns of Polish Prussia and Great Poland, the other half was composed of the Orthodox population of Lithuania. The dissidents had no political rights, and their religious liberties had also been unjustly restricted. For these persons, mainly agricultural labourers, artisans, and petty tradesmen, Repnin, in the name of the empress, demanded absolute equality, political and religious, with the Catholic population of Poland. He was well aware that an aristocratic and Catholic assembly like the *sejm* would never concede so preposterous a demand.

Early in 1767 the malcontents, chiefly conservative magnates supported by Repnin, formed at Radom a confederation whose first act was to send a deputation to St. Petersburg, petitioning Catherine to guarantee the liberties of the republic. With a *carte blanche* in his pocket, Repnin proceeded to treat the *sejm* as if it were already the slave of the Russian empress. But despite threats, wholesale corruption, and the presence of Russian troops outside and even inside the Chamber of Deputies, the patriots, headed by four bishops, offered a determined resistance to Repnin's demands. Only when brute force in its extremest form had been ruthlessly employed, when two of the bishops and some other deputies had been arrested in full session by Russian grenadiers and sent as prisoners to Kaluga, did the opposition collapse. The delegation of the *sejm* accepted the so-called fundamental laws: the *liberum veto* and all the other ancient abuses were now declared unalterable parts of the Polish constitution, which was placed under the guarantee of Russia. All the restrictions against the dissidents were, at the same time, repealed.

Confederation of Bar.—This shameful surrender led to a Catholic patriotic uprising, known as the Confederation of Bar (q.v.), which was formed in 1768 at Bar in the Ukraine, by a handful of squires. It never had a chance of permanent success, though, feebly fed by French subsidies and French volunteers, it lingered on for four years, until finally suppressed in 1772. Insignificant in itself, the Confederation of Bar was the cause of great events.

Some of the Bar confederates, scattered by the Russian regulars, fled over the Turkish border, pursued by their victors. The Turks, already alarmed at the progress of the Russians in Poland and stimulated by Charles Gravier, comte de Vergennes, at that time French ambassador at Constantinople, at once declared war against Russia. Seriously disturbed at the prospect of Russian aggrandizement, the courts of Berlin and Vienna conceived the idea that the best mode of preserving the equilibrium of Europe was for all three powers to readjust their territories at the expense of Poland. Negotiations led to no definite result at first; then Austria took the first step by occupying, in 1769, the county of Spisz (Szepes, Zips), which had been hypothecated by Hungary to Poland in 1411 and never redeemed. This act decided the other powers; in June 1770 Frederick II of Prussia threw a military cordon, ostensibly to keep out the cattle plague, around those of the Polish provinces which he coveted. Catherine's consent had been previously obtained.

First Partition, 1772.—The first treaty of partition was signed at St. Petersburg between Prussia and Russia on Feb. 17, 1772; the second treaty, which admitted Austria also to a share of the spoil, was signed on Aug. 5 of the same year. The consent of the *sejm* to this act of brigandage was extorted by bribery and force in 1773. Russia obtained the palatinates (*wojewodztwa*) of Vitebsk, Polotsk, Mscislaw: 35,907 sq.mi. (92,999 sq.km.) of territory, with a population of 1,300,000. Austria got Little Poland without Cracow and also Lwow, Tarnopol (Ternopol), and Halicz (Galich) and, by extending the name of the last, called the new province Galicia: 31,622 sq.mi. (81,901 sq.km.), with a population of 2,650,000. Prussia received the palatinate of Pomorze minus Gdansk, the palatinate of Chelmno minus Torun, the northern half of Great Poland, and the palatinates of Malbork (Marienburg) and Warmia, calling the new acquisition West Prussia: 14,015 sq.mi. (36,299 sq.km.), with a population of 580,000. The total area of Poland before 1772 was about 283,200 sq.mi. (733,485 sq.km.), with an estimated population of 11,420,000.

The partitioning powers presented Poland with a new constitution. The elective monarchy and the *liberum veto* were of course retained. Poland was to be dependent on its despoilers, but they evidently meant to make it a serviceable dependent. The government was henceforth to be in the hands of a permanent council of 36 members, 18 senators and 18 deputies, elected biennially by the *sejm* in secret ballot, subdivided into the five departments of Foreign Affairs, Police, War, Justice, and the Exchequer, whose principal members and assistants, as well as all other public functionaries, were to have fixed salaries. The royal prerogative was still further reduced. The king was indeed the president of the Permanent Council, but he could not summon the *sejm* without its consent and in all cases of preferment was bound to select one out of three of the Council's nominees. Still, the new organization made for order and economy and enabled Poland to develop and husband its resources and devote itself uninterruptedly to the now burning question of national education.

The shock of the first partition had a certain salutary effect on national mentality. Already in the darkest days of Saxon rule, important educational reforms had been carried out in the schools of the Piarist order by Stanislaw Konarski (*q.v.*). Now, the dissolution of the Society of Jesus in 1773, putting its rich possessions and the system of schools conducted by it into the hands of the state, gave Poland opportunity to secularize as well as to modernize the whole educational fabric of the nation. This huge task was admirably performed by the Commission of National Education, the first Ministry of Education in Europe. It reorganized both the program of teaching and the structure of the schools—including the decayed universities of Cracow and Wilno—in a thoroughly modern and enlightened way. Less progress was made with the cause of constitutional reform: the chancellor Andrzej Zamoyski indeed drafted a new comprehensive code of laws, in which a beginning was made with the emancipation of the peasant serfs and of the town population, but this was rejected by the gentry in the *sejm* (1780).

In the meantime, events in the international field seemed to give Poland another chance of reasserting its independence against its despoilers. The death of Frederick II in 1786 loosened the bonds of the alliance between Prussia and Russia. Russia, drawing nearer to Austria, undertook, jointly with Austria, a war against Turkey which proved unexpectedly hard; and Russia was at the same time attacked by Sweden. Prussia, having changed its policy and concluded an alliance against Russia with Great Britain and Holland, was now emboldened by Russia's difficulties to go further: it invited Poland also to forsake the Russian alliance and offered to place an army corps of 40,000 men at its disposal.

The Constitution of May 3, 1791.—It was under these exceptional circumstances that the "four years' *sejm*" assembled (1788). Its leaders, Stanislaw Malachowski, Hugo Kollataj (*qq.v.*), and Ignacy Potocki, were men of character and capacity, and its measures were correspondingly vigorous. Within a few months of its assembling it had abolished the Permanent Council, enlarged the royal prerogative, raised the army to 65,000 men, established direct communications with the Western Powers, declared its own session permanent, and finally settled down to the crucial task of reforming the constitution on modern lines. But the difficulties of the patriots were commensurate with their energies, and it was not till May 1791 that the new constitution could safely be presented to the *sejm*. Meanwhile, Poland endeavoured to strengthen its position by an alliance with Prussia. Frederick William II stipulated at first that Poland should surrender Gdansk and Torun; but the Poles proving obstinate and Austria simultaneously displaying a disquieting interest in Poland's welfare, Prussia on March 19, 1791, concluded an alliance with Poland which engaged the two powers to guarantee each other's possessions and render mutual assistance in case either were attacked.

But external aid was useless so long as Poland was hampered by its anarchical constitution. The most indispensable reforms had been frantically opposed; the debate on the reorganization of the army alone had lasted six months. It was only by an audacious surprise that Kollataj and his associates contrived to carry through the new constitution. Taking advantage of the Easter recess, when most of the malcontents were out of town, they suddenly, on May 3, brought the whole question before the *sejm* and demanded urgency for it. Before the opposition could remonstrate, the marshal of the *sejm* produced the latest foreign dispatches, which unanimously predicted another partition, whereupon, at the solemn adjuration of Ignacy Potocki, King Stanislaw exhorted the deputies to accept the new constitution as the last means of saving their country; and he set the example by swearing to defend it.

The constitution of May 3, 1791, converted Poland into a hereditary limited monarchy, with ministerial responsibility and biennial parliaments. The *liberum veto* and all the intricate and obstructive machinery of the anomalous old system were forever abolished. All invidious class distinctions were done away with. The towns, in a special bill confirmed by the new constitution, got full administrative and judicial autonomy, as well as a certain measure of parliamentary representation; the personal privileges of the gentry, such as possession of land and access to office in the state and in the church, were thrown open to the townsmen. The peasants were placed under the protection of the law, and their serfdom was mitigated. Absolute religious toleration was established. Provision was made for further periodical reforms by subsequent Parliaments.

The Confederation of Targowica.—The constitution of May 3 had scarcely been signed when Stanislaw Feliks Potocki, Seweryn Rzewuski, and Ksawery Branicki, three of the chief dignitaries of Poland, hastened to St. Petersburg and there entered into a secret convention with the empress, whereby she undertook to restore the old constitution by force of arms but at the same time promised to respect the territorial integrity of the republic. Entering Polish territory with Russian troops, the conspirators on May 14, 1792, proclaimed a confederation at the little town of Targowica in the Ukraine, protesting against the new constitution as tyrannous and revolutionary; four days later, the new Russian minister in Warsaw presented a formal declaration of war to the king and the *sejm*.

The *sejm* met the crisis with dignity and firmness. The army was at once dispatched eastward to meet the invading Russians;

the male population was called to arms, and Ignacy Potocki was sent to Berlin to claim the assistance stipulated by the treaty of 1791. The king of Prussia, in direct violation of all his oaths and promises, declined to defend a constitution which had never had his "concurrence." Thus Poland was left entirely to its own resources. The little Polish Army of 46,000 men, under Prince Jozef Antoni Poniatowski, nephew of King Stanislaw II, and Tadeusz Kosciuszko (q.v.), did all that was possible under the circumstances. For more than three months they kept back the invader, and, after winning three pitched battles, retired in perfect order on the capital (see Poniatowski). But the king, and even Kollataj, despairing of success, now acceded to the confederation; hostilities were suspended; the indignant officers threw up their commissions; the rank and file were distributed all over the country; the reformers fled abroad; and the constitution of May 3 was abolished by the Targowicians as a "dangerous novelty." As the Russians occupied all eastern Poland, the Prussians, at the beginning of 1793, alarmed lest Catherine should appropriate the whole republic, seized Great Poland; and a diminutive, debased, and helpless *sejm* met at Grodno in order, in the midst of a Russian Army Corps, "to come to an amicable understanding" with the partitioning powers.

Second Partition, 1793.—After every conceivable means of intimidation had been unscrupulously applied, the second treaty of partition was signed at three o'clock on the morning of Sept. 23, 1793. By this *pactum subjectionis*, as the Polish patriots called it, Russia got all the eastern provinces of Poland, extending from Livonia to Moldavia, comprising a territory of 96,602 sq.mi. (250,199 sq.km.), while Prussia got Dobrzyn, Kujavia, Great Poland, Torun, and Gdansk (22,046 sq.mi. [57,099 sq.km.]). Poland was now reduced to 83,012 sq.mi. (215,001 sq.km.), less than one-third of its original dimensions, with a population of about 4,000,000.

Kosciuszko and the Third Partition.—The focus of Polish nationalism was now transferred from Warsaw, where the Targowicians and their Russian patrons reigned supreme, to Leipzig, where the Polish patriots, Kosciuszko, Kollataj, and Ignacy Potocki among the number, assembled from all quarters. From the first they meditated a national rising, but their ignorance, enthusiasm, and simplicity led them to commit blunder after blunder. The first of such blunders was Kosciuszko's mission to revolutionary France in January 1793. He was full of the idea of a league of republics against the league of sovereigns; but he was unaware that the Jacobins themselves were already considering the best mode of detaching Prussia, Poland's worst enemy, from the anti-French coalition. Kosciuszko received an evasive reply and returned to Leipzig empty-handed. In the meantime, certain officers in Poland had revolted against the reduction of the Polish Army to 15,000, imposed upon the country by the partition treaty. Kosciuszko himself condemned their hastiness; but the march of events forced his hand, and on March 23, 1794, he went to Cracow, proclaimed a national insurrection and assumed the powers of a dictator. He called the peasants to arms, and they responded nobly, in return for which he supplemented the provisions of the constitution of 1791 by a manifesto giving them personal freedom and limited obligation toward the gentry. At first, Kosciuszko's arms were almost universally successful. The Russians were defeated in pitched battles, three-quarters of the ancient territory was recovered, and Warsaw and Wilno were liberated by popular uprisings.

The first serious reverse at Szczekociny was outweighed by the defense of Warsaw against the Russians and Prussians (July 9–Sept. 6). But even during that heroic defense the mood of the Warsaw mob became more radical, and violent dissensions in the Supreme Council and in the army, notwithstanding the extension of the rising to Great Poland, began to complicate the dictator's task. The appearance of overwhelming masses of Russian troops, together with the open hostility of Austria as well as Prussia, did the rest, and Kosciuszko's insurrection received its deathblow on the battlefield of Maciejowice, where he himself was wounded and taken prisoner. Warsaw was taken amid a terrible massacre in the suburbs of Praga, and the remainder of the troops capitulated a few weeks later.

TERRITORIAL CHANGES IN POLAND DURING THE 18TH CENTURY

The greed of the victorious powers nearly led to a rupture between Austria and Prussia, but, after some dissension, the third partition of Poland was effected by treaties in 1795 and 1796. Austria had to be content with Lublin, Siedlce, Radom, and Kielce (18,147 sq.mi. [47,001 sq.km.]), while Prussia took Suwalki, Bialystok, Lomza, and Warsaw (18,533 sq.mi. [48,000 sq.km.]). Russia annexed all the rest (46,332 sq.mi. [120,000 sq.km.]) and was afterward to tear even parts of their booty from the two others. Thus the name of Poland was wiped from the map of Europe.

The estimated population of Poland in 1795 (in 1772 frontiers) was 13,500,000; of that number Prussia subjected 3,105,000 (23%), Austria 4,320,000 (32%), and Russia 6,075,000 (45%). Of the territory of Poland in 1772 Prussia annexed 19.5%, Austria 17.5%, and Russia 63%. Almost all lands ethnically Polish fell under Prussian or Austrian domination.

The destruction of the Polish state supervened on a period of regeneration and of political, economic, and cultural revival. The reign of Stanislaw II Poniatowski, so lively in the political and social field, had seen a growth of the rural economy, as the peasant's condition became better, and the towns—especially Warsaw—had prospered. Grain exports had increased, despite Prussian restrictions; industrial plants had appeared in various parts of the country; and in the towns trading and banking had risen. In the field of general culture the results of education and wealth were apparent.

The partitions of Poland forced the separated parts of the nation to live under three different political, constitutional, and economic regimes. The gentry, and especially the magnates, having lost their former political role, tried to adjust themselves to life under the new conditions, but the towns and economic life as a whole fell into a decline, except in Austrian Poland, where the reforms introduced by Joseph II protected the peasants from abusive exploitation by the landowners.

(R. N. B.; R. Dy.; A. Wy.)

D. The Duchy and Foreign Rule

After the third partition, the more high-spirited Poles, chiefly officers and soldiers of Kosciuszko's army, emigrated and formed, on Italian soil, the Polish Legions, hoping to return to Poland with the revolutionary French Army. During the next ten years they fought the battles of the French republic and of Napoleon all over Europe and even outside it, from Egypt to the West Indies. They were commanded by Jan Henryk Dombrowski (q.v.), one of Kosciuszko's ablest generals; but Kosciuszko himself stood aloof, distrusting Napoleon.

1. The Duchy of Warsaw.—In 1806 and 1807, when Napoleon defeated Prussia and engaged in a war with Russia, Polish soldiers once more appeared on Polish soil, and the hopes of the nation seemed near fulfillment. In fact, the Peace of Tilsit resulted in the reconstruction of a Polish state out of the central provinces of Prussian Poland; but Napoleon's anxiety to conciliate Russia effectually prevented him from making his new creation large enough to be self-supporting. The Duchy of Warsaw, as it was called, consisted in 1807 of territories taken by Prussia in the second and third partitions, with three exceptions: Gdansk (Danzig) became a free city; the district of Bialystok was given to Russia; the so-called Notec (Netze) district, annexed by Prussia in the first partition, was added to the duchy. In 1809 the duchy was increased by the territory which Austria had seized in the third partition. The total area of the duchy was then about 59,382 sq.mi. (153,799 sq.km.), with a population of 4,350,000.

The constitution of July 22, 1807, was dictated by Napoleon; it was framed on the French model and on very advanced lines. Equality before the law (implying personal freedom of the peasant), absolute religious toleration, and highly developed bureaucracy were its salient features. The king of Saxony, Frederick Augustus I (previously elector as Frederick Augustus III; grandson of Augustus III of Poland), whom Napoleon made duke, took the initiative in all legislative matters, but the administration was practically controlled by the French. In spite of being subject to most burdensome financial and military exigencies for the purposes of Napoleon's continuous wars, the duchy contrived, during the few years of its existence, to do much productive, organizing work. The country's economic position worsened because production was geared for military purposes, but the middle class profited from its new legal and social status.

Poland's hopes for greater things revived once more when Napoleon announced his war against Russia (1812), as his "second Polish war." The duchy, by an immense effort, put an army corps of nearly 98,000 men into the field. But the calamity that overtook Napoleon in Russia also sealed the fortunes of the duchy. The remainder of the Polish troops faithfully followed Napoleon in his campaign of 1813–14, during which the heroic leader of the Poles, Prince Jozef Antoni Poniatowski, perished in covering the emperor's retreat from Leipzig. The duchy was occupied by the Russians.

2. The Congress Kingdom and Russian Rule.—The Russian emperor Alexander I had been united by youthful friendship to the most eminent Polish noble of his time, Prince Adam Jerzy Czartoryski, and had even made him, on his accession, foreign minister of the Russian empire. On Napoleon's downfall the Poles, to whom Alexander did not spare promises and flatteries, entertained the highest hopes.

It was not Alexander's fault, indeed, if the Congress of Vienna, because of jealousy among the great powers and the entanglement of the Polish question with that of Saxony and other territories, did not lead to a reunification of Poland, even under the Russian sceptre, but confirmed the division of the country among the three partitioning powers. Only Cracow, with a small surrounding territory (449.2 sq.mi. [1,163 sq.km.], with a population of 95,000), was erected into a free republic. Great Poland, with Poznan for its centre, was left to Prussia as the Grand Duchy of Posen (11,178 sq.mi. [28,951 sq.km.], with a population of 776,000). Austria remained in possession of a slightly reduced Galicia (30,212 sq.mi. [78,249 sq.km.], with 3,500,000 inhabitants). The eastern borderlands, from Lithuania and Belorussia to the Ukraine, continued to be incorporated in Russia. The remnant of central Poland only (49,217 sq.mi. [127,472 sq.km.], with a population of 3,300,000) was constituted as the so-called Congress Kingdom under the emperor of Russia as king of Poland. Guarantees of home rule in all parts of the divided country and of free communication between them were given by all powers concerned, only to prove soon more or less futile.

Alexander, who had a sentimental regard for freedom, so long as it meant obedience to himself, had promised the Poles a constitution. That constitution was soon duly drafted and signed. It provided that the Kingdom of Poland was to be united to Russia in the person of the emperor, as a separate political entity. Lithuania and the Ruthenian palatinates continued to be incorporated with Russia as the Western Provinces and were divided from the Congress Kingdom by a customs barrier till the reign of Nicholas I. The Poland thus defined was to have at its head a lieutenant of the emperor (*namiestnik*), who must be a member of the imperial house or a Pole. The first holder of the office, Gen. Jozef Zajaczek (1752–1826), formerly a political radical but now a conservative, was a veteran who had served Napoleon.

Roman Catholicism was recognized as the religion of the state, but other religions were tolerated. Liberty of the press was promised, subject to the passing of a law to restrain its abuses. Individual liberty, the use of the Polish language in the law courts, and the executive employment of Poles in the civil government were secured by the constitution. The machinery of government included a council of state (at which the imperial government was represented by a commissioner plenipotentiary) and a *sejm* divided into a Senate, composed of the princes of the blood, the palatines and councillors named for life, and a House of Deputies elected for seven years. Poland retained its flag and a national army based on that which had been raised by and had fought for Napoleon. The command of the army was given to the emperor's brother Constantine (*q.v.*), a man of somewhat erratic character, who did much to offend the Poles by violence.

The *sejm* met three times during the reign of Alexander, in 1818, in 1820, and in 1825, and was on all three occasions opened by the emperor. But Alexander and the *sejm* soon quarreled. The third session of the *sejm* (May 13 to June 13, 1825) was a mere formality. All publicity was suppressed, and one whole district was disfranchised because it persisted in electing candidates who were disapproved of at court. All Europe at the time was seething with secret societies organized to combat the reactionary governments of the Holy Alliance. In Poland the National Freemasonry, or National Patriotic Society as it was afterward called, had a large membership, especially among the students and the younger officers. Outside Congress Poland, a similar student movement arose in the University of Wilno. Severe measures—imprisonment, deportation, and exile—were taken against students and graduates of Wilno (including the poet Adam Mickiewicz), and

FRONTIERS OF THE DUCHY OF WARSAW (1807-1809-1815)
KINGDOM OF POLAND UNDER RUSSIAN RULE
POZNANIA—RETURNED TO PRUSSIA IN 1815
REPUBLIC OF CRACOW (1815-46) BEFORE ITS ANNEXATION BY AUSTRIA
DISTRICT OF BIALYSTOK CEDED TO RUSSIA IN 1807
INTERNATIONAL FRONTIERS AFTER 1815
BOUNDARY OF THE FREE CITY OF DANZIG (1807-14)

THE DUCHY OF WARSAW AND THE POLISH KINGDOM

they added to the excitement in Warsaw. No open breach occurred during the reign of Alexander I, nor for five years after his death in 1825. His successor, Nicholas I, soon became entangled in a war with Turkey.

Austria, as usual, desirous of profiting by Russia's difficulties, began to court the favour of the Poles. Nicholas was crowned king of Poland in Warsaw in 1829 and personally opened the *sejm* in 1830. But the *sejm* already in 1828 had refused to sentence to death a group of Polish conspirators accused of dealings with the Russian Dekabrists who had plotted Nicholas' overthrow, and in 1829 there was even an abortive Polish plot to murder him at his coronation in Warsaw. Fresh excitement was created in Poland by the outbreak of the Revolution in France in July 1830 and the revolt of Belgium; a rumour was current—not without justification—that Nicholas, acting in concert with the other autocrats of the Holy Alliance, intended to use the Polish Army to coerce the French and Belgian revolutionaries.

During the period of the Congress Kingdom, economic life and education were developing rapidly. The government aimed at strengthening the economy by a system of protection and state investment. The Land Credit Society (1825) and the Bank of Poland (1828) created by Ksawery Drucki-Lubecki, minister of the treasury, secured credits for municipal investments and for the development of communications. Mining, metallurgy (in the Kielce district), and the textile industry (Lodz, Zyrardow) were growing, while in agriculture the big farms were intensifying their production at the cost of the peasants' lands. In Warsaw a university (1816) and a college of engineering (1830) were founded to train specialists, while in the Russian provinces the Polish University of Wilno flourished.

The Rising of 1830.—On Nov. 29, 1830, a military insurrection broke out in Warsaw. It was started by the young hotheads of the officers' training school. Regiments of the army and masses of the civilian population began to join the rising; the weakness of Constantine allowed it to gather strength. He evacuated Warsaw and finally left the country. The war lasted from January to September 1831. The Poles began with some chances of success; they had a well-drilled and well-equipped army of about 30,000 men, which they increased by recruiting to about 80,000. Against this, the Russians, with considerable difficulty, succeeded in putting only about 114,000 men into the field. Their ultimate success resulted partly from the friendly attitude of Prussia, partly from the fact that the Polish *sejm,* having proclaimed the deposition of the Russian king at an early stage of the conflict, received no response to its appeal for Western European protection. But to a large extent the defeat of the insurrection was caused by certain faults on the Polish side: want of ability and decision on the part of the generals; a succession of rapid changes in the command of the army; fierce party strife within the civil government in the capital; a naïve hope for an agreement with the emperor instead of a vigorous military action, as recommended by a section of the insurrectionary government; and, finally, an irresolute attitude of the insurrectionary parliament toward the peasant claims.

The failure of the insurrection was followed by the exile of about 10,000 political leaders and soldiers—the "Great Emigration," which was concentrated mainly in France but was also represented in England, Belgium, and Switzerland. Soon the Emigration became divided into different political groups, of which the right wing, led by Prince Adam Czartoryski, undertook energetic diplomatic action aimed at interesting the Western powers in the Polish question. The left wing of the exiles established ties with the international revolutionary movements, seeking to prepare a new insurrection in Poland and hoping to win the peasants' support. With the Great Emigration, moreover, was associated the creative work of the most prominent Romantic poets.

After the suppression of the insurrection, certain remnants of a constitution were still granted to Russian Poland by the "Organic Statute" of 1832, but they were soon rendered illusory; the administration avowedly aimed at destroying the nationality and even the language of Poland. The universities of Warsaw and Wilno were suppressed; the Polish students were compelled to go to St. Petersburg and Kiev. After the disbanding of the Polish

Army, recruits from Poland were distributed in Russian regiments, and the use of the Russian language was enforced as far as possible in the civil administration and in the law courts. The customs barrier between Lithuania and the former Congress Poland was removed, in the hope that Russian influence would spread more easily over Poland. A hostile policy was adopted against the Roman Catholic Church. But though these measures cowed the Poles, they failed to achieve their main purpose. Polish national sentiment was intensified. The Poles in Russia, whether at the universities or in the public service, formed an element which refused to assimilate with the Russians. In Poland itself much of the current civil administration was left in the hands of the nobles, whose power over their peasants was hardly diminished and was misused as of old. The Polish exiles who filled Europe after 1830 maintained a constant agitation from abroad. The stern government of Nicholas I was, however, so far effective that Poland remained quiescent during the Crimean War, though the country was seething with plots and secret preparations for an insurrection.

Alexander II and the Rising of 1863.—The reign of the new emperor Alexander II began with certain concessions to Poland in the political and educational field. Exiles were allowed to return, administrative pressure was lightened, the church was propitiated, an Agricultural Society was allowed to be formed and to discuss important affairs of the community, a medical faculty and, later on, a complete university were reestablished in Warsaw. Finally, even a Polish council of state and a Polish administrative apparatus for the kingdom began to be organized. In their later stages these reforms were the work of Count Aleksander Wielopolski, who was installed in high office and stood for a national policy of loyal union with Russia. But his autocratic temper lost him the sympathies of the moderate elements of the gentry, while on the ardent minds of the young his methods acted like fuel heaped on fire. Religious ceremonies were used as the occasion for demonstrative political processions, there were collisions with the Russian troops, and victims fell in the streets of Warsaw. Wielopolski had the unhappy idea of causing the revolutionary youth of the cities to be recruited *en masse* for the Russian Army; the plan became known, numbers of the young people fled into the forests, and a revolutionary committee on Jan. 22, 1863, proclaimed an insurrection and announced, as its first decision, that the peasants were granted ownership of the land that they held.

The struggle of the ill-equipped and ill-organized insurgent bands against the Russian garrisons dragged on in the form of guerrilla warfare throughout the country for nearly two years. A secret national government was set up in Warsaw and the movement spread successfully into Lithuania. But the assistance promised by the French emperor Napoleon III never became effective; the rising was crushed; wholesale executions, confiscations, and deportations followed its suppression; and Poland was now definitely turned into a Russian province.

Russification.—All self-government in Congress Poland was suppressed in 1863; all education was russified in 1869, justice in 1873. On the other hand, the abolition in 1851 of the customs frontier between Russia and Poland had laid the foundation for an extraordinary industrial expansion: Russian Poland, with its great textile factories at Lodz, with the coal and iron-foundry centre at Dabrowa Gornicza, became the chief industrial region for all Russia. Its vast market in agricultural Russia was protected against Western competition by high tariffs; the Russian government took every possible measure (such as the introduction of specially favourable railway tariffs) to assist this expansion. The Poles, being excluded from state service in their own country, busied themselves with productive occupations, and the upper and middle classes achieved a well-being far superior to anything enjoyed by their cousins in Galicia. A second result of this expansion was the growth in Congress Poland of a large and radical proletariat which made common cause with the Russian Social Democratic movement. In the country districts, the agrarian policy of the Russian government was expressly calculated to stir up ill-feeling between the Polish peasants, whom the government demonstratively took under its protection, and the country gentry, whom it was determined to punish in every way for their leading part in the insurrections. In March 1864 the Russian government promulgated an agrarian reform in Russian Poland by which all peasants, whatever their tenure had been, and the mass of the landless proletariat became freeholders, on a far more generous basis than the Russian peasants in 1861. The landlords received compensation in Russian treasury bonds, which stood far below par, and the peasants got the right to use the landlords' pastures and woods. The agrarian reform accelerated the development of the towns, with industry, trade, and banking. The new social structure produced both financiers who exploited the great possibilities of the Russian market and a class of workers among whom the first socialist organizations began their secret activity.

In the sphere of education, the most thoroughgoing system of russification set in after 1864. All the revived Polish schools of the Wielopolski period were made Russian again, including the University of Warsaw, and no effort was spared to produce in the minds of youth a distorted image of Poland's past. Secret patriotic education, however, counteracted this policy both in town and country, and kept the Polish cultural tradition alive.

The civil government of Russian Poland was reorganized strictly on the model of the rest of the Russian empire, the Poles being debarred, however, from certain liberal institutions which the Russians by that time possessed, such as municipal self-government and trial by jury. The Russian language was made compulsory in all official relations and at a later time even in the records of private institutions. A corrupt Russian bureaucracy filled all government offices, censorship strangled every free utterance of the nation in the press and in literature, and a police regime kept the prisons filled with political offenders.

After Russia's defeat in the Japanese War of 1904, the outbreak of a revolution in 1905, which also engulfed the territory of the Congress Kingdom, kindled Polish hopes once more. A constitution was granted to the Russians, and 36 Polish deputies sat in the first Russian Duma. The peasants of Russian Poland spontaneously introduced the Polish language in their self-governing bodies. In the Duma itself, the Liberals were not averse to granting Poland a large measure of autonomy within Russia. At the same time, persecution in Prussian Poland increased under Prince Bernhard von Bülow, while the Ukrainian national movement, developing in Austrian Poland especially since the grant of universal suffrage in 1907, was unwelcome both to Poles and to Russians. Under these circumstances, Russian propaganda, reviving the pan-Slav ideals of 30 years ago, could count on some success even among the Poles. There were gestures of reconciliation at two Slav congresses, in 1908 and 1910, the Czechs willingly acting as mediators. The idea of uniting all Poles, with autonomy, within the Russian empire was widely preached; it became the program of the National Democratic, or all-Polish, Party, led by Roman Dmowski (q.v.), the head of the Polish representation in the second and third Dumas.

Opposed to Dmowski there stood the irreconcilable revolutionaries, led by Jozef Pilsudski (q.v.). Both the insurrectionary movement started by Pilsudski in 1905 and the constitutional endeavour of Dmowski and his friends in the Duma were soon stifled by the Russian reaction. Pilsudski took refuge in Galicia and began to organize armed resistance to Russia from that base. In the Duma, the Polish representation was lowered from 36 to 10 deputies. In the country, all the liberties gained after 1905 soon disappeared. The government's purchase of the railway line from Warsaw to the Austrian frontier resulted in the removal of all Polish railwaymen from the service and was a great blow to the Polish element. In 1912 the separation of the district of Chelm, in the southeast of Russian Poland, from the body of the province and its incorporation in Russia proper was received with indignant protests by Polish opinion as a new partition of Poland.

3. Prussian Poland.—The regime in Prussian Poland during the first 15 years after the Congress of Vienna had been endurable. A Polish nobleman related by marriage to the Prussian dynasty—Prince Antoni Radziwill—was appointed lieutenant governor of the Poznan province; and there were a provincial assembly and local representative bodies both urban and rural. The landowners were allowed to organize for economic purposes, and the peasants were fully enfranchised in 1823. After the insurrection of 1830, a

period of more oppressive government by a German provincial *Oberpräsident,* Eduard Heinrich von Flottwell, set in; he revived Frederick II's method of German colonization of the Polish province, and he began to germanize the administration and the school system. A period of new concessions to the Poles under Frederick William IV was interrupted by the revolution of 1846–48. The constitution with which Prussia emerged from the revolution put an end to the self-government of Prussian Poland. Another interval of relaxation, in the first years of William I, was soon succeeded by the period of Bismarck's and Bülow's resolutely anti-Polish policy—characterized by the *Kulturkampf,* the Commission on Colonization, the Wrzesnia scandal, the schools' strike, the Law of Expropriation and the like, for an account of which *see* POZNAN. The result of the Prussian methods was to create a sturdy class of peasants and a *bourgeoisie,* economically and culturally advanced; and a fellow feeling arose between the peasants and the landowning gentry hardly known in other parts of Poland.

4. Austrian Poland.—After the insurrection of 1830–31, no remnant of Poland's independent political existence had been left except the minute republic of Cracow, created by the Congress of Vienna. For 30 years this miniature state led a flourishing existence. When the ferment of the approaching European revolution of 1848 was stirring most continental countries to their depths, there were active preparations for another rising both in Austrian and in Prussian Poland. For Austria the menace was diverted by a peasant revolt in Galicia in February 1846, which led to a massacre of about 2,000 landowners by the peasantry incited by the Austrian governor-general Baron Krieg von Hochfelden. At the same time, Austria availed itself of the unrest among its Poles to obtain the consent of Russia and Prussia to the suppression of the republic of Cracow. After a short-lived insurrection, Cracow was finally occupied by Austrian troops in March 1846 and incorporated into Galicia.

Austria under the old autocratic regime oppressed its Polish province politically and exploited it economically in the most ruthless fashion. The revolution of 1848 brought a change, but not until the defeat of Austria by Prussia in 1866 was it realized at Vienna that only a more liberal policy could hold the tottering, mixed monarchy together. The relation with Hungary having been placed on a federal footing, concessions had to be granted to the strong Polish element in Austria. The Poles began to be active in Austrian politics. The numerical strength of Polish deputies in the Vienna Parliament was such that no Austrian government could be formed without it. Galicia (as Austrian Poland was officially called), containing a large Ukrainian element in its eastern half, was granted a special minister to represent its interests in the Vienna cabinet. It also got a provincial legislative assembly and a governor, who was invariably appointed from the ranks of the Polish aristocracy. With purely Polish administration, schools, and courts of law, Galicia became indeed almost an independent Polish state within Austria and successfully defied the centralizing efforts of the Vienna bureaucracy.

The Polish landowning class, which practically governed the country for the next few decades, managed its affairs in a one-sidedly agrarian spirit; the interests of the towns were not properly considered, hardly any attention was given to the development of industries, and Galicia remained economically backward. On the other hand, political and cultural activities had more scope than in the two other parts of Poland; Galicia became the "Piedmont" of Polish nationalism in the form of the radical agrarian movement, and Cracow, with its old university and new Academy of Sciences, an intellectual, artistic, and literary centre for the whole nation. With the growth of a new educated class and the introduction of universal suffrage in Austria (1907) the social structure of the country began to change, its politics were strongly democratized, new economic tendencies got the upper hand, and Galicia was at last on the road to material advance when World War I began.

(R. Dy.; A. Wy.)

E. THE POLISH QUESTION DURING WORLD WAR I

The Polish political groupings did not react to the outbreak of World War I in uniform manner. In all three parts of Poland the Conservatives were loyal to the partitioning powers; the moderate Socialists and Peasant parties supported Germany and Austria-Hungary; the National Democrats rather sympathized with Russia, though they were engaged on Russia's side officially only in Russian Poland; and the left-wing Socialists took an anti-war position. A Supreme National Committee, striving for the unification of the Austrian and Russian parts of Poland in the Habsburg monarchy, came into being in Galicia on Aug. 16, 1914. Volunteer Polish Legions were set up at the side of the Austro-Hungarian Army under the supreme command of Austrian officers. Pilsudski became the commander of a brigade in these legions. In Congress (*i.e.*, Russian) Poland, in November 1914, the Polish National Committee was established under the leadership of Dmowski: it called for support of Russia for the sake of unification of Poland under the sceptre of the emperor and in the name of common Slav interests. In a proclamation on Aug. 14, 1914, the Russian commander in chief, the grand duke Nikolai Nikolaevich, promised unification of Poland and autonomy within the Russian empire after a victorious war. The Central Powers exhorted the Poles to fight for freedom against Russia.

In the first year of World War I the front passed through the Russian and Austrian parts of Poland; in the summer of 1915 Congress Poland and nearly all of Austrian Poland were in the hands of the Central Powers. The military operations had caused great damage to Polish industry, agriculture, communications, and housing. About 800,000 persons had been evacuated into Russia. In the first year of the war more than 1,000,000 Poles were mobilized in the armies of the partitioning powers, and by the end of the war more than 2,000,000 were mobilized. The behaviour of the military authorities, especially of the Germans, toward the civilian population in the occupied territories was ruthless.

After occupying Russian Poland, the Central Powers divided it into two military occupation zones with a German governor-general in Warsaw and an Austro-Hungarian one in Lublin. The Germans pursued a ruthless requisition policy, carrying off industrial equipment and raw materials and agricultural produce. Several hundred thousand persons were deported to Germany to work there.

The Polish National Committee moved to Petrograd (Leningrad) while their supporters who remained in Congress Poland assumed a passive attitude. A difference of opinions appeared among the supporters of the Central Powers. On Pilsudski's inspiration, in Congress Poland the Polish Socialist Party, the Peasant, and the Democratic groups on Dec. 18, 1915, set up the Central National Committee, which fought against the policy of the Supreme National Committee and opposed further enlistment for the legions until the Central Powers made a decision about the future of Poland.

It was not until the summer of 1916 that, in connection with the loss of all hope for a separate peace with Russia and in view of the need of increasing their military potential, Germany and Austria-Hungary decided to create a Polish buffer state, dependent on them economically, politically, and militarily. On Nov. 5, 1916, the German and Austrian emperors issued proclamations setting up a Polish kingdom on the territory of Congress Poland. The governors-general named on Nov. 26 a provisional council of state of 25 members to represent the Polish people, but only with advisory powers. The council consisted in the main of right-wing supporters of the Central Powers, though the minority included representatives of the Central National Committee as well. Pilsudski became the chairman of the council's Military Board. The Pilsudski group unsuccessfully demanded that he be named commander in chief of the Polish Army and that a Polish government be formed.

On March 27 (new style; old style March 14), 1917, after the overthrow of the Russian imperial regime, the Petrograd Soviet of Workers' and Soldiers' Deputies unanimously recognized Poland's right to independence. The Russian provisional government of Prince G. E. Lvov confirmed this right on March 29 (N.S.; O.S. March 16) but at the same time insisted on a military union of Poland with Russia. Organization was begun of a Polish Army Corps in Russia under the command of Gen. Jozef Dowbor-Musnicki (1867–1937). But in view of the Russian military disinte-

gration and the fear of the radicalism of the Revolution, the Polish leaders who opposed Germany turned their hopes toward the Western Allies. The Polish National Committee in Petrograd was dissolved and several days later, on Aug. 15, 1917, a body under the same name was founded at Lausanne, Switz. Later established in Paris, it was headed by Dmowski; and on Sept. 20 it was recognized by France as the official mouthpiece of Polish interests. Recognitions by Great Britain (Oct. 15), Italy (Oct. 30), and the United States (Dec. 1) followed. Ignacy Jan Paderewski (*q.v.*) was the committee's delegate in the United States. Meanwhile, on June 4, 1917, a Polish Army had come into being in France. Volunteers, including emigrants from the United States and Canada, enlisted in it.

At a conference in Berlin on March 27, 1917, Austria-Hungary recognized Congress Poland as an area of German influence. On April 10 the legions were put under the supreme command of the German governor-general. In fear of the Russian Revolution, some of the Conservative supporters of Russia in the Congress Poland associated themselves with the Central Powers. Social radicalism and dislike for Germany grew intense in the workers' and peasants' groupings. Pilsudski strove for *rapprochement* with the National Democrats who remained faithful to the anti-German line. On July 2, 1917, he left the provisional council of state in opposition to the renewed oath of allegiance given by the legions to the Central Powers. He was arrested on July 22 and interned in Germany. Some of the legionaries were interned and others were incorporated into the Austro-Hungarian Army and dispatched to the Italian front. Those who had given the oath were again placed under the Austro-Hungarian command as the Polish Auxiliary Corps. In the face of the indignation of the people the provisional council of state resigned on Aug. 25. In Galicia, in May 1917, the National Democrats, the Socialists, and the Polish Peasant Party had entered into an agreement; the Polish deputies to the Austrian Parliament and the Galician Diet adopted a resolution demanding the creation of "an independent Polish state, comprising all Polish lands with access to the sea."

On Sept. 12, 1917, the Central Powers decided to set up in Congress Poland a regency council, a Polish government, and a council of state of 110 members (half of them elected) as a provisional Parliament. The Regency Council consisted of Mgr. Aleksander Kakowski (1862–1938), archbishop of Warsaw, Prince Zdzislaw Lubomirski (1865–1941), and Count Jozef Ostrowski (1850–1924), a landowner. The first government was formed on Dec. 7 by Jan Kucharzewski (1876–1952).

After the Bolsheviks had taken power Soviet Russia began negotiations with the Central Powers at Brest-Litovsk (*see* BREST-LITOVSK, TREATIES OF). In order to embarrass the Soviet delegation Germany and Austria-Hungary on Feb. 9, 1918, concluded a separate peace treaty with the nationalist Ukrainian government, giving them the Chelm Province, which had a primarily Polish population. This infuriated Polish opinion in all three parts of Poland. On Feb. 11 the Kucharzewski government resigned in protest. The Polish Auxiliary Corps, under the command of Colonel Jozef Haller (1873–1960), broke through the front into the Ukraine and joined the units being formed there of Polish soldiers of the former Russian Army.

After a short time the Conservatives resumed their cooperation with the Central Powers. The National Democrats, foreseeing the coming defeat of Germany and Austria-Hungary and fearing Soviet Russia and the increasingly radical Polish Socialist movement, cooperated with the Regency Council in building a Polish administration in Congress Poland. They did not, however, engage in political action together with the occupying powers. The supporters of the interned Pilsudski kept building up the illegal Polish military organization (Polska Organizacja Wojskowa, POW) and were preparing to take power the moment the Central Powers were defeated.

In Belorussia and the Ukraine three Polish Corps were formed but were disarmed during the advance of the armies of the Central Powers to the east. Only the II Polish Corps under Haller was smashed in battle (at Kanev, on the Dnieper), but some of its officers and men reached France where, on Oct. 4, Haller was appointed by the Polish National Committee to be commander in chief of the Polish Army, recognized by the Allies as "allied and belligerent."

The U.S. Pres. Woodrow Wilson, in his tentative peace message of Jan. 22, 1917, called for the creation of a "united, independent, and autonomous Poland." In a message to the U.S. Congress on Jan. 8, 1918, in his 13th point, he urged the formation of "an independent Polish state" with "a free and secure access to the sea." On June 3, 1918, Great Britain, France, and Italy declared they were in favour of "an independent and united Poland." On Aug. 29, 1918, Soviet Russia abrogated the partition treaties concerning Poland, concluded by tsarist Russia with Prussia and Austria.

F. Independence Restored

1. The Reemergence of the State.—In the face of the defeat of the Central Powers the Regency Council on Oct. 6, 1918, issued a manifesto to the nation, declaring the aspiration for an independent and united Poland, the convocation of a *sejm,* and the formation of a representative national government. After negotiations with the National Democrats the Regency Council on Oct. 23 set up a government sympathetic to the Western Allies under Jozef Swiezynski (1868–1926), but on Nov. 3, it dismissed this government. In Galicia, on Oct. 28, in agreement with all the Polish political parties, a "liquidation commission" was set up; and, in view of the disintegration of Austria-Hungary, it assumed power in western Galicia. The moderate Socialist and Peasant parties, with the backing of the Polish military organization, formed a government in Lublin on Nov. 7 with Ignacy Daszynski (*q.v.*) as prime minister. In Congress Poland the left-wing Socialists began forming councils of workers' delegates and advanced a program of socialist revolution.

Released by the German government, Pilsudski arrived in Warsaw on Nov. 10, 1918. On Nov. 11 the German troops in Warsaw and other places of Congress Poland were disarmed. The Daszynski government and the Regency Council turned power over to Pilsudski and dissolved themselves. The Polish liquidation commission in Galicia also subordinated itself to Pilsudski. On Nov. 14, the Supreme People's Council came into being in Poznan as the representative of the Polish people in Prussian Poland, which was still under German control. The National Democrats, adversaries of Pilsudski, had the decisive voice in the Poznan council. On Dec. 27 an uprising against the Germans broke out in Poznan and within a few days it engulfed almost the entire province. On Feb. 16, 1919, an armistice was concluded and a provisional demarcation line was established.

On Nov. 18, 1918, Pilsudski appointed a government that was similar to the Lublin one and was headed by Jedrzej Moraczewski (1870–1944), a Socialist devoted to him. On the left the revolutionary Socialist groupings opposed the government and in December they created the Communist Party of Poland (KPP). On the right, the government was opposed by the National Democrats, who strove to seize power. As provisional head of state, Pilsudski in December began talks with envoys of the Polish National Committee in Paris, Stanislaw Grabski (1871–1949) and Paderewski. On Jan. 16, 1919, he dismissed the Moraczewski government and appointed a new one with Paderewski as prime minister. This government was recognized by the Supreme People's Council in Prussian Poland, by the Polish National Committee in Paris, and by the Allies. On Jan. 26 elections to the *sejm* were held in Congress Poland and western Galicia. The *sejm* elected Pilsudski provisional head of state and reappointed Paderewski as prime minister. The government firmly combated the Communist movement: in June 1919 the councils of workers' delegates were broken up.

Poland's position after World War I was most difficult. The state was coming into being through the unification of three parts which had formerly been incorporated by the partitioning powers. These lands had different levels of political, economic, and cultural development and different traditions. The former Russian and Austrian parts had suffered serious devastation during the war. The industrial plant of Congress Poland had been carried off to a great extent to Russia or Germany; where it remained there was

a lack of raw materials causing widespread unemployment. Agriculture was ruined and a great proportion of the livestock had been requisitioned during the war. Famine reigned and epidemic diseases spread. In various parts of the country there were different currencies (German marks and two types of occupation marks, Austrian crowns, and Russian rubles), but all were of low and uncertain value. A Polish civil administration had existed previously only in Galicia and on a small scale, since 1917, in Congress Poland. The army came into being out of various units: besides Pilsudski's organization, there were Polish units previously formed by the Austrians and Germans, groups of volunteers from former army corps organized in Russia, and then the several classes called up. In April 1919 units of the Polish Army in France returned to Poland.

There were many political groupings, mostly small. The greatest political influence was wielded by the National Democratic Party (ND), which was supported by urban middle and upper classes, the landowners, the clergy, and a considerable proportion of the peasants, especially in the former Prussian Poland. In the former Austrian and Russian part of Poland there was a peasant political movement split up into left-wing groups cooperating with the Socialists and the moderate Polish Peasant Party (PSL) led by Wincenty Witos (1874–1945). Active among the workers were the Polish Socialist Party (PPS) and the Communist Party of Poland. The nationalist workers' organizations united in 1920 as the National Workers' Party. The national minorities organized their own political parties. The left-wing peasant parties, the PPS, and, in part, also the National Workers' Party supported Pilsudski, whom they regarded as a champion of democracy; Pilsudski was opposed mainly by the National Democrats.

In mid-1919, after by-elections, there were 394 deputies in the *sejm,* 140 of them representing the ND and allied groupings, 46 from the PSL, 71 from left-wing peasant parties, 35 from the PPS, 32 from the National Workers' Party, and 13 from the national minorities.

The ND took a firmly anti-German position and through diplomatic contacts tried to obtain the most advantageous Polish-German frontier possible. Its eastern program envisaged the incorporation into Poland not only of all Galicia, including its eastern part inhabited mainly by Ukrainians, but also of areas situated to the east of Congress Poland, though only insofar as they contained major centres of Polish population. This incorporation program planned a progressive polonization of the Belorussian and Ukrainian populations. Pilsudski and the parties supporting him were in agreement with the ND's aspirations for the best possible frontier with Germany, but their foreign policy was definitely anti-Russian: it aimed at separating Belorussia and the Ukraine from Russia and joining these countries and Lithuania with Poland in a federation, with Poland maintaining the leading economic, military, and political role. Paderewski's government resigned on Dec. 9, 1919, being followed by those headed by Leopold Skulski and, from June 23, 1920, by Wladyslaw Grabski (1874–1938). On July 24, 1920, at a critical moment of the Russo-Polish War (*q.v.*), Witos, with Daszynski as deputy premier, formed a coalition government.   (J. Hr.; A. Wy.)

2. The Treaty of Versailles and Frontier Problems.—On June 28, 1919, on behalf of Poland, Dmowski and Paderewski signed the Treaty of Versailles, which, however, left the major part of the country's frontiers undefined. Poland regained part of eastern Pomorze and almost all Poznania, but in East Prussia and Upper Silesia the Polish-German frontier was to be decided by plebiscite. Gdansk (*see* Danzig) was to be a free city under the protection of the League of Nations but was to be included within the Polish customs frontier in order to provide Poland with a free and secure access to the sea; in addition, Poland was to have free, unrestricted use of the port and to undertake the conduct of the free city's foreign relations. There was a Polish-Czechoslovakian dispute over Teschen (Cieszyn or Tesin) and also over the territories of Orawa (Orava) and Spisz. Of the eastern frontiers of Poland art. 87 of the treaty stated that they would be "subsequently determined by the principal Allied and Associated Powers."

East Prussia.—Two plebiscite zones were established, that of Kwidzyn (Marienwerder), an area of 1,036 sq.mi. (2,683 sq.km.) with 174,000 inhabitants, and that of Olsztyn (Allenstein), about 4,800 sq.mi. (12,432 sq.km.) with 565,000 inhabitants. All Prussian civil servants were left in the plebiscite areas and the presence of German security police precluded freedom of speech.

The vote was taken on July 11, 1920, when Soviet forces were at the gates of Warsaw. In the Olsztyn zone 363,209 votes were cast for Germany and 7,980 for Poland, in the Kwidzyn zone 96,923 for Germany and 8,018 for Poland. Making the utmost of a stipulation that not only residents but also persons born in the area had the right to vote, the Germans sent to the plebiscite zones 202,700 "emigrants," who constituted nearly half of the voters, while 40% of the qualified residents abstained from voting. Thus the plebiscite, lost by Poland, could scarcely be described as a fair expression of the popular will.

Upper Silesia.—The plebiscite area of Upper Silesia was 4,250 sq.mi. (11,000 sq.km.) with 1,942,200 inhabitants. Out of 706,-820 votes cast for Germany on March 20, 1921, emigrant voters were responsible for 182,288; Poland obtained 479,414 votes. In all, 682 communes voted for Poland and 792 for Germany, but the Poles secured preponderance in the southeastern plebiscite area, which economically was the most important. Disregarding the treaty provisions for the partition of the area according to the wishes of the inhabitants expressed by communes, Germany claimed the whole of Upper Silesia, while Wojciech Korfanty (*q.v.*), the leader of the Silesian Poles and Polish plebiscite commissioner, demanded that 59% of the area, in which 673 communes voted for Poland and 230 for Germany, be awarded to Poland.

The Inter-Allied Commission failed to agree on a unanimous proposal to the Supreme Council of the principal Allied Powers, the British and Italian commissioners favouring cession to Poland of only the two southern agricultural districts of Rybnik and Pszczyna (Pless) while the French commissioner proposed a frontier less favourable than the Korfanty line but leaving the industrial basin to Poland. Learning of this basic disagreement, the Polish military organization, of which Michal Grazynski (1890–) was one of the chief organizers, thought that only an insurrection could save the Polish cause. Korfanty agreed and gave the order for a rising, which broke out on May 3, 1921. In a few days almost all the area within the Korfanty line was occupied. Taken by surprise, the Germans were thrown back. After six weeks' fighting the Inter-Allied Commission effected a cessation of hostilities on June 24, and both the belligerents withdrew their troops.

The Supreme Council assembled in Paris on Aug. 8–12 failed to draw a new frontier across Upper Silesia because David Lloyd George was anxious to save for Germany as much of the industrial area as possible. The only way out of the deadlock was to submit the question to the Council of the League of Nations, where Great Britain was represented by Arthur James Balfour. The council's verdict, given on Oct. 12, 1921, was endorsed by the Allied Powers eight days later. The new frontier divided the industrial area: Poland was awarded 1,241 sq.mi. (3,214 sq.km.) with about 996,000 inhabitants, 76% of the coal production, 22 out of 37 blast furnaces, and 9 out of 14 steelworks. Thus a basis for economic independence was assured. (*See also* SILESIA.)

Teschen (*Cieszyn, Tesin*).—On Nov. 5, 1918, close upon the final dissolution of the Habsburg monarchy, the Polish and Czech National Council of Teschen Silesia concluded an agreement dividing the four districts of the province into two ethnographic entities. On Jan. 23, 1919, however, on orders from Prague, the Czech forces fell unexpectedly upon insignificant Polish forces in the area and occupied the greater part of the province. The government of Prague argued that Teschen was historically a Czech land and, moreover, that the new Czechoslovakia needed its coal.

The fighting was stopped by the Supreme Council on Feb. 3, 1919. After a vain attempt to reach agreement by direct negotiation, the Supreme Council decided on Sept. 27 that the dispute should be settled by plebiscite. On July 10, 1920, Poland, whose existence was menaced by the Soviet offensive, agreed at Spa that the Conference of Ambassadors should draw a final frontier. On

July 28 less than half of Teschen Silesia was awarded to Poland (390 sq.mi. [1,011 sq.km.] out of 881 sq.mi. [2,283 sq.km.], with a population of 142,000 out of 435,000). Czechoslovakia secured all coal mines. No Czechs were left on the Polish side of the new frontier, but on the opposite side were 140,000 Poles. The decision relating to Orawa and Spisz was likewise disadvantageous to Poland, which kept 27 villages; the 44 villages awarded to Czechoslovakia had a Polish population of 45,000.

Eastern Galicia.—Of 4,743,000 inhabitants of Eastern Galicia (18,245 sq.mi. [47,255 sq.km.]), Ukrainians formed 52.7%, Poles 39.3%, and Jews 7.2%; there was, however, a considerable Polish majority at Lwow (64% of a population of 300,000) and in some other towns. Enabled by the Austrian authorities to assume control of the whole area, the Ukrainians on Nov. 1, 1918, proclaimed at Lwow (Lvov) an independent republic of the Western Ukraine. Thereupon the local Polish population organized military formations, which succeeded in freeing the city by Nov. 22. In May 1919, after the fighting had continued for six months, the Polish Army occupied the whole of the disputed province.

In March 1919 the Commission on Polish Affairs at the Paris Peace Conference considered the following alternatives regarding the future of Eastern Galicia: (1) a Polish mandate over the whole territory for 25 years, after which its fate was to be settled by plebiscite; (2) partition between Poland and a Ukrainian state. There were alternative demarcation lines in connection with these schemes: line A to run east of Przemysl, if the whole territory were to be entrusted to Poland under a mandate; and line B, which would leave Lwow and the Drohobycz (Drogobych) oil fields to Poland in the event of the creation of a Ukrainian state. On June 25 the Supreme Council accepted line A and authorized Poland to occupy the whole area; on Nov. 21, it approved the draft of an autonomous statute for the area with a 25-year mandate; on Dec. 22, 1919, giving satisfaction to Polish demands, the Supreme Council rescinded its previous decision and allowed Poland to incorporate the whole area (*see also* GALICIA).

The Polish-Soviet Frontier.—Under the terms of the Armistice of Nov. 11, 1918, the German Armies had to evacuate western Russia and Poland. As the Germans withdrew, the Soviet Army was advancing westward. In Nov. 1918 it was still on the Dnieper, but by Feb. 1919 had moved forward to the Bug. Soviet Russia needed territorial contact with revolutionary Germany and this could only be won across Poland. The Soviet government hoped, of course, that the Polish workers and peasants would greet its armies as liberators, and was greatly dismayed when they did not. (*See also* RUSSO-POLISH WAR.)

A counteroffensive launched by the Polish Army under Pilsudski brought the Polish-Soviet front, by the end of 1919, along the Berezina River in Belorussia, and in the Ukraine Novograd-Volynski, Staro-Konstantinov, and Bar were in Polish hands. Although in no haste to decide on Poland's eastern frontiers, the Supreme Council, on Dec. 8, 1919, authorized Poland to organize a regular administration within a temporary line of demarcation "on the territories of the former Russian empire"; *i.e.*, not encroaching upon the formerly Austrian territory of Galicia. The declaration of Dec. 8 stated explicitly that the line fixed was a provisional minimum frontier, without prejudice to later terms which might be designed to fix the final eastern frontier of Poland.

On Jan. 28, 1920, V. I. Lenin, Georgi Chicherin, and Lev Trotski handed a peace proposal to the Polish government suggesting the actual front as the armistice line. Pilsudski doubted the sincerity of this offer because he had information that the Soviet command was concentrating new divisions on the front and Trotski himself, in a letter to three prominent French Communists, had written shortly before: "When we have finished with Denikin, we are going to attack the Poles" (*Internationale Communiste*, Dec. 15, 1919). When, however, on March 27, 1920, the Polish government decided to open negotiations the Soviet government's rejection of Borisov, near the front, as a suggested meeting place confirmed Pilsudski's suspicion of a threatened Soviet offensive. On April 21, 1920, he accordingly signed a treaty of alliance with Symon Petlyura (*q.v.*), head of a Ukrainian government at Kamenets-Podolski, and three days later a Polish offensive started in the Ukraine. (*See* also UKRAINIAN SOVIET SOCIALIST REPUB-LIC: *History*.) On May 7 the Poles occupied Kiev, but on June 8 the Soviet Cavalry under Semen (later Marshal) Budenny broke through the Polish line southwest of Kiev, and on July 4 Mikhail (later Marshal) Tukhachevski attacked north of Borisov. The military situation of Poland became critical. On July 6 W. Grabski, the prime minister, went to Spa, Belg., where the Supreme Council was assembled to ask for immediate help in the shape of war supplies.

With the assent of representatives of France and Italy, the British prime minister Lloyd George undertook to act as mediator. He suggested an armistice along the line of Dec. 8, 1919; in Eastern Galicia the armies were to stand on the line reached on the date of the armistice. Grabski agreed, and on July 11 Lord Curzon, the British foreign secretary, suggested an armistice to Moscow and the Polish Army's withdrawal to the line of Dec. 8, 1919, and in Eastern Galicia to the line A (*see* above), an obvious discrepancy with the agreement reached the previous day. Thus was born the "Curzon line." (*See* also SPA, CONFERENCE OF.)

Meanwhile the situation on the front gradually changed. By mid-August Pilsudski's counteroffensive brought a decisive victory. Poland was saved, but not only Poland. "By attacking Poland," said Lenin in Moscow on Oct. 8, 1920, "we are attacking also the Allies. By destroying the Polish army we are destroying the Versailles settlement." A Soviet-sponsored government for "liberated" Poland, headed by Julian Marchlewski, Feliks Dzerzhinski, and Feliks Kon, which had already established itself at Bialystok, had to flee back to Moscow. A Polish-Soviet peace treaty, concluded on March 18, 1921, at Riga, Latvia, added to Poland an area of 51,762 sq.mi. (134,064 sq.km.) E of the line of Dec. 8, 1919.

The Wilno Dispute.—The Polish Army captured Wilno (Vil-

nius) on April 20, 1919, and Pilsudski issued a proclamation suggesting the creation of a federation of Poland with the lands of the former Grand Principality of Lithuania. On July 27 the Supreme Council approved a demarcation line between Poland and Lithuania, leaving Wilno on the Polish side. During the advance of the Soviet armies westward, the Soviet government "ceded" Wilno to Lithuania by a peace treaty signed on July 12, 1920. The city was evacuated by the Russians during their general retreat following the Polish victory and on Aug. 26 was entered by Lithuanian troops. The Poles appealed to the League of Nations and a partial armistice was signed at Suwalki on Oct. 7. Pilsudski was still inclined toward a federal solution of the dispute, with Wilno and its region providing an independent link between Poland and Lithuania. Gen. Lucjan Zeligowski (1865–1947) accordingly occupied Wilno on Oct. 9 and set up a local government. Pilsudski's scheme, however, was incompatible with the prevailing temper of the Poles and Lithuanians. On Feb. 20, 1922, therefore, the democratically elected Regional Assembly of 106 members voted the incorporation of the whole province in the Polish republic; 96 members voted for the incorporation, 6 abstained, and 4 were absent. It remained only to obtain the approval of the principal Allied Powers. The Soviet government had declared in the Riga Treaty its disinterestedness in the Polish-Lithuanian dispute.

The Council of the League of Nations was no longer interested and on Feb. 3, 1923, adopted a final resolution fixing the Polish-Lithuanian line of demarcation. On March 15, 1923, the Conference of Ambassadors, requested by both the Polish and Lithuanian governments to use their right to fix the frontier, recognized the demarcation line of Feb. 3 as the final frontier between the two states.

By the same decision the Conference of Ambassadors recognized

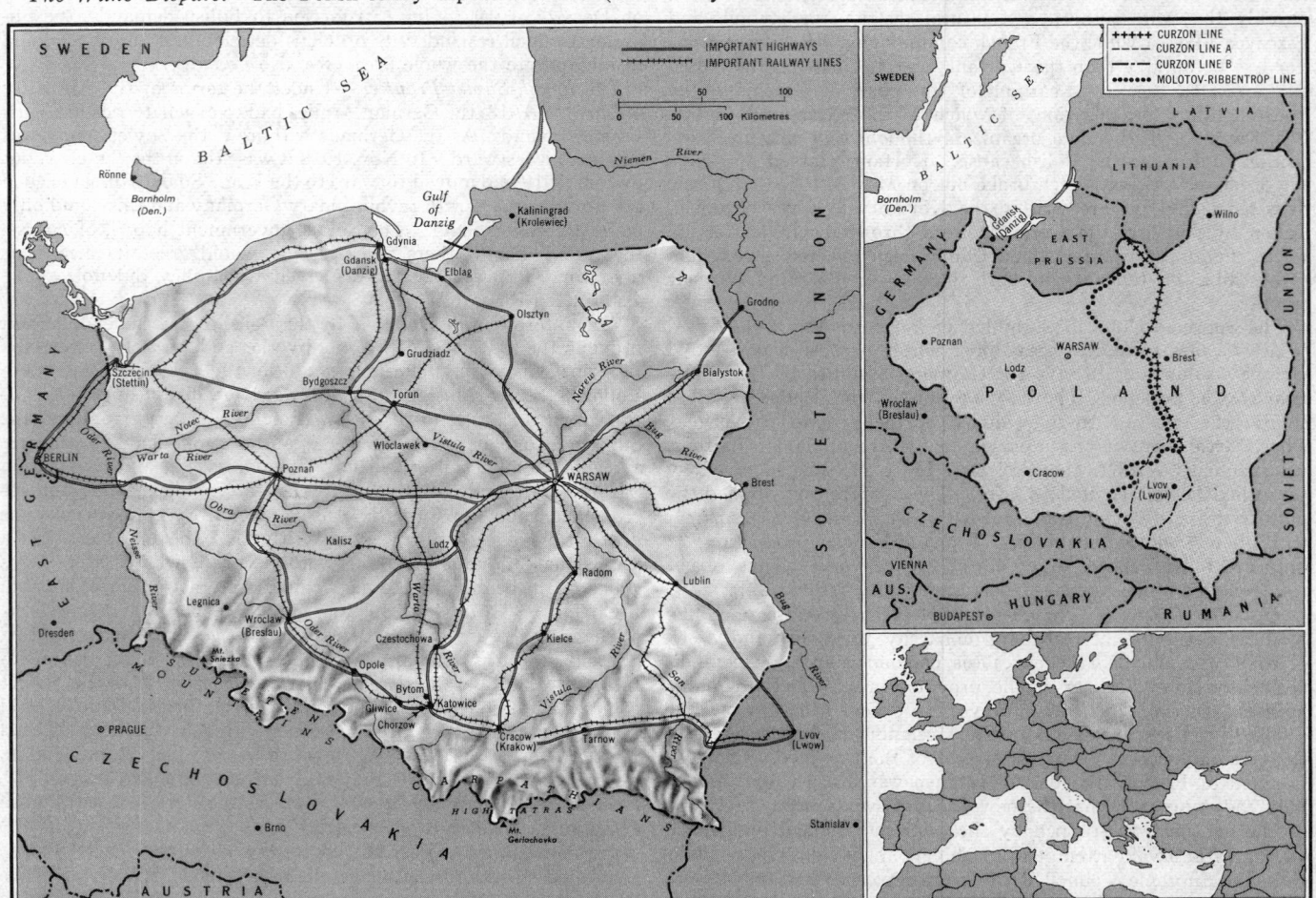

POLAND IN THE 20TH CENTURY: (LEFT) LIMITS OF THE COUNTRY SINCE 1951, SHOWING PRINCIPAL CITIES AND PHYSICAL FEATURES; (TOP RIGHT) POLAND'S BOUNDARY CHANGES BETWEEN 1919 AND 1937 (*see* TEXT)

as final the Polish-Soviet frontier fixed by the Treaty of Riga. On April 5, 1923, both Polish-Soviet and Polish-Lithuanian frontiers were recognized by the government of the United States. The long series of territorial disputes which handicapped Poland's foreign policy and its internal reconstruction was definitely settled, both legally and in fact. The new Poland had a total area of 150,052 sq.mi. (388,634 sq.km.) with an approximate population of 27,200,000. (K. SM.)

3. Internal Affairs, 1920–26.—The Witos government continued its duties until Sept. 13, 1921, but after the resignation of Daszynski (Jan. 4) it had lost its character of a national coalition. The social and political struggle flared up in the country. In February and March of 1921 there were a railwaymen's strike and a general strike. Particularly acute contradictions appeared in connection with the constitution's being prepared. The left wing in Parliament wanted to stress the role of the president of the republic and expected Pilsudski to be elected to the post. The National Democrats strove for a senate, in addition to the *sejm*, and wanted this chamber to be appointed without general elections.

In the end the constitution of March 17, 1921, was a compromise by both sides and was modeled after the French constitution of 1875. In the Polish republic the legislative power was wielded by the *sejm* and the Senate but the latter had no right to initiate legislation. Both chambers were elected for five years by a system of proportional representation. The *sejm* by a two-thirds majority could dissolve itself before the expiration of its term, but the president could dissolve the *sejm* only with the consent of three-fifths of the Senate. The president and the Council of Ministers were the executive. The president was elected for a seven-year term by both chambers. He nominated and dismissed the prime minister and the ministers, but the government was responsible to the *sejm* and at its demand the cabinet or any minister had to resign. The president promulgated laws and government acts but together with the prime minister and the appropriate minister who bore the full responsibility. He also represented the state externally and was the commander in chief of the armed forces in peacetime, but in wartime, at the recommendation of the government, he had to appoint a commander in chief. The Council of Ministers had the right to initiate legislation.

The president appointed judges who were independent in carrying out the duties of their office. Civic rights were guaranteed. Property was under the care of the state and the abolition or limitation of property by legislation could be effected only with compensation. Citizens had the right to work or to social insurance. Roman Catholicism was accorded a special position, and the state's relations with the church were to be determined in a concordat with the Holy See. Education in state and local government schools was to be free.

Administratively Poland was divided into voivodeships (*wojewodztwa*), these in turn into districts (*powiaty*), and the latter into communes (*gminy*). The Silesian voivodeship had partial autonomy and it elected its own local *sejm*. At first the old legislation of the partitioning powers remained in effect in the several parts of the country; gradually, however, unifying work was carried out in the field of judicial administration and codification, but by 1939 it was not completed.

The adopted constitution complicated the solution of the urgent agrarian problem. According to the census of 1921 the landed estates accounted for 47.3% of the total arable land. There were 1,100,000 peasant farms under 2.5 ac. (1 ha.) in size. As early as July 10, 1919, the *sejm* passed a law calling for agrarian reform and on July 15, 1920, during the Russo-Polish War, it passed an act providing for the compulsory partition of the large estates among the peasants. The opponents of that law acted to prevent its implementation by referring to the constitutionally guaranteed property rights. It was not until Dec. 28, 1925, that the *sejm* passed a new law which made provision primarily for voluntary partition of the estates.

In addition to the agrarian question, there was the problem of national minorities. According to the census of 1921 the latter constituted 30.8% of the population, including Ukrainians 14.3%, Jews 7.8%, and Belorussians and Germans 3.9% each. The Ukrainians, mainly under the influence of nationalist organizations, opposed the Polish government with particular vigour. Among the Polish population there developed anti-Semitism fostered by the National Democrats; among the Jews there grew separatism.

Parliamentary elections were held on Nov. 5–12, 1922. Of the 444 seats in the *sejm*, the ND and its allies won 166, Polish Peasant Party 70, the left-wing Peasant parties 42, the National Workers' Party 18, the PPS 41, the Communists 2, the crypto-Communists 15, the national minorities 81, and others 9. The previous head of state Pilsudski, declined to stand for the office of president in view of its merely representative nature. The votes of the PPS, the Peasant parties and the national minorities elected Pilsudski's old friend, Gabriel Narutowicz (1865–1922), formerly minister of foreign affairs. The ND launched a violent campaign against the president and a week after this election, on Dec. 16, 1922, a sympathizer of this party assassinated him. The same parties which had elected Narutowicz elected Stanislaw Wojciechowski (1869–1953), on Dec. 20. On Dec. 16 Gen. Wladyslaw Sikorski (*q.v.*) had become prime minister. Pilsudski (a marshal from March 19, 1920) took the position of chief of the general staff.

In 1922 the policy of the Polish Communist Party changed. Its leadership, headed by Maria Koszutska (pseudonym Wiera Kostrzewa; 1879–1939), emphasized patriotic slogans and the movement's need to make its decisions independently. The leadership strove to ease the acuteness of the conflict with the parliamentary left wing and advanced a program, not of direct struggle for a socialist revolution, but of agrarian reform, improvement of the living conditions of the workers, and the strengthening of democracy against the attacks from the right. In 1924 Koszutska and the leaders working with her were removed by the Comintern. From 1925 on, however, they again played a certain role in the leadership of the party.

The steadily growing inflation reached a peak in 1923 and disorganized the life of the country. On May 28, as a result of an understanding between the ND and the PSL, the Witos government took office, and two days later Pilsudski resigned as chief of the general staff, formally retiring from political life. A wave of strikes culminated in a general strike in November, combined with armed uprisings, above all in Cracow (Nov. 6). There was a split in the PSL; the government lost its majority in the *sejm* and resigned on Dec. 14.

The next government was headed by W. Grabski, who also became minister of finance. The government vacillated between the ND and the supporters of Pilsudski. In order to stabilize the currency (74% of budgetary expenditure in 1923 had been covered by the printing of money), Grabski increased tax revenues and cut expenditure. The attempts to make foreign loans brought little result. A British adviser, Edward Hilton Young (later Lord Kennet) was asked to come to Poland, but Grabski did not agree to the formation of a permanent mission of British financial advisers in Poland. On Feb. 1, 1924, a new currency, the zloty, was inaugurated, to be backed up to 30% by gold and hard foreign currencies. On April 28 the Bank of Poland opened its doors: it was a private limited company controlled by the state, with a capital of 100,000,000 zl. subscribed by 52,000 Polish citizens. From February 1925, however, state expenditure again began to exceed the revenues. The economic situation was worsened when in June 1925 Germany began applying trade restrictions against Poland, a move which resulted in both sides engaging in a "tariff war." The inability to overcome the financial crisis induced the Grabski government to resign on Nov. 14, 1925.

While the Grabski government was in office a concordat was signed with the Vatican on Feb. 10, 1925, ensuring for the Roman Catholic Church complete internal freedom with only the nominations to the higher church posts having to be agreed with the government. The church properties were exempted from the agrarian reform. The teaching of religion in state and private schools was organized by the church and the teachers of religion in state schools approved and paid by the state.

Grabski was followed by Aleksander Skrzynski (1882–1931) who formed a government of national coalition. The financial crisis continued, the salaries of state employees were cut, and treasury notes were printed to cover expenditures. Attempts to obtain foreign loans failed. The PPS ministers opposed the dismissals of workers, the reduction in old age pensions, and the rise in taxes levied on working people; accordingly they left the government, which resigned on May 5, 1926. The government crisis came at a time when there was universal dissatisfaction caused by the instability of the currency, the rise in prices, and also by the endless changes of government.

4. Foreign Policy, 1921–26.—In the first years of Polish independence France's support was Poland's greatest asset. In February 1921 Marshal Pilsudski, as head of state, visited France, and talks led to the signing in Paris, on Feb. 19, of a political agreement. It provided that the two governments should take concerted measures for the defense of their territories if either or both should be attacked without provocation. Circles close to Pilsudski studied the possibility of *rapprochement* with Great Britain, but without success.

Pilsudski also strove to build an alliance of states bordering with the U.S.S.R. on the west. A conference of representatives of Poland, Latvia, Lithuania, Estonia, and Finland, meeting in Helsinki, Fin. (Jan. 15–22, 1920), yielded no results. On March 3, 1921, in Bucharest, Rum., Poland and Rumania signed a treaty of alliance, providing for mutual assistance in the event of an aggression. On March 17, 1922, Warsaw was the venue of the signing of a political treaty by Poland, Latvia, Estonia, and Finland, but it was not ratified by the latter. This treaty envisaged consultation on countermeasures in the event of aggression against one of the contracting countries. The relations between Poland and Lithuania were bad, since Lithuania continued to claim Wilno.

The National Democratic Party wanted to tie Poland with the Little Entente (*q.v.*). This seemed possible after a visit to Prague, Czech., by the Polish foreign minister, Konstanty Skirmunt (1866–1949), and the signing on Nov. 6, 1921, of a political agreement on joint action in the implementation of international treaties signed by both countries. This referred particularly to the treaties of Versailles, Saint-Germain, and Trianon. It was in the interests of Poland to stress the anti-German character of the Little Entente, which had hitherto been directed chiefly against Hungary. In June 1923, the Polish foreign minister, Marian Seyda (1879–   ), proposed the transformation of the Little Entente into a quadruple alliance with Poland's participation, but he got no support from the countries of the Little Entente. Correct Polish-Czechoslovakian relations, however, were maintained and the Czechoslovakian foreign minister, Edvard Benes, visited Poland in April 1925.

The Dawes Plan was received in Poland with some anxiety as an expression of a desire to rebuild Germany, and this anxiety was deepened by the policy of Gustav Stresemann, linking Germany's power aspirations with *rapprochement* to Great Britain and France. The treaties initialed at Locarno, Switz., on Oct. 16, 1925 and signed in London on Dec. 1 guaranteed the borders of the western neighbours of Germany, but the borders of its eastern neighbours were left without safeguards. The danger was only lessened by two additional treaties concluded at the same time (1) by Poland and Germany on the peaceful settlement of disputes and (2) by France and Poland, giving a French guarantee for the Polish western border.

Locarno weakened the position of the National Democratic Party as an anti-German and pro-French force and strengthened the position of Pilsudski, a statesman with relatively high prestige in Germany. In international and Polish political circles Pilsudski was regarded as being capable of reducing the tension in Polish-German relations and of getting Poland a more advantageous position in the new balance of power.

5. The May Coup d'État and Pilsudski's Rule.—After the fall of Skrzynski's government there was a new understanding between the National Democrats and the PSL and, as in 1923, a government headed by Witos was formed on May 10, 1926. This was a challenge both to Pilsudski and to the left-wing parties. At the head of army units led by his supporters, Pilsudski marched on Warsaw and after fighting on May 12, 13, and 14, he took control of the city. On May 14 the Witos government and Pres. Wojciechowski resigned. In keeping with the constitution Maciej Rataj

(1884–1940), the speaker of the *sejm*, assumed supreme power. The Pilsudski *coup d'état* took place under the slogan *sanacja*, or the moral "cleansing" of society and the state, a fight against corruption, for the restriction of the parliamentary regime, and for the strengthening of the executive power. Pilsudski was backed by the left-wing Peasant parties, by the Socialists, and for several days even by the Communists. The army was split between supporters of Pilsudski and opponents, the latter headed by Gen. Tadeusz Rozwadowski (1866–1928), while General Sikorski remained neutral.

Rataj called to office a government with Kazimierz Bartel (1882–1941) as prime minister and Pilsudski as minister of military affairs. The members of the cabinet were linked with the victorious camp, but they did not belong to any of the large parties supporting Pilsudski. On May 31, 1926, Pilsudski was elected president of the republic by the votes of the parties which backed the coup and of some of the representatives of the PSL who, headed by Witos, were disposed to come to an understanding with Pilsudski. However, Pilsudski refused to accept the election and proposed the candidacy of a prominent scientist, Ignacy Moscicki (*q.v.*), who was elected president on June 1.

One month after the coup Pilsudski inspired a project to change the constitution so as to restrict the power of the *sejm*. The president could dissolve both Houses of Parliament and issue decrees with the force of laws. This second change was opposed by the Socialists, but the constitution was revised by an enormous majority. On Oct. 2, 1926, Pilsudski himself became head of the government, retaining the portfolio of minister of military affairs and, as from Aug. 27, also taking over the office of inspector general of the armed forces, a newly formed post. Socialist and Peasant leaders closest to Pilsudski were also in the government. Two portfolios went to representatives of the Conservative landowners from the eastern regions of the country. On Oct. 25–26 Pilsudski called on the most powerful aristocratic family, the Radziwills, at their estate in Nieswiez. His *rapprochement* with the Conservatives led to a drop in his support from the parliamentary left wing. In September 1927, Col. Walery Slawek (1879–1939), a close friend of Pilsudski, concluded a pact with the Conservatives at Dzikow. The pact provided for the strengthening of the role of the Roman Catholic Church, acceptance of the principle of social solidarity and, in the long run, the introduction of a monarchy. The Polish Socialist Party and the Peasant parties went more and more sharply into the opposition and the groups most closely linked with Pilsudski in 1927 and in 1928 either left these parties or were expelled.

In spite of the tense relations between the *sejm* and the government, Pilsudski did not want to dissolve Parliament before its term of office expired; but he treated it with demonstrative disregard. Presidential decrees restricted the freedom of the press. There were few cases of naked abuse of power, but the authorities disclaimed any responsibility for several political murders and acts of violence against anti-Pilsudski military men and political leaders. The mood of the people was affected by the improvement in the country's economic situation. On Oct. 13, 1927, Poland received an international (mainly U.S.) stabilization loan of $72,000,000. A stabilization plan was worked out by U.S. adviser Edwin W. Kemmerer, and another U.S. adviser, Charles S. Dewey, sat on the board of directors of the Bank of Poland. There was an increased influx of foreign capital into Poland. An important development in improving the situation was an enormous increase in coal exports, because of a six-month strike by British miners (1926).

In the elections to the *sejm* on March 4, 1928, the nonparty bloc of Pilsudski's supporters won 130 seats, the National Democrats obtained 37, the Christian Democrats 19, the Polish Peasants 21, the Peasant left wing 66, the National Workers' Party 14, the Socialists 63, the Communists 8, and the national minorities 86 (of which 11 were close to the Communists). The administration supported the government lists and the nonparty bloc received considerable government funds for propaganda purposes. The *sejm* elected as speaker the Socialist leader Daszynski over the Pilsudski candidate, Bartel. However, Bartel formed on June 27 a new government composed almost the same as the previous one.

The struggle between Pilsudski and the *sejm* grew sharper and on March 20, 1929, the *sejm* decided to refer to the High Court of Justice the case of Gabriel Czechowicz (1876–1938), minister of finance, who was charged with having transferred state funds to the nonparty bloc before the elections. On April 14 the first so-called colonels' government was formed by Kazimierz Switalski (1886–1961). On Oct. 31, when 50 officers in uniform came to the opening of the *sejm*, Daszynski refused to open the meeting. The left-wing and centre opposition to Pilsudski, from Socialists to Christian Democrats, who had formed the centre-left bloc, with the backing of the National Democrats and the Communists, overthrew the government when the *sejm* session opened on Dec. 5, 1929. This was only a demonstration, since the opposition was aware that the Pilsudski dictatorship could not be overthrown by parliamentary means. The next Bartel government was unable to ease the situation, and a new strong-arm cabinet formed by Slawek on March 29, 1930, aggravated the situation.

On June 29, 1930, the centre-left bloc convened a congress in Cracow and decided to go over to a mass protest campaign. Pilsudski became head of the government on Aug. 25 and Parliament was dissolved on Aug. 30. In September about 70 deputies of the Polish and national minority opposition parties were arrested and the most prominent, including Witos, Korfanty, and the Socialist Herman Lieberman (1870–1941), were imprisoned in the fortress of Brzesc (Brest). The persons arrested were subjected to physical maltreatment. At the same time the areas inhabited by Ukrainians were the scene of military "pacification" by searches, economic repressions, and violence.

In the *sejm* elections on Nov. 16, 1930, according to official returns, the nonparty bloc received 44.7% of the votes, gaining 247 seats. The National Democrats won 62 seats, Christian Democrats 15, Polish Peasants 15, left-wing Peasants 33, National Workers' Party 10, the Socialists 24, the Communists 5, and the national minorities 33. From then on the cabinets headed by successive prime ministers (Slawek, Aleksander Prystor, Janusz Jedrzejewicz, Leon Kozlowski, and Slawek again) had a majority in the *sejm* but not enough to change the constitution.

The economic crisis of 1929–33 again engulfed industry and agriculture alike. The value of industrial output in 1932 was only 54% of what it had been in 1928. According to the census of 1931, meanwhile, 21.5% of the workers were unemployed. The prices paid to agricultural producers in 1933 were a mere 40% of those of 1928.

The influence of the formally banned Communist Party grew during the years of the crisis; from 1928, when the Koszutska group had been removed from the leadership, the Communists had cut themselves off even more sharply from the other opposition forces. The centre-left bloc fell apart, the slogans of the Polish Socialist Party became more radical, and so did those of the Peasant Party (SL) which came into being on March 15, 1931, as a result of the unification of all the peasant groups under Witos' leadership. In the right-wing opposition, there were growing reflections of Italian Fascism; these tendencies were represented by those of the National Democrats who, from December 1926, were organized in the Camp for a Great Poland, set up by Dmowski. The activities of all forms of opposition were weakened by the restriction of parliamentary activities, by repressions, and by the censorship of the press.

On Jan. 26, 1934, the nonparty bloc took advantage of the fact that the opposition deputies had walked out of the chamber and, with a dubious interpretation of the rules, passed the draft of a new constitution. With some amendments adopted by the Senate, Pres. Moscicki promulgated it on April 23, 1935. The constitution entrusted supreme power to a president responsible "to God and to history." The legislative powers of the *sejm* and the Senate, as compared to the constitution of 1921, were cut back by the president's right to issue decrees. Both chambers were elected for five years, the *sejm* by a general election. One-third of the senators were appointed by the president, and the manner of election of the remainder was to be specified in an election act. The president called elections for Parliament and dissolved it. He

also exercised executive power and the government was politically responsible to him. If both houses demanded it, the president had to dismiss the government or dissolve Parliament. The candidate for the presidency was chosen by a college of electors, most of whom were to be selected from the deputies and senators. If the outgoing president nominated another candidate, there were general elections, otherwise the candidate of the college of electors became president for a seven-year term.

The constitution made provision for freedom of conscience, speech, and assembly, but made the reservation that the limit of these freedoms was the "common good" of all the citizens. The government could declare a state of emergency with the president's consent and this state was lifted only if the Senate endorsed the *sejm's* bill to this effect.

6. Pilsudski's Successors.—On May 12, 1935, Pilsudski died at the age of 68. His death caught the government camp at a time of increased pressure by the opposition. In 1935 the Communists called for a popular front and defense of the independence of Poland against the menace from Nazi Germany; and these slogans evoked a response from the left-wing Socialists and some Peasant leaders. The leadership of the PPS and the Peasant Party rejected an alliance with the Communists, but the antigovernment agitation was intensified. In 1936 and 1937 the country was swept by a wave of political demonstrations and strikes by workers and peasants. Among the intellectuals, the campaign conducted by the Communists and left-wing Socialists was joined even by some writers and scientists who had previously been under the spell of Pilsudski. The activity of the Polish Communists, however, decreased from the end of 1936 in connection with the arrest of their leaders in the U.S.S.R. In March 1938 acting on Stalin's orders, the Comintern dissolved the Communist Party of Poland, branding its leaders as provocateurs and agents of capitalist intelligence services. Many of them were shot.

On the extreme right, on March 17, 1934, the National Radical Camp (ONR) came into being; in the same year it was dissolved by the government, but it continued its activities in two factions. It took up the totalitarian slogans and acquired an overwhelming influence among the university students. Sikorski, Paderewski, Haller, and Witos strove to create a bloc of moderate opposition forces and were particularly active in this respect in 1936–38, but with no result worth mentioning. The Ukrainian movement, which was primarily nationalist, grew more intense even though the government tried to suppress it by new "pacifications."

In the fight for the political heritage of Pilsudski were Pres. Moscicki, Gen. Edward Smigly-Rydz (1886–1941), inspector general of the armed forces, and Slawek, the leader of the nonparty bloc, which had been dissolved on Oct. 30, 1935. Before the dissolution of the bloc, elections had been held. The new electoral law for the *sejm* restricted the nomination of candidates; and for the Senate only citizens with higher education or an officer's rank, teachers, and members of certain institutions were to be eligible. The opposition parties boycotted the elections. On Sept. 8, 1935, according to the official returns, 45.9% of the electorate cast their votes, the figure for Warsaw being only 29.4%. It was generally felt that the elections had been falsified.

Moscicki appointed a government headed by Marian Zyndram-Koscialkowski (1892–1946); and on May 15, 1936, after an understanding with Gen. Smigly-Rydz, he named a cabinet headed by Gen. Felicjan Slawoj-Skladkowski (1885–1962), which remained in office until September 1939. On July 15, 1936, there appeared a government circular which declared that Smigly-Rydz, "in keeping with the will of the President," was his first collaborator, to whom the government and state officials should give obedience. On Nov. 10, 1936, Smigly-Rydz was made a marshal.

In June 1936 the ruling groups called to life the Camp of National Unity (OZN). Slawek was ignored, but there were sharp differences between Moscicki and Smigly-Rydz. The presidential group tried to ease the opposition on the part of the Peasant Party. The head of the Camp, Col. Adam Koc (1891–1969), and Smigly-Rydz decided in 1937 to enter into an alliance with the right wing of the National Radical Camp. However, this alliance soon disintegrated.

In the years 1935–39 there was an improvement in the economic situation. Eugeniusz Kwiatkowski (1888–   ), minister of finance, implemented a policy of a moderate planned economy. By mid-1936 the government published a four-year investment plan. The main aim was to build a central industrial region in the Sandomierz area to work primarily for national defense. This caused some rise in employment, but the economic balance sheet in industrial and agricultural production was finally still unsatisfactory. In many branches of industry less was produced in 1938 than in 1913, though new industries had been developed; and agricultural production was stagnant. Implementation of the agrarian reform lagged far behind the timetable foreseen in the act of 1925.

7. Foreign Policy, 1926–39.—After the May *coup d'état* of 1926, Pilsudski influenced Poland's foreign policy. He suggested that August Zaleski (1883–   ) should be the foreign minister, and the latter kept this portfolio for more than six years. The Franco-Polish alliance was maintained, though some loosening of it resulted from repeated attempts, both from Berlin and from Paris, at a Franco-German reconciliation. In September 1926 Germany joined the League of Nations, with a permanent seat in its council. Poland demanded the same privilege, but obtained only a semipermanent seat. The Polish government tried without success to achieve a *détente* with Germany as well as to increase contacts with Great Britain. Poland signed the Kellogg-Briand Pact of July 24, 1929, considered as a sort of additional guarantee against German aggression.

Soviet-Polish relations became strained after Pilsudski's return to power, but a *détente* followed when on Feb. 9, 1929, Poland, Rumania, Latvia, and Estonia signed with the U.S.S.R. a protocol outlawing wars of aggression. On July 25, 1932, a five-year Polish-Soviet nonaggression treaty was signed; and in December 1934 it was prolonged for ten years. Zaleski resigned on Nov. 2, 1932, and was succeeded by Col. Jozef Beck, formerly Pilsudski's *chef de cabinet*. A Polish-German ten-year nonaggression treaty was concluded with Germany on Jan. 26, 1934. There was of course a reservation that the new treaty was not to affect Poland's previous engagements, particularly its alliance with France.

After Pilsudski's death (May 12, 1935) Beck continued his master's difficult policy of holding the balance between the U.S.S.R. and Germany. When on March 7, 1936, Hitler reoccupied the demilitarized zone of the Rhineland, violating the treaties of Versailles and of Locarno, Poland assured France that it was ready to fulfill the duty of an ally. During the critical year 1938 Poland twice declared its readiness to use force to settle local disputes: on March 17 it demanded and obtained from Lithuania the establishment of normal diplomatic relations (*see* LITHUANIA: *History*); and on Sept. 30 it demanded and obtained from Czechoslovakia the cession of that section of the Czech part of Teschen Silesia in which Polish population remained predominant (*see* above).

From October 1938, Germany increased its political pressure on Poland, demanding consent to the annexation of the Free City of Gdansk to the *Reich* and the construction of exterritorial highways between the *Reich* and East Prussia across Poland. Regarding these demands as the first step toward the subjugation of Poland to Germany, the Polish government rejected them. On March 31, 1939, Neville Chamberlain, the British prime minister, speaking also on behalf of France, announced that Poland would receive help if its independence were threatened. Beck went to London and after talks with him Chamberlain said on April 6 that Poland and Great Britain would conclude a treaty of mutual assistance. During the talks Beck gave the assurance that the Polish government treated the pledge of mutual assistance as a bilateral one. On April 28 Hitler abrogated the nonaggression treaty with Poland. The Germans started organizing provoking incidents in Gdansk and on the Polish-German frontier.

The military negotiations between Great Britain, France, and the U.S.S.R. in Moscow in August were broken off when Poland rejected the proposal that Soviet troops should march across its territory in the event of a conflict with Germany. On Aug. 23, in Moscow, Joachim von Ribbentrop, the German foreign minister, and V. M. Molotov, the Soviet people's commissar for foreign affairs, signed a nonaggression treaty. A secret protocol provided, in the event of "a territorial and political transformation of the territories belonging to the Polish state," for mutual respect of the spheres of interest bordered by the Pisa-Narew-Vistula-San line. On Aug. 25 a Polish-British treaty of alliance was signed in London.

G. POLAND DURING WORLD WAR II

On Sept. 1, 1939, without declaration of war, German troops marched into Poland from the north, the west, and the south. Two days later, Great Britain and France declared war on Germany. The Polish forces, weaker numerically and technically, were overcome by the German superiority of arms in spite of fierce resistance. By mid-September the main Polish forces were smashed, Warsaw was surrounded, and German troops were occupying Bialystok and Brest and approaching Lwow (Lvov). On Sept. 17 Soviet troops crossed the eastern Polish border without encountering any notable resistance. Pres. Moscicki, the commander in chief, Marshal Smigly-Rydz and the government, who had left the capital on Sept. 6 and 7, entered Rumania, where they were interned. Encircled Warsaw, bombed from the air and bombarded by artillery, surrendered on Sept. 27 after heroic resistance by the army, backed by the civilian population. The Polish campaign was ended on Oct. 5, when the group of Gen. Franciszek Kleeberg (1888–1941) capitulated near Kock, southeast of Warsaw.

In a protocol signed in Moscow on Sept. 28, 1939, Ribbentrop and Molotov established a new border between the Soviet and German spheres of interests. On the territory which had hitherto belonged to the Polish state it ran along the San and Bug rivers, and then westward of Bialystok. The Germans annexed to the *Reich* that part of the occupied territories which included Poznan, Gdynia, Bydgoszcz, Katowice, Lodz, and Plock, while the rest was set up as a *General-Gouvernement* with four districts—Cracow, Warsaw, Lublin, and Radom. The governor-general, Hans Frank, resided in Cracow. About 1,000,000 Poles and Jews were deported from the annexed territories, primarily into the *General-Gouvernement*. Part of the population was deported to Germany to do forced labour or concentrated in special "reserves." With the Jews, mainly townspeople were deported. The Polish population which was left, chiefly in Pomorze and Silesia, was subjected to a policy of germanization. At the same time the lands annexed to the *Reich* were settled by more than 700,000 Germans.

In the *General-Gouvernement* the administration was in German hands. Polish secondary schools and institutions of higher learning were closed. The teaching of Polish history and the history of Polish literature in primary schools was forbidden. However, clandestine education was conducted at all levels. From the very first days of the occupation persecution of the Poles began. On Dec. 27, 1939, there was a mass execution of civilians at Wawer near Warsaw. In November 1939 several dozen professors of the University of Cracow were sent to concentration camps, where some of them died. In June 1940 prominent political leaders—among them Rataj and the Socialist leader Mieczyslaw Niedzialkowski (b. 1893)—were shot; and the infamous concentration camp was set up at Oswiecim (Auschwitz). Other camps were also established.

The area occupied by the U.S.S.R. was annexed to Soviet Belorussia and the Ukraine; the territories bordering on Lithuania, including Wilno (Vilnius), were transferred to it, but on Aug. 3, 1940, Lithuania was declared a constituent republic of the U.S.S.R. Mass deportations carried Poles deep into the U.S.S.R., often at random, though in principle these measures were to involve persons suspected of political activity and employees of the former Polish administration. Some Polish professors, however, were allowed to lecture at institutes of higher learning.

After the German invasion of the U.S.S.R., Eastern Galicia was joined to the *General-Gouvernement*. The Bialystok region was incorporated into the *Reich*. The remaining eastern provinces which had belonged to Poland until 1939 were later incorporated into the *Reichskommissariat Ukraine* and *Reichskommissariat Ost*. Immediately upon entering these provinces the Germans began to persecute Poles and Jews there, and in this they received support from Ukrainian nationalist organizations. In Lwow, 21 professors of the university and the higher school of engineering were shot in July 1941.

It is estimated that the death of more than 6,000,000 persons was caused by the Germans within the 1939 Polish frontiers. More than 600,000 died directly as the result of military operations, including about 500,000 civilians. Of the persons murdered 3,200,000 were Jews. As early as October 1939 the Germans began to organize walled ghettos for the Jews in the towns. From autumn 1941 to autumn 1943 nearly the entire Jewish population was transported to death camps. In the face of the danger of extermination, the Warsaw ghetto on April 19, 1943, took to arms, and this rising was suppressed only after three weeks of bitter fighting. Jews from Poland were taken to be exterminated at Oswiecim-Brzezinka, Majdanek, Chelmno, Treblinka, Belzec, and other camps. Poles were sent to camps at Oswiecim-Brzezinka, Majdanek, Ravensbrück, Sachsenhausen, Dachau, Stutthof, and elsewhere. About 200,000 Polish children from 6 to 10 years of age, who were classified as "racially valuable," were sent to the *Reich* and subjected to germanization. Approximately 2,500,000 Poles were taken to Germany for forced labour.

After the campaign of 1939, a Polish government in exile was set up in France. Pres. Moscicki, interned in Rumania, appointed Wladyslaw Raczkiewicz (1885–1947) as his successor. Gen. Sikorski became commander in chief of the Polish Army formed in France out of wartime refugees from Poland and other Poles abroad. He also became prime minister of the government, which represented all political parties and allowed greater influence than before to the prewar opposition. The Polish Army in France amounted to about 85,000 men. One brigade took part in the Battle of Narvik during the Norwegian campaign, two divisions fought in Champagne and Lorraine during the French campaign of 1940. After the fall of France, the Polish government and about 20,000 soldiers managed to get to Great Britain. Polish airmen took part in the Battle of Britain. A Polish brigade which came into being in Syria in 1940 passed to Palestine after the capitulation of France. In 1941 it took part in the fighting in Egypt and Libya, including the defense of Tobruk.

The Polish underground resistance movement began to take shape immediately after the defeat in 1939. On Sept. 27 the Victory of Poland Service came into being, and in January 1940 it was transformed into the Union for Armed Struggle. Political parties began illegal activities. In August 1940 a delegate of the London government in exile was appointed in Poland. The resistance movement soon began sabotage and subversive activities.

Shortly after the German attack on the U.S.S.R., a Polish-Soviet agreement for cooperation during the war and for the creation of a Polish Army in the U.S.S.R. was signed in London on July 30, 1941. The Soviet government declared that the Soviet-German agreements of 1939 dealing with territorial changes in Poland were no longer valid. On Aug. 14, 1941, a Polish-Soviet military convention was signed in Moscow, and the organization of an army started under the command of Gen. Wladyslaw Anders (*q.v.*). On Dec. 4, 1941, in Moscow, Sikorski and Stalin signed a declaration on the participation of the Polish Army in the fighting on the eastern front. (J. HR.)

The Katyn Massacre.—The Polish Army was to consist of seven divisions, not a difficult number to make up since, as a result of Soviet intervention in September 1939, there were 9,361 officers and 181,223 other ranks interned in the U.S.S.R. as prisoners of war. The officers were confined in three camps, at Kozelsk, Starobelsk, and Ostashkov, together with some 6,000 members of the Polish intelligentsia. Great was Anders' surprise and anxiety when he was informed by the Soviet authorities that he could count on only 448 officers collected at Gryazovets in April 1940 at the time of breaking up of the three camps. When Sikorski asked Stalin in Moscow on Dec. 3, 1941, where the missing officers were, Stalin replied that they had escaped to Manchuria. During 1942, as a result of an agreement between Churchill and Stalin, 75,000 Polish soldiers were evacuated from the U.S.S.R. to the Middle East. On April 13, 1943, the Germans announced the discovery in the Katyn Forest of mass graves of Polish officers.

The names published by the Germans were those of Kozelsk inmates; the most recent entries in their diaries dated from April 1940. What had happened to those detained at Starobelsk and Ostashkov remained a mystery. On April 15 the Soviet government alleged that Polish prisoners of war who in 1941 were engaged in construction work west of Smolensk had been executed by the Germans. On April 17 the Polish government asked the International Committee of the Red Cross to examine the situation on the spot. On April 25 the Soviet government, accusing the Polish government of contact and accord with Hitler, severed diplomatic relations with them. (K. SM.)

On July 4, 1943, Sikorski died in an aircraft crash near Gibraltar. The new prime minister was Stanislaw Mikolajczyk (1901–66), leader of the Peasant Party, and the new commander in chief was Gen. Kazimierz Sosnkowski (1885–1969). The Polish Army that had been evacuated from the U.S.S.R. was re-formed in Iraq and Palestine; and as the II Corps it took part in the fighting in Italy from May 1944. A Polish Armoured Division in Great Britain (under Gen. Stanislaw Maczek [1892–   ]) participated from August 1944 in the fighting on the western front, including the Battle of Falaise. A Polish parachute brigade (under Gen. S. Sosabowski [1892–1967]) took part in the Arnhem operation.

On the Soviet government's severance of diplomatic relations with the Polish government in London, the Union of Polish Patriots, led by the Communists Wanda Wasilewska (1905–64) and Alfred Lampe (1900–43), came into being in the U.S.S.R. at the end of April 1943. The formation of a Polish division began under the command of Gen. Zygmunt Berling (1896–   ), formerly chief of staff of 5th Division in the Anders Army. This division was transformed into an army corps in August 1943 and into the 1st Polish Army in March 1944. In October 1943 the 1st Polish Division distinguished itself in fighting at Lenino, near Mogilev.

The rupture between the Soviet government and the Polish government in London brought up the question of the future Polish-Soviet frontier, which had not been raised officially before. At the Teheran conference (Nov. 28–Dec. 1, 1943) Franklin D. Roosevelt, Winston Churchill, and Stalin began to concert the views of the Allied Powers on this matter. On Feb. 2, 1944, in the House of Commons, Churchill spoke in favour of transferring the lands east of the Curzon line (*see* above) to the U.S.S.R. and of compensating Poland with territory in the west and the north.

The London government's delegate in Poland, Jan S. Jankowski (1882–1953) on April 26, 1944, was appointed deputy premier of that government. Three other ministers were appointed, and together with Jankowski they constituted the Home Council of Ministers, which had the Council of National Unity, representing all political parties, as its advisory body. The Union for Armed Struggle became the Home Army under the command of Gen. Stefan Rowecki (1895–1944), known as Grot, on Feb. 14, 1942, and under that of Gen. Tadeusz Komorowski (1895–1966), known as Bor, after Rowecki's arrest. The armed organizations of parties associated with the London government, which previously had been independent, also joined the Home Army.

In January 1942 Polish Communists founded the Polish Workers' Party (Polska Partia Robotnicza or PPR), which undertook a political struggle against Germany. The successive secretaries-general of the PPR were Marceli Nowotko (1893–1942), Pawel Finder (1904–44) until his arrest in November 1943, and finally, Wladyslaw Gomulka (*q.v.*). In May 1942 the People's Guard, the military organization of the PPR, began action. The People's Guard, and in its footsteps the Home Army, developed more and more intensive guerrilla warfare against the Germans from mid-1942 and especially from spring 1943. On Jan. 1, 1944, on the initiative of the PPR, the National Home Council came into being under the chairmanship of Boleslaw Bierut (1892–1956) and with the participation of the left-wing Socialists and some leaders of the Peasant and Democratic parties. At the same time the People's Army was organized under the command of Gen. Michal Zymierski (1890–   ), known as Rola. Its core consisted of the previous People's Guard.

When the Soviet Army, with the Polish Army formed in the U.S.S.R., crossed the Curzon line on July 21, 1944, the Polish

Committee of National Liberation (PCNL) was established; and when the Germans were driven out of Lublin, that city became its seat. In a manifesto on July 22 the PCNL declared itself the sole legal Polish executive power and proclaimed that the constitution of 1921 was in force. It called for a continued struggle against Germany in alliance with the U.S.S.R., for settlement of the Polish-Soviet frontier according to the principle of nationality, and for a westward realignment of the Polish-German frontier. The committee announced the restoration of democratic rights, agrarian reform, and the introduction of provisional state administration of heavy industry. On July 22 a decree united the Polish Army in the U.S.S.R. and the People's Army into a single force.

On Aug. 1, 1944, the Home Army began a rising in Warsaw in an effort to take over the city before the Soviet Army could occupy it. However—either as a political maneuver or because of German resistance (an issue still debated)—the Russians failed to relieve the Polish home army. The insurgents found themselves in a disastrous situation. The Germans gradually reconquered the city, bombarding it from the air and by artillery fire. The insurgents and the civilian population were murdered or deported to concentration camps or to forced labour in the *Reich*. After a heroic resistance of more than two months Warsaw capitulated on Oct. 2. The insurgents, with their commander in chief, were taken prisoners; the entire population of the city was evacuated and the city itself almost totally gutted by fire.

Mikolajczyk visited Moscow early in August 1944, but his negotiations with Stalin and with the PCNL did not lead to any understanding; equally inconclusive were the negotiations during Mikolajczyk's next visit in October, when Churchill was in Moscow. On Nov. 24 Mikolajczyk resigned and a new London government was formed by an opponent of negotiation, Tomasz Arciszewski (1877–1955), a senior Socialist leader who until July 1944 was the chairman of the underground Council of National Unity in Warsaw.

H. THE PEOPLE'S REPUBLIC

Poland came out of World War II with enormous losses of population, industry smashed, and agriculture devastated. Warsaw had almost ceased to exist. The people were divided between rival political camps. A consolidating bond, however, was the hatred felt for the Germans. There was general approval for the battles fought by the Polish forces in the final stages of the war, first on lands to be incorporated into Poland, later in Germany proper till Berlin was captured. In these final stages, two Polish armies of about 150,000 men fought alongside the Soviet forces.

The PCNL was composed of Communists, left-wing Socialists, left-wing Peasant leaders, and representatives of the Democratic Party. It was headed by the left-wing Socialist, Edward Osobka-Morawski (1909–). The National Home Council functioned as the provisional Parliament. On Dec. 31, 1944, the PCNL was transformed into a provisional government. The decisive role was played by the PPR, led by Gomulka who became deputy premier. After the winter offensive by the Soviet forces the provisional government took control of all of Poland in the early months of 1945. Political groups connected with the government in London remained partly underground; some took up arms. Gen. Leopold Okulicki (1898–1946), who had succeeded Komorowski as commander in chief of the Home Army, Jankowski, and their ten colleagues were arrested on March 20, 1945, by the Soviet military authorities on charges of conducting armed action against them. They were tried in Moscow on June 21: Okulicki was sentenced to ten years' imprisonment, Jankowski to eight, the others to terms varying from five years to four months.

1. The Provisional Government of National Unity.—At the Yalta conference in February 1945, Roosevelt, Churchill, and Stalin decided that a new "Polish Provisional Government of National Unity" should be formed, based on the existing provisional government (which on Feb. 1 had moved from Lublin to Warsaw), but also including "other Polish democratic leaders from Poland and from abroad"; then democratic elections to the *sejm* should be held as soon as possible. Only a small part of the Polish émigré leaders took part in the roundtable conference which began in

Moscow on June 17. On June 28 a Provisional Government of National Unity was formed with 16 ministers from the old provisional government and five new ones, with Osobka-Morawski as premier and Gomulka and Mikolajczyk as deputy premiers. In the reorganized presidium of the National Home Council, Bierut remained president, and Wincenty Witos (who died shortly after) and Stanislaw Grabski became vice-presidents. On July 5 the new government was recognized by the United States and Great Britain, who withdrew their recognition from the London government. However, this government tried to continue its activities.

2. The New Frontiers.—In February 1945, at Yalta, the Allied Powers established in principle Poland's eastern frontier more or less identical with the Curzon line. On Aug. 16, 1945, in Moscow, Poland and the U.S.S.R. signed a treaty demarcating the new Polish-Soviet frontier. The overwhelming proportion of the Polish population on Soviet territory moved to Poland. Small changes in the Polish-Soviet frontier were made on Feb. 15, 1951.

On Aug. 2, 1945, in Potsdam, U.S. Pres. Harry S. Truman, Clement Attlee, and Stalin issued a declaration establishing a new *de facto* western frontier of Poland along the Oder and Lusatian Neisse rivers. Poland took over the administration of lands previously held by Germany to the east of this line, with the exception of the northern part of East Prussia, which was incorporated in the U.S.S.R. Gdansk was also turned over to Poland. Like Czechoslovakia and Hungary, Poland was authorized by the Potsdam conference to transfer the German population to Germany (for details *see* GERMANY: *History: Germany After World War II, 1945–49*). On July 6, 1950, the Oder-Neisse frontier was recognized as final in a treaty signed in Zgorzelec (Görlitz) by the German Democratic Republic and Poland. The Polish-Czechoslovakian frontier was identical with that of July 28, 1920; in other words, the disputed territories taken by Poland in 1938 were restored to Czechoslovakia. Poland's territory was reduced in the east by 69,290 sq.mi. (179,460 sq.km.), and increased in the west and north by 39,597 sq.mi. (102,556 sq.km.), the new area amounting in all to 120,359 sq.mi. (311,730 sq.km.).

3. Social and Economic Reforms.—The PCNL undertook fundamental social reforms. The major industrial establishments which had been under German management during the war were put under Polish state management. On Sept. 6, 1944, the committee issued a decree on land reform, which was implemented immediately in the territory under the committee's power and subsequently by the government for the rest of Poland. Farms of more than 123.5 ac. (50 ha.) of arable land and farms of more than 247 ac. (100 ha.) overall size were subject to expropriation without compensation. Former German farms and farms left by Ukrainians who were repatriated to the U.S.S.R. were taken over for the agrarian reform as well. Peasants, chiefly smallholders, and agricultural workers received 5,891,000 ac. (2,384,100 ha.) in the old Polish territories and 9,107,000 ac. (3,685,600 ha.) in the new ones. Forests were nationalized, and part of the arable land of the former private estates became state farms. On Jan. 3, 1946, the National Home Council passed a bill nationalizing those industrial establishments which employed more than 50 workers per shift and all former German property. The settling of the new western and northern territories, partly with Polish people from prewar eastern territories, started immediately after the war. The reconstruction of Warsaw began.

On Nov. 10, 1945, the Central Planning Office was set up; it was transformed into the State Planning Commission in 1949 and into the Planning Commission of the Council of Ministers in 1956. On Sept. 22, 1946, the National Home Council promulgated a three-year plan for economic reconstruction (1947–49).

4. Internal Affairs, 1945–48.—The Provisional Government of National Unity consisted of representatives of all legally authorized political parties. In addition to the Polish Workers' Party (PPR), the Polish Socialist Party (PPS, with some Socialists who had previously collaborated with the London government), the Peasant Party, and the Democratic Party, there were also the new Polish Peasant Party (PSL) led by Mikolajczyk and the Christian-Democratic Labour Party. While remaining in the government, the PSL enjoyed the support of all the legal and illegal opposition forces. On Aug. 2, 1945, the government issued a decree of amnesty for all members of illegal military and political organizations. More than 44,000 persons took advantage of this amnesty. However, some members of the illegal organizations remained in the underground, concentrated chiefly around the Association for Freedom and Independence, set up in place of the Home Army. The illegal groups, with a membership of about 22,000, carried on propaganda activities and some terrorist activities as well. Apart from these, there were nationalist Ukrainian groups with about 6,000 members.

The Democratic bloc, consisting of the PPR, the PPS, the Peasant Party and the Democratic Party, favoured close cooperation with the U.S.S.R. and the introduction of a socialist system. The PSL gravitated toward the Western Powers and the retention of the capitalist system, though officially it supported the land reform and nationalization of industry as envisaged by the decisions of 1944 and 1946.

Elections to the *sejm* took place on Jan. 19, 1947. The PPR and the three parties allied with it came out with a joint list for the Democratic bloc. The only opponent of the bloc was the PSL. The official returns were that 80.1% of the votes were cast for the bloc. On Feb. 5, the new *sejm* elected Bierut president of the republic. The new government was headed by Jozef Cyrankiewicz (1911–) of the PPS, Gomulka becoming deputy premier. On Feb. 19 the *sejm* passed the so-called "Small Constitution." Backed by the Democratic bloc, opposition to Mikolajczyk within the PSL increased; and on Oct. 21, 1947, he fled to England.

5. The Eclipse of Gomulka, 1948–55.—In the first months of 1948 preparations began for the unification of the PPR and the PPS. These preparations ran into opposition on the part of the Socialists who wanted to maintain the independence of their party and had hitherto treated cooperation with the PPR as a necessity. They were also distrustful of the Soviet system of government. Gomulka emphasized the necessity of the political link with the U.S.S.R., but also the need of independent internal policy. He accepted the formation of the Communist Information Bureau, known as Cominform (*see* COMMUNISM), in September 1947 with reservations, but in 1948 he opposed the condemnation of Yugoslavia and the beginning of the collectivization of agriculture in Poland. Gomulka was removed from the post of secretary-general of the PPR, and on Sept. 3, 1948, his place was taken by Bierut. The Cominform's recommendations were accepted in full and a purge took place in the PPS. On Dec. 15, 1948, the PPR and the PPS merged into the Polish United Workers' Party (*Polska Zjednoczona Partia Robotnicza* or PZPR) led by Bierut.

The merger Congress adopted the basic economic premises of the 1950–55 six-year plan which was later approved by the *sejm*. The plan provided for the rapid industrialization of the country, especially the extension of heavy industry. During these six years the economic reconstruction of formerly German lands east of the Oder-Neisse line was in principle completed. The rapid industrialization, however, took place in part at the expense of a reduction in the standard of living: rises in wages and salaries did not compensate for the rises in prices for some groups of working people. On Oct. 28, 1950, a drastic currency revaluation was introduced: savings accounts and all bank deposits up to 100,000 zlotys were revalued at the ratio of 100 to 3; wages and prices were reduced at the same ratio; but all deposits over 100,-000 zlotys were exchanged at the rate of 100:1. In the countryside collectivization under administrative pressure yielded small results: by the end of 1953 there were about 8,000 producers' cooperatives owning 9% of arable land, and agricultural production was stagnant. The one-sided expansion of heavy industry and the situation in agriculture led to an undermining of the market equilibrium, most markedly in the years 1951–53.

Within the ruling PZPR the main decisions were made by a political bureau of about a dozen persons. In addition to Bierut the greatest influence was wielded in the bureau by Jakub Berman (1906–) and Hilary Minc (1905–). Gomulka and his closest friends, Gen. Marian Spychalski (1906–) and Zenon Kliszko (1908–), were removed from the bureau in November 1949; and

UPI COMPIX

FIRST SECRETARY OF THE POLISH COMMUNIST PARTY WLADYSLAW GOMULKA (RIGHT) FACES SOVIET PARTY CHIEF NIKITA KHRUSHCHEV (LEFT) ACROSS THE CONFERENCE TABLE AT MEETING IN MOSCOW, NOV. 15, 1956, TO DISCUSS ANTI-SOVIET UPRISING IN POLAND. OTHER PARTY LEADERS REPRESENT POLAND (RIGHT) AND THE U.S.S.R. (LEFT)

in July 1951 they were arrested. Marshal Zymierski, the minister of national defense, resigned on Nov. 6, 1949, and was replaced by a Polish-born Soviet marshal, Konstanty Rokossowski (1896–1968), who on May 8, 1950, was co-opted to the political bureau of the PZPR. In addition to Communists suspected of the "rightist-nationalist deviations," a considerable number of non-Communist political leaders and senior military men were arrested and sometimes tortured. Several political trials were staged. The other political groupings outside of the PZPR did not play any noteworthy role in political life. On Nov. 29, 1949, the peasant parties combined into the United Peasant Party. The Christian-Democratic Labour Party was dissolved in July 1950, some of its members going into the Democratic Party. The "Pax" association, which cooperated with the three parties, comprised Catholic activists with a right-wing political past; it was sharply opposed by the Catholic Church hierarchy. Relations between the hierarchy and the government were tense and on Sept. 27, 1953, Stefan Cardinal Wyszynski (1901–), the primate of Poland, was interned. On Dec. 17, 1953, the bishops took an oath of loyalty to the Polish state.

On July 22, 1952, the *sejm* passed a new, Soviet-type constitution. The president of the republic was replaced by the Council of State, of which Aleksander Zawadzki (1899–1964) became chairman. The new government was formed by Bierut, but on March 19, 1954, he resigned to become first secretary of the PZPR. Cyrankiewicz was again appointed premier. Stalin's death, however, led to changes in Polish political life. The turning point came after the 20th congress of the Communist Party of the Soviet Union and the report delivered on Feb. 25, 1956, by Nikita S. Khrushchev.   (J. HR.; A. WY.; X.)

6. Gomulka's Return and Fall.—The year 1956 was one of great upheaval, which some described as a successful bloodless revolution. Khrushchev's denunciation of Stalin's crimes fell on the PZPR leadership like a thunderbolt. Some of the Polish Stalinists, or Moscovites, so-called because they had nearly all stayed in the U.S.S.R. during World War II, had indeed sensed the coming termination of their power two years earlier when Jozef Swiatlo, a former high official of the Ministry of State Security, fled to the West in December 1953 and began broadcasting to Poland in September 1954. He made sensational disclosures about the inhumanity of the Polish political police and about the luxury of party leaders' private lives. This campaign brought results: not only were some officials of the political police arrested and sentenced "for using forbidden methods of investigation," but numbers of innocent people were released from prisons and labour camps. And, just before Khrushchev's speech in Moscow, the erstwhile Communist Party of Poland—the KPP, founded in December 1918 and dissolved by the Executive Committee of the Comintern in 1938—was formally rehabilitated.

News followed from Moscow that Bierut, head of the ruling Polish triumvirate, had died there on March 12, 1956. No member of the Political Bureau had any real prestige, but on March 20 the party's Central Committee elected Edward Ochab (1906–) as its first secretary, with the concurrence of Khrushchev, who came to Warsaw for the occasion and who considered that Ochab would be able to control the process of "liberalization."

Already in September 1954 Gomulka had been secretly released from prison on Beirut's order. On April 6, 1956, Ochab announced Gomulka's rehabilitation, while still condemning his nationalist views. Soon, however, Ochab and Cyrankiewicz realized that the mood of the Polish people was such that something more drastic than restoring Gomulka's political respectability—or dismissing Berman, another member of the triumvirate, from the Political Bureau (May 6)—was necessary to appease the workers, the peasants, and the intelligentsia. While they hesitated, an event of historic significance overtook them on June 28. Industrial workers in Poznan staged a general strike, and a procession 50,000 strong demanded bread and freedom. Riots followed in which a security police officer was lynched. Cyrankiewicz denounced the rioters as instigated by an imperialist plot, and the following day Rokossowski ordered the local commander to quell the revolt by force: 53 people were killed and about 200 wounded.

Addressing the Central Committee on July 18 Ochab admitted that the authorities' lack of understanding and not imperialist agents' plotting was the chief cause of the revolt. In the contest that followed three trends were apparent: the Stalinist group recommended strict censorship of the press and the curtailment of liberalization; they were opposed by those reformed Moscovites who now wanted the thaw to continue; between these two groups stood the realists led by Ochab and Cyrankiewicz who supported change, but sought to achieve it without provoking a Soviet reaction. They also came to the conclusion that Gomulka was the only man who could restore party unity and authority. On Aug. 4 the former first secretary was readmitted to the party. On Oct. 9 Minc, his chief accuser and the last of the triumvirate, was dismissed from the Political Bureau.

On Oct. 19, when the Central Committee assembled to elect a new Political Bureau, Khrushchev, accompanied by Marshal Ivan Konev, commander in chief of the armed forces of the Warsaw Treaty powers, arrived in Warsaw unexpectedly. At the same time Soviet divisions stationed in Silesia were marching on Warsaw, allegedly on maneuvers. Having co-opted Gomulka as a member, the Central Committee decided that the old Political Bureau—but with Gomulka—would discuss Polish-Soviet relations with the Soviet guests. The meeting, which was held in the Belweder Palace on the night of Oct. 19–20, was stormy. Brave words were pronounced by Gomulka and his supporters, and they

succeeded in convincing Khrushchev that they wished to keep Poland within the Socialist camp, but as an equal and sovereign member. Reassured that the return of Gomulka to power would not mean an estrangement in Soviet-Polish relations, Khrushchev returned to Moscow. On Oct. 21 the Central Committee elected a new Political Bureau and Gomulka as its first secretary.

In a speech broadcast to the nation, Gomulka acknowledged that the working class of Poznan had given a lesson to the party's leadership. He promised workers' participation in the management of industrial enterprises, announced the end of compulsory collectivization of agriculture, and reiterated his belief that there were many roads to socialism. On Nov. 13 General Spychalski (created marshal on Oct. 1, 1963) succeeded Rokossowski as minister of defense. Censorship became more liberal. Cardinal Wyszynski was released from internment and on Oct. 28 returned to Warsaw; by an agreement of Dec. 5 appointment of bishops according to canonical law was guaranteed.

On Jan. 20, 1957, a new *sejm* was elected. Although there was still only one list per constituency (but with three candidates for every two seats), nine-tenths of registered electors voted for Gomulka, who was then at the height of his popularity, in the hope that he would lead the country on a "Polish road to socialism"—a socialism with free elections. Such a course, however, was never contemplated by Gomulka, who had always believed in democratic centralism at home and in proletarian internationalism within the Socialist camp.

Except that he left more than four-fifths of the arable land in the peasants' hands, Gomulka went back on many of his October promises. He tightened press censorship, picked fresh quarrels with the Roman Catholic Church, and continued to impose economic plans and reforms which the workers resented as measures of exploitation.

By 1967 criticism of Gomulka within and especially outside the PZPR had become general. Inside the party two significant groups were noticeable: the Partisans and the Technocrats. The former were led by Mieczyslaw Moczar (1913–), minister of the interior since December 1964. During World War II the Partisans of the People's Army had been a minority as compared with the huge Home Army; since the early 1960s, however, the Partisans had been able to achieve a measure of collaboration among all combatants who had fought the Germans on any front. For their part, the Technocrats comprised a loose assemblage of industrial administrators and technicians aiming to achieve efficient and profitable management of the national economy; they needed a political leader and saw one in Edward Gierek (1913–), a mining engineer, who from March 1957 was first secretary of the PZPR in the highly industrialized Katowice *wojewodztwo* and from March 1959 was a member of the party's Political Bureau.

In order to distract from the criticism emanating from these two groupings, Gomulka, in June 1967, attacked the "Zionist circles" of Polish Jews who had applauded Israeli "aggression" against the Arabs. A more violent campaign against Zionists flared up in the spring of 1968. It began as a result of the student demonstration protesting against the suspension of a 19th-century play containing a few anti-tsarist lines which had become the occasion for expressing of anti-Soviet feelings. The government expelled from Warsaw University two alleged ringleaders, the sons of prominent party members of Jewish origin, as being under revisionist influence, and a protest meeting of 4,000 students was dispersed by militia. The protest movement spread to other cities, and subsequently about 1,800 students were arrested, many being drafted into the Army and some receiving short prison sentences. Gomulka tried to stem the tide and in a speech to the Central Committee (July 9) said that the anti-Zionist campaign had gone out of hand and that revisionism should be unmasked, not dressed up in the name of Zionism; he added that those Jews who wished to leave Poland could do so, and some Jews made use of this opportunity.

At the fifth congress of the PZPR, held in Warsaw in November 1968, the Partisan-Technocrat alliance failed to dislodge Gomulka. Leonid Brezhnev, general secretary of the Soviet party, was present at the congress and did not conceal his preference. Moczar

TANKS FILE PAST REVIEWING STAND IN PARADE SQUARE, WARSAW, JULY 22, 1966, DURING MILITARY CELEBRATIONS OF 1,000TH ANNIVERSARY OF THE FOUNDING OF POLAND

ceased to be minister of the interior and became a candidate member of the Political Bureau, while disappointed Gierek returned to Katowice. The attempt to oust Gomulka was put off to another occasion.

Gomulka himself provided the occasion, following the adoption (May 1970) by the Central Committee of the new five-year plan for 1971–75, the aim of which was to close the wasteful era of extensive growth and to begin a period of intensive growth, with a complex system of economic incentives related to technological progress. When the functioning of the plan was explained to the workers they saw that during the coming five years there was no hope of obtaining any appreciable increase in wages. To cap this, on Dec. 12, Gomulka ordered price increases from 10 to 30% on 46 items of basic foodstuffs, fuel, and clothing. On Dec. 14 the workers from the Gdansk shipyards went on strike and held protest meetings against the price increases. Gomulka proposed to use the Army in what he considered to be a counterrevolutionary situation, but Gen. Wojciech Jaruzelski (1923–), minister of defense since April 1968, refused to act. The workers from the shipyards in Gdynia and Szczecin joined the strike movement, while antisocial elements started looting shops. On Dec. 17 the militia was ordered to use firearms, street fighting resulted, in which at least 45 persons were killed and 1,165 injured, and buildings were destroyed by fire. Brought back to power as a result of bloodshed in Poznan 14 years earlier, Gomulka was now forced to quit the political scene after an even bloodier tragedy.

7. Gierek in Power.—On Dec. 20 at a dramatic session of the Central Committee in Warsaw, Gomulka, Spychalski (chairman of the Council of State from April 1968), Kliszko, and two other members resigned from the 12-man Political Bureau. They were replaced by Moczar, Piotr Jaroszewicz (1909–), deputy premier from 1952, and three other younger members of the Central Committee, while General Jaruzelski was elected candidate member of the Political Bureau. Gierek, elected first secretary of the PZPR, declared in a broadcast to the Polish people that he would abandon ill-conceived past economic policies and revise the 1971–75 plan in consultation with the workers. On Dec. 23 Cyrankiewicz resigned from the premiership and was elected chairman of the State Council by the *sejm*. On the same day Jaroszewicz was elected as the new head of government, while Gierek announced that the government would appropriate 7,000,000,000 zlotys to make it possible to raise the lowest wages and pensions. Another meeting of the Central Committee was held on Feb. 6–7, 1971, at which Gierek, in his first major speech, presented a candid analysis of the December drama. Gomulka, because of his "serious mistakes," was suspended as a member of the Central Committee, and two more members of the Political Bureau resigned. Following the strike of 10,000 cotton workers in Lodz, Jaroszewicz announced on Feb. 15 that foodstuffs prices would revert on March 1 to their previous lower level, while price reductions of industrial consumer goods, introduced on Dec. 12, would remain in effect. These economic decisions, as well as many personal changes at party and government levels, introduced a spirit of confidence between the leadership and the people.

8. Foreign Policy from October 1956.—In his first public speech Gierek said that there would be no change in foreign policy. In this domain nobody disputed Gomulka's achievements. He reinforced Poland's security by improving the working of the Polish-Soviet alliance as early as November 1956. His foreign minister, Adam Rapacki (1909–70), proposed in 1958 that in a zone comprising Poland, Czechoslovakia, and the two German republics no nuclear weapons should be manufactured or stockpiled, and in December 1964, speaking at the General Assembly of the United Nations, launched the idea of a European security conference with the participation of the U.S.S.R. and the U.S.

The establishment of normal and friendly relations with the German Federal Republic on the basis of the existing territorial status quo was a constant aim of Poland's foreign policy, but until 1969 the response from Bonn had always been negative. When Brandt became the head of the new West German government he announced in the *Bundestag* on Oct. 28, 1969, that he would propose to the Polish government the opening of bilateral negotiations

on issues previously touched upon by Gomulka. These negotiations began on Feb. 5, 1970, and the resulting Polish-West German treaty was solemnly signed by Chancellor Brandt and Premier Cyrankiewicz in Warsaw on Dec. 7. In this document the West German government declared that the existing Oder-Neisse borderline, determined at Potsdam on Aug. 2, 1945, formed the western state frontier of Poland, and affirmed its inviolability. The U.S., British and French governments approved the Warsaw Treaty.

IV. POPULATION

The first census (1921) after the restoration of the Polish state revealed a total population of 27,176,717; the second (1931) a total of 32,107,252, and an official estimate for September 1939 put the total at 35,339,000 (excluding the Cieszyn disputed territory). Between World Wars I and II Poland was not a homogeneous national state. At the 1931 census just under one-third of the population gave their mother tongue as other than Polish.

Poland: Administrative Units

Province (wojewodztwo)	Area (sq.mi.)*	Population	
		(1960 census)	(1967 est.)
Warsaw (city)	172	1,139,189	1,283,000
Warsaw	11,340	2,314,930	2,483,000
Bialystok	8,937	1,090,231	1,177,000
Bydgoszcz	8,030	1,708,298	1,871,000
Cracow (city)	89	481,296	540,000
Cracow	5,927	1,990,359	2,159,000
Gdansk	4,239	1,222,769	1,393,000
Katowice	3,675	3,274,512	3,585,000
Kielce	7,517	1,815,667	1,910,000
Koszalin	6,940	687,915	774,000
Lodz (city)	82	709,698	750,000
Lodz	6,589	1,595,021	1,675,000
Lublin	9,586	1,801,304	1,920,000
Olsztyn	8,106	881,332	973,000
Opole	3,670	929,033	1,027,000
Poznan (city)	85	408,132	447,000
Poznan	10,318	1,992,758	2,159,000
Rzeszow	7,203	1,586,157	1,720,000
Szczecin	4,895	757,884	872,000
Wroclaw (city)	87	430,522	487,000
Wroclaw	7,269	1,806,310	1,994,000
Zielona Gora	5,604	782,332	866,000
Total	120,359	29,775,508	32,065,000

*1 sq.mi. = 2.59 sq.km.
Source: *Rocznik Statystyczny 1964* (369,779 people not included in the above mentioned administrative units) and *1968*.

No part of Europe was more profoundly affected by the great displacements of population that occurred in and immediately after World War II and for a few years afterward. Polish citizens were deported by both occupying powers during the German-Soviet partition and by the Germans over the whole of Poland after June 1941. Of Poland's 3,351,000 Jews (1939 est.) some 85% were murdered at Oświęcim (Auschwitz) and other extermination camps, and only about 100,000, hidden by Poles at risk of death, survived the German occupation. After the liberation of Poland by the Soviet armies the number of Jews in Poland increased probably to 500,000 by those who returned from the U.S.S.R., but the great majority of them emigrated later to Israel, to Western Europe, or to the U.S.

The territories annexed by the U.S.S.R. had in 1939 a population of 10,864,000; by June 1949, 1,503,800 persons of Polish nationality had been transferred from Soviet territory to the new Poland, while 518,200 Ukrainians, Belorussians, and Lithuanians had been moved from Poland to their respective Soviet republics. A smaller repatriation of Polish citizens from the U.S.S.R. took place between 1955 and 1959 when about 275,000 returned.

According to the German census of May 17, 1939, the population of the then German lands east of the Oder-Neisse line incorporated into Poland in 1945 amounted to 8,372,700. To this total must be added the German population of the Free City of Danzig (392,000 in 1939) and the German minority in the pre-1939 frontiers of Poland (741,000), but there must be subtracted 1,011,700 Poles living between the Versailles and Potsdam frontiers of Poland. Theoretically, the total number of Germans living within the frontiers of 1945 Poland was about 8,494,000. In fact, toward the end of 1944, they were more than 10,000,-000, because their number was increased by the repatriation of the Germans from the Baltic states, Bukovina, and Bessarabia (353,000); by the German personnel of the civil and military administration sent there after occupation (470,000); and by 725,000 evacuees from central and western German cities bombed by the British and U.S. Air Forces. The majority of those Germans fled westward before the advancing Soviet armies and in May 1945 only about 4,400,000 remained.

According to the census of February 1946 the population of Poland within its new frontiers was 23,929,757, including 2,288,300 Germans. By the end of 1948 a further 2,170,866 Germans had been repatriated from Poland to the Soviet, British, and U.S. zones of occupied Germany, while 2,266,000 Polish forced labourers, prisoners of war, and demobilized soldiers returned to Poland from Germany and from western Europe. The Polish census of December 1950 revealed a total population of 25,008,179; that of December 1960 a population of 29,775,508. The estimated population at the end of 1968 amounted to 32,400,000. It was overwhelmingly Polish, although small national minorities, which enjoyed cultural autonomy, were (1963 est.): Ukrainians 180,000; Belorussians 165,000; Jews 31,000; Slovaks 21,000; Russians 19,000; Lithuanians 10,000; Germans 3,000; Czechs 2,000; others (gypsies, Greeks, etc.) 22,000.

The natural increase in the years 1950–56 was on the average 19.1 per thousand; by 1968 it had fallen to 9.6 per thousand. In 1950 the female population constituted 52.3% of the total, but in 1960 this proportion fell to 51.6%. The density of population in 1960 was 247 per sq.mi. (236 in 1939), and approximately 49% of the people were classified as urban (27% in 1931). This increase in urban population does not reflect a steady growth of towns. Many towns, particularly Baltic and Silesian, suffered damage and population loss during World War II but most of them had regained their former size by the 1960s. Warsaw, for example, had a population of 937,000 in 1921, 1,289,000 in 1939, 479,000 in 1946, and 1,283,000 on Dec. 31, 1967 (est.).

Poles abroad are divided into two categories: the autochthonous Poles inhabiting alien territory contiguous with the political frontiers of Poland, and the emigrants or refugees. Between the two World Wars the largest groups of autochthonous Poles were in eastern Germany, their number being estimated in 1939 at more than 1,000,000. Nearly 1,220,000 lived in the Ukraine, Belorussia, Lithuania, Latvia, Rumania, and Czechoslovakia. The situation changed radically after World War II. According to the Soviet estimate for 1962 there were 1,430,000 Poles in the U.S.S.R., mainly in the Ukraine, in Belorussia, and in Lithuania. Poles in the German Federal Republic (mostly in the Ruhr basin) numbered about 132,000. Their number in Czechoslovakia (1961 census) was 84,500.

The largest number of emigrants from mid-19th century to 1939 settled in the United States. In the early 1960s, 6,372,000 Americans were estimated to be of Polish descent; and an additional 178,000 Poles had entered the U.S. between 1941 and 1962 as displaced persons, refugees, or immigrants. The 1940 census revealed that there were 2,416,320 persons in the United States whose mother tongue was Polish—the largest non-English-speaking group after the German and Italian speakers. According to the 1960 census 747,750 of the U.S. population were born in Poland. These loyal U.S. citizens were proud of their origin and maintained a strong interest in Polish culture through their own Polish-speaking educational and religious organizations. In the 1960s nearly 60 Polish periodicals appeared in the United States, including daily and weekly newspapers. Other groups of Polish emigrants in the 1960s included: 450,000 in Brazil, 324,000 in Canada, 120,000 in Argentina, and 100,000 in Australia. The largest group of emigrant Poles in Europe after World War I went to France, settling for the most part in the northern and eastern mining areas. In the early 1960s they numbered about 750,000, mostly French citizens. A Polish daily and a few Polish journals were published.

A significant change brought about by the political consequences of World War II was the establishment of a Polish colony in Great Britain. The majority of the 140,000 Poles in that country, including 46,000 naturalized British (1968), was constituted by former servicemen and their families. Many cultural, social, professional, and trade organizations were established. There were in the late 1960s one daily newspaper and more than 20 Polish periodicals published in Great Britain.

V. ADMINISTRATION AND SOCIAL CONDITIONS

1. Constitution and Government.—The first constitution after the restoration of the Polish state, promulgated in March 1921, was modeled on the French system. The first *sejm,* or Chamber of Deputies, elected under a system of proportional representation, contained 16 parliamentary groups, four of which represented national minorities. A new constitution promulgated in April 1935 increased the power of the president of the republic, but the *sejm* fixed the budget and had the right to demand the resignation of the government. Under art. 24, in time of war the president had the right to appoint his successor.

After World War II the Warsaw provisional government promulgated (in February 1947) a temporary constitutional act which was formally democratic but never became effective, and a new constitution was passed by the *sejm* in July 1952. Under this the supreme organ of state authority was the Council of State (*Rada Stanu*), composed of a chairman, 4 deputy chairmen, secretary, and 11 members. The supreme organ of state administration was the Council of Ministers appointed by and responsible to the *sejm,* or to the Council of State if the *sejm* were not in session. The electoral law adopted by the *sejm* in August 1952 accorded the franchise to all citizens of 18 years, including members of the armed forces; citizens of 21 years were eligible for election to the *sejm.* In every constituency there could be only one list of candidates nominated by the National Front, which grouped the three existing political parties. The Communists always managed to obtain an absolute majority in the *sejm.*

2. Local Government.—From June 1950 the number of provinces (*wojewodztwa*) was increased to 17 by the creation of three new provinces in the western territories. The five largest cities (Warsaw, Poznan, Lodz, Wroclaw, and Cracow) formed separate administrative units (*see* Table). Each province is divided into a number of districts (*powiaty*).

3. Taxation.—In Poland, as in every other people's democracy, direct taxation is small and (including taxes and duties from the private sector) amounts to about 11% of the national budget revenue; the main direct tax is that on wages. Indirect taxation is high and is included in the price of goods produced by the socialized economy and supplied to the population in state-owned stores and shops.

4. Living Conditions.—*Employment.*—In prewar Poland, according to the 1931 census, there were 4,881,500 persons employed, including 3,452,600 outside agriculture and forestry (1,781,500 in mining and industry).

In postwar Poland, with a different area and a smaller population, total employment in the national economy rose between 1949 and 1967 from 4,309,000 to 9,044,000. In the socialized sector employment rose from 3,960,000 to 8,901,000, and in mining and industry alone from 1,617,000 to 3,729,000. In addition, there were about 300,000 persons employed in 159,570 private handicraft establishments.

Housing.—In prewar Poland most houses were built privately and up-to-date housing was accessible only to those who could afford to pay high rents. After 1945 the great bulk of housing construction was taken over by the state. The share of rent (plus utilities rates) in the family budgets of working people dropped substantially as compared to the prewar period. At the end of 1966 there were in Poland 4,046,200 dwelling houses with 20,208,900 rooms; these totals included 2,940,900 houses in the countryside with 9,430,100 rooms; the average number of persons per room amounted to 1.41 in towns and to 1.66 in the countryside.

5. Social Welfare.—Medical care was provided in the 1960s free of charge to all workers and their families, that is, to about 60% of the population. Connected with this was the expansion of hospital facilities and of the medical and nursing staff. Though there was a substantial increase in all fields, much was still to be done. Between 1938 and 1967 the number of doctors rose from 12,917 to 43,201, that of dentists from 3,686 to 12,329.

All workers have the right to paid holidays. After one year of employment white-collar workers receive a 30-day holiday; physical workers are entitled to 12 days after one year, 15 days after three years, and 30 days after ten years of employment. The Workers' Holiday Fund, functioning under the supervision of the Central Council of Trade Unions, helps the workers to arrange their vacations. The fund has more than 1,500 rest homes and about 500,000 persons benefit yearly from these holidays.

6. Justice.—Administration of justice is assured by the Supreme Court, 19 provincial courts, 5 city courts, and 331 district courts. According to the constitution judges are independent, and are elected, except those of the Supreme Court who are appointed by the State Council for five years. Since 1964, with the abolition of private practice, all lawyers have had to belong to a "legal collective." In 1967 about 400,000 offenses were reported, mainly larceny and robbery, but also 400 cases of homicide and some 40,000 offenses against public order and authority.

7. Education.—The policy of the post-1945 Polish government was the gradual replacement of the old system of state, municipal, and private establishments by a uniform, secular state educational system at every level. All private and independent institutions had by 1952 been closed or subjected to governmental supervision. Primary education is compulsory for all children of 7 to 15 years of age. The state created no obstacles for parents who wished their children to be taught the principles of religion, but religious teaching should be given out of school. There are various types of secondary schools, such as the four-year general secondary school, the three-year vocational school, and the five-year technical school. Institutions of higher education include universities, colleges of engineering, medical academies, schools of agriculture, of economics, teachers' colleges, etc. Education at all schools and higher institutions is free, but admission to a secondary or high school requires the passing of preliminary examinations. In 1967–68 there were 26,600 primary schools with 5,604,000 pupils, and 862 secondary schools with 311,200 pupils. Between 1937 and 1968 institutions of higher education increased from 32 to 76 and students from 49,534 to 304,600.

The University of Cracow is one of the oldest in Europe (*see* CRACOW), but the loss of the eastern territories deprived Poland of its old universities of Wilno (Vilnius), which was founded by Stephen Báthory in 1578, and of Lwów, (Lvov), founded by John Casimir in 1661. There were also in pre-1939 Poland state universities in Warsaw and in Poznan, and a Catholic university in Lublin. Five new state universities were founded after 1945, in Wroclaw, Torun, Lodz, Lublin, and Katowice. The Catholic university in Lublin survived, the only institution of its kind in a Communist country. Before 1939 there were two colleges of engineering (Warsaw and Lwów); in the late 1960s there were 17.

In January 1949 an act to eliminate illiteracy was passed. As a mass phenomenon illiteracy ceased to exist in Poland. Various opportunities were provided for adults to pursue their education and attain higher standards of skill.

8. Defense.—Between the armed forces of pre-1939 Poland and those established after 1945 there was no continuity; personnel, organization, training, and equipment were completely changed. The Polish Army suffered catastrophically from the German and Soviet invasions, although certain Naval, Army, and Air Force units escaped abroad and made an important contribution to the Allied war effort from the Polish headquarters in Britain.

Including the forces of the interior (frontier guards and security troops), the Polish Armed Forces were estimated in the late 1960s at 319,000. There were three military areas (Warsaw, Bydgoszcz, and Wroclaw). The Army (185,000 men) comprised 15 divisions (5 armoured divisions, 8 motorized rifle, 1 airborne, and 1 amphibious assault). There were 2,800 tanks in the land forces, mostly T-54s and T-55s. The Air Force (70,000 men) had 750 combat and 300 training aircraft. It comprised 6 tactical bomber squadrons (with Il-28s), 45 fighter squadrons (with PZL-15s, MiG-19s, and MiG-21s), and 14 ground support and reconnaissance squadrons (with MiG-17s and Su-7s). In addition the Air Force had 40 transport aircraft and 40 helicopters. The Navy (19,000 men including marines) had 3 destroyers, 5 submarines, 25 coastal escorts, 24 coastal minesweepers, about 75 other auxiliary craft, and 50 naval aircraft (MiG-17s).

Since 1963 military service has been universal and compulsory between the ages of 19 and 50. According to the law of Jan. 30, 1959, active service was two years for the Army, three years for the Air Force and the Navy, two years for antiaircraft units, and 27 months for the forces of the interior. In March 1963 the *sejm* cut the period of service in the Army from 24 to 18 months, but lengthened it in a number of specialized units, which use modern weapons and equipment. (K. SM.)

VI. THE ECONOMY

The economic development of Poland following its emergence as a modern independent state after World War I was greatly influenced by its vulnerable position in a continent riven with deep national and political antagonisms. Economic viability in the interwar years was complicated by the widely contrasted social conditions in the areas inherited from Germany, Russia, and Austria, while the new, sinuous frontiers caused severe disruption of former trading patterns and induced great economic and political tensions in areas such as Upper Silesia and the so-called Polish Corridor. Political dismemberment and massive destruction of human and physical resources during World War II (two-fifths of the total national wealth and one-fifth of the population were

GRAIN HARVESTING AT PTASZKOWO IN POZNAN PROVINCE

HENRYK HERMANOWICZ, KRAKOW

FARMLANDS GIVE WAY TO STEEL MILLS AT NOWA HUTA, A SUBURB OF CRACOW

destroyed) bequeathed serious problems of postwar reconstruction and resettlement to a country which was territorially displaced westward while being ideologically incorporated in the Socialist camp. The transformation of economic conditions which subsequently occurred owed much to the acquisition of new resources and to Communist policies such as emphasis on heavy industrialization and on the attempted collectivization of peasant agriculture. Important modifications of economic planning, particularly in agriculture, occurred after the political changes of October 1956.

A. PRODUCTION

1. Agriculture.—Between World Wars I and II Poland was a predominantly agricultural country. Agricultural land accounted for two-thirds of the total area and arable land alone nearly half. After World War I large estates of 124 ac. (50 ha.) and more accounted for about one-quarter of the total area (those exceeding 1,235 ac. [500 ha.], one-fifth), the remainder being divided into smaller estates, of which nearly one-third were less than 5 ac. (2 ha.) and a similar proportion between 5 and 12 ac. (2 and 5 ha.). In 1920 a land reform act was passed to encourage redistribution of land, with compensation, under state control. By the end of 1938 one-quarter of the land belonging to the large estates had been distributed and the amount of land which had by then passed from the large estates to the small farmers and landless peasants equaled the area of all the arable land in England and Wales. In this interwar period more than 700,000 people received land in this way, yet Poland continued to suffer from rural overpopulation, particularly in the central provinces.

Although Poland was one-fifth smaller after 1945 than before 1939, arable land was reduced proportionately less, for it occupied a smaller share in the east than in the west. Thus agricultural land still accounted for about two-thirds of the total area, but the share of arable land alone rose to nearly three-fifths. By its decree of Sept. 6, 1944, the Polish Committee of National Liberation expropriated without compensation all private holdings exceeding 124 ac. (50 ha.), except church land, although that too was confiscated in the reform of March 20, 1950. In all, by January 1949, in the territories which were part of Poland before 1939, more than 2,965,200 ac. (1,200,000 ha.) of arable land were received by about 400,000 peasants, while in the recovered territories in the west 9,884,000 ac. (4,000,000 ha.) were shared out and about 480,000 new small holdings were created.

The land reform increased, in number and proportion, both the very small farms of under 5 ac. (2 ha.), which were economically unsound, and the larger holdings between 25 and 124 ac. (10 and 50 ha.) owned by the richer peasants. The economic and political problems thereby posed to the government, which was anxious to

rationalize agriculture as a means of releasing labour for the industrialization program, led to efforts to collectivize peasant holdings in producers' cooperatives. By June 1956 there were nearly 10,000 cooperatives occupying one-tenth of the agricultural land. Collectivization proceeded fairly rapidly in most of the recovered territories, but in the older areas of Polish peasant farming the policy met with stronger resistance (less than 2% of Kielce and Cracow *wojewodztwa* were collectivized). Another one-eighth of the agricultural area was administered by about 6,500 state farms, established predominantly in the recovered territories on the basis of the large prewar German estates. Following the political upheaval of October 1956 the unpopular cooperative farms were largely disbanded; by the late 1960s only about 1,220 survived, accounting for little more than 1% of the agricultural land. The state farms, in contrast, were maintained.

In 1959 approval was given to a seven-year plan for Polish agriculture which involved a gross increase in output of 30% between 1958 and 1965 and stressed the need for mechanization and for a reduction in the number of horses. A new form of cooperation was defined in terms of "agricultural circles" entitled to financial help, particularly for mechanization, from an agricultural development fund. By the early 1960s there were about 25,000 such circles, with a membership (including that of the rural housewives' associations) approaching 1,000,000, and utilizing 190,267 ac. (77,000 ha.) of agricultural land.

Crops.—Climate and soil combine to give Poland a mixed type of farming. The main crops are grains (rye, oats, wheat, and barley, in that order of importance), potatoes, sugar beet, and fodder crops. By the late 1960s agricultural production was two-thirds larger than that of 1934–38. The average yearly harvest of the four main cereals amounted to 15,500,000 tons, while the yield rose from 11.4 to almost 21 quintals per hectare in 1968, the highest yield in the history of Polish agriculture. The average yield for 1965–68 was 19.7 quintals.

Livestock.—Dairy and poultry farming and the raising of pigs are found in most areas of the country. In the late 1960s there were 10,900,000 head of cattle (an increase of 3.5% in comparison with 1938), and 14,000,000 pigs (almost twice as many as in 1938).

Postwar Trends.—The 1950s witnessed a growing concentration on foodstuffs of value to the export market, such as sugar, poultry products, bacon, and ham. By the late 1960s sugar production, for example, was three times the prewar figure. The demands of the export drive and the victualing of the considerable armed forces imposed heavy demands on agriculture. Moreover, production was hindered by changes in the agrarian system, lack of incentives for farmers, and locally by the diversion of agricultural labour into industrial employment. At the beginning of the 1930s the agricultural population had been three-fifths of the total, but in the late 1960s the proportion was one-third. Internal food shortages became apparent in 1948 and have been intermittently experienced since. From 1953 Poland had to import large quantities of grain, whereas before World War II there had been both grain and potato surpluses for export.

2. Forestry.—More than one-quarter of Poland was afforested by the late 1960s, compared to 21% at the end of the war. The proportion of the forest area covered by the state forest administration rose to over 80%, compared to only 37% in prewar years. The growth of industrial demand for timber, for example in construction and chemicals, encouraged a major afforestation program on poorer land, which was planned to increase the total area under forests to 27% of the country by 1975. Most of the forested regions are on the sandy, lighter soils of the lowlands, notably in Zielona Gora and Olsztyn *wojewodztwa*, and in the upland and mountainous areas of the southern margins, where afforestation is further encouraged by flood prevention requirements.

3. Fishing.—The growing role of Poland as a maritime power since 1945 is reflected in the increasing importance of fishing, in terms both of catch and of building vessels. By the late 1960s Poland had become a major exporter of fishing vessels, and was second only to Japan in their construction. The annual catch of sea fish rose between 1946 and 1966 from 23,300 to 316,500 tons.

4. Industry.—After World War II a short-term (1947–49) recovery plan was drawn up to make good the war losses and to adjust the economy to the conditions presented by major frontier changes. The total capital expenditure envisaged was nearly $2,000,000,000, of which two-fifths was for industry and one-quarter for transport. Rapid industrialization, however, was hindered by the inability of the U.S.S.R. to spare capital goods and by the growing reluctance of the Western industrialized countries to supply capital (and potentially strategic) goods to Communist countries. Supplies valued at $471,000,000 were provided by the UN Relief and Rehabilitation Administration, and $42,000,000 of Polish gold and other assets in U.S. and British banks were released in 1946–47. However, following Poland's rejection, at the behest of the U.S.S.R., of the European Recovery Program, the six-year industrialization plan (1950–55) was compelled to rely for its capital largely on internal or other Communist sources. This imposed severe strains upon the economy, and, with the worsening of East-West relations forcing further investment funds into heavy strategic industries at the expense of consumer goods and housing, general living standards remained low or even deteriorated. In 1950 the industrial targets of the plan were revised upward drastically, the proposed increase in industrial output for the period being put at 158% instead of the 95% originally envisaged.

Although the ambitious targets of the six-year plan were not always realized, substantial progress was recorded. Over a rather longer period, 1949–57, total industrial output increased about three times, with an increase in industrial employment of only two-thirds. In 1956 a new five-year plan was introduced, envisaging a great expansion of the chemical industry, the doubling of production of machinery and metal products, and a further increase of one-third in nonagricultural employment in the nationalized economy. In 1957 work was begun on a long-term (1961–75) plan to serve as a general framework for the more detailed five-year plans, and in 1959 it was announced that during these 15 years industry's contribution to the national income would rise from 46 to 57%. By 1968 the value of Poland's industrial production in constant prices was 12 times larger than in 1938.

The targets set in the 1956–60 plan were generally achieved, with a total increase in gross industrial production of 58%. Iron ore production rose by 32%, while the new copper field near Glogow provided an increase of over 70% on the 1955 output of copper ore. The production of sulfur, calcinated soda, insecticides, and pharmaceuticals more than doubled. The growth of employment during the same period was relatively small (11%), indicating substantial increases in industrial productivity.

The main objective of the 1961–65 plan was to encourage such increase in productivity by modernization and technological advances. The gross increase in industrial production was to be 52% (compared with only 22% in agriculture), with particularly high rates of growth planned for electricity, chemicals, iron and steel, and building materials. About 600 new industrial plants were included in the investment program, and by 1964 industrial employment had risen by about 380,000 (12% above 1960) to reach 3,390,000.

Coal Mining.—Postwar boundary changes led to the inclusion of the whole of the Upper Silesian coalfield within Polish territory, while further gains included the smaller but valuable coking coal deposits near Wałbrzych. By 1968 hard coal extraction reached 128,600,000 tons, almost three times more than in 1938. The extraction of brown coal, insignificant before World War II, reached 26,900,000 tons in 1968. Brown coal was playing an important role in the generation of electricity, and it was intended that this function should figure prominently during the period 1970–80 when long-term plans envisaged a total brown coal output of about 110,000,000 tons.

Metal Industries.—Communist planning has placed great emphasis on the growth of the heavy-metal industries, notably iron and steel, and an early spectacular example of this priority occurred during the six-year plan with the construction of the Nowa Huta steelworks (capacity 3,500,000 tons annually) immediately east of the historic capital of Cracow. Steel production was also expanded at Czestochowa and at centres such as Zabrze in the Upper Silesian Industrial District (Gornoslaski Okreg Przemyslowy, or G.O.P.). Between 1938 and 1968 steel production increased from 1,441,000 to 11,007,000 tons. Zinc production reached 202,500 tons in 1968, twice the pre-1939 average. While the zinc industry was an old one, the aluminum and copper industries started from scratch after World War II. Production of electrolytic copper began in 1950 reaching 43,600 tons in 1968; that of aluminum commenced in 1955 attaining 93,500 tons by 1968.

Power.—The expansion of electric-power production was rapid after 1945, and from less than 4,000,000,000 kw-hr. in 1938 it rose to 55,500,000,000 kw-hr. in 1968. Many new power stations were installed, notably the Turoszow plant based on lignite in the extreme southwest of the country. Coal continued to provide the overwhelming bulk of Poland's power requirements, but there was a growth too in the production of oil and natural gas with the discovery of new oil deposits in the Carpathian foothills and of rich natural gas fields in the Lubaczow region.

Chemicals.—Since 1955 this has been one of the conspicuous growth industries of Poland. The traditional centres of the industry were in the south, related to the fossil-fuel deposits in particular, but new centres have appeared at Płock and Puławy on the Vistula, whose primary materials were to be supplied by pipelines from the Soviet Union. The Płock oil refinery receives oil from the Volga field (the Romashkin area), and the Puławy nitrogen combine was using natural gas from the Soviet fields north of the Carpathians. The Puławy combine was intended to improve the productivity of Polish agriculture. The Płock refinery was one of several consequences of the completion of the oil pipeline in late 1963, which would help satisfy a national oil consumption expected to rise from 4,000,000 tons in 1963 to 9,000,000 tons in 1970. Other major chemical plants, based also on natural gas, were expanded during the 1960s at Oświęcim, Tarnów, and Blachownia Slaska. At Tarnobrzeg the intensive development of sulfur mining, which started in 1960, permitted an increase in the production of sulfuric acid from 189,000 to 1,315,000 tons between 1938 and 1968. Particular emphasis was also placed on the production of plastics, rubber, man-made fibres, and detergents. Production of cement rose between 1938 and 1968 from 1,719,000 to 11,600,000 tons.

B. TRADE AND FINANCE

1. Foreign Trade.—The transition from a mixed to a Communist economy was paralleled by important changes in Poland's economic relations. Before World War II its main trading partners were Western European countries and the United States, but after the war there was a very pronounced shift of trade toward the Socialist camp, especially after the formation in January 1949 of the Council for Mutual Economic Assistance (*q.v.*; Comecon), whose main aim was to increase barter trade between the U.S.S.R. and the people's democracies, an exchange based on bilateral agreements and coordinated with the respective national economic development plans.

Polish imports rose between 1950 and 1966 from 2,672,600,000 zl. ($668,100,000) to 9,976,200,000 zl. ($2,494,100,000). Polish exports increased during the same period from 2,537,000,000 zl. ($634,000,000) to 9,088,400,000 zl. ($2,272,100,000). Despite this fourfold increase, the proportion of Polish trade with the Socialist countries remained more or less constant; they were supplying two-thirds of Polish imports and taking an equal amount of Polish exports, the U.S.S.R. being the chief supplier and customer, handling about half of Poland's trade with all the Comecon states. In the late 1960s the U.S.S.R. was supplying Poland with 88% of its crude petroleum, 65% of iron ore, 79% of manganese ore, and 60% of cotton, while buying from Poland 66% of the annual production of shipping, 70% of railway passenger cars, and 33% of freight cars. The German Democratic Republic and Czechoslovakia occupied the second and third positions respectively as Poland's trading partners, while Great Britain was fourth (but first among the capitalist countries). Polish-British trade rose between 1950 and 1966 from £22,750,000 to £57,160,000 in exports to Poland, and from £19,000,000 to £51,800,000 in imports from Poland. Poland's fifth, sixth, and seventh trading partners were the German Federal Republic, Hungary, and the United States. Polish imports from the U.S. increased between 1950 and 1966 from $5,025,000 to $44,550,000, while exports to the U.S. rose from $11,200,000 to $79,225,000.

Concerned about improving material standards of living, the Polish government was trying, especially after October 1956, to develop trade links with Western Europe and the U.S. The creation of the EEC in 1958, and of EFTA in 1960 implied a threat of trade discrimination against Poland. In 1964, however, Poland joined GATT (the General Agreement on Tariffs and Trade) and was one of the 53 countries that took part in the "Kennedy Round" negotiations at Geneva. They ended on May 15, 1967, in agreement on tariff reductions of up to 50% on industrial commodities to become effective by 1972 between participating countries.

Another transformation of Polish commercial relations in the postwar period sprang from the structural changes effected in the economy. Before 1939 Polish exports consisted predominantly of agricultural products and raw materials such as coal and timber. In the late 1940s postwar disorganization of agriculture was partly responsible for a greater dependence on coal exports, though these exports declined rapidly after 1956. The replacement of livestock losses resulted in a steady increase in the export of meat products during the 1950s, but the decade was more notable for the growth in industrial exports. The new shipbuilding industry began to play an increasing role, and by the late 1960s the sale of machines and fully equipped industrial plants amounted to almost two-fifths of the total value of exports. Changes in imports also reflected the development of industrialization. Iron ore imports, mainly from Krivoi Rog, U.S.S.R., increased fivefold between 1946 and the late 1960s.

2. Banking and Currency. —The Narodowy Bank Polski was created as a state issue bank by a decree of Jan. 15, 1945, and a uniform currency for the whole country was introduced. In 1948 a major reform produced three state banks, the Narodowy (or National) Bank, the Investment Bank, and the Agricultural Bank. These banks handle exclusively the credit requirements of socialized enterprises, and thereby act in a controlling capacity within the planning mechanism. The bulk of credit and clearing operations is handled by the National Bank, while 75% of the national financial resources are kept on account with the National Bank. Its role was further defined in 1958, and in 1960 a further law defined the legal status of the other banks. The Agricultural Bank, for example, finances and controls the management and investments of state farms, cooperative farms, and state forestry enterprises. Another state bank was the Powszechna Kasa Oszczednosci, which handles the savings of the public.

The monetary unit is the zloty, with a foreign trade exchange rate of 4 zl. to U.S. $1, or (from November 1967) 9.60 zl. to £1 sterling, and a tourist rate of 24 zl. to U.S. $1, 57.60 zl. to £1.

3. National Finance. —From 1950 Poland had a comprehensive Soviet-type budget including not only all government revenues and expenditures but also those of the whole nationalized economy. Between 1951 and 1969 national budget revenue rose from 63,616,-000,000 to 353,600,000,000 zl. More than half the revenue came from the turnover tax and tax on non-commodity operations of socialized enterprises, and about one-sixth was collected from payments arising from their profits. Expenditure was as a rule slightly smaller than the revenue. About 55% of the revenue was invested in national economy, about 30% covered social and cultural services, while 9% was spent on national defense.

German reparations were expected to assist the industrialization of Poland. In 1945 the U.S.S.R. undertook to settle reparations to Poland by the allocation of 15% of all reparations received by the Soviet Union from Germany. In 1950, however, when the Soviet government estimated that the German Democratic Republic had paid $3,658,000,000 (Western calculations put the figure much higher), it announced, in agreement with the Polish government, the reduction of the remaining demands by half to $3,171,-000,000. In 1953 both countries renounced further payments. The amount of the Polish share was not published.

In November 1956 the Soviet government agreed to consider as settled Poland's indebtedness for the credits already granted (amounting to 2,300,000,000 rubles or $575,000,000), thus indirectly recognizing the Polish claim that, by delivering to the

FREIGHTERS AND HARBOUR CRAFT AT GDYNIA, BALTIC PORT AND NAVAL BASE WHICH, WITH DANZIG, IS THE PRINCIPAL SHIPPING CENTRE OF POLAND

Soviet Union during 1946–53 about 50,000,000 tons of coal at a nominal price of $1.25 a ton, Poland had lost about $740,000,000.

C. Transport and Communications

1. General.—The restored Poland inherited in 1918 three differing systems of communications, of which the Prussian was most highly developed, the Russian least so. The damage resulting from World War I and the Polish-Soviet War was great. Roads were ill-provided, a disadvantage from which the country was still to suffer despite continuous road building between 1921 and 1939.

The shift of frontiers in 1945 enriched the system of communications by bringing in the industrial areas of German Silesia and their outlet through the Oder Valley. War damage was, however, higher than in World War I, and the period 1945–50 was occupied mainly with the work of reconstruction and the improvement of existing facilities. Destruction was estimated at two-fifths of main railway tracks and locomotives, more than two-thirds of large railway bridges, almost all the freight cars, nine-tenths of passenger cars, all the motor trucks, nearly one-third of road surfaces, and four-fifths of boats and barges on inland waterways. Among the more spectacular achievements after 1945 were the rebuilding of an east-west thoroughfare through Warsaw and the electrification of the major trunk lines. By the late 1960s, of a total standard-gauge railway length of more than 14,292 mi. (23,000 km.) more than 1,800 mi. (2,900 km.) were electrified. On 74,564 mi. (120,000 km.) of hard-surfaced roads more than 350,000 passenger cars and 240,000 trucks were in use.

Poland's merchant marine made a phenomenal increase; in the late 1960s its total tonnage approached 1,300,000 tons gross (ships over 100 tons), being 13 times the tonnage before World War II. Foreign trade through the main ports (Danzig, Gdynia, and Szczecin) reached 32,000,000 tons in 1968.

2. Inland Waterways.—The inland waterways have always been of considerable importance to Poland. By far the greatest stretches of inland navigation are provided by the Vistula and Oder and their main tributaries. The low sandy banks, the fast-flowing streams, and the tendency to flood after the spring thaw necessitated regulation and canalization. The interconnecting glacial valleys provided means of linking by short canals a whole series of east-west tributaries and so, eventually, the main river systems of Germany, Poland, and the U.S.S.R. Thus the Oginski and Royal canals (built in the 18th century, north and west of Pinsk, now in the U.S.S.R.) and the Augustów Canal (1825) joined the Vistula and Bug with the Neman, Pripet, and Dnieper. The Bydgoszcz (Bromberg) Canal (1773–74) was used for barge traffic between Germany and East Prussia; it linked Königsberg (now Kaliningrad in the U.S.S.R.) with the Oder and central Germany by way of the sheltered lagoons of the Baltic coast, the canalized Nogat distributary of the Vistula, and the Brda and Noteć rivers. This canal was linked in 1949 through Lake Goplo with the canalized Warta River. In 1959 a short canal was opened between Warsaw and the lower Bug to avoid the navigational hazards at the confluence of that stream with the Vistula. In the 1960s the Vistula River between Warsaw and Torun was being canalized. The Upper Silesian coalfields are served by the Gliwice Canal leading into the Oder.

3. Air Services.—The Polish state-owned airline, LOT, provided in the late 1960s services to and from 26 foreign capitals, including Moscow, Paris, Brussels, Copenhagen, Amsterdam, Athens, Cairo, Istanbul, and Beirut, while regular internal services linked Warsaw with Szczecin, Poznan, Danzig, Wroclaw, Katowice, Cracow, and Rzeszów. In 1968 LOT transported 773,800 passengers, two-thirds of them on domestic lines.

4. Postal Services and Telecommunications.—All these services are state controlled. By the late 1960s there were more than 7,400 post offices, more than 1,100,000 telephones, more than 5,700,000 radio-receiving sets, and about 3,500,000 television receivers. (G. W. S.; K. Sm.; Ed. Br.)

Bibliography.—*General*: E. de Martonne, "La Pologne," in part 2 of *Europe Centrale*, vol. iv of *Géographie Universelle*, ed. by L. Gallois and P. Vidal de la Blache (1931); S. Lencewicz and J. Kondracki, *Geografia Fizyczna Polski*, 2nd ed. (1959).

The People: B. Chlebowski, W. Walewski and T. Sulimirski, *Słownik geograficzny* ("Geographic Dictionary"), 15 vol. (1880–1902); A. Fischer, *Polacy—Etnografia słowiańska* (1934); K. Moszyński, *Kultura ludowa Słowian*, 3 vol. (1929–39); J. Bystroń, *Wstęp do ludoznawstwa polskiego* ("An Introduction to Polish Ethnography"), 2nd ed. (1939); T. Lehr-Spławiński, *O pochodzeniu i praojczyźnie Słowian* (1946); J. Czekanowski, *Polska-Słowiańszczyzna* ("Poland-Slavdom") (1948) and *Wstęp do historii Słowian* ("An Introduction to the History of Slavs"), 2nd ed. (1957). (J. Cz.)

History: General, in Polish: R. Grodecki, S. Zachorowski and J. Dabrowski, *Dzieje Polski średniowiecznej* ("History of Medieval Poland"; 1926); W. Konopczyński, *Dzieje Polski nowożytnej, 1506–1795*, 2 vol. ("History of Modern Poland"; 1936); M. Kukiel, *Dzieje Polski porozbiorowej 1795–1921* ("History of Partitioned Poland"; 1961); Polish Academy of Sciences, Institute of History, T. Manteuffel *et al.*, *Historia Polski*, 3 vol. (1957–60); W. Czaplinski and T. Ladogorski, (eds.), *Atlas Historyczny Polski* (1967).

History: General, in Foreign Languages: The *Cambridge History of Poland*, 2 vol. (1941–50); *Recueil des actes diplomatiques, traités et documents concernant la Pologne*, vol. i, K. Lutostanski (ed.), *Les Partages de là Pologne* (1918), vol. ii, S. Filasiewicz (ed.), *La Question polonaise pendant la guerre mondiale* (1920); K. M. Smogorzewski, *La Pologne restaurée* (1927); R. Machray, *The Poland of Pilsudski* (1937); Gen. M. Norwid-Neugebauer, *The Defence of Poland: September 1939* (1942); J. Ciechanowski, *Defeat in Victory* (1948); A. Bliss Lane, *I Saw Poland Betrayed* (1948); Gen. W. Anders, *An Army in Exile* (1949); T. (Gen. Bor) Komorowski, *The Secret Army* (1951); J. Beck, *Dernier rapport: politique polonaise, 1926–1939* (1951); T. Komarnicki, *Rebirth of the Polish Republic, 1914–1920* (1957); Count E. Raczyński, *In Allied London* (1963); A. Gieysztor *et al.*, *History of Poland* (1968).

German-Polish Relations: K. M. Smogorzewski, *La Silésie polonaise* (1932) and *Poland's Access to the Sea* (1934); W. J. Rose, *The Drama of Upper Silesia* (1935); E. Wiskemann, *Germany's Eastern Neighbours* (1956); J. Kokot, *The Logic of the Oder-Neisse Frontier* (1959); Anna M. Cienciala, *Poland and the Western Powers 1938–1939* (1968); W. Jędrzejewicz, ed., *Diplomat in Berlin 1933–1939: Papers of J. Lipski* (1968).

Polish-Russian Relations: Z. L. Zaleski, *Le Dilemme russo-polonais* (1920); A. Żółtowski, *Border of Europe* (1950); Z. Stypułkowski, *Invitation to Moscow* (1951); J. K. Zawodny, *Death in the Forest: the Story of the Katyn Forest Massacre* (1962); S. Kot, *Conversations with the Kremlin and Dispatches from Russia* (1963); Gen. Sikorski Historical Institute, *Documents on Polish-Soviet Relations*, 2 vol. (1961–67).

Population: G. Frumkin, "Pologne: dix années d'histoire démographique," *Tr. Inst. Nat. Etudes Démographiques* (Oct.–Dec. 1949); J. Zubrzycki, *Polish Immigrants in Britain: a Study of Adjustment* (1956); B. O. Jeżewski, *Yearbook and Directory: Poles Abroad* (1958); J. Wytrwal, *America's Polish Heritage* (1961); B. Gruchman *et al.*, *Polish Western Territories* (1959); *Rocznik Statystyczny* and *Rocznik Polityczny i Gospodarczy,* both annual. (K. Sm.)

POLARIMETRY is the science of measuring the angle of rotation of the plane of polarized light (*see* Light: *Polarization and Electromagnetic Theory*).

Polarimetry is primarily of interest to the chemist, because many compounds, either in the pure state or in solution, possess the power of rotating the plane of polarization of a beam of polarized light. The phenomenon is displayed by compounds which lack a centre of symmetry in their molecular or crystalline structure, such that the compound and its mirror image are not superimposable. This situation most commonly results from the presence of a carbon atom which is covalently bound to four different atoms or groups of atoms. The angle through which the plane is rotated varies directly with the length of the light path through the sample and, in the case of solutions, with the concentration. For a given path length and concentration, the angle depends on the wavelength of the light, the temperature, and the nature of the sample and its solvent, if any. Substances which are capable of producing this effect are said to be optically active. They are characterized by a constant known as the specific rotation, designated by the symbol $[\alpha]$, usually accompanied by a subscript letter to indicate the wavelength and a superscript number for the temperature. Thus, $[\alpha]_D^{20}$ means that the value was determined at 20° C with the D-line of sodium as light source. The specific rotation is defined by the relation,

$$[\alpha] = \frac{a}{dc}$$

where a is the observed angle of rotation in degrees, d is the length of light path through the sample in decimetres, and c is the concentration in grams per millilitre.

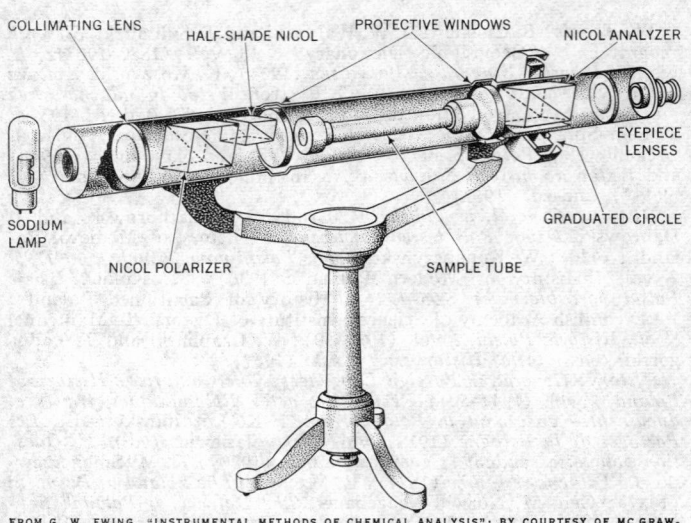

COLLIMATING LENS   HALF-SHADE NICOL   PROTECTIVE WINDOWS   NICOL ANALYZER

EYEPIECE LENSES

SODIUM LAMP

NICOL POLARIZER   SAMPLE TUBE   GRADUATED CIRCLE

FROM G. W. EWING, "INSTRUMENTAL METHODS OF CHEMICAL ANALYSIS"; BY COURTESY OF MC GRAW-HILL BOOK CO., INC.

DIAGRAM OF A CONVENTIONAL POLARIMETER

The angle of rotation is measured with a polarimeter (*see* figure). Monochromatic radiation, polarized by a Nicol prism (*see* LIGHT, fig. 13), is passed through the sample and a second Nicol (the analyzer) to the eyepiece for visual observation. Between the first Nicol and the sample a small, auxiliary Nicol is so placed as to cause a slight modification of the polarization angle of one-half of the light beam. This permits visual balance of the two half-beams at an intermediate level of intensity between dark and light, as the eye is most sensitive under such conditions. Several manufacturers offer completely automatic or semiautomatic recording instruments which operate on similar principles.

The chief application of polarimetric analysis is in the sugar industry, since sucrose has a much greater specific rotation than impurities likely to be present. Many other compounds, principally organic, are optically active; some are of biological and pharmacological significance.

BIBLIOGRAPHY.—F. J. Bates, *et al., Polarimetry, Saccharimetry, and the Sugars,* National Bureau of Standards Circular C440 (1942); George W. Wheland, *Advanced Organic Chemistry,* 2nd ed., pp. 130 ff. (1949); Galen W. Ewing, *Instrumental Methods of Chemical Analysis,* 2nd ed., pp. 151 ff. (1960).   (G. W. E.)

POLAROGRAPHY (POLAROGRAPHIC ANALYSIS, VOLTAMMETRY), an electrochemical method of analyzing solutions of reducible or oxidizable substances, was invented by Jaroslav Heyrovsky at Charles University, Prague, Czech., in 1922.

The majority of the chemical elements can be determined by polarographic analysis, and the method is applicable to the analysis of alloys and to various inorganic compounds. Polarography is also used to identify many types of organic compounds, and to study chemical equilibria and rates of reactions in solutions.

The solution to be analyzed is placed in a glass cell containing two electrodes. One electrode consists of a glass capillary tube (internal diameter about 0.05 mm., or 0.002 in.) from which mercury slowly flows in drops (dropping mercury electrode), and the other is a pool of mercury or some other nonpolarizable electrode. The cell is connected in series with a galvanometer (for measuring the flow of current) in an electrical circuit that contains a battery, or other source of direct current, and a device by means of which the voltage applied to the electrodes can be varied from zero up to about two volts. With the dropping mercury electrode connected (usually) to the negative side of the polarizing voltage, the voltage is increased by small increments and the corresponding current is observed on the galvanometer. The current is very small until the applied voltage is increased to a value large enough to cause the substance being determined to be reduced at the dropping mercury electrode. The current increases rapidly at first as the applied voltage is increased above this critical value, but gradually attains a limiting value and remains more or less constant as the voltage is increased further. The critical voltage required to cause the rapid increase in current is characteristic

of, and serves to identify, the substance being reduced (qualitative analysis). Under proper conditions the constant limiting current is governed by the rate of diffusion of the reducible substance up to the surface of the mercury drops, and its magnitude is a measure of the concentration of the reducible substance (quantitative analysis). Limiting currents also result from the oxidation of certain oxidizable substances when the dropping electrode is the anode.

In 1925 J. Heyrovsky and M. Shikata invented an instrument called the polarograph, which automatically applies an increasing voltage to the dropping electrode cell and photographically records the resulting current-voltage curve. Curves thus recorded are called polarograms.

When the solution contains several substances that are reduced or oxidized at different voltages, the polarogram shows a separate current increase (polarographic wave) and limiting current for each. The method is thus capable of detecting and determining several substances simultaneously, and is applicable to relatively small concentrations, *e.g.,* 10^{-5} up to about 0.01 moles per litre, or approximately 1 to 1,000 parts per 1,000,000.

In recent years specialized measuring techniques, using superimposed alternating or pulsed voltage impulses, have been used to study mechanisms of reactions at the dropping mercury electrode.

See I. M. Kolthoff and J. J. Lingane, *Polarography,* 2nd rev. ed., 2 vol. (1952); G. W. C. Milner, *Principles and Applications of Polarography and Other Electroanalytical Processes* (1957).   (J. J. LE.)

POLAR REGIONS: *see* ANTARCTICA; ARCTIC, THE.

POLDING, JOHN BEDE (1794–1877), English Benedictine, first Roman Catholic bishop in Australia, first archbishop of Sydney, and a man full of zeal for the spiritual welfare of the isolated settlers of the new continent and of the numerous convicts who were constantly being shipped from England, was born at Liverpool on Oct. 18, 1794. He became a Benedictine monk and quickly rose to positions of influence and trust in his order. Consecrated as the first Australian bishop, he arrived at Sydney in September 1835. There were but four Roman Catholic clergymen to meet him. The new bishop vigorously set to work dividing up his territory into missionary districts and providing priests, churches, and schools as rapidly and extensively as he could. Visits to Europe enabled him to procure help for his people in various ways. From one of these visits he returned in March 1843 as archbishop of Sydney (appointed April 10, 1842). Nevertheless his kindness and humility were more evident than his administrative gifts. He died on March 16, 1877.

See P. F. Moran, *History of the Catholic Church in Australasia,* (1894); H. N. Birt, *Benedictine Pioneers in Australia,* 2 vol. (1911).   (E. McD.)

POLE, the name of two families famous in English history. The de la Poles, earls and dukes of Suffolk, were descended from SIR WILLIAM DE LA POLE (d. 1366), of Kingston-upon-Hull, the richest English merchant of his age. The parentage of Sir William, his elder brother, SIR RICHARD (d. 1345), and his younger brother, JOHN, remains uncertain; they may have been sons of Sir Lewis de la Pole (d. 1294) and grandsons of Gruffydd ap Gwenwynwyn (d. 1286), prince of Powys.

Sir Richard, vintner of Hull and London, made loans to Roger Mortimer's government (1327–30) and later to Edward III; he was king's butler from 1327 to 1331 and from 1333 to 1338. Joan, Lady Cobham (d. 1434), whose fourth husband was the Lollard Sir John Oldcastle, was the daughter and heiress of Sir Richard's grandson, Sir John de la Pole (d. 1380).

Sir William (d. 1366), first mayor of Hull (1332–33) following the grant of a royal charter in 1331, represented the borough in five parliaments between 1332 and 1338. At the beginning of the Hundred Years' War, he was Edward III's chief financial agent and in just over a year (1338–39) he loaned the king more than £100,000; in 1339 he was made 2nd baron of the exchequer and created knight banneret. De la Pole was among those arrested in December 1340 after the king's return from Flanders and charged with frauds in connection with the wool transactions; his lands and goods were forfeited and he remained in prison until May 1342. He organized the "English Company" which was granted a monopoly of the wool export trade in 1343. Despite his losses in 1340–41, he possessed great wealth and was the first English financier to found a noble house. His eldest son, MICHAEL DE LA POLE (*c.* 1330–89), acquired estates in Suffolk by his marriage with Katharine, daughter of Sir John Wingfield, and was summoned to Parliament as a baron before his father's death. He served in France under Edward the Black Prince and John of Gaunt, and in 1380 led the embassy which arranged Richard II's marriage with Anne of Bohemia. In 1383 he became chancellor of England, and his heir, MICHAEL (d. 1415), married Katharine, daughter of Hugh, 2nd earl of Stafford, a descendant of Edward I. When the earldom of Suffolk was revived in de la Pole's favour in August 1385, a royal grant gave him the East Anglian lands formerly held by the De Ufford earls of Suffolk. His opponents, led by the king's uncle, Thomas, duke of Gloucester, obtained his dismissal from the chancellorship in the Parliament of October 1386, and he was impeached, convicted, and imprisoned. Richard II soon released his fallen minister and Suffolk was the leader of the court party in the struggle that followed. After being charged with treason by the victorious lords appellant in November 1387, Suffolk escaped abroad and was sentenced to death and forfeiture in the Merciless Parliament of February 1388. He died in exile in Paris in 1389.

After Richard II's triumph in 1397, the sentence on Suffolk was reversed and in the Shrewsbury Parliament of January 1398, his son, Michael, was restored to the earldom. (For his descendants, see SUFFOLK, EARLS AND DUKES OF; SUFFOLK, WILLIAM DE LA POLE, Duke of; POLE, RICHARD DE LA.)

Another family of the name of Pole, perhaps distantly related to the house of Suffolk, owed their advancement and their fall to a match with a princess of the royal house. SIR RICHARD POLE (d. 1505), a Buckinghamshire knight, was the son of Geoffrey Pole, a squire of Welsh descent whose wife, Edith St. John, was half sister to Henry VII's mother, Lady Margaret Beaufort. About 1491 Sir Richard married the Lady Margaret, daughter of George, duke of Clarence (d. 1478), a brother of Edward IV.

In 1513 Henry VIII created Sir Richard's widow countess of Salisbury, as some amends for the judicial murder of her brother, Edward, earl of Warwick, in 1499. Her eldest son, HENRY (d. 1539), henceforth styled Lord Montague, was summoned to Parliament as a baron in 1529. Until the king's marriage with Anne Boleyn (1533), the countess of Salisbury was governess of her godchild, the Lady Mary (afterward Mary I). When her third son, Reginald, Cardinal Pole (d. 1558), published his *Pro ecclesiasticae unitatis defensione*, the whole family fell under the displeasure of the king, who resolved to make an end of them. The Lord Montague was the first victim, beheaded in 1539 on a charge of treasonable conversations, on evidence exacted from his brother, SIR GEOFFREY POLE (d. 1558). In 1541 the aged countess, attainted in 1539 with her son Montague, was also executed; a woman of great piety, she is among the English martyrs who have been beatified. Sir Geoffrey Pole joined the cardinal in exile and returned with him at Mary's accession. His sons ARTHUR and EDMUND, taken in 1562 as plotters against Queen Elizabeth, were committed to the Tower of London, where they died after eight years of imprisonment. *See also* POLE, REGINALD.

BIBLIOGRAPHY.—C. Frost, *Notices Relative to the Early History of the Town and Port of Hull* (1827); G. Poulson, *The History and Antiquities of the Seigniory of Holderness* (1840–41); H. A. Napier, *Historical Notices of the Parishes of Swyncombe and Ewelme in the County of Oxford* (1858); G. O. Sayles, "The English Company of 1343," *Speculum*, vol. vi (1931); A. S. Harvey, *The De La Pole Family of Kingston-upon-Hull* (1957). (T. B. P.)

POLE, REGINALD (1500–1558), English cardinal and archbishop of Canterbury, who, at the accession of Mary I, reconciled England with the Holy See and became a close counselor of the queen, was born at Stourton castle, Staffordshire, in March 1500, the third son of Sir Richard Pole and Margaret, countess of Salisbury, a niece of Edward IV. Intended for the church, he spent five years at the grammar school founded by John Colet at Sheen, where his kinsman Henry VIII contributed to the cost of his education. In his 13th year he went to Oxford, matriculating from Magdalen college. Thomas Linacre and William Latimer were among his tutors. He took his B.A. in 1515. In 1518 the

king appointed him to the deanery of Wimborne and then to two prebends in Salisbury cathedral. In 1521 he went, with an annual grant of £100 from the king, to continue his studies at Padua, where during the next few years he corresponded with Desiderius Erasmus and formed friendships with Pietro Bembo, Christophe de Longolius, and other prominent humanists. He paid a brief visit to Rome for the 1525 jubilee.

Two years later he returned to England and was appointed dean of Exeter. He showed, however, little desire to desert his studies for a more active career; and it is possible that Thomas Cromwell, by recommending to him the precepts of Niccolo Machiavelli, helped to encourage this distaste for public life. When the question of Henry VIII's "divorce" from Catherine of Aragon arose, Pole at first sought to avoid taking part on either side. In 1529 he obtained the king's leave, and £100, to continue his studies at the University of Paris. The following year, however, by the king's order he helped to secure that university's pronouncement in favour of the divorce. On returning to England he was offered the archbishopric of York, vacant by Thomas Wolsey's death, but was required first to declare his opinion about the divorce, Henry not wishing to confer so great an honour upon an adversary. Pole suggested that he was ready to satisfy the king, but then apparently changed his mind, for in a stormy interview at York place he roundly denounced the royal policy. He later wrote to Henry, explaining his reasons against the divorce, and in January 1532 he received permission to go abroad again, without losing the revenues of his benefices. After a brief stay at Avignon, he settled once more at Padua and devoted himself to the serious study of theology. These studies soon led him to become a prominent member of the group of Catholic reformers, headed by Gasparo Cardinal Contarini, Giovanni Giberti and Giampietro Carafa, who were eager to reform ecclesiastical abuses but regarded the maintenance of papal supremacy as necessary to preserve the unity of Catholic Christendom.

At this point in his development his relations with Henry VIII reached their crisis. In February 1535, after the king's final break with Rome, Pole was called upon to make a formal statement of his opinion about the divorce and the royal supremacy. The executions of Bishop John Fisher and Sir Thomas More (June and July 1535) gave him grim warning of the fate which his answer might bring upon his family as well as upon himself; and the task of answering was not made easier by the genuine admiration which hitherto he had felt for Henry or by his reluctance to abandon all hope of reconciliation. Thus he took a year to write his reply and by the time it was dispatched to England (May 1536) it had grown into a full-sized book. Although later published, without Pole's consent, under the title *Pro ecclesiasticae unitatis defensione* (usually known as *De Unitate*), it was meant for the king's eye alone. It contained a severe attack on the royal policy and a strong defense of the pope's spiritual supremacy.

In July 1536, Paul III summoned Pole to Rome to serve with Contarini, Giberti, Carafa and others on the commission to consider the reform of church discipline. After some hesitation, caused by letters from his mother and brother emphasizing the dangers that his conduct might lead them into, he eventually obeyed this papal call. In December he was made a cardinal and by February 1537 the commission's report, *Consilium de emendanda ecclesia*, was completed. This most important document trenchantly summarized the outstanding abuses in the church and pointed to the remedies with plain-spoken directness. Pole's share in this notable work was hardly completed when a new task was thrust upon him. Paul III, who had already prepared a bull of deposition and excommunication against Henry VIII, now appointed Pole legate *a latere* for England and sent him to persuade the Catholic powers to take advantage of the difficulties created for Henry by the Pilgrimage of Grace. The mission was ill-timed and quite unsuccessful. The pilgrimage had been crushed almost before Pole left Rome (February 1537); Francis I refused to let him stay in France; Charles V's representative would not admit him to the Netherlands; Henry would not negotiate with him in his capacity as papal legate; and in August 1537 the pope recalled him to Rome. A second mission in 1538–39 to persuade Charles and Francis to enforce the bull resulted in an equally humiliating failure and Pole, his life threatened by Henry's agents, sought refuge with his old friend Jacopo Sadoleto at Carpentras before returning to Rome at the end of 1539. Meanwhile the royal vengeance had fallen upon his family in England. His eldest brother, Lord Montague, and his cousin, the marquess of Exeter, were executed in 1538; his mother and he himself were attainted in 1539; and his mother executed in 1541.

On Aug. 21, 1541, Pole was appointed legate of the *Patrimonium Petri,* the oldest of the papal states, and took up his residence at Viterbo. There he gathered around him a group which included Marc-Antonio Flaminio and Vittoria Colonna, the poetess and friend of Michelagelo. With them he discussed many of the great theological questions raised by the German reformers and by the Spanish reformer Juan de Valdes. Justification by faith, the burning question of the day, was a special subject of discussion. Pole's own attitude at this time may be best summed up in his advice to Vittoria Colonna, that she should believe as though she could be saved by faith alone and act as though she could be saved by works alone. His open-mindedness, the leniency of his rule at Viterbo, and his reluctance to abandon all hope of healing the divisions of Christendom were, however, by now beginning to separate him from Carafa and those who felt that, after the failure of Contarini's negotiations with the Lutherans at Ratisbon (Regensburg) (1541), the time had come for sterner measures to defend and define the Catholic faith. Indeed, after the conversion to Protestantism in 1542 of Vittoria's friend Bernardino Ochino and of Peter Martyr, whom Contarini had defended, the newly established Roman Inquisition, headed by Carafa, regarded the entire Viterbo circle as no better than heretics.

Nevertheless Pole was one of the three legates appointed in 1542 to open the Council of Trent and, when the council eventually met in December 1545, he was one of the three who presided over its session, after journeying to Trent by a devious route for fear of assassins hired by Henry VIII. He urged the council very strongly to reform the abuses as well as to define the doctrines of the church and when the question of justification came up for discussion he entreated the fathers to study the subject well before committing themselves to a final decision. Soon after this discussion began, however, his health broke down and he retired to Padua (June 1546). There is no reason to believe that this was a feigned illness. It is true that the council did not accept the compromise on justification that Contarini had put forward at Ratisbon and which Pole still favoured. But Pole kept in touch with its proceedings by letter; his view was well represented in the discussions by Seripando; and he accepted readily enough the decree that the council finally passed.

On the death of Paul III (November 1549) Pole, thanks to Charles V's support, came near to election as pope. After hesitating to let himself be acknowledged by acclamation before all the French cardinals had arrived, he just failed to obtain the necessary two-thirds of the votes. In the end the French and imperialist factions compromised by electing Julius III. Under him reform made little headway. Pole lost his legacy at Viterbo (1550), was openly (though vainly) denounced by Carafa for heretical leanings, and about 1553 retired to the monastery of Maguzzano on Lake Garda.

However, on the accession of Mary Tudor (July 1553), the pope at once appointed Pole legate for England. Yet even now his course was not smooth. He had often been spoken of as a possible husband for Mary—he was still only in deacon's orders, so that a papal dispensation might have been obtained—and Charles V was therefore determined to keep him out of England until Mary's marriage to his own son Philip had been arranged. Moreover Pole himself thought this marriage a mistake, although he failed to convince the pope. Even when Philip and Mary were safely married (July 1554), other obstacles remained, notably the English parliament's insistence upon adequate guarantees that lay holders of confiscated church lands should not be disturbed. Thus it was not until Nov. 20 that he landed at Dover. Ten days later he formally absolved the realm and received it back into the Roman fold. On Dec. 24 he issued a decree guaranteeing holders of church property against all ecclesiastical censures, though he would

not add that they might hold it with a clear conscience. On Philip's departure in September 1555, Mary turned more and more to Pole for advice on all matters. He was not responsible for the religious persecution that disfigured the last four years of her reign, although he did nothing to stop it and occasionally himself issued commissions to repress heresy. First and foremost he was still the Catholic reformer. In November 1555 he assembled at Westminster a national synod of the two convocations, which quickly agreed to measures to enforce clerical residence, reduce pluralism, increase preaching, compel priests to set a good example to their flocks, and to provide a new book of homilies and a new translation of the New Testament. On Thomas Cranmer's deposition, Pole became archbishop of Canterbury (March 1556), after being ordained priest two days before, and sought to enforce these decrees by a metropolitical visitation. He also attempted to refound some of the monasteries and sent commissioners to carry out a visitation of the universities. All this work, however, went forward too slowly to take any firm root within the few short years of Mary's reign.

Moreover, Pole was thwarted by the papacy itself. In May 1555 Carafa had become pope as Paul IV. He adopted a violent anti-Spanish policy which soon brought renewal of the war between France and the Habsburgs. Pole's efforts to prevent the conflict only infuriated Paul. In April 1557 he was deprived of his legatine authority and in June, after England's declaration of war on France, he was summoned to Rome, the aged William Peto being appointed legate in his place. At the same time the Pope inveighed against Pole as a heretic and handed his friend Cardinal Morone over to the Inquisition. Doubtless Pole would have shared this fate had Mary not prevented the delivery of the pope's summons. Instead, he remained in England until, broken as much by the unmerited blow of the papal disgrace as by ill health, he died at Lambeth on Nov. 17, 1558, 12 hours after Mary. He was buried at Canterbury, near the site of the shrine of St. Thomas à Becket.

BIBLIOGRAPHY.—G. Quirini's *Epistolarum R. Poli collectio,* 5 vol. (1744–57), also contains the life written in Italian by Pole's secretary Beccatelli, which Andrew Dudith translated into Latin (*Vita Poli cardinalis,* 1563). *See* also A. Zimmermann, *Kardinal Pole, sein Leben und seine Schriften* (1893); W. Schenk, *Reginald Pole, Cardinal of England* (1950). (R. B. WM.)

POLE, RICHARD DE LA (d. 1525), claimant to the English crown, was the youngest son of John de la Pole, 2nd duke of Suffolk (d. 1491/1492), and Elizabeth, sister to King Edward IV. Since Edward IV's brother and successor Richard III died childless, and since Edward's own sons disappeared in the Tower (probably murdered by their uncle's orders), the de la Poles inherited the Yorkist claim to the throne, a claim strengthened when Richard III named Suffolk's eldest son John (d. 1487), earl of Lincoln, as his successor. The claims of the attainted line of Clarence, represented by the young earl of Warwick, were passed over under Richard III but were sufficiently alive under Henry VII to postpone the full assertion of the de la Pole claim until Warwick's execution in 1499. After the accession, in 1485, of the first Tudor, Henry VII, the family therefore lived under suspicion, nor did it help that Lincoln joined Lambert Simnel's rebellion (1487), which cost him his life. The claim thus devolved upon the second brother, Edmund, earl of Suffolk (d. 1513). After years of waiting, the earl fled abroad in 1499; and though he returned briefly he fled again in 1501, this time accompanied by his brother Richard. The brothers tried to interest the emperor Maximilian in their cause, but in 1502 Maximilian agreed with Henry VII on terms which included dropping the Yorkist claimants. Edmund, attainted as a traitor in 1504, was imprisoned in Burgundy in that year and surrendered to Henry in 1506, on condition that his life be spared. He lived a prisoner in the Tower until Henry VIII carried out the old sentence against him in 1513.

Meanwhile Richard had led an adventurous life, escaping (1504) the pressing attentions of his brother's creditors at Aachen, taking service with King Ulászló II of Hungary, and establishing something of a reputation as a *condottiere.* After Edmund's death he took over the claim to the crown, calling himself duke of Suffolk. In 1512, the outbreak of war between France and England encouraged him to seek French help, and he was given an army that he might have used against England if time had served. However, when peace was concluded in 1514, Louis XII of France at once dropped him and forced him to leave the country. He went to live at Metz, but maintained his contacts with France. Louis XII's successor Francis I found him useful both as a man of military capacity and as a weapon in his complex diplomacy. In 1523, when he wished to prevent English assistance to the Habsburgs, he encouraged an intrigue which was meant to restore the Yorkist claimant to England with the help of an exiled claimant to the Scottish throne. Though nothing came of this, Richard de la Pole remained in Francis' service, accompanied him to the war in Italy, and was killed in the Battle of Pavia (1525). His death terminated the claims of the main Yorkist line and ended a threat to the Tudor throne.

See J. D. Mackie, *The Earlier Tudors, 1485–1558* (1952).

(G. R. E.)

POLE AND POLAR, in mathematics. If from a point *P* outside a circle the two tangents to the circle be drawn, the line joining the points of contact is called the polar of the point *P*, and *P* is called the pole of the secant line. If *P* is on the circle, the two tangents coincide and the polar of *P* is the single tangent at *P*. For *Q*, a point inside the circle, draw two secants to the circle through it. The line joining their poles is called the polar of *Q*. If the polar of *P* passes through *Q*, the polar of *Q* passes through *P*. In the figure shown, $\overline{AB}$ is the polar of P_1; $\overline{CD}$ is the polar of P_2; line P_1E is the polar of *A*; P_1P_2 is the polar of *Q*. The same principle applies to any conic. In space there is a corresponding theory of points and polar planes as to a sphere or any fixed quadric surface. The idea is due to C. J. Brianchon, who first applied it in 1806, but it was developed by J. V. Poncelet, and presented in final form in 1829. Later the concept was extended to other curves and surfaces, and to other configurations.

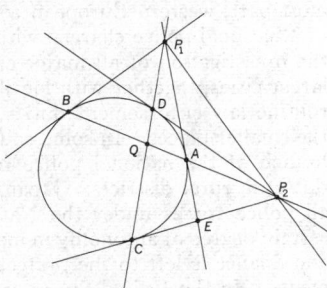

DIAGRAM ILLUSTRATING THE THEORY OF POLE AND POLAR PLANES

POLECAT (FITCH), a weasellike carnivore of the family Mustelidae, which also includes the weasel, mink, otter, etc. Polecats (*Mustela putorius*) are confined to the northern hemisphere, being found in the central and northern parts of the European continent, east to Siberia and Mongolia and south to the Himalayas. The polecat is well known in its domesticated, albino variety as the ferret. The wild polecat is brownish above and black below, the face being variegated with white. The fur is long, coarse and of little commercial value. This polecat is more powerful than the marten (*q.v.*) but less active, and rarely climbs trees. Its food consists of small mammals and any birds it can catch, especially poultry. It also eats snakes, lizards, frogs, fish and eggs. It is extremely bloodthirsty and hunts at night. From three to eight young are produced in April or May, after a two months' gestation. It is tenacious of life and has a fetid smell.

On the central plateau of the United States is found the black-footed ferret, *M. nigripes*, a related species with creamy-yellow fur, brown legs and black feet and tail. A related genus, *Vormela*, whose fur is white marbled with reddish spots above, extends from east Poland to Afghanistan. These animals resemble *M. putorius* in habits. In the United States, the name polecat is often applied to skunks. *See also* FERRET; WEASEL.

POLE STAR (POLARIS), the (naked-eye) star nearest the north celestial pole, is the brightest star in the constellation Ursa Minor (*q.v.*), hence its Bayer designation, α Ursae Minoris. The closeness of the star to the pole (minimum distance about 27′ in the year 2102) causes its apparent position to remain nearly constant all night and all year. The location and moderate brightness of Polaris make it a convenient object for navigators and surveyors to use in determining latitude and north-south direction in the northern hemisphere.

Polaris, a single star to the naked eye, is a system of three stars.

A faint companion is visible in a small telescope; spectrographic observations indicate the presence of a third star very close to the brighter of the visual pair.

The bright star is a pulsating variable of the classical Cepheid type, undergoing changes in diameter and in brightness during a four-day period.   (EH. R.)

POLESYE (Polish POLESIE; meaning "cleared forest land"), a region in the western U.S.S.R., is the largest swamp and bog area in Europe, covering the major part of the basin of the Pripyat (Pripet; Polish Prypeć) River, a tributary of the Dnieper River, with its marshes (*see below*). It has roughly the form of a triangle with its apex near Brest and its base between the points where the Berezina in the north and the Teterev in the south join the Dnieper. Polesye was settled relatively early because food was abundant (fish in the rivers and the lakes, game in the forests) and because the area was easy to defend. The oldest known inhabitants were the Dregovichi, a Slavonic tribe, whose neighbours to the northwest were Lithuanians and to the southeast other Slavs—ancestors of the modern Ukrainians. In the 11th century the local principality of Turov (on the Pripyat) was part of Kievan Russia. Conquered by Lithuania in the 14th century, it became part of Poland after the Polish-Lithuanian union of 1569. At that time Polesie formed the Polish *wojewodztwo* (province) of Brzesc Litewski (Brest). After the partitions of Poland the country was divided among the Russian *guberniyas* (provinces) of Grodno, Minsk, and Volhynia. When Poland was restored after World War I, western Polesie became a *wojewodztwo,* while eastern Polesye was divided between the Belorussian and the Ukrainian Soviet Socialist republics; after World War II the whole of Polesye was divided between the two latter republics.   (K. SM.; X.)

POLESYE (PRIPET) MARSHES lie in the basin of the Pripyat River and cover the greater part of Brest and Gomel *oblasti* of the Belorussian Soviet Socialist Republic and the northern parts of Volyn, Rovno, and Zhitomir *oblasti* of the Ukrainian S.S.R., an estimated 10,000,000 ac. (4,000,000 ha.). Into the flat Pripyat Basin flow a number of rivers from the Belorussian Ridge to the north and the Volyno-Podolsk Upland to the south. The deposition of fluvioglacial sands complicated the drainage, and man contributed to the formation of swamps by building fish- and milldams. There are small areas of sphagnum peat bog, but the swamps are for the most part reed or grass marsh or swamp-forest associations with willow and alder. The only dry areas are "islands" formed by sand dunes or by remnants of a former, higher river terrace. In 1872 drainage of the swamps was started by a state-organized "western expedition for the drainage of swamps." Over the next 25 years more than 3,000 mi. (4,830 km.) of canals were built, and extensive areas were reclaimed. During World War I and the following years, when the region was divided politically between Poland and the U.S.S.R., much of this work was destroyed or fell into disuse. After 1939 further drainage operations were undertaken. The chief towns are Mozyr in the east and the seats of ancient princedoms, Turov and Pinsk, all on the Pripyat River. (R. A. F.; X.)

POLE VAULTING, the art of jumping over an obstacle with the aid of a pole. Originally a means of clearing objects, such as ditches, brooks, and fences, pole vaulting for height, clearing a bar supported by two uprights, became a competitive sport. In competition, each vaulter is given three chances to clear a specified height. The bar, which rests on the uprights set not less than 12 ft. apart, is raised progressively until a winner emerges. Ties are broken by a "count back" based on fewest failures and fewest attempts throughout the contest. The pole may be of any material (fibre glass became the most effective, and popular, in the early 1960s) and of any length or diameter. A slideway, or box, is sunk into the ground, the back of which is placed directly below the crossbar. The pole is thrust into this box. A soft pit, generally of sawdust or foam rubber, is provided for the vaulter's landing.

Requirements of the athlete include a high degree of coordination, timing, speed, and gymnastic ability. The modern vaulter approaches the takeoff with great speed, carrying the pole with his hands about 2½ ft. apart. As the stride next before the spring is completed, he performs the shift, which consists in advancing the pole toward the slideway (known as the advance) and at the same time allowing the lower hand to slip up the pole until it reaches the upper hand, and raising both hands as high above his head as possible before leaving the ground. He is thus enabled to exert the full pulling power of both arms to raise his body and help the swing-up of his legs. There are two factors the pole-vaulter bears in mind—one is height and the other is carry. Height gives him the elevation, and carry takes him across the bar.

The modern pole-vaulter generally uses the following techniques: A long run of approximately 100 to 150 ft., great speed down the runway, and exact timing when the shift takes place, so that his hands are extended high above his head at the instant of the takeoff. He then runs off the ground (he does not jump) leaving his body hanging by the hands as long as possible, not pulling too soon. He then lets his legs swing upward and to the side of the pole. The athlete's feet should reach a point well above the crossbar, in an attempt to actually make a handstand. At this stage the vaulter shoots his legs high above the crossbar by means of a strong arm pull on the pole. He next turns his body face downward and converts his pulling force into a pushing force. The bar lies in the concavity of the stomach, so that his feet are on one side and his head and shoulders are on the other side. The athlete finally carries his body across the crossbar by what is known as the carry, which is the speed he has acquired from his run.

Astounding improvements in performance are best illustrated as follows: (1) H. H. Baxter (New York Athletic Club), in 1883, 11 ft. $\frac{1}{2}$ in. (using old style), the first man to vault over 11 ft.; (2) Norman E. Dole, 1904 world's record, 12 ft. $1\frac{1}{4}$ in., the first man to vault over 12 ft.; (3) Robert A. Gardner (Yale University), at the Intercollegiate Association of Amateur Athletics of America games in 1912, 13 ft. 1 in., the first man to vault over 13 ft.; (4) Sabin W. Carr (Yale University), at the IC4-A games in 1927, 14 ft., the first man to vault 14 ft.; (5) Cornelius Warmerdam (Olympic Club), at Berkeley, Calif., in 1940, 15 ft. $1\frac{1}{8}$ in., the first man to vault 15 ft.; (6) John Uelses (U.S. Marine Corps), using a fibreglass pole, at Santa Barbara, Calif., in 1962, 16 ft. $\frac{1}{4}$ in., the first man to vault 16 ft.; (7) John Pennel (Northeast Louisiana State College), at Miami, Fla., in 1963, 17 ft. $\frac{3}{4}$ in., the first man to vault 17 ft.; (8) Christos Papanicolaou, at Athens, Greece, in 1970, 18 ft. $\frac{1}{4}$ in., the first man to vault 18 ft. Introduction of a bamboo pole, used with modern technique, added approximately a foot to the records; Warmerdam used a bamboo pole. Don Bragg achieved his world record of 15 ft. $9\frac{1}{4}$ in. (1960) with an aluminum pole. However, with mastery of the different timing and technique of fibre-glass poles, vaults of over 17 ft. became commonplace. *See* OLYMPIC GAMES; TRACK AND FIELD SPORTS; SPORTING RECORD.

BIBLIOGRAPHY.—H. A. Meyer, *Track and Field Athletics* (1964); Richard I. Miller, *Fundamentals of Track and Field Coaching* (1952); R. L. Quercetani, *A World History of Track and Field Athletics 1864–1964* (1964); G. H. G. Dyson, *The Mechanics of Athletics* (1962).
(A. C. G.; N. D. McW.; Sv. S.)

POLICE. In a broad sense, the term police (Lat. *politia*, the state) connotes the maintenance of public order and the protection of persons and property from the hazards of public accidents and the commission of unlawful acts; specifically, it applies to the body of civil officers charged with maintaining public order and safety and enforcing the law, including preventing and detecting crime. In its wider aspects, the term at one time also included such "public health" activities as street paving and lighting, or scavenging and sanitation, as well as applications broad enough to comprehend the entire range of government domestic policies. In modern usage, it includes various inspectional, licensing, and other regulatory activities.

A special use of the word is involved when authoritarian states set up secret political police organizations that operate independently of the regular civil police establishments. Political police are always highly centralized agencies. The Nazi Gestapo and *Schutzstaffel*, the tsarist Okhrana, the Soviet Cheka, OGPU, and NKVD, and Mussolini's Ovra all had common characteristics sharply distinguishing them from other civil police. Their governments may be called police states. Though democratic governments may need to protect themselves against subversion, they do not hesitate to entrust this protection to police forces charged with law enforcement in general. Lest private rights be infringed, police authority is then carefully limited and numerical strength is held within modest bounds. Under some systems the policeman bears a heavy responsibility for the manner in which he performs his law-enforcement functions, and he is personally answerable in the criminal and civil courts for abuses of his authority. With increasing experience in police management, the maintenance of adequate safeguards for both the state and its citizens is coming closer to realization, though reconciling the two will continue to require attention under all forms of government that support the exercise of substantial civil rights.

Popular governments permit much local autonomy in police administration while authoritarian states tend to centralize police control, but other factors also may produce centralized police control even in democratic countries. England, Wales, and Scotland have scores of local police forces, whereas the Republic of Ireland and the government of Northern Ireland each maintains a single police establishment. Belgium has dual police systems for the national and local levels, with municipal forces that are almost completely autonomous, whereas in Denmark all police activities are administered by functionaries of the crown. For the most part, western European countries follow the French pattern of a national police charged with the maintenance of public order, the investigation of all major crimes, and the full policing of the larger cities, together with locally recruited forces concerned with routine law enforcement duties, including local traffic control, in the smaller places. In some countries, such as France and Italy, a branch of the national police force also performs routine police duties in rural districts. Japan, under a law of 1954, centralized all police forces under the National Defense Force; even so, a certain degree of autonomy in matters of authority, administration, and finance is left to the prefectural and larger municipal departments. In the United States and Canada, national and state (or provincial) police parallel the local police systems.

Police administration in the English-speaking countries has six major aspects: uniformed patrol, criminal investigation (detection of criminals), traffic regulation, special measures for controlling commercial "vice" (narcotics, prostitution, and gambling), regulation of the sale and consumption of intoxicating liquor, and procedures and facilities for dealing with women offenders and juvenile delinquents. (In this connection, *see* GAMBLING; INVESTIGATION, CRIMINAL; JUVENILE DELINQUENCY; LIQUOR LAW. For a general discussion *see* CRIME.)

United States.—Strictly speaking, the United States has no police system. It has about 40,000 police jurisdictions represented by the federal government, the states, the sheriffs and deputy sheriffs of 3,000 counties, a handful of county police forces independent of the sheriffs' offices, the police of 1,000 cities, and occasional constables in more than 20,000 townships, magisterial districts, or county districts, together with other minor forces in 15,000 villages, boroughs, and incorporated towns. In addition, there are a number of special districts concerned with the patrol of parks, parkways, tunnels, bridges, and aqueducts. In short, police administration follows the jurisdiction of the civil governments, whether federal, state, or local. This produces serious internal strains since in a given area there may be as many as five or six levels of police administration. It also unduly complicates the task of coordinating investigations and other police activities. However, central clearinghouses for crime records, criminal identification, and police training, and the vast interstate networks of police teletype and radio, serve in part to overcome some of the more flagrant defects. The total numbers of all full-time and part-time police, including administrative and clerical employees, in the service of these many jurisdictions in the 1960s was around 340,000, compared with an estimated 198,000 in 1940. The increase in police numbers was roughly proportionate to the population growth in the same period. The well-defined trend is away from part-time police, particularly the township constables and deputy sheriffs; but when these are found to be inadequate, state and local governments tend to create new and additional police bodies without eliminating the outworn agencies.

Local police agencies range in size from only one or two part-

POLICE

153

time employees to a highly developed force of thousands in the largest cities. The ratios of police to population generally are highest in the largest cities and decline by graduated steps. Thus, in cities of more than 250,000 population the ratio of full-time police to population was approximately 1:420 in the mid-1960s, while in places of less than 10,000 population the ratio was only about 1:770. The crime index also has been consistently higher in large metropolitan centres than in smaller cities or rural areas. Similar variations appear geographically. New England has the highest police ratios for cities over 250,000 population, the Pacific Coast for places under 25,000. Lowest ratios are most commonly found in the central states. Police strength thus is not only disproportionately greater in those parts of the country having large urban centres but it is in large degree actually concentrated in the big cities. Of the total number of police employed in about 3,700 urban places, more than half were concentrated in less than 50 cities with populations exceeding 250,000.

The inherent weakness of the smallest police establishments and the abdication of police authority by many rural functionaries combined to produce inadequate policing throughout most of the U.S. countryside. For many years this condition was ignored, but the advent of the motor age brought with it so many problems of crime control and traffic regulation that the ancient sheriff-constable system was quickly overwhelmed. A new type of police agency thereupon emerged—one destined to have a far-reaching influence upon the development of police in the United States and upon the distribution of functions among local and state governments. The 19th century witnessed several limited and tentative experiments in state police administration—in Texas, Massachusetts, and Connecticut—but it was not until 1905 that Pennsylvania established its state police force; and when New York and other large states followed at about the time of World War I, success of the state police idea was assured. Because these agencies were in fact wholly new, they did not inherit the old United States police tradition, parts of which were thoroughly bad. Furthermore they were able to experiment with new devices for selection, training, promotion, and discipline.

By the time of World War II every state had acquired a police agency of its own. Some of these were rudimentary in conception and limited in both authority and number of personnel. Some were charged merely with the patrol of state highways for traffic law enforcement. Others had broad enforcement powers exercised throughout populous states but especially in the rural areas where local policing was least adequate. Without exception, state police forces represented a break with the past and with the tradition of local autonomy in police management. But their numbers were nowhere great and their establishment was not accompanied by any large-scale abandonment of outworn and outdated local police units.

The federal government also was drawn more and more into the police field, because it could not be expected indefinitely to entrust the enforcement of many federal statutes to local and state police bodies. The stresses of the American Civil War brought several rudimentary investigative agencies into existence while the expansion of federal regulation encouraged the development of others. In all but a mere handful of these, law enforcement was either auxiliary to other administrative activities or was performed within a narrowly restricted area or involved in the conduct of military or naval operations.

General police jurisdiction at the national level is exercised only by the Federal Bureau of Investigation, the FBI. (*See* FEDERAL BUREAU OF INVESTIGATION.) This select corps of criminal investigators has had repeated additions to the scope of its responsibilities. The central services performed by the FBI for state and local law-enforcement agencies include maintenance of extensive crime laboratories and a uniform system of crime reporting for all jurisdictions in the United States and its possessions.

In a special category are the police organizations maintained by such federal agencies as the Treasury Department and the Tennessee Valley Authority. The police department of Washington, D.C., is wholly unique; commissioners appointed by the president administer the governmental affairs of the federal district and accordingly are responsible for law enforcement within its boundaries.

Great Britain.—Modern police administration in Great Britain stems from the establishment in 1829 of the metropolitan police in the sprawling urban and suburban area surrounding the City of London by the home secretary, Sir Robert Peel. (The popular term "bobby" to denote a policeman stems from his name.) Today the metropolitan police enforce the law in a wide circle of 700 sq.mi., most of it lying within a radius of 15 mi. from Charing Cross. The ancient City, however, which is only 1 sq.mi. in area, has only a small resident population but boasts great wealth and importance, has never been a part of the Metropolitan Police District. Under the London Government Act 1963, the Metropolitan Police District consists of Greater London (excluding the City and the Inner and Middle Temples) and parts of Essex, Hertfordshire, and Surrey.

Headquarters of the metropolitan force are at New Scotland Yard in the borough of the City of Westminster on the Thames embankment, close to the offices of the national government and the Houses of Parliament. The police commissioner of the metropolis is appointed by the crown, with the Home Office occupying the position of responsible police authority in all metropolitan police matters. The home secretary exercises direct control over this critically important law-enforcement agency. (*See* also SCOTLAND YARD.)

The commissioner of the City of London police is chosen by the mayor and aldermen, while in other cities and boroughs having their own police establishments the Watch Committee of the city or borough council appoints the chief constable. Each county constabulary is under the control of a standing joint committee, consisting of specially designated members of the county council and justices of the peace, which selects the chief constable; but the choice of chief constable must in all cases be ratified by the Home Office.

The early county constabularies were created around 1840, primarily for the protection of rural areas, but many now are also charged with responsibility for policing towns in their areas, some of them of considerable size. This process of consolidation, which had gone on for many years, was speeded up greatly by the exigencies of World War II. Further absorption of 45 of the 47 noncounty borough forces followed application of the terms of the Police Act of 1946. Another trend toward integration is marked by the device of placing a single chief constable in command of two or more neighbouring forces.

The authorized strength of the London Metropolitan Police in the 1960s was about 20,000 but the actual strength was around 17,000; the figures for the City of London Police were about 1,000 authorized but 700 actual. The strength of the total county, city, and borough forces in England, Wales, and Scotland was approximately 92,000 authorized, 81,000 actual. Ratio of police to population throughout England, Wales, and Scotland was about 1:600, but this uniform ratio conceals great local differences due to differing population densities, differing conditions in town and country, the nature or value of property to be guarded, and any circumstances making such property unusually vulnerable.

Although the British police system is deeply imbedded in local political institutions, the national government nevertheless maintains a certain degree of surveillance over the administration of even the smallest borough forces and county constabularies and extends financial and technical aid in various important ways. This represents an effort to introduce some degree of unity and coherence into a system that in most respects is wholly decentralized. Hence, the home secretary (for England and Wales) and the secretary of state for Scotland may enforce standards of efficiency in all police establishments. They also control the conditions of police employment (appointment, promotion, discipline, compensation, etc.) through widely ranging regulations. Such controls are made effective by the grant-in-aid annually made to each police establishment, totaling one-half of the net cost of each force, including pensions. The various forces are thereby made largely dependent upon the national exchequer, for it is provided that the grants shall be made only to those meeting the required standards.

Annual visitations by her majesty's inspectors of constabulary (five for the Home Office, including one woman, and one for the Scottish Office) operate to enforce compliance.

The national government provides various central facilities. It operates seven forensic science laboratories (in addition to the metropolitan police laboratory at New Scotland Yard), district recruiting offices, regional networks for wireless communication, and eight training centres serving a number of neighbouring forces in England and Wales, with a ninth serving Scotland. It also bears a special relationship to the metropolitan police that springs from the unique position and character of that force. For example, the Metropolitan Police Force through its Special Branch is charged with certain duties in the U.K. and British colonies not readily performed by any other existing body. It is responsible for the protection of the royal family, the ministers of government, and distinguished foreign visitors; for traffic and maintaining order in the vicinity of the Houses of Parliament; for guarding government buildings and taking special precautions at state functions; and for protecting against political agitators and sabotage. A special contribution of £100,000 a year is made from the exchequer for these purposes.

The Metropolitan Police Force performs a widely heralded and generally misunderstood function in investigating certain crimes committed outside the metropolitan area. For the most part these excursions are confined to cases of murder; and since they are authorized only upon the request of the local chief of police, their number in any one year is small. A new branch was formed in 1954 to cooperate on country crimes committed by London criminals. The Metropolitan Police Force also operates the Criminal Record Office, a national registry of crimes and criminals, and publishes the daily *Police Gazette* which carries details of persons wanted for crime and of stolen property; this publication is distributed without charge to British and certain European police forces.

Commonwealth of Nations.—Canadian local police forces, unlike those in the United States, are usually under the jurisdiction of police boards or commissions comprised of the mayor, the county judge, and a police magistrate. While the county judge and police magistrate are appointed by the central and provincial governments respectively, in practice they are regarded as servants of the local community. For Canada's extensive federal police system *see* ROYAL CANADIAN MOUNTED POLICE. The RCMP act as provincial police except in Ontario and Quebec, which have their own provincial police forces, and as municipal police in many small communities.

Australia has a small Commonwealth police force, with restricted federal duties, but the various states maintain their own police forces. These are the smallest units; there are no separate city forces, though Canberra, the capital, has a detachment of about 25 men from the Commonwealth force. Commonwealth duties such as the registration and control of aliens, firearms, the drug traffic, and the trade in obscene literature are left to the state forces; these, however, cooperate so closely and confer so frequently that national uniformity is maintained.

(BR. S.; L. GU.)

European Countries.—The main police forces in France are the Préfecture de Police and the Sûreté Nationale, both controlled by the Ministry of the Interior, and the Gendarmerie Nationale, a military force controlled by the minister for armed forces but made available to the Ministry of the Interior for police work. The Préfecture provides the "preventive" police force for Paris and the Seine *département;* its uniformed members, known as *gardiens de la paix,* are responsible for traffic and crowd control and are highly motorized. By contrast, their "plain clothes" members, who are known as the directorate of judicial police, investigate all serious crime throughout France. Their work frequently overlaps, not without occasional friction, that of the *juges d'instruction* in the early stages of a prosecution for crime. The Sûreté Nationale operates throughout the country and supervises the municipal police of provincial towns with over 10,000 inhabitants (each town having a *commissaire de police*). It has two rigidly distinct functions—"preventive" police work and criminal investigation, the latter being the concern of a Sûreté Urbaine.

The Gendarmerie polices rural areas and small towns, its duties including those of military police. (*See also* FRANCE: *Administration and Social Conditions.*)

The state police (*Bundespolizei*) of West Germany are controlled by the Ministry of the Interior; and except in Baden-Württemberg, Bavaria, and Hesse there are no local police forces throughout the provinces of the union. Among the subdivisions of the state police, a National Boundary Guard (*Bundesgrenzschutzpolizei*) patrols the frontier of the German Democratic Republic, and a Criminal Investigation Department (*Bundeskriminalamt*) maintains a central information index, links with Interpol, technical laboratories, and specialist officers for dealing with particular crimes. All criminal investigation work is governed by a code of criminal process, arrests being permissible only under rigidly prescribed conditions, which vary to some extent in the various provinces. (*See also* GERMANY: *Administration and Social Conditions.*)

The Italian Corps of Agents of Public Safety (*guardia di pubblica sicurezza*), a part of the national armed forces, is responsible to the Ministry of the Interior for the protection of life and property and the prevention of crime throughout Italy. It has three sections: the territorial, operating from fixed police stations, with a central bureau (*questura*) in each province; the *mobile,* heavily armed and specially trained for dealing with strikes, riots, and revolutionary movements; and the special section, which controls road traffic and railways and guards the frontiers. The larger towns, such as Rome and Milan, have city police forces, but their duties are confined to traffic control. The Agents of Public Safety enforce all the major laws and are responsible for public safety. The Ministry of the Interior also maintains a Carabinieri, which has ordinary police duties but is also a military corps. (*See also* ITALY: *Administration and Social Conditions.*)

U.S.S.R.—The MVD (*Ministerstvo Vnutrennykh Del*) is the nationwide police system at union-republic level. The MVD of the U.S.S.R. guides the activities of the MVD's of the autonomous republics. It polices the rural districts and the provincial cities of the larger republics and is entrusted with the security of public order and the protection of state property; many of its preventive purposes are achieved by installing secret agents in factories and offices. The Moscow militia, which has 134 militia precincts, comes under that city's own administration of internal affairs—a department of the executive committee of the Moscow Soviet of Working People's Deputies. It maintains law and order, investigates crimes for the district prosecutors, enforces passport regulations, and controls road traffic.

For the international police network known as Interpol, *see* INTERNATIONAL CRIMINAL POLICE ORGANIZATION. *See also* MILITARY POLICE; and references under "Police" in the Index.

(C. H. R.)

BIBLIOGRAPHY.—Brian Chapman, articles on French and European police in *Public Administration* (spring 1951), *The Journal of Criminal Law, Criminology, and Police Science* (Nov.–Dec. 1953), and *The Manchester Guardian* (Aug. 25 and 27, 1955), also ch. 1 in his *The Profession of Government* (1959); Police College, Japan, *The Japanese Police* (1954); Bruce Smith, *Police Systems in the United States,* 2nd rev. ed. by Bruce Smith, Jr. (1960); Sir John Moylan, *Scotland Yard and the Metropolitan Police* (1934); J. M. Hart, *The British Police* (1951); Charles Reith, *A New Study of Police History* (1956); John Coatman, *Police* (1959), a general treatment concerning police in English-speaking countries, France, and Germany; Sir Percy Sillitoe, *Cloak Without Dagger* (1955), memoirs of a British intelligence officer, providing much information on modern police history; Philip John Stead, *The Police of Paris* (1957); James Cramer, *The World's Police* (1964); Geoffrey Marshall, *Police and Government* (1965); Leon Radzinowicz, *A History of English Criminal Law and Its Administration From 1750* (1956); *Final Report of the Royal Commission on the Police* (1962); Michael Banton, *The Police in the Community* (1964); Benjamin Whitaker, *The Police* (1964). For police administration *see* Orlando Winfield Wilson, *Police Administration* (1950) and *Police Planning,* 2nd ed. (1958); "New Goals in Police Management," Bruce Smith (ed.), *The Annals* (Jan. 1954).

See also Her Majesty's Inspectors of Constabulary, *Police: Counties and Boroughs, England and Wales* (annual reports); also *Reports of Her Majesty's Inspector of Constabulary for Scotland* (annual); Federal Bureau of Investigation, *Uniform Crime Reports for the United States* (annual, together with quarterly preliminary releases of crime data).

(BR. S.; L. GU.)

POLICE POWER is a term used in U.S. constitutional law to describe the permissible scope of state legislation. In spite of its importance, police power is not mentioned in the U.S. constitution; the concept was created by the courts to reflect the conclusion that an approved law did not violate specific constitutional prohibitions—especially the 14th amendment's provision that no state may "deprive any person of life, liberty or property without due process of law."

During the decades immediately preceding 1937, while the U.S. supreme court was forcefully using the due process clause to outlaw social and economic controls, such as minimum wage and maximum hour laws, an important step in the court's reasoning was a narrow definition of the police power. The freedom of labour to bargain was thought of as a liberty protected under the due process clause; an invasion of this liberty could be justified only by a proper exercise of the police power. The critical point in the court's reasoning was the further assertion that the state's police power existed only for certain limited objectives which the court frequently described as the promotion of "health, safety and morals."

Under this formula much social and economic legislation could be outlawed. Limiting the hours of work might not directly affect health, except in unusual situations such as underground mines and smelters; through this approach the supreme court in 1905 invalidated New York's 60-hour maximum work week for bakers. The court similarly concluded that minimum wage legislation did not fit under any of the permitted headings of the police power. Thus in 1923, the court invalidated the establishment of minimum wages for women, observing: "It cannot be shown that well-paid women safeguard their morals more carefully than those who are poorly paid." Even in cases where the police power was said to extend to "health, safety, morals and welfare," the court's early decisions indicated that it was physical, rather than economic or social, welfare which fell within the permissible scope for legislation.

In 1937, notably first in a decision upholding a Washington state minimum wage law (*West Coast Hotel Co.* v. *Parrish,* 300 U.S. 379), the supreme court sharply altered its approach to allow wide latitude for social and economic legislation; in the course of this development the court virtually abandoned the police power concept as a means of limiting legislative power. For example, in the 1952 *Day-Brite* case upholding a state law which required that workers be paid for time spent going to the polls on election day, the court's opinion declared that the police power "is not confined to a narrow category" but "extends to all the great public needs." Although the validity of aesthetics as a goal of regulation was once in doubt, the court in 1954 sustained a program of urban development, declaring that the state may legislate to make the community "beautiful as well as healthy"; the goals of legislation may be "spiritual as well as physical, aesthetic as well as monetary."

While police power as a concept for limiting governmental objectives thus was virtually abandoned by the supreme court, state supreme courts in construing their own state constitutional provisions in many cases continued the earlier approach which requires that legislation be justified under distinct and traditional headings.

Police power has occasionally been invoked to sustain rather than to invalidate legislation. This has been true in dealing with laws which impair the value of property, *e.g.,* by shutting down a still on the advent of prohibition or by restricting the use of property through zoning; the court has sustained such legislation on the ground that effective exercise of the police power justified the restriction. But this reference to police power is only another way of saying that constitutional provisions for the protection of property, such as those of the 5th and 14th amendments, cannot have been intended to block the necessary processes of government even though some financial loss may result. In similar manner, the police power has been invoked in deciding whether laws, such as those suspending mortgage obligations in times of economic depression, violate the constitutional prohibition against impairing the obligation of contracts. In all these cases, resolving the question whether public or private interest must yield has called for balancing delicate and elusive considerations applicable to each individual case; the general concept of police power, although often invoked, has not in reality supplied the specific materials for decisions.

See also AMERICAN LAW: *Public Law;* CONSTITUTION AND CONSTITUTIONAL LAW: *United States.*

See E. Freund, *Police Power* (1904); C. B. Swisher, *American Constitutional Development,* ch. 32, 33, 37, 2nd ed. (1954). (J. O. Ho.)

POLIGNAC, a noble family of France.

The first viscounts of Polignac (in the modern *département* of Haute-Loire) were practically independent rulers of Velay, the country where the Loire rises, at least from the 1050s, perhaps from 860. Their ultimate heiress, VALPURGE, was married in 1349 to Guillaume III de Chalençon, whose descendants assumed the Polignac name in 1421. The actual power of the house declined as feudalism broke down, but it maintained its exalted rank in the nobility; and in the ninth generation after Guillaume de Chalençon it emerged into political prominence with MELCHIOR (1661–1741), known first as the abbé, then as the cardinal de Polignac. Early experienced in diplomatic affairs between France and Rome, the abbé was sent as Louis XIV's ambassador to Poland in 1693. There he procured the abortive election of François Louis de Bourbon, prince de Conti (*q.v.*), as king of Poland in 1697. After a temporary disgrace, he was elected to the French Academy in 1704. During the War of the Spanish Succession he played a major part in the negotiations at Gertruydenberg (1710) and at Utrecht (1712) before becoming a cardinal (creation *in petto* 1712, published 1713). He was exiled for participation in the Cellamare plot of 1718 (*see* MAINE, LOUIS AUGUSTE DE BOURBON, DUC DU), but was French *chargé d'affaires* in Rome from 1724 to 1732 and was made archbishop of Auch in 1726. He died in Paris on Nov. 21, 1741. His long Latin poem, *Anti-Lucretius,* first printed in 1747, largely against Pierre Bayle's philosophy, went through many editions and translations.

The cardinal's grandnephew, ARMAND JULES FRANÇOIS (1745–1817), was married in 1767 to Yolande Martine Gabrielle de Polastron. She became a great favourite of Queen Marie Antoinette, and he was created duc de Polignac (1780). Their influence was savagely denounced in pamphlets during the Revolution.

JULES DE POLIGNAC (1780–1847), the 1st duc's second son, went from England back to France, with his elder brother ARMAND (1771–1847; later 2nd duc), to conspire against Napoleon in 1804, but they were arrested. Released in 1813, Jules was made a peer at the Bourbon Restoration (1815), but refused at first to take the constitutional oath as he thought it derogatory to the Holy See's rights. For this the Holy See granted him the Roman title of prince (1820; recognized in France 1822). His ultramontanism and extreme royalism appealed to Charles X (*q.v.*), who appointed him minister of foreign affairs on Aug. 8, 1829, and prime minister on Nov. 17. Responsible for the ordinances which provoked the July Revolution of 1830, he was arrested and, in December 1830, sentenced to life imprisonment. Released but banished in November 1836, he finally returned to France in 1845. The Bavarian monarchy in 1838 extended the title of prince to all his descendants, and as his elder brother died childless (March 2, 1847), he inherited the ducal title as well just before his own death on March 29. The comtes de Polignac descend from the 1st duc's third son, CAMILLE MELCHIOR HENRI (1781–1855). One of them, Comte PIERRE (1895–1964), was the father of Prince Rainier of Monaco.

Prince EDMOND MELCHIOR (1834–1901), fifth son of Jules, was a composer. In 1893 he married Winnaretta Singer (1865–1943), who, as Princesse Edmond de Polignac, was the outstanding Parisian patroness of *avant-garde* music in the first half of the 20th century.

POLIOMYELITIS (INFANTILE PARALYSIS) is an acute infectious disease caused by a filterable virus and characterized by symptoms that range from a mild nonparalytic infection to an extensive flaccid paralysis of voluntary muscles.

History.—There is evidence that the disease has existed for many centuries. However, the first clear description of poliomyelitis came from Jakob von Heine in 1840. It was not recognized in its epidemic form until Oskar Medin in 1887 reported observations on an outbreak in Sweden. In addition to the usual spinal form, he described the bulbar and certain less common types of the disease. C. S. Caverly, in 1896, recognized that the disease may occur in an abortive or nonparalytic form, a fact confirmed by others later. While earlier outbreaks centred largely in Sweden, epidemics have occurred in many parts of the world and became particularly prominent in the United States after the beginning of the 20th century.

Incidence.—Severe epidemics have been reported in many countries and islands including North, Central and South America, Europe and Africa. The disease reached epidemic proportions in some region of the United States almost every year after the beginning of the 20th century until vaccine became available. The greatest recorded sustained incidence in the United States was in 1942–53; in 1950, for example, there were 33,344 cases in the United States. In 1952 severe epidemics occurred in Denmark, Germany and Belgium. With the advent of the Salk and Sabin vaccines after 1955, the incidence of the disease showed a remarkable decline, especially in those countries with an intensive immunization program. In 1967, for example, the United States and Canada reported a total of only 47 cases. Sharp outbreaks in 1967, however, were reported in a number of countries with warm climates in Latin America and Africa and in Turkey and Spain, possibly because of a letup in their immunization programs.

Symptoms.—The commonest early complaints consist of mild headache, fever, sore throat, nausea, vomiting, diarrhea, restlessness and drowsiness. The temperature rises slowly, reaching its peak in two to three days, and then rapidly subsides. Fortunately more than two-thirds of the patients who develop these early symptoms recover and remain well without any signs of muscle weakness. When the disease is severer, the patient develops pain in the back and limbs, muscle tenderness, stiff neck, irritability and fretfulness.

Paralytic Forms.—*Spinal Poliomyelitis.*—This is the commonest type of paralytic poliomyelitis and is caused by infection of the spinal cord. At about the third day of the illness, the patient develops weakness of the limbs. The paralysis may be of all grades of severity from transient weakness that soon disappears to complete and permanent paralysis. The lower limbs are more often affected than the upper limbs. Within a few months after the development of paralysis, the involved muscles begin to atrophy.

Respiratory Poliomyelitis.—The muscles of the chest that control breathing receive their nerve supply from the upper part of the spinal cord. When the virus injures this part of the spinal cord, the patient develops difficulty in breathing. Acts such as coughing, sneezing and sniffing cannot be carried out. When there is a definite loss of function to these muscles, it is essential that some mechanical device be used to aid respiration.

Bulbar Poliomyelitis.—That part of the nervous system situated just above the spinal cord is called the bulb or brain stem. In this region are situated the nerve centres that control swallowing and talking, and when poliomyelitis affects this area the patient has difficulty with these actions. Secretions collect in the throat. The voice becomes hoarse and develops a nasal twang. The accumulation of secretions in the throat may block the airway, causing the patient to suffocate. If this obstruction to the airway is not relieved, the patient loses consciousness and will die.

Diagnosis.—In the preparalytic stage of the disease, the diagnosis must depend on strong clinical suspicion supported by certain laboratory observations on the spinal fluid. This is particularly true of patients who become ill in the late summer and autumn in an area where poliomyelitis is prevalent. In 1951 a rapid method for identifying the infection became available, based on the direct inoculation of tissue cultures with stools of ill patients. Virus growth is manifested within 24 hours by a breakdown of the growing tissue culture cells.

Prognosis.—Of all patients who develop poliomyelitis, more than 80% recover within three to four days without the development of paralysis. When paralysis has occurred, considerable restoration of normal muscle powers may take place, although some residual weakness remains in almost half these patients. The over-all fatality rate in the United States was estimated in the 1960s at between 1% and 4%, while a death rate of 30% has been reported in Europe during periods of low prevalence.

Treatment.—Treatment during the preparalytic stages includes complete bed rest, isolation and careful observation. The patient should be permitted to assume whatever position he wishes. It is important to check carefully for evidence of limb paralysis or breathing or swallowing difficulty.

If paralysis occurs, good nursing care is of primary importance. The bed should be firm with a board under the mattress. Passive movement of the limbs can be used to avoid deformities. Moist heat usually makes the patient more comfortable. As muscle strength returns, exercises are increased. (See *Orthopedic Aspects*, below.)

When there is paralysis of the breathing muscles, some form of mechanical breathing aid is necessary. The one most commonly used is the tank respirator, or "iron lung." The patient is placed in the tank respirator with only his head emerging, and by a rhythmical increase and decrease of the pressure within the tank his chest is expanded and relaxed. In less severe cases it is possible to use a respirator that fits to the chest only (cuirass respirator) or a rocking bed.

When the patient develops difficulty in swallowing, with accumulation of secretions in the throat, it is important that the airway be kept open by removal of the secretions. This can be done by a mechanical suction machine. If suction of the machine is not adequate an artificial airway must be made from the outside into the throat (tracheotomy).

Etiology.—In 1909 Karl Landsteiner and Constantin Levaditi showed that the causal agent of poliomyelitis is a filterable virus. This virus cannot be cultivated on ordinary lifeless media since it grows only in media containing living tissue cells. It is fairly resistant to physical and chemical agents and is able to survive for some time in water, milk and sewage.

When the virus comes in contact with the defense mechanism of the body it elicits the formation of specific antibodies that act to neutralize its infectivity. Of importance, however, is the fact that not all strains are antigenically or immunologically alike. Many strains have been isolated from patients with poliomyelitis from all parts of the world; they can be divided into three immunologically distinct types, and infection with one type does not protect against reinfection with one of the other types. The three types are known as type I, or Brunhilde; type II, or Lansing; and type III, or Leon.

Up to 1939 the virus could be transmitted to monkeys only. In that year, however, Charles Armstrong succeeded in transmitting the Lansing strain to eastern cotton rats and from these animals to white mice. In 1949 J. F. Enders and his associates demonstrated that the virus could be isolated and grown in tissue culture on nonnervous tissue cells, thus making it possible to study and grow this virus without the use of living animals. This inexpensive method of working with the virus greatly facilitated research and was directly responsible for the development of poliomyelitis vaccine.

Pathology.—The virus probably enters the body through the throat and intestinal tract, since large quantities are excreted in the stools for a number of weeks before and after an attack of poliomyelitis. The disease is probably spread from person to person by intimate human contact. It has been postulated that the virus migrates from the throat and intestines to the central nervous system along the peripheral nerves. However, more recent studies have suggested that the virus may spread from the alimentary tract into the blood and lymphatics, whence it is disseminated widely throughout the body, including the nervous system. Within the central nervous system it spreads along nerve pathways (axonal transmission) and eventually reaches the more sensitive motor nerve cells in the spinal cord, medulla or brain. These are destroyed in varying numbers, and the destroyed cells are not replaced since nerve cells lack the power of regeneration. Not all cells attacked are destroyed, however, and those not severely injured recover their normal function in time. To the extent that they do recover a corresponding restoration of muscle function may be expected to take place.

Predisposing Factors.—Individual differences in the degree of natural susceptibility appear to exist. Many persons have acquired antibodies in their blood without having knowingly gone through a poliomyelitic infection. The disease commonly attacks those who seem to be in the best of health, so that undernutrition or faulty health do not appear to be predisposing factors.

It is generally held that a lasting immunity follows recovery from the disease. Second attacks are known to occur, however, some of which may be caused by strains differing immunologically from those that caused the first attack.

Among other predisposing factors, age has always been considered the most important. In early epidemics (*i.e.*, before *c.* 1945), most cases occurred in children under ten years of age. Later, however, there was a definite shift to the beginning of adult life.

Geographic areas appear to play little role in the disease. Although the majority of cases occur in temperate climates, the disease has a world-wide distribution and has been reported in the tropics as well as in Iceland and Alaska. Although the disease persists throughout the year, the highest incidence is in the late summer and early fall. Active cases may extend into early winter.

Strenuous exercise, sudden chilling and pregnancy all seem to predispose to the disease. It is generally accepted that removal of the tonsils at the time when the disease is prevalent predisposes to the severer forms of the disease. There is also suggestive evidence that injections of any type (vaccinations) may predispose to the disease, particularly when it is prevalent.   (A. B. Br.)

Control.—From 1955 on the use of two different vaccines in the prevention of poliomyelitis reduced the incidence of the disease almost miraculously. The first of these was introduced in 1955 by Jonas Salk whose vaccine consists of a combination of three types of poliovirus strains that are inactivated by treatment with formalin. This vaccine must be administered by parenteral injection, preferably in infancy. Opinions differ regarding the number of injections required but most agree that a minimum of four, given over a period of at least a year, are necessary. Some have maintained that the primary course should be followed by yearly doses of up to as many as six or eight for adequate maintenance of immunity. In popular parlance these injections became known as "Salk shots." In areas where the inactivated vaccine was used efficiently, which includes quite a few parts of the world, the incidence of poliomyelitis underwent a remarkable reduction. Not only was this due to protection afforded to the individual but there was evidence that the prevalence and circulation of strains of poliovirus were greatly diminished in areas where a substantial number of the population were protected by vaccination, notably in Sweden.

In 1961–62 another, and presumably more efficient, vaccine, developed by Albert B. Sabin, was introduced. Known as the live attenuated poliovirus vaccine, it exerts its effect by inducing a harmless immunizing infection of the intestinal tract, thus simulating natural infection without causing any disease. The live-virus vaccine has certain advantages over the killed Salk type, including ease of administration, for it is given by mouth. It also has the ability to induce immunity very rapidly, a property particularly valuable in the face of an epidemic. When given to a significant proportion of a population it is efficient in producing community protection by rendering the alimentary tract of those vaccinated resistant to reinfection by polioviruses. The use of the Sabin-type vaccine, which is given in three separate doses—one for each poliovirus type—or as a trivalent preparation in two to three doses, was followed by a further sharp reduction in the incidence of poliomyelitis in the United States to approximately a scant 100 cases annually in the mid-1960s.

There is evidence that the immunity resulting from live-virus vaccine persists for years. It is therefore rather well agreed that once the three-dose schedule has been completed (plus a "booster" after one year for infants), oral immunization does not have to be repeated—the individual is probably protected for life. Whether killed- or live-virus vaccine is used, however, constant vigilance is required on the part of practicing physicians, baby clinics and

the like, as well as local health officers, to see that all children are immunized, including new babies born into the community and susceptible immigrants moving into the area.   (J. R. Pa.)

Orthopedic Aspects.—The orthopedic management of a paralytic patient is directed toward the prevention of deformities, correction of those that cannot be prevented and restoration of bodily function. Actually, 80% of patients with poliomyelitis require little more than general nursing care and recover without significant paralysis. Of the remaining 20%, not all require intensive orthopedic care. During the acute phase of the disease the patient must be kept at absolute bed rest. Attention is given to the prevention of joint contractures by proper positioning of the extremities. As long as the patient is bedridden care must be taken to prevent the development of decubitus ulcers (bedsores).

As muscle pain subsides active motion is begun. Frequently patients require assistance in certain movements to neutralize the opposing force of gravity. However, it is only through active contraction by the patient himself of the muscle groups still intact that sufficient strength can be restored to permit normal function of the part. In selected cases, supported walking or exercise in a water tank is of value. Other aids to the restoration of muscle power may occasionally be utilized. The relatively small group of patients who fail to regain enough muscle power to function independently can usually be taught to walk with the support of braces or crutches.

It is not until a permanent plateau of function is reached—usually 12 to 18 months after the acute illness—that surgical measures are considered. Surgery in poliomyelitis may be undertaken to (1) stabilize an unsupported joint; (2) correct fixed deformities; (3) adjust leg length inequalities; or (4) restore function. A common stabilizing procedure involves arthrodesis (fusion) of a joint. In such cases motion is sacrificed for position and strength. Extensive fusion is sometimes the treatment of choice in scoliosis (spinal curvature) resulting from postparalytic imbalance of the spinal musculature. Another useful type of surgical operation involves transplantation of one end of a functioning but expendable muscle in the region involved to a new insertion where its contraction will then produce a movement or perform a joint-stabilizing function formerly performed by a paralyzed muscle group. Leg length inequality, rarely considerable enough to require treatment, may, when necessary, be compensated for by a growth-arresting procedure on the uninvolved extremity at an age calculated to permit equalizing but not excessive growth of the shorter leg. Clearly the purpose of surgical treatment, whatever the type, is to restore the paralytic patient to as nearly normal function as possible and free him from the use of artificial supports.   (J. Dy.)

Bibliography.—Ludvig Hektoen and Ella Salmonsen (comps.), *A Bibliography of Infantile Paralysis, 1789–1949*, ed. by Morris Fishbein, 2nd ed. (1951); J. F. Enders, T. H. Weller and F. C. Robbins, "Cultivation of Lansing Strain of Poliomyelitis Virus in Cultures of Various Human Embryonic Tissues," *Science*, 109:85–87 (1949); J. E. Salk, "Principles of Immunization as Applied to Poliomyelitis and Influenza," *Amer. J. Public Health*, 43:1384–98 (1953), "Persistence of Immunity After Administration of Formalin-Treated Poliovirus Vaccine," *Lancet*, 2:715–723 (Oct. 1, 1960); E. R. Alexander, "The Extent of the Poliomyelitis Problem," *J.A.M.A.*, 175:837–840 (March 11, 1961); "Living or Dead?" *Lancet*, 2:1011–12 (Nov. 4, 1961); A. B. Sabin, "Present Position of Immunization Against Poliomyelitis With Live Virus Vaccine," *Brit. Med. J.*, 1:660–663 (1959), "Oral Poliovirus Vaccine," *Roy. Soc. Health J.*, 82:51–59 (March–April 1962); University of Michigan Poliomyelitis Vaccine Evaluation Center, *Evaluation of the 1954 Poliomyelitis Vaccine Trials* (1955); J. R. Paul, "Status of Vaccination Against Poliomyelitis With Particular Reference to Oral Vaccination," *New Eng. J. Med.*, 264:651–658 (1961). *See* also the reports of the International Poliomyelitis Conference (1948 *et seq.*), International Conference on Live Poliovirus Vaccines (1959 *et seq.*), World Health Organization expert committee on poliomyelitis and the Soviet-American Polio Conference, Moscow (May 1960).

POLISH LANGUAGE. Polish, the mother tongue of probably 30,000,000 speakers, belongs to the western group of the Slavonic (Slavic) languages (*q.v.*). Its first written records consist of proper names in Latin documents of the 12th century, and extant manuscripts containing any considerable amount of connected Polish text go back no earlier than the 14th century. The modern literary language may be dated from the 16th century, when the ferment of Reformation, Renaissance and Counter-Reformation produced the first outstanding Polish writers, such as Mikołaj Rej, Jan Kochanowski, Piotr Skarga and others associated with the Golden Age of Polish literature. Under their cultivation, Polish developed with astonishing rapidity into the refined instrument of literary expression that it has since remained.

Foreign influences on Polish have been numerous, but (except for the macaronic aberrations of the late 17th and early 18th centuries) have been easily absorbed without harm to the integrity of the language. The introduction of Christianity brought not only Latin, but also Czech, the language of the first missionaries, into living contact with Polish. As an already developed literary language, Czech continued to enjoy high prestige among the Poles as late as the 14th and 15th centuries, and there are still Polish words whose form betrays their Czech origin, such as *hańba* "disgrace," *brama* "gate," *władać* "to rule." The large medieval German immigration and settlement in Polish cities is reflected in an extensive layer of the vocabulary, such as *ratusz* "town hall," *burmistrz* "mayor," *malarz* "painter," *handel* "trade," *rachunek* "account," *gmach* "building," *szlachta* "nobility" and many others (compare German *Rathaus, Bürgermeister, Maler, Handel, Rechnung, Gemach, Geschlecht*). Italian (at the time of the Renaissance), French (in the 17th and 18th centuries) and English have supplemented the Polish vocabulary. In addition, special mention should be made of White Russian and Ukrainian influences, particularly as they penetrated into Polish through the works of writers from the eastern borderlands.

Polish shares with other West Slavonic languages a number of notable phonological characteristics, such as: (1) fixed stress accent—in Polish, on the penultimate syllable of the word; (2) non-palatalization of Common Slavonic (CS) velars in forms like *kwiat, gwiazda*—compare Czech *květ, hvězda* and contrast Russian *cvet, zvezdá;* (3) the development of CS *tj, dj* to hissing sounds, as in *świeca, miedza* (<CS **světja, *medja*)—compare Low Sorbian *sweca, mjaza* and contrast Russian *svečá, mežá;* (4) š (spelled *sz*) resulting from the second palatalization of CS *x*, as in *wszystek, wszak*—contrast the hissing sibilant in Russian *ves', vsjákij;* (5) preservation of dental stops before *l*, as in *wiódł, mydło*—compare Czech *vedl, mýdlo* and contrast Russian *vël, mylo.*

More or less peculiar to Polish, particularly in contrast to Czech and Slovak, are such phenomena as: (1) nasal vowels (spelled *ę, ą*), indirectly continuing the nasal vowels of CS, as in *mięso, trząść*—contrast Czech *maso, třásti;* (2) dispalatalization of CS *e, ě, r̝* to *o, a, ar* before nonpalatalized *t, d, n, s, z, r* and *ł* as in *żona, wiara, twardy*—contrast Czech *žena, víra, tvrdý;* (3) palatalization of consonants (indicated in the spelling by *i* following the consonant letter) before *e* from CS front *jer*—contrast, for example, Polish *pies, dzień* and Czech *pes, den.*

The dialects, whose differences cause no practical difficulties in understanding, are customarily grouped into a few major types, notably Great Polish and Pomeranian, Silesian, Little Polish and Mazovian. In addition, Cassubian has come to assume the role of a Polish dialect although, historically speaking, it is not. The dialect base of the literary language, which displays some features associated with Great Polish and others associated with Little Polish, is still a matter of dispute.

BIBLIOGRAPHY.—*Grammars:* H. Grappin, *Grammaire de la langue polonaise,* 2nd ed. (1949); T. Benni, J. Łoś, K. Nitsch, J. Rozwadowski, H. Ułaszyn, *Gramatyka języka polskiego* (1923); W. Doroszewski, *Podstawy gramatyki polskiej I* (1952); St. Szober, *Gramatyka języka polskiego,* 4th ed. (1957). *Dictionaries:* K. Bulas and F. J. Whitfield, *Kościuszko Foundation Dictionary I, English-Polish* (1959); K. Bulas, L. L. Thomas and F. J. Whitfield, *Kościuszko Foundation Dictionary II, Polish-English* (1960); J. Stanislawski, *English-Polish and Polish-English Dictionary* (n.d.); S. B. Linde, *Słownik języka polskiego,* 2nd ed., 6 vol. (1854–60; repr. 1952); J. Karłowicz *et al., Słownik języka polskiego,* 8 vol. (1900–27; 1952); T. Lehr-Spławiński, *Słownik języka polskiego,* 2 vol., A–N (n.d.); W. Doroszewski, St. Skorupka *et al., Słownik języka polskiego Polskiej Akademii Nauk* (1958 *et seq.*); Fr. Stawski, *Słownik etymologiczny języka polskiego* (1952 *et seq.*). *History:* J. Łoś, *Gramatyka polska,* 3 vol. (1922–27); T. Lehr-Spławinski, *Język polski: pochodzenie, powstanie, rozwój,* 2nd ed. (1951); Z. Stieber, *Rozwój fonologiczny języka polskiego* (1952); Z. Klemensiewicz, T. Lehr-Spławiński, St. Urbańczyk, *Gramatyka his-toryczna języka polskiego* (1955). *Dialectology:* St. Urbańczyk, *Zarys dialektologii polskiej* (1953); J. Karłowicz, *Słownik gwar polskich,* 6 vol. (1900–11). *Polish in the United States:* W. Doroszewski, *Język polski w Stanach Zjednoczonych Ameryki Północnej* (1936). *Manuals:* M. Corbridge-Patkaniowska, *Essentials of Polish Grammar* (1944) and *Teach Yourself Polish* (1950); J. A. Teslar, *A New Polish Grammar,* 5th ed. (1947); Z. M. Arend, *A Polish Phonetic Reader* (1921).

(F. J. Wd.)

POLISH LITERATURE.

POLISH LITERATURE. Although Poland has been part of Christian Europe from the 10th century, Polish literature was slow to emerge, partly because of Poland's remoteness from cultural centres and the difficulties that assailed the young state, frequently attacked by plundering invaders and weakened by division into small principalities; and partly because of the domination of foreign priests, which resulted from the action of Mieszko I, prince of Poland, who, accepting Christianity in 966, placed his lands in the pope's hands. *See* POLAND: *History.*

THE MIDDLE AGES

Writings in Latin.—As in other European countries, Latin was at first the only literary language. Early writings in Latin included saints' lives and annals and chronicles written by monks and priests. An anonymous writer known as Gallus (probably a Benedictine monk from Provence) recorded the exploits of the Piast dynasty, and of Bolesław III Wrymouth in particular, to 1113 in a chronicle written in the style of the French *chansons de geste* (*q.v.*). Wincenty Kadłubek (1160–1223), a Polish bishop who had studied in Paris, wrote the *Chronica Polonorum* as an allegorical, devotional romance in an artificial, florid style. A chronicle known as the *Kronika Wielkopolska* (written *c.* 1295; published 1730), probably by a priest called Baszko, relates events to 1271. The masterpiece among chronicles, however, is the *Annales seu Cronicae Incliti Regni Poloniae* (the *Historia polonica*) by Jan Długosz (*q.v.;* 1415–80), first printed (in part only) in 1615. It was the first, and, for centuries, the only, attempt at a systematic and scholarly history of medieval Poland. Długosz was also the author of a revision (published 1511) of one of two 13th-century accounts of the life of Stanisław of Szczepanów (*see* STANISLAW, SAINT). The first history of Poland to be printed (1519) was the *Chronica polonorum,* by Maciej of Miechów (1457–1523). The 15th century also produced the first lay writer, and the first official critic of the papacy and priesthood, Jan Ostroróg (*c.* 1436–1501), author of *Monumentum . . . pro Reipublicae ordinatione* (1475), a treatise attacking ecclesiastical power and urging reform of church and state. Stanisław Ciołek (1382?–1437) wrote court poetry modeled on that in other European countries.

Writings in Polish.—Use of the vernacular was first allowed by the church only where Latin could not meet particular needs—in prayers, sermons, and songs, for instance. The oldest surviving literary text in Polish is a song in honour of the Virgin Mary, *Bogurodzica* (printed 1506), in which language and rhythm are used with high artistic craftsmanship. The earliest manuscript dates from 1407–08, but it was probably written much earlier.

Preaching in Polish became established toward the end of the 13th century. The earliest known example of Polish prose, the *Kazania świętokrzyskie* ("Sermons of the Holy Cross"), dating from the end of the 13th or the beginning of the 14th century, was discovered in 1890 and published in 1891. Of the six surviving sermons, five are fragmentary. *Kazania Gnieźnieńskie* ("Sermons of Gniezno"; published 1857), another notable example of early Polish prose, dates from the late 14th century. The first extant translation of the psalms, the so-called *Psałterz królowej Jadwigi* ("Psalter of Queen Jadwiga") or *Psałterz Floriański* ("Florian's Psalter"; published 1834), also dates from the end of the 14th century: the text is in Latin, German, and Polish, the Polish text being probably a copy of an earlier manuscript. Part of a translation of the Bible, made in 1455 by Jędrzej of Jaszowice for Queen Sofia, widow of Władysław II Jagiełło, has also survived. Lives and legends of the saints were also written in Polish during the 14th and 15th centuries.

Secular works began to appear toward the end of the 15th century. Satirical verse is represented by the *Pieśń o Wiklefie* (dating from *c*. 1449; published 1816), directed against the "Roman antichrist" (the pope) by Jędrzej Gałka, a follower of John Wycliffe and John Huss. A high literary standard was achieved in a morality verse dialogue, the satirical and grotesque *Rozmowa mistrza Polikarpa ze Śmiercią* ("Dialogue Between Master Polycarp and Death"), dating from the second half of the 15th century, and first published in 1886. The style of the medieval period lasted late in Poland. Marcin Bielski (1495–1575) represented this late medievalism in his *Kronika wszytkiego świata* ("Chronicle of the World," 1551), the first general history in Polish.

Most surviving examples of medieval Polish literature long remained unknown, but the complex technical organization of the best examples implies a continuous literary tradition. Moreover, although its themes are those of the common European heritage, Polish writing of this period can be intensely personal within its anonymous framework. Devotional lyrics in particular, such as the fine *Żale Matki Boskiej pod krzyżem* ("Lament of the Mother of God Under the Cross," dating from *c*. 1470; published 1826) and the rich tradition of carols, reach a high poetic level, and help to account for the rapid flowering of the language during the 16th century.

The groundwork for the leap into the ranks of major literatures was laid during the reign (1333–70) of Casimir III the Great (*q.v.*), who in 1364 founded the University of Cracow, and who promoted the entry of new ideas from west and south by his contacts with the courts of Hungary and Bohemia.

THE RENAISSANCE PERIOD

The Renaissance reached Poland comparatively late and lasted for a shorter time than elsewhere. It flourished abundantly, however, and is known as the Golden Age of Polish literature. External security, constitutional consolidation, and the ferment of the Reformation contributed to this flowering; and the rapid development of printing in the early 16th century facilitated stabilization of spelling. The first permanent press was established at Cracow by Jan Haller at the turn of the 15th century, and the first book printed entirely in Polish, the devotional *Raj duszny* ("The Soul's Paradise"), by Biernat of Lublin, was issued *c*. 1513. The modern literary language dates from this time (*see* POLISH LANGUAGE).

The first generation of writers influenced by the Italian Humanists wrote in Latin. Among them were Jan Flachsbinder (Joannes Dantiscus; 1485–1548), courtier, diplomat, and author of incidental verse, love poetry, and panegyric; Andrzej Krzycki (Cricius; 1482–1537), archbishop and primate, who wrote witty and frivolous epigrams, courtly panegyrics, political verse, and religious poems; and Klemens of Januszkowo (Janicki, Janicius; 1516–43), a peasant who studied at Padua and became poet laureate and the first original Polish poet. His elegies in the manner of Tibullus and Ovid bear the stamp of his emotional, melancholy personality.

A writer who combined medieval and Renaissance aspects was Mikołaj Rej of Nagłowice (1505–69). Self-educated, and of great vitality and literary force, he was the first idiomatically Polish talent and the first widely read writer of his time; he is known as "the father of Polish literature." His numerous works in verse include satirical epigrams, *Figliki* ("Trifles," 1574); but more important are his prose works, especially *Postilla* (1557), a collection of Calvinist sermons; and the *Żywot człowieka poczciwego* ("Life of an Honourable Man," 1558), a description of the life of an ideal nobleman, which contains a unique account of customs

MARBLE BUST OF JAN KOCHANOWSKI BY AN UNKNOWN SCULPTOR, LATE 16TH CENTURY; FROM HIS TOMBSTONE AT A CHURCH IN ZWOLEN, NEAR KIELCE

and conditions in 16th-century Poland. It forms one section of *Zwierciadło* (1568), a larger work modeled on the medieval *Speculum*. Rej's verse *Krótka rozprawa między panem, wójtem a plebanem* ("Short Debate Between the Landlord, the Bailiff, and the Priest," 1543) treats topical themes in a medieval manner and is the only Polish example of the medieval dialogue.

The second generation of Humanist poets, and indeed the whole Renaissance period, is dominated by Jan Kochanowski (1530–84). The son of a country squire, he studied at Padua and Paris and was encouraged to write in the vernacular by the example of Pierre de Ronsard (*q.v.*). Kochanowski was the first Polish writer to attempt heroic satirical poetry and classical tragedy (in *Odprawa posłów greckich*, 1578; *The Dismissal of the Greek Envoys*, 1918, on a subject from the Iliad). His lyrical works, however, surpass these experiments. His adaptation of the Book of Psalms, *Psalterz Dawidów* (1579), illustrates his mastery of form and metrical versatility; and his *Fraszki* ("Trifles," 1584) are typical of the Renaissance in their vigorous joy in life and their epigrammatic precision.

Kochanowski's collection *Pieśni* (1586; *Chants*, 1932) includes love songs, patriotic and festive songs, and reflective lyrics, often revealing a Horatian outlook. His crowning achievement, the first Polish work to equal the great poems of Western Europe, is his *Treny* (1580; *Laments*, 1920), inspired by despair after the death in 1579 of his infant daughter, Ursula, and his final recovery of spiritual harmony. In Kochanowski's poetry the archaisms still apparent in Rej's work have almost disappeared: language and idiom are modern. The flexibility and assurance of his poetic genius was immediately recognized as a sign that the literary language had attained its maturity; his diction remains a model of harmony and purity.

The most notable of Kochanowski's followers was Szymon Szymonowic (Simonides; 1558–1629). A burgher of Lwów (Lvov), educated at Cracow and abroad, in his *Sielanki* ("Eclogues," 1614) he introduced a poetic genre that was to retain its vitality until the end of the 19th century. These pastoral idylls, influenced by Theocritus and by Virgil, exemplify the processes of imitation, adaptation, and assimilation by which Renaissance writers brought foreign models into the native tradition.

The numerous poems, in Latin and Polish, of Sebastian Klonowic (1545–1602) are of interest for their description of contemporary life. In the Latin poem *Roxolania* (1584), he gives the first full account of the geography, landscape, and people of Ruthenia; and in *Flis* (1595; *The Boatman*, 1958) he vividly describes the valley of the Vistula and the life and customs of the raftsmen. *Worek Judaszów* ("Judas' Sack," 1600) is a satirical and didactic poem on the life, especially the folly and vice, of Lublin, of which he was mayor.

The prose of the 16th century ranks with its poetry in vitality and range. The most eminent writer in Latin was Andrzej Frycz Modrzewski (1503–72). In his *Commentariorum de republica emendanda libre quinque* (incomplete 1551; complete 1554) he evolved a bold social and political system extending far beyond the accepted ideas of his time, based on the principle of man's equality before God and the law. Another notable writer in Latin was Marcin Kromer (1512–89), scholar, Humanist, historian, and Catholic apologist, who studied in Italy, Germany, and France. His *Polonia sive de origine et rebus gestis polonorum* (1555) and *Polonia sive de situ, populis, moribus, magistratibus et Republica Polonici* (1577) are important for their detailed account of Polish history, geography, institutions, people, and customs; and for their

MIKOŁAJ REJ OF NAGŁOWICE, A WOODCUT FROM HIS ZWIERZYNIEC, CRACOW, 1562. IN THE BRITISH MUSEUM elegant style. Of his theological and controversial works, most interesting is the Polish *Rozmowy dworzanina z mnichem* ("Dialogues Between the Courtier and the Monk"; 1551–54), a defense of Catholicism. Other outstanding prose writers of this period are Stanisław Orzechowski (Orichovius; 1513–66), Łukasz Górnicki (1527–1603), and Piotr Skarga (Powęski; 1536–1612). Orzechowski, a controversialist in Latin and Polish, commanded a keen and artistically sure range of expression for a great diversity of intellectual attitudes. Górnicki, in *Dworzanin polski* ("The Polish Courtier," 1566), his free version of Castiglione's *Il Cortegiano* (transplanted to Polish soil and adapted to Polish conditions), created in aristocratic prose the ideal of Renaissance manhood. Skarga, a militant Jesuit and the first Polish representative of the Counter-Reformation, wrote the popular *Żywoty świętych* ("Lives of the Saints," 1579) and the famous political treatises *Kazania sejmowe* (1597). In the form of sermons to the assembled diet, these advocate curtailment of parliamentary rights and a strengthening of royal authority.

The 16th century produced a wealth of historical writings, though none to compare with those of Długosz. It also saw the beginnings of polemical writing, much of it inspired by the rise of Socinianism (*see* SOCINUS; UNITARIANISM). Socinian writers, as well as engaging in polemic, produced notable works, in Latin and Polish, on social, moral, and religious problems. After the Polish Brethren were expelled from Poland (1658) many settled in Amsterdam, and there published the *Bibliotheca Fratrum Polonorum* (1666–68), which exerted some influence on the political thought of Spinoza and Locke.

Many translations of the Bible were published. The Catholic translation (*Nowy Testament,* 1593; complete Bible, 1599) by Jakub Wujek (1541–97) came to occupy in Poland a position comparable to that of the Authorized (King James) Version (1611) in England, and is an outstanding literary work.

In this period Polish literature became a national literature expressing a fully awakened national consciousness, the ethos of a people. It reflected Poland's position as a great power with far-flung boundaries, the evolution of the nobility as a ruling class, and the country's economic prosperity. Its influence spread east, above all to Moscow; Rej's *Postilla* was translated into Russian and Lithuanian. To the west the culture of the Polish Renaissance was represented by men of such high repute as Copernicus (*q.v.*).

THE BAROQUE PERIOD

The Baroque period began very early in Poland. In 1564 Poland invited the Jesuits to settle in the country, and from about 1570 Protestant influence began to wane. The Baroque style and outlook were congenial to the Polish spirit; the period was one of considerable literary output, in spite of almost incessant wars. Indeed perhaps it mirrored, in its stylistic tension, the external strife characteristic of the 17th century.

A forerunner of Baroque poetry was Mikołaj Sęp-Szarzyński (1550–81), who left only one volume, *Rytmy ...* (1601), containing predominantly religious poetry akin to that of the English metaphysical poets. In the Baroque period itself satire and pastoral were the most popular forms. Foremost among satirists was Krzysztof Opaliński (1609–55), prince palatine of Poznań. His *Satyry* (1650), modeled on Juvenal, are bitter, pessimistic, and wide-ranging. The pastoral is represented by Samuel Twardowski (1600–61), author of the pastoral epic *Daphnis ...* (1638) and the romance *Nadobna* ("Enchanting") *Pasqualina* (1655), a paradoxical tale of sacred and profane love in which Polish Baroque achieves perhaps its most finely wrought splendour. The collection of love songs with a Ruthenian setting, *Roksolanki* (1654), represents a further achievement in lyric poetry. Long attributed to the poet Szymon Zimorowic (1608–29), they are now known to have been written by his brother, Bartłomiej Józef (1597–1677), who also, in his *Sielanki* ("Pastorals," 1663), introduced original, dramatic elements of topical reference, often with macabre effect, into the traditional form of the pastoral idyll, superimposing images of war and death upon the pastoral background with typical Baroque incongruity.

A parallel but less formalized rustic genre produced much verse celebrating rural life. One of the more successful examples is the *Votum* by Zbigniew Morsztyn (*c.* 1627–89), whose finest achievement, however, is in religious poetry. His *Emblemata* (first complete edition 1954) are the only known examples of the emblem tradition (*see* EMBLEM BOOK) in Polish literature. In contrast to his writings is the work of his cousin, Jan Andrzej Morsztyn (*c.* 1613–93), whose language is marked by the extravagant "conceited" style of the Italian *Seicento*. The formal complexity and skill of his verse, most of it unpublished until the 19th century, is unsurpassed; and his translation (1661) of Corneille's *Le Cid* remains the standard Polish version. The Jesuit Maciej Kazimierz Sarbiewski (Sarbievius; 1595–1640) was internationally celebrated for his Latin poems; his *Lyricorum libri* (1625) went through 36 editions.

The age was characterized by ambition to write heroic epics—a preoccupation to be explained perhaps by historical events: wars with Sweden, Russia, and Turkey, internal revolts, and attempts to introduce constitutional reforms. The *Pharsalia* of Lucan (*q.v.*) attracted both translators and adapters. Torquato Tasso's *Gerusalemme liberata,* brilliantly translated (1618) by Piotr Kochanowski (1566–1620), inspired attempts at epics on national themes. Among the more notable is the vigorous *Wojna chocimska* ("The War of Chocim," written 1670; published 1850), describing the Turkish onslaught through Moldavia in 1621, by Wacław Potocki (1621?–96). Potocki was more famous for his epigrams, collected in *Ogród Fraszek* ("Garden of Rhymes," written 1670–95; published 1907), which give a lively picture of ideas and manners. Another epic, the *Psalmodia polska* (1695), by the poet and historian Wespazjan Kochowski (1633–1700), was written under the impact of John III Sobieski's victory over the Turks at Vienna in 1683, at which Kochowski was present; the work is interesting both for its style, which is based on biblical parallelism, and as the first example of a theme developed by writers of the Romantic movement—the messianic interpretation of Poland's destiny.

The prose of the period does not rise to the level of its poetry. It is notable, however, for its wealth of diaries and memoirs. Outstanding are the memoirs (*Pamiętniki;* published 1836) of Jan Chryzostom Pasek (*c.* 1630–1701), a country squire and soldier. Written in a lively, humorous style, they give a vivid description of the life of a man of independent personality. Other notable prose writers are Stanisław Żołkiewski (1547–1620), author of an impressively direct account of the campaign against Moscow (*Początek i progres wojny moskiewskiej,* published 1833); Andrzej Maksymilian Fredro (1620–79), writer of skeptical aphorisms, *Przysłowia ...* ("Proverbs ...," 1658); Stanisław Herakliusz Lubomirski (1642–1702), notable for his political treatises; and Łukasz Opaliński (1612–62), author of polemical works. The last three wrote in Polish and Latin.

The period was also notable for the emergence of the letter as a literary form. The letters of John III Sobieski to his wife (published in parts, 1823 and 1860; first collected edition, *Listy do Marysieńki*—"Letters to Mary"—1962) are remarkable for their passion and tenderness, and their day-by-day account of his experiences of battles and diplomacy. Their style combines elegant ease with feeling, and they are among the best letters in the language. Another interesting development was the rise of a popular anonymous literature, exemplified by the so-called "komedia rybałtowska" ("ribald comedies"). These are generally popular satiric comedies and broad farces about bachelors, clerics, beggars, court officials, and soldiers, written mainly by playwrights of plebeian birth. Of the few whose names are known, most notable is Piotr Baryka (fl. 1600–56), author of the "carnival comedy" *Z chłopa król* ("The Peasant-King"; performed 1633, published 1637), which develops the theme of the induction to Shakespeare's *The Taming of the Shrew.* Some 30 anonymous examples of this type of comedy survive, among them *Peregrynacja dziadowska* ("The Beggar's Wanderings," 1612), the *Komedia rybałtowska nowa* ("A New Ribald Comedy," 1613–14), *Wyprawa plebańska* ("The Curate's Journey," 1590), and *Mięsopust* ("Shrovetide Carnival," 1622). These plays, consisting of strongly realistic depictions of popular customs and grotesquely humorous situations, are of interest in that they provide a parody on the lofty themes of "official" literature, and so express an indirect protest against social inequality.

The last stage of Baroque literature (c. 1675–c. 1750), from 1697 called the "Saxon period" because of the accession to the throne, as Augustus II, of the elector of Saxony, displays a long process of decline, marked only by the emergence of the first women writers (e.g., Elżbieta Drużbacka, 1695–1765; author of popular romances and moral and religious verse) and by the important figure of Stanisław Konarski (q.v.; 1700–73), a reformer of education, literature, and the political system. Konarski wrote poetry in Latin (Opera lyrica, 1767); a tragedy, in the classical French style, in Polish (Tragedia Epominondy, published 1880); and political treatises in clear, incisive prose.

It was not until the mid-20th century that the literature of the Baroque period was fully appreciated. It may well be regarded as the most enduring of Polish styles, for many of its features recur in the Romantic period and in modern writing.

THE ENLIGHTENMENT

Close contact with Western Europe, especially France and, to a lesser extent, England, characterized the literature of the Enlightenment period. Certain general ideas and tendencies of the second half of the 18th century coincided with Poland's political situation. The country, exhausted by wars and burdened with a corrupt political system, was menaced by aggressive neighbours (see POLAND: History: The Elective Kings). Literature was imbued with a desire to improve and reform, to strengthen the state against collapse, or at least to save the national culture from the effects of partition and foreign rule. Literary developments include the rise of drama; introduction of the periodical and the novel; publication of the first Polish dictionary; the application to historical writing of scholarly methods; and, in poetry, introduction of dumy (ballads).

Drama.—Drama was established late in Poland, although Rej, Kochanowski, and Szymonowic had attempted it, and didactic plays were performed in Jesuit colleges throughout the 17th century (see DRAMA: Modern Drama: Jesuit School-Drama). The earliest significant event was the inauguration of the national theatre (Teatr Narodowy) in Warsaw in 1765, on the initiative of the last king of Poland, Stanisław II Poniatowski, a patron of literature and the arts. The principal dramatists (much influenced by French models) were Franciszek Bohomolec (1720–84), Wojciech Bogusławski (1757–1829), and Franciszek Zabłocki (1752–1821). Bohomolec, in adaptations of Molière, satirized the ignorance and folly of the Polish aristocracy. Bogusławski wrote plays adapted from foreign originals and the popular national comic opera Krakowiacy i Górale ("Cracovians and Mountaineers," 1794) based on Polish folklore. In 1783 he became director of the Teatr Narodowy and after the partitions toured the country with a traveling company. Zabłocki, a prolific playwright, produced two works of lasting value, Fircyk w zalotach ("The Dandy's Courtship," 1781) and Sarmatyzm (1785), the latter introducing the "foray" theme developed by Adam Mickiewicz (q.v.; 1798–1855) in his Pan Tadeusz. The comedies of Aleksander Fredro (1793–1876) appeared when the Romantic movement was already underway and in them the influences of Molière and Carlo Goldoni are assimilated to the native idiom, as, for example, in Zemsta ("The Revenge," 1834). They are remarkable for their brilliant "type" characterization, ingenious construction, and metrical facility. (See also DRAMA: Modern Drama: The Late 18th Century.)

BY COURTESY OF POLSKA AKADEMIA NAUK, INSTYTUT SZTUKI

ALEKSANDER FREDRO, AN 1828 LITHOGRAPH AFTER THE DRAWING BY A. LAUB. IN THE POLSKA AKADEMIA NAUK, INSTYTUT SZTUKI

Prose.—Didacticism permeated most of the period's prose writing. The first modern periodicals appeared at this time (e.g., the Monitor, 1765–85; modeled on the English Tatler and Spectator). Several men of great intellectual gifts wrote on contemporary issues, among them Stanisław Staszic (1755–1826), who, in Przestrogi dla Polski ("Warning to Poland," 1790), presented a grim picture of the country's social and economic depredation; and the statesman, Hugo Kołłątaj (q.v.; 1750–1812), whose style in his political treatises is distinguished by its forcefulness and clarity.

From the spirit of the Enlightenment and its educational and social reforms sprouted a new, widespread cultural movement typified by compilation of the first Polish dictionary (Słownik języka polskiego, 6 vol., 1807–14) by Samuel Bogumił Linde (1771–1847).

Poetry.—The first poet of the Enlightenment period was the bishop Adam Naruszewicz (1733–96). His poetic works—fables, satires, pastorals—considered chronologically, reflect the transition from Baroque to Classical. He also wrote the first history of Poland to use modern methods of scholarship—the Historia narodu polskiego (7 vol., 1780–86), recording events to the end of the 14th century. The period's central poet was Count Ignacy Krasicki (1735–1801), prince-bishop of Warmia (Ermeland), of European outlook and modern, skeptical intellect whose diverse writings include two mock-heroic poems, Myszeis (1775) and Monachomachia (1778), Satyry (1779), and the Bajki i przypowieści ("Fables and Moral Tales," 1779), remarkable for concise expression, formal elegance, and wit. Krasicki also introduced the novel with Mikołaja Doświadczyńskiego przypadki ("The Adventures of Mikolaj Doświadczyński," 1776), which shows the influence of Swift and Rousseau.

Two other outstanding poets of the Enlightenment were Stanisław Trembecki (1739–1812), the favourite and poet laureate of Stanisław August (Stanisław III Poniatowski); and Tomasz Kajetan Węgierski (1756–87). Trembecki, rationalist and libertine, wrote fables, satires, odes, poetic epistles, and descriptive poems (e.g., Sofiówka, 1806): though many of the characters are of only topical interest, and the treatment is panegyrical, his works have an important place in the poetry of Polish classicism as models of stylistic fluency. Węgierski, a freethinker and admirer of Voltaire, expressed his rationalistic philosophic outlook in his mock-heroic poem Organy (1784), published anonymously and dedicated to Krasicki.

Lyrical poetry continued to develop. Two writers are outstanding: Franciszek Karpiński (1741–1825), who developed features of the Baroque style in his popular pastorals and religious songs; and Franciszek Dyonizy Kniaźnin (1750–1807), a conscious experimenter, who rewrote much of his earlier work to achieve stylistic uniformity. His verse, cool and intellectual in quality, anticipated certain Romantic themes—e.g., folk poetry, popular superstition, and gypsy life.

The personality of Julian Ursyn Niemcewicz (q.v.; 1757?–1841), whose writings were inspired by patriotism and concern for social and political reform, bridges the gap between the eras before and after the partitions. He was the first Polish writer to know English literature thoroughly. His early translations of English Romantic ballads influenced Mickiewicz, and his original dumy were the first of their kind in Poland. He also introduced the historical novel to Poland with Jan z Tęczyna (3 vol., 1825), which shows the influence of Sir Walter Scott. His comedy Powrót posła ("The Envoy's Return," 1790), written during a recess of the four-year diet to propagate the cause of the Reform Party, was immediately successful, and is one of the best dramatic works of the period; and his Śpiewy historyczne ("Historical Songs," 1816), a song-cycle on themes from Polish history, was one of the most widely read books in Poland in the 19th century.

After loss of national independence, resulting from the last of the three partitions, in 1795–96, the tradition of patriotic poetry was continued by the émigré soldier-poets in the Polish legions of Napoleon's army under Gen. Jan Henryk Dąbrowski (Dombrowski). Among them was Józef Wybicki (1747–1822), author of the popular patriotic song Mazurek Dąbrowskiego, written in Italy in

1797, which begins *"Jeszcze Polska nie zginęła . . ."* ("Poland has not died yet . . ."); in 1918 it was adopted as the national anthem.

A second, distinct period of Polish classicism, less fruitful than the first, and called pseudoclassicism, covers the years of the duchy of Warsaw (created by Napoleon in 1807–09) and the Congress kingdom under Russian rule established by the Congress of Vienna. In general pseudoclassical writing, constricted by its own rigid canons of taste, lacks freshness. During the Enlightenment period literature reestablished contact with the West and became the mouthpiece of national consciousness. Although it was the literature of a community undergoing a severe political crisis, it exercised an influence on neighbouring countries; Krasicki, especially, influencing Russian, Czech, and Rumanian writers.

ROMANTICISM

The Romantic period began later than in England or Germany, but it lasted longer than elsewhere, and is regarded as the greatest period in Polish literature. The rise of Romanticism coincided with a tragic moment—the loss of independence—and the great writers found in it an expression of their own mood. Their writings, imbued with a prophetic quality, express Romantic despair and aspiration with grandeur. The need to interpret their country's destiny gave to the work of the three great Romantic poets—Adam Mickiewicz (*q.v.;* 1798–1855), Juliusz Słowacki (*q.v.;* 1809–49), and Zygmunt Krasiński (1812–59)—visionary power and moral authority, and they were regarded as national bards, apostles of the movement for national freedom. Writing in exile, they kept alive their country's faith in the restoration of Polish independence, and their concern with political and historical problems gave the literature of the Polish Romantic movement its strength and spiritual passion.

Writers in Exile.—Mickiewicz is regarded both as the greatest Polish poet and as the leader of the Romantic movement, and publication of his *Poezye* (2 vol., 1822–23) was the first major literary event of the period. The first volume, containing ballads and romances, begins with an important preface explaining his admiration for these Western European forms and his desire to transplant them to Polish soil. In the second volume were included parts ii and iv of his *Dziady,* in which he combined folklore and mystic patriotism to create a new kind of Romantic drama. Mickiewicz' greatest works, however, were written after 1824, when he was deported to Russia for his revolutionary activities as a student: they include the *Sonety Krymskie* ("Crimean Sonnets," 1826); the visionary third part of *Dziady* (1833); the messianic interpretation of Poland's past and future destiny *Księgi narodu i pielgrzymstwa polskiego* (1832; *Books of the Polish Nation and its Pilgrimage,* 1925), written in a biblical prose; and the great poetic epic, *Pan Tadeusz . . .* (1834; trans. 1962).

The suppression of the insurrection of 1830–31 drove the cultural elite into exile in France: among poets whom Mickiewicz joined there were Słowacki, Krasiński, and Cyprian Norwid. Słowacki, a Romantic in the fullest sense, who in all his work shows poetic genius, wrote verse-narratives in the style of Byron (most outstanding being *Beniowski,* 1841) as well as accomplished lyric poetry. Like Mickiewicz, though in a very different style, he was inspired by patriotic themes: his *Kordian* (1834), a drama of conspiracy and the problems of commitment, is the counterpart of Mickiewicz' *Dziady;* and *Anhelli* (1838) was inspired by the *Books of the Polish Nation.* Słowacki imbued traditional forms with new aesthetic content. *W Szwajcarii* (1839; *In Switzerland,* 1953) is a transformed pastoral, exalted to an unprecedented degree of subtlety, and probably the finest lyrical work in Polish. Much of Słowacki's work is in dramatic form, and although it was not intended for production, and he lacked experience of the stage, it laid the foundations of Polish tragic drama. His plays show the influence of French Romantic drama (*Maria Stuart,* 1833; *Mazepa,* 1840); Shakespeare (*Balladyna,* 1839; *Horsztyński,* published 1909); classical tragedy (*Lilla Weneda,* 1840; a symbolic drama of Polish legendary history); and Calderón (*Książę niezłomny,* 1844; a creative adaptation of *El príncipe constante,* and *Sen srebrny Salomei,* "The Silver Dream of Salomea," 1844). The last years

ADAM MICKIEWICZ, PORTRAIT IN OILS BY ALEKSANDER KAMINSKI, 1850. IN THE POLSKA AKADEMIA NAUK, INSTYTUT SZTUKI

of his life were devoted to writing the unfinished *Król-Duch* ("The Spirit King," 1847), a lyrical and symbolic epic describing the history of a people as a series of incarnations of the essential spirit of the nation.

Zygmunt Krasiński, when only 23, published (anonymously, as all his works) *Nieboska komedia* (1835; *The Undivine Comedy,* 1924). This play presented, for the first time in Europe, the struggle between two social classes, and the opposed worlds and cultures of the aristocracy and the disinherited masses, which yet share the characteristic of spiritual despotism. *Irydion* (1836; trans. 1927), his second play, is an allegory of Poland's fate presented as a conflict between the Greeks and the Romans. In *Przedświt* ("The Moment Before Dawn," 1843), he developed the messianic interpretation of Polish history foreshadowed by Kochowski's *Psalmodia polska* (*see* above), and this conception of Poland as "the Christ among the nations" is also expounded in his *Psalmy przyszłości* ("Psalms of the Future," 1845). The introduction of fantastic or supernatural elements into a realistic setting is characteristic of many Polish Romantic works, and facilitates a type of symbolic expression that established itself in Polish literary tradition.

The genius of Cyprian Kamil Norwid (*q.v.;* 1821–83) was not fully recognized until the 20th century. Belonging to the second generation of post-1830 poets, he became one of the most tragic of them. During his lifetime he was misjudged and obscure. This resulted partly from the duality of his attitude (he accepted some of the ideas of Romanticism while criticizing others), but even more from his ironic intellectual reserve, which enabled him to distinguish between false and genuine ideological coinage too acutely for his contemporaries' comfort. Few of his works were published in his lifetime, a notable exception being the verse dialogue on aesthetics, *Promethidion* (1851), which expounds a theory of the social and moral function of art anticipating that of Ruskin (*q.v.*). The authentic text of his most important lyrical collection, the *Vademecum,* was first published in 1947 (new complete edition, 1962). He experimented with free verse and the rhythms of natural speech, and foreshadowed the French Symbolists in his analogical method of presenting the poetic concept.

The lesser *émigré* talents of Romanticism formed the so-called Polish Ukrainian school. The most outstanding of them was Antoni Malczewski (1793–1826), author of a single poem, the

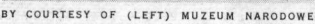

(LEFT) JULIUSZ SŁOWACKI, AN 1838 ENGRAVING BY JAMES HOPWOOD AFTER A PORTRAIT IN OILS BY J. KUROWSKI. IN THE MUZEUM NARODOWE, WARSAW. (RIGHT) CYPRIAN KAMIL NORWID, A DRAWING BY TYTUS MALESZEWSKI, 1857. IN THE POLSKA AKADEMIA NAUK, INSTYTUT SZTUKI

Romantic verse-narrative *Maria*... (1825; trans. 1935), a Byronic tale of love and treachery with a Ukrainian setting, remarkable for its original diction, dramatic tension, and unity of mood. Others belonging to the group were the radical conspirator Seweryn Goszczyński (1801–76), also influenced by Byron; and Józef Bohdan Zaleski (1802–86), who wrote naively stylized folk songs.

There were fewer prose writers than poets among the exiles. Among novelists, mention must be made of Zygmunt Miłkowski (pseudonym, Teodor Tomasz Jeż; 1824–1915), who wrote on a wide range of subjects, including folklore and the history of the Balkan countries. The literary criticism of Maurycy Mochnacki (1804–34), a passionate advocate of Romanticism and the first Polish critic to define the part to be played by literature in the spiritual and political life of society, and to link literature with Poland's political progress, exercised a strong and not wholly beneficial influence on literary theory. The history of Poland by the scholar and patriot Joachim Lelewel (*q.v.*; 1786–1861) is an impressive example of the prose of the period.

Writers in Poland.—As a result of partition, Romantic poetry in Poland was limited to closed provincial circles. In Warsaw a group of young, exuberant poets, the "Warsaw Bohème," was formed, but its activities were restricted by political pressure. Its most fully developed talent was that of Teofil Lenartowicz (1822–93), who sang the praise of the countryside and peasantry of central Poland. In Poznań, under Prussian domination, Ryszard Wincenty Berwiński (1819–79) made a meteoric appearance as a poet of social radicalism (*Poezje*, 2 series, 1844). His prose *Studia o literaturze ludowej* ("Studies on Folk Literature," 1854) marks a step away from Romantic nationalist interpretations, and stresses the international community of folk tradition.

Among other provincial poets were Kornel Ujejski (1823–97), a native of Galician Podolia, whose *Z dymem pożarów* ("With the Smoke of Fires"), written after the Galician massacre in 1846, became the national anthem of Austrian Poland; Wincenty Pol (1807–72), also a Galician, who wrote unsophisticated and effective songs about the 1830–31 rising that captured the hearts of the people and were praised by Mickiewicz for their directness and vigour; and Ludwik Kondratowicz (pseudonym, Władysław Syrokomla; 1823–62), a Lithuanian who described episodes from rural life in *gawędas* (verse tales in a conversational style), and was at his best in the shorter tales, bitterly satirizing the sorrow and hardship of peasant life.

Prose was more popular with writers in Poland than with those in exile. Henryk Rzewuski (1791–1866), a true artist, belonged spiritually to the 18th century. His *Pamiątki Seweryna Soplicy* ("Memoirs of Seweryn Soplica," 1839), discursive narratives on 18th-century themes, evokes the atmosphere of the Baroque tradition. Toward the end of the period signs of a realistic tendency are discernible in the work of Józef Korzeniowski (1797–1863), particularly in the novels *Spekulant* (1846) and *Kollokacja* (1847), portraying the life of the impoverished gentry in a remote countryside. The woman novelist Narcyza Żmichowska (pseudonym, Gabryella; 1819–76) produced the strange *Poganka* ("The Pagan," 1846; revised 1861), the tale of a man demoniacally possessed by an ideal love that finally destroys him. A psychological allegory, it anticipates 20th-century sensibility in its subtle analysis of feeling.

The dominant figure among prose writers was Józef Ignacy Kraszewski (*q.v.*; 1812–87), a literary giant whose output runs into hundreds of volumes of fiction, history, ethnography, criticism, etc. His imaginative writings reflect the change of literary styles during his long career. Banished to Dresden by the Russian authorities in 1863, he continued to influence Polish writers at home and in exile, maintaining the Polish cause, both in politics and letters, by his manifold contacts and activities.

The Influence of Romanticism.—Polish Romanticism, conscious of its role as the torch of the national spirit, retained its force as a mode of thinking beyond the period of the political circumstances that fostered it. It produced works of the highest artistic value, which excited the interest of foreign writers. Mickiewicz, for example, considerably influenced Lamennais

(*q.v.*) and the Slavonic literatures; and was compared by George Sand with Goethe and Byron. Słowacki's poetic technique proved of fundamental importance to writers at the end of the 19th century, and that of Norwid was increasingly felt in the mid-20th century. The artistic achievements of the period therefore stood the test of time, though the political implications of the Romantic movement led to the insurrection of 1863, which ended in Poland's absorption as a province of Russia.

POSITIVISM

The literature of the period following the 1863 uprising is called "positivism," and reflects a mood of practical thinking and action and a rationalist reaction against Romanticism and domination of life by literary theory. Politically, the positivist mood led to renunciation of armed resistance and to concentration of energy on retrenchment, preservation of the ideological and cultural assets of the nation, and development of material prosperity. The rise in Russian Poland of an urban intelligentsia formed from the impoverished members of the gentry who moved to the towns after the emancipation of the peasants in 1864 acted as the leaven in this ferment. Popular journals and periodicals were of particular importance in dissemination of new ideas, especially the widely read *Tygodnik Ilustrowany* ("Illustrated Weekly"), founded in 1859.

The natural consequence of the positivist outlook was the predominance of prose, particularly journalistic prose, over poetry. With other writers of the Warsaw school, of which he was leader, Aleksander Świętochowski (1849–1938) voiced anticlerical and antiaristocratic views in his weekly paper *Prawda* (1881–1902), and in novels, plays, and short stories. Bolesław Prus (pseudonym of Aleksander Głowacki; 1847–1912), a journalist with experience of proletarian conditions, ranks high among Polish short-story writers and is one of the most considerable Polish novelists. *Lalka* ("The Doll," 1890) gives a complex picture of bourgeois life in Warsaw toward the end of the century; and *Faraon* (1897; *The Pharaoh and the Priest*, 1902) is an ambitious evocation of ancient Egypt with a strangely equivocal approach to the theme of power.

Eliza Orzeszkowa (*q.v.*; 1841–1910), a campaigner for social reform, wrote novels concerning women's emancipation, the ignorance and superstition of the peasants, and the Jewish problem; and, in her three-volume epic, *Nad Niemnem* ("By the Niemen," 1889), gave a realistic description of the life of the Polish gentry. In this, and in books on less topical subjects—*e.g.*, *Cham* ("The Boor," 1888)—she shows psychological penetration and a fine sense of style.

Another popular novelist, and winner of the Nobel Prize for Literature in 1905, was Henryk Sienkiewicz (*q.v.*; 1846–1916). His early critical works propounded positivist aesthetic theories, and that he was aware of the social function of art is clear from his statement that his historical trilogy (1884–88) was written "to fortify the hearts" of his countrymen, but in choice of subject and style he is not typical of his period. His early short stories, however, show acute awareness of the contemporary situation and a stark realism.

A more flexible Naturalism gained ground toward the end of the period. The transition is seen in the novels and short stories of Adolf Dygasiński (1839–1902), famous for his realistic but sympathetic portrayals of animal life—*e.g.*, in his novel *Zając* ("The Hare," 1900)—which can be compared with those of Rudyard Kipling. A notable personality of the later part of the period was Gabriela Zapolska (1857–1921), a critic of social hypocrisy in her Naturalistic novels and lively comedies. Trained as an actress, she excels in dialogue and power to present dramatic situations in such plays as *Moralność Pani Dulskiej* ("The Morals of Mrs. Dulska," 1907).

The period produced only two poets of importance: Adam Asnyk (1838–97), a reflective lyricist of formal dexterity but limited imaginative range; and Maria Konopnicka (*née* Wasiłowska; 1842–1910), prolific author of sentimental verses on the underprivileged. Some of her less characteristic work (*e.g.*, the cycle *Italia*, 1901) has distinction.

THE "YOUNG POLAND" MOVEMENT

The "Young Poland" movement was similar to contemporary trends in other Western European countries. The name is used to describe several different groups and tendencies united only by opposition to positivism. The movement was dominated by a desire to return to the expression of feeling and imagination in literature, and from this acquired its other name, neo-Romanticism. In aiming to free the arts from utilitarianism, it showed affinities with French Symbolism, and with certain aspects of French Naturalism. Among its pioneers were the poet Antoni Lange (1861–1929) and Zenon Przesmycki (pseudonym, Miriam; 1861–1944), editor of the important Symbolist review *Chimera* (1901–07), who helped to reestablish a closer contact between Polish and foreign literature, particularly in poetry. Both made translations from a number of other languages; both expressed their aesthetic theories in critical essays. Przesmycki's most influential contribution to the development of modern literature, however, was his rediscovery of Norwid.

The lyrical poet Kazimierz Tetmajer (1865–1940) early achieved popularity with his nostalgic and pessimistic *Poezye* (8 series, 1891–1924). The self-conscious, generalized melancholy of much of his verse, however, is less impressive, when seen in the perspective of time, than his prose, which is characterized by greater vigour and precision of observation. The five volumes of *Na skalnym Podhalu* (1903–10; *Tales of the Tatras*, 1941) were conceived with epic intent and contain some effectively stylized folk material; they are probably his most enduring work. A more interesting poet, Jan Kasprowicz (1860–1926), was of peasant origin; he presented themes from his personal experience directly and without the sentimentality of such earlier writers as Lenartowicz. His principal contribution to Polish literature, however, lies in the structure of his longer lyrical poems; the penitential poems in the volume *Ginącemu światu* ("To the Dying World," 1901), especially the impressive *"Moja pieśń wieczorna"* ("My Evening Song"), employ a technique of association, quotation, musical repetition, and free metre that anticipates the early style of such poets as T. S. Eliot. He also made many translations from English literature, ranging from Chaucer to 20th-century writers. Tadeusz Miciński (1873–1918), regarded as a forerunner of Expressionism and Surrealism, wrote philosophical and mystical poems and plays in which flashes of brilliantly imaginative imagery alternate with a disordered extravagance. His most notable works are the collection of poems *W mroku gwiazd* ("In the Darkness of the Stars," 1902), and the play *Kniaź Patiomkin* ("Prince Potemkin," 1906). The lyrical poet Leopold Staff (1878–1957), whose work shows great variety and technical dexterity, was at this period associated with the "Young Poland" movement. His first volume, *Sny o potędze* ("Dreaming of Power"), was published in 1901. Some of his finest work, however, was written after World War II (*see below*).

A leading exponent of the movement's new aesthetic theories was Stanisław Przybyszewski (1868–1927), who in 1898 became editor of the Cracow literary magazine *Życie* ("Life"). His mannered novels and plays, luridly exploiting psychological themes, enjoyed a meteoric but short-lived success. Stephen (Stefan) Żeromski (*q.v.*; 1864–1925), possibly the most widely read early 20th-century novelist in Poland, reveals his passionate concern for social justice and national freedom in novels, plays, and short stories in which the characters are shown in conflict with circumstance, paying for adherence to principle by loss of personal happiness. An excess of realist documentation, however, with an overblown lyricism of style, frequently vitiates the power of his later work. Władysław Stanisław Reymont (*q.v.*; 1867–1925), himself of peasant stock, adapted the Naturalistic technique to create a vision of peasant life, epic in scale, in his novel cycle *Chłopi* (4 vol., 1902–09; *The Peasants*, 1924–25), for which he received the Nobel Prize in 1924. Another writer who used his experience of peasant life in his novels was Franciszek Smreczyński (pseudonym, Władysław Orkan; 1875–1930), who in *Komornicy* ("The Tenant Farmers," 1900) and *W Roztokach* ("In Roztoki," 1903), for example, described with mature realism the life of the people living in the country at the foot of the Carpathians. One of the

most effective novels of the period, *Żywot i myśli Zygmunta Podfilipskiego* ("The Life and Thought of Zygmunt Podfilipski," 1898) by Józef Weyssenhoff (1860–1932), presents an ironic portrait of the egoist in society. Wacław Berent (1873–1940) parodies the positivist ideal in *Fachowiec* ("The Professional Man," 1895). In *Próchno* ("Rotten Wood," 1903) he portrays with biting irony the late 19th-century decadence of life and art through vivid evocation of various typical "Bohemian" groups—artists, poets, musicians, journalists; and in *Ozimina* ("Autumn Sowing," 1911), in many respects a Symbolist novel, he foreshadows the associative structure and narrative technique of James Joyce's *Ulysses* (1922). His *Żywe kamienie* ("The Living Stones," 1918), a stylized re-creation of the life of the 14th-century wandering scholars, stresses the unity of medieval culture and Poland's place within it. A bold experiment in form and structure, antedating the development of the psychoanalytical novel in Western Europe by several years, was *Pałuba . . .* (1903; new edition 1948) by Karol Irzykowski (1873–1944). In it motivation and behaviour are presented at several "subjective" levels and from different viewpoints, ingeniously cemented by the author's own analyses and cross-references, as in a scientific study. Irzykowski was also a penetrating critic of modern Polish literary theory, and the first to give serious attention to the cinema as an art form in *Dziesiąta muza* ("The Tenth Muse," 1924).

Stanisław Brzozowski (1878–1911), an outstanding critic who developed an original philosophy of the relationship between art and life, stressed the moral function of art and the need for the critic to represent the "moral consciousness" of his age. In *Legenda Młodej Polski* ("The Legend of Young Poland," 1909), he analyzed the weakness of the period's literature and expounded his view of the unity of all work—physical, technical, intellectual, and artistic. He opposed both positivist utilitarianism and the aestheticism of the "Young Poland" movement; his penetrating critical analyses of Polish culture remain of value.

Stanisław Wyspiański (*q.v.*; 1869–1907), painter, draftsman, designer of stained glass, and typographer, was also a dramatist of genius. His plays show the influence of Maeterlinck and Wagner, and of his interests as a graphic artist, with their emphasis on static mood and search for a synthesis of pictorial, musical, and dramatic elements. In them, he reforged elements from classical tragedy and mythology, Polish Romantic drama, and national history in a complex whole. *Wesele* ("The Wedding," 1901) is a visionary parable of Poland's past, present, and problematical future presented in the symbolic but realistic terms of a marriage in his native region of Cracow. Cast in the form of the traditional puppet-theatre (*szopka*) play, it is a masterpiece of evocative allusion, tragedy, and humour.

STANISŁAW WYSPIAŃSKI, A SELF-PORTRAIT IN PASTELS, 1894. IN THE MUZEUM NARODOWE, WARSAW

The literature of the period as a whole is characterized by close contact with Western European literatures, but in their search for a new poetic language writers such as Wyspiański turned to the Polish Romantics, especially to Słowacki and the newly rediscovered Norwid.

RESTORED INDEPENDENCE

The restoration in 1918 of independence decisively affected Polish literature. Taken as a whole, the period between 1918 and 1939 was characterized by richness and variety, and by increasing contact with other European literatures. The publication of many translations, from French, German, and English especially, was a sign of the revival of interest in Western literary developments.

Poetry.—For nearly the whole decade after 1918 lyrical poetry predominated. The periodical *Zdrój* ("The Fountainhead"), published in Poznań, 1917–20, showed affinities with German Expressionism. During the first stage of his career Józef Wittlin (1896–) was a member of this group. His stirring *Hymny* (1920) depict the horrors of war, and in the novel *Sól ziemi* (1936; *Salt of the Earth*, 1939) he portrays wartime experience through the eyes of a man of the people.

The Skamander Group.—In Warsaw several young poets of different tendencies formed a group called *Skamander*, from the name of their monthly publication. The group had no general program, but was held together by the enthusiasm of its members, and their desire to forge a new, poetic language, attuned to the experience of modern life. It was headed by Julian Tuwim (1894–1953), a lyrical poet of emotional power and linguistic sensitivity, whose very facility, however, in time blunted the edge of his originality. Two of his many collections of verse are the early *Czyhanie na Boga* ("Lurking God," 1918) and *Biblia cygańska* ("The Gypsy Bible," 1933). During World War II, in Brazil and the United States, he wrote a long, discursive, autobiographical poem in the nine-syllable line, *Kwiaty polskie* ("The Polish Flowers," 1949). Kazimierz Wierzyński (1894–), in *Laur olimpijski* ("Olympic Laurels," 1927), sang the praise of sport, health, and physical beauty. The poetry of Jan Lechoń (pseudonym of Leszek Serafinowicz; 1899–1956) treats intellectual and national subjects in a balanced classical form. Antoni Słonimski (1895–1969) reveals in his writing his discursive, rhetorical temperament.

Among sympathizers with *Skamander* was Maria Pawlikowska-Jasnorzewska (1894–1945), who had an exceptional gift for concentration, precision, and control in the formulation and expression of emotion. Also connected with the *Skamander* group at this period was Władysław Broniewski (1897–1962). A poet of great power and feeling, with strong left-wing sympathies, he became the master of the revolutionary lyric, and in his popular poetry used traditional metres and forms to express concern with current social and ideological problems.

A writer of great importance was Bolesław Leśmian (1878–1937). His symbolic, Expressionist poetry, containing elements of fantasy and fable, is remarkable for the inventiveness of its vocabulary, its sensuous imagery, and its philosophic content, which in some ways anticipates Existentialism. Although his output was small—he published only three notable collections: *Łąka* ("The Meadow," 1920), *Napój cienisty* ("The Shadowy Drink," 1936), and *Dziejba leśna* ("Woodland Tale," 1938)—he has been increasingly recognized as the most outstanding 20th-century Polish lyrical poet.

The Awangarda.—Among other experimental movements active at this time the *Awangarda* followed the revolutionary trends in poetry, particularly Futurism, in France, Italy, and Spain. This group, led by Tadeusz Peiper (1891–), produced few finished works of art, but had a widespread influence on the regeneration of poetic technique. One of its adherents, Julian Przyboś (1901–70), ranks among the outstanding poets of the post-World War II period; as does Adam Ważyk (1905–), who was loosely connected with the *Awangarda* movement, and a poet, essayist, prose-writer, and brilliant translator. Józef Czechowicz (1903–39) assimilated traditional and regional elements to the new style to produce the concentrated lyricism of such collections as *Dzień jak codzień* (1930).

Prose.—Prose writing reached ascendancy in the second decade of independence. The early novels and short stories of Zofia Nałkowska (1884–1954)—*e.g., Kobiety* ("Women," 1906)—belonged to the "Young Poland" movement, and aimed to reveal the feminine psyche. Later she turned to other themes, striving for narrative objectivity and technical simplicity, and in such novels as *Romans Teresy Hennert* ("The Romance of Teresa Hennert," 1924), *Granica* ("The Frontier," 1935), and *Węzły życia* ("The Threads of Life," 1948–54) developed her talent for psychological analysis but applied it to the revelation of reality. Ferdynand Goetel (1890–1960) wrote of his experiences in Russia during the Revolution in *Kar-Chat* (1923; trans. 1930) and *Z dnia na dzień* (1926; trans. as *From Day to Day*, with intro. by John Galsworthy, 1931), a novel interesting for its use of the diary form

within the main narrative as a means of exploring character. Two women novelists of distinction are Zofia Kossak-Szczucka (1890–1968), noted for her historical novels—*e.g., Krzyżowcy* (4 vol., 1935; trans. as *The Crusaders*, 1947)—and Maria Kuncewiczowa (1899–), who writes psychological novels—*e.g., Cudzoziemka* (1936; *The Stranger*, 1944). Juliusz Kaden-Bandrowski (1885–1944) evolved an individual style marked by experimental realism. His *Generał Barcz* (1923), *Czarne skrzydła* ("Black Wings," 1928–29), and *Mateusz Bigda* (1933) are outstanding examples of a prose style both Naturalistic and Expressionistic, and treat social and political themes with power. Michał Choromański (1904–) achieved success with *Zazdrość i medycyna* (1932; *Jealousy and Medicine*, 1946), which uses experimental methods of narrative sequence and is remarkable for its clinical analysis of character. A writer skilled in reflecting subtleties of perception is Bruno Schulz (1892–1942), author of *Sklepy cynamonowe* (1934; *Cinnamon Shops*, 1963), which presents the mystery of existence in a style combining Expressionism and Surrealism. His prose is reminiscent of that of Kafka, whose works he translated into Polish. Jarosław Iwaszkiewicz (1894–), co-founder of *Skamander*, wrote many novels and short stories in a vivid, succinct prose style, and also critical studies of Chopin and Karol Szymanowski (*q.v.*).

Tadeusz Boy-Żeleński (1874–1941), who had begun his career in the 1890s with songs and light verse, became one of the period's most important literary critics. His attitude was influenced by his knowledge of French literature—he translated more than 100 volumes from French, ranging from the *Chanson de Roland* to Proust, in the Polish style most appropriate to each, and in his introductions and commentaries provided a survey of French literature. In treating Polish writers, he showed interest in biographical and psychological rather than literary considerations, and provided revaluations of most of the great figures of the past. His theatrical reviews and journalism reveal his critical acumen and originality and his hatred of hypocrisy and cant.

The essay form is represented by Jan Parandowski (1895–), whose main theme is the classical culture of Greece and Rome.

SOVFOTO
MARIA DĄBROWSKA PHOTOGRAPHED IN 1960

Parandowski is also a novelist, his best-known works being a biographical novel about Oscar Wilde, *Król życia* ("King of Life," 1930), and *Dysk olimpijski* (1933; *The Olympic Discus*, 1939). A subversive attack on intellectual and social conventions was launched in *Ferdydurke* (1937; Eng. trans. 1961), a novel by Witold Gombrowicz (1904–69) which displays a satirical talent reminiscent of such writers as Alfred Jarry (*q.v.*). The taste for the cyclic novel was satisfied by several novelists: for example, Maria Dąbrowska (1889–1965), with *Noce i dnie* ("Nights and Days," 4 vol., 1932–34), the outstanding modern Polish example of a chronicle novel in epic style, about the development of the Polish intelligentsia of upper-middle class origin during the period 1863 to 1914.

Drama.—The drama was the weakest of the literary forms during this period. Włodzimierz Perzyński (1878–1930), a novelist who wrote realistic comedies, and Karol Hubert Rostworowski (1877–1938), author of poetic dramas, both belong to the previous period. Toward the end of his career Rostworowski began writing prose plays on social and moral problems which at times attained the monumental grandeur of classical tragedy. Jerzy Szaniawski (1887–1970) tried to revive the Symbolist drama. The novelist Zofia Nałkowska wrote two successful plays that have remained in the repertory. The experimental dramas of Stanisław Ignacy Witkiewicz (1885–1939) are of interest chiefly for their expression of his antirealist, aesthetic theories. Witkiewicz, also a painter, novelist, and critic, developed many of the ideas of the *Awangarda*, and applied the principles of "pure form" to painting and drama. He was, moreover, the main exponent of a movement in Polish literature known as "catastrophism." Obsessed with the idea of the disintegration of European culture, endangered by totalitarian ideologies and the attempt to impose the uniformity of a "mass society," he developed his ideas in plays combining elements of Surrealism, grotesque misrepresentation, and what later became known (in the plays of Eugène Ionesco, for example, whose work Witkiewicz to some extent foreshadowed) as the Theatre of the Absurd; and in such philosophical novels as *Pożegnanie jesieni* ("Farewell to Autumn," 1927) and *Nienasyconie* ("Insatiability," 1930). After World War II his work attracted great interest abroad, and began to appear in translation in several Western European countries.

LITERATURE AFTER WORLD WAR II

The impact of the war, the tragic experience of occupation, and the establishment in 1945 of a people's republic decisively affected the character of literature in Poland, and also led to the development of an *émigré* literature, written by Poles who, though widely scattered, struggled to preserve their national identity.

Writers in Exile.—Among *émigré* writers were many who had become famous between the wars: lyrical poets of the *Skamander* group—Wierzyński, Lechoń, Stanisław Baliński (1899–)—and former associates of the *Awangarda* movement, among them Józef Łobodowski (1909–), Jerzy Brzękowski (1903–), Marian Czuchnowski (1909–), and Czesław Miłosz (1911–). The last two were also notable as prose writers: Miłosz won the *Prix Littéraire Européen* for *Zdobycie władzy* (published as *La Prise du pouvoir*, 1953; in Polish, 1955; *The Usurpers*, 1955).

Many *émigrés* wrote of their experiences in German or Soviet prisons and forced labour camps. The most accomplished as literature was *Inny świat* (*A World Apart*, 1951; in Polish, 1953) by Gustav Herling-Grudziński (1919–). *Sprawa Józefa Mosta* (1953), by Herminia Naglerowa (1890–1957), a distinguished novelist of the period between the wars, re-creates and projects as art her experiences in a Soviet prison. Jerzy Pietrkiewicz (1916–), poet, novelist, and literary historian, whose early work was published in Poland during World War II, later wrote mainly in English (*e.g.*, the novels *The Knotted Cord*, 1953; *Isolation*, 1959). Other writers in exile included the essayists Jerzy Stempowski (pseudonym, Paweł Hostowiec; 1894–) and Stefania Zahorska (1894–1961); and the literary historians Tymon Terlecki (1905–), Wiktor Weintraub (1908–), and Maria Danilewiczowa (1907–), who also wrote novels. Witold Gombrowicz (*see above*) also published his postwar work abroad, and became famous, particularly in France, with the novels *Trans-Atlantyk* ("Ocean Liner," 1953), *Pornografia* (1960; Eng. trans. 1966), and especially *Kosmos* (1965; *Cosmos*, 1967), which won him the 1967 International Prize for Literature. He also published abroad the play *Ślub* (1953, "The Wedding") and two volumes of diaries (*Dzienniki*, 1957–62). In all these works, especially the novels, Gombrowicz treats philosophical and psychological themes in a satirical narrative style in which, by emphasizing the grotesque and irrational elements in human nature, he presents an exposé of the conventions of modern life and culture.

Writers in Poland.—In Poland, the years immediately after World War II were notable for publication of works written during the occupation or by writers who had been in concentration camp or prison. The dominant theme was the attempt to come to terms with Fascism and with the experiences of war. This is exemplified particularly in the short stories of Tadeusz Borowski (1922–51), a prisoner at Auschwitz who in collections published in 1948, *Pożegnanie z Marią* ("Farewell to Mary") and *Kamienny świat* ("World of Stone"), explored the depths of human depravity and degradation; and in those of Adolf Rudnicki (1912–), who treated moral and philosophical themes in lyrical prose, and described, in such collections as *Szekspir* ("Shakespeare," 1948) and *Ucieczka z Jasnej Polany* ("Flight from Jasna Polana," 1949), the wartime fate of the Jewish community in Poland. (Selected stories in English translation in *Ascent to Heaven*, 1951, and *The

PHOTO BY MAREK HOLZMAN, BY COURTESY OF POLONIA PUBLISHING HOUSE

JERZY ANDRZEJEWSKI

Dead and the Living Sea and Other Stories, 1957.) Another theme, shown, for example, by the novel *Popiół i diament* (1948; *Ashes and Diamonds*, 1962) by Jerzy Andrzejewski (1909–), was the examination of the moral controversies that accompanied the political and social changes of the postwar period, especially the tragic situation of young conspirators involved in the struggle against the new regime.

"Social Realism."—During 1949–54 the literature of "social realism" gained ground. Writers were concerned with depicting the social changes taking place in Poland. In form, they attempted to emulate the great 19th-century realist writers. A new type of hero was created (the so-called "positive" hero)—the ordinary man or woman actively engaged in "productive" work—and those elements in the social scene that served to present the idea of revolutionary progress were accentuated. The main writer of the "social realist" movement was Leon Kruczkowski (1900–62), a prewar exponent of the Marxist novel—*e.g.*, in his historical novel *Kordian i Cham* ("Kordian and the Boor," 1932)—whose outstanding plays *Niemcy* ("The Germans," 1949) and *Pierwszy dzień wolności* ("The First Day of Freedom," 1960) were successfully performed abroad. Kazimierz Brandys (1916–), whose development typifies postwar tendencies in Polish literature, published the epic novel cycle *Między wojnami* ("Between the Wars," 1947–51), and in 1954 published a "social realist" novel, *Obywatele* ("Citizens"). Brandys and other writers regarded in the early 1950s as being representatives of "social realism"—*e.g.*, Igor Newerly (1903–) and Julian Stryjkowski (1905–)—later ceased to develop this tendency.

Among writers of the "social realist" period who stood aside from political involvement were the poet Konstanty Ildefons Gałczyński (1905–53), who combined lyricism with grotesque fantasy; and the reflective poet and essayist Mieczysław Jastrun (1903–), who in his later work—*e.g.*, the verse collection *Intonacje* ("Intonations") and the series of essays *Mit Śródziemnomorski* ("Mediterranean Myth"), both published in 1962—moved toward Existentialism. A group of Catholic writers opposed to "social realism" included Antoni Gołubiew (1907–), author of the epic novel cycle *Bolesław Chrobry* (1947–55); the prose writer and dramatist Jerzy Zawieyski (1902–69); and the historical novelist, Hanna Malewska (1911–).

Teodor Parnicki (1908–) used a background of conflict between cultures for a penetrating analysis of contemporary philosophical and political problems in historical novels set mainly in the early Christian period: *Koniec "Zgody Narodów"* ("End of 'The Agreement Between the Nations,'" 1955); *Nowa baśń* ("A New Fairy-Tale," 5 vol., 1962–68); and *Tylko Beatrycze* ("Only Beatrice," 1963).

Reaction Against "Social Realism"; The Thaw.—The weakness of the "social realist" movement—its attempt to impose a political pattern on creative writing, its avoidance of themes arising from contemporary social, political, and moral conflicts—resulted in part from the stranglehold of the Stalinist regime. In the period beginning in 1954–55 writers began to criticize these weaknesses and to oppose them. Andrzejewski, for example, presented contemporary ideas and problems in two novels combining historical and metaphorical treatment—*Ciemności kryją ziemię* (1957; *The Inquisitors*, 1960), and *Bramy raju* (1960; *The Gates of Paradise*, 1963). Brandys criticized Stalinism in his novel *Matka Królów* (1957; trans. as *Sons and Comrades*, 1961). The short stories of the young Marek Hłasko (1933–69) in *Cmentarze: Następny do raju* ("The Graveyard: Next Stop Paradise," 1958) showed a new, pessimistic type of realism.

The political "thaw" after 1956 made it more possible for writers to renew contacts with the West. As a result Polish literature was enriched and stimulated, and a period of development and experiment began. In prose, although traditional realistic treatment of social and psychological themes continued in the work of Wilhelm Mach (1917–65), whose *Góry nad czarnym morzem* ("Mountains by the Black Sea," 1961) was an attempt to translate into Polish terms the French "anti-novel," the development of the essay as a vehicle for philosophical and intellectual discussion and comment and the rise of satire showed the tendency to experiment. Among essayists were Brandys (*e.g.,* his series *Listy do Pani Z,* 1958–63), and Tadeusz Breza (1905–70), who analyzed contemporary life and ideas in a prose of Proustian subtlety in, for example, *Spiżowa brama* ("The Bronze Gate," 1960), a penetrating description of life in the Vatican. And despite the passage of time, that writers continued to be concerned with the problems of World War II and the occupation is shown by such novels as *Czarny potok* ("Black Stream," 1954) by Leopold Buczkowski (1905–), *Kolumbowie-rocznik 20* ("The Columbuses—Generation of 1920," 1957) by Roman Bratny (1921–), and *Tren* ("Threnody," 1961) by Bohdan Czeszko (1923–). Moreover, many writers chose as their theme the contemporary consequences of wartime experience, as, for example, Tadeusz Konwicki (1926–) in *Sennik współczesny* ("The Contemporary Nightmare," 1963). In *Głosy w ciemności* ("Voices in the Dark," 1956) and *Austeria* ("Austerity," 1966), Julian Stryjkowski (*see* above) returns to the theme of the feeling of the Orthodox Jewish Polish community that the world has already ended, and gives it a universal application.

Many writers of the 1950s and 1960s attempted to depict the realities of contemporary life in prose works ranging from the political novels of Jerzy Putrament (1910–) to the psychological novels of manners of Stanisław Dygat (1914–); while the novels of Stanisław Lem (1921–), leading Polish representative of serious science fiction, look to the future. Young writers such as Marek Nowakowski (1935–), in their search for a moral basis for life, often penetrate into the worlds of those on the fringes of society—social outcasts and misfits.

One of the most interesting younger writers, whose work is well known outside Poland, is Sławomir Mrożek (1930–), who, with others, went into exile after the political crisis of 1968. Both in his plays—*Policja* (1958; *The Police*), *Na pełnym morzu* (1961; *Out at Sea*), *Karol* (1962; *Charlie*), *Strip-tease* (1962), *Zabawa* (1963; *The Party*), *Czarowna noc* (1963; *Enchanted Night*), and above all in *Tango* (1965; trans. 1966), his most outstanding and widely known work—as well as in the stories collected in *Słoń* (1957; *The Elephant,* 1962) and *The Ugupu Bird* (1968), he shows an acute sense of satire and the grotesque, which he uses to express a philosophy of life both topical and timeless. His comedy belongs essentially to the Theatre of the Absurd, and is distinguished by the subtlety of its parody and its highly stylized language. (The first six plays mentioned are translated by N. Bethel in *Six Plays by Sławomir Mrożek,* 1967.)

The poetry of the "second" postwar period is also notable for expression of philosophical thought. Stanisław Jerzy Lec (1909–66) was a satirical poet famous for his skeptical philosophical aphorisms, *Myśli nieuczesane,* published in series from 1957 (posthumous collected edition, 1968; trans. as *Unkempt Thoughts,* 1962). An outstanding representative of the new intellectual poetry is Zbigniew Herbert (1924–), whose most notable collection is *Studium przedmiotu* ("Study of a Subject," 1961); a selection has been translated into English in *Selected Poems,* with introduction by A. Alvarez (1968).

Perhaps the most interesting of the postwar poets, however, is Tadeusz Różewicz (1921–), who has had a profound influence on younger lyrical poets. From *Niepokój* ("Trouble," 1947), his first collection, to *Głos Anomina* ("The Nameless Voice," 1961), his work has shown a preoccupation with moral themes; he often looks back to the tragic experiences of World War II. Stylistically, he has developed the forms of the *Awangarda* poets in an individual way. Różewicz has also written plays, resembling those of Ionesco: *Świadkowie albo Nasza mała stabilizacja* ("Witnesses,

or Our Little Stability," 1962) and one published with poems in *Kartoteka* ("The Card Index," 1961). Contemporary modern problems also dominate the intellectual, ironic poetry, expressed in brief aphorisms, of Wisława Szymborska (1923–), collected in *Sól* ("Salt," 1962) and *Sto pociech* ("The Hundred Consolations," 1967).

The lyrical poetry of the generation of poets born about 1930 or after is characterized by a wide range of aims and styles. On the one hand the controversial work of such poets as Miron Białoszewski (1922–) shows extreme linguistic and formal experimentalism; on the other hand, a poet such as Ernest Bryle (1935–) reasserts traditional bourgeois morality in traditional poetic forms. Some poets—*e.g.,* Tadeusz Nowak (1930–), Jerzy Harasymowicz (1933–)—have turned for inspiration to the ancient sources of peasant culture; others, among them Jerzy S. Sito (1934–) and Jarosław M. Rymkiewicz (1935–)—two outstanding translators of English and American poetry—have based their poetic program, following the example of T. S. Eliot, on a return to Baroque and neoclassical forms, and have developed an erudite, allusive poetry. Perhaps the most representative of the poets of this new generation is Stanisław Grochowiak (1934–). Grochowiak has created an expressive poetic style based on sudden contrasts and deliberate emphasis on the grotesque aspects of life.

Several writers of the prewar period have continued to publish; among them the poets Leopold Staff and Kazimiera Iłłakowiczówna (1892–); Maria Dąbrowska, who enhanced her reputation with a collection of short stories, *Gwiazda zaranna* ("Morning Star," 1955) and a series of critical essays on Conrad, *Szice o Conradzie* (1959); the novelist Maria Kuncewiczowa; and the novelist, poet, and dramatist Jarosław Iwaszkiewicz, whose fame was increased by the epic novel *Sława i chwała* ("Fame and Praise," 1956–62).

Critics and essayists include Artur Sandauer (1913–); Jan Kott (1914–), whose *Szkice o Szekspirze* (1961; trans. as *Shakespeare Our Contemporary,* 1964) has been widely translated and discussed; Kazimierz Wyka (1910–); and, from the younger generation, Jan Błoński (1931–).

BIBLIOGRAPHY.—*Bibliographies and Histories:* The fundamental biobibliographical work on Polish literature from its beginnings to the end of World War I is the *Bibliografia literatury polskiej "Nowy Korbut,"* 19 vol. (1963– ; 7 vol. published by 1968), a collective work by the Institute of Literary Research of the Polish Academy of Sciences. For the period 1918–57, the basic work is *Słownick współzesnych pisarzy polskich,* 4 vol. (1963–66), also a collective work of the Institute of Literary Research, and in some respects a continuation of the *"Nowy Korbut."* *See* also, on postwar Polish literature abroad, T. Terlecki (ed.), *Literatura polska na obczyznie 1940–1960,* 2 vol. (1964–65). The standard history, by an outstanding scholar of Polish literature, is J. Kleiner, *Zarys dziejów literatury polskiej,* vol. 1 (1932), vol. 2 (1939; 7th ed. 1968). For a modern reassessment *see* J. Kryżanowski, *Dzieje literatury polskiej. Od początków do czasów najnowszych* (1968). K. Krejči, *Geschichte der polnischen Literatur* (1958), is a German translation of a valuable history of Polish literature by a Czech scholar. M. Herman, *Histoire de la littérature polonaise des origines à 1961* (1963) is a valuable textbook by a well-known French Polonist. *See* also R. Dyboski, *Periods of Polish Literary History* (1923), and *Modern Polish Literature* (1924); G. Korbut, *Literatura polska,* 4 vol. (1929–31) with addenda (in English) by M. Danilewiczowa, in *The Year's Work in Modern Language Studies* (1951–); J. Krzyżanowski, *Polish Romantic Literature* (1930), and *Historja literatury polskiej: Od średniowiecza do XIX wieku* (1939; 3rd ed., 1966); B. Chlebowski, *La Littérature polonaise au XIX⁰ siècle,* ed. by M. Kridl (1933); W. Lednicki, *Life and Culture of Poland as Reflected in Polish Literature* (1944); K. Czachowski, *Obraz współczesnej literatury polskiej, 1884–1933,* 3 vol. (1934–36); Marina Bersano Begey, *Storia della letteratura polacca* (1953); M. Kridl, *A Survey of Polish Literature and Culture* (with full bibliography; 1956); S. Marcel, *Histoire de la littérature polonaise des origines au début du XIX⁰ siècle* (1957); R. Matuszewski, *Portraits of Contemporary Polish Authors* (1959); H. Kunstmann, *Die moderne polnische Literatur, 1918–60* (1962).

Collections: W. Borowy (ed.), *Od Kochanowskiego do Staffa,* an anthology of lyric poetry, 2nd ed. (1954); M. Kridl (ed.), *An Anthology of Polish Literature,* in Polish, with Eng. commentary and notes (1957); J. Pietrkiewicz and B. Singer (eds.), *Five Centuries of Polish Poetry, 1450–1950,* an anthology of translations (1960); K. Dedecius (ed.), *Lektion der Stille, neue polnische Lyrik* (1959); G. Hagenau (ed.), *Polen erzählt,* a collection of translated stories (1961); M. Kuncewiczowa (ed.), *The Modern Polish Mind,* a collection of translated stories and essays (1963); *Obraz literatury polskiej XIX i XX wieku,*

21 vol. (1965– ; 5 vol. published by 1968), a collective work by the Institute of Literary Research of the Polish Academy of Sciences, contains monographs on writers, selections from their works, and bibliographies; C. Jelenski (ed., preface by Cz. Miłosz) *Anthologie de la poésie polonaise*, selections from the 15th century to modern times (1965); A. Gillon and L. Krzyżanowski (eds.), *Introduction to Modern Polish Literature: an Anthology of Fiction and Poetry* (1964); Cz. Miłosz (ed. and trans.), *Postwar Polish Poetry: an Anthology* (1965); C. Wieniewska (ed.), *Polish Writing Today* (1967).

(J. W.; Ju. K.)

POLISH NATIONAL CATHOLIC CHURCH, a denomination which arose among Polish immigrants in the United States who separated themselves from the Roman Catholic Church. It is in intercommunion with the Old Catholic, Anglican, Episcopal, and Orthodox churches and has its headquarters in Scranton, Pa. In the mid-1960s, it numbered more than 280,000 members in more than 160 parishes.

Roots of the movement date to the 1870s when "independent" parishes detached themselves from Roman Catholic hierarchical jurisdiction mainly over internal disputes and dissatisfaction with pastors. The influence of clerical converts to Old Catholicism who advocated national churches with Catholic liturgy, the 1884 Baltimore Council ruling which gave bishops title to diocesan properties, the lack of a bishop of Polish birth or descent in the American hierarchy, and resentment of "Americanization" urged by some of the bishops furthered secessions and the emergence of "independent" sects.

In 1896, members of the Sacred Hearts of Jesus and Mary parish in Scranton unsuccessfully protested against the arbitrariness of their pastor to the diocesan bishop. Their former curate, The Rev. Francis Hodur, advised them to found a new parish and hold title to its property. In March 1897 a petition requesting consecration of the new parish's church and installation of Father Hodur to its pastorate was rejected by the bishop. Father Hodur secured a second petition bearing about 5,000 signatures calling for: (1) ownership by Polish parishes of property built by their members, (2) parish-wide elections of administrators of such property, and (3) no appointment by bishops of non-Polish pastors to such parishes without their parishioners' consent.

After returning from an attempt to petition Pope Leo XIII in Rome, Father Hodur held a meeting of his parishioners at which it was voted that the parish remain independent. Excommunication followed. Father Hodur's parish became the nucleus of a movement which took in other seceded congregations. He linked it spiritually to the Protestant and pre-Protestant reformers (especially Huss and Savonarola), to Sts. Cyril and Methodius, whose followers had won converts to Christianity in Poland before its ruler had accepted it from Rome, and, also, to 19th-century romantic Messianic poets who prophesied Poland's resurrection from death under partition.

In September 1904 a synod of the "independent" parishes in Scranton voted to form one body and chose the name Polish National Catholic Church. It also adopted a constitution, elected a lay-clerical Supreme Council, and unanimously elected Hodur bishop. On Sept. 29, 1907, he was consecrated in Utrecht, Neth., by bishops of the Old Catholic Church, and through them established a claim to apostolic succession.

The Polish National Catholic Church proselytized actively; after World War I, it extended its mission to Poland.

Liturgically, the Polish National Catholic Church resembles the Roman Catholic Church. From 1900, masses were in Polish. By 1960, however, one mass in English was permitted each Sunday in parishes where two-thirds of the parishioners desired it. Doctrinally, the church is based on the Scriptures, tradition, decrees of the four councils before the split of 1054, and decrees of its own synods. Up to 1967, the Nicene Creed was recited with the *filioque* clause, but afterward without it (*see* CREED: *Nicene Creed: Filioque Clause*). There is also an expanded confession of faith.

"The Word of God" is enumerated as one of the church's seven sacraments (baptism and confirmation are considered one sacrament but administered separately as in the Roman Catholic Church). In 1922 the requirement of clerical celibacy was abolished. General rather than auricular confession is made by adults.

The Polish National Catholic Church holds quadrennial synods called by the prime bishop and Supreme Council. The synods consist of all clergy, one layman for each 50 parishioners, and representatives of church organizations and of the Polish National Union (Spójnia). They rule on doctrinal matters and elect bishops. Executive power between synods rests with the prime bishop and Supreme Council which consists of all bishops and the seminary rector, plus a lay and a clerical representative from each of the church's five dioceses.

Parishes have governing committees elected at annual parish meetings and with executive power in temporal affairs. Parish meetings also vote on acceptance and rejection of pastors (candidates are designated in lists submitted by diocesan bishops). Each parish holds title to its property but must turn over funds and records to the prime bishop if it dissolves.

Associated with the Polish National Catholic Church in the late 1960s were Czechoslovak and Lithuanian parishes (the former under jurisdiction of a separate bishop).

In 1951 the movement in Poland severed hierarchical ties with the movement in the United States and renamed itself the Polish Catholic Church.

BIBLIOGRAPHY.—Paul Fox, *The Polish National Catholic Church* (1957), the standard general English-language history of the church; T. Andrews, *The Polish National Catholic Church in America and Poland* (1954); Robert W. Janowski, *The Growth of a Church* (1965).

(Jo. W. W.)

POLISH ORTHODOX CHURCH was originally part of the Russian Orthodox Church but became independent after World War I when large numbers of Orthodox faithful found themselves part of the new Polish state. Most of the Orthodox people lived on the eastern borders of Poland and were incorporated into the U.S.S.R. at the end of World War II; this reduced the numbers of the church from about 4,500,000 (1939 est.) to about 350,000 (1948 est.).

On June 14, 1922, the Episcopal Synod of the Polish Church proclaimed its independence, a decision which evoked protests from the Russian Orthodox Church. On Nov. 13, 1924, the church was officially recognized as autocephalous by the ecumenical patriarch of Constantinople. The canonicity of this act was disputed by the Russian Church on the ground that Orthodox custom requires the consent of the mother church before a church can become autocephalous.

At the end of World War II Metropolitan Dionysius of Warsaw was head of the Polish Church, and he declined to submit to the Russian Church. He was therefore prevented on May 4, 1948, from fulfilling his functions by the Polish authorities, and an ecclesiastical delegation went to Moscow asking for autocephalous status on the ground that the 1924 decision was invalid. This was granted by the Russian Church on June 22, 1948. In 1951 at the request of the Polish Church a Russian bishop was nominated to be its head because no suitable Polish churchman could be found. The patriarch of Constantinople did not recognize these actions and continued to regard Dionysius as head of the church, although he was unable to function. This dispute was one example among others of unresolved differences as to the limits of the authority of the various patriarchs. *See also* ORTHODOX EASTERN CHURCH.

(H. M. W.)

POLISH SUCCESSION, WAR OF THE, the European war that broke out in 1733, so named because the rivalry between two candidates for the kingdom of Poland was taken as the pretext for hostilities by governments whose real quarrels with each other had in fact very little connection with Polish affairs.

Poland was an elective monarchy; and Augustus II (*q.v.*) of Poland, who was also elector of Saxony as Frederick Augustus I, died on Feb. 1, 1733. Thereupon Austria and Russia decided that their interests would best be served if Augustus II's son, Frederick Augustus II of Saxony, were to become king of Poland as Augustus III (*q.v.*). Most Poles, however, favoured a candidate of their own nationality, Stanislaw Leszczynski (*see* STANISLAW I). The latter had not only been king of Poland under Swedish protection from 1704 to 1709 (while Augustus II was temporarily deposed), but also had subsequently become the father-in-law of Louis XV of France.

Louis XV, despite the cautious objections of his chief minister, the cardinal de Fleury, had more grounds than those of kinship with Leszczynski for opposing Austria. The Austrian archduchess Maria Theresa, whom the Holy Roman emperor Charles VI had made heiress to the Habsburg lands by his Pragmatic Sanction (q.v.), was about to marry Francis Stephen, duke of Lorraine (see FRANCIS I, Holy Roman emperor); and this marriage threatened to establish Habsburg interests in Lorraine to France's disadvantage.

Spain was ready to make war against Austria for the aggrandizement of the infante Don Carlos (see CHARLES III, king of Spain) in Italy. Don Carlos had already got the duchies of Parma and Piacenza and was expecting to succeed to Tuscany, as Gian Gastone, the last Medici grand duke, was childless; but his mother, Isabella (q.v.) Farnese, coveted Austria's kingdom of Naples-Sicily for him also, as well as Austrian Lombardy (Milan and Mantua). Sardinia-Savoy also had designs on Austrian Lombardy.

Antonio Felice de Monti, France's ambassador to Poland, propped Leszczynski with promises and money and reconciled the houses of Potocki and Czartoryski (qq.v.) in his interests. Leszczynski was elected king by a sejm (parliament) of 12,000 in Warsaw on Sept. 12, 1733, but had to take refuge in Gdansk as a Russian army 30,000 strong was already approaching Warsaw. Then a puppet sejm of 3,000, dominated by the families of Radziwill and Sapieha (qq.v.), elected Augustus III on Oct. 5.

France signed the Treaty of Turin with Sardinia-Savoy on Sept. 26, 1733, declared war against Austria on Oct. 10, and made the first "Family Compact" of the two Bourbon kingdoms by alliance with Spain on Nov. 7. The French overran Lorraine to attack the Austrian Rhineland and sent their marshal Villars with an army over the Alps to invade Lombardy in cooperation with the Savoyards; and a small force was dispatched by sea to relieve Gdansk. The French marshal Berwick (q.v.), however, was killed besieging Philippsburg; Prince Eugene (q.v.) of Savoy, on the Austrian side, defended southern Germany effectively; the invaders in Lombardy were unable to take Mantua; and on June 28 Gdansk fell to the Russians. Escaping to Prussian Königsberg (Kaliningrad), Leszczynski in August appealed to the Poles to continue the struggle, and in November a confederation to support him was formed at Dzikow, near Sandomierz, with Adam Tarlo as its leader.

Meanwhile, Don Carlos and a Spanish army of 40,000 under the conde de Montemar (José Carrillo de Albornoz) had marched across Tuscany and the Papal States to Naples. His victory over the Austrians at Bitonto (May 25, 1734) enabled Don Carlos to proceed to Sicily to be crowned king at Palermo. The Austrian field marshal C. F. von Mercy attacked Parma in the absence of Don Carlos but was defeated and killed in battle there (June 29).

Dissension between Spaniards and Savoyards made the Italian campaign of 1735 inconclusive, and Fleury feared that the British and the Dutch might intervene to help Austria. Accordingly the preliminary Peace of Vienna, between France and Austria, was signed on Oct. 3, 1735. This stipulated that Don Carlos should keep Naples-Sicily but should renounce Parma and Piacenza to Austria and his claims on Tuscany to Francis Stephen of Lorraine; Francis Stephen should renounce Lorraine to Stanislaw Leszczynski, on whose death it should pass to France; Augustus III should be recognized as king of Poland; and Sardinia-Savoy should have Novara and Tortona from Lombardy. The final Franco-Austrian Peace of Vienna (Nov. 18, 1738) confirmed this general post, France also conditionally guaranteeing the Pragmatic Sanction. Since Leszczynski had renounced his crown (Jan. 26, 1736), the Dzikow confederacy had recognized Augustus, and Augustus in 1737 granted Courland as a fief to the Russian empress Anna's favourite, E. J. Biron (q.v.). The outstanding belligerents acceded to the peace in 1739.

POLITIAN (ANGELO AMBROGINI) (1454–1494), Italian poet and humanist, the friend and protégé of Lorenzo de' Medici, and one of the foremost classical scholars of the Renaissance, was born at Montepulciano, Tuscany, on July 14, 1454. He was the eldest of five children of Benedetto Ambrogini, a doctor of law, and Antonia Salimbeni. From the Latin name of his birthplace, *Mons Politianus,* he derived the name (Politianus; Italian form,

Poliziano; anglicized as Politian) by which he is generally known. The murder of his father in May 1464 left the family poverty-stricken, and not later than 1469 Politian was sent to Florence to live with a cousin. To find a patron he started to write Latin epigrams in praise of various Florentine citizens, and attracted the attention of Lorenzo de' Medici (see MEDICI family), to whom he dedicated the first two books of his Latin translation of the *Iliad.* In c. 1473 he entered the Medici household, but without specific duties, and was thus able to study in the Medici library until, in 1475, he was entrusted with the education of Lorenzo's eldest son, Piero, then aged three. In 1477 he was given as a benefice the priory of San Paolo. In Florence he attended the lectures in philosophy given by Marsilio Ficino (q.v.) and the university courses of Cristoforo Landino and of the Greek masters John Argyropulus (q.v.), Demetrius Chalcondyles (see under CHALCONDYLES, LAONICUS), and Andronicus Callistus. Although influenced by Ficino's Neoplatonic ideas, he was more attracted by poetry and philology. His translation of the *Iliad,* books ii–v, into Latin hexameters (1470–75) brought him his first renown. Between 1473 and 1478 he produced Latin verses which are among the best examples of humanist poetry: they include elegies, odes, and epigrams (of particular merit are the elegies *In violas* and *In Lalagen* and the ode *In puellam suam*); to the same period belong the poetic invectives *In Mabilium* and the *Sylva in scabiem* (written 1475, but unpublished until 1954), in which he describes realistically the symptoms of scabies.

His poetic masterpiece of this period is, however, a vernacular poem in ottava rima, *Stanze per la giostra del Magnifico Giuliano de' Medici,* composed between 1475 and 1478, which is one of the great works of Italian literature. The poem describes the love of "Julio" (*i.e.,* Giuliano de' Medici), for "Simonetta" (*i.e.,* Simonetta Cattaneo; d. 1476, wife of Marco Vespucci) by means of a poetic transfiguration in which beauty is glorified according to humanist ideas. Stylistically it is influenced by Latin epic and encomiastic poems, and reveals the author's taste for refined poetry. It was interrupted at book ii, stanza 46, probably because of Giuliano's death in 1478.

Politian was, with Lorenzo de' Medici, one of those mainly responsible for the revaluation of vernacular literature. It is generally believed that it was he who wrote the dedicatory letter, tracing the history of vernacular poetry and warmly defending it, which accompanied the so-called *Raccolta Aragonese,* a collection of Tuscan verse sent by Lorenzo de' Medici to Federico d' Aragona, the second son of the king of Naples, in c. 1477. Although there is no definite evidence of Politian's authorship, there can be little doubt that he must have acted as Lorenzo's adviser in the constitution of this collection, which had great importance in the diffusion of Tuscan literature in southern Italy in the late 15th century.

Politian was with Lorenzo and Giuliano when the latter was killed by the Pazzi on April 26, 1478; on this episode he wrote a dramatic report in a Sallustian style, *Pactianae coniurationis commentarium* (1478). In May 1479, as a result of a quarrel with Lorenzo's wife, Clarice Orsini, he was expelled from the Medici household. In December, instead of accompanying Lorenzo on a difficult diplomatic mission to Naples, he undertook a series of journeys in northern Italy. In Venice he met the famous humanist Ermolao Barbaro, and the two became friends. In Verona he expounded Catullus with much success. Then, attracted to Mantua by the splendour of the Gonzaga court, he found a new patron in

MANSELL—ALINARI

PORTRAIT OF POLITIAN, DETAIL FROM "ZACCHARIAS AND THE ANGEL" BY GHIRLANDAJO; 1490–94

POLITICAL PHILOSOPHY

Cardinal Francesco Gonzaga. It was for a court occasion that
he wrote in Mantua the *Favola d'Orfeo* (1480), a short dramatic
composition in the vernacular based on the myth of Orpheus and
Eurydice, and inspired by the same humanist ideal of beauty
which pervades his *Stanze*. The *Favola* is less refined than the
Stanze, but it nevertheless reveals the author's poetic genius. During his stay in Mantua Politian repeatedly wrote to Lorenzo asking
to be recalled to Florence, and in August 1480 he was at last invited to return and was again entrusted with Piero's education.
Thanks to Lorenzo he was appointed to the Florentine chair of
Latin and Greek (November 1480), but was not readmitted to the
Medici household and went to live at his priory of San Paolo.

At the Florentine university he gave four inaugural lectures
in verse (*Sylvae*): *Manto* (1482), on Virgil's poetry; *Rusticus*
(1483), on the bucolic poems of Hesiod and Virgil; *Ambra* (1485),
on Homer; and *Nutricia* (1486), on the different genres of Greek
and Latin literature. In opposition to the predominant Ciceronianism of his contemporaries, he maintained that modern writers
should elaborate the classical tradition in their own way.

In 1488 he took part in a diplomatic mission to Pope Innocent
VIII; and in 1491 he traveled to Bologna, Padua, and Venice to
trace manuscripts for the Medici library. Otherwise he spent the
last years of his life in Florence. His writings of this last period
include a Latin translation of Epictetus' *Manual* (1479); a collection of *Detti piacevoli* (witty sentences), composed in the vernacular between 1477 and 1479; Greek epigrams; a number of
vernacular *Canzoni a ballo* and *Rispetti* which show his taste for
popular poetry; and Latin letters on problems of style and literature.

His most important work on classical philology is the *Miscellanea* (1489), a collection of 100 notes (*centuria*) on classical
texts: this work marked a turning point in the history of classical
philology. The autograph of an uncompleted second *centuria*
of the *Miscellanea* was discovered in 1961 and is in the Fondazione
Cini Library, Venice. Politian died at Florence on the night of
Sept. 28–29, 1494.

See also ITALIAN LITERATURE: *The 15th Century*; RENAISSANCE.

555555555BIBLIOGRAPHY.—*Editions, etc.*: *Angeli Politani: Opera* (1553);
Epigrammi greci, ed. by A. Ardizzoni (1951); *Sylva in scabiem* (1954)
and *Coniurationis commentarium* (1958), both ed. by A. Perosa; *Le
Stanze, L'Orfeo e le Rime*, ed. by G. Carducci, 2nd ed. (1912); *Stanze*,
critical ed. by V. Pernicone (1954). For bibliographical references see
B. Maier in *I classici italiani nella storia* critics, ed. by W. Binni, vol. i,
pp. 231–56 (1945); B. Maier, "La critica polizianesca del Novecento"
in *La rassegna della letteratura italiana*, lxviii, pp. 377–90 (1954); R. Lo
Cascio, "Sul Poliziano," in *Cultura e Scuola*, vi, pp. 17–25 (1963).

English Translations: L. E. Lord, *A Translation of the "Orpheus"
of Angelo Politian and the "Aminta" of Torquato Tasso* (1931); translations from Politian's poems in J. A. Symonds' *Sketches and Studies in
Italy* (1879).

Biography and Criticism: G. B. Picotti, "Tra il poeta e il lauro," in
Giornale storico della letteratura italiana, lxv–lxvi (1915); Istituto
Nazionale di Studi sul Rinascimento, *Mostra del Poliziano nella Biblioteca Medicea Laurensiana: Manoscritti, libri rari, autografi e documenti. Catalogo*, ed. by A. Perosa (1954), and *Il Poliziano e il suo
tempo. Atti del IV Convegno internazionale di Studi sul Rinascimento*
(1957); V. Branca, "La incompiuta Seconda Centuria dei 'Miscellanea'
di Angelo Poliziano," in *Lettere Italiane*, xiii, pp. 137–77 (1961); A.
Perosa, "Febris; a poetic myth created by Poliziano," in *Journal of the
Warburg and Courtauld Institutes*, vol. ix, pp. 81 ff. (1946); *Dizionario
Biografico degli Italiani*, vol. ii, pp. 691–702 (1960).   (G. A.)

POLITICAL PHILOSOPHY. The traditional problems of
political philosophy have been the nature and the justification of
political obligation and authority. There are here two essentially
different sets of questions. First, there are the questions how
men came together under governments and what were the motives
which originally influenced them to do this and which still prevail
to keep them obedient to government orders. These are questions of fact and they are properly studied by social historians,
sociologists and psychologists; but before sociology and psychology were established as independent sciences, many political
philosophers included speculations on these historical and psychological topics in their works. The second question is that of the
ethical justification of obedience to government; or, if we look at
it from the point of view of the rulers, that of the moral basis of
their authority. This question is the proper concern of political

philosophy. In this article some representative answers to it are
considered.

Force.—One answer is that there is no ethical justification for
government. Rulers govern because they have the power and consequently they govern in their own interest. Subjects obey because
they cannot help it; they are the tools of the rulers. Greek sophists,
of whom Thrasymachus in Plato's *Republic* is an example, first
gave this answer, but it is still alive, for it was the view of the
19th-century anarchists and is still the official Marxist doctrine.
"The State is nothing more than a committee for the administration of the affairs of the ruling class" (*Communist Manifesto*);
and "With the disappearance of classes the State too will disappear" (Friedrich Engels). How far this is a complete answer will
depend on the merits of the alternative answers which follow.

The Organic Theory.—The state has been likened to an organism, the citizens to its organs: "We are members one of another." As an eye is good when it best serves the organism as a
whole, so the good citizen is he whose whole life is dominated by
the ideal of state service. If he fails to perform his civil functions
he should be liquidated ("If thine eye offend thee, cut it out . . .").
The government is the brain of the state, the organ whose function
is the control of the other organs in the interest of the whole body.

The difficulties in this theory are these. First, it tends to assume that actual states are ideal, that their governments do control the citizens in the interest of the whole. Secondly, it assumes
that there is something correctly described as "the interest of the
whole state," to which individual interests can be sacrificed. But
there is no such thing: the interests of some can be sacrificed to the
interests of others, but the good of the state must be analyzed
without remainder into the goods of individual men (as must public health or social welfare). Thirdly, this theory assumes
that the state is the only form of association, as was the Greek
city-state in the time of Plato and Aristotle when the theory first
appeared. But the scriptural quotations cited above stressed the
unity and organic character not of the state but of the church.
Nowadays, with the vast multiplication of associations, it is impossible for one type of association, the political, to claim the complete self-sufficiency, the overriding authority and the undivided
loyalty which the organic theory of the state requires.

The General Will.—On this view it was argued that a moral
rule, to be moral, must be self-imposed, and the problem of political authority thus became that of self-government. At first sight
this leads straight to democracy as the only legitimate form of
government. We have an obligation to obey laws only if we ourselves have made them. But in Jean Jacques Rousseau, who
originated this theory, the argument took a different direction, in
which it was further developed by Hegel and his followers (*e.g.*,
Bernard Bosanquet, *The Philosophical Theory of the State*).
My real good must be distinguished from what at the moment I
actually want. My permanent aim, if I am reasonable, is my real
good, though my passing desires may thwart and impede it. This
distinction between ends or aims is then carried over as a distinction between two selves within me, my rational, true, permanent,
higher self and my lower, fluctuating, impulsive, desiring self.
When a law compels me to abstain from murder or blackmail it
expresses my higher against my lower self. Thus when I obey the
law, I am obeying my own real will, the law is self-imposed, and
I am "forced to be free" (Rousseau). Since "the good" is the
same for all rational men, the real selves of all will be identical,
and the state can be said to have (or be) a single will; the general
will. There is thus attributed to the state a unity of a type higher
even than that of an organism, the unity of a self. In Hegel and
his successors this led to a kind of deification of the state as "the
march of God upon earth" (Hegel) and as the sole source of moral
right and the sole centre of human devotion.

Parallel objections to those against the organic theory are valid
here. What is called "the will of the state" is in fact the will of
the government, and governments are just as capable as individuals
of making irrational decisions based on desire or short-term interest. A state decision is in any sense my responsibility only if
I have had some actual share in bringing it about. Much of
morality and much of human value is no concern of the state at

all. Finally it may be objected that, even if all this theory were literally defensible, what is said of the state could be said of any other association: trade unions, colleges, churches and athletic clubs would have (or be) general wills too.

Pluralism.—From this last criticism there emerged a theory called pluralism in contrast with the "monistic" theory of Rousseau and the Hegelians with their single supreme association. The pluralists varied in their attitude to the state. Some of them found no rational function for the state to perform (except making wars). There they joined hands with the Marxists, who were pluralists so far as they substituted for the state a complex of voluntary associations. Others held that there were certain functions which the state should perform, but these gave it no supremacy over other associations, no monopoly of loyalty, no right to stand as the sole source of morality and no claim to obedience beyond the affairs which were its special charge.

The Liberal View.—These theories have now few defenders; the living issues in politics are to be sought elsewhere. They are here considered under labels which are not used with any suggestion that they correspond to the lines between political parties. The views here considered are distinguished by the divergence between their basic principles and between the elements in politics on which they lay most stress. We have seen how the pluralists asked what was the function of government, what purposes the state in particular among all other associations was alone or best fitted to achieve. This question is the way in which the problem has been seen by the English tradition from Hobbes through Locke and J. S. Mill; and it is on the whole characteristic of British and American thought to look at government in this practical and utilitarian light.

First, government is needed to provide security of life, as Hobbes insisted. No individual is strong enough to guarantee his own security unaided. No voluntary association is sufficiently inclusive or wields the sort of weapons needed to keep violence at bay. But security of life is not all that men need. Security of other interests (especially property, said Locke) and security from all kinds of damage by blackmail, arson, rape, assault, etc. (this was Mill's view) require government action. This is the field of criminal law. The Communist says that the state will wither away at the establishment of a classless society; but Marx and Engels nowhere explain what is to be done about crimes of violence. Lenin does face this problem in one place; he says:

> We are not utopians, and do not in the least deny the possibility and inevitability of excesses on the part of *individual persons,* or the need to suppress *such* excesses. But, in the first place, no special machine, no special apparatus of suppression is needed for this; this will be done by the armed people itself, as simply and as readily as any crowd of civilized people, even in modern society, interferes to put a stop to a scuffle or to prevent a woman from being assaulted (V. I. Lenin, *The State and Revolution,* ch. 5, sec. 2, in *Lenin, Selected Works,* vol. ii, pt. i, pp. 293–294, Lawrence and Wishart, London, 1951).

But crowds do not part combatants and men do not violate women when there is a crowd standing by. Lenin's recipe is lynch law, and lynch law is notoriously incapable of dealing with most crimes or of dealing justly with those which it does assail. Here then is a clear case for government action.

Secondly, government is required to settle disputes which are not amenable to direct compromise or agreed settlement. This is the province of civil law. If government were to wither away, the victory in every dispute would go to the stronger or to the possessor. Things would be little better if a voluntary society undertook to adjudicate, for some disputants would not fall under its authority, nor could it enforce its awards.

These two functions of protection and of settlement of disputes exhausted the functions of the state as seen by the classic English tradition. Here the work of government is essentially negative: its force is applied only against bad men or against the side in a dispute which has the weaker case; and its only duty to the good and peaceable citizen is to leave him alone, except to the extent that it must tax him and perhaps enlist his services as juryman or soldier to enable it to perform its protective and arbitral functions.

The Socialist View.—English and American governments up to the middle of the 19th century restricted themselves to those minimal negative protective functions. But they performed two jobs which were the seeds of a more positive doctrine of state action. The state protected men's rights from invasion by other men. But there was one right for which it did more than that. On the Hobbes-Locke view, the state's concern with the right to life was to prevent other men at home or abroad from endangering my life. But what if my life is endangered by starvation (not because an ogre has shut me in a dungeon but because I cannot work or cannot find work to do)?

On the strict liberal or protective view, governments should agree with Arthur Hugh Clough:

> Thou shalt not kill, but need'st not strive
> Officiously to keep alive.

But in fact government did so strive, through poor relief and casual wards. Over no other right did government assume this paternal care, but this is obviously the thin end of a very thick wedge. The "right to work" was originally taken to mean the right to do whatever work I can find (and to stop doing it) without interference; and this was how the right was interpreted and protected by English law. But what of the unemployed? Unemployment pay ensured their right to life, not their right to work. It is only since the state undertook the provision of schemes of work and adopted a full-employment policy that the supply of work has been accepted as a government responsibility.

The first seed in fact grew into the welfare state. Not only life, but education, health and pensions have become government responsibilities. It might be thought that there can be no limit to this extension, and the phrase welfare state encourages this idea. But even its strongest supporters would not propose state-guaranteed supplies of tobacco, cosmetics, television sets or theatre seats. "To each according to his needs"—not his wants—is the socialist slogan: the state should ensure the supply of those things from which, it is thought, no human being should be debarred by accident of birth or wealth or dwelling place. The welfare state really appeals to a principle of justice, not of welfare—to the view that it is unfair that some men should be deprived of things without which life is not worth living (health, education, work) because they cannot afford them.

Though the welfare state is not usually extended to supply luxuries there is sometimes invoked another principle, in addition to that of justice, which would work in that direction. It is the principle of equality—not merely equality of opportunity (which the principle of justice achieves) but an equality more fundamental still. It is thought wrong that some people should have automobiles, television sets or vacations which others cannot have. On this principle the aim of state education is not merely to provide educational opportunities for those who cannot afford them but to equalize education for all. The aim of taxation is not merely to raise money for necessary and justifiable services but to redistribute and to equalize incomes. It is held to give a child an unfair advantage not only if other children have no education but also if he has parents who can afford to send him to a better school or if he has the ability to pass examinations earlier than other children.

The second seed of a theory much wider than the negative liberal one to be found in 19th-century government was the postal service. For here was the idea that a certain service was required which could not be effectively supplied to all who needed it unless it was supplied by government. This seed has grown into the program of nationalization. This program too has tended to operate on a distinction between needs and wants. There are some services which every citizen in a civilized community has a right to enjoy: roads; drainage; and a clean water supply. All of these used to be supplied by individual enterprise or by private persons or companies working for profit. But this meant that many poor people or people living in remote areas could not have these services or had to pay a prohibitive price for them. But the list has grown to include railways, gas and electricity, where it is more doubtful whether these are needs to which all men have an equal right and which must therefore be state-supplied. We noticed above how the principle of justice was supplemented and in places supplanted by the principle of equality. Here too another basic principle has come in to promote the development of state services: the principle that no man's labour should be exploited for the profit of another man, or, put the other way round, that no man should enjoy income unearned by his own efforts. On this principle there are no limits to nationalization as an ideal, since whenever any industry is nationalized the employment of labour for profit is correspondingly diminished; it ceases to matter whether services nationalized are necessary for civilized existence or whether the nationalization benefits the workers or the public.

The Conservative View.—In opposition to the liberal and socialist principles, it has been objected that they overemphasize human reason. No citizen regards his state in this cool, calculating way as an association existing to do certain jobs for him. "The state ought not to be considered as a partnership agreement in a trade . . . to be taken up for a little temporary interest or to be dissolved on the fancy of the parties" (Edmund Burke). To regard the moral claims of one's country in this light is like doing one's best for one's friends or one's children solely from a lively expectation of favours to come. Around these centres—country, family, friends—gather a loyalty and a devotion, traditions of fellowship and service which mere utility can never explain or exhaust.

Nor is reason an adequate guide for the rulers either: no human individual or committee can be trusted to change a society or to plan its future. The garnered wisdom of centuries expressed in custom, tradition, laws and constitutions, the slow process of unconscious change, adapted perhaps empirically here and there to some immediate problem—these form a better guide than the blue books and blueprints of the planners. The conservative tradition respects the individual, not the abstract identical individuals of liberal theory, the bearers of universal rights, but the individual in his rich variety. It would rather have things done in an illogical, confused and piecemeal way, provided that this allowed individual variety and individual enterprise, than in an efficient, streamlined way through uniform leveling and dragooning. It sees state provision and state management in human terms. State or "free" education means education at the taxpayer's expense. It will not deny occasional justice to the Robin Hood ethic of robbing rich Peter to pay poor Paul, but it will require strong justification for it in each case. It sees state control as control by politicians and civil servants. Such control, the conservative would say, may on occasion be justified but there is no such inherent merit in it as to justify rejoicing in its every advance, as the nationalizers do.

Politics and Morals.—The aim of the preceding sections has been to show how political ideals rest on certain moral principles or judgments of value. To work out these connections is the task of political philosophy. But it may be doubted whether it is the task of political philosophy to decide between these principles or the systems erected upon them. Here political thinking is driven back on a fundamental issue in ethics. Some would hold that moral values are subjective: each man must make his own decision between them; none of them can be rationally defended against its rivals. If so, political philosophy cannot claim to do as it once did, to lay down the best kind of state or the best laws.

Analysis.—Developments since the middle of the 19th century have thus tended to diminish the function of political philosophy. Factual questions have been removed from it and handed over to sociology and to psychology. Its nonfactual arguments have been driven back into ethics, and ethical principles in their turn have been removed from the field of rational discussion. By the middle of the 20th century, however, philosophical movements were showing a great positive interest in linguistic analysis, and here, it would seem, there was another remaining field for political philosophy. The analysis of language about politics, of such terms as government, sovereignty, law, rights and punishment, remained to be achieved.

See also references under "Political Philosophy" in the Index.

BIBLIOGRAPHY.—T. H. Green, *Lectures on the Principles of Political Obligation* (1895), reprinted from *Philosophical Works,* vol. ii (1885); B. Bosanquet, *The Philosophical Theory of the State* (1899); L. T. Hobhouse, *The Metaphysical Theory of the State* (1918); G. D. H. Cole, *Social Theory* (1920); T. D. Weldon, *States and Morals* (1946); J. D. Mabbott, *The State and the Citizen* (1948).   (J. D. M.)

POLITICAL SCIENCE, a term most broadly understood to mean the systematic study of government processes by the application of scientific methods to political events. More narrowly, and more traditionally, it has been thought of as the study of the state and of the organs and institutions through which it functions. In the United States, as in most countries, political science is thought to be a single discipline, but the plural form is used in France, as in the name of L'École Libre des Sciences Politiques, founded in 1871, the first school of its kind in Europe. There is some tendency both within and without the United States to be agnostic about the scientific character of the discipline, which is sometimes referred to as "political studies." Although speculation about political subjects is not unknown in other ancient cultures, such as that of India, most students agree that the roots of political science are to be found in the earliest sources of western thought. Sir Frederick Pollock wrote of Aristotle that "he has been recognized as the founder of political science by the general voice of posterity."

The origins of contemporary political science are to be found in the 19th century's enthusiasm for the development of social sciences, an enthusiasm that had been stimulated by the rapid growth of the natural sciences. This enthusiasm reinforced an existing interest in the subject in the United States and created a generation of U.S. political scientists, including Theodore Dwight Woolsey, John W. Burgess, Woodrow Wilson, W. W. Willoughby, and Frank Goodnow. In 1903, to signalize the professional nature of the new political science, the American Political Science Association was organized with Frank Goodnow as its first president.

Although the study of political science in U.S. universities and colleges surged in the last half of the 19th century, attention to systematic politics had been by no means unknown before that, although the subject was usually taught in conjunction with moral philosophy. At Harvard College, under Henry Dunster, its first president, the curriculum in 1642 provided instruction on Mondays and Tuesdays in "*Ethicks* and *Politicks,* at convenient distances of time." Politics as an academic subject was made independent of moral philosophy when Theodore Dwight Woolsey, president of Yale University (1846–70), first introduced a course in "political philosophy" in 1847–48. The first chair of history and political science was created at Columbia University in 1857 and was occupied by Francis Lieber, who had earned a reputation as a political philosopher while teaching in South Carolina. Political science, free of any connection with moral philosophy, fusion with history, or submergence in political economy, may be said to date from 1880 when John W. Burgess, after studying at L'École Libre des Sciences Politiques, succeeded in establishing a separate school of political science at Columbia University. Although political science faculties appeared in increasing numbers after 1900, the growth was uneven and in some major institutions separate departments were not created until after World War I. In England, the emergence of political science as a subject was recognized in the establishment of the London School of Economics and Political Science in 1895 and by the founding of a separate politics chair at Oxford in 1912.

Though political science may be distinguished from political philosophy, the distinctions must be unsatisfactory inasmuch as they lack categorical rigour. In the most usual distinction, political philosophy is thought to be concerned primarily with the study of political ideas, often within the context of their times. It is strongly normative in its thrust and disposition, and rationalistic in its method. Political science, to the contrary, concerns itself with institutions and behaviour, eschews normative judgments as much as possible, and attempts to derive principles from objective facts with as much quantification as the evidence will allow. Thus political philosophy speculates about the place and order of values, the principles of political obligation—why men should or should not obey political authority—and the nature of such terms as "right," "justice," and "freedom." Political science, on the other hand, seeks to establish by observation (and, if possible, by measurement) the existence of uniformities in political behaviour—how governments and people in political situations actually conduct themselves—and to draw correct inferences from these data. The stated differences between political philosophy and political science are less than is sometimes supposed, for the most empirical scholar in both the social and natural sciences makes use of unproved postulates, hunches, and intuitions; and the most rationalistic philosopher employs conceptions that embody empirical statements.

Because political science deals with some aspects of human behaviour, it is closely allied to other social sciences that also deal with human behaviour. For example, numerous theories of the state have drawn inspiration from the human being as model, as in the *Policraticus* of John of Salisbury (1159) in which the physiology of the body and that of the state are compared; or in the *Republic* of Plato in which the elements of the human personality prefigure the class structure of the state; or in Rousseau's *Contrat Social* in which the political order is animated by a *General Will* (will being a human attribute); or in the work of Hegel in which the state is exalted as a person.

Besides biological and psychological theories of the state, there have been anthropological theories like that of Gumplowicz, which ascribes the origin of the state to the struggle of races for domination, and those of De Gobineau and Houston Chamberlain, which assigned primacy in politics to a master race. Economic theories of the state are to be found in Harrington's *Commonwealth of Oceana* and in the works of Marx and Lenin. Sociological theories of the state are available in Pareto's *Mind and Society* and Karl Mannheim's *Ideology and Utopia*. Sociological theory with a core of geographical determinism led the Swedish political scientist, Rudolf Kjellén, to a theory of politics which he named "geopolitics." Cybernetics supplies a modern model for the study of political systems as communications networks, resembling that of the brain and the nervous system in the human body.

Among the other social sciences with which political science has been historically related, a special place is occupied by law. A close connection between the state and law was made in the 16th century in Jean Bodin's theory of sovereignty, which supposed the necessary existence in each state of a supreme authority to make the law. This theory gave rise to numerous juristic theories of the state, especially among German publicists of the 19th century who sought to define the nature of federation and empire. Although the doctrine of sovereignty made most sense as a statement of the power of monarchs to make the law in simple unitary political systems, earnest writers forced the facts of federation and empire to fit the theory, and often ignored those that did not.

The relatively narrow and somewhat culture-bound view that the state is the focus of political science has been questioned by some scholars who feel that the concept has limited analytical use. For some of these, the subject matter of political science is power in human relations, a phenomenon that may be studied in forms of human association other than the state, and with somewhat better claims to the attribute of universality, which is one of the elements of science. G. E. G. Catlin, an English scholar, in his *Science and Method of Politics* has expressed this view. Bertrand Russell, the English philosopher, and Bertrand de Jouvenal, the French writer, have contributed to the literature on political power; and Harold Lasswell, the American political scientist, has brought to the analysis of power strong supporting insights from the field of psychology.

The inadequacy of mere institutional description and the failure of ethnocentric categories to be truly comparative have led still others to employ such various definitions of the research field as political process, decision-making, community studies, and political systems. For those interested in political process as the significant research situation in political science, a principal analytical technique has been the group concept derived most directly, in U.S. political science, from Arthur F. Bentley's *Process of Government* (1908), and reinforced by contributions from sociology. This has led to an increasing understanding of interest groups in the political process, an understanding which has been enriched since World War II by new research by scholars in England, Yugoslavia, and Australia. Research into decision-making uses the techniques of game theory (*see* GAMES, THEORY OF); and the investigation of political systems has been greatly stimulated by the rise of former colonies to independence. It has also been suggested by some that political science is one of the "policy sciences" and that its proper concern is the objective selection of alternative public policies according to consequences predicted for them by the political analyst.

The question as to whether political science is a "science" is largely inconsequential because the problem is primarily one of definition. If the term science is to be applied to any body of systematically organized knowledge based on facts found by empirical methods with as much measurement as the material allows, then political science is a "science," just as are the other social disciplines. If, on the other hand, the term science is to be limited to those disciplines in which the scholar can control the materials to be studied, can perform experiments that others can reproduce under the same conditions, and in which predictability is possible, then the label is less appropriate, although not entirely misapplied. Thorstein Veblen denied that political science was anything more than a "taxonomy of credenda," but Lord Bryce, although of the opinion that politics could not be as precise as mechanics, said, in his presidential address to the American Political Science Association in 1909, that it was at least as much a science as meteorology.

The method of political science varies with the subject matters that make up the topics of the discipline. Thus institutional analysis is conventional in the study of the formal agencies of government; structural-functional analysis which was developed by sociologists has been employed in the study of the political systems of non-Western countries; and the methods of legal reasoning are those customarily brought to the study of international, constitutional, and administrative law. The techniques of statistics are applied to the measurement of public opinion and the voting activities of the electorate, and some attempt has been made to apply them to the study of the behaviour of courts and judges. The techniques of historical analysis and of conceptual inquiry are principal approaches to political philosophy and theory. Other subjects of political science using combinations of all of these techniques are public administration, state and local government, political parties and interest groups, governmental regulation of the economic order, and international relations and politics.

Although political science is primarily an academic discipline, it has applications in the government service, journalism, business enterprise, and professional politics. Political scientists have been called to advise on the size, shape, and staffing of governmental agencies, the design and installation of public administration programs, the behaviour of ethnic, social, and economic groups, the analysis of policy alternatives in national security and other public affairs, the refinement of principles of constitutional and administrative law, the establishment of the optimum conditions for new governments such as those of Puerto Rico or Japan or West Germany, the development of governmental programs for the regulation of business enterprise, and the prescription of rules for the more efficient conduct of the business of legislative bodies.

Though empirical approaches to the study of political events have been more widely used in the United States than elsewhere, significant work has been done in several countries. In France, where constitutional law and history have been abundant and politics often has been viewed from legal perspectives, André Siegfried introduced the geographical and historical study of elections as early as 1913, and Jean Stoetzel the scientific study of public opinion in 1943. The latter was not a field study but a discussion of method. In the field of political parties the work of Maurice Duverger and François Goguel has been notable. England has made many creative contributions to political theory and law throughout its history, as have other European countries, and it has also produced substantial work that can be classified as positive political science. Among these are the studies of R. T. McKenzie and David E. Butler in the field of political parties, S. E. Finer on interest groups, Uwe Kitzinger on German elections, and Herman Finer and Denis Brogan in the field of comparative government. Early work by Graham Wallas drew attention to the importance of psychology in an understanding of politics. In Australia, teaching and research in political science have developed in the years since 1945. Strong interest has been shown in parties and elections, and attention has been given to the study of interest groups. (E. LA.)

POLITIS, NIKOLAOS SOKRATES (1872–1942), Greek jurist and diplomat, a brilliant champion of the peaceful settlement of disputes and of disarmament, was born at Corfu on Feb. 7, 1872. After holding professorships in the faculty of law at Aix-en-Provence, at Poitiers, and at Paris, he was in 1914 summoned by Eleutherios Venizelos to reorganize the Greek Ministry of Foreign Affairs, of which he became director general. Appointed minister of foreign affairs in 1916, he went to the peace conference of 1919 as the delegate of Greece. In the League of Nations, where he was also the Greek delegate, he wrote the report on the Geneva Protocol (1924). As vice-president of the Disarmament Conference, he drew up the definition of the aggressor there propounded. His lucid, powerful, and eloquent speeches put him in the first rank of the delegates to the League.

Politis published a number of books of jurisprudence, including *La Justice internationale* (1924) and *Les Nouvelles Tendances du droit international* (1927; Eng. trans., *New Aspects of International Law*, 1928). These showed him to be at once a thinker of far-reaching interests and a passionate believer in the future of international law. The foundation of the Academy of International Law at The Hague was largely the result of his efforts. In 1937 he was made president of the Institute of International Law. He died at Cannes, France, on March 4, 1942. (CH. D. V.)

POLK, JAMES KNOX (1795–1849), 11th president of the United States, was born in Mecklenburg County, N.C., on Nov. 2, 1795. At the age of 11 he accompanied his family to Tennessee, settling in what is now Maury County. In his childhood formal schooling was impossible because of ill health, but at the age of 20 he successfully passed the entrance requirements for the second-year class of the University of North Carolina. As an undergraduate his record was "correct, punctual, and industrious." As a graduating senior in 1818 he was the Latin salutatorian of his class—the pre-eminent scholar in both the classics and mathematics.

Early Career.—With this academic background he began to read law in the office of Felix Grundy in Nashville, Tenn., to associate with leading public figures in the state, and to make political speeches. In 1820 he was admitted to the bar. Since he was a confirmed Democrat and an unfailing supporter of Andrew Jackson, and since his style of political oratory became so popular that he was characterized as the "Napoleon of the stump," his political career was assured. With him in his rapid rise to political power was his wife, Sarah Childress Polk (1803–1891), whom he married Jan. 1, 1824, during his service in the state house of representatives (1823–25).

Mrs. Polk's home was Murfreesboro, Tenn., the temporary state capital. The social prominence of her family and her personal charm were distinct assets for a politically ambitious lawyer. As an official hostess she won the admiration and esteem of the leading figures of the day. For 25 years she was her husband's close companion in state and national politics. In the long period of her widowhood she maintained Polk Place in Nashville as a shrine.

James K. Polk was by nature a student of government, by experience a legislator and by force of circumstance an administrator. He was not an easy man to know or to like. Boon companions did not relish his austerity. Associates tolerated but did not approve his inflexible living standards. He had many acquaint-

POLK, DAGUERREOTYPE BY MATHEW BRADY

ances, but very few friends. One friend was Andrew Jackson, who encouraged and advanced Polk and whose influence carried him from the Tennessee house of representatives to the U.S. house of representatives, where he served from 1825 to 1839. From 1835 to 1839 he was speaker of the house. In that service in Washington Polk acquired a reputation as a constant, undeviating supporter of Jacksonian principles. In 1839 he left the house to become governor of Tennessee. Two defeats for a second term (1841, 1843) by small majorities convinced him that to strengthen his party he should return to Washington in some capacity.

Polk's nomination for president at Baltimore on the Democratic ticket in 1844 was unsought by him, for the party had more prominent sons in Martin Van Buren, Lewis Cass, and James Buchanan. However, they could not reconcile their differences and a compromise candidate had to be found; since the campaign was to be run on issues and not on personalities, it was decided that Polk would do. He is regarded as the first "dark horse" nominee in the history of the presidency. He was a party man from the west, and his experience as a legislator, it was thought, would make possible the realization of legislative and executive co-operation and understanding in the functioning of the national government. While speaker of the house he had decided many procedural questions and had usually been sustained on appeal by majorities composed of the leaders of both parties. His party feeling was intense, but his integrity was unquestioned. He knew the rights and privileges of the house and he also knew its responsibilities.

Campaigner Polk surprised the country by taking a positive stand on two burning issues of the day. While other candidates hedged on Texas, he demanded annexation. While other candidates evaded the Oregon problem he openly advocated a drastic change in policy in the boundary dispute with Great Britain represented by the slogan "54°40′ or fight." His election was close, but it was decisive—a popular plurality of about 38,000 and 170 electoral votes against 105 for Henry Clay.

Presidency.—Not yet 50 years of age, Polk was the youngest successful presidential candidate up to that time. He entered the presidency full of vigour and with an expressed zeal to serve his country to the best of his ability. He left it four years later exhausted and enfeebled by the efforts he had made. In office he demonstrated remarkable skill in the selection and control of his official advisers. In his formal relations with congress his legislative experience served him well. When his party was united, he yielded to the wishes of congress. When he disagreed with congressional policy and made an issue of it, he fortified his position with recognized precedent and established practice. His formal disapprovals (two message vetoes and one pocket veto) were questioned, but the two returned measures failed to command the necessary two-thirds majority for repassage.

The Polk administration was marked by large territorial gains. The annexation of Texas as a state of the union was concluded—resulting in a two-year war with Mexico. As a consequence of that war the southwest and far west (California), by conquest and by purchase, became part of the U.S. domain. During this period the northwest boundary became fixed by treaty, and the continental United States emerged a recognized reality. Additional achievements included a treaty with New Granada (Colombia) clearing up the problem of right of way for U.S. citizens across the Isthmus of Panama; establishment of a warehouse system which provided for the temporary retention of undistributed imports; and the passage of the Tariff Act of 1846. As these helped foreign trade, so the reenactment of the independent treasury system helped in the solution of domestic financial problems.

The expansion of the country westward caused the creation of a new agency, the Department of the Interior. The Polk administration should also be credited with the establishment of the U.S. Naval Academy at Annapolis, Md., and the authorization of the Smithsonian Institution.

Polk's influence over his congresses may be gauged from the results of the recommendations of four annual messages and ten significant special messages to one or both houses. His control of legislative policy in bitterly partisan congresses must be judged in terms of results, not oratory or parliamentary delay. He recommended with a high degree of success: settlement of a trade dispute with Great Britain; an increase in U.S. armed forces; war with Mexico; peace with Great Britain over Oregon, making available finances to expedite peace conclusions; organization of the Oregon Territory; peace with Mexico providing for limited conquest; and a revised treasury system. As an executive he refused information desired by Congress (on the ground that it was incompatible with the public interest), recognized a new French revolutionary government, and proclaimed the validity of the Monroe doctrine. These pronouncements were recognized by succeeding presidents.

The diary kept by Polk during his term of office stressed the presidential burden. Day after day, week after week, he recounted in his diary his experiences with the hosts of office seekers who infested Washington and who occupied so much of his public time. Again and again there was evident a note of despair in his writings. He knew from personal experience what an evil an unlimited executive patronage can become. Nevertheless, he felt powerless to change its obligations and too conscientious to avoid its duties. At the close of his term, March 4, 1849, Polk retired to his home in Nashville, where he died on June 15, 1849.

The office of chief executive under Polk was well filled. He maintained it with dignity, with integrity, and with an extraordinary sense of duty. His great influence over congress was due to the justness of his policies and the persistence of his efforts in having the members see the questions not as interests of district or section but as matters of national welfare. It was his sturdy character and unblemished reputation that gave weight to his counsels and strengthened his pleas. History may not rate James K. Polk as one of the greatest of U.S. presidents, but for the accomplishments of his short time in office he cannot be rated among the least influential.

BIBLIOGRAPHY.—The following references are highly selective as to source material and to availability: M. M. Quaife (ed.), *The Diary of James K. Polk, 1845–1849* (1910), an almost complete printing of the manuscript material and a revelation of the mind of a president; E. I. McCormac, *James K. Polk: a Political Biography* (1922); C. G. Sellers, *James K. Polk, Jacksonian, 1795–1843* (1957).   (G. C. Ro.)

POLKA, a lively dance in 2/4 time of Bohemian origin, characterized by three quick steps and a hop. Introduced in Paris about 1843, it became an extraordinary craze in the ballroom and on the stage, sweeping rapidly across Europe and the United States. Frequently introduced in ballets, such as F. Ashton's *Façade,* it has also retained considerable popularity as a social dance.

(LN. ME.)

POLLAIUOLO, the name of two Florentine brothers, Antonio, who was a sculptor, painter, engraver, and goldsmith, and Piero, who was a painter and sculptor.

ANTONIO POLLAIUOLO (*c.* 1430–1498) was trained by his father as a goldsmith, and his most outstanding work in this field is the base for the silver reliquary of St. Giovanni (1457–59, now in the Opera del Duomo, Florence). Yet his chief claim to fame rests on his works in bronze, such as a lively small group of "Hercules and Antaeus" (Bargello, Florence), which once belonged to the Medici. Called to Rome in 1484, he executed with the assistance of his brother the lavish bronze tombs of Pope Sixtus IV (now in the SS. Grotte of St. Peter's) and of Innocent VIII (St. Peter's). The latter, with the enthroned figure of the pope giving his blessing, had a considerable influence on later papal tombs. It seems that Antonio learned the technique of painting from his brother and completed a number of pictures in collaboration with him, among them the altarpiece in the chapel of the cardinal of

ALINARI

"HERCULES AND THE HYDRA", A PAINTING BY ANTONIO POLLAIUOLO. IN THE UFFIZI GALLERY, FLORENCE

Portugal in S. Miniato, Florence, and the "Martyrdom of St. Sebastian" (National Gallery, London). Antonio's chief interest was the human figure in motion; he is supposed to have been one of the first artists to concern himself with dissection and anatomical studies. Hence his engraving "Battle of the Nudes" as well as his drawings took for his and later generations the place of pattern books. He died in Rome on Feb. 4, 1498.

PIERO POLLAIUOLO (1443–1496), born in Florence in 1443, was probably a pupil of Alessio Baldovinetti. He painted six of the "Virtues" for the Mercanzia of Florence (1469–70, Uffizi, Florence). His principal work, "Coronation of the Virgin," was painted for S. Agostino, S. Gimignano (now in the cathedral). He died in Rome in 1496.

BIBLIOGRAPHY.—Maud Cruttwell, *Antonio Pollaiuolo* (1907); Attilio Sabatini, *Antonio e Piero Pollaiolo* (1944); L. D. Ettlinger, "Pollaiuolo's Tomb of Pope Sixtus IV" in *Journal of the Warburg and Courtauld Institutes,* vol. xvi (1953).   (L. D. ER.)

POLLARD, ALBERT FREDERICK (1869–1948), English historian of the 16th century, was born at Ryde, Isle of Wight, on Dec. 16, 1869, and was educated at Felsted School and Jesus College, Oxford. In 1893 he was appointed to the editorial staff of the *Dictionary of National Biography,* to which he contributed about 500 entries. During that period he wrote one of his biographical volumes, *England Under Protector Somerset* (1900). Quitting the *Dictionary of National Biography* in 1901, he was elected to the chair of constitutional history at the University of London in 1903; he held that position until his retirement in 1931. At the University of London he firmly established the history degree course and strove to promote postgraduate research. The Institute of Historical Research, of which he was chairman (1921–39), was largely his achievement. He was the leading Tudor scholar of his day; his volume in the *Political History of England* series and his books on *Henry VIII* (1902) and *Wolsey* (1929) were models of careful and enduring work. He died on Aug. 3, 1948, at Milford-on-Sea, in Hampshire.

POLLEN COUNT, an estimate of the concentration of pollen grains in the air, gives some indication of the relative discomfort that may be experienced by sufferers from hay fever and allergenic asthma. The count is based on the accumulation of pollen grains on a collection device (grease-coated microscope slide, cellophane tape, etc.) during successive 24-hour periods (although spot checks are often also made). The collected grains are viewed under a microscope for identification and counting, the count being given in grains per cubic metre of air. The pollen count is higher during the day; it is highest during dry, windy weather and lowest after a rainfall. *See also* HAY FEVER; ASTHMA.

POLLEN GRAINS. In the biology of the plant, pollen grains are the structures that produce the male sex cell (sperm), which in turn effects bisexual reproduction by union with the female sex cell (egg). In the evolution of higher plants pollen grains are derived from asexual reproductive structures called spores, and in certain groups of plant, both living and fossil, the distinction between pollen and spore is arbitrary since they both perform a similar function in reproduction. The term pollen is usually restricted, however, to the male reproductive structure of seed-bearing plants, including the gymnosperms—conifers, cycads, ginkgo, etc.—and the angiosperms—all the flowering plants. Genetically the pollen grain is a minute plant, the cells of which bear one-half the chromosome number (the haploid number) found in the parent plant (which has diploid cells). Botanically the pollen grain is the male counterpart of the haploid female embryo sac in the ovule, the potential seed.

Transfer of pollen is carried out by wind, water, insects and other agents. After a pollen grain has made contact with the female reproductive structure—the moist stigma of the pistil—it sends out a pollen tube, which travels down through the pistil and into the ovules, within the ovary. The pollen tube works into the ovule and fertilizes the egg cell within the embryo sac. After fertilization the ovule begins to develop into a seed. (For further details on pollination *see* POLLINATION.)

The role of pollen grains in the reproduction of plants was known empirically to several ancient cultures. The earliest is

PHOTOMICROGRAPHS OF POLLEN GRAINS: (LEFT) DAY LILY MAGNIFIED ABOUT 65 TIMES; (RIGHT) PINE MAGNIFIED ABOUT 400 TIMES

perhaps that of the Assyrians, who employed hand pollination to ensure full yields of date palm fruits. Since pollen grains are minute in size—although produced in prodigious numbers in some plants and therefore visible as a dust—knowledge of their structure and details of their biologic function awaited the discovery of the microscope. The early microscopists Nehemiah Grew and Marcello Malpighi studied and drew pollen grains.

Because of their remarkably symmetrical structure and surface patterns pollen grains are readily recognizable under the microscope. The structure of the wall of a pollen grain is oftentimes so characteristic that in some cases species may be identified by pollen grains alone. On the other hand there are cases in which pollen grains of very like structure occur in quite unrelated plant families.

Because of their high resistance to decay, their widespread dispersal by wind and water and their abundant production by plants, pollen grains are very common constituents of geologic sediments, both recent and ancient. In view of these features pollen grains have provided much information on the origin and geologic history of terrestrial plant life (see PALYNOLOGY).

Pollen is produced in such quantities that it is a significant component of the airborne constituents of the earth's atmosphere, especially in areas over continents. The proteinaceous substance in many pollen grains (namely, ragweed and many grasses) induces an allergic reaction commonly known as hay fever (q.v.). See also references under "Pollen Grains" in the Index.

BIBLIOGRAPHY.—G. Erdtman, *Pollen Morphology and Plant Taxonomy* (1952) and *An Introduction to Pollen Analysis* (1943); K. Faegri and J. Iversen, *Textbook of Modern Pollen Analysis* (1950); R. P. Wodehouse, *Pollen Grains* (1935).   (EL. S. B.)

POLLENTIA (mod. POLENZA), an ancient town in the territory of the Statielli in Liguria, northern Italy, 10 mi. N of Augusta Bagiennorum (Vagienna) on the Tanarus (Tanaro) River. Its position on the road from Augusta Taurinorum (Turin) to the coast at Vada Sabatia (Vado), where a road diverged to Hasta (Asti), gave it military importance. Decimus Brutus managed to occupy it an hour before Mark Antony in 43 B.C.; and it was there that Stilicho on Easter Sunday, April 6, A.D. 402, fought the battle with Alaric which, though indecisive, led the Goths to evacuate Italy. Pollentia was noted for its pottery and wool. Remains survive at the village of Polenza.   (H. H. SD.)

POLLINATION, a botanical term for the transference of pollen, the dustlike powder produced by the stamen of seed plants, to the stigma (the receptive surface) of the ovary of the flower. (See also FLOWER; POLLEN GRAINS.) Pollination brings about the fertilization of the ovules in the ovary and their subsequent development into seeds. As the pollen-bearing parts of the stamens are rarely in contact with the stigma at the time when both of these are ripe, usually wind or insects, though sometimes other agencies such as water or birds, bring the pollen to the stigma. The great variety in the form, colour and scent of flowers was developed in relation to the particular agency of insects. Apart from the mechanism of pollination we can distinguish two types—self-pollination, in which pollen is transferred from anther to stigma in the same flower or between flowers of the same plant; and cross-pollination, in which pollen is transferred from an anther on one plant to a stigma on another plant, whether of the same species or not, and whether done by wind, insect, hummingbird, or man.

Cross-Pollination.—Cross-pollination is the only possible method in the case of unisexual flowers because these flowers have only stamens or pistils, not both. In hermaphrodites, *i.e.*, in flowers bearing both stamens and pistils, either self-pollination or cross-pollination can occur. It is interesting to note, however, that many flowers have special arrangements to ensure that the pollinating mechanism, whatever it may be, allows cross-pollination and not self-pollination. One of the commonest methods to achieve this is a separation in time of the sexes—the stamens burst and shed their pollen either before or after the stigma is receptive. This separation in time—and it may apply to the separate male and female flowers on the same plant—is known as dichogamy. When the stamens ripen first it is known as protandry, the more common case; when the stigma is ready first, it is known as protogyny. Protandry is very common in insect-pollinated (entomophilous) flowers, as in nearly all members of the Compositae (*q.v.*) and Umbelliferae, many Labiatae (such as dead nettle [*Lamium*] and *Salvia*), the Caryophyllaceae, the great willow herb (*Epilobium angustifolium*), etc. Protogyny is found in the horse chestnut (*Aesculus*), the autumn crocus (*Colchicum*), many Araceae, and in wind-pollinated (anemophilous) flowers such as plantain (*Plantago*), meadow rue (*Thalictrum*) and many grasses, though here separation in time is very short and many are self-pollinated, such as wheat, barley and oats.

Another structural feature that is a bar to self-pollination is heterostyly. It is seen at its simplest and clearest in the primrose. About half the population of this plant has flowers with long styles, which bring the stigmas to the mouth of the corollas as little "pinheads." The stamens lie halfway down the tubes. In the other half the style is short and the stamens form a "thrum-head" at the mouth of the corolla. Visiting bees transfer pollen from one type of flower to the other. An equal balance of the population is maintained by a special genetic system. Species of *Linum*, *Oxalis* and *Lythrum salicaria* (loosestrife) are other examples. The most complete bar to self-fertilization is self-sterility, which is known to be widespread. This condition is brought about by failure of the pollen tube to grow properly on styles of the same plant, though it can do so on styles of most other plants of the species.

Cross-pollination gives two distinct results, one short-term and the other long-term. It tends to give more and better seed and more vigorous progeny—a result well known in the production of outbred maize. The long-term effect is on the process of evolution. Crossing maintains and replenishes the pool of mutations, patent and latent, on which natural selection acts. Crossing also brings about new combinations of mutations. It has a major effect on the rate at which species can evolve.

INSECT POLLINATION (ENTOMOPHILY)

The special characteristics of entomophilous flowers are the attractive colour of the floral envelope, the presence of scent and of nectar, and of pollen that is not powdery but sticky and is present in comparatively small quantities. The entomophilous is the most common type of pollination in flowering plants, and special floral conformations and irregularities adapted to insect visitors are characteristic of the higher families of flowering plants, as will be seen below. The evolution of flowers and of insects must have gone hand in hand; such groups as Lepidoptera (butterflies and moths) and Hymenoptera (bees, wasps, etc.) could not have existed without the more elaborate and honey-bearing flowers. The plants with such elaborate flowers are cross-pollinated only by insects with highly specialized organs for sucking nectar and gathering pollen.

Types of Insects.—Five classes of insects visit flowers. The

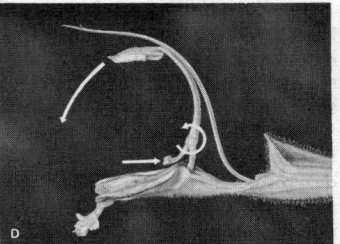

HERMANN EISENBEISS

INSECT POLLINATION OF SALVIA GLUTINOSA

(A, B, C) Honeybee triggering the mechanism; (D) corolla removed from flower to show details. Arrows indicate force upon and reaction of parts

Hemiptera (bugs) are unimportant. The Coleoptera (beetles) are frequent visitors, eating pollen and licking nectar with short tongues. The Diptera (flies) are important and varied visitors; many have only short tongues but some, *e.g.*, the hoverflies, are moderately long-tongued and suck concealed nectar. The Hymenoptera include the most important flower visitors. Many bees have long tongues and can manipulate complex floral mechanisms. The Lepidoptera are also important visitors. They include the longest-tongued insects which alone can reach the most deeply concealed nectar.

Classes of Flowers.—The entomophilous flowers can be divided into nine classes based on the structure of the flower and its relation to particular insects.

1. Class A, flowers with exposed nectar: in this class come most Umbelliferae, many Saxifragaceae, the bedstraws (*Galium*), ivy, and such trees as maple, elder and linden. The flowers are wide open and usually small, and the visitors are mostly short-tongued.

2. Class AB, flowers with partially concealed nectar: in this class fall the buttercups, the Cruciferae, the strawberry and the willows. The nectar is protected and concealed by the position of the stamens, by the development of hairs or scales, or by the flower being partially tubular.

3. Class B, flowers with fully concealed nectar: in this class are the flowers of many Caryophyllaceae, wild geranium, phlox, blackberry, eyebright (*Euphrasia*), mint, heather. In these the nectar may be concealed by the stamens, by the calyx, by the receptacle becoming hollowed or by the petals being united to form a sympetalous corolla. The insect visitors are the smaller bees and a few of the longer-tongued flies.

4. Class B′ is an extension of Class B and includes the flowers of the Compositae, most Dipsaceae and some Campanulaceae, in which the flowers have the same length of tube, etc., as Class B, but are in clusters.

5. Class F, lepidoptera flowers, includes those flowers in which the floral tube is so deepened that in many cases only Lepidoptera can reach the nectar. The alpine moss campion (*Silene acaulis*), for example, is adapted to butterflies, while the bladder campion (*Silene inflata*) is adapted to moths and emits a scent at night.

6. Class H, bee flowers, are those that are visited mostly by long-tongued bees, the depth of the tube being 6 to 15 mm. The flowers are also often markedly irregular, providing a landing place for the bee.

7. and 8. The D and K classes of flowers include those adapted to small insects; they are pollinated by flies, beetles and small bees.

9. Class Po, pollen flowers: these provide no nectar, but abundant pollen for which the flower is visited, mainly by bees. Examples: *Clematis*, *Spiraea*, rockrose (*Helianthemum*), dog rose (*Rosa canina*), poppy.

Food, Colour and Scent.—The insect visits the flower for nectar or pollen. Nectar is produced by special glands, the nectaries, which may occur on any of the floral organs. In many flowers nectar collects at the bottom of the corolla tube or in a special spur. It is a solution of the sugars glucose, fructose and sucrose at a concentration ranging from 8% to 70%. Pollen is rich in proteins and oil.

It seems obvious that scent and brightness must be the guides for the visiting insect. Whether the insect perceives colour as such or only brightness was long in doubt, as were the details of its reactions. Exact knowledge dates from the work of K. von Frisch, begun in 1914. He studied the special senses of the honeybee, a domestic animal that lends itself to controlled experiment. The bees of a hive can be trained to visit a piece of blue paper with a watch glass of sugar water on it. They continue to visit the paper for a time after the sugar is removed. This fixation is the basis of the bee's habit of mass visits to one type of flower in nature. Moreover, the bee can pick out the blue paper from a series of graded grays, some of which must have the same brightness. It perceives blue colour as such. It also perceives white and yellow; but it cannot distinguish red from green, dark gray or black. It is significant that, where insect pollination is predominant, flowers show white, yellow, purple and blue colours, but very rarely red.

By other similar experiments, Frisch showed that bees can distinguish between scents in very much the same way as man can. The sense of scent is used by scout bees to inform their fellows in the hive of the kind of flower available for mass visiting. This extraordinary proceeding and the subject of the bee "language" lies in the domain of insect physiology.

F. Knoll carried out similar studies on other insects in the field as well as in the laboratory. He came to the conclusion that colour is the important "distant" signal for the bee and that scent is a "near" signal, which aids in the final selection of a flower. He studied the behaviour of one of the long-tongued flies, the bee fly (*Bombylius fuliginosus*), as it visited the flowers of the starch grape hyacinth (*Muscari racemosum*) in Dalmatia. It flew from one spike to another of this one species of flower. It would dip to a piece of blue paper placed between the plants, and could pick out blue from surrounding grays. It also visited yellow flowers. If a spike of flowers was covered by a clear inverted test tube the fly would approach and circle the tube but would not try the opening, a short distance removed, from which the strong scent welled out.

In another group the hummingbird hawk moth (*Macroglossum stellatarum*) also visits the grape hyacinth, perceiving its blue colour. At close quarters it is able to find the mouth of the corolla by perceiving the pattern of white petal tips on the blue ground. Here is a distant reaction to blue and a near reaction to white circle on blue ground. The same insect flies from a distance to the yellow flowers of the toadflax, perceives at close quarters a pattern of orange blotch on yellow and is able to probe the narrow entrance to the deep spur with great speed and accuracy, and while in flight. Such colour patterns are frequent in flowers; *e.g.*, the dark streaks on pansy petals and the orange eye on blue ground of the forget-me-not. They are called honey guides. Their recognition is responsible for the accuracy with which insects probe sources of concealed nectar.

The hawk moth has a deficient sense of smell, but it is certain the night-flying moths perceive odours. J. H. Fabre showed that they can react to flower scents at a distance of more than 100 yd. Some flies and beetles react to stinks like that of rotten meat. Such odours are given off by the clubs of many aroids and the flowers of some asclepiads. The colour of these is often a dull red. In the case of the South European *Arum nigrum* (a close relation of *Arum maculatum*, the lords-and-ladies), Knoll showed that the insects reacted to the smell and not to the lurid colour.

In this curious plant pollen-dusted small flies and beetles slide down the slippery hood and are trapped by a fringing "wall" of hairs among the ripe female flowers. After a day or two the stigmas shrivel, the anthers open and release pollen, the stiff hair "wall" shrivels and the newly dusted insects escape.

The Form of the Flower and Floral Mechanisms.—The form and size of the flower and the degree of concealment of nectar determine the kind of insect visitor. The structure of the flower often imposes a particular course of visit that favours cross-pollination. There is very great variety of detail and the variety of structure gives the elegant range of floral form.

In the flowers of Class A the visits of small insects are haphazard. The small flowers of the hedge parsley (*Anthriscus sylvestris*) are showy in the massed umbel. The nectar is freely exposed on lobed nectarial disks in the centre of the corolla. Small flies and beetles lick the nectar and transfer pollen at random. But the stamens are withered before the stigmas are ripe, and cross-pollination is favoured.

The buttercup is an example of the more advanced flowers of Class AB. There is a nectary at the base of each petal and it is covered by a little scale. There is no definite manner of visit, but larger flies and small bees tend to settle on the centre of the flower where they touch the stigmas first. Willows are the earliest mass source of nectar in the spring, and are much visited by bees. The flowers are small and simple but are so close-set in their catkins that small insects cannot reach the nectar. They are dioecious; *i.e.*, with staminate and pistillate flowers on different plants.

In Classes B, B', F and K are found the most elaborate examples of the relation of floral structure and insect visit. Some idea of the range is given in the following examples.

Sage.—Such a plant as the sage (*Salvia pratensis*) has a typical bumblebee flower. The bee alights on the platform formed by the lower lip of the corolla and pushes its head down the tube to reach the nectar at the bottom. Each of the two stamens is of special shape; the connective is very large and two-armed, and is hinged to the short filament. The longer arm bears a half anther and the short arm is sterile, the whole stamen having a lever mechanism. The bee, in probing for the honey, comes in contact with the short arm of the lever and in pressing this down brings the half anther at the end of the longer arm down upon its back where the pollen becomes deposited. The flower is protandrous and in a later stage the style elongates and is brought into the same position as occupied by the back of the bee when in contact with the anther.

Papilionaceous Types.—The Leguminosae show a very interesting series of pollination mechanisms. In this familiar type of flower, to which the pea and gorse belong, the essential parts of the flower are enclosed in the keel. The nectar is secreted by the inner sides of the lower part of the staminal tube; one of the ten stamens is usually free and at its base are two openings leading to the nectar. The nectar is thus not only carefully concealed but is also at a considerable depth. These flowers are bee flowers. An insect visiting the flower alights on the wings, thus depressing them and, as they are joined to the keel, this is depressed also. The stigma and stamens are thus forced out, the stigma usually first so that it has the chance of brushing off pollen from the underside of the bee and thus being cross-pollinated.

There are four different types. (1) Flowers in which the stamens and stigma return within the keel so that repeated visits are possible; examples are the clovers, melilot and laburnum. (2) Flowers that are explosive, since the style and stamens are confined under tension in the keel and when it is depressed they are released with suddenness, thus scattering pollen on the undersurface of the bee. Only one insect visit is thus effective. Examples are broom (*Genista*), gorse (*Ulex*), and lucerne (*Medicago*). (3) Flowers that display a piston mechanism—the pollen is shed early and the heads of the five outer stamens act as pistons so that the weight of the bee on the keel squeezes a narrow ribbon of pollen through the pore at the apex of the keel. A further pressure causes a protrusion of the stigma, which is thus brought in contact with the bee. Examples are lupin (*Lupinus*), restharrow (*Ononis*) and bird's-foot trefoil (*Lotus corniculatus*). (4) Flowers with a brush

mechanism, in which the pollen is again shed early and the style, which is provided with a brush of hairs, sweeps the pollen in small portions out of the tip of the keel. An example is the bean (*Vicia faba*).

Orchids.—The orchids show many and complicated adaptations to pollination by insects. A great impetus to their study was given by the publication in 1862 of Charles Darwin's monograph on the various pollination mechanisms exhibited by this group. As is well known, in this flower there is generally only one stamen, which is two-lobed, and the pollen is in the form of two-stalked masses, the pollinia, which the insect carries away stuck to its head. As the insect flies away, the pollinia, if not already properly oriented, execute such a movement as brings them into position to touch the sticky stigma of the next flower that is visited. There are, however, a great many variations in the details of this process. Nectar is not usually secreted by the orchid flower, but to obtain a sweet juice the insect has to pierce a special tissue, usually that of the labellum (the posterior petal), which is often spurlike. (*See also* ORCHID.)

Honeysuckle.—The honeysuckle (*Lonicera periclymenum*) is a moth flower. It is pale in colour and becomes highly scented in the evening. Probably the scent is here the distant guide and the pale colour, showing up in half light, acts at close quarters. The tube is so long that it can be plumbed only by moths, which suck in flight. Stamens and style project from the mouth of the corolla. On the first evening of opening, the style is folded down on the lower lip and only the stamens are touched. On the second evening the stamens are withered and empty and the style stands out, exposing the stigma.

BIRD POLLINATION (ORNITHOPHILY)

Pollination by insects is the basic type in flowering plants, but there has gradually accumulated a great deal of evidence that pollination by birds is widespread throughout the tropics and in some warm temperate regions, such as western Australia and parts of South America. In Brazil one-third of the plant families investigated were found to include ornithophilous species. The birds concerned are mostly hummingbirds and honey birds, creatures that may be no larger than a bumblebee. They suck nectar through a closed bill with the tongue acting as a piston. They usually suck in flight and are rough visitors, not so exact or so thorough as the bees. They require large quantities of liquid. They have little sense of smell. Their colour sense differs from that of the bee in that they distinguish reds, yellows and greens, but not blues. Corresponding to these characteristics of the bird are distinctive adaptations in the flowers frequented.

The most notable is the frequency of brilliant reds. Of 160 South American species known to be bird pollinated, 134 or 84% are red. Garish colour contrasts are frequent. The bird-of-paradise flower (*Strelitzia reginae*) is blue and yellow, appearing to the eye of the bird as a pattern of black and yellow. The flowers of *Billbergia* are pink and green. The stamens and styles stand clear of the corolla and resist rough treatment by their stiffness. The flowers have no landing platform, spurs or such features. When birds perch they usually do so on bracts or other strong structures near the flower. In the Chilean *Puya* the tip of the inflorescence forms a rigid, flowerless perch. The flowers have no scent, but nectar is very abundant, even welling from the mouth of the corolla.

These features may be seen in some plants commonly grown in European greenhouses and gardens. *Strelitzia* is prized as a greenhouse plant for its brilliant colour display. The garden fuchsia (*Fuchsia magellanica*) has flowers of crimson and blue. Style and stamens are stiff and project far out of the corolla. The nectar is so abundant that it can be shaken from the flower in drops. Even more interesting is *Salvia splendens*, the scarlet sage, extensively used as a bedding plant. It may be contrasted with the culinary sage described above. Apart from the colour it can be seen that the hooded petal and the broad landing stage are absent and that stamens and style are no longer enclosed but protrude from the corolla. It is a fine example of the way a flower fitted for bird pollination has evolved from the insect-pollinated type.

There can be no doubt that ornithophily is a later development than entomophily and that the bird flower has evolved from insect-pollinated ancestors.

POLLINATION BY OTHER ANIMALS

A remarkable arrangement exists between the yucca moths (*Tegeticula*) and yucca plants or Spanish bayonets, members of the lily family, found in the southwestern U.S. through Mexico and into Central America. Different species of the moth are adapted for pollinating different species of yucca. The female moth collects pollen from several stamens, then drills a hole through the wall of a yucca ovary and deposits her eggs among the undeveloped seeds. She then carries the collected pollen to the top of the pistil and forces it down the long, hollow style to the stigmatic surface where the pollen grains can germinate and thus fertilize the ovules. The relationship between plant and moth is mutualistic and absolutely obligatory, the plant being wholly dependent on the moth for pollination and the moth being wholly dependent on the yucca for feeding its larvae (some but not all of the developing seeds of the yucca being eaten by the larvae).

Among the bats some species of leaf-nosed bats in the new world and a group of flying "foxes" in the old world have evolved suctorial tongues and feed on nectar. They act as pollinators. The bat is night flying, clings to the flowers with its claws and is a rough visitor. Bat-pollinated flowers tend to stand away from the stems or to hang in free bunches: they are a dirty white in colour and have a peculiar smell. Details of visits by quick-flying nocturnal animals are naturally difficult to obtain. The extent to which bats effect pollination can be gauged by the fact that, in Java alone, 31 species of plants have been identified as bat pollinated.

In Australia about a dozen species of small marsupials—the honey mice—are nectar feeders and pollinate the flowers of species of *Eucalyptus, Protea* and other trees.

Various other animals, including snails, have been observed transferring pollen.

POLLINATION BY WIND (ANEMOPHILY)

The conifers, more primitive than the flowering plants, are all wind pollinated. The pollen is not transferred to a stigma, for these are naked-seeded plants. The ovule is exposed and the pollen is caught in a drop of liquid exuded from the micropylar opening of the integument. There is an enormous wastage of pollen drifting in air currents, and very great quantities are produced. A male yew shaken in February fills the air with "yew smoke." Lakes in the vicinity of pine woods may have their surface covered with a yellow film of pollen. The pollen is very light and powdery, in contrast to the sticky pollen of insect flowers. In the conifers male and female organs are always in separate cones and sometimes on separate trees.

There are many wind-pollinated flowering plants. They, too, produce light, powdery pollen in large quantities—as any sufferer from hay fever knows. The corolla is either little developed and green, or absent. There is neither scent nor nectar. Attractive characters are wanting. The lack of corolla is a positive advantage as it allows the free exposure of stamens and stigmas. The flowers stand well above surrounding foliage in the grasses, and appear before the leaves in such trees as the hazel and elm. The stigmas are often large and feathery, or covered with hairs acting as pollen traps. The individual stamen in the plantain and grasses, and the whole inflorescence in the hazel, is easily shaken, so that the pollen is readily dispersed when the air is in motion. Protogyny occurs, as in the plantain, and protandry, as in the grasses. Stamens and carpels occur in separate catkins in hazel, oak and beech.

The salad burnet (*Poterium sanguisorba*) in the Rosaceae and the meadow rues (*Thalictrum*) in the Ranunculaceae are examples of wind-pollinated flowers in families normally insect-pollinated. There is no doubt that these and others like them do not show a primitive condition but were evolved from insect-pollinated ancestors. The great group of wind-pollinated plants, which includes the grasses, sedges and rushes, may also exhibit a derived

HERMANN EISENBEISS

PINE TREES ARE WIND POLLINATED. IN THIS PHOTOGRAPH, TWO MALE CONES ARE SHAKEN TO ILLUSTRATE THE FINENESS OF THE POLLEN

condition. There is evidence to suggest that the most specialized family, the grasses, evolved through sedgelike and rushlike ancestors from showy-flowered plants of the lily type. The other great group of wind-pollinated plants, which comprises many forest trees such as the oak, birch, hazel and alder, offers a more difficult problem. It is possible that they are primitive types that have retained a primitive pollinating mechanism.

Pollination by the agency of water currents is very rare: an example is the grass wrack (*Zostera marina*).

SELF-POLLINATION (AUTOGAMY)

Self-pollination frequently takes place at the end of the life of a flower, ensuring fertilization if cross-pollination failed. It is often brought about by movements of the stamens or style. It is well seen in the Compositae where the branches of the style curl back and bring the stigmas into contact with their own pollen. There is great variety of detail in other flowers.

Some flowers never open and are said to be cleistogamous. They are small and budlike and petals are reduced or absent. The wood sorrel (*Oxalis acetosella*) and the sweet violet (*Viola odorata*) are examples.

APPLICATIONS

The fig is pollinated by a small wasp that passes from male to female flowers. The two are borne on separate trees and the male fig, which bears no fruit, is called a goat fig or caprifig. It was known in Greece in the time of Aristotle that goat figs must be planted near the fruiting trees, or branches placed in their crowns: the practice is known as caprification and still goes on. When the Smyrna fig was introduced into California at the end of the 19th century the goat fig and its wasps had to be brought in as well.

FROM GILBERT SMITH ET AL., "A TEXTBOOK OF GENERAL BOTANY," © 1953; REPRODUCED BY PERMISSION OF THE MACMILLAN CO.

TWO TYPES OF FLOWER OF THE CHINESE PRIMROSE ILLUSTRATING A STRUCTURAL BARRIER TO SELF-POLLINATION: (A) PINHEAD TYPE; (B) THRUMHEAD TYPE

The date is another Mediterranean fruit tree that has been artificially pollinated from time immemorial by hanging male inflorescences among the female. The peach, when grown in the greenhouse, is usually pollinated by hand, using a brush or hare's foot; so is the melon. In the orchard it is often an advantage to make sure of adequate pollination by having beehives among the trees.

Red clover, which can be pollinated only by bumblebees with their heavy bodies and very long tongues, was a failure when first introduced into New Zealand but succeeded when the bee was successfully established.

Artificial pollination is essential in all breeding work. When crosses are made it is usual to remove the stamens before they are ripe and to enclose the flower or inflorescence in a paper bag to avoid chance pollination. The most suitable technique must be worked out for each plant and an intimate knowledge of the development of the flower is required. When growing crops for seed production it is necessary to make sure that crossing with other varieties, and consequent impurity in the seed stock, does not occur. The cereals give little trouble in this respect, for they are almost entirely self-pollinated. With other crops—such as cabbages and beets—this is not so. Plots must be isolated by distance, by hedges or otherwise. Exact knowledge of pollination agencies is the basis of such precautions.

See also references under "Pollination" in the Index.

See P. Knuth, *Handbook of Flower Pollination,* trans. by J. R. Ainsworth Davis, 3 vol. (1906–09), which includes an account of the work of such pioneers as C. K. Sprengel, C. Darwin and H. Müller; B. J. D. Meeuse, *The Story of Pollination* (1961).   (V. H. B.; M. SE.)

POLLIO, GAIUS ASINIUS (76 B.C.–A.D. 4 or 5), Roman orator, poet and historian whose contemporary history, although lost, provided much of the material for Appian and Plutarch. Born into a leading Marrucine family—his grandfather had been an Italian general in the Social War—Pollio moved in the literary circle of Catullus and entered public life in 56 by supporting the policy of Lentulus Spinther (*q.v.*). In 54 he impeached unsuccessfully the tribune C. Cato, incurring Pompey's displeasure. In the Civil War he joined Caesar at the Rubicon and campaigned in Africa with Curio and (49–45) in Greece, Africa and Spain with Caesar, for whom he held a praetorian command in Spain against Sextus Pompey (44). On Caesar's death he followed Antony, for whom he governed Transpadane Gaul. There he was friendly with Virgil and in distributing land to veterans saved the poet's property from confiscation. He stood aloof from Fulvia, Antony's wife, and L. Antonius in the Perusine War, but held his army firmly in Antony's interests, and shared in the negotiations leading to the pact of Brundisium between Antony and Octavian in 40. In that year he was consul, and Virgil addressed his Fourth Eclogue to him. In 39 Pollio subdued the Parthini, an Illyrian people, and celebrated a triumph (Oct. 25). From the booty he built the first public library in Rome, in the Atrium Libertatis, which he restored. With full honours he then retired from public life. Unwilling to join Antony in the east, hoping for nothing from Octavian, he took no part in the Actium campaign (31) and subsequently maintained a position of republican dignity and independence. He gave hospitality to the rhetorician Timagenes, when the latter was in disgrace with Augustus. This was the main period of his activity as an advocate, and he devoted himself to the support of literature, organizing public recitations. He died in his villa at Tusculum.

Pollio was a distinguished orator, combining, according to Tacitus and Seneca, careful composition and dry Atticist elegance in strict presentation of his argument. His style displeased Ciceronian critics such as Quintilian and his speeches are lost. As a poet he was accepted by Catullus, Helvius Cinna and Virgil and wrote tragedies, which Virgil and Horace praised, but he ceased to write serious verse when he turned to history shortly after 35. His *Historiae* covered the period from 60 probably to 42 (hardly as late as 35 or 31), that is, from the First Triumvirate to Philippi—the period in which the Roman republic fell. To this contemporary work ("a work full of perilous hazard"), Pollio brought personal experience, independent judgment and a sober style that aided historical analysis. Pollio may be ranked with Sallust and Tacitus. A stern critic of men and style, he corrected Caesar, attacked Cicero, praised Brutus, and reprimanded Sallust for archaism and Livy for *Patavinitas* (probably "provincialism"). Above all, he defended Roman *libertas* under the *principatus* of Augustus. His three letters to Cicero (*Ad Cam.* x, 31–33) bring him closer to the reader than any other work.

BIBLIOGRAPHY.—For references to Pollio in classical literature see *Oratorum Romanorum fragmenta,* ed. by H. Malcovati, 2nd ed., pp. 516–518 (1955); *Historicorum Romanorum reliquiae,* ed. by H. Peters, vol. ii, pp. 67–70, pp. lxxxiii–lxxxvvii (1906). *See also* R. Syme, *The Roman Revolution,* p. 5, 91 (1939), and *Tacitus,* p. 136 (1958); E. D. Pierce, *A Roman Man of Letters* (1922); J. André, *La vie et l'oeuvre d'Asinius Pollion,* with bibliography (1949); E. Gabba, *Appiano* (1956).   (A. H. McD.)

POLLOCK, the name of a great English legal family. The best-known members are:

SIR JONATHAN FREDERICK POLLOCK (1783–1870), chief baron of the exchequer, was born on Sept. 23, 1783, in London, the son of David Pollock, saddler, of Charing Cross. He was educated at St. Paul's and Trinity college, Cambridge, and was called to the bar in 1807. He took silk in 1827, and in 1831 became member of parliament for Huntingdon. In 1834 he became attorney general and was knighted. His party lost office in 1835, but he was again attorney general from 1841 until in 1844 he succeeded Lord Abinger as chief baron of the exchequer. In 1866 he retired with a baronetcy, and on Aug. 22, 1870, he died at Hatton, Middlesex.

SIR FREDERICK POLLOCK (1845–1937), 3rd Bart., a grandson of the chief baron, and a notable author, was born in London on Dec. 10, 1845. He was educated at Eton and Trinity college, Cambridge, where he became a fellow in 1868. He was called to the bar by Lincoln's Inn in 1871 and for several years he practised, though with little success. After holding various teaching posts, from 1883 to 1903 he was Corpus professor of jurisprudence at Oxford. In 1885 he played a leading part in founding the *Law Quarterly Review,* the distinguished learned legal periodical of the common-law world, which he edited for the first 34 years. He also edited the *Law Reports* from 1895 to 1935. In 1911 he was made a privy councilor and in 1914 judge of the admiralty court of the Cinque Ports, an office with only nominal duties. In 1920 he became one of the first of the few academic lawyers to be made a king's counsel. He died in London on Jan. 18, 1937.

Sir Frederick Pollock's *Principles of Contract* was in many ways the first of the modern textbooks with a critical, analytical and learned approach, concentrating on principles rather than details. For over half a century his writings, especially in the *Law Quarterly Review,* exerted an influence on the development of English law that was unprecedented for an academic lawyer. Yet Pollock was no mere lawyer; he was a true scholar who was widely read in many tongues, both in law and other subjects, especially philosophy. Although somewhat reserved in his manner, he could be an effective speaker; and he was kindness itself to the serious student. Much of his remarkable personal and intellectual friendship of over 60 years with Justice Oliver Wendell Holmes, Jr., is revealed by their correspondence, published in 1941 and edited by M. de W. Howe.

Sir Frederick Pollock's works include *Principles of Contract* (1876; 13th ed., 1950); *Digest of the Law of Partnership* (1877; 15th ed., 1952); *The Law of Torts* (1887; 15th ed., 1951); *Possession in the Common Law,* with R. S. Wright (1888); *The History of English Law Before the Time of Edward I,* 2 vol., with F. W. Maitland (1895; 2nd. ed., 1898); *Spinoza, His Life and Philosophy* (1880; 2nd. ed. reissued with additions, 1912).

BIBLIOGRAPHY.—Lord Hanworth (grandson of the chief baron), *Lord Chief Baron Pollock* (1929); Sir F. Pollock, 2nd Bart., *Personal Remembrances* (1887); *Law Quarterly Review,* vol. 53, pp. 151–206 (1937).   (R. E. MY.)

POLLOCK, JACKSON (1912–1956), U.S. abstract painter, one of the founders of a loose movement called Abstract Expressionism or Action painting in the U.S. and *tachisme* in France, was born at Cody, Wyo., on Jan. 28, 1912. After a period of realism after the style of Thomas Hart Benton, Pollock's first paintings in the new style, in 1943, mingled energetic linear invention and a subconscious imagery derived from Surrealism. His later work was entirely abstract, characterized by an intense activism of surface and by the interweaving of whipped lines. After 1947, Pollock employed aluminum paint and commercial enamels, dripping and spattering them over the canvas surface. This radical technical innovation brought him unfavourable publicity, but also helped identify him in the minds of many young American artists as the most revolutionary artist of an older generation of innovators. Pollock died at East Hampton, L.I., N.Y., on Aug. 11, 1956. Abstract Expressionism became one of the dominating international tendencies after the close of World War II. Its aesthetic principle is based upon free and expressive handling and unarranged, chance pictorial effects, which seem to arise spontaneously under the brush stroke. (S. Hu.)

POLLS, PUBLIC OPINION: *see* PUBLIC OPINION.

POLL TAX, a tax of a uniform amount levied on each individual or "head" (middle English *polle*, "a head"). This tax has long been abandoned by most countries and is not an important source of revenue in any tax system in the world.

The most famous poll tax in English history is the one levied in 1380, which led to the revolt of the peasants under Wat Tyler in 1381, but the first instance was in 1377, when a tax of a groat a head was voted by both clergy and laity. In 1379 the tax was again levied, but on a graduated scale. John of Gaunt, duke of Lancaster, paid ten marks, and the scale descended from him to the peasants, who paid one groat each, every person over 16 years of age being liable. In 1380 the tax was also graduated, but less steeply. For years after the rising of 1381 money was raised in this way only from aliens, but in 1513 a general poll tax was imposed. This produced only about £50,000 instead of £160,000 as was expected, but a poll tax levied in 1641 resulted in a revenue of about £400,600. During the reign of Charles II, money was obtained in this way on several occasions. For years after 1688 poll taxes were a favourite means of raising money for the prosecution of the war with France.

Although a few U.S. states at mid-20th century still levied the tax for revenue purposes, most discussion of the tax centred around its use as a voting prerequisite in the Southern states. Ten Southern states made payment of the poll tax a voting prerequisite between 1889 and 1902; an 11th, Georgia, had enacted the requirement many years earlier. In its origins the tax is associated with the agrarian unrest of the 1880s and 1890s, which culminated in the rise of the Populist Party in the West and the South. The Populists, a low-income farmers' party, gave the Democrats in these areas the only serious competition they had experienced since the end of Reconstruction. The intensity of competition led both parties to bring the Negro back into politics and to compete for his vote. Once the Populists were defeated the Democrats amended their state constitutions or drafted new ones to include various disfranchising devices. The poll tax was one of these. Its purpose was to disfranchise Negroes and possibly also to weaken politically the poor whites who had made up the backbone of the Populist Party.

Beginning in 1920 the poll tax was abolished by state action in North Carolina, Louisiana, Florida, Georgia, South Carolina, and Tennessee. In 1937 the Supreme Court unanimously upheld the constitutionality of a Georgia poll tax. Constitutional amendments to abolish the tax were submitted to the voters in Arkansas, Virginia, and Texas, but failed to pass. The tax still prevailed in these states as well as in Alabama and Mississippi at mid-century; the rate ranged from $1 to $2 per year. In Texas and Arkansas, failure to pay merely disfranchised a person for that year only and did not create an obligation that had to be paid in subsequent years if he wished to vote. In Alabama, Virginia, and Mississippi the tax was in some degree cumulative. As a requirement for voting for federal offices, however, the poll tax was prohibited in 1964 by the 24th Amendment to the U.S. Constitution. A poll tax that was not a requirement for voting, as in New Hampshire, was not affected by the amendment. An amendment to the Arkansas constitution ratified in 1964 repealed the poll tax as a voting prerequisite. In 1966 federal courts ruled the poll tax unconstitutional in Texas and Alabama, and later in the same year the Supreme Court went beyond the 24th Amendment by ruling that under the "equal protection" clause of the 14th Amendment states could not levy a poll tax as a prerequisite for voting in state and local elections, thus outlawing the tax in Virginia. This decision rendered appeals from Texas and Alabama futile. When the case involving the Mississippi tax was decided in conformity with this decision, the poll tax was dead. (D. S. Sg.)

POLLUCITE, a rare mineral consisting of hydrated cesium aluminum silicate, is the richest source of cesium, the oxide being present to the extent of 30% to 36%. Cesium, together with rubidium, is important in the manufacture of photoelectric cells, scintillation counters, and optical instruments and devices. Pollucite occurs sparingly, associated with the mineral petalite (*q.v.*) in cavities in the granite of Elba, and with beryl in pegmatite dikes at Andover and Hebron, Me., and in the pegmatite mines of the Black Hills, S.D. It also is found in Brazil, South West Africa and South Africa.

The composition of pollucite is $CsAlSi_2O_6 \cdot H_2O$. It is closely related to leucite, $KAlSi_2O_6$. It crystallizes in the cubic system, is colourless and transparent and has a vitreous lustre. There is no distinct cleavage and the fracture is conchoidal, so that the mineral closely resembles quartz. The hardness is 6.5 and the specific gravity 2.90. *See* also CESIUM. (L. S. Rl.; X.)

POLLUTION, ENVIRONMENTAL. The environment includes the complex of physical, chemical, and biological factors surrounding an organism or an ecological community. Such factors act and interact with various species of organisms to affect their form, growth, and survival. Since an environmental element that is a pollutant with respect to certain species may be a desirable nutrient to other species, the definition of pollution and contamination often becomes difficult. The terms are especially difficult to define in relation to so complex an organism as man. The simple fact that man or any other organism lives gives rise to environmental pollution by the release and buildup of metabolic excretion products unless such materials are utilized by other organisms to balance the ecology. Moreover, in converting energy and matter into usable products, man is frequently inefficient, wasteful, and inconsiderate, thus giving rise to contaminants of industrial origin. The modern problems of environmental pollution, then, are essentially those of rapid human population growth and expanding technology.

So much has been written and spoken about the environment, pollution, population, and resources in recent years that the general public in well-developed countries has become aware of ecological problems. A number of environmentalists and ecologists have caught the public attention with prophecies of doom. Scientists have properly pointed to pictures of Earth taken from a lunar spaceship and reminded us that we are all astronauts riding a spaceship called Earth. This ship of ours has long been blessed with a reasonably well-balanced life-support system, so massive that it can supply the needs of billions of humans. How long and to what extent the balance of this life support may remain favourable to man poses questions of enormous technological, political, and religious complexity. Although industrialization of human cultures is essential to development of an adequate level of living for all members of the culture, it is increasingly difficult to utilize matter and energy efficiently and to achieve such a goal without producing waste—and waste is the source of pollution.

Cultural development and industrialization are products of mankind and as such are directly related to population. The history of human population growth is not primarily a story of changes in birthrate, but rather of changes in death rate. It is thought that the total human population at the time of Christ was around 200,000,000 to 300,000,000 people, and that it had increased to about 500,000,000 by A.D. 1650. By 1850 it had doubled to 1,000,000,000 and doubled again to 2,000,000,000 by 1930. World population was estimated at more than 3,600,000,000 at the beginning of the 1970s and has a doubling time of approximately 35–37 years.

Population growth may be calculated from the exponential equation $P_t = P_o e^{Kt}$ in which P_o is the population at any starting time designated as zero, P_t is the population after any elapsed time t, e

is the base of the Naperian or natural logarithm system (2.718 ...), and K is a growth rate constant calculated on the basis that the frequency at which some increment of growth occurs is infinitely often and that the relative size of the change in population is infinitely small. Since births represent additions and deaths represent subtractions from the population, we may approximate the value of K by subtracting the death rate plus emigrations from the birthrate plus immigrations. Obviously, if deaths and emigrations exceed births and immigrations, the value of K is negative and the population is declining rather than growing. The growth rate constant for the world is presently between $+0.0187$ and $+0.0198$ per year. For a natural system of logarithms the growth rate constant and the growth rate are practically synonymous. Thus it may be stated that the current world growth rate is between 1.87 and 1.98% per year. By comparison, the 1969 growth rate of the United States has been estimated to be 1.03% per year, of which one-fifth has been due to net immigration. Considering only that net growth attributable to births minus deaths, the doubling time of the United States would be about 86 years.

The doubling time of a nation or other political entity may be computed by setting $P_t/P_o = 2 = e^{Kt}$. For this special case the doubling time $t_2 = 0.693/K$. An easily remembered method for estimating doubling times is to divide 70 by the annual percent growth rate of a population. Thus a short table illustrating the relationship between annual percent change and the doubling time may be developed. For decreasing populations the tabulated per-

TABLE I. *Relationship Between Annual Growth and Doubling Time*

Annual percent increase	Doubling time (years)
0.0	infinite
0.5	140
0.8	87
1.0	70
2.0	35
3.0	24
4.0	17

cent increases are, of course, negative and the corresponding doubling times become half-lives of exponential decay.

Excessive population density has long been recognized by engineers and other environmentalists as a major factor in environmental pollution on a local or regional basis. It is now quite clear that the time has come for humanity to take a careful look at its resources, its ideals, its political objectives, and its numbers so as to make meaningful adjustments about population size not only for cities and regions but for individual countries and for the world as a whole. Relative to resources alone, optimum population is not a simple figure to establish. The size, climate, and location of a land area and its possibilities for exchange with other areas must be considered. The question of how long the population is to be maintained also is important.

An area must be considered overpopulated if it is being supported by rapid consumption of nonrenewable resources. It must also be considered overpopulated if the activities of the population are leading to a steady deterioration of the environment. Determinations of optimum population sizes relative to resources alone may be straightforward in principle; however, material standards are only part of the problem. Political pressures, acquisitiveness, religious beliefs, and desired life styles all would contribute to the problem. With the passage of time, both technological innovation and cultural evolution will inevitably change the setting of optimal population sizes. Should political structures be developed capable of realistically setting optimum population, all governments, including a world government, would have to be established so as to influence appropriate population trends just as they now intervene in attempts to produce desired economic conditions.

Much of the human population growth of the past century and a half may be attributed to the technological developments of man relative to food production and the control of disease. The industrialized countries of the world have enjoyed a century of death control arising primarily from mass sanitation and good nutrition. In contrast, widespread introduction of public sanitation and mass

immunization programs to the underdeveloped countries was not made until after World War II. The traditionally high birthrates of underdeveloped countries have remained more or less constant, but death rates, particularly among infants and young children, have declined rapidly. The net result of application of public health measures in already overpopulated underdeveloped countries has been to increase the population growth and aggravate existing problems of poverty, pollution, and poor productivity.

The control of waterborne diseases has largely been accomplished by the provision of disinfected water for public consumption on a mass basis. Disinfection of public water supplies has been achieved most effectively by chlorination; i.e., the addition of chlorine to water in concentrations that kill most pathogenic organisms but are harmless to man. Since overpopulation with its attendant pollution problems may only be alleviated by reducing births, increasing emigration, or increasing deaths, some widespread mass means of reducing the degree of human fertility is needed; especially since the latter two methods of population control are generally unacceptable or impractical. What has been suggested as needed now is a chemical substance that could be distributed via public drinking water and which would reduce fertility levels to approximately 10 to 50% of current human fecundity. To be acceptable such a chemical should be uniformly effective, free of adverse side effects, and have no harmful effects on pets, livestock, or plants. Ideally, such a substance should be easily and economically neutralized so that any member of the population has freedom of choice to return to a full normal fertility level or achieve sterility by such medical or surgical means as are acceptable to him or her. The foregoing ideas are at present speculative; no such fertility depressant exists today.

The ultimate population supportable by the planet Earth has been the subject of many estimates and speculations. Seemingly reasonable values range from 1,000,000,000 to 20,000,000,000. The lower estimate is based on the assumptions that the current industrial and agricultural exploitation of the world can be maintained without serious ecological disturbances and that the average U.S. level of living would become worldwide. That estimate indicates that the Earth is already overpopulated by 2,600,000,000 people. The higher estimate is based on an energy budget of 600,000,000 British thermal units (BTU) per person per year for at least 2,000,000 years utilizing uranium-238 or thorium-232 in catalytic nuclear burners, the so-called breeder reactors. Six-hundred million BTU per person per year is equivalent to 20 kilowatts thermal (kwt) per person and is twice the per capita energy consumption in the United States for all uses. The Population Commission of the United Nations has indicated that 15,000,000,000 people is about the maximum life-support burden of the planet.

That the population of Earth with its attendant pollutional load needs to be stabilized seems beyond controversy. The maximum population acceptable without drastic political upheavals (nuclear warfare) or severe ecological imbalances (mass starvation or elimination of man as the prime species on Earth) is very controversial. Pan-disciplinary efforts of physical and behavioural scientists of all types as well as engineers and politicians will be needed to establish both an upper bound and workable optimal levels. Although members of the scientific community may tend to look askance at the alarming prophecies of doom, warnings sounded should not go unheeded, especially concerning the need for greater knowledge on environmental effects. A great need exists for continuing education of the public in the relationships among environment, population, and pollution so as to obtain political consent and public implementation of both population and pollution control measures. Alarmist tactics, on the other hand, result in loss of credibility and failure to obtain public support, especially when unrealistic standards or goals are set. *See* further, for projections, POPULATION; also FOOD SUPPLY OF THE WORLD; NATURAL RESOURCES.

Elements of Pollution.—Environmental contaminants include products of combustion; human excreta; expired air; dusts; pathogenic organisms; vapours; gases; industrial solvents; extremes of temperature; agricultural fertilizers; infrared, ultraviolet, and even visible light; ionizing radiations; radioisotopes; noise; ultrahigh-frequency sound; and certain microwave electromagnetic radiations. Presence of such biological, chemical, or physical agents per se, however, does not necessarily make them pollutants. Quantitative evaluation as to time, place, amount, and detrimental effect is required to adequately define pollution.

Contaminants present in great enough concentration to pose an immediate threat to life or to cause frank cases of disease or acute poisoning are usually readily apparent, and experience has led to the development of adequate, but by no means perfect, environmental control measures. Although accidents attributable to such pollutants still occur with disturbing frequency, preventing them is largely a matter of education and regulation. With new products of science and industry, though they are frequently tested for toxicity and hazard, untoward effects from pollution may not be immediately apparent.

The effects of environmental contaminants are related to time as well as concentration or intensity. Thus such factors as duration of exposure, frequency of repetition, and recovery period are significant. Time factors become increasingly important when low concentrations of contaminants do not produce ill effects until after months or years of exposure. If the concentration is so low that no harmful effect is measured after a full lifetime of exposure, the level may be considered negligible, at least in regard to life processes. But with contaminants that are offensive even though they produce no measurable health problems, the nuisance, economic, and aesthetic values are of considerable moment; in the general outdoor environment they still appear to outweigh directly measurable health effects. In confined work space, however, permissible contaminant criteria are usually based upon human health considerations.

Problems of Control.—The question naturally arises, "Why permit any of these pollutants to contaminate our work and living spaces?" For such a simple question, the answer is complex. First of all, there is no such thing as absolute zero as far as the existence of matter and energy is concerned. It can only be approached. For example, the specification of a zero tolerance of pesticide residues on foodstuffs really means that no measurable amount of the pesticide may be present, not that absolutely none is present; it would be absurd to reject foodstuffs because of harmless traces of contaminants. Next, various types of matter and energy are harmful or beneficial depending largely upon concentration, time of exposure, physical state, and opportunity for contact. For example, the lead in ordinary fishing sinkers is toxic when vapourized and inhaled for appreciable periods at concentrations much in excess of 0.2 mg. per cubic metre of air. Lesser concentrations of lead are considered harmless for industrial exposures as well as those exposures arising from typical concentrations of lead in food and drink. The otherwise harmless sugars in waste waters from wood-pulping processes can through bacterial action readily deplete the oxygen in water, thus destroying fish life and even converting some streams into open septic tanks. Thus contaminants or pollutants are usually useful substances that have many beneficial applications; it is only when they are used so as to produce excessive concentrations in the environment, that pollution really occurs.

Restriction and reclamation of waste is the crux of environmental pollution control. Unfortunately, the economy of highly industrialized nations is predicated upon a philosophy of waste in connection with many products. This is especially true where raw materials are abundant. Thus with plastic products manufactured from polyethylene, polypropylene, or other nonbiodegradable polymers, there is a solid-waste-disposal problem. On the other hand, matter and energy left over from industrial processes, commercial manufacture, or conversion of fuels to motive power, electricity, light, or heat are considered as wastes only because they have little recovery value. Such waste products create problems in the home, work place, outdoors, in rivers, lakes, oceans, the atmosphere, and even nearby outer space.

Control of environmental pollution requires efficient manufacturing and energy-conversion processes; conscientious efforts to eliminate waste at the source; the measurement of effects on human health, plants, animals, and structures; the ability of natural processes to cope with waste discharges; economic evaluations; political and legislative actions; and the education of policy makers to obtain realistic support of abatement measures. Panic peddling does not obtain continuing support. These generalities apply to air pollution, water pollution, air and water resource management, industrial hygiene, food sanitation, nuclear waste disposal, radiological health protection, and solid waste disposal.

WATER POLLUTION

Water Resources.—Water is our most abundant resource. Worldwide there are about 1.4×10^{21} litres of water. If it could be evenly allocated, this would provide approximately 420,000,000,000 litres (110,880,000,000 U.S. gal.) per person. Most of this water is contained in the oceans and, as far as most human use is concerned, is contaminated with a wide variety of dissolved salts in relatively high concentrations. Use and reuse of this vast store of water for freshwater purposes depends mainly upon natural desalinization. Though several industrial processes exist for desalinization of sea or brackish water, they are not competitive economically with natural water-supply developments or reclamation of soiled fresh water, such as domestic sewage, except in unusual geographic locations.

So-called shortages of water are not caused by a short supply of water itself but rather by excessive demands being made upon water resources and by lack of adequate storage, treatment, and distribution facilities. The amount of water in existence on Earth is increasing at the rate of 5×10^{12} litres each year due to the combustion of petroleum fuels alone. Resynthesis of this water to form fossil fuels is essentially nil, although photosynthetic generation of new plant matter and free oxygen may be appreciable. As far as technological capabilities are concerned, water of nearly any desired quality may be supplied to almost any place at any time in adequate quantities—for a price. Though water is the most used and usually the cheapest commodity required by man, the problems of obtaining sufficient lead time and funds for developing water supplies and protecting water resources from pollution are frequently of major importance. Water and waste-water projects, because of their magnitude and social nature, are frequently supported by municipal, state or provincial, or national governments. The extent of such support reflects public understanding and political foresight based upon sound engineering projections.

Water Supply and Waste-Water Disposal.—Of the various areas of environmental health engineering, water supply and waste-water disposal are the most sophisticated and most widely developed (see WATER SUPPLY AND PURIFICATION; SEWAGE DISPOSAL). Historically the design, construction, and management of public water supplies and waste-water disposal systems were allied to the growth of capital cities and religious or trade centres. Remnants of large and complex installations stand as monuments to early engineering. Notable among the ancient structures are the aqueducts and sewers of Rome. Sextus Julius Frontinus, water commissioner of Rome (A.D. 97), reported the existence of nine aqueducts supplying water to Rome, varying in length from 10 to more than 50 mi. (16 to 80 km.) and in cross section from 7 to more than 50 sq.ft. (0.65 to 4.6 sq.m.). The aggregate capacity of the Roman aqueducts has been estimated at 320,000,000 litres (84,500,000 U.S. gal.) per day. The ancient peoples were well aware of the relationships between pure water, excreta disposal, and good health, though not in terms of modern microbiology, chemistry, and physics, and they adopted civic and religious laws pertaining to water uses and excreta disposal.

Since the mid-19th century the effectiveness of environmental health engineers in providing potable water to well-developed areas has been so great that most people in North America and Europe are no longer aware of waterborne agents of disease. Although engineers are faced with the problem of refining lake, river, and groundwaters containing more and more contaminants, the emphasis in water supply has shifted from health considerations to considerations of quantity and economics. The various aspects of water quality and quantity, however, are interrelated, and as large uncontaminated stores of water become increasingly hard to preserve, due to human population growth and industrial burdens, better and more reliable water purification processes will be needed. There will also be a need for purifying waste waters and raw waters, since natural processes can no longer do most or all of this.

Despite the widespread delivery of potable water and consequent decline in emphasis on health considerations, neglect to apply available knowledge can give rise to an untoward incidence of disease, as was attested by an epidemic of gastroenteritis that occurred in the spring of 1965 in Riverside, Calif. During a one-month period more than 1,500 cases of gastroenteritis, including 3 deaths, were reported to health officials before the widespread, sporadic nature of the epidemic led to the suspicion that the disease was waterborne. It was later estimated that as many as 10,000 to 15,000 persons may have been affected. The epidemic reached its peak on May 22, but it was not until seven days later that the cause was finally traced to the water supply, which was found to contain the bacterium *Salmonella typhimurium*. The community water supply, from deep wells inside and outside the city, had never been chlorinated. Even though water at the source of supply may meet sanitation standards, the opportunities for subsequent contamination in the distribution system of a city the size of Riverside (pop. [1970] 140,089) are so frequent during maintenance and operation that a disinfection method must be used that provides residual power throughout the entire network.

Pollutants.—Although water pollutants can be classified generally as physical, chemical, or biological, several categories are of particular concern.

Excreta and Organic Industrial Wastes.—Human excreta are discharged to water carriage systems of waste collection for subsequent discharge to receiving streams or other bodies of water. Organic constituents in these excreta products serve as food for indigenous microorganisms that carry out oxidative processes. If the organic constituents are excessive after the treated or untreated waste water is diluted by discharge into the receiving body of water, the biochemical oxygen demand of the stabilizing organisms may deplete the available oxygen in the water, thereby upsetting normal ecological conditions and producing pollution. Ordinary organic constituents from food-processing plants, paper manufacturing, malting and distilling processes, and various other industries also contribute to the biochemical oxygen demands made upon natural waters.

Infectious Agents.—Sewers receive almost every type of pathogenic organism known to man and probably some that have yet to be identified. Fortunately the aquatic environment in sewers and in waste treatment plants is hostile to most pathogens, and extinction occurs within a reasonable period of time. Surviving species of pathogenic bacteria have been successfully prevented from contaminating potable waters by various treatment and disinfection processes. As far as bacterial waterborne diseases are concerned, testing for a few species of microorganisms of enteric origin as indicators of fecal contamination provides excellent control. These coliform organisms, hardier and more numerous than associated enteric pathogens, can be detected and estimated numerically by relatively simple bacteriological procedures. If a population density of less than ten coliform organisms per litre of water is found, the possibility that bacterial pathogens are present is negligible. A so-called negative coliform test, however, does not preclude contamination with viruses. Good, easily applied control tests for virological contaminants are needed.

Plant Nutrients.—In well-developed nations such as the United States, Great Britain, France, and Germany, more than 75% of the people reside in cities. A constant flow of foodstuffs produced largely through photosynthesis of soil minerals is required to feed them. Unfortunately the nitrogen, phosphorus, and other elements essential to life are not returned to the land for completion of the ecological cycle but instead are discharged to watercourses in waste waters or disposed of locally as garbage. To replenish minerals in agricultural areas, vast amounts of fertilizers, not commonly thought of as pollutants, must be used. If significant quantities of fertilizers are carried by rainwater runoff or ground-water seepage into lakes or streams, however, lush growths of algae may occur. In normal amounts such algae contribute to the

oxygen balance in lakes and streams, and they also serve as food for fish. But with excessive amounts of nitrogen and phosphorus, several species of algae are capable of growing so rapidly in a favourable aquatic environment that they crowd out other populations of organisms, overgrow, and finally die because of exhaustion of available nutrients and autointoxication. Various species of bacteria then begin to decay and putrefy the dead algal bodies, which in turn depletes the oxygen resources of the lake or stream and gives rise to offensive odours.

Organic Pesticides.—Toxic chemicals have long been employed to control or eliminate insects, vermin, and weed plants that destroy crops, harm domestic animals, or spread disease (*see* SPRAYS AND DUSTS IN AGRICULTURE). Since 1930 the armamentarium of pesticides, insecticides, and herbicides has grown by leaps and bounds. They have had a tremendous influence upon agricultural productivity and have now become essential to nearly every food-producing activity. The toxic character of pesticides has resulted in the development of a wealth of toxicological data. Governmental regulations in a number of countries require rigorous testing of newly developed pesticides before they are released for use. The widespread use of pesticides and the universal nature of water made it inevitable that pesticides would appear as stream pollutants and even as contaminants in drinking water. Although the incidence of human poisoning from regulated sources of public water supply has been essentially nil since mid-20th century, occasional instances have occurred as a result of cross connections of industrial-process piping or tanks with potable water distribution lines. Moreover, stream pollution from pesticides has occurred, and concern about the long-range effects of low concentrations of these toxic chemicals is justifiable, especially since new and more effective pesticides are being developed rapidly. Chemical and physical methods for detecting and measuring such substances in water are available, and standards of permissible concentrations in streams, lakes, and drinking water should be established.

Waste Minerals and Chemicals.—Untreated industrial wastes discharged into lakes and streams can result in serious problems of water pollution. Dissolved minerals, especially calcium and magnesium salts, cause hard-water problems for industrial and municipal water supplies. Toxic chemicals may alter normal biological activity of streams, and many chemicals react with water to raise the acidity or alkalinity of streams to a point where the water becomes corrosive and living organisms are killed. Chemicals with a high oxygen demand add to the problems of deoxygenation. Although upper limits for drinking water have been developed regarding the concentrations of several chemicals such as arsenic, barium, chromium, cyanide, lead, and phenols, no general rules exist for the treatment of industrial wastes because of the wide variety of organic and inorganic waste materials involved.

By the late 1960s stringent regulations regarding the chemical and physical qualities of both industrial and municipal waste discharges had been promulgated by a variety of governmental agencies. In addition to waste-water effluent standards, criteria regarding the acceptable future quality of rivers, streams, lakes, and estuaries had been set so as to require adequate levels of waste-water purification by both industries and municipalities. The enforceability of these standards is now being tested in the courts and becomes exceedingly complex when jurisdictional disputes arise between regulatory agencies or when the pollution control operations of one industry or even a municipality interfere with those of another industry.

In the past, most large cities placed general restrictions on the nature and chemical concentrations of liquid wastes acceptable for discharge into their sewers. They are now in the process of developing acceptance criteria for concentrations of specific categories of chemical substances such as cyanides and compounds of mercury. The environmental engineering involved in establishing such criteria requires a knowledge of the toxicity of the chemical and its compounds to humans, fish, aerobic organisms responsible for biological stabilization of organic waste waters, and anaerobic organisms involved in sewage sludge digestion. In addition, the engineer must be able to estimate limits on the transfer of chemicals from liquid to gaseous or solid phases through an understanding of chemical and physical kinetics and biological mechanisms.

Mercury.—On March 19, 1970, Norvald Fimreite, a graduate student in zoology at the University of Western Ontario, London, Ont., wrote to the federal Department of Fisheries and Forestry describing his findings of mercury of up to seven parts per million (ppm) in pickerel from Lake St. Clair and the St. Clair River. This information arose from Fimreite's doctoral research on mercury pollution and triggered quite a furor regarding mercury contamination of fish. The Canadian Food and Drug Directorate had set 0.5 ppm as the maximum permissible concentration of mercury in fish flesh. Within days the Department of Fisheries and Forestry had confirmed Fimreite's findings of high mercury and acted to ban export of Lake St. Clair pickerel, most of which goes to the United States. They also promptly prohibited commercial and sport fishing of Lake St. Clair only a few days before the season was to open and cited the chlorine-caustic operations of a chemical manufacturer at Sarnia on the St. Clair River as the main source of the mercury pollution.

Widespread concern about mercury pollution of aquatic environs has developed. It has been estimated that 75,000,000 kg. of mercury have been consumed in the United States since 1900; in 1969 alone it amounted to 2,700,000 kg. Little is known about the final disposition or storage of mercury at specific points in the environment. Methyl mercury, which is the principal form of the element found in food fishes, is highly toxic and causes neurological damage and chromosomal aberrations. Mercury-bearing waste waters, particularly from industrial plants, that are discharged directly into lakes and rivers are substantial contributors to the problem. A case that was reported to have occurred in one area of Japan showed that, between 1953 and 1960, 111 persons were seriously affected because of having eaten fish and shellfish taken from mercury-polluted waters. Of the 111, 45 died and 19 babies born to mothers who had eaten the fish had congenital defects. Although methyl mercury tends to associate with red blood cells and nerve tissue, it passes easily through the placenta to the fetus and can cause chromosomal disorders. Findings of elevated mercury concentrations in tuna and, especially, swordfish further complicate the problem by raising questions regarding man's role in the natural process of concentrating mercury.

Sediments.—Sediments from waste waters contribute to the turbidity of lakes and streams, affecting their surface-water quality. Sediments also form banks of sludge that can eventually dam or fill up narrow or shallow channels. Anaerobic decomposition of the sludge materials draws heavily on the oxygen content of the water and results in the release of noxious gases.

Radioactive Substances.—While a number of radioisotopes, the radioactive forms of chemical elements, occur naturally, their relative abundance in nature is usually small. With the discovery of nuclear reactions and the development of methods by which they can be controlled and utilized on a large scale, radioisotopes are being produced in large quantities, not only in natural forms that had previously been identified but also as new mutants of the various chemical species (*see* ISOTOPE). Many of the man-made radioisotopes are quite valuable and are useful in industry, agriculture, and in medical diagnosis and treatment. In the production of energy from nuclear reactions, however, quantities of fission products are produced far in excess of current demands for such radioactive elements. Thus a potentially serious problem attends the disposal of radioactive wastes. Materials that emit ionizing radiations are capable of producing cancer, disrupting basic biological processes, and causing genetic changes in various types of organisms, including man.

As with practically all other wastes, the disposal of nuclear wastes, whether gaseous, liquid, or solid, has classically followed two divergent paths: "CC," which stands for concentrate and confine, or "DD," dilute and disperse. However, both methods have their shortcomings. Dilution leads to contamination of more and more waters to the point where radioactive decay cannot keep up with the discharge of new radio contaminants. The alternate method, though relatively costly, is the method

that must be used if widespread utilization of nuclear energy is to be achieved.

Heat.—As with all things out of place or out of balance, heat can be a water pollutant. Electrical power plants, petroleum refineries, chemical process plants, steel mills, coke ovens, and nuclear reactors all use large quantities of water and return it at elevated temperatures. Heated water alters the existing ecology, sometimes enough to drive out or kill desirable species of fish or to cause rapid oxygen depletion. Since the exponential rate of increase of energy consumption for the world is currently about 3.5% per year (doubling time is 20 years), heat pollution is apt to develop into a major problem unless more efficient energy utilization is employed. This is especially pertinent for the U.S., which is increasing its electrical power generation at 7.2% per year.

About two-thirds of the U.S. states and territories, as well as Washington, D.C., have adopted water quality standards regarding permissible heat discharges to surface waters. These standards are mainly in the form of proscribed temperature maxima and increases above ambient levels in the vicinity of discharge. Some agencies, however, restrict the rate of temperature change. Temperature limits and changes reflect the geographic locations, stream conditions, and climatology of the areas and vary widely. Among those agencies adopting temperature increase above ambient as a criterion for controlling waste heat discharge, values range from 2° to 10° F, the most frequent value being 5° F. In applying temperature measurements to the control of heat discharges, the location of temperature measurements must be clearly defined.

Due to the influence of temperature on biological processes, a great deal of controversy has arisen regarding the setting of temperature standards for cooling waters discharged from power generating plants into lakes which might be subject to eutrophication. Criteria should be set that conserve natural resources while at the same time permitting industries and utility companies to provide for the cultural needs of the population.

Fluorides.—The concentration of fluorides in potable water deserves special mention because both upper and lower limits for it have been recommended. The proper amount of fluoride affords resistance to tooth decay, while too much fluoride in water produces dental fluorosis, a mottling of the tooth enamel. The recommended limits for fluoride in drinking water range from 0.7 to 1.2 mg. per litre, depending upon the annual average of maximum daily air temperatures of the community to which the water is supplied. Any potable water supply bearing less than 0.6 mg. of fluoride per litre should be considered deficient, while one containing more than 1.7 mg. per litre may produce an occasional case of mottled enamel.

Spills.—The physical, biological, and chemical agents mentioned as possible pollutants under the foregoing categorical headings are usually encountered as wastes intentionally discharged or discarded. Accidental spillage of large quantities of valuable materials requires mention because of the gross pollution that may result from the rupture of storage or transport vessels. The largest, most notorious episode of oil spillage began on March 18, 1967, when the "Torrey Canyon," with a cargo of 118,000 tons of crude oil, was reported aground on the Seven Stones reef between the Scilly Isles and Land's End, Eng. Some 60,000 tons of oil spilled into the sea. Despite attempts to destroy it, the oil reached the coasts. It began to arrive on March 25 and continued for several weeks. Detergents were then employed to clean the beaches.

Except for the immediate danger to rescue, salvage, and antipollution crews during the episode, no human health hazards were anticipated from this oil spill, and both deepwater fish and shellfish were reported as essentially unaffected. The St. Agnes Bird Observatory (in the Scilly Isles) estimated that 40,000 seabirds died as a result of the episode.

Oil spills are not new. The unique feature of the "Torrey Canyon" spill was its size, which dwarfed previous spills. Tankers nearly twice as big as the "Torrey Canyon" are now at sea; 300,000-ton vessels are under construction; and one-half megatonners are feasible. Environmental engineering plans to cope with future wrecks of such ships in coastal waters are being developed. Those aimed at speedy recapture and reclamation of the oil are most desirable. Pumping the oil into air-dropped bladders or into another ship would probably be the best solution; burning, however, seems to be the next best answer, even though it contributes to air pollution. Except in quiet waters, containment booms have not worked out well. Detergents or dispersants result in dilution of the oil or sinking to the bottom where it may cause harm to benthic organisms. Since the "Torrey Canyon" incident, oil production activities in coastal waters have given rise to large losses of oil in areas where much desirable marine productivity is concentrated. Severe fines have been levied against responsible oil companies for failure to install safety cut-off valves in such situations. It has been estimated that leakage of oil into the oceans as a result of man's activities is currently in excess of 3,000,000 tons a year.

Although the rediscovery of the environment in comparatively recent times has led some regulatory officials to strive toward "zero risk" standards with no concern for economic or other costs, an extreme of water pollution developed in July 1969 in the Cuyahoga River when a portion of it became so covered with oil and debris that the surface caught fire in the Cleveland, O., factory area and damaged two railroad bridges.

AIR POLLUTION

Air pollution, like other forms of environmental pollution, is directly related to fuel usage, increased industrialization, and growing urban populations. This historical relationship is perhaps somewhat more direct and apparent for atmospheric than for water pollution. The first smoke abatement law was passed in England in 1273, during the reign of Edward I, in response to a popular belief that food cooked over burning coals would cause illness and even death. In 1306 the concern about air pollution was so great that a royal proclamation prohibited the burning of coal in London. The first recorded penalty imposed for violating an air pollution code occurred when a manufacturer who had disobeyed the proclamation was tried, found guilty, and beheaded.

In defining air pollutants it is common to consider only those substances added in sufficient concentration to produce a measurable effect on man, animals, vegetation, or inanimate materials. Pollutants may therefore include almost any natural or artificial composition of matter capable of being airborne. They may occur as gases, liquid droplets, or solid particles, or in various mixtures. It is convenient to consider two groups of air pollutants: (1) primary emissions from identifiable sources; and (2) products formed in the air by interaction between two or more primary contaminants or by reaction with normal atmospheric constituents, with or without photochemical activation.

Primary Contaminants.—Although it is possible to determine the kinds and amounts of primary contaminants emitted from each source in a community, their end products and effects cannot be predicted with certainty from these data alone. Such data define the primary reactants and, after reaction chains are identified, enable abatement of primary emissions. Primary emissions include: fine solids less than 100 μ in diameter; coarse particles greater than 100 μ in diameter; sulfur compounds; organic compounds; nitrogen compounds; oxygen compounds; halogen compounds; and radioactive compounds.

The fine aerosols include carbon particles, metallic dusts, silicates, fluorides, resins, tars, pollen, fungi, solid oxides, nitrates, sulfates, chlorides, aromatics, and a host of other chemical species that overlap many of the more specific categories. As particles they scatter light according to established physical laws, and they afford opportunity for catalysis of otherwise slow interactions among adsorbed pollutants due to their finely divided state. As carriers of electrostatic charges they influence the condensation and coalescence of other particles and gases. As chemical species some of them are highly toxic to plants and animals or are corrosive to metals. To the extent that they are radioactive they increase the normal radiation dosage and may be cancer- or mutation-producing factors. Finally, as plain dust, they soil clothing, buildings, and bodies, and are a general nuisance.

Coarse particles 100 μ in diameter and larger present similar problems but in a greatly diminished degree because of their rather prompt removal from the air by gravitational attraction. Their size also prevents significant quantities from entering human or animal lungs. However, their soiling effect may be more evident than that of the fine particles because they are not widely dispersed but rather are deposited quickly around the source of discharge.

Interest in sulfur compounds has been intense for a long time because of the irritating effects of sulfur oxides and the high toxicity of hydrogen sulfide. Organic compounds released to the atmosphere include a large number of hydrocarbons, together with their combustion products and halogenated derivatives. These contaminants are mainly emitted as vapours, though some may occur as droplets or particles. Among these hydrocarbons, a number, notably the polynuclear aromatics, have been associated with carcinogenesis in mammalian test animals. The majority, though, have relatively low potential for serious air pollution effects so long as they retain their specific identities. Nitrogen compounds most abundantly generated and released to the atmosphere are nitrogen oxides and ammonia. Oxides of nitrogen are produced in high-temperature combustion and other industrial operations. Although nitrogen dioxide is irritating at fairly low concentrations, the major interest in nitrogen oxides as air contaminants is related to their participation in atmospheric photochemical reactions.

Large amounts of carbon dioxide and carbon monoxide arise from the complete and partial combustion of carbonaceous fuels. The production of carbon monoxide in Los Angeles County, Calif., has been estimated to exceed 10,000 tons (10,000,000 kg.) daily, at least 80% of it arising from incomplete utilization of the carbon in automobile gasolines. Carbon dioxide in high concentrations affects the human respiratory control mechanism, but the concentration required is too great to be of much significance. Although the doubling time for fuel consumption in the world is presently 20 years, statistically significant evidence of a buildup in atmospheric carbon dioxide concentrations has not been established, even though the burning of carbonaceous matter has produced great quantities of carbon dioxide. Measurements during the past century, however, indicate that worldwide they may be increasing. Concern has been expressed by some scientists about such an occurrence, since carbon dioxide is an excellent absorber of infrared radiant energy. Recent calculations indicate that a doubling of the carbon dioxide concentration in the atmosphere would cause an average rise in the Earth's surface temperatures of about 6.5° F (3.6° C). A temperature shift of this magnitude would have far-reaching hydrological and meteorological effects; the polar ice masses would be reduced and the ocean levels would rise. Although the carbon dioxide theory has plausibly explained the climatic oscillations of geologic time, accompanied by the coming and going of glacial periods, the present annual production of carbon dioxide by fuel combustion is only enough to raise the global atmospheric concentration by 1 or 2 parts per million, approximately less than 0.0002% if not counterbalanced by plant photosynthesis. Since the carbon dioxide concentration of the atmosphere is about 300 parts per million (0.03%), the production over a few years would appear to be insignificant. Furthermore, the available sinks of marine and terrestrial plant life capable of reducing carbon dioxide seem entirely adequate to maintain the ecological balance for centuries unless other factors come into play. Concern has been expressed by some meteorologists over the possible reduction in solar energy reaching the Earth due to the production of water vapour by the fuel combustion of jet aircraft flying at high altitudes. This effect, if any, would be opposite to that of its companion product of combustion from hydrocarbon fuels; i.e., carbon dioxide. The problem of air pollution with carbon dioxide therefore does not seem to be alarmingly great. Quantitatively, however, knowledge is lacking. Carbon monoxide, unlike carbon dioxide, deserves status as a primary pollutant due to its ability to impair the oxygen-carrying capacity of hemoglobin in blood.

Inorganic halogen compounds are produced from metallurgical and other industrial processes. Among these, hydrogen fluoride and hydrogen chloride are corrosive and irritating in themselves, and the metallic fluorides have toxic properties that have precipitated intricate and costly legal actions between operators of factories and nearby residents whose crops and cattle have been damaged. Radioactive contaminants have not presented any major practical problems beyond the vicinities of nuclear energy generation, development, and research installations. That they will do so with increased use of nuclear power and industrial and medical applications is certain. Statistical associations between infant mortality and nuclear tests reported (1969) by Ernest J. Sternglass of the University of Pittsburgh, Pa., called for further study in this area of health hazard analysis.

Secondary Contaminants.—The contaminant-containing air mass over a populated area is both chemically and physically unstable, and the ensuing reactions give rise to secondary pollutants. The reaction rates, routes, and intermediate steps involved in generating new pollutants are influenced by many factors, such as concentrations of reactants, extent of photoactivation, meteorological forces, local topography temperatures, and relative amounts of moisture. Of important consequence is the formation of sulfates from sulfur dioxide and nitric oxide plus free oxygen radicals from nitrogen dioxide. The latter substances are able to initiate sustained free radical reaction chains. Secondary pollutants, which are among the most troublesome to control, include ozone, formaldehyde, organic hydroperoxides, and other very reactive compounds and free radicals.

Major Disasters.—Although serious incidents of air pollution are infrequent, four major disasters have been recorded. The first occurred in the Meuse Valley between Seraing and Huy, Belg., between Dec. 1 and 5, 1930, when a large number of persons became ill and more than 60 died. Elderly persons who had medical histories of heart or lung impairments accounted for most of the deaths. The symptoms, mainly those associated with a respiratory irritant, included chest pain, cough, shortness of breath, and irritation of the mucous membranes and of the eyes. The episode occurred in an area approximately 15 mi. (24 km.) long and 1.5 mi. (2.4 km.) wide, surrounded by hills 330 ft. (100 m.) high. Within the area were steel mills, power plants, glassworks, lime kilns, zinc refining plants, a coking plant, a sulfuric acid plant, and a fertilizer plant. Most of the homes and buildings in the area were heated with coal, which added to the pollution load. Later it was revealed that more than 30 contaminants had probably been present in the atmosphere at the time of the disaster. After checking all available data, it was concluded that the contaminants most likely to have caused the symptoms were sulfur compounds.

The second well-known air pollution disaster occurred between Oct. 27 and 31, 1948, at Donora, Pa. During this period 20 persons died and 6,000 became ill. Like the Meuse Valley, Donora was heavily industrialized and located in a topological basin. Meteorological inversion and stagnation occurred while large amounts of various air contaminants were being discharged. Investigations indicated that, while no single substance was responsible for the disaster, the adverse effects could have been produced by a combination or summation of the action of two or more of the contaminants. Oxidation products of sulfur dioxide, together with particulate matter, were significant factors.

At Poza Rica, Mex., on Nov. 24, 1950, when the third much-publicized air pollution episode occurred, 22 persons died and 320 were hospitalized. In this incident, a sulfur removal unit used in petroleum refining had been put into operation on Nov. 21. Although during the "shakedown" period an overflow of amine solution had partly plugged the gas lines to the pilot lights on the flare stacks of the unit, this had gone unnoticed by operating personnel, and on Nov. 24, at 2:00 A.M., operation of the plant at full-rated capacity was begun. By 2:30 A.M. the desired flow rate was reached, but at approximately 4:00 A.M. operational difficulties were encountered, with the probable result that large quantities of hydrogen sulfide were vented unburned into the air. Meteorological data indicated that a pronounced low-altitude temperature inversion prevailed at the time. The onset of acute illnesses began at 4:50 A.M. and ended at 5:10 A.M., and the victims were all directly downwind of the unit's vent stacks. The onset, symptoms, and pathological findings were consistent with hydrogen sulfide poisoning. Unlike other acute air pollution incidents, a single toxic substance and source were responsible.

In London, between Dec. 5 and 9, 1952, the fourth and largest air pollution disaster occurred. Most of the British Isles were covered by fog, and there had been a temperature inversion. Characteristically the illnesses were sudden in onset and tended to begin on the third or fourth day of the episode. In the one-month period that followed, the number of deaths in Greater London in excess of normal totaled more than 3,500. The peak death rate occurred on Dec. 13, when it was 2.5 times as high as the norm for the preceding five years for that time of year. Although increased mortality was experienced by every age group, persons in their 60s and 70s had the highest increase. More than 80% of the deaths occurred among persons with known heart and respiratory diseases. Although this was the first air pollution episode in which air sampling was conducted before, during, and after the event, the general nature of the pollution problem was such as to preclude development of specific cause-and-effect relationships. Autopsies did not reveal any characteristic mode of death other than evidence of respiratory tract irritation.

Confined Space Pollution.—Contaminants may occur or build up in enclosed spaces such as houses, factories, office buildings, and space vehicles. Volatile liquids and substances that are gaseous at normal temperatures are more likely to produce contamination than solids, although even solids have measurable vapour pressures and, if toxic enough, can produce pollution problems in poorly ventilated places. Finely divided liquids and solids dispersed into confined spaces must also be considered as potential pollutants, as must unusual releases of all types of energy. With the increasing development of chemical products and devices for use in the home, the potential for accidental poisoning—both acute intoxications and long-term chronic effects—has risen. Health hazard evaluation and control of confined space contamination have been developed mainly in industry.

Wherever matter is handled or energy is utilized or converted, some of the substances, by-products, or energy will escape into the surrounding environment either directly or indirectly. The toxicity or detrimental effects of atmospheric contaminants is closely related to the amount that may occur in spaces occupied by workers, and many occupations have been found to have injurious effects on the physical health of workers. Fortunately, the number of chemical, physical, and biological agents to which any one worker may be exposed at any one time is often limited, and only one of these may be of critical significance. Thus, based upon human experience, measurable physiological responses, and toxicological data derived from test animals, lists of permissible concentrations have been developed to serve as a guide in making health hazard evaluations of industrial environments. The most widely used of these is the list of threshold limit values published by the American Conference of Governmental Industrial Hygienists, which names approximately 500 substances that may occur in the work environment as gases, vapours, mists, fumes, or dusts. The concentrations refer to average values for a normal work exposure of eight hours a day, five days a week. They represent levels of atmospheric contamination to which it is believed that nearly all workers may be repeatedly exposed, day after day, without adverse effects. These threshold limit values are reviewed annually. Depending upon the physical state of the substance that may occur as a contaminant, threshold limit values (see Table II) are expressed as parts of vapour per million parts of air (ppm), milligrams of substance per cubic metre of air (mg/m³), or millions of particles per cubic foot (mppcf).

TABLE II. *Threshold Limit Values of Common Industrial Contaminants*

Substance	ppm	mg/m³	mppcf
Acetone	1,000	2,400	—
Benzene	25	80	—
Carbon monoxide	50	55	—
Ethyl alcohol	1,000	1,900	—
Hydrogen sulfide	10	15	—
Mercury*		0.1	—
Ozone	0.1	0.2	—
Zinc oxide fume	—	5	—
Asbestos dust	—	—	5
Talc dust	—	—	20
Portland cement dust	—	—	50

*Subject to change.

These limits must be combined with considerations of many other factors and should be applied and interpreted only by qualified persons. They are primarily applicable to single-substance exposure of workers in industry and are not intended for use in the evaluation or control of community air pollution or in estimating the toxic potential of continuous exposures. When two or more hazardous substances are present, their combined effect rather than that of either individually should be considered. Mathematical approximations of threshold limit values for mixtures can be made but must be applied with caution since synergism or potentiation may occur in the organism.

Besides threshold limit values, emergency exposure limits have been developed by the American Industrial Hygiene Association for a few common contaminants for exposure periods ranging from 5 to 60 minutes. Exposure concentrations permissible for short periods are normally, of course, several times greater than those for long-term work routines. There are, however, important exceptions in which ceiling values no more than 1.25 to 3 times the 8-hour-day, 40-hour-week threshold limit values should be enforced, even for quite short exposure periods.

Other limits of exposure relative to radioisotopes, noise levels, heat stress, and various ionizing and nonionizing radiations have also been developed for industrial application.

Of all of the areas of concern regarding environmental pollution, most success has been achieved in establishing reasonable levels of exposure for workers in enclosed spaces. There have been developed exposure limits for chemicals and dusts, damage risk criteria, and audiometric techniques for controlling noise exposures, heat stress indices for hot work, and various other guides, which when intelligently applied not only protect the health of the worker but permit him to make beneficial use of the resources that are being continually released by an expanding technology.

LEGISLATIVE CONTROL MEASURES

Efforts to control environmental pollution have met with varying degrees of success and have been limited to some extent by problems of legislative jurisdiction. Frequently the problems of pollution require a many-faceted attack.

Although many communities have enacted effective legislation to control pollution, the problem continues. For example, Chicago began to be concerned about smoke as early as 1874, when a citizens' association became interested in the problem, and in 1881 the Chicago City Council adopted the first smoke ordinance in the United States. While this and similar ordinances successfully reduced pollution from smoke, the problem of pollution persisted from other contaminants, such as noxious motor-vehicle fumes. Moreover, polluted air or water does not respect, city, state or provincial, national, or even continental boundaries. Smoke emanating from the steel mills of Gary, Ind., less than 30 mi. (48 km.) from Chicago but in another state, cannot be controlled by Chicago's City Council or even by the Illinois state legislature. In Europe, long rivers that flow through many countries present similar problems of pollution and legislative control.

Although many communities have enacted legislation dealing with pollution, national legislation has assumed increasing importance, as evidenced by passage of the Clean Air Act (1956) in England and, in the United States, by the adoption of the Clean Air Act of 1963 (amended 1965) and the Water Quality Act of 1965. The regional abatement plan adopted for the Ruhr River in West Germany concerns a cooperative venture aided by the federal government and involving compulsory membership of the industries and municipalities that use the Ruhr water supply. The tax-deductible effluent fee paid by the 1,200 members of the Ruhr River Valley Association provides funds for operating more than 100 sewage-treatment plants serving about 1,700 sq.mi. (4,403 sq.km.) of the river's drainage area.

Further efforts have been made to control pollution on an international basis. In June 1964 experts from the United States and Japan and from 17 European countries (members of the Council of Europe) met in Strasbourg, France, to plan a common offensive against air pollution, and in August of the same year the second International Conference on Water Pollution Research was held

in Tokyo. Studies begun in 1965 with the introduction of the International Hydrological Decade promised to develop further international cooperation in the area of water resources development and control. *See* also references under "Pollution, Environmental" in the Index.

BIBLIOGRAPHY.—G. M. Fair and J. C. Geyer, *Water Supply and Waste-Water Disposal* (1954); American Institute of Chemical Engineers, *Pollution and Environmental Health* (1961); National Society for Clean Air, London, *Clean Air Year Book* (1961); Stanford Research Institute, *Chemical Reactions in the Lower and Upper Atmosphere* (1961); A. V. Kneese, *Water Pollution* (1962); A. C. Stern (ed.), *Air Pollution,* 2 vol. (1962); A. R. Meetham, *Atmospheric Pollution,* 3rd rev. ed. (1964); R. N. Rickles, *Pollution Control* (1965); O. C. Herfindahl and A. V. Kneese, *Quality of the Environment* (1965); E. R. Hermann, "Environmental Aspects of Energy Development," ch. viii in A. B. Cambel *et al., Energy R & D and National Progress* (1965); Editorial Outlook, "The Continuing Tale of the Torrey Canyon," *Environmental Science and Technology* (May 1967); Paul R. and Anne H. Ehrlich, *Population Resources Environment* (1970); H. R. Hulett, "Optimum World Population," *BioScience,* vol. 20, no. 3 (Feb. 1, 1970); A. M. Weinberg and R. P. Hammond, "Limits to the Use of Energy," *American Scientist,* vol. 58, no. 4, pp. 412–418 (July–August 1970); G. Hardin, "The Tragedy of the Commons," *Science,* vol. 162, no. 3859, p. 1243 (Dec. 13, 1968); Gordon Young, "Pollution, Threat to Man's Only Home," *National Geographic,* vol. 138, no. 6 (Dec. 1970); American Conference of Industrial Hygienists' TLV Committee, "Threshold Limit Values of Airborne Contaminants for 1970"; Ernest J. Sternglass, "Infant Mortality and Nuclear Tests," *Bulletin of the Atomic Scientists* (April 1969).   (E. R. HE.)

POLLUX, JULIUS (2nd century A.D.), Greek scholar and rhetorician of Naukratis in Egypt, was the author of an *Onomasticon,* a Greek thesaurus of terms. The emperor Commodus appointed him to a chair of rhetoric in Athens. The *Onomasticon,* his only surviving work, is in ten books. It is incomplete, having undergone abridgment and interpolation in antiquity. The work contains rhetorical material (*e.g.,* collections of synonyms and compounds) and technical terms pertaining to a wide variety of subjects, as well as citations from literature. The material on music and the theatre is of special interest. Editions include that by W. Dindorf (1824) and by E. Bethe in the Teubner *Lexicographi Graeci,* three volumes (1900–37).   (G. Do.)

POLLUX, in astronomy, the brightest star of the zodiacal constellation Gemini (*q.v.*). This reddish first-magnitude star and the slightly less bright blue star Castor mark the heads of the celestial Twins, whose feet are in the Milky Way across from Orion. Pollux is 35 light-years distant and is intrinsically 33 times as luminous as the sun. The Twin stars are not far from overhead in the early evenings of early spring for observers in middle northern latitudes.   (R. H. BR.)

POLO, MARCO (1254–1324), Venetian traveler, whose descriptions of his journey across the world from Venice to China and back, and of his experiences in the vast dominions of the Mongol emperor Kublai, make one of the greatest books of all time. This remarkable work, *The Book of Marco Polo, Citizen of Venice, Called Million, Wherein Is Recounted the Wonders of the World,* is a forerunner of scientific geography. Its author was the first to inform the West of the extent and power of China, and the first to give an intelligible account of the ways thither. He made known a host of places hitherto hidden from European cartographers. Granted the prejudices of his age, in which, for instance, Christians and Muslims knew each other's faith only in travesty, his judgments reveal an open mind. The value of his observations on the events of his time is recognized by modern Orientalists, and the problems posed by variations in the reading of his book have inspired much scholarly research in the attempt, still in progress, to reconstruct the original text. Yet *The Book of Marco Polo* did not become a widely read work until the 19th century, since when it has been translated into many languages.

Journey of Niccolo and Matteo Polo.—Marco Polo was born either at Venice, or perhaps at Korcula (Curzola), a Venetian outpost on an island off the Dalmatian coast, in 1254. His father, Niccolo Polo, and his father's brother Matteo were members of a noble family of Dalmatian origin, though we do not know whether their remote forebears were Italian or Slav. When Marco was still a child, his father and uncle set out for the East; they were

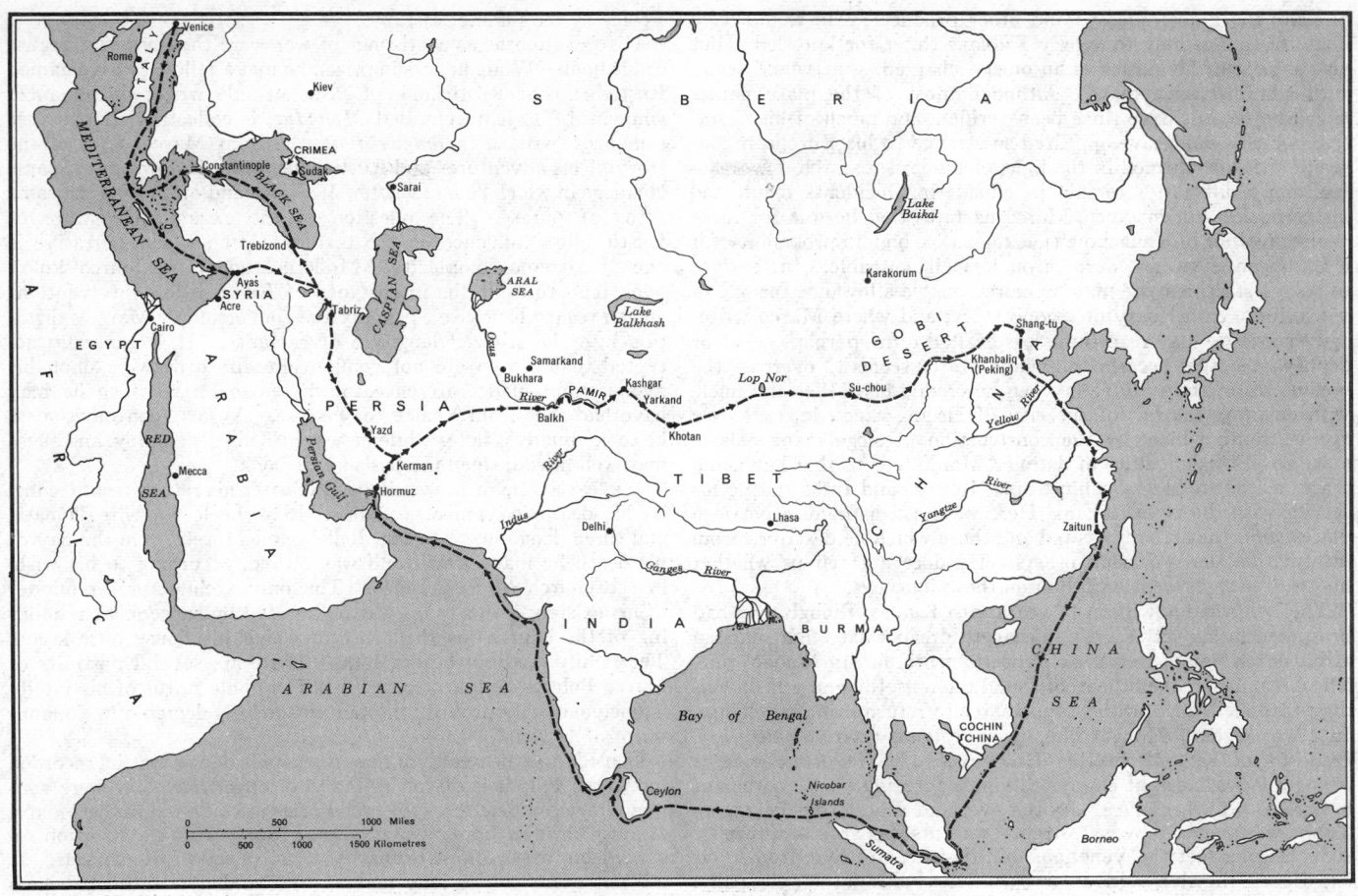

ROUTES TRAVELED BY MARCO POLO BETWEEN 127? AND 1295

merchants and had commercial interests in Constantinople. From there they sailed in 1261 to pursue their trading operations at Sudak, a Venetian colony on the southeastern coast of the Crimea, where they seem to have had a branch of their business. From there they went on to Sarai (Chaucer's "Sarra in the land of Tartarie"), the capital of the western Kipchak horde whose prince, Berke (Barka Khan), warmly received them. They remained in Sarai for a year. The outbreak of war between Berke and Hulagu, the Mongol ruler of the Persian region of the former Abbasid Arab Empire, blocked their way back to Europe, so they chose a safer but much longer route round the Caspian Sea and on to Bukhara in central Asia where they made another prolonged halt, this time for three years. While they were at Bukhara some envoys returning from a mission from Hulagu to his brother Kublai, the Great Khan of China, persuaded the brothers to accompany them to Kublai's court at Khanbaliq, the modern Peking (Peiping), or Shang-tu, the Xanadu of Samuel Coleridge's poem *Kubla Khan*. The extension of the area of Mongol conquest from the Pacific Ocean to the gates of Europe had given this immense tract a political unity and a security along its roads which it had never possessed before, and this circumstance permitted a few enterprising travelers from the West to penetrate behind the barrier which Islam had long raised against European contacts with the Far East. The Polo brothers were among the first Europeans in medieval times to enter China. Kublai welcomed them and asked them many questions about Christendom. They stayed for several years at the court of the Great Khan but unfortunately left no record of their experiences there. At last the Great Khan allowed them to return to their home and gave them letters to the pope asking him to send learned missionaries to instruct his subjects in the tenets of Christianity, for Kublai's attitude toward the great religions was still experimental and fluid. The Venetians once more took the road and traveled over the length of Asia to Acre (Akko) where, in 1269, having learned that no new pope had been elected

since the death of Clement IV, in 1268, they decided to return to Venice, there being no pope to whom they could deliver their letters in Rome.

Marco Polo's Journey.—Two years passed before the brothers resolved to start again on their travels, and this time they took with them Niccolo's son Marco, then 17 years old. They prudently armed themselves with letters justifying their delay in Europe, but hearing after they had arrived on the Syrian coast that the papal elections had taken place and a new pope, Gregory X, had been enthroned, they returned to Italy to carry out Kublai's mission. Gregory could supply only two Dominicans, men poor in spirit who soon turned back, glad to be relieved of so arduous an apostolate. In 1271 the brothers left Ayas (Yumurtalik, known as Ajuzzo or Laiazzo to the Italian merchants), a small town on the Gulf of Iskenderun, and rode overland by Yazd and Kerman to Hormuz on the Persian Gulf with the intention of taking ship to China. For some reason unknown to us the party abandoned its plan for a sea voyage and stolidly turned northward and made its way through Persia to Balkh, and from there ascended the upper Oxus (Amu-Darya) to Wakhan and crossed the plateau of the Pamir, a name which Marco was the first European to record. They then descended from the high plateau and journeyed through Kashgar (Shufu), Yarkand, and Khotan (Ho-t'ien), regions which remained closed to Western knowledge until the 19th century. From Khotan they passed near Lop Nor, crossed the Gobi Desert and entered China by way of Su-chou (Kiuchüan) and Ch'ang-an (Sian). At length, in 1275, after a journey lasting three years, they presented themselves to Kublai Khan at his summer palace at Shang-tu.

Marco records that he made rapid progress in the Great Khan's favour; he studied the Mongol language and was entrusted by the emperor with various missions to different parts of his realm. As he became an astute man of business, Marco made careful notes of his itineraries, the state of the cities, the customs of the people, and the kinds of crops and other products. He would have done this not merely to satisfy Kublai's thirst for knowledge but also as part of his duties as an official charged, so it would seem, with administrative tasks. Although most of the place names which he records have since been verified, and much of his narrative, which would have appeared so strange to his European contemporaries, confirmed in the light of modern research, nevertheless many difficulties remain in elucidating incidents mentioned in the book. For instance, Marco narrates that he was for three years governor of Yangchow (Chiang-tu), a high improbability for a European, even if it were chronologically possible. In the face of such a statement we may make reasonable allowance for his, or his scribe's, embroidery of a good story, and where Marco writes "governor" we may read some less exalted term, perhaps agent or deputy. Another occasion on which Marco seems to overpass the boundaries of the credible is when he credits his father and uncle with ensuring the fall of the city of Hsiang-yang, during a war against south China, by the construction of siege mangonels, a story beset by difficulties of dating. Marco tells us that he visited places as far afield as Cochin China, Burma, and India during his service with the Great Khan. Here we must distinguish between places which he actually visited and those which he describes from information derived from others. He does not tell us whether his two relations went with him on these journeys.

The Polos had now been 17 years with Kublai; though they had prospered in his service, they began to dread what might happen at his death, for there was no dynastic continuity in Mongol rule. The Great Khan liked them, or found them useful, and was unwilling to let them go, and the opportunity to return came by chance. In 1286 Arghun, Mongol ilkhan, or regional ruler, of Persia, a grandson of Kublai's brother Hulagu, lost his favourite wife, a Mongol lady, and sent envoys to China to bring back another of her tribe to fill her place. As the overland route from Peking to Tabriz was menaced by war, Arghun's agents prepared to return by sea. Having met the Venetians and desiring to profit from their experience, they begged Kublai to send the Polos in their company. The Great Khan consented; he ordered junks to be fitted out for the voyage, and he gave the Polos friendly messages to the potentates of Christendom, including the pope and the kings of France and England. Early in 1292 the mission sailed from Zaitun, probably the modern Chin-chiang in Fukien, then one of the chief Chinese ports for foreign trade, and navigated a course which took them through the straits of Singapore and Malacca to the Nicobar Islands, Ceylon, Malabar, and on, hugging the coast where they could, to Hormuz, where they arrived in 1294. The long voyage involved vexatious delays on the coasts of Sumatra and south India. Some tragedy, possibly a disease such as scurvy, caused the death of many on board, including two of the envoys and most of their suite, but the young bride and the three Venetians survived. Arghun Khan had died in 1291, before the party left China; the bride thereupon married his son, Ghazan Khan. After nine months at the Persian court the Polos started on the last lap of their journey, traveling from Tabriz over the mountains to Trebizond (Trabzon) where they took ship for Constantinople and Venice. They arrived home after an absence of 25 years. Giovanni Battista Ramusio of Treviso, the Venetian diplomat who composed an edition of Marco's book two centuries later, mentions that the travelers' relations failed to recognize them. They were said to have brought back much wealth, though Marco did not die a rich man by the standards of his time.

We next hear of Marco Polo as a naval officer, a *sopracomito* or gentleman commander of a galley in a Venetian fleet commanded by the admiral Andrea Dandolo. War had broken out between the republic and Genoa, and a Genoese fleet under Lamba Doria had sailed into the Adriatic on a raid into Venetian home waters. In a battle off Curzola (Korcula) Island in Sept. 1298 the Venetians were routed and, according to one source, Marco was taken prisoner, though he himself is silent on the circumstances of his capture. Another source suggests that he was captured in an earlier clash with the Genoese. Whatever the cause of his imprisonment at Genoa, the victors treated their distinguished captive with kindness; his captivity lasted less than a year and he was back in Venice by the summer of 1299.

His few months as a prisoner of war were the immediate cause of his book. While he was in prison he met a fellow captive named Rustichello, or Rusticiano, of Pisa, an able writer of romances who, in 1271, had compiled *Meliadus,* a collection of chivalric romances, written in *langue d'oïl.* To him Marco dictated the story of his adventures and Rustichello wrote it down in the same language in which he had written *Meliadus* and often with the same turns of phrase. The question of the extent and nature of Rustichello's influence on the text of Marco Polo's narrative is one of extreme complexity. Modern students of Marco Polo's book tend to limit the importance of Rustichello's interventions and to regard his share as simply the conversion of Marco's dictation into the stylized language of romance. It is generally accepted that Marco did not confine himself to drawing upon his memory but made reference to written material which he may have had sent from Venice for his use. As has been mentioned, he took abundant notes while he was in Kublai's employ, and these may well have formed the basis of his book.

We learn little of Marco Polo's life after his return from Genoa. At his death in Venice on Jan. 8, 1324, he left a wife Donata, and three daughters, Fantina, Bellela and Moreta. On the day of his death he made a will and was buried, according to his wish, in the church of S. Lorenzo. The only architectural reminder of his existence—his tomb was obliterated by subsequent rebuilding of the church—is the court in which his house once stood. The family died out before 1500. There are several portraits of Marco Polo, none taken from life. The noble status of his family is documentarily proved; the family shield is depicted in a manuscript of 1424.

Considering the wealth of new geographical information recorded by Marco Polo it is disconcerting to discover how slow were contemporary cartographers to embody this information in their maps. It must however be remembered that Marco Polo's generation regarded his descriptions primarily as a collection of marvels. It did not occur to the map makers to abandon traditional beliefs and to apply scientific criteria to geographical discoveries. The first map in which Marco Polo's influence is abundantly evident is the great Catalan Atlas of about 1375 which drew freely upon his book for the topography of central Asia and the Far East. It was not until the age of the great ocean voyages of the later 15th century that Polo's material was widely used. Columbus, for instance, whose destination was Polo's Cathay, heavily annotated a printed copy of Ramusio's Latin version in his possession. The popular ascription to Marco Polo of the introduction to the West of gunpowder, the mariner's compass, and block printing is now discredited.

The Texts.—In different countries the book of Marco Polo has customarily received different titles. In Britain it has been persistently called *The Travels of Marco Polo,* while the Italians insist on calling it *Il Milione* and apply this title both to the book and to the author. Indeed the significance of this curious title has given rise to much conjecture, though with inconclusive result. According to some, Marco, and hence his book, were thus called by his fellow citizens by reason of the exaggerated magnitude of the wonders which he recounted. Later opinion advances the possibility that *Milione* may not be a nickname after all, but rather Marco's real name, a variant of Emilio.

Over 140 manuscripts of *The Book of Marco Polo* have been located, and these fall into groups according to their dependence on the following key texts: (1) an early 14th-century version, written in Italy, in italianate French, and first published in Paris in 1824 (not without errors of transcription) by the Société de Géographie of Paris as *Voyages de Marco Polo* in *Recueil de Voyages et de Mémoires,* i, and known as the "Geographic" text; (2) another early 14th-century version written in French and printed by J. P. G. Pauthier in Paris, 1865, as *Le Livre de Marco Polo;* (3) a version in Tuscan Italian, dated perhaps 1305 and printed by G. B. Baldelli Boni in Florence in 1827 as *Il Milione di Marco Polo;* (4) a version in Venetian Italian, early 14th-century, printed in Studi Romanzi, iv, Rome (1906); (5) a Latin version by Fra F. Pipino of Bologna, dated between 1307 and 1314, and made from (4); (6) an Italian version, edited by G. B. Ramusio, printed in Navigationi Viaggi, ii, in Venice (1559), and derived from (1) and from another manuscript, possibly (7); (7) a Latin version in the cathedral chapter house at Toledo, written probably in Italy about 1470, a translation of a text older than (1) and known as the "Z" text from the surname of Cardinal F. X. de Zelada (1717–1801), a papal secretary of state who gave the manuscript to the library. Of these seven manuscripts, (1), (6), and (7) are usually held to be the most important.

The original text that Marco Polo dictated to Rustichello was almost certainly written in French. The work is divided into two parts: the first a narrative of the Polos' two journeys, the second a series of descriptions of administrative, economic, and political facts and notable occurrences in the lands which he describes. The original text is believed to have been destroyed, and the quest for a text as near as possible to the original has taxed the ingenuity of scholars ever since W. Marsden first applied the critical method in his translation, *The Travels of Marco Polo* (London, 1818). Sir Henry Yule's magnificent translation, *The Book of Ser Marco Polo*, published in London in 1871 (third edition, revised and augmented by H. Cordier, London, 1903), though slightly marred by lapses into somewhat precious English, remains the most compendious source of information on Marco Polo. This was followed by H. Cordier's *Ser Marco Polo, Notes and addenda to Sir Henry Yule's edition* in 1920. Both Yule's edition and that of A. J. H. Charignon, *Le livre de Marco Polo* (published in Peking in 1924–28), a modern French translation of Pauthier's text of 1865, suffer from having been based on texts of unascertained authenticity. The first to present a reconstructed, authenticated text was L. F. Benedetto in his *Marco Polo, il Milione* (Florence, 1928); Italian translation by L. F. Benedetto (Milan, 1932); English translation by A. Ricci with introduction by Sir E. Denison Ross (London, 1931). Textual reconstruction was carried a stage further with the discovery by Sir Percival David in Toledo in 1932 of the "Z" text, published by A. C. Moule and P. Pelliot in London in 1938 as *Marco Polo, the Description of the World*, of which volume i consists of an English translation, with critical apparatus, of the "Geographic" text together with collated passages drawn from other important manuscripts, and volume ii of a transcription of the "Z" text. Among more recent editions of outstanding merit is a Polish translation by A. L. Czerny, with notes by M. Lewicki, *Marko Polo, opisanie swiata*, published in Warsaw in 1954.

See also references under "Polo, Marco" in the Index.

BIBLIOGRAPHY.—There is a large literature of shorter studies concerned with Marco Polo; *e.g.,* G. Orlandini, "Marcò Polo e la sua famiglia," *Archiv. Veneto-Tridentino,* ix (1926); R. Almagià, "A proposito di recenti studi su Marco Polo e i suoi viaggi," *Riv. Geogr. Ital.,* vol. lxii (1955); A. C. Moule, *Quinsai, With Other Notes on Marco Polo* (1957). The 700th anniversary of Marco Polo's birth was marked by several popular works and special articles including the symposium *VII centenario della nascita di Marco Polo* (1955).   (R. L. HL.)

POLO is played on horseback with stick and ball, and takes its name from the Tibetan *pulu,* "ball." The earliest records of polo are Persian; there is evidence that it was played in the time of King Darius the Great (522–486 B.C.). Persian polo is described in Sir Anthony Sherley's *Travels to Persia* (1613). From Persia it spread to Constantinople, and eastward through Turkistan to Tibet, China and Japan, and from Tibet to India, where it flourished throughout the Mughal dynasty (early 16th to mid-18th century). Then for 100 years there are no records of it in India proper though the game continued to be played in the feudal states on the northwestern and northeastern frontiers.

The first Western polo players were British tea planters in Assam, who learned the game in nearby Manipur, on the Indo-Burmese border. They formed the first European's polo club in 1859 at Silchar and drew up the first rules. The Calcutta Polo Club was formed in the early 1860s. In 1869 the 10th Hussars started to play polo in England after reading an account of the game in India. In 1871 the first recorded match took place on Hounslow Heath between the 9th Lancers and the 10th Hussars, with eight players to a side; in 1873 the numbers were reduced to five and in 1882 to four. The Hurlingham Polo Association, which be-

came the leading association in Great Britain, was founded in 1874. Polo was first played in the United States in 1883 and the U.S. Polo Association was founded in 1890.

The Game.—Polo is played with four players on each side. The small light ball is made of willow or bamboo root and is not more than $3\frac{1}{4}$ in. in diameter, weighing between $4\frac{1}{4}$ and $4\frac{3}{4}$ oz. The stick is made of cane and is from 48 to 54 in. long. It has a narrow wooden head measuring $8\frac{1}{2}$–$9\frac{1}{2}$ in. which is set on it at a slight angle. The ball is struck not with the forward face (as in croquet) but with the long side of the head. The total weight of the stick is about one pound.

A full-sized polo field is 300 yd. in length by 200 yd. in width, if unboarded; and 300 yd. in length by 160 yd. in width, if boarded. The goals must not be less than 260 yd. apart, and each goal is 8 yd. wide. The object of the game, as in so many others, is to pass the ball between the goalposts. A match lasts about an hour, divided into periods of play known as chukkas (chukkers; from the Indian word denoting one full turn of a wheel); intervals between chukkas, when ponies are changed, are of 3 min., with 15 min. at half time. Six chukkas of $7\frac{1}{2}$ min. are usual in a full match. Ends are changed every time a goal is scored. The players are designated no. 1 and no. 2 (forwards), no. 3 and no. 4 (backs).

The two mounted umpires, one for each side of the field, consult together after each infringement and impose a penalty only if they agree. If they do not agree a decision is given by the referee, who watches the game from the sidelines or the grandstand. The referee also gives judgment on any question of the rules which arises outside the actual play.

The most important rules are those concerning the safety of men and ponies. Chief of these are the crossing and riding-off rules. No player may cross the line of another in going for the ball, and the last man to strike it has right-of-way. Other players may legitimately "ride him off," however. This means impinging, pony to pony, on a converging course in the manner of a shoulder charge in football. Hooking of sticks is also permitted. In a game played at the gallop, hazards are equally shared; consequently the rules are carefully observed, such transgressions as occur being mostly accidental.

PERSIAN PRINCES PLAYING POLO: A MINIATURE FROM AN ILLUMINATED MANUSCRIPT OF 1472

BY COURTESY OF (TOP, BOTTOM LEFT) THE OAK BROOK POLO CLUB; PHOTOGRAPH, (BOTTOM RIGHT) ACME

(TOP) PLAYER AT RIGHT IS ATTEMPTING AN OFFSIDE FOREHAND SHOT OF A BOUNCING BALL. (BOTTOM LEFT) PLAYER IN FRONT HAS JUST MADE A NEARSIDE BACKHAND SHOT UNDER THE NECK OF HIS PONY. NOTE THE CLOSENESS OF THE TRAILING PONY TO THE FRONT PONY AS ITS RIDER TRIED TO GET INTO POSITION TO BLOCK THE SHOT. (BOTTOM RIGHT) THE THONG ATTACHED TO THE HAFT OF THE MALLET IS WOUND TIGHTLY AROUND THE PLAYER'S WRIST. BALL IS HIT WITH THE SIDE OF THE MALLET

side. For instance, a handicap of 10 goals, which is the highest ever given, implies a player of the greatest talents and in constant practice; such a handicap is supportable only by a man who plays or practices polo daily. In modern conditions most 10-handicaps are held by South American players. A few are held in the United States. The difficulty of obtaining constant practice in Britain, and the temporary reduction in the number of tournaments in India and Pakistan, have made 10-goal players from these countries rare. The lowest handicap possible is —2.

Handicaps are applied in matches by adding together the ratings of the players on either side; the lesser team total is then subtracted from the greater, and the resultant number of goals is allowed to the weaker side as a "start." The idea of handicaps originated in the United States as long ago as 1891 and, besides making play more interesting, had the immediate effect of raising standards with surprising speed. Not only did the handicap idea enable less-experienced and younger players to take part in the same matches as top-class performers, but it compelled the latter always to play at their best and hardest.

Handicaps also serve to grade the standard of a polo tournament. An "8-goal tournament," in which no team with a greater total handicap than 8 may compete, implies competence only, since the average rating is 2 goals per man; a "12-goal tournament" indicates fair quality performers; a "20-goal tournament," the highest class.

Polo is an expensive game. Behind each player must be an organization of ponies and grooms, the maintenance of which involves continuous expenditure on feed, equipment, and wages in and out of season. Transportation from tournament to tournament is likewise costly. Not surprisingly, the game has always depended on the participation of wealthy men. However, there have always been, in every polo-playing country, a small proportion of players for whom polo has provided a livelihood, some as the permanent guests of team captains. Others, if very fine horsemen, are employed in buying and training ponies: this work keeps them in constant practice and develops their game so that they are always sure of their place in a team. Such professional players traditionally were recruited from among the British officers of the old Indian Army. Latterly, professional players have been drawn from such diverse sources as North American cowboys, South American gauchos, and the princely families of the Indian subcontinent.

A polo player requires a strong seat on a horse, a good eye for hitting a ball, a powerful wrist, dash, determination, great physical stamina, and experience. The latter is so important that, although polo is the most strenuous of summer games, few players reach

The American game, borrowed from the British, developed independently for 30 years, with certain fundamental differences from the game as played elsewhere. Some of these differences, combined with the U.S. handicapping system, dating from 1891, and the ready supply of suitable ponies, went far toward establishing an American world supremacy.

Attack has always been stressed in play in the U.S. After the U.S. won its first victory in the Westchester Cup international series with England in 1909, the rules of the two countries were assimilated. The U.S. adopted the English rule permitting the hooking of sticks, and the English abandoned the offside rules and adopted the handicap system. After World War I England followed the U.S. lead in abolishing the size limit for polo ponies (see below).

Players.—All polo players competing in tournaments are given a handicap by the governing bodies in their own countries. By international agreement these handicaps, in effect a ranking list, are accepted in all other countries. The system is based on a national estimate of the number of goals a player is worth to his

their best form until they are aged 40 or more, and the prime of life for polo is between 45 and 55.

Ponies.—The term "polo pony" has become a misnomer. There is no longer any height limit on the mounts used in polo and the only criteria for selecting a pony are that it should be both large enough to carry its rider without loss of pace and small enough to be handy. Obviously it is easier to hit a moving ball from the back of a small mount than from a large one. Obviously, too, a small animal is the more maneuverable and can turn more quickly. On the other hand, the longer the stride the greater the speed, and the stouter the build the greater the weight that can be carried. Most polo ponies are really small horses, 15–15.2 hands high, and some of them are taller. (A horse under 14.2 hands is defined as a pony.)

In the past the size of the ponies was restricted. In Manipur the game was played on ponies of 12 hands. The English, being larger than the Indians, raised the limit to 13.2 hands, then to 14.2 hands, and finally, in 1919, abolished it altogether to conform with the earlier decisions (by 1918) of the United States and Argentina. Polo ponies are predominantly grade Thoroughbreds, descending from a series of racehorse sires bred with mares of different local bloods. In the East the mares were chiefly Arabian; in Great Britain, one of the native pony breeds; in the United States and Australia, free-running ranch ponies; and in Argentina, the hardy native pampas pony.

Because the game is very hard on the ponies—they may gallop as much as three miles in each chukka and the sudden stopping and turning imposes considerable strain—no pony plays two successive chukkas except in an emergency, and each player generally rides at least three ponies in the course of a six-chukka match. With careful training ponies develop keenness and skill and show great cleverness in anticipating the run of the ball and in placing themselves at the best distance from it for the rider to make his stroke. A pony needs sagacity, a nerveless temperament, quick reflexes to respond instantly to his rider's aids, very sound legs for galloping on hard grounds, and great muscular power so as to be able to stop and turn from full gallop.

Injuries to ponies and riders are few. The ball is too light to inflict much damage; sticks are less stoutly made than appears to be the case and even a vigorous accidental blow is unlikely to break a bone.

Championship and International Polo.—Before World War II the two most important trophies for polo were the Hurlingham Champion Cup, an international contest inaugurated in 1876, and the Westchester Cup, a contest between Great Britain, represented by a Hurlingham team, and the United States, represented by a Meadow Brook team, inaugurated in 1886. Great Britain won in 1886, 1902, and 1914; the U.S. in 1909, 1911, and 1913, and in 1921, 1924, 1930, 1936, and 1939. Argentina and the United States met four times, 1928–50, for the Copa de las Americas, won by the U.S. in 1928 and 1932, and by Argentina in 1936 and 1950; and Mexico and the United States met three times, once in 1941 and twice in 1946, for the General Manuel Ávila Camacho Cup, the U.S. winning each time.

After World War II it looked as if polo in England were finished. But the remnants of the prewar players were determined to carry on. The small Ham Club was the first to start, and then Viscount Cowdray began a great revival with the Cowdray Park Polo Club. Other old clubs revived and new ones started, and some began to maintain trained ponies for hire.

In the second half of the 20th century Argentina and the U.S. had become the leading polo-playing countries, followed by South Africa and England. High-class polo had developed rapidly in Mexico and in Chile, Colombia, and in other parts of South America as well. Polo has flourished in India and Pakistan, and players appear regularly in English teams. India has sent a touring side to Great Britain and the British Army has sent a side to India.

In the United States, interest in polo increased markedly after World War II, with play in the seven circuits: Northeastern, Southeastern, Central, Mid-States, Northwestern, Southwestern, and Pacific Coast, and intercircuit and national championships.

One of the world's finest polo centres was established by Paul Butler at Oak Brook, near Chicago, and another by Robert A. Uihlein at Uihlein Field, near Milwaukee. In 1963 these fields were the scenes of the first international competition between the United States and the United Kingdom since 1939. Cowdray Park of the United Kingdom defeated a Milwaukee team in two matches for the Robert A. Uihlein International Cup and defeated Tulsa, the U.S. Open Champions, in the Butler National Handicap.

Organization.—Outside the United States the governing body of polo is the Hurlingham Polo Association. The associations of many other countries and regions are affiliated to it and have representatives on the council. In the 1960s the following were members: India, Pakistan, Assam, New Zealand, Australia, South Africa, Rhodesia, Zambia, Kenya, Nigeria, Malaya, Jamaica, Malta, Cyprus, the Republic of Ireland, Northern Ireland, Accra, Aden, Tangier, Hong Kong, and the Rhine Army Polo Club. The United States Polo Association is the governing body in American polo.

Polo has been included intermittently in the Olympic Games, the last time being at Berlin in 1936. In some countries, notably Great Britain and the United States, women are allowed to participate and several of them have played regularly in low- and medium-goal tournaments. Popular variants of the game are arena polo, which is played indoors in the winter in North America, and paddock polo, which is played with a soft ball by children in Great Britain.

For outstanding players, *see* SPORTING RECORD: *Polo.*

BIBLIOGRAPHY.—R. Weir and J. M. Brown, *Riding and Polo,* Badminton Library, rev. by T. F. Dale, new ed. (1905); J. M. Brown, *Polo,* 2nd ed. (1896); Beauvoir de Lisle, *Polo in India* (1890), rev. ed. (1924); *Tournament Polo* (1897); T. F. Dale, *The Game of Polo* (1897); T. B. Drybrough, *Polo,* 2nd ed. (1906); E. D. Miller, *Modern Polo,* 6th ed. (1929); W. Buckmaster, *Hints on Polo Combination* (1910); W. C. Forbes, *As to Polo* (1920); W. B. Devereux, *Position and Team Play in Polo* (1924); "Marco" (Earl Mountbatten of Burma), *An Introduction to Polo,* 4th ed. (1960); J. Board, *Polo* (1956); W. G. H. Vickers, *Practical Polo* (1959); Hurlingham Polo Association, *Laws and Bye-Laws of Polo* (1912–   ); National Pony Society, *The Polo Pony (and Riding) Stud Book* (1894–1913), *National Pony Stud Book* (1915–   ); *The Polo Monthly and Racing Review* (1909–39); *Baily's Magazine of Sports and Pastimes* (1889–1926); yearbooks of the Hurlingham Polo Association, the American Polo Association, and the Indian Polo Association. (J. R. C. G.; W. S.)

POLOCK, MOSES (1817–1903), U.S. publisher and bibliophile, is chiefly remembered as the first rare-book dealer to devote himself solely to Americana. Born in Philadelphia, Pa., on May 14, 1817, he was apprenticed to the firm of McCarty and Davis, an old Philadelphia house of bookdealers and publishers. Polock succeeded to the ownership of the firm in 1851 and from 1853 the business was conducted under his name. The store was frequented by well-known literary figures of the time.

Notable among his publications was the first collected edition of the works of Charles Brockden Brown (*q.v.*), earliest U.S. novelist, which appeared in 1857. He was also responsible for the first U.S. collection of children's literature; he specialized in books on Benjamin Franklin and George Washington. He became an authority on the early history of Philadelphia and Pennsylvania. Polock died on Aug. 16, 1903.

See W. Brotherhead, *Forty Years Among the Old Booksellers of Philadelphia* (1891); A. S. W. Rosenbach, *Books and Bidders* (1927).

POLONAISE, a dignified ceremonial dance, in 3/4 time. It frequently served, from the 17th to 19th century, to open court balls and other royal functions. Originally a folk dance or warriors' triumphal march, it was adopted by the Polish nobility as a formal march as early as 1573. In its aristocratic form the dancers, in couples, walked around the ballroom in stately procession, with slightly accented steps.

As a musical form, the polonaise was occasionally employed by Beethoven, Mozart, and Handel, and was highly developed by Chopin. The polonaise has been introduced in opera (Mussorgsky's *Boris Godunov*) and ballet (Tchaikovsky's *The Sleeping Beauty*). (LN. ME.)

POLONIUM, a radioactive element, the first to be discovered by the radiochemical method. In 1898 Pierre and Marie Curie, after finding that the radioactivity of Joachimsthal pitchblende was much greater than could be predicted from the content of uranium and thorium, undertook to extract the substance causing this anomaly. Since the only known property of the hypothetical substance was its radioactivity, the Curies developed and used a new method for separating the various substances in the mineral and measuring the radioactivity of each portion. The Curies quickly found that the activity became concentrated, partly with the alkaline earths and partly with the sulfides precipitated from acid solution. They were soon able to confirm the existence of two new radioelements: one a higher homologue of tellurium, to which they gave the name polonium in honour of Marie Curie's native land, Poland; the other, a homologue of barium, was radium. (*See also* RADIOACTIVITY.)

The chemical symbol of polonium is Po and its atomic number is 84. Twenty-seven isotopes are known; all are radioactive, some naturally and the others artificially (*see* NUCLEUS). The isotope discovered by the Curies was Po^{210}, the most important of the isotopes and the one generally referred to as polonium. It belongs to the natural radioactive family of the uranium-radium system, whose members are as follows:

$$^{238}UI \xrightarrow{\alpha} UX1 \xrightarrow{\beta} UX2 \xrightarrow{\beta} UII \xrightarrow{\alpha} Io \xrightarrow{\alpha} Ra \xrightarrow{\alpha} Rn \xrightarrow{\alpha} RaA \xrightarrow{\alpha}$$

$$RaB \xrightarrow{\beta} RaC \begin{smallmatrix} \beta \nearrow RaC' \searrow \alpha \\ \searrow \alpha \; RaC'' \nearrow \beta \end{smallmatrix} RaD \xrightarrow{\beta} RaE \xrightarrow{\beta} RaF \xrightarrow{\alpha} RaG \text{ (stable lead)}$$

Note: Io is the symbol for ionium, a radioactive isotope of thorium.

The Po^{210} isotope was produced artificially for the first time in 1936 by J. J. Livingood, who bombarded bismuth with accelerated deuterons.

Natural Occurrence and Preparation.—Polonium (Po^{210}) is found in much smaller amounts than is radium in minerals containing uranium. About 2,900 kg. of uranium element are in radioactive equilibrium with 1 g. of radium and 0.22 mg. of polonium (1 curie). It can therefore be estimated that 1,000 kg. of Joachimsthal pitchblende containing 65% of uranium also contains about 0.05 mg. of polonium. Its abundance in the earth's crust is of the order of $10^{-13}\%$.

The half life of polonium is long enough so that it can be ex-

Isotopes of Polonium

Isotope	Half life	Manner of disintegration	Manner of production
192 . . .	0.5 sec.	α	Bi + p
193 . . .	4 sec.	α	Bi + p
194 . . .	13 sec.	α	Bi + p
195 . . .	30 sec.	α	Bi + p
196 . . .	1.9 min.	α	W + Ne
197 . . .	$\cong$ 4 min.	α	Bi + p
198 . . .	$\cong$ 6 min.	α	Bi + p
199 . . .	$\cong$ 11 min.	α	Bi + p
200 . . .	$\cong$ 8 min.	e, α	Bi + p
201 . . .	18 min.	e, α	Bi + p
202 . . .	44 min.	e, α	Bi + p
203 . . .	45 min.	e	Bi + p
204 . . .	3.8 hr.	$e, \alpha \; (e/\alpha \cong 99)$	Bi + p
205 . . .	1.8 hr.	$e, \alpha \; (\sim 0.074\%)$	$Pb^{204} + \alpha$
206 . . .	8.8 days	$e, \alpha \; (e/\alpha \cong 19)$	$Pb^{204} + \alpha$
207 . . .	5.7 hr.	$e, \alpha \; (0.01\%)$	$Pb^{206} + \alpha$
208 . . .	2.93 yr.	α	$Pb^{206,207} + \alpha$; Bi + p; Bi + d
209 . . .	103 yr.	$\alpha, e \; (\alpha/e \cong 9)$	Bi + p; Bi + d
210 (RaF) .	138.4 days	α	natural; Bi + d; Bi + n; Pb + α
211 (AcC') .	0.52 sec.	α	natural
212 (ThC') .	3.0×10^{-7} sec.	α	natural
213 . . .	4.2×10^{-6} sec.	α	Rn^{217}; $Bi^{213} \xrightarrow{\beta}$
214 (RaC') .	1.637×10^{-4} sec.	α	natural
215 (AcA) .	1.83×10^{-3} sec.	$\alpha; \beta \; (\cong 5.10^{-4}\%)$	natural
216 (ThA) .	0.158 sec.	α	natural
217 . . .	<10 sec.	α	$Rn^{221} \xrightarrow{\alpha}$
218 (RaA) .	3.05 min.	$\alpha; \beta \; (\cong 0.04\%)$	natural

e, electronic capture; p, proton; d, deuteron; α, alpha particle; Ne, neon ions; n, neutron.

tracted directly from uranium minerals. This process has been used but is of little practical value. Polonium is usually extracted either from radioactive lead, which is a by-product of the extraction of radium from uranium minerals, or from radium D, obtained

by washing old radon tubes that contain the long-lived active deposit, radium D+E+F; radium D also may be extracted from old preparations of radium salts. The extraction of polonium from solutions of radium D, as well as the preparation of strong sources (up to about one to two millicuries per square millimetre) of this radioelement, usually is by electrochemical deposition on silver or nickel from a weak solution of acetic (CH_3CO_2H), nitric (HNO_3), or hydrochloric acid (HCl). On silver, Po is deposited spontaneously free from RaE and RaD; on nickel, Po and RaE are deposited from hot solution almost free from RaD.

Ponderable quantities of polonium can be produced artificially by bombarding bismuth or lead with neutrons (n) or accelerated charged particles. For example:

$$Bi^{209} + n \longrightarrow Bi^{210} + \gamma; \; Bi^{210} \xrightarrow{\beta} Po^{210}$$
$$Pb^{208} + He^4 \longrightarrow Po^{210} + 2n$$

When polonium is obtained by neutron irradiation of bismuth in a nuclear reactor, it can be separated from the bismuth by volatilization, either directly by heating the irradiated metal or after enrichment achieved by spontaneous deposition of polonium in a hydrochloric solution on a small quantity of bismuth; the bismuth may be either pulverized or in needle form. One can also dissolve the bismuth in acid solution and co-precipitate the polonium by stannous chloride with tellurium added in the form of telluric acid. Afterward, it is separated from the tellurium by precipitation of the latter from hydrochloric solution by hydrazine or by sulfur dioxide.

Polonium can be purified by extraction from its acid aqueous solutions with tributyl phosphate, diisopropyl ketone, mesityl oxide, dithizone (diphenylthiocarbazone) in chloroform solution, etc. Anodic deposition on gold in dilute nitric acid is recommended in order to obtain very pure polonium. Finally, very pure sources of high density of activity can be obtained by volatilization at red heat, in a quartz tube, of polonium that is drawn along by a current of hydrogen, nitrogen or argon and is collected on a cooled metallic surface or on a plastic pellicle.

Radioactive Properties.—Polonium disintegrates with emission of alpha rays to give radium G, a stable isotope of lead (Pb^{206}). Its half life is 138.4 days. The range of the alpha rays is 3.87 cm. in air at 15° C. and at a pressure of 760 mm. of mercury, which corresponds to an energy of 5,298 Mev. The range in nuclear photographic emulsion is of the order of 21μ and in aluminum of 22μ. Each alpha particle of Po^{210} produces along its path in air 152,000 pairs of ions. It is estimated that the quantity of polonium corresponding to a saturation current of 1 electrostatic unit (E.S.U.) in an ionization chamber using all the ions produced in the angle of 2π is equal to 1.67×10^{-10} g., *i.e.*, $\frac{1}{1.340}$ millicurie of Po^{210}. The heat loss per hour of 1 curie of Po^{210}, which is equivalent to the kinetic energy of the alpha rays and of the recoil atoms, is equal to 27.24 cal., which corresponds to 0.143 w. per milligram. The alpha radiation, which is essentially monokinetic, is accompanied by very weak gamma radiation (1.25 quantum of 0.8 Mev per 10^5 alpha particles). Marie Curie and A. Debierne were able to determine directly Avogadro's number by measuring the volume of helium corresponding to a known number of alpha particles emitted by a polonium source. The alpha radiation of polonium can cause the decomposition of water, the ozonization of air, and also can affect photographic plates. It excites the fluorescence of polonium compounds and of glass and quartz plates on which these have been placed. It has a toxic effect on living organisms. A rabbit into which 500 E.S.U. of polonium have been injected wastes considerably and dies a few days afterward. Polonium concentrates itself chiefly in the spleen and in the ganglions. According to the national bureau of standards, the maximum permissible dose for a human being in the mid-1960s was 0.02 microcuries (4.5×10^{-12} per gram).

Physical Properties.—The study of the physical and chemical properties of polonium was restricted for many years to the application of radiochemical methods to very small quantities (of the order of 10^{-11} to 10^{-9} g.) of Po^{210}. Since Po^{210} has been prepared artificially, experiments on the milligram scale have been carried out.

The metal, of 9.4 density, is silver-gray or black. There are two crystalline varieties: α-Po, cubic, and β-Po, rhombohedral; the transition point is about 36° C. The melting point is close to 255° C. Judging by measurements of its vapour pressure, the boiling point is likely to be about 960° C. The speed of vaporization, in vacuum, of polonium deposited in minute quantities on nickel is already measurable at 108° C., and a heat treatment of 5 minutes at 350° C. releases 90% of the polonium atoms. On platinum, volatilization begins toward 350° C.; on gold it starts at a slightly lower temperature, and on palladium only at 500°–560° C. The vaporization temperature increases with the time that elapses after preparation. It varies, too, with the method of preparation of the sources and also according to the nature of the gaseous atmosphere in which the volatilization is carried out. The diffusion coefficient of polonium at room temperature in aluminum, iron, nickel, copper, silver, gold and lead is less than 10^{-14} sq.cm. per day. In gold and in platinum it is, at 470° C., close to 10^{-14} sq.cm. per second. In bismuth the diffusion coefficient reaches the value of 5×10^{-11} sq.cm. per second at 150° C. and 5×10^{-10} sq.cm. per second at 200° C.

Between 1.920 Å and 3.975 Å, 147 rays of the high-frequency spectrum of Po and 48 rays of its arc spectrum have been identified. From these measurements the ionization potential of the neutral polonium atom is estimated at 8.43 v.

Chemical and Electrochemical Properties.—From a chemical point of view, polonium, which is the higher homologue of tellurium and the neighbour of bismuth in the periodical classification, is related to these two elements. It is more metallic than is tellurium. When exposed to air the metal is slowly covered by a yellow oxide film. It reacts with chlorine and bromine and dissolves in acids.

Like tellurium, polonium is tetravalent in its most stable state. The existence of two other valencies, $+2$ and -2, also is certain; that of valency $+6$ is probable; an unstable valency of $+3$ is possible. In its tetravalent state, polonium tends to form complex ions with such anions as chloride, nitrate, phosphate, acetic, tartaric, etc. The yellow ammonium hexachloropolonite $(NH_4)_2$-$[PoCl_6]$ is the isomorph of the similar compounds of Te^{4+}, Pb^{4+}, Sn^{4+} and Pt^{4+}.

In the absence of the formation of complexes, polonium compounds have, in a nearly neutral aqueous solution, a strong tendency to hydrolyze with the formation of basic salts and of a yellow insoluble hydroxide, $PoO(OH)_2$. This hydroxide, which has colloidal properties, is amphoteric; it dissolves in sufficiently concentrated solutions of caustic soda or potash, resulting in a polonite, Na_2PoO_3 or K_2PoO_3, that is similar to the tellurites. The oxide (PoO_2), obtained by the action of oxygen at 250° C. on metal or by the thermal decomposition of nitrate, is yellow and has a face-centred cubic structure. The tetrachloride has been prepared by dissolving the metal in hydrochloric acid or by heating the metal with chlorine at 200° C.; and also from PoO_2 with hydrochloric acid. It is of bright yellow colour (m.p. = 294° C.; b.p. = 390° C.). Tetrabromide is bright red (m.p. = 330° C.); dark-gray tetraiodide sublimes at 200° C. with partial decomposition. The solubility of nitrate in nitric acid, even when this is concentrated, is very slight (3.7×10^{-3} mole per litre in HNO_3 7.8N at 25° C.). In dilute hydrochloric acid, polonium forms a black sulfide, PoS, that is insoluble in ammonium sulfide (differing in this respect from tellurium but resembling bismuth). With pyrogallol polonium likewise gives an insoluble compound. Reducing agents such as hydrazine, hydroxylamine or sulfur dioxide in an acid medium bring tetravalent polonium into the bivalent state (by contrast with tellurium, which precipitates in a metallic state). The chloride $(PoCl_2)$ is a red solid that melts at 170°–180° C. when heated in a sealed tube. Solutions in dilute hydrochloric acid are pink in colour and oxidize rapidly under the effect of the proper alpha radiation of polonium. Dibromide aqueous solutions are purple. Strong reducing agents, e.g., stannous chloride, sodium hydrosulfite, alkaline solutions of hydrazine, etc., reduce polonium compounds to the metallic state (by analogy with tellurium). Polonium in nitric, hydrochloric or acetic solutions 0.1 to 0.5N deposits spontaneously on silver, tellurium, bismuth, nickel and on the less noble metals. Under the action of an electric current polonium is deposited, in acid or alkaline solution, on the cathode in metallic form and partially on the anode, probably as the peroxide, PoO_3. The normal potential of the Po/Po^{4+} electrode in nitric solution is $E_h^°$ (normal potential of a hydrogen electrode at 0° C.) = $+0.76$ v. In acid solutions, the critical potential of the cathodic deposit is lowered if the electrolysis is carried out in the presence of different reducing agents, e.g., oxalic acid, oxygenated water. The normal potential of the Po^{2+}/Po^{4+} couple should be $E_h^° = +0.91$ v. Strong oxidizing agents such as bichromate or ceric salts transform tetravalent polonium compounds into a state of higher valency, most likely $+6$. The potential of the Po^{4+}/Po^{6+} couple in HCl or HNO_3 6N is about $+1.5$ v. Moreover, polonium forms a volatile hydride, PoH_2, and polonides with sodium, mercury, lead, beryllium, calcium, zinc, silver, nickel and platinum, which indicates the existence of the anion Po^{2-}. Finally, several organic compounds of polonium that can be extracted with solvents have been prepared: polonium dibenzyl, acetylacetonate, diethyldithiocarbamate, oxinate and dithizonate. Polonium dimethyl, which is volatile at room temperature, is also known.

Applications.—Polonium is used in nuclear physics as a source of alpha radiation that is practically exempt from penetrating rays. Irène Curie and her husband, F. Joliot-Curie, discovered artificial radioactivity in 1934 by bombarding aluminum, boron and magnesium with alpha rays of Po. Mixtures of polonium with beryllium and other light elements are used as sources of neutrons. Polonium also has been used to ionize air, mainly in order to avoid the accumulation of electrostatic charges.

BIBLIOGRAPHY.—M. Curie, *Radioactivité* (1935); I. Joliot-Curie, *Les Radioéléments naturels* (1957); M. Haïssinsky, *Le Polonium* (1937), *Nouveau Traité de chimie minérale*, vol. xiii of the series published under the direction of P. Pascal (1958); K. W. Bagnall, *Chemistry of the Rare Radioelements* (1957). (I. J.-CE.; G. Bs.)

POLONNARUWA, an ancient capital of Ceylon that long lay deserted but has again become a thriving town. It is the administrative centre of its district. Polonnaruwa first became a royal residence in A.D. 368 when the tank of Topawewa was formed, and succeeded Anuradhapura (q.v.) as the capital in the middle of the 8th century. The principal ruins date chiefly from the time of Parakramabahu (1153–86). The most imposing pile remaining is the Lankatilaka Vihara, a building 170 ft. (52 m.) long with walls about 80 ft. high and 12 ft. thick. Many other great buildings have been carefully excavated and preserved.

Modern Polonnaruwa (pop. [1963] 5,921) owes its rise to the restoration, in 1938–42, of the great irrigation tank known as Parakrama Samudra (Parakrama's Sea), which now irrigates more than 18,000 ac. (7,285 ha.) of rice. Road and railway construction have destroyed its isolation, and it is now a market centre of more than local significance.

POLONNARUWA DISTRICT had a population (1963) of 114,104, compared with 7,907 in 1931. This increase came about largely through the government-organized colonization of former wasteland now irrigated under the Parakrama Samudra and other large schemes. The principal product is rice; tobacco is also grown. Irrigation will be further improved when the Mahaweli Ganga Project is completed (see MAHAWELI GANGA).

See also CEYLON: *History.* (B. H. F.)

POLOTSK, a town of Vitebsk Oblast of the Belorussian Soviet Socialist Republic, U.S.S.R., on the Western Dvina at its confluence with the Polóta. Pop. (1969 est.) 64,000. First mentioned in 862, Polotsk is one of the eight Russian towns known to have existed in the 9th century. It was the seat of an early Russian princedom. Its position on a main route between Russia and the west ensured both commercial importance and a remarkably stormy history. After the 13th-century Tatar (Mongol) invasion, Polotsk fell under the control of the grand dukes of Lithuania. In 1498 the town was granted self-government. After many attacks by Russia, Polotsk was captured by Ivan IV (the Terrible) in 1563, but lost again to Lithuania-Poland under Stephen Báthory in 1579. Russia finally acquired the town by the first partition of Poland in 1772. In 1812 it was the scene of an engagement during the Napoleonic invasion. In World War II German forces occupied Polotsk and severe damage was suffered.

After its liberation in 1944 it was an *oblast* administrative centre until 1954. Survivals of the past are part of the ancient walls, the 12th-century cathedral of the Spaso-Yevfrosinyevski monastery and the Sofia cathedral, built in 1044–66 and reconstructed in the 18th century. Modern Polotsk has glass-fibre, timberworking, and food-processing industries. Its satellite town of Novopolotsk is one of the largest oil-refining centres of the U.S.S.R., with associated petrochemical industries, using oil piped from the Volga-Urals field.   (R. A. F.)

POLTAVA, an *oblast* of the Ukrainian Soviet Socialist Republic, U.S.S.R., formed in 1937, lies along the left bank of the middle Dnieper and is drained by the Dnieper tributaries Sula, Psel, and Vorskla. Area 11,120 sq.mi. (28,800 sq.km.). Pop. (1970 prelim.) 1,706,000. It is almost wholly within the forest-steppe zone, only the extreme south lying within the true steppe. Except on the meadows of the Dnieper floodplain, soils are everywhere fertile chernozems (black earths). The natural grass and forest vegetation has been very largely removed by plowing, and soil erosion is serious. Surviving groves of oak or pine cover only 6% of the surface.

In 1970, 60% of the population was rural, reflecting the agricultural importance of the *oblast*. The 679,000 urban dwellers lived in 12 towns and 21 urban districts, all of which are small, except Poltava (220,000) and Kremenchug (148,000). Agriculture is dominated by grains (wheat and maize [corn]), sugar beets, and sunflowers. Industry is chiefly concerned with processing agricultural produce. Natural gas and petroleum are found in several areas and oil is refined at Kremenchug. Iron ore is mined at Komsomolskoye near Kremenchug.   (R. A. F.)

POLTAVA, a town and the administrative centre of Poltava Oblast in the Ukrainian Soviet Socialist Republic, U.S.S.R., on the right bank of the Vorskla River, 180 mi. (290 km.) ESE of Kiev. Pop. (1970 prelim.) 220,000. Although the first documentary reference to the town is in 1174, archaeological evidence shows a town existed as early as the 8th–9th centuries. At first known variously as Oltava, Ltava, or P'ltava, by the 15th century the name Poltava was established. In the 17th century it was the chief centre of a Cossack regiment. In 1709 Peter the Great inflicted a crushing defeat on Charles XII of Sweden outside the town. In 1802 it was made the seat of a *guberniya* (province).

Lying in the fertile chernozem (black earth) zone, Poltava is the focus of a rich agricultural region, and its industries are mainly concerned with processing farm products: flour milling, canning, and the manufacture of footwear. A cotton-spinning mill and knitwear and clothing factories represent the textile industry. Engineering is important, with machine-building and locomotive-repair works.

Poltava is a key railway junction of the Kharkov–Kremenchug and Kiev–Donbass lines. It has pedagogic, agricultural, and agricultural engineering institutes.   (R. A. F.)

POLYAENUS (2nd century A.D.), a Macedonian living in Rome as a rhetorician and pleader, was the author of a work entitled *Strategica* (or *Strategemata*), which he dedicated to the emperors Marcus Aurelius and Lucius Verus on the outbreak of the Parthian War (162–165). This work, still extant, is a historical collection of stratagems and maxims of strategy written in Greek and strung together in the form of anecdotes; it includes also examples of wisdom, courage, and cunning from civil and political life. Comprising eight books (parts of the sixth and seventh are lost) it originally contained 900 anecdotes, of which 833 are extant. Despite its many errors of judgment and fact, its contents have some historical value. Evidently highly esteemed by the Roman emperors, it was handed down by them as a sort of heirloom, and passed to Constantinople, being diligently studied by Leo VI who himself wrote a work on tactics. It was also used by Stobaeus and in the Suda lexicon.

See for the text, E. Wölfflin and I. Melber (eds.) in the Teubner series, 2nd ed. (1887); Eng. trans. by R. Shepherd (1793).

POLYANDRY, the system under which a woman is married to several men at the same time (Gr. *polys*, "many," and *aner*, *andros*, "man"). Polyandrous institutions include cases in which (1) children recognize more than one man as having the status of

true father; (2) a woman bears legitimate children to several different fathers in succession; (3) a legitimately married woman regularly cohabits with several men, none of whom rate as father to her children; and (4) a single legitimate husband allows other men sexual access to his wife. It is debatable how far any of these varieties may properly be described as polyandrous marriage.

Type 1 occurs in Ceylon, parts of India, and Tibet; the fathers in question are usually, but not always, full brothers (in the latter case called adelphic or fraternal polyandry). An unusual version was reported from the Lele of the former Belgian Congo, where certain women are regarded as common wife of all men in the village. The child of such a woman is a "child of the village" and has a special exalted status. Type 2 is strictly polyandrous only if the successive fathers simultaneously have the status of husband, as seems to be the case among the Toda (*q.v.*) of south India and among certain peoples of northern Nigeria. Such cases may be hard to distinguish from those in which each child is born of a different marriage separated from the last by a divorce. The classic example of type 3 is that of the Nayar (*q.v.*) of south India. Formerly every Nayar girl, before attaining puberty, went through a form of marriage with one husband designated by astrology. After three days the marriage was dissolved and the husband returned to his home. The wife then took visiting mates who had a recognized status but were not regarded as the legal fathers of her children. If she had several such mates at one time they cohabited with her but did not reside with her. In this matrilineal society the initial marriage ceremony serves to make a woman's children legitimate, but these children belong to the matrilineage (*taravad*) of the mother; the social status of father is repudiated altogether.

Polyandry of type 4 includes wife lending, which may be simply an expression of hospitality and which serves a purpose among families liable to be separated over long periods, as among the Australian Aboriginals and the Eskimo. Type 4 also includes cicisbeism (male concubinage): the woman has only one legal husband and her children have only one legal father, but her other sexual partners have a recognized and respectable status. Institutions of this kind have occurred sporadically thoughout history: Caesar is a witness for the ancient Britons; Herman Melville for the Marquesas islanders; about 1716 it was fashionable at the court of Vienna. The distinction between cicisbeism, slavery, and prostitution is not always easy to draw (*see* CONCUBINAGE; PROSTITUTION).

Why some societies should approve of polyandry and others not has not been satisfactorily explained. Some polyandrous peoples are said to have more men than women and their polyandry has sometimes been directly attributed to this fact, but the evidence on this point is unconvincing. Tibetan polyandry is alleged to check the increase of population in regions from which emigration is difficult, but since most adult Tibetan women bear children this can hardly be the case. The view that polyandry is designed to prevent the dispersal of family property has greater plausibility for some cases. Personal relations within polyandrous families are often markedly free from jealousy. The polyandry of the Nayar is linked historically not only with their matrilineal ideology but also with their military organization, which prevented the men from living the ordinary life of a husband and father of a family. Polyandry may coexist with monogamy and polygyny (*q.v.*).

See also MARRIAGE, PRIMITIVE: GROUP MARRIAGE.

BIBLIOGRAPHY.—W. H. R. Rivers, *The Todas* (1906); E. R. Leach, "Polyandry, Inheritance and the Definition of Marriage," *Man,* vol. 55 (1955); Mary Trew, "A Form of Polyandry Among the Lele of the Kasai," *Africa,* vol. 21 (1951); M. G. Smith, "Secondary Marriage in Northern Nigeria," *Africa,* vol. 23 (1953); E. Kathleen Gough, "Changing Kinship Usages . . . Among the Nayars of Malabar," *J. Roy. Anthrop. Inst.,* vol 82 (1952); H. T. Fischer, "Polyandry," *Int. Arch. Ethnogr.,* vol. 46 (1952); H.R.H. Prince Peter of Greece, *A Study of Polyandry* (1963); S. J. Tambiah, "Polyandry in Ceylon" in C. von Fürer-Haimendorf, ed., *Caste and Kin in Nepal, India and Ceylon* (1966).
                                                              (E. R. L.)

POLYBIUS (*c.* 200–after 118 B.C.), the Greek historian of 3rd- and 2nd-century Rome, was born at Megalopolis in Arcadia; his father Lycortas was a distinguished Achaean statesman. The dates of his birth and death have to be inferred. His reference to measurements along the Via Domitia in Narbonese Gaul (iii, 39,

8) suggests that he was still alive in 118, when this road was constructed; if he died from a fall from his horse at the age of 82, as stated in the pseudo-Lucian's *Macrobii*, he was probably born about 200 B.C. This would fit Plutarch's description of him (in his *Philopoemen*) as a boy when he carried Philopoemen's ashes to burial in 182, and also the fact that when appointed ambassador to Egypt in 180 he was under the legal age, which was probably 30 (xxiv, 6, 5; xxix, 24, 6).

Polybius received the upbringing appropriate for a son of rich landowners. His youthful biography of Philopoemen reflected his admiration for the great Achaean leader; and an interest in military matters found expression in his lost book on *Tactics* (ix, 20, 4). He enjoyed riding and hunting, but his knowledge of literature was rather specialized (apart from the historians) and his acquaintance with philosophy superficial. Between 180, when the Egyptian embassy was canceled because of Ptolemy V's sudden death, and 170/169, when he was hipparch in the Achaean confederation, nothing is known of his career. But he then became involved in critical events. Encumbered by their war with Perseus of Macedonia, the Romans were watching for disloyalty in the Greek states. Although Polybius declared for open support of Rome and was sent with the cavalry to the consul Q. Marcius, Achaean help was rejected (xxviii, 12–13). After Perseus' defeat at Pydna (168 B.C.) Polybius was one of 1,000 eminent Achaeans who were deported to Rome at the instigation of the pro-Roman Callicrates, and detained in Italy without trial.

At Rome Polybius had the good fortune to attract the friendship of L. Aemilius Paulus' two sons Q. Fabius Maximus Aemilianus and P. Cornelius Scipio Aemilianus; he became the latter's mentor and through his family's influence was allowed to remain in Rome when the other detainees were distributed into custody throughout Italy (xxxi, 23, 5). It is probable that Polybius accompanied Scipio to Spain in 151, went with him to Africa (where he saw the Numidian king Masinissa) and crossed the Alps in Hannibal's footsteps on his way back to Italy (iii, 48, 12). In 150, through Scipio's influence and Cato's acquiescence, the 300 surviving internees were allowed to return home (xxxv, 6). Shortly afterward Polybius joined Scipio at Carthage and was present at its siege and destruction in 146; and it is likely that he then undertook a voyage of exploration in the Atlantic as related in Pliny's *Naturalis historia*. Meanwhile hostilities had broken out between Achaea and Rome, and Polybius was in Corinth shortly after its destruction (146). He devoted himself to securing as favourable a settlement as possible for his countrymen, and to re-establishing order (xxxix, 5); and, as the geographer Pausanias states, Achaean gratitude found expression in the erection of statues in his honour at Tegea, Pallantium, Mantinea, Lycosura—where the inscription declared that "Greece would never have come to grief, had she obeyed Polybius in all things, and having come to grief, she found succour through him alone"—and Megalopolis, where it was recorded that "he had roamed over all the earth and sea, had been the ally of the Romans, and had quenched their wrath against Greece." The inscribed base of a statue erected to him by Elis was discovered at Olympia in 1877; and in 1880 a relief showing Polybius himself in idealized form was found at Clitor (reproduced in F. W. Walbank, *Commentary*, frontispiece; see *bibliography*), and above it a couplet recording that the city raised this

POLYBIUS, RELIEF FOUND AT CLITOR IN 1880

most beautiful statue to Polybius, son of Lycortas, in recognition of his noble deeds. Of Polybius' life after 146 little is known. At some date he visited Alexandria and Sardis (xxi, 38, 7). He is known to have discussed political problems with Scipio and Panaetius of Rhodes. He wrote a history of the Numantine War, evidently after 133 B.C., and also a treatise on the habitability of the equatorial region; but when he composed the latter is unknown.

Scope of the History.—The history on which his reputation rests consisted of 40 books, the last being indices. Books i–v are extant. For the rest there are excerpts in the collection of passages from Greek historians assembled for Constantine Porphyrogenitus in the 10th century, rediscovered and published by various editors from the 16th to the 19th centuries; excerpts from books i–xvi and xviii, first published at Basel in 1549; and citations and extracts in numerous authors writing between the 1st and 6th centuries A.D., and from the Suda lexicon and that of Stephanus of Byzantium.

Polybius' original purpose was to narrate the history of the 53 years (220–168 B.C.)—from Hannibal's Spanish campaign to the battle of Pydna—during which Rome had made itself master of the world. Books i–ii form an introduction covering Roman history from the crossing into Sicily against the Carthaginians in 264 and including events in various other parts of the world (especially Achaea) between 264 and 220. In book iii, 4, Polybius sketches a modified plan, proposing to add an account of how the Romans exercised their supremacy down to the destruction of Carthage in 146.

These events of 168–146 were related in books xxx–xxxix. Probably Polybius conceived his revision after 146, having by this date completed his narrative down to the end of the Second Punic War. At least books i–vi seem to have been published by about 150; there is no information as to when the rest of the work, including the revised plan in book iii, appeared.

Conception of History.—"All historians," according to Polybius (i, 1, 2), "have insisted that the soundest education and training for political activity is the study of history, and that the surest and indeed the only way to learn how to bear bravely the vicissitudes of fortune is to recall the disasters of others." Practical experience and fortitude in facing calamity are the rewards of studying history, and are stressed repeatedly throughout the work. History is essentially didactic. Pleasure is not to be wholly excluded; but the scale comes down sharply on the side of profit. To be really profitable history must deal with political and military matters; and this is *pragmatike historia,* in contrast to other sorts of history (ix, 1–2)—genealogies and mythical stories, appealing to the casual reader, and accounts of colonies, foundations of cities and ties of kindred, which attract the man with antiquarian interests. Its nature is austere, though it may include contemporary developments in art and science, for instance the fire-signaling perfected by Polybius himself (x, 47). It stands in contrast to the sensationalism of many of his predecessors, who confuse history with tragedy. His remarks on Phylarchus are characteristic (ii, 56, 7 ff.): "In his anxiety to excite his readers' pity and secure their sympathy for what he is describing, he introduces women clinging to altars, their hair dishevelled and their breasts uncovered, and crowds of both sexes together with children and aged parents weeping and lamenting as they are led away to slavery. . . . A historian should not try to astonish his readers by such sensationalism, nor, like the tragic poets, seek after men's probable utterances and enumerate all the possible consequences of the events under consideration, but simply record what really happened and was said, however commonplace. For the object of history is the very opposite of that of tragedy. The tragic writer seeks by the most plausible language to thrill and charm the audience temporarily, the historian by real facts and real speeches to instruct and convince serious students for all time. There it is the probable that counts, even though it be false, the object being to beguile the spectator; here it is the truth, the object being to benefit the student."

This attack on Phylarchus is not isolated. Similar faults are castigated in other historians guilty of sensationalism (*cf.* ii, 16, 13–15; iii, 48, 8; vii, 7, 1–2; xv, 34, 1–36). Nor are these their only weaknesses. Many historians are prone to exaggeration—and that for a special reason. As writers of monographs whose subjects are simple and monotonous, they are driven "to magnify small matters, to touch up and elaborate brief statements and to transform incidents of no importance into momentous events and actions" (xxix, 12, 3). In contrast Polybius stresses the universal character of his own theme, which is to narrate "how and thanks to what kind of constitution the Romans in under 53 years have subjected nearly the whole inhabited world to their sole government—a thing unique in history" (i, 1, 5). Apart from a general preference for a comprehensive view of history, Polybius had a particular reason for adopting it at that point. "Hitherto the affairs of the world had been as it were dispersed . . . ; since this date (220 B.C.) history has formed an organic whole, and the affairs of Italy and Africa have been interlinked with those of Greece and Asia, all tending towards one end" (i, 3, 3–4). Indeed, only universal history is capable of adequately treating Rome's rise to world power—the historian's synoptic view matches the organic character of history itself: "What gives my work its peculiar quality, and is nowadays most remarkable, is this. Tyche (Fortune) having guided almost all the world's affairs in one direction and having inclined them to one and the same goal, so the historian must bring under one conspectus for his readers the operations by which she has accomplished her general purpose. For it was chiefly this consideration, coupled with the fact that none of my contemporaries has attempted a general history, which incited and encouraged me to undertake my task" (i, 4, 1–2).

The role here allotted to Tyche is somewhat unusual. For clearly the value of history as a source of practical lessons is diminished if cause and effect are at the mercy of an incalculable and capricious power. Usually, although Polybius uses Tyche to cover a variety of phenomena ranging from pure chance to something very like a purposeful providence, much of the apparent inconsistency springs from his use of purely verbal elaboration or the careless adoption of current Hellenistic terminology, which habitually made Tyche a goddess. Here, however, Tyche seems to be a real directive power, which raised Rome to world dominion —because Rome deserved it. Normally Polybius lays great emphasis on causality, and his distinction (iii, 6) between the causes of an event (*aitiai*) and its immediate origins (*archai*) is useful up to a point, though it is more mechanical than that of Thucydides, and allows nothing for the dialectical character of real historical situations. An important place in Polybius' work is occupied by his study of the Roman constitution and army and the early history of the city in book vi. His analysis of the mixed constitution, which had enabled Rome to avoid the cycle of change and deterioration to which simple constitutional forms were liable, is full of problems, but it has exercised widespread influence from Cicero's *De republica* down to Machiavelli and Montesquieu.

Sources of Information.—Polybius defines the historian's task as the study and collation of documents, acquaintance with relevant geographical features and, finally, political experience (xii, 25e); of these the last two are the most essential. Polybius practised what he preached; he possessed good political and military experience and he traveled widely throughout the Mediterranean and beyond; as he explains, "I sustained the perils of journeys through Africa, Spain and Gaul and of voyages on the sea adjoining these lands on the outside, in order to correct the errors of my predecessors and make known those parts of the world also to the Greeks" (iii, 59, 7). He did not neglect written sources, however; indeed for his introductory books (i–ii), covering the period from 264 to 220, they were essential. His discussion of Aratus and Phylarchus, his sources for Greece, and of Fabius Pictor and Philinus, those for the First Punic War (i, 14–15; ii, 56, 2; iii, 26, 3–4), indicates his critical approach. For the main part of his history, from 220 onward, he consulted many writers, Greek and Roman; but following precedent he rarely names them. An exception is Zeno of Rhodes, whom he criticizes harshly (xvi, 14–19).

He had access to private sources, for instance Scipio Africanus' letter to Philip V of Macedonia, describing the capture in Spain in 209 B.C. of New Carthage (x, 9, 3) and that of Scipio Nasica to some Hellenistic king about the campaigns of the Third Mace-

donian War (xxix, 14, 3). He almost certainly consulted the Achaean record office (*cf.* xxii, 9, 10) and must have drawn on Roman records for such material as the treaty between Carthage and Philip V (vii, 9). That he had access to the Rhodian records has not been proved. His detailed figures for Hannibal's troop formations in Italy came from an inscription left by Hannibal, which he found in the temple of Juno on the Lacinian promontory (iii, 33, 18).

Polybius himself regarded oral sources as his most important, and questioning witnesses as the most vital part of a historian's task (xii, 4c, 2–5); indeed this is one reason why he chose to begin his main history at 220. Anything else would be "hearsay at one remove," a safe foundation for neither judgments nor statements (iv, 2, 3). Of the thousands whom he must have questioned few names can be isolated; but at Rome he had opportunities of meeting men from all parts, including internees, ambassadors and visitors.

His purpose was to ascertain the truth. "Truth is to history," he writes (i, 14, 6), "what eyesight is to the living creature"; and in the main Polybius achieves this standard. There are exceptions. His prejudice against Aetolia is easily detected and disallowed; and there is some rancour against Boeotia (xx, 5–7). But no serious charges can be leveled against his reliability; and he has stated his own position very frankly: "That historians should show partiality for their own country I would allow, but not that they should make statements about it that contradict the facts. There are enough errors of ignorance to which historians are liable and which a man may hardly avoid. But if we write falsely from intention—be it for country or for friends or for favour—what better are we than those who make their living by such means? . . . Readers should keep a watchful eye on this tendency, and historians themselves should be on their guard against it" (xvi, 14, 6–10).

Style and Qualities as a Historian.—Writing in the 1st century B.C. as a strict Atticist, Dionysius of Halicarnassus reckons Polybius among those who "have left behind them compositions which no one endures to read to the end"; that his successors shared this view of Polybius' style is confirmed by the failure of his works to survive except in an incomplete form. The infelicity of Polybius' Greek (which frequently reproduces the conventional phrases of the Hellenistic chancelleries familiar from contemporary inscriptions) lies in its awkward use of long and cumbersome circumlocutions, vague abstract nouns and pedantic repetitions. To the scholar his style is, however, no great obstacle; and though in his anxiety to improve his reader he moralizes and labours the obvious, the perennial interest and importance of his theme will always insure him a following among those who can enjoy a historian who is accurate, serious and sensible, understands the events of which he writes, and above all who asks the right questions.

BIBLIOGRAPHY.—*Editio princeps,* bk. i–v, by V. Opsopaeus (1530) (Latin trans. by N. Perotti, 1473); later editions include F. Hultsch, 4 vol. (1870–92); T. Büttner-Wobst, Teubner series, 5 vol. (1889–1905); and J. L. Strachan-Davidson, *Selections From Polybius* (1888). Text with Eng. trans. by W. R. Paton, Loeb series, 6 vol. (1922–27). Eng. trans. by E. S. Shuckburgh, *Histories of Polybius,* 2 vol. (1889). See also R. von Scala, *Die Studien des Polybios* (1890); O. Cuntz, *Polybios und sein Werk* (1902); J. B. Bury, *Ancient Greek Historians* (1909); C. Wunderer, *Polybios* (1927); T. R. Glover, *Cambridge Ancient History,* vol. viii (1930); E. Mioni, *Polibio* (1949); K. Ziegler in Pauly-Wissowa, *Real-Encyclopädie,* vol. xxi, col. 1440–1578 (1952); A. Mauersberger, *Lexicon Polybianum,* vol. 1 (1956); F. W. Walbank, *Historical Commentary on Polybius,* vol. 1 (1957).   (F. W. WA.)

POLYCARP, SAINT (A.D. 70/82–156/168), bishop of Smyrna in Asia Minor, who died a martyr at the age of 86, and whose importance is adequately expressed by the words of the crowd, which are preserved in the moving account of his martyrdom (*Martyrdom of Polycarp,* xii, 2): "This is the teacher of Asia, the father of the Christians, and the destroyer of our gods." Establishing the precise year of Polycarp's death is difficult and represents a famous and inveterate topic of scholarly discussion. The date suggested by the *Martyrdom of Polycarp* is 156, the year given by Eusebius 167/168 (the seventh year of Marcus Aurelius). St. Polycarp's day is Jan. 26.

Better and more reliable information is available about Polycarp than about any other person in the history of the Christian Church in the same period. The earliest mention comes from Ignatius, bishop of Antioch (*c.* A.D. 110), who on his way to Rome had visited Smyrna, and upon reaching Troas dispatched two letters to Smyrna, one of them to Polycarp personally. There is also extant an Epistle of Polycarp, actually a composition of two epistles, one of them written shortly after Ignatius' departure. Although extant Greek manuscripts give only the text of the first nine chapters of Polycarp's Epistle, missing parts can be supplied from Eusebius, who quotes from it verbatim in his *Ecclesiastical History* (iii, 36, 13–15), and from a Latin translation. Furthermore, the account of Polycarp's martyrdom, written not long after his death, is the oldest and most valuable martyrological account surviving from the ancient church (even if, in its present form, it has been subject to revisions and interpolations in later centuries). Both the Epistle of Polycarp and the *Martyrdom* are customarily counted among the writings of the Apostolic Fathers (*q.v.*).

In addition to these sources information is supplied by Irenaeus, who as a boy had seen Polycarp and speaks of him several times; and by Eusebius of Caesarea, who preserved parts not only of Polycarp's Epistle but also of the *Martyrdom* in a text more reliable than present manuscripts and who provides additional information concerning the date of his death.

Smyrna (modern Izmir, Turk.) was in Roman times an important trading centre in the province of Asia, in population second only to Ephesus. As bishop of this city, Polycarp was in a very influential position. Since he held the post for more than half a century, and since he possessed extraordinary qualities, Polycarp became the most commanding church leader in the province of Asia and beyond throughout the first half of the 2nd century. This is already evident in the letters of Ignatius, who commends his younger colleague as a pillar of true Christian belief and as an exemplary churchman and bishop with respect to virtue, commitment, and true faith. Ignatius also entrusts Polycarp with the task of sending a messenger to the church in Antioch in order to forward copies of his letters, and of writing himself to other churches which Ignatius was unable to visit.

Shortly afterward, still without any confirmation of Ignatius' death as a martyr in Rome, Polycarp answered a request from the church in Philippi for copies of Ignatius' Epistles, which Polycarp had collected. This collection is the direct basis for the only Greek manuscript that preserves the original text of six of the Ignatian Epistles. The Epistle of Ignatius to the Romans, which could not have been available to Polycarp at that time, is missing from this manuscript. The covering note which Polycarp sent along to Philippi with the epistles is preserved as a part of the extant Epistle of Polycarp (ch. xiii).

Epistle of Polycarp.—The larger part of this epistle (ch. i–xii and probably xiv) is (as P. N. Harrison has shown) a letter which Polycarp sent to the Philippians a few years or even decades later. The letter shows that Polycarp meanwhile had visited Philippi himself. One of the reasons for his writing is that he wants to give instructions concerning the case of the presbyter Valens, who, with his wife, apparently had embezzled funds (xi, 1–4). Accordingly, exhortations concerning avarice, together with admonitions to lead a virtuous life and special instructions for church officers, make up most of the content. At the same time, however, this epistle, in which Polycarp presents himself as a man of receptive rather than creative qualities of mind, is an important source for the development of tradition, doctrine, and organization of the church at this time. In the preservation and continuation of such traditions and institutions, Polycarp must have had a considerable part; thus, for later generations, he has become an important link between the apostolic age and the early Catholic Church with respect to apostolic tradition and succession.

Although Ignatius writes to Polycarp as "the bishop of the church of the Smyrnaeans," Polycarp, in the Epistle to the Philippians, seems to present himself only as one of the presbyters of that church. In Philippi also he presupposes a college of presbyters (or bishops) and deacons, rather than a monarchial episcopate as it was propagated by Ignatius. Therefore, it would seem, the constitution of the churches in Asia had not yet developed a monarchial structure, though it allowed already for the leadership of such men as Polycarp.

But even if the constitution of Polycarp's church was more primitive than that of Ignatius, his use and evaluation of the authorities of the Christian tradition is further developed than it is in Ignatius' writings or in I Clement (dating from near the end of the 1st century). In the former are sayings of Jesus drawn from the Gospels of Matthew and Luke, whereas Ignatius and I Clement still depend upon oral tradition. Polycarp also includes the oldest quotations from such books of the New Testament as Acts, I Peter and I John, along with the first quotations from such postapostolic writings as I Clement and the first references to the Epistles of Ignatius.

Of primary importance, however, is the way in which Polycarp refers to the apostle Paul. Not only does he repeatedly quote from the Pauline writings, but also he stresses the importance of the apostle's person (*cf., e.g.,* iii, 2; ix, 1). It must be remembered that in the time of Polycarp the great apostle to the gentiles had become a primary authority for the Gnostic heretics. Polycarp, following in the footsteps of Ignatius, reclaims Paul as a treasured possession of the church. Paul is referred to side by side with the other apostles and is obviously included in their number when they are compared with the prophets of the Old Testament and Christ himself as the church's primary authorities (vi, 3). It is apparently to some extent to Polycarp's credit that this disputed apostle has become a theologically respectable part of the tradition entrusted to the church.

Polycarp's obvious dependence upon written sources raises some doubts with respect to Irenaeus' statement (quoted by Eusebius) that Polycarp had personally known John and others of the original apostles of Jesus; Irenaeus may have wanted a link with the apostolic age, although he actually lived one and a half centuries later. Even if he was born in A.D. 70, it is unlikely that Polycarp could have known any of the first-generation apostles. But Irenaeus may be right in saying (in *Adversus Haereses*) that it was Polycarp's influence which prevented the heretic Marcion from settling in the province of Asia. At any rate, Polycarp's Epistle (vii, 1) contains a classical formulation of a doctrine or creed, opposing the Gnostics' denial of the reality of incarnation and crucifixion, their perversion of the sayings of the Lord, and their rejection of resurrection and judgment, a statement that Irenaeus understood to be coined against Marcion as the "first-born of the devil." Noteworthy in this context is H. von Campenhausen's attempt to interpret the Pastoral Epistles as an anti-Marcionite work of Polycarp. It seems to be clear at least that these deutero-Pauline Epistles from Asia Minor must have been written under the influence of Polycarp. With him they share the theological concern for the apostle Paul as the model church leader, the anti-Gnostic thrust, the concept of the constitution and tradition of the church, and even such details as specific lists of virtues and peculiarities of literary style.

The last information about Polycarp's life that comes to us through Irenaeus pictures very persuasively his qualities of leadership and the high estimation in which he was held outside his own diocese. For years a controversy about the date of the Easter festival had vexed the church and threatened to result in a schism between Asia and Rome. Polycarp, already at the advanced age of 80, undertook a journey to Rome to settle this problem with the Roman bishop Anicetus. Although they could not reach an agreement, they did not break off communion with each other, and as a mark of special honour Anicetus (according to Irenaeus) allowed Polycarp to celebrate the Eucharist in his church.

BIBLIOGRAPHY.—P. N. Harrison, *Polycarp's Two Epistles to the Philippians* (1936); H. von Campenhausen, "Polykarp von Smyrna und die Pastoralbriefe" in *Aus der Frühzeit des Christentums*, pp. 197–252 (1963); C. J. Cadoux, *Ancient Smyrna*, pp. 315–366 (1938); P. T. Camelot in *Sources Chrétiennes*, vol. x, 2nd ed. (1951); J. B. Lightfoot, *Apostolic Fathers*, vol. ii, 3 (1889); J. A. Kleist in *The Ancient Christian Writers*, vol. vi (1948); J. A. Fischer in *Die Apostolischen Väter* (1956); H. Koester, *Synoptische Ueberlieferung bei den Apostolischen Vätern*, pp. 112–123 (1957); N. Bonwetsch in *New Schaff-Herzog Encyclopedia of Religious Knowledge*, vol. ix (1911); P. Meinhold in Pauly-Wissowa, *Real-Encyclopädie der classischen Altertumswissenschaft*, vol. 42 (1953); A. Vööbus in *Twentieth*

Century Encyclopedia of Religious Knowledge, vol. ii (1955). On the discussion about his martyrdom: C. H. Turner, "The Day and Year of St. Polycarp's Martyrdom," *Studia biblica et ecclesiastica,* 2, pp. 105–155 (1890); E. Schwartz, *De Pionio et Polycarpo* (1905); H. Grégoire and P. Orgels in *Analecta Bollandiana,* 69, pp. 1–38 (1951), and H. I. Marrou, *ibid.,* 71, pp. 5–20 (1953); H. von Campenhausen, "Bearbeitungen und Interpolationen des Polykarpmartyriums" in *Aus der Frühzeit des Christentums,* pp. 253–301 (1963).   (H. H. Ko.)

POLYCLITUS (POLYCLEITUS), the name of two Greek sculptors of the school of Argos; the first belonging to the 5th century B.C., the second to the earlier part of the 4th.

The elder, better-known Polyclitus (fl. 5th century B.C.) was a contemporary of Phidias and in the opinion of the Greeks his equal. Whether he was a pupil of Ageladas is disputed; at least he carried on the Argive tradition. He made a figure of an Amazon for Ephesus which was regarded by later Greek writers as superior to the Amazon of Phidias made at the same time. His colossal Hera of gold and ivory which stood in the temple near Argos was considered as worthy to rank with the Zeus of Phidias. Balance, rhythm, and the minute perfection of bodily form, which were the great merits of this sculptor, appealed especially to the Greeks of the 5th century. Polyclitus worked mainly in bronze.

In regard to his chronology there are data in a papyrus published by B. P. Grenfell and A. S. Hunt containing lists of athletic victors. From this it appears that he made a statue of Cyniscus, a victorious athlete (464 or 460 B.C.), of Pythocles (452), and of Aristion (452). He thus can scarcely have been born as late as 480 B.C. His statue of Hera is dated by Pliny to 420 B.C. His artistic activity must therefore have been long and prolific. His two great statues, ideal or heroic types rather than portraits, are the Diadumenus ("Man Tying on a Fillet") and the Doryphorus ("Spearbearer"), copies of both of which survive. The Doryphorus was known as "The Canon," because it embodied the correct proportions of ideal male form. The most complete copy is from Herculaneum. There are Roman copies in marble of the Diadumenus in London and New York, giving a good basic impression but only a general idea of the finish of Polyclitus' work in bronze. At Delos, French excavators discovered a Diadumenus of more pleasing type and greater finish, a Hellenistic transformation of the Polyclitan type into a youthful Apollo. Among the bases of statues found at Olympia were three signed by Polyclitus, still bearing on their surface the marks of attachment of the feet of the statues. This gives us their pose, and critics such as A. Furtwängler identified several extant statues as copies of figures of boy athletes victorious at Olympia set up by Polyclitus. Among these the Westmacott athlete in the British Museum is probably a copy of the "Cyniscus."

The Amazon of Polyclitus survives in many copies, among the best being the Lansdowne statue in the Metropolitan Museum of Art, New York. The masterpiece of Polyclitus, his Hera in gold and ivory, has disappeared, but coins of Argos give us the general type. A marble head in the British Museum gives a Greco-Roman version of this type, treated in general terms.

The want of variety in the works of Polyclitus was brought as a reproach against him by certain ancient critics. Varro says that his statues were square and almost of one pattern. Excepting the statue of Hera, the work of his later years, he produced scarcely any notable statue of a deity. His field was narrowly limited; but in that field he was unsurpassed.

The younger Polyclitus (fl. 4th century B.C.) was of the same family as the elder. Sculptures by him have been difficult to identify among existing copies. Some bases bearing the name, however, are inscribed in characters of the 4th century, when the elder sculptor cannot have been alive. He was also an architect of note. His best-known buildings are the tholos (in ruins) and the theatre (now restored) of Epidaurus (360–330 B.C.).

BIBLIOGRAPHY.—G. M. A. Richter, *The Sculpture and Sculptors of the Greeks,* 246 ff. (1950); G. Lippold, *Handbuch der Archäologie,* iii, 1, 162 ff. (1950); R. B. Bandinelli, *Policleto* (1938).   (C. C. V.)

POLYCRATES, tyrant of Samos, in the Aegean Sea, *c.* 535–522 B.C., took advantage of a festival of Hera which was being celebrated outside the walls to make himself master of the city. After getting rid of his brothers Pantagnotus and Syloson, who had at first shared his power, he established a despotism, equipped a fleet of 100 ships and so became master of the Aegean basin. His numerous acts of piracy made him notorious throughout Greece; but his real aim was the control of the archipelago and the mainland towns of Ionia. He maintained an alliance with Lygdamis of Naxos and dedicated to Apollo of Delos the neighbouring island of Rheneia (Rinía). He also defeated a coalition of Miletus and Lesbos. He made an alliance with Ahmose (Amasis) II, king of Egypt, but when the Persians advanced against Egypt in 525 he abandoned his ally and sent a squadron of 40 ships to join the Persian fleet. He took the opportunity to send his main political opponents with this squadron, but they deserted the Persians and attempted to dislodge Polycrates. After a defeat by sea, he repelled an assault upon the walls, and subsequently withstood a siege by a joint force of Spartans and Corinthians assembled to aid the rebels. He maintained his ascendancy until about 522, when Oroetes, the Persian governor of Sardis, lured him to the mainland and put him to death.

Besides the political and commercial preeminence which he conferred upon Samos, Polycrates was also a patron of letters; the poet Anacreon lived at his court.   (R. ME.)

POLYGLOT BIBLES are Bibles that contain side-by-side versions of the same text in several languages (Gr. *polys,* "many," *glotta,* "tongue"). The most important polyglots are editions in which the Hebrew and Greek originals are exhibited along with the great historical versions. The famous *Hexapla* of Origen (*q.v.*), in which the Old Testament Scriptures were written in parallel columns, probably suggested the later polyglots, but though it gives six texts it is itself in only two languages.

In the 16th and 17th centuries polyglots became a favourite means of advancing the knowledge of Eastern languages as well as the study of Scripture. The most celebrated of these is the Complutensian Polyglot (1522), produced under the inspiration of Cardinal Francisco Jiménez de Cisneros and published in six volumes at Alcalá (Roman *Complutum*) in Spain; it had the Old Testament in Hebrew, Greek, and Latin, the New in Greek and Latin. The Antwerp Polyglot (eight volumes, 1569–72), published by Christophe Plantin (*q.v.*) and edited by Benito Arias Montano, added the Syriac New Testament, with a Latin translation. The Paris Polyglot (ten volumes, 1629–45) added the Arabic, with Latin translation, and the so-called Samaritan Pentateuch, a Hebrew version that differs slightly from the standard Masoretic text and that had first become known in Europe only a few years earlier. The London Polyglot (six volumes, 1657), edited by Brian Walton, added other versions as well as several Targums and readings from the Codex Alexandrinus, which had reached England in 1627.

POLYGNOTUS (*c.* 500–440 B.C.), Greek painter, son of Aglaophon, was a native of Thasos who soon moved to the Greek mainland and eventually acquired Athenian citizenship. His fame was based on large, monumental wall paintings in the severe style, admired by posterity but now totally lost. The following titles are mentioned by ancient writers: (1) Plataeae, entrance porch of the temple of Athena Areia: "Ulysses after the punishment of the suitors"; (2) Athens, Painted Hall ("Poikile"): "The taking of Ilium"; (3) Athens, Temple of the Dioscuri ("Anakeion"):

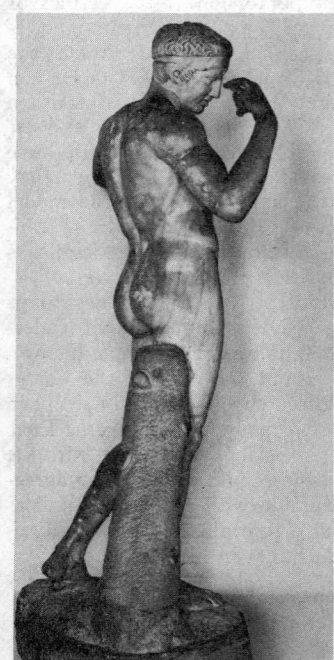

DIADUMENUS ("MAN TYING ON A FILLET") BY POLYCLITUS, GRECO-ROMAN COPY IN MARBLE FOUND IN VAUCLUSE, FRANCE, IN 1862. IN THE BRITISH MUSEUM

"Wedding of the daughters of Leucippus"; (4) Athens, Acropolis ("Pinacotheca"): "Achilles in Scyrus"; (5) Same as no. 4: "Nausicaa"; (6) Delphi, Hall ("Lesche") of the Cnidians: "Departure of the Greeks from Ilium"; and (7) Same as no. 6: "Ulysses visiting Hades."

Pausanias left an account of the last two paintings (Paus. x, 25-31) from which, with occasional support of other sources, the following characteristics of Polygnotus' style are deduced. Figures approximating life-size were freely distributed within the composition, near the lower border and higher. In Greek painting of the first half of the 5th century B.C. this method represents an innovation, though precedents existed elsewhere, notably in Assyrian art. It constitutes a break with the ancient Greek principle of arranging figures on a single base line; Polygnotus replaced the horizontal base lines by irregular, mounting or descending terrain lines. Comparable representations can be found in contemporary vase paintings, perhaps under his influence. There was no unifying perspective in the modern sense: the individual figure remained the focus of interest even when several figures were grouped together. Stateliness was paired with subtlety of detail: delicate headdresses of women, transparent garments, mouths with parted lips uncovering the teeth. Sharp foreshortenings were not lacking. Coloration consisted of four basic colours: black, white, red and ochre. None of the last named characteristics can be claimed for Polygnotus alone: he was merely the outstanding representative of the severe style in Greek monumental painting. The "ethos" which later critics, including Aristotle, valued so highly in his work indicates a concept of character as an innate disposition, governing the actions and manifest in a person's outward bearing.   (O. J. Bl.)

POLYGON, in classical geometry, a simply connected plane region bounded by straight line (q.v.) segments (its sides) which meet in corners of the region (its vertices). In modern mathematics the word usually denotes only the boundary (sides and vertices); the region is called a polygonal region. A region is called simply connected if any two points within it can be joined by a continuous path lying wholly within it, and if any such path can be continuously deformed into any other that joins the same two points, remaining within the region throughout (see Topology, General).

If there are n vertices the polygon is called an n-gon; when $n = 3, 4, 5, 6, \ldots$ it is called a triangle, a quadrangle, a pentagon, a hexagon, . . . , accordingly. The vertices can be written in order, say $A_1 A_2 \ldots A_n$, so that the n sides are $A_i A_{i+1}$ (for $i = 1, \ldots, n-1$) and $A_n A_1$. If a sense or orientation is attached to any segment XY by regarding it as described from X to Y (so that YX denotes the same segment with the opposite orientation), this specification of the sides, the end of each being the beginning of the next, gives a continuous description of the polygon. This is then said to be oriented, the orientation being positive or negative according to the position of the region to left or to right of the boundary as it is described; i.e., according to whether travel around it is counterclockwise or clockwise. The orientation does not depend on the vertex (in this case A_1) chosen to begin and end the description. If no sense is attached to the sides the polygon is unoriented. Thus ABC, BCA, CAB denote the same oriented triangle, with sides BC, CA, AB, while ACB, CBA, BAC denote the same triangle oppositely oriented, and all denote the same unoriented triangle.

More generally, if $A_1, \ldots, A_n$ are any n points, the closed path consisting of the segments $A_i A_{i+1}$ $(i = 1, \ldots, n-1)$ and $A_n A_1$ is called a polygon (oriented if the segments are so) even if it crosses itself or is not in one plane. In the latter case it is called a skew polygon as opposed to a plane polygon. It is called simple if it is in fact the boundary of a plane region, and convex if the region is so (which means that the line segment joining any two points of the region lies wholly within it). If one side be omitted, say $A_n A_1$, the others form a continuous path (oriented or not) joining A_1 to A_n, which is called a polygonal line.

Angles of a Plane Polygon.—Generalizing the familiar idea of an internal angle of a polygonal region and its supplement, the external angle, the following definitions are made for any oriented plane polygon (the first two definitions agreeing with the elementary notions if the polygon is simple and positively oriented):

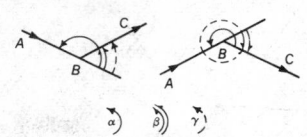

FIG. 1.—POLYGONAL ANGLES

if AB, BC are any two consecutive sides (fig. 1), the internal angle α at B is the least positive angle from the direction BC to the direction BA; the external angle β is the absolutely least angle (positive or negative) from the direction AB to the direction BC; and the peripheral angle γ is the least positive angle from the direction AB to the direction BC. These (measured in radians) satisfy $\alpha + \beta = \pi$ in all cases, and $\gamma = \beta$ or $\gamma = \beta + 2\pi$ according as α is less or greater than π (see Radian Measure). If α', β', γ' are the corresponding angles when the orientation is reversed, then $\alpha' = 2\pi - \alpha$, $\beta' = -\beta$, $\gamma' = 2\pi - \gamma$. The algebraic sums of these angles over all the vertices of an n-gon are $\Sigma\alpha = (n - 2p)\pi$, $\Sigma\beta = 2p\pi$, $\Sigma\gamma = 2q\pi$, where p,q are integers; p can have any value absolutely less than $\frac{n}{2}$ (positive, negative, or zero) and q any value from 1 to $n - 1$. If the polygon is simple, $p = \pm 1$; and a necessary and sufficient condition for it to be convex and positively oriented is that $p = q = 1$.

Classification of Plane Polygons.—If no two nonconsecutive sides of a plane polygon intersect it is "simple," and if in addition the external angles all have the same sign it is "convex." The specification of the intersections (if any) of nonconsecutive sides and of the changes of sign of the external angle in going around the polygon defines for each n a finite number of types of plane n-gon such that two polygons are of the same type if and only if one can be continuously deformed into the other, remaining in the plane, without any vertex crossing over a side and without two consecutive sides becoming collinear during the process. Omitting intermediate cases in which some side contains a vertex other than its end points, there are 1, 3, 11, 70, . . . types of unoriented triangle, quadrangle, pentagon, hexagon, . . . respectively, most of which correspond to two oriented types. These types are

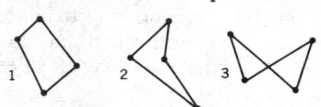

FIG. 2.—TYPES OF QUADRANGLE

partly characterized by the numbers p,q above; thus the three types in fig. 2 (the first two positively oriented) have respectively $p = q = 1$; $p = 1$, $q = 2$; $p = 0$, $q = 2$. On the other hand these numbers do not provide a complete basis for the classification, as in fig. 3. They have the same values for types 3 and 4, 6 and 7, and 8, 10, and 11.

The Encircling Coefficient.—If O is any point in the plane of an oriented polygon (but not in any of its sides) the angle subtended at O by a side AB is defined as the absolutely least angle (positive or negative) from the direction OA to the direction OB. The algebraic sum of the angles subtended at O by all the sides of an oriented n-gon is of the form $2k\pi$, where k is an integer (positive or negative) absolutely less than $\frac{n}{2}$, which is called the encircling coefficient of the polygon at O. In a sense k is the number of times that O is encircled counterclockwise in describing the polygon.

The sides of any plane polygon divide the whole plane into a number of nonoverlapping polygonal regions and one infinite external region. The integer k has the same value at all points of any one such nonoverlapping region, and is zero at any point of the external region. If the polygon is simple, $k = \pm 1$ (according to the orientation) at any point within it.

Area of a Polygon.—It is convenient to regard the area of the region bounded by) an oriented simple plane polygon as being positive or negative according to the orientation of the polygon. With this convention let O be any point in the plane; each oriented side of the polygon, say AB, determines with O an oriented triangle OAB; and the algebraic sum of the areas of the n oriented triangles thus determined by all the sides of an oriented n-gon can be shown to be independent of O; this sum is in fact the area of the n-gon. If O is chosen at a vertex of the n-gon, two of these triangles vanish, and there is a dissection of the n-gon into $n - 2$

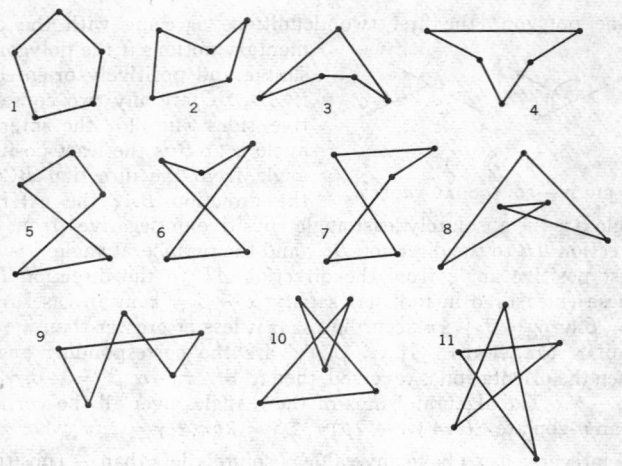

FIG. 3.—TYPES OF PENTAGON

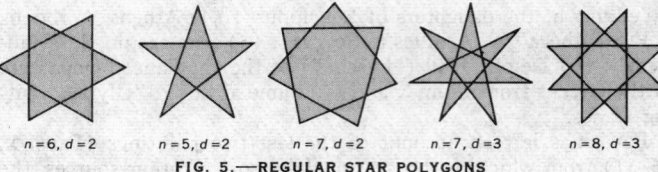

n = 6, d = 2   n = 5, d = 2   n = 7, d = 2   n = 7, d = 3   n = 8, d = 3

FIG. 5.—REGULAR STAR POLYGONS

triangles by means of $n - 3$ diagonals; this is the classical method of finding the area.

If the plane n-gon is not simple, it can still be proved that the algebraic sum of the areas of these n oriented triangles is independent of O; and this is accepted by definition as the area of the polygon. It is in fact the sum of the areas of the polygonal regions into which the sides of the polygon divide the plane, each multiplied by the corresponding encircling coefficient.

If O is the origin of a cartesian coordinate system, and A_i has coordinates (x_i, y_i) $(i = 1, \ldots, n)$, this leads to the expression $\frac{1}{2}(x_1y_2 - x_2y_1 + x_2y_3 - x_3y_2 + \ldots + x_{n-1}y_n - x_ny_{n-1} + x_ny_1 - x_1y_n)$ for the area of the oriented n-gon $A_1 \ldots A_n$.

Polygonal Approximation.—Study of polygons is valuable to mathematics in general largely because polygonal regions and polygonal lines can be used to achieve as close an approximation as desired to most ordinary plane regions and curved lines. People in ancient times, for instance, obtained very good approximate values for π by comparing a circle (q.v.) with inscribed and circumscribed regular polygons that have a large number of sides

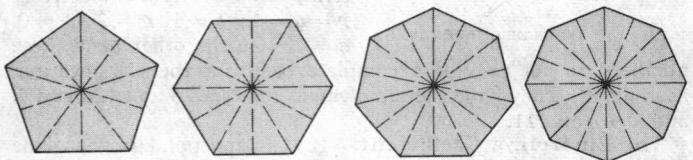

FIG. 4.—REGULAR CONVEX POLYGONS

(*see* LIMIT).

A polygonal approximation to a closed curve is a polygon with vertices that are all on the curve in the same order as in the polygon, so that if AB, BC are consecutive sides of the polygon, then B and no other vertex is in one arc AC of the curve. The shorter the longest side of the polygon, and the greater consequently the number of its vertices, the closer the approximation. An arc of a curve is similarly approximated by a polygonal line joining its end points. A plane region is often approximated by superimposing on the plane a mesh of squares (like ordinary graph paper) and by constructing a polygonal region as the aggregate of all squares of the mesh that are wholly inside the given region. Here, the finer the mesh the closer the approximation.

In wide classes of cases as close an approximate value as may be required can be obtained for the length of a curve or arc, or for the area of a plane region, by considering a sufficiently close polygonal approximation—often indeed an exact value. For instance, for a given curve, if it can be shown, as it often can, (1) that the perimeter (sum of the lengths of the sides) of every polygonal approximation is less than some fixed length s, but (2) that by taking the approximation close enough, in the sense explained above, the perimeter can be made to differ from s by as little as may be required, then it is justifiable to accept s as the length of the curve. Similar considerations apply to area. The technique

of this process, and the determination of the cases to which it is applicable, belong to integral calculus (*see* CALCULUS, DIFFERENTIAL AND INTEGRAL).

Regular Polygons.—A polygon is called regular if all its sides are equal in length and all its internal angles are equal (when, of course, all its external angles are likewise equal). All the vertices lie on one circle, the circumcircle, and all the sides touch another, the incircle. These have the same centre, called the centre of the polygon. A regular triangle is called equilateral, and a regular quadrangle is a square; fig. 4 shows the next four convex cases.

Besides these convex polygons there are (for values of n greater than 4) nonsimple regular n-gons (called regular star polygons) constructed as follows: if $A_1 \ldots A_n$ is a regular convex n-gon, the sides of a new polygon are obtained by joining each vertex A_i, not to the next A_{i+1}, but to the dth following A_{i+d} (or A_{i+d-n} if $i + d$ is greater than n); where d is any integer less than $\frac{n}{2}$, and

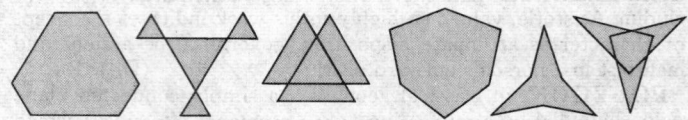

FIG. 6.—SEMIREGULAR HEXAGONS

has no common factor with n except 1. The number d is called the density of the star polygon, and is equal to its encircling coefficient at the centre; $d = 1$ of course gives the convex n-gon. (If d, n have any common factor this construction gives more than one polygon, as in the first example in fig. 5.)

Regular skew polygons are also defined; these always have an even number of vertices, lying alternately on two equal circles in parallel planes, and the projection onto any plane parallel to these is a regular plane polygon.

Symmetry.—A regular plane n-gon is made to coincide with its former position if it is either (1) rotated about its centre through an angle that is any multiple of $\frac{2\pi}{n}$, or (2) reflected in any one of n lines through the centre (axes of symmetry), each joining two points that are either vertices or midpoints of sides (fig. 4); these reflections however reverse the orientation. Both kinds of operation are called the symmetry operations of the polygon. The symmetry operations of a regular skew $2n$-gon are of four kinds: (1) rotation through angles that are all multiples of $\frac{2\pi}{n}$ about a principal axis perpendicular to the planes of the two circles containing the vertices and joining their centres; (2) rotations through the angle π about each of n axes perpendicular to this, joining the midpoints of opposite sides; (3) reflection in each of n planes, each joining the principal axis to a pair of opposite vertices; and (4) rotation about the principal axis through angles that are all odd multiples of $\frac{\pi}{n}$, combined with reflection in the plane perpendicular to this axis, which contains the midpoints of all sides. Operations of types (2) and (3) reverse the orientation.

A plane polygon is sometimes called semiregular if it has an even number of vertices and either (1) the internal angles are all equal and the vertices lie on one circle but alternate sides have two different lengths and touch two concentric circles, or (2) all sides are equal and touch one circle but the angles have two different values alternately, and alternate vertices lie on two concentric circles (fig. 6). A semiregular $2n$-gon has the same symmetry operations as a regular n-gon.

Ruler and Compass Construction.—The construction of regular polygons by (ungraduated) ruler and compass only is a classical problem; its solution for the triangle is Euclid's first proposition; he also solved it for the square and the pentagon. The problem can be proved to be equivalent to that of finding the ratio of two lengths that determine the shape of the figure, such as the side and the radius of the circumcircle, by solving one or more quadratic equations (*see* Geometry: *Greek Geometry*).

It is a remarkable result, due to C. F. Gauss, that this can be done for the regular *n*-gon if and only if the odd prime factors of *n* are all different, and all of the form $2^{2^k} + 1$, where *k* is an integer. The first five prime numbers of this form are 3, 5, 17, 257 and 65,537; and there is reason to conjecture that there are no others. *See also* Triangle; Square; Quadrilateral; Figurate Numbers; Mensuration.

Bibliography.—M. Brückner, *Vielecke und Vielflache . . .* (1900); H. G. Forder, *The Foundations of Euclidean Geometry* (1927); E. Steinitz, *Enzyklopädie der mathematischen Wissenschaften* (1922); O. Veblen and J. W. Young, *Projective Geometry,* vol. ii (1946); C. Wiener, *Über Vielecke und Vielflache* (1864); H. S. M. Coxeter, *Regular Polytopes,* 2nd ed. (1963).   (P. Du V.)

POLYGONACEAE, the buckwheat family of dicotyledonous plants of about 40 genera and 800 species, consisting chiefly of herbs, although shrubs, vines and even trees occur.

Among the important cultivated food plants in the family are buckwheat (*q.v.; Fagopyrum esculentum*) and rhubarb (*q.v.*) or pieplant (*Rheum rhaponticum*). Ornamentals include several old world species of *Polygonum* such as silver lace vine (*P. auberti*), coral vine (*Antigonon*) from Mexico and the sea-grape (*Coccoloba uvifera*), whose fleshy sepals form an edible berrylike structure.

Common weeds that belong to this family are knotweed (*q.v.*) or knotgrass (*Polygonum aviculare*), the vine, black bindweed (*Polygonum convolvulus*), and dock or sorrel (*qq.v.*) (several species of *Rumex*). In this last genus, the three inner sepals, known as valves, enlarge and surround the fruit.

To the Polygonaceae belong such wild plants as mountain sorrel (*Oxyria digyna*), smartweed and water pepper (several species of *Polygonum*), canaigre (*Rumex hymenosepalus; see* Dock), whose root is a source of tanning material and dye, and California buckwheat (*Eriogonum fasciculatum*), an important bee plant in its native range.

The stems are often swollen at the nodes (whence comes the genus name *Polygonum*, referring to the many joints or knees). The leaves are alternate, usually simple and entire, and stipules at the base of the leaves usually form a highly characteristic sheathing growth (ocrea) around the stem. The flowers, often borne in clusters, are radially symmetrical, lacking petals, and usually small. The calyx generally consists of five or six separate or united sepals. These are usually green or white, but other colours such as rose and yellow also occur. The stamens vary in number from five to nine and the achenelike fruit is one-celled, one-seeded and usually three-carpellate and three-sided. The single seed is erect and attached at the base of the fruit. The flowers, usually bisexual, are wind- or insect-pollinated (depending on the genus), or sometimes self-pollinated. The family is so distinct from its nearest relatives that it is placed in a separate order, the Polygonales.

The apparently basic type of flower has six sepals (two whorls of three), nine stamens and three united carpels: such a flower is usual in *Eriogonum*. Although examples with the flower parts in fours occur, the usual variation is a reduction in number of one or all of the parts. Five sepals and five to eight stamens are frequent in *Polygonum;* two whorls of two (2 + 2) sepals and two united carpels characterize *Oxyria*.

The family occurs primarily in the northern hemisphere. As is true in many plant families, the geographic distribution of the genera often provides interesting problems. *Polygonum* (about 200 species) is widely distributed, whereas *Rheum* is strictly Asian, and *Muehlenbeckia* (15 species) is unusual because it is limited almost entirely to the southern hemisphere. *Coccoloba*, with 125 species, is confined to the American tropics and subtropics. Several small genera (*e.g., Gilmania, Hollisteria, Mucronea*) are limited to California, while the one species of *Koenigia*, in addition to being circumboreal, is found also in the Himalayas and in Tierra del Fuego. Of the two species of *Brunnichia*, one occurs in the southeastern part of the United States, the other in west Africa.

The tribe *Eriogoneae* is strictly American and occurs almost entirely in the western portion of the United States. It is unusual in lacking the ocreae so characteristic of the family. Besides several small genera, the tribe includes *Chorizanthe* (60 species) and *Eriogonum*, nearly 200 species.   (G. J. G.)

POLYGYNY, the system under which a man is married to several women at the same time, a type of polygamy or plural marriage. Polygyny is nowhere the exclusive form of marriage, and among most peoples who permit it the large majority of men live in monogamy. It may be modified in a monogamous direction both from the social and the sexual point of view. Frequently one of the wives, generally the one first married, holds a higher position than the rest or is regarded as the principal wife. In some cases this position implies certain sexual privileges; but more often it is the custom for the husband to cohabit with wives in turn, or this is actually required of him.

Primitive Societies.—Among preliterate peoples polygyny does not seem to be practised on a large scale by the hunters and food collectors, except some Australian and Bushman tribes, nor by any incipient agriculturists. On the other hand, a considerable number of these hunting and slightly agricultural tribes—such as some of the South American Indians, the aboriginal tribes of the Malay peninsula, most of the Andaman Islanders, the Veddas of Ceylon, certain tribes in the Malay archipelago, most of the Negritos of the Philippine Islands and some at least of the central African pygmies—are represented as monogamous. Among more well-to-do hunters polygyny is more frequent, although in the majority of their tribes it is practised only occasionally; and exclusive monogamy is rare, though perhaps not unknown. Among pastoral peoples there seems to be none that can be regarded as strictly monogamous; and both among them and the higher agriculturists polygyny is undoubtedly more frequent than among the hunters and incipient agriculturists, although cases of regular monogamy are more frequent among the higher agriculturists than among the higher hunters. The cases in which polygyny is represented as general are comparatively much more numerous among African than non-African pastoral peoples and higher agriculturists. Polygyny is at its height in Africa, both in point of frequency and in number of wives. King Mutesa of Uganda and the king of Loango each are said to have had 7,000 wives.

Ancient Civilizations.—Polygyny, or a sort of concubinage hardly distinguishable from genuine polygyny, was found among most peoples of archaic civilization. In China there were, besides the legal principal wife, so-called wives "by courtesy" or lawful concubines. In Japan concubinage of the Chinese type existed as a legal institution until 1880. In ancient Egypt polygyny seems to have been permitted but to have been unusual, except in the case of kings. The Babylonian code of Hammurabi assumed that marriage should be monogamous; yet "if a man has married a wife and a sickness has seized her," he might take a second wife; and if she remained childless he might take a concubine. Among the Hebrews a man could in any circumstances have a plurality of wives, and there was no difference in the legal status of different wives, nor was there any limit to the number of wives a man might take. In Arabia Mohammed ordained that a man's legal wives should be not more than four. Polygyny has been permitted among many of the Indo-European peoples—among ancient Slavs and Teutons, the ancient Irish and the Vedic Indians—though it seems to have been as a rule confined to kings or chiefs or nobles. None of the Hindu lawbooks restricts the number of wives a man is allowed to marry; yet some preference is often shown for monogamy, and most castes object to their members having more than one wife, except for some cogent reason. On the other hand, there can be little doubt that monogamy was the only recognized form of marriage in Greece; concubinage existed in Athens, but it was well distinguished from marriage, conferring no rights on the concubine. Roman marriage was strictly monogamous; liaisons between married men and mistresses were not uncommon, but such a relation was not considered lawful concubinage.

Modern Times.—Polygyny has been found even in Christian Europe. No obstacle was put in the way of its practice by kings in countries where it had occurred in the times of paganism. In the middle of the 6th century Diarmait, king of Ireland, had two queens and two concubines. Polygyny was frequently practised by the Merovingian kings. Charlemagne had two wives and many concubines; and one of his laws seems to imply that polygyny was not unknown even among priests. In later times Philip of Hesse and Frederick William II of Prussia contracted bigamous marriages with the sanction of the Lutheran clergy. In 1650, soon after the peace of Westphalia, when the population had been greatly reduced by the Thirty Years' War, the Frankish *Kreistag* at Nürnberg passed the resolution that thenceforth every man should be allowed to marry two women. The Anabaptists as well as the Mormons once advocated polygyny with much religious fervour.

Causes.—One cause of polygyny can be an excess of marriageable women in certain age groups. But while the existence of available women makes polygyny possible, the direct cause of it is generally the man's desire to have more than one wife. There are various reasons for this desire. Among many of the simpler peoples the husband has to abstain from his wife during her pregnancy, or at least during the latter stage of it, and after childbirth until the child is weaned, which often means an abstinence lasting for a couple of years or more. Other contributing factors are the attraction of youth and beauty, the desire for many children— which is one of the principal causes of polygyny in the east—and the fact that polygyny may contribute to a man's material comfort or wealth, and thereby his social importance. But it should also be noted that the paying of a dowry, the amount of which is influenced by economic conditions, makes it possible for certain men to acquire several wives while others can acquire none at all.

See Marriage; Marriage, Primitive; Polyandry; Social Anthropology; Sororate; *see* also references under "Polygyny" in the Index.

Bibliography.—L. T. Hobhouse, G. C. Wheeler and M. Ginsberg, *The Material Culture and Social Institutions of the Simpler Peoples* (1915); Nobushige Hozumi, *Ancestor-Worship and Japanese Law* (1913); P. W. Joyce, *A Social History of Ireland*, vol. ii (1903); J. Jolly, *Recht und Sitte* (1896); L. Beauchet, *Histoire du droit privé de la République Athénienne*, vol. i (1897); T. Mommsen, *Römisches Strafrecht* (1899); E. Westermarck, *The History of Human Marriage*, vol. iii (1921); R. Briffault, *The Mothers*, reprint (1963); G. P. Murdock, *Social Structure* (1949); J. R. Christianson, "Contemporary Mormons' Attitudes Toward Polygynous Practices," *Marriage and Family Living* (May 1963).   (E. W.; X.)

POLYMERIZATION, in chemistry, was originally considered to be any process in which two or more molecules of the same substance unite to give a molecule (polymer) with the same percentage composition as the original substance (monomer), but with a molecular weight which is an integral multiple of the original molecular weight. A special case exists when the monomer and polymer are so easily interconvertible that their isolation and chemical distinction are difficult; this condition is usually considered to be association (*see* Association, Chemical).

The term "polymerization" now applies when the monomer and polymer are easily distinguished; it applies also to preparations of some polymers which do not conform to the original definition (*see* below). Polymerization is the process by which plastics, resins and rubber are synthesized.

This article is concerned with the general principles of polymerization processes, particularly with the processes that produce polymers of high molecular weight (high polymers).

Addition Polymerization.—This process occurs when monomer units simply join together to form polymers. The process usually requires a double or triple bond in the structural formula of the monomer. Although a carbon-oxygen or carbon-nitrogen multiple bond will serve (*see* Formaldehyde), most examples involve carbon-carbon double bonds, particularly olefins with $>C=CH_2$ groups (*see* Chemistry: *Organic Chemistry* for many terms used here). Some polymers contain only two or three monomer units (*see* Terpenes), some contain many, and some monomers yield more than one kind of polymer. Phosphonitrile chloride, $P \equiv NCl_2$, is an inorganic monomer yielding several addition polymers.

The polymerization of styrene (*q.v.*) illustrates addition polymerization. The monomer is a colourless, mobile liquid. On standing for several weeks at room temperature, for a few days at 100° C., or for a shorter time at higher temperatures, the liquid polymerizes, becoming first an increasingly viscous solution of polymer in monomer, and finally a clear, odourless, glassy solid. The polymer is a mixture of molecules of the formula $(C_8H_8)_n$, where n has a wide range of values and averages several thousand. When the monomer is warmed with 1% or less of an initiator such as benzoyl peroxide, C_6H_5—CO—O—O—CO—C_6H_5, a similar polymer is formed, but in minutes or hours instead of days or weeks. These processes are chain reactions, starting when styrene is activated thermally, or when the initiator decomposes, to give electrically neutral fragments of molecules, with free or unsaturated valences (free radicals with trivalent carbon atoms). Such a fragment, R —, adds easily to the double bond in the monomer

$$R- + H_2C=CH-C_6H_5 \rightarrow R-CH_2-CH(C_6H_5)-$$

forming a larger radical with the free valence now on the styrene unit. This new free radical adds to another double bond, and so on, so that many monomer units become linked together in a linear (threadlike) polymer. Thousands of steps in a single reaction chain may occur in a second, the reaction ending when two radicals interact and mutually destroy their free valences.

Similar polymerizations are industrially important both with liquids (*e.g.,* vinyl acetate, acrylic esters, acrylonitrile) and with gases under pressure (*e.g.,* ethylene, butadiene and vinyl chloride). Such polymers have a wide range of physical properties (*see* Plastics; Ethylene; Butadiene). To avoid difficulties in handling large masses of hard or viscous polymer, large-scale polymerizations are frequently carried out in emulsion or suspension in water to produce synthetic latex or beads.

Initiators which do not produce free radicals may also be employed. Some metal halides (aluminum chloride or boron trifluoride), sulfuric acid, metal alkyls (from sodium, lithium or aluminum; *see* Organometallic Compounds) and strong bases (sodamide) also cause addition polymerization of some olefins, but here the growing chains are usually ion pairs. These initiators require anhydrous conditions since the polymer ions are destroyed by water. Although styrene and butadiene are polymerized by all the initiators mentioned, the choice of initiators for most monomers is limited.

Considerable heat is evolved when high polymers are formed, and the process can become violent. The driving force in the polymerization is the conversion of the double bond in each monomer to two single bonds in the polymer. In a sense, the strain in the double bond is thus relieved. However, in the polymer, the monomer units are crowded together and restricted in their motions. These restrictions become more important at increasing temperatures, and high polymers made from larger monomers begin to revert to monomer above 200° C. Polymers from smaller monomers hold together better, but at 300°–400° C. they also break up, yielding complex mixtures and rather little monomer.

When a mixture of two monomers is subjected to polymerization, the product may contain both monomers in each polymer molecule (*i.e.,* copolymerization of two monomers yields a copolymer), or it may contain only one kind of monomer in each polymer molecule, depending on the monomer and type of initiator. Many commercial polymers are actually copolymers, a wider range of properties being possible than with single monomers.

Two polymers may have atoms joined together in the same sequence, but still have different physical properties because of different spatial relations among the atoms (*see* Stereochemistry: *The Stereochemistry of Carbon*). Lowering the temperature of polymerization for SBR synthetic rubber from 50° to about 5° C. has resulted in the improved "cold rubber." Natural rubber has been duplicated by polymerizing isoprene with specific organometallic catalysts. Similar catalysts have produced crystalline modifications of polystyrene and polypropylene which melt above 150° C., instead of softening below 100°.

Condensation Polymerization.—This is the process of making products, commonly called polymers, with the formation of a small, easily removed molecule (often water) for each step in the process. For making high polymers, the general method is to choose a simple and clean organic reaction, to make it possible for this reaction to take place at each end of every molecule, and to force the reaction to completion by removing the water (or other volatile condensation product) from the reaction mixture. Reactions which give amides or esters are particularly useful. For example, a polyamide can be made either from an amino acid, $H_2N—(CH_2)_x—CO_2H$, or from an equimolecular mixture of a dibasic acid, $HO_2C—(CH_2)_y—CO_2H$, and a diamine, $H_2N—(CH_2)_z—NH_2$. Proteins are polyamides assembled from many amino acids in a very specific manner by enzymes. Starch and cellulose can be considered to be made similarly from glucose units. The condensation of a dihydroxysilane produces a silicone (*q.v.*) polymer. (*See* also AMIDES; ESTERS; PROTEINS; STARCH; CELLULOSE.)

For polymerization to occur, each molecule must contain two potential open ends and the monomer units must join end-to-end into linear polymers. Such polymers are usually soluble in suitable solvents, soften (reversibly) on heating, and are termed thermoplastic. However, if the monomers contain more than two sites of reaction (*e.g.*, butadiene, glycerol, phenol, tribasic acids), then net-like (cross-linked) instead of threadlike molecules result. When the networks grow large enough, they become equivalent to many linear polymer molecules joined together in a single network. At this stage, the polymers are insoluble and infusible and are termed thermosetting. *See* PLASTICS: *Causes of Resinification; Synthetic Resin Plastics;* RESINS: *Synthetic Resins;* RUBBER: *Development of Synthetic Rubber; see* also references under "Polymerization" in the Index.

See P. J. Flory, *Principles of Polymer Chemistry* (1953); R. W. Lenz, *Organic Chemistry of Synthetic High Polymers* (1967). (FK. R. M.)

POLYNESIA, the islands scattered over the eastern Pacific ocean within the vast triangle formed by the state of Hawaii to the north, New Zealand to the south and Easter Island to the east. Samoa Islands and Tonga are located at the western edge of this triangle and the Society Islands (with Tahiti the largest of the group) at the centre. Northeast of the Society Islands are the Marquesas Islands and between them the Tuamotu archipelago stretches eastward to the Mangareva Islands. The Cook Islands lie to the west of the Society Islands and the Tubuai Islands to the south. What follows is an exposition of the physical and cultural anthropology of Polynesia. (For a discussion of such aspects as geography, geology, climate, wild life and modern government *see* PACIFIC ISLANDS.) Polynesian peoples, because of their pleasing appearance, natural graces and traditionally simple life among enchantingly fabled islands, have long exerted a strong appeal on outsiders. Efforts to account for their presence in such remote land areas have been the pursuit of many authors and a continuing subject of scientific research.

Genetic and Linguistic Affinities.—People with Polynesian genetic traits have not been found outside of Polynesia except in some islands to the west which were more recently settled by Polynesians. The article OCEANIA describes with the aid of a map how successive hybridization of people of different racial strains moving out from Asia seems to have resulted in the formation of the populations met by the European explorers of the Pacific. The languages spoken by the Polynesians are so similar from island group to island group as to constitute one close-knit family. This in itself is abundant evidence of the recent and rapid spread of their culture through the islands of Polynesia without encountering any other languages. Very important for considerations of origin is the fact that the languages of Fiji and a number of adjacent islands in the Melanesian area to the west of Fiji can be grouped in a family, which, with the Polynesian languages, is derived from a common language, termed proto-East Oceanic. This family is a sub-group of the great Austronesian group of languages stretching from Easter Island in the east to Madagascar off the east coast of Africa (*see* MALAYO-POLYNESIAN LANGUAGES). The divisions of the Polynesian family into Tongan and Samoan for West Polynesia, and Marquesan and Tahitian for East Polynesia point to a settlement pattern consistent with archae-ological evidence. This pattern would have Tonga settled first, then Samoa, then the Marquesas from Samoa, followed by Tahiti from the Marquesas. Easter Island and Hawaii appear to have been first settled from the Marquesas, and New Zealand from Tahiti. Subsequent arrivals in Hawaii from Tahiti, and in New Zealand from the Marquesas, would account for later developed and uniquely shared features between each of these two areas.

The remarkable genetic homogeneity of the Polynesian people also argues for their having spread through the islands without encountering racially different populations. In prehistoric times migrants to these distant islands would, perforce, have come in such small numbers that they would have been absorbed by any established groups, whose physical type and language would then in all probability persist and predominate (*see* RACES OF MANKIND).

American Indian Influence.—The presence of the sweet potato in Polynesia, which botanists agree could only come from South America, has raised the question of what else may have been derived from the Americas, and how and when. In 1947 it was demonstrated by Thor Heyerdahl that balsa rafts such as were employed by the Inca Indians of Peru could reach Polynesia (*see* SHIP). A number of cultural parallels between ancient Peru and eastern Polynesia may be the result of cultural diffusion from that area. Advocates of the theory of a basic American-Indian origin for the Polynesians have offered details from myths and traditions which are too nebulous to be relied upon, and have seized upon cultural parallels from widely scattered parts of the Americas and Polynesia as if they constituted proof of historical connections. Most of this evidence will not bear careful scrutiny as demonstrating such connections. Polynesian-speaking people from the islands to the west of the triangle, however, must have firmly established themselves first in Polynesia as far east as Easter Island (within 2,000 miles of Peru); otherwise the language relationships would not be what they are. The argument that the islands of Polynesia could not be reached from the west because they lie in the face of prevailing winds and currents is untenable in the light of the numerous elements which could only have come directly from the direction of Asia.

Polynesian Vessels and Dates of Arrival.—The Polynesians' twin-hulled sailing vessels, their genius for organizing and equipping settlement expeditions, and their skill in guiding themselves across the open sea by means of the stars, winds and ocean currents enabled them to settle the whole of Polynesia in a relatively short time, once the movement had begun. Archaeological excavations, through radiocarbon dates obtained on charcoal from fireplaces, have determined that Viti Levu, the main island in the Fijian group, was inhabited on both the northern and southern coasts by 1200 B.C. (*see* GEOCHRONOLOGY; RADIOCARBON DATING). In adjacent West Polynesia, a radiocarbon date of 420 B.C. has been obtained from the island of Tongatabu in the Tongan group and of 200 B.C. from the island of Upolu in the Samoan group. For East Polynesia the earliest dates obtained are 124 B.C., and A.D. 200, from the Marquesas Islands, indicating that these were the first to be settled in the east. The dates from Easter Island, the easternmost island inhabited by Polynesians, indicate the time for its settlement was about A.D. 600. The numerous radiocarbon dates from the northernmost and southernmost islands reached by Polynesians—Hawaii and New Zealand—indicate settlement had taken place in these areas by about A.D. 750. Apparently by A.D. 1000 all the widely scattered island groups of East Polynesia were well occupied. No archaeological evidence has been uncovered of any substratum of culture attributable to migrants from the Americas.

Indications point to Tahiti and the Marquesas as having been settled several centuries before the Christian era, implying an earlier date (500 B.C. at the very least) for western Polynesia. It seems most improbable that Peruvians had developed their maneuverable sailing raft at this early time. On the other hand, ocean-sailing canoes typical of Oceania certainly had been developed by then; these are far superior in speed and maneuverability to anything American Indians produced. The twin-hulled sailing canoes of the Polynesians are entirely of Oceanic origin in design and in the terminology of their parts. (*See* BOAT: *Existing Boat Types.*)

Social and Political Organization.—In Polynesia the extended family was an almost self-sustaining unit with the head of the family being the oldest-born of the oldest-born (*see* KINSHIP TERMINOLOGY: *Distribution of Types of Terminology: Indonesia and Oceania*). The blood tie was all-important in social relations. Ideally the ruling chief of an independent population was the most direct descendant in the senior line from the head of the family which established itself on the land by virtue of first occupancy or conquest. A chief ruled through members of his family appointed as lesser officers. Independent chiefs rarely ruled over more than a district or a single island.

The families of the chiefs established themselves as a class apart from commoners and their position became hereditarily fixed. Their genealogies provided connections with creator gods from whom they derived their mana (*q.v.*); *i.e.*, sacred and superior qualities. Rigid tabus (restrictions), the infringement of which often involved the death penalty, were laid down to protect the chief from being familiarly approached by those not of his blood or rank, and to uphold the religious system which supported him (*see* TABU). A supreme chief in Hawaii and Tahiti owned all the land under his jurisdiction and had absolute power over his people.

In those islands where priests or talking chiefs participated in the government they wielded great influence. The Christian missionaries succeeded in overthrowing ancient religious practices only after they had converted the chiefs. Since chiefly power was deeply rooted in the old religion and made effective through religious tabus, the chiefs lost much of their hold on the people through this change. Those who let their land be taken over by foreigners lost even more power and prestige. In the 1960s Tonga and Samoa were practically the only Polynesian areas where hereditary chiefs retained even a degree of control. Throughout the islands governors or administrators have replaced the high chiefs, and ideas of democratic government are followed. However, in remote communities the family is still important politically, and family heads control local affairs.

Religion and Myths.—Considering their isolation, Polynesians had a most remarkable idea of the creation of the world. Chants honouring their chiefs trace their ancestors back to the major gods who were born of Mother Earth and Sky Father and who put the world in its present order. The chants relate that earth and sky have sprung out of a void and darkness where existed the Source or the Foundation (Te Tumu). Through the pairing of mental and natural phenomena, such as rumbling-foundations with shaking-foundations, and memory with reflection, emerge Earth and Sky. Born of the union of Earth and Sky in darkness were the gods Tane, Tu, Rongo and Tangaroa. Tane is a leader in separating this primal pair and bringing in the world of light. All this is dramatically and poetically expressed in beautiful cosmogonic chants. Myths, legends and traditions are embodied in chants whose meaning is often quite obscured through references to lost lore (*see* MYTHOLOGY, PRIMITIVE).

Chiefs approached the major gods at open-air temples with offerings and prayers for the well-being and success of themselves and their people. Favourable or unfavourable answers were determined by cloud omens and other signs of nature. In Hawaii and Tahiti the ritual of worship became so elaborate as to require schools of priests to carry them out. Human sacrifices were required for the war gods. Some chiefs, upon death, were deified and thus continued to be called upon for aid. Each family and each profession had its own tutelary gods. No project was undertaken without enlisting the assistance of the gods. Sorcery was widespread and sorcerers greatly feared. Upon conversion of Polynesians to Christianity the ancient mythology was altered to agree with Biblical accounts. In New Zealand a Christianized native withdrew from his congregation to found a school of an esoteric cult around a god named Io, who took on attributes of Yahweh, but functioned ritualistically like the ancient gods.

Material Culture.—The garment of Polynesian men was a loincloth or kilt and of the women a kilt made of fibres, fine matting or bark cloth. For protection against the cold, the Maori wore dogskin or bird-skin cloaks, or cloaks woven of flax. Some Polynesian chiefs had feather headdresses or helmets. A few Polynesian groups pierced their ears for ornaments.

Human hair necklaces supporting a whale tooth or pearl shell adorned those of rank; Hawaiians had bracelets of pig tusks. The European word tattoo for the art of tattooing (*q.v.*) is derived from the Polynesian term *tatau,* for the practice which was everywhere in evidence.

Houses were one-room buildings with thatched roofs and screened or open sides; several composed the household of a chief. People sat on the floor which was furnished with mats and head rests (*see* DWELLINGS, PRIMITIVE: *Oceania*). Cooking was done mainly in ground ovens, the food wrapped in leaves; it was served with wooden bowls and platters, and eaten with the fingers. Eastern Polynesians used stone food pounders. Pottery was absent except in Tonga, prehistoric Samoa and the Marquesas Islands. Tools were hafted stone adzes, hammerstones, grindstones, digging sticks, carrying poles, pumice, coral or lava rubbing stones for shaping wooden objects, and coral or stone files for shaping fishhooks.

The main weapons were wooden spears and clubs, and the sling; the bow and arrow were not used in warfare. The outrigger canoe, which could negotiate shallow lagoons, land over reefs, and be easily hauled ashore, was essential to island life. When a second canoe was substituted for the outrigger float, the craft became a double canoe. Both the single canoe and the double canoe were often equipped with mat sails. Very large double canoes for interisland communication or for settlement expeditions were seaworthy double-hulled vessels 60 or 70 ft. long, decked over and supporting a thatched house. These were capable of transporting families, domesticated animals, and plants over great ocean stretches.

Economics.—Fishing and agriculture maintained the people; their regular diet was supplemented by the flesh of dogs and fowl, and on special occasions by pork. In a few of the islands human flesh was sometimes eaten, but as a gesture of bravado (*see* CANNIBALISM). Kava (*q.v.*), a narcotic beverage made from a variety of pepper plant, was a favourite of the chiefs and was served ceremonially. The cultivation of taro (*q.v.*) involved terracing and irrigation; sweet potato, banana, breadfruit and sugarcane were grown around the dwelling or in isolated, small gardens tended by family members.

Experts in the arts of canoe making, house thatching, bird catching, adze making, healing, dancing and other activities handed down their skills in their families. The best practitioners were drafted into the service of the high chiefs. The ruler levied taxes in the form of products of all sorts (such as bark cloth, dogs, pigs, food and feathers) for the support of his court, his priests and his professional soldiers. Both within the extended family and outside of it, goods were exchanged solely through gifts; stinginess in reciprocation was considered the meanest trait.

Arts and Crafts.—In what they fashioned Polynesians showed themselves to be consummate craftsmen and artists. Their finest skill and artistry was displayed differently in each island group. In Hawaii it was revealed in their magnificent feather cloaks and helmets; New Zealand was noted for carved meeting houses, Easter Island for gigantic stone statues and Samoans lavished their talents on the ornamental lashings of their council houses. Polynesian canoes reflected great resourcefulness in utilizing materials at hand and in adapting to island conditions of fishing and travel. The graceful war canoes of the New Zealanders were ornamented with bow and stern pieces intricately carved with open-worked double spirals.

Wooden images made by eastern Polynesians showed a complete mastery of sculpture. Because the images were grotesque symbols of idolatry to the Christian missionaries, their destruction was ordered; consequently few have survived. The western Polynesians, with one or two minor exceptions, did not carve images but produced elegantly shaped ceremonial bowls supported on legs. The polished and carved war clubs of the Marquesans are among the prized possessions of museums. In Hawaii single whale teeth were fashioned into artful hook-shaped pendants to be worn by chiefs on human hair necklaces of hundreds of strands of fine square braid. (*See* Wood Carving: *Primitive Peoples;* Jade and Other Hard Stone Carvings: *New Zealand.*)

The bark cloth manufactured by beating out the inner bark of the paper mulberry plant was of fine quality. In Samoa and Tonga it was decorated by rubbing designs raised on a plaque placed beneath the cloth and by painting other designs on in freehand. In Hawaii the bark cloth (tapa) was given watermark patterns in the final beating with heavy, carved mallets. Delicate geometric patterns were tastefully printed on tapa with bamboo stamps (*see* Bark Cloth).

The feather cloaks of Hawaii represented a phenomenal amount of effort in the gathering of thousands of small, rare feathers, arranging them in tufts, and tying them in overlapping rows onto a fabric of exceedingly fine netting. The red, yellow and black feathers were arranged in triangle, diamond or crescent patterns in an over-all design. They were the most valued possessions of the Hawaiian chiefs and constituted the finest gift they could offer to distinguished visitors. Consequently more than 150 of these feather cloaks and capes have been preserved. The fact that no two have the same design is a tribute to the versatility of the Hawaiian artist. (*See* also Primitive Art.)

Music and Dance.—The ancient vocal music of Polynesia consisted of chants using one to four tones with one tone predominating; emphasis was on rhythm and pattern of words. Composers carefully set words together so that they would be most agreeable to the tongue and ear as well as appropriate to the theme. Love songs were rendered with irregular changes in pitch approaching melody; dance songs were initiated with calls. The popular musical instrument of the eastern Polynesians was the sharkskin-covered drum and of the western Polynesians, the wooden slit-gong; complicated and stirring rhythms were beaten on them. Also in accompaniment to dances, sticks were rhythmically beaten together, lengths of bamboo thumped on the ground, and gourds struck with the palm of the hand; in Hawaii only were gourd rattles brought into play. A bamboo nose flute was a popular serenading instrument; shell trumpets were used mainly to announce coming events. (*See* also Music, Primitive.)

Stylized group dances were staged for the entertainment of visitors and returning friends or relatives. Teen-agers gathered at sequestered places in the evening for dances which gave expression to their emotions. In Hawaii dancing was so important that it became a profession under the training of experts in dancing, chanting and drumming, and rated a tutelary goddess. Performers took their positions standing or seated and usually kept them throughout the dance. While hip movements were important, conventional hand motions interpreted words. In Hawaii the movements were slow and graceful, but in most parts of Polynesia they were rapid and took abrupt turns.

As soon as the Polynesians became acquainted with European music they acquired melodic freedom, harmony and elements of western form. However, the rich quality of their voices, their keen sense of tone and rhythm, and fondness for improvisation brought modifications which have set their music apart. Ancient dances are still known and followed, but most are lost; in their place have appeared dances with borrowings from far and wide accompanied by modern music, but still possessing the Polynesian flavour and serving some of the same functions.

See Cook Islands; Easter Island; French Polynesia; Hawaii; New Zealand; Samoa Islands; Tahiti; Tonga Islands; *see* also references under "Polynesia" in the Index.

Bibliography.—E. S. C. Handy, *Polynesian Religion* (1927); J. Hornell, *Canoes of Oceania,* Bishop Museum Special Publ. 27, vol. 1 (1936); E. G. Burrows, *Western Polynesia,* Ethnological Studies, Gothenburg Ethnological Museum (1938); H. L. Shapiro, "Physical Differentiation in Polynesia," *Pap. Peabody Mus., Harvard University,* vol. 20 (1940); F. M. Keesing, *Social Anthropology in Polynesia* (1953); S. H. Elbert, "Internal Relationships of Polynesian Languages and Dialects," *SWest. J. Anthrop.* (1953); W. Goodenough, "A Problem in Malayo-Polynesian Social Organization," *Am. Anthrop.* (1955); M. D. Sahlins, *Social Stratification in Polynesia* (1958); K. P. Emory (ed.), "Pacific Islands: Area 21," no. 1, 2, and 3, Survey and Bibliography, *Council for Old World Archaeology Survey* (1958, 1960, 1965); G. W. Grace, *The Position of the Polynesian Languages Within the Austronesian (Malayo-Polynesian) Language Family* (1959); K. P. Emory, "Origin of the Hawaiians," *J. Polynes. Soc.,* vol. 68 (1959), *Kapingamarangi* (1965); R. C. Suggs, *The Island Civilizations of Polynesia* (1960); C. A. Sharp, *Ancient Voyagers in Polynesia* (1964); J. Barrau, *Plants and the Migrations of Pacific Peoples* (1963); G. A. Highland *et al.* (eds.), *Polynesian Culture History* (1967); A. P. Vayda (ed.), *People and Cultures of the Pacific* (1968); *see* also *J. Polynes. Soc.* and *Oceania.* (K. P. E.)

POLYNESIAN LANGUAGE is spoken by fewer than 1,000,000 persons living among a group of Pacific islands which covers a larger segment of the globe than that encompassing the native speakers of any other single language. This one language has more than 60 closely related dialects and subdialects, but contrasts markedly with the many related Melanesian, Micronesian and Indonesian languages of the Austronesian (or Malayo-Polynesian) family of language, itself a member of the over-all Austric group. The Polynesian speech area is bounded by Kapingamarangi and Nukuoro Islands in the west through Hawaii to the north and New Zealand in the south through Easter Island to the east. The best known of the dialects include Hawaiian, New Zealand Maori, Samoan, Tongan, Tahitian, Niuean, Mangarevan and Tuamotuan.

Intensive exploration of the Pacific ocean by Capt. James Cook and his contemporaries of the last quarter of the 18th century accompanied a general awakening of interest in linguistic studies. The early discoverers collected vocabularies for both practical and scientific purposes. Following this period of discovery a world-wide expansion of Christian missionary activity and an accompanying need for translation of the Bible into native tongues led to a more systematic study of many of the Polynesian dialects. By the middle of the 19th century there were dictionaries, grammars and a full translation of the Bible for the most important island groups. Continuing interest in Polynesian history and culture has resulted in this language becoming one of the best known of the non-Indo-European languages from the standpoint of morphology and the techniques of translation.

Phonology.—Because of the paucity of consonants and the presence of at least ten meaningfully distinct vowel sounds, Polynesian is frequently termed a "vowel language." Each of the positional variant sounds /a/, /e/, /i/, /o/ and /u/ has up to five recognizable variants of length in ordinary speech. For orthographic purposes these may be clustered together in two groups, distinguished by the use of the macron (¯) over the longer variants, as in New Zealand Maori *mata* "the face" and *mātā* "a heap." The many variant vowel lengths are patterned in relation to their linguistic environment, but exact rules of pronunciation have not been worked out. There are indications that the meaningful distinction between short and long vowels is a relatively recent phenomenon related to the loss of consonants with or without the coalescence of two or more shorter vowels.

Considerable alternation exists between certain vowels, notably /i/ ⟷ /u/ and /a/ ⟷ /e/. This shift may be freely variable within one dialect, as Hawaiian *imu*⟷*umu* "earth-oven." Frequently it is fixed between dialects, as Rarotongan *meitaki* and Tahitian *maita'i* "excellent," but is never an established sound shift in the same sense that consonants are found to vary between dialects.

A comparison of data from 50 dialects suggests the following reconstruction of the proto-Polynesian consonantal system:

	Bilabial	Labiodental	Alveolardental	Velar	Glottal
Continuant	M	V	N	ŋ	
Stop	P		T	K	'
Fricative		F	S		H
Flap			L/R*		

*Whether or not the sound was /L/ or /R/ or whether both existed as distinct meaningful sounds is not clear.

No modern dialect retains all of the original sounds, and there has been a marked tendency toward reduction in the number of consonants, especially in Eastern Polynesia. Only seven consonants appear to be present in Rurutuan, contrasting strongly with Tongan, the most conservative in the retention of consonants. Regular shift of consonants between dialects and the complete loss of certain consonants are characteristic of most dialects. Hence, the variations between dialects may be predicted and ancient or modern forms within one dialect may be derived with a fair degree of confidence. In Rarotongan when one finds that the term for proto-Polynesian (PPN) *ahi* "fire" is *a'i*, and that PPN *faka* the causative prefix is *'aka*, then it may be assumed that the term for PPN *tahi* "one" will be *ta'i*, as the shift from the PPN fricative to the glottal stop is obvious. Likewise, when it is determined that Rarotongan *tayata* "person" and *tapu* "sacred, forbidden" are in Hawaiian *kanaka* and *kapu* then it may be predicted that Hawaiian *maka* "face" will be *mata* in Rarotongan.

In some cases the sound shift was only partially completed at the time of European arrival, as in Mangaian where the velar stop /k/ has shifted to the glottal stop /'/ only in certain words. In other cases there has been an irregular but complete loss of a sound, as in Hawaiian *'uala* and Mangaian *'uara* from PPN *kumara* "sweet potato," as well as in such words as PPN *tasi* "sea" which becomes *tai* in much of Polynesia.

There are no such distinctive voiced sounds as English /b/, /d/ and /g/, although in the past European recorders have misspelled terms such as *tapu* "forbidden" as *tabu*, and the island of *Porapora* as *Borabora*. Polynesians cannot distinguish between the English speaker's "bad" and "bat," "tab" and "tap." Other than the apparently mnemonic device of the controversial Easter Island "talking boards" there was no pre-European system of writing. Those English and French missionaries who developed the present Polynesian systems of writing attempted to use their own European orthography. In most cases they did not understand the significance of the distinction between short and long vowels and the importance of the glottal stop, hence these were not provided for in the alphabets. These omissions seriously affect the ability to read aloud or to translate from the literature in most areas other than New Zealand.

Many foreign words have been adapted by the various dialects. The sound changes involved bring the new words into conformance with the Polynesian sound system by shifting any voiced sounds to sibilants or stops and by adding vowels to closed syllables; hence English "broom" and "towel" become Tahitian *purumu* and *tauera*.

Morphology.—The seemingly inexhaustible vocabulary is derived from a relatively limited number of basic words, which are capable of being used individually or combined with other basic words and frequently also with a small number of prefixes and suffixes. These basic words are usually, but not invariably, disyllabic in nature. The New Zealand Maori base word *tupu* "to grow" when combined with the causative prefix *whaka* becomes *whakatupu* "to cause to grow"; *turipona* "the knee joint" is derived from *turi* "the knee" and *pona* "a knot, joint." All syllables end in vowels although the initial sound may be consonant or vowel. Stress or "accent" varies between areas and appears to be absent from certain dialects, notably Tahitian; traditionally it is stated to be upon the penultimate syllable, with certain exceptions related to vowel length.

Basic words and syllables are frequently duplicated to form diminutives, pluralatives, frequentatives, and other variants of the base, as *paki* "to pat," *pakipaki* "to pat frequently," *papaki* "to clap together"; or *manu* "a bird, small insect," *manumanu* "a very small insect." A few words are composed of a single sound or syllable, as New Zealand Maori *ā* "to compel, drive," *ki* "to be full."

Syntax.—Sentences are generally brief, and when spoken in full are composed of an initial predicative phrase followed by a subject, which may or may not be followed by one or more locative, directive or possessive phrases. The predication is the most significant part of the sentence and is spoken even when the nature of the situation permits the rest of the sentence to remain unsaid, as in Rarotongan *E kai! E kai ra!* "Eat! Eat on!"

Phrases are composed of one or more central "full words,"

usually (but not always) preceded and in some cases also followed by particles. Full words are those innumerable terms which have definable meanings within themselves. The very limited number of particles do not in themselves convey meaning, but serve only to place the predication or substantive as to identity, location and duration of the time, place or type of possession. A simple analogy would be to a brick wall, the bricks being similar to the full words of a sentence, the mortar similar to the particles which serve to bind the individual units into the whole structure. The Rarotongan base term *'aere* "to go" (without connotation of direction) and *au* "I, ego" may be combined with particles as follows: *Kua 'aere au* "I went," *Ka 'aere au* "I shall go," *Tē 'aere nei au* "I am (in the process of) going."

Terms may be classified as full words or particles on the basis of specific meaning or function, but not individually as the traditional noun, verb and the like. A more useful classification relates to their use and position within the phrase or sentence. Many Polynesian full words may serve as predicative, substantive or the modifier of either. The initial full word of a phrase is invariably the most significant term with respect to meaning, and the words which may follow or the surrounding particles serve only to modify the basic concept. The first full word of the initial phrase of a sentence is the basis of the predication and the first full word of the second phrase is the subject, as *Kua tupu te taro* "The taro grew" and *Kua oti te tupu* "The growth stopped."

Polynesian predicatives lay greater stress upon the state of being than do English verbs and many of them must be preceded in translations by the phrase "was in the state of being." A particular source of confusion relates to the fact that a predicative may be either active or passive in nature as well as transitive or intransitive in any one of the four possible combinations. The full word involved may be modified by the passive suffix, one of a number of prefixes and by the intransitivizing particle. A secondary source of confusion relates to the sentence initial particle *E*, which is frequently mistranslated as equivalent to the English indefinite nominalizing particle "a, an," but in reality it is a predicative equational particle best translated as "is, am, was," as in Rarotongan *E tayata tikai koe* "You are truly a man."

Polynesian full sentences may be analyzed as follows (particles are in small capitals, full words are italicized):

In Hawaiian

UA *ho'ohiu* 'IA / KA *moku* / I *luna* O KE *alahukimoku*
predicative phrase   subject   locative phrase
The ship was lifted (was lifted the ship) on to (on top of) the marine railway.

In Tahitian

'UA *papa'i* HIA / TE *rata* / Ē *au*
predicative phrase   subject   agentive phrase
The letter was written (was written the letter) by me.

Semantics.—Studies utilizing the technique of glottochronology reveal that Polynesian is possibly the most changeless of languages known to scholars. During more than 2,000 years following the settlement of Polynesia about 90% of such basic vocabulary terms as "fish," "fire" and "water" have retained the same form as that of the proto-language. The recording and translation of Polynesian has been considerably hampered by the lack of adequate orthography, and many dictionaries give the false impression of lack of precision of terminology as a result of having entered meanings belonging to several orthographically separate words under a single form. Despite the conservatism and the preciseness of vocabulary meanings, Polynesian makes extensive and truly complex use of analogy and imagery in oratory, poetry and folk lore. Despite the lack of written language there was an elaborate oral literature, with great stress upon preciseness of memorization and usage. Feats of memory witnessed by early explorers and later by anthropologists seem little short of phenomenal. Much of the memorization involved ancient prayers, religious ceremonies, folk tales and legends, but the most significant of all (and still a vital force in court cases) was the recounting of genealogy and secret family chants. This type of knowledge was the sole patent to land rights and verbal knowledge ruled in the event of dispute.

Together with other Oceanic languages Polynesian utilizes a

complex system of differentiating persons, with the individual distinguished from two persons as well as from a plurality, and the further differentiation of whether or not the person spoken to is included in the reference. Furthermore, the system of particles distinguishes persons and personified places or things from all others. All phenomena are divided into category of implicit and explicit connection when spoken of in the possessive sense, where for example one's blood kin are considered to be intimately a part of the speaker, hence are intrinsic, and one's wife is much less so and therefore explicitly "possessed."

Polynesian dialects, together with languages such as Javanese, utilize a form of courtesy reference or "chiefly language," as it is called in Samoa where its use is most elaborated. This vocabulary is used by commoners in addressing chiefs and their families and by upper classes among themselves. The terms are frequently simple analogies, as when chiefly women of Samoa are referred to as "flowers," but in other cases represent retention of archaic terms. In central Polynesia a distinct vocabulary was also used for theological purposes by priests, enabling them to perform ceremonies and render prayers not understood by noncommunicants. Learned aged men still are able to converse among themselves, to the bafflement of the young.

BIBLIOGRAPHY.—Songs, tales, chants, genealogies have been preserved in the *Journal of the Polynesian Society,* Wellington, New Zealand; the *Memoirs* and *Bulletins* of the Bernice P. Bishop Museum, Honolulu, Hawaii; and in the *Bulletin de la Société des Études Océaniennes,* Papeete, Tahiti. The most important dictionaries include C. M. Churchward, *Tongan Dictionary* (1959); Herbert W. Williams, *A Dictionary of the Maori Language,* 6th ed. (1957); Mary Kawena Puki and S. H. Elbert, *Hawaiian-English Dictionary* (1957); J. Frank Stimson with Donald Stanley Marshall, *A Dictionary of Some Tuamotuan Dialects of the Polynesian Language* (1960). See also R. C. Green and A. Pawley, *The Linguistic Subgroups of Polynesia* (1966). (D. S. ML.)

POLYNOMIAL is used in elementary algebra to denote an expression that is the sum or difference of simpler expressions called monomials. Thus $x^2 + 2xy^3 + 5$ and $\sqrt{2x^3} - (1/x) + a^2b$ would be called polynomials, while $2xy^3$ and $1/x$ would be called monomials. For greater clarity this discussion follows the definitions of higher mathematics, in which monomial means the product of several variables raised to positive integral powers, and multiplied by a real or complex number (q.v.) called the coefficient; accordingly, $ax^py^qz^r$ is a monomial, where x, y, and z are the variables (there could be more or less than three), p, q, and r are positive integers, and a is the coefficient. The degree of the monomial is the sum of the exponents, here $p + q + r$; the degree of the monomial with respect to x alone is p. By definition a polynomial in several variables x, y, z, . . . , is a monomial or sum of monomials in these variables. The degree of the polynomial is the largest degree of any of the monomials occurring in it. Polynomials of degree one are called linear, of degree two quadratic, and of degree three cubic. Each monomial occurring in a polynomial is called a term of that polynomial. If the monomial is just a number, it is called the constant term of the polynomial. To illustrate these definitions: the expression $2x^2y - \sqrt{3x} + a^4b + c$, where a, b, and c represent numbers, is a polynomial of degree three in two variables, with three terms including the constant term $a^4b + c$; the expression $2 + 1/x + 3 \sin x$ is not a polynomial, since neither of the last two terms is a monomial of the accepted form. Occasionally the usage is relaxed to call such an expression as $a(1 + \sqrt{x})^2 + b(1 + \sqrt{x}) + c$ a polynomial of degree two in $(1 + \sqrt{x})$, or $\sin^3 x - \sin x$ a trigonometric polynomial in $\sin x$.

Polynomials are added, subtracted, and multiplied by the usual laws of algebra and the result is always another polynomial. In general, however, when one polynomial is divided by another, the result is not a polynomial.

Algebraic Aspects.—In elementary algebra (q.v.) attention is (as a rule) confined to polynomials in only one variable. If $f(x)$ denotes the polynomial $a_0x^n + a_1x^{n-1} + . . . + a_n$, where the coefficients a_i are real or complex numbers and a_0 does not equal zero, then a basic problem (the main subject of the theory of equations) is to determine those real or complex values of x for which $f(x)$ is zero (see EQUATIONS, THEORY OF). Such values are called the roots of the equation $f(x) = 0$. The so-called funda-

mental theorem of algebra states that there always exists a root α of the equation $f(x) = 0$. From this it follows that $x - \alpha$ is a factor of $f(x)$; by repeated use of the fundamental theorem it can be shown that the polynomial has exactly n roots (not necessarily distinct) and that it can be written in the factored form $f(x) = a_0(x - \alpha_1) (x - \alpha_2) . . . (x - \alpha_n)$, where the factorization, except for the order of the factors, is uniquely determined.

Such a factorization of $f(x)$ into a product of linear polynomials of the form $x - \alpha_i$ may not be possible if the domain of the coefficients α_i of the linear polynomials does not consist of all complex numbers. Thus the polynomial $f(x) = x^2 - 2$ cannot be factored if the coefficients of the factors are restricted to the domain of rational numbers, but it can be factored if the coefficients are allowed to be real numbers, since $x^2 - 2 = (x + \sqrt{2}) (x - \sqrt{2})$, and $\sqrt{2}$ is real but not rational. From this point of view, the fundamental theorem of algebra says that any polynomial with complex coefficients may be factored into linear polynomials, provided the factors are allowed to have complex coefficients; it would be false if a smaller coefficient domain were specified.

In modern algebra the problem of factorization is studied using as coefficient domain an arbitrary field (see FIELDS). It is proved that any polynomial in n variables with coefficients from a fixed field may be factored uniquely into the product of irreducible (not further factorable) polynomials with coefficients in that field.

Geometric Aspects.—Consider a polynomial $f(x,y)$ in two variables x and y with real coefficients. If a and b are two real numbers such that the polynomial becomes zero when a is substituted for x, and b for y, then the pair (a,b) is called a zero of $f(x,y)$. The set of all zeros of $f(x,y)$ defines a plane curve; the properties of the polynomial are reflected in the geometric properties of the curve and conversely. For example, if the polynomial is of the first degree, $ax + by + c$, then the associated curve is a straight line given by the equation $ax + by + c = 0$. If it is of the second degree, $ax^2 + bxy + cy^2 + dx + ey + f$, the curve is a conic section (q.v.). The zeros of a polynomial in three variables define in general a surface in three-dimensional space; if two such polynomials are considered together, their surfaces intersect in a curve in three-dimensional space. The natural generalization of these ideas to the study of the common zeros of a set of polynomials in n variables (viewed then as a locus in n-dimensional space) is the subject of algebraic geometry (q.v.).

Polynomials in Number Theory and Logic.—Diophantine analysis, a branch of number theory, is concerned with finding a set of integer zeros of one or more polynomials with integer coefficients (see DIOPHANTINE EQUATIONS; NUMBERS, THEORY OF). In geometric terms the problem is to find those points in space represented by integer coordinates that lie on the locus of zeros of the polynomial. Diophantine problems have an extensive literature going back to the Egyptians and Greeks, and have given rise to some of the most famous problems of mathematics (e.g., see FERMAT'S LAST THEOREM).

There are striking modern applications of polynomials to mathematical logic, computer design, and allied problems. For example, information is usually transmitted over long distances in the form of sequences of digits (see INFORMATION THEORY). Disturbances in the line can alter some of the transmitted digits, and the garbled message may be unintelligible. Techniques of encoding have been developed in which the meaning of the message does not depend on each digit (just as in written material, sm of the lttrs can be left out without disturbing the intelligibility). The successive members of a sequence of $n + 1$ digits are thought of as the coefficients of a polynomial of degree n. The encoding and decoding processes are then given as algebraic operations on these polynomials which produce new polynomials.

Analytic Aspects.—Polynomials in one variable are important in analysis (q.v.) because they form an especially simple class of function (q.v.). The derivatives and integrals of polynomials are themselves polynomials, and are readily calculated from simple formulas. Computation with polynomials does not require tables as do other simple functions (such as trigonometric and exponential functions). Such properties of polynomials make them useful for approximating other functions. An applied mathematician or engineer who has empirical information in tabular or graphical form will frequently try to fit a polynomial to these data; *i.e.*, will seek a polynomial of conveniently low degree whose values reasonably approximate those given, or, equivalently, one with a graph that lies close to the empirical curve. The data can then be handled conveniently through their polynomial approximation, rather than as an original table or graph susceptible only of numerical treatment. Formulas of numerical integration depend on fitting such polynomials to data (*see* CALCULUS OF DIFFERENCES). If the graph of the polynomial need only pass through a few points, the Lagrange interpolation formula, with which a polynomial of degree n is passed through $n + 1$ given points, can be used (*see* INTERPOLATION AND EXTRAPOLATION).

In theoretical and applied work it is frequently useful to expand a real function into a series of polynomials $p_i(x)$, where the ith polynomial is of degree i. A series (*q.v.*) representation for a given smooth function $f(x)$ can be written $f(x) = c_0 p_0(x) + c_1 p_1(x) + c_2 p_2(x) + \ldots$ to be valid in some interval of values for x. Here the coefficients c are chosen so that (if the series is broken off after the nth term) the resulting polynomial $c_0 p_0(x) + \ldots + c_n p_n(x)$ will be the "best possible" approximation to $f(x)$ by a polynomial of degree n. A theorem due to K. T. W. Weierstrass states that an arbitrary continuous function can be uniformly approximated by a polynomial with any assigned degree of accuracy; the greater the desired accuracy, the higher the needed degree of the polynomial. For example, if $p_i(x)$ is taken to be $(x - \alpha)^i$ for some fixed real number α, a Taylor series results; if $\alpha = 0$, a Maclaurin series (*see* TAYLOR'S THEOREM). In either case the coefficients are given by $c_i = f^{(i)}(\alpha)/i!$ where $f^{(i)}(\alpha)$ denotes the ith derivative of $f(x)$, evaluated at α. If the function $f(x)$ arises as the solution to a differential equation (as is frequent in physical problems), other sets of polynomials are often more natural, and the corresponding coefficients c_i give a better description of $f(x)$ than the Taylor series coefficients. For example, problems of steady-state temperature or electrical charge distribution on a sphere may lead to Legendre's differential equation, and the solutions are expanded in terms of the Legendre polynomials (*see* SPHERICAL HARMONICS). Hermite and Chebichev polynomials are yet other classes of special polynomials arising as solutions to second order differential equations (*see* FUNCTIONS, SPECIAL: *Orthogonal Polynomials*).

See also references under "Polynomial" in the Index.

BIBLIOGRAPHY.—D. Jackson, *Fourier Series and Orthogonal Polynomials* (1941); M. S. Knebelman and T. Y. Thomas, *Principles of College Algebra* (1942); W. V. D. Hodge and D. Pedoe, *Methods of Algebraic Geometry*, vol. 1 (1947); R. Courant, *Differential and Integral Calculus*, 2 vol. (1936, 1937); G. Birkhoff and S. MacLane, *A Survey of Modern Algebra*, rev. ed. (1953); G. B. Thomas, *Calculus and Analytic Geometry*, 3rd ed. (1960); R. Courant and H. E. Robbins, *What is Mathematics?* (1941); J. D. Mancill and M. O. González, *Modern College Algebra* (1960).   (A. P. M.)

POLYP, in medicine, is a general term used to designate any growth projecting from the wall of a cavity lined with a mucous membrane. This growth may have a broad base, in which case it is called sessile; or it may have a long narrow neck, the characteristic of a pedunculated polyp. The surface of a polyp may be smooth, irregular, or multilobular. The commonest locations of polyps in the human body are the nose, the bladder, and the gastrointestinal tract, especially the rectum and colon. Symptoms of polyps depend upon their location and size. There may be no symptoms, or there may be symptoms resulting from pressure or from mechanical obstruction of all or part of a lumen, such as the nose or bowel; they may occasionally bleed. Usually polyps are simple, benign growths, but a small percentage may be either precursors to cancers or may actually contain cancers. It is for this reason that it is best, when possible, to remove all polyps and examine them microscopically to determine whether further treatment is necessary.   (J. A. RR.)

POLYP, in zoology, is the name commonly applied to animals that bear tentacles and that are in some way attached to the substrate. In its broadest usage, the name applies to the individuals of such diverse animal phyla as the Bryozoa (Ectoprocta), the Endoprocta, the pterobranch Hemichordata and the sessile members of the Coelenterata. More strictly the term is ordinarily applied only to members of the latter group. The word itself seems to have come into English from the French word *poulpe* ("octopus"). Polyps are illustrated and discussed in the articles COELENTERATA; HYDROZOA; ANTHOZOA; and SEA ANEMONE.

In the phylum Coelenterata the polyp represents one of the two body forms known in that group, the other being the medusa, or jellyfish. Polyps are of columnar form in general and with few exceptions are attached to the substrate or burrow into it. The attached end may be called the base. The free end of the polyp has a centrally located mouth, surrounded by tentacles in most instances. While most polyps have many tentacles—some large sea anemones have thousands—certain hydroids are exceptions: *Hydrichthys*, parasitic on fish, and the minute hydralike polyp *Protohydra* have no tentacles; *Monobrachium* has a single tentacle; and *Proboscidactyla* has two.

The coelenterate polyp is not only morphologically different in the different classes but represents different stages in the life history of those animals. For example, the polyps of the Hydrozoa, the hydroids, are morphologically quite simple. They usually have small numbers of tentacles, as indicated above, are of small size and have a coelenteron (the gut) that is a simple sac. These polyps are usually the immature, attached stages of medusae, representing the adult, sexually reproducing form. Within the Hydrozoa, however, not all polyps bud off free medusae, and many polyps are known that are themselves the sexually reproducing stage. In almost all instances where hydroid polyps represent sexual adults, it can be shown nonetheless that the gonads develop in association with structures that represent reductions of the medusa. Thus it seems to be a safe generalization that the polyp of the Hydrozoa represents an immature stage in the life history of the members of that class.

Much the same seems to be true for the class Scyphozoa, whose members are the large medusae, or jellyfish, of marine waters. The polyps here are simple, but the coelenteron is divided into four compartments by four mesenteries, membranes that arise at right angles along the inner body wall. These polyps bud off the sexual medusae (the adults) much as in the Hydrozoa, and the polyps seem to represent only an attached immature stage in the life history of the group.

In the Anthozoa, on the other hand, no medusae are known, and the polyps represent the adult individuals. Here the polyps may grow to very large sizes, up to about three feet in diameter, and internally become very complex through the possession of many mesenteries, which subdivide the coelenteron into many radially distributed compartments.

Polyps may occur as solitary individuals as in the fresh-water *Hydra* and many sea anemones, or they may occur as colonial aggregations. These colonies result from asexual reproduction by budding from the original polyp. Buds may arise apically, laterally or from stoloniferous growths from the basal region. Associated with colony formation, in many instances, especially among the marine hydroids, individual polyps in the colony assume different morphologies and have differing functions. Thus some individual polyps may be specialized for feeding (gastrozooids), for protection (tentaculozooids and dactylozooids) or for reproduction (gonozooids). Colonies possessing more than one type of polyp are said to be polymorphic; a good example is the common hydroid *Hydractinia* or *Podocoryne*. Another excellent example of a polymorphic colonial coelenterate is to be found in such organisms as the Portuguese man-of-war or any of its relatives (Siphonophora). Commonly among these free-floating colonial hydroids medusalike individuals may also occur that function as locomotory structures for the colony.

Polyps may occur as naked individuals or colonies, or they may have skeletons of various sorts. Among the hydroids, tough but flexible chitinous exoskeletons are common, and in many cases the polyp can contract completely within the surrounding skeletal cup. Skeletons of calcium carbonate or lime are also known among marine hydroids; the colonial polyps possessing these are called hydrocorals. The true corals, which are anthozoan polyps, also have skeletons of lime (see CORAL). The polyps here, as in the hydrocorals, live in cups on the surface of the limy skeleton; when disturbed, the animals can contract into these protective structures. In the Anthozoa a number of colonial polyps are known, such as sea fans and sea pens, that have an axial, internal skeleton around which the colony grows.

Coelenterate polyps possess nematocysts (see COELENTERATA), with the aid of which they are able to capture other animals as food. Contact of a potential food organism, such as a small worm, mollusk or fish, with the tentacles of a polyp causes the nematocysts to discharge. Once a food item has been caught, the tentacles bend toward the mouth and the mouth opens in preparation to receive the food. Primary digestion of the food takes place in the coelenteron, where strong protein-splitting enzymes break the food down to minute particles. The cells lining the coelenteron then engulf these particles and final digestion takes place within the individual cells.

Polyps are for the most part restricted to marine habitats. In fresh water hydras are abundant and minute polyps of the freshwater medusa *Craspedacusta* are found occasionally. The only other coelenterate polyp seen in fresh water is the widely distributed colonial hydroid, *Cordylophora*, which, while commonest in brackish waters, does occasionally appear in lakes and reservoirs. In marine habitats coelenterate polyps are abundant nearly everywhere. The open ocean supports many different siphonophores, while along the shores of the world hydroids, anemones and corals flourish, the last group, however, being most conspicuous in tropical waters. Somewhat below the reach of the lowest tides occur veritable gardens of sea fans and sea pens, particularly in warm waters, while even at the greatest depths of the oceans anemones and hydroids may still be found. The tallest hydroid polyp known, *Branchiocerianthus,* is usually restricted to waters more than one-half-mile deep, and the largest specimens recovered have been more than six feet long. See JELLYFISH; see also references under "Polyp" in the Index. (C. HA.)

POLYPHEMUS, the most famous of the Cyclopes, son of Poseidon and the nymph Thoösa. Odysseus, having been cast ashore on the coast of Sicily, fell into the hands of Polyphemus, who shut him up with 12 of his companions in his cave and blocked the entrance with an enormous rock. Odysseus at length succeeded in making the giant drunk, blinded him by plunging a burning stake into his eye while he lay asleep, and with six of his friends (the others having been devoured by Polyphemus) made his escape by clinging to the bellies of the sheep let out to pasture. See ACIS; CYCLOPS; ODYSSEUS.

POLYPHONY, a musical term, deriving from the Greek *polys*, "many," and *phonos*, "sound," used of music in which the parts are independent of each other though forming an acceptable harmony. It is thus a synonym of counterpoint (*q.v.*), though the term counterpoint is generally associated with the technique of polyphonic music. The term polyphony is used of vocal works of the 16th century, *e.g.*, a polyphonic chanson, madrigal, or motet, as opposed to homophony (*q.v.*), used of music in which the conception is predominantly harmonic. It is also the converse of monophony, music consisting of one part alone, and monody (*q.v.*), a solo song with continuo. See also references under "Polyphony" in the Index.

POLYPTYCH: *see* ALTARPIECE.

POLYTECHNIC SCHOOL, generally a postsecondary school or institute in which the emphasis is on training in technology and applied science. The polytechnics of London derive from the institute founded (1882) by Quintin Hogg (*q.v.*). See TECHNICAL EDUCATION; *see also* VOCATIONAL EDUCATION.

POLYTONALITY, a term in music meaning the simultaneous use, common at the beginning of the 20th century, of different tonalities. Usually two different tonalities were used—this was known as bitonality—as in the passage for trumpets in C and F♯ minor in the second tableau of Stravinsky's *Petrouchka* (1911), expressive of the puppet's pathos. Alfredo Casella's *Pezzi infantili* are among the children's pieces in which this device was used. S. Prokofiev's *Sarcasms* for piano boldly juxtaposes the keys of F♯ minor in the right hand and B♭ minor in the left, while Darius

Milhaud's *Saudades do Brazil* has a melody in C with an accompaniment in A♭ major. Such combinations of tonalities may also be analyzed as highly inflected forms of chromatic harmony, the dissonances of which are eventually resolved. The passage from *Petrouchka* may be said to be based on the harmony of C♯ minor, to which it resolves, and the passage from Milhaud's work on the key of the accompaniment, in A♭. The simultaneous combination of three or more keys leads to harmonic or contrapuntal combinations that are even more difficult to define and which belong to the technique of atonality. The technique of polytonality was first analyzed by Milhaud, who maintained that it could be traced back to the simultaneous use of two keys in a canon at the fourth of J. S. Bach.

See D. Milhaud, "Polytonalité et atonalité," *La Revue Musicale* (Feb. 1921).

POLYXENA, in Greek mythology, a daughter of Priam, king of Troy, and his wife Hecuba (Hekabe). After the fall of Troy, she was claimed by the shade of Achilles, the greatest of the Greek warriors, as his share of the spoils and was therefore put to death at his tomb. In postclassical times this story was elaborated to include a love affair between Polyxena and Achilles before the latter was killed.

POMBAL, SEBASTIÃO JOSÉ DE CARVALHO E MELLO, MARQUÊS DE (1699–1782), Portuguese statesman, master of the government throughout King Joseph's reign, and a reformer who ruthlessly exercised his despotic power, was born in Lisbon on May 13, 1699. Known for most of his life as Sebastião de Carvalho, he began reading law at Coimbra University, then embarked briefly on a military career, but eventually took up the study of politics and history on his own account and was appointed a fellow of the Royal Academy of History by King John V in 1733. After being ambassador in London (1738–43), he was sent on a diplomatic mission to Vienna in 1745, where he married Gräfin Eleonora von Daun (his former wife, Thereza de Noronha e Bourbon, had died in 1739). He returned to Portugal in December 1749.

On Joseph's accession (1750), the favour of the queen mother, Mariana of Austria, together with a recommendation by one of the former ministers, Luis da Cunha, brought Carvalho into the government as secretary for war and foreign affairs (from August 1750). Winning the king's confidence, particularly by his measures after the great earthquake (1755), he became chief minister in 1756. He was created conde de Oeiras in 1759 and marquês de Pombal (the name to be used in the rest of this article) in 1769.

Pombal claimed absolute power for the king. Atrocious sentences were pronounced by extraordinary tribunals: in 1757 on the people of Oporto who had rioted against the monopoly granted to the wine company; and in 1759 on the great nobles accused of complicity in the Sept. 3, 1758, attempt against the king's life, all of whom were tortured to death (though some were innocent). The whole Society of Jesus, apart from individual members who were arrested, was expelled from the Portuguese dominions (Sept. 3, 1759), and the church was subjected to royal control (1759 and 1764). All who opposed Pombal were thrown into prison.

Pombal nevertheless promulgated many economic and educational reforms. He promoted new industries and developed existing ones; *e.g.*, glass and textile manufactures, especially silk. He fixed the wages of peasant labourers (1756) and the size of agrarian properties (1769 and 1773). Chartered companies created by him were the General Company for Agriculture and for Wines of Alto Douro (1756), to handle the port wine trade; the companies of Pará and Maranhão (1754) and of Pernambuco and Paraíba (1759), for trade with Brazil; and the Algarve Fisheries Company (1773). He initiated commercial education (1759) and radically modernized the university (1772).

Joseph's death (February 1777) changed everything. Under the new queen, Maria I, political prisoners were freed; and Pombal, having resigned his ministry, faced charges of having abused his powers. He was severely interrogated during a judicial inquiry (October 1779–January 1780) and was found guilty; but the queen remitted all punishment save exile from Lisbon (August 1781). He died at Pombal on May 8, 1782. (DA. A. P.)

POMEGRANATE, the fruit of *Punica granatum,* a bush or small tree of Asia, which with a little-known species from the island of Socotra constitutes the family Punicaceae. Throughout the Orient this fruit has since earliest times occupied a position of importance alongside the grape and the fig.

King Solomon possessed an orchard of pomegranates; and when the children of Israel, wandering in the wilderness, sighed for the abandoned comforts of Egypt, the cooling pomegranates were

JOHN H. GERARD

(LEFT) WHOLE AND CUT FRUIT AND (RIGHT) LEAVES AND FLOWERS OF THE POMEGRANATE (PUNICA GRANATUM)

remembered longingly. Centuries later, the prophet Muhammad remarked sententiously: "Eat the pomegranate, for it purges the system of envy and hatred." It will thus be seen that this fruit is of exceptional interest because of its historic background.

While the pomegranate is considered to be indigenous in Iran and perhaps neighbouring countries, its cultivation long ago encircled the Mediterranean and extended through Arabia, Afghanistan, and India. The juicy subacid character of the ripe fruit makes it particularly agreeable to inhabitants of hot arid regions—precisely those areas in which the pomegranate attains its greatest perfection.

The ancient Semitic name *rimmon* was adopted by the Arabs as *rumman,* from which the Portuguese in turn formed *romão* or *roman.* From the early Roman names *malum punicum* (apple of Carthage) and *granatum* have come the modern botanical binomial and the common name *granada,* used in Spanish-speaking countries.

The plant, which may attain 15 or 20 ft. in height, has elliptic to lance-shaped, bright green leaves about 3 in. long, and handsome axillary orange-red flowers borne toward the ends of the branchlets. The calyx is tubular, persistent, 5- to 7-lobed; the petals lance shaped, inserted between the calyx lobes. The ovary is embedded in the calyx tube and contains several locules in two series, one above the other.

The fruit is the size of a large orange, obscurely six-sided, with a smooth leathery skin that ranges from brownish yellow to red; within, it is divided into several cells, containing many thin, transparent vesicles of reddish juicy pulp, each surrounding an angular elongated seed. The subtle flavour of the fruit is described by some Westerners as being delicately delicious, by others as insipid.

Presumably the plant was introduced into the New World by the early Spanish colonists. It is commonly cultivated in gardens from the warmer parts of the United States to Chile. Small commercial plantings have been made in California. Though the pomegranate will grow in a wide range of climates, good fruit is produced only where high temperatures and dry atmosphere accompany the ripening period. Deep, rather heavy loams appear to be the best soils. Seeds can readily be grown, but choice varieties are reproduced by cuttings and layerings. Commercial propagation is by hardwood cuttings 10 to 12 in. long, which can be rooted in the open ground.

The varieties of the pomegranate are numerous. Ibn al-Awam, a Moor who wrote in the 13th century, described about ten that were grown in southern Spain at that time. Varieties cultivated commercially in the United States include Wonderful, Sweet, and Acid. Several dwarf forms are grown for their handsome scarlet flowers. (W. Po.)

POMERANIA: *see* POMORZE.

POMO, a group of North American Indians who occupied California from the upper reaches of San Francisco Bay northward about 80 mi., and from the Pacific Ocean inland approximately 80 mi. The population is estimated to have been from 8,000 to 16,000 at the time of first European contact. By the 1960s about 900 Pomo were reported living in California. The many autonomous villages, each with its own territory and its own language distinct from the others, were interrelated by trade, warfare, a common religion, and a chiefly language of the Hokan (*q.v.*) family unintelligible to the general population.

Pomo women are reputed to have made the finest basketry in the world. The baskets had many purposes, including cooking and housing; the finest were used as higher denominations of money (*see* BASKET: *Primitive Basketry*). The Pomo practised professions that required a lifetime of training; some of these were fishing, deer hunting, gambling, doctoring (including a highly developed psychotherapy), and money manufacturing. There was a formal economic and monetary system. They were well fed on a wide variety of foods, most important being acorns and horse chestnuts (leached before eating), fish, and deer. The hunters commonly knew every deer in the territory and maintained a balance between the herds and the available vegetation to keep the animals from straying outside Pomo territory. Their religion included the idea of a separate creation of their territory, animals, vegetation, and the Pomo people, as well as accounts of destruction by their gods and reestablishment afterward. *See* also MAIDU.

BIBLIOGRAPHY.—S. A. Barrett, *Pomo Myths* (1933), *Material Aspects of Pomo Culture* (1952); E. W. Gifford, *Clear Lake Pomo Society* (1926); E. M. Loeb, *Pomo Folkways* (1926); C. Clark and T. B. Williams, *Pomo Indian Myths . . .* (1954); B. W. Aginsky, "The Pomo: a Profile of Gambling Among Indians," *Annals of the American Academy of Political and Social Science* (May 1950); United States Department of the Interior, *United States Indian Population and Land* (1961). (B. W. A.)

POMONA, Roman goddess of tree fruit—apples, cherries, etc. (*i.e., poma*). She is obviously an old Italian goddess, for she had a special priest at Rome, the *flamen Pomonalis.* Although there is no festival in her honour in the calendar, there was a sacred area, the Pomonal, 12 mi. from Rome in the direction of Ostia. Ovid tells the story (*Metamorphoses* XIV, 623 ff.), perhaps of his own making, that she spurned all her woodland would-be suitors. The god Vertumnus, however, after wooing her in many disguises finally gained his suit. She is also said to have been associated with the agricultural deity Picus.

BIBLIOGRAPHY.—G. Wissowa, *Religion und Kultus,* 2nd ed., pp. 198 ff. (1912); W. Ehlers, "Pomona," in Pauly-Wissowa, *Real-Encyclopädie der classischen Altertumswissenschaft;* A. M. Young, *Legend Builders of the West* (1958). (R. B. Ld.)

POMONA or MAINLAND (the latter is the more correct name), the central and largest island of the Orkneys, Scot. Pop. (1961) 13,495. Area, including smaller adjacent islands, 201.6 sq.mi. (522 sq.km.). It is irregularly shaped, and Kirkwall bay and Scapa Flow, cutting into the land on the north and south respectively, at one point reduce the width to less than 2 mi. The western coast is almost unbroken, but the eastern and southern shores are considerably indented. Ward hill (881 ft. [269 m.]) in the south is the highest peak in the island. There are numerous lakes, some of considerable size and most of them abounding in trout. Kirkwall (*q.v.*), the capital of the Orkneys, and Stromness (*q.v.*) are the only towns. Antiquities include Pictish *brochs,* chambered mounds, and weems, or underground dwellings afterward roofed in. Northeast of Stromness, and within a mile of the standing stones of Stenness, lies the great barrow or chambered mound of Maeshowe. It is a blunted cone 300 ft. (91 m.) in circumference, and at a distance of 90 ft. (27 m.) from its base is encircled by a moat. The ground plan shows that it was entered from the west by a passage, leading to a central apartment, the walls of which ended in a beehive roof. The barrow is variously ascribed to the Stone Age and to 10th-century Norsemen. The stone circles forming the Ring of Brogar and the Ring of Stenness, traditionally pagan temples, lie 4½ mi. (7 km.) NE of Stromness. The former stands on a raised circular platform of turf, surrounded by a moat and a grassy rampart. The ring originally comprised 60 stones, varying from 9 to 14 ft. (3 to 4 m.) in height, set up at intervals of 17 ft. (5 m.). Only 27 are now erect. The Ring of Stenness is of similar construction, and 150 yd. (137 m.) N of it formerly stood the monolith called the Stone of Odin, pierced by a hole at the height of 5 ft. (1½ m.), through which persons swearing a particularly binding oath clasped hands. At the bay of Skaill is the Neolithic village of Skara Brae (*q.v.*), where evidence has been found of more than one occupation, with perhaps hundreds of years between. On Marwick Head stands the Kitchener memorial, erected to the memory of Lord Kitchener, drowned off Mainland in 1916. *See also* ORKNEY ISLANDS.

POMONA, a city of California, U.S., is in Los Angeles County, 30 mi. E of Los Angeles. A group of promoters purchased lands for town and agricultural development in 1875. The settlement, which the founders named Pomona for the Roman goddess of fruit, grew slowly until after 1880, when the sinking of deep wells provided a dependable source of irrigation water and made it the centre of a prosperous farming and fruit-raising region. The southern California real estate boom of 1887 brought rapid growth to Pomona; the town was incorporated in 1888 and the census of 1890 recorded a population of 3,634. Pomona remained the trading centre for a growing region which produced oranges, lemons, and walnuts as well as deciduous fruits, field crops, and livestock. The Southern Pacific, Santa Fe, and Union Pacific railroads, which passed through or near it, gave a wide outlet for its crops. Pomona's agricultural character was recognized by the location of the extensive grounds of the Los Angeles County Fair there.

World War II and the years following brought major changes to Pomona. Its population, which had been 20,695 in 1930, grew to 87,384 by 1970. (For comparative population figures *see* table in CALIFORNIA: *Population.*) This was partly due to the expansion of Los Angeles, which brought Pomona into commuting range of the city. It was even more the result of the industrialization of Pomona itself. There had been some manufacturing in Pomona since 1902, notably of water pumps necessary for the irrigation of the fruit groves. During and after the war, however, the number and size of industrial plants increased steadily. Naval ordnance, guided missiles, aircraft parts, pumps, paper products, and tile were manufactured. Hundreds of acres of orange groves were replaced by single-family dwellings, and citrus culture was no longer the prime activity of the region. The Kellogg-Voorhis campus of the California State Polytechnic College was established in 1938 just west of Pomona. The city has a council-administrator form of government, in effect since 1949.   (J. H. K.)

POMORZE (POMERANIA), the southern coastland and hinterland of the Baltic Sea from the lower Vistula in the east to the lower Oder in the west. The Slavonic name (*po,* "along," *morze,* "sea") was latinized first as Pomorania, later as Pomerania, and germanized as Pommern. Political developments contributed in extending the name west of the Oder as far as Stralsund, with the island of Rügen (Rugia).

Physical Geography.—Pomorze is a flat country lying generally about 300 ft. (91 m.) above sea level, though its centre is traversed by a west-east range of morainic ridges rising in many places to 650 ft. (198 m.), at some points to more than 975 ft. (297 m.) and at one, the Wiezyca Hill (near Koscierzyna), to 1,079 ft. (329 m.). Off the west coast, which is irregular, lie the islands of Uznam (Usedom) and Wolin (Wollin); the eastern coast is smooth in outline, but behind the dunes or accumulations of silt there are many lakes. Altogether, hundreds of lakes, large and small, are to be found, the largest being Lebsko, Dabie, Miedwie, and Gardno. There are many small rivers, some of which flow into the Baltic (Leba, Slupia, Parseta, Rega), some into the Vistula (Wda), some into the Notec (Brda, Glda, Drawa), and some into the Oder (Ina, Plona).

The soil is for the most part thin and sandy, with patches of good land along the river valleys; there are also rich meadows and pastures and, on higher ground, dense forest, mainly coniferous. Poland's ports are situated in Pomorze: in the chief ports, Gdánsk (Danzig), Gdynia, and Szczecin (Stettin), important shipbuilding industry is concentrated, while Kolobrzeg (Kolberg), Darlowo (Rügenwalde), and Ustka (Stolpmünde) are mainly centres of fishing industry.

History.—In prehistoric times the southern coast of the Baltic seems to have been occupied by Celts, who made way for various tribes of Germanic stock. These in turn were replaced, about the end of the 5th century A.D., by Slavs: the Pomorane or Pomorzanie settled between the Vistula and the Oder, while the Polabs were occupying the land between the Oder and the Elbe (Labe).

Almost the whole of Pomorze was included in the territory of Mieszko I (d. 992), Poland's first historical ruler; and his successor Boleslaw I the Brave (992–1025) founded a Polish bishopric at Kolobrzeg in A.D. 1000.

At that time there existed a local dynasty that ruled over the whole of Pomorze and also in what was later known as Mecklenburg. Swiatobor or Svantibor, duke of Pomorze, who died in 1107, divided his land among his three sons: Boguslaw (Bogislaw or Bogislav) received the eastern part (Pomerania Ulterior, later known as Hinterpommern), with Gdánsk; Warcislaw (Wratislaw) received the western part (Pomerania Citerior, or Vorpommern), with Wologoszcz (Wolgast); while Ratibor was the ruler of the central part, with Szczecin. The dukes recognized Polish suzerainty during the reign of Boleslaw III (1102–38); and about 1119 eastern Pomorze was included in the Polish Kujawy diocese of Kruszwica. Later this episcopal see was transferred to Wloclawek. In 1140 a new bishopric for western and central Pomorze was created at Wolin, and in 1176 it was transferred to Kamien (Kammin), replacing that of Kolobrzeg.

In 1181 both western and central Pomorze had to accept the protection of the German *Reich,* and in 1225 the Kamien diocese was transferred from the Polish archbishopric of Gniezno to the German archbishopric of Magdeburg. In the following five centuries these two parts of Pomorze were united under a single duke for two periods (1264–95 and 1478–1532) but generally remained separated under two branches of the same family. From the 13th century the country was opened to German immigrants, and this resulted in the germanization of the towns and later of the nobility and of the countryside.

In eastern Pomorze (Gdánsk), Duke Msciwoj I (1209–20) was succeeded by his son Swietopelk (1220–66), who had to defend his lands against the Teutonic Order, which in 1226 succeeded in establishing itself east of the lower Vistula. Swietopelk's son, Msciwoj II, having no issue, agreed in 1282 that after his death his dukedom should become part of Poland; and this came about in 1294. In 1308, however, eastern Pomorze was conquered by the Teutonic Order; but Poland's reconquest of it (1454) was recognized by the Order in 1466.

Western and central Pomorze remained under the suzerainty of the German *Reich.* In 1625 Boguslaw XIV once more united the duchies of Wolgast and Stettin, but he died without issue in 1637 and the whole succession passed to Brandenburg. At the peace of Westphalia in 1648 it was again divided with Sweden, which took Vorpommern, that is, the part west of the Oder, with Stettin, leaving the remainder, Hinterpommern, as far as the frontiers of Poland, to Brandenburg. In 1720 Stettin and the southern part of Vorpommern, as far as the Peene (Piana) River, were ceded to Brandenburg, but the northern part, with Greifswald, Stralsund, and Rügen, remained Swedish until 1815.

In the meantime, Polish Pomorze was annexed by Brandenburg-Prussia in 1772 and renamed West Prussia (Westpreussen). It was recovered by restored Poland in 1919, with somewhat smaller boundaries, and until 1939 constituted the province of Pomorze, with its chief town at Torun. Its area was 6,327 sq.mi. (16,387 sq.km.) and in 1921 it had 939,000 inhabitants.

In 1815 Vorpommern and Hinterpommern were united in one Prussian province of Pommern, with its chief town at Stettin. That province had an area of 11,663 sq.mi. (30,207 sq.km.) and its population in 1926 was 1,897,166.

After 1945 almost the whole of historic Pomorze, except its section west of the Oder, became part of Poland. It was then divided into three provinces (*wojewodztwa*) of Gdánsk, Bydgoszcz, and

Szczecin. On June 1, 1950, a fourth province of Koszalin was formed in the eastern part of that of Szczecin. The four provinces of Pomorze cover together an area of 24,103 sq.mi. (62,427 sq.km.). Their population in 1946 was 2,041,170, including 619,287 Germans. In 1960 it was 4,367,400, practically all Poles. (K. Sm.)

POMPADOUR, JEANNE ANTOINETTE POISSON, MARQUISE DE (1721–1764), fourth and most famous of the acknowledged mistresses of Louis XV of France, was born in Paris on Dec. 29, 1721. Of lower middle-class parentage, she owed her fortune in the first instance to her father's misfortune and her mother's devotion and resource. Her father, François Poisson, had been employed by the Páris brothers, influential army contractors and bankers; and in 1725, when they were involved in a temporary financial failure, he had to flee abroad, where he remained for eight years. In the interval his wife, to support her family, found a rich protector in C. F. Le Normant de Tournehem, who gave her daughter an expensive education and arranged her marriage, in March 1741, to his nephew, C. G. Le Normant d'Étioles. The young girl was by then already remarkable for

THE BETTMANN ARCHIVE

MARQUISE DE POMPADOUR, DETAIL OF PORTRAIT BY MAURICE QUENTIN DE LA TOUR

her beauty: although tall, her figure was perfect, her complexion clear, her hair chestnut, and her eyes animated and expressive. Her talents as a hostess in the world of finance and fashion, her intellectual interests, her musical and acting ability soon attracted attention in Paris, where she entertained some of the leading writers of the day, including Voltaire, Montesquieu, Fontenelle, and the elder Crébillon.

Early in 1745, Madame d'Étioles attracted the attention of Louis XV at a masked ball at Versailles. During his absence in the summer on the Fontenoy campaign, he created her marquise de Pompadour; and after his return she was formally presented to the queen at Versailles in September and so recognized as the king's *maîtresse en titre.*

Though the dauphin, the aristocratic court, and the Jesuits frowned on her, Madame de Pompadour soon established her ascendancy over Louis XV. She provided him with distractions from the affairs of state, sharing his mania for building and landscape gardening, introducing amateur theatricals to the court, and giving a stimulus to art and literature. She continued and increased her contacts with the *philosophes*—securing Voltaire the post of historiographer royal and admission to the Académie Française, having François Quesnay, founder of the Physiocratic School of economists, as her physician, and affording protection and encouragement to the editors of the *Encyclopédie.* Her exquisite taste was shown in the interior decoration of her various residences, particularly that of Bellevue, near Saint-Cloud, in the enlargement of the Hôtel d'Evreux (now the Élysée palace), and in the building of the École Militaire by J. A. Gabriel. She also took a personal interest in the supervision of the state china manufactory at Sèvres and was responsible for the appointment of her brother, Abel Poisson, as supervisor of buildings (1751); he proved extremely competent, and was created marquis de Marigny in 1754. Her political influence has been exaggerated: it was mainly exerted in internal affairs, in the appointment and dismissal of ministers, and in the animus that she displayed against the Jesuits. Though Austria's secret negotiations for the reversal of alliances which began the Seven Years' War were initially conducted through Madame de Pompadour's agent, the abbé François Joachim de Bernis, her responsibility for the Austrian treaties of alliance with France in 1756 and 1757 was much less than formerly supposed. Her physical liaison with the king had terminated about 1751, but she still continued as his friend and adviser till her death, at Ver-

sailles, on April 15, 1764.

In her later years Madame de Pompadour became more devotional in her habits and acquired a securer status at court after her appointment in 1756 as lady-in-waiting to the queen.

BIBLIOGRAPHY.—P. de Nolhac, *Louis XV et Madame de Pompadour* (1928) and *Madame de Pompadour et la politique* (1930); H. Carré, *La Marquise de Pompadour,* 1937; Nancy Mitford, *Madame de Pompadour* (1954); G. P. Gooch, *Louis XV* (1956).   (A. Gn.)

POMPANO, any of a number of coastal fishes in the jack family (Carangidae), especially several species of *Trachinotus.* Pompanos occur in all warm seas. They are deep-bodied with smooth sides. The first dorsal fin is composed of seven or fewer very low spines; the second dorsal and anal fins are of about equal length and longer than the abdomen, and their highest rays are usually more than three-fourths the length of the head.

The common pompano of eastern America (*Trachinotus carolinus*) ranges from North Carolina to Brazil; it reaches a length of about 18 in. and a weight of about 2 lb. It is perhaps the most delicious of the pompanos, and one of the most costly food fishes of the United States. The African pompano (*Alectis ciliaris*), another carangid, has long streamers, extending from its dorsal and anal fins, which disappear with age. *Diapterus olisthostomus,* of the mojarra family (Gerridae), is called the Irish pompano; it occurs from the West Indies to southern Florida. The Pacific, or California, pompano (*Palometa simillima*) is of the butter-

NEW YORK ZOOLOGICAL SOCIETY

LONG-FINNED POMPANO OR PALOMETA (TRACHINOTUS GLAUCUS)

fish family (Stromateidae); it occurs from San Diego to Puget Sound.   (L. A. Wd.)

POMPEII, an ancient city of Campania, Italy, 14 mi. SE of Naples, near Mt. Vesuvius, built on a spur formed by a prehistoric lava flow to the north of the mouth of the Sarnus (modern Sarno) River. Pompeii was destroyed, together with Herculaneum and Stabiae (*qq.v.*), by the eruption of Vesuvius in A.D. 79; the circumstances of their preservation make their remains a unique document of Greco-Roman life. The modern town of Pompei (pop. [1961] 20,142) lies to the east; it contains the basilica of Sta. Maria del Rosario, a pilgrimage centre.

History.—Pompeii was a suitable occupation site for the first Oscan inhabitants of Campania, and from the 8th century B.C. the Sarnus mouth must have offered a good anchorage to the earliest Greek navigators. However, archaeological evidence does not go back beyond the 6th century, when, to judge from the remains of an archaic Doric temple in the triangular forum, Pompeii came under the rule of the Greeks of Cumae. The Etruscan occupation mentioned by Strabo has not been conclusively proved by excavation. Toward the end of the 5th century Campania was invaded by Samnite peoples. Pompeii was conquered and thereafter rebuilt in Italic style, its constitution, language (Oscan), customs, and religion being those of the Samnites.

In 310 B.C. a Roman fleet landed at Pompeii but was driven off. The Pompeians took little part in the Samnite and Hannibalic wars, but they intervened vigorously in the Italic revolt against Rome (the Social War, or war of the *socii*); in 89 Pompeii was besieged, and probably captured, by L. Cornelius Sulla. In 80 B.C. it became a Roman colony with the name of Colonia Cornelia Veneria Pompeianorum, from Sulla's name and the cult of Venus Pompeiana. Publius Sulla, the dictator's nephew, was put in charge of the new organization of the colony; an echo of this troubled period survives in Cicero's defense of Publius Sulla.

Pompeii soon became romanized in language, constitution, and architecture. In A.D. 59 a riot in the amphitheatre between Pompeians and Nucerians resulted in several deaths, and the Roman Senate banned gladiatorial shows there for ten years. The city was the commercial, agricultural, and maritime centre of the Sarnus valley, with a population estimated at 20,000–22,000, when, in 62 (or possibly February 63—Tacitus and Seneca give different dates), it suffered a disastrous earthquake. Reconstruction was still in progress when, on Aug. 24, 79, there followed the violent eruption of Vesuvius described in two letters (vi, 16 and 20) from an eyewitness, Pliny the Younger, to the historian Tacitus. Pliny the Elder, commander of the Roman fleet, rushed from Misenum to help the stricken population and to get a close view of the volcanic phenomena, and died at Stabiae. Falling lapilli, pumice, and hot scoriae (for terms, *see* VOLCANO) covered Pompeii over six feet deep, causing the roofs of the houses to fall in. A rain of ashes followed, reaching a depth of five to six feet and preserving in a pall of ash the bodies of the inhabitants who perished sheltering in their houses or trying to escape toward the coast or by the roads leading to Stabiae or Nuceria; many were suffocated by the ash. Thus Pompeii remained buried under a layer of lapilli and ash 12 ft. or more deep, overlaid in time by a further 6 ft. of fertile earth.

History of the Excavations.—In the late 16th century, buildings and paintings in the hill called La Civita were discovered during the construction of a water channel from the Sarno. Systematic exploration was begun in March 1748 by the king of Naples, Charles of Bourbon (later Charles III of Spain). The finds of the excavations carried out before 1763 were limited to the area of the amphitheatre, the Via delle Tombe, the Villa of Julia Felix, the so-called Villa of Cicero outside Porta Ercolano, and the Temple of Isis. In 1763 the discovery of an inscription identified the ruins as those of Pompeii.

At first the excavators looked mainly for paintings, statues, and precious objects. But a real interest in the architecture was awakened with the discovery of the first large public buildings, the fine houses, and above all the forum. More systematic excavation, together with preservation and restoration, began in 1860 under the direction of G. Fiorelli, who also originated the method of obtaining impressions of the bodies of the victims by pouring plaster of paris into the hollows left in the ash, a system also adopted for wooden house frameworks, domestic furniture, and trees. After 1895, paintings and mosaics were left *in situ,* including those of the House of the Vettii, the House of the Silver Wedding, the House of the Golden Cupids, the House of M. Lucretius Fronto and, more recently, the houses and shops in the Via dell' Abbondanza, the Villa of the Mysteries, the House of the Menander, and the great *palaestra* (sports ground). Among the restorations of architectural interest which have been carried out is that of the *tribunal* of the basilica.

After World War II, in 1951, intensive excavation was resumed south of the Via dell' Abbondanza, as far as the inner rampart of the walls, bringing to light some fine houses, such as the House-Villa of Julia Felix (excavated and buried again in the 18th century), the House of Venus Marina, the House of the Fruit Orchard, the House of the Beautiful Impluvium, and numerous minor rustic and commercial dwellings. Also since 1951 the external line of the walls has been largely freed from the debris of former excavators outside it. As a result, the Porta di Nocera

and a monumental cemetery flanking the road from Pompeii to Nocera Inferiore have been discovered. More than three-fifths of the city has been uncovered, not counting the villas and cemeteries outside it.

Topography and Construction Periods.—Pompeii was built upon a lava flow that sloped sharply down from north to south; in the south and west the lava flow formed a steep wall which constituted a natural bulwark toward the sea. The city was level in the southwestern sector, in which were the forum and the more important public and religious buildings. There were other minor terraces, for instance around the Temple of Venus in the southwest and the triangular forum in the southeast (*see* plan). The extreme southeastern section of the perimeter wall was reserved, because of its flat surface, for the construction of the amphitheatre; in the other parts of the city the construction of buildings had to overcome the slope of the ground by means of embankments and cryptoporticoes with arches.

The Via Stabiana, which crosses the city from northwest to southeast, from Porta Vesuvio to Porta Stabia, passes along the line of the steepest slope and is crossed at right angles by two other main streets, the Via di Nola and the Via dell' Abbondanza. Corresponding with the main roads there are seven gates, named according to their position: Porta Marina, Porta Ercolano, Porta Vesuvio, Porta di Nola, Porta di Sarno, Porta di Nocera, and Porta Stabia; the existence of the Porta di Capua in the north is still doubtful. The town is conventionally divided into nine regions, each consisting of several *insulae* (blocks) which normally include several dwellings; consequently every building in Pompeii is known by the number of its region, its *insula,* and the room with the main entrance.

The plan of the town is less uniform geometrically than those of Neapolis (Naples) and Herculaneum; presumably at Pompeii the building plan evolved gradually from an Oscan nucleus, subsequently enlarged during the periods of Greek, Etruscan, and Samnite influence.

The construction periods can be divided approximately into the following:

1. Pre-Samnite (500–420 B.C.), in which limestone materials, almost exclusively from alluvial deposits of the Sarnus, were used, and building was in *opus quadratum* (stone blocks; *see* ROMAN ARCHITECTURE: *Building Techniques*). The Doric temple in the triangular forum and the pre-Samnite walls belong to this period.

2. First Samnite (420–250 B.C.), in which mainly limestone was used and construction in tufa was begun, employing *opus quadratum* and *opus incertum* (concrete faced with irregular pieces of stone) techniques. This period includes the restoration of the perimeter walls, the construction of houses with limestone atria, the regular plan of some quarters of the town, and the completion

EDWIN SMITH

VIA STABIANA

of the network of roads, besides the building of the Temple of Jupiter.

3. Second Samnite (250–80 B.C.), in which tufa is chiefly used, while Hellenistic Greek influence is noticeable in the architecture. In this period took place the second and third restorations of the walls, with the addition of the towers, the building of the forum, the large theatre, and, later, the porticoes of the forum, the Temple of Apollo, the triangular forum, the small *palaestra* and the Stabian baths. The original foundations of the basilica and the decoration of the floors of the houses with mosaics also fall within this period.

4. Beginning of Roman colonization (80–*c.* 23 B.C.), when *opus reticulatum* (concrete faced with regular pieces of stone) and brick facing were first employed. The forum baths were built, as well as the *odeon* (small theatre), the amphitheatre, the Temple of Venus and the Temple of Zeus Meilichios.

5. Augustan and Julio-Claudian (23 B.C.–A.D. 62), in which *opus reticulatum* was extensively used. Marble was used for the facing of buildings, while the houses were rich in decorative features and paintings with Greek subjects. New public buildings were constructed along the southern and eastern sides of the forum, and existing buildings were freshly decorated.

6. First Flavian (A.D. 62–79), in which there was a marked use of *opus latericium* (brick-faced concrete) in the reconstruction of the buildings damaged in the earthquake of 62. The Temple of Isis was rebuilt and the central baths and the *aulae* of the curia were begun.

Public and Private Buildings.—The most important public monuments of Pompeii, except for the baths and the amphitheatre, were grouped round the civil forum and the smaller triangular forum. The civil forum was rectangular and surrounded by a portico with a gallery above it. Around it are: the Temple of Jupiter, sacred to the Capitoline triad (Jupiter, Juno, and Minerva) after Pompeii became a *colonia*, severely damaged by the earthquake; the Temple of Apollo, the best preserved in Pompeii; the basilica, seat of the law court, preceded by a *chalcidicum* (vestibule) with tufa pillars, and divided inside into three naves by a magnificent colonnade; on the inner wall rises the pillared front of the *tribunal*, inspired by the purest models of Hellenistic Greek architecture, while the covered court of the basilica already fore-

shadows the Vitruvian style; the *sacrarium* dedicated to the *lares* of the city; the Temple of the *genius* of Augustus (sometimes called Temple of Vespasian); the *curia* (council house), opposite the Temple of Jupiter; the *macellum* or covered market; the great building of Eumachia, seat of the corporation of the manufacturers and cleaners of cloth.

The triangular forum is one of the oldest centres of the city. In it, along the side of the terrace of the 6th-century Doric temple, was developed, between the 3rd and the 1st century B.C., a group of buildings intended for public entertainment, particularly the small *palaestra*, the large theatre, and the small covered theatre, or *odeon*. Thus the triangular forum has the noncommercial character of a Hellenistic city quarter, while the civil forum was built in a markedly Italic and Roman style and was the centre of the daily life of the city.

At the extreme southeast angle of the built-up area rose the amphitheatre, perhaps the oldest so far known (*see* AMPHITHEATRE). Great flights of stairs in a double ramp constructed externally lead to the top row, where there are large stone rings to receive the framework for the support of the *velarium* (canopy). To the west of it is the great *palaestra*.

The baths (*thermae*) of Pompeii include the Stabian baths, the forum baths, and the unfinished central baths, besides many private baths preserved in the nobler houses of the city; they are important examples of both architecture and decoration (*see* BATH).

In Pompeii it is possible to follow the evolution of the ancient house through at least five centuries, from the primitive Italic house, closed externally and open on the inside, overlooking the atrium, which is surrounded by the living rooms, to the house clearly showing Hellenistic influence in both its decorative and functional elements. The House of the Surgeon, near Porta Ercolano, of Italic type, yielded a large set of surgical instruments. Houses of the Samnite period, enlarged or improved in the republican and imperial periods, include the House of the Faun, which covers a whole *insula* and has two entrances and two atria; the House of the Labyrinth, in which the architectural decoration of the walls is a background for the main architecture, an example of the second style of painting (*see* below); the House of Meleager; the House of the Silver Wedding; the House of the Centenary; and the House of Cornelius Rufus.

EDWIN SMITH

GENERAL VIEW OF EXCAVATIONS
Looking north from Region I across the Via dell' Abbondanza to Region IX. Farm rising behind excavations is at ground level

In the last republican period and in the Augustan age stucco facing of the houses began and porticoes had pictorial decoration. Brick columns also began to appear, evidence of the prevalence of commerce in Pompeii, which built up an enriched middle class with more exacting if perhaps less refined tastes than those of the Samnite and Roman patricians. The problem of space brought about the transformation of the old indivisible patrician house into small houses, alternating with small shops; it led also to habitation on the upper floor, reached by means of wooden staircases, lighted by open balconies, and divided up by light wooden-frame partitions. Examples of such crowding are the House of the Vestals, the House of the Anchor, the House of the Dioscuri, the House of the Citharist. On the other hand there are houses which reflect the taste of cultured Pompeian society, such as the House of the Menander, the House of the Lovers, the House of the Ephebus (which takes its name from a

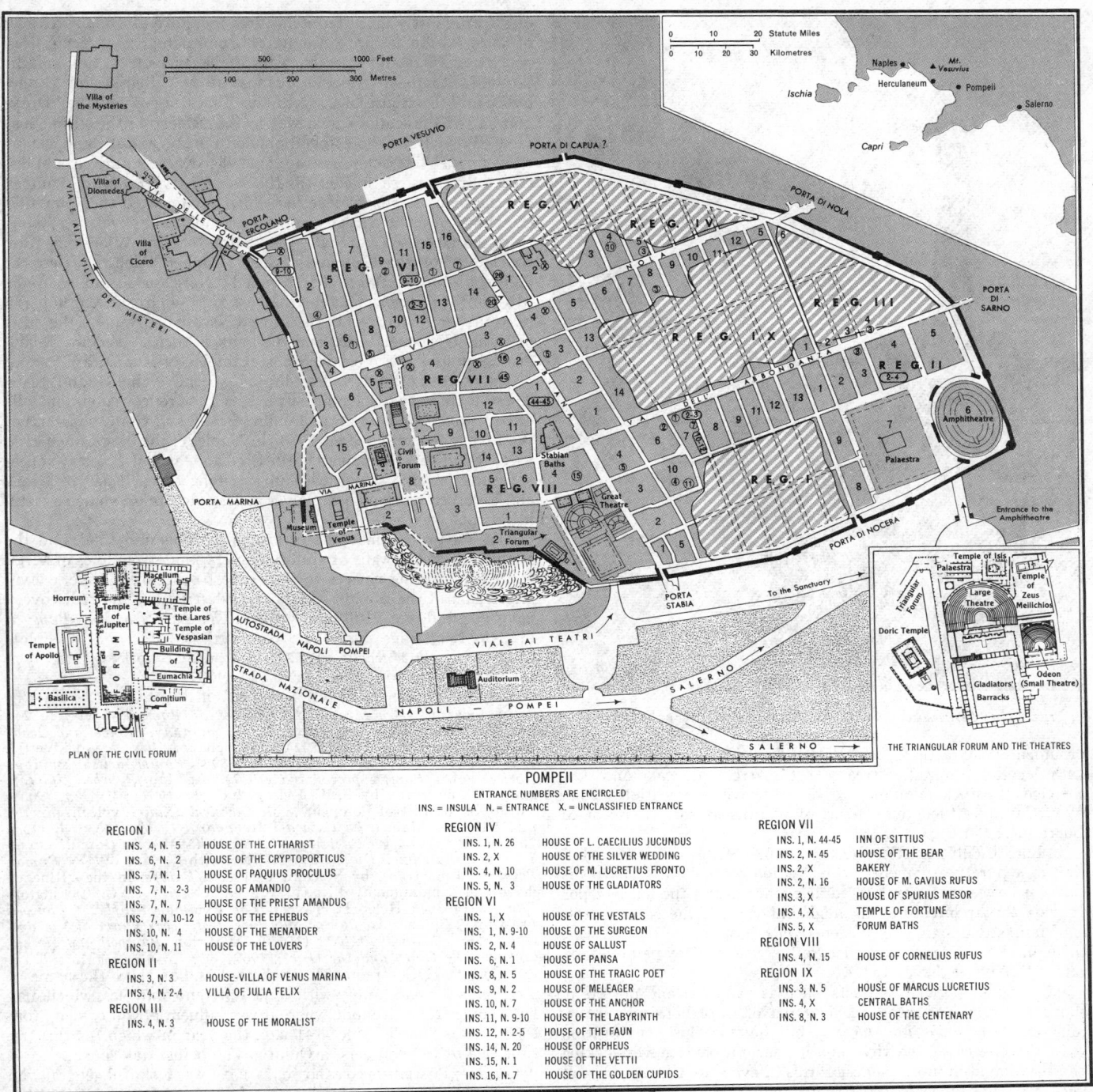

POMPEII
ENTRANCE NUMBERS ARE ENCIRCLED
INS. = INSULA   N. = ENTRANCE   X. = UNCLASSIFIED ENTRANCE

REGION I		
INS. 4, N. 5	HOUSE OF THE CITHARIST
INS. 6, N. 2	HOUSE OF THE CRYPTOPORTICUS
INS. 7, N. 1	HOUSE OF PAQUIUS PROCULUS
INS. 7, N. 2-3	HOUSE OF AMANDIO
INS. 7, N. 7	HOUSE OF THE PRIEST AMANDUS
INS. 7, N. 10-12	HOUSE OF THE EPHEBUS
INS. 10, N. 4	HOUSE OF THE MENANDER
INS. 10, N. 11	HOUSE OF THE LOVERS

REGION II
| INS. 3, N. 3 | HOUSE-VILLA OF VENUS MARINA |
| INS. 4, N. 2-4 | VILLA OF JULIA FELIX |

REGION III
| INS. 4, N. 3 | HOUSE OF THE MORALIST |

REGION IV		
INS. 1, N. 26	HOUSE OF L. CAECILIUS JUCUNDUS
INS. 2, X	HOUSE OF THE SILVER WEDDING
INS. 4, N. 10	HOUSE OF M. LUCRETIUS FRONTO
INS. 5, N. 3	HOUSE OF THE GLADIATORS

REGION VI
INS. 1, X	HOUSE OF THE VESTALS
INS. 1, N. 9-10	HOUSE OF THE SURGEON
INS. 2, N. 4	HOUSE OF SALLUST
INS. 6, N. 1	HOUSE OF PANSA
INS. 8, N. 5	HOUSE OF THE TRAGIC POET
INS. 9, N. 2	HOUSE OF MELEAGER
INS. 10, N. 7	HOUSE OF THE ANCHOR
INS. 11, N. 9-10	HOUSE OF THE LABYRINTH
INS. 12, N. 2-5	HOUSE OF THE FAUN
INS. 14, N. 20	HOUSE OF ORPHEUS
INS. 15, N. 1	HOUSE OF THE VETTII
INS. 16, N. 7	HOUSE OF THE GOLDEN CUPIDS

REGION VII		
INS. 1, N. 44-45	INN OF SITTIUS
INS. 2, N. 45	HOUSE OF THE BEAR
INS. 2, X	BAKERY
INS. 2, N. 16	HOUSE OF M. GAVIUS RUFUS
INS. 3, X	HOUSE OF SPURIUS MESOR
INS. 4, X	TEMPLE OF FORTUNE
INS. 5, X	FORUM BATHS

REGION VIII
| INS. 4, N. 15 | HOUSE OF CORNELIUS RUFUS |

REGION IX
INS. 3, N. 5	HOUSE OF MARCUS LUCRETIUS
INS. 4, X	CENTRAL BATHS
INS. 8, N. 3	HOUSE OF THE CENTENARY

FROM A. MAIURI, "POMPEII," 1962

GENERAL PLAN OF POMPEII

fine bronze statue converted into a lampstand, found in 1925), the House of Loreius Tiburtinus (or of D. Octavius Quartio), the House-Villa of Julia Felix, with a bath for public use, installed by the owner-tenant, announced by a notice affixed to the entrance.

Finally, there are modest middle-class houses, such as the House of Amandio, the House of the Priest Amandus, and the House of the Moralist, and working-class houses. Visitors to Pompeii for reasons of trade found accommodation in the *hospitia* (inns), situated at various points of the city, usually near the gates.

Painting, Mosaic, Sculpture, and Minor Arts.—Pompeii, together with Herculaneum and Stabiae, has preserved the richest evidence extant of ancient painting, used extensively in the decoration of houses and villas, evidence the more precious because the Greek painting which inspired the Campanian is virtually lost.

The wall decoration of Pompeii, from the mid-2nd century B.C. to the day of the eruption, is conventionally divided into four styles:

1. First (incrustation) style (180–80 B.C.), in which the stucco decoration imitates in various colours the plaster or marble facing of the walls (House of Sallust, House of the Faun).

2. Second (architectural) style (80 B.C.–A.D. 14), in which the decoration by the use of perspective creates the illusion of an architectural composition two or more planes in depth; figured compositions appear in the large pictures of mythological, heroic, or religious subjects as well as in the smaller pictures inserted as panels between the architectonic features (House of the Silver Wedding, House of the Cryptoporticus, Villa of the Mysteries).

3. Third (ornamental and Egyptianizing) style (*c.* A.D. 14–62), in which the architectural wall schemes are flat and assume a chiefly

EDWIN SMITH
THE TEMPLE OF APOLLO WITH MT. VESUVIUS IN THE BACKGROUND

ornamental character; columns, bands, and friezes are enriched with decorative minutiae treated with extreme delicacy and skill; the central painting dominates the decorative composition (House of L. Caecilius Jucundus, House of Spurius Mesor, House of M. Lucretius Fronto).

4. Fourth (illusionist) style (c. A.D. 62–79), in which the whole wall is a purely ornamental composition without any sharp distinction between the architectural elements and the subject portrayed; the architecture, although linked with the second style, is of fantastic design, overburdened with ornamental motifs, while the figured paintings are true decorative panels, often painted separately (House of the Vettii).

Paintings of popular subjects, such as paintings and posters on shops, portrayals of scenes in hostelries or workshops, pictures of religious ceremonies and *lararia,* fall outside this classification.

In the houses of the rich, mosaic decoration is never lacking, and it is found in more modest forms in even the humblest dwellings in a wide range of types from *opus signinum,* in terra-cotta fragments, passing on to *lithostraton,* consisting of white pebbles interspersed with coloured stones, to true mosaic in white, black, and polychrome tesserae, with a rich variety of geometrical designs, often of scenes drawn from mythology or from nature. (*See* also MOSAIC.) The mosaic of the Battle of Issus, found in the House of the Faun and now in the Museo Nazionale at Naples, is of great artistic value, being a copy of a lost Hellenistic painting (*see* GREEK ART: *The Hellenistic Period* [*c.* 330–*c.* 30 B.C.]: *Hellenistic Painting*). Other mosaics of particular artistic value are those discovered in the so-called Villa of Cicero (in the Naples museum) of scenes and sketches of life of the people in Hellenistic settings; one of these bears the signature of Dioscurides of Samos. In the Flavian era mosaic is replaced by floors in inlay or *opus sectile.*

Pompeii has also yielded a valuable range of bronze and marble sculptures, besides gold, silver, bronze, terra-cotta, glass, bone and ivory household objects of every type; the most precious works

of art are mostly imported items, but there are also many articles of local workmanship. Among the more important sculptures, which testify to the eclectic taste of the ancients in art, are the "Apollo Citharoedus" from the House of the Citharist; the "Ephebus" from the House of P. Cornelius Tages; a copy of the "Doryphoros" of Polyclitus which was in the *palaestra;* the "Ephebus" of the Polyclitan school found outside Porta Vesuvio; and a copy of Lysippus' "Heracles Epitrapezios" discovered in the coastal district. But most significant for the art and civilization of Pompeii are the many bronze statuettes which ornamented the fountains, the nymphaea, the gardens, and the triclinia; the "Dancing Faun" from the House of the Faun, the "Satyr with the Wineskin" from the House of the Centenary, the "Drunken Silenus" from the House of the Marbles, the so-called "Narcissus," and so forth. Most of the statues, including the busts and some excellent imperial portraits, are preserved in the Museo Nazionale, Naples: the busts of Gaius Norbanus Sorex and the banker Lucius Caecilius Jucundus are among the most vigorous examples of Roman art.

Toilet and table articles display special richness and taste. These include two splendid silver services from a suburban villa at Boscoreale (mostly in the Louvre, Paris) and from the House of the Menander (discovered 1930; in Naples); the blue cameo glass vase, found in a tomb near Porta Ercolano, also at Naples; and finally the jewelry, which without attaining the delicacy of Greek and Etruscan craftsmanship gives a clear picture of women's tastes in Pompeii.

The finds of ordinary objects such as tools and food, and the abundance on the walls of graffiti of every kind, from lines of Virgil and electioneering notices to the crudest obscenities, give a vivid impression of the life of the city. Its destruction and rediscovery have inspired, *e.g.,* Bulwer-Lytton's *The Last Days of Pompeii* (1834), Leopardi's poem "La Ginestra" (1836), and Théophile Gautier's *Arria Marcella* (1852); more recent works include Jack Lindsay's *The Writing on the Wall* (1960).

See also references under "Pompeii" in the Index.

BIBLIOGRAPHY.—F. Mazois, *Les Ruines de Pompéi,* 4 vol. (1824–38); Sir William Gell, *Pompeiana: the Topography, Edifices and Ornaments of Pompeii,* 2 vol. (1832); A. Sogliano, "La Casa dei Vetti," *Monumenti antichi,* vol. viii, pp. 234 ff. (1898), *Pompei nel suo sviluppo storico,* vol. i, *Pompei preromana* (1937); A. Mau, *Pompeii, Its Life and Art,* Eng. trans. by F. W. Kelsey, 2nd ed. (1902); F. Day, "Agriculture in the Life of Pompeii," *Yale Classical Studies,* vol. iii, pp. 165 ff. (1932); A. Maiuri, *La Casa del Menandro,* 2 vol. (1933), *Pompei,* 2nd ed. (1943), *La Villa dei Misteri,* 2nd ed. (1947), *La Casa di Loreio Tiburtino e la villa di Diomede in Pompei,* with R. Pane (1947), *Roman Painting,* Eng. trans. by S. Gilbert (1953), *Pompei* in the "Itinerari dei musei e monumenti d'Italia," 8th ed. (1956); R. C. Carrington, *Pompeii* (1936); Helen H. Tanzer, *The Common People of Pompeii* (1939); V. Spinazzola, *Pompei alla luce degli scavi nuovi di Via dell' Abbondanza, anni 1910–1923* (1953); M. Brion, *Pompeii and Herculaneum: the Glory and the Grief* (1960).   (A. MA.; X.)

POMPEIUS (frequently anglicized as POMPEY), the name of a plebeian Roman family with three different branches, which may have come from Picenum, where it was influential and owned property; it was "noble" since 141 B.C., the year in which for the first time one of its members, a Quintus Pompeius, was consul.

GNAEUS POMPEIUS STRABO (d. 87 B.C.) was a skilful general who as consul in 89 campaigned successfully in the Social War (the war of the Italian *socii,* "allies"), captured Asculum, and celebrated a triumph; he carried the law (*lex Pompeia*) granting Latin status to the inhabitants of Cisalpine Gaul north of the Po River, which may have been the charter by which Cisalpine Gaul was constituted a province. He evaded an attempted prosecution for treason (*maiestas*) and retained command of his army in 88 in Picenum after it had murdered the consul Quintus Pompeius Rufus who was sent to supersede him. Though in 87 he obeyed the Senate's summons to come with his army to defend Rome against the attack of Cinna and Marius, he declined at the critical point to drive home his military advantage. He was perhaps intriguing with Cinna in the hope of using his army to secure dominant power for himself; but in an epidemic which killed large numbers of his troops he died. He was described by Cicero in 65 B.C. as "a man hated by the gods and the nobility."

GNAEUS POMPEIUS MAGNUS (POMPEY THE GREAT) (106–48 B.C.), son of the preceding, an exact contemporary of Cicero, celebrated a triumph and commanded armies before he was even a member of the Roman Senate, conquered Mithradates VI of Pontus, and was generally esteemed the greatest general and administrator of the late Roman Republic until his defeat by Julius Caesar at Pharsalus in 48. He served under his father in the Social War; joined, then in 84 abandoned, the popular cause of Cinna; raised three legions from clients and veterans of his father in Picenum to fight for Sulla on his return to Italy in 83. He married Sulla's stepdaughter Aemilia and in 81 and 80 recovered Sicily and Africa for Sulla. In Africa his army saluted him, perhaps not as *imperator* but as *Magnus* ("great"), by which name—no doubt because of his supposed likeness to Alexander the Great—he was probably called already in his camp. Sulla addressed him by this name on his return to Italy, after being forced to tolerate Pompey's refusal to disband his army in Africa. It was more like a Hellenistic royal

MARBLE HEAD (c. 60–50 B.C.) OF POMPEY THE TRIUMVIR; IN THE NY CARLSBERG GLYPTOTEK, COPENHAGEN

name than a Roman one, and had something in common with Sulla's name of *Felix;* it embarrassed Pompey for some years after Sulla's death.

He celebrated a triumph on March 12, 79. After the death of Sulla, with whom at the end he was not on good terms, he received extraordinary military commissions from the Senate to help in suppressing the risings of Lepidus in Italy in 78/77—this was when he broke his word and executed the father of M. Brutus, the later assassin of Julius Caesar —and of Sertorius in Spain (77– 71). In Italy he defeated the

remnants of Spartacus' army on his return in 71, was elected consul for 70 with strong popular support (though he was not even a senator nor of the proper age), and triumphed on the last day of the year. Crassus was his colleague as consul; their relations, ever since Sulla had shown his preference for Pompey, were consistently bad.

From 70 until his return from the east in 62 he had strong popular and equestrian support (*see* EQUITES) and was suspected and feared as a possible subverter of republicanism by the conservative element in the Senate, the Optimates, particularly Q. Lutatius Catulus (consul of 78). The most unpopular of Sulla's constitutional changes were revoked in his consulship; in 67 by the *lex Gabinia* he received a three-year commission (which he executed in three months) to eliminate piracy from the Mediterranean, and in 66 by the *lex Manilia* he was given command in the war against Mithradates in which Lucullus (*q.v.*) had recently been superseded. Mithradates was defeated at Nicopolis (modern Purk in northeastern Turkey), and driven to the Crimea, where he died in 63; his son-in-law Tigranes I of Armenia submitted to Pompey. Pompey proceeded, with ostentatious disregard of arrangements made previously by Lucullus and the senatorial commission sent out to assist Lucullus, to make far-reaching administrative arrangements affecting the whole area of his conquests. The province of Cilicia was enlarged; two new provinces, Bithynia-Pontus and Syria, received charters (the *lex Pompeia*, the constitution of Bithynia, was still effective in the 2nd century A.D.); and in Palestine he deposed King Aristobulus and appointed Hyrcanus high priest and ethnarch of Galilee, Judaea, and Peraea. On returning to Italy in late 62, he disbanded his army at Brundisium (instead of repeating Sulla's march on Rome, as alarmist Optimates had anticipated), and celebrated his third prodigious triumph on Sept. 28/29, 61.

In politics from 61 to 50 he showed neither courage, determination, nor policy. Never having served the apprenticeship of a junior senator, he did not feel at home in politics or with politicians. His guarded and ambiguous utterances were susceptible to, and received, the most varied and often sinister interpretations. Like Cicero, he was isolated, accepted wholeheartedly by neither

Populares nor Optimates (among whom he had offended the Metelli and their connections by his divorce in 62 of his third wife Mucia, mother of his two sons and of his daughter). Only his administrative genius remained unimpaired until his serious illness in early summer 50.

Understandably piqued by Pompey's refusal to countenance a senatorial debate on his eastern settlement, the Senate delayed making land allotments to Pompey's troops. His acts were in the end confirmed and land allotments made through bills promoted by Caesar as consul in 59, the outcome of the pact (which modern historians conventionally call "the first triumvirate") by which Pompey, Crassus, and Caesar joined forces in politics for their separate purposes in 60, Pompey marrying Caesar's daughter Julia (very happily, as it transpired) in 59 (*see* CAESAR, GAIUS JULIUS; CRASSUS). From 58 to 56, Caesar being in Gaul, Pompey, who had disliked the violence with which Caesar's measures were carried in 59 and for whose alliance Optimate politicians were starting to bid, was frightened and excluded from politics in Caesar's interest and at Crassus' instigation, through the belief, carefully fostered by Clodius (*q.v.*), that his life was threatened. So he did nothing to prevent Cicero's exile in 58, but in 57 he played a large part in securing Cicero's recall, and directly afterward, in September, he received a special commission to reorganize the corn supply of Rome (*cura annonae*). There was opposition in the Senate and, organized by Clodius, outside it, to the suggestion of his being commissioned early in 56 to restore Ptolemy XII Auletes to the throne of Egypt. At Luca in April 56 Pompey, Crassus, and Caesar settled their differences and in 55, the year of the dedication of his splendid theatre, Pompey and Crassus were consuls together for the second time. Pompey was given the governorship of the two provinces of Spain for five years and, perhaps because of the corn commission, was allowed to remain in Italy (outside Rome) and to govern his provinces through deputies (*legati*). His ties with Caesar were broken when Julia died in 54 and Crassus was killed at Carrhae in 53. In the wild disorder which followed the murder of Clodius, Pompey was made sole consul just before the beginning of March 52; later in the year his new father-in-law, Q. Metellus Scipio (*see* METELLUS), became consul with him. He was ruthless in ensuring Milo's condemnation for the murder of Clodius, and passed a number of laws for the enforcement of law and order and to check opportunities of corruption in magisterial administration. (For their bearing on Caesar's position, *see* CAESAR). His Spanish governorship was reconferred for a further five years, and the Optimates were forced, however reluctantly, to rely on him as their only hope of checking the now evident ambitions of Caesar, who was expected back from Gaul in 49. The crisis over Caesar's return developed at the end of 50, and on Dec. 2 the consul Gaius Marcellus hysterically placed a sword in Pompey's hand and called on him to defend the state. Whatever the outcome of victory in the civil war might have been, it seems clear that at this moment, as indeed in the whole period since his return from the East, Pompey was instinctively a constitutionalist, and had no ambition for personal domination of an unconstitutional kind.

Caesar invaded Italy on Jan. 11, 49. Pompey was hampered by sharing his command with the consuls (which fact partly explains the failure of Caesar's attempts to negotiate with him), and by the obstinate refusal of L. Domitius Ahenobarbus to comply with his general strategy for withdrawal of the government and its armed forces through Brundisium to Illyricum. Had he pressed his advantage, he would have defeated Caesar when Caesar tried to blockade him at Dyrrhachium in spring 48; he withdrew to the east, and at Pharsalus in Thessaly he was persuaded against his better judgment to engage, and was defeated on Aug. 9. He fled from the battlefield to his wife Cornelia in Lesbos; then to Egypt, where on Sept. 28 he was murdered on landing.

When in his *De republica* (54–52 B.C.) Cicero (*q.v.*) made provision for a "moderator" in his ideal republic, he was not unmindful of Pompey, disappointed though he was at all stages of his career at the failure of his personal hopes for effective political cooperation with Pompey. Pompey's career, indeed, provided Augustus with a number of convenient republican precedents for the new constitution of the principate, in particular Pompey's position in 52, when he was consul in Rome and governor (*proconsul*) of the Spains, which he administered through *legati*. In the lost books of his *History* Livy wrote so sympathetically of Pompey that Augustus jokingly called him a Pompeian. For portrait *see* article ROMAN HISTORY.

GNAEUS POMPEIUS MAGNUS (*c.* 76–45 B.C.), the elder son of Pompey the Great and of Mucia. In 49/48 B.C. during the civil war he commanded the Egyptian section of his father's fleet in the Adriatic. After the Battle of Pharsalus he set out for Africa with the remainder of the Pompeian party but, meeting with little success, crossed over to Spain. He collected an army of 13 legions, which was increased by the Pompeians (including his brother Sextus) who fled from Africa after the Battle of Thapsus (46). Caesar, who regarded him as a formidable opponent, set out against him in person. At Munda (*q.v.*) on March 17, 45, the Pompeians were defeated. Gnaeus escaped, but was soon (early April) captured and put to death.

SEXTUS POMPEIUS MAGNUS (who in the end called himself MAGNUS POMPEIUS PIUS) (?66–35 B.C.), the younger son of Pompey the Great and of Mucia. After his father's death he continued the struggle first against Caesar, then against Octavian (later the emperor Augustus) and Antonius (Mark Antony). From Cyprus, where he had taken refuge, he made his way to Africa and, after the defeat of the Pompeians at Thapsus (46), crossed over to Spain. After Caesar's victory at Munda (45), he abandoned Corduba (Córdoba), though for a time he held his ground in the south, and defeated Asinius Pollio, the governor of the province. After Caesar's murder he came to terms with Antony and the Senate, but in 43 he was proscribed by the triumvirate and put himself at the head of a fleet manned chiefly by slaves or proscribed persons, with which he made himself master of Sicily, and from there ravaged the coasts of Italy. Rome was threatened with a famine, as the corn supplies from Egypt and Africa were cut off by his ships, and it was thought prudent to negotiate a peace with him at Misenum (39), which was to leave him in possession of Sicily, Sardinia, and Achaea, provided that he would allow Italy to be freely supplied with corn. But the arrangement could not be carried into effect, as Sextus renewed the war and gained some considerable success at sea. In 36, however, his fleet was defeated and destroyed by Agrippa at Naulochus off the north coast of Sicily. After his defeat he fled to Mytilene, and from there to Asia Minor. In an attempt to make his way to Armenia he was taken prisoner by Antony's troops and put to death at Miletus.

BIBLIOGRAPHY.—Pompeius Strabo: *Ancient sources:* A. H. J. Greenidge and A. M. Clay, *Sources for Roman History 133–70 B.C.*, 2nd ed. rev. by E. W. Gray (1960). *Modern works:* H. Last and R. Gardner in *Cambridge Ancient History*, vol. ix, ch. 4, 6 (1932); F. Miltner in Pauly-Wissowa, *Real-Encyclopädie der classischen Altertumswissenschaft*, xxi, 2254–2262 (1952); E. Badian, *Foreign Clientelae*, ch. 10 (1958).
Pompey the Great: *Ancient sources:* Cicero, *Letters, Ad familiares*, v, 7, and *Ad Atticum*, viii, 11b (Cicero to Pompey), *Ad Atticum*, vii, 11a (Pompey to Cicero), 12a-d (dispatches from Pompey; 49 B.C.); Sallust, *Histories*, ii, 98 M (purporting to be a letter from Pompey in Spain to the Senate in 75 B.C.); Cicero, *passim*; Caesar, *De bello civili*; Velleius Paterculus, ii, 29–53; Plutarch, *Pompey*; Dio Cassius, books xxxvi–xlii; Appian, *Bellum civile*, books i–ii; Strabo, xii, 555–560; Lucan, *Bellum civile*.
Modern works: E. Meyer, *Caesars Monarchie und das Principat des Pompejus*, 3rd ed. (1922); T. Rice Holmes, *The Roman Republic*, 3 vol. (1923); H. Last *et al.* in *Cambridge Ancient History*, vol. ix, ch. 6–8, 12, 15–16 (1932); R. Syme, *The Roman Revolution*, ch. 3 (1939); M. Gelzer, *Pompeius* (1949); F. Miltner in Pauly-Wissowa, *Real-Encyclopädie der classischen Altertumswissenschaft*, xxi, 2062–2211 (1952); J. van Ooteghem, S.J., *Pompée le Grand* (1954). *Early career:* E. Badian, *Foreign Clientelae*, ch. 11 (1958). *Pompey in the East:* D. Magie, *Roman Rule in Asia Minor*, ch. 15 (1950). *Pompey and Clodius:* L. G. Pocock, *A Commentary on Cicero in Vatinium*, pp. 1–28, 146–160 (1926).
Sextus Pompeius: *Ancient sources: Bellum Hispaniense* (which was certainly not written by Caesar); Dio Cassius, books xlii–xlix; Appian, *Bellum civile*, iv, 83–117; v, 2–143; Plutarch, *Antony. Modern works:* T. Rice Holmes, *The Roman Republic*, vol. iii, ch. 24 (1923), *The Architect of the Roman Empire*, vol. i, ch. 1–2 (1928); M. Hadas, *Sextus Pompey* (1930); F. E. Adcock in *Cambridge Ancient History*, vol. ix, ch. 16–17 (1932) and M. P. Charlesworth in vol. x, ch. 1–2 (1934); F. Miltner in Pauly-Wissowa, *Real-Encyclopädie der classischen Altertumswissenschaft*, xxi, 2211–2250 (1952). (J. P. V. D. B.)

POMPIDOU, GEORGES JEAN RAYMOND (1911–), teacher, bank director, and statesman, became president of the French Republic in June 1969. Born on July 5, 1911, at Montboudif in the Cantal *département*, the son of schoolteachers, Pompidou attended the École Normale Supérieure, where he won first place (1934) in the Agrégation des Lettres. He began his teaching career at the Lycée St. Charles in Marseilles, but moved to the Lycée Henri IV in Paris for a short while before the outbreak of World War II. During the war he served as an infantry lieutenant and won the Croix de Guerre.

When, late in 1944, a former fellow student, René Brouillet (then De Gaulle's chief personal assistant), introduced him to the general, head of the provisional government, Pompidou was a complete stranger to politics and had not even a record of work in the Resistance. He proved to be a natural Gaullist, however, adept at interpreting and presenting the general's policies. He served on De Gaulle's personal staff from 1944 to 1946 and remained a member of the general's "shadow cabinet" after De Gaulle's sudden resignation of the premiership in January 1946. Assistant to the general commissioner for tourism (1946–49), Pompidou also, with no legal qualifications, held the post of maître des requêtes at the Conseil d'État, France's highest administrative court, where he worked on disputed claims (1946–57). In 1955 he entered the Bank of Rothschild in Paris where, again without specific professional qualifications, he rose rapidly to become director-general (1959).

De Gaulle had never lost touch with Pompidou, and on his return to power at the time of the Algerian crisis (June 1958), took Pompidou as his chief personal assistant (June 1958–January 1959). Pompidou played an important part in drafting the constitution of the Fifth Republic and in preparing plans for economic recovery. When De Gaulle became president (January 1959), Pompidou resumed his private occupations, although he became a member of the Constitutional Council. In 1961 he was sent to establish contact with the Algerian Front de Libération Nationale (FLN), a mission that led to the cease-fire signed at Évian-les-Bains in March 1962.

The Algerian crisis resolved, De Gaulle decided to replace Michel Debré as premier and appointed Pompidou, then virtually unknown to the public, in his place (April 1962). Defeated in a vote of censure in the National Assembly (October 1962), Pompidou resumed office after De Gaulle's victory (October) in the plebiscite on the election of the president by universal suffrage. The second Pompidou administration (December 1962–January 1966) was succeeded by the third (January 1966–March 1967), and the fourth (April 1967–July 1968). Pompidou had thus been premier for six years and three months, a phenomenon that De Gaulle noted had been unknown in French politics for four generations.

The reduction of the Gaullist majority in the elections of March 1967 put Pompidou on his mettle and he developed more positive policies. His standing was probably highest at the time of the 1968 May riots. Hastily returning from a visit to Afghanistan, he persuaded De Gaulle to grant the necessary reforms and concluded with both sides of industry the Grenelle Agreement (May 27) which finally ended the strikes. Meanwhile, De Gaulle dissolved the National Assembly. In the elections of June 30, 1968, following a brilliant government campaign, organized by Pompidou, for the restoration of law and order, the Gaullists won a majority of unprecedented size. Pompidou's part in the triumph was notable, and his sudden replacement as premier by Maurice Couve de Murville caused a major sensation. Nevertheless, De Gaulle's answer to Pompidou's formal letter of resignation gave some hope for the future; stressing his continued high regard for Pompidou, the president wrote: "I hope that you will remain in readiness to carry out any mission and take up any office which the nation may one day call on you to assume."

The hope was fulfilled unexpectedly soon, when De Gaulle abruptly resigned as president, following the adverse vote in the referendum of April 27, 1969, on proposals for reorganization of local government and reform of the Senate. Pompidou campaigned for the presidency on a basis of continuing Gaullist policies, but with greater flexibility and realism. Gaining a distinct lead over his major opponents in the first round of the election (June 1), he won 58.2% of the votes cast in the second round (June 15), against the 41.8% accorded to his sole remaining rival, Alain Poher. Described by the Socialist leader Guy Mollet as the most intelligent member of De Gaulle's circle, yet more adaptable than his predecessor, Pompidou seemed likely to frame French policy more in accord with the country's actual needs and capacities.

In early 1970 Pompidou visited Washington on his first official trip overseas, and made side trips to New York and Chicago.

A scholar and writer of style and distinction, Pompidou has produced three notable works, *Étude sur Britannicus* (1944), a study of H. A. Taine's *Les Origines de la France contemporaine* (1947), and *Pages choisies, romans d'André Malraux* (1955). He also compiled an anthology of French poetry (1961).

BIBLIOGRAPHY.—P. Rouanet, *Pompidou* (1969); M. Bromberger, *Le destin secret de Georges Pompidou* (1965); P. Viansson-Ponté, *Les Gaullistes, rituel et annuaire* (1963), *Après de Gaulle, qui?* (1968). (J. M. KN.)

POMPONAZZI, PIETRO (1462–1525), Italian philosopher and a leading representative of Renaissance Aristotelianism as it had developed at the Italian universities (*i.e.*, in conjunction with medicine rather than with theology) after the end of the 13th century. He was born in Mantua on Sept. 16, 1462, studied philosophy and medicine at Padua and taught philosophy in that university (1487–1509, with interruptions), at Ferrara, and finally at Bologna (1512–25), where he died on May 18, 1525. Pomponazzi was thoroughly versed in Aristotle and his commentators, especially Averroës and St. Thomas Aquinas. His questions and lectures on Aristotle are still for the most part unpublished. His treatise on the immortality of the soul, *De immortalitate animae* (1516), was violently attacked but not officially condemned, and the author was allowed to defend his position in his *Apologia* (1518) and *Defensorium* (1519). He contended that the immortality of the individual soul cannot be demonstrated on the basis of Aristotle or of reason but must be accepted as an article of faith. In developing this view, he maintains that the end of human life consists in moral action and that virtue is its own reward, vice its own punishment. This moral virtue constitutes the peculiar dignity of man. Pomponazzi's largest treatises, *De incantationibus* and *De fato*, were published posthumously (1556 and 1567). The former proposes a natural explanation of several reputedly miraculous phenomena. The latter defends the Stoic doctrine of fate against Alexander of Aphrodisias and adds a subtle philosophical discussion of predestination and free will.

BIBLIOGRAPHY.—*P. Pomponatii Mantuani tractatus . . . mere peripatetici* (1525); *Opera* (1567); *Tractatus de immortalitate animae*, ed. by W. H. Hay (1938) and by G. Morra (1954); E. Cassirer *et al.* (eds.), *The Renaissance Philosophy of Man* (1948); F. Fiorentino, *Pietro Pomponazzi* (1868); A. H. Douglas, *The Philosophy and Psychology of Pietro Pomponazzi* (1910); B. Nardi, *Studi su Pietro Pomponazzi* (1965); P. O. Kristeller, "Two Unpublished Questions on the Soul of Pietro Pomponazzi," *Medievalia et humanistica*, vol. viii, pp. 76–101 (1955). (P. O. K.)

PONCA CITY, a city of Kay County, Okla., U.S., 90 mi. NE of Oklahoma City. It was established in 1893. Prior to the opening of the historic Cherokee strip on Sept. 16 of that year (*see* OKLAHOMA: *History*), 2,300 $2 certificates were sold by a private group, entitling each holder to participate in forming the new town and in acquiring a lot. More than 2,000 people gathered at the proposed site, and on Sept. 21 the drawing for lots was held and a provisional government was organized by popular assembly.

The name is from the Ponca tribe of Indians, moved in 1879 to a reservation located south of the townsite. Although the name Ponca City had always been in popular use, the post-office name was Ponca until 1913. The city has a council-manager form of government, in effect since 1954.

Ponca City is an important petroleum centre; two large refineries have a combined daily capacity of more than 100,000 bbl. There is also an annual production of 75,000,000 lb. of carbon black. Other industries in the city process agricultural products; manufacture oil-drilling bits, farm equipment, ceramics, decorative wreaths, vacuum cleaners, and composite cans; and service diesel engines.

The city is the home of the famous "Pioneer Woman" statue and Pioneer Woman State Park, presented to the people of Oklahoma by Gov. E. W. Marland, and is the location of the Pioneer Woman Historical Museum.

Pop. (1970) 25,940. For comparative population figures *see* table in OKLAHOMA: *Population*. (GE. H. S.)

PONCE, the largest and most important city on the southern coast of Puerto Rico and the second city in size and importance on the island. In 1960 the population of the city was 114,286. Ponce's official history dates from 1692 when a town council was established and a mayor appointed. In 1877, because of its growth and importance, the Spanish government elevated Ponce to the category of a city.

The warm, dry climate on the south coast is most agreeable. The average annual temperature is 79° F (26.1° C), and the yearly rainfall is 36 in. Constant breezes coming off the mountains and from the Caribbean Sea assure comfortable living. As Puerto Rico's principal shipping port on the Caribbean, Ponce trades with the islands of the Lesser Antilles, Colombia and Venezuela. Extensive improvements of the excellent harbour were made under the direction of U.S. agencies. Cement, iron, shoes, candy, textiles, and paper products are some of the more important industrial goods manufactured in Ponce. To the west on the coast is located a large oil refinery. To the east well-irrigated plains produce high-grade sugarcane. Five banking firms have offices in Ponce. There are four radio stations, two television stations, and one daily newspaper.

Excellent highways connect the city with other coastal towns, and two well-kept paved roads lead up over the mountains to the interior and the north coast. The city is also connected with San Juan (*q.v.*) by regular commercial air service. Ponce's parks, plazas, public buildings, and private residences are well-kept and attractive. In addition to first-class hotels, the city has an ultra-modern tourist hotel.

The Roman Catholic Church maintains the University of Santa Maria with facilities for over 3,000 students. (T. G. Ms.)

PONCE DE LEÓN, JUAN (1460–1521), Spanish explorer and discoverer of Florida, was born in Tierra de Campos (Palencia), Spain, in 1460. After service in the Moorish wars, he reached the New World with Columbus in 1493. From 1508 to 1509 he explored and settled Puerto Rico. Royal orders to search for new lands and a belief in the legend of a Fountain of Youth on Bimini Island in the Bahamas led Ponce de León to the discovery of Florida at Easter time in 1513. The region was named "Florida" from the name of the day in the calendar. Landing near the site of modern St. Augustine, he coasted southward, sailed through the Keys called "The Martyrs," and ended his search near Charlotte Harbor. Though named in 1514 governor to colonize Bimini and Florida, Ponce de León first campaigned against the Carib Indians and occupied Trinidad. Finally, in 1521, he left for Florida with two ships and 200 men, landing near Charlotte Harbor. He was wounded during an Indian attack and died soon after in Havana. *See also* FLORIDA: *History*. (A. B. T.)

PONCELET, JEAN VICTOR (1788–1867), French mathematician and engineer, one of the founders of modern projective geometry, was born at Metz on July 1, 1788. From 1808 to 1810 he attended the École Polytechnique and afterward, until 1812, the *école d'application* at Metz. He then became lieutenant of engineers and took part in the Russian campaign during which he was taken prisoner and confined at Saratov, on the Volga, until 1814, when he returned to France. During his imprisonment he began his researches on projective geometry which led to his great treatise on that subject. This work, the *Traité des propriétés projectives des figures* (1822; 2nd ed., 2 vol., 1865–66), is occupied with the investigation of the projective properties of figures and entitles Poncelet to rank as one of the greatest of those who took part in the development of the new geometry of which G. Monge was also a founder (*see* GEOMETRY: *Projective Geometry*). Poncelet developed the principle of duality and discovered the circular points at infinity. From 1815 to 1825 he was occupied with military engineering at Metz, and from 1825 to 1835 he was professor of mechanics at the *école d'application* there. In 1834 he became a member of the Académie; from 1838 to 1848 he was professor to the faculty of sciences at Paris and from 1848 to 1850 commandant of the École Polytechnique, with the rank of general. He died at Paris on Dec. 22, 1867.

See Eric T. Bell, *Men of Mathematics* (1937); M. Kerker, "Sadi Carnot and the Steam Engine Engineers," *Isis* (Sept. 1960); J. R. Newman (ed.), *The World of Mathematics*, pt. 1, reprint (1962).

(O. Oe.)

PONCHIELLI, AMILCARE (1834–1886), Italian composer best known for his opera *La Gioconda*, was born at Paderno Fasolaro, near Cremona, on Aug. 31, 1834. He studied at Milan and produced his first opera, *I Promessi Sposi*, based on the novel of Alessandro Manzoni, at Cremona (1856). In a revised version it was frequently given in Italy and abroad. Between 1873 and 1875 he wrote two ballets and four operas and became the most important of Verdi's Italian contemporaries. *La Gioconda* (La Scala, Milan, 1876), on a libretto by Arrigo Boito based on Victor Hugo's *Angelo*, achieved wide success at the end of the 19th century. Later it was chiefly known for its ballet "Dance of the Hours," but returned to the repertory of Italian opera houses in the 1950s. From 1881 to 1886 Ponchielli was musical director at Bergamo Cathedral; there he wrote several sacred works. He died in Milan on Jan. 16, 1886.

See A. Damerini, *A. Ponchielli* (1940). (Dy. H.)

POND, JOHN (1767–1836), English astronomer who reorganized the Royal Observatory on modern lines, was born in London in 1767. After leaving Trinity College, Cambridge, he traveled abroad, making astronomical observations. He returned to England and settled at Westbury, Somerset, about 1798. There he began to determine star places with a fine altitude and azimuth circle of $2\frac{1}{2}$-ft. diameter. His demonstration of deformation in the Greenwich mural quadrant as a result of age made it necessary to introduce astronomical circles into the equipment at the Royal Observatory, Greenwich. In 1807 he was elected a fellow of the Royal Society and in the same year he married and went to live in London. In 1811 he succeeded Nevil Maskelyne as astronomer royal.

At Pond's instigation the instrumental equipment at Greenwich was completely changed and the number of assistants increased from one to six. The superior accuracy of his determinations was attested by S. C. Chandler's discussion of them in the *Astronomical Journal* (1894). Pond published *Astronomical Observations made at the Royal Observatory* from 1811 to 1835, translated P. S. Laplace's *Système du monde* (2 volumes, 1809), and contributed 31 papers to scientific collections.

Pond's catalog of 1,112 stars (1833) was of great value, and he received many academic honours. He retired in 1835 and died at Blackheath, Kent, on Sept. 7, 1836.

BIBLIOGRAPHY.—*Memoirs of the Royal Astronomical Society*, x, pp. 357–364 (1838); *Proc. Roy. Soc.*, iii, pp. 434–435 (1837); *Annual Biography and Obituary*, vol. xxi (1837); R. Grant, *History of Physical Astronomy*, p. 491 (1852); E. W. Maunder, *The Royal Observatory, Greenwich* (1900).

PONDICHERRY (French PONDICHÉRY from Tamil *puddu cheri*, "new village"), the name of a centrally administered state of India and of its capital, and of the chief settlement of former French India. On Nov. 1, 1954, on the basis of a vote of the elected representatives of French Indian municipalities, the administration of French India was transferred to the Republic of India; central control was initiated through a chief commissioner with headquarters at Pondicherry; and on Jan. 6, 1955, the four settlements together were designated the state of Pondicherry. A treaty for the *de jure* transfer was formally signed on May 28, 1956, and ratified in July 1962. (For early history, *see* INDIA-PAKISTAN, SUBCONTINENT OF: *European Settlements*.)

The state thus comprises: the town and settlement of Pondicherry on the Coromandel Coast (*q.v.*) and geographically in the South Arcot district of Madras; Karikal (*q.v.*), an enclave in the Thanjavur (Tanjore) district of Madras; Mahé (*q.v.*) on the Malabar Coast in the Cannanore district of Kerala; and Yanam in the East Godavari district of Andhra Pradesh. Area 185 sq.mi. (479 sq.km.); pop. (1961) 369,079.

There are three colleges, including one for medicine, a teacher's training centre, an arts and crafts school, a research institute, and a general educational institute, all in Pondicherry town. The chief food crops of the territories are paddy and a variety of millet; cash crops include peanuts, coconuts, cotton, tobacco and chillies. There are a number of textile mills and oil presses in Pondicherry town and toymaking and handmade matches are some of the cottage industries. The various units of the state are well served by road or rail.

PONDICHERRY TOWN lies 122 mi. (196 km.) SSW of Madras City by rail. Pop. (1961) 40,421. (G. Kn.; X.)

PONIATOWSKI, a great Polish family, with princely rank from 1764. Jan Ciolek (d. *c.* 1676), having inherited the property of Poniatow, took the name Poniatowski and founded the family, which settled in the district of Cracow.

STANISLAW PONIATOWSKI (1676–1762), Jan's grandson, was born on Sept. 15, 1676. After serving with his brother Jozef as a volunteer in the Austrian Army against the Turks, under the command of Gen. Michal Sapieha, he accompanied Sapieha to Lithuania in 1697 and settled there. During the Northern War (*q.v.*), together with the Sapiehas, he sided with the Swedes. Major general in the army of Charles XII of Sweden, he rendered great services to Stanislaw Leszczynski (STANISLAW I, *q.v.*), but after Charles XII's death he was reconciled with Augustus II of Poland. He was appointed grand treasurer of Lithuania in 1722 and palatine (*wojewoda*) of Mazovia in 1731. From 1728 he was commander in chief of the Polish Army. In 1752 Stanislaw received the highest dignity in the Senate, castellan of Cracow. He was a partisan of constitutional reforms. He died Aug. 3, 1762, at Ryki.

Stanislaw's second son, STANISLAW AUGUST, became king of Poland as Stanislaw II (*q.v.*) in 1764; and his brothers, Kazimierz, Andrzej, and Michal (*see* below), received princely titles.

KAZIMIERZ (1721–1800), from 1742 grand chamberlain of Poland, was a close adviser to Stanislaw II at the beginning of his reign, trying to curb the influence of his Czartoryski uncles and to bring about a rapprochement between Poland, Austria, and France against the policy of the Russian empress Catherine II. After the first partition of Poland (1772) he withdrew from political life.

ANDRZEJ (1734–1773) as a young man served in the Austrian Army and during the Seven Years' War was promoted lieutenant general in 1760. In the years 1765–66 he was engaged in official and secret missions to Vienna. From Austria he finally received the title of prince (in the Kingdom of Bohemia).

MICHAL (1736–1794) was from 1773 bishop of Plock and from 1784 archbishop of Gniezno and primate of Poland. After the first partition of Poland he became one of the closest political advisers of King Stanislaw II. From 1776 he headed the Commission of National Education. In favour of submissiveness toward Russia, he opposed the alliance with Prussia (1790).

JOZEF ANTONI (1763–1813), Polish general and marshal of France, was born in Vienna on May 7, 1763, the son of Andrzej. He served in the Austrian Army, but in 1789, at the request of his uncle, King Stanislaw II, he was transferred to the Polish Army. Appointed lieutenant general, he fought the Russian invaders in 1792. When the king acceded to the Confederation of Targowica (*see* POLAND: *History*) he gave up his commission and went to Vienna. In 1794 he joined the insurrection led by Tadeusz Kosciuszko. After the third partition (1795) he lived in Warsaw in retirement. During the Napoleonic Wars (*q.v.*), when the Prussians left Warsaw in 1806, he became commander of the Polish National Guard. Adhering to Napoleon, he was appointed minister of war of the Duchy of Warsaw in 1807. In Napoleon's campaign of 1812 against Russia he commanded the V (Polish) Army Corps. After the retreat from Moscow he remained faithful to Napoleon and formed a new Polish Army Corps, with which he contributed to the victory at Lützen (May 2, 1813). A marshal of France from Oct. 16, 1813, he fought brilliantly at Leipzig; but on Oct. 19, having been five times wounded, he perished in the Elster River when trying to swim it on horseback. He is buried in the Wawel Cathedral in Cracow.

STANISLAW (1754–1833) was the son of Kazimierz. Grand treasurer of Lithuania from 1784, he was Stanislaw II's candidate for the succession to the Polish crown. After the destruction of

Poland in 1795 he settled in Vienna, but later moved to Rome and then to Florence. By a marriage with Cassandra Luci he had two sons, Charles (1811–87) and Joseph (*see* below), who obtained the Tuscan title of Principi di Monte Rotondo in 1847 and the Austrian princely title of Poniatowski in 1850.

JOSEPH (1816–1873), born in Rome on Feb. 20, 1816, was the envoy of Tuscany in London (1849) and in Paris (1853). He also composed many operas, produced in Florence, Paris, and London. A friend of Napoleon III, he became senator of the French Empire in 1855. Having accompanied Napoleon to England in 1871, he died in London on July 3, 1873.

Joseph's son STANISLAS (1835–1908), who had been equerry to Napoleon III, left a son ANDRÉ (1864–1954), who prospered in business and finance and described his eventful life in *D'un siècle à l'autre* (1948). This André's sons STANISLAS (1895–), CASIMIR (1897–), and ANDRÉ (1899–) served during World War I in the French and later in the Polish army. MARIE ANDRÉ (1921–1945), son of the last-named André, served in World War II in the Polish Army from 1940 and was killed in the Netherlands.

See S. Mnémon, *L'Origine des Poniatowski* (1913); S. Askenazy, *Fürst Joseph Poniatowski* (1912). (EM. R.)

PONSARD, FRANÇOIS (1814–1867), French dramatist who, with Émile Augier, advocated a return to a moral and socially conscious literature after the extravagances of Romanticism, and so represents the *École du bon sens*. He was born on June 1, 1814, at Vienne (Isère) and studied law. After translating Byron's *Manfred* (1837), he wrote *Lucrèce*, performed in 1843, the year in which the failure of Hugo's *Les Burgraves* marked the end of Romantic triumphs in the French theatre. *Lucrèce* was classical in style as well as subject, though not entirely uninfluenced, technically, by Romantic innovations. Notable among Ponsard's later plays were *Agnès de Méranie* (1846), *Charlotte Corday* (1850), *L'Honneur et l'argent* (1853), *Le Lion amoureux* (1866), and *Galilée* (1867), which aroused considerable clerical opposition. Ponsard was elected to the Académie Française in 1855, and was highly regarded by Napoleon III. He died in Paris on July 7, 1867.

See *Œuvres complètes* (1865–76); C. Latreille, *La Fin du théâtre romantique et F. Ponsard* (1899). (W. D. Hн.)

PONSONBY, the name of an English family, seated at Ponsonby and elsewhere in Cumberland since before the 13th century, a branch of which has been connected with Ireland since 1649. Honours held by the family have been the baronies of Bessborough, County Kilkenny (from 1721), of Ponsonby of Sysonby in Leicestershire (from 1749), of Ponsonby of Imokilly, County Cork (1806–66), and of de Mauley of Canford in Dorsetshire (from 1838); the viscountcies of Duncannon of Fort Duncannon, County Wexford (from 1723), and of Ponsonby of Imokilly (1839–55); and the earldom of Bessborough (from 1739).

The family's Irish connection began when JOHN PONSONBY (1608–1678) of Hale in Cumberland, who raised a regiment of horse and fought for Oliver Cromwell in Ireland in 1649, was given Kildalton Castle, which he renamed Bessborough after his second wife Elizabeth. His numerous descendants by his first marriage remained in Cumberland, many later emigrating to Tasmania. His eldest son by his second marriage, WILLIAM (1659–1724), held Londonderry against James II (1689–90). He was created Baron Bessborough in 1721 and Viscount Duncannon in 1723. His eldest son, BRABAZON (1679–1758), was created earl of Bessborough in 1739 and Baron Ponsonby of Sysonby (peerage of Great Britain) in 1749.

Brabazon's third son, JOHN (1713–1787), was speaker of the Irish House of Commons from 1756 to 1771. One of his sons, WILLIAM (1744–1806), was created Baron Ponsonby of Imokilly in 1806; another, GEORGE (1755–1817), was lord chancellor of Ireland. William's son JOHN (1771–1855), created Viscount Ponsonby in 1839, was ambassador to Constantinople (1832–41) and to Vienna (1846–50). On his death without issue the viscountcy became extinct and the barony passed to his nephew WILLIAM (1816–1861), son of his brother WILLIAM (1782–1815), the major general who served in the Peninsular War and fell at Waterloo. The barony became extinct on the death of WILLIAM BRABAZON

(1807–1866), cousin and successor of the 3rd baron.

JOHN WILLIAM (1781–1847), 4th earl of Bessborough, was home secretary in the first ministry (1834) of Viscount Melbourne, the husband of his sister CAROLINE (1785–1828). His brother, WILLIAM FRANCIS SPENCER PONSONBY (1787–1855), married the heiress of the barony of De Mauley and was created Baron de Mauley in 1838. His great-grandson HUBERT WILLIAM PONSONBY (1878–) is 5th baron. A nephew of the 4th earl, SIR HENRY PONSONBY (1825–1895), was Queen Victoria's private secretary from 1870 until his death.

The 10th earl of Bessborough is FREDERICK EDWARD NEUFLIZE PONSONBY (1913–).

See Sir John Ponsonby, *The Ponsonby Family* (1929).
(E. A. MacL.)

PONTA DELGADA, the capital of an administrative district comprising the islands of São Miguel and Santa Maria in the Portuguese archipelago of the Azores. Pop. (1960) 22,740. Ponta Delgada is on the south coast of São Miguel, in 37° 45′ N and 25° 40′ W. Its mild climate and the fine scenery of its mountain background render it attractive to visitors; it is the most populous town and the most important commercial centre of the archipelago. The harbour has a breakwater 4,900 ft. (1,500 m.) long. Fueling, supply, and minor repair facilities are available for ships. A local shipping line maintains regular commercial services with Portugal, northern Europe, and the United States. (J. Ao.)

PONTA GROSSA, a city in the central portion of the state of Paraná, Braz. It is connected by highway and rail with the state capital, Curitiba, and is a station on the north-south railroad that connects Pôrto Alegre and São Paulo. Pop. (1960) 77,803. Ponta Grossa is a major distribution centre of western Paraná, a region that produces maté (Brazilian tea), cereals, tobacco, rice, and livestock. The city also has a lumber industry. A settlement of Russians, Poles, and Germans, established there about 1898, has prospered. Ponta Grossa began as a supply town on the old colonial cattle trail from the state of Rio Grande do Sul to São Paulo. (J. J. J.)

PONTANO, GIOVANNI (JOVIANUS PONTANUS) (1422 or 1426–1503), Italian humanist whose voluminous and wide-ranging work illustrates the diversity of the Renaissance scene, was born at Cerreto, in Umbria, on May 7, 1422 or 1426. At about the age of 21 he went to Naples, where he spent the rest of his life. In 1471, on the death of the scholar Antonio Beccadelli (Panormita), he became head of the Neapolitan humanist academy, called after him Accademia Pontaniana. In 1461 he married Adriana Sassone, who bore him one son and three daughters and died in 1490. From 1486 until 1495 he was the effective political leader of the kingdom of Naples as adviser, military secretary and chancellor to the kings of the Aragonese dynasty. He died in September 1503.

Pontano's extensive literary output, all in Latin, includes a historical work (*De bello Neapolitano*), philosophical treatises (*De prudentia, De fortuna*), an astrological poem (*Urania*), five dialogues dealing with such widely differing subjects as morals and religion, philology and literature (*Aegidius, Actius, Asinus, Antonius, Charon*) and many lyrics on love, nature, family life and scenes from Neapolitan life (*Lepidina, Amorum libri, Eridanus, Hendecasyllabi, De amore coniugali, Jambici, Tumuli*). His erudition embraced all fields of knowledge, but neither as a thinker nor as a poet did he display a powerful personality. The importance of his work for the cultural and, even more, the social history of the Renaissance, lies not so much in its erotic originality as in the fact that it synthesizes and reproduces, more completely perhaps than that of any other humanist, the diverse elements of the period.

BIBLIOGRAPHY.—C. M. Tallarigo, *Giovanni Pontano e i suoi tempi* (1874); M. Scherillo, "Il Rinascimento" in *Le origini e lo svolgimento della letteratura italiana*, parte i, pp. 76–122 (1926). (G. P. G.)

PONTCHARTRAIN, a lake in southern Louisiana, U.S., 40 mi. (64 km.) long and 25 mi. (40 km.) wide, with an area of 625 sq.mi. (1,619 sq.km.) and a mean depth of from 10 to 16 ft. (3 to 5 m.). Lying due north of a bend of the Mississippi, it is in places only 5 mi. (8 km.) distant from the river. More a lagoon than a lake, since it connects eastward with the Gulf of Mexico by a narrow passage called the Rigolets, Pontchartrain is brackish and teems with game fish. It was discovered by Pierre le Moyne, sieur d'Iberville, in 1699. New Orleans, founded on the Mississippi, now extends to the lake, on which there are a state park and many small resorts. Pontchartrain causeway, a 24-mi. multispan concrete bridge, crosses the lake north from New Orleans.   (W. A. Ro.)

PONTE, JACOPO DA: *see* under BASSANO.

PONTEFRACT, a market town and municipal borough in the West Riding of Yorkshire, Eng., 25 mi. (40 km.) SSW of York and 13 mi. (21 km.) SE of Leeds by road; it is served by three railway stations. Pop. (1969 est.) 30,820. An ancient Brigantian settlement existed there, to be succeeded by the Saxon town of Kirkby; the name was changed to Pontefract at some date prior to 1140, when the death in the town of Archbishop Thurstan was recorded. The building of the famous castle was begun in 1069 by Ilbert de Lacy. In the 14th century the much-altered castle and manor passed by marriage to Thomas, earl of Lancaster. Henry IV held his court there for many years after deposing Richard II, and within the castle dungeons Richard was imprisoned until his death in 1400. There too, after the Battle of Agincourt (1415), Charles, duke of Orléans, was imprisoned for more than 20 years. In 1541 Henry VIII made a visit to the north with the object of pacifying the northern counties after the disturbances occasioned by the Pilgrimage of Grace, in the course of which the castle had been taken by Robert Aske, leader of the Pilgrimage, in 1536. Elizabeth I also visited the castle and repaired the chapel, the remains of which can still be seen within the walls. During the Civil War the castle sustained three sieges. It was the last Royalist stronghold to be reduced by Cromwell, who had it dismantled. Sufficient of its walls, towers, and dungeons still remain to give some idea of its former grandeur.

The town was the site of several important monastic settlements, including the priory of St. John, which was later demolished upon the orders of Henry VIII. The material recovered from the demolition was used for the building, about half a mile away, of the New Hall, itself reduced to ruins (which may still be seen) during the Civil War. In Southgate is an ancient hermitage and oratory cut from the solid rock and dating from 1368. The Butter Cross in the market place was erected in 1734 by the widow of the Spaniard Solomon Dupier with whose collaboration Gibraltar had been taken by Adm. Sir George Rooke.

The Church of All Saints, under the castle, was probably built in the 13th century. Ruined in the Civil War, it had its central portion repaired and it is still in use. The Church of St. Giles, first mentioned in a charter of Henry I, became the parish church after the ruin of All Saints.

There are several ancient almshouses. The old town hall (18th century) contains the original plaster cast from which was made the panel depicting the death of Lord Nelson, at the foot of the column in Trafalgar Square, London. The King's School, whose foundation was confirmed by Edward VI in 1549, is now housed in modern buildings. Three miles away, at Ackworth, is the well-known Society of Friends School, founded in 1778. Other principal buildings are the market hall, the courthouse, the barracks (containing a military museum), the assembly rooms, and the municipal offices. There is a racecourse in the park.

The principal industries are those of licorice confectionery, nowadays made chiefly from imported licorice (the town being the home of the celebrated "Pomfret cakes," so named from the old but still current pronunciation of Pontefract), coal mining, furniture making, iron founding, tanning, textiles, and engineering. The market rights are exercised under a charter granted by Roger de Lacy in 1194, while the first mayor was appointed pursuant to a charter of Richard III in 1484. From the end of the 13th century to the Reform Act of 1832 Pontefract returned two members to Parliament. In the 1960s the parliamentary constituency of Pontefract, which includes the borough of Castleford and Featherstone urban district, returned one member. The Pontefract Court of Quarter Sessions has an unbroken history from 1640 to the present day, and the town gives its name to a bishop suffragan in the Wakefield diocese.

PONTEVEDRA, capital of the province of the same name,

region of Galicia, northwestern Spain, is situated on the Lérez River at its entry into an inlet, the Ría de Pontevedra, 31 km. (19 mi.) NNE of Vigo by rail. Pop. (1969 est.) 65,532 (mun.). Noteworthy buildings include the Plateresque church of Santa María la Mayor (1520–59), the 14th-century Gothic convents of San Francisco and Santa Clara, the rococo Santuario de la Peregrina (1778–92), and the ruins of the 14th-century convent of Santo Domingo, now an archaeological museum. Pontevedra is on the railway from La Coruña to Vigo and Portugal. Industries include the manufacture of cloth, hats, leather, pottery, fertilizers, timber, and cellulose and there is an active trade in grain, wine, and fruit. Legend says that Pontevedra was founded by a Greek, Teucro, who called it Helenes, but more likely it was of Roman origin, hence its name (*pons vetus,* "old bridge"), from the 11-arch bridge which, with modifications, still exists and spans the Lérez River. Its port and shipyards were important in the Middle Ages and it is probable that Columbus' ship, the "Santa Maria," was built there. It has also been claimed as the birthplace of Columbus.

PONTEVEDRA PROVINCE, smallest of the four Galician provinces, is mountainous, with a coastline deeply indented by the picturesque *rias bajas* of Arosa, Pontevedra, and Vigo. Area 1,729 sq.mi. (4,477 sq.km.). Pop. (1969 est.) 772,151. Granite is widely used in building construction. Numerous traditional fiestas are held throughout the province and contribute, with the scenic beauty and fine beaches, to its attractions for tourists. Cattle, timber, agricultural produce, fish, and shellfish are exported. Vigo, with one of the best harbours in Europe, is an important port of call for transatlantic shipping. Other ports are Villagarcía (also a resort) and Marín (with a naval academy). Inland communications are good and all the mountain ranges are crossed by roads. There are airports at Peinador and La Lanzada.

(J. A. F. A.)

PONTIAC (*c.* 1720–1769), chief of the Ottawa Indians and leader in the "Conspiracy of Pontiac" in colonial America in 1763–64, was born about 1720, probably on the Maumee River, in what is now northwestern Ohio. His father was an Ottawa and his mother an Ojibwa. By 1755 he had become a chief of the Ottawa and a leader of the loose confederacy of the Ottawa, Potawatomi, and Ojibwa. In 1760 he met Maj. Robert Rogers, famed colonial ranger, then on his way to occupy Michilimackinac and other forts surrendered by the French, and agreed to let the English troops pass unmolested on condition that he be treated with respect. Like other Indians he soon realized the difference between French and English rule—that the Indians were no longer welcomed at the forts and that they would ultimately be deprived of their hunting grounds by encroaching English settlements. There was also widespread resentment among the Indians because of the refusal of the English to continue giving them presents. French hunters and traders encouraged Indian disaffection with vague promises of help from France; and in 1762 Pontiac enlisted the support of practically all the Indian tribes from Lake Superior to the lower Mississippi for a joint move to expel the British. He arranged for each tribe to attack the fort nearest to it in May 1763, and then to combine to wipe out the undefended settlements. Pontiac himself decided to capture Detroit, but his carefully laid plans for a surprise attack on May 7 were betrayed to the commanding officer, and he was forced to lay siege to the fort. The Indians were not used to making long sieges and, after a few months, several of the associated tribes made peace. With his own Ottawa, Pontiac continued to camp around Detroit until Oct. 30, when, hearing that no aid from the French could be expected, he withdrew to the Maumee River.

Pontiac's larger plan was more successful. Of the 12 fortified posts attacked by the Indians, all but 4 were captured; most of the garrisons were massacred; several relief expeditions were nearly annihilated, and the frontiers were desolated and plundered. An English officer, Col. Henry Bouquet, succeeded in defeating the Indians at Bushy Run when on his way to relieve Forts Pitt and Ligonier, and in 1764 he led a second expedition into Ohio from Pennsylvania and forced the Indian tribes to sue for peace and release their prisoners. Pontiac still hoped to arouse other tribes to continue the fight, but after another year he saw that the English were the real masters of the situation and, on behalf of the tribes lately banded in his league, he concluded a treaty of peace and amity with Sir William Johnson at Oswego, N.Y., July 25, 1766.

Pontiac, laden with gifts from the enemy, returned to his home on the Maumee. Contemporary sources credit several versions of Pontiac's death, the most likely being that he was assassinated in 1769 by an Illinois Indian who was bribed by an English trader to murder him at Cahokia, Ill. (nearly opposite St. Louis). His death occasioned a bitter war among the Indians, and the Illinois group was all but annihilated by his avengers.

Historians are not in full agreement as to Pontiac's role in the famous conspiracy, for the evidence is fragmentary. There is, however, no doubt that he was one of the most remarkable American Indians in American history, possessing a commanding energy and force of mind combined with subtlety, craft, and organizational ability.

BIBLIOGRAPHY.—Francis Parkman, *The Conspiracy of Pontiac*, 2 vol. (1907); H. H. Peckham, *Pontiac and the Indian Uprising* (1947); W. R. Jacobs, *Diplomacy and Indian Gifts* (1950); M. M. Quaife (ed.), *The Siege of Detroit in 1763: the Journal of Pontiac's Conspiracy and John Rutherfurd's Narrative of a Captivity* (1958).

PONTIAC, the seat of Oakland County, Mich., U.S., 26 mi. NW of Detroit (*q.v.*) and within the Detroit metropolitan area, is an important automobile-manufacturing city in the midst of a residential area, with hundreds of lakes and many public parks. Named for the famous Ottawa chief, Pontiac was settled in 1818 by the Pontiac Company, organized in Detroit; the site was the intersection of the Clinton River and the Saginaw Trail, which formed part of the Indian route from the Straits of Mackinac to northern Ohio. In the 19th century, Pontiac was the shopping centre for a prosperous agricultural area. It was chartered as a city in 1861; in 1877 its population of about 4,000 supported newspapers, banks, mercantile establishments, hotels, and blacksmiths, gunsmiths, mills, foundries, and small factories.

Its river location made available water power essential to the rise of factories. Most important for its future were the wagon and carriage works, which, with the invention of the automobile, turned to production of cars and parts; in the 20th century, Pontiac's economy has depended largely upon the automobile industry. Pontiac established a commission-manager form of government in 1920. Pontiac State Hospital and the Moses Wisner Home, a historic house, are in the city; nearby are the Cranbrook institutions (private schools, museum, and art academy) and Oakland University. The population of the city in 1970 was 85,279; for comparative population figures *see* table in MICHIGAN: *Population*. (E. S. AD.)

PONTIANAK, a port and the capital of West Kalimantan Province (of Borneo), Indonesia, lies on a tongue of land at the junction of the Kapuas and Landak rivers, 14 mi. (23 km.) from the western Borneo coast. Pop. (1961) 150,220, including many Chinese. The town was formerly the capital of the sultanate of Pontianak, founded in 1772 by Abdul Rahman, who gained the support of the Dutch East India Company (*q.v.*) in claiming the area from the sultan of Bantam (Java). Under Abdul Rahman the town of Pontianak became a trading station, and later it was to be the chief gold town of Borneo. The main industry is shipbuilding. A large factory manufactures palm oil for export, and there are also rubber- and sugar-processing concerns. Houses are built on piles to avoid the regular flooding. Large warehouses store goods for transshipment to other parts of Indonesia and abroad.

Products of the surrounding area include copra and palm oil from the coconut palm groves along the coast, and pepper and rubber which are grown to the north of the city. Rice, maize (corn), cassava, tobacco, and sugar are also grown. The hinterland is tropical forest, with swamplands in between, and the whole area is one of great humidity.

PONTIANUS, SAINT (d. after 235), pope from 230 to 235, is said in the *Liber pontificalis* to have been a Roman by birth. He convened the synod that confirmed Demetrius of Alexandria's condemnation of Origen (*q.v.*). At the beginning of the persecu-

tion under the emperor Maximinus in 235, Pontianus was exiled to Sardinia, together with the theologian and antipope Hippolytus (*q.v.*), who had maintained opposition to the official leadership of the church since the elevation of Calixtus to the papacy in 217/218. While sharing their exile Pontianus and Hippolytus became reconciled. On Sept. 28, 235, Pontianus abdicated the papal office, and died, with Hippolytus, at Sardinia sometime after, traditionally in consequence of ill treatment.

Pontianus was venerated as a martyr, and his feast day is Nov. 19. His epitaph in the cemetery of St. Calixtus was found in 1909; the inscription of the date of his resignation of the papacy is noted as the first specific date in papal history.

See E. Caspar, *Geschichte des Papsttums*, vol. i, pp. 43–46 (1930). (D. AR.; X.)

PONTIFEX, literally "bridge-builder," hence originally a Roman priest whose main duty was no doubt to appease the wrath of the Tiber at having a bridge, the very ancient Pons Sublicius, built over him. This was done by the immemorial ceremony of the *Argei* (a name the derivation of which is uncertain), in which once a year, on May 14, puppets representing men in archaic costume were flung into the water off the bridge.

The *pontifices* originally numbered three and were advisers of the king. In republican times their numbers were increased till they reached 16 at the time of Julius Caesar's dictatorship. They formed the chief group of the college of pontiffs (*collegium pontificum*), which also included the *rex sacrorum*, *flamines* (*see* FLAMEN), and vestal virgins (*see* VESTA). At their head was the *pontifex maximus*, the chief priest of Roman religion. Originally, on the death of a pontiff his place was filled by co-option, but from some time in the 3rd century B.C. the *pontifex maximus* and from 103 onward all the pontiffs were elected by a minority of the tribes (17 out of 35), the members of the college retaining the right to nominate candidates. Under the empire, the emperor was always *pontifex maximus* until certain Christian emperors refused the post.

The duties of the college included the performance of sundry rites, not always in Rome itself; if any change in the existing regulations was thought advisable, it was up to the government of the day to take the necessary steps: the pontiffs themselves had no executive but only advisory powers on the matter, though no doubt their expert opinion carried great weight. But generally speaking they, and especially the chief pontiff, supervised the sacral law (*ius divinum*), including the act of "taking" (*capere*) a new flamen Dialis or a vestal virgin. They kept records, the fragments of which (*commentarii pontificum*) are a valuable source for the study of Roman religion. They also kept and published brief accounts of the events of each year, *annales*.

Nothing prevented a pontiff from being also a secular magistrate; Rome had priests, but no priestly class or caste, and secular magistrates regularly had certain sacral functions, whether they were pontiffs or not. The only priest absolutely debarred from magistracies was the *rex sacrorum*.

Pontifex is one of the styles by which the pope (*q.v.*) is designated.

See G. Wissowa, *Religion und Kultus der Römer*, vol. ii, pp. 501 ff. (1912); G. Rohde, *Die Kultsatzungen der römischen Pontifices* (1936). (H. J. R.)

PONTINE MARSHES (now known as AGRO PONTINO), an area of about 290 sq.mi. (750 sq.km.) southeast of Rome between the Alban Hills, the Lepini Mountains, and the Tyrrhenian Sea, which was reclaimed by the Italian government before World War II. It is known that two tribes, the Pomptini and the Ufentini, lived in this area in early Roman times, but the region was already marshy and malarial during the later years of the Roman Republic, and the Appian Way traversed it, using the higher, eastern section of the area. The first attempt at reclamation was made in 160 B.C., and subsequently numerous other attempts were made without success.

The Pontine Marshes throughout modern history was a region of malaria, inhabited by a handful of shepherds, with small fields on the eastern edge where peasants from towns high on the Lepini Mountains cultivated wheat. Rough pasture and maquis covered most of the area. In 1932–34 the Fascist government launched a spectacular drive to drain the marshes, clear the vegetation, and settle several hundred families. Towns were built in what was wilderness: Latina (earlier Littoria) was established in 1932, Sabaudia in 1934, Pontinia (1935), Aprilia (1937), and Pomezia (1939); rural service centres were constructed, and on the eve of World War II the only areas where the original vegetation remained were in the Monte Circeo National Park. Damage done to the farms and to the drainage works during the fighting in 1944 was later repaired.   (G. KH.)

PONTOISE, a cathedral town of the Paris area, *préfecture* of the *département* of Val-d'Oise (created 1964), lies on the right bank of the Oise where the Viosne joins it, 32 km. (20 mi.) NW of Paris by road. Pop. (1962) 14,898. The convent of the Cordeliers, restored in the 18th century, forms part of the *hôtel de ville.* The Tavet Museum nearby is a 15th-century building. The tower (1547) of St. Maclou, a 12th-century church (restored in the 15th–16th centuries), now a cathedral, dominates the town. The church of Notre Dame (16th century) contains the tomb of St. Gautier, founder of the abbey of St. Martin de Pontoise. Remains of the 13th-century Cistercian abbey of Maubuisson are on the left bank of the Oise. A fair is held on Martinmas (Nov. 11). Pontoise, on the Paris–Dieppe railway, is an important market centre and is becoming an important satellite town of Paris.

The town was acquired by Philip I in 1064 and became the capital of the French Vexin. It played a conspicuous part in the wars between the French and the dukes of Normandy and in the Hundred Years' War. The English captured it in 1419 and again in 1437. In 1441 Charles VII took it after a three months' siege. Allied to the Holy League, Pontoise was taken by Henry III and the king of Navarre in 1589. The parliament of Paris met there several times: in 1652 (when it offered a refuge to Louis XIV and Cardinal Mazarin) and in 1720 and 1753. Pontoise passed to the prince of Conti in 1749. It was occupied by the Germans in 1870–71 and was damaged in World War II.   (J. M. HA.)

PONTOPPIDAN, HENRIK (1857–1943), Danish writer whose novels and short stories present an unusually comprehensive picture of his country and his epoch, was born at Fredericia on July 24, 1857. His father was a clergyman, and it was partly in revolt against his environment that he began to study engineering in Copenhagen in 1873. In 1879 he broke off his studies and became for several years a teacher. His first collection of stories, *Staekkede Vinger,* was published in 1881, and thereafter he supported himself by writing, until 1900 partly as a journalist with various Copenhagen papers. In 1917 he shared the Nobel Prize for Literature with Karl Gjellerup. Pontoppidan died at Ordrup on Aug. 21, 1943.

Pontoppidan's output, mainly of novels and short stories, stretches over half a century and covers most aspects of Danish life and the social, political and religious problems of the period. As a poet he belonged to the naturalist school, though he showed a characteristically critical independence and an agile, dialectic, ironic mind. An individualist and an apostle of the cult of personality, he yet had strong ties with his nation and his compatriots, for whom he had great affection although he criticized them severely.

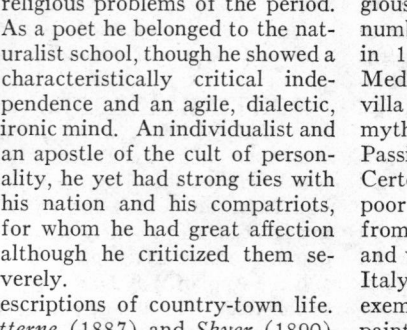

HENRIK PONTOPPIDAN

His first books were mainly descriptions of country-town life. *Landsbybilleder* (1883), *Fra Hytterne* (1887) and *Skyer* (1890) are all characterized by social indignation though also by ironic appreciation of the complacency and passivity of country people. The trilogy *Det forjaettede Land* (1891–95; Eng. trans., *Emanuel or Children of the Soil,* 1892, and *The Promised Land,* 1896) describes the religious controversies in country districts. The chief

character is a pastor from Copenhagen, a dreamer who tries, unsuccessfully, to gain the confidence of the peasants. In the 1890s Pontoppidan wrote a number of short novels on psychological, aesthetic and moral problems (*e.g., Nattevagt,* 1894; *Den gamle Adam,* 1895; and *Højsang,* 1896). These were followed by a major work, the novel *Lykke-Per* (1898–1904), in which the chief character bears some resemblance to Pontoppidan himself. He is a clergyman's son who rebels against the puritanical atmosphere of his home and seeks his fortune in the capital as an engineer. But his religious background inhibits him and he loses interest in success and wealth, separates from his Jewish fiancée (who with her strength of will and pride probably represents Pontoppidan's ideal), and after an unsuccessful marriage ends his life in complete loneliness. The book's theme is the power of environment, and national tendencies toward daydreaming and fear of reality are condemned.

Deeper problems are touched on in the shorter novels *Borgmester Hoeck og Hustru* (1905) and *Den kongelige Gaest* (1908), after which follows a third great novel, *De Dødes Rige* (1912–16). This covers the first decade of the 20th century and shows dissatisfaction with political developments after the liberal victory of 1901, and anxiety for the future. It sounds a warning against the barrenness of the new era. Anxiety for the country's destiny also lies behind the bitter novel *Mands Himmerig* (1927), which describes neutral Denmark during World War I and attacks carefree materialism.

The cold, aloof, epic style which Pontoppidan had developed during his career is also a feature of his last important work, the four volumes of memoirs which he published between 1933 and 1940 and which appeared in a collected and abridged version entitled *Undervejs til mig selv* (1943).

BIBLIOGRAPHY.—V. Andersen, *Henrik Pontoppidan* (1917); P. C. Andersen, *Henrik Pontoppidan, En Biografi og en Bibliografi* (1934); C. M. Woel, *Henrik Pontoppidan,* 2 vol. (1945); Knut Ahnlund, *Henrik Pontoppidan* (1956).   (S. M. K.)

PONTORMO, JACOPO DA (JACOPO CARRUCCI) (1494–1557), Italian painter, one of the creators of Florentine Mannerism, was born at Pontormo, near Empoli, on May 24, 1494, the son of Bartolommeo Carrucci, a painter. According to Vasari he was apprenticed to Leonardo da Vinci and afterward to Albertinelli and Piero di Cosimo. At the age of 18 he entered the workshop of Andrea del Sarto, and it is this influence that is most apparent in his early works. In 1518 he completed the altarpiece (still in the church of S. Michele Visdomini, Florence); its agitated—almost neurotic—emotionalism marks a departure from the balance and tranquillity of the High Renaissance and makes it one of the first Mannerist pictures. His painting of "Joseph in Egypt" (*c.* 1515; National Gallery, London), one of a series for Pier Francesco Borgherini, suggests that the revolutionary new style appeared even earlier.

Pontormo was primarily a religious painter, but he painted a number of sensitive portraits and in 1521 was employed by the Medici family to decorate their villa at Poggio a Caiano with mythological subjects. In the Passion cycle (1522–25) for the Certosa near Florence (now in poor condition) he borrows ideas from Dürer, whose engravings and woodcuts were circulating in Italy. His mature style is best exemplified in the "Deposition" painted soon after this for Sta. Felicità, Florence.

Pontormo became more and more of a recluse in later life. A diary survives from 1554–57, but the important frescoes in S.

ALINARI

THE "DEPOSITION" BY JACOPO DA PONTORMO, IN THE CHURCH OF STA. FELICITÀ, FLORENCE

Lorenzo on which he worked during the last decade of his life are now known only from drawings; in these the influence of Michelangelo is apparent. Numerous drawings survive and paintings are to be found in various galleries in Europe and America, as well as in Florence. Pontormo was buried in Florence on Jan. 2, 1557.

BIBLIOGRAPHY.—F. M. Clapp, *Jacopo Carucci da Pontormo* (1916); E. Berti Toesca, *Il Pontormo* (1943); Florence, Palazzo Strozzi, *Mostra del Pontormo* (1956).

PONTRESINA, a village in the upper Engadine, canton of Graubünden, Switz., 6 km. (3¾ mi.) E of St. Moritz by rail. Pop. (1960) 1,067, mostly Romansh-speaking. Situated at about 6,000 ft. (1,800 m.) above sea level at the junction of the Bernina and Roseg valleys, it is an important winter and summer resort. It is the starting point of the spectacular Bernina railway into Italy. The tourist trade is the town's chief industry. Settled by Celts and Ligurians in the 5th century B.C., the area was invaded in the first century A.D. by Saracens from southern Spain.

(OT. A. L.)

PONTUS, in ancient geography, a district in northeastern Asia Minor, bordering on the Black Sea (Greek *Pontos*). At first it was reckoned as part of Cappadocia; then, in order to differentiate it from inland Cappadocia, it was described as Pontic (*i.e.,* "maritime") Cappadocia; the name Pontus was a later simplification.

Several mountain chains run through the region in lines from east to west, roughly parallel to the Black Sea coast, divided from one another by the valleys of rivers. The more important rivers are the Halys (modern Kizil Irmak), the Lycus (Kelkit), and the Iris (Yesil Irmak). The fertile ground lies chiefly along the latter two. The higher ground was in ancient times well wooded and contained at certain places rich mineral deposits. Along the coast Greek colonies were established from Miletus at Sinope (Sinop) and Amisus (Samsun) in the 7th century B.C.; subsequently Cotyora (Ordu), Cerasus (Giresun), and Trapezus (Trabzon) were colonized from Sinope. The major centres of native settlement were near the great temples: that of Ma at Comana; that of Men Pharnaku at Cabira; and that of Anaitis at Zela. It was not until the time of the Roman occupation in the late 1st century B.C. that true cities developed in the interior of Pontus.

It may be supposed that the same kind of feudal society as existed in Cappadocia prevailed also in Pontus. The population was very mixed. Apart from the native Cappadocian people and the Iranian settlers who came to the country after the Persian conquest, there were several tribes of separate races occupying various districts. Of the latter the Chalybes, in tradition the first workers of iron (Greek *chalyps*), the Tibareni, the Mossynoeci, and the Macrones are mentioned in the ancient accounts.

The emergence of the region as a political unit of international importance dates from the end of the 4th century B.C. when a Persian nobleman or dynast Mithradates (*q.v.*) founded there a small kingdom. The capital of the dynasty was at first at Amasia (Amasya) on the Iris, where the rock-cut tombs of four of the kings have been recognized; later the capital became Sinope after that city had been annexed to the kingdom (183). The kings gradually built up the strength of their country, while obtaining from other states the recognition that they had become members of the Hellenistic concert of powers. Many Greeks were employed at the court and in the army, and, like many oriental rulers of the age, the Pontic kings fostered at least a superficial Hellenism throughout their dominions.

In the early 2nd century B.C. an aggressive policy was followed by the king Pharnaces I; Sinope, Cerasus, and Cotyora were annexed by him. But it was not until the accession of the eighth king Mithradates VI Eupator (*see* MITHRADATES) that the great expansion of the Pontic kingdom began. During his long reign (*c.* 115–63 B.C.) the kingdom reached its zenith. But his disastrous wars with Rome brought about the loss of most of the kingdom, only the overseas province of the Crimea and its adjoining districts being left to him at the end. Under Pompey's settlement (63–62 B.C.) the western part of the kingdom was attached to Bithynia to form the province of Bithynia and Pontus; and the eastern part was assigned to the Galatians. After 40 B.C. the Pontic kingdom was revived in the eastern districts, but only as a Roman protectorate; it was finally reannexed in A.D. 64–65, and was thereafter known as Pontus Polemoniacus (after its former kings Polemo I and II).

See D. Magie, *Roman Rule in Asia Minor,* 2 vol., especially ch. 8 (1950). (R. H. SI.)

PONTYPOOL, an urban district in Monmouthshire (*q.v.*), England, situated approximately in the centre of the county, about 10 mi. (16 km.) N of Newport by road. Pop. (1961) 39,930. It lies in the valley of the Lwyd, a tributary of the Usk River. This north-south valley, colloquially known as the Eastern Valley, divides the mountainous industrial area of the west from the low agricultural country in the east of the county. Pontypool owes its industrial development to its position on the eastern edge of the South Wales coalfield. The first ironworks were erected in 1577 by Edmond Brode, a partner of Richard Hanbury whose name figures so largely in local history. Pontypool was the pioneer in sheet rolling and tin plating and it became famous for wire, cast-iron gates, etc. Specially lacquered decorated ironware was known in the 18th century as Pontypool Japan. The old forges have given place to modern works producing special steel products, glass, and rubber. There are also toy factories and a large nylon plant.

(H. CK.)

PONTYPRIDD, an urban district of Glamorgan, Wales, is situated on the Taff at its junction with the Rhondda, and on the Glamorgan Canal, 12 mi. (19 km.) NW of Cardiff by road. Pop. (1961) 35,494. It received its name from the remarkable single-span stone bridge over the Taff, erected by William Edwards in 1750. The town has a biweekly street and covered market. On the opposite bank of the Taff is the suburb of Ynysangharad with its fine public park. After the opening of the Taff Vale Railway in 1840, Pontypridd became the railway junction for the Merthyr, Aberdare, and Rhondda valleys. Mainly industrial in character, its manufactures include steel, electrical equipment, chains, and cables, besides its traditional coal-mining industry. An effective balance between the last named and lighter industries was achieved with the establishment in 1937 of the Treforest Industrial Estate (160 ac. [65 ha.]), 2 mi. (3 km.) from the town.

PONY EXPRESS, the name applied in U.S. history to a system for providing fast mail service between St. Joseph, Mo., and Sacramento, Calif., from April 1860 to October 1861. The pony express was established by the freighting and stagecoach firm of Russell, Majors, and Waddell. Expert riders chosen from boys and small men rode fleet horses in relays. They carried half-ounce letters bearing a $5 pony express stamp and a 10-cent U.S. stamp. A specially designed square of leather, called a *mochila*, was thrown over the saddle, with a hole for the saddle horn and a slit for the cantle. The letters were carried in four sole-leather boxes attached to the corners of the *mochila*. The goal of ten-day service between St. Joseph and Sacramento was sometimes achieved.

The route at the outset covered 1,838 mi. and included 157 stations from 7 to 20 mi. apart. "Home stations" were located at intervals of 75 to 100 mi. Each rider changed horses from six to eight times on his scheduled ride from one home station to another. After a rest period he carried the mail in the other direction.

The route followed in general the Oregon-California Trail and passed through Ft. Kearney, Julesburg, Ft. Laramie, South Pass, Ft. Bridger, Salt Lake City, and Carson City. Indians burned stations, killed employees, and otherwise disrupted service in the summer of 1860 during the Paiute War.

Among the best-known pony express riders were William ("Buffalo Bill") Cody and "Pony Bob" Haslam. Joseph A. Slade was a hard-driving division superintendent. Russell, Majors, and Waddell had introduced the pony express in the hope of winning a mail contract that would save their tottering transportation empire from bankruptcy. In this they failed. Sensational though it was, the pony express was a financial failure when completion of the transcontinental telegraph line in October 1861 ended all need for it.

See Raymond W. and Mary L. Settle, *Saddles and Spurs* (1955); Arthur Chapman, *The Pony Express* (1932). (T. A. LN.)

PONZA (ancient PONTIA), the name of a small group of islands off the west coast of central Italy about 65 km. (40 mi.) SW of Gaeta. The islands, lying between Rome and Naples, include Ponza (the largest), Palmarola, and Zannone in a western cluster and Ventotene and Santo Stefano in an eastern group. Their total area is 10.9 sq.km. (4.2 sq.mi.); their population (1964 est.) 5,732. Regular steamer services connect Ponza with Naples and, during the summer, with Anzio and Formia. The highest point on the island of Ponza is Monte della Guardia (283 m.; 928 ft.). Kaolin and bentonite are mined on the islands; and they have lately become popular as summer resorts. The island of Ventotene has a prison; under the Fascist regime Ponza was used as a place of banishment for political prisoners.   (G. KH.)·

POOL: see BILLIARDS.

POOLE, WILLIAM FREDERICK (1821–1894), U.S. bibliographer, was a pioneer in U.S. periodical indexing and library administration. He was born in Salem, Mass., Dec. 24, 1821. As a student at Yale he became librarian of a literary society; his *An Alphabetical Index to Subjects Treated in the Reviews and Other Periodicals, to Which No Indexes Have Been Published* (1848) appeared a year before his graduation. A second edition of what became *Poole's Index to Periodical Literature* (1887–1908) appeared in 1853. Poole was an assistant in the library of the Boston Athenaeum in 1851; was librarian of the Boston Mercantile Library Association (1852–56); of the Boston Athenaeum (1856–69); served two years as a library consultant; was librarian at the Cincinnati Public Library, which he organized (1871–73); of the Chicago Public Library (1874–87), building it to the largest circulation in the U.S.; and organized the reference library of the Newberry Library, Chicago, where he remained until his death, March 1, 1894, in Evanston, Ill. History was his avocation and he published widely, especially in the *North American Review*.

POOLE, a municipal and parliamentary borough, a county of a town, a port, and seaside resort in Dorset, Eng., 24 mi. (39 km.) E of Dorchester and 5 mi. (8 km.) W of Bournemouth by road. Pop. (1961) 92,111. The name alludes to the remarkable situation of the old town on a peninsula between the almost landlocked Holes Bay and the tidal waterway (7 mi. by 4½ mi. [11 km. by 7 km.]) to the north of Purbeck known as Poole Harbour. A chain ferry operates between South Haven and Sandbanks at the entrance to the harbour, and a lifting bridge to Hamworthy crosses the entry to Holes Bay. On the east, Poole includes Parkstone and Branksome and extends to Bournemouth. It is a great yachting centre and its good sands have gained it popularity as a holiday resort. The southeast coast is formed by chalk cliffs scored by several of the chines characteristic of those parts. Largest of the islands in Poole Harbour is Brownsea (a bird sanctuary, given to the National Trust in 1962) where in 1907 was held the experimental camp from which sprang the Boy Scout movement. There is an old-established pottery, and other industries include boatbuilding, chemicals, agricultural implements, and engineering. Coal, timber, oil, and general merchandise are imported; exports include clay and tar.

Poole, not mentioned until after the Domesday survey, was granted its charter in 1248. It is uncertain when the burgesses obtained their town at the fee-farm rent of £8 13s. 4d. mentioned in 1312. In 1372 they obtained assize of bread and ale and right to hold courts of the lord of the manor. Elizabeth I made it a separate county in 1569.

POONA (PUNE), a city, district, and division of Maharashtra, India. The city, headquarters of the district and division, lies at the confluence of the Mutha and Mula rivers, 1,850 ft. (564 m.) above sea level and 119 mi. (192 km.) SE of Bombay on the Central Railway. Pop. (1961) 597,562, excluding cantonment. It has a temperate and pleasant climate, and is known as the "Queen of the Deccan" because of its historical associations, its picturesque surroundings, and its importance as a cultural, educational, and political centre. It was the centre of the Mahratta (Maratha) Empire for more than 100 years and the monsoon capital of the Bombay presidency under British rule. The old government house at Ganeshkhind is now the home of Poona University (founded 1948). It has 14 central departments and a large number of constituent and affiliated colleges, including those of arts and science,

medicine, commerce, agriculture, law, and engineering.

Several departments of the Maharashtra government have headquarters at Poona, which is also the headquarters of the southern command of the Indian Army and of the Poona subarea. The Indian National Defence Academy is at Khadakvasla, 10 mi. (16 km.) from the city. The College of Military Engineering and the Armed Forces Medical College are also in Poona. The Indian naval and mechanical training establishment, the I.N.S. "Shivaji," with its engineering college, is at Lonavla, 40 mi. (64 km.) NW of Poona. Other institutions are the Institute of Armament Studies and the Artificial Limb Centre, the only one of its kind in India. Poona is supplied with water from the Khadakvasla dam and electricity comes from the Tata group of hydroelectric works in the hills nearby.

The city has a municipal corporation consisting of 65 corporators who annually elect their mayor. A civilian officer of the Maharashtra government functions as the chief executive officer of the corporation and is known as the municipal commissioner. The cantonments of Poona (pop. [1961] 65,838) and Kirkee or Khadki (58,496) adjoin the city area.

In the city of Poona itself and in the adjoining cantonments are a number of places of historical association: e.g., the remains of the famous Shaniwarwada Palace of the peshwas and the Aga Khan's palace where M. K. Gandhi was held in custody in 1942. To the southwest of the city is Parvati Hill, so named after the temple of Durga, or Parvati, on its summit. Public gardens include the Bund Gardens, laid out beside the stone *bund* (dam) on the Mula River, the Empress, and the botanical gardens. There are a number of museums and churches, a synagogue, and several hospitals. Poona has a cotton mill, a paper mill, and a few metal and engineering factories. The National Chemical Laboratory and the meteorological department observatory are also at Poona. Kirkee contains a large ammunition factory, and there is a penicillin factory at Pimpri, a few miles away. Poona is an important rail and road junction.

POONA DISTRICT has an area of 6,033 sq.mi. (15,625 sq.km.); pop. (1961) 2,466,880. Toward the west the country is undulating and numerous spurs from the Western Ghats enter the district; to the east it opens out into plains. The region is liable to drought. The two most important irrigation works are the Mutha Canal, with which the Poona waterworks are connected, and the Nira Canal. The main crops are jowar and paddy. Jaggery is produced in great quantities from sugarcane, and there are several sugar factories. The district is traversed by the Central Railway and also by the Southern Railway, which runs southward from Poona city to Miraj and Belgaum.

The district contains a number of historical places which include the Shivneri Fort, the birthplace of Sivaji (*q.v.*), and the well-known Karli (*q.v.*) caves.

POONA DIVISION comprises the districts of Poona, Ahmednagar, Satara, Sangli, Kolhapur, and Sholapur. Area 28,909 sq.mi. (74,-874 sq.km.). Pop. (1961) 10,360,282.   (D. G. K.)

POOR CLARES, the Second Order of St. Francis, an order of contemplative nuns founded in 1212 by St. Clare (Clara) of Assisi.

See FRANCISCANS: *Second Order;* CLARE, SAINT.

POOR LAW. A series of enactments culminating in the English Poor Law of 1601 provided for minimal relief for the destitute through a poor rate levied on all householders, thus for the first time establishing secular and legal obligations to aid the unfortunate, in addition to the previously recognized moral and religious duties to give alms for the poor. Though the causes of this development were many, they were all basically connected with the breakdown of the medieval economy and social structure of western Europe, which both destroyed the traditional framework of charity and produced new types of poverty.

For the origins of charitable institutions, the early influences of Buddhism, Islam, Judaism, and Christianity and the development and decline of medieval philanthropic institutions *see* PHILANTHROPY. For the development of modern programs to aid those in need *see* CHILD WELFARE; SOCIAL SECURITY; SOCIAL SERVICE; SOCIAL WELFARE.

ENGLAND AND WALES

In medieval England poverty had been largely due to an under-developed economy in which famine and pestilence were recurring phenomena. By the beginning of the 16th century this kind of destitution was giving place to the "dearth in the midst of plenty" which so perplexed contemporaries. Enclosure for pasture was blamed for unemployment, depopulation, and vagrancy. The rising price level, resulting from a complex combination of the influx of treasure from the New World and the disastrous monetary debasements of Henry VIII and Edward VI, was popularly attributed to the mania for sheep farming. The breakdown of the medieval rural economy, deplorable as it seemed to contemporaries, must not be exaggerated; the areas affected by enclosure for sheep were very limited. It was the expansion of the woolen industry, with its close dependence on foreign markets, which was often responsible for this kind of unemployment. The cycle of boom and slump had come to add a new element of instability to the economic life of England. Of less importance in the creation of Tudor poverty is that cause which loomed so large in early accounts of the origin of the poor law, the dissolution of the monasteries. By 1536 many of these were too embarrassed financially to do more than relieve the local beggars their presence attracted. The legend that hordes of monks and nuns were turned adrift to beg their bread has not been substantiated by later research.

This new type of poverty was not confined to England; it was appearing in all the more economically advanced countries of western Europe. It is customary to attribute the pattern of early Tudor legislation to the influence of Juan Luis Vives' *De subventione pauperum sive de humanis necessitatibus*, published in 1526. This formed the basis of the experiment of dealing with poverty by municipal action undertaken at Ypres in 1525, an account of which appeared in an English translation in 1535. But foreign influences may have been overestimated; similar causes were everywhere likely to suggest similar remedies. That the crown evinced any interest in the destitute was attributable to politics, not compassion. Vagrants spread disaffection and might provide the raw material for a rebel army. The early efforts of the government, therefore, were directed to stamping out vagrancy. The relief of poverty was left, with some general directives, to local authorities. The first statute dealing specifically with poor relief was that of 1531, which merely empowered justices to license aged and impotent persons to beg within their own neighbourhood. The interlocking problems of destitution, unemployment, and vagrancy seem to have been under discussion in 1535, as in that year draft proposals outlined revolutionary suggestions for dealing with them, including the employment of the able poor on public works and the setting up of both central and local administrative machinery. The statute of 1536, as finally passed, was less drastic and concentrated largely on the organization of voluntary funds for the relief of those unable to work. Despite its lack of administrative machinery, it, like the previous draft, illustrates the new approach to the problem and for this reason is often regarded as the first English poor law. In line with continental opinion it prohibited begging and indiscriminate charity, and attempted to classify the poor into the aged and impotent needing relief, and poor children who should be apprenticed. In practice, lacking administrative machinery, it could be put into effect only where the municipal authorities had the organization to finance and implement its provisions. London, Norwich, and York were among those towns confronted with turning theory into fact.

London took the lead. A serious attempt to deal with the City's poor soon showed that funds provided by voluntary contributions were insufficient, and in 1547 the corporation decided to impose a compulsory poor rate. A new administrative device of the greatest importance was thus introduced, and there was a decisive break with the medieval conception of charity as a religious duty. Other expedients of a modern character followed rapidly. By 1553 a comprehensive scheme for the treatment of the poor was in existence. They were now classified as the poor by impotency, the poor by casualty, and the thriftless poor, and appropriate institutional treatment was to be provided, as far as resources would allow, for each group. Similar programs were initiated by other cities, particularly those whose connection with the fluctuating fortunes of the woolen industry increased the instability of employment. By the end of the 1570s many of them had evolved workable schemes based on classification, some measure of institutional treatment and compulsory rates.

Before 1572 the state provided little legislation to underpin this system and it looked as if the relief of poverty would become the responsibility of the towns rather than of the nation. Indeed a characteristic feature of the English poor law is the way in which national legislation followed, rather than initiated, local experiment. This, until the adoption of the civil parish as the unit of poor law administration, was dictated by the fact that the central authority had no effective machinery through which to administer statute law locally. It was only in the sphere of providing funds, therefore, that a few fumbling advances were made by the acts of 1551–52 and 1563. Not until 1572 was a straightforward, compulsory rate imposed on a national scale. By then it was clear that the state would have to take a more active part in enforcing on local authorities some responsibility for destitution. The same act also ordered the compilation of a comprehensive register of persons needing relief and instructed justices in rural areas and mayors in towns to appoint collectors and overseers. It also, like the earlier draft of 1535, recognized the fact that not all the unemployed were work-shy; local authorities were now encouraged to use funds left over from the relief of the aged, sick, and infant poor to set the able-bodied pauper "on work" (*i.e.*, provide work for the able-bodied). In 1576 this permission was transformed into compulsion. All local authorities were to provide funds for the purchase of raw materials for this purpose.

The "Old Poor Law" (1601).—The codification of 1597–98, reenacted in 1601 with minor changes and finally made permanent in 1623, completed the first stage of the poor law (sometimes known as the Elizabethan poor law or the "old poor law" in contradistinction to the "new poor law" set up after 1834). The parish, the smallest unit of local government, was finally and decisively acknowledged as the normal unit of administration. This was entrusted to overseers, appointed annually by the local justices and forced to serve under penalty of a fine, who, together with the churchwardens, were to assess and levy a poor rate on all householders which, when ratified by the justices, was compulsory. With these funds the aged were to be relieved and provided, if necessary, with cottages on the waste, or common, poor children were to be apprenticed, and the able poor set "on work." This codification was at once a synopsis of previous urban experience and a break with urban experiments, since the parish, a smaller but ubiquitous unit, was now the basis of the national system. Though later the parish was to prove too small, it is difficult to see what else could have been done. Experience had shown that poor relief confined to the towns put too heavy a burden on them and distributed rather than relieved destitution.

The subsequent period, from 1597 to 1644, is of fundamental importance in the history of the poor laws; in these years the privy council succeeded in building up an administrative hierarchy to make the earlier acts effective. It is easy for the modern citizen to forget how great was the gap between enactment and enforcement in Tudor England and to assign to early acts a practical importance which they could not possess. After 1597 the exertion of pressure on the justices and the sending of directives became more frequent. Sometimes these took the form of general orders, such as those sent to all high sheriffs and courts of quarter sessions in 1598 to explain the new legislation; sometimes they were concerned with particular problems and were sent to individual authorities. Until 1622 this kind of pressure was irregular, being called into being in response to a sudden crisis, either local or national. The failure of the harvests in 1621 and 1622 and in 1629–31 apparently converted an occasional expedient into a regular routine. Since 1597 the privy council had had experience in dealing with the regulation of grain supplies under scarcity conditions and in 1631 it applied this experience to its system of supervision of the local poor law authorities. The system was both practical and detailed. The justices of each county were to divide themselves into groups, so many being responsible for each subdivision, or hundred (*q.v.*). They were to hold monthly meetings with the church-wardens and overseers of the parishes within their respective hundreds, to punish neglect by these officers of their statutory duty, and to report what had been done every three months to the high sheriff. These reports were sent to the justices of assize and finally submitted to the privy council. In this way it was possible, at least in theory, for the central government to get a picture of the way in which the local authorities were carrying out their tasks.

The general impression is one of real but geographically patchy success. Where the pressure of work was not great, or where local charity and endowments were adequate, or the parish remote and difficult to supervise, the poor, if assisted at all, were helped without much reference to the letter of the law. For example, the parish of Sawston in Cambridgeshire levied no regular poor rates until 1658. In contrast, where towns and cities had long been grappling with the problem, or in those rural areas where the justices were accessible to pressure, parishes seem to have been relieving the aged and sick, apprenticing their children and even complying with the obligation to have a "town stock" of raw materials with which to set the poor "on work."

With the outbreak of civil war and the determined attack of the Long Parliament on the coercive power of the privy council, the situation altered. Authorities were once again left to their own devices. The statutory obligations remained but the encouragement and supervision disappeared, not to return until the creation of the poor law commissioners in 1834. Nevertheless, the pressure of the previous 40 years was not without results. The habit of appointing overseers, levying rates, relieving the poor, had become something of a social tradition. It might not be well done, and the difficult task of organizing employment was often dropped, but the laws, far from falling into abeyance, were gradually extended into parishes and areas where earlier they had been little observed.

Parish Organization of Poor Relief, 1662–1795.—The next milestone in the history of the English poor law came with the restoration of the monarchy. There was no attempt to revive the control of any central authority, but in 1662 the responsibility of each parish was defined by an act usually known as the Law of Settlement and Removal. Its preamble contained the statement that "by reason of some defect in the law, poor people are not restrained from going from one parish to another, and do therefore endeavour to settle themselves in those parishes where there is the best stock, the largest commons or wastes to build cottages and the most woods for them to burn and destroy." To remedy this defect the act provided that any person coming into a parish who neither rented a house of the annual value of £10 (which was a rental completely outside the economic resources of the craftsman or labourer) nor was able to give security against becoming a burden on the rates at any future time, could be moved back to his or her place of settlement within 40 days on application made by the overseers to two local justices for a warrant of removal. There was nothing very new in this act except in the precise definition of the occasion and method of removal. The piecemeal legislation of the Tudors, before the final codification of 1601, contained assumptions that the right to relief was a local one, that parishes were entitled to some defense against an influx of strangers and need not relieve, might indeed even remove, "aged, lame or impotent persons" of less than three years' residence. Sixteenth-century municipal authorities had been zealous in removing persons likely to become chargeable. The act of 1662 thus gave national force to existing local custom.

The legal basis for the custom however had never been clearly defined, though most communities seem to have felt that people had a right to relief only where they lived and were known. Charity both began and ended at home. Even so, why the task of definition should have been undertaken just when it was has been something of a puzzle to historians. The general upheaval and unsettlement of the years after the Civil War and interregnum is usually adduced as the most likely cause. The growth of population may well have been an additional reason.

However it may be, the act of 1662 with its subsequent amendments was thenceforth the hub around which the administration of the poor law revolved. In 1685 it was amended so that the 40 days' residence necessary to gain a settlement only began from "the time of his or her Delivery of a Notice in Writing of the house of his or her Abode, and the Number of his or her Family, if he or she have any, to one of the Churchwardens or Overseers of the said Parish." In 1693 the regulations were further tightened by the stipulation that the notice in writing had to be read in the parish church at the time of divine service. After this there was little chance of a stranger's gaining a settlement without the consent of the general body of the ratepayers. In an attempt to make the act work in a reasonable way, the same statute also defined other methods of gaining a settlement. These were by serving an apprenticeship within the parish, by being hired as a servant for a year, by executing some parochial office for the same period, or by paying parochial rates. In addition, women gained a settlement on marriage, and legitimate children took that of their father until they reached the age of seven, when they could acquire one of their own. Illegitimate children were settled where they were born.

Effects of Settlement Laws.—Between 1662 and 1795, after which date no person could be removed until he was actually chargeable, the attempts of parish officers to take advantage of the settlement laws distorted almost every aspect of the poor laws except the granting of relief to those aged and sick paupers who were, beyond all doubt, the settled poor of the parish. Despite the condemnation of Adam Smith, the purely economic effect of this legislation appears to have been slighter than might have been expected. Some elasticity was given by an act of 1697, which gave legal sanction to the existing practice by which parishes gave testimonials to parishioners seeking work elsewhere: these were, in effect, promises to take them back should they ever become chargeable. Moreover it was clearly impossible to remove every newcomer, particularly where there was a demand for labour. In practice, able-bodied men, so long as they took no steps to obtain a settlement by presenting a notice in writing, rarely seem to have been removed unless they were actually chargeable. Rural parishes appear to have concentrated on removing married couples, particularly those "overburdened with children." Single women, women with children, and orphans were equally unpopular. In industrial areas where young and old could be employed, the family unit was less economically vulnerable. Here women, particularly those with children, were the main victims. In any case the changing distribution of the growing population of the 18th century makes it clear that mobility could not have been unduly restricted.

If the economic consequences of the Law of Settlement were not notably harmful, the social consequences can be more justifiably condemned. Apprenticeship, originally intended to give a child a start in life, was now often used to change its settlement. Children could be compulsorily bound out in their own parishes or, with funds provided from the poor rate, elsewhere. In this case no one questioned the suitability of the master or the trade selected, or the treatment the child received. In this matter the urban parishes appear to have been the chief offenders. The result was many runaway apprentices and much misery. Another unfortunate result was the restriction on the building of new cottages on the commons, which led to overcrowding and the retarding of marriage. Unmarried mothers were treated with great harshness. An act of 1576 had made it an offense to beget an illegitimate child which was likely to become chargeable, and the father, if known, could be forced to give security "to save the parish harmless." Little proof beyond the woman's oath was required, and many men, guilty or innocent, found refuge in flight. In such cases the overseers, faced with the responsibility for the child, forced or bribed the woman to take to the roads. Yet whether this widespread distortion of the poor laws really saved parish funds may be doubted. Removals were expensive and often contested at quarter sessions; sometimes they were taken on appeal to higher courts. Moreover, though each parish struggled to save itself expense, it was in turn the victim of similar practices by other parishes.

The best-administered part of the poor law appears to have been the relief of those aged and sick persons who were unquestionably settled inhabitants. Indeed, care had to be taken to keep this kind of relief within bounds. After 1693 none was to be given, except in case of emergency, without the authority of a justice, the names of such persons to be entered in a book and reviewed annually. Paupers whose claims were allowed received small monthly pensions, though by the act of 1697 they were ordered to wear a large red or blue P on their outer garment. Often their rent was paid and they got occasional gifts of fuel and clothes. Sick paupers were looked after, medical attention that ranged from the services of a bonesetter to those of the local doctor was provided, and, if death followed, the parish paid funeral expenses.

The Workhouse.—The obligation to set the poor "on work" was the most difficult of all the burdens placed on the parish by the act of 1601. To manage a parish stock at a profit was well-nigh impossible. Municipal experiments on the lines of the London Bridewell tended to peter out, while the houses of correction, which an act of 1607 ordered to be set up in every county, were increasingly regarded as penal establishments for the idle rather than as places of employment. Once the supervision of the privy council disappeared, the first phase of the attempts to employ the poor came to an end in 1644. After the Restoration the increasing interest taken in political economy refocused attention on this failure to employ the poor. Emphasis was now placed on the loss to the national income sustained through the waste of labour, and many pamphleteers, among whom were John Bellars, Richard Haines, and Thomas Firman, outlined schemes for the organization of corporations to employ the poor on a commercial basis. For this purpose stock was to be subscribed and workhouses erected. Most schemes were quite impracticable, but John Cary started a new chapter in poor law history when he persuaded the Bristol parishes to apply for a local act to set up a "Corporation of the Poor" in 1696. This was to be responsible for the poor of the entire city and provide employment for them in a well-run workhouse. At first the experiment appeared successful, and Bristol's example was followed by other towns. These early hopes were not maintained, but workhouses became established institutions largely for their deterrent value. In 1723, indeed, a permissive general act allowed parishes to build and manage workhouses and to refuse relief to those who would not enter them. Though useful in keeping down the poor rate, such workhouses made no effective contribution to setting the poor on profitable work. During the 18th century they rapidly degenerated into mixed receptacles of misery where every class of pauper, vicious or unfortunate, young or old, sick, well, or lunatic, was dumped. Sometimes they were managed by parochial officials, often they were let out to contractors, either for a lump sum or on a capitation basis. Many parishes fluctuated from one method to the other but neither led to any satisfactory employment of the poor.

Humanitarians were increasingly troubled by the abuses of the general mixed workhouse, while there were increasing complaints about the inadequacy of the parish as a unit for poor law administration on the grounds that it was too small (particularly in the towns) for effective action, and that its unpaid, annually appointed, untrained officers were either lazy or corrupt. Indeed, some parishes, though without legal sanction, were already employing a salaried overseer. An act of 1782 permitted parishes to unite for the purpose of building institutions to house all classes of the destitute, except the able-bodied. For the able-bodied the overseers, in vague terms, were directed to provide relief or work outside the house. This meant a complete reversal of earlier policy in a revulsion from its failure.

Speenhamland System (1795).—Between 1782 and 1793 economic depression, poor harvests, and frictional unemployment caused by agricultural developments and the early stages of industrialization combined to make life difficult for the labouring poor. Wages often were traditional and bore little relation to changing conditions. Yet, to men steeped in mercantilist thought, it appeared plain folly to raise wages to meet what, to contemporaries, must have seemed a temporary crisis. It had long been the practice to help poor men "overburdened with children" by making them some allowance from the parish. In the same way temporarily soaring prices, caused by a failure of the harvest, were commonly met by *ad hoc* emergency relief measures rather than by raising wages. In line with this tradition the justices of

Berkshire, meeting at Speen in the district of Speenhamland in 1795, decided that wages below what they considered an absolute minimum should be supplemented by the parish in accordance with the price of bread and the number of dependents a man had. Their example was widely followed and the practice received parliamentary confirmation in 1796. Yet another phase of English poor law history, the so-called Speenhamland system, had begun.

(D. ML.)

The word "system" is misleading, for the Speenhamland decision was a makeshift, grounded in existing social theory and practice, rather than a deliberate proposal for a general poor law policy. Even in Berkshire itself, the decision did not result in any substantial changes in local administration. Parishes continued to maintain their own workhouses, to give or to withhold casual relief, to distribute cheap food, and to fix bread prices. During the Napoleonic Wars, however, there was a great extension of the allowance system, or various types of allowance systems, in the southern counties of England, and contemporaries found it convenient to describe this as part of one general process. Most historians have agreed with contemporary critics that the spread of the allowance system was "momentous" and "disastrous."

The "system" had three possible abuses. First, it might lead to the subsidization of wages out of the poor rate. In *The State of the Poor* (1797), Sir F. M. Eden claimed that the larger farmers were able to take advantage of the magistrates' benevolence by forcing the smaller ratepayers, who were not themselves employers of labour, to augment wages. The charge may have been exaggerated, for some tenant farmers were able to pass on the increase in poor rates to their landlords, but such a transfer was not general and did not prevent the poor rate from becoming a redistributive tax. Second, it might entail the general pauperization of large numbers of employed workers on the land. It was argued that the system made the poor careless and indifferent, checked their incentive to save, encouraged improvident marriages, and engendered a large increase in population which, according to Malthusian theory, would inevitably create a new mass of poverty. Some opponents even went so far as to argue that all poor laws should be abolished; as Thomas Chalmers put it, "no evil genius could have designed a system of greater malignity for the corruption of the race." Third, it sharpened the contrast between industrial north and agrarian south and perpetuated the division of the labour market into two sectors, the one depending upon a contractual wages system, the other depending upon status and protection. Controversy centred on these points not only during the Napoleonic Wars but also after 1815, when agrarian discontent was accompanied by industrial expansion.

Between 1815 and 1830 contemporaries were mainly concerned, however, with the burden of poor law expenditure, particularly in the area south of the Wash-Severn line. In 1785 the total cost of poor law administration was a little less than £2,000,000; by 1803 it had increased to a little more than £4,000,000; and by 1817 it had reached the total of almost £8,000,000. This final figure represented a cost of about 13s. 3d. per head of the population or about one-sixth of total public expenditure. Although the total fell a little in the subsequent 15 years, it did not fall as much as the price level, and in 1832 it stood at about £7,000,000, or 10 s. per head of the population. Some parishes were particularly affected by the burden. One Buckinghamshire village, for instance, reported in 1832 that its expenditure on poor relief was eight times what it had been in 1795 and more than the rental of the whole parish had been in that year. In face of statistics of this kind, the Whig government decided to intervene, and in the year of reform, 1832, a royal commission was appointed to inquire into the whole "system." Its recommendations served as the basis of the reforms embodied in the Poor Law Amendment Act, 1834.

New Poor Law (1834).—The new act was not merely a return to severity after a period of benevolence; it was inspired by new principles and set up new administrative machinery. The case for abolition of the poor laws was not accepted, but on Benthamite lines it was laid down that poor relief should be granted to able-bodied poor and their dependents only in well-regulated workhouses under conditions inferior to those of the humblest labourers outside. As the commissioners had argued, "every penny bestowed that tends to render the condition of the pauper more eligible than that of the independent labourer is a bounty on indolence and vice." The machinery also was Benthamite. The hitherto independent parishes were grouped into unions, each under an elected board of guardians, with a strong central authority—the Poor Law Commission—to enforce a uniform policy.

On paper, the act of 1834 introduced order into the poor law system; in the words of Nassau Senior, one of its chief architects, it was "a measure of social policy." Poverty was considered a crime, which merited a stigma, and the poor were poor not because Providence had ordained them to be so but as a result of their own failings. Such a harsh philosophy, which was sharply criticized by traditionalists and helped to rouse the Chartist movement, was nonetheless better suited to the mood of an industrial age than Speenhamland. One of the purposes of the act was to stimulate free trade in labour by driving workers onto the labour market. The abolition of outdoor relief was intended to provide an incentive to workers to seek regular employment. Unfortunately, however, when the poor law commissioners attempted to apply the act in the north of England in 1837, there was much genuine industrial unemployment.

Less Eligibility.—The inadequacies of the act were demonstrated very clearly during the subsequent 30 years. The first and most dramatic crisis in its administration came in 1847 at Andover. The workhouse there was so efficient in applying the principle of less eligibility (*i.e.,* that the condition of the poor should be made "less eligible" than that of the labourer) that labourers were willing to accept as little as 5s. or 6s. a week rather than enter the workhouse, for work conditions imposed on inmates were intolerably cruel. A committee set up to investigate conditions at Andover condemned its internal administration and led to the setting up of a new Poor Law Board (1847), directly responsible to Parliament, in place of the Poor Law Commission. The president of the board was now eligible to sit in Parliament. Some improvement in workhouse conditions followed the Andover scandal, but in 1852 an experienced lawyer, Robert Pashley, maintained that "the workhouse as now organized is a reproach and disgrace peculiar to England: nothing corresponding to it is to be found throughout the whole Continent of Europe."

There was an inevitable reaction in the middle of the century against the excessive harshness of poor law administration. The attempt to treat as one group all children, women, and men in need of assistance was bound to create social as well as administrative difficulties. To place under the same stringent discipline the young, the sick, the aged, and the able-bodied proved as much of a strain to the administrators as it was a grievance to the poor themselves. The new poor law, in consequence, became almost as subject to local variation as the old poor law of the 17th and 18th centuries. In many parts of the country it proved impossible totally to abolish outdoor relief; in other parts, separate poor law institutions were created for the young and the sick; and in some districts, boards of guardians continued to pay small weekly doles to old men and women incapacitated from work. Such signs of "sentimentalism" were bitterly attacked by the faithful supporters of the principles of 1834. The development of democracy, however, associated as it was with the growth of humanitarian feeling, and, after 1880, the development of more scientific methods of dealing with destitution, helped to mitigate the harshness of poor law administration.

Extension of the Franchise.—The extension of the franchise in 1884 (which extended the household and lodger franchise to the counties, nearly tripling the county electorate; *see* PARLIAMENT: *The Franchise*) was an important turning point in the approach to the poor. From that date onward a move away from the principles of 1834 can clearly be traced. In 1891 supplies of toys and books for workhouses were permitted; in 1892 tobacco and snuff could be provided; in 1893 visiting committees of ladies were allowed to inspect the workhouses; in 1894 guardians were given the right to distribute dry tea, milk, and sugar for women to make their own afternoon tea; in 1897 trained nurses could be employed for the care of the sick poor; and in 1900 a government circular recom-

mended the grant of outdoor relief for the aged of good character.

In addition to these deviations from the principle of less eligibility, changes were made in the fiscal and administrative machinery for supervising the poor laws. In 1871 the Poor Law Board was abolished and central authority passed directly to the Local Government Board. The new body was as much concerned as the old one had been with fiscal surgery as well as social policy, and throughout its existence it emphasized the most important social bulwark of 1834, the assertion that poverty deserved a stigma. Men and women in receipt of relief under the poor law were not only subject to a special discipline and compelled to wear pauper uniforms as a symbol of their inferiority; they were robbed of their civil and political rights, including the right to vote. The poor law treated the claims of the poor not as an integral part of the rights of the citizen, but as an alternative to them—as claims which could be met by society only if the claimant ceased to be a full citizen of the community. It was not until 1918 that the pauper disability of disfranchisement was removed, and even after that signs of the stigma still remained.

Criticism and Reform.—The changed approach both to poverty and to the poor law began with a new inquiry into the facts of destitution in the last 20 years of the 19th century. Charles Booth's *Life and Labour of the People in London,* the first volume of which was published in 1889, was the first great landmark. It was followed by other important books, such as Seebohm Rowntree's *Poverty: A Study of Town Life* (1901), which gave a new precision to the concept of poverty. Further evidence collected by official committees, particularly the Royal Commission on the Aged Poor, which reported in 1895, helped to direct attention both to existing practices and to basic presuppositions about the poor. The way was prepared for setting up the Royal Commission on the Poor Laws in 1905.

Unlike the commission of 1832, that set up in 1905 was not the outcome of any sustained agitation, nor did its members start with any common theory to apply to the contemporary situation. "There is no one directing purpose shaping the enquiry to a predetermined end," wrote Beatrice Webb, one of the members, in the middle of the deliberations, "which of the many conflicting or diverging purposes will prevail remains to be seen." But the commission included many experts in dealing with the poor. Some, like Sir Charles Loch, had experience with both poor law and voluntary charity; some, like Charles Booth, Helen Bosanquet, and Beatrice Webb herself, had been leaders in social study and research; others, like George Lansbury and Francis Chandler, were representatives of the new labour upsurge as well as experienced guardians; and finally there was Octavia Hill, who had done more than any other woman for the welfare of the London poor. If these distinguished members of the commission had been unanimous, they would, said Canon S. A. Barnett, have been invincible.

In fact no single purpose prevailed and two reports were produced by the commissioners. The majority (16) recommended that the boards of guardians should be replaced by statutory committees of the county and county borough councils, that the new committees should be called "public assistance authorities" with a number of subordinate public assistance committees working under them in subareas, and that general workhouses should be abolished and different classes of the destitute should be relieved in specialized institutions. The able-bodied poor should, as far as possible, be found work, but outdoor relief could be provided after strict inquiry, under supervision, and on a uniform basis.

The minority (four) were not content with this retreat from the principles of 1834. They argued that the poor law system was fundamentally bad. It was the business of the community to try to prevent destitution and not merely to palliate it when it occurred. In consequence, the poor law should be broken up, and in its place the state and the local authorities should provide specialized social services to deal with separate categories of poor people. Already administrators had been compelled to note the existence of the sick, the feeble-minded, the aged, and pauper children as well as the able-bodied. Now the able-bodied should be placed in charge of a national unemployment authority and the other categories should be transferred to the local authorities.

Both majority and minority expressed themselves strongly against the views of the surviving supporters of 1834, particularly J. S. Davy, the principal officer of the poor law division of the Local Government Board. There was a remarkable measure of agreement in the condemnation of the past and the assessment of the present. There were two distinct views of the future, however, each of which was to prove influential. The minority report, drafted with skill and driven by passion, advocated optimum social services maintained by specialists, the boundaries of whose activities would be set by the boundaries of perfection in their own expert techniques. In the middle of the picture would be a registrar of public assistance for each local authority, coordinating the various schemes. The majority report, building on the social situation as it existed in 1905, was more concerned with minimum social security than with the optimum, and more conscious of the continued role of voluntary action, maintained by an army of trained general or family caseworkers. If the minority report seemed to point more clearly toward the welfare state, it was opposed to the insurance principle on which the welfare state was to be constructed.

Breakup of the Poor Law.—No action was taken in 1909 to implement the proposals of either the majority or the minority reports, although Beatrice Webb set up the National Committee for the Promotion of the Break-up of the Poor Law, and Lord George Hamilton created an alternative National Poor Law Reform Association.

The government did not respond to the arguments of this agitation, and within the poor law structure itself undertook merely a mild so-called revolution by administration. It did, however, herald a genuine revolution in welfare policy, and by introducing such measures as old age pensions without "the stigma of pauperism" and national insurance it placed the poor laws in a new legislative and administrative context.

It was not until 1929, however, after a period of prolonged enquiry and economic and political disturbance during the 1920s, that the Local Government Act implemented the main recommendation of both the 1909 reports by replacing the boards of guardians by local authorities. The Poor Law Act, 1930, consolidated previous legislation. The minister of health was charged with the central direction and control of all matters relating to the administration of poor relief; in the localities, most authorities appointed separate public assistance committees, consisting of elected members of the council plus (optionally) a number, not exceeding one-third of the total, of persons co-opted from outside the council. In addition there were subordinate guardians' committees for appropriate workhouse areas in the counties, although they had no power to appoint or dismiss officers without the approval of the public assistance committees. The chief local administrator of the poor law was the public assistance officer, who sometimes was also the clerk of the council. He was assisted by the district relieving officer, the direct descendant of the Elizabethan parish officer.

The passing of the new legislation coincided with an alarming increase in the number of unemployed and the darkest period of industrial distress in the whole of English history. The break up of existing social policy in the 1930s was the prelude to reforms introduced during and after World War II, which marked a radically new approach to social welfare (q.v.). (A. BRI.)

UNITED STATES

Public provision for the care of persons in economic need in the United States is as much a part of North America's English heritage as the right of trial by jury. Before the first year at Plymouth ended, it was necessary for members of the colony to call upon their experience in the homeland to assure food, shelter, and clothing to the least fortunate members of the colony. The Elizabethan Poor Law of 1601 was a codification of many various acts and decrees dating back to the 14th century, and the colonists drew upon this experience to deal with their own community problems.

Classification of the Needy.—As in England, two principal classes of needy persons were recognized: (1) the able-bodied, and (2) children plus the permanently incapacitated. Able-bodied adults were to be put to work, and children were to be trained for self-support through apprenticeship. The lame, the sick, and the aged were given what in that age was regarded as humane care. In New England each town was responsible for its own poor. The classical poor law formula was less commonly used in the South, partly because of indenture, slavery, and the plantation system.

Local Administration.—The Elizabethan Poor Law was an act of the national government, but it was administered by the local authorities. The American adaptation was at first simply a derivative from the English law, but eventually it became part of the colonial codes and still later part of the statutes of the several states. Hence, the problem of the "settlement" of the needy arose. Where did he live and, therefore, who was responsible for him and his family? From the earliest colonial days a needy person had to apply for assistance in the local governmental unit in which he had settlement. The ancestor of poor law settlement was the medieval doctrine that every man had a master and was bound by rights and obligations to some feudal domain. The growth of population disturbed the validity of this assumption. The rise of the doctrine of a free labour market in the 18th century, supplemented by the population theory of Thomas R. Malthus, dealt settlement doctrine a staggering, though not fatal, blow.

Criterion of Need.—During the 19th century in the United States as in Great Britain, to be eligible for assistance the recipient had to have less income than he could earn at the lowest-paid job in the community, and the rule was that he should not be given as much as he could earn at such a job if one were available. This was the doctrine of "less eligibility."

During the period since 1930 a new phrase has been used to indicate the amount of assistance to be given, namely, that necessary to maintain "health and decency." For one thing this took account of all members of the family in terms of what was required for physical health and respectable appearance. The operational definition of "health and decency" is made by the local assistance agency. The tendency has been to remove fixed maximum amounts of money to be paid to needy persons. Some agencies are generous, but others are restrictive and still make grants within the tradition of less eligibility.

Multiplication of Categories of Assistance.—Instead of the two categories in the old poor law, needy persons since 1900 have been classified into several administrative categories: mothers and dependent children, the aged, the blind, the permanently disabled, and then the residue. Illinois adopted the first Mother's Aid Law in 1911, and Montana set up a special old age pension scheme in 1923. Both of these categories derive from the "unemployable" category of the old poor law. Under the Federal Social Security Act a national system is administered through the states but usually still by town or county agencies. The "health and decency" criterion is more or less in use.

A new system of categories came into existence with the first social insurance laws in Germány in the 1880s, later in Great Britain, and still later in the United States. Benefit under social insurance is payable, not because somebody is necessarily in economic need, but because an "insurance event" has occurred. Money is paid according to a scale from funds accumulated for the purpose. Social insurance for the unemployed, the aged, survivors, the disabled, the blind, and the sick provides a substitute for earned income to prevent or reduce need for public assistance.

General assistance is nearer to the old poor law than are the categories. Only economic need must be shown to establish eligibility, and it is determined on the basis of all members of the household.

The Poor Law Transformed.—The poor law in purpose and to a considerable extent in method has been transformed into social service and social welfare (qq.v.). Hence, it may be said "that the primary objective of public welfare services is to develop, restore, or maintain working capacity, to promote sociopsychological adjustment, to provide humane care of the incapacitated, and to establish facilities for the attainment of these ends, and in so doing to maintain a morale and a sense of security which are necessary to an orderly government." (R. Clyde White, *Ad-*

ministration of Public Welfare, p. 7, American Book Company, 1950.)

See also POVERTY, and entries under "Poor Law" in the Index.
(R. C. WE.)

BIBLIOGRAPHY.—S. and B. Webb, *English Poor Law History*, vol. vii–ix of *English Local Government* (1927–29); Sir G. Nicholls, *A History of the English Poor Law*, 3 vol., new ed., with 3rd vol. by J. Mackay (1898–99); Sir F. M. Eden, *The State of the Poor*, 3 vol. (1797); E. M. Leonard, *The Early History of Poor Relief* (1900); B. Tierney, *Medieval Poor Law* (1959); D. Marshall, *The English Poor in the Eighteenth Century* (1926); F. R. Salter, *Some Early Tracts on Poor Relief* (1926); E. M. Hampson, *The Treatment of Poverty in Cambridgeshire, 1597–1834* (1934); D. Marshall, "The Old Poor Law," *Economic History Review*, vol. viii, no. 1 (1927); W. A. Robson (ed.) *Social Security*, 3rd ed. (1948); T. H. Marshall, *Citizenship and Social Class, and Other Essays* (1950).

Official Publications: *Report of the Commissioners for Inquiring into the Administration and Practical Operation of the Poor Laws, 1834* (1835); *Report of the Royal Commission on the Poor Laws and the Relief of Distress, Parliamentary Papers*, vol. 37 (1909–13); *Report of the Local Government Committee of the Ministry of Reconstruction* (1918); *Ministry of Health Provisional Proposals for Poor Laws Reform* (1925); *Annual Reports* of the Poor Law Commission, the Poor Law Board, the Ministry of Health, the National Assistance Board, and the Ministry of National Insurance.   (D. ML.; A. BRI.)

Edith Abbott, *Public Assistance*, vol. i (1940); Sophonisba P. Breckenridge, *Public Welfare Administration in the United States* (1938); Eveline M. Burns, *The American Social Security System* (1949); John J. Clarke, *Social Administration*, 2nd ed. (1935); Nathan E. Cohen, *Social Work in the American Tradition* (1958); Margaret D. Creech, *Three Centuries of Poor Law Administration* (1936); *Social Security Bulletin* (monthly); Amos Warner, Stuart A. Queen, and Ernest Harper, *American Charities and Social Work* (1930); R. Clyde White, *Administration of Public Welfare*, 2nd ed. (1950).   (R. C. WE.)

POORWILL, the name (from its cry) of a North American bird (*Phalaenoptilus nuttallii*) of the nightjar family (Caprimulgidae). It is about eight inches long; the primaries are rusty gray, barred with black. It breeds in arid country west of the Mississippi north to British Columbia and south to southern California.

Poorwills are cited as classic examples of hibernation among birds; they cling to the walls of rock crevices and remain in a torpid state during the unfavourable winter months. *See* also BIRD: *Natural History and Habits: Resting, Sleeping, and Hibernating.*

POPAYÁN, a city in southwestern Colombia, capital of the department of Cauca, is located on a tributary of the Cauca River. The city lies on a deep deposit of volcanic debris from adjacent Puracé Volcano (16,306 ft. [4,970 m.]) and from other nearby volcanoes, such as Sotará (14,550 ft. [4,435 m.]) and Pan de Azúcar (15,321 ft. [4,670 m.]). Founded in 1537 by Sebastián de Belalcázar, the city has always been a seat of government of secondary rank. During colonial times many great landowners and entrepreneurs in placer mining resided there, and Popayán became a major cultural and religious centre. It is still important for its educational institutions. The changing pattern of economic activity in Colombia since independence has reduced Popayán's significance, although the city has contributed major political, religious, and literary figures to the nation. Its population (58,500 in 1964) has fallen far behind that of such cities as Cali and Pasto which were once subordinate to it. Situated off the main lines of modern commercial traffic, Popayán is now a minor industrial and transportation centre. Its industrial activity is largely focused on food and beverage preparation, clothing, and building materials. Coffee and sugar are produced in the surrounding area. Popayán is on both the Pacific Railway and the Simón Bolívar Highway, a part of the Pan-American Highway connecting the Cauca Valley with Ecuador. The city lies at the centre of an extensive departmental road network.   (R. L. GE.)

POPE (Latin PAPA, from Greek PAPPAS, "father"), an ecclesiastical title expressing affectionate respect, formerly given, especially from the 3rd to the 5th century, to any bishop and sometimes to simple priests, still used in the East for the Orthodox patriarch of Alexandria and for Orthodox priests, but since the 9th century reserved in the West exclusively for the bishop of Rome, in his capacity as sovereign pontiff or head of the Roman Catholic Church (as distinct from his lesser offices and dignities: patriarch of the Western Church, primate of Italy, archbishop and metropolitan of the Roman province, local bishop of the diocese of Rome, sovereign of the Vatican City-State). Even in the case of the sovereign pontiff the word pope or *papa* (abbreviated PP.) is officially used only as a less solemn style: though the ordinary signature and heading of briefs, encyclicals, and other lesser documents is, *e.g.*, "Paulus PP. VI," the signature of solemn documents such as bulls is *Paulus episcopus ecclesiae catholicae,* and the heading, *Paulus episcopus, servus servorum Dei,* this latter formula going back to the time of Pope St. Gregory the Great (d. 604). Other styles met with in official documents are *Pontifex, Summus pontifex, Romanus pontifex, Sanctissimus, Sanctissimus pater, Sanctissimus dominus noster, Sanctitas sua, Beatissimus pater, Beatitudo sua;* while the pope is addressed in speaking as "Sanctitas vestra," or "Beatissime pater."

According to Roman Catholic doctrine, whoever succeeds St. Peter in the see of Rome holds, by the plan of Christ himself, Peter's primacy—the full and supreme power of ruling and teaching the entire church (hence not a primacy merely of honour or inspection or direction). The bishop of Rome is therefore, like Peter, Christ's vicar, the visible head of the church on earth, while Christ remains its invisible and one chief head. In virtue of his primacy, the Roman pontiff has full and supreme jurisdiction over the whole church in all matters pertaining to faith, morals, church government, and discipline. This papal jurisdiction exceeds the power not only of any individual bishop but also of all the bishops taken collectively (without the pope). It can be exercised in dioceses outside Rome at any time, and not only through the bishops of those dioceses but also directly upon the individual flocks and individual members of those flocks. Because of this direct pastoral authority over the entire church the pope is sometimes called "the bishop of the Catholic Church." Included in his primacy is the supreme power of teaching the whole church in matters pertaining to faith and morals. This power is employed above all (though not only) when the pope speaks *ex cathedra,* in which case he is infallible, that is, cannot make a mistake and teach error (*see* INFALLIBILITY). These primatial powers of ruling and of teaching, even infallibly, having been claimed and exercised by the popes in the course of centuries, were solemnly defined at the first Vatican Council (July 18, 1870), which reiterated, clarified, and amplified earlier conciliar pronouncements.

For the history of the papacy and associated questions, *see* PAPACY; CONCLAVE; CARDINAL; VATICAN; and biographies of the different popes. *See* also references under "Pope" in the Index.

BIBLIOGRAPHY.—Article "Pope" in *The Catholic Encyclopedia;* G. C. Van Noort, *Christ's Church,* trans. and rev. by J. J. Castelot and W. R. Murphy (1957); C. Butler, *The Vatican Council,* 2 vol. (1930).
(G. W. SH.)

POPE, ALEXANDER (1688–1744), the most distinguished of the classical poets of the Augustan age and the most accomplished verse satirist in English,

THE BETTMANN ARCHIVE
ALEXANDER POPE, ENGRAVING BY J. PESSELWHITE FROM A PORTRAIT BY THOMAS HUDSON

was born in Lombard Street, London, on May 21, 1688. His father, a wholesale linen merchant, retired from business in the year of his son's birth, and in 1700 went to live at Binfield in Windsor Forest. The Popes were Roman Catholics, and at Binfield they came to know several neighbouring Catholic families who were to play an important part in the poet's life. Pope's religion procured him some lifelong friends, notably the wealthy squire John Caryll (who persuaded him to write *The Rape of the Lock*, on an incident involving Caryll's relatives) and Martha Blount, to whom Pope addressed some of the most memorable of his poems—the second *Moral Essay, To Mrs. M. B. on*

Her Birthday, and *An Epistle to Miss Blount with the Works of Voiture*—and to whom he bequeathed most of his property. But his religion also precluded him from a formal course of education; he was trained at home by Catholic priests for a short time and attended Catholic schools at Twyford, near Winchester, and at Hyde Park Corner, London; but he was mainly self-educated. He was a precocious boy, eagerly reading Latin, Greek, French, and Italian, which he managed to teach himself, and an incessant scribbler, turning out verse upon verse in imitation of the poets he read. The best of these early writings are the "Ode on Solitude" and a paraphrase of St. Thomas à Kempis, both of which he claimed to have written at the age of 12. But perhaps in later life he believed himself to have been more precocious than he was.

Early Works.—Windsor Forest was near enough to London to permit Pope's frequent visits there. He early grew acquainted with former members of Dryden's circle, notably William Wycherley, William Walsh, and Henry Cromwell, the recipients of his earliest surviving letters, which are devoted to a somewhat mannered discussion of the art of poetry. By 1705 his "Pastorals" were in draft and were circulating amongst the best literary judges of the day. In 1706 Jacob Tonson, the leading publisher of poetry, had solicited their publication, and they took the place of honour in his *Poetical Miscellanies* in 1709.

This early emergence of the man of letters may have been assisted by Pope's poor physique. As the result of too much study, so he thought, he acquired a curvature of the spine and some tubercular infection which limited his growth, and seriously impaired his health. His full-grown height was four feet six inches; but the grace of his profile and fullness of his eye attracted numerous painters (such as Sir Godfrey Kneller and Charles Jervas) and sculptors (such as John Michael Rysbrack and Louis François Roubillac), who have transmitted his likeness in such variety as to make his iconography more extensive than that of any other English writer before Dr. Johnson. He was a lifelong sufferer from headaches and his deformity made him abnormally sensitive to physical and mental pain; but though he was able to ride a horse and delighted in travel, he was inevitably precluded from much normal physical activity, and his energetic, fastidious mind was largely directed to reading and writing.

When the "Pastorals" were published Pope was already at work on a poem in an equally well-established tradition, on the art of writing. This was *An Essay on Criticism*, published in 1711. Its brilliantly polished epigrams (*e.g.*, "A little learning is a dangerous thing," "To err is human, to forgive divine," and "For fools rush in where angels fear to tread"), which have become part of the proverbial heritage of the language, are readily traced to their sources in Horace, Quintilian, Boileau, and other critics, ancient and modern, in verse and prose; but the charge of plagiarism, so often made in the past, obscures Pope's success in harmonizing a century of conflict in critical thinking and in showing how Nature may best be mirrored in Art.

Following the well-deserved success of the *Essay on Criticism* came a wider circle of friends, notably Richard Steele and Joseph Addison, who were then collaborating in *The Spectator*. To this journal Pope contributed the most original of his pastorals, *Messiah* (1712), and perhaps other papers in prose. He was clearly influenced by its policy of correcting public morals by witty admonishment, and in this vein wrote the first version of his mock-epic, *The Rape of the Lock* (two cantos, 1712; five cantos, 1714), to reconcile two Catholic families. A young man in one family had stolen a lock of hair from a young lady in the other. Pope treated the dispute that followed as though it were comparable with the mighty quarrel between Greeks and Trojans which had been Homer's theme. Telling the story with all the pomp and circumstance of epic made not only the participants in the quarrel but also the society in which they lived seem ridiculous. But though it was a society where

> . . . Britain's statesmen oft the fall foredoom
> Of foreign tyrants, and of nymphs at home;

as if one occupation concerned them as much as the other; and though in such a society a young lady might do equally ill to

> . . . Stain her honour, or her new brocade,
> Forget her pray'rs, or miss a masquerade;

Pope managed also to suggest what genuine attractions existed amidst the foppery and glitter. He acknowledged how false the sense of values was that paid so much attention to external appearance; but ridicule and rebuke slide imperceptibly into admiration and tender affection as the heroine Belinda is conveyed along the Thames to Hampton Court, the scene of the "rape":

> But now secure the painted vessel glides
> The sunbeams trembling on the floating tides,
> While melting music steals upon the sky,
> And soften'd sounds along the waters die.
> Smooth flow the waves, the zephyrs gently play,
> Belinda smil'd, and all the world was gay.

A comparable blend of seemingly incompatible responses—love and hate, bawdiness and decorum, admiration and ridicule—is to be found in all Pope's later satires.

Pope had also been at work for several years on *Windsor Forest*. In this poem, completed and published in 1713, he proceeded, as Virgil had done, from pastorals to georgics, and celebrated the rule of Queen Anne as the Latin poet had celebrated the rule of Augustus. By choosing for its background a region so rich in historical associations, he was enabled to prophesy the greater glories of regenerate and peaceful society.

In yet another of these early poems, *Eloisa to Abelard*, Pope borrowed the form of Ovid's "heroic epistle" (in which an abandoned lady addresses her famous lover) and showed remarkable imaginative skill in conveying the struggle between sexual passion and dedication to a life of celibacy.

Translation of Homer.—These poems, with *Verses to the Memory of an Unfortunate Lady* (modeled on the elegies of Ovid and Tibullus), some translations from the classics, and a few shorter pieces, were collected in the first volume of Pope's *Works* in 1717. This is a volume of experiments in various poetical kinds; it might almost be called a volume of juvenilia. When it was published, he was already far advanced with the greatest labour of his life, his verse translation of Homer. He had announced his intentions in October 1713, and had published the first volume, containing *Iliad*, Books I–IV, in 1715. The *Iliad* was completed in six volumes in 1720. The work of translating the *Odyssey* (vol. i–iii, 1725; vol. iv and v, 1726) he shared with William Broome, who had contributed notes to the *Iliad*, and Elijah Fenton (*qq.v.*). The labour had been great, but so were the rewards. By the two translations he cleared about £10,000 and was able to claim that, thanks to Homer, he could ". . . live and thrive/Indebted to no Prince or Peer alive."

The merits of Pope's *Homer* lie not in the accuracy of translation nor in representation of the spirit of the original, but in the achievement of a heroic poem as his contemporaries understood it, a poem Virgilian in its dignity, moral purpose, and pictorial splendour, yet one which consistently kept Homer in view and alluded to him throughout. Pope offered his readers the *Iliad* and the *Odyssey* as he felt sure Homer would have written them had he lived in early 18th-century England.

Political considerations had affected the success of the translation. As a Roman Catholic his affiliations were Tory rather than Whig, and though he retained the friendship of such Whigs as William Congreve, Nicholas Rowe, and Charles Jervas the painter, his ties with Steele and Addison grew looser owing to the political animosity at the end of Queen Anne's reign, and he found new and lasting friends in Tory circles, Swift, John Gay, John Arbuthnot, Thomas Parnell, the earl of Oxford, and Viscount Bolingbroke (*qq.v.*). With the first five he was associated (1713–14) in the Scriblerus Club (*see* LITERATURE, SOCIETIES OF) to write joint satires on pedantry, later to mature as *Peri Bathous; or the Art of Sinking in Poetry* (1728) and the *Memoirs of Martinus Scriblerus* (1741); and these were the men who encouraged his translation of Homer. The Whigs, who associated with Addison at Button's Coffee-House, put up a rival translator in Thomas Tickell, who published his version of *Iliad*, Book I, two days after Pope's. Addison preferred Tickell's manifestly inferior version; his praise increased the resentment he had already given Pope by a series of slights and misunderstandings; and when Pope heard gossip of further malice on Addison's part, he sent him a satirical view of his character published later as the character of Atticus, the insincere arbiter of literary taste in the *Epistle to Dr. Arbuthnot* (1735), but with the most topical couplet omitted:

> Who when two wits on rival themes contest,
> Approves them both, but likes the worst the best.

The stages in this famous quarrel and the partial reconciliation that followed remain obstinately obscure; but Pope's subsequent praise of Addison in the verse epistle first published in Addison's works and in the *Epistle to Augustus* is generous and genuine.

"The Dunciad."—Even before the Homer quarrel, Pope had found that the life of a wit was a perpetual warfare. There were few years between 1711 and 1718 when either his poems or his person were not objects of attacks from the critic John Dennis, the notorious bookseller Edmund Curll (*qq.v.*), the historian John Oldmixon, and other writers of lesser fame. The climax was reached over his edition of Shakespeare. He had emended the plays, in the spirit of a literary editor, to accord with contemporary taste (1725); but his practice was exposed by the scholar Lewis Theobald (*q.v.*) in *Shakespeare Restored* (1726). Though Pope had ignored some of these attacks, he had replied to others with squibs in prose and verse. But he now attempted to make an end of it, and defended his standards, which he aligned with the standards of civilized society, in the mock-epic, *The Dunciad* (1728). Theobald was represented in it as the Goddess of Dullness' favourite son, a suitable hero for those leaden times; and others who had given offense were preserved like flies in amber. Even if the individuals can no longer be recognized, what they stand for can usually be appreciated. Thus to conclude the "heroic" games in Book II, the Goddess prescribes a gentler exercise to discover

> . . . What author's heaviness prevails,
> Which most conduce to soothe the soul in slumbers,
> My Henley's periods, or my Blackmore's numbers?
> Attend the trial we propose to make:
> If there be man who o'er such works can wake.

Three Cambridge undergraduates are summoned to read from these prescribed authors, and so soporific is the effect that even the most clamorously persistent scribblers amongst the audience are forced into silence:

> As what a Dutchman plumps into the lakes,
> One circle first, and then a second makes,
> What Dullness dropt among her sons imprest
> Like motion, from one circle to the rest;
> So from the midmost the nutation spreads
> Round, and more round, o'er all the sea of heads.
> At last Centlivre felt her voice to fail,
> Old James himself unfinish'd left his tale,
> Boyer the state, and Law the stage gave o'er,
> Nor Motteux talk'd, nor Naso whisper'd more;
> Norton, from Daniel and Ostrœa sprung,
> Blest with his father's front, and mother's tongue,
> Hung silent down his never-blushing head;
> And all was hush'd, as Folly's self lay dead.

In this and several other passages Pope dispatches his victims with such sensuousness of verse and imagery that the reader is forced to admit that if there is petulance here, as has often been claimed, it is, to parody Wordsworth, petulance recollected in tranquillity. Pope reissued the poem in 1729 with an elaborate mock-commentary of prefaces, notes, appendices, indexes, and errata; this burlesque of pedantry whimsically suggested that *The Dunciad* had fallen a victim to the spirit of the times and been edited by a dunce.

His Life at Twickenham.—Pope and his parents had moved from Binfield to Chiswick in 1716. There his father died (1717), and in 1718 he and his mother rented a villa on the Thames at Twickenham, at that time a small country town where several Londoners had retired to live in rustic seclusion. This was to be Pope's home for the remainder of his life. There he entertained with studied modesty such friends as Swift (who returned from Ireland in 1726, and stayed with Pope while seeing to the publication of *Gulliver's Travels*), Bolingbroke, Oxford, and Jonathan Richardson, the painter, regaling them on gudgeons and flounders from the Thames at his door and on figs and walnuts from the little garden which he took such pains to design and cultivate. The famous grotto, which provided a tunnel under the main highway and formed a study, ornamented by Pope with rare minerals, is all that survives. He kept his own boatman to row him downstream on his frequent visits to London, and his own coach to take him on his customary round of summer visits to country houses, the duke of Argyll's at Adderbury, Lord Bathurst's at Cirencester, Lord Cobham's at Stowe, Ralph Allen's at Prior Park, Bath, and Lord Peterborough's at Southampton. These friends were all enthusiastic gardeners, and it was Pope's pleasure to advise and superintend the laying out of their grounds on the best romantic principles, formulated in his verse *Epistle to the Earl of Burlington* (1731). This poem, now known as *Moral Essay, Epistle IV*, is one of the most characteristic works of his maturity, a rambling discussion in the manner of Horace on false taste in architecture and design, with some suggestions for the worthier employment of a nobleman's wealth.

"Essay on Man" and Related Poems.—Pope now began to meditate a new work on the relations of man, nature, and society. This was evidently to be such another grand organization of human experience and intuition as Milton had attempted in the 17th century, and Wordsworth was to attempt in the 19th; but he was destined never to complete it. He told Joseph Spence that the following lines, later incorporated in the *Essay on Man*, would have conveyed its dominant tone and interest:

> Laugh where we must, be candid where we can,
> But vindicate the ways of God to man.

An Essay on Man (1733–34) was intended as the introductory book discussing the grand design. The poem has often been charged with shallowness and philosophical inconsistency. There is indeed little that is original in the thought, almost all of which can be traced in the work of the great thinkers of western civilization. It is not strictly an argumentative poem so much as a discourse, or extended monologue delivered by the poet to a friendly auditor. As becomes a good conversationalist, he alters his mood from time to time, now grave, now gay, colloquial at one moment, formal at another, now affirmative, now quizzical. He deliberately prefers the middle flight to the sublime; but within that range he uses all the arts of diction and versification, the charm of imagery, and variation of rhythm to effect his persuasion. Subordinate themes were treated in greater detail in *Of the Use of Riches, an Epistle to Allen Lord Bathurst* (1732), *An Epistle to Richard Lord Cobham, Of the Knowledge and Characters of Men* (1733), and *Of the Characters of Women, an Epistle to a Lady* (1735), later rearranged as *Moral Essays*, III, I, and II, respectively. He was deflected from this "system of ethics in the Horatian way" by the renewed need for self-defense. The character of "Timon," an ostentatious nobleman in the *Epistle to Burlington*, was reported to represent the duke of Chandos, who had generously subscribed to Pope's *Homer*. Though the report was malicious, it was plausible enough to rouse Pope's apprehensions. This attack and others of a like nature drove him to consider his position as satirist. He chose to adapt for his own defense the first satire of Horace's second book where the ethics of satire are propounded, and after discussing the question in correspondence with Dr. John Arbuthnot (*q.v.*), he addressed him an *Epistle* in verse (1735), one of the finest of his later poems, in which were incorporated fragments written over several years. His case was the satirist's traditional case, that depravity in public morals had roused him to stigmatize outstanding offenders beyond the reach of the law, concealing the names of some and representing others as types, that he was innocent of personal rancour and habitually forbearing under attack.

"Imitations of Horace"–"New Dunciad."—The success of his first *Imitation of Horace* (1733) led to the publication (1733–38) of ten more of these paraphrases of Horatian themes adapted to the contemporary social and political scene. Pope's poems followed Horace's satires and epistles sufficiently closely for him to print the Latin on facing pages with the English; but whoever chose to make the comparison would notice a continuous enrichment of the original by parenthetic thrusts and compliments as well as by the freshness of the imagery. Thus Horace declares that he is a peace-loving fellow, "but he who provokes me (better not touch me, I cry) will weep for it and be well-known in song throughout the city"; while Pope, in following him, not only glances at Sir Robert Walpole and his French counterpart, Cardinal Fleury (at that time both anxious for peace), but enlivens the whole passage:

> Peace is my dear delight—not Fleury's more:
> But touch me, and no Minister so sore,
> Whoe'er offends, at some unlucky time
> Slides into verses, and hitches in a rhyme,
> Sacred to ridicule his whole life long,
> And the sad burden of some merry song.

The series was concluded with two dialogues in verse, republished as the *Epilogue to the Satires* (1738), where, as in the *Epistle to Dr. Arbuthnot* (1735), Pope ingeniously combined a defense of his own career and character with a restatement of the satirist's traditional apology. These *Imitations* and dialogues show Pope at his easiest and most genial in manner. In them he directed his attack upon the materialistic standards of the commercially minded Whigs in power and upon the corrupting effect of money, while restating and illustrating the old Horatian standards of serene and temperate living. His anxiety about prevailing standards was shown once more in his last completed work, *The New Dunciad* (1742), reprinted as the fourth book of a revised *Dunciad* (1743), in which Theobald was replaced as hero by Colley Cibber (*q.v.*), the poet laureate and actor-manager, who had not only given more recent cause of offense but seemed a more appropriate representative of the degenerate standards of the age. In *Dunciad*, Book IV, the culture of the city of London was seen to overtake the court and seat of government at Westminster, and the poem ends in a magnificent but baleful prophecy of anarchy. He had begun work on *Brutus*, an epic poem in blank verse, and on a revision of his poems for a new edition, but neither was complete on his death at Twickenham on May 30, 1744.

Personality, Poetic Genius, and Reputation.—In the *Epistle to Dr. Arbuthnot* and the *Imitations of Horace* Pope had presented himself to his readers as he would have them see him. He supplemented this defense of his character by editing a selection of his letters. To publish them himself seemed an offense against modesty; he therefore arranged for copies to be placed in the hands of Curll, a bookseller whose taste for piratical publication ensured that a "surreptitious" edition would be produced. The stratagem succeeded (1735), and enabled Pope to complain that he was injured in his reputation and must bring out a correct and authentic edition (1737). Other stratagems were required to secure the publication of his letters to Swift (1741) without his open connivance. Collation of the printed texts with such manuscripts as have survived shows that Pope published a text not substantially different from that which his correspondents read, though he felt himself free to repair his syntax and to readdress a few letters from correspondents who had kept many to correspondents who had kept none. These and his many other surviving letters reveal him at first as a young man labouring successfully to be a wit in the Restoration manner, but show him later in a more sympathetic light as a dutiful son, a kind and thoughtful friend, a well-bred host, a disinterested critic of society, warm in wishes for his country's good, patient under attack, a man of plain living, high thinking, and unimpeachable integrity. Not every critic of Pope has been able to accept this picture; his friendliest critics could wish that he had been less accustomed to equivocation and devious dealings; but when allowances have been made for this and for the too relentless pursuit of some who had injured him—Lady Mary Wortley Montagu, for example, though why Pope came to hate this famous "blue-stocking" for whom he had once expressed a gallant admiration is still obscure—the picture obtained from the letters is convincing, though somewhat conscious in its pose. The picture is paralleled in the later poems, where Pope frequently describes himself as a model of modest, honourable,

contented living, a survival of old Roman simplicity in an age of degenerate taste.

Pope's favourite, but not invariable metre, was the ten-syllable rhyming ("heroic") couplet. He handled it with increasing skill and adapted it to such varied purposes as the epigrammatic summary of the *Essay on Criticism*, the pathos of *Verses to the Memory of an Unfortunate Lady*, the mock-heroic of *The Rape of the Lock*, the discursive tones of the *Essay on Man*, the rapid narrative of the Homer translation, and the Miltonic sublime of the conclusion of *The Dunciad*. But his greatest triumphs of versification are found in the *Epilogue to the Satires*, where he moves easily from witty, spirited dialogue to noble and elevated declamation, and in the *Epistle to Dr. Arbuthnot*, which opens with a scene of domestic irritation suitably conveyed in broken rhythm:

> Shut, shut the door, good John! fatigu'd, I said,
> Tie up the knocker, say I'm sick, I'm dead!
> The Dog-star rages! nay 'tis past a doubt,
> All Bedlam, or Parnassus, is let out:
> Fire in each eye, and papers in each hand,
> They rave, recite, and madden round the land;

and closes with a deliberately chosen contrast of domestic calm, which the poet may be said to have deserved and won during the course of the poem:

> Me, let the tender office long engage
> To rock the cradle of reposing age,
> With lenient arts extend a mother's breath,
> Make languor smile, and smoothe the bed of death,
> Explore the thought, explain the asking eye,
> And keep a while one parent from the sky.

His command of diction is no less happily adapted to his theme and to the type of poem, and the range of his imagery is remarkably wide. He has been thought defective in imaginative power, but the case cannot be sustained in view of the invention and organizing ability shown notably in *The Rape of the Lock* and *The Dunciad*. His standing as a poet was not only recognized at home. He seems to have been the first English poet to enjoy contemporary fame in France, Italy, and Switzerland, and to see translations of his poems into modern as well as ancient languages. Soon after his death different standards began to prevail; but even when his stock was at its lowest, in the 19th century, he found such champions for his poetry as Byron, Lamb, and Hazlitt, and for his letters as Thackeray; and he has long been restored to the esteem if not to the preeminence he enjoyed in his lifetime.

See also references under "Pope, Alexander" in the Index.

BIBLIOGRAPHY.—*Editions, Correspondence, and Selections:* Pope published the first collected ed. of his poems in 1717, adding a 2nd vol. in 1735. Thereafter not a year passed until his death (1744) without some of his earlier writings being reissued. His literary executor, William Warburton, later bishop of Gloucester, published *The Works*, with Pope's corrections, additions, and improvements, 9 vol. (1751); though it purported to be complete, every subsequent editor has added some piece to the canon. The standard edition of the poems is the Twickenham Edition, general editor, John Butt, 6 vol. (1939–61), to be completed with the translation of Homer in 4 vol. (1966). There is a one-vol. version of the complete text of the first six vol. with selected notes, ed. by John Butt (1963). *The Prose Works of Alexander Pope, 1711–20*, vol. 1, was ed. by Norman Ault (1936). The standard ed. of Pope's *Correspondence* is by George Sherburn, 5 vol. (1956). There are convenient selections of his poetry in Everyman's Library, ed. by Bonamy Dobrée (1956); in the Globe Library, ed. by A. W. Ward (1869); and of his letters, ed. by John Butt (1960), in the "World's Classics Series." *See* also *Selections from Pope*, ed. by George Sherburn (1929; reissued as *The Best of Pope*, 1931). Still briefer selections are *Pope: Poetry and Prose*, ed. by H. V. D. Dyson (1933); *Poems*, selected by Douglas Grant for the Penguin Poets (1951); *Selected Poetry and Prose*, ed. by W. K. Wimsatt (1951); *Selected Poems and Letters*, ed. by R. P. C. Mutter and M. Kinkead-Weekes (1961). The translation of Homer is reprinted in the "World's Classics Series," 2 vol. There are separate editions of the *Memoirs of Martinus Scriblerus*, by C. Kerby-Miller (1950) and of *The Art of Sinking in Poetry* (*Peri Bathous*), by E. L. Steeves (1952).

An important development has been the production of Pope's poetical manuscripts in facsimile, with transcript and editorial notes. The following had been published by 1964: *Windsor Forest*, ed. by R. M. Schmitz (1952); the *Epistle to Bathurst*, ed. by E. R. Wasserman (1960); *An Essay on Criticism*, ed. by R. M. Schmitz (1962); *An Essay on Man*, ed. by Maynard Mack (1963). *See* also John Butt, *Pope's Poetical Manuscripts* (1954).

Bibliography: The standard bibliography is R. H. Griffith, *Alexander Pope: a Bibliography,* 2 vol. (1922–27).

Biography: The best of the early biographies was that of Dr. Johnson, in his *Lives of the Poets* (1781); he had access to the most important primary document (apart from Pope's letters), J. Spence's *Anecdotes* of his conversations with Pope and others, which was eventually published, ed. by S. W. Singer (1820); a much fuller edition from the manuscripts, by J. M. Osborn appeared in 1965. New facts were gathered by R. Carruthers in his *Life,* 2 vol. (1853; rev. ed. 1858); by C. W. Dilke, whose papers, mainly on the authenticity of Pope's letters, were published as *The Papers of a Critic,* 2 vol. (1875); and by Norman Ault in *New Light on Pope* (1949). The standard biography so far as it goes (1727) is George Sherburn's *The Early Career of Alexander Pope* (1934). Edith Sitwell, *Alexander Pope* (1930), and Bonamy Dobrée's short *Alexander Pope* (1951) are sympathetic studies, using already known facts.

Criticism: The first substantial study of Pope's poetry was by Joseph Warton in *An Essay on the Writings and Genius of Mr. Pope* (vol. 1, 1756; vol. 2, 1782). The best early critical appreciation is by William Hazlitt, in *Lectures on the English Poets* (1818). Of 20th-century assessments, the most important are G. Tillotson, *On the Poetry of Pope* (1938; rev. ed. 1950), and *Pope and Human Nature* (1958); and R. A. Brower, *Alexander Pope: the Poetry of Allusion* (1959). Of many shorter studies the most rewarding are by George Sherburn, "Pope at Work," in *Essays on the Eighteenth Century Presented to David Nichol Smith* (1945); and by Maynard Mack, "'Wit and Poetry and Pope': Some Observations on His Imagery," in *Pope and His Contemporaries: Essays Presented to George Sherburn* (1949) and "The Muse of Satire," *Yale Review,* vol. 41 (1951). On specific poems the following studies are noteworthy: E. N. Hooker, "Pope on Wit: *The Essay on Criticism*," in *The 17th Century: Studies by R. F. Jones and Others* (1951); D. Knight, *Pope and the Heroic Tradition* (1951), on the *Iliad;* Aubrey L. Williams, *Pope's Dunciad* (1955); Robert W. Rogers, *The Major Satires of Alexander Pope* (1955). There is a useful reprint of critical studies entitled *Essential Articles for the Study of Alexander Pope,* ed. by Maynard Mack (1964).   (J. E. Bt.)

POPE, JOHN (1822–1892), Union general in the American Civil War, was born in Louisville, Ky., March 16, 1822. He graduated from the U.S. Military Academy at West Point, N.Y., in 1842 and served as an engineer until the outbreak of the Mexican War, in which he served with distinction. At the outbreak of the Civil War he was named a brigadier general of volunteers. His success with a small independent command in the campaign to open the Mississippi River in the spring of 1862 led Pres. Abraham Lincoln to call him east to lead the Army of Virginia in the defense of Washington, D.C., and to cooperate in Gen. George B. McClellan's peninsular campaign against Richmond. Partly because of lack of experience and tact, Pope failed to enlist the wholehearted support of his subordinates. McClellan's abandonment of the peninsular campaign enabled Gen. Robert E. Lee to turn his full attention to Pope's army before McClellan could join him and to defeat him disastrously at the second Battle of Bull Run (Aug. 29–30). He was relieved of command and held no important post during the remainder of the war. He served competently until his retirement in 1886, rising to the rank of major general in 1882. He died at Sandusky, O., on Sept. 23, 1892.
                    (C. W. Te.)

POPISH PLOT: *see* Oates, Titus.

POPLAR, the name commonly applied to several species of trees comprising a subgeneric group of the genus *Populus,* belonging to the willow family, the Salicaceae (*q.v.*). Aspens (*q.v.*), also members of the genus *Populus,* comprise a second subgeneric group. Several of the poplars are better known in some areas as cottonwoods. This name alludes to their minute, air-borne, hairy-tufted seeds, which are released in profusion, and which in accumulations suggest cotton. Others, with fragrant, balsamic-resinous winter buds, are commonly called balsam poplars. (Buds of aspens are essentially nonresinous.)

Populus comprises a group of about 35 species of rapid-growing but short-lived softwood trees, and a number of natural hybrids. These are widely distributed through the northern hemisphere and range from northern Africa through Eurasia and North America; a few species extend even beyond the Arctic circle.

The leaves of poplars are alternate, deciduous, and are mostly triangular to oval in outline, with finely to coarsely toothed margins and long, cylindrical and tapering, or laterally compressed petioles. The sexes are separate in poplars, with the flowers of both sexes borne in long drooping catkins (aments) in advance of leaf emergence. Flowers on staminate (male) trees consist of 12 to 60

stamens inserted in a cuplike disk subtended by a many-fingered bract (those of the aspens with but 6 to 12 stamens). Flowers from pistillate (female) trees are composed of a single two- to four-cell ovoid to globular ovary surmounted by a large spreading stigma, and are similarly inserted on a disk with bract attached. The fruit, a thick-walled (thin-walled in aspens) two- to four-

JOHN H. GERARD

(LEFT) CATKINS AND (RIGHT) LEAVES AND COTTONY SEED MASSES OF EASTERN COTTONWOOD (POPULUS DELTOIDES)

valved capsule, contains many minute seeds clothed in cottony pubescence.

There are about a dozen poplars and cottonwoods, including stable varieties and natural hybrids, indigenous to and widely distributed through North America, exclusive of central and southern Mexico.

The eastern cottonwood (*P. deltoides*), a large tree with coarse, deeply furrowed bark and triangular-shaped leaves, which are about as broad as long, often attains a height of 150 or more feet and a diameter of 48 to 96 in. Ranging from Quebec westward to Montana and south to Florida and Texas, it is not only a pulpwood and timber tree of major importance, but it is also planted in many localities as a street and shade tree. Numerous forms of this poplar are ornamentals in both Europe and America, several of which are hybrids with the European black poplar (*P. nigra*) or one of its varieties. Among these are the Carolina poplar (*P.* × *canadensis* [hybrid between *P. deltoides* × *P. nigra*]), a vigorous tree with strongly ascending limbs, widely used in parks and streets; and the Eugene poplar (*P. canadensis eugenei* [hybrid between *P. deltoides* × *P. nigra italica*]), a tree of narrow-pyramidal habit that originated in France in 1832. Pistillate trees of the two forms have never been found.

The black cottonwood (*P. trichocarpa*) is the largest of the American poplars, and not infrequently attains a height of more than 200 ft. and a diameter of more than 80 in. It is found along the Pacific slope from southern coastal Alaska to Lower California, and eastward in Canada to Alberta and in the United States to western Montana and Nevada, but is most abundant at low elevations. Reaching its maximum development on deep, moist alluvial or sandy soils, it is often the first tree species to become established on newly formed sand bars and flood plains. While very abundant in some areas, the black cottonwood was unexploited for many years, due in large measure to a preponderance of readily accessible softwood timber of higher quality throughout its range. Since the early 20th century, however, it has been harvested in ever increasing quantities for use in the production of lumber, slack cooperage, excelsior, veneer and paper pulp.

The balsam poplar or the tacamahac (*P. balsamifera* [*tacamahaca*]), the "liard" of the early Canadian *voyageurs,* is a large tree of transcontinental distribution, with a pyramidal crown and shallow root system. Essentially a Canadian tree, it occurs along the northern border of the United States from New England westward through the lake states and northern Rocky mountains to Oregon and Washington. Northward it ranges from Labrador westward across nearly all of Canada to beyond the Arctic circle in Alaska. The balm of Gilead poplar, once widely used ornamentally throughout much of the northeastern U.S. and southern Canada, is now generally regarded to be either a clone from a pistillate tree of the heartleaf balsam poplar (*P. balsamifera* var. *subcordata*) or a hybrid between the balsam poplar and the eastern cottonwood.

The principal poplar of the swamps and river bottoms of the coastal plains and the Mississippi river drainage basin is the swamp cottonwood (*P. heterophylla*). In the Mississippi valley, where they reach their maximum development, these trees are often 80 to 90 ft. tall and 36 to 42 in. in diameter.

The plains cottonwood (*P. sargenti*) is often seen in the otherwise essentially treeless areas of the central U.S. Narrowleaf cottonwood (*P. angustifolia*) is a tree of the Rocky mountains and adjacent plains to the east. The ranges of these two species overlap, and at least one natural hybrid between them has become well established: the lanceleaf cottonwood (*P.* × *acuminata* [hybrid between *P. angustifolia* × *P. sargenti*]).

Fremont cottonwood (*P. fremonti*) and its variety, Rio Grande cottonwood (*P. fremonti* var. *wislizenii*), are two tree forms not infrequently found along the margins of streams and water holes in the semiarid areas of the southwestern United States. Palmer cottonwood (*P. palmeri*) is a little-known tree of central and the trans-Pecos regions of Texas and northern Mexico.

Of the European forms, the white poplar, or abele (*P. alba*), is probably the most important. This is a large tree with rounded and spreading crown composed of several massive, curved branches, which, like the trunk, are clothed with grayish-white bark. Its leaves are ovate to nearly circular, with deeply wavy or more or less lobed margins and heart-shaped bases. The foliage, although dark green above, is clothed below in dense, white pubescence, as are also the young shoots, which, with the bark, give a rather hoary aspect to the tree. Of its several varieties, *P. alba* var. *pyramidalis* (Bolleana poplar), a tree of narrow columnar habit, probably enjoys the greatest ornamental use. A closely related species, the gray poplar (*P. canescens*), with grayish deltoid leaves, is equally well known. Some taxonomists, however, regard this form as a hybrid between the white poplar and the European aspen (*P. tremula*). Both trees have extended ranges through Europe and Asia, and often attain a height of 90 or more feet. Their white, soft, even-grained timber is used in quantity in the construction of boxes and crates. Both are also ornamental, although the white poplar produces root suckers some distance from the tree, restricting its use as an ornamental specimen.

The black poplar (*P. nigra*), a tree of 100 or more feet in height, with smooth, dark-green, deltoid leaves and dark, deeply furrowed bark, is a Eurasian species of wide distribution. Its almost universally known variety, the Lombardy poplar (*P. nigra* var.

italica), is easily identified by its narrow-pyramidal crown composed of many closely appressed and vertically ascending branches. Its origin appears to have been in Iran or some adjacent country. From remote times it has been found in Kashmir, Punjab and Iran, where it is still commonly to be observed along roadsides and in formal gardens. It was probably brought to southern Europe from one of these countries, and derives its common name from its abundant use along the rivers of Lombardy. It was introduced into Great Britain in the early 18th century, and somewhat later into the U.S. Lombardy poplar's value lies chiefly in its ornamental use, since its rapidly tapering bole, densely clothed in branches for the greater part of its length, is incapable of producing any appreciable volume of utilizable lumber. This tree often makes very rapid growth, and can attain a height of 100 or more feet.

The white, black and Lombardy poplars are widely planted in eastern United States and Canada; the first two of these have become naturalized in many areas. *P. euphratica*, believed to be the weeping willow of the Scriptures, is a large tree remarkable for its variability in the shape of its leaves. It is a native of northern Africa and western and central Asia. Yellow poplar (*Liriodendron tulipifera*), an unrelated species of the magnolia family, is one of the most important hardwoods of eastern United States. *See* TULIP TREE. (E. S. HR.)

POPLAR BLUFF, a city of southeastern Missouri, U.S., 156 mi. S of St. Louis on the Black River; the seat of Butler County. Situated in the Ozark perimeter above a broad alluvial plain that forms the rich delta land of one of Missouri's most prosperous farming areas, Poplar Bluff is essentially a farm marketing centre with diversified light industries. It is located at the intersection of two main transcontinental highways and is served by a major railroad.

Founded in 1850 and named for a forest of yellow poplars in the lowlands of the Black River, the city was almost destroyed by guerrilla and troop foragers during the American Civil War. Its subsequent development gained impetus with the construction of the St. Louis, Iron Mountain, and Southern Railway (Missouri Pacific) in 1872. Agricultural growth followed a lumbering boom and reclamation of vast swamplands between the St. Francis and Black rivers. The county produces cotton, soybeans, rice, grain, livestock, and lumber. Pop. (1970) 16,653. For comparative population figures *see* table in MISSOURI: *Population*. (W. E. RO.)

POPOV, ALEKSANDR STEPANOVICH (1859–1906), Russian physicist and electrical engineer, among the earliest scientific investigators of electromagnetic waves (as later used in wireless communication), was born on March 16, 1859, in a mining village in the Ural Mountains where his father was a priest. He graduated from St. Petersburg University in 1883 and became an assistant in the physics laboratory, later joining the staff of the torpedo school at Kronstadt, where he subsequently became head of the physics department. Popov became interested in the work of H. R. Hertz (*q.v.*), and began to develop a device for receiving electromagnetic waves (*q.v.*). To detect the oscillations resulting from these waves he made various modifications to the coherer, a primitive radio receiver. This apparatus was used for detecting lightning discharges at a distance and was demonstrated at a meeting of the St. Petersburg Physical Society in May 1895. Later, it was connected to a lightning conductor and used for the study of atmospheric electrical discharges. In March 1896 Popov showed the transmission of Hertzian waves between different parts of the university buildings.

In June 1896 Guglielmo Marconi took out the first patent granted for wireless telegraphy based on the use of electric waves. The news of this aroused Popov to fresh activity, and working in conjunction with the Russian navy he effected ship-to-shore communication over distances of about 6 mi. by 1898. This was increased to about 30 mi. by the end of the following year. Unfortunately Popov's work was not sufficiently appreciated and supported by the Russian government, and in 1901 he returned to St. Petersburg as professor at the electrotechnical institute, of which, a few years later, he was elected director. Popov died on Jan. 13, 1906 (new style; Dec. 31, 1905, old style).
(R. L. S.-R.; X.)

L. W. BROWNELL

(LEFT) LEAVES AND (RIGHT) CATKINS OF THE WHITE POPLAR (P. ALBA)

POPPY, common name for plants of several genera of the poppy family (Papaveraceae), especially the type genus *Papaver*. This genus comprises annual and perennial erect herbs containing a milky juice, with lobed or cut leaves and generally long-stalked regular showy flowers, which are nodding in the bud stage. The greenish sepals, usually two in number, fall off as the flower opens; the four (very rarely five or six)
petals, which are crumpled in the bud stage, also fall readily. Numerous stamens surround the ovary, which is surmounted by a flat or convex rayed disk bearing the stigmas. The ovary develops into a short many-seeded capsule, opening by small valves below the upper edge. The valves respond to an increase in the amount of moisture in the atmosphere by closing the apertures. In dry weather the valves open, and the small seeds escape through the pores when the capsule is shaken by the wind.

GIANT SALMON VARIETY OF ORIENTAL POPPY (PAPAVER ORIENTALE)

Papaver contains about 100 species, mostly natives of central and southern Europe and temperate Asia. Of the five species that occur in Great Britain, *Papaver rhoeas,* the corn or field poppy, is also found in fields in the U.S. Cultivated forms of this, with exquisite shades of colour and without any blotch at the base of the petals, are known as Shirley poppies. *P. somniferum,* the opium (*q.v.*) poppy, with large white or blue-purple flowers, is native to Greece and the Orient; it is widely cultivated for medical uses, although it is often grown illicitly. The oriental poppy (*P. orientale*) and its many varieties are fine garden plants, having huge bright crimson flowers with black blotches at the base. Many hybrid forms of varying shades of colour have been raised, especially in the U.S. The Iceland poppy (*P. nudicaule*) is one of the showiest species, with gray-green pinnate leaves and flowers varying in colour from pure white through pink and yellow to deep orange-yellow and red shades.

The Welsh poppy (*Meconopsis cambrica*) is a perennial herb with a yellow juice and pale-yellow poppylike flowers. It is found in the southwest and north of England, Wales, Ireland, and western Europe. The prickly poppies belong to the related tropical American genus *Argemone. A. grandiflora* is a popular Central American annual with large white or yellow flowers. The horned or sea poppy (*Glaucium flavum*), found on sandy seashores along the Mediterranean and naturalized in the U.S., is characterized by the waxy bloom of its leaves and large golden-yellow short-stalked flowers. The plume poppies (*Macleaya;* often listed misleadingly as *Bocconia*) are ornamental plants with long terminal flower clusters. The snow poppy (*Eomecon chionantha*) is a native Chinese perennial with roundish slightly lobed leaves and pure-white flowers about 2 in. across. The Mexican tulip poppy or golden cup (*Hunnemannia fumariaefolia*), a perennial usually grown as an annual, has very showy yellow flowers. The celandine poppy is *Stylophorum diphyllum; Hydrocleis nymphoides* is the water poppy of ponds and aquaria.

The poppy family is well represented in western North America, especially in California, where about 20 native species, together with numerous varieties, are found. The best known is the California poppy (*Eschscholtzia californica*), an annual with brilliant, orange-coloured flowers, widely grown in gardens and extensively naturalized in Australia and India. Other noteworthy Californian species, more or less cultivated, are the tree or bush poppy (*Dendromecon rigida*), a rigid, leafy shrub, 2 to 10 ft. high, with golden-yellow flowers, about 2 in. across; the Matilija poppy (*Romneya coulteri*), a widely branched subshrub, 3 to 8 ft. high, with large white fragrant flowers, 6 in. across; the cream-cups (*Platystemon californicus*), a low, delicate annual, with light-yellow flowers,
1 in. across; and the flaming poppy or wind poppy (*Meconopsis* or *Stylomecon heterophylla*), bearing brick-red flowers 2 in. across.

The common garden poppies (*Papaver* species) grow well when provided with rich well-drained soil in an open sunny location; they require supplementary watering only during dry spells. Some varieties of *P. orientalis* have enormous flowers in nearly all colour shades, but are short-lived and useless as cut flowers. Seed should be sown where plants are to grow, for poppies, especially the annuals, do not transplant well.   (N. Tr.; X.)

POPULAR MUSIC. "Popular music" is music inhabiting the broad domain that lies between musical folklore and fine art music. This domain has no clearly defined frontiers. At one extremity it merges into folk music; at the other, it merges into art music. However, for the most part, the distinction between folk, popular, and art musics is clear enough.

In general, popular music—unlike folk music proper—is produced by professionals, and mainly in the towns. At the same time —unlike art music—it is in many cases diffused by oral means. In some important areas, such as Spanish flamenco, Central European gypsy music, and a great deal of jazz, it flourishes without the aid of print. These three considerations, professionalism, urbanism, and relative orality, have for centuries affected the nature of popular music in many parts of Eastern and Western Europe, North and South America, and much of Asia. After the mid-20th century, with the global expansion and dominance of Western music from Los Angeles to Laos, from Prague to Peking, a worldwide uniformity of popular music began to show, mainly derived—even in the Communist bloc—from U.S. models.

Antiquity to the Middle Ages.—In antiquity, between the music of the peasantry and that of the upper classes, another layer of music interposed. Cities such as Rome and Alexandria attracted Greek minstrels, Syrian dancers, Negro musicians, singers from the Italian countryside, and former slaves or smallholders who made a living by providing music for the urban crowds at circuses or in theatres, in processions or dances. The phenomenon of the popular "hit" song, spreading from the theatre into the streets, was already familiar in Roman times. Suetonius tells us that when Galba was made emperor, the entire audience in a theatre roared out a song in vogue at that moment, satirizing Galba's avarice. When, in 6th-century Europe, the by then degenerate theatre of antiquity finally disappeared during the barbarian invasions, dispossessed professional musicians were driven afoot to mingle with the bards of various peoples, Teutonic, Celtic, Slav, etc., in that miscellaneous body of entertainers who haunted the towns and thoroughfares of the Middle Ages. Before long, a general European popular music idiom began to show itself, in which the national differences between, for example, music of Spanish, Italian, German, and Polish origin were to some extent masked by a stylization that resulted from the cosmopolitanism of the professional musicians' calling. To some extent only: if the popular performances of medieval Europe were far more "international" in character than the performances of folk music (which often varied enormously in style not merely from country to country but from province to province), there were nevertheless certain characteristic differences between the analogous melody forms and utterances of northern French *trouvères*, Provençal troubadours, German *Minnesänger*, Spanish *juglares*, and English minstrels. A 14th-century proverb of French origin indicates the manner of popular singing among various nations: "Galli cantant, Angli jubilant, Hispani plangunt, Germani ululant, Itali caprizant," which has been translated as "The French sing, the English carol, the Spaniards wail, the Germans howl, the Italians bleat." In the High and Late Middle Ages, popular music covered a wide social and artistic range. Minstrels might be of the court or the tavern, they might be large landowners or beggars, wandering scholars or illiterates, virtuosos or strummers. The repertory ranged from aristocratic hero ballads, through lyrical songs, courtly or crude, to rustic dance tunes. Musicians' earnings varied as widely as their grades, and the wealthy troubadours were as scornful of the ragged jongleurs as *Minne-* and *Meistersänger* were of the itinerant *Spielleute* of the German countryside and back streets. The fortunes of popular musicians in the Middle Ages were subject to the same ups and downs as those experienced by the star performers today. Thus the talented *jongleur* Bernart de Ventadour, a baker's son, attained the courtly rank of troubadour and entered the aristocracy; on the other hand, the equally gifted Rambaut de Vaqueyras, a dispossessed nobleman, sank down into the ranks of the *joglars*, playing and singing on fairgrounds and in market squares.

International traffic in popular music, exemplified in modern times in the worldwide spread of jazz and rock 'n' roll, was already foreshadowed in the Middle Ages by itinerant professional musicians who might wander anywhere within a territory bounded by Edinburgh, Santiago de Compostela, Cyprus, and Tallin (Reval) on the Baltic. Paris-based minstrels would operate between Roncesvalles and Metz; Nürnberg-based musicians might be in Cracow for the summer and in Verona for the winter. French, Italian, Spanish, and Portuguese minstrels were frequent guests in England. In the towns on the Adriatic coast, Serbian, Greek, and Croatian musicians played alongside instrumentalists from the German principalities and from Transylvania. French popular musicians, settled in the Hungarian wine-growing districts, accompanied the annual Tokay caravans through Slovakia and across the Carpathians into central Poland. All these musicians would be exchanging melodies, musical ideas, and instrumental techniques. Nor should the influence of the Orient be forgotten. Urban popular music of Arabic-Persian origin was early spread over parts of southwest Europe by the Moors in Spain, southern France, and southern Italy (from this culture came the short-necked lute with bent-back peg-box, the instrument now popularly associated with medieval minstrels). Later, with the Turkish invasions and occupations, music of similar provenance was spread among occupational musicians in the towns of southeast Europe, notably Bulgaria, Rumania, Serbia, Bosnia, and Albania. It was carried into central Europe mainly by gypsy professional entertainers, where it mingled with the local musical stock to create the peculiar hybrid semioriental kind of popular music of which, in a later age, Mozart availed himself in his *alla turca* compositions.

The Renaissance.—As feudalism merged into early capitalism (in Western Europe in the 15th and 16th centuries, later elsewhere), popular musicians became more settled, and generally only those in the lowest reaches of the profession remained itinerant. An active traffic between town and country culture became the normal condition of popular song. Some of the agents of this process were amateur composers among the rural middle class, making formalized arrangements of folk tunes; domestic servants bringing village music into towns and taking town music back into the villages with them; fairground and marketplace singers; street showmen; booth theatre actors; pedlars of cheap songbooks and broadsides (from the 16th century onward). Various institutions helped in the formation of popular music idioms. In England, from Tudor times, the municipalities employed "town-waits," instrumentalists who combined the functions of perambulating night watchmen and town bandsmen. They played for official visits, for the mayor on market days, and for summer evening concerts from the guildhall roof or a roadside scaffolding; in Coventry, for instance, they also played softly at various corners of the city five days a week between midnight and 4 A.M., for the reassurance of citizens. Their repertory consisted mainly of adapted folk melodies, humble amateur compositions, popular dance tunes, theatre music, and marches. In France, from the time of Villon and Rabelais onward, popular city cabarets were putting into circulation a large number of songs, sentimental, satirical, or comic, most of which enjoyed only a brief vogue, though some proved lasting. An even more powerful source of popular music was the secular theatre that established itself firmly in France, Spain, and Italy during the 15th and 16th centuries, with performances of short plays, often four pieces in an evening, acted usually on open platforms of a movable kind by companies consisting partly of professionals, partly of amateurs, including women and sometimes children. Many of these plays began and ended with a song, in the manner of an overture-finale frame, and most of them were punctuated with *chansons, villancicos,* and *villanelle* during the course of the action. Some of the actors would be instrumentalists and at times would play pieces from the regular minstrel repertory, in the absence of music specially written for the theatre. In Germany where, following the Reformation, printed music, the popular choral movement, and the activities of educated amateur musicians, parsons, schoolmasters, etc., worked with specially powerful effect on lower-class music making, a vast amount of folk song was transformed into popular song by the imposition of the conventions and usages of art music (by simplifying rhythms, converting old modes into modern scales, tidying up the structure of melodies, encouraging a standard kind of voice production, etc.). A characteristic institution of the early capitalist period in Germany was that of the *Meistersänger*, mostly small merchants, artisans, and tradesmen who assembled, usually in the guildhall on Sunday afternoons, to practise their new, often homemade, songs that belonged firmly to the realm of popular music, being neither folk song nor fine art compositions.

The Baroque.—In 17th-century England, the powerful expansion of bourgeois ways of life and manners of thought was accompanied by a flourishing of urban popular music that became equally as important as folk music and art music. Significant landmarks were the extremely successful publication of John Playford's *The English Dancing-Master*, a collection of *contredanse* tunes, many of them based on popular song and ballad airs that ran into 17 editions between 1650 and 1728, and Henry Playford's *Wit and Mirth. An Antidote against Melancholy*, published in 1682 and gaining great fame when it was re-edited in 1699 with the subtitle of *Pills to Purge Melancholy*. Rather unjustly, Thomas D'Urfey gets the most credit for this collection of popular songs, serious or saucy, of aristocratic, bourgeois, or lower-class origin. To it, new volumes were added over the years and reprintings constantly ordered. By 1720, the work had grown to six volumes containing more than 1,000 songs giving a wide view of the popular music of the time in parlour and kitchen, tavern and pleasure-garden. The pleasure-gardens that sprang up, notably during the 18th century, in the cities and spas, gave an important stimulus to popular music through their evening entertainments. Thousands of songs were written specifically for performance in these places and, at least from the middle of the century, were profusely printed on leaflets or in books. Between 1769 and the early years of the 19th century, at least one, sometimes two or three, books of Vauxhall Gardens songs were published annually; so too with songs from Marylebone Gardens. Mainly for the "gardens crowd," James Hook (1746–1827) wrote more than 2,000 songs; Charles Dibdin (1745–1814) wrote nearly 1,000; several other composers were scarcely less diligent. A comparable flood of lyrical popular music flowed from the (slightly later) beer-garden entertainments of the German and Austrian towns. Meanwhile, in most of the larger towns of 18th-century continental Europe, popular comedies with music were to be seen in the puppet and marionette tents, and on the fairground or back-street stages, often with stereotyped figures derived from the Italian *commedia dell'arte*—Pantaloon, Harlequin, Pulcinella, and the rest. A report from 1711 tells that at the fairs of Saint-Germain and Saint-Laurent in Paris, the theatre audiences habitually joined with the actors in singing the favourite songs of the day; the actors had only to sing the opening bars of the song, and the audience sang the rest. Later in the century, when the Royal Opera, on grounds of privilege, forbade actors to sing in the popular theatres, the actors would cause a scroll to unfurl each time they came to a song, the instrumentalists would introduce the melody, and the entire audience would roar out the song, reading the words from the scroll. Usually, in this kind of performance, the text was more important than the music, which more often than not was derived or adapted from well-known tunes, similar to the ballad opera. Probably the most important of the ballad operas, and one that had great effect internationally, was *The Beggar's Opera* by John Gay (1685–1732), an aggressively satirical piece and a huge favourite with the populace. It was first staged in 1728 and was an immediate success; within a few years it had been played on countless stages in England, Ireland, and Scotland, and was even seen on the island of Minorca. In 1733 it was performed in Jamaica, and in 1750 in Paris and

New York. Its triumph encouraged others. By the end of 1729 London had seen 15 ballad operas, and by 1733, 70. A painstaking survey by W. Barclay Squire showed that some 700 popular tunes were used in these works, with librettos sometimes by hack writers, sometimes by eminent literary men such as Swift, Fielding, and Sheridan. In later years, this form of light Baroque lyrical theatre was to have considerable influence on continental popular music, notably in Germany.

The French Revolution.—The years of the French Revolution comprise a singular period in the history of popular music. Admired singers such as Bellerose and Beauchant would set up their little platforms in the squares or by the bridges of Paris, to amuse the public of an evening by singing topical songs. In many parts of the city, the audiences were so large (travelers noted crowds of at least 1,000 round Beauchant's stand) that coach and wagon traffic was seriously hindered and the municipal authorities were at length obliged to provide special vantage points where the singers might perform. During the height of revolutionary enthusiasm there was hardly a gathering of any kind where patriotic, satirical, or general popular song was not heard. Constant Pierre reports: "For a certain period the theatres were literally invaded and treated as an annexe of the public highway; the audiences displayed their opinions by themselves singing songs of political tendency or by demanding performances, there and then, of their preferred ditties." The singing invaded the National Convention itself, with one deputation after another announcing its revolutionary fervour and then singing its favourite song to the accompaniment of drums and other instruments brought along for the purpose. Deputies had the habit of standing up in the Convention and intoning lengthy ballads written around some topical point or other until, at last, in March 1794, Danton proposed a resolution "That henceforth this platform hears nothing but reason in prose." The motion was carried, and from then on, singers were rarely heard in the Convention Hall unless by invitation. The course of the torrent of revolutionary popular songs is not without interest. In 1789 a mere 100 songs on political or social themes were published. In the enthusiasms of 1793 the number rose to 590, and in 1794, 701 such songs were issued. With the reaction that set in after the execution of Robespierre, the numbers declined steeply. Only 137 new songs on topical themes were issued in 1795, and by the end of the century, the flow of directly political songs had to all intents ceased. This example serves to remind us that popular music is far more sensitive to the important moments of history than either fine art or folk music, at least in the Western tradition. Thus, the American Revolutionary and Civil wars both produced a flood of popular songs, but only a few occasional pieces for the concert hall, while—contrary to general belief—the reflection of these events in folk song proper was minimal.

The 19th Century.—The period of industrial capitalism saw the greatest spread of specifically popular music. The growth of large towns meant bigger audiences, which in turn gave rise to an entertainment industry of vast scope; at first in Europe, later in the Americas, and then in Africa and Asia. Conditions favouring an oral culture weakened, and the immense mass of working people evolved away from self-made folk song toward the products of music hall, dance hall, and popular theatre.

Particularly in the early part of the 19th century in Western and central Europe and the Americas, popular social song developed enormously in all its forms—sentimental, patriotic, comic, satirical, etc. The remarkable evidence of the democratization of musical life after the period of the French Revolution and with the growth of the industrial proletariat was the appearance of the British music hall, which was to have an even more decisive influence on the trends of popular music than the cabarets of Paris or the operetta theatres of Vienna. The music halls first sprang up in the big industrial cities as workingmen's beer halls with entertainment. Gradually, during the second half of the 19th century, the entertainment became more important than the drinking, and the beer halls evolved into theatres-with-a-bar, providing shows that largely consisted of humorous, social-critical, or sentimentally emotional songs mainly of lower-class life. In the earlier years of the 19th century, visiting entertainers from the British music

halls were considerably instrumental in stimulating the American entertainment industry that in a later time, in the domain of popular music, as in other fields, was to become the dominant influence throughout the world.

Even in the less developed parts of Europe, as in Central and South America, popular musics were expanding and undergoing transformation. In Spain, flamenco music was growing progressively more showy and exotic in the cabarets and small theatres that sprang up around the middle of the century, notably in the Andalusian seaports. In the Balkans, about the same time, the emancipation of serfs and the weakening of the Turks' grip meant that many private orchestras belonging to nobles and officials—playing an orientally tinged music—were broken up, resulting in a flood of popular instrumentalists seeking employment in the restaurants and night spots of the towns and cities. The result was the stylized, urbanized idiom loosely called "gypsy music," in which—as with flamenco—the exotic aspects are often exaggerated to satisfy the customers. In Latin America the great developments in popular music were in the domain of the dance. Fashionable travelers from Europe brought to Havana, Rio de Janeiro, Buenos Aires, and Lima the minuets, gavottes, schottisches, polkas, and waltzes of Paris and Vienna. In the upper-class ballrooms, these dances would be performed as received, but as they seeped down to the lower classes—which, from the Caribbean to Rio Grande do Sul, were mainly comprised of Negroes and mulattoes—the dances and the music accompanying them became altered and hybridized with the choreography, melody, and rhythm current among the working people, producing the rumbas, sambas, congas, etc., that were later to invade the ballrooms and dance halls of North America and Europe, and were to have great influence on urban popular music over a great part of Africa.

In the United States, an important development toward the middle of the 19th century was the emergence of the blackface minstrel shows with white performers comically disguised as Negroes, and presenting mainly a burlesque of Negro song and humour. Touring groups such as Dan Emmett's "Virginia Minstrels," who made their debut in 1843, and the Christy Minstrels, who followed very shortly after, gave widespread currency to a vast number of popular songs, some of which are still in use. Companies such as these, and the growing number of vaudeville theatres in the U.S. towns, promoted on a vast scale the compositions of such songwriters as Stephen Foster (1826–64), the composer of "Oh! Susanna," "Old Folks at Home," etc., Henry Clay Work (1832–84), who wrote "Marching Through Georgia" and "The Year of Jubilo," and George F. Root (1820–95), whose best-known songs are "The Battle-cry of Freedom" and "Tramp, Tramp, Tramp, the Boys Are Marching." A more peripheral but ultimately very influential development was the emergence of a stratum of rural musicians who became entertainers with medicine shows and on the country town vaudeville circuits, playing a stylized music of folklore origin. It was these minstrels who laid the foundations for the powerful hillbilly "industry" and its subsequent analogues, country-western, bluegrass, etc., in the mid-20th century.

The 20th Century.—In the early years of the 20th century, in London and New York, musical comedy established its importance in the world of formal popular music, and began to overshadow heavily the operettas of Paris, Berlin, Vienna, and Budapest. But undoubtedly the most powerful development was the emergence of jazz as a commercially viable entertainment for the public. Like the urban popular music of Cuba and Brazil, jazz developed first of all as a synthesis of European ballroom and brass-band music and the songs of Negro workers. At first it was the kind of pieces that were more European than African that enjoyed the greatest vogue, though subsequent taste allowed more prominence to specifically Negro ingredients. W. C. Handy, Duke Ellington, Hoagy Carmichael, George Gershwin are notable among light-music composers who profited from the discoveries and inventions of a great stream of more or less anonymous jazz musicians, Negro and white.

The 20th century has seen a vast expansion of the entertainment industry, which has developed massive corporations largely concerned with the production and exploitation of popular music "hits." This concern has been much intensified by the emergence of the phonograph, radio, talking motion picture, and television, as a means of earning greater profits from successful compositions and performances.

At the same time, particularly from the beginning of the "swing" era of the 1930s, a number of players and critics attempted to raise the level of popular music almost in defiance of big business. Jazz, flamenco, "gypsy music," and the urban popular musics of the Caribbean, Brazilian, and Andean areas acquired a following of more or less expert devotees concerned with levels of expression not hitherto reached by the products of mass entertainment. For the first time, light music began to be studied as an academic discipline. In general, however, commercial considerations are paramount in the development of light music. In the years following World War II, the growth of a profitable market among adolescents coincided with the invention of electronic instruments, allowing the fairly easy production of a powerful and impetuous sound leading to the enormous diffusion of simple musics such as rhythm-and-blues, rock 'n' roll and their neo-primitive successors, folk-rock, etc., found irresistible by young people.

Conclusion.—Initially formed mainly in the south and west of Europe, Western popular music has gradually spread throughout the entire world, at first to the ends of Europe, then to the colonized Americas, then to the cities of the Orient, and now into the maize and paddy fields and even the jungles of peoples who had hitherto remained primitive. The rise of the United States to a position of enormous economic and political power has greatly accelerated the process by which Western popular music replaces the proper musical arts of Asians, Africans, and other civilized or primitive peoples, a process already begun with the weakening of feudal traditions and religious rites, and the introduction of formal education through Western colonialism. Missions, schools, trade, radio, films, development aid projects, have all played a part in encouraging a taste for Western popular music. At the same time, throughout the Communist world, sovietization carried the more formal idioms of popular European music across a vast area of the globe, acclimatizing it by means of political rather than commercial propaganda.

Throughout the Communist world, popular music has become mainly identified—at least officially—with stylized folk music performed in a diluted manner, while in the Western world and throughout the sphere of Western influence, jazz music has seemed progressively to shrink into an intellectually rarified atmosphere, being replaced in the affections of the younger mass audiences by the emotional and musical simplifications of rock 'n' roll and its successors. Musical comedy, in theatre and in motion pictures, was still vital in the 1960s, but salon music was fading. For the global intrusion of Western popular music, the Orient extracts a mild revenge, with the introduction of one or two Eastern instruments (such as the sitar) and a few tentative Oriental intonations into popular instrumental ensembles of the large U.S. and European cities.

BIBLIOGRAPHY.—E. Forel, *Les Jongleurs en France* (1910); W. Chappell, *Popular Music of the Olden Time*, 2 vol. (1855–59); J. C. Bridge, "Town Waits and Their Music," *Proceedings of the Royal Music Association* (1928); E. M. Gagey, *Ballad Opera* (1937); R. Nettel, *Seven Centuries of Popular Song* (1956); S. G. Spaeth, *History of Popular Music in America* (1948); W. MacQueen-Pope, *Melodies Linger On: the Story of Music Hall* (1950); W. Wiora, *The Four Ages of Music*, Eng. trans. by M. D. Herter Norton (1965); W. L. Woodfill, *Musicians in English Society from Elizabeth to Charles I* (1953).

(A. L. Ll.)

POPULATION. The population of the world rose from about 1,000,000,000 in 1850 to 2,000,000,000 in 1930 and 3,000,000,000 in 1960. It is expected to be in the vicinity of 4,000,000,000 persons in 1980, according to estimates by the staff of the UN. It is now increasing at the rate of about 2% per year. This rate, which if continued would double the population before the end of the century, is well above that prevailing in any previous epoch. According to widely accepted estimates, the average rate of increase had risen from less than 0.1% per year in ancient and medieval times to about 0.3% at the beginning of the 18th century and about 0.6% during the middle decades of the 19th century. The acceleration of population increase in the 20th century was the result of a progressive worldwide lowering of mortality.

TABLE I.—*Percentage Population Increase
(Estimated 1920–60; Projected 1960–2000)*

Period	World	Africa	Asia	Europe	Latin America	North America	Oceania	U.S.S.R.
1920–40	22	32	42	16	41	24	28	24
1940–60	29	39	61	11	55	35	39	11
1960–80	39	57	81	13	65	29	40	28
1980–2000	37	62	66	10	59	33	38	26

Source: United Nations, *Provisional Report on World Population Prospects, as Assessed in 1963* (1964). Medium estimates.

Differences in population trends among the various regions of the world are strongly affected by differences in fertility. Estimates of population increases and projected trends, by continents, prepared by the United Nations Secretariat, are shown in the accompanying graph. The graph shows that for the world as a whole about 950,000,000 persons were added by the excess of births over deaths from 1900 to 1950. The expected increase during the second half of the 20th century is nearly 3,800,000,000, about four times that during the previous 50 years. The term "population explosion" is frequently used to emphasize the extraordinary force of this trend and its possible threat to human welfare. (*See* also ECOLOGY; ECONOMIC DEVELOPMENT: *Population Growth and Development*.)

No population projections are prophetic. Projected trends for the continents having less-developed countries may be modified by social changes affecting births and deaths, the discovery of new techniques for the control of fertility or in other ways. Trends in the more-developed countries, where mortality at early ages is very low and fertility is already subject in large measure to voluntary control, are peculiarly sensitive to changes in economic conditions and cultural values. The projections merely show the expected effects of processes already in force if these continue without drastic modification. Projections were made on several sets of hypotheses; those shown on the accompanying graph follow from a central assumption of medium, or average, fertility and mortality.

Some idea about variations in population trends among particular countries is given by the information on countries with more than 30,000,000 inhabitants presented in Table II.

KNOWLEDGE ABOUT POPULATION

The scientific study of population, known as demography, began with investigations by John Graunt in the 17th century. Graunt was one of a group of associates in London who were fired with enthusiasm for observations and experiments and received a charter as the Royal Philosophical society, the first scientific academy in the modern world. Graunt, who was a haberdasher by trade, discovered many significant regularities in a series of periodic records of christenings and burials, with reports on the apparent causes of deaths, issued by parish clerks. He published his findings in a pamphlet, *Natural and Political Observations . . . Made upon the Bills of Mortality* of London (1662). This

TABLE II.—*Population of Countries with 30,000,000 or More Inhabitants, 1966*

Country	Population (in 000,000)	Average annual rate of increase 1958–64	Persons per square mile
China, People's Rep. of	690*	1.5	186
India	499	2.3	395
U.S.S.R.	232	1.6	27
United States	196	1.6	54
Indonesia	108	2.2	147
Pakistan	104	2.1	285
Japan	99	1.0	692
Brazil	85	3.1	26
Germany, Fed. Rep.	59	1.3	618
Nigeria	59	2.0	161
United Kingdom	55	0.7	578
Italy	53	0.7	455
France	49	1.3	233
Mexico	42	3.2	55
Philippines	33	3.3	289
Spain	32	0.8	163
Poland	32	1.3	263
Turkey	33	2.8	104
Thailand	33	3.0	154
U.A.R.	30	2.7	78

*Estimate 1964 by United Nations.
Source: Population from individual country sources. Rate of increase from United Nations *Statistical Yearbook, 1965*.

pamphlet, in which Graunt had sketched a hypothetical life table to show the proportions of persons born alive who live to successive ages and the expected years of future life at each age, attracted the attention of scientists in England and on the continent and stimulated other inquiries.

In 1693 Edmund Halley, the astronomer, constructed the first

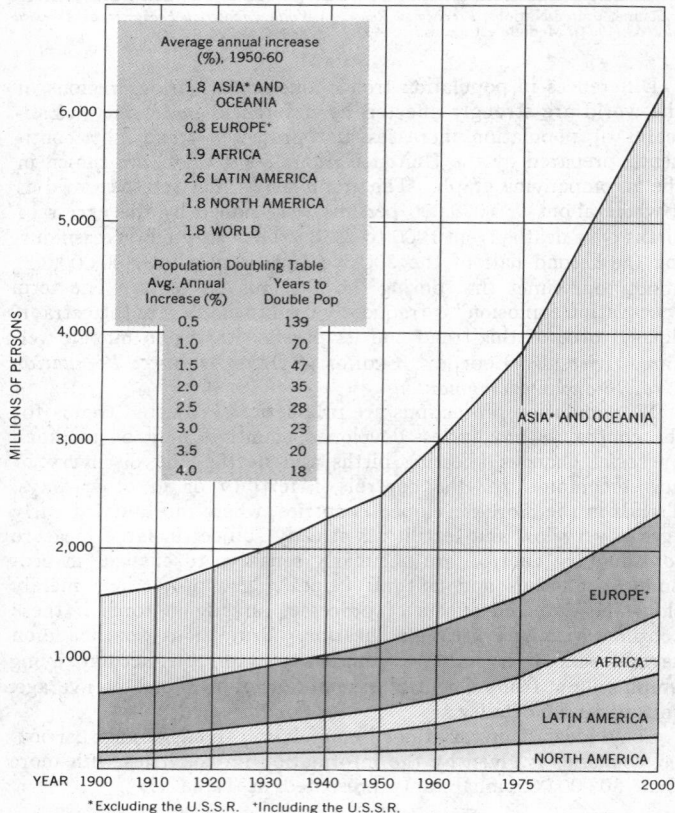

Average annual increase (%), 1950-60

1.8	ASIA* AND OCEANIA
0.8	EUROPE*
1.9	AFRICA
2.6	LATIN AMERICA
1.8	NORTH AMERICA
1.8	WORLD

Population Doubling Table

Avg. Annual Increase (%)	Years to Double Pop
0.5	139
1.0	70
1.5	47
2.0	35
2.5	28
3.0	23
3.5	20
4.0	18

*Excluding the U.S.S.R.   †Including the U.S.S.R.

FROM THE UNITED NATIONS, "THE FUTURE GROWTH OF WORLD POPULATION," POPULATION STUDIES, NO. 28, 1958; UNITED NATIONS, "DEMOGRAPHIC YEARBOOK," 1960

ESTIMATED WORLD POPULATION 1900–60, AND POPULATION PROJECTIONS, 1960–2000

empirical life table on the basis of information about deaths by age in Breslau, Ger., which had been forwarded to the London Philosophical society by Leibniz. The measurement and analysis of mortality engaged the attention of scientists in many countries through successive decades. Eventually their investigations led to the systematic exposition of possible interrelations among births, deaths and the age structure of populations. Alfred J. Lotka developed the classic formulation of these relations.

Censuses.—The major source of basic information on population during the 18th century was the civil register of vital events, established in most European nations to supersede reliance in legal affairs on church records of christenings, marriages and burials. There had already been occasional countings of people in some nations, but these early censuses were sporadic. Usually there was neither a complete tabulation of the returns nor any publication of the results. Quite different opinions were often entertained about the population of a country, even as to whether its population was increasing or decreasing. Scientists investigating these questions experimented with new methods of observation and analysis.

The constitution of the United States prescribed representation in congress on the basis of a periodic census of the population beginning in 1790. Periodic censuses were initiated both in England and in France in 1801. Since that time censuses have gradually spread through the world and supply basic information on most of the world's inhabitants. The greatest gap was apparently closed by the census of China, 1953–54, though its results must be accepted with some reservation. Three-fourths of the popula-

tion of Africa has been described by complete enumerations or national inquiries on the basis of scientific sampling. However, the scope and reliability of censuses differ greatly among nations. (*See also* VITAL STATISTICS.)

Information on births, deaths and migration is less satisfactory. In the United States, the registration of births and deaths was still very defective in most states at the beginning of the 20th century. Federal birth and death registration areas, initiated at that time, were first extended to include all states in 1933. Before the 1950s reliable vital statistics were lacking for countries containing more than half the world's population; *i.e.*, Asia (except Japan, Formosa, Ceylon and Israel), most of Africa and much of Latin America. By the 1960s many countries in these areas, stimulated by the United Nations World Census programs, had conducted censuses (*see* CENSUS).

Estimates of fertility and mortality can sometimes be obtained by the systematic exploitation of indirect and fragmentary information, but even the critical and skilful use of incomplete information is not a satisfactory substitute for adequate basic data. The measurement of migration, especially within nations, is inherently difficult. Census inquiries are used in many countries to obtain some information on this subject.

MORTALITY

The risk of death varies with age and sex. In general the risk at any given age is less for females than for males, though under some conditions the death rates of women in the childbearing ages may be above those of men at the same ages. The risk of death is high immediately after birth and, with diminishing force, through early childhood; it decreases to a minimum at 10 to 12 years of age. The risk then rises again until at late ages it surpasses that in the first year of life. So the crude death rate of a population (usually expressed as deaths per year per 1,000 persons) is powerfully influenced by its age composition. For comparative purposes, the effect of age composition must always be taken into account in the measurement of mortality. Various standardized death rates have been devised for this purpose, but each is subject to certain technical objections. The expectation of life at birth, as given by a life table, is the most efficient index of the general level of mortality of a population. This is a hypothetical figure. It shows the average years of life to be expected at birth if the risks of death at particular ages in a specified year continue in effect. In Table III the calculated expectations of life at birth are shown for certain countries at particular times.

Mortality Levels.—The range in levels of mortality, shown in Table III, mainly reflects degrees of progress in technology, especially in sanitation and medicine. Prior to the 18th century, the range in levels of mortality was much narrower, except at times of famine, plague or war. In normal times the mean expectations of life at birth were then in the vicinity of 25 to 30 years.

Death rates declined gradually in Europe and North America from the late 17th century onward, at first due mainly to advances in economic conditions and then more rapidly with progress in medicine and sanitation, to the point where further increases in longevity have become largely dependent on the control of organic diseases. Meanwhile, dramatic increases in the chances of survival from birth to late ages have been achieved in countries where the expectation of life at birth was formerly low (*see* Table III). This has been effected mainly by measures to control malaria and epidemic diseases even where, as in Mauritius and Ceylon, there has been little change in nutrition or general levels of living. As a result, the wide differences in mortality among nations have been considerably narrowed during the 20th century. Nevertheless, differences in living conditions still have an important influence on health and longevity between and within nations.

Class Differences.—There are still important differences among social classes within technically advanced nations in levels of mortality, especially in infancy and early childhood. This is indicated by the differences between the figures for whites and nonwhites in the United States (*see* Table III) and by other information concerning families at different economic levels. However, such differences have generally been narrowed in North

TABLE III.—*Life Expectancy at Birth in Selected Countries*
(in years)

Country	Dates	Males	Females
United States	1959–61	67	73
	1939–41	62	66
Whites	1959–61	68	74
	1939–41	63	67
Nonwhites	1959–61	61	66
	1939–41	52	56
Mexico	1960	57	60
	1940	38	40
England and Wales . .	1961–63	68	74
	1930–32	59	63
France	1964	68	75
	1933–38	56	62
Netherlands	1956–60	71	75
	1931–40	66	67
U.S.S.R.	1962–63	65	73
	1926–27	42	47
Japan	1964	68	73
	1935–39	47	50
India	1951–60	42	41
	1941–50	32	32
Ceylon	1954	60	59
	1946	44	42
Mauritius	1961–63	59	62
	1942–46	32	34
Congo, Republic of . .	1950–52	38	40

Source: Official publications; United Nations *Demographic Yearbook, 1965.*

America and in Europe, especially since World War II. On the other hand, differentials in mortality between males and females have generally widened—notably in the United States. Various reasons for this phenomenon have been advanced, but none has as yet won a clear consensus among scientists.

Effect on Population Growth.—The lengthening of the span of life is due chiefly to the control of infectious diseases which are especially dangerous in infancy and early childhood. Where the expectation of life at birth is only 30 years, about half of the new-born infants die before age 25 years; but where the expectation is 70 years, over 95% of those born alive pass the 25-year point. Past progress in lowering mortality and that now going on in under-developed countries, therefore, exerts a powerful influence on rates of population increase. Future progress in the extension of life in technically advanced countries, being largely dependent on the reduction of deaths at late ages, may be relatively slow.

FERTILITY AND REPRODUCTION

The word fertility is used to denote the actual production of offspring, whereas fecundity refers to biological capacity. The average capacity of a population for reproduction cannot be precisely measured; it varies to an unknown degree under different conditions and perhaps among different stocks. The average capacity of couples under widely prevalent conditions has been estimated at 8.5 to 10 or more births; some couples can have more than 20 births, but others in every society are sterile or become so after the birth of one or several children. In any case, reproduction in human societies is always influenced by customs affecting the frequency of and ages at marriage, divorce and separation, the remarriage of widowed and divorced persons, prohibitions against sexual intercourse under particular conditions, and in many other ways. Various practices, largely magical, both to promote fertility and under certain conditions to prevent conception or induce abortion, are found in most preliterate societies, but they usually have little effect on actual performance. Among technically advanced societies, variations in levels of fertility are determined mainly by attitudes and practices; they have little relation to possible variations in fecundity—though post-World War II increases of birth rates in Europe and North America may have been due in small part to a reduction in the frequency of complete or partial sterility.

Reproduction Ratios.—In most of Asia (except Japan), in Africa and in America from Brazil north through Mexico, each woman who lives through the childbearing years has on the average about six children—though there is, of course, some variation among regions. Between 48% and 49% of all babies are girls. So the average number of daughters born alive per surviving woman (gross reproduction ratio) under these conditions is about three. If the number of children which newborn female infants might eventually bear (if all lived through the childbearing period) is cut in half by premature deaths (between birth and successive adult

ages), there will still be about 150 daughters in each generation per 100 daughters in the previous generation (net reproduction ratio). The population will then tend to increase by 50% during an intergeneration interval, usually somewhere between 25 and 30 years. In past times, this tendency was checked by recurrent disasters. With the same gross reproduction ratio (three) but improvement in sanitation so that only one-third of the potential reproduction is lost by mortality, the net reproduction ratio becomes two. In other words, the population then doubles in each generation. Due to reductions in mortality and the persistence of high fertility, the population of the less-developed countries is generally moving toward, or has already exceeded, this reproductive level. This statement, in the absence of reliable vital statistics, is necessarily based on inferences from census data, investigations in various localities and other indirect evidence; but it is supported by cumulative evidence from many sources.

The general level of fertility in Europe prior to the Industrial Revolution, and perhaps throughout medieval times, was significantly below that now generally prevalent in Asia, Africa and Middle America. The moderation of fertility in preindustrial Europe was not due to the control of fertility within marriage but to social restraints on marriage or procreation at early ages —associated with an emphasis on the nuclear family (husband, wife and children) as contrasted with the larger kinship groups in many societies. These restraints on early marriage were eased among

TABLE IV.—*Estimated Birth Rates by World Regions, 1960–64*

Region	Per 1,000 population per year	Region	Per 1,000 population per year
World . . .	34	Oceania . . .	27
Africa . . .	47	U.S.S.R. . . .	23
Middle America .	44	North America . .	23
Southeast Asia .	43	Southern Europe . .	21
Southwest Asia .	42	Central Europe . .	18
South Central Asia	41	North and Western Europe	18
South America .	38	Japan . . .	17

Note: The speculative estimate for East Asia, which includes the People's Republic of China, is omitted.
Source: United Nations *Demographic Yearbook, 1965.*

settlers in the new world, so that fertility in colonial America was much higher than in Europe. Different social conditions, also, led to some reduction of fertility in premodern Japan, but in this case by resort to abortion and infanticide.

Control of Fertility.—The growth of commerce, new opportunities for individuals to achieve higher levels of living, the withdrawal of children from economic production and provisions for their education stimulated a new interest in the control of fertility within marriage. At the same time, the lowering of mortality increased the probability that most infants would survive to maturity. Then, too, the progress of science and education fostered rationalistic behaviour in the pursuit of personal goals. Incidentally, it seems that men were at least equally and probably more insistent than women on the control of births. So a trend toward the regulation of births within marriage began in France and in the U.S. near the beginning of the 19th century. Later it spread through all western and central Europe and then eastward and southward and from cities into rural areas. The control of fertility was at first achieved through an intensification of ancient folk practices, but it was later facilitated by mechanical and chemical means of contraception. It first gained momentum in professional and commercial classes and then spread more slowly through the families of skilled and unskilled workers. This pattern brought wide differences in fertility among the social classes.

As the regulation of fertility has become more nearly universal in Europe, North America, Australia and New Zealand, social class differentials in fertility have been narrowed, though they have not entirely disappeared. The trend toward the regulation of fertility in these regions was apparently approaching completion, in the sense of bringing fertility more or less into conformity with the personal interests of couples, when the world-wide economic depression generated a wave of anxiety to avoid, or at least to postpone, the enlargement of families. Wartime opportunities for employment and postwar prosperity brought a shift toward earlier marriages, a reduction in the frequency of childless or one-child families and some increase in the number of subsequent births to couples who already had two children—notably in North America, Australia and New Zealand and, to a lesser extent, in Europe. Assuming 1.057 male births per female birth, with 95% of the female infants living to the centre of the childbearing period, of whom 90% marry, an average of 2.16 births per woman living through the childbearing years, or 2.4 births per ever-married woman, will maintain a constant population. Around 1960 fertility was well above this level in North America and Oceania and in some European countries; in some other European countries it was fluctuating in this vicinity. Fertility in the Soviet Union was then similar to that in the United States. The rapid decline of fertility in Japan brought it into line with the low-fertility countries in Europe. In both instances, sharp declines were initially effected by widespread resort to abortion, with a gradual shift toward increased reliance on contraception.

Meanwhile fertility remained fairly constant in most of the underdeveloped countries. Except in periods of rapid change, crude birth rates usually give a fair indication of levels of fertility (in contrast to crude death rates, which are strongly influenced by differences in age composition). Estimated birth rates by world regions are shown in Table IV. See also BIRTH CONTROL.

AGE AND SEX STRUCTURE

The age and sex composition of a population is determined, apart from the effects of migration, by the frequencies of births in previous years, the sex ratio at birth and the proportions of male and female infants living to successive ages. The age and sex composition of a closed population (not affected by migration) in which the relative frequencies of vital events (births, deaths by age and by sex, and the sex ratio at birth) have been constant for a long time can be calculated mathematically from information on these vital rates. The effects of particular changes in vital rates, although more complex, can also be calculated.

A population with persistently high fertility has a large proportion of children and a small proportion of aged persons. A population, such as that of France, in which fertility has been low for a long time, has a smaller proportion of children and a larger proportion of aged persons. Changes in fertility have an immediate effect on numbers of children, but 15 years must pass before the change affects the numbers above this age, and 60 years before it affects the numbers of older persons. Therefore, a population that has experienced a recent decline in fertility tends to have relatively small numbers both of children and of aged persons and a large proportion of adults in the middle ages. An upswing in births will again bring an increase in the proportion of children. Thus the rise of fertility in France during the post-World War II period increased the proportion of children in its population while the proportion of aged persons remained relatively high. In technically advanced countries reductions in mortality at late ages may be expected to increase the proportions of aged persons. (A systematic exposition of these principles is given by Ansley J. Coale,

"The Effect of Changes in Fertility and Mortality on Age Composition," *The Milbank Memorial Fund Quarterly*, 34:79–114 [Jan. 1956].)

The age distributions of population in different countries (*see* Table V) are mainly due to differences in the levels and trends of fertility. They have also been influenced in varying ways by migrations, war losses and differences in mortality—though these effects are generally less important than the influence of variations in fertility. The migration of young adults, who bring children with them or soon have children in the area to which they move, is likely to swell the numbers both of adults in the middle ages and of children in the receiving country while the proportion of aged persons remain low—with reverse effects on the population of an area from which there is a large net out-movement.

The division by sex of a population, or of its component age classes, at any moment is determined quite simply, apart from the influence of migration, by the ratio of males to females at birth and the relative proportions of males and of females who have survived from birth to successive ages. See SEX.

MIGRATION

It is possible to distinguish three major kinds of spatial population movements: tribal wanderings and expansion by conquest into new lands—a process continued in the form of military occupation and colonization; forced transfers of people, including the acquisition of captives, the movement of slaves and the expulsion of minorities for political reasons; and the free movement of individuals. (The movement of indentured or contract labourers, which in some situations includes an element of force or fraud, is somewhat intermediate between the last two types.) Migration usually refers to the free movement of individuals; but other types of movement have been important forces in determining the present distribution of the world's population, and the 20th century has been plagued by forced movements on a large scale (*see* MINORITIES; REFUGEES).

The free movement of individuals is directed mainly toward the adjustment of people to economic opportunities—though it is influenced by diverse motives and has complex social and cultural aspects. Migration as a process of economic adjustment is often impeded by ignorance, attachment to habitual sites, the costs and risks of migration, and political barriers. Moreover, the sheer magnitude of population and the force of natural increase in the major regions of limited opportunity exclude the possibility that international migration can be a major factor in raising the levels of living of these regions. Migration seems to have been economically most effective when great resources held by small populations have been open to migrants, or there has been a great expansion of economic activities in which prospective migrants could be absorbed, and when migration has been associated with other transitional economic and demographic processes in the countries of origin.

The second of these relations is illustrated by the progressive shift southward and eastward of the areas of overseas emigration from Europe, with a spontaneous diminution of outflows from western and northern Europe as their industries expanded and their birth rates declined. It is also illustrated by the post-World War II movement of Puerto Ricans to the U.S. mainland, associated with the formation of new economic enterprises, progress in education and an initial trend toward modification of fertility.

Although migration varies greatly in magnitude and significance under different conditions, some approaches have been made to the formal analysis of internal migration (within nations) and the magnitudes of various streams of international migration at different times have been estimated. There is also much information about the characteristics of migrants and their adjustments, but this is not easily summarized. Overseas migrants passing from Europe to the Americas, Oceania and Africa from 1800 to World War II numbered about 60,000,000, of whom about two-thirds to three-fourths remained abroad. These immigrants and their descendants have increased more rapidly than the people in the countries of origin so that their number approaches that of the population of Europe outside the Soviet Union. There were also smaller

TABLE V.—*Age Distribution of Enumerated Populations in Selected Countries*

Country and date of census	Per cent in specified classes		
	0–15 years	16–45 years	over 45 years
Mexico, 1960	46.4	40.1	13.5
Philippines, 1960 . . .	45.7	41.8	12.5
Ecuador, 1962	45.1	40.9	14.0
Thailand, 1960	45.0	41.7	13.3
South Korea, 1960 . . .	44.9	40.6	14.5
Ghana, 1960	44.6	43.0	12.4*
India, 1961	42.9	43.8	13.3
United Arab Republic, 1960	42.8	40.4	16.8
Canada, 1961	34.0	41.0	25.0
Australia, 1961	31.8	41.1	27.1
Japan, 1960	31.8	46.8	21.4
United States, 1960 . .	31.1	39.6	29.3
Netherlands, 1960 . . .	30.7	60.6	8.7†
Argentina, 1960	29.0	52.5	18.5‡
France, 1962	27.4	39.2	33.4
Belgium, 1961	23.7	39.0	37.3
United Kingdom, 1961 .	23.4	39.4	37.2*
Germany, Fed. Rep., 1961	22.6	40.8	36.6
Sweden, 1960	22.0	40.5	37.5

*0–14, 15–44, over 44.   †0–14, 15–64, over 64.   ‡0–13, 14–49, over 49.
Source: National censuses.

but important movements from China, Japan and India to other continents, as well as within Asia.

The partition of India in 1947 involved the forced movement of some 17,000,000 persons. World War II uprooted 25,000,000 to 30,000,000 people in Europe, and there was a net overseas migration of more than 4,000,000 persons from Europe during the first postwar decade, 1946–1955. There were 600,000 displaced persons on the rolls of the International Relief organization in 1946. These were absorbed in new situations; but, because of unresolved political conflicts, the Arabs displaced by the formation of Israel in 1948 remained in refugee camps into the 1960s.

Postwar emigrants from Italy, Spain and Portugal went mainly to Latin America. Most of those from northern and western Europe, including Germany, went to the United States or to Canada, Australia, New Zealand, South Africa or Israel. Migrants from eastern Europe, mostly displaced persons, were widely dispersed; but they contributed a large contingent to the formation of the population of Israel. *See also* MIGRATION.

THEORIES AND POLICIES

The movement and structure of a population involves the formation of new lives and their persistence through spans varying from a moment to a century. These demographic processes can be measured, and possible interrelations among them can be analyzed in abstraction; but they are essentially biological processes and in human societies they are largely controlled by economic, social and psychological conditions. Moreover, population movements in turn influence all other human affairs. They have social determinants and consequences. The objective study of population in its biological and social context, therefore, can aid in the formation of realistic public policies.

Turning to aspects of population theory that are related to social issues, mention still must be made of the century-old debate between the exponents of two conflicting dogmas, expounded by Thomas Malthus and by Karl Marx, about relations between population and economic conditions. Each of these dogmas contains sufficient truth to inspire disciples, but each is a gross oversimplification and distortion of actual situations.

Malthus, who in 1798 published the first edition of *An Essay on the Principle of Population as It Affects the Future Improvement of Society, with Remarks on the Speculations of Mr. Godwin, M. Condorcet, and Other Writers,* held that the increase of population enforced by "the attraction between the sexes" constantly tends to exceed the resources for its sustenance and is always subject to the "positive checks" of famine, war and disease. Each advance in the arts is absorbed by a consequent increase of population, thus preventing any rise in the general level of living. This is, indeed, a fair statement of the situation in much of the world prior to the time of his essay and in some areas at later times. But he proceeded on the fallacious assumption that increases in production could never exceed, or even equal, increases in population. He later modified this position by suggesting that under some conditions population might be brought into a more favourable balance with production through the "preventive check," by which he meant the postponement or avoidance of marriage and procreative activity. He repudiated M. Condorcet's suggestion that fertility might be controlled within marriage not only on moral grounds but also for economic reasons because he viewed poverty as a necessary stimulus to economic activity. Some later proponents of birth control who drew support from his economic doctrine called themselves Neo-Malthusians. Malthus applied his exposition of "the population principle" in opposing certain welfare measures which he viewed as futile and dangerous and, in general, repudiated the idea of improving the condition of mankind through changes in economic and social institutions. Marx viewed revolutionary changes in economic and social institutions as inevitable and as leading toward an ideal society. He violently attacked Malthusian theory, just as Malthus had attacked the utopian socialism of Condorcet and Godwin. He equated overpopulation with actual, or latent, unemployment; he described relative overpopulation in this sense as essentially and purely a phenomenon of the capitalist system. Exponents of Marxist doctrine have generally viewed the control of population and changes in economic institutions as alternative and incompatible approaches to the advancement of levels of production and income.

Most contemporary demographers and economists view constructive changes in economic institutions, the advancement of education and the control of fertility as essentially complementary processes—none of which can alone be effective in the long run. They point to specific ways in which rapid increase of population in low-income countries hampers economic and social development. This type of analysis was well summarized in the following quotation from a statement prepared by the UN Secretariat.

To sum up, population enters into the problem of achieving satisfactory standards of living in the under-developed countries in three principal ways. First, their high birth rates create a heavy load of dependent children per adult. This makes it difficult to save enough, over and above what is required for the support of the workers and their dependents, for needed investments in equipment for economic development. It also seriously complicates the problem of providing the children with the education that is essential for social and economic progress in the long run. This aspect of the population problem is common to all the under-developed countries. Second, falling death rates with high birth rates bring about a rapid increase of population. Large investments must be made to keep the growing numbers of workers equipped even with the same inadequate amounts of working equipment per man as they have had in the past. So the possibilities for investments which would improve the equipment and raise productivity per worker are diminished. This speeding up of population growth, aggravating the shortage of capital, is now taking place in very many under-developed countries, wherever successful public health campaigns have greatly reduced death rates. Third, many of the under-developed countries have an excessive density of agricultural population in relation to the area of cultivated land. The average farmer has too little land to make a satisfactory living for himself and his family. Not all under-developed countries face this difficulty, but it exists in some which have large amounts of unused land, as well as in those where nearly all the cultivable land is fully occupied. At least some of the countries now suffering from acute agricultural over-population might be able to employ all their numbers to good advantage, and benefit in the long run from a substantially larger population, if they were better equipped to utilize the land resources which they possess, or if they could industrialize. But neither the necessary improvements of agriculture nor the development of industry can easily be accomplished, and the difficulties are increased by high birth rates and rapid population growth. It appears that even in a country where population growth would be economically advantageous in the long run, economic progress will be hindered if the birth rate is so high and if the population grows so rapidly as to put an excessive strain on the economy. (From *Population Growth and the Standard of Living in Under-Developed Countries,* a summary of relevant chapters of UN Dept. of Social Affairs, *The Determinants and Consequences of Population Trends,* UN Population Studies no. 20 [1954].)

The social aspects of population have generally received much less attention than the economic aspects, though in some situations they may be even more important. For example, there are important relations between population trends and education. A high ratio of children to adults, characteristic of many poor areas with high fertility, requires a larger expenditure per adult to maintain a given standard of schooling than where the proportion of adults is higher, and may hamper the recruitment of qualified teachers. Again, the character of the adult population in areas of heavy inmigration, *e.g.,* most cities, is strongly affected by levels of education in other regions. This reinforces the thesis that education is not purely a matter of local concern. Moreover, if the less-educated elements in a population are more reproductive than those with higher education, the cultural force of education in successive decades is weakened. This trend may be largely a transitional phenomenon; but the extent to which it may reflect persistent conditions requires greater attention. On the other hand, the advancement of education may be a potent force in promoting the regulation of births. These brief comments suggest larger and more complex problems on which as yet there is little knowledge. The distribution of genetic factors is inevitably affected by differences in reproduction rates. But, again, this is a momentous issue on which present knowledge is sadly deficient. Some governments, including among others those of Sweden, the Soviet Union, Japan and many of the state governments of the United States, have taken special measures (sterilization) to control fertility by persons handicapped by defects or diseases that frequently involve genetic factors.

During the late 1920s and the 1930s, when birth rates were falling rapidly in Europe, North America and Oceania, there was much alarm about "the retreat from parenthood"—reinforced in some countries by considerations of national security. Demographers were to some extent responsible for exaggerating the dangers in this situation through misplaced confidence at that time in the net reproduction ratio as an index of intrinsic population trends. Moreover, some economists viewed the slackening of population growth as tending to cause economic stagnation and chronic unemployment. It was, in any case, apparent that demographic changes were increasing the proportion of aged persons in the population.

These considerations led to the advocacy of measures for promoting the maintenance and growth of population as a matter of public policy. Quite different measures to this end were advanced in different countries and by different groups within the same country. In France concern about population trends, in conjunction with other interests, led eventually to a comprehensive system of family allowances and related measures, in which the government still makes a large investment each year, which actually offset at least in large part the costs of additional children in many French families. Some programs of financial aid to families with children have been adopted in most European and many non-European countries, including Canada. These programs are usually designed to serve various ends, and it is often difficult to say to what extent they express population policies. Moreover, most governments have been reluctant to authorize expenditures on a scale comparable to that accepted in France. More blatant but less expensive pronatalist measures were inaugurated by the Italian Fascist and the German National Socialist regimes.

Laws against the promotion or sale of contraceptives, as such, as well as stringent legislation against abortion are supported in some countries by demographic as well as religious considerations. The qualitative aspects of population trends were taken explicitly and seriously into account in general population policies only in Sweden. And even there the early program, which included this emphasis along with other welfare features, has been revised in favour of direct subsidies to families with children. Many governmental programs designed to promote fertility without much expenditure of public funds had practically no effect.

It is now generally recognized that the rapid increase of population in the less developed countries, at rates of 2 to $3\frac{1}{2}\%$ per year, impedes their economic and social development. This principle is accepted by all responsible students of population though there are wide differences in emphasis and interpretation. Communist theoreticians who formerly denied or ignored this problem now tend merely to insist that changes in economic institutions are fundamental and that such changes will induce a spontaneous response toward controlled fertility. The Soviet Union and most of the Eastern European nations have legalized abortion and promote contraception, though in theory this is intended only for the welfare of the individual families rather than as a means of population control. Moreover, the Communist regime in China, according to a statement of Premier Chou En-lai (Feb. 1964), encourages delayed marriage and the control of births within marriage as a factor in achieving its economic objectives. Leading Roman Catholic theologians also recognize the serious economic and social consequences of the persistence of high fertility in association with declining mortality in nations with limited resources. They accept the regulation of fertility as a family goal, but insist that the means of achieving this goal must conform to approved moral principles.

Many of the governments of the less developed countries, following the lead of India in its first five-year plan (1951–56), now promote planned parenthood as a national policy—either directly through public agencies or through public assistance to private agencies. Besides India and mainland China, the list includes Pakistan, Ceylon, Singapore, Malaysia, South Korea, Taiwan (Formosa), Turkey, Egypt, Tunisia, Morocco, Mauritius, Kenya, Honduras, Puerto Rico, and Chile. The General Assembly of the United Nations in 1962 adopted a resolution calling attention to the importance of population problems; a specific clause authorizing the provision of technical assistance in this field was deleted on the ground that it was unnecessary because the secretary-general has the authority to consider any requests for assistance by member governments. The UN Economic and Social Council in 1965 voted to increase "the amount of technical assistance in population fields available to governments of developing countries upon their request." The World Health Organization in 1965 also gave limited approval to this principle. The United States government, under Presidents J. F. Kennedy and L. B. Johnson, moved from official indifference to questions of population policy toward positive action in several ways in that country and the extension of technical assistance to other countries at their request.

The results of official programs, notably in India, were at first discouraging. The obstacles to changes in personal behaviour in a vast illiterate population dispersed in small villages are obviously enormous. Subsequent events have provided grounds for greater optimism. Methods of organization and communication have been improved on the basis of early experimentation. The appropriation for this work was increased in India from 1,500,000 rupees in the first five-year plan to 265,000,000 in the third plan and 950,000,000 in the fourth plan (1966–71). Equally intensive programs have been inaugurated in some other countries. Moreover there has been a large response in various low-income populations to new contraceptive techniques, notably intra-uterine devices and pills to regulate ovulation (see BIRTH CONTROL), that are more effective and more acceptable than those previously available. Therefore, it now appears that family planning programs may have an important influence on future population trends. If so, this success will not in itself assure great advances in the well-being of people who are now impoverished, but it will remove one of the major obstacles to such progress and facilitate more rapid and sustained economic and social development.

See also references under "Population" in the Index.

BIBLIOGRAPHY.—International journals of demography: *Population Index* (Princeton), an annotated bibliography of current books and articles on population; *Population Studies* (London); *Population* (Paris). United Nations: *Demographic Yearbook;* also "Population Studies" (a series of monographs). Philip M. Hauser and Otis Dudley Duncan (eds.), *The Study of Population, An Inventory and Appraisal* (1959). The American Assembly, *The Population Dilemma* (1963).

(F. Lo.)

POPULIST PARTY, a short-lived minor political party that flourished in the United States in the 1890s. Officially named the People's Party of the United States of America, it was founded at Cincinnati, O., May 21, 1891, by a mass convention of delegates representing the discontented farmers of the Northwest and the South. The Populists met in national convention at Omaha, Neb., on July 4, 1892, and nominated James B. Weaver of Iowa for president and James G. Field of Virginia for vice-president. In the presidential election of that year they polled 22 electoral votes and more than 1,000,000 popular votes. By fusing with the Democrats in certain states the Populists were able also to elect several members of Congress, three governors, and hundreds of minor officials and legislators, nearly all in the Northwest. In the South most of the farmers refused to endanger white supremacy by voting against the Democratic Party.

Populist gains in the midterm elections of 1894 were considerable, but when the Democrats nominated William Jennings Bryan in 1896 on a free silver platform, the Populists endorsed him, although nominating their own vice-presidential candidate, Thomas E. Watson of Georgia. After Bryan's defeat, most Populists became Democrats. A small residue known as "fusionists" endorsed Bryan, the Democratic candidate, again in 1900, while another element of the party nominated Wharton Barker of Philadelphia. A splinter group supported "middle-of-the-road" tickets, both state and national, as late as 1912.

See J. D. Hicks, *The Populist Revolt* (1931); Richard Hofstadter, *The Age of Reform* (1955).   (J. D. H.)

PORCELAIN ENAMELING. A porcelain enamel is a thin layer of glass fused to a metal to enhance its beauty, to prevent corrosion, or both. Porcelain-enameled iron is used extensively for both domestic and industrial articles. In addition to its use for kitchenware (see *Enamelware,* below), bathtubs and sinks, it is used extensively for table tops, refrigerators, washing machine tubs and stoves. Industrially, it is used for advertising signs, chemical and food tanks of large sizes, hospital furniture, grocery, meat market, supermarket and restaurant equipment, and has found application in architecture for the facing of the outsides of buildings. A porcelain enamel, being a glass, has the properties of glass; namely, its hard, glossy surface and resistance to solution, corrosion and scratching. The metal backing and design greatly influence its strength and resistance to damage. The quality of porcelain enamels varies greatly, depending upon the glass used, the design and the manufacturing technique.

History.—Although the term porcelain enameling (also called vitreous enameling or enameling) did not come into common use until about 1929, enamels were used far back in the early history of man, first as glass beads fused onto metal, later as medallions and finally, in the first half of the 18th century, as a protective surface. Although jewelry enamels, art pieces and photographs in enamels are still made and highly prized (for cloisonné, champlevé, etc., see ENAMEL; JEWELRY), enamels on sheet steel and cast iron constitute the principal part of the modern industry.

Manufacture.—Although the early developments took many years, the transition of enameling from an art to an industry in the early part of the 19th century proceeded very rapidly. Cast-iron dry-process enamels were the first to be used on a large scale. In this process, the castings, such as bathtubs, were first sandblasted to give them a clean surface. The grip or ground coat was then applied. This ground coat consisted of a powdered glass, clay and water suspension with a consistency about like that of cream. This was dipped, slushed or sprayed on the cool casting and allowed to dry. The ware was then introduced into a furnace at about 900° C. and allowed to come to the temperature of the furnace. The hot ware was withdrawn from the furnace and powdered glass dusted through a screen over it. This powdered glass melted as it fell on the hot ware and formed a continuous layer of enamel. Several applications were generally made, the ware being returned to the furnace for reheating before each application. This process is particularly applicable to the manufacture of heavy castings.

Another process which has come into common use is that of wet-process cast-iron enameling. This is used on lightweight or thin castings and has been adopted extensively in the stove industry. In this process, the ground coat is generally applied as a suspension of the glass with clay in water, dried and then fired in a furnace

Typical Enamel Compositions

Component	Ground coats (%)		White cover enamel (%)
	A	B	C
Borax	35.0	35.0	—
Feldspar	21.0	21.0	—
Quartz	28.0	21.0	41.5
Soda ash	4.5	6.0	—
Soda nitre	4.0	4.5	5.7
Fluorspar	5.0	10.0	—
Cobalt oxide	0.5	0.5	—
Nickel oxide	0.5	0.5	—
Manganese dioxide	1.5	1.5	—
Dehydrated borax			22.6
Titanium dioxide			17.6
Potassium silicofluoride			8.0
Sodium silicofluoride			1.3
Monosodium phosphate (dehydrated)			3.3
Totals	100.0	100.0	100.0

Mill additions	Ground coat (parts)	Cover coat (parts)
Frit A	40% }100	
Frit B	60% }	5
Enamel clay	7	5
Water	40	40
Frit C	—	100
Electrolytes	Various	Various
Totals	147	145

at about 750° C. The ware is removed from the furnace, cooled, the second coat applied and then refired. This process is sometimes known as the U.S. process for enameling cast iron.

Sheet-steel enameling has become the process most widely used for porcelain enamels. In this process, the sheet steel is fabricated and put through a cleaning and pickling process which pre-

pares the surface for enameling. Sheet-steel enameling requires a ground coat containing a small percentage of cobalt to give it adherence. This ground coat is applied by the wet process, dried and then fired in a furnace at about 830° C. After the ware has been removed from the furnace and cooled, a second coat of cover enamel is applied by the wet process. This cover coat may be of any desired colour and may have special properties depending upon the use to which the ware is to be put. It is commonly sprayed or dipped onto the ware, allowed to dry and then fired at about 830° C. Additional coats of enamel are sometimes applied, and finally the decoration is applied and fired into the last coat.

Although enameling is an important industry in most countries, the use of automatic equipment, technical control and mass production is outstanding in the United States.

Enamelware.—Metal kitchenware, such as pots and pans, the surface of which is protected and decorated by a thin layer of porcelain enamel is known as enamelware. Prior to the advent of enamelware such utensils were made of pottery, copper, cast iron and to some extent tinned sheet iron. Aluminum and stainless steel, introduced in the 19th century, have come into common use.

In the kitchenware industry, enamelware is produced chiefly in large modern plants, with machine operations and a great deal of automation and control. Ware made in the second half of the 20th century is far superior to any of that made prior to World War II. In the manufacture of enamelware a good grade of low-carbon sheet iron is formed in the shape of the utensil by pressing or drawing, by spinning and by trimming; the handles, spouts and ears are welded in place by spot or resistance welding. The ware is then cleaned in a chemical detergent bath, rinsed in water, pickled in acid (usually 5% sulfuric acid), rinsed and neutralized in a bath of sodium hydroxide, borax or sodium cyanide. In some cases the ware is treated in a nickel sulfate bath prior to neutralizing to improve enamel adherence. The shapes are finally dried, sorted and inspected.

Enamel glasses are prepared by melting the raw materials together and quenching in a water spray and bath. These operations are called smelting and fritting, and the product, which is broken glass, is called frit. The frit is dried and weighed with mill additions such as water, clay and special suspending agents. This mill batch is charged into ball mills of about 1,000- to 3,000-lb. capacity and ground to a fineness of about 2% on a 200-mesh sieve. The product is a thick slurry called slip, the properties of which must be accurately controlled.

Enamel usually is applied in two coats each being fired separately. The first coat, called a ground coat, is an enamel containing cobalt. A typical composition is shown in the accompanying table. It usually is applied to the shapes by dipping, the properties of the slip being such that the excess drains off or is thrown off in the special handling of the ware just after it is removed from the slip bath. After drying it is fired, usually in a continuous conveyor furnace, at about 1,500° F., with four minutes in the hot zone of the furnace.

The ground-coated ware is next coated with the slip of the cover enamel (see table) in a similar manner, dried and fired. Where white is desired, the cover enamel is usually an acid-resistant titanium opacified enamel. Special compositions are needed for the colours, for the bead on the rim or for handles. In very special cases a third firing is used for special decorations.

Enamelware is usually acid-resistant, withstanding fruit and vegetable acids to a high degree. When made under modern conditions, it is very resistant to impact. The enamel fails only when the piece is subjected to a deformation of the iron, which results in a cracking of the glass coating. Enamelware is very resistant to thermal shock, but cold water should not be put in a hot dry pan. Enamelware will withstand all temperatures used in cooking. It has a hard, scratch-resistant surface and can be cleaned with all common cleaning materials, but harsh abrasives such as sand should not be used, as they scratch any glass surface.

BIBLIOGRAPHY.—A. I. Andrews, *Enamels* (1935); A. I. Andrews and R. L. Cook, *Enamel Laboratory Manual* (1941); American Society for Testing Materials, *Symposium on Porcelain Enamels and Ceramic Coatings as Engineering Materials* (1954). (A. I. A.)

PORCH, originally a roofed structure, usually open at the sides, to protect the entrance of a building; loosely used of any projecting portico, or even of any colonnade and, in the United States, of any roofed structure open at the sides and front, attached to a house or other building; synonymous with veranda or piazza. A sleeping porch is such a structure usually opening from an upper story.

Of the porch proper there are few extant remains prior to the classic period, although Egyptian wall paintings seem to indicate their occasional use with houses. The most important Greek porches are those of the Tower of the Winds at Athens (1st century B.C.), in which two columns of a simple Corinthian order carried a pediment. A similar porch exists in the so-called villa of Diomed at Pompeii. Houses in Rome sometimes had long colonnades facing the street which served as porches. During the Romanesque period simple projecting porches covering the western doors of churches are found instead of the earlier basilican colonnaded narthices. Especially interesting are the projecting porches of the Italian Romanesque, such as that of S. Zeno Maggiore at Verona (12th century), in which the columns are carried on marble lions (as frequently in Lombard work) and at Modena (12th century) and Parma (13th century). In Apulia there are many similar porches of distinct Lombard character.

In France, especially in Burgundy, an even greater development of the porch occurred, in which it became a vaulted structure of great height and importance, two or more bays long and sometimes as wide as the entire church. The great porch of the abbey church at Vézelay (1132-40), sometimes termed an antechurch, is the largest and richest.

The English love of picturesqueness sometimes developed the porch to such an extent that it became almost a separate building which was called a "galilee," like that at Durham (1175). Galilees in medieval churches are supposed to have been used sometimes as a court of law, or a place where corpses were placed before interment, but the galilee probably served chiefly as a chapel for penitents before their admission to the body of the church. Many fantastically rich projecting porches occur in French Flamboyant churches, such as that of the church of Notre Dame at Alençon (c. 1500), the pentagonal porch of St. Maclou at Rouen (c. 1520) and the side entrance of the cathedral at Albi (early 16th century).

The same richness of porch design is not found in English Gothic churches, where western doors are often small and unimportant. The other type of porch, the small projecting gabled feature projecting from the north or south walls of the nave, was, however, highly developed throughout the course of English Gothic.

In the larger city churches there was frequently a room over the porch, sometimes known as a porch chamber and sometimes incorrectly termed a parvis. These seem to have been used sometimes as vestries, sometimes as treasuries and sometimes as chantry chapels. Similar porches, with chambers above, occur occasionally in Tudor mansions.

In Germany churches of the Flamboyant Gothic period are frequently decorated with western porches of the most fantastic richness, with a great use of cusping, pierced tracery and canopy work. Such are the double-arched entrance of the cathedral at Ulm (c. 1390) by Ulrich von Ensingen and the triangular porch

PORCH OF SAN ZENO MAGGIORE, VERONA. 12TH-CENTURY ITALIAN ROMANESQUE

of the cathedral at Regensburg by M. Roritzer (1482-86).

During the Renaissance the porch was usually treated as a portico, but simple porches of two or four columns were exceedingly common features of the late 18th-century houses of England and the United States. (T. F. H.)

PORCUPINE, a name loosely applied to large, quill-bearing terrestrial rodents of the suborder Hystricomorpha. The New World porcupines belong to the family Erethizontidae, which consists of four genera: *Erethizon*, the North American porcupine found in wooded areas south of the tundra in Canada and the U.S. to northern Mexico; *Coendou*, the prehensile-tailed tree porcupines from southern Mexico to South America; *Echinoprocta*, the short-tailed porcupine found only in Colombia; and *Chaetomys*, the aberrant, thin-spined porcupine found only in Brazil.

The typical North American porcupine, *Erethizon dorsatum*, has a heavy, compact, arched body, about two feet long; the thick, muscular tail is an additional seven inches or so. The three-inch-long quills—hairs modified to form stiff, hollow spines—are interspersed among the dark, coarse, sparse guard hairs and brown-black underfur of the upperparts and the tail. The quills are black tipped and white based; they are erectile like the hairs.

Porcupines are slow moving, clumsy, methodical, and show little fear of other animals. They eat plant materials only and prefer the tender cambium layer directly beneath the bark, sometimes completely girdling a tree as they feed. Buds, tender twigs, and leaves are also eaten. Porcupines are solitary but not antisocial; several may be found in an especially suitable den site. Usually one young is born in the spring after about 209 days gestation.

Its spiny investure has made the porcupine unpopular prey. It presents its rear to an enemy, and, if attacked, drives its powerful tail against the attacker. The quills are easily detached from the skin and remain with the barbed ends embedded in the assailant. The porcupine does not throw its quills at will, although they may become loose and be detached when the animal shakes itself. Because of their food habits porcupines are sometimes destructive of commercial timber. These prodigious gnawers also have a taste for other substances; many a woodsman has had his well-handled ax handle or canoe paddle destroyed by a "quill pig" who was after the salt and oil it contained. The flesh of the porcupine is tasty but fat; it is a godsend to persons lost in the woods.

The Old World porcupines belong to the family Hystricidae. They are also placed in four genera: *Hystrix*, the typical porcupines; *Thecurus*; and *Atherurus* and *Trichys*, the brush-tailed porcupines. *H. cristata*, the crested porcupine, is the largest terrestrial rodent of Europe; it ranges over southern Europe and the northern half of Africa. It has two types of quills, the longer ones measuring up to 1½ ft. long. Little hair is present in the quilled

NORTH AMERICAN PORCUPINE (ERETHIZON DORSATUM)

areas of the skin. Crested porcupines are nervous, shy, and nocturnal. When disturbed they shake their bodies, thus rattling the hollow quills and producing a surprising amount of noise. Like their American counterparts, they display a wide variety of vocal sounds: grunts, squeaks, chatterings, and whines. One or two young are produced following a gestation of 63 to 112 days.

A number of other species are widespread over Asia and adjacent islands and Africa, some species having only poorly developed quills. *See* RODENT. (K. R. KN.)

PORDENONE (GIOVANNI ANTONIO DE' SACHIS) (*c.* 1483–1539), a north Italian painter who, although basically influenced by Venetian painting, shows an element of violence which probably derives from Germany. He was born at Pordenone, in Friuli, in about 1483; however, the date of his birth rests only on the statement by G. Vasari that he died in 1540 (instead of 1539) at the age of 56. Pordenone was a pupil of Pellegrino da S. Daniele and other Friulian masters, but his style is founded on Venetian models and in particular on Titian; later he was influenced by Correggio and also by the Roman works of Michelangelo and Raphael and it is assumed, therefore, that he went to Rome, probably about 1515/16.

He worked in Treviso, Mantua, Genoa and Cremona as well as in Friuli and all over northern Italy. Even in Venice his work was so popular that for a short time he was a serious rival to Titian himself, and on one occasion the senate of Venice gave him the preference for a commission. Unfortunately, his frescoes in Venice have perished, but he painted a dome in Piacenza in the illusionistic manner of Correggio (1529–31). He was invited to Ferrara by Ercole II but died there soon after his arrival and was buried on Jan. 14, 1539. There are many documented and dated works by Pordenone, the earliest being a fresco at Valeriano, signed and dated 1506.

See C. Ridolfi, *Le Maraviglie dell' Arte,* etc. (1648; ed. by Hadeln, 1914–24); G. Fiocco, *Giovanni Antonio Pordenone,* 2nd ed. (1943). (P. J. MY.)

PORDENONE, a town of Udine Province, Friuli-Venezia Giulia region, northeast Italy, lies on a small tributary of the Meduna, 31 mi. (50 km.) WSW of Udine by road, and in a plain about halfway between the Alps and the Adriatic coast. Pop. (1961) 37,204 (commune). Pordenone has many Romano-Gothic and Venetian palaces along its main street, and the 13th-century campanile of S. Marco is a national monument. There are fine modern buildings as well. Pordenone is on the railway from Treviso to Udine. Machinery, textiles, ceramics, and wood products are made. There are few Roman remains. The medieval river port (Portus Naonis) was a bulwark of the Trevigiani in their war against Aquileia. The latter destroyed it in 1233. It later became a fief of the Holy Roman Empire, passed to Venice in 1508 and became part of the kingdom of Italy in 1866. (PI. P.)

PORGY, a name applied to various perchlike marine fishes of the family Sparidae, sometimes called sea breams. The body is oblong with the back more or less elevated; the jaws are armed with strong teeth, those in front being prominent and conical or incisorlike, those on the sides molarlike. Porgies are shore dwellers, occurring around the world, chiefly in warm seas. South Africa is especially rich in species, many of which are popular angling fishes. One temperate species, the northern porgy, commonly called scup (*Stenotomus chrysops*), ranges on the Atlantic coast from South Carolina to Maine. Scup grow to be about 18 in. long and 4 lb. in weight. They migrate northward and shoreward in spring, and southward and into deeper water in fall. They feed near the bottom on a variety of invertebrates and young fish. Scup spawn chiefly during the summer. The edible red porgy (*Pagrus pagrus*) of southern Europe and tropical America is believed to be the *Pagrus* referred to with much appreciation in ancient literature. (L. A. WD.)

PORIFERA, a phylum of the animal kingdom comprising the sponges. *See* SPONGE.

PORISMS, the title of a treatise written by Euclid (*c.* 300 B.C.), the author of the *Elements*. This book, no longer extant, is known only through the account given by Pappus of Alexandria (*q.v.; c.* A.D. 320) in the seventh of the eight books of his *Collection.* Translated from the Greek into Latin toward the close of the 16th century, this work of Pappus was the subject of study by scholars who endeavoured to reconstruct the original, an effort not unconnected with the development of projective geometry.

The word porism (from *porizein*, "to carry" or "to produce") has several shades of meaning. In Euclid's *Elements* there are instances when a theorem (*q.v.*) is followed by the words "Porism. From this it is manifest that . . ." and a statement that is a corollary to the theorem. For example:

Euclid III, 1. *To find the centre of a circle. Porism* . . . if in a circle a straight line cuts a straight line into two equal parts and at right angles, the centre of the circle is on the cutting line.

Euclid IV, 15. *In a given circle to inscribe an equiangular and equilateral hexagon. Porism* . . . the side of the hexagon is equal to the radius.

Euclid VII, 2. *Given two numbers not prime to one another, to find their greatest common measure. Porism* . . . if a number measure two numbers, it will also measure their greatest common measure.

Pappus, quoting "older writers," gave three classes of propositions:

A *theorem* is directed to *proving* what is proposed.
A *problem* is directed to *constructing* what is proposed.
A *porism* is directed to *producing* or *finding* what is proposed.

T. L. Heath suggests that the usual porism was "to prove that it is possible to find a point with such and such a property or a straight line on which lie all the points that satisfy given conditions." Tobias Dantzig summarizes the matter in these terms:

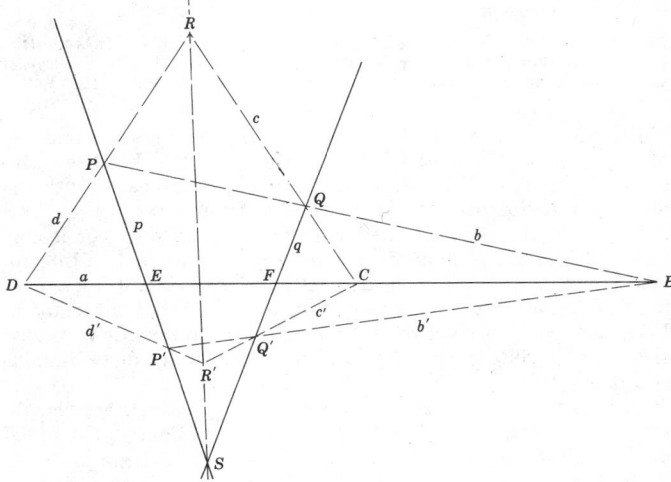

FROM B. L. VAN DER WAERDEN, "SCIENCE AWAKENING" (P. NOORDHOFF LTD.)

ILLUSTRATION OF THE FIRST OF EUCLID'S PORISMS. SOLID LINES INDICATE THOSE THAT ARE FIXED IN POSITION. BROKEN LINES SHOW TWO POSITIONS OF THE VARIABLE LINES

"The only thing certain about the *Book of Porisms* is the title, and even here there is no general agreement as to the sense in which Euclid used the term" (*Bequest of the Greeks,* p. 36, Charles Scribner's Sons, New York, 1955).

Pappus states that the *Porisms* contained 171 propositions and 38 lemmas. He gives examples of a few of the propositions and adds 38 lemmas of his own. He begins by stating a proposition that he says epitomizes the first ten of Euclid's porisms. It reads:

If in a system of four straight lines which cut one another two and two, three points on one straight line be given, while the rest except one lie on different straight lines given in position, the remaining point also will lie on a straight line given in position.

Thus in the accompanying diagram, three points of intersection of the lines *b, c, d* lie on *a,* namely *D, C, B.* Two other points *P* and *Q* are on the fixed lines *p* and *q,* with *p* and *q* intersecting *a* at *E* and *F,* respectively. In a second position the variable lines *b', c', d'* intersect the lines *p* and *q* at *P'* and *Q',* respectively. It follows that the remaining point of intersection *R'* lies on the line that passes through the join of *p* and *q* and the point *R.* Pappus stated that this theorem is true of any number of straight lines intersecting two by two.

B. L. van der Waerden discusses the 13 lemmas that Pappus added to this porism, noting first that when two different positions of the variable lines are drawn, as is the case in the accompanying diagram, it is the theorem of Desargues (1636):

If two triangles are so situated that the lines joining pairs of corresponding vertices are concurrent, then the points of intersection of pairs of corresponding lines are collinear, or, as it appears in projective geometry, if two triangles are perspective from a point, they are perspective from a line, and conversely.

The lemmas that follow include the seeds of the ideas of the theorem of the complete quadrangle, of six points in involution, of four harmonic points and a special case of Pascal's hexagon.

Pappus' *Collection* was translated from the Greek into Latin by Federico Commandino (1509–75). Several editions of this work appeared, and in 1660 there was a revision of it by Carlo Manolesse. The Latin and Greek text with notes was published by F. Hultsch in 1876–78.

The problem of reconstructing the *Porisms* from the evidence offered by Pappus is a challenging one. H. W. Turnbull describes it as being like trying to follow a chess game by listening to the comments of an intelligent onlooker. Pierre de Fermat (1601?–65) was one of the first to attempt the reconstruction; Michel Chasles (1860) made a notable effort. In the course of this work Chasles was led to the important idea of anharmonic ratios. In his opinion, the *Porisms* belong to the modern theory of transversals and to projective geometry. H. G. Zeuthen (1886) suggested that the *Porisms* may have been corollaries to a fully developed projective geometry of conics. *See also* GEOMETRY: *Projective Geometry.*

BIBLIOGRAPHY.—T. L. Heath, *The History of Greek Mathematics,* 2 vol. (1921), and *Manual of Greek Mathematics* (1931) ; B. L. van der Waerden, *Science Awakening,* Eng. trans. by A. Dresden (1954).

(V. Sᴅ.)

PORK, the edible flesh of swine, is the most versatile and one of the most popular meats. Since ancient times it has been consumed by most of the omnivorous peoples of the earth with the notable exception of Orthodox Jews and Muslims (*see* PIG). Like other meats, pork is consumed as a cooked fresh meat, or it may be cured (or salted) to produce many types of products. In combination with other meats, or by itself, it is the principal ingredient in innumerable types of sausages (*q.v.*) and other meat foods. Pork and pork products are among the most nutritious foods; their caloric value is high and they are a good source of B vitamins and minerals.

Pork is usually derived from young animals which are slaughtered before reaching puberty. In this respect it differs from beef or horsemeat and is perhaps more comparable to lamb and veal than other meats. Carcasses of mature swine, such as cull sows, are generally used in sausage trimmings.

Swine produce more edible meat per pound of feed consumed than any other of the mammalian livestock species generally used

TABLE I.—*United States Standards for Pork: Average Back Fat Thickness by Grade*
(in inches)

Carcass weight or carcass length	U.S. No. 1	U.S. No. 2	U.S. No. 3	Medium	Cull
Under 120 lb. or under 27 in.	1.2–1.5	1.5–1.8	1.8 or more	0.9–1.2	less than 0.9
120–164 lb. or 27–29.9 in.	1.3–1.6	1.6–1.9	1.9 or more	1.0–1.3	less than 1.0
165–209 lb. or 30–32.9 in.	1.4–1.7	1.7–2.0	2.0 or more	1.1–1.4	less than 1.1
210 lb. or over, or 33 in. or longer	1.5–1.8	1.8–2.1	2.1 or more	1.2–1.5	less than 1.2

as food. (Rabbits have an even higher feed efficiency but are not so generally consumed.) This high feed efficiency is the economic basis for pork's place as the meat of the common man, and also explains why it has been said that the average hog provides enough meat for two people and enough lard (*q.v.*) for three. Animal husbandrymen throughout the world are working successfully toward the general adoption of swine which produce carcasses with a larger percentage of lean meat and a smaller percentage of fat.

To facilitate marketing and give some indication of potential quality, pork carcasses are usually separated into grades according to length of carcass, back fat thickness, or some other measurement which is considered to be closely correlated with the amount of edible meat. The United States and Canada both use a combination of length and back fat thickness while Denmark, Britain, and countries which primarily produce Wiltshire bacon (*see* below)

TABLE II.—*Danish Bacon Grading (October 1964)*

Measurement	Danish AA	Danish A	Danish B
	Maximum		
Back fat thickness—on the point of the neck where the back fat is thickest . . .	4.0 cm.	4.7 cm.	5.2 cm.
Back fat thickness—on the central point of the middle and extending 7 cm. on both sides of the point which is halfway between the other two measurements	2.0 cm.	2.9 cm.	3.4 cm.
Back fat thickness—on the top of the muscle which arches out above the loin into the back fat	2.0 cm.	2.7 cm.	3.2 cm.
Slight of lean measurement—taken 8 to 9 cm. from the edge of the back fat in line with the last rib	2.9 cm.	2.9 cm.	3.5 cm.

also include a "slight of lean" measurement or a measure for loin muscle area in their grading. Grading standards in the United States and Denmark in the 1960s are shown in Tables I and II.

A U.S. No. 1 hog carcass is one which is considered to have an ideal amount of fat for its weight or length. A No. 2 or No. 3 carcass is somewhat more fat than desirable, while medium or cull carcasses have too little fat to satisfy the demands of the trade for a firm carcass that will handle properly on the block when cut. Some authorities think that less fat would be acceptable in the No. 1 carcass; others feel that the present standards result in roast pork that is somewhat too dry because it lacks enough fat for succulence. The tables presented here are examples of grading systems rather than an indication of any exact values. The values upon which a system is based—including, for example, consumer preference—vary from country to country and from time to time; and any system represents a compromise of all the factors involved.

In the U.S. individual pork cuts, unlike beef or lamb, are not graded. In Canada and the United States pork carcasses are divided into separate cuts as shown in the figure. In European countries a similar system is used, except for Wiltshire sides. The latter consists of the whole side of pork with the head and feet removed. The Wiltshire side is used for Wiltshire bacon and is an important item of export in Denmark, Poland, Ireland, Holland, Sweden, and to some extent in other continental countries.

Except for the making of Wiltshire bacon, the hams, shoulders, and bacon are generally cured, while the loins are eaten as fresh pork. A notable exception is socalled Canadian bacon, which consists of the cured loin muscle.

Curing and Cured Pork.— Most pork consumed in Great Britain is cured as Wiltshire bacon; in the rest of the world somewhat more than half the pork produced is cured. In the United States and Canada the

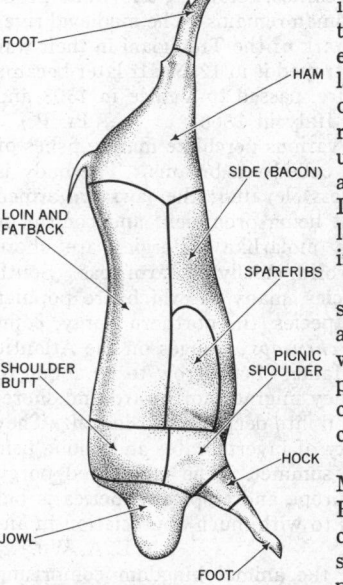

FOOT
HAM
SIDE (BACON)
LOIN AND FATBACK
SPARERIBS
SHOULDER BUTT
PICNIC SHOULDER
HOCK
JOWL
FOOT

U.S. METHOD OF CUTTING PORK

ham, shoulder, shoulder butt, bacon (belly), and some of the loin is generally cured. Curing takes many forms. Originally it was developed as a means of preserving meat for consumption weeks or months after slaughtering and dressing. It is a very ancient art; salting of meat is mentioned by Homer, and it was probably common before that. With the development of rapid distribution and the wide use of refrigeration, the preservative action of heavy curing is not so necessary, and the process has gradually changed.

The two traditional curing procedures are called dry curing and brine curing, depending on whether the curing ingredients are applied in a dry state or in solution. The curing ingredients are sodium chloride (common salt), sugar, and either sodium or potassium nitrate ($NaNO_3$ or KNO_3). A typical mixture consists of about 8 lb. of salt, about 2 lb. of sugar, and about 2 oz. of $NaNO_3$ per 100 lb. of meat. For dry cures the salt mixture is rubbed over the surface of the pork, and for brine cures the ingredients are dissolved in a suitable amount of water. Salt is absorbed rapidly by the meat and affects the flavour and chemical characteristics of the muscle proteins. It also acts as a bacteriostatic agent, retarding spoilage. Sugar has an effect on flavour which is said to reduce the harshness of the salt, although excellent cured meats may be made without its use. The nitrate is reduced to nitrite by microorganisms and, to a lesser extent, by other substances in pork tissue, and combines with the myoglobin (the red pigment of muscle) to form the relatively insoluble pink or red pigments of cured meats. This fixed colour, which is one of the important attributes of modern cured meats, is called nitrosohemochromogen. After a suitable time of exposure to the curing substances, the meat is washed briefly with a shower of water, allowed to dry, and then heated in a smokehouse. The time in smoke varies widely for different products. The essential results are the hardening of the exterior surfaces of the meat due to heat coagulation of the protein, the drying effect of the warm atmosphere, a further fixation of the pigment probably due to heat denaturation of the protein portion of the pigmented substance, and finally, the deposition of chemicals from the smoke on the meat. These smoke chemicals (aldehydes, phenols, polycyclic compounds, and others) have both an antioxidant effect, which protects the meat from becoming rancid, and some bacteriostatic action which helps further to retard spoilage.

In the early 1900s it occurred to scientists that the curing process could be accelerated and made more certain if some nitrite, such as sodium nitrite ($NaNO_2$) were added to the cure. This would promote rapid colour fixation without waiting for bacterial reduction of nitrate. This has become general practice and most countries now permit the use of nitrite in cures.

A further and more dramatic speedup of the curing process occurred in the early 1930s with the development of artery pumping. It consists of introducing the curing brine into the arterial system of a ham or other pork cut. In the case of hams, brine equal to about 10% of the weight of the ham is forced, at rather high pressure, into the femoral artery with a large hypodermic needle and a pump. Following pumping, the cuts may be subjected to further curing by submerging in cover pickle or by rubbing with a salt mixture.

The modern so-called ready to eat or fully cooked ham of the American market is often cured by brine pumping followed by immediate smoking. The temperature of the ham is raised to about 155° F in the smokehouse. The whole procedure from fresh ham to cured and cooked product, ready for the market, may take as little as ten hours. This sort of product may be contrasted with a Smithfield-type ham which is cured by a dry salt mixture and a very long cool smoke. Such hams may remain in cure for about 3 days per pound of weight (thus a 15-lb. ham would be cured for 45 days), and in the smokehouse for another 25 to 30 days of intermittent smoking. Long cured or regular hams are cured for about 14 to 30 days in brine and smoked to an internal temperature of 140° F. Table III shows some of the chemical and nutritional properties of the lean meat of several types of ham.

The figures in Table III are averages of several samples but should not be regarded as more than a comparison between types. Curing methods differ so widely and change so frequently and there is such great variation among pork carcasses that the figures cannot be considered specifically accurate for any ham other than the ones analyzed. It is important, however, to note the high free-fatty-acid content, high salt content, and low moisture content of

TABLE III.—*Composition of Lean Meat of Several Ham Types*

Type	Moisture (%)	Protein (%)	Fat (%)	NaCl (%)	Free fatty acid (%)	Thiamin*	Ribo-flavin*	Niacin*
Canned	65.0	18.3	12.3	3.5		29.0	14.0	250
Ready to eat	68.6	20.8	6.4	3.6	.41	29.5	8.3	168
Long cured	67.1	21.3	5.9	5.2	.64	29.7	8.6	173
Smithfield	51.0	27.7	11.2	8.4	9.3	26.2	10.4	248

*Values given in micrograms per gram of protein.

the aged Smithfield ham as compared to the other three. The Smithfield ham owes much of its distinctive flavour to its high free-fatty-acid content.

Bacon.—In Canada and the United States the term bacon means the cured belly or abdominal wall of the hog. The flat abdominal musculature gives the alternate streaks of lean and fat in the bacon slice. Bacon may be cured in many ways, but in most modern plants it is given a quick cure with a machine which injects the bacon with curing brine through a large number of needles arranged in gridlike pattern. After a period in brine cure of from a few hours to several days, depending on the practices of the particular plant, the bacon sides are washed and given a light smoke. The usual American practice is to market bacon as packaged slices. Bacon slabs have all but disappeared from the general market.

Wiltshire Bacon.—In Europe, the entire Wiltshire side and the cuts obtained from it are referred to as bacon. In manufacturing this product, the pork sides (after chilling and removal of the head, feet, etc.) are pumped with the brine and then piled in vats holding from a dozen to several hundred sides. When a vat is filled, usually with one day's kill, brine is pumped into the vat from another which is ready to be emptied. Brine for Wiltshire bacon is not made up fresh for each batch of meat, as it is in American practice, but is reused as long as possible. Salt and nitrate and nitrite are added to the brine from time to time to bring it up to strength (about 23–24% NaCl) and the brine is brought back to volume. Wiltshire bacon is cured in brine for a period of seven to ten days, and then the sides are piled in another part of the curing cellar for "maturation." It is claimed that this process, which may take from three days to two weeks at a controlled temperature, distributes the salt more evenly and produces better colour and flavour. Following maturation, the sides may be sold smoked, or "green," i.e., unsmoked. The hind leg portions from Wiltshire sides are termed gammons and are frequently sold separately. The shoulders ("fore ends") are also often sold as separate cuts, but the rest of the side is normally sliced for sale.

A modern innovation, called "slice curing," consists of a process for slicing the raw "middles" (the sides minus hams and shoulders) and passing the slices on a conveyor through a brine tank. The resultant slices, which are cured in little more than an hour, are vacuum-packed in a plastic film for sale. This product is said to have better colour than, and to be as acceptable to consumers as, the traditional product that may take as much as three or four weeks to produce.

Public Health Aspects.—Swine may suffer from the parasitic disease trichinosis and pork may harbour the cysts of the parasite, *Trichinella spiralis*. To guard against the infection of humans, the meat inspection laws of the various countries contain provisions to prevent the consumption of infectious pork. In the United States and Canada, all pork products which are likely to be eaten without further cooking (such as ham) must be either heated to 140° F, or frozen, or salted in a specified manner which will kill the parasite. The trichina larvae are killed by heating to 137° F, and the common stricture to cook pork well done allows for more than an ample safety factor. In many European countries where the number of hogs handled by a plant is not nearly so large as in the United States and Canada, an actual microscopic inspection for trichina is conducted on each hog carcass. In these countries many pork products are prepared which are not cooked and such laborious inspection is necessary.

Like other meat products, pork products may become contaminated by food poisoning bacteria—especially during slicing or handling under adverse conditions. Pork products, particularly cooked products, should therefore be handled under hygienic conditions and kept under refrigeration.

BIBLIOGRAPHY.—Lloyd B. Jensen, *Meat and Meat Foods* (1949); American Meat Institute Foundation, *The Science of Meat and Meat Products* (1960); B. K. Watt and A. L. Merrill, "Composition of Foods," U.S. Department of Agriculture *Agriculture Handbook No. 8* (1963); N. E. Gibbons, *Wiltshire Bacon* (1953).   (W. L. SU.)

POROS (anc. Greek CALAURIA), an island off the east coast of the Peloponnese, Greece (area 9 sq.mi. [23 sq.km.]; pop. [1961] 4,422), included in the *nomos* (department) of Attica. It is separated at its western end by a narrow channel (*poros*) from the mainland at Troezen and consists of a mass of limestone joined by a sandy isthmus to a smaller mass of trachyte on the south, where the modern harbour town Poros stands.

Calauria was famous for its temple of Poseidon, the centre at an early date of an amphictyony (*q.v.*) of maritime states—Hermione, Epidaurus, Aegina, Athens, Prasiae, Nauplia, and Orchomenus in Boeotia; later Argos replaced Nauplia and Sparta took the place of Prasiae. Demosthenes took sanctuary there and poisoned himself to avoid arrest (322 B.C.). The Doric temple lay on a ridge inland, commanding a view of Athens and the Saronic Gulf; it was excavated in 1894 by the Swedes S. Wide and L. Kjellberg. Traces of porticoes and other buildings were also found.

English, French, and Russian plenipotentiaries met at Poros in 1828 to discuss the future of the new Greek state, and in 1831 the Greek admiral Andreas Vokos Miaoulis (*q.v.*) attempted to hold the town against Kapodistrias and blew up the "Hellas" in Poros Harbour.

PORPHYRIA. The term porphyria embraces a group of diseases characterized by marked overproduction and excretion of porphyrins (red pigments), their colourless porphyrinogens, and/or their precursors, δ-aminolevulinic acid (ALA) and porphobilinogen (PBG).

Two main groups of porphyria are recognized: (1) erythropoietic and (2) hepatic. In the first the overproduction occurs in relation to hemoglobin synthesis by erythroid cells in the bone marrow; in the second the disturbance is in the liver. There are two principal types of erythropoietic porphyria: (*a*) Classical congenital uroporphyria (Günther's disease) in which large amounts of uro- and coproporphyrin type I are excreted, the former mainly in the urine, the latter in the feces. The hemoglobin protoporphyrin is of the normal type III. The two isomer series (H. Fischer's "dualism") are formed independently from PBG. The great increase of blood porphyrins results in photodynamic injury to light-exposed skin, due to photooxidation of protein. Vesiculobullous (blistering) reactions eventually result in scarring and severe mutilation. The teeth and bones are reddish brown. Enlargement of the spleen and hemolytic anemia are frequently noted. Some cases are benefited by splenectomy. The genetic abnormality is of autosomal recessive type. (*b*) Erythropoietic protoporphyria in which large excesses of free protoporphyrin of isomer series III are excreted in blood and feces, but not in urine. Skin photosensitivity is again the dominant symptom, but more often erythematous or eczematoid than vesiculobullous in type. Overproduction of protoporphyrin may occur in liver as well as erythroid cells. The genetic abnormality is autosomal dominant.

There are three types of hepatic porphyria: (*a*) In acute intermittent (AIP) the autosomal dominant biochemical abnormality is largely represented by the precursors ALA and PBG, in the liver and urine. These, particularly PBG, are probably related to disturbance of the nervous system and produce a wide variety of symptoms: abdominal pain and vomiting; hypertension; pain and weakness or paralysis of the extremities; respiratory paralysis; hypothalamic (electrolyte) disturbances; hysteroid or psychotic behaviour; coma. Diagnosis depends largely on demonstration of excessive urinary PBG by appropriate use of the Ehrlich reaction. The excess often persists during remission though generally at a lower level than in relapse. Attacks are often precipitated by "porphyrogenic" chemicals such as barbiturates. (*b*) Clinically "mixed" or "variegate" porphyria (VP) is also an autosomal dominant genetic error. This form is especially common in the white population of South Africa but occurs in other parts of the

world. The acute attacks of VP are indistinguishable from those of AIP and similarly precipitated. Skin photosensitivity and fragility with bullous lesions are observed in the same individuals or families. This is correlated with the large amounts of free porphyrins of the blood plasma and feces. Urinary PBG is generally normal in remission, increased in varying degree with the acute attack. (*c*) The onset of *porphyria cutanea tarda* (PCT) is in later life, usually 4th–8th decades, with lack of the overt hereditary character noted in types *a* and *b*. Nevertheless, careful study of family members has at times revealed evidence of familial occurrence. The skin photosensitivity and sequelae are entirely similar to those of VP. Many patients with PCT are found to have used alcohol excessively.

Liver function impairment is common and cirrhosis relatively frequent. The liver contains large amounts of uroporphyrin, with a usual excess of iron. Since most alcoholics with or without cirrhosis do not develop porphyria, it seems probable that a constitutional or occult genetic hepatic abnormality is represented. PCT is characterized by marked sensitivity to chloroquine, with fever and vomiting.

A complex of porphyrin and chloroquine is believed to cause transitory liver injury with release of porphyrins in large amount after which a remission of the disease may occur. Remission is also produced by repeated bloodletting, the presently accepted method of treatment.   (C. J. WA.)

PORPHYRY (234–*c*. 305), Neoplatonist philosopher and scholar who is important as both editor and biographer of Plotinus (*q.v.*) and because of the influence of his logical works on medieval thought, was born at Tyre (or Batanaea in Palestine). He originally bore the Syrian name Malchus ("king"), hellenized by Longinus into *Porphyrios* ("purple") in allusion to the colour of the imperial robes. He studied under the great scholar Cassius Longinus (*q.v.*) at Athens. In the year 262/263 he went to Rome and attached himself to Plotinus, the founder of Neoplatonism, with whom he remained for five years. These years were the decisive period in his life. Owing to severe overstrain which led him to contemplate suicide (very sympathetically and sensibly dealt with by Plotinus) he had to leave his master and retire to Sicily. But Plotinus had made him his literary executor, and 33 years later, in 301, at the age of 68, he produced what is incomparably his most important piece of work, an edition of the writings of Plotinus, the *Enneads,* to which he prefixed a biography of his master which is a noble testimony to the continuing devotion which the latter inspired in his pupil and is unique among ancient lives of philosophers for its informativeness and reliability. Apart from this publication little is known of the later life of Porphyry. He returned to Rome some time after the death of Plotinus (though he probably did not engage in any organized philosophical teaching there; the school of Plotinus had come to an end with the last illness of the master). Late in life he married a philosophically inclined widow called Marcella.

Porphyry was a voluminous writer, not original but well-read and careful to give the names of his authorities. He has thus preserved in some of his works (notably the *De abstinentia*) important fragments of earlier philosophy. His extant works, besides the biography of Plotinus already referred to, are:

1. Philosophical and religious: *Aphormai pros ta noeta* (*Sententiae ad intelligibilia ducentes*), a collection of philosophical aphorisms borrowed or adapted from Plotinus; *Peri apoches empsychon* (*De abstinentia*), on vegetarianism; *Pros Markellan* (*Ad Marcellam*), a work of edification addressed to his wife; the *Pros Anebo epistole,* an extremely skeptical "open letter" to Anebo on theurgy; the *Pythagorou bios* ("Life of Pythagoras"), probably part of a larger history of philosophy, written in Porphyry's youth; the introduction to and commentary on Aristotle's *Categories,* which played an important part in the development of medieval logic; the introduction (*Isagoge*) in a Latin translation by the Christian philosopher Boethius became a standard medieval textbook. Porphyry's great work *Kata Christianon* ("Against the Christians") was condemned to be burned in 448 and only fragments survive, from which it is clear that it was a scholarly and intelligent attack on Christianity. Fragments survive also of a

PORPHYRY

work *Peri agalmaton* ("On Images") and of the *Peri tes ex logion philosophias* ("Philosophy from Oracles"), which may be identical with the work referred to frequently by St. Augustine as *De regressu animae* ("On the Return of the Soul"). Some fragments of the *Symmikta zetemata* ("Various Investigations") also survive.

2. Philological: *Homerika zetemata* (*Quaestiones Homericae*); *Peri tou en Odysseia ton nymphon antrou* (*De antro nympharum*), an example of the allegorical interpretation of Homer.

3. Scientific: a commentary on Ptolemy's *Harmonica* (incomplete); an introduction (*Isagoge*) to Ptolemy's *Tetrabiblos* (or *Apotelesmatica*); *Pros Gauron*, a work on embryology, dedicated to Gaurus, formerly attributed to the physician Galen, but now generally agreed to be by Porphyry.

BIBLIOGRAPHY.—There is no complete edition of the works of Porphyry. Biography of Plotinus in all editions of the *Enneads* of Plotinus (*q.v.*); text with German translation and commentary by R. Harder, *Plotins Schriften*, vol. Vc, 2nd ed. (1958); *Sententiae* ed. by B. Mommert (1907); *Opuscula selecta*, containing *Vita Pythagorae, De antro nympharum, De abstinentia, Ad Marcellam* ed. by A. Nauck, 2nd ed. (1886); works on Aristotle's logic ed. by A. Busse, *Commentaria in Aristotelem graeca*, vol. 4, part 1 (1887); letter to Anebo in G. Parthey's edition of Iamblichus' *De mysteriis* (1857); fragments of work against Christians ed. by A. von Harnack in *Abhandlungen der Königlichen Preussischen Akademie der Wissenschaften*, philos.-hist. Klasse (1916) and in *Sitzungsberichte der Preussischen Akademie der Wissenschaften* (1921); fragments of the "Philosophy from Oracles" ed. by G. Wolff (1856) and *see* also J. J. O'Meara, *Porphyry's Philosophy from Oracles in Augustine* (1959); fragments of *Symmikta Zetemata* ed. by H. Dörrie (1959); *Homerika Zetemata* ed. by H. Schrader (1880–90); commentary on Ptolemy's *Harmonica* ed. by I. Düring (1932); introduction to Ptolemy's *Tetrabiblos* ed. by H. Wolf (1559) and *cf. Catalogus codicum astrologorum Graecorum*, vol. 5, part 4, pp. 190–228 (1940); *Pros Gauron* ed. by K. Kalbfleisch in *Anhang zu den Abhandlungen der koniglichen Akademie zu Wissenschaften zu Berlin* (1895) and French trans. by A. J. Festugière, *La Révélation d'Hermès Trismégiste*, vol. 3 (1953).

See also J. Bidez, *Vie de Porphyre* (1913; reprinted 1964); R. Beutler in Pauly-Wissowa, *Real-Encyclopädie der classischen Altertumswissenschaft*, vol. 22, col. 275–313 (1953). (A. H. Ag.)

PORPHYRY, a beautiful red or purplish rock used by the ancients for ornamental purposes when cut and polished. The name porphyry (Greek *porphyreds*, "purple") was derived from the older name porphyrites, which in the time of Pliny was applied to purplish and reddish rocks mottled with light spots. Although most of this material was of igneous (volcanic or shallow intrusive) origin, the early Italian sculptors erroneously considered it a variety of marble, of metamorphosed sedimentary origin. The famous red porphyry (*porfido rosso antico*) came from Egypt where it was used in sculpture. Its beauty and decorative value were recognized by the Romans in the time of the emperor Claudius. For a long time the knowledge of its source was lost, but the original locality of the ancient quarries was rediscovered on the west coast of the Red Sea, where it forms a dike 80 or 90 ft. thick.

In a dark-red groundmass, porphyry contains many small white or rose-red plagioclase feldspars, black shining prisms of hornblende, and small plates of iron oxide. The red of the feldspars and of the groundmass arises from the partial conversion of the plagioclase feldspar into thulite (*see* ZOISITE) and manganese epidote (*q.v.*). These minerals also occur in thin veins crossing the rock. Many specimens show effects of crushing, which in extreme cases has produced brecciation.

Applications of Term.—In petrography the term porphyry is used to designate an igneous rock characterized by abundant relatively large crystals (phenocrysts) set in a matrix or groundmass of fine-grained to amorphous (apparently without crystal structure) material. The porphyries belong to a larger group of rocks, all of which possess a porphyritic texture (phenocrysts and groundmass). Thus, all porphyries have a porphyritic texture, but by no means are all porphyritic rocks true porphyries. Most generally perhaps, the term porphyry is restricted to those porphyritic rocks in which the phenocrysts abound or predominate and which consolidated at shallow depths beneath the earth's surface (hypabyssal rocks). Hence, the true porphyries are most commonly found in sills, dikes, and other minor intrusive bodies. Not uncommonly, however, the term is also applied to certain highly

porphyritic volcanic rocks, which may resemble the intrusive porphyries.

In the United States the term porphyry is used chiefly in a textural sense. A simple and rather precise scheme is to modify the term by prefixing the common rock name which the porphyry most closely resembles chemically or mineralogically. Thus, granite porphyry, diorite porphyry, etc., are porphyries, compositionally equivalent to the plutonic (coarse-grained) rocks, granite, diorite, etc., respectively. Rhyolite porphyry and andesite porphyry, for example, correspond in composition respectively to the volcanic rocks rhyolite and andesite.

A distinction is to be made, however, between such terms as porphyritic granite and granite porphyry. The former is a true granite; that is, its texture is phaneritic (constituent grains visible without magnification). The latter is not a granite, because its groundmass is aphanitic (constituent grains indiscernible without magnification). A similar distinction is to be made between such terms as porphyritic rhyolite and rhyolite porphyry. Generally the porphyritic rhyolite has a higher proportion of groundmass, which is in itself finer grained or richer in glassy constituents, than the rhyolite porphyry.

The early petrographers (particularly in Europe), in their studies of porphyries and related hypabyssal rocks, placed great emphasis upon the mineral composition of the large crystals, the geologic age of the rocks, and the degree to which the rock had been altered. As a result a very complex and confusing nomenclature evolved. Some petrographers prefer to restrict the term porphyry to those types in which the large crystals are principally feldspar (with or without quartz) and to place those types with abundant, large crystals of olivine, pyroxene, amphibole, and mica under the lamprophyres.

It is the general practice outside the United States to subdivide the highly porphyritic rocks with an aphanitic groundmass into two classes. Those in which potash feldspar is dominant are called the true porphyries, whereas the plagioclase feldspar types are called porphyrites. The porphyries, under this scheme, are essentially equivalent compositionally to the granites, syenites, and nephelite syenites, whereas the porphyrites are compositional equivalents of the diorites and gabbros. In the United States the term porphyrite is nearly obsolete.

Origin.—Theories of origin of porphyries are manifold, and it is highly probable that different porphyries have formed in equally different ways. Many porphyries may have had an interruption in their course of crystallization. The phenocrysts may have formed largely at depth (intratelluric crystals), where cooling of the magma (molten rock material) proceeded slowly, permitting the growth of large scattered crystals. Before complete congelation, however, the magma, with its suspended crystals, was erupted to higher levels and injected as dikes and sills into colder rocks. The cooling effect upon these thin injected sheets was so marked that the liquid phase was rapidly transformed to a fine-grained or aphanitic groundmass.

In other porphyries the large crystals may have developed mainly subsequent to injection. Certain minerals may have developed well-formed crystals before the viscosity of the melt increased sufficiently to retard and restrict diffusion. Changes in pressure on the magma and the loss of dissolved volatiles may have contributed to the formation of porphyritic textures. The role of certain trace elements in controlling crystal growth rates is of possible importance and needs further investigation. Inoculation and incorporation of foreign crystals may explain the porphyritic character of some rocks. (For processes of crystallization *see* GEOCHEMISTRY: *Geochemistry of the Lithosphere*.)

Occurrences.—Porphyries occur abundantly as dikes and sills, satellitic to larger masses of compositionally equivalent plutonic rock. Thus, granite porphyry and quartz porphyry are exceedingly common in regions where granitic intrusive rocks occur. Nephelite- and leucite-rich porphyries, though rare, are associated with larger intrusions of nephelite syenite and leucite syenite. Diorite porphyries (porphyrites) accompany plutonic masses of diorite. Coextensive masses of porphyry may extend as veinlike projections and offshoots from larger parent masses of plutonic rock.

Some porphyries, furthermore, appear as marginal phases of the larger intrusions. In such cases the plutonic masses and associated porphyries were probably derived from a common magma.

See A. Johannsen, *A Descriptive Petrography of the Igneous Rocks*, vol. iii (1937).　　　　　　　　　　　　　　　　(C. A. Cn.)

PORPOISE, the common name often applied to any of the smaller, round-muzzled toothed whales, but properly restricted to the genus *Phocaena.* Porpoises, along with dolphins and whales, are included in the mammalian order Cetacea. There is no sharp scientific distinction between porpoises and dolphins, but, generally speaking, the porpoise is smaller and does not have the characteristic beak nose of the dolphin. In North America "porpoise" is generally used to indicate the bottle-nosed dolphin (*see* Dolphin).

Like most other mammals, these superficially fishlike forms breathe air directly and bear live young which they suckle. The adult porpoises mate in late summer, and the female bears a single calf, almost a yard long, in about a year. Their life expectancy has been estimated at 30 years. Porpoises feed on schooling fish, such as herring and mackerel, as well as on squid and other marine animals.

The wide mouth is bounded by stiff, immobile lips, and the underjaw projects slightly. The teeth number between 80 and 100. In colour, the porpoise is black or dark gray above and white below, with black flippers. A single dorsal fin is triangular in shape and low.

The common, or harbour, porpoise (*Phocaena phocaena*) attains a length of 4–6 ft. It prefers coastal waters to the open sea and inhabits the North Atlantic area, entering the Baltic in summer; it is rare in the Mediterranean. A distinct form of the common porpoise appears in the Black Sea; one or two other species are found in the South Atlantic. The Pacific porpoise is a distinct species. The black finless porpoise (*Neophocaena phocaenoides*) inhabits the warm coastal waters of the Indian Ocean.

Porpoise has been used for food—the flesh resembles pork but has an odour somewhat disagreeable to most persons. The oil obtained from the soft fat of the head and jaw of the common porpoise has been used as a lubricant in the manufacture of watches, clocks, and other delicate mechanisms made of hard steel. The value of the oil lies chiefly in the fact that it is free from a tendency either to gum or thicken by oxidation, or to corrode metal, and in its ability to withstand exposure to very low temperatures without freezing or thickening to any great extent. The oil was also formerly used in lamps. *See also* Whale.　　　(K. P. S.; X.)

PORPORA, NICOLA ANTONIO (1686–1768), Italian opera composer and singing teacher, was born at Naples on Aug. 17, 1686. His first three operas were produced at Naples; others followed in Rome, Vienna, and Venice. He taught in Naples and Venice: among his pupils were the celebrated *castrati* Antonio Uberti (known as "Porporino"), Farinelli, and Caffarelli, and the poet and librettist Pietro Metastasio. After visiting Vienna in 1725 Porpora settled for a while in Venice where he taught at the Ospedale degli Incurabili, a famous music school for girls. In 1733 he went to London as a rival to Handel and as chief composer of the "Opera of the Nobility" at the theatre in Lincoln's Inn Fields and at the King's Theatre in the Haymarket. While in London he wrote five operas, among them *Polifemo, Davide e Bersabea,* and *Ifigenia in Aulide,* with parts for his remarkable pupil Farinelli. In 1737 he was teaching at Venice and two years later at Naples, where he also produced two comic operas. In 1747 he taught singing at Dresden and the following year was appointed *Kapellmeister* there. Later he was at Vienna where he gave composition lessons to the young Haydn. He died in poverty at Naples on March 3, 1768.　　　　　　　　　　(Cs. Ch.)

PORRES, SAINT MARTÍN DE (1579–1639), the Peruvian national patron of social justice, was born in Lima, the illegitimate son of a noble Spaniard, Don Juan de Porres, and a Negro woman, Ana Velázquez. As a youth, he was taken by his father to Ecuador and placed in school there. When official duties transferred the father to Panama, the boy returned to the care of his mother in Lima, and the remainder of his life was spent in that city.

When he was about 15 years old, Martín was apprenticed to a barber surgeon. In 1601 he became a Dominican oblate, his first duties being to care for the sick friars in the monastery of Santo Domingo. It was not customary at that time to permit a mulatto to enter a religious order in Peru, but because of the exceptional qualities and virtue exhibited by Martín, he was ordered to become a lay brother in the Dominican Order in 1610. As a friar, Martín was noted for his kindness to all persons but especially to the poor and the unfortunate; animals also found in him a friend of rare understanding. His greatest sympathy was won by the youth of Lima, for whom he established an asylum and a school, considered by some to be his monument. He died on Nov. 3, 1639, was beatified in 1837, and canonized in 1962; his feast is celebrated on Nov. 5.

See Cyril Martindale, *Blessed Martín de Porres* (1920).
　　　　　　　　　　　　　　　　　　　(A. S. Tr.)

PORSON, RICHARD (1759–1808), one of the greatest of English classical scholars, was born on Dec. 25, 1759, at East Ruston, Norfolk, the son of a weaver. The vicar of the parish recognized his promise, gave him tuition, and interested the local gentry in him, so that he was able to go to Eton (1774) and subsequently to Trinity College, Cambridge (1778), of which he became fellow in 1782. In 1792 his fellowship came to an end, because he was unwilling to fulfill the statutory requirement of taking holy orders within seven years of his M.A. degree and the master of Trinity declined to appoint him to a lay fellowship which he had reason to expect. When his fellowship ceased his friends subscribed enough to produce an annuity of £100, and later in the same year he was appointed to the professorship of Greek at Cambridge, which then carried a salary of £40 and was virtually a sinecure.

From 1792 Porson lived in London, in chambers in the Temple. Among his friends was James Perry, editor of the *Morning Chronicle,* to which Porson contributed anti-governmental lampoons and *jeux d'esprit,* and in 1796 he married Perry's sister, Mrs. Mary Lunan. She died a few months after the marriage. For the last two years of his life Porson was for the first time in easy circumstances, with his appointment in 1806 as librarian to the London Institution with a salary of £200. He died in London on Sept. 15, 1808, and was buried in the chapel of Trinity College, Cambridge.

Porson drank to excess, was addicted to late hours, took no care of his health or his appearance, and could be rude and boorish in company. But there was an attractive, even a noble, side to his character. His friends delighted in his wit and learning and his store of anecdotes and quotations and admired him for his devotion to truth, his indifference to worldly success, and his readiness to communicate his knowledge. He had a remarkable memory, a love of literature ancient and modern, and a gift for satire and parody. But he was content for the most part to devote his talents to Greek scholarship (*see* Classical Scholarship).

His earliest interest was Aeschylus. Shortly after taking his degree he began work on an edition, but the project was abandoned. In 1792, however, he arranged for an edition to be printed by Andrew Foulis of Glasgow. In 1795 Foulis published a folio edition from his text without his consent, and in 1806 after long delays Porson grudgingly agreed to the publication of the octavo edition. His notes on the Suda lexicon were published as an appendix to the 1790 edition of J. Toup's *Emendationes in Suidam.* In the same year appeared the *Letters to Mr. Archdeacon Travis in Answer to His Defence of the Three Heavenly Witnesses, 1 John v. 7,* the substance of which had already appeared in the *Gentleman's Magazine.* In these letters, written with wit and polemical vigour as well as learning, Porson effectively demolished the case which Travis had put for the authenticity of a verse now universally acknowledged to be interpolated. In 1797 he published his edition of the *Hecuba,* intended as the first volume of a complete Euripides. In fact only three more plays were published, the *Orestes* in 1798, the *Phoenissae* in 1799, and the *Medea* in 1801. A second edition of the *Hecuba,* with an important supplement to the preface, appeared in 1802.

Porson was the most brilliant of the English school of scholars who, following where Richard Bentley had pointed the way, devoted themselves to the task of freeing the Greek texts from corruption. His work, though limited in range and in quantity, has a quality which raises him above his contemporaries. His special strength lay in his insight into Greek metre, his skill in emendation, and his appreciation of the niceties of Attic diction. In the preface to the *Hecuba* he threw new light on the metres of Greek drama, and in particular enunciated "Porson's law," which forbids a break in the fifth foot of the iambic senarius after a long syllable (*see* PROSODY, CLASSICAL). As a textual critic he combined brilliance with carefulness, and many of his emendations have been accepted. He was scrupulously honest and interested only in discovering the truth; while he did not ignore manuscript evidence, he was mainly guided by his sense, at once instinctive and based on careful study, of Greek usage and versification. His work is marked by a sureness of touch and economy of expression which give the impression of effortless ease and conceal the learning and hard work which lay behind it.

Porson took a delight in calligraphy and was specially interested in Greek script. The admirably clear and readable Greek type which bears his name was long used by the English university presses.

BIBLIOGRAPHY.—Reviews and minor works ed. by T. Kidd, *Tracts and Miscellaneous Criticisms of Richard Porson* (1815), which contains bibliography of his works, including publications of other scholars to which he contributed notes; unpublished notes and emendations ed. by J. H. Monk and C. J. Blomfield, *Adversaria* (1812), and by P. P. Dobree, *Notae in Aristophanem* (1820). *Correspondence* ed. by H. R. Luard (1867). *See also* J. S. Watson, *Life of Porson* (1961); M. L. Clarke, *Richard Porson* (1937), with bibliographies; D. L. Page, "Richard Porson," *Proceedings of the British Academy,* vol. xlv (1960).

(M. L. CE.)

PORT, a place where goods, passengers, and mail are transferred to, from, or between carriers of the same or different modes. In this article, the term is confined to places where carriers by water, either ocean, inland, or both, are involved. Nearly all ports include portions of one or more harbours where the configuration of the shore, either naturally or with artificial improvement, offers protection to vessels. A harbour may serve a single port or, as in the case of a large harbour such as San Francisco Bay, several ports, or, as in the cases of London, Chicago, and Sydney, several harbours may serve one port. Ports are gateways leading to and from inland areas, or hinterlands, connecting them with other areas, sometimes called forelands, by means of ocean and inland waterway carriers. Associated with the waterfront terminals are complexes of services and facilities ashore, such as local roads, railway terminals, ship repair facilities, and numerous offices concerned with the operation and maintenance of vessels and the movements of cargoes and passengers, all of which are also included within port areas. Many industries located in and near the port areas are wholly or largely dependent upon the port for receipt of raw materials and fuels and for shipment of their products; other industries and commercial establishments depend upon a port-related labour force as part of their markets. Because all of these activities require large labour forces in or near the port areas, ports are usually associated with cities.

The primary objective of port development and operation is to move traffic through the port quickly and economically. Other things being equal, large ports, with a greater variety of routes and services, will offer the shipper greater frequency of ship sailings and will generate sufficient traffic to justify a larger number of calls by vessels. The volumes of cargo and of ship services, therefore, are reciprocally related, and the larger and more efficient ports, because of economies of scale, tend to grow more rapidly than smaller ones with traffic volumes less able to justify the efficiency and variety of services and facilities. An important measure of port efficiency is "turnaround time": the time a vessel or a shipment spends in port. In the case of a vessel, this includes the time required for it to move from the harbour entrance to its berth, to process the various documents associated with the movement of the vessel and its cargo and passengers, to take on fuel and load, and to proceed out of the harbour on its return or subsequent leg of its voyage; in the case of cargo, the turnaround time is the time required for the shipment to arrive at and depart from the port area. A port with a good harbour and with adequate physical equipment and services will attract traffic from a hinterland that is also served by competitive ports even though inland distances and rates may be somewhat disadvantageous. In many industrialized and urbanized regions, such as northwestern and central Europe and the northeastern United States, port competition is intense, and to secure an increasing share of the traffic many port organizations maintain extensive trade development and promotional activities, as well as staffs to protect and enhance their competitive position with respect to inland and overseas rate structures and services.

Port Location.—The location of a port is a major consideration with regard to its economic functions. Geographers consider location in terms of site and situation. Site refers to the characteristics of the area occupied by the port, including the harbours and adjacent landward areas occupied by the port functions; situation refers to the relations of the port location to the hinterland and to overseas areas or forelands with which the port has connections.

Site.—Among the important site characteristics of a port are the existence of adequate protection from the fetch of waves and wind across open water, an entrance sufficiently wide and deep for the largest vessels expected to use the port, a sufficient depth of water in the harbour to permit use by vessels of deep draft, a climate that does not present unusual difficulties, and shorelines and nearby land areas that are sufficiently level and with adequate topographic and foundation conditions for landward access and for building foundations. Few ports have all of these characteristics, but in many instances extensive modification of the natural conditions is possible by dredging, building of protective breakwaters, and extension of land areas by artificial fill, or leveling and excavation of land areas. As the average draft of vessels increases and a higher proportion of the world's ships are of deeper draft, ports must either resign themselves to decline as they become accessible to fewer vessels, with increasing concentration at fewer but deeper harbours, or they must engage in extensive and expensive dredging and harbour extension projects, which, in many instances, cannot be justified by the potential traffic. Most modern ports used by oceangoing ships have minimum depths of 32 to 40 ft. (9.8 to 12.2 m.) at low tide in their entrance channels and alongside their principal terminals. A typical 12,000-ton dry-cargo vessel will have a draft, fully loaded, of about 30 to 34 ft. (9.1 to 10.4 m.); while by the end of the 1960s supertankers were in operation with loaded drafts of nearly 80 ft. (24.4 m.) with larger vessels in prospect. In entrance channels and harbours, an additional 1 to 5 ft. (0.3 to 1.5 m.) must be allowed under the vessel's keel to allow for squat and roll.

The simplest type of harbour is an open roadstead in which the shoreline provides little or no protection from winds and waves. Where the direction of the winds and waves is rather constant, an open roadstead to the lee is usable most or all of the time; among examples of this type are many ports on the west coasts of South America and Africa. When strong winds or heavy seas from other than an offshore direction occur, vessels must "lay to" and are not free to load or discharge. At most open roadsteads loading and discharge of cargo is done by means of lighters and of passengers by tenders, small shallow-draft vessels that have access to wharves with insufficient depth alongside to accommodate the larger vessels. The use of lighters and tenders involves extra time, expense, and handling; if substantial volume of traffic develops at such a port it becomes necessary eventually to seek an alternative location for the port or to provide an artificially protected harbour by construction of breakwaters. Both of these alternatives were utilized in the 1960s with the substitution of a breakwater-protected harbour at Tema for the open roadstead at Takoradi in Ghana, and of the new port of Ashdod for the open roadstead at Tel Aviv in Israel.

With the development of supertankers of 100,000 to 300,000 tons and more, it became impracticable to provide harbours with adequate depth in many areas; open roadsteads are used, connected to shore by submarine pipelines from vessels tied up to pilings or other offshore structures, as in many of the Persian Gulf ports. The opening up of the oil fields of northern Alaska and the prospect of direct supertanker movements to East and West Coast ports of the United States in the 1970s, together with the demonstrated dangers of oil pollution of the ocean waters, focused much research on the potentialities and limitations of offshore terminals, while the growth in size of dry-bulk vessels in the ore, grain, and coal trades stimulated investigation of the possibility of new types of offshore loading and unloading facilities, far from shore on the continental shelves. Experiments with the use of helicopters for transfer of cargoes between ship and shore, in connection with military operations in Vietnam and elsewhere, demonstrated that, while such transfers are technically possible, the high cost prevents their use commercially.

A more promising possibility for direct offshore cargo interchange independent of shore-based facilities along coastlines is in the LASH (lighter-aboard-ship) concept, in which barges, collecting and distributing cargoes along inland waterways and coastwise, are lifted aboard oceangoing ships tied up offshore. Such transfers do not require direct access to port facilities, while the barges make available direct access to river ports, as along the Mississippi and Rhine systems from such ports as New Orleans and Rotterdam, Neth., respectively. With several major shipping companies developing extensive fleets of oceangoing ships and barges designed to be loaded into them, the competitive threat to major ports handling large volumes of general cargo and located at or near the lower reaches of extensive river systems was clearly evident late in the 1960s.

Many ports are located on rivers, and on estuaries, the lower portions of river valleys that have been drowned by geological changes in the relative levels of land and sea. In the case of estuaries with relatively narrow entrances and wide expanse, such as Chesapeake Bay in the U.S., the tides are distributed throughout the estuary so that the daily tidal range is small and adaptation of shoreside terminal facilities is relatively simple. Where the estuary is funnel-shaped with a wide entrance and gradually narrows, as in the case of many of the estuaries of the British Isles and northwestern Europe as well as the Bay of Fundy, the tides are accentuated. The great tidal range at such ports, augmented by irregularities of river levels, necessitates the provision of various devices to keep a relatively constant level between the vessels and the shoreside facilities. Similarly, inland river ports, as along the Mississippi River and many of its tributaries, require special facilities to minimize the effects of wide fluctuations in river level. At ports such as London and Liverpool, Eng.; Le Havre, France; and Antwerp, Belg., large artificial basins are provided, separated from the estuary by locks. These basins can be constructed economically only where the shores are relatively low and where soft unconsolidated materials permit easy excavation for dock construction. These basins, or "wet docks," are connected to the estuary by locks, usually having two sets of gates that permit the water level within the basin to be constant, while the level within the lock can be raised and lowered, permitting vessel movement between the constant level within the basin or dock and the fluctuating level of the estuary or river. If the lock gate is single, vessels can move in or out of the basin only when the water level of the river or estuary is the same as the level of water in the basin. The provision of basins is also necessary where a large tidal range or river flow induces strong currents; at Liverpool, Eng., with a rise of 27 ft. (8.2 m.) currents with velocities up to 6 knots occur; this condition would make the handling of cargo at an open wharf a difficult operation. Because of delays in movement of vessels in and out of the basins, many estuary ports that handle substantial volumes of passenger, mail, and express freight traffic have, in addition to the terminal facilities along the margins of the basins, landing stages or floating terminals outside the basins. These facilities, connected to the shore by means of ramps or bridges, maintain a constant level relative to the vessels. Among the best known are the St. Pauli landing stage at Hamburg, Ger.; the Princes landing stage at Liverpool; and the passenger landing stage at Tilbury near London. Similar floating structures, known

as wharf boats, are utilized in rivers where the fluctuations in water level are great, as along the Ohio and Mississippi rivers, where many of the major barge terminals are on floating structures.

Many ports on rivers and canals, where the changes in water level are not great, are provided with artificial basins not separated by locks from the river or canal. These are called tidal, or outer, basins, and are entered directly from the river, since the water level in the basin is the same as that of the river. Commonly their entrances are so located as to enable vessels to enter or leave without the necessity of turning sharply, thereby minimizing or eliminating the use of tugs. Among ports of this type are Rotterdam, Neth.; Hamburg and Bremen, Ger.; Glasgow, Scot.; Manchester, Eng.; and Stockton, Calif., as well as many of the barge ports along the Rhine such as Düsseldorf, Duisburg-Ruhrort, Ger.; and Basel, Switz.

Marginal wharves parallel to the shore are characteristic of many ports; among those accessible to oceangoing ships are New Orleans and Albany, N.Y., the former in the lower reach of a river and the latter at the inland head of navigation for oceangoing ships. With the increasing size of vessels and the need for faster turnarounds, vastly increased volumes of cargo can be handled with fewer ships, so that the amount of available land area per berth is becoming more important than the length of berthage available for vessels. As a result, the long narrow "finger" piers, characteristic of many of the older portions of ports—especially such U.S. ports as Boston, New York, Philadelphia, and San Francisco—are rapidly disappearing, to be replaced by marginal wharves, which make more extensive land areas available adjacent to the ship berths, for receiving, sorting, and storage of goods. Commonly this situation has intensified the need for relocation of the port facilities away from the congested and older portions of cities, in favour of locations on the urban peripheries, where more extensive land areas are available for terminals, port-associated industries, and access and circulation by motor trucks and railway cars, as well as for "tank farms" for storage of liquid bulk commodities. Thus, the old piers of Manhattan in New York City have become the sites of shoreline redevelopment projects, not directly associated with the port, on landfill, while the Port of New York Authority has developed extensive terminal facilities in other parts of the metropolitan area, most notably in New Jersey at Port Newark and Elizabeth. Similarly, in the 1960s the Port of San Francisco declined relative to Oakland, across the bay, where more extensive land areas were available. The growth of unitized cargo handling, and particularly containers, gave many of the larger ports the opportunity to develop extensive new facilities at some distance from the older installations close to the centres of the respective port cities.

Many ports have been developed where no natural harbours existed, or where they were far from adequate to handle the vessel traffic. Artificial breakwaters protect the installations and provide shelter for vessels. Such ports include Long Beach, Calif.; Marseilles, France; Naples and a major part of the harbour of Genoa, Italy; and many of the Great Lakes ports, including Chicago, Calumet Harbor, Milwaukee, and Cleveland. In some instances, locations well situated with regard to traffic-generating hinterlands but lacking suitable natural harbours have become the sites of important ports as the result of construction of completely artificial harbours.

Large ports commonly include combinations of several of the above types of harbour configurations. The Port of New York, for example, includes development along several rivers and bays with piers, slips, marginal wharves, and artificial basins; London has a number of wet docks or basins in addition to landing stages and marginal wharves along the Thames.

Situation.—The situation of a port refers to its location relative to the port hinterland and to the open waters of the sea, lake, or river that provides access to its foreland. Since ships and inland waterway barges are the most economical form of transportation for most goods, it has been advantageous to carry the goods for the maximum possible distance by water on the largest possible vessel, assuming the volume of traffic is sufficient to justify employment of large vessels. Ports therefore have tended to develop as far inland as large vessels could operate. An additional advantage is that an inland port can command a hinterland in every direction. For these reasons many of the major ports of the world have been developed at considerable distances from the sea, in spite of the necessity to improve or construct and maintain canals and channels leading from the sea to the port. Houston, Tex., and Manchester are connected to the sea by artificial ship canals; Albany is at the head of a 143-mi. (230 km.) artificially deepened channel in the Hudson River. The St. Lawrence Seaway was constructed to open up a waterway to Chicago and Duluth, each more than 1,000 mi. (1,600 km.) from tidewater and over 2,000 mi. (3,200 km.) from the ocean.

With the significantly greater drafts of oceangoing vessels that were developed during the later 1960s, and subsequently particularly with the large supertankers and dry-bulk carriers, many ports found themselves accessible to only a decreasing proportion of the world's ocean ships because of dimensional restrictions, particularly depths, in the channels connecting them to the sea and alongside the terminals. Development of higher-speed and more sophisticated, and hence more costly, general cargo vessels, including ships designed for the transportation of containerized cargo, together with rapidly increasing costs of shipboard and shoreside labour, increasingly emphasized in the 1970s the advantages of fast turnaround. Many ports in inland locations and reached by channels requiring slow vessel speeds, particularly around bends and through bridges, were in the 1960s disadvantaged in the competition for calls by the larger ships. With improvements in land transportation, the economies of scale achieved by use of fewer but larger and more efficient ports, and the competitive pressures to maximize the utilization of the ships, the handicaps of inland port location were increased, and many port installations were developed seaward of the older ones. In many instances, the new locations had the additional advantage of more extensive land areas for port-associated facilities and industries. A noteworthy example is Europoort, seaward from the older portions of the Port of Rotterdam. Europoort handles very large tankers and bulk carriers, in a location close to the entrance to the New Waterway, a distributary of the Rhine, while the older Port of Rotterdam with its numerous basins 15 mi. (24.1 km.) inland continues to handle the general cargo liners, which are generally smaller, and the transatlantic passenger ships. Hook of Holland, also close to the sea, is the location of the terminals for the "short sea" ferries connecting with England. This complex of ports, together, handled the heaviest volume of traffic, both seaborne and on inland waterways, in the world, having surpassed the Port of New York in the early 1960s.

Many ports some distance inland have outports closer to the sea, and commonly, if the respective ports are separated by sufficient distance, twin cities tend to develop. Hamburg, Ger., for example, has an outport, Cuxhaven, at the North Sea entrance to the Elbe, serving vessels for which fast turnaround is important or whose draft does not permit them to proceed upstream to Hamburg; similarly Bremerhaven, Ger., at the entrance to the Weser, serves as the seaward outport for Bremen. Much of London's container ship and passenger liner traffic is handled at Tilbury, about 30 mi. (48 km.) seaward. Although Houston, Tex., handled a considerable volume of cargo liner traffic in the late 1960s, Galveston remained a major port, and was seeking additional traffic, particularly for container ships which require fast turnaround. The development of Albany did not have any major effects upon the Port of New York. The St. Lawrence Seaway, with draft restrictions of 25 ft. 9 in. (7.85 m.), was not usable by many of the larger cargo and passenger vessels, which continued to turn around at Montreal; and the Great Lakes ports, reached through the Seaway, were increasingly disadvantaged as vessel drafts continued to increase. With improvements in railway service, including fast piggyback (motor truck trailers on flatcars) and container trains, even Montreal had to compete with the ports of the Maritime Provinces, which have the dual advantage of location closer to the open sea and freedom from ice conditions in winter.

Functional Types of Ports and Terminal Facilities.—Ports may specialize in the handling of a single type of bulk cargo, such as an ore; in several bulk cargoes; in general cargo (merchandise); in passengers; or in combinations of any or all of these. Most major world ports are comprehensive, handling a variety of types of traffic, although the various facilities within the ports are specially designed for particular kinds of traffic.

General cargo consists of discrete packages or items, such as bales, boxes, crates, machines, etc., which vary in size, shape, and weight, and which require considerable labour in their handling.

From the 1960s on, a significant portion of the general cargo traffic came to be handled in standardized containers, with vessels especially designed to handle such containers either exclusively or in combination with "break bulk" general cargo handled by conventional means. Large container ships, handling 1,000 or more containers, operated in transatlantic and transpacific services, as well as between northwestern Europe and Australia, New Zealand, and Japan, serving a limited number of ports in each range or terminal region. Containers are transferred between shore and ship by means of specially designed cranes mounted on shipboard, or, more commonly, on the wharf; such cranes are extremely complex and can transfer between ship and shoreside truck or railway car as much as 2,000 tons of containerized cargo per hour. Modern container ships are typically turned around in a well-equipped port in a single working day, as contrasted with the conventional general cargo liner, with half the capacity, which may take a week or more to unload and load; the result is that a single container ship may replace the equivalent of four or more conventional general cargo ships. This acceleration of port turnaround time requires much more extensive land areas per ship berth than formerly, with much reduced demand for wharfage. The typical container ship berth requires from 15 to 25 ac. of land area to handle the cargo arriving at and departing from the terminal by motor truck or railway. Such extensive areas can usually only be acquired and developed at some distance from the older and more congested portions of the port cities. Furthermore, the investment in sophisticated ships and shoreside facilities and the need for fast turnaround result in concentration of container traffic in fewer ports than the older methods of general cargo handling required. As a result, many of the ports handling general cargo but not well located for rapid access and turnaround began to witness rapid decline or cessation of their general cargo traffic in the late 1960s. The reduction and dislocation of the port labour force became a serious problem in some port areas, and, following extensive strikes and negotiations, many agreements were made between port terminal operators and labour unions by which the workers received partial compensation for the economies in labour utilization achieved by the new method of cargo handling.

In spite of the rapid growth of containerization, many trade routes continued to be served primarily or exclusively by conventional "break of bulk" ships for general cargo, especially those serving developing regions where extensive capital investment in shoreside container terminal facilities might not be justified, or where landward connections by railway, highway, and inland waterway were not adapted to the handling of heavy container traffic.

Conventional methods of general cargo handling include sideport horizontal transfer between ship and shore by means of forklift trucks and other mechanical devices, or, more typically, by cranes and cargo booms operating vertically through hatches. In most European ports and overseas ports developed by Europeans, the cranes are typically onshore; while in the United States and Canadian ports and overseas ports developed by American interests, the cargo is generally handled by ships' gear, consisting of cargo booms and winches permitting both vertical and horizontal movement between wharf and ships' hold; the typical boom has a lift capacity of about five tons, and two booms may be operated simultaneously to double the lift capacity. The reasons for the distinction between European and American practices in the handling of general cargo are not clear, but they probably include the fact that many ports of northwestern Europe are served by inland waterway vessels that transfer cargo directly to and from ships, so that the ship's gear can work cargo over the water side of the vessel, while the shoreside cranes transfer cargo between ship and shoreside wharf. Also, many ports of the eastern United States were originally developed with their general cargo terminals supplied by private interests, including the railways, whereas European ports were developed by public authorities able to supply the capital for extensive shoreside mechanical cargo-handling equipment.

General cargo is typically handled in liner vessels, whether break-of-bulk, containerized, or mixed, as distinguished from tramp vessels, which predominate in the bulk trades; liner vessels operate on regular routes between ports or ranges of ports, on regular schedules, and their services are available to all shippers. Important general cargo ports are served by many shipping lines connecting with many regions of the world. For example, the Port of New York had approximately 175 shipping lines in the early 1970s, New Orleans about 125, and Chicago and other Great Lakes ports about 50. Major ports typically have several competitive lines serving each of the more important regions with which it has traffic, so that the shipper using the port has frequent service and a choice of carriers. The auxiliary services associated with regular cargo liner operation constitute major parts of the economic base of port cities.

Ports that can offer, in addition to general cargo, bulk cargoes such as grain to fill out the unused space or weight capacity of liners offer additional inducements for liner services and may grow at the expense of ports not offering such bulk traffic; many cargo liners take advantage of the availability of bulk cargoes to "bottom out" their capacity, which may be available near scheduled departure time. Many general cargo piers and wharves at ports such as Boston, Philadelphia, Baltimore, New Orleans, Montreal, and Vancouver offer direct access to grain elevators by means of conveyor belts so that vessels can load grain at the same time that they load general cargo. In addition pipelines at some ports connect the general cargo berths with liquid bulk storage facilities so that vessels may load and discharge such commodities as vegetable oils concurrently with the loading or discharge of general cargo.

Bulk cargoes, in contrast with general cargoes, consist of commodities that can be handled by continuous flow, by means of pipes, chutes, conveyor belts, and other similar devices. Such cargoes are usually moved in privately owned vessels or in tramps, which do not operate on regular schedule but are chartered by the voyage or time in accordance with changing cargo demands. Bulk-carrying vessels may be "dry" bulkers, or tankers specializing in liquid bulk transportation, although many vessels by the early 1970s could be adapted to either type of commodity, depending upon the demand; tankers frequently engage in the grain trade when demand for liquid transportation is slack, and some "oil-ore" bulk vessels find economic employment as a result of their suitability to carry return loads, whereas if they were designed exclusively for dry or liquid bulk commodities, they would have to spend a substantial part of their time in ballast without producing revenue.

In many parts of the world, bulk-handling ports have been developed to serve centres that produce raw materials, foodstuffs, or fuels. If such centres are located inland, rail, pipeline, or highway connections are provided to transport the commodities to the port area. Many such ports handle single commodities, such as, for example, the many oil ports of the Persian Gulf area, some of which are pipeline terminals from which crude oil moves out in tankers, and others of which are refinery sites, from which petroleum products are transported by the tankers. Along the coasts of South America and Africa are many ports built to handle the outputs of individual mines or groups of plantations.

On the other hand, many industrial ports located in and near the major population centres and consuming regions serve specific industries, or they may serve many industries for receipt of raw materials and fuels and shipment of products. In the U.S., Gary and Burns Waterway Harbor, Ind., for example, are individual ports, each with its harbour, serving the steel mills adjacent to the harbours, in contrast to Duluth-Superior and Taconite Harbor, Minn., ports primarily shipping iron ores. At most bulk-receiving

industrial ports in the manufacturing areas, a high proportion of the traffic terminates at plants along the waterfront, requiring no further inland transportation prior to processing. Industrial establishments requiring direct waterfront access for transportation purposes generally need extensive land areas; most such plants have highly developed specialized facilities for large-scale handling of bulk commodities, and they are generally located beyond the highly built-up urban areas, or, in some instances, in locations where urbanization has spread to them.

The increasing size of bulk-carrying vessels, and particularly the great drafts, severely limited the number of ports at which they could call by the early 1970s. The huge supertankers carrying Middle Eastern oil around the Cape of Good Hope after the closing of the Suez Canal in 1956 could discharge in northwestern Europe only at a few ports, including particularly Bantry Bay, Ire., Milford Haven, Eng., and Europoort, Neth., and even those few ports could not be expected to deal with the generation of supertankers being planned in the early 1970s. Similarly, the prospect of exploitation of the oil resources of northern Alaska and the opening of the passage north of North America following the voyage of the tanker "Manhattan" in 1969 focused attention on the prospect that very large vessels might have to load and discharge far offshore, and thereby not be directly dependent upon shoreside terminals. General cargo as well as bulk cargoes carried in barges aboard LASH-type vessels, which began to operate commercially in 1970, furnish direct all-water access to inland river ports, with the loading and unloading of the barges aboard ship not dependent upon the facilities of the traditional ports. The possibility that such operations can be carried on offshore caused much concern to the major ports in the 1960s, and, by 1970, stimulated research on the developmental and ecological problems associated with offshore cargo handling, both with respect to effects upon traditional ports and the possibility of pollution of the waters of the continental shelves.

A special type of port, particularly characteristic of northwestern Europe but also common in the Mediterranean, in Japan, on the shores of Lake Michigan, and elsewhere, is the ferry or packet port. Such ports may be regarded essentially as "way stations" along land routes interrupted by short sea passages, and they may be located where sites are not especially favourable, but where minimization of the sea passage is critical. Many harbours at such ports are completely artificial, protected by breakwaters, as at Dover, Holyhead, Harwich, Eng., Calais, France, and elsewhere, and they have facilities especially designed for end-loading or side-port loading and discharge of automobiles and, in some instances, railway rolling stock, at all stages of the tide or river level.

Evolving from the vehicular and railway ferries, the oceangoing "Roll On-Roll Off" (RoRo) type of vessel was introduced on some routes in the 1960s. Some exclusively RoRo ships operate to Puerto Rico and elsewhere; others, including several in transatlantic service, combine RoRo with large capacity for containers. These vessels require special ramps for loading of trucks, truck trailers, and other wheeled vehicles that are driven aboard.

In 1968, cross-channel service by Hovercraft, operating on a cushion of air a short distance above the water, began between Dover, Eng., and Boulogne, France, and called for construction of "hoverports," with concrete ramps leading between the water and the terminal buildings, not unlike the loading ramps associated with airport terminals.

Hinterlands and Freight Rate Structures.—There usually is strenuous competition for the business of port hinterlands. The principal exceptions are those of ports that export bulk cargoes and were developed for the purpose of serving one or more inland establishments, such as mines, logging camps, plantations, etc. Each of the major industrialized regions of the world is served by many ports in competition with each other. The major factors determining the success or failure of a port to capture traffic of a competitive hinterland are the inland freight rates and services, the efficiency and costs of transfers within the port, and the availability of ship sailings to and from the port.

Few large ports can exist for very long if they handle only the traffic of their own metropolitan areas. Ports are gateways, and the cost and efficiency of inland transportation between port and hinterland are basic considerations. Even within the port city or metropolitan area the competition of other ports is often felt. For example, in the 1970s ports such as Philadelphia, Baltimore, and Boston had fewer scheduled liner services than New York. Often the same vessels called inbound at New York before, and outbound after, making calls at the other ports, with the result that those cities had difficulty in attracting shipments to and from their own metropolitan areas in competition with New York.

In such regions as North America and Western Europe that have extensive networks of inland transportation, many ports compete for the traffic of a common hinterland on the basis of relative inland rate advantage and quality of service. In many instances rates through "ranges" or groups of ports are equal, or nearly equal. For example, rates on many shipments to and from the midwestern United States are equal through North Atlantic ports from Canada to the Virginia capes, and these in turn are equalized with inland rates to and from southern Atlantic and Gulf of Mexico ports. Until 1963, Philadelphia, Baltimore, and other North Atlantic outports had inland rates below those through New York; earlier, rate equalization of these ports had been a major issue before regulatory bodies. Ocean liner rates are commonly equalized through all ports of a range, but ports within that range may have different inland rates. On the other hand, several ranges of ports may compete for the traffic of a common hinterland, as, for example, in the midwestern United States where ports of the Great Lakes, the North Atlantic range, and the Gulf Coast are in competition for the traffic. Similarly, in much of west-central Europe, ports of the Mediterranean and of the Bordeaux-Hamburg range are in competition with each other.

In addition to the basic inland rates by rail, highway, inland waterway, pipeline, and sometimes by air, there are many other cost items in which ports compete for traffic. For example, "free time," i.e., the number of days allowed by the inland carriers between arrival of the shipment at a port and the unloading from the railway car, truck, or barge before charges for storage or demurrage, may differ among the various ports. Costs of local cartage in the port area may vary. Stevedoring charges, for handling of goods between ship and shore, may vary, as may also the port dues assessed for use of the facilities and, in some countries, for maintenance of channels and other navigation facilities by the port authority. Some ports, such as portions of New York, have many of their terminals across water from their major hinterland areas, and the absorption of transfer or lighterage charges may be an important consideration in enabling such ports to compete with other ports not so disadvantaged. Another important element in the inland competitive rate structure is the availability of inland waterway transportation at some ports, tending to give the ports so favoured a rate advantage over those without the competitive waterway transportation, which may tend to force lower overland rates on routes paralleling the waterways.

Port Organization and Finance.—Many different types of organizations construct and operate ports and port terminals. Some ports are completely owned by governments; others are completely owned and operated by private industries to serve their own needs; still others represent combinations of public and private ownership and operation. In many instances, harbours are maintained and improved by public agencies while the shoreside terminals may or may not be publicly owned and operated. In the United States nearly all harbours and navigable waterways are improved and maintained by the federal government, with actual construction and maintenance carried on by the Army Corps of Engineers under congressional authorization and appropriation, either directly or by employment of civilian contractors. Provision of terminal facilities and maintenance of depths of water alongside is a local responsibility. In Canada many of the harbours are maintained by the Department of Transport, which also operates some terminal facilities although most are under private operation. In Great Britain there is a diversified pattern of ownership and operation, with some harbours and terminal facilities owned, maintained, and operated by public authorities, including, in some instances, the British Railways, and others by private interests; a proposal was made in 1969 to bring all of the operations at the larger ports of that country under the national government. The worldwide tendency during the 20th century has been to bring an increased proportion of the port and terminal facilities under public ownership and control.

Although most harbours in the United States are maintained and improved by the federal government, there is no uniform pattern with regard to the terminal facilities. In most of the larger ports, including New York, Boston, Philadelphia, Hampton Roads, New Orleans, Houston, San Francisco, Portland, and Seattle, as well as in such Great Lakes ports as Chicago, Cleveland, and Toledo, some terminal facilities are publicly owned and operated and others are under private ownership and management. In many ports, such as the larger ones on the Atlantic Coast, extensive waterfront facilities were developed by railroads that offered free or low-cost berthage to vessels that supplied the owner railroads with traffic, although in some ports, notably Boston and Baltimore, many of the railroad waterfront terminals had been taken over by public authorities by the early 1970s. In some instances, as at the ports of New York and Chicago, more than one public authority owns or operates port terminals.

Public authorities concerned with port development and operation may be national, state, and local governments, including counties and municipalities, or specially created port authorities that may or may not have general taxing powers within the port districts. Examples of municipally owned and operated facilities in the United States are those of the Milwaukee lakefront; in 1969 the San Francisco piers were transferred from state to municipal control. In 1968 the major lakefront terminals at Cleveland (Ohio) were transferred to a county port authority by the city. In New York, the Port of New York Authority owns many of the waterfront facilities, while the City of New York also owns some; many are leased to railroads, shipping companies, and private terminal operators. An example of a county-owned facility is that of Port Everglades, Fla., which competes with newly developed facilities nearby controlled by the City of Miami. Los Angeles and Long Beach have many municipal port terminal facilities, some of them leased for operation, while others are operated directly by the municipal authorities. Examples of state-owned port terminals are found in Mobile, Ala.; Wilmington and Morehead City, N.C.; Charleston and Brunswick, S.C.; and Hampton Roads, Va.

Public terminal facilities are rarely self-liquidating, but their construction and operation are usually justified by the indirect economic benefits to the local community, region, and nation. The deficits are charges against the tax base of the community, and the facilities are commonly financed by general obligation bonds backed by the faith and credit of the governments concerned. Some of the specialized public port authorities finance their facilities by revenue bonds that are retired by rentals to private operators or, in the case of direct public operation, by charges made against the traffic using the facilities; such charges may be absorbed by the carriers and not passed on directly to the shippers or passengers. One advantage of the specialized port authority, independent or partly independent of the general government, is its freedom to incur debts beyond the legal limit of the city, county, state, or national government for purposes of building, acquiring, leasing, and operating the facilities. In many instances the revenues of the port agencies are insufficient to cover amortization, interest, depreciation, operation, and maintenance expenses so that public subsidy is required. In other instances the port authority is really a general transportation authority, as in the case of the Port of New York Authority, which operates a variety of facilities not directly associated with maritime transportation, including airports, inland truck terminals, bridges, tunnels, a bus terminal, a rapid transit railway, and a large office building complex. That authority, created in 1921 by interstate compact, has many self-liquidating operations that have established its credit so that it can more easily finance its maritime terminal developments.

Port Labour.—Technological innovations in waterfront handling of general cargo and increased automation and efficiency in the handling of bulk cargoes had by the late 1960s substantially reduced the amount of labour required on the waterfronts, in spite of increased volumes of traffic at the larger ports. The land and site requirements for handling of ships and cargoes and for expeditious landward access to the port areas, furthermore, had produced shifts in the location of many of the port areas. The dislocations and reductions of the waterfront labour forces frequently met with resistance from the organizations representing longshoremen and other labour interests within the ports. In many instances, nationwide strikes involving several or many ports disrupted their operations. Much of the trouble springs from the casual nature of many of the port operations, and in some instances, as on the Great Lakes and in some Baltic ports, from seasonal closure of the ports in winter. Day-to-day fluctuations in demand for many types of waterfront labour are great, depending upon the volume of traffic to be handled. The development of containerization, which made possible through movement of goods between overseas and inland points with substantial reductions in the amount of goods handling at the ports, aggravated the dislocations of the labour force, with reductions in the ports adversely affected by the scale economies of the larger ones and the need for new and higher levels of skills, involving operation of complex equipment, at the larger and more successful ports. These conditions were reflected in the organization of the labour force into strong unions and in the regulation of hiring at many of the larger ports. Jurisdictional disputes among waterfront labour unions caused difficulties in many ports; in the New York port area the transfer of major general cargo handling from the older portions of the port to the new container terminals in New Jersey caused many adjustments in the labour force; similarly the development of modern cargo-handling facilities at Tilbury and the consequent reductions in the older docks of the Port of London caused serious dislocations, and strikes at Tilbury seriously retarded the introduction of container services at the latter location. On the Pacific Coast of the United States, the development of container traffic was possible on large scale only after agreement was reached for payment of some of the savings in handling costs into special funds maintained by the labour organizations, and in the New York area all shipments in containers originating less than 50 mi. from the waterfront were required to be reloaded within the port. There, as elsewhere, the effects upon the labour force of improved methods of cargo handling continued to be a major issue.

Port Planning.—In major metropolitan areas with important port functions, a substantial part of the local and regional economic base is attributable directly and indirectly to the existence of the port. It follows, therefore, that the accommodations of the demands of the port activities to the other elements of the industrial and commercial patterns of the port cities constitute a challenge to city planners. In many cities, the changing requirements of the ports have permitted the release of much centrally located waterfront land for new uses not directly associated with port activities, and the determination of the best uses of such waterfront areas in the light of the total city pattern is a matter of great concern. In Manhattan, downtown Boston, Philadelphia, Baltimore, Jacksonville, and many other port cities, the movement of major port activities from central to peripheral areas has opened up space for spectacular redevelopment of strategically located downtown sites for waterfront parks, civic centres, and apartment house developments. On the other hand, the increasing demand for extensive areas on the peripheries of cities to accommodate the modern efficient terminals for both bulk and general cargoes demands that the areas to be devoted to such terminals and to the port-associated industries be properly related to metropolitan-wide traffic circulation facilities, local transportation of the labour force between areas of residence and of employment, access by railway and truck to the waterfront terminals and to the hinterland, and, in many instances, resolution of the conflict between the demands for scarce waterfront land on the part of port-associated activities and other uses, such as park, boulevard, and residential. Port planning is an integral part of city and metropolitan planning, and coordination between the port authorities and the general city, metropolitan, and regional planning bodies has become essential.

In most developing nations, national planning of the ports is essential in order to maximize the utilization of the scarce national resources. In the more urbanized and industrialized nations, national planning of ports is carried on in some instances, and in others it is resisted. In Great Britain, where some of the ports are under control of the railways, a national organization, many of the larger ports are under special *ad hoc* bodies, such as the Port of London Authority, although there were, in the late 1960s, several proposals for nationalization of the larger ports. In the United States, Congress authorizes improvements of individual waterways and channels serving the ports, but there has not been study of the total number, sizes, and locations of the ports required to serve the national interest; and proposals for overall studies of the national port requirements have been strongly resisted by such organizations as the American Association of Port Authorities, which advocates competitive development. The increasing emphasis upon fast turnaround in handling of general cargo and cargo liner vessels, including container ships, the increasing size of ships and deeper channel requirements in the bulk trades, and the extensive financial requirements of modern terminals all indicate that many of the smaller and less efficient ports may become redundant; on the other hand, efficient terminal facilities may so reduce the costs of transfers between large ships and smaller carriers by water, land, and air that small ports may benefit from "feeder" services, including LASH-type ship-barge movements, while improved highways and inland waterways will spread the benefits of increased port efficiency widely into the hinterlands. The extent of concentration of port activities and the problems of adjustment to changes of scale and location of them constitute major challenges to the carriers, local and national governments, and the users of the transportation services.

BIBLIOGRAPHY.—*Ports of the World* (annual); *Jane's Freight Containers* (annual); M. L. Fair, *Port Administration in the United States* (1954); G. G. Weigend, "Some Elements in the Study of Port Geography," *Geographical Review*, vol. 48, no. 2, pp. 185–200 (April 1958); A. H. J. Brown, C. A. Dove, and E. S. Tooth, *Port Operation and Administration*, 2nd ed. (1960); G. Alexandersson and G. Norström, *World Shipping: an Economic Geography of Ports and Seaborne Trade* (1963); R. B. Oram, *Cargo Handling and the Modern Port* (1965); W. P. Hedden, *Mission: Port Development* (1967); R. H. Gilman, "Cargo Handling," *Scient. Am.*, vol. 219, no. 4, pp. 80–88 (Oct. 1968).
(H. M. M.)

PORTA, GIACOMO DELLA (*c.* 1537–1602), Italian architect whose work represents the development in style from late mannerism to early Baroque, was born and died at Rome. He was the chief Roman architect during the latter third of the 16th century. Della Porta continued two of Michelangelo's greatest architectural projects, the Piazza del Campidoglio and St. Peter's in the Vatican at Rome, whose dome, with a more pointed profile than Michelangelo intended, became the prototype of the Baroque dome. In a similar manner the facade he added to Giacomo da Vignola's church of Il Gesù at Rome was the model for the typical Baroque church facade.   (D. R. Cn.)

PORT ADELAIDE: *see* ADELAIDE.

PORTALES, DIEGO JOSÉ VICTOR (1793–1837), Chilean politician and *caudillo*, was born at Santiago on June 26, 1793. By 1824 he had built a profitable commercial firm that held a monopoly on tobacco in return for servicing a public loan contracted in England. When the Chilean government abrogated his contract, he threw himself into politics as an ultraconservative. In 1830 the conservative Joaquín Prieto became president, but Portales as chief minister ruled from behind the scenes and identified the objectives and defined the methods of the new power elite. He speedily silenced his liberal opponents, forced the military to submit to civilian dominance, and reestablished Chile's credit standing abroad. The constitution of 1833, which reflected his political doctrines, created a highly centralized state controlled by and for the landed oligarchy and the Roman Catholic Church. It provided 60 years of social stability and political order unequaled in Latin America. In 1836 he forced war on the Peru-Bolivian confederation in order to distract attention from his repressive domestic measures. He was assassinated at Valparaíso on June 6, 1837, while reviewing troops preparing to embark for Peru. Hated and feared alive, in death he became a hero around whom the Chilean people rallied to win the war in 1839. Chile then entered a period of aggressive nationalism and cultural flowering in the 1840s under Manuel Bulnes.

See also CHILE: *History.* (J. J. J.)

PORTALIS, JEAN ÉTIENNE MARIE (1746–1807), French lawyer and statesman, one of the chief architects of the *Code Civil*, was born at Bausset in Provence on April 1, 1746. He practised at the bar of Aix and in 1778–81 was one of the assessors or administrators of Provence. In November 1793, after the First Republic had been proclaimed, he came to Paris and was promptly imprisoned as the brother-in-law of Joseph Jérôme Siméon, the leader of the Federalists in Provence. Upon his release he resumed practice in the capital, but in 1795 was elected deputy to the *Conseil des Anciens,* later becoming its president. As a leader of the moderate party opposed to the Directory he was proscribed at the *coup d'état* of Fructidor, and escaped to Switzerland. In 1800, when Napoleon became first consul, he returned to Paris and was appointed by Napoleon a *conseiller d'état* and a member of the commission charged with the drawing up of the *Code Civil.* As this body's most industrious member, he sought to permeate the code with the ideas of Roman law; many of the most important titles, notably those on marriage and succession, are his work. (*See* FRENCH LAW: *The Civil Code* [1804].)

In 1801 he was placed in charge of *cultes,* or public worship, and was chiefly responsible for drawing up the provisions of the concordat between Napoleon and Pius VII. He entered the French Academy in 1806 and died in Paris on Aug. 25, 1807.

(L. N. B.)

PORT ARTHUR (LÜ-SHUN), city and naval base in Liaoning province, China, at the southern extremity of the Kwantung peninsula of Manchuria. On the only part of the Manchurian coast line that is ice-free throughout the year, it occupies a strong strategic position, commanding the entrance to Po-hai wan, a gulf of the Yellow sea. Until the Chinese-Japanese war of 1894–95 Port Arthur was the chief Chinese naval base. It fell in 1894 to Japan, which was, however, forced to return it to China under European pressure. Russia was anxious to obtain an ice-free port for its Pacific fleet, and the capture of Chiao-chou (Kiaochow) by the Germans in 1897 provided the occasion for Russian ships to occupy Port Arthur and the near-by commercial port of Dairen (*q.v.*). In 1898, by agreement, Russia acquired from China the entire Kwantung peninsula for 25 years and the right to build a railroad to connect with the Trans-Siberian railway. Port Arthur was made an apparently impregnable stronghold.

During the Russo-Japanese War (*q.v.*), Port Arthur was the scene of a victorious Japanese siege from the landward that undoubtedly had considerable influence on the outcome of the war. In May 1904 the Japanese 2nd army landed at P'i-tzu-wo and gained control of the isthmus that connects the Kwantung peninsula with the mainland. Dairen was seized without fighting and its port was used to debark the Japanese 3rd army in June. The following month the Japanese broke through the outer defenses of Port Arthur and forced the Russians, under Gen. Anatoli M. Stössel, to withdraw to the main defense works of the base. Costly Japanese assaults were repeatedly frustrated during the next four months, until the key Russian position on 203-Metre hill was finally overcome in late November. The Russian garrison capitulated Dec. 20, 1904. Even before the start of the siege, the Russian far eastern squadron, consisting of 7 battleships, 7 cruisers and 25 destroyers, had been bottled up in Port Arthur by a blockading Japanese naval force and fell to the Japanese at the time of the capitulation.

By the Treaty of Portsmouth (1905) Port Arthur was transferred to the Japanese, who called it Ryojun. Japan retained control over the base and the entire Kwantung lease until the end of World War II. Soviet forces seized Port Arthur in Aug. 1945. By treaty arrangements with the Chinese Nationalists and, later, with the Communists, the Soviet Union secured joint Soviet-Chinese control over Port Arthur until 1955, when the naval base passed to exclusive Chinese Communist use.

Port Arthur became part of the joint municipality of Port Arthur-Dairen, known in Chinese as Lüshun-Talien, or simply Lü-ta, with its seat at Dairen. The population of Port Arthur in the 1953 census was 126,000; that of Lü-ta (1958 est.) 1,590,000.

See also references under "Port Arthur" in the Index.

(T. SD.)

PORT ARTHUR, a major deepwater port of east Texas, U.S., is on the northwest shore of Sabine Lake, 9 mi. from the Gulf of Mexico. The city is 16 mi. (26 km.) SE of Beaumont (*q.v.*) and 17 mi. SW of Orange (*q.v.*), the three points of the Golden Triangle, site of an important petrochemical industry. Pop. (1970) 57,371; Beaumont-Port Arthur standard metropolitan statistical area (Jefferson and Orange counties), 315,943. For comparative population figures *see* table in TEXAS: *Population.*

The area, known in 1840 as Aurora, was an important base for a considerable illegal African slave trade into Texas during the mid-19th century. In the 1890s Arthur E. Stilwell, for whom the city was named, decided to use the port as the southern terminus for the Kansas City Southern railroad which he was promoting. Stilwell bought 53,000 ac. of land in the area in 1895, organized a town and arranged in 1899 for the dredging of a deep-sea canal to bring vessels directly to the city's docks.

In 1901 oil prospectors discovered the remarkable oil well known as Spindletop a few miles from Port Arthur. This event marked the birth of the Texas oil industry. James Stephens Hogg, a former governor of Texas, and the promoter and financier John W. ("Bet-a-Million") Gates stepped in to exploit the area and the port became a major sea outlet for a fabulous oil industry. Gates, in gratitude for a fortune made in the area, left the city funds for a library, art gallery, hospital, and an industrial college.

Port Arthur has a council-manager form of government, in effect since 1932. (E. W. F.)

PORT-AU-PRINCE, capital, chief port, and commercial centre of the Republic of Haiti, situated on a magnificent bay at the apex of the Gulf of La Gonâve, which strikes inland for about 100 mi. between the two great peninsulas of the west coast, with its upper recesses protected by the island of Gonâve (30 mi. [48 km.] long and 2 mi. [3 km.] broad). Pop. (1968 est.) 340,175. The National Palace, rebuilt in 1918, the army barracks, and an imposing statue of Jean Jacques Dessalines dominate the Champs-de-Mars in the centre of the city. The most picturesque site is the Iron Market, where the merchants are almost exclusively women. Other notable buildings include the National Archives, the National Library, and the National Museum. It is the centre of the political and intellectual life of the nation and is the seat of the University of Haiti (established 1944), but Haiti's poverty makes the city one of the most unsanitary and backward capitals in the Western Hemisphere. During the U.S. occupation, 1915–34, sanitary conditions were improved. The climate is warm and humid, average 81° F (27° C) with little seasonal change.

Port-au-Prince is linked by railroad to Saint-Marc, about 45 mi. NW, and by paved road to Cap-Haïtien; buses run on irregular schedules to all parts of the country. There are air services to most of the Caribbean islands and to New York. During the 1950s several luxury hotels were built to accommodate tourists. Textiles, cottonseed oil, flour and sugar mills are located in or near the capital.

The city was first laid out in 1749 by the French, and its bicentenary was commemorated in 1949 by an international exposition, the site of which is now a pleasant palm-fronted promenade. In 1751, and again in 1770, it was destroyed by earthquakes; in subsequent years the city was ravaged frequently by fire.

(R. W. LN.)

PORT CHESTER, a village in Westchester county, N.Y., U.S., on Long Island sound at the mouth of the Byram river, which separates it from Connecticut.

Port Chester's earliest history began with Peter Disbrow's purchase of the southern part of its present site on Jan. 3, 1660, from the Siwanoy Indians, a Mohegan tribe. In 1661 he and his associates proclaimed Charles II their lawful monarch in defiance of the claims of the Dutch West India company (*see* LONG ISLAND: *History*). As early as 1732 the settlement was known as Saw

Pit because of its important shipbuilding trade. On March 11, 1837, the name was changed to Port Chester, and the village was incorporated under that name on May 14, 1868.

Although Port Chester is a residential suburb, there were in the 1970s more than 300 establishments making or selling such products as candy, cough drops, plastics, porcelainized products, electronics, airplane parts, women's hats, and men's shirts.

Pop. (1970) 25,803. For comparative figures *see* table in New York: *Population*. (M. D. Hн.)

PORTE, SUBLIME, the name once given to the Turkish government, is a European translation of the Turkish *Babiâli,* the High Gate or Gate of the Eminent. This was the official name of the gate giving access to the block of buildings in Istanbul which housed the principal state departments. Early in the history of the Ottoman Empire the grand viziers became powerful but it was only in the 17th century that they acquired the official residence, *Babiâli,* which became the real centre of government. There, too, were the offices of the foreign ministry and the council of state; hence the application of the term to the government as a whole. In the early 1970s the buildings were the seat of the provincial governorate, and the nearby street was the "Fleet Street" of Istanbul. (A. D. A.)

PORT ELIZABETH, a seaport situated on Algoa Bay, 436 mi. (702 km.) by sea east of Cape Town in Cape Province, Republic of South Africa. The total population in 1960 was 245,985, of whom 84,505 were whites, 106,162 Bantu, 51,453 Coloured, and 3,865 Asian.

Port Elizabeth was settled after Fort Frederick was founded in 1799 and developed rapidly with the completion of the Kimberley Railroad (1873). It lies midway between Cape Town and Durban, and is the third port of South Africa. The area south of the harbour has become a seaside resort possessing some of the finest beaches in South Africa and extensive residential development. The main business centre of the town is situated immediately inland from the harbour, with further residential areas stretching about 12 mi. inland. To the north of the town more than 3,000 ac. of land have been developed with industries, the largest establishments being those of the automotive industry; and in the 1960s further industrial expansion over an area of more than 1,000 ac. was projected.

Like other South African ports, the port is owned by the government but administered by South African Railways. The harbour, with a water area of 314 ac., is enclosed and has three quays, one 3,540 ft. long and the others each 1,700 ft. long. The depth of the water in the harbour is 36 ft. above low-water ordinary spring tides and is capable of taking any ocean-going liner. The port handles a large proportion of the imports for Zambia and Southern Rhodesia by virtue of its excellent rail communication system with the hinterland. Ample cold storage facilities exist to handle the increased citrus exports. Ore-loading and discharging berths of 1,200 ft. take ships of up to 65,000 tons and there are storage facilities for 180,000 tons. This project cost R.5,500,000 and was undertaken after World War II when the industries of Port Elizabeth developed more rapidly than those of any other town in the republic. By the 1960s there were more than 500 factories engaged in more than 80 types of industrial activity.

PORTEOUS, JOHN (d. 1736), captain of the city guard of Edinburgh, whose name is associated with the riots of 1736, which provided the plot for Sir Walter Scott's novel *The Heart of Midlothian,* was the son of Stephen Porteous, an Edinburgh tailor. He served in the army in Flanders in the War of the Spanish Succession and upon the outbreak of the Jacobite Rebellion in Scotland in 1715 was appointed as drillmaster to the city guard of Edinburgh. By January 1726 he had risen to be one of the three captains lieutenant in the guard. On April 14, 1736, a smuggler, Andrew Wilson, who had won popular sympathy in Edinburgh by helping a friend to escape from prison, was hanged. A riot broke out at the execution and the city guard fired into the crowd. Porteous, who was accused of giving the order to fire, and of firing himself, was brought to trial in July and sentenced to death. After he had sent a petition for pardon to Queen Caroline, then acting as regent in the absence of George II, his execution was postponed.

On the night of Sept. 7, 1736, an armed mob broke into the Tolbooth prison in Edinburgh, seized Porteous, and hanged him from a signpost in the street. The government in London ordered an inquiry, but no one was ever convicted of the murder. In 1737 a harsh Pains and Penalties Bill was introduced, but in its final form was much modified. The city of Edinburgh was fined £2,000 and the lord provost was disqualified from holding any other office.

See W. Roughead (ed.), *Trial of Captain Porteous* (1909); P. H. Brown, *History of Scotland,* vol. iii (1911).

PORTER, COLE (1892–1964), U.S. composer of musical comedies and popular songs, was born in Peru, Ind., on June 9, 1892. He studied at the Harvard School of Music and during World War I served in the French Army. Among his successful musical comedies, combining sentimental appeal with sophisticated satire, were *Anything Goes* (1934), *Dubarry Was a Lady* (1939), *Panama Hattie* (1940), *Kiss Me, Kate* (after Shakespeare's *The Taming of the Shrew*) (1948), *Can-Can* (1953), and *Silk Stockings* (1955). His popular songs include *Begin the Beguine* and *Night and Day*. All his musical comedies and songs were written to his own words. He died in Santa Monica, Calif., on Oct. 15, 1964. (N. Sʏ.)

PORTER, DAVID (1780–1843), U.S. naval officer who commanded the frigate "Essex" on her famous expeditions during the War of 1812, was born in Boston, Mass., on Feb. 1, 1780. His father, David, commanded U.S. ships in the American Revolutionary War. In 1796 he accompanied his father to the West Indies; on a second and on a third voyage he was impressed on British vessels, but he escaped. He became a midshipman in the U.S. navy in April 1798; served on the "Constellation" and was midshipman of the foretop when the "Constellation" defeated the "Insurgente"; was promoted lieutenant in Oct. 1799 and was in four successful actions with French ships in that year.

In 1803, during the war with Tripoli, he was first lieutenant of the "Philadelphia" when that vessel grounded, he was taken prisoner and was not released until June 1805. He was commissioned master commandant in April 1806; from 1807 to 1810 he served about New Orleans, where he captured several French privateers, and in 1812 was promoted captain. He commanded the "Essex" in her famous voyage (1812–14). In the Atlantic he captured seven brigs, one ship, on Aug. 13, 1812, the sloop "Alert," the first British war vessel taken in the War of 1812. Without orders from his superiors he then (Feb. 1813) rounded Cape Horn, and in the South Pacific captured many British whalers and took formal possession (Nov. 1813) of Nukuhiva, the largest of the Marquesas Islands. The United States, however, never asserted any claim to the island, and in 1842, with the other Marquesas, it was annexed by France. During most of February and March 1814 he was blockaded by British frigates in the harbour of Valparaiso, and on March 28 was defeated. Released on parole, he sailed for New York.

He was a member of the new board of naval commissioners from 1815 until 1823, when he commanded a squadron sent to the West Indies to suppress piracy. One of his officers, who landed at Fajardo (or Foxardo), Puerto Rico, in pursuit of a pirate, was imprisoned by the Spanish authorities on the charge of piracy. Porter, without reporting the incident or awaiting instructions, forced the authorities to apologize. He was recalled (Dec. 1824), court-martialed and suspended for six months. In Aug. 1826 he resigned his commission, and until 1829 was commander in chief of the Mexican navy, then fighting Spain. Pres. Andrew Jackson appointed him consul general to Algiers in 1830, and in 1831 created for him the post of chargé d'affaires at Constantinople, where in 1841 he became minister. He died in Pera on March 3, 1843.

He wrote a *Journal of a Cruise Made to the Pacific Ocean in the U.S. Frigate "Essex" in 1812-13-14* (1815; 2nd ed., 1822), and *Constantinople and Its Environs* (1835), which is a valuable guidebook.

See the *Memoir of Commodore David Porter* (1875), by his son, Adm. David D. Porter; R. Wheeler, *In Pirate Waters* (1969).

PORTER, DAVID DIXON (1813–1891), U.S. naval officer, who held important commands during the American Civil War, was born in Chester, Pa., on June 8, 1813. His first voyage, with his father, Capt. David Porter, in West Indian waters (1823–24), was terminated by the Fajardo affair (*see* PORTER, DAVID). In April 1826 he entered the Mexican navy, of which his father was commander in chief, and which he left in 1828 after the capture by the Spanish of the "Guerrero," on which he was serving under his cousin, David H. Porter (1804–28), who was killed before the ship's surrender. He became a midshipman in the U.S. navy in 1829 and was in the coast survey (1836–42). Porter became a lieutenant in Feb. 1841 and served at the naval observatory from 1845 to 1846, when he was sent to the Dominican Republic to report on conditions there. During the Mexican War he served as lieutenant and then as commanding officer of the "Spitfire," a paddle vessel built for river use, and took part in the bombardment of Veracruz. In 1855 and in 1856 he made trips to the Mediterranean to bring to the U.S. camels for army use in the southwest. In April 1861 he was assigned to the "Powhatan," and was sent under secret orders from the president for the relief of Ft. Pickens, Pensacola. Porter was promoted commander on April 22, and on May 30 was sent to blockade the Southwest pass of the Mississippi. Upon his return to New York in November he urged an expedition against New Orleans (*q.v.*), and recommended the appointment of Comdr. D. G. Farragut (*q.v.*), his foster brother, to the chief command.

In the expedition Porter himself commanded the mortar flotilla, which, when Farragut's fleet passed the forts on the early morning of April 24, 1862, covered the passage by a terrific bombardment that neutralized the fire of Ft. Jackson. At Vicksburg Porter's bombardment assisted Farragut to run past the forts (June 28). On July 9 Porter was ordered, with ten mortar boats, to the James river, where McClellan's army was concentrated. On Oct. 15 he took command of the gun vessels and had a share in the capture of Arkansas Post (Jan. 11, 1863). In the operations for the capture of Vicksburg in 1863 unsuccessful attempts were made by Porter's vessels to penetrate through connecting streams and bayous to the Yazoo and reach the right rear of the Confederate defenses on the bluffs, but the fleet ran past the Vicksburg batteries, mastered the Confederate forts at Grand Gulf and made it possible for Grant's army to undertake the brilliant campaign which led to the fall of the place (*see* AMERICAN CIVIL WAR and VICKSBURG). Porter received the thanks of congress for "opening the Mississippi river" and was promoted rear admiral. He co-operated with Maj. Gen. N. P. Banks in the Red river expeditions in March–May 1864, in which his gunboats, held above Alexandria by shallow water and rapids, narrowly escaped isolation. On Oct. 12, 1864, he assumed command of the North Atlantic blockading squadron, then about to engage in a combined military and naval expedition against Ft. Fisher, N.C. Porter claimed that his guns silenced Ft. Fisher, but Maj. Gen. B. F. Butler, in command of the land forces, refused to assault, asserting that the fort was practically intact.

After Butler's removal, Porter, co-operating with Maj. Gen. Alfred H. Terry and commanding the largest fleet assembled at any one point during the war, took the fort on Jan. 15, 1865; for this he again received the thanks of congress. From 1865 to 1869 he was superintendent of the U.S. Naval academy, Annapolis, which he greatly improved, his most notable change being the introduction of athletics. On July 25 he became vice-admiral. From March 9 to June 25, 1869, while Adolph E. Borie (1809–80) of Pennsylvania was secretary of the navy in President Grant's cabinet, Porter was virtually in charge of the navy department. In 1870 he succeeded Farragut in the grade of admiral. He died in Washington, D.C., Feb. 13, 1891.

Porter wrote a *Life of Commodore David Porter* (1875), gossipy *Incidents and Anecdotes of the Civil War* (1885), a none too accurate *History of the Navy During the War of the Rebellion* (1887), two novels, *Allan Dare* and *Robert le Diable* (1885; dramatized, 1887) and *Harry Marline* (1886), and a short "Romance of Gettysburg," published in *The Criterion* in 1903.

See J. R. Soley, *Admiral Porter* (1903).

Admiral Porter's three brothers were in the service of the United States: WILLIAM DAVID PORTER (1809–64) commanded the "Essex" on the Tennessee and the Mississippi in the Civil War and became commodore in July 1862; THEODORIC HENRY PORTER (1817–46) was the first officer of the U.S. army killed in the Mexican War; and HENRY OGDEN PORTER (1823–72) resigned from the U.S. navy in 1847, after seven years' service, fought under William Walker in Central America, returned to the U.S. navy, was executive officer of the "Hatteras" when she was sunk by the "Alabama" and received wounds in the action from the effects of which he died several years later.

PORTER, ENDYMION (1587–1649), English courtier, the most trusted of Charles I's personal attendants, and a patron of art and literature, was born at Mickleton, Gloucestershire, in 1587. From 1605 to 1612 he was in Spain, where he had family connections, and on returning to England, entered Edward Villiers' service. In 1617 or 1618 he became master of horse to Edward's half brother, George, later duke of Buckingham, and in 1619 he married Buckingham's niece, Olivia Boteler. In 1621 he became personal attendant to Prince Charles. He took part in the secret negotiations for the Spanish marriage (1622) and accompanied Charles and Buckingham on their clandestine visit to Madrid (1623).

On Charles' accession (1625), Porter was made a groom of the bedchamber. He continued to be employed in diplomacy with Spain, but his main duties were concerned with the arts. He negotiated many of the purchases that made the royal collection one of the finest in Europe, and acquired a notable private collection of his own. He knew Rubens and was a friend of Van Dyck, who painted portraits of him. Sir William Davenant owed his rise to Porter, and addressed 13 poems to him and his family, and Herrick praised his learning, wit, and "sweet temper." He acquired considerable wealth in the 1630s, through royal gifts, fines, wardships, leases on crown lands, patents, monopolies, and commercial enterprises under royal license.

Porter sat in the Long Parliament for Droitwich, and in January 1642 left London with the king, to whom he remained a faithful servant during the Civil War. Of the 11 Royalists exempted from the pardon offered by Parliament in September 1642, he was the only one not in high office—a tribute to his confidential position, his Spanish connections, and his wife's Catholicism. After the Battle of Naseby (1645) he was sent to France with letters for the queen, and remained in exile, in Paris and Brussels, until the winter of 1648–49. In April 1649 he appeared at the Court of Compounding in London, and was permitted to compound for his delinquency by a fine. Exhausted by the hardships of the war years, he died in London in August 1649.

See G. Huxley, *Endymion Porter* (1959).

PORTER, HENRY (*fl.* 1589–1599), English dramatist, author of *The Two angrie women of Abington* (publ. 1599), may have matriculated at Brasenose College, Oxford, on June 19, 1589. Entries in Philip Henslowe's *Diary* between Dec. 16, 1596, and April 16, 1599, suggest that Porter was successful but needy. He collaborated with Henry Chettle and Ben Jonson on *Hot Anger Soon Cold* (1598) and with Chettle on *The Spencers* (1599); neither has survived. In 1598 Porter provided the Admiral's Men with a lost play, *Love Prevented*. In February 1599, they performed the second part of *The Two angrie women* and he contracted to write them *The Two merrie women of Abington*. Porter was wounded in a duel by John Day (possibly the dramatist) on June 6, 1599, and died the next day. He wrote lively, coherent prose and verse dialogue and had a talent for comic plot and character.

BIBLIOGRAPHY.—*The Two Angry Women of Abingdon*, ed. by C. M. Gayley in *Representative English Comedies* (1903), and by W. W. Greg for the Malone Society (1912). *See also* J. M. Nosworthy, "Henry Porter," in *English*, vol. vi, no. 32 (1946). (B. L. J.)

PORTER, KATHERINE ANNE (1890–   ), U.S. writer of fiction, whose best-known novel, *Ship of Fools*, appeared in 1962, was born May 15, 1890, at Indian Creek, Tex., and educated at Southern convent schools. For many years she lived abroad—in Mexico, where she did much to stimulate interest in Mexican art and culture, and in Paris and Berlin. These experiences as well as those of her girlhood in the South are reflected in her stories. Though she wrote early and voluminously, she made no attempt to publish until about 1925. The appearance in 1930 of her first collection of stories, *Flowering Judas*, won her immediate critical acclaim. *Hacienda* followed in 1934 and in 1939 *Pale Horse, Pale Rider: Three Short Novels*. This volume established her as one of the foremost short-story writers of the period, but it was not until 1962 that *Ship of Fools* first brought her a truly wide circle of readers.

Critics have praised her for the extraordinary purity and concentration of her style, but her style never becomes a mere preciosity: it is made to serve her vision of life whether her theme is the individual's fight to maintain spiritual integrity or the vicissitudes of growing up or the attempt to discover the meaning of one's past. Other works by Miss Porter include *The Leaning Tower, and Other Stories* (1944) and *The Days Before* (essays and reviews) (1952).

See Edward Schwartz, *Katherine Anne Porter: a Critical Bibliography* (1953).   (C. Bs.)

PORTER, WILLIAM SYDNEY: see HENRY, O.

PORTES GIL, EMILIO (1891–   ), Mexican provisional president (1928–30) and statesman, was born in Ciudad Victoria, Tamaulipas, on Oct. 3, 1891. After teaching for two years (1910–12) he entered law school and was in Mexico City when the revolution led by Venustiano Carranza began. After late 1914 Portes Gil served the revolution in various legal capacities in Mexico City, in Sonora, and in Tamaulipas. He supported Alvaro Obregón in 1920, and after Obregón's victory over Carranza in that year Portes Gil became provisional governor of Tamaulipas. He served parts of four terms in the National Congress, was governor of Tamaulipas (1925–28) and minister of government (1928) prior to his election by Congress to the provisional presidency, in which he served from Dec. 1, 1928, to Feb. 5, 1930. He then was elected president of the official political party (National Revolutionary Party), but dissension forced his resignation and he was sent to France as minister in 1931; while in Europe he also was delegate to the League of Nations. Returning in 1932 Portes Gil became attorney general, from which post he moved to minister of foreign relations in 1934. In 1936 he retired from political life, devoting his time to private affairs and to encouraging intellectual and artistic development in Mexico.   (C. C. Cu.)

PORT GLASGOW, a large burgh of Renfrew, Scot., on the south bank of the Firth of Clyde, 19 mi. (31 km.) WNW of Glasgow by road. Area 1.8 sq.mi. Pop. (1968 est.) 22,095. It is continuous with Greenock. Industries include large shipbuilding and engineering works and sawmills. The area of the docks, both wet and graving, is 16½ ac. The graving dock (1762) was the first dock of the kind in Scotland. The first Clyde steamship, the "Comet," was built at Port Glasgow in 1812. In 1775 it was made a burgh of barony. Nearby are the ruins of 16th-century Newark Castle.

PORT HARCOURT, the second port of Nigeria, Africa, lies about 41 mi. (66 km.) from the sea on the Bonny River, an eastern distributary of the Niger, in an area of mangrove swamps and rain forest. The climate is hot and humid with an annual rainfall of 94 in., largely between April and November. The most congenial months are January and December. Pop. (1963 est.) 179,563. It covers about 12 sq.mi. between the Bonny River (west), the Amadi (east), and the Nwatugbo (south) creeks. First marked out in 1912 on a derelict site known as Obomotu, and linked by rail in 1916 with the Enugu coalfields, the port has continually expanded. The main streets are wide, with modern-style buildings, and the principal commercial and residential houses are grouped around a central area known as The Circle, though there are new residential quarters to the northwest and southeast. The many open spaces include Jubilee Memorial Park and a sports stadium.

Port Harcourt is the capital of the Rivers State and is the terminus of the eastern branch of Nigerian railways; it is linked by road and internal air services with the rest of the republic. The airport is 7 mi. NE on the Aba Road. Local industries include an oil refinery and cement, cigarette, and metal window-frame and door manufacture. The port has deepwater berths and bulk palm oil storage plants. Increasing traffic necessitated a further large ex-

pansion of the port facilities in the late 1950s. Its exports are mainly palm oil and kernels, cocoa, coal, tin, peanuts, and mineral oil from the oil fields of the Niger Delta.   (W. H. I.)

PORT HURON, a city of southeastern Michigan, U.S., 57 mi. (92 km.) NE of Detroit at the lower end of Lake Huron on the St. Clair River, opposite Sarnia, Ont., with which it is connected by a railway tunnel and the Bluewater International Bridge. It is a part of the St. Lawrence Seaway and is close to the St. Clair County Airport. Port Huron, the seat of St. Clair County and the centre of a thriving agricultural community, has many industries and is a popular summer resort and the site of St. Clair County Community College (1923). It has a commission-manager form of government. Pop. (1970) 35,794. For comparative population figures see table in MICHIGAN: *Population*.

In 1686 Ft. St. Joseph was built within the present city limits by Daniel Greysolon, Sieur du Lhut (Dulhut), a French trader and explorer; the British took possession in 1761 and the Americans built a fort on the site in 1814, naming it Ft. Gratiot for Capt. Charles Gratiot, who supervised its construction. The settlement, which had grown up around the fort, was incorporated as the village of Fort Gratiot in 1840; in 1893 it joined the other communities along the St. Clair River which had formed the city of Port Huron in 1857. Thomas A. Edison (*q.v.*) lived there as a boy.   (V. A.)

PORTICI, a seaside town of the province of Napoli (Naples) in the region of Campania, south Italy, is 5 mi. (8 km.) SE of Naples, with Mt. Vesuvius to its northeast and the buried Roman town of Herculaneum nearby. Pop. (1968 est.) 67,888 (commune). The chief buildings are the 18th-century church of S. Ciro with pictures by Luca Giordano, and the ornate Palazzo Reale, begun in 1738 by Charles of Bourbon (later Charles III of Spain), which houses mosaics, etc., from Herculaneum and the agriculture faculty of the University of Naples. Portici is on the Naples–Salerno railway and near the Naples–Castellammare motorway. Fishing is carried on and apples, pears, olives, nuts, and hemp are grown. Wine and fertilizers are made. The port is fairly busy.

As a medieval fief, Portici was owned by various princely families; it later passed to the kingdom of Naples. The town was completely destroyed by the eruption of Vesuvius in 1631. Italy's first railway (Portici–Naples) was inaugurated there in 1839.
                                                    (M. T. A. N.)

PORT JACKSON: see SYDNEY.

PORT KEMBLA, a town and port of New South Wales, Austr., lies 55 mi. S of Sydney and forms part of Greater Wollongong (see WOLLONGONG). Pop. (1961) 7,830. Since the establishment of iron and steel works in 1926, Port Kembla has developed into an important industrial centre, producing about 2,600,000 tons of steel ingots annually.

Other industries include the smelting and refining of copper and other metals, and the manufacture of tin plate, wires and cables, sulfuric acid, fertilizers, and metal products. There is also a large power station.

The artificial harbour has grown from a jetty built in 1883 to ship coal mined at Mount Kembla in the Illawarra Range to the west; after 1960 a new harbour was built to provide many more berths, with a depth of 32 ft. at low water. The chief imports are ironstone, limestone, and liquid fuels; iron and steel products and coal are the chief exports.

PORTLAND, HANS WILLEM BENTINCK, EARL OF (1649–1709), Anglo-Dutch statesman, was a close friend of Prince William III of Orange, afterward King William III of England, and for 30 years his *alter ego* in politics, diplomacy, and war. He was born on July 20, 1649, the fourth son of Bernhard Bentinck of Diepenheim, a member of the Gelderland nobility. He made his career at Prince William's court, where he was page of honour and, from 1672, gentleman of the bedchamber, and in the army, becoming colonel of horse guards in 1675. In 1677 he preceded William to England to make a formal request on his behalf for the hand in marriage of Princess Mary, daughter of James, duke of York (later James II). He returned on missions of compliment in 1683 after the failure of the Rye House plot and in 1685 after the duke of Monmouth's rebellion. On each occasion he was entrusted with highly confidential negotiations, with Charles II to try to enlist his support against Louis XIV of France, and with James II to dissipate suspicions that William had favoured Monmouth. Bentinck corresponded with William's supporters in England in 1687 and 1688 and supervised the arrangements for William's expedition to England in 1688. As a reward for his services, in 1689 he was appointed to the privy council, made groom of the stole, and created earl of Portland.

Portland fought at the Boyne (1690), Landen (1693), and Namur (1695), and William used him extensively as an intermediary with his English ministers. He had an important share in the conclusion of the Treaty of Rijswijk (1697), was English ambassador to France (1698), and on William's behalf, but unknown to the English Parliament, he signed with Louis XIV the two treaties, of 1698 and 1699, for the partition of the Spanish Empire. When the treaties were made public in 1701, Portland was impeached (April), but the proceedings were discontinued in July when the danger of war with France became a more important issue. Like all William's Dutch advisers, Portland was unpopular in England; in 1695 the House of Commons prevented him from obtaining a large grant of crown land in Denbighshire, and the Act of Resumption in 1700 deprived him of the large estates in Ireland which he had received after the suppression of the rebellion in 1691. From 1697 his jealousy of William's favourite, Arnold Joost van Keppel, 1st earl of Albemarle, poisoned his relations with the king, and after provoking a series of quarrels with William, he resigned all his offices in 1700 and virtually retired from court. However, he was finally reconciled to the king on William's deathbed two years later. He was occasionally employed on public business under Queen Anne but was more often in Holland than in England. He died at Bulstrode, Buckinghamshire, on Nov. 23, 1709.

See M. E. Grew, *William Bentinck and William III* (1924); A. S. Turberville, *History of Welbeck Abbey and Its Owners,* vol. ii (1939).
(J. P. K.)

PORTLAND, WILLIAM HENRY CAVENDISH BENTINCK, 3RD DUKE OF (1738–1809), English statesman, prime minister from April to December 1783 and from 1807 to 1809, was born on April 14, 1738, at Bulstrode, Buckinghamshire, the eldest son of William, 2nd duke of Portland. He was educated at Westminster and Christ Church, Oxford, and succeeded his father as 3rd duke in 1762. From July 1765 to December 1766 he was lord chamberlain of the household. In the marquess of Rockingham's second ministry he was appointed lord lieutenant of Ireland (April 1782), but resigned (August 1782) after the earl of Shelburne became prime minister. On Shelburne's fall, Portland was selected by Lord North and Charles James Fox as nominal head of their coalition ministry. He was dismissed in December 1783 when Fox's India Bill was, under the king's influence, thrown out by the House of Lords. Regarded as leader of the Rockingham Whigs, Portland lived in semiretirement until the progress of the French Revolution and the outbreak of war with France led him to support William Pitt's administration. He was secretary of state for the home department from July 1794 until July 1801, when he became lord president of the council. He relinquished that office in January 1805, but remained in the cabinet during the last year of Pitt's second ministry. On Pitt's death in January 1806 he retired, but was brought back as prime minister in March 1807. The dominating figures in his second ministry were Viscount Castlereagh and George Canning. Troubled by their disagreements and by persistent ill health, he resigned in September 1809. He died at Bulstrode on Oct. 30, 1809.

See A. S. Turberville, *A History of Welbeck Abbey and Its Owners,* vol. ii (1939).
(A. Al.)

PORTLAND, the largest city in Maine, U.S., the seat of Cumberland County and a port of entry, is located on Casco Bay 110 mi. (177 km.) NE of Boston. The city is built largely on two hilly peninsulas which command arresting views of Casco Bay and its many islands. Pop. (1970) 65,116; Portland standard metropolitan statistical area (comprised of the cities of Portland, South Portland, and Westbrook, and the towns of Falmouth, Cape Elizabeth, Cumberland, Gorham, Scarborough, and Yarmouth)

(141,625). For comparative city population figures *see* table in MAINE: *Population.*

Portland was first settled in 1632 by the Englishmen Richard Tucker and George Cleeve. During its early years it was known by several names and suffered various disasters. It was destroyed in 1676 by Indians and in 1690 by French and Indians. In 1775 a British fleet bombarded the settlement as punishment for patriotic activities. It was rebuilt and then was incorporated as a town in 1786, when it took the name of Portland. When Maine became a state in 1820 Portland served as the capital until 1832. It also was incorporated as a city in 1832. A fire which resulted from an Independence Day celebration destroyed much of the centre of the city on July 4 and 5, 1866.

Reconstruction soon took place, however, and the city continued to grow. Portland's traditional fishing, shipping, and commercial activities were increasingly supplemented by the development of manufacturing industries. The city was important in the building and operation of naval ships in both World Wars I and II. It has a council-manager form of government which it adopted in 1923.

Portland is the transportation and commercial centre of southwestern Maine. It has an excellent harbour, which is served by several steamship lines. It is a major petroleum port and is the eastern terminus of the Portland–Montreal oil pipeline. The metropolitan area has a diversified manufacturing base. Among the chief products are pulp and paper, a variety of canned and processed foods, textiles, lumber and wood products, furniture, footwear, chemicals, metal goods, and various types of machinery. There is also considerable shipbuilding, printing, and publishing in the area. Fishing is an important source of employment.

Educational facilities include the University of Maine at Portland-Gorham and Westbrook, a private junior college for women. Two museums, an art gallery, and music and drama groups contribute to the area's cultural activities.
(H. A. PE.)

PORTLAND, the largest city of Oregon, U.S., and the seat of Multnomah County, is in the northwestern part of the state. Its original site was a shallow bench of land between low but steep wooded hills and the west bank of the Willamette River, 10 mi. (16 km.) from its entrance into the Columbia River. This remains the financial and commercial centre of the city. Zoned residential, commercial, and industrial developments have spread out to occupy the plain on the east side of the Willamette, extending to the Columbia. From the city's heights, to the east, can be seen an encirclement of low foothills climaxed in the snow-capped summit of Mt. Hood, 48 mi. (75 km.) away, and in the farther distance, the peaks of Mt. St. Helens and Mt. Adams in Washington. To the west lie the Tualatin Valley, the Coast Range Mountains, and beyond, less than 100 mi. away, the Pacific Ocean. Pop. (1970) city 382,619; standard metropolitan statistical area (Multnomah, Washington, and Clackamas counties, Oregon; Clark County, Washington) 1,009,129. For comparative population figures *see* table in OREGON: *Population.*

History.—Portland was founded in 1845 and was named for the city in Maine. Deep water for oceangoing vessels and the opening of a road to the wheat producing farms of the Tualatin Valley in the early 1850s gave it commercial advantages over rival town sites. By 1860, when its population was less than 3,000, it was the largest town in the Pacific northwest and remained so until outstripped by Seattle at the turn of the century. Between 1850 and 1870 Portland was the outfitting point and supply centre for northwest gold rushes and interior settlement. Thrifty and conservative businessmen, many originally from New England, invested capital earned during these prosperous times in real estate and transportation facilities. Locally owned stern-wheelers navigated the rivers and carried agricultural traffic to Portland; after 1880 it became one of the nation's chief grain exporting ports. In the 1860s and 1870s Portland's residents invested heavily in railroad lines to California and in the Northern Pacific Railway Company which gave them their first transcontinental connection in 1883. By 1910 all major western steam railroad lines entered Portland.

In 1889 a local company brought electric power to Portland

from Oregon City, 14 mi. up the Willamette, over the world's first long-distance transmission line. With the completion of Bonneville and other dams on the Columbia beginning in 1940, the availability of hydroelectric power attracted metallurgical and chemical industries to the metropolitan area.

Local residents early advertised Portland as the city of homes as well as "the city of roses," celebrated in an annual rose festival. Multiple-unit dwellings were slow to develop until the urban rènewal projects, a new airport, and the building of expressways changed the appearance of the city.

Government.—Portland is governed by an elected, nonpartisan board of five commissioners and a mayor. It operates only minimum public utilities. An important administrative change occurred in January 1971 when the Portland Commission of Public Docks merged with the Port of Portland, an action that had been approved earlier by the voters. The merger saw the beginnings of such improvements as expansion of pier facilities and the grain terminal.

Educational and Cultural Activities.—Institutions of higher education in the city include Cascade, a private, interdenominational college chartered in 1918 as the North Pacific Evangelistic Institute; Lewis and Clark, a Presbyterian college founded in 1867; Reed, a private, nonsectarian college opened in 1908; the University of Portland, a coeducational institution established in 1901; the medical and dental schools of the University of Oregon; and the Museum Art School (1909). Portland State University (which grew out of Vanport Extension Center, established in 1946) became a degree-granting college in the Oregon state system of higher education in 1955. Cultural institutions include a library, art museum, historical society, and symphony. In 1925 one of the first junior symphonies in the nation was founded in Portland. The Multnomah County Library, with headquarters in Portland, operates a number of branches and several bookmobiles.

The city school district, a separate taxing agency, operates elementary and high schools and a radio station and provides special programs for exceptional children.

Parks and Recreation.—Portland has over 100 park and recreational areas, including rose and zoological gardens, totaling over 6,000 ac. Forest Park, 3,500 ac., is a primitive area within the city limits.   (D. O. J.)

PORTLAND, ISLE OF, a craggy peninsula on the coast of Dorset, Eng., is connected to the mainland by the Chesil bank, or beach, an unbroken ridge of shingle about 30 ft. high and 200 yd. wide, stretching 17 mi. W as far as Bridport. Pop. of urban district (1970 est.) 13,270. Four miles long and nearly 1¾ mi. wide in extreme breadth, its area is 4.5 sq.mi. and its precipitous shores render the island virtually inaccessible from the sea except toward the south. Its highest point is Verne Hill (490 ft.) in the north, and the southern tip is Portland Bill with its storm-worn caves, a raised beach, and the Pulpit Rock. The dangerous Portland race, where the tides meet, flows toward the Shambles sands 4½ mi. to the east and is marked by the Shambles lightship.

The substratum of the island is Kimeridge clay overlain by beds of sand and strata of oölitic limestone—the famous Portland stone used extensively in the London architectural masterpieces of Sir Christopher Wren and many other well-known buildings. Because of a similarity in colour, the stone gave its name to Portland cement (see CEMENT). In the dirt bed on the oölitic strata are numerous specimens of petrified wood, some of great size.

The island is a royal manor whose court leet still functions. On it are the famous convict prison, converted in 1921 to a borstal institution, and the Verne Prison, formerly a barracks. Portland Castle, built by Henry VIII in 1520, is open to the public. The remains of the Norman Bow and Arrow Fortress (Rufus Castle) stand on the eastern cliffs in the grounds of Pennsylvania Castle which was built about 1800 by James Wyatt for John Penn, governor of the island and grandson of William Penn, founder of the state of Pennsylvania. Avice's cottage, facing the castle, is a local museum. The peninsula has been described by Thomas Hardy as the "Gibraltar of Wessex" and "The Isle of Slingers."

Portland's breakwaters, constructed by convict labour, enclose **the great roadstead of Portland Harbour which was started by the**

Admiralty in 1847–62. A breakwater stretching northward from the northeastern corner of the island partially enclosed a large area of water naturally sheltered on the south and west. An inner arm ran nearly east from the island to a masonry head and fort, and an outer detached arm bent north to a circular fort, a narrow entrance for shipping being left between the two. Two new breakwaters, built after 1895, closed the gap between the end of the outer breakwater and the Bincleaves rocks near Weymouth. The completely enclosed harbour covers 2,233 ac. to the one-fathom line, of which 1,500 ac. have a depth of not less than 30 ft. at low water.

After World War II a further naval establishment was built toward Portland Bill. There is a well-known local breed of small black-face sheep. Round the coast lobsters and crabs are caught.
                                                    (C. P. BN.)

PORTLAND CEMENT: see CEMENT.

PORTLAOISE (MARYBOROUGH), the county town of Leix (Laoighis), Republic of Ireland, lies on the Triogue River, 52 mi. (84 km.) SW of Dublin. Pop. (1966) 3,434. A sand and gravel esker runs northward from the town to Mountmellick and thence to Tullamore. Portlaoise, established as Fort Protector during the reign of Mary I (hence its common English name), was granted its charter in 1570, and a bastion of the castle still remains. The main industries are flour milling and the manufacture of worsted goods. On the Rock of Dunamase (the Fort of Masg), 3 mi. E, are the ruins of an old castle, the former seat of the kings of Leinster (q.v.). It was destroyed in 1650 by Oliver Cromwell's army.

PORT LOUIS, the capital and port of Mauritius (q.v.), is built round a small, well-sheltered harbour on the northwestern coast, and backed by an almost semicircular ridge of mountains which form part of an extensive range stretching toward the centre of the island. Because of these protective mountains, the town and harbour are almost entirely cut off from the normal east and southeast trade winds, and this makes Port Louis one of the hottest places in Mauritius in summer. The town covers an area of 2.1 sq.mi. (5.4 sq.km.). Pop. (1962) 89,096.

Port Louis was founded in about 1736 by the French governor, Mahé de La Bourdonnais, and considerably improved in 1770. In appearance it seems a curious and fascinating assemblage of ancient and modern, Oriental and European, shabby and luxurious. Its streets are laid out in a rectangular network and it is dominated by an old fortress, the Citadel (1838), built on a hill almost in its centre. Port Louis possesses two cathedrals, St. Louis (Roman Catholic) and St. James (Anglican), and two fine Roman Catholic churches, a stately town hall, a natural history museum and art gallery, two public libraries, a theatre, a large public hospital, and several colleges. A small racecourse lies on the southeastern extremity and a public park on the northeastern seaboard. The Grand River North West, which runs on the outskirts, furnishes part of the freshwater supply.

The port, which is the main harbour on the island, has one deep-sea quay. From the Central Railway Station and clearing yard lines branch off to all parts of the island. Port Louis contains no large industrial establishment. Its industrial activity, besides that connected with docks and warehousing, is restricted to minor mechanical workshops, small food and wine manufactures, oil extraction and refining, sawmilling, printing, etc. On the outskirts of the town proper, however, are a big tobacco warehouse, a modern cigarette factory, a thermal power station, and a railway workshop. As the central collecting and clearing ground for all merchandise imported or exported from the island, the commercial activity of Port Louis is extensive in wholesale and retail sales. The main export is sugar (98% of domestic exports in value).   (M. V. M. H.)

PORTO: see OPORTO.

PÔRTO ALEGRE, a city and port in southern Brazil, the capital of the state of Rio Grande do Sul. Pop. (1968 est.) 932,-801. It is located 670 mi. SW of Rio de Janeiro and 150 mi. NNE of the seaport of Rio Grande at the entrance to the lake. Pôrto Alegre is at the northern end of the Lagôa dos Patos on an arm of the lake known as the Rio Guaíba. Into this end of the lake five short but deep rivers empty their waters: the Gravataí, Sinos, Caí, Jacuí and its tributary the Taquarí. Since the lower courses of these rivers are all navigable, Pôrto Alegre has become the most important centre of inland navigation in all of Brazil. The outlet of the Lagôa dos Patos, near Rio Grande, is too shallow to accommodate ships of more than 16½-ft. draft. The lake and rivers, however, provide a fine system of inland waterways to serve the chief area of concentrated settlement in the state. The city is built on a ridge of high ground on the edge of the lake. It is located about 30° south of the equator and its climate is one of mild winters and hot summers, with abundant rainfall (average of 50 in.). In winter cold waves from the south bring occasional frosts.

In addition to its function as administrative centre of the state Pôrto Alegre is also the chief commercial centre serving the whole of this southernmost part of Brazil. From the rural hinterland come a variety of agricultural and pastoral products: meat and hides, wool, rice, tobacco, grapes, cereals, manioc meal and maize. From the forests lumber is produced. In the city are many business and financial establishments serving this economically active region. Educational institutions include two universities, a medical school, a normal school and a school of agronomy and veterinary medicine. The city also ranks high among the industrial centres of Brazil. Manufacturing industries are chiefly those engaged in processing the products of the farms, forests and ranches; they include meat packing, lard refining, leather tanning, the weaving of woolen yarn and cloth and the manufacture of clothing, the brewing of beer and the manufacture of cigarettes, furniture, soap, candles, macaroni, farinha (manioc flour) and a variety of preserves and wines. There are also metal factories producing stoves, furnaces and iron safes and a shipbuilding and ship repair works. The city is provided with electric power by a large steam-electric plant making use of coal from the nearby mines at São Jerônimo, brought to Pôrto Alegre by river barge. Although this coal has a high ash content and requires the use of especially designed grates, it is cheaper than imported coal.

The city is connected by rail with the Uruguayan railroads at Sant'Anna do Livramento and with the Argentine railroads at Uruguaiana. From the junction of Santa Maria, a rail connection exists all the way to São Paulo and Rio de Janeiro. Modern all-weather highways also connect Pôrto Alegre with the rest of Brazil and with neighbouring countries. Regular air connections tie the city to these same countries and regions.

Pôrto Alegre was founded in 1742–43 by immigrants from the Azores and was first known as Pôrto dos Cazaes. In 1825 the first German immigrants were settled in the country north and northwest of the city; later Italian settlers also came into this region. The administrative centre of Rio Grande do Sul was moved from Rio Grande to Pôrto Alegre in 1773; it was officially named capital of Rio Grande do Sul in 1807. (P. E. J.)

PORTO BELLO (Puerto Bello), a village on the Caribbean, 18 mi. N.E. of Colón, Panamá. Columbus named its site "beautiful harbour" in 1502; the city was founded March 20, 1597, by Francisco de Valverde y Mercado. As a point of transshipment and exchange for the colonial merchandise of Spain and South America it was famous for its annual fairs and notorious for its high prices, congested quarters and tropical fevers. Once the busiest city in the new world and target of concentrated wealth, it was attacked by the English buccaneers Sir Francis Drake (who was buried in Porto Bello bay), William Parker, Sir Henry Morgan and Edward Vernon. In 1713 Spain opened it to the trade of one British ship annually. The abandonment by Spain in the 18th century of the fleet system and fairs, the building of the Panama railroad in the 1850s and the opening of the Panama canal brought about its eclipse. It has ruins of great historic interest. Pop. (1960) 591. (A. R. W.)

PORTOFINO, a picturesque fishing village on the Riviera di Levante in Genova province, Liguria, Italy, 20 mi. (32 km.) S.E. of Genoa by road. Pop. (1961) 1,096 (commune). It stands on the small peninsula of Portofino whose evergreen-clad hills descend steeply to the Rapallo gulf. Brightly colour-washed houses line both sides of a deep inlet at the head of which is a small port where

yachts and sailing boats cluster. To the north (1½ mi.) is the monastery of La Cervara. Pope Gregory XI rested there on his way from Avignon back to Rome (1377) and Francis I of France was imprisoned there (1525) after the battle of Pavia. Southeast is the church of S. Giorgio, said to contain the relics of St. George brought by the crusaders from the Holy Land. Portofino has much tourist traffic. Pillow lace is made to traditional 18th-century patterns. (M. T. A. N.)

PORT-OF-SPAIN, the capital city and chief port of Trinidad and Tobago in the West Indies, lies on the west coast of Trinidad, below the northern peninsula, on the Gulf of Paria, which separates the island from the northeastern coast of Venezuela. Pop. (1960) 93,954.

On the hills behind Port-of-Spain are residential suburbs, such as Goodwood Park, and the city itself is well laid out with parks and squares. Woodford Square is the principal one, situated in the business district near Holy Trinity Cathedral. Queen's Park Savannah is at the centre of the city and from it radiate many of the most important streets, including Frederick Street, the main shopping thoroughfare, Charlotte Street, with its markets and small shops, and Cipriani Boulevard, Marli Street, and St. Clair Avenue, which are residential. Around Queen's Park Savannah are several buildings of historical and architectural interest: the former Government House which stands in the grounds (63 ac. [25 ha.]) of the Royal Botanical Gardens; Whitehall, which houses the office of the prime minister of Trinidad and Tobago; the palace of the Roman Catholic archbishop of Port-of-Spain; Knowsley House, which accommodates some government ministries; All Saints Church; and the Red House near Woodford Square, which houses the supreme court and government offices. Among educational institutions are Queen's Royal College (which is also used for evening classes of the government polytechnic institute), Fatima College, and St. Mary's College. The college of engineering and tropical agriculture of the University of the West Indies is situated at St. Augustine, 8 mi. (13 km.) E of the city.

Port-of-Spain is a commercial and retail centre and has in its vicinity a variety of industries, including the production of rum, bitters, beer, margarine and oils, cigarettes, plastics, and building materials. There are also sawmills, textile mills, and citrus canneries; and the tourist industry has increased. A hotel and catering institute and several technical institutes train workers for various industries, and government policy aims to attract new factories to the town.

Port-of-Spain is linked by good roads with other parts of Trinidad. It is the island's centre of broadcasting and publishes the main newspapers. The port has a key position on world shipping routes and is a centre of trade within the West Indies. The sheltered harbour accommodates medium-sized ships at eight berths, and there are smaller wharves and jetties. The main imports are food, timber, cotton, fertilizers, and manufactured goods; principal exports include crude petroleum and gasoline products, sugar, citrus fruit and juice, asphalt, cocoa, and coffee. The airport at Piarco, 16 mi. (26 km.) E of the city, is the chief airport of the Caribbean and is used by many of the world's principal airlines. (H. E. Cn.; O. C. Ma.)

PORTOLÁ, GASPAR DE (c. 1723–c. 1784), commander of the expedition sent from New Spain to colonize Upper California, was born about 1723 in Balaguer, Catalonia. At the age of 11, according to his military record, he became an ensign in the dragoon regiment of Villaricosa. He was promoted to lieutenant of dragoons and grenadiers in the Numancia regiment, where he served 21 years, and later was made captain of the España regiment and took part in the campaign against Portugal.

After José Gálvez was sent to New Spain in 1765 as *visitador*, he became aware of British and Russian interest in the Pacific coast of North America, an area which Juan Rodríguez Cabrillo in 1542 and Sebastián Vizcaíno and Bruno Heçeta later had visited and partially charted in behalf of Spain. He secured the appointment of Portolá, then of noble rank and unmarried, as governor of the Californias. Portolá took office in October 1767 and, after organizing an expedition, sailed from San Blas and landed at La Paz, Lower California, on July 6, 1768. His first duty there was to remove the Jesuits from their missions and replace them with Franciscans.

For the colonization of Upper California he prepared both land and sea expeditions with the intention that they were to rendez-vous at San Diego and later advance to Monterey, a harbour which had been reported in 1603 by Vizcaíno. Portolá led the land force, taking with him Fathers Junípero Serra, Juan Crespi, and several other priests to establish missions. He arrived at San Diego on July 1, 1769, after an arduous journey of four months from Loreto. On July 14 Portolá began the trip to Monterey but, failing to recognize the bay, he passed on to San Francisco Bay. There, realizing that the party had gone too far, he turned back on Nov. 11 and arrived in San Diego on Jan. 24, 1770. Within a few months he tried again and was successful in reaching and identifying Monterey, where a settlement was made. Portolá re-turned by sea to Mexico, surrendering his governorship in September 1770.

He became governor of the city of Puebla on Feb. 23, 1777. In 1784 the viceroy of New Spain reported that he had advanced Portolá 12 salary payments to enable him to return to Spain, but whether or not he ever attempted to make the journey remains unknown.

BIBLIOGRAPHY.—"Diary of Gaspar de Portolá during the California Expedition of 1769–70," *Academy of Pacific Coast History,* i, 33–89 (1909); "Narrative of the Expedition by Miguel Costansó," *ibid.,* i, 93–159; Francisco Palóu, *Historical Memoirs of New California,* ed. by H. E. Bolton, 4 vol. (1926); G. P. Hammond, *Noticias de California* (1958). (R. G. RR.)

PORTO MAURIZIO: *see* IMPERIA.

PORTO-NOVO, capital of the Republic of Dahomey, West Africa, is built above the coastal lagoon on the edge of a plateau. Pop. (1965 est.) 69,500. The town was probably founded in the late 16th century, as the centre of a kingdom, by the merging of two villages, Aklon and Djassin. Portuguese sailors and traders were the first to establish themselves there and the slave trade flourished. The French did not settle there until the 19th century. A protectorate treaty was signed in 1863 by King Dé Sodji in order to oppose the English. The existence of this small, inde-pendent kingdom, protected by the French, was at the root of their conflict with Béhanzin, sovereign of the well-developed king-dom of Abomey; the struggle lasted until 1894, when Béhanzin surrendered to the French.

Porto-Novo has retained a distinctive appearance from its early European occupation. There are still numerous buildings in the colonial or Portuguese style, with balconies of carved wood, and some old African palaces, more or less in ruins. The European quarter is cramped but pleasant, with its long avenues planted with flame trees (*Delonix regia*) and flanked by modern buildings. The centre of the African town is animated, with its guilds of artisans, potters, dyers, tanners, and smiths. On the shore of the lagoon are an old-established fishermen's quarter and stone quarries. The old urban populations live on the east side; to the north and west the people are farmers. Porto-Novo, although the administrative centre, is a town of the past; Cotonou is the com-mercial and industrial metropolis of Dahomey. (J. D.)

PORTO-RICHE, GEORGES DE (1849–1930), French dramatist celebrated as the author of *Amoureuse* (1891), the best of a collection of four plays called *Théâtre de l'Amour,* was born at Bordeaux on May 20, 1849. His theme is sensual love, which he studies mainly in the maladjusted married couple, even in his war play *Le Marchand d'estampes* (1917). The theme is broad-ened in *Le Vieil Homme* (1911), in which the husband and wife are also a father and mother. "The father of few plays but the grand-father of many," as he said himself, he possessed originality, which had a far-reaching influence on his contemporaries. His first and last plays, *Un Drame sous Philippe II* (1875) and *Les Vrais Dieux* (1929), are historical dramas. In 1923 he was elected to the Académie Française. He died in Paris on Sept. 5, 1930.

See H. Brugmans, *G. de Porto-Riche* (1934). (D. Ks.)

PORTO RICO: *see* PUERTO RICO.

PORT PHILLIP: *see* MELBOURNE.

PORT PIRIE, a city and seaport of South Australia on the eastern shore and toward the northern end of Spencer Gulf, 136 mi.

(219 km.) NNW of Adelaide by rail. Pop. (1966) 13,947. It is the natural port for the export of ore from Broken Hill (about 220 mi. NE). Most of this ore is smelted at Port Pirie and the main product is lead. The city's main exports are lead, ores, and wheat. It has a 51-cell wheat silo with a capacity of 3,300,000 bu. and an output rate of 400 tons per hour. In the mid-1960s Port Pirie was considered the second port of South Australia. It also has metallurgical and light industries. Port Pirie was made a rural city in 1953. (R. W. Fu.)

PORTRAIT PAINTING. A portrait is a record of certain aspects of a particular human being as seen by another. The sitter may be deified or merely flattered by the painter, satirized or even maligned but, as long as some sense of his individuality remains, a painting of him will be a portrait. The artist may be interested only in the sitter's physical appearance, his social position, his soul or his unconscious problems, but again, as long as the sitter's iden-tity remains, the artist will have painted his portrait. Finally the painter may paint him with a concern for precision of detail or with apparent abandon, with an interest in photographic realism or with a composition of cubes; but still, whatever the style is, as long as the artist can suggest some aspect of a particular person, the work will be a portrait. (It may not be a very good portrait but that is another problem.)

The Portrait and History.—By its very nature the portrait grows out of a respect for the differences between human beings; therefore it is only in periods primarily interested in individual dif-ferences that portrait painting thrives. In classical Greece, where the ideal mattered more than human particularities, portraiture had no place. In the middle ages, when man should ideally have lost his identity in the contemplation of God, again portraiture had an insignificant role. In the 20th century, portrait painting, with certain exceptions, has not been an important art form, perhaps because photography has provided an inexpensive substitute or perhaps because the norm is worshiped more than specific human characteristics.

The reasons for a concern with the individual and a subse-quent desire for portraits vary according to the period. The wish to have a portrait may be for religious reasons; *e.g.,* the ancient Egyptians needed a durable portrait in stone enough like the body of the dead person with which it was buried to suggest his authority and thus deceive his Ka so it would reside in the image and not haunt the survivors. At other times the moving force may have been a conviction of the importance of the individual to the family's prestige, as it was for the noble Romans or for the great of Georgian England. The cult of the hero, whether knight or courtier, grew up in the late middle ages and was developed in the Renaissance; his individual virtues had to be recorded. In contrast to this, the 19th and 20th centuries have observed the human being realistically, almost critically; portrait painters (as well as novel-ists) have emphasized his physical peculiarities and his psycho-logical problems. Circumstances such as these have helped determine the character of the portrait historically.

The Painter and the Sitter.—In a portrait the personality of the sitter is obviously of primary importance. It may not be equally apparent that the personality of the painter is just as signifi-cant, and that the character of the relationship between them is perhaps most relevant of all. When a fashionable patron com-missions a portrait from a fashionable painter the relationship between painter and sitter may be a formal one, and the work will reflect that formality. When an artist instead chooses to paint a portrait from his own affection or interest the relationship between the painter and the sitter becomes intimate and revealing. A por-trait may reveal the shyness, the apprehension, the arrogance, the amusement or the casualness with which the sitter regarded the artist.

The great moments in the history of portraiture are probably those when the personality of the artist can most completely com-prehend his sitter's—when a Hans Holbein is capable of identify-ing himself with the merchant Gisze or a Diego Velázquez can meet the challenge of the realism of an Innocent X or a Jean Ingres can love the vulgarity of a Mme Moitessier. Out of such a rap-port the greatest portraits are painted.

HISTORY

The beginning of the Renaissance, about 1400, introduced the first consistent tradition of portrait painting in the west. The Egyptians and the Romans who, unlike the Greeks, were portraitists, preferred sculpture. During the middle ages interest in the individual's mortal life had a lesser place; it was only toward the end of this period that a donor felt a need to have his individual piety recorded—not just by a symbol, his coat of arms perhaps, used to decorate some object he had given—but by having his own features reproduced as he knelt in devotion before the Virgin Mary.

The Sitter's Piety.—In the late middle ages Richard II (1367–1400) of England was painted kneeling, under the protection of his three patron saints, before a Madonna and Child surrounded by a circle of angels who look and point toward the suppliant king. There is some question whether this work, the "Wilton Diptych," was painted during Richard's lifetime or was commissioned by some admirer after his death. Whatever the circumstances were, the artist was not interested in visual probability; rather he imposed upon the scene the traditional conception of religious decorum by making the Virgin Mary appropriately larger than the three patron saints, who are bigger than the king, and by isolating Richard and the three saints in the left of the two panels which form the diptych.

The artist imposed the same medieval conventions in the portrait of Richard that he did in the arrangement of the whole. Richard's kneeling body has no apparent existence under the heavy robes which enclose it. All that is exposed are the head and the hands. The hands are held apart in a rather uncertain suppliant gesture before the Madonna to emphasize the humility of the king. That he is king is indicated by his crown and his gold brocaded robes, that he is Richard by the white hart with which his robe is decorated and which also hangs as an emblem around his neck. Finally, instead of using the three-quarter view of the face as he did for most of the other figures, the artist chose the position in which a person's features are most easily remembered—the profile. Richard's face is smooth, bland and young, its features delicate and somewhat pointed, his expression content. As long as he was identifiable, perhaps as much by the heraldic symbols as by his features, the purpose of the painting was served. The artist had clearly achieved the suggestion of the piety of this particular king.

RENAISSANCE

The Sitter Seen.—The convention of including the portrait of a donor in a religious work continued into the 17th century, but early in the 15th century during the Renaissance in both Italy and northern Europe independent portraits became common as an expression of the renewed interest of the Renaissance in the individual human being. One of the greatest portrait painters of the time was the Flemish artist Jan van Eyck (1385?–1441), and his most remarkable portrait was of an Italian merchant, Giovanni (or Jan) Arnolfini, and his wife. This painting has been shown to be more than a double portrait; it is a witness to the marriage of the Arnolfinis, which Van Eyck shows taking place, and is full of late medieval symbolism referring to the event: the single candle in the candelabra burning in daylight represents the unity of marriage; the fruit, so casually placed on the chest by the window sill, suggests the state of man before the fall; the dog represents domestic bliss; etc. The painting is more important as a portrait, however, because it is a rare attempt in the 15th century to paint a full standing figure and because both these figures are placed in their own familiar setting, no matter how fraught with symbolism it may be.

Although the garments the Arnolfinis wear are full they do not conceal their figures entirely; so Jan van Eyck, more than the artist of the "Wilton Diptych," makes use of their bodies to enrich his interpretation. The Italian merchant has narrow, sloping shoulders, he stands with his legs apart and his feet outspread; there is no suggestion of classical beauty or power. His body is, still in medieval terms, unimportant. He holds himself erect like an ascetic, somewhat aloof from his wife at whom he does not look,

his head and his lifted right hand concentrating upon the troth he is pledging. His wife is a gentler figure; her shoulders are bent, her head is modestly lowered in her husband's direction. Although Jan van Eyck proved here that full figures could be used meaningfully in a portrait, it was another hundred years before the practice became common.

The Arnolfini portrait is also remarkable in its effort to make the figures seem very natural in their environment. Their slippers, the wooden planks of the floor, the bed, the opened window with the warm sunshine streaming through it, the obvious details of a prosperous 15th-century home can be seen. Although the Arnolfinis are quite large for the scale of the room, the slippers and the dog in front of them seem to place them convincingly back into it. This position, combined with the visual interest demonstrated in the textures, in the quality of light and shadow and even in the reflection of the mirror (all of which the new technique of oil painting made more possible) makes this work a step toward a greater naturalism, a desire to give the illusion of the Arnolfinis as they might actually be seen in their own drawing room. This interest in the thing seen is apparent in Van Eyck's choice of the three-quarter view of the heads, which also brings the two sitters, particularly Jan, into a closer relationship with the spectators.

This portrait is in some respects essentially a tour de force which had no imitators; however, it displays a visual realism, characteristic of all Jan van Eyck's work, which became an integral part of northern Renaissance painting, particularly in the work of such gifted followers of Van Eyck as Rogier van der Weyden (c. 1400–64), Petrus Christus (c. 1420–72/73) and Hans Memling (c. 1430–94).

The Sitter of Authority.—In Italy in the 15th century portraiture took a somewhat different form. Federigo da Montefeltro, duke of Urbino (1422–82), might have the Umbrian painter, Piero della Francesca (c. 1420–92), paint him kneeling piously before the Madonna and Child but he also felt quite free to have himself painted as the symbol of authority over the world he ruled, without any of the implicit humility which Van Eyck's work still possessed. Like the painter of the "Wilton Diptych," Piero imposed relationships upon the work which are rational rather than visual. However, the basis for his reasoning was quite unlike the medieval painter's. The duke of Urbino is exaggeratedly and imposingly large in relation to the countryside, his own territory, behind him; Piero has made it quite clear that his sitter was master over nature rather than, like Richard, small and humble before God. In describing the silhouette of the duke's head and shoulders Piero used firm, clear contours which grow even more abrupt in the face—quite unlike the delicate, continuous lines which describe the figure of Richard. Their very severity suggests the harshness of the duke whose portrait is being painted to record his power rather than his piety. At the back of this small panel painting there is another study of the duke as part of a classically inspired triumphal procession; this makes the motivation for the portrait quite clear since, crowning the duke of Urbino, is the allegorical figure of Fame.

This portrait is a profile portrait. Since the duke had lost his right eye in the same tournament which had given his nose its distinctive shape, a profile portrait was probably mandatory. However, it was the position most characteristically chosen for Italian 15th-century portraits. One reason it was so popular may have been the authority of classical medals and gems. It is also possible that these artists may have felt, like the painter of the "Wilton Diptych," that the profile could most clearly characterize the distinctive features of a sitter's face. The profile places the emphasis upon the head as we know it or remember it to be rather than upon the visual impression which interested Jan van Eyck. Consistently the head is built up of separate facts, like the features revealed in the profile or in each curling strand of hair, rather than upon the visual unity of the whole; the imperfections of the moles and wrinkles, for example, do not destroy the alabaster smoothness of the skin.

Although the duke possessed the supreme kind of self-confidence which did not demand that a painter flatter him, indeed permitted

Piero to enumerate any facts with brutal honesty, the ultimate purpose was not a record of his appearance—but rather of his authority. And it is generally true of 15th-century Italian portraiture that, although the painter recorded the anatomical features of his sitters as he knew them to be, he was primarily concerned with the ideal to which these sitters aspired. Therefore as Piero in painting the duke suggested his worldly power, Domenico Ghirlandajo (1449–94) in painting Giovanna Tornabuoni degli Albizzi would emphasize her female dignity or Gentile Bellini (c. 1429–1507) in painting a doge would show his keen intelligence—qualities represented in their most perfect form.

The Sitter Idealized.—*"Mona Lisa."*—In Florence, at the turn of the 16th century, painters and sculptors were not so interested in Piero's unequivocal realism of detail. An artist as renowned as Leonardo da Vinci (1452–1519) was seldom willing to paint a portrait and, when he did, it seems to have been because his sitter could be made to represent an ideal rather than a particular human being. The most famous portrait painting by his hand is of the wife of Francesco del Giocondo, the "Mona Lisa." (For an illustration of this painting, *see* LEONARDO DA VINCI.) This work, from 1504, not only makes it clear that Leonardo was interested in idealization but also that he was perhaps sufficiently tempted by the technique of oil painting to want to achieve the illusionary effects for which Jan van Eyck had also strived.

More even than Van Eyck, Leonardo, in his portrait, makes the transitions so subtle that the illusion of a body of flesh and blood occupying space is almost complete; however, in spite of the fact that she seems so physically convincing, the "Mona Lisa" remains aloof. Her dress is simple but the bearing of her head, the position of her hands and the triangular form she occupies make her seem imposing and regal. The face which, more than mere flesh and blood, seems to radiate with an inner warmth is so provocative, so eternally enigmatic in its expression that it has tantalized the millions who have seen it in the Louvre or in reproduction. The landscape behind her increases the mystery; it is so much sheer fantasy that it seems related to the world of imagination rather than fact. The "Mona Lisa" is so generalized that it is perhaps not even a portrait; rather she is characteristic of the short-lived High Renaissance desire to concentrate upon the ideal rather than the particular.

The ideal which the "Mona Lisa" represents, no matter how illusive it is, is certainly a matter of inner life rather than physical externals; it radiates through her flesh and skin. The best portraits by Raphael (1483–1520) have somewhat the same quality. However, the inner spirit within a Raphael is neither so enigmatic nor so timeless; e.g., in the portrait of Julius II (1445–1513) in the Uffizi the inner spirit can show the effects of age and care. Raphael's ideal, at least in this portrait, was of a dignified and noble maturity. The weary shoulders, the head weighed forward, the white beard, the shadows under the eyes, the wrinkles enhance that effect. And the simple pyramidal composition, of the kind Raphael had studied in Leonardo's work, contributes to the sense of the pope's dignity.

In Venice about 1520 Titian (c. 1490–1576) painted a portrait of an unknown young man which shows another aspect of the search for the ideal in the portraiture of the Renaissance. This young man, whose elegance Titian proclaimed in the relaxed pose, the long fingers, the gloves and particularly by the extended "V" of his white shirt, has at the same time a youthful vulnerability. Instead of idealizing the dignity of old age, as Raphael did in his "Julius II," Titian is reminding us of the potentialities of youth; this is a man who may yet form himself into a maturer ideal. Although it is this suggestion of anticipation that makes this work most characteristic of the High Renaissance, it is the elegance of the man and the visual beauty of the arrangement within the painting that had most influence. Artists later in the 16th century, in the style called Mannerist rather than Renaissance, developed this self-conscious grace in paintings of polished and affected beauty. The type spread throughout Europe so that such Italians as Jacopo da Pontormo (1494–1556), Parmigianino (1503–40) and Bronzino (1503–72), such Frenchmen as François Clouet (c. 1515/20–1572), such Flemings as Sir Anthony More (c. 1512–

75) and such Englishmen as Nicholas Hilliard (1547–1619) painted Mannerist portraits.

During the Renaissance artists like Leonardo, Raphael and Titian had positions as courtiers rather than as artisans. This increase in social prestige helped to make the artist more conscious of his own personality. This consciousness accomplished two things: it encouraged the artist to paint portraits of himself and it made him impose himself in some fashion upon portraits he painted of others. Leonardo, Raphael and Titian did not efface themselves before their sitters as did Piero or Van Eyck; instead they revealed their own preoccupations by making these men conform to their particular ideals.

The Self-Conscious Sitter.—The same change in the social position of the artist took place in the north, with the same effects. The German Albrecht Dürer (1471–1528), at 13, was sufficiently aware of himself to make an exquisite silverpoint self-portrait. He later revealed his personal ambitions in paintings of himself. The self-portrait of 1498 (in the Prado, Madrid) shows Dürer in the costume of an elegant young man. Proudly displayed in the background are the Alps the painter had crossed on his way to Italy. In 1505, conscious of the religious troubles of his time, Dürer painted a self-portrait which showed another ideal—the desire to lead a life in imitation of Christ.

Dürer's compatriot, Hans Holbein the Younger (1497?–1543), excelled in superb and rather detached portrait drawings and paintings. His paintings show a desire for elegance, an enjoyment of the description of textures and a delight in the surface of the panel. A portrait such as that of the "Merchant Gisze" may at first seem cold and objective. Like Van Eyck in the portrait of the Arnolfinis, Holbein indicates the man's environment, his occupation (he is a Hanseatic merchant in the Steelyard in London) and even his habits by the details of the setting, and suggests his dignity and his position by the merchant's bearing and costume. However it soon becomes evident that Holbein is as much concerned with the nature of this man as with such externals. Here there is none of the easy grace of Titian's "Man With a Glove." Indeed Gisze holds himself rather tensely; he looks far to his right, well beyond us, not casually but with an expression which shows apprehension. Holbein uses the ingredients of the setting masterfully, building them around the Merchant Gisze in space so that he is hemmed in one corner. This position, combined with the dark shadow he casts, makes even the gesture of his opening the envelope a furtive one. On the wall is inscribed his appropriate motto: "No Joy Without Sorrow." Holbein tries to remain objective but within the formal restraint he gives his portraits strong emotional overtones which ask the spectator to respond as he once presumably responded before his sitter.

El Greco (1541–1614) did not feel as much need to discipline his responses to his sitters 66 years later. A comparison of his "Cardinal Guevara" with Raphael's "Julius II" shows how differently from a Renaissance artist this painter approached an important ecclesiastic. El Greco does everything to destroy the pyramidal order and calm of Raphael's work by choosing an elongated canvas, emphasizing its verticality, showing the figure full length and by giving the red silk of the robe an independent life by the angular and dynamic play of the folds. The cardinal does not sit with the heavy gravity of the pope; instead he perches on the edge of his chair, his feet nervously protruding from beneath his robes, his right hand conspicuously relaxed, the left toying with the arm of the chair. The piece of paper at his feet helps destroy any sense of self-containment. Nor is there any suggestion of spiritual contemplation, for the cardinal looks out with great wariness through his black-rimmed spectacles. He has more in common with Holbein's "Merchant Gisze" although he is painted more freely and the emotions are much intensified. In the works of both El Greco and Holbein, like the best 16th-century portraiture after 1530, the emotions in the relationship between sitter and artist predominate.

BAROQUE AND ROCOCO

The Whole Man.—The artists of the late middle ages were interested in man as a symbol; those of the early Renaissance in

Left panel of the "Wilton Diptych" by an unknown artist, late 14th or early 15th century. 18 × 11½ in.

"Federigo da Montefeltro, Duke of Urbino" by Piero della Francesca, c. 1472. 18½ × 13 in. In the Uffizi Gallery, Florence

"Arnolfini and His Wife" by Jan van Eyck, 1434. 32¼ × 23½ in.

EARLY PORTRAITS

Medieval portraits, like that of King Richard II of England, above, may have been painted to record their subject's piety. The king is shown kneeling in supplication and surrounded by his patron saints in the left panel of the "Wilton Diptych"; the Madonna and Child are depicted in the right-hand panel (not shown). With the renewal of interest in the individual that characterized the Renaissance, it became fashionable for wealthy men, like the young Italian merchant who appears with his bride, at bottom right, to have their portraits painted in as lifelike a manner as possible. Though the couple stands somewhat stiffly and the seemingly casual details that fill the scene constitute a rebus of medieval symbols of the marriage sacraments, the portrait, by Jan van Eyck, in its brilliant rendering of texture, detail, and the effects of natural light, hints at the naturalism that was to follow. In 15th-century Italy this increasing interest in accurate rendering was put to a new purpose: the glorification of the ideal to which the sitter aspired. Thus Piero della Francesca's portrait of the duke of Urbino (top right) is a highly realistic representation which also conveys the absolute temporal power of a Renaissance prince

PLATE II   PORTRAIT PAINTING

"Portrait of the Artist" by Albrecht Dürer, 1498. 20½ × 16⅛ in.

"Merchant Gisze" by Hans Holbein the Younger, 1532. 37½ × 33½ in.

"Man with a Glove" by Titian, c. 1520. 39 × 35 in. In the Louvre, Paris

"Julius II" by Raphael, c. 1511–12. 42 X 32 in. In the National Gallery, London

RENAISSANCE PORTRAITS

Portrait painters of the High Renaissance were increasingly intrigued by the abstract ideals which their sitters could be made to personify. Meticulous attention to specific detail of the kind that characterized the work of Van Eyck (Plate I) became less important than the search for the generalized ideal, and Late Renaissance portraits still manage to convey to the modern eye the ideals that inspired them. Thus, the serene and contemplative gaze of the militant Pope Julius II by Raphael (above) still evokes the weary dignity of old age, while the "Man with a Glove" by Titian (Plate II, bottom) conveys the promise of youth in his graceful pose and eager look. Enhanced social prestige helped make the Renaissance artist increasingly aware of, and fascinated by, his own personality. His emotional reactions to the sitter, favourable or unfavourable, became of great importance to him, causing Hans Holbein to paint a Hanseatic merchant (Plate II, top left) as he saw him rather than as the sitter saw himself, and El Greco (right) to paint a frank portrait of an ostensibly spiritual cardinal. Albrecht Dürer's 1498 self-portrait (Plate II, top right) shows, in its elegant dress and introspective look, the Renaissance spirit of self-awareness.

"Cardinal Don Fernando Niño Guevara" by El Greco (1541–1614).
67¼ × 42½ in.

PLATE IV

PORTRAIT PAINTING

"Innocent X" by Diego Velázquez, 1650. 55¼ × 47¼ in. In the Galleria Doria, Rome

BAROQUE PORTRAITS

Baroque portraitists, in seeking to present the total man, synthesized the aims of the artists who preceded them. They sought simultaneously to render accurately, record their own emotional responses to the sitter, and express the ideals which their sitters seemed to personify. Thus, Velázquez in his portrait of Innocent X (left) portrayed a pope who is at once ugly and magnificent, Rembrandt evoked the spiritual beauty within an unattractive woman (Plate V), and Anthony van Dyck (below) made an elegant figure of a powerful king

"Charles I" by Anthony van Dyck, c. 1638. 107 × 83½ in. In the Louvre, Paris

"Lady with a Pink" by Rembrandt van Rijn, c. 1655. 36¼ × 29⅜ in.

PLATE VI   PORTRAIT PAINTING

"Baron Schwiter" by Eugène Delacroix, 1826.   85¾ × 56½ in.

"Mme Moitessier (Seated)" by J. A. D. Ingres, 1856.   47¼ × 36¼ in.

"Victorine Meurend" by Édouard Manet, c. 1875.   17 × 17 in.

18TH- AND 19TH-CENTURY PORTRAITS

The English 18th-century portraitists, of whom Thomas Gainsborough (Plate VII, top right) was among the most gifted, sought, through flawless execution and graceful pose, to increase the sitter's stature.   John Singleton Copley (Plate VII, bottom right), Gainsborough's American contemporary, represented a different and more realistic strain, painting straightforward likenesses without flattery.   Just as Gainsborough and Copley represented the romantic and realistic poles in the 18th century, so to a considerable degree did Eugène Delacroix (top left) and J. A. D. Ingres (above) represent them in the 19th.   However, Delacroix tempered his essential romanticism with some characteristically realistic touches (like the shy vulnerability of his otherwise elegant subject) while Ingres, though meticulously exact in rendering his sitter's likeness, emphasized her feminine curves and relaxed pose to produce an essentially seductive effect.   Édouard Manet (left), like other painters associated with the Impressionists, was interested neither in flattery nor realism but rather in the purely visual problems that a portrait posed.   John Singer Sargent (Plate VII, left) carried the fashionable romantic tradition of elegant flattery into the early 20th century

"Mrs. Graham" by Thomas Gainsborough, c. 1777. 93½ × 60¾ in.

"Madame X (Mme Gautreau)" by John Singer Sargent, 1884.
82½ × 43¼ in.

"Mrs. Seymour Fort" by John Singleton Copley, c. 1780. 24 × 19 in.

PLATE VIII   PORTRAIT PAINTING

"Duke and Duchess of Morbilli" by Edgar Degas, c. 1865.   20 × 17 in.

"Jacques Lipchitz and His Wife" by Amedeo Modigliani, 1916.   31½ × 21 in.

"Portrait of a Lady" by Pablo Picasso, 1937.   24 × 11 in. Owned by the artist

LATE 19TH- AND EARLY 20TH-CENTURY PORTRAITS

The three portraits on this Plate show the increasing interest in psychological complexity that has characterized much modern portraiture. In the Edgar Degas portrait of the Duke and Duchess of Morbilli (top left), painted in c. 1865, may be seen a conscious effort to portray both individuals as well as something of the relationship between them.   Amedeo Modigliani (top right), about 50 years later, in 1916, felt free to eliminate superfluous detail and concentrate on the essentials that reveal more completely the personalities of the sitters, sculptor Jacques Lipchitz and his wife.   A comparison of these portraits with the Van Eyck portrait of Arnolfini and his wife, which appears on Plate I, shows how far inward artists have turned since the Renaissance.   In the portrait by Pablo Picasso (left), the artist has radically altered the appearance of the sitter for his own artistic ends, portraying her from several vantage points at once, as if simultaneously to reveal as many facets of her personality as possible

the facts of his appearance and position; those of the High Renaissance in him as an expression of an ideal and the Mannerist painters of the 16th century in his emotional responses. But it was not until the 17th century, in the period called the baroque, that any artist tried to embrace all these approaches in a single portrait. Certainly the Flemish Peter Paul Rubens (1577–1640) and the Dutch Frans Hals (*c.* 1580–1666) accomplished this—but it was the Spaniard Diego Velázquez (1599–1660) who succeeded most impressively in his portrait of Innocent X. The pope in his dress, in his throne and in his bearing is a symbol of papal authority if not of infallibility. The facts of his appearance, no matter how ugly, are recorded here although they in no sense destroy the total impression. The ideal that Innocent X represents is far from the Renaissance ideal—but it is a magnificent expression of the physical and intellectual and moral force to which the baroque aspired. Velázquez is as much concerned as Holbein or El Greco with emotional relationships, but his are not so subtle or so strained; Innocent X challenges us with his penetrating look. Velázquez, with his remarkable ability to give the illusion of this dynamic man in space, has made a characteristically baroque effort to present the total man.

Velázquez' contemporary in Protestant Holland, Rembrandt van Rijn (1606–69), normally painted far gentler, humbler people but also tried to arrive at the synthesis of the complete man or woman. One of his late paintings, "Lady With a Pink," records the facts of his sitter's weariness and age and, by the position of her head and hands, suggests her shyness and humility. Like Leonardo, Rembrandt was interested in the spirit within such a woman, but here this radiates warmly and not coquettishly through a physical shell which in itself is a revelation of this woman's experience. Her beauty seems completely spiritual, the result of a moral life rather than of a physical ideal; Rembrandt expresses it in the gentle, worn face, the large, tender eyes and particularly in the light which seems to be the equivalent of her soul. Rembrandt's judgment of his sitters is ultimately a moral one.

One of the most influential portrait painters in Europe in the 17th century was the Flemish Sir Anthony Van Dyck (1599–1641). Like Rembrandt and Velázquez, Van Dyck was interested in an illusion of the total man revealed in a moment of contact. However, his ideal was more like that of the early Titian whose work he admired.

As can be seen in his portrait of Charles I of England (1600–49), to whom Van Dyck was court painter, he could suggest the easy grace, the elegance and the arrogance of this man through the swing of the body, the texture of the dress, the haughty expression of the features. The casual landscape setting, the grooms with the horse, also contribute to the sense of the grace of the king, so accidentally discovered with them. Van Dyck brought this tradition of the courtly portrait from 16th-century Venice to England where it was developed in the 18th century by such painters as Sir Joshua Reynolds and Thomas Gainsborough.

The Sitter Romanticized.—France had several artists in the 18th century, including Jean Baptiste Chardin (1699–1779), Maurice Quentin de La Tour (1704–88) and Jean Baptiste Perroneau (1715–83), who drew sensitive heads in pastel (*q.v.*) which show a lightness of touch which was appropriate for the period called rococo. But it was England that had the most substantial sequence of portrait painters; their names form an imposing list: William Hogarth, Sir Joshua Reynolds, Thomas Gainsborough, Joseph Highmore, Allan Ramsay, Sir Henry Raeburn and George Romney. Of these, Reynolds (1723–92) was the most verbally articulate and, before the Royal Academy of which he was the first president, he made a series of discourses about art in general with several asides on portraiture which he, like his age, regarded as a form of art inferior to history painting. During his fourth discourse he said of the portrait painter: "He cannot make his hero talk like a great man, he must make him look like one." And essentially this was the attitude of most of these English portrait painters—to emphasize, with certain visual conventions and exaggerations, the stature of the sitter. Reynolds did it himself, most convincingly in his portraits of such men as Samuel Johnson.

Gainsborough (1727–88) was perhaps the most gifted of these painters and, although many of them were influenced by Van Dyck, his style was closest. He applied paint with the fluidity of Van Dyck. His work has a similar luminosity which seems, in itself, to give his portraits great distinction. Like Van Dyck he normally painted his sitters out-of-doors—although for the landed aristocracy of 18th-century England those parklike settings probably had more meaning in terms of prestige than they had had a century earlier. And he took certain conventions which Van Dyck had used to flatter his sitters and exaggerated them further to give the most aristocratic impression. In his portrait of "Mrs. Graham," for example, Gainsborough emphasized her proud dignity by elongating her body and by emphasizing the vertical through her long, graceful throat, the right arm and even the supporting pillar. She is spatially and psychologically sufficiently removed to remain appropriately remote. Her beauty is suggested by her exquisite features and by the shimmer of her garments, echoed in the romantic light of the sky. Finally the casualness of such an aristocratic ideal is indicated by the informal way Mrs. Graham leans on the pillar and looks without concern in another direction.

Eighteenth-century England was invaded periodically by American artists. Two talented portrait painters remained there. One of them, Benjamin West (1738–1820), became president of the Royal Academy. The other, John Singleton Copley (1738–1815), painted good, straightforward paintings which seem far removed from Gainsborough's romanticized portraits. When Copley painted "Mrs. Seymour Fort" he may have used the device of the baroque red curtain in the background and shown her in a position of considerable dignity—but with the crocheting in her hand, her solid body and good-humoured face, she represents all the most sensible middle-class virtues, presented without flattery, satire or rationalization.

19TH AND 20TH CENTURIES

Realism.—In France during the first half of the 19th century there were two strains in painting comparable with those Gainsborough and Copley had represented in the 18th. Eugène Delacroix (1798–1863), when he painted his 21-year-old friend, the Baron Louis Schwiter, continued the strain in European painting which runs from the Venetians through Van Dyck to Gainsborough. Consistently he painted the full figure of this rather elegantly dressed young man, standing in a park with a poetic light breaking across the sky. However at the same time with a characteristically 19th-century realism Delacroix portrays the baron's essential vulnerability. His hands and the position of his feet, the untidy hair and collar convey his helplessness. And because he stands so simply and directly and because Delacroix has raised the horizon so that, unlike a portrait by Van Dyck or Gainsborough, the viewer is put almost on a level with him, the impression is given that this rather gentle, shy figure of Baron Schwiter has been exposed because he has been too passive to resist or to care. In the very lack of assertiveness or definition, which makes it possible for him to be such a harmonious part of the idyllic setting, the baron seems to represent at least one romantic ideal.

Just as Copley's "Mrs. Seymour Fort" is the antithesis of Gainsborough's "Mrs. Graham," so "Mme Moitessier" by Jean Auguste Dominique Ingres (1780–1867) is the antithesis of Delacroix's "Baron Schwiter." As substantial as Mrs. Fort and as elaborately dressed, Mme Moitessier is decisive, assertive and meets our eyes with a challenge. Ingres, with the examples of Roman painting and of Raphael in mind, found every excuse for curves which would emphasize the firmness and roundess of her body; these combined with the relaxed pose make Mme Moitessier essentially seductive. Throughout his career Ingres painted and drew many portraits as meticulous and direct.

The portraitist in the second half of the 19th century in France who perhaps most completely understood both Delacroix and Ingres, and learned from each, was Edgar Degas (1834–1917). His early portrait of his sister and brother-in-law, "Duke and Duchess of Morbilli," shows an indebtedness to Ingres in the relative precision and boldness of the work but also something of the quality of Delacroix in the hesitancy of both husband and wife before the spectators. However, Degas was most conscious of the psychological complexities and tensions in the relationship of two human beings to each other—and in their relationship to the world. Although the work possesses almost the formality of a daguerreotype, Degas makes use of the positions of the figures in relation to each other and in space, their expressions and particularly their gestures to make the nature of their adjustment to each other and to society quite clear. Later Degas found a more personal visual vocabulary to convey the same kind of meaning in his portraits, which influenced such painters as Vincent van Gogh (1853–90) and Henri de Toulouse-Lautrec (1864–1901).

Degas' contemporary and friend Édouard Manet (1832–83) painted portraits which are psychologically uncomplicated, straightforward, but most remarkable, like all his paintings, for their sheer visual beauty. Like Manet, other painters associated with the Impressionists were less concerned with subject matter than with certain visual problems. Even Paul Cézanne (1839–1906), who painted some beautiful portraits, was only incidentally concerned with recording the appearance, personality or virtues of any particular person; his paintings had another function. It might be argued that the decline in the interest of the finest painters in portraiture was a result of the decline in patronage.

However, at the same time that Degas and his friends were receiving little encouragement, there were fashionable portrait painters throughout Europe who made fortunes from this form of art. Perhaps the best of these was the U.S. expatriate, John Singer Sargent (1856–1925). Sargent may have suffered somewhat from his generous patronage; indeed he eventually reacted against it and refused to paint more portraits. Whereas the most creative artists of the 19th century—Goya, David, Corot, Daumier, Millet, Courbet, Whistler, Eakins, Renoir, besides those already mentioned—revealed an underlying realism and a desire to present the sitter as unpretentiously as possible, Sargent fulfilled his sitters' desires to be ravishingly beautiful or forcefully handsome. In such paintings as "The Wyndham Sisters" he succeeded in giving an illusion of the most beautiful and animated of young women in a work of great brilliance and bravado. Sargent has survived the criticisms of the 20th century more satisfactorily than such fashionable rivals as Giovanni Boldini (1845–1931) or Philip Alexius Laszlo de Lombos (1869–1937). However, a market for their kind of portraiture still exists.

The 20th Century.—In the first half of the 20th century, even more than during the 19th, the most penetrating portraits have not been the result of commissions of the kind Sargent received. Amedeo Modigliani (1884–1920), an Italian living a poverty-stricken and bohemian life in Paris, painted many of the most successful portraits of this period—but usually of his friends; they might pay him, but he demanded only a paltry sum. The sculptor Jacques Lipchitz (1891–   ) has written that when he was newly married and he and his wife decided to have their portrait painted by Modigliani, the painter asked ten francs a sitting and insisted it was finished after the first. Lipchitz, in his embarrassment, persuaded Modigliani to work on it longer; however, the sculptor acquired his portrait for a modest sum.

Lipchitz has also written that the pose for this double portrait was inspired by their wedding photograph; this makes it particularly appropriate to compare it with Degas' portrait of the Morbillis, which must have been based upon some daguerreotype. Probably a comparison of the photographs, as much as a comparison of the paintings, would reveal how much more casually and informally the Lipchitzes were living than the Morbillis had three decades earlier. It is not just that the sculptor wears a turtle-neck sweater or has a hand cockily in his pocket or that the picture behind him on the wall is tilted precariously. It comes out in their perfect ease with the spectators, and even more tellingly in their casual intimacy with each other. Lipchitz places his hand protectively on her shoulder and she leans her head back on his chest with supreme confidence in him and in herself. None of the tensions of the Degas portrait seems to exist.

There is nothing photographic about this double portrait even if a photograph was the source for the composition. Modigliani

makes use of visual abstractions, particularly pattern, to interpret this husband and wife. The beautiful oval of the woman's face opens up sensually whereas the features of the husband's face are smaller, cramped and more ingrown. In depending upon such abstractions Modigliani was able to eliminate irrelevant detail, to simplify the work and therefore to concentrate upon those essentials which could suggest their separate personalities, their relationships to each other and to the rest of the world more perfectly than any wedding photograph could.

Twentieth-century portraiture, like all 20th-century art, has been affected by the Freudian analysis of the personality, as is seen in "A First Sketch for the Spectre of a Genius" by the Swiss painter Paul Klee (1879–1940). The work is a pathetic commentary upon the lack of balance in emotional, physical and spiritual growth of the genius.

Of all 20th-century painters Pablo Picasso (1881–   ) has been the most creative in the discovery of new visual vocabularies to convey the character of a sitter. He has drawn and painted as meticulously and as representationally as Ingres or he has departed as far from the conventional as it seems possible for a painter to do without losing a sense of the thing portrayed. His responses to people in his portraits have been sentimental, cynical, calm, analytical or morally indignant, in each case representing an attitude characteristic of a part of 20th-century society.

In his "Portrait of a Lady" (1937) Picasso continued, as he had for 30 years, to destroy the conventional integrity of the body for his own expressive purposes. With colour, pattern, line and important allusions to anatomy, Picasso makes it apparent that a classically beautiful woman is seated, with a certain aplomb, in brilliant sunshine. She seems a typical 20th-century sophisticate in her informality, the smart dress, the lacquered nails and the hand which toys with her long hair. But Picasso was not content to describe her only socially; he designed her dress so that her jacket opens to reveal lines like stamens fanning out to her petal-like breasts; this floral motif seems carried out in the hands. It does not seem improbable that Picasso, with great restraint, is suggesting her sexual urges. But the most startling area is the face. The eye on the left is the strange and frightening red of something possessed; the quieter green eye on the right seems to have turned on itself to regard the other with disturbance and surprise. It is as if this woman, so suave externally, has suddenly become aware of the unknown world of her unconscious. Picasso, like the 20th-century novelist or psychologist, makes the accepted breakdown of the barriers between the normal and the abnormal, the unconscious and the conscious quite explicit. The Surrealists, such as Giorgio de Chirico (1888–   ), Max Ernst (1891–   ) and Yves Tanguy (1900–55), delved even more obviously into Freudian realms.

The Judgment of Quality in Portraiture.—How can the quality of a contemporary portrait be determined without the selective critical process of generations? A great portrait painting must be, first of all, a great work of art; this means that every brush stroke will have a structural role in the total painting and will, at the same time, express the attitude of artist toward sitter.

The abstract elements must have a vitality of their own which seems to be the consequence of the creative activity of a painter whose whole being is absorbed in the process. As completely different as such artists as Piero della Francesca, Velázquez or Picasso may be, every part of their work operates in producing visual relationships which make their sitters seem physically and spiritually alive. The portrait, a very difficult form of art, presents other problems about which it is perhaps rash to generalize. However, in all great portrait paintings the suggestion of the intelligence of the sitter seems to surmount the handsome costumes, elaborate settings or an unusual style. Even in Picasso's portraits from the most difficult of all his periods, analytical Cubism, the sense of the particular intelligences of sitters, as in his portraits of Ambroise Vollard, Wilhelm Uhde and Daniel Henry Kahnweiler, is finally triumphant. The great portrait, whatever the period, seems to be the product of the painter's imagination before a sitter whom this painter, because of his temperament and background, is fully able to understand. Being the product of the painter's imagination, it is thus strange to his contemporaries and impossible to anticipate.

See also OIL PAINTING, TECHNIQUE OF; see also references under "Portrait Painting" in the Index.

BIBLIOGRAPHY.—M. J. Friedländer, *Landscape, Portrait, Still-Life* (1949); F. Wormwald, "The Wilton Diptych," *Journal of the Courtauld and Warburg Institutes*, 17:191 (July–Dec. 1954); M. Wheeler, *Twentieth Century Portraits* (1942); *A.L.A. Portrait Index* (1906); Jacob Burckhardt, *Das Portrait* (1908); Herbert Fuerst, *Portrait Painting* (1927); Ludwig Goldscheider (ed.), *Five Hundred Self-Portraits* (1936). *See* also bibliographies of the articles on the individual painters and of PAINTING. (J. S. Bs.; X.)

PORT ROYAL, an island of Beaufort County, S.C., U.S., 50 mi. (80 km.) SW of Charleston, one of the Sea Islands. It is about 17.5 mi. (28 km.) long and 7.5 mi. (12 km.) wide. The principal city is Beaufort, a port of entry and seat of Beaufort County. The town of Port Royal is on the southern tip of the island, 5 mi. S of Beaufort; its population is less than 1,000. Major occupations include fishing, shrimp and crab processing, cypress and pine lumbering, cattle and cotton farming, and employment at nearby Parris Island, a U.S. Marine Corps installation. Old plantation homes, vast oaks covered with Spanish moss, and nearby beaches make Port Royal an exotic resort area.

The port was named Santa Elena by Spanish explorers in the early 16th century. In 1562 the French Huguenot Jean Ribault, seeking a haven for French Protestants and a privateering base against Spanish shipping, renamed it Port Royal and left 30 settlers on Parris Island, three miles from the present town of Port Royal. Neglected by Ribault, after two years the settlers killed the commander he had left in charge, built a tiny ship and returned to Europe. The Spanish occupied the area more or less continuously from 1566 to 1650, maintaining garrisons and Indian missions. English claims to Carolina grew with the settlement of Charleston in 1670, and in 1684 Henry Erskine (Lord Cardross) led 51 Scottish Covenanters to Stuart's Town, 1 mi. N of the present town of Port Royal. Charlestonians looked upon the Scots as trade rivals and ignored pleas for help when Stuart's Town was destroyed by Spanish and Indians in 1686. Gradually planters moved into the area, and in 1710 Henry Somerset (duke of Beaufort) established the present town of Beaufort. In Jan. 1779, during the American Revolution, the British occupied the area but were dislodged the following month. After the Revolution the Port Royal environs became the centre of opulent rice and cotton plantations, and scores of magnificent ante-bellum homes attest to this golden age. Early in the American Civil War, on Nov. 6–7, 1861, a fleet of 56 Union vessels, and 12,000 men under Gen. Thomas W. Sherman, reduced the Confederate fortifications and used the port as a Union coaling and repair station for the remainder of the war. Northern idealists, supported by the U.S. government, conducted the Port Royal experiment during and immediately after the war, confiscating the lands abandoned by white planters and seeking, with mediocre success, to educate the former slaves of the area and give them control over local lands and government. *See* also SEA ISLANDS. (G. H. CT.)

PORT ROYAL (PORT-ROYAL DES CHAMPS), a celebrated abbey of Cistercian nuns, was the centre of Jansenism (*q.v.*) and of literary activity in 17th-century France. It was founded about 1204 as a Benedictine house by Mathilde de Garlande on a low, marshy site in the valley of Chevreuse, seven miles south of Versailles. Its church was built in 1230.

In 1609 the young abbess Jacqueline Marie Angélique Arnauld began a much-needed reform. However, the unhealthiness of the site drove her, in 1626, to establish her community in Paris, in the Faubourg Saint-Jacques, where new buildings were erected, including a Baroque church. In 1638 the deserted building was occupied by the *Solitaires* (hermits), pious laymen or secular priests living without vows or definite rule under the spiritual guidance of Jean Duvergier de Hauranne (*q.v.*), abbot of Saint-Cyran and friend of Cornelius Jansen. Among them were several members of the Arnauld (*q.v.*) family. Several times the *Solitaires* were forced by persecution to leave. In 1648 a group of nuns returned to occupy the buildings; the *Solitaires* moved to Les Granges nearby and there started the Petites Écoles de Port Royal, which provided a type of education differing in important ways from that of the Jesuits. Jean Racine was a pupil there.

In 1665 most of the nuns of Port-Royal de Paris, having refused to sign the fomulary condemning Jansen, were sent to Port-Royal-des-Champs, where they underwent a kind of captivity, deprived of all sacraments. The *Solitaires* were dispersed and went into exile or hiding. However, in 1669 the Peace of Clement IX, or Peace of the Church, was concluded and ten years of calm followed. The houses of Paris and Les Champs were finally separated, and the latter enjoyed the protection of the duchesse de Longueville, cousin of Louis XIV. After her death in 1679 persecution was renewed, the community was forbidden to receive novices, and it declined in numbers. The last abbess but one was Agnès de Sainte-Thècle, aunt of Racine. In 1705 the bull *Vineam domini* of Clement XI renewed measures against Jansenists, and the remaining 17 nuns refused to submit. On Oct. 29, 1709, the community was dispersed and the nuns exiled to various other convents. In 1711 the buildings and cemetery were completely destroyed and the bones of the buried thrown into a hole in the cemetery of Saint-Lambert.

In 1824 the land was bought by the lawyer Louis Silvy out of devotion to the memory of Port Royal. After his death the property was transferred to the Society of St. Augustine, which became the Society of Port Royal. The ruins of the church were uncovered and a small museum built. Port-Royal-de-Paris became a prison during the Revolution. In the 19th century the Hôpital de la Maternité was installed there. The buildings are in perfect state of preservation and both chapter house and choir have been restored. *See* also JANSENISM, with bibliography.

BIBLIOGRAPHY.—The following books deal with Port Royal primarily as a historical monument: L. P. Hérard, *Recherches archéologiques sur l'abbaye de Port-Royal des Champs* (1881); H. Mabille, *L'Église de Port-Royal des Champs* (1901); A. Hallays, *Le Pélerinage de Port-Royal* (1925); C. Gazier, *Histoire du monastère de Port-Royal* (1929). *See* also R. A. Knox, *Enthusiasm* (1950). (L. CO.)

PORTRUSH, an urban district and seaside resort of County Antrim, Northern Ireland, lies 6 mi. (9.7 km.) N of Coleraine at the end of the Antrim Coast Road. Pop. (1961) 4,265. It is situated on the basaltic peninsula of Ramore Head, with magnificent sandy beaches and deep bays on either side. There is a harbour on the western side. Out to sea lie the Skerries (rocks) forming a natural breakwater. The Giant's Causeway (*q.v.*) is 7 mi. (11.3 km.) E along the coast beyond the White Rocks, with their caves, and Dunluce Castle (14th century), standing on a rock separated by a chasm spanned by a footbridge. Portrush caters principally to tourists; it has three golf courses and spacious recreation grounds. There are salmon fisheries and a whitefish trade.

(H. M. A.)

PORT SAID (BUR SA'ID), the second seaport and one of the four urban *muhafazat* (governorates) of Egypt (United Arab Republic), is situated at the northern end of the Suez Canal, 145 mi. (233 km.) NE of Cairo by rail. Pop. (1966) 282,977. The town lies on the western side of the canal on the low sandy strip of land that separates the Mediterranean from Lake Manzala (Buhayrat al Manzilah). This land was raised and extended by the draining of part of the lake and by material excavated from the inner harbour and main channel. Port Fouad (Bur Fu'ad) on the opposite bank between the Mediterranean and Al Mallaha Lagoon (Tawwal al Mallahah) is a residential quarter of more recent growth. The outer harbour, or roadstead, is about 4 mi. (6.4 km.) long and is formed by two protective jetties, or breakwaters, the western one carrying a lighthouse 174 ft. (53 m.) high. The main channel of the port, $2\frac{1}{2}$ mi. (4 km.) long and flanked by open basins, curves through a 40° angle to the beginning of the canal, where for $1\frac{1}{2}$ mi. (2.4 km.) there is a parallel second channel.

Port Said, named after Said Pasha, dates from 1859, the year in which the construction of the canal was begun. Originally it depended entirely upon the canal traffic, becoming the largest coaling station in the world and later an important oil–bunkering port. After 1902 increasing quantities of raw cotton and subsequently rice were exported from the eastern provinces of the delta, the cotton traveling by boat from Al Matariyah across Lake Manzala. Since 1904, when the standard-gauge railway from Cairo was completed, Port Said has been in a position to compete with the main

J. ALLAN CASH

THE WATERFRONT OF PORT SAID

port of Alexandria. There is a separate fishing harbour. The main workshops of the canal administration are there.   (A. B. M.)

PORTSMOUTH, a city, county and parliamentary borough, the premier naval base of the British Commonwealth, and (with Southsea) a popular holiday resort, in Hampshire, Eng., lies 73 mi. (117 km.) SW of London by road. Pop. (1961) 215,077. It is the seat of an Anglican and a Roman Catholic bishop.

The naval station and Royal Dockyard (known colloquially as "Pompey") occupy the southwestern part of Portsea Island, which lies between Portsmouth Harbour and Langstone Harbour, inlets of the English Channel. The island is connected to the mainland by road and railway bridges. Portsmouth Harbour opens into Spithead, the eastern end of the Solent (q.v.), which separates the Isle of Wight from the mainland. The four conspicuous masonry forts in Spithead were built in the 1860s as part of the port defenses. Portsmouth Harbour widens inward in bottle form, with Portsmouth on the east shore and Gosport (q.v.) on the west. Hayling Island lies east of Langstone Harbour.

Portsmouth extends to the northern mainland, including Cosham, Paulsgrove, Drayton, Wymering, and Farlington, north of which the chalk ridge of Portsdown (400 ft. [122 m.]) commands a view of the city and harbours. Portsmouth suffered severe bomb damage in World War II, but substantial clearance and rebuilding have taken place. The dockyard, which is the principal employment centre, dates from 1496, when the town was already a naval station. It was greatly expanded after 1698 and now covers more than 300 ac. (121 ha.), with four large dry docks and 75 ac. (30 ha.) of fitting and repairing basins. There are numerous naval establishments, and a Royal Marine headquarters at Eastney.

Portsmouth owes its origin to the retreat of the sea from Portchester at the head of Portsmouth Harbour. No town existed until 1194, when the strategic importance of Portsea Island induced Richard I to build one and to grant a charter, fair, and market to the inhabitants. The borough is governed by a charter granted by Charles I in 1627, modified by later municipal acts.

The holiday and tourist trade, which is centred primarily on Southsea, attracts more than 150,000 staying visitors and 500,000–800,000 day tourists annually. The resort area, with a broad sweep of grassland (Southsea Common) adjoining the beach and promenades, includes two piers, fine seafront gardens, and sports areas. Industries include shipbuilding, aircraft engineering, and the manufacture of corsets, cardboard boxes, brushes, refrigerators, sweets, and baby products. The commercial port at Camber Docks near the harbour entrance and the airport in the northeast part of Portsea Island are municipal.

Lord Nelson's flagship at the Battle of Trafalgar, HMS "Vic-

tory," occupies a small dry dock in the dockyard and is a major tourist attraction, and the nearby Victory Museum contains many relics of Nelson. The spacious guildhall, reconstructed after having been gutted by enemy action in 1941, was reopened by Queen Elizabeth II in 1959. It serves as civic headquarters and as a concert and conference hall. Other notable buildings include the cathedral (the former parish church, dating in part to the 12th century), several dignified buildings of the 18th and early 19th centuries in the dockyard, Southsea Castle, and the birthplace of Charles Dickens at 393 Commercial Road (now a museum). Other distinguished natives of Portsmouth were George Meredith, Sir Walter Besant, Isambard Brunel, the philanthropist Jonas Hanway, and the cobbler John Pounds who started a "ragged school."

Passenger steamers and car ferries from Portsmouth serve Ryde and Fishbourne, Isle of Wight. The parliamentary borough is divided into Langstone, South, and West divisions, each returning one member. Portsmouth became a county borough in 1888 and a city in 1926, with a lord mayor in 1928.   (C. A. Gt.)

PORTSMOUTH, a city of New Hampshire, U.S., named after Portsmouth, Eng., is New Hampshire's oldest settlement, second oldest city, first capital and only seaport. Situated on the Piscataqua river near its entrance into the Atlantic ocean, it is about 60 mi. N. of Boston, Mass., and about 50 mi. S.W. of Portland, Me. Known as the Old Town by the Sea and the Queen of the Piscataqua, it is rich in historic associations and on its winding streets, tree-shaded and narrow, there are still examples of prerevolutionary architecture, ranging from the earliest simple salt-box style to the dignified 18th-century mansions, tall and square, built on the profits of the city's 18th-century shipbuilding and sailing trade.

Only three years after the Pilgrims settled at Plymouth a fishing settlement was planted 2 mi. E. of the present city. The next year (1624) settlement was made at Portsmouth proper, called successively Piscataqua and Strawbery Banke and finally in 1653 incorporated under its present name. Portsmouth was the seat of the provincial government of New Hampshire and the home of the famous Wentworth family which furnished two royal governors. Adjacent New Castle was the scene of one of the earliest military events of the Revolution in the patriot capture of Ft. William and Mary from the British in 1774.

In the first half of the 19th century Portsmouth suffered a gradual decline of its commerce and settled down to its present status of a trading centre and home of small industry. The continuance of one of the first U.S. navy yards, dating from the 1790s, has been important as a major economic support for the area. Although it is actually on Seavey's Island in the river (and so in Kittery, Me.), the establishment is known as the Portsmouth Navy yard. There, in 1905, treaty negotiations ended the Russo-Japanese War. In the 20th century the yard became a centre for the building and repair of submarines. Connected with it are a naval hospital and a naval prison. The development of the large Pease air force base in Newington, just outside Portsmouth, has also been of great economic advantage to the area. A unique urban renewal project—Strawbery Banke, Inc.—approved in 1960 and continued in the mid-1960s, was very active in the restoration of a number of the old houses and public buildings in Portsmouth.

Portsmouth is on a coastal highway, and for more rapid travel north and south the New Hampshire and Maine turnpikes are easily accessible. The city has a council-manager form of government. Pop. (1970) 25,717. For comparative population figures see table in New Hampshire: Population.   (A. R. F.)

PORTSMOUTH, a port city in southeastern Virginia, U.S., on the south shore of the Elizabeth River (an estuary of Hampton Roads), opposite the city of Norfolk (q.v.), with which its history has been closely associated; the seat of Norfolk County until the latter became part of the newly organized city of Chesapeake in 1963. Pop. (1970) 110,963. Norfolk-Portsmouth standard metropolitan statistical area (see Norfolk) 680,600. For comparative city population figures see table in Virginia: Population.

Portsmouth was settled in 1752 by people interested in trade but after the American Revolution the town refused to permit the settlement of British merchants. The Norfolk Navy Yard was established in Portsmouth by the U.S. government in 1801. In 1855 the population was decimated by yellow fever. When Federal troops evacuated the Navy Yard in 1861 the South fell heir to great stores of equipment and built the Confederate ironclad "Virginia" from the hull of the scuttled USS "Merrimack." The yard was recaptured by the Federals in 1862. Portsmouth received a city charter in 1858 and has a council-manager form of government, in effect since 1917.

Portsmouth is connected to other ports serving the Hampton Roads area by a belt-line railway. The city is an important research centre for the Navy, whose facilities include the navy yard and the naval hospital, the Navy's oldest. Portsmouth manufactures chemicals, wood products, sail and power boats, apparel, and peanut butter, and has a large steam-generating plant. The Intracoastal Waterway runs southward past Portsmouth to Dismal Swamp, a haven for hunters and naturalists. The city has a community theatre group, a concert association, a naval museum, and a minor league baseball team. Trinity Church (1762) is an attraction. Tidewater Community College (1969), a private coeducational college, is in Portsmouth. (G. M. Be.)

PORT SUDAN, the principal seaport of the Republic of the Sudan, lies on the west coast of the Red Sea, about 700 mi. (1,127 km.) S of Suez by sea and 490 mi. (789 km.) NE of Khartoum by rail. Pop. (1965 est.) 78,940, half being Arab or Nubian Sudanese (many of Nile Valley origin), with large numbers of indigenous Beja and West Africans, and a small European minority; Asian traders are prominent. Port Sudan was built in 1908 to replace Sawakin, the historic Arab port on a lagoon farther south (now coral-choked and in ruins). The harbour is in the mouth of a gulf continuing seaward through the fringing reefs in a straight, coral-free channel, 10 to 14 fathoms deep, marked by two lighthouses. On the northeast side of the inlet are the customhouse, dockyard, main quays (depth 30–35 ft. [9–11 m.]) with cranes and railway sidings, offices, and warehouses; new deepwater berths were constructed in the 1950s and early 1960s. The fuel dock is on the west side of the inlet, south of the town. A causeway carries a road and railway from the main docks to the town, from which the Nile Valley at Atbara is 295 mi. (475 km.) by rail. Kassala (343 mi. [552 km.]) and the Gezira are directly served by a branch line and a new road to Kassala and Khartoum was opened in 1962. There is an airport with regular services to Khartoum, Atbara, Cairo, Jidda, and Beirut.

Port Sudan has a hot, near-desert climate. Fresh water is piped from Khawr (Khor) Arba'at in the Red Sea Hills, and there are salt-evaporating pans and irrigated market gardens. Among imports cotton textiles have been displaced from first importance by machinery, vehicles, fuel oil, and building materials—commodities vital to development in the republic. The chief exports are cotton, gum, oilseeds, peanuts, hides and skins, and senna. (M. T. P.)

PORT TALBOT, a municipal borough in the Aberavon parliamentary division of Glamorgan, Wales, on the Avon (Afon) near its mouth in Swansea Bay, 31 mi. (50 km.) WNW of Cardiff by road. Pop. (1961) 51,322. Area 36.6 sq.mi. (95 sq.km.). Port Talbot docks were opened in 1837 and enlarged in 1898 when, after the coming of the railways, coal from the Afon valley was carried by rail for export from the docks. With the passing of the Railways Act in 1921, the Great Western Railway Company took over the docks, and Port Talbot became one of the south Wales chain of ports for coal from the Rhondda and other valleys. It suffered severely in the depression of the 1930s. The docks are now used for the export of coal and coke, iron and steel, tin plate, etc., and the import of iron ore, timber and other mainly heavy-class goods.

In 1947 the gigantic Abbey steel works at Margam were built by four companies as a reconstruction project for bringing up to date the sheet steel and tin plate industries of south Wales. This led, in turn, to the adaptation of the docks to meet the additional traffic. The steel works are named after Margam Abbey, a Cistercian Foundation of 1147, on which land they are built near the ruins of the abbey and also near Margam Castle and the docks.

Margam urban district and Aberavon town were amalgamated in 1921 under the name of Port Talbot.

Besides workers in steel, oxygen, industrial solvents, and on the docks, Port Talbot has a farming community. Two agricultural shows and a horticultural show are held annually as well as open and local shows of the Port Talbot Cage Birds Society. The Aberavon Fair (formerly a flannel fair) is held twice yearly under the 13th-century charter of Hugh le Despenser. On the beach, with its fine stretch of sand, is a pleasure fair near the promenade. On reclaimed marshland to the west of the town the large housing estate of Sandfields was constructed. Open spaces include the Talbot and Vivian Memorial parks, each of 12 ac. (5 ha.).

PORTUGAL, a country of southwestern Europe and a republic since 1910, flanks the western side of the Iberian Peninsula. It has an area of 35,340 sq.mi. (91,530 sq.km.), roughly rectangular in shape, with a breadth varying from 140 mi. (225 km.) in the north to about 70 mi. (113 km.) in southern Alentejo, and a north-south extent of about 360 mi. (579 km.). The Atlantic island groups of the Azores and Madeira (area 1,201 sq.mi. [3,111 sq.km.]) are included within metropolitan Portugal. They had 595,875 inhabitants in 1960 when Portugal proper had 8,255,414. The sea is the horizon from every Portuguese summit, the coast stretching for a distance of about 500 mi. (805 km.). The land frontiers with Spain are either along stretches of the major rivers, the Minho, Douro, Tagus, and Guadiana, or in rugged, sparsely populated mountains.

This article contains the following sections and subsections.

I. Physical Geography
  1. Structure and Relief
  2. Climate
  3. Vegetation
  4. Animal Life
II. Geographical Regions
III. The People
  1. Racial Types
  2. Religion
  3. Language
  4. Customs and Culture
IV. History
  A. Pre-Roman, Roman, Germanic, and Muslim Periods
  B. The County and Kingdom of Portugal (to 1383)
  C. The House of Avis, 1383–1580
  D. Medieval Social and Economic Development
  E. The Discoveries and the Empire
  F. Union of Spain and Portugal, 1580–1640
  G. The House of Braganza, 1640–1910
    1. The 18th and 19th Centuries
    2. Constitutionalism
    3. Social and Economic Conditions
  H. The Republic, from 1910
    1. Evolutionists, Unionists, and Democrats
    2. The "New State"
V. Population
VI. Administration and Social Conditions
  1. Constitution
  2. Government
  3. Local Administration
  4. Taxation
  5. Living Conditions
  6. Welfare Services
  7. Justice
  8. Education
  9. Defense
  10. Overseas Provinces
VII. The Economy
  A. Production
    1. Agriculture
    2. Forestry
    3. Fisheries
    4. Mining
    5. Power
    6. Industries
  B. Trade and Finance
    1. Foreign Trade
    2. Banking and Currency
    3. National Finance
  C. Transport and Communications

I. PHYSICAL GEOGRAPHY

1. Structure and Relief.—Relief divides Portugal along the Tagus Valley into a mountainous north and a lowland south. Of the land above 1,300 ft., more than 90% lies to the north of the Tagus, and about 60% of the land below 650 ft. is to the south, providing the fundamental contrast of the country. Seven-tenths of the country belongs to the ancient block of the Meseta, folded in Hercynian times and fractured by the later Tertiary movements. About 40% of the total area consists of hard slates, schists, and granites, which are an essential feature of northern Portugal. The well-marked pattern of the valleys in the northern highlands, guided by the lines of fracture and warping, is also a characteristic. The western appendage of the Central Cordillera, the Serra da Estrêla, 6,532 ft. (1,911 m.), has the highest relief, forming the backbone of Beira. The next highest mountains frame the Galician border: Serra do Gerez (4,944 ft.), Larouco, 5,003 ft. (1,525 m.), and Nogueira near Braganza or Bragança (4,324 ft.). North of the Douro, the ancient block touches the seacoast along a well-defined line of fracture, permitting only a narrow coastal plain. Between the Douro and the Mondego, the mountain blocks of Montemuro (4,534 ft.) and the Serra do Caramulo (3,514 ft.) separate the high plateaus of Beira from the broad coastal plain and Ria de Aveiro. To the south, the Mesozoic limestones and sandstones are folded into rolling, hilly relief in Estremadura and part of Ribatejo.

Most of southern Portugal represents a stable ancient block, gently lowered so that the Tertiary surfaces of the southwestern Meseta continue uninterrupted across the monotonous schistose and granitic plains of lower Alentejo. Even the higher plateaus

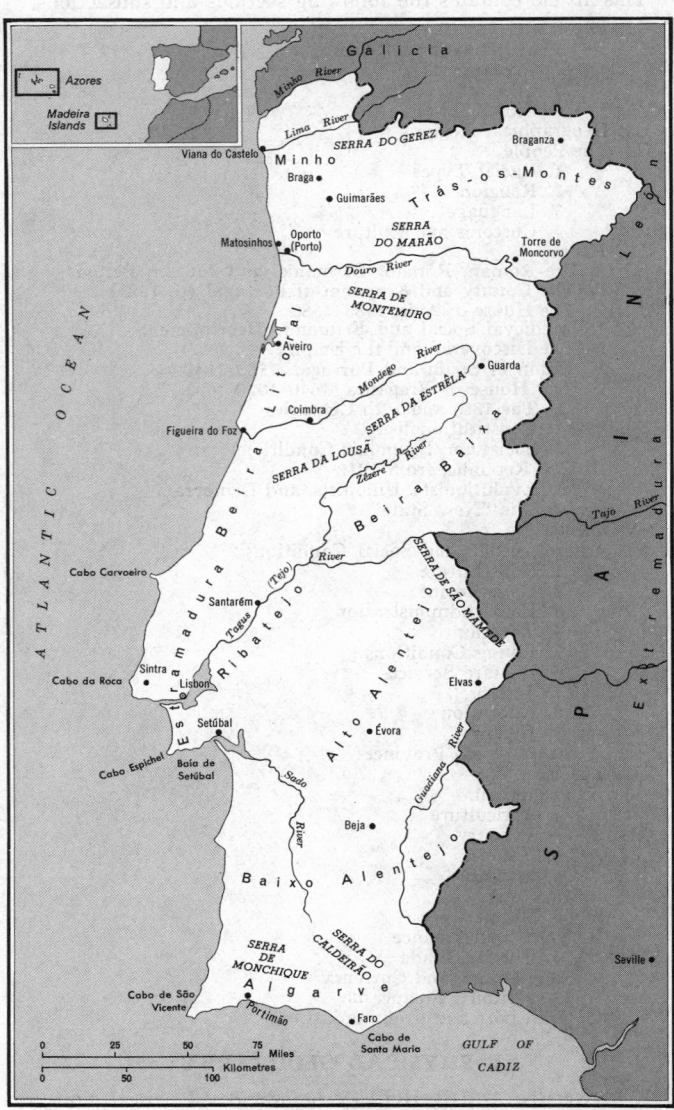

PHYSICAL FEATURES, CITIES, AND GEOGRAPHICAL REGIONS OF PORTUGAL

of upper Alentejo (São Mamede, 3,363 ft.), a continuation of the mountains of Toledo, and the Caldeirão (1,893 ft.), the extension of the Sierra Morena, preserve the surface. To the north and west the lower Tagus and Sado represent faulted troughs infilled with Tertiary and Quaternary sediments. The folded hills of Arrábida, 1,644 ft. (501 m.) north of the lower Sado and the more extensive scarps and hills behind the Algarve coast comprise Mesozoic limestones and sandstones. The highest relief of Algarve is in the Monchique (2,959 ft.), a dissected syenite massif.

All the main rivers of Portugal flow from Spain over the edge of the Meseta in a series of defiles and gorges. Consequently none of them is navigable between the two countries (with the possible exceptions of the lower Minho and Guadiana) and Portugal and Spain have turned their backs on each other, though several rivers do have local traffic, notably the Douro. Sandbars at the mouths of many rivers are further disadvantages, so that Lisbon is the only obvious choice for a large port. The changing fortunes of the ports of Algarve have reflected the variations of silting along the coast, while the past history of ports in Beira Litoral has been similar. It is somewhat paradoxical that much of the Portuguese coast south of the Mondego should be relatively sparsely populated when the sea has played such an important role in the country's history and there is an average of one mile of coast for every 68 sq.mi. of territory.

2. Climate.—The extreme southwesterly position of Portugal in Europe explains its mild, moist winters and its relatively equable and dry summers. Its position through the latitudes 37° to 42° N gives it transitional features between west temperate and Mediterranean conditions. In winter the northern half of Portugal is dominated by the polar front, and in summer the Azores high-pressure system advances northward over the country. In January there is a gentler gradient of sea level temperature, averaging from 11° C (52° F) in the southwest to about 9° (48°–49°) in the northeast. Severe cold is usually associated with the incursion of high-pressure conditions from the Spanish Meseta or from Siberian anticyclones. The highest mountains of Serra da Estrêla have less than 7° (45°) and snow lies on the mountain summits for several months between November and April; but there is no snow line. In summer the oceanic influence is marked; the fact that no part of the interior is more than 134 mi. from the sea is significant. In July the isotherms therefore run north-south, with a steep thermal gradient which rises from 18° (64°) on the west coast, to 27° (80°) or more along the Spanish frontier. Sea breezes at evening temper the summer heat of the coastal zone; e.g., the *nortada* at Lisbon.

Northern Portugal receives considerable rainfall and everywhere on the coast the humidity is relatively high for the latitude. Near the Galician frontier summer drought is not pronounced, but toward the northeast, and especially south of the Tagus, the intensity of summer drought is increased; Oporto (Porto) has a mean annual rainfall of 45 in., falling within 137 rain days; Lisbon 24 in. in 99 days; Lagos 15 in. in 90 days. Relief too plays its role and the Serra da Estrêla has over 110 in., with comparable precipitation in the mountains of the northwest. The leeward position of Trás-os-Montes and the Douro Valley explains partly their lower rainfall of 30–40 in. in 90–130 rain days.

3. Vegetation.—Portugal has been deservedly called "the Garden of Europe." It has more than 2,700 plant species and 53% of all those found in Spain, which is so much more extensive in area. The chief characteristic is the mingling of Atlantic deciduous flora with Mediterranean and African evergreens; about two-thirds are European species, about one-third Iberian and African. North of the Mondego Valley the European and Mediterranean species represent 57% and 26% respectively. Between the Mondego and Tagus these percentages are 38 and 42, and it is there that the mingling is most marked, especially in the lovely woodlands of Sintra and Serra do Bussaco. The soil conditions there are influential, for on the calcareous soils the Mediterranean species increase to 56%, whereas on the siliceous soils they are scarcely 36%.

Two species of pine (*Pinus pinaster* and *P. pinea*) and three species of oak (*Quercus robur*, *Q. toza*, and *Q. lusitanica*) predominate in the northern half of Portugal, with notable concentrations of maritime pine in the coastal lands and the Toza oak more confined to the drier northeast. The chestnut, Barbary oak (*Q. bellota*), linden, elm, and poplar are widespread. South of the Tagus there are four significant concentrations of tree species. In western Alentejo the cork oak estates predominate, mixed with evergreen oak to the east, and umbrella pines in the Sado basin. Lower Algarve is renowned for its groves of carobs, almonds, and figs. The olive, once concentrated in the south, is now widespread, with significant extent in Algarve, central Portugal, and the Douro Valley. The Australian eucalyptus flourishes in the ill-drained valleys of the Tagus and Sado. Noted specialized flora are the aquatic plants of the Aveiro lagoons, the Mediterranean species of the Serra de Arrábida, the alpine flora of Serra da Estrêla, and the numerous exotics of Sintra.

4. Animal Life.—The fauna of Portugal closely resembles that of Spain (*q.v.*). It is largely an admixture of central European and North African types but there are some species indigenous to the Iberian Peninsula that probably originated in earlier geological times. Apart from wild goats, wild boars, and deer found in the mountains, there no longer exist any of the larger wild animals. Probably the last bear was shot in the Serra do Gerez in 1650. Wolves are still found in the remoter parts of the Serra da Estrêla and the lynx in the cistus scrub of Alentejo, while the fox, rabbit, and the Iberian hare are ubiquitous.

There are fewer reptiles than in Spain, but one species of snake (*Pelias berus*) is dangerously poisonous. There are numerous species of grass snake. The chameleon is rare, but it occurs in Algarve, and the amphibian salamander is found occasionally in the mountains. A genus peculiar to the Iberian Peninsula is the slug *Geomalacus;* the spotted variety *G. maculosus* is limited to Portugal and a very restricted area near the Kenmare River in southwest Ireland.

Fish are plentiful, especially the young pilchard (sardine) which comprises over one-third by weight of the total landed, and tunny fishing is important from the ports of Algarve. Crustacea are common on the northern rocky coasts, and there are extensive oyster beds in the Ria de Aveiro, the estuaries of the Tagus, and especially the Sado.

As in Spain, there is a rich bird life, since the peninsula lies on the winter migration routes of western and central European species. In spring, north African species fly northward along the Portuguese coast. Very few birds, however, remain throughout the year in Portugal. Indigenous species include a blue magpie, particular varieties of a cuckoo, an owl, and a red partridge. Vultures, kestrels, and eagles nest on the rocky heights, while the stork (protected by special legislation), snipe, and quail are common in the coastal marshes.

Much of the wild life was destroyed during the Middle Ages when the king and the nobility created extensive preserves (*contadas*). Modern conditions controlling hunting and shooting are based on the Civil Code of July 1, 1867, but some municipalities also have local restrictions. The close season is roughly between Feb. 15 and Sept. 1, though quail shooting begins on Aug. 1.

II. GEOGRAPHICAL REGIONS

Since the Middle Ages six provinces have clearly divided the country: Minho, Trás-os-Montes, Beira, Estremadura, Alentejo, and Algarve (*qq.v.*). These were divided in 1833 into 17 districts, each named after its chief town, with the district of Setúbal subsequently added. In 1933, 11 new provinces were created on a geographical and economic basis. Provincial names survive for geographical designation but the 18 districts of continental Portugal are now the largest administrative subdivisions.

The landscapes of Portugal are more diverse than these administrative regions would suggest. The granite country of the Minho with its misty blue skies, green bocage, and intense polyculture, the terraced vineyards of the Douro Valley, the treeless plateaus and nucleated villages of Trás-os-Montes, the mountain splendour of Beira, the "dutch" landscape of the Ria de Aveiro, the orchards and vineyards of Estremadura, the lush pastures of the Tagus in Ribatejo, the monotonous cereal lands of Alentejo, and the dusty orchards of Algarve are only a few of its varied vignettes.

In the past the contrasts between the lands north and south of the Tagus were sharper than they now appear. The spread of the olive and vine, the rapid development since the 16th century of the maize (corn) plant, and the advance of the pine forests, have tended to obliterate some of the native contrasts between the Atlantic and Mediterranean facades of Portugal. Further transformation has taken place since the beginning of the 20th century, with the colonization of waste in Alentejo for cereal lands, reducing to some extent the contrast between the densely settled lands of the north, and the relatively sparse population of the southern half of Portugal. Only the northeast, remote and poor, has preserved archaic and traditional forms of life. (J. M. Ho.)

III. THE PEOPLE

Although western Iberia has been occupied for a long time, relatively few remains of Paleolithic man have been found. Neolithic and Bronze Age discoveries are commoner, among them many dolmens. Some of the earliest permanent settlements were the northern *citanias* or *castros,* hill villages first built by Neolithic farmers who began clearing the forests of western Iberia. Incoming peoples, Phoenicians, Greeks, and Celts, intermingled with the settled inhabitants, and celticized natives occupied the fortified *citanias.* For 200 years these were centres of resistance against Roman legions. Subsequently the Romans, Suebi (Suevi), Visigoths, Moors, and Jews exerted various influences over the territory which in the 13th century acquired the frontiers of modern Portugal.

1. Racial Types.—Portugal's situation at the western extremity of Europe made it a gathering ground for invaders by land, and its long coastline invited settlement by seafarers. Although formed of different elements, the population of Portugal is one of the most homogeneous in Europe, and has physical characteristics which are common to circum-Mediterranean peoples. Most Portuguese are of slightly lower than average stature (the average height of the adult male is 1,640 mm. [5 ft. 5 in.]), have brown eyes, dark wavy hair, and a pallid or brunet skin. The average cephalic index is 76–78.

2. Religion.—The largest part of the Portuguese population traditionally follows the Roman Catholic Church. Though freedom of worship is permitted, followers of other creeds are few, including about 3,000 Jews. The country is divided into three ecclesiastical provinces, Lisbon, Braga, and Évora. The archbishop of Lisbon is the metropolitan for all Portugal, with the title of patriarch, and is vested with the dignity of cardinal. The church is separated from the state and a concordat regulates the relations of Portugal with the Holy See.

3. Language.—Portuguese is one of the richest Romance languages and has a greater variety of sounds than Spanish. Although rooted in Latin, it has a few words of Germanic and Semitic origin introduced after the decline of the Roman power, when the Iberian Peninsula, or part of it, was for some centuries under the domain of the Visigoths and the Moors. The language is remarkably uniform throughout the country, including the Azores and Madeira. Differences in the speech of the provinces are mainly phonetic; differences in vocabulary, where they exist, are minor and limited to a confined area, so that there is no question of any different dialects. Only at Miranda do Douro, in the northeastern corner of Portugal, is there a true dialect, which is now indeed recognized as a linguistic curiosity. Portuguese is also spoken in the overseas provinces and in Brazil, and the literary language is there preserved in its purity. (*See* PORTUGUESE LANGUAGE.)

4. Customs and Culture.—In spite of certain affinities with the neighbouring Spaniards, the Portuguese have their own distinctive way of life. The geographical variety of the country has evoked different responses but there is less regionalism than in Spain. Dancing and singing play a prominent part in the life of the people. Almost every village has its own *terreiro* or dancing floor of beaten earth. Many popular dances are lively, and the *verdegaio, cana verde, malhão, vira, chula, fandango, corridinho, bailarico,* etc., may be seen at *romarias* or pilgrimages which combine religion with the attractions of a fair. Each region has its own style of dances and songs; most traditional songs are of a slower rhythm than those in Spain. Small accordions are often used to accompany dances and Portuguese guitars accompany the *fado* and other songs. Fiddles, drums, and triangles are popular, and bagpipes are played in some regions.

Bullfighting is a popular sport which is conducted differently from bullfights in Spain. The bulls are not killed and often their horns are sheathed to prevent injury to the horses.

Differences in environment cause variety in styles of building and dress, some distinctive garments being the *capucha,* a hooded cape worn in mountain areas, and the *palhoças,* a rain cape made of reeds and worn in the Douro Valley area. The staple diet is one of fish, vegetables, and fruit. Meat is seldom eaten, although village farmers each keep a few pigs which are killed for special occasions. In general wine is consumed sparingly.   (X.)

IV. HISTORY

Portugal became an independent monarchy in the 12th century A.D. Its name derives from Portus Cale, a pre-Roman or Roman settlement near the mouth of the Douro River. The southern part of the Roman province of Gallaecia was occupied by a Germanic people, the Suebi, in A.D. 415, and Portucale (Oporto) was held by them. They were subdued by the Visigoths, whose state was overthrown by the Muslim invasions in the 8th century. A Christian territory of Portugal was constituted in 868; it later became a county and was extended to Coimbra. Afonso Henriques assumed the title of king (1139), and annexed Lisbon. His successors took Alentejo and Algarve from the Muslims (by 1252). Portugal includes the "adjacent islands" of Madeira and the Azores, first settled in the 15th century.

A. Pre-Roman, Roman, Germanic, and Muslim Periods

The earliest human remains found in Portugal are Neanderthal-type bones from Furninhas. Most Peninsular Paleolithic industries are represented, but a distinct culture first emerges in the Mesolithic middens of the lower Tagus Valley, dated *c.* 5500 B.C. Neolithic cultures entered from Andalusia. There are varied types of beehive huts and passage graves: agriculture, pottery, and the working of soft metals followed by the same route. In the first millennium B.C., Celtic peoples entered the peninsula by the Pyrenees and many groups were projected westward by natural pressure. Hallstatt cultures brought iron-working to the Tagus Valley. Phoenician and later Carthaginian influence reached southern Portugal in the same period. By 500 B.C. Iron Age cultures predominated in the north. Celtic hill-top settlements (*castros, citânias*) retained their vitality after the Roman conquest.

After the Second Punic War (218–201 B.C.), Rome dominated the eastern and southern seaboards of the peninsula, and Celtic peoples who had partially absorbed the indigenous population occupied the west. A Celtic federation, the Lusitani, resisted Roman penetration under the brilliant leadership of Viriathus; but after his assassination (139 B.C.), Decimus Junius Brutus was able to march northward through central Portugal, cross the Douro, and subdue the Gallaeci. Julius Caesar governed the territory for a time. In 25 B.C. Augustus founded Augusta Emerita (Mérida) as capital of Lusitania, which incorporated the present central Portugal. Gallaecia, to the north of the Douro, was erected into a separate province under the Antonines. In Roman times the region of Beja and Évora was a wheat belt. The valley of the Tagus was famous for its horses and farms, and there were important mines in Alentejo. Notable Roman remains include the Temple of Diana at Évora and the site of Conimbriga (Condeixa). Christianity reached Lusitania in the 3rd century and in the 4th Gallaecia, where the heretical teaching of Priscillian long held sway.

With the collapse of the Rhine frontier (406), barbarian peoples forced their way into Gaul and crossed the Pyrenees. A Germanic tribe, the Suebi (*q.v.*), was settled in southern Gallaecia, their rulers residing at or near Bracara Augusta (Braga) and Portucale. They annexed Lusitania and for a time overran the rest of the peninsula, but the Visigoths were sent to subdue them and extinguished their monarchy (469). The records are silent until *c.* 550, when the Suebic monarchy had been restored and was reconverted to Catholicism by St. Martin of Dum. The Visigoth

Leovigild again overthrew the Suebic monarchy and annexed the territory, but it remained distinct from Gothic Spain. St. Martin's church grouped together the bishoprics of the Suebic territory until *c.* 660, when the ecclesiastical divisions were adjusted to the old Roman provincial system and the region to the south of the Douro was restored to Lusitania. With the Muslim invasion of 711, the only serious Gothic resistance was made at Mérida; on its fall the northwest submitted. Berber troops were placed in central Portugal and Galicia, but with the revolt of the Berbers and famine (740–750) the latter was evacuated. Braga was abandoned, but the rural population remained or was restored. When Abd-al-Rahman I set up the Omayyad monarchy at Córdoba (756), there was some resistance in the west, and he perhaps stationed Berber allies at Mérida and Coimbra. Lisbon was independent for a few years (*c.* 805). The restoration of the Christian sees of Galicia, the discovery of the supposed tomb of St. James, and the erection of his shrine at Santiago de Compostela were followed by the organization of the frontier territory of Portucale (868) by Vimara Peres; Coimbra was annexed by the Christians, but later lost again.

B. The County and Kingdom of Portugal (to 1383)

By the 10th century the county of Portugal (north of the Douro) was held by Mumadona Dias and her husband Hermenegildo Gonçalves and their descendants, one of whom was tutor and father-in-law to the Leonese ruler, Alfonso V. But when this dynasty was overthrown by the Navarrese-Castilian house of Sancho III the Great, the western county lost its autonomy. Sancho's son, Ferdinand I of Castile, reconquered Coimbra in 1064, but entrusted it to a Mozarabic governor. When the African Almoravids annexed Muslim Spain, Alfonso VI of León (1065–1109) and Castile (1072–1109) provided for the defense of the west by calling on Henry, brother of Duke Eudes (Odo) of Burgundy, whom he married to his illegitimate daughter Teresa and made count of Portugal. From 1095, therefore, Henry and Teresa (who used the title of queen) ruled Portugal and Coimbra. On the death of Alfonso VI, his realms passed to his legitimate daughter Urraca and her little son Alfonso (VII). Henry of Portugal sought power, but had achieved little when he died in 1112, leaving Teresa with an infant son, Afonso Henriques. Teresa's intrigues with her Galician favourite, Fernão Peres of Trava, lost her the support of the Portuguese barons, and in 1128 followers of her son defeated her and drove her into exile. Thus Afonso Henriques became count of Portugal. Though at first obliged to submit to his cousin Alfonso VII, he began to use the title of king, traditionally because of a victory over the Muslims at Ourique (July 25, 1139; but perhaps a symbolic legend). In 1143 his cousin accepted his autonomy, but the title of king was only formally conceded in 1179, when Afonso Henriques placed Portugal under the direct protection of the Holy See, promising an annual tribute. He had captured Santarém (March 1147) and Lisbon (October 1147), the latter with the aid of English, French, German, and Flemish crusaders bound for Palestine. An English priest, Gilbert of Hastings, became first bishop of the restored see of Lisbon. Although the new Moroccan dynasty of the Almohads (*q.v.*) struck back (1179–84), when Afonso I died (Dec. 6, 1185) the Portuguese frontier was firmly established on the Tagus. The new military orders, the Templars, those of Calatrava (from *c.* 1156), and of Santiago (from *c.* 1170), etc., governed castles and territory on the frontier, and the Cistercians introduced agriculture and architecture in central Portugal (Alcobaça).

Although Afonso Henriques began to grant charters to new settlements, it was his son Sancho I (1185–1211) who enfranchised many municipalities (*concelhos*), especially in eastern and central Portugal. The privileges of these communities were embodied in charters (*forais*), which attracted settlers from the more feudal north. Even Muslims were enfranchised, though on the other hand many of them were enslaved. Assisted by passing crusaders, Sancho captured Silves in Algarve (1189); but in 1190 an Almohad army from Africa advanced to the Tagus and, although Lisbon, Santarém, and Tomar stood firm, the Muslims recovered Silves in 1191 together with most of the land south of the Tagus. In his later years Sancho was involved in a quarrel with Pope Innocent III over the payment of tribute due to the Holy See, and with the bishop of Oporto, who received Innocent's support. But peace was made before his death, and it was left to his son Afonso II, the Fat (1211–23), to endeavour to strengthen the throne at the expense of the church.

Though Afonso II was an unwarlike king, his followers were beside the Castilians at the great Christian victory of Las Navas de Tolosa in 1212 and, again assisted by crusaders, recovered Alcácer do Sal in 1217. Meanwhile Afonso repudiated the bequests of large estates made by his father to his brothers and accepted those to his sisters only after a war with León and in a form settled by the pope which recognized Afonso's sovereignty. In the first year of his reign, Afonso called a meeting of the *Cortes* at Coimbra, to which the nobility and prelates were summoned (representatives of the commoners were not to appear until 1254). Both estates obtained important concessions; in fact the position of the church and the orders was now so strong that Afonso II and his successors were involved in recurrent conflicts with Rome. Afonso himself instituted (from 1220) *inquirições* or royal commissions to investigate the nature of holdings and recover whatever had been illegally taken from the crown. In his last years Afonso quarrelled with the archbishop of Braga who was supported by Pope Honorius III, defied the papacy, and was excommunicated.

Little is known of the reign of his son Sancho II (1223–45), but the reconquest of Alentejo was now completed and much of Algarve was reduced. On his accession, Sancho found the church in full ascendancy as a result of the agreement made before his father's death. Conflicting reports exist of Sancho's own government, but in his later years the kingdom seems to have slipped into anarchy. At all events his younger brother Afonso, who had become count of Boulogne by his marriage (1235) with Matilda, daughter of Count Raynald I of Dammartin, was granted a papal commission (1245) to take over the government, and Sancho was ordered to be deposed by papal bull. When Afonso reached Lisbon (late 1245 or early 1246), he received the support of the church and of the inhabitants of Lisbon and other towns. After a civil war lasting two years, Sancho II retired to Toledo, dying there in January 1248.

On his arrival the count of Boulogne had already declared himself king as Afonso III, and the death of Sancho without issue gave his usurpation the mantle of legality. He brought together the divided kingdom, completed the reconquest of Algarve, transferred the capital from Coimbra to Lisbon, and, fortified by the support of the towns, summoned the *Cortes* at Leiria at which for the first time commoners representing the municipalities made their appearance (1254). His conquest of Algarve aroused the jealousy of Castile. Two campaigns were fought (1250 and 1252), Afonso probably being worsted, and peace was made by means of a marriage pact. Although still the husband of Matilda of Boulogne, Afonso married Beatriz, illegitimate daughter of Alfonso X of Castile, holding the disputed territory of Algarve as a fief of Castile until such time as the eldest son of the marriage should reach the age of seven, when Algarve was to return to Portugal. This marriage led to a dispute with the Holy See, in which Afonso was placed under an interdict. Despite his early connection with Rome, Afonso refused to give way, and in 1263 the bigamous marriage was legalized and his eldest son, Diniz (Denis), legitimized. Shortly afterward, Afonso launched *inquirições,* as a result of which the church was deprived of much property. The prelates protested and most of them left the country. Although Afonso was excommunicated and threatened with deposition, he defied the church until shortly before his death early in 1279.

The achievements of Afonso's reign—the completion of the reconquest, the assertion of the royal power before the church, and the incorporation of the commoners in the *Cortes*—indicate important institutional advances. Under his son Diniz (1279–1325), Portugal was to come into closer touch with Western Europe and to acquire a university, the elements of a national literature, and a navy. The chartering of fairs and the increased use of minted money bear witness to the growth of commerce, and the planting of pine forests to hold back the sand dunes near Leiria illustrates

Diniz' concern for shipbuilding and agriculture. In 1317 Diniz engaged a Genoese admiral, Emmanuele di Pezagna (Manoel Pessanha), to build up his navy, having already adopted various measures to stimulate foreign trade. He founded the University of Coimbra (at first in Lisbon) in 1290 and was both a poet and patron of literature. Yet he was especially famed as the "farmer king" (*rei lavradór*) for his interest in the land.

Despite his attachment to the arts of peace, Portugal was several times involved in strife during the reign of Diniz. In 1297 the Treaty of Alcañices with Castile confirmed Portugal's possession of Algarve and provided for an alliance between Portugal and Castile. In the later years of his reign, his son, the future Afonso IV, rebelled more than once, being persuaded to submit by the influence of his mother Isabella, daughter of Peter III of Aragon. This remarkable woman, later canonized as St. Elizabeth of Portugal and popularly known as *a Rainha-Santa,* successfully exercised her influence in favour of peace on several occasions.

Afonso IV (1325–57) was also involved in various disputes with Castile. Isabella, who had retired to the Convent of Santa Clara at Coimbra, continued to intervene in favour of peace; but on her death in 1336 war broke out, and terms were not made till 1340, when Afonso himself with a Portuguese army joined Alfonso XI of Castile in the great victory over the Muslims on the Salado River in Andalusia. Afonso's son Pedro was married (1336) to Constanza (d. 1345), daughter of the Castilian infante Juan Manuel de Peñafiel, but soon after the marriage he fell in love with one of her ladies, Inês de Castro (*q.v.*), by whom he had several children. Afonso was persuaded to countenance the assassination of Inês in 1355, and one of Pedro I's earliest acts on his accession was to take vengeance on her murderers. During his short reign (1357–67), Pedro devoted himself to the dispensation of justice; his judgments, which he executed himself, were severe and often violent, and his iron rule was tempered only by fits of revelling.

Pedro's son by Constanza, Ferdinand (1367–83), inherited a wealthy throne almost free of external entanglements; but the dispute between Pedro the Cruel and Henry of Trastámara (later Henry II) for the Castilian throne was raging, and on the murder (1369) of the former, several Castilian towns offered to Ferdinand their allegiance, which he was unwise enough to accept. Henry II duly invaded Portugal in 1369, and by the Peace of Alcoutim (1371) Ferdinand was constrained to renounce his claim and to promise to marry Henry's daughter. However, he instead took a Portuguese, Leonor Teles, although she was already married and in spite of the protests of the commoners of Lisbon. He also made alliance (1372) with John of Gaunt, duke of Lancaster, who had married the elder daughter of Pedro the Cruel and claimed the Castilian throne. In 1372 Ferdinand provoked Henry II, who invaded Portugal and besieged Lisbon. Unable to resist, Ferdinand was forced to repudiate his alliance with John of Gaunt and to act as an ally of Castile, surrendering various castles and persons as hostages. It was only on the death (1379) of Henry that Ferdinand dared openly to challenge Castile again. In 1380 the English connection was resumed, and in the following year John of Gaunt's brother, Edmund of Langley, earl of Cambridge (afterward duke of York), took a force to Portugal for the invasion of Castile and betrothed his son Edward to Ferdinand's only legitimate child, Beatriz. In mid-campaign Ferdinand came to terms with the enemy (August 1382), agreeing to marry Beatriz to a Castilian prince. She did in effect become the wife of John I of Castile, and when Ferdinand died, prematurely decrepit, Leonor Teles became regent and Castile claimed the Portuguese crown.

Leonor had long been the paramour of the Galician João Fernandes Andeiro (*q.v.*), count of Ourém, who had intrigued with both England and Castile and whose influence was much resented by Portuguese patriots. Opponents of Castile chose as their leader an illegitimate son of Pedro, John, mestre de Avis, who killed Ourém (December 1383) and, being assured of the support of the populace of Lisbon, assumed the title of defender of the realm. The regent fled to Alenquer and thence to Santarém, and the king of Castile came to her aid, soon, however, relegating her to a Spanish convent. Lisbon was besieged for five months (1384), but an outbreak of plague obliged the Castilians to retire.

C. The House of Avis, 1383–1580

The legitimate male line of Henry of Burgundy ended at Ferdinand's death, and when the *Cortes* met at Coimbra (March–April 1385) John was declared king and became the founder of a new dynasty. This result was not unopposed, for many of the nobility and clergy still considered the queen of Castile the rightful heiress; but popular feeling was strong, and John I had valuable allies in Nuno Álvares Pereira (*q.v.*), "the Holy Constable," his military champion, and João das Regras, his chancellor and jurist.

A number of towns and castles still held out for Castile when in August 1385 John I of Castile and a considerable army made their appearance in central Portugal. Although much outnumbered, the Portuguese won the great Battle of Aljubarrota (Aug. 14, 1385) in which the Castilian chivalry was dispersed and John of Castile himself barely escaped. The victory, followed by secondary successes won by Nuno Álvares, assured John I of his kingdom and made him a desirable ally. A small force of English archers had been present at Aljubarrota. Now the Treaty of Windsor (May 9, 1386) raised the Anglo-Portuguese connection to the status of a firm, binding, and permanent alliance between the two crowns. John of Gaunt duly went to the Peninsula (July 1386) and attempted an invasion of Castile in conjunction with John I. This was not successful, but the Portuguese king married Gaunt's daughter Philippa of Lancaster (1387), who introduced various English usages into Portugal and became the mother of five sons and one daughter, the *inclita geração*. The truce arranged with Castile in 1387 was prolonged at intervals until peace was finally concluded in 1411.

The victory of John of Avis may be regarded as a victory of the national spirit against the feudal attachment to established order. As much of the older nobility had adhered to Castile, John rewarded his followers at their and at the crown's expense. Meanwhile, commerce prospered, and the marriage of John's daughter Isabella to Philip the Good of Burgundy was to be followed by the growth of close trading relations between Portugal and Philip's County of Flanders. With the conclusion of peace with Castile, John found an outlet for the activities of his frontiersmen and of his own sons in the conquest of Ceuta (1415), from which may be dated the great age of Portuguese expansion.

During the short reign of John's eldest son Edward (Duarte), (1433–38), an unsuccessful attempt was made to conquer Tangier in 1437 by Prince Henry the Navigator and his younger brother Ferdinand, who was captured by the Moors and died, still unransomed, in 1443. On Edward's death his son Afonso V was still a child, and his brother Pedro, duke of Coimbra, had himself made regent (1440) instead of the widow, Leonor of Aragon. But Pedro's own regency was later challenged by the powerful Braganza family, descended from Afonso, illegitimate son of John of Aviz and Beatriz, daughter of Nuno Álvares Pereira. This family continued to set the young king against his uncle, who was forced to resign the regency, driven to take up arms, and killed at Alfarrobeira (May 1449). Afonso V (1438–81) proved unable to resist the demands of the Braganzas, who now became the wealthiest family in Portugal. Having married Joan, daughter of Henry IV of Castile, Afonso laid claim to the Castilian throne and became involved in a lengthy struggle with Ferdinand and Isabella in the region of Zamora and Toro, where he was defeated in 1476. He then sailed to France to entreat the aid of Louis XI, in which he failed, and on his return concluded with Castile the Treaty of Alcáçovas (1479), abandoning the claims of his wife Joan. Afonso never recovered from this reverse, and during his last years his son John administered the kingdom.

John II (1481–95) was as cautious, firm, and jealous of the royal power as his father had been openhanded and negligent. At the first *Cortes* of his reign he exacted a detailed oath of homage which displeased his greatest vassals. A suspicion of conspiracy enabled him to arrest Fernando II, duke of Braganza, and many of his followers; the duke was sentenced to death and executed (1483) at Évora, and John himself stabbed James (Diogo), duke of Viseu (1484). As well as attacking the power of the nobility, John lessened the effects of the unfavourable treaty with Castile. Calculating and resolute, he received the epithet of "the Perfect."

John II was predeceased by his legitimate son and therefore succeeded by his cousin, the duke of Beja, as Manuel I (1495–1521), known as "the Fortunate." Manuel, who assumed the title of "lord of the conquest, navigation, and commerce of India, Ethiopia, Arabia, and Persia," inherited, because of the work of John II, a firmly established autocratic monarchy and a rapidly expanding overseas empire. Drawn toward Spain by the common need to defend their overseas interests as defined by the Treaty of Tordesillas (1494; *q.v.*), Manuel nourished the hope of joining the whole peninsula under the house of Avis; he married Isabella, eldest daughter of Ferdinand and Isabella, who, however, died (1498) in giving birth to a son, Miguel da Paz. This child was recognized as heir to Portugal, Castile, and Aragon, but died in infancy. Manuel then married Isabella's sister Maria (d. 1517) and thirdly Eleanor, sister of the emperor Charles V.

As a condition of the marriage with Isabella, Manuel was required to "purify" Portugal of Jews. John II had admitted many Jewish refugees expelled from Spain (1492) and had taxed them heavily, but was also to supply ships for them to leave Portugal within eight months. This was not done, and Manuel now ordered all Jews to leave by October 1497. On their assembly in Lisbon, every effort was made to secure their conversion by promises or by force. Some who resisted were allowed to go, but the rest were "converted" under promise that no inquiry should be made into their beliefs for 20 years. As "Christians" they could not be forced to emigrate, and they were indeed prohibited from leaving Portugal. In April 1506 a large number of these "new Christians," or *marranos,* were massacred in Lisbon during a riot, but Manuel afterward protected them and allowed many to emigrate to Holland, where their experience of Portuguese trade was put at the service of the Dutch.

If Manuel failed to realize his dream of ruling Spain, his son John III (1521–57) lacked the power to resist Castilian influence. A pious, dull man, he was ruled by his wife, Queen Catherine, sister of the emperor Charles V, and encouraged the installation of the Inquisition (1536); the first auto-da-fé was held in 1540. The Society of Jesus, established in 1540, soon controlled education in Portugal. In 1529 the settlement by the Treaty of Saragossa of a dispute over the possession of the Moluccas removed an obstacle to Portuguese-Spanish understanding, and the line of Tordesillas was matched by a similar line in the Pacific; all the countries in the New World were in theory divided between Spain and Portugal, while the Reformation (as well as the discoveries) had come between the latter and its English ally.

John III was succeeded by his grandson Sebastian (1557–78), then a child of three. As a boy Sebastian became obsessed with the idea of a crusade against Morocco. Fanatically religious, he had no doubts of his own powers and listened only to flatterers. He visited Ceuta and Tangier in 1574 and began in 1576 to prepare a large expedition against Larache (El Araish); this departed in June 1578 and on Aug. 4 was utterly destroyed by the Moors at the Battle of the Three Kings near Alcazarquivir. Sebastian himself was killed, 8,000 of his men are said to have died and 15,000 were captured. Only a handful escaped.

Sebastian was succeeded by his great-uncle, Cardinal Henry (1578–80), a brother of John III. His age and celibacy made it certain that the Portuguese throne would soon pass from the direct line of Avis. Philip II of Spain, nephew of John III and husband (by his first marriage) of John's daughter Maria, had already made his preparations and, on the death of the cardinal-king (Jan. 31, 1580), summoned the authorities to obey him. An army under the great duque de Alba (*see* Alba, Fernando Álvarez de Toledo, duque de) entered Portugal in 1580, the resistance of Antonio the prior of Crato (illegitimate son of John III's brother Luís), acclaimed Antonio I at Santarém, collapsed, and Philip II of Spain became Philip I of Portugal (1580–98). The claims of the duchess of Braganza (Catherine, daughter of John's brother Edward) were disregarded.

D. Medieval Social and Economic Development

Medieval Portugal comprised regions of considerable diversity. In the north the old aristocracy of Leonese descent owned large estates worked mainly by serfs. In the south, the territory of the Reconquest, there were many towns, often separated by districts almost barren and depopulated. The initiative in settling these areas was taken by the Cistercian monks who had reached Portugal by 1143; later kings such as Sancho I and Afonso III established *concelhos* (municipalities), granting to them by the issue of *forais* (charters) many privileges designed to attract population. Tax concessions were often given and freedom was promised to serfs or to Christian captives after a year's residence. But in the south the *concelhos* were burdened with defense duties, the *cavaleiros-vilãos* (villein knights) being obliged to horse and arm themselves and the *peões* or less substantial men to serve as foot soldiers in defense of the country and perhaps also on a *fossado* (raid) into Muslim territory.

At court the king was advised by his *curia regis* (court or council), comprising the *majordomus curiae*, the head of the administration, the military chief or *signifer*, the *dapifer curiae* (steward of the household), the chancellor (an official whose origins in Portugal were Burgundian rather than Visigothic), and any members of the greater aristocracy, the *ricos-homens*, who might be at court. This class also comprised the bishops and abbots and masters of the orders of knighthood; many held private civil or military authority. The lesser nobility were without such rights. Below them came various classes of free commoners, such as the *cavaleiros-vilãos* and the *malados*, men who had commended themselves to protectors. There were numerous serfs and slaves.

By the end of the medieval period several shifts in the social structure had occurred. Many of the old aristocracy lost their position at the advent of the house of Avis and the new nobility, exemplified in the house of Braganza, was often of bureaucratic or ministerial origin. The privileges granted to *concelhos* forced landlords to compete for labour and by the time of Afonso III money payments had largely replaced labour services on the estates. Representatives of the commoners, first attending the *Cortes* in 1254 on behalf of the *concelhos*, took an increasing part in politics. The *Cortes* were very frequently called in the reigns of John I, Duarte, and Afonso V; but the avenues of power had become wider by the 16th century and John III's proposal (1525) to call them only every ten years aroused no opposition. Although the trade guilds were slow in developing, they took some part in determining local taxation in the 13th century. Trade increased, Portuguese merchants having connections with the Low Countries from the time of Afonso Henriques and with England from the early 13th century. A coin shortage in the 13th century and debasements in the late 14th and early 15th centuries caused widespread difficulties and unrest, however.

E. The Discoveries and the Empire

The idea of expansion into Africa was a logical result of the completion of the Reconquest in the Peninsula, and the conquest of Ceuta in 1415 probably provided the impulse toward further expansion. The simple idea of fighting the Muslims on their own soil was linked with more complicated motives: the search for a Christian ally, Prester John (*q.v.*); the desire to explore in a scientific sense; the hope of finding a way to the rich spice trade of the Indies; and the impulse to spread the Christian faith. These purposes were gradually molded together into a national enterprise, though at first they represented the hopes and aspirations of one man, Prince Henry (*see* HENRY the Navigator). The third son of John I and Philippa of Lancaster, known rather inaccurately as "the Navigator" (he himself never went farther afield than Tangier), Henry became (1420) master of the Order of Christ, which King Diniz had founded (1319). The resources of the Order were used to draw together skilled geographers and navigators and to equip a series of expeditions that only gradually began to bear fruit.

The date of Prince Henry's earliest expedition is not exactly known, but appears to have been about 1418, when the island of Porto Santo was visited; the first call at Madeira probably dates from 1419. An attempt was made to settle in the Canaries, and between 1427 and 1431 the Azores were visited by Portuguese seamen. Both the Azores and Madeira were then uninhabited, and

their colonization proceeded fairly rapidly from *c.* 1445. Sugar was exported to Europe and gave the islands great economic importance. Meanwhile, Prince Henry's ships were probing the African coast, passing Cape Bojador in 1434 and Rio de Oro (1436). The unsuccessful expedition against Tangier (1437) was followed by a break in the discoveries; but in 1439 Prince Henry was authorized to colonize the Azores, and from 1440 further expeditions equipped with a new and lighter ship, the caravel, reached the Bay of Arguin (1443), Cape Verde (1444), and by Henry's death (1460) had explored the coast as far south as Sierra Leone.

Under Afonso V three military expeditions were sent against Morocco (1458, 1461, and 1471); by the last of them Tangier and Arzila were captured. The African explorations were not entirely neglected, but it remained for John II, with his sharp sense of the national interest, to found a fortress and trading post in the Gulf of Guinea at Elmina (São Jorge da Mina, 1481–82). Diogo Cam (Cão) discovered the mouth of the Congo in 1482 and then advanced to Cape Cross, 200 leagues southward (1486). A native tribe, the Manicongo, sought conversion and alliance with the Portuguese: its first Christian king, Afonso I (1505–40) made Mbanza a centre of Portuguese influence, but the "kingdom of Congo" fell into internal strife and Portuguese interests were transferred to the neighbouring kingdom of Angola. Paulo Dias de Novais founded Luanda, the first city in West Africa south of the Equator, in 1576. In 1488 Bartolomeu Dias de Novais at length rounded the Cape of Good Hope and reached the East African coast, and the seaway to India lay open. His return was followed in 1493 with the news that Christopher Columbus had, as he thought, discovered Asia by sailing west across the Atlantic. Much as this news must have perturbed the Portuguese, Columbus brought no news of the spiceries or the cities of the East, and John II ordered the preparation of an expedition to India by way of the Cape of Good Hope, though this sailed only after his death. John also contested the Spanish claim to all lands discovered west of the Atlantic, and by the Treaty of Tordesillas (June 7, 1494) Spain's rights were limited to what lay more than 370 leagues west of the Cape Verde Islands. Thus the territory that was to become Brazil was reserved for Portugal.

The Treaty of Tordesillas had confirmed Portugal's rights to the exploration of Africa and the seaway to India. In July 1497 Vasco da Gama set sail with four ships on the first expedition to India. They reached Calicut (Kozhikode) the following spring, and the survivors put into Lisbon in the autumn of 1499 with specimens of Oriental merchandise. A second fleet was at once prepared under Pedro Álvares Cabral, who touched the Brazilian coast (April 22, 1500) and claimed it for Portugal. One of Cabral's ships, under Diogo Dias, discovered Madagascar in 1500; João da Nova discovered Ascension in the following year, and St. Helena in 1502. Tristão da Cunha sighted the island named after him in 1506 and went on to explore Madagascar. Meanwhile, trading posts in India had been established by Cabral at Cochin and Calicut (1501) and by João da Nova at Cannanore. In 1502 Vasco da Gama made tributary to Portugal the ruler of Kilwa (Quiloa) in East Africa.

In 1505 Francisco de Almeida arrived as viceroy of India, strengthening the African station at Kilwa and supporting the ruler of Cochin against the *samorin* of Calicut. The control of sea trade now instituted became the chief source of Portuguese wealth in the East. It was assured by the defeat of Muslim naval forces off Diu in 1509. Almeida's successor Afonso de Albuquerque (*q.v.*) conquered Goa (1510), which he made the seat of Portuguese power, and Malacca (1511); sent two expeditions to the Moluccas (1512 and 1514); and captured Ormuz in the Persian Gulf (1515). Soon after Fernão Pires de Andrade reached Canton in China; in 1542 Portuguese merchants were permitted to settle at Liampo (Ningpo), and in 1557 they founded the colony of Macao (Macau).

Albuquerque was responsible for this conception of a system of strong points which secured the trade of the Orient to Portugal for nearly a century. Goa soon became the chief port of western India; Ormuz controlled the Persian Gulf and Malacca the gateway from the Indian Ocean to the South China Sea, while a string of fortified trading posts secured the coast of East Africa, the gulf and the shores of India and Ceylon. Farther east, less fortified settlements were set up with the consent of the native rulers from Bengal to China, and the trade of the principal spice islands was in Portuguese hands. The preservation of the whole system was entrusted to a governor, who sometimes held the rank of viceroy, at Goa; and although Portuguese arms had both triumphs and reverses, their control of the Oriental trade remained substantial, if never complete, until the 17th century, when the Dutch, at war with the joint crown of Portugal and Spain and deprived of their traditional trade with Lisbon, began to seek spices from their source and effectively demolished the Portuguese monopoly.

F. Union of Spain and Portugal, 1580–1640

After Philip II of Spain had occupied Portugal in 1580, the island of Terceira in the Azores held out for António of Crato, who himself sought alliances in England and France. In 1582 a French expedition to establish him in the Azores was defeated, and in 1589 an English attempt upon Lisbon, led by Sir Francis Drake and Sir John Norris, failed dismally. But although António died in Paris in 1595, the true symbol of Portuguese independence was not the prior of Crato but King Sebastian himself. The Portuguese people refused to believe that he was dead and nourished a messianic faith in his reappearance, of which four pretenders sought to avail themselves, the last as late as 1600 and as far afield as Venice.

Meanwhile, Philip arrived in Portugal and was accepted as King Philip I (1580–98) by the *Cortes* held at Tomar (1581). He undertook to preserve Portuguese autonomy, to consider the union as a personal one like that of Aragon and Castile under Ferdinand and Isabella, to appoint only Portuguese to the administration, to summon *Cortes* frequently and to be accompanied by a Portuguese council in Madrid. These undertakings were, however, neglected by Philip II (III of Spain, 1598–1621) and completely violated by Philip III (IV of Spain, 1621–40). Portuguese resentment against Spanish rule was increased by the failure of these kings to visit Portugal, the appointment of Spaniards to Portuguese offices, the loss of trade consequent on Spain's foreign wars, and the levying of taxation to sustain these wars. In 1624 the Dutch seized Bahia in Brazil, only to be expelled by a joint Spanish and Portuguese expedition (1625). But in 1630 they occupied Pernambuco and the adjoining sugar estates, which they held for a generation. The final straw was the conde-duque de Olivares' plan (1640) of using Portuguese troops against the equally discontented Catalans. Two Portuguese insurrections in 1634 and 1637 had failed to attain dangerous proportions, but in 1640 Spain's powers were extended to the utmost by war with France and revolt in Catalonia. Richelieu already had agents in Lisbon, and a leader was found in John, duke of Braganza, a grandson of the duchess Catherine (niece of John III) whose claims had been overridden in 1580 by Philip II of Spain. Taking advantage of the unpopularity of the governor, Margaret of Savoy, duchess of Mantua, and her secretary of state Miguel de Vasconcelos, the leaders of the party of independence carried through a nationalist revolution on Dec. 1, 1640. Vasconcelos was almost the only victim; the Spanish garrisons were driven out; and on Dec. 15 the duke of Braganza was crowned as John IV (1640–56).

G. The House of Braganza, 1640–1910

Although the *Cortes* confirmed the accession of the dynasty of Braganza and John's coronation on Jan. 28, 1641, the success of the new regime was not finally assured till 1668, when Spain at last recognized Portuguese independence. Faced with the threat of a Spanish invasion, John had sent missions to the courts of Europe in quest of alliances. France now refused a formal treaty. The Dutch, having seized northern Brazil, accepted a truce in Europe and proceeded to capture Angola from Portugal. John made a treaty (1642) with Charles I of England, which was made void by Charles' execution (1649). Meanwhile, the Portuguese defeated the Spaniards at Montijo (May 26, 1644) and warded off several invasions. In 1654 they negotiated a treaty with the English Commonwealth, obtaining aid in return for commercial concessions. The Dutch were now finally expelled from Pernambuco. By a secret article of the Treaty of the Pyrenees (1659) France

promised Spain to give no further aid to Portugal, but in 1661 Portugal signed a treaty of alliance with the restored English monarchy. In 1662 Charles II of England married John's daughter Catherine of Braganza and, in return for a large dowry, including the cession of Bombay and Tangier, provided arms and men for the war with Spain. Portuguese defense was organized by the German soldier Friedrich Hermann von Schönberg (later duke of Schomberg); in June 1663 Sancho Manuel, count of Vila Flor, defeated Don John of Austria at Ameixial, and in June 1665 von Schönberg won the important victory of Montes Claros. Peace was finally made by the Treaty of Lisbon early in 1668.

On the death of John IV his second son Afonso VI (1656–83) was 13 years of age. Afonso's mother Luisa de Guzmán acted as regent until, in June 1662, he began to rule. Afonso himself was feebleminded, but the country was capably governed by Luiz de Vasconcelos e Sousa, conde de Castelo Melhor, until 1667. The French princess, Marie Françoise Elisabeth de Savoie-Nemours, who had married Afonso in the previous year, now entered into an intrigue with his more personable brother Pedro (afterward Pedro II). They contrived to dismiss Castelo Melhor and to have Marie Françoise' marriage annulled. She at once married Pedro (1668), who was declared regent. Afonso was imprisoned until his death. During the reign of Pedro II (1683–1706), Portugal recovered from the strain of the Spanish wars and began to feel the effects of the discovery of gold and precious stones in Brazil. The first strike of gold in Minas Gerais took place in 1693, and in the last years of the 17th century considerable wealth was being extracted; however, it was not until 1728 that diamonds were discovered and the wealth of Brazil came to form an appreciable part of the revenue of the Portuguese crown.

1. The 18th and 19th Centuries.—The War of the Spanish Succession (1701–13) saw Portugal's recent friends, England and France, on opposing sides; and although Pedro sought at first to remain neutral, Portugal joined the Anglo-Austrian Grand Alliance in 1703, by which it afforded a base for the archduke Charles (later the emperor Charles VI) to conduct his war for the Spanish throne. In the same year (Dec. 27) the English envoy, John Methuen, also concluded the treaty which bears his name, by which the exchange of port wine for English woolens became the basis for Anglo-Portuguese trade. Although the treaty of 1654 had secured great privileges for English merchants in Lisbon, neither it nor the treaties of 1642 and 1661 by which the traditional alliance was restored had created trade. This was now done, and by reason of the wealth that soon poured into Lisbon from Brazil, the English merchants gained a commanding position in the trade of Portugal. The political treaties of 1703 proved less fruitful. The Portuguese general, Antonio Luís de Sousa, marquess of Minas, entered Madrid in 1706, but French and Spanish forces were victorious at Almansa (1707), and in 1711 the French admiral René Duguay-Trouin sacked Rio de Janeiro. At the end of the war Portugal made a peace treaty with France (April 1713), but did not conclude peace with Spain until February 1715.

Under Pedro's son John V (1706–50) Portugal attained a degree of prosperity unknown since the restoration. The royal fifth levied on the precious metals and stones of Brazil gave the monarchy an independent source of wealth. The *Cortes*, which had met irregularly since 1640, were no longer summoned, and government was carried out by ministers appointed by the king. John V himself showed little interest in administration, though he did not fail to convert his wealth into papal and other dignities. The archbishop of Lisbon became a patriarch (1716) and Pope Benedict XIV in 1749 gave John the title "his most faithful majesty"; and royal academies, palaces, and libraries were inaugurated. But in his later years his ministers proved inadequate and the kingdom sank into stagnation. However, on John's death his son Joseph (1750–77) appointed as minister Sebastião José de Carvalho e Mello, later conde de Oeiras and marquês de Pombal (*q.v.*), who soon gained a complete ascendancy over the king and endeavoured to replace the stagnant absolutism with a more active type of despotism which, with some qualifications, deserves the epithet "enlightened." His full powers date from his efficient handling of the crisis caused by the disastrous Lisbon earthquake of November

1755; but even before this he had reformed the sugar and diamond trades, set up a national silk industry (1750), and formed one chartered company to control the sardine- and tunny-fishing industry of Algarve and another to trade with northern Brazil. In 1756 he founded the *Junta de Comércio,* a board of trade with powers to limit the privileges enjoyed by the English merchants under the treaties of 1654 and 1661, and set up the General Company for Agriculture and for Wines of Alto Douro to control the port wine trade. Industries for the manufacture of hats (1759), cutlery (1764), and other articles were set up with varying success.

Pombal's methods were arbitrary and his enemies numerous. His reform of the wine industry provoked a riot in Oporto (1757) which was savagely repressed; but his principal victims were the Jesuits, expelled in 1759 from all the Portuguese dominions, and the nobility, in particular José Mascarenhas, duque de Aveiro, and the Távora family, who were accused of an attack on the king (Sept. 3, 1758), condemned, and executed (Jan. 12, 1759). Having eliminated the Jesuits from the educational system, Pombal applied regalist principles in the reform of the University of Coimbra (1772) and the royal board of censorship (1768), which directed lower education from 1771.

While Pombal succeeded in modifying the ascendancy of the British merchants in Portugal, he invoked the English alliance in 1762 when Spain, prompted by the renewal of the Bourbon Family Compact Alliance with France, invaded Portugal. The Portuguese Army was reformed by Wilhelm von Schaumburg-Lippe, and an English force was led by James O'Hara, 2nd Baron Tyrawley, and John Campbell, 4th earl of Loudoun. Peace was signed in February 1763 at Fontainebleau. On the death of Joseph (Feb. 24, 1777), his daughter Maria I (1777–1816), who had married his brother, her uncle (Pedro III), acceded; Pombal was dismissed (1777) and eventually was condemned on several charges. His successors restored the Jesuits and made peace with Spain by the Treaty of San Ildefonso (1777).

Maria I suffered from melancholia after the loss of her consort (1786) and eldest son John (1788). In 1792 her mental balance was further disturbed, probably by the news of the French Revolution, and she ceased to reign. Her son, who on her death became John VI (1816–26), then ruled in her name and in 1799 became prince regent. In 1793 Portugal joined England and Spain against France, sending a naval division to assist the English Mediterranean fleet and an army to the Catalan front. The Peace of Basel (July 1795), by which Spain abandoned its allies, left Portugal still at war. Although subjected to pressure from the French Directory and from the Spanish minister, Manuel de Godoy, Portugal remained unmolested until 1801, when Godoy sent an ultimatum and invaded Alentejo. By the Peace of Badajoz (June 1801) Portugal lost the town of Olivenza and paid an indemnity.

From the Peace of Amiens (1802) until 1807 Portugal was once more immune from attack, though subjected to continuous pressure to break off the English connection. By the Berlin decree of Nov. 21, 1806, Napoleon sought to close all continental ports to British ships. Portugal endeavoured to maintain neutrality, but the secret Franco-Spanish Treaty of Fontainebleau (October 1807) provided for its eventual dismemberment by Napoleon I and Godoy. Already Gen. Andoche Junot was hastening across Spain with a French army, and on Nov. 27 the prince regent and the royal family and court embarked on a fleet lying in the Tagus River and were escorted by British vessels to Brazil; the court remained 12 years at Rio de Janeiro. Junot declared the Braganzas deposed, but his occupation of Portugal was challenged in August 1808 by the arrival of Sir Arthur Wellesley (later duke of Wellington) and 13,500 British troops in Mondego Bay. Winning the victories of Roliça (Aug. 17) and Vimeiro (Aug. 21), Wellesley enabled his superiors to negotiate the Convention of Sintra (Aug. 31) by which Junot was allowed to evacuate Portugal with his army. A second French invasion (1808–09) led to Sir John Moore's death at Corunna (January 1809) and the reembarkation of the British forces. In February William Carr (later Viscount) Beresford was placed in command of the Portuguese Army, and in March Marshal N. J. de Dieu Soult advanced from Galicia and occupied Oporto. Wellesley returned

to Portugal in April, drove Soult from the north, and after his victory of Talavera de la Reina in Spain (July) withdrew to Portugal. The third French invasion followed in August 1810 when Marshal André Masséna with Marshal Michel Ney and Junot entered Beira province. Defeated by Wellington in October at Bussaco near Coimbra, the French found themselves facing the prepared lines of Torres Vedras, north of Lisbon, where they wintered amid great privations. By the spring of 1811 they could only retreat and, on March 5, began the evacuation of Portugal, harassed all the way by English and Portuguese attacks and crossing the frontier after a defeat at Sabugal (April 3).

Portugal made peace with France on May 30, 1814. It was represented at the Congress of Vienna but played little part in the settlement. However, the series of Anglo-Portuguese treaties concluded between the years 1809 and 1817 was important insofar as it extended many of the conditions of the Anglo-Portuguese alliance to Brazil and had an influence on the future of Africa. England's efforts to get Portuguese collaboration in suppressing the slave trade resulted in the treaty of Jan. 22, 1815, and in the additional convention of 1817, by reason of which Portugal's claims to a considerable part of Africa were admitted.

2. Constitutionalism.—The Napoleonic campaigns had caused great devastation in Portugal, and the absence of the royal family and the presence of a foreign commander (Beresford) combined with revolutionary agitation and the influence of Spanish liberalism to produce an atmosphere of discontent and restlessness. On Dec. 16, 1815, Brazil was raised to the rank of a kingdom united with Portugal, and John VI, who succeeded in March 1816, showed no desire to return to Portugal. In 1817 Beresford suppressed a conspiracy in Lisbon, and the Masonic leader Gen. Gomes Freire de Andrade was executed. Unrest increased, and when Beresford himself went to Brazil (March 1820) to press John to return, a constitutionalist revolution began in Oporto (Aug. 24, 1820), spread over the country and led to the formation of a junta in Lisbon (Oct. 4). On Beresford's return (Oct. 10) he was not allowed to land, and British officers were expelled from the army. A constituent assembly was summoned which drew up a very "democratic" constitution, thus confronting John VI with an accomplished fact.

John's reluctance to return was at last overcome and he left his elder son Pedro to govern Brazil, landing at Lisbon on July 4, 1821. He swore to uphold the constitution, but his wife, Carlota Joaquina, and their second son, Dom Miguel, refused to take the oath and were sentenced to banishment, though this was not carried out. The Portuguese constitutionalists, not appreciating the determination of Brazil not to yield up its status as a kingdom, sought to compel Pedro to return; but he, rather than sacrifice the rule of the Braganzas in Brazil, declared for Brazilian independence (Sept. 7, 1822) and became emperor of Brazil as Pedro I. This enabled his brother Miguel to appeal to absolutist forces in Portugal to overthrow the constitutionalists, and an insurrection led by Miguel almost succeeded (April 30, 1824); but through the action of the foreign ministers John VI was restored and Miguel went into exile in Vienna (June 1824).

John VI acknowledged the independence of Brazil in 1825, assuming *pro forma* the imperial title and then yielding it to Pedro, but when John died (March 10, 1826) no provision had been made for the succession except that his daughter Maria Isabel was now named regent. Pedro, as Pedro IV of Portugal, issued from Brazil a charter providing for a parliamentary regime by the authorization of the monarchy and not based on the sovereignty of the people. He then made a conditional abdication (May 1826) of the Portuguese throne in favour of his daughter Maria da Glória, aged seven, provided that she should marry her uncle Miguel and that he should swear to accept the charter. This compromise could not be effective. The absolutists had hoped that Pedro would resign all rights to the Portuguese crown, and the council of regency hesitated to publish the charter until Gen. João Carlos de Saldanha (later duque de Saldanha) forced their hand. In October 1827 Miguel took the oath and was appointed regent, landing in Lisbon in February 1828. His supporters at once began to persecute the liberals. A form of *Cortes* met in Lisbon, and in July 1828 repudi-

LISBON, LOOKING TOWARD ROSSIO SQUARE AND THE DONA MARIA II THEATRE. THE STATUE IN THE SQUARE HONORS PEDRO IV

ated Pedro's claims and declared Miguel rightful king.

Only the island of Terceira in the Azores sustained the liberal cause. In June 1829, however, a regency on behalf of Maria da Glória was set up in Terceira, and in 1831 Pedro, having abdicated the Brazilian throne, went to Europe and began to raise money and men for the conquest of Portugal. In February 1832 the expedition sailed to Terceira and in July the liberals, led by Pedro, disembarked at Mindelo near Oporto, which city they soon occupied. However, the rest of the country stood by Miguel, who besieged the liberals in Oporto for a year (July 1832–July 1833). By now Miguelite enthusiasm had waned, and António José de Sousa Manuel, duque de Terceira, and Capt. (later Sir) Charles Napier, who had taken command of the liberal navy, made a successful landing in Algarve (June 1833). Terceira advanced on Lisbon, which fell in July 1833, and Miguel capitulated at Évora-Monte in May 1834.

The War of the Two Brothers ended with the exile of Miguel (June) and the death of Pedro (Sept. 24, 1834). Maria da Glória became queen as Maria II (1834–53) at the age of 15. While Maria necessarily came under the influence of the successful generals of the civil war, her chief aim was to defend her father's charter (which had been *octroyée, i.e.,* granted by the king) from those who demanded a "democratic" constitution like that of 1822, asserting the sovereignty of the people. In September 1836 the latter, thenceforth called Septembrists, seized power. The chartist leaders rebelled and were exiled, but by 1842 the Septembrist front was no longer united and António Bernardo da Costa Cabral restored the charter. In May 1846 the movement of Maria da Fonte, a popular rising against certain improvements in industry and reforms in public health in which almost all parties joined, put an

end to Costa Cabral's government but left Portugal divided between the Septembrists, who held Oporto, and Saldanha, now in Queen Maria's confidence, in Lisbon. Saldanha negotiated for the intervention of other members of the Quadruple Alliance (formed in April 1834 by England, France, Spain, and Portugal), and a combined British and Spanish force received the surrender of the Oporto junta in June 1847 and ended the war with the Convention of Gramido (June 29, 1847). Saldanha governed until 1849, when Costa Cabral resumed office only to be overthrown in April 1851. Saldanha then held office for five years (1851–56), and the period of peace at length permitted the country to settle down.

Maria II was succeeded by her eldest son by her second husband, Ferdinand of Saxe-Coburg, Pedro V (1853–61), who married Stephanie of Hohenzollern-Sigmaringen in 1858. He gave promise of being a capable and conscientious monarch, but died of typhoid fever on Nov. 11, 1861. His brother Luís I (1861–89) seemed to have inherited a country that had recovered from the Napoleonic invasions and from civil wars, political strife, and pronunciamentos. But although the main parties were now defined as Historicals (*i.e.,* radicals) and Regenerators (or moderates), the alternation of governments gradually ceased to reflect popular feeling, and in the last years of Luís' reign republicanism was already gaining ground.

With the accession of Carlos I (1889–1908), a serious dispute with Great Britain occurred. Portugal's possessions in Africa had been recognized by Great Britain in the treaty of 1815; but more recently Germany and Belgium had entered the colonial field and at the Conference of Berlin (1885) the definition of "effective occupation" was adopted as the basis for possession of colonial territories. A colonial movement had gained momentum in Lisbon, and a Portuguese scheme, known as the "Rose-Coloured Map," which laid claim to a colony stretching across Africa from Angola to Mozambique, was recognized by France and Germany (1886). Although the marquess of Salisbury registered a protest (1888), the Portuguese foreign minister Henrique de Barros Gomes sent Maj. Alexandre de Serpa Pinto to the Shiré Highlands in Nyasaland, with a view to their annexation. He became involved in a fight with the Makololos, who were under British protection, and a series of communications between London and Lisbon ended in the dispatch of the British ultimatum of Jan. 11, 1890, demanding the withdrawal of all Portuguese from the Shiré. Amid great popular excitement Barros Gomes had no alternative but to comply, and the government resigned. The incident caused the deepest resentment in Portugal, not only against the ancient ally but also against the monarchy, which was menaced by a republican revolution in Oporto (Jan. 31, 1891).

During the following years, the Portuguese African colonies were defined as a result of the Anglo-Portuguese treaty of July 1891, but the financial position of the country was so bad that it seemed unlikely that the efforts to consolidate the African colonies would succeed. In 1897 it became clear that Portugal would require a considerable loan, and Germany demanded to partake in any assistance that was offered. On Aug. 30, 1898, A. J. (later the earl of) Balfour, temporarily in charge of the British Foreign Office, concluded a secret Anglo-German convention assigning spheres of influence in the Portuguese colonies to Great Britain and Germany in the event of such a loan. This was, however, denounced by the prime minister, Lord Salisbury, and in 1899 when the Germans endeavoured to persuade the Portuguese to accept a loan, Salisbury's action and the imminent danger of a conflict in the Transvaal caused an Anglo-Portuguese approximation. On Oct. 14, 1899, the ancient treaties of alliance were reaffirmed in a secret declaration, later made public (the so-called Windsor Treaty).

Meanwhile, the financial situation showed little improvement, and the republicans continued to progress. In 1906 João Franco, formerly a Regenerator, came to power as champion of the failing monarchist cause. Unable to obtain the support of the other monarchists, he began to govern by decree. Although Franco bravely undertook to reform the finances and administration, he was accused of illegally advancing money to the king. These scandals were followed by rumours of plots, and on Feb. 1, 1908, Carlos and his heir, Luís Filipe, were assassinated as they rode in an open carriage in Lisbon. Whether or not the regicides were isolated fanatics or agents of a wide organization such as the *Carbonarios,* a republican secret society, the deed was applauded by the republicans, who now prepared for a final attack on the monarchy.

King Manuel II (1908–10) found no unity among the monarchist politicians. The general election of August 1910 showed republican majorities in Lisbon and Oporto, and on Oct. 3 the murder by a madman of one of the republican leaders, the distinguished physician Miguel Bombarda, offered the pretext for a rising that was already organized. Armed civilians, soldiers, and the men aboard some ships in the Tagus began the republican revolution on Oct. 4 and, after faltering, their movement, in which António Machado dos Santos played the predominant part, succeeded on Oct. 5. Manuel escaped to Ericeira and thence by sea to Gibraltar and to England. On his death in 1932 his body was returned to Portugal.

3. Social and Economic Conditions.—From the time of the Portuguese overseas conquests the flow of wealth from the new territories and trading posts, although never sustained, was yet sufficient to discourage the building of a sound home economy. The favourable financial position of the late 15th century, derived from trade in slaves, gold, and spices, did not long survive into the 16th century, when the expenses of maintaining some far-flung and unproductive foreign stations and the depredations of pirates quickly absorbed any surpluses. There were few native industries. Not only were manufactured goods such as cloth, tapestry, and metalware imported, but also basic foodstuffs, salt meat, cured fish, poultry, and dairy produce. Agriculture was little regarded and insufficient land was available for small holdings. During the years of Spanish domination the ports were closed to English merchants and by the time they were reopened after 1640 the flow of trade had found new channels and the Dutch and English had outstripped Portugal as colonial powers. The discovery of gold in Brazil at the end of the 17th century brought about a revival in the country's economy, but gold production was in decline by 1750, while the diamond market was saturated. The later 18th century saw a series of protectionist measures, many introduced by Pombal. The Methuen Treaty with England (1703) had strengthened the port wine trade at the expense of Portuguese cloth; later further attempts were made to improve the export value of port wine. Support was also given for the production of woolen goods, linen, paper, porcelain, and cutlery, and to the tunny and sardine fisheries. But the absence of an educated *bourgeoisie* made real development in industry and commerce very difficult and Portugal had to wait until the 20th century for any sustained attack upon its economic difficulties.

H. The Republic, from 1910

The new regime formed a provisional government under the presidency of Teófilo Braga, a well-known writer. This in turn issued a new electoral law giving the vote to all adult Portuguese and presided over the election of a constituent assembly which opened on June 19, 1911. The constitution was passed on Aug. 20, and the provisional government surrendered its authority on Aug. 24 to the new president, Manuel José de Arriaga.

1. Evolutionists, Unionists, and Democrats.—Although a monarchist invasion was unsuccessfully attempted by Henrique de Paiva Couceiro in October 1911, the main danger to the new regime came from its internal divisions. For the moment, it was fairly united in denouncing monarchism and persecuting the church. The religious orders were expelled (Oct. 8, 1910) and their property confiscated. The teaching of religion in primary schools was abolished and the Roman Catholic Church disestablished. The conditions under which Catholics and monarchists were imprisoned attracted attention abroad, and it was only gradually that this legislation was modified. New universities were founded at Lisbon and Oporto, but the task of destruction proved easier than that of construction, and before long the republicans were divided into Evolutionists (moderates), led by António José de Almeida; Unionists (centre party), led by Manuel Brito Camacho; and Democrats (the left wing), led by Afonso Augusto da Costa. A number of prominent republicans had no specific party. The whirligig of republican political life offered little improvement on the monarchist regime, and in 1915 the army showed signs of rest-

lessness. Gen. Pimenta de Castro formed a military government and permitted the monarchists to reorganize, but a Democratic revolution (May 14) led to his arrest and consignment to the Azores. President Arriaga resigned and was succeeded by Braga and then by Bernardino Machado (Oct. 5, 1915–Dec. 8, 1917). The Democratic regime, in which Costa was paramount, was ended by the revolution (December 1917) of Maj. Sidónio Pais, who established a "New Republic" of a right-wing tendency, supported at first by the Unionists. On their withdrawal (March 1918) a new National Republican Party gained control. Sidónio Pais' "presidentialist" regime was abruptly ended with his assassination on Dec. 14, 1918, when, after the provisional presidency of Adm. João de Canto e Castro, power passed gradually back to the Democrats.

Meanwhile, on the outbreak of World War I, Portugal had proclaimed its adhesion to the English alliance (Aug. 7, 1914), and on Nov. 23 committed itself to military operations against Germany. On Sept. 11 a first expedition left to reinforce the African colonies, and there was fighting in northern Mozambique, on the Tanganyika frontier, and in southern Angola, on the frontier of German South West Africa. In February 1916 Portugal seized German ships lying in Portuguese ports and Germany declared war (March 9). A Portuguese expeditionary force went to the western front in 1917, under Gen. Fernão Tamagnini de Abreu e Silva; on April 9, 1918, they were under heavy German attack in the Battle of Lys. By the Treaty of Versailles (1919) Portugal received 0.75% of the indemnity payable by Germany and the Kionga (Quionga) area captured by Portuguese forces in East Africa.

Almeida completed his term of office as president (Oct. 5, 1919–Oct. 5, 1923), but ministries succeeded one another in rapid succession. In 1921 the founder of the republic, António Machado Santos, was among those murdered by enemies of Sidónio Pais; and although António Maria da Silva contrived to govern in the Democratic interest for a year and nine months, his fall in November 1923 was followed by a number of short-lived ministries. Revolutionary movements grew more frequent as the Democratic Party lost its cohesion, and there were signs in the army of impatience with the political turmoil. Although the Democrats obtained a clear majority in 1925 and Manuel Teixeira Gomes (1923–25) yielded the presidency to Bernardino Machado without incident, a military revolt occurred in Lisbon on Feb. 2, 1926. It was quelled, but on May 28 Commander José Mendes Cabeçadas and Gen. Manuel de Oliveira Gomes da Costa rebelled at Braga. Machado was deposed, and a provisional government was formed.

2. The "New State."—At first Cabeçadas was head of the provisional government and Gomes da Costa minister of war; but the former was regarded as too close to the politicians, and Gomes da Costa unseated him. Within a few weeks he too was deposed and his place taken by his foreign minister, Gen. (later Marshal) António Oscar de Fragoso Carmona (July 9, 1926). Elected president of the republic in March 1928, he remained in office until his death in April 1951. After an attempt at revolution in February 1927, which resulted in considerable bloodshed, Carmona's government was not seriously interrupted. The program of the military regime was merely to restore order. To remedy the financial plight of the country, it had been proposed to borrow money from the League of Nations, but the conditions offered included supervision of the finances, which was regarded as offensive to national sovereignty. The loan was, therefore, rejected, and Carmona in 1928 called on António de Oliveira Salazar to take the Ministry of Finance.

Salazar, professor of economics at Coimbra University, fully controlled all expenditure and revenue and embarked on a complete overhaul of the administration. As minister of finance from 1928 to 1940 he produced an unbroken series of budgetary surpluses, which restored Portugal's financial credit. As prime minister from 1932 he ushered in the new Constitution of 1933 (*see* below); as minister of colonies in 1930, he prepared the Colonial Act governing the administration of Portugal's overseas provinces; and as minister for foreign affairs (1936–47) he guided Portugal through the difficulties caused by the Spanish Civil War, and during World War II practised a form of neutrality compatible with the Anglo-Portuguese Alliance. In May 1940 a concordat was signed with the Vatican, which clarified the position of the Catholic Church in Portugal. The church was reconfirmed in its possession of most of the property it had held before 1910, religious instruction was restored in state schools, private church schools were allowed, and church marriages were to be recognized. On the death of Carmona in 1951, Salazar assumed under the constitution the attributes of the presidency, until Gen. Francisco Craveiro Lopes was sworn in as president in August 1951.

By 1953 Salazar had been a member of the government for 25 years. His "New State," as defined by the Constitution of 1933, provided for a president elected for a period of seven years, who appointed a prime minister and a variable number of ministers; a national assembly of deputies elected quadrennially as a block, meeting for at least three months annually; and a corporative chamber consisting of representatives of trades and professions acting as a consultative assembly. At general elections from 1934 onward, all seats in the National Assembly went to government (National Union Party) supporters, although in 1949, 1953, and 1957 there were a few opposition candidates. General Craveiro Lopes was succeeded (1958) as president by Rear Adm. Américo Rodrigues Tomás, elected by a large majority over Brig. H. Delgado, who shortly afterward went into exile. Meanwhile, the determination of the Indian government to annex Portuguese India led to India's severing diplomatic relations with Portugal (July 1955) and to mass invasions of the Portuguese possessions by Indian "passive resisters," who were repelled. In 1955 Portugal entered the United Nations, and in February 1956 referred the question of free access across Indian territory to the enclaves of Dadrá and Nagar Aveli (Havili) to the International Court of Justice, which in April 1960 recognized Portugal's right of passage to the enclaves and India's control of the surrounding territory. On Dec. 18, 1961, India invaded Goa, Diu, and Damão; the subsequent debate in the UN was stifled by the U.S.S.R.'s veto.

Salazar had made it plain that "decolonization" was not a possible policy for him. Shortly afterward, northern Angola was invaded from the Congo and a number of settlers and others were murdered. Attempts were later made to invade Guinea and Mozambique, involving a substantial Portuguese military commitment. In Portugal a small rising at Beja failed in January 1962.

The New State pressed on with electrification schemes (the most important being that of the Douro), industrialization (steelworks, assembly of motor vehicles, shipbuilding, etc.), and public works (the Salazar Bridge at Lisbon, the largest in Europe). Many new schools were built. Internal migration swelled the population of the cities, especially Lisbon.

In September 1968 Salazar suffered a serious stroke, and the president, after consulting the Council of State, asked Marcello Caetano, former minister and rector of Lisbon University, to form a government. Salazar, who died in July 1970, was never informed of the change.   (H. V. L.)

V. POPULATION

The population of Portugal with the Azores and Madeira was 9,234,000 in 1965, giving a density of 101 per sq.km., localized mainly around Lisbon (17.1% of the total population) and Oporto (14.8%). The overseas provinces, with an area of 804,292 sq.mi. (2,083,107 sq.km.), had a population of just over 13,000,000 in 1965. In the same year the population of the main towns of metropolitan Portugal was: Lisbon 802,300; Oporto 386,960; Coimbra 46,300; and Setúbal 44,400.

The Portuguese population is increasing rapidly in relation to the size of the country, at a rate of 102,000 per year. The population is unevenly distributed, all but one-seventh inhabiting the provinces north of the Tagus, which are thus seriously overpopulated. There cultivation and marketing methods are antiquated and the land is uneconomically subdivided; people are thus leaving the countryside for industry and the cities (or to more highly-paid centres abroad) in growing numbers, escaping from irregular employment, inadequate wages, and a low standard of living. There has long been considerable emigration of Portuguese, mainly to Brazil but also to the United States and Canada,

Population Distribution of Portugal

District	Area (sq.mi.)*	Population (in 000s)		Density (per sq.mi.) 1965
		1960 census	1965 est.	
Aveiro	1,046	522.2	555.5	531.1
Beja	3,954	268.9	275.6	69.7
Braga	1,054	593.6	632.1	599.7
Braganza	2,527	230.3	239.9	94.9
Castelo Branco	2,588	310.7	319.0	123.3
Coimbra	1,527	433.6	439.5	287.8
Évora	2,855	215.2	223.0	78.1
Faro	1,958	312.5	314.9	160.8
Guarda	2,122	276.5	276.1	130.1
Leiría	1,326	400.3	416.7	314.3
Lisbon	1,066	1,402.6	1,487.2	1,395.0
Oporto	881	1,191.5	1,284.9	1,458.4
Portalegre	2,274	183.8	185.8	81.7
Santarém	2,583	462.1	471.6	182.6
Setúbal	1,989	376.1	410.0	206.1
Viana do Castelo	814	275.3	282.2	346.7
Vila Real	1,637	322.6	334.2	204.2
Viseu	1,938	477.5	486.2	250.9
Total	34,139	8,255.4	8,634.4	252.9

*1 sq.mi. = 2.59 sq.km.

other parts of Latin America, and under government sponsorship to the African possessions. Since the 1950s, emigration has mainly been directed to France and Germany. Portugal lost more than 500,000 people by legal emigration in 1957–67 and probably as many again illegally. In 1965, 89,056 workers left legally (the largest number since 1912), plus roughly 40,000 clandestinely. This figure of over 100,000 emigrants represents about 3% of Portugal's working population and equals the annual natural increase.

VI. ADMINISTRATION AND SOCIAL CONDITIONS

1. Constitution.—The Portuguese state in the 1960s remained organized according to the Constitution of 1933, approved by plebiscite and modified by subsequent laws. The constitution has 181 articles which fall into two sections: (1) fundamental guarantees; (2) political organization of the state. It is in force throughout the national territory, which comprises the mother country and the overseas provinces. In the Portuguese view there are no colonial territories subject to the metropolitan community; there is a single national community covering a territory which is juridically one despite geographical separation.

2. Government.—The Portuguese state is a unitary and corporate republic. Sovereignty is vested in the nation and its exercise is delegated to the head of the state (the president of the republic), the National Assembly, the government, and the courts of justice. The president of the republic is elected for seven years by the nation, through an electoral college consisting of members of the National Assembly and the Corporative Chamber, and representatives of the municipalities and of the legislative or governing councils of the overseas provinces. He chooses the head of the government and appoints ministers whom the latter proposes. He has the power to convene and dissolve the assembly.

The president is assisted by the Council of State (with merely consultative powers but with important functions of verification) composed of 15 members, 5 ex officio and 10 appointed for life. The government is composed of the chairman of the council of ministers and of the ministers. Ministers are responsible to the chairman of the council. The government can issue decree laws having the force of law and is independent of the vote of parliament. The chairman of the council is the delegate of the head of state and, as such, holds the power of government.

The National Assembly consists of one chamber composed of 130 members elected by universal and direct suffrage for four years. Members have the right to remuneration. Ministers who are members of the assembly may not take part in its proceedings (except for committees), but the government selects a member to represent its point of view in debates. The parliamentary session is normally for three months annually, beginning on Nov. 25. Both the government and members of the assembly have the right to initiate legislation, but members may not introduce bills which would involve increases in state expenditure or decreases in state revenue. Besides the discussion of political and administrative measures and the voting of bills after consulting the Corporative Chamber, the assembly has certain specific functions such as the approval of the general principles of the organization of national defense and of the law courts, and the creation of banks.

The Corporative Chamber represents interests of an administrative, economic, spiritual, and moral character. Its functions are consultative and advisory and its duties include reporting on draft bills and proposals before their discussion by the National Assembly. The chamber normally functions through sessions of one or more of its 12 sections (each of which represents a separate interest), but exceptionally it may meet in plenary session.

3. Local Administration.—The basic unit of the Portuguese local administrative structure is the *concelho,* or municipality, the lineal descendant of the medieval councils. The *concelho* is composed of parishes (*freguesias*), each with its administrative board, and *concelhos* are grouped into districts (18 in all), each with a board. Since 1959 the province has not been an administrative unit, though the provincial names are retained for regional designation. The municipal council comprises representatives of its parishes, of the guilds and syndicates (wage earners, salaried employees, and members of the liberal professions), of the agricultural corporative bodies, and of welfare institutions, etc. Its executive body is the Câmara Municipal, whose president is also the representative of the government. The district board is headed by a civil governor, who represents governmental influence in local administration. Each overseas province has a governor, assisted by governmental and legislative councils, who is subject to the Overseas Ministry of the Portuguese government.

4. Taxation.—Various taxes are levied on different forms of income brought in by property, trade and industry, capital gains, etc., and employed persons are taxed not on their actual income but on an assumed average income. There is also a supplementary personal tax, which is progressive and designed to correct anomalies in normal taxation.

5. Living Conditions.—More than 40% of the working population is employed in agriculture, though the development plan for 1959–64 foresaw a displacement of many farm workers. Few skilled workers are unemployed, but an incidence of unemployed unskilled, seasonal workers is sometimes recorded, causing authorities to create employment through public works projects. The country's excess of unskilled labour and lack of skilled technical and scientific workers is being remedied by extending and improving training facilities.

Wages.—Collective agreements between trade unions and employers' associations establish minimum salaries in given grades of employment and the number of employees to be included in each grade. Wages have been keeping pace with rising domestic prices; thus, the wages of farm workers rose by 89% from 1960 to the end of 1966 and those of factory workers by 39%. Nevertheless, these rises are much less than in industrialized Western European countries, and this is an important attraction for foreign investment. The average income per head in 1967 in metropolitan Portugal was only £134 (compared with £520 in the U.K.).

Housing.—The problem of housing has been much eased by intensive building of modern houses and blocks of apartments, with special attention to housing for the lower income groups in cooperation with the corporative organizations and social welfare bodies. New residential areas have been opened up with houses at low rentals which can become the property of the tenants. Loans are provided to workers for building their own homes.

6. Welfare Services.—The Constitution of 1933 laid down the general principle that the state should promote and encourage provident institutions, and the National Labour Statute of 1933 furthered this aim. The first practical measures were taken from 1935 onward. From the early 1960s four classes of social insurance institutions were recognized: (1) institutions covering the compulsory insurance of employed persons, including the Social Providence Organization for employees (and their dependents) in industry and commerce; People's Centres (Casas do Povo) which catered for the rural population, providing benefits and social centres; Fishermen's Centres, providing education and training as well as other benefits; (2) pension and provident schemes for the various professions; (3) provident institutions for state and local government servants (civil and military); (4) voluntary mutual

J. ALLAN CASH

MODERN APARTMENT BUILDING IN LISBON

aid (or friendly) societies, which inherit an older tradition; they are private but subject to government inspection. Benefits in the above institutions vary but those included are for sickness, disablement, maternity, and special risks, and also family allowances and old age and widows' pensions. Each industry, trade, and profession (and many individual enterprises) has its own corporative organization which provides social benefits and arbitrates for it in labour tribunals. Both employers and employed are equally represented in the corporative organizations, which are also linked with public life through the Corporative Chamber on which they are represented.

Health.—Portugal is divided into three hospital zones based on Lisbon, Oporto, and Coimbra. These are subdivided into regions and subregions, providing a network of general and specialized hospitals, sanatoriums, and clinics. About 80% of patients in central hospitals receive free treatment and the state covers about 80% of the expenses of central hospitals. The main hospitals, medical institutions, and sanatoriums are in Lisbon, Oporto, and Coimbra, and number about 30.

7. Justice.—Judges are independent of the legislature and government; they are appointed for life, after an examination by legal experts, by the Higher Council of the Judicature which is composed of the president of the Supreme Court of Justice and the presidents of the appeal courts. There is a distinction between the courts of justice, which deal with civil, criminal, and commercial cases, and the administrative tribunals, which deal with the legality of administrative authorities' decisions. There are separate civil, criminal, commercial, labour, and juvenile courts. Military tribunals deal with offenses by members of the armed forces. All cities have a "court of first instance" and there are also municipal courts in some boroughs and parishes. Higher courts of appeal ("courts of second instance") sit regionally in Lisbon, Oporto, Coimbra, Luanda, and Lourenço Marques. The Supreme Court of Justice sits in Lisbon and has jurisdiction over the whole of Portuguese territory. The attorney general is represented in all courts and tribunals. The minister of justice is the intermediary between the judicature and the government and coordinates the necessary services such as attorney general's office, judicial police, prison services, etc.

8. Education.—Educational standards in Portugal are not such as can easily respond to the demands of a technological age. Education is compulsory only from the age of 7 to 11. Thereafter, children may attend a secondary technical school, which has five-year industrial and commercial courses, or a secondary high school (*liceu*) which has a seven-year course directed toward university entrance. In the early 1960s only 13% of children proceeded to the former and 7% to the latter. The state Portuguese Youth Organization is concerned, through extrascholastic activities, with the moral and political training of all primary and secondary school pupils. At these levels both private and state schools are found. Higher education is provided by the Universities of Lisbon (founded 1290; reestablished at Lisbon 1911), Oporto (1911), and Coimbra (1290); by the Technical Universities of Lisbon and Oporto; and by various technical institutes, both officially and privately financed. The main official bodies coordinating international scientific relations are the Institute for Higher Culture and the Scientific Research Council for the Overseas Provinces. At the national level research is coordinated by the National Board for Scientific and Technological Research, set up in 1967. There are now more than 80 public bodies engaged in these fields.

9. Defense.—The Ministry of Defense coordinates the activities of the Army and Navy Ministries through a general secretariat for national defense under the direction of the Chief of the General Staff of the Armed Forces.

Besides the Army, Navy, and Air Force there are the National Republican Guard, the Fiscal Customs Guard, and the Portuguese Legion (a voluntary patriotic organization). Military service is compulsory and though nominally lasting 18 months, in the present state of hostilities in the African provinces it may be prolonged up to four years. The Portuguese Youth Movement, the Military School, and the Army Pupils Organization provide some paramilitary training.

Continental Portugal in the 1960s was divided into five military regions: Oporto, Coimbra, Tomar, Évora, and Lisbon; and there were separate commands in Madeira and the Azores. There were commands also in each of the overseas provinces. The Navy comprised destroyers, frigates, submarines, and light vessels. Portugal had three air regions: Lisbon, Luanda, and Lourenço Marques. The Air Force was equipped with various types of U.S. aircraft and contributed to the NATO Air Forces.

10. Overseas Provinces.—Portugal has five separate provinces in Africa, one in Asia (Macao or Macau), and one in Oceania (Portuguese Timor). The Portuguese State of India (Goa, Damão, and Diu) is still regarded by the Portuguese as belonging to Portugal (*see* PORTUGUESE INDIA). Angola (Portuguese West Africa) and Moçambique or Mozambique (Portuguese East Africa) on the African mainland comprise more than 90% of the total area of the overseas provinces. Portuguese Guinea, the Cape Verde Islands, and São Tomé e Príncipe are the remaining African provinces. In China the promontory of Macao on the Canton (Pearl) River lies near Canton and Hong Kong. Timor, the largest of the Lesser Sunda Islands, is divided between Portugal and Indonesia. All of these provinces are described in separate articles.   (JN. N.)

VII. THE ECONOMY

Portugal is in an anomalous position with respect to its economy. It is associated with some of the most prosperous nations in Europe, as a member of the European Free Trade Association (EFTA). Yet it is one of the poorer nations of the world, with the lowest per capita standard of living in Europe. Portugal is one of the smallest nations, and yet it has preserved its vast colonial empire, equivalent in area to two-thirds of Europe. Its social inequalities are greater than those of other southern European states, and yet it has a robust cohesion as a nation. It has a demographic problem that can be met only by a very heavy

rate of emigration to other lands, and yet it has one of the highest rates of infantile mortality in Europe.

To speed up its slow industrial growth and improve on the use of its resources, Portugal has embarked on three national plans since 1953. The first plan (1953–58) chiefly involved investments by the public sector, with some emphasis on the utilization of its rivers by the development of hydroelectric power. With the country's rapid increase of population, the second plan (1959–64) doubled the national investment in the infrastructure, to raise the GNP by 27% and the production per capita by 22%. A further boost to the development of hydroelectric power was given, but some effort was also made to modernize the archaic character of agriculture, notably by means of irrigation in Alentejo. Heavy industry was also promoted by mining expansion, the establishment of iron and steel mills and shipbuilding yards, and by the improvement of communications and port facilities, etc. The third six-year plan (1968–73) envisaged quadrupling the previous expenditure with main emphasis on industry, followed by transport and communications, energy, agriculture and forestry, and tourism. To boost this ambitious program, an interim development plan for 1965–67 was introduced, at a time when drought had affected agricultural production and hydroelectric supplies to industry.

A. PRODUCTION

1. Agriculture.—The long-term stagnation of Portugal's agricultural output and productivity continues to be a major drag on the economy, which only agrarian reform can effectively alter. As many as 95% of the farms are under 10 ha. in size, occupying about one-third of the cultivated area, especially in the north. But in the south a further 40% of the cultivated area is taken up by large estates. Neither system is adequately productive, because of fragmented and uneconomical holdings, and extensive methods, respectively. Thus Portugal continued to make the poorest showing of agricultural production in southern Europe, and its output was not helped by short-term events such as poor climatic conditions during the 1960s. Yet agriculture still employs about 37% of the active population to contribute only 18% of the gross domestic product.

Crops.—More than one-third of Portugal is arable land, a great part of which is devoted to cereals. Alentejo and Estremadura produce more than four-fifths of the wheat crop; Minho, Beira Alta, and Beira Litoral two-thirds of the maize (corn);

YAN—RAPHO

LOADING CORK ONTO CARTS OUTSIDE SETÚBAL IN THE ESTREMADURA REGION

and Trás-os-Montes e Alto Douro and Beira Baixa half the rye. With relatively low yields, production has been increased by extending the arable area on poor, marginal lands, where soil erosion has often ensued. Fallow land still accounts for one-fifth of the total arable area. One-tenth of the productive area is under tree crops, chiefly olives and vines. The table wines of Estremadura, the port wine of the Douro Valley, and the acid *vinho verde* of the northwest are famous. Olive groves are scattered widely, though Estremadura, Ribatejo, and Alentejo produce among them three-fifths of the total. Fruit and vegetables now comprise more than a quarter of the agricultural exports, notably developed in Ribatejo, Estremadura, and Algarve. A major irrigation project to reclaim 170,000 ha. of land in Alentejo, with water from the Tagus and Guadiana rivers, is now in its first stage. A large part of the reclaimed area will be for horticulture.

Livestock.—Lacking mechanization, a very high proportion of the existing cattle herd is being used for draught purposes. This however is at the expense of a considerable loss of milk and meat production, for Portugal has the lowest milk production in Europe. Beef cattle are also poorly developed. Alentejo has one-third of all the sheep and goats of the country.

2. Forestry.—Ecologically, much of Portugal is suited to a program of afforestation. The actual forest area is 3,200,000 ha., 43% of it under pines and 23% under cork oak. Portugal is the world's leading producer and exporter of cork. It is also a foremost producer of naval stores, more than two-thirds of which are exported.

3. Fisheries.—Fish is still an important Portuguese source of food and livelihood. In 1966 the zone of fishing rights was extended from 6 to 12 mi. off the coast. The sardine catch, which was 54,835 tons in 1966, is concentrated in the ports of Matosinhos (the chief cannery centre), Setúbal, Portimão, and Olhão. Tunny is landed in Olhão and Faro on the south coast.

4. Mining.—Portugal is moderately rich in some minerals, chiefly sulfur, iron and copper pyrites, wolfram, uranium, and iron ore. It lacks coal, three-quarters of its coal needs having to be imported. The anthracite mines of Pejão and Este near Oporto, and the iron pyrites mines of Aljustrel in Alentejo are the largest operators. Tin and iron are mined in Torre de Moncorvo (Braganza).

5. Power.—Until 1955 barely one-third of Portugal's electricity supplies came from its ample water resources, and about four-fifths of its thermal power was dependent upon imported coal and oil. Since then an ambitious program of building new dams on the Douro, Cávado, Zêzere, Ponsul, and Sado rivers has radically altered the situation. Per capita electricity consumption increased from 60 kw-hr. in the 1930s to 700 in 1967. However, the rather excessive emphasis on hydroelectric sources, together with weak policies in planning the sequence of developments, and the unreliability of the rivers, have all indicated the need to install more thermoelectric plants. In 1967 the first stage of a new thermal plant was initiated at Carregado near Lisbon, which eventually would produce 500,000 kw., a third of Portugal's total generating capacity (in 1967).

6. Industries.—The industrial sector contributes about 45% of the GNP. Three main groups—food, textiles, and metals—account for more than half of the country's total industry, and employ about 55% of the labour. The cotton industry is the most developed, concentrated in and around Oporto, with new factories built by foreign companies engaged in man-made fibres at Portalegre, Espinho, Trofa, etc. A major development in the iron and steel industry is the Aldeia de Paio Pires factory opposite Lisbon, with neighbouring shipyards being developed to absorb some of its capacity. The first and only oil refinery was built at Cavo Ruivo in 1940, near Lisbon, but a new petrochemical plant is being planned near Oporto, associated with improved port facilities at Leixões to receive oil tankers of 100,000 tons. Dam construction has promoted the cement industry, which has several large plants in the Lisbon area. Despite these developments, Portuguese manufactures are still largely associated with small plants and family workshops, and even when plants are large there is some underutilization of plant capacity.

PAUL ALMASY

BARRELS OF PORT WINE FOR EXPORT ON THE DOCKS OF OPORTO. THE WINE IS PRODUCED IN THE DOURO VALLEY

B. TRADE AND FINANCE

1. Foreign Trade.—Because of the weakness of the agricultural sector and the lack of manufacturing activities, Portugal has to import both food and expensive manufactures. There would be an enormous deficit in the trade balance but for the benefits of its colonial trade. About one-quarter of its export trade is with its colonies but only one-tenth of its imports come from them. Invisible earnings have increased significantly from emigrants' remittances, and since 1963 there has been a major growth of tourism that is creating considerable financial benefit to the economy. Principal imports in order of value are machinery, fuels and oils, vehicles, iron and steel, cotton, and grain. Major exports are cotton, cork, meat and fish preparations, and wine.

2. Banking and Currency.—The Portuguese monetary unit is the escudo (100 centavos), with the conto equivalent to 1,000 escudos. The official exchange rate was stabilized in 1949 at U.S. $1 to 28.75 escudos. The sole bank of issue is the Bank of Portugal, founded in 1846; its statutes were revised in 1931. More than 20 commercial banks operate in Portugal and the islands of Madeira and the Azores. In 1959 the Bank of Development was set up to act as an investment bank for both metropolitan and overseas territories. Portugal is a member of the International Monetary Fund, the International Bank for Reconstruction and Development, and the Organization for European Cooperation and Development.

3. National Finance.—The maintenance of price stability has been the chief aim of monetary policy. Taxation of industry is moderate compared with that of other countries, with provision for a high rate of depreciation on equipment. The channeling of savings to long-term investment is still a weak feature of the monetary system.

C. TRANSPORT AND COMMUNICATIONS

Although transport and communications have been seriously neglected in the past, there has been in recent decades a strong effort to improve this sector of the economy. The railway system consists of 2,234 mi. (1,760 mi. of wide gauge [5′6″] track, and 474 mi. of narrow gauge [3′3″] track). The main Lisbon-Oporto line was electrified in 1965. Bus services operate on about 15,200 mi. of roads (c. 10,550 mi. hard surfaced). Two new bridges have been built: the Arrabida Bridge over the Douro at Oporto in 1963, and the Tagus suspension bridge at Lisbon in 1966. Air transport is increasingly important, Transportes Aereos Portugueses serving a network of internal airports, as well as to the overseas provinces. Lisbon's Portela Airport is a major European air terminal.

Portugal is an important international gateway for cable and radio connections, operated by Companhia Portuguesa Rádio Marconi and the Eastern Telegraph Co. There are about 38 radio and 2 television stations, with transmitters reaching 98% of the population.

See also references under "Portugal" in the Index.

(J. M. Ho.)

BIBLIOGRAPHY.—Geography and General: "Portugal: Das Land als Ganzes," Ergänzungsheft 213 Petermanns Mitt. (1932), "Portugal: Die portugiesischen Landschaften," Ergänzungsheft 230 Petermanns Mitt. (1937), Bibliografia geográfica de Portugal, additions by M. Feio (1948); A. de Amorim Girão, Geografia de Portugal (1942); O. Ribeiro, Portugal, o Mediterrâneo e o Atlântico (1945), Portugal, vol. 5 of Geografia de España y Portugal, ed. by M. de Terán (1955); P. Birot, Le Portugal: Étude de Géographie régionale (1950); D. Stanislawski, The Individuality of Portugal (1959); E. de Castro Caldas, Modernizaçao da Agricultura Portuguesa (1960); Government of Portugal, Plano de Fomento para 1953–58 (1953), Relatório Final Preparatório do Plano II di Fomento (1958); Instituto Nacional de Estatística, Bibliografia sobre a Economia Portuguesa, 1948–1955, ed. by A. D. Guerreiro, vol. 1–7 (1958–64); F. Pereira de Mouta, Problemas Fundamentais da Economia (1962); V. Xavier Pintado, The Structure and Growth of the Portuguese Economy (1964); A. Pasquier, L'Economie du Portugal (1961).

History: General histories of Portugal in English are Charles E. Nowell, A History of Portugal (1952); H. V. Livermore, A History of Portugal (1947), A New History of Portugal (1966); H. Morse Stephens, Portugal (1891; with additional chapter, 1908). In Portuguese the most complete modern history is the monumental História de Portugal, ed. by Damião Peres and others, 8 vol. (1928–35); Fortunato de Almeida's História de Portugal, 6 vol. (1922–29), is valuable for its bibliography. Other general works covering various aspects of Portuguese history are: Fortunato de Almeida, História da Igreja em Portugal, 4 vol. (1910–22), and Padre Miguel Augusto de Oliveira, História eclesiástica de Portugal, 2nd ed. (1948); J. Lucio de Azevedo, Épocas de Portugal económico (1929); the História da expansão portuguesa no mundo, 2 vol. (1937–42). See also E. Prestage, "The Anglo-Portuguese Alliance," Transactions of the Royal Historical Society, 4th series, vol. xvii (1934) and (ed.), Chapters in Anglo-Portuguese Relations (1935).

Early and Medieval Portugal: José Leite de Vasconcelos, Religiões da Lusitânia (1924); Adolf Schulten, Viriato, Port. trans. by A. Ataide, 2nd ed. (1940); A. A. Mendes Corrêa, Raizes de Portugal, 2nd ed. (1944); Damião Peres, Como nasceu Portugal, 2nd ed. (1942). For the early monarchy, see Alexandre Herculano de Carvalho e Araujo, História de Portugal, 4 vol. (1846–53), 7th ed., 8 vol. (1914–16), going to the death of Afonso III in 1279; Padre Luis Gonzaga de Azevedo, História de Portugal, 5 vol. (1935–42). For the documents of Afonso Henriques' chancery see Rui P. de Azevedo, Documentes Régios (1958–62). The English narrative of the conquest of Lisbon is edited and translated by C. W. David, De expugnatione Lyxbonensi (1936). Karl Erdmann, Papsturkunden in Portugal (1927), deals with early relations between Portugal and Rome. For the 14th-century crisis see P. E. Russell, The English Intervention in Spain and Portugal in the Time of Edward III and Richard II (1955). See also E. Prestage, Royal Power and the Cortes in Portugal (1927), and Visconde de Santarém, Memorias e alguns documentos para a história e teoria das côrtes geraes . . . , new ed. (1924), which deal with early institutions. H. da Gama Barros, História da administracão pública em Portugal nos séculos XII a XV, 3 vol. (1885–1914), new ed. by T. de Sousa Soares (1945 et seq.), deals with administration. See also A. de Sousa Silva Costa Lobo, História da sociedade em Portugal no século XV (1903); Virgínia Rau, Subsídios para a história das feiras (1943), As sesmarias medievais portuguesas (1946).

The Age of the Discoveries: For the domestic history of Portugal, see the general histories already mentioned and the chronicles of John II by Ruy de Pina, Damião de Gois and Garcia de Rèzende; of Manuel by Damião de Gois; of John III by Frei Luiz de Sousa and Francisco de Andrade; and of Sebastian by Frei Bernardo da Cruz. See also Alfredo Pimenta, D. João III (1936); I. D. M. Ford (ed.), Letters of John III, king of Portugal, 1521–1557 (1931); J. M. de Queiróz Veloso, D. Sebastião: 1554–1578, 3rd ed. (1945), and A Perda da independência, vol. i, O Reinado do Cardeal D. Henrique (1946). Alexandre Herculano de Carvalho e Araujo, History of the Origin and Establishment of the Inquisition in Portugal, Eng. trans. by J. C. Branner (1926); Mário Brandão, O Colégio das Artes, 2 vol. (1924–33), and Cardinal M. Goncalves Cerejeira, Clenardo (1926), afford useful introductions to the Renaissance in Portugal. For the Portuguese in the

East, see C. R. Boxer, Fidalgos in the Far East, 1550–1770 (1948), The Christian Century in Japan, 1549–1650 (1951) and "The Portuguese in the East, (1500–1800)" in Portugal and Brazil, ed. by H. V. Livermore and W. J. Entwistle (1953). For the discoveries, see E. Prestage, The Portuguese Pioneers (1933); B. Diffie, Prelude to Empire (1960); D. Peres, História dos descobrimentos portugueses (1943–46).

The Late 16th, 17th, and 18th Centuries: A. Danvila y Burguero, Don Cristóbal de Moura (1900); M. Martins d'Antas, Les Faux Don Sébastian (1866); J. Lúcio de Azevedo, A Evolução do Sebastianismo, 2nd ed. (1947).

For the restoration see E. Prestage, The Diplomatic Relations of Portugal and England from 1640 to 1668 (1925), and contemporary authorities such as Luis de Menezes, História de Portugal restaurado, 2 vol. (1679–98). For the life of D. Luisa de Gusmão see Hipólito Raposo, Dona Luisa de Gusmão, duquesa e rainha (1613–1666) (1947). António Baião studied the marriage of Afonso VI in his Causa de nulidade (1925); Damião Peres, A Diplomacia portuguesa e a sucessão de Espanha: 1700–14 (1931), deals with Portugal in the War of the Spanish Succession; Eduardo Brazão, Relacões externas de Portugal: reinado de D. João V, 2 vol. (1938), with the reign of John V. For the age of Pombal see Marcus Cheke, Dictator of Portugal (1938); the most convenient introduction in Portuguese is J. Lúcio de Azevedo, O Marquês de Pombal e a sua época (1909 and 1922). See also Caetano Beirão, D. Maria I, 1777–92, 2nd ed. (1934); C. R. Boxer, The Golden Age of Brazil (1962); A. D. Francis, The Methuens and Portugal (1966); T. D. Kendrick, The Lisbon Earthquake (1956).

The 19th and 20th Centuries: M. de Oliveira Lima, Dom João VI no Brasil, 1808–1821, 3 vol., 2nd ed. (1945); Oliveira Lima, D. Miguel no trono 1828–1833 (1933); Maria Amélia Vaz de Carvalho, Vida do duque de Palmela, 3 vol. (1898–1903); Júlio de Vilhena, D. Pedro V e o seu reinado, 3 vol. (1921); Luis Vieira de Castro, D. Carlos I, 3rd ed. (1943); Jesús Pabón, La Revolución Portuguesa, 2 vol. (1941–45); P. B. Warhurst, Anglo-Portuguese Relations in South-Central Africa, 1890–1900 (1962); A. Pasquier, L'Economie du Portugal (1961); R. J. Hammond, Portugal and Africa, 1815–1910 (1966).

For the regime of Salazar, see F. C. C. Egerton, Salazar, Rebuilder of Portugal (1943); Antonio Ferro, Salazar: Portugal and her Leader, Eng. trans. by H. de Barros Gomes and J. Gibbons (1939); Luis Teixeira, Perfil de Salazar, su vida y su tiempo (s.d.); also Salazar's own Discursos (1928–50) and Doctrine and Action: Internal and Foreign Policy of the New Portugal, 1928–1939, Eng. trans. by R. E. Broughton (1939). Michael Derrick, The Portugal of Salazar (1938), is a general account. Current history and statistics are summarized annually in Britannica Book of the Year.

PORTUGUESA, a state of Venezuela, occupies the northeast section of the western llanos (q.v.). The state takes its name from the Portuguesa River, which is a part of the Orinoco River drainage system. Portuguesa has an area of 5,869 sq.mi. (15,200 sq.km.). With an increase in population from 34,000 in 1941 to 203,707 in 1961, it is one of the most rapidly growing states of Venezuela. The capital, Guanare, founded in 1591, had a population of 18,476 in 1961. Acarigua is the principal commercial centre of the state. Livestock raising dominates the economy and rice, coffee, cotton, tobacco, cocoa, and corn (maize) are grown. At Turén, in the district of the same name, the national government sponsored a planned agricultural community which was expected to establish the best means of bringing the vast llanos under cultivation. The Virgin of Coromoto, patron of Venezuela, is associated with the parish church in Guanare, and thousands annually visit the city to pay homage to the venerated image. (J. J. J.)

PORTUGUESE EAST AFRICA (MOZAMBIQUE; officially PROVÍNCIA DE MOÇAMBIQUE), an overseas province of Portugal and the most populous and second largest (after Angola) of the five Portuguese African possessions, lies on the east coast of Africa between Tanzania and South Africa. Its area is 297,846 sq.mi. (771,124 sq.km.), about seven times the size of Portugal itself and about the size of Texas. From north to south it is about 1,300 mi. (2,100 km.) long. The frontier is very irregular, and the territory varies in width from 56 mi. (90 km.) in the south to 400 mi. (640 km.). It takes its name from the island and town of Moçambique or Mozambique (q.v.), formerly the capital. The modern capital is Lourenço Marques (q.v.).

PHYSICAL FEATURES

The coastline extends from 10°27′ S to 26°52′ S and makes a double curve on a northeast-southwest axis. Its length is about 1,736 mi. (2,795 km.). In the extreme south, about 40 mi. (64 km.) N of the South African frontier, is the great basin of Delagoa Bay (q.v.; officially Baía de Lourenço Marques) on which stands the capital. North of this the coast is low-lying and sandy or swampy as far as the deep indentation of the Zambezi Delta. From the Zambezi northward the coast is studded with small islands, mainly of coral formation, on one of which is the town of Mozambique. North of this are high rocky headlands and rugged cliffs. Porto Amélia stands on the great natural harbour of Pemba Bay. The territory is rich in rivers, about 50 of which flow into the Indian Ocean, including the Zambezi in the centre, the Limpopo in the south, and the Ruvuma in the north.

The Zambezi divides the province in two. To the south the coastal plain is much deeper, and only a small part of the high plateau falls in Portuguese territory. In the centre Mt. Gorongoza reaches 6,112 ft. (1,863 m.), and farther north there are several ranges. Niassa District has more than 20 groups of mountains more than 4,000 ft. (1,200 m.) high, and Namuli Peak reaches 7,936 ft. (2,419 m.). Southeast of Lake Nyasa (part of the eastern shore of which is in Niassa District) is a high range which drops 3,000 ft. (900 m.) in 6 mi. to the level of the lake. The highlands along the Rhodesian border reach about 9,000 ft. (2,700 m.).

Geology.—The central plateau consists of gneisses, granites, and schists which in part or in whole belong to the Archean System. Rocks of the Karroo Period occur in the Zambezi Basin, where at Tete they contain workable seams of coal and have yielded plant remains of Upper Carboniferous age. Sandstones and shales, possibly of Upper Karroo age, form a narrow belt at the foot of the plateau. Upper Cretaceous rocks crop out from beneath the superficial deposits along the coastal belt between Delagoa Bay and Mozambique. The highest Cretaceous strata occur in Conducia, where they contain the huge ammonite *Pachydiscus conduciensis.* The Eocene formation is well represented in Gaza District by the nummulitic limestones which have been found to extend for a considerable distance inland. Basalts occur in the Zambezi Basin.

Climate.—There are two meteorological zones. North of the Zambezi seasons are monsoonal, October–March being hot and wet, April–September cooler and dry. To the south, where an anticyclonic regime prevails, seasons are similar, but less well defined. Lourenço Marques, in the extreme south, has an annual mean temperature of 72° F (22.2° C). Quelimane, in the centre near the coast, has an annual mean of 85° F (29.4° C), while at Tete, in the interior, about 260 mi. (418 km.) up the Zambezi, the annual mean is 78° F (25.6° C). The annual extremes are much greater on the coast than in the interior. The range is similar in the north. On the uplands and plateaus the climate is more temperate.

Average annual rainfall figures (in inches; millimetres in parentheses) are: Lourenço Marques 31 (787); Beira 60 (1,524); Quelimane 56 (1,422); Mozambique 31 (787); Tete 21 (533); and Vila Cabral 44 (1,127).

Vegetation.—The soils of Mozambique are predominantly poor and sandy. Three-quarters of the territory is covered with open woodland mixed with savanna and steppe, which can be subdivided into three types of vegetation: (1) moderately dry with much *Brachystegia* and *Julbernardia;* (2) relatively drier undifferentiated types; and (3) especially dry types, dominated by *Colophospermum mopane.* The first type is general throughout the northern half of the territory.

Six palms are found, including the coconut, which is common in the coastal regions, and the date palm, mostly in marshy ground and near rivers. A kind of cedar is found in the lower forests, and ironwood (suitable for high-class furniture) and ebony are common. A large African mahogany (*Khaya senegalensis*), found in ravines and by riverbanks, affords durable and easily worked timber; other timbers include pod mahogany, used for furniture and vehicles; *m'bila* (*Pterocarpus*) or bloodwood; *ziba* (*Dialium schlechteri*), a valuable hardwood; and *monhe* or *gone* (*Adina*), similar to teak. Several varieties of *Vitex* and of *Ficus,* notably the sycamore fig (*Ficus sycomorus*), bear edible fruit.

Excellent hardwood is obtained from a species of *Grewia.* Other characteristic trees are the mangrove (along the seashore), sandalwood, gum copal, baobab, and bombax, and, in the lower plain, dracaenas (dragon trees), many species of creepers and flowering shrubs, and several prickly shrubs. Acacias are numerous, including the gum-yielding variety, while *Landolphia* rubber vines grow

freely in the forests. The bamboo is common, and spear grass is abundant along the riverbanks and the edges of the marshes.

Animal Life.—Among the commoner mammals are the elephant, black rhinoceros, lion, leopard, spotted hyena, jackal, serval, civet cat, genet, hunting dog, and mongoose. The rivers and marshes are the home of hippopotamuses, though they have deserted the lower Zambezi. The wart hog and the smaller red hog are common in open country. A species of zebra is plentiful, and herds of buffalo are numerous in the plains and in open woods. Many antelopes are found, and the giraffe, though scarce, also occurs. Scaly anteaters are fairly numerous, and rodents are common. There are several kinds of monkeys and lemuroids. Crocodiles, lizards, chameleons, and land and river turtles are all very numerous, as are pythons, cobras, puff adders, and vipers. Centipedes, scorpions, and insects abound. Among insects, mosquitoes, locusts, tsetse and hippo flies, cockroaches, phylloxera, termites, and soldier ants are common plagues.

Flamingoes, cranes, herons, storks, pelicans, and ibises are found, including the beautiful crested crane and the comparatively rare saddle-billed stork. The eagle, vulture, kite, buzzard, and crow are well represented, and guinea fowl, partridge, bustard, quail, teal, widgeon, and mallard are all common. Gregarious small green parrots move through the trees in search of fruit.

Gorongoza National Park (1,150 sq.mi. [2,979 sq.km.]) is one of the finest game parks in southern Africa. There are four other game reserves in the territory: Ruvuma, Gilé, Marromeu, and Maputo. Of these, only Gorongoza is open to tourists, but 16 tourist zones have been set aside for safari hunting.

THE PEOPLE

The 1960 census showed the total population of Mozambique to be 6,578,604, of whom 6,430,530 were African, 97,268 European, 31,465 mixed, 17,243 Indian, and 2,098 others. The number of Europeans had grown from 48,910 in 1950 to 65,598 in 1955 to 97,-268 in 1960, primarily as a result of immigration from Portugal.

Intermarriage between Europeans and Africans has not been encouraged, although miscegenation has probably been greater than the census figures indicate. While many mulatto children are accepted as family members by the Portuguese parent and raised without discrimination in Portuguese society, there are limitations to the fulfillment of political and administrative ambitions.

Theoretically, there is no colour bar in Mozambique, the only legal criterion for social acceptability being that the individual is "civilized." For the African this means becoming literate in Portuguese, acquiring a Portuguese education, and being Christian. In 1955 only 4,554 individuals, less than 0.1% of the African population of Mozambique, were so assimilated. The official estimate for 1960 envisaged only 5,020 *assimilados.* The influx of Portuguese settlers that began in the 1950s, together with the further entrenchment of the white populations of southern Africa, is creating a situation in Mozambique where the culture bar is virtually synonymous with the colour bar.

The mean population density (1960 census) is 22.1 persons per square mile, but the distribution is irregular, ranging from 6.0 in Niassa District to 111.6 in Lourenço Marques District. Of the Europeans, 63.8% live in Lourenço Marques and Manica e Sofala districts, where they are concentrated primarily in the cities of Lourenço Marques and Beira. African population density is greatest in the districts of Zambézia and Moçambique. (For district populations and densities, *see* below, *Administration and Social Conditions.*)

Tribal Distribution.—The main peoples in the north are the Yao, between Lake Nyasa and the Msalu River; the Makonde in the extreme northeast; and the Makua-Lomwe, who dominate the districts of Cabo Delgado, Moçambique, and Zambézia, numbering about 2,500,000. All these people are matrilineal, as are the Malawi groups who live north of the Zambezi in Tete District. South of the Zambezi and north of the Sabi River are the patrilineal Shona groups, including the Manyika and Ndau. South of the Sabi are the patrilineal Hlengwe, Thonga, Ronga, and the Chopi. The African population of the Zambezi Valley is ethnically mixed, it being a transition zone between the matrilineal people to the north and the patrilineal people to the south. Swahili live on the coast from Cape Delgado down to António Enes.

Religion.—The Africans mainly practise their traditional religions, but an estimated 800,000 are Muslims. There are nearly the same number of African Roman Catholics and some 200,000 Protestants. The position of the church is defined by the Portuguese-Vatican concordat and missionary agreement of 1940, which created a metropolitan see at Lourenço Marques, to which the four dioceses of Beira, Quelimane, Nampula, and Porto Amélia are suffragan. There is freedom of worship, and Lourenço Marques has, in addition to the modern Roman Catholic cathedral, an Anglican procathedral, a Methodist church, a synagogue, a mosque, and a Chinese temple.

Languages.—Portuguese is the official language, but many European inhabitants also speak English, mainly because the hinterland is surrounded by English-speaking areas. French is widely spoken among the upper levels of Portuguese society. All the Africans are Bantu-speaking. (H. V. L.; A. A. G. P.; E. A. A.)

HISTORY

Early Exploration and Trade.—Between the 11th and the 15th centuries the Mozambique coast as far south as Sofala was linked politically and commercially to the coastal city-states north of Cape Delgado. Arab and Swahili traders penetrated inland from Sofala and up the Zambezi into what later became Manica e Sofala District. This was the situation the Portuguese found when Vasco da Gama put in at Mozambique Island early in March 1498. Just before this he had discovered and landed at what he called the Rio do Cobre (the Inharrime) and the Rio dos Bons Sinais (the Quelimane, the northern outlet of the Zambezi). Da Gama left Mozambique for India at the end of March, accompanied by a pilot lent by the sultan. In July 1500 Pedro Álvares Cabral, on his way to India, saw Sofala, and on his return it was visited by a squadron of his ships under Sancho de Toar, who made inquiries about its legendary gold trade. Between 1500 and 1502 either Cabral or João da Nova visited Lourenço Marques Bay. A Portuguese settlement was made at Sofala to exploit the fabled gold trade from the empire of Monomotapa (*q.v.*), which was centred in Rhodesia but extended into Mozambique. The Portuguese in 1507 occupied Mozambique Island to serve as a way station to India.

Attempts to reach the monomotapa were disappointing, though a convict named António Fernandes explored much of his territory before 1514. The Portuguese soon realized that they could not control the trade of the interior from Sofala alone, as Arab and Swahili merchants were making increasing use of the Zambezi route. Accordingly, after 1531 the Portuguese established settlements on the Zambezi banks at Sena and Tete, respectively 160 mi. (257 km.) and 260 mi. (418 km.) upstream. In 1544 a post was founded at Quelimane to guard the river delta. At the same period, the Portuguese began to trade at Inhambane and Lourenço Marques Bay, though no permanent settlement was set up at either place for some time. Portuguese efforts at Mozambique centred on the gold of the monomotapa; it was only there that they involved themselves seriously in African affairs. In 1561 the Jesuit Gonçalo da Silveira reached the head village of the monomotapa, whom he baptized. The Arabs and Swahili seeing their commercial position threatened by the Portuguese, convinced the chief that Silveira's intentions were evil, and he had the Jesuit strangled.

The death of Silveira was followed by the dispatch (1569) of an expedition from Lisbon to seize the monomotapa's mines. The expedition ended unsuccessfully in 1575, but despite this setback the Zambezi Valley and the monomotapa's country remained the focus of Portuguese attention until the late 19th century. Elsewhere, the Portuguese limited themselves, or were limited by African opposition, to scattered settlements along the coast. Nevertheless, the arrival of the Portuguese in East Africa had a vital impact on African trade to the north of the Zambezi.

Taking advantage of factional strife the Portuguese in 1629 negotiated a vassalage treaty with Monomotapa Mavura, who thereby recognized Portuguese sovereignty over his kingdom. Portuguese ascendancy was short-lived, however, and at the end of 17th century the expansion of the Rozvi kingdom of Guruhuswa,

ruled by Changamire, eclipsed the power of both the monomotapa and the Portuguese to the south of the Zambezi.

In 1752 Mozambique, after being subordinated to the Portuguese administration at Goa in India, was separated and given an independent governor. In the 18th century the slave trade became an important factor in Mozambique for the first time. The demand came first from French slavers from the Mascarene Islands and later from the Brazilians. Slave trading by Europeans continued into the 1850s, and an active slave trade to Madagascar was carried on by Arabs and Swahili for several decades more.

Colonization.—Until the mid-19th century the most serious attempt to colonize Mozambique was the *prazo* system. This system of crown grant estates, which had its roots in the late 16th century, was formalized by the Portuguese government in the middle of the 17th. It failed as a colonization scheme, because the estate holders (*prazeros*) amassed large personal fiefdoms. In the 19th century a series of wars was waged by the government against these virtually autonomous rulers. A similar though less ambitious attempt was made to colonize the Kerimba Islands, which extend from Cape Delgado almost to Porto Amélia. There, too, the estate holders became independent lords.

No further colonization plans were contemplated until the 20th century. Several pilot projects failed in the 1930s and 1940s, but since the 1950s an attempt to settle immigrant Portuguese peasant cultivators, either in cooperatives or on small individual family holdings, has been pursued in the south. The most ambitious of these is centred in the lower Limpopo Valley, another is proposed for the upper reaches of the Revué River. The Mozambique government, unlike its counterpart in Angola, has kept to a minimum the influx of poor unskilled white immigrants.

Portugal v. Other European Powers in Africa.—At the beginning of the 17th century the Portuguese beat off three attempts by the Dutch to seize the port of Mozambique. The Austrians seized Lourenço Marques in 1777, but Portuguese sovereignty was reestablished in 1782. During the Napoleonic Wars the French attacked Lourenço Marques, Inhambane, Mozambique, and the Kerimba Islands. During the same period these islands suffered more seriously at the hands of Sakalava raiders from Madagascar.

In the 19th-century partition of Africa among the European powers, Portugal maintained rights based on the discovery of most of the African coast, in the face of the doctrine of effective occupation. Until the Berlin Conference (1884) Portugal hoped to preserve a continuous belt of territory from coast to coast, uniting modern Angola with Mozambique. The acquisition of British rights in the area frustrated this design. The Portuguese proposed to submit the question to arbitration, but Britain refused and delivered an ultimatum to Lisbon (1890). A treaty in 1891 defined the frontiers of British and Portuguese possessions.

Colonial Rule.—The establishment of effective colonial rule in the interior began in the 1890s and was not completed in the northwest until 1912, when the Yao chief Mataka was subdued. The Makombe Rebellion (1917), which embraced much of the country south of the Zambezi, was the last traditional manifestation of African opposition to Portuguese rule.

The Companhia de Moçambique was incorporated by royal charter in 1891 for a term of 50 years. Much of its capital was foreign, and it exercised sovereign rights over the territories of Manica and Sofala until they were entrusted to direct Portuguese administration in 1942. The Companhia do Niassa acquired a charter for the administration of lands north of the Lurio River in 1894. Development was comparatively slow, and in 1929 the Portuguese government took over administration of the area.

Under the Treaty of Versailles (1919) the German East African territory between the mouth of the Ruvuma River and Cape Delgado (the Kionga or Quionga triangle) was added to Mozambique.

Railway building led to a rapid expansion of Mozambique's economy, and conventions with the countries of the hinterland were signed covering the question of transit trade and the recruitment of Africans from Mozambique to work in the South African Rand mines. In 1901 a modus vivendi governing these matters was concluded with the Transvaal government. This was replaced by the Transvaal-Mozambique Convention in 1909, which lapsed in 1923 and was replaced in 1934 by a new treaty which ran until 1939; it was then prolonged for five years and later remained in force subject to 12 months' notice of termination by either party.

A measure of autonomy was granted to the colony under the Portuguese republic, and this was extended in 1920. After the Portuguese revolution of 1926 this system was brought to an end, and within the provisions of the Colonial Act (1930) a much more centralized system was adopted. Mozambique was designated an overseas province of Portugal in 1951.

African Nationalism.—In the 1960s various African nationalist parties were formed in exile. These were united as the Frente de Libertação de Moçambique (Frelimo; Mozambique Liberation Front) in 1962 under the presidency of Eduardo Mondlane, a former professor of anthropology at Syracuse (N.Y.) University. Fighting between Frelimo forces and Portuguese troops broke out in northern Mozambique on Sept. 25, 1964, the day celebrated as marking the beginning of the Mozambique people's struggle for freedom, and has continued. There are several small rival organizations, but only Frelimo is recognized by the Liberation Committee of the Organization of African Unity. (A. A. G. P.; E. A. A.)

ADMINISTRATION AND SOCIAL CONDITIONS

Administration.—Constitutionally, Mozambique is an integral province of Portugal; it has 7 representatives in the Portuguese National Assembly, elected on a restricted basis depending on Portuguese literacy and income. It is administered by a governor general who is appointed by the Council of Ministers in Lisbon and is directly responsible to the minister for overseas provinces. He is assisted by a Legislative Council, composed of 16 elected and 8 appointed members; and is advised by a Government Council composed of 12 members, including the secretary-general, the four provincial secretaries, the chief military commanders, the attorney general, the director of the treasury, and two elected members of the Legislative Council who are chosen by the governor-general. There is also an Economic Coordination Council which includes 11 representatives of the private sector. The few principal areas with European, half-caste, and *assimilados* majorities are designated as communes and have elected councils.

There is only one political party, the government's União Nacional (National Union).

Mozambique is divided into nine districts (*distritos*; see table), each administered by a governor. These are divided into *concelhos* (municipalities), subdivided into *freguesias* (parishes), and into *circunscrições* (circumscriptions, or rural subdistricts), sub-

Administrative Divisions of Mozambique

Districts and capitals	Area (sq.mi.)	Population		
		1950 census	1960 census	Density (1960; per sq.mi.)
Cabo Delgado (Porto Amélia) .	30,313	494,974	542,165	17.9
Gaza (Vila de João Bela) .	33,750	681,602	675,150	20.0
Inhambane (Inhambane) .	25,589	571,625	583,772	22.8
Lourenço Marques (Lourenço Marques) . .	4,009	199,067	441,363	110.1
Manica e Sofala (Beira) . .	52,268	711,584	781,070	14.9
Moçambique (Nampula) .	30,815	1,317,631	1,444,555	46.9
Niassa (Vila Cabral) . . .	46,242	260,413	276,810	6.0
Tete (Tete)	36,041	337,656	470,100	13.0
Zambézia (Quelimane) . .	38,819	1,164,359	1,363,619	35.1
Total	297,846	5,738,911	6,578,604	22.1

divided into *postos administrativos* (rural administrative posts).

A judicial system, comprising a court of appeals and courts of preliminary investigation in ten judicial divisions, maintains separate sections for African cases and applies the Portuguese law.

Mozambique is a military command of overseas Portugal. Military and naval headquarters are at Lourenço Marques, which is also the headquarters of one of Portugal's air regions.

Living Conditions.—Of the total working population of about 1,600,000, three-quarters are employed in agriculture and about one-tenth in industry; at least another one-tenth work in neighbouring countries (although some estimates go as high as 450,000 migrant labourers), especially in the Rand mines. Workers first went to South Africa when diamonds were discovered at Kimberley in

the mid-19th century, and the numbers increased after the discovery of gold in 1886.

The ethics of Portuguese colonial theory demands labour of the African as a moral obligation. Africans are consequently recruited by licensed companies to work on contract for European-owned agricultural and industrial enterprises. Wages are very low, about Esc. 5 a day allowing for food and lodging. Contract employment averages about 300 days a year, the annual wage being about $52.50 U.S., compared with about $70 (Esc. 2,000) annual average earnings by Africans cultivating their own cotton. Wages are considerably higher in industry than in agriculture. Europeans are employed (chiefly in the higher grades) in commerce, the public services, communications, and transport. The Chinese and half-castes devote themselves to agriculture and commerce; most of the traders are Indians.

Development plans in hand, especially in the Revué, Limpopo, and Zambezi valleys, include the resettlement of Africans, construction of new villages, and improvement of living conditions.

Health.—Malaria and other diseases are prevalent, especially on the lower ground. Great progress has been achieved in making Lourenço Marques and the other main centres healthful, and medical and preventive services have been much extended, especially in combating malarial mosquitoes at their breeding grounds. Endemic focuses of sleeping sickness have been verified at various places, and tsetse fly is found in several districts. Schistosomiasis (bilharziasis) is widespread among the African population. There are three central hospitals (Lourenço Marques, Beira, Nampula), several regional hospitals, and about 500 smaller installations. Mozambique in the 1960s had one doctor to 20,000 inhabitants, one infirmary to 5,000, and 1.4 hospital beds to 1,000.

Education.—All instruction is given in Portuguese. Primary education of Africans, which normally lasts four or five years, is entrusted to the Roman Catholic missions, which run more than half of the primary schools with the help of a state subsidy. There are also about 2,500 pre-primary schools, almost all subsidized mission establishments. In 1961 there were six secondary and eight technical schools. About 400,000 children are in primary schools, compared with about 4,000 in secondary. While there is no university, and students usually go to Portugal for higher education, a program of general university studies was created in 1963, although it is confined to science, technology, and teacher training.

THE ECONOMY

Mozambique is one of the least developed parts of Africa. It can be divided into three economic zones. (1) The northern zone (Cabo Delgado, Niassa, and Moçambique districts), which is served by the port of Nacala and a developing railway to Lake Nyasa, is dominated by agriculture and has many Asian traders. (2) The central zone (Zambézia, Tete, and Manica e Sofala districts), with several railways leading from the hinterland to Beira, depends on transit trade. (3) The southern zone (Inhambane, Gaza, and Lourenço Marques districts) depends both on transit trade and on the migration of 150,000 Africans a year to the Rand mines. Lourenço Marques and Beira have developed industrially.

The development of the territory was greatly assisted by the transit trade of the Transvaal, Zambia, Malawi, and the Congo (Kinshasa), though this in some ways hindered the growth of internal communications. The hiring of African labourers to the Rand mines has also contributed much to the territory's prosperity, though the absence of so many workers affects its own agriculture. The requirements of the transit trade have led to a continuous development of the ports and railways, and the construction of railways into the interior has given rise to new townships in the hinterland of the capital and of Beira. Agricultural production has steadily increased, and Portuguese industrialists have introduced a number of manufactures. British and South African interests are represented in transport services, distribution, and agriculture, and United States, French, Belgian, and West German capital has also been invested in the territory.

Agriculture.—Though about a third of the country is suitable for agriculture, only about 1% is actually cultivated. A number of important European companies produce sugar (approaching

200,000 tons in the 1960s) and bagasse, tea (8,000 tons), sisal (30,000 tons), copra (60,000 tons), and vegetable oils (15,000 tons), all mostly for export. Sugar is cultivated in the Zambezi, Buzi, and Komati (Incomati) valleys and around Inhambane; tea near Milange and Guruè; sisal near Quelimane and Nampula, and in the districts of Cabo Delgado, Inhambane, and Manica e Sofala; and coconuts between the mouth of the Zambezi and Mogincual Bay (south of Mozambique).

African agriculture is chiefly subsistence, the main crops being corn (maize), peas, peanuts, manioc, sesame, and vegetables. Among cash crops, Africans account for virtually all the production of cotton, which is the territory's chief export (around 40,000 tons annually; though, as an indication of the province's underdevelopment, it ranks only fifth among African countries in cotton exports). Africans also account for nearly all the rice (30,000 tons husked), which meets local needs and leaves a surplus for export; and cashew nuts (119,000 tons of unprepared nuts), which are uncultivated but also an important export. Both cotton (around Beira, and in Quelimane and Niassa) and rice are cultivated under European supervision, under a concessionary system. Between 1940 and the mid-1950s the productivity per acre of cotton was trebled. There are great possibilities for the expansion of rice growing, nearly half the territory being suitable for it.

In contrast to Angola, there are no white small farmers except on the Chimoio Plateau, where they cultivate tobacco, citrus fruit, wheat, oilseeds, and a little cotton. In the early 1960s, after irrigation had begun in the Limpopo Valley, settlement of several thousand families from Portugal was started there. Encouraging results had already been achieved in the valley with long-staple cotton and wheat. It was hoped to follow this experiment with the settling of the large, rich basin of the Revuè River (west of Beira).

Animal husbandry is little developed, and the Africans typically own no cattle. The province has about 1,000,000 oxen, 400,000 goats, 100,000 sheep, and 100,000 pigs.

Forestry.—Though exports of timber and wood products have expanded greatly beyond what they were before World War II, the potentialities for forestry are still far greater, particularly behind Beira. (See also *Vegetation*, above.)

Mining.—The mineral resources of the province are still inadequately known, though the Mines Department started a full survey in the mid-1950s. A little gold is mined near Vila de Manica and Tete, and there are alluvial deposits near Vila de Manica and Alto Ligonha (Zambézia). Coal is the only mineral produced in other than negligible quantities, more than 250,000 tons being taken annually from the Moatize field in the Zambezi Valley near Tete. Coal resources there are estimated at 700,000,000 tons, and coal has also been discovered near the Limpopo Railway and in the Nyasa Basin. The Companhia Carbonifera de Moçambique, with Belgian capital, supplies the railway and the port of Beira and exports some coal to Malawi, although coal is also imported from South Africa. Iron ore exists at Moatize near the coal mines. The Alto Ligonha Company, with exclusive rights over part of Zambézia, mines beryl, mica, columbite, and bismuth. Quantities of graphite exist near Nacala and in Angónia, but extraction is irregular. Radioactive minerals exist in the Tete and Moçambique districts; prospecting concessions for these are granted only through the Portuguese government. Prospecting for petroleum had yielded no positive results by the later 1960s, except at Pande, 160 mi. SW of Beira. Diamonds were found for the first time in 1966, near the Rhodesian border.

Fisheries.—The Mozambique coast is very rich in shellfish and certain fish. A large fish-processing plant was established at Porto Amélia and five subsidiary plants were being built along the coast to act as feeders. The Anglo American Corporation of South Africa was reported in the late 1960s to be planning large investments in the fishing industry. There was also great hope for developing this industry in the inland waters.

Power.—Industry obtains most of its energy from thermal power stations, using imported fuel, and only about one-fifth of its supply comes from hydroelectric plants. However, the centre of the country obtains much of its power from the Mavúdzi Dam at the Revué Falls on the Revué River, from which the government

has also undertaken to supply power to Umtali, in Rhodesia. Other development works include a dam at Chicamba Real Gorge, also on the Revué River near Mavúdzi, and on the Limpopo and Komati rivers and on the Zambezi, all of which involve agricultural development as well as power supply.

Manufacturing.—Less than one-tenth of the working population is employed in manufacturing industries, chiefly in Beira and Lourenço Marques. The largest numbers work in sugar, sisal, cotton, and tea factories, but there are also tobacco, oil, and soap factories, potteries, flour mills, and cement works.

Finance and Trade.—The chief sources of revenue are customs duties, income tax, and license and stamp duties. There was a surplus of income over expenditure after 1937, so that large sums were devoted to public works.

The monetary unit is the Mozambique escudo of 100 centavos, equal in value to the Portuguese escudo (about Esc. 80.20 = £1 sterling; Esc. 28.75 = $1 U.S. or Esc. 1 = about 3.5 cents.

Imports in 1963 totaled Esc. 4,077,000,000 and exports Esc. 2,896,000,000. Re-exports, largely minerals from South Africa, were valued at Esc. 6,000,000,000 annually in the early 1960s and transit traffic at Esc. 8,000,000,000. Portugal accounts for about 30% of imports and about 35% of exports. South Africa supplies around 12% of imports, and the U.K., West Germany, and the U.S. are also important trading partners, while India and Rhodesia are important customers. The chief imports are cotton textiles, railway equipment, agricultural and other machinery, iron and steel, and table wines. (For exports see *Agriculture*, above.)

Transport and Communications.—The road system is satisfactory in the settled areas, though many parts of the territory are still inaccessible by road, and much surfacing and bridge building is necessary to make the existing roads suitable for use all the year round. Of 15,000 mi. (about 24,000 km.) of fully constructed road in the province in the 1960s, 6,500 mi. (10,500 km.) were described as main roads, 2,300 mi. (3,700 km.) being first class. Metaled roads are limited to the capital and Beira, but the chief towns are linked by good gravel roads. The main international routes run from Lourenço Marques to Swaziland and to Johannesburg, S.Af., from Beira to Salisbury, Rhodesia; from Tete to Blantyre, Malawi, and Fort Jameson, Zambia; from Quelimane, Lumbo, and Nacala to Blantyre; and a smaller coastal road north to Tanzania.

The railway system owes its existence to the transit trade, but there is still little rail connection between the chief centres of the territory itself. The total internal length is about 2,000 mi. (3,300 km.), mostly state owned. There are lines from Lourenço Marques to Johannesburg and to Bulawayo, Rhodesia. The port of Beira is connected with Blantyre and Salisbury. A railroad running from Lumbo is intended to reach Lake Nyasa.

The province is served by about 40 shipping lines, which link Lourenço Marques with the main South and East African, European, Indian, and U.S. ports. Coastal shipping also uses harbours at Quelimane, Inhambane, Chinde, Mozambique, António Enes, Porto Amélia, and Nacala. Lourenço Marques is possibly the best shelter on the East African coast between Suez and Cape Town, and improvements are in progress there and at the ports of Beira, Quelimane, Nacala, and Porto Amélia. In 1962, 7,093,316 tons of goods were transported through Lourenço Marques, and 3,085,592 tons through Beira.

An oil pipeline runs from Beira to Umtali, in Rhodesia. In April 1966 considerable British diplomatic pressure was brought to bear on the Portuguese not to permit oil to be piped through this line to the rebel regime in Rhodesia (*q.v.*). At the same time, a British naval patrol was mounted to intercept any vessels intending to discharge oil for Rhodesia at Beira. In December, responding to the UN Security Council resolution imposing economic sanctions, including oil imports, on Rhodesia, Portugal announced that it did not mean to supply oil to Rhodesia but that it would not attempt to control such provisions to Rhodesia. The interests of the Portuguese in Mozambique, however, clearly lay in maintaining white rule in Rhodesia, and the traditional policy of good neighbourliness continued. The Zambezi is navigable by light-draft steamers throughout its course in Mozambique, with a break at the long

Quebrabasa Rapids above Tete. (*See also* ZAMBEZI.) There is a direct steamer and railway connection with Lake Nyasa via the Shiré River.

There are regular air services from Lourenço Marques to Mocimboa de Praia in the north and to Tete, and international services to Johannesburg, Salisbury, and Durban. The airports at Beira and Nampula also handle international traffic. Most local services are operated by the Directorate of Harbours, Railways, and Transport, but private companies operate air taxi services.

The province is connected with Europe by telegraph via South Africa and via Zanzibar. A cable connects Mozambique with Madagascar and is linked with the Aden-Durban cable. There are land lines between Lourenço Marques and Johannesburg and between Beira and Salisbury, an internal radio system for communication between the main centres, and an external radio system for communication with Portugal. The Radio Clube de Moçambique at Lourenço Marques (which controls several transmitters) is the official broadcasting agency, and Emissôra de Aero Clube (commercial) and Radio Pax (religious) are privately owned.

(H. V. L.; A. A. G. P.; E. A. A.)

BIBLIOGRAPHY.—A. Lobato, *A Expansão Portuguesa em Moçambique de 1488–1530*, 3 vol. (1954–60), and *Evolução Administrativa e Económica de Moçambique, 1752–1763*, part I (1957); E. V. Axelson, *Portuguese in South-East Africa, 1600–1700* (1960); J. Duffy, *Portuguese Africa* (1959), and *Portugal in Africa* (1962); J. de Oliveira Boleo, *Moçambique* (1951); A. Rita-Ferreira, *Agrupamento e Caracterização Étnica dos Indígenas de Moçambique* (1958); N. B. Valdez dos Santos, *O Desconhecido Niassa* (1964); Instituto Superior de Ciências Sociais e Política Ultramarina, *Moçambique, Curso de Extensão Universitária* (1965); C. F. Spence, *Moçambique* (1963).

PORTUGUESE GUINEA

PORTUGUESE GUINEA (GUINÉ PORTUGUESA), a Portuguese overseas province on the West African coast, extends from Cape Roxo to the Cajet estuary (the western arm of the Cogon estuary) at Tristão Island, being enclosed inland by the republics of Senegal and Guinea. Its area is 13,948 sq.mi. (36,125 sq.km.). The capital is Bissau.

Physical Characteristics.—A line along the Geba Valley to its junction with the Corubal River, and from there to the extreme south, separates the two main geological features of the territory: to the west the sediments of the Tertiary Gulf of Senegal and to the east the Paleozoic formations of Fouta Djallon. Almost the whole country is lowland, with many swamps and pools, the only high ground being in the southeast (about 800 ft. [244 m.]). The main rivers are the Cacheu, Mansôa, Geba, and Corubal (Rio Grande), the last two uniting in a large estuary. The coast is heavily indented by deep inlets, or gulfs, including the Rio Tombali, Rio Grande de Bolola, and Rio Cacine. Off the coast many islands are separated from the mainland only by creeks, although the Bijagós (Bissagos) Islands, of which there are about 25, lie up to 30 mi. (48 km.) offshore.

Climate.—During the dry season, December–May, the hot

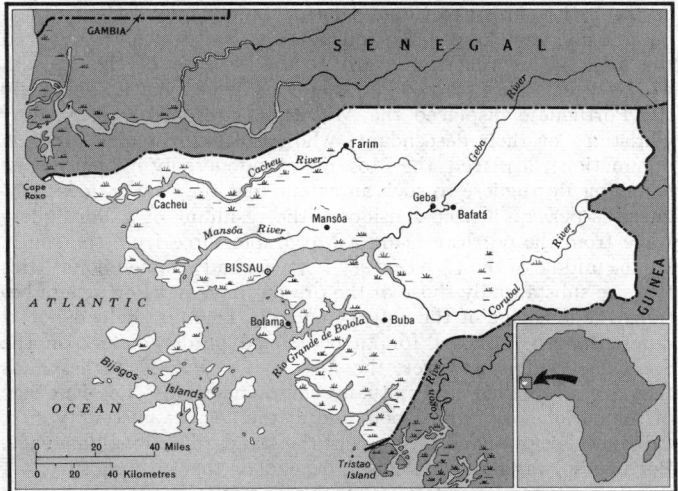

PRINCIPAL COMMUNITIES AND RIVERS OF PORTUGUESE GUINEA

northerly harmattan (*q.v.*) blows from the desert. The maximum monthly mean temperature is 85° F (29.5° C) in May and the minimum 77° F (25° C) in January. The whole rainfall (average 75 in. [191 cm.]) occurs in the wet season, June–November, one-third of it in August.

Vegetation and Animal Life.—The coastal region and the islands are covered with forests and palm trees, the valleys being swampy and the coasts and gulfs bordered by mangroves. The rest of the country, interspersed with swamps, is less forested. The chief trees are the cotton tree, the African mahogany (*Khaya senegalensis*), the copaiba balsam tree, the baobab, and many varieties of acacia. Fruit trees include the pawpaw, guava, mango, banana, and orange. The fauna includes water buffaloes, deer, antelopes, leopards, monkeys, many varieties of snakes, and in the south a few elephants. Crocodiles and sharks abound in the estuaries. Birds include the pelican, heron, marabou, trumpet bird, egret, and several parrots. (H. V. L.; A. T. DA M.)

History.—By the 13th century A.D. the coast of Portuguese Guinea was occupied by iron-using agriculturists such as the Barhun, Casanga, Papel, Balante, and Bijago. They were particularly skilled in the production of both irrigated and dry rice and were also the major suppliers of marine salt to the adjacent areas of the western Sudan. From the 13th century these coastal farmers came increasingly into contact with the outside world, first from the landward side and later from the seaward. The earliest recorded influences from the interior are associated with the breakup of the Ghana Empire when Nalu and Landuma peoples sought refuge near the coast. Later the region was loosely drawn into the sphere of the Mali Empire and regional governors called *farims* were appointed to obtain some form of allegiance to the great Mande ruler.

The earliest overseas contacts of the Guinea coast were opened by the Portuguese, probably from the 1440s. Guinea played an important role in the colonization of the Cape Verde Islands from this period. Slave labour was first used to establish plantations of cotton and indigo and then skilled Guinea craftsmen were introduced to establish a weaving and dyeing industry. Much of the cloth was sent back to the mainland for the purchase of slaves destined for the Americas. The transatlantic slave trade was facilitated by Portuguese and mulattoes called *Lançados* who acted as intermediaries between the Guinean rulers and the visiting slave ships. In the 16th century the expansion of Mande-speaking peoples into the Upper Guinea coast area caused wars which greatly increased the number of prisoners available for export as slaves. In addition to the slave trade the country had a spasmodic trade in salt, kola nuts, and food to the interior and ivory, wax, dyewood, and hides overseas. The main overseas buyers came from Portugal, Britain, Holland, and France.

During the next four centuries, when the slave trade was the main economic activity of the country, the people of Guinea had little difficulty in preventing or restricting the attempts of foreign powers to establish territorial claims. A post established at Cacheu by Cape Verde traders in 1588 was given periodic support by the Lisbon government during the 17th century but did not expand. In 1687 a Portuguese post was established at Bissau in an attempt to limit French commercial competition by political, diplomatic, and military means, but that too failed to survive. In 1792 the English briefly and disastrously held a settlement at Bolama. Meanwhile the Portuguese had reestablished a base at Bissau and during the 19th century increasingly came to regard the coast on either side as their sovereign territory.

The Portuguese territorial claim in Guinea was disputed by both the British and the French. Spasmodic negotiations first of all excluded the British (1870) and then settled the boundaries with the French-claimed territories (1886 and 1902–05). These frontier agreements were followed by the slow and sometimes violent imposition of Portuguese colonial rule. The final "pacification" campaigns were fought by João Teixeira Pinto in 1913–15. These wars were followed by nearly half a century of predominantly peaceful Portuguese administration. But with the rise of African nationalism after World War II and the gaining of independence by the neighbouring territories, Guineans again began to challenge their colonial rulers. War against Portugal broke out in 1962.

Population.—The total population at the 1960 census was 521,336. The main groups are the Balante, Papel, and other agricultural peoples of the coastal belt. Inland are the seminomadic Fulani (*q.v.*) cattle-keeping peoples and the sedentary Mandingo agriculturalists. These two peoples are mainly Muslim in contrast to the coastal peoples. In 1950 there were about 4,000 mulattoes, mainly Creoles from the Cape Verde Islands who held most of the minor administrative and commercial posts in the country. Cape Verde Creole is the *lingua franca* although Portuguese is the official language of administration. There were also about 2,000 Europeans in 1950.

After the outbreak of war in 1962 the population pattern was altered by the exodus of refugees to Senegal and Guinea (Conakry) and by a large influx of Portuguese troops to support the Bissau administration.

Administration and Social Conditions.—Information about the administrative situation after the outbreak of war in 1962 was hard to come by in the late 1960s. It seemed that about half the territory, centred on the main towns of Cacheu, Bissau, Mansoa, Bafata, and Bolama, was still being administered as an overseas province of Portugal. The theoretical administration consisted of a governor, responsible to the Portuguese minister for overseas territories, who took executive and legislative decisions in conjunction with a ten-man advisory council. The *de facto* administration was thought to be the Portuguese Army which might have been 20,000 or more strong and was responsible for patrolling the roads and garrisoning the administrative posts in the central part of the country.

The remainder of the country was administered by the PAIGC (African Independence Party for Guinea and Cape Verde), a nationalist movement which was seeking by means of guerrilla warfare to oust the Portuguese and establish a unified independent country. The political leader of this movement was Amilcar Cabral. As in the Portuguese-held half of the country a very close link existed between the civil administration and the military authorities.

Owing to the war conditions little information was available about the state of the country's schools, missions, hospitals, and disease eradication campaigns.

The Economy.—In 1960 the value of exports from Portuguese Guinea amounted to $5,800,000 (166,000,000 escudos). Three-quarters of the exports consisted of peanuts. Lesser items of export were coconut, timber, and beeswax. These were mainly exported to Portugal in exchange for cotton materials, wine, foodstuffs, and machinery. The currency used is the Portuguese overseas escudo of the Banco National Ultramarino. The chief ports are Bissau, the capital, which also has an international airport and a radio station, Farim, and Bolama.

The major economic activity is subsistence farming. Important crops include rice and palm nuts, neither of which was exported in significant quantities in 1960. Cattle, pig, and goat rearing are also important. The country has no railways and relies for communications on light aircraft, river vessels, and road transport.

Before 1960 Guinea was a small but marginally viable tropical producer within the Portuguese Empire. Since 1962 the escalating war increased the cost of administration while reducing the revenue from export surpluses. In the late 1960s Portugal continued to bear the resulting increased burden on its economy because of its reluctance to create a precedent for retreat which could harm its interests in the economically more significant wars which it was fighting in Angola and Mozambique.

BIBLIOGRAPHY.—Walter Rodney, "A History of the Upper Guinea Coast," Ph.D. dissertation, London University (1966); A. Teixeira da Mota, *Guiné Portuguesa*, 2 vol. (1954); J. Barreto, *História da Guiné* (1938); G. Chaliand, *Lutte armée en Afrique* (1967).   (D. Bi.)

PORTUGUESE INDIA (ESTADO DA ÍNDIA), a name once used for those parts of India which were under Portuguese rule from 1505 (Goa 1510) to December 1961. It consisted of several isolated tracts: (1) the territory of Goa with the capital, a considerable area in the middle of the west coast of India; (2) Damão or Daman, with the separated territories of Dadrá and Nagar Aveli (Nagar Havili), north of Bombay and lying between the Indian states of Maharashtra and Gujarat; (3) Diu with Pani Kota Island on the southern coast of Kathiawar Peninsula in Gujarat State. The total area was 1,619 sq.mi. (4,193 sq.km.) and the population in 1960 was 625,831. Of this total Goa accounted for 1,394 sq.mi. (3,610 sq.km.) with 589,120 persons. About 60% of the total inhabitants are Hindus, about 37% Christians, and the rest are Muslims. The whole formed a single administrative province under a governor general and a single ecclesiastical province subject to the archbishop of Goa who is also Primate of the East.

History.—For almost a century (1500–1600) the Portuguese had a monopoly of European exploration and trade in the Indian Ocean. Their interests on the west coast of India were largely determined by sailing conditions; in Goa they found a defensible island site with excellent harbour facilities on either side and, captured by Affonso de Albuquerque in 1510, it became the main Portuguese base, which it remained for four and a half centuries. With the end of the British raj in India in 1947, and the quiet handing over of former French settlements in 1949–54 (*see* FRENCH INDIA), there was a natural desire of the Republic of India to absorb the Portuguese territories also. The position, however, was somewhat different. Four and a half centuries marked by much intermarriage and under the influence of the Catholic Church produced a distinctive racial, cultural, religious, and linguistic group, especially in Old Goa itself, which was not yet ready to throw in its lot with India. However, India's continuous demand for the cession of the Portuguese territories and Portugal's unwillingness to negotiate led to India's taking Goa, Damão, and Diu by force, Portuguese resistance ceasing on Dec. 19, 1961. The territories, constituted as the Union Territory of Goa, Daman, and Diu, are centrally administered by the government of India.

Economy.—The evaporation of seawater to produce salt is an industry in all three territories. Since its discovery in 1906 there has been a considerable production and export of manganese ore from deposits near Mormugão. Otherwise the economy depends largely on the transit trade of Mormugão from which there is an export of iron pyrites, manganese ore, coconuts and copra, fresh and dried fish, spices, cashew nuts, and salt. Remittances home from the many Goanese resident abroad played a large part in the colony's finances.

See also GOA; DAMÃO; DIU.   (L. D. S.)

PORTUGUESE LANGUAGE, one of the Romance languages (*q.v.*), is the language of Portugal, including the Madeiran and Azorean archipelagos, and of Brazil. It is also the official language of Portugal's overseas provinces in Africa and the east. Spoken by about 100,000,000 persons, it is the end product of the evolution of the Romance dialect that was spoken in the county of Portugal, awarded by the king of León and Castile at the end of the 11th century to Count Henry of Burgundy. Henry's son became the first king of an independent Portugal and advanced the area of his rule southward at the expense of the Muslim Moors who then governed the region. The language spoken by the Portuguese displaced the Mozarabic presumably spoken by Christians or their descendants who were living under Moorish domination; displaced, the Mozarabic undoubtedly influenced the emerging Portuguese to such an extent that the new national language is perhaps better considered the resultant of a Portuguese force from the northwest and a Mozarabic force from the south. By the middle of the 13th century Portugal had attained boundaries that are substantially those of the present day, and Portuguese became the language of the entire country. There is slight dialectal differentiation. Except for an occasional border dialect on the Spanish frontier, however, the *falares regionais portugueses*, as they are now called, are mutually comprehensible. The language of the nation's capital, Lisbon, and of the ancient university city, Coimbra, has provided the basis of the standard national language. Portuguese was first written at the end of the 12th century. A standard written language was quickly formulated. It has changed little since the 13th century, virtually not at all since the 16th.

Portuguese was established as the official language of Brazil soon after Pedro Álvares Cabral's discovery of the continent in 1500. In its subsequent development it proved to be, on the whole, more conservative than the language of Portugal. Although regional pronunciations have developed, they do not hinder intercommunication. Moreover, the Brazilians and Portuguese communicate with ease despite an instantly recognizable accent. The influence on the Portuguese of Brazil of native American languages, African languages of imported slaves and Spanish of adjacent countries to the south has probably been negligible except for certain items of vocabulary.

Vasco da Gama initiated the Portuguese influence in the orient. The language of the Portuguese discoverers, colonizers, merchants and missionaries spread rapidly and Portuguese words are today far more disseminated than the area of Portugal's political control would suggest. They are found on Ceylon, for example, and even in Japan. Thus in the latter country the Portuguese *têmporas* "Ember days" is used for fried seafood.

In its evolution since the establishment of the Portuguese monarchy, Portuguese has developed more or less independently of the Romance dialects that ultimately became the language of Spain. In Galicia, however, the local dialect was originally very similar to Portuguese and has occasionally been used as a literary language. Several features of Portuguese distinguish it markedly not only from Spanish but also from other Romance languages.

Phonology.—There are five distinctive nasal vowels, as in *sim, lenço, sã* and *lanço, som* and *dom*, and *dum*, and a series of nasal diphthongs, as in *pão, põe* and *bem*. Final *em*, as in the latter word, is pronounced [ẽĩ] in standard Portuguese but as [ẽ] in many regions of Portugal and in Brazil. Among the oral vowels the distinction between closed and open *e* and *o* is meaningful: *sê-sé, pôde-pode*, the circumflex indicating closeness, the acute accent openness. Final unstressed vowels are weak and tend to disappear, especially in Portugal. In most regions *s* before a consonant is [ʃ] or [ʒ], depending on whether the consonant is voiceless or voiced (*casta, Lisboa*); intervocalic *s* is [z]. In the Rio de Janeiro area *t* and *d* before [i] become affricates approaching [tʃ] and [dʒ]. Historically, Latin intervocalic *l* and *n* have in many situations disappeared (*só*, Spanish *solo; lua*, Sp. *luna*). Because of the history of *l* and *ll*, the Portuguese definite article is simply *o, a, os* or *as*. Although the intervocalic *n* tended to disappear as a consonant, it often nasalized a preceding vowel. Thus, the singular noun ending *ão*, as in *mão, alemão, nação*, corresponds to three plural endings, *mãos, alemães, nações*. Comparison with Sp. *manos, alemanes, naciones* clarifies the endings and confirms that today's *ão* represents a convergence of earlier *ão, am* and *om*. Latin stressed *e* and *o* did not diphthongize (*pé, terra, roda, porta*, contrasted with Sp. *pie, tierra, rueda, puerta*), nor has initial *f* disappeared (*filho*, Sp. *hijo*).

Forms.—Portuguese is most different from Spanish in the verb system. It retains the Latin pluperfect as a pluperfect (1st and 3rd sg. *cantara*, used alternatively with a compound *tinha cantado*). It has a conjugated or personal infinitive and a future subjunctive. They have identical endings, those of the former being added to the infinitive, those of the latter to the preterite stem (3rd pl. *cantarem*, but *fazerem-fizerem*). Portuguese has two forms for "two," masc. *dois* and fem. *duas*, and maintains vowel harmony in such groups of words as demonstrative *isto*, a neuter pronoun, and *êste* and *esta*, masculine and feminine demonstrative adjectives, respectively, the *e* of *esta* being [ɛ].

Syntax.—As suggested above, *ter* (Lat. *tenere*) is today the normal verbal auxiliary, and not *haver* (Lat. *habere*). Object pronouns are normally placed after the verb in Portugal, although in spoken Brazilian they usually precede. In the future tense, today used chiefly in the written language, they are inserted between infinitive and ending (*dar-lhe-ei o livro* "I shall give the book to him"). The combination of preposition and article is common (*do, da, dos, das*, for *de* + *o*, etc., and similarly *no, em* + *o*, and *pelo, por* + *o*). Forms of direct address are elaborate, ranging from *V.ª Ex.ª* (*Vossa Excelência*) through *o Senhor* and *a Senhora* and a more familiar *Você* to *tu;* all but the latter take the so-called "third-person" verb forms. In Brazil *V.ª Ex.ª*

is restricted to the most formal discourse, its use otherwise being considered distinctly Portuguese.

Vocabulary.—An outstanding feature of Portuguese is the use of the church's designations for the days of the week, Monday *segunda-feira*, Tuesday *têrça-feira*, Wednesday *quarta-feira*, Thursday *quinta-feira* and Friday *sexta-feira*. Saturday and Sunday are the common *sábado* and *domingo*. Portuguese shares with Spanish many words of Arabic origin, yet also has several not found in standard Spanish, such as *alface* "lettuce," *alfaiate* "tailor." The language of Brazil contains many words, particularly designations for native animals, flowers, foods and the like, that have not entered the language of Portugal or other Romance languages.

BIBLIOGRAPHY.—*General statement with basic bibliography not repeated below:* William J. Entwistle, "The Portuguese and Brazilian Language" in H. V. Livermore (ed.), *Portugal and Brazil* (1953). *Additional general works:* Manuel de Paiva Boléo, *Introdução ao estudo da filologia portuguesa* (1946); Serafim Silva Neto, *Introdução ao estudo da língua portuguêsa no Brasil* (1950); *Manual de filologia portuguêsa* (1957); *História da língua portuguêsa* (in fascicules, 1952 ff.); Antenor Nascentes, *Dicionário etimológico da língua portuguêsa*, 2 vol. (1932–52). *Miscellaneous works:* Kimberley S. Roberts, *An Anthology of Old Portuguese* (1956); F. M. Rogers, "Gonçalves Viana and the Study of Portuguese Phonetics," *Bol. de Filol.*, vii, 17–29 (1940); Armando de Lacerda, *Características da entoação portuguesa*, 2 vol. (1941–47); J. Mattoso Camara, Jr., *Para o estudo da fonêmica portuguêsa* (1953); Helmut Lüdtke, "Fonemática portuguesa," *Bol. de Filol.*, xiii, 273–288 (1952), xiv, 197–217 (1953); Sebastião Rodolfo Dalgado, *Influência do vocabulário português em línguas asiáticas* (1913), English trans., "Gaekwad's Oriental Series," lxxiv (1936); David Lopes, *A expansão da língua portuguesa no Oriente durante os séculos XVI, XVII e XVIII* (1936); Leo Pap, *Portuguese-American Speech: an Outline of Speech Conditions Among Portuguese Immigrants in New England and Elsewhere in the United States* (1949). *Current periodicals:* Boletim de Filologia (1932 ff.); Revista de Portugal, series A, Língua portuguêsa (1942 ff.); Revista Portuguesa de Filologia (1946 ff.); Revista do laboratório de fonética experimental (1952 ff.); Revista Brasileira de Filologia (1955 ff.). (F. M. R.)

PORTUGUESE LITERATURE. The literature of Portugal is distinguished by a wealth and variety of lyric poetry, which has characterized it from the beginning; by its medieval lack of and later achievement in the national epic; by its wealth of historical writing; and by its relative slightness in drama, biography, and the essay. The early *cancioneiros* evidence a school of love poetry which spread, with the language, to Spain at a time when Spanish was as yet undeveloped for lyrical purposes. The *romanceiro* or balladry on the other hand was much influenced by that of Spain, though not sharing the latter's predilection for the heroic. *Amadís de Gaula* (q.v.), prototype of the romance of chivalry, was in its primitive version almost certainly Portuguese, as was, later, the *Diana* of Jorge de Montemôr (Montemayor), the masterpiece of the pastoral novel (*see* below; *see also* PASTORAL; ROMANCE). The *Lusíadas*, by Camões, may be held at once the most successful of the many Renaissance epics cast in the classical mold and the most national of great poems in any modern literature, and the many outstanding works of history and travel of the 16th and 17th centuries are worthy of a race of explorers who carried their flag, their faith, and their speech to the ends of the earth. Though Gil Vicente, in the early 16th century, was a dramatist of great gifts, no other appeared until Almeida Garrett in the 19th, and Portugal never developed a national drama.

This literature, which until the 19th century lay largely unstudied and unknown, has from the beginning been much exposed to foreign influences. The earliest was Provençal, and Provençal taste ruled for more than a century. Then came Castilian, with a court poetry which provided models until the Renaissance saw the triumph of that of Italy and the classics of antiquity. In the 17th century with political domination Spain again imposed its literary standards, followed in the 18th century by France. The Romantic movement reached Portugal from both France and England, two countries whose influence, joined in a lesser degree by that of Germany, persisted long after. The closeness of contacts with Spain, reinforced by dynastic marriages which often brought to the court at Lisbon a predominantly Spanish atmosphere, explains why for two centuries and more after 1450 nearly every Portuguese writer of note was bilingual and wrote also in Spanish, so that some, like

Montemôr and Manuel de Melo, are numbered among the classics too of Spanish letters. Portuguese literature retains nonetheless a distinct individuality which contrasts strikingly with that of Spain alike in the nature of its development and in the divergent kinds where lie its major achievements; in it may be seen reflected the differing ethnical constitution of its people and the distinctive paths along which their lot has been cast. The medieval lyric, the chronicles of Fernão Lopes, the plays of Gil Vicente, the *História trágico-marítima*, the bucolic verse and prose of the 16th century and, above all, the *Lusíadas*, are several expressions of a clearly defined national temperament which early carved out for itself original expression. (*See* also PROVENÇAL LITERATURE; SPANISH LITERATURE; FRENCH LITERATURE.)

Early Period.—Though no literary documents belonging to the first century of Portugal's history as a nation have survived, there is evidence of the existence of an indigenous popular poetry both sacred and profane. Provençal influences were for long to mold the manifestations of poetical talent, but they did not originate them. A few compositions from before 1200 survive; one, attributed to Sancho I (1185–1211), is the earliest extant *cossante*, the name now given to brief lyrical poems which are almost immobile in their repetitiveness and are marked by a wistful sadness which is never wholly absent from Portuguese literature. The accession in 1248 of Afonso (Alphonso) III, who had lived 13 years in France and returned home, bringing poets in his train, to play the role of patron of letters, inaugurated a period of poetic activity illustrated in the *Cancioneiro da Ajuda,* the oldest collection of Peninsular verse. Soon all the norms of Provence and of northern France were current, subtlety of form and device taking precedence in them over thought or emotion. Three main types of *cantiga* were recognized, all often practised by the same poet: *de amor, de amigo,* and *de maldizer.* The second, put into the mouth of the lady lamenting her lover's absence, commonly betrays a truer feeling than the first; in the third the poet vents satire on his rival or enemy.

The apogee of this palace poetry dates from the early years of the reign of Afonso's son Diniz (Denis; 1279–1325), who had been educated by a Frenchman, Aymeric of Cahors. Diniz, grandson and imitator in his services to culture of Alfonso the Learned of Castile, founded his country's first university in Lisbon (later removed to Coimbra) in 1290 and stimulated the translation into Portuguese of outstanding works from Spanish, Latin, and Arabic. He thus ranks as the founder of vernacular prose in Portugal; but he was also a true poet, technically accomplished and with genuine feeling, and was esteemed the best poet of his age in the Peninsula. To his court came troubadours and *jograis* from León, Castile, and distant Aragon to enjoy the last afterglow of a cult already dying or dead elsewhere, and about 2,000 poems by its 200 poets are preserved in the three great *Cancioneiros da Ajuda, da Vaticana,* and *Colocci-Brancuti* (or *da Biblioteca Nacional*). In the main this poetry forms monotonous reading today, because of its poverty of ideas and conventionality of metrical form and expression; in it poets served an apprenticeship to their craft, and the language developed its rare musical qualities against the birth of more individual inspiration.

In contrast with the restricted horizons of courtly verse, themes of adventure, war, and chivalry mingled with love, religion, and the sea in the considerable collection of ballad poetry known as the *romanceiro.* Differing in subject matter from the ballad in Spain, which drew heavily on the native epic tradition, the *romanceiro* still derived in all probability from across the border and exploited the popularity of the form—the octosyllable with assonance in alternate lines—in more congenial directions. Few if any of these romances can be dated earlier than the 15th century; they belong to the close of the Middle Ages, an anonymous collective poetry kept alive by oral transmission, with a late artificial flowering, from the pens of known poets, in the 16th and 17th centuries. Heroes and incidents of the French and Spanish epos were reflected in numerous derivative ballads: of native Portuguese epic we can point at most to a *Poema da batalha do Salado* (1340) by one Alphonso Giraldes concerning which the brief surviving fragment allows no firm inferences.

Prose literature took much longer than verse to perfect its instrument. Religious writings (fragments of the Bible, lives of saints, and monastic rules), brief annals of the early kings, and *livros de linhagens,* or books of descent, constitute the earliest texts; they date from the late 12th century onward and interest the student of language rather than of literature. The *Livro de linhagens* of Pedro, count of Barcelos (1289–1350), raised the last-named kind to the height of literature, and therein constitutes a landmark, by a concern that went beyond genealogy to history and legend. The early popularity of the *matière de Bretagne* is attested both here and elsewhere, as in the five songs based on Breton *lais* with which the *Cancioneiro Colocci-Brancuti* opens: the ideals of chivalry and the spirit of sentimental adventure associated with the knights of the Round Table clearly made strong appeal to the Portuguese temperament. The *História dos cavaleiros da Mesa Redonda e da demanda do Santo Graal,* an adaptation from the French dating from the early 14th century, is the chief relic of a considerable activity in this field, out of which derived *Amadís de Gaula,* progenitor of a long succession of romances of chivalry in Spain and Portugal. While the authorship and country of this are still in debate, the balance of probability inclines to a Portuguese original, at least for the first three books of *c.* 1350, from the pen possibly of one Vasco de Lobeira.

The 15th Century.—Under John (João) I (1385–1433), founder of the new dynasty of Avís, the court became once again a centre of literary culture. The king himself wrote a *Livro da montaria,* or treatise on the chase. His son Edward (Duarte) collected a rich library of the ancients (some translated by his order, as was also John Gower's *Confessio amantis*), and of medieval poems and histories, and composed a moral treatise, *Leal Conselheiro, c.* 1430, which revealed a great and conscious stylist. His brother Pedro's *Tratado da Virtuosa Benfeitoria* was a version of Seneca's *De beneficiis;* Cicero and Vegetius were among other authors translated by this much-traveled prince or at his instance. But the great distinction of the age was its chronicles, for which much credit falls to Edward who as king created in 1434 the office of Cronista Mor do Reino and appointed to it Fernão Lopes (*q.v.*), the father of Portuguese historiography—Robert Southey called him the best chronicler of any age or nation—and author of chronicles of the first ten kings of Portugal, of which only those of Peter (Pedro) I, Ferdinand (Fernando) I, and John I survive. Earlier he had, perhaps, written the biography of the hero of Aljubarrota, the constable Nuno Álvares Pereira. Vividness of style and character portrayal combined with serious documentation and a high sense of principle and responsibility to produce in Lopes the finest achievement of medieval Portuguese prose.

His successor in office, Gomes Eanes de Zurara (*q.v.*), adding to the seriousness a constant parade of erudition, continued the chronicle of John I on a lower level of artistry with an account of the 1415 expedition to Ceuta and the early period of expansion in North Africa. His chief work, born of admiration for Prince Henry the Navigator, was his *Crónica do descobrimento e conquista da Guiné.* Rui de Pina (*c.* 1440–*c.* 1523), if likewise not of the stature of Lopes either as historian or as artist, was free from the rhetorical defects of Zurara, and his chronicles of Duarte, Afonso V, and John II were characterized by a notable frankness: the people, who in Lopes had occupied the foreground, here yielded pride of place to the monarch. To Pina's reworking of Lopes' narratives of the six reigns from Sancho I to Afonso IV is owed the irreparable loss of the original text; his own chronicle of John II was in its turn reworked, and spiced with much anecdotal gossip, by Garcia de Resende (*q.v.*).

Poetry had suffered a long eclipse after the spate of activity reflected in the *cancioneiros,* and when in the mid-15th century it was once more cultivated, much had changed. The dominant influence came now from Spain, and where once Spanish poets had written in Galician-Portuguese, Portuguese poets initiated the long chapter of fealty, in theme and language alike, to Spain. Apart from the romances, popular poetry had disappeared along with that of the troubadours, whose legacy stood reduced to a set of metrical devices and another of conceits on the topic of courtly love (*q.v.*). The constable Dom Pedro de Portugal (1429–66), son of the prince of that name already referred to, was led by the accidents of his own storm-tossed life—he lived for seven years in exile in Castile and died as king of Aragon—to initiate the fashion of writing in Castilian. As one of the first likewise to adopt the new Spanish trend away from the Provençal manner in favour of allegory and the cult of classical antiquity derived from Italy, his influence on his compatriots was doubly important. His own poems were inspired by deep feeling and much reflection on life. It was to him that the Marqués de Santillana (*q.v.*) addressed, *c.* 1449, his historic letter dealing with the origins of Peninsular verse. The constable was one of almost 200 poets represented in the *Cancioneiro Geral* (1516) of Garcia de Resende, covering the preceding three-quarters of a century. The main subjects of these 1,000-odd poems, in Portuguese and Castilian, are love, satire, and epigram. Discovery and conquest in the East hardly find an echo, even in the verse of those who had taken part in them. Instead theme and tone are predominantly trivial and treatment artificial; the compositions that reveal genuine feeling or serious intent are very few. Resende was himself a better poet than most of his contributors, notably in his stanzas on the death of Inês de Castro. Some names were destined notwithstanding to count among the foremost in Portuguese literature: Bernardim Ribeiro, Gil Vicente, Francisco de Sá de Miranda (*qq.v.*), Cristóvão Falcão. These typify the transition from the 15th-century Spanish school to the Italianate school of the 16th century. Ribeiro and Falcão, introducers of the bucolic style, poured new life into old forms and by their eclogues and *redondilhas* gave models which later writers worked by but rarely equaled.

Gil Vicente and Early Drama.—The emergence of the drama from its medieval swaddling clothes to the threshold of the modern play may be traced in the works of Gil Vicente (*q.v.*), court dramatist and greatest name in the Portuguese theatre, who, having no forerunners in Portugal, drew for his first pastoral-religious plays on Spain, chiefly on Juan del Encina (*q.v.*). Eleven of his 44 plays were written wholly, and another 17 partly, in Spanish. The trilogy of the *Barcas* (1517–19) reveals his dramatic power in serious vein, but even here can be seen his fondness for comic relief, by way of which he arrived at pure comedy and the study of character. In this lay his strength, in construction his weakness; and the latter consideration, not remedied by his successors, had its bearing on the phenomenon of a potential national theatre that may be said to have died with its founder. His real influence was felt in Spain. In centres where Vicente's plays were known and acted, writers for the stage did spring up, in number sufficient to allow afterward the term *Escola Velha*, or old school, of Gil Vicente, but none had the talent to compare with his achievement. The best known were Afonso Álvares in the religious vein, António Ribeiro Chiado, an unfrocked friar who wrote farces with a strong satirical bent, and his brother Jerónimo Ribeiro, likewise a satirist. António Prestes evinced in his plays more knowledge of folklore than dramatic competence. Baltasar Dias, a blind poet from Madeira, wrote simple religious plays which for long retained their popularity. One of the last of the school was Simão Machado, whose *Comédia de Dio* and *Comédia da pastora Alfea* possessed something of Vicente's lyrical facility and skill in portraying peasant scenes.

By the time of Vicente's death, *c.* 1536, court favour had been withdrawn from the stage. The Inquisition, introduced into Portugal in that year, early declared war on the popular theatre on the charge of grossness, to counter which the Jesuits encouraged the writing of Latin tragicomedies or dramatized allegories for performance at religious or scholastic festivals. Vicente's own plays, which figure on the Spanish Index of 1559, were reduced in number to 35 and sadly mutilated in the second edition of 1586, and no new edition appeared for another 250 years. (*See also* DRAMA: *Modern Drama*.)

The Renaissance.—The movement commonly called the Renaissance reached Portugal both indirectly through Spain and directly from Italy, with which country there had been close cultural relations through the 15th century. Afonso V had Matthew of Pisa as tutor and summoned Justus Balduinus to his court to write the nation's history in Latin, while John II corresponded with

Politian. In the following century many famous humanists took up their abode in Portugal. Nicolas Cleynaerts taught Prince Henry, later cardinal and king, and lectured on the classics at Braga and Évora; Vassaeus directed a school of Latin at Braga; and George Buchanan accompanied other foreign professors to Coimbra when in 1547 John III reformed the university. Many distinguished Portuguese teachers returned from abroad to assist the king in his task, among them Aires Barbosa from Salamanca, André de Gouvêa of the Parisian college of Ste. Barbe, whom Montaigne called *"sans comparaison le plus grand principal de France,"* Aquiles Estaço, and Diogo de Teive.

At home Portugal produced its scholars of note, André de Resende, author of *De antiquitatibus Lusitaniae*, Francisco de Holanda, painter, architect, and author of *Quatro Diálogos da pintura antiga,* and many another. Women took a share in the intellectual movement of the time. The sisters Luisa and Angela Sigéa, Joana Vaz, and Paula Vicente, daughter of the dramatist, constituted an informal female academy under the presidency of the Infanta Maria, daughter of King Manuel. Luisa Sigéa (*c.* 1518–60) was both orientalist and poetess in Latin; Lianor de Noronha, of noble family, served letters by her encouragement of translations.

The Italianate School.—The return in 1526 of Francisco de Sá de Miranda (*q.v.*) after a six years' stay in Italy initiated a literary reform of far-reaching effect, though his *Obras* only appeared posthumously in 1595. Like his contemporary Garcilaso in Spain, he introduced and acclimatized the new poetic forms of sonnet, *canzone*, ode, and epistle in hendecasyllabic ottava rima and in tercets. At the same time he gave fresh vigour to the national octosyllable or *medida velha*, through his *Cartas* and *Sátiras* which, with the *Éclogas*, some in Portuguese, others in Castilian, are perhaps his most successful compositions. His chief disciple, António Ferreira (*q.v.*), a convinced classicist, wrote sonnets superior in form and style, along with odes and epistles too obviously reminiscent of Horace. Pero de Andrade Caminha, Diogo Bernardes, Frei Agostinho da Cruz, and André Falcão de Resende continued the erudite school which, after some opposition, definitely triumphed with Luís Vaz de Camões (*q.v.*). The *Lima* (1596) of Bernardes contains beautiful eclogues, while the religious poems of his brother Frei Agostinho are full of charm. Camões, for all his eminence in the epic, was greater still as a lyric poet: were the *Cem melhores poesias líricas da língua portuguesa* true to its title, wrote the compiler, D. Carolina Michaëlis de Vasconcelos, it would contain no other name. Here a profound classical education combined with perfect mastery of his instrument and a lifetime of checkered experience on which the poet had reflected deeply to produce in sonnets, eclogues, odes, elegies, and *canções* the greatest poetry in the language. *Os Lusíadas* ("The

TITLE PAGE OF THE 1ST EDITION OF LUÍS DE CAMÕES' OS LUSÍADAS, 1572

Portuguese"), his epic narrative of Portuguese achievement in the East, with which was interwoven the whole story of the nation and much else, took rank on its appearance in 1572 as the national poem par excellence and the greatest of all Renaissance epics after the Virgilian pattern. Of the many who were moved to emulation by its success none approached Camões in inspiration or poetic gifts. The least unsuccessful was perhaps Jerónimo Corte-Real with his lengthy prosaic accounts of the *Segundo Cêrco de Dio* (1574) and the *Naufrágio de Sousa de Sepúlveda* (1594). Most of these poems, like the *Elegíada* (1588) of Luís Pereira Brandão on the disaster of Alcácer-Kebir, the *Primeiro Cêrco de Dio* (1589) of the chronicler Francisco de Andrade, and even the *Afonso Africano* (1611) of Vasco Mousinho de Quevedo, for all their futile allegory, contain vigorous descriptive passages.

In the drama Sá de Miranda and his followers protested against the name *auto*, restored that of comedy, and substituted prose for verse. Taking Terence commonly as their model, they produced not Portuguese characters but conventional Romano-Italian types. This revived classical comedy, artificial alike in subject and style, won the favour of humanists and the nobility, though its influence was to be short-lived. Plautus and Ariosto were present as well to Sá de Miranda when, avowedly to combat the school of Vicente, he wrote *Os Estrangeiros*, the first prose comedy, and *Os Vilhalpandos*, both actions being set in Italy. His *Cleopatra*, a first classical tragedy, is lost. António Ferreira (*q.v.*), a greater dramatist, likewise attempted both kinds: *O Cioso*, Italian even to the names of the personages, came nearer to being a comedy of character, but his fame rests chiefly on *Inês de Castro* (*c.* 1557), which treated the most moving tragic theme in the nation's history by reference not to Seneca but to Sophocles and Euripides. From Jorge Ferreira de Vasconcelos (*c.* 1515–85) came a "new invention" of another kind with *Eufrosina*: written under the influence of the Spanish novel *La Celestina* (*c.* 1499), which enjoyed a great vogue in Portugal, it was close kin to the Spanish school though essentially Portuguese in characters and general atmosphere. This and his other plays, *Ulissipo* and *Aulegrafia*, resemble novels in dialogue and contain a treasury of popular lore and wise and witty sayings introduced with a moral purpose.

16th-Century History.—Discovery and conquest in Africa, Asia, America, and on the ocean inspired historians as well as poets, and many achieved distinction in narrating these events. The best had themselves seen Portugal's new greatness in the building and were moved by patriotism to write of it, so that their records gain in vividness what they may lose in scientific detachment. In the three "Decades" of his *Ásia* (1552–63) João de Barros (*q.v.*), the Livy of his country, told in simple, vigorous language the deeds of his compatriots overseas down to 1526. His first "decade" undoubtedly influenced Camões, and together, one by his prose, the other by his verse, the two fixed the written language. This work, continued by the more critical and incisive Diogo do Couto (1542–1616), may claim to rank as the noblest historical monument of the century. The manuscript of Do Couto's *Décadas 4–12*, carrying the story to the end of the century, suffered shipwreck, fire, theft, and official delays, and reached publication piecemeal in partial and very unequal form. In his *Soldado prático* he added some acute observations on the causes of Portuguese decadence in the East. Ten years of investigation in India underlay the *História do descobrimento e conquista da Índia* (1552–54 and 1561) of Fernão Lopes de Castanheda (*c.* 1500–59), covering the first 40 years, a work which ranks close to those of Barros and Do Couto. António Galvão, a governor of the Moluccas who died at home a pauper, left a brief *Livro dos descobrimentos das Antilhas e Índia* (1563) full of curious observations cast in the form of annals. Gaspar Corrêa (*c.* 1495–*c.* 1565) likewise embodied intimate knowledge of the manners and customs of India in the picturesque prose of his *Lendas* or *Crónica dos feitos da Índia* (1551), a work remarkable for the vividness of its effects. Among other historical works dealing with the East were the *Comentários de Afonso d'Albuquerque* (1557), an account of the great captain and administrator by his son, and the *Tratado das cousas da China e de Ormuz* (1570) of the missionary Frei Gaspar da Cruz.

DAMIÃO DE GÓIS, PORTRAIT BY ALBRECHT DÜRER

From this spate of writing on expansion overseas attention returned, by way of chronicles of the monarchs who presided over it, to the history of Portugal itself. Damião de Góis (*q.v.*), diplomatist, traveler, humanist, and intimate friend of Erasmus, possessed an encyclopaedic mind and one of the most critical spirits of the age: his *Crónica* (1566–67) of Manuel the Fortunate, preceded by one of his son, later John III, is most valuable where the author's own feelings or experience come into play. Like Francisco de Andrade's uncritical *Crónica de D. João III* (1613), it still allowed Eastern affairs to overshadow events at home; so too did Jerónimo Osório, "the Portuguese Cicero," whose *De rebus Emmanuelis regis Lusitaniae* (1571), based on Góis and written in Latin in order to make the story known *per omnes reipublicae Christianae regiones*, achieved considerable fame abroad. Frei Bernardo da Cruz, who was with his king at the disaster of Alcazarquivir, told the story of the reign in a *Crónica de D. Sebastião;* Miguel Leitão de Andrade, taken prisoner in the battle, related his experiences along with popular traditions and customs in his wide-ranging *Miscelânea*.

Works of travel likewise abounded and derive a particular importance from the fact that their authors were often the first Europeans to visit or at least to study the countries in question. Among the more noteworthy were the *Verdadeira informação das terras do Preste João* (1540) by Francisco Álvares, the *Itinerários* (1560 and 1565) of António Tenreiro and of Martim Afonso, the *Itinerário da Terra Santa* (1593) by Frei Pantaleão de Aveiro, the *Etiopia oriental* (1609) by Frei João dos Santos, and a much-translated classic, the *História da vida do padre Francisco Xavier* (1600) by Padre João de Lucena. Important both as history and as human documents were the *Cartas* written home by Jesuits in China and Japan, of which collections were published in 1570 and 1598. An anonymous *Descobrimento da Frolida*, or Florida, and the *Tratado descritivo do Brasil em 1587* of Gabriel Soares de Sousa are reminders that Portugal was also present and active in the new world to the west. In all this literature of travel the palm is still held for curious interest by the *Peregrinação* (1614) which Fernão Mendes Pinto (*q.v.*), prince of adventurers throughout the East, composed in his old age for his children's reading, and for tragic pathos by the *História trágico-marítima*, a collection first printed as such in 1735–36 of 12 contemporary narratives, told by survivors or based on their accounts, of the more notable disasters which befell Portuguese ships between 1552 and 1604, among them the stories of the "São João" wrecked on the Natal coast in 1552, which inspired Côrte-Real's epic poem as well as some poignant stanzas in the *Lusíadas*, and of the "São Bento" which foundered when homeward bound in 1554 after carrying Camões to India.

The Novel and Other Prose.—Bernardim Ribeiro (*q.v.*), whose five eclogues introduced pastoral poetry to Portugal, was

HYSTORIA DE MENINA E. MOÇA, POR BERNALDIM RIBEYRO AGORA DE NOVO ESTAMPADA E CON SVMMA DELIGENCIA EMENDADA.

E assi algūas Eglogas suas com ho mais que na pagina seguinte se vera.

En Ferrara. 1554.

TITLE PAGE OF THE 1ST EDITION OF BERNARDIM RIBEIRO'S MENINA E MOÇA, 1554

[caption on left column:]

Asia de Joam de Barros/dos fectos que os Portugueses fizeram no descobrimento e conquista dos mares e terras do Oriente.

Impressa per Germão Galhard em Lisboa: a. xviij. de Junho anno de. m.v.lij.

TITLE PAGE OF JOÃO DE BARROS' ÁSIA, 1552

equally an innovator in the pastoral novel with his *Saudades,* better known by its opening words *Menina e Moça* (published 1554–57). This tale of rustic love and melancholy, chivalresque elements mingling with the pastoral and lyric songs with the prose, transferred themes and emotions previously held the preserve of poetry to a new medium and explored them with scant concern for plot. From it Jorge de Montemôr (Montemayor; *q.v.*) drew some part of his inspiration for the *Diana* (*c.* 1559) which, written in Spanish, started a fashion subscribed to by Cervantes and Lope de Vega among many others and represents one of the outstanding contributions of Portugal to the neighbouring literature. Both countries shared in the new enthusiasm of the 16th century for the romance of chivalry, in an age when imperial enterprise to east and west was such as to blur the dividing line between fact and the most improbable flights of the imagination. The first work of João de Barros (*q.v.*), historian of empire, was in fact his *Crónica do Imperador Clarimundo* (1520), written purposely to develop his style for more serious tasks and serving, through the adventures of this fictitious progenitor of the kings of Portugal, his consistent aim of glorifying his native land. In the *Palmeirim de Inglaterra* (1544) Francisco de Morais naturalized one branch of the Spanish descent of Amadís with an imaginative luxuriance and a purity of style which caused Cervantes to bracket it with the works of Homer. Its own Portuguese progeny, the *Dom Duardos* (1587) of Diogo Fernandes and Baltasar Gonçalves Lobato's *Dom Clarisol de Bretanha* (1602), were of an inferior order. The dramatist Ferreira de Vasconcelos kept alive memories of the Arthurian cycle with his *Sagramor* or *Memorial da segunda Távola Redonda* (1567). A very different type of fiction entered with the *Contos de proveito e exemplo* of Fernandes Trancoso, containing 38 tales derived from tradition or imitated from Boccaccio and others, which won and held favour for more than a century.

Among moralists three at least rank as masters of prose style: Frei Heitor Pinto for his *Imagem da Vida Cristã* (1563), Bishop Amador Arrais for his ten *Diálogos* (1589) on religious and other topics, and Frei Tomé de Jesus for his mystic and devotional treatise *Trabalhos de Jesus* (1602–09). The maxims of Joana da Gama entitled *Ditos da freira* (1555) form a curious if unsubtle psychological document. The roll of scientists includes the cosmographer and mathematician Pedro Nunes, inventor of the nonius, and the botanist Garcia da Orta, whose *Colóquios dos simples e drogas* (1563) was the first book to be printed in the East (Goa); while the form of Aristotelian scholastic philosophy professed at Coimbra had a succession of learned exponents, mainly in Latin, in which language also Francisco Sanches wrote his notable treatise *Quod nihil scitur* (1581).

The 17th Century.—From a literary as from a political point of view the new century found Portugal in a lamentable state of decadence. Long before the loss of independence to Spain in 1580 Spanish influence had brought about the introduction of the Inquisition, and with it censorship of books and the preparation of an Index; among its early victims was George Buchanan, at the instance of the Jesuits, into whose hands passed between 1552 and 1555 control of higher education. Cultism, inseparable at bottom from classical education, was already present—as in Camões and Ferreira de Vasconcelos—before Luis de Góngora y Argote (*q.v.*); but with the exhaustion of the national spirit that underlay political eclipse the influence of Góngora penetrated deeply. Its extent may be seen in the five volumes of the *Fénix renascida* (1716–28), which anthologizes the poetic production of the preceding century and reveals in the very titles of poems the emphatic futilities to which good talents could devote themselves. The trend, reinforced by the new fashion out of Italy of literary academies, survived the throwing-off of the Spanish yoke in 1640; Portuguese editions of Góngora appeared in 1646, 1647, and 1667. In 1649 there was founded the Academia dos Generosos, numbering many illustrious by rank and learning, and in 1663 the Academia dos Singulares.

In the bucolic vein a worthy disciple of Bernardim Ribeiro arose in Francisco Rodrigues Lobo (*q.v.*), whose long pastoral romance *A Primavera* (3 parts, 1601–14) showed, with the same delicate perception of nature, a gentler melancholy still and even more sluggish action, interspersed with songs which, with his

Éclogas (1605), earned him the title of the Portuguese Theocritus. Livelier and more varied interest attaches to the same author's *Côrte na aldeia e noites de inverno* (1619), a late flowering of Castiglione's *Cortegiano.* The foremost literary figure of the age was the encyclopaedic Francisco Manuel de Melo (*see* MELO, FRANCISCO MANUEL DE), at once a classic of Spanish and—with his *Epanáforas de vária história portuguesa* and *Apólogos dialogais*—of Portuguese literature, who strove hard, more successfully in prose than in verse, to free himself from subservience to Spanish form and style. Most lyricists of the period remained steeped in Gongorism or, writing in Spanish, have no place here. It suffices to mention Soror Violante do Céu, an exalted mystic praised as "the tenth muse," or the poems of Frei António das Chagas, who is better represented by his *Cartas espirituais* (1684–87). Satirical verse had two cultivators of merit in Tomás de Noronha and António Serrão de Castro, author of *Os Ratos da Inquisição,* a facetious fruit of his imprisonment by the Holy Office; the adherents of Gongorism were pilloried by Diogo de Sousa Camacho. Epic poets continued active, but few of their productions were more than rhymed chronicles. Their works span the century, from the *Condestabre de Portugal* (1610) of a poet already mentioned, Rodrigues Lobo, to the *Viriato trágico* of Brás Garcia de Mascarenhas, published posthumously in 1699; those falling between include the *Ulissea* (1636) of Gabriel Pereira de Castro, the *Malaca conquistada* (1634) of Francisco de Sá de Meneses, and the *Ulissipo* (1640) of Sousa de Macedo.

History, Oratory, and Drama.—Frei Bernardo de Brito (1569–1617), beginning his ponderous *Monarquia lusitana* (1597–1609) with the Creation, reached only to the founding of the monarchy. His work is a mass of legends lacking in foundation or critical sense, but both here and in the *Crónica de Cister* (1602) he proved himself a great stylist. Of the four continuers of the former work, the last three were no better equipped; the first, Frei António Brandão, who covered the period from Afonso Henriques to John II, wrote as a man of high intelligence and a learned and conscientious historian; his parts three and four appeared in 1632, parts five to eight between 1650 and 1727. Other historical works deserving of mention are the *Discursos vários políticos* (1624) of Manuel Severim de Faria, the *Crónica da Companhia de Jesus* (1645–47) of Padre Baltasar Teles, and the *Portugal restaurado* (1679–98) of Luís de Meneses, Conde de Ericeira. Baltasar Teles also edited in 1660 an *História geral da Etiopia a alta ou Preste João* of his fellow-Jesuit, the missionary Manuel de Almeida; and, although travel literature compares ill with that of the preceding century, note should be made of the *Itinerário da Índia por terra* (1611) of Frei Gaspar de S. Bernardino and of the *Relação do novo caminho . . . da India para Portugal* (1665) of Padre Manuel Godinho. Frei Luís de Sousa, a typical monastic chronicler, won lasting fame as a stylist with his *Vida de Frei Bartolomeu dos Mártires* (1619) and the *História de S. Domingos* (1623). Another notable biography, one of the best-known works of the century, was Jacinto Freire de Andrade's *Vida de D. João de Castro* (1651). Manuel de Faria e Sousa, a voluminous writer on Portuguese history and commentator of Camões, wrote in Spanish, as did Melo in his classic account of the 1640 *Guerra de Cataluña.*

The Jesuit António Vieira (*q.v.*), missionary and diplomatist and regarded for his *Cartas* as one of the greatest of all writers in Portuguese, repeated his triumphs of Bahia and Lisbon in Rome, which proclaimed him the prince of Catholic orators. Dying, Vieira considered the language safe in the hands of Padre Manuel Bernardes (1644–1710), a humble priest and recluse whose sermons and oratorical works *Luz e Calor, Nova Floresta,* and *Exercícios espirituais* breathed a calm serenity and naturalness alien to Vieira and exerted a powerful influence in freeing the language from the now outworn conceits of the *culteranos.* Padre Ferreira de Almeida's translation of the Bible (*Novo Testamento,* 1681; *Velho Testamento,* 1748–53) has considerable linguistic importance.

The popular theatre lived on obscurely in the *comédias de cordel,* mostly anonymous and never printed. Such plays as have survived are mainly religious and show the common Gongoristic abuse of metaphor and conceit. All through the century dramatists who aspired to be heard wrote, like Jacinto Cordeiro and João de Matos Fragoso, in Spanish, with an occasional exception such as Melo's witty *Auto do Fidalgo Aprendiz* (1646). The court after 1640 preferred Italian opera, French plays, and Spanish *zarzuelas* to dramatic performances in the vernacular, to the detriment alike of native drama and of acting.

The 18th Century.—The 18th century, in Portugal as in Spain, was to be predominantly prosaic, even in poetry. In the opening decades bad taste was still rampant, but gradually signs appeared of a literary revolution which developed eventually into the Romantic movement. Men of liberal ideas went abroad to France and England, and to their exhortation and example were largely due the reforms which by degrees invaded every branch of letters. Of such were Alexandre de Gusmão, Xavier de Oliveira, Ribeiro Sanches, Correia da Serra, Avelar Brotero, and Francisco Manuel do Nascimento (*q.v.*). Earlier, Luís António Verney had poured scorn on prevailing methods of education in his *Verdadeiro método de estudar* (1746). New literary societies, variously called academies or "*arcádias*," cooperated in the task of reform. In 1720 John V, an imitator of Louis XIV, established the Academia da História; in its *Memórias* (15 vol., 1721–36) may be seen the excellent work done by its members, who included Manuel Caetano de Sousa, author of a colossal *História genealógica da casa real portuguesa* (1735–49), Barbosa Machado, compiler of the invaluable *Biblioteca Lusitana* (1741–58), and Soares da Silva, chronicler of the reign of John I.

FRANCISCO DO NASCIMENTO, ENGRAVING FROM HIS OBRAS COMPLETAS

The Academia Real das Ciências, founded in 1779 by the Duque de Lafões, showed particular interest in language and literature and initiated specialized research and the study of Portuguese literary history (*Memórias de literatura,* 8 vol., 1792–1812). In its ranks were found nearly all the scholars of note at the end of the century, such as the ecclesiastical historian Frei Manuel do Cenáculo, the scientist of many parts Ribeiro dos Santos, Caetano do Amaral, a patient investigator into the origins of Portugal, João Pedro Ribeiro, who has been called his country's first modern historian, and the critics Francisco Alexandre Lobo, bishop of Viseu, Cardinal Saraiva, and Frei Fortunato de S. Boaventura.

The Arcádias.—In 1756 António Dinis da Cruz e Silva (*q.v.*) established with others the Arcádia Ulissiponense (or Lusitana), its first aim being the uprooting of Gongorism and Spanish influence generally; an indifferent poet himself in odes, elegies, and sonnets, his mock-heroic *O Hissope,* inspired by Boileau's *Le Lutrin,* was a telling satirical document. Pedro António Correia Garção (*q.v.*), the most prominent Arcadian, was a devotee of Horace and technically accomplished rather than inspired. The bucolic verse of Domingos dos Reis Quita signified a return to the native tradition of two centuries earlier. Sincerity and suffering spoke in the justly more famous *Marília,* a volume of love lyrics in a pastoral setting, of Tomás António Gonzaga (*q.v.*). In 1790 a Nova Arcádia came into being, its two most distinguished members the rival poets Manuel Maria Barbosa du Bocage (*q.v.*), a would-be second Camões in his life and in his lyrics who overspent himself and lives by a few sonnets, and José Agostinho de Macedo (*q.v.*), in whom inspiration fell below a notable industry, chiefly in the epic. Curvo Semedo was the only other "New Arcadian" of merit. Outside the Arcádias stood the "Dissidents," who numbered at least two writers of distinction. Few Portuguese satirists have possessed such equipment for the office as Nicolau Tolentino de Almeida (1740–1811), who painted the customs and follies of his day with devastating accuracy and distributed attacks or begged favours in the same sparkling verse. Francisco Manuel do Nascimento addressed himself perseveringly, at home and through 40 years of exile, to the purifying and enrichment of the language and to restoring the cult of the *quinhentistas* (16th-century poets). A convert to romanticism shortly before his death, he prepared the way for its triumph in Portugal.

Early in the century authors sprung from the people attempted a revival of the drama at the Bairro Alto and Mouraria theatres in Lisbon, where numerous pieces of low comedy were staged. The *Óperas portuguesas* of António José da Silva (*q.v.*), produced between 1733 and 1741, owe their name to the interspersing of the prose dialogue with arias, minuets, and *modinhas* (popular, light songs); if unremarkable in plot, style, or language, they have a certain comic force of invention. Nicolau Luís was a fertile adapter from the Spanish and Italian, his best play, on the ever-appealing tragic theme of *D. Inês de Castro* (1772), being an imitation of Vélez de Guevara; lifeless characters and conventional passions notwithstanding, his comedies long held the stage. Meanwhile the Arcádia Lusitana sought to raise the tone of the stage, finding its ideals in the classics of antiquity or of the 16th century but immediate inspiration in the contemporary French theatre. Its efforts failed from lack of dramatic talent and of popular appeal. Correia Garção led the way with two satirical comedies in blank verse, *Teatro Novo* and *Assembleia ou partida,* but did not persevere. Manuel de Figueiredo, setting out to write pieces "morally and dramatically correct," produced 14 volumes of plays in prose and verse (*Teatro,* 1804–15) on national subjects; utterly lacking in life, they were never acted. The three Greek tragedies of the bucolic poet Reis Quita, *Astarto, Megara, Hermione,* proved likewise stillborn; to them he added yet another *Inês de Castro,* reduced to the three unities, and a pastoral drama *Licore.*

Romanticism and After.—The 19th century witnessed a general revival of letters; again the initial stimulus came from abroad, but this time it proved more congenial to the native temperament. The chief exponents of romanticism were in poetry and the drama João B. de Almeida Garrett (*q.v.*) and in prose Alexandre Herculano (*q.v.*), both formed in exile, the price of their political liberalism. Almeida Garrett read contemporary foreign literature in England and France and, imbued with patriotic fervour, introduced his fellow countrymen to the new movement through two epics, *Camões* (1825) and *Dona Branca* (1826). His poetry, subjective in the short lyric, historical in longer compositions, remained always sincere and natural. António Feliciano de Castilho (*q.v.*), a gentle Romantic who still looked back to the Arcádias and beyond, exercised much influence over a younger generation of poets: João de Lemos and the group associated with him in *O Trovador* (1848), Soares de Passos, and Tomás Ribeiro, who won fame with his ardently patriotic *Dom Jaime* (1862). Mendes Leal, outstanding in the heroic vein, Francisco Gomes de Amorim, and Raimundo António de Bulhão Pato belong more or less to the same school.

In 1865 romanticism received a frontal attack in a revolt against the primacy of Castilho led by Antero de Quental, a student of German philosophy and poetry, and Teófilo Braga (*qq.v.*), disciple of Auguste Comte and author already of an epic of humanity, *Visão dos tempos* (1864). Literature gained considerably therefrom, and especially poetry. Quental enshrined his metaphysical pessimism and agony of thought in finely wrought sonnets, *Odes modernas* (1865), *Sonetos* (1881), which place him near to Heinrich Heine and Giacomo Leopardi. The *Campo de flores* (1893) of João de Deus (*q.v.*) contains some of the finest short poems in the language, of a spontaneous simplicity. Abílio Manuel Guerra Junqueiro (*q.v.*), heir to Victor Hugo, was a would-be social revolutionary swayed by grandiose ideas and overprone to grandiloquence (*A Morte de D. João, A Velhice do Padre Eterno, Finis Patriae*); in *Os Simples* (1892) he turned to the portrayal of peasant life in sonorous stanzas that, lit by his powerful imagination and pantheistic tendencies, constitute his finest poetry. Akin to him on a lower level was Duarte Gomes Leal (*q.v.*), a militant anti-Christian in *Claridades do Sul* (1875) and antimaterialist in *O Anti-Cristo* (1886), whose declamatory excesses could likewise yield to a quiet sincerity on humble themes. Cândido Gonçalves Crespo (1846–83), in his slender harvest of delicately chiseled verse,

Miniaturas and *Nocturnos*, stood out as the first of his country's Parnassians. By contrast Cesário Verde (1855–86) addressed himself in unaffected style to surprising the poetic essence of common realities; through the posthumous *Livro de Cesário Verde* he became one of the rediscoveries of a later generation. The *Só* (1892) of António Nobre (*q.v.*) was intensely Portuguese in themes, mood (an all-pervading *saudade*), and rhythms; he typifies, with the sincere but nebulous pantheist Teixeira de Pascoais (*q.v.*), a cult of *saudosismo* that was to inspire a whole school of northern poets, and his influence went deep. French Symbolism found an enthusiastic adept in Eugénio de Castro (*q.v.*); in a long series of volumes from *Oaristos* (1890) to *Camaféus Romanos* (1921) and beyond he sought to fill his verse with imagery and colour while emptying it of all personal element, and was admitted for a period, after the death of Junqueiro, as the greatest of contemporary poets. Afonso Lopes Vieira (1878–1946) brought the rhythm of the sea as well as many traditional notes into his *Ilhas de bruma* (1918) and showed a rare artistry in his retellings of two earlier classics, *Amadís* and *Diana*.

Drama, the Novel, and History.—Almeida Garrett, seeking early to reinvigorate the drama, found that he had to create alike theatre, plays, actors, and audience. In *Um Auto de Gil Vicente, O Alfageme de Santarém*, and especially in *Frei Luís de Sousa*, a tragedy of fatality and pathos, all written in prose as admirable as his poetry, he proved himself, after Vicente, his country's most notable dramatist. The historical bent was continued by José Mendes Leal (1818–86), Gomes de Amorim (1827–91), and Manuel Joaquim Pinheiro Chagas (1842–95), all three inclined to ultraromanticism. António Enes (1848–1901) dramatized questions of the day in a spirit of combative liberalism, Ernesto Biester (1829–80) wrote social drama, and Fernando Caldeira (1841–94), also no mean lyric poet, comedy. Good dialogue and sparkling wit marked the comedies of Gervásio Lobato (1850–95), some of the most popular of them written in collaboration with João da Câmara (1852–1908), who for his plays historical, social, and fanciful—*Afonso VI, A Rosa engeitada, Os Velhos*—was accounted the outstanding dramatist of his day. Other historical playwrights include Henrique Lopes de Mendonça, Marcelino Mesquita, and the admirably gifted Júlio Dantas (1876–1962), remarkable for the wit, lightness of touch, and sense of atmosphere with which he reconstructed the past (*A Severa, Santa Inquisição, A Ceia dos Cardeais, Rosas de todo o ano*). With these plays of the early 20th century may be mentioned António Patrício's *Dinis e Isabel* (1919) and *D. João e a Máscara* (1924), the *Egas Moniz* (1918) of Jaime Cortesão, and *O Gebo e a Sombra* (1923), a tragedy of unrelieved gloom and considerable power by Raul Brandão.

Herculano, returning from exile with an enthusiasm for the Waverley Novels, launched the historical romance with *O Monasticon* (1844–48) and *Lendas e Narrativas* (1851). Many took up the kind, Oliveira Marreca, Arnaldo da Gama, Pinheiro Chagas, the most popular being *A última corrida de touros em Salvaterra* and *A Mocidade de D. João V* by Rebelo da Silva, and João de Andrade Corvo's *Um ano na côrte*. This was the great age of the novel: Camilo Castelo Branco (*q.v.*), J. G. Gomes Coelho (better known as Júlio Dinis; *q.v.*), José Maria Eça de Queirós (*q.v.*) are names which would stand high in any country. The first, a great Impressionist, described to perfection the domestic and social scene (*Amor de Perdição, Amor de Salvação*, the various *Novelas do Minho*). Gomes Coelho depicted country life and scenery with much charm, as in *As Pupilas do Senhor Reitor*; *Uma Família Inglesa* describes English society in Oporto with a detail suggestive of Charles Dickens. Eça de Queirós introduced Naturalism with his powerful novel *O Crime do Padre Amaro*, followed by *O Primo Basílio* and *Os Maias;* he was the greatest of the realists, though his materialism was always tempered by a sensitive imagination, and his last novels, *A Ilustre Casa de Ramires* and *A Cidade e as Serras*, place him rather with the regionalists. Naturalism claimed too Lourenço Pinto, Luís de Magalhães, and the much greater Francisco Teixeira de Queirós (1849–1919), who sought to lay bare contemporary society in the 15 volumes of his two series *Comédia do campo* and *Comédia burguesa*. Antero de Figueiredo, a stylist who excelled in regionalist sketches (*Jornadas*

em Portugal, Senhora do Amparo), showed historical imagination of a high order in his fictionalized biographies *D. Pedro e D. Inês* (1913), *Leonor Teles* (1916), *D. Sebastião* (1925). Raul Brandão in *Os Pobres* (1906) and *Os Pescadores* (1923) brought a poignant realism to the description of the sufferings of humble folk.

With his magnum opus the *História de Portugal* (1846–53), on a scale which allowed it to reach only to 1279, and the *História da Inquisição em Portugal* (1854–59) Herculano established himself as the leader of modern Peninsular historians; in 1856 he initiated the important series *Portugaliae Monumenta Historica*. Historiography flourished with names such as the Visconde de Santarém, historian of the *cortes*, José Simão da Luz Soriano of constitutionalism, L. A. Rebelo da Silva of the period of Spanish rule under the Philips, and José Maria Latino Coelho of the dictatorship of Pombal; if all four have been overtaken by later research, the two latter still rank highly as stylists. Henrique da Gama Barros (1833–1925) and António da Costa Lôbo (1840–1913) followed in the footsteps of Herculano, the first with his erudite *História da administração pública em Portugal nos séculos xii a xv*, the second with the unfinished *História da sociedade em Portugal no século xv*, both monuments of scientific objectivity. The works of J. P. de Oliveira Martins (*q.v.*), if not similarly grounded in original research, gave proof of psychological imagination, a notable capacity for general ideas, and the gift of picturesque narration; at once the most artistic and most philosophically minded historian of his generation, he left in his numerous writings a vast portrait gallery of the great figures of his country (*História da civilização ibérica, História de Portugal, Portugal contemporâneo, Os Filhos de D. João I, A Vida de Nun'Álvares*). The 20th century has seen accentuated the trend toward scientific documentation and objectivity. Fortunato de Almeida followed up an *História da Igreja em Portugal* with a masterly *História de Portugal* (6 vol., 1922–27). The monumental *História de Portugal* edited by Damião Peres and others (8 vol., 1928–38) provides an exhaustive treatment of the whole field.

The 20th Century.—The passage from monarchy to republic in 1910 was accompanied by a revisionary urge in literature associated chiefly with Oporto and self-styled the *Renascença portuguesa*. Leonardo Coimbra (1883–1936) was its philosopher, António Sérgio de Sousa (1883–1969) its critic and historian. Its poets—Mário Beirão (*Ó último Lusíada*, 1913), Augusto Casimiro (*A Vitória do Homem*, 1910; *A Evocação da Vida*, 1912), and João de Barros (*Oração à Pátria*, 1917)—adopted the *saudosismo* of Teixeira de Pascoais (*see* above) as key to the nation's soul and so to the recovery of greatness, though the inadequacy of mere nostalgic regret for the past as a principle of action was soon realized. Against this the "Integralist" school reacted from 1913 onward in favour of Catholic monarchist tradition, under the leadership of the historian and poet António Sardinha (1888–1925); among his followers were the Conde de Monsaraz and Hipólito Raposo. The formula of Afonso Lopes Vieira, another sensitive traditionalist, *reaportuguesar Portugal tornando-o europeu* (an almost untranslatable phrase expressing the intention to make Portugal really Portugal again by making it once more truly European), synthesized in some degree the objectives of both schools, and received impetus from Portugal's intervention in World War I. Less was heard thereafter of the cult of the past, and poetry, while responsive to developments abroad, grew personal and introspective in a vein that proclaimed its affinity with that of Cesário Verde and António Nobre. Fernando Pessoa published in his lifetime only *Mensagem* (1934); posthumously he stood revealed as a complex personality responsive to all winds that blew, and gained acceptance as the most inspired poet of his generation. His influence enriched poetry's moods and resources without imposing a poetic school. Prominent among later poets were José Régio (1901–   ) and Miguel Torga (1907–   ). Régio, poet, novelist, and dramatist, established himself in a dozen volumes, from *Poemas de Deus e do Diabo* (1925) to *El-Rei Sebastião* (1949), as a religious, if sorely perplexed, poet of power, and the most outstanding dramatist of his time. Torga's works, from the verse in *Ansiedade* (1928) to the eighth volume of his *Diário* (1960), reveal a less introspective mind, with a robust faith in the primitive virtues of mankind.

Among novelists, Aquilino Ribeiro (1885–1963) was a vigorous personality and prolific writer with wide-ranging lexical and stylistic resources, and themes often centring on his native province of Beira. In Ribeiro the delight of life in all its aspects—gay, carnal, harsh—stands close to awareness of inevitable decay and death (*Jardim das Tormentas*, 1913; *A Via Sinuosa*, 1916; *Caminhos Errados*, 1947; *A Casa Grande de Romarigães*, 1957). J. M. Ferreira de Castro (1898–   ), author of *A Selva* (1930; *Jungle*, 1934), a brilliant evocation of his early years as a worker in an Amazonian rubber plantation; and of *Terra Fria* (1934) and *A Lã e a Neve* (1947), is deeply concerned with social problems. The widely traveled J. Paço de Arcos (1908–   ) is a readable and penetrating observer, particularly of the upper levels of Lisbon society from the end of World War I onward (*Ana Paula*, 1938; *Ansiedade*, 1940; *Tons Verdes em Fundo Escuro*, 1946). J. Rodrigues Miguéis (1901–   ) united social and psychological trends in *Páscoa Feliz* (1932) and *Onde a Noite se acaba* (1946). Novelists who treat African colonial questions include Castro Soromenho (1910–   ; *Terra Morta*, 1950). An important woman novelist of the postwar period is Agustina Bessa Luís (1922–   ), whose *A Sibila* (1955) is a complex psychological study.

Notable work has also been done in history (Damião Peres, J. M. Queirós Veloso, Luís Gonzaga de Azevedo, David Lopes) and in literary criticism (F. de Figueiredo, Manuel Rodrigues Lapa, Hernâni Cidade, A. J. Saraiva, J. Gaspar Simões). Through their work, Portugal's long and distinguished record in action and letters has at last become more adequately known.

For the literature of Brazil in Portuguese, see IBERO-AMERICAN LITERATURE; see also references under "Portuguese Literature" in the Index.

BIBLIOGRAPHY.—*Histories:* T. Braga, *História de literatura portuguesa*, 11 vol. (1896–1907); J. Mendes dos Remédios, *História da literatura portuguesa*, with anthology (1930); A. F. Bell, *Portuguese Literature* (1922); F. de Figueiredo, *História da literatura classica*, 3 vol. (1917–24), *Historia de la literatura portuguesa* (1927), *Historia literária de Portugal* (1944); A. Forjaz de Sampaio (ed.), *História da literatura portuguesa ilustrada*, 3 vol. (1929–32); G. Le Gentil, *La Littérature portugaise* (1935); A. J. Saraiva and O. Lopes, *História da Literatura Portuguesa* (1956); J. do Prado Coelho (ed.), *Dicionário das Literaturas Portuguesa, Galega e Brasileira* (1960); Francisco F. del Riego, *História de la Literatura Gallega* (1951); B. Varela Jácome, *História de la Literatura Gallega* (1951).
Anthologies: A. F. Bell (ed.), *Oxford Book of Portuguese Verse*, 2nd ed. rev. by B. Vidigal (1952); J. J. Nunes (ed.), *Florilégio da literatura portuguesa arcaica* (1932), *Crestomatia arcaica*, 3rd ed. (1943); G. Young (ed.), *Portugal, an Anthology,* with English versions (1916). *Texts:* Colecção de Classicos Sá da Costa (1937–   ).
Bibliographies: Barbosa Machado, *Biblioteca lusitana*, 4 vol. (1741–58; 2nd ed. 1930–35); Inocêncio da Silva et al., *Dicionário bibliográfico português*, 22 vol. (1858–1914), suppl. by Martinho Fonseca, *Aditamentos* (1927); F. de Figueiredo, *A Crítica literária como ciência*, 3rd ed. (1920); A. F. Bell, *Portuguese Bibliography* (1922); H. Thomas, "English Translations of Portuguese Books Before 1640," in *The Library* (June 1926, continued to 1950 by Carlos Estorninho in *Portugal and Brazil; an Introduction* (1953).
Criticism: F. de Figueiredo, *Características da literatura portuguesa* (1915; Eng. trans., 1916), *Estudos de literatura*, 5 vol. (1917–51), *A Épica portuguesa no século xvi*, rev. ed. (1950), *Pyrene* (1935); A. F. Bell, *Studies in Portuguese Literature* (1914); H. V. Livermore and W. J. Entwistle (eds.), *Portugal and Brazil: an Introduction* (1953); M. Rodrigues Lapa, *Das Origens da poesia lírica em Portugal na idade-média* (1929), *Lições de literatura portuguesa: época medieval*, 3rd ed. (1952); P. Le Gentil, *La Poésie lyrique espagnole et portugaise à la fin du moyen âge*, 2 vol. (1949–53); J. Ruggieri, *Il Canzoniere di Resende* (1931); studies of Fernão Lopes, Gil Vicente, Gaspar Corrêia, Camões, Diogo do Couto (all by Bell), and Manuel de Melo (by Prestage), in *Hispanic Notes and Monographs* (1921–24); M. Bataillon, *Études sur le Portugal au temps de l'humanisme* (1952); Hernâni Cidade, *A crise mental do século xviii* (1929), *Tendências do lirismo contemporâneo*, with anthology, 2nd ed. (1939), *Lições de cultura e literatura portuguesas*, I, 3rd ed. (1951), II (1940); *O Conceito da poesia como expressão da cultura* (1945); *A Literatura Portuguesa e a expansão ultramarina*, 2nd ed. (1963).   (W. C. AN.; N. J. L.)

PORTUGUESE MAN-OF-WAR, any of the large floating hydrozoan coelenterates of the genus *Physalia*, belonging to the group Siphonophora. *Physalia* has a large gas-filled float that may be as long as 10 or 12 in. and is commonly seen in tropical or subtropical waters of all oceans. These animals are sometimes blown ashore in large numbers, and their bright blue, red and some-

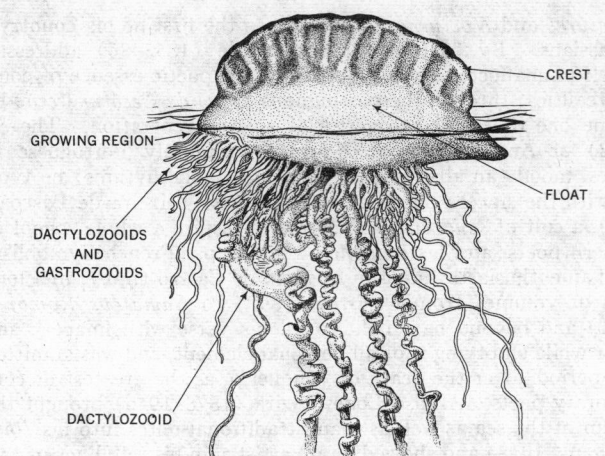

FIG. 1.—YOUNG SPECIMEN OF PHYSALIA

times greenish coloured floats can hardly be overlooked. Beneath the float there hang numerous polyps of a highly polymorphic nature; they may be described as protective, nutritive and reproductive (*see* POLYP).

The protective polyps (dactylozooids) are of two sorts, large ones with very long tentacles and more numerous small ones with small tentacles. The large dactylozooids possess tentacles specialized as fishing or food-catching tentacles that may be from several feet to several yards long. It is these fishing tentacles, heavily armed with nematocysts, that enable the Portuguese man-of-war to capture animals, including fish, up to its own size. The nematocysts of *Physalia* are larger than those of most coelenterates and contain potent toxins; the sting is extremely painful and, in the extreme, can cause death in man.

The feeding or nutritive polyps (gastrozooids) occur in clusters, and the individual zooids do not have tentacles. Once food has been captured by the fishing tentacles, those tentacles contract and carry the food up beneath the float where the gastrozooids can reach it. The gastrozooids apply their mouths to the surface of a food item and will swallow the item if it is small. If it is a large food organism, such as a fish, the mouths of many gastrozooids will spread out over the surface of the captured animal, sometimes completely covering the whole organism. Digestion is believed to be similar to that in other coelenterates.

The remaining zooids, the reproductive ones, are more complex than the others. They are complexly branched structures, perhaps representing many individual zooids. These structures, called gonodendra, are made up of clusters of male reproductive units (male gonophores), clusters of female reproductive units (the medusoid female gonophores), long gelatinous processes called gelatinous zooids and short finger-like processes called gonopalpons. Sometimes, but apparently not always, the medusoid female gonophores may be released at sexual maturity. The early stages in the development of *Physalia* are not known, but once the first polyp appears, part of it becomes

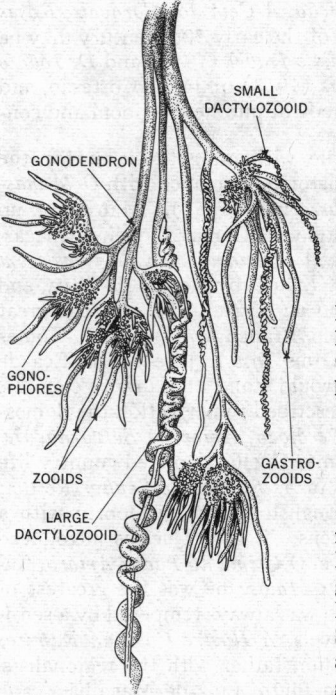

FIG. 2.—CLUSTER OF POLYPS FROM SEXUALLY MATURE PHYSALIA

the float while an intermediate position, presumably homologous to the stem of most siphonophores, differentiates as a budding region from which the rest of the colony develops.

The zooids are set at an angle beneath the float and act like the keel of a ship; thus, instead of simply blowing about the ocean's surface with the wind, these animals tack at an angle to the wind. The relationship of the float to the zooids is different in Northern and Southern Hemisphere representatives of this animal, such that those in the north tack to the left of the wind and those in the south to the right of the wind. The same phenomenon is also known for the colonial hydroid *Velella* (the by-the-wind sailor), whose sail is differently set in the two hemispheres.

The float of *Physalia* has a pore through which the contained gas may escape, allowing the animal to sink. In a short while, the gas-secreting tissues of the float will refill it and the animal will again return to the surface.

The Portuguese man-of-war commonly is accompanied by a fish, *Nomeus*, which lives among the tentacles of the hydroid and is said to share the food *Physalia* catches. *Nomeus* has also been reported to eat the tentacles of *Physalia*. As long as *Nomeus* is healthy and has no wounds it is not harmed by *Physalia*, and the presence of the fish does not cause discharge of the nematocysts. However, once wounded, *Nomeus* too falls prey to its host just as does any other fish. The nature and origin of the immunity of this fish to the potent nematocysts of *Physalia* is not understood. See Hydrozoa.

BIBLIOGRAPHY.—L. H. Hyman, *The Invertebrates*, vol. i, *Protozoa Through Ctenophora* (1940); C. E. Lane and E. Dodge, "The Toxicity of Physalia Nematocysts," *Biol. Bull.*, 115(2):219–226 (1958); A. K. Totton, "Siphonophora of the Indian Ocean," *Discovery Reports*, 27:1–162 (1954). (C. Ha.)

PORTUGUESE TIMOR (Cólonia de Timor): see Timor.

PORTUGUESE WEST AFRICA: see Angola.

PORTULACACEAE, the purslane family of plants, containing 16 or more genera and more than 500 species of widely distributed rather fleshy annual or perennial herbs or subshrubs. The family is characterized by simple, often cylindrical leaves and flowers with usually two green herbaceous sepals and from four to six petals (sometimes fewer).

A few members are grown for ornament, among them rose moss (*Portulaca grandiflora*), spring beauty (*Claytonia*), and fameflower (*Talinum*). A very troublesome weed in many sections of the United States is the garden purslane or pusley (see Purslane).

PORTUNUS (Portumnus), in Roman cult originally a god either of gates and doors (from *porta*) or harbours (from *portus*), eventually associated with both. In the former capacity he was probably connected with Janus (q.v.), but the degree of their association is conjectural. At Rome he had his own priest, the *flamen Portunalis*, and a festival, the Portunalia, celebrated on Aug. 17 in his temple near the *pons Aemilius*. He was similarly worshiped at Ostia. The conjecture that he is the god of the gates and keys of granaries may explain the location of his shrine near the storehouses of the Tiber and his festival in the harvest season. He was, however, definitely connected with the guiding of ships to harbour (Virgil, *Aeneid*, v, 241; cf. Cicero, *Nat. deor.*, ii, xxvi), and he came to be associated with the Greek marine deity Palaemon-Melicertes. He is represented as a youth bearing keys.

BIBLIOGRAPHY.—W. W. Fowler, *Roman Festivals*, pp. 202–204 (1899); H. Papenhoff in Pauly-Wissowa, *Real-Encyclopädie der classischen Altertumswissenschaft*, s.v.; Platner-Ashby, *Topographical Dictionary*, s.v. Portunium. (R. B. Ld.)

PORTUS (now about a mile inland) was the harbour town of Rome in the late empire, 2½ mi. (4 km.) N of Ostia (q.v.) at the mouth of the Tiber. The republican river harbour had proved increasingly inadequate because of the sandbar at the mouth and the narrowness of the river; the emperor Claudius therefore built an artificial harbour to the north and connected it by canal with the Tiber and so with Rome. Two long moles were built out to sea enclosing about 160 ac. (65 ha.); and a giant merchantman, filled with concrete, was sunk to provide the foundation for a great lighthouse. The work, begun A.D. 42, was completed in

Nero's reign, but in 62 a bad storm wrecked 200 ships in the harbour. Trajan added an inner hexagonal basin (97 ac.), connected by canal with the Claudian harbour and with the Tiber. The double harbour was able to handle a considerably increased tonnage in greater security.

Very little is known of the building associated with the Claudian harbour, but most of the plan of Trajan's harbour can be restored. Part of the area between the two harbours was reserved for an official residence; the rest of the basin was surrounded by large standardized warehouses for corn, oil, and other commodities. At first the harbour was controlled from Ostia; most of the workers lived in the old town, and some of the smaller ships continued to use the river harbour. But when trade declined the emphasis shifted. Constantine recognized realities when he made Portus an independent community in the early 4th century. Residential quarters had developed to the east and south of the harbour. Among the cults already attested are those of Liber Pater, Bona Dea, Cybele, Sarapis, Isis, Mithras, and Marnas; by the end of Constantine's reign at the latest there was a Christian bishop. The main cemeteries were developed outside the eastern gate along the Via Portuensis which led to Rome and, on the south side of the canal, along the road which led to Ostia. A substantial sector of the latter cemetery has been excavated, revealing an interesting and well-built series of mainly 2nd-century tombs of harbour workers. Portus was sacked by Alaric (408), but quickly recovered. It was still inhabited, with at least seven churches, in the 11th century, but by the 9th century the harbour and canal were silted up and out of use. The river harbour again became Rome's port until Trajan's canal was cleared and reopened in 1618.

The site was bought by the Torlonia family in 1856, and private excavations have unearthed parts of buildings, inscriptions, and sculpture, most of which can be seen in the Torlonia Museum in Rome. The building of a new airport at Fiumicino has revealed more clearly the main outlines of the Claudian harbour.

BIBLIOGRAPHY.—G. Lugli and G. Filibeck, *Il Porto di Roma imperiale e l'agro Portuense* (1935); G. Calza, *La necropoli del Porto di Roma nell' Isola Sacra* (1940); R. Meiggs, *Roman Ostia*, esp. ch. 8 (1960); O. Testaguzza, "The Port of Rome," *Archaeology*, 17:173–179 (1964). (R. Me.)

PORUS (4th century B.C.), an Indian prince, ruler of the country between the Hydaspes (Jhelum) and Acesines (Chenab) rivers at the time of Alexander the Great's invasion (327–326 B.C.). In the battle of the Hydaspes (q.v.) he offered a desperate resistance and Alexander, struck by his independent spirit, allowed him to retain his kingdom, which he increased by the addition of territory. Thenceforth a loyal supporter of Alexander, Porus held the position of Macedonian satrap when he was assassinated some time between 321 and 315 B.C.

The name Porus, which is not known in Indian sources, has been conjecturally interpreted as standing for Paurava; i.e., the ruler of the Purus, a tribe known in this region from Vedic times.

See Arrian, v, 8, 4 ff.; Plutarch, *Alexander*, 60 ff. (J. Br.)

PORVOO (Swedish Borgå), a seaport in Uusimaa *lääni* (county), Fin., lies about 35 mi. (56 km.) NE of Helsinki by road, to which it is also linked by rail. The population (11,875 in 1960) is predominantly Swedish-speaking. Porvoo possesses a beautiful Gothic cathedral built in 1414–18, the old school building (1760) which now serves as the chapter house, and the home of the national poet Johan Ludvig Runeberg. Since 1723 Porvoo has been the seat of a bishopric. There are several educational institutions and industrial enterprises. Porvoo was granted town rights in 1346. It was there in 1809 that the Russian tsar Alexander I, having summoned a special Finnish diet, granted Finland a constitution as a semiautonomous grand duchy with the tsar as grand duke. (E.-S. Ku.)

POSADA, JOSÉ GUADALUPE (1851–1913), Mexican print maker, was born on Feb. 2, 1851, in Aguascalientes. As a child he worked as a farm labourer and in a pottery factory. He taught school for a short time and then began to draw, inspired largely by posters for the Rea circus. Gradually he was attracted to print making and became a kind of pictorial journalist with the publication of thousands of broadside illustrations and popular book and song covers. He may be regarded as one of the greatest popular artists of all time. Contrary to belief, most of his works were not executed in woodcut, but engraved or etched in relief on type metal. Posada died Jan. 20, 1913, in Mexico City.

See Carl O. Schniewind and Hugh L. Edwards, *Posada: Printmaker to the Mexican People* (1944). (H. Es.)

POSEIDON, in Greek mythology, god of the sea and of water generally. Originally he was probably a supreme deity, who was later fitted into a more specialized place in the Hellenic pantheon. Philologists interpret his name as meaning either "husband of Earth" or "lord of the earth." Homer tells the myth that he was a son of Cronus (*q.v.*) and Rhea and brother of Zeus and Hades. When the three brothers deposed their father, the kingdom of the sea fell by lot to Poseidon, whom Homer represents as dwelling in a palace in the depths of the Aegean. His weapon was the trident which he used to raise storms and also to split rocks, but it seems originally to have been a long-handled fish spear.

Beside these marine aspects, Poseidon was the god of earthquakes, his oldest titles being *gaieochos* ("holder of the earth") and *enosichthon* ("land-shaker") or *enosigaios* ("earth-shaker"). His oldest places of worship in Greece itself were many of them inland: in Thessaly, in Boeotia, and particularly in Arcadia, where he was associated as mate with Demeter (*q.v.*). Also in these places and elsewhere he was closely associated with horses. His union with Demeter was said to have been in this shape, their offspring being the horse Arion, and he was by Medusa the father of Pegasus, the winged horse. Modern scholars have rejected the idea that Poseidon's connection with horses was derived from association with rushing streams or the white crests of waves; in-

MANSELL—ALINARI

MARBLE STATUE OF POSEIDON FROM MELOS, 2ND CENTURY B.C., IN THE NATIONAL MUSEUM, ATHENS

stead they usually agree that he came to Greece as the god of the earliest Hellenes who also introduced the first horses to the country. This theory fits well with Poseidon's prominence as god of the Ionians, who must have taken him with them when they colonized Asia Minor after the Dorian invasion. There they held a joint festival, the Panionia, at which bulls were sacrificed to Poseidon. The association of bulls with the god suggests a link with Minoan Crete. At Ephesus the attendants at his worship were called *tauroi* ("bulls").

In Athens the myth told how Poseidon and Athena contested the sovereignty of Attica. The decision of the citizens was to be determined by the gifts bestowed by the divinities. Poseidon with a blow of his trident created a salt spring on the Acropolis (or, according to another version, caused a war-horse to spring from the ground), but Athena triumphantly produced beside it the first olive tree, which the citizens declared to be the more acceptable gift. However, Poseidon received worship in Attica, particularly at Colonus as *hippios* ("of horses"). Elsewhere he was associated with freshwater springs, as for instance in the Argolid at Amymone, named after a nymph whom he had loved. The importance of water in fertility may partly explain the connection with Demeter.

Poseidon was not as prominent as Zeus in Greek mythology. He was the father of Pelias and Neleus by Tyro, the daughter of Salmoneus, and thus became the divine ancestor of the royal families of Thessaly and Messenia. But otherwise his offspring were mostly giants and savage creatures such as Orion, Antaeus, and Polyphemus, which expressed the general view of his character as violent. In the *Iliad* Poseidon is on the side of the Greeks because of his hostility to King Laomedon (*q.v.*), who defrauded him of his reward for building the walls of Troy. In the *Odyssey* his persistent hostility to Odysseus is explained by the latter's blinding of his son Polyphemus. According to Hesiod, Poseidon was married to Amphitrite, one of the Nereids.

The chief festival in Poseidon's honour was the Isthmia, celebrated in alternate years near the Isthmus of Corinth and the scene of famous athletic contests (*see* GAMES, CLASSICAL). But his character as a sea-god, which tended to develop at the expense of other aspects, became the most prominent in art, where he is shown with the attributes of the trident, the dolphin, and the tunny fish. The contest with Athena was carved on the west pediment of the Parthenon (now in the British Museum, London). Sculptures of Poseidon usually represent him as resembling Zeus, but less dignified and more tousled. The Romans, ignoring his other aspects, identified him as sea-god with Neptune (*q.v.*).

See also references under "Poseidon" in the Index.

See P. Schachermeyr, *Poseidon und die Entstehung des griechischen Götterglaubens* (1950); E. Wüst in Pauly-Wissowa, *Real-Encyclopädie der classischen Altertumswissenschaft,* vol. 17, col. 446–557 (1953). (H. W. PA.)

POSEIDONIUS (POSIDONIUS) (*c.* 135–*c.* 50 B.C.), nicknamed "the Athlete," Stoic philosopher, the most learned man of his time and perhaps of all the school. A native of Apamea in Syria and a pupil of Panaetius, he spent many years in travel and scientific researches in Spain (particularly at Gades), Africa, Italy, Gaul, Liguria and Sicily and on the eastern shores of the Adriatic. When he settled as a teacher at Rhodes his fame attracted numerous scholars; next to Panaetius he did most, by writings and personal intercourse, to spread Stoicism in the Roman world, and he became well known to many leading men, such as Marius, Rutilius Rufus, Pompey and Cicero. The last-named studied under him (78–77 B.C.) and speaks as his friend.

The titles and subjects of more than 20 of his works, now lost, are known. In common with other Stoics of the middle period, he displayed eclectic tendencies, following the older Stoics, Panaetius, Plato and Aristotle. Unquestionably more of a polymath than a philosopher, he appears uncritical and superficial. His inquiries, however, were criticized by Strabo as alien to the Stoic school. In natural science, geography, natural history, mathematics and astronomy he took a genuine interest. He sought to determine the distance and magnitude of the sun and to calculate the diameter of the earth and the influence of the moon on the tides. The history by Poseidonius of the period 146–88 B.C., in 52 books, must have been a valuable storehouse. Cicero made much use of his writings.

See also STOICS.

BIBLIOGRAPHY.—For the fragments *see* J. Blake (ed.), *Posidonii Rhodii reliquiae* (1810) and C. Müller (ed.), *Fragmenta historicorum graecorum,* vol. iii (1849). General works include: E. V. Arnold, *Roman Stoicism* (1911; new ed. 1958); E. R. Bevan, *Stoics and Sceptics* (1913); E. Zeller, *Philosophie der Griechen,* vol. iii, 5th ed. (1923); M. Pohlenz, *Stoa und Stoiker* (1950). *See* also R. Hirzel, *Untersuchungen zu Ciceros philosophischen Schriften,* 3 vol. (1877–83); C. Thiaucourt, *Essai sur les traités philosophiques de Cicéron et leurs sources grecques* (1885); A. Schmekel, *Die Philosophie der mittleren Stoa* (1892); I. Heinemann, *Poseidonios' metaphysische Schriften* (1921); K. Reinhardt, *Poseidonios* (1921) and *Kosmos und Sympathie: neue Untersuchungen über Poseidonios* (1926); P. Schubert, *Die Eschatologie des Posidonius* (1927); L. Edelstein, "The Philosophical System of Posidonius," *Amer. J. of Philos.,* vol. lvii (1936).

POSITIVISM, a philosophical term which, in its broader sense, may be applied to any system that confines itself to the data of experience and excludes a priori or metaphysical speculations. In this sense the term is commonly applied to the empirical philosophers, although in fact reservations ought to be made (John Locke and David Hume accept mathematics, Locke and George Berkeley accept a knowledge of the soul and of God, on nonempirical grounds). John Stuart Mill's "experience philosophy" is positivistic in this sense. Positivists have usually held that theological and metaphysical questions arise but cannot in fact be answered by any method available to men. Others, however, have dismissed such questions as meaningless. This second view connects with pragmatism and with logical positivism (*qq.v.*) and also with the hints to be found in Berkeley and in Hume of an experience test of meaning. Positivism emphasizes the achievements of science; but questions arise even within the sciences which do not seem to be answerable by experimental methods. Ernst Mach attempted to assign an experience meaning to such theoretical questions and to relate theories directly to the evidence for them.

More narrowly, the term describes the philosophy of Auguste Comte (*q.v.*), who held that human thought had passed inevitably through a theological stage into a metaphysical stage and was passing into a positive or scientific stage. Comte held that the religious impulse would survive the decay of revealed religion and ought to have an object. He projected a worship of man, with churches, calendar and hierarchy. Disciples (F. Harrison, R. Congreve, *et al.*) founded such a church in England, but Mill, who inclined to accept the religion, repudiated Comte's organization.

See also references under "Positivism" in the Index.

See Thomas Whittaker, *Comte and Mill* (1908).   (K. W. B.)

POSSE COMITATUS, an ancient English institution consisting of the shire's force of able-bodied private citizens summoned to assist in maintaining public order. This "power of the county," originally raised and commanded by the sheriff, became a purely civil instrument as the sheriff's office early lost its military functions. From time to time legislation gave authority to other peace officers and magistrates to call upon the power of the county.

While Blackstone stated that liability to serve extended to every person over the age of 15 and under the degree of peer, judicial interpretation (of a riot act of Henry IV) excluded also women, clergymen, and the infirm. Failure to respond to the call subjected one to fine and imprisonment. The English sheriff ceased in the 19th century to be a police officer, but an act of 1887 still required every person in the county to be ready and apparelled (*i.e.,* armed) at the sheriff's command to arrest a felon or to assist if there were resistance to the execution of a writ. In the U.S., the posse comitatus was perhaps most important on the frontier, but it has been preserved as an institution in many states through the middle of the 20th century. Statutes confer on sheriffs and other peace officers authority to summon the power of the county. Some have made it a crime to refuse assistance. In general, its members have been privileged to use force if necessary to achieve a posse's legitimate ends, but states' laws differ as to the legal liability of one who in good faith aids an officer himself acting beyond his authority.   (V. No.)

POSSESSION, a state in which the behaviour of a person is interpreted as evidence that he is under the direct control of an external supernatural power. Symptoms of possession include violent, unusual movements, shrieking, groaning, and uttering disconnected or strange words (*see* TONGUES, GIFT OF). Occasionally a normally pious member of a religious body becomes incapable of prayer, utters blasphemies, or exhibits terror or hatred of sacred persons or objects. Christianity and some other religions allow for the possibility that some of these states have an evil transcendental cause (*see* EXORCISM). Most scientific studies treat them as psychophysical manifestations to be dealt with medically or in terms of social psychology. Conditions historically termed demonic possession (*see* DEMON) have come to be treated as epilepsy, hysteria, somnambulism, schizophrenia, or other forms of natural illness (*see* NEUROSES; PSYCHOSES).

In some forms of possession the person becomes ill and is regarded by his community as having committed some spiritual transgression; recovery is held to require expiation of his sin, often by sacrifice. In other types the possessed person is conceived as a medium for the spirit controlling him, functioning as an intermediary between spirits and men. His major role is usually to diagnose and heal spirit-afflicted patients (*see* SPIRITUALISM; SHAMANISM). In such case the trance behaviour of the medium is often self-induced (autohypnotic); it may be stimulated by drugs, drumming, or collective hysteria. In his trance the medium appears genuinely insensible to ordinary stimuli. Faking the possessed condition to perform the therapeutic role (and collect the fee) seems rare.

The phenomena of possession are known among civilized as well as primitive people, and instances have been reported from societies as far apart in space and time as those of ancient Greece, China, and Western Europe. Apart from its therapeutic function, possession may take the form of religious ecstasy and so offer mystical satisfactions and psychological release to those possessed. Thus possession cults flourish in modern times—the outstanding example being the Voodoo (*q.v.*) cults of Haiti—even in communities that adhere to Christianity or some other major religion. *See* also ANIMISM; DEVIL; PSYCHICAL RESEARCH; RELIGION; LYCANTHROPY.

BIBLIOGRAPHY.—J. L. Nevius, *Demon Possession and Allied Themes* (1897); M. Bouteiller, *Chamanisme et guérison magique* (1950); M. Eliade, *Le Chamanisme et les techniques archaïques de l'extase* (1951); A. Wiesinger, *Occult Phenomena; In the Light of Theology* (1957); A. Métraux, *Voodoo in Haiti* (1959); P. M. Yap, "The Possession Syndrome," *J. Ment. Sci.,* 106:114–137 (1960); S. A. Freed and R. S. Freed, "Spirit Possession as Illness in a North Indian Village," and J. H. M. Beattie, "The Ghost Cult in Bunyoro," *Ethnology,* vol. 3 (April 1964).   (R. F.)

POSSESSION (IN LAW) signifies that a person has acquired, with the intention to own, either a very considerable degree of physical control over a physical thing, such as land or a chattel, or the legal right to control intangible property, such as a credit. With respect to land and chattels, possession may well have started as a physical fact, but possession today is often an abstraction. For instance, a servant or an employee may have custody of an object, but he does not have possession; his employer does, even though he may be thousands of miles from the object he owns. Furthermore, except in the most abstract way, it is not possible to speak of the "possession" of intangible property.

In the development of the Roman legal system, possession tended to assume more importance than proprietary rights, and the same is true of the Anglo-American system. Thus possession tends to be regarded as *prima facie* evidence of the right of ownership; it gives this right against everyone except the rightful owner. Mere possession by a finder is sufficient to provide good grounds for an action against one who deprives him of the object with no better right than his own.

See PERSONAL PROPERTY; REAL PROPERTY AND CONVEYANCING, LAWS OF.   (A. DM.)

POST, EMILY PRICE (1872–1960), U.S. writer whose name was to become synonymous with proper behaviour and the rules of etiquette, was born in Baltimore, Md., on Oct. 27, 1872, and as a young girl moved with her family to New York City, where her father, Bruce Price, achieved eminence as an architect. She was privately educated and in 1892 was married to Edwin M. Post. When circumstances impelled her to earn an income, she turned to the writing of magazine articles and light fiction, beginning with a novel, *The Flight of a Moth* (1904). *Etiquette* (1922), which she undertook at the request of the publisher, was an immediate success and established her as the outstanding authority on the subject; at the time of her death, in New York City on Sept. 25, 1960, it was in its 10th edition and 90th printing. Quantities of letters requesting advice on specific situations led to her syndicated newspaper column, and for a number of years she also had her own successful radio program.

See E. M. Post, Jr., *Truly Emily Post* (1961), a biography by her son.   (E. M. P.)

POST, PIETER (1608–1669), Dutch architect and painter, one of the principal architects of the Dutch golden age, was born at Haarlem and died at The Hague. He was a contemporary of Rembrandt and secretary to Constantijn Huygens. Though Post began his career as a painter, he had by 1633, in collaboration with Jacob van Campen, designed the exquisite Mauritshuis at The Hague, thus showing his mastery of the typical Dutch Baroque style. In 1645 he became architect to the stadtholder Frederick Henry. With Campen he designed the House in the Wood (Huis ten Bosch) at The Hague (1645–47) and, independently, Swanenburg House (1645), Nieuwkoop almshouses at The Hague (1658), and the weighhouse in Leiden (1658). Post's town hall at Maastricht (1656 ff.) is one of the outstanding buildings of the 17th century in the Netherlands. Post and Campen are notable for anticipating some of the architectural refinements of 18th-century France and for the influence they exerted on English architecture.

BIBLIOGRAPHY.—*Les Ouvrages de Pierre Post*, engravings (1715); G. A. C. Blok, *Pieter Post* (1937); F. A. J. Vermeulen, *Handboek tot de geschiedenis der Nederlandsche bouwkunst*, vol. iii (1941).

                                          (H. Mn.)

POST, WILEY (1898–1935), one of the most colourful figures of the early years of U.S. aviation, was born on Nov. 22, 1898, on a farm near Grand Saline, Tex., and grew up in the oil country of Texas and Oklahoma. Of natural mechanical bent, young Post worked first on well-drilling rigs, then became interested in gasoline-driven engines and in the airplane flights of the barnstormers who performed at county fairs. He began his career as a featured parachute jumper in tours throughout the U.S. Determined to purchase his own airplane, he returned to oil drilling to earn money. While working as a driller, he suffered an accident to his left eye, which was removed, but this did not prevent him from learning to fly. Backed by a wealthy Oklahoma oilman, F. C. Hall, for whom he became personal pilot, Post purchased the Lockheed monoplane "Winnie Mae" and proceeded to set an astonishing series of records, culminating in his solo round-the-world flight July 15–22, 1933. He covered a total of 15,596 mi. in 7 days, 18 hr., and 49 min. On this flight Post proved the value of navigation instruments, including the automatic pilot, that later came into common use in airline service. He had made an earlier round-the-world trip in the same airplane June 23–July 1, 1931. On that flight he had been accompanied by Harold Gatty as navigator.

Post also did pioneering work in high-altitude flying. Convinced of the feasibility of flying at increased speed in the rarefied air of the sub-stratosphere, he designed and tested a flying suit that would maintain low-altitude pressure while flying at great height. This suit was the prototype of those later used by military pilots.

In August 1935, while flying in Alaska accompanied by the humorist Will Rogers, Post and his famous passenger were killed in a plane crash near Point Barrow.

See W. Post and H. Gatty, *Around the World in Eight Days* (1931).   (S. P. J.)

POSTAL SERVICES (in British usage simply "posts"), the receipt and delivery of letters, postcards, and small packages by a government agency for a small fee paid for each item by the sender. In highly industrialized countries the post office makes use of a complex network of communications extending to all parts of the

country, and to foreign lands, to provide fast, dependable, and inexpensive postal service. In such countries the post office achieves the status of a big business and makes an important contribution to the economic and cultural life of the nation. Because of the existence of post offices in every town and city, many governments have assigned to their post-office departments a variety of miscellaneous functions such as banking, selling licences and revenue stamps, selling government stock, and handling payments under specific welfare programs.

This article is divided into the following main sections:

I. GREAT BRITAIN

A. GENERAL HISTORY

The history of postal services goes back to the early days of the great empires of the East, when the maintenance of political control over a wide area was seen to depend on rapid and frequent communication. The postal service of the Persian Empire under the successors of Cyrus the Great is the first great example. The Roman Empire brought the official postal service to a high standard that was maintained until the Western empire collapsed.

During the Middle Ages such postal services as existed were maintained by the universities or by the guilds of merchants. With the Renaissance the need for private communication forced itself upon the notice of the governments of the day. There were three motives underlying the development of governmental policy: the desire to ensure an official control or censorship, mainly of international correspondence; the need for additional sources of revenue; and the wish to provide an efficient service.

1. Early Proclamations.—In England, the first motive was prominent in a proclamation of Queen Elizabeth I dated 1591, which prohibited the carrying of letters to and from "the Countreys beyond the seas" except by messengers duly authorized by the Master of the Posts. This was directed against the private posts maintained by the foreign merchants in London and seems to have been effective at the time in ending them. In 1609 James I extended the prohibition to the inland post. The importance of state control emerged again during the protectorate, and in Oliver Cromwell's Post Office Act of 1657 stress was laid on the importance of a centralized post office as a means not only of promoting trade but also of discovering and preventing "many dangerous and wicked designs which have been and are daily contrived against the peace and welfare of this Commonwealth, the intelligence whereof cannot well be communicated but by letter of script." (Postal censorship, long discontinued, was briefly revived during World Wars I and II.)

The Post Office as a public service under the royal monopoly was first constituted in 1635 by a proclamation of Charles I "for the settling of the Letter-Office of England and Scotland." The task of setting this up was given to Thomas Witherings, the "postmaster of England for foreign parts." Witherings organized posts that traveled night and day on each of the great post roads, covering a minimum distance of 120 mi. a day, with branch posts working to and from the post towns on the way. A letter could be thus sent from London to Edinburgh and a reply received in six days—an enormous improvement on anything previously attempted. A regular tariff of rates was established, based on the "single letter," *i.e.*, one sheet of paper. This method of charging and the zone system of postage rates remained until the reforms of (Sir) Rowland Hill. Witherings' rates for the single letter ranged from 2*d.* for 80 mi. in England to 9*d.* from England to Ireland; and there was an additional charge for use of the branch posts.

In 1653 the government decided, for revenue purposes, to let the posts out to farm, *i.e.*, have them handled by a private organization that paid the government £10,000 per year for the privilege of carrying on the business. This arrangement was continued until 1716. The revenue of the Post Office, however, was not considered simply as a contribution to the general expenses of government. In 1663 it was settled on the duke of York and his male heirs, reverting to the crown in 1685 on the accession of the duke as James II. The proclamation of 1657 marked the first attempt to regulate the postal service by statute. It affirmed a government monopoly, provided for the post of postmaster general, regulated the treatment of letters brought by private ship, and prescribed the rates of postage, both inland and foreign.

In 1653 Louis XIV of France had authorized the establishment of a local post in Paris at a charge of one sou. Profiting no doubt by this example, a London merchant, William Dockwra, brought into existence in 1680 the London penny post as a private business enterprise. A rate of 1*d.*, to be prepaid, was charged on all packets up to one pound in weight, the packets being insured up to £10. Several hundred receiving offices were opened, from which an hourly collection was made, the letters being brought into six central sorting offices. There were 4 to 8 deliveries a day in the greater part of London and 10 or 12 in the business centres. There was also a daily delivery, for which an additional 1*d.* was charged, to places 10 or 15 mi. from London. For some time Dockwra struggled with serious financial difficulties, and no sooner had his penny post begun to show a profit than the duke of York asserted his monopoly. Dockwra was condemned to pay damages and his undertaking was incorporated in the General Post Office.

Another Post Office Act was passed in 1711. This united the post offices of England and Scotland, which had been separated in 1695, regulated the postal service in the West Indies, New York, and the other British colonies in America, prohibited Post Office officials from taking part in politics, and increased substantially the rates of postage to provide for the expenses of the War of the Spanish Succession.

A difficult administrative problem had now arisen—that of the crossposts, or letters exchanged between one town and another without passing through London. In 1719 Ralph Allen, postmaster of Bath, offered to farm them at a rent half as large again as the current net receipts, and he managed them successfully for nearly 50 years at a constantly increasing rent. The net revenue of the Post Office increased by two-thirds between 1724 and 1769.

2. First Mail Coach, 1784.—The later years of the 18th century were marked by a great development of the main roads and a consequent improvement in speed of communication. A proposal to establish regular mail coach services was brought to the personal notice of William Pitt, who saw its merits and ordered its adoption. The coaches were all to leave London at the same time—8 P.M.—and to return together as far as possible. The security of the mails was to be provided for by armed guards. The first mail coach was established between London and Bath in 1784, and within two years coaches were running to Norwich, Nottingham, Liverpool, Manchester, Leeds, Milford Haven, Holyhead, Exeter, and other places. By 1797 there were 42 mail coach routes in operation. Examples of times taken were: London to Holyhead 27 hours, to Edinburgh 43 hours, to Falmouth 29 hours.

The development of the post was hampered by the need to obtain revenue to finance the war with Napoleonic France, and the rates of postage were periodically increased until in 1812 they were higher than ever before. These high rates were retained for 25 years after Waterloo, and when Rowland Hill published his pamphlet on uniform postage in 1836 he had behind him a substantial volume of public discontent. Hill argued that the postal administration was conducted on principles which were in effect an obstacle to the development of postal business. The principal features of his scheme were: the abolition of postage rates based on distance and the number of sheets, and substitution of rates based simply on weight; the prepayment of letters by postage stamps; and the adoption of a uniform minimum rate of 1*d.* for a one-half ounce letter. (For information on stamps *see* PHILATELY.)

3. Rowland Hill's Success, 1840.—It was only after four years of agitation and parliamentary inquiry that uniform penny postage was finally established in 1840. This was the most signal service Great Britain rendered to the cause of postal progress, and from the point of view of developing social relations and business communications it was an unqualified success; the standard established was one which it became the ambition of the rest of the world to attain. This success, however, had to be paid for in another way. Post Office revenue fell by two-thirds between 1839 and 1840, and it took 35 years for it to recover to the 1839 level.

For several years after the introduction of uniform penny postage the Post Office introduced no more reforms and devoted itself to developing its existing services. The effect of the new rate on the volume of correspondence was immediate and continuous. In 1840 the number of letters posted was more than double that of the previous year. In ten years it had almost quadrupled, and by 1870 had increased tenfold. Penny postage disappeared in 1918.

In 1968 the new inland letter service was introduced superseding some of the existing services such as the sample post, and giving all posters a choice between a fast and a slower, but cheaper, service. The rates fixed for mail up to 4 oz. were 5*d.* in the first-class and 4*d.* in the second-class service (with decimalization of the coinage in February 1971 these rates became 2½p and 3p, respectively). There is a maximum weight limit of 1½ lb. on second-class postage.

4. Newspapers.—In 1840 newspapers were by statute carried free of postage. This, however, was not equivalent to the free postage given on a more or less extended scale in other countries; from the time of Queen Anne all newspapers had contributed to the revenue through the stamp duty which was levied on every copy. This continued until 1855 when the duty was made optional, the privilege of free postage being continued for such newspapers and even periodicals as chose to pay the duty; other newspapers were forwarded by book post (*see* below). In 1870 the position was altered by an act of Parliament which established a small flat rate, irrespective of weight, for each publication registered at the General Post Office as a newspaper; the privilege of registration was granted only to papers that were published at intervals of not more than seven days and complied with certain specified conditions. The principle of a flat rate irrespective of weight was abandoned when the rate was increased in 1915.

5. Book (Now Printed Paper) Post.—The first special rate of postage introduced after 1840 was the book post, instituted in 1848. This was intended to benefit education and literature and was fixed at 6*d*. a pound. By the time the minimum charge was reduced to ½*d*. per 2 oz. in 1870, circulars had been admitted at the special rate. The service was extended in 1906 to include practically all formal, partly printed documents, but in 1968, with the introduction of the new inland letter service, it was continued only for items between 1½ and 2 lb.

6. Postcards.—The Austrian Post Office introduced the inland postcard in 1869. It won immediate success and was adopted in Great Britain in 1870, the postage rate being originally ½*d*. For many years only officially provided postcards were allowed. The admission of private cards paid at the same rate, first allowed in 1894, encouraged the development of the picture postcard. The separate postcard rate was abolished in 1968 on the introduction of the new inland letter service and postcards were thereafter charged on the same basis as letters.

7. Sample Post.—This classification was established in 1863 to allow a special rate to bona fide trade patterns and samples. The rate fixed at that time was 3*d*. for 4 oz., rising to 1*s*. 6*d*. for 24 oz., the maximum weight then permitted. Because of the restriction of the sample post to bona fide samples it was always found in practice extremely difficult to operate and was finally abolished in 1968.

8. Parcel Post.—An international parcel post was established by the Postal Union Conference of Paris in 1880. In Great Britain an inland parcel post service was started in 1883; the maximum weight for parcel post service was then seven pounds with a scale of charges from 3*d*. to 1*s*. according to weight. The maximum weight was raised to 11 lb. in 1886, to 15 lb. in 1935, and to 22 lb. in 1963. Numerous changes have taken place in the rates over the years.

9. Articles for the Blind.—Reduced postage rates for articles for the blind were introduced in 1906 and with some variations continued until 1965 when they were superseded by free postage facilities.

10. Registration.—A parliamentary commission in 1838 recommended a uniform system of registration, but the reform of postage rates caused the postponement of the scheme and it was not until 1841 that a general registration system came into being, and then only in an attenuated form, no responsibility being accepted in the event of loss. The service was not attractive, but it was not until 1878 that compensation was introduced for loss and extended in 1886 to cover damage. The liability accepted was originally £2, but was gradually increased. The minimum registration fee in the inland service now covers compensation up to £100, and the maximum fee compensation up to £400. The service is extensively used for both letters and parcels.

11. Recorded Delivery.—This service, which is available for most classes of inland postal packets except parcels, was introduced in 1961 as a cheaper alternative to registration for items such as legal documents which have little intrinsic value but for which the sender may wish to have a record of posting and delivery. A receipt is given at the time of posting and a signature is taken from the recipient on delivery. A recorded delivery packet is not permitted to contain articles exceeding £2 in total value (the limit of compensation in the service); and some articles, such as money or jewelry, are prohibited.

12. Philatelic Bureau.—This bureau was set up at Post Office headquarters in 1963 to provide (1) a central point from which all stamps on sale at post offices would be available at face value by post for customers in Great Britain and abroad (including, for example, regional stamps and phosphor-lined stamps on sale only at certain offices); (2) specialized services for philatelists (including, *e.g.*, first day cover services, credit accounts, regular mailing list facilities). It moved to Edinburgh in 1966.

B. MAILS BY RAIL

1. Letter Mails.—The first important railway passenger service in England was established between Manchester and Liverpool in 1830. Mails were carried from that year but the first Conveyance of Mails Act was not passed until 1838. Under this act, the provisions of which were, in essentials, perpetuated in the Post Office Act 1953, the postmaster general was empowered to call on the railway companies to convey mails and guards in all trains, and, if required, to provide a whole car for the purpose of sorting letters. The only financial provision in the act was that the railway companies should receive "reasonable remuneration" for their services; any disputes which could not be settled amicably were to be referred to arbitration.

Even at this early stage it was seen that the value of the railways to the Post Office lay not only in their speed but in the facilities they afforded for doing in transit the work of sorting letters. The first traveling post office ran between Birmingham and Liverpool in 1838. Later in the same year another traveled between London and Preston. The speeds on the early railways were comparatively slow. The journey from London to Birmingham took five and a half hours, and from London to Manchester or Liverpool nine and a half. These times were, however, less than half those taken by the London mail coaches, the last of which was withdrawn in 1846. In spite of the great improvements they offered in the mail service, the railways entailed a much heavier cost on the Post Office than the mail coaches, and for several years after their establishment the companies and the Post Office disagreed on the question of payment.

At the outset mails not carried in a traveling post office were dispatched by train in charge of a post-office guard. The system worked well enough for the small mails of the 1830s; but the great growth in the number of letters which followed the introduction of penny postage soon made this arrangement inconvenient and costly, and in 1848 statutory powers were obtained under which the railway companies were obliged to convey mails by train in charge of their own guards; this remains the normal procedure for the great bulk of the mails sent by railway.

Far-reaching as are the statutory powers of the Post Office with regard to the railways, in practice they are not invoked; the arrangements with the railway authorities are settled by negotiations and are laid down in contracts. An important requirement of the contracts is the running of certain trains at times convenient to the mail service, and these times cannot be altered without the consent of the Post Office. Great Britain is covered by an intricate network of mail trains providing direct and speedy communication between all parts of the country. On the route to Scotland there is a special train devoted entirely to the Post Office, running nightly in each direction between London and Edinburgh, Glasgow, and Aberdeen. This successor of the original London-Preston traveling post office is the trunk main line mail service of Great Britain. A similar special train runs in each direction between London and Penzance. In all other cases the mail trains carry passengers as well as mails.

2. Parcels.—The Post Office Parcels Act of 1882 provided that the Post Office should pay to the railway clearinghouse 55% of the postage received on all parcels conveyed by railway, the distribution of the sums thus received among the railway companies being undertaken by the clearinghouse. This arrangement enabled the Post Office to maintain the principle of flat rates of postage according to weight for the whole country.

It soon became evident that for short distances it was possible to convey parcels by road at a lower cost than the payment to the railway companies provided under the act, and, very shortly after the establishment of the parcel post, parcel coaches were established by the Post Office. These road services developed further with the coming of the internal-combustion engine. The higher speed and greater capacity of the motor van made a large extension of the coach system practicable, and by the outbreak of World War I parcels were being carried by road during the night between large towns up to a distance of 120 mi.

Following fresh negotiations with the railway companies, it was enacted by the Post Office Parcels Act of 1922 that the share of the postage payable to the railway companies should be reduced to 40%, the Post Office for its part agreeing that the railway companies should be entitled to claim a revision of the basis of their remuneration if the number of parcels conveyed otherwise than by railway exceeded 10% of the total number transmitted by post. Under these arrangements, many of the road services were terminated as being no longer remunerative. Beginning on Jan. 1, 1951, the arrangements between the railways and the Post Office were based on a contract between the parties which superseded the arrangements laid down in the Post Office Parcels Acts. While the bulk of mail was still carried by rail, changes in the patterns of both postal and rail services led to a reversion to conveyance by road in certain areas. A large-scale experiment for the conveyance of parcels by road began in East Anglia in 1963.

C. Mails by Sea

The first regular government mail packet service was established during Charles I's reign between Holyhead, Wales, and Dublin, Ireland. At that period, however, foreign communications were of greater postal importance than those with Ireland, and, when a postmaster for foreign parts was appointed, it became incumbent on the Post Office to provide a regular means of communication with foreign countries. In 1633 Witherings, who subsequently reformed the inland post, began his career by establishing efficient and regular communication with France by hired boatmen engaged to carry the mail between Dover, Eng., and Calais, France.

For the next 50 years the service appears to have been somewhat unsatisfactory and development slow; but in 1666 a regular service was established by government packet between Harwich and the Netherlands, followed in 1690 by a service from Falmouth to Corunna, Spain, and in 1703 by a weekly service from Falmouth to Lisbon, Port.

The growth of British overseas possessions in the 18th century led to further developments. After an unsuccessful attempt at the beginning of the century, regular packet service from Falmouth to the West Indies was established in 1702; packets also ran to North America and by the end of the 18th century they served a great part of the world. The packets themselves were small, being only 150 tons, but, according to a report of 1788, they were considered fit to go to any part of the world.

The next important event in the history of the packets was the introduction of the steamship. Steamship communication with Ireland was established in 1818, and in 1821 a mail packet of 205 tons burden was put on this service, being followed in the next year by a steamship on the Dover-Calais route. It soon became evident, however, that mails could be carried more advantageously by private companies than by the government, and in 1838 the principle of inviting tenders for the mail service from private companies was introduced.

In the earlier part of this period the government definitely adopted the policy of subsidizing steamship companies in order to establish regular communication on routes where ordinary traffic would not have justified the requisite expenditure, and to ensure the provision of a better type of vessel. The first contract was made with Samuel Cunard in 1839 for a subsidy of £55,000 a year and was speedily followed by others. The subsidy policy, however, proved in practice costly; the expenditure in 1853, when it became the subject of a parliamentary inquiry, had reached the considerable sum of £825,000. Thereafter the principle of the subsidy gradually disappeared; its object had been fulfilled by the establishment of such far-reaching mail services as those of the Peninsular and Oriental Steam Navigation Company, the Royal Mail Steam Packet Company, and the Cunard White Star Line.

The use of noncontract ships for mail service was, in fact, a return to an earlier epoch in the history of the overseas mail service. The government packets in the 17th and 18th centuries were far from covering the whole field; for example, Africa and Asia were never touched by them, and for correspondence to and from a great part of the world the only means of transport was the private ship. The Post Office for a long period made only a feeble attempt to secure control of this means of communication. The measures taken were not effective, and as late as 1827 certain coffeehouses, which had customarily kept bags for the acceptance of overseas mail, were still collecting letters in defiance of the law. The general improvement in the postal service, and in particular the effective measures taken to establish regular mail services by private ships whenever such a course was advantageous, gradually abolished the incentive to forward letters by other means than through the Post Office.

D. Mails by Air

The history of airmails in Great Britain began in 1911 when, to celebrate the coronation of King George V, an airmail service was run between Hendon and Windsor. Twenty-one trips were made and thousands of postcards and letters were carried; but the service was irregular and did not hold out much promise of the development which came a few years later as a result of the great progress made by aviation during World War I. After the Armistice an experimental service between Folkestone and Cologne, Ger., was set up for the benefit of the army of occupation; it was followed in November 1919 by a regular service between London and Paris, on which the air fee, originally fixed at the high rate of 2s. 6d. an ounce in addition to postage, was soon reduced to 2d. an ounce. Other regular services to European countries followed (including an air parcel service between London and Paris in 1921); airmail services spread further afield, the England-India service begun in 1929 being the first stage in extending airmail services from the United Kingdom to the rest of the Commonwealth of Nations.

During the 1930s the United Kingdom Post Office introduced in the service to many European countries the so-called "all-up" system, whereby first-class mail was sent by air at normal rates of postage whenever it would thereby secure earlier delivery. An all-up system at a postage rate of $1\frac{1}{2}d.$ per $\frac{1}{2}$ oz. was also introduced on the Commonwealth air routes to the Union of South Africa and Australia. During this period regular airmail services over internal routes were also begun. In some instances special air fees were charged; in others the mail was carried at the ordinary postage rates.

The outbreak of World War II led to the suspension of many airmail services and the reintroduction of air fee services on other routes. Aircraft capacity was at a premium and, to meet the urgent needs of military personnel in particular, an airgraph service, both from and to the United Kingdom, was introduced in 1941. Airgraph messages (known in the U.S. as V-mail) were written on special forms which were handed in at post offices. The forms were photographed on a strip of film 100 ft. long by 16 mm. wide. The film strip, containing 1,700 messages and enclosed in a cardboard container, weighed only $5\frac{1}{2}$ oz., whereas a similar number of letters by ordinary post would have weighed about 50 lb. After being forwarded to their destination by air, prints prepared from the photographed messages were delivered to the addressees in the ordinary way. More than 350,000,000 airgraph messages were conveyed during the four years in which the service operated. A lightweight air letter service between military personnel abroad and correspondents in the United Kingdom was also introduced in 1941–42.

At the end of the war, airmail services were reintroduced throughout the world, and it became possible to send both first-class and second-class mail from the United Kingdom to practically any place in the world. The air letter form was retained as a specially inexpensive form of airmail service and this type of communication was internationally recognized by the Universal Postal Union in 1952 under the name of "aerogram." The all-up service to European destinations was reintroduced and extended, but the high cost of air transport in the postwar period precluded its introduction on the intercontinental routes. Air parcel services were introduced to most destinations.

Inland air mail services were also extended after the war and by 1961 links between London, Manchester, Edinburgh, Glasgow, and Belfast and services to the Scottish Islands, the Isle of Man, and the Channel Isles were playing a valuable part in speeding the mail.

E. Postal Mechanization

Conventional mechanization in transport, conveyance systems, lifts, self-service machines, etc., and various mechanical aids have been exploited to an increasing extent since the early 20th century. Between World Wars I and II, conveyor systems were introduced at all large sorting centres for bulk transfer of mail. No machinery existed, other than stamp-cancelling machines, for process mechanization although both in the Post Office and in industry attempts were made to construct machines particularly for letter sorting.

In 1927 the 6½-mi. Post Office London railway, running between Liverpool Street and Paddington stations, was opened. Seven main sorting offices were linked, the largest being Mount Pleasant which became by 1934 one of the most highly mechanized in the world.

Until the 1960s all the major processes on mail, letter facing, and segregation from packets, letter sorting and parcel sorting remained completely manual. Development work aimed at mechanizing these processes started in the Post Office Research Station in 1937 but was interrupted by war; the work recommenced in 1945. Post Office engineers studied the letter processes in detail and experimental machines were built to advance the technology of letter handling. The design of suitable machinery for handling pieces of mail is complicated by the great variety of shape, size, and weight of the items.

A practical letter-sorting machine was soon produced and among its novel features was the ability to adjust its speed to the natural requirement of the operator for each individual item. On this machine the operator seated at a keyboard was able to sort twice as fast as in hand sorting and into three times as many selections. By 1960 several offices were equipped with these machines but the economic advance was insufficient to justify further investment.

The next phase of research and development aimed at separating the operator from the sorting machine. This arrangement allowed the latter to run at a much higher speed, about six times as fast as manual sorting and into three times the number of selections. By mid-1969, after several years of intensive development, an experimental installation at Norwich of the new system—known as code-sorting—had proved operationally acceptable and a phased program of introduction commenced.

Other machines were developed to prepare letter mail for the sorting machinery and by the end of the 1960s these were being installed as standard equipment in large centres. The first machine, the Segregator, separates packets and large letters and prepares standard-size letters for the next machine in line, the Automatic Letter Facing Machine (ALF). The facing machine locates and identifies the stamp, cancels it, and stacks each letter into one of two separate streams according to class. Success with all these precision-made machines had depended upon the application of modern electronic control systems to satisfy the highly complex requirements of the postal circulation and delivery service.

A prerequisite to the successful operation of the code-sorting system is that a postcode should be allocated to every address and for maximum efficiency and economy the public should use the code as part of the normal address. The postcode consists of five, six, or seven alphanumeric characters and is in two parts; e.g., YO2 4HB. The first part represents the town (in this case York with the figure 2 denoting the district) to which the letter has first to be sent, and the second part (4HB) represents the particular place to which the letter is to be delivered; i.e., a street, part of a street, or an individual large user of the post. Following a successful experiment in Norwich postcoding in all other areas was begun in November 1966 and by 1969, 7,000,000 addresses had been coded. The remaining 11,000,000 addresses including the whole of London would be coded by 1971–72.

In June 1965 a range of envelope sizes, internationally agreed as suitable for mechanical handling, was introduced into the U.K. as "Post Office Preferred" (POP).

Parcel sorting also received attention and a standard machine based on a tilted conveyor band and controlled through a keyboard became available for sorting up to 50 selections, and was in use in 12 offices by 1969.

The large-scale use of industrial bulk-materials-handling equipment integrated with the new specialized-process machinery was the basis of the pattern for the program of modernization and mechanization of all large postal centres.

F. Miscellaneous Services

In addition to the general postal service, special facilities have been made available for speedier or more convenient delivery. The most important is the express delivery, established in 1891. The most useful variety of express delivery is perhaps that by which a letter or packet may, when messengers are on duty, be dispatched by special messenger to its destination on payment of a mileage fee. Living animals are accepted for express delivery if a suitable receptacle or leash is supplied and provided the sender takes precautions to safeguard the messenger from injury. A further service provides for the immediate delivery, at the request of the sender, of letters or parcels received at the Post Office in the ordinary mails; the same service is provided at the request of an addressee who is expecting an important letter.

When a quicker transmission is required than that of ordinary mail, the Railex service provides for letters to be accepted at many post offices for conveyance by messenger to the railway station for dispatch by the next available train. A messenger will meet the train and deliver the packet to the addressee.

When correspondence is regularly required earlier than the normal delivery time, anyone may rent a private post office box from which he or his messenger may obtain his letters and parcels on application. Large users may have their correspondence or parcels collected free by the Post Office; and, when postings are so large that the application of postage stamps becomes inconvenient, postage may, subject to certain conditions, be paid in cash. Another method of avoiding the use of postage stamps is by means of postal franking machines, used under licence from the Post Office. These machines impress the correspondence with a red franking stamp which is accepted as the equivalent of a postage stamp. Some machines are provided with meters, which are set from time to time at the Post Office, postage being prepaid in cash on the number of impressions which the meters are set to register. Other machines use special-value cards, which are bought from the Post Office, to unlock them and which enable the machines to print as many impressions as the value of the card permits.

There are two services—business reply service for letters, cards, etc., and postage forward parcel service—where postage has not been prepaid by senders but is charged to the special deposit accounts of addressees when delivery of the items is made. These services operate under licence, an additional fee is charged, and a special envelope or label has to be used.

G. The Post Office and Banking

1. National Giro Service.—The word "giro" is derived from the Greek word *guros*, meaning ring or circle, which aptly describes any system concerned with the circulation of money. The decision to open a giro service in the United Kingdom was the culmination of research by the Post Office following the recommendation in 1959 (by the Radcliffe Committee on the Working of the Monetary System) that there was a case for considering the setting up of a service similar to the giro systems already in operation in many European countries. The National Giro Centre was opened in October 1968 to provide a money transfer service and current account banking facilities for those people and organizations who wish to avoid the inconvenience, expense, or delay of payment by cash or by other methods. There are, however, two fundamental differences from the current account banking services provided by other banks. In the first place, all the accounts of customers are centralized in one place, namely, at the National Giro Centre, Bootle, Lancashire. Secondly, transfers between Giro accounts are carried out virtually simultaneously. These differences stem from the basic principle under which all giro systems operate, namely, to provide a method of transferring money from one person to another as simply, as quickly, and as cheaply as possible. The centralization of all accounts and processing equipment obviates the need for a clearing system and immediately facilitates speed and economy. The National Giro provides its account holders with readily accessible and acceptable facilities for depositing and withdrawing cash (using the counter services of more than 20,000 post offices), for making payments to and receiving payments from non-account holders, and for moving funds to and from other banking institutions. It is a system which will help to reduce the many problems and risks attendant upon the handling of cash and which extends the advantages of current account banking for paying bills and transferring money to a great number of people who hitherto have not enjoyed such facilities.

2. Money Orders.—The original purpose of the "money letter" plan when it was introduced toward the end of the 18th century was to prevent the theft of money carried in letters. There was some doubt whether such a service could be established by the Post Office under its existing powers, so by a curious compromise certain officers of the Post Office were allowed in 1792 to set up a service on their own account, the cost of advertising it being borne by the postmaster general. The money order service was taken over by the Post Office in 1838. The rates of commission charged to the public varied from time to time, and the maximum for which a single order may be issued increased to £50. Notwithstanding competition of the less expensive postal order (*see* below), the money order appeals because of the security afforded by the special feature of the service—the advice note which is sent to the office of payment and against which the order is checked before payment.

The overseas money order service came into being in 1856 when arrangements were made for sending orders to Britain from army post offices at Constantinople, Scutari, Alban., and Balaklava, Crimea, this plan being extended to Gibraltar and Malta the following year. The first two-way service was with Canada in 1859, and services with other colonies soon followed. In 1868 the first foreign money order service was started with Switzerland. The service was extended gradually to cover most parts of the world in which an inland money order service operated. A telegraph money order service was started with Germany in 1898 and was extended to many other countries. Since 1939 the overseas money order service has been subject to exchange control regulations.

3. Postal Orders.—A reduction in 1871 of the commission charged on money orders under £1 was followed by an increased demand for the low-value orders, and by 1875 the service was being run at a loss. The comparatively high charges which would have been necessary to avoid this loss caused the Post Office to consider the alternative of introducing a new method of remittance for smaller amounts which would dispense with the advice note, an expensive feature of the money order service. As a result the postal order (originally styled postal note) was introduced in 1881. These orders were for fixed denominations up to 21*s*.; after 1951 orders for £2, £3, £4, and £5 were added to the range. Odd amounts can be made up by attaching postage stamps. The orders must be made payable to a particular person, preferably at a particular office, and can be cleared for payment through a bank. The simplicity, low cost, and convenience of the postal order made it an immediate success. Great use is made of this form of remittance in connection with football pools and newspaper competitions.

The convenience of the postal order soon led to a proposal to extend its use, and in 1903 all dominions, colonies, and dependencies were invited to participate in a scheme for making postal orders available for remittances to and from the United Kingdom, between one part of the empire and another, and within the participating country. Most of the Commonwealth, with the notable exceptions of Australia and Canada, are part of this scheme.

4. Department for National Savings.—Under the Post Office Act, 1969, the Post Office Savings Department separated from the Post Office and became the Department for National Savings, responsible for the administration of the National Savings Bank (formerly Post Office Savings Bank), the Savings Certificate Office, the Bonds and Stock Office (including premium savings bonds), and the "Save as You Earn" scheme. The Post Office acts as an agency in carrying out all types of Department for National Savings' transactions.

5. Savings Bank.—The Savings Bank was set up in 1861, as a result of legislation introduced by William Ewart Gladstone. The object was to encourage thrift among poorer people, and limits were therefore set to the amount of money which could be deposited. In ordinary accounts the maximum amount which may be deposited by any individual is £10,000. Interest is allowed on complete pounds at the rate of 2½% and is added to the balance at the end of each calendar year. All accounting is centralized but a depositor may pay in or withdraw money at any of the 21,000 post offices in the country at which savings bank business is transacted. On certain conditions, a withdrawal on demand up to £10 at a time may be made at any savings bank post office. To make larger withdrawals a notice has to be sent to headquarters and an authority to pay is issued to the office named by the depositor. Within certain limits withdrawals may be made by telegram. All deposits are handed over to the national debt commissioners, by whom they are invested for the National Savings Bank Fund. An investment account, which provides a higher rate of interest, may be opened by any depositor having not less than £50 in an account in the ordinary series. Deposits must be of £1 or more and the maximum amount which may be deposited is £10,000. Withdrawals are subject to one month's notice in writing.

6. Insurance and Annuity Business.—In 1864 the Post Office was authorized to set up an insurance and annuity business through the Savings Bank, but this business was never of more than moderate dimensions. Insurance business was discontinued in 1928 and the sale of government annuities ceased in 1962.

7. National Savings Stock Register.—A much more successful development was instituted in 1880 when facilities were given to depositors in the Savings Bank to purchase government stock up to a limit of £300. There is now no overall limit to the amount of stock that may be held, but purchases are limited to £5,000 nominal value of any stock at any one time. A simple method of purchase was devised at a low rate of commission, and dividends were credited to the purchaser's savings bank account. From 1915 it was no longer necessary to be a savings bank depositor in order to hold stock through the Post Office, nor did dividends need to be paid into a savings bank account. During World War I the machinery proved of great value to the government in making it possible for the small investor to purchase or subscribe to government stock. For many kinds of government stock there was a Post Office as well as a Bank of England issue, and subscriptions could be made at most post offices. The most outstanding development occurred during World War II when a special issue of defense bonds was introduced. The bonds made an appeal to all classes; although initially a maximum of £1,000 was set to each holding, the peak holdings of the bonds exceeded £1,000,000,000. National development bonds replaced defense bonds in 1964 and were themselves superseded by British savings bonds in 1968, in which the maximum amount which may be invested is £10,000.

8. Savings Certificates.—A further simple and popular method of investment managed by the Department for National Savings is the national savings certificate. Originally issued in 1916, it proved attractive to all classes during World War I as a means of helping the war finance, and at the end of 1918 the value of the certificates held exceeded £200,000,000. By the beginning of the 1970s the figure was more than ten times as great.

The early certificates were based on a unit of £1, which was the value given to the certificate after it had been held for a number of years. The purchase price varied from time to time according to the rate of growth and the number of years before the value reached £1. Interest on the certificates is not paid separately but is included in the value when the certificate is repaid. Certificates are repayable at any time after a few days' notice. The accrued interest is free from income tax. Limits are imposed on the number of certificates held by one individual.

9. Premium Savings Bonds.—Premium savings bonds, issued through the Department for National Savings by the Treasury, were put on sale in 1956. They differ from other securities offered to the small saver in that instead of earning interest they have, after a qualifying period of a few months, chances of winning cash prizes free of U.K. tax. A draw is held every month for prizes ranging from £25 to £5,000. Every week there is also a draw for a single prize of £25,000. Each unit bond gives the holder one chance in every drawing for which it qualifies. A novel feature of the scheme was the method of drawing winning bond numbers electronically and entirely at random by ERNIE (Electronic Random Number Indicator Equipment) which was built specially by the Post Office engineers.

10. Savings Stamps.—Various aids have been introduced from time to time to encourage the saving of quite small sums; *e.g.*, home safes (until 1942) and slips to which postage stamps could be affixed (until 1959); but the method of national savings stamps became the main as well as the most popular method. The stamps can be used for the purchase of savings certificates, British savings bonds, and premium savings bonds, or for deposit in the savings bank, but they can also be cashed at post offices subject to a minimum value of £1.

11. Save as You Earn.—Under the "Save as You Earn" scheme, in return for regular monthly savings over five years a tax-free bonus equal to one year's savings is paid when the savings are returned at the end of the period. If the savings are left in for a further period of two years, without further contributions being made, a bonus equal to two years' savings is paid.

H. Post-Office and Social Services

One of the most striking developments in the 20th century has been the assignment to the Post Office of functions that have no connection whatever with its primary purpose but rely on its widespread network of local offices having day-to-day financial dealings with the public. This development began with the use of the Post Office for the collection of local or national revenue by means of licence duties. For example, dog, gun, and game licences are available at most post offices and motor vehicle licences (renewals) at selected post offices.

This is, however, a comparatively small item of business and is far exceeded by business connected with the social services. When the Old Age Pension Act of 1908 came into operation the Post Office became the paying agent. This was extended to payments under the Widows', Orphans', and Old Age Contributary Pensions Act of 1925 and under the National Insurance Act of 1946. Similarly, war pensions, service allowances, supplements to pensions, and family allowances are paid by the Post Office.

A considerable number of stamps are sold for other than postal purposes. Certain inland revenue duties may be paid by postage stamps (*e.g.*, receipt duty); in addition, the Post Office has long assisted the inland revenue authorities by selling such inland revenue and fee stamps as are in general use. There is also a large sale of stamps for the various state insurance schemes culminating in the National Insurance Act, 1946. The Post Office also sells broadcast (sound and television) receiving licences. Records are maintained of the persons who hold such licences and steps are taken to ensure that the licences are renewed as necessary.

I. Postal Staff

Until October 1969, when the Post Office became a public corporation, the bulk of the Post Office staff enjoyed the usual civil service conditions of permanence of employment and pensionability. The clerical and professional staff generally belonged to grades common to the civil service as a whole. The manipulative staff—postmen, telegraphists, telephone operators, and postal and telegraph officers—were recruited either by interview and selection or by competition. Members of the manipulative staff had opportunities for advancement and promotion to higher ranks, including some appointments in other civil service grades. Pay and conditions of service were settled generally by negotiations with the staff associations or, failing agreement, by awards of the civil service arbitration tribunal, subject to the overriding authority

of Parliament. (The Post Office Act, 1961, set up a new financial basis for the Post Office as a whole by creating and placing under the postmaster general's control a self-contained fund into which all income would be paid and from which all expenses would be met.) In 1969, however, the Post Office ceased to be a government department run by civil servants and controlled by the postmaster general. By the Post Office Act, 1969, it became a public authority and, in effect, a nationalized industry. It is headed by a chairman and board of control, appointed by and responsible to a minister, the minister of posts and telecommunications.

The difficulties that trade unionism met in outside employment were reflected in the history of the postal staff, and it was not until 1899, after two partial strikes, that the duke of Norfolk as postmaster general consented to receive representations from the Postmen's Federation. Thereafter many associations were formed covering the various grades of staff. In the late 1960s there were about 20 separate associations officially recognized.

Since 1920 general questions common to the Post Office and the rest of the civil service have been discussed on the national Whitley Council (*see* INDUSTRIAL RELATIONS), but the Post Office has its own headquarters departmental councils (working largely through smaller joint committees) to discuss general matters affecting the staff, and local committees in head post offices, etc., to discuss local matters. This machinery has in no way superseded the functions of the separate unions, which continue to negotiate independently on matters such as wages.

The Trade Unions Act of 1927 forced the Post Office unions to sever their connections with the Trades Union Congress, but, with the passing of the Trade Disputes and Trade Unions Act of 1946, some of the unions affiliated with the TUC.   (G. H. V.)

II. UNITED STATES

Until 1971, the postal system in the United States was known as the Post Office Department, headed by a postmaster general who was a member of the Cabinet. On July 1, 1971, by an act of the U.S. Congress, the department became an independent agency of the government, the U.S. Postal Service, still headed by a postmaster general but no longer of Cabinet rank.

A. History: Post Office Department

"Neither snow, nor rain, nor heat, nor gloom of night stays these couriers from the swift completion of their appointed rounds." So wrote the Greek historian Herodotus (*c.* 430 B.C.) in describing the mounted couriers used by King Xerxes of Persia. Although the Post Office Department did not have an official motto, many persons came to consider the above inscription, which appeared on several post-office buildings throughout the United States, as the official motto of the letter carrier.

The first postal system in America was legalized in 1639 by the colonial legislature of Massachusetts. All mail brought from overseas was to be left at the home of Richard Fairbanks in Boston, who would have it transmitted to its destination. Fairbanks was allowed one penny for the transmission of each letter. In 1672 Gov. Francis Lovelace of New York established a monthly postal service between New York and Boston over what later became the Boston Post Road—U.S. Highway No. 1. In 1683 Gov. William Penn of Pennsylvania established a post office in Philadelphia where Henry Waldy, the first postmaster, was authorized to send mail weekly between Philadelphia and New Castle, Del., and to supply the riders with horses. In 1691 Andrew Hamilton of Edinburgh, Scot., was appointed postmaster general for the American colonies, and the first advance toward establishing an organized intercolonial service was made on Feb. 17, 1692, when a patent was granted to Thomas Neale to establish post offices in North America. An office was established at Philadelphia and rates were fixed for sending mail to most of the colonies, but receipts did not cover expenses and in 1707 the government purchased the rights.

In 1737 Benjamin Franklin was appointed postmaster at Philadelphia and later (in 1753) became co-deputy postmaster general of the British colonies in North America. He served in this office until 1774. The next year, on July 26, 1775, Franklin was appointed head of the American postal system by the Continental

Congress at a salary of $1,000 a year; he served until Nov. 7, 1776. To Franklin, in great measure, belongs the credit for establishment of the U.S. postal system. He increased the number of post offices, introduced stagecoaches, started a packet service to England, and put the service on a sound financial basis.

The federal Constitution drafted in 1787 gave to Congress authority "To establish Post Offices and Post Roads." During his first term as president, George Washington, on Sept. 26, 1789, appointed Samuel Osgood of Massachusetts to serve as postmaster general. At that time the postal service was part of the Treasury Department and it remained so until 1829, when Andrew Jackson invited his selection for postmaster general, William T. Barry of Kentucky, to become a member of the president's Cabinet; it was not until June 8, 1872, that Congress passed a law making the Post Office an executive department of the government. In 1789 there were only 75 post offices; by 1901 the number had increased to 76,945, an all-time high; thereafter the number gradually decreased, amounting to more than 32,000 by 1971. In 1790 there were only 1,875 mi. of post routes; by the 1960s there were more than 2,250,000 mi. of post routes.

As railroads and steamboats appeared on the scene in the 19th century they were utilized to carry mail. Many communities, particularly those in the West, were remote from such means of communication and were served instead by "star routes," so called because they were identified with stars on the Post Office Department's lists. On these routes the mail was not carried by postal employees but by private contractors using horses and wagons. Fraudulent administration of some of these star-route contracts cost the U.S. government millions of dollars before it was exposed in the early 1880s. After that time the Post Office Department continued to make contracts for carrying mail on star routes and actually increased the number of such routes as rail service to some communities was curtailed and improved highways for motor vehicles were built.

Under the broad powers granted to Congress by the Constitution, a vast and important public service was established and developed. Post offices were established as rapidly as possible, speedy transportation of mails was provided, and service was extended to distant parts of the country. From its small beginnings in 1789 the postal service developed into the largest business in the world. By 1971 the postal service employed more than 720,000 workers to process and deliver 413 pieces of mail annually for every man, woman, and child in the United States, a total of more than 84,000,000,000 items.

Post offices were established in every U.S. city, town, and village for the receipt and delivery of mail and for other special services appropriate to the community's size and importance. These offices, each with a postmaster, were divided into four classes, depending upon their annual receipts. Postmasters of the first three classes were appointed by the president with the advice and consent of the Senate and those of the fourth class by the postmaster general. By 1969 there were 4,979 first-class, 7,340 second-class, 12,650 third-class, and 7,095 fourth-class post offices.

In colonial times the policy was to make a profit from the postal service, but this policy was changed as the nation developed and pushed westward. It was felt that the Post Office Department should render service to the public in all parts of the country—with due regard for cost—but it was maintained that such service should not always be self-sustaining. This policy continued throughout the years and deficits became common. By the end of the 1960s the revenues of the Post Office Department exceeded $5,600,000,000 annually and expenditures amounted to $6,800,000,000, resulting in gross operating deficits of about $1,200,000,000.

In 1967, when the Post Office deficit exceeded $1,000,000,000, Congress enacted rate increases in order to reduce the traditional government subsidy. In a reaction to rising costs and rapid changes in transportation and techniques, a presidential committee was appointed to study the possibility of making the postal department into a nonprofit government corporation. In 1968 the Kappel Commission recommended in favour of the new plan, and in 1971 the plan was fully implemented with the establishment of the U.S. Postal Service, an independent agency of the government.

1. Expansion of Services.—One of the first major advances in the postal service was the use of adhesive postage stamps for prepayment of postage. Legislation was enacted on March 3, 1847, authorizing the postmaster general to issue stamps, and they were placed on sale in New York on July 1, 1847, seven years after being introduced in England. (*See* PHILATELY.) The next new service and the first special mail service to be adopted by the U.S. Post Office was the registry system, inaugurated in 1855 to provide for greater security of valuable letters. The registration service began with a simple fee of five cents for each item; it was applicable only to first-class mail and provided no indemnification or liability for loss. This service was later extended to all classes of mail. In 1898 a nominal indemnity, not to exceed $10, was added and from then on this protective feature was gradually extended.

The establishment of a parcel post system in 1913 raised the question of providing registration for the anticipated avalanche of parcels. It was felt that the burden would be too great for the registration facilities then available. This situation led to the inauguration of a system of insurance designed especially for parcel post mailings. In 1924, when the distinction between third- and fourth-class mail was placed on a weight basis, the insurance service was extended to third-class mail. At first, the maximum indemnity was $50 but over the years it was increased to $200. By payment of a small additional fee a return receipt could also be requested by the mailer.

Collect on delivery (COD) service was also inaugurated in 1913 as an accessory to parcel post. At first, COD was available only on fourth-class matter, but it was later extended to third-class and to all classes of sealed mail bearing postage at first-class rates. COD proved to be invaluable to the shipper who did not wish to extend credit and to the buyer who did not wish to make advance payment. This service also included an indemnity feature against loss or damage; a registry service could be obtained on payment of an additional fee.

Special delivery on a limited scale was first offered in 1885. It was simply another manifestation of the public's desire for faster delivery of mail. By payment of an extra fee the sender was assured that his mailing would be dispatched promptly and would be delivered by a special messenger at its destination. Special delivery service is not to be confused with special handling, which was started in 1925 and consisted only of expeditious treatment in transit and did not include immediate delivery at office of address. Special delivery was available for all classes of mail; special handling was available only for fourth-class matter.

In June 1955, a certified mail service was inaugurated. This service was designed to accommodate senders who, when mailing documents or other items that have no intrinsic value, desired proof of delivery. At the time the certified mail service was established, no-value registered mail was discontinued.

2. Transportation and Delivery.—In its earliest years, mail in the United States was transported by horseback riders, stagecoaches, and steamboats. The opening of the West and the movement of settlers to new lands broadened the demand for postal service and the advent of railroads in the 1830s introduced a new means of mail transportation.

With the discovery of gold in California in January 1848 and the rush of thousands of people westward, the postal service kept pace by sending mail overland to Monterey, Calif., by way of Fort Leavenworth, Kan., and Santa Fe, N.M.; the first overland mail arrived in Los Angeles in May 1848. The pony express (*q.v.*), a private enterprise, was inaugurated in 1860 to provide faster mail transportation to and from the Pacific Coast, but with the advent of the telegraph the service was discontinued in 1861.

From 1789 to 1863, letter mail rates did not include city delivery service. Mail patrons had the option of using the service or not, as they saw fit. The carrier collected two cents for the delivery of each letter, and a similar fee for each letter received by the carrier for deposit in the post office. All fees collected were kept by the carrier. In 1858 street letter boxes were introduced so that postal patrons would not have to pay such fees or have to go to post offices to mail their letters. In 1863 free delivery was inaugurated in 49 cities and 440 carriers were employed the first year. By 1970 there were more than 6,200 communities throughout the country enjoying this service, and the number of carriers exceeded 155,000. Village delivery service was established at certain second- and third-class offices in 1912 and developed rapidly until most such services were consolidated with city services. Rural free delivery (RFD), generally regarded as one of the most far-reaching developments in mail service, was inaugurated on Oct. 1, 1896, when five routes were placed in operation in West Virginia. By 1971 there were more than 31,000 RFD routes serving 39,000,000 persons, and rural letter carriers were traveling more than 2,000,000 mi. daily.

Until 1862 all mail carried on trains was distributed in post offices; in that year the postmaster of St. Joseph, Mo., tried out a method of sorting and distributing mail on a moving train between Hannibal, Mo., and St. Joseph in an attempt to avoid delays in mail departures for the West. The experiment was successful, and on Aug. 28, 1864, the first officially sponsored test of a railway post-office car was made between Chicago and Clinton, Ia. On Dec. 22 of that year the Post Office Department appointed a deputy in charge of railway post offices and railway mails. This marked the beginning of the railway mail service, later designated postal transportation service.

As early as 1930, officials of the Post Office Department, anticipating the continued decline in passenger train service, prevailed upon Congress to authorize the establishment of highway post offices throughout the country. Operated on the same basis as the railway mail service, the mails on these highway post offices were transported in large bus-type vehicles that were equipped with facilities for sorting, handling, and dispatching mail. The first route, established Feb. 10, 1941, ran between Washington, D.C., and Harrisonburg, Va. By 1960 there were more than 175 highway post offices and the system had proved highly satisfactory, but by the late 1960s the number had decreased to 95.

3. Other Services.—In 1864 the money order system (*see* MONEY ORDER) was placed in operation in 139 post offices, mainly to accommodate soldiers who were desirous of sending money to their homes. The service was extended to foreign countries in 1867. Postal notes, which were placed on sale for the first time at post offices throughout the country on Feb. 1, 1945, as an experiment to determine whether card money orders were feasible, were withdrawn from sale on March 31, 1951. It was found that the method of bookkeeping employed to keep track of postal notes received and sold at post offices was too complicated to make their continuance desirable.

An important addition to first-class mail was the government postal card, first used in 1873. The original denomination was one cent. It was provided as a convenient means of transmitting brief messages at a rate less than that for a letter in an envelope. By 1970 the Post Office Department was selling over 3,000,000,000 postal cards each year. As early as 1852 Congress had enacted special legislation authorizing the postmaster general to provide suitable stamped envelopes to be sold as nearly as possible at the cost of procuring them.

The postal savings system was established in 1911 to provide a convenient and safe depository for savings and to encourage thrift. Eventually it made the Post Office Department a major U.S. savings bank, deposits reaching a peak of almost $3,400,000,000 in 1947. Mainly because of the 2% limit on interest paid, deposits declined, and in 1966 Congress discontinued the system. The original maximum account of $500 ultimately reached $2,500.

The establishment of the parcel post system on Jan. 1, 1913, constituted a major extension of the postal service. It answered the popular demand for an efficient means of shipping small packages. Because transportation cost per mile is an important factor in the shipment of packages, distance was considered in setting parcel post rates. The eight zones established in 1913 continued to serve as the basis of the graduated rates for parcel post.

4. Airmail.—Airmail service was established on May 15, 1918, by the Post Office Department in cooperation with the War De-

partment, which furnished the planes and the pilots; the mails were first flown between Washington, D.C., and New York City, a distance of 216 mi. Great interest was aroused and Pres. Woodrow Wilson left the White House to witness the departure of the first mail plane from the nation's capital.

On May 15, 1919, airmail service was established between Cleveland, O., and Chicago, with a stop at Bryan, O., the first step in what a year later became the transcontinental route linking New York City and San Francisco, Calif. The first transcontinental night flight began at San Francisco on Feb. 22, 1921, and ended at Hazelhurst Field on Long Island, N.Y., 33 hr. 21 min. later. By July 1924 regular 24-hr. transcontinental airmail service was in operation. With the passing of the pioneering stage the time had arrived for the Post Office Department to discontinue government operation of the service and turn the airmail routes over to private contractors. This action played an important part in the development of commercial aviation. The funds received by airlines for carrying mail were frequently their most important source of revenue. In fact, the first commercial use of the airplane as a means of conveyance was to carry the mail.

Shortly after completion of the coast-to-coast air route, the postal service awarded its first contract for carrying mail by air to a foreign country. The route ran between Seattle, Wash., and Victoria, B.C., a distance of 74 mi., and the service was inaugurated on Oct. 15, 1920, although it was not until 1927 that regular foreign airmail service was in operation. In 1935 another milestone in overseas air transport was marked with the inauguration of transpacific airmail service from San Francisco to the Philippine Islands by way of Hawaii, Midway, Wake, and Guam. This route was extended to Hong Kong on April 21, 1937, and to Singapore on May 3, 1941. Transatlantic airmail service was inaugurated on May 20, 1939, from New York via Bermuda and Portugal to Marseilles, France. Another route between New York and Great Britain by way of Canada and Newfoundland began operation on June 24, 1941. Direct air service to Africa was made possible by the establishment of a route from Miami, Fla., to the Belgian Congo. After World War II there was a tremendous increase in foreign air transport, and direct airmail service to every continent was afforded by U.S. carriers.

The first airmail rate was established in May 1918 at 24 cents an ounce, including special delivery. By November of the same year the rate was reduced to six cents an ounce without the provision for special delivery. The many changes in postal rates for airmail during the period from the inauguration of the service to 1928 reflected the rapidly changing conditions that surrounded the phenomenal development of transportation by air. By 1928 the rates became stabilized, and thereafter ranged only from 5 to 11 cents per ounce. On April 29, 1947, the 10 cent air letter sheet, mailable to any country in the world, was made available to postal patrons by the Post Office Department as a convenient, economical means of sending communications to foreign lands. The charge for such letters increased to 13 cents in the late 1960s.

Large metropolitan areas continued to present a problem in dispatching mail to and from the airport. In numerous instances the time saved in sending mail long distances by air was lost by the time consumed in surface transportation. It was thought that the helicopter, because of its ability to land in a small area, on the ground or rooftop, might prove the solution to the problem. Tests of the carrying of mail by helicopter were conducted in the Los Angeles area in July 1946, in Chicago in October 1946, and at New York City in February 1947. As a result, the world's first experimental helicopter airmail service was inaugurated in the Los Angeles area on Oct. 1, 1947, over a route linking communities to the north directly with the airport. Shuttle service between the airport and the Los Angeles terminal annex post office was instituted the same day. The route was expanded until by 1956 it served about 50 cities and towns in the Los Angeles Metropolitan Area. Similar service was inaugurated later in other cities.

Domestic air parcel post service was begun Sept. 1, 1948, including parcels weighing more than 8 oz. and not more than 70 lb. Zone rates varied according to the distance flown.

International air parcel post service was inaugurated in 1948 between the United States and Europe, the North Atlantic area, South America and the Pacific area. Air parcel post service became available to more than 60 countries throughout the world. Hundreds of planes flown by U.S. carriers in the early 1970s were operating over 300,000 mi. of foreign routes, transporting in a matter of hours mail that less than 20 years before had taken weeks to deliver.

Late in 1953 the Post Office Department initiated the experimental carrying of regular letter mail by air between New York, Chicago, and Washington, D.C., at no extra charge. European countries had previously pioneered this practice. The new service supplemented, but did not displace, regular airmail. Airmail letters were guaranteed transportation by plane but other mail was carried by air only when space was available for it. By 1960 this experimental airlift service had well-defined routes in several regions of the U.S., and by the late 1960s a nationwide airlift network connected 500 cities for the movement of first-class mail. During the same period, air-taxi services were established, connecting smaller communities to main transportation centres; these quickly proved expeditious. Of first-class mail posted at the end of a business day, 90% was delivered within two days, the majority of first-class matter traveling 225 miles or more being carried by air. About 549,000,000 lb. of mail were being airlifted annually, exclusive of airmail.

5. Classifications of Mail.—In the early years of the U.S. postal system there was not sufficient diversity of mail matter to require formal mail classification. The act of 1792 recognized only letters, packets, and newspapers as mail matter. Magazines and pamphlets were recognized in 1799 and unbound journals in 1825. Lithographed circulars, handbills or advertisements, and every other kind of printed or other matter were recognized as mailable in 1845. In 1851 bound books were made mailable, with a weight limit of four pounds. In 1861 maps, engravings, photographic prints, photographic paper, letter envelopes, cards, blanks, seeds, and cuttings were made mailable and the weight limit for each was fixed at four pounds. The following four classes of mail were established in 1879:

First-Class Mail.—As letter mail has always ranked first in terms of revenue and number of pieces, letters of a personal or written nature were designated as the "first" class when mail matter was classified in 1863. In the early period, letter rates varied not only on the number of sheets in a letter but also on the basis of the distance the letter was to travel. There was a constant tendency to reduce the number of distance graduations. By 1845 the move to a uniform rate was advanced when the five-zone schedule was reduced to two zones. Six years later the only distance differential remaining was under and over 3,000 mi. Finally, in 1863 a uniform rate regardless of distance was established.

From 1879 on there were relatively few changes in the rate structure of first-class mail. Among the most important were the inauguration of the postcard service in 1898; an increase in the weight limit in 1916 from four pounds to the weights applicable to fourth-class matter; and the initiation of business reply cards and letters in 1928. With the exception of a brief period during World War I, nonlocal letters were carried at a rate of two cents an ounce between 1883 and 1932. In 1932 the rate was increased to three cents an ounce, in 1958 to four cents, in 1962 to five cents, in 1968 to six cents, and in 1971 to eight cents.

Congress vested in the Post Office Department a monopoly in the conveyance of letters, but did not extend this monopoly to any other class of mail matter.

Second-Class Mail.—Prior to 1863 there was no "second" class of mail. Separate rates of postage existed for newspapers and magazines, and when additional printed matter was admitted to the mails it was charged the same rate as magazines. With the establishment of three classes of mail in 1863, newspapers, magazines, and other periodical publications came under second-class rates and other printed matter under third class.

Since 1879 the most important change in the second-class rate structure was the introduction of a distance factor in levying separate charges on the advertising portions of second-class mat-

ter. This change took place in 1918, the parcel post zones being used as a basis of a graduated schedule of rates. The rates for the editorial portions of publications remained relatively stable in spite of the many changes that took place in both postal and publishing operations. Eligibility for the second-class privilege was redefined on several occasions in order to reduce administrative difficulties and help eliminate abuses of a subsidized service.

Third-Class Mail.—Before the "third" class of mail was also established in 1863, circulars, handbills, and other material were charged the same postage rates as magazines. For all practical purposes third-class mail between 1863 and 1879 became a catch-all category. Within the classification was a miscellany of matter, some of which was accorded special rates. With the designation of a fourth class of mail in 1879 some of the matter that was embraced by the former third class was shifted to fourth class. Printed matter other than regular newspapers and periodicals remained third class, while merchandise and other mailable matter became fourth class. Later the distinction between third and fourth classes was changed from type of matter to a weight basis. First, in 1914, parcels of miscellaneous printed matter, if weighing over 4 lb., were shifted to fourth class; in the same year books over 8 oz. were also placed in fourth class. In 1925, all matter not in the first or second classes weighing 8 oz. or less was placed in the third class and that weighing over 8 oz. in the fourth class; in 1958 the dividing line between third and fourth classes, in terms of weight, was changed from 8 to 16 oz.

The most important change in the third-class rate structure occurred in 1928 when a special "bulk rate" was made applicable to separately addressed identical pieces of third-class matter mailed at one time in quantities of at least 20 lb. or 200 pieces. Facing and separation by states, cities, etc., was required of the mailer.

Fourth-Class Mail.—The "fourth" class of mail was established in 1879, with a single flat rate of one cent per ounce. This rate remained in effect until the major revision that established the parcel post system. By the Parcel Post Act of Aug. 24, 1912, the scope of fourth-class matter was enlarged, and it marked the end of the 4-lb. weight limit on mail matter. At the start, in 1913, the weight limit was established at 11 lb. Within a year, in response to public needs, weight limits of 50 lb. for nearer points and 20 lb. for more distant points were established. Later the weight limit was increased to 70 lb., with the limit of size not more than 100 in. in length and girth combined, except at first-class post offices, where the limitations were set at 72 in. and from 20 to 40 lb., the latter depending upon the zone to which the parcel post matter was shipped. Fourth-class mail was the only postal service that by law had to be operated on a self-supporting basis.

(L. W. Co.; X.)

6. Technical Progress.—Having embarked in 1953 on a program to modernize and streamline postal operations, in 1955 the postal administration launched a plan for the replacement and rehabilitation of obsolete and deteriorated post office buildings throughout the country. The project was implemented largely through the department's commercial leasing program and through the Lease-Purchase Act of 1954. The latter provided for construction of post office buildings by private builders and their purchase by the Post Office Department on the installment plan. In addition, private industry constructed several thousand new postal facilities that were financed by private capital and leased to the Post Office. These remained under private ownership, with the owner paying local real estate taxes.

Great progress was made in the mechanization and automation of actual methods of mail handling within 20 years after the first measures were initiated. By 1960 many major improvements had been made, especially in more rapid handling of the mails. At several large post offices machines had been installed that mechanically culled, face-cancelled, and sorted letters into 1,000 different separations. In the 1960s, however, such machinery was outdated by even more sophisticated electronic equipment capable of reading and sorting letters with printed or typed addresses at the rate of 36,000 pieces per hour. The first of these went into use in Detroit and Baltimore in 1965. In the mid-1960s the Post Office Department established a new system of zone coding to facilitate mail sorting. After an extensive publicity campaign, the department finally succeeded in eliciting a reasonably widespread acceptance of the Zone Improvement Plan (ZIP) Code. Users of the mails were requested to include in all addresses a five-digit number, of which the first three digits identified the section of the country to which the item was destined and the last two digits the specific post office or zone of the addressee. The new code's primary long-range objective was to fully exploit the potential of electronic reading and sorting equipment. By the late 1960s all gummed stamps were being printed with luminescent inks enabling electronic sensing devices to locate indicia faster in the process of facing and cancelling mail. In the early 1970s a system was perfected that automatically scanned machine-readable addresses and encoded them on the envelopes for swift handling by other machines. The first computer-directed sorting device went into operation in New York City in 1969.

Another technical advance was the fully automated post office, the first of which was opened at Providence, R.I., in 1960. An installation large enough to accommodate two football fields and theoretically capable of handling 2,000,000 pieces of mail per day, it contained the most sophisticated automatic devices then available, linked by more than 15,800 ft. of conveyor belts. Similar post offices were later established in other key locations. By the mid-1960s a number of self-service postal facilities were also in operation; supplementing regular post office service, they enabled patrons to mail letters, buy stamps, postcards, envelopes, and minimum insurance, weigh and mail packages, and get change—at any hour of the day or night.

B. United States Postal Service

The Postal Reorganization Act of 1970 established the United States Postal Service as an independent agency within the executive branch of the government. The service replaced the Post Office Department, which had been an executive department since 1872. The basic proposal for the setting up of the agency came in May 1969 and the Congress was asked to pass an act calling for the creation of a self-supporting corporation wholly owned by the federal government. It also called for the removal of the postmaster general as a member of the Cabinet. Other provisions were: adequate financing authority; removal of the system from politics to assure continuity of management; collective bargaining between postal management and employees; and the setting of postal rates by the service after hearings before a rate panel. The bill was signed into law Aug. 12, 1970, and on July 1, 1971, the U.S. Postal Service began operation.

The Postal Service is directed by an 11-member Board of Governors—9 members appointed by the president, with the advice and consent of the Senate, for staggered nine-year terms, who in turn select the postmaster general and deputy postmaster general, making the 11 members. An Advisory Council, composed of four representatives from postal labour, four from the major mailers, and three from the general public, counsels the service. A five-member Postal Rate Commission, presidentially appointed, recommends rates and classifications for adoption by the Board of Governors. The governors may accept or reject the recommendations or modify them, and may establish temporary rates if the Rate Commission fails to make a recommendation within 90 days.

Reporting directly to the postmaster general are the assistant postmasters general of finance and administration, facilities, personnel, operations, research and engineering, and planning and marketing, and a general counsel and a chief postal inspector.

The previous 15 postal regions were reduced to 5, each headed by a regional postmaster general, and each fully responsible for postal operations within its territory.

An Office of Consumer Affairs, headed by a consumer advocate who represents the interests of the mail customers and reports to the postmaster general, was an innovation in the new system.

The new service was to be funded by a general public service subsidy through 1979 in an amount equal to 10% of the appropriations to the Post Office Department in 1971. The Postal Service was also authorized to borrow from the general public in the form of bonds up to $10,000,000,000.

III. OTHER COUNTRIES

1. Australia.—The Australian Post Office, the nation's biggest business undertaking, handles over 2,700,000,000 articles of mail a year. Most of this mail passes through the six capital city mail exchanges, one of which, the Sydney Mail Exchange, is the largest in the world using an electronic letter-sorting system. A four-digit postcode to be added to addresses was introduced in mid-1967 and is borne on nearly 90% of Australian mail.

Letters are carried by air, free of surcharge, within Australia and its territories. Over 1,400 places have regular air services. Services now include special despatch mail for guaranteed overnight service between capital cities, discounted rates for bulk presorted mail, low-rate householder mail service for blanket deliveries in specified areas, and "Post Office-preferred" sizes of envelopes.

Australian postal engineers have since 1930 been in the forefront of design of mechanized mail-handling systems. Some of their designs, such as parcel-sorting systems and electronic letter-sorting equipment, have been adapted in other countries.

2. Canada.—The postal service commenced in the French regime in 1705. It expanded under the British crown and in 1763 Benjamin Franklin established post offices at Quebec, Trois Rivières, and Montreal. The Post Office continued to establish offices and mail services as villages were founded. There are now over 10,000 post offices and 8,000 transportation services handling some 5,000,000,000 pieces of mail annually.

Domestic airmail not exceeding 25 lb. in weight and prepaid at the first-class rate is carried by air. Airmail connections are available to most countries in the world. The Canada Post Office has introduced improved mail-handling techniques and equipment to keep abreast of the rapid growth in the volume of mail handled.

3. Federal Republic of Germany.—The Deutsche Bundespost is run as a federal administration with its own administrative structure. Its head is the federal minister of posts and telecommunications, responsible to Parliament; he is assisted by the Administrative Council of the Deutsche Bundespost. Below come the medium-level federal authorities comprising the 21 regional postal directorates and the directorate of Land Berlin, a Telecommunication Engineering and Research Centre, a Postal Engineering Centre, a Welfare Office, and two Engineering Academies. They control the lower-level authorities; i.e., about 26,500 offices in both postal and telecommunication services.

Article 87 of the Basic Law of the Federal Republic and a new Postal Law of 1969 form the legal basis for the postal services. By law, the federal capital available to the Deutsche Bundespost and acquired in the administration of its services is separated from all other federal funds. Because of its financial autonomy, the Deutsche Bundespost has to cover from its own revenues the expenditure necessary to fulfill its functions. In addition, a contribution of $6\frac{2}{3}\%$ of the yearly operating revenues has to be paid to the federal government.

Postal services comprise the usual mail, telecommunications, and financial services, as well as pension payments and sale of social security contribution stamps. These functions are executed with modern technical means (automation, mechanization, electronic data processing, rationalization). The Deutsche Bundespost uses the most rapid means of transportation for the conveyance of mail and has the largest motor vehicle fleet in Europe.   (X.)

4. France.—The date of the creation of a state postal service in France is generally given as that of the Edict of Luxies promulgated by Louis XI in 1464, but the authenticity of this edict is disputed by some historians. Over the centuries the organization of the service was modified by different sovereigns, always tending to reduce the privileges enjoyed by private messengers and to strengthen the control of the royal power over the postal service. The culmination of this policy was the consuls' edict of the 27th Prairial, Year IX (June 16, 1801), of which the sections establishing the foundations of the postal monopoly are still valid. The system of leasing out the postal service was maintained until the Revolution. It was abolished in 1792 and the service was raised to the status of a national agency. A law of 1848 fixed a uniform inland postage rate and introduced postage stamps for prepayment.

Apart from the use of balloons for transporting mail from the besieged Paris in 1871, the first experimental air link was effected in 1913 between Paris and Pauillac. Following the creation of the first air transport company in 1918, France was quickly linked with Morocco, Senegal, and South America. An inland air service began in 1933 but there was no real network until after World War II.

In the course of the 19th century and the first half of the 20th, various services were attached to the postal administration, notably money orders (1817), telegraphs (1878), National Savings Bank (1881), telephones (1889), and postal checks (1918). The traditional classification of mail and tariff rates of postal charges were changed on Jan. 13, 1969, when they were reframed on the basis of speed of delivery required by the sender.

(J.-P. G.)

5. India.—The postal system of India dates back to 1837. In 1947, the British left behind a well-knit postal system. Since then the postal services have made further strides, and India has perhaps the largest number of post offices among the countries of the world: in 1969 there were 102,477 post offices, of which over 90% were, thanks to the government's liberal policy with regard to the opening of post offices even at loss, in backward and rural areas. A post office serves an area of 11.7 sq.mi. and a population of 4,350 as compared with an area of 57 sq.mi. and population of 16,000 in 1947; 320,000 villages get daily delivery of mails. The rapid industrialization of the country has in its turn led to an increase in postal traffic which has imposed a heavy strain on the postal services. To cope with this, a large number of branch and extradepartmental offices have been converted into departmental sub-offices, besides 16 mobile and 69 night post offices having been opened in urban areas. Better training facilities have been developed and some projects for postal mechanization have also been initiated.

India has arrangements for air parcel services with most countries. The Post Office also discharges certain agency functions such as savings bank, sale of Post Office certificates, collection of wireless licence fee, postal life insurance, etc.

India is a pioneer in the field of airmail, the mail having been flown by air as far back as 1911. The night airmail service and the all-up scheme introduced immediately after independence have effected improvements in delivery. India is one of the first countries to carry all first-class mail by air without surcharge and to have introduced a uniform rate of postage for airmail postcards and aerograms. (H. N. V.)

6. Italy.—In 1862 the Italian government reserved to itself the right to collect, carry, and deliver mail, introduced the uniform tariff, and established the registered mail service. Express mail was started in 1890. The first traveling post offices began their activities in 1854. Surface transportation by sea was introduced in 1862 and by rail in 1865. The first official mail transport was effected in 1917.

The Posts and Telecommunications Administration has a monopoly for the forwarding of parcels up to 20 kg. (44 lb.) weight (1923) but private individuals and/or companies may operate such service under licence. They also may freely collect, carry, and deliver printed matter and newspapers, this monopoly having ceased in 1873.

The postal savings service was established in 1875 for booklets and in 1924 for bonds. It is operated on behalf of the Deposit and Loan Fund in competition with the banks.

Postal money orders, already in use in the Kingdom of Sardinia (only for military personnel) since 1818, were extended to civilians in 1849 and to united Italy from 1862. Checking accounts were established in 1917. The postal administration contributes to the implementation of social welfare programs by paying out government pensions and INPS (National Welfare Institute) pensions and making disbursements on behalf of other government agencies and welfare institutions.

In 1965 the night airmail service was established; it provides for the forwarding-on of mail and parcels by air without requiring additional airmail postage. As from Oct. 1, 1967, Italy introduced postcode numbers based on a five-figure code.

A minister is in charge of the Posts and Telecommunications Administration. He is assisted by a director general. (A. P.)

7. Japan.—Japan's modern postal service came into being in 1871 when a regular transportation of mail between Tokyo-Kyoto-Osaka was commenced with squads of foot carriers in relay, who made the distance of 550 km. (340 mi.) in 78 hr. The following year saw the service cover the entire country, and in 1873 the postal service was made the monopoly of the government.

The Post Office savings and remittance services were begun in 1875, and in 1877 Japan joined the Universal Postal Union. The Post Office life insurance and annuities services were inaugurated in 1916.

The telegraph service, which began in 1870, was taken over by the Postal Ministry in 1885, and the telephone service was introduced in 1890. But these services were severed from the Postal Ministry in 1949, and are now conducted by the Japan Telegraph and Telephone Public Corporation and the International Telegraph and Telephone Company, over whose activities the Ministry of Postal Services exercises supervisory function, as over radio activities in general.

The country is divided into 10 regional postal directorates. As of June 1969, the postal ministry has under it 20,310 post offices, including their branches and agencies, with a total of 320,000 employees.

Standardization of letter mail and construction of centralized post offices specializing in the processing of bulk and parcel mails in major cities have been undertaken. The automatic letter culling-facing-cancelling machine and the zip code reader-sorter, the latter capable of reading the handwritten code figures optically and doing the sorting accordingly, have come to be of practical use in coping with the mounting increase of mail. (S. Eg.)

8. New Zealand.—In 1831, the postmaster-general of New South Wales appointed a representative, William Powditch, in the Bay of Islands. In 1840, the first official New Zealand post office was established at Kororareka (now Russell). By 1858, when the Post Office was separated from the Customs Department, there were 73 separate offices, by 1860 there were 107, and toward the end of the 1960s there were about 1,400. Adhesive postage stamps, first printed in England, were introduced in 1855. By 1860, the government was printing its own stamps at Auckland. Penny postage was introduced in 1901 including service with the rest of the Commonwealth and many foreign countries. Airmail services were inaugurated between the larger centres of the country in 1936 and between Auckland and Sydney, and New Zealand and North America, in 1940.

In 1881 the first telephone exchange, with 27 subscribers, was installed at Christchurch. In 1963 New Zealand was linked with Great Britain by the Commonwealth undersea telephone cable system, "Compac."

Since 1867 the Post Office has provided savings-bank facilities. In this it acts as agent for Treasury, and all of its funds are made available to government for national development work. The New Zealand Post Office also acts as agent for such departments as agriculture, customs, social security, and transport. It also does agency work for the N.Z. Broadcasting Corporation, the State Advances Corporation, and Government Life Insurance Office.

In New Zealand, many postmasters are registrars of electors, and registrars of births, deaths, and marriages. (G. C. H.)

9. Pakistan.—The foremost problem faced by Pakistan, when created in 1947, related to maintenance of efficient communications between its two zones separated by 1,000 mi. of Indian territory. This was solved by having an all-up airmail service between the two zones for letters, postcards, and money orders. The surcharge on other correspondence was also very much reduced and at the same time the sea route was quickly developed. The sailings between Karachi and Chittagong range between 5 to 7 a month either way. The second urgent challenge was to reorientate communications to help develop rural areas where 80% of the population lives. This has been met by expansion without regard to immediate profitability. The total number of post offices at the beginning of the 1970s was 13,537 as against 6,446 in 1947.

Karachi and Chittagong are linked by both sea and air to practically all the countries of the world. Having secured the basic requirements, Pakistan progressed toward modernization of services. Electromechanical letter-sorting machines, franking and letter-cancelling machines, etc., have been extensively brought into use, and Post Office mail motor fleets have been established in large towns. (K. A. R.)

10. South Africa.—The first regular postal service was introduced in South Africa in 1803 when communication was established between Cape Town and the important centres by Hottentot postboys. These foot messengers were replaced by horsed post orderlies, and subsequently the development of railways made rapid communication possible on an extensive scale. Later the internal air services provided a means of transmission for letters. The four states of South Africa maintained their separate post offices until the formation of the Union in 1910, when a centralized postal administration was formed. (X.)

11. Sweden.—The Swedish Post Office was founded in 1636 by a royal ordination. In 1820 the Post Office started to forward newspapers. The forwarding of printed matter began in 1864. In 1834 an organized special conveyance of parcels was introduced. Forwarding by rail was organized in 1860. In 1920 mail for the first time carried by air.

The Post Office is entrusted with the payment of national old-age pensions and child allowances and it takes tax payments. Ballots for the general elections can also be delivered there. The Post Office Bank was inaugurated in 1883 and the postal giro in 1924. The postal giro conducts payments but it also undertakes the payment of salaries, collection of rents and such things for companies and government organizations. The Post Office Bank is divided into the savings bank and the postal giro and is one of the biggest credit granters on the Swedish capital market.

The Post Office is an agency managed by a director general who is chairman of a board constituted by the king in council. The agencies are subordinate to the king in council and must obey directives, given as orders in council. A minister may not give orders directly to an agency. The Post Office central administration is divided into three parts. The country is for administrative purposes divided into seven postal areas, each managed by a director.

For the forwarding and distribution of post the country is divided into about 40 sorting areas, whose boundaries mainly coincide with those of the local government areas. (NI. H.)

12. U.S.S.R.—The Soviet Post Office is one of the oldest in Europe, and in the 13th century the so-called carriage express (postal stations with horses and drivers for the transport of couriers) was created. Gradually the carriage express was changed into an organized service. In the second half of the 19th century railways and steamboats provided a new technical basis for the development of a postal network. By 1913 there were 7,618 communication centres in the Russian Empire, but more than four-fifths of them were in European Russia and many centres of population were more than 50 mi. from the nearest post office.

By 1960 the number of postal communication centres in the U.S.S.R. had increased eight times in comparison with 1913. More than three-quarters of them were in rural areas, as compared with only 3% in 1913. Between 1913 and 1969 the length of railway postal routes had increased ten times and that of water routes six times; the volume of mail carried by train had increased nine times and that by water five times. Besides road transport, express trains, airplanes, and steamboats, use was made of fast launches, hydrofoils, and airscrew-driven sledges. The sorting and handling of mails and parcels was becoming fully mechanized. Over 6,000,000,000 letters and printed matter were handled, 148,000,000 telegrams forwarded and delivered in 1968, as well as 600,000,000 money orders and pensions worth 67,000,000 rubles. Deliveries of newspapers and magazines reached 30,000,000,000 copies.

The U.S.S.R. Ministry of Communications is in charge of the postal system organized on the radial-centre principle including 80,000 post offices and centres of which about 60,000 are in the countryside. (X.)

IV. INTERNATIONAL POSTAL SERVICE

1. Early History.—The importance of the international mail service is evident from the earliest days of postal history, but the working of the service is somewhat obscure. In the 16th century a regular service seems to have been provided between London and Calais, France. In 1670, a regular postal treaty was concluded between England and France. This was renewed in 1698 after the conclusion of the Treaty of Rijswijk. The postal treaty provided that the mail being sent from London to Paris and from Paris to London was to leave twice a week. Between Dover and Calais the English Post Office provided the mail packets in both directions; the service beyond Calais was provided by France. Letters could be prepaid to only three destinations—Paris, Rouen, or Lyons; any charges for further transmission were collected from the addressee. This treaty, soon interrupted by further hostilities, was again renewed in 1713. The new version contained the germ of the international system of accounting for transit mails which lasted with but slight alteration until the latter part of the 19th century. On letters for Italy, which could be franked to Turin, England was to pay France at the rate of 21 sols per single letter; on letters for Spain franked to Bayonne the payment was 19 sols; on letters for Turkey franked to Marseilles, 17 sols. The accounting between the two offices was based on the sum of the amounts due on the separate letters, mail by mail. The principles adopted in the 17th century showed little change in the 18th, and a treaty concluded with France in 1802 showed comparatively little variation from its predecessors of more than a century before.

As time went on the postal treaties required for the establishment of a gradually expanding foreign service became more and more numerous and complicated. The postage depended on the sums payable to the national post offices concerned in the transit of the letters, and these were often based on their own internal rates and units of weight. The result was an extraordinary variety of rates. Prepayment was in some cases compulsory, in some cases optional; but compulsory prepayment covered conveyance only up to a certain point, all charges beyond that point being collected from the addressee. In 1856 the lowest postage in force was that between England and France, which was 4d. per ¼ oz. A letter from England to Belgrade, Serbia, via France, weighing over three-quarters of an ounce and up to one ounce, cost 4s. 4d.; a half-ounce letter to California via Panama cost 2s. 4d., in addition to a further charge on delivery. Even to Spain the postage was 2s. 2d. per ½ oz., plus a charge on delivery.

From the point of view of post-office management, the industrial development of the 19th century and the constant growth of correspondence caused the service to become so complex that rapid and accurate handling of the mails was practically impossible. Almost the only advance made over 17th-century procedure was that letters were weighed in bulk instead of singly. The example of a simple and uniform tariff had been set by the establishment of internal penny postage, but the principle which underlay this (viz., that the cost of conveyance of a letter represented only a small fraction of the total cost of its treatment) was far from being applicable to the conditions of the international post.

2. Formation of the Universal Postal Union.—The first step in the direction of reform was taken by the United States, which in 1862 suggested a conference for the purpose of considering the improvement and simplification of international postal relations. The conference met in Paris in 1863 and adopted a code of 31 articles, intended to serve as the basis of bilateral international conventions. Further progress was delayed first by the American Civil War and then by the Franco-German War.

In the meantime, however, another great postal reformer, Heinrich von Stephan of the North German Postal Confederation, had prepared a plan for a universal postal union, based in part on the conclusions of the conference and in part on the experience of Germany, which several years before had formed a postal union including Prussia, Austria, and all the other German states, nearly 20 in number. The Swiss government, at the instance of Germany, summoned a conference to meet at Bern to consider the proposal to form a general postal union.

The Congress of Bern in 1874 was attended by the representatives of 22 countries, including all the countries of Europe plus the United States and Egypt. The result was the signature of the first International Postal Convention, which created the General Union of Posts and replaced the plethora of bilateral arrangements. Membership increased rapidly and in 1878 the name was changed to the Universal Postal Union.

Ten years after its foundation the Union included 55 member countries and by the end of the 19th century nearly all parts of the world were included. At the beginning of the 1970s the Union had about 140 members.

3. Principles of the Union.—The international convention, which from 1875, with comparatively little modification, remained the foundation of the international postal service, set forth five main principles. The first and fundamental principle was contained in a striking article which stated that for the purposes of postal communication all the signatory countries formed a single territory. The practical application of this principle lies in the doctrine of liberty of transit; every member of the union binds itself to transmit the mails entrusted to it by every other member by the best means of communication which it employs for its own mail. Thus each country has in effect the full and unrestricted use of the transportation services of the whole world, and any improvement made by any member of the Union is placed at the disposal of any other which desires to utilize it.

The second principle was the uniformity of postage rates and of units of weight. The Congress of Bern adopted the rate of 25 gold centimes per 15 grams for letters, but permitted a certain variation within a definite maximum and minimum, and the rate of 7 gold centimes, with a similar variation, per 50 grams of printed papers. In 1878, however, standard uniform rates in gold centimes were adopted for letters, postcards, and printed papers; these rates were retained unaltered until 1920. The only variation allowed was the addition of a surtax when heavy costs for sea transport were incurred. The conditions following World War I swept away the uniformity which had prevailed for 40 years and brought about a reversion to the original principle of a maximum and a minimum rate; this has been maintained ever since. The only change in the units of weight has been the raising of the letter unit from 15 to 20 g., or to one ounce for English-speaking countries.

The third principle was the classification of postal correspondence into three groups—letters, postcards, and other matter (including printed papers, commercial papers, and samples). Definite conditions of acceptance, as well as separate rates of postage, were adopted; the delicate distinctions between what can be sent at the cheap rate and what must be charged as a letter depend on international decisions binding on individual countries. By the end of the 1960s there was, however, a trend toward simplification in this field as the category "commercial papers" was abolished and transmission speed rather than contents of the items became the determining factor for tariffication.

The fourth principle was the adoption of definite payments to be made by the country which dispatched mails by the trains or steamships of another country for the use of those services. The only exception to this principle is that no payment is made to the country of destination, the flow of correspondence in each direction being assumed to be approximately equal.

The fifth principle was the universal adoption of a system of registration and compensation. International registration differs from internal registration in one important particular: the compensation payable is a fixed amount and is allowed only in the event of the entire loss of the registered item and not for damage to or loss of contents. This principle the Union has steadily maintained from its inception.

4. Later Changes.—The original convention applied only to letter mails, but supplementary agreements were soon adopted at successive congresses for various extensions of the postal service. In 1878 an agreement for an international money order service was signed by a considerable number of countries. At the same time an insurance service, which provided for payment of compensation for loss or damage of letters containing documents of value (paper money, etc.), was established. This was later extended to cover insured boxes containing valuables such as gold or jewelry. The amount insured varies with the fee paid, and the maximum varies in different countries.

A further important advance was made in 1880 when 19 countries concluded a parcel post agreement. The original agreement was limited to parcels not exceeding three kilograms; it prescribed a simple procedure and fixed rates of payment for both terminal and transit countries. The scope of the service expanded considerably and provided for insurance and cash on delivery. These supplementary agreements were not adopted universally throughout the Union, but, where separate agreements had to be concluded, they generally followed with only slight variations the principles sanctioned by the Union. In 1947 the Union became a specialized agency of the United Nations.

5. The Postal Union Organization.—Most questions are settled between the countries immediately concerned, serious disputes being dealt with by a system of compulsory arbitration. For matters in which the whole Union is concerned, however, an International Bureau is maintained at Bern, Switz. This serves as a centre of information and consultation and, if required, as a clearinghouse in the settlement of accounts. It is the only permanent organ of the Union and acts as a general secretariat for the higher organs. A congress meets, usually every five years, to review the Union's legislation, every member being invited to send delegates. A 27-member Executive Council meets annually in Switzerland to maintain contact with the United Nations and other international organizations, supervise the International Bureau and appoint the higher officials of the Bureau.

A Consultative Committee for Postal Studies (CCPS) was created in 1957 to undertake a more thorough study of economic, technical, and operational problems in the postal service. The Management Council of the CCPS also meets annually and comprises 26 countries.

6. Commonwealth Preferential Postage.—The idea of adopting preferential postage rates on political grounds began to develop in the era following the establishment of the Universal Postal Union, and it was decided in 1897 that the postal union convention should permit the establishment, by agreement, of rates below the standard postage. This decision, coinciding with a growth of the feeling of the unity of the Commonwealth of Nations, led to the introduction by the United Kingdom in 1899, following a special conference, of "imperial penny postage" at a rate of $1d$. per $\frac{1}{2}$ oz. to Canada, India, South Africa, and the crown colonies generally; it was extended to New Zealand in 1901 and Australia in 1905. Certain foreign countries, including the United States, which were closely linked with the United Kingdom by tradition or trade, were subsequently included in the scheme, but the preferential rate to these countries was withdrawn in 1957 for financial reasons. Throughout the various changes in letter postage brought about by World Wars I and II the principle of maintaining the initial Commonwealth letter rate at the same point as the initial inland rate has been uniformly observed.

(R. A. Le.; X.)

Bibliography.—Rowland Hill, *Post Office Reform: Its Importance and Practicability*, 4th ed. (1838); *Report of Secret Committee on the Post Office* (1844); *Annual Reports* of the postmaster general (1854–1915); W. Lewins, *Her Majesty's Mails*, 2nd ed. (1865); H. Joyce, *The History of the Post Office* (1893); A. H. Norway, *History of the Post-Office Packet Service* (1895); H. Swift, *A History of Postal Agitation* (1900); *The Post Office: an Historical Summary* (1911); J. C. Hemmeon, *The History of the British Post Office* (1912); *Handwörterbuch des Postwesens* (1927); Sir George E. P. Murray, *The Post Office* (1927); E. Vaillé, *Histoire générale des postes françaises* (1947); H. Robinson, *The British Post Office* (1948); *Britain's Post Office* (1953); *Postal Union Convention* (1952); *Convention of the Pan-American Postal Union* (1955); *The Universal Postal Union: Its Foundation and Development* (1955); annual *Rapports de gestion* of International Bureau and *Statistiques générales* of the Postal Union; parliamentary *Reports* on the post office, *passim;* Kenneth Ellis, *Post Office in the Eighteenth Century* (1958); Frank Staff, *Transatlantic Mail* (1956); W. E. Fuller, *R.F.D., the Changing Face of Rural America* (1964).

POSTCARD, a card for transmitting a message that can be mailed without an envelope. The first government-issued cards were the straw-coloured Austrian *Korrespondenz Karte* (with a two-kreuzer stamp) issued in October 1869.

In the United States John P. Charlton of Philadelphia in 1861 obtained a copyright for privately printed cards decorated with a border pattern; the copyright later passed to his fellow townsman, M. L. Lipman. The U.S. government issued postal cards with imprinted stamps in May 1873. Until 1898 privately printed souvenir cards required a two-cent stamp (double the amount of the government card) if they bore a message.

Germany, Switzerland, and Great Britain followed Austria's example in supplying postcards through the post offices. The British buff and violet cards, imprinted with the halfpenny stamp, were issued in October 1870 and sold 76,000,000 in the first year.

Various claims to the invention of the picture postcard have been made. The best known is perhaps that of Léon Besnardeau of Sillé-le-Guillaume, near Le Mans, France, who devised a card for Breton soldiers during the Franco-German War. These postcards bore an engraving of the battlefield, with stacked arms, around a space for the address.

Postcards bearing small engraved views appeared in the 1870s in Germany and Austria, but in Great Britain their publication was not possible until 1894, when the post office relinquished the right to charge the letter rate on any card other than the official one. Designers were hampered by the rule forbidding correspondence on the side that carried the address. This rule was waived in Britain in 1897, in France in 1903, in Germany in 1905, and in the U.S. in 1907.

Artists who designed postcards at the beginning of the 20th century included Alphonse Mucha, Phil May (*q.v.*), and Louis Wain. Photomontage (superimposition of photographs) and the combination of drawing and photography were introduced for postcards. At first coloured by hand, colour printing of photographs was adopted by Edwin Bamforth, whose "song and hymn" cards became very popular during World War I.

Collecting picture postcards was an immensely popular hobby in the first decade of the 20th century. Societies and journals dealing with postcards existed in most countries, while a number of societies continued in the U.S. in the second half of the century. The postcard remains an important item of stationery trade.

See R. C. Carline, *Pictures in the Post: the Story of the Picture Postcard* (1959); J. R. Burdick (ed.), *Pioneer Post Cards* (1957); C. Lauterbach and A. Jakovsky, *A Picture Postcard Album,* trans. by J. Bradley (1961).   (R. C. Ca.)

POSTER. A poster is an announcement publicly exhibited which is designed to be understood at a glance. Advertising an event, product or service, the poster must combine immediate visual effectiveness with concise communication of a message; it must compete for attention in visually confusing surroundings and yet inform the spectator or communicate the advertiser's message to him. The design of posters is a challenge to the artist, and besides their value as commercial objects many posters are of aesthetic interest. Some noted artists have designed posters, and their work has been studied and collected by students of the arts.

History and Development.—A kind of advertising closely related to the poster is the signboard or shop sign, hand painted on a wall or on a piece of wood. Signboards of this kind are still used widely, and they have been present in cities and towns through the ages. In their use of a striking symbol rendered in bold shapes and colours, with wording kept to a minimum, these signs are undoubtedly among the ancestors of the modern poster. But in modern times most posters are printed, and identical copies are posted in many different locations joining familiarity with visual impact in the advertising campaign for which the poster is used.

Printing (*q.v.*), as it now exists, dates from the middle of the 15th century. The first posters which have been preserved date from the early years of printing. Composed almost entirely of text, these posters carried notices of royal proclamations, tax assessments, fairs, markets and newly printed books. From a note on the bottom of one such poster (issued by an English printer and bookseller) it is known that these were meant to be left posted in public places, and hence they were an economical means of

CAXTON'S ADVERTISEMENT, PRINTED 1477, THE EARLIEST PRINTER'S ADVERTISEMENT IN ENGLISH

The handwriting ("Pray, do not pull down the Advertisement"), a later addition, translates the statement in Latin at the end of the notice

carrying a message to great numbers of persons.

Illustrations appear on posters from the early period of printmaking. Handbills often illustrated with crude but spirited woodcuts were used as broadsides which recounted notable happenings; these were essentially newssheets in poster form. The widespread use of posters to advertise products for sale (other than books) does not seem to occur before the early years of the 19th century.

Beginnings of the Modern Poster.—In the 19th century the expansion of industry gave new impetus to poster advertising. Now wealthy patronage was available, and there had also been devised a new method of printing—lithography (*q.v.*)—which allowed brilliantly coloured posters to be produced cheaply and easily. Since the process allows the image to be drawn directly onto the printing surface, and does not physically alter the drawing in preparing it for printing, artists soon saw in lithography a medium which allowed them to design posters freely and simply. The firm of Rouchon in Paris was one of the pioneers in poster printing, and boldly coloured lithographic posters issued from it as early as 1845. Among the earliest French artists whose work was utilized for posters are Paul Baudry and Denis Auguste Raffet.

But it was not until 1867 that the first of the great modern poster artists began his career. Jules Chéret left Paris as a young man, in 1856, to study colour lithography in London. When he returned ten years later, he immediately became interested in the problem of designing theatrical posters. In 1867 Chéret's first poster was published, announcing the appearance of Sarah Bernhardt in the play *La Biche au Bois*. Chéret's style immediately attracted great interest; he used clear, rather pastel colours and shimmering, vignetted backgrounds, against which he placed delicate and elegant figures. His lettering was bold and gaily coloured, and the whole effect of his posters is extremely arresting. The visual impact of Chéret's work, coupled with the fact that he was a prolific worker (he designed about 1,000 posters), makes his designs a major influence on later 19th-century posters. But there were other developments as well. During the last quarter of the 19th century there was an expansion of the realm of the fine arts. Artists no longer felt constrained to work only in painting or sculpture, but turned as well to designing furnishings, books, textiles and other useful things. Posters were not neglected. Painters such as Edouard Manet, Pierre Bonnard, Edouard Vuillard, and Henri de Toulouse-Lautrec all worked in the field, and the last-named is one of the great masters of the medium.

Toulouse-Lautrec was a master of trenchant characterization, and the means he used in his posters were bold and simple. Inspired by the work of Manet and Edgar Degas, as well as by Japanese colour woodcuts, Toulouse-Lautrec rendered his designs in large, interestingly shaped areas of bold colour and simple values. He used an exceedingly restricted range of colours and textures, carefully combining his shapes with line for maximum visual effectiveness. His line was bold, but sinuous and sensitive, and his backgrounds were the utmost in simplicity—often consisting of the blank paper itself carefully worked into the design of the whole poster. The lettering of Toulouse-Lautrec's posters was kept to a minimum, and the style of letter he used picked up

BY COURTESY OF THE VICTORIA AND ALBERT MUSEUM

(LEFT) COLOURED LITHOGRAPH POSTER BY T. A. STEINLEN FOR THE AMBAS-SADEURS CABARET IN PARIS ADVERTISING THE NIGHTLY PERFORMANCE OF YVETTE GUILBERT, (1894); (RIGHT) COLOURED LITHOGRAPH POSTER BY HENRI DE TOULOUSE-LAUTREC FOR "DIVAN JAPONAIS," (1892)

curving rhythms and colours from the illustrations, welding the entire poster into a unified design. He produced his first poster in 1891, after more than ten years' work at painting and drawing. Between 1891 and 1899 he produced about 30 posters—among them several for clients in England and in the United States.

A contemporary of Toulouse-Lautrec whose work is closely related in style is T. A. Steinlen. The two men worked for some of the same clients, and in fact Steinlen's style seems to have been one of the influences upon Toulouse-Lautrec's early posters. The boldness of their work made Toulouse-Lautrec and Steinlen pioneers of a new movement in poster design, and their influence was felt in every European country and in the United States during the 1890s.

The imprint of these French artists can be found in the work of Edward Penfield and Will Bradley in the U.S. The posters of the "Beggarstaff Brothers" (William Nicholson and James Pryde) in England carry boldness and simplicity even further. Another English artist, Aubrey Beardsley, designed a few posters which had an impact comparable to Toulouse-Lautrec's. Beardsley's elegantly curved thin line, equally elegant solid shapes, and his elaborate linear and dotted textures created a mood of luxurious and almost mysterious sensuousness. Around 1900 many young artists found this attractive, and Beardsley must join Toulouse-Lautrec as one of the main sources in poster and illustrative art for the so-called *art nouveau* (*q.v.*). England and the U.S. had begun to produce illustrated posters in the 1870s, and with the addition of a style of illustration deriving from the popular painting of the time (*i.e.*, the adaptation of Sir John E. Millais' "Bubbles" into a soap poster in England), the posters designed in these countries generally followed French developments. Artists in other European countries produced work along similar lines.

20th-Century Posters.—Around 1900 several new movements in art were forming in the Netherlands, in Germany and in Austria. In the field of poster design, France had previously been a leader, but now for the first time its supremacy as a source for innovation was challenged. Developing further some of the ideas first enunciated by John Ruskin and William Morris, these artists showed an interest in crafts, techniques and in machine-made forms; this interest motivated them to make use of simple colour schemes based on primary colours, geometrically derived patterns, etc. Their efforts culminated in the work of the Bauhaus at Weimar and Dessau (1919–28) in Germany. The Bauhaus was an art school, and the work of both professors and students gave a new direction to design in posters and in every other field. Although its posters were actually of little significance in themselves, and despite the fact that its more radical innovations were subsequently abandoned, the Bauhaus (*q.v.*) remained the major

influence through the mid-20th century. Artists such as Herbert Bayer, Josef Albers, Gyorgy Kepes and later E. McKnight Kauffer organized lettering and pictorial matter into clearly defined rectangular and curved areas. Elaboration of colour and of letter forms was kept to a minimum, and some designers even gave up the use of mixed upper- and lower-case letters to avoid distracting variations in size and shape.

With the growth of the advertising industry in the 20th century, the poster assumed greater importance than ever. Cassandre, Carlu and Savignac were typical of the better French poster designers of the generation following World War I; their work combined simplicity and visual force with genuine wit, and the fame of their posters became world-wide. During World Wars I and II, the major powers involved paid tribute to the effectiveness of the poster in according it many tasks: armed forces were recruited, bond issues advertised, participation in the war effort maintained, all by use of large-scale poster campaigns. James Montgomery Flagg and Ben Shahn were typical of the artists who designed posters for the United States in World Wars I and II, respectively.

Another widespread use of posters is to advertise the services of transportation companies. A pioneer in this field was the London Transport company in England, which began in 1908 not only to advertise its services but also to commission prominent and promising artists to design posters describing places which could be reached using the facilities of London Transport. Undoubtedly the entire travel-poster industry owes much to the initiative of the directors of London Transport. By the 1930s virtually every major transportation company was publishing and distributing posters. With the increase in the use of posters in the 20th century, it became necessary to institute measures for the control and limitation of public advertising. Laws to control the dimensions and placement of hanging signs were instituted as early as the 18th century both in England and in France, and similar regulations exist in modern times in many countries the world over. In the 20th century city governmental authority has been exercised to limit the placement of posters on walls, and there exist standardizing and limiting measures to govern the use of free-standing billboards. *See also* ADVERTISING.

BIBLIOGRAPHY.—E. McKnight Kauffer (ed.), *The Art of the Poster, Its Origin, Evolution and Purpose* (1925), *Art for All: London Transport Posters From 1908 to 1949* (1949, 1950); Bernard Champigneulle, "The Earliest Known Colour Posters" in *Graphis # 50* (1953); W. von zur Westen, *Reklamekunst aus zwei jahrtausenden* (1925); Ervine Metzl, *The Poster: Its History and Its Art* (1963); Hellmut Rademacher, *Das Deutsche Plakat* (1965); *Outdoor Advertising Association News; Graphis; Gebrauchsgraphik; Journal of Advertising Art* (periodicals). *See also* numerous monographs on individual poster designers.
(A. M. FN.)

POSTIMPRESSIONISM is a collective designation for isolated trends that arose in late 19th-century French painting out of dissatisfaction with the formlessness and limited aims of Impressionism (*q.v.*). In no sense a movement, it is summed up in the individual researches of Cézanne, Seurat, Van Gogh, and Gauguin, whose achievements, if unvalued in their own time, became signposts for the main directions of the modern movement.

After a phase of uneasy dissension among the Impressionists, Paul Cézanne (*q.v.*) withdrew from the movement in 1878, in order "to make of Impressionism something solid and durable like the art of the museums." In 1884, at the Salon des Artistes Indépendants, Georges Seurat (*q.v.*) revealed a like intention with his picture "Une Baignade-Asnières." Cézanne studied indefatigably to present nature in terms of advancing and receding planes (*see also* CUBISM). Seurat's investigations into the science of colour and into aesthetic theories led him to develop the Pointillist technique, his unerring sense of relationships between tones, intervals and accents reinforcing his Impressionist subject matter with a secure scaffolding and a harmonious unity.

Cézanne worked in isolation at Aix; his solitude was matched by that of Paul Gauguin (*q.v.*) in the Pacific and of Vincent Van Gogh (*q.v.*) at Arles. Gauguin, after he had exhibited at the eighth and final group show of the Impressionists in 1886, renounced "the abominable error of naturalism" and began to paint imaginative concepts, as distinct from imitations, of form. He set out for the South Seas where his search for simplicity culminated in a richly coloured and decorative symbolism. Van Gogh arrived in Paris in 1886 and was attracted to Impressionist colour and the Pointillist technique. In his remaining years, he made use of these influences, not as techniques of recording, but for expressing his acutely felt emotions. *See also* MODERN ART.

BIBLIOGRAPHY.—C. L. Hind, *The Post-Impressionists* (1911); R. E. Fry, *Characteristics of French Art* (1932); J. Laver, *French Painting and the Nineteenth Century* (1937); J. Rewald, *Post-Impressionism: From Van Gogh to Gauguin* (1956); J. Canaday, *Mainstreams of Modern Art* (1959).   (F. W. W.-S.)

POSTLIMINY, a technical term that applies to the status of a government in its own territory when this territory has been reacquired from an invading enemy. The territory reacquired may have been the whole territory of the invaded country or merely a part. Originally the term was applied to a different situation. A Roman citizen lost all his civil property and matrimonial rights if he became the prisoner of war of an enemy. If he returned he was automatically restored to all his previous rights and obligations and that restoration was called postliminy. Some writers use the term in the old Roman sense, and a few apply it to other postwar restoration problems. An example of the latter would be the return of German assets sequestrated in the United States during World War II. (*See* ALIEN PROPERTY.)

Postliminy in its chief meaning, which applies to returning sovereigns, operates immediately, long before the peace treaty. Normally, in the international law of war, all final settlements are postponed until peace treaties are made. Under postliminy, however, the returning sovereign may act immediately as if the government had never been absent. Public property seized by the enemy is immediately reacquired. Enemy legislation may be canceled, even with retroactive effect. Property the enemy has seized and sold may be restored to the owner. Traitors and collaborationists may be punished. The logical implications of postliminy are so extreme that other rules of international law and morality have to operate against extreme abuses. For instance, it would be going too far under postliminy to annul all criminal sentences, to carry actions against collaborationists to the point of imposing standards of martyrdom on the population, or to collect debts and taxes already collected by the enemy.

BIBLIOGRAPHY.—Ernst H. Feilchenfeld, *The International Economic Law of Belligerent Occupation,* pp. 144–151 (1950); Kirchenheim, "Postliminium," in Karl Strupp, *Wörterbuch des Völkerrechts und der Diplomatie,* pp. 295–299 (1925); J. M. Spaight, *War Rights on Land,* pp. 366–367 (1911); Luigi Amironte, *Captivitas e postliminium* (1950).   (E. H. F.)

POST-MORTEM EXAMINATION: *see* AUTOPSY.

POSTULATE, a proposition assumed without proof in founding a mathematical discipline. Though the propositions of a particular mathematical discipline, or branch of mathematics, are generally established by proof, there must be some unproved first principles, if the process of basing one proposition on others from which it is proved is not to be an infinite regress. Similarly, although the terms used are generally introduced by definition, there must be some undefined terms. These unproved first principles are the *postulates,* and the terms not defined are the *primitive terms.* (*See* AXIOM; LOGIC, HISTORY OF.)

For example, in the case of Peano's postulates for arithmetic (so called after Giuseppe Peano, who proposed them as first principles of arithmetic, though the postulates themselves are due rather to C. S. Peirce and Richard Dedekind), the primitive terms are "0," "number" (in the sense of non-negative whole number) and "successor" (in the sense that $x + 1$ is the successor of x). And the postulates themselves are: (1) 0 is a number. (2) Every number has a number as its unique successor. (3) Two numbers having the same successor are identical. (4) 0 is not successor of any number. (5) If 0 belongs to a class $F,$ and if whenever a number x belongs to F the successor of x belongs also to $F,$ then all numbers belong to $F.$

These may be expressed in logistic notation (*see* LOGIC) by using an individual constant 0, and two functional constants N and S ("$N(x)$" to mean "x is a number," and "$S(x, y)$" to mean "y is successor of x"). However, the implicit assumption that it is only numbers that have successors is best represented by defining

$N(x)$ to stand for $(\exists y)S(x, y)$ (and $N(y)$ to stand for $(\exists x)S(y, x),$ etc.), so that the number of primitive terms is reduced to two. The statement of some of the postulates may then be simplified, and the second postulate is also conveniently divided into two parts: (1) $N(0).$ (2_1) $S(x, y) \supset N(y).$ (2_2) $S(x, y) \supset .$ $S(x, z) \supset y = z.$ (3) $S(y, x) \supset . S(z, x) \supset y = z.$ (4) $\sim S(x, 0).$ (5) $F(0) \supset . F(x)S(x, y) \supset_{xy} F(y) \supset . N(x) \supset_x F(x).$ The postulates have to be added to an underlying logic, which in this case must be a functional calculus of at least second order (*see* LOGIC) to make definitions possible of addition and multiplication of numbers.

Another familiar example of mathematical postulates is that of the postulates for elementary geometry. As in other cases, the postulates for a particular discipline are not uniquely determined, and various alternative systems of postulates are known. The original axioms and postulates of Euclid are the prototype of axiomatic treatments of geometry, and are in a certain sense still standard, though they do not satisfy modern requirements of rigour. For modern systems of postulates for geometry *see* the works of Hilbert and of Veblen, cited in the bibliography below.

According to the view now usual, the postulates constitute a definition of the particular mathematical discipline; and a change of one of the postulates to something different or contrary would not be wrong, but would merely lead to the definition of a different discipline. This contrasts with an older view according to which the postulates of arithmetic or of Euclidean geometry are a priori truths. The abandonment of the older view was brought about largely by the discovery of non-Euclidean geometry (*see* GEOMETRY, NON-EUCLIDEAN; MATHEMATICS, FOUNDATIONS OF), since Euclid's parallel postulate and its contradictory lead to two geometries which not only are equally sound logically but, in the absence of experimental evidence against the Euclidean postulate, would be equally applicable to physical space.

A set of postulates is called *consistent* if, in the mathematical discipline which the postulates determine, not both A and $\sim$ A are ever theorems. A particular postulate is *independent* if it is not a theorem of the discipline determined by the remaining postulates.

In general, a mathematical discipline based on a consistent set of postulates can be strengthened (without adding to the list of primitive terms) by adding new, independent postulates in various alternative ways. But if the set of postulates is *categorical,* there is a sense in which this is not possible. (*See* CATEGORICAL.)

Use of axioms and postulates for a rigorous account of the foundations of a branch of natural science is less usual than in mathematics, and its appropriateness is still the subject of controversy. Some reject the postulational form for theoretical science altogether. And some regard it as an ideal to which the development of a science approaches, not yet attained except in the case of applied geometry and possibly mechanics, and not a useful form in at least the present stage of most sciences. But a noteworthy attempt to apply the axiomatic method in biology is contained in the writings of J. H. Woodger, whose book (cited below) may be consulted both for this and for an expository account of the axiomatic or postulational method in general.

BIBLIOGRAPHY.—D. Hilbert, *Grundlagen der Geometrie* (1899, with later editions) and *The Foundations of Geometry,* Eng. trans. by E. J. Townsend (1902); O. Veblen, "A System of Axioms for Geometry," *Trans. Amer. Math. Soc.,* vol. 5, pp. 343–384 (1904); J. H. Woodger, *The Axiomatic Method in Biology* (1937).   (Ao. C.)

POTASSIUM, a silvery white metal with a brilliant lustre, is one of the most reactive of the metallic elements. This property is illustrated when it is dropped into water; hydrogen is displaced and both the hydrogen and the potassium take fire, burning with a violet flame that usually culminates in a slight explosion.

Potassium is not found in a free state in nature, but in combined form is distributed in nearly all soils and terrestrial waters and many rocks. It is important for the nutrition of plants, and its compounds are contained in most plant and animal tissues.

Potassium chloride is an important fertilizer. Other potassium compounds have a wide range of industrial and pharmaceutical applications. Metallic potassium has few uses, the most important being the preparation of potassium superoxide (KO_2) used in protective breathing equipment. In the rebreather gas mask, the KO_2 reacts with the exhaled air to liberate oxygen and remove carbon dioxide and water. A eutectic alloy of potassium and sodium containing 77.2% of potassium has been suggested as a liquid coolant for nuclear reactors. A potassium-sodium alloy is used to reduce titanium tetrafluoride, TiF_4, to the metal.

The symbol of potassium is K (from kalium, a Latinized form of the Arabic word for alkali). Its atomic number is 19, atomic weight 39.102.

Historical Background.—The history of potassium is closely linked to that of sodium. Materials containing their compounds, particularly carbonates and nitrates, were known and used in some of the earliest civilizations. Native sodium carbonate was used by the Egyptians for making glass as early as the 16th century B.C.; records originating in lower Mesopotamia and dating from the 17th century B.C. mention the use of saltpetre for making glazes. However, the ancient technicians and artisans who used these materials, having no knowledge of the chemical and physical methods of analysis and identification, did not distinguish between similar sodium and potassium compounds. The terms used were often general and implied the source rather than the chemical content of the material. Alkali (q.v.) originally referred only to the material obtained from the ashes of plants, sodium, and potassium carbonates. The term soda, of unknown etymology, was first applied to any alkali and later to the ash of sea plants, while the term potash (pot-ash) was applied to the ash of land vegetations, both of which generally contained a greater proportion of potassium carbonate. The two alkalies, soda and potash, were successively designated as natural and artificial and as mineral and vegetable. In the first decade of the 15th century, potassium salts were being produced in Scotland from the ashes of seaweed. Finally in the 18th century, after it was shown that the "mineral alkali" occurred in the ashes of sea plants and the "vegetable alkali" in a number of minerals, the terms soda and potash were properly applied to specific substances. Since the chemical nature of these common alkalies had not yet been determined, they were believed by some to be elements. A. Lavoisier did not include them in his list of elements, "because," he stated, "these substances are evidently compounds, although however, the nature of the principles which enter into their composition is still unknown." This problem was finally solved in 1807 by the brilliant young English chemist Sir Humphry Davy, who decomposed both the alkalies, obtaining the metals potassium and sodium. It was he who coined the word "potassium"—a Latinized version of "potash."

Since potassium is one of the strongest reducing agents known, it cannot be isolated by chemical reduction without resorting to unusual conditions which favour the necessary equilibrium shift and permit the removal of the product from the system as it is formed. It is therefore not surprising that potassium and the other alkali metals were prepared only after the discovery of current electricity (1800) and the subsequent development of electrolytic methods. Davy prepared potassium by the electrolysis of molten potassium hydroxide using platinum electrodes. He described the experiment:

A small piece of pure potash . . . was placed upon an insulated disc of platina, connected with the negative side of the battery . . . ; and a platina wire, communicating with the positive side, was brought in contact with the upper surface of the alkali. . . . The potash began to fuse at both its points of electrization. There was a violent effervescence at the upper surface; at the lower or negative surface, there was no liberation of elastic fluid, but small globules having a high metallic lustre . . . appeared, some of which burnt with explosion and bright flame, as soon as they were formed, and others remained, and were merely tarnished, and finally covered with a white film which formed on their surfaces. These globules, numerous experiments soon showed to be the substance I was in search of and a peculiar inflammable principle the basis of potash.

Occurrence and Production.—It is estimated that potassium constitutes about 2.59% of the igneous rocks of the earth's crust, ranking seventh in order of abundance of elements. Its compounds are widely distributed in the primary rocks, the oceans, the soil, plants, and animals. Although nearly as abundant as

sodium, it is less accessible, and relatively few workable mineral deposits are available; these contain saline residues formed by the evaporation of inland seas which existed in past geological eras. The largest known deposit was found in southeastern Saskatchewan, Can. The beds, which are several hundred feet thick and at a depth of 2,800–3,500 ft., contain 25–35% of K_2O (equivalent) in the minerals carnallite, $KCl \cdot MgCl_2 \cdot 6H_2O$, and sylvinite, $KCl \cdot NaCl$. The estimated amount above a depth of 3,500 ft. is 5,000,000,000 tons of K_2O equivalent and possibly 30,000,000,000 tons in reserve. The deposit at Stassfurt, Ger., contains the following minerals: carnallite, kieserite, $MgSO_4 \cdot H_2O$; polyhalite, $K_2SO_4 \cdot MgSO_4 \cdot 2CaSO_4 \cdot 2H_2O$; as well as kainite, $MgSO_4 \cdot KCl \cdot 3H_2O$. Important deposits at Wittelsheim in Alsace and in eastern Galicia, Spain, contain sylvinite. One near Kalusz in the Ukrainian S.S.R. contains sylvite, KCl; langbeinite, $K_2SO_4 \cdot 2MgSO_4$; and kainite. Additional saline deposits are at Carlsbad, N.M., Cardona, Spain, Searles Lake in California, the Dead Sea in Palestine, Tunis, Lake Elton in the Urals, and Chile. The above minerals are soluble in water and consequently are easily extracted and readily amenable to chemical operations. They represent, however, only a very small fraction of the total quantity of potassium in the earth's crust, the great bulk of which is found in the igneous rocks.

Potassium occurs as an alkali constituent in a number of alumino-silicate minerals, examples of which are: leucite, $KAl(SiO_3)_2$; muscovite mica, $KAl_3Si_3O_{10}(OH)_2$; orthoclase feldspar, $KAlSi_3O_8$; and biotite, $KHMg_2Al_2(SiO_4)_3$. These and other silicate minerals are insoluble in water and, with the exception of leucite, are not processed for their potassium content. In the weathering of igneous rocks, feldspar, for example, is decomposed into clay and soluble potassium salts; it might be expected that the latter would be ultimately carried to the sea by the surface waters. However, the potassium salts are retained by the soil to a large extent, more so than those of sodium, and are utilized by plants. The retention of the potassium ions by the soil may be a result in part of an ion exchange between potassium and the sodium salt of a complex sodium aluminum silicate which belongs to a class of compounds known as zeolites; e.g.,

$$2K^+ + Na_2(Al_2H_4Si_3O_{12}) \rightarrow K_2(Al_2H_4Si_3O_{12}) + 2Na^+$$

Soluble potassium salts which are present in all fertile soils are drawn into the roots of plants and accumulate in the plant structure. In the process of plant metabolism part of the inorganic potassium salts are converted into potassium salts of organic acids (e.g., tartrates and oxalates), which, when the plants are burned, are in turn converted to potassium carbonate. All plant structures are therefore potential sources of potassium compounds. The proportion of potassium present in the total plant or animal organism varies widely, but in most vegetation and in higher animals the potassium content is greater than that of sodium. In sea vegetation the balance is more in favour of sodium, but the potassium content is high and in some seaweeds is in excess of that of sodium. Sugar cane and sugar beets contain significant quantities of potassium salts, but the bulk of it (90%) is extracted with the sugar.

The bulk of the potassium salts of industry is obtained from salt deposits and only a very small fraction (approximately 1%) from plant and animal sources. There remains a vast potential source in the silicate minerals such as leucite, wyomingite, and glauconite if economic processes of recovery can be developed.

A number of processes for the preparation of potassium metal by electrolytic reduction and by chemical reduction have been proposed. In 1808 Joseph Gay-Lussac and Louis Thénard obtained the metal by reducing the hydroxide with iron; the materials, including iron wire or turnings, were packed in a gun barrel which was coated with clay and heated to white heat. During the same year F. R. Curaudau prepared potassium by a somewhat similar procedure in which he reduced potassium carbonate with carbon:

$$K_2CO_3 + 2C \rightarrow 2K + 3CO$$

This reaction was studied by various chemists during the following 50 years, for it was necessary to devise a method for the separation and rapid cooling of the products in order to prevent the formation of the explosive compound $K_6C_6O_6$. These processes were the forerunners of a number of methods in which potassium compounds were reduced by metals such as magnesium and aluminum, or by calcium carbide, hydride, or silicide. With the later development of high-vacuum techniques, the use of calcium for reduction of potassium in a vacuum yields the pure metal; the similar use of sodium vapour as the reducing agent has been fairly successful.

Electrolytic methods include the decomposition of the fused hydroxide, the cyanide, and a potassium oxysalt dissolved in a fused potassium halide. The Castner cell, developed in 1890 for the manufacture of sodium (q.v.), was modified for the more difficult potassium operation, but the results were not entirely satisfactory. During the first half of the 19th century, metallic potassium was used to produce aluminum by the reduction of the chloride; magnesium, boron, and silicon were produced by a similar method. It was shown in 1854 that sodium, which can be produced more cheaply, would serve as well as potassium for the production of magnesium and aluminum, and sodium was subsequently used for these purposes until electrolytic processes were developed. Similarly, sodium replaced potassium in many other industrial processes in which the latter was used. However, potassium is used in certain organic syntheses that involve reduction, dehalogenation, condensation, and polymerization reactions.

Properties.—Naturally occurring potassium consists of three isotopes of mass numbers 39, 40, and 41 with relative abundances 93.10%, 0.0118%, and 6.88%, respectively. The least abundant isotope, K^{40}, is radioactive with a half-life of 1.31×10^9 years emitting beta particles (electrons):

$$_{19}K^{40} \rightarrow {}_{20}Ca^{40} + e^{--}$$

and, to a lesser extent, gamma radiation by electron capture:

$$_{19}K^{40} + e^{--} \rightarrow {}_{18}Ar^{40} + \gamma$$

The ratio of the potassium to the argon content is used to estimate the ages of rocks and minerals, including meteorites. For example, some of the rock samples brought from the moon were found by this method to be about 3,100,000,000 years old. It is also thought that the abnormally high amount (1%) of argon in the atmosphere is due to K^{40} decay by electron capture.

Potassium belongs to the group of alkali metals (Group I of the periodic system) and closely resembles the other elements of the group, lithium, sodium, rubidium, cesium, and the short-lived radioactive element francium. The atoms of potassium and the other alkali metals each have a single valence electron which is easily removed whereas the remaining electrons are tightly held by the nucleus in completely filled orbitals. Consequently these elements are the most reactive of all the metals and are the strongest reducing agents known. Their valence or oxidation state is uniformly +1 in all their compounds.

When exposed to air, potassium rapidly tarnishes and becomes coated with a film of oxide or hydroxide. At room temperatures it is soft and pliable and can be cut with a knife, but below 0° C it is hard and brittle. The vapour of potassium, which is mainly monatomic, contains a small fraction (about 1%) of diatomic molecules which are indicated by a characteristic band spectrum. The solid metal has a body-centred cubic structure with $a = 5.25$ Å. The vapour of potassium is green and it imparts a violet coloration to the flame of a Bunsen burner. The emission spectrum shows a double line (7,699 Å and 7,665 Å) near the infrared and another near the ultraviolet (4,047 Å and 4,044 Å).

Additional physical and atomic properties are listed in Table I.

TABLE I.—*Properties of Potassium*

Outer electron configuration.	$3s^2\ 3p^6\ 4s^1$	Heat of hydration of gaseous ions, kcal. per mole	77
Density of solid at 20° C, g. per cc.	0.862	Electronegativity	0.8
Atomic volume of solid, cc.	45.36	Specific heat at 25° C, cal. per gram	0.177
Melting point, °C	63.65		
Boiling point, °C	774.0	Specific electrical resistance at 20° C ohm-cm.	7×10^{-6}
Ionization potential, volts	4.34	Metallic radius, Å	2.025
Potential for $K \rightleftarrows K^+ + e$	2.925	Ionic radius in crystals, Å	1.33

Many of the physical and chemical properties of potassium may

be correlated with its atomic structure. The difference in the atomic radius and the ionic radius is significant; the volume of the atom is nearly four times as great as that of the ion, the valence electron accounting for nearly three-fourths of the total volume. The potassium atom is the largest of the first 36 elements. The valence electron is therefore at a relatively great distance from the nucleus and is easily lost to other atoms in chemical reactions. In the solid metal the valence electrons hold the atoms together; but there are not enough of them to form stable electron pairs, so the binding of an atom to its neighbours is relatively weak and the valence electrons can easily pass from one ion to another. Accordingly potassium is soft, has a low melting point, and is a good conductor of electricity.

The chemistry of potassium is relatively simple; it has a valence of +1, it does not form complex ions, and it is joined to other elements or groups of elements in its compounds by ionic bonds. Potassium is more reactive than sodium and lithium. It inflames spontaneously in moist air, forming a mixture of oxides. Potassium reacts vigorously with water, liberating hydrogen and forming potassium hydroxide. The reaction is:

$$2K + 2H_2O \rightarrow 2KOH + H_2$$

Potassium reacts with nearly all the electronegative elements, including the halogens, sulfur, and phosphorus, forming the corresponding halides, the sulfide, and phosphide, respectively; with arsenic and antimony forming K_3As and K_3Sb; and with hydrogen to form the hydride. It reacts with organic compounds containing reactive groups (alcohols, halides, etc.); e.g.,

$$2K + 2C_2H_5OH \rightarrow 2C_2H_5OK + H_2$$

and vigorously with acids. When heated gently in the presence of dry ammonia gas, potassium reacts to form the amide:

$$2K + 2NH_3 \rightarrow 2KNH_2 + H_2$$

The amide decomposes into the nitride and ammonia when heated strongly:

$$3KNH_2 \rightarrow K_3N + 2NH_3$$

Potassium dissolves in liquid ammonia, forming a highly conductive blue solution.

The alloying properties of potassium have not been fully investigated. It does not alloy appreciably with lithium nor with gold, iron, zinc, or aluminum, but is mutually soluble with sodium. An alloy containing 22.7% of sodium remains liquid at a minimum temperature of −12.5° C. Potassium reacts vigorously with mercury; a number of compounds of the two elements have been identified, among them KHg_2. A compound of cadmium, $Cd_{12}K$, and one with thallium, KTh, have also been reported.

COMPOUNDS

The compounds of potassium are mostly ionic, and their chemical properties in solution are those of the potassium ion and the respective anions. Practically all the potassium compounds are soluble in water, the exceptions being the perchlorate, $KClO_4$ (slightly soluble); the chloroplatinate, K_2PtCl_6; the acid tartrate, $KHC_4H_4O_6$; the fluosilicate, K_2SiF_6; and the cobaltinitrite, $K_3Co(NO_2)_6$. In this and other respects the salts of potassium resemble those of the ammonium ion, NH_4^+.

Oxides.—Potassium forms three oxides and a fourth of less certain existence has been reported. The monoxide, K_2O, may be prepared by heating the metal in a limited supply of air or by heating the nitrate with potassium:

$$2KNO_3 + 10K \rightarrow 6K_2O + N_2$$

It is a white solid, yellow at high temperatures, and combines with water to form potassium hydroxide, KOH. The peroxide, K_2O_2, an orange-coloured solid, is prepared by the reaction of oxygen and the metal, either dry or in liquid ammonia solution. It is not a common substance for it reacts violently with oxygen to form the superoxide. Potassium superoxide, KO_2, the commonest of the superoxides, first prepared by Gay-Lussac and Thénard, is made by heating the metal in air at 180°–200° C or by treating a liquid ammonia solution of the metal with oxygen at $-50°$ C. It is decomposed by water:

$$2KO_2 + 2H_2O \rightarrow 2KOH + H_2O_2 + O_2$$

and oxidizes carbon monoxide to the dioxide below $100°$ C. At room temperatures it is an orange-yellow solid which turns black when melted. The melting point is $380°$ C and the density is 2.15 g. per cc. The compound was for many years formulated as K_2O_4, but X-ray studies show the potassium ions and superoxide ions, O_2^-, to be arranged in tetragonal structure. It is paramagnetic with a susceptibility corresponding to one unpaired electron spin; thus the simpler formula, KO_2, is indicated. A trioxide, K_2O_3, has been reported, but its behaviour suggests that it may be a mixture of the peroxide and the superoxide, $K_2O_2 \cdot 2KO_2$.

Potassium hydroxide, or caustic potash, KOH, was formerly prepared by the reaction of an aqueous solution of potassium carbonate with slaked lime (calcium hydroxide):

$$K_2CO_3 + Ca(OH)_2 \rightarrow CaCO_3 + 2KOH$$

The insoluble calcium carbonate was removed by filtration or sedimentation and the hydroxide recovered by evaporation. This was the primitive process whereby the alkali was obtained for soap-making, wood ashes being the source of the carbonate. It was also the standard industrial method until the end of the 19th century, when it was superseded by the electrolytic process. Potassium hydroxide is now manufactured by the electrolysis of an aqueous solution of potassium chloride, whereby chlorine and hydrogen are also produced. The cell used for this electrolysis must be constructed so as to prevent the intermingling of the hydroxide and the chlorine, which react to give the hypochlorite at low temperatures and the chlorate at higher temperatures. The Nelson cell has a graphite anode which is immersed in the salt solution contained in a perforated double-walled steel vessel which serves as a cathode. The vessel is lined with an asbestos diaphragm through which the solution seeps at a rate which prevents the hydroxide, formed at the cathode, from migrating to the anode region. The Castner-Kellner process utilizes a mercury cathode at which the potassium ion is discharged to form an amalgam and the amalgam, in turn, reacts with water to form the hydroxide solution. In either process the chloride and other impurities are removed from the solution containing the hydroxide by crystallization and the hydroxide is recovered by complete evaporation.

Potassium hydroxide is a white solid, stonelike in appearance and brittle with a fibrous crystalline fracture. The density is 2.04 g. per cubic centimetre and it melts at $380°$ C. It is deliquescent and is sometimes used as a drying agent; if exposed to air, it absorbs water and carbon dioxide. It is very soluble in water; a saturated solution, for example, contains 52.8% of KOH at $20°$ C and the solubility increases with the temperature. Solutions of potassium hydroxide are never saturated at the boiling point, which rises steadily with increasing concentration.

Potassium hydroxide is a strong base, being almost totally ionized in dilute solutions. It reacts with the various acids and acid oxides, forming the corresponding salts. As it is more expensive than sodium hydroxide, its use, other than for the manufacture of liquid soaps, is somewhat limited.

Potassium hydride, KH, is prepared by the reaction of hydrogen on the heated metal. It is a white, saltlike compound with a density of 1.43 g. per cubic centimetre and possessing a cubic structure of the sodium chloride type. In the electrolysis of the molten hydrides of this type the hydrogen migrates to the anode, indicating that it is the negative ion. The compound is a strong reducing agent, acting violently on water and liberating hydrogen:

$$KH + H_2O \rightarrow KOH + H_2$$

It inflames in air.

Potassium carbonate, K_2CO_3, was formerly obtained almost exclusively by lixiviating plant ashes. The first method used to manufacture this salt on an industrial scale was an adaptation of the Leblanc process, previously developed in France for the production of sodium carbonate. The Solvay process, used to manufacture sodium carbonate, is not applicable to potassium carbonate

production because of a difference in the solubility of the two bicarbonates. The crucial reaction in this process takes place because sodium bicarbonate precipitates from a concentrated solution whereas potassium bicarbonate, which is about three times as soluble, does not precipitate under similar conditions.

Potassium carbonate is now made either by the reaction of carbon dioxide on potassium hydroxide,

$$2KOH + CO_2 \rightarrow K_2CO_3 + H_2O$$

or by the Engel-Precht process. In the latter process, carbon dioxide is passed into a concentrated solution of potassium chloride containing a suspension of hydrated magnesium carbonate. A double salt of magnesium carbonate and potassium bicarbonate precipitates:

$$3(MgCO_3 \cdot 3H_2O) + 2KCl + CO_2 \rightarrow 2(MgCO_3 \cdot KHCO_3 \cdot 4H_2O) + MgCl_2$$

The double salt decomposes when heated:

$$2(MgCO_3 \cdot KHCO_3 \cdot 4H_2O) \rightarrow 2(MgCO_3 \cdot 3H_2O) + K_2CO_3 + CO_2 + 3H_2O$$

The magnesium carbonate is removed by filtration and the potassium carbonate crystallized by evaporation of the solution.

The density of potassium carbonate is 2.29 g. per cubic centimetre; the melting point, $881°$ C; the solubility in 100 g. of water at $0°$ C, 105.5 g.; and at $100°$, 156 g. Anhydrous potassium carbonate is a white, somewhat deliquescent salt. The hydrate, $2K_2CO_3 \cdot 3H_2O$, crystallizes in monoclinic form from a concentrated solution; below $-6°$ C the hydrate $K_2CO_3 \cdot 6H_2O$ crystallizes.

Although stable toward heat, potassium carbonate is decomposed by steam at red heat temperatures:

$$K_2CO_3 + H_2O \rightarrow 2KOH + CO_2$$

When a saturated solution of the carbonate is treated with carbon dioxide, crystals of the less soluble bicarbonate are precipitated:

$$K_2CO_3 + H_2O + CO_2 \rightarrow 2KHCO_3$$

The normal carbonate of a high degree of purity may be obtained by decomposition of the recrystallized bicarbonate at $190°$ C:

$$2KHCO_3 \rightarrow K_2CO_3 + H_2O + CO_2$$

Potassium carbonate is used in the manufacture of hard glass, liquid soaps, and numerous inorganic chemicals.

Halogen Compounds.—The halides of potassium and of the other alkali metals are typical salts, predominantly ionic and soluble in water. A number of their properties are given in Table II.

TABLE II.—*Properties of the Potassium Halides*

Property	KF	KCl	KBr	KI
Melting point, °C	846	768	728	693
Boiling point, °C	1,498	1,417	1,376	1,330
Densities, g. per cc., 0° C	2.48	1.99	2.76	3.13
Heats of formation, kcal. per mole	134.5	104.4	94.07	78.9
Interatomic distances in crystals, Å	2.66	3.14	2.94	3.23

Potassium fluoride, KF, may be prepared by neutralizing potassium carbonate or hydroxide with hydrofluoric acid, and upon evaporation cubic crystals of the salt are obtained. It forms the acid fluoride, KHF_2, when dissolved in hydrofluoric acid solution. Upon heating the acid salt decomposes:

$$KHF_2 \rightarrow KF + HF$$

The more complex salts KH_2F_3 and KH_3F_4 have been reported. Potassium fluoride, unlike the other potassium halides, forms hydrates, $KF \cdot 2H_2O$, and $KF \cdot 4H_2O$.

Potassium chloride, KCl, the most abundant of the naturally occurring potassium salts, closely resembles sodium chloride. It is a constituent of a number of minerals found in the Stassfurt and other deposits, some of which are hydrated double salts; e.g., kainite, $MgSO_4 \cdot KCl \cdot 3H_2O$. Potassium chloride is used for the preparation of many other potassium compounds, including the hydroxide and the carbonate. More than 90% of the potassium chloride produced is used as a fertilizer.

Potassium bromide, KBr, is prepared by the reaction of bromine and potassium hydroxide:

$$3Br_2 + 6KOH \rightarrow 5KBr + KBrO_3 + 3H_2O$$

The bromate decomposes upon heating to form more of the bromide:

$$2KBrO_3 \rightarrow 2KBr + 3O_2$$

Another method of preparation utilizes a solution of ferric and ferrous bromides, a by-product from one of the technical processes for the production of bromine. The iron bromides react with potassium carbonate solution,

$$FeBr_2 + 2FeBr_3 + 4K_2CO_3 \rightarrow 8KBr + Fe_3O_4 + 4CO_2$$

and the ferrosoferric oxide is removed by filtration. Potassium bromide is also obtained from natural brines. It is used in the preparation of photographic emulsions, in process engraving, and in medicine as a sedative.

Potassium iodide, KI, is prepared by the reaction of iodine and potassium hydroxide solution:

$$3I_2 + 6KOH \rightarrow 5KI + KIO_3 + 3H_2O$$

Upon evaporation and further heating, usually after the addition of some charcoal, the iodate decomposes, yielding more iodide. The iodate may also be reduced to the iodide in solution by bisulfite ion, stannous ion, or a suitable metal such as iron. Iodine dissolves in solutions of potassium iodide by forming the complex tri-iodide, KI_3; higher polyiodide ions containing an odd number of atoms, I_5^-, I_7^-, and I_9^-, are formed in very concentrated solutions. Upon evaporation of the KI_3 solution, dark-blue or black crystals of the salt are obtained. Potassium iodide is used in the manufacture of photographic emulsions, in organic chemical syntheses, in animal and poultry feed, in table salt, and in some drinking waters. In medicine it is used with iodine for the treatment of hyperthyroidism, and the salt containing radioactive iodine is used in the study and treatment of thyroid cancer. (For the oxyhalogen salts *see* BROMINE; CHLORINE; IODINE.)

Sulfur Compounds.—Potassium sulfate, K_2SO_4, a constituent of a number of saline minerals, is a colourless or white compound crystallizing in the rhombic form. Its density is 2.66 g. per cc., melting point 1,067° C, refractive index 1.4947, and solubility 24.1 g. per 100 g. of water at 100° C. It is used in fertilizers, as an antiflash agent in smokeless powders, and in the manufacture of potassium alums, potassium carbonate, and glass.

Potassium bisulfate, $KHSO_4$, is a white, deliquescent substance with a density of 2.24 g. per cc. and melting point of 197° C. At a high temperature it is converted to the pyrosulfate:

$$2KHSO_4 \rightarrow K_2S_2O_7 + H_2O$$

It is soluble in water, the solution being somewhat acidic because of the ionization of the HSO_4^- ion. Electrolysis of the solution yields the sparingly soluble potassium peroxydisulfate, $K_2S_2O_8$. Potassium bisulfate is used as a flux in the analysis of ores and as a chemical intermediate.

Potassium sulfite, K_2SO_3, is prepared by saturating a solution of potassium hydroxide or carbonate with sulfur dioxide. It exists in the anhydrous form, the monohydrate and the dihydrate, $K_2SO_3 \cdot 2H_2O$, the latter being the commonest. The solubility of the salt is fairly constant over a wide range of temperature.

Potassium sulfide, K_2S, is a white crystalline substance. It may be prepared by the direct combination of potassium and sulfur or by the reduction of potassium sulfate with carbon or hydrogen. In water solution it is strongly alkaline because of the extensive hydrolysis of the sulfide ion. Upon treatment with sulfur, polysulfides, K_2S_x, with as many as six sulfur atoms are formed. The salt has little use except as a laboratory reagent and a depilatory. (*See* SULFUR.)

Potassium nitrate, KNO_3, also called nitre or saltpetre, is a white crystalline salt with a density of 2.11 g. per cc., a melting point of 333° C and a refractive index of 1.5038. It decomposes at 400° C to potassium nitrite, KNO_2, and oxygen. Since the quantity of the salt obtained from natural deposits is limited, it is prepared by the reaction either of synthetic nitric acid and potas-

sium hydroxide or of naturally occurring potassium chloride and sodium nitrate. It is used in the manufacture of fireworks, gunpowder, fluxes, and glass and for curing meats, pickling, tempering steel, and impregnating candle wicks. (*See* NITRIC ACID AND NITRATES; NITROGEN.)

Determination.—Potassium may be identified by its emission spectrum or by the violet colour which its compounds impart to the Bunsen flame; if sodium is present the violet flame is masked and can be observed only through a suitable filter such as cobalt glass. Potassium may be identified and gravimetrically determined in the presence of the alkali metals by precipitation as potassium cobaltinitrite, $K_3Co(NO_2)_6$. Ammonium cobaltinitrite is insoluble and similar in appearance to the potassium salt. It is therefore necessary to eliminate ammonium ion from a sample before testing for potassium. Other gravimetric methods involve the precipitation of potassium perchlorate or of potassium chloride. The flame photometer is also used to quantitatively determine potassium. Another procedure involves the elution of the sample with hydrochloric acid in an ion exchange column. The potassium ion moves through the column at a characteristic rate and the solution carrying it is collected, evaporated, and weighed as potassium chloride.

PHARMACOLOGY

The principal salts and preparations of potassium used in medicine are the following:

Potassium p-aminobenzoate is used in fibrositic skin disorders. Potassium bicarbonate is used as a gastric antacid; potassium bromide as a sedative and an antiepileptic. Potassium chloride is used as a prophylaxis and in the treatment of hypokalemia, digitalis intoxication. Potassium citrate is used as a prophylaxis and in treatment of hypokalemia; as expectorant, sudorific, diuretic, urinary alkalizer, and gastric antacid. Potassium gluconate is used as a prophylaxis and in treatment of hypokalemia. Potassium iodide is used chiefly as an expectorant and in mycotic infections. Potassium perchlorate is used in hyperthyroidism; potassium permanganate as a topical astringent, antiseptic, and antidote for some poisons. Potassium phosphate, dibasic, and potassium sodium tartrate are used as saline cathartics. Potassium tetraiodomercurate II and potassium triiodomercurate II are used as topical antiseptics and disinfectants.

See ALKALI MANUFACTURE; *see* also references under "Potassium" in the Index.

BIBLIOGRAPHY.—F. A. Cotton and G. Wilkinson, *Advanced Inorganic Chemistry* (1966); J. W. Mellor, *A Comprehensive Treatise on Inorganic and Theoretical Chemistry,* vol. ii (1922); J. W. Mellor, *Comprehensive Treatise on Inorganic and Theoretical Chemistry,* supplement 3 (1963); J. F. Suttle, *Comprehensive Inorganic Chemistry,* vol. vi (1957), ed. by M. C. Sneed and R. A. Brasted.   (J. B. Ps.)

POTATO. The potato, common potato, white potato, or Irish potato, is one of the eight main food crops of the world, differing from the others in that the edible part of the plant is a tuber, *i.e.*, the swollen end of an underground stem.

The word potato derives from the Spanish *patata* (itself derived from *batata,* the American Indian word for the sweet potato, *Ipomoea batatas,* of which the succulent tuberous roots are eaten). It first referred to the sweet potato (*q.v.*), which was known in England in the 16th century before the common potato; the term was then used indiscriminately for both sweet and common potatoes; and, by the end of the 17th century, almost always for the common potato, which was by then better known to English-speaking people. This article describes the potato, and discusses its cultivation and use throughout the world, as follows:

POTATO

I. BOTANICAL CLASSIFICATION

The cultivated potato, considered by many to be a native of the Peruvian-Bolivian Andes, is one of approximately 150 tuber-bearing species of the genus *Solanum*. The name *Solanum tuberosum esculentum* was given to it in 1596 by Gaspard Bauhin, after its introduction into Europe. Linnaeus in 1753 called it *Solanum tuberosum*, and described it from what presumably were tetraploids (*i.e.*, plants with doubled sets of chromosomes). The great majority of cultivated potatoes are tetraploids (with 48 chromosomes), but an appreciable proportion of those grown in South America are diploids (with 24 chromosomes). Triploids, heptaploids, and hexaploids also exist. Potato cultivation in South America dates back at least to the 2nd century A.D.—probably much earlier—as evidenced by the finding of dried potatoes and pottery decorated with potato motifs in graves of that age. Interbreeding and progeny selection from species taken into cultivation, and from polyploids arising from these, have led, in the course of centuries, to the sharing of a common genetic "pool" by nearly all cultivated potatoes wherever they are grown: and this forms the basis for the cultivated species *S. tuberosum*. Members of it exhibit considerable variation, depending upon which of the pool-derived characters are dominant, but there is no consistent basis for separating them into more than one species (although this has been attempted, *e.g.*, by establishing a species, *S. andigenum*, to include potatoes growing under short-day conditions in the north of South America). *See* EVOLUTION, ORGANIC: *Early Theories of Evolution: Mutation Theory*; PLANTS AND PLANT SCIENCE: *Morphology of Plants*.

II. DESCRIPTION

1. Structure and Composition of the Tuber.—A potato tuber consists of about 10,000,000–100,000,000 cells, each 0.1–0.2 mm. in diameter and joined by pectin, gaps between them giving interconnected airspaces amounting to 1–2% of the volume. Aeration by these spaces maintains concentrations of about 18% oxygen and 3% carbon dioxide at the centre of an average tuber respiring at 0.2 millilitre per 100 grams' weight per hour at 10° C (50° F). Most cells consist of a cellulose wall lined with protoplasm, in which are insoluble constituents such as starch grains, surrounding an aqueous solution of the soluble constituents. The tuber has a corky skin pierced by lenticels through which occurs gaseous exchange. Metabolism continues at a slow rate after harvest and during storage. The vascular system through which the materials for the growth of the tuber were conveyed is discernible 0.5–1 cm. below the skin, rising to the surface at the "eyes" and at the point of attachment to the plant. Starch occurs in highest concentration adjacent to this system.

The content of dry matter of a tuber normally ranges from 18 to 28%, depending upon the variety (responsible for half of the variation), and upon maturity and growing conditions. Average figures for some important constituents, expressed as percentage of dry weight, are: starch, 70–75%; sugars, both reducing and nonreducing, approximately 0.5–1% each (but reaching over 10% if the tuber is immature or stored below 5° C); total nitrogen, 1–2%; protein nitrogen, 0.5–1%; ascorbic acid (vitamin C), 0.02–0.04%, but partly lost during storage; and citric acid, 2–5%.

2. Description of the Plant.—The potato is a herbaceous plant, 0.5–1 m. high. Its stems, usually angular in section, vary in posture, thickness, branching, colour (from green to deep purple), pubescence, and other characters. Leaf arrangement is spiral; leaves are compound and 20–30 cm. long, consisting of a terminal leaflet and two to four pairs of leaflets, each from about 6 to more than 10 cm. long, varying in shape and symmetry, but at least half as broad as they are long; there is also a variable number of small secondary leaflets. The inflorescence, on a stalk up to 20 cm. long, consists of several flowers on pedicels 1–4 cm. long. Frequency and duration of flowering are extremely variable. The corolla of the flower is wheel-shaped, five-lobed, 2–3 cm. in diameter, and varies in colour from white or pale yellow to deep reddish or bluish purple, often tipped or striped with white. There are five erect stamens, with large (about 7 mm. long) anthers converging around the pistil. They open by terminal pores, and

(LEFT) J. HORACE MCFARLAND CO., (RIGHT) FROM BAILLON, "HISTOIRE DES PLANTES" (BONNAIRE)

POTATO (SOLANUM TUBEROSUM) SHOWING (LEFT) UNDERGROUND STEMS AND TUBERS, (RIGHT) FLOWER AND FRUIT

(A) Single flower. (B) Fruit cut across to show placenta and developing ovules. (C) Longitudinal section through flower. (D) Ripe anther opening and shedding pollen. (E) Longitudinal section through ovary. (F) Fruit

vary in symmetry and also in colour, from pale yellow (associated with male sterility) to deep orange. The ovary is two-celled, the style single, the stigma bilobed. The fruit is a globular berry, green to purple and poisonous, 15–25 mm. in diameter, with 100–300 seeds, embedded in mucilage. Underground stems (stolons) extend from the stem below ground. The roots are fibrous, adventitious, arising in groups of 3 at the stolon nodes (though seedlings from true seed have a tap root). The ends of the stolons may enlarge greatly to form a few to more than 20 tubers, of variable shape and size, usually ranging in weight up to 300 g. but occasionally to more than 1.5 kg.; their total weight may be more than 2 kg. Their skin varies from brownish white to deep purple in colour, and their flesh normally from white to yellow, but it is occasionally purple. The tubers bear spirally arranged buds ("eyes") in the axils of aborted leaves, of which scars remain. These buds may remain dormant after the tuber is fully grown, even under conditions favourable to their development, for up to more than 10 weeks. They grow into plants identical with the plant that bore the tubers (except for occasional aberrant forms). Vegetative propagation of desired characteristics is thus possible; and this method is always used commercially because of the great variation that results when plants are grown from true seed. True seed is used only for the production of new varieties.

3. Varieties.—Plants grown from potato seeds, even from the same berry, may be very different not only in morphological features but also in commercially important characteristics, such as their response to climatic factors, their time of maturity, yield, disease resistance, cooking quality, suitability for industrial use, and keeping qualities. Commercially successful varieties have arisen in the past from the seeds of casual and often unknown crosses. This has become rare, however, because established varieties of reasonable quality and yield no longer "degenerate" and disappear from commerce as was once the case (*see* below); and hence a new variety must compete with the best of the surviving old ones, some of which have been on the market since the 1890s. The modern potato breeder is usually a geneticist who is trying to introduce some definite character—such as resistance to *Phytophthora* (late blight)—and selects his breeding material accordingly. From the progeny of his crosses he selects those uniting the quality he is seeking with the best combination of other characters, and propagates them vegetatively for some years, until a sufficient quantity of seed-tubers has been built up for the commercial introduction of the variety. Some varieties so introduced become established; others show unsuspected defects in cultivation and disappear in a few years.

Varieties are grouped according to their response to climatic conditions; the purposes for which they are fitted; and their earliness or otherwise in producing a crop. Most commercial varieties yield best in temperate climates with long summer days. Others yield best under tropical, short days, if at high altitudes where temperatures are not excessive. Some are grown for industrial use, the main requirement being a high content of starch; others are for the table. Some are early varieties that form a crop after a short growing season, providing the first fresh potatoes of the year; others are late varieties, but giving a higher yield. Intermediately come second early and midseason or early main-crop varieties.

Rarely, varieties may be of international importance. Although the number in commerce in the 20th century must have been of the order of 1,000, relatively few were important. Even these cannot here be enumerated, but examples of categories of modern long-day varieties are:

Industrial: Stärkeregis, Irene, Deodora, Voran.

Culinary, early: Erstling (or Duke of York), Juli, Irish Cobbler, Arran Pilot.

Culinary, second early: Bintje, Eigenheimer, Cherokee, Craig's Royal.

Culinary, midseason: Alpha, Record, Chippewa, Majestic.

Culinary, late: Birgitta, Ackersegen, Russet Burbank, Kerr's Pink.

III. HISTORY OF POTATO GROWING

The potatoes cultivated on high ground in South America 1,800 years ago probably consisted of a haphazard mixture of varieties; as they do in parts of the same area today, where, though tetraploids are the most numerous, any type from diploid to hexaploid may be grown in the same field, and all be harvested and marketed together. Potatoes were not introduced into Europe from South America until the second half of the 16th century, having earlier been encountered and described by Spanish invaders. The exact date and source of their introduction is unknown. Judging from material in old herbariums, the original tubers were probably tetraploids from the north of South America. They possibly were shipped to Spain from Cartagena, Colombia. European herbalists were growing and describing the potato plant at the end of the 16th century, and during the next half-century it spread throughout the physic gardens of Europe. It was supposed to possess, among other vices and virtues, some potency as an aphrodisiac; and even to this day a slice of potato may be carried in the pocket, or even the handbag, by some who cling to the belief it has powers as a specific against rheumatism.

The staple food crops in Europe were rye, wheat, oats, and barley, grown in quantities normally adequate for the population. The potato was first added to this list in Ireland. There, as the systems of land tenure and inheritance led to farms of inadequate size, the introduction of a high-yielding crop was favoured, for the yield of the potato was many times that of any grain, and, despite its high water content, the food value obtained per acre of land was greater also. Moreover, political unrest and local warfare, in which whole areas were sometimes devastated, often caused the destruction of standing crops, or prevented the harvesting of any that survived; but the potato was little harmed, and could be dug when required. By the end of the troubled 17th century it was a major crop in Ireland; by the end of the 18th century (probably as a result of Irish experience) it was a major crop in continental Europe, particularly Germany, and in the west of England. The Irish economy itself had become dependent on it. A typical Irish peasant family consumed an average of more than 3.5 kg. (about 8 lb.) of potatoes per person per day. In other parts of the world where European settlement was proceeding, *i.e.*, North America, Africa, India, Java, and Australasia, the potato was introduced as a food crop, and, where conditions were suitable for its culture, assumed some importance. It continued to spread during the first four decades of the 19th century; but the disastrous failures of the Irish crop in 1845 and 1846, due to late blight (*Phytophthora infestans*), and the ensuing famine and disease, led to a more cautious attitude toward it. (*See* IRELAND: *History: The Union: The Great Famine.*) Its cultivation subsequently decreased in areas which had been dependent upon it.

In the early 1960s annual world production was about 280,000,000 metric tons, of which, in round figures, 30% was grown in the U.S.S.R., 15% in Poland, and 10% in West Germany; 5% in East Germany, in France, and in the United States; about half this latter amount in the United Kingdom and in Czechoslovakia; and smaller quantities throughout the rest of the world. Production per head of population was greatest in Poland—about 1,200 kg. (2,646 lb.).

IV. YIELD

Under good growing conditions, with good cultivation and fertilizing, yields of 30–35 metric tons per hectare (ha.; 2.471 ac.) are common. Much of the world's production is necessarily on soils and in climates which are not ideal, and includes the results of inefficient as well as efficient agricultural systems. The average yield over the whole world is about 11 metric tons per hectare, national averages ranging from under 6 metric tons per hectare in Peru to 25 metric tons per hectare in Ireland and the Netherlands.

1. Environmental Requirements.—*Light.*—Tubers are formed from starch synthesized by the foliage in the light, surplus to the foliage's own requirements. Under daylight lasting 15–17 hr. (up to 24 hr. within the Arctic Circle) the foliage is large and long-lived, with initially large demands on its starch production and late formation of tubers which then grow rapidly because of the large photosynthesizing surfaces of the foliage. Under short daylight (about 12 hr.) the foliage is smaller and short-lived, with early formation of tubers, which then grow more slowly owing to the lesser photosynthesis of the smaller foliage. Varieties differ in the length of daylight at which they strike the best compromise between these opposing effects and give maximum yield. Potato production is mainly in areas with 15–17 hr. of daylight during the growing season, and most commercial varieties have been selected to give maximum yields under these conditions.

A fully exposed potato leaf photosynthesizes carbon dioxide at a rate dependent upon the light intensity, rising from zero at dawn to 20–25 milligrams (mg.) per square decimetre (dm.) of exposed leaf surface per hour for some hours in the middle of a clear day and falling to zero again at dusk. Shading of one leaf by another reduces the maximum rate, averaged over the whole foliage, to about 15 mg. per dm.^{2} per hr. On a cloudy, though bright, day it is further reduced to about 10 mg. and on a very dull day to about 1 mg. If the crop is irrigated, the yield is greater, depending upon light intensity, because of enhanced photosynthesis; but in the absence of irrigation, the positive effect of light on yield may be obscured by the negative effect of water shortage, which often accompanies prolonged clear weather.

Water.—Normally 3–5 mm. of rain or irrigation water are required to replace the water removed from moist soil by potato plants and lost to the atmosphere through evapotranspiration. Replacement by rain involves overcast or cloudy periods, during which photosynthesis and tuber growth are slow. But without regular rain or irrigation the soil dries out, leading to incipient wilting and closing of the pores of the leaves: absorption of carbon dioxide ceases, causing lack of growth. If rain is the only water supply, about 10 mm. per week provides the best compromise between these opposed effects. Supplemental irrigation twice a week to bring the daily average of water to 3–5 mm. gives better yields. Supplemental irrigation is preferable to an excess of rainy weather. (*See also* IRRIGATION: *Supplemental Irrigation.*)

Temperature.—Temperatures fluctuating between 20° C (68° F) during the day and 14° C (about 57° F) during the night are best. Yield may be negligible at mean temperatures as high as 25° C, although short daylight hours partly counteract this effect. Daylight hours as long as those within the Arctic Circle necessitate low temperatures if any potato crop is to be obtained.

Soil.—The soil should be friable and uniform, without rock formations and stones, for these obstruct root and stolon growth and cause formation of uneven tubers and difficulties in cultivation and harvesting. Water retention should be good; hence sands, and soils with sand or gravel subsoil, are not among the most suitable. Rich silts are best.

2. Fertilizer and Manuring.—Every metric ton of potatoes harvested removes from the soil about 4 kg. of nitrogen and potassium, 0.4 kg. of phosphorus, and smaller quantities of many other elements, some essential to growth. A good crop removes far more than can be replaced naturally; and if the plants (as in the wild state) are not manured, the weight of tubers produced is small, and adequate only for the natural function of vegetative reproduction. Such a crop is useless commercially; manuring may increase it more than tenfold.

Elements are leached out of or fixed by soil in different proportions varying with the soil and the locality. The best proportions in which to add elements vary, therefore; but on most types of soil they are about 1 part of nitrogen, 0.4 of phosphorus, and 0.8–1.6 of potassium. On heavy fen or marsh soils the proportion of phosphorus should be increased to 0.9–1.3. Some soils in the western United States need no added potassium, and some muck soils no nitrogen. Broadly speaking, applications of fertilizer may be calculated from the above proportions, taking nitrogen as 190 kg. per ha. on good potato soils and as 125 kg. per ha. on soils that are poor for reasons other than lack of nutrients (e.g., because of scanty water supply) and on which, therefore, heavy fertilizer applications are wasted.

The elements are added in forms such as the following: ammonium sulfate (20–21% nitrogen); crude potassium sulfate (c. 40% potassium) or chloride (muriate of potash; 50% potassium); superphosphate (8%–9% phosphorus); and dung (0.6% nitrogen and potassium, 0.15% phosphorus—but only a fraction of each of these is available in the first year after application). Manure, though an inefficient source of the major nutrients, has beneficial effects on soil texture and on water retention; when used, 25–50 metric tons of it should be applied per hectare, supplemented by chemical fertilizers. Where agriculture is mechanized and stock-farming unimportant, applications of manure are often reduced or omitted. Compost, a plowed-in green crop (or, in coastal areas, seaweed) sometimes replace it. Manure is plowed in, either in the fall, or (where the annual rainfall exceeds 75 cm.) preferably in the spring. Chemical fertilizers may be broadcast and worked into the soil during spring cultivations before planting; but the preferred method is to place them in bands beside and beneath the seed-pieces at the time of planting. In many countries, compound potato fertilizers are available, providing nitrogen, potassium, and phosphorus in proportions best suited to the local soil. Many other elements are required in smaller quantities; they are usually present in the crudely purified chemical fertilizers, in manure, or as the produce of soil weathering; but any deficiency in them will have adverse effects on yield. Calcium (which may be deficient on acid soils, particularly if rainfall is high and application of potassium is lavish) is artificially added as lime; but this should not be done immediately before the potato crop is grown as it increases infection by scab. Magnesium deficiency in acid peat and sandy soils can be cured by applying magnesian limestone. Calcareous soils with free drainage may exhibit iron deficiency, which is treated by spraying the foliage with 0.2–1% ferrous sulfate. Deficiency in manganese and boron sometimes occurs in soils low in clay; the manganese deficiency can be rectified by spraying the foliage with 1% manganese sulfate, and the boron deficiency by plowing in borax in a proportion of about 20 kg. per ha.

In view of the frequent presence of chlorides in fertilizers, it is of interest that every 100 kg. of chloride added per hectare may reduce yield by nearly 450 kg. per ha.

(See also FERTILIZERS AND MANURES.)

3. Planting, Cultivation, and Harvesting.—Seed-tubers of about 50–60 g. weight are best for planting; but larger tubers cut into seed-pieces may be used. Planting is done as soon as conditions are suitable. Maximum yield from each individual plant would be obtained by spacing at a minimum of about 0.7 m. apart; but this would result in insufficient plants for best use of the land. In practice, the ground is cultivated and drawn into furrows, spaced, according to soil, climate and local custom, at 60 to 100 cm. apart. In these the seed-pieces are placed 15 to 60 cm. apart, according to the characteristics of the seed and the type of crop

desired; and the ridge is split over them. Usually, the larger the seed-piece the more tubers it will produce; and, if these tubers are to grow to marketable size, the plants must be spaced farther apart. If the crop is being grown for seed, however, close spacing is employed to give the maximum yield of suitably small tubers. Varieties differ in the number of stems and tubers produced from a seed-piece of given size—though this characteristic may be modified by adjusting the storage conditions of the seed. Optimum spacing therefore also differs according to the variety. Depth of planting varies from 5 to 10 cm., the former being usual if rapid emergence is desired.

In some regions, planting is done by hand; in others, plowing, placement of the fertilizer, planting, and covering of the seed are all done by one machine.

Cultivation after planting to control weeds is held to a minimum to avoid damaging the plants. It is possible to control weed growth by preemergence herbicides, and cultivation is then unnecessary (see also WEED). In that case the ridges are sometimes harrowed down before the plants emerge and the crop is grown "on the flat." This has the advantage of hastening emergence and, on dry soils, of conserving moisture.

In regions where infection or damage is likely, the crop is sprayed or dusted against blight, and against pests such as aphids and Colorado beetle. If the foliage is diseased or likely to interfere with harvesting, it is destroyed, either mechanically or by spraying with a herbicide before harvest is begun.

Harvesting methods vary from digging by hand (in peasant communities); through plowing up, followed by lifting of the tubers by hand; to mechanized harvesting (in which the tubers, separated from soil, are delivered into a trailer). Even complete harvesting machines, however, need a crew to remove diseased and damaged tubers, stones, and clods of earth.

In regions where the climate permits, two crops of potatoes may be grown in one year.

(See also FARM MACHINERY; SPRAYS AND DUSTS IN AGRICULTURE.)

4. Diseases and Pests.—Most diseases exist in several strains, to each of which potatoes may be susceptible in differing degrees. Resistance to disease may take the form of hypersensitivity of the potato, which removes foci of infection by rapid death; or of biochemical depression by the potato of the growth and reproduction of the causative agent. The seriousness of diseases and pests varies in different regions and in different years according to the prevailing weather.

Foliage Destruction.—Late blight (*Phytophthora infestans*), the most widespread and destructive disease, may rapidly destroy the whole foliage when the weather is humid and daytime temperatures fluctuate between 10° and 25° C (about 50° and 78° F). Early blight (*Alternaria solani*) may be equally destructive under hot, dry conditions—the optimum temperature for it is about 27° C—but at lower temperatures it usually only produces brown "target spots" on the leaves. The progress of both diseases may be delayed by frequently spraying or dusting the foliage with copper sulfate or various dithiocarbamates; preferably the latter. Many countries operate a local radio warning service, based on weather reports, in order that spraying against late blight may be started in time. (See also PLANT DISEASES; FUNGI.)

Insect pests may eat the foliage, the seriousness of this varying with both pest and weather conditions. The potato flea beetle (*Epitrix cucumeris*), for instance, may eat holes in the leaves, giving a shot-hole appearance; but the Colorado potato beetle (*Leptinotarsa decemlineata*) will, if uncontrolled, eat the whole foliage except the stems (see POTATO BUG). Tuberworms (the larvae of a moth, *Gnorimoschema operculella*), burrow in the stems and leaf midribs. Leafhoppers (*Empoasca fabae*), in feeding on the leaves, introduce toxins which cause necrosis (hopper burn) at the tips and margins of the leaflets: in hot dry weather the whole plant may be destroyed. Insect pests are controllable by, for example, DDT-containing sprays.

Stunting of the Plant or Shortening of Its Life.—Stunting, often accompanied by crinkling and yellowing of the leaflets, is a symptom of secondary virus infection, i.e., it is the result of growing crops from tubers from infected plants. There are several causative viruses (designated as A, X, Y, leaf-roll virus, etc.), disseminated, with one main exception (X, which may spread by contact), by insects feeding first on diseased and then on healthy plants; the chief insects are aphids, flea beetles, and leafhoppers. It is therefore wisest to produce seed-tubers in localities where sources of infection, or the insect vectors, are not prevalent; and this is a major feature in seed certification schemes. Widespread infection of seed stocks, with consequently stunted plants and negligible yields, has caused "degeneration" of varieties. Recognition of this cause in the second decade of the 20th century, and the subsequent introduction of seed certification, were major factors in its eradication.

Stunting and premature death also result if the root system or conducting strands are attacked, with resultant obstruction of water and nutrient supply. Examples are infection by the fungi *Pellicularia filamentosa* (which normally may only produce black scurf on the tubers), *Sclerotinia sclerotiorum*, *Verticillium albo-atrum*, *Fusarium oxysporum* and *F. solani* var. *eumartii;* infection by the bacteria *Pectobacterium carotovorum* var. *atrosepticum* (blackleg), *Pseudomonas solanacearum* (brown rot) and *Corynebacterium sepedonicum* (ring rot); and attack by the eelworms *Heterodera rostochiensis* and (less frequently) *Ditylenchus dipsaci*.

Biochemical Interference with Photosynthesis or Conduction.—Photosynthesis may be reduced by lack of chlorophyll, as in several secondary virus infections; and by lack of carbon dioxide in plants that have wilted because of interference with water supply (as mentioned above). Failure of the synthesis of sucrose, in which form carbohydrates are translocated from leaves to tubers, is a symptom of primary leaf roll infection.

Interference with Channels of Conduction to the Tuber.—This obviously leads to loss of yield, and may result in the formation of aerial tubers from carbohydrates that accumulate above ground. Infection by the fungus *Pellicularia filamentosa* may give this result.

Destruction of the tuber is caused by the fungi *Synchytrium endobioticum* (wart, or black wart), *Phytophthora infestans* (late blight), several species of *Fusarium* (dry rot), *Phoma foveata;* and by the bacteria *Pectobacterium carotovorum*, *Pseudomonas flourescens*, *Pseudomonas solanacearum,* and *Corynebacterium sepedonicum.*

Damage to the tuber is caused by slugs, potato tuberworm, wireworm (*q.v.*), the fungi *Streptomyces scabies* (common scab) and *Spongospora subterranea* (powdery scab); and by mild attacks from the destructive organisms mentioned above.

(*See also* PLANT DISEASES; PLANT QUARANTINE.)

5. Quality and Use.—In countries where an appreciable quantity of potatoes is grown, annual consumption per head varies from 27 kg. (Bulgaria) to 240 kg. (Poland). Annual consumption in the United States is 47 kg. and in the United Kingdom 88 kg.; in these two countries, most potatoes are grown for eating. In the chief producing regions of Europe, however, a large proportion of the crop is grown for stock feed and for industrial use.

One hundred grams of cooked potato, without addition of fat, provide about 70 calories (an equal quantity of bread gives about 200 calories); and about 10–30 mg. of ascorbic acid, depending upon how long the potatoes had been stored. This, in view of the large quantities regularly eaten, makes the potato an important source of vitamin C; and outbreaks of scurvy followed shortages of potatoes in Ireland in 1847, in Norway in 1904 and 1912, and in the United States in 1916. Hydrolysis of potato protein yields all the amino acids essential for nutrition, though the content of protein is variable. On the average, nitrogen equilibrium could be attained by the daily consumption of about 3 kg. potatoes (which, incidentally, would provide the total requirements of thiamin and nicotinic acid).

The cooking quality can be judged largely from the texture and colour of the cooked flesh. Mealiness is directly correlated with the percentage of dry matter, and so is partly dependent on the variety, as is the yellowness or otherwise of the flesh and any proneness to graying after cooking. The colour of fried potatoes depends mainly upon the content of reducing sugars, which are caramelized during frying. A low content of these sugars, *i.e.,* about 0.2% fresh weight, gives the usually desired pale colour.

Inferior potatoes are often used as stock feed; but potatoes are often grown especially for this and for industrial use. For both purposes they are inefficient, because of their low dry matter content; but the yield of dry matter per unit area of ground is greater than that of most crops. When this is more important than industrial efficiency, potatoes are used as a source of starch, and hence also of dextrins, alcohol, and other derivatives.

6. Storage.—Potatoes may be stored simply by piling them in the field in a long heap about 1 m. high, and by covering them with straw, 15 cm. thick, laid vertically from ground to ridge. This covering is capped with straw bent over it, and with a layer of soil 15–30 cm. thick. In cold climates the cover may be duplicated. A storage cellar is commonly used for home storage.

Where potatoes are grown commercially, it is more usual to store the crop in buildings. These should be weatherproof, insulated to prevent frost penetration and to enable the potatoes to be held at the desired temperature. Storage may be in one large mass, 3 m. or more high (1 metric ton of potatoes occupies about 1.6 m³.); in 50–100-ton bins; or in crates holding 1 ton or less. Ventilation ducts are frequently placed under the potatoes, often with provision for forced ventilation, with outside air, air recirculated in the building, or a combination of both. Refrigeration is sometimes necessary in hot countries. (*See also* FARM BUILDINGS: *Crop Storage.*)

At storage temperatures below 4° C (about 40° F), rotting and sprouting are negligible, but marked sweetening occurs. At temperatures of 8–15° C, which retains the sugar at a desirable level, both rotting and sprout growth present problems. For the latter, chemical suppression may be used; by previously spraying the growing crop; by dusting the harvested tubers; or by ventilating them with the vapours of suppressants. Prevention of rotting takes precedence over other storage requirements, and, if disease is present, may require much more forced ventilation, and a lower temperature, than would be used if the tubers were healthy.

Potatoes, being alive, respire, producing about 10 kilocalories of heat per metric ton per hour—more when freshly harvested, immature, sprouted, or diseased—and this, if they are heaped together, raises the temperature of the mass. This in turn causes convective air exchange between the stack and the surrounding air, which removes heat, and, with healthy mature potatoes, a balance is eventually struck in which the heat is removed by this convection as fast as it is produced. At this stage, the maximum temperature, and the convection activated by it, are dependent upon the height of the potato stack. (If the height is h metres, the maximum potato temperature is about 1.5 $h°$ C above the 24-hr. average temperature of the surrounding air.) The minimum temperature is about 1° C above average ambient temperature. With forced ventilation, the temperature range in the stack is much reduced, temperatures throughout being held within about 1° C of that of the surrounding air.

Weight is lost, otherwise than through rotting, mainly by evaporation of water, which is highest just after harvest, and when sprouting has occurred. With storage in bulk without forced ventilation, loss is restricted while with forced ventilation, the loss is increased. If the potatoes are in crates, air exchange is so free that temperatures are uniform and not much above that of the surrounding air; but weight losses are equal to the losses with continuous forced ventilation.

See also references under "Potato" in the Index and the *Agriculture* sections of country articles.

BIBLIOGRAPHY.—R. N. Salaman, *Potato Varieties* (1926), *The History and Social Influence of the Potato* (1949); E. Hellbo and H. Esbo, *Våra Potatissorter,* 2nd ed. (1942); W. G. Burton, *The Potato* (1948); T. Whitehead, T. P. McIntosh and W. M. Findlay, *The Potato in Health and Disease,* 3rd ed. (1953); W. F. Talburt and O. Smith, *Potato Processing* (1959); R. Schick and M. Klinkowski (ed.), *Die Kartoffel* (1961); D. S. Correll, *The Potato and Its Wild Relatives* (1962).

See also *American Potato Journal* (1926–); *European Potato Journal* (1958–); *Kartoffelbau* (1950–); and various official publications, such as those of the U.S. Department of Agriculture and U.S.

state agricultural experiment stations; the English and Irish ministries of agriculture; the British Agricultural Research Council; the Scottish Department of Agriculture, etc.   (W. G. Bu.; D. S. Cl.)

POTATO BUG, an agricultural pest (*Leptinotarsa decemlineata*), also known as the Colorado potato beetle, which attacks the leaves of potato plants. This leaf beetle (family Chrysomelidae), native to the western United States, originally fed upon a wild plant of the potato family, *Solanum rostratum*, abounding in the Rocky mountain region. With the westward movement, the cultivation of potatoes was brought to the beetle's

LYNWOOD M. CHACE
COLORADO POTATO BEETLE (LEPTI-NOTARSA DECEMLINEATA)

neighbourhood, and the insect at once took to the cultivated plant and began an eastward spread. By 1864 or 1865 it had crossed the Mississippi river into Illinois, and in 1874 it reached the Atlantic seaboard. As it progressed, certain predatory insects and various birds became accustomed to it, and as early as 1869 the insecticide paris green was used against it; so that by the time the beetle reached the Atlantic, potato growers in the midwest were able to control it. From 1945 the annual loss caused by the Colorado potato beetle has ranged about $40,000,000.

Upon the advance of this pest great alarm was expressed in Europe. The German government early in 1875 issued a decree against the importation of U.S. potatoes. Similar action was taken the same year by Belgium, Spain, France, Russia, Italy, Hungary and Austria, and by Portugal and Sweden the following year. In spite of the German decree, the beetle was discovered in a potato field near Hamburg, but was exterminated by radical measures.

In 1922 the beetle was found to have been introduced near Bordeaux, France, in a region where there had been large numbers of American troops. From that region it has since spread, rather slowly, and infestation by the Colorado potato beetle is now general in France, the Netherlands, Luxembourg, Germany and Spain. It also occurs in much of Portugal and Switzerland and in parts of Austria, Yugoslavia, Czechoslovakia and Poland. It has been found sporadically in England, but repressive measures are believed to have exterminated the species.

The adults are oval shaped, about $\frac{3}{8}$ in. long, and are orange coloured with black stripes running lengthwise along the wing covers. Both the adult beetles and the larvae feed upon potato leaves. The extensive work of the insect on the foliage may often affect the quality of the tuber, and at one time it was difficult to obtain potatoes that were not watery when cooked. The adult beetles pass the winter underground, and in the spring emerge about the time that potato plants come through the ground. Females lay from 300 to 500 eggs over a five-week period on the undersides of leaves; there are one to three generations per year, depending on the latitude.

The leaf-feeding larvae always descend to the ground to turn into pupae. The insect feeds on nearly all plants of the potato family, including eggplant, tomato and tobacco. The tender-leaved varieties of potato are most affected however.

Many chemical mixtures such as DDT or arsenical compounds control the adults and larvae. Some growers apply DDT in combination with the recommended fungicide for their area. Resistance of the beetle to DDT has been reported in some localities.

Information may be obtained from the U.S. department of agriculture or agricultural experiment stations in affected areas.

BIBLIOGRAPHY.—F. H. Chittenden, "The Colorado Potato Beetle," U.S. Department of Agriculture *Circular* 87 (1907); C. L. Metcalf and W. P. Flint, Destructive and Useful Insects, 3rd ed., rev. by R. L. Metcalf (1951); U.S. Department of Agriculture, "Insects" *1952 Yearbook of Agriculture* (1952).   (R. E. Bl.; J. C. Dy.)

POTATO WAR: *see* BAVARIAN SUCCESSION, WAR OF THE.

POTAWATOMI, an Algonkian tribe of North American Indians whose name connotes firemakers (with flints or a one-stringed bow). Their culture, language, and particular traditions unite them to prehistoric Ojibwa (*q.v.*) and Ottawa of the eastern woodlands, as is affirmed by 17th-century Jesuit accounts. Like other Algonkians, the Potawatomi migrated west from the Atlantic seaboard, partly under Iroquois pressure (*see* ALGONKIAN TRIBES). Observed in 1670 on islands around Green Bay, Wis., they spread south into lands that became Michigan, Wisconsin, Illinois, and Indiana. In the 1700s the tribe joined the French against the Iroquois and was allied with Pontiac (*q.v.*) in his uprising; it aided British forces in the American Revolution and opposed England in the War of 1812. Crowded by settlers, the so-called Potawatomi Nation moved west of the Mississippi River; some in Indiana escaped from the U.S. military into Canada. In 1846 most Potawatomi were removed by U.S. soldiers to a Kansas reservation where they became known as the Prairie Band of their tribe. During the westerly trek, they borrowed such alien Plains lifeways as communal bison hunts (replacing pursuit of woodlands game and fish), associated camp organizations, and the intertribal sign language that was generally understood throughout the Plains area (*see* PLAINS INDIANS).

In 1861 most of the Kansas band decided to take and sell their lands in severalty; after disputes, many moved (1868) to Oklahoma Indian Territory and were called Citizen Potawatomi. Despite the schism and the Citizens' assimilation to the dominant U.S. life, the two groups have maintained contact with each other, with the impoverished Forest (or "Stray") Potawatomi who fled to Wisconsin, and with the Huron Potawatomi who went to Michigan (1830s). Separation favoured social and linguistic differences among the bands, though many Citizens returned to the Kansas reservation. The Prairie Band cherishes its reservation as a home for aboriginal culture, which actively blends crafts and values with aspects of colonial and contemporary white culture. A resurgence of traditional religion and magic (dating from the 1930s) and a general acculturation were proceeding vigorously during the 1960s. At that time the U.S. government reported Potawatomi reservation population as follows: Kansas 830, Oklahoma 277, Wisconsin 246, and Michigan 134.   (R. La.)

POTEMKIN, GRIGORI ALEKSANDROVICH, PRINCE (1739–1791), Russian army officer and statesman, for two years the lover of the empress Catherine II and for 17 years the most powerful man in the empire, was born at Chizevo in Belorussia, on Sept. 24 (new style; 13, old style), 1739, the son of a nobleman of Polish descent (Potempski was the original family name). Educated at Moscow University, he entered the horseguards in 1755. He took part in the *coup d'état* of 1762, which brought Catherine II to power as empress; and Catherine made him a *Kammerjunker* and gave him a small estate. He distinguished himself in the Turkish War of 1768–74, and in March 1774 he

GRIGORI POTEMKIN, ENGRAVING DATED 1789

became Catherine's fifth favourite. She bestowed on him the highest honours, including the post of commander in chief and governor-general of "New Russia" (Ukraine). In 1776 he was superseded in the empress's amorous graces by Zavadovski; but relations between her and Potemkin continued friendly, and his influence was never seriously disturbed by any of her later favourites.

Potemkin was deeply interested in the question of Russia's southern boundaries and so in the fate of the Turkish Empire. In 1776 he sketched the plan for the conquest of the Crimea, which was subsequently realized; and he was busy with the so-called Greek project, which aimed at restoring the Byzantine Empire under one of Catherine's grandsons. In many of the Balkan lands he had well-informed agents. After he became field marshal, in 1784, he introduced many reforms into the army and built a fleet in the Black Sea, which, though constructed of bad materials, did excellent service in Catherine's second Turkish War (1787–92). His stupendous activity had admirable results: the arsenal of Kherson, begun in 1778, the harbour of Sevastopol, built in 1784, and the new fleet of 15 ships of the line and 25 smaller vessels, were monuments of his genius. But there was exaggeration in all his enterprises. He spared neither men, money, nor himself in attempting to carry out a gigantic scheme for the colonization of the Ukrainian steppes; but he never calculated the cost, and most of the design had to be abandoned when but half finished. Even so, Catherine's tour of the south in 1787 was a triumph for Potemkin, for he disguised all the weak points of his administration (hence the apocryphal tale of his erecting artificial villages to be seen by the empress in passing). On this occasion he received the title of prince of Tauris.

When the second Turkish War began, the founder of New Russia acted as commander in chief. But the army was ill-equipped and unprepared, and Potemkin, in a hysterical fit of depression, would have resigned but for the steady encouragement of the empress. Only after A. V. Suvorov had valiantly defended Kinburn did he take heart again and besiege and capture Ochakov and Bender. In 1790 he conducted the military operations on the Dniester and held his court at Iași with more than Asiatic pomp. In 1791 he returned to Saint Petersburg, where, along with his friend A. A. Bezborodko, he made vain efforts to overthrow the new and last favourite, Platon Zubov. The empress grew impatient and compelled him (1791) to return to Iași to conduct the peace negotiations as chief Russian plenipotentiary. He died on Oct. 16 (N.S.; 5, O.S.), while on his way to Nikolayev.

Potemkin was indubitably the most extraordinary of all Catherine's favourites. He was an able administrator, licentious, extravagant, loyal, generous, and magnanimous. Nearly all the anecdotes related of him by the Saxon diplomat G. A. W. von Helbig and freely utilized by later biographers are worthless.

See Theresia Adamczyk, *Fürst G. A. Potemkin* (1936); G. Soloveytchik, *Potemkin,* 2nd ed. (1949). (R. N. B.; X.)

POTENTILLA, the generic name for the cinquefoils, plants of the rose family (Rosaceae, q.v.), comprising more than 300 species, mostly herbs, widespread in North Temperate and Arctic regions, many being cultivated as border and rock garden plants. Various species bear brilliant flowers in white, yellow, or red, and graceful foliage. A good loamy soil, enriched with rotted manure, is most suitable.

Cinquefoils are easily propagated by seed or by division of the rootstocks; rootstocks, separated in early autumn or early spring, will generally produce blooms the succeeding growing season. Some perennial species are used in the garden border—*P. argyrophylla,* with whitish hairs on the underside of the leaves; *P. grandiflora,* with large, showy, golden yellow flowers; *P. tormentilloformosa,* a much cultivated hybrid, with trailing stems and yellow flowers with a red centre—while others are good in the rock garden—*P. nitida,* a mat-forming species barely two inches high, with pink or white flowers one inch across; *P. multifida,* a spreading type up to four inches high, with small yellow flowers, two or three in a cluster. The shrubby cinquefoils, *P. fruticosa* and its varieties, provide a number of attractive flowering small shrubs for the garden.

POTENZA, chief town of the province of the same name in the region of Basilicata, south Italy; and an episcopal see. It stands 2,700 ft. above sea level in the Apennines near the upper Basento River, 56 mi. (90 km.) E of Salerno. Pop. (1961) 44,063

J. HORACE MCFARLAND CO.

PURDOM BUSH CINQUEFOIL (POTENTILLA PURDOMI)

(commune). Notable churches are the cathedral (rebuilt 1799); the Romanesque S. Michele (11th–12th century); S. Francesco (1274), with Gothic apse and priceless carved wooden doors; and the small 15th–16th-century church of S. Rocco. The town has several times been rebuilt after earthquakes. The Museo Provinciale Lucano has an important archaeological collection. Potenza is a railway junction on the Salerno–Taranto line. The inhabitants are mostly engaged in agriculture and much of the abundant market gardening and orchard produce is exported.

Roman Potentia (founded *c.* 2nd century B.C.), which stood on a lower site than the modern town, was an important road junction and became a flourishing imperial *municipium*. In the 6th century it passed to the dukes of Benevento and thereafter to a succession of feudal owners. In 1806 the French made Potenza capital of Basilicata. In 1860 it was the first south Italian town to drive out the Bourbons. (*See also* BASILICATA; LUCANIA.)

POTENZA PROVINCE is watered by the upper courses of the Agri, Basento, Bradano, and Sinni rivers, and is traversed by the Apennines. Area 2,527 sq.mi. (6,545 sq.km.). Pop. (1961) 414,968. Agricultural products include cereals, fruit, olives, and grapes; and there is stock raising (sheep and goats). The province has many mineral springs and lignite and marble deposits. It was, until 1927 when Matera Province was detached, coextensive with Basilicata. (M. T. A. N.)

POTGIETER, ANDRIES HENDRIK (1792–1852), a Boer leader in the Great Trek, best known for his part in establishing Boer settlement in the Transvaal, was born in the eastern Cape Colony on Dec. 19, 1792, and with his trekker party left the colony late in 1835. Joined by other trekkers, they halted near Winburg, north of the Orange River (February 1836). As commandant and leader, Potgieter treated with local Bantu tribes to establish Boer title to the land. He clashed with the hostile Matabele (1836–37) and won the battle at the Marico River (November 1837), which opened the high veld interior to the Boers. After the massacre of Piet Retief (February 1838), he joined an unsuccessful expedition in Natal against the Zulu king Dingaan, but returned to Winburg in May 1838, convinced that the destiny of the trekkers lay northward. His ideal was an interior republic, remote from British influence, but linked commercially with the Portuguese at Delagoa Bay. He founded three settlements in the Transvaal: Potchefstroom (1838) in the southwest, Andries Ohrigstad (1845) in the northeast, and one in the Zoutpansberg (1848), the northernmost region colonized in the Great Trek. Partly through his efforts, Boer republicanism enjoyed a continuous history in the Transvaal during this period, in contrast to its fate in Natal and the future Orange Free State. As a leader Potgieter exercised authority along local, military, and patriarchal lines. In the conflicts within the Transvaal trekker community (*see* TRANSVAAL: *History*), as head commandant he supported the military party against the *volksraad* (elected council) and favoured local autonomy rather than the establishment of a centralized state. When Great Britain recognized the independence of the Transvaal Boers in the Sand River Convention (Jan. 17, 1852), he held aloof from the negotiations, which were conducted on the Boer side by his rival Andries Pretorius, but in March he ratified the Convention. He died in the Zoutpansberg on Dec. 16, 1852.

See C. S. Potgieter and N. H. Theunissen, *Kommandant-Generaal Hendrik Potgieter* (1938). (N. G. GA.)

POTGIETER, EVERHARDUS JOHANNES (1808–1875), Dutch prose writer and poet, who tried to set new standards and encourage national consciousness in his journal *De Gids* (founded 1837), and anticipated the literary revival of the 1880s, was born at Zwolle on June 27, 1808. His initial optimism is evident in *Jan, Jannetje en hun jongste kind* (1842), an allegory satirizing the people's mental inertia; in *Het Rijksmuseum* (1844), a homage to 17th-century Holland and to the prose style of P. C. Hooft (*q.v.*) which it follows; and in *Liedekens van Bontekoe* (1840), songs in the 17th-century manner.

The resignation of the historian Bakhuizen van den Brink from the editorial board of *De Gids* in 1843 left Potgieter with a sense of frustration and gloom until his confidence in the possibility of a literary revival was restored by the critic Conrad Busken Huet (*q.v.*). His subsequent work includes *Onder weg in den regen* (1864), the best of many subtle and often humorous sketches and short stories; *Florence* (1868), a long poem in tercets written after a visit to the city for the Dante centenary; and *De Nalatenschap van de Landjonker* (1875), a poem cycle by a fictitious aristocrat which amply justifies the trouble required to master his highly individual style. He died on Feb. 3, 1875.

BIBLIOGRAPHY.—*De Werken van E. J. Potgieter*, 18 vol. (1885–86); J. H. Groenewegen, *Bibliographie der werken van E. J. Potgieter* (1890); G. M. J. Duyfhuizen, *E. J. Potgieter's Florence* (1942); T. Weevers, "Goethe and Holland" in *Publications of the English Goethe Society,* vol. xviii (1949): J. Smit, *E. J. Potgieter* (1950).
(P. K. K.)

POTHIER, DOM JOSEPH (1835–1923), French monk and scholar who, together with his contemporaries, reconstituted the Gregorian chant (*see* PLAINSONG). Born at Bouzemont, near Saint-Dié, on Dec. 7, 1835, he took vows as a Benedictine monk at Solesmes in 1860. He was prior of Ligugé in 1893 and in 1898 was appointed abbot of Saint-Wandrille. Soon after he entered Solesmes he collaborated with Dom Paul Jausions on a new edition of the choir books based on manuscripts of the Gregorian chant. Dom Jausions died in 1870 but his contribution was acknowledged in the preface to Dom Pothier's publication *Les Mélodies grégoriennes d'après la tradition* (1880), which became the standard work on the subject. In 1883 he published the *Liber gradualis,* which also included research earlier undertaken by Dom Jausions and which, with the *Mélodies grégoriennes,* marked the beginning of a reform in liturgical chant. In 1889 he was associated with his disciple Dom André Mocquereau (1849–1930) in the foundation of the publication *Paléographie musicale* for the dissemination of medieval liturgical manuscripts. In 1904 Pope Pius X appointed him chairman of a commission for the reconstitution of the music of the Roman Catholic Mass. Many of the controversial theories regarding the intervention of Gregorian chant were published in the *Revue du chant grégorien* (1892–1914), of which Dom Pothier was editor. He died at Conques, Belg., on Dec. 8, 1923.

See M. Cocheril, "Dom Joseph Pothier," *Encyclopédie de la musique,* ed. by F. Michel, vol. iii (1961); Abbé M. Blanc, *L'Enseignement musical de Solesmes et la prière chrétienne* (1953).

POTI, a town and port of the Georgian Soviet Socialist Republic, U.S.S.R., on the Black Sea at the mouth of the Rioni River, on the site of the ancient Greek colony of Phasis. Pop. (1967 est.) 46,000. The modern town developed only in the 19th century, when in the 1880s an artificial harbour and a rail link to the main Trans-Caucasus Railway at Mikha Tskhakaya were built. Its chief exports are manganese from Chiatura, cotton, and citrus fruits; coal, grain, sugar, and fertilizers are the main imports. There is a fishing fleet and fish-processing works. Dredgers are built at Poti, and there is a flour mill, a meat-packing plant, and a refrigeration plant. (R. A. F.)

POTLATCH, meaning giveaway in Chinook (*q.v.*) trade jargon, the public distribution of property as uniquely and elaborately institutionalized among American Indians of the North Pacific Coast. The potlatch existed in the following cultures, reading from southern Alaska to northern Oregon: Tlingit, Tsimshian, Haida, Bella Coola, Northern and Southern Kwakiutl, Nootka, Coast Salish, and Lower Chinook. Although each group had its characteristic version, the potlatch had certain general features. Ceremonial formalities were observed in inviting guests, in speechmaking, and in the distribution of goods by the donor according to the social rank of the recipients. The size of the gatherings reflected the rank of the donor; often large, they tended to include guests from a wide territory. Great feasts and generous hospitality accompanied the potlatching, and the efforts of the kin group of the host were exerted to maximize the liberality. The proceedings gave wide publicity to the social status of donor and recipients since there were many witnesses.

Nonutilitarian prestige property was most appropriate for such distributions; useful goods were given in quantities far beyond normal needs. A potlatch was given by an heir or successor to assert and validate his newly assumed social position. Important steps such as marriage were frequent occasions for potlatches, but just as often such trivial events as the first time a baby's hair was singed served equally well. The main purpose was the validation of any and all claims to social rank. Among the Tlingit the potlatch centred around mourning the death of an important chief; among the Tsimshian and Haida the potlatch memorialized a chief and established his successor. The Kwakiutl and Nootka potlatched for these and other reasons, most frequently to affirm and reaffirm social rank. They also had the face-saving potlatch to wipe out such losses of dignity as falling into the water in public view, and the competitive potlatch in which two rivals in social rank vied even to the point of destroying property. Coast Salish potlatches were usually given by established village leaders as reconfirmation of their worth.

The potlatch reached its most elaborate development among the Southern Kwakiutl from 1849 to 1925. The whole culture focused on the institution; their potlatches were the most frequent, distributed the greatest amount of property, and were the most complex financially. Interest-bearing loans, and coppers (shield-shaped pieces of copper) serving as negotiable checks for credit and property, were native inventions supporting the potlatch.

The recipient had to return greater value when it came his turn to potlatch; in their expanding economy these prosperous people distributed extraordinary amounts of property. In ceremonies lasting days, thousands of blankets and other European goods including motorboats, sewing machines, enamelware, clothing, flour, and sugar were distributed along with such native goods as masks and canoes. The donor of such a potlatch required several years to prepare, earning Canadian money (usually in commercial salmon-fishing), and making loans to fellow Kwakiutl probably for their own potlatching. Considering the lengths to which they went to make potlatching their most absorbing institution, the Southern Kwakiutl burlesque through a play potlatch is remarkable. By the 1960s traditional potlatching had virtually ceased, even where enthusiasm for it had run highest. Economic factors were more to blame than were interests working for Indian assimilation.

See also GIFT EXCHANGE; INDIANS, NORTHWEST COAST; KWAKIUTL; NOOTKA (AHT).

BIBLIOGRAPHY.—F. Boas, "The Social Organization and the Secret Societies of the Kwakiutl Indians," *Rep. U.S. Nat. Mus. 1895* (1897); G. P. Murdock, "Rank and Potlatch Among the Haida," *Yale Publ. Anthrop.,* 13:1–20 (1936); H. G. Barnett, "The Nature of the Potlatch," *Amer. Anthrop.,* vol. 40 (1938); H. Codere, *Fighting with Property: a Study of Kwakiutl Potlatching . . .* (1950); P. Drucker, *Indians of the Northwest Coast* (1955); W. Suttles, "The Persistence of Intervillage Ties Among the Coast Salish," *Ethnology* (Oct. 1963).
(HE. C.)

POTOCKI, the name of a Polish aristocratic family known in southern Poland since the 13th century. Its seat was Potok, near Jedrzejow. The founders of the family's power were the sons of MIKOLAJ (1517–1572), namely JAN (1555–1611), ANDRZEJ (d. 1609), JAKUB (1554–1613), and STEFAN (d. 1631), who distinguished themselves in wars against the Tatars. During the Zebrzydowski insurrection (1606–07; *see* POLAND: *History*) they fought at the side of King Sigismund III.

MIKOLAJ (d. 1651), son of Jakub and hetman of the crown, was in command of the Polish forces at the victorious Battle of Beresteczko (1651; *see* UKRAINIAN SOVIET SOCIALIST REPUBLIC: *History*). STANISLAW (1579–1667), son of Andrzej, was also hetman of the crown, and took part in battles against Wallachians, Muscovites, Cossacks, Turks, and Swedes. In 1660 he defeated the Muscovites at Cudnow; and in 1662 he founded the city of Stanislawow (Ivano-Frankovsk). His sons ANDRZEJ (d. 1692) and FELIKS KAZIMIERZ (d. 1702), both hetmans, took part in the Turkish wars of King John III Sobieski.

In the 18th century the Potockis were among the most prominent "republicans" opposing Kings Augustus II and Augustus III and the Familia (party of the Czartoryskis and the Poniatowskis). JOZEF (d. 1751), son of the hetman Andrzej, was a partisan of Stanislaw Leszczynski during the Northern War (*q.v.*) and was made hetman by him. Since his baton was taken away during the restoration of Augustus II, he again supported Leszczynski during the interregnum of 1733. Having formally reconciled himself with Augustus III, he became again hetman in 1735. Leader of the "republicans," he sought French, Turkish, and Prussian support against the Saxon dynasty. In this he had the help of his distant cousin TEODOR (1664–1738), primate of Poland from 1722, who as *interrex* in 1733 had procured Leszczynski's election as king.

FRANCISZEK SALEZY (d. 1772), grandson of Feliks Kazimierz, palatine of Kiev from 1756 and the richest magnate of his times, became reconciled with the court after the break between Augustus III and the Familia; but under King Stanislaw II Poniatowski the Potockis were again in opposition.

The firmest supporter of the "republican" tradition was STANISLAW SZCZESNY or FELIKS (1752–1805), the son of Franciszek Salezy and heir to immense estates in Ukraine. He dreamed of transforming Poland into a federal republic (without a king), following the example of the United States of America. He was palatine of Ruthenia and later general of the crown artillery. In 1785–89 he was grand master of Polish freemasonry. In favour of friendly relations with Russia, he opposed the alliance with Prussia (1790) and the monarchical constitution of May 3, 1791. Head of the Confederation of Targowica, which was formed with the Russian military aid in 1792 to annul the enactments of the "Four Years' *sejm*", he did not foresee the second partition of Poland (1793). Disillusioned and branded as a traitor, he retired to his Tulczyn estates.

IGNACY (1751–1809), great-grandson of Feliks Kazimierz, was prominent in the Commission of National Education from 1773 and grand master of Polish freemasonry from 1781 to 1784. He advocated a reform to subordinate the government to a sovereign *sejm*. During the "Four Years' *sejm*," from 1788, he was a leader of the patriotic faction and promoted the alliance with Prussia and the constitution of May 3, 1791. After the Confederation of Targowica he emigrated to Dresden (1792–94) and helped to prepare Tadeusz Kosciuszko's insurrection (1794). Having directed the foreign policy of the insurrectionary government, he surrendered to the Russians after the fall of Warsaw and was sent to St. Petersburg. On his return to Poland (1796) he settled at Klimontow and devoted himself to political writing. He died in Vienna in 1809, having gone there to present to Napoleon I a petition for the incorporation of Galicia in the Duchy of Warsaw.

STANISLAW KOSTKA (1755–1821), many times deputy to the *sejm* and an outstanding orator, followed the politics of his elder brother Ignacy. After creation of the Duchy of Warsaw (1807) he was president of the council of state. Between 1812 and 1821 he was grand master of Polish freemasonry. In the Polish kingdom created by the Congress of Vienna he served as minister of education and church affairs (1815–20). He wrote many literary and political works, the most famous being the anticlerical *Podróż do Ciemnogrodu* ("Journey to Backwash Towns"; 1820), for which he was dismissed from office.

JAN (1761–1815), explorer in Asia and Africa, archaeologist, historian, novelist, and journalist, first appeared as a deputy to the "Four Years' *sejm*." He wrote some notable historical works and travel books in French and also a fantastic novel, *Manuscrit trouvé à Saragosse* (new edition 1958).

ALFRED (1817–1889), a member of the Lancut-Antoniny branch of the Potockis (made counts by Austria in 1768), served as Austrian prime minister in 1870–71 and as governor of Galicia in 1875–83. ADAM (1812–1872), deputy to the Vienna Parliament, became the leader of the Polish Conservative Party in Galicia, loyal to Austria. His son ANDRZEJ (1861–1908) was governor of Galicia from 1903 till a Ukrainian nationalist student shot him. The younger ALFRED (1886–1957), son of Roman and grandson of the Austrian prime minister Alfred Potocki, took over the *majorat* of Lancut and left memoirs published as *Master of Lancut* (1959). His brother JERZY (1889–1961) served as Polish ambassador to Turkey (1933–35) and to the United States (1936–40). Their uncle JOZEF (1862–1922), Roman's brother, administered the estates of Antoniny in the Ukraine; his title of count was confirmed by Russia in 1890. His son JOZEF (1895–   ), a member of the Polish diplomatic service from 1919, was ambassador to Spain in World War II.   (EM. R.)

POTOMAC, a river in the east central United States, rises in the Appalachian mountains of West Virginia and flows southeastward into Chesapeake bay, draining an area of approximately 14,500 sq.mi. Its two headwaters, the north and the south branch, join about 15 mi. below Cumberland, Md. From there to the bay it is 287 mi. long, 117 of which are tidal. At Harpers Ferry it receives the Shenandoah river from the Appalachian valley to the south and after traversing the easternmost mountain chains through a series of spectacular watergaps it is joined by the Monocacy river in the Piedmont region and by the Anacostia or east branch at Washington, D.C. Together with its north branch, it forms the boundary between Maryland and West Virginia from its source to Harpers Ferry, and from there to its mouth it is the boundary between Maryland and Virginia. The District of Co-

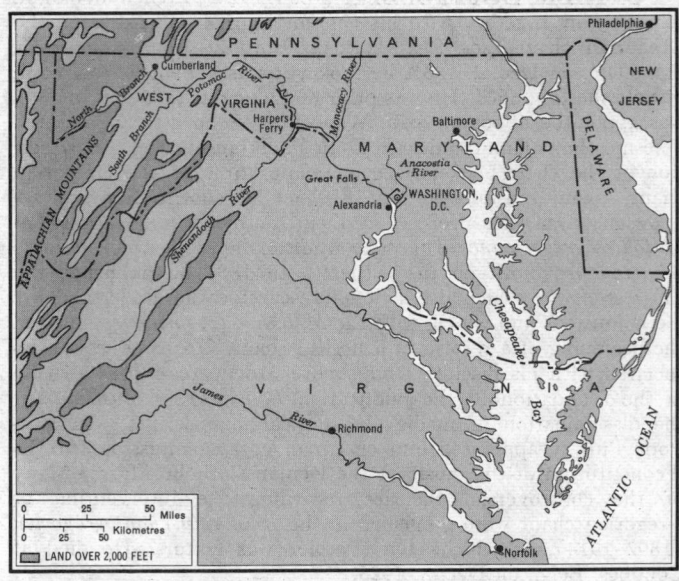

COURSE OF THE POTOMAC RIVER

lumbia lies on its left bank at the head of tidewater. Navigability of the tidal portion is assured by channels dredged to a depth of 18 and 21 ft. at Washington and of 24 ft. through all the shoals. Washington and Alexandria (Va.) possess minor port facilities; the lower Anacostia is navigable to Bladensburg, Md., for small craft. For a stretch of about 12 mi. upstream from Washington the Potomac descends from the Piedmont to the coastal plain in a series of rapids and falls, of which Great Falls contains a cataract about 35 ft. high. The Chesapeake and Ohio canal, paralleling the Potomac, was completed in 1850 from Georgetown to Cumberland; traffic ceased at the beginning of the 20th century but the canal remains a scenic and recreational asset.

                        (F. O. A.)

POTOSÍ, a department of Bolivia, bounded north by Oruro and Cochabamba, east by Chuquisaca and Tarija, west by Chile and south by Argentina. Pop. (1961 est.) 608,000. Area 45,644 sq.mi. Situated in the southwest of the country, it ranks second in population and fourth in territorial area among Bolivia's departments. Potosí (*q.v.*) is capital of the department and of the province of Cercado. Indians, mestizos and people of European descent make up the population.

The department is noted for its great mineral wealth and its high physical altitude. The surface is extremely rugged, being traversed by the eastern branch of the Andes, and the climate is rigorous. Elevations range from about 6,000 ft. to more than 20,000 ft. above sea level. The capital city stands at an altitude of over 13,700 ft., and the temperature there seldom exceeds 59° F. Livestock grazing and agriculture are carried on, chiefly at lower elevations owing to the harsh natural environment of the Altiplano. Vegetation is scarce and there is little water for irrigation. The region is drained mainly by the affluents of the Pilcomayo. The department is also deficient in fuels, a significant obstacle to industrial development.

The Spanish mining industry in Bolivia began in 1540 with the operation of the silver mines of Porco (now the province of Quijarro) by Gonzalo Pizarro and Diego Centeno. The discovery in 1545 of Cerro Potosí, a conical mountain rising 15,680 ft. above sea level, established Potosí as the foremost silver producing region in the world. It is estimated that the region subsequently produced $1,000,000,000 worth of silver. The Cerro is composed of one of the richest ore bodies yet discovered, an ore containing tin, bismuth and tungsten in addition to silver.

Potosí declined in importance as a mining area as a result of the diminution of the more readily available ores and of progress in technology which made feasible the use of lower quality ores in more accessible locations. The exploitation of Bolivia's tin ores which began shortly before the end of the 19th century restored mining activity in the department. The construction of a railway from Antofagasta to the centre of the plateau in 1892 made it possible to ship out ores of lesser value than those of silver; newly discovered uses for tin created an expanding market for that metal. Lead, zinc, antimony, copper, bismuth, sulfur, gold, silver and wolfram, are also worked in the region. Among the 13 provinces of the department, those notable for minerals comprise Sud Chichas (regarded as the richest), Cercado, Chayanta, Bustillo, Charcas, Linares, Alonso de Ibañez, Nor and Sud Lipez and Nor Chicas. Extensive deposits of solid salt, the Salar de Uyuni (3,500 sq.mi.) and Copaisa, Chiguana and Empexa, south of Lake Poopó, are also exploited.

Air, railroad and highway facilities are available within the department. A branch line of the Antofagasta-La Paz railway extends to the city of Potosí from the junction at Río Mulato. This line (15,705 ft. above sea level at Condor) is one of the highest railways in the world. (J. L. TR.)

POTOSÍ, a city in Bolivia, capital of the department of Potosí, is located on a cold and barren plateau 275 mi. S of La Paz. Pop. (1969 est.) 63,590. One of the highest cities of the world (altitude over 13,700 ft.), it stands in the shadow of the fabulous Cerro Potosí and its 5,000 mines. The temperature seldom exceeds 59° F. Legend attributes the name to "potojchi," Quechua word meaning "thunder," on account of rumblings inside the mountain. The city came into existence after the discovery of silver in the *cerro* by the Indian Gualpa, whose master Juan de Villaroel registered the first claim April 21, 1545. Charles V conferred upon it the title Villa Imperial (1547). Philip II chartered the university (1571) and the mint (1572). So great was the wealth of the mines that "as rich as Potosí" became a current expression. About 200 merchants supplied the city with luxuries from all parts of the world. It was a turbulent city full of factions, such as the Vicunas and Vascongados, who waged full-fledged civil war, 1623–26. Population fluctuated with the mineral production. Of the estimated 160,000 residents in 1650 only 8,000 remained when Simón Bolívar liberated the area in the final battle of the Wars for Independence, Oct. 5, 1825. Rich tin deposits replaced the diminishing silver lode and 20th century Potosí became the leading industrial city of Bolivia. Iron, steel, shoes, soft drinks, beer, furniture, electric products, and mosaics supplemented mining (tin, lead, copper, silver) and refining industries.

Although flood and earthquake have taken their toll, Potosí retains its colonial charm. The city is laid out in squares with narrow, sometimes winding streets originating in the central plaza, around which are grouped the government house, city hall, national college, mint, treasury, and cathedral, dating back to colonial times. Potosí is on a highway, and the Sucre-Potosí Railway connects with the Antofagasta-Bolivia line.

See Lewis Hanke, *The Imperial City of Potosí* (1956). (G. B. Co.)

POTSDAM, a town of East Germany, the headquarters of the *Bezirk* (district) of the same name, in the German Democratic Republic. It is situated on the Havel, divided there into lakes, and is adjacent to the southwest boundary of Berlin. Pop. (1964) 110,083. It was first mentioned in the 10th century as a Slav settlement and received its municipal charter in the 14th century. Under the Great Elector, Frederick William, it became a garrison town in 1640, and from the time of Frederick the

FRITZ ESCHEN

SOUTH FACADE OF SANSSOUCI PALACE

Great, to whom it owes many of its fine buildings, it was the summer residence of the Hohenzollerns. The Stadtschloss (reconstructed 1745–51, with splendid rococo interiors) and the nearby Garrison Church (1731–35) as well as most of the town centre were severely damaged by bombing attacks during World War II but restoration was later undertaken. The Brandenburg Gate (1770) stands near the entrance to the Sanssouci Park in which is the Sanssouci Palace (1745–47), the one-storied summer residence of Frederick the Great, a masterpiece of German rococo. The Neues Palais (1763–69) is now a teachers' training college. Other buildings of interest are Babelsberg Castle, built 1834–49 in the English Tudor style, the Friedenskirche (Church of Peace), erected in 1845–49 in the style of an early Christian basilica, and the Nikolai Church (1830–37).

Potsdam is an industrial town with scientific institutes, including the German academy of political science and law, the college of finance, the German academy of film art, and institutes connected mainly with agriculture and medicine. There are also the Einstein Observatory, a meteorological observatory, and a theatre. In Babelsberg (an incorporated suburb) are film studios, and the town has important industry including locomotive works, textile mills, and pharmaceutical factories.

For the Potsdam Conference (July 17–Aug. 2, 1945) *see* WORLD WARS: *World War II: Potsdam.*

POTTER, ALONZO (1800–1865), U.S. Protestant· Episcopal bishop and educator, who by writing and lecturing did much to extend and improve public school education, was born at Beekman (now La Grange), N.Y., July 6, 1800. He graduated in 1818 at Union College, where he became tutor and then professor of mathematics after a brief period spent in studying theology at Philadelphia. He was a rector of St. Paul's, Boston, from 1826 to 1831, when he returned to Union as professor of philosophy and political economy, becoming vice-president of the college in 1838. He was consecrated bishop of Pennsylvania on Sept. 23, 1845. Potter died on board ship in San Francisco Bay on July 4, 1865.

Potter's chief work (with G. B. Emerson) was *The School and the Schoolmaster* (1842). He was particularly interested in work for young men and in temperance reform. As a legislator in the church he was wise and progressive. He established the Philadelphia Divinity School (1863) and laboured for the hospital of the Protestant Episcopal Church in Philadelphia.

See M. A. De Wolfe Howe, *Memoirs of the Life and Services of the Rt. Rev. Alonzo Potter, D. D.* (1870).

POTTER, (HELEN) BEATRIX (1866–1943), English writer and illustrator of books for young children, the creator of "Peter Rabbit," "Benjamin Bunny," "Jemima Puddle-Duck," "Mrs. Tiggy-Winkle," and other famous animal characters, was born in South Kensington, London, on July 6, 1866. Her father, a barrister, had never practised; both parents came of hard-headed Lancashire stock and had inherited cotton fortunes. Even by mid-

Victorian standards they were conventional and authoritarian, and Beatrix, their only daughter, spent a lonely and repressed childhood, enlivened only by annual holidays in Scotland or the Lake District. These gave her her first experience of the country and developed her artist-naturalist talent for drawing hedgerow animals, which she kept as pets and used as models for both naturalistic and imaginative watercolour drawings.

When she was 27, still living at home, she began sending illustrated letters to the sick child of a former governess, telling him stories about Peter Rabbit, Benjamin Bunny, and her tame hedgehog, Mrs. Tiggy-Winkle. These letters gave such pleasure that she decided to make Peter Rabbit into a book. *The Tale of Peter Rabbit* (1902) was privately published, as was *The Tailor of Gloucester* (1903). She eventually found a publisher, Frederick Warne & Co., who in the next 30 years brought out 23 of the little books which made her famous.

Despite strong parental opposition, in 1905 she became engaged to Norman Warne, the son of her publisher, and after his sudden death a few months later spent much of her time alone at Hill Top, a small farm in the village of Sawrey in Lancashire, bought with the proceeds of a legacy and the royalties from her books. In 1913 she married William Heelis, a solicitor from Ambleside, Westmorland, and spent the last 30 years of her life extending her farm property and breeding Herdwick sheep. She bequeathed her land to the National Trust, which maintains her original farmhouse as it was when she lived in it. She died at Sawrey on Dec. 22, 1943. After her death the Tate Gallery, London, acquired her watercolour illustrations to *The Tailor of Gloucester*. The only known portrait of her is in the National Portrait Gallery.

Beatrix Potter's books have been loved by generations of children and have been widely translated. They combine a deceptively simple prose, concealing a dry north-country humour, with illustrations in the best English watercolour tradition. In old age, as her sight deteriorated, she lost much of her freshness of vision, and her last few stories, written for publication in the United States, were poor both in style and draftsmanship. The best of these later works, *The Fairy Caravan,* was published in New York in 1929 and in London in 1952; it does not in any sense compare with her earlier masterpieces. In these, her animal characters are described with shrewd economy, and their homes and backgrounds—hedgerows, gardens, cabbage-patches, farmhouse kitchens—in the precise and homely detail that children love. There is nothing sentimental about her themes; there is even a macabre strain occasionally, for she is not squeamish and her eye is faithful to nature. Though her rabbits may wear shoes and jackets and her hedgehog a mobcap and pinafore, they are fundamentally true to their animal nature. Poetic vision and a robust regard for truth go hand in hand.

See M. Lane, *The Tale of Beatrix Potter* (1946); L. Linder and W. A. Herring, *The Art of Beatrix Potter* (1955).   (M. LA.)

POTTER, PAUL (PAULUS) (1625–1654), Dutch painter and etcher, celebrated chiefly as an animal painter, son of the painter Pieter Potter, was born at Enkhuizen in 1625. He entered the Guild of St. Luke at Delft in 1646. In 1649 he moved to The Hague, where in the following year he married Adriana, daughter of the architect Claes van Balkeneynde. In 1652 he settled in Amsterdam, where he died on Jan. 15, 1654. Potter probably received his early training from his father, but his style shows little dependence upon that of earlier masters. Animals appear prominently in all of Potter's characteristic works, sometimes singly (the "Grey Horse," dated 1653, Hamburg), more usually in small groups silhouetted against the sky, or in greater numbers with peasant figures and rustic buildings in an extensive landscape. So lifelike is his portrayal of cows, horses and other domestic animals that many critics tend to regard this as his only talent, and to treat him as one of the minor Dutch masters—charming, but limited in range. This is an undervaluation of Potter's genius. His range of subject matter is limited by his own choice, but within that range he displays powers far above many contemporaries who are usually judged to be more eminent. No Dutch painter of his time was more sensitive to the passing moods of nature, or to the countryside's timeless harmony of beast, landscape

BY COURTESY OF THE SALZBURGER RESIDENZGALERIE

"EARLY MORNING" BY PAUL POTTER, 1647

and weather, and none gives the impression of having observed the landscape of his country with deeper love or understanding. In addition, Potter possessed a remarkably developed feeling for design, expressed in the grouping of his forms and in his use of eloquent silhouette, dark on light or light on dark. All of these qualities can be admired in the superb "Early Morning" (1647, Salzburg museum), which is possibly his most perfect masterpiece. This is a fine, open composition, painted with a small, but firm and lively touch; the light of early morning—and of early spring—is deliciously rendered, and there is a keen understanding of both animal and human behaviour. Like most of his really successful pictures it is on a small scale, and painted on panel.

In so tragically short a career there was naturally little development in style between the earlier and the later works, but 1647 seems to mark a peak in his achievement, for many of the finest paintings bear this date. Characteristic works are: "Cattle in a Stormy Landscape" (1647; National gallery, London); "Horses Tethered at a Cottage Door" (1647 or 1649; Louvre, Paris); "Peasant With Cattle" (1648; Cassel) and "Cattle Reflected in Water" (1648; Mauritshuis, The Hague). Among works which depart from his normal scale or style, the huge "Young Bull" (1647; The Hague), which is on the scale of life, is his most celebrated though surely not his finest work, while "Orpheus Charming the Beasts" (1650; Rijksmuseum, Amsterdam), is an untypical excursion into a poetic world reminiscent of Roland Savery. Potter's etchings of animals show all the skill and sympathy of his paintings.

See T. van Westrheene, *Paulus Potter, Sa vie et ses oeuvres* (1867); C. H. de Groot, *Catalogue of . . . Dutch Painters,* etc., vol. iv (1912).   (R. E. W. J.)

POTTERIES, THE, a name applied to a district of north Staffordshire, the principal seat of the china and earthenware industry in England. It lies in the upper part of the Trent basin. For a distance of 9 mi. from southeast to northwest and about 3 mi. from northeast to southwest, the district resembles one great town, but the chief centres are Burslem, Hanley, Longton, Stoke-on-Trent, Fenton and Tunstall (except Fenton, the "Five Towns" of Arnold Bennett's novels). These towns were amalgamated in 1910 as one municipal borough under the name of Stoke-on-Trent (*q.v.*), which was made a city in 1925. Newcastle-under-Lyme, though not sharing in the staple industry, may also be reckoned in the district. In 1769 Josiah Wedgwood founded potteries at Etruria, by the Trent and Mersey canal; they are now at Barlaston. Wedgwood and Minton are the two most famous family names connected with the china industry of the district. Coal, from the north Staffordshire coal field, and coarse clay are the only local natural products used in the industry, the finer clay and other ingredients being brought from elsewhere.

POTTER'S CLAY: see KAOLIN.

POTTERY AND PORCELAIN. Pottery in its widest sense includes all objects made from clay and hardened by fire; the term porcelain applies only to certain kinds of pottery. The following article outlines the history of the art and manufacture of the principal types of pottery and porcelain throughout the world and is arranged as follows:

I. INTRODUCTION

"Pottery" and "porcelain" are technical terms referring to the composition and method of manufacture of the material in question. Both terms require some explanation. Clay, the basic material of both pottery and porcelain, has two distinctive characteristics: it is plastic (*i.e.*, it can be molded and will retain the shape imposed upon it); and it hardens on firing to form a brittle, but otherwise virtually indestructible, material which is not attacked by any of the agents that corrode metals or organic materials. Also if a sun-dried clay vessel is filled with water it absorbs the liquid, becomes very soft, and eventually collapses, but if it is heated chemical changes that begin to take place at about 500° C preclude a return to the plastic state no matter how much water is later in contact with it. At extremely high temperatures, which are difficult to achieve in any kiln, the clay will eventually "vitrify," or fuse to form a glassy, nonporous substance. If, however, the clay is mixed with suitable proportions of more easily fusible material, the vitrification temperature can be lowered to around 1,200° C. The fusible material melts and seals the pores of the unfused clay which retains the original shape of the vessel. (For this reason the Chinese refer to the clay as "the bones" of the vessel, and to the vitrifying substance as "the flesh.") At temperatures between 1,250° and 1,450° C the vitrified substance becomes translucent.

The terms describing the end products of firing are sometimes used very loosely. In this article, all objects that are made from clay and hardened by fire are termed "ceramics," a word derived from the Greek *keramos* ("potter's earth"). This meaning corresponds with the French *céramique* and the German *Keramik*. "Pottery" is used synonymously with "earthenware" to denote all ceramic substances which are not vitrified. These are, in consequence, slightly porous and are coarser than vitrified materials, which may belong to one of two classes, "stoneware" or "porcelain." The line of demarcation between the last two is extremely vague. In Europe porcelain is usually defined as a translucent substance—when held to the light most porcelain will be found to have this property—and stoneware is regarded as partially vitrified material which is not translucent. The Chinese, on the other hand, define porcelain as any ceramic material which will give a ringing tone when tapped. None of these definitions is completely satisfactory: for instance, some thinly potted stonewares are slightly translucent if they have been fired at a high temperature, whereas some heavily potted porcelains are opaque. Therefore the application of the terms is often a matter of personal preference and they should be regarded as descriptive without being definite.

Earthenware, stoneware, and porcelain are all found in glazed and unglazed forms and, in the case of the first two, the type of glaze is often used as the basis for further classification within each category.

1. Types of Earthenware.—Primitive races made vessels of sun-dried clay which could be used only for storing cereals and similar dry materials. Early fired vessels held water, but, because they were still slightly porous, the liquid percolated slowly to the outside where it evaporated, cooling the contents of the vessel. Thus the porosity of earthenware was, and still is, sometimes an advantage in hot countries and the principle is utilized in the 20th century in the construction of domestic milk and butter coolers and some food-storage cupboards.

Porosity, however, had many disadvantages—*e.g.*, the vessels could not be used for storing wine or milk—and a remedy eventually was devised. This consisted of covering the surface with a thin layer of glass, termed a "glaze." The art of glazing for decorative as well as practical purposes followed speedily upon its introduction (see *Primitive Pottery,* below).

There are two main types of glazed earthenware: the one is covered with a transparent glaze, and the other with an opaque white glaze.

Apart from some glazes made from feldspar which are, in effect, natural glasses, glazes in normal use are indistinguishable from manufactured glass. Some of the earliest glazes fall into much the same divisions as old glass (*i.e.,* soda glass or potash glass) but the introduction of lead as a flux, probably in the 1st century B.C., gave a glaze more suitable for soft earthenware because it fused at a much lower temperature. Lead glazes were employed in the 18th century in soft porcelain manufacture. Modern technology has produced new glazes which fall into none of these categories while remaining a type of glass.

Opaque white glazes are made by adding stannic oxide, one of the oxides of tin, to the glaze material. Wares thus decorated are often referred to as "tin enameled" or "stanniferous." Other terms in common use are "majolica" (Italian, *maiolica*), "faience," and "delft." These, again, are used by various authorities with different meanings and the position needs clarification. The art of tin enameling was discovered by the Assyrians who used it to cover courses of decorated brickwork. It was revived in Mesopotamia about the 9th century A.D. and spread to Moorish Spain, whence it was conveyed to Italy by way of the island of Majorca or Maiolica. In Italy tin-enameled earthenware was called *maiolica* after the place where it was mistakenly thought to have originated. The wares of Italy, particularly those of Faenza, were much prized abroad and early in the 16th century the technique was imitated in southern France. The term "faience," which is applied to French tin-enameled ware, is undoubtedly derived from "Faenza." Wares made in Germany, Spain, and Scandinavia are known by the same name. Early in the 17th century a flourishing industry for the manufacture of tin-enameled ware was established at the town of Delft, Holland, and Dutch potters brought the art of tin enameling to England together with the name of delft, which now applies to wares manufactured in the Netherlands and England. Some misleading uses of these terms include that of applying *"maiolica"* to wares made outside Italy but in the Italian style, and "faience" to Egyptian blue-glazed ware and certain kinds of Near Eastern earthenware. *Fayence-Porcellaine* was a term sometimes used in 18th-century Germany to describe faience decorated with enamel colours applied over the glaze, as on porcelain.

Tin enamel was undoubtedly devised in the first place to hide faults of colour in the body, for most clays contain a variable amount of iron which colours the body from buff to dark red. Tin-enameled wares look somewhat as though they have been covered with thick white paint. They sometimes received the addition of a lead glaze, known in Italy as *coperta* and in the Netherlands as *kwaart.*

Defects of body colour also suggested the use of slip, a mixture of clay and water with a creamlike consistency which is washed over the vessel before firing. Slips may be either white or coloured. A common mode of decoration is to incise a pattern through the slip revealing the body colour beneath, a technique which has received the generic term of *sgraffito* ("scratched") ware. Slip, too, is sometimes dotted and trailed in much the same way as a confectioner decorates a cake with icing sugar; the English slipwares of the 17th and 18th centuries are typical of this kind of work. Earthenware washed over with a white slip and covered with a colourless glaze is sometimes difficult to distinguish from lead-glazed tin enamel. In consequence it has sometimes been wrongly called faience. The term for French earthenware decorated in this way (in imitation of Wedgwood's creamware, is *faience fine* and in Germany it is called *Steingut. Mezza-Maiolica* (Italy) and *Halb-Fayence* (Germany) refer to similar white earthenware with incised decoration.

2. Types of Stoneware.—Although glazed stoneware does not fall into such definite categories as glazed earthenware, to some extent it can be classified according to the kind of glaze used. The fine Chinese stonewares of the Sung dynasty (A.D. 960–1279)

were covered with a glaze made from feldspar, the same vitrifiable material as was later used in both the body and glaze of porcelain. Stoneware covered with a lead glaze is not uncommon, but perhaps the majority of extant glazed wares are salt glazed. In this process a shovelful of common salt (sodium chloride) is thrown into the kiln when the temperature reaches its highest. The salt splits into its components, the sodium combining with the silica in the clay to form a "smear" glaze of sodium silicate, the chlorine escaping through the kiln chimney. Salt glazes have a pitted appearance similar to that of orange peel. A little red lead is sometimes added to the salt, which gives the surface an appearance of being glazed by the more usual means.

A fine white stoneware, conventionally glazed, was made in Staffordshire, Eng., during the early years of the 19th century, and was termed "Ironstone China."

Of the unglazed stonewares, the most familiar are the Chinese teapots and similar wares from I-hsing in Kiangsu Province, the red stoneware body made at Meissen in Saxony during the first three decades of the 18th century and revived in modern times, and the ornamental basaltes and jaspers made by Josiah Wedgwood and Sons since the 18th century.

In the mid-20th century stoneware was used mostly for utility articles such as drainpipes and laboratory ware, and also by artist-potters such as Bernard Leach and his followers.

3. Types of Porcelain.—Porcelain is classified not by the type of glaze used, as is the case with earthenware and stoneware, but by the composition of the body. It was first made in a primitive form in China during the T'ang dynasty (A.D. 618–906). The kind most familiar in the West was not manufactured until the Yüan dynasty (A.D. 1280–1368). It was made from kaolin (white china clay) and petuntse (a feldspathic rock), the latter being ground to powder and mixed with the clay. During the firing, which took place at a temperature of about 1,450° C, the petuntse vitrified, while the refractory clay ensured that the vessel retained its shape. It was extremely difficult to attain an even distribution of heat throughout the kiln, and in some parts the temperature rose to a point where even the clay vitrified. The vessels that warped or melted to shapeless lumps are known as "wasters." All old pottery and porcelain factories accumulated "wasters," many of which have been subsequently excavated. They provide the most reliable evidence of the types of ware made, and the position of sherds in the heap enables a system of sequence dating to be established.

In medieval times isolated specimens of Chinese porcelain found their way to Europe where they were much prized, principally because of their translucency. European potters made numerous attempts to imitate them and, since at that time there was no exact body of chemical and physical knowledge whereby the porcelain could be analyzed and then synthesized, experiments proceeded strictly by analogy. The only manufactured translucent substance then known was glass, and it was perhaps inevitable that glass made opaque with tin oxide (the German *milch-glas,* for example) should have been used as a substitute for porcelain. The nature of glass, however, made it impossible to shape it by any of the means used by the potter, and a mixture of clay and ground glass was eventually tried. Porcelain made in this way resembles that of the Chinese only superficially and is always termed "soft" or "artificial" porcelain. The date and place of the first attempt to make soft porcelain is debatable, but some Middle Eastern pottery of the 12th century was made from glaze material mixed with clay and is occasionally translucent (see *Islamic Pottery: Egypt,* below). Much the same formula was employed with a measure of success at Florence about 1575 at workshops under the patronage of Duke Francesco de' Medici. Specimens of this "Medici" porcelain are now very rare. No further attempts of any kind appear to have been made until the mid-17th century, when Claude and François Révérend, Paris importers of Dutch pottery, were granted a monopoly of porcelain manufacture in France. It is not known whether they succeeded in making it or not, but certainly by the end of the 17th century porcelain was being made in quantity, this time by a factory at Saint-Cloud, near Paris.

The secret of "true," or "hard," porcelain similar to that of China was not discovered until about 1707 in Saxony when Ehrenfried Walter von Tschirnhaus, assisted by an alchemist called Johann Friedrich Böttger, substituted ground feldspathic rock for the ground glass in the soft porcelain formula. Since its discovery hard porcelain has been the body preferred on the European continent.

The terms "soft" and "hard" porcelain refer to the "soft" firing (about 1,150° C) necessary for the first, and the "hard" firing (about 1,450° C) necessary for the second. By coincidence they apply also to the physical properties of the two substances: for example, soft porcelain can be cut with a file, whereas hard porcelain cannot. This is sometimes used as a test for the nature of the body.

In the course of experiments in England during the 18th century a type of soft porcelain was made in which bone ash was added to the ground glass. Josiah Spode the Second later added this bone ash to the true, hard porcelain formula and the resulting body, known as bone china, has since become the standard English porcelain. Soft porcelain, always regarded as a substitute for hard porcelain, was discontinued because it was uneconomic; kiln wastage was excessive, occasionally rising to nine-tenths of the total. Hard porcelain is strong, but its vitreous nature causes it to chip fairly easily and, unless specially treated, is usually tinged slightly with blue or grey. Bone china is slightly easier to manufacture than hard porcelain. It is strong, does not chip easily, and the bone ash confers an ivory-white appearance widely regarded as desirable. Generally, bone china is most popular for table-services in England and the United States, although connoisseurs of the finer qualities of old porcelain usually prefer the hard variety.

4. Methods of Fashioning Ceramics.—The earliest vessels were modeled by hand. Almost as early, pots were made by smearing clay round the inside of a basket or coarsely woven sack. The

HAND-MODELED VESSELS

(Left) Polished red-ware, black-topped vase; Egypt, about 4000 B.C. Height: 21 in. (Above) Gray earthenware bowl; Nihavand, western Iran, about 2500 B.C. Height: 12½ in. In the Victoria and Albert Museum

matrix was consumed during firing, leaving the finished pot. It is not unusual to find imitations of the marks of a basket or textile weave incised as decoration into pottery made by other means.

Coiled pottery was the next development. Long strips of clay were coiled in a circle, layer upon layer, until the approximate shape had been attained and the walls of the vessel were then finished by scraping and smoothing. Some remarkably fine early pots were made in this way.

It is impossible to say when the potter's wheel was introduced. A pot cannot be made by hand modeling or coiling without the potter either turning it or moving round it and, as turning involves the least expenditure of human effort, it would obviously be preferred. The development of the "slow," or hand-turned, wheel as an adjunct to pottery manufacture led eventually to the

introduction of the "kick" wheel, rotated by foot, which became the potter's principal tool. The potter now centred the clay on a rapidly rotating disc and shaped his pot by manipulating it with both hands. This is a considerable feat of manual dexterity which led to much greater exactness and symmetry of form. Perhaps the most skilful of all potters have been the Chinese. Excellent examples of their virtuosity are the "double gourd" vases, made from the 16th century onward, which were turned in separate sections and afterward joined together. By the 18th century the wheel was no longer turned by the potter's foot but by small boys, and since the 19th century the motive power has been mechanical.

The use of molds is very ancient. The basketwork pottery described above is molding of a kind. A more advanced method, used by the Greeks and others, is to press the pottery body into molds of fired clay. Though the early molds were comparatively simple, they later became more complex, a tendency best seen in those molds used for the manufacture of pottery figures. The unglazed earthenware figures of Tanagra (Boeotia, central Greece) were first modeled by hand, then molds of whole figures were used, and finally the components—arms, legs, heads, and torsos—were all molded separately. The parts were often regarded as interchangeable, so that a variety of models could be constructed from a limited number of components. It is interesting to note that no improvement on this method of manufacture had been devised by the 18th century: the European porcelain factories made their figures in precisely the same way.

Plaster of paris molds were introduced into Staffordshire about 1745. They enabled vessels to be cast in slip, for when the slip was poured into the mold the plaster absorbed the water from it and thus deposited a layer of clay on the surface of the mold. When this layer had reached a sufficient strength and thickness, the surplus slip was poured off, the cast was removed and fired, and the mold was used again. This method is still in common use in the mid-20th century.

More recent methods of large-scale production are discussed in the section *Modern Manufacturing Techniques*, below.

5. Ceramic Figures.—Figures were made in ancient times, the most notable being those of Tanagra, mentioned above, and those of the T'ang dynasty of China. For the most part they were intended for religious purposes, particularly for placing in tombs as a substitute for the servants and cattle which earlier burial customs had demanded. In the 18th century A.D. figures became important again though this time they were used for purely ornamental purposes. The first serious attempt at modeling is a series of large animals from Meissen made for the Japanische Palais of Augustus the Strong. Small figures came into vogue as a result of the fashion for elaborate table decoration, which had hitherto been supplied by confectioners who worked in sugar. The most eminent of the modelers, and the man who secured for porcelain figures a popularity they have never lost, was J. J. Kändler of Meissen. Toward the mid-century all kinds of decorative ware were made in the form of figures and even practical articles such as candlesticks and vases were thus embellished. Today, such figures are sought by collectors as the chef-d'oeuvre of the factories responsible for them.

6. Decoration.—Even the earliest pottery is usually embellished in one way or another. The most primitive kind of decoration is that which is scratched into the raw clay with a pointed stick, chevrons being a particularly common motif. Finger marks are sometimes used, as well as impressions from rope, or from a "beater" bound with straw. The beater was used to shape the pot in conjunction with a pad held inside it. Basket and textile motifs have been mentioned above. Decoration which has been engraved after firing is much less usual, but the skilful and accomplished engraving on one fine Egyptian pot of the predynastic period (*i.e.*, before *c.* 3100 B.C.) suggests that the practice may have been more frequent than was previously suspected.

The addition of separately modeled ornament, known as "applied" ornament, came somewhat later. The earliest known examples are found on Mediterranean pottery made at the beginning of the 1st millennium.

Painted designs are an early development, some remarkably fine

CHINESE STONEWARE

(Above) White stoneware jar with impressed chevron decoration; Shang dynasty, late An-yang, 14th–12th century
B.C. Height: 13 1/16 in. In the Freer
Gallery of Art. (Right) Vase of black-
glazed stoneware; probably Tz'u Chou
ware, 13th century. Height: 18 in. In
the Victoria and Albert Museum

work made before 3000 B.C. coming from excavations at Ur and elsewhere in Mesopotamia, as well as urns from Pan-shan in Man-churia which date back to 2000 B.C.

Colour.—The earliest pottery colours appear to have been achieved by using slips stained with various metallic oxides. At first these were undoubtedly oxides which occurred naturally in the clay; later they were added from other sources. From early times right up to the 19th century, when pottery colours began to be manufactured on an industrial scale, the oxides commonly used were those of tin, cobalt, copper, iron, manganese, and antimony. Tin oxide supplied a useful white and was much used in making tin-enamel glaze (see *Types of Earthenware,* above). Cobalt blue is an extremely stable and reliable colour which yields similar results under both high- and low-temperature firings. For this reason it appears on pottery and porcelain alike and was used more than any other colour. Cupric oxide gives a distinctive series of blues, cuprous oxide a series of greens, and, in the presence of an excess of carbon monoxide, which the Chinese achieved by throwing wet wood into the kiln, cupric oxide yields a bluish red. This particular colour is known as "reduced" copper, and the kiln is said to have a "reducing" atmosphere. The colours obtained from ferric iron range from pale yellow to black, the most im-portant being a slightly orange red, referred to as "iron red." Ferrous iron yields a green which can be seen at its best on Chinese celadon wares. Manganese gives colours varying from the bright red purple similar to permanganate of potash to a dark purplish brown which can be almost black. The aubergine purple of the Chinese was derived from this oxide. Antimony provides an ex-cellent yellow.

Ceramic colours are used in two ways—under the glaze or over it. Earthenware and stoneware were usually decorated in under-glaze colours. After the body was manipulated into the desired shape it was fired. It was then painted, dipped into, or sprayed with glaze and fired again. The second firing was at a lower temperature than the first, being just sufficient to fuse the glaze, the vitrification point of which may have been further lowered by the addition of certain substances known as fluxes. In the case of tin-enameled wares the fired object was coated with the tin glaze and then painted, glaze and decoration being subsequently fired together. The painting needed exceptional skill since it was executed on the raw glaze and erasures were impossible. The addition of a lead glaze over the enamel needed a third firing.

The body and glaze of most hard porcelain were fired in one operation since the fusion temperature of body and glaze is roughly the same. Although the Chinese made some use of copper red, un-derglaze painting is more or less limited to cobalt blue, since only this pigment will bear the full heat of the kiln satisfactorily. On soft porcelain, manganese was sometimes used under glaze, but examples are rare. All other porcelain colours were painted over the fired glaze and fixed by a second firing.

Underglaze pigments and those used with tin enamel are known as high-temperature colours, or colours of the *grand feu.* Simi-larly overglaze colours are known as low-temperature colours or colours of the *petit feu.* Other terms for overglaze colours are "enamel colours" and "muffle colours," the latter name being de-rived from the type of kiln, known as a muffle kiln, in which they are fired. Enamel colours consist of pigments mixed with glaze material suspended in a medium such as gum arabic, with an alka-line flux added to lower the melting point below that of the glaze. Enamel colours were used in Persia on pottery (*minai* painting) in the 12th century, and perhaps at the same date on Chinese stone-ware made at Tz'u Chou. In the 18th century they were applied to European tin-enameled wares, for example the *Fayence-Porcel-laine* of Germany mentioned above.

A third method of applying colour to ceramics is to add colour-ing oxides to the glaze itself. Coloured glazes have been widely used on earthenware, stoneware, and porcelain and have led to the development of special techniques in which patterns were incised, or outlined with clay threads, so that differently coloured glazes could be used in the same design without intermingling, for ex-ample the *lakabi* wares of the Middle East.

Lustre decoration is carried out by applying a colloidal suspen-sion of finely powdered gold, silver, platinum, or copper to the glazed and fired object. On a further, gentle, firing, gold yields a purplish colour, silver a pale straw colour, platinum retains its natural hue, and copper varies from lemonish yellow to gold and rich brown.

Lastly, ceramics may be gilded or silvered. The earliest gilding was done with gold mixed with an oil base. The use of gold ground in honey may be seen on the finest porcelain from Sèvres during the 18th century, as well as on that from Chelsea. Toward the end of the same century gold was applied as an amalgam, the mercury subsequently being volatilized by heating. Silver was used occasionally for the same purposes as gold, but with time has nearly always turned black through oxidation.

7. Ceramic Marks.—Most porcelain and much earthenware bear marks or devices for the purpose of identification. Stone-wares, apart from those of Wedgwood, are not so often marked. Ceramic marks are recorded in such standard works as W. Chaffers' *Marks and Monograms on Pottery and Porcelain* (1876, and many later editions) and W. B. Honey's *Dictionary of European Ceramic Art* (1952). Chinese porcelain marks usually record the dynasty and the name of an emperor, but great caution is necessary before accepting them at their face value. The Chinese frequently used the mark of an earlier reign as a sign of venera-tion for the products of antiquity, and, in recent times, for financial gain. Most books on Oriental porcelain include a list of the com-monest marks.

The majority of European factories adopted a device—for ex-ample, the well-known crossed swords of Meissen taken from the electoral arms of Saxony, or the royal monogram on Sèvres porce-lain—but these, also, cannot be regarded as a guarantee of authen-ticity. Not only are false marks added to contemporary forgeries, but the smaller 18th-century factories often copied the marks of their more august competitors. If 18th-century European porce-lain is signed with the artist's name it generally means that the painting was done outside the factory. Permission to sign factory work was rarely given, and usually it indicates a test piece, or something of the sort. Concealed signatures are sometimes to be noted.

On earthenware, a factory mark is much less usual than on porcelain. Workmen's marks of one kind or another are frequently to be seen, but signatures are rare. There are a few on Greek vases.

8. Forgeries.—Fine examples of pottery and porcelain have always commanded high prices in the salesrooms and this, in turn, has encouraged the making of forgeries and reproductions. Most of these are not close enough to deceive a reasonably expert eye because until recently it has been impossible to procure materials in a pure state and potters used natural deposits whose impurities, for good or ill, often affected the final result. In all but a few isolated instances (some German stoneware reproductions, for example) the forger no longer has access to these original sources, and he has to imitate the effect of the impurities as best he may. Although the best forgeries are remarkably close to the originals, they are few in number, and the best safeguard against them is an acquaintance with genuine examples. Scientific methods of detecting forgeries are discussed in the next section.

9. Scientific Analysis.—Because of forgeries and the absence of documentation, physical and chemical tests are used to reinforce less exact methods of comparison and analogy generally used in assessing the date and provenance of doubtful specimens. Chemical analysis and examination under ultraviolet radiation are the two techniques most commonly employed, but analysis by X-ray spectroscopy, and testing for magnetic polarity, have also been used to a limited extent. Ultraviolet radiation is extremely useful for detecting restorations and repairs and for identifying certain types of wares.

Whether carried out by chemical means or by X-ray spectroscopy, analyses of unknown specimens are helpful only if they can be compared with analyses of objects which can be attributed with certainty. Since factories tended to draw raw materials from a well-tried source and having once evolved a satisfactory formula to go on using it, the compositions of the various types of ware are fairly consistent, although they show some minor variations.

The example which follows is a chemical analysis of early porcelain from Bow, in London: silica 55.1%, alumina 16.5%, quicklime 15.12%, magnesia 0.4%, iron oxide—a trace, phosphoric acid 11.5%, potash (potassium oxide) and soda (sodium oxide) 1.01%. This formula is recognizable immediately as 18th-century English soft porcelain containing bone ash. The bone ash is revealed by the high percentage of phosphoric acid, calcined bones yielding from 65 to 85% of basic calcium phosphate. The silica and alumina are both constituents of clay, about 50% of silica to 33% of alumina being average. Some glass contains silica, potash, and lime, the latter also being present in bone ash, while another variety of glass contains lead but omits the lime. Some early English soft porcelain of the glassy variety contains a considerable proportion of lead, the highest (about 17%) being found in a class which was perhaps made at Chelsea. In the Bow formula both magnesia and iron oxide are present accidentally. In Worcester porcelain, on the other hand, magnesia appears in great quantity (about 12% or more), indicating the presence of soaprock, a kind of steatite. A true porcelain analysis should read somewhat as follows: silica 72.29%, alumina 19%, lime 0.1%, magnesia 0.53%, alkalis 4.46%, iron oxide 0.62%, 3% lost on ignition. Here the important ingredients are the silica and alumina contained in the clay and the fusible feldspathic rock. The other substances are present in fractional amounts with the exception of the alkalis. These may have been added to assist fusion, or they may have been present in the raw materials.

Examination by ultraviolet radiation ("black light") depends for its effectiveness on the phenomenon of fluorescence. The colour of any light depends upon its wavelength, violet light having the shortest wavelength of any visible light and red the longest. If the waves are extremely short, the light is no longer visible to the human eye, and is called "ultraviolet." Certain substances, however, possess the property of converting the invisible waves into visible light by lengthening the wavelength, and the object is then said to fluoresce. Fluorescence and phosphorescence are the same thing in principle, but the former disappears when the radiation which excited it has been shut off, whereas the latter persists for a while.

The usual source of ultraviolet radiation for ceramic investigations is a quartz tube filled with mercury vapour. This gives an intense visible illumination which is also rich in invisible ultraviolet radiation. The visible illumination is unwanted, and it is therefore screened off as far as possible by the interposition of a filter of suitably dyed glass. A little red and violet light passes the filter, and the general appearance is of a subdued violet illumination.

It has been found that some specimens of old pottery and porcelain exhibit colours ranging from yellow to deep violet under ultraviolet radiation. Not all the effect is due to fluorescence. Some of it is a reflection of the red and violet light passing the filter, but this reflection also has peculiarities of its own which vary according to the nature of the glaze. In many cases the effect is reasonably characteristic of the material under examination. A certain class of Chelsea porcelain, for instance, invariably shows a distinctive peach colour, while other classes exhibit a violet colour which is mainly a reflection, but is also fairly distinctive. Because so much depends on an individual's reaction to colour the ultraviolet lamp is a very personal tool, and the results need to be interpreted in the light of the operator's experience. Restorations can always be detected immediately. The restored area almost invariably fluoresces with a brilliant yellow which stands out plainly from the unrestored porcelain glaze.

The other techniques mentioned are comparatively new but analysis by X-ray spectroscopy (*q.v.*) may, in time, replace chemical analysis, since the latter always means sacrificing part of what may be a valuable specimen. Some interesting work on Chinese porcelain utilizing X rays has been done in the United States by the Far Eastern Ceramic group. Magnetic polarity tests are applicable only to archaeological specimens.

10. Collections.—In the Far East both pottery and porcelain have always been treasured by collectors. When Chinese porcelain began to be exported in the 14th century, important collections were assembled in the Middle East, and later, from the 15th century onward, in Turkey, where a notable collection from this period still survives in Istanbul. In Europe the collecting of pottery and porcelain has been a pursuit of the leisured and wealthy classes since the early part of the 17th century, and latterly it has become more generally fashionable. Before 1600, although isolated examples of Chinese porcelain were regarded as among the treasures of kings and princes, there was little collecting in the modern sense. The fashion seems to have started with the appearance of Chinese and Japanese porcelain in larger quantities than hitherto. The first shipment of any size was brought into a Dutch port in the "San Jago," captured from the Portuguese, in 1602, and both Henry IV of France and James I of England bought part of the cargo. Soon the Dutch started to trade directly with China and were granted a monopoly of trade with Japan in 1641.

Cardinal Mazarin (1602–61), minister to Louis XIV, had a large collection of Chinese works of art which included porcelain, and Louis himself had a similar collection. Augustus the Strong (1670–1733) of Saxony and Poland spent 100,000 thalers (about £25,000) on porcelain in the first year of his reign alone, and is said to have exchanged a regiment of dragoons with Frederick I of Prussia for a set of Chinese vases. In the late 17th century a collection of Japanese porcelain brought to England by William III and Queen Mary II was lodged at Hampton Court. This made collecting fashionable in English court circles. During the middle years of the 18th century collections of Chinese porcelain and the products of Meissen and the royal factory at Sèvres were the vogue. Both Louis XV and Louis XVI were excellent salesmen of their factory's products, and Mme de Pompadour is reputed to have remarked that not to buy the porcelain of Sèvres was to prove oneself a bad citizen.

Until the French Revolution, however, most art collections were an assemblage of all kinds of rare and valuable objects which were more or less unrelated. A vast collection of this nature, much of it acquired from the sales of the royal French collections during the revolution, was gathered together by the English eccentric William Beckford of Fonthill Abbey near Salisbury. It was dispersed at an enormous sale in 1823.

Modern collectors tend to specialize in the wares of a certain period or country, and most of them do not include wares made later than the 18th century. Modern collecting dates, perhaps, from the days of Charles and Lady Charlotte Schreiber who, in the latter half of the 19th century, made a specialist collection of

English pottery and porcelain which is now in the Victoria and Albert Museum, London. Other important collections made since include Mortimer Schiff's collection of Italian *maiolica*, dispersed at the Parke-Bernet Galleries, New York, in 1946, and that of George Eumorfopoulos, who was mainly responsible for the fashion for early Chinese wares which prevailed in the 1920s. The latter is now in the British Museum, London. The important collection of Chinese porcelain formed by Sir Percival David is now housed in the Percival David Foundation in London. The collection of English porcelain made by Sigmund J. Katz, eventually to be housed in the Boston Museum of Fine Arts, will probably remain unsurpassed for its wealth of early wares, while that of Irwin Untermeyer in New York is remarkable for a magnificent display of the finest work of Meissen, Chelsea, and other important factories, and an especially notable collection of German porcelain has been formed by Siegfried Ducret of Zurich. Early Japanese porcelain is probably best represented by the collection belonging to Gerald Reitlinger of Sussex, Eng., which is also rich in Persian pottery. The principle notable public collections include those of the Sèvres Museum on the outskirts of Paris, the Hetjens Museum (Düsseldorf), the Kunsthistorisches Museum (Vienna), the State Hermitage Museum (Leningrad), the Metropolitan Museum of Art (New York), the Smithsonian Institution (Washington, D.C.), Colonial Williamsburg (Va.), and the Victoria and Albert Museum and the British Museum (London).

II. HISTORY OF CERAMICS

A. Foreword

The pages which follow are a miniature, and therefore necessarily lacunary, history of the ceramic art of the world. Since every historical work must adopt a frame of reference, the subject is here discussed from the viewpoint of Europe and the United States. The section on the ceramic art of Asia not only provides information on the Far Eastern wares themselves but shows how strong has been the influence of the East on European potters. A preliminary reading of this section, therefore, ought to be undertaken by anyone seeking to understand the development of European wares from the early 17th century onward.

The first section of this history deals with the techniques of primitive pottery, the basis of all subsequent skills, many of which are found all over the world. The next section discusses the very early wares of Anatolia and the Near and Middle East. The first European pottery to be considered is that of the northern Mediterranean. Apart from some indebtedness to Egypt and Mesopotamia during the early part of the 1st millennium B.C., both form and motif are European. Most of the wares show a high degree of artistry and skill. After the decline of the Roman Empire, there was a long period in Europe in which pottery was unfashionable, metal being the preferred medium for table dishes and ornaments. Meanwhile in the Middle East from the 8th century A.D. onward there was a revival of the ceramic art, and it was the Islamic wares which reached Italy from Moorish Spain in the 14th century that eventually reawakened interest in Europe. In spite of this Moorish influence and the fact that the technique for glazing Italian *maiolica* was borrowed from the Middle East via Spain, ceramic styles during the Renaissance remained predominantly European.

From the beginning of the 17th century onward, however, Eastern influences grew progressively stronger. Toward the end of the 18th century, in the Neoclassical period, the styles of Greece and Rome returned to favour but the influence of China remained as firmly entrenched as before, and even today it is often to be noticed in modern commercial decorations. This is not surprising: ceramics have always been regarded as an important art form in most Eastern countries—in China, for example, they have a known and continuous history from about 1500 B.C.—and, until the last century, China has also been ahead of Europe in technical matters.

The pottery and porcelain of the Americas before 1800 is discussed in a separate section, below. American Indian pottery has no obvious relationship with that of any other part of the world and post-Columbian wares are mostly derived from those of Europe, partly because settlers brought with them the styles of

their own country and also because competition with European suppliers from the mid-18th century onward compelled the newly established factories to provide comparable wares. The article concludes with an account of modern manufacturing techniques.

It is possible to draw a fairly clear line between those wares made in the West before 1800 and those made afterward. The work of the 19th and 20th centuries is therefore discussed separately. The old tradition of craftsmanship, already weakened by the Industrial Revolution, hardly survived the Napoleonic Wars, and the growth of the factory system enforced the use of mechanical methods which, for many years, made it doubtful whether ceramics could survive as an art. Later years have seen a revival of the artistic traditions of this ancient craft, for example, by Bernard Leach and others, and the work of the larger factories has shown some improvement.

1. Importance of Ceramics in Historical Studies.—It is often desirable to identify the provenance and the date of manufacture of specimens of pottery and porcelain as closely as possible. Not only does such information add to the interest of the specimen in question and increase understanding of the ceramic art as a whole, but it often throws fresh light on historical questions or the social habits and technical skills of the time it was made. Since ceramics are not affected by any of the agents which attack metal, wood, or textiles, they are often found virtually unchanged after being buried for thousands of years while other artifacts from the same period are partially or completely destroyed. For this reason archaeologists use pottery extensively; for example, to trace contacts between peoples, since vessels were often widely distributed in course of trade, either by the people who made them, or by such maritime nations as the Phoenicians. Scientific methods of investigating ceramics have been discussed above.

2. Decorative Motifs.—The history of the ceramic art is much concerned with the origin of patterns, for decorative motifs from one place were freely adopted by others and once the source of a pattern is known both date and provenance of the copy can often be ascertained. Patterns were borrowed from countries with

DISH PAINTED IN BROWNISH LUSTRE PIGMENTS; VALENCIA, SPAIN, ABOUT 1430. DIAMETER: 21 IN. IN THE VICTORIA AND ALBERT MUSEUM

which there was a trading connection, and the fact that they were borrowed at all perhaps suggests that those who supplied the inspiration were artistically in advance of those who took it. The copies were often free adaptations to which something of value was added, but many were done without understanding. Typical examples of the latter are the Moorish patterns on late Spanish lustre pottery, forms based on Arabic calligraphy which degenerated in the hands of Spanish workmen who neither spoke nor read Arabic. Much the same fate awaited the Chinese motifs copied by the European potters who transposed them to suit Western tastes and conventions and were ignorant of any symbolic meanings.

3. Provincial Wares.—The often considerable difference between wares made at a centre of manufacture where technical knowledge was advanced and contemporary, but rougher, wares from the provinces frequently tempts one to date the less well-finished specimen to an earlier period. Some of the provincial Chinese porcelain of the 18th century, for example, has been erroneously awarded an early Ming date. When pottery is excavated there are often other factors which enable the date to be estimated fairly closely, but isolated specimens often present difficult problems.

B. Primitive Pottery

The methods of pottery making used by primitive peoples are very much alike, and there is little difference between the tech-

WARES FROM ENGLAND AND FRANCE

(Left) Portrait of Charles II, gray stoneware, probably modeled by Grinling Gibbons. Fulham, London; about 1680. Height: 8 in. In the Victoria and Albert
Museum. (Right) "Le Jaloux," white biscuit porcelain, after a model by Vau-
drevolle. Vincennes, France; about 1725. Height: 11 in. In the Wadsworth
Atheneum

niques in use today and those of Neolithic times. However, comparatively little primitive pottery is being made in the mid-20th
century, owing to improved communications and the opening up
of vast tracts of land in Africa and elsewhere, and the interest of
this section tends to be historical.

Pottery making is not universal. It is rarely found among
nomadic tribes, since potters must live within reach of their raw
materials. It has been absent from large regions of America, and
in other parts of the world it is no longer practised. If there
are gourds, skins, and similar natural materials which can be made
into vessels without trouble, there is no incentive to make pottery.

Clay frequently needs to be "seasoned" before use; this is done
by exposing it to the action of the weather. Clays which are excessively plastic crack and become distorted during drying and
firing unless they are "opened" by mixing them with sand or some
other material. Even chopped grass, animal dung, and cinders are
used occasionally for this purpose, the last being found in some
early British pottery.

Primitive methods of forming pottery vessels have been discussed in the introductory section *Methods of Fashioning Ceramics,* above. Generally speaking, the method most frequently used
is coiling, although among a few primitive peoples baskets are still
used as molds and sometimes the belly of the pot is shaped over
a ring of vegetable fibre. The Hausa of Nigeria use an old pot
as a mold by inverting it and then forming a sheet of clay over
it in such a way that the mold can be withdrawn. Two or three
sections shaped in this way may be joined to form a simple vessel.
The neck and shoulders are then finished by hand. In some areas
vessels are hand modeled from a ball of clay, the simplest method.

Most primitive peoples can make excellent pots by these various means, and the wheel is rarely used. It is a more difficult tool,
and needs long apprenticeship. An example of the achievements
of the primitive potter without the wheel can be seen in the Chinese
Neolithic urns from the Pan-shan cemetery in Manchuria.

The finished pot is first dried to "leather" hardness and then
it is fired. Primitive "beehive" kilns have been observed in the
lower Congo, but elsewhere the pots are simply stacked in a shallow depression or a hole in the ground and a pyre of wood is built
over them. Charcoal is often used for firing.

Decoration is effected, more often than not, by incising lines
into the raw clay with a pointed stick or with the thumbnail. The
impression of rope can sometimes be seen; patterns of this kind
occur on the Japanese Jōmon ware of the 1st millennium B.C. A
more advanced technique was to use wooden stamps to impress the
design, and in some places these were developed into rollers similar
in principle to the Babylonian cylinder seal. Basketwork patterns
are found on pots molded over baskets and are sometimes imitated
on pots made by other methods.

Most designs are geometric, the chevron being particularly
common, but animal, plant, and human forms appear occasionally
on the more sophisticated wares. They are usually drawn in a
stylized manner—which might be regarded as inevitable on primitive work were it not for the naturalism of some of the cave paintings executed at much earlier dates. Incised designs on a dark
body are sometimes filled with lime which effectively accents the
decoration. Examples can be seen in some early work from Cyprus
and in some comparatively modern work from primitive tribes.

Applied ornament is unusual. When it does occur it is in the
form of knobs, scrolls, or even crudely modeled figures. Raised
designs are produced by pressing out the wall of the vessel from
inside, a technique which resembles the *repoussé* method adopted
by metalworkers.

The colour of the pot is dependent to a great extent on the
composition of the body. Iron is almost ubiquitous in clay and
under the usual firing conditions it oxidizes, giving a colour ranging from buff to dark red according to the amount present. In a
reducing atmosphere (*i.e.,* one where a limited supply of air causes
the presence of carbon monoxide) the iron gives a colour varying
from grey to black, although a dark colour may also occur as a
result of the action of smoke. Both of the colours which result
from iron in the clay can be seen in the black-topped vases of
predynastic Egypt. Slip was not commonly used among primitive
peoples and painted decoration is extremely rare.

Glazing is an advanced technique which is not found in primitive pottery and its introduction is discussed later (see *China:
Han Dynasty,* below). However, varnishes of one kind or another
are often applied to overcome the porosity of low-fired earthenware. They are made from resins, gums, fat, or gelatinous substances. Varnished pots of this
kind were made in Fiji, and
specimens are not uncommon.
When the clay is exceptionally
fine, it is sometimes polished or
burnished after firing, as in the
case of the Pan-shan urns mentioned above.

Apart from vessels of various
sorts—dishes, jars, vases, and the
like—figures are made (often for
some magical or votive purpose)
and also tobacco pipes, drums,
and other practical objects.

Primitive pottery making has
usually been done by women,
and in some cases men have even
been prohibited from approaching while the operation was in
progress. When the wheel was

**SUSQUEHANNOCK POTTERY JAR FROM
CAYUGA COUNTY, NEW YORK.
HEIGHT: 4¾ IN. IN THE MUSEUM
OF THE AMERICAN INDIAN**

adopted, however, it became a male prerogative. The making of
pots was often limited to certain families or to certain districts.
The former practice was noticeable in China and Japan until recent
times; the latter was probably due to the geographical location of
the raw materials.

C. ANATOLIA, MESOPOTAMIA, AND EGYPT

It used to be thought that the first pottery came from the Middle East. However, in the early 1960s, excavations at a Neolithic
settlement at Çatal Hüyük on the Anatolian Plateau of Turkey
by James Mellaart revealed a variety of crude, soft earthenware
estimated to be approximately 9000 years old. A more advanced
variety of handmade pottery, hard-fired and burnished, has proved
to be as early as 6500 B.C. The use of a red slip covering and
molded ornament came a little later.

Sir Leonard Woolley found handmade pottery at Ur, in Mesopotamia, below the clay which he termed "the Flood deposit."
Immediately above the Flood deposit, and therefore dating from
a time soon after the Flood (about 3000 B.C.), was wheel-made,
decorated pottery of a type usually called Al 'Ubaid after a nearby
site which was the first to be cleared. Perhaps the most richly
decorated pottery of the Middle East, remarkable for its fine

painting, comes from Susa (Shushan) in southwest Iran. The motifs are partly geometric, partly stylized but easily recognizable representations of waterfowl and running dogs, usually in friezes. They are generally executed in dark colours on a light ground. Vases, bowls, bowls on feet, and goblets have been found, all dating from about 3200 B.C. By 3000 B.C. pottery is no longer decorated, but earthenware statuettes belong to this period, and a vessel (in the Louvre Museum, Paris) with a long spout based on a copper prototype is the ancestor of many much later variations on the same theme from this region in both pottery and metal. The body of this pottery contains a very large quantity of lime (37%), and it was fired at approximately 1000° C.

Remarkable glazed brick panels have been recovered from the ruins of Khorsabad (Dur-Sharrukin), Nimrud (Kalakh), Susa, and Babylon. They provide the first instance of the use of tin enamel, although the date of its introduction cannot be certainly determined. A well-known fragment from Nimrud in the British Museum belongs to about 890 B.C., and by the 5th century B.C. extremely large friezes, one of them about 11 yd. long, were being erected at Susa. The presence of lead in the blue glazes derived from copper suggests that the lead may have been added deliberately as a flux, and that this glazing technique, like that of tin enameling, was forgotten—to be recovered only at a much later date. In Egypt pottery was made in great variety in the predynastic period (up to c. 3100 B.C.), and a hard-fired ware of good quality was attained. Wares deteriorate in quality during the 1st dynasty (c. 3100–c. 2890 B.C.) but improve again by the 3rd (c. 2686–c. 2613 B.C.). The earliest forms of decoration were geometrical, or stylized, animal or scenic motifs painted in white slip on a red body. Comparatively little variation is to be noticed until the 26th dynasty (c. 664–525 B.C.), when clay was probably imported from Greece. Most artifacts are vessels of one kind or another, although pottery figures of variable quality were made, some of the later examples (after 500 B.C.) showing signs of Greek influence.

The so-called "faience" of Egypt is an unfired ware and thus, strictly speaking, falls outside our definition of pottery. It contained about 94% of sand, 2% of clay, soda and lime in varying proportions, and perhaps also an organic binder such as gum arabic. As early as the 1st dynasty, figures, vases, and tiles of this material were covered with a fired glaze (probably fused from powdered marble, soda, and sand) which was coloured turquoise and green with copper oxide. Later, the colouring materials common to the Egyptian glassmaker, including cobalt and manganese, were added. (G. Se.)

GLAZED BRICK PANEL DEPICTING AN ARCHER: SUSA (SHUSHAN), IRAN, 5TH CENTURY B.C. SIZE: 27½ X 76½ IN. IN THE BRITISH MUSEUM

D. THE AEGEAN AND GREECE

1. Neolithic Period (c. 6000–3000 B.C.).—The potter's art first reached the Aegean in the New Stone Age. All Neolithic vases are handmade and the best are highly polished: in other respects, the various local schools have little in common, since communications were severely limited in this remote period. The main centres of ceramic production lay in Thessaly and Crete. Thessalian potters favoured a red monochrome ware but occasionally attempted simple painted decoration consisting of rectilinear patterns, with a vertical or diagonal emphasis. The Neolithic pottery of Crete is remarkable for its finely burnished surface, any decoration being usually incised.

2. Early Bronze Age (c. 3000–2000 B.C.).—On the mainland the ceramic initiative passed from Thessaly to the Peloponnese and Boeotia. The Early Helladic wares from these two areas show how quickly pottery fell under the influence of the new craft of metalworking: the two leading shapes, the "sauceboat" and the high-spouted jug, both have metal prototypes. Painted ornament is rare before the final stage (Early Helladic—usually represented by the initials "EH"—III); in the central phase (EH II) the surface is coated with a dark pigment formed from a solution of the clay. This type of paint, later much improved by the Athenians (see *Attic Black-Figure and Red-Figure*, below), remained the normal medium of decoration on all Aegean pottery until the adoption of a true silicate glaze in Byzantine times.

The contemporary wares of the Cyclades are similar, but more use is made of incised ornament: spirals are common motifs, while some vases bear primitive representations of ships. The pottery of Early Minoan Crete bears simple geometrical patterns, at first in dark paint on a light clay ground (EM I–II), and subsequently in white over a coat of dark paint (EM III). On the ware of Vasiliki in eastern Crete (EM II) a bichrome effect is obtained by placing the fuel up against the vase in the kiln so that the surface assumes a mottled red and black appearance. The commonest Early Minoan shapes are high-spouted jugs, and long-spouted drinking jars resembling teapots.

3. Middle Bronze Age (c. 2000–1580 B.C.).—After the conquest of the mainland by the first Greeks in the Middle Bronze Age the local schools of pottery developed on widely different lines. The Minyan ware introduced by the newcomers (named after the legendary Minyans of Orchomenos, where it was first found) is an unpainted monochrome fabric thrown on a fast wheel and fired in a reducing kiln to an uniform gray colour which penetrates right through the biscuit (the term generally applied to ware fired without a glaze); the surface is then highly polished, and feels soapy to the touch. The shapes are all strongly carinated and probably derive from metalwork. The simultaneous appearance of Minyan pottery at Troy VI suggests that the Greek invaders arrived from a northeasterly direction. With them, too, had come the knowledge of the potter's wheel, already used at Troy II (2600–2300 B.C.).

Equally characteristic of this period are the matt-painted wares, which are mainly handmade: here rectilinear patterns are applied in dull black or lilac to a porous white surface. This fabric, although native to the Cyclades, was also widely imitated on the mainland; in the latest stage the ornament falls increasingly under the influence of the polychrome and curvilinear style of Middle Minoan Crete.

By far the most sophisticated pottery of this epoch was made in Crete, contemporarily with the first palaces at Knossos and Phaistos. The finest ware (Middle Minoan II) is confined to these two royal capitals together with the Kamares cave-sanctuary whence the style derives its name. Over a dark lustrous ground the ornament is added in red and white, the carefully composed designs striking a subtle balance between curvilinear abstract patterns and stylized motives derived from plant and marine life. The decoration sometimes takes the form of appliqué molded ornament, or barbotine knobs. By the time of MM II the use of the fast wheel had become general, imparting a new crispness to the profiles. Among the commonest shapes are carinated cups (often of eggshell thinness), small round jars with bridged spouts, and large storage jars (*pithoi*). In the course of MM III the fashion for polychrome schemes gradually died out, but at the very end of the period (MM III B) a new naturalistic style was born, inspired by the floral and marine frescoes on the walls of the second palaces. The wide distribution of MM pottery illustrates the vigour of Cretan commercial enterprise; several Minoan emporia were founded in the Aegean Islands, while exports also reached Cyprus, Egypt, and the Levant.

4. Late Bronze Age (*c.* 1580–1100 B.C.).—Aegean civilization now reached new heights of prosperity, displayed in the luxurious life of the Minoan palaces and the splendid treasures of the shaft graves at Mycenae. Potters were much influenced by work in richer and more spectacular media: many of their shapes can be traced to originals in gold and bronze found in Cretan palaces and Mycenaean tombs. Their decoration owes much to contemporary wall painting, although the motifs are always carefully adapted to the shape of the vase.

With the spread of Minoan culture round the shores of the Aegean, Cretan potters exercised a profound influence on the other local schools, and for the first two centuries of this period the vases of the mainland (known as Late Helladic or Mycenaean) are closely related to Minoan models. In the 16th century (LM I A) Cretan potters reversed their colour scheme, and returned to dark-on-light decoration. Their repertoire includes some abstract motifs (*e.g.*, running spirals and vertical ripples) but is mainly derived from nature, a continuation of the figurative style of MM III B: flowers, grasses, and olive sprays are drawn with charm and spontaneity. After 1500 (LM I B) marine creatures are much in evidence, rendered with alarming realism: in a setting of coral and seaweed are often found argonauts, starfish, dolphins, and, above all, the octopus, wrapping his tentacles round the vase. However, on the palace style amphoras of the late 15th century (LM II) there is a reaction against this extreme naturalism: plants and marine life continue but in a more stylized and symmetrical form.

AEGEAN AND ATTIC POTTERY

(Top) *Krater* (mixing bowl) with bull and bird motif; Late Helladic III B, 13th century B.C. Height 10½ in. (Bottom) Pitcher in the Geometric style; Attic, about 750 B.C. Height: 8½ in. In the British Museum

After the fall of Knossos in *c.* 1400 B.C., the artistic initiative passed to Mycenae and remained with it until the end of the Bronze Age. In the 14th and 13th centuries (LH III A and B) Mycenaean vases were widely exported, not only to Egypt and the Levant, but also as far west as Italy and Sicily. In the interests of commerce pottery was mass-produced, and the Mycenaean colonies on Rhodes and Cyprus were as prolific as the mainland. Some shapes, like the stirrup-vase, were imported for their contents of oil and unguents; others, such as the tall stemmed goblets, were prized for the excellence of their fabric. Yet in spite of their high technical standards, the decoration shows a strange lack of invention. In the absence of any new ideas, the old floral and marine motifs are subjected to an ever-increasing degree of stylization: the flowers degenerate into chevrons and dashes, the octopus into wavy lines. At the same time there is a new tendency to concentrate the decoration into a single focal zone, in anticipation of later Greek pottery. A few large jars bear crude representations of human figures in chariot scenes, probably derived from palace frescoes: no less schematic are the painted female figurines found in tombs and shrines of this period. In the pottery of the 12th century, which saw the collapse of Mycenaean civilization (LH III C), there is an abrupt decline in fabric as well as in artistic imagination.

5. Early Iron Age.—*Geometric Pottery* (*c.* 1100–*c.* 725 B.C.).—Pottery was the first art to recover its standards after the Dorian

invasion and the overthrow of Mycenae. Athens escaped these disasters and in the ensuing dark age became the chief source of ceramic ideas. For a short time Mycenaean motifs survived in debased form, but on new shapes. However, this "Submycenaean" ware soon gave place to the style known as Protogeometric (*c.* 1050–900 B.C.) by a natural process of evolution which converted the decaying Mycenaean ornament into regular geometrical patterns: thus the slovenly spirals were transformed into neat sets of concentric circles, always drawn with a compass fitted with a multiple brush. These circles are the hallmark of Protogeometric decoration which, like the latest Mycenaean, is confined to the handle zone; in the final stage the rest of the surface is covered with a thick black paint remarkable for its high lustre. Many shapes were inherited from Submycenaean, but all were tautened and vastly improved: the drinking vessels rest on high conical feet, while the closed vases have graceful ovoid bodies. After its invention in Attica the Protogeometric style spread to other parts of the Aegean world.

In the early 9th century Athenian potters introduced the full Geometric style by abandoning circular for rectilinear ornament, the key meander assuming the leading role. At first decoration is restricted to a small reserved area surrounded by the lustrous dark paint; later, as the style approaches maturity, more decorated zones are added until the potter achieves a harmonious balance between light and dark. In the 8th century, after nearly 400 years of abstract decoration, living creatures appear once again, although their style is hardly less angular than the geometric ornament that supports them. Geometric pottery reached its fullest development in the gigantic amphoras and kraters that served as grave monuments in the Athenian Dipylon cemetery; here a funerary scene, showing the corpse on the bier surrounded by mourners, occupies the main panel, while other friezes contain chariot processions, battles on land and sea, rows of animals, and linear geometric designs. The creators of these monumental vases established a continuous tradition of figured painting which persisted on Greek pottery until the end of the classical period; the immediate consequence of their innovation was a loss of interest in purely abstract design, which became increasingly perfunctory on the latest Geometric vases.

6. Period of Oriental Influence (*c.* 725–*c.* 600 B.C.).—After several centuries of isolation, the renewal of contact with the Near East provided a welcome stimulus to the Greek potter. In art, as well as in commerce, it was Corinth who now led the way. Unlike the Athenians, her potters specialized in small vases and especially in the tiny aryballos, or scent bottle, which found a ready market all round the Mediterranean. Hence arose the miniature style called Proto-Corinthian, which borrowed much of its repertoire from the fauna and flora of Syro-Phoenician art. Processions of animals, both real and legendary, are placed in the main friezes, while lotus flowers and palmettes serve as subsidiary ornament. When human beings appear, mythical scenes can often be recognized, reflecting the early diffusion of Homeric epic poetry. It was on Proto-Corinthian vases that the technique known as "black-figure" was first applied: the figures are first drawn in black silhouette and are then marked with incised detail; further touches are added in purple and white. The pottery of Corinth reached the peak of its excellence in the middle of the 7th century; later, in the course of the Ripe Corinthian style (*c.* 625–550), quality is sacrificed in the interests of mass production.

Other notable "Orientalizing" styles arose in Attica ("Proto-Attic"), the Cyclades, Laconia, and Rhodes, regional differences in pottery becoming more clearly marked as the Hellenic city-states grew into self-conscious political units. The Athenians still did their best work on large funerary vases. At first they cultivated a wild and grandiose manner in which the figures of men and animals were elaborated in outline; later the idea of incised ornament was introduced from Corinth, and imposed a salutary discipline. Cycladic potters also attempted the grand manner; Laconian work, on the other hand, is confined to a small scale, and owes comparatively little to Oriental influence. The Rhodians rarely progressed beyond animal friezes drawn in outline; their style is known as "wild goat," after their favourite quadruped. Each of these local schools could match the vitality of Proto-Corinthian drawing, but none could excel its purity of line.

7. Attic Black-Figure and Red-Figure.—*Archaic Period (c. 600–c. 480 B.C.).*—By c. 550 B.C. Athens had once again become the principal centre of pottery manufacture in Greece, having ousted its Corinthian rivals from the overseas markets. Its success is at least partially due to a sudden improvement in fabric, for its potters had by now learned how to obtain the familiar orange-red surface of their vases by mixing a proportion of ruddle, or red ochre, with their clay. The Corinthians tried to imitate this Attic colour by adding an orange slip to their pale yellow clay, but in vain. As the main medium of decoration, the Athenians perfected a shiny black pigment that was more lustrous than anything that had been achieved hitherto. The nature of this black pigment has been much disputed, and it has been variously described as a "glaze" and as a "varnish." Technically, it is neither. It lacks the glossiness and vitreous nature of a true glaze, while the fact that it was fired makes it unlike a varnish. Research by Theodor Schumann in the 1940s has shown it was achieved by painting the vase with a mixture of an iron-containing clay (such as was commonly found in Attica) and potash. Sour wine or urine was added to the mixture to prevent it from running during firing, and when the pot was fired in a reducing atmosphere a glossy black surface appeared, due to the formation of ferrous oxide.

In these centuries most of the more important vases were painted either in the black-figure, or in the slightly later red-figure technique, so that some explanation of the essential difference is necessary. Perhaps the closest analogy is to say that the two classes resemble a photographic negative and a print, the black-figure style being the negative. Such figures were painted in the glossy black pigment on the orange-red polished surface, appearing in silhouette; details, as mentioned above, were indicated by incised lines, and by the occasional use of white and purple, the female figure, especially, being painted in white. Decoration on the red-figure vases was first outlined in black; the remaining surface was then completely covered by the black pigment, leaving the figures reserved in red. Details were added in black, and in dilutions of the black pigment which appear as brown; purple is occasionally found at first, but dies out in mature red-figure work. The use of white is revived on the gaudier vases of the 4th century, where yellow brown, gold, and even blue, are sometimes used.

The Attic black-figure style was well developed by the beginning of the 6th century. Among the most favoured subjects were the labours of Hercules and Theseus and the revels of Dionysus with his attendant train of satyrs and maenads. The practice of signing vases, already begun in the 7th century, now became more common. The signatures, always in black paint, record either the potter or the painter, or in some cases both. The inscription on the celebrated François vase in the Museo Archeologico in Florence ("Ergotimos made me; Kleitias painted me") supplies our first positive evidence that the two functions had become separate, although occasional signatures such as "Exekias painted and made me" are to be noted. The name of Pamphaios appears on finely decorated vases in both the black- and red-figure styles. When the name of a recognizable painter is not known from an inscription, it has become the fashion to name him after the potter with whom he usually worked: thus the "Amasis painter" is the habitual colleague of Amasis the potter. The forms of Attic black- and red-figure tend, in the course of centuries, to be limited to certain well-defined types, the most usual of which are pictured in outline in fig. 1–14; the name of each is given, as well as a note of its function. It is worth observing that when the black-figure style reached maturity Attic artists were no less at home in miniature work than in scenes on a large scale; the best painters, however, preferred to specialize in decorating either large pots or small cups.

The finest Attic black-figure vases were made between 550 and 520 B.C., the figures being rendered in a mature Archaic style, much influenced by contemporary developments in sculpture. This is the generation of Exekias, the greatest master of the technique. He excelled in painting and in finely engraved detail; he also succeeded, where others had failed, in endowing his figures with mood and emotion, as well as the capacity for action. With Exekias the possibilities of black-figure were virtually exhausted, and after the invention of red-figure (c. 530 B.C.) it is not surprising that the best artists soon turned to this new technique, which allowed a greater freedom of expression, and a more naturalistic treatment of the human frame. After c. 500 B.C. the only important vases in black-figure are the amphoras presented to victors at the Panathenaic Festival; these have a figure of Athena standing between two pillars, and are usually inscribed "I am one of the prizes from Athens."

The early red-figure artists were not slow to exploit the advantages of the new system. Benefiting from the experience of relief sculptors, they had mastered the problems of foreshortening by the end of the 6th century; but since they still avoided any suggestion of depth in their grouping, they were able to convey the illusion of a third dimension without doing violence to the two-dimensional surface of the vase. The most successful work was done in the final years of the Archaic period (c. 500–c. 480 B.C.) when the style of the figures, with their formal and elaborate patterns of drapery, was still decorative rather than naturalistic. Monotony was avoided

ATTIC LEKYTHOS (OIL FLASK) IN THE WHITE-GROUND TECHNIQUE BY THE THANATOS PAINTER, SHOWING SLEEP AND DEATH RAISING THE BODY OF A WARRIOR: ABOUT 440 B.C. HEIGHT: 19¼ IN. IN THE BRITISH MUSEUM

ATTIC KYLIX (DRINKING CUP) PAINTED BY EPIKTETOS IN THE RED-FIGURE STYLE; ABOUT 520 B.C.

(Above) Exterior showing Hercules slaying Busiris. (Right) Interior showing a flute player and a dancer. Height: 4¾ In., diameter: 12¾ in. In the British Museum

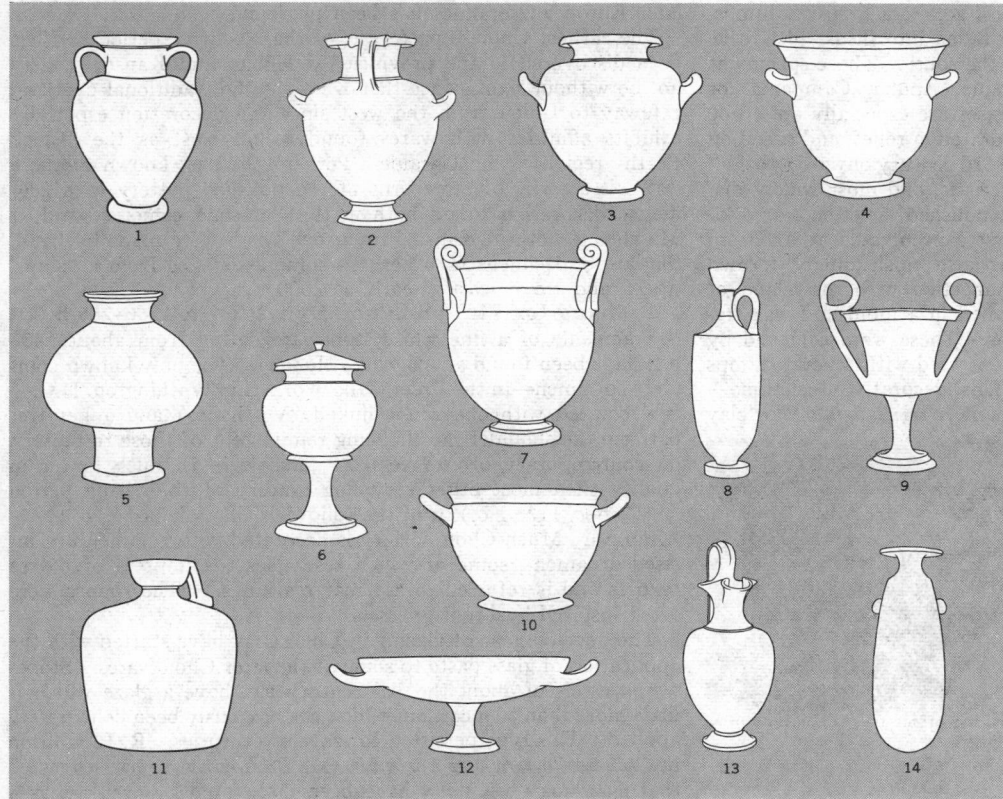

FIG. 1–14.—ATTIC BLACK- AND RED-FIGURE FORMS

(1) *Amphora:* two-handled jar for storing liquids. Those with a pointed base are designed to stand in sand. (2) *Hydria:* three-handled jar for carrying water. (3) *Stamnos:* wine jar. (4) Bell *krater:* large bowl for mixing wine and water; the bell krater is confined to red-figure. (5) *Psykter:* wine cooler. (6) *Lebes:* cauldron, sometimes provided with a stand, as here. (7) Volute *krater:* large bowl for mixing wine and water; named for its handles, it is found throughout the black- and red-figure styles. (8) *Lekythos:* oil flask, often used for funerary purposes. (9) *Kantharos:* drinking cup with two high vertical handles. (10) *Skyphos:* drinking bowl with two horizontal handles. (11) *Aryballos:* small unguent bottle. (12) *Kylix:* shallow drinking cup, usually provided with a pedestaled foot. (13) *Oinochoe:* wine jug with a trefoil lip, revived during the Renaissance and in the 18th-century neoclassical period. (14) *Alabastron:* small unguent bottle with rounded base

through the use of a wide variety of poses and simple devices for rendering character and mood. At the same time the repertoire of subjects was greatly enlarged; besides the old heroic and Dionysiac themes, many scenes from daily life (especially riotous banquets) now took their place.

The Classical Period (c. 480–c. 330 B.C.) saw a progressive decline in Attic vase painting. Owing to the very limitations imposed by the pot surface, the vase painter could no longer keep pace with the rapid advance toward naturalism in the major arts, and the occasional attempts at perspective and depth of grouping simply detracted from the shape of the vessel (a mistake repeated in some painting on Italian *maiolica* in the late 16th century A.D.). Furthermore, much of the later Attic vase painting shows a saccharin sentimentality and triviality of thought in both the choice of subject and its treatment which is much at variance with the earlier wares. But here we must admit a distinguished exception in the funerary *lekythoi* of the late 5th century, decorated in subdued matt colours on a white background. The figures on these vases, isolated and statuesque, share the serenity and restraint of the Parthenon sculptures and allow us to visualize something of the grandeur of classical free painting, nearly all of which is now lost. In the 4th century the figured decoration of pottery had become a degenerate art and it had died out in Attica by c. 320 B.C.

In addition to their black- and red-figure vases, the Athenians manufactured plain black-painted wares in great quantity; these follow the shapes of the figured pottery. There was also a limited vogue for plastic vases, in the shape of human or animal heads, which sometimes bear painted decoration in the style of the period.

8. Hellenistic Period (c. 330–c. 30 B.C.).—After the end of red-figure, Greek pottery is undistinguished. Painted decoration is virtually limited to festoons of ivy, laurel, and vine in white or yellow over a black ground; the black pigment loses its lustrous sheen, and assumes a dull metallic texture. A class of hemispherical bowls, known as "Megarian," was made in molds, and bears relief decoration in imitation of metal bowls. Altogether more remarkable are the contemporary terracotta figurines; among the most accomplished are the draped women from Tanagra in Boeotia, whose artistic value is sometimes marred by excessive sentimentality. (J. N. Co.)

E. ITALY

At the beginning of the Iron Age the pottery of the Villanovan culture was incised with rectilinear patterns somewhat reminiscent of Geometric Greece; the resemblance, however, is fortuitous, since there is no trace of Greek contact with Italy at this time (*c.* 900 B.C.). The most characteristic vessel is the cremation urn; this is usually biconical in shape, but sometimes takes the form of a primitive hut, decorated with quasi-architectural ornament in relief.

1. Etruria.—The first pottery of importance is the black Etruscan ware called *bucchero* which, like Middle Helladic Minyan (*see* above), was fired in a reducing kiln. The earliest examples of the 8th century B.C., for which the wheel was rarely used, were decorated with incised or engraved ornament in the form of geometric patterns. By the 6th century lively and stylized birds and animals were engraved, modeled, or applied, in conjunction with such geometric patterns as reentrant spirals, or in friezes. Later relief ornament was often executed by rolling a cylinder with design recessed in intaglio over the soft clay, the principle being the same as that used to make Babylonian cylinder seals. Vases with covers in the form of a human head, with arms slipped through fixed ring handles, were made for funerary purposes until about the mid-6th century.

In the late Archaic period the Etruscans excelled in life-size terra-cotta sculptures, of which the outstanding examples are the menacing figure of Apollo, from his temple at Veii, and the large sarcophagi from Caere with couples of banqueters reclining on the lid. Some large figures of warriors have since been recognized as forgeries, and at least one forged sarcophagus is in existence. Figures, heads, and busts continued to be made in the Hellenistic period.

2. Greek Influence.—Proto-Corinthian ware was copied with great exactness by Greek colonists as early as 700 B.C. at Cumae, near Naples. The Etruscans soon learned to use the Greek black pigment, and stylized human and animal figures appear in red, black, and white on a light clay or on the *bucchero* surface. Copies of the black-figure vases were soon so accomplished that it is not always easy to tell exactly where a specimen was made. The red-figure class, however, is rarely difficult to separate from Greek work. The decoration is much more flamboyant and elaborate, and the reverse is often carelessly executed. Many Greek vases were imported and used for funerary purposes. These have frequently been recovered intact, or almost so, from Etruscan tombs.

Long after the red-figure style had fallen into disuse in Greece it lingered on in Italy, particularly in the south. Those specimens most usually seen came from Lucania, Apulia, Campania, or Paestum. Campanian and Apulian vases are especially apt to be profusely decorated. Black ware decorated in relief, and based on metal vases, was made from about the 3rd century onward.

3. Roman Empire.—The characteristic, and most widely dispersed, type of pottery was the red, polished Arretine ware, so-called because manufacture was at first concentrated at Arretium (modern Arezzo). It is sometimes also misleadingly termed "Samian ware," from a supposed connection with the island of Samos. The body was generally formed in a mold and was frequently decorated with raised designs. These were achieved by using a mold which had itself been impressed with several stamps arranged in the desired pattern. This decorative technique— which gave to the ware yet another name, *"terra sigillata"* ("clay

ITALIAN POTTERY

(Left) Etruscan *amphora* of *bucchero* ware decorated with a frieze of horsemen in relief; 6th century B.C. Height: 20½ in. (Above) Roman bowl of Arretine ware with a design of the seasons in relief. Made in the factory of Cn. Ateius in about 10 B.C. Height: 7½ in. In the British Museum

impressed with designs")—was borrowed from metalwork. The patterns also were often influenced by metalwork and include floral and foliate motifs, mythological scenes, and scenes from daily life. The potteries at Arretium, which were organized on factory lines, operated between about 30 B.C. and A.D. 30, their products being highly prized and widely exported. Wares were stamped with the name of the potter and, probably for the first time, the name of his employer. Manufacture in Italy seems to have ceased very suddenly and was taken up, in the 1st century A.D., in southern and then in central Gaul. At first Gaulish pots resemble those of Arretium; later the body becomes rougher, the designs less disciplined, and trailed slip was sometimes added as decoration. From the 2nd to the 6th centuries the ware was also made in the eastern Mediterranean and North Africa.

Lead glazing perhaps originated or was rediscovered (the Assyrians having used it) in Egypt. Certainly it was established in the Near East by the 1st century B.C. The glazes were generally stained with copper to yield a greenish colour, and were used over relief decoration which, like the designs on Arretine ware, betrays the influence of metalwork. The technique had reached Italy and France by the 1st century A.D.

Of the other varieties of Roman pottery, lamps made either in a buff or a dark gray clay are exceptionally common, and usually have an impressed or molded design. A few depicting Christian motifs or gladiatorial combats were prized a little more highly than most specimens, but, generally, they are of little value, monetarily or otherwise. Molded terra-cotta plaques with reliefs of mythological and other subjects borrowed from Greece were often used to decorate buildings.

F. CHINA

Nowhere in the world have pottery and porcelain assumed such importance as in China, and the influence of Chinese porcelain on later European ceramics has been profound.

The earliest Chinese pottery is of the Neolithic period and has been discovered in the provinces of Honan and Kansu; it may not be without significance that Kansu is the traditional overland gateway to China from the west since the decoration especially exhibits affinities with wares found as far west as the "Black Earth" region of the Ukraine. Perhaps the best known of these wares is a series of large urns of red polished pottery with geometric decoration found both in the Pan-shan cemetery and at Ma-ch'ang, both in Kansu Province. These were made by hand, the latest specimens with perhaps some assistance from a "slow" wheel, and are at least as early as 2000 B.C.

1. Shang (or Yin) and Chou Dynasties (c. 1766–256 B.C.). —Fragments of a fine white stoneware dating from about 1400 B.C. have been found at An-yang (Honan). The only known complete specimen—in the Freer Gallery of Art in Washington, D.C.— is decorated with chevrons (linked "V"-shapes) and a key-fret pattern, the shoulder motifs being reminiscent of those to be seen on contemporary bronze vessels. This ware is much better in quality than most other surviving pottery of the Shang period (c. 1766–c. 1123 B.C.) or of the following Chou dynasty (c. 1122– 256 B.C.). Much Chou pottery is decorated with rudimentary incised ornament, some of which resembles the impress of coarse textiles and is referred to as "mat markings." The shapes were often inspired by bronze vessels.

The development of glazing in China may have started with the application of glass paste to some of the later Chou wares. Stoneware vessels of about the 3rd century B.C. have a glaze which is little more than a smear, but which has obviously been deliberately applied. This type persisted for several centuries. R. L. Hobson in *Chinese Pottery and Porcelain* (see *Bibliography*) has suggested that glaze may originally have been discovered by accident as a result of wood ash coming into contact with the surface of the pot during firing; the potash in the wood ash would then act as a flux forming a glaze from the silica in the clay. This explanation is likely enough.

2. Han Dynasty (202 B.C.–A.D. 221).—The first pottery to survive in appreciable quantities belongs to the Han dynasty and most of it has been excavated from graves. Perhaps the commonest form is the *hu*, a baluster-shaped vase copied from bronze vessels of the same name, and sometimes decorated with relief ornament in friezes taken directly from a bronze original (see METALWORK, DECORATIVE). The "hill" jar, which has a cover molded to represent the Taoist "Isles of the Blest," is another fairly frequent form and many models of servants, domestic animals, buildings, wellheads, dovecots, and the like also have been discovered in graves. Some of this pottery is unglazed, or decorated with cold (*i.e.*, unfired) pigments, but much of it is covered with a glaze which varies from copper green to yellowish brown which has often become iridescent during its long burial. The body is usually a dark red and approaches stoneware in hardness.

Han glaze is more glasslike than that of the Chou period and is of an excellent quality, obviously carefully regulated. It contains lead and was frequently coloured green with copper oxide. It has been suggested that it was introduced from western Asia, and was ultimately derived from the Roman green glazed pottery mentioned in the preceding section; at the time, there were well-established contacts with Rome where Chinese silk, under the name of Coan silk, was especially valued. On the other hand, it is now recognized that glass was made in China much earlier than was once thought—slightly before the Han period in fact—and glazes of this kind may have developed independently.

Celadon.—Yüeh *yao* ("ware") was first made at Yüeh-chou in Chekiang Province during the Han dynasty, although all surviving specimens are later. These have a stoneware body and an olive or brownish-green glaze and belong to the family of celadons, a term which looms large in any discussion of early Chinese wares. It is applied to glazes ranging from the olive of Yüeh to the deep green seen on later varieties. These colours were due to a wash of slip containing a high proportion of iron which was put over the body before glazing. The iron interacted with the glaze during firing and coloured it.

CHINESE CERAMICS OF THE HAN AND T'ANG DYNASTIES

(Left) Watchtower with pale green glaze; Han dynasty (202 B.C.–A.D. 221). Height: about 25½ in. (Right) Lady and a phoenix headdress; T'ang dynasty (A.D. 618–906). Height: about 17½ in. In the Museum of Fine Arts, Boston

3. Six Dynasties (A.D. 221–589).—Most Yüeh ware belongs to the Six dynasties, a period of strife about which little is definitely known. To the same period belong some tomb figures, often in a dark grey body with traces of unfired pigment. The Han green glaze was also still in use.

4. T'ang Dynasty (A.D. 618–906).—Chinese ceramics reach an important stage in their development during the T'ang dynasty. Nearly everything which has survived has been excavated from tombs, many of them found accidentally by railway engineers and latterly by more systematic excavations. Perhaps the most important single development was the use of coloured glazes, either as monochromes, or splashed and dappled.

The influence of Persian metalwork of the Sassanid period (3rd–7th centuries) is seen in some of the shapes used and in the occasional use of engraved decoration. Greek influence can also be traced in some examples of T'ang pottery; it reached China by way of the province of Bactria (Balkh) in Afghanistan, and was the delayed result of the conquests of Alexander the Great in the Middle East.

Excavations at Samarra on the Tigris, a pleasure resort built by the caliph al-Mu'tasim (son of Harun al-Rashid) in A.D. 838, have uncovered many fragments of T'ang wares of all kinds. Since Samarra was more or less abandoned in 883, wares found on this site can be dated with a certain amount of confidence. Perhaps the most important finds from a historical viewpoint are the fragments of what is undoubtedly porcelain. An Islamic record of travels in the Far East, written in 851 and attributed to Ibn Wahab, records "vessels of clay as transparent as glass." There can be little doubt, therefore, that translucent porcelain was made in the T'ang period, although it was not until the Yüan dynasty (1280–1368) that it began to resemble the type with which we are now most familiar.

The T'ang wares commonest in Western collections have a highly absorbent, buff, earthenware body, and are covered either with monochrome or dappled glazes. The latter were usually applied with a sponge and include blue, dark blue, green, yellow, orange, straw, and brown colours. These glazes normally exhibit a fine crackle, and often fall short of the base in an uneven wavy line, the unglazed surface area varying from about one-third to two-thirds of the vessel. Dappled glazes are also found on the magnificent series of tomb figures with which this period is particularly associated. Similar figures were made in unglazed earthenware,

and were sometimes decorated with cold pigment.

Although the unglazed specimens, or those covered only with the straw-coloured glaze, are occasionally modeled superbly, many are crude and apparently made for the tombs of the less affluent and influential. Most of the glazed figures are much better in quality, and occasionally reach a large size; figures of the Bactrian camel, for instance, are particularly impressive, some being nearly three feet high. The Bactrian pony, introduced into China about 138 B.C., is to be found in many spirited poses. The fashion for tomb figures fell into disuse at the beginning of the Sung dynasty (A.D. 960–1279), but was revived for a short while during the Ming period (1368–1644) when T'ang influence is noticeable.

"Marbled" wares are seen occasionally. The effect was achieved either by "combing" slips of contrasting colours (*i.e.*, mingling the slips after they had been put on the pot, by means of a comb), or by mingling differently coloured clays. Another type of T'ang ware had a stoneware body with a dark brown glaze streaked by pale blue. It probably came from Honan. A few wares known from literary references, of which Ch'ai *yao* is an example, still remain unidentified.

Most vessels stand on a flat base and although later T'ang wares sometimes were given a footring, for the most part this can be regarded as evidence in favour of a Sung dating. At this point it is worth remarking that many Chinese ceramics cannot be dated with certainty since there were traditional and persisting types which overlapped and, quite often, these dynastic labels cannot be regarded as more than an indication of the affinities of the object under discussion.

5. Sung Dynasty (A.D. 960–1279).—The wares of the Sung dynasty are those most highly regarded by Chinese and Japanese connoisseurs, and by many in the West. They are particularly noted for brilliant feldspathic glazes over a stoneware body, and their emphasis on beauty of form. Decoration is infrequent but may be incised, molded, impressed, or carved; a certain amount of painted decoration was done at Tz'u Chou in Chihli (now called Hopeh) Province (*see* below). The esteem accorded to the Sung wares accounts for the relatively large number which have survived. Literary references, too, are greater in number and more exact than previously, although the habit of referring to vessels in poetic language sometimes makes identification with existing specimens difficult. The principal varieties are Ju, *Kuan, Ko,* Ting, Lung Ch'üan, Chün, Chien, Tz'u Chou, and *ying ch'ing.*

Ju yao has a buff stoneware body and is covered with a dense greenish-blue glaze which sometimes has a fine crackle. It was made in Honan at an imperial factory which apparently had a

 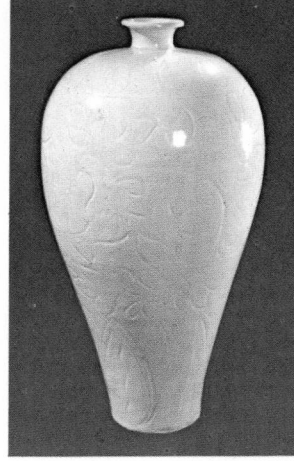

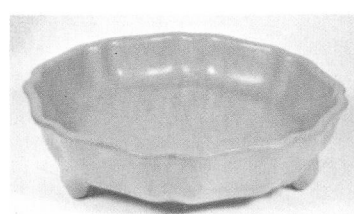

WARES OF THE SUNG DYNASTY; A.D. 960–1279

(Top left) Ju ware: buff-white porcelaneous ware with greenish-blue glaze netted with a fine crackle. Diameter: 6.6 in. Percival David collection. (Bottom left) *Kuan* ("official") ware: an 18th-century copy in the Victoria and Albert Museum. Diameter: 8½ in. (Right) Ting ware: grayish-white porcelain with a warm ivory-white glaze covering carved design of lotus flowers and foliage. Height: 14½ in. Percival David collection

life of about 20 years, starting in 1107. For years it was known only from literary references, and it was, at one time, tentatively identified with *ying ch'ing* ware (*see* below). The reader is referred to "A Commentary on Ju Ware" by Sir Percival David in *Transactions of the Oriental Ceramic Society, 1936–1937*.

Kuan is another imperial ware which is also exceedingly scarce. The name means "official." It was probably first made in the north, the kilns being reestablished at Hangchow in Chekiang Province about 1127 when the court fled southward to escape the Chin Tatar invaders. The body is of stoneware washed with brown slip while the glaze varies from pale green to a lavender blue with a wide-meshed crackle emphasized by the application of brown pigment. Chinese references to "a brown mouth and an iron foot" can be identified with the colour of the rim and the footring.

Ko yao is closely related to *Kuan* ware. It has a dark stoneware body and a grayish-white glaze with a well-marked crackle, which was induced deliberately for its decorative effect and is well controlled. *Ko* ware was extensively copied in the 18th century in a porcelain body.

Ting wares are white in colour. Some exhibit an orange translucency, while the coarser varieties are opaque. The finest examples are called *pai* Ting ("white" Ting). On the exterior of bowls and similar vessels *pai* Ting glaze is apt to collect in drops, called "teardrops." Many articles, particularly bowls, were fired mouth downward, leaving an unglazed rim which was afterward bound with a band of copper or silver. (Bands appear occasionally on other Sung wares, notably *ying ch'ing*, and were sometimes used to conceal damage rather than an unglazed rim.) Coarser varieties are known as *fen* Ting ("flour" Ting) and *t'u* Ting ("earthen" Ting), and there are also references to brown, black, and red Ting, although only a few examples of black Ting now survive and the others have not been identified. As in the case of *Kuan yao*, the kilns are said to have been removed southward in 1127, but it has so far proved impossible to differentiate between the northern and southern varieties. Other white wares made elsewhere during the period include those of Tz'u Chou, and a variety covered with a white slip over a grayish body from Chü-lu Hsien, both in Chihli Province.

Lung Ch'üan. The celadons of Lung Ch'üan are, perhaps, the most common of the classic Sung wares. The town is in the province of Chekiang, near the capital of the southern Sung emperors at Hangchow. The kilns probably date back to the 10th century. The glaze, which is superb in quality, is a transparent green in colour. It is thick and viscous, usually with a well-marked crackle. The glaze on early specimens is less transparent and more dense. The body is gray to grayish white, best seen at the rim where the glaze tends to be thin, and unglazed parts burned to a dark brownish red. A bluish-green variety of celadon is sometimes called *kinuta seiji*, a Japanese term meaning "mallet" celadon. It is applied to a favourite shape which resembles a fuller's mallet, the colour of which is much prized in Japan. Another variety, *tobi seiji*, has isolated spots of brown in the green glaze. By far the most frequent surviving examples of Lung Ch'üan celadon are large dishes for which there was a thriving export trade, due in part to the superstition that a celadon dish would break or change colour if poisoned food were put into it. Bowls and large vases, both of which are scarce, were also made with this glaze. Decoration is usually incised but molded decoration is also found. On some pots the molding was left unglazed so that it burned to a dark reddish brown—an effective contrast to the colour of the glaze. The more finely potted wares are the scarcest, and often the oldest. The heavier varieties were intended to withstand the rigours of transport to overseas markets and probably most of them belong to the following Yüan dynasty (1280–1368), when the export trade was considerably extended.

Of the other celadons of the period, it is desirable to mention the northern group. These have an olive-green glaze, and the decoration is carved or molded, usually with foliate motifs. Their relationship to Yüeh *yao* (see *Han Dynasty*, above) is fairly obvious, but there are a number of differences. Most Yüeh specimens, for instance, show signs of having rested on little piles of sand in the kiln, whereas this feature is absent from northern

celadons. Tung *yao*, known from Chinese literary sources, may be related to this group.

The kilns of Lung Ch'üan were transferred to Ch'ü-chou not far away at the beginning of the Ming dynasty (1368–1644). The suggestion that an unglazed band inside the footring may be a sign of Ch'ü-chou manufacture is not an entirely trustworthy one.

The celadon glaze was used at Kingtechen (Ching-te-chen), in Kiangsi (Chiang-hsi Sheng) Province, over a white porcelain body from the Ming period onward, and at the kilns in Kwangtung Province over a dark stoneware body during the same period. Figures of Kuanyin (Bodhisattva of Compassion) in a shrine are usually of Kwangtung manufacture.

Chün ware is more popular with Western collectors than it is in China. It comes from the K'ai-feng Fu District of Honan Province, and the body is a grayish-white hard-fired stoneware covered

DISH OF CHÜN WARE; SUNG DYNASTY (A.D. 960–1279). DIAMETER: 7⅜ IN. IN THE VICTORIA AND ALBERT MUSEUM

with a thick, dense, lavender blue glaze which is often suffused with crimson purple. This is the first example of a reduced copper, or *flambé*, glaze (which is also known as a "transmutation" glaze, the more familiar colours derived from copper being blues and greens). Conical bowls are especially numerous, and dishes not unusual, but the finer specimens are usually flowerpots, sometimes said to have been made for Imperial use. Characteristic are barely perceptible channels or tracks caused by the parting of the viscous glaze; these are called "earthworm tracks" by the Chinese. The kilns probably continued to produce this ware until the 16th century, and it is difficult to separate some of the later productions from the earlier. Imitations are numerous, some fairly close approximations being made in a white porcelain body in the reign of Yung Cheng (1723–35). The footring was washed over with brown to simulate that of the earlier ware. The impressed seal of the reign was sometimes added, but has frequently been ground out later by someone anxious to pass the vessel off as being made in the Sung period. "Soft Chün" has a dense, opaque, glaze which is markedly turquoise in colour. Most of it belongs to the Ming period, although isolated specimens may be earlier. "Fatshan" Chün, which is not a particularly good imitation, was made in the Canton area.

Chien-yao is called after the original place of manufacture, Chien-an, in Fukien Province. Manufacture was later moved to Chien-yang nearby, probably during the Yüan period. The glaze is very dark brown, approaching black, over a dark stoneware body, and it usually stops short of the base in a thick treacly roll.

Many variations in the colour of the glaze are to be observed. Streaks in lighter brown are referred to by the Chinese as "hare's fur." Silvery spots on the glaze are called "oil spots." The most usual surviving form is the teabowl; these were much esteemed by the Japanese under the name of *temmoku* and were later used in the Tea Ceremony. The black glaze was imitated in Honan Province where the glazes were used on a variety of wares.

Tz'u Chou. The kilns of Tz'u Chou are now in Hopeh Province, although they were formerly in Honan. The earliest surviving examples are referable to the T'ang dynasty and the kilns were still working in the 1960s. The finer varieties of this ware are sought by Western collectors and have inspired a certain amount of modern English studio pottery but, generally, they have not been esteemed very greatly in China. In the Sung period vases, wine jars, and pillows were the most usual products. The body is usually a hard-fired grayish-white stoneware which was first covered with a wash of white slip and then with a transparent glaze. For the first time painted decoration appears under the glaze, perhaps as a result of influence from the Middle East. Decoration is nearly always in brown or black; the motifs are usually floral and display a singular freedom of line which is very attractive. (The inclusion of human and animal figures suggests a Yüan or a Ming dating, at the least.) The slip covering was sometimes carved away leaving a pattern in contrasting colour, a technique also used in conjunction with a dark brown glaze. A "hare's fur" glaze, similar to that of Chien wares, was also employed. A blue glaze with painted decoration in black beneath it was obviously inspired by contemporary Persian pottery decorated in the same way. Another innovation, perhaps derived from the same source, is the use of enamel colours applied over the glaze. These are limited to primitive reds and greens and yellows. The dating of Tz'u Chou wares is frequently difficult, and depends principally upon style.

Ying ch'ing. An important and not uncommon ware is *ying ch'ing* ("shadowy blue"). However, little is definitely known about it as there seem to be no contemporary references to it, a strange lacuna considering its wide distribution. It was manufactured both in the south (Kiangsi) and the north (Hopeh). Moreover, it was extensively exported, and has been found as far west as the ruins of Al Fustat (Old Cairo). The body is pale buff in colour, usually translucent, and thinly potted, breaking with a sugary fracture. Most genuine examples seem to belong to the Sung and Yüan periods, but it is probable that, at any rate in the north, manufacture started late in the T'ang dynasty, and lasted well into the Ming period. Bowls of conical form are the commonest survival, and many are decorated with incised floral and foliate motifs. Lightly molded decoration occurs, as well as "combing" of the clay. The *mei p'ing* vase is found with this glaze; it has a tall, rather straight body with a short narrow neck and was intended to hold a single spray of prunus blossom. Stem cups, deep bowls, and ewers have also been noted, though some of the ewers which have appeared in Europe latterly are forgeries. Bowls sometimes have the rim bound with copper.

Identification of Sung Ware.—Because of the many later copies of Sung wares, and in particular those of the Yung Cheng period, it will be profitable at this point to mention the work of Robert T. Paine Jr. and W. J. Young of the Boston Museum of Fine Arts on the "bubble" structure of some of these glazes (Boston Museum of Fine Arts, *Far Eastern Ceramic Bulletin*, vol. v, no. 3 [1953]). From the Sung period the majority, of which *Kuan* is a typical example, contain a large number of bubbles which can be seen under a good magnifying glass. These, together with crystals which form on cooling, made the glaze appear dense, and, in extreme cases, almost opaque. By means of photomicrography Paine and Young have shown that various glazes exhibit a characteristic pat-

BY COURTESY OF VICTORIA AND ALBERT MUSEUM; PHOTOGRAPH (BOTTOM), WILFRID WALTER

WARE OF THE SUNG AND YÜAN DYNASTIES

(Top) Tz'u Chou ware: vase of *mei p'ing* shape, green glazed with carved floral decoration; Sung dynasty (A.D. 960–1279). Height: 15 in. (Bottom) *Ying ch'ing* ware: porcelain vase; about 1350, Yüan dynasty (1280–1368). Mounts of German origin; about 1720. Height: 10 in. In the Victoria and Albert Museum

tern which, in conjunction with other indications, can be used to determine the date of manufacture with a reasonable degree of accuracy. The bubble structure of northern celadons, for instance, is distinctly different from that of Yüeh ware, and both are distinguishable from Lung Ch'üan glazes. Whatever the surface resemblances between the Sung *Kuan* glaze and that of the 18th-century copy, magnification shows an unmistakable difference.

6. Yüan Dynasty (1280–1368).—The Yüan, or Mongol, dynasty is often regarded as being no more than transitional between the Sung and Ming dynasties. This is not entirely true. Undoubtedly many Sung types were continued, just as T'ang types were continued at the beginning of the Sung dynasty, but there are other wares which are a new departure. The manufacturing centre of Kingtechen increased in importance and first manufactured the white translucent porcelain which was to have a revolutionary effect on Chinese wares. The use of painted decoration, begun during the Sung period at Tz'u Chou, also became much more widespread, and the two techniques were combined in a manner which later affected the course of porcelain manufacture throughout the world.

The *Ko-ku-yao-lan* of 1387 refers to *shu fu* ware, a type of white porcelain which sometimes bears the characters representing *shu fu* ("central palace"), probably because of its imperial associations. This has been identified with existing specimens of white porcelain covered with a fairly dense bluish glaze. It appears to be related to the earlier *ying ch'ing* ware and probably developed from it. The base is unglazed. Decoration in relief, painted in slip or engraved, is to be seen on most surviving examples. Much more unusual is the appearance of a few specimens, almost certainly of Yüan date, which are painted with reduced copper red under the glaze. This technique was certainly not derived from the Middle East, but it is possible that it came originally from Korea. As mentioned above, the potters of Chün Chou had achieved this colour but only in the glaze.

The use of underglaze blue was definitely introduced from the Middle East where it was used at least as early as the 9th century, specimens thus decorated having been recovered at Samarra. The best-known example of Yüan porcelain decorated in this manner, which is usually referred to as blue and white, is a pair of vases in the Percival David collection in London. They bear a date equivalent to 1351. The accomplished handling of the decorative motif implies an advanced technique rather than a recent introduction, and suggestions that blue painting of this kind may have been done during the latter part of the Sung dynasty are therefore easier to accept than formerly. A pair of vases in the collection of Mrs. Alfred Clark have been dated to this earlier period.

As mentioned above the wares of Tz'u Chou are notoriously difficult to date accurately, but many of the brown-glazed wares with carved decoration belong to the Yüan, rather than to the Sung, period. Some of the painted wares, too, have certainly been awarded too early a date. It is almost as difficult to differentiate between late Sung, Yüan, and early Ming celadons. The Mongol conquests led to an opening of trade with many parts of the world to the west of China, and goods of all kinds were freely exported. It must, therefore, be assumed that manufacture of the exportable kinds of pottery was on a much larger scale at this time, and more specimens are likely to have survived from this than from the Sung period. The makers of celadons—one of the principal export wares—were distinctly conservative. However, some variations in form during the Yüan dynasty are noticeable, and the peony scroll, carved or in applied relief, is a typical motif, also appearing on some early blue-and-white wares.

7. Ming Dynasty (1368–1644).—The Mongol emperor Shun Ti was defeated in a popular uprising, and the first Ming emperor, Hung Wu, succeeded him in 1368. When the country had recovered from these internecine struggles the ceramic art took a new lease of life, though under somewhat changed conditions. The Sung monochrome wares, the celadons, Chün wares, etc., went out of favour and the old factories sank into obscurity, while the fame and importance of the great porcelain town of Kingtechen, near the P'o-yang Lake in Kiangsi Province, overshadowed all the rest. The imperial factory there was rebuilt and reorganized to keep the court supplied with fine white porcelain; Chinese ceramic writers thenceforward speak of Kingtechen and little else.

The neighbourhood of Kingtechen had long been noted for its excellent ceramic wares. All that the industry required in the way of material was lavishly supplied by the neighbouring hills, kaolin (china clay) for the body of the porcelain, petuntse (china stone) to mix with it and to form the glaze, and wood ashes for fluxing purposes. The staple product of Kingtechen is the fine white porcelain which has made "china" a household word throughout the world; and as this ware lent itself peculiarly well to painted decoration, the vogue for painted porcelain rapidly replaced the old Sung taste for monochromes.

Some blue-and-white specimens exist with the four-character mark of Hung Wu, and although R. L. Hobson comments that they seem unduly advanced for the period, the present antedating of the use of underglaze blue makes them much more acceptable. The reign of Yung Lo (1402–24) is remarkable for some extremely thin-walled pieces, referred to as *t'o t'ai,* or "bodiless ware." Engraved examples are known, and the Chinese commentaries refer to specimens decorated in red, agreeing with the mid-20th century attribution of the use of underglaze copper red to the Yüan dynasty. Some white bowls of conical shape are also ascribed to this reign.

SEATED LOHAN; 16TH CENTURY, MING DYNASTY (1368–1644). HEIGHT: ABOUT 27½ IN. IN THE STAATLICHE MUSEEN, BERLIN

After this early period Ming wares, generally, are fairly easily recognizable. Porcelain replaced stoneware as the usual medium, and polychrome decoration became widely employed. The wares lack much of the precision of the porcelain made during the following Ch'ing period (1644–1912), when a kind of factory system grew up which divided the work into a large number of repetitive operations. Little trouble was taken to smooth over imperfections of manufacture and footrings are often finished summarily. The glaze, too, frequently has minor defects, and articles such as vases are often slightly distorted and carelessly finished. The shape of many examples can fairly be described as "massive," in spite of the fact that most of them were made for export and the difficulties of transporting them must have been considerable. None of these factors ought to be regarded as evincing a lack of skill, especially as the potters were quite capable of technical virtuosity when they wished to display it—some of the most thinly potted of all Chinese porcelain belongs to this period. It seems that the Ming potters disdained the attitude of mind which treated blemishes as important, and occasional distortions were regarded as lending interest to an object. The Chinese did not carry this aesthetic creed to the same lengths as the Japanese, but the difference seems to be largely one of degree. Ming wares can fairly be described as masculine, in contrast to the more feminine qualities of the later Ch'ing wares.

The largest single group of Ming porcelain is that painted in blue underglaze, and much of the pigment used was imported from Middle Eastern sources. The Chinese sources of cobalt were adulterated with manganese, and the colour was defective. Persian cobalt, on the other hand, was inclined to run, and the best results were obtained from a mixture of the two. Supplies of this so-called "Mohammedan blue" (*hui hui ch'ing*), which came from the Kashan District of Persia, were not always obtainable and were interrupted on more than one occasion. The quality of the blue painted wares, however, remained to a great extent dependent on its use until the end of the 16th century when methods of refining native cobalt were devised.

Reign of Hsüan-te (1425–35).—In this reign the arts were particularly fostered and a high level of achievement attained. The blue painting was blackish in colour, with dark spots at intervals where thick blobs of pigment were deposited by the brush—the "heaped and piled" effect referred to by the 19th-century commentator, Lan Pu (see *Bibliography*). This style was deliberately copied in the 18th century, often with the appropriate reign mark, but its contrived nature is usually apparent. The motifs were floral and foliate, with the occasional use of fish and waterfowl. Sometimes vessels are bordered by a pattern of conventional rocks amid waves—the "Isles of Immortality"—usually referred to as the "Rock of Ages" pattern. This may have been first used during the 14th century, and it appears frequently throughout the Ming period and later. It can also be seen on Persian copies of Ming blue-and-white wares and, in a much debased form, on some pottery from Iznik (Anatolia) during the 16th and 17th centuries. The cobalt pigment said to have been exclusively used during this reign and the preceding reign of Yung Lo was neither from Middle Eastern nor native sources. It was referred to as *su-ni-po,* or *su-ma-ni,* and is discussed in the *Shih-wu Kan-chu* by Huang Yi-cheng, published in 1591. *Su-ni-po* has tentatively been translated to mean "Sumatra" as it appears that envoys from that country brought tributes of cobalt blue to China from 1426 to 1448. Supplies of cobalt also reached China from East Africa, probably from Zanzibar, and it may well be that "Zanzibar" would be a better reading.

References to underglaze copper red become much more definite in contemporary commentaries. It is often called "sacrificial red" for some reason which cannot be determined. To a great extent sacrificial red was abandoned later in the dynasty in favour of overglaze iron red, although it was used again during the reign of the Ch'ing emperors, K'ang-hsi (1661–1722) and Yung Cheng (1723–35), and appears in a rather primitive form from some provincial kilns. Most existing examples of Hsüan-te types such as the stem cups with three fish in silhouette are 18th-century copies. Both cobalt blue and copper red were used as monochromes, and occasionally together, but since these pigments required a slightly different firing temperature one or the other is usually deficient in quality.

The use of enamel colours was rare and the technique had by no means been fully mastered although some specimens decorated in primitive red, green, and yellow enamels had been made at Tz'u Chou as early as the Sung period.

Ch'eng Hua (1464–87).—Records between the time of Hsüan-te and Ch'eng Hua are meagre, and specimens which can be attributed to it with any degree of accuracy are few. Most enameled decoration, however, can be attributed with a reasonable measure of certainty to the reign of Ch'eng Hua, the finest examples being, perhaps, the "chicken" cups, so called because they are decorated with chickens. Their decoration is outlined in underglaze blue and filled in with soft enamels called *tou ts'ai,* or "contrasted colours." These were much imitated later. Ku T'ai in the *Po wu yao lan,* a commentary published in 1627, refers to Ch'eng Hua enamels as being thin, subdued in colour, and pictorial in effect, which accords with the little now known about them. He also mentions that the *su-ni-po* blue was no longer available and that the blue and white was poorer in quality.

The practice of enameling directly on to unglazed porcelain (biscuit) instead of on to a glazed and fired body is sometimes thought to have begun in this reign, though that of Chia Ching (1521–66) is the more likely. Ming specimens are, in any case, extremely rare, and most belong to the reign of K'ang-hsi (1661–1722) in the Ch'ing dynasty. The enamel covers the whole of the biscuit surface, and the difference between the two techniques is marked. The style of decoration, too, is different, although this was sometimes imitated in overglaze enamels.

Like the mark of Hsüan-te, that of Ch'eng Hua has been much copied later, and true examples are exceedingly scarce.

Hung Chih and Cheng Te (1487–1521).—The first use of a coloured overglaze ground can be attributed to the reign of Hung Chih (1487–1505), when a yellow of variable shade first appears. The blue-and-white motifs of the reign of Cheng Te (1505–21)

show the influence of the Muslim palace eunuchs who supervised the imperial kilns. "Mohammedan blue" was again available, and arabesques and Arabic inscriptions appear on some examples of porcelain made at Kingtechen. The "Mohammedan scroll" is composed of somewhat formal flowers joined by S-shaped stems, with scroll-like leaves at intervals along them. The earliest versions of this theme, which seems originally to have come from a textile pattern, are the least stiffly drawn. The linear style of painting previously employed altered to one where outlines were filled in with flat ungraduated washes.

Chia Ching (1521–66).—This reign is notable for a deterioration in the quality of the porcelain body, offset by the use of rich dark blue. The latter may have been due to fresh imports, or to the discovery of native deposits at Jui-chou (Kao-an) in Kiangsi Province. The technique of using this colour had obviously been mastered, because there is no sign of running. Enameled wares, too, were executed in good colours, with well-marked outlines. A characteristic colour, the opaque tomato-coloured iron red (*fan hung*), was used as a monochrome with gilt traceries over it on bowls which sometimes had interior decoration in underglaze blue. Various wares have decoration in red and green, a scheme which became more familiar later. A yellow glaze is found in conjunction with incised decoration (usually a dragon) in green. Very rarely was a green or blue monochrome used.

Lung Ch'ing and Wan Li (1566–1620).—The styles of Chia Ching were, to some extent, continued in the following reigns of Lung Ch'ing (1566–72) and Wan Li (1572–1620). A palette which contained underglaze blue in conjunction with green, yellow, aubergine purple, and iron red (the precursor of the later Ch'ing *famille verte* palette), was known as *wan li wu ts'ai* or "Wan Li five-colour ware." Continuation of the red and green decoration is also to be seen, and vast quantities of blue-and-white porcelain were produced for export. The body is quite unlike that used earlier in the dynasty, being thin, hard, crisp, and resonant. It is the commonest of all Ming wares in the West.

During this reign much pierced work (*ling lung*) was done. It is sometimes called *kuei kung* ("devil's work") in allusion to the almost supernatural skill needed. Pierced objects range from small brush pots to vases covered with coloured glazes, and their artistic importance is usually in inverse ratio to the amount of time and manual dexterity lavished on them.

The Ming dynasty ended in 1644. The wares of the last three emperors, for the most part, had followed styles already established though perhaps an exception can be made for blue and white, which shows a number of new departures in both form and decoration. Many of the vases are without a footring and stand on a flat base. Forms based on European wares were obviously made for export. A few examples with cyclical dates (*i.e.*, inscriptions referring to one of the 60 year "cycles" rather than to the reign of an emperor) enable these wares to be dated accurately. These transitional wares are discussed in detail by Soame Jenyns in "The Wares of the Transitional Period Between the Ming and the Ch'ing, 1620–1683," *Chinese Art Society of America,* ix (1955).

Provincial and Export Wares.—The wares hitherto discussed were made, for the most part, in the Kingtechen area; it remains to consider the other wares of the period. The export of celadons went on, not only to the countries west of China but also to Japan where they were much esteemed. Vast collections of these and other Ming wares gathered together by the sultans of Turkey are still at Istanbul and have given particularly valuable assistance in dating. Most celadons attributable to the Ming period have incised under the glaze floral and foliate decoration of a kind which also appears on blue painted wares, and the drawing is distinctively Ming in style.

The Tz'u Chou kilns continued working, the traditional nature of their styles once again making it difficult to date wares accurately. The forms of the vessels are probably the safest guide. Many of the pillows (which are more comfortable than they appear) belong to the Yüan and Ming periods. Decoration which includes Taoist figures can probably be placed to the reign of Chia Ching, when Taoism was in the ascendant. It is difficult to sepa-

rate Ting wares made after the Sung dynasty from some of those made earlier. A type known as Kiangnan Ting from Anhwei, which is creamy in colour and sometimes has a brown tinge in the glaze, was made during Ming times and continued into the Ch'ing period. Some of the Chün wares made during Ming times may be wrongfully attributed to Yüan or Sung, and the "soft Chün" types probably belong almost exclusively to the Ming period. *Temmoku* wares were undoubtedly continued.

The fine porcelain of Te-hua in Fukien Province was first made, perhaps, in the early part of the dynasty, although some authorities are inclined to regard it as later. Most of this porcelain was left undecorated, and received the name in Europe of blanc de chine. The glaze is exceptionally thick and lustrous, and early examples are often slightly ivory in tone, although this can by no means be relied upon to identify them. Enameling is infrequent; and virtually all enameled specimens, figures or vessels, have been decorated in Europe, usually in the Netherlands. Figures especially were made here, the Buddhist goddess Kuanyin being a favourite subject. Most examples belong to the 17th and 18th centuries, and even later. Detachable hands and heads probably indicate an early date.

The stoneware of I-hsing in Kiangsu Province is extremely important and its teapots were much valued in 17th-century Europe where tea was newly introduced. It was known in the West as

BY COURTESY OF VICTORIA AND ALBERT MUSEUM

SAN TS'AI (THREE-COLOURED WARE); MING DYNASTY, 1368–1644
Potiche (vase with separate cover) decorated with coloured glazes separated by clay threads in the so-called cloisonné technique; about 1525. Height: 12¼ in. In the Victoria and Albert Museum

boccaro ware and was copied and imitated at Meissen, Ger., in Staffordshire, Eng., and in the Netherlands by Arij de Milde and others. The wares of I-hsing are unglazed, the body varying from red to dark brown. The molding is extremely precise and was often sharpened by grinding on a lapidary's wheel. The body was sometimes polished in the same way. Copies of Chün, *Ko*, and *Kuan* glazes were made at the same kilns.

The kilns of Kwangtung also copied some of the Sung glazes, the most notable being the Chün types of which "Fatshan" Chün has already been mentioned (see *Sung,* above). Some celadons are also reputed to come from this district.

Most of the Ming stoneware ridge tiles and roof finials were made at kilns near Peking. Many of them are decorated in green, yellow, turquoise, and aubergine purple glazes, recalling the wares of the T'ang dynasty. A Ming date is exceedingly optimistic for most of them. To this group belong, perhaps, a few large figures which have sometimes been doubtfully awarded a T'ang date.

The provincial tile kilns also manufactured the so-called *san ts'ai,* or "three-colour wares," perhaps originally a product of the Tz'u Chou kilns. These were decorated with coloured glazes which were often kept from intermingling by threads of clay (the so-called cloisonné technique), or were used in conjunction with the *ling lung* technique. Others have engraved designs under the glazes. Most existing specimens are large vases, barrel-shaped garden seats, and the like. The best are extremely handsome and imposing, turquoise and dark-blue glazes being particularly effective. Copies have been made in Japan in modern times.

"Swatow" plates are a provincial type, perhaps made in Fukien for export. They are notable for a poor finish, often with a sandy base, and are decorated with sketchy but vigorous painted designs in underglaze blue, or, less often, in a limited range of enamel colours—usually red and green.

8. Ch'ing Dynasty (1644–1912).—The Ch'ing dynasty marks the beginning of the immense vogue for porcelain in Europe which was to reach its height during the first half of the 18th century. Its wares differ, for the most part, from those of the Ming period in a fairly distinctive manner. Potters now had their medium under almost complete control and their products are much more

precisely finished. Their finesse contrasts sharply with the struggles of potters in Europe where porcelain manufacture did not emerge from the purely empirical stage until the 19th century. Ch'ing wares are treated at somewhat greater length than those of the preceding periods, partly because of their greater diversity, but also because many varieties are fairly common in the West.

Dating is assisted by literary sources such as two letters of 1712 and 1722 written by Père d'Entrecolles, a Jesuit missionary who spent some years at Kingtechen. He not only described the various processes of manufacture in some detail but added many comments of considerable use and interest to the ceramic historian and collector. He records that some pieces were handled by as many as 70 men, each contributing a small part to the total effect, and this must surely be one of the reasons why many Ch'ing wares lack the freshness and spontaneity of Ming decoration. An important early collection was made by Augustus the Strong, elector of Saxony and king of Poland, who patronized the Meissen factory. The collection, much of which was acquired between 1694 and 1705, was at first housed in the specially acquired Japanische Palais, but was later transferred to the Johanneum, both in Dresden. Much of it was returned to Dresden by the government of the U.S.S.R. in 1959, but some had been destroyed by bombardment during World War II.

The most famous contemporary Chinese commentaries are the *T'ao Shuo* ("A Description of Pottery") by Chu Yen, published in 1774, and the *Ching-tê Chên T'ao-Lu* ("The Potteries of Ching-tê Chên") by Lan Pu published in 1815. However, even the best translations (see *Bibliography*) are not easy to read without a considerable fund of practical knowledge, and even this is not sufficient to penetrate the obscurity of some passages.

The 18th Century: Kingtechen.—The imperial kilns of Kingtechen were fortunate in their directors during the reigns of K'ang-hsi (1661–1722), Yung Cheng (1723–35), and Ch'ien-lung (1736–96), and these directors were still more fortunate in the support they received from the palace. K'ang-hsi, in particular, was a patron of the arts on a considerable scale.

Underglaze Blue and Red.—The blue painted porcelain of the Ch'ing dynasty has been somewhat neglected in the 20th century. This is probably due to the ridiculously high value placed on it during the latter years of the 19th century, when it was usually called "Nanking" ware. Even the best, which belongs to the reign of K'ang-hsi, hardly bears comparison with the finer Ming wares though its influence on European porcelain was far-reaching. Blue-and-white porcelain was exported to Europe in vast quantities, and much has survived. Many of the forms were especially made for export; the condiment ledge on plates and dishes, for instance, which had first appeared in the reign of Wan Li had been added for Western customers: the Chinese use the saucer-dish. The blue and white of the K'ang-hsi period has an extremely white body and the blue is exceptionally clear and pure. It is variable in shade and the design is executed in graduated washes within lightly drawn outlines, a point of difference from Ming wares. Many of the designs of the Ming period were still in use and, of the later patterns, those illustrating literary and historical themes, sometimes with an inscription and a cyclical date added, are probably the best.

Ginger jars decorated with prunus blossom reserved in white on an irregular blue ground, intended to represent the cracked ice of spring and sometimes described as "pulsating," were once valued exceptionally highly, although in the mid-20th century a more realistic attitude was taken toward them. During the 18th century, copies were made of the blue-and-white wares of Hsüan-te and Chia Ch'ing (1796–1820); pains were taken to make them as accurate as possible, even to an imitation of the "heaped and piled" effect, and many were marked falsely.

Underglaze copper red was also used during the period under review. Despite statements to the contrary, it is becoming apparent that this pigment was never entirely abandoned, but merely became unpopular. The stem cups of the Yung Cheng period with three fruit or three fish in silhouette, which imitate those of Hsüan-te, are much better known than the wares they copied. Copper red also appears in conjunction with underglaze blue, and a greenish-toned glaze is common with pieces thus decorated. The designs are those of the period.

Underglaze blue was sometimes used as a monochrome ground colour. It was blown on to the surface in powder form before glazing, a bamboo tube, closed with gauze at one end, being employed for the purpose. For obvious reasons, it is called powder blue, or, in Chinese, *ch'ui ch'ing* ("blown blue"), and is distinct from the sponged blue grounds of the Ming dynasty. It was later used at several of the porcelain factories in Europe. Clair de lune (*yüeh pai,* or "moon white") is a cobalt glaze of the palest blue.

Coloured Glazes.—Copper red appears in monochrome form as

BY COURTESY OF VICTORIA AND ALBERT MUSEUM; PHOTOGRAPHS, WILFRID WALTER

WARES OF THE CH'ING DYNASTY; 1644–1912

(Top left) Vase with *flambé* glaze of reduced copper; Ch'ien-lung (1736–96). Height: 17 in. (Top right) Jar of "Batavian" ware with "dead leaf" brown glaze and decorated with floral sprays in the *famille rose* palette; about 1720. Height: 15½ in. (Bottom left) Flask with a turquoise glaze; Ch'ien-lung. Mounted in France during the reign of Louis XVI. Height: 17½ in. (Bottom right) Vase with a ground of underglaze blue painted with fish in iron red (*fan hung*) with added gilding; Ch'ien-lung. Height: 19 in. In the Victoria and Albert Museum

lang yao (the *sang-de-boeuf,* or "oxblood," of the French). *Lang* was probably the name of a potter; *yao,* of course, means ware. This glaze was also known to the Chinese as *ch'ui hung* ("blown red"). It was certainly used as a monochrome in early Ming times and possibly even earlier. It was the direct ancestor of the showy *flambé,* or transmutation, glazes of the Ch'ien-lung period which are referred to as *yao pien* and which are often vividly streaked with unreduced copper blue. These glazes are, of course, also related technically to the purple-splashed Chün wares of the Sung dynasty, and to some of the glazes used on Kwangtung stoneware.

Another variation, no doubt at first accidental, is the glaze known in the West as "peach bloom," a pinkish red mottled with russet spots and tinged with green. The Chinese have various names for it, of which, perhaps, the commonest is *p'in kuo hung*, or "apple red." It is used on a pure white body. Most objects glazed in this way are small items for the writer's table.

Monochromes of all kinds are a distinct and important section of Ch'ing wares, and many reproductions of Sung monochromes were made. The use of iron as a pigment can be seen in a revival of the celadon glaze. The Kingtechen celadons have, generally, a pale green glaze over white porcelain, the white footring being given a wash of brown to simulate the old ware. Meanwhile, celadons of the Lung Ch'üan type were still being made and Père d'Entrecolles describes their manufacture. It is probable, therefore, that the kilns of Ch'ü Chou were still working in the old tradition. As well as the celadon glaze, iron was used to produce colours varying between café au lait and pale yellow, and also "dead leaf" brown. Sometimes panels were reserved in white and painted in enamel colours. Specimens thus glazed appear in the old Dutch catalogues as "Batavian" ware, because the wares were imported via the Dutch entrepôt at Batavia (modern Jakarta or Djakarta) in Java. They are also related to "mirror black" (*wu chin*), a lustrous colour obtained by the addition of manganese, and sometimes further decorated with gilding or even, as in at least one extant specimen, with both gilding and silvering. "Imperial" yellow, a lead glaze often used over engraved dragons and similar designs, was revived during the 19th century.

Brilliant turquoise glazes derived from copper have been produced up to the mid-20th century although later examples seldom have the quality of the earlier ones. The glaze is usually covered with a network of fine crackle and some examples have engraved decoration under it. Related glazes are the copper greens, for example leaf green and cucumber green, the latter being speckled with a darker colour. Apple green is an enamel colour used as a ground and applied over a cracked gray glaze. Most greens are relatively late.

Purple, or aubergine, glazes derived from manganese are seen occasionally. *Brinjal* bowls, decorated with engraved flowers, have an aubergine ground in conjunction with dappled green and yellow glazes. "Brinjal," in fact, means aubergine (eggplant) which is a favourite food in parts of the East. Bowls with engraved dragons and a combination of only two of these colours are somewhat better in quality.

Enamels.—These were sometimes used as monochromes. The use of iron red (*fan hung*) is an excellent example of the technique. It is sometimes called coral red, and it varies a little in shade. The surface is usually glossy but occasionally matt. The *rose* colour, discussed below, was certainly used in this way, and as a ground colour.

The wares enameled on biscuit are a much sought-after group. They are a development of the Ming *san ts'ai* wares, which were still being made during the Ch'ing period. The effect of painting directly on to biscuit was to produce a soft and distinctive colouring, which is extremely attractive. The outlines were first painted directly on to the unglazed surface in brownish black; some of the colours were then painted within these outlines and others were washed over them. Red or blue enamels, when they appear, are usually provided with a patch of glaze underneath them. The practice seems hardly to have survived the K'ang-hsi period, except for deliberately made later copies.

During the reign of K'ang-hsi the enameled wares were painted in the *famille verte* palette, usually over a white glaze. The name *famille verte* ("green family") is derived from the dominant distinctive green, but the wares are in fact a development of the Wan Li five-colour ware, the most important difference being the replacement of the earlier underglaze blue by an enamel blue. On most genuine examples it is possible to see a distinct "halo" round the enamel blue, but its absence does not necessarily condemn it as not genuine. The *famille noire* has the *verte* palette in conjunc-

tion with a black ground; the *famille jaune* uses the same colours, but with a yellow ground. In each case the white porcelain disappears under the enameling, and modern taste is inclined to award them a far lower aesthetic position than was once the case.

Toward the close of the reign of K'ang-hsi an opaque *rose* enamel appears. This and its related colours were called *yang ts'ai* or "foreign colours." It was discovered by Andreas Cassius of Leiden, Neth., and introduced about 1685. It is sometimes referred to as the "purple of Cassius," particularly in older works. It soon formed the characteristic colour of a group of wares, referred to as the *famille rose,* which was particularly developed

FAMILLE ROSE WARE OF THE YUNG CHENG PERIOD, 1723–1735
Saucer dish decorated with a quail in colours of the *famille rose* palette. Diameter: 8 in. In the Victoria and Albert Museum

during the reign of Yung Cheng. It more or less replaced the *verte* palette although combinations of the *verte* and *rose* palettes can sometimes be found. The translucent enamels of the earlier period tend to become opaque, and painting is more feminine in style.

White Wares.—During the 18th century the white wares of Kingtechen were made mostly for the home market although a few were exported. They include examples of the *t'o t'ai*, or "bodiless ware," and the *an hua* (literally "secret language"). The latter has designs lightly incised or painted with white slip. The body is white, and the whole is covered with clear glaze. The decoration can only be seen plainly if light be allowed to shine through it. This style is copied from a traditional Yung Lo (1402–24) type. *Ling lung* (pierced work) was revived in certain rare pieces inspired by jade; the use of piercing filled with glaze is derived from Persian Gombroon ware.

European Influence and the Export Trade.—Before mid-18th century some European wares had found their way to China, as witness certain copies of early Meissen porcelain. The taste of the European trader, though hardly representative of the more cultured section of Western civilization, also began to have considerable influence. Much decoration was done in studios in and around the port of Canton, white porcelain being sent from Kingtechen for the purpose. Enormous quantities of *famille rose* porcelain were painted there, including most of the so-called rubybacked dishes which are completely covered on the reverse, except for the interior of the footring, with a ground of opaque *rose* enamel. These often have an elaborate arrangement of minutely delineated border patterns round the central subject (usually pretty women) demonstrating the new, and later widespread, idea that the beauty of an object is directly proportional to the amount of decoration on it. This theory was to be one of the causes of the degeneration of later Chinese and Japanese wares; it was, however, by no means confined to the Orient and can be seen in most 19th-century European porcelain. Its probable cause is discussed in the section *19th and 20th Centuries,* below.

The Yung Cheng painters were the first to carry foliate decoration over on to the back of the dish, usually as a prolongation of the stem. This was repeated later during the reign of Tao Kuang (1821–51). The European tendency to draw flowers in a naturalistic manner also appears in China from the Yung Cheng period onward, although it was not carried to the same lengths.

An attempt to imitate the European method of enameling, in which enamels were applied in flat washes which partly sank into soft porcelain glazes, can be seen in the so-called Ku Yüeh Hsüan ("Ancient Moon Pavilion") wares. These sometimes have a European subject, such as a Watteau shepherdess, but Chinese subjects were also used.

Of the wares more directly due to European intervention perhaps the best known is "Oriental Lowestoft," more correctly known as Chinese export porcelain. The first name is due to an error on the part of William Chaffers, who persisted in attributing these wares to the small English factory at Lowestoft. If this porcelain is important at all, it is as a curiosity; the artistic value is nearly always negligible. The styles are usually based on those of European ceramics or metalwork, or on a combination of Western and Oriental motifs in an unpleasing *mélange confus*. The designs were provided by Western traders and coats of arms are comparatively common. The importance of this kind of decoration is that it enables a piece to be dated and traced to its origin with a measure of certainty. Another variety, known as "Jesuit" porcelain, was painted with crucifixions, nativities, and the like in sepia with a little gilding. Much rarer are specimens painted with secular subjects, which can usually be traced to a contemporary engraving. They are executed in a careful linear style which makes their origin obvious. Such wares are, however, a peculiarly unprofitable bypath in any study of Chinese ceramics.

Other wares connected with the export trade are those decorated with the so-called Mandarin patterns, which came from the Cantonese studios and were introduced toward the end of the 18th century. These have figure subjects in panels, which are surrounded with coloured grounds and an excess of floral and other ornament in unprepossessing combinations of colours.

Some specimens of *ling lung* imitate European pierced work, which was, in turn, copied from contemporary silver. Much white porcelain was sent to Canton to be decorated, but much, too, was shipped to Europe for the same purpose. Many examples were painted by German *Hausmaler* ("home painters") such as Preussler, by Dutch enamelers, and by English "outside decorators" such as James Giles. Decorated wares, usually those sparsely painted in underglaze blue, sometimes have added enamel decoration. Most of these were done by Dutch enamelers, and are usually termed "clobbered"—a word perhaps of Dutch origin. Dutch glass engravers also cut designs into some brown-glazed examples, a technique known as *Schnittdekor*.

Europe, of course, was not the only export market open to the Chinese. Much blue and white was exported to the traditional markets in Persia and the Near East, and Arabic inscriptions can be seen on some specimens. Of the other markets, India, Thailand, Burma, and Tibet deserve mention.

Other Kilns.—The wares discussed so far have been principally those of Kingtechen. Those of Te-hua in Fukien Province, however, are also important. Figures of Kuanyin in particular were exported in enormous quantities, and the *an hua* and pierced decorations often came from here. Vessels such as libation cups with applied prunus sprigs were copied by European factories in the 18th century, notably by those at Meissen (Ger.), Chelsea and Bow (London), and Saint-Cloud (France). The body is usually white, sometimes with an ivory tone, and the glaze is thick, rich, and lustrous. European forms are to be seen occasionally, and most coloured examples have been decorated in the West. The kilns of I-hsing also continued making the traditional wares.

19th and 20th Centuries.—The 19th century has little to offer which is new, or of good quality. Snuff bottles painted with miniature designs were first made toward the end of the 18th century, but most belong to the reign of Chia Ch'ing (1796–1820) and Tao Kuang (1821–51). The former reign can be regarded as an extension of the Ch'ien-lung period, although an increasing degeneration is obvious. Bowls with circular medallions painted in enamel colours with yellow or *rose* grounds are, perhaps, among the finer wares. Also of good quality are bowls covered with an opaque ground, *rose* or yellow, with designs engraved into it. These were first made in the 18th century and extend to the reign of Tao Kuang. The technique is referred to as *graviata*.

Most of the wares of Tao Kuang are poor in quality, although some examples in the style of Yung Cheng are a little better. The glaze has a "musliny" texture similar to that seen on some early Ming wares, and on Japanese porcelain from Arita. Translucent enamels over underglaze blue are a Yung Cheng type revived at this time. The *rose-verte* palette was commonly used.

In 1853 the T'ai P'ing Rebellion led to the destruction of the kilns at Kingtechen, and these were not rebuilt until 1864. The reign of T'ung Chih (1862–75) is principally notable for poor

copies of some of the earlier monochromes, including the "peach bloom" glaze. Nearly all wares from this time onward are slick copies of older work. Criticism is chiefly directed against them on the ground that they are sometimes passed off as genuine, but as decoration they are often much more pleasing than many 20th-century European wares.

9. Marks.—It is difficult to give much practical assistance on the question of Chinese marks. Most of them give the name of the dynasty and that of the emperor, and reference to any of the standard books on the subject will enable the reader to ascertain the meaning. However, many of them have been used so inconsequentially that unless the period can also be assigned with reasonable certainty by other means, it is better to disregard them. The most abused are those of Hsüan-te and Chia Ching. Hardly less abused in the 19th century is the mark of Yung Cheng. Although not unknown, the genuine mark of K'ang-hsi is comparatively rare since it was thought that to put the name of the emperor on something like porcelain, which might be broken, was sacrilege. Reign marks do not often appear before the Ming dynasty, although there are a few earlier examples. Studio marks and devices are seen occasionally, and most of them are given in the better books of marks (see *Bibliography*). Inscriptions were often used as decoration, and sometimes include cyclical dates, which are to be found in some books of marks. There is a distinct difference between Ming and Ch'ing calligraphy which will be apparent to anyone familiar with Chinese ideograms.

10. Symbolism.—Chinese decoration is usually symbolic and often exploits the double meaning of certain words: for instance, the Chinese word for bat, *fu*, also means "happiness." Five bats represent the Five Blessings—longevity, wealth, serenity, virtue, and an easy death. Longevity is symbolized by such things as the stork, the pine, and the tortoise, the *ling chih* fungus, and the bamboo, all reputed to enjoy long life. The character *Shou*, which also denotes longevity, is used in a variety of ornamental forms. Together the peach and the bat represent *fu shou*, long life and happiness. The "Buddha's hand" citron, a fruit with fingerlike appendages, is a symbol of wealth, and each month and season is represented by a flower or plant. The *Pa Kua*, consisting of eight sets of three lines, broken and unbroken in different combinations, represents natural forces. They are often seen in conjunction with the *yang-yin* symbol which represents the male-female principle, and which has been well described by R. L. Hobson as resembling "two tadpoles interlocked." The dragon is too well known to need description, but generally it is a mild and beneficent creature. It is a symbol of the emperor, just as the *fêng-huang* (a phoenix-like creature) symbolizes the empress.

ENAMELED WARE OF THE K'ANG-HSI PERIOD, 1661–1722

Winepot in the form of the character *Shou* (longevity); enamel on biscuit porcelain. Height: 15½ in. In the Victoria and Albert Museum

There are three principal religious systems in China: Confucianism, Taoism, and Buddhism. The Taoist gods, in particular, appear frequently on porcelain as decoration. The most important, Lao Tzu, has a large and protuberant forehead. He is usually accompanied by the Eight Immortals (Hsien) and these are sometimes modeled as sets of figures. The eight horses of the emperor Mu Wang (Chou dynasty) are also frequently represented. The Buddhist goddess, Kuanyin, and the Eighteen Lohan, disciples of Buddha, were also modeled. The Eight Buddhist Emblems appear fairly frequently, as well as the Eight Precious Things, and a collection of instruments and implements used in the arts known as the Hundred Antiques. The Lions of Buddha (often miscalled dogs) are frequently represented, as well as the kylin (properly the *ch'i-lin*) which is a composite animal, not unlike a unicorn,

Spouted jar in the polychrome Kamares style. Middle Minoan II, about 1850–1700 B.C. Height: 9½ in.

AEGEAN AND GREEK POTTERY

The jars at top are from the palace workshops at Knossos, where floral and marine motifs were effectively exploited. The flowers on the jar above are woven into a symmetrical pattern in which it is hard to see where nature ends and abstraction begins. Closer to nature are the formally arranged lilies of the amphora at right. The aryballos (centre) is a miniature masterpiece of the orientalizing period: the lion's head follows a neo-Hittite model, while the battle scene reflects the early diffusion of epic poetry. The black-figure technique, already attempted on the aryballos, reaches perfection in the amphora below by Exekias, who endowed his figures with mood and emotion. The psykter shows the wider variety of pose and greater freedom of drawing made possible by the red-figure technique

Three-handled amphora (storage jar) in the palace style, decorated with stylized lilies. Late Minoan II, about 1450–1400 B.C. Height: 27½ in.

Aryballos (scent bottle) with mouth in the form of a lion's head. The three zones contain a hoplite battle, a horse race, and a hare hunt. Proto-Corinthian, about 650 B.C. Height: 2½ in. In the British Museum

Amphora in the black-figure style, signed by Exekias, showing Achilles slaying Penthesilea. Attic, about 530 B.C. Height: 16¼ in. In the British Museum

Psykter (wine cooler) in the red-figure style, signed by Douris, showing reveling satyrs. Attic, about 480 B.C. Height: 11¼ in. In the British Museum

PLATE II   POTTERY AND PORCELAIN

Painted urn of red polished pottery with geometric decoration, from the Pan-shan cemetery, Kansu Province; about 2000 B.C. Height: 15¼ in. In the Victoria and Albert Museum

CHINESE POTTERY AND PORCELAIN

These two plates give a brief survey of Chinese ceramic art from Neolithic times to the 18th century. A period of 400 years stretched between the making of the Han censer (top right) and the T'ang figure (right). These four centuries—turbulent, characterized by western-nomad raids and the rise of Buddhism—were not favourable to ceramic art. Only during the T'ang dynasty were the nomads beaten back; the empire expanded greatly and contacts with the West resumed. The Sung dynasty, though another turbulent era, was the classic period of Chinese art. Sung pottery (bottom right) emphasized form and employed coloured glazes of great beauty and variety. Invading Mongols overthrew the Sungs and established the Yüan dynasty; the traditional Chinese white translucent porcelain decorated in underglaze blue, first produced under this dynasty, reached its peak under the Mings (below)

"Hill" jar, or censer, with a cover representing the Taoist "Isles of the Blest"; Han dynasty (206 B.C–A.D. 221). Height: 9½ in. In the Victoria and Albert Museum

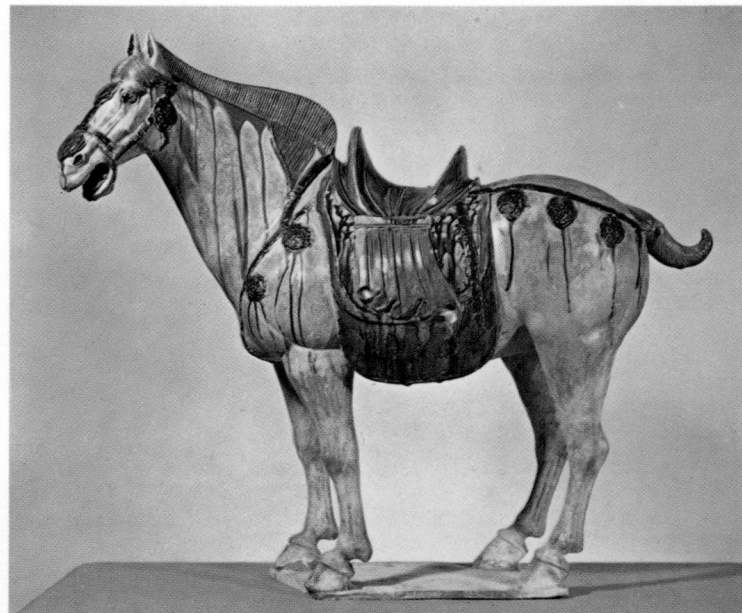

Tomb figure decorated in characteristic coloured glazes; T'ang dynasty (A.D. 618–906). Height: about 2 ft., 4 in. In the Victoria and Albert Museum

Flask decorated with a dragon and wave scrolls in underglaze blue; Ming dynasty (1368–1644), 14th century. Height: 14½ in. In the Victoria and Albert Museum

Dish of Lung Ch'üan celadon with incised decoration and four fish left unglazed; Sung dynasty (A.D. 960–1279). Length: 12⅜ in. In the Victoria and Albert Museum

Pear-shaped bottle with "garlic" mouth, painted in underglaze blue and overglaze enamels; Ming dynasty (1368–1644), signed on the lip with six-character mark of Wan Li (1572–1620). Height: 21 in.

Vase of the *famille noire* painted with flowers of the seasons; reign of K'ang-hsi (1661–1722), Ch'ing dynasty (1644–1912), with mark of Ming emperor Ch'eng Hua (1464–87). Height: 18¼ in. In the Victoria and Albert Museum

Trumpet-shaped vase with floral decoration on background of green enamel, *famille verte;* reign of K'ang-hsi, Ch'ing dynasty. Height: 29 in. In the Victoria and Albert Museum

CHINESE PORCELAIN

If the Sung dynasty is regarded as China's classic period, then the Ming dynasty might be termed its baroque phase. The technical advances in production and decoration, the more extensive use of painting, and the great diversity of forms that characterized Ming ceramics may be seen in the exceptional example at top left. The Manchu Ch'ing emperors of the middle 17th and 18th centuries fostered the art of porcelain making and encouraged experimentation. This patronage led to such ambitious schemes of decoration as the *famille noire* (above), the better-known *famille verte* (top right) and the *famille rose* (left), the pigment for which was introduced from Europe and generally used to decorate wares made for export. The practice of painting on biscuit (right) was a development of the Ming *san ts'ai* wares which were still being produced during the Ch'ing period

Buddhist figure painted with *famille rose* enamels; reign of Ch'ien-lung (1736–96), Ch'ing dynasty. Height: 17 in. In the Victoria and Albert Museum

Vase of lobed form painted on biscuit with a yellow ground; reign of K'ang-hsi, Ch'ing dynasty. Height: 12¼ in. In the Victoria and Albert Museum

PLATE IV   POTTERY AND PORCELAIN

Japanese lobed dish with a bouquet of chrysanthemums in a paper holder; Kakiemon ware from Arita, about 1700. Diameter: 7 in.

Bottle of Japanese white porcelain decorated with enamel colours at Delft, the Netherlands; about 1730. Height: 20 in.

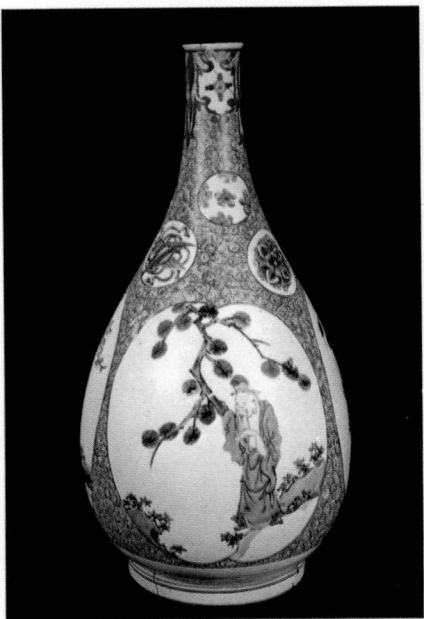

Pear-shaped bottle of Japanese Kutani porcelain decorated in characteristic enamel colours; about 1685. Height: 16 in.

JAPANESE AND KOREAN PORCELAIN

Japanese ceramics were strongly influenced by those of Korea and China. An exception was Kakiemon ware, originating in the 17th century, which made innovations in design and, in turn, influenced 18th-century porcelain makers in Europe. Kakiemon ware (top left) is noted for its white porcelain surface which enhances the asymmetrically placed painting. Much Japanese white porcelain (top right) was exported to Europe where it was decorated in enameling studios. Kutani porcelain (above), seldom seen in European collections, is rich in colour, bold in design. The Korean bottle (right) exemplifies the rare and uniquely Korean technique of *mishima*, inlaying decoration under glaze

Korean bottle with a celadon glaze and *mishima*, or inlaid decoration; Koryo dynasty, 13th century. Height: 13⅝ in. In the Victoria and Albert Museum

BY COURTESY OF (BOTTOM RIGHT) THE VICTORIA AND ALBERT MUSEUM, (OTHERS) GERALD REITLINGER; PHOTOGRAPHS, WILFRID WALTER

Turkish jug characteristically decorated with a scale pattern, tin enamel glaze; Iznik (Anatolia), about 1575. Height: 11 in. In the Victoria and Albert Museum

Two examples of Persian pottery. (Left) Bowl painted in black and cobalt over a white slip; from Kashan, Iran; about A.D. 1200. Diameter: 7⅜ in. (Right) Blue-glazed Seljuk bowl with carved decoration; about A.D. 1150. Diameter: 7¼ in. In the Victoria and Albert Museum

Persian jar with fish painted in black under a turquoise glaze; Sultanabad. Height: 11¼ in. In the Victoria and Albert Museum

Persian bowl painted with overglaze colours (*minai* technique); late 12th century. Diameter: 8⅜ in. In the Victoria and Albert Museum

ISLAMIC POTTERY

All Islamic pottery is earthenware, usually fired at comparatively low temperatures and therefore extremely fragile. Perfect excavated specimens are very rare; the condition of the plate (top centre) is typical of the state in which most vessels are recovered. Abstract patterns and designs based on Kufic inscriptions are common decorative motifs; naturalistic representations of human beings and animals are found in Persian pottery but are rare elsewhere. The rediscovery of tin enamel (top left), lost since Assyrian times, was the major Islamic contribution to ceramic history and inspired the development of the European faience industry. Enameling on glaze, *minai* (above), was also an Islamic discovery, later copied in China during the Sung dynasty

PLATE VI POTTERY AND PORCELAIN

Large Italian *maiolica* dish decorated with hunting scenes; signed by the potter and painter, dated 1594. From the Modena workshop. Diameter: 30 in. In the Hastings Museum

French dish painted in the *istoriato* style of Urbino; from Lyons, about 1575. Diameter: 15 in. In the Victoria and Albert Museum

EUROPEAN POTTERY
TO THE END OF THE 18TH CENTURY

Italian *maiolica* or tin-enamel ware (top left), noted for its technically brilliant painted decoration, was the distinctive pottery of the Renaissance. Influenced directly by the developing art of easel painting and by rediscovered classical motifs, *maiolica* set a fashion copied elsewhere in Europe, as in the French dish above, which was inspired by the *istoriato* style of pottery from Urbino. Seventeenth-century stoneware of the Rhineland (left), made to endure use in tavern and inn, was principally Late Gothic in style. English pottery figures owed little to continental sources. Lively and amusing figures, such as the one below, are typical of English preindustrial work

Gray stoneware jug decorated with cobalt and salt glaze; from the Westerwald region, Germany. Early 17th century, English silver mounts dated 1652. Height: 9½ in.

An Astbury figure of a mounted dragoon; Staffordshire, Eng., about 1740. Height: 7⅞ in. In the Victoria and Albert Museum

Teapot with decoration in underglaze blue; Saint-Cloud, France, about 1720. Height: 5⁵⁄₁₁ in. In the Museum of Fine Arts, Boston

Porcelain plaque with portrait of Empress Maria Theresa; Doccia, Italy, about 1750. Height: 12½ in. In the Victoria and Albert Museum

EUROPEAN PORCELAIN OF THE 18TH CENTURY

The development of artificial or soft-paste porcelain was primarily French and began in 1664 with the granting of a royal privilege for its manufacture to the Révérend brothers. Soon porcelain factories in several cities were producing distinguished works. Notable were the wares from the factory of the widow Chicaneau at Saint-Cloud (above). The early porcelain of Chantilly (right) imitated the Japanese Kakiemon style but also introduced an important innovation, the use of tin-enamel glaze over a ceramic body. The royal factory at Sèvres made porcelain of great richness and subtlety of colour (bottom right), well suited to the luxurious court life of the time. The French royal family, which owned the Sèvres factory, tried to maintain its monopoly by royal decree. It did not succeed entirely, as evidenced by the rare jug below, made at Mennecy, an unauthorized factory

Cachepot with flower painting in the Kakiemon style of Arita, Japan; Chantilly, France, about 1740. Contemporary mounts. Height 9¾ in. In the Victoria and Albert Museum

Covered jug painted in enamel colours and mounted in ormolu (simulated gold); Mennecy, France, about 1760. Height: 9½ in. In the Victoria and Albert Museum

Vase and cover decorated in reserved panels by Morin; Sèvres, France, 1780. Made for presentation to King Gustavus III of Sweden. Height: 19½ in. In the Victoria and Albert Museum

PLATE VIII   POTTERY AND PORCELAIN

Wine cooler with floral decoration; factory of Claudius Innocentius du Paquier, Vienna, Aus., about 1740. Height: 6⅝ in. In the Victoria and Albert Museum

EUROPEAN PORCELAIN OF THE 18TH CENTURY

Eighteenth-century German and Austrian porcelain reflected both Baroque and Rococo influences. The vigorously modeled Harlequin (left) and the richly painted wine cooler (above) are both masterpieces in the Baroque tradition. The Columbine (bottom centre) is an excellent example of south German Rococo, displaying the grace and charm characteristic of the period as well as an asymmetrical scrollwork base of unusual delicacy and restraint. While notable Rococo porcelain was made in England (bottom left and right), the Rococo style never became fashionable there as it conflicted with the two stronger influences of the classical tradition and of Italy

Harlequin, from the *commedia dell'arte*, modeled by Johann Joachim Kändler; Meissen, Ger., about 1738. Height: 6½ in. In the Victoria and Albert Museum

"The Dancing Lesson," after a design by François Boucher; a superb example of the work of the period of the gold anchor at Chelsea, about 1763. Height: 18 in. In the London Museum

English vase in the French Rococo style of Sèvres with mazarine blue ground and painted in reserved panels by John Donaldson; Chelsea, about 1760. Height: about 20 in. In the Victoria and Albert Museum

Columbine, from the *commedia dell'arte*, modeled by Franz Anton Bustelli; Nymphenburg, Ger., about 1760. Height: 7¾ in. In the Victoria and Albert Museum

Pre-Columbian stirrup vase in the form of a portrait head; Mochica culture, Peru. Height: 8½ in. In the British Museum

POTTERY AND PORCELAIN OF THE AMERICAS

Pre-Columbian pottery (above) developed independently of outside influences, achieving a high level of quality. It declined with the coming of the Spanish in the 16th century. The first notable pottery to show European influence, Mexican faience (right), appeared about 1650. European immigrants, like the German settlers in Pennsylvania, used their own techniques and materials as much like those used in Europe as they could find (bottom right). Apart from a few attempts in the 18th century, American porcelain manufacture began with the fine wares of William Tucker (below)

Mexican faience (tin-enameled) jar in the style of the Spanish potters of Talavera de la Reina, New Castile; about 1775–1800. Height: 10⅜ in. In the Metropolitan Museum of Art

Porcelain pitcher by William E. Tucker; Philadelphia, about 1830. Height: 9½ in. In the Brooklyn Museum

Red earthenware pie plate with *sgraffito* decoration, the design scratched through the slip; Pennsylvania-German style, early 19th century. Signed by David Spinner. Diameter: 11½ in. In the Brooklyn Museum

PLATE X   POTTERY AND PORCELAIN

"Virginian Cardinal and Orange Blossom," from a series of American birds by Dorothy Doughty; Worcester Royal Porcelain Co., Worcester, Eng., 1938. Height: 11½ in.

Porcelain service plate decorated by Scottie Wilson; Worcester Royal Porcelain Co., 1965. Diameter: 10 in.

20TH-CENTURY POTTERY AND PORCELAIN

In Europe the art of porcelain making declined after the 18th century, largely because it was unsuited to the Neoclassical style then in fashion. In the ensuing years, Wedgwood's cream-ware and stoneware (below left) grew in popularity and gained an important position in the ceramic market. The renaissance of porcelain did not become apparent until after World War II, but its origin may be traced back to the 1930s when Dorothy Doughty designed a series of American birds (above). Some indication of the wide variety of styles that characterized post-World War II porcelain may be seen in the service ware (top right) decorated by the primitive painter Scottie Wilson, and the seal (right) from the Royal Copenhagen Porcelain factory

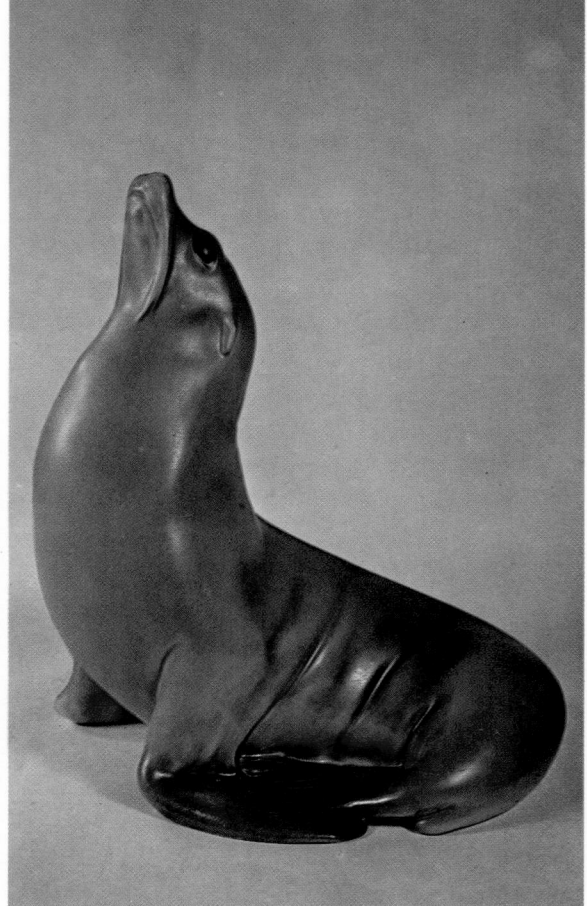

Modern coffeepot of traditional stone-ware; Josiah Wedgwood & Sons, 1964. Height: 10½ in.

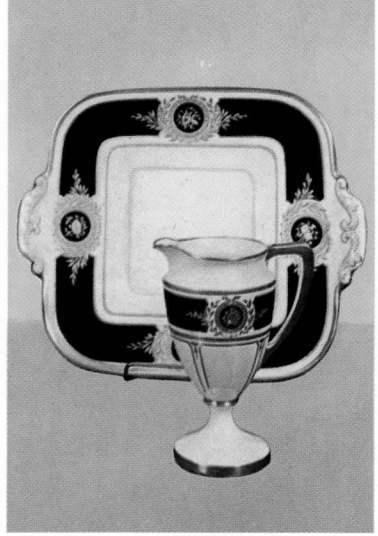

Porcelain plate and pitcher from the Sèvres coffee service designed by Frank G. Holmes, 1913. Lenox, Inc. Size, plate: 8¾ in. sq.; height, pitcher: 5½ in.

Seal; Royal Copenhagen Porcelain Co., 1906. Height: 11½ in.

BY COURTESY OF (TOP LEFT AND RIGHT) WORCESTER ROYAL PORCELAIN CO., (BOTTOM LEFT) JOSIAH WEDGWOOD & SONS, (BOTTOM CENTRE) LENOX, INC., (BOTTOM RIGHT) THE ROYAL COPENHAGEN PORCELAIN CO. LTD.; PHOTOGRAPHS, (ALL EXCEPT BOTTOM CENTRE) WILFRID WALTER

which has a fierce appearance but gentle disposition.

Most of these symbols were not used in ceramic decoration before the Ming dynasty, although both the dragon and the *fêng-huang,* as well as some floral motifs, are earlier. The *lei-wên,* however, which resembles the Greek key fret and is sometimes used on the later ceramic wares, appears on bronzes as early as the Shang and Chou dynasties, where it is called the "cloud and thunder" fret. The *t'ao t'ieh,* a grotesque mask of uncertain origin, also appears on early bronzes, and on later pottery and porcelain. Decorations based on Chinese literary sources are usually extremely difficult to trace to their origin.

G. KOREA

The chronology used in discussing Korean wares is comparatively simple. The early period, the Silla dynasty (57 B.C.–A.D. 935), is roughly contemporary with that period in Chinese history which runs from the Han to the T'ang dynasty. The Koryo dynasty (918–1392) covers approximately the same period of time as the Sung and Yüan dynasties, and the Yi dynasty (1392–1910) almost exactly parallels that of the Ming and Ch'ing. Precise dating of almost all existing specimens, however, is virtually impossible.

Korea lies to the north of China and close to the islands of Japan. It has, therefore, usually formed a cultural link between the two countries. For instance, during the Japanese invasion of 1592 many Korean potters were taken to Japan, where they were set to work making Tea Ceremony wares which had hitherto been imported, and they later helped to found the porcelain industry.

1. Silla Dynasty (57 B.C.–A.D. 935).—It is difficult to distinguish some Korean wares from those made in the northern provinces of China. The wares of the Silla period include some which are reminiscent of those of the Chou dynasty. Specimens of stoneware, obviously based on metalwork, are distantly related to some of the Han bronzes. Patterns on these wares are geometric, and incised in the clay before firing. An olive-green glaze was introduced later in the Silla dynasty, probably about the 9th century, while some unglazed gray vessels with incised or impressed decoration are sometimes said to recall T'ang wares, but the resemblance is extremely slight. Roof tiles and finials have a brown or a green glaze, and may be contemporary with the Han dynasty.

KOREAN COVERED DISH ON A HIGH FOOT; SILLA DYNASTY (57 B.C.–A.D. 935). HEIGHT: 5½ IN. IN THE MUSEUM OF FINE ARTS, BOSTON

2. Koryo Dynasty (918–1392).—The wares of the Koryo dynasty exhibit a much greater diversity, and fall into rather more clearly defined groups. The attribution of certain black-glazed *temmoku* types is controversial, but it seems that at least some were made in Korea. Many celadons, too, have typical Korean lobed forms, based on the melon or the gourd. These are also to be seen in porcelain, much of which has a bluish-white glaze. Some lobed boxes, usually circular, are decorated with impressed designs and are probably always Korean.

One of the difficulties in the study of Korean pottery is that practically everything has been recovered from tombs; few actual kiln sites have been discovered. Nevertheless, one such excavation at Yuch'on-ri has disclosed sherds of both the celadon glaze and of white porcelain from which it seems evident that white porcelain resembling both the *ying ch'ing* and Ting types was made (see *China: Sung Dynasty,* above). The earliest vessels were probably fairly close copies of Chinese styles, and the distinctive Korean style of many examples followed rather later. A crazing of the glaze and a certain amount of flaking are characteristic. A mere handful of specimens, some fragmentary, of inlaid white porcelain

have survived. They are best represented by a vase in the Prince Yi Museum in Seoul, which has panels of black-and-white inlay beneath a celadon glaze. Decoration on much Korean porcelain of the period is either incised (foliage being a frequent motif), combed, or molded in shallow relief.

Korean celadons are mentioned in Chinese writings of the 12th and 14th centuries. They have a stoneware body covered with a glaze which varies from bluish green to a putty colour, and some are obviously analogous to the celadons of Yüeh-chou discussed in the section *China: Han Dynasty.* Characteristic of Korean pots are the "stilt" or "spur" marks to be seen on the otherwise glazed base; these are the points on which it rested in the kiln. Many of the forms are lobed. Perhaps the most important divergence from the usual Chinese celadon is the presence of inlaid decoration beneath the glaze of many specimens, later examples of which are often referred to as *mishima.* (*Mishima* is a Japanese term, sometimes said to have been borrowed from a Japanese town of the same name whose almanacs bore characters similar to the design on the pots; another, and more likely, explanation is that *Mishima,* or *mitsu-shima,* which means three islands, was a harbour on the sea route between Korea and Japan.) The designs were first incised into the clay, and the incisions were then filled with black-and-white clay in the form of slip. This technique seems to date from the 13th century, and was probably derived originally from attempts to paint in white slip under a celadon glaze; one or two rare examples of Chinese celadons from Lung Ch'üan thus decorated have survived. The inlaid patterns are diverse but most of the subjects are floral; birds are to be seen occasionally. Isolated flowers with symmetrically radiating petals are also found, principally on boxes.

3. Yi Dynasty (1392–1910).—While most Korean wares of this period are distinctly rougher than those of China, the decoration is often magnificent in quality. Most can be clearly distinguished from Chinese wares by their forms, which show distinct differences in almost every case. Lobed forms suggested by the melon are very characteristic, and the pear-shaped bottle differs in its proportions from that of the Chinese. The large rugged jars with high shoulders are not so precisely potted as similar jars from China, often showing a marked degree of asymmetricality. "Twisted rope" handles are also peculiar to Korea. Many of the ewers in particular are obvious adaptations from metalwork.

Painting in brownish black beneath a celadon glaze, which had begun in the Koryo dynasty and has an obvious relationship to some of the work or Tz'u Chou, continued in the Yi dynasty. Inlaid decoration was also executed during the early part of this period, the pattern often being engraved by stamps rather than incised freehand. *Sgraffito* decoration, in which patterns were incised through a grayish-white slip, is also seen occasionally.

Some excellent painted designs in an underglaze blue of variable colour, but usually distinctly grayish in tone, were executed on a rough porcelain body which is almost stoneware. They are particularly notable for great economy of brushwork and superb drawing. Their affinities are much more with Japanese pottery than with contemporary Chinese wares. A typical Japanese technique, *hakeme* (from *hake,* "brush"), or brushed slip, is used in conjunction with painted decoration in the early part of the dynasty, but later it is used alone. Korean influence on Japanese pottery was probably at its strongest during the ascendancy of the Japanese warrior Toyotomi Hideyoshi (1536–98) who invaded Korea. Although it is difficult to date Yi wares pre-

KOREAN VASE PAINTED IN UNDERGLAZE COPPER RED; PROBABLY 15TH CENTURY, YI DYNASTY (1392–1910). HEIGHT: 11⅝ IN. IN THE VICTORIA AND ALBERT MUSEUM

cisely, it is unlikely that much important work was done in Korea itself after this invasion.

H. Japan

Japanese ceramics have not received such close attention in the West as those of China, and interest has been chiefly centred on its porcelain.

Since Japan is a well-wooded country, wood has always been used for domestic utensils of all kinds, either in a natural state or covered with the sap of the *Rhus vernicifera* tree in the form of lacquer. Until recent times, therefore, pottery and porcelain were not employed extensively for general domestic use, but were reserved for such special purposes as the Tea Ceremony (*see* below). In pottery the Japanese especially admire accidental effects which resemble natural forms. Objects which appear misshapen and glazes which exhibit what would normally be regarded as serious imperfections in China or the West are admired by the Japanese connoisseur. The Western student has to learn and adopt new criteria of judgment which are, nevertheless, equally valid. The Japanese potter liked his work to reveal the impress of the hand which had made it. Marks such as the ridges left by the fingers in a newly-thrown vessel were frequently accentuated instead of being obliterated, and marks made by tools were often left untouched. Hand modeling was practised long after the wheel was known, and asymmetries and irregularities of form were purposely sought. Similar accidental effects were encouraged in glazing: coloured glazes were allowed to run in streaks and were irregularly applied. They were often thick, with many bubbles, and with a semifluid or treacly appearance. Crackled glazes and those deeply fissured (the latter being termed "dragon skin" or "lizard skin") were deliberately induced. Painted decoration, frequently blue, brown, or iron red, is often summary, and almost calligraphic in its simplicity. The aim was to give an overall effect which resembled natural objects, such as stones, in being totally uncontrived.

From the 15th century onward the art of the potter was also affected by the elaborate Tea Ceremony (*q.v.*). In fact this ceremony (the *cha-no-yu*) assumed such importance that a brief description is necessary. In its original form it was probably introduced from China by Zen priests, but at the court of the Shōgun Yoshimasa (1435–90) in Kyōto it developed into a fixed ceremonial pattern. It is held in a small room or pavilion, usually with a carefully laid out garden surrounding it. When the guests are summoned they enter a sparsely furnished room through a very low doorway. In a recess called the *tokonoma*, a picture mounted on brocade or silk is hung, and the guests bow to this in appreciation. The Tea Master puts a little powdered tea in a bowl and pours on it hot water which has been heated over a charcoal brazier. The tea is whipped to a froth with a bamboo whisk, and then passed from hand to hand. The various utensils (the teabowl, tea caddy, water container, boxes, plates, and iron tea kettle) have been carefully selected by the Tea Master and are often of great age. The tea drinking is followed by a discussion and appreciation of their qualities. The bowls are valued for their heat-retaining properties and the way in which they fit the hand as well as for their appearance. Sometimes a newly acquired work of art is produced by the host for the delectation of his guests. Possibly the ceremony was first exploited as a means of settling feudal disputes, and the fact that guests must crawl into the room is thought to have prevented them from concealing a sword under their robes. Since the Tea Masters were the aesthetic arbiters, their influence on Japanese ceramics was profound.

1. Early History.—The early history of Japan is considerably more obscure than that of China. The first Japanese pottery belongs to the Jōmon period (*c.* 2500–250 B.C.) and has a black body. Decoration is usually an impressed representation of coiled rope or matting, and *jōmon* actually means "coiled." At one time this pottery was thought to have been made by the Ainu people who migrated from Siberia and were the first inhabitants of Japan, but this is now doubtful. Jōmon-*shiki* ("pottery") is widely distributed throughout the islands but complete specimens are very rare. It was followed by Yayoi pottery, so called because the

first specimens were discovered in the Yayoi quarter of Tokyo in 1885. Specimens of this, too, have since been excavated throughout Japan. The body is somewhat finer in quality than Jōmon pottery and is usually red or gray. Decoration is simple, and forms sometimes show the influence of Korean pottery of the period. It ceased to be made about the 6th century A.D. Meanwhile, from about the 3rd to the 6th century A.D. large tombs were constructed in the form of oval or circular tumuli from whose bases have been recovered the so-called *haniwa* (*hani*, "clay"; *wa*, "circle") figures of warriors, women, horses, and so forth. These are hollow and are more primitive than analogous figures from China though they are vigorously modeled.

In the Asuka or Sueki period (A.D. 560–710) which followed wares are much more sophisticated. Unlike the preceding types, they were made with a wheel and firing took place in a rudimentary kiln at a much higher temperature than previously. Widespread manufacture persisted through the Nara period (710–784) and the early part of the following Heian, or Fujiwara, period (784–1185). Some examples have a smear glaze, no doubt at first caused accidentally by wood ashes coming into contact with the surface. Three colours of glaze—green, yellowish brown, and white—were used either alone or in combination and resemble those of T'ang china. Pottery of this kind has been found around Ōsaka and Kyōto. Examples can also be seen in the Shōsō-in, which is a windowless pavilion in the grounds of the Temple of the Great Buddha at Nara. This contains a large collection of various works of art given on the death of the emperor Shomu, in 756—possibly the earliest instance of an art collection being left to posterity and still surviving. The principal pottery productions of the period were vases, dishes, bowls, and bottles of various kinds. The influence of Korea and of T'ang china is noticeable, and many of the objects in the Shōsō-in come from China, and some from much farther west. Toward the end of the Heian period contacts with China were severed, and there was a corresponding decline in the art of pottery; even the traditional Sueki-type ware disappeared.

2. Kamakura and Muromachi Periods (1186–1573).—A revival in the Kamakura period (1186–1335) followed the visit of the potter Kato Shirozaemon (Toshiro) to China in 1223, in company with a Zen monk named Doyen. Here Toshiro learned the secrets of pottery making, and he later established himself at Seto, in Owari (now Aichi Prefecture), which speedily became a large centre of manufacture. There were soon about 200 kilns in the vicinity making a variety of wares, some of which were glazed in black in imitation of the so-called *temmoku* wares of China. The early wares were mainly for ritual purposes, but by the beginning of the Muromachi, or Ashikaga, period (1335–1573) teabowls, plates, jars, and saucers of domestic utility were also being made. Wares of the Kamakura period are decorated with incised designs, or with impressed or applied ornament. The Muromachi wares are much plainer, due to the growing influence of the Tea Ceremony, especially the *Wabi* school of the cult which concentrated on rustic simplicity. The latter, too, have a feldspathic glaze which is more even in quality, the earlier glazes tending to run in rivulets. A transitional type has a soft yellowish glaze, and a dark brown glaze is sometimes called Seto *temmoku*.

A large number of kilns were in use, the more important being known as the "six pottery centres of ancient Japan." These were Seto; Tokoname (also in Aichi Prefecture) which may have exceeded Seto in the size of its production; at Bizen (Okayama Prefecture), which has produced an excellent unglazed stoneware from the Heian period to the mid-20th century; at Tamba (Kyōto Prefecture); at Shigaraki (Shiga Prefecture); and at Echizen (Fukui Prefecture). The wares of Seto, especially those made for Buddhist ceremonies, are regarded as the finest, and *seto-mono* is sometimes used as a generic term for pottery and porcelain.

3. Momoyama Period (1574–1603).—*Seto-Mino Wares.*—Production had been interrupted during the civil wars of the 15th and 16th centuries, and toward the end of the latter century the Seto kilns were removed for a time to the Gifu Prefecture of Mino Province where they received the protection of the *daimyo* of Toki. The Mino pottery was founded by Kato Yosabei Kagemitsu, and his sons started other potteries in the vicinity, notably that under the aegis of the Tea Master Furata Oribe Masashige. The later wares of these kilns are much less austere than those attributed to the Muromachi period since the cult of the Tea Ceremony, though now widespread, had lost something of its earlier simplicity. New kilns were also built and pottery, as well as retaining its importance in the Tea Ceremony, became much more widely used for ordinary purposes. The inspiration for most of its shapes and designs came from the Mino region. Characteristic Tea Ceremony wares of the early years of the 17th century are *Shino*, which has a thick, crackled glaze and is sometimes summarily painted in blue or brown; *ki-Seto*, or yellow Seto, whose crackled yellow glaze covers a stoneware body; and, at Narumi in the adjoining Owari region, a ware of the kind associated with Oribe (which had become a generic term for pottery influenced by the Tea Master of that name) which is glazed in white, straw colour, yellowish green, and pinkish red, with sometimes the addition of slight painting in brown. *Shino* traditionally takes its name from the Tea Master, Shino Ienobu, while *ki-Seto* is reputed to have been discovered by a descendant of Kato Shirozaemon.

BY COURTESY OF MUSEUM OF FINE ARTS, BOSTON, HOYT COLLECTION

JAPANESE CERAMICS OF THE 18TH CENTURY
(Left) *Shino* ware dish. Diameter: about 11 in. (Top right) *Raku* ware water jar and cover; Tokyo. Height: 8 in. (Bottom right) Tea bowl signed by Kenzan. Height: about 3¾ in. In the Museum of Fine Arts, Boston

Toward the end of the 16th century the Tea Ceremony was reformed by Sen-no-Rikyu (1520–91), the Tea Master to Toyotomi Hideyoshi (*q.v.*), who was principally responsible for the replacement of the hitherto much admired *temmoku* bowls from China by others influenced by unsophisticated Korean wares; his influence has persisted to the 20th century. In the 1590s Hideyoshi twice invaded Korea, and as a result of these wars many Korean potters were taken to Japan, where their influence was considerable.

Raku Ware.—A tilemaker named Ameiya, who is said to have been a Korean, introduced a new type of ware which was covered with a lead glaze and fired at a comparatively low temperature. His son Tanaka Chojirō and his family extended this technique to the Tea Ceremony bowl and their wares were brought to the notice of Hideyoshi about 1588, who awarded them a gold seal engraved with the word *raku* ("felicity"). These *raku* made in Kyōto by the Chojirō family are among the most famous of all Japanese wares. The shape of the vessels was extremely simple, a wide straight-sided bowl being set on a narrow base. At first the glaze was dark brown, but a light orange red was developed later, to be followed in the 17th century by a straw colour. Still later green and cream and other colours were introduced. Teabowls attributed to the first Chojirō are greatly valued in Japan, and numerous copies exist.

Karatsu Ware.—The kilns of Karatsu and district in the north of Hizen Province may have been established by Korean potters at this time since the influence of Korea is perceptible in some of them. The term Karatsu ware encompasses a great variety of shapes and styles: *muji-garatsu* ("undecorated"), *e-garatsu* ("painted"), *madara-garatsu* ("speckled"), *Chosen-garatsu* ("in the Korean style") which has a thick opaque glaze, and *Seto-garatsu* ("in the style of Seto") which has a white glaze. The earliest Karatsu ware belongs probably to the end of the 16th century, although it is sometimes awarded a still earlier date. Most surviving examples belong to the 17th century. The most valued pieces are those made for the Tea Ceremony.

4. Edo Period (1603–1867).—According to tradition the first Japanese porcelain was made at the beginning of the 16th century after Goradoyu-go Shonzui brought back the secret of its manufacture from Kingtechen. Another account claims that a Korean potter called Risampei, who was brought to Japan by Hideyoshi, discovered porcelain clay in the Izumi mountain, near Arita (Saga Prefecture); this version is feasible since no porcelain made before the end of the 16th century has been identified.

The first Arita manufacture was decorated in blue underglaze, and this is simple and excellent in quality. Specimens soon found their way to Europe in Dutch ships and the Dutch were awarded a trading monopoly in 1641. Some of these early Japanese wares are based on contemporary European metalwork and faience. They have, in the past, frequently been mistaken for Chinese export porcelain of the 17th century, and no doubt many such specimens are still misattributed.

The family of Sakaida is especially connected with the Arita kilns. The first recorded member, born about 1596, worked in underglaze blue until the family learned the secret of using enamel colours. According to tradition it was told to them by a Chinese met by chance in the port of Nagasaki. Sakaida Kakiemon I perfected this overglaze technique at Arita in the Kan'ei era (1624–43). It was continued by his family and, since many of them were also called Kakiemon, the style has become known by that name. The palette is easily recognized—iron red, bluish green, light blue, yellow, and sometimes a little gilding. Many examples have a chocolate-brown rim, and octagonal and square shapes are especially frequent. Themes of decoration are markedly asymmetrical, with much of the white porcelain surface left untouched. This technique and style spread rapidly to other provinces and is of considerable importance in any historical examination of the ceramic art. It is not always realized that its influence on European porcelain manufactured during the first half of the 18th century was at least as great as that of Chinese porcelain. Augustus the Strong of Saxony had a large collection and named the building to house it the Japanische Palais. The style was much copied at Chantilly, France, where the prince de Condé collected it, and at Chelsea in England. A later Kakiemon development in which *nishikide* ("brocade") patterns in compartments were used at the suggestion of Dutch traders is less pleasing.

These later coloured wares from Arita became known as "Imari," the port from which they were shipped. An interesting development is the practice of shipping white wares to Europe where they were decorated by Dutch and other European enamelers.

Of considerable importance, but more rarely seen in Europe, was the porcelain called Kutani which was made from clay discovered at Kutanimura (Ishikawa Prefecture) by Gotō Saijirō. The kilns were founded about 1652 and operated for approximately 60 years, being reopened briefly in the 19th century. Old-, or ko-Kutani porcelain is greatly valued and can be placed among the finest of the Japanese wares. The body is heavy, approaching stoneware, and the designs were executed boldly and in rich colours. At Okochi, near Arita, a factory was founded about 1660 by the prince Nabeshima with the aid of Korean potters using Arita materials. This ware was rarely exported, and is purely native in style. The Mikawachi kilns under the protection of the princes of Hirado made porcelain principally for his use. The delicate very white body is usually decorated in miniature style with underglaze blue. Kyōto imitated Sung celadons and the Ming green and red wares. Seto made no porcelain until about 1807; the first production was decorated in underglaze blue and enamel decoration dates from about 1835. Outrageously large and hideously decorated vases were made here for export during the 19th century.

The manufacture of pottery was continued during the 17th and 18th centuries and much of it is notable for its decoration. Toward the end of the 17th century Ninsei (Nonomura Seisuke) began work at Kyōto and was responsible for much finely enameled decoration on a cream earthenware body covered with a finely crackled glaze. Also at Kyōto, the work of Kenzan, who used rich and subtly coloured slips often as a background for plant motives, and of the Dohachi family, famous for their enamels, are among the wares which are much sought in Japan, although it is extremely difficult to refer specimens to them with any certainty. Most signed examples can only be said to be in their style.

5. 19th and 20th Centuries.—Japanese productions during the 19th century, in common with those in most other parts of the world, greatly deteriorated in taste. A typical product of the period is the so-called "Satsuma" pottery, most of which was not made at Satsuma, but at Kyōto and was then sent to Tokyo to be decorated especially for export. The designs are overcrowded and debased, and its popularity undoubtedly retarded a true appreciation of work in the Japanese taste among Western students and collectors.

Like Western pottery and porcelain manufacture in the mid-20th century that of Japan is largely industrialized, most products being derivative and likely to appeal only to uninformed taste. However, the Japanese tradition of pottery making in small, and private kilns continues. Japanese potters have gone to England to work and a few Western artist-potters, notably Bernard Leach of St. Ives, Eng., have worked in Japan and have been influenced by Japanese traditions.

The Arita kilns began to revive the old styles after 1830 and modern versions of porcelain in the Kakiemon style have appeared in Europe. Recent work in the manner of Nabeshima—a porcelain always exceedingly rare in the West—has provided material for controversy among collectors. These are all of relatively high quality. A great deal of porcelain decorated in a debased Imari style was exported during the 19th century, but manufacture seems to have been discontinued.

At the former Russian port of Dalny, which is now Dairen in Manchoukuo, a Japanese pottery makes poor copies of Chinese celadons of the 12th century, and much better imitations of the early wares of Tz'u Chou, some of which are marked with an impressed stamp. Imitations of old Chinese porcelain are still coming from the Japanese islands, but the factories cannot be identified.

I. THAILAND AND ANNAM

Pottery was made in the old Siamese capitals of Sukhothai and Sawankhalok. It is also thought that potteries persisted at Ayutthaya until the 18th century. Little is known of the early history of the region, and definite information on its pottery is almost nonexistent. Dating for the most part has been by analogy with related Chinese wares, which greatly influenced Siamese work. It cannot be doubted that Chinese potters migrated southward, taking their knowledge with them.

Kilns have been excavated on the site of old Sawankhalok, about 200 mi. N of Bangkok. The principal type of ware is a grayish-white stoneware covered with a translucent celadon glaze which is usually grayish green in colour. The glaze is commonly crackled, and this appears to be fortuitous. Little trouble was taken to achieve a precise finish. Decoration is often of roughly scored vertical flutes, with incised circles at the shoulder to accentuate the form. The latter is particularly common. Decoration of a more definite kind is always incised under the glaze and is usually floral. Flowers are stylized, sometimes with combed lines on the petals. Covered bowls, dishes, ewers, and bottles with two small loop handles at the neck are the most usual forms. Another type of ware has a rather treacly-brown glaze, but the forms are similar. Some well-modeled animals are also found with this glaze. Tiles and bricks with crudely modeled figures in relief can also be seen. These objects are analogous in form and technique to Chinese pottery of the Sung dynasty, and they are generally regarded as being contemporary with the Sung or Yüan period. While poor quality porcelain enameled with Siamese subjects was made in China for export, some small covered jars of a gray porcelaneous ware, summarily decorated with stylized floral and foliate patterns, seem to have been made at Sawankhalok, and the date is probably equivalent to that of the early Ming period. These wares were widely exported throughout the East, one of the ports from which they were shipped being Martaban in Burma. As a result the term "Martabani" ware was sometimes used synonymously with "celadon" in the East.

Little is known of wares made in Annam, but some brownish celadons are regarded as likely to have been made there, as well as some small covered jars painted in a poor underglaze blue.

J. ISLAMIC POTTERY OF THE NEAR AND MIDDLE EAST

The Islamic pottery of Syria, Egypt, Mesopotamia, Persia, Afghanistan, and Anatolia occupies an important place in the history of ceramic art. In quality it rivals even the wares of the Far East, and its influence on the development of European ceramics was more profound than that of any other region except China. In China, too, Islamic innovations were adopted while the Islamic potter, in his turn, owes an incalculable debt to the Chinese.

Near and Middle Eastern pottery was at its greatest between the 9th and 13th centuries and its history is closely linked to the fortunes of the caliphate. Each dynasty was surrounded in its capital by a wealthy and beauty-loving court which patronized artists and artisans. When one dynasty fell and another established itself elsewhere it seems that the finest potters emigrated to the new capital carrying with them their special, and often secret, skills. At first the principal centres of manufacture were Baghdad, Al Fustat (Old Cairo), and Samarkand; later they shifted to Raqqah on the Euphrates and to Ray (Rhages) and Kashan, both in northern Iran.

Most of the pottery in our possession has been excavated and consequently is fragmentary. Little made before the 14th century has survived above ground, and tombs, often rich depositories of undamaged wares in other regions of the world, are fruitless because Muslims do not bury pottery with their dead. Only one or two discoveries of undamaged wares have been made: for

STONEWARE VASE WITH PALE GRAY-GREEN CELADON GLAZE AND WELL-DEFINED BROWNISH CRACKLE; SAWANKHALOK. 14TH CENTURY. HEIGHT: 6¼ IN. IN THE GLASGOW ART GALLERY AND MUSEUM

POTTERY AND PORCELAIN

example, at Gurgan, Iran, which was looted by the Mongols in 1221, entire specimens were found carefully packed in large earthenware jars. They had probably formed part of the stock of merchants, who buried them and fled before the invaders.

Excavated fragments are often pieced together by dealers, and frequently unrelated fragments are married to make a slightly more complete specimen and false inscriptions are added. The ultraviolet lamp is the finest weapon in the collector's armoury against this kind of chicanery, revealing such additions ruthlessly. As complete and undamaged specimens are such rarities, some sort of restoration must obviously be attempted but the only satisfactory method is to set the fragments into a plaster matrix which repeats the original form. The missing decoration can, of course, be lightly indicated if thought desirable.

Until recently properly controlled excavations have been rare and many Persian and Armenian dealers who carried out excavations were anxious, somewhat naturally, to conceal the source of their finds. Therefore, although names such as Ray, Sultanabad, and so forth have been given to specific groups of ware, it is not always certain that they were made at these places. They are, however, convenient labels, and are entitled to remain unless they can be replaced by something better.

The glaze of much Islamic pottery is iridescent owing to deterioration through burial. In this it resembles Roman and Near Eastern glass. The iridescence sometimes obscures decoration but if the glaze is dampened with a little water, the underlying painting often becomes visible temporarily. A smear of Vaseline usually has a more permanent effect of the same kind. In the case of a badly-obscured glaze in conjunction with serious deterioration it is often best to remove the glaze altogether, but the job is one for an expert and needs both care and skill.

1. Early Period.—There is little pottery of merit from the period of the Omayyad caliphate (661–750). At this time the capital was at Damascus and the chief interest of the pottery lies in its mingled Mediterranean and Middle Eastern derivation; for example, attempts were made to synthesize the formal repetitive style derived from the ancient Babylonian and Assyrian civilizations with naturalistic ornament in the Greco-Roman style. When the Abbasids overthrew the Omayyads and moved the capital to Baghdad the European influence on ornament waned although good use continued to be made of Western techniques, particularly of lead glazes which had been employed by Greek and Roman potters since the 3rd century B.C. The advantage of lead glaze is that, unlike the more brilliant alkaline glazes known to the ancient Egyptians and still sometimes used at the time in Egypt and Syria, it will adhere to ordinary potter's clay. Its disadvantage is that it blurs all but a few underglaze pigments when it is fired, and consequently the palette which can be used beneath it is very restricted.

2. 9th and 10th Centuries.—An event which had a profound effect on the development of Middle Eastern pottery was the presentation of a number of T'ang porcelain bowls to the caliph Harun al-Rashid about A.D. 800 (see *China: T'ang Dynasty*, above). Shortly after this the first fine pottery was produced in Baghdad and elsewhere. Thus it seems possible that it was through the example of the Chinese that ceramics came to be regarded as an artistic medium instead of a purely utilitarian one. This supposition is borne out by the fact that T'ang wares were in great demand and were imported in large quantities after this date: they and early Islamic imitations, particularly of the mottled T'ang glazes, have been found in various parts of Mesopotamia and as far apart as Egypt and eastern Persia. However, unlike their contemporaries in China, Islamic potters aimed primarily at richness of colour and decoration rather than beautiful shapes and textures. Nearly all their pottery is glazed and is painted with elegant, rather stylized, motifs. Floral and foliate ornaments predominate although complex geometrical patterns are also characteristic. In theory there was a religious ban, formulated in the Hadith ("Traditions" of the Prophet), on all representations of animal life, which were thought to encourage idolatry. In practice, particularly in Persia, the limitation was often disregarded except in the decoration of mosques. The animal figures on pot-

BY COURTESY OF VICTORIA AND ALBERT MUSEUM; PHOTOGRAPH, (BOTTOM RIGHT) WILFRID WALTER

ISLAMIC POTTERY

(Above) White earthenware bowl painted in gold lustre showing a Coptic priest; signed by the potter Sa'd. Egyptian, Fatimid dynasty; first half of the 12th century. Diameter: 8⅝ in. (Above right) White earthenware bowl painted in lustre with an animal figure. Mesopotamian; 10th century. Diameter: 7½ in. (Bottom right) Large dish painted in lustre pigments. Persian, from Ray, Iran; 12th century. Diameter: 14¼ in.

tery are spirited and rhythmical while the human ones tend to be stiff, resembling those in contemporary miniatures. Arabic script was commonly and effectively used, both the Neskhi, or running script, and the angular Kufic.

The Islamic potters were responsible for a number of important technical innovations, the most influential of which was possibly the rediscovery of tin enamel in the 9th century A.D. Tin enamel is a lead glaze rendered white and opaque by the addition of stannic oxide, one of the oxides of tin. Coloured pigment can be painted onto the unfired glaze and both are then fixed in one firing. Though tin enamel was first used by the Assyrians and according to some authorities was discovered as early as 1100 B.C., it had fallen into disuse. The Abbasid potters first used it in an attempt to imitate the texture of T'ang wares but soon it became the vehicle for characteristically Middle Eastern decoration. From Mesopotamia and Persia the technique was later taken to Moorish Spain and then to Italy and other parts of Europe where it was employed for a number of important wares—*maiolica*, faience, and delft (see *European Pottery to the End of the 18th Century*, below). The Chinese occasionally used an opaque white enamel in the 18th century but they never adopted tin glaze.

Like that of tin enameling the technique of lustre painting was perfected (and probably invented) by Islamic potters. Again, like tin enameling, it later passed to Muslim Spain but not to the Far East. Its origin is obscure but it may first have been used in Egypt during the 8th or 9th century for painting on glass. The date at which the technique was extended to pottery is also uncertain; the 9th century is likely although the earliest dated example is a bottle from Ray made in 1179 (now in the British Museum, London). Probably lustre on pottery was first used to cover entire vessels and may have been employed to evade the sumptuary laws laid down in the Hadith which, by proscribing the use of gold and silver vessels, sought to preserve the earlier simplicity of Muslim life. The metallic pigments employed in lustre-work painting were probably silver and copper in combination, although an occasional ruby glint suggests that gold may sometimes have been included. After firing, the painting can be dull yellow, golden brown, or olive, tinged with green or red. The colouring is, in fact, extremely variable, indicating that the results were partly a matter of chance because materials with unknown and differing proportions of impurities were employed. The metals were applied in the form of oxides, finely powdered and mixed with sulfur. They were painted on to a glazed and fired vessel and were themselves fixed by a light firing. Kiln wastage was probably high.

Extensive use was always made of slip. Wares such as the early *Gabri* type of the 11th century and later had a reddish body washed over with white slip. Designs were executed by scratching through the slip to the body beneath (*sgraffito*). On some later specimens the background was cut away to leave a raised design in white slip (the champlevé technique) or the design was incised through the white slip as before and then was itself painted with green and brown slips. Yellowish or green lead glazes were used. The usual motifs are large floral forms, animals, and bold inscriptions. *Sgraffito* ware became common throughout the Middle East and appears in Egypt and Syria in the 13th century.

The site of Samarra on the Tigris, where the Abbasids built their summer palaces in the 9th century, is of great importance both to the student of Middle Eastern wares and to the Chinese ceramic historian, for many fragments of Chinese pottery and porcelain have been found there (see *China: T'ang Dynasty,* above). Among the native wares are some made in a buff body decorated in relief under a green glaze; others with monochrome green, white and yellow glazes, or with glazes mottled in imitation of a well-known type of T'ang decoration; and others painted with cobalt blue (perhaps the earliest use of underglaze blue) and further embellished with lustre of various colours. The discovery of lustre painting on a 9th-century site helps to fix the date of its introduction.

3. Samanid Pottery.—To the northeast, beyond the Oxus (modern Amu-Darya) River, the Samanid dynasty (874–999) became practically independent of the caliphate at Baghdad and fostered a national artistic and literary revival. Samanid pottery, which has been found chiefly at Samarkand and Nishapur, differs from the pottery of more westerly regions in technique and style. The best pieces have a reddish body covered with a white, vivid red-brown or purplish-black slip which was then painted and fired under a lead glaze. The function of the slip, besides providing colour, was to prevent the pigments of the painting from running when the lead glaze was applied. The colours used in painting were the same as those of the slips with the addition of yellowish green and browns. The designs often consisted of the angular Kufic characters used in a simple and effective manner or of stylized birds and floral motifs. The shapes were plain—usually either plates or rather shallow bowls—and the total effect is both bold and elegant.

4. Egyptian Pottery of the Islamic period was at its best during the Fatimid dynasty (969–1171). Wares were at first coarser than those of Mesopotamia because of the poor quality of local materials, and the shapes were less refined since Chinese influence was absent. Lustre painting was, nevertheless, excellent in quality. The exact date of its introduction cannot be determined but the middle of the 10th century is probable. A typical feature is the painting on the backs of dishes, a practice derived from Baghdad and later copied by the Moorish potters of Spain. Signed specimens of lustre ware and tin-enameled wares are known, the best coming from a potter named Sa'd.

Toward the end of the period a much whiter type of ware, with a compact body which was given a harder firing, came into use and thereafter became common throughout the Middle East. An important group of wares, popular until the 14th century, has decoration carved and incised into the body and covered with transparent glazes. This type, too, was widespread, and patterns suggest the influence of some of the Sung wares of China decorated in a similar technique.

5. 11th to 13th Century in Mesopotamia and Persia.—In the 11th century the Seljuk Turks overran Persia and Mesopotamia, and their ascendancy lasted until the advent of the Mongols during the 13th century. As the Seljuks had no capital the most flourishing cities during this time were those on the trade routes. In the 12th century very fine pottery was made in the new white body recently developed in Egypt; this was decorated with bold carving, occasional piercing and translucent glaze. Most of these wares are said to have been found at Ray near Teheran where many other beautiful wares have been excavated, although the kiln sites have not yet been discovered, if, indeed, they existed. Wares with a sandy body and a clear glaze were painted with a golden-brown lustre, often in conjunction with blue. These seem not to have been made after the city was sacked by Genghis Khan in 1220. Especially associated with Ray are examples of *minai* painting of uncommon quality. The *minai* technique, a Persian discovery of the 12th century, was a method of decoration in which enamel colours were painted onto a glazed and fired pot and then fixed by refiring the pot at a comparatively low temperature. The advantage of the process was that many colours which would not have withstood the heat of the first firing could now be used. The technique may perhaps have influenced the rare examples of enamel decoration on late Sung or Yüan wares from Tz'u Chou although it did not come into common use in China until the early part of the 15th century (see *China: Ming Dynasty,* above).

At Ray the glaze is cream or turquoise, and the palette included blue, turquoise, purple, red, green, and white, with the addition of gold leaf. All these colours, except the blue, are matt in appearance, and the style strongly recalls that of the Persian manuscript illuminations of the 13th century.

Another technique employed at Ray was the use of silhouette decoration. The pot was covered with a thick black, or blue and black, slip and the design was carved out with a knife. The glazes were applied without colour or stained with copper to yield a brilliant turquoise.

Raqqah was a prosperous trading city until it was sacked by the Mongols in 1259. Most of its pottery, which can be dated between the 9th and 14th centuries, is rougher, and the designs bolder than those of Ray. The body is white, inclining to buff, and is covered with a siliceous glaze. Some of the Raqqah fragments are painted with a brownish lustre. Others have designs in relief, sometimes covered with an opaque turquoise glaze, or with a bluish-green translucent glaze. In the 12th and early 13th centuries bold designs were executed in underglaze black with pale blue glazes and more frequently in blue and black under a clear glaze. Occasionally the glazes were stained purple with manganese. Like the Egyptian wares in the same style, but unlike those of Ray, the slips used were fluid enough to be applied with a brush.

Kashan is chiefly famous for its tiles, in fact the words *kashi* or *kashani* ("of Kashan") are commonly used as a synonym for tile (and have been incorrectly applied to tilework from India). Lustre painted tiles had been made since at least the 9th century and were used mostly on the walls of mosques and public buildings. Those of Kashan, particularly in the 13th and 14th centuries, are distinguished by their fine workmanship, brilliance, and intricacy of design. In shape they are square, rectangular, or interlocking cross or star shapes, each carrying a small part of the total design. The relief inscriptions are frequently picked out with blue pigment.

Also associated with Kashan are the *lakabi* ("painted") wares made in the 12th century. The term, a misnomer, refers to a variation of the *sgraffito* technique mentioned above: an incised design was decorated with different coloured glazes which were kept apart by the intervening threads of clay. The colours used were blue, yellow, purple, and green. Although a number of *lakabi* wares were also made at Raqqah, the technique was soon abandoned at both places as the glazes always tended to run out of their compartments during firing, giving a smudged effect.

Both the site of Sultanabad and the nature of the wares which may have been made there are extremely uncertain. The modern town is situated on the road between Hamadan and Isfahan. Principally associated with it are wares decorated with relief molding under a turquoise or dark blue glaze, or painted in black slip under a clear turquoise glaze. They date from the second half of the 13th century onward. Toward the end of the 12th century the glaze material was frequently mixed with the white-burning clay when in use. In the more highly fired specimens the product is not unlike a primitive soft porcelain, and occasional specimens are slightly translucent. Although this was undoubtedly an attempt to reproduce the porcelain of the Chinese, it is doubtful whether the translucency was ever more than the result of accidental aggregations of glassy substances. These wares probably inspired the attempts to make porcelain at Florence (see

European Porcelain, below). Neither stoneware nor true porcelain was ever made in Persia.

6. Later Persian Pottery.—After the Mongol conquests of the 13th century the production of pottery practically ceased except at Kashan. A slow revival began about 1295 and although pottery in the Near and Middle East never again reached its former height, some fine wares were made at Sultanabad in the 14th century. Good use was made of the rich sombre colours beloved by the Mongols, particularly dark blues, grays, and blacks.

Since the whole of Central Asia now lay under the Mongol domination, overland trade with China greatly increased and by the 15th century Chinese influence, particularly that of Ming blue and white, was predominant, and the older styles were tending to die out. A group of blue-and-white wares belonging to the 15th and early 16th century are known as "Kubachi" wares because large numbers of them survived above ground in this town in the Caucasus; their place of manufacture remains uncertain. They have a very soft body, a brilliant crackled glaze, and are notable for the rhythmical and spontaneous qualities of their design. The later "Kubachi" blue and white is closer to the Chinese originals. Polychrome appears about 1550 and the palette includes a red, related to, though lighter than, the Armenian bole introduced about the same time in Turkey (see *Turkish Pottery,* below). The best polychrome painting was done on tiles. Tabriz has been suggested as the real centre of manufacture, but although it seems likely that Tabriz was a manufacturing town, in view of its tiled mosques and the fact that Tabriz potters were famous abroad (and indeed were either invited or carried off to Turkey on two occasions), no kiln sites have been found there.

The location of later kiln sites in Persia is equally uncertain, one of the few known ones being Kerman, which was the leading pottery centre in the 17th century. Its wares are characterized by a very strong bright blue and a wavy, rather bubbly, glaze. Pseudo-Chinese marks were frequently added to the blue and white. The most usual colours on Kerman polychrome wares are blue, green, browns, and a bright red similar to Armenian bole. The quality of production declined considerably during the 18th century.

Lustre painting was revived during the second half of the 17th century and perhaps lasted into the 18th century. Its place of manufacture is not known. Most of the objects decorated in this manner are small bottles or spittoons and their cramped designs are timid and fussy. The lustre is warm brown, often with a strong red tinge, and was sometimes used in conjunction with blue glaze. Another early technique revived at the same time was that of piercing, formerly practised in the Seljuk era. There are a number of delicate pierced white wares covered with a colourless glaze, which were imitated in China during the reign of Ch'ienlung. Persian pottery of this period was often known in Europe as Gombroon ware, the name of the port (now Bender 'Abbas) from whence it was shipped.

BY COURTESY OF VICTORIA AND ALBERT MUSEUM

PERSIAN AND SYRIAN POTTERY

(Top) Persian tankard with decoration cut through a black slip and covered with a turquoise glaze; 12th century, found at Sultanabad. Height: 5 in. (Bottom) Syrian jar of white earthenware painted in underglaze blue and black; 14th century. Height: 15 in. In the Victoria and Albert Museum

Chinese celadon was imitated, not very successfully, from the 14th century. In the 16th century other monochrome glazes were produced at Kerman and elsewhere. These and the celadon were frequently decorated with painted or incised ornament—a practice quite foreign to the Chinese style.

During the 18th century most of the pottery produced in Persia was inferior blue and white. In the 19th century the standard declined still further with the adoption of the *famille rose* palette, and only a group of wares made at Teheran between 1860 and 1890 can command any respect. Some excellent peasant pottery with a buff body and lead glaze was made in Turkistan.

7. Syrian Pottery.—The potters from Al Fustat and Raqqah may have migrated to Damascus after their potteries were destroyed, for lustre painting continued in Syria throughout the 13th and 14th centuries when it had ceased elsewhere in the Middle East. The lustre ranges in colour from silver to yellow and dull brown and is often used in conjunction with a blue glaze on big, heavy jars and albarelli. Characteristic are gold designs arranged in panels with much use of inscriptions and heraldic devices. The body material is coarse and grayish and the glaze sometimes has a wide crackle. Lustre painting fell into disuse in Syria about 1400 and might have died out altogether had not the secret meantime been carried from Egypt to Spain (see *European Pottery to the End of the 18th Century,* below). The commonest type of Syrian pottery in the 14th century is a blue-and-black style similar in shape and design to the lustre ware. Rather uncertainly drawn animals appear on some of the vessels.

The earliest-known Middle Eastern copies of Chinese blue and white were made in Syria and can be assigned with certainty to the end of the 14th century. (This has helped to date the introduction of blue and white in China.) Blue and white became commoner on both vessels and tiles in the first half of the next century. Later the potteries seem to have fallen into disuse until the new mosque built in Damascus by Suleiman I in the mid-16th century provided a fresh impetus for the industry. The polychrome tiles of the 16th century have at first designs with a hard black outline; later a more flowing foliate style was developed. A soft purple replaces the Armenian bole of Iznik (see *Turkish Pottery,* below). Vessels and tiles, gradually declining in quality, continued to be made in Damascus till the end of the 18th century.

8. Turkish Pottery.—A branch of the Seljuk Turks occupied Anatolia from 1078 to 1300 and was succeeded by the Ottoman Turks who first extended their lands westward, conquering Byzantium in 1453 and in the 16th century became masters of much of southeastern Europe and the lands lying to the east and south of the Mediterranean. The first notable ceramics from Turkish lands were the tiles and bricks covered with coloured glazes made in Anatolia for architectural purposes in the 13th century. Mosques in particular were decorated in this way and Persian influence in decoration suggests the presence of potters from that region. The art of tile mosaic apparently died out after 1300 and was not reintroduced until about 1415 when Persian craftsmen were brought from Tabriz to decorate the mosques at Bursa and Edirne. Apart from tilework, pottery appears to have received little encouragement until the late 15th century by which time the chief centre of production was firmly established at Iznik (earlier called Nicaea). Iznik was selected because of deposits of suitable clay in the neighbourhood, and there may have been potteries here, and at Ismit not far away, as early as the 12th century.

The great era of Turkish pottery (c. 1500–c. 1580) coincides with the expansion of Ottoman power. Decoration was strongly influenced by 15th-century Ming blue-and-white porcelain. The earlier designs were probably taken at second hand from Persian sources, since a distinctly Persian flavour is usually evident. Their intricacy and minuteness, their arrangement in bands, and the shapes of some of the vessels all indicate the influence of metalwork. At one time the wares in this style, which lasted until about 1525, were thought to come from Kutahiya in central Anatolia and are still sometimes known by that name.

At this and later periods the body of Iznik pottery was soft and sandy. It was made from grayish-white clay covered with a thin slip which was usually white, although occasionally red or blue was used on later wares. Decoration was carried out in high temperature colours under a transparent siliceous glaze. The commonest shapes are flat dishes, but jugs, dishes with a high foot, and bowls are also found. Cylindrical vessels with small rectangular handles set halfway down are flower vases not tankards. A rare form is a pottery version of a mosque lamp. A number of dated pieces exist.

During the next period (c. 1525–50), whose wares have been erroneously attributed to Damascus, Iznik pottery was at its finest. Ming blue and white was now copied directly; for example, the central motif of grapes to be seen on a dish in the Victoria and Albert Museum in an almost exact imitation of a well-known and mid-15th century Chinese motif. (It is interesting to note that somewhat similar patterns of grapes appear on the back of bronze mirrors of the T'ang period, and also on some Roman mirrors in the same material.) On the same dish can be seen a characteristic border pattern which was called the "Ammonite" scroll border since it was thought to resemble the coiled shell of the fossil ammonite but which is certainly a debased version of the Ming "Rock of Ages" pattern. This scroll border appears often; a slightly later version, which incorporates large "S"-shaped scrolls and is sometimes known as the "dollar" pattern, would be difficult to recognize as derived from the "Rock of Ages" border without knowledge of the intervening stage.

The palette was gradually expanded to include turquoise, sage green, olive green, purple, and black. Most of the blue and turquoise specimens are painted with flowers. The Chinese floral motifs tended to be replaced by tulips, poppies, carnations, roses, hyacinths, and cypresses which appeared in the form of fairly symmetrical sprays springing from a single point. The earliest flowers are often rather more stylized than the later, perhaps because the representation of living things was prohibited by Koranic tradition. Even on comparatively late examples, floral designs are sometimes stylized to the point of abstraction, and it is possible that decorators suited their patterns to the religious susceptibilities of their customers. An effective abstract pattern is formed from a series of overlapping scales which are usually carefully drawn. The same ground was later imitated in Italy on *maiolica,* and may have indirectly inspired the series of wares with scale grounds made at Worcester, Eng. The latter factory probably took the idea from certain Meissen and Berlin *mosaik* patterns, and it is noteworthy that a faience factory in Berlin copied the work of Iznik. This is an excellent example of the transfer of ideas, often by indirect routes, from one place to another. Trading connections with Turkey at the end of the 16th century were well established and we find examples of Iznik pottery with contemporary English silver mounts.

After about 1550 Iznik pottery enters its third stage. The most notable technical innovation is the use of Armenian bole ("sealing-wax" red), a thick pigment which stands out in slight relief from the surface of the vessel.

The other great change is that tiles which had previously

BY COURTESY OF VICTORIA AND ALBERT MUSEUM

TURKISH POTTERY FROM ANATOLIA

(Top) White earthenware dish painted in blue and turquoise in imitation of Chinese porcelain of the Ming dynasty. The border is a debased version of the Ming "Rock of Ages" pattern. From Iznik; first half of 16th century. Diameter: 15½ in. (Bottom) Dish showing St. Michael saving a man's soul, inscribed in Armenian. From Kutahiya; dated 1719. Diameter: 8⅝ in. In the Victoria and Albert Museum

been made in small numbers, became all important until the early 17th century. They were used to provide lavish decoration for the new mosques built at Istanbul by Suleiman I the Magnificent (1520–66). Once again potters were brought from Tabriz to begin the work. Much use is made of copper green and the new red, the colours appearing very brilliant on the glossy white ground. The tiles, usually square, make up flowing repeating patterns or long high pictures with elaborate borders.

On pottery symmetrical sprays of flowers continued to be used as decoration until about 1600. Paintings of animals and birds are found occasionally and were probably executed by Persian workmen since their resemblance to Persian wares is strong. The rare specimens with human figures were probably painted by Greeks or Armenians for export to the West. Turkish sailing vessels sometimes appear and are an effective decorative motif.

In the 17th century the quality of Iznik wares declined and manufacture had ceased by 1800. At Kutahiya pottery making had begun by 1608 and continued into the middle of the 20th century. The wares, though inferior, have some resemblance to those of Iznik with the addition of a yellow pigment.

K. European Pottery to the End of the 18th Century

The wares made in Europe before the 19th century fall into three main categories: lead-glazed earthenware, tin-enameled earthenware, and stoneware.

Lead-glazed earthenware was made from medieval times onward and owes little to outside influences. The body is generally reddish buff in colour and the glazes are coloured yellow and brown from iron compounds, purplish from manganese, or green from copper. The wares are usually vigorous in form but are often crudely finished. Lead-glazed wares fell out of favour when tin glaze became widely known toward the end of the 15th century, but they returned to popularity nearly 300 years later. The body of this later earthenware is white or cream in colour, the glaze is clear and transparent like glass, and the forms are precise.

The first important tin-enameled wares came from Italy during the Renaissance, and these colourful examples of the painter's art exerted a profound influence on later work elsewhere. Manufacture spread rapidly, first to France, then to Germany, Holland, England, and Scandinavia. Under the name of *maiolica,* faience, or delft it enjoyed immense popularity until the advent of Wedgwood's creamware shortly after the middle of the 18th century, after which the fashion for tin-enameled ware declined rapidly.

Stoneware is first to be seen in Germany during the 16th century; its manufacture was developed in England during the 18th century, culminating in the unglazed ornamental jaspers and basaltes of Wedgwood.

Two other types of ware, less common than these already discussed, are slipware and lustre ware. Slip was applied both as a covering over an earthenware body and in the form of decoration, for example on the *sgraffito* wares of Italy (which owe a good deal to similar wares from Byzantium) and the dotted and trailed slips of 17th- and 18th-century England. Lustre pigments were used in Spain, where they are the principal decoration on the magnificent series of wares referred to as Hispano-Moresque; in Italy, where they supplement other modes of decoration; and much later, in England—although in the last case they are no longer artistically important.

1. Byzantium.—In A.D 330 Byzantium became the imperial capital of the Roman Empire and was renamed Constantinople. The term Byzantine, however, is applied to the period which ended only in 1453 when Constantinople was captured by the Ottoman Turks (since when the city has been known as Istanbul).

It was not a Christian custom to bury pottery with their dead and in consequence few wares survive and chronology is difficult. Most of the surviving wares fall into two classes: one is a red-bodied type, sometimes with stamped relief decoration under a clear glaze; the other, a *sgraffito* type with human figures, animals, birds, monograms, foliate designs, the Greek cross, and the like, engraved through a white slip and covered with yellow and green glazes. The latter is the commonest technique after the 12th century. Both styles were fairly widespread, and have been recovered in fragmentary form from excavations at Istanbul, and in Greece, Cyprus, and the Crimea.

2. Spain.—The wares of Spain can be divided into two classes: lustred pottery and tin-enameled wares.

Lustre Ware.—The lustre technique spread to Moorish Spain by way of Egypt, but it is impossible to say exactly when it arrived.

The body of Hispano-Moresque pottery is usually of fairly coarse clay, which has burned to a pinkish buff, covered with a tin enamel containing lead in varying proportions. The lustre, added overglaze, varies in colour from golden to a pale straw, and a coppery lustre almost invariably indicates at least a 17th-century date. Many dishes were also painted in blue and, less often, with manganese.

Most surviving wares of the early period are dishes of various shapes. Less often seen are *albarelli*, waisted drug jars which were based on a Middle Eastern form. Vases based on the old Iberian *amphora* but with two massive wing handles are very rare; a superb specimen (the Alhambra vase) is in the Museo Español de Antiguedades in Madrid. The decoration is predominantly Moorish on early examples, but specimens of this kind are unlikely to be later than 1525. Subsequently, Spanish artists repeated the Moorish designs but they often degenerate in their hands and the Kufic script, frequently used by Moorish potters, becomes meaningless. The early designs are, for the most part, plant forms and arabesques, both the vine leaf and the bryony leaf being used. A little later we find magnificently drawn animals in heraldic form, principally lions and eagles. The deer and the antelope, which may owe something to Persian sources, are still later. Dishes with coats of arms of noble families surrounded by vine- and bryony-leaf ornament are not only unusually fine but are of some assistance in dating in cases where the arms can be traced.

HISPANO-MORESQUE WARE

Spanish *albarello* (drug jar) painted with lustre on a blue ground; Valencia, about 1460. Height: 10⅞ in. In the British Museum

Many of them were made in and around Valencia for Italian families. A feature of many of the dishes is the lustre decoration on the reverse. Although often no more than a series of concentric circles, the superb eagles and other animals occasionally found on dishes from Valencia are even finer than the obverse designs, and are drawn with great economy by a sure hand.

It is not always easy to say where pieces of lustre ware were made. Málaga was probably working until the beginning of the 16th century, but after this the principal centre was Valencia and its suburb of Manises. Valencian pottery was particularly popular in Italy (*see below*).

In the 17th century much lustred pottery was made for the cheaper markets. The painting is executed in a lustre pigment of deep coppery hue, and while this ware is not important in comparison with the early wares, it is often decorative. It was freely exported to England, and fragments dredged from Bristol docks once caused it to be attributed mistakenly to potteries in that city.

Other Tin-Enameled Ware.—Although the influence of lustre pottery on later Italian *maiolica* is obvious, the wares of Paterna, near Valencia, were hardly less influential in the 14th century. They were decorated in green and manganese, often with motifs taken from Moorish sources, and this combination of colours is to be seen in early Italian pottery from Orvieto and elsewhere.

Much tin-glazed pottery of excellent quality was made at Talavera de la Reina, in New Castile, during the 17th and 18th centuries. The palette is characteristic; green and manganese again play a distinctive part, frequently combined with touches of orange-red and gray. The *istoriato* style of Urbino, discussed in the next section, was copied here, and the Italian painter and engraver Antonio Tempesta (1555–1630) provided a source of inspiration for some of the painting. Alcora, in Valencia, made much faience of excellent quality during the 18th century and used designs after Jean Bérain (1637–1711) in the manner of the French factory at Moustiers (properly Moustiers-Sainte-Marie). Later it produced some cream-coloured earthenware in the style of Wedgwood.

Tilework was particularly common in Spain from the earliest period and, according to one proverb, only a really poor man had "a house without tiles." At first the tiles were made with a typically Persian technique in which thin slabs of tin-glazed pottery were sawed into pieces and embedded in a kind of mortar (tile mosaic). The *cuerda seca* method followed about 1500: outlines were drawn on the tile in manganese mixed with a greasy substance which prevented the coloured glazes used from mingling. Tiles made by the *cuenca* technique had deeply impressed patterns whose compartments were filled up with coloured glazes. Tiles were also decorated with lustre pigments.

3. Italy.—The pottery of Italy is extremely important not only in itself but for its subsequent influence on production in other European countries. Indeed, its influence may have spread even farther afield, because a few specimens of Ming porcelain have motifs which may have been inspired by it.

There are two well-defined classes of Italian wares: *maiolica*, or tin-enameled ware, and pottery decorated in the *sgraffito* technique, sometimes called *mezza-maiolica*.

Maiolica.—Tin enameling was introduced from the Middle East through the Muslim civilization in southern Spain, wares being shipped from there to Italy by Majorcan traders. The term *maiolica* was at first applied to this Hispano-Moresque lustre ware, but in the 16th century it came to denote all tin-enameled ware.

Italian *maiolica* is principally noteworthy for its painted decoration, which excelled in technical competence anything which had been produced in Europe since classical times. It was often called Raffaele ware, a tribute to the influence of the painter Raphael (1483–1520) although he, in fact, never made any designs for pottery. In particular the *maiolica* painters copied his *grotteschi* motifs adapted from those on imperial classical ruins (principally the *thermae* ["baths"] of Titus and the Golden House of Nero) and so named because they were first rediscovered in the grottoes there. They are usually fantastic combinations of human, animal, and plant forms.

Much of the technical information about Italian pottery comes from a manuscript written *c.* 1548 by Cipriano Piccolpasso (1524–79) of Castel Durante, in the province of Pesaro e Urbino; it is entitled *Le tre libri dell'Arte del Vasaio*, and the author discusses such questions as the preparation of the clay, the glazes and the colours, as well as methods of applying the last two. The painting was executed in high-temperature colours on the dry but unfired enamel glaze. Great skill was needed since the surface absorbed the colour like blotting paper absorbs ink and erasures were therefore impossible. The best wares were given a final coating of lead glaze, called *coperta*. The range of colours was comparatively limited: cobalt blue, copper green, manganese purple, antimony yellow, and iron red formed the basic palette, while white was provided by the glaze material. The use of white can be seen in examples painted in this colour on a bluish-white glaze (*bianco sopra bianco*, or "white on white"), or on a light blue ground (*berettino*). A dark blue ground was used in the same way.

Lustre pigments were introduced from Spain and were used for a short time on wares made at Cafaggiolo in Tuscany, and in two Umbrian towns, Gubbio, where the best-known painter was Maestro Giorgio Andreoli (*c.* 1462–*c.* 1553), and Deruta. The lustre is often the golden yellow colour derived from silver, but the ruby lustre of Andreoli suggests the use of gold. The silver lustre often developed a nacreous effect known as *madre perle* ("mother-of-pearl").

Forms are few and comparatively simple. For the most part

they were dictated by the necessity for providing a surface on which the painter could exercise his skill and for this reason dishes form the greater part of surviving wares. It is doubtful whether most *maiolica* was ever intended for general use. Dishes, for instance, were displayed on sideboards and buffets far more often than they were placed on the table. Gaily coloured drug jars were a fashionable decoration for pharmacies and include the albarello shape for dry drugs, copied from Spain, and a spouted jar for wet drugs. Ewers with a trefoil spout, derived from the Greek *oenechoe*, were made as well as massive jars represented by Florentine work of the 15th century.

The earliest *maiolica* is decorated in green and manganese purple in imitation of the Paterna ware mentioned above. Much work of this kind was done at Orvieto, in Umbria, and jugs with a disproportionately large pouring lip are characteristic. "Orvieto" ware has almost become a generic term for anything in this style although similar vessels were made at Florence, Siena, and elsewhere. It was current in the 14th century and continued in the 15th century, when other colours were added to the palette. The decorative motifs are Gothic, with some traces of Eastern influence.

Also from Florence came a series of wares painted in a dark, inky, *impasto* (or "very thick") blue. These, too, have Gothic ornament, particularly oak leaves which came into use sometime before 1450. Heraldic animals also appear on some specimens. This kind of decoration was obviously inspired by Spanish pottery and a few examples are hardly more than copies. Soon after 1500 Florentine production was concentrated in the castle of Caffagiolo and came under the patronage of the Medici family, whose arms appear frequently. A notable addition to the palette here was a bright red pigment, a most difficult colour to attain and one which was not often used.

Gothic ornament was gradually displaced by classical motifs such as arabesques, trophies, and the like, which themselves gave way to the *istoriato* style. This style, no doubt inspired by the achievements of contemporary painting, imitates the easel picture closely. Its realism, including the use of perspective, is quite unlike any previous ceramic decoration. The subjects were often classical, but biblical subjects, some taken from the woodcuts of Bernard Salomon (*c.* 1506-61), are frequently represented. The works of Raphael, Dürer, and Andrea Mantegna were also borrowed, often through engravings made by Jacopo Ripanda (Jacopo da Bologna; d. *c.* 1530) and Marcantonio Raimondi (d. *c.* 1534); some specimens are almost exact copies, others are freer interpretations. The paintings sometimes occupy the centre of the dish with a border of formal ornament surrounding them but in many instances, notably those from Urbino, they cover the entire surface. It is often impossible to regard the pottery body as anything more than a surface for the painting, its pictorial or narrative subject having been executed with little or no consideration for the nature of the object it decorated. Although ceramic decoration is rarely successful unless it is designed to en-

BY COURTESY OF VICTORIA AND ALBERT MUSEUM; PHOTOGRAPHS, WILFRID WALTER

ITALIAN MAIOLICA

(Top) Dish painted with a rabbit surrounded by formal borders; Tuscany, probably Florentine, about 1450. Diameter: 17¾ in. (Bottom) Polychrome inkstand, inscribed "Urbino"; Fontana factory, about 1550. Height: 15 in. In the Victoria and Albert Museum

hance, or at least not to detract from, the shape of the body, an exception must be made for some of these colourful wares: at their best they are highly ornamental.

The *istoriato* style probably developed about 1500 at Faenza (Emilia), one of the earliest and most important centres which had been manufacturing *maiolica* since before 1450. Almost as early are some examples from Cafaggiolo. Castel Durante adopted the same style, where it is particularly associated with the name of Nicola Pellipario (d. *c.* 1542), the greatest of the *maiolica* painters. He also painted grotesques similar to those of Deruta and elsewhere; these are rather more stylized than the grotesques introduced later in the 16th century at Urbino, which was probably the largest centre for the manufacture of *maiolica* at the time. Many wares from Urbino have survived. The industry there was under the patronage of the Della Rovere family, whose name, meaning "oak tree," led to the adoption of the oak-leaf motif in wreathed form. The later Urbino grotesques are in a humorous vein, and full of movement. They are often used as a surround to an interior medallion in the *istoriato* style.

Among the early factories, that of Deruta is of considerable importance and may have been made under the patronage of Cesare Borgia. *Maiolica* has been made there from medieval times and manufacture continues in the mid-20th century. Deruta potters were the first to use lustre pigment, which was of a pale yellow tone, and they also adopted the Spanish practice of painting designs on the reverse of dishes. They covered only the obverse with tin-enamel, and applied a lead glaze to the reverse—again, a typically Spanish practice. The best work was done before 1540.

The use of lustre pigments at Gubbio probably started soon after it began at Deruta, and the quality of the work was such that *maiolica* was sent from Castel Durante, Faenza, and even from Deruta itself for this additional embellishment.

An interesting series of dishes is that painted with the portraits of young women, often with the addition of a terse and appreciative comment, such as *"Bella."*

Maiolica was manufactured in Venice between the 16th and 18th centuries. As might be expected in an important seaport with worldwide trade, its *maiolica* often shows Eastern influence. The designs of Iznik were sometimes copied (as they were, in fact, on other Italian wares of the period) and imitations of Chinese porcelain of the Ming period gave rise to a style known as *alla porcellana* ("in the manner of porcelain").

Of the later potteries, that of Castelli, near Naples, did excellent work from the 16th century onward, although its wares tend to become pedestrian. *Istoriato* painting was revived there in the 17th century in a palette which is paler in tone than that of early work in this style. Much *maiolica* survives from Savona, in Liguria region, a good deal of which is painted in blue in Oriental styles. There were also many small centres during the 16th and 17th centuries whose work can hardly be identified. Many of them copied better-known wares with varying success.

Sgraffito Wares.—These are comparatively rare. The technique was derived from Byzantine sources by way of Cyprus, which was under Venetian rule from 1472 to 1570. Manufacture was confined to northern Italy, the largest centre being at Bologna. The body was covered with a slip of contrasting colour, the decoration then being scratched through to the body beneath and the whole covered with a lead glaze. Often the incised designs were first embellished with high-temperature colours (blue, green, purple, brown, and yellow), which tended to run during firing. The lead glaze has a yellowish tone. The manufacture of these wares died out finally at the end of 18th century, but some important work of the kind was done in the late 15th and 16th centuries.

Later Wares.—A number of factories were founded during the 18th century, but the distinctive style of the earlier wares can no longer be seen. A factory in Turin, for instance, imitated the work of Moustiers, and the Rococo style was generally adopted.

Forgeries.—Forgeries of Italian *maiolica* of the best period are fairly common, and many European factories tried to imitate it during the 19th century when it was especially popular. The work of Urbino, Castel Durante, Faenza, and Gubbio was copied freely, and, to a lesser extent, the wares of Orvieto and Florence received similar attention. Most are not particularly deceptive to anyone acquainted with genuine examples.

4. France and Belgium.—The medieval pottery of France is difficult to date and classify with accuracy, but the lead glaze was in common use by the 13th century at the latest. Some examples, especially those with yellow and green glazes, are reminiscent of English pottery of the same period, and the knowledge of glazing probably reached England from France. Proficient *sgraffito* decoration was done at Beauvaisis (Oise) and at La Chapelle-aux-Pots (Charente-Inferieur).

Lead-Glazed Wares of the 16th Century.—Bernard Palissy (*q.v.*) began to experiment with coloured glazes about 1539 and, after much difficulty, succeeded in producing his "rustic" wares in 1548. For the most part these are large dishes made with wavy centres intended to represent a stream, with realistically modeled lizards, snakes, and insects such as dragonflies grouped thereon. They are decorated on the obverse with blue, green, manganese purple, and brown glazes of excellent quality, while the back is covered with a glaze mottled in brown, blue, and purple. Palissy later turned his attention to classical and biblical subjects which he molded in relief. After his death in 1589, work in his style was continued at the Avon pottery, near Fontainebleau.

Almost contemporary with Palissy's rustic ware is a type of pottery which was made in the style of the metalwork of the period. It was made at Saint-Porchaire and is sometimes called,

16TH-CENTURY FRENCH LEAD GLAZED WARES

(Above) "La Fécondité," dish by Bernard Palissy; about 1580. Length: 19 in. (Right) Candlestick made at Saint-Porchaire, sometimes erroneously called *Henri Deux* ware; about 1540. Height: 13 in. In the Victoria and Albert Museum

erroneously, *Henri Deux* ware, or *faience d'Oiron*. The body is ivory white, and covered with a thin glaze. Before firing, designs were impressed into the clay with metal stamps like those used by bookbinders, and the impressions were then filled with slips of contrasting colours. This technique resembles the *mishima* mode of decoration in Korea.

Faience, or Tin-Enameled, Ware.—This dates from the early part of the 16th century. The art of tin enameling was learned from Italy, the wares of which were much admired. Italian potters were established at Lyons in 1512 and attributions, at one time controversial, were confirmed when a dish inscribed "Lyon 1582," was discovered in 1959 (now in the British Museum, London). By the end of the 16th century, painting in the manner of Urbino was well established there. Faience, the designs of which were influenced by Italian *maiolica*, was also made at Rouen, probably as early as 1526, and Nevers started work toward the end of the 16th century.

A new factory was established at Rouen about 1656 by Edmé Poterat, probably assisted by workmen from Nevers. Edmé's son, Louis, introduced a decoration of *lambrequins*, ornament with a jagged or scalloped outline based on drapery, scrollwork, lacework ornament, and the like, which was used in much the same way as the German *Laub- und Bandelwerk*. *Lambrequins* were extremely popular and were copied at other porcelain and

FRENCH FAIENCE WARE

Dish painted in blue with *lambrequins* decoration; Rouen, early 18th century. Diameter: 22½ in. In the Victoria and Albert Museum

faience factories. The faience of Nevers, too, is extremely important, and shows the Baroque style at its best. In the second half of the 17th century the porcelain of both China and Japan became increasingly well known in Europe, and many designs were borrowed from Chinese sources by potters at Nevers and elsewhere.

The factory of Moustiers in the Basses-Alpes was founded by Pierre Clérissy in 1679. During the early period frequent use was made of the engravings of Antonio Tempesta (1555–1630) as well as biblical scenes. Later came a series of dishes decorated with designs after Jean Bérain (1637–1711) whose work greatly influenced French decorative art at the time. These designs usually include grotesques, *baldacchini* ("canopies"), vases of flowers, and the like, linked together by strapwork in a typically Baroque manner.

In 1709, when Louis XIV and his court melted down their silver to help pay for the War of the Spanish Succession, the nobility looked for a less expensive medium to replace it. In consequence faience gained in popularity and importance. A great deal was manufactured in the region of Marseilles, the factory of the Veuve Perrin being particularly noted for enamel painting in the Rococo style, but perhaps the most influential factory was that of Strasbourg, in Alsace (which had officially become part of France in 1697). The factory here was started by C. F. Hannong in 1709, and the wares painted in blue, in other faience colours and in enamel colours, were much copied elsewhere. The latter were introduced about 1740, the first recorded use in France of tin-enameled pottery. Brilliant *indianische Blumen* (flower motifs which were really Chinese in origin but which were thought to be Indian because they were imported by the East India companies) were painted in a palette which included a carmine similar to the "purple of Cassius," the Chinese *rose* enamel. A characteristic copper green was also used. *Deutsche Blumen* ("German flowers") were introduced, perhaps by A. F. von Löwenfinck, about 1750, and inspired similar painting elsewhere. Figures by J. W. Lanz, who also worked in porcelain here and at Frankenthal, are to be seen. Much work was done in the fashionable Rococo style, including objects such as clock cases, wall cisterns, and tureens in the form of fruit and vegetables. Both faience and porcelain in a variety of decorative forms were used for the banqueting table and, in Germany, it was the custom to serve dessert at a separate table also decorated in this way.

The wares of Niderviller, in Lorraine, were much influenced by those of Strasbourg. The earlier figures are reminiscent of those of Lanz. The later ones were probably modeled by the sculptor Charles Gabriel Sauvage, called Lemire (1741–1827), and were sometimes taken from models by Paul Louis Cyfflé (1724–1806). At Lunéville, not far away, Cyfflé worked in a pleasant but sentimental vein,

FAIENCE WARE FROM NIDERVILLER, FRANCE

Figure of Louis XV painted in enamel colours; after a model by Paul Louis Cyfflé, about 1760. Height: 10¾ in. In the Victoria and Albert Museum

and used a semiporcelain biscuit body known as *terre-de-Lorraine*, which was intended to resemble the biscuit porcelain of Sèvres. He was later copied by modelers in Staffordshire, notably Jean Voyez. The work of both Sauvage and Cyfflé is extremely skilful.

Faience was made at Tournai (now in Belgium) and at Brussels during the 17th century. Their styles were mainly derivative, but Brussels made some excellent tureens in the form of poultry, vegetables, fruits, and so forth during the Rococo period.

Only some of the more important factories have been mentioned since the number operating during the 18th century was very large. The products of the smaller centres were mostly based on the wares discussed above, and in some cases were merely copies. Porcelain, too, affected the decoration of faience, not only in the adoption of enamel colours (as at Strasbourg and Marseilles) but much more directly, as in some of the work at Sceaux, which is some 5 mi. S of Paris. Wedgwood's creamware was imitated at many of the French factories toward the end of the 18th century, and Apt, in Vaucluse, made an excellent agateware, as well as lead-glazed pottery modeled on contemporary silver. After 1800 there was a distinct tendency to concentrate on the manufacture of porcelain.

5. Germany and Austria.—While Germany is principally noted for its superb porcelain (described in the section *European Porcelain*, below), the stoneware of the Rhineland is, in its own way, no less noteworthy. A great deal of faience was also made though this was less important.

Hafner Ware.—The earliest type of ware made in Germany was the *Hafnergeschirr* (*Hafner*, "stovemaker"; *geschirr*, "vessel"). Originally the term referred to tiles, molded in relief and usually covered with a green glaze, which were built up into the large and elaborate stoves needed to make the mid-European winter tolerable. Jugs and other vessels made by these stovemakers, however, came to be called Hafner ware by extension when their manufacture began about the mid-16th century. The work of Paul Preuning of Nürnberg is an example of this kind of ware. He decorated his pottery with coloured glazes kept apart by threads of clay. In Silesian Hafner ware, on the other hand, the design is cut out with a knife and the incisions prevent the coloured glazes from mingling. The earliest German stove tiles date back to about 1350, and are lead glazed. Tin glazes came into use about 1500.

After these beginnings, German pottery developed in two distinct classes: stoneware and tin-enameled earthenware.

Stoneware.—The stoneware (*Steinzeug*) came mainly from the Rhineland, and in particular from Cologne, Westerwald, Siegburg, and Raeren (the latter now in Belgium). Manufacture probably began in Cologne about 1540. The body is extremely hard, and varies from almost white (Siegburg) to bluish gray (Westerwald), while a brown glaze over a drab body is also to be seen (Raeren). The surface was glazed with salt and was no more than a "smear" glaze, pitted slightly like orange peel. A smooth, though still very thin, glaze was achieved by mixing the salt with red lead. Particularly popular at Cologne in the late 16th century was the *Bartmannkrug* ("bearded-man jug"), a round-bellied jug with the mask of a bearded man applied in relief to the neck. This type was sometimes called a "Bellarmine," the mask being regarded as a satire on the hated Cardinal Robert Bellarmine (Bellarmino), but there is no authority for this assumption. In England, where they were imported in large quantities, they were also known as "graybeards." A mottled brown glaze over the grayish body was common and gave rise to a second term, "tigerware."

Some of the earliest German stoneware is notable for its remarkably fine molded decoration in the Gothic style. Oak-leaf and vine-leaf motifs were common, as were coats of arms on medallions. The applied relief and stamped decoration was, at times, most elaborate and the thin glaze lent it additional sharpness and clarity. Reliefs of biblical subjects appear on tall, tapering tankards (*Schnellen*), which were provided with pewter or silver mounts. The *Doppelfrieskrüge* were, as the name implies, jugs with two molded friezes round the middle; they usually portray classical subjects. They and the *Schnellen* were made in Raeren

brownware by Jan Emens, surnamed Mennicken, in the last quarter of the 16th century. Emens also worked in the gray body which was used at Raeren at the turn of the century, in this case employing blue pigment to enhance the decoration. Figures were sometimes set in a frame reminiscent of Gothic architectural arcades, and inscriptions of one kind or another are fairly frequent. A few signed and dated examples are known. At a later date, blue and manganese pigments were used together and this practice continued throughout the 17th century.

The style of the stonewares gradually fell into line with the prevailing Baroque style, particularly toward the end of the 17th century. At Kreussen, in Bavaria, a grayish-red stoneware was covered with a brown glaze and the molded decoration was picked out with opaque overglaze colours which had a tin-enameled base. This was the first time enamel colours had been used on pottery in Europe. The technique, learned from Bohemian glass enamelers, was to have some influence in France as well as Germany.

German stoneware was extremely popular abroad; during the 17th century, for instance, Sieburg even exported to Japan.

An extremely important type of stoneware was first made shortly before 1710 at Meissen, in Saxony. It was discovered by E. W. von Tschirnhaus (1651–1708) and J. F. Böttger (1682–1719) during their researches into the secret of porcelain manufacture. It usually varies from red to dark brown in colour, due to the presence of iron oxide, and is the hardest substance of its kind known. An almost black variety was termed *Eisenporzellan* ("iron porcelain"), and a black glaze was devised by Böttger to cover specimens of defective colour. Decoration is usually effected by means of applied reliefs, although the black-glazed specimens are sometimes decorated with lacquer colours, probably by Martin Schnell (d. *c.* 1740), as well as with gold and silver. Silvering was not uncommon, and was also practised in other German centres during the early part of the 18th century on both stoneware and porcelain. It has nearly always oxidized to black, and grave risks attend any attempt to revive the original colour. Böttger obviously intended, at first, to imitate the wares of I-hsing (see *China: Ming Dynasty*, above), and a few surviving examples are direct casts from Chinese originals, but the court goldsmith, J. J. Irminger (d. *c.* 1722), soon influenced the style in the direction of contemporary metalwork.

A particular feature of Meissen stoneware is the decoration done by lapidaries. Many specimens were engraved with coats of arms, and grinding into facets (the *Muscheln* pattern) was also practised. The same methods were used to give a plain surface a high polish. Engraved decoration was sometimes executed on stoneware at a later date, usually to increase the value, and considerable knowledge is sometimes needed to detect the fraud.

Metal mounts, common on Rhenish stoneware, also were sometimes accompanied by precious and semiprecious stones set in the stoneware body.

Because of the vogue for porcelain stoneware manufacture declined in the 18th century and it was finally abandoned about 1730. It was copied early in the 18th century at Plaue an der Havel, and a brown-glazed stoneware with decoration in gold and silver from Bayreuth was obviously made with the same end in view. Modern reproductions have also been attempted.

Tin-Enameled Ware.—Faience factories were so numerous that it is only possible to mention the most important. Perhaps the earliest tin-glazed wares other than stove tiles are the amusing jugs in the form of owls which came from Brixen (Bressanone), in the Tirol. Their detachable heads formed a cup and their shape and style no doubt inspired the later owl and bear jugs made in England during the 18th century which had similarly versatile heads. These *Eulenkrüge* were, at first, used as prizes in archery contests, and were sometimes repeated in Rhenish stoneware. The first manufacture of faience on a considerable scale, however, took place at Nürnberg, and some dishes in the Italian style still survive. The earliest specimen which can reasonably be attributed to it is dated 1526, and it is possible that Nürnberg actually preceded Brixen in point of time.

Much more is known of the productions of Kreussen. This factory started at the beginning of the 17th century, when it was

under the direction of Lorenz Speckner, and is chiefly of interest for its blue-and-white faience jugs. The outline of flowers painted in blue is almost cross-sectional in style and terminates in a small spiral—hence the name "spiral family."

A factory at Hanau, near Frankfurt am Main, was started in 1661 and remained in operation until about 1806. Many of the early wares were decorated with Chinese motifs. A type of jug with a narrow neck, the *Enghalskrug,* was made in Hanau. (Those with a globular body were sometimes copied in China and Japan in blue painted porcelain.) Others have a spirally fluted body and a twisted handle. Pewter or, less often, silver covers were common. The painting includes coats of arms, landscapes, and biblical subjects. Groups of dots amid strewn flowers (*Streublumen*) are characteristic and help to identify some of the faience. Realistically painted German flowers (*deutsche Blumen*) appear shortly before mid-18th century. Most painting is in blue, manganese, and the other high-temperature faience colours. Enamels do not seem to have been used.

A factory in Frankfurt am Main itself was founded in 1666. Imitations of Chinese motifs were very popular, as well as biblical subjects. The blue is brilliant, and the surface usually suggests the use of an overglaze. *Enghalskrüge* were commonly made and are sometimes difficult to distinguish from those of Hanau. This centre closed about 1740. At Nürnberg a factory was established about 1712, continuing until about 1840. Most of the subjects used at Frankfurt and Hanau were repeated, as were designs based on the Rococo engravings of J. E. Nilson (1721–88), which were also popular at many of the porcelain factories. The Rococo style, which spread from France to Germany about the second quarter of the 18th century, is reflected both in the forms and the decoration.

The wares of Bayreuth are particularly interesting. Early products were painted with a misty blue, but enamel colours were speedily adopted. *Laub-und-Bandelwerk* was a much used type of motif and excellent work was done by A. F. von Löwenfinck, whose work on porcelain is well known, and J. P. Dannhofer. Perhaps the finest 18th-century faience was made by the factory at Höchst, near Mainz, which also manufactured porcelain. Decoration was usually in enamel colours, and landscapes, figure subjects, *deutsche Blumen,* and *chinoiseries* are of a much higher quality than elsewhere. Faience thus decorated was termed *Fayence-Porcellaine* during the 18th century.

An important aspect of both faience and porcelain decoration in Germany is the work of the *Hausmaler* ("home painters"). These men bought undecorated faience and porcelain from the factories and painted it at home, firing the decoration in small muffle kilns. For this reason, their work was done in enamel pigments over the glaze. At first they mostly used the *Schwarzlot* technique—decoration in a black, linear style which was nearly always based on line engravings. Faience thus decorated dates from about 1660 and is the work of Johann Schaper (d. 1670) who had been a Nürnberg glass painter, J. L. Faber, and others. Polychrome enamel decoration was developed by another glass painter, Abraham Helmhack (1654–1724), who mastered the technique as early as 1690, many years before it was adopted by the factories. Undoubtedly in Europe the use of enamel colours on faience and porcelain was derived from glass painting. Another illustration of this borrowed technique is the use of enamel colours on Kreussen stoneware mentioned above.

Toward the end of the 18th century a number of German factories, including some already making faience, made lead-glazed earthenware in imitation of Wedgwood, while a factory at Königsberg (now Kaliningrad) imitated Wedgwood's black basaltes body.

6. The Netherlands.—Most Dutch pottery is covered with a tin-enamel glaze. Of the medieval lead-glazed wares found in the Netherlands, most are imports from Germany, although there are a few instances of manufacture in the territory itself. During the 17th century red stoneware was made by Arij de Milde of Delft and others in imitation of the wares of I-hsing (see *China: Ming Dynasty,* above). Creamware was manufactured at several places at the end of the 18th century. Enamel decoration was added to porcelain imported from China, Japan, and, occasionally, from Meissen. Salt-glazed wares from Staffordshire, as well as a certain amount of English creamware, were decorated in the same way. Much ware sparsely decorated in blue was also overpainted with enamels, a practice known as "clobbering."

Italian potters had settled in Antwerp by 1525, and surviving examples of tin-enameled ware from this period are in the Italian style. Manufacture was concentrated to a great extent in Delft soon after the beginning of the 17th century. By about 1650 the large brewing industry began to decline, and the old buildings were taken over by potters who retained such names as "The Three Golden Ash-Barrels," "The Four Roman Heroes," and "The Double Jug" for their potteries. The craftworkers of the town were organized into the Guild of St. Luke which exercised a considerable amount of control over apprenticeships and the like and established a school of design.

In the 17th century the Dutch East India Company, chartered in 1602, imported Chinese and Japanese wares in great quantities, and the taste for Eastern decoration rapidly ousted Italian fashions. For the greater part of the 17th century decoration was in blue and Chinese porcelain was closely imitated. In wares of the best quality this imitation is so exact that, without a fairly close inspection, it is possible to mistake them for the originals. Biblical scenes were still extremely common, and landscapes and seascapes are often well painted. These and the many genre scenes are in the same styles as the paintings of the period. Tilework was frequently undertaken and many individual tiles have survived although the large panels made up of many tiles are very rarely complete. Blue painting was followed by the use of the usual faience colours, the outline (known as *trek*) being first drawn with blue or manganese and then filled in. Before firing the object was covered with the additional lead glaze known as *kwaart,* which made the surface more brilliant. Red was a difficult colour; often when it was to be used an unpainted space was left during the first firing and it was applied afterward and fired at a lower temperature. Gilding is found on the finer specimens and required a further firing. Enamel colours were introduced by Zacharias Dextra about 1720, and the *famille rose* patterns

were frequently imitated. Among the rarer and more showy examples of Delft may be numbered the *delft dorée* on which gilding is lavish, and the *delft noir* which has a black ground, suggested by Chinese lacquer work, in conjunction with polychrome decoration. Work of this kind is often attributed to Adriaen Pijnacker.

Marks on Dutch delft are extremely unreliable for many later copies were given the earlier marks of important potteries, especially during the 19th century.

7. Britain.—*Medieval Pottery.*—The medieval pottery of England was affected little by outside influences. Poor communications prevented the industry from concentrating in any one place, and most wares, therefore, are made of local clay by local craftsmen. The potters worked either alone or in extremely small groups and their tools were few and simple. There are almost no records of consequence before the 16th century, and it is therefore impossible to find sufficient information on which to base a systematic classification of the wares in question. The clay used for the body contains iron, and it ranges from buff to red, or, when it was fired in a reducing atmosphere, from gray to almost black. The clay was commonly mixed with sand, and, as in much Japanese pottery, little effort was made to disguise the method by which the vessel was formed, pronounced ridges frequently being visible. Both relief and inlaid decoration is found, especially on tiles, and brushed slip was also used to add simple patterns.

Unglazed ware was common, especially in the early period, but a soft lead glaze came into more general use later, the knowledge probably being derived from France. The glaze varied between yellow and brown according to the iron content of the clay, although a group having a particularly rich brown glaze was made by first washing the pot with slip containing manganese. The use of copper oxide to give a rich green of variable colour dates from the 13th century. The green, buff, and brown glazes were used in conjunction. "Cistercian" wares, made in the monasteries before their dissolution in 1536–39, are more precisely finished. They have a dark brown glaze over a stoneware body and are sometimes decorated with white slip, or incised. By far the greater number of surviving specimens are jugs and vessels for storing liquids, and since they have almost always been excavated, a reasonably perfect specimen is a rarity.

Tin-Enameled Ware.—Lead-glazed wares tended to die out after tin glaze reached England via the Netherlands about 1550. At first it was called "gallyware," but the name was later changed to "delftware" with the rise of the Dutch manufacturing centre at Delft. Its popularity was due to the fact that it could be painted in bright colours. The earliest surviving examples are the Malling jugs, so called because an early specimen of the kind was preserved in the church at West Malling, in Kent. These were almost certainly made in London, and usually have silver or pewter mounts. The colour varies from turquoise to black, while a variety with a blue ground flecked with orange was probably suggested by the "tigerware" from the Rhineland. Similar mounts, often of English manufacture, are to be seen on Rhenish jugs imported into England, and occasionally on Turkish jugs of about the same period.

By 1628 a flourishing factory had been established at Southwark, in London, and dated specimens are known from this time onward. Many are decorated in blue with birds amid floral and foliate motifs based on some blue-and-white porcelain of the reign of Wan Li (1572–1690). Inscriptions with the name of the owner are relatively common, as they are on English wares of all kinds. Almost contemporary are some large dishes painted in polychrome high-temperature colours. The earliest, which is in the London Museum, is dated 1600 and bears the following couplet:

> The rose is red and leaves are grene
> God save Elizabeth our Queene.

The dish has a border of blue dashes and is a forerunner of the so-called "blue dash" chargers which were popular later in the century and were decorated with biblical scenes (that of Adam and Eve being a special favourite), crude portraits of the kings of England, ships, armorial bearings, and the like. The influence of Italian *maiolica* is also to be seen.

Many wine bottles are extant, often with the name of the wine ("Sack," "Claret," etc.) painted in blue, with the date. Others are more elaborately decorated and a few are in polychrome.

Toward the end of the 17th century painting becomes more colourful and service ware more frequent (although tea ware is now scarce). Blue and white was still made in large quantities but the high-temperature palette is much more in evidence and the influence of Dutch potters is often obvious.

Chinese influence, which had been particularly strong in the early part of the 18th century tended to persist, particularly at Bristol. Rococo decorations were used to a limited extent. Later some not very successful attempts were made to utilize the Neoclassical style. Overglaze enamels appear after the middle of the century but were probably only used at Liverpool. Also from Liverpool are many specimens, including tiles, decorated with transfer printing by John Sadler (*c.* 1720–89) and Guy Green (retired 1799). They claimed to have evolved this technique independently of John Brooks of London who is generally credited with discovering it about 1753.

The main centres of production were in London (Southwark and Lambeth), Bristol, and Liverpool, although there were smaller potteries elsewhere. Wincanton in Somerset made frequent use of manganese. The tin glaze fell into disuse about the turn of the 18th century, its place having been taken by Wedgwood's creamware. In the mid-20th century manufacture has been successfully revived at Rye, in Sussex.

Slipware.—Wares decorated with dotted and trailed slip were made at Wrotham, in Kent, and in London during the first half of the 17th century. Wrotham is noted principally for drinking mugs with two or more handles, known as tygs, and London for dishes with pious exhortations obviously inspired by the Puritans, for example "Faste and Pray." In the same century manufacture was started in Staffordshire and many surviving examples were signed by the potter in slip. The work of Thomas Toft is particularly valued although dishes signed by other potters, including another member of the Toft family called Ralph, are known. The best work of this kind was done before the end of the 17th century and although it may fairly be described as "peasant ware" many of the earlier specimens are vigorously decorated and amusing. Manufacture continued until the end of the 18th century.

ENGLISH SLIPWARE DISH BY THOMAS TOFT; ABOUT 1685. DIAMETER: 17¼ IN. IN THE VICTORIA AND ALBERT MUSEUM

17th-Century Stoneware.—The popularity of Rhineland stonewares in England, as well as that of the newly imported Chinese teapots from I-hsing kilns, led to attempts to imitate both forms of this medium. Patents for making copies of Rhenish stoneware were granted as early as 1626, but the first known to have been exercised was awarded to John Dwight (1640–1703) of Fulham in 1671, both for porcelain and for the so-called "Cologne" ware. As well as "German" stoneware he made a brown-glazed stoneware decorated with stamped ornament which was continued at Fulham after his death and has been extensively reproduced since. He probably never made any porcelain but he mentions "red china," which can only refer to imitations of the I-hsing stoneware. His misuse of the term "china" is probably accounted for by the fact that a few specimens of thinly-potted stoneware are slightly translucent. Some remarkably fine figures in drab-coloured stoneware have survived, reputedly modeled by the sculptor and wood-carver Grinling Gibbons.

The brothers John Philip and David Elers, of German origin, made "brownware" and "red china" at a factory not far from that of Dwight in Fulham. They later moved to Bradwell Wood in Staffordshire where they found a vein of suitable clay and continued to make red stoneware. Their monopoly in Staffordshire was short-lived, and it is difficult to separate their work from that of Dwight, on the one hand, and that of their Staffordshire imitators, on the other. Most wares are decorated with stamped reliefs, the Chinese prunus blossom being comparatively common. The tendency to utilize patterns from silverwork which is apparent on some examples may be connected with the fact that the Elers had been silversmiths. The Elers' migration to Staffordshire perhaps can be regarded as the starting point for the large modern industry which has grown up in that area. Certainly from this time onward Staffordshire wares tend to lose their "peasant" character and to approach a factory-made precision which was to be general by the end of the 18th century.

The earlier red- and brown-glazed stonewares were replaced about 1690 by a salt-glazed stoneware which was regarded as an acceptable substitute for porcelain. This varies in colour from drab to off-white, the glaze on later specimens often having a richer, more glassy appearance due to the addition of red lead. One of the earliest varieties is decorated with stamped reliefs on pads of clay which were applied to the surface.

18th-Century Developments.—The "scratched blue" class of white stoneware dates from about 1730, and is decorated with incised (or scratched) patterns usually touched with blue. Decoration is floral, and inscriptions and dates are fairly frequent. Its manufacture survived until about 1775.

From the 1730s molded patterns in relief were popular, the clay being pressed into molds of metal, wood, or fired clay. The introduction of plaster of Paris molds (see *Introduction: Methods of Fashioning Ceramics,* above) devised by Ralph Daniel of Cobridge about 1745 gave much greater scope and led to the development of intricate shapes in the finer varieties of white stoneware. The patterns greatly increased in sharpness and complexity; silver patterns especially were copied and elaborate piercing is to be seen.

As mentioned above, transfer printing was first used about 1755. The earliest enameled painting belongs to the same period—previously white wares had been sent to Holland for decoration. The man who first mastered the technique was William Duesbury. He was established as a decorator in London by 1751 and, while he concentrated on painting porcelain (*see* further *European Porcelain: Britain,* below), it appears from his surviving account books that he also enameled stoneware from Staffordshire. Some extant brilliantly enameled figures are probably from his studio, in some cases copies of contemporary models from Meissen. A little earlier than Duesbury's enameled figures are the "Pew" groups which consist of two or three figures seated on a high-backed settle or pew, modeled in a primitive and amusing fashion.

Enameling in Staffordshire is thought to have been introduced by two Dutchmen who were at Hot Lane, Cobridge, about 1755: however, little is known of them and the name of Willem Horologius, sometimes associated with them, is apocryphal. A rich blue ground is often called Littler's blue after William Littler, the man who is thought to have invented it. He was one of the partners at Longton Hall where a porcelain factory, which also made salt-glazed stoneware, was established in 1751 and made much use of the blue. The attribution has been confirmed from fragments and "wasters" discovered on the site of the old factory by Bernard Watney in 1955.

John Astbury is particularly associated with a type of brown-glazed ware decorated with stamped pads of white clay. A surviving example depicting the victory of Admiral Vernon at Porto Bello is dated 1739 (Victoria and Albert Museum, London). Some of the earliest Staffordshire figures in brown and white clay covered with a lead glaze have been attributed to Astbury. It is probable that his son Thomas experimented with the lead-glazed earthenware which was later to be known as creamware and, improved by Wedgwood, eventually renamed Queen's ware. It was developed from the earlier white stoneware body and covered with a lead glaze.

Thomas Whieldon (1719–95) of Fenton Low, Staffordshire, manufactured "agateware"—that is, ware made by combining differently coloured clays or by combing together different colours of slip. In the former method the clays were usually laid in slabs,

one on the other, and beaten out to form a homogeneous mass in which the colours were inextricably mingled. Agatewares seem to have been made between 1725 and 1750, the earlier specimens being salt-glazed while the later ones were covered with a colourless lead glaze. Whieldon is most famous for his use of coloured glazes which were mingled to give a clouded or tortoiseshell effect and were used on an earthenware body, sometimes over molded decoration. A few naively modeled figures with this type of glaze are attributed to him. From 1754 to 1759 he was in partnership with Josiah Wedgwood, who developed the fine green and yellow glazes to decorate molded wares in the form of pineapples, cauliflowers, and the like. A rich black glaze, sometimes decorated with gilding, was made by Whieldon and at Jackfield, in Shropshire.

Coloured glazes were also used by Ralph Wood (1715–72) of Burslem, Staffordshire, for decorating an excellently modeled series of figures in a creamware body, the finest being perhaps a mounted Hudibras in the Victoria and Albert Museum. Many of these figures are attributed to the modeler Jean Voyez, who was much influenced by the work of P. L. Cyfflé at Lunéville (see *France,* above). Enoch Wood, another member of the family, started work on his own account in 1783 as Enoch Wood & Co. He made most of the wares current in Staffordshire at the time, as well as some excellent figures decorated with overglaze colours.

Josiah Wedgwood (1730–95), the most famous of all the Staffordshire potters, is chiefly celebrated for his fine jasper and black basaltes stonewares but his creamware was undoubtedly the more influential. It was well finished and clean in appearance with simple decoration in good taste, often in the popular Neoclassical style. His wares appealed particularly to the rising bourgeois class, both in England and abroad, and porcelain and faience factories suffered severely from competition with him. Surviving factories switched to the manufacture of creamware (*faience fine* or *faience anglaise*) and the use of tin enamel died out. Even Sèvres and Meissen found themselves in difficulties financially. Wedgwood's jasper wares were imitated in biscuit porcelain at Sèvres, and Meissen produced a glazed version which they called *Wedgwood-arbeit.*

Wedgwood secured the patronage of Queen Charlotte for his creamware in 1765, and renamed it Queen's ware. Much of it was transfer printed by Sadler and Green at Liverpool. Evidence of its popularity and importance is provided by the enormous service of 952 pieces made for Catherine the Great's palace of La Grenouillière in St. Petersburg.

The basaltes ware, also called black porcelain or Egyptian ware, was a type of stoneware introduced about 1768. Like the jasper which followed, it was used almost entirely for ornamental work; vases, ewers, candlesticks, plaques, medallions, and tea and coffee ware were made. Some of it was painted in what Wedgwood called "encaustic" enamel, but most of the decoration was either molded and applied, or incised by turning on a lathe.

Jasper was introduced about 1775. It is a fine-grained white unglazed stoneware, which is slightly translucent when thinly potted. Undoubtedly it was inspired by the biscuit porcelain of Sèvres. Its name derives from the fact that it resembles the natural stone in hardness. At first the body was stained blue with applied decoration in white. Other colours followed speedily. Like basaltes, jasper was used mainly for ornamental wares, but perhaps the most interesting products are the portrait medallions of contemporary notabilities. Vases do not appear to have been made until after 1780, and in 1790 Wedgwood produced the first

MOUNTED HUDIBRAS BY RALPH WOOD; CREAMWARE BODY DECORATED WITH COLOURED GLAZES. STAFFORDSHIRE, ENGLAND; ABOUT 1765. HEIGHT: 11¾ IN. IN THE VICTORIA AND ALBERT MUSEUM

copies of the Portland vase, a magnificent Roman vase of dark blue glass decorated with white figures, at that time owned by the duke of Portland but now in the British Museum (*see* GLASS). The vase was extensively copied in later years, particularly in Victorian times. Toward the end of the 18th century Sèvres began to copy Wedgwood's reliefs on vases and plaques for furniture decoration. Less influential were the red stoneware (*rosso antico*), which sometimes had an enameled decoration of classical subjects, and caneware, a buff stoneware, old specimens of which are fairly common.

Wedgwood's productions were extensively copied by William Turner, William Adams, Enoch Wood, and others, and forgeries of one kind or another are numerous.

Lustre Pigments, introduced into England toward the end of the 18th century, are used in a manner quite different from the earlier styles of other countries. To simulate silverwork wares were completely covered with platinum lustre which remains unchanged in colour after firing (silver itself yields a pale straw colour), the amount of metal used, of course, being extremely small. Such wares were known as "poor man's silver." Wares were also painted or stenciled with lustre patterns. The most valuable type commercially are the "resist" lustres which have a lustred background and the pattern reserved in white. They were made by painting or stenciling the pattern on the glaze with shellac which "resisted" the subsequent application of the metallic pigment. Silver lustre was rarely used but gold lustre, which gives variable colours from pink to purple, was fairly common. Copper, whose colour remains more or less unchanged in its lustre form, was used throughout the 19th century for common wares.

Scotland.—There were three pottery-making centres of minor importance in Scotland. A factory for the manufacture of tin enamel was established in Glasgow in 1748, but only one specimen can now be identified with certainty. In the 19th century the principal factory belonged to J. & M. P. Bell and was noted for blue painted earthenware and Parian statuettes of good quality. Pottery was made at Prestonpans in the 17th century, and in the 18th century figures, punch bowls, and similar items were produced by Watson's factory. Ornamental pottery of all kinds was produced at Porto Bello from about 1786 onward. In 1810 a Staffordshire potter became a partner, after which the factory's work begins to resemble that of Staffordshire; its wares were copied by a factory at Tunstall, Staffordshire, in the 1820s.

8. Scandinavia.—The faience industry spread to Scandinavia mainly because of migratory workmen from Germany. There were a number of factories located in Denmark, Norway, and Sweden during the 18th century which made faience, and creamware in the English manner. Bowls in the shape of a mitre were made for a kind of punch called "bishop," and these are a distinctive Scandinavian production. The most important factories are those of Rörstrand and Marieberg (Koja) in Sweden. A Rörstrand workman later at Marieberg, Anders Stenman, is reputed to have discovered the art of transfer printing independently, and the manager of the Marieberg factory, Pierre Berthevin, later went to Frankenthal, where he experimented with this form of decoration. Berthevin was, at one time, at the French factory at Mennecy, and the influence of Mennecy can be seen in the wares of Marieberg.

BY COURTESY OF VICTORIA AND ALBERT MUSEUM; PHOTOGRAPH, WILFRID WALTER

WEDGWOOD JASPER WARE

Blue and white jasper ware vase by Josiah Wedgwood; Staffordshire, England, about 1785. Height: 18 in. In the Victoria and Albert Museum

A typical Rococo concept to come from Marieberg is the "terrace" vase. This has a vase standing at the top of a winding flight of steps, often with a rabbit or some other animal at the bottom.

A factory at Kiel, Ger., under the direction of J. S. F. Tännich, formerly of Strasbourg, did excellent work. There were two factories operating in Copenhagen, and one at Herrebøe, in Norway. Ulfsunda, in Sweden, made many close copies of Wedgwood's basaltes ware and the *rosso antico*.

L. EUROPEAN PORCELAIN TO THE END OF THE 18TH CENTURY

1. General Outline.—*Soft Porcelain.*—The manufacture of soft porcelain was essayed in Italy under the patronage of Francesco de' Medici. Similar attempts were made elsewhere in Italy about the same time, and manufacture is supposed to have been continued at Pisa, and at Candiana, near Padua. However, no specimens from these factories are known, and the first production of soft porcelain on a considerable scale did not take place until toward the end of the 17th century in France.

Hard Porcelain.—In Saxony about 1675 Ehrenfried Walter von Tschirnhaus started experiments to make porcelain from clay mixed with fusible rock. Almost certainly, he had made hard porcelain by the end of the century but manufacture did not become a practical commercial proposition until the year of his death in 1708. Experiments were continued by his assistant, an alchemist named Johann Friedrich Böttger, who is sometimes credited with von Tschirnhaus' discovery. The factory was established at Meissen about 1710, and the first porcelain sales of any consequence took place at the Leipzig Fair in 1713. Early production was divided between the red stoneware, which had been discovered in the course of the experiments (see *European Pottery: Germany,* above) and hard porcelain, the latter becoming the sole manufacture after about 1730.

Styles.—Style is of great assistance in dating 18th-century European porcelain. The early porcelain, when it is not copied from Chinese or Japanese wares, is Baroque in form and decoration. Some of the figure modeling at Meissen shows a typical Baroque exaggeration of gesture. The *lambrequins* and the *Laub- und Bandelwerk* which appear on both the faience and porcelain of the time are characteristic forms of Baroque ornament, as are the designs of Jean Bérain.

The early part of the 18th century saw the first essays in the Rococo style which developed from Baroque. Its name is derived from the French *rocaille,* or "rockwork," probably because the earliest motifs were based on wave, rock, and shell patterns. The first important Rococo work in porcelain—the Swan service, made at Meissen for the director, the Graf Heinrich von Brühl—was started in 1737, the decorative motifs being swans, nereids, tritons, etc. Later Rococo ornament is characterized by scrollwork whose asymmetry contrasts with the symmetrical Baroque use of similar motifs.

In Rococo pieces form is often subsidiary to ornament. Porcelain figures appear on bases profusely ornamented with scrollwork and occasionally, as for example on those from Frankenthal, the scrollwork is carried upward, dwarfing the figures themselves. The backs of figures and groups tend to be sketchily finished, and since many such figures were derived from engravings, it seems that the modeler had no clear idea of what ought to be on the other side.

Rococo had run its course by the middle of the 18th century and was followed by a revival of classical motifs as a result of the excavations at Pompeii and Herculaneum in the mid-18th century. The resulting style has come to be known as "Neoclassical" and is often referred to in England as the Adam style because the brothers Adam were its principal exponents. In France the earliest, or Louis Seize (Louis XVI), phase retained some of the elements of the Rococo. Later the style became increasingly severe, especially during the French Revolution. In the early part of the 19th century, under Napoleon, it was transformed into the Empire style which was little more than a pompous and ostentatious copy of imperial Roman art.

In Germany Neoclassicism took a slightly different course since it became mingled with the Romantic movement. Its sentimental vein is well illustrated by the figures and groups of the Meissen modeler Michel Victor Acier, and in England by the work of the painter Angelica Kauffmann and others. In the 19th century a revival of the Rococo style incorporated the worst elements of both.

Both the Baroque and Rococo are satisfactory styles for porcelain. Neoclassicism, however, was suited neither to this medium nor to faience. It found its ideal material in the creamware of Wedgwood, the most important exponent of Neoclassicism in the field of ceramics.

Many imitations were made of Chinese wares, but perhaps the most important Far Eastern influence during the first half of the 18th century was that of Arita (see *Japan*, above). The designs of the Kakiemon family were copied at almost all the porcelain factories, in particular at Meissen and at Chantilly.

2. France.—In the second half of the 17th century much interest was taken in both faience and porcelain although the technique of making soft-paste porcelain (*pâté tendre*) had yet to be mastered, and the secret of hard-paste, or "true," porcelain manufacture was not discovered till the 18th century. In 1664 a privilege had been granted to Claude and François Révérend for the manufacture of porcelain. A similar privilege was granted to the faience maker Louis Poterat of Rouen in 1673, yet from contemporary records it seems that little porcelain was manufactured. Some specimens decorated in the manner of Rouen faience, or with the armorial bearings of local families, have been attributed to Poterat but it is possible that some of these, as well as some rare examples hitherto tentatively attributed to Révérend, may have been made by M. Morin who had moved to Saint-Cloud. In 1698 Martin Lister visited Saint-Cloud and records that Morin had been experimenting with soft porcelain for 20 years, but had only achieved success 3 years before.

Another factory at Saint-Cloud, which was probably a separate establishment, was founded by Pierre Chicaneau in the 1670s and was afterward directed by his son's widow and her second husband, Henri Charles Trou. Its wares were yellowish in tone, and heavily potted. Much use was made of molded decoration, which included sprigs of prunus blossom copied from the blanc de chine of Te-hua. Particularly common was a molded pattern of overlapping scales. Most examples are small but there are some large *jardinières* which are extremely handsome. The early painted wares were decorated in underglaze blue with typically Baroque patterns, including the *lambrequins* introduced at Rouen. Motifs derived from the designs of Jean Bérain are also to be seen. Polychrome specimens, some of which were decorated in the style of Kakiemon, date from about 1730.

A small quantity of porcelain which is sometimes difficult to separate from that of Saint-Cloud was made at Lille, and an offshoot of the former factory at the Rue de la Ville l'Evêque in Paris also made similar wares. Saint-Cloud itself finally closed about 1768.

At Chantilly the first porcelain was decorated almost entirely in the Kakiemon style, and the body was invariably covered with a tin-enamel glaze—a fact which makes it easy to recognize. The Japanese period ended about 1740. For some years thereafter Meissen styles were copied, in particular the *deutsche Blumen*. In 1753 an edict in support of the newly established factory at Vincennes forbade all other factories to manufacture porcelain or to decorate faience in polychrome; much Chantilly porcelain of the later period is creamy white decorated only with slight flower sprigs in blue underglaze. A transparent glaze was introduced in 1751. The presence at this factory of the erstwhile Meissen painter A. F. von Löwenfinck has been noted.

A factory at the Rue de Charonne in Paris was started by François Barbin in 1735, and removed to Mennecy in 1748 where it came under the protection of Louis Francois de Neufville, duc de Villeroy. The early productions were in the manner of Saint-Cloud and the prunus sprig motif is found. *Lambrequins* painted in underglaze blue as at Rouen and Saint-Cloud were also used. Later, some excellent flower painting was done and a few imitations of the early work of Sèvres have also been recorded. Figure modeling was excellent in quality. Small porcelain boxes from

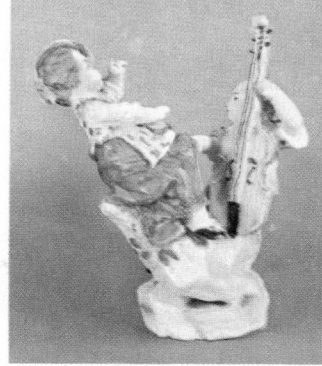

GROUP OF CHILDREN, PORCELAIN FIGURINE FROM MENNECY, FRANCE; ABOUT 1760. HEIGHT: 6⅝ IN. IN THE VICTORIA AND ALBERT MUSEUM

Mennecy, often in the form of animals, are now much sought. The work of a small factory at Crépy-en-Valois is similar, and some confusion has occurred. Mennecy was removed to Bourg-la-Reine in 1773, where it came under the protection of the comte d'Eu.

The most important of the French factories was established at Vincennes about 1738 and removed to a new building at Sèvres in 1756. The moving spirit behind the original factory was Orry de Fulvy, brother of the minister of finance, who was at first assisted by two workmen from Chantilly, Gilles and Robert Dubois. They achieved no success until 1745 when porcelain was at last made with the aid of François Gravant, also from Chantilly. Louis XV was a large shareholder in the original company and the factory eventually passed to the crown in 1759. It became state property in 1793, and has so remained to the present day.

The early work at Vincennes consisted of porcelain vessels decorated with naturalistic flowers and often elaborately mounted in gilt bronze by the court goldsmith, Claude Thomas Duplessis, and others. Meissen was also copied for a short period, but the factory soon evolved its own style which remained partly dependent on the use of gilt-bronze mounts of the highest quality. A few glazed and painted figures were made. These gave place to figures of biscuit porcelain. Figures in this material were first made in 1751, and in 1757 the sculptor Etienne Maurice Falconet was appointed to take charge of modeling, a position he retained until 1766. Designs by François Boucher were frequently used by Falconet and others, and Boucher's influence is particularly strong during the lifetime of Mme de Pompadour who took much interest in the factory. Later, some excellent work in this medium was done by the sculptors Augustin Pajou and Louis Simon Boizot.

Both at Vincennes and Sèvres much use was made of coloured grounds in conjunction with white panels, which were used for decorative painting of the highest quality. These panels were surrounded by rich and elaborate raised gilding which was engraved and chased. The most usual ground colours were *gros bleu* (a dark underglaze blue introduced in 1749) and the brighter *bleu*

18TH-CENTURY FRENCH PORCELAIN

(Left) *Vaisseau à mât* (masted vessel) from Vincennes; about 1755. Height: 19½ in. In the Wallace collection. (Right) *Jardinière* (flowerpot holder) with *rose Pompadour* ground painted in reserved panels by Robert Dubois; Sèvres, 1761. Height: 7½ in. In the Victoria and Albert Museum

de Roi (an enamel blue which followed in 1756). Also used were turquoise blue (1752), yellow (1753), green (1756), and the *rose Pompadour* (1757) probably invented by the painter Xhrouet and discontinued on the death of the marquise in 1764. This last colour is often miscalled *rose du Barry* in England. Many examples bear a device by which the painter may be identified as well as a factory mark.

The porcelain of Sèvres was made to harmonize with the exotic and luxurious style of interior decoration which characterized French court circles. The soft-paste body was of superb quality, and the extremely fusible glaze partly remelted in the enameling kiln causing the colours to sink into it in a way which is hardly ever seen elsewhere. Forgeries, usually in hard-paste porcelain, are particularly numerous and the mark of the factory has been much abused. White porcelain, usually with slight defects, was sold by the factory on several occasions before the end of the 18th century and decorated by outside enamelers in its own styles.

The factory prosecuted the search for the ingredients of hard porcelain with vigour, and these were found after a prolonged search at Saint-Yrieix-la-Perche, near Limoges, in 1769. The new body was first manufactured soon after 1770, although for some years it was only used for biscuit figures. Later, it was employed for services and vases decorated in a severely classical style. The director, Alexandre Brongniart, who was appointed in 1800, discontinued the manufacture of soft porcelain and sold off the stocks remaining in white.

A large number of smaller factories making hard porcelain sprang up, chiefly in and around Paris, in the second half of the 18th century. Some were patronized by members of the royal family, including Marie Antoinette. A number of provincial factories were also engaged in the same manufacture. Principally deserving of mention is that of Paul Antoine Hannong in Strasbourg, where porcelain of good quality was first made in 1751. The factory was removed to Frankenthal in the Palatinate in 1753 in consequence of the royal edict on behalf of Vincennes.

3. Germany and Austria.

The factory at Meissen was under the patronage of Augustus the Strong. Its earliest porcelain is smoky in tone but some improvements were made in 1715, and others in the following decade. Many early specimens were painted with a limited range of enamel colours of good quality, including a pale violet lustre derived from gold which remained in use until about 1730. In 1720 a painter from Vienna, Johann Gregor Höroldt, was appointed chief painter (*Obermaler*) to the factory, and he was responsible for introducing a new and much more brilliant palette, as well as some ground colours (*Fond-Porzellan*). The earliest ground colour to be noted is a coffee brown termed *Kapuzinerbraun* which was invented by the kilnmaster, Samuel Stölzel. Difficulty was experienced in using blue underglaze, and little work of the kind was done. Enamel painting, on the other hand, was of fine quality and includes topographical subjects, figure subjects which were based either on the harlequins, pierrots, and other characters of the Italian comedy or on the style of Watteau and his followers, and flowers in the Oriental style, mistakenly called *indianische Blumen* as well as native flowers taken from books of botanical illustrations (*deutsche Blumen*). A series of harbour scenes from engravings of Italian ports were mostly executed by C. F. Herold (cousin to the *Obermaler*) and J. G. Heintze. Perhaps the most important early wares are the *chinoiseries*, European delineations of the Chinese scene with a strong element of fantasy. They appear in great variety. The first work of the kind, much of it painted by the *Hausmaler*, Bartholomäus Seuter, is in gold silhouette. This was followed by a type in which the figures are painted in three-quarter length. *Indianische Blumen* motifs were used and Arita decorations, particularly those of Kakiemon were closely copied.

Little figure modeling was done until about 1727 when Johann Gottlob Kirchner was appointed *Modellmeister* and asked to make some colossal figures of animals for the Japanische Palais. The medium was unsuited to work of this kind, and most of the surviving examples are spectacular and magnificent failures. Another sculptor, Johann Joachim Kändler (*q.v.*), was employed in 1731 to assist Kirchner but soon replaced him. After the death of

Augustus the Strong in 1733 the large-scale modeling was practically discontinued and Kändler turned his attention to small figures suitable for the dining table.

Helped by Johann Friedrich Eberlein, Friedrich Elias Meyer, Peter Reinicke, and others, Kändler soon made the figures of Meissen fashionable throughout Europe and they were extensively copied elsewhere, particularly in England. The Rococo style appears in Saxony after 1737 when Kändler started to make the Swan service—perhaps the best known of all porcelain services—for Graf Heinrich von Brühl. Rococo speedily became fashionable.

Meissen was the most influential European factory until the beginning of the Seven Years' War in 1756 when it was taken by the Prussians. From then until 1763 it was operated by nominees of Frederick the Great, who virtually looted the factory. By the end of the war leadership had passed to Sèvres, and the work of Meissen in the Academic period (1763–74), and under the directorship of Count Camillo Marcolini (1774–1814), is much less important than formerly. The transitional Louis Seize style of the former period is typified by the figure modeling of Michel Victor Acier who came to the factory to share the position of *Modellmeister* with Kändler in 1764. During the latter period the designs of Sèvres and of Wedgwood (*Wedgwood-arbeit*) were copied, and the Neoclassical style was increasingly used.

The other German factories of the period were, for the most part, established with the aid of runaway workmen from Meissen and also from Vienna, where Claudius Innocentius du Paquier had started a factory in 1719 with the aid of two men, Christoph Konrad Hunger and Samuel Stölzel, who were themselves from Meissen. Early Vienna wares are highly prized. Much use was made of *Laub- und Bandelwerk* ("leaf and strapwork") patterns and excellent work was done in *Schwarzlot* ("black monochrome"). The factory passed to the state in 1744, and its later work is competent without being distinguished. Under Konrad von Sorgenthal (1784–1805) it became noted for elaborate gilding and coloured grounds, with minutely detailed painting after Angelica Kauffmann and others in reserved white medallions.

The Vienna factory provided a number of wandering "arcanists" (men who possessed the *arcanum* or "secret" of porcelain manufacture), two of whom, Johann Benckgraff and J. J. Ringler, helped to establish the Höchst factory which began manufacture about 1752. It is principally noted for excellent figures in the Louis Seize style by Johann Peter Melchior, who left in 1779 to work at Frankenthal, and for the work of Simon Feilner.

Also in the early 1750s a factory was established in Berlin by a merchant named Wilhelm Kaspar Wegely, who received some assistance from Benckgraff. It closed in 1757 after failing to obtain a subsidy from Frederick the Great but another factory, started in 1761, was acquired by Frederick in 1763 when he re-

BY COURTESY OF VICTORIA AND ALBERT MUSEUM; PHOTOGRAPHS, WILFRID WALTER

18TH-CENTURY GERMAN PORCELAIN

(Left) Group of peasants by Simon Feilner; Höchst, about 1752. Height: 8⅞ in. (Right) Group emblematic of sculpture, model by Wilhelm Christian Meyer; Berlin, about 1775. Height: 12¼ in. In the Victoria and Albert Museum

linquished his hold on Meissen. The painted decoration of the second factory was of high quality and made much use of *mosaik* patterns—detailed diapers painted over a coloured ground. A large service made in 1819 for presentation to the duke of Wellington and decorated with scenes from his battles is now in Apsley House, London.

Much interest now centres on the figure modeling of Franz Anton Bustelli (*q.v.*), who worked at Nymphenburg, a suburb of Munich. The factory, which was still in operation in the mid-1960s, was started about 1753 with the assistance of Ringler, and was under the direction of the Graf Sigismund von Haimhausen. Bustelli became *Modellmeister* in 1754 and retained the position until his death in 1763. His magnificent series of figures based on the Italian comedy are the most important expression of Rococo in German porcelain. Another modeler of note was D. J. Auliczek. The painted wares of the factory were also of fine quality.

Some excellent figures were made at Fürstenberg, where porcelain was first manufactured in 1753 with the aid of Benckgraff, and at Frankenthal, to which the Strasbourg factory was removed in 1753 (see *France*, above). Frankenthal employed some notable modelers; *e.g.*, J. W. Lanz (from Strasbourg), the cousins J. F. and K. G. Lück, and Konrad Linck, the latter working in the Louis Seize style. Ludwigsburg, started in 1756, was taken over by the Duke Karl Eugen of Württemberg in 1758. The porcelain was grayish in colour, and more suitable for figure modeling than for service ware. The figures of artisans by an artist known as the *Modeller der Volkstypen* ("modeler of folktypes") are original and pleasing, and the sculptor, J. C. W. Beyer, did good work in the Louis Seize style. A factory founded at Fulda by Prince-Bishop Heinrich von Bibra did some distinguished figure modeling while smaller factories at Onolzbach (now Ansbach), Ottweiler, Cassel, Pfalz-Zweibrücken, and Kelsterbach, for the most part produced competent imitations of work from the larger factories. A number of factories in the Thüringer Wald made provincial wares which often have a good deal of charm.

Much important work was done in the early period by the *Hausmaler*—independent decorators who bought white porcelain and painted it at home. The more important are Johann Aufenwerth and Bartholomäus Seuter of Augsburg, J. F. Metszch of Bayreuth, the Bohemians Daniel and Ignaz Preussler, and Ignaz Bottengruber of Breslau. The work of the latter is particularly esteemed. Christoph Konrad Hunger, who was at Meissen and Vienna, devised a method of using raised gilding in conjunction with translucent enamels, a technique which can also be seen on some early French porcelain and on enameled copper from Alex Fromery of Berlin. An unusual technique was devised by A. O. E. von dem Busch, canon of Hildesheim, who engraved his designs in the glaze with a diamond, subsequently filling the incisions with black pigment.

Few marks have been so consistently abused as that of the crossed swords of Meissen. During the 18th century the Thüringian factories belonging to the Greiners adopted marks which could easily be mistaken for it, and it has since been added to all kinds of unlikely specimens. Many reasonably good copies of Meissen figures have been made at Potschappel (Pottschapplitz) near Dresden and in Paris, and variations in colouring are sometimes the only serious points of difference. The Meissen factory, too, occasionally used its old molds at a later date. Crude copies of an early design were made in Dresden during the 1870s by Helena Wolfsohn, who used the royal monogram (AR for Augustus Rex) as a mark. Their tawdry nature is always apparent.

4. Britain.—A factory for porcelain manufacture, using a body similar to that of Saint-Cloud, was established in Chelsea in 1743 by Charles Gouyn and Nicolas Sprimont. The rare surviving specimens include jugs molded in the form of goats and further decorated with an applied bee, a style based on one current in silverwork some 15 years earlier. These, the so-called "Goat and Bee" jugs, are often marked with an incised triangle, which was then the mark in use. About 1750 Gouyn retired. A new body was adopted, together with the familiar mark of an anchor, which was raised on a small medallion until about 1752, painted in red until about 1756, and executed in gold thereafter. The work of

BY COURTESY OF VICTORIA AND ALBERT MUSEUM

ENGLISH PORCELAIN FROM CHELSEA
Figure of a carpenter; period of the raised anchor mark, about 1752. Height: 7¾ in. In the Victoria and Albert Museum

the Chelsea factory was extensively influenced by Meissen until about 1756, the styles of Sèvres superseding it in the gold anchor period. Wares marked either with the raised or the red anchor are the most highly valued, and painting is excellent in quality. Some of the best were painted by the Irish miniaturist, Jeffryes Hamett O'Neale, whose work is much more frequent on Worcester porcelain at a later date. The gold anchor marked wares are noted for rich gilding and some fine coloured grounds which, on occasion, rivaled those of Sèvres. The figures in the later Rococo style are generally inferior to those of the early period. Some Chelsea porcelain from 1760 onward was painted in the studio of James Giles of Clerkenwell, whose work, like O'Neale's, is much more frequent on Worcester porcelain. The factory was bought by William Duesbury of Derby in 1770 and entered a phase known as the Chelsea-Derby period. The Neoclassical style was introduced together with the figures in the biscuit porcelain made fashionable by Sèvres. It closed finally in 1784.

A group of figures, the best-known examples of which are those portraying the "Girl in a Swing," were possibly made at Chelsea but more probably at a short-lived factory directed by Charles Gouyn and staffed by workmen who had seceded from Chelsea. They can be dated with reasonable certainty to the early 1750s. No complementary service ware has been positively identified.

A factory was established in Derby about 1750, and a class of figures characterized by a retraction of the glaze from the base— "dry-edged" figures—are attributed to it. It appears that this first enterprise petered out and that another factory in Derby was started by Duesbury in 1756. It advertised itself as "the second Dresden" and is principally noted for the excellence of its painting toward the end of the century, the artists being Zachariah Boreman, William Billingsley, and others.

The Bow factory (London) was started as early as 1744 with the aid of clay brought from Virginia by the American settler Andrew (André) Duché, who had discovered the secret of manufacture quite independently some years before. An amusing and primitive class of Bow figures was executed by an anonymous artist known as the "Muses Modeler" because the most typical figures portray the muses. Generally speaking Bow wares are unsophisticated and the factory obviously catered for prosperous tradesmen, a market ignored by Chelsea. An important technical innovation took place at Bow in 1750 when calcined bones were added to the porcelain body. This was the first major departure from the French soft-porcelain formula, which was fundamentally a mixture of clay and ground glass. Bone ash was added to soft porcelain by Chelsea about 1755, by Lowestoft (which mainly copied Bow styles) in 1758, and by Duesbury in 1770 when he purchased the Chelsea factory. About 1800 at his factory at Stoke-on-Trent, Staffordshire, Josiah Spode the second added calcined bones to the hard porcelain formula to produce the standard English bone-china body.

Longton Hall in Staffordshire was started about 1750, one of the partners being a salt-glaze potter named William Littler. The figures are naive, and much of the service ware was molded in the form of leaves. A rich blue ground (Littler's blue) was used on porcelain and salt-glazed ware alike. The factory closed in 1758.

Another variation on the original soft-porcelain body was introduced at a factory in Bristol started by Benjamin Lund about 1748. Clay was mixed with a fusible rock called steatite (hydrous magnesium silicate), the principle being similar to that used in the manufacture of hard porcelain. This factory was transferred to Worcester in 1752, and was still in operation in the mid-20th century. In the 18th century "scale" grounds, which consisted of patterns of overlapping scales in various colours, were particularly popular. Transfers taken from engraved plates were also extensively used for decoration. Worcester was bought by Thomas Flight in 1783, and later wares show a progressive decline in taste. Small factories using a similar body were established at Liverpool, and at Caughley, in Shropshire. A second factory was established at Worcester by Robert Chamberlain in 1786 (see *19th and 20th Centuries in the West,* below).

William Cookworthy (*q.v.*) discovered the secret of hard porcelain independently after many years of experiment. He opened a factory at Plymouth in 1768, and this was transferred to Bristol in 1770. He made figures in the style of Bow and Longton Hall. Richard Champion acquired the patent in 1772 and manufactured tableware which is Neoclassical in style and excellent in quality. The patent was bought by a syndicate which established a factory at New Hall, Staffordshire, in 1782 and made a humbler variety of wares for about 40 years.

5. Other European Countries.—*Switzerland.*—A factory started near Zürich in 1763 was directed by Adam Spengler, formerly a painter at Höchst. Both faience and porcelain were made, and, after 1790, creamware was also manufactured. Delicate figures, some modeled by J. V. Sonnenschein from Ludwigsburg, and good quality service ware were produced. A factory at Nyon, founded about 1780, made porcelain in the style of the Paris factories.

Belgium.—The Tournai factory which began to make porcelain in 1751 enjoyed the patronage of the empress of Austria, Maria Theresa, and during the early period exchanged several artists with the English Chelsea factory. Here, and in the associated factory at Saint-Amand-les-Eaux, the work of Sèvres was imitated on a considerable scale. Tournai porcelain sold "in white" was decorated at The Hague.

Denmark and Sweden.—After a number of attempts a factory, which used clay from the island of Bornholm, was established in Copenhagen. In 1760 it was directed by Louis Fournier, a modeler from Vincennes and Chantilly, and a type of soft porcelain was made, few examples of which survive. The manufacture of true porcelain began in 1774 with the aid of workmen from Fürstenberg, and the factory was acquired by King Christian VII of Denmark and Norway in 1779. In 1789 the factory started to make an enormous service, originally intended for Catherine the Great, each piece of which was painted with detailed picture of a Danish flower. This service, the *Flora Danica,* is now in Rosenborg castle, Copenhagen. Numerous skilfully made figures were also produced. The factory continues to produce fine porcelain. A factory at Marieberg (Koja), near Stockholm, started in 1766, and its early work was strongly influenced by that of Mennecy. Quality began to deteriorate after about 1770, and the factory closed in 1788.

Russia.—The factory of St. Petersburg was established about 1745. Later production was on a fairly large scale, and the work of Sèvres and Meissen was freely copied. Some good original work was also done, and well-modeled figures of Russian peasants were made toward the end of the century. Even better figures were made at a factory in Moscow which had been founded in 1758 by an Englishman named Francis Gardner. Another factory near the same city was started by A. Popoff in 1806. A number of small factories elsewhere in Russia were established during the 19th century.

Italy.—There are only about 50 surviving pieces of the porcelain made in Florence at the time of the Medicis, and little is known of its actual production. Giorgio Vasari, in his *Lives of the Painters,* refers to experiments in porcelain manufacture and contemporary records mention a "Levantine" assistant, who may have been a Persian with knowledge of Near Eastern experiments in mixing clay with glaze material. A formula is preserved in the Biblioteca Nazionale Centrale, in Florence, which helps to confirm this supposition. The earliest definite date for manufacture is 1581, a flask in the Sèvres Museum being so dated. Painting

BOTTLE OF MEDICI PORCELAIN; ABOUT 1580. HEIGHT: 6⅞ IN. IN THE VICTORIA AND ALBERT MUSEUM

is nearly always in blue with manganese outlines; a polychrome specimen is doubtfully attributed. Most decorative motifs are derived from China, Persia, or Turkey, and the forms usually copy those of Urbino *maiolica.* Specimens are to be found in most important museums.

No hard porcelain was made in Italy until Francesco and Giuseppe Vezzi's factory was established in Venice in 1720 with the aid of Christoph Konrad Hunger. It made fine hard porcelain whose body has a slightly smoky colour. The style is Baroque and the palette is notable for a brownish red. Another factory, that of Gemminiano Cozzi, started in 1764, was the one where most Venetian porcelain was made. Cozzi worked in the Meissen and Sèvres styles, and produced some good figures.

The factory at Doccia, near Florence, which was still in production in the mid-1960s, was founded by Marchese Carlo Ginori in 1735. Coffeepots in the Baroque style, sometimes painted with coats of arms, are characteristic of the early period. Equally fine figures were made during the 18th century. Porcelain with figure subjects in low relief was made only at Doccia although it has been repeatedly attributed to the soft porcelain factory established in the royal palace of Capodimonte by Charles III of Naples in 1743. As well as extremely well-painted service ware, Capodimonte is renowned for its figures. The factory was transferred to Buen Retiro, near Madrid, in 1759 when Charles became king of Spain. Another factory at Naples was established in 1771 by Ferdinand IV of Naples but its wares are not of very great importance.

Other factories at Le Nove (near Bassano), Vinovo (near Turin), and Treviso (near Venice) produced interesting and competent wares.

Spain and Portugal.—The early porcelain made at Buen Retiro has been justly compared to that of Saint-Cloud. The quality of the ware was good, and some skilful figure modeling was done by Giuseppe Gricci, who had previously worked at Capodimonte. The factory closed in 1808, but manufacture was revived at La Moncloa (Florida, near Madrid) in 1817 and lasted until 1850. Porcelain was also made at the Alcora faience factory from 1774, but production was artistically undistinguished. The same is true of the wares from the factory at Vista Alegre, near Oporto, in Portugal, which was still in production in the second half of the 20th century.

M. THE AMERICAS TO THE END OF THE 18TH CENTURY

1. Indian Pottery.—The extent to which the original inhabitants of the Americas developed in isolation from the Old World is a controversial question but one in which the researches of the ceramic historian may assist the ethnographer. The American Indians are of Asiatic descent and their route to the New World was from Siberia into Alaska across the Bering Straits. The usually quoted period of their migration is between 40,000 and 10,000 years ago. Since they were nomadic peoples, it is unlikely that they brought the knowledge of pottery making with them. When pottery making did begin, it was fundamentally unlike any known work from the Old World and the few remote resemblances to Oriental motifs are almost certainly fortuitous. The wheel remained unknown until the arrival of Europeans, although there is reason to think that a turntable or "slow" wheel may have been used occasionally. Most of the pottery was made by coiling, which is so obvious a method that even young children sometimes use it without tuition; there is therefore no need to assume Asiatic influence. Molding was used for certain vessels but, like coiling, this technique undoubtedly could have arisen spontaneously. It is therefore probable that the art of pottery developed in complete isolation. It is likely that most of the work was done by women. This is nearly always the case when the wheel is not used, and furthermore Pueblo Indian women still do this kind of work.

Slips were used to cover the body, and coloured slips provided the material for much of the painted freehand decoration. Glazes are rare although examples can be found among the Pueblo Indians of New Mexico from about A.D. 1300 onward, on a few vessels from the Chimú area in the Andes, and occasionally in Central America. The effect of a "reducing" atmosphere was understood, so that gray and black pots are found as well as the red and brown ones which were fired in an oxidizing flame. Undecorated surfaces were often highly polished.

North America.—The most important North American pottery was made in the southwest—an area which includes Arizona, New Mexico, and parts of Utah and Colorado. The people who inhabited the plateau land from about 100 B.C. are often referred to as the Anasazi, a Navaho Indian word meaning "ancient people." They are the ancestors of the Pueblo who began to emerge about A.D. 700. The Anasazi were nomadic hunters and although they did not make pottery, they did make excellent baskets. Fixed dwellings appear about A.D. 50, and this probably marks the beginning of pottery manufacture. The earliest pots were probably baskets smeared with clay and dried in the sun. Next came basket-shaped wares coiled in a gray body. These were used principally for cooking. They were followed by more decorative bowls and pots with striking black-and-white geometric designs which seem to have been executed about A.D. 700. Slightly later there is another type of ware which has black decoration on a red slip. After the 12th century the earlier types began to dis-

BY COURTESY OF (LEFT) INDIAN ARTS FUND COLLECTION, SCHOOL OF AMERICAN RESEARCH, MUSEUM OF NEW MEXICO, (RIGHT) ARIZONA STATE MUSEUM, THE UNIVERSITY OF ARIZONA, TUCSON, ARIZONA

NORTH AMERICAN INDIAN POTTERY

(Left) Pueblo jar with black-and-white geometric design, from New Mexico. Height: 15 in. In the Museum of New Mexico. (Right) Hohokam storage jar with red-on-buff decoration, from southern Arizona. Height: 19½ in. In the Arizona State Museum

appear and were replaced by polychrome wares decorated with stylized birds, feathers, animals, and human figures amid the geometric patterns. The principal colours are yellow and red. A small quantity of glazed ware was made in the Zuñi area of New Mexico.

The Hohokam tribes (a Pima word meaning "those who have gone") lived in the desert of southern Arizona, and were approximately contemporary with the Anasazi. They made pottery figures for religious purposes, usually of crudely modeled naked women. Some of this pottery is a gray ware, but most of it is buff with decoration in iron red which lacks the stiffness of the Pueblo designs.

The Mogollon culture of New Mexico produced, during the Mimbres period of the 11th and 12th centuries, a ware which is remarkable for its lively black-and-white decoration depicting human, animal, and insect forms in a much less stylized manner than the paintings on most other wares from the southwest.

There is little pottery of importance from other parts of the United States. Primitive pots have been found on the Atlantic coast, in Georgia and Florida, on the Gulf Coast, and elsewhere, some of which are based on basketwork. Geometric decoration, usually incised, is the rule. Eskimo pottery, which is generally rather crude, bears some resemblance to early Asiatic types.

Central America.—The pottery of Mexico and the rest of Central America is of considerable interest but the wares are so diverse that it is impossible to summarize them adequately. They probably date from the 2nd millennium B.C. onward and were made by the Mayas, the Zapotecs, the Toltecs, and the Aztecs. Generally speaking, geometric patterns are common, and slips in black, brown, white, or red were frequently used. A curious Central American technique somewhat resembles the *batik* method of dyeing textiles. The surface of the pot was first coated either with wax or gum. This was then scraped away in part to form a predetermined pattern, and the whole surface was covered with pigment. In firing, the gum burned away, leaving only the scraped parts in colour. This process may have been adopted from South America. Ornament carved in low relief after firing is to be seen occasionally and has few parallels outside the Americas. An unusual technique from the Mexican highlands consisted of covering the whole surface of the pot with a kind of thick slip, most of which was then scraped away leaving only thin partitions. These compartments were filled with slips of a contrasting colour. The commonest shapes are bowls and wide-mouthed vases; many of these were made with legs, usually three in number so that they could be set down on uneven ground. Figurines, which may be painted, are also found.

By about 600 B.C. the Mayas were making an excellent polychrome pottery in which designs in red and black were painted on a cream or orange slip. This was continued until about A.D. 1000. Between roughly the 4th and the 10th centuries A.D. the Zapotecs, whose chief ceremonial site was Monte Albán in Oaxaca State, made urns in the form of the gods which are extremely striking in appearance. An orange-coloured pottery, decorated in a great diversity of styles, is associated with the Toltecs, as is a dark-coloured pottery with a glossy appearance and incised ornament ("plumbate" ware). Both these types were widely distributed throughout Central America from the 11th to 14th centuries. Little is known of the Aztecs until about 1325, the date of the foundation of Tenochtitlán (Mexico City). Much of their pottery utilizes an orange-burning clay which was painted with black curvilinear geometric motifs in contrast to the earlier rectilinear style. During the period of Montezuma I in the 15th century, designs became more naturalistic, and birds, fish, and plant forms were freely used. European motifs appear after the conquest and such techniques as tin enameling were used from the 17th century onward. Examples can be seen in the Metropolitan Museum of Art, New York City, and elsewhere.

South America.—Most South American pottery was made at centres in the Andes and on the west coast, particularly in Bolivia and Peru. Pottery of lesser importance comes from Ecuador, Colombia, northwest Argentina, and northern Chile. In some places a very high degree of skill was attained, particularly in the central Andes where the earliest wares seem to date from the end of the 2nd millennium B.C. Much of the pottery was made in molds. A characteristic feature is the stirrup-shaped spout on many jars. The *batik* type of decoration already mentioned was also used. Vessels were modeled in the shape of animal or human figures, which were also used as motifs for painted decoration. The puma god worshipped by the early peoples appears in many forms.

The work of the Mochica (Mochicha) culture which flourished around the northern coast of Peru is at its best about the 7th century A.D. Jars in the form of human heads, some of which may be portraits, are remarkable both for the naturalism of the treatment and the skill of the potter. These have the stirrup spout. Painted decoration is often stylized, but with a considerable degree of realism and the subjects are nearly always ceremonial or religious.

The pottery of the Nazcas who lived on the southern coast of Peru at much the same period is noted for its painting. A varied palette included several shades of red and blue, yellow, orange, green, brown, black, gray, and white. The stirrup spout here becomes two spouts joined by a flat bridge. The earliest painting is on a red ground, white grounds becoming more common later. Geometric patterns are to be seen in conjunction with stylized birds, human heads, and the like. The naturalistic portrait jars of the Mochica do not appear, but there are some vessels in the form of figures modeled in a much more conventional style and characteristically painted. Puma's heads are often applied in relief with the body of the animal completed in brushwork. The centipede god is a motif which does not appear elsewhere.

The people of Tiahuanaco, who lived in the region around Lake Titicaca, were influenced by the Nazca wares though painted decoration, often carried out on a red slip ground, is more limited in colour than the Nazca types. The puma head was used as a motif and decoration generally is extremely stylized with a strong geometric flavour.

The Chimú culture succeeded the Mochica in the northern area and lasted until the arrival of the Incas. The most familiar ware is in a body which varies from gray to black, although a red polished ware, sometimes painted in white slip, was also made. The influence of the Mochica tradition can be seen in the retention of the stirrup spout on some jars; others have the double spout connected by a flat bridge. The modeled wares of the Mochica culture were also revived, but are generally inferior.

The Incas originally settled in Cuzco, the old capital of Peru at the end of the 11th century. During the 15th century they established themselves firmly over a wide area including the territory of the Chimús. They were principally soldiers and administrators with small inclination toward luxury and their pottery, particularly in the 15th century, is of excellent quality, being designed in good taste without an excess of decoration. Most Inca pottery is red polished ware. It is usually painted with geometric designs in red, white, and black, although relief decoration is also to be seen on black ware, especially from the Chimú region. The commonest surviving form has been called an aryballos, although its resemblance to the Greek form is remote and fortuitous. It has a conical base, and the neck finishes in a flaring mouth. Two loop handles are set low down on the body. The assumption that this vessel was made for carrying water on the back seems a little doubtful in view of its shape and the disposition of the handles. Little fine pottery was made after the arrival of the Spaniards in the 16th century.

2. The 17th and 18th Centuries.—We have little detailed information about the pottery made by the early European settlers in North America. Most of it was manufactured locally for local needs and from the clays that were nearest to hand. Since most of these contained iron in varying quantities, the pottery body burned to colours between buff and red. As kilns capable of reaching a high temperature were not constructed manufacture was limited to earthenware. Lead glazes were commonly used. Slips, both as a wash and as "trailed" decoration, were employed, and *sgraffito* decoration is known. Most of this pottery was made for practical rather than decorative purposes. A few potteries were established in the 17th century in Virginia, Massachusetts, and New Jersey, and German settlers started work in eastern Pennsylvania as early as 1735, making slip-painted and *sgraffito* ware in their own traditions.

Perhaps the most important development in colonial America took place in Savannah, Ga., where Andrew Duché, of Huguenot descent, started a pottery about 1730. He interested himself in the manufacture of porcelain and discovered the china clay (kaolin) and feldspathic rock (petuntse) necessary to its manufacture. By 1741 he appears to have made a successful true porcelain, but failed to gain adequate financial assistance to develop it. He therefore traveled to London, arriving in 1744, and endeavoured to sell the secret to Edward Heylyn and Thomas Frye, the founders of the Bow factory in London. Their interest is certain, since the patent specification subsequently filed specifically mentions *unaker,* said to be the Cherokee name for china clay. Duché returned to Virginia by way of Plymouth and there spoke with William Cookworthy, later to be the first manufacturer of true porcelain in England. In the early 1960s it was still not known to what extent Duché actually manufactured porcelain, but the Cherokee clay was shipped to England from time to time during the 18th century, and the *Bristol Journal* for Nov. 24, 1764, refers to the import of some specimens of porcelain made in Georgia. There is little doubt, therefore, that the first porcelain to be made in an English-speaking country came from North America. Wedgwood imported several tons of Cherokee clay which was used in the development of the jasper body, and on June 12, 1950, a marker was placed on Highway 28, five miles north of Franklin, N.C., to mark the site of the pit and to commemorate Wedgwood's use of this clay.

By 1765 potteries were being established on a sufficient scale to warrant an attempt to recruit workmen from Staffordshire. Wedgwood wrote at the time: "They had an agent amongst us hiring a number of our hands for establishment of new Pottworks in South Carolina." As early as 1769 a workman named Gousse Bonnin, reputed to have come from the Bow factory, and a certain George Morris advertised porcelain for sale in Philadelphia, but manufacture appears to have ceased there in 1774. A specimen of Bonnin's work is in the Henry Francis du Pont Winterthur Museum at Winterthur, Del. Potteries for the manufacture of creamware were also established in and around Philadelphia.

PORCELAIN BASKET BY GOUSSE BONNIN AND GEORGE MORRIS; PHILADELPHIA, 18TH CENTURY. HEIGHT: 2¾ IN., DIAMETER: 8⅜ IN. IN THE HENRY FRANCIS DU PONT WINTERTHUR MUSEUM

N. THE 19TH AND 20TH CENTURIES IN THE WEST

There is a fundamental difference between work done before the Industrial Revolution, the effect of which began to be felt in the ceramic industry before 1800, and that done subsequently. A student of the older wares, particularly those of the East, may find much of the later work difficult to accept because of its machine finish. When an object is made by hand it is never exactly the same as any other object; also the processes by which it has been formed and decorated are not disguised. Consider, for example, a Sung pot or a specimen of Japanese Tea Ceremony ware, whose so-called imperfections of finish by factory standards are an integral part of their beauty and character, or the glaze of a *Kuan* vase, which would lose its individuality if it possessed the smooth finish of a factory-made specimen. The technical precision of the 19th century, which made its products indistinguishable from one another, and the careful concealment of the means by which the end had been achieved, were both unprecedented and deleterious. Style and craftsmanship degenerated steadily in the factories and the situation was aggravated by the Great Exhibition of 1851 which encouraged manufacturers throughout Europe to vie with each other in producing wares which displayed virtuosity unhampered by questions of taste; for example, from as far afield as St. Petersburg, hitherto outside the mainstream of European development, there came some particularly hideous and colossal vases in a debased Neoclassical style—which, incidentally, were described by a contemporary writer as "second to few of the productions of Dresden and Sèvres for beauty of outline and perfection of finish."

It would, however, be unfair to blame only the factories for this degradation of taste; the citizens who bought their wares must bear some of the responsibility. Before the advent of mass communications in the 20th century, new fashions originated in the wealthiest stratum of society, which was usually the most cultivated, and filtered downward. An example of this process is the popularity of pottery figures in the outmoded Rococo style among the labouring classes in England in the late 18th and early 19th century. As a result of the political and economic effects of the Seven Years' War (1756–63), in combination with the beginning of the Industrial Revolution, the European *bourgeoisie* prospered and their wealth enabled them to become patrons and arbiters of taste. Having little taste and fewer traditions, they were primarily interested in the arts as a method of display or as a "status symbol," and thus they demanded an excess of intricate and expensive ornament. In the Far East the same process of degeneration began at this time, at least partly as a result of the large number of export orders received. This pernicious influence was kept at bay by the emperor Ch'ien-lung, who stigmatized the English as cultural barbarians, but became much more pronounced in the 19th century. Similar tendencies may be seen in Japanese ceramics after 1853, when many factories worked almost entirely for export to the West in styles demanded by their customers.

1. Britain.—*19th-Century Porcelain.*—The Neoclassical style, which had been popular during the middle years of the 18th century, gradually lost its earlier simplicity. In France the rise of Napoleon brought in its train the ostentatious Empire style, which was copied, for the most part, from the decorative art of imperial Rome and had some influence in England during the Regency period (1811–20). It is noticeable on the porcelain vases made at Worcester, Derby, Rockingham, and elsewhere. These were often decorated with well-painted topographical subjects which were no longer confined by frames but ran round the vase as a continuous landscape. Flower painting was often of excellent quality and was much influenced by the work of William Billingsley, a flower painter who worked at Derby toward the end of the 18th century and who later started a factory of his own at Nantgarw, Glamorgan. It seems likely that he received his soft-porcelain formula from Zachariah Boreman, a Chelsea workman who had become a landscape painter of note at Derby. His porcelain was, perhaps, the last survival of the 18th-century tradition and was much used by London decorating establishments for work in the style of Sèvres.

At Worcester a factory which had been established by Robert Chamberlain in 1786 produced porcelain decorated in a debased Japanese style. Because of its gaudy colour—iron red and underglaze blue coupled with lavish gilding—it is sometimes called the "thunder and lightning" pattern by collectors. Similar "Japan" patterns were being employed at Derby and at the Worcester Royal Porcelain Factory although much of the work of the latter was more restrained. Some of the best painting at the old factory at Worcester was executed by Thomas Baxter, who used marine shells as a subject, and by the figure painter James Pennington.

It has been said, unfairly, that Josiah Wedgwood (*q.v.*), by developing the factory system, was largely responsible for the degradation of the ceramic art; Wedgwood wares have usually been in good taste even if they have not always been particularly adventurous. A far more malign influence was that of John Rose of Coalport (Salop), who took over the virtually bankrupt Nantgarw factory in 1819. Rose admired the work of Sèvres and proceeded to imitate it, buying or borrowing specimens to copy and using such ground colours as the *rose Pompadour,* which became popular under the inaccurate name of *rose du Barry.* He was one of the first English exponents of the revived Rococo style, which appeared about 1830, and made much porcelain encrusted with applied flowers. His work has been erroneously regarded as a close copy of Sèvres. Rose is also said to have made some copies of Chelsea, notably of the "Goat and Bee" jugs, and of tureens in the form of vegetables, principally cabbages. Coalport flower painting, however, is very fine in quality and much in the style of Billingsley, who actually worked at the factory for some years, although it would be dangerous to attribute any surviving work to his hand.

Josiah Spode the Second invented bone china about 1800 and at first made good use of it. Some of his later wares became increasingly pretentious copies of French styles, with highly coloured grounds, lavish gilding, and an excess of applied ornament. The factory was taken over in 1833 by William Taylor Copeland, Jr., whose father had been in partnership with Spode and who with Minton and others did much to expand the industry.

The firm of Minton's was founded at Stoke-on-Trent in 1793 by Thomas Minton, a Caughley engraver said to have devised for Spode the Broseley Blue Dragon and Willow patterns which are still in use. Like Coalport, the factory was much occupied in copying the work of Sèvres. From 1848 to 1895 they employed a Frenchman, Joseph François Léon Arnoux, as art director and under his tutelage French artists were brought to England; for example, the sculptor Albert Carrier-Belleuse and also Marc Louis Solon, who was responsible for introducing *pâté-sur-pâté* decoration into England (*see* below).

The Derby tradition of fine painting was carried into the 19th century during which time the flower designs became somewhat overblown although landscapes remained on a high level. The sets of so-called *Campaña* vases (more properly *Campagna*), distantly derived from Italianate copies of the Greek *krater,* were often decorated with landscapes by the brothers Robert and John Brewer, and others. The Brewers were pupils of the topographical painter Paul Sandby whose exact and realistic style also influenced Boreman. A colourful character, "Quaker" Pegg, produced some meticulous botanical representations of flowers because his Puritan conscience forbade anything more decorative. Thomas Steele painted fruit and flowers, sometimes on porcelain plaques intended for framing—a singular misuse of porcelain copied from Paris and Vienna.

About 1840 the Parian body, an imitation of Sèvres biscuit porcelain, was introduced by Copeland and Garrett (formerly Spode) and a great many figures, some of them extremely large, were made in this medium. Most of them are either sentimental subjects or quasi-erotic nudes such as were popular in Victorian art. A specialist in the latter mode was Thomas Bott of Worcester whose nudes, painted in white enamel on a deep blue ground, were intended to imitate the earlier Limoges enamels on copper. Parian ware had some success in America where it was manufactured by Norton and Fenton.

BY COURTESY OF VICTORIA AND ALBERT MUSEUM AND W. T. COPELAND & SONS LTD.

FIGURE OF MUSIDORA, AFTER W. THEED, IN PARIAN PORCELAIN. COPELAND, STOKE-ON-TRENT, STAFFORDSHIRE; 1857. HEIGHT: 14½ IN. IN THE VICTORIA AND ALBERT MUSEUM

19th-Century Stoneware and Earthenware.—Side by side with these developments in the manufacture of porcelain, the production of earthenware and stoneware for the cheaper market continued on an ever-increasing scale. Lustre decoration which had been revived in the preceding century was used more frequently than before. A type of stoneware obviously inspired by Wedgwood's jasper ware was made at Castleford, in Yorkshire. "Ironstone" china, a type of opaque stoneware sometimes called "opaque porcelain," was introduced early in the 19th century. Its development is usually credited to Miles Mason, although the patent granted to Turners of Lane End, Staffordshire, in 1800 may have been the starting point. Pseudo-Chinese and "Japan" patterns were frequently used to decorate it.

By 1830 new underglaze colours had been pressed into service for transfer printing. These new colours were particularly used by Ridgway and Co. of Hanley, Staffordshire. Transfer-printed earthenware in blue, which became increasingly popular after 1810, was soon being produced in enormous quantities. It was much used by Spode, who often used American subjects for wares exported to the United States; these are now prized by collectors. Polychrome transfer printing, essayed tentatively at Liverpool during the 1760s, was also mastered.

Earthenware figures were made in large quantities in Staffordshire and elsewhere, the best being associated with Enoch Wood. They were intended as chimney ornaments, and the subjects range from bullbaiting to sentimental shepherdesses. Many of them are copied more or less directly from Derby porcelain figures, and they are a sad but accurate reflection of the times during which they were made.

The Great Exhibition completed the degeneration which had been started by the revival of the Rococo style. Technical progress allowed the manufacturers ever-increasing elaborations with which they bludgeoned the few remaining sensibilities of their customers. Past styles were indiscriminately and clumsily copied. Minton's made an earthenware decorated with coloured glazes which they miscalled *maiolica*. It was used not only for decorative wares but for other domestic articles—even umbrella stands—and for architectural

ENGLISH WARES OF THE 19TH CENTURY

(Left) Dish by William de Morgan, probably painted at Merton Abbey, 1882–88. Diameter: 14⅜ in.   (Right) Earthenware dish painted by Émile Lessore, about 1857. Wedgwood: Etruria, Staffordshire. Diameter: 15 in. In the Victoria and Albert Museum

purposes. At Minton's, too, Palissy's work was badly imitated and Charles Toft, one of the modelers, laboured to produce copies of the *Henri Deux* ware of Saint-Porchaire—surely the least rewarding of all such derivations.

The Paris exhibitions of 1867 and 1878 brought Japanese pottery and porcelain once more to the attention of European manufacturers, but it was not the superb porcelain of Arita which had had so much influence in the previous century. This time the Japanese exported cream-coloured earthenware with a closely crackled surface and lavish painting of poor quality, rightly judging that it would appeal to Western taste. It became extremely popular under the name of "Satsuma" and was copied avidly at Worcester and elsewhere. Gothic wares, distantly echoing some of the old Rhineland stonewares, were made by Meigh and Co. at Hanley, Staffordshire, and, as Geoffrey Bemrose has remarked in his admirable survey of 19th-century wares (see *Bibliography*, below), it is surprising that no enterprising firm thought of giving the world pottery designs in Japanese Gothic as had been done in furniture.

By 1860 a few people had become profoundly disturbed by the level to which popular taste had sunk. Among them was William Morris (*q.v.*), who founded a firm of interior decorators and manufacturers in 1861. One of his pupils, William de Morgan, started a pottery at Fulham (London) in 1888 and made dishes and tiles inspired by Persian, Hispano-Moresque, and Italian wares. De Morgan used brilliant blues and greens and a coppery red pigment. His designs are a great improvement on those of the factories, although they are still derivative.

After about 1860 Doultons of Lambeth (London) copied 18th-century brown stoneware, making small figures and repeating earlier designs. The incised decoration by Hannah Barlow is both pleasant and competent. From a Fulham pottery owned by the brothers Martin came grotesque and often amusing stoneware vases which were sometimes decorated with coloured slips.

20th Century.—In the early part of the 20th century Bernard Moore experimented with Chinese glazes, producing some successful *flambé* and *sang de boeuf* glazes on a stoneware body at his small factory in Stoke-on-Trent. He worked in association with William Burton of Pilkington pottery in Manchester, which also made experimental decorative ware of all kinds.

The fact that increasing attention was being paid to ceramics is shown by the opening of the Omega workshops in 1913 by the art critic Roger Fry. This promising venture failed because of lack of trade during World War I and closed in 1919.

The artist-potter has had an important influence on modern design from the time that Bernard Leach (1887–   ) established the St. Ives pottery in 1920. Leach spent many of his early years in the Far East and learned the art of making *raku* and stoneware

in Japan. He began working at a time when interest in early Chinese wares had greatly increased and much of his work is obviously influenced by the work of Tz' u Chou as well as that of Japan. It is, nevertheless, strongly individual. One of Leach's pupils, Michael Cardew, has done good work in stoneware, which he often decorates with vigorous patterns drawn with a pleasing economy of outline. William Staite Murray, at one time the head of the ceramic department of the Royal College of Art, has made some important and interesting stoneware and has influenced many younger potters. Excellent work has been done by continental potters working in England, among them Lucie Rie from Vienna and by Hans Coper. Amusing figures have come from Marion Morris who was trained in Budapest.

Development after World War II was much hindered by a heavy purchase tax on ceramics. Its relaxation in the early 1950s allowed the movement to resume its progress. By the 1960s many art schools included pottery making in their curriculum and students were rapidly increasing in numbers.

Design in factory-made wares has improved considerably. The work of Wedgwood, in particular, deserves mention. During the 19th century, Wedgwood wares, exemplifying the value of a sound tradition, had always been in better taste than that of their contemporaries. Bone china was made between 1812 and 1816, and manufacture was revived in 1878. A noted decorator of creamware in the mid-19th century was the French artist Émile Lessore. Jasper ware was unpopular for a short period during the first half of the 19th century, but it was revived with success in 1850, when some busts of contemporary celebrities in black basaltes were done by the sculptor C. F. Wyon, and has been made ever since. At the beginning of the 20th century the factory extended its already considerable business in the United States and a service of

STONEWARE COVERED BOWL BY BERNARD LEACH; ENGLISH, 1950. ST. IVES, CORNWALL. DIAMETER: 12 IN.

nearly 1,300 pieces was supplied to the White House during the presidency of Theodore Roosevelt (1901–09).

Between 1918 and 1939 Keith Murray and Eric Ravilious did excellent work in keeping Wedgwood design at a high level, and their work was continued by Victor Skellern, who became art director in 1935. In 1936 the factory moved to its present site at Barlaston, Staffordshire, when the historic site at Etruria, Staffordshire, was abandoned, and it is now one of the most modern in the world. As with most other firms, both the factory and the museum can be visited by the public by appointment.

A new development in decorative porcelain is to be seen in the designs of Dorothy Doughty for the Worcester Royal Porcelain Company in England, and in those of Edward Marshall Boehm at Trenton, N.J. Characteristic of this kind of work are the American birds of Dorothy Doughty issued in limited editions by the Worcester Company. These are especially remarkable for technical advances in preparing the article for firing, which allow the material to be treated with much greater freedom than hitherto. Porcelain becomes very soft when it reaches the point of vitrification but, using an elaborate series of props to support free-floating parts, the Worcester technicians having succeeded in firing designs which would have been completely impossible earlier. Associated with these models are exact reproductions of natural flowers which also excel in complexity anything which has been made in the past.

2. The European Continent.—In the 19th century Meissen and Sèvres continued to be the two principal factories and leaders of fashion, although at both places, as elsewhere, artistic standards declined considerably.

Meissen.—At the end of the 18th century Meissen was in grave financial difficulties and its situation was aggravated after Dresden was bombarded in 1813 in the course of the Napoleonic Wars. For some years afterward it struggled along producing wares in a version of the Empire style which is also reflected in the ornate and cumbersome lines of the Biedermeier period (*see* NINETEENTH-CENTURY ART).

Later, the revived Rococo style was adopted under the chief modeler Ernst August Leuteritz, and a large export trade with England was renewed. This was the period of the sentimental Dresden shepherdess, formerly much admired in England and the

BY COURTESY OF VEB STAATLICHE PORZELLAN-MANUFAKTUR, MEISSEN

HERCULES AND THE ERYMANTHEAN BOAR, PORCELAIN FROM MEISSEN, GERMANY; 1922. HEIGHT: ABOUT 16 IN.

United States, to the neglect of German figures made during the early 18th century. Heinrich Gottlob Kühn, who was appointed director in 1849, restored much of the factory's former prosperity, and it was moved from the old Schloss Albrechtsburg to the present site at Triebischtal in 1860. Productions during this period include large and ornate candelabra, overdecorated mirror frames, clock cases, and the like, as well as vases and tureens based on the old Rococo models.

From about 1870 styles altered somewhat and are afterward referred to as those of *die Neuzeit* ("the New Period"). Some of the figures and groups illustrating contemporary subjects throw an amusing sidelight on manners and customs of the time. Meissen celebrated its bicentenary in 1910 with a massive illustrated history of the factory by K. Berling (see *Bibliography*).

After World War I, advances were made under the directorate of Adolf Pfeiffer, and figure modeling worthy of the old tradition was done by Paul Scheurich, Max Esser, Paul Börner, and others. The early red stoneware was also revived. This renaissance was halted temporarily by World War II, but production had been resumed by 1950. In the early 1960s the wares which were being exported from the German Democratic Republic into western Europe were excellent in quality.

Sèvres.—In the early part of the 19th century the gaudy Empire style was current. As a result of Napoleon's campaign in Egypt and the newly aroused interest in that country, the style incorporated many Egyptian motifs which were somewhat incongruously translated into porcelain. Also many porcelain plaques with minutely detailed enamel painting in imitation of easel pictures were executed during the first decades of the century. In 1804 the new director, Alexandre Brongniart, discontinued the

manufacture of soft paste which was, however, revived under Ebelmen in the middle of the century. The later soft paste is decorated in the old styles, a turquoise-blue ground in conjunction with flower painting in reserved panels being especially common.

Technical improvements include the introduction, in about 1855, of *pâte-sur-pâte*, a process later popular in England and particularly at Minton's. The design was painted in white slip on to a surface of coloured, lightly-fired clay. Each coat of slip was allowed to dry, and another superimposed upon it, until the desired degree of relief had been attained. Finally it was scraped, smoothed, and incised by metal tools and the whole object glazed and fired.

The sculptor Albert Carrier-Belleuse was appointed art director in 1876 and, at about the same time, Oriental porcelain was freely imitated and experiments with *flambé* glazes undertaken. Théodore Deck, who influenced the work of Bernard Moore in England, became director in 1887. He introduced a variety of soft porcelain and promoted the use of stoneware for architectural purposes. Many new underglaze colours were also introduced. The sculptor Auguste Rodin was employed at Sèvres for a short time but does not seem to have left any enduring marks of his presence. Artistically speaking, Sèvres ware has not been very distinguished since the 18th century. The factory possesses an excellent museum of French ceramic art.

Other Continental Factories.—The Royal Porcelain works at Copenhagen has made a great deal of porcelain with simple patterns in underglaze blue derived from Chinese sources by way of Meissen. Molded fluted shapes are characteristic. The well-known biscuit figures after the sculptor Bertel Thorwaldsen (1768–1844) were not produced until 1867, and the factory later introduced a slightly amber-coloured biscuit which was used for figure modeling by A. Malinowski and others. Painting on a grayish-toned crackled glaze led to experiments with celadons since, technically, the two have much in common. Other glazes inspired by early Chinese work followed. The firm of Bing and Gröndahl was established in 1853, and excellent and imaginative work has been done there. In later years, too, such factories as that of Rörstrand in Sweden and Arabia Oy. in Finland have achieved a growing reputation for excellent design in the modern idiom.

A factory which has preserved its traditional reputation for fine porcelain is that of Nymphenburg, at Munich, now the Staatliche Porzellan-Manufaktur Nymphenburg. After many vicissitudes in the early part of the 19th century, it was taken over by Albert Bäuml, and under his able directorship the factory was put on a sound commercial basis. At the beginning of the 20th century, it began to use a wider range of underglaze colours with the aid of colour-chemists from Sèvres and, about the same time, reissued some of the old figures and services of Bustelli and Auliczek which are appropriately marked. Attention was soon turned to services of fine quality in the modern idiom, and excellent figures by Resl Lechner and others were produced. The former artist succeeded in adapting the 18th-century styles to 20th-century purposes in a manner which is an object lesson to those manufacturers who insist, even today, in adding the scrolls and flourishes of the Rococo.

In this brief discussion it is impossible to describe in detail the work of the artist-potters on the continent. They tend to be less conservative than their English counterparts and many new and interesting developments have occurred. The modern fashion for

BY COURTESY OF STAATLICHE PORZELLAN-MANUFAKTUR NYMPHENBURG

PORCELAIN FIGURE OF A YOUNG BERNESE WOMAN BY RESL LECHNER; CONTEMPORARY. NYMPHENBURG, GERMANY. HEIGHT: 6½ IN.

abstraction in art is particularly favourable to development, since the potter understood its principles long before the 20th-century artist came to it.					(G. Se.)

3. The United States.—Although Andrew Duché had succeeded in making porcelain as early as 1741, the first man to produce porcelain in any quantity was William Elias Tucker of Philadelphia. At first he was a decorator of whiteware, but started to manufacture both creamware and bone china about 1826. Judge Joseph Hemphill became a partner in 1832, and workmen were imported from Europe. Copies of Sèvres porcelain and other European wares were made about this time in a fine white porcelain body. The first factory at Bennington, Vt., was founded by Capt. John Norton in 1793. He made domestic wares, including salt-glazed stoneware. The factory was removed to Bennington Village by his son, Judge Lyman Norton, in 1831, and creamware and a brown-glazed ware were produced. In 1839 the factory became Norton and Fenton and later the manufacture of Parian ware began. This unglazed near-white soft porcelain named after Parian marble had been first made in England by Copeland and Garrett. John Harrison of Copeland's was employed and brought with him a number of molds. An ironstone china called graniteware or white granite was also made.

The East Liverpool, O., industry was established in 1838 by James Bennet, an English potter. The first products made there were "Rockingham" and yellow-glazed ware. In the decade following the Civil War, William Bloor, Isaac Watts Knowles, and others introduced the production of whiteware. By the last decade of the 19th century production had grown until it was the largest pottery-producing area in the world.

At about the same time Zanesville, O., was developing as a pottery centre. First production was salt-and-slip-glazed stoneware. At a later date much artware was produced in plants operated by Samuel Weller, J. B. Owens, George Young, and others. Zanesville artware established the basis for a sizable modern interest in collecting. Another important centre during the 19th century was located at Trenton, N.J., where the first factory was established in 1852. Connected with it was William Bloor, who had some responsibility for putting the industry on a successful footing in East Liverpool. Trenton, like East Liverpool, produced fine, skilfully decorated whiteware.

A close study of the technical side of manufacture was not undertaken until Edward Orton, Jr., succeeded in getting support for the establishment of a department of ceramics at Ohio State University in Columbus in 1894. The New York State College of Ceramics at Alfred, N.Y., was started soon afterward with Charles F. Binns as its director. Binns was a member of an English family connected with the manufacture of porcelain at Worcester and Derby during the 19th century, and had himself held a supervisory position at Worcester. Similar departments were added to other universities soon afterward, and Orton took the lead in forming the American Ceramic Society in 1898. In this way knowledge was put on a more scientific basis, and the trained ceramists who soon became available to the industry were responsible for many technical improvements. Nevertheless, the artistic direction of the factories did not reach a high standard.

Toward the end of the century it became fashionable for American women to study the art of painting on European pottery and the Cincinnati Pottery Club was founded in 1879 to promote sound pottery design. As a result of its work, the Rookwood Pottery was established in 1880 by Maria Longworth Storer. Rookwood wares show a distinct Japanese influence and have excellent red and yellowish-brown glazes.

The National Ceramic Association was organized in Chicago in 1891 for much the same purpose as the Cincinnati Pottery Club. The National League of Mineral Painters, founded by S. S. Frackelton of Milwaukee, Wis., encouraged the art of enameling on pottery. The American Ceramic Society came into existence in 1898.

The most important regular exhibition is organized and circulated biennially by the Everson Museum of Art. It was originated by its predecessor, the Syracuse Museum of Fine Arts, in 1932 as the Robineau Memorial Ceramic Exhibition and held annually, excepting the war years, until 1952. These exhibitions have been instrumental in making American pottery more widely known in Europe.

The pottery and porcelain of the United States now bears comparison with that of any other country, and standards are constantly improving. Technically, the U.S. is perhaps ahead of the rest of the world. The growing appreciation of good ceramic design has led national, state, and local governments to sponsor pottery making as an art. There is also a ceramic experimental station in the Tennessee Valley. Meanwhile the number of enthusiasts who collect early wares from other parts of the world is steadily increasing. Many important private collections are now in the United States and significant contributions have been made to scholarship.					(M. M. F.; G. Se.)

III. MODERN MANUFACTURING TECHNIQUES

1. Composition and Preparation of Clay.—Clay is formed by the gradual decomposition of feldspar, a crystalline mineral which is the chief constituent of igneous rocks, for example granite and gneiss. Feldspar contains alumina and silica in combination with another metallic oxide, usually that of potassium. Over very long periods it decomposes into true clay, or kaolinite (*q.v.*) as a result of mechanical disintegration together with the chemical action of carbonic acid and water. These conditions are most often found where rock has been kept from contact with atmospheric oxygen by overlying marshland.

Raw clay consists primarily of true clay particles and undecomposed feldspar mixed with other components of the igneous rocks from which it was derived, usually appreciable quantities of quartz and small quantities of mica, iron oxides, and other substances. The composition, and thus the behaviour and plasticity of clays from different sources, is therefore slightly different. The composition of a fine white clay, known as china clay or kaolin, is approximately as follows: silica 50%, alumina 33%, iron oxides 2%, magnesia 1%, alkali 2%, water 12%. At the start of the manufacturing process coarse clays are washed with water or "levigated," a process which separates the gross particles but not the particles of quartz and feldspar of a similar weight. Washing has no effect on finer clays.

Kaolin is the only type of clay which yields a white material when fired. Porcelain is made from kaolin mixed with fusible rocks, such as feldspar and silicas. When the mixture is raised to a high temperature it "vitrifies" or fuses to form a glasslike substance; if heated still further it becomes translucent. For example, porcelain composed of 50% clay, 50% feldspar will vitrify at 1,200° C, become translucent at 1,250° C, and will melt completely at 1,400° C. (Porcelain manufacture is discussed in detail in the article CHINAWARE.)

Earthenware is not vitrified; it is fired only to the temperature where point-to-point attachment of particles occurs and in consequence remains porous. Earthenware bodies are made by mixing plastic clays with flint and feldspar. In the mid-20th century in England ball clay, common in Devon, is included for its plasticity. It is grayish blue in colour, and becomes white when fired at a moderate temperature. The proportions of the constituents vary according to the purpose for which the body is required, but a typical example is as follows: blue ball clay 43%, china clay 24%, flint 23%, pegmatite 10%. The firing temperature of such a body would be in the region of 1,150° C; that of softer varieties of earthenware about 1,000° C.

Stoneware is fired to the point of vitrification, but not to that of translucency, although overfired specimens may be slightly translucent if they are also thin. Its constituents are similar to those of earthenware, a typical example consisting of 30% ball clay, 32% china clay, 15% flint, and 23% Cornish stone. Vitrifiable clays, which naturally contain fluxes such as alkali and lime, are used when they are available, but they often need additional silica without which they tend to collapse in the kiln. Stoneware bodies vitrify at between 1,000° and 1,200° C according to their composition.

The function of the flint is to "open" the material, preventing cracking and warping during firing. Being itself a refractory material it is unaffected by the temperature. It is added to the mixture in the form of a fine powder which is achieved by heating and then quenching the material when it becomes white and easily crushed. The feldspar, which acts as a flux (a substance which lowers the vitrification temperature), is usually added in the form of Cornish stone or pegmatite. Like the flint it must be very carefully ground. If the particle size is small, its fluxing property is increased while deformation during firing becomes increasingly likely. If, however, the particle size is too great, the porosity of the ware is increased. The raw material is therefore carefully sieved before being added to the mixture.

Before mechanization the clay was prepared for use by exposing it to the disintegrating action of sun, rain, and frost ("weathering"). It is now broken down, mixed, and made homogeneous by machines such as the de-airing pugmill. This blends the clay and also frees it from air pockets by shredding it into thin strips in a vacuum: in the past small pockets of air were often left in the clay and as they expanded when heated, they left cavities in the body after firing, causing the so-called "moons"—patches of greater translucency—to be seen in some early European porcelains. Another innovation is the use of magnetic devices to remove gross particles of iron from the clay. The body is finally diluted to the consistency of slip from which the excess water and gross impurities are removed by filter presses.

2. Shaping the Clay.—Earthenware bodies are usually extremely plastic and can be shaped by many methods. Porcelain and stoneware bodies are usually less plastic, and sometimes present difficulties which have to be overcome in various ways. The methods in use before the advent of mass production have been already discussed (see *Introduction*, above). Both throwing on the wheel and slip casting are still used, but not to the same extent as formerly. The jolly, introduced during the 18th century, is much used for making cups and circular plates. It is similar to the wheel in appearance except that the head consists of a plaster mold. As it revolves, the interior of the plate is shaped by pressing the clay against the head, while the exterior, including the footring, is shaped by a profile brought into contact with the clay. Machines which make both cups and plates automatically on this principle have now been introduced. Small parts, such as cup handles, are made separately by pressing clay into molds, and are subsequently attached to the vessel by "luting," the term used when clay slip is used as an adhesive. Extrusion, which consists of pressing the clay body through a shaped mouthpiece (like toothpaste from a tube) is used in brickmaking and for pipes, rods, and so forth. Pressing with steel dies is becoming more common; the body can be in a wet, semiwet, or dry state.

Lathe turning, which can only be used when the article has dried to "leather" hardness, is occasionally employed for finishing touches such as grooving and undercutting. Like most hand op-

erations, it was tending to disappear in the early 1960s except on the more ornamental and expensive objects.

3. Drying and Firing.—Newly shaped articles were formerly allowed to dry slowly in the atmosphere. This stage has now been speeded up by the introduction of automatic dryers, often in the form of hot, dry tunnels through which the ware passes on a conveyor belt. Infrared dryers have been particularly used in the United States. Another method, which has found some application in the making of porcelain insulators and similar equipment for the electrical industry, is to expose the clay to a rapidly alternating electric field ("high-frequency" drying).

Kilns, too, are no longer the coal- or wood-fired ovens which were once universal. In England the disappearance of such fuels has been accelerated by the institution of "smokeless zones." Both gas and electricity are now used as fuels and although coal is still employed, its disappearance is only a matter of time. Many improvements have been made in the design of "intermittent" kilns, in which the ware is stacked when cold and then raised to the desired temperature. However, they remain extravagant on fuel and are awkward to fill or empty if they have not had time to cool completely. For these reasons they are being replaced by "continuous" kilns, the most economical and successful of which is the tunnel kiln. The wares are conveyed slowly from a comparatively cool region at the entrance to the full heat in the centre. As they approach the exit after firing they cool gradually. These kilns were developed independently in Germany and the United States at the end of the 19th century, and by the mid-1960s had been installed by almost all of the larger factories. Normally they burn either coal- or producer-gas or oil, but coal is used occasionally.

In the U.S., natural gas is more plentiful than in Europe and is often employed as an alternative fuel, particularly during the summer as the price is lower than in the winter. Electricity is being increasingly used and has many advantages, although it is costly unless the factory is close to a source of hydroelectric power. It is often used for small kilns, and for tunnel kilns in which glaze and decoration are fired on. Wedgwood's factory at Barlaston, Staffordshire, is now operated entirely by electricity, and the traditional soot-laden atmosphere of Staffordshire is beginning to disappear.

Since the success of the firing operation depends upon the kiln temperature, exact methods of ascertaining and controlling it are essential. In early times this depended on the skill of the kilnmaster who removed a small plug from the kiln and judged the temperature by the colour of the glowing interior—the whiter the glow, the higher the temperature. Empirical methods of this kind have been replaced by devices such as the Seger cone invented by Seger of the Staatliche Porzellan-Manufaktur, Berlin. These are small three-sided cones made of ceramic materials which soften

MANUFACTURING TECHNIQUES

(Left) Throwing, or shaping, on a potter's wheel. This method, which has remained essentially unchanged for 5,000 years, is still used but not to the same extent as in the past. (Centre) Transfer printing. Pottery is often decorated by transfers taken from an engraved copper plate. (Right) Decoration. The application of small, molded ornament to the ledge of a plate is being done by hand

and bend over at known temperatures. Several cones, each made to bend or "squat" at a different degree of heat, are set side by side and watched through a plug in the kiln wall. As the intervals between the temperatures registered by the cones are arranged so that they are in the region of 20°–30° C the heat of the kiln can be gauged with considerable accuracy. In the U.S. Orton cones replace Seger cones. They are similar in principle but register a different set of temperatures.

4. Decoration.—*Glazes.*—Until the 20th century, glazes were similar in composition to lead glass or soda glass. The usual method of application was to grind the glass to a fine powder and to make a suspension of the particles in water. The fired object was then dipped into the mixture, and the fine particles covering the surface fused into an amorphous, glasslike layer during a second firing, which was at a lower temperature than that used to fire the body. The most common practice is to spray the object with glaze material, although the older method is still practised occasionally.

Some fusion usually occurs between glaze and body and it is therefore essential that both should shrink by the same proportion and at the same rate on cooling. If there is a discrepancy, the glaze will either develop a network of fine cracks, or will peel off altogether. This "crazing" of the glaze sometimes develops at the time of manufacture, but sometimes many weeks afterward. It has been used decoratively by the Chinese.

The disadvantage of lead glazes is that very poisonous lead compounds are evolved during firing. (After firing such glazes are, of course, quite harmless.) Safe ways of handling this substance have been developed, but leadless glazes, the first of which was developed in England about 1820, are now the more frequently used in commercial production.

Fluxes are added to glazes to lower the melting point, since it is essential that this should not approach or exceed the firing temperature of the body.

Matt and semiopaque glazes are achieved by using materials— for example, certain silicates—which tend to crystallize. These can be very decorative. The substance first used to opacify glaze was stannic oxide, which yields a completely opaque, glossy white glaze. This process, known as tin enameling, has had great influence on the development of ceramic art. Bone ash (calcium phosphate) also acts in the same way when added to glaze material and, in modern times, zirconium oxide and antimony oxide have been used for this purpose.

Patterns.—Rubber stamps, inked with ceramic colours, are used to apply simple decoration and trademarks. Transfers from copper plates, introduced during the 18th century, are still in common use, as are lithographic and other processes, for example silk-screen printing, which consists of rubbing the colour through a patterned screen of textile material. Methods of decorating by hand differ little from those of earlier times but they are rarely practised because the high cost of labour makes them expensive and skilled workmen are now almost unprocurable. For the most part, uninformed public taste is satisfied by monotonous mechanical methods of decoration; indeed hand-painted wares are sometimes rejected as incompetent because the result is less precise than mechanical decoration.

5. Industrial Uses.—In the 20th century ceramics, especially stoneware and porcelain, have become much more widely used in industry. The electrical industry, in particular, is dependent on the porcelain factories for supplies of equipment. Porcelain insulators, for example, are used in domestic power plugs, transformers, and overhead lines. The fact that ceramics can withstand an intense degree of heat has led to experiments with mixtures of metallic and ceramic substances in certain parts of gas turbines and rocket motors. Similar mixtures have been applied to metal components as a protective layer against the corrosive effect of gases at high temperatures. Developments in this particular field are undoubtedly in their infancy.

See also references under "Pottery and Porcelain" in the Index.

BIBLIOGRAPHY.—*General:* E. Hannover, *Pottery and Porcelain*, 3 vol. (1925); W. B. Honey, *European Ceramic Art*, 2 vol. (1949–51), *The Art of the Potter* (1955); K. Clark, *Practical Pottery and Ceramics* (1964); L. Danckert, *Handbuch des europäischen Porzellans* (1954), B. H. Leach, *A Potter's Book*, 2nd ed. (1940); G. Savage, *Porcelain through the Ages* (1963), *Pottery through the Ages* (1963); E. J. Bourry, *Treatise on Ceramic Industries* (1920); W. Chaffers, *Marks and Monograms on Pottery and Porcelain* (various editions from 1876 onward). Articles on various aspects of the subject are contained in the published transactions of a number of societies, principally the following: *Transactions of the British Ceramic Society, Bulletin of the American Ceramic Society, Transactions of the English Ceramic Circle, Transactions of the Oriental Ceramic Society;* A. Lane, *Guide to the Collection of Tiles* (Victoria and Albert Museum) 2nd ed. (1960).

Scientific Analysis: H. Eccles and B. Rackham, *Analysed Specimens of English Porcelain*, HMSO (1922); *Far Eastern Bulletin*, vol. v, no. 3 (1953); A. L. Hetherington, *Chinese Ceramic Glazes* (1937); J. King, "Lead in Glass and Glaze," *Museums Journal*, vol. lvi, no. 12 (1957); J. A. Radley and J. Grant, *Fluorescence Analysis in Ultra-violet Light* (1935); J. J. Rorimer, *Ultra-violet Rays and Their Use in the Examination of Works of Art* (1931); G. Savage, *18th-Century English Porcelain* (1952).

Anatolia, Mesopotamia and Egypt: J. Mellaart, "A Neolithic City in Turkey," *Scientific American* (April 1964); H. Frankfort, *Art and Architecture of the Ancient Orient* (1954); W. Andrae, *Coloured Ceramics from Assur* (1925); H. Wallis, *Egyptian Ceramic Art* (1900); W. S. Smith, *The Art and Architecture of Ancient Egypt* (1958).

The Aegean, Greece and Italy: H. B. Walters, *History of Ancient Pottery*, 2 vol. (1905); C. Seltman, *Attic Vase-Painting* (1933); V. R. d'A. Desborough, *Protogeometric Pottery* (1952); G. M. A. Richter, *A Handbook of Greek Art*, 2nd ed. (1960), *The Craft of Athenian Pottery* (1923), *Attic Red-figured Vases: a survey*, 2nd ed. (1958); A. Lane, *Greek Pottery* (1948); R. M. Cook, *Greek Painted Pottery* (1960); T. B. L. Webster, *Greek Terracottas* (1950); P. A. Arias, M. Hirmer, and B. B. Shefton, *History of Greek Vase Painting* (1962); T. Schumann, "Oberflachenverzierung in der antiken Topferkunst," *Berichte der deutschen Ceramischen Gesellschaft*, Bd. 23, Heft 11 (1942); R. J. Charleston, *Roman Pottery* (1955); G. Dennis, *Cities and Cemeteries of Etruria*, rev. ed., 2 vol. (1848); G. M. A. Richter, *Ancient Italy* (1955); J. D. Beazley, *Etruscan Vase Painting* (1947).

China: Books in European Languages: B. Gray, *Early Chinese Pottery and Porcelain* (1953); A. L. Hetherington, *Early Ceramic Wares of China* (1922), *Chinese Ceramic Glazes*, 2nd ed. (1948); R. L. Hobson, *Catalogue of the George Eumorfopoulos Collection* (1929–30), *Chinese Pottery and Porcelain* (1915), *The Wares of the Ming Dynasty* (1923), *The Later Ceramic Wares of China* (1925), *Handbook of the Pottery and Porcelain of the Far East in the British Museum*, 3rd ed. (1948), *A Catalogue of Chinese Pottery and Porcelain in the Collection of Sir Percival David* (1934), with A. L. Hetherington, *The Art of the Chinese Potter* (1924); B. Rackham and W. King, *Chinese Ceramics in Private Collections* (1931); W. B. Honey, *The Ceramic Art of China and Other Countries of the Far East* (1945), *Guide to Later Chinese Porcelain: K'ang Hsi, Yung Chêng, and Ch'ien Lung*, Victoria and Albert Museum (1927); S. Jenyns, *Later Chinese Porcelain* (1951), *Ming Pottery and Porcelain* (1953); E. Zimmermann, *Chinesisches Porzellan*, 2nd ed. (1923); Ching-ting Wu, *Prehistoric Pottery in China* (1938); Fujio Koyama and J. Figgess, *Two Thousand Years of Oriental Ceramics* (1961). *Chinese Sources Easily Available:* Chu Yen, *T'ao Shuo* (1774), Eng. trans. *Description of Chinese Pottery and Porcelain* by S. W. Bushell (1910); Lan Pu, *Ching-tê-Chên T'ao-Lu* (1815), Eng. trans. *The Potteries of China* by G. R. Sayer (1951); Liu Ch'ên, *T'ao Ya* (1906), Eng. trans. *Pottery Refinements* by G. R. Sayer (1959). *Chinese Marks:* W. Burton and R. L. Hobson, *Handbook of Marks on Pottery and Porcelain* (1928). Most books on Chinese wares have a short list of the more important marks. *Chinese Symbolism:* W. F. Mayers, *Chinese Reader's Manual* (1874); A. de C. Sowerby, "The Flora of Chinese Art," *China J.* (June 1937); E. T. C. Werner, *Myths and Legends of China* (1924); W. P. Yetts, "Symbolism in Chinese Art," *Trans. China Soc.* (London) (1912), "Notes on Flower Symbolism in China," *J. R. Asiat. Soc.* (January 1941).

Korea: G. St. G. M. Gompertz, *Korean Celadon* (1963), with Chewon Kim, *The Ceramic Art of Korea* (1961); W. B. Honey, *Corean Pottery* (1948), *Ceramic Art of China and Other Countries of the Far East* (1945); Prince Yi Household Museum at Seoul, *Album of Photographs: Pottery* (1932); Victoria and Albert Museum, *Catalogue of the Le Blond Collection of Korean Pottery* by B. Rackham (1918), *A Picture Book of Corean Pottery* (1932); Fujio Koyama and J. Figgess, *Two Thousand Years of Oriental Ceramics* (1961).

Japan: M. J. Ballot, *La céramique Japonaise* (1926); J. Harada, *English Catalogue of Treasures in the Imperial Repository Shosoin* (1932); R. L. Hobson, *Handbook of the Pottery and Porcelain of the Far East in the British Museum*, 3rd ed. (1948); W. B. Honey, *The Ceramic Art of China and Other Countries of the Far East* (1945); B. Leach, *A Potter's Book* (1940); T. Mitsuoka, *Ceramic Art of Japan* (1949); *Pageant of Japanese Art*, vol. iv, Tokyo National Museum (1952); Oriental Ceramic Society, *Japanese Porcelain* (Exhibition Catalogue) (1956); Fujio Koyama and J. Figgess, *Two Thousand Years of Oriental Ceramics* (1961).

Thailand and Annam: W. B. Honey, *Ceramic Art of China and Other Countries of the Far East* (1945); Fujio Koyama and J. Figgess, *Two Thousand Years of Oriental Ceramics* (1961). This apart, the literature of the subject is mostly in the form of magazine articles and papers; these are listed by Honey in the work cited above.

Islamic Pottery: M. S. Dimand, *A Handbook of Muhammadan Art,* 3rd ed. (1958); R. L. Hobson, *A Guide to the Islamic Pottery of the Near East in the British Museum* (1932); A. Lane, "The Early Sgraffito Ware of the Near East," "Sung Wares and the Saljuq Pottery of Persia," *Transactions of the Oriental Ceramic Society* (1937–38) and (1946–47), *Early Islamic Pottery,* 4th imp. rev. (1958), *Later Islamic Pottery* (1957), *Islamic Pottery from the 9th to the 14th Centuries in the Collection of Sir Eldred Hitchcock* (1956); A. U. Pope and P. Ackerman (eds.), *A Survey of Persian Art,* vols. ii and v (1938–39); G. Reitlinger, "Sultanabad," *Trans. O.C.S.* (1944–45); Victoria and Albert Museum, *Turkish Pottery* (1955).

European Pottery to the End of the 18th Century: Byzantium: D. T. Rice, *Byzantine Art* (1954). *Spain:* A. W. Frothingham, *Catalogue of Hispano-Moresque Pottery in the Collection of the Hispanic Society of America* (1936), *Talavera Pottery, with a Catalogue of the Collection of the Hispanic Society of America* (1944), *Lustreware of Spain* (1951); A. Van der Put, *Hispano-Moresque Ware of the 15th Century,* 2 vol. (1904); Victoria and Albert Museum, *Hispano-Moresque Pottery* (1957). *Italy:* J. Chompret, *Répertoire de la Majolica Italienne* (1949); B. Rackham, *Guide to Italian Maiolica* (Victoria and Albert Museum) (1933), *Catalogue of Italian Maiolica* (Victoria and Albert Museum), 2 vol. (1940), *Italian Maiolica* (1952). *France and Belgium:* C. Damiron, *La Faïence Artistique de Moustiers* (1919), *La Faïence de Lyon* (1926); J. Giacometti, *French Faïence* (1963); H. Haug, *Les Faïences et Porcelaines de Strasbourg* (1922); A. Lane, *French Faïence* (1948); F. Poncetton and G. Salles, *Les Poteries Françaises* (1929). *Germany and Austria:* O. von Falke, *Das Rheinische Steinzeug* (1908); F. H. Hofmann, *Geschichte der Bayreuther Fayencefabrik* (1928); K. Kötschau, *Rheinisches Steinzeug* (1924); A. Meyer, *Böhmisches Porzellan und Steingut* (1927); G. E. Pazaurek, *Deutsche Fayence- und Porzellan-Hausmaler* (1925), *Steingut: Formgebung und Geschichte* (1927); A. Klein, *Rheinisches Steinzeug des 15. bis 18. Jahrhunderts* (n. d.; c. 1963). The most comprehensive work is that of O. Riesebieter, *Die Deutschen Fayencen des 17. und 18. Jahrhunderts* (1921). Little has been published in English but mention should be made of E. Hannover, *Pottery and Porcelain,* 3 vol. (1925); G. Savage, *Pottery through the Ages* (1963); and W. B. Honey, *European Ceramic Art from the End of the Middle Ages to about 1815,* 2 vol. (1949–51). *The Netherlands:* H. Harvard, *La Céramique Hollandaise* (1909); F. W. Hudig, *Delfter Fayence* (1929); C. H. De Jonge, *Oud-Nederlandsche Majolika en Delftsch Aardewerke* (1947); E. Neurdenberg, *Old Dutch Pottery and Tiles,* Eng. trans. by B. Rackham (1923); B. Rackham, *Early Netherlands Maiolica* (1926). *Britain:* H. Barnard, *Chats on Wedgwood Ware* (1925); F. H. Garner, *English Delftware* (1948); J. E. and E. Hodgkin, *Examples of English Pottery Named, Dated, and Inscribed* (1891); W. B. Honey, *English Pottery and Porcelain* (1933), *Wedgwood Ware* (1948); L. Jewitt, *The Ceramic Art of Great Britain* (1878); E. M. Nance, *The Pottery and Porcelain of Swansea and Nantgarw* (1942); W. J. Pountney, *The Old Bristol Potteries* (1920); B. Rackham, *Medieval English Pottery* (1948), *Early Staffordshire Pottery* (1951), *Catalogue of the Schreiber Collection of English Earthenware in the Victoria and Albert Museum* (1930), with H. Read, *English Pottery* (1924); G. W. Rhead, *The Earthenware Collector* (1920); G. B. Hughes, *English and Scottish Earthenware* (1961); J. A. Fleming, *Scottish Pottery* (1963). *Scandinavia:* K. Huseler, *Geschichte der Schleswig-Holsteinischen Fayencen im 18. Jahrhundert* (1919), *Die Kieler Fayence-Manufakturen* (1923).

European Porcelain to the End of the 18th Century: General: L. Danckert, *Handbuch des europäischen Porzellans* (1954); E. Hannover, *Pottery and Porcelain,* 3 vol. (1925); W. B. Honey, *European Ceramic Art from the End of the Middle Ages to about 1815,* 2 vol. (1949–51); G. Savage, *Porcelain through the Ages* (1955); R. Schmidt, *Das Porzellan als Kunstwerk und Kulturspiegel* (1925). *France:* E. Bourgeois, *Le Biscuit de Sèvres au XVIIIe Siècle* (1909); Comte X. de Chavagnac and Marquis A. de Grollier, *Histoire de Manufactures Françaises de Porcellaine* (1906); W. B. Honey, *French Porcelain of the 18th Century* (1950); G. Savage, *Seventeenth and Eighteenth Century French Porcelain* (1960); P. Verlet, S. Grandjean and M. Brunet, *La Porcelaine de Sèvres* (1953). *Germany and Austria:* F. H. Hoffman, *Das Porzellan der Europäischen Manufakturen im 18. Jahrhundert* (1932); W. B. Honey, *Dresden China* (1947), *German Porcelain* (1947); G. E. Pazaurek, *Deutsche Fayence- und Porzellan-Hausmaler* (1925); Max Sauerlandt, *Deutsche Porzellanfiguren des 18. Jahrhunderts* (1923); G. Savage, *18th-century German Porcelain* (1958). *Britain:* W. B. Honey, *Old English Porcelain* (1948); W. King, *English Porcelain Figures of the 18th Century* (1925); B. Rackham, *Catalogue of the Schreiber Collection of English Porcelain, Earthenware, Enamels, and Glass in the Victoria and Albert Museum* (1930); G. Savage, *18th-century English Porcelain* (1952); B. Watney, *Longton Hall Porcelain* (1957); F. A. Barrett, *Worcester Porcelain* (1953); J. L. Dixon, *English Porcelain of the 18th century* (1952). *Other Countries:* S. Ducret, *Zürcher Porzellan des 18. Jahrhunderts* (1944); E. L. Soil de Moriame and L. Delplace de Formanoir, *Les Porcelaines de Tournay* (1937); G. Lukomsky, *Russisches Porzellan: 1744–1923* (1924); A. Lane, *Italian Porcelain* (1954); G. Morazzoni, *Le Porcellane Italiane* (1935); B. Rackham, *Spanish Art* (1927).

American Indian Pottery: G. H. S. Bushnell and A. Digby, *Ancient American Pottery* (1955); H. Ubbelohde-Doering, *The Art of Ancient Peru* (1952); G. C. Vaillant, *The Aztecs of Mexico* (1941). *Colonial America:* J. Ramsay, *American Potters and Pottery* (1939); E. A. Barber, *Tulip Ware of Pennsylvania-German Potters* (1903); W. E. Cox, *Book of Pottery and Porcelain,* vol. ii (1947).

The 19th and 20th Centuries in the West: W. B. Honey, *The Art of the Potter* (1955); B. H. Leach, *A Potter's Book,* 2nd ed. (1940); E. Rosenthal, *Pottery and Ceramics* (1949); G. Bemrose, *Nineteenth-century English Pottery and Porcelain* (1952); M. Rose, *Artist-Potters in England* (1955); W. Mankowitz and R. G. Haggar, *Concise Encyclopedia of English Pottery and Porcelain* (1957); A. Levy (ed.), *L'Art Décoratif Française* (1918–25); G. Migeon, *Préface à l'Exposition de l'Oeuvre Céramique du Potier E. Chaplet* (1910); K. Berling, *Festschrift der Königlichen Sächsischen Porzellanmanufaktur Meissen, 1710–1910* (1910), Eng. trans., *Publication to commemorate the 20th Jubilee of the oldest European Porcelain factory* (1910); R. Borrmann, *Moderne Keramik* (1902); O. Pelka, *Keramik de Neuzeit* (1924); H. Meyer, *Böhmisches Porzellan und Steingut* (1927); E. Poche, *Bohemian Porcelain* (1957); W. Rochowansky, *Wiener Keramik* (1923); H. E. van Gelder, "Pottenbakkerskunst" *De Toegepaste Kunsten in Nederland,* no. xvi (1927); A. Hayden, *Chats on Royal Copenhagen Porcelain* (1918); E. Wettergren, *The Modern Decorative Arts of Sweden* (1928); J. Ramsay, *American Potters and Pottery* (1939); W. E. Cox, *Book of Pottery and Porcelain,* vol. ii (1947); G. Savage and D. Doughty, *The American Birds of Dorothy Doughty* (1963).

Manufacturing Techniques: E. Bourry, *Treatise on Ceramic Industries* (1911); E. Rosenthal, *Pottery and Ceramics* (1949). (G. SE.)

POTTHAST, AUGUST (1824–1898), German historian who compiled the monumental *Bibliotheca historica medii aevi* (1862, 1868; new enlarged edition, 1895–96), a guide to the sources of European history in the Middle Ages. The work, in the form of an index, gives particulars of practically all the historical writers of Europe and their work between 375 and 1500. Potthast was born at Höxter on Aug. 13, 1824. He assisted G. H. Pertz (*q.v.*), the editor of the *Monumenta Germaniae historica,* and edited the *Regesta pontificum romanorum, 1198–1304* (1874–75). From 1874 to 1894 he was librarian of the German *Reichstag.* He died on Feb. 13, 1898, at Leobschütz.

POTTO, the name for small primates of forested areas of equatorial Africa. In common with the lorises, which they resemble, pottos are slow-moving tree dwellers that forage about at night in search of fruit, insects, and any small animals they can creep up on. Their deliberate pace is quickened only in emergencies. Pottos have large, staring eyes, stublike second fingers and second toes, and a peculiar ridge of spines formed of extensions of the backbone. The common pottos (*Perodicticus*), squirrel sized, with round faces, grizzled brownish fur, and a furry tail, are reputed to have the strongest hand grip of any animal their size. The smaller Calabar or golden pottos, also called angwantibos (*Arctocebus*), have stubby tails concealed in fur and smaller eyes closer set on a foxy face. *See* PRIMATES: *Lemurs.*

POTTSTOWN, a borough of Montgomery County, Pa., U.S., on the Schuylkill River, about 38 mi. NW of Philadelphia, is the trading centre for a prosperous farm, dairy, and industrial region. Hill School, a college-preparatory school for boys, is located there. The borough has a council-manager form of government, in effect since 1945. Steel fabricators and the manufacture of tires, tubes, and related products are the largest industries. Other manufactures include universal joints and axles, pipe fittings, gray iron castings, boilers, dresses and shirts, dairy and bakery products, paper boxes, and clay and concrete pipes.

In the immediate area of Pottstown iron was manufactured by 1717. The first cold-blast iron furnace in America was erected by Thomas Potts and Thomas Rutter in 1720, and the Coventry forge produced the first commercial steel in Pennsylvania in 1732. The prosperity of Pottstown was based mainly on the production of iron and steel until about 1918, when fabrication replaced the reduction of ores.

John Potts, ironmaster and merchant, laid out the town in 1752 under the name of Pottsgrove. Arthur St. Clair was a resident of Pottsgrove when he was elected president of the Continental Congress. In 1815 the town was incorporated as the borough of Pottstown. For comparative population figures *see* table in PENNSYLVANIA: *Population.* (L. A. GR.)

POTTSVILLE, a city of Pennsylvania, U.S., on the Schuylkill river, 93 mi. N.W. of Philadelphia; the seat of Schuylkill county. It is a picturesque town at the gap of the Schuylkill river through Sharp mountain and has many narrow and extremely steep streets. The shopping centre is extensive and attractive, serving a retail-trade area with a population of more than 100,000. Pottsville is located on the southern edge of the Pennsylvania anthracite coal region, and after the opening of the Schuylkill canal in 1824 the prosperity of the city was closely related to anthracite prosperity. The steady decline of the anthracite industry in the mid-20th century brought problems of chronic unemployment and of loss in population. (For comparative population figures *see* table in PENNSYLVANIA: *Population*.) The Greater Pottsville Industrial Development corporation experienced some success in bringing new industries to the area. Besides extensive mining industries and railroad shops, manufactures produce aluminum extrusions, plastics, dresses and shirts, an assortment of steel products, shoes, beer, concrete products and paper boxes.

Permanent settlers came to the site of Pottsville about 1795 and soon established a furnace for the production of raw iron. John Pott acquired and expanded the local iron furnace and set the stage for an important iron and steel industry that lasted until the 1920s. He laid out the town of Pottsville in 1816. It was incorporated as a borough in 1828, became the county seat in 1851 and was chartered as a third-class city in 1911. In the 1860s and 1870s Pottsville was a rallying point of the Molly Maguires (*q.v.*).

(L. A. GR.)

POUGHKEEPSIE, a city of New York, U.S., on the east bank of the Hudson River, midway between New York City and Albany, the seat of Dutchess County, a rich dairy-farming area. The city is the shopping centre of the mid-Hudson Valley and contains many diversified industries. Among the largest are an electronic research and assembly centre for computers, a dairy machine company, and a printing and lithography company. Other manufactures include clothing, chemicals, cough drops, and ball bearings. Among the nationalities represented in the city are Italians, Poles, Irish, Germans, and Dutch. Pop. (1970) 32,029. For comparative population figures *see* table in NEW YORK: *Population*.

The name Poughkeepsie was derived from Indian words meaning "the reed-covered lodge by the little water place." The town was settled by the Dutch in 1687 and temporarily served as the capital of New York State in 1778. A thriving river port in the early 19th century, from which ships carried grain to New York, it suffered a decline after the completion of the Erie Canal and turned to industry and commerce. Poughkeepsie was incorporated as a city in 1854 and in 1952 adopted the council-manager plan.

Vassar College was founded there in 1861 as a private college of liberal arts for women. Its founder, Matthew Vassar, conceived the idea "to build and endow a college for young women which shall be to them what Yale and Harvard are to young men." The college was incorporated as Vassar Female College, but under the influence of the intrepid feminist Sarah J. Hale, editor of *Godey's Ladies Book*, "Female" was deleted in 1867. In the fall term of 1970 Vassar became coeducational, admitting its first freshman class of both men and women. From 1925 Vassar has conducted a Summer Institute of Family and Community Living for parents and their children, social workers, and teachers. Also in Poughkeepsie is the Dutchess Community College, a junior college affiliated with State University of New York, opened in 1958, and Marist College, founded in 1946. Extensive medical facilities are offered at Vassar and at the Hudson River State Hospital for mental illness.

The Hudson River near Poughkeepsie for many years was the scene of the annual Poughkeepsie regatta of the Intercollegiate Rowing Association, one of the most famous rowing events in the world. Established in 1895, it was held annually until 1949 except for 1898 when it was at Saratoga Lake and for 1917–19, 1933, and 1942–46, when no competition was held. In 1950 the regatta was moved from Poughkeepsie to Marietta, O., and later to Onondaga Lake, Syracuse, N.Y. (*see* ROWING). (E. M. A.; X.)

POULENC, FRANCIS (1899–1963), French composer whose work illustrates a sophisticated trend in French music after World War I, was born in Paris on Jan. 7, 1899. He studied the piano with Ricardo Viñes and in 1917 produced *Rapsodie nègre,* followed in 1918 by *Trois Mouvements Perpétuels* and the *Sonata* for piano duet, and in 1919 by songs on poems by Guillaume Apollinaire and Jean Cocteau. In 1920 he was one of the group known as "Les Six," sponsored by Cocteau and Erik Satie and including, besides Poulenc, Georges Auric, Darius Milhaud, Arthur Honegger, Germaine Tailleferre, and Louis Durey. (The name of the group was taken from an article, "The Five Russians, the Six Frenchmen, and Satie," by the critic Henri Collet, comparing the French composers with the Russians led by M. A. Balakirev, though they were not united by aesthetic affinities.)

From 1921 to 1924 Poulenc studied composition under Charles Koechlin. His ballet *Les Biches* was produced by Sergei Diaghilev in 1924. Settings of poems by Ronsard and *Chansons gaillardes* (1926) began a series of song cycles, chiefly on poems by Apollinaire and Paul Éluard. In 1928, at the suggestion of Wanda Landowska, he wrote *Concert champêtre* for harpsichord and orchestra. In the following year his *Aubade,* a choreographic concerto for dancer, piano, and chamber orchestra, was performed. In 1934 he gave the first of his joint recitals with the singer Pierre Bernac, with whom he later toured Europe and the United States. *Litanies à la Vierge Noire de Rocomadour* (1936), the first of his religious choral works, was followed by the Mass (1937). During World War II he wrote the cantata *Figure humaine* on poems by Éluard, inspired by the spirit of the resistance movement; it was first performed in London in 1945. In 1947 his comic opera *Les Mamelles de Tirésias,* on a farce by Apollinaire, was produced at the Paris Opéra-Comique. In 1951 he wrote *Stabat Mater,* and between 1953 and 1956 the opera *Dialogues des Carmélites* on a libretto by Georges Bernanos (La Scala, Milan, 1957). His one-act opera, *Voix humaine,* on the monodrama by Cocteau, was produced at the Opéra-Comique in 1959. Poulenc died in Paris on Jan. 30, 1963.

Predominantly lyrical and traditional in harmony, Poulenc's music revived the ironic spirit of Emmanuel Chabrier and also the elegance of the French 18th-century composers. His religious works are urbane. His songs, which number over 100, show his melodic sense and his gifts for parody and for musical prosody.

See F. Poulenc, *Entretiens avec Claude Rostand* (1954); H. Hell, *Francis Poulenc,* Eng. trans. by E. Lockspeiser (1959). (E. LR.)

POULTRY AND POULTRY FARMING. Few agricultural enterprises are as widespread as poultry farming for the production of meat and eggs for table use, and in a number of countries, including the United States, Canada, the United Kingdom, Denmark, and Australia, the poultry industry is one of the leading branches of agriculture. Within each country egg and chicken production is by far the most important aspect of the industry.

In some areas each farmer raises a few chickens that live on table scraps and what food they can find about the house and neighbourhood; such eggs and live birds are usually consumed by the farmer and his family or sold on the local market. At the other extreme are large commercial operations, raising thousands of birds and employing the most modern of food marketing and distribution systems.

Although the greater part of the world's poultry output is based on the domestic chicken, in some countries—the United States and the United Kingdom, for example—turkeys have substantial importance. There are also locally important industries of ducks and geese. Turkeys and geese are raised only for their meat; ducks are raised sometimes for eggs, sometimes for meat. Formerly it could be said that egg and meat production mostly went together, the meat coming from hens that had completed their life as layers or from surplus male birds specially fattened. This is still true in many less developed countries and in the remoter areas of more advanced ones. After about 1950, however, especially in North America and Western Europe, egg and meat production evolved as two separate, virtually unconnected industries. The techniques there developed have been transplanted to many other countries, so that nuclei of poultry production showing at least some elements of advanced systems are to be found scattered in many parts of the world.

POULTRY AND POULTRY FARMING

This article discusses the different types of bird, their rearing and utilization, as follows:

I. DOMESTIC FOWL AND THEIR USES

Breeds of the domestic fowl are descended from the jungle fowl (*Gallus gallus,* see FOWL) of India and neighbouring countries. It has been domesticated for not less than 4,000 years. King Solomon's table was supplied with "fatted fowl"; but these may have been geese (I Kings 4:22, 23). The Greeks and Romans were poultry farmers and raised distinctive breeds of their own. Modern breeds are numerous, but only a few are kept pure for commerce. Most pure breeds and varieties are kept by fanciers solely for their decorative appearance and for competitive exhibition. The breeds that are of commercial value for either egg production or meat production—rarely for both—are maintained in a pure state by a few breeders only in each country. In some places they are used commercially as pure stock; but they also provide the basic genetic material for the "hybrids" that after the mid-1950s became widely used for commercial production.

The breeds known today can be divided into five classes based on their origin: English, Asiatic, American, Mediterranean, and Continental European. The breeds of Mediterranean origin are used in the makeup of a number of commercial laying hybrids, because of their superior production of eggs and their low food consumption, besides the characteristics of nonbroodiness (*i.e.,* disinclination to incubate their eggs) and small body size. (They are thus, however, not suitable for meat production.)

English and American breeds are of the heavy variety with good fleshing qualities. Some are also good egg producers. Asiatic and Continental European classes include both light and heavy breeds which are not generally economic, although many are decorative.

No brief summary can indicate the place of the various breeds in the highly diversified world poultry industry. In many undeveloped agricultural areas the fowls kept may belong to no definite breed, being the product of casual mating. In other areas poultry industries may be built on one or more well-known breeds (listed below). However, in North America and Western Europe, the bulk of the poultry industry has been built up on hybrid birds created by geneticists to meet specific needs. The basic genetic characters—such as body size, colour of egg, rate of growth, etc.—are drawn from parents belonging to different breeds and are combined as required. These methods produce large numbers of uniform offspring. In many countries, hybrids are marketed under trade names that give no indication of the breeds contributing to their makeup. An illustration of the development of these techniques is the fact that, for the production of meat poultry, male parents are bred to combine one set of characteristics and female parents to provide the others, often by different firms.

All birds within a given breed have the same shape, while varieties within a breed differ in plumage, colour, or shape of comb. The majority of the so-called fancy breeds are miniatures, *i.e.,* bantams. Although there are well over 100 breeds and varieties of fowls only a few are of economic importance; the main ones are discussed below.

Australorp.—This breed originated in Australia from Black Orpingtons imported from England. It was developed for egg production and enjoyed popularity in Australia and South Africa.

Cornish.—Originally an English breed, this was recognized as important only after it had been imported into the United States in 1887. It has excellent meat qualities and has probably contributed to the makeup of many of the proprietary broiler hybrids.

Dorking.—This was one of the oldest English breeds, but is important only for its part in the makeup of the modern Light Sussex breed.

Leghorn.—There are 12 varieties of Leghorns, which are grouped in the Mediterranean class. Of these, the single-combed White is the most important, though Blacks and Browns are favoured in some areas for egg laying. The Whites have been bred to a high level of egg production in England, Canada, Australia, and the United States, and have been used in the makeup of many of the light-type laying hybrids. Their white-shelled eggs suit North American taste, but may be at some disadvantage in Great Britain, where brown eggs are preferred.

New Hampshire.—This breed was developed in the United States from the Rhode Island Red (*see* below). It gives a good average egg yield, and has meat qualities which have been drawn on in the production of some broiler strains.

Plymouth Rock.—There are seven varieties of this American breed, but only one, the White Rock, is important. This is a good meat producer and has contributed to broiler strains. Buff and Barred Rocks are found locally.

Rhode Island Red.—This American breed is among the most popular of the heavy breeds because of its good egg production, both as a pure breed and in hybrids and first crosses. (A first cross is the offspring of one pure breed mated with another pure breed.) The Rhode Island Red is especially useful because, when mated with certain breeds, for instance the Light Sussex, it gives chicks whose sex can be distinguished by the colour of their down when one day old (females are darker).

Sussex.—Of the several varieties of this English breed the Light Sussex is the most important, because of the sex-linkage characteristic mentioned above and its good meat production. Its white skin suits the English market; the egg production of some strains is good, though food consumption is high.

Other Breeds and Varieties.—Breeds such as the Orpington and Wyandotte were once popular, especially in England, but their commercial importance declined greatly. Some of the French breeds, such as the Faverolle, which has feathered shanks, and Bresse, are good meat producers but have the disadvantage of maturing slowly. Indian Game birds, obtained by crossing English with Indian and Sumatran game fowls, were formerly used for production, but they mature late and their fertility tends to be low. The Asian breeds are the most decorative, possibly as a result of infusion of genes from wild fowl living in the same area, and are popular for competitive showing.

A. BREEDING

The majority of poultry producers in the United States and Western Europe no longer attempt to breed and rear their own stock for either meat or egg production, but buy them, generally at one day old. Chicks can travel long distances at this age without food or water, provided they are in a suitable temperature. Commercial hatcheries can produce large numbers of chicks and dispatch them to their customers by air, road, or rail in special boxes. Techniques for separating the sexes at day old have been developed giving 75–98% accuracy, so that pullets for laying can be sold alone. Chicks for meat production are usually sold straight run, or "as hatched," *i.e.,* with the sexes mixed, but can be sexed for separate selling if required.

Meat Production.—Chicken is marketed in several forms, mostly, in North America and Great Britain, as broilers and fryers. These are chickens, both male and female, of specially developed strains, reared to about nine weeks of age, and about 3½ to 4 lb. average live weight. Profit margins are so small that these chickens must grow fast and gain weight well for the feed they consume, as feed costs are at least 60% of the total costs of broiler production. Broilers are reared in one house only for the whole of their short life, in conditions as nearly ideal as knowledge permits. Very large-scale broiler production is found in the United States, the United Kingdom, and most countries of continental Europe, and there is local production in the U.S.S.R. and many other countries.

There is also poussin, capon, and roaster production. Poussins are very small chickens reared to six weeks of age for sale to some branches of the catering industry. This production is not common, for the demand for this type of bird is small.

Capons and roasters are heavier cockerels, formerly bred especially for Christmas and other festivals, kept to about 20 weeks of age and marketed at about 5 to 8 lb. weight. They may be either broilers or surplus birds of heavy breeds or heavy crosses reared especially for the table. They may spend part of their life in fields on corn stubbles after harvest. Rock Cornish hens obtained by crossing Cornish and white Plymouth Rock fowls are popular in the United States as small roasters.

Meat Production Standards.—A number of characteristics are used for selecting breeding stock for meat producers. The father of the broiler chick comes of a heavy, "meaty" male line, and its mother of a fairly meaty but not-so-heavy female line. This is because the egg production of the lighter-weight females is better than that of the very heavy females; so that the cost of each chick is reduced. Breeders select for: (1) rapid growth to marketing time; (2) low food consumption per unit of body weight; (3) good finish to the carcass at the weight at which the progeny will be marketed; (4) good, deep breast for heavy meat deposition; (5) quick growth of feathers to protect the body against scars and bruises; (6) good health and form of the bird; (7) fairly prolific female line; (8) skin colour suited to the market —usually white for the English market and yellow for North America and much of continental Europe.

Egg Production.—In the United States, the United Kingdom, most of Europe, in places in the U.S.S.R. and many other countries with commercialized agricultural industries, it is the rule to buy pullets (young hens) at day old from hatcheries. Some hatcheries control the breeding farms that supply them with hatching eggs. The customers for the hatched chicks are either egg producers who rear their own replacement stock, sometimes under contract with larger producers; or farmers who specialize in rearing pullets, who may seek customers for their birds at various ages from about 8 weeks up to "point of lay," *i.e.*, about 18–20 weeks.

Successful hybrids are introduced into many countries from the one where they were developed. For example, many American strains were introduced into Europe in the late 1950s and early 1960s and competed strongly with local breeds and strains. Many countries operate strict quarantine arrangements to prevent the transmission of diseases. Consequently, rather small quantities of foundation stock are usually introduced at first into a new country. Sometimes a new business is established for this purpose, or an agreement may be made with an established organization.

Egg Production Standards.—The basic characters that are considered in selecting stock are: (1) high egg production (an average of 220 eggs per year per hen housed at the start of the season should be obtainable); (2) low food consumption; (3) sexual maturity at a stage suited to the type; (4) eggs up to standard weight after not more than six weeks' production; (5) continuous production of good-quality eggs for at least 12 months after the first egg; (6) little or no broodiness; (7) health and vigour of the stock throughout their life. Many other characters also may be taken into account, *e.g.*, the shape and strength of the eggs, their hatchability, etc.

The large breeders may test great numbers of birds in the course of selection and use electronic computers to handle the very large amounts of data assembled. Various breeding systems are used; best results are obtained by crossing two independently inbred lines to produce the commercial fowls. *See* EGG: *Edible Eggs.*

B. MANAGEMENT

Renewing the Flock.—Most birds lay 20% fewer eggs in their second year than in their first. But a few producers keep a flock of hens for a second year if they lay a large egg and there is a local market for large eggs.

In most countries with a commercialized poultry industry, broody hens are allowed to hatch only bantam and fancy breed eggs. All flock replacements are hatched in incubators of a cabinet or walk-in type. The walk-in incubators run by the large hatcheries will hold up to 100,000 eggs each. Hatching can be organized to take place from once or twice to five or six times a week. A rigid program of hygiene is followed both on the farms producing the hatching eggs and in the hatchery itself to ensure that only healthy chicks are sold.

Rearing Chickens.—Only very small numbers of chicks can be brooded under hens, so that most of the large numbers required are brooded artificially. Broilers can be brooded in groups of 1,000 or more, but pullets do better if reared in groups of not more than 600. Artificial brooding makes it possible to rear chicks the year round for meat and egg production.

There are several types of brooders, varying according to size, design, and the kind of fuel used for heating. They range in size from those that can take 25 chicks to those accommodating several thousand, and are usually heated by fuel oil, paraffin oil (kerosene), butane, natural or liquid gas, or electricity.

For the first few days of the chicks' lives the temperature is kept at about 95° F (about 35° C) at a height of two inches above the floor of the brooder. The temperature is reduced by about 5° F each week, depending on the weather outside; it is not allowed to sink below about 70° F (about 20° C) for the first four or five weeks. The first two weeks are the critical period. By about six weeks of age the chicks should be weaned off heat. Litter should be kept dry to prevent the spread of disease.

Poultry need to have adequate trough space for food and water at all stages of their lives. Food troughs can be either circular or long. The standard circular unit, about one-foot across, is provided in a ratio of three or four per hundred birds according to age. With long troughs, half an inch to one inch per bird is allowed from day old to four weeks of age, rising to three and one half inches per bird by the time adulthood is reached and to four or five inches for layers. Automatic feeding has been introduced in large units. Drinkers also can be automatic. The number required depends on the variety of bird. No feeder or drinker should be more than about 10–12 ft. walking distance away from a bird.

The total area allotted for rearing chicks is calculated on a basis of half a square foot per bird from one to four weeks of age up to two square feet per bird for adults, with up to four square feet per bird in laying houses (*see* FARM BUILDINGS: *Poultry Brooders and Houses*). A number of large producers rear pullets in tier batteries which accommodate more birds. These tier houses are heated by the same fuels as are other brooders, and the pullets are already accustomed to wire floors ready for battery egg-laying accommodation.

Housing Adult Birds.—Under the battery system, housing consists of wire cages, in each of which one or more birds may be kept. Feed and water may be distributed by hand but in large units the distribution is mechanical. In fully automatic systems the cages are cleaned mechanically.

There are other systems of housing which leave the birds loose on a communal floor. Such houses may be insulated, with temperature and light control, or they may be little more than roofs with wire-netting walls; the choice of arrangement is largely according to climate. Artificial lighting is used to stimulate egg production, especially during the autumn and winter seasons (*see* RURAL ELECTRIFICATION). Birds used to be customarily kept on free range, and small flocks are still kept in this way in many countries. However, this system requires much labour and leaves the birds exposed to bad weather and predators, which puts it at a disadvantage in comparison with closely controlled systems for commercial poultry raising.

Broilers are usually raised in houses where they are free to move about the floor. However, for them, too, construction varies greatly. In England, Germany, and other continental European countries rather elaborate houses are usual; in the southern United States very simple ones serve a large industry.

Nutrition.—A newly hatched chick can survive for up to two days on the yolk ingested from the egg, but it needs to be fed as soon as possible with a mash, or with crumbs containing a source of good quality protein. Broilers, which need to grow fast all their lives, are fed on a good quality, energy-giving mash and good quality protein. Replacement pullets, once off to a good start, can be gradually weaned on to a growers' mash or pellets, the process being complete by the time they are eight weeks of age. Growers' feed has more fibre and less protein and energy-giving qualities. A hundred chicks will eat 10–20 lb. of feed in their first week and 10–20 lb. more each week for the next eight or nine

Australorp rooster

Australorp hen

Old English black-breasted game cock

Barred Plymouth Rock hen

Barred Plymouth Rock rooster

Light Sussex rooster

Light Sussex hen

EXAMPLES OF PUREBRED POULTRY

PHOTOGRAPHS, (CENTRE LEFT, CENTRE RIGHT) ESTHER HENDERSON FROM RAPHO-GUILLUMETTE, (OTHERS) GRANT HEILMAN

PLATE II

POULTRY AND POULTRY FARMING

New Hampshire rooster

New Hampshire hen

Buff Orpington rooster

Silver Pencilled Wyandotte rooster

Speckled Sussex rooster

Buff Orpington hen

Silver Pencilled Wyandotte hen

Speckled Sussex hen

EXAMPLES OF PUREBRED POULTRY

PHOTOGRAPHS, (CENTRE TOP, CENTRE BOTTOM) ESTHER HENDERSON FROM RAPHO-GUILLUMETTE, (OTHERS) GRANT HEILMAN

White Plymouth Rock rooster

Broiler male at eight weeks of age

White Plymouth Rock hen

Dark Cornish rooster

Dark Cornish hen

White Leghorn hen

Commercial layer, a hybrid four-way cross
of highly inbred lines

White Leghorn rooster

COMMERCIAL BROILERS AND LAYERS (U.S.)

BY COURTESY OF (BOTTOM CENTRE) HY-LINE POULTRY FARMS; PHOTOGRAPHS, (TOP CENTRE, CENTRE RIGHT) GRANT HEILMAN, (OTHERS) ESTHER HENDERSON FROM RAPHO-GUILLUMETTE

Plate IV

POULTRY AND POULTRY FARMING

Khaki-Campbell drake

Muscovy drake

Indian Runner drake

Aylesbury duck

Pekin drake

Broadbreasted Bronze tom

Beltsville White tom

DUCKS AND TURKEYS

PHOTOGRAPHS, (BOTTOM LEFT, BOTTOM RIGHT) H. ARMSTRONG ROBERTS, (OTHERS) ESTHER HENDERSON FROM RAPHO-GUILLUMETTE

weeks. The actual amount depends on the type of chick, the energy content of the feed, and the chicks' rate of growth. A broiler chick eats about $8\frac{3}{4}$ lb. food in eight weeks to reach 4 lb. in weight. A pullet eats about 4 lb. in its first eight weeks and about 20 lb. to point of lay.

Laying birds are always fed mash or pellets in troughs. In the United Kingdom this mash contains 17% protein, and in the United States 15% protein. Its value to the fowls depends on the source of the protein. There is sufficient calcium for eggshells in the rations of most laying hens provided they are below 75% production. Hens laying more than this are fed supplementary calcium. Insoluble grit is also provided, in separate feeders. Some strains of birds reach their peak at 90% production. If the hens are to be fed a scratch feed of corn, a grain balancer diet is fed. This is made up with a high protein and low energy-giving content to counteract the effect of the added grain.

The only birds that will benefit from free-range foraging without subsidiary feeding are cockerels that are to be fattened for the table; these can survive for a few weeks on stubbles. With the development of intensive feeding systems, careful compounding of diet is required. This is done by national compounders; by local compounders serving an area of countryside (on specifications drawn up by the national mills); or by the poultry farmers themselves. This last arrangement usually pays only if the mixing equipment can be used for large quantities of stock and the grain is homegrown. Concentrates of all the essential minerals and vitamins and any extra protein required can be bought and added at predetermined levels to recommended proportions of cereals to give a balanced ration for a given class of stock. Corn (maize) and wheat are the usual grains, with milo (a grain sorghum) in the United States. Biochemists and food manufacturers conduct research into the food requirements of all types and classes of stock, so that more efficient and economical feeds can be compounded. Drugs for controlling disease often are added to commercial feeds. Antibiotic feed supplements are frequently used to increase growth rates. In the United States recommended ration formulas, continuously revised on the basis of research, are prepared by the advisory service of each state. The use of compounded feeds was at first largely confined to the sizable poultry farms of North America and Western Europe; later the small producers who formerly fed their stock from their own farm produce came to be regular buyers of compounded feeding stuffs, because they were more reliably beneficial, perhaps especially to the newer type of hybrid.

C. DISEASES AND PARASITES

All species of poultry are subject to both internal and external parasites, many of which can be controlled by appropriate drugs and disinfectants if their presence is accurately diagnosed in time; however, chemicals are no substitute for good management. External parasites—mites, lice, and fleas—can be controlled by appropriate application of nicotine sulfate, sodium fluoride, or insecticidal sprays.

Internal parasites include worms in the alimentary tract, but these are not a major problem for healthy birds. Coccidiosis (q.v.), a disease caused by a protozoan parasite, which affects birds while they are still growing, is potentially much more serious. It can be controlled by rearing the birds on wire floors so that they are not infected from their own or other birds' feces. Customarily, also, a coccidiostat (i.e., a drug controlling the disease) is given in the feed during the early stages of the chicks' lives.

Most fungal and bacterial diseases no longer present problems to the poultry farmer. The salmonella organisms are the principal members of this group causing disease, especially in young chicks. They can be controlled by good hygiene; but, if an outbreak is suspected, effective drugs are available. Since 1935 the U.S. Department of Agriculture has conducted the National Poultry Improvement Plan to control pullorum disease (bacillary white diarrhea) and typhoid. Flocks of participating hatcheries are tested to assure that the disease will not be transmitted to chicks.

Virus diseases are the principal causes of death and loss of production. There are no effective drugs, and once an outbreak has taken hold of a flock, control is extremely difficult. Good hygiene, including the segregation of birds of different ages, is the only means of avoiding the danger. The principal virus diseases are the fowl leukosis (leukemia) complex, including fowl paralysis (range paralysis, or neurolymphomatosis), Newcastle disease (fowl pest), and some respiratory diseases. Leukosis and fowl paralysis are extremely important in most countries with commercial poultry industries. They probably account for one-fifth of the total deaths of adult stock in Great Britain. There is no known cure or vaccination.

Newcastle disease, which is often difficult to distinguish from other respiratory diseases, must be reported in Great Britain, where a subsidized killed-virus vaccine is available for injecting into all birds throughout the country; in the United States both live-virus and killed-virus vaccines are available, and either dosed into drinking water or sprayed or dusted over the birds, thus eliminating the need to handle stock. Newcastle disease does not kill adult birds, but causes grave losses of production.

With intensive systems of poultry rearing, great care has to be taken to provide sufficient suitable ventilation lest respiratory diseases get a hold. Antibiotics and drugs can sometimes be used against them with moderate success provided that the originating cause is at least partially removed. New diseases have appeared in several countries, possibly in association with environmental changes.

Finally, there are various deficiency diseases, often with characteristic symptoms. For example, rickets, in which the bones are malformed, is caused by shortage of vitamin D; while a characteristic form of paralysis, in which the toes are curled, is caused by shortage of riboflavin.

D. MARKETING

Eggs.—Marketing systems vary as widely as do production systems. Even in countries where egg production is industrialized, a significant proportion of eggs passes direct from producer to consumer. The remainder are collected from the farms, taken to packing stations where they are candled to assess internal quality, graded, and packed in containers, often 15 or 30 dozen to a box. Retail boxes containing 6 or 12 eggs are increasingly used. Large quantities are processed and frozen or dehydrated (see EGG: *Edible Eggs*).

Before World War II a substantial international trade in eggs had grown up. Part of this was in shell eggs, of which Denmark, the Netherlands, Ireland, and Australia were among the major exporters; part was in egg products, e.g., broken-out shell eggs for cold storage in cans, in which China was prominent. The United Kingdom was a major importer of shell eggs and egg products. This situation was disrupted, not only by the effects of war but also by the technological changes in the poultry industry, and by the action of a number of importing countries, e.g., the United Kingdom and Germany, to protect their own egg-producing industries to the disadvantage of the exporting countries. By the 1960s, many countries were acutely embarrassed in their search for markets for a product so well suited to the small peasant farmer.

Meat.—Poultry meat also is marketed in various ways. In many countries, producers with a few cockerels or old hens sell them live to local shops or to individual consumers. Many more are collected by dealers, who dispose of them live through markets. Large producers handle their birds in specially built plants, in which they are stunned, bled, defeathered, and cooled while being moved mechanically from one part to another of the plant. They may also be eviscerated and frozen. They are then distributed: chilled, wrapped and frozen, jointed, and even cooked. There is a substantial international trade in frozen birds.

Organization of Marketing.—The scale and complexity of the poultry industry, and the large proportion of a country's production which may be controlled by a few firms, represent a break with traditional farming practice in most countries. In several countries, breeding firms can number their chick sales in terms of tens of millions a year. Individual firms may have outputs representing one-quarter or more of the total for their section of the industry; the six biggest firms in a country may account for two-thirds or three-quarters of the national output.

Those sections of the modern poultry industry that require very heavy capital expenditure, highly skilled scientific knowledge, or experienced management, bear most of the responsibility for its success. Partly owing to the interdependence of businesses in supplying one another's raw materials, or outlets for one another's products, links have developed such that a single firm may control by contract or actual ownership two or more stages in the industry. For example, a feed manufacturer, by means of contracts with farmers on the one hand and with hatcheries on the other, may control the production of meat chickens right up to the stage where the birds are ready to kill.

Details of organization vary greatly throughout the world; but the "vertical integration" described above is especially widespread in North America, the U.K., Germany, and Italy. Not only the largest firms are involved. For example, in parts of the U.S. and some continental European countries in the 1960s, meat birds were raised by small farmers in small units, although these farmers were under contract to large firms. However, these are not the only arrangements under which poultry producers have operated. The marketing of eggs by farmers' cooperative societies has played an important role, for example, in Denmark, Canada, the U.S., and the U.K. But the cheapness of the individual bird still renders poultry-keeping feasible for even the smallest producer. Consequently, unorganized production—though, possibly, with sophisticated hybrid stock—may be found not only in countries where agriculture is still managed largely on traditional lines but also where it has become a network of big businesses.

II. DUCKS

Duck raising is practised on a limited scale in nearly all countries, for the most part as a small farm enterprise. The flocks once kept in England are much reduced, the demand for eggs being greatly lessened, though there is still a limited market. Khaki Campbell and Indian Runner ducks are prolific layers and can average 300 eggs a year each. In the U.S. many commercial plants have been developed exclusively for duck-meat production, especially on Long Island. There are also local industries in the Netherlands and England, the favourite breed in England being the Aylesbury. This has white flesh, and can reach 8-lb. weight in eight weeks. In the U.S. the favourite is the Pekin duck, which is slightly smaller than the Aylesbury and is yellow fleshed. It is marketed at about nine weeks of age.

III. TURKEYS

The industry of raising turkeys for meat (see TURKEY) underwent technical development after World War II. Well-fleshed types, which mature at different ages, have been developed. Bronze strains reach slightly heavier weights than whites, but the latter are preferred because they are of better appearance when ready for cooking. Generally speaking, stag or tom (i.e., male) turkeys reach 26-lb. weight in 26 weeks, while hen turkeys mature earlier and rarely exceed 20–22 lb.

It is now known that turkeys require a feed richer in protein at the start of their lives than do chicks. They can be reared on either wire or litter flooring, but preferably on litter, providing disease is kept under control.

Large stag (tom or gobbler) turkeys may achieve 50-lb. weight. The largest are used for catering and the smaller ones for families. Although turkey is generally eaten on festivals such as Thanksgiving and Christmas, the industry has been attempting to encourage year-round sales. In the United States smaller birds such as fryer-roasters produced from Beltsville Small Whites have gained in popularity. Besides fattening, a production of day-old "poults" also is carried on from stock developed for the purpose. These young birds are supplied to rearers who contract with packing stations. Once the young turkeys have been encouraged to start eating, there is not much risk of substantial loss of stock, although in former times turkeys had the reputation of being extremely difficult to rear, and much folklore surrounded the feeding methods that were believed to be successful. Turkey poults are, however, very susceptible to damp, and are prone to respiratory

diseases, which often affect their sinuses. The congestion can be relieved by injecting antibiotics directly into the sinuses. Poults are also susceptible to blackhead, a disease caused by a protozoan parasite, which can now be controlled by drugs.

IV. GEESE

Goose raising is a minor farm enterprise in practically all countries, but in Germany, Austria, some eastern European countries, parts of France, and locally elsewhere there is important commercial goose production. The two outstanding meat breeds are the Toulouse, predominantly gray in colour, and the Embden, which is white. Geese do not appear to have attracted the attention of geneticists on the same scale as the meat chicken and the turkey, and no change in the goose industry comparable to that in the others has occurred or seems to be in prospect. In some commercial plants, geese are fattened by a special process resulting in a considerable enlargement of their livers, which are sold as a delicacy. See GOOSE.

V. GUINEA FOWL

Guinea fowl (q.v.) are raised as a sideline on a few farms in many countries. In Italy there is a fairly extensive industry. They are reared in yards with open-fronted shelters. In England they are usually marketed at 16–18 weeks of age and in the United States at about 10–12 weeks of age. The market weight is usually about 2½–3½ lb. but their food conversion is poor.

VI. SQUABS

Pigeons are raised not only as messengers and for sport (see PIGEON; PIGEON FLYING) but also for the meat of their squabs (nestlings). Squab production is carried on locally, but is rare in most countries with established poultry industries. A pair of pigeons can rear six pairs of squabs a year, and they are marketed at three to four weeks of age.

See also FARM BUILDINGS: *Quarters for Animals: Poultry Brooders and Houses;* FEEDS, ANIMAL; FARM MACHINERY; FOOD PREPARATION: *Entrees: Poultry and Game;* FOOD SUPPLY OF THE WORLD; GAME BIRDS.

See also references under "Poultry and Poultry Farming" in the Index.

BIBLIOGRAPHY.—G. H. Biddle and E. M. Juergenson, *Approved Practices in Poultry Production* (1963); L. E. Card and M. C. Nesheim, *Poultry Production,* 10th ed. (1966); A. A. McArdle, *Poultry Management and Production,* rev. ed. (1966); W. O. Wilson, "Poultry Production," *Sci. Amer.,* 215:56–64 (July 1966); G. J. Mountney, *Poultry Products Technology* (1966); H. E. Biester and L. H. Schwarte (eds.), *Diseases of Poultry,* 5th ed. (1965); World Poultry Science Conference, *Reports;* Organization for European Co-operation and Development, *Marketing Meat Poultry with Special Emphasis on Broilers* (1961); A. L. Roy, *Contract Farming* (1962). (K. E. H.; X.)

POUND, EZRA LOOMIS (1885–), U.S. poet and a profoundly generative influence on 20th-century writing in English,

EZRA POUND PHOTOGRAPHED IN 1964

was born on Oct. 30, 1885, in Hailey, Ida., but immediately taken to the eastern seaboard. Educated at the University of Pennsylvania and at Hamilton College, in Clinton, N.Y., he first visited Europe as a graduate student of Romance literature, and after a brief experience as a teacher at Wabash College, in Crawfordsville, Ind., returned in January 1908 to Europe, where he made his home, first in London (1908–20), then in Paris (1920–24), finally in Italy (1924–45, and after 1958). He was confined in St. Elizabeth's Hospital, Washington, D.C. (1946–58), as mentally unfit to answer indictments for treason arising from his broadcasts from Rome between 1941 and 1945. When released, he wrote further installments of what he called "an epic poem which begins 'in the dark forest,' crosses the purgatory of human error, and ends in light . . . among the masters of those who know." This is *The Cantos,* of which the first installment appeared in 1917 and the latest in 1959 (*Thrones;* Cantos 96–109). For *The Pisan Cantos* (1948), composed in 1945–46 when Pound was in a U.S. military prison in Italy, he was awarded the 1949 Bollingen Prize in Poetry. He had declared himself dissatisfied with the poem as a whole, and in the late 1960s was said to be revising it. By then he was in failing health, and seldom spoke, but continued to travel.

Homer's *Odyssey* and Ovid's *Metamorphoses* shape *The Cantos* hardly less than does Dante's *Divina Commedia.* Many of them review past periods of world history, paying polemical attention to the fiscal policies of ancient and modern states. The moral and philosophical attitudes which Pound esteems, he has found mainly in Confucian China:

> this breath wholly covers the mountains
>   it shines and divides
> it nourishes by its rectitude
> does no injury
> overstanding the earth it fills the nine fields
>   to heaven
> Boon companion to equity
>   it joins with the process
>   lacking it, there is inanition
> When the equities are gathered together
>   as birds alighting
> it springeth up vital
> If deeds be not ensheaved and garnered in the heart
> there is inanition

(Ezra Pound, *Cantos.* © 1948 by Ezra Pound. Reprinted by permission of New Directions Publ. Corp. and Faber & Faber, Ltd., London)

In this passage, governed by submerged reference to four Chinese characters in a passage by Mencius, the suppression of punctuation is characteristic, as is the procedure, fruitfully influential to the present day, of directing rhythm by typographical spacing—a procedure feasible only when composing on the typewriter. Equally characteristic is the deliberately archaic and stilted or stylized diction. Though Pound uses colloquial, even slangy language (*see* his Sophoclean translation, *The Women of Trachis,* 1956), he has readily, ever since the beautifully Browningesque or Pre-Raphaelite archaism of his earliest poems, departed far from currently spoken English.

This has determined his practice as a verse-translator—from the Old English (*The Seafarer,* 1912); from the Italian of Cavalcanti (1912, but also later, and within *The Cantos*); from the Provençal (1919–20); from the Japanese (the *Noh* plays, 1916); and from the Chinese (*Cathay,* 1915; but also *The Classic Anthology Defined by Confucius,* 1954). Pound does not agree that the translator must be a modernizer, and he has urged the translator to depart from current English, when necessary, so as to hint at the melody of the original, whether melody inherent in the words or (almost more important, since Pound has championed the tradition of European song) the melody of musical accompaniment. Often included with Pound's translations is his *Homage to Sextus Propertius* (written 1917; published 1919), but this belongs in another category, the imitation; by wittily reordering Propertius' elegies, Pound makes Propertius register the Roman imperial twilight as, in his own *Hugh Selwyn Mauberley* (1920), he himself had registered the British.

Especially during his London years Pound was a polemicist, a patron and impresario for other writers, and indeed for practitioners of other arts. It was his admiration of the French sculptor Henri Gaudier-Brzeska (*q.v.*), killed in World War I, that led him, in a memoir of Gaudier-Brzeska, to expand and elaborate his own program for Imagism (*q.v.*) into Vorticism, a theory of poetry that places it in relation to other arts, for instance the sculpture of Gaudier and the painting of Percy Wyndham Lewis (*q.v.*). Not only the youthful T. S. Eliot but also the senior and already established poet W. B. Yeats were content to take instruction from Pound, not just as to the publication of poems but as to the writing of them. Yeats, however, whose early achievement in poetry had been the principal reason for Pound's coming to London, certainly taught Pound as much as he learned from him.

Another older writer whom Pound readily acknowledged as his master was the novelist, poet, and editor Ford Madox Ford (*q.v.*). Other writers who profited from Pound's exertions on their behalf were James Joyce and Robert Frost. Pound has insisted always that the idea of *l'atelier,* of the master instructing and assisted by his pupils, is as natural a medium for the transmission of tradition in poetry as it is in other arts like painting.

After the death of T. S. Eliot (1965) and of Ernest Hemingway (1961), both his friends and one-time protégés, Pound saw himself as lone survivor of the American expatriate generations in Europe, the last heir of Henry James. William Carlos Williams (*q.v.*), however, a friend since student days, censured Pound for living abroad and so losing touch with American 20th-century reality, especially American speech.

BIBLIOGRAPHY.—Donald Gallup, *A Bibliography of Ezra Pound* (1963; revised reissue 1969); *Letters of Ezra Pound 1907–41,* ed. by D. D. Paige (1950); H. Kenner, *The Poetry of Ezra Pound* (1951); Clark Emery, *Ideas into Action* (1959); N. Stock, *Poet in Exile* (1964); D. Davie, *Ezra Pound: Poet as Sculptor* (1964); H. M. Meacham, *The Caged Panther* (1967). (D. A. DE.)

POUND, ROSCOE (1870–1964), U.S. jurist, one of the most influential figures in U.S. legal education, and a leading exponent of the reform of judicial administration, was born in Lincoln, Neb., Oct. 27, 1870. He studied at the University of Nebraska, where he received a B.A. degree in botany in 1888. In 1889 he received his M.A. degree in the same subject. He studied law at Harvard for one year (1889–90), passed the Nebraska bar without his law degree, and until 1907 practised law in that state. He taught at the University of Nebraska (1890–1903) and was commissioner on uniform state laws for Nebraska (1904–07). During that time he had earned a Ph.D. (1897) in botany from the university and directed the botanical survey of the state (1892–1903), during which he discovered the rare lichen *Roscopoundia* which was named for him. After teaching at Northwestern University and the University of Chicago, Pound went to Harvard as professor of law, and in 1916 he became dean of the Law School. Resigning as dean in 1936, he received a "roving professorship" and taught a variety of subjects until his retirement in 1947. After his retirement he was active in numerous legal, editorial, and educational positions. He spent a few years in Formosa reorganizing the Nationalist Chinese government's judicial system.

Many fields of the law, including jurisprudence, Roman law, equity, and criminal law, were enriched by his writings and teaching. He directed the Cleveland Survey of Criminal Justice in 1922 and was a leader in the cause of efficient court administration. He died on July 1, 1964, in Cambridge, Mass.

BIBLIOGRAPHY.—P. L. Sayre, *The Life of Roscoe Pound* (1948); F. C. Setaro, *Bibliography of the Writings of Roscoe Pound* (1942); G. A. Strait, *Bibliography of the Writings of Roscoe Pound, 1940–1960* (1960). (L. HL.)

POUND. The basic unit of weight in English-speaking countries is the avoirdupois pound. By agreement between Australia, Canada, New Zealand, the Republic of South Africa, the United Kingdom, and the United States, the pound is defined for international purposes at 0.45359237 kg. But in each country the standard pound as determined by the national laboratory differs slightly from the international pound.

The earliest weight in the English system was the Saxon pound, subsequently known as the tower pound from the old mint pound kept in the Tower of London. It weighed 5,400 gr. and this weight of silver was coined into 240 pence or 20 shillings, hence pound in the sense of an English money of account (*see* MONEY). The pound troy, probably introduced from France, was in use by 1415. In 1527 an act of Henry VIII substituted a pound troy of 5,760 gr. (the "pounde Troye which exceedeth the pounde Tower in weight iii quarters of the oz.") as the legal standard for gold and silver, abolishing the tower pound. In use at the same time were two merchant's pounds of 6,750 and 7,200 gr. for goods sold by weight, *avoir de pois.* The official avoirdupois pound was in use in the reign of Edward I but Henry VIII changed it from 15 oz. troy to 16 oz. avoirdupois. The overlap in the avoirdupois and merchant's pounds led Elizabeth I to discard the latter and establish Henry VIII's avoirdupois pound as the only legal avoirdupois pound at 7,000 gr. divided into 16 oz. (437.5 gr. to the ounce).

The standard troy pound and the standard yard, in the custody of the clerk of the House of Commons since 1758, were destroyed in 1834 at the burning of the Houses of Parliament. In 1841 the report of a commission on the restoration of the standards led to the substitution of the pound avoirdupois of 7,000 gr. for the pound troy as the standard. A new standard pound avoirdupois was made in 1844, by comparison with authenticated copies of the original standard, and was legalized in 1855. The standard avoirdupois pound is made of platinum, in the form of a cylinder nearly 1.35 in. (3.43 cm.) high and 1.15 in. (2.92 cm.) in diameter, and is marked "P.S. 1844. 1 lb.," P.S. meaning parliamentary standard. It is preserved at the Standards Office, in the custody of the Board of Trade. The term "troy pound" was abolished in 1878 but the decimal multiples and submultiples of the ounce troy continue in use for gold, silver, and medicines.   (L. C. Po.)

POUSSIN, NICOLAS (1593/94–1665), considered the greatest and most characteristic French painter of the 17th century, and the leading exponent of pictorial classicism of that period, was born near Les Andelys, Normandy. At about the age of 17 he moved to Paris, working under various Mannerist artists and studying in the royal collections of painting, sculpture and engraving. At the court of the queen mother he met his first important patron, the Italian poet G. Marino, who commissioned a series of drawings illustrating Ovid's *Metamorphoses*.

In 1624 Poussin reached Rome, where Marino introduced him to Marcello Sacchetti, through whom he met Francesco Cardinal Barberini. His style during this period is not easy to define as he was experimenting in various directions at once; but one important influence was that of the Bolognese classical artist, Domenichino. The culminating work of this phase was a large altarpiece for St. Peter's representing the "Martyrdom of St. Erasmus" (1629; Vatican gallery). However, it was a comparative failure and Poussin never again tried to compete with the Italian masters of the Baroque on their own ground. Thereafter he painted only for private patrons and confined his work to a format rarely more than five feet in length. From 1629 to about 1633 Poussin took his themes from classical mythology and from Torquato Tasso,

BY COURTESY OF THE NATIONAL GALLERY OF IRELAND

"THE HOLY FAMILY" BY NICOLAS POUSSIN. IN THE NATIONAL GALLERY OF IRELAND

and his style became romantic and poetical under the influence of the Venetians, especially Titian; examples are "The Arcadian Shepherds" (1629; Chatsworth, Derbyshire), "Rinaldo and Armida" (*c.* 1629; Dulwich) and "Cephalus and Aurora" (*c.* 1630; National gallery, London).

In the mid-1630s he began deliberately to turn toward Raphael and antiquity for his inspiration and to evolve the purely classical idiom which he retained to the end of his life. He also included religious themes once more, beginning with stories which offered a good pageant (*e.g.*, "The Worship of the Golden Calf," *c.* 1636; National gallery), but going on to choose incidents of deeper

moral significance in which human reactions to a given situation constitute the main interest. The most important work which exemplifies this phase is the series of "Seven Sacraments" painted for Cassiano del Pozzo, secretary to Francesco Barberini, of which five are now in the duke of Rutland's collection; in connection with another, "The Gathering of Manna" (1639; Louvre, Paris), Poussin wrote that it should be possible to "read" the emotions of all the various figures in the composition.

In 1640 Poussin was summoned to Paris by the king and Cardinal Richelieu, and among his commissions was the decoration of the long gallery of the Louvre. However, disillusionment set in, the local artists intrigued against him and he returned to Rome in 1642. The most valuable result of his visit to his native country had been the friendships which he formed with his French patrons, notably Fréart de Chantelou, whose interest in Stoic and Epicurean philosophy appealed strongly to Poussin. Both his religious and secular paintings of the 1640s and 1650s are concerned with moments of crisis or difficult moral choice, and Poussin's heroes are always those who reject vice and the pleasures of the senses in favour of virtue and the dictates of reason; *e.g.*, Coriolanus, Scipio, Phocion, Diogenes. His style was consciously calculated to express such a mood of austere rectitude. Thus in the "Testament of Eudamidas" (1644–48; Copenhagen) there are only five figures, all painted in dull or harsh colours against the severest possible background. Even in his landscapes, a form which Poussin first took up about 1645 and which he used for the stories of Diogenes and Phocion, the disorder of nature is reduced to the order of geometry, and trees and shrubs are made to approach the condition of architecture. The second series of "Seven Sacraments," executed for Chantelou (1644–48; earl of Ellesmere's collection), has a solemnity which is relatively lacking in the more picturesque first series. In each case the composition is conceived very carefully, not only on the surface but also in depth, recalling the methods of Raphael and reflecting Poussin's own practice at this time of supplementing his preparatory drawings with a three-dimensional model made of wax figures set in a boxlike stage.

Poussin believed in reason as the guiding principle of artistic creation and he was an artist who, in Sir Joshua Reynolds' phrase, was "naturalized in antiquity," yet his figures are never merely cold or lifeless. Though in pose they may resemble figures used by Raphael or in ancient Roman sculpture, they have a strange and unmistakable vitality of their own. Even in his late period, when all movement, including gesture and facial expression, had been reduced to a minimum, his forms are instinct with life. The devotion he has inspired in so many later French artists, among them David and Ingres, Cézanne and Picasso, bears eloquent testimony to this. Poussin died in Rome on Nov. 19, 1665.

BIBLIOGRAPHY.—G. P. Bellori, *Le Vite de' Pittori, scultori ed architetti moderni* (1672); W. Friedlaender, *Nicolas Poussin* (1914), *The Drawings of Nicolas Poussin* (1939–53); O. Grautoff, *Nicolas Poussin* (1914); P. du Colombier (ed.), *Lettres de Poussin* (1929); A. Blunt, *Art and Architecture in France, 1500–1700* (1953), *Nicolas Poussin*, 2 vol. (1966).   (M. W. L. K.)

POVERTY is an insufficiency of goods and services measured by the standard of a given society at a given time. Poverty is thus a relative condition. Who shall be counted as poor is a moral, not a technical, question. The distribution of wealth and income in a population is a matter of fact, but a poverty line drawn across the distribution implicitly argues that the people below that line ought to be raised above it.

Since the distribution of income and wealth in the world is highly structured by geographic location, occupation, social class, nationality, race, education, and age, among other factors, the poor generally differ from the non-poor in predictable ways. The penalties of poverty are always severe. Compared with their contemporaries, the poor appear always to have shorter lives, more illness, more physical and mental defects, more personal crises, less education, and less protection from hazards.

Internationally, Asiatic and African countries are poor compared to Latin-American countries, which in turn are poor compared to Europe or North America. Eastern Europe is poor compared to Western Europe, Mexico compared to the United States, mainland Asia compared to Japan.

In most countries, the rural population is poor, on the average, compared to the urban population. Manual workers are poorer than white-collar workers, the old are poor compared to adults of working age, large families are poorer than small families, and the uneducated much poorer than the educated. In countries with racially mixed populations, nonwhites are poorer than whites, often very much poorer.

Although poverty is a phenomenon as old as human history, its significance has changed rapidly in the second half of the 20th century. Under traditional conditions of production, widespread poverty had been accepted as inevitable. The total output of goods and services, if equally distributed, would still have been insufficient to give the entire population a standard of living that was comfortable by prevailing standards. This became no longer the case in highly industrialized countries, whose national outputs were sufficient to raise the entire population to a comfortable level if the necessary redistribution could be arranged without adversely affecting output. The world as a whole was in a less favourable situation. Because of differing standards, an egalitarian redistribution of world output would abolish poverty in Africa but make it universal in North America. Rates of economic development in the 1960s, however, foreshadowed spectacular increases of world output before the end of the 20th century. From 1960 to 1966, with the world's population increasing at an annual rate of 1.9%, the global production and consumption of energy increased at an annual rate well over 5%, according to the United Nations. In the circumstances, poverty no longer appears as an inevitable feature of the human condition. It will more likely be treated as a defect in the social machinery, to be corrected as quickly as possible.

For convenience of discussion, several types of poverty may be distinguished which are, in real life, closely interrelated: class poverty, case poverty, cyclical poverty, and regional poverty.

Class Poverty.—Class poverty is the condition of a social class or stratum in which low income and a degraded status are closely associated and perpetuate each other.

Every large-scale premodern society appears to have had a distinct stratum of disreputable poor; in Imperial Rome, Elizabethan England, and Mogul India, for example, they were probably a majority of the population. The French peasants observed by Arthur Young in the late 18th century appeared scarcely human to outsiders. The factory workers of England and New England in the early 19th century were regarded as scarcely human by their employers. Even the Marxists waxed furious about the irregularly employed urban workers whom they called the *Lumpenproletariat* and described as shiftless, immoral, and politically unreliable. The stigma of disreputable poverty was carried in turn by each arriving population that entered the United States in large numbers beginning with the Irish and ending with the Puerto Ricans. In nearly all of the world's biracial and triracial societies, the lowest ranking ethnic group is both poor and disreputable, its disrepute perpetuated by poverty and its poverty maintained by discrimination in education, housing, employment, and social opportunities of all kinds.

This mechanism was described in the first full-scale sociological study of the Negro's situation in the United States, Gunnar Myrdal's *An American Dilemma* (New York: Harper and Row, 1944):

White prejudice and discrimination keep the Negro low in standards of living, health, education, manners and morals. This, in its turn, gives support to white prejudice. White prejudice and Negro standards thus mutually "cause" each other.

A more universal form of the same theory was advanced by Oscar Lewis in his introduction to *The Children of Sánchez* (New York: Random House, 1961), the collective autobiography of a Mexico City slum family. According to Lewis, there is a distinct "culture of poverty" among the peasant masses of the underdeveloped countries and in the urban and rural slums of the developed countries which transcends regional differences. Its economic traits include

the constant struggle for survival, unemployment and underemployment, low wages, miscellaneous unskilled occupations, child labor, the

absence of food reserves in the home, the pattern of frequent buying of small quantities of food many times a day as the need arises, pawning of personal goods . . . and the use of second-hand clothing and furniture.

The social and psychological characteristics of the culture of poverty include

living in crowded quarters, a lack of privacy, gregariousness, a high incidence of alcoholism, frequent resort to violence in the settlement of quarrels, frequent use of physical violence in the training of children, wife-beating, early initiation into sex, free unions or consensual marriages, a relatively high incidence of the abandonment of mothers and children, a trend towards mother-centered families and a much greater knowledge of maternal relatives, the predominance of the nuclear family, a strong predisposition to authoritarianism, and a great emphasis upon family solidarity—an ideal only rarely achieved.

All of these traits have been repeatedly recorded in studies of slum life elsewhere in the Americas. Whether the pattern is universal among the poor of Europe, Asia, and Africa remains to be determined.

Some of the industrially advanced countries have made considerable progress toward the elimination of class poverty. In the Scandinavian countries, the Netherlands, and Switzerland, for example, there was by the 1970s no longer a large stratum of the population stigmatized by poverty. In England, France, Japan, West Germany, Czechoslovakia, Australia, and the Soviet Union, the economic and cultural disadvantages of the poor were spectacularly reduced, although not eliminated, in the period following World War II. The United States, which has the highest per capita wealth and income of any country, made relatively less progress in assimilating its hereditary poor, presumably because a large proportion of them are nonwhite.

The official recognition of the poor in the United States and of the necessity for governmental action on their behalf is largely traceable to the influence of a single book by a nonacademic sociologist, Michael Harrington's *The Other America* (1962). The American poor had not previously been visualized as a distinct or permanent class; the United States was often described in the 1950s as an affluent society whose principal economic problem was the imbalance between the prosperity of the private consumer and the relative impoverishment of public institutions and facilities. *The Other America* attacked this complacent assumption without challenging the facts on which it was based. Harrington identified between 40,000,000 and 50,000,000 Americans, nearly a quarter of the total population, as poor. He admitted that they were better off than the poor in nations where poverty is associated with starvation; but he maintained that some of them suffered from real hunger, that they lacked adequate housing, education, and medical care, and that they were more pessimistic and unhappy than the majority of the population suspected. Since they lacked the necessary education and skills for more complex jobs, technological progress tended to diminish their chances of obtaining steady employment and to lock them more tightly into a vicious circle of inadequate earnings and disorganized family life that condemned their children in turn to substandard education and occupational marginality. Harrington asserted that the resources of the affluent society were more than sufficient to raise the entire population to a comfortable standard of living and that the persistence of poverty was a national scandal.

Less than three years later, the first of a series of antipoverty programs was launched by the federal government, and the Johnson administration had committed itself to a "War on Poverty" whose active phase was launched with the passage of the Economic Opportunities Act of 1964 with provisions for youth programs (the Job Corps), state-operated youth camps, work-training programs, work-study programs, urban and rural community action programs (general programs, adult basic education programs, the volunteer programs for needy children), rural antipoverty programs, employment and investment incentives, and work experience programs, together with provisions for the administration, coordination, and financing of all these activities. Antipoverty provisions were also contained in the Older Americans Act of 1965, the Housing and Urban Development Act and the Appalachian Regional Development Act of 1965, and the Child Nutrition Act of 1966. These measures paralleled the involvement of the Johnson administration in a vast civil rights campaign that culminated in the passage of the Civil Rights Act of 1964 and the Voting Rights Act of 1965. Toward the end of 1966, the War on Poverty began to be pushed aside by escalation of the war in Vietnam and although existing antipoverty programs were continued with varying success, no major new steps were taken until President Nixon's 1969 proposal for the enactment of a nationwide guaranteed minimum income in place of the existing welfare system.

About 10,000,000 Americans, approximately 5% of the total population, received welfare payments at one time or another in the late 1960s. The relief system was a vast patchwork of separate programs, mostly supported by federal funds but locally administered. Eligibility requirements, operating procedures, and benefits varied sharply among states and localities. Indigent children, their mothers, and a few of their fathers comprised more than half the relief population; the aged and handicapped accounted for most of the rest. At least half of the persons classified as poor under varying income standards proposed by public agencies and private experts received no welfare payments of any kind; all of them would be affected by a guaranteed income plan.

A 1968 study, *Families on Welfare in New York City,* by Lawrence Podell showed that this population, comprising about one-tenth of the nation's welfare recipients, was 50% Negro, 40% Puerto Rican, and 10% white. More than seven out of ten families were headed by women, four of the seven separated from their husbands, two unmarried, and one divorced or widowed. Two out of three welfare families had three or more children; fully half of the women over 30 had borne five or more children. The majority did not anticipate remarrying or leaving the welfare rolls in the near future. These figures seem to substantiate the belief that the welfare system encourages family disorganization and a type of hereditary dependency. Whether these effects would be eliminated by a guaranteed minimum income remained to be seen, but by the early 1970s, there was hardly any overt opposition in the United States to the policy of reducing class poverty and the various stigmas attached to it by means of governmental programs.

Case Poverty.—Case poverty (or indigence) is the inability to support oneself, even at a low standard of living, without outside assistance. Case poverty is affected, of course, by collective poverty in one form or another. In a poor region, an underprivileged stratum, or a bad year, the risk of indigence for marginal wage earners will be very much greater than in a more prosperous setting. But the categories of persons with a high risk of indigence are nearly the same in all large-scale societies—the helpless aged, the fatherless children, the blind or crippled, the chronically ill, the chronically intoxicated, the mentally defective, and the relatives of institutional inmates. All of these conditions are associated with the collective forms of poverty and with each other so that agencies engaged in programs of assistance give much of their attention to multiproblem families.

The earlier students of poverty attached great importance to the question of whether indigent persons were responsible for their plight. In his *Inquiries Concerning the Poor* (1782), the Reverend John McFarlan of Edinburgh wrote that

in tracing the causes of poverty, I have endeavoured to show that the greatest number of those who are now objects of charity are either such as have reduced themselves to this situation by sloth or vice, or such as, by a very moderate degree of industry and frugality, might have prevented indigence.

Somewhat later it became a scholarly game to estimate the exact proportions of blameless and blameworthy paupers. Late in the 19th century, Amos G. Warner concluded that 25% of the poor in the United States owed their condition to laxness, shiftlessness, and insobriety while the remaining three-quarters were victims of misfortune. British studies of the same period estimated about half of the poor to be innocent and the other half culpable. The first scientifically respectable study of the causes of individual poverty was made in the last two decades of the 19th century by the tireless Charles Booth, who analyzed 4,076 cases of indigence in London. For 62%, the principal cause of poverty was ill-paid or irregular employment; 23% of his sample had been reduced to misery by large families or illness. The remaining 15% were said to be drunken, thriftless, or lazy. In subsequent British investigations by B. Seebohm Rowntree and by Sir Arthur Lyon Bowley and A. R. Burnett-Hurst, the attempt to find a single cause of poverty was abandoned. Among low-paid factory workers, illness or temporary unemployment was likely to impose bitter hardship on families with many children. The same contingencies threatened only moderate hardship for single wage earners or small families. The death of a wage earner usually meant impoverishment of a family.

Poverty could also be explained by the varying number of dependents whom the worker had to support during his lifetime taken in relation to his varying earning power from youth to old age. Rowntree, whose three social surveys of the English town of York (in 1900, 1936, and 1950) were the most detailed empirical investigations made in this field, described a typical career pattern for the industrial worker. It is characterized by two periods of sufficiency above the poverty line, in youth and in middle age, when the worker enjoys full earnings but has no dependent children; and by three episodes of poverty, as a dependent child, as an overburdened young father, and as a dependent old man. Something like this individual career pattern can probably be traced in every social stratum although it is a little difficult to establish with precision in the highly dynamic economies of the 20th century in which the conditions prevailing during the worker's childhood will have changed considerably before he reaches old age.

A good deal is known about the style of life of families living at a level below their previous minimum. Available cash tends to be used for the purchase of food, and there is a continuous depletion of savings, family capital, and credit. In the 1930s, Carle C. Zimmerman studied the living conditions of Cuban families who had incomes of less than one dollar per day. Practically all of their resources were devoted to food. In less favourable climates, the need for shelter at the level of living where all income is spent for food is likely to elicit community action. The history of such measures may be briefly summarized:

In the preindustrial era the care of paupers was everywhere a local responsibility, and everywhere reluctantly discharged. The role of the central government, as illustrated in the famous Poor Law (*q.v.*) of Elizabeth I (1601) and the edicts of Colbert concerning the treatment of vagabonds, was limited to seeing that local responsibilities were more or less carried out. Less extreme cases were generally handled by private action and some elements of aid to the poor fell into the sphere of the church. In the industrial era, with the coming of large-scale urbanization, this traditional local responsibility collapsed, and for a while, nothing took its place except sporadic repression by the police. As Anatole France remarked, "The law, in its majestic equality, forbade the rich and poor alike to sleep under bridges." Beginning with the social insurance program established in Germany between 1878 and 1891, the rest of the 19th century and the 20th century saw the enactment, at uneven rates and in various fashions, of a more or less complete program of welfare measures in every industrialized country, designed to provide minimum subsistence to the victims of each category of poverty. In the United States the enactment of such measures was one of the central themes of the New Deal. It included unemployment insurance, pensions for the aged, aid to widows and dependent children, and special provisions for the blind and the handicapped. The main outlines of this system were embodied in the Social Security Act of 1935 and its many later amendments. In Great Britain earlier legislation along these lines was strongly supplemented by the enactment after World War II of most of the features of the "cradle to grave" protection proposed by the 1942 Beveridge Report.

Modern urban conditions generate some novel forms of case poverty. In the United States and in a few other countries, the cost of medical services is so disproportionate to the resources of the average patient that a single major illness or injury may permanently impoverish a middle-income family. Other individuals are impoverished by narcotics addiction, uninsured automobile accidents, forced retirement from industrial occupations because of automation or from agriculture because of mechanization, expulsion from a war zone, and by political or religious persecution; it is estimated that the number of refugees forced to flee from various disturbed areas in the 50 years following the end of World War I exceeded 100,000,000.

Cyclical Poverty.—In the preindustrial world, economic crises were accompanied by high prices. Prices rose periodically because of scarcities of food, which brought widespread misery. (Although famine was extremely common in the preindustrial world, the last major crisis in Western Europe due entirely to natural causes was that of 1709. However, hunger has appeared at many times and places since then. Even in the United States, which has never known a general famine, there has not been a year in which some areas, such as the mountain counties of Kentucky, did not experience widespread hunger.) After the Industrial Revolution, the typical crisis was caused by overproduction and accompanied by low prices. The sign of crisis and the characteristic type of cyclical poverty in economically advanced countries is mass unemployment.

The business cycle in its modern form, with mass unemployment during periods of depression, developed gradually in the 19th century. While the severity of successive crises varied, their consequences broadened as national economies became more dependent upon each other. There was also an irregular tendency for crises to last longer. The Great Depression which began about 1930 persisted for the better part of a decade in most of the countries involved. In 1935 the number of unemployed in the United States approached 20,000,000 and about one-third of the population was receiving public relief or assistance. The impact of the crisis was equally severe in western and central Europe where it was further complicated by the political unrest that eventually led to World War II. Unemployment decreased very gradually from the high point of the 1930s, and it was not until after the outbreak of war in 1939 that the surplus manpower was absorbed.

Although the business cycle has been closely studied and the entire pattern of events is well understood, economists are not unanimous about how to control it. The remedies are of two kinds. First, through control of production or through the manipulation of market mechanisms, the state may intervene to interrupt the deflationary spiral of falling prices and decreasing employment before it acquires momentum. Second, the victims of unemployment may be partially protected by social security (*q.v.*) or governmental subsidies in cash or kind, or by employment on public works. All of these devices were finally adopted by the governments of all of the countries involved in the Great Depression, although with many variations in detail. In Great Britain the principal reliance was upon direct assistance, commonly known as the "dole." In the United States, after some experimentation, the federal government established the huge public enterprise known as the Works Progress Administration. During the same decade, a great deal of experimentation was carried on with devices for controlling the cycle itself. In England, France, Italy, and the Scandinavian countries, government participation in heavy industry was increased. In the United States, Canada, Germany, and some other countries, the central supply of bank credit began to be vigilantly supervised and controlled.

Whether these devices have effectively restricted the business cycle must for some time remain uncertain. Conditions in the period after World War II did not permit a clear-cut test. A high rate of productive activity throughout the world was associated with heavy military expenditures and with a number of unusual circumstances that facilitated economic cooperation among the nations.

Even in the absence of widespread mass unemployment, cyclical unemployment continued to present local problems in many parts of the world. The alleviation of unemployment by insurance benefits or other forms of relief became a standard practice in advanced countries. Such aid is sufficient only to cushion the unemployed against homelessness and starvation. It cannot prevent other kinds of family hardship, including the loss of savings, the thwarting of plans, and the experience of insecurity.

Regional Poverty.—One of the most conspicuous features of the modern world is the enormous disparity between regions (con-

tinents, subcontinents, countries, parts of countries) at different levels of development with respect to the per capita supply of goods and services available to their populations.

Table I shows the per capita consumption of energy (measured in equivalent units of kilograms of coal per capita) in 66 countries having populations over 5,000,000 in 1965. This is an excellent, simple indicator of industrialization, but it is only one of a large cluster of closely related variables. The ranking shown in Table I has been found to closely correlate with the proportion of the population urbanized in the same countries, the proportion of literate adults, the proportion of the school-age population in school, the per capita volume of communications, the average life expectancy, the per capita availability of medical care, and literally dozens of similar indicators.

There is no significant correlation, however, between national size and level of development, and this is one of the major sources of disequilibrium in the contemporary international system. The nations with the most political and military power, like the United States and the Soviet Union, are large and highly developed. The weakest nations are small and underdeveloped. In the range between there is no coherent relationship between a nation's military and political power and its level of development.

The distribution of countries in Table I reflects the history of industrialization and national development in the past two or three centuries. Industrialism as a culture pattern originated in northern and western Europe and was diffused thence by emigration, colonialism, and commercial contact until it penetrated all but the remotest parts of the world. The array of countries in Table I reflects this process. The leading countries in the upper tercile (developed countries) are those of northern and western Europe plus three large countries originally settled from that region, with the peripheral regions of Europe trailing somewhat behind. Japan is the only Asiatic country to appear in the first tercile and South Africa the only African country. The second tercile (developing countries) includes most of Latin America, a few relatively backward European countries, and a number of Asiatic and African countries that have been exposed to intensive European influence. The third tercile (underdeveloped countries) includes the remaining major countries of Asia and Africa with, at the very bottom of the list, the only four countries (except for Japan) that never fell under extended European control—Afghanistan, Ethiopia, Yemen, and Nepal.

TABLE I.—*Per Capita Energy Consumption in 66 Major Countries, 1965*

Country	Per capita Energy consumption*	Rank	Country	Per capita Energy consumption*	Rank
First tercile (developed countries)			Second tercile (developing countries)		
United States	9,201	1	China	461	35
Canada	7,653	2	South Korea	445	36
Czechoslovakia	5,676	3	Rhodesia	399	37
East Germany	5,460	4	Iran	391	38
United Kingdom	5,151	5	Turkey	348	39
Australia	4,795	6	Brazil	347	40
Belgium	4,724	7	Malaysia	338	41
Sweden	4,506	8	Saudi Arabia	311	42
West Germany	4,234	9	Egypt	301	43
U.S.S.R.	3,611	10	Algeria	300	44
Poland	3,504	11			
Netherlands	3,271	12	Third tercile (underdeveloped countries)		
Venezuela	2,974	13			
France	2,951	14	Philippines	209	45
Hungary	2,812	15	India	172	46
South Africa	2,716	16	Morocco	153	47
Switzerland	2,668	17	Kenya	124	48
Austria	2,630	18	Ceylon	114	49
Bulgaria	2,571	19	Indonesia	111	50
Rumania	2,035	20	Thailand	110	51
Italy	1,787	21	Mozambique	106	52
Japan	1,783	22	Ghana	104	53
			Pakistan	90	54
Second tercile (developing countries)			Congo	83	55
Argentina	1,341	23	South Vietnam	73	56
Yugoslavia	1,192	24	Sudan	69	57
Chile	1,089	25	Tanzania	55	58
Spain	1,023	26	Burma	47	59
Mexico	977	27	Nigeria	44	60
Cuba	950	28	Malagasy		
Greece	784	29	Republic	42	61
Taiwan	654	30	Uganda	42	62
Peru	588	31	Afghanistan	25	63
Iraq	581	32	Ethiopia	10	64
Colombia	532	33	Yemen	10	65
Portugal	521	34	Nepal	8	66

*In equivalent kilograms of coal per capita.

In a set of countries, as in a domestic population, the establishment of a poverty line is an arbitrary procedure, but hardly anyone would quarrel with the designation of the countries in the lowest tercile of Table I as poor. The per capita consumption of energy in the leading country of this group, the Philippines, is barely 2% of the per capita consumption of energy in the United States. The consumption of energy in the poorest country of the group, Nepal, is less than 4% of that of the Philippines. These figures provide a rough but convincing picture of the enormous disparities involved.

Table II shows additional differences between the United States and the Philippines in the per capita availability of goods and services in 1965. The differences in food supply and in social services are relatively much smaller than the differences in manufactured goods and in services requiring mechanical equipment.

TABLE II.—*Comparative Availability of Certain Goods and Services in a Developed Country and an Underdeveloped Country, 1965*

Goods and services per capita	United States	Philippines
Commodities:		
Food consumed, calories per capita per day	3,140	2,170
Steel used, kilograms per capita per year	656	24
Transportation:		
Motor vehicles registered per 1,000 population	442	8
Air travel, kilometres per capita per year	473	19
Communication:		
Telephones in service per 1,000 population	478	5
Printing paper used, kilograms per capita per year	33	1
Social Services:		
Primary and secondary teachers per 100,000 population	100	56
Physicians in practice per 100,000 population	148	75

The rank order of national development is not readily susceptible to change. The worldwide complaints that in the second half of the 20th century the rich countries were getting richer and the poor countries poorer does not seem to be supported by any objective evidence. Almost all of the world's countries—and all of its major regions—were getting richer rapidly. For example, among the 39 countries for which the United Nations gathered information on iron production from 1953 to 1966, not a single country failed to increase its production substantially; the average increase for the 13-year period was 96%. Between 1950 and 1965 the per capita availability of physicians in the world increased from around 28 to around 42 per 100,000 of the population. The available supply of mechanical energy in the world approximately doubled—from about 4,000,000,000 to about 8,000,000,000 equivalent metric tons of coal—between 1960 and 1970.

Similar figures may be cited for all of the indicators mentioned above and for many others as well. On the other hand, a poor country has very little hope of catching up with a rich country. Although it is relatively easy to mount the ladder of development, it is very difficult to pass one's neighbour on the next higher rung if only because he must be overtaken on 20 ladders at once. Between 1950 and 1965 the consumption of steel in the Philippines rose 243%, bringing the per capita availability of steel in that country to the U.S. level of 1890. But by the time the Filipinos bridge the remaining gap, the United States, barring a cessation of its development, will have moved far ahead. Although there is every prospect of universal improvement, there is no real prospect of international equalization for the time being. Once a pound of steel enters the economy of a developed country most of it circulates there indefinitely, with a mean cycle of only about 25 years between fabrications. Meanwhile, new metal is constantly added to the circulating supply. To catch up, the poorer country must add steel—and everything else—to its system at a faster per capita rate, although its productive capacity is lower. The same problem inhibits equalization with respect to the intangible resources of a national system, like education and industrial skill.

Within countries also, some regions are poorer and less developed than others. All of the technologically advanced countries contain depressed regions that are relatively underdeveloped and whose populations do not enjoy the same standard of living as their compatriots. Calabria and Sicily are depressed regions in Italy, Brittany in France, and Northern Ireland in the U.K. The most conspicuous depressed regions in the United States are Appalachia and the Deep South. Per capita income in those areas is only about two-thirds of the national average, housing and public services are generally of inferior quality, and unemployment remains relatively high even in periods of prosperity.

In principle, the poverty of poor regions in a rich country ought to be easily alleviated since such regions have a better claim on the total resources of the nation than poor countries have on the total resources of the world. In practice, the problems of poor regions have been astonishingly persistent. Thirty years after the New Deal addressed itself to the special problems of Appalachia through the Tennessee Valley Authority and the Farm Resettlement Administration, the region was still in desperate need of outside assistance. Five years after the passage of the Appalachian Regional Development Act of 1965, the poverty of Appalachia had been only slightly ameliorated. Nevertheless, the long-term prospects are much brighter for national than for international equalization.

Current Trends.—Because poverty is a relative rather than an absolute condition, there is no way it can be abolished except by total equalization of access to resources, a measure never yet attempted in any country and nearly inconceivable for the world as a whole. But if poverty cannot be abolished, it can be mitigated by raising the minimum standard of living, and much progress has already been made in this direction. Although the ultimate value of this progress may be challenged, it is absurd to deny its existence. There is hardly any useful commodity whose per capita consumption had not increased in a spectacular way by the second half of the 20th century. The poorest regions of the world had infant mortality rates and life expectancy rates more favourable than those of the richest regions around 1900. The poorest countries reported an appreciable fraction of their school-age populations in school and literacy was practically universal among the poorest classes of the developed countries.

The increasing protest in the 20th century from the poor throughout the world is at least partially attributable to this same progress. The necessity of poverty is no longer apparent, and that is probably the reason why the existing patterns of unequal access to goods and services are increasingly challenged by those who are excluded from affluence by accidents of birth or location.

BIBLIOGRAPHY.—John McFarlan, *Inquiries Concerning the Poor* (1782); Friedrich Engels, *The Condition of the Working Class in England* (1845); Charles Booth, *Life and Labour of the People of London,* 17 vol. (1889–1903); Anton von Kostaneki, *Arbeit und Armut* (1909); B. Seebohm Rowntree and G. R. Lavers, *Poverty and the Welfare State* (1951); Theodore Caplow, *The Sociology of Work* (1954); John Kenneth Galbraith, *The Affluent Society* (1958); Richard Titmuss, *Essays on the Welfare State* (1959), *Income Distribution and Social Change* (1962); William Cottrell, *Energy and Society* (1960); Jean Fourastié, *The Causes of Wealth* (1960); Angelo Pagani, *La Linea Della Povertà* (1960); Oscar Lewis, *The Children of Sánchez* (1961); Michael Harrington, *The Other America; Poverty in the United States* (1962); R. Buckminster Fuller *et al.*, *Inventory of World Resources, Human Trends and Needs* (1963); Bureau of Applied Social Research, Columbia University, *A Matrix of Modernization* (1964); Herman Miller, *Rich Man, Poor Man* (1964); Bruce M. Russett *et al.*, *World Handbook of Political and Social Indicators* (1964); Alan B. Batchelder, *The Economics of Poverty* (1966); J. Ten Broek *et al.* (eds.), *The Law of the Poor* (1967); L. Rainwater and W. L. Yancy, *The Moynihan Report and the Politics of Controversy* (1967); Report of the President's Commission on Income Maintenance Programs (1969); L. Podell, *Families on Welfare in New York City* (1969); *Statistical Abstract of the United States*; *United Nations Statistical Yearbook*. (T. Cw.)

POWDER METALLURGY, the fabrication of useful items from a metal powder or a mixture of powders, differs from most metallurgical techniques, which initially involve the solidification of a molten metal. Fabrication by powder metallurgy techniques is usually employed for one of two reasons: (1) Such techniques may be the only feasible or practical means of producing certain metals, alloys, or mixtures of two or more metals and/or nonmetals having desirable physical or mechanical properties. This is the case in producing metals having very high melting points, such as tungsten; in making alloys of two metals or materials that cannot normally be mixed together, such as copper and graphite; and finally, in producing parts with controlled amounts and types of usable porosity, such as stainless steel filters. (2) Powder metallurgy may be the cheapest method of manufacture, as is often the case where a large number of identical parts, such as gears for calculating machines, are required. Powder-metallurgy techniques can be used to form such parts directly to shape, with little or no finishing or machining required. Also, scrap losses are minimized and raw-material inventory for production consists of only a few grades of metal powder.

BONDING OF METAL POWDER

In order to bond powder particles into a mass solid enough to withstand the stresses encountered in service, the powder must be heated, or sintered. This process may require from a few minutes to two or three hours for completion. Special protective atmospheres are required during sintering.

There are two distinctly different types of sintering in powder metallurgy. The most common one is described as solid state sintering: the sintering temperature is such that there is no molten metal present during the major portion of the sintering period. One of the constituents of the powder being sintered may melt initially when the powder is first heated, but if this molten metal alloys with the solid particles present and thus disappears during the course of sintering, the process is considered to take place with essentially no liquid present. A second type of sintering, known as liquid phase sintering, is carried out with a mixture of low- and high-melting-point metal powders. The sintering temperature is above the melting point of the lower melting component so that molten metal is present during the entire sintering period. The molten metal wets the remaining solid particles and rapidly flows around them and into the spaces between them if enough of the liquid metal is present, in some cases dissolving a portion of the solid powders. When the powder is cooled from the sintering temperature, the molten metal solidifies and bonds the solid particles together. By contrast, in solid state sintering, the solid particles of metal must be allowed to bond themselves together through the rather slow motion or diffusion of individual metal atoms within the solid.

Solid state sintering is analogous to the coalescence of small drops of water to form a single large drop. A finely divided material, either solid or liquid, will tend to reduce its exposed surface area as much as possible. In the case of a metal, the strength of the particles resists this tendency unless the temperature is high enough to allow the atoms of the metal to move about to some extent within the particles. Temperatures well in excess of one-half the melting point of the solid are necessary to achieve sintering in reasonable times.

The time required for sintering to take place in the solid state depends on the condition of the powder, the size of the particles, and the sintering temperature. The closer the packing of the powder particles, the smaller the particle size, and the higher the temperature, the shorter the time required for sintering. To keep the sintering time within reasonable limits, the powder is generally compacted under high pressures to bring the particles as close together as possible. The average particle size ranges from about 0.006 to 0.00001 in. in diameter, and the powder contains both large and small particles in order to have as many points of contact between particles as possible. Their shape is usually quite irregular. Thus, the concept of a particle diameter, corresponding to a spherical shape, is only an approximation.

During liquid phase sintering, the proportion of liquid to solid metal must not get too high, or the part will lose its shape, or distort badly. The amount of molten metal present should not exceed about 30% of the total volume of liquid and solid together. The time required for sintering in this instance generally depends on the condition and size of the solid particles and upon the temperature, just as in solid state sintering. The greater the amount of liquid metal present during sintering, however, the shorter will be the sintering time.

One other variety of sintering is actually intermediate between the two types described above. If a metal powder is partially sintered in the solid state, it will contain interconnected holes or pores between the solid metal particles. If the partially sintered metal is placed in contact with a molten metal that will wet the sintered powder but not completely alloy with it, then the molten metal will infiltrate the sintered powder and, if enough liquid is present, fill up the pores.

In most sintering processes the dimensions of the mass of powder change during the sintering. This change may be a shrinkage or expansion; the former is likely for powders of simple composition. The amount of the change depends chiefly on the composition of the powder, the particle size and shape, the amount of compression to which the powder has been subjected before sintering, and the time and temperature of sintering. Dimensional changes vary from 1 or 2% up to about 25%. This change must be allowed for in the design of parts which are to be made directly to shape and size.

MANUFACTURE OF METAL POWDERS

In general, metal in powdered form is a premium product, since energy must be expended to obtain a metal in a finely divided condition. Also, powders for powder metallurgy must often meet certain specifications as to particle size, shape, and other properties. To meet these, careful precautions may have to be taken during manufacture of the powder. There are two classes of methods used to manufacture metal powders: mechanical and chemical.

Chemical methods of producing metal powders are adaptable to a large number of metals. In reduction, the most widely used method, a compound of the metal (generally an oxide, although sulfides and chlorides are also employed) is reduced by a chemical agent, either a gas, liquid, or solid, which breaks down the compound into particles of the desired metal and some by-product that must be removed or separated from the metal itself. If the original metal compound is a solid, the size of the particles of the resultant metal depends largely on the condition of the solid compound; a finely divided compound will yield small metal particles. Most solid metal compounds, like oxides, are brittle and can be milled to a fine particle size, so with these the reduction method can produce a finely divided metal powder.

Where the by-product of the reduction of a metal compound and a chemical agent is a gas, its removal is simple and requires only some form of vacuum pump or a continuous flow of an inert or reducing gas to sweep the by-product away. An example is the reduction of copper oxide with hydrogen gas at 350° C (662° F) to form copper metal and steam. The steam is easily removed by continually passing fresh hydrogen over the solid copper oxide. The by-product may, however, be a solid or a liquid that solidifies on cooling from the reduction temperature, as in the case of the reduction of titanium tetrachloride with magnesium at 900° C (1,652° F). The by-product formed along with the titanium metal is molten magnesium chloride, which solidifies around and between the titanium particles. The magnesium chloride must be dissolved away from the titanium with dilute acid or removed by melting and distillation in a vacuum.

Reduced type powders generally consist of irregular particles containing isolated and/or interconnected porosity. Significant amounts of impurities are usually present, such as unreduced oxides.

Another widely used chemical method is the electrolysis of a liquid solution that contains the desired metal. Many metal compounds may be dissolved in water at room temperature or in a molten metal compound at elevated temperatures. An electric current is passed through the solution, and the metal is deposited on the cathode. This process is similar to electroplating, but the conditions of current and temperature are adjusted to produce a porous, flaky, or brittle deposit of metal. This coating is

TABLE I.—*Sintering Temperatures and Times, and Melting Points*

Metal	Sintering temperature, °C	Sintering time, minutes	Melting point, °C
Aluminum	540–640	15–30	660
Bronze (90% Cu–10% Sn)	760–870	10–20	999
Copper	840–900	12–45	1,083
Iron	1,000–1,150	8–45	1,530
Nickel	1,000–1,150	30–45	1,455
Stainless steel	1,100–1,300	30–60	approximately 1,375
Molybdenum	2,050	120	2,610
Tungsten	2,340	480	3,410

scraped off or broken up to obtain the powder. If the powder is required to be ductile, it is generally heated in an inert or other protective atmosphere to soften the metal. Copper powder is often made by this process from aqueous solutions. Titanium and zirconium powders are made by electrolysis of fused chlorides.

A few miscellaneous chemical methods are used to produce minor amounts of metal powders. Some metals, like copper, are readily obtained as water solutions of their compounds. If clean scrap iron or steel is placed in these solutions, copper metal will be precipitated while iron dissolves in the solution. Since copper is more valuable than steel, this process is economically sound for copper production. Iron and nickel form gaseous compounds with carbon monoxide at elevated temperatures and pressure. These compounds are called carbonyls, and they may be broken down into metal particles and carbon monoxide again at low pressures. This technique allows the formation of high purity spherical particles of iron and several irregular types of particles of nickel.

Mechanical methods are applied to either solid or liquid metals. The most widely used method for solids is milling by power-driven hammers (hammer milling) or balls in a rotating container (ball milling). If the metal is brittle, it will easily break into many small, equiaxed particles. Milling times may run from 1 or 2 to 100 hours or more, with the longer times resulting in very finely divided powder. This type of particle can be used in powder-metallurgy products. Annealing (heating) of the powder may be necessary, however, to remove the effects of the mechanical treatment and produce softer powder particles. If the metal is ductile, however, and can be readily deformed, it will form small, flat flakes when pounded. This type of particle is not well adapted to fabrication of items by powder-metallurgy techniques but finds use as pigment for inks and paints. Solid metals can also be cut or machined to produce fine chips.

Liquid metals can be subjected to atomization, a process that breaks up the metal into droplets that are allowed to solidify in air, water, or an inert gas. In most of these methods a stream of liquid metal is broken up by an air blast or a stream of water

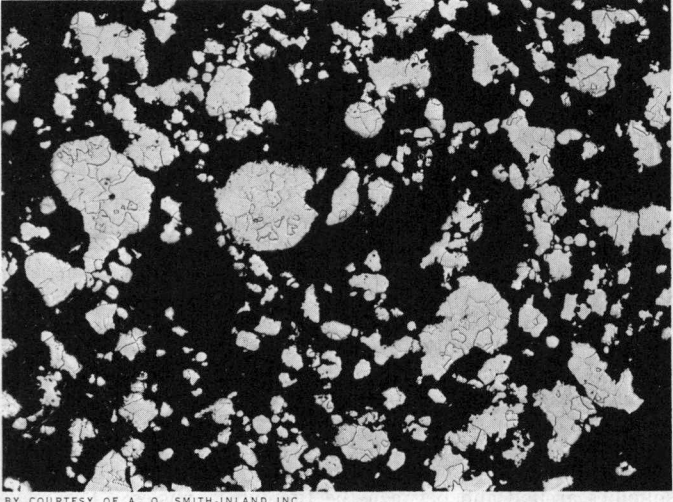

COMMERCIAL GRADE OF ATOMIZED STEEL POWDER, SHOWING CROSS SECTIONS OF PARTICLES. NOTE IRREGULAR SHAPE, DISTRIBUTION OF PARTICLE SIZES, AND POLYCRYSTALLINE (GRAIN) STRUCTURE OF INDIVIDUAL PARTICLES. MAGNIFIED 100 TIMES

and the air or water also cools, or freezes, the metal droplets. Another method consists of having a stream of molten metal fall onto a rotating wheel simultaneously cooled by air or water. These processes are applicable to any metal or alloy that can conveniently be melted. This method is widely used to produce high purity pure metal and alloy-type powders. In the latter each particle is analogous to a casting of the true alloy.

One advantage of mechanical methods of powder production is that alloy powders containing two or more constituents can be produced. Such alloys as brass (copper-zinc), bronze (copper-

tin), and steel (iron-carbon) can be produced in powder form in this way, which is not generally true of the chemical methods of powder production. The greatest disadvantage of milling methods is that these are restricted to brittle metals or alloys, and most useful metals, like copper and iron, as well as their alloys, are ductile. This problem can sometimes be avoided by intentionally embrittling a normally ductile material, pulverizing it while in the brittle condition, and then treating the powder to restore its ductility, if ductility of the powder is required. Certain magnetic iron-nickel alloy powders are made in this fashion.

Table II is a list of some metals used in powder metallurgy, along with the processes which can be used to produce each.

TABLE II.—*Metal Powder Manufacturing Processes*

Metal	Processes
Tin	Atomization
Aluminum	Atomization
Silver	Atomization, electrolysis, precipitation
Copper	Reduction, atomization, precipitation, electrolysis
Brass	Atomization
Bronze	Atomization
Beryllium	Reduction, electrolysis
Iron	Reduction, atomization, electrolysis
Steel	Atomization
Titanium	Reduction, atomization
Molybdenum	Reduction
Tantalum	Electrolysis
Tungsten	Reduction

PROCESSES AND PRODUCTS

The majority of processes used in powder metallurgy can be divided into three general classes, depending on the types of metal used in each: those involving metals of relatively low melting point that are ductile, such as silver, copper, and iron; those processes involving the so-called refractory metals of high melting point, such as tungsten, molybdenum, and titanium; and the processes for the production of materials known as cemented carbides, which contain tungsten carbide.

Ductile Metals.—Parts made from ductile metal powders generally are produced directly to the shape in which they will be utilized. Most of these parts produced by powder metallurgy consist of an alloy of two or more materials such as iron and carbon (steel), copper and tin, or a mixture of two or more metals that do not alloy and that cannot normally be mixed together, such as copper and tungsten. If an alloy part is the final product, it is often made by starting with the separate constituents and allowing alloying to take place during the sintering operation, rather than starting with alloy powder. The former approach is generally used when medium to high densities are required; alloyed powder particles are too resistant to deformation and densification during forming of the shaped part.

The production starts with the mixing or blending together of the required constituent powders and usually a solid lubricant, very similar to a soap, such as zinc stearate; this lubricant allows the powder particles to flow easily and also is necessary to reduce friction when the powder mixture is pressed to shape. The loose powder at this point has a density of about 30 to 60% of the density of a similar mass of solid, nonporous metal of the same composition.

A pressing, briquetting, or compaction operation forms the metal powder to the desired shape at room temperature. A die of strong, hard material, generally a high-quality steel or carbide material, and several punches or plungers are used. Pressure may be applied through both the upper and lower punches in order to achieve uniform densities in parts that are not extremely small. This method of forming parts has several limitations that must be borne in mind in the design of parts to be made from ductile metals by powder metallurgy. The die must have straight sides and cannot be undercut, since metal powder, even though it is blended with a lubricant, will not flow readily into an undercut portion of the die cavity that is not directly subjected to pressure from the punch. In addition, the powder tends to adhere to the inside walls of the die cavity. This effect is called die-wall friction and acts to decrease the pressure available to compact the powder. Despite lubricants blended in with the powder, die-wall friction prohibits the compaction of parts whose height is more than about three times their width, so that tall, narrow shapes are not easily made by pressing. Die-wall friction also causes wear of the die; the lifetime of a die is of the order of 150,000 pressings even when the surface of the die cavity is made as hard and wear resistant as possible.

The pressures used to compact ductile metal powders range from about 10 to 60 tons per square inch, depending on the shape of the part and the type of metal used. After pressing, the part is removed from the die, and the pressure used must have been sufficient to give the compacted powder enough strength to withstand this removal and subsequent handling. If only a few parts are being made on an experimental basis, simple hand-operated hydraulic presses are used. If many thousands of parts are to be made, automatic presses, either mechanical or hydraulic, are necessary; the former have maximum capacities of about 100 tons total force and can produce parts at rates up to 100 per minute, while the hydraulic presses are capable of exerting up to 5,000 tons total force at a rate of one to five pressings per minute. The tonnage capacities of such presses limit the size of parts that can be made to about 2 in. square in mechanical presses or about 100–200 in. square in hydraulic presses. One type of automatic mechanical press known as the rotary press compacts several small batches of powder simultaneously and is capable of a maximum output rate of several thousand parts per minute.

Automatic presses measure the correct amount of powder into the die cavity, compact the powder, eject this compacted powder, and then repeat their cycle. Either the total amount of compaction of the powder or the total force exerted on the powder may be controlled, depending on the type of press.

During pressing, the metal powder is compacted by a ratio from 2:1 to 3:1, so that the compacted powder is about 60 to more than 90% as dense as a similar mass of solid metal. Only ductile metals of rather high purities can be subjected to a compaction of this magnitude. Brittle powders usually have a high strength that prevents such a considerable compression at practically attainable pressures, and even if they could be compressed by the application of a high enough pressure, the particles of a brittle material would fracture and not interlock or flow around each other as do the particles of a ductile metal powder. This last feature is particularly important, since it means that the interlocked particles of a compacted ductile metal powder will have appreciable strength after pressing. The powder after pressing is called a green compact and should have a strength of at least a few hundred pounds per square inch to allow normal handling. Green strength is promoted by particles having an irregular shape; spherical powders are usually incompactible and not usable for molding applications. The exterior surface of the green compact after it has been ejected from the die will have almost exactly the same shape and be slightly larger in size (due to elastic expansion upon ejection) than the cavity of the die in which it was formed. To develop strength to withstand the stresses encountered in service, however, it must be sintered to bond the individual particles together.

Sintering of green compacts of ductile metal powders generally takes place with no liquid phase present, since this method of sintering results in the least distortion of the shape of the green compacts as well as permitting the highest degree of dimensional control. Many iron-powder parts, however, are sintered in contact with molten brass or copper, so that the liquid metal infiltrates the partially sintered iron structure. The furnaces used for sin-

BY COURTESY OF AMPLEX DIVISION, CHRYSLER CORP.

BRIQUETTING PRESS SHOWING (LEFT) PART EJECTED FROM THE DIE AND (RIGHT) METAL POWDER FROM WHICH PARTS ARE MADE

tering ductile metals show as much variation in size and type as do presses for compaction. Sintering furnaces have one characteristic in common: they must protect the heated metal powder that is being sintered from contact with the air if production of a clean, oxide-free part is desired. Gaseous furnace atmospheres commonly used for this purpose are carbon monoxide-carbon dioxide mixtures with varying amounts of nitrogen, pure hydrogen, and hydrogen-nitrogen mixtures. The carbon monoxide-carbon dioxide mixtures are made from the partial combustion of coke or natural gas; hydrogen is made by electrolyzing water into its constituents and is readily available commercially; and hydrogen-nitrogen mixtures are obtained by the dissociation of ammonia gas. The sintering atmosphere is usually enclosed in a muffle that is heated externally by burners or electric-resistance elements. Electric heating is often used because it is clean and easy to control.

The smaller furnaces used for sintering may be only a few feet long and of the pusher type in which an operator places green compacts in trays and pushes these slowly through the furnace from one end to the other. This type will sinter only a few hundred parts per hour. Large furnaces are employed where many parts must be sintered, and may be of the pusher type with automatic and mechanized operation, the roller-hearth type with rollers along the bottom of the muffle over which trays of parts are passed, or the belt-conveyor type which has an endless heat-resistant alloy belt passing continually through the furnace. This latter type of furnace can sinter thousands of parts per hour. (See FURNACE, METALLURGICAL.)

The strength and toughness of a sintered compact of a ductile metal powder will be somewhat less than those of a cast material of the same composition due to porosity inherent in the powder-metallurgy part. Infiltration of a partially sintered part, the use of specific alloying elements, and the use of repressing and re-sintering operations to increase density, however, can be used to increase its strength. Also steel parts made from some types of powder mixtures can be heat-treated after sintering to develop higher strengths than would be obtained from as-sintered material. In general the good strength and lower toughness of pressed and sintered parts must be considered for projected applications. Fully dense materials can be made by mechanically working (forging or extruding) sintered compacts; these have properties equal or superior to conventional wrought products.

Many ductile metal compacts experience a shrinkage of about 1 to 5% in their dimensions during sintering. When this is properly allowed for in the design of dies, sintered parts can be produced that will have their dimensions equal to any specified size within a tolerance of from 0.1 to 1%. Many parts produced to such tolerances can be used as is, with no further treatment necessary. This dimensional tolerance may not meet all design requirements, however, so that some postsintering operation is necessary. The most common procedure is to make parts slightly oversized as regards the exterior dimensions and then compress the part slightly in a split or sectional die to bring it to the correct size. This repressing is known as sizing or coining, and no metal is removed from the part in this operation. Interior dimensions, some exterior contours, and such features as an internally threaded hole that cannot be pressed to shape require machining operations on the sintered part. Sintered parts may also receive treatments other than coining or machining. Parts designed for use as bearings are

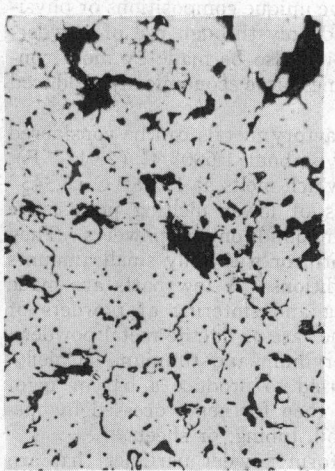

BY COURTESY OF PRESMET CORP.

SURFACE OF POROUS BRONZE BEARING MADE FROM METAL POWDER; POLISHED, NOT ETCHED. DARK AREAS REPRESENT VOIDS IN THE METAL BEARING. MAGNIFIED 250 TIMES

usually impregnated with lubricating oil or a solid antifriction material by means of a vacuum treatment. The oil in the pores of the bearing serves as a reservoir for lubrication during the lifetime of the bearing. Parts may also be electroplated or may be steam treated to provide a more corrosion-resistant or a more attractive surface.

A few types of powder-metallurgy products made from ductile metals do not follow the exact cycle of pressing and sintering which has been described. Metal-powder filters are one example of such parts. In some cases the powder is not pressed. Instead the powder is poured into suitable forms of graphite or ceramic and heated while still confined in these forms. The sintering of the particles is allowed to take place to develop reasonable strength in the filter, but not to the extent where the pores between the particles are closed up due to shrinkage. Special powdered additions termed pure formers may be mixed in with the metal powder to help control the amount and nature of the porosity. These are burned off prior to or during sintering. Alloy powders, such as bronze or stainless steel for corrosion-resistant purposes, are generally used in the manufacture of metal-powder filters.

The pressing operation may also be replaced by other compacting procedures. Ductile metal powder can be fed between a pair of rotating rolls which compact the powder into a wide, continuous sheet. Or metal powder can be extruded through a shaped, wear-resistant alloy nozzle called an extrusion die. This process is much like that of pressing paste through a tube, except that higher pressures are required. Extrusion is particularly successful in fabricating parts from very ductile powders. (*See* also Die Casting.)

TABLE III.—*Items Made from Ductile Metals*

Description	Composition	Uses
Small structural parts, such as gears, cams, retainers .	Iron, brass, bronze, iron infiltrated with copper, aluminum, steel	Machine parts where strength is not extremely important
Structural parts . . .	Steel	High-strength machine parts
Porous bearings . . .	Bronze, copper-graphite, lead-bronze, iron	Bearings or bushings (often impregnated with lubricating oil)
Electric conductors . .	Copper-tungsten, silver-molybdenum, copper-graphite	Switch contacts, current collectors in rotating machinery
Friction linings . . .	Copper-graphite, copper-silica-lead	High-friction material for heavy-duty clutches and brakes
Filters	Bronze, iron, stainless steel, nickel alloys	Rigid filters, corrosion-resistant filters
Heavy metal . . .	Tungsten-nickel	High-density material for weights and radiation shielding

Table III is a list of some of the items made from ductile metal powders. Some of these have unique compositions or physical properties that can be attained only through use of powder-metallurgy techniques. Others could also be made by more conventional processes but are sometimes more economically produced by powder metallurgy.

Refractory Metals.—The refractory metals can be considered as those with melting points above about 1,600° C (2,912° F), with the exception of beryllium, which melts at 1,285° C (2,345° F). These metals, unlike metals of lower melting points, are generally obtainable from their compounds only as powders. They are usually utilized in the pure form or with only small amounts of other elements as alloying additions. A few parts are made directly to shape by the pressing and sintering of powders of the refractory metals, just as in the case of ductile metal powders. This is particularly true with beryllium and titanium. Chiefly, however, powder metallurgy is used to produce a bar or ingot of the refractory metal, which is then further processed by mechanical working to make wire, rod, tubing, or sheet.

Since most refractory metals form powder particles that are either too brittle or too hard to be compacted like the ductile metals, they can be compacted at room temperature only with a binder to hold the particles together. Examples are niobium, tantalum, molybdenum, and tungsten. Production starts with the blending of the metal powder with from ½ to 2% of a binder, such as paraffin wax, dissolved in a volatile solvent. The solvent is evaporated by gentle heating to leave a coating of binder on each powder particle. The powder is then compressed at pressures of up to 50–75 tons per square inch in a rigid die, as in the case described previously, or in a mold made from a flexible, rubbery material. In the latter case the mold is placed within a pressure vessel. Pressure is transmitted to the powder through the pressurized fluid from all directions. This isostatic type of compaction is well suited for hard powders and long, narrow types of compacts or ingots. The binders used do not have much strength so that the compacted powder is quite fragile and must be handled carefully to prevent breakage.

The green compact is presintered in a protective atmosphere at about 1,000° C (1,832° F) to volatilize the binder and to give the compact enough strength to withstand further sintering. The second sintering must be carried out at high temperatures that would be difficult to obtain in conventional furnaces (*see* Table I). Heating of the ingots to accomplish sintering is carried out by passing a heavy electric current through the metal. Heat is generated directly within the ingot because of the resistance it offers to the current flow. (See Furnace, Electric.) The amount of the current is carefully controlled to bring the temperature of the ingot close to its melting point to carry out sintering in the shortest possible time. Distortion of the ingots is pronounced under these conditions but is not important, since the ingot is mechanically worked by hot forging or other processes after sintering.

The atmosphere used for sintering of the refractory metals not only must prevent oxidation of the metal but also must not react detrimentally with the metal itself. For molybdenum and tungsten purified hydrogen gas makes a satisfactory atmosphere. Since niobium and tantalum are embrittled by heating in a hydrogen atmosphere, they are sintered in vacuum.

Molybdenum and tungsten sintered ingots are brittle, although strong, after sintering, in contrast to niobium and tantalum. Some amount of ductility can be produced in the former by proper mechanical working of the ingots, which also closes up the pores remaining in the ingot after sintering, to make a completely dense material. The sintered ingots must first be forged hot, then forged or rolled at successively lower and lower temperatures until deformation, such as cold-rolling into sheet or drawing into wire, is possible at room temperature.

To make ingots or certain shapes of refractory metals from powders, the processes of pressing and sintering can also be combined into a single operation known as hot-pressing, actually compaction of the metal at an elevated temperature. Extrusion is a more satisfactory process to achieve compaction than is pressing in a die because of the problem of finding a die material that can withstand the high temperature encountered in hot-pressing. In extrusion the process is so rapid that the extrusion die does not become too hot during the process except at the surface immediately in contact with the hot metal powder. Hot extrusion has been applied chiefly to beryllium, zirconium, and titanium in the refractory metal class, and to nickel base superalloys. Since these metals would oxidize if exposed to air when hot, the powders are placed in a thin-walled steel container that is evacuated by means of vacuum pumps. The container and powder are then heated, and the hot assembly is extruded in presses of up to 1,000 tons capacity. The steel container is removed after extrusion by machining. The result of extrusion is a rod or tube with a diameter of up to 2 or 3 in., which is almost completely dense. A rod can be further mechanically worked by rolling or other processes, while tubes are used for applications requiring piping that has to withstand corrosive or other conditions for which these metals are suited. In this connection, it should be noted that beryllium and zirconium are both particularly useful in the production of nuclear energy, since these metals have a very low neutron absorption, and parts made from them can be used in the interior construction of nuclear reactors.

Hot-pressing with a die is most feasible with refractory metal powders if the powder is placed in the die and heated by passing a current through the powder itself. If the rate of heating of the powder is high enough, the die will not become hot throughout but only at the surface in contact with the powder. This technique requires that the powder be insulated electrically from the die wall by some type of high-resistance lining so that the die will not short-circuit the heating current around the powder.

Table IV lists some of the uses of relatively pure refractory metals made by powder metallurgy. Porous refractory metals infiltrated with a lower-melting-point metal are used for a number of unique applications such as silver-infiltrated tungsten rocket nozzles.

TABLE IV.—*Refractory Metals*

Metal	Use
Beryllium	Construction of nuclear reactors, windows for X-ray tubes, lightweight panels for space vehicles, aircraft brake systems
Zirconium	Construction of nuclear reactors, corrosion-resistant parts
Titanium	Lightweight aircraft parts, corrosion-resistant parts
Molybdenum	Vacuum-tube components, electrical resistors, electrical contacts
Tantalum	Highly corrosion-resistant parts, vacuum-tube components, electrical capacitors
Tungsten	Vacuum-tube filaments and parts, electrical contacts, glass-to-metal seals, rocket nozzles, nose cones, and ion engines

Cemented Carbides.—The so-called cemented-carbide materials made by powder metallurgy contain as their principal constituent powder of the compound of tungsten and carbon known as tungsten carbide. Other refractory metals, notably titanium and tantalum, also form similar compounds, and these are often used along with tungsten carbide powder. The carbides have extremely high melting points and are very hard. The principal use of cemented carbides is as metal-cutting tools and as parts that must resist wear or abrasion.

The melting point of carbides is so high that pure tungsten carbide powder cannot be satisfactorily sintered. The carbide particles must be bonded or cemented together with another metal; cobalt is generally used for this purpose in amounts ranging from 3 to 25%. The manufacture of cemented-carbide materials starts with the blending of carbide powders and cobalt powder. The blended powders are mixed with a binder, as in the case of the refractory metals, and pressed to shape in a die and punch set. A presintering treatment at about 900° C (1,652° F) evaporates the binder and results in a material that has about the strength and consistency of chalk. The material in this condition can now be shaped by machining or grinding to provide the shape necessary in the finished part. The machining operation must be carried out at this point in the manufacture because the final product is so hard as to defy most cutting or grinding operations except those using the hardest of abrasives. The use of ferrous powders in place of cobalt, however, can allow machining after sintering; this is followed by heat treatment that hardens the material considerably.

After the presintered compact is shaped to size, it is sintered at a temperaure of 1,450°–1,550° C (2,642°–2,822° F). During this sintering process the metal melts so that molten metal completely surrounds the carbide particles. Shrinkages of up to 25% in the dimensions of the compact take place during sintering, and this shrinkage must be carefully allowed for in the shaping of the presintered compact.

The furnaces used for sintering cemented carbides are fairly small. Many utilize a ceramic muffle tube and an electric-resistance heater made either from one of the refractory metals, such as molybdenum, or from graphite. Some furnaces consist of a graphite muffle tube surrounded by a water-cooled coil of copper tubing, with a high-frequency electric current passing through the tubing (3,000–100,000 cycles per second). This arrangement is known as an induction-heating furnace, since the high-frequency current in the coil induces an electric current in the graphite tube within the coil. The induced current, in turn, heats up the graphite to a high temperature. In both types of furnace, purified hydrogen gas is generally used as the furnace atmosphere to protect the carbide and the metals from oxidation and also to protect the heater of an electric-resistance furnace or the graphite of an induction-heating furnace. To accomplish this, the entire furnace, heater and muffle alike, is surrounded by an enclosure which contains the furnace atmosphere. Electric-resistance furnaces used for sintering cemented carbides are of the pusher type, while induction-heating furnaces are usually of a batch type that must be loaded with presintered compacts, heated to the sintering temperature, cooled, emptied of their charge, and then reloaded. The heating and cooling rates of an induction-heating furnace are high enough so that this procedure is feasible.

The sintered carbide material may be utilized as is or subjected to further operations. In the manufacture of cutting tools for high-speed metal-cutting machines, such as lathes, milling machines, and drill presses, the cemented carbide is needed only for the tip of the cutting tool. A steel shank, a rod or rectangular piece of tough steel, is used to hold a small piece of the sintered carbide material. This piece may typically be only a fraction of an inch in thickness and half an inch square. Small pieces of cemented carbide of this type are fastened to the steel shank by brazing or soldering with copper or silver alloys. This technique can be used to fasten cemented-carbide tips to lathe cutting tools, drills, saw blades, and almost any other type of cutting tool. The advantage of cemented carbide over tool steel as a cutting tool stems from its ability to cut while red hot.

If the cemented carbide is to be used as a wear-resistant material, it may be inserted in a hole made in a heavier piece of steel. The dimensions of the carbide and the hole should be such that carbide can be pressed into the hole under pressure. Another method of getting a good fit is to cool the carbide to below room temperature, while the steel is heated to cause expansion. If the dimensions of the carbide and the hole are correct, the chilled carbide can easily be inserted in the hole in the warm steel, and when the whole assembly reaches room temperature, the steel will have contracted around the cemented carbide to grip it tightly.

A few types of small cemented-carbide parts are made by hot-pressing in dies, as in the case of refractory metals. This process offers some advantage in rapidly producing parts of somewhat lower quality than those made by pressing and sintering.

Carbide powders can also be used to provide hard, wear-resistant coatings on large areas of a softer metal without going through the pressing and sintering cycle. For this purpose, carbide powder and metal powder are forced into a hollow nickel or iron tube about one-quarter inch or larger in diameter. Twelve-inch lengths of this carbide-filled tubing can be used as arc-welding electrodes to provide a hard facing of carbide particles bonded with a cobalt-nickel-iron alloy on any electrically conducting surface. The process consists of striking an electric arc between the electrode and the surface to be plated, just as in arc welding. The heavy electric current in the arc (50–200 amp.) causes melting of the end of the tube, the cobalt, and the surface layer of the work being plated. Tungsten carbide and molten metal drop from the end of the electrode to the surface of the work and solidify there to produce a material much like a cemented carbide. Thus a tough base metal may be coated with an extremely wear-resistant coating about one-sixteenth to one-eighth inch thick. In another version of this process, a hot mixture of tungsten carbide and cobalt powders is projected forcibly onto a base-metal surface by a gas explosion to produce very thin wear-resistant coatings on the base metal.

Much effort has been devoted to the development of heat-resistant materials that can operate under stress at high temperatures, as, for example, in gas turbines or jet engines. These materials have been made experimentally from powdered compounds of refractory metals with carbon, boron, and silicon. These elements form carbides, borides, and silicides, respectively, with most of the refractory metals. Powder particles of these compounds can be bonded together with a metal, as in the manufacture of cemented carbides. The major shortcoming of such materials is their poor resistance to mechanical shock.

The same may be said of metal-ceramic combinations made from ceramic powders that are bonded with a metal (*see* METALLURGY: *Powder Metallurgy: Cermets*). But ceramic parts of silicon carbide and aluminum oxide are produced by pressing and sintering on an industrial scale for unique application.

Among the metal carbides that have been developed for high-temperature operation are those of titanium and chromium, with nickel or a nickel-base alloy as the binder. These were developed primarily for use in jet-engine components, with high resistance to oxidation at temperatures from 870° to 1,200° C (about 1,600° to 2,200° F). These carbides also are sometimes referred to as cermets. In addition to jet-engine components they have been used in high-speed tools, dies, and other high-temperature applications. Chromium carbides with nickel, nickel-chromium, or nickel-cobalt as binder are resistant to oxidation and corrosion at temperatures up to 980° C (about 1,800° F). Commercial applications include dies, punches, and valve components. Carbides of molybdenum, vanadium, and hafnium with metal binders of cobalt, nickel, iron, or chromium have been developed for specialized uses, as in rocket nozzles.

BIBLIOGRAPHY.—J. S. Hirschhorn, *Introduction to Powder Metallurgy* (1969); R. L. Sands and C. R. Shakespeare, *Powder Metallurgy Practice and Applications* (1966); P. Schwarzkopf and R. Kieffer, *Cemented Carbides* (1960); W. D. Jones, *Fundamental Principles of Powder Metallurgy* (1961).   (J. S. HI.)

POWELL, CECIL FRANK (1903–1969), British physicist, who was awarded the 1950 Nobel Prize for Physics "for his development of the photographic method in the study of nuclear processes and for his discoveries concerning mesons," was born at Tonbridge, Kent, Dec. 5, 1903. After studying natural science at Sidney Sussex College, Cambridge, he worked for two years as a research student in the Cavendish Laboratory. In 1928 he was appointed research assistant to A. M. Tyndall, director of the Wills Physical Laboratory at the University of Bristol; there he remained as lecturer, reader and, after 1948, as Melville Wills professor of physics. His experiments led to many fundamental discoveries. The most important of these was the development of a photographic method of observing the tracks of elementary particles. The method was subsequently applied to the study of the particles occurring in the primary cosmic rays which come from outer space. This was done by exposing plates coated with a special emulsion on high mountains and in special balloons made of a thin plastic material. One consequence of this work was the discovery in 1947 of new forms of matter, the heavy mesons. Powell was elected a fellow of the Royal Society in 1949, and was given its Royal Medal in 1961. He died near Milan, Italy, on Aug. 9, 1969. In collaboration with G. P. S. Occhialini he wrote *Nuclear Physics in Photographs* (1947), and with P. H. Fowler and D. H. Perkins, *Study of Elementary Particles by the Photographic Method* (1959).   (W. J. BP.)

POWELL, JOHN WESLEY (1834–1902), U.S. ethnologist and geologist, the founder of the United States Bureau of American Ethnology, is remembered both for his pioneer classification of American Indian languages and for his surveys of the Rocky Mountain region. He was born in Mount Morris, N.Y., on March 24, 1834. He began his professional career in geology with his appointment, in 1865, as professor of geology and curator of the museum at Illinois Wesleyan University, and afterward at Illinois Normal College. In 1867 Powell began a series of expeditions to the Rocky Mountains and the canyons of the Green and Colorado rivers during which, in 1869, he made a daring boat trip of three months through the Grand Canyon. For the Smithsonian Institution, in which he founded and directed the Bureau of American Ethnology, he also made ethnological studies that resulted in the first definitive analysis of North American Indian languages. His able work led to the establishment of the U.S. Geographical and Geological Survey of the Rocky Mountain Region, with which he was occupied from 1870 to 1879. This survey was incorporated with the U.S. Geological and Geographical Survey in 1879, the year in which Powell became director of the Bureau of American Ethnology. He died in Haven, Me., on Sept. 23, 1902.

See F. S. Dellenbaugh, *A Canyon Voyage* (1962); M. T. Place, *John Wesley Powell: Canyon's Conqueror* (1963).

POWER. The word "power," as used by the engineer, indicates energy under human control and available for doing mechanical work. The principal sources of power are the muscular energy of men and animals; the kinetic energy of the winds and of streams; the potential energy of water at high levels, of the tides and of waves; the heat of the earth and of the sun; and heat derived from the combustion of fuels. Of these sources of power the winds, waves and solar heat suffer the disadvantage of being essentially intermittent and therefore requiring some method of storage of power if the demand for power is continuous. From the point of view of the size and cost of the power plant, when large amounts of power are required, windmills, wave motors and solar engines are not adaptable to large-scale power generation; tidal power, while it may be developed in certain places for large power, usually entails excessive first cost; volcanic power or natural steam is used in Italy and Iceland; hydraulic turbines and heat engines alone permit the construction of compact plants of practically unlimited capacity and of moderate first cost. The commonly accepted unit of power is the horsepower, which was defined by James Watt (1736–1819) in 1783 as the equivalent of 33,000 foot-pounds (f.p.) of work per minute. This is about ten times as much work as can be done per minute by a labourer working eight hours per day.

The use of domesticated animals was the first enlargement of the power of man and the beginning of his civilization. The use of the wind for sailing vessels was an early development, but its use in operating windmills dates from about the 12th century. Water wheels were known in Greek times and are described by Vitruvius, but their capacity was very small. To the end of the 18th century the largest water wheels for industrial use did not exceed 10 h.p. The earliest operative heat engine was the cannon, used first at the end of the 13th century. The social consequences of its invention were momentous; it had a great part in the destruction of the feudal system. It represented a greater concentration of power than had been possible previously. Its indirect influence in stimulating the development of the art of cutting metals is of prime importance in the history of the heat engine.

The special incentive which gave birth to the steam engine was the desire to remove water from mines (particularly the tin mines of Cornwall). In 1698 Capt. Thomas Savery's engine was patented and a number of his engines were built. They were found to be extravagant in their use of coal. Four years later the first steam engine using a cylinder and piston was devised by Thomas Newcomen.

It was while repairing a model of this engine that James Watt made the improvements that resulted in the modern steam engine. In 1782 Watt patented a double-acting rotative engine which, for the first time, made steam power available for driving all kinds of mechanism. The result of this invention was the factory system and the Industrial Revolution. It became possible also to apply steam power to navigation and to railroads.

The next important advance in power generation was the invention by Benoît Fourneyron of the hydraulic (reaction) turbine in 1827, for utilizing the energy of water available under high heads. Impulse water turbines of the Pelton type, adapted to use the highest heads, were developed in California about 1860. Hydraulic turbines reached a high degree of perfection, giving efficiencies in excess of 90%.

The thermal efficiency of a heat engine is a function of the maximum and minimum temperatures of the working substance and also of the cycle of operations. The cycle of maximum efficiency for given temperature limits is the Carnot cycle. Combustion, which is the source of heat in heat engines, may occur either outside the engine (external combustion) or inside the engine (internal combustion). In external-combustion engines the working substance is distinct from the products of combustion, and heat travels to it by conduction through containing walls, such as boiler heating-surface. The maximum temperature of the working substance is then limited by the strength of the containing walls at high temperature. With internal combustion the products of combustion are used as the working substance, and there is no maximum temperature limit, since the containing walls, piston and valves can be water-cooled. The theoretical thermal efficiency of the steam turbine is about 36%, of the diesel engine about 50%. The brake thermal efficiencies actually realized are considerably lower. The internal-combustion engine is compact, of light weight, instantly available for use, has low labour cost and no stand-by losses. One of its principal disadvantages is that it uses a fuel more costly than coal except in diesel engines utilizing the cheapest grades of oil.

The first practical internal-combustion engine was that of E. Lenoir (1860). Two years later Beau de Rochas showed that for good efficiency it is necessary to compress the explosive mixture before igniting it, and in 1876 this idea was effectively realized in a successful explosion engine by N. A. Otto. The Otto cycle is the standard cycle in automobile, airplane and many stationary and marine engines. The fuel used by Lenoir and Otto was coal gas, but in 1883 Gottlieb Daimler substituted volatile liquid hydrocarbon fuel (gasoline or petrol) and thereby made the engine available for automotive purposes. The use of less volatile hydrocarbon fuels (kerosene, fuel oil, etc.) was first successfully developed by Hornsby in the Hornsby-Ackroyd engine of 1894. A year later Rudolf Diesel built his first engine, in which the air is brought up to the temperature of ignition of the fuel by the work of compression alone and fuel is injected in a finely atomized state after the compression is completed. It is possible to burn in it any fuel that can be atomized by high-pressure air injection, by spraying under very high pressure through small openings, or by other means. It offers the combination of the cheapest fuel and the highest efficiency of utilization. The diesel engine was slow in development at first because of many practical difficulties, especially from heat stresses. It came into wide use, however, in ships, railway locomotives and motorbuses.

The principal uses for power up to about 1890 were for driving shafting, pumps, compressors and hoists, for locomotives and for marine propulsion. With the improvements that had recently been made in the use of electricity the power station appeared. Electricity is a means for transmission of power and the only means which is economical for long distances and for complicated systems. The earlier power-transmission systems by rope drives, compressed air and water under pressure were too costly and cumbersome to survive.

See ATOMIC ENERGY; AUTOMOBILE; DIESEL ENGINE; GENERATOR, ELECTRIC; ELECTRIC POWER; HORSEPOWER; INTERNAL-COMBUSTION ENGINE; MOTOR, ELECTRIC; NUCLEAR ENGINEERING; POWER TRANSMISSION; SOLAR ENERGY, UTILIZATION OF; TURBINE; WINDMILL; see also references under "Power" in the Index.
(L. S. MA.; X.)

POWERS, HIRAM (1805–1873), perhaps the most famous U.S. sculptor of the middle of the 19th century, was born in Woodstock, Vt., on June 29, 1805. In 1826 Powers began to frequent the studio of Frederick Eckstein where he received some instruction, and at once became strongly attracted to the art of sculpturing. About 1829 he discovered his talent for modeling while working as a general assistant and artist in a waxworks museum in Cincinnati. His ingenious representations of scenes from Dante's *Inferno* met with extraordinary success.

At the end of 1834 Powers went to Washington, D.C., where he soon attracted much attention. During his stay in that city he modeled a portrait of Andrew Jackson (now in the Metropolitan Museum of Art, New York City), which is probably the best portrait he ever made. In 1835 Powers set out for Italy to become a sculptor and in 1837, after a few months residence in Paris, he settled in Florence, where he remained until his death. While he found it profitable to devote the greater part of his time to busts, his best efforts were bestowed on ideal work. In 1839 his statue "Eve" excited much admiration, and in 1843 he produced his most famous work "Greek Slave" (Corcoran Gallery, Washington, D.C.), a female nude, completed in 1843, which caused a sensation when it was exhibited at the Crystal Palace Exposition in London in 1851; it was this work that placed him among the leading sculptors of his time. High prices were paid for his work. He produced many portrait busts of the prominent American visitors to his studio, where he charmed them with his lively conversation. Powers died in Florence on June 27, 1873.

See Albert Ten Eyck Gardner, *Yankee Stonecutters* (1945); Lorado Taft, *History of American Sculpture* (1924).   (A. T. G.; X.)

POWER TRANSMISSION. The appliances for the utilization of natural sources of energy may be classified into three groups: (1) Prime movers, by means of which the natural form of energy is transformed into mechanical energy. To this group belong all such devices as water, gas and steam turbines, steam engines, internal-combustion engines, etc. (2) Machinery of any kind which is driven by energy made available by the prime mover. To this group belong all machine tools, textile machinery, pumping machinery, cranes—in fact every kind of machine which requires any considerable quantity of energy to drive it. (3) The appliances by means of which the energy made available by the prime mover is transmitted to the machine designed to utilize it.

In many cases the prime mover is combined with the machine in such a way that the transmitting mechanism is not distinctly differentiated from either the prime mover or the machine, as in the case of the locomotive. In other cases the energy made available by the prime mover is distributed to a number of separate machines at a distance from the prime mover, as in the multiple pulley-and-belt drives used in early factories. In this case the transmitting mechanism has a distinct individuality.

Finally, prime movers may be located in places where the natural source of energy is abundant (near waterfalls or in the neighbourhood of coal fields), and the energy made available is transmitted in bulk to factories, etc., at relatively great distances. In this case the method and mechanism of distribution become of paramount importance, since the distance between the prime mover and the places where the energy is to be utilized is limited only by the efficiency of the mechanism of distribution.

This article deals with power transmission by mechanical and hydraulic means. For a discussion of the generation, transmission and distribution of electricity, see ELECTRIC POWER.   (X.)

MECHANICAL POWER TRANSMISSION

Mechanical power transmission refers to the transfer of power through and among machines by means of mechanical devices, such as shafts, gears, belts and clutches. Other methods of power transmission, *e.g.*, electrical, are generally used to convey power over long distances. Power can also be transmitted by means of vibrating media, such as sound and electromagnetic waves—as, for instance, in the tremendous force that is effected by an explosive charge. Any moving mass possesses energy and, therefore, power. A flowing river or a blowing wind each possesses power which is available anywhere along its path of travel.

POWER AND ITS MEASUREMENT

Power.—Power is the time rate of doing work. When a body weighing 5 lb. is raised vertically a distance of 4 ft., 20 ft-lb. of work are performed. In general, work is done whenever a force is moved through a distance; work is the product of force times displacement. Either the force or the displacement must be effective; *i.e.*, either the displacement must be the component parallel to the force direction or the force must be the component parallel to the displacement path.

In fig. 1, for example, the applied force makes an angle of 30° with the direction of motion of the box along the floor. Thus the component parallel to the floor—the effective force—is 100 × cos 30°, or 86.6 lb. The work, then, is 86.6 × 5, or 433 foot-pounds (ft-lb.). The downward component, 100 × sin 30°, or 50 lb., per-

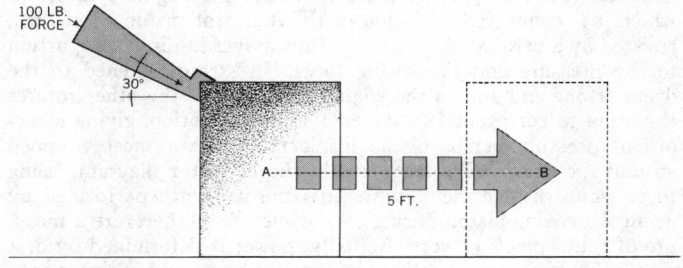

FIG. 1.—WORK SHOWN AS A RESULT OF FORCE (THRUST OF 100 LB. AT AN ANGLE OF 30°) AND DISTANCE (OBJECT MOVED 5 FT., A TO B)

forms no work because the box does not move in the vertical direction.

The factor of time is not considered in this example. On a slick floor the box might have moved 5 ft. in 3 seconds, while on a rough floor the time might have been 30 seconds. The difference is due to the frictional force between floor and box. What the frictional force does is also work, but the energy is wasted in heating the floor or the box, or both. Less of the total work is left in the second case, and so the box moves (accelerates) slower. The point is that the same amount of work is expended in each case but over a different period of time. In the first case, work is performed at 433/3 or 144.3 foot-pound/seconds (f.p.s.), and in the second case at 433/30 or 14.43 f.p.s. These figures are a measure of power—the time rate of doing work (see Power; Horsepower).

Mathematically, the time rate of work is expressed as dW/dt—the first derivative of work, W, with respect to time, t. This is the power at any given instant; the average power during some particular time interval is the total work divided by the time consumed: $P_{avg} = W/\Delta t$.

Work performed by a force F on a body which is thereby displaced a distance ds in the direction of the force is Fds; the power P is Fds/dt. Since ds/dt, the time rate of displacement, is velocity, power equals force times velocity, or $P = Fv$. Thus, force multiplied by effective velocity is an expression of power.

A torque or moment M_t applied to a body will cause it to rotate. That is, the body will undergo an angular displacement $d\theta$ during the time dt. The power involved here is: $P = dW/dt = M_t d\theta/dt = M_t\omega$, where ω is the angular velocity. Power is thus the result of force translation along a straight line, torque rotation about a plane, or some combination of the two.

These fundamental definitions can be used to derive the power involved in any particular case. When the force, or torque, and velocity are constant, power is computed, using the finite expressions. When either or both vary, the infinitesimal expressions are applied and integrated. Such cases can become quite complicated, mathematically.

Power Measurement.—Power-delivering machines must be evaluated, because the amount of power being delivered is most important. In numerous cases, power output can be measured at different places. For instance, in the case of an automobile, power can be measured at the output end of the engine or at the wheels. Thus it is possible to measure and identify power in many ways, such as indicated horsepower, brake horsepower, shaft horsepower and friction horsepower (see Horsepower).

In steam, gasoline and diesel engines, the working substance, resulting from the fuel combustion outside or inside the cylinder, exerts a varying force on a moving piston. In a reciprocating compressor and pump, power supplied to the shaft is transmitted to the piston and, in turn, to the working substance. In either case the piston force is variable. This variation must somehow be measured if the power delivered to or by the piston is to be determined. A special device called an indicator is used, and indicated horsepower (i.h.p.) is thus measured.

Of the many types of indicators, probably the most common is the piston type, often called a steam-engine indicator (it was originally designed to measure the power of steam engines). In a device of this type, the piston within the body of the indicator is actuated by the varying pressure within the engine cylinder to which it is connected. Motion of the indicator piston is, in turn, resisted by a calibrated spring and thus moves in direct proportion to the pressure and the spring force. A string fastened to the drum at one end and to the engine crosshead at the other rotates the drum to correspond to the engine-piston motion, giving a record of pressure versus piston displacement on a sheet wrapped around the drum. The area within the indicator diagram, being force times displacement, represents the net work performed by or on the engine piston during each cycle. It is therefore a measure of the engine's power. Actually, power is determined by first computing the mean effective pressure (m.e.p.)—the diagram area divided by the diagram length. The calculation yields the equivalent constant pressure which defines the same amount of work.

When the m.e.p. is multiplied by the piston area, the total force is found. This force multiplied by the stroke L and the number of cycles per minute n, and divided by the horsepower factor, yields the indicated horsepower:

$$\text{i.h.p.} = \frac{(\text{m.e.p.})ALn}{33,000} \text{ per piston face}$$

The result, of course, must be multiplied by the number of cylinders (or faces when each side of each piston develops power) present in the engine. Other indicators differ in the type of pressure-sensing unit or recording device; electrical, optical and diaphragm principles have been used.

Power may also be measured at the output end of an engine. A dynamometer, such as the Prony brake, is used for this purpose. The Prony brake is an energy-dissipating device in which friction generates heat. Some dynamometers use fluid friction in place of solid friction; e.g., hydraulic and air dynamometers. In other types, power is converted to electrical energy and dissipated in resistors as heat. Still another type is the torque transmission dynamometer, which measures the power actually being delivered. The power passes through the dynamometer without waste and is delivered by it to the work shaft. It is the angular twist occurring in the dynamometer shaft which is measured; this twist is directly proportional to the torque and so can be used to obtain the shaft horsepower (s.h.p.). Another transmission dynamometer uses electric strain gauges to sense the twist in the shaft, the strain gauge output being calibrated to yield the torque, which then can be converted into shaft horsepower (see Dynamometer).

Whenever one body slides or rolls over another, friction develops. Friction consumes power, and the power thus lost is called friction horsepower. Friction horsepower is not easy to measure. It can be determined, however, by measuring the power input at zero load; the entire input must be friction power, since external work is not being done. Friction horsepower can also be found by the method of difference: both input and output power, e.g., indicated and brake horsepower, are measured; the difference between the two is loss and so represents friction horsepower.

Any power wasted in friction becomes unavailable to do the machine's work, and thus the machine becomes less efficient. Mechanical efficiency, therefore, can be stated as the ratio of input to output horsepower. It is a measure of an engine's capacity to keep the externally usable power at a maximum; alternatively, it is also a measure of the ability of a machine to use the power supplied it to do useful work.

POWER PRODUCTION

Prime Movers.—Prime movers are power-generating devices, the output of which is used to operate machines. It is immaterial how the power is developed within the prime mover. In some, the energy is created chemically, as the burning gases in the internal-combustion engine; others convert one form of energy into another by physical means. For instance, steam is expanded to yield shaft power in the reciprocating steam engine; i.e., heat is transformed into mechanical power.

The terms prime mover, power source and power plant are often used interchangeably, but differences may exist. A prime mover provides the immediate energy needed to run the machine: the tiny motor powering an electric shaver is a prime mover. A power plant generates power within itself: the automobile engine is a power plant, but it also acts as a prime mover, turning the rear wheels of the car.

Fundamentally, the sun is the source of all power; the equivalent of the energy obtained from 2×10^{14} tons of coal reaches the earth as solar energy each year. If man knew how, he could produce 1 h.p. from the solar energy striking each square yard. Some of this energy is naturally consumed for man's welfare: evaporation and climatic differences, which bring about rain and winds, supply water, water power and wind power; vegetation feeds both man and animal and so generates muscular power; and the vegetation of past ages is available as coal and petroleum.

For practical purposes, discussion must be limited to power

sources found on earth in sufficient quantity for man's use. These are muscle, water and wind power, wood, coal, petroleum and natural gas. The direct use of solar energy constitutes another, although as yet minor, source (*see* SOLAR ENERGY, UTILIZATION OF). Atomic power is a source man has learned to harness only recently, and nuclear reactors are now used as the heat source in steam-power plants and marine propulsion. The only major difference between the ordinary and the nuclear steam-power plant is the replacement of the boiler by the reactor (*see* ATOMIC ENERGY; NUCLEAR ENGINEERING).

A typical list of prime movers might include: (1) muscles; (2) windmills; (3) sails; (4) water wheels; (5) reciprocating steam engines; (6) spark-ignition engines; (7) diesel engines; (8) hydraulic turbines; (9) steam turbines; (10) gas turbines; (11) jet and rocket engines; (12) electric motors; and (13) springs. The first four are industrially no longer important in much of the world, although they were in the past; however, in technically undeveloped nations they still provide the major portion of the power consumed.

MECHANICAL TRANSMISSION ELEMENTS

Devices which transmit the power output of prime movers to the place of use are transmission elements. Power involves time, force or torque, and velocity. The same power can result from a large force at low velocity or from a small force at high velocity. In one place on a machine one combination may be required; at an adjoining place, the other combination. If both locations are to be supplied by the same prime mover, many transmission elements may have to be interposed. Therefore, the elements may be numerous and complex.

Mechanical transmission elements include such devices as shafts, gears, belt drives, chain drives, couplings, clutches, brakes, power screws, cams, linkages, flywheels and bearings.

Shafts.—The various designs of shafts may be classified for convenience into two groups: transmission and machine shafts. Transmission shafts are those used outside the machine to bring power to it. These may be relatively long and supported at several places. Line shafts and countershafts, so common in older manufacturing plants, were of this type, distributing the power from a single prime mover to machines throughout the plant. In modern plants the single prime mover has been replaced by individual prime movers, one in each machine. Therefore any shafting needed becomes an integral part of the machine and so falls into the second group, machine shafts.

Basically there is no difference between machine and transmission shafts. Both transmit power, and they differ only in length and the number of stations at which power is withdrawn. The diameter depends upon the torque being transmitted and may be just as large on a short shaft as on a long one. In addition to the torque, shafts are subjected to bending forces (transverse to the shaft), if only due to their weight. Thus, flexure, as well as torsion stresses, is always present.

Since shafts are often critical members, they must be properly designed. The amount of twist, as well as the stress, must remain within safe limits. Generally, shafts are made of plain carbon and alloy steels. When greater strength is required, particularly at higher speeds, nickel, nickel-chromium and chrome-vanadium alloy steels are used. Shafts are hot-rolled to standard sizes, and for use under severe fatigue conditions, they are turned and ground or polished to eliminate all surface defects. In addition, they often are given special heat-treatments.

Most shafts are solid and of circular cross section, although they may be hollow, *e.g.*, to carry lubricants on an inner, concentric shaft, and occasionally a power shaft may have a cross section other than circular (*see* SHAFT, DRIVING).

Keyways and keys are an integral part of power shafting. Sometimes a shaft alone is used between the prime mover and load; more often, however, shafts have many other power-transmission elements attached to them. The elements must be fixed rigidly to the shaft, and to assure this, fasteners, such as keys, pins, cotters and splines, are used. These devices are interposed between the shaft and transmission elements to prevent relative motion between them. This often involves keyways along the shaft, as well as fasteners (*see* KEYS AND KEYWAYS).

Gears.—When teeth are placed around the surface of a cylinder, cone or hyperboloid, the member becomes a gear, another power-transmission element. Gears can transfer power from one shaft to another, and the shafts may be intersecting, as well as parallel. The transmission is positive because gears provide meshing surfaces which do not depend upon friction as the driving medium. Power must be transferred at a constant velocity ratio, quietly and with a low friction loss. Such requirements are not easily satisfied. Thus, gear teeth must be of proper profile, dimension, tolerance and finish. Gears having standard profiles but differing in other details are needed to connect the many shaft directions and satisfy other conditions arising in power transmission. The following types have been developed: spur, bevel, hypoid, helical, herringbone, planoid and worm. Descriptions and applications may be found in the article GEARS.

Belt Drives.—Belts are convenient power connectors when shafts are some distance apart and when an absolutely constant velocity ratio is not essential. Belts usually are used to connect shafts that are parallel, but the flexibility of belts permits other arrangements. Belt-connected shafts can be made to turn in opposite directions by crossing the belt.

A necessary part of the belt drive is the pulley over which the belt rides. Iron, steel, wood, compressed fibre, and plastic laminates are all used to make pulleys. Split as well as solid pulleys are common, the split type being easy to fasten to a long shaft because the halves can be placed over the shaft and clamped to it. When it is required to stop and start the driven shaft while the driving shaft continues its rotation, a tight-loose pulley combination is useful; the belt is shifted from one pulley to the other by means of a lever arrangement.

V-belts are made endless and in a sufficient number of standard sizes to meet most needs. Stretch in these drives is taken up by idler pulleys or pivoted motor bases. A more recent belting development is the toothed, or positive-drive, belt, with teeth on its inner surface to engage corresponding spaces on axially grooved pulleys. This arrangement approximates the positive gear drive, and it can be used when a flexible drive capable of synchronizing the shafts is needed. (For mechanics, applications and construction of belt drives *see* PULLEY AND BELT.)

Chain Drive.—When positive power transmission between shafts too far apart for gear connection is desired, chain drives become useful. The greater elasticity of chain drives also provides better shock absorption and wear is reduced because of the larger contact area.

A chain is a combination of close-tolerance links, pins and rollers. Standard chains are made in two forms: roller chain and silent chain, and they are manufactured in many sizes. Three principal dimensions define the chain: the pitch (length between rollers), the inside width of the chain and the outside diameter of the roller. A special link, easy to assemble and disassemble, is used to fasten the chain ends. Chains ride on sprockets or toothed wheels, the teeth being shaped to mesh precisely with the chain links.

A less refined but equally practical chain drive can be obtained by running a common link chain over a sprocket designed in the form of a pulley with its rim shaped to interlock with the links.

BY COURTESY OF LINK-BELT

A 12-IN.-WIDE SILENT CHAIN WITH 1-IN. PITCH THAT DRIVES A CENTRIFUGAL EXHAUST FAN AT FOUR SPEEDS UP TO 363 RPM

This type of drive is especially useful when heavy loads must be lifted without danger of slippage, as in the anchor windlass and in the differential chain hoist used in maintenance shops. (*See* CHAIN.)

Couplings.—Couplings are used to join shafts. In general, a coupling is considered a permanent connector, although it can be disconnected for repairs. Both rigid and flexible couplings are made; the latter allow for slight shaft misalignments. Couplings are made in many different styles, the most important of which are discussed in the article COUPLING.

Clutches.—The clutch is a device designed to connect and disconnect a power source from its load. Mechanical-contact clutches are of the positive friction type. Positive clutches contain protruding jaws which engage when the two halves are brought together. The jaws are either square (in which case rotation in either direction may be handled) or spiral (in which case only unidirectional rotation is possible).

The positive clutch is simple, slip-free and light. It does not develop appreciable heat and so can be engaged and disengaged frequently. On the other hand, the sudden engagement and release subjects not only the clutch but also the attached machinery to much shock and wear.

The friction clutch contains two friction surfaces, one on the driving element, the other on the driven element, and some form of linkage to engage and disengage the friction surfaces. Probably the chief advantage of the friction clutch is its ability to slip slightly when first engaged, thus cushioning shocks and reducing wear and stresses. The most common types are discussed in the article CLUTCH.

Brakes.—The mechanical brake, like the clutch, contains two friction surfaces and a mechanism which brings them into contact. The brake absorbs kinetic energy by generating and dissipating heat. Block, band, disk and shoe brakes are common. (*See* BRAKE.)

Power Screws.—Threaded rods (screws) are often used to transmit power. Lathes, presses, jacks and materials-testing machines are typical of devices employing power-transmission screws. Screw drives are not very efficient, but for slow, powerful motion, they are convenient. The lathe tool-carriage screw (*see* MACHINE TOOLS) is illustrative of an important trait of the power screw: its ability to convert a rotational force (torque) into a powerful linear (translational) force.

Cams and Linkages.—A cam transmits power by means of a follower in direct contact with it. The contact is either sliding or rolling. The cam itself can take many forms and can impart an infinite variety of reciprocating or oscillating motions to the follower. Because it can be designed to provide nearly any complex motion, it finds much use in automation devices, computers and servomechanisms. (*See* CAM.)

Like cams, linkages primarily transmit motion, although in some applications they may push or pull a load and in transmitting power become machines. For instance, the power generated at the piston of an internal-combustion engine is transmitted to the crankshaft by means of the connecting rod. The combination is one of the two basic link mechanisms: the slider crank and the four-bar chain. Important linkages of one type or the other are devices like the Scotch yoke, the Whitworth quick-return mechanism, the Geneva wheel, escapements, toggle joints, Hooke's coupling and the straight-line mechanisms. (*See* LINKAGES.)

Flywheels, Bearings.—These two devices only assist in power transmission; they do not in themselves actually transmit power. Flywheels are attached to a shaft and, because of the large mass involved, absorb and release energy to maintain a more uniform rotation. For example, during the power stroke of a punch press the kinetic energy of the flywheel provides some of the power suddenly needed. Therefore, shaft rotation is reduced but not stopped, as it might be without the flywheel.

Bearings permit motion of one part relative to another with a minimum of friction or power loss, while simultaneously supporting the load on the moving element. They are necessary machine elements in a power-transmission system but do not themselves transmit useful power. (*See* BEARINGS.)   (J. P. V.)

HYDRAULIC POWER TRANSMISSION

A variety of machines use some liquid for developing a push or pull, for moving some object or for controlling some action. Oil, water or some other liquid can be used, but oil is the most common. For practical purposes, it does not change its volume when the pressure is increased. Thus, if oil fills a hydraulic system completely (leaving no air or gas pockets), the motion of a piston can be controlled conveniently and within close limits by the oil flow. Oil lubricates the sliding parts and also prevents rust.

Many complicated hydraulic systems have been developed; however, most of these are essentially combinations of certain simple hydraulic circuits. A study of these simple systems is helpful in understanding the more complicated systems.

Hydraulic Press.—The simple system in fig. 2 illustrates the action of many devices, including the hydraulic press. The two

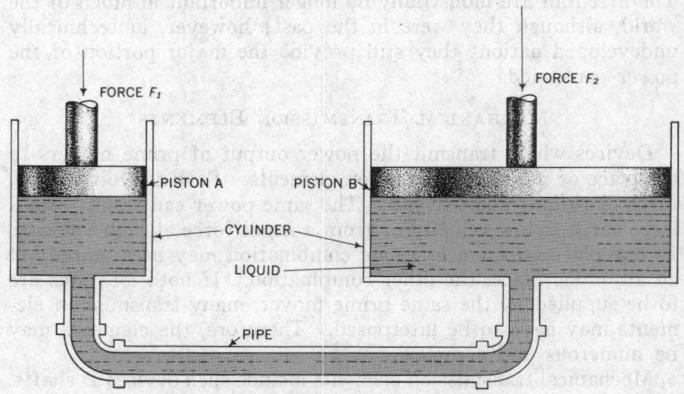

FIG. 2.—HYDRAULIC PRESS

cylinders are connected by a pipe. There is a close-fitting piston in each cylinder, and liquid in the pipe and cylinders. Assuming no leakage past the piston, the pressure of the fluid is the same in all parts—a statement of Pascal's law (*see* MECHANICS, FLUID). Essentially the same fluid pressure acts on the face of each piston. Thus a small force F_1 on piston A (small area) can balance a large force F_2 on piston B (large area). In principle, the hydraulic press is analogous to the mechanical lever.

Hydraulic System.—Fig. 3 is an example of a hydraulic system. Oil from a reservoir flows through a pipe into the pump, which increases the pressure of the oil. The oil then flows through a pipe into the control valve, which regulates the flow to the cylinder.

A relief valve, pre-set at some safe maximum pressure, is provided for the protection of the system; if the oil pressure should rise above the safe maximum, the relief valve will open and relieve the pressure. Oil entering the cylinder acts on the piston, and this action develops a force on the piston rod which can be used to operate some device. Oil from the cylinder returns to the

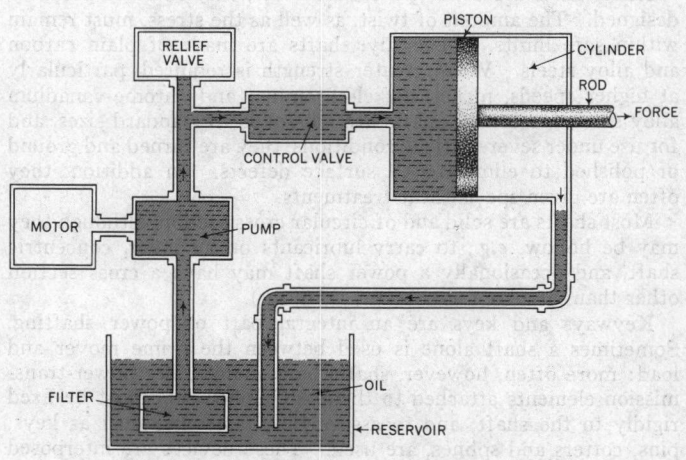

FIG. 3.—COMPONENTS OF A HYDRAULIC SYSTEM

reservoir. A filter in the circuit removes dirt and foreign matter from the oil.

As an illustration, assume that the oil pressure produced by the pump is 1,000 lb. per square inch (p.s.i.) and that the piston area over which the oil pressure acts is 3 sq.in. The force on the piston then is $3 \times 1,000$, or 3,000 lb. Thus, a relatively small pressure, acting on a small cylinder, produces a relatively large force to act on some load.

Fig. 3 also illustrates the principle of the hydraulic amplifier. Assuming that the pump produces a pressure of 1,000 p.s.i. in the system, as above, and that a force of 8 oz. is required to move the control valve through its entire range, from fully closed to fully opened, the 8-oz. force can be used to vary the output force on the piston through a range of 0–3,000 lb.

General Features of Hydraulic Systems.—There are three basic parts in the typical hydraulic system: (1) an oil pump; (2) a cylinder or chamber having an actuating piston driven by the liquid; and (3) valves and piping to control the flow of the liquid. The actuating piston can be given any motion desired for control and power. Straight-line reciprocating motion is common, and rotary motion of the driven unit can be accomplished with different hydraulic motors. With these basic features in mind, it is possible to develop different combinations of the simple system.

Hydraulic Pumps and Motors.—In the electric generator, mechanical energy is converted into electrical energy. In the fluid pump, mechanical energy is converted into fluid energy. Therefore, the electric generator and the pump are analogous. Likewise, both the electric motor and the hydraulic motor produce mechanical work, the former from electrical energy, the latter from mechanical energy. The fluid motor may be of either the reciprocating or the rotary type.

Hydraulic machines are of two principal kinds: the dynamic or velocity machine and the positive-displacement or static-pressure machine. In the dynamic or velocity type the action between some mechanical part and a fluid involves significant changes in fluid velocity. The electric fan and the automobile torque convertor are examples of the dynamic type.

In the positive-displacement or static-pressure machine the characteristic action is a volumetric change or a displacement action. The hand bicycle pump is an example of the displacement type of hydraulic machine. A positive-displacement machine may have either a fixed or a variable displacement. For example, the internal-combustion engine involves a crank, connecting rod, and piston; the piston displaces a certain fixed volume in the cylinder with each revolution of the crank. If the stroke could be varied, then the displacement could be varied.

The basic hydraulic machine is the plunger pump. It consists of a cylinder fitted with a reciprocating piston, and valves for directing the liquid to and from the cylinder. When acting as a pump, the piston does work on the liquid; the pressure is increased. When functioning as a motor, the liquid does work on the piston.

In a rotary hydraulic pump, work is done by a rotating member on the fluid; the pressure at the outlet is higher than the pressure at the inlet. In a rotary hydraulic motor, fluid pressure is higher at the inlet than at the outlet; the difference in fluid pressure is absorbed by the rotating member to turn the output shaft. Rotary machines are usually classified into three main types, according to the design of the rotating element: gear, vane or piston.

The hydraulic gear pump or motor has a pair of meshing gears in a casing. As the gears rotate, liquid passing through the inlet is trapped between their teeth and the casing and is carried around to the outlet. During each revolution of the gears a certain volume of liquid is transferred from inlet to outlet, so this is a fixed-displacement machine.

The hydraulic vane pump or motor has a rotating member fitted with sliding vanes and set off-centre in a casing. The entering liquid is trapped between the vanes (which ride on the inside of the case) and is carried to the discharge. Both the gear machine and the vane machine are described further in the article PUMP.

Fig. 4 shows the design principles of a hydraulic radial-piston pump or motor. The reaction ring, or housing, and the rotating cylinder block have centres which do not coincide. As the cylin-

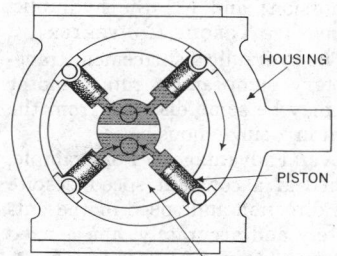

ROTATING CYLINDER BLOCK

FIG. 4.—HYDRAULIC RADIAL-PISTON PUMP OR MOTOR

der block rotates, the pistons in the cylinder block execute a reciprocating motion in a radial direction. By means of a valve arrangement, the liquid moves in and out of the machine at the centre of the cylinder block. The displacement of this machine can be varied by altering the distance between the centres of the cylinder block and the housing.

Various arrangements of axial-piston machines have been devised. Fig. 5 illustrates the features of one arrangement of a hydraulic axial-piston pump or motor. The pistons move back and forth in the cylinder block in a direction parallel to the axis of rotation of the cylinder block; this explains the term "axial-piston." The liquid enters and leaves the piston chambers, or bores, at the left end of the cylinder block, which is suitably arranged with a valve plate. The axis of the rotating shaft (either driver or driven) is set at an angle with respect to the axis of rotation of the cylinder block. As the shaft rotates, the piston connector actuates the piston; in one revolution of the shaft, each piston has reciprocated back and forth. This machine can be arranged for a variable displacement by varying the angle.

Standard gear pumps and motors are available for pressures of 2,000 p.s.i. or more, and gear motors are rated to deliver up to

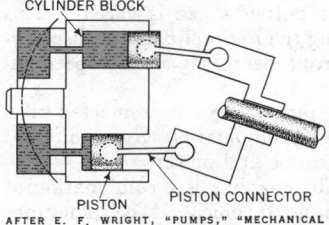

CYLINDER BLOCK

PISTON   PISTON CONNECTOR

FIG. 5.—HYDRAULIC AXIAL-PISTON PUMP OR MOTOR

20 h.p. Vane pumps and motors are made for the same pressures, and vane motors will deliver up to 125 h.p. Rotary piston pumps and motors are built for pressures of 5,000 p.s.i. or more, and the motors have outputs of as much as 150 h.p.

Valves.—In hydraulic systems one of the most common types of valve is the piston or spool valve (fig. 6). As shown in the figure, fluid enters port A, passes through the valve body and leaves at port B. By sliding the valve stem, the ports A and B could be blocked by a spool. Various arrangements of ports and spools can be used to get different types of flow control.

Accumulators.—Some hydraulic systems include an accumulator, which is a device for storing fluid energy. An air accumulator is a closed chamber, partly filled with air, into which the pump supplying hydraulic power to a machine delivers liquid while the machine is not working at full capacity. Such an air cushion is used on many reciprocating water pumps. The main purpose of the accumulator is to allow hydraulic machines, such as lifts and presses, to work for a short time at a greater rate than the pump can supply energy. The accumulator acts as a pressure regulator; it serves to damp out pressure surges and shocks in the system.

Hydraulic Transmissions.—Various methods can be used to connect two rotating shafts. In many cases purely mechanical connectors are suitable: gears, chain drives, clutches. In other applications, however, service requirements are best met with some form of hydraulic connector or transmission. In practice two types of hydraulic transmissions are commonly found: (1)

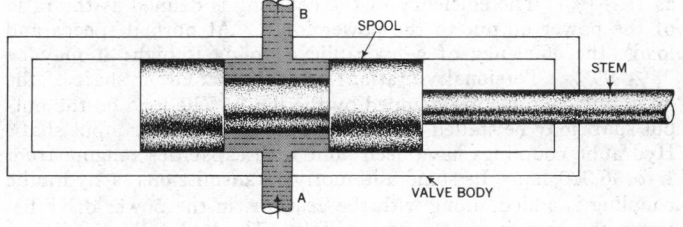

B   SPOOL   STEM

A   VALVE BODY

FIG. 6.—PISTON OR SPOOL VALVE

the static or displacement transmission; and (2) the hydraulic, hydrodynamic or dynamic coupling (*see* Torque Converter).

Displacement Transmission.—The hydraulic displacement transmission is a combination of a rotary pump and a rotary motor connected by piping. The pump may be some distance from the motor, or the two may be mounted in a single housing.

This type of transmission has several advantages. For example, the output shaft can be maintained at a constant speed despite a varying input-shaft speed. The direction and speed of the output shaft can be controlled remotely and accurately, and a fixed power output can be maintained over a range of speeds. Automatic overload protection can be maintained, and power consumption can be kept low.

There are four major combinations of pump and motor in a displacement-type transmission.

In the first, a variable-displacement rotary pump is connected to a fixed-displacement hydraulic motor. For a constant work load, a variation in the output-shaft speed will result in an almost constant output torque and variable power. Constant-torque hydraulic transmissions are used on machine tools and conveyors.

A second arrangement couples a fixed-displacement rotary pump with a fixed-displacement rotary motor; there is a flow-control valve in the connecting line to vary the rate of oil flow to the motor. If the load on the output shaft is constant, the output torque will be constant and the power will vary proportionally with the speed.

In a third arrangement, a fixed-displacement pump is connected to a variable-displacement motor. There are various applications, as in machine-tool spindle drives, in which it is desired to maintain constant output power as the output speed is varied. This condition can be realized by varying the hydraulic motor displacement; in this case the output torque decreases as the speed increases.

Finally a variable-displacement pump may be connected to a variable-displacement motor. This combination gives different variations in output-shaft speed, torque and power.

Hydraulic Coupling.—A hydraulic coupling is a combination of a centrifugal pump and a hydraulic turbine. It is sometimes called a hydraulic flywheel, primarily because it reduces torsional vibrations. The action of a hydraulic coupling can best be illustrated by two ordinary electric fans set facing each other. One fan is started by switching on the electric current; its blades rotate, the air flow turning the blades of the other fan. In the hydraulic coupling, the rotating input or primary shaft drives a centrifugal-pump runner or impeller. This usually has straight radial vanes or blades; in construction it resembles a grapefruit half, with the fruit removed. As the pump runner builds up speed, kinetic energy is added to the fluid, which flows outward along the vanes, crosses a gap and enters the turbine runner. Usually the turbine runner is similar in construction to the pump impeller, with straight radial blades. After sufficient energy has been developed, the liquid turns the turbine runner, which is connected to output or secondary shaft. There is no mechanical connection between the input and output shafts; the linkage between them is solely through the medium of the moving fluid.

Since there are no torque-reacting members in the hydraulic coupling other than the pump impeller and the turbine runner, the output torque always equals the input torque for steady operating conditions. The speed of the input shaft always exceeds that of the output shaft. At the start of operation, the input shaft rotates while the output shaft remains stationary; the "slippage" is 100%; at normal speeds and loads, the slip may be low as 1%–4%. The efficiency of the coupling is defined as the ratio of the power output to the power input. At normal speeds and loads, the efficiency of a hydraulic coupling is high; it may be 95%–99%. Torsional vibrations or shocks on either shaft of the hydraulic coupling are damped by the fluid. The load on the output shaft may be stalled without stalling the driver or input shaft. Hydraulic couplings have been built with capacities ranging from 1 to 36,000 h.p. In some automotive transmissions, a hydraulic coupling is added, along with the gearbox, in the power drive between the engine and the rear wheels. The hydraulic coupling is

not a substitute for the gearbox: the gearbox is used to change the torque, whereas the hydraulic coupling does not change the torque. The hydraulic coupling merely serves to cushion shocks.

A variant of the hydraulic coupling is the electromagnetic clutch, which contains a fluid suspension of paramagnetic particles (*e.g.,* a compound of iron). When an external magnetic field is applied, the fluid suspension becomes almost solidified and capable of transmitting torque.   (R. C. Br.)

Bibliography.—Abbott P. Usher, *A History of Mechanical Inventions,* rev. ed. (1954); C. W. Ham *et al.*, *Mechanics of Machinery,* 4th ed. (1958); R. E. Hampton, *Introduction to the Basic Mechanisms* (1956); H. H. Mabie and F. W. Ocvirk, *Mechanisms and Dynamics of Machinery* (1957); H. L. Stewart and F. D. Jefferis, *Hydraulic and Pneumatic Power for Production* (1955); W. Ernst, *Oil Hydraulic Power and Its Industrial Applications* (1949); I. McNeil, *Hydraulic Operation and Control of Machines* (1955); J. J. Pippenger and R. M. Koff, *Fluid-Power Controls* (1959); W. E. Wilson, *Positive-Displacement Pumps and Fluid Motors* (1950); H. G. Conway, *Fluid Pressure Mechanisms* (1949); R. Hadekel, *Hydraulic Systems and Equipment* (1954); R. C. Binder, *Fluid Dynamics and Fluid Machinery* (1964).

POWHATAN. This group of Algonkian Indian tribes in the tidewater portion of Virginia and southern Maryland had been welded into a confederacy, by the conquests of an able chief known by the same name, shortly before the settlement of Jamestown in 1607. His daughter Pocahontas (*q.v.*) married John Rolfe. After Powhatan's death the Indians massacred 347 British settlers in 1622. Fourteen years of relentless warfare followed until the Indians submitted, only to rise again in 1644 and slay 500 whites. The war that followed broke them, and though in 1669, 2,100 remained of the original 8,000, they dwindled to about 700, mixed with Negroes and whites, and were known as Chickahominy, Pamunkey and by other tribal names. In the 1960s an estimated 3,000 Powhatan were reported, largely scattered along the Virginia coast. *See also* Algonkian Tribes.

See J. R. Swanton, *The Indian Tribes of North America* (1952); F. W. Hodge (ed.), *Handbook of American Indians North of Mexico* (1959).   (A. L. K.; X.)

POWIS, EARLS AND MARQUESSES OF. The Welsh principality of Powis, comprising the county of Montgomery and parts of the counties of Brecknock, Radnor, Shropshire, Merioneth, and Denbigh, was subject to the princes of North Wales from about the 9th to the 13th century. In about 1200 it was divided into North and South Powis. It seems clear, however, that Owen ap Gruffydd ap Gwenwynwyn (d. 1293), who succeeded his father in 1286, held his lands in South Powis of Edward I as an English barony. Owen's only son, Gruffydd ap Owen (d. 1309), died without issue, and the lands and the lordship of Powis went with Owen's daughter Hawise to her husband John de Cherleton or Charleton (d. 1353). Their great-grandson, Edward, died in 1421 without male issue and the barony fell into abeyance between Edward's two daughters.

Sir Richard Grey (1436–1466), of "Pole" (Welshpool), as "Dominus de Powes" swore allegiance in Parliament to Henry VI in July 1455. On the death without legitimate issue of his great-grandson Edward Grey, in 1551, the barony fell into abeyance or became extinct. However, Edward instituted his illegitimate son Edward universal heir; this Edward in 1587 alienated the lordship and castle of Powis to Sir Edward Herbert (d. 1595), second son of William Herbert, earl of Pembroke. Edward Herbert's son, William (*c.* 1573–1656), was created Baron Powis of Powis on April 2, 1629. During the English Civil War he held the castle for Charles I. His grandson, William (*c.* 1626–1696), was created earl of Powis on April 4, 1674, and Viscount Montgomery and marquess of Powis on March 24, 1687. From 1678 to 1685 he was in the Tower of London, accused of complicity in the Popish plot. In 1688 he followed James II into exile and was created duke of Powis by the dethroned king. William (*c.* 1665–1745), 2nd marquess, also suffered as a Jacobite. When his son William (*c.* 1698–1748) died unmarried, the titles became extinct. In 1748 Henry Arthur Herbert (*c.* 1703–1772), who had been made Baron Herbert of Chirbury in 1743, was created Baron Powis and earl of Powis. The title again became extinct at the death of his son George Edward Henry Arthur in 1801, but George's only surviving sister Henrietta Antonia married

EDWARD CLIVE (1754–1839), Baron Clive of Plassey (son of the soldier Robert Clive), who was created Baron Powis and earl of Powis on May 14, 1804. The title has remained with his descendants, who took the surname Herbert, and the present holder, EDWARD ROBERT HENRY HERBERT (1889–), 5th earl of Powis is his great-grandson.

POWYS, the name of three outstanding English writers, sons of the Rev. C. F. Powys. JOHN COWPER POWYS (1872–1963), was born at Shirley, Derbyshire, on Oct. 8, 1872, and educated at Sherborne School and Corpus Christi College, Cambridge. He was a university extension lecturer for some 40 years, 30 of them in the United States. He died at Blaenau Ffestiniog, Merioneth, North Wales, on June 17, 1963. His works include poetry, philosophy, literary criticism, a striking *Autobiography* (1934), and the series of long, panoramic novels on which his fame chiefly rests, including *Wolf Solent* (1929), *A Glastonbury Romance* (1932), *Owen Glendower* (1940), and *Porius* (1951).

THEODORE FRANCIS POWYS (1875–1953), was born at Shirley on Dec. 20, 1875, and died at Mappowder, Dorset, on Nov. 27, 1953. He was educated privately and became a farmer, soon abandoning this to live on a small private income. He began to write early, but was slow to publish; two small essays in philosophy attracted little attention, but in 1923 *The Left Leg* introduced him to a wider public; thereafter his short stories were collected at intervals—*The House with the Echo* (1928), *The White Paternoster* (1930), and others—and he published eight novels, of which *Mr. Weston's Good Wine* (1927) is the best known; this beautiful allegory of the wines of Love and Death is unique in English fiction. T. F. Powys had also a gift for ironic humour, best seen in *Kindness in a Corner* (1930).

LLEWELYN POWYS (1884–1939), was born at Dorchester, Dorset, on Aug. 13, 1884, and died at Clavadel, Switzerland, on Dec. 2, 1939. He was educated at Sherborne and Corpus Christi, Cambridge. Though early stricken with tuberculosis he lived a full life, traveling widely and commenting on all he saw, in such books as *Ebony and Ivory* (1923), *The Verdict of Bridlegoose* (1926), *A Pagan's Pilgrimage* (1931), and *Earth Memories* (1934). He wrote mainly in essay form, hedonistic reflections on life, sensitive reflections on nature and country manners, and appreciations of idiosyncratic writers like Thomas Deloney and Sir Thomas Browne. His last and best book was the "imaginary autobiography" *Love and Death* (1939), a love story distilling the reflections of a lifetime.

No three writers could be more dissimilar. John Cowper works on a vast canvas crowded with characters, and Theodore within the confines of a Dorset hamlet, his cast a few villagers. John Cowper works out complex permutations of character, interweaving motive and event; Theodore sees all in black and white, good or evil, without compromise. His style is spare and strange, full of beauty, irony, and horror, deceptively simple. John Cowper's style is eloquent and rhetorical, a great spate of words which cannot be stemmed. Llewelyn Powys, almost entirely neglecting fiction, was the most consciously propagandist, proclaiming the delights of the senses and the bounty of the sun.

Others in this remarkable family of 11 children were Littleton (1874–1956), a headmaster of Sherborne Preparatory School, author of two volumes of autobiography; Gertrude (1877–1952), a painter; Albert Reginald (1881–1936), an architect long associated with the Society for the Protection of Ancient Buildings; Marian (1882–), an internationally celebrated expert on lace; and the poet and novelist Philippa (1886–1963).

BIBLIOGRAPHY.—J. C. Powys, *Poems,* ed. by K. Hopkins (1964); L. Marlow, *Welsh Ambassadors* (1936); M. Elwin, *Life of Llewelyn Powys* (1946); H. Coombes, *T. F. Powys* (1960); G. Wilson Knight, *The Saturnian Quest: a Study of the Prose Work of J. C. Powys* (1965). (K. Ho.)

P'O-YANG, a lake in northern Kiangsi Province, China, is a rapidly silting up flood reservoir for the Yangtze River at the northern end of the basin, the drainage of which coincides with the area of Kiangsi Province in central China. The lake covers an area of 1,073 sq.mi. (2,780 sq.km.) and is 70 ft. (21 m.) deep at high water, but shrinks greatly during the dry winters. Through its flood plain flows its chief river, the Kan Chiang, from the south,

the Lo-an Shui and Hsin Chiang from the east, and the Hsiu Shui from the northwest. River steamers navigate between the lower reaches of these and the narrow northern P'o-yang arm to reach the Yangtze at Huk'ou. (H. J. Ws.)

POYNINGS, SIR EDWARD (1459–1521), lord deputy of Ireland from September 1494 to December 1495, mainly remembered for the laws, called after him, which subjected the Irish Parliament to the control of the English king and council, the son of Robert Poynings and grandson of Robert, 4th Baron Poynings, was probably born at Southwark. His mother was Elizabeth, daughter of William Paston. A rebel (1483) against Richard III, Poynings attached himself to Henry Tudor, earl of Richmond, who employed him after his accession as Henry VII in military offices at Calais and elsewhere. Yorkist pretenders against Henry VII having secured support in Ireland even from the lord deputy Gerald Fitzgerald, 8th earl of Kildare, Henry decided to experiment with a regime of military and financial experts who would attack the Yorkists in the field, take statutory steps to prevent the king's government in Dublin being utilized against him, and endeavour to revive the king's revenue which had virtually disappeared. In 1494 Poynings was put in charge of this program (*see* IRELAND: *History*).

From the military standpoint, Poynings was successful in driving the Yorkist pretender, Perkin Warbeck, out of Ireland. He was less successful against the Ulster Irish lords, and was obliged to abandon his military expedition, thereby losing any chance of reducing the whole of Ireland to obedience.

Poynings' legislative measures earned him a lasting, if unsought fame. As part of the policy of imposing upon the English colony in Ireland laws now enforced in England, 49 statutes were passed at a parliament held at Drogheda in the years 1494–95. Of these, two measures subsequently came to be associated with the name of Poynings. The first applied all recent English public laws to Ireland; the second and more famous one subjected the meetings and legislative drafts of the Irish Parliament to the control of the English king, and of his English council (but not of the English Parliament). Thereafter until 1782 Parliament could not legally meet in Ireland until licensed to do so by the English lord chancellor, and until the causes for the meeting and the bills to be put before it had first been approved by the king and his English council. Moreover, as draft legislation had to be approved by the king in council before being put before the Irish Parliament, amendments to government measures could not be introduced in Ireland.

The measures taken to revive revenue were not successful. The Dublin administration actually became too costly for Henry VII, who ultimately decided to recall Poynings (December 1495); Poynings was subsequently appointed warden of the Cinque Ports. Under Henry VIII he helped to negotiate the Holy League in 1513. He died at Westenhanger, Kent, in October 1521.

See A. Conway, *Henry VII's Relations with Scotland and Ireland, 1485–1498* (1932). (R. D. Es.)

POYNTING, JOHN HENRY (1852–1914), British physicist, discoverer of Poynting's vector that describes energy flow, and experimenter in gravitation, was born at Monton, near Manchester, on Sept. 9, 1852. He studied at Owens College, Manchester, and at Trinity College, Cambridge. He was bracketed third wrangler in 1876. Poynting went as demonstrator in physics to Owens College, but returned to Cambridge in 1878 on his election as fellow of Trinity College. In 1880 he was appointed professor of physics at the Mason College, which afterward became the University of Birmingham. He retained this post until his death at Birmingham on March 30, 1914.

Poynting carried out experiments over a period of 12 years to determine the gravitational constant and the mean density of the earth. He used a balance method and during the course of his experiments added considerable knowledge to the technique of accurate weighing. (*See* GRAVITATION: *Poynting's Experiment.*) Poynting's best-known work is that in the papers "On the Transfer of Energy in the Electromagnetic Field" (*Phil. Trans. A.,* 1884) and "On the Connection between Electric Currents and the Electric and Magnetic Induction in the Surrounding Field" (*Phil.*

Trans. A., 1888). In the first paper Poynting showed that the flow of energy at a point could be expressed by a simple formula in terms of the electric and magnetic forces at that point. This is known as Poynting's theorem and the vector is also called by his name. Poynting also wrote papers on radiation and the pressure of light and several books.

BIBLIOGRAPHY.—*Collected Scientific Papers* (1920); *The Pressure of Light* (1907, 1910); *The Earth* (1913); with J. J. Thomson, *University Textbook of Physics*, 11th ed., rewritten by J. H. Awberry (1952).

POZNAN (Polish POZNANSKIE) is the second largest *wojewodztwo* (province) in Poland, with an area of 10,318 sq.mi. (26,-723 sq.km.) and a population (1960) of 1,992,758. The province lies within the north European plain. The Kocie Mountains, to the south, rise only to 932 ft. (284 m.) above sea level. The region has natural east to west communications; its central axis is the Warta River, navigable from the mouth of the Prosna. Lakes of glacial origin occur mainly in the northern and western parts of the province, most of them in Kujavia, near Goplo Lake. The postglacial soils are not particularly fertile, but careful cultivation and artificial fertilizers produce some of the highest yields in Poland. Agriculture and livestock breeding employ about four times as many people as do industry and crafts. Pig breeding is of the highest quality in Poland. The large amounts of agricultural and animal produce support the local food industry (sugar, meat products, potatoes, fruit and vegetable products, and distilling) and provide exports.

The chief mineral wealth is brown coal, rock salt, and potash, which occur (the salt as salt plugs) in the comparatively recent Kujavia and Pomerania anticline formations, (*see* BYDGOSZCZ). A new industrial region was established in 1949–55 near Konin, based on brown coal and potash salt from the region of Klodawa. The long-established building-material industry and glass and porcelain manufacture are based on local Pliocene loam and postglacial sands. The metal and machine industries, both well developed since World War II, are important.

Settlements are evenly distributed throughout the province. About 35% of the population is urban. The largest towns include Poznan, Kalisz, Gniezno, Ostrow Wielkopolski, and Pila (*qq.v.*).
(K. M. WI.)

History.—Poznania is the cradle of the Polish state. From very early times it has been known as Wielkopolska, or Great Poland, as opposed to Malopolska, or Little Poland, to the southeast. From 1138 to 1314 Wielkopolska was one of the autonomous Polish principalities within a form of a federal Polish state. After the reunification of the Kingdom of Poland under Wladyslaw I (Lokietek), Poznania shared the fate of the united country.

At the first partition of Poland, in 1772, the districts to the north of the Notec River fell to the share of Prussia. The rest of the province followed in 1793. In 1807, after the Peace of Tilsit, the province was incorporated in the Duchy of Warsaw, but in 1815 it reverted to Prussia as the grand Duchy of Poznan. During the first decades after the Congress of Vienna the Prussian regime was, on the whole, conciliatory, and Prince Antoni Radziwill, a Polish nobleman, was appointed lieutenant governor of the province; there was a provincial assembly and local representative bodies. At the end of 1830, however, a new policy was inaugurated with the presidency of E. H. von Flottwell: the experiment of settling subsidized German colonists on Polish soil (started by Frederick the Great after the first partition of Poland) was resumed, and the Polish language was deprived of its position of equality with German in the government offices, law courts, and schools.

In 1848 Poznania revolted against Prussian rule, but this armed rising was suppressed and a policy of stricter germanization was applied. In the period of Kulturkampf, 1872–74, German became the language for all teaching. Polish was not allowed except for religious instruction and in the two first classes of the primary schools. In 1900 Polish was completely eliminated by the decision that even the catechism must be taught in German. This measure provoked, in 1901, the incident of Wrzesnia (the protest of Polish mothers who took the part of their children when the latter were beaten by the schoolmasters for refusing to say the Lord's Prayer in German) and, in 1903, the famous children's strike, which lasted for more than a year.

The sharpest battle that the Poles had to sustain in defense of their nationality was the struggle for the soil. It was marked by three laws: the Colonization Law (April 26, 1886); the law forbidding building (Aug. 20, 1904); and the Law of Expropriation (March 20, 1908). In enforcing these laws Germany spent 1,300,-000,000 gold marks (mainly in Poznania, but also in Pomorze and Upper Silesia) between 1886 and 1914. Bismarck established the form of this policy, and Bernhard von Bülow continued it. But the Poles would not give in. The report of the Commission on Colonization (*Ansiedlungskommission*), prepared in 1906, on the 20th anniversary of its foundation, stated: "Incontestably the Poles have increased their material force. Their national consciousness has become stronger."

In 1910 the Provinz Posen, as it was called, covered an area of 11,193 sq.mi. (28,990 sq.km.) and had a population of 2,099,831, of which, according to the German census, only 61% were Poles. Those "61%," however, shortly after the Armistice of Nov. 11, 1918, rose on Dec. 27 and shook off German domination.

The Treaty of Versailles did not restore Poznania to Poland according to its historic frontiers, but left certain border districts in Germany. This newly defined Poznania had an area of 10,242 sq.mi. (26,527 sq.km.) and a population of 1,967,865 (1921 census), including 327,846 Germans. Ten years later the total population was 2,106,500, including 173,500 Germans. A change in the administrative division of Poland took place on April 1, 1938. Certain northern districts of Poznania (for instance, Bydgoszcz) were given to Pomorze, while certain others, which had previously belonged to the province of Lodz (Kalisz, Kolo), were added to Poznania. As a result, its area was increased to 10,899 sq.mi. (28,228 sq.km.) and its population (1931 census) to 2,339,600.

During World War II Germany annexed the whole of western Poland. Poznania was called Gau Wartheland, and even Lodz (renamed Litzmannstadt) was added to it. After the war, when the formerly German lands east of the Oder-Neisse frontier were included in Poland, the province of Poznania was temporarily extended westward up to the Oder, but on July 6, 1950, when a new province of Zielona Gora was created in the west, Poznania returned, with a few exceptions, to its 1938 boundaries. (K. SM.)

POZNAN, one of the oldest cities of Poland, is the capital of the Poznan *wojewodztwo* (province) and the seat of a Roman Catholic archbishopric. Pop. (1960) 408,132. The city lies in the great Polish plain, halfway between the Sudety (Sudeten) Mountains and the Baltic Sea and on the navigable course of the Warta River, a tributary of the Oder. In this sector the Warta flows northward, linking two parallel east-west valleys (*pradoliny*), a natural communication which has always served commercial functions throughout the history of Poznan. The city today is on the direct rail and road routes between Warsaw and Berlin and has rail links with all the larger Polish towns. It has air services to Szczecin (Stettin), Warsaw, and Lodz, and an inland port on the Warta.

The oldest part of the city lies in the fork formed by the two arms of the Warta and the Cybina, its right-bank tributary. It became known as the Cathedral Island or Ostrow Tumski. There in 968 the first Roman Catholic cathedral of Poland was erected, in Romanesque style. It was rebuilt in Gothic style in the 14th and 15th centuries, and again in the 18th century. Badly damaged during the 1945 fighting, it was again rebuilt in Gothic style. The Golden Chapel (1837), a Raczynski foundation, escaped destruction; it contains the tombs of the first two kings of Poland, Mieszko (Mieczyslaw) I and Boleslaw I the Brave. The smaller Gothic St. Mary's Church (1434) and the Baroque archbishop's palace (1732) stand nearby.

In the 13th century a new town (now known as the Old Town or *Stare Miasto*) began to grow on the left bank of the Warta. Its centre was occupied by the Old Market Place with a town hall built about 1300 in Gothic style; after the great fire of 1536 it was rebuilt in 1556–60 in Renaissance style; destroyed in 1945, it was restored to its former magnificence to become a museum.

Toward the end of the 18th century the city grew farther westward. New streets were constructed around a wide rectangular square (1803), named Freedom Square in 1919. The most remarkable building facing the square is the Neoclassic Raczynski Library (1829); this, too, was destroyed in 1945; it was rebuilt in 1956. In 1905–10 William II, the German emperor, built in the western part of the city a neo-Romanesque castle, which after Poland's restoration housed some faculties of the university and became the new city hall after 1945. The city walls, built by the Germans in the mid-19th century, were dismantled in 1902 and replaced by a green belt, but the citadel on the north side remained. The town area was increased by including the suburbs of Srodka (east), Wilda (south), Jezyce and Lazarz (west), and Gorczyn (southwest).

Poznan is a cultural and scientific centre for the whole of western Poland. It has seven higher educational establishments including the Adam Mickiewicz University (founded 1919) and many other cultural and educational institutions. It contains Poland's oldest zoological garden, one of the largest collections of palms in Europe, and a fine botanical garden.

The city is one of the largest industrial and trade centres in Poland. The International Poznan Trade Fair, inaugurated in 1921, is held there annually, as well as local trade fairs. The industry of Poznan employs nearly half of all those employed in industry in the Poznan *wojewodztwo*. The chief industry is metallurgy, and agricultural implements are manufactured. Also well developed are chemical, clothing, food, and printing industries.

(K. M. Wɪ.)

History.—Poznan was founded as a fortified place with a castle in the 10th century. It became the see of the first Polish bishop (968) and the first (together with Gniezno) capital of Poland. In 1253 Poznan was granted municipal autonomy, and in 1394 King Wladyslaw II Jagiello gave the city staple right for all wares passing from Poland into Germany and from Germany into Poland. The German settlers, who began to arrive about 1250, were gradually assimilated. From the mid-15th century to the beginning of the 17th century the city prospered and became a centre of the Polish Renaissance and Reformation movement. The Lubranski Academy, the first humanist institution of higher education in Poland, was founded there in 1519.

The Swedish wars of the mid-17th century and the Northern War at the beginning of the 18th century ruined the city. Its revival at the end of the 18th century was interrupted by its annexation by Prussia at the second partition of Poland in 1793. From 1807 to 1815 Poznan was part of the Duchy of Warsaw, afterward reverting to Prussia.

Under the German regime, especially during 1830–48, the city was a centre of Polish cultural and social progress and political conspiracy. After the unsuccessful rising of 1848 measures of repression against Polish organizations followed, but a resolutely anti-Polish and anti-Roman Catholic policy on a large scale was originated by Otto von Bismarck, and was carried out after 1871. Poznan then became the bulwark of the Poles in their successful struggle against germanization. In 1886 the Commission on Colonization was established in the city to buy up Polish land for German colonists. The Poles countered by cooperative credit organizations in which both peasants of the countryside and the middle class of the town took a prominent share. Aleksander Jackowski (1816–1905) and Father Piotr Wawrzyniak (1849–1910) were the main organizers of this economic resistance movement; soon the Poles succeeded in buying more land than they lost.

In 1894 the creation of a subsidized *Deutscher Ostmarkenverein* (nicknamed H.K.T. by the Poles from the initials of its three founders) for the promotion of German advance in the east, the great increase of the funds at the disposal of the Commission on Colonization, and the financing of a campaign against the Polish middle class all proved insufficient, and Bernard von Bülow, the German chancellor, brought, in 1904 and 1908, new legislative means to bear. They were, however, largely rendered futile by the disciplined organization of the entire Polish element, as well as by its continuous growth. Poznan and its countryside shared in the material progress of Germany after 1871. Between that year and 1910 the city's population increased from 56,000 to 156,000.

On Dec. 27, 1918, the city rose against the Germans, shaking off a 103-year occupation. In September 1939 the Germans returned to Poznan for more than five years. In January–February 1945 the city became a battlefield for the retreating Germans and the victorious Soviet forces. By the 1950s the city's rebuilding was completed. Although remaining the chief town of the province, Poznan in 1956 became an independent administrative unit. The famous strike at the Cegielski metallurgical plant on June 28, 1956, was the beginning of a national process of liberalization.

(Jz. A. Z.; H. J. Z.)

POZZO DI BORGO, CARLO ANDREA, Count (1764–1842), Corsican nobleman who became a Russian diplomat and was a conspicuous champion of French interests after the Napoleonic Wars, was born at Alata, in Corsica, on March 8, 1764, four years before Genoa's cession of the island to France; he was educated at Pisa. On the outbreak of the French Revolution he was one of two delegates sent to the National Assembly in Paris to demand the political incorporation of Corsica in France; and he was subsequently a Corsican deputy to the Legislative Assembly (1791–92). In early life, through his family, he had been closely associated with Napoleon and Joseph Bonaparte, but on his return to Corsica he found himself in opposition to them: he took the side of Pasquale Paoli (*q.v.*) while the Bonapartes were veering to the Jacobin side. Elected official chief of the civil government, he was summoned, with Paoli, to appear before the Convention in Paris, but ignored the summons and favoured the English protectorate over Corsica (1794–96), during which he was president of the council of state under Sir Gilbert Elliot. When the French occupied Corsica, he fled to Italy, then to England. Having accompanied Elliot (by then Lord Minto) on an embassy to Vienna in 1798, he stayed there for most of the following six years.

In 1804, through the influence of Prince Adam Czartoryski, Pozzo served as Russian commissioner with the Anglo-Neapolitan army in 1805 and with the Prussian in 1806 and was entrusted with an important mission to Constantinople in 1807, before the Tilsit alliance between the Russian emperor Alexander I and Napoleon. This alliance caused Pozzo to retire to Vienna and thence to London. He was recalled by Alexander in 1812 and went on a successful mission to obtain Sweden's collaboration against the French. In 1814, on the downfall of Napoleon and the entry of the Allies into Paris, Pozzo, now a Russian general, became high commissioner to the provisional government of France; and at the Bourbon restoration he was appointed Russian ambassador to the French court. He was present at the Congress of Vienna and joined Louis XVIII of France in Belgium during the Hundred Days in 1815. There he negotiated with the duke of Wellington, who objected strongly to Alexander's idea of consulting the people of France about their future form of government.

In Russia, Pozzo's attachment to the Bourbon dynasty was considered excessive, and indeed during the early years of his residence in Paris he laboured constantly to lessen the burdens laid on France by the Allies and to shorten the period of foreign occupation—so much so that the French government made him a count (1825) and that it was even suggested that he should become France's foreign minister.

The accession of Charles X of France, whose reactionary tendencies he had always disliked, undermined Pozzo's influence in Paris; but after the Revolution of 1830, he smoothed relations between France and Russia when Nicholas I was reluctant to recognize Louis Philippe as king of the French. Fear lest Pozzo's Francophile sympathy should damage Russian interests ultimately led to his being transferred to London (1835). There his health suffered; and on retiring from the Russian service (1839) he moved to Paris, where he died on Feb. 15, 1842. His diplomatic correspondence with the Russian minister Karl Nesselrode was edited by Charles Pozzo di Borgo in two volumes (1890–97).

See A. Maggiolo, *Corse, France et Russie: Pozzo di Borgo, 1764–1842* (1890); P. Ordioni, *Pozzo di Borgo . . .* (1935). (G. A. Lɴ.)

POZZUOLI, an ancient seaside town in the Province of Napoli (Naples), region of Campania, south Italy, lies 5 mi. (8 km.) W of the city of Naples, and is an episcopal see. It stands on a promontory of volcanic tuff, almost marking the centre of the Gulf of Pozzuoli separating Cape Posillipo (east) from Cape Miseno (west). Pop. (1961) 52,640 (commune). The intense volcanicity characteristic of this area has given rise to thermal springs and to changes in the level of the land which has caused buildings to be submerged beneath the sea. The countryside is fertile and picturesque and the climate is mild.

Many traces of the Roman city of Puteoli remain nearby, including a well-preserved amphitheatre (1st century A.D.); baths; and a necropolis with stuccoed and painted underground chambers. The cathedral of S. Procolo incorporates several columns of the Temple of Rome and Augustus. In it is buried the composer G. B. Pergolesi (1710–36), who died at the neighbouring monastery of S. Gennaro (St. Januarius). Temple porticoes along the shore have been drowned by the sea as a result of earth movements. Semisubmerged is the old Roman market (erroneously called the Temple of Sarapis) of the 1st century A.D., which consists of a quadrangle with central courtyard and an arcade with merchants' booths. Inland, to the northeast, is the famous solfatara (called by the Romans the Forum of Vulcan), a semiactive volcano which exhales sulfurous vapours and gives vent to liquid mud and hot mineral springs. Along the coast to northwest is the Monte Nuovo, a volcanic cone which arose after eruptions in 1538.

Pozzuoli is on the Rome-Naples railway line. The people engage in fishing; food processing based on the abundant local fruit and vegetable produce; and the manufacture of machinery. The local volcanic material is used for making the fine cement called pozzolana from the name of the town (see CEMENT).

Ancient Puteoli was founded c. 529 B.C. by Greek emigrants and called by them Dikaiarkeia, "city of justice." Rome captured it in the Samnite wars; it was vainly besieged by Hannibal in 214. From 194 it had the status of a colony. Its port made it a leading commercial centre and, indeed, a cosmopolitan city. In A.D. 60 St. Paul spent a few days at Puteoli while on his way to Rome as a prisoner (Acts 28:13, 14), and found a Christian group already in existence there. The town's fortunes declined with those of the empire, and local volcanic and seismic activity caused most of the people to move to Naples.   (M. T. A. N.)

PRABHU, a member of a group of important scribe castes of Maharashtra (q.v.) in western India, numbering about 30,000 in the 1960s. More than 20,000 of these were Chandraseni Kayastha Prabhus concentrated in Thana and Kolaba districts and in Bombay city; the smaller Pathare Prabhu and Dhruv Prabhu castes respectively are located mainly in Bombay and Poona cities. Prabhus are the equivalent of the Kayastha writer castes in Bengal and northern India. Like the northern Kayasthas, Prabhus claim membership in the Kshatriya (q.v.) varna (class) of rulers and warriors by descent from Prince Arjuna of the Mahabharata epic; they name Chitragupta, the Brahman (q.v.) accountant for the god of death, as a maternal ancestor. Prabhus have claimed historical ties with classical rulers of Oudh and Bihar, but are first clearly documented as accountants in Muslim service during late medieval times. Administrators and soldiers for the Maratha (q.v.) kings and peshwas, the Prabhus were landlords, civil servants, and practitioners of modern learned professions under British rule. They approximate Maharashtrian Brahmans in social organization and religion. They imitate Brahman clan (gotra) names, but without claiming descent from Vedic sages. They prohibit marriage among sapindas (see INDIAN LAW: Hindu Law: Marriage) and until recently forbade the remarriage of widows. They employ Brahman priests fully and take the sacred thread (see HINDUISM: Everyday Religious Life). See also CASTE (INDIAN).   (M. Ma.)

PRACTICE AND PROCEDURE. Law is sometimes said to consist of two parts, substantive law and adjective law. The former is concerned with the definition of legal rights, the latter with the modes of enforcing them. This article discusses the machinery of the courts and the methods by which both the state and the individual (the latter including societies, whether incorporated or not) enforce their rights in the several courts. For the composition and powers of these courts, see COURT. Procedure is a self-explanatory term; practice may be defined as the rules of procedure, these being one part of the system of adjective law.

The other principal part is the law of evidence (q.v.); i.e., the rules governing proof of the facts by means of which a party seeks to establish his claims or to rebut those of his opponents.

Emphasis in this article is placed on practice and procedure in the English courts; practice and procedure in United States federal and most state courts and in the Canadian courts derive from the same source as in England, namely, the rules of common law and equity. Scotland has different rules and different nomenclature from England, because the main roots of the Scots system is Roman law. (See SCOTS LAW.) The main principles of Anglo-American practice and procedure will be discussed as follows:

  I. England
    A. Criminal Prosecution
      1. The Prosecutor
      2. Indictable Offenses and Summary Offenses
      3. Magistrates' Court Proceedings
      4. Trial of Indictable Offenses by Higher Courts
      5. Appeals
    B. Civil Procedure
      1. Protection and Enforcement of Legal Rights
      2. High Court Procedure
      3. Magistrates' Court Procedure
  II. United States
      1. History of the Code Reform
      2. Federal Rules of Civil Procedure
      3. Status of Pleading Systems
      4. Course of Proceedings in a Civil Action
      5. Criminal Procedure
  III. Canada
      1. Selection of the Forum
      2. Beginning Actions and Pretrial Procedure
      3. Trials
      4. Enforcement of Judgment

I. ENGLAND

It is convenient to distinguish at the outset between, on the one hand, the rules applicable to proceedings the object of which is to maintain public order or to punish breaches of it; and, on the other hand, the rules applicable to proceedings whose object is to establish or enforce civil rights, whether public or private. Therefore the two following sections deal consecutively with procedure in criminal prosecutions and civil procedure.

A. CRIMINAL PROSECUTION

1. The Prosecutor.—Prosecutions are undertaken in the name of the crown, but they may be started by private individuals or by corporate bodies (e.g., British Rail, which has to initiate a vast number of prosecutions for such offenses as pilfering on the railways or traveling without a ticket). There are, however, certain offenses for which prosecutions may not be instituted without the authority of the attorney general, such as incest, except where the director of public prosecutions has instituted the proceedings, and offenses under the Official Secrets Act of 1911.

The director of public prosecutions has particular duties in relation to a number of offenses. He must institute, undertake, or carry on criminal proceedings in any case involving the death penalty; in any case, referred to him by a government department, in which he considers that criminal proceedings should be instituted; and in any case which appears to him to be of importance or difficulty or otherwise to require his intervention. Chief officers of police have to report to the director a number of offenses allegedly committed within their districts. These include incest and other serious sexual offenses, forgery, coinage offenses, sedition, conspiracies to pervert the course of justice, corruption by a public official, obscene or indecent libels, and offenses against the Extradition Act of 1870 and the Fugitive Offenders Act (1881). The director's duties in relation to most classes of cases are not, however, exclusive; i.e., there is no question of others being forbidden to prosecute if he decides not to. A private individual may prosecute in cases other than those in which prosecution may be initiated only on the order of a judge of the Queen's Bench Division, on the authority of the attorney general or on that of the director of public prosecutions, if the director does not choose to prosecute; as, for example, in a murder charge.

However, while the director of public prosecutions undertakes the more difficult and important cases and private prosecutors intervene on a limited number of occasions, most charges are preferred and most prosecutions are undertaken by the police. Any constable may prosecute, but in practice the authority of a superior officer is obtained before proceedings are undertaken in a case of any seriousness.

2. Indictable Offenses and Summary Offenses.—Before considering further the procedure in criminal trials, it is necessary to distinguish between indictable offenses and summary offenses, because the procedure differs accordingly. An indictment is a written accusation signed by the clerk of a court of assize or quarter sessions charging a person or persons accused of an indictable offense with such an offense; the indictment may, by means of separate counts, charge him or them with more than one offense. An indictable offense, if committed by an adult, is triable on indictment, while summary offenses are triable only summarily (by magistrates sitting in a court of petty sessions without jury).

In effect, indictable offenses are those offenses which are tried by a jury in a court of assize or quarter sessions. From this point of view, there are three classes of offense: (1) those triable only on indictment; (2) those triable only summarily (*i.e.*, by magistrates' courts without a jury); and (3) those triable either on indictment or summarily, at the option either of the prosecution or of the accused. For example, a charge of causing death by dangerous driving is triable on indictment only; a charge of driving without due care and attention can be tried only summarily; and a charge of simple dangerous driving (*i.e.*, without causing death) or of driving under the influence of drink or drugs can be tried either way, at the choice of either prosecution or defense.

The defendant has a right to trial by jury (*i.e.*, by indictment) if the offense (unless it is an assault or comes under s. 1 of the Vagrancy Act, 1898) carries a maximum sentence of more than three months' imprisonment. A prosecutor's right to demand that the accused be tried by jury depends on a number of enactments dealing with specific offenses. The prosecutor will normally claim trial by jury where he considers that the offense merits a severer penalty than a magistrates' court is competent to impose (although petty sessions have the power to send an offender convicted before them to quarter sessions for sentence); whereas a defendant will choose a jury trial if he considers that he has a better chance of being acquitted by a jury than by magistrates.

Most criminal cases tried in England and Wales are tried by magistrates' courts. Criminal proceedings in such courts are initiated by information, as distinct from civil proceedings, which are initiated by complaint. An information, apart from any statutory requirement to the contrary, need not be in writing, but is generally required by the courts to be so; but where a warrant has been issued for an arrest, the information must be in writing and substantiated by oath. A warrant may be issued only where the offense charged is an indictable one (for the question of arrest, *see* below).

3. Magistrates' Court Proceedings.—*By Way of Information.*—As has been said above, most proceedings in criminal cases are by way of information, and for the majority even of indictable offenses this procedure is followed because the cases are decided by magistrates' courts rather than by the higher courts.

The first step in the judicial process is the laying of an information before a justice of the peace, who has to decide whether the matter is within the scope of his jurisdiction (*e.g.*, whether the offense was committed within the county or borough for which he is a justice) and whether it is otherwise proper for a prosecution to proceed. If he decides these questions in the affirmative, he has next to decide whether to issue the defendant a summons to appear before the court or whether to issue a warrant for his arrest. He will not as a rule issue a warrant in the first place unless the charge is serious or unless a summons is likely to be disobeyed; but he has power to issue a warrant in respect of any indictable offense. A warrant cannot be issued in respect of an offense which is triable only summarily; and before it can be issued at all the information must be put into writing and substantiated on oath.

The summons must state briefly the substance of the charge and must be signed by the justice issuing it; it must state the time and place at which the defendant must appear to answer the charge.

A single summons may be issued in respect of several informations. A summons may be served in person, left with some person at the defendant's last known address, or sent there by registered post. The Magistrates' Courts Act, 1952 (s. 3), provides for the jurisdiction of justices where offenses have been committed on jurisdictional boundaries or have been started in one jurisdiction and finished in another. Such offenses may be treated as having been committed in either jurisdiction.

When the case comes for trial the court, if the accused appears, states to him the substance of the information and asks him whether he pleads guilty or not guilty. A procedure has come into existence whereby, on charges that are triable only summarily, the accused can at his option plead guilty in writing, setting out any grounds of mitigation that there may be; and the court may thereupon convict and sentence him. Equally, a defendant who is absent may plead guilty through solicitor or counsel representing him, and the court may thereupon proceed to pass sentence. If the accused does not appear, and it is established that he has had reasonable notice of the trial (or, on an adjourned trial, that he has previously failed to appear), the court can decide to hear the case in his absence; or, if the information has been substantiated on oath and the offense is considered to be of sufficient gravity to justify it, can issue a warrant for his arrest.

If the information charges the defendant with an offense that is triable either summarily or on indictment, the mode of trial to be selected depends on a number of factors. If the accused has a right of trial by jury, he must be informed of his right before he is called on to plead guilty or not guilty. If he should not have this right, or should he, having it, decide not to exercise it, the procedure to be followed depends mainly on the course adopted by the prosecution. If the prosecution applies to have the case tried summarily, the court may decide to grant the application (though, before doing so, if the offense is within the jurisdiction of quarter sessions, the magistrates should inform the accused that, if he is convicted and they are of opinion that he merits a more severe punishment than petty sessions can impose, they may send him to quarter sessions for punishment). This gives him a further opportunity to choose trial by jury. Thus, in effect, it is as a rule only at the option of both prosecutor and defendant that an accused, charged with an offense triable either summarily or on indictment, will be tried summarily. An important exception is made if the accused is a child under 14. Such a child will be tried summarily unless he is charged with homicide; or, if he is accused jointly with a person who has attained the age of 14, the court, if it considers this in the interests of justice, may commit them both for trial. The court also has power to deal summarily with any offense other than homicide with which an accused under 17 is charged, though if he is between 14 and 17 it is not bound to do so.

Summary Trial.—Once it is decided that the trial shall be a summary one, the procedure is the same whatever the offense. The prosecutor calls his witnesses, addressing the magistrates if he considers it necessary; and the defense does likewise, both prosecutor and defense being limited as a rule to one speech. The court is composed either of a minimum of two lay justices, or of one stipendiary magistrate where provision for such exists. If, as in the vast majority of magistrates' courts, the magistrates are laymen, their clerk (who is normally, though not necessarily, a solicitor—he may be a barrister, or even have no legal qualification, though this last is unusual) gives them such guidance as they may require on questions of law. He should not, however, retire with them to form their conclusions on the questions of fact which they have to decide. The chairman, finally, announces the decision of the court and the sentence it has decided to impose.

The proceedings are in open court. There are, however, some important differences for the trial of an accused under 17 years of age. He is tried by a juvenile court whose members are drawn from a special panel of justices. The proceedings are in private, the sittings are in a room apart from the adult court sitting on the same day, and the press is not allowed to publish reports.

4. Trial of Indictable Offenses by Higher Courts.—*Pretrial Procedure.*—When a trial is not to proceed summarily, the functions of the justices are to hear and record the evidence presented by the prosecution, and by the defense, if any. By virtue, however, of s. 1 and 2 of the Criminal Justice Act, 1967, written statements are admissible in committal proceedings to the like extent as oral evidence, provided that certain conditions are satisfied. The effect of these provisos is that the statements must be properly authenticated, that copies have been made available to the other parties, and that none of these objects to the statements being so tendered. A statement made by a person under 21 years of age must give his age. The justices must then either commit the accused for trial at one of the higher courts, if they consider that there is a case for him to answer, or else discharge him. When sitting for this purpose the justices are described as examining justices (these functions can be discharged by a single justice). Examining justices are not bound to sit in open court, although in fact they generally do so. Section 3 of the Criminal Justice Act, 1967, prohibits the publication or broadcasting of committal proceedings, with some specified exceptions, other than where the magistrates' court determines not to commit the defendant or defendants for trial, after it so determines, or after the conclusion of his trial or, as the case may be, the trial of the last to be tried: unless an application to the contrary is made on behalf of the defendant, or any of the defendants, and is granted by the court. The court has to bind each witness (other than the accused himself and any witness to his character only) to attend and give evidence before the court by which the accused is to be tried; and it also has to bind the prosecutor by a recognizance to prosecute before that court.

When it appears to the court that the attendance of a given witness at the trial is not required, either because of some statement made by the accused or because the witness's evidence is merely formal, the court may bind him over to attend the trial conditionally, if he has not already been bound over; or direct that he shall be treated as having been so bound over, if he has already been bound over. The effect is that it is not necessary for the witness to attend the trial unless the court requires him to do so, and that at the trial his evidence may be read instead of being given by himself in person.

If any witness refuses to enter into a recognizance, the court may commit him into custody until he does so enter, or, if he continues to refuse, until the trial. He must be released if the court decides to discharge the accused.

If the court decides to commit the accused for trial, it may either commit him into custody or grant him bail; in other words, allow him to be free, subject to giving such recognizances as the court may require for his appearance at the trial. Committal is normally either to the next quarter sessions (if the charge is within the jurisdiction of quarter sessions) or to the next assizes. There are, however, provisions authorizing the court to commit to assizes if the gravity of the case warrants it, even if the charge is technically within the competence of quarter sessions; and also to commit to quarter sessions or assizes other than the local ones on grounds either of hardship or of general convenience. Having started inquiries into any information relating to an offense that is triable either summarily or on indictment, the justices may, if they think proper, try the case summarily on application made either by the prosecutor or by the accused.

Trial Procedure.—The courts to which magistrates may commit defendants for the trial of indictable offenses, *i.e.*, in general, assizes (to which judges come on circuit) and quarter sessions (*see* QUARTER SESSIONS, COURT OF), include certain courts where the trial of criminal cases is to some extent centralized, such as the Central Criminal Court at the Old Bailey in London, and the Crown Court in Manchester, where a judge of the High Court of Justice presides over the most important trials. The chairman's part in trials at quarter sessions is precisely the same as that of the recorder or as that of the judge at an assize court except that, when the defendant is convicted, the chairman and the justices sitting with him will confer as to the sentence.

Trial in all these courts is conducted in the same way. Its essential feature is that it is trial by jury. A judge conducts the trial, gives any rulings on law that are necessary in the course of it, and passes sentence (after consultation with lay justices at

county sessions) on any convicted prisoner; but the jury, as judges of fact, agree on the verdict, which before the Criminal Justice Act, 1967, had to be unanimous, on each count of the indictment. By virtue of s. 13 of this act of 1967 the verdict of a jury in criminal proceedings need not be unanimous if, where there are not less than 11 jurors, 10 of them are agreed, or where there are 10 jurors, 9 of them are agreed; but a court may not accept a majority verdict unless the jury has had not less than two hours for deliberation or such longer period as the court thinks reasonable. The trial usually begins with the clerk of the court reading each count and asking each accused person to plead either guilty or not guilty to it. If there is any objection to the form of the indictment, or it is sought to make any amendment thereto, this matter must be disposed of by the court before the prisoner is called upon to plead. If there is more than one prisoner, and all or some of the pleas are of not guilty, it will be decided whether the prisoners are to be tried separately or together after the taking of their pleas. If the pleas are all of guilty, counsel for the prosecution outlines the prosecution case and calls evidence—normally from the police officer in charge of the case—as to the antecedents of the accused. The accused or his counsel calls any evidence as to the accused's previous good character or as to the difficulties of his situation; and addresses the court, as is said, "in mitigation"—that is, in order to persuade the court to take the most lenient view possible of the offense. Thereafter, when the prisoner has said anything that he wishes, the court passes sentence. The same procedure is followed after a verdict of guilty as after a plea of guilty.

When the court proceeds to trial after a plea of not guilty, the clerk calls on each member of the jury by name (either prosecution or defense may object to any individual juror; *see* JURY). After a jury of 12 has been empaneled without objection, the clerk administers an oath to the jurors collectively that they will try the issues according to the evidence, and then reads to them the contents of the indictment. Prosecuting counsel next addresses the jury, outlining the nature of the charge or charges and the evidence which he intends to call in proof. At the conclusion of his speech, he calls his witnesses and examines them; the defense then cross-examines them so far as is considered necessary or useful; and the prosecutor thereafter examines them again, if he deems it expedient, on any matters raised in the course of cross-examination. When he has finished reexamining his last witness, he says to the judge, "That is the case for the prosecution."

At this stage (if the defense considers that there are gaps in the prosecution evidence which justify such a course), the defense may submit to the judge that there is no case for the jury to consider. Should the judge accept this submission in relation to any of the counts, he directs the jury to bring in a verdict of not guilty in relation to them. If the verdict or verdicts so reached should dispose of the whole indictment, the prisoner is discharged and the trial is at an end. Otherwise, or if there is not a submission of no case, the defense will deploy its own case.

The course this takes will depend on the nature of the defense evidence; if the defense calls no evidence, counsel (or the accused himself, if, as seldom happens with the development of the legal aid system, he is unrepresented) will forthwith address the jury. If there is only one defense witness, or the evidence is short and simple, the defense testimony will be called for at once. If the defense case involves more than one witness, and counsel deems this course to be warranted, he will address the jury in order to explain the general nature of the defense before witnesses are called. They will be examined, cross-examined, and reexamined in the same way as the prosecution witnesses. The defendant himself may choose whether to give evidence on oath, or not on oath and without leaving the dock, or to remain silent. If he elects to give evidence on oath, he leaves the dock and testifies, like the other witnesses, from the witness-box. If he does not give evidence on oath, the prosecution may not comment on his not doing so, although the judge may.

At the conclusion of the evidence for the defense, the prosecution may apply to call evidence in rebuttal should any unexpected defense evidence justify this course; the judge will not allow this except in unusual circumstances. Both prosecution and defense counsel have then the opportunity to address the jury, first the former, then the latter. Finally, the judge sums up, his summing up consisting partly of a legal direction to the jury and partly of a review of the facts in which it is essential that he should put to the jury the defense against each charge. At the conclusion of the summing up the jurors retire to consider their verdict or verdicts. When they return to the court their foreman (whom they have elected) announces the verdicts they have found. If these are all not guilty, the prisoner is discharged. Otherwise, the same procedure is followed as that described above as if the accused had pleaded guilty. In either case, the court has normally to consider a social inquiry report made by a probation officer or other authorized person before passing sentence.

5. Appeals.—Appeals in criminal cases can be classified under three heads: (1) appeals on questions of fact, from magistrates' courts to quarter sessions; (2) appeals, whether on questions of fact or of law, from the higher courts (i.e., assizes and quarter sessions) to the Court of Appeal, and, ultimately, with leave, to the House of Lords; (3) appeals, on questions of law only, to the divisional courts from magistrates' courts or from quarter sessions (when sitting in an appellate capacity only; appeals from quarter sessions exercising their original jurisdiction go to the Court of Appeal, as stated above).

Appeals in the first two of these three categories can be initiated by the defendant only, except that the prosecutor may appeal, with leave, on a question of law only, from the Court of Appeal to the House of Lords. Appeals in the third category can be initiated on behalf of either defendant or prosecutor; and the divisional court, where a prosecutor's appeal is successful, may either send the case back to the lower court with a direction to convict or may order a rehearing.

Appeals from Magistrates' Courts to Quarter Sessions.—Notice of appeal has to be given within 14 days, although this time can be, and often is, extended by leave of quarter sessions. Appeal may be against either conviction or sentence. The procedure is by way of rehearing, the respondent opening his case first and calling his witnesses (if the appeal is against conviction), just as in the lower court, and the appellant following. Speeches are limited to one each, unless some question of law is involved. Fresh evidence (i.e., evidence not called in the court below) may be called on appeal.

Appeals from Higher Courts to Court of Appeal.—An appeal lies as of right on a question of law, but by leave either of the court of first instance or of the Court of Appeal (Criminal Division) on a question of fact. A notice of appeal setting out the grounds of appeal has to be submitted to the court within 14 days (except on capital charges, where there is no time limit). When a notice is given (which may be with an application for extension of time), a transcript of the shorthand note of the evidence, of the summing up, and of any rulings on law that the judge may have made, is submitted with the notice to one of the judges of the Court of Appeal, who may himself grant the application for leave to appeal. If he does, the court (of three judges, or, in an exceptionally important or difficult appeal, five) then proceeds to hear the appeal. If he does not, the court may hear the application and grant it, often treating this as though it were the appeal itself, which the court may allow or dismiss—it may, of course, simply refuse the application for leave to appeal. An appeal may be against conviction or sentence or both. When the court dismisses an appeal against conviction it (or the House of Lords) may certify that there is a point of law of exceptional public importance, and it (or the House of Lords) may then grant leave to appeal to the House of Lords. The certificate does not of itself entitle the appellant to leave to appeal to the House of Lords, but is a necessary prerequisite of such leave.

The appeal is by way of rehearing; but this normally consists of the reading of relevant parts of the transcript by the appellant's counsel and argument thereon. The respondent's counsel follows, and the appellant's counsel has a right of reply. Evidence not used in the court below is in practice only admitted by the appeal court when it has not been available at the trial; but the appeal court is empowered to hear oral evidence. After long controversy, the

court was authorized to order a new trial instead of directing the entry of a judgment and verdict of acquittal; but it is still permitted to deal finally with a matter. A retrial may take place only in respect of (1) the offense of which the appellant was convicted at the original trial and in respect of which his appeal is allowed; (2) any offense of which he could have been convicted at the original trial on an indictment for that offense (e.g., an attempt instead of the complete offense originally charged); (3) an offense charged in an alternative count of the indictment on which the jury was discharged from giving a verdict at the trial.

Appeals to the Divisional Court.—These are by way of case stated: the party intending to appeal asks the chairman of the magistrates' court or of the court of quarter sessions to prepare a statement of the relevant facts and of the grounds of the decision. In practice, the appellant will generally prepare the case through his legal advisers and ask the chairman to agree to it and sign it. If the court refuses to state a case, the appellant may apply to the divisional court for an order of mandamus directing the lower court to state a case. Appeal lies from the divisional court, with leave, to the House of Lords. *See* APPEAL.

B. CIVIL PROCEDURE

1. Protection and Enforcement of Legal Rights.—Criminal proceedings have been considered above; i.e., those in which some breach, or alleged breach, of public order is involved, whether it be a crime of violence or of dishonesty or both; or whether it be some offense creating conditions of physical danger or inconvenience to the public (as do motoring offenses, or even such comparatively trivial breaches of public order as riding a pedal cycle without lights or stopping a railway train by pulling the communication cord without good reason).

The procedure now to be discussed concerns cases in which the rights of an individual (or of a corporation, such as a county council or a limited company) are invaded by some act or omission on the part of another; and in which action is taken in the courts to redress the matter by (1) obtaining compensation (damages); (2) restraining repetition of unlawful conduct by means of an injunction (q.v.) addressed by the court to the wrongdoer; (3) commanding performance of a specific action where a party to a contract, for example, is failing to carry out his part of the bargain. There are cases, too, in which a party to a contract seeks to ascertain or clarify his legal rights, when he may seek from the courts a declaration or rectification of the written contract.

There is a class of cases where a party seeks from the High Court of Justice (q.v.), one of whose essential attributes is unlimited jurisdiction, the protection or enforcement of his rights either against an inferior court (in the sense of a court of limited jurisdiction; e.g., a county court or a magistrates' court); or against a government department or a local authority which, for the purposes of particular legislation (such as the Town and Country Planning acts), has judicial or quasi-judicial powers. The High Court, although it is only a court of appeal from such courts when so established by statute, has a general, supervisory jurisdiction to see that they comply with and keep within the law. It carries out these duties by three types of order: mandamus, certiorari, and prohibition. An example of mandamus has been given above, where a party seeks an order to a magistrates' court that it shall state a case to enable the High Court to consider the legal correctness of its decision.

An order of certiorari is made where the award of a judicial or quasi-judicial tribunal either constitutes an excess of its jurisdiction or contains an error on its face. An order of prohibition forbids an inferior court or an authority with judicial or quasi-judicial powers to act outside its lawful scope—as when a tribunal has evidenced its intention of hearing a cause outside its jurisdiction (*see* ABATEMENT).

Other cases which come under this head are matrimonial causes. Although now all petitions for divorce have to be initiated in county courts with divorce jurisdiction, but may be transferred to the High Court thereafter, the Probate, Divorce, and Admirality Division of the High Court alone has jurisdiction to grant decrees of nullity of marriage and of judicial separation. It, too, alone has unlimited powers to order a divorced or separated person to maintain his spouse or former spouse. (But the magistrates' courts also exercise matrimonial jurisdiction over a very wide field; they can, for example, order a husband to maintain his wife and children.)

The proving of wills (*see* PROBATE) and the granting of letters of administration where wills cannot be found, so that the estates of deceased persons can be distributed, are other functions of the courts. This jurisdiction inheres in the Probate, Divorce, and Admiralty Division of the High Court, but the county courts have powers to deal with smaller estates. Much of this work is non-contentious.

Parallel with the division of jurisdiction over matrimonial causes between the Probate Division of the High Court, the county courts, and the magistrates' courts is that among the Chancery Division of the High Court, the county courts, and the magistrates' courts over the guardianship of infants. The Chancery Division and the magistrates' courts likewise divide between them provision for claims by mothers against putative fathers for the maintenance of illegitimate children; and jurisdiction in relation to adoption orders is again divided among the Chancery Division, the county courts, and the magistrates' courts.

These categories of types of proceedings that can be brought in the civil courts are by no means exhaustive. No mention has been made, for example, of the Restrictive Practices Court, with its important jurisdiction under the Restrictive Trade Practices Act, 1956, and the Resale Prices Act (1964). They perhaps indicate sufficiently the field of work covered by the civil courts.

2. High Court Procedure.—*Initiation of an Action.*—There are four means of starting proceedings in the High Court: by writ, by originating summons, by originating motion, and by petition. Each of these has its own uses, although at some points they overlap. The writ has to be used in claims based on tort (*i.e.*, on civil wrong—other than trespass to land, fraud, or breach of duty, whether contractual, statutory, or otherwise) where the damages claimed are in respect of the death of or injury to any person or in respect of damage to property. Actions for trespass to land may be begun either by writ or by originating summons; and probate actions and certain admiralty actions also may be initiated by writ. An originating summons must be used where an application (other than in pending proceedings) is made under any act, except where some other procedure is expressly required or authorized. Except where otherwise specifically required, proceedings may be begun either by writ or by originating summons, as the plaintiff (*i.e.*, the party initiating the proceedings) considers appropriate. Proceedings in which the principal issue is likely to be the construction of an act of Parliament or of some document, or in which there is unlikely to be any substantial dispute of fact, are appropriate for the use of originating summons unless the plaintiff intends to apply for summary judgment. Proceedings may only be begun by motion or petition when this is expressly authorized by the rules of the Supreme Court. An example of procedure by motion is the apportionment of salvage in the Admiralty Division. The petition is best known for its use in matrimonial proceedings, but it is also used in the Chancery Division in certain types of company and bankruptcy proceedings.

Proceedings may be begun and carried on by the plaintiff or petitioner either in person or through his solicitor.

Preparation of an Action for Trial.—The rules of the Supreme Court of Judicature govern procedure. They are framed by the Rules Committee and cannot take effect until laid before Parliament. These rules are not here analyzed or even summarized; but a general picture is given, seen in its most complete and perhaps most complex form in the action started by writ. The issue of a writ sets in motion a lengthy but logical sequence of steps that have to be taken if each party to the action contests it to the stage at which it is tried. These steps have each to be completed within a certain time; what these times are can be ascertained by reference to the rules themselves. In each case, the times allowed can be extended either by consent of the parties or by leave of the court.

Writs and Endorsements.—The writ itself consists of a direction from the sovereign to the defendant which, after setting out the names of the parties, commands the defendant to enter an appearance within eight days of its service, and warns him that in default of his doing so the plaintiff may proceed and that judgment may be given against him (the defendant) in his absence. Before the writ is issued it has to be endorsed with a statement of the nature of the plaintiff's claim. This may be either a general endorsement, as, for example, "The plaintiff's claim is for damages for breach of contract"; or a so-called special endorsement, which, under the subheading of "statement of claim," sets out in more detail what is the contract alleged and how the defendant is said to be in breach. It is also open to the plaintiff, if the writ is endorsed generally and not specially, to deliver the statement of claim at the same time as he serves the writ. The writ must in either event be endorsed with the name and address of the plaintiff or of any solicitor serving it on his behalf, and with a statement showing that it has been served, together with the date of service. Various methods of serving the writ are prescribed, but the ordinary method is by personal service on the defendant, or, if the latter has so authorized, upon his solicitor. The next step is incumbent upon the defendant: namely, to enter an appearance, which can be done by either delivering it or posting it to the Central Office of the Royal Courts of Justice. After an appearance has been entered by or on behalf of the defendant, the plaintiff, if he has not already done so, has to deliver his statement of claim.

Applications for Summary Judgment.—If the writ is specially endorsed, or if the statement of claim is delivered at the same time as the writ is served and the claim is for debt, for liquidated damages (*see* DAMAGES), or for the specific performance of a contract, the plaintiff may swear an affidavit to the effect that there is no defense to the action, and apply for summary judgment. This step is taken by means of a summons to appear before one of the masters of the Supreme Court. The masters are subordinate judicial officers who are entrusted, subject to the right of appeal to a judge sitting in chambers (as distinct from open court), with the supervision of all interlocutory and procedural matters and who have certain defined and limited powers to give judgment. In the Chancery Division it is not, technically, a question of an appeal, but the hearing of the particular stage in the proceedings is transferred from the master to the judge. An application for summary judgment may be either granted or refused outright, or the master may make some other order directing the trial of the matter. Whatever order he makes is subject to an appeal to the judge in chambers, or, with leave, from the judge to the Court of Appeal: there is, however, no appeal to the Court of Appeal from a decision refusing summary judgment.

The Pleadings.—Should summary judgment not be claimed or be refused, the next step is the delivery of a statement of claim, should this not have been taken already. This should set out the material facts on which the plaintiff bases his claim, though not the evidence by which he intends to prove it. The defendant has in his turn to deliver a statement, called the defense, which in its turn sets out the material facts on which he relies; in default of defense the plaintiff may apply for judgment. The statement of claim and the defense are each called "the pleadings." There may be further pleadings if it cannot be presumed, for example, that the plaintiff traverses all matter in the defense, so that there may be a reply, a rejoinder, and even a surrejoinder (though these last two are most exceptional). It is open to either party to apply to strike out his opponent's pleading, or part thereof, on the ground that it discloses no cause of action or of defense, as the case may be, and on certain other grounds; the effect of a successful application of this sort may be to dispose of the matter. It is likewise open to either party to apply for further particulars of his opponent's pleading on the grounds that this does not sufficiently disclose the case he has to meet; and the delivery of further and better particulars may be ordered.

The above is a simple example in which one plaintiff sues one defendant for one cause of action. The rules make provision for the joinder both of parties and of causes of action. Further, if a defendant (1) claims against a person not already a party to the action any contribution or indemnity; (2) claims against such a person any relief or remedy relating to or connected with the original subject matter of the action, and substantially the same as some relief or remedy claimed by the plaintiff; (3) requires that any question or issue relating to or connected with the original subject matter of the action should be determined not only as between himself and the plaintiff but also as between either or both of them and a person not already party to the action: he may issue a notice, called a third party notice, containing both a statement of the nature of the claim made against him, and a statement either of the nature and grounds of the claim made by him or of the questions or issues to be determined. The leave of the court is required for the issue of a third party notice, unless the action is begun by writ and the notice is issued before delivery of the defense. A third party has the same rights against the defendant as the latter has against the plaintiff; and he may bring in a fourth party, and the fourth party a fifth party, and so on.

Discovery and Inspection.—When the process of exchanging pleadings has been concluded and the pleadings, under the rules, are deemed to be closed, the parties normally have to serve on the other parties lists of the relevant documents which are, or have been, in their possession, custody, or power. This process is known as discovery and is followed by inspection.

Summons for Direction.—After either the close of pleadings (or in the actions in which discovery is necessary) after discovery, the plaintiff has to take out what is known as a summons for directions. The object of this, in the words of the rule, is to provide "an occasion for the consideration by the court of the preparations for the trial of the action, so that: (a) all matters which must or can be dealt with on interlocutory applications and have not already been dealt with may so far as possible be dealt with; and (b) such directions may be given as to the future course of the action as appear best adapted to secure the just, expeditious, and economical disposal thereof."

There are certain classes of actions to which the rule as to the summons for directions does not apply—*e.g.,* cases where directions have already been given in an application for summary judgment; actions referred for trial to an official referee (a judge who deals with actions in the High Court involving detailed inquiries into figures); and actions for the infringement of a patent.

The matters to be considered at the hearing of the summons for directions include the place and mode of trial. It must be decided whether there is to be a jury or not, and whether the case is suitable for transfer to a county court, to an official referee, or to the commercial list (where it can be tried, rather more expeditiously, by a judge with special experience of commercial matters). The court (which means for these purposes a master of the Supreme Court) has also to consider whether the writ or any of the pleadings requires amendment; whether in any respects documentary or affidavit evidence should be allowed instead of oral evidence; and whether there should be any limitation of the medical or expert evidence to be called. The court has also to try to secure that the parties make all admissions and all agreements that appear to be reasonable, as to the conduct of the proceedings; and the parties have to try to dispose of all interlocutory business that may be necessary before trial, such as any applications to administer interrogatories (which have to be answered on oath) to any other party to the action.

When the interlocutory business has been disposed of, the plaintiff has to set the action down for trial; and, should he fail to do so within a reasonable time, the defendant may apply to the court for the action to be dismissed for want of prosecution.

The Trial.—At the trial the procedure followed is broadly similar to that in a criminal trial, although there are differences, some of which depend on whether or not there is a jury. The plaintiff (generally, of course, through his counsel) will open his case with an address outlining the issues and the evidence he proposes to call. The defendant may at the conclusion of the plaintiff's evidence submit that it discloses no case; but if he does so he has to stand on his submission—that is, he is precluded from calling evidence in support of his own case. If he does not make such a submission, the defendant will decide whether to make an opening address or not, will call his evidence, and will conclude his case by a speech, to which the plaintiff will reply. If there is a jury, the

judge will then sum up to it (probably, if the case is of any complexity, putting to it a number of questions, frequently agreed with counsel for the parties, to which the jury has to give the answer). If there is no jury, the judge will deliver a judgment setting out his findings on the facts and the legal conclusions he draws from them—announcing, in fact, the result of the action. If damages are claimed in the action, and there is a jury, it decides the amount of the damages, if any; if there is no jury, the judge does so. He also decides and announces his award as to costs; *i.e.,* as to who must pay the costs of the action.

Costs are in the discretion of the judge; but this discretion has to be exercised judicially, and the normal rule is that costs follow the event. The judge will then simply direct that the successful party shall have the costs of the action, and these will then be submitted to a process known as taxation. The matter will be remitted to one of the court officials called taxing masters, who will quantify the amount to be paid by the unsuccessful to the successful party, applying the principle that the latter is entitled to such costs as were reasonably necessary for the prosecution of the action. In practice, the taxing master will generally reduce quite drastically the successful party's bill. His decision is subject to appeal by either party should he err in principle. Different scales of costs are applicable to different classes of action, the most usual scale being known as "party and party," where costs are taken into account from, but not before, the issue of the writ.

If damages have been awarded, and the party against whom they are awarded indicates his intention to appeal, the judge may order (in whole or in part) a stay of execution. The effect of this is that the successful party may not take steps to enforce payment of the damages until after the appeal, or until the time allowed for entering a notice of appeal has expired.

A formal judgment embodying the order of the court has to be prepared and signed.

The procedure outlined above is particularly applicable to actions in the Queen's Bench Division of the High Court. Differences exist, both among kinds of action, especially when started otherwise than by writ, and among divisions of the High Court. Clearly, where the main issue is the construction of a document, the processes of preparing for trial (the chief complexities of which derive from the necessity of submitting and proving, whether orally or by documentary evidence, those facts which are relevant and legally admissible) will need to be less elaborate. Likewise, in the county court, where the subject matter of the action is less weighty than in the High Court (*see* COURT), to apply the identical principles with the same elaboration as in the High Court would be not only uneconomic but in effect a denial of justice if the stakes involved were less financially valuable than in a High Court case. For details of procedure, see *The Annual Practice* (for proceedings in the High Court) and *The County Court Practice* (for proceedings in the county courts).

3. Magistrates' Court Procedure.—Civil proceedings in magistrates' courts are initiated by the making to the court of a complaint, which need not be in writing or on oath, followed by the issue of a summons if the complaint shows that the subject matter is within the jurisdiction of the court. At the hearing the court has to state to the defendant, if he appears, the substance of the plaint, and then to hear the evidence. If the complaint is for an order for the payment of a civil debt or for the variation of any order for periodical payments (or, it would seem, for any matter within the court's competence), the court may, with the defendant's consent, make an order without hearing evidence.

Much of the civil jurisdiction of magistrates' courts is concerned with domestic proceedings as defined by the Magistrates' Courts Act, 1952 (s. 56); these include cases under the Guardianship of Infants acts (1886, 1925), and the Summary Jurisdiction (Separation and Maintenance) acts 1895 to 1949, among others. The court for these purposes has to consist of not more than three justices, of whom if possible at least one shall be a man and at least one a woman. The public has no right to be present and the court may order the withdrawal of all, including press, who are not directly concerned, during the taking of indecent evidence.

For information on appeals, *see* APPEAL; COUNTY COURT.

In order to initiate an appeal, a notice of appeal has to be given, setting out the grounds. The appeal is by way of rehearing, but this is carried out by reading of the transcripts of evidence taken in the lower court; only in exceptional circumstances, when the court is satisfied that important evidence is available that was not available at the hearing at first instance, will leave be given for fresh evidence, oral or documentary, to be heard. For an appeal to the House of Lords, more elaborate documentary preparation is required, and the parties to the appeal have to prepare a detailed statement of their case. An appellate court may order a new trial if that is considered appropriate.

Appeals from magistrates' courts in civil cases are governed by the same procedure as appeals in criminal cases. A case stated to the High Court is considered by a divisional court of the appropriate division; for example, a matrimonial appeal by way of case stated will be heard in the Probate, Divorce, and Admiralty Division, and an appeal under the Guardianship of Infants acts in the Chancery Division.

See also SETTLEMENT.   (W. T. Ws.)

II. UNITED STATES

Though shorn of many of the trappings of the English tradition, the practice and procedure of all the courts of the United States except those of Louisiana are derived from the English system. But since each state and territory, and the federal government also, has its own system of courts and its own procedure, considerable diversity exists.

In general, the United States courts have benefited from a reform of court procedure similar to that made in England during the 19th century, owing to Jeremy Bentham, Lord Langdale, and others (Bentham's influence in the United States was strong); but the extent of the reform varies among the different jurisdictions. The most far-reaching change was that of the so-called code reform of procedure which was fathered by the code of civil procedure adopted in New York State in 1848; this code was eventually followed in substance in 40 U.S. states and territories and in the federal system. A later reform was that of the Federal Rules of Civil Procedure, adopted in the federal courts in 1938 and copied in many of the states, as noted below.

1. History of the Code Reform.—In 1847 the New York legislature instructed a commission "to provide for the abolition of the present forms of actions and pleadings in cases at common law; for a uniform course of proceeding in all cases . . . and for the abandonment of all Latin and other foreign tongues, so far as . . . practicable, and of any form and proceeding not necessary to ascertain or preserve the rights of the parties" (N.Y. laws, 1847, C. 59, § 8). The commission reported a code which was adopted April 12, 1848. This measure, largely the work of David Dudley Field (*q.v.*), a member of the commission, is often called the "Field Code"; it served as the model for other codes in the United States.

The most fundamental part of the code is its single form of action for all civil cases. The distinctions among various common-law actions and among their forms were abolished; the separation in procedure of equitable from legal relief was abandoned. Prior to adoption of the codes, most American states, following the English example, distinguished, in varying degrees, "legal" and "equitable" actions. These two systems offered distinctive remedies and followed distinctive procedures. Equitable relief includes all remedies which historically were available only in the courts of equity. As a substitute, the codifiers planned a system combining law and equity, with only one form of action—the civil action. This same step was taken in England a generation later in the Judicature Act of 1873; thereby English law may be said to have borrowed from its child.

The full benefits of this reform were not attained in all the states, for many courts clung to the ancient forms of action, holding them to rest upon distinctions fundamental in the law. Furthermore, some courts were hostile toward the attempted union of actions at law and suits in equity. In these cases the history and tradition of the separate systems of law and equity were strong obstacles to a complete amalgamation. It has therefore often been held that the theory of the action, whether legal or equitable,

must be pointed out in the pleadings. In fact, however, the difference between law and equity actions is chiefly in the remedy granted, and this should not be an objection to the single action or the simpler forms of pleading.

Perhaps one obstacle has seemed greatest to the courts in preventing a complete union of law and equity: this is the requirement in all the state constitutions that the right of trial by jury shall remain inviolate. This is construed to mean a preservation of that right substantially as it was when each state's constitution was adopted. As a result, jury trial is a matter of right in cases which would formerly have been actions at law, while in equitable claims no such right exists. Some courts, in protecting the constitutional right, continue to divide all actions into "law actions" and "equity actions." A more convenient rule, and one more in keeping with the code principle, is followed in many states, where the question of the form of trial is not allowed to affect the pleading in advance of the trial. If an issue arises at the trial whether there is a right to jury trial, it is decided by the nature of the issues developed in the pleadings in the light of the historical method of trying such issues.

Another important characteristic of the code is its emphasis upon pleading facts, not evidence or conclusions of law. Fact pleading was substituted for the issue pleading of the common law. This part of the code reform has been comparatively unsuccessful, because no clear line of demarcation exists between statements of fact and statements of law. An additional change wrought by the code was the adoption of the equity principles of greater freedom of joining parties (combining different suits) and of rendering judgments in part for and in part against the various parties, as the justice of the case may require (the "split judgment" of equity).

In spite of the fact that the code reform has not had the same degree of success in all the states, it seems in general to have been in accord with the desires of the people for simpler procedure. Modern plans for further reform are all in the direction of greater simplification of practice through authorized rules of court.

2. Federal Rules of Civil Procedure.—Modern reform plans were embodied in the Federal Rules of Civil Procedure, adopted by the Supreme Court of the United States to regulate the practice in the U.S. district courts. The rules were the culmination of a long struggle carried on by leaders of the bar for reform in the federal system. Traditionally the procedure in these trial courts had been divided, although a single judge sat in both law and equity cases. In equity the practice was uniform in the many district courts under rules laid down by the Supreme Court. But on the law side, each district court was supposed to conform to the practice in the courts of the state where it was sitting, subject, however, to a considerable and constantly increasing number of federal statutes dealing with details of procedure.

The resulting hodgepodge led the American Bar Association, from 1912 on, to press with vigour for complete rule-making authority to be given to the Supreme Court, so that a uniform system might be developed. No advance was made, however, for several years because of opposition from U.S. senators convinced of the need of preserving the local practice in their individual states. At length, after the Rule-Making Act of 1934 became law, the Supreme Court appointed an advisory committee of lawyers and law teachers to prepare a draft of rules. The committee consulted many members of the bar and bench and many teachers in the law schools and, after the publication and revision of preliminary drafts, made its final report, which the court accepted in 1937. The set of rules was reported to and lay before Congress for a full session, as then required by statute, and became effective Sept. 16, 1938. The committee remained active, recommending amendments from time to time. Among these were amendments, effective March 19, 1948, that made extensive reforms; and another, effective Aug. 1, 1951 (Rule 71A, Condemnation of Property), that added a rule governing the taking of property by eminent domain—the power of the federal and state governments to take private property for public use without the owner's consent.

The Supreme Court discharged the original committee in 1955. A statute enacted in 1958 gave the Judicial Conference of the

United States the responsibility of making a continuing study of all federal procedure and recommending additions or amendments to the rules in the interest of simple and effective administration of law. In 1960, at the request of the conference, the chief justice of the United States appointed advisory committees for civil, criminal, admiralty, bankruptcy, and appellate procedures, together with an overall standing and supervising committee on practice and procedure. In 1963 an additional advisory committee to draft rules of evidence was authorized. Thus the continuity of court rule making in the federal system is assured. On recommendation of these committees, certain minor amendments of the civil rules were adopted effective July 19, 1961, and a more extensive series of amendments was adopted effective July 1, 1963. Further amendments of the civil rules and amendments of other systems of procedure within the rule-making power were under study.

The federal system of procedure, as regulated by rules of the court made in this way, became a model for reform in most of the states. Those which adopted the federal system are noted below; but hardly one of them has not been affected by the reform in some degree or at least had its bar fired with zeal for far-reaching improvement. The system employs all the best features of English and U.S. state practice acts or codes, and it is generally regarded as ensuring, to a large extent, simple, flexible, and effective court administration. Notable features include a simple and generalized statement of claim and the various devices of discovery and pretrial procedure noted below.

3. Status of Pleading Systems.—The states are often classified as "code" or "non-code," depending on whether or not they adopted the Field Code established in New York in 1848. The lines of distinction, however, became blurred, particularly after 1938 when the federal rules began to be felt. By that time code pleading had been adopted in the following 31 jurisdictions: Alaska, Arizona, Arkansas, California, Colorado, Connecticut, Illinois, Indiana, Iowa, Idaho, Kansas, Kentucky, Minnesota, Missouri, Montana, Nebraska, Nevada, New Mexico, New York, North Carolina, North Dakota, Ohio, Oklahoma, Oregon, Puerto Rico, South Carolina, South Dakota, Utah, Washington, Wyoming, and Wisconsin. The adoption of the federal rules brought into this group all the vast federal system, with its 86 district or trial courts and the courts of the District of Columbia, the Canal Zone, Guam, and the Virgin Islands. And the spread of the federal rules to the states, while occurring for the most part in jurisdictions already having code pleading, brought into this group certain other states, notably Maine, New Jersey, and West Virginia. In nearly all of these jurisdictions the law and equity procedures have been fully merged, though in Arkansas, Iowa, and Oregon a formal distinction, and in Illinois a formal labeling, of actions at law and suits in equity are maintained in the same court.

In the mid-1960s the following jurisdictions had fully adopted the federal rules: Alaska, Arizona, Colorado, Delaware (separately for the chancery and law courts), District of Columbia, Hawaii, Idaho, Kansas, Kentucky, Maine, Minnesota, Missouri, Montana, Nevada, New Jersey, New Mexico, North Dakota, Puerto Rico, Utah, Washington, West Virginia, and Wyoming. Furthermore, the federal rules have been followed extensively, although not completely, in revisions of practice in Florida, Iowa, Louisiana, Michigan, New York, and Texas. Also, specific sections or separate rules have been adopted in Alabama, Arkansas, California, Connecticut, Georgia, Illinois, Louisiana, Maryland, Nebraska, New York, Ohio, Pennsylvania, South Dakota, Texas, and Vermont. Hardly a jurisdiction, however, remains unaffected; thus the important Rule 16 for pretrial conferences is universal. Only one state has turned backward; in Nebraska the rules were adopted in 1943, only to be repealed at once by the state legislature.

With respect to the non-code states, now few in number, the old classification into "quasi-code" and "common-law" jurisdictions based on the nearness of approach to code pleading is no longer useful. The practice in states such as Georgia, Massachusetts, New Hampshire, and Virginia is relatively simple and uncomplicated. There is less trace of the modern approach in Mississippi, Rhode Island, and Tennessee, although even these can hardly be termed "common-law" jurisdictions, since the an-

cient practice has been improved in many ways, as by breaking down the old distinctions between law and equity. It is true, however, that the surface diversity among U.S. jurisdictions is accentuated by the fact that an attorney of one state cannot appear as counsel in the courts of another except by special permission of the court for an individual occasion. Underneath, however, is a substantial similarity of objective which could be more easily and fully achieved by uniform rules. Adoption of the federal rules by additional states is a desirable trend toward such uniformity.

4. Course of Proceedings in a Civil Action.—Notice to the defendant at the institution of suit and an opportunity to present his side of the case are essential to the U.S. system of justice. In many of the states the traditional practice is followed of issuing a writ in the name of the state directing the sheriff to make the summons to a defendant to appear in court to answer a suit against him. In others, however, a simple written summons to appear, signed by the plaintiff or his attorney, is used instead; it is served upon the defendant by anyone not a party to the suit—usually by a clerk of the plaintiff's attorney. Even in these jurisdictions, however, when the plaintiff claims some extraordinary or provisional remedy, such as attachment of the defendant's property, arrest of the defendant, or an injunction, notice is given in the form of a court order served by some public officer, such as the sheriff.

Proper service of the summons is essential; unless the defendant is legally notified of the action, no jurisdiction is acquired over his person. Moreover, the action has to be brought to the proper court, the one that has jurisdiction over the subject matter.

Next come the pleadings, the first step being the filing by the plaintiff or his attorney of his complaint or petition. This contains the names of the parties and the court, a statement of the facts making up the plaintiff's cause of action, and a demand for the judgment to which he thinks he is entitled. The complaint is served upon the defendant with the summons, or after the parties are in court, or else is supplied to the defendant by the court clerk.

If the defendant desires to defend, his first move is to enter an appearance, which may be done, without his presence in court, by a written notice of appearance by his attorney or by filing an answer to the complaint. By demurring, the defendant may question the legal sufficiency of the complaint—he asserts that the law provides no remedy for the factual situation stated in the complaint. Where demurring does not exist, as in Illinois and New York, he moves for judgment and thus raises the same issue. In the defendant's answer he may deny the plaintiff's allegations; alternatively, he may admit them and allege new matter in his defense or as a basis for a counterclaim against the plaintiff. To this the plaintiff under most codes may file a reply. At this stage the pleadings are generally required to come to an end. The actual trial follows, with the production of evidence by the parties, followed by the verdict, if a jury is present, and culminating in judgment. If the defeated party so desires he may then take an appeal to some appellate tribunal. (*See* APPEAL.) When the judgment is finally effective—it can be stayed in many cases by an appeal—extensive proceedings are available to secure its enforcement.

The federal system is substantially the same, but with some change of emphasis from formal pleadings of fact to short and succinct statements of claim or defense, ending with the answer or with a reply to a counterclaim. The demurrer has been abolished, and objections may be presented either by answer or by a motion, including a motion for summary judgment, supported by affidavits or depositions on the merits. Stress is placed on reaching the merits quickly. Hence, so that each party may be thoroughly informed of all elements of the case at once and may thus be in a position to prepare his case completely in advance of trial, there is an extensive system of discovery by the taking of depositions, generally by witnesses; by submission of interrogatories (written questions to witnesses or parties to the suit); by requests for admissions (formal statements of relevant facts); and by the production of documents, and so on. Pretrial conferences, which are optional, are widely used. Their object is to settle the issues (the points affirmed by one side and denied by the other) and to dispense with formalities of proof of detail. They add to the sense of full preparation for trial and often facilitate settlements out of court. There is practically complete freedom of joinder of actions, both of parties and of suits, as well as of counterclaims. New parties may be summoned to answer claims developed in the case. This system is rounded out by provisions governing trials; these include waiver of jury trial by failure to ask for it within a set time and the simplifying of appeals.

The procedure described is that followed in the trial courts of general jurisdiction, usually but not always called district courts. In the states, there are usually other courts, with limited jurisdiction, inferior to the trial courts. These are known by such names as county court, municipal court, justice of the peace court, small claims court, conciliation court, and the like. Even within a single state, there frequently is a bewildering hodgepodge of these, and their procedures are as varied as the courts. Commonly the defeated litigant in a minor court may have his case tried again in the district court, but this depends on the state and on the nature and size of the claim.

A movement looking to further reform, supported by the American Bar Association, advocates improved court structure and administration. The main feature would be a unified court which would sit in various divisions as required. The chief justice, assisted by an administrative director, would supervise the system and there would be centralized administrative responsibility along businesslike lines. The movement for an integrated court—indeed the whole stress upon better administration of the courts—promises to be the outstanding trend of law reform in the decade commencing in the mid-1960s; in about three-fourths of the states there are responsible movements in the profession, the bar associations, and the legislature toward this end. Outstanding reforms have been achieved in Connecticut (P.A. 1959, C. 28), New Jersey (Const. 1947, Art. 6), Puerto Rico (Judiciary Act, 1952), and Wisconsin (Sess. Laws 1959, C. 315).

5. Criminal Procedure.—Here again the English practice is the source. For capital crimes and many other serious offenses, indictment by a grand jury is still an essential step in a criminal prosecution in many jurisdictions. This body varies in number in different jurisdictions but is usually made up of not less than 12 and not more than 23 persons. The indictment is usually prepared beforehand by the prosecutor and is given to the grand jury for its consideration. A majority of this body must concur in presenting an indictment, which then serves at the trial as the prosecution's complaint. The grand jury may also act upon its own knowledge, upon an information (similar to an indictment) of the prosecutor, or upon a complaint made under oath by a private person before a committing magistrate (one who has authority to conduct preliminary hearings in the case of serious crimes).

A number of technical rules apply to the indictment, making criminal procedure very rigid. Thus, in many jurisdictions, unless the indictment describes the offense with great detail, including its time and place of occurrence and the accused's name, it may be quashed. Authorities today advocate a procedure requiring only that reasonable notice of the ground of complaint be given the accused. In a considerable number of states an information by the prosecutor has been substituted for the indictment by the grand jury. An information suffices in the federal courts except in offenses punishable by more than one year's imprisonment. Trial by jury is usually a constitutional guarantee except for minor offenses. But in Maryland and Connecticut the accused may choose to be tried without a jury.

The American Law Institute, an organization of judges, lawyers, and law teachers with headquarters in Philadelphia, Pa., recommended an advanced and simplified Model Code of Criminal Procedure (1931), which has been adopted in some states. More lately the Supreme Court reformed its criminal procedure, following the method of drafting first employed for the civil rules. Its Advisory Committee on Rules of Criminal Procedure recommended, and the court approved, the Federal Rules of Criminal Procedure; these became effective throughout the federal system March 21, 1946. And, as noted above, a continuing advisory committee has been organized to recommend changes or additions to the federal rules. Thus there is promise that reform in criminal procedure, which has lagged far behind that occurring in civil procedure, is now at hand.

See ADMIRALTY JURISDICTION; APPEAL; ARBITRATION; CRIMINAL LAW; EVIDENCE; JUDGMENTS AND DECREES; PROBATE; SUPREME COURT OF THE UNITED STATES, THE. (C. E. Cl.)

III. CANADA

The potential for diversity in procedure in Canadian courts has been enormous. Under the British North America Act, Canada's constitution, 11 legislatures, one of which (Quebec) operates nominally under a civil-law system (*see* CIVIL LAW), have competence to create systems of courts with their own procedure. Further, procedure in all criminal matters in Canada is controlled by the federal government by virtue of s. 91 (27) of the act. In general, however, there is remarkable uniformity in this branch of the law, and such differences as occur are differences of detail rather than principle.

The principal reason for this has been, no doubt, the extremely close relation of the Canadian legal profession and system to that of England. With a common heritage, as well as the fact that the Privy Council was the final court of appeal for Canada until 1949, it was natural for procedural innovations in Canada to spring from the great reforms that occurred in England in the late 19th century. The English Judicature Act of 1873, by which common-law and equity jurisdictions were fused, has served as a pattern to all Canadian legislatures. (Parenthetically, because of the influence of United Empire Loyalists and other U.S.-trained lawyers in the Maritime Provinces, the merger of equity and common law was completed in Nova Scotia in 1855, many years before this happened in England.) There was, however, powerful opposition to this change in Ontario, a stronghold of conservatism, where originally common law and equity were administered by separate courts using old forms of English procedure. Nevertheless, after several abortive attempts to overcome the opposition of the bar, a Judicature Act modeled on the prevailing English legislation was finally enacted in 1881. Initially, the results of this move were not satisfactory; but slowly, due to modifications of the code in 1888, 1896, and 1913 and more acquaintance with the new procedure by lawyers, the changes became acceptable. Once the battle had been won in Ontario the other provinces followed suit, the last being Prince Edward Island in 1929.

The similarities between procedure in the common-law jurisdictions and in Quebec are especially striking. English influence was felt in Quebec as early as 1763, when at the prompting of the attorney general, Francis Maseres, courts of King's Bench and Common Pleas were established. Maseres, born in London of French Huguenot parents, exerted great influence on the development of law in Quebec and was responsible for much of the English content in Quebec law. Since 1777, when certain aspects of English procedure were introduced by ordinance, most of the basic concepts of procedure in the common-law jurisdictions have been included in Quebec's Code of Civil Procedure.

There is no marked difference in Canada between civil and criminal procedure; the latter is essentially civil procedure where the crown acts as plaintiff and rules of evidence are more strictly enforced. Therefore there has been virtual uniformity in the principles of procedural law, those being the principles of the English law on the subject. The following section deals only with those areas of the law which substantially differ from English practice.

1. Selection of the Forum.—The first procedural problem in any litigation is the choice of the court in which to bring action. In most federal countries this poses serious problems. In Canada the British North America Act provided for a dual system of courts, one for the provinces, which may establish their own courts (s. 92 [14]), and one for the Dominion (s. 101). In practice, however, this has not resulted in federal courts for federal matters and provincial courts for provincial matters. Generally, most matters have been dealt with, at least initially, by the provincial courts that were in existence at the time of confederation. Each province has a superior court of general jurisdiction from which appeals are taken to the provincial court of appeal. In most cases these are both branches of the province's Supreme Court, the former being called the Supreme Court, the High Court of Justice, or the Court of Queen's Bench, the latter the Court of Appeal or the Appellate Division of the Supreme Court. Below these are various levels of minor courts, the chief being the County and District Courts which try civil and criminal actions by either judge or judge and jury as well as accept appeals from certain inferior courts within the county or district. At the bottom of the judicial hierarchy there exist a multitude of minor courts such as the surrogate courts for the probating of wills and estates; division courts for civil actions involving small sums of money; magistrates' courts for trials of minor offenses and preliminary inquiries; justices of the peace for the issuance of warrants and summonses; and family and juvenile courts for matters involving the family relationship exclusive of divorce.

Superimposed on this have been the federal courts. The federal government, although having the power to establish a federal system of courts, has never created one of general jurisdiction except in very limited matters. In fact, it has established only two significant courts: the Supreme Court of Canada and the Court of Exchequer in 1875. The former court, which since 1949 has been the final court of appeal in Canada, exercises an almost completely appellate and extremely wide jurisdiction. If more than $2,000 is involved, almost any case can go to it. This is a completely different approach from that in the United States, where the Supreme Court will hear only cases of national significance. The Exchequer Court is a court of original but not general jurisdiction, dealing with patent and trademark, admiralty, and tax cases, suits against the crown, and certain other lesser federal matters. Thus, the Canadian court system, though not unitary in the English tradition, varies from the federal model supplied by the United States.

This refusal to adopt a completely dual system of federal and provincial courts seems justified on practical grounds and is, perhaps, inevitable in a sparsely populated country. There are obvious advantages in avoiding the duplication of courts and personnel. Also federal control over the appointment of provincial judges (s. 96) and review by the Supreme Court of Canada ensures, to a great extent, conformity in the interpretation of federal legislation by provincial courts. The absence of any federal court of both original and general jurisdiction, besides causing the greatest part of litigation in Canada to be dealt with in provincial courts, also means that there is virtually no problem of conflicting jurisdictions between provincial and federal courts as there is in the United States. The few jurisdictional problems stem from the legal notion that each province is an autonomous sovereign state. Thus, the intricacies of private international law are introduced into intraprovincial litigation. Fortunately, geography, population, and economics all work against the occurrence of a great many of these situations.

2. Beginning Actions and Pretrial Procedure.—Whether the cause of action is based on common law or equity, most civil actions in Canada are begun by writ of summons. In certain classes of actions, such as actions for liquidated demands, enforcement of mortgages or dower, the writ may be specially endorsed and become subject to summary judgment procedure. Thus, the plaintiff may specially endorse his writ with a statement of claim requiring the defendant to file an affidavit stating his belief that he has a valid defense on the merits. If such document is not filed, the plaintiff may immediately have judgment signed against him. When such an affidavit is filed the plaintiff may examine him upon it and move for judgment, but such motions are rarely successful. In many cases, however, such affidavits are not filed; hence this device has been widely used by litigants.

There are certain exceptions to this method of commencing actions. For example, in actions to enforce mechanics' liens the proceedings are begun by the filing of a statement of claim and proceeding immediately to trial and judgment before an official referee in a summary manner. Again, actions for the administration of a deceased person's estate or for the partition of an estate

are started by the service of an originating notice of motion, returnable in chambers, on the party from whom an account is claimed, or, in case of partition, on some of the parties interested, and the judgment may be granted or refused. Where a judgment is granted, the officer to whom the cause is referred adds all other necessary parties as defendants, and these persons are given an opportunity to contest the decision.

As a result of general acceptance of the fundamental conception of the adversary system, Canadian pretrial procedures seek to compel the parties to disclose the issues and merits of their case. Since litigation is expensive and its results uncertain, great emphasis has been placed on pretrial procedures to expedite settlements. To this end, parties have been required only to state the material facts relied upon, and courts have been given liberal powers of amendment to remedy errors in pleading. This has meant that greater importance is attached to subsequent examinations than to the preliminary statement. Examination upon discovery has become the most important aspect of pretrial procedure, and in almost all jurisdictions, except some in the Maritimes, oral discoveries have replaced discovery by interrogatories. Because the rules permit questioning on any issues pleaded, these examinations have become as broad as those at trial.

Where witnesses are aged, infirm, or outside the province, discovery may also be had through taking evidence from witnesses *de bene esse* (conditionally) for use at trial. Although the primary purpose of this is to preserve testimony, it also discloses it and thus facilitates settlements. Provision is also made for examination of relevant, nonprivileged documents, or property, and, in personal injury cases, of the injured person.

Criminal actions are begun by summons in the case of lesser offenses and by warrant in the case of more serious offenses, both summons and warrant being obtainable from a justice of the peace. In five provinces (Ontario, Nova Scotia, New Brunswick, Prince Edward Island, and Newfoundland) the grand jury has been retained, and its approval must be obtained to institute prosecution of indictable offenses.

3. Trials.—Trials in Canada, whether by judge and jury or judge alone, follow the English pattern. The traditional adversary system, with its sharp division of functions among judge, jury, and counsel, has been maintained rigidly. The only variant has been the gradual replacement of trial by judge and jury to trial by a judge alone. The only civil cases where a right to a jury trial still exists are the common-law actions of libel, slander, criminal conversation, seduction, malicious arrest or prosecution, and false imprisonment; there is no right to a jury in equitable actions; and in the remaining actions the judge is given discretion to exclude a jury. In practice, juries are empaneled in less than 2% of cases. Unfortunately, no comparable changes have been made in the procedural rules stemming from the adversarial theory, especially as it relates to matters of evidence. This has been at the root of many criticisms of the judicial system in Canada.

Similarly, in criminal cases, juries play a continually smaller role. In almost all indictable offenses, except for a relatively few minor offenses tried by a magistrate or judge alone, the accused is entitled to a jury. In only about 3% of these cases does the accused elect for a jury trial. In cases involving more serious offenses, such as rape or motor manslaughter, however, the accused must be tried by jury.

4. Enforcement of Judgment.—The last stage of a civil trial is the execution of judgment. In theory, execution of judgment should be an executive rather than a judicial act carried out by the crown rather than the individual; indeed, a writ of execution, by its terms, is a command by the crown to a sheriff to execute the judgment. In practice, however, the sheriff does nothing until spurred to action by the successful party. Thus, as the individual rather than the crown enforces the judgment, this concluding phase of litigation with its emphasis on regulated self-help is merely another example of the adversarial principle carried to its ultimate and rather abstract conclusion.

The problems which face the judgment creditor are almost entirely procedural because virtually all forms of property, whether legal or equitable, tangible or intangible, real or personal, are now exigible. Discovery in aid of execution is provided in most jurisdictions to assist the creditor in his search, and generally this has worked well. His problems begin, however, when he attempts to seize the assets so found, because there is no unified procedure for all types of assets.

In practice, the commonly used procedures are by way of the writ of *fieri facias* and the garnishment order *nisi*. The first works a notional seizure from the date it is filed with the sheriff, but, except for realty, it requires actual seizure to be effective against bona fide purchasers. Of necessity this involves many additional expenses. Garnishment procedure, although simple in theory, has not worked well in practice, because to successfully garnish money there must be a "present indebtedness" of the garnishee to the primary debtor. This means, in the case of wages, the sum must not only have been earned but also be payable. Thus, if the wages are paid in advance they are not earned, and if they have been handed to the primary debtor they are not payable; in both cases the creditor's garnishment is ineffective because the requirement of a "present indebtedness" is not satisfied. The rationale for the existence of these rules is found in history rather than utility. In practice they only make the execution process expensive, haphazard, and inequitable, the procedural niceties providing opportunities for error to the creditor and evasion to the debtor. This is probably the least satisfactory phase of judicial administration in Canada.

In criminal cases and cases involving the custody of children there has been a tendency to place increasing reliance on reports of social workers, psychiatrists, psychologists, and other professional persons. Outside the sphere of criminal law, however, there has been little uniformity in this, and many experts have expressed doubts as to whether judges place much reliance on the material supplied them. (EA. E. P.)

BIBLIOGRAPHY.—*England:* A. S. Diamond *et al.* (eds.), *The Annual Practice;* J. F. Archbold, *Pleading, Evidence and Practice in Criminal Cases,* 35th ed. by T. R. Fitzwalter Butler and M. Garsia (1962, with supplements); Sir Edgar Dale, R. C. L. Gregory, and D. Fearn (eds.), *The County Court Practice, 1963–1964* (1964); S. Stone, *Stone's Justices' Manual, 1963–1964,* ed. by J. Whiteside and J. P. Wilson (1964). *United States:* C. M. Hepburn, *Development of Code Pleading* (1897); C. E. Clark *et al., Handbook of the Law of Code Pleading,* 2nd ed. (1947); W. W. Blume, *American Civil Procedure* (1955); R. W. Millar, *Civil Procedure of the Trial Court in Historical Perspective* (1952); C. A. Wright, *Minnesota Rules* (1954), *Handbook of the Law of Federal Courts* (1963); G. H. Dession, *Criminal Law, Administration and Public Order* (1948); Roy Moreland, *Modern Criminal Procedure* (1959); W. W. Barron and Alexander Holtzoff, *Federal Practice and Procedure, with Forms,* ed. by C. A. Wright (1958–   ); J. W. Moore, *Federal Practice,* 2nd ed. (1948–60). The Judicial Administration Series, 8 vol., by recognized authorities, under the auspices of the National Conference of Judicial Councils (1939–52), covers the topics of civil, criminal, and appellate procedure, court organization, judicial selection, and standards of judicial administration. There are many editions, official and nonofficial, of the Federal Rules of Civil Procedure and Federal Rules of Criminal Procedure and Advisory Committees' Notes; special case series include *Federal Rules Service* (1939 *et seq.*) and *Federal Rules Decisions* (1941 *et seq.*). *Canada:* L. A. Audette, *The Practice of the Exchequer Court of Canada,* 2nd ed. (1909); *The Canadian Bar Review,* vol. 33, no. 1 (January 1955), devoted to procedure under the Criminal Code; D. G. Kilgour, "Procedure and Judicial Administration in Canada" in E. McWhinney (ed.), *Canadian Jurisprudence: the Civil Law and Common Law in Canada* (1959); D. A. MacRae (ed.), *Holmested and Langton on the Judicature Act of Ontario,* 5th ed. (1940); A. E. Popple, *Criminal Procedure Manual,* 2nd ed. (1956).

PRAED, WINTHROP MACKWORTH (1802–1839),

English author and politician remembered chiefly for his humorous verse, was born in London on July 26, 1802, and educated at Eton (where he founded a celebrated periodical, *The Etonian*) and at Trinity College, Cambridge, where he had a brilliant career. He was called to the bar in 1829, and entered Parliament in 1830, representing successively St. Germans, Great Yarmouth, and Aylesbury in the Tory interest. In 1834 he was appointed secretary to the Board of Control, a step in government office which was confidently expected to lead him to great heights, and in 1838 he became deputy high steward of Cambridge University and recorder of Barnstaple—various recognitions of his ability which his death from consumption on July 15, 1839, in London, brought to nothing. Praed engaged a good deal in miscellaneous journalism (his

Essays were collected in 1887), but his literary reputation rests on the most accomplished body of *vers de société* in English, such pieces as "The Vicar" and "Good Night to the Season" being unsurpassed in their subtle blending of humour, sentiment, and light satire:

> Good night to the Season!—the dances,
> The fillings of hot little rooms,
> The glancings of rapturous glances,
> The fancyings of fancy costumes;
> The pleasures which fashion makes duties,
> The praisings of fiddles and flutes,
> The luxury of looking at Beauties,
> The tedium of talking to mutes;
> The female diplomatists, planners
> Of matches for Laura and Jane;
> The ice of her Ladyship's manners,
> The ice of his Lordship's champagne.

Praed shared with Southey a talent for grim humour, as in "The Red Fisherman," and his verse epistles are the best since Swift. He wrote many political squibs, some of which, for example "Stanzas to the Speaker Asleep," have a bantering grace, the effect of which is moving as well as comic.

See W. M. Praed, *Selected Poems,* ed. by K. Allott (1953); D. Hudson, *A Poet in Parliament* (1939). (K. Ho.)

PRAEMUNIRE,

in English law, an offense so called from the introductory words, *Praemunire facias A.B.* ("cause A.B. to be forewarned"), of the writ of summons issued to the defendant. The word came to be used to denote the offenses, usually ecclesiastical, prosecuted by means of such a writ, and also the penalties they incurred. From the 13th century papal encroachment increased, especially in two forms. One was the disposal of ecclesiastical benefices to men chosen at the papal Curia: this was the practice of provision (*q.v.*). The other involved judicial actions in the papal court, which either ran counter to decisions in the English royal courts or drew to the Curia business thought by royal lawyers to fall outside papal jurisdiction. The first Statute of Provisors (against provision) of 1351 was followed in 1353 by the Statute of Praemunire, which provided that any subject of the king who had litigated "out of the realm" in a matter properly belonging to the king's court should be allowed two months in which to answer for his contempt.

This statute was revised in 1365 and was followed, in 1393, by the so-called "great" Statute of Praemunire, primarily directed against Pope Boniface IX. In the 16th century it acquired great importance and was used by Cardinal Thomas Wolsey against William Warham, archbishop of Canterbury, in 1518. In 1529 Wolsey himself was found liable to the penalties of praemunire. The statute was used in 1530–31 by Henry VIII to obtain the submission of the English clergy.

The Royal Marriages Act of 1772 is the last which subjects anyone to the penalties of a praemunire.

See E. B. Graves, "The Legal Significance of the Statute of Praemunire of 1353," *Anniversary Essays in Mediaeval History by the students of Charles Homer Haskins,* ed. by C. H. Taylor (1929); W. T. Waugh, "The Great Statute of Praemunire," *English Historical Review,* vol. xxxvii (1922). (J. R. L. H.)

PRAENESTE

(modern PALESTRINA), a very ancient city of Latium, lies 23 mi. (37 km.) ESE of Rome on the Via Prenestina, on a spur of the Apennines facing the Alban Hills. On the summit of the hill (2,471 ft. [753 m.]), at Castel San Pietro, nearly a mile from the later Sullan settlement and the modern town of Palestrina, stood the ancient citadel, the site of which is now occupied by the church of San Pietro and a ruined medieval castle of the Colonna family. Portions of the southern wall of the ancient citadel, built of very massive blocks of limestone, are still to be seen; and two walls (also of polygonal masonry), which descended from the citadel to the town, can be traced. Praeneste's foundation was traditionally assigned to the mythological period (Virgil, *Aeneid* vii, 678); Odysseus' son Telegonus was one of the supposed founders. By the 7th century B.C. Praeneste was rich, powerful, and civilized with an etruscanized culture. Its wealth is shown by the contents of the Barberini and Bernardini tombs, now in Rome in the Villa Giulia Museum. Tombs of the 6th and 7th centuries have not yet been found, but those of the 4th and 3rd are known. Praeneste was famous for its *cistae* or bronze toilet chests of the 4th and 3rd centuries B.C., which in the beauty of their engravings reach a high level of artistic achievement. Reliefs in ivory also have been found.

In 499 B.C., according to Livy, Praeneste formed an alliance with Rome; during the 5th century it was exposed to attack by the Aequi. After Rome had been weakened by the Gallic invasion (390), Praeneste frequently fought against Rome and joined in the great Latin War of 340–338. It was punished by the loss of part of its territory, and it became an ally of Rome, possessing the right of exile (*ius exilii*); *i.e.*, persons banished from Rome might live at Praeneste. The city remained loyal to the Roman cause, resisting both Pyrrhus and Hannibal. After 90 B.C. it received Roman citizenship and became a *municipium*. In the civil wars the younger Marius was blockaded in the town by the Sullans (82 B.C.); on its capture the male inhabitants were massacred in cold blood, and a colony of Sulla's veterans was settled on part of its territory, while the city was removed from the hillside to the lower ground at the Madonna dell'Aquila, and the temple of Fortuna was reconstructed. Under the empire Praeneste, from its elevated position and healthy air, became a favourite summer resort of wealthy Romans, whose villas studded the neighbourhood. Horace ranked it with Tibur and Baiae, though in fact it never rivaled Tibur or the Alban Hills as a fashionable residence. Still, Augustus resorted to it; here Tiberius recovered from an illness, and Hadrian and Marcus Aurelius had villas. Among private owners were the younger Pliny and Symmachus. The nuts of Praeneste were famous and its roses were among the finest in Italy. The Latin spoken there was somewhat unusual, and was ridiculed by Romans such as Plautus. A calendar, set up by the grammarian M. Verrius Flaccus in the forum of Praeneste, was discovered in 1771.

Its greatest claim to fame, however, was its great temple to Fortuna Primigenia (*i.e.*, the first-born of Jupiter) and the oracle connected with the temple, known as the "Praenestine Lots" (*sortes Praenestinae*); these responses were given on slips of wood. An immense complex of buildings rose up the hillside like a pyramid in terraces, linked by ramps or stairs, and covered the area occupied by the medieval town. The higher section was later incorporated into the Palazzo Colonna-Barberini (begun in 12th century A.D.); in 1944 during World War II this was severely damaged by bombing, which revealed much of the ancient structure. This area has been restored (1952–55) and a museum housed in the palace. The lower buildings, near the cathedral, include the so-called "antro delle sorti," with marine mosaics, a temple, and the famous Nile mosaic. Little idea can be given here of the grandeur and complexity of the temple site. The cult was flourishing by 241 B.C., but the period of great building remains controversial: many (*e.g.*, G. Lugli) would assign it essentially to Sulla, but Fasoli and Gullini (*see* below) date it *c.* 150 B.C. Moreover, while the complex is normally explained as upper and lower parts of a sanctuary, some believe that the lower buildings were not part of the *area sacra*. This immense and imposing sanctuary, probably the largest in Italy, was visible from a great part of Latium, from Rome, and even from the sea.

BIBLIOGRAPHY.—H. C. Bradshaw, *Papers of the British School at Rome*, vol. ix, pp. 233–262 (1920); Pauly-Wissowa, *Real-Encyclopädie der classischen Altertumswissenschaft*, vol. xxii, ii, 2, 1549–55 (1954) and supplementband viii, 1241–59 (1956); F. Fasolo and G. Gullini, *Il santuario della Fortuna a Palestrina*, 2 vol. (1953); and a brief guide by G. Iacopi, *Il santuario della Fortuna e il museo archeologico prenestino* (1959).　　　　　　　　　　　　　　　(H. H. Sd.)

PRAESTÖ, an *amt* (county) of Denmark, embracing southeastern Sjaelland (Zealand), the island of Mön, and islets including Bogö and Nyord, is centred on the small town of Praestö. Area 654 sq.mi. (1,694 sq.km.). Pop. (1960) 121,976. Its gently undulating morainic surface with fertile clay loams forms an important mixed farming district. Impressive limestone cliffs occur at Stevns Klint and Möns Klint. The ports of Naestved (pop. [1960] 19,617) and Vordingborg (11,780) are the principal settlements.　　　　　　　　　　　　　　　　　　　　　(HA. T.)

PRAETOR (derived from Latin *prae-ire*, "to lead, to precede") was the title borne by the consuls in the early republic of Rome (*see* CONSUL). Its military connotations remain in the adjective *praetorius*, in such phrases as *castra praetoria* and *cohors praetoria* and its translation into Greek with the word *strategos*, "general." The praetorship was instituted as a patrician office for the administration of the civil law in 366 B.C. when the consulship was first held by a plebeian (*see* PATRICIANS). The praetor (later called *urbanus* when other praetors were added) was elected by the centuriate assembly (*see* COMITIA) as a junior colleague of the consuls, whose *imperium* (authority) was superior to his. He could hold military command, summon the senate in the absence of the consuls, and perform other public functions, but could not legally hold a consular or a praetorian election. The office was first held by a plebeian in 336.

Increases in the number of foreign traders and residents made necessary the creation of a second praetor (*praetor peregrinus*) to judge suits between foreigners and between citizens and foreigners, under whom considerations of equity began to relieve the strict application of the civil law. About 227 two praetors were added to govern the provinces of Sicily and Sardinia. The organization of the two Spanish provinces led to the addition of two more in 197, a number which remained fixed until L. Cornelius Sulla (dictator 81–79). The praetor had six lictors (two in the city), as well as the *toga praetexta* and the curule chair, while the praetors in Spain, such as Aemilius Paullus in 191–189, who had 12 lictors, usually received a consular *imperium*. Additional provinces and the creation of new courts to deal with extortion (149), treason (103), and murder (before 98) added to their duties. Finally, Sulla raised the number to eight and placed the series of courts regularly in their charge (extortion, bribery, embezzlement, treason, murder, and forgery), while continuing the *urbanus* and the *peregrinus*, each being allotted his jurisdiction before entrance upon office. This meant in practice that praetors served a year in Rome before proceeding to provinces as propraetors or proconsuls. Julius Caesar raised the number to 16, Augustus reduced it to 8, but added 2 new praetors of the treasury and raised it temporarily to 16 again. Later numbers vary according to fields of competence, sometimes, as with Agricola, too many for the fields to be allotted. Claudius abolished the praetors of the treasury, but two were created to deal with trusts (*fidei commissa*), another to deal with disputes between the fiscus (*q.v.*) and private citizens (Nerva), another as a guardian for minors (Marcus Aurelius), one in charge of the *centumviri* (*q.v.*; Augustus), and one for cases involving freedom of slaves.

Under the principate elections became a form determined by imperial commendation of candidates and the process of *destinatio*, but the magistracy remained an important stage in a senatorial career, as the command of a legion and of provinces of second rank were reserved for ex-praetors. The urban praetor's responsibility under the republic for the games of Apollo became a general praetorian responsibility for the major games.

From early in the history of the magistracy the praetor as a civil administrator issued an edict on entering office stating the procedure by which he would be guided. This edict, accepted and modified by succeeding praetors, became one of the most important factors in molding and adapting the Roman law to new conditions and the demands of equity and good faith. Under Hadrian this development ended when the "perpetual edict" was codified and published in definitive form, but praetorian jurisdiction in both civil and criminal law had already been circumscribed by imperial responses, judgments of the imperial consilium, and the jurisdiction of the emperor, the senate, and the urban and praetorian prefects.

In the late empire most praetorships disappeared but the *praetor urbanus* remained with the heavy burden of providing games, and also those who were guardians of minors and those who judged questions of freedom. The office became a *munus* ("public duty") instead of an *honor*.

Praetor was the title of the elected head of the Latin League, and of the chief magistrate in some Latin and Italian towns.

BIBLIOGRAPHY.—T. Mommsen, *Römische Staatsrecht*, vol. ii, 193 ff. (1887); G. Wesenberg in Pauly-Wissowa, *Real-Encyclopädie der classischen Altertumswissenschaft*, 1581–1606 (1954); A. N. Sherwin-White, *Roman Citizenship* (1939); F. Pringsheim, "The Legal Policy and Reforms of Hadrian," *Journal of Roman Studies*, 24, 141 ff. (1934);

H. F. Jolowicz, *Historical Introduction to the Study of Roman Law*, vol. ii, pp. 208, 367 (1952).　　　　　　(T. R. S. B.)

PRAETORIAN GUARD, the household troops of the Roman emperors. By the 2nd century B.C. Roman generals had a bodyguard known as the praetorian cohort (*cohors praetoria*). After the Battle of Philippi (42 B.C.) 8,000 veterans who refused discharge were formed into praetorian cohorts and shared between M. Antonius (Mark Antony) and Octavian, who later, as the emperor Augustus, stationed a number of cohorts (probably 9) in and around Rome, and in 2 B.C. appointed two equestrian prefects to command them (*see* PREFECT). Tiberius' powerful prefect Sejanus concentrated the praetorians in A.D. 23 in fortified two-story barracks on the Viminal Hill, just outside the walls of Rome to the northeast; the site is at present occupied by the Caserma Macao. The barracks were shared with the three (later four) urban cohorts, a police force under the *praefectus urbi*.

The cohorts were increased to 12 by either Gaius (Caligula) or Claudius. Vitellius enrolled 16 briefly in 69, but Vespasian returned to 9; later, possibly under Domitian, they were raised to 10 again and remained so until Diocletian. There is some doubt whether there were originally 500 or 1,000 men to a cohort; 1,000 is certainly the figure later on. A few cavalry were attached to them, but they themselves were foot soldiers. Their pay was roughly three times a legionary soldier's, and they served 16 years instead of 20. They were recruited from Italy and the romanized provinces until 193, when Septimius Severus disbanded the existing praetorians and replaced them with picked men from the legions; even before this their officers had as a rule had at least brief service with a legion.

The emperor's actual bodyguard was a separate smaller body, often of non-Romans, but the praetorians performed guard duties at the imperial palace (for which they wore the civilian toga), and a part of them was always with the emperor. Hence some of them served in foreign wars; Nero even sent a contingent of praetorians on a reconnoitering expedition into Nubia. They also acted on occasions as a political police, carrying out arrests and executions, and had various ceremonial duties.

Although the frontier legions took as much part in appointing emperors, the praetorians figure in such sensational incidents as the accession of Claudius (41), the disorders of 68–69, the lynching of Domitian's murderers (97), and, in 193, the murder of Pertinax and the subsequent auction at the praetorian camp, where the Roman Empire was knocked down to Didius Julianus for a bounty of 6,250 denarii per praetorian. This last incident probably influenced Septimius Severus in his decision to reorganize them. After this they murdered Elagabalus (222), and Balbinus and Maximus (238). Diocletian reduced their numbers. Many of them fell with Maxentius at the Battle of the Milvian Bridge (312), and in the same year Constantine finally disbanded them (but not the urban cohorts).

See R. Durry, *Les Cohortes prétoriennes* (1938); A. Passerini, *Le coorti pretorie* (1939).

PRAETORIUS, MICHAEL (1571–1621), German music theorist and composer, highly regarded by his contemporaries, was born in Kreuzberg (Thuringia) on Feb. 15, 1571. He adopted the latinized form of the German name Schultheiss. After studying at Frankfurt an der Oder he was organist and *Kapellmeister* to the bishop of Halberstadt, and from 1612 was *Kapellmeister* at the court of Wolfenbüttel until his death there on Feb. 15, 1621.

Praetorius was extremely zealous for the advancement of music. An admirer of Italian music, he had a predilection for rich and varied settings for voices and all kinds of instruments. His output was considerable and various. The most important collections of his works are the settings of evangelical church songs called *Musae Sioniae* (nine parts, 1605–10), partly for 8 to 12 voices in the Venetian double choir style, and partly in simple four-part style; and the *Puericinium* (1621), where the hymn strophes receive very varied treatment, foreshadowing the choral cantata. Praetorius published much music other than his own, and in his collection *Terpsichore* (1612) he introduced several hundred foreign dance pieces to Germany.

The three surviving parts of Praetorius' great work *Syntagma Musicum* (1614–18) comprise a Latin treatise on music theory, a lavishly illustrated account of instruments, and an exposition of musical forms and methods of performance; the fourth part, on counterpoint, was not completed.　　　　　　(C. P. Co.)

PRAGMATIC SANCTION, a pronouncement by a sovereign on a matter of prime importance, such as the relationship between church and state or the dynastic succession.

The Pragmatic Sanction of Bourges (July 7, 1438) was issued by Charles VII of France after an assembly had examined the decrees of the Council of Basel (*q.v.*). It established the "liberties" of the Gallican Church (*see* GALLICANISM), in particular by declaring that the successors to vacant prelacies in France should be elected by their chapters or convents unless the vacancy arose from the previous occupant's death *in curia*, that is, on a visit to Rome, in which case the pope could nominate his successor. In practice, election usually meant the election of the French king's nominee. Revoked by Louis XI in 1461, but reasserted from time to time later, the Pragmatic Sanction was ultimately superseded by the Concordat (*q.v.*) of Bologna between Francis I and Pope Leo X (1515).

The Holy Roman emperor Charles VI (*q.v.*) designed his Pragmatic Sanction of April 19, 1713, to preserve the integrity of the Habsburg inheritance (*see* AUSTRIA, EMPIRE OF; HABSBURG). It stipulated that if Charles left only daughters, the undivided heritage should go to the senior one and then to her descendants by primogeniture; and that if Charles died childless, it should go to his deceased brother Joseph I's daughters or their descendants, likewise in order of primogeniture. Charles laboured for years to induce the estates of the various Habsburg lands, the German princes, and the other European powers to assent to this Pragmatic Sanction; and the Peace of Vienna (1738–39), after the War of the Polish Succession, seemed to guarantee it, with Maria Theresa (*q.v.*) as the prospective beneficiary. When Charles died (1740), however, the War of the Austrian Succession (*q.v.*) broke out.

In Spain, by his Pragmatic Sanction of March 29, 1830, Ferdinand VII (*q.v.*) promulgated his predecessor Charles IV's unpublished decision of 1789 revoking the Salic law of succession (*q.v.*), so that the subsequent birth of Ferdinand's daughter, the future Isabella II, deprived his brother Don Carlos (*q.v.*) of his right as heir presumptive. The first Carlist War broke out on Ferdinand's death (1833).

PRAGMATISM, a term of philosophy (from Greek *pragmata,* "acts," "affairs," "business") chosen by the U.S. logician C. S. Peirce (*q.v.*; 1839–1914), apparently in the course of discussions with William James and others in the 1870s, to stand for a way of making our ideas clear or, more accurately, for "a method of logic, a method of determining the meanings of intellectual concepts, that is, of those upon which reasoning may hinge" (*Collected Papers of Charles Sanders Peirce,* ed. by Charles Hartshorne and Paul Weiss, vol. 5, p. 464; Cambridge, Mass.: Harvard, 1935). Pragmatism was popularized by the writings of James during the first decade of the 20th century; but the later publication of Peirce's *Collected Papers* showed that the two fathers of the doctrine diverged considerably in their interpretations of it.

Peirce's original formulation of the pragmatist principle was: "Consider what effects, that conceivably might have practical bearings, we conceive the object of our conception to have. Then our conception of these effects is the whole of our conception of the object" (*Collected Papers,* vol. 5, p. 2). A more readily intelligible and apparently equivalent formula of James is that "the whole meaning of a conception expresses itself in practical consequences, either in the shape of conduct to be recommended or in that of experience to be expected if the conception is true, which consequences would be different if it were untrue, and must be different from the consequences by which the meaning of other conceptions is in turn expressed" (William James in James Mark Baldwin, *Dictionary of Philosophy and Psychology,* New York, Macmillan Company, 1902). Both statements make a point which is closely related to the central teaching of British empiricism (*see* EMPIRICISM); but where traditional empiricism has taught that none of our conceptions (or the verbal expression of them) has a meaning unless it has been derived from some elementary sensory impression, pragmatism teaches that no conception has meaning unless it can be applied, directly or indirectly, in the location and description of something of a kind that might be revealed to our senses.

Regarded in this way, the positive content of pragmatism is simple enough; viz., that all our conceptions, even the most abstract, derive their peculiar point or meaning from things or from differences in such things as we can actually observe and point to. But pragmatism has certain features which constitute a further important development of traditional empiricism. Two things differ practically, or differ for us, insofar as we find ourselves compelled to treat them differently or to expect different reactions from them. Similarly, according to pragmatism, two words (or conceptions) have different meanings not because of some direct relation between word and thing in either case but in virtue of their different uses; *i.e.*, in virtue of the different ways in which they help to express or communicate different procedures—involving expectation and adjustment—with regard to the things in question. Thus pragmatism contains, or rests upon, what might be called a procedural theory of meaning. Moreover, Peirce's principle has proved a most searching tool of criticism. We are all liable to confuse highly abstract and erudite conceptions, not only in metaphysics but also in the mathematical and natural sciences; but if one conception does not differ "practically" (in Peirce's sense) from a second, then our employment of it adds nothing to our employment of that second conception. Again, we are sometimes tempted to engage in speculations which have no assignable "practical bearings"; but in that case, according to pragmatism, our thoughts and words have no assignable meaning. Men of science, Peirce claimed, have always unconsciously applied the pragmatist method to distinguish better conceptions which common sense treats as one or to identify conceptions which common sense has traditionally regarded as several. Unfortunately philosophers have not made much use of the method.

Thus far Peirce and James were in agreement; the grounds of their divergence were more complex than either of them appreciated. In the first place, for example, James wished to use the pragmatist method to vindicate—not simply to elucidate—our basic moral and religious beliefs by reference to their beneficial practical consequences on our conduct and temper. Peirce was on the whole averse to applying the pragmatist method to moral or to religious concepts, which seemed to him of a kind that could not be made clear; and certainly he was flabbergasted by some of James's ventures in this field. Second, as the basis, to a large extent, of these ventures, there was James's "pragmatist" account of our conception of truth, his view that a belief or theory is true insofar as it "works" or "pays." To be sure, James has often been cruelly misunderstood in this connection, yet it is questionable whether his account of truth can be regarded as an inevitable —and still more questionable whether it can be regarded as the one and only possible—result of applying the pragmatist method to our normal uses of the word "true." Third, underlying most of James's applications of the pragmatist method (including the case of "truth") was his strong prejudice in favour of whatever is concrete and particular and against whatever is abstract and general. This finds expression in his statement that the meaning of any proposition "can always be brought down to some particular consequence in our future experience . . . the point lying rather in the fact that the experience must be particular, rather than in the fact that it must be active" (William James, *Collected Essays and Reviews,* p. 412; New York: Longmans, Green & Co., 1920). Peirce explicitly repudiated this view. Fourth, the last-named prejudice of James was closely connected with his hankering after that form of metaphysics—"radical empiricism" he called it—according to which the fundamental reference of all discourse is "pure experience," something which is in itself neutral as between mind and matter and which is exemplified in the content of our sensations and the felt transitions between our sensations. (For example, "truth" on this view stands for certain experienceable transitions between one "bit" of experience and other bits with which it can be brought into harmonious and successful relation.) James openly confessed that he was attracted to pragmatism be-

cause he thought it would help him to vindicate his radical empiricism—of which indeed it seemed to him to be simply the logical facet. Peirce on the other hand vehemently rejected the suggestion that any doctrine of logic should be preferred for its metaphysical affinities. "Pragmatism is no doctrine of metaphysics."

Of these four grounds of divergence the last two are fundamental. In them we see the transition from Peirce's account of the meaning of a term or statement as an attribute of certain prescribable and justifiable procedures to James's account of it as an attribute of certain describable, because individually experienced, processes. The illegitimacy of this transition seemed plain to Peirce from the fact that his pragmatist principle was put forward, as has been said, as a method of "determining the meanings of intellectual concepts, that is, of those upon which reasoning may hinge." For all reasoning is, in Peircian phrase, subject to "logical control" (*i.e.*, to agreed logical canons); but whatever is amenable to control by rules must be in the nature of a habit or general procedure of action. Hence it can only be to concepts (or their verbal expression) which are irreducibly general (*i.e.*, such that they can be employed by any rational being in any situation of appropriate general kind) that the pragmatist principle can apply. Alternatively we can say: Pragmatism, according to Peirce, teaches that our descriptions of things are to be understood as ways of dealing with those things—but of dealing with them from the standpoint, in some respects highly specialized, but in other respects entirely general, of reasoning; *i.e.*, of finding out how observation, hypothesis, deduction and checking of consequences shows them to behave. But while making this protest against James's misuse of his pragmatist principle, Peirce was no less strenuous than James in emphasizing its empiricist purpose; only insofar as an intellectual concept (or its verbal expression) refers to "compulsory perceptions" of a certain sort—perceptions forced upon anyone who uses it—does it possess distinctive and genuine meaning.

Largely because of these disagreements between its originators, partly also because of their respective literary failings—James's writings at their worst are intolerably slapdash, Peirce's at their worst distressingly obscure—pragmatism was subjected during the first quarter of the 20th century to scathing criticisms from philosophers both of the realist and of the idealist schools. For later readers, the annals of this interschool battle are neither lively nor illuminating.

But the inner vitality of Peirce's pragmatist teaching is sufficiently shown by the variety of first-class minds that subsequently described themselves or allowed themselves to be described as pragmatists. Among these may be mentioned the English philosopher F. C. S. Schiller, whose very uneven writings contain some admirable expositions of the "question-and-answer" character of all purposive thinking; John Dewey (*q.v.*), whose "instrumentalist" theory of knowledge owes much to Peirce and whose naturalistic metaphysics of experience would have appealed greatly to James; G. Mead, who developed in the most suggestive manner Peirce's conception of inquiry as a socially controlled activity. C. I. Lewis drew on Peirce's teaching to restate the Kantian distinction between a priori and empirical elements in knowledge.

See also references under "Pragmatism" in the Index.

BIBLIOGRAPHY.—C. S. Peirce, *Collected Papers,* ed. by Charles Hartshorne and Paul Weiss, 6 vol. (1931–35), especially vol. v, and *The Philosophy of Peirce,* ed. by J. Buchler (1940); W. James, *The Will to Believe* (1897) and *Pragmatism* (1907); J. Dewey, *Essays in Experimental Logic* (1916); F. C. S. Schiller, *Humanism* (1903); G. H. Mead, *Mind, Self and Society* (1934); C. I. Lewis, *Mind and the World-Order* (1929); W. B. Gallie, *Peirce and Pragmatism* (1952); Manley H. Thompson, *The Pragmatic Philosophy of C. S. Peirce* (1953); J. D. Butler, *Four Philosophies and Their Practice in Education and Religion* (1957). (W. B. Ge.)

PRAGUE (Czech PRAHA), the capital city of Czechoslovakia, is situated along both banks of a large meander of the Vltava (Ger. Moldau), a tributary of the Elbe. The Vltava is there crossed by 13 bridges. Prague lies 650 ft. (198 m.) above sea level and is approximately 160 mi. (255 km.) NW of Vienna and 75 mi. (120 km.) SE of Dresden. Area 72 sq.mi. (186 sq.km.). Pop. (1961) 998,493.

The modern town has spread along the winding riverbanks, up

CAMERA PRESS—PIX FROM PUBLIX

VIEW OF PRAGUE ACROSS CHARLES BRIDGE AND VLTAVA RIVER, WITH HRADCANY PALACE AT UPPER RIGHT

the steep terraced hill slopes, and into the side valleys as well as the surrounding high ground. The hilly position of the town forms a serious barrier to modern communications but adds greatly to its beauty which is enhanced by the many medieval and Baroque buildings with their towers and spires and by the numerous parks, of which Stromovka and the Petrin orchards and gardens are the most extensive. A few industrial districts are situated on the left bank, but the chief factories are along the right bank in the northwestern part of the town (Vysocany-Liben) and a new industrial quarter is growing up in the eastern sector. The residential quarters and new housing estates lie farther from the centre and form part of greater Prague, which has engulfed the surrounding towns.

The historical parts of the town, which have retained their ancient appearance, are kept up by the state. The vast 16th- to 17th-century fortified palace on Hradcany Hill, now the residence of the president of the republic and formerly that of the ancient kings of Bohemia, dominates the entire town. The castle has a number of halls including Vladislav Hall in Late Gothic style and the Spanish Hall in 17th-century Baroque. In the inner castle yard stands St. Vitus Cathedral, begun in 1344 and finally completed in 1929. Other important buildings on the castle hill include the Romanesque basilica of St. George (912) and the Renaissance Belvedere. The Little Quarter below the castle is a district of picturesque streets overshadowed by the Baroque dome of St. Nicholas' Cathedral (1703). Overlooking the many fine squares and narrow streets stand numerous palaces, now used for public purposes. The Little Quarter is joined to the Old Town by the Charles Bridge (1357), now flanked by Baroque statues. The Old Town abounds in monuments and relics of the history of the district. Its most remarkable features include the Old Town Square with the ruins of the town hall, burned down during the 1945 uprising, and the ancient clock of the seasons. Opposite them is the 14th-century Tyn Church, in the Prague Gothic style, containing the tomb of Tycho Brahe, the Danish astronomer. The church was the religious centre of the Hussite movement and in the centre of the square is a monument (1915) to John Huss. Nearby are the remnants of the old Josef's town (the Jewish ghetto) and a 13th-century Jewish cemetery and synagogue.

Passing out of the Old Town through the 15th-century gate, or Powder Tower, to Prikopy, the site of the former moat around the old walls, there is a change from ancient beauty to modern, commercial life with department stores, hotels, restaurants, and offices. The centre of the modern town is Wenceslas Square with the statue of St. Wenceslas (1913) and the National Museum (1894). Other sights worth mentioning include the Tyl Theatre, where Mozart's *Don Giovanni* was first performed; the National Theatre (1883); Vysehrad Hill with the church of St. Peter and St. Paul and the poets' corner; the national monument at Zizkov with the mausoleum; and the statue of the Hussite leader Jan (John) Zizka by Bohumil Kafka (1950).

Education and Culture.—Prague University, founded by Charles IV in 1348, was the first in central Europe. The Technical University (1707) has developed a great number of faculties. Other centres of learning include the Prague School of Economics, the arts and crafts school (1885), the Academy of Graphic Arts (1799), the Academy of Music, Dancing and Film (1948), the Conservatoire (1811), and the Institute of Physical Training. The Czechoslovak Academy of Sciences carries out its research in numerous buildings.

Besides the National Museum (founded 1818) there are a technical, an ethnographical, an arts and crafts, and a Jewish museum, and museums of Czechoslovak literature and of the Working Class Movement. The National Gallery contains pictures and sculptures by famous Czech, Slovak, and foreign artists and has a unique collection of Gothic art. The Art Gallery of Prague Castle, opened in 1965, displays the remnants of the once famous art collection of Rudolf II. In addition to the central municipal library there is the university library which owns a collection of precious manuscripts and old prints. Prague has 26 theatres, including 3 belonging to the National Theatre, where drama, opera, and ballet are performed, special theatres for children (puppets), and a theatre of recorded music. A number of symphony orchestras are headed by the Czech Philharmonic.

Industry and Communications.—As a capital, Prague is the seat of the ministries, foreign trade corporations, the chamber of commerce, and the highest church dignitaries. Though the main town of the Central Bohemian region and housing its regional administrative offices, the town has autonomous status on a par with a region. For purposes of local administration it is divided into ten independent districts. It is also a big industrial town and with its surroundings now forms the largest centre of engineering in the entire country. Most of the industries are highly specialized, with more than half the production capacity devoted to heavy and precision engineering. All works have been greatly expanded and brought up to date since nationalization in 1945, and many new factories have been built. Products include automobiles, motorcycles, buses, airplanes, railway engines and coaches, machine tools, boilers, mining and foundry equipment, cranes, electrical equipment, turbines, machinery for the chemical industry, etc. Other important industries include food processing (mills, breweries, a refrigeration plant, dairy produce, and meat products) and the manufacture of clothing and chemical and pharmaceutical products. There are also printing works, phonograph and film industries, and tanneries.

The electric power for the city is brought by grid from the brown coal basin in northwestern Bohemia, which also supplies gas. There are hydroelectric power stations on the Vltava at Orlik, and Stechovice, at Vrane, and at the Slapy Dam (1955).

Prague is the meeting place of rail and air routes joining the north and south of Europe and, especially, the east and west. There are three main-line railway stations. The airport, Ruzyne, is 7 mi. (11 km.) from the centre of the town. Local transport services (streetcars, trolley buses, buses) extend over 100 mi. (160 km.), with an additional 60 mi. (96 km.) of local railway lines. Holesovice, the inland harbour, is the terminus of Elbe-Vltava shipping.

History.—There is evidence that the site on which Prague stands has been inhabited since Paleolithic times. Its fertile soil and mild climate (average temperature 1.6° C [35° F] in January, 19.4° C [67° F] in July), its easy fords across the river and the possibilities of defense and of trade, favoured the growth of a town which later became the political centre of Bohemia (q.v.). The ruling dynasty of the Premyslids (until 1306) succeeded in defeating all foreign attempts at subjugation and preserved the territorial integrity of the country.

The earliest settlements, documented from about the 9th century, were found at the foot of the ancient castles built on two dominating hilltops, Vysehrad on the right bank of the river and Hradcany on the left, which were residences of the Bohemian princes and later kings. On the right bank a small settlement formed the market centre for the isolated homesteads in the neighbourhood. This developed into Stare Mesto (Old Town), and on the opposite bank King Premysl Otakar II founded Mala Strana (Little Quarter) in 1257. Under Charles IV, king of Bohemia (1346–78) and Roman emperor, Nove Mesto (New Town) was built adjacent to the old town, and the ghetto was also developed.

In the 14th century Prague was already one of the most important towns in central Europe. It was a vital crossroad of trade routes running from north to south and from east to west, and it was also a centre of culture, its university attracting scholars and students from all over Europe. Charles IV, besides founding the university, was personally responsible for extensive building activities in the town according to an elaborate plan. Outstanding examples are the Charles Bridge joining the Little Quarter to the Old Town, the Carolinum (the central auditorium of the university), and the town hall as well as several churches and monasteries in the New Town.

Foreigners who came to settle in Prague contributed toward its growth, and the German and Italian merchants grew into a rich patriciate who ruled the town. They could usually rely on the support of the king in all measures designed to curb the guilds formed by Czech craftsmen. Many conflicts arose between the two social groups and were conducted with an eye to nationality. Disputes between guild masters and their journeymen incited numerous town paupers to minor uprisings, which went on prior to and throughout the period of the Hussite Wars.

Among the scholars of the university, John Huss soon assumed a leading role in the struggle that ended with the Kutna Hora decree (1409), in which Wenceslas IV granted the Czechs a predominant position in the university. Huss, basing his criticism on the theoretical writings of Wycliffe which he developed further, publicly voiced sharp criticism of the church and the secular power it exerted as well as the sinful life of the clergy. His sermons, delivered in the Bethlehem Chapel (restored to its original appearance in 1954), gained him support among the common people. Repressive measures on the part of the church and the patriciate led to violent uprisings in 1419 during which the radical elements, led by John Zelivsky, rose to power. Prague came to the aid of the people's uprisings in the countryside, which were led by the Hussite supporters, who had established a model community at Tabor in southern Bohemia. The Taborites, led by Zizka, helped Prague and gained a decisive victory in the Battle of Vitkov Hill in 1420. After the defeat of the radicals the city patriciate and the rich burghers gradually changed sides until, toward the end of the Hussite Wars, Prague stood in the ranks of the opponents. (See HUSSITES.)

The town's significance grew under the rule of George of Podebrady and the Jagiello dynasty, during which Prague was enriched by the building of churches and halls (e.g., Vladislav Hall) in Late Gothic style. The following centuries witnessed the growing opposition to the Habsburgs who had become kings of Bohemia on the death of Louis II of Hungary and were endeavouring to reintroduce Catholicism by force. Opposition to those measures and attempts to put an end to the feudal might and Catholic influence of the monarchy and the church led to the Defenestration of Prague (May 23, 1618), one of the steps leading to the Thirty Years' War (see BOHEMIA: Habsburg Rule, 1526–1918).

During the Hussite Wars the town was a Czech stronghold, but after the defeat of the Protestants at the Battle of the White Mountain in 1620, and after the public execution of Czech noblemen and Prague commoners on the Old Town Square in 1621, the German predominance increased again. Prague ceased to be the chief town of the German empire and its significance began to wane. At the very end of the Thirty Years' War the town was partially occupied by Swedish armies and shared in the general chaos and decline suffered by the whole of central Europe for many decades after the cessation of hostilities. During the Seven Years' War (q.v.) the neighbourhood of Prague was the scene

(May 1757) of the Battle of Prague in which Frederick II the Great defeated the Austrians.

In the Baroque period, rich merchants and the mainly foreign nobility (German, Spanish, Italian) who had settled in Prague and its surroundings invited some outstanding architects and artists, who were later aided by Czech masters, to embellish the town. At the time when Mozart lived in Prague, it had large gardens, aristocratic palaces, and Baroque churches, especially in the Little Quarter.

Prague's most rapid expansion, however, came with the advent of industrialization which took advantage of the proximity· of coal mines and ironworks at neighbouring Kladno and Kraluv Dvur. The population, which was only 140,000 in 1843, was 849,000 in 1930. Efforts are being made to prevent the further growth of the town. In the 19th century, with the rapidly changing social and economic relations within its population, Prague became the centre of a great cultural drive for the revival of the Czech national heritage. During the revolutionary wave of the year 1848, a Slav congress was convened at Whitsuntide, and the townspeople attempted to resist the repressive measures of the Austrian generals, but the fighting on the barricades ended in surrender. Nevertheless, Czech feeling and cultural life gained in significance and in 1861 the Czechs won a majority in the town administration. At the conclusion of World War I the independent republic of Czechoslovakia was established with Prague as its capital city. In March 1939 the country was occupied by the Germans, and Hitler established a protectorate with a puppet government. On May 5, 1945, the citizens of Prague rose against the German occupying forces, erecting barricades and holding out against superior German forces until the entry of the Soviet army four days later. Prague once again became the capital of the Czechoslovak Republic. (T. GR.)

PRAGUERIE, a revolt of princes and other nobles against Charles VII of France in 1440, so named in allusion to contemporary movements at Prague and elsewhere in Bohemia. As early as April 1437 a number of princes, excluded from the royal council, had unsuccessfully plotted to reassert their influence. In 1439 the king, inspired by the constable de Richemont (see ARTHUR III, of Brittany), issued the first of his great ordinances for military reform, which forbade the raising or maintenance of troops without his permission. The king's action strengthened the princes by bringing to their support those mercenary captains whose existence was threatened. Charles I, duc de Bourbon, and Jean II, duc d'Alençon, were the real leaders of the revolt, though the 16-year-old dauphin, later Louis XI, was induced to put himself at its head. They were abetted by John V of Brittany; by Louis, comte de Vendôme; by Jean IV, comte d'Armagnac; by Jean, comte de Dunois; and by Georges de La Trémoïlle, Richemont's old enemy. Alençon and the dauphin began the revolt in Poitou in February 1440, but were soon outgeneraled by Richemont. They then withdrew to Bourbon territory, but the king's artillery reduced their strongholds, and in July peace was made at Cusset, on very generous terms.

The rebels had proposed peace with England and a lessening of taxation, but the towns and the people stood loyally for the king. An attempt to renew the Praguerie through an assembly at Nevers in 1442 was brought to nothing by Charles VII's diplomacy.

PRAIRIE, the grassland biome (formation) of North America, the main body extending from southern Alberta to Texas and from the western arid desert eastward to contact with the humid forests. Other grasslands are the desert plains, extending southward from western Texas and Arizona into Mexico; the California prairie of central California; and the Palouse prairie of the northwestern states of the U.S. Grasslands ecologically equivalent to various prairies, including the steppe of the U.S.S.R., the veld of South Africa, and the pampas of South America, occur on all continents.

Perennial grasses gave the prairies their special character, but numerous colourful flowering plants, particularly legumes and composites, were conspicuous in spring and autumn. Bison and pronghorn antelope, grazing animals originally abundant on the prairies, disappeared in the earliest days of exploration and settlement. The coyote, jack rabbit, badger, prairie dog, prairie chicken, and many kinds of grasshoppers, robber flies, and other insects are representative of a rich variety of animal life.

Prairie climate is marked by low, irregular rainfall, high summer temperatures, strong winds, high rates of evapotranspiration, and intense late summer drought, and is increasingly rigorous from east to west. Along this gradient of decreasing water supply tall grass prairie, of sod-forming grasses 8–10 ft. high, occupied the more humid eastern area to about the 100th meridian, where it graded into the mixed prairie of bunch and sod grasses reaching heights of about 4 ft. Westward, on the high plains leading to the Rocky Mountains, sod grasses only a few inches high characterized the short grass plains.

Deep, fertile, organic soils and climate favourable to grain farming led to early destruction of most prairies; only vestiges remain in the highly productive corn and wheat belts.   (M. E. B.)

PRAIRIE CHICKEN (Prairie Hen), the name for two species of North American grouse that inhabit the west- and south-central prairies from Louisiana (rarely) and Texas to Manitoba and Alberta. The brownish, chicken-sized greater prairie chicken (*Tympanuchus cupido*), of which the extinct heath hen (*q.v.*) was a subspecies, has a short, rounded tail and dense barred patterning on the underparts. The male has a neck tuft of ten or more dark, rounded feathers that are raised when the orange air sacs are inflated during the community courtship display. The females, enticed by the performance, gather about and choose their mates. After mating, the female deposits about a dozen eggs in a cleared area and incubates them for about three weeks. The lesser prairie chicken (*T. pallidicinctus*), a smaller and paler version, is largely restricted to the central part of the range. Prairie chickens are fine game birds but are not important economically.

WALTER DAWN

MALE GREATER PRAIRIE CHICKEN (TYMPANUCHUS CUPIDO) IN COURTSHIP DISPLAY

PRAIRIE DOG, the name for heavy-bodied, short-tailed burrowing rodents of the genus *Cynomys,* of the squirrel family, formerly abundant throughout the plains of the western United States and northern Mexico but now greatly restricted. These gregarious animals live in colonies, or "towns," formed of elaborate burrows and raised entry mounds.

Of the several species known, the black-tailed prairie dog (*C. ludovicianus*) has the widest range, occurring sparsely over the Great Plains. It weighs about 2 lb. and measures about 16 in., 3 to 4 in. of which is tail. The pelage is mainly cinnamon brown; the terminal one-third of the tail is black and the underparts are buffy white. Two to ten pups are born in late spring or early summer after a gestation period of about a month. They mature at about two years of age and live about another six years.

The prairie dog modifies its environment in building its towns: fast-growing vegetation for food is encouraged and elimination of dense cover favourable to predators such as bobcats and coyotes is effected. The funnel-shaped entry mounds, 1–2 ft.

JOHN H. GERARD

PRAIRIE DOG (CYNOMYS)

high and 5–6 ft. across, provide high and dry access to burrows and serve as elevated lookout posts. Territories, or coteries, within a town are well defined and defended by members. Recognition "kissing" and grooming afford the frequent contact necessary to maintain the social structure of each coterie. The prairie dog's bark (its only resemblance to a dog) is a short nasal yip, varied to convey alarm, urgency, or security (the territorial call).

The smaller, white-tailed prairie dog (*C. leucurus*) differs further from the black-tailed in living at higher elevations, in building smaller colonies, and in hibernating. *See also* Rodent.

PRAIRIE DU CHIEN, the seat of Crawford County in southwestern Wisconsin, U.S., owes its existence to the historic military and economic importance of its site, a point on the Mississippi River about 3 mi. above the mouth of the Wisconsin River. The French and British each maintained a trading post and fort there before the territory became part of the United States in 1783. Ft. Crawford, erected in 1816, was for the next four years a link in the chain of military outposts guarding the Indian frontier. After 1820, when the American Fur Company erected a depot there, the settlement continued to be the area's trading centre. The development of varied industries ensured its permanence and in 1872 it received its city charter. Campion Academy, located in the city, is a widely known residential high. school for boys. Villa Louis, home of Hercules Dousman, a factor of the American Fur Company, is maintained by the state historical society as a museum. For comparative population figures *see* table in Wisconsin: *Population.*   (R. F. F.)

PRAIRIE PROVINCES, the three Canadian provinces of Manitoba, Saskatchewan, and Alberta, located in the northern Great Plains region of North America. The prairie provinces form the great wheat-producing region of Canada and are its chief source of petroleum and natural gas. *See* Alberta; Manitoba; Saskatchewan. *See also* Canada: *Geographical Regions.*

PRAKRIT LANGUAGES, in its widest sense, denotes those languages of India which chronologically are Middle Indo-Aryan as distinguished on the one hand from Old Indo-Aryan, *i.e.,* Vedic and Sanskrit, and on the other hand from Modern Indo-Aryan, *i.e.,* the present-day languages of north India and Pakistan (*see* Indo-Aryan Languages). It is thus used by modern scholars both in the west and in India. In this sense it includes the literary Prakrits and Apabhraṁśas used by Hindu, Jain, and Buddhist writers, the languages of many inscriptions and other non-literary documents ranging from the 3rd century B.C. to the 4th century A.D., the Pali language of Southern Buddhism, and Buddhist Hybrid Sanskrit, in which the Northern Buddhist scriptures were written. The word Prakrit has been used in more restricted senses, especially by the scholars of medieval India. Some have included only the four most important literary Prakrits; others have extended the list greatly, some even to include the Dravidian literary languages, which are not Indo-Aryan at all but have borrowed many Indo-Aryan words. In general these Indian scholars have included only the literary Prakrits used by Hindu and Jain writers, excluding the Buddhist languages and the inscriptional Prakrits. They have listed and characterized briefly many varieties which are claimed to be vernaculars, but of which nothing is otherwise known. There was a tendency to exclude the Apabhraṁśa dialects.

Several etymologies have been given of the Sanskrit word *prākṛta* which denotes these languages. One is that it is derived from *prakṛti* "nature" and means "the natural language" as opposed to Sanskrit (*saṁskṛta*), "the refined (or literary) language." Another involves *prakṛti* in its meaning "basis"; *prākṛta* is then "derived from the basis (Sanskrit)." In either case it is implied that Sanskrit is the norm and the Prakrits are departures from the norm and in a way inferior.

Two slightly differing dialects of Old Indo-Aryan became literary languages in the last two millennia B.C. One is that of the Vedas. The other is. classical Sanskrit as formulated by a succession of grammarians ending with Pāṇini (probably 5th century B.C.). From a very early period other dialects were already developing, differing from these two in the direction of Middle Indo-Aryan. The literary languages after their standardization remained practically unchanging in usage, but the vernaculars continued to diverge. As time went on, the users of the literary languages composed in the literary forms but spoke normally in dialects which were closer to Middle Indo-Aryan. There are even traces of their vernaculars, *i.e.*, Prakritisms, to be found in their literary compositions.

The Prakrits in their turn began to be written, and many of them received literary cultivation. The early chronology is very uncertain, but it may be that the earliest literature is the religious texts of the Buddhists and Jains. The Buddha (6th–5th centuries B.C.) directed that each of his disciples should teach in his own vernacular dialect. It is thought that in the first few generations after the Buddha numerous Middle Indo-Aryan dialects were used in preaching and teaching. This state of affairs seems to be reflected in the multiplicity of Prakrit dialects found in the religious inscriptions of the Buddhist emperor Aśoka (3rd century B.C.). As certain Buddhist centres gained influence, the dialects of these centres came to be used as literary languages to the exclusion of the others, although it is notable that there was much dialect mixture. These teaching dialects, like Sanskrit itself, became standardized, and gradually the spoken vernaculars diverged from them. Of the Buddhist languages, Pali became the standard language of Southern Hīnayāna Buddhism and the vehicle of a great body of canonical and exegetical literature. Other Buddhist schools, including many of the Mahāyāna schools, which are known as Northern Buddhism, seem to have used another Prakrit for a voluminous literature. As controversy with Hinduism began to flourish, Sanskrit came to be used by Buddhists, especially in polemic philosophical discourses. The use of Sanskrit infected this Prakrit, and resulted in a partial sanskritization of the prose written in it and even of verse texts. The result is that there survive no pure examples of this hypothetical Prakrit; the texts that survive are all more or less sanskritized, and the language is generally known now as Buddhist Hybrid Sanskrit (BHS). Both chronology and locality are very uncertain. It may be that BHS originated in a more westerly Prakrit dialect and Pali in a more easterly one, which however is still to be identified as central or west central in the Ganges valley. Crystallization of both dialects was complete in the pre-Christian period. A version of one Buddhist text, the Dharmapada (Pali and Prakrit Dhammapada), was found in a central Asian excavation at the end of the 19th century, written in a Prakrit which was different from that at the base of BHS and which belonged originally to northwest India. In all probability there were in the early centuries of Buddhism literatures in other Prakrits than these three that have survived.

For the Jain religion the situation is somewhat similar. The canonical texts of the Śvetāmbara (Shvetambara) sect are in two dialects of Ardhamāgadhī. Later texts, especially commentaries on the canon, but also others such as the epic *Paümacariya* of Vimala Sūri (perhaps 4th century A.D.) are in Jain Māhārāṣṭrī. The Digambara sect used Jain Śaurasēnī.

In the literature of the Hindus, also, Prakrit in several dialects came to be used probably at the end of the pre-Christian era. Later, Māhārāṣṭrī was especially used in composing lyric poetry, possibly on the basis of a popular oral lyric in the dialect; it began to flourish in the 3rd–4th centuries A.D. The most important independent work of this kind that is preserved is an anthology by Hāla, called the *Sattasaī* (Sanskrit title *Saptaśatī* "the 700 verses"); it was compiled between the 3rd and 7th centuries. Māhārāṣṭrī is the language of the lyric verses in the classical period of the Sanskrit drama beginning (in what survives to the present) with Kālidāsa. In this dialect there were also composed epics of the *kāvya* or belles-lettres type. The most important specimens are the *Rāvaṇavaha* or *Sētubandha* (attributed to Pravarasēna, possibly 6th century A.D. dealing with the subject of the Rāmāyaṇa, and the *Gaüdavaha* of Vākpati (8th century A.D.), celebrating the conquest of Bengal by Yaśovarman, king of Kanauj. Others exist, including the *Kumārapālacarita*, or the last eight cantos of the poem *Dvyāśraya-mahākāvya* written by Hemacandra (12th century A.D.) to serve as a series of illustrations to his Sanskrit and Prakrit grammar, the *Siddha-hemacandra*. These cantos in Prakrit illustrate the Prakrit section of the grammar.

The Sanskrit drama is an important source for knowledge of Prakrit. From its beginning its dialogue must have been intended as a realistic linguistic picture. In it educated men, like kings and Brahmans, spoke and also sang in Sanskrit, the literary language par excellence. All others, with few exceptions, spoke the vernacular; *i.e.*, Prakrit. It must have been the case, however, that people of various classes or castes spoke differing dialects, and that people of different localities appeared in the plays speaking their own local dialects. By the time of the earliest specimens now preserved conventions had begun to harden, and by the time of the classical theatre of Kālidāsa and his successors various types of characters were always provided with dialogue in the dialects which were considered appropriate and which had taken on conventional, unchanging forms. Most women, if not of low caste, speak Śaurasēnī, but sing in Māhārāṣṭrī; some children and various other characters, including the Brahman clown, speak Śaurasēnī. Various types of servants, fishermen, lowcaste men and many others speak Māgadhī. Other dialects appear in the drama. Unfortunately, after the grammarians had prescribed the forms of the dramatic Prakrits, the dramatists seem to have composed according to rule rather than from any real knowledge of the dialects as living forms of speech.

A Prakrit called Pāiśācī is known through grammarians' statements. According to literary tradition it was the language in which Guṇāḍhya's *Bṛhatkathā* was composed, before A.D. 500 and possibly in the 1st or 2nd century A.D. This work is known through much later reworkings, especially Sōmadēva's *Kathāsaritsāgara* (11th century A.D.), but unfortunately the Pāiśācī text has not yet come to light.

Of nonliterary materials in Prakrit there are early coin inscriptions and inscriptions on stone (3rd century B.C. to 4th century A.D.). Beside the inscriptions of Aśoka, which are the earliest, the most interesting are probably the materials from Niya in Chinese Turkestan. These are official documents from the Kroraina kingdom and date from the 3rd century A.D. Their Prakrit is close to that of the Dhammapada. The original home of the language was northwest India, probably the region of Peshawar; it seems to have been the administrative and literary language of the Kushan empire and its central Asiatic offshoots.

Some of the other Prakrits may be located geographically with some accuracy. Śaurasēnī was the dialect of Śūrasēna, the country around Mathurā (Muttra). It was the language of the Gangetic Doab, and probably extended westward as far as Lahore and eastward as far as the confluence of the Jumna and the Ganges. Its use extended also to Rajputana and Gujarat. Māgadhī was spoken in the eastern half of the Ganges valley, extending westward probably as far as Varanasi (Benares). Māhārāṣṭrī was the language of Mahārāṣṭra, the "great Kingdom" south of the Nerbudda river, where in modern times Marāṭhī is spoken. Not all the dialects may be located with equal exactitude. Pāiśācī, for example, may have been spoken in the northwest, although the Vindhya region south of the Ganges valley seems more probable.

Because of the literary pre-eminence of Māhārāṣṭrī, it is the Prakrit described at greatest length by the Indian grammarians, *e.g.*, by Vararuci (before A.D. 700, perhaps much earlier) and Hemacandra (12th century A.D.). The other Prakrits used in the dramas, as well as numerous others which never appear in the literature, are described sketchily in terms usually of their deviations from Māhārāṣṭrī.

After various Prakrits had been given standard literary form, the vernaculars continued to diverge from these standards. Again at a later period various dialects received literary form; the earliest reference to a literary use of these seems to be in the 7th century A.D. They are known by the name apabhraṁśa, ("departure from correct speech"). One dialect, western apabhraṁśa, belonged to the region of Śaurasēnī Prakrit, and is represented by numerous texts, most of them by Jain authors, such as Dhaṇavāla's *Bhavisattakaha* (probably 10th century A.D.), Haribhadra's *Sanatkumāracaritam* (A.D. 1159), and Somaprabha's *Kumārapālapratibodha* (A.D. 1195). There are also texts in a southern apabhraṁśa, corresponding to Māhārāṣṭrī, and a few in an eastern apabhraṁśa, corresponding to Māgadhī.

The apabhraṁśa dialects are the immediate predecessors of the modern Indo-Aryan vernaculars, the older stages of which seem to have been recognized by the Indian grammarians as early as the 12th century A.D. The relations, however, between the various Middle Indic dialects and the modern languages are not yet clearly known in detail.

Characterization of the Languages.—The Middle Indo-Aryan languages are marked by progressive changes from the type of the Old Indo-Aryan languages. (Skt. = Sanskrit; Ś = Śaurasēnī; M. = Māhārāṣṭrī.)

Phonetic change is conspicuous. The complex consonant clusters of Skt. are simplified, most frequently by assimilations or losses, sometimes by insertions of vowels, e.g., putra "son" > putta, ratna "jewel" > Ś. radaṇa, Māgadhī ladaṇa. Stop consonants between vowels were liable to many sorts of changes. Voiceless stops (k, t, p) remained in Pali, became voiced (g, d, v) in some dialects, e.g., Ś and apabhraṁśa, but were lost in M., e.g., Skt. śata "100" > Pali sata, Ś. sada, M. saa. The cumulative effect of all changes was to produce words which are very far from their Skt. origins, e.g., Vappaïrāā = Skt. Vākpatirājā "king Vākpati"; prākr̥ta "Prakrit" > Ś pāūda, M. pāūa.

Noun morphology tends toward simplification; e.g., by loss of the dual number. The eight-case system of Skt. is reduced by loss and amalgamation of cases. Dative forms are completely lost in some dialects; syntactically the dative merges with the genitive. In feminine stems in ā, the instrumental, genitive, and locative singular have identical forms. In the apabhraṁśa stage case declension had gone a long way toward the Modern Indo-Aryan system of practically only two cases, absolute and oblique. The system of three genders remains intact until in apabhraṁśa masculine and neuter came near to a complete merging. The numerous declensional types of Skt. are somewhat reduced in number. Especially, the consonant stems tend to add vowels and merge with the vocalic declensions.

Verb conjugation shows even greater departures from the Skt. system. With some exceptions, the Skt. consonantal conjugation has been replaced in Prakrit by the conjugation type in which a vowel appears between the final consonant of the root or stem and the inflectional suffix. In Middle Indo-Aryan the vowel is often -a- as in Skt., but there has been a great extension of use also of -ē-, which derives from -aya- of the Skt. causative and denominative conjugations. The causative stem on the other hand often has a suffix -vē-, in which v represents Skt. p which in Skt. appears in only a few verbs. Exceptional remnants of the Sanskrit consonantal conjugation include the highly irregular enclitic verb "to be", e.g., mhi "I am" (< asmi), si "you are" (< asi), etc.; the 3rd singular form atthi (< asti) is not enclitic. The past tenses are completely remade into one fairly well unified system in Pali, but in the Prakrit dialects very little remains of them, except such forms as āsī "was, were" (< āsīt). The present tense has an imperative and an optative. The future remains, usually formed with a suffix -issa- or -ihi- (< Skt. -iṣya-) added to the present stem. Passive stems either derive from Skt. passive stems, with Skt. -y- appearing in M. as -jj- (e.g., dijjaī "it is given" < Skt. dīyate), or add a suffix (Ś -ia-, M. -ijja-) to the present stem. Infinitives, gerunds, gerundives and present participles all survive from Skt., with many phonetic and other changes. Most important is the past participle, which is passive in transitive verbs and active in intransitive verbs. Syntactically, it occurs most frequently with an instrumental case of a noun, to replace the old past tense and its subject; this is the precursor of the peculiar past tense of Modern Indo-Aryan. Very frequently the past participle shows a suffix Ś. -ida-, M. -ia- (< Skt. -ita-) added to the present stem. This part of the verb system shows more irregularities of form than any other, because of inheritance of old forms from Skt., e.g., Ś. gada, M. gaa- "gone" (< Skt. gata-) beside present stem gacch-; Ś. kida-, M. kaa- "made" (< Skt. kr̥ta-) beside present stem kar-; Ś. ṇāda-, M. ṇāa- "known" (< Skt. jñāta-) beside present stem jāṇ-.

The vocabulary of Prakrit is in general derived from Old Indo-Aryan, but there are also many words not so derivable, called dēśī or "provincial" words. Lists of these were produced by the Indian grammarians.

See also SANSKRIT LANGUAGE; PALI LANGUAGE.

BIBLIOGRAPHY.—General grammars: R. Pischel, Grammatik der Prākritsprachen (1900); Madhukar Anant Mehendale, Historical Grammar of Inscriptional Prakrits (1948); Gajanan Vasudev Tagare, Historical Grammar of Apabhraṁśa (1948). Introduction to the study of the Prakrits: H. Jacobi, Ausgewählte Erzählungen in Māhārāshtrī (1886); Alfred C. Woolner, Introduction to Prakrit (1928). Editions of some of the Indian grammars: E. B. Cowell's of Vararuci's Prākrta-prakāśa (1868), R. Pischel's of Hēmacandra (1877–80). For dēśī words: Muralydhar Banerjee, The Deśīnāmamālā of Hemacandra (1931). For Buddhist Hybrid Sanskrit: Franklin Edgerton, Buddhist Hybrid Sanskrit Grammar and Dictionary and Buddhist Hybrid Sanskrit Reader (1953). For the Prakrit Dhammapada: H. W. Bailey, "The Khotan Dharmapada," Bulletin of the School of Oriental and African Studies, vol. 11, pp. 488–512 (1945); the bibliography is important. For the Northwestern Prakrit of Central Asia: T. Burrow, The Language of the Kharoṣṭhi Documents from Chinese Turkestan (1937); A Translation of the Karoṣṭhi Documents from Chinese Turkestan (1940). For apabhraṁśa texts published in the West: H. Jacobi's editions of Dhanavāla's Bhavisatta-kaha (1918) and Haribhadra's Sanatkumāra-caritam (1921), and Ludwig Alsdorf's edition of Somaprabha's Kumārapālapratibōdha (1928). For nonreligious Prakrit texts: A. Weber, Das Saptaçatakam des Hāla (1881); S. Goldschmidt, Rāvanavaha oder Setubandha (1880–83); S. P. Pandit, The Gaüdavaho by Vākpati (1887) and The Kumārapālacharita (1900). (M. B. E.)

PRAKRIT LITERATURE.

The greatest contribution to Prakrit literature was made by the Buddhists, who wrote in a Prakrit language called Pali; their writings are described in the article PALI LITERATURE. This article discusses the literature that was written in Prakrits other than Pali (see PRAKRIT LANGUAGES) and which is chiefly important as the literature of Jainism (q.v.).

Canonical Literature.—The canon of the Śvetāmbaras (Shvetambaras), one of the two Jain sects, is composed entirely in Prakrits. It was fixed in its present form by the 6th century A.D., although some portions may date from the 3rd century B.C. It contains a mixture of monastic rules, dogmatics, philosophy, cosmology, gnomic sayings, folktales, encyclopaedic enumerations, and legends about Jain devotees. Its literary value varies greatly, and some of the older texts, such as the Āyāraṁga, Sūyagaḍaṁga and Uttarajjhayaṇa-sutta, sometimes reach a high poetic standard, while others, such as the Anuttarovavāiya-sutta, consist of little more than a series of stereotyped accounts of how devotees starved themselves to death.

The earliest commentaries on this canon, the nijjuttis, cūrṇis, and bhāṣyas, are written in a Prakrit, and are noted for the wealth of ancient historical and semihistorical tradition and the mass of folktales they contain. Many of these Prakrit stories are incorporated in the later Sanskrit commentaries of Haribhadra (8th century) and Devendra (11th century).

The early quasi-canonical texts of the other Jain sect, the Digambaras, were also written in a Prakrit and are mainly on philosophical and polemic themes. One of the earliest Digambara authors is Kundakunda (perhaps 1st century A.D.), whose works include the Pavayaṇasāra, Samayasāra, and Niyamasāra. Later Digambara philosophical writings include the Yogasāra and Paramātmaprakāśa by Yogīndra (6th to 10th century).

Narrative Literature.—There is a rich Prakrit narrative literature, for the Jains appropriated many of the themes of the common Indian literary inheritance for their own religious purposes. The earliest Prakrit epic is probably the Paümacariya of Vimala Sūri (perhaps 3rd or 4th century A.D.), based largely on Vālmīki's Rāmāyaṇa (see SANSKRIT LITERATURE). Other Jain versions of the Rāma story are the Vasudevahiṇḍi of Saṅghadāsa (before the 7th century), the Paümacariu of Svayambhū (before the 10th century), and the Mahāpurāṇa of Puṣpadanta (10th century). The authors' claim to be great epic poets is not entirely unjustified, for they show an ability to compose in a highly ornate style, based on Sanskrit models. Their main aim, however, is not literary but religious, and their narrative is often interrupted by long instructive discourses on religion and morality. The protagonists are finally converted to Jainism and attain nirvāna.

The Mahābhārata (q.v.) story is similarly adapted for Jain purposes. Portions of the story are already found in the Śvetāmbara canon, but the earliest Jain version of the story as a whole is the *Harivaṁsapurāṇa* of Jinasena (8th century). Non-Jain epics include the *Rāvaṇavaha* by Pravarasena (perhaps 6th century) which is based on the Rāma story, and the *Gaüḍavaha* by Vākpati (8th century), which relates the story of the conquest of Bengal by Yaśovarman, king of Kanauj.

The *kathānakas* ("minor stories"), of the type found in the commentaries on the canon, also exist as separate works. These are stories of a more popular nature, intended both to instruct and to amuse, and their language is usually simple, with occasional passages of high-flown poetic imagery. The *dhammakahās* ("religious stories"), such as the *Samarāiccakahā* by Haribhadra and the *Bhavisattakahā* by Dhanavāla (perhaps 10th century), differ from this more popular literature in being more pretentious and aiming at a more poetic style.

Jain Prakrit literature is rich in hagiographical works. Lives of the *tirthānkaras* (or *jinas*), the 24 spiritual conquerors, appear in the canon, and later formed the subject of independent works called *cariyas*. The *Cauppannamahāpurisacariya* of Śīlāṅka (9th century) is a collection of biographies of the *jinas* and other heroes. Biographies of individual *jinas* or other Jain personages include the *Jasaharacariu* of Puṣpadanta and the *Karakaṇḍacariu* of Kanakumāra (11th century). A nonreligious work of this type is the *Kumārapālacarita* by Hemacandra (12th century), written to illustrate the rules of his Prakrit grammar while describing the achievements of his royal patron Kumārapāla.

Didactic, Dramatic, and Technical Literature.—Didactic poetry has a prominent place in the Jain canon, but of noncanonical works the *Uvaesamālā* by Dharmadāsa (before the 9th century) is probably the oldest. The *Kumārapālapratibodha* by Somaprabha (12th century) is a didactic poem which includes a collection of tales reputedly used to illustrate the sermons by which Hemacandra converted Kumārapāla to Jainism.

Dramatic works were mainly written by non-Jains. In the earliest extant dramas, those of Aśvaghoṣa (perhaps 1st century A.D.) and Bhāsa (perhaps 2nd century A.D.), the humbler characters already speak in various Prakrits (see SANSKRIT LITERATURE: *Drama*). Kālidāsa (*q.v.*; fl. *c.* 400) seems to have been the first to use Māhārāṣṭrī Prakrit in a play, possibly introducing it from lyric poetry where its long-established use is shown by the anthologies, in particular the *Sattasaī* of Hāla (3rd to 7th century), and the *Vajjālagga* of Jayavallabha (8th to 13th century). Dramas were sometimes written in which all characters, even the king, spoke in a Prakrit; *e.g.*, the *Karpūramañjarī* by Rājaśekhara (perhaps 9th century).

The considerable amount of technical literature written in various Prakrits includes the cosmological works *Tiloyapaṇṇatti* of Jadivasaha (5th to 7th century) and *Jambudīpapaṇṇattisaṁgaha* of Paümanandi (perhaps 11th century). Grammars of Prakrit include the *Prākṛtaprakāśa* of Vararuci (before A.D. 700), the *Prākṛtalakṣaṇa* of Caṇḍa (of unknown date) and the eighth chapter of the *Siddha-hemacandra* of Hemacandra. The grammarians also compiled dictionaries of *deśī* words (*i.e.*, those not derivable from Sanskrit). These include the *Pāiyalacchīnāmamālā* of Dhanavāla (10th century) as well as the *Deśīnāmamālā* of Hemacandra.

The Last Stages of Prakrit.—After the 12th century Prakrit began to develop into the New Indo-Aryan vernaculars, and Prakrit literature shows signs of this change (see INDIAN LITERATURE). It is debatable whether such a work as the *Kīrtilatā* of Vijjāvai (14th century), which presents a form of Apabhraṁśa influenced by the developing Maithilī vernacular and strewn with Arabic and Persian words, is to be considered as Prakrit literature or not. Nevertheless, some authors continued to write technically correct examples of Prakrit composition according to the rules laid down by grammarians hundreds of years before. The last period of Prakrit literature includes such works as the drama *Candralekhā* of Rudradāsa (17th century), in which all the characters speak in Prakrits, and the epic poems *Kaṁsavaha* and *Usāṇiruddha* of Rāma Pāṇivāda (18th century).

BIBLIOGRAPHY.—Extensive bibliographical references to Jain canonical and noncanonical literature are given by M. Winternitz, *History* *of Indian Literature*, vol. 2 (1933), and W. Schubring, *Die Lehre der Jainas* (1935). Other editions of Prakrit works include *Two Prakrit Versions of the Maṇipaticarita*, ed. by R. Williams (1959), and publications in the *Singhi Jain Series* (Bombay, 1936–   ), *Jīvarāja Jaina Granthamālā* (Sholapur, 1951–   ), *Prakrit Text Society Series* (Varanasi, 1957–   ) and other series. See also the bibliography for PRAKRIT LANGUAGES.　　　(K. R. N.)

PRANDTL, LUDWIG (1875–1953), German physicist famous for his work in aeronautics, was born at Freising, Bavaria, on Feb. 4, 1875. He qualified at Munich in 1900 with a thesis on elastic stability, and was professor of applied mechanics at Göttingen from 1904 until his death there on Aug. 15, 1953. In 1925 he became director of the Kaiser Wilhelm Institute for fluid mechanics. His discovery (1904) of the "boundary layer" which adjoins the surface of a body moving in air or water led to an understanding of skin friction drag and of the way in which streamlining reduces the drag of airplane wings and other moving bodies. His work on wing theory, published in 1918–19, which followed that of F. W. Lanchester (1902–07) but was carried out independently, elucidated the flow over airplane wings of finite span. This body of work is known as the Lanchester-Prandtl wing theory (see AERODYNAMICS).

Prandtl made decisive advances in boundary layer and wing theories, and his work became the basic material of aerodynamics. He also made important contributions to the theories of supersonic flow and of turbulence, besides contributing much to the development of wind tunnels and other aerodynamic equipment. In addition he devised the soap-film analogy for the torsion of noncircular sections and wrote on the theory of plasticity and on meteorology.　　　(H. B. S.)

PRASEODYMIUM is a moderately soft, silvery metal of the rare-earth (*q.v.*) group. It is oxidized slowly by air at room temperature and reacts rapidly with hot water, liberating hydrogen. The metal is a component of Misch metal (see CERIUM), which is used for cigarette lighter flints and as an alloying addition in magnesium alloys of high strength and creep resistance used principally for jet engine parts. (The use of an alloying constituent consisting primarily of praseodymium and neodymium in place of Misch metal gives a magnesium alloy of still higher strengths at all temperatures.) A mixture of praseodymium and neodymium is used in sunglasses and in goggles for glassblowers and welders. Glass containing cerium and praseodymium gives total optical filtration of all blue, violet, and ultraviolet radiation. Praseodymium imparts colour to glass ranging from bright yellow to green; its oxide also produces a yellow ceramic colour on a zirconium oxide base.

The element was discovered by C. A. von Welsbach in 1885 when he separated a "didymium" salt fraction into praseodymium and neodymium. The name is derived from *praseodidymium*, meaning "green didymium," because of the green colour of the salts. Praseodymium occurs in many rare-earth minerals; the chief commercial source is monazite (*q.v.*). It is also one of the products of atomic fission. The classical methods for the separation and purification of the element were fractional crystallization and precipitation, but ion-exchange techniques have been used since World War II for commercial production.

The symbol for praseodymium is Pr, atomic number 59, atomic weight 140.907; there is only one stable isotope Pr^{141}. Praseodymium is one of the three rare earths which exhibit an oxidation state of plus four (the others are cerium and terbium). A black oxide obtained by heating a salt in air has the approximate formula, Pr_6O_{11}. The dioxide PrO_2 and the double fluoride K_2PrF_6 are examples of the higher oxidation state. Praseodymium also forms a series of green salts and solutions in which the metal is trivalent. Solutions show discrete absorption peaks in the visible and ultraviolet regions of the spectrum which are useful for quantitative analysis. Due to the presence of unpaired electrons, the trivalent Pr^{+3} ion is paramagnetic.

The metal is prepared by electrolysis of the fused anhydrous halides or by thermoreduction of these salts by alkali or alkaline earth metals. The melting point is 935° C and the density of the hexagonal close-packed structure is 6.782 g. per cc.; other forms are known. See RARE EARTHS.　　　(LD. B. A.; J. B. Ps.)

PRATAPGARH (formerly PARTABGARH), a town and district in the Fyzabad division of Uttar Pradesh, India. The town, headquarters of the district, lies about 25 mi. (40 km.) N of Allahabad, on the Varanasi-Lucknow railway.

PRATAPGARH DISTRICT (area 1,458 sq.mi. [3,776 sq.km.]; pop. [1961] 1,252,196) lies in the southeast of Uttar Pradesh with the Ganges forming its southwestern boundary. The general aspect of the district is that of a richly wooded and fertile plain, relieved by gentle undulations and ravines near the rivers and streams. Smallish barren tracts impregnated with saline efflorescence (reh) occur in places. The only mineral products are salt, saltpetre and *kankar* (nodular limestone). Main crops are rice, barley, pulse, millets, and sugar cane; hemp and hides are also produced.

PRATAPGARH is also the name of a town in Chittorgarh district of Rajasthan, India, and of a former princely state. The walled town lies 75 mi. (121 km.) SE of Udaipur. Pop. (1961) 14,573. It was founded in 1698 by Maharawat Pratap Singh and became the capital of the princely state, which was once tributary to Indore (Holkar). It came under British protection in 1818 and was merged with Rajasthan in 1948. The people are mostly Bhils and other aborigines (*see* BHIL). Pratapgarh was once well known for its engraved gold enameled work inlaid on emerald-coloured glass.   (S. M. T. R.)

PRATO (PRATO IN TOSCANA), a town of the Province of Firenze, region of Tuscany, central Italy, lies on the Bisenzio River at the foot of the Monti della Calvana, 10 mi. NW of the city of Florence. It is the seat of a bishopric. Pop. (1961) 111,-112 (commune). Old Prato, which is still surrounded by a wall (*c.* 1330), has narrow streets with many medieval buildings. Outstanding is the cathedral, a harmonious fusion of Romanesque and Gothic; the nave, by Guidetto (begun 1211), is the Romanesque portion and the transepts (1317–20, perhaps by Giovanni Pisano) the Gothic portion. The campanile is 13th–14th century. The facade is adorned with a splendid pulpit (1434–38) by Donatello and his partner Michelozzo. Interior works include the frescoes of Filippo Lippi in the choir (1456–66). Another church, one of the finest of the Tuscan Renaissance, is Sta. Maria delle Carceri (1485–92), the masterpiece of Giuliano da Sangallo. The 13th-century Castello dell' Imperatore was built by the Holy Roman emperor Frederick II. Notable also is the 18th-century Collegio Cicognini. The town has modern and expanding suburbs.

Prato is connected by rail with Florence, Pistoia, and Bologna, and is served by the Florence-coast motorway. It is a leading centre for wool manufacture, which has been traditional to it for many centuries. Textile machinery and cement also are made.

The origin of Prato is uncertain. It became a free Italian commune in the 11th century; was later drawn into the orbit of Florence (which succeeded in purchasing its overlordship despite the famine and plague of 1347–48); and was brutally sacked by the Spanish Army in 1512 during the campaign to restore the Medici. In 1653 it obtained the rank of city. Prato's subsequent existence was uneventful, until, in the 19th century, it became a lively centre of political activity during the Risorgimento.   (G. N.)

PRATT, EDWIN JOHN (1882–1964), the leading Canadian poet of his time, was born at Western Bay, Nfd., on Feb. 4, 1882, the son of a Methodist clergyman. After a preparatory education in Newfoundland and some experience in teaching, he went to Victoria College in the University of Toronto, where he graduated in 1911. He then studied theology and published, in 1917, *Studies in Pauline Eschatology* (developed from his Ph.D. dissertation), but his interests turned to psychology—he was for several years a psychologist on the staff of the university—and finally to English literature, which he taught at Victoria College from 1919 until his retirement as professor emeritus in 1953.

His first collection of poems, *Newfoundland Verse* (1923), drew on his early impressions, especially of the hardships and courage of the fishermen in their constant battle with the sea. Even when lyrical, the poems show an interest in and a distinctive command of the techniques of narrative, to which Pratt turned in *The Witches' Brew* (1925) and *The Titans* (1926), the second of which is made up of two long poems, "The Cachalot," and "The Great Feud." "The Cachalot," an account of a whale hunt, is

one of his most brilliant and widely read poems. All three are in octosyllabic couplets, and show a lively humour and the free play of an exuberant imagination that marked Pratt out as a strikingly original poet in a new genre. Pratt's fascination with themes of shipwreck broadened and deepened in *The Roosevelt and the Antinoe* (1930) and *The Titanic* (1935), where a more sombre sense of the indifference of nature to human values prevails.

With *Brébeuf and His Brethren* (1940), a blank-verse chronicle of the martyrdom of Jesuit missionaries by the Iroquois, Pratt was established as Canada's most influential poetic personality. (For the importance of his influence *see* CANADIAN LITERATURE [ENGLISH]). Three volumes after *Newfoundland Verse* contain the bulk of his shorter poems: *Many Moods* (1932), *The Fable of the Goats and Other Poems* (1937), *Still Life and Other Verse* (1943). Many of these poems are still concerned with the sea and seafaring life, but there is a growing awareness of the poet's social responsibilities, reflected in the title poem of *Still Life*, in some bitter anti-Nazi satire, and in some philosophical verse, notably *The Iron Door* (1927) and the remarkable dialogue "The Truant" in *Still Life*.

After the outbreak of World War II, Pratt turned mainly to topical themes, as in *Dunkirk* (1941). His *Collected Poems,* with a preface by William Rose Benet, appeared in 1944 (U.S. edition, 1945; 2nd ed., 1958). *Behind the Log* (1947) commemorates the heroism of the Canadian convoy fleet in running supplies to Murmansk through the war, and *Towards the Last Spike* (1952) tells of the building of the Canadian Pacific Railway (1870–85). Many features of Pratt's work made him not simply a respected but a genuinely popular poet in Canada: his preoccupation with the Canadian scene, both historical and geographical; his power of storytelling; his unforced use of the imagery of machinery and technology. Pratt was awarded the highest civilian honour in Canada, the companion of the Order of St. Michael and St. George, in 1946. He died in Toronto on April 26, 1964.

BIBLIOGRAPHY.—W. E. Collin, *The White Savannahs* (1936); E. K. Brown, *On Canadian Poetry* (1943); C. F. Klinck and H. W. Wells, *Edwin J. Pratt, the Man and His Poetry* (1947); Thelma Lecocq, "Ned Pratt—Poet" in *Our Sense of Identity*, ed. by Malcolm Ross (1954); John Sutherland, *The Poetry of E. J. Pratt* (1956); W. C. D. Pacey, *Ten Canadian Poets* (1958).   (No. F.)

PRAXITELES, of Athens, greatest of the Attic sculptors of the 4th century B.C., was active from perhaps *c.* 370 B.C. to 330 B.C. Ancient writers sing his praises, and they are borne out by what would seem to be the only major original work that has

survived, *i.e.,* the marble statue of Hermes carrying the infant Dionysus. It was found at Olympia in the temple of Hera, in the very place where it was seen and described by Pausanias (v, 17, 3). The delicate modeling and exquisite finish of the surface enable one to add these qualities in one's imagination to the other works by him that exist only in Roman copies. His most celebrated work was the Aphrodite which he made for Cnidus, considered by Pliny not only the finest statue by Praxiteles but in the whole world. Numerous copies have been recognized— statues, heads and statuettes (in the Vatican and in the Terme museum in Rome; in the Louvre, Paris; at Toulouse; etc.).

Many other statues, both of marble and bronze, are mentioned by ancient writers as works by Praxiteles, but comparatively few have been identified in Roman copies. Chief among them are: the Apollo

BY COURTESY OF THE VATICAN MUSEUM AND GALLERIES

"APHRODITE OF CNIDUS" BY PRAXITELES: A ROMAN COPY IN THE VATICAN MUSEUM

Sauroctonus, in which the god is shown as a boy leaning against a tree trunk, about to kill a lizard with an arrow; the Artemis Brauronia perhaps reproduced in the charming Artemis of Gabii in the Louvre; and several Erotes and Satyrs.

Two sculptures that can be connected with Praxiteles stand apart. One is a base decorated with Marsyas and the Muses described by Pausanias as in a temple at Mantinea and supporting the statues of Leto, Apollo and Artemis by Praxiteles. Three slabs of this base have actually come to light, and, though probably not executed by Praxiteles himself, for the execution is cursory, they presumably reproduce his design. The other work is the bust of a youth, found at Eleusis. It seems to be an original Greek work of the 4th century and has by some been thought to be the Eubuleus known to have been made by Praxiteles. It approximates, though it does not equal, the workmanship of the Hermes.

According to Pliny, when Praxiteles was asked which of his statues he valued most highly, he replied "those to which Nicias (a famous painter) has put his hand; so much did he prize the application of colour (circumlitio) of that artist." To visualize the sculptures of Praxiteles it is well to remember how much this colour must have added to the general effect.

Praxiteles was one of the most original of Greek sculptors. He transformed the 5th-century style of detachment and majesty into one of gentle grace and sensuous charm. His favourite material was marble, of which he was perhaps the greatest exponent. Diodorus says of him that "with consummate art he informed his marble figures with the passions of the soul." It is indeed this subtle, personal element, combined with an exquisite finish of surface, that imparts to his figures their singular appeal.

The influence of Praxiteles was widespread. Figures standing in graceful, sinuous poses and lightly leaning on some support became favourite representations and were later further developed by the sculptors of the Hellenistic age. *See also* GREEK ART.

BIBLIOGRAPHY.—J. Overbeck, *Die antiken Schriftquellen*, no. 1190–1300 (1868), for the ancient sources; G. E. Rizzo, *Prassitele* (1932); G. M. A. Richter, *The Sculpture and Sculptors of the Greeks*, rev. ed., pp. 259–267 (1950); G. Lippold, *Die griechische Plastik*, pp. 234–243 (1950); C. Picard, *Manuel d'archéologie grecque*, iv, 2, pp. 236–410 (1954).   (G. M. A. R.)

PRAYER, man's personal directing of himself toward and intercourse with the transcendental reality, whether in word or in thought. Many theologians and scholars of comparative religion regard prayer as the central phenomenon of religion, a position others claim is held by sacrifice (*q.v.*). These two views can be correlated by pointing out that at its highest level sacrifice is absorbed into prayer, insofar as sacrificial giving of oneself to God takes place spiritually by means of prayer.

Private Prayer.—At its lower levels prayer is closely related to spells or incantations, from which it must be carefully distinguished. Incantation may be regarded as the mere expression of a wish; it appears in various forms as a blessing (a good wish), a curse (an evil wish), or an oath (a conditional curse which is to recoil on the maker if it later appears that he has lied or broken faith). All incantations, however, are meant to have their effect without the help of a superhuman being. Prayer, on the other hand, even in its primitive form, is addressed to another being, who is considered to be in some sense personal, or similar to man, on whom man knows he depends, and whom man regards as on the whole kindly disposed to him and ready to help, though sometimes angry. Somewhere between prayer and incantation lies conjuration, whereby some fundamentally evil and hostile spiritual being is compelled either to appear or to depart.

Communication with divine beings in prayer is carried on in the same way as ordinary social intercourse, whether the divine being is a natural force (*e.g.*, a rain god), a patron of human activity (*e.g.*, a goddess of childbirth), an ancestor, or the highest power of all, the god of heaven and the creator. Thus the terms of address "Father," "Mother," "Lord," "King," are used in prayer, as are such forms of speech as confession of sins, requests, thanks, praise, reference to presents (sacrifice), or the promise of presents (a vow) if a request made in prayer is fulfilled. In all these ways man tries to influence the deity: to win him over, to change

his mind, or to appease him. A characteristic feature of prayer at its primitive level is the desire to be free from earthly ills and dangers and to gain earthly goods.

As a blessing or a curse can be approximated to a prayer ("May God bless" or "curse so-and-so"), so conversely on the primitive level prayer takes on forms similar to magical formulas or to oaths when it is thought of as having magical or compulsive power. This combination of the personal address to a divine being with impersonal magic is apparent also in the bodily attitudes (standing, kneeling, crouching, prostration) and position of the hands (raised, folded, crossed, clasped) of the person praying. Such attitudes too have a social character, for they express submission, homage, and devotion, while at the same time, because of their disarming nature, they are a defense against a taboo or against a danger from the superhuman being.

This primitive prayer, whose simple forms are found among preliterate peoples, lived on into the ancient civilizations, where it developed from its spontaneous and free expression into fixed formularies. Another development was the hymn, which gradually escaped from ritual rigidity and formality into pure contemplation of God's working in nature and reached its highest point in the hymns to the sun of the Egyptian king Ikhnaton.

Prayer, directed to a person, seems to have originated independently of magic, which is wholly impersonal, although their paths perpetually crossed and indeed intermingled as they developed. The common assumption that magical formula preceded prayer and that prayer owed its origin to a failure in magic cannot be proved.

As religion became more spiritual and moral, man's prayer life developed comparably. Requests for earthly goods assumed much less importance and in some cases disappeared completely, while prayers for spiritual and moral qualities, for the knowledge and love of God, and for union with him, came to the fore. Confession of sin, praise and thanksgiving, expressions of trust and acceptance of the will of God, also predominated. Whereas in primitive prayer man with his needs and desires puts himself at the centre, in higher forms of prayer God is at the centre. "You shall pray for nothing else than God himself," warns St. Augustine. Further, prayer expressed in words is replaced by wordless prayer, called "spiritual prayer" or "prayer of the heart," the holy silence, which mystics experience as the purest form of reverent adoration of the deity. For great religious figures, whether mystics, prophets, apostles, or reformers, prayer is not only a regular turning to God but it becomes their whole life ("Pray constantly"; I Thess. 5:17). St. Francis of Assisi is said by his biographer Thomas of Celano not so much to have prayed as to have turned into prayer. Above all, prayer is regarded as a gift of grace from God, not as an independent activity of man: "we do not know how to pray as we ought, but the Spirit himself intercedes for us with sighs too deep for words" (Rom. 8:26).

This higher form of prayer is found in Judaism, Christianity, Islam, Buddhism, Brahmanism, and Hinduism. In all these religions, but particularly in the first three, two types of prayer appear side by side. One is a simple, spontaneous "outpouring of the soul" (*e.g.*, in Ps. 42:4, and in many other Old Testament passages). The other is more elaborate, frequently marked off in ascending steps, and described with psychological accuracy. The goal of this second type is mystical union, whether this is thought of as leading to identity of the worshiper with the deity or as a spiritual marriage between them. Such mystical prayer is often connected with a material pledge of the divine presence, as for instance the images of gods in Buddhism and Hinduism and the Eucharist and icons in Christianity. In earlier Buddhism, which had no real concept of God, absorption into one's own inner being in meditation and contemplation takes the place of the mystical "prayer of the heart." Although in Buddhism in its original form this prayer is not directed toward a personal deity, its aim is Nirvana, which is not only the state of deliverance but also a mystical "highest good."

Communal Prayer.—Public as well as private prayer is found at all stages in the development of religion. Among primitive peoples communal prayer takes the form of responses by the community to the prayers of their representative, who may be the head of a household, a chieftain, or a priest (see Priesthood). The most elaborate development of such communal prayer is found in Judaism after the destruction of the Second Temple (A.D. 70) and in Christianity, which carried on the Jewish tradition. Prayer in public worship is, first and foremost, praise of God for the creation and for the redemption. The highest point of such praise in Christian worship is the preface in the Eucharist, which is introduced by the dialogue "Lift up your hearts . . ." between priest and people and concludes with the threefold *Sanctus* ("Holy, Holy, Holy . . .") taken from the Jewish Temple liturgy (Isa. 6:3).

After praise comes intercessory prayer for the needs of God's people and of all mankind. The apogee of communal prayer is the Lord's Prayer (q.v.), which combines the chief petitions used by Jesus' Jewish contemporaries. Its central feature is the prayer for the coming of the Kingdom of God. A parallel prayer in Buddhism is the following: "May every living thing, movable or unmovable, tall, big, or medium-sized, clumsy or refined, visible or invisible, near or far, already born or aspiring to birth—may all beings have a happy heart."

Obligatory Prayer.—The four prophetic religions, Judaism, Christianity, Islam, and Zoroastrianism, teach the observance of a daily set form of prayer for certain individuals, in addition to spontaneous private prayer and public worship in common. Every male Jew must twice a day recite the Shema, the commandment to love Yahweh as the only true God ("Hear, O Israel . . ."; Deut. 6:4), and the so-called Prayer of 18 Requests ('Amida), also simply called "prayer" (Tefilla), which combines praise, thanksgiving, and petition. The latter must be recited three times a day by women, slaves, and children, as well as by men. (See also Liturgy, Jewish.)

The canonical hours of the Christian Church, which developed out of these obligatory Jewish prayers, are said or sung communally by monks and nuns in convent chapels and said privately by secular priests. In the Anglican Communion and in Lutheran churches a simplified form of the canonical hours is used as a congregational service (see Liturgy, Christian).

The Islamic *salat*, more closely related to the obligatory Jewish prayers, is performed five times a day (at dawn, at midday, in the afternoon, immediately after sunset, and about two hours later) after the call to prayer made from the minaret. Ritual ablutions take place before the prayer. Strict regulations govern both the recital of the texts (the first *sura* of the Koran, a prayer of praise, a confession of faith, a benediction of the prophet and the faithful) and the bodily postures (standing, bowing, prostration, crouching, raising or stretching out the hands, etc.). Similar recitations of formulas take place in Zoroastrianism (see Parsees: *Ritual*). In all these religions, further, the repetitions of obligatory prayer formulas are regarded as particularly meritorious.

Philosophical Problems.—The philosophical problems raised by prayer were seriously studied in the ancient world, and this criticism has been further developed by modern philosophers. Any prayer for earthly good fortune seems to the philosopher unworthy of address to God. In particular, the idea that man's prayers can influence God seems incompatible with a philosophical conception of the deity. This criticism of course concerns only the lower forms of prayer, not mystical prayer or the classical Christian theories of prayer. The early Christian theologian Origen said that to pray for earthly things was disobedience to God. Augustine pointed out that prayer was intended not to instruct God but to elevate man, not to make God change his mind but to bring man round to what he ought to desire. Prayer for Thomas Aquinas is concerned only with awaking trust in man and with contemplation of God's love. Meister Eckhart regards each prayer as a part of the eternal foresight of God and of his eternal predestination.

The philosophical problems of prayer have become more involved since the advent of modern astronomy, which has no place for a heavenly ruler enthroned high above the earth but only for the creative force which permeates the immeasurable universe. This cosmic viewpoint had been anticipated by the mystics' concept of infinity, though the mystics always stressed the immanence of God as well as his transcendence. (See Mysticism.) Thus, the infinitely great God of the cosmos dwells in the heart of man; not only can he hear man's cry but this cry is but the echo of the call of God that preceded it; however many desires expressed in prayer remain unfulfilled, the faithful believer knows that no prayer goes unheard. The Islamic poet Jalal-ud-din Rumi tells in his *Mathnawi* (2:195–197) how a bewildered man complained that when he cried "O God" God did not reply "Here am I"; and how he then received from God this consoling revelation: "That 'O God' of thine is my 'here am I' and that supplication and grief and ardour of thine is my messenger to thee. Thy shifts and attempts to find a means of gaining access to me were in reality my drawing thee towards me. . . . Thy fear and love are the noose to catch my favour: beneath every 'O Lord' of thine is many a 'Here am I' from me" (Eng. trans. by R. A. Nicholson, ed., *Mathnawi*, vol. 2, 1926).

Bibliography.—*Collections of Prayers:* R. F. Merkel, *Gebete der Völker* (1946); P. W. Scheele, *Opfer des Wortes, Gebete der Heiden* (1960).
General: Max Müller, "On Ancient Prayer" in G. A. Kohut (ed.), *Semitic Studies in Memory of Alex Kohut*, pp. 1–41 (1897); F. Heiler, *Das Gebet* (1918; 5th ed., 1923), abbreviated Eng. trans. *Prayer* (1932; reissued 1958); D. V. Steere, *Prayer and Worship* (1938); T. Ohm, *Die Gebetsbärden der Völker* (1948).
Primitive Prayer: L. R. Farnell, *The Evolution of Religion*, pp. 163–231 (1905); R. R. Marett, *The Threshold of Religion*, pp. 33–84 (1909); G. A. Reichard, *Prayer the Compulsive Word* (1944).
Judaism: J. Hempel, *Gebet und Frömmigkeit im Alten Testament* (1922); A. Wendel, *Das israelitisch-jüdische Gebet* (1932); E. Munk, *The World of Prayer* (1954); A. J. Heschel, *Man's Quest for God* (1954).
Christianity: G. A. Hamman, *La Prière*, vol. i, *Le Nouveau Testament* (1959); W. Emery Barnes, *Early Christians at Prayer* (1924); J. M. Nielen, *Gebet und Gottesdienst im Neuen Testament* (1937); F. Cabrol, *Liturgical Prayer* (1922); M. Marx, *Incessant Prayer in Ancient Monastic Literature* (1946); E. Behr-Siegel, *Prière et sainteté dans l'église russe* (1950).
Islam: Max Grünert, *Das Gebet in Islam* (1911); E. Mittwoch, *Zur Entstehungsgeschichte des islamischen Gebets und Kultes* (1913); C. E. Padwick, *Muslim Devotions* (1961).
Buddhism: F. Heiler, *Die buddhistische Versenkung*, 2nd ed. (1922); E. Conze (ed. & trans.), *Buddhist Meditation* (1956).
Problems of Prayer: B. H. Streeter *et al.*, *Concerning Prayer, Its Nature, Its Difficulties, and Its Value* (1916); Friedrich von Hügel, *The Life of Prayer* (1929); Francis Underhill, *Prayer in Modern Life* (1929); F. Ménégoz, *Le Problème de la prière*, 2nd ed. (1932); A. Hodge, *Prayer and Its Psychology* (1931); E. Eller, *Das Gebet, Religionspsychologische Studien* (1937); G. A. Buttrick, *Prayer* (1942); A. de Quervain, *Das Gebet* (1948). (F. J. He.)

PRAYING MANTIS: *see* Mantis.

PREACHING, a term popularly applied to any type of authoritative moral exhortation. Even in its ecclesiastical sense and in its Christian form, which alone is considered in this article, it is not patient of clear and precise definition. It will be convenient to start from the distinction indicated by New Testament scholars between *kerygma* and *didache*, proclamation and instruction. First the gospel must be proclaimed or preached; then the catechumen must be instructed in the Christian tradition and the Christian way of life. "Preaching" is thus distinguished from "teaching." But in practice the distinction wavers, for preaching is undoubtedly a form of instruction, and instruction in Christian doctrine or Christian practice may often in fact, if not in form, be preaching.

The distinction is parallel to that in the Old Testament between the functions of the prophet and the priest. The prophet from his own insight or inspiration says, "Thus says the Lord"; the priest gives instruction in the Torah, the tradition. But, again, the distinction is not absolute. The Book of Deuteronomy, for instance, is part of the Torah, the Law, but it is also prophetic literature. It is teaching quickened by prophetic insight.

History.—The New Testament contains much catechetical instruction, but the ground plan of the apostolic preaching (*kerygma*) is not in doubt:

The prophecies of the Old Testament have now been fulfilled. This has happened in the ministry, death and resurrection of Jesus. He has now been exalted to God's right hand as Messiah and Lord. This belief has been confirmed by the gift of the Holy Spirit. Jesus will return to bring God's purposes to their consummation. Meanwhile men have an opportunity to repent and to receive forgiveness and the gift of the Holy Spirit (pp. 37–38 from *The Apostolic Age,* by G. B. Caird, Gerald Duckworth & Co. Ltd., London, 1955).

The primitive church distinguished between the offices of prophet and of teacher (*cf*. Eph. iv, 11). "Prophecy" roughly corresponded with "preaching." But soon, under stress of pressures from within and without, "prophecy" fell into disfavour, and charismatic ministries came to be regarded with suspicion. The bishop was designated the guardian of the apostolic tradition, and "preaching" gradually gave place to "teaching," a function of officials.

At the Eucharist in the 2nd century, as Justin Martyr says, after the reading of the memoirs of the apostles and the writings of the prophets the president gave "the instruction and exhortation (*nouthesian kai paraklesin*) to the imitation of these noble things." This must presumably have been teaching rather than preaching; the evangelistic or missionary work of the church must have been in the hands of laymen such as Justin himself. In those days the purpose of philosophy was deemed to be "the salvation of the soul," as the Neoplatonist Porphyry says, and Justin was the Christian philosopher comparable to the Stoic and Cynic preachers of the day.

In the early days of eastern Christianity there were notable preachers such as Gregory of Nazianzus and Basil in the 4th century and Theodoret in the 5th. But after the Council of Chalcedon (451) preaching became largely a matter of compilation and quotation concerned with asceticism, legends of the saints, angels, the cult of the Virgin Mary, icons and the like. A notable exception was Simeon the New Theologian (9th–10th centuries), but even he addressed almost exclusively a monkish audience. The reasons for this are twofold. On the one side was the pressure of the imperial interest and later of Islam. On the other was the nature of the Orthodox liturgy; for whereas rhetoric was widely studied in the Byzantine empire, in respect of worship "we do not consider God, we experience him." In the 20th century a revival of preaching has occurred in Orthodox churches, but the relative disparagement of preaching continues because of the view that the central rite of the Eucharist is itself the proclamation or preaching of the gospel.

With the collapse of the western Roman empire and the irruption of the barbarians, preaching, apart from cloistral meditations given to monks and nuns, became largely a fierce denunciation of sin and a threatening of hell-fire. Certainly the "preaching" of the crusades cannot be regarded as a republication of the apostolic gospel. But in the west during the 11th and 12th centuries, after the foundation of the Franciscan and Dominican preaching orders, there was a notable revival of preaching, and vast crowds gathered to hear the preachers.

At the end of the middle ages in the west there was a sad decline of preaching into the burlesque-scholastic, but with the Reformation came a great revival. This was inevitable, for *verbum, inquam, et solum verbum, est vehiculum gratiae*, said Luther: "The Word, and the Word alone, is the vehicle of grace." Sacrament and sermon were the two modes of the operation of the Word, but there was to be no sacrament without the preaching of the apostolic gospel.

Within the Roman Catholic Church there was a revival of preaching also. The Council of Trent laid great stress upon the importance of frequent preaching; Charles Borromeo, himself a famous preacher, set up a school of preaching in Milan in the 16th century, and there were many notable Roman Catholic preachers, such as François Fénelon and Jean Baptiste Massillon in the 17th–18th centuries.

In the Anglican Church the sermon, on the whole and with many notable exceptions, has conformed to the type of homily or pastoral teaching rather than the proclamation of the gospel. This is, perhaps, connected with the transference of the sermon from the communion service, where it belongs in the Book of Common Prayer, to the noneucharistic offices of matins and evensong. In the Reformed churches which stem from Geneva public worship is in principle eucharistic even where there is no celebration of the Supper. According to the theory of these churches, therefore, the sermon is, as it were, the monstrance in which Christ is held up before the congregation for their worship and adoration; it is the counterpart of "the breaking of the bread" and its distribution to the congregation. While, in fact, many Anglicans preach powerfully in the full sense of *kerygma* or the apostolic gospel, and many representatives of traditional Protestantism emit sermons which barely fall under the category of *didache* or teaching, the concept of the sermon and of preaching differs in these two traditions.

Types of Preaching.—It would be both tedious and invidious to attempt a catalogue of the most famous preachers, but powerful sermons fall into several overlapping categories, which may be illustrated by an almost arbitrary selection of great names.

First, there are the natural orators such as John Chrysostom, bishop of Constantinople in the 4th century, whose eloquence was such that he had to deprecate the applause he often elicited from his congregation; the 17th-century French bishop J. B. Bossuet; his contemporary Isaac Barrow, the preceptor of Isaac Newton and master of Trinity college, Cambridge, who has been styled "the English Bossuet"; the 18th-century George Whitefield, of whom the orator Bolingbroke wrote, "He has the most commanding eloquence I ever heard in any person" and of whom Hume said that it was worth going 20 miles to hear him preach.

But of these Chrysostom was an expositor of Scripture; Bossuet's most famous sermons are rather panegyrics upon the dead than declarations of the gospel; Barrow was at different times professor of Greek, of geometry and of mathematics; and Whitefield was an itinerant preacher of the gospel. If the excellence of preaching be judged by its effect, a sermon cannot be estimated by the oratorical prowess of the preacher or the literary felicities of his manuscript. One may criticize the style or content of J. H. Newman's Anglican sermons and wonder why they have been so extravagantly praised, but there can be no doubt about the profound impression they made upon the hearers. Indeed, many a sermon imperfect in literary form and unsatisfactory in logical presentation has achieved greatness because its conclusion, driven home by the earnestness of the preacher and some divine concursus of the Holy Spirit, has achieved an effect beyond the reach of eloquence. One can estimate the power better than the technical eloquence of such missionary preachers as Ulfilas in the 4th century, Columba in the 6th, Boniface in the 8th or Ansgar who evangelized Sweden in the 9th century.

Second, beside the great orators of the pulpit may be set those who were rulers of peoples. Such were Savonarola, who dominated Florence by the passion of his eloquence at the end of the 15th century; and the two Reformation leaders John Calvin, the master of Geneva, and John Knox in Scotland. Of Knox, James Melville recorded in his diary for 1571:

Of all the benefetes I haid that yeir was the coming of that maist notable profet and apostle of our nation, Mr. Jhone Knox to St. Andro. I hard him teatche ther the prophecie of Daniel, that simmer and the wintar following. I haid my pen and my litle book, and tuk away sic things as I could comprehend. In the opening upe of his text he was moderat the space of an halff houre; but when he enterit to application, he maid me sa to grew and tremble, that I could nocht hald a pen to wryt.

By 1574 Knox was physically so weak that he had to be "lifted upe to the pulpit whar he behouit to lean at his first entrie . . . bot for he haid done with his sermont, he was sa active and vigorous, that he was lyk to ding that pulpit in blads and flie out of it."

Third, there are the systematic expositors of Scripture. The Greek Fathers fall into this category, as in the west does St. Augustine of Hippo. Medieval exegesis was perhaps too fanciful to come under the heading of systematic exposition. The reformer John Calvin and the 18th-century English Nonconformists Matthew Henry and Philip Doddridge were eminent expositors of the whole Bible, and outstanding among such preachers in the 19th and 20th centuries were Alexander Maclaren, Alexander Whyte and George Adam Smith.

Fourth, the type of preaching that most closely corresponds to the apostolic *kerygma* is that of the evangelists. Luther's doctrine of justification by faith, with its corollary that "these two words, grace and peace [Gal. i, 3], do contain in them the whole sum of Christianity," was not intrinsically new, but he saw and experienced it with such power and vividness that it became for much of Christendom a republication of the apostolic gospel. In his passionate and searching proclamation of the mercies of God he was followed, after a period of Protestant scholasticism, by such preachers as John Wesley, the founder of the Methodist movement; Charles Simeon, who from King's college and Holy Trinity in Cambridge exercised an immense influence upon the Church of England and was one of the founders of the Church Missionary society; the 19th-century Baptist Charles Haddon Spurgeon, whose sermons in spite of their traditional Calvinist theology deserve study for their simple, nervous English; and his United States contemporary the traveling missioner Dwight L. Moody, who, being asked after three nights of preaching why he had not discoursed upon the wrath of God, promised that he would come to that subject when he had finished speaking of the love of God. Such men could say of themselves as the 17th-century Puritan Richard Baxter said:

> I preach'd, as never sure to preach again,
> And as a dying man to dying men!

It was primarily with evangelistic preaching that the churches followed up the expansion of the population westward in the United States and Canada. North America has proved fertile in the production of evangelistic preachers, among whom in the 20th century John R. Mott, "Billy" Graham and Edwin Orr have been outstanding examples. The publication in the mid-20th century of *The Interpreter's Bible* is perhaps the most notable U.S. contribution to expository preaching.

A fifth type of preaching is the very simple, colloquial and dramatic. Illustrations of this are the sermons of Peter Waldo of Lyons in the 12th century, of Bertold von Regensburg in the 13th, the famous discourse of the Reformation bishop Hugh Latimer on the playing cards and on the plow; the *Village Sermons* (1849) of Charles Kingsley; and the *Dorfpredigten* (1899–1902) of Gustav Frenssen, the German novelist who prepared his sermons as he walked through the village street and visualized the lives and hopes and fears of those who lived in the cottages he passed.

Sixth, there are the sermons more philosophical in form, such as those preached in the 17th century by the Cambridge Platonists; or in the 18th century the *Astronomical Discourses* of Thomas Chalmers and the sermons of Jonathan Edwards; and in the 19th the sermons of F. D. E. Schleiermacher, the father of modern Protestant theology, and those of James Martineau and Horace Bushnell.

Finally there is the mystical type of discourse such as the expositions of the Song of Songs by Bernard of Clairvaux in the 12th century and the sermons of Bonaventura in the 13th century, of Jean de Gerson and the Dominican Johann Tauler in the 14th, and of Peter Sterry, chaplain to Oliver Cromwell, in the 17th.

Many of the great names of the pulpit cannot be fitted easily into any of these categories, and many could be accommodated in more than one. Preaching is at once an impossible task—for what mortal man may dare to say "Thus saith the Lord God"?—yet it is a necessity laid upon many consciences: "His word was in mine heart as a burning fire shut up in my bones, and I was weary with forbearing, and I could not stay" (Jer. xx, 9). It is on the human side the most tremendous exercise of the whole personality. It may be surmised that all those whose preaching has been great in the sense of *kerygma* or proclamation might agree with the words ascribed to the notable 19th-century U.S. minister Henry Ward Beecher:

To preach the Gospel of Jesus Christ; to have Christ so melted and dissolved in you, that when you preach your own self you preach Him as Paul did; to have every part of you living and luminous with Christ, and then to make use of everything that is in you . . . all steeped in Jesus Christ, and to throw yourself with all your power upon a congregation—that has been my theory of preaching the Gospel . . . I have felt that man should consecrate every gift that he has got in him that has any relation to the persuasion of men and to the melting of men—that he should put them all on the altar, kindle them all, and let them burn for Christ's sake.

Sermon Construction.—Every preacher has his own style, and the varieties of form and manner among the acknowledged masters of pulpit eloquence are so great that it might seem foolish to suggest that there is any literary pattern to which all preaching conforms or should conform or any rules for the construction of a sermon. Yet in very general terms a common, if not universal, pattern can be found.

The middle ages knew rules and conventions of sermon construction. First, a text must be selected; this is to be, as it were, the acorn from which the whole tree of the discourse is naturally to emerge. Then a brief ante-theme should be composed, the purpose of which is to catch the attention of the audience; it may be accompanied by an invitation to prayer. The theme itself is then introduced and divided into three parts which in due course are to be developed. They are then to be confirmed by arguments from reason and from Scripture. Finally comes the *dilatatio* or peroration. Great stress was laid upon the use of *exempla* or illustrations.

This somewhat redoubtable plan does not conform to the practice of many exemplary preachers. But there is a simpler paradigm which, if it offers no binding rules, underlies the practice of many or most and carries its inherent logic. Preaching is a proclamation of the gospel from the text of Scripture; the sermon is to be an exposition of the chosen text. Its announcement is preceded or followed by a short exordium designed to indicate to the hearers that what follows is of interest and importance to them. The text, whether it refers to an event or a saying, arises always from a concrete situation. This historical situation is to be presented to the congregation with all possible vividness, so kindling their imaginations that they can visualize the scene or overhear the words of the text in their historical setting. Underlying every concrete historical situation is some principle of universal significance and application.

After his exposition of the scene the preacher therefore enlarges upon such underlying principle or principles and illustrates his argument from Scripture, from history, from literature, from imagination or any other source. In a final section the preacher brings home the significance of this exposition to the hearts and consciences of his hearers.

Such may be deemed the simple, general but flexible outline or schematism of the sermon. It may be observed that it is closely parallel to the traditional rules for the making of a meditation. First comes the exercise of the imagination, a visualizing of the scene; second follows an exercise of reflection or thought, an attempt to understand the permanent and universal principle implicit in the scene thus visualized; finally comes the exercise of the will and the decision of heart and conscience.

BIBLIOGRAPHY.—C. H. Dodd, *The Apostolic Preaching and Its Developments* (1936); B. Reicke, "A Synopsis of Early Christian Preaching," in A. Fridrichsen *et al.*, *The Root of the Vine* (1953); G. R. Owst, *Preaching in Medieval England* (1926), *Literature and Pulpit in Medieval England* (1933); John Brown, *Puritan Preaching in England* (1900); C. Smyth, *The Art of Preaching: a Practical Survey of Preaching in the Church of England, 747–1939* (1940); E. C. Dargan, *A History of Preaching, 70–1572* (1905); R. Rothe, *Geschichte der Predigt von den Anfängen bis auf Schleiermacher* (1881); H. C. Fish, *History and Respository of Pulpit Eloquence*, 2 vol. (1857); A. E. Garvie, *The Christian Preacher* (1921); R. F. Horton, *Verbum dei* (1893); P. T. Forsyth, *Positive Preaching and Modern Mind* (1907); C. S. Horne, *The Romance of Preaching* (1914); Horton Davies, *Worship and Theology in England*, vol. iii and iv (1962), *Varieties of English Preaching 1900–1960* (1963).   (N. Mi.)

PRECAMBRIAN TIME. The Precambrian, as the name implies, includes all geologic time before the Cambrian Period and all rock formations older than the basal beds of the Cambrian System (*q.v.*), the earliest period of the Paleozoic Era, as indicated on the accompanying geologic time chart. (*See also* GEOLOGY: *Historical Geology.*)

In much geologic literature the early part of Precambrian time is designated the Archeozoic or Archean Era, and the later part the Proterozoic Era; and these terms are retained in *Encyclopædia Britannica* articles dealing with areas where they remain in general use (*i.e.*, Africa, Australia). In this article Precambrian time is divided into *Early Precambrian* and *Late Precambrian*. This terminology recognizes that the total time involved is too immense and the records in all continents are too complex for meaningful division into two formal eras. The general classification of the rock units as Early and Late Precambrian is based on stratigraphic and structural relationships. A basic requirement is regional evidence that the rocks in both groups are older than strata dated by contained fossils as Lower Cambrian. Separating the older rock units into Early and Late Precambrian must rest on regional evidence for widespread unconformity between the two, generally with more pronounced metamorphism in the lower unit.

Following are the main divisions of this article:

I. CHARACTERISTICS

Throughout most of the world, wherever the contact of Cambrian with older rocks is exposed, there is a great unconformity or gap in the sequence of formations. In a few regions, however, there seems to be no unconformity, the Cambrian beds grading downward without interruption into strata believed to be of Precambrian age. Most of the Cambrian and younger strata contain numerous fossils that give evidence of varied and abundant life. The comparatively few fossils known in Precambrian rocks represent simple forms such as calcareous algae, microscopic fungi, trails and burrows of worms or wormlike creatures, and possible fragments of arthropods, foraminifera, and radiolarians. The oldest fossil forms so far reported came from rocks in South Africa for which analysis by the rubidium-strontium method indicates an age more than 3,000,000,000 years. The tiny bacterium-like forms, revealed and studied by optical and electron microscopy, indicate that life began much earlier in Precambrian time than had been supposed.

Wherever erosion has removed the Paleozoic and later formations, Precambrian rocks are usually present. They are exposed over one-fifth of the land surface of the earth and, except where intruded by igneous rocks of later age, exist everywhere at depth beneath Paleozoic and later strata. They are exposed in areas of two kinds: (1) the deeply denuded parts of mountain chains where they have been uplifted by mountain building; and (2) in widely extended areas of relatively low elevation, called shields because of their gentle outward slopes resembling roughly the surface of a shield. The exposures in mountain chains are much more restricted in extent than in the shield areas.

The formations of the Precambrian are, for the most part, highly folded and intruded by masses of granite, granite gneiss, and other igneous rocks, most of which came in at depth as the Precambrian mountain-building was in progress. On the margins of the Precambrian shield areas, Cambrian and later beds in many places lie on the upturned edges of Precambrian strata. This relationship shows that, prior to the Cambrian, the Precambrian mountains were worn down to a relatively low land area over which the Cambrian seas advanced.

Although most Precambrian rocks have been subjected to the deformation and alteration that accompanies mountain-building, many of the shield areas have suffered little change through all the later eras; and original structures even of the earliest Precambrian have been remarkably well preserved. It has been found possible in many Precambrian regions, by means of detailed mapping, to determine the structural succession of formations over considerable areas. Only a relatively small part of the Precambrian has been mapped in this way; and because of the absence of diagnostic fossils, much intensive geological work will be necessary before

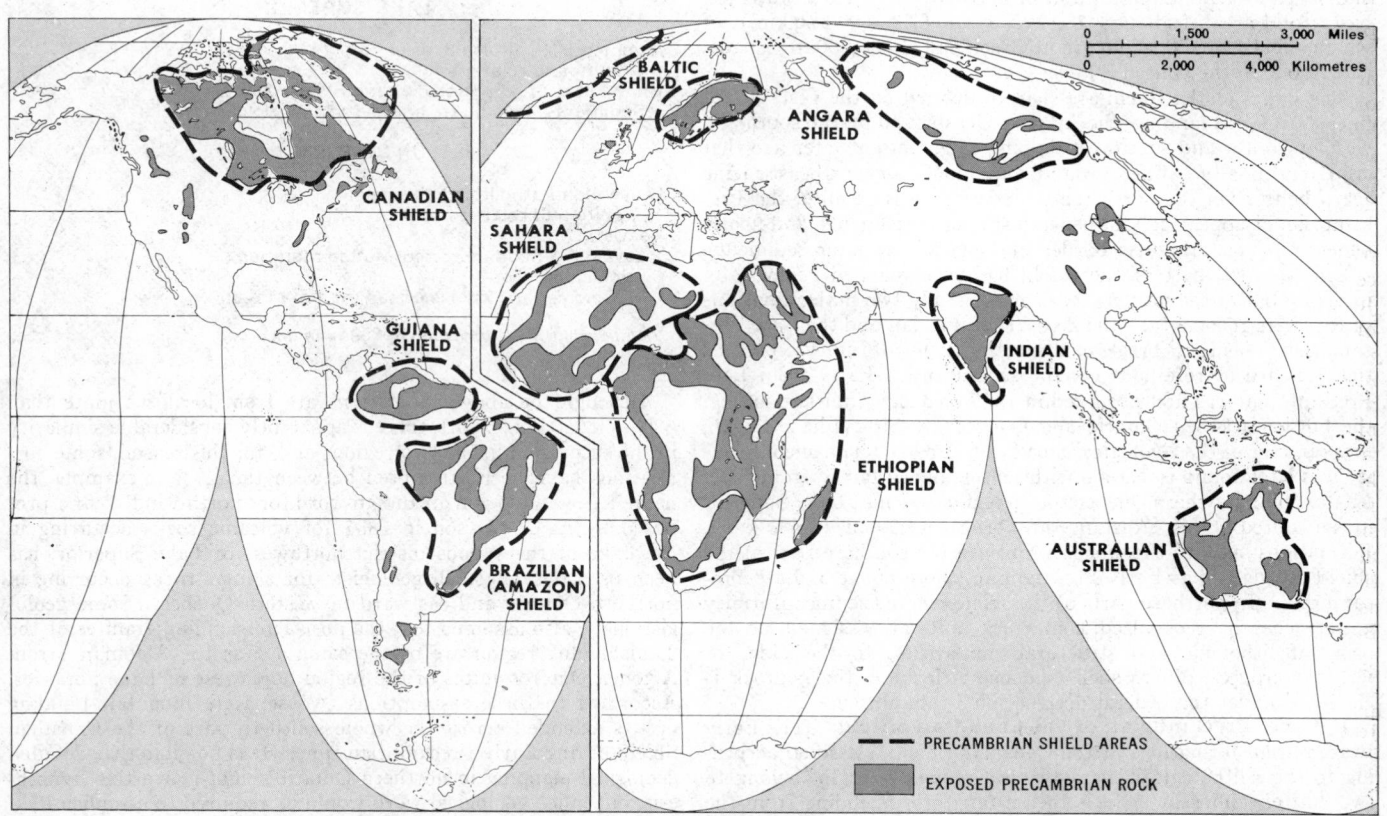

PRINCIPAL PRECAMBRIAN OUTCROP AREAS SHOWN IN GRAY; BROKEN LINES INDICATE SHIELD AREAS

the rocks can be correlated with certainty even within most of the separate Precambrian areas.

1. Dating.—The discovery that radioactive elements slowly disintegrate into other elements affords a way in which the approximate age of Precambrian rocks can be determined. Thus from the time a uranium-bearing mineral is formed, its uranium slowly breaks up into helium and isotopes of lead.

Since the rate of disintegration of the uranium is known, it is possible to determine the age of the mineral from the amounts of lead isotopes relative either to one another or to the uranium present. Many pegmatites and other igneous rocks of the Precambrian contain uranium-bearing minerals, the oldest of which has been determined to have an age of more than 3,500,000,000 years. The rocks in which these occur, however, are intrusive into older formations, and it has been estimated that the oldest Precambrian rocks on the earth's surface have an age of more than 4,000,000,000 years. (*See also* GEOCHRONOLOGY.)

2. The Precambrian World.—For all of Precambrian time for which there is a geological record, conditions on the surface of the earth appear to have been similar in most respects to those of later eras. Mountain-building and volcanic activity recurred as in the later periods of the earth's history; water played the same role as it does today; rocks were deeply eroded; and conglomerates, sandstones, and other sediments were deposited in the same manner as at the present time. There is evidence also that great ice sheets similar to the one now covering most of Greenland existed in Canada, India, South Africa, Australia, and elsewhere.

II. THE PRECAMBRIAN RECORD

A. NORTH AMERICA

Precambrian rocks occur in North America mainly in the Canadian Shield that occupies most of the northeastern part of the continent. They occur also in numerous scattered areas in the western or Cordilleran part and in places in the eastern belt of folded rocks that extends northward from Alabama to Newfoundland.

The Canadian Shield has the world's largest area of exposed Precambrian rocks. It includes most of northeastern Canada and the greater part of Greenland, and extends into the United States west and south of Lake Superior and in northern New York State. It has a total area of about 2,780,000 sq.mi. (7,200,000 sq.km.), of which about 800,000 sq.mi. are in Greenland, 1,905,000 in Canada, and 75,000 in the United States.

The limits of the shield are sharply defined on the east, except in eastern Greenland, by the Atlantic Ocean; and on the south and west by south- and southwest-dipping sediments of later age that crop out in alternating lowland and north- or northeast-facing scarp belts. On the north the boundary is less definite, the Precambrian disappearing first beneath scattered remnants, and finally beneath a most irregular border of Paleozoic or later sediments.

Only a small part of the shield has been mapped geologically in detail, but at the present stage of the study two major divisions of rocks are recognized—the Early Precambrian and the Late Precambrian. A major break in deposition (unconformity), used as the standard of reference for the separation of Early from Late Precambrian, was first observed in 1845 on Lake Timiskaming, on the border between Ontario and Quebec, by Sir William Logan, first director of the Geological Survey of Canada. The unconformity was later found to extend with reasonable certainty from Lake Mistassini in northern Quebec to the region south of Lake Superior in the United States, a distance of more than 900 mi. (1,450 km.). Formations beneath this unconformity in the southern part of the shield are classed as Early Precambrian, those above as Late Precambrian. In northern parts of the shield where the unconformity is not generally recognized, some rock units are assigned, on the basis of lithologic and structural similarities, to the older or younger group. Where such evidence is lacking, the bedrock is classified under the general designation Precambrian.

1. Early Precambrian of the Canadian Shield.—The Early Precambrian formations of the Canadian Shield, classified according to their lithological character and mode of origin, belong to two entirely different types. In the territory extending from the north end of Lake Huron to the Strait of Belle Isle, the Adirondack

region in New York State, Baffin Island, and Greenland, the rocks are limestone and associated sediments of the types laid down in the sea adjacent to land of low relief; whereas elsewhere in the shield limestone is almost wholly absent and the predominant formations are lava flows and clastic sediments (that is, composed of fragments of preexisting rocks), characterized by features that suggest deposition either on land or in the sea adjacent to mountains.

Information is far too incomplete for setting up a single tabular classification of the Early Precambrian rocks of the shield that would hold for its entire area; but in the Timiskaming region of northeastern Ontario and western Quebec, where an area of about 2,600 sq.mi. (6,750 sq.km.) has been mapped geologically in detail, the succession in descending order (*i.e.,* from youngest to oldest strata) is as follows:

EARLY PRECAMBRIAN ROCKS IN TIMISKAMING REGION

GREAT UNCONFORMITY

Batholithic intrusives
    Granite and related rocks
Intrusive masses, dikes, and sills
    Diorite, gabbro, peridotite, and related rocks
Timiskaming
    Conglomerate, graywacke, and volcanic rocks

UNCONFORMITY

Pre-Timiskaming batholithic intrusives
    (represented only by pebbles in Timiskaming conglomerate)
Pontiac and Hoyle groups
    Graywacke, lava flows, and fine-grained volcanic ejecta
    (tuff)
Keewatin
    Lavas, volcanic fragmental rocks (agglomerate), and tuff

In the region northwest of Lake Superior the Early Precambrian succession from youngest to oldest is the following:

EARLY PRECAMBRIAN ROCKS NORTHWEST OF LAKE SUPERIOR

Algoman batholithic intrusives
    Granite and related rocks
Knife Lake, Steeprock Lake, and Seine River series
    Sediments, lava flows, and pyroclastic volcanic rocks

UNCONFORMITY

Laurentian batholithic intrusives
    Granite and related rocks
Keewatin
    Lavas and Soudan iron formation member
Coutchiching*
    Mica schist and gneiss of sedimentary origin

Relationship of Coutchiching to Keewatin uncertain

Although the above tabulations are from localities more than 600 mi. (950 km.) apart, there is apparently considerable similarity in the succession in the two regions and, for this reason, some correlations have been attempted between them. For example, the name Keewatin (from an Indian word for "north wind"), first proposed by A. C. Lawson in 1885 for volcanic rocks occurring in the Lake of the Woods district northwest of Lake Superior, has been used by almost all geologists for similar rocks occurring in northern Ontario and eastward in western Quebec. Some geologists have also assumed that the post-Timiskaming granites of the Timiskaming region are of the same age as the Algoman (from Algoma, Ont.) granites of the region northwest of Lake Superior. According to these assumptions two separate mountain-building uplifts extended across the whole southern part of the Canadian Shield during Early Precambrian time. It is possible that detailed geological mapping in northern Ontario might prove this hypothesis, but much geological work would be required to establish it.

In the southeastern part of the Canadian Shield, where the

Grenville (Grenville, Ont.) sediments, believed to be of marine origin, occur, the most complete succession of formations is in southeastern Ontario. A tabular statement of the sequence of formations in this region is as follows:

EARLY PRECAMBRIAN ROCKS IN SOUTHEASTERN ONTARIO

Batholithic intrusives
    Granite, granite gneiss, syenite, and related rocks
Diorite, gabbro, and related rocks
Hastings series
    Limestone, dolomite, graywacke, mica schist, conglomerate

UNCONFORMITY

Batholithic intrusives
    (represented only by pebbles in Hastings conglomerate)
Grenville series
    Crystalline limestone, dolomite, quartzite, garnet gneiss, mica schist, lava flows, pyroclastic volcanic rocks

Except for the presence of the Hastings (Hastings County, Ont.) series and the Grenville volcanic rocks restricted mainly to southeastern Ontario, the above succession is similar to that throughout most of the Grenville subprovince that extends from the north end of Lake Huron and the Adirondack region northeast to the Strait of Belle Isle. However, at Mt. Wright and Wabush Lake about 220 mi. (350 km.) north of the lower St. Lawrence, recrystallized iron-bearing sediments are believed to be a southern part of the Labrador-Quebec Late Precambrian sedimentary belt.

2. Late Precambrian of the Canadian Shield.—Late Precambrian rocks occur extensively in the southern part of the Canadian Shield south and northwest of Lake Superior and in the territory extending northeast from the north shore of Lake Huron to Lake Timiskaming. In the region south of Lake Superior in 1935 they were called Algonkian type and classified by C. K. Leith, R. J. Lund, and A. Leith in descending order as follows:

LATE PRECAMBRIAN ROCKS SOUTH OF LAKE SUPERIOR

KEWEENAWAN	Acidic intrusives Basic intrusives Sandstone, shale, conglomerate, lava flows

UNCONFORMITY

UPPER HURONIAN—Sediments, iron formation, volcanic rocks

UNCONFORMITY

MIDDLE HURONIAN—Basic intrusives, iron formation, sediments

UNCONFORMITY

LOWER HURONIAN—Dolomite and quartzite

UNCONFORMITY

In the region northwest of Lake Superior, F. F. Grout, J. W. Gruner, G. M. Schwartz, and G. A. Thiel in 1951 classified the younger group of rocks as follows:

LATE PRECAMBRIAN ROCKS NORTHWEST OF LAKE SUPERIOR

KEWEENAWAN	Upper—Sandstone, other sediments Middle—Acid, basic intrusives, lavas Lower—Conglomerate, sandstone

UNCONFORMITY

ANIMIKIE—Slate, iron formation, and quartzite

UNCONFORMITY

In the Lake Huron-Lake Timiskaming region in northern Ontario the Late Precambrian rocks are classified as follows:

LATE PRECAMBRIAN ROCKS IN NORTHERN ONTARIO

Acid and basic intrusive rocks
Whitewater series

UNCONFORMITY

Cobalt series

UNCONFORMITY

Bruce series

UNCONFORMITY

Of the above, the Bruce series is probably the eastward continuation of the Lower Huronian of the region south of Lake Superior. The Cobalt series, although believed to be, in part, of glacial origin, is usually classified as Middle Huronian. The correlation of the Whitewater series is in doubt. It was formerly thought to be Keweenawan or possibly Animikie, but in 1956 J. E. Thomson suggested that this series might be considerably older.

In the vast northern part of the shield, extending from the Strait of Belle Isle to Great Bear Lake and the Arctic Ocean, the Late Precambrian rocks belong to three main classes: (1) in the northern part of the shield west of Hudson Bay, extensive separate areas of flat-lying conglomerate, sandstone, and lava flows known from place names as the Coppermine River, Et-then, Dubawnt, and Athabasca groups; (2) in the eastern part of the shield, areas or belts of partly folded and partly gently dipping iron formation, dolomite, and clastic sediments of the Belcher Islands, Richmond Gulf, Labrador-Quebec, or similar groups; and (3) in the northwestern part of the shield unconformably beneath the Coppermine River and Et-then rocks, zones of folded dolomite, limestone, quartzite, and graywacke called the Great Slave, Snare, and Nonacho groups. The rocks of class 1 are similar to the Keweenawan of the Lake Superior region; those of class 2 to the Animikie northwest of Lake Superior; and those of class 3 to the Huronian south of Lake Superior.

3. Other North American.—In the western Cordilleran part of North America, the best known section of Precambrian rocks is that exposed in the Grand Canyon of the Colorado River in Arizona. The most extensive occurrence, however, is that of the Late Precambrian Beltian (Little Belt Mountains, Mont.) formations. These occupy an area 300 mi. (475 km.) wide in northern Idaho, Montana, and Washington, and extend discontinuously northwest with a maximum width of about 100 mi. (160 km.) through British Columbia to the Yukon in Canada.

In addition to occurrences in the Grand Canyon area, Precambrian rocks are widely scattered in southern, southwestern, and western parts of Arizona. In the Grand Canyon gorge the oldest rocks, known as the Vishnu schist, are classed as Early Precambrian. They consist of igneous gneisses and altered sedimentary rocks. They are cut by dikes of granite and pegmatite. A younger group of Precambrian rocks 12,000 ft. (3,600 m.) thick, the Grand Canyon series, composed mainly of sediments, rests unconformably on the Vishnu schist. In other parts of Arizona the older Precambrian rocks are known as the Yavapai or Pinal schist, and the younger as the Apache group.

The rocks of the Beltian System include argillite, impure limestone, quartzite, and other sediments. They are estimated to have a thickness up to 35,000 ft. (10,700 m.) in the United States. In Canada, according to H. M. A. Rice, they have a total thickness of 67,000 ft. (20,400 m.) and occur in two series separated by an important unconformity.

In the belt of folded rocks that lies parallel with the east coast of North America, there are Precambrian rocks in eastern Newfoundland, in southeastern Nova Scotia, along the northwest shore of the Bay of Fundy in New Brunswick, and in zones within or adjacent to the eastern part of the Appalachian Mountains from the Canadian border to Georgia. In southeastern Pennsylvania and adjacent parts of New York, New Jersey, and Maryland, the

Geologic Time Chart

System and Period	Series and Epoch	Distinctive Records of Life	Began (Millions of Years Ago)
CENOZOIC ERA			
Quaternary	Recent (last 11,000 years)		
	Pleistocene	Early man	2+
	Pliocene	Large carnivores	10
	Miocene	Whales, apes, grazing forms	27
Tertiary	Oligocene	Large browsing mammals	38
	Eocene	Rise of flowering plants	55
	Paleocene	First placental mammals	65–70
MESOZOIC ERA			
Cretaceous		Extinction of dinosaurs	130
Jurassic		Dinosaurs' zenith, primitive birds, first small mammals	180
Triassic		Appearance of dinosaurs	225
PALEOZOIC ERA			
Permian		Reptiles developed, conifers abundant	260
Carboniferous			
Upper (Pennsylvanian)		First reptiles, coal forests	300
Lower (Mississippian)		Sharks abundant	340
Devonian		Amphibians appeared, fishes abundant	405
Silurian		Earliest land plants and animals	435
Ordovician		First primitive fishes	480
Cambrian		Marine invertebrates	550–570
PRECAMBRIAN TIME		Few fossils	more than 3,490

Precambrian includes sedimentary and igneous gneisses overlain unconformably by crystalline limestone, dolomite, quartzite, sedimentary gneisses, and schists. The older group of rocks is known as the Baltimore gneiss; the younger as the Glenarm series. Farther south the schists and gneisses of the Blue Ridge and the (Piedmont) plateau belts have been classed as Precambrian by most geologists who have examined them.

B. SOUTH AMERICA

Precambrian formations crop out in South America mainly in two regions: (1) in elongated zones here and there in the western Cordilleran belt of mountains extending from Venezuela to Chile; and (2) in broad masses or scattered areas in the eastern part of the continent, but most extensively in Brazil, southeastern Venezuela, French Guiana, Surinam, and Guyana. The territory in northeastern South America underlain by Precambrian rocks lying south of the Amazon basin is known as the Brazilian or Amazon Shield; that north of the Amazon basin as the Guiana Shield. The zones of the Cordilleran region consist mainly of granite, schists, and gneisses, which have been classed as Early Precambrian largely because of their highly altered condition. The succession of formations in central and southeastern Minas Gerais State, Brazil, is believed to be typical of the Amazon Shield. The oldest rocks of this region include gneisses and schists, presumably transformed sediments, overlain successively by two groups of Late Precambrian sediments: the Minas series, composed mainly of quartzite, slate, dolomite, conglomerate, and iron formation called itabirite; and the Itacolumi series, consisting chiefly of quartzite. All of these have been affected by mountain-building, as shown by their highly folded condition and intrusion by granite.

The oldest rocks of the Guiana Shield are crystalline schists, limestone, gneisses, and granite of Early Precambrian age. These are overlain in unconformable succession by two groups of Late Precambrian rocks: (1) the Balling series, composed of lava flows with interbedded iron formation and other sediments; and (2) the Orapu, a sedimentary series consisting of conglomerate, quartzite, and slate. Mountain-building and granitic intrusion followed the deposition of both the Balling and Orapu formations.

Important mineral deposits occur in both the Amazon and Guiana shields. These include hematite iron ore, manganese, gold, mica, and diamonds in Brazil; gold in Guyana; and hematite-magnetite iron ore in Venezuela.

C. EUROPE

Small areas or zones of Precambrian rocks occur widely scattered in Europe wherever deeply eroded folded rocks of mountains or former mountains are present, but by far the largest area underlain by Precambrian formations is that known as the Baltic Shield (Baltica or Fennoscandia), which occupies a large part of Norway, and most of Sweden, Finland, and northwestern U.S.S.R. west of the White Sea. There are also considerable areas of Precambrian in the Highlands of Scotland and northeastern Ireland that may be parts of a western extension of the Baltic mass.

The most important mineral deposits in the Precambrian of Europe are in the Baltic Shield. These include magnetite iron ore at Kiruna in Sweden and apatite (phosphate rock) in the Kola Peninsula of the U.S.S.R.

1. Fennoscandia (Baltic Shield).—The Precambrian area of Fennoscandia or the Baltic Shield extends from the Arctic Ocean to the island of Bornholm in the Baltic Sea and from the eastern extremity of the Kola Peninsula in the U.S.S.R. to the westernmost tip of Norway. In the 1930s J. J. Sederholm classified the Precambrian rocks of this region into four divisions: (1) Sivonian; (2) Bothnian; (3) Jatulian-Kalevian; and (4) Jotnian, each of which he believed was separated from the underlying and overlying divisions by great unconformities. He also believed that the intervals of erosion represented by these unconformities in every case were preceded by mountain-building and intrusion of granitic rocks which were laid bare by erosion before the succeeding formations were deposited. Finnish and Swedish geologists have concluded from later work, however, that mountain-building did not intervene between the Sivonian and Bothnian rocks, and that these belong to a single group. This Sivonian-Bothnian succession of formations includes abundant altered sandy sediments, conglomerate, limestone, and interbedded volcanic rocks. They are intruded by basic igneous rocks and post-Bothnian granite. The Jatulian-Kalevian group is composed of conglomerate, ripple-marked quartzite, dolomite, and greenstones that have been transformed by folding and intrusion of granite. During the Late Precambrian the peculiar Rapakivi granite was intruded, after which the Jotnian sandstone was deposited. Since the earlier work of Sederholm, considerable progress has been made in the study of the granitic rocks of Fennoscandia; and some Finnish geologists, notably P. Eskola, have concluded that these igneous intrusions are related to two mountain-building uplifts: (1) the Svecofennidic or post-Sivonian; and (2) the Karelidic or post-Kalevian. According to Eskola, the Svecofennidic mountain chain extended east-west through central Sweden and southwest Finland; the Karelidic mountain-folding trended northwest from Lake Ladoga through eastern Finland and Lapland. In the folded Caledonian Mountains of Norway, thick sandy sediments, known as the Sparagmite or Eocambrian formation, occur extensively at the top of the Precambrian succession.

2. Scotland.—The Precambrian of Scotland lies north of the great fault that marks the southern border of its Highlands. In this region there are four main rock groups of Precambrian or possible Precambrian age. These are: (1) The Lewisian (from Lewis-and-Harris Island in the Outer Hebrides) complex, consisting of sediments that have been transformed into gneisses and schists, and intruded by granite, igneous gneisses, pegmatite, and ultrabasic rocks. It occurs in the northwest Highlands and in the Hebrides Islands. (2) The Moine series, composed of metamorphosed sediments, ultrabasic or basic intrusive rocks, and banded gneisses formed by the intrusion of granite into schist. (3) The Dalradian (from the region of Dalradia, Scot.) series, a metamorphic group of rocks mainly of sedimentary origin. It occurs in the southeast Highlands north of the Highland boundary fault. (4) Unaltered conglomerate, sandstone, grit, and shale—the gently folded Torridonian (from Loch Torridon, Scot.) sediments. They rest unconformably on Lewisian gneiss in the northwest Highlands, in the Hebrides, and other adjacent islands, and are overlain with structural unconformity by Cambrian sediments.

The Lewisian presumably belongs to the Early, and the Torridonian to the Late Precambrian. The Moine sediments have been variously classified as Lewisian, post-Lewisian but pre-Torridonian, Torridonian, or early Paleozoic transformed by Caledonian mountain-building. According to James Phemister, the post-Lewisian pre-Torridonian age is probably the most generally accepted hypothesis. The Dalradian rock group is of uncertain age. Some geologists think it Precambrian but others maintain that it belongs wholly or in part to the Cambrian.

D. Asia

Rocks that are positively known to be Precambrian, or are probably Precambrian, are widespread in Asia wherever eroded mountains occur. The most extensive areas, however, are in eastern Siberia, northeastern China, Korea, India, and Arabia.

1. Siberia.—The Precambrian Angara Shield of Siberia occupies two extensive areas in the headwater parts of the Yenisei and Lena river basins. The northeasterly of these is called the Anabar Massif and that to the southeast the Aldan Plateau. The rocks in the central parts of these ancient land masses include crystalline limestone, quartzites and other metamorphosed sediments, schists, gneisses, and intrusions of granite. In their border zones, notably in the Lake Baikal region, the Early Precambrian complex is overlain unconformably by a folded succession of two Late Precambrian structurally unconformable, metamorphic series. The lower of these consists of schists, conglomerate, and quartzites; the upper of phyllites, sandstone, and interbedded lava flows. In parts of the region Cambrian strata rest on the Early Precambrian complex, and Late Precambrian strata are absent. Geologists of the U.S.S.R., noting the wide zone of unfolded Paleozoic rocks that commonly encircle the Precambrian shield areas, designate the combined shield and surrounding undeformed formations as platforms.

2. China.—In China Precambrian rocks occur widely from Mongolia southeast, east, and northeast to the Siberian border. They belong to three unconformably separate groups: (1) the Tai-Shan (Early Precambrian) complex of gneisses, schists, and altered sediments, intruded by granite and basic igneous rocks; (2) the Wu-T'ai System composed of dolomite, conglomerate and other sediments metamorphosed to schists, interbedded greenstones—probably altered volcanic rocks—and gneisses intruded by granite; and (3) the Sinian System consisting of limestone, quartzite, shale, and other sediments. The Wu-T'ai is compared by some authors with the Huronian of North America. The Sinian is similar in many respects to the Beltian sediments of western United States and Canada. In Manchuria and Korea the names Lia-ho and Keirin have been given by Shintaro Nakamura to rocks believed to be the equivalent of the Wu-T'ai and Tai-Shan systems. Geologists conclude that Precambrian granitic rocks of three ages occur in north China and Korea.

3. India.—The bedrock surface of peninsular India and the adjacent island of Ceylon is composed mainly of highly folded, crystalline schists and gneisses intruded by granite and granite-gneiss, and a widespread group of igneous rocks containing the mineral hypersthene and known as the Charnockite series. This complex was called Vedic and correlated with the Early Precambrian by Sir Thomas H. Holland. It includes an abundance of crystalline limestone, and other highly altered sediments, which, as noted by F. D. Adams in Ceylon, resemble the Grenville series in the southeastern part of the Canadian Shield.

In parts of the peninsula the sediments and schists of sedimentary origin within the complex are known as the Dharwar System. These Early Precambrian rocks are overlain unconformably by great thicknesses of little-disturbed rocks called Purana. They contain no fossils and are believed to be of Late Precambrian age. The Purana sediments have been variously named in different parts of the peninsula. In central India they are divided into two series separated by an unconformity, the Gwalier and Vindhyan. The gold-bearing veins of the Kolar goldfields in Mysore intersect schists of the Dharwar System. Deposits of white mica (muscovite) occur in pegmatite dikes cutting the Dharwar or similar rocks in several provinces of India. The graphite of Ceylon occurs in veins cutting the older gneisses.

E. Africa

Precambrian rocks occur in many places in Africa but are most widespread in an irregular zone extending longitudinally from Arabia and Egypt to Cape Province in South Africa, and transversely from the Gulf of Aden almost to the western extremity of the continent. They also underlie most of the island of Madagascar and occur discontinuously in a narrow belt adjoining the west coast from the Gulf of Guinea southward. In most of these regions they are not in contact with Cambrian formations but are overlain with great unconformity by Devonian, Permo-Carboniferous, or later strata. Their classification as Precambrian is, therefore, based largely on their metamorphic condition and lithological character.

In most of the Precambrian areas of Africa, a highly deformed basal group of schists and gneisses, usually called the Basement, is overlain with great unconformity by one or more less altered rock series. A multitude of local names have been given to these various rock groups but only those occupying extended areas can be mentioned. In the Sahara region of North Africa, two major rock divisions have been observed; the lower is known as Suggarien and the upper, Pharusien. To the southwest, in former French West Africa and Ghana, the names Dahomeyan, Birrimian, and Tarkwaian have been used over a large area.

In Kenya and Tanganyika, which are predominantly underlain by Precambrian rocks, the Precambrian formations are classified into three main groups: the Basement, Nyanzian, and Kavirondian systems. Extensive areas of gneiss and granite intervening in age between the Basement and Nyanzian systems have been mapped as the Granitoid Shield by G. M. Stockley.

The major Precambrian divisional names in southeast Africa are included in the following table:

Precambrian Divisional Names, Southeast Africa

Waterberg System ....Conglomerate, quartzite, shale, volcanic rocks

Transvaal System
  Pretoria series ......Conglomerate, quartzite, shale, and lavas
  Dolomite series .....Dolomite, chert, and quartzite
  Black reef series ....Conglomerate, quartzite, and shale

Ventersdorp System ...Conglomerate, quartzite, chert, shale, and volcanic rocks

Witwatersrand System
  Upper division .....Conglomerate, grit, and quartzite
  Lower division .....Conglomerate, arkose, quartzite, slate, lavas

The Witwatersrand rocks are of special interest because they contain the world's largest known deposits of gold. They have a total thickness of more than 24,000 ft. (7,300 m.). The gold occurs in conglomerate beds known as bankets or reefs. In South West Africa and western South Africa, a succession of conglomerates, quartzites, dolomite, and limestone called the Nama System, because of lithological similarity, has been correlated tentatively with the Transvaal rock group. One of the outstanding features of the South African Precambrian is the widely extended assemblage of volcanic and intrusive igneous rocks known as the Bushveld complex that occurs in central Transvaal. This igneous activity occurred mainly between late Pretoria and Waterberg deposition. Considerable amounts of tin and chrome ore are found in the intrusive phases of the Bushveld complex.

F. Australia and New Zealand

The Precambrian formations of Australia and New Zealand occur in either (1) relatively small scattered areas or zones in the cores of mountains or highlands in New South Wales, South Australia, northern Queensland, western Tasmania, and southwestern New Zealand; or (2) in the widely extended shield area of western and central Australia. In most of these regions an older group of schists, gneisses or volcanic rocks, and intrusive granite is overlain unconformably by less deformed sediments or lavas. At Broken Hill in New South Wales highly altered sandy, argillaceous, and calcareous sediments of the Early Precambrian Willyama series are overlain unconformably by the Late Precambrian Torrowwangee series composed of limestone, shale, and boulder beds.

In New South Wales the older sediments of the Hutchison series and granite gneisses are overlain unconformably by folded limestone, quartzite, and slate of the Adelaide series. In the Mount Isa region of western Queensland, the Precambrian is represented by four rock groups separated by unconformities. The two older of these, the Kalkadoon-Argylla and Soldier's Cap series, are assigned to the Early Precambrian; and the two younger, the Mount Isa and Mount Quamby series, to the Late Precambrian. The Mount Quamby rocks, in contrast with the underlying formations, are only gently dipping. In the shield area of western and central Australia, the Precambrian rocks are classified into two major divisions: (1) a basal group of mainly volcanic rocks but including some interbedded sediments, the Yilgarn-Kalgoorlie system; and (2) the younger Nullagine series composed of gently folded unmetamorphosed conglomerate and other sediments, lavas, and fragmental volcanic rocks. Masses of granite intrude the older system and are overlain unconformably by the Nullagine series.

A considerable part of the gold of Australia has been obtained from lodes and veins occurring in the Precambrian Shield of west and middle Australia. The silver-lead-zinc ores of Broken Hill in New South Wales are in intensely altered Precambrian rocks; iron ore is mined from the Early Precambrian rocks of the Middleback Range in South Australia.

G. Antarctica

The continent of Antarctica, with its margin generally concentric to the South Pole, has an area almost half that of Africa. An ice cap with average thickness of many thousands of feet covers the greater part of the bedrock surface. Geologically, the continent is divided in a general way into West Antarctica, which lies south of South America, and East Antarctica, which lies south of Australia and Africa. For general description and geology of both West and East Antarctica see Antarctica.

East Antarctica is regarded as a shield area. The known bedrock consists of an elevated Basement complex of schists, gneisses, and granitoid intrusives, overlain by little-deformed clastic sedimentary rocks of Paleozoic and Mesozoic age with included basic sills and dikes. Steep faults bound and offset some mountain blocks, but no folds of consequence are exposed. Surveys along lines crisscrossing the continent have given exact altitudes on the ice at numerous stations and, by use of seismic equipment, have determined thicknesses of the ice cap. Resulting profiles on the bedrock indicate a surface of low relief similar to that of eastern Canada. This indication of the general surface form, coupled with evidence that a complex of metamorphic rocks is widespread beneath little-deformed Paleozoic strata, leads to a logical supposition that much or all of East Antarctica is a Precambrian shield.

Much of the reliable geologic evidence on Antarctica has come from intensive exploration by field parties from several nations, starting in the International Geophysical Year, 1957. See International Geophysical Year.

III. ECONOMIC IMPORTANCE

Because most valuable mineral deposits are found in association with igneous rocks of deeply denuded mountainous or formerly mountainous regions, the Precambrian parts of the earth's surface are of special economic importance. Most of the world's largest gold mines, including those of the Transvaal and Rhodesia (Africa), South Dakota (U.S.), northern Ontario and Quebec (Canada), Brazil, and western Australia, are in Precambrian rocks.

The important iron deposits of the Lake Superior region in the United States, the iron deposits of Labrador-Ungava, the iron ores of Brazil and northern Sweden, the great nickel-copper ore masses of Sudbury, Ont., the silver-bearing cobalt-nickel veins of Cobalt, Ont., the occurrences of uranium in South Africa and Canada, and many important copper deposits belong to the Precambrian. It also includes a great variety of useful nonmetallic minerals. Among these are garnet, talc, mica, graphite, feldspar, and magnesite.

See also references under "Precambrian Time" in the Index.

Bibliography.—General: C. O. Dunbar, Historical Geology, 2nd ed. (1960); A. O. Woodford, Historical Geology (1965).

North America: G. H. Ashley, "A Syllabus of Pennsylvania Geology and Mineral Resources," Bull. Pa. Geol. Surv. (1931); M. E. Wilson, "Pre-Cambrian," in Fiftieth Anniversary Volume, Geological Society of America, pp. 269–305 (1941); J. V. Lewis and H. B. Kummel, "The Geology of New Jersey," Bull. N.J. Div. Geol., 50 (1940); F. J. Alcock, "Problems of New Brunswick Geology," Trans. Roy. Soc. Can., vol. 42, sec. 4, pp. 1–15 (1948); F. F. Grout et al., "Pre-Cambrian Stratigraphy of Minnesota," Bull. Geol. Soc. Amer., 62:1017–78 (1951); C. A. Anderson, "Older Pre-Cambrian Structure in Arizona," Bull. Geol. Soc. Amer., 62:1331–46 (1951); J. M. Harrison, "The Canadian Shield, Mainland," Geology and Economic Minerals of Canada, pp. 19–122, Geological Survey of Canada (1957).

South America: W. F. Jenks (ed.), Handbook of South American Geology, Mem. Geol. Soc. Amer., 65 (1956).

Europe: J. J. Sederholm, "On the Geology of Fennoscandia with Special Reference to the Pre-Cambrian," Bull. Comm. Géol. Finl., 98 (1932); P. Eskola, "Glimpses at the Geology of Finland," J. Manchr. Geol. Ass., vol. 11, pt. 1, pp. 61–79 (1950); E. B. Bailey, "The Structural History of Scotland," Report of International Geological Congress (18th sess., Great Britain), pt. 1, pp. 230–254 (1950); O. Holtedahl, "The Structural History of Norway and Its Relation to Great Britain," Quart. J. Geol. Soc. Lond., vol. 108, pt. 1, no. 429, pp. 65–98 (1952); A. Simonen, "Stratigraphy and Sedimentation of the Svecofennidic Early Archaean Supracrustal Rocks in Southwestern Finland," Bull. Comm. Géol. Finl., 160 (1953).

Asia: L. L. Fermor, "An Attempt at the Correlation of the Ancient Schistose Formations of Peninsular India," Mem. Geol. Surv. India, vol. 70, pt. i (1936); "Neogene of the U.S.S.R.," in Stratigraphy of the U.S.S.R., ed. by A. D. Arkhangelsky, vol. 12, pp. 601–642 (1940); J. M. Weller, "Outline of Chinese Geology," Bull. Amer. Assn. Petrol. Geol., 28:1417–29 (1944); L. J. D. Fernando, "The Geology and Mineral Resources of Ceylon," Bull. Imp. Inst., Lond., 46:303–325 (1948); S. I. Tomkeieff, "The Rhiphaean System and the Structure of the Russian Platform," Proc. Geol. Soc., Lond., no. 1501, pp. 108–112 (1953).

Africa: W. Pulfrey, "The Geology and Mineral Resources of Kenya," Bull. Imp. Inst., Lond., 45:277–299 (1948); G. M. Stockley, "The Geology and Mineral Resources of Tanganyika Territory," Bull. Geol. Surv. Tanganyika, 20 (1948); F. Dixey and E. S. Willbourn, "The Geology of the British African Colonies," Report, International Geological Congress (18th sess., Great Britain, 1948), pt. 14, pp. 87–117 (1951); H. M. E. Schurmann, "The Pre-Cambrian of the Gulf of Suez Area," Report, International Geological Congress (19th sess., Algeria, 1952), sec. 1, f. 1, pp. 115–135 (1953); M. Lelubre, "Stratigraphy of the Pre-Cambrian of the Sahara," Bull. Soc. Géol., Fr., ser. 6, 3:547–577 (1953); A. L. Du Toit, Geology of South Africa, 3rd ed. (1954); N. R. Junner, "Notes on the Classification of the Pre-Cambrian of West Africa," Report, International Geological Congress (19th sess., Algeria, 1952), pt. 1, f. 20, pp. 115–127 (1954); E. S. Barghorn and J. W. Schopf, "Microorganisms Three Billion Years Old from the Precambrian of South Africa," Science, vol. 152, pp. 758–763 (1966).

Australia and New Zealand: R. T. Prider, "Igneous Activity, Metamorphism and Ore-Formation in Western Australia," J. Roy. Soc. W. Aust., 31:43–84 (1948); T. W. E. David, Geology of the Commonwealth of Australia, ed. by W. R. Browne, vol. 1 (1950); F. G. Forman, "The Geological Structure of the Shield in South Western Australia," Geology of Australian Ore Deposits, publication of 5th Empire Mining and Metallurgical Congress, 1:65–78 (1953).

Antarctica: John J. Anderson, "Bedrock Geology of Antarctica: a Summary of Exploration, 1831–1962," pp. 1–70 in Geology and Paleontology of the Antarctic, vol. 6 in the "Antarctic Research Series," American Geophysical Union (1965).   (M. E. Wn.; C. R. L.)

PRECESSION OF THE EQUINOXES, in astronomy, an effect connected mainly with a gradual change of the direction of the earth's axis of rotation. There is a general resemblance between the motion of the earth and that of a spinning top. It is well known that when a spinning top is slightly disturbed its axis gyrates, or precesses, round the vertical so that it traces out a cone; the earth's axis similarly describes a cone at the rate of one revolution in about 26,000 years. In applying this analogy the ecliptic (i.e., the plane of the orbit of the earth round the sun) must be taken to correspond to the horizontal; the axis about which the earth spins is inclined at $23\frac{1}{2}°$ to the "vertical," and, keeping this inclination, it turns slowly round the "vertical." It must be emphasized, however, that this correspondence between the earth and a top is superficial, the cause of the precessional motion being governed by different principles.

In this way the North Pole of the celestial sphere describes among the constellations a circle of $23\frac{1}{2}°$ radius, making a revolution in 26,000 years. At present it is near the star α Ursae Minoris, which is therefore called the polestar; but it has traveled a considerable distance within historic times. About 3000 B.C. the star α Draconis would have served as polestar; in 13000 B.C., also in A.D. 13000 Vega would be near enough to the pole to mark roughly its position. By this displacement the part of the sky visible from a particular terrestrial station gradually changes; certain constellations cease to rise above the horizon and others appear for the first time. In the time of the early Chaldean astronomers it was not necessary to travel so far south to see the Southern Cross as it is now.

Cause of Precession.—This was first explained by Isaac Newton. It is due to the attraction of the sun and moon on the equatorial protuberance of the earth, the moon being responsible for about two-thirds and the sun for one-third of the motion—the same proportion as the lunar and solar tides. Treating the equatorial bulge as an extra ring of matter surrounding a spherical earth, the attraction of the sun and moon on this ring forms a couple that tends to turn the ring into the plane of the ecliptic, since both disturbing agents are in or near the ecliptic. If the earth were not spinning this would turn the earth over until the equator coincided with the ecliptic, but the spinning earth behaves like a gyrostat, so that its axis moves at right angles to the plane of the couple—just as the couple, which would upset a top at rest, gives the axis of the spinning top a conical motion.

The moon's orbit is inclined at about 5° to the ecliptic, but it does not remain still; its nodes travel round the ecliptic in 18.6 years. Averaged over a long period of time the deviations of the moon from the ecliptic cancel out; however, at any moment the precession caused by the moon may be greater or less than the average, according to the position at the time of the lunar orbit. In fact the path of the pole among the stars is a slightly sinuous curve. Astronomers distinguish the average secular motion as precession and the periodic fluctuations or sinuosities as nutation.

As the pole (corresponding to the equator) moves round the pole of the ecliptic, so the equinox or intersection of the equator and ecliptic moves round the ecliptic once in 26,000 years. Both right ascensions and longitudes are reckoned from the equinox as zero point; stellar longitudes on this account increase steadily by nearly a minute of arc every year; the effect on the right ascensions is more complicated, but these also continually increase. The vernal equinox is commonly called the first point of Aries, but it has already moved away from that constellation and is now in Pisces. It should be understood that the precession of the equinoxes has no effect on the seasons, and, for example, has no connection with the gradual departure of the spring equinox from March 21 which occurred in the old Julian calendar.

Planetary Precession.—Besides the foregoing lunisolar precession, a phenomenon of much smaller magnitude, known as planetary precession, is recognized. It is due to perturbations by the planets which cause slow changes in the plane of the earth's orbit. Planetary precession changes the position of the ecliptic, whereas lunisolar precession changes the position of the equator; either change affects the equinox, which is the intersection of the two planes. Corrections for precession and nutation are of great importance in most branches of positional astronomy.

PRECIPITATION, in meteorology, denotes all forms of water falling upon the earth's surface. It includes rain (*see* RAIN-FALL) and snow (*q.v.*) and their various modifications such as drizzle, freezing rain, sleet, snow pellets and hail. Precipitation is considered to be one of the most important of all meteorological elements since it is the only important source of fresh water.

The essential difference between a precipitation particle and a cloud particle is one of size. An average raindrop has a mass equivalent to several million cloud droplets. Because of their large size, precipitation particles have significant falling speeds and are able to survive the fall from the cloud to the ground. (*See* CLOUD.)

Precipitation Formation.—The transition from a cloud containing only cloud droplets to one containing a mixture of cloud droplets and precipitation particles involves two basically different steps: formation of incipient precipitation elements directly from the vapour state; and subsequent growth of these elements through aggregation and collision with cloud droplets. The initial precipitation elements may be either ice crystals or chemical solution droplets.

Development of precipitation through the growth of ice crystals depends upon the fact that cloud droplets usually do not freeze at temperatures warmer than about $-40°$ F ($-40°$ C). (The reduction of cloud droplets to temperatures below the normal freezing point is termed supercooling.) Within supercooled clouds, ice crystals may form through sublimation of water vapour upon certain atmospheric dust particles known as sublimation nuclei. In natural clouds, ice crystals form at temperatures colder than about $+5°$ F (about $-15°$ C). The exact temperature of ice-crystal

formation depends largely upon the physical-chemical nature of the sublimation nucleus. (*See also* DUST.)

Once they are formed within a supercooled cloud, ice crystals will continue to grow as long as their temperature is colder than freezing. The rates of growth depend primarily upon the temperature and degree of vapour saturation of the environmental air. The crystals grow at the expense of the water droplets. As the crystals grow, the droplets evaporate by virtue of the fact that the saturation vapour pressure over an ice crystal is less than over a supercooled water surface at the same temperature. In favourable conditions, *e.g.,* in a large, rapidly growing cumulus cloud, an ice crystal will grow to a size of about 0.005 in. in three to five minutes after formation. At this size, the rate of growth through sublimation slows down and further growth is largely through aggregation and collision with cloud droplets.

Small solution drops are also important as incipient precipitation particles. The atmosphere contains many small particles of soluble chemical substances. The two most common are sodium chloride, swept up from the oceans by spray and bubbles, and sulfate-bearing compounds formed through gaseous reactions in the atmosphere. Such particles, known as giant condensation nuclei, collect water because of their hygroscopic nature and, at relative humidities above about 80%, exist as solution droplets. In tropical maritime air masses the number of giant condensation nuclei frequently is very large. Clouds forming in such air may develop a number of large solution droplets long before the tops of the clouds reach temperatures favourable for the formation of ice crystals.

Regardless of whether the initial precipitation particle is an ice crystal or a droplet formed on a giant condensation nucleus, the bulk of the growth of the precipitation particle is through the mechanisms of collision and coalescence. Because of their larger size, the incipient precipitation elements fall faster than cloud droplets. As a result they collide with the droplets lying in their fall path. The rate of growth of a precipitation particle through collision and coalescence is governed by the relative sizes of the particle and the cloud droplets, the size and number of cloud droplets, the fraction of the droplets in the fall path which are actually hit by the precipitation particle and the fraction of these droplets which actually coalesce with the particle after collision. Under ordinary cloud conditions it takes between 10 and 20 minutes for an incipient precipitation element to grow into a large raindrop or a large snowflake.

The efficiencies of the natural precipitation processes are known to be rather low. Although vast amounts of vapour are condensed into cloud droplets to form clouds, most of this water re-evaporates without becoming involved in the precipitation processes. Precipitation particles also suffer considerable loss from evaporation in falling from the cloud bases to the ground. Studies carried out on thunderstorms in the humid eastern part of the United States show that only about 20% of the condensed water reaches the ground as rain. In the arid regions, the bases of clouds may be so far above the ground that most of the rain is evaporated between the clouds and the ground. (*See* CLIMATE AND CLIMATOLOGY.)

Measurement of Precipitation.—Rain gauges and snow gauges are used for measuring precipitation. The amount of precipitation is expressed in terms of the total equivalent amount of liquid water. Thus snow, caught in a gauge, is melted before measurement. In regions where snow forms an important fraction of the precipitation, it is customary to measure the amount of snow by means of a snow survey. (*See* SNOW.) In snow surveys it is necessary to determine the density as well as the depth of the snow in order to determine the water content.

The data from rain gauges and snow surveys are subject to large sampling errors, particularly during periods of shower and thunderstorm activity. The spacing between gauges usually is several times the size of the shower rain area. Over a period of several weeks or months errors due to rain-gauge spacing tend to be averaged out.

Precipitation measurements, when collected from many places, form the basis for estimating the amount of rain falling in a region. Such data are available for regions all over the globe. Because of the problems of sampling rainfall and because of variations in rainfall from one year to the next, climatologists desire at least 40 years of record for computing average annual precipitation amounts.

The development of centimetre wave-length radar during World War II gave the first means of accurately identifying and locating precipitation areas. (*See* RADAR METEOROLOGY.) When combined with a few scattered rain gauges, radar enables meteorologists and hydrologists to determine the amount of precipitation falling on a given area more accurately than with the rain gauges alone.

Artificial Control of Precipitation.—Throughout recorded history, there have been attempts to control precipitation. Early societies employed various forms of magic in their efforts to increase rainfall. During the latter part of the 19th century, experiments using cannon shots, explosions and large fires were carried out for the same purpose. During World War I it was not infrequently observed that rain occurred during or immediately following major battles, and it was believed by many that the sounds of the cannons were responsible for causing the clouds to release the rain. Subsequent findings disproved this idea.

The first series of systematic experiments designed to discover the physics of precipitation and thereby find a means of producing precipitation were carried out by Vincent J. Schaefer in 1946. These experiments, ultimately involving seeding clouds with silver iodide smokes, were successful in causing light snow to fall from supercooled stratified clouds.

Experiments to increase precipitation rest upon the hypothesis that natural precipitation is limited by a shortage of natural precipitation nuclei. Silver iodide smokes, produced by burning a silver iodide-acetone solution, will supply sublimation nuclei effective at temperatures colder than about 23° F (about −5° C). A different approach to the problem of increasing rain involves the release of giant condensation nuclei, or small waterdrops, into suitable clouds in order to initiate rain through the collision-coalescence mechanisms.

Whether or not the amount of precipitation at the ground can be increased through any of these techniques depends largely upon large-scale meteorological factors governing the formation, growth, duration and dissipation of the clouds.

Because of the fact that natural rain is highly variable in time and space, very carefully designed experiments are necessary in order to determine the efficacy of any given rain-making technique. When rain falls from a seeded cloud, one naturally asks whether or not it would have fallen had the cloud not been seeded. When rain fails to fall, one asks whether seeding prevented it. Because of this uncertainty it is impossible to estimate the effect of cloud seeding from a few isolated experiments or from experiments which do not include a group of randomly selected, nonseeded control cases, as statistical methods would require.

From the extensive experiments carried out between 1946 and 1956, it was learned that it is possible to modify some clouds and in some very favourable conditions to cause more precipitation to fall than would have fallen through natural processes. The magnitudes of these increases are not known, although they are usually thought to be less than 10%.

See also references under "Precipitation" in the Index.

See Horace R. Byers, *General Meteorology* (1944); John C. Johnson, *Physical Meteorology* (1954).   (R. R. Bм.; X.)

PRECIPITATION, ELECTROSTATIC, is a process for removing small particles, smoke and fumes from air and gases. The precipitation of smoke by electricity was described in 1824 by M. Hohlfeld, a teacher of mathematics in Leipzig, Ger., but only after it was independently rediscovered and critically studied by Sir Oliver Joseph Lodge about 1884 did it attract general attention and lead to attempts at industrial applications. At the time, however, these proved unsuccessful because of the lack of modern equipment. It was not until 1906, following experiments by F. G. Cottrell at the University of California, Berkeley, that the process was commercially successful.

The first installation was at the Selby Smelting works, near San Francisco, Calif., where it was used for the removal of sulfuric acid mist from about 5,000 cu.ft. (142 cu.m.) of gases per minute. Later the process was successfully extended to the removal of cement dust at nearly red heat from 1,000,000 cu.ft. (28,317 cu.m.) of gas per minute at the Riverside Portland Cement company, a mill in the heart of the California orange groves threatened with legal closure as a nuisance because of the dust emitted.

The method removed 98% of the dust, the daily catch being about 100 tons. Dust removal efficiency in modern industrial plants rarely exceeds 99%. Although first applied purely to mitigate nuisances, the demand for the process is primarily based on the greater profit to be derived from the cleaned gases or the material removed. At one time the Riverside plant was making even more profit from potash incidentally recovered in its dust than from its cement.

The Process.—Technically the process consists in securing a uniform, copious but nondisruptive corona discharge of electricity from small electrode surfaces of one polarity into a stream of cloudy gas. The fine solid or liquid particles composing the dust, fumes or smoke are attracted to, and deposited on, large electrode surfaces of opposite polarity, the particles having become charged from the depletion or gain of electrons on their surfaces; *i.e.*, ionization.

Several variations on the process have been incorporated into the original Cottrell design, which, in principle, consists of a single-stage discharge and collection unit. This design as well as those having two stages—one for discharge and a second for collection—may have automatic washing systems which permit continuous operation.

Another type of precipitator is based upon the collection of ionized particles on electrostatically charged dry filters, such as cellulose mats, which have a large surface area and great dirt-holding capacity. Still another design relies solely on the ability of dust particles to be trapped on electrostatically charged filters without a prior ionization or discharge step. One advantage to these designs is that mechanical filtering is available in case of failure of the electrical system; however, filters offer resistance to air flow, especially under dirty or humid conditions, and must be replaced periodically.

In the Cottrell type of precipitator a single vertical tube or bank of tubes is commonly used. Each tube has a wire electrode suspended axially and insulated so that a voltage may be maintained between the wire and the tube. Relatively high D.C. potentials of 12,000 v. or more are generally employed, and the collection of suspended particles occurs on the tube walls. Single-stage precipitators are thus characterized by the collection of particles in the same electric field that produces the charged particles. During operation a countercurrent flow is set up so that while gas is passing through the tube or tube bank in one direction, the dust or liquid collected on the tube walls falls or drains into a bin or similar collection unit at the tube base. Precipitators are usually installed so that fans pull rather than blow air through the units, and typical operating velocities are in the range of 300 to 500 ft. per minute (f.p.m.). The electrical power consumption of precipitators is relatively low, being of the order of 50 w. per 1,000 cubic feet per minute.

A typical two-stage precipitation process is illustrated diagram-

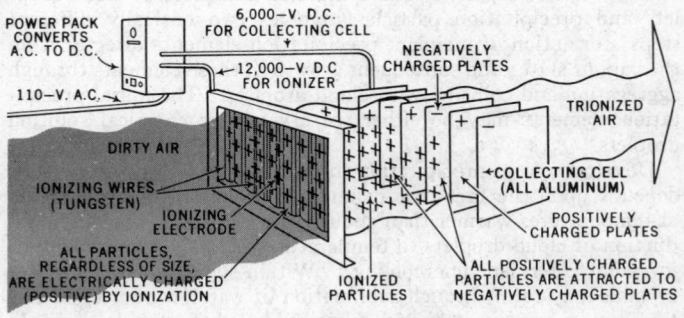

THE TWO-STAGE METHOD OF CLEANSING AIR BY COLLECTION OF IONIZED PARTICLES ON ELECTRICALLY CHARGED PLATES

matically in the figure. This type of precipitator is commonly called the plate type, and its operation may be enhanced by mechanical prefilters or perforated plates in order to ensure a uniform distribution of air. In a typical operation, dirty air is passed through fine tungsten wires maintained at a positive potential of 12,000 v. D.C. This is the ionizing step. The ionized particles then flow past a set of plates spaced about ⅜ in. apart. Alternate plates are charged with a positive potential of about 6,000 v.

Upon contact with the negative collecting plates, the positively charged ions gain electrons and stick to the plates. The voltage on the wires in the ionizing chamber is regulated to secure as strong a glow as possible without passing over into the disruptive discharge; i.e., a spark or arc. The two-stage unit is used most frequently for dry dusts, and the gas flow is horizontal. Dust collected on the plates is either washed, blown or mechanically agitated into drains, bins or conveyers for easy removal.

Electrostatic precipitators for heavy-duty industrial applications differ in design but not in principle from the types of precipitators already described. Potentials of 25,000 to 100,000 v. D.C. are maintained in the operation of both single-stage and two-stage devices, although two-stage units with horizontal air flow are the commonest; air velocities range from 250 to 480 f.p.m., and mechanical filters for large particles are generally employed in series with the precipitation units.

Factors in Design.—Most units are designed with electrodes of opposite polarity spaced two to six inches apart. The size of the installation is determined primarily by the volume of gas to be treated and the amount of suspended matter to be removed, although in many cases the amount, type and size of the particles of suspended matter are of minor consequence. The air cleaners employed in ventilation, air-conditioning and heating systems usually must process air containing no more than four grains of suspended matter per 1,000 cubic feet. Industrial air and gas cleaners, however, frequently encounter loadings of 100 to 20,000 gr. per 1,000 cubic feet.

The materials of construction, including the collecting electrodes, vary from aluminum, iron and lead to reinforced concrete and vitrified earthenware, depending upon the composition and temperature of the gas stream to be processed. High-voltage equipment produces ozone and nitrogen oxides, and operating temperatures in excess of 370° C. (698° F.) are generally avoided. In comparison with dry filters, which in moderate-sized cleaning operations can be thrown away or cleaned, the high initial cost of electrostatic precipitators is generally offset by low maintenance costs.

Industrial Uses.—The earliest applications of the process were to the smelting and sulfuric acid industries. Precipitators at cement mills were fewer in number but handled large volumes of gas and large tonnages of precipitate. Other important applications are in the detarring of coke-oven gases, the cleaning of producer and iron blast-furnace gas, the cleaning of ventilating air in crushing, grinding and polishing mills, the recovery of acid fumes in petroleum refineries and chemical plants, the recovery of dust from coal dryers and the removal of ash from the stack gases of large power plants burning powdered coal.

BIBLIOGRAPHY.—Evald Anderson, *Trans. Amer. Inst. Chem. Engrs.*, vol. xvi, pp. 69–86 (1925), describing theory of comparative efficiencies of the electrical and other methods; H. J. Bush, *J. Soc. Chem. Ind., Lond.*, vol. xli, pp. 22T–28T (1921), giving history, theory and British practice; F. G. Cottrell, *J. Industr. Engng. Chem.*, vol. iii, pp. 542–550 (1911), also *Annual Report*, Smithsonian Institution, pp. 653–685 (1913) (chiefly historical); R. Durrer, *Stahl u. Eisen*, vol. xxxix, pp. 1377–85, 1423–30, 1511–18, 1546–54 (1919), historically very complete and fully illustrated; A. B. Lamb, G. L. Wendt and R. E. Wilson, *Trans. Amer. Electrochem. Soc.*, vol. xxxv, pp. 357–369 (1919), application to gas masks and bacteria; "Air Pollution Symposium," *Iron Steel Engr.*, vol. xxx, pt. 2, pp. 91–110 (1953); W. H. Carrier, R. E. Cherne and W. A. Grant, *Modern Air-Conditioning, Heating and Ventilating*, 2nd ed. (1950); *Heating, Ventilating and Air Conditioning Guide*, vol. 35, pp. 831–852 (1957).   (R. E. Ge.)

PREDESTINATION, the doctrine that God has eternally chosen those whom he intends to save. As the term is understood in modern usage, predestination is distinct both from determinism or fatalism and from the doctrine of divine providence, because it applies to the eternal destiny of man rather than to all the individual events of his life on earth. Thus one may teach that these events are subject to the free decision of man's moral will, but teach at the same time that salvation is due entirely to the eternal decree of God. In its fundamentals the problem of predestination is as universal as religion itself, but the emphasis of the New Testament on the divine plan of salvation has made the issue especially prominent in Christian theology.

Christian doctrines of predestination may be read as a series of glosses upon the words of the apostle Paul (Rom. 8:29–30):

> For those whom he [God] foreknew he also predestined to be conformed to the image of his Son, in order that he might be the first-born among many brethren. And those whom he predestined he also called; and those whom he called he also justified; and those whom he justified he also glorified.

On the basis of these words, three types of predestinarian doctrine, although with many variations, have arisen in the history of Christian thought. One theory—associated with Semi-Pelagianism (q.v.), some forms of Nominalism (q.v.), and Arminianism (q.v.) —makes foreknowledge the ground of predestination, teaching that God predestined to salvation those whose future faith and merits he foreknew. At the opposite extreme is the doctrine of double predestination, commonly identified with John Calvin but more officially associated with the Synod of Dort, and appearing also in some of the writings of St. Augustine and Martin Luther and in the thought of Gottschalk and the Jansenists; according to this doctrine, God has determined from eternity whom he will save and whom he will damn, regardless of their faith, love, or merit—or lack thereof. A third doctrine—set forth in other writings of Augustine and Luther in the decrees of the Council of Orange (529), and in the thought of Thomas Aquinas—ascribes the salvation of man to the unmerited grace of God and thus to predestination, but attributes divine reprobation to man's sin and guilt. Pressed to their ultimate implications, however, all three types leave the mystery unanswered. For even if God bases his predestinating action upon his foreknowledge of faith and merit, such faith or merit is in turn dependent upon grace (q.v.), which God gives to some and not to others.

Thus the doctrine of predestination appears in Christian theology as a corollary of the doctrine of grace, protecting the freedom and sovereignty of God while at the same time declaring his love. Beyond this neither biblical revelation nor theological speculation provides a reliable guide. *See also* DETERMINISM; FREE WILL: *The Theological Problem;* and references under "Predestination" in the Index.

BIBLIOGRAPHY.—Augustine, *On the Predestination of the Saints;* Thomas Aquinas, *Summa Theologica,* I, Q. 23; Martin Luther, *The Bondage of the Will;* John Calvin, *Institutes of the Christian Religion,* III, ch. 21–24; Karl Barth, *Church Dogmatics,* II-2.   (J. J. Pn.)

PREDICABLES, in scholastic logic, a term referring to certain relationships which may obtain between the predicate of a simple statement and its subject. The traditional list of these relationships is derived from Boëthius' Latin version of Porphyry's *Eisagoge* and consists of five items: genus, species, differentia, property and accident. It is based upon a similar classification set forth by Aristotle in the *Topics* (a, iv–viii), differing only by having species where the Aristotelian list has definition.

Aristotle's treatment of the matter is concerned only with statements of the form "*A is B*," where the subject and predicate terms are both universal. He notes that in every true statement of this type the predicate will either be convertible with the subject (i.e., "*B is A*" will follow from "*A is B*") or it will not. If the predicate is convertible with the subject and states its essence, then it is the definition of the subject; while if it is convertible but does not state the essence, it is a property of the subject. On the other hand, if the predicate is not convertible with the subject but is part of the definition, it is the genus or differentia of the subject, for a definition always consists of genus and differentia. If the predicate is not convertible and is not part of the definition, it is an accident of the subject. In attempting to understand these distinctions one is handicapped by Aristotle's failure to indicate clearly whether he is speaking of relations between linguistic expressions or between the meanings of such expressions. Thus, although definition is explicitly described as a phrase which means the essence, the remaining four predicables seem all to be treated primarily as nonlinguistic. Some Aristotelian examples may be mentioned. In the true statement "Man is a rational animal," the predicate is convertible with the subject and states its essence. Therefore, "rational animal" is the definition of man. The statements "Man is an animal" and "Man is rational," while true, are not convertible. Their predicate terms, however, are parts of the definition and hence are the genus and differentia of man. On the other hand, the statement "Man is capable of learning grammar" is true and convertible, since all men are capable of learning grammar and whatever is capable of learning grammar is a man. But "capable of learning grammar" does not state the essence of man. It is therefore a property of man. For an example of an accident, take the predicate of the true statement "Man is featherless." This predicate is not convertible with its subject, nor is it part of the definition. Accordingly, it expresses only an accidental characteristic of man. Porphyry gives the following examples: of genus, animal; of species, man; of differentia, rational; of property, risible; of accident, white.   (B. Ms.)

PRE-ELEMENTARY EDUCATION. Education outside the home of children under compulsory school or kindergarten age is provided under institutional arrangements identified in a wide, and at times confusing variation of terms. Prevalent are such terms as infant school, nursery school, and day nursery (Great Britain), crèche and *école maternelle* (France), *casa dei bambini* (Italy), kindergarten (Germany), preschool, nursery school, day care centre, pre-primary, pre-kindergarten, and co-operative nursery (U.S.). Beginning in 1965 in the United States, federally sponsored programs have used the titles Head Start, Child Development Center, Parent and Child Center, and Follow Through. Schools or day care centres for children from two to four and a-half or five years are variously supported by philanthropic funds, tuition fees, public monies, or combinations of these. Variations in the age of compulsory school entrance are to be found in the U.S. as well as in Western Europe and elsewhere, the range being from five to seven years.

Kindergartens, which enroll children between the ages of five and six or seven years, have been generally accepted as an integral part of the elementary school (*see also* ELEMENTARY EDUCATION) although the source of aid for their support differs from country to country and state to state. This article is concerned with schools or centres for children from two to five years of age.

HISTORY

Historically, the training of children before they entered primary school was considered to be solely the province of the family. An occasional philosopher or educational reformer contemplated the possibilities of improved education of toddlers and young children but the early schools appear to have been philanthropic in purpose, established primarily as substitutes for home care rather than as supplements to the educational functions of the home. In general these early institutions were set up to provide custodial care, safety, and health services to destitute and homeless children and those whose mothers could not care for them in the home. These institutions were frequently in the hands of religious orders. To some extent these generalizations still hold. However, as developments in medical science, psychology, and education led to better understanding of the nature and needs of the young child (*see* CHILD PSYCHOLOGY), there was increasing concern for making provision for the optimum development of young children in all aspects of their growth—physical health, emotional security, social and intellectual development.

In 1767 Johann Friedrich Oberlin, an Alsatian Lutheran pastor, opened in his parish, Waldersbach, in the upper valley of the Bruche River (the Steintal or Ban de la Roche), the first day nursery in the Western world for young children whose mothers worked in the fields. The writings and life work of Friedrich Froebel (*q.v.*) focused attention on the possibilities of educating children before the age of seven. In 1837 he opened the first kindergarten and demonstrated that children could learn through play and without formal instruction. Since Froebel's day other edu-

cators (*e.g.,* Maria Montessori in Italy, Ovide Decroly in Belgium, Margaret McMillan in Great Britain, Harriet Johnson in the United States) have viewed the preschool years as a period of great educational possibilities. In the 20th century the preschool program came to be viewed increasingly as a desirable supplement to the home—as an agency that can give effective support to parents in the rearing of children as well as offer to the children themselves appropriate experiences that will contribute to harmonious growth and to a healthy, joyous, and intellectually stimulating existence.

Great Britain.—In 1816 Robert Owen, a cotton mill owner in Scotland, founded a "preparatory school for infants" (age range of the pupils was from one to six years) where children were not to be given formal lessons but were permitted to play. His aim was "to prevent children from acquiring bad habits, to give them good ones, and to form their dispositions to mutual kindness." The idealism of Robert Owen and the enthusiasm of others in the years following resulted in the founding of many of these infant schools throughout the country and had an influence on the movement toward infant schools and day nurseries on the continent and in the United States. In time (1870) the infant schools became an integral part of the state system of education in Great Britain, the age of five being adopted as the age of entry to infant school and the age of three fixed as the minimum age at which children in attendance could count for a government grant.

As the years passed the infant schools lost their "nursery" character and developed more and more a scholastic tradition in which little provision was made for physical activity, sleep, and play. Children of three, four, and five years were required to sit still in rows in large galleries—with arms folded and without conversing with one another—reciting lessons in which pictures and museum specimens took the place of living plants and animals and spending hours on the "three R's" and on needlework. Outside the official system, experiments in childhood education were being tried, notably the introduction of the views and methods of Froebel in the setting up of kindergartens for fee-paying pupils and the institution of schemes for the training of kindergarten teachers. The realization came generally that enlightened and psychologically sound methods of early childhood education ought to be used with all children irrespective of parents' ability to pay fees, and out of this realization developed the British nursery schools. After 1918 such schools were a recognized part of the national school system with standards for nursery schools defined by law.

Miss McMillan and Grace Owen were pioneers in the movement to improve the health of young children and to provide a suitable environment for their growing minds. Both these leaders saw the nursery school as an extension of home life and as an institution which could improve through education the standard of home care of children. They further maintained that a nursery school is not a place for formal education but rather a community nursery where children up to the ages of five or six years may have appropriate opportunities for physical, mental, and social growth through playing in small groups under the supervision of qualified teachers. Miss McMillan outlined a plan for a three-year course for training teachers for these schools, maintaining that only trained personnel should work with children of these ages. Training centres at Manchester (under Miss Owen), at London (under Lillian DeLissa), and at Deptford (under Miss McMillan) supplied nursery teachers for the entire Commonwealth as well as for the early nursery schools in the United States. The older infant-school system was modified in the light of principles underlying the nursery school experiments, for the nursery school movement in England was from the first both vigorous and articulate. (*See also* DAY NURSERY.)

Continental Countries.—By 1779 Oberlin had founded a number of schools for young children, which he called *écoles à tricoter* (knitting schools). These were philanthropic in purpose, with religious and moral training constituting their chief objectives. Crèches and *salles d'asile* were also being established about this time in the cities, more with the aim of protecting children from the dangers of the streets than of educating them. The *salles d'asile* changed from private to state-supported institutions in 1833 when they were made part of the national educational system. These establishments henceforth carried the designation of *écoles maternelles*. The objective of these schools is to work toward well-rounded development of the young child, without fatigue, restraint, or force.

In Italy around 1835 a Catholic priest, Abate Ferrante Aporti, working to establish elementary schools became dissatisfied with the progress made by the children and was led to investigate the conditions under which their preschool years had been passed. As a result he drew up a plan for the establishment of an infant school in which moral habits, intellectual cultivation, and physical faculties were all to be emphasized. Early in the 20th century Maria Montessori (*q.v.*) began her experiments with children three to six years of age. She was a physician who first became interested in the educational problems of mentally defective children, but soon also became impressed with the learning potentialities of the normal preschool age child. Her first *casa dei bambini* was established in connection with a tenement-improvement project in Rome. In this school the children were given special educational apparatus (*see* MONTESSORI SYSTEM). Self-education was the keynote of the plan; a large measure of individual initiative and self-direction characterizing the Montessori philosophy, the teacher would withdraw to the background and merely supervise the use of the apparatus, or "didactic material." This material was not designed to encourage children to play together. What opportunity there was for group activity occurred in connection with the housekeeping activities which the children shared: *i.e.*, keeping the rooms in order, serving the meals, etc. In 1928 Dr. Montessori was invited by the Italian government to institute a six-month training course in the use of her method for religious and lay teachers. In the latter years of her life she traveled extensively in Europe and Asia, and her ideas regarding the education of children under six had an important influence on the development of pre-elementary education in many parts of the world.

The United States.—Beginning around 1920 in the United States, nursery schools developed as the outcome of interest that may be traced to a variety of sources: (1) a scientific interest in early childhood, resulting from new applications in the fields of psychology and medicine; (2) a rapidly expanding background of educational theory; (3) experimental efforts in the fields of psychiatry, child guidance, and parent education; and (4) the efforts of individuals and agencies to improve the educational programs of day nurseries already established for the care of children of working mothers. Because the nursery-school movement sprang from such a variety of social forces, no one type of school may be singled out and described as representative of the movement.

Interest in systematic research into the abilities and development of young children increased rapidly after 1920 and a number of nursery schools were organized in universities to provide laboratories for the study of normal young children. Children two to six years of age were enrolled to furnish subjects for research, but soon it was recognized that such laboratories had an obligation to provide an educational program for the children enrolled and to demonstrate what good educational programs for preschool children entailed. Nursery schools were also established as laboratories in which high school and college girl students could study child care and development in preparation for their future roles as mothers. As more nursery schools were founded, colleges also instituted programs for the training of teachers. Prior to 1935 some nursery schools were also set up in conjunction with guidance clinics (as a parent-education effort) and in hospitals as an effort to encourage the recovery of the convalescent child.

Widespread unemployment and economic distress in the early 1930s resulted in the authorization, by the Federal Emergency Relief Administration, of nursery schools to provide jobs for unemployed teachers, nurses, and affiliated workers and to promote better morale among parents through fostering the physical and social well-being of their children. These nursery schools, under the control of the public-school system, were for the most part housed in public-school buildings and served to draw the attention of the general public to the desirability of school services for children below school age.

During World War II federal legislation (1942) made funds available to provide facilities for the day care of the many children whose mothers were employed in industries necessary for war production. Supervision of these child-care projects was under local or state departments of education or welfare. When the war was over, federal funds began to be withdrawn from these projects and by mid-1946 all federal support had been withdrawn.

In the years after the war there was steadily growing concern for the need for day care services as the working mother continued to be more and more a part of the urban-industrial scene. Many centres were operated as commercial ventures, and many more were supported by social welfare and local community agencies. Cooperative nurseries, established and maintained with professional staffs by groups of parents for their children, increased markedly in number. In many communities churches established nurseries, *i.e.*, weekday preschool programs, some offering religious instruction to the children enrolled, others without emphasis on religious training and enrolling children from differing religious backgrounds. Especially in metropolitan areas, specialized programs, often relying heavily on voluntary contributions, were organized to offer group experiences to preschool children who are mentally retarded, physically handicapped, blind, deaf, or emotionally disturbed. Teachers in such programs may be specially trained to give appropriate therapy to the children in addition to giving them a satisfying experience with peers and adults beyond the family circle. In many instances such schools are also centres for research in the educational problems of the handicapped. Finally, in 1962, federal child welfare services were expanded to provide for day care for children of working mothers, on a limited basis.

DEVELOPMENTS AND TRENDS

The preschool programs discussed above, while they emerged primarily in response to the needs for day care, emphasize opportunities for physical, emotional, and intellectual growth consonant with each child's capacity. In the 1960s there was an upsurge of interest in young children's cognitive development. This interest was evidenced by the amount of research undertaken and the number of new experimental programs reported in the literature. Common to these experimental programs was a focus on a more highly structured, cognitive-task-oriented approach to learning. Psychologists and educators increasingly reflected upon the developmental psychology of Jean Piaget, with its focus upon cognitive development, and explored its implications for educational application. A related phenomenon was a revival of interest in the Montessori method and materials.

A major development in pre-elementary education in the U.S. was the inauguration in 1965 of Project Head Start, a preschool program for economically and culturally disadvantaged children, as a part of the country's War on Poverty. Funds were allotted through the federal Office of Economic Opportunity and, beginning in the summer of 1965 and in many communities continuing in year-round programs, provisions were made for teacher-training and for medical and dental services, psychological services, and social services. These efforts emphasized educational programs designed to supplement and enrich children's experimental backgrounds and the involvement of their parents and local community members in further development and support of the projects. Head Start was intended to give preschool children the beginnings of an understanding of basic concepts prior to entering school. In 1967 two additional programs were instituted on a limited experimental basis: Follow Through programs designed to extend the enriched experiences of the Head Start children into the kindergarten or first grade; and Parent and Child Centers to provide services for disadvantaged families with one or more children under the age of three.

Services to young children and their families in Great Britain and Europe appear to be more highly institutionalized than in the

U.S. For principal programs in Great Britain *see* DAY NURSERY. In many countries day care facilities are associated with the mother's place of work. In Czechoslovakia, Poland, and France the crèche or infant nursery for children between three months and three years of age is quite common. Hungary, which began day nurseries in 1936, now has 3,000 centres. In the Soviet-bloc countries, *e.g.*, Hungary and the U.S.S.R., education of the young child has been reported as rigid and doctrinaire with emphasis on rules and conformity. Since 1965 the reported trend in Hungary has been toward greater freedom for children aged three to six years. Children are now encouraged to do things for themselves and they are no longer compelled to sing, to play with certain toys, or to participate in group projects. Children are considered as individuals with different capabilities, responses, and problems. Soviet educators appear to be reversing policy by now giving the home a greater role in educating their young children. Children attending nursery school and kindergarten are increasingly being offered reading and mathematics instruction (children in the U.S.S.R. begin first grade at seven).

PRINCIPLES AND GUIDELINES

The nursery school has long been viewed as an extension upward or outward of the home and family rather than an extension downward of the elementary school. These schools exist not to substitute for the home but to supplement it. Essential to any meaningful nursery school experience for a child is the quality of relationship and sharing between home and school, parents and teacher.

The program of a nursery school is based on child development principles and understanding of the teaching-learning process. It has also been based on the belief that young children learn best from firsthand, concrete experiences with people, things, events, and processes. The program is therefore focused on direct experiences for the child with his peers, adults, creative materials, science and nature, music and dance. Increasing emphasis is being placed on helping children learn how to learn.

The teachers of young children are challenged to provide an environment which supports the individual child's needs, interests, and capabilities and at the same time offers him various opportunities to share in common interests. They must know how to provide a setting appropriate to the physical, social, emotional, and intellectual skills of the children and must take into account changes in behaviour and increasing skills, fluctuations in independence and dependence, confusion between fantasy and fact. They must be sensitive to children's verbal facades and their tendency to use the teacher as their primary and most efficient source of information. Their skills in assessing the children's understanding of words and concepts and their ability to encourage divergent thinking and problem solving can contribute significantly to the children's cognitive growth and attitudes toward learning.

In essence, schools for young children offer learning experiences for children, their families, and their teachers, as well as those who observe them. It is important that younger children have opportunities to explore and experiment in the worlds in which they live not only through self-initiated activities but also with adults. Their abilities to cope with an ever-changing world and their feelings of self-worth can be enhanced by teachers who are understanding and consistent in their expectations, realistic and sincere in their praise for effort as well as achievement, and skillful in sharing their insights and knowledge of growth and development with other adults significant to the child.

Common problems relating to pre-elementary education exist throughout the world. There continues to be a shortage of trained teachers along with a lack of agreement as to what constitutes adequate education and training for effective teachers. Financial support for day care centres and nursery schools for all children under compulsory school age is not yet available; licensing and supervision of centres and schools by informed responsible agencies do not yet apply to all existing units. While in some places physical facilities and adequate outdoor play area for nursery schools continue to leave much to be desired, architects and planners are increasingly interested in creative designing of buildings, playgrounds, and equipment.

The problems associated with assessing the influence of nursery school attendance on increased intellectual productivity, improved school readiness, effect on later school grades, changes in parental child-rearing practices, and so forth, are well-documented. It appears that involvement of parents in nursery school programs, directly or indirectly, may provide an influence that is not easily measured. *See* also EDUCATION, HISTORY OF.

BIBLIOGRAPHY.—Maria Montessori, *The Montessori Method* (1912); Susan Isaacs, *The Children We Teach* (1932); Harriet Johnson, *Children in the Nursery School* (1928); Ruth Updegraff *et al.*, *Practice in Preschool Education* (1938); Louise Woodcock, *Life and Ways of the Two-Year-Old* (1941); Millie Almy *et al.*, *Young Children's Thinking* (1966); Katherine Read, *The Nursery School: a Human Relationships Laboratory*, 4th ed. (1966); F. Hechinger, *Pre-school Education Today* (1966); Anne Schulum, *Absorbed in Living, Children Learn* (1967); A. Kadushin, *Child Welfare Services* (1967); United Nations Educational, Scientific and Cultural Organization, *Mental Hygiene in the Nursery School* (1953).
See also other publications of UNESCO, *e.g.*, *International Yearbook of Education* (annual); World Organization for Early Childhood Education, Reports of Conferences; and publications of National Association for Education of Young Children. (D. HT.)

PREESTABLISHED HARMONY, in the philosophy of Leibniz, constitutes the explanation of the coordination of change in substances which are not causally related.

Leibniz asserts for logical reasons that the universe consists of monads, indivisible substances which develop in time. Every characteristic of a monad (the events which happen to it being included among characteristics) is deducible from its own nature. There is thus no causal link between different monads. They are "windowless." Nevertheless everything happens as if by mutual influence, and Leibniz accounts for this by postulating that God created the monads in such a way that each represents the universe from its own point of view. The changes in them are thus necessarily coordinated.

The preestablished harmony was most highly valued by Leibniz as affording a solution to the mind-body problem posed by Cartesianism. Descartes's insistence on the complete qualitative difference between mind and body, together with his account of causation, made interaction impossible, although Descartes himself did not appreciate this. His followers, who were acutely aware of the difficulty, introduced the theory of occasionalism, by which the appearance of interaction is explained by the intervention of God on appropriate occasions. For Leibniz the mind is one monad and the body, a group of monads, so that the two are not completely disparate; but his theory of substance precluded him from allowing causal connection, and he substituted for the recurrent miracle of the occasionalists the single creative act of God by which harmony between monads is once and for all established.

See LEIBNIZ, GOTTFRIED WILHELM.   (M. KE.)

PREFECT (*PRAEFECTUS*), a title given in ancient Rome to an officer appointed by a magistrate as his deputy or subordinate.

1. A prefect of the city (*praefectus urbi*) was in the early republic appointed by the consuls when both were to be absent from Rome. When in 367 B.C. a praetor was instituted he took charge of the city in the consuls' absence, and a prefect of the city was henceforth appointed only for the annual Latin festival, when all the higher magistrates left Rome for a few days. The emperor Augustus revived the office in a new form, appointing a prefect of the city in 26 B.C. and again in 16 B.C. when he left Rome, although there were still a consul or consuls and praetors in the city. Toward the end of his reign, when owing to old age he took little part in public affairs, the office became permanent, even when he was himself in Rome, and it so continued under Augustus' successors. The post was given, normally for life, to a very senior senator. The prefect commanded the urban cohorts and was responsible for the maintenance of law and order in the city. He acquired a police jurisdiction, which developed into a full criminal jurisdiction, extending to the hundredth milestone from the city. Under the later empire the prefect became responsible for the entire government of Rome. The post was normally assigned to members of the great aristocratic families, and was held for a

brief term only (about a year). It ranked very high in official precedence, immediately below the praetorian prefects. In A.D. 359 a similar prefecture of the city was instituted for Constantinople.

2. Two praetorian prefects (*praefectus praetorio*) were appointed by Augustus in 2 B.C. to command the praetorian guard. The post was thereafter usually assigned to a single man, sometimes shared between two; the holders were almost invariably of equestrian rank. The praetorian prefect, being responsible for the safety of the emperor, rapidly acquired great power, and his office became the summit of the equestrian career. Many were virtually prime ministers to the emperor, and some ruled the empire in the name of a weak emperor. Two, Marcus Opellius Macrinus (*q.v.*) and Marcus Julius Philippus (*see* PHILIP the Arabian), seized the throne for themselves. The functions of the office were ill-defined. Praetorian prefects occasionally were given the command of armies; Cornelius Fuscus, for instance, was commander of the Roman forces in Domitian's Dacian War. They also acquired important judicial functions as delegates of the emperor; in the Severan period several eminent lawyers—Papinian, Ulpian, Paulus—held the office. In the late 3rd century, the praetorian prefect also acquired functions of a financial character; for as the money revenue dwindled owing to the inflation of the currency, and requisitions in kind were used to supply the court, army, and civil service, it was the praetorian prefects who as quartermasters general to the emperor directed and organized these requisitions.

Under Diocletian each emperor had his praetorian prefect, who combined military, judicial, financial, and general administrative functions. He was a chief of staff and adjutant general, controlling the discipline and recruitment of the armies, and often assuming the supreme command. He was, next to the emperor himself, the supreme judge, receiving appeals from the courts of provincial governors; his sentences were declared by Constantine to be inappellable. He organized the indiction (*q.v.*), the taxation in kind which supplied the bulk of the empire's needs. Through his deputies (*vicarii*) he controlled the provincial governors. Constantine by the creation of the *magistri militum* deprived the praetorian prefects of their military powers, but they retained their judicial and financial functions and remained the highest officers of the empire. The three sons of Constantine had each a prefect but when Constans conquered Constantine II he kept two prefects, and when Constantius II reunited the empire he retained three prefects or sometimes four. From 395 four territorial prefectures became stabilized: of the Gauls (Britain, Gaul, the Seven Provinces, and Spain); of Italy (Pannonia, Italy, the city of Rome, and Africa); of Illyricum (Dacia and Macedonia); and of the East (Thrace, Asiana, Pontica, Oriens, and Egypt). When Justinian reconquered Africa he created a separate praetorian prefecture for it.

3. An equestrian prefect of the corn supply of Rome (*praefectus annonae*) was appointed by Augustus toward the end of his reign. The office continued into the later empire, when Constantinople also acquired its *praefectus annonae*.

4. An equestrian prefect of the fire brigade and night watch of Rome (*praefectus vigilum*) was appointed by Augustus in A.D. 6. This office also survived in the later empire, and was transplanted to Constantinople.

5. Equestrian *praefecti vehiculorum* were instituted, probably by Hadrian, to manage the public post in Italy and the provinces.

6. When Augustus annexed Egypt, he did not put it under a governor of senatorial rank, since he feared to place a possible rival in control of a province so rich, so militarily impregnable, and so vital for the corn supply of Rome, but appointed an equestrian prefect (*praefectus Aegypti*) with the powers of a proconsul; he commanded three legions. Under Diocletian's reorganization the prefect of Egypt became merely civil governor of one of the three provinces into which Egypt was divided, but under Valens, when Egypt became a separate diocese, the title of *praefectus Augustalis* was given to its civil administrator.

7. Augustus appointed equestrian prefects to govern small but turbulent areas, such as the Alpine districts, Raetia or Corsica.

The title was replaced by that of procurator under Claudius. Septimius Severus placed Mesopotamia with its two legions under an equestrian prefect.

8. Under the republic judicial prefects (*praefecti juri dicundo*) were appointed by the urban praetor to administer justice in the towns of the Roman territory. Four of these (*praefecti Capuam Cumas*) were by exception elected by the assembly from 211 B.C.

9. Consuls and praetors (and proconsuls and propraetors) appointed an equestrian *praefectus fabrum*, originally a chief engineer, later a chief of staff. They also appointed *praefecti* to command allied contingents and fleets. Under the principate the equestrian commanders of auxiliary cavalry units were styled prefects (*praefectus alae*), as were the commanders of the fleets (*praefectus classis*). Each legionary camp had a quartermaster styled *praefectus castrorum*, usually a former centurion. In Egypt the legions were commanded by equestrian *praefecti* instead of senatorial *legati*, as were the Mesopotamian legions under Severus. From the reign of Gallienus, when senators were generally excluded from military commands, prefect became the normal title of legionary commanders.

10. Various senatorial commissioners instituted by Augustus bore the title of prefect. Such were the two *praefecti aerarii Saturni*, who managed the treasury from 28 to 23 B.C. and again from A.D. 58; the three *praefecti aerarii militaris*, who managed the military treasury established in A.D. 6; and the *praefecti frumenti dandi*, responsible for the distribution of the corn dole in Rome. From the time of Trajan or Hadrian there were also *praefecti alimentorum*, who managed the funds for the maintenance of children in the various regions of Italy.

On the praetorian prefect *see* L. L. Howe, *The Praetorian Prefect from Commodus to Diocletian* (1942); J. R. Palanque, *Essai sur le préfecture du prétoire du Bas-Empire* (1933). On the prefecture of the city of Rome in the later empire, *see* A. Chastagnol, *La préfecture urbaine à Rome sous le Bas-Empire* (1960). (A. H. M. J.)

PREFECT (FRENCH). A prefect (*préfet*) in France is a high government official. A similar official (*praefectus*) existed under the Roman Empire, and in France a comparable official (*intendant*) existed under the *ancien régime*. The French prefectoral corps was created in 1800 by Napoleon, who raised it to a position of great prestige and influence. The prefects were the administrators of the *départements;* they were responsible for public order, for good government, and for ensuring that the central government's policy was effectively carried out throughout the country. Napoleon called them *empereurs à petit pied.*

Under succeeding regimes the power of the corps increased but its prestige declined. Dependent for office on the whim of the government, the prefects became primarily concerned with police and elections, and one of their principal functions was to ensure the government a safe parliamentary majority. They reached the height of their power under the Second Empire. During the first decades of the Third Republic the prefects' position was weakened by the frequent nomination of new men by successive governments. However, prefects then became increasingly concerned with social and economic problems, and after World War II, while retaining responsibility for public order and good government, they became the dynamic element in the provinces for promoting and coordinating social policies.

In addition to the prefects, each of whom was responsible for a *département*, the prefectoral corps in the 1960s consisted of secretaries-general, who were second in command; subprefects, who were responsible for the *arrondissements;* and *chefs de cabinet*, who were the prefects' personal assistants. Under the 1958 constitution (art. 13) prefects were appointed by the president of the republic with the approval of the council of ministers and on the recommendation of the minister of the interior, to whom they were responsible. They could be dismissed at any time without cause or notice, but in the second half of the 20th century they enjoyed in fact considerable security of tenure. Sweeping changes were likely only when there was a major change of political direction or regime.

Conditions of service in the corps were laid down in a special statute of June 19, 1950. A prefect has a wide variety of powers accrued haphazardly over the years; according to one estimate there are as many as 4,000 separate sources of his legal authority. The prefect is constitutionally responsible for "coordinating the activities of state officials, the representation of national interests, and the administrative supervision of local authorities." He is the sole legal representative of the government and the state in the *département;* when a minister delegates his powers, he is required by law to delegate them to the prefect and not directly to his own officials in the field. The prefect, therefore, acts as the agent through which all powers are transmitted from the centre to the periphery.

The prefect is the general administrator of the *département,* the chief executive officer of the elected departmental authority (the *conseil général*), the principal police authority, and the supervisor of the communes in the *département.* His approval is required for many administrative acts of local authorities.

In Paris the prefect of the *département* of the Seine also exercises the municipal powers normally possessed by the mayor of a commune, there being no popularly elected mayor of Paris. There is, in addition, a special prefect of police whose jurisdiction covers the whole Paris conurbation.   (B. CN.)

PREGL, FRITZ (1869–1930), Austrian chemist who received the 1923 Nobel Prize in Chemistry for his work on the microanalysis of organic substances, was born in Laibach on Sept. 3, 1869, and was graduated from the *Gymnasium* in that city. He received his M.D. degree from the University of Graz in 1894. After teaching in the Physiological institute at Graz for several years, he went to Leipzig in 1904, where he studied methods of physical chemistry with Wilhelm Ostwald and then went to Berlin where he worked with E. Abderhalden. He returned to Graz in 1904 as professor of physiological chemistry at the Medico-Chemical Institute. During the year that followed he investigated the components of albuminous bodies and the analysis of bile acids. From 1910 to 1913 he was professor at the University of Innsbruck, returning to Graz in 1913 as director of the Medico-Chemical Institute.

Lack of material in Pregl's work with bile acids had impelled him to look for methods requiring smaller amounts when making quantitative analyses of elements in compounds. By 1912 he was able to make measurements of carbon, hydrogen, nitrogen, sulfur and halogen, using only 5 mg.–13 mg. of starting material with results as accurate as those obtained by existing methods. Later he perfected his techniques so that as little as 3 mg.–5 mg. were adequate for measurements at least as exact as the results of macroanalysis. The development of chemical microanalysis (*see* CHEMISTRY: *Microanalysis*) marked a great advance in organic elementary analysis. In addition to the general factor of economy, it became indispensable in many research problems of pure science, physiology, medicine, and industry. Pregl also contributed a number of micromethods for measuring atomic groups and a sensitive microbalance. In 1917 he published *Die quantitative organische Mikroanalyse* (6th ed., 1949), a monograph. Pregl also perfected the Abderhalden dialysis test for the presence of enzyme, so that less serum was needed for a reaction; invented a simple method for determining the functional capacities of the kidneys; and added to medicine an iodine solution, named for him, which is a mild but effective antiseptic. He died at Graz on Dec. 13, 1930.

PREGNANCY. Life has its beginning in the egg cell or ovum. These minute cells, which measure about $\frac{1}{120}$ in. (0.2 mm.) in diameter, are contained in the two ovaries, which lie in the abdomen, one on either side of the uterus (womb). During healthy reproductive life one ovum is shed each month from one or the other ovary (ovulation) about the middle (12th–14th day) of a menstrual cycle. Average cycles—measured from the first day of one period to the first day of the next—occupy 28 days and in health are regular within a day or two. For each day that the period is prolonged beyond the average 28 days, ovulation is delayed for one day, so that if the cycle is 32 days, the ovulation will be between the 16th and 18th days. Expressed in other words, ovulation tends to occur about 14 days before the next period regardless of the interval between the periods. After being shed the ovum enters the Fallopian tube, along which it

passes to the uterus. If it is not fertilized it succumbs quickly. Since the sperm cells also have a short maximum life-span (two–four days), though somewhat longer than that of the ovum, it thus follows that there is only a short critical interval in the cycle during which fertilization is possible; on either side of this critical period is an interval when intercourse is unlikely to be fertile (the so-called safe period). If the ovum is not fertilized it escapes in the next monthly loss of blood. If it is fertilized by a sperm cell (spermatozoon), pregnancy has begun.

Reproductive Physiology.—A brief summary of some matters of reproductive physiology is essential for an understanding of the complex changes which occur during pregnancy. The first factor is the pituitary gland (*q.v.*), the front part of which (the anterior pituitary) plays a dominant role in the initiation and maintenance of the rhythmic functions of the sexual glands and breasts in the female and of the sex glands in the male. It is also concerned with the functioning of the thyroid and adrenal glands. Specific hormones of the anterior pituitary are responsible for the periodic functioning of the ovary and the rhythmic shedding of ova. The pituitary energizes the ovary to produce hormones (estrogen and progesterone) which prepare the uterine bed for the reception of the ovum should fertilization occur, preparations which in the nature of things are only relatively rarely required.

During reproductive life the ovaries shed between them from 300 to 400 ova. The ovary through its hormones controls the imbedding of the fertilized ovum in the uterine wall, and this control continues for about 12 weeks, after which it is taken over by the placenta (*q.v.*), the organ through which the embryo draws its nourishment from the maternal blood. Its vessels ramify freely around the uterine vessels in the placenta, where there is a constant diffusion of nutritive elements from maternal to fetal blood and of waste products in the opposite direction. The fetal blood passes to the placenta along the two arteries in the umbilical cord and, after it has been replenished and purified, it passes to the fetus via the umbilical vein. In addition to these combined nutritional and excretory functions the placenta takes over the hormonal functions which are in large part abdicated by the pituitary and ovaries.

A special anterior pituitary hormone (prolactin) acts on the breasts and stimulates the production of milk. Prolactin is produced in large amounts after labour, and its production continues as long as the infant is suckled. The hormonal mechanism by which the active secretion of milk from the breast is delayed till after labour is not well understood. There is some reason for the view that so long as the hormones of the placenta (estrogen and progesterone) are circulating in the blood the lactogenic influence of prolactin is inhibited and that this inhibition is not removed until the placental hormones are excreted in the days following labour. (*See* also HORMONES: *Ovarian and Placental Hormones.*)

Among the other physiological changes that are evoked by pregnancy one of the most important is an increase in weight. On the average a pregnant woman gains 24 to 28 lb. (10.9 to 12.5 kg.) but there are wide differences; some women enjoying apparent health may gain much less, others much more. The organs of reproduction—the uterus and its contents and the breasts—contribute an average of 11 lb. (5 kg.) to the total increase in weight. Under normal conditions the weight increase in pregnancy is quickly lost after labour, but in some instances this does not occur, and many women retain their weight gain and may even acquire active obesity dating from childbirth.

A considerable part of the normal weight gain of pregnancy is due to the retention in the body of water which is required for the increase in the total volume of the circulating blood; by the 36th week of pregnancy the total amount of blood in the heart and the blood vessels is increased by about 30% over that in the nonpregnant state. The greater part of this increase is used up in filling the greatly expanded arteries and veins of the womb. The solid elements of the blood—the red blood corpuscles carrying the hemoglobin—are also increased, but not to the same degree. While the fluid part of the blood (the plasma) is increased by

40%, the red blood cells are increased by only about 15%; the result is the so-called physiological anemia of pregnancy.

Duration of Pregnancy.—There is a small but appreciable elevation of the body temperature at the time of ovulation, and this, by pinpointing the date of ovulation, has provided a method of determining the interval between ovulation and childbirth. Usually this lies between 266 and 270 days, with extremes of 250 and 285 days. The usual method for determining the date of childbirth is to add seven days to the first day of the last menstrual period and count forward nine calendar months. Thus, if the last period began on March 10, the estimated date of childbirth is Dec. 17. This gives a figure of roughly 280 days or ten lunar months. As ovulation occurs about the 14th day of the cycle, it follows that this estimate is in reality about 14 days longer than the true average duration of pregnancy as estimated by the temperature method.

Not infrequently the law courts are required to pronounce on the legitimacy of a child born after an interval that is greatly in excess of the average figure or, on the other hand, that is much shorter than this figure. Some countries recognize upper and lower limits.

Diagnosis of Pregnancy.—A woman normally recognizes that she is pregnant by the cessation of menstruation (amenorrhea; *see* MENSTRUATION), and within a short time this is confirmed by the increasing swelling of the abdomen. But menstruation may cease and the abdomen increase in size apart from pregnancy, and the doctor often has to adopt other criteria for his diagnosis.

There are, indeed, only three unmistakable signs of pregnancy. The first is the hearing of the fetal heartbeat, which is audible beginning about the 16th to 18th week of pregnancy. It is heard by placing a stethoscope on the lower abdomen; the sound resembles in quality the ticking of a watch beneath a pillow. At the sixth month its rate is 150–160 per minute, while at the end of pregnancy it is 120–140. The second positive sign, the demonstration of the fetal skeleton by X-ray examination, is possible by the 16th week, when the fetal bones are visible, but such an examination is rarely required and should not be routinely used. The third positive sign is the recognition of the kicking movements of the fetus, usually noticeable by the 18th to the 20th week. By this time the woman often feels the movements herself; this is the so-called "quickening" that reveals to the mother that her pregnancy has reached its halfway stage.

There are several probable signs and symptoms of pregnancy. Amenorrhea, however, can occur apart from pregnancy in anemia, chronic infections such as tuberculosis, or after mental shocks; *e.g.,* the mental shock associated with the death of a relative, or the anxiety of a woman who has exposed herself to the risk of pregnancy. There is a reverse of this latter condition in false pregnancy (pseudocyesis), when a childless woman with a fervent desire for motherhood develops, though she is not pregnant, the signs and symptoms of pregnancy, such as amenorrhea and increasing size of the abdomen; at the end of the term, she may actually go into "labour."

Nausea, with or without vomiting and usually more evident in the morning ("morning sickness"), is a common symptom. It generally occurs between the 6th and 12th week of pregnancy. In some women it is such a constant feature in pregnancy that they regard it as a sure sign of their state. The sickness is sometimes associated with the development of an acute dislike of some ordinary article of food. (An unusual craving for certain foods may occur in the latter part of pregnancy.) Morning sickness in some cases may be severe enough to require hospital treatment.

A sense of fullness in the abdomen is often felt from the early weeks, and by the end of the third month the uterus can be felt where it rises from the pelvis. It reaches the level of the navel about the fifth lunar month. In the last weeks there is commonly a sinking down of the womb when the woman may feel more comfortable from relief of pressure ("lightening").

Enlargement and tenderness of the breasts are especially evident in women pregnant for the first time (primigravidae). In women who have had a previous pregnancy these changes are

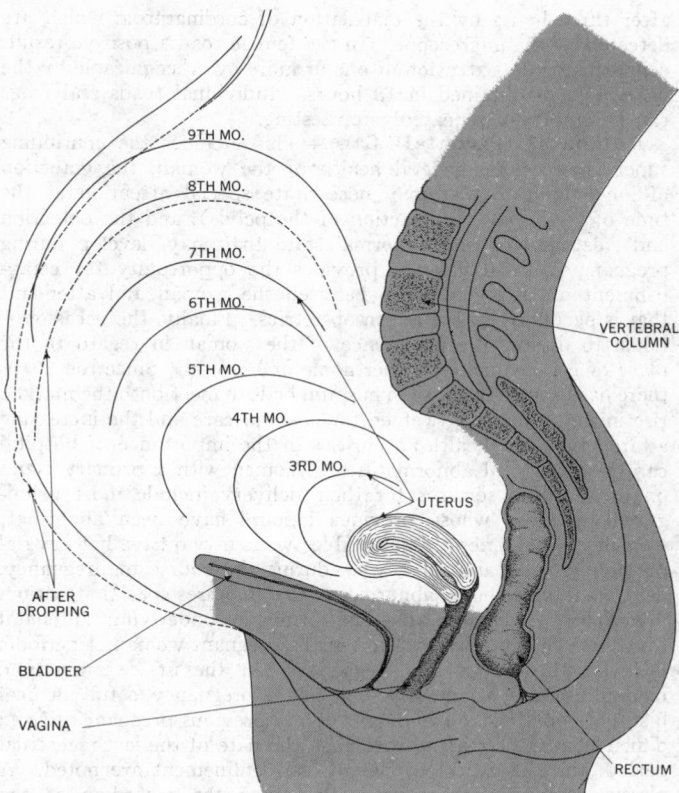

9TH MO.
8TH MO.
7TH MO.
6TH MO.
5TH MO.
4TH MO.
3RD MO.
AFTER DROPPING
BLADDER
VAGINA
VERTEBRAL COLUMN
UTERUS
RECTUM

"DORLAND'S ILLUSTRATED MEDICAL DICTIONARY," 23RD EDITION, PHILADELPHIA, W. B. SAUNDERS COMPANY

UTERINE LEVELS DURING PREGNANCY

often less evident, though in the second half of pregnancy there is in most women a marked dilatation of the superficial veins and there is fluid in the breast which can be easily expressed from the nipple. In many women, especially brunettes, there is a dark pigmentation of the area around the nipple, which deepens with the advance of pregnancy. Pigmentary changes in other parts of the skin are sometimes found; *e.g.,* the abdomen, where there is often a dark streak (linea nigra) extending from the pubic hair upward as far as and, sometimes, beyond the navel, while some women develop areas of pigmentation on the face, especially the forehead. This pigmentation is believed to be due to stimulation of the pigment cells by secretions of the anterior pituitary.

As the result of stretching of the abdominal walls there are often formed the striae gravidarum (pinkish or purple streaks) where the superficial and less active layer of the skin has failed to keep pace with the generalized stretching of the abdominal wall. The streaks mark where the deeper and more vascular areas are thus exposed.

Further evidence for the diagnosis of pregnancy is gained by internal examination, by which the physician can find enlargement of the uterus as early as the eighth or tenth week.

Biochemical tests for pregnancy depend upon the fact that chorionic gonadotropin or HCG, one of the hormones produced by the placenta, is excreted in the urine of the pregnant woman. When a small quantity of urine containing HCG is injected under the skin of female mice it produces characteristic changes in the ovaries of the animals. Young virgin mice so treated are killed at the end of 100 hours and the test is positive if characteristic "blood points" are present in the ovaries. The method, called after its inventors the Aschheim-Zondek test, is accurate in 98% of cases and may reveal a pregnancy that has advanced only four days beyond the first period missed. At such an early stage, however, the output of hormone may be small and it is better to wait for a further two or three weeks before having recourse to the test.

Toads or frogs are also commonly used in pregnancy testing. In a male frog the injection of urine containing HCG is followed after three hours by the ejaculation of spermatozoa, which are detected by the microscope. In the female toad a positive result, consisting of the extrusion of one or more ova recognizable by the naked eye, is obtained in 18 hours. Individual toads and frogs can be employed repeatedly for testing.

Antenatal (Prenatal) Care.—This includes the continuing supervision of the general health of the woman, the detection of any condition that may necessitate special attention at the time of birth (*e.g.*, contraction of the pelvis), and the detection and treatment of any abnormal state that may develop during pregnancy. In addition it provides the opportunity for establishment of that confidence between the woman and attendant that is peculiarly important in obstetrics. Finally, the occasion is taken to discuss the preference of the woman in regard to the place of confinement, whether home or hospital. Since the 1930s there has been an increase in hospital beds to meet both the marked rise in the demand by women for hospital care and the increasing awareness of the health authorities of the importance of hospital care in obstetrical abnormalities. Women with a primary claim on the hospital services for their delivery include most primigravidae; those whose previous labours have been abnormal; women whose homes are unsuitable; women who have had several previous births; and those who, during the course of pregnancy, develop an unexpected abnormality that requires special attention.

Periodic Examinations.—The principle underlying antenatal care is the medical examination of the pregnant woman at periodic intervals throughout her pregnancy. At the first examination, made preferably at an early stage of the pregnancy, a full medical history is obtained. The details of any previous pregnancies (*e.g.*, difficulty at the birth and toxemia), the date of the last menstrual period, and the expected date of the confinement are noted. A physical examination is made, including the recording of the weight and blood pressure. The urine is examined for abnormal constituents, especially albumin and sugar. The heart and lungs are examined and a sample of blood is removed from a vein to be tested for anemia, for syphilis (Wassermann test), and for the Rhesus and ABO grouping (*see* below). The next examinations are generally made at four-week intervals up to the 30th week, at three-week intervals to the 36th week, and weekly from then onward. At each of the later examinations the weight, blood pressure, and state of the urine are recorded, and the abdomen is palpated to determine that the position of the fetus in the womb is correct, for at this stage a faulty position often can be rectified. Excessive enlargement of the abdomen may indicate twins, which will demand special care at the delivery; or there may be excessive fluid in the womb (hydramnios). At the 34th week an estimate of the pelvic shape and size is made with special reference to the discovery of any contraction that may require special care at birth or, in a severe abnormality, Caesarean section (*q.v.*).

Nutrition in Pregnancy.—The diet of a pregnant woman should contain 2,400–2,500 calories (*i.e.*, 400–500 more calories than are in the diet in the nonpregnant state) and that of the nursing mother should contain 3,000 calories. In general a woman who is ordinarily accustomed to a well-balanced diet will not require adding more to this regimen than is dictated by the normal, steady increase in appetite that is especially marked from the third month onward. (*See* NUTRITION.) Such a diet will contain red meat, eggs, and seafood two or three times weekly; and green vegetables, fresh fruit, and at least one pint of milk daily.

Drugs Harmful in Pregnancy.—Until the late 1950s it had been assumed that the fetus was adequately protected from the effects of drugs given to the mother during pregnancy. Events have shown that this is not so; the fetus is peculiarly sensitive to damage during the first 12 weeks of its existence. There is evidence that a large number of drugs, if given during this period, are capable of causing malformations. The most dramatic episode of this type was the production of phocomelia ("seal limbs") in the infants of mothers who had taken thalidomide as a sedative or anti-emetic during early pregnancy. The main deformities in this condition are a shortening or absence of the limbs; important associated defects include absence or malformation of the external ear, fusion defects of the eye, and absence of the normal openings of the gastrointestinal tract. It was estimated that between 2,000 and 3,000 such babies were born in West Germany and 500 in Great Britain between 1959 and the beginning of 1962. In the U.S., thalidomide never was distributed for clinical use. (*See* also MONSTER.)

Another group of drugs harmful in pregnancy is the androgenic (masculinizing) compounds, which have produced in female infants external genitalia showing a variable degree of deviation toward the male type of anatomy. Not only will frankly androgenic drugs such as testosterone produce this effect, but also those with androgenic side effects; for example, the anabolic steroids, and many of the compounds with a progesteronelike activity which are used in threatened or habitual abortion.

Cortisone and related drugs given to experimental animals in early pregnancy will produce cleft palate in the offspring, but this has only rarely occurred in man. However, a transient depression of adrenal function in the mother may occur in the neonatal period (the first 28 days following birth) if she has been receiving large doses of cortisone throughout pregnancy.

After the early 1960s greater care was exercised in the screening of new drugs before they were considered safe for clinical use in pregnancy. The screening included, among other things, tests on pregnant animals of a number of species.

Toxemias of Pregnancy.—Among the most prominent of the abnormal conditions that make the periodic examination essential are the toxemias. They are of two kinds. The commoner is preeclampsia, which, unless recognized early and vigorously treated, may pass into a grave, convulsive form (eclampsia). The other kind is characterized by severe and persistent vomiting (hyperemesis gravidarum). Because of their superficial resemblance to a toxic state, these diseased conditions have been classified as toxemias, despite the fact that in neither case has intensive research revealed the existence of a causative toxic agent.

Preeclampsia usually develops insidiously in the latter half of pregnancy. The first sign may be a swelling of the ankles and legs and sudden increase in weight, but, while they should always arouse suspicion, these signs are often present without toxemia. Commonly the first significant sign is an elevation of the blood pressure, detected at a routine antenatal visit. The presence of albumin in the urine is the second most important sign.

In the milder forms of toxemia ambulant home treatment, consisting of rest, is often permissible on the understanding that the patient visits the clinic or is seen by a doctor or midwife at short intervals. Where the initial signs are marked or where there is a progressive worsening of the state, the patient is admitted to a hospital or nursing home. In the graver manifestations termination of the pregnancy is called for in the interest of both mother and child.

Rhesus Factor.—One of the reasons for an examination of the pregnant woman's blood at the first antenatal visit is to determine her blood group. About 85% of Caucasians, and almost all non-Caucasians, contain in their blood an antigen similar to that present in the Rhesus monkey and are therefore classed as Rhesus positive (Rh+); the remaining 15% of Caucasians have no such antigen and are classed as Rhesus negative (Rh−). If the father is Rh+, the baby may be Rh+; if, in such a case, the mother belongs to the Rh− group, the bloods of mother and baby are "incompatible." In the placenta the Rhesus antigen passes into the maternal blood and stimulates the formation in the mother of antibodies which enter the fetal circulation and destroy the red blood cells by agglutination and hemolysis, with the production of anemia or jaundice or both (erythroblastosis fetalis). The risk is small during a first pregnancy, unless the mother has by mischance previously received an incompatible transfusion; *i.e.*, of Rh+ blood. With each succeeding pregnancy in which the fetus is Rh+ the antibodies in the mother's blood increase, and with them the risk to the fetus. In cases where the woman's blood is Rh− the husband's blood group is determined; if it is positive the woman's blood is tested for antibodies monthly from the sixth month onward. Where the child is erythroblastotic the sole effective treatment is the replacement of the child's blood by compatible blood from a donor. Mother-fetus incompatibility similar to that found in the Rhesus blood group occurs with other types of antigen; *e.g.*, the ABO group. (*See* BLOOD GROUPS.)

Exercise and Relaxation.—Walking in the open air should be a daily routine for the pregnant woman, but too long walks or exhausting exercise of any kind should be avoided. Women vary greatly in these respects, and any advice given is weighed against the woman's natural habits. Much can be said in favour of the so-called relaxation classes organized in relation to antenatal clinics. These classes are a valuable addition to the educational functions of the clinic. There the care of the body can be discussed and the facts of labour explained, so that the expectant mother is encouraged to forsake her fear and to adopt a more confident attitude toward pregnancy and labour.

For further clinical and anatomical information *see* EMBRYOLOGY AND DEVELOPMENT, ANIMAL: *Human Development;* FETAL DISORDERS; GYNECOLOGY; OBSTETRICS; PLACENTA AND FETAL MEMBRANES, DISEASES OF; RADIATION: BIOLOGICAL EFFECTS: *Exposure of the Embryo and Fetus.* For termination of pregnancy *see* ABORTION; BIRTH, HUMAN; MULTIPLE BIRTHS; PREMATURE BIRTH. For social aspects of the subject *see* BIRTH CONTROL; ILLEGITIMACY; MATERNAL AND CHILD HEALTH. *See* also references under "Pregnancy" in the Index.

BIBLIOGRAPHY.—Grantly Dick Read, *Introduction to Motherhood* (1950); F. J. Browne and J. C. McClure Browne, *Antenatal Care and Postnatal Care,* 9th ed. (1960); I. Donald, *Practical Obstetric Problems,* 3rd ed. (1964); J. B. De Lee, *Obstetrics,* 12th ed. by J. P. Greenhill (1960); F. E. Hytten and I. Leitch, *The Physiology of Human Pregnancy* (1964). (J. Y.)

PRE-HELLENIC ARCHITECTURE.

This article deals with the architecture that developed around the Aegean sea and in the near east from earliest times through the Archaic period of Greece (6th century B.C.). The architecture of the subsequent period is discussed in GREEK ARCHITECTURE. Though belonging within the greater context of this discussion, the architectural history of Egypt will be found in EGYPTIAN ARCHITECTURE.

The maritime kingdom of Crete, by virtue of its central position between Europe, Asia and Africa, had early contacts with Egypt and the ancient near east and seems to have played an important intermediary role in the transmission of architectural influences to Greece. It is for this reason that near eastern architectural development is included here. The architecture of Achaemenid Persia, contemporary to early Greek architecture and therefore not strictly speaking pre-Hellenic, is included here also for the sake of geographic unity.

Since the chronology of pre-Hellenic times in the regions discussed in this article is subject to controversy, the dates given here are not necessarily identical with those given in other articles. In each case the author's dates are used. For further historical information *see* the articles about the specific places involved (*e.g.*, BABYLONIA AND ASSYRIA; CRETE; etc.).

MESOPOTAMIA

Mesopotamian civilization was theocratic; consequently it is in religious buildings that the architecture of this region finds its earliest and fullest expression. (*See* BABYLONIA AND ASSYRIA.) The beginnings of mud-brick architecture in the Ubaid period (4th millennium B.C.) may be seen in the earliest temples at Abu Shahrain in the south of Mesopotamia and Tepe Gawra in the north. Platforms, buttresses and recessed portals, perennial traits of Mesopotamian architecture down to the Hellenistic period, were already established at both sites. A recessed portal is part of the entrance façade of the earliest temple at Tepe Gawra, and at Abu Shahrain a similar building was placed on a platform and approached by a flight of steps.

These characteristics were repeated at Uruk (Erech, mod. Warka), with the added development that the platform of Abu Shahrain was replaced by the ziggurat (*q.v.*), a tall staged tower with outside staircases and a shrine at the top.

Walls and columns of early Mesopotamian temples were covered with a patterned facing of coloured clay cones that were inserted into the mud plaster; this primitive decorative technique gave rise to the later Assyrian practice of covering entire walls with richly polychrome glazed and molded brickwork. The arch was used in Mesopotamia, and false, or corbeled, vaults (*i.e.*, vaults constructed of successive series of projecting courses) were occasionally employed for tombs.

The transition to the Early Dynastic period (*c.* 3000–2340 B.C.) brought with it certain innovations. The plano-convex brick, flat on one side and curved on the other, was invented. Both religious and secular buildings were built around a central court; the entrances to temples were generally flanked by towers and approached by a stairway.

The oval temple precinct at Khafajah is a typical example of Early Dynastic architecture. There, as at Abu Shahrain, the whole layout was elevated on a low platform. A flight of steps led up to an outer gateway flanked by two high towers. A small forecourt led to another gate which opened upon a spacious inner court, containing a well, several shallow ablution basins and the sacrificial altar. The temple proper, which probably had buttresses and recessed walls, was placed on a second platform approached by another flight of steps. Basically, this is also the type of complex at Tell Asmar and Tell Agrab. Later the square or oblong plan became more common.

Little is known about the architecture of the Akkadians, a Semitic dynasty which assumed power over Mesopotamia in the middle of the 3rd millennium B.C. This dynasty was ousted by the Guti, who were, in turn, driven out of Mesopotamia by the Sumerians at the end of the 3rd millennium, which began a time of great architectural activity.

The city of Lagash (mod. Telloh) flourished under King Gudea, but few remains of his architecture have come to light. Ur-Nammu, the first king of the 3rd dynasty of Ur (*c.* 2250 B.C.), erected a great ziggurat at Ur, his capital. It stands within an oblong court and is oriented to the points of the compass. Buttresses on its outer face give it added strength. Three monumental stairways with bastions in their angles converge at the first stage from which a single stairway ascends to the top of the second stage. A temple no doubt crowned the summit of the structure, but this has disappeared without a trace.

The 3rd dynasty of Ur is also represented by buildings at Uruk, Nippur, Mari (mod. Tell el Hariri), Ashur and Tell Asmar. The temple-palace of Gimil-Sin at Tell Asmar deviates little from the development already described. The temple portion of the complex consists of a square central court, with the cella at the far end, surrounded by massive buttressed walls and entered by a towered gateway. The palace of the local ruler joins this temple at an angle and consists of antecella, cella, central court, throne room and great hall. Surrounding these large ceremonial spaces were small administrative offices; the living quarters seem to have been situated on a second floor.

Ur fell early in the 2nd millennium B.C., and the succeeding phase is known as the Isin-Larsa period (2025–1763 B.C.). The temple of Ishtar-Kititium at Ishchali belongs to this period. Although related to, and developed from, the Early Dynastic complex at Khafajah, the original single-chambered shrine at Khafajah was there elaborated into an architectural complex with forecourt, court and cella.

A palace at Mari has been tentatively identified with the reign of Hammurabi (probably 18th century B.C.), the ruler and lawgiver of the 1st dynasty of Babylon which flourished contemporaneously with Isin and Larsa to the south.

A foreign dynasty, the Kassites, invaded southern Mesopotamia in about 1600 B.C. Their accession to power inaugurated a new era of building activity at Ur, Uruk and Dur-Kurigalzu, the new capital 20 mi. to the west of modern Baghdad.

While the Assyrians in general adhered closely to established architectural schemes, they also brought about several important deviations from the early Mesopotamian norm. The latest Ishtar temple at Ashur and the Ashur temple at nearby Tukulti-Ninurta, built during the reign of Tukulti-Ninurta I (*c.* 1250–1210 B.C.), established the type that became characteristic for Assyrian temples.

The Ashur temple at Tukulti-Ninurta was built against a ziggurat, as at Mari, and incorporates a dual entrance system: one entrance faces the cella as in earlier buildings; the other enters at a right angle. The cella is on a podium that lies in front of a recess cut out of the body of the ziggurat, and the ziggurat itself no longer incorporates a staircase. The practice of setting a series of stone slabs, called orthostates, at the bottom of a wall below the mud-brick upper parts became common in the Assyrian period and was seen again in Hittite architecture.

During the Late Assyrian age (c. 1000–612 B.C.), Ashur, Babylon, Nineveh, Nimrud, and Dur-Sharrukin (mod. Khorsabad) flourished as royal residences, but since only Ashur and Dur-Sharrukin have been at all fully excavated, we shall confine our remarks to the palace of Sargon II (722–705 B.C.) in Dur-Sharrukin.

The palace area occupies about 7¾ ac., of which two-thirds are given over to the palace proper and the temple, the remainder being occupied by a large ziggurat probably composed of seven stages with an external spiral ramp. Basically, this plan is an elaboration of the traditional units that occur at Tell Asmar: square court, throne room, great hall. Each side of the court measures 300 ft., and its walls were revetted with monumental reliefs. In addition, great stone sculptures of monsters and genii, such as those that flanked the doorways, must also be considered as part of the architecture.

The final rebuilding of Babylon by Nebuchadrezzar II (605–562 B.C.) marks one of the greatest building achievements ever attempted by man. Excavations during the first decades of this century by R. Koldeway and the German Orient society revealed no less than four gigantic castles on this site. It was during the reign of Nebuchadrezzar II that the fabled "hanging gardens" were built. The Ishtar gate of Nebuchadrezzar's palace, decorated with lively bulls and dragons executed in molded and glazed brick, has survived well and ranks as the finest monument of this great period. Of the ziggurat of Babylon, the biblical Tower of Babel, little remains today other than the ground plan and a description of the Greek traveler and historian, Herodotus.

MINOAN CRETE

The great maritime civilization of Crete (q.v.) crystallized around the palaces such as exist at Knossos, Phaistos, Hagia Triada, Mallia and Tylissos. The immensely important "Palace of Minos" at Knossos, excavated and reconstructed early in the 20th century by Sir Arthur Evans, offers evidence of unbroken architectural and artistic development from Neolithic beginnings, culminating in a brilliant display of building activity during Middle Minoan III (1700–1580 B.C.), and continuing until the invasion of the Achaeans in the 12th century. However, the palace is essentially a structure of the last two Middle Minoan periods (1800–1580 B.C.). It no doubt rivaled near-eastern and Egyptian palaces in monumentality. As in these, a quadrangular complex of rooms and corridors is grouped around a great central court, at Knossos roughly 175 ft. × 100 ft. At the northern end, toward the sea, a grand portico of 12 pilasters gave access to the central court. At this end, also, is situated the grand theatrical area, a rectangular open-air theatre perhaps used for ritual performances. The east wing of the palace is divided into two parts by a long east-west corridor and rose four or five stories above the slope of the valley. The southeast portion of the palace contains domestic apartments elaborately supplied with plumbing and flushing facilities as well as a sanctuary. A wide stairway led to an upper story which no longer exists. The northeast portion of the palace is occupied by offices and storerooms. The west portion is again divided by a long corridor, over 200 ft. long, running north and south. Behind this corridor was discovered a series of long narrow storerooms containing great numbers of pithoi, or man-size storage vessels for oil. On the other side of the corridor, toward the central court, are the rooms of state, including the throne room with its unique gypsum throne and world-famous griffin frescoes.

Light was supplied from above by an ingenious system of "light wells," and several colonnaded porticoes provided ventilation during the hot Cretan summers. Brilliantly hued frescoes played an important part in both the interior and the exterior decoration of the palace.

The development of the other Minoan palaces (Phaistos, Mallia, Hagia Triada, Tylissos) roughly parallels that of Knossos. Each has its special interest, and Phaistos is particularly fascinating, due to extensive Italian excavations. Maritime hegemony enabled the Cretan sea kings to build these palaces in low and unprotected places; consequently there is a conspicuous absence of fortification walls, as contrasted to the great walls of Mesopotamian palaces. Since Cretan worship seems to have been largely in the open air, there are no real temples as in the near east. Yet, the disposition of the various parts of the palace around the central court and the avoidance of outside windows as much as possible are characteristics that seem to indicate an early contact with the near east. A taste for long, straight palace corridors, as well as a highly developed water-supply system, may also have been inherited from older civilizations to the east. The column made its first European appearance in the Cretan palace, where it is often employed individually to divide an entrance way.

The development of funerary architecture in Crete proceeds from the old chamber ossuaries of the Early Minoan period (2750–2000 B.C.) to the developed tholoi or beehive tombs of the Mesara plain and the elaborate temple-tombs of Knossos at the end of the Middle Minoan period.

On the crest of Minoan prosperity came the great crash. An invasion from the mainland c. 1400 B.C. destroyed the palaces and resulted in the removal of power to Mycenaean Greece. Architectural remains in Crete which are pre-Greek and yet subsequent to this catastrophe are very rare. Several country shrines belong in this postdestruction period, and at Prinias a unique temple building may be as late as 700 B.C. The doorway of this temple is now in the Candia museum and has low reliefs on its architectural members. The opening above the lintel is flanked by seated figures, while the lintel itself is carved on its underside with figures of a goddess and of animals. That the Minoan tradition was not entirely extinct is indicated by the column which seems to have stood in the middle of this doorway, as at the "palace of Minos." (For a further discussion of Minoan palatial architecture, towns, sanctuaries and tombs, see CRETE: Archaeology.)

MYCENAEAN GREECE

The sudden architectural awakening of the Mycenaean Greek mainland is intimately connected with the zenith and decline of Minoan Crete and can only be understood against the background of a long Cretan development. Unlike Minoan Knossos, the archaeological remains on the mainland are fragmentary. In order to obtain an idea of Mycenaean architecture, we must draw on our knowledge of at least three sites: Mycenae, Tiryns and Pylos. Since the important architectural monuments visible today date largely from Late Helladic times (1580–c. 1100 B.C.) and since little earlier architecture is preserved, our brief survey shall be confined to this period. (See also AEGEAN CIVILIZATION.)

Fortification.—The tremendous building activity of the 14th century B.C. reflects an age of warfare, when powerful Greek-speaking kings built fortresses in key defensive positions on the mainland. The cyclopean walls of Mycenae and Tiryns (i.e., the walls in which great blocks of untrimmed stone were employed) and the strategically placed Lion gate at Mycenae were constructed in this period. The latter consists of two colossal door jambs that support a monolithic lintel. The wall above the gate is so constructed as to form a relieving triangle over the lintel, and this empty space is blocked with the famous relief panel of two heraldic lions, which has given the gate its name. This method of construction provides an ingenious substitute for the arch which was unknown to the Mycenaeans.

Also justly famed are the concealed galleries of Tiryns, where the primitive corbeled vault makes its first appearance in mainland Europe.

Palaces.—Mycenaean palaces have been unearthed at Mycenae, Tiryns, Pylos, Gla and Phylakopi (Cyclades). The palace at Pylos is a typical mainland palace of the Heroic Age as described in the poetry of Homer. The characteristic plan comprises four elements: (1) a narrow court on which the structure fronts; (2) a double-columned entrance portico; (3) a vestibule (prodomos); and (4) the richly frescoed domos, or hall proper. The latter had

View of the ruins of Babylon, with the foundations of the Ishtar gate in the foreground

Painting of a reconstruction of the Ishtar gate, Babylon

Reconstructed model of the city of Babylon showing the famous ziggurat

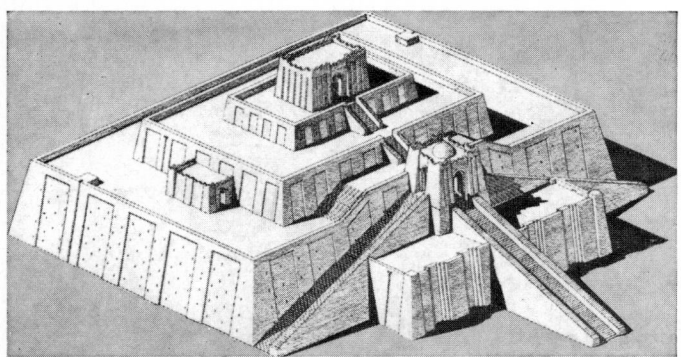

Above, reconstruction of the ziggurat at Ur. Below, ruins of the ziggurat at Ur, erected by King Ur-Nammu c. 2250 B.C.

Ancient archway made of brick in ruins of Babylonian city in Iraq

ANCIENT ARCHITECTURE OF MESOPOTAMIA

BY COURTESY OF (TOP LEFT) THE ORIENTAL INSTITUTE, THE UNIVERSITY OF CHICAGO, (TOP RIGHT, CENTRE RIGHT, CENTRE LEFT, BOTTOM LEFT) INSTITUTE OF ARCHAEOLOGY, LONDON: PHOTOGRAPH, (BOTTOM RIGHT) RADIO TIMES HULTON PICTURE LIBRARY

PLATE II

PRE-HELLENIC ARCHITECTURE

Stair ramp and wall in a palace at Persepolis, one of the capitals of the Achaemenid dynasty of ancient Persia

Rebuilt portion of the north entrance to the Palace of Minos at Knossos, Crete

Lion gate at Mycenae, Greece, constructed during the 14th century B.C.

Untrimmed stones form the gallery and casemates in the east bastion of the palace at Tiryns, Greece

Throne room in the Palace of Minos at Knossos, showing the gypsum throne and griffin frescoes

Monumental columns at Persepolis

ARCHITECTURE OF MINOAN CRETE, MYCENAEAN GREECE AND ACHAEMENID PERSIA

BY COURTESY OF (SECOND ROW CENTRE) INSTITUTE OF ARCHAEOLOGY, LONDON; PHOTOGRAPHS, (TOP LEFT, BOTTOM RIGHT) KEYSTONE PRESS AGENCY LTD., (TOP RIGHT, CENTRE LEFT, BOTTOM LEFT) TONI SCHNEIDERS

a fixed throne at one end and a central fixed hearth between four wooden columns that supported an open towerlike structure rising above the roof for light and ventilation. Archives, comparable to those of the Hittite kings at Bogazkoy, were associated with this palace. Private houses, such as have been discovered at Mycenae, exhibit similar features as well as the basement storage magazines mentioned by Homer.

Tombs.—The earliest royal burials known from Mycenae are those of the two grave circles, the first discovered by H. Schliemann in 1876 and the second by A. J. B. Wace in 1951. These grave circles have no architectural character, consisting essentially of vertical shafts cut into the bedrock.

More important architecturally are the tholoi or beehive tombs. The evolution of these family sepulchres began in Minoan Crete, but culminated in the so-called "treasury of Atreus" at Mycenae, now believed to have been constructed as late as *c.* 1250 B.C. This most impressive monument of the Mycenaean world is a pointed dome built up of overhanging (*i.e.*, corbeled) blocks of conglomerate masonry cut and polished to give the impression of a true vault. The diameter of this tomb is almost 50 ft.; its height is slightly less. The enormous monolithic lintel of the doorway weighs 120 tons and is $29\frac{1}{2}$ ft. long, $16\frac{1}{2}$ ft. deep and 3 ft. high. It is surmounted by a relieving triangle similar to that over the Lion gate and decorated with relief plaques in a manner not yet established with certainty. A small side chamber hewn out of the living rock contained the burials, whereas the main chamber was probably reserved for ritual use. Two engaged half-columns of Cretan type (now in the British museum) were secured to the façade which was approached by a dromos, or ceremonial passageway, revetted with cyclopean blocks of masonry and open to the sky. Other tholoi, though not as excellently preserved, exist at Mycenae and Orchomenos.

TROY

Excavations at Troy (mod. Hissarlik, on the eastern shore of the Dardanelles) have distinguished no less than nine stratified levels extending from prehistoric into Roman times.

Houses at Troy I (*c.* 3200–2600 B.C.) and Troy II (*c.* 2600–2300 B.C.) were formed of long narrow groups of rooms that already seem to bear a relationship to the rectangular megaron, or large hall, of the Mycenaean dwelling, sharing, as they do, the fixed hearth, deep vestibule and most of the other architectural features of megara on the Mycenaean mainland. Defensive gates flanked by towers at Troy II recall the military architecture of Hittite Anatolia to the east.

Troy VI (*c.* 1900–1300 B.C.), the immediate predecessor of Homer's Troy, was largely demolished by leveling operations in Roman times and at the end of the 19th century by Schliemann. This city possessed a symmetrical layout, impressive walls and, like Troy II, gate towers of splendid masonry that could be the prototype of Mycenaean as well as classical Greek propylaea. A large megaron of Troy VI incorporates a row of three columns along a central axis in its plan, again anticipating a development of Greek architecture (*e.g.*, the first temple of Hera at Samos).

Another feature of interest at Troy is the un-Mycenaean use of sun-baked brick for walling, probably a link with the construction techniques of Mesopotamia.

As more becomes known about the peculiar un-Minoan Bronze-Age civilization of Troy, other parallels with the architectural evolution of pre-Hellenic and Hellenic Greece will no doubt emerge. It is not unlikely that Troy will eventually take its place as an important intermediary for the transmission of ideas from the ancient near east to the younger cultures of the west. (*See also* TROY.)

HITTITE ANATOLIA

Because of recent excavations at Bogazkoy, Alaca Huyuk and Kultepe in Turkey, it is now possible to talk with a good deal of certainty about Hittite architecture. These three cities possess the earliest remnants of Hittite civilization. Their architecture is of a rude and primitive kind, yet not uninfluenced by the more developed architecture of older civilizations in Syria and Mesopo-

tamia. Stones of colossal dimensions were employed in corbeled vaults for the construction of tunnels, gates and tombs. Monolithic orthostates, often decorated with reliefs, are common. At Bogazkoy (anc. Hattusas or Khattushash), the capital and most important city of the Hittites, as well as at other Hittite sites, such carved orthostates form the lowest masonry courses of palaces and temples. The absence of the column, employed by all neighbouring cultures, is conspicuous in Hittite architecture, square pillars serving in their stead. Also noticeable in the architecture of the Hittites is an apparent lack of axial planning. Hittite temples and palaces are built on an agglomerate principle, with rooms of varying dimensions grouped in tiers around a rectangular court. Internal communication must have been difficult.

Few buildings of architectural distinction remain from the Early Hittite period (1650–1460 B.C.), although from this period are the beginnings of monumental architecture on the Anatolian plateau. The flowering of Hittite architecture takes place during the three centuries of imperial expansion (1460–1190 B.C.), when the might of the Hittite kings was felt as far abroad as Egypt.

From this period date the great Hittite temples. Five such temples have been uncovered at Bogazkoy. In each of these, many small rooms are disposed about a large central courtyard. It was in this courtyard that the worshipers assembled. The cult statue was hidden in a remote holy of holies and seems to have been accessible only to the priesthood. In Temple I at Bogazkoy, this holy of holies projects from the core of the temple building, apparently in order that the cult statue could be illuminated by side windows. Numerous subsidiary rooms seem to have served administrative and storage purposes.

Architecturally, the palaces are closely related to the temples. As in the temples, the rooms of the palaces were grouped around a central courtyard. In contrast to the tightly organized palace-complexes of Crete and Mesopotamia, the palace of the Hittite kings at Bogazkoy consists of a number of isolated structures loosely disposed in a semicircular formation. Most of these buildings were multistoried, and, in addition to the royal habitation, an archive and a palace shrine have been identified. Two other excavated Hittite palaces of this period, at Kultepe and Huyuk, do not seem to differ substantially from that at Bogazkoy. The collapse of the Hittite empire at about 1200 B.C. is marked by destruction levels at these three sites. Subsequently, a short afterblossoming of Hittite culture took place in northern Syria at several centres where displaced Hittites, Aramaeans and nomads reassembled; and considerable architectural remains of this period have been uncovered at Carchemish, Tell Halaf and Zincirli in the foothills of the Taurus.

The employment of carved orthostates to adorn the lower part of a wall is a characteristic feature that unifies the architecture of these scattered sub-Hittite principalities and relates it to that of the Hittite empire at the height of its expansion. Another feature of the conglomerate architectural style that distinguishes these petty autocracies seems to be of Syrian, rather than Hittite, origin. This is the *bit hilani,* or pillared porch, the supports of which often rested on animal bases. (*See also* HITTITES.)

ACHAEMENID PERSIA

The origins of the monumental architectural style that appeared in Persia with the foundation of the Achaemenid empire in 539 B.C. are disputed. (*See* IRAN: *Archaeology: Achaemenid Period.*) It has been suggested that the Persians learned the art of cyclopean building from the Urartaeans of Lake Van to the north; other elements of Persian architecture are often traced to Mesopotamia and even Egypt. It is known for certain that Greeks were among the foreign craftsmen employed in the construction of the great Achaemenid residences. The presence of horizontally fluted column bases in the Achaemenid palace at Pasargadae, similar to those of the Archaic Greek temples at Samos, Ephesus and Naukratis, is only one of several examples of their influence.

Yet, notwithstanding the presence of such foreign elements, it cannot be denied that the architecture of Achaemenid Persia is remarkably original. Veritable forests of columns and square halls of vast proportions radically differentiate Achaemenid buildings from the contemporary architecture in Greece and are more reminiscent of the native Persian development in Islamic times.

A great columned hall exists already in the palace of Cyrus at Pasargadae, the earliest of the three Achaemenid dynastic residences (other two: Persepolis and Susa). This palace was elevated on a series of man-made platforms and approached by a system of impressive stairways. A colonnaded gatehouse fronted by Assyrianizing bull-monsters gave access to the parklike enclosure in which stood the numerous pavilions and subsidiary buildings that comprised the palace. Among these there was the audience hall surrounded by four porticoes, each with a double row of pillars. Another building, believed to be the palace proper, has double porticoes flanking an almost square hall containing 30 columns arranged in 5 rows of 6 columns each distributed over the entire space.

The best-known, best-preserved and most spectacular of the Persian palaces is that at Persepolis (c. 521–388 B.C.). This enormous complex of buildings, terraces and stair ramps consisted, among other elements, of the palace of Darius I (522–486 B.C.), Xerxes I (486–465 B.C.) and Artaxerxes III (359–338 B.C.), a harem, a treasury, the Gate of Xerxes, the Hall of the Hundred Columns and a number of other buildings.

The Hall of the Hundred Columns at Persepolis is 225 ft. square, though its columns are only 37 ft. high as compared to 67 ft. in the smaller Hall of Xerxes at the same site. The gateways of the Hall of Xerxes are flanked by colossal winged genii similar to those associated with Assyrian palaces; flanking the stairway leading to the Audience Hall of Darius were discovered the famous reliefs of tribute bearers that have since found their way into museums throughout the world. Everywhere, sculpture was combined with architecture to produce a total effect of grandeur hardly surpassed by the great architectural complexes of Egypt.

At Susa, the palace is in part similar to that at Persepolis, in part related to the palace of Nebuchadrezzar at Babylon. The widespread use of glazed coloured bricks in the architecture of Susa also associates this palace with the earlier architecture of nearby Mesopotamia.

The aniconic religion of the Persians required only simple open-air fire altars for the perpetuation of its rites. Consequently, there is no temple architecture, and only tombs remain to be mentioned. At Pasargadae, an early Achaemenid tomb, probably correctly identified as that of King Cyrus, consists of a rectangular single-roomed sarcophagus chamber with a gable roof recalling the tombs of Caria and Lycia in southwestern Turkey. The entire structure and the pedestal of six steps on which it stands are built of great blocks of well-dressed masonry and were formerly surrounded by a colonnade. Later Persian monarchs were interred in the cliff-hewn tombs at Naksh-i-Rustam near Persepolis. *See* also TEMPLE ARCHITECTURE; ETRUSCANS; and references under "Pre-Hellenic Architecture" in the Index.

BIBLIOGRAPHY.—*Mesopotamia:* H. Frankfort, *The Art and Architecture of the Ancient Orient* (Pelican History of Art, 1954).
Minoan Crete: F. Matz, *Die Ägäis* (Handbuch der Archaeologie, vol. ii, 1954; bibliography); J. D. S. Pendlebury, *The Archaeology of Crete* (1939); E. Bell, *Prehellenic Architecture in the Aegean* (1926; good general account, though no longer up to date); Sir A. J. Evans, *The Palace of Minos*, 4 vol. (1921–35; index 1936).
Mycenaean Greece: F. Matz, *Die Ägäis* (Handbuch der Archaeologie, 1954); E. Bell, *Prehellenic Architecture in the Aegean* (1926); A. W. Lawrence, *Greek Architecture* (Pelican History of Art, 1957); G. E. Mylonas, *Ancient Mycenae* (1957; bibliography); A. J. B. Wace, *Mycenae* (1949; excellent account, but already outdated by new discoveries); C. W. Blegen, "The Palace of Nestor at Pylos," in *American Journal of Archaeology*, vol. 57 (1953) and *Illustrated London News*, pp. 86 ff. (Jan. 16, 1954); R. Rodenwaldt, *Tiryns* (1912, et seq.).
Troy and Hittite Anatolia: R. Naumann, *Die Architektur Kleinasiens* (1955; bibliography); O. R. Gurney, *The Hittites* (1952; on Hittite civilization in general); E. Bell, *Early Architecture in Western Asia* (1924; good general account, but outdated by subsequent excavation).
Achaemenid Persia: A. U. Pope, *A Survey of Persian Art*, vol. i (1938); R. Girschman, *Iran* (English version in Pelican series, 1954); E. F. Schmidt, *Persepolis*, 2 vol. (1953–57).   (H. HN.)

PREHNITE, a relatively uncommon calcium and aluminum hydrous silicate mineral, is generally light green in colour and occurs in rounded masses of crystals. The individual crystals are not usually distinct to the unaided eye. Prehnite resembles certain varieties of the hydrous zinc silicate hemimorphite (*q.v.*). It can be distinguished from that mineral most readily by its lower specific gravity and by its type of geologic occurrence and associated minerals.

Prehnite occurs most commonly as crystal masses lining cavities in mafic (basic) igneous rocks such as basalt and diabase. Characteristically associated with it are calcite, quartz, zeolites, datolite and pectolite. Prehnite also occurs less commonly and less strikingly in other types of rocks, such as schists, amphibolites and metamorphosed sedimentary carbonate rocks. The composition of prehnite is expressed by $Ca_2Al_2Si_3O_{10}(OH)_2$. Small amounts of ferric iron (Fe^{3+}) may be present in place of some of the aluminum.   (D. M. H.)

PRELATE, an ecclesiastical dignitary of high rank. In the modern practice of the Roman Catholic Church, prelates, properly so-called, are those who have jurisdiction in the external forum; *i.e.,* those who exercise the public power of the church. This true prelacy is defined as "preeminence with jurisdiction," and true or real prelates are distinguished as: (1) greater prelates, possessing episcopal jurisdiction, *e.g.,* patriarchs, archbishops and bishops; and (2) lesser prelates, possessing a quasi-episcopal or other jurisdiction, *e.g.,* abbots and prelates "of no diocese" and religious superiors, withdrawn from the ordinary diocesan jurisdiction.

In some of the Protestant churches the title of prelate was retained after the Reformation. In the Church of England it is restricted to bishops.

See J. A. Abbo and J. D. Hannan, *The Sacred Canons* (1952).
    (F. R. McM.)

PREMATURE BIRTH is defined as birth at less than 37 weeks after conception. Prematurity occurs in about 7–9% of pregnancies in white women in the United States, and in 10–12% of those in Negro women; the rate in the latter is higher probably because of poorer socioeconomic conditions. In the U.S. prematurity is directly or indirectly responsible for at least 50% of all deaths of newborn infants.

A presumptive reason (usually multiple pregnancy, maternal toxemia or hypertension, abnormal attachment of the placenta or congenital malformation of the infant) can be found for 40–60% of premature births, but fully half those of single infants are of unknown cause. Poor maternal health, hygiene, and nutrition increase the likelihood of prematurity; maternal accidents and acute illnesses are insignificant as causes. The chief specific causes of death among premature infants are respiratory disturbances (hyaline membrane disease, atelectasis), infections (usually pneumonia), and hemorrhages, especially into the brain or lungs and often not caused by injury. With good care about 85% of all premature infants born alive should survive. In the large group born at 4½–5½ lb. (2,000–2,500 g.), 95% or more should survive. Chances of survival decrease in direct proportion to lower weight.

Prevention of premature birth is not yet possible. Treatment of the infant begins with skilful obstetric management under minimal anesthesia during premature delivery, followed by specialized nursing and pediatric care in an environment approved as a premature infant nursery by public health authorities. This must provide the space, equipment, and trained personnel for isolation against infection, regulation of temperature and humidity, feeding of special mixtures (often by special means), and prompt relief of respiratory crises. Subsequently, instruction of the mother, supervision of home care, and special attention to the nutritional requirements of rapid growth are needed.

Prematures weighing over four pounds (1,800 g.) at birth are usually born after 32 weeks, and they have much the same outlook for later growth and development as do term infants. Those of three pounds (1,350 g.) or less, especially if born before 28 weeks, are more liable to reduced stature and disturbed neuromuscular development.

See also FETAL DISORDERS; INCUBATOR; BIRTH, HUMAN.

See H. N. Bundesen *et al., Progress in the Prevention of Needless Neonatal Deaths* (1951); W. A. Silverman (ed.), *Dunham's Premature Infants,* 3rd ed. (1961).   (C. A. SM.)

PREMCHAND (pseudonym of DHANPAT RĀY ŚRĪVĀSTAV) (1880–1936), Indian writer. Until about 1914 he wrote chiefly in Urdu, and thereafter usually in Hindi; his work consolidated the position of the novel and short story as Hindi literary genres (*see* HINDI LITERATURE; URDU LITERATURE). Born on July 31, 1880, at Lamahī, Premchand first worked as a teacher, becoming a sub-inspector of schools, but gave up teaching to join Gandhi's non-cooperation movement in 1921. He died on Oct. 8, 1936, at Banāras (Varanasi).

Much of Premchand's best work is to be found among his 250 or so short stories, collected in Hindi under the title *Mānasarovar* ("The Holy Lake"). Compact in form and style, they draw, like his novels, on a notably wide range of northern Indian life for their subject matter. Premchand's approach to his material is basically realistic, but a strong, conflicting vein of idealism also runs through most of his work. As a result, the novels particularly are of uneven literary merit, though not necessarily less valuable as a record of the life and mood of the northern India of the time. His 12th and last complete novel, *Godān* (1936; English translation 1956), is his best: in its main section he presents Indian village life and character vividly, refusing to sacrifice realistic detail to uncritical idealism; a less well-realized section, however, poses an artificial contrast between the values of village and urban life, and this mars the novel as a whole.

See English translation of part of *Godān* and a short story, "The Shroud," in *A Treasury of Modern Asian Short Stories,* ed. by D. L. Milton and W. Clifford (1961). (R. S. McG.)

PREMONSTRATENSIANS (ORDO PRAEMONSTRATENSIUM, O. PRAEM.; or CANONICI REGULARIUM PRAEMONSTRATENSIUM, C.R.P.), called in America NORBERTINES, in England WHITE CANONS, a Roman Catholic order of canons regular, following the Rule of St. Augustine. The members are engaged in the solemn public enactment of the liturgy and in the apostolate of preaching, pastoral work and education.

The Premonstratensian order was founded in 1120 by St. Norbert, who, with 13 companions, established at Prémontré in Aisne a monastery that became the cradle of a new order. Though they followed the Rule of St. Augustine (*see* AUGUSTINE OF HIPPO, RULE OF ST.), their supplementary statutes made their life one of great austerity. St. Norbert was a friend of St. Bernard of Clairvaux and was much influenced by Cistercian ideals in both the manner of life and the government of his order. The order was approved in 1126 and quickly spread over western Europe. Later, after its austerity had been relaxed, reforms were undertaken and a number of more or less independent congregations were created. The order was nearly destroyed by the French Revolution. Its modern centre of strength is in Belgium, where there are restored medieval Norbertine abbeys at Averbode and Tongerlo. Norbertine houses in the English-speaking world are located at Kilnacrott, Ire.; De Pere, Wis.; Storrington, Eng.; and Perth, Austr.

A second order of contemplative nuns and a third order of active sisters are affiliated with the canons. There are four provinces, called *circaries;* the world centre is the Norbertine generalate in Rome. The habit is all white. *See* also NORBERT, SAINT; ORDERS AND CONGREGATIONS, RELIGIOUS; MONASTICISM.

See C. J. Kirkfleet, O. Praem., *History of St. Norbert* (1916); H. M. Colvin, *The White Canons in England* (1951). (S. M. KI.)

PREPARATORY SCHOOL, a term usually restricted to schools whose special task is to prepare students for entrance to another educational institution. In Europe, where publicly maintained secondary education is selective, preparatory schools are frequently private and often cater to pupils wishing to enter the academic secondary schools. In North America, where secondary education is less selective and entry to it less competitive, preparatory schools tend to prepare students for college; *i.e.*, higher education (*see* COLLEGE).

In Britain the preparatory or "prep" schools form an integral part of the "public school" (*i.e.*, independent school) system. Boys enter the preparatory schools at about the age of 8 and usually leave between the ages of 11 and 13, often to attend one of the some 200 institutions regarded as public schools. Before

Thomas Arnold in the 1830s excluded boys under 12 from Rugby School there were few preparatory schools in England. By the middle of the 20th century over 500 preparatory schools were members of the Incorporated Association of Preparatory Schools founded in 1892. Conditions of membership require that the headmaster or the assistant headmaster is academically well-qualified, that the school has more than 35 boys (all under 15 years of age), that it prepares them for public schools, and that it is recognized as being efficient by the ministry of education. Cooperation between the preparatory schools and the public schools is very close. A joint committee is responsible for the common entrance examination to the latter and papers are set in English, mathematics, Latin, Greek, and general subjects. The curriculum of many preparatory schools includes all these subjects, although Greek is no longer compulsory. Preparatory schools are found in many English-speaking parts of the Commonwealth of Nations and in Brazil and Peru. As high schools for girls developed in Great Britain preparatory schools for them were established with aims similar to those of the boys' preparatory schools.

In the United States, a very high proportion (over 90% in some cases) of preparatory school graduates enters college or university. The age of enrollment is about 15, and the four- or five-year course is usually geared to meet the requirements of either the college entrance examination board or a particular institution. The growth of the private or semi-public secondary schools in the United States is usually traced back to the suggestions made by Benjamin Franklin in 1743 in his *Proposals Relating to the Education of Youth in Pennsylvania*. His academy in Philadelphia, which later became the University of Pennsylvania, was the first of many. The period of greatest growth was the first half of the 19th century. Most of the academies were founded by religious bodies, were semi-public, provided a broader, more vocationally oriented curriculum than the Latin schools, and extended education to girls. After 1850 when the public high school movement gained momentum the number of academies gradually declined. Those surviving tended to become private independent schools, nonsectarian in outlook and concentrating on college entrance. In the second half of the 20th century about 1,800 institutions in the United States (of about 3,000 private schools) were listed as college preparatory schools. Admission tests usually include a general school ability test, largely in arithmetic, a reading test, and an English test. Co-operation between the schools and the private colleges has always been close. In 1885 the New England Association of Colleges and Preparatory Schools was formed to promote common interests. Later, other state and regional associations of this kind were established which have helped to standardize criteria for college entrance. There have been for many years student exchanges between certain of the U.S. college preparatory schools and certain English public schools.

Preparatory schools are found in many other countries. In Japan, after World War II, the number of upper secondary school graduates going to special private preparatory schools for a year or two prior to entering the university rose steadily. In Europe there has been a reduction in the number of private elementary preparatory schools or state schools for which fees are charged. In Sweden a few such schools remain in some large towns. The elementary private preparatory schools (*Vorschulen*) in Germany were abolished shortly after World War I by the Weimar Republic. In France, the preparatory classes (*classes préparatoires*), attached to the state *lycées*, were formerly fee paying. The differences between these and primary classes in other schools were abolished so that primary education became identical everywhere. *See* also EDUCATION, HISTORY OF; SECONDARY EDUCATION.

BIBLIOGRAPHY.—*Preparatory Schools' Review,* issued by the Incorporated Association of Preparatory Schools (London, thrice yearly); IAPS, *Foundations: a Reconsideration of the Aims of Teaching in Preparatory Schools* (1959). *See* also articles in *Times Educational Supplement* (March 1962, Sept. 1962, Jan. 1963).
United States: Office of Education, *The State and Non-Public Schools* (1958); Ernest B. Chamberlain, *Our Independent Schools* (1944); Allan V. Heely, *Why the Private School?* (1951). (BR. H.)

PRE-RAPHAELITE BROTHERHOOD, the name adopted in 1848 by a group of young English artists who reacted violently against contemporary academic painting and sought to set new standards in their own work. Although its active life lasted at most ten years, the Brotherhood's influence on painting in England, and ultimately on the decorative arts and interior design, was profound. The members, all very young men, were seven, but in the initial stage they were only three, William Holman Hunt, John Everett (later Sir John Everett) Millais, and Dante Gabriel Rossetti (qq.v.), all painters. The painter James Collinson, the painter and critic F. G. Stephens, the sculptor Thomas Woolner, and the critic W. M. Rossetti (q.v.; Dante Gabriel's brother) joined them by invitation.

Hunt, Millais, and Rossetti, students at the Royal Academy schools, were deeply dissatisfied with the anecdotal and unimaginative paintings which formed the bulk of the display at the academy's annual exhibitions, and determined to set a new example in their own work. Insisting that most contemporary painting was derivative and basically untrue to nature, they stated their aims as: (1) to have genuine and lively ideas to express; and (2) to paint always directly from nature and never at secondhand. They tried to look at things as if they had never seen them before and in their best work the vivid quality resulting from this keen sense of purpose survives with remarkable freshness.

The term Pre-Raphaelite occurred to them almost incidentally. They had none of them been to Italy and they could have seen in England very few Italian pictures painted before Raphael's time. They were, however, deeply impressed by a set of engravings from the frescoes in the Campo Santo at Pisa and they knew of the revival of the early Italian style in the work of a group of German painters, called the Nazarenes, especially that of Peter von Cornelius and Friedrich Overbeck (qq.v.). They believed that the pursuit of the conventional resulted from the academic example set by Raphael which had dominated teaching in the schools and academies of Europe since his time. Hence their decision to call themselves the Pre-Raphaelite Brotherhood (indicated by the monogram PRB), and the gesture of defiance which this monogram implied.

The initiation of the Brotherhood was followed by production of some of its most significant work: Rossetti's "Ecce Ancilla Domini" (1850); Millais' "Christ in the House of His Parents" (1850) which was savagely criticized by Dickens on the grounds of lack of reverence; and Hunt's "The Hireling Shepherd" (1851). They frequently took their subjects from literature (e.g., Millais' "Ophelia," 1852), and Rossetti had a penchant for all things medieval, but perhaps their most representative work is that in which they were able to make a reference to the life of their own times and preach a sermon from it (Hunt, "The Awakening Conscience," 1854; Millais, "The Blind Girl," 1856). Ford Madox Brown, although never a member of the Brotherhood, produced pictures of this kind which were wholly Pre-Raphaelite in style in "The Last of England" (1852–55) and "Work" (1852–65); and a number of other young painters such as Arthur Hughes, Walter Deverell, and W. L. Windus also worked in the Pre-Raphaelite style. The work of the Brotherhood as a whole came in for severe criticism in its early days but it had a stout champion in John Rus-

kin (q.v.); and the members were never wholly without patrons, a number of whom were industrialists from the Midlands and North.

In 1858 Rossetti helped to organize a team of young men, Edward Burne-Jones and William Morris (qq.v.) among them, to paint a series of murals representing scenes from the Arthurian legend. From this association developed what is now known as the aesthetic movement; but it is important to remember that Morris and Burne-Jones belonged to a new generation and that their work is totally un-Pre-Raphaelite in character. Indeed, after 1858, first Rossetti and then Millais gradually abandoned PRB principles, and some of Millais' later great successes, such as "The North-West Passage" (1874) and "Cherry-Ripe" (1879), are the antithesis of all he was aiming at in the 1850s. Hunt alone pursued the same style fairly consistently. His masterpiece, and perhaps the masterpiece of the movement, is "The Scapegoat" (1854).

BIBLIOGRAPHY.—Percy H. Bate, The English Pre-Raphaelite Painters (1899); W. H. Hunt, Pre-Raphaelitism and the Pre-Raphaelite Brotherhood, 2 vol. (1905); R. Ironside and J. A. Gere, Pre-Raphaelite Painters (1948). (K. J. G.)

PREROGATIVE, in English law, means the residue of discretionary powers and legal immunities that are left in the hands of the sovereign (throughout this article generally referred to as "the queen").

As regards immunities a distinction has to be made between those peculiar to the queen in her "natural" capacity and confined to her (such as the rule that she is personally exempt from all jurisdiction and cannot be sued for debt) and those that belong to her political capacity and as such extend to the whole government carried on in her name (such as the immunity at common law of "the crown" from being sued by ordinary civil process, before the Crown Proceedings Act [1947]). English law, however, has never clearly distinguished between the two capacities, so that the sovereign has been completely identified with the state—indeed, modern British constitutional law does not employ the term "the state," although it is found in statutes, as, for example, in the Official Secrets Act, which refers to the "safety or interests of the State." All writs run in the queen's name.

As regards the prerogative powers of the sovereign (as distinct from powers conferred on the sovereign by statute) these can generally be exercised by the sovereign only on the advice of ministers or in particular forms and by the use of particular instruments. In foreign relations the queen has the exclusive power of making war and of declaring peace. The power is usually exercised by a proclamation and an order in council and, as such, it is binding on the courts. In practice the power is never exercised except with the approval of Parliament. The queen can make what treaties she pleases. (Whether she can cede British territory by negotiation of such a treaty is more doubtful and has been much disputed; but she can extend British territory; e.g., by incorporating an area of the open sea into territorial waters.)

The queen's prerogative in respect of foreign relations does not entitle her, whether pursuant to treaty or otherwise, to deprive the subject of his rights, as was decided in the case of Attorney-General v. Nissan (1969). It rests with the crown alone to "recognize" foreign governments as de jure governments. Such recognition is binding on the courts and, by a logical sequence, so is a declaration by the crown that a particular person is entitled to the status of a foreign sovereign and as such is immune from the jurisdiction of the courts. So, too, with the status of an ambassador and the diplomatic immunity of himself and his suite. The queen is head of the naval and military forces of the country and can alone recruit them. However, the raising, recruiting, and discipline of the armed forces are regulated by statute.

The requirement that the queen assent to a bill passed by both houses of Parliament before it can be enacted may be regarded as an aspect of the royal prerogative in that the queen may, in law, withhold her assent. This prerogative is not dead but it has not been exercised since the reign of Queen Anne. In the case of colonies this prerogative still exists and may be exercised; for example, by a governor acting in the queen's name.

It is the sole prerogative of the queen to summon, prorogue, and

"THE SCAPEGOAT," 1854, BY WILLIAM HOLMAN HUNT

dissolve Parliament. This is an executive, not a legislative, act and is performed only on the advice of ministers. It may be regarded as an accepted constitutional convention, at any rate since 1924, that the sovereign cannot refuse to dissolve Parliament when requested to do so by a prime minister. But the queen might still dissolve Parliament against the wishes of her prime minister under certain circumstances; e.g., should a prime minister, having been defeated on a direct vote of confidence in the Commons, refuse either to resign or to ask for a dissolution.

The theory of the law is that the government of the country is still a matter of prerogative; although many, if not most, of the executive powers now exercised by the crown have been conferred upon it by statute—in particular the power of making statutory rules and orders to carry a statute into effect. (See STATUTE LAW: Delegated Legislation.) All ministers are appointed by the queen —on the nomination of the prime minister—and "kiss hands," or, as in the case of secretaries of state, receive their seals from the queen herself.

In the choice of a prime minister the queen has in law, and may have in fact, a discretion; the latter situation was shown by the selection of Harold Macmillan to succeed Sir Anthony Eden in 1957. All military and naval officers and governors of colonies are appointed by a "commission" from the queen. And as she appoints, so she can dismiss from every office under the crown, except that those of the judges, the comptroller and auditor general, and the parliamentary commissioner for administration are held "during good behaviour," subject to removal on addresses from both Houses of Parliament. The general view is that servants of the crown have, apart from statute, no legally enforceable right to pay, pension, or security of tenure, but hold their employment "at the pleasure of the crown."

The queen is the supreme landowner, a relic of feudal doctrines, which means that, in the case of a man dying intestate and without next of kin, his estate goes to the crown. The queen also is the depositary of the prerogative of mercy: she can pardon those who offend against her "peace." This prerogative is now exercised exclusively on the advice of the home secretary. She is the sole grantor of titles such as peerages, baronetcies, and knighthoods, but "honours" are rarely conferred by her except on the advice of ministers. She is the "supreme governor" of the Church of England in virtue of the Acts of Supremacy and Uniformity.

In the course of English history, Parliament frequently has intervened to abolish some particular prerogative, and since the Revolution of 1689 it has never been doubted that such a statute binds not only the monarch who actually assents to it but all his successors as well. It was for long a matter of considerable doubt and speculation whether a statute could curtail a prerogative in the absence of express words to that effect; but it was decided in the case of Attorney-General v. De Keyser's Hotel (1920) that when Parliament has by statute regulated "the whole field of the prerogative," then that particular prerogative can be exercised in no other way than that prescribed by the statute.

See CONSTITUTION AND CONSTITUTIONAL LAW.

BIBLIOGRAPHY—F. W. Maitland, Collected Papers, vol. iii, 3 vol. (1911); A. V. Dicey, Introduction to the Study of the Law of the Constitution, ed. by E. C. S. Wade, 10th ed. (1959); W. R. Anson, The Law and Custom of the Constitution, vol. ii, The Crown, ed. by A. B. Keith, 4th ed. (1935); D. L. Keir and F. H. Lawson, Cases in Constitutional Law, 5th ed. (1967); E. C. S. Wade and G. Godfrey Phillips, Constitutional Law, 7th ed. by E. C. S. Wade and A. W. Bradley (1965). (J. H. Mo.; N. S. M.; W. T. Ws.)

PRESBYTERIANISM. The term Presbyterian distinguishes a group of Christian churches which took form during the British Reformation and which have since given rise to other churches bearing the same name in the Americas, Asia, and Africa. It is also the specific name of a form of church constitution or polity which claims its origin in the church during apostolic times and reformulation during the Swiss Reformation. Subsequently, this system was adopted, with variations, by many churches in other countries, some of which use the original name "Reformed Church," others the name "Presbyterian Church," and others other names. Generally speaking, the churches of British origin use some form of the name Presbyterian, while those of continental origin use some form of the name Reformed. This article is con-

cerned with the former group; for the latter, see REFORMED CHURCHES.

The Protestant Reformation in all the churches that became Reformed and Presbyterian arose partly from local roots and partly from outside influences. None of these churches received the Reformation as a finished system of faith and order which they had only to accept and adopt. Rather, each, over a span of years, sought to reform its faith, order, and life in the light of its understanding of the failures of the past.

As the Protestant Reformation in general got under way, these churches at first saw no real differences between themselves and the Lutheran churches. In the early period the influence of Luther, Philipp Melanchthon, and other "Lutherans" was often felt in these churches. However, after 1529–30 the churches of northern Germany and of the Scandinavian countries began drawing together as a distinct Lutheran group on the basis of one single uniform pattern of faith and order (see LUTHERANISM). The Reformed and Presbyterian churches continued as before to work out their reforms largely in terms of their local situations. Each of these churches drew up its own creeds, catechisms, orders of church government, and liturgies; and most of them made new translations or editions of the Bible adapted to the needs of their people. What bound these churches into a family, therefore, were certain general convictions regarding the Christian faith, the right ordering of the church, the service of God among men, and the conduct of the Christian life. It has become customary in many countries to call these churches Calvinistic, because of their debt to John Calvin (q.v.), the reformer of Geneva. But Calvin was the great expounder of what these churches already believed; he did not teach them things before unknown.

The term Presbyterian requires, therefore, discussion under two aspects: the Presbyterian churches of Christendom and the Presbyterian system, or manner of thinking about Christianity— i.e., doctrines, polity, worship, etc.

HISTORY OF THE PRESBYTERIAN CHURCHES

ENGLAND

In the English-speaking world Presbyterian ways of thinking first emerged in England. Even so, as events fell out, Presbyterianism became in time almost synonymous with "Scottish" and "Scotch-Irish," and English Presbyterianism was to lose its great bid to control the English Church, even at one period coming close to extinction.

Reformation.—The Reformation was late in taking hold in England and Scotland. The church in England remained unchanged in the Roman faith and obedience till 1534, the year in which Henry VIII's breach with Rome was completed. Yet that year marked only a hesitant beginning of reformation in England, and it was not till 1558 that Protestantism became at all secure. During the years before 1534 reforming influences were felt from several sources, among them the Christian humanists, the Lutherans, and the reformers of north Switzerland—Huldreich Zwingli and John Oecolampadius—and Martin Bucer and others of Strasbourg. The earliest English reformers, William Tyndale, John Frith, George Roye, John Rogers, Robert Barnes, Miles Coverdale, and others, began largely under humanist (Erasmian) influences, then were deeply attracted to Luther's work. But by the time (1529) Luther and his followers broke with the reformers of Switzerland and southern Germany, only Barnes, and perhaps Rogers, continued a straight Lutheran line. Since the outlook of the Swiss and south German reformers was that which is designated as Reformed, or Presbyterian, the major continental influence upon the English Reformation as a whole after 1530 was to be Reformed-Presbyterian.

Henry VIII tried to hold the church in England to a royally dominated nonpapal Catholicism. Under his son Edward VI (1547–53) Protestantism had a brief period of successful development. The leaders of the church, Thomas Cranmer, Nicholas Ridley, Hugh Latimer, and others, held it to a middle position between Catholicism and Protestantism, to the discontent of many who wished a more decisively Protestant position. These persons were greatly encouraged when several of the leading Reformed theologians of south Germany and Switzerland were brought into England by Cranmer in 1549–50 (Bucer, Pietro Martire Vermigli, Paul Fagius, and others). Yet Edward VI died before any drastic change in a Reformed-Presbyterian direction had taken place.

Under Mary's reign (1553–58) Roman Catholicism was restored and 800 of the younger Protestant leaders fled to the continent, where they came under strong Reformed influences. These influences, plus considerations of English policy, made some of the refugees more English than ever and more determined to pursue an "English" Reformation. Others saw in the continental churches which sheltered them that type of Reformed-Presbyterian doctrine, polity, and character which they had already come to accept intellectually but which they had not yet succeeded in instituting in England. These exiles became more convincedly Reformed-Presbyterian than ever.

Elizabeth I (1558–1603) restored Protestantism to England, but it was the Protestantism of the middle way, now proclaimed to be the English way. Few of the returning exiles had wished for quite as much of a compromise as Elizabeth and her counselors forced upon them, though gradually most of their leaders acquiesced, largely because of fear that the only possible alternatives were worse. Those who refused to accept these compromises as final, and who sought to secure further reforms, became known by the spite name Puritans. (*See* PURITANISM.) They lost their first encounter, the vestment controversy of the mid-16th century, a concerted attack on the external aspects of the Elizabethan settlement. Then came a frontal attack by a group of Puritans who came to be known as the Presbyterian party.

Thomas Cartwright led a powerful movement (1570–73) aimed at eliminating the entire episcopal system through which Elizabeth worked. He advocated a presbyterian system, modeled on the system of Calvin, in which the people chose their own pastors and then elected lay elders to share with the pastor in governing the local church. Central authority was vested in representative bodies of ministers and laymen who were chosen by the churches themselves or by the lower judicatures.

This first Presbyterian attempt at reforming the church was defeated. However, it did set in motion endeavours which shortly resulted in the working out, by Cartwright and others, of a coherent and comprehensive understanding of Christianity which formed the basis for all subsequent forms of Presbyterianism. Its underlying structure was that

THOMAS CARTWRIGHT (c. 1535–1603), LEADER OF THE PURITAN MOVEMENT UNDER ELIZABETH I

of covenant-contract, now in a much more fully worked out form, having its nearest likeness in the covenant system of the Rhineland-Netherlands reformers (*see* COVENANT THEOLOGY). Its church government theory was most nearly paralleled by Calvin's theory. Its austerity, its "blue laws," and its theocratic outlook have often been traced to Calvin, yet medieval England and medieval Geneva had known blue laws, and Calvin's own attitudes had come to him from Zürich via Strasbourg.

The Presbyterians were sabbatarian and antiliturgical, as were the Rhineland-Netherlands reformers; Calvin was the reverse. The Puritan and Presbyterian "prophesyings" were borrowed from Zürich. On decisive doctrines such as faith, repentance, law and gospel, the church, the ministry, and the two sacraments the Presbyterians stood nearest to the Rhineland-Netherlands reformers, not to Calvin or Luther. Politically their closest continental counterparts were the Huguenots.

Episcopal–Puritan–Presbyterian–Independent. — Though none of the contending groups in England realized it, the entire nature of the struggle, as well as the whole character of the English Reformation, was changing. The events which followed the excommunication of Elizabeth by Pope Pius V in 1570 terminated any real Romanist-Protestant controversy within England. Moreover, the rise of another generation within the Protestant group brought new issues to the fore. Such men as John Whitgift and Richard Bancroft led the episcopal party into a defense of the Elizabethan settlement on the grounds of divine right and royal authority. The Puritan group developed new tensions and alignments. The presbyterians demanded parliamentary establishment of their system, for which divine right was asserted. The Independents (later Congregationalists) became divided between those who desired the establishment of their system and those who wished a wholly free church with no established church of any kind. Moreover, other issues, baptism, "inner light," the ministry, etc., divided this latter group of Independents.

Each of these contending parties and groups sought control of the church in order to preserve or institute its own ideals. Each sought for allies—religious, political, and economic. As the struggle went on into the reigns of James I and Charles I it became, more and more, a barren power conflict, and theological or religious issues became secondary. Yet great theological changes were occurring. Within the royal-episcopal party a form of Arminianism (*q.v.*) became entrenched. Among the Puritans federalism (the perfected covenant theology) gained complete control—only to see Puritanism break up into three wings: (1) a right wing (presbyterian) stressing the objective, given character of the biblical revelation; the fundamental, given character of the natural law; the due authority of representative governing bodies in church and state; etc.; (2) a left wing (Brownist-sectarian) stressing the guidance of conscience, individual freedom, and the tentative nature of all external order and authority; (3) a centre wing (Independent-congregational) stressing the same general outlook as the presbyterian wing but wishing to vest all authority in local groups rather than in a powerful central authority. As the problem of power, or authority, dominated the entire struggle, all factions tended to lose sight of other events that were taking place. Accordingly, when the English Civil War began (1642) most men were unprepared for what they found to be the actual state of affairs. (*See* CIVIL WAR, ENGLISH: *Background to the War.*)

Beginning with the "Root and Branch Petition" to Parliament (1640), events moved steadily toward control of England by the presbyterian-parliamentary party. Charles was driven to accept a bill removing bishops from all temporal offices, and depriving them of their powers of arrest and imprisonment. This move satisfied many. The presbyterian-parliamentary party drove on, however, for a complete victory. By several overzealous acts they alienated the moderate nobles and others who had not yet declared for the king. Moreover, the Scots became neutral. Meanwhile Parliament abolished prelacy in the church and began preparations to institute presbyterian forms. An Assembly of Divines was summoned to advise Parliament in religious matters. Two ministers from each county of England were appointed, plus 10 peers, and 20 commons. A majority were Puritans of the right wing, a few were royal-episcopalians but they took no part; five were Independents.

The excesses of the king in 1642–43 drove the Scots once more into an alliance with his enemies. The parliamentary party now signed (1643) the Solemn League and Covenant with the Scots, pledging the civil and religious unity of England, Scotland, and Ireland under a presbyterian-parliamentary system. The Parliament now ordered the Assembly of Divines to proceed, with the aid of six Scottish advisers, to the drafting of a completely new religious constitution for the three kingdoms.

The assembly (called the Westminster Assembly because its meetings were held in Westminster Abbey) then elaborated (1643–49) a Confession of Faith, a Larger and a Shorter Catechism (*see* WESTMINSTER CONFESSION; CATECHISM: *Presbyterian*), a Form of Government, and a Directory of Public Worship. These documents, the results of years of debate by many able scholars, put in classic form a consistent federalism. The Westminster Assembly was merely an advisory committee of the English Parliament, however, and its constitutional documents met an odd fate. The Scottish Church and the Scottish Parliament accepted them promptly. The English Parliament delayed accepting them because of the growing power of the Independents. The English Church never had an opportunity to consider them.

Even with the aid of the Scots the military fortunes of the parliamentary party were unfortunate. It became necessary, at length, to allow Oliver Cromwell to create the New Model Army, which, although it proved invincible against the king, also proved invincible as the Independent-left-wing Puritans' force against the right-wing presbyterian Puritans. The army, not Parliament, became supreme in England. Its political-religious program alienated the Scots and the right-wing Puritans. Some right-wing leaders began to have intelligence with the king, believing that a government of law and order, though despotic, was better than army rule by sectaries. Eventually, in 1648, Col. Thomas Pride's soldiers "purged" Parliament of all presbyterians (140) leaving about 60 Independent Puritans in the Commons. This "Rump Parliament" tried and executed Charles I, set up a military dictatorship under Cromwell, terminated the Presbyterian establishment, and granted freedom to all religious groups while giving special privileges to Congregationalism under a modified form of establishment.

As the meaning of the left-wing movement became clearer the right-wing Puritans revolted completely. Many protested the execution of the king and the establishment of the dictatorship. Opposition was hampered seriously, however, by the now evident inner weakness of the right-wing movement. The presbyterian-Puritans had lost their popular following. Despite the large place accorded to the laity in the general structure of the presbyterian system, circumstances had led to the formation of only a ministerial party and not to the formation of a Presbyterian Church. Fear of the Independents and reliance upon Parliament and upon strong political figures had been disastrous. Few of the several thousand congregations held by the presbyterians ever had elders or any lay leadership. Moreover, the controversy with the episcopal party had come to involve almost exclusively issues of greatest moment only to the clergy. The right-wing Puritan-parliamentary party, accordingly, was without enough popular support to take any decisive action.

Restoration, Revolution, and After.—Hopeless chaos reigned after Cromwell's death. Gen. George Monck reassembled the Long Parliament, thus putting great powers in the hands of the presbyterian-parliamentary group formerly purged by Colonel Pride. They reestablished presbyterianism, although granting tolerance to other Protestant bodies. Something better than army rule, however, was needed. Hence, all the right-wing groups, parliamentary and presbyterian, royalist and episcopal, joined in restoring Charles II unconditionally. Charles quibbled briefly with the presbyterians, who were now in full control of the church with about 8,000 beneficed ministers and professors. These ministers offered to accept a modified form of episcopacy first elaborated by Archbishop James Ussher. Charles, realizing that his real supporters were the royalist-episcopal group, rejected this offer and demanded capitulation. About 6,000 ministers accepted reordination, unqualified oaths of obedience to bishops and king, abjuration of the Solemn League and Covenant. Two thousand were ejected, of whom approximately 1,500 were presbyterian and 500 Independent. Later, many of these (about 500) conformed to the episcopal terms.

The Revolution of 1688 brought to the throne a king genuinely friendly to presbyterianism. In view of the total situation, however, no more was gained by his accession than a measure of toleration for all Protestants. Under this toleration and its subsequent enlargements, a number (often given as high as 500) of Presbyterian congregations existed. In almost no recorded instances did any of these churches have elders or any lay leadership. Ministerial thought continued to develop along extremely autocratic and High Church lines. Such presbyteries as existed were almost exclusively ministerial. Since many of the stronger churches became endowed, actual control of them passed into the hands of the minister and a few trustees. Laymen lost all part in them. In the early part of the 18th century many of these ministers became Unitarians and numerous others conformed to the Anglican establishment. The greater number of those who cherished the older Puritan ideals became Independent-Congregationalist under the influence of the movement known as the United Brethren, organized under the Heads of Agreement of 1691. By the close of the 18th century English Presbyterianism had become virtually extinct.

Scots began coming into England in increasing numbers after the union of 1707. Many of these were Seceders, hence rigorous Presbyterians. Soon they had several congregations. In 1847 these, together with certain of the surviving English Presbyterian congregations and other Scottish groups, merged as the United Presbyterian Church. This body joined with the remaining English Presbyterians and most of the other Scots churches in England to form in 1876 the Presbyterian Church of England. It then had 259 congregations with about 50,000 members. A theological college was founded at London in 1844 and later moved to Cambridge under the name of Westminster College. In the late 1960s the Presbyterian Church of England had 315 congregations and 68,000 members. (*See also* ENGLISH HISTORY.)

SCOTLAND

Although Presbyterianism as such took form in England, and there received its definitive theoretical delineation by the Westminster Assembly, it was in Scotland that Presbyterianism was to take its deepest roots. Moreover, although the Scottish Reformation was begun under essentially Genevan Calvinistic patterns, it adopted in time, and became the very incarnation of, the patterns of English Presbyterianism. It was able, however, to give to laymen a real place in the life of the church. Consequently in no country did Presbyterianism so deeply affect the national life as it did in Scotland. In many ways Scottish history provides the best available illustration of Presbyterianism at work.

John Knox.—Scotland's first reforming martyr was Patrick Hamilton (1504–28), who had been influenced by personal contact

CULVER PICTURES, INC.

JOHN KNOX (c. 1514–72), ENGRAVED BY H. T. RYALL FROM THE ORIGINAL PORTRAIT AT THE PALACE OF HOLY-ROODHOUSE, EDINBURGH

with Luther, Tyndale, and other reformers. George Wishart, burned in 1546, had traveled in England and Switzerland; his ideas were essentially Zwinglian. His assistant, John Knox (*q.v.*), was to become the real leader of the Reformation in Scotland. Before long Knox had to flee and found refuge in England. During the reign of Edward VI he was an active leader in the English Reformation. When Queen Mary restored Roman Catholicism, Knox fled to the continent with the English reformers and eventually became pastor of an English refugee church at Geneva. In 1555–56 he visited Scotland and preached vigorously in the interests of the Reformation. The next year, certain nobles, the "Lords of the Congregation," led the Scottish reforming group in signing the first great covenant binding themselves to support the Reformation. Knox returned permanently to Scotland in 1559. A year later the reforming group, through English pressure on the Scottish regent, gained its first great victory. The Scots Confession (*Confessio Scoticana*) of 1560 was drawn up and accepted by Parliament. A Book of Common Order (Knox's Liturgy; see LITURGY, CHRISTIAN), a Metrical Psalter and a Book of Discipline (The First Book of Discipline, 1561) were also drawn up by the reformers. Parliament did not ratify these, but the church was deeply influenced by a rather general acceptance of them.

These documents were all decisively Genevan in character. Knox, who had been deeply influenced by Calvin, was the leader in their framing. The Book of Discipline was an advance on Calvin's system in that it applied Genevan ideals on a national scale, following a lead given by the Huguenots. A General As-

EARLY SCOTTISH MARTYRS: (LEFT) GEORGE WISHART (c. 1513–46), EN-
GRAVED BY S. FREEMAN; (RIGHT) PATRICK HAMILTON (1504–28). BOTH
FROM ORIGINAL PORTRAITS IN THE UNIVERSITY OF GLASGOW

sembly was instituted as the national meeting of representatives of the church. Here, in free debate, issues were to be determined by a body of ministers and laymen met under their own chairman and at their own call. Also a governing body, the Church Session, was instituted for each local church. This body consisted of elders elected by the people and had as its chairman the pastor of the church. The people themselves were given the right to elect their pastor, and this election, rather than ordination by other ministers, made a man a minister. Episcopacy was abolished, but several superintendents were named to itinerate in areas without ministers and to have some limited administrative duties. The religious prerogatives and authority of bishops were not given to them, however, and they did not preside over the church courts.

The last four decades of the 16th century witnessed the defeat of the Reformed, or Presbyterian, Scottish Church in spite of several notable temporary victories. In 1581 the Presbyterians gained parliamentary sanction for their Second Book of Discipline and for the so-called Negative Confession of Faith, better known as the King's Confession. Moreover, regional church governing bodies, the presbyteries, began to be set up. Yet, the Parliament of 1584 placed bishops in control of most of the church and the more prominent Presbyterian leaders were forced to flee to England. In 1592 the Presbyterians were able to extort from the king sanction for a parliamentary law which has ever since been regarded as the Magna Carta of Scottish Presbyterianism. Five years later the king, working through bishops forced upon the church, gained almost complete control of the entire church, a control which lasted until the first of the Bishops' Wars in 1639.

After the Union.—James VI of Scotland became king of England also in 1603 and then set out to make the Scottish Church the principal instrument of his absolutism in Scotland. Between 1603 and 1612 he brought the church wholly under the power of his bishops. From 1612 until his death he was occupied in shaping the life and work of the church to serve his general policies. At his death Scotland was under an unqualified absolutism.

Charles I (reign 1625–49) continued the Tudor-Stuart policy of using the episcopacy as an instrument in the furtherance of royal absolutism, with Archbishop John Spottiswoode his chief agent in Scotland. When, however, Charles, Archbishop William Laud, and Spottiswoode attempted to force the last degree of submission upon the Scottish Church, namely "Laud's liturgy," popular resentment came to the aid of the church. In a wave of public feeling expressing opposition to the whole of Stuart absolutism, the covenant of 1557 was "renewed" by signatures of all classes all over Scotland. Spottiswoode and all but 4 of his 50 fellow bishops fled to England. In the two Bishops' Wars which followed the Scots demanded, basically, free parliaments and free general assemblies. Charles lost the wars and granted the demands. Parliament and the General Assembly abolished the entire episcopal regime and restored Presbyterianism as of its "Magna Carta" of 1592.

In 1643 the two parliaments signed the Solemn League and Cove-

nant between England and Scotland. Upon this basis of a union of England, Scotland, and Ireland in state and church, the two presbyterian-parliamentary groups worked together in opposing the episcopal-royalist absolutism. One aspect of this cooperation was the adoption by the Scottish Church of the religious constitution framed by the Westminster Assembly. Scottish Presbyterianism thus passed from a Genevan-Calvinistic pattern to a Puritan-federalist pattern. When the Independents gained control in England, purged the presbyterians and executed Charles I, many of the Scots objected and proclaimed Charles II. Cromwell defeated the Scots' armies and held the country under military occupation. During this occupation the church was not persecuted. It had, moreover, a great series of religious awakenings under Covenanter leadership. (*See* COVENANTERS.)

Charles II, at the Restoration, brought back the episcopacy as an instrument of royal absolutism into Scotland as well as into England. Under Archbishop James Sharp a veritable Inquisition reigned in Scotland, "the killing times," as the Covenanter movement was wiped out. When William and Mary came to the throne in 1689 presbyterianism was restored finally by constitutional act. However, despite some opposition, most of the former episcopal clergy retained their pastorates.

Presbyterian Scotland.—After 1689 Scotland was unquestionably Presbyterian, but new problems arose. Within the established state church were now two parties—one a group of convinced Presbyterians who had only recently been terribly persecuted by king and bishop, the other a group who had served the persecutors and now served the current regime with no great concern for it or against it. The next generation saw the rise of a large group of essentially professional clergymen known as Moderates, whose deepest interests were in social life, in culture, and in their prerogatives within a state establishment. An Evangelical group sought to promote the older Reformation ideals. In 1707 the Scottish and English parliaments were united. Five years later the Parliament restored patronage in Scotland. This meant that the local landowner had the right of nominating the minister for the congregation, and the people lost the right of electing their pastors. This system of patronage quickly brought the Church of Scotland under the control of the Moderate ministers and the wealthy landowners. As many protests were made against patronage, the Moderates claimed supreme powers for the General Assembly, which they controlled, and did not hesitate to resort to the use of military escorts and to the imprisonment of dissenting ministers to enforce their dictates.

By 1733 resistance to the Moderates and to patronage led to the deposition of four ministers. Led by Ebenezer Erskine they formed a secession church, the Associate Presbytery (the Seceders). This body "renewed" the Solemn League and Covenant in 1742 and 1744. Even so some members desired greater attachment to the old covenanting ideals and withdrew to form the Reformed Presbytery (1743). In 1811 this group became the Reformed Presbyterian Church (*see* CAMERONIANS). Within the Seceder group also the covenanting principle raised the problem of their relation to the state, which supported the church from which they had separated themselves. In 1747 they divided into two groups, known after 1788 as the General Associate Synod (Antiburgher; *i.e.*, against taking the burgher's oath in various cities) and the Associate Synod (Burgher; *i.e.*, willing to take the oaths). By 1799 and 1805 the problem of the civil government's authority in religious matters broke both these bodies into Auld Licht ("old light") and New Licht sections.

Meanwhile patronage and the Moderate party caused further discontent. In 1761 Thomas Gillespie (deposed in 1752 for resistance to the General Assembly) founded the Presbytery of Relief, a tolerant, evangelical, non-Covenanter body designed to provide relief for ministers and congregations who wished to withdraw peacefully from the establishment. In 1773 it assumed the name of Relief Church of Scotland.

These new groups grew rapidly, and were greatly strengthened by the evangelical revivals, the Sunday School movement, and the new missionary spirit. In 1820 a United Secession Church was formed by certain segments of secession bodies, and in 1827 others formed the Associate Synod of Original Seceders. These unions involved Burghers, Antiburghers, Auld Lichts and New.

From 1833 to 1843 a severe struggle took place within the Church of Scotland between the Moderates and the Evangelical group, now greatly strengthened by the revivals and the Sunday schools. Finally when the government in London supported on legal grounds the entire Moderate structure, the Disruption led by Thomas Chalmers (*q.v.*) took place. A Free Church of Scotland

CULVER PICTURES, INC.

THOMAS CHALMERS (1780–1847), LEADER OF THE DISRUPTION OF 1843 AND FIRST MODERATOR OF THE FREE CHURCH OF SCOTLAND

was formed by 474 ministers and thousands of lay people, free of state control, free of patronage, and zealously evangelical. All but one of the Church of Scotland's missionaries, and most of its best scholars, joined the Free Church. Thereafter the Free Church led all Christian causes in Scotland.

The United Presbyterian Church was founded in 1847 by the union of the Relief Church with the United Secession Church. In 1852 about half of the Associate Synod of Original Seceders joined the Free Church of Scotland. The year 1876 witnessed the union of the majority of the Reformed Presbyterians with the Free Church. Union negotiations between the United Presbyterian Church and the Free

Church raised many problems. A small group left the Free Church in protest against the union and formed the Free Presbyterian Church. Eventually, in 1900 the United Free Church of Scotland was formed by a merger of the Free Church and the United Presbyterians. A small group, the "Wee Frees," remained outside as the Free Church of Scotland. In many ways the United Free Church was the most vigorous religious body in Scotland.

Before long, attempts were made to unite the United Free Church and the old Church of Scotland. Patronage had been abolished in 1874, and the old Moderate party had given way to a better leadership in the Church of Scotland. The issue of an established state church proved insoluble, however, until after World War I. Both churches had drawn closer together in the meanwhile. In 1921 the state by law severed its old relation with the Church of Scotland, leaving it "the national church" but not the established state church. This allowed union negotiations to make progress, and in 1929 the two churches united under the original name of the Church of Scotland. A small group remained outside and continued the name United Free Church.

Vast changes, meanwhile, had greatly altered the total religious situation in Scotland. The Lowlands had become industrialized and had brought in large numbers of Irish workmen, most of whom were Roman Catholics. The Highlands were being depopulated by changing economic conditions. Presbyterianism as a whole enrolled only a fourth of the population of Scotland, and three-fifths of the Scots were nominally in no church. The Church of Scotland had lost heavily among the labouring classes and in the rural areas.

Various movements were under way, each seeking in some measure to improve conditions: a High Church liturgical movement; a movement to bring together in the church the labouring classes and student groups (Iona group); and a movement for the recovery of a more adequate theology. The Church of Scotland continued to be active in missionary work and to take a leading part in the ecumenical movement among the Protestant churches throughout the world. A move to affiliate the Church of Scotland with the Church of England was defeated in 1959.

Five Presbyterian bodies remain in Scotland (figures are approximate, for the late 1960s): (1) Church of Scotland, 1,250,000 members, 2,200 congregations; (2) United Free Church, 25,000 and 100; (3) Free Church of Scotland, 5,500 and 160; (4) Re-

formed Presbyterian Church (Cameronians), 550 and 5; (5) Free Presbyterian Church, 800 members.

See also SCOTLAND: *History;* SCOTLAND, CHURCH OF; SCOTLAND, FREE CHURCH OF; UNITED FREE CHURCH OF SCOTLAND; UNITED PRESBYTERIAN CHURCH.

IRELAND AND WALES

Ireland.—Except for scattered Puritan groups, Irish Presbyterianism began with the Irish plantation of 1610. These Presbyterians were first in the established church under the tolerant Archbishop Ussher. Charles I and Archbishop Laud drove them out. During the English Civil War they suffered vicissitudes much like those of the Scottish Presbyterians. William III gained for them only partial toleration. Until 1869 their harsh lot led hundreds of thousands to migrate to North America.

Scottish controversies usually had their counterparts in Ulster. Seceders appeared in 1741 and organized in 1750; Reformed Presbyterians came in 1752 and organized in 1792. The Synod of Ulster was the main Presbyterian body, but it did not include the Presbyterians in Dublin and south and west Ireland, which formed the Synod of Munster. Severe doctrinal controversies occurred in the 18th and 19th centuries. Each time a Unitarian group left the church. Consequently Irish Presbyterianism became very conservative in theology. In 1840 the Secession Church and the Synod of Ulster merged as the Presbyterian Church in Ireland. The Synod of Munster joined them in 1854.

Two Presbyterian bodies remain in Ireland: (1) Presbyterian Church in Ireland, with (late 1960s) about 144,000 communicants and 570 congregations; (2) Reformed Presbyterian Church, with about 3,400 members.

Wales.—The Presbyterian Church of Wales, known also as the Calvinistic Methodist Church, grew out of the evangelical revival of the 18th century. Howel Harris and other friends of George Whitefield led the movement and gave to it the general society character of the Wesleyan societies but the doctrinal convictions of Calvinistic Puritanism. Its earliest organization outside the Church of England in Wales took place in 1811 on a Presbyterian form of polity.

CULVER PICTURES, INC.

HOWEL HARRIS (1714–73), OF THE WELSH CALVINISTIC METHODIST CHURCH

Two synods, or associations, were formed, one for South Wales and one for North Wales. Twelve years later a Calvinistic, Presbyterian creed was officially adopted. In 1864 a General Assembly was formed to unite, but not to control, the two associations. About one-fourth of the congregations use the English language in some measure. In the late 1960s it had about 123,000 communicants. (*See* CALVINISTIC METHODISM.)

COMMONWEALTH OF NATIONS

Canada.—Presbyterianism first took real root in Canadian territory after the Treaty of Paris of 1763. Settlement of Scots in Nova Scotia brought many Presbyterians there. In 1817 the various elements united as the Synod of Nova Scotia in Connection with the Church of Scotland. Then, in 1835, the Synod of New Brunswick in Connection with the Church of Scotland was formed. These bodies were all at work in eastern Canada.

Farther to the west the Church of Scotland was also sending ministers and aid. Secession groups had already organized, in 1826, the United Presbytery of Canada. In 1831 the Synod of the Presbyterian Church of Canada in Connection with the Church of Scotland was organized. These two bodies united in 1840.

The Disruption of 1843 in the Church of Scotland caused parallel ruptures in all the Canadian Presbyterian churches. In 1845 there were seven separate bodies. Thirty years later, in 1875, all had reunited in the Presbyterian Church in Canada, with several colleges and a strong body of congregations and ministers.

The 20th century brought new problems to Canada, theological as well as social and economic. Roman Catholicism was growing. The sparse population of the Canadian prairies put a severe drain on all Protestant home mission efforts. The changing scene in Canada had made Protestantism too exclusively urban. As early as 1890 projects for uniting Canadian Protestants had been broached rather widely. The Church of England in Canada quickly dropped out of these negotiations, but the two largest Protestant bodies, the Presbyterians and the Methodists, together with the much smaller Congregational Church, united as the United Church of Canada in 1925. A sizable minority of Presbyterians refused to enter the union and continued as the Presbyterian Church in Canada.

The United Church of Canada continued to maintain official connections with other Presbyterian and Reformed churches throughout the world. In government it is essentially Presbyterian, although in doctrine and other matters it allows great latitude to points of view traditionally non-Presbyterian, because of its Methodist and Congregational constituencies.

The two churches are represented as follows: (1) United Church of Canada (mid-1960s), about 1,000,000 members, 2,700 churches; (2) Presbyterian Church in Canada, 192,000 members, 770 churches. (*See* also UNITED CHURCH OF CANADA.)

Australia.—Australian Presbyterianism was essentially Scottish in origin and character. The first organized body was founded in 1826 by Church of Scotland ministers. During the stormy years following, the divisions of the homeland had their counterparts in Australia. Reunions of fragments formed the Presbyterian Church of New South Wales in 1865; the Presbyterian Church of Victoria in 1870; and smaller bodies in Queensland, Western Australia, South Australia, and Tasmania. A federal union of most of these bodies was formed in 1886, and in 1901 all united in the Presbyterian Church of Australia. Considerable local autonomy was granted each of the regional bodies. From 1918 to 1923 strenuous efforts were made to achieve a union among Presbyterians, Methodists, and Congregationalists similar to that achieved in Canada, but without success. The Presbyterian Church of Australia in the 1960s had about 104,000 members.

New Zealand.—Presbyterianism in New Zealand arose in two distinct migrations. To the northern regions came Church of Scotland ministers as early as 1840. The first presbytery was founded at Auckland in 1856 and later grew into the Presbyterian Church of New Zealand. In the southern area Scottish Free churchmen founded a model religious colony at Dunedin in 1848 which grew first into the Presbytery of Otago (1854), then the Presbyterian Church of Otago and Southland. In 1901 these bodies united as the Presbyterian Church of New Zealand. It had about 75,000 members in the 1960s.

UNITED STATES

There are ten Presbyterian bodies in the United States. Six of these, embracing 88% of all U.S. Presbyterians, are parts of one mainstream which is essentially American in origin and character. The other four (12%) are bodies which have sought to continue in the American scene certain specifically Scottish movements. The United Presbyterian Church in the U.S.A., the largest single body, is a union (1958) of two bodies of different backgrounds, the Presbyterian Church in the U.S.A. and the United Presbyterian Church of North America. The united church in the late 1960s had about 3,300,000 members in more than 9,000 churches. Since the backgrounds of the two merged bodies are so different, an account will be given of each group prior to the merger.

The Presbyterian Church in the U.S.A.—The earliest Presbyterian churches in the American colonies were planted on Long Island by New England Puritans who preferred the presbyterian way to the congregationalist. Very soon after, Scotch-Irish, English, and other settlers formed Presbyterian churches in Maryland, Delaware, and Pennsylvania. In 1706, some of these joined in a loosely organized presbytery which in 1716 was expanded to a synod of three presbyteries. The church continued to be a blend of New England Puritan Presbyterians and Ulster Presbyterians, plus Welsh and other elements.

Because this new body was not attached to a parent body in Great Britain, it had to form its own character and constitution. The Scotch-Irish element regarded doctrine as the basis of the church, strove for unqualified subscription to the Westminster Confession and for centralized church authority able to enforce conformity. The New England element regarded the Christian life as the basis of the church, accepted creeds as expressions of the faith held by the church, and wished the superior church courts to have only limited and fixed powers. The revivals of the Great Awakening broke the church in two in 1741. The New England (pro-revival) element, called the New Side, trebled in the next few years, and the Scotch-Irish (anti-revival), called the Old Side, declined. In 1758 the two groups reunited on a compromise. At that time the New England element greatly outnumbered the Scotch-Irish. Beginning in 1760, however, several hundred thousand Scotch-Irish immigrants came to the colonies. Many of these joined the Presbyterian Church, and its character gradually changed to the Scotch-Irish pattern.

In the struggles leading up to the American Revolution the Presbyterians took a vigorous part. They formed an alliance with the Congregationalists of New England in order to prevent the settling of Anglican bishops on the colonies, because they feared an intolerant establishment was contemplated. The struggle for colonial independence was, in time, called a Christian cause. In personnel and property the church suffered heavily in the war. The near triumph of deism among Americans after the war came as a staggering blow to the church. During the years 1785–88 a General Assembly was founded with an explicit constitution. Some resistance was offered by those who feared extreme centralization. In the constitution, therefore, all reserve powers were left with the presbyteries, and the higher, central, courts were given limited and fixed powers only. Doctrinal subscriptions continued to be flexible.

The church took up frontier missions, benevolent work, the founding of schools, etc., with vigour. A series of revivals greatly increased its strength, despite some concurrent problems. Charles G. Finney and Lyman Beecher were active evangelistic leaders of the second quarter of the 19th century.

In 1801 the church entered into a Plan of Union with the New England Congregationalists. Though the churches did not merge, they federated their home missionary work on the frontier. This drew the two denominations closer together everywhere, and raised again the old Scotch-Irish versus New England antipathies of the 18th century. Moreover, New England theology was restless and inquiring, while the Scotch-Irish tended to consider theology a finished structure which must be protected against innovation.

In the South the church was almost wholly Scotch-Irish, and proslavery sentiment there kept most Northern Scotch-Irish Presbyterians either proslavery or neutral. The Presbyterians of New England background were generally antislavery.

After years of turmoil a majority in the assembly of 1837 abrogated the Plan of Union, expelled illegally all the federated churches, and demanded subjection by all to the assembly. During the ensuing year nearly half of the church refused to recognize these acts and joined the expelled group in declaring themselves to be the genuine Presbyterian Church and the group that had ousted them to be schismatic. The civil lower courts declared them to be the continuing church, but the appellate court reversed the decision. They continued the name Presbyterian Church in the U.S.A. and added "New School." The other group took the same name but added "Old School."

The New School denomination continued, as before 1837, to work in close cooperation with the Congregationalists in home and foreign missions, in antislavery, temperance, and other work. Though it had a few congregations in the South (these withdrew in 1856–57), it was largely a Northern church. The Congregationalists abrogated the Plan of Union in 1852, though the two churches continued some joint work. Even so, the abrogation was a setback for the Presbyterians. In frontier missions, education, and benevolent work they made great contributions. Union Theological Seminary in New York City became their great centre.

During the American Civil War the church was active on the Northern side.

The Old School Presbyterians built a well-organized church on the basis of their doctrinal, racial, and social homogeneity. Though spread over all the nation, their great strength was among the Scotch-Irish and Scottish groups. Princeton Seminary became their focal point. A solid denominational structure enabled them to make great strides in missions, colleges, and Sunday School work. The Civil War brought new issues. The Old School Assembly of 1861 passed the Gardiner Spring resolutions which so wholly committed the church to the Northern view that the entire Southern section of the church seceded to form the Presbyterian Church in the Confederate States of America.

After the war the North-South groups of the two churches could not agree to reunite. Unions took place instead of New School and Old School to form in the South the Presbyterian Church in the United States (see below) and in the North the Presbyterian Church in the U.S.A.

The Northern reunited church took up frontier mission work anew, built new colleges and institutions, expanded Sunday School, youth, and benevolent work, as the nation moved westward. A quarter of a century of achievement was interrupted by a major controversy which arose as a result of the influence of the new scientific views upon Christian thought. There came first (about 1892) a long struggle over biblical criticism, followed (about 1910) by the organization, on an international scale, of an interdenominational group, strongly Presbyterian, to defend the "fundamentals" of the faith. By World War I the Fundamentalist-Modernist controversy was intense. Moderate groups pleaded for comprehension within the church of all essentially Christian views, but without success. The struggle now assumed a new form. The Fundamentalist group attacked various boards and institutions of the church as unorthodox and founded within the church rival institutions of their own to compete with the church's institutions. This brought judicial process in the church courts against J. Gresham Machen and other Fundamentalist leaders. Most Fundamentalists then drew back from the controversy. A few, however, joined with Machen in founding the Presbyterian Church in America (see FUNDAMENTALISM).

Between World Wars I and II the Presbyterian Church in the U.S.A. came to have one of the largest foreign missionary enterprises in the world. In the U.S. the church sponsored more than 50 colleges and 9 theological schools. As national and international cooperative ventures among churches were launched the Presbyterians took an active part. Negotiations for union were undertaken with other Reformed and Presbyterian bodies and with the Methodists and the Episcopalians. The major part of the Cumberland Presbyterian Church (see below) reunited with the U.S.A. Presbyterians in 1906. The Welsh Calvinistic Methodists merged with the Presbyterians in 1920. Attempts to reunite the U.S. Presbyterians and the U.S.A. Presbyterians failed. In 1958 the United Presbyterian Church of North America merged with the U.S.A. Presbyterians. At the time of the merger the U.S.A. Presbyterians had 2,809,603 members and 8,658 churches.

United Presbyterian Church of North America.—Covenanters, or Reformed Presbyterians, began coming to North America, principally from Ireland, before 1750, and in 1774 their first presbytery was founded. Seceder Presbyterians organized a presbytery in 1758. Both groups were located principally in Pennsylvania. In 1782 the Reformed Presbyterians and some of the Associate (Seceder) Presbyterians united, and these together with other Secession groups united to form in 1858 the United Presbyterian Church of North America. Covenanter and Secession backgrounds made this church very conservative in doctrine and worship. At first it practised closed communion, sang only psalms in public worship, adhered to the Solemn League and Covenant, etc. Gradually, however, changes came as the memory of Scottish issues faded. The church was early active in the antislavery cause and in other significant reform movements. Due to its solid Scottish and Scotch-Irish background, its main strength lay in Pennsylvania, Ohio, New York, Illinois, and Iowa. When in 1958 the church merged with the U.S.A. Presbyterians it had 251,344 mem-

bers and 833 churches.

The Presbyterian Church in the United States.—This body, commonly called the Southern Presbyterian Church, came into being during the Civil War, when the Old School churches in the Confederate states seceded from the Presbyterian Church in the U.S.A. to form the Presbyterian Church in the Confederate States of America. The war also cut off other Southern Presbyterian bodies from their Northern brethren. Older lines of cleavage lost their meaning. In 1864 the United Synod of the South (largely New School) merged with the Confederate Presbyterians, as also did certain small units of Seceders and Covenanters. Border state Presbyterian bodies, at first neutral, joined also: Synod of Kentucky, 1869; Synod of Missouri, 1874. After the war, the name Presbyterian Church in the United States was adopted.

The church continued to devote its energies to the Southern states, Texas, Arkansas, and Missouri marking in general its western boundaries. It is essentially Scottish and Scotch-Irish in membership and traditions. Its homogeneity ethnically, geographically, and socially makes it a very close-knit body. Traditionally the church divides between a spiritual and a political approach to problems, always rejecting the latter. As a result the church has been very conservative on all religious, political, and social issues. Yet in educational and benevolent enterprises it has long been a leader in the South, its educational and missionary ventures being especially significant. In its polity great care has been taken to promote local initiative and to restrict the powers of all central agencies. The church in the late 1960s had nearly 1,000,000 members in about 4,000 churches.

The Cumberland Presbyterian Church.—The Cumberland Church grew out of a purely American situation—frontier conditions. Differences of opinion regarding the great Kentucky revival of 1799–1802; impatience with high educational requirements for a frontier ministry and with excessive ecclesiastical authority; differences on the subject of predestination, etc., brought about a separation, in 1810, from the Presbyterian Church in the U.S.A. of a group on the Kentucky-Tennessee frontier. The Cumberland Presbyterian Church they founded stressed evangelism, repudiated predestination, avoided highly centralized authority, etc. Early in the 20th century negotiations for reunion with the Presbyterian Church in the U.S.A. began, and a majority of the Cumberland Presbyterians rejoined the older church in 1906. Others, however, have continued as a distinct group under the Cumberland name, with about 80,000 members in nearly 1,000 churches in the late 1960s.

Until the Civil War, Negroes, lay and ministerial, had a very real place in the Cumberland Church. In 1869, however, they separated to form the Colored Cumberland Presbyterian Church. In 1940 this body was joined by a presbytery in Liberia. Later renamed the Cumberland Presbyterian Church in the U.S. and Africa, it has about 20,000 members and 200 churches.

Churches Continuing the Covenanter-Secession Tradition.—There are four of these bodies (statistics are for the late 1960s and are approximate):

1. The Associate Reformed Presbyterian Church (General Synod): 28,000 members, 150 congregations.

2. The Associate Presbyterian Church of North America: 650 members, 4 congregations.

3. The Reformed Presbyterian Church of North America (Old School): 6,000 members, 70 congregations.

4. The Reformed Presbyterian Church, Evangelical Synod, formed in 1965 by union of the Reformed Presbyterian Church in North America (General Synod) and the Evangelical Presbyterian Church: 10,000 members, 110 congregations.

Bodies Formed Later.—The Fundamentalist-Modernist controversy of the 20th century led to the formation in 1936 of the Presbyterian Church in America (see above). Further doctrinal controversy broke this group into two distinct bodies a year later:

1. The Orthodox Presbyterian Church, a body stressing classical Presbyterian orthodoxy and extremely conservative in worship, organization, and practice. In the late 1960s it had about 13,000 members in 110 congregations.

2. The Bible Presbyterian Church, a body stressing revival

evangelism and Bible institute work; it is more loosely organized than the parent body. Members numbered about 5,000 in 68 churches in the 1960s.

Presbyterian Bodies on Former Mission Fields.—Presbyterians have long been active in foreign missionary work. Especially in the years since World War II, the older European and American bodies have aided their mission-founded congregations in becoming self-governing indigenous churches, while continuing to provide them with money, personnel, and technical assistance. In Africa, Latin America, and Korea, most of these "younger churches" are Presbyterian bodies. In a number of countries of the Near East and Far East, the Presbyterians have merged with other Protestants to form united churches.

The Book of Confessions.—The Presbyterian-Reformed churches are "confessional churches"; that is, for them a true and valid church is one that holds and follows the one common faith in Jesus Christ across all the centuries and across all cultures. Such matters as uniformity in liturgy, in organization, or in officers such as bishops are regarded as nonessential and to be arranged and changed to fit local needs. Presbyterian-Reformed confessionalism took the form of many regional confessions, each of which arose out of the immediate situation of a particular church. When it became necessary to support or interpret any one of these creeds, the usual procedure was to revise the old creed or to write a new one. In this way, more than 40 Presbyterian-Reformed creeds were published between 1530 and 1600. The various churches agreed to recognize each other on the grounds that, despite local differences in these many creeds, all agreed on the essentials.

Theological controversy and intellectual and cultural changes during the centuries after the Reformation brought about a shift in the attitudes of the Presbyterian-Reformed churches toward their confessions. The creeds came to be regarded as anchors for a church threatened by change, pluralism, and relativism. The assurance with which the Reformation churches had thrust their creeds out to "the whole world" was replaced by the churches' anxious use of creeds as defenses against "the outside world." The more outmoded the old creeds became, the more anxiously the churches tended to cling to them. The creeds thus came to be regarded as timeless truth rather than as the truth for the times.

American Presbyterians found it especially difficult to remain a confessional church. The Westminster Confession, which they had inherited from 17th-century English and Scottish Presbyterianism, had been written by and for state churches that intended to direct the religious life of entire kingdoms. In the United States there were many denominations and many creeds instead of one dominant church and a few small "sects." Because American Presbyterians were also, by and large, well educated, they were fully exposed to cultural change and scientific discovery. Throughout the 18th and 19th centuries controversy persisted over the need for creedal revision, but as late as 1903–06 only a few minor adjustments had been achieved; *e.g.*, on the doctrine of predestination. The Fundamentalist-Modernist controversy of the 1920s and '30s made further changes as difficult psychologically as they were mandatory theologically and intellectually.

The union that formed the new United Presbyterian Church, U.S.A., in 1958 had stipulated that the new church would draft "a brief contemporary statement of faith." A committee of 15 began work on the project in 1959. The assumption had been that this new statement would be a brief and simple version of the Westminster Confession. The committee soon found that a contemporary statement could not be a simplified version of a 300-year-old confession. Permission was then granted the committee to develop a "Book of Confessions" that would deal adequately with the problem of continuity and tradition and would include a contemporary creed.

The Book of Confessions, as proposed and adopted in 1967, includes: the Nicene Creed, the Apostles' Creed, the Scots Confession (1560), the Heidelberg Catechism (1563), the Second Helvetic Confession (1566), the Westminster Confession and Shorter Catechism, the (theological) Barmen Declaration (1934), and a new Confession of 1967. (*See* CREED; CONFESSIONS OF FAITH,

PROTESTANT; WESTMINSTER CONFESSION; BARMEN, SYNOD OF.) The Confession of 1967 was so named in order to emphasize the temporary character of any human attempt to comprehend the whole of the Christian faith and life. The three Reformation creeds included were selected because of their excellence and their wide acceptance among the Presbyterian-Reformed churches.

The Confession of 1967 was designed explicitly to presuppose, continue, and supplement the historic creeds of the Book of Confessions, without repeating their contents. The major concern of the new creed is with the task of the church, Presbyterian or any other, in the modern world. It assumes that the greatest problem of the contemporary Christian Church lies in its own confusion about its role or mission. By definition Christianity is a religion of salvation. Until the early 20th century, all Christians understood this salvation in terms of healing, saving, redeeming back something that had become unnatural because of sin. Inevitably this view led the church to look for a restoration of that which was natural, or for the recovery of an original condition, and made the vast changes of modern culture difficult to fit into the Christian scheme. The emphasis upon change that is characteristic of Marxist thought, evolutionary thought, and other modern views seemed to many Christians to be relativistic, manipulative, and nihilist. Yet recent Christian theology had come to realize that the biblical view of redemption in Christ is that of a "new man in Christ," a "new heaven and a new earth," and "the coming of the Kingdom of God." The gospel directs men's thoughts and hopes forward to what God is yet to do and not backward to a return to Eden.

The Confession of 1967, however, does not interpret the Kingdom of God, or the new man in Christ, in terms of a utopian new world order. Rather, it asserts that the redeeming work of Christ is an act of reconciliation of God to man, man to God, and man to his fellow man, which takes place in the midst of good, evil, sin, change, disaster, and progress but is not to be identified with any of these. Reconciliation is necessitated because relationships have been broken, whether by wrong, by change, or by unequal good. The confession at this point presupposes the classic doctrines of the earlier creeds regarding the reconciliation of God to man in Christ (the atonement) and focuses attention upon the mission of the church based upon the atonement of Christ (II Cor. 5:18–20). The cumulative consequences of good and sin, change, disaster and progress, cannot be done away with by the reconciliation of persons. But the reconciliation of man to God and to his fellow man does create a new kind of personal relationship among men, based upon a new awareness of each other and a new conception of the goals of human life.

American Christians, Presbyterians especially, the Confession admits, tend to fall out among themselves and with others over the proper goals for human life. Traditionally, these goals have been discussed in terms of right and wrong, good and bad, true and false. The Confession asserts that in personal relations the Bible points not to a code of perfection, to which all should conform, but to forgiveness, to reconciliation, and to the sin and failure that prevail in all men. Too often the traditional interpretations of right and wrong have been more concerned with social stability, peace, and progress than they have been with removing injustices and inequalities. If these traditional interpretations of right and wrong had in fact been eternal and unchanging they would have been obligatory for all classes and all races, and the dominant group could not have asked the less privileged to accept their unequal status. Reconciliation in Christ, the confession asserts, must mean the willingness to reexamine even the contemporary church's conceptions of right and wrong. The confession illustrates this point briefly by reference to the modern problems of racism, war, poverty, and breakdown of personal relations.

The Confession of 1967 also expresses clearly the contemporary church's conviction that critical study of the Bible is an aid to, rather than an attack upon, the use of the Bible in the church. It states also that when other religions are under discussion by the church a distinction must be drawn clearly between, on the one hand, popular religiosity and those cultural forms and expressions that grow up around any and all religions—including the many forms of Christianity—and, on the other, that which the church affirms as the uniqueness of Jesus Christ.

THE PRESBYTERIAN SYSTEM

The Presbyterian way of ordering the life of the church intends to be no more than a systematic and consistent attempt to follow the general principles laid out in the New Testament. It is confessed that the New Testament presents no one, definite, complete pattern. However, the very nature of what is there said of the gospel, the church, the ministry, etc., is taken by those who hold this system as an adequate indication of the basic elements essential to the ordering of the church's life. Not all who have called themselves Presbyterian or Reformed have ever followed Calvin in all things, but the system is best described by reference to his presentation of it.

The Church.—Calvin's view of the church was shaped by his understanding of the gospel. The gospel was the "good news" of God's forgiveness of man and the call to man to return, to be reconciled, to God; *i.e.*, to repent. Forgiveness and reconciliation were inseparably bound together. Men were to be reconciled to God by receiving his forgiveness and to be reconciled to their fellow men by their mutual forgiveness. To be reconciled to God was to come into his fellowship, and to be reconciled to one's fellows was to come once again into their fellowship. On that basis there could be no private or individualistic salvation. Salvation was intensely personal, because the Christian became a responsible actor, but never a matter involving only the individual soul and God. Calvin, therefore, was much opposed to mysticism and its view that each individual sought God alone and directly: "Outside the church there is no salvation."

This sense of community, or fellowship, in Calvin's opinion, was to be seen also in God's method of redeeming men. It was God who sought men rather than men who sought God. Yet God did not work directly but through agents, through means. God redeems men through the agency of their fellow men. God's love, which brought men to himself, was given to men through other men, thereby forming a bond of unity among them greater than any other conceivable bond. God was the source of all good, spiritual and temporal. But because he dispensed this good to men by the labours of others, each owed to the other that which he had received. Therefore, mutual sharing was necessary. This was part of reconciliation and love.

The church, then, according to Calvin, had as its sole function the task of telling men of God's forgiveness and of leading them to reconciliation with God and their fellows. This involved several other things. Men could not accept forgiveness and agree to be reconciled to God and man without confessing that they were in need of doing so. Moreover, to be reconciled meant to be reconciled to the service of God among one's fellow men. The Christian life was to be lived among God's people for their good and God's glory, not for any selfish desire for temporal or eternal gains. Ethics, therefore, were always part of theology in Calvin's thinking. Political and moral problems dominated his activities. Though the economic application was stated in principle, it was never as fully worked out.

Since there is only one Christ, or head, Calvin declared, there can be only one church or body. Wherever Christ is present, redeeming men in a manner essentially agreeable to the pattern he himself laid down, there, men are to know, is the church. Wherever a religion contrary to Christ's own pattern was being offered to men, there, men were to know, was no church of Christ. This was the one basic difference between the papacy and the reformers. The unity, continuity, universality of the church were all to be found in the redeeming presence of Christ, not in any particular form of government, doctrine, leadership, or lineal descent. The church was the body of Christ on earth among men, and therefore plainly visible to all.

Yet because it is all too human there are senses in which it is impossible for men to mark out its exact boundaries, etc. In that sense the church is invisible, and we are "to believe the church," Calvin said; *i.e.*, we are to believe that this very imperfect community is truly the body of Christ.

The Ministry.—Two aspects of the nature of the church, Calvin said, provide the occasion or reason for the ministry, namely, that the church is a community and that its own life and felicity are not the reasons for its existence. It exists for the service of God. Consequently direction and leadership are needed, and this the government or ministry of the church is instituted to provide.

The one head of the church is Christ and no one is ever his substitute or vicar. However, Christ moves his people to elect from their membership various persons to discharge the various aspects of the church's function. Some are to preach, some to teach, some to care for the poor and sick, some to exercise discipline, etc. As Calvin believed, God himself called his ministers, but he did it through the church. The ministry does not exist parallel to or prior to the church. God, working through the people's election, calls the ministry. The ministry is not then a sacred or spiritual "order" of men. It is a group of officeholders within the body of Christ.

The church ordered its life in the service of God, then, in Calvin's thinking, by means of a ministry exercised by a variety of officeholders: pastors, teachers, elders, and two types of deacons. The pastors were to preach the gospel, to administer the sacraments, and to serve as presidents of the other officers. Because they had the most responsible office within the total ministry, they might be called "the ministers." The teachers were to devote their whole time to teaching. Elders were to share with the pastors the spiritual oversight of the church. Deacons, men and women, were to care for the poor and the sick. No one was to exercise any function to which he had not been elected, and election to an office by the people was the sole necessary qualification. No matter to what office a man had been elected, he remained merely one of the brethren. Any distinction between clergy and laity was one of function alone.

God's call, made known through election by the people, was for Calvin all that was needed to make anyone the holder of any office in the ministry. Ordination by other ministers, he asserted, could not make anyone eligible to serve any office. When the ceremony of ordination was used, he declared that it meant no more than that the ministers led the people in a solemn prayer that God would recognize as his act that which they had done in electing the man in accord with what they believed was his will.

Those who hold offices in the ministry do so only within the church. They have no personal authority or virtue, Calvin said. Consequently, they may act only on the authority and prerogatives given them.

Government.—Though Calvin believed that the system of church government which was used by himself and his associates in Geneva, Strasbourg, Zürich, etc., was based upon the Bible and the experience of the church, he did not claim for it exclusive divine right. He acknowledged the English Church under Archbishop Thomas Cranmer and the Lutheran churches of Germany under their consistorial system as true and complete churches. Cranmer and the Lutherans also acknowledged the Reformed churches.

The primary elements of Calvin's theory of church government may be summed up in three. The church is a community or body in which Christ only is head and all other members are equal under him. The ministry is given to the whole church and is there distributed among many officers according as God has gifted and called them. All who hold office do so by election of the people whose representatives they are. The church is to be governed and directed by assemblies of officeholders, pastors, and elders, chosen to provide just representation for the church as a whole.

Since the Reformation the various Reformed churches have made many adaptations of this basic structure, but without departing from it in essentials. In the Presbyterian churches of British-American background, there are usually four categories of church courts, or judicatories, outlined below.

Session, Deacon, Trustees.—On the congregational level, there are the session, the deacons, and the trustees. The session is made up of the elders and the pastor, who is also the moderator, or chairman. To the session belongs the care of all religious, or strictly churchly, jurisdiction. It supervises the calling and election of pastors, receives and dismisses members, determines the order of the services, and exercises church discipline. The deacons, over whom the pastor is also the moderator, care for the poor and any other temporal affairs assigned to them. The trustees, under their own chairman, have charge of the property and fiscal and legal obligations of the congregation. All these officers are elected by the congregation. The elders and deacons are ordained to their offices by the pastor. Ordination is for life, but the exercise of the office is often for a term of years. The trustees serve for stated terms and are not ordained.

Presbytery.—All of the ministers, in pastorates or not, of a given area, together with certain elders deputed by the churches of that area, form a presbytery. In their hands rests authority for ordaining, installing, removing, or transferring ministers. Ordinarily the people may elect their own pastor, but the presbytery must sanction their choice and install him in office. Once installed, the pastor may not be dismissed by the people, or leave the people, without consent of the presbytery. The presbytery also has religious, financial, and legal authority over all the congregations. It serves as a court of appeal for cases coming up from the congregational courts. It meets as often as it wishes. The moderator is elected annually.

Synod.—The synod is made up of several presbyteries. It may be a delegated synod to which only a few representatives from each presbytery are sent, or it may be a synod to which all the members of all the presbyteries belong. In either case its jurisdiction in modern times is slight. It is a court of appeal in judicial matters, and it has a certain coordinating role in church program matters among the presbyteries. A synod usually meets only annually, and its moderator is elected annually.

General Assembly.—The General Assembly is an annual meeting of commissioners, ministers, and elders, elected by all the presbyteries (not by the synods) in number according to their total church memberships. This body elects its own officers, the moderator for one year only, the stated clerk for a longer term. It has charge of all the general concerns of the church's faith, order, property, missions, education, and the like. The missionary, benevolent, educational, and publishing work of the denomination are under boards elected by the assembly. The assembly also functions as the final court of appeal on all cases coming up from the lower courts.

In Presbyterian churches of British background the assembly is the seat of ultimate authority and the lower courts are regarded as descending from it. In churches of American background the presbytery is regarded as the basic unit. The synods and the assembly are regarded as formed by the presbyteries, and the congregations are considered dependent upon the presbytery.

WORSHIP

The Christian humanist movement prior to the Reformation had been highly anticlerical and bitterly opposed to the increasing elaboration of symbol and ceremonial in church worship. Even men such as Sir Thomas More, later a Roman Catholic martyr, and Erasmus had urged drastic simplification of the liturgy. Some even urged the removal of organs and choirs from the churches. Elaborate vestments also came under severe attack. Most Christian humanists agreed with Erasmus that a clergyman was essentially a teacher of Christ's philosophy of life.

In varying ways every Protestant reform movement incorporated some part of this older protest. The Reformed and Presbyterian churches attempted radical reform, although the pattern of action was not everywhere the same. Emphasis was put upon the congregational character of worship. The people all participated rather than acted as a mere audience. Symbolism had been intended to teach the unlearned. A better teaching ministry could now supersede the images, incense, gestures, and lights. Since all believers were alike in Christ, the clerical vestments which symbolized the religious distinction between clergy and laity were rejected. Only garb symbolic of offices and duties was to be used. Clerical choirs were to be supplanted by congregational singing. Luther had developed a Protestant popular hymnody welding folk tunes and evangelical texts. The Reformed churches used popular melodies but confined themselves to psalms and other biblical texts. In part this was a carry-over from the psalm singing of the anticlerical humanist circles of France from which many of the Calvinistic leaders came.

Liturgically, no Protestant group in the 16th century advocated wholly free worship. Since all were struggling to win people away from the Roman Mass, all believed that a proper and required form of service was necessary. All the Reformed and Presbyterian churches, therefore, began with some form of stated liturgy. The churches of northern Switzerland and Holland had perhaps the simplest forms. The churches of French-speaking Switzerland, the Huguenots and the earlier Scots and English Puritans followed a fuller form derived from Martin Bucer's service at Strasbourg and modified by Calvin. In this form the service opened with a salutation, followed by the common confession of sin, the words of assurance of pardon through faith, and a psalm of praise and thanksgiving. Then came the preaching and hearing of the Word of God which involved a prayer for the right understanding of the Word, the Scripture lesson, and the sermon based on that lesson. Attention then shifted to concern for others as the prayer of intercession for all sorts and conditions of men followed. Next came the Apostles' Creed as an expression of oneness with all other Christians through the ages. The Lord's Prayer, again common to the universal church, a psalm, and the benediction closed the service. Probably the alms for the relief of the poor came after the creed. In later Scottish Presbyterianism the alms were often taken up as the congregation left the church to signify that they were given for fellowman rather than as a sacrifice to God, who needed nothing.

Perhaps the most striking feature of the service when it included the Lord's Supper was that the stress fell upon the redemptive work of Christ to which the sacrament testified rather than upon the sacrament itself. To that end there was no consecration of the elements nor any focus upon them. In Zürich and north Switzerland the ministers and elders brought the bread and wine to the people in the pews. In Holland and Scotland tables in the aisles, or even out-of-doors, enabled the congregation to "sit at the Lord's Table." In Geneva the people received the communion standing before the table. Pew communion is today regarded as the most meaningful way of expressing the congregational or community aspect of the Lord's Supper.

See also LITURGY, CHRISTIAN.

PRESBYTERIAN THOUGHT

In the early decades of the Protestant Reformation none of the major groups influenced by it thought of itself as a "denomination" with ideas which were "Lutheran," "Anglican," "Presbyterian," or "Reformed." Rather, each professed to be seeking to understand and to follow the one Christian faith. But just because their situations and circumstances were so different, these groups soon found themselves, though with large areas of agreement, also with stubborn spots of disagreement.

The Presbyterian and Reformed churches have characteristically maintained certain attitudes toward their differences with other Evangelical or Protestant churches. They have insisted that the Christian faith must be confessed in the specific and local circumstances and that only on the great essentials is complete uniformity required among churches. Therefore these churches have no one creed or liturgy or polity which unites them internationally, as in Lutheranism or Anglicanism. In ecumenical relations they regard all other evangelical denominations as they do themselves, namely as particular expressions of a common faith. They wish to practise intercommunion with other churches and to receive from or to transfer to them members and ministers on the basis of mutual recognition.

The Bible.—The Protestant Reformation was in part a consequence of the revitalization of biblical studies among the Christian humanists, who demanded that the church be reformed by a return to the teachings of Jesus, of the Bible, and of the early Church Fathers. Since many of the Protestant reformers had begun as humanists, they followed the same pattern of thinking. The Bible represented original Christianity. It was older and more universal than the papacy. The early Church Fathers understood Jesus and the Bible better than the medieval scholastics did.

Whereas the Christian humanists had understood the Bible primarily in terms of the ethic of the Christian life, the Protestant reformers read it primarily as the theological interpretation of God's redemptive work among men. Among the Reformed and Presbyterian leaders the entire Bible was read as the record of one history of redemption stretching over many centuries, culminating in Jesus Christ. While Christ was the key to understanding the Old Testament, it was necessary to retain the Old Testament in the Christian church in order to understand the history of God's dealings with men.

The Christian humanists had agitated for reform and had defined many areas of church and society that needed reform. But they had urged that action must come from the traditional authorities in church and state. The Protestant reformers, by forcing the issue of practical reform, inevitably raised the question of authority. Luther and many early Reformed thinkers such as Zwingli urged that the civil government must assume all authority in both church and state. Other Reformed leaders, especially the Huguenots, the Dutch Calvinists, the English Puritans, and the Scots Presbyterians, followed the lead of Calvin in demanding that the church be allowed to retain many of its old institutions and prerogatives and be supported in their use by the state. This early form of separation of church and state in jurisdiction raised many serious problems. Since it went beyond previous European experience the question arose as to what patterns to use. The New Testament writers and the early Church Fathers had lived under persecution, hence they set no patterns for the new Protestant state churches to imitate. Those who followed Calvin's lead, therefore, sought these patterns in the Old Testament. Yet, the Genevan "theocracy" in its attempts to reform and control moral conduct was usually motivated by medieval attitudes toward the "flesh." Its novelty lay in its insistence upon one inflexible standard for clergy and laity alike.

The Old Testament had profound influence upon the political thought of these churches. The tendency to use it as a code book to which appeal could be made against traditional church or civil authority led directly to making the political theory of fundamental law, or constitutional law, a religious tenet. Law stood over the ruler. Likewise, the Old Testament idea of a covenant (q.v.) between God and his people which bound even the king and the high priest made the then obscure contract theory of political authority (see SOCIAL CONTRACT) a sacred cause among these churches. Since in the Old Testament wicked kings were repudiated, the growing assertion of the divine right of kings was rejected by the Reformed churches as non-Christian. Eventually most of them espoused the right of a people to rebel against an unjust ruler.

The fact that in the Old Testament God's redemptive work among the Israelites was presented as going on through many centuries, and reaching a climax in the historical work of Christ among men, aroused among some Reformed leaders (as Bullinger, Jud, and Pellicanus) the beginnings of an interpretation of history which was to culminate in the influential 19th- and 20th-century "history of salvation" (*Heilsgeschichte*) theory of biblical hermeneutics.

The Work of Christ.—All Protestant groups in the 16th century agreed that man's salvation was wholly the work of Jesus Christ and that it was in no way the result of, or dependent upon, human merit. Yet, the manner in which one understood the work of Christ had important bearings upon how one understood its consequences in the life of a Christian. Technically, the discussion of the work of Christ under the ancient categories of prophet, priest, and king, which Calvin popularized in all the Reformed and Presbyterian churches, need not have caused differences with the Lutherans. But the fact that Calvin insisted upon distinguishing what Jesus Christ did as man from what he did as God had far-reaching consequences. All agreed that Jesus in his human life revealed what man ought to be and to do. Luther felt, however, that so great was man's fall that not much empirical

change would come over him as a Christian. The believer would love God and seek to serve him out of gratitude, but his actual renewal would be slight and fluctuating. Calvin believed that in salvation the believer was united to Jesus Christ by faith. By the power of the Holy Spirit he would be enabled to live in some measure according to the standard of Jesus Christ. Sanctification, therefore, played a greater role in Reformed and Presbyterian theology than it did in Lutheran thought. Likewise, because of a greater emphasis upon Christ's victory over sin and death in his resurrection and ascension, there was a greater stress upon the possibilities in the believer's life as he shared in Christ's victory. Tendencies toward activism among the Reformed and toward quietism among the Lutheran groups therefore emerged.

Predestination.—The doctrines of election and predestination have played so large a role in Reformed and Presbyterian thought that often they are regarded as peculiar to these churches. The problem, however, is rooted in the relationship of the freedom of God to the freedom of man, and as such it troubled biblical figures such as Jeremiah and Paul, early Church Fathers such as Augustine, and medieval churchmen as different as Aquinas, Bradwardine, and Wycliffe. Unless the God revealed in Jesus Christ is the ultimate God, completely free of any fate, destiny, or other external necessity, then there is no assurance that the Christian gospel of love and forgiveness represents more than an optimistic hope in the face of unknown odds. But when the questions of man's freedom, of his responsibility, and of his aspirations are raised, the freedom of God seems to deny or to override man's freedom. Man seems to become merely a pawn in God's purposes. Throughout Christian history the debate has gone on among those who argued for the primacy of the divine freedom, for the primacy of human freedom (or usually human responsibility), or for various mediating positions. Luther, in debate with Erasmus, pushed the freedom of God almost to the extent of asserting a psychological determinism for man. William Tyndale, the English Bible translator, defended a rigorous Augustinian type of predestination against Sir Thomas More, the English humanist. Among all the early Protestant reformers it was regarded as axiomatic that the current Roman Catholic teaching about man's claim upon God by way of his merits undercut the whole Christian gospel.

Calvin's role in the doctrine of predestination was similar to his role in many Protestant ideas, that of a systematizer. Leaning heavily upon Augustine, he pushed the idea of God's freedom to the extent of saying that God was wholly free to save or to damn any man without regard to what men thought was just under the circumstances. This doctrine of "double predestination" was regarded by him as the only possible assurance a Christian could have that despite his sins and failures God would in the end save him. Later Calvinism pushed these ideas further, in the so-called doctrine of the decrees, to where it became the explanation of how and why men act as they do in history. As such it came close to determinism. Modern Protestantism seeks a solution of the problem in terms of the concurrent activity of God and man.

The Sacraments.—Because, Calvin asserted, it is God who seeks his prodigal children rather than they who seek him, and because it is God who directs his church in the life which it lives in his service, public worship is primarily the assembling of the people of God to hear what he has to say to them. They do not assemble to seek him but to meet him and to hear his word. When this takes place, they respond by receiving his love, his grace, his fellowship; and they present their prayers and petitions. The action of public worship was the hearing of the gospel and the joyful communion with God to which that gospel summoned men. By preaching and teaching, the gospel was to be made known and understood in the church. In the sacraments there were provided ways whereby men could actually appropriate and receive the grace offered in the gospel.

The sacraments in themselves possessed no particular powers. Whatever man received, he received by faith. The sacraments, therefore, are not independent of faith. They are rather a "lively preaching" intended to call forth faith. By this very fact they could not be considered necessary to salvation. Yet, since Christ commanded the church to carry out its mission in this manner, and since he did by means of the sacraments truly call forth faith, it was the duty of the church faithfully to use these "means of grace." Preaching and the sacraments could never be separated. A sacrament had three elements: the promise of God, its attestation or seal which showed that it had been fulfilled, and man's reception by faith of that which God had promised.

Baptism.—The promise of God in the gospel, Calvin said, is that God will forgive and receive into his fellowship those who have forsaken him. That promise was fulfilled, or sealed, when Jesus Christ came and was crucified and raised from the dead for man's redemption. What remains to be done is that man must actually return to the fellowship of God and become a member of the community of believers who make up the church, the body of Christ. This must be done as an act of faith, and under normal circumstances it is to be done through receiving baptism. Baptism symbolizes the death, burial, and resurrection of Christ. By accepting baptism, in an act of faith, men confess that they hope for salvation only in Christ and that they do in fact return to God. This is their part in the sacrament. God, then and there, "incorporates" the believer into the body of his Son, the church.

Calvin elaborated not a doctrine of infant baptism but a doctrine of Christian baptism, and then urged that children as well as adults might receive it. Children were to be given the promise held out in baptism and then brought up to exercise such faith as their growing years and perception might enable them to do. Until they exercised faith their baptism would be incomplete. Yet, Calvin thought, since their salvation depended upon God's love and not upon baptism itself, they were safe in God's care while unable to exercise faith. Baptism was intended by God as an aid to faith, not as an indispensable rite necessary for salvation. God could, therefore, dispense with it if he chose. Men, however, were never to omit it, unless unable to use it.

Baptism could be administered by any method, immersion, sprinkling, etc., provided only that the method used clearly symbolized and proclaimed the death and resurrection of Christ. Baptism ought to take place only in the midst of the public worship of the church because it symbolized entrance into the Christian communion. Also, only those who lead in public worship should baptize. There could be no private baptism because there was no private salvation. There could be no "emergency baptism" because baptism had no such character about it as to create any emergency.

The Lord's Supper.—The Lord's Supper, Calvin believed, was instituted by God to support, nourish, and increase the faith of the Christian church. It was rooted in the event of Christ's death on the cross and symbolized that death. It proclaimed, therefore, the fact that God had fulfilled his promise and that men had been forgiven. Moreover, it invited men to "take," to receive, the offered mercy of God. Receiving the sacrament in an act of faith meant that one believed that God truly held out something to man in it and that man truly received in it just what God offered, namely, forgiveness, reconciliation, continued fellowship, and communion with God.

The elements (bread and wine) themselves had no particular merit or significance beyond their historical connection with Christ's last supper with the disciples. Nothing in the ritual changed the elements in any way. Christ was indeed present during the sacrament as he was present in preaching or in baptism. But his presence was not associated with the bread and wine. He was present to meet with and commune with his followers.

The setting for the sacrament demanded a table, Calvin said. Thus Christ instituted the sacrament, and thus it should be continued. The table symbolized the fact that God is offering to man and that man is to come, to receive; the altar, on the contrary, symbolized that man is offering something to God. Also, the sacrament belongs to the whole church, not to the ministers. It is to be administered only in the public worship of the congregation. All were to be invited to come. Any who feared they were "unworthy" were to know that only the confession of need could constitute worthiness. Those who came inwardly ungodly and unrepentant rejected God's mercy in the sacrament just as they rejected it when they heard it preached. Calvin believed that private communion, even for the sick, obscured the true nature of the church as a community and fostered superstitious ideas about the sacrament.

See further CALVIN, JOHN: *Theology;* CALVINISM; REFORMED CHURCHES; *see* also references under "Presbyterianism" in the Index.

BIBLIOGRAPHY.—T. M. Lindsay, *History of the Reformation,* 2 vol., rev. ed. (1922); A. H. Drysdale, *History of the Presbyterians in England* (1889); W. T. Latimer, *History of the Irish Presbyterians* (1902); W. H. Roberts, *A Concise History of the Presbyterian Church in the United States of America* (1920); L. J. Trinterud, *Forming of an American Tradition, a Re-examination of Colonial Presbyterianism* (1949); W. W. Sweet, *Story of Religion in America,* 2nd rev. ed. (1950); J. N. Ogilvie, *The Presbyterian Churches of Christendom,* rev. ed. (1925); John Calvin, *Institutes of the Christian Religion,* trans. by H. Beveridge, 2 vol. (1959); J. L. Ainslie, *Doctrines of Ministerial Order in the Reformed Churches of the 16th and 17th Centuries* (1940); A. Barclay, *Protestant Doctrine of the Lord's Supper* (1927); George S. Hendry, *The Westminster Confession for Today* (1960); Eugene C. Blake (ed.), *Presbyterian Law for the Local Church,* 6th rev. ed. (1960); *The Proposed Book of Confessions of the United Presbyterian Church in the United States of America* (1966).   (L. J. T.)

PRESCOTT, WILLIAM HICKLING (1796–1859), U.S. historian noted chiefly for his dramatic accounts of the Spanish conquest of Mexico and Peru, was born in Salem, Mass., on May 4, 1796. His family had been prominent in Massachusetts history and was financially well off. After entering Harvard College in 1811 Prescott suffered an injury that caused him to lose the sight of his left eye; his other eye was later weakened by an infection, leaving him virtually blind. In spite of this handicap he determined to embark upon a literary career after he graduated from college. Prescott turned to the study of Spanish history and in 1837 published a three-volume work entitled *History of the Reign of Ferdinand and Isabella, the Catholic.* This work was followed by *History of the Conquest of Mexico* (1843), which eventually became one of the most widely read histories in the English-speaking world, and by *History of the Conquest of Peru* (1847). *History of the Reign of Philip the Second, King of Spain* was incomplete at the time of his death on Jan. 28, 1859.

With his vivid historical imagination, Prescott breathed life into the chronicles of the early Spaniards, yet he was passionately devoted to historical truth. His approach to history as a dramatic art had its shortcomings, such as lack of attention to certain details and occasional verbosity. Later anthropological research has corrected minor portions of Prescott's work on Mexico and Peru but on the whole his histories have stood the test of time and critical examination by scholars.

BIBLIOGRAPHY.—William Charvat and Michael Kraus, *William Hickling Prescott* (1943); George Ticknor, *Life of William Hickling Prescott* (1864); W. H. Munro (ed.), *Works of Prescott,* 22 vol. (1904).   (W. R. J.)

PRESCOTT, seat of Yavapai County in west central Arizona, U.S., about 100 mi. NW of Phoenix, is in a mile-high basin among pine-dotted mountains rich in minerals. Gold mining brought the first settlers; farmers and cattlemen followed. Ft. Whipple was built in the 1860s about 17 mi. N of the present city, and in 1864 the first government of Arizona territory was set up near it. Later that year the fort and the government were moved to the area of the present city and the first legislature met. The location of the capital alternated between Prescott and Tucson until 1889, when Phoenix was made the state capital. A railroad reached Prescott in 1893 and was extended to Phoenix in 1895.

Prescott is a trade centre for cattle ranches and farms in the valleys; mining also continues to be important, and small industries are increasing. The city was named for the historian William Hickling Prescott; founded in 1864, it was incorporated as a city in 1881 and in 1955 adopted a council-manager form of government. The inhabitants of Prescott boast that the rodeo staged by competing cowboys on July 4, 1888, was the first public rodeo to be given anywhere; over the years the celebration developed into a lively three-day event—Prescott Frontier Days. For comparative population figures *see* table in ARIZONA: *Population.*   (A. M. PE.)

PRESCRIPTION, in both domestic and international law, is the effect of the lapse of time in creating and destroying rights;

it is also used in some philosophical writing such as Edmund Burke's to describe what legal philosophers would now call custom —that is, long-continued usage or habit as a source of law. Burke used long-continued beneficent working as the basis of law to refute the claim of philosophers of the French Revolution that the source of law is the present generation of people. The historical school of jurisprudence developed by Friedrich Karl von Savigny (*q.v.*) is similar. (*See also* JURISPRUDENCE.)

In law, custom as a source of law and prescription as a source of rights were originally two aspects of the same thing. They both required usage from time immemorial (beyond the memory of living man) as proof. In England and the United States, custom still continues as a source of law, but the phrase "time immemorial" in England has come to mean usage since 1189, the first year of the reign of Richard Coeur de Lion.

In Anglo-American law, prescription is distinguished from adverse possession; that is, the rights acquired from long-continued possession rather than use, such as a right-of-way acquired from use or a right to view as in Ancient Lights (*q.v.*) in England, which are called easements by prescription. English law gave a right of use if there was long-continued use, but on a legal fiction: if usage existed for a period as long as that prescribed in the statute of limitations for adverse possession, then it was presumed that there had once existed a now lost grant to use from the rightful owner. Most jurisdictions now have statutes just as applicable to long-continued usage as to long-continued possession, and the fiction of a lost grant, although available in some jurisdictions, is not used.

Modern justification of the concept of prescription is usually placed on three elements: law should reward the vigilant against the slothful; judicial administration should avoid the difficulties of proof, which long-continued delay in the assertion of rights occasions; and long-continued use does permit the inference of ownership, since right and use usually go together.

International law also has a concept of prescription: it recognizes a nation's claim to be valid by reason of long-continued assertion, and finds an abandonment of a claim by reason of long-continued failure to assert it. (A. DM.)

PREŠEREN, FRANCE (1800–1849), the outstanding Slovene poet of the Romantic movement, was born at Vrba, near Lake Bled, Slovenia, on Dec. 3, 1800, the son of a farmer. He studied law in Vienna, where he acquired the familiarity with the mainstream of European thought and literary expression which, through him, reinvigorated Slovene literature. He later held posts in Ljubljana and Kranj as a civil servant and lawyer. His life was one of struggle and disappointment, and in 1835 the sudden death of his close friend, Matija Čop, and his unhappy love for Julija Primic, brought him to the verge of suicide. He died at Kranj on Feb. 8, 1849.

Although Prešeren was not a prolific writer, his work gave new life to Slovene literature, the development of which had been checked by political and social conditions (*see* YUGOSLAV LITERATURE: *Slovene Literature*). The themes and prosodic structure of his verse set new standards for Slovene writers, and his lyric poems are among the most sensitive, original, eloquent, and aesthetically perfect works in Slovene. The varied poetic forms and metres, derived from foreign literatures, which he deliberately cultivated in his earlier lyrics, imposed no restraint on his own inspiration.

In his *Sonetni venec* ("Garland of Sonnets," 1834), inspired by his unhappy love, as in his later lyrics, he expresses the national consciousness which he sought to stimulate in his compatriots. His later lyrics (1841–43) are closer in rhythm to Slovene folk-poetry. He also wrote satirical verses (1845) on contemporary literary conditions in Slovenia. The epic poem, *Krst pri Savici* ("The Baptism by the Savica," 1836), dedicated to the memory of Matija Čop, treats the conflict between paganism and the early Slovene converts to Christianity, and illustrates Prešeren's patriotism, pessimism, and resignation.

See *Selection of Poems by France Prešeren*, trans. and ed. by W. K. Matthews and A. Slodnjak (1954). (V. J.)

PRESERVING OF FOODS: *see* FOOD PRESERVATION (IN THE HOME).

PRESIDENT, a term widely used to designate a person appointed or elected by a group or an organization to preside over its meetings and perform whatever managerial duties may be assigned to him. In the United States, president is the almost universal title of the head of a college or university. In Great Britain, though it is not so commonly used for that purpose, it does designate the heads of four of the colleges of Oxford and one of Cambridge's colleges. In the United States it is the title of the chief executive officer of business corporations, clubs, professional societies, and—most important of all—the federal government.

In early modern times the title came to be applied to the head of a division of a country, such as a dependency, city, or colony. Thus the title of the chief magistrate in some of the British colonies in North America was president. Such a colonial president was always associated with a colonial council to which he was elected and was therefore denominated president of the council of the colony. This title of president in the North American colonies was carried over into some of the state governments that were organized after the American Revolution. The title of president was used for the chief executives of the state governments of Delaware (1776–92), New Hampshire (1784–92), Pennsylvania (1776–90), and South Carolina (1776–78). Since 1792, however, the title of the chief executive of every state in the United States has been governor.

With rare exceptions the title president is used in republics throughout the world to designate the officer in whom the executive power is vested. The president of a republic inevitably has some of the functions of the head of a monarchical government and is, in fact, the chief of state. The title "President of the United States" is even older historically than the office of president of the United States, the chief executive prescribed by the Constitution framed in Philadelphia in 1787. It was applied to the officer who presided over the sessions of the Continental Congress and of the Congress under the Articles of Confederation. As this officer had no executive duties, the office was in no proper sense a predecessor of the present office of president of the United States. The framers of the Constitution in 1787 adopted the title president to designate the very different office in which they vested the authority of the chief executive of the United States.

UNITED STATES

The framers of the federal Constitution provided for the office of president in one succinct sentence: "The executive power shall be vested in a President of the United States of America" (Art. II, sec. 1). The very brevity of this provision has afforded ample opportunity for the evolution of the presidency into the extraordinary office it has become.

Election.—The Constitution provided for the election of the president by special presidential electors. Each state was to appoint "in such Manner as the Legislature thereof may direct, a Number of Electors, equal to the whole Number of Senators and Representatives to which the State may be entitled in the Congress" (Art. II, sec. 1). Every state legislature has surrendered its right to choose electors and has provided that its electors shall be chosen by popular election on a general ticket nominated by each party. Whichever party receives the most votes for its list of candidates for presidential electors wins all the electoral votes of that state.

The Constitution requires that the presidential electors shall vote by ballot for president and vice-president in their respective states and send the certified result of their balloting to the president of the U.S. Senate. According to a 1934 act of Congress, the electors vote on the first Monday after the second Wednesday in December. The votes are then counted before a joint session of the Senate and House of Representatives and the candidates receiving a majority for president and vice-president are declared elected. In case no candidate for president receives a majority, the House of Representatives votes on the three candidates receiving the highest number of electoral votes, with each state delegation casting a single vote. The Senate—each member casting one vote—elects the vice-president if no candidate for that office receives a majority of the electoral votes.

An almost inflexible custom since the election of 1800 had induced presidential electors to cast their ballots automatically in accordance with the expectation of the voters who had elected them, but since 1948 that usage has not been universally followed. In the 1960 election 15 Democratic presidential electors cast their ballots for Sen. Harry F. Byrd of Virginia instead of for the presidential candidate of the Democratic Party, Sen. John F. Kennedy.

With rare exceptions, such as the Hayes-Tilden election in 1876 and the Cleveland-Harrison election of 1888, the electoral college has elected the candidate with either a majority or at least a plurality of the popular vote. The majority cast by the electoral college is almost always much greater for the victor than his popular majority or plurality. In 1960, for example, Kennedy's popular vote was less than two-tenths of one percent greater than his opponent's but his vote in the electoral college was almost 16% greater.

Candidates for president are nominated by each major party at a national nominating convention consisting of more than 1,000 delegates representing party members in every state, the District of Columbia, and the possessions. The delegates convene in some selected city during the summer preceding the presidential election. Aspirants to the presidency usually have participated in preconvention campaigns in states holding presidential primary elections, seeking to win delegates who will support them in the national convention. Each convention adopts a party platform before the balloting of the delegates to select its presidential and vice-presidential candidates. (*See* NATIONAL CONVENTION, POLITICAL.)

The strategy of each party is to endeavour to win the big blocs of electoral votes of the more populous states such as New York, Illinois, or California in order to accumulate the majority of electoral votes necessary to elect. As a result, presidential candidates are usually nominated from such states. Following the nominating conventions, the presidential candidates tend to concentrate their campaigning in these populous states, especially those that have a habit of swinging from one major party to the other. Half the candidates for president in the century following the American Civil War were or had been governors of such states.

Requirements and Salary.—The Constitution requires that the president be a natural-born citizen of the United States and be not less than 35 years old. A president must have been a resident of the United States for 14 years at the time of his inauguration, though such residence need not have been continuous. The Constitution also provides that the president shall receive a compensation for his service that shall neither be increased nor diminished during his term. Congress in 1969 fixed the presidential salary at $200,000 a year, taxable, plus a nontaxable allowance of $50,000 to assist in defraying expenses resulting from official duties. The president may also draw up to $40,000 a year for travel expenses and official entertainment, and this sum is also not taxable. Former presidents are provided with a lifetime pension of $25,000 a year and a $50,000 expense fund. Widows of presidents receive $10,000 per year.

Two-Term Limit.—The president is elected for a four-year term but the Constitution originally placed no limit on the number of terms a president might serve. Alexander Hamilton, in *The Federalist,* argued for unlimited reeligibility. Washington opposed placing any limit on the number of terms a president might serve and, by retiring at the end of his second term, he had no intention of setting a precedent. Thomas Jefferson was the first president (1801–09) who favoured setting a precedent for only two terms and during the next 130 years the two-term limit was assumed to be permanently established by an inflexible custom.

As the presidential campaign of 1940 drew near, however, the electorate became deeply concerned over the threat to the security of the United States by the war then raging in Europe. Pres. Franklin D. Roosevelt's second term was drawing to a close. The Democratic national convention nominated him for a third term, apparently on the assumption that a change of administration would not be prudent in the midst of a world crisis that might suddenly involve the United States in war. Roosevelt was elected for a third term in 1940 and for a fourth term in 1944, thereby shattering the long-standing two-term precedent.

As part of the postwar reaction against strong executive leadership, the 22nd Amendment to the Constitution was adopted in 1951 to limit the president to two terms. "No person shall be elected to the office of the President more than twice, and no person who has held the office . . . , or acted as President, for more than two years of a term . . . shall be elected to the office . . . more than once." Pres. Harry S. Truman was exempted.

Inauguration.—On assuming office the president takes the oath of office prescribed by the Constitution: "I do solemnly swear (or affirm) that I will faithfully execute the Office of President of the United States, and will to the best of my Ability, preserve, protect and defend the Constitution of the United States." This oath is administered by the chief justice of the United States. Since Washington's day every newly inaugurated president has delivered an inaugural address describing the basic policies he plans to follow.

Impeachment.—The president is not subject to judicial process despite the silence of the Constitution on the matter. This immunity is derived by judicial interpretation from the implied separation of powers of the Constitution, which signifies that the judiciary may not interfere with the executive. However, the president, along with other civil officers of the United States, may be impeached and, if convicted, removed from office. The House of Representatives initiates impeachment proceedings against the president by passing resolutions consisting of articles of impeachment charging him with "Treason, Bribery, or other high Crimes and Misdemeanors." "Managers" appointed by the House of Representatives prosecute the accused president on trial before the Senate sitting as a court, with the chief justice presiding when the president is on trial. The president is not present in person but is defended by his legal counsel. Conviction requires a two-thirds vote of the senators. The only penalty the Senate can impose is removal from office. Pres. Andrew Johnson (*q.v.*) was impeached and tried but the Senate, by a margin of a single vote, did not find him guilty. The trial of Johnson was so manifestly animated by passion and prejudice that it severely damaged the device of impeachment as a check on the president.

Vice President.—The vice-president is elected with the president and for the same term. The Constitution provides for vice-presidential succession to the presidency when that office is vacant. It also originally provided that: "In Case of the . . . Inability [of the president] . . . [his] Powers and Duties . . . shall devolve on the Vice President . . . ." But no authority to determine inability was named. Thus, during the invalidism of President Garfield in 1881 and of President Wilson in 1919, and the illnesses of President Eisenhower, official functions of the president were virtually suspended. To provide for both offices becoming vacant, Congress in 1947 determined the succession goes first to the speaker of the House of Representatives, next to the president pro tempore of the Senate, and then to cabinet members in the order their departments were created. In 1967 the 25th amendment provided that the vice-president succeeds to the presidency if the president declares his inability to the president pro tempore of the Senate and the speaker of the House, or if the vice-president and a majority of the cabinet declares the inability. Presidential notice of no inability goes to the same congressional officers and is effective unless contested by the vice-president and a majority of the cabinet, or a body designated by Congress; then a two-thirds majority of both houses can overrule the president. If the vice-presidency is vacant the president appoints a vice-president subject to confirmation by a simple majority of both houses. Succession on the simultaneous vacancy of both offices remains governed by the act of 1947.

President as Chief Executive.—The Constitution makes the president the nation's chief executive with this succinct injunction: ". . . he shall take Care that the Laws be faithfully executed" (Art. II, sec. 3). He performs this duty through the elaborate system of executive agencies created by Congress under its constitutional power "To make all Laws which shall be necessary and proper for carrying into Execution" the powers vested in Congress and other powers vested in the other branches of the federal government by the Constitution.

As the president is responsible for seeing to it that the laws are faithfully executed, the Constitution vests in him the power to nominate and, by and with the advice and consent of the Senate, to appoint all but inferior executive officers. He may "fill up all Vacancies that may happen during the Recess of the Senate, by granting Commissions which shall expire at the End of their next Session." Usually, but not always, the Senate confirms these recess appointments. Customarily the Senate confirms the president's nominations of cabinet appointees without question. The Constitution is silent as to the president's power to remove appointees without the consent of the Senate. The first Congress (1789–91) assumed without legislative action that he could not be held responsible for enforcing the laws unless he had the unrestricted power to remove subordinates in whom he did not have confidence. This interpretation was not definitively determined by the U.S. Supreme Court until 1926 (*Myers* v. *United States, 272 U.S. 52*). Congress has, however, created a number of independent agencies such as the Federal Trade Commission and invested them with quasi-legislative and quasi-judicial functions. The president's power to remove members of these commissions is somewhat restricted.

The Constitution provides that "The President shall be Commander in Chief of the Army and Navy of the United States, and of the Militia of the several States, when called into the actual Service of the United States" (Art. II, sec. 2). He is commander in chief in time of peace as well as in time of war. He has at all times unlimited authority to direct movements of land, sea, and air forces. This unlimited discretion enables a president to direct movements of the armed forces that may provoke hostilities with a foreign nation and leaves Congress no alternative but to declare that a state of war exists. Thus President Polk in 1846 ordered U.S. troops into disputed territory at the Mexican border where a clash with Mexican troops initiated the Mexican War.

President Lincoln gave the commander in chief power an extraordinarily broad interpretation during the American Civil War as he utilized armed forces to fulfill his constitutional obligation to "take care that the laws be faithfully executed" throughout the entire nation. To this end he suspended the privilege of the writ of habeas corpus, increased the personnel of the Army and Navy, acquired vessels for the Navy, proclaimed emancipation of the slaves, and initiated his own plan of reconstruction of the states whose citizens had been in rebellion—all powers generally assumed to belong to Congress. Lincoln asked Congress to authorize retroactively some of his acts, and it did so. Clinton L. Rossiter has summed up the situation by saying that since the Supreme Court "regards the war powers of Congress as limited only by the necessities of the case, which are for Congress to ascertain, there is apparently nothing the President cannot do *constitutionally* if war should strike the country." (*The Supreme Court and the Commander in Chief*, pp. 101–102, Cornell University Press, Ithaca, New York, 1951.)

The Constitution empowers Congress "To provide for calling forth the Militia [of the states] to execute the Laws of the Union, suppress Insurrections and repel Invasions" (Art. I, sec. 8). The president may have in the meantime also used the federal armed forces for these purposes. There was no federal army when Congress enacted the legislation in 1794 that enabled President Washington to assemble 15,000 state militiamen and suppress the revolt in western Pennsylvania against collection of the federal excise tax on whisky stills. In 1861 President Lincoln interpreted the secession movement in the very phrases of the statutes of Washington's administration when he called upon the governors of the states for 75,000 militiamen to suppress combinations obstructing the enforcement of federal laws in states that had passed ordinances of secession. In 1957 President Eisenhower, utilizing the power Congress had authorized, mobilized the militia of Arkansas under his power as commander in chief, thereby taking it out of the control of Gov. Orval Faubus, who had been defying a federal court order. President Eisenhower then utilized federal armed forces to prevent further interference with the court order which directed limited desegregation in a school at Little Rock, Ark.

Foreign Relations.—The Constitution invests the president with "Power, by and with the Advice and Consent of the Senate, to make Treaties, provided two thirds of the Senators present con-

cur" (Art. II, sec. 2, clause 2). Usage has established the practice that the president, either directly or through his agents, negotiates treaties and submits them to the Senate for action. In addition to treaties the president frequently negotiates with foreign governments executive agreements which are not referred to the Senate but have all the effect of treaties.

"The President is the sole organ of the nation in its external relations and its sole representative with foreign nations," declared John Marshall as a member of the House of Representatives in 1799. The Constitution provides that the president, "by and with the Advice and Consent of the Senate, shall appoint Ambassadors, other public Ministers and Consuls" (Art. II, sec. 2), who become, in effect, the president's personal diplomatic representatives abroad. Only the president can "receive Ambassadors and other public Ministers" whereby foreign governments are recognized and diplomatic relations with them are maintained. Only the president can dismiss foreign diplomatic representatives.

Pardons and Reprieves.—The Constitution provides that the president "shall have Power to grant Reprieves and Pardons for Offenses against the United States, except in Cases of Impeachment." A "reprieve" suspends the penalties of the law while a "pardon" remits the penalties. The president may not grant a pardon before the commission of an offense but may do so at any time after its commission. Since impeachment and conviction of officers of the United States is an exclusive function of Congress, the president is forbidden the power of pardon in such convictions. In like manner Congress may not interfere with the president's power of pardon.

Cabinet.—The president's cabinet grew unexpectedly out of the provision of the Constitution that the president "may require the Opinion, in writing, of the principal Officer in each of the executive Departments, upon any Subject relating to the Duties of their respective Offices" (Art. II, sec. 2). President Washington at first followed this provision explicitly and obtained the opinions in writing. Later, with no idea that he was initiating a cabinet, he began holding informal conferences with these heads of the executive departments. In the course of time these random conferences became habitual and regular meetings and thus the cabinet as an institution was firmly established. The president's cabinet constitutes a purely advisory group with no collective authority. The weight of its influence varies greatly with the theory and practice of different presidents. President Lincoln ignored its opinion whenever he chose, while President Pierce is said to have based some decisions on a majority vote of his cabinet.

Ceremonial Duties.—With the passage of time the president has become increasingly burdened with ceremonial duties. The elaborate ritual of his inauguration, suggestive of a royal coronation, is but the first of such activities. He awards medals to military heroes, buys the first poppy at the annual Veterans of Foreign Wars sale, greets delegations of firemen, Boy Scouts, Elks, Eagles, Daughters of the American Revolution, and other organizations, issues the Thanksgiving Proclamation, lays a wreath on the Tomb of the Unknowns, lights the White House Christmas tree, and receives visiting monarchs. Nor can it be doubted that these acts of the chief of state strengthen the powers of the chief executive. More than once the electorate has chosen as president a symbol rather than one who, by an appropriate apprenticeship in public administration, has been prepared for the presidency.

Origin and Early History.—Historically the office of chief executive of the states at the time of the framing of the Constitution of the United States, the state governors, provided the model for the office of president; the framers lifted several provisions for the office of governor from state constitutions and put them in Article II, which prescribes for the presidency. For example, just as the constitution of every state made its governor commander in chief of its military forces, so the president was made commander in chief of the armed forces of the nation.

No sooner had President Washington been inaugurated than the office began its evolution, continuous ever since, shaped by the influence of events and the personalities of the presidents. Washington's secretary of the treasury, Alexander Hamilton, with Washington's willing acquiescence, assumed bold headship of the executive departments. He drafted and promoted passage through Congress of the administration measures known ever since as the Hamiltonian program. But Hamilton's competent and aggressive leadership, no less than the very nature of the legislation he had enacted, aroused a determined opposition. Rallying around Thomas Jefferson, this opposition formed the first Republican Party, elected Jefferson president in 1800, and brought about a striking change in the very nature of the presidency. The centre of gravity in the federal government passed from the executive to the Congress, with President Jefferson managing congressional legislation through his personal influence as an astute party leader. Jefferson had initiated what turned out to be a quarter century of congressional government under the "Virginia dynasty" of three two-term presidents: Thomas Jefferson (1801–09), James Madison (1809–17), and James Monroe (1817–25). By the 1820s the president seemed to have become practically the agent of Congress.

Late in the 1820s, with white manhood suffrage almost universal, the voters rallied under and elected president a military hero, Gen. Andrew Jackson, who assumed that he was a tribune of the common man and had a mandate to act as his protector. Jackson imposed his imperious will on the Congress and so shifted the centre of gravity in the government back to the executive branch, where it had been in Washington's administration. The presidency had taken another sharp turn. To this day the office bears the impress made on it by the personality of President Jackson (1829–37). But even more than Jackson, President Lincoln (1861–65), in the crisis of the American Civil War, utilizing the unexplored power of commander in chief, reshaped the presidency into an instrument of extraordinary power for resolving crises and great emergencies, all with a confident touch and an incomparable ingenuity in dealing with them. Historians, with virtual unanimity, rank Lincoln first among all the presidents.

20th Century.—With the beginning of the 20th century the presidency, after a generation-long decline of the high prestige Lincoln's hand had given the office, experienced a revival of the executive leadership in legislation which Hamilton had given it in the first years of the republic. Pres. Theodore Roosevelt (1901–09) believed that "a good Executive under present conditions of American life must take a very active interest in getting the right kind of legislation." As a consequence of his extraordinary ability to dramatize public issues and bring public opinion to bear on Congress, the number and importance of legislative accomplishments in his administration had scarcely been surpassed by any previous administration.

It was Pres. Woodrow Wilson (1913–21) who brought to the presidency a well-matured and clear-cut formula for presidential leadership in legislation. Utilizing the hitherto neglected provision of the Constitution that the president "shall from time to time give to the Congress Information of the State of the Union, and recommend to their Consideration such Measures as he shall judge necessary" (Art. II, sec. 3), he proceeded to demonstrate his legislative leadership by getting an unprecedented program of important measures, regulative of business, enacted by Congress in his first term. Wilson gave a dramatic touch to his leadership by resuming the delivery of presidential messages in person, something that had not been done since the administration of John Adams 112 years earlier. In the 1920s Howard L. McBain was to note the new trend in the unqualified statement: "The prime function of the President is not executive. It is legislative." The proof of this is demonstrated by the fact that presidential campaigns are primarily competitions between the two major party candidates for president, each trying to outbid his opponent on policies he proposes to induce the Congress to enact into law if he is elected.

Pres. Franklin D. Roosevelt (1933–45) introduced new features into the pattern of presidential leadership in legislation. There was the "fireside chat," an informal talk broadcast by radio to the nation; its purpose was to encourage the public to induce Congress to enact measures in the president's program. It became an established device and was fortified in later years by the use of television. Franklin D. Roosevelt also initiated the practice of accompanying a proposal for legislation with an already prepared bill. Although patronage is no longer so abundant, what is available is still utilized by resolute presidents to reward administration supporters of their programs by appointing their constituents to desirable federal jobs while withholding patronage from dissident party members.

If the president decides not to sign a bill passed by both houses of Congress but to veto it, that is, return it to the house in which it originated along with his objections to it as the Constitution directs, it may still become a law by a two-thirds vote of both houses. In the hands of a shrewd president this veto power may become a decisive and even positive force in legislation; if the president is known to be ready to veto certain measures the legislators may decide to reshape them to meet his objections. No one can say just how much a president's known or even suspected objections to this or that provision of a pending bill may induce a congressional committee to recast it in the hope of avoiding a possible veto.

The Constitution provides that the president "may, on extraordinary Occasions, convene both Houses, or either of them, and in Case of Disagreement between them, with Respect to the Time of Adjournment, he may adjourn them to such Time as he shall think proper" (Art. II, sec. 3). The president has never had occasion to adjourn Congress. The Senate has frequently convened immediately after inauguration of a new president to consider and confirm his nominations of officers, especially his cabinet. The House of Representatives has never been called into session alone.

The sudden growth in magnitude of the presidency in mid-20th century constitutes a landmark in the history of the office. With the sharp decline in isolationism in the late 1930s and after World War II, and the sudden plunge of the United States into the midst of world politics, the very nature of the presidency underwent a profound change. War, both hot and cold, had shifted the centre of gravity of the presidency from the domestic field into the vortex of world problems with the attention of the human race centred on the president of the United States. Questions of foreign aid designed to rescue the critical economies of recent allies from impending collapse, of whether to meet Communist aggression with armed force in Korea or to use it in the Near East, whether to rescue Greece and Turkey from impending inclusion in the Communist sphere, or even to be ready at any moment to order the use of nuclear weapons—all this and more put on the presidency an unprecedented burden of responsibility. Meanwhile new domestic issues with worldwide implications such, for example, as desegregation riots, added to the president's responsibilities.

Some measure of the growing burden of the presidency can be seen in the fact that Pres. Grover Cleveland in the 1880s managed the office with a single secretary—when he had any at all—and answered the telephone in person. In 1960 the executive office of the president comprised half a dozen agencies with a total personnel of 2,814, while one of the agencies, the White House Office—the president's immediate staff and thus the counterpart of Cleveland's single secretary—had a personnel of over 400. With it all, the president is overburdened. Whatever responsibility the Constitution vests in him cannot be shifted.

LATIN AMERICA

Latin-American governments provide the most numerous examples of presidential government since that type was initiated by the Constitution of the United States. The single exception to the presidential type of government in South America is Uruguay, whose executive consists of a council of nine. Some Latin-American constitutions show a slight trace of a parliamentary system where they prescribe that cabinet members, in contrast with those in the United States, may appear on the floor of the legislature to speak and explain their programs. Actual premiers, however, are conspicuously absent in Latin America.

Latin-American presidents are elected either indirectly by electoral colleges after the general pattern of the United States or directly by the voters. The presidential term of office in Latin-American republics varies from nation to nation with the number of terms of office frequently limited and successive consecutive terms sometimes forbidden. Often these presidents are genuine political leaders functioning in the democratic tradition as duly elected public officials after the manner of strong presidents of the United States. Other Latin-American presidents have been military adventurers ambitious for power who after election have seized control and continued in office beyond their constitutional term under the pretense of emergency. Sometimes the president is an ambitious civilian who prolongs his term arbitrarily. There have been Latin-American presidents who were obviously virtual puppets of the army or of powerful economic interests, or of some clique which put them in office and made decisions for them.

The legal authority of a Latin-American president consists of the power vested in him by the constitution and laws. His main responsibility is to head and direct the executive branch of the government. He has the authority to nominate major executive officials under him, usually with the requirement of confirmation by a branch of the legislature. He recommends measures to the legislature, receives foreign ministers, and carries on relations with foreign nations. He is dependent on the legislature for appropriations and for ratification of the international agreements he makes, and he is subject to impeachment by the legislature. He is commander in chief of the nation's armed forces and has the power of pardon. The Latin-American presidency is modeled after that of the United States no matter how differently it functions in an alien culture.

FRANCE AND OTHER COUNTRIES

France's imitation of the U.S. office of president was a consequence of the Revolution of 1848 when the government of King Louis Philippe was overthrown and the Second Republic was established with a constitution that provided for a president elected by universal manhood suffrage for a term of four years. Louis Napoleon, a grand-nephew of the first Napoleon, was elected first president, but before the end of his four-year term arbitrarily extended his term to ten years and less than a year later directed a plebiscite which voted him emperor for life (1852). But when, in the short Franco-German War (1870–71), France was overwhelmed, Napoleon III was utterly discredited and the French conception of the office of president was profoundly affected by Napoleon's conduct following his election to it by popular vote.

The constitution of the Third Republic that followed the collapse of the Second Empire rejected popular election of the president and provided for his election by a joint vote of the two houses of parliament. The term was set at seven years with no limit on reeligibility. The new constitution gave the president an imposing list of powers, none of which he could exercise except on the advice of his ministers. His every official directive had to have the countersignature of a minister in order to be valid. The folly of President Louis Napoleon had thus emasculated the office of president in France. As Sir Henry Maine put it: "The constitutional King . . . reigns but does not govern. The President of the United States governs but does not reign. It has been reserved for the President of France that he neither reigns nor rules." France had, in fact, turned from the presidential type of government of the United States and Latin America and returned to parliamentary government. In the absence of significant authority the presidents of France, during the Third and Fourth republics, had to rely upon the use of whatever influence and political skill they had.

The constitution of the Fifth Republic of France, adopted in 1958, created a formidable office of president under the influence of Premier Charles de Gaulle. As the framers of the U.S. Constitution in 1787 had shaped the office conscious of the fact that General Washington would be its first incumbent, so the constitution of the Fifth Republic shaped the presidential office in France for General de Gaulle. It therefore stands in sharp contrast with the president elected by and subservient to parliament. At first elected by the members of the two houses of parliament, the general councils of the departments (virtually counties), and representatives of the municipal counties, totaling in all more than 80,000 electors, the president, after an amendment in 1962, is elected by direct universal suffrage.

The president of the Fifth Republic of France appoints the premier, who then nominates a ministry or cabinet that the president appoints. When a ministry falls as a consequence of an adverse vote of parliament the president accepts the premier's resignation. He has a suspensive veto over acts of parliament. This veto merely requires parliament to reconsider its vote, but repassage by a majority vote validates the act. If parliament so proposes, the president may submit a bill to a referendum. The constitution gives the president the power to dissolve a parliament, but he may not exercise this power during the first year after its election. While the president must consult the premier and the presidents of the assemblies on a decision to dissolve a parliament, he need not heed the advice. Under a resolute president the power of dissolution may be very significant. The president of France has the power to appoint high civil and military officials. He is commander in chief of the armed forces of France. He is authorized to send messages to parliament which it must debate at once, and he may convene parliament in special session to hear and consider a message. Emergency power is vested in the president of France "to take those measures which circumstances demand when the institutions of the Republic, its independence or the integrity of its territory or the fulfillment of its international obligations threaten a grave crisis and when the regular functioning of constitutional authority is interrupted."

Next to the president of France the most significant office of that title in Europe is the president of the Federal Republic of Germany. This office is almost a replica of the weak presidency of France during the Third and Fourth republics. He is elected by a special convention composed of the *Bundestag* (lower house of parliament) plus an equal number of delegates elected by the popular branch of the *Länder* (states) of the federal union. The president's term of office is five years and he may be reelected only once. The influence of earlier French constitutions is seen in the provision that official acts of the German federal president must be countersigned by the chancellor (prime minister) or other appropriate minister. The president appoints and dismisses the chancellor but these acts require the approval of parliament.

With rare exceptions the titular head (and sometimes actual chief executive) of nearly all other European governments bears the title of president. The constitutions of Finland and Portugal provide for the election of the president by electoral colleges while in Austria and Italy he is elected by the parliament. In contrast to the republics of North and South America, European republics weaken the presidential power by vesting executive authority in cabinets responsible to parliaments. The president of Switzerland is in reality the president of the federal executive council, which is elected by the assembly and is invested with the executive power of the nation. However, the Swiss president may make decisions in the name of the federal council in cases of emergency, and he exercises general supervision of federal administration. In the communist governments of Europe, designated as people's republics, the head of the state bears the title of president.

BIBLIOGRAPHY.—E. S. Corwin, *The President: Office and Powers, 1787–1957* (4th ed. 1957); C. L. Rossiter, *The American Presidency* (1960); R. E. Neustadt, *Presidential Power: the Politics of Leadership* (1960); W. E. Binkley, *President and Congress* (1947) and *Man in the White House: His Powers and Duties* (1959); H. J. Laski, *The American Presidency: an Interpretation* (1940); Sidney Hyman, *American President* (1954); Herman Finer, *Presidency: Crisis and Regeneration* (1960). (W. E. By.)

PRESIDENTE HAYES, the southernmost of the three departments which make up the Paraguayan Chaco, is for 250 mi. adjacent to the Argentine province of Formosa, from which it is separated by the Pilcomayo River. The latter is the longest of many parallel watercourses draining the department eastward to the Paraguay River. Although mainly a marshy plain with thickets of scrub forest, the department contains alluvial areas adjacent to the Paraguay near Asunción which produce sugar, corn, and cotton. Villa Hayes, the capital, is named (as is the department) after Rutherford B. Hayes, the U.S. president whose arbitration settled the boundary between the Argentine and Paraguayan Chacos. The department has an area of 22,579 sq.mi. Population ([1962] 31,572) is sparse and communications are poor.

(G. J. B.)

PRESOV (Hung. Eperjes), the third largest town of Slovakia, in the East Slovak *kraj* (region), Czech., lies on the Torysa River 25 mi. (40 km.) N of Kosice. Pop. (1961) 37,534. Presov's position in the Kosice Basin is its main asset, since this region provides an easy approach from the south northward to the Carpathians.

The town was founded in the 12th century by German immigrants, and was one of the group of 24 settlements (Spis or Zips) along the trade route from east Hungary to Poland. Most of Presov was rebuilt after a devastating fire in 1887, but the medieval oval-shaped marketplace remains. There is a fine 18th-century Greek Catholic cathedral, and the town is traditionally a meeting place and cultural centre of the Slovaks and Ruthenes; the emphasis on Ruthenian culture remains.

Presov's industrial activity is new; its traditional economy was that of trade in wheat, cattle, and salt. The salt mines at Solivar nearby supply about one-fourth of Czechoslovakia's needs. At Dubnik, 15 mi. E, is the only opal mine in Europe (now abandoned). Presov has grown vigorously since World War II with the industrial development of electrical engineering, textile production, and food processing. The town is an important rail and road junction for the Carpathians and Poland, and there are regular air services to Prague and Bratislava.   (H. G. S.)

PRESS ASSOCIATION: *see* News Agency.
PRESSBURG: *see* Bratislava.
PRESS SYNDICATE, an organization formed to spread the cost of expensive features among as many newspapers (subscribers) as possible. Press syndicates sell the exclusive rights to a feature to one subscriber in each territory in contrast to the wire news services (*see* News Agency), such as the Associated Press, United Press International, and Reuters, which offer their reports to all papers in a given area.

Irving Bacheller of Brooklyn, N.Y., started the first modern syndicate in 1883; it offered and distributed fiction and articles about housekeeping. In 1884 S. S. McClure (who later established *McClure's Magazine*) founded the syndicate that still bears his name. He first offered fiction and secured the rights to several stories by Rudyard Kipling which were widely published. He also helped to introduce the stories of Sir Arthur Conan Doyle and others into the United States.

The features then offered were mostly literary material and pictures (*see* Photojournalism: *Syndicates and Agencies*). An important change came in 1896, however, when the big New York Sunday newspapers began to produce and publish comic pages such as "Foxy Grandpa," "The Yellow Kid" (originally called "Hogan's Alley"), and "Li'l Mose." In 1907 the comic strip (*see* Caricature and Cartoon) in daily papers was introduced. Two artists, "Bud" Fisher and George Herriman, were credited with drawing the first strips, though an earlier strip by Clare Briggs had a brief run in Chicago. This form of art gradually changed the whole character of the business and made it more profitable. The strips were shipped in matrix form to the subscribers for simultaneous publication. Originally they were truly "comics" in that they were intended to make readers laugh, but later many became continued stories with no humour. When Fisher's "Mutt and Jeff" was first bought and published in England in 1920 many British readers scoffed at the idea. It proved successful and English editors later originated many strips in competition with the U.S. products. By the latter 1950s U.S. comics were being translated into several languages and sold all over the world.

Before the modern syndicate was developed there had been a few sporadic efforts to distribute political and fashion letters. In 1875 A. N. Kellogg of Chicago began to sell stereotyped plates carrying literary and pictorial material to weekly papers. Kellogg was followed in this technique by Major O. J. Smith in England (1882) and by directors of political parties and factions in Germany.

In the 1960s a great variety of material was available from press syndicates, including columns on a wide range of subjects, dress patterns, crossword puzzles with substantial prizes offered for the correct solution, etc. Several newspaper chains had their own syndicates.

The leading syndicates in the 1960s were King Features, owned by the Hearst Papers; United Features, an offspring of Scripps-Howard; Bell-McClure Syndicate; A.P. Newsfeatures; General Features; and Chicago Tribune-New York News Syndicate. Prominent British syndicates were Central Press, Exchange Telegraph Co., Ltd., and Incorporated Press of Great Britain.
(F. L. Mt.; J. N. W.)

PRESSURE CHEMISTRY is the study of the pronounced influence of pressure on both the physical and chemical states of matter and on the changes that matter undergoes in industrial chemical processes. The Haber process for the synthesis of ammonia from hydrogen and nitrogen, developed in Germany prior to World War I by the Badische Anilin und Soda Fabrik, was the first industrial chemical process to use high pressure for a chemical reaction. Many other substances are manufactured under conditions which include elevated pressure. These include methanol, ethanol and other alcohols; phenol, polyethylene, amines, and naphtha or gasoline from coal or gas. Pressure, which ordinarily changes a gas or vapour into a liquid, is used in the production of oil from wells, in purification and separation operations and in changing carbon into diamond.

Pressure performs several functions. It has an effect on some chemical reactions so that at equilibrium a greater amount of product is formed. It causes some reactions to take place at a faster rate, so that much more of the desired product is formed in a given time. It may maintain water or organic substances in a liquid state at a higher temperature than would be possible under ordinary pressure. This is beneficial in some chemical reactions.

Chemical Equilibrium.—According to H. L. Le Châtelier's principle, when a system at equilibrium is subjected to a constraint, the system will change in a manner to oppose the constraint. Thus, when a system in chemical equilibrium is subjected to pressure it will react to reduce its volume. Pressure favours a chemical reaction in which the volume of the products is less than that of the reactants. The effect of pressure on chemical equilibrium may be stated more precisely in terms derived from thermodynamics, *e.g.*, the reaction of hydrogen and nitrogen to form ammonia is favoured when it is carried out under elevated pressures. This reaction is $1/2 N_2 + 3/2 H_2 \rightleftharpoons NH_3$. Each mole of ammonia is formed from two moles of hydrogen and nitrogen and, according to Le Châtelier's principle, the reaction is favoured by elevated pressure. The fugacity f may be considered as a corrected pressure for each of the elements and compounds involved in the reaction. The ratio of the fugacities, as expressed below, must have a value fixed by the temperature according to the equation by Samuel Glasstone:

$$RT \ln \left[\frac{f\,NH_3}{f_{H_2}^{3/2} f_{N_2}^{1/2}} \right] = 9,130 - 7.46T \ln T + 3.69 \times 10^{-3}T^2 - 0.235 \times 10^{-6}T^3 + 12.07RT,$$

where R is the gas law constant in cal./(gram-mole×°K.) and T is in °K. From this equation the extent to which the reaction proceeds may be determined. Starting with a mixture of 3 moles of hydrogen to 1 mole of nitrogen, the resulting mixture will contain 3.85% ammonia at equilibrium under 10 atm. pressure, 25.1% under 100 atm. and 79.8% under 1,000 atm., all at 400° C. This illustrates the effect of increasing pressure in forming more ammonia at equilibrium.

Pressure has a similar effect on the equilibrium between carbon monoxide and hydrogen to form methanol, according to the reaction $CO + 2H_2 \rightleftharpoons CH_3OH$.

Rate of a Chemical Reaction.—A chemical reaction may reach equilibrium slowly or quickly. In many industrial processes it is important that reactions take place quickly, and pressure sometimes increases the rate of reaction.

For example, when ammonia is formed in a reactor under identical conditions except that the pressure is varied, the rate of formation is 1 mole/(hr.×cu.ft. of catalyst) at 100 atm. and 10.5 mole/(hr.×cu.ft.) at 300 atm., representing a 10.5-fold increase in the rate of the chemical reaction as a result of a 200 atm. increase in the pressure.

Effects on the Physical State.—A pressure of 5,000 p.s.i.

(pounds per square inch) is used to maintain a mixture of chloro-benzene and sodium hydroxide solution in a single liquid phase at 360° C. Under these conditions, a reaction occurs which produces sodium phenolate. The latter is neutralized with hydrochloric acid to produce phenol. In this process the caustic soda solution and chlorinated benzene are mixed and passed through a heated pipe autoclave under pressure. The pressure increases the mutual solubility of the components of the reaction mixture and provides suitable conditions for the hydrolysis of the chlorobenzene. This illustrates the action of pressure in maintaining a liquid phase.

The phase relation between liquids and vapours in equilibrium is often complex when mixtures of several components are considered. Mixtures of hydrocarbons under pressures as high as 10,000 p.s.i. are found in oil and gas wells. Normally, a vapour phase is formed when the pressure on a liquid mixture is decreased or when the temperature is increased. A liquid is formed from a vapour by the reverse procedure. However, for many mixtures there are limited ranges of pressure and temperature near the critical point where retrograde condensation occurs. Within these ranges a liquid phase is formed when the pressure is lowered. Repressuring operations that take advantage of this situation are conducted in the oil fields. The pressure in the underground structure is not allowed to decrease beyond a certain point. This pressure maintains a single gaseous phase underground. The single phase is brought to the surface where the pressure is reduced somewhat and a liquid phase separates. The remaining gas phase is returned to the ground to maintain the high pressure there. (*See* PHASE EQUI-LIBRIA.)

Synthetic Ammonia Process.—The synthesis of ammonia is an example of a high-pressure chemical process. Pressure increases the amount of ammonia formed from hydrogen and nitrogen at equilibrium. However, the reaction takes place too slowly to be of commercial importance unless a catalyst is used. In the presence of a catalyst, increased pressure also increases the

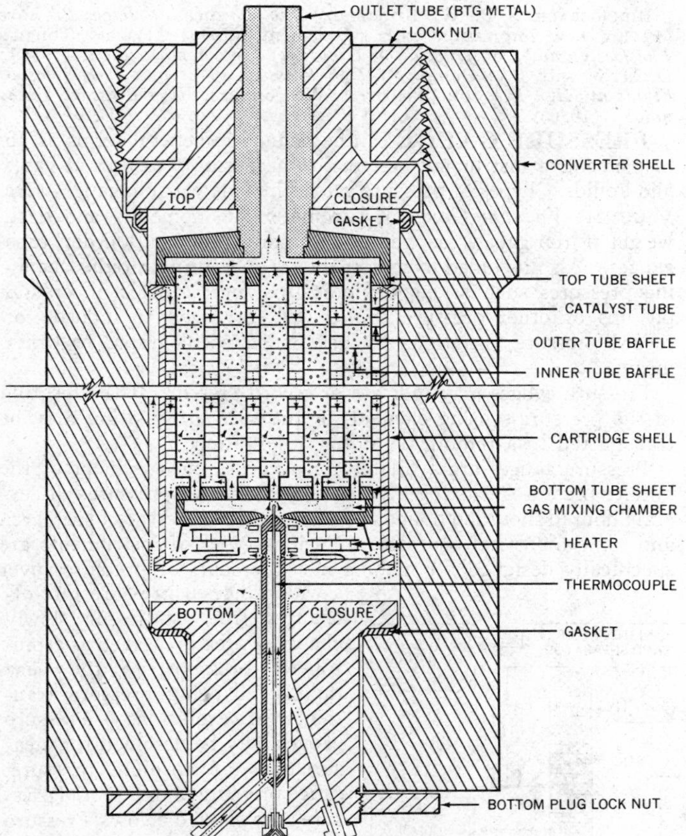

OUTLET TUBE (BTG METAL)
LOCK NUT
CONVERTER SHELL
TOP
CLOSURE
GASKET
TOP TUBE SHEET
CATALYST TUBE
OUTER TUBE BAFFLE
INNER TUBE BAFFLE
CARTRIDGE SHELL
BOTTOM TUBE SHEET
GAS MIXING CHAMBER
HEATER
THERMOCOUPLE
BOTTOM
CLOSURE
GASKET
BOTTOM PLUG LOCK NUT
COLD SHOT GAS INLET
NORMAL GAS INLET

FIG. 1.—AMMONIA SYNTHESIS CONVERTER FOR OPERATION AT 1,000 ATM.
(After H. L. Thompson, P. Guillaumeron and N. C. Updegraff)

rate of reaction. The process is then commercially successful. The catalyst is iron, but the method of preparation and the nature of the iron surface on which the reaction takes place are of great importance. A smooth iron surface or iron shavings are ineffective. Other noncatalytic agents should also be present in the iron to promote its activity. A typical catalyst, before it is made active, contains 66% Fe_2O_3, 31% FeO, 1.0% K_2O and 1.8% Al_2O_3. These materials must be free from impurities which would act as catalyst poisons. The mixture is fused into a solid mass by passing an electric current through it. Then it is broken up and screened, and the —3 to +6 mesh (per inch) fraction is used, although it must be activated before it will produce ammonia. Activation consists of reducing the iron oxides by passing the hydrogen and nitrogen synthesis gas over them according to a predetermined time schedule, with gradually increasing temperature. After the catalyst is activated it cannot be exposed to air and must be kept continuously in a reducing atmosphere. Impurities such as sulphur, phosphorus and arsenic will poison the catalyst permanently, reducing its activity, while oxygen, water vapour and carbon oxides are temporary poisons and reduce the activity only as long as they are present in the synthesis gas stream.

The synthesis reaction is carried out in a large complicated pressure vessel called a converter. The catalyst is maintained at a temperature in the range from 750° to 1,050° F., according to the process and the condition of the catalyst. The high temperature is confined to the inner regions of the converter; the walls which must withstand the pressure are at a much lower temperature, not over 120° F. in some cases. The synthesis gas entering the converter is relatively cool and is heated to the reaction temperature by heat exchangers within the converter. The heat generated by the reaction in the catalyst bed must be removed to prevent overheating and damage to the catalyst.

A typical converter designed for operation in the high-pressure range, at about 1,000 atm., is a thick-walled carbon steel vessel containing a basket, or cartridge, which includes both a heat-exchanger and tubes of catalyst. (*See* fig. 1.) The heat exchange is carried out in the same region as the catalytic reaction. The cold incoming gas enters at the bottom and moves upward through a narrow passage between the inside of the converter wall and the cartridge, keeping the wall cool. The catalyst tubes are arranged in closely spaced concentric circles and are fitted with internal baffles to aid in removing the heat of reaction. The region outside the tubes also is provided with baffles to improve the gas flow distribution and provide local high velocity and turbulence to improve the heat transfer. Synthesis gas enters the cartridge near the top, flows downward around the catalyst tubes and into a mixing chamber where it may be heated electrically if necessary. It then flows upward through the catalyst tubes. The reaction is rapid in the lower part of these tubes and slow in the upper part so the gas is cooled considerably before it leaves the catalyst. Each converter contains about 16.5 cu.ft. of catalyst and produces from 250 to 400 lb. of ammonia per hour per cubic foot of catalyst.

For use at lower pressures, in the range from 250 to 350 atm., the walls of the converter are made of medium-carbon steel and are kept cool by a portion of the cool synthesis gas entering at the top and flowing down through an annular space inside the converter wall. The main flow of synthesis gas enters at the bottom and, after mixing with that from above, flows upward around the tubes of a heat exchanger. There it receives heat from the hot gases which have just left the catalyst and are flowing down inside the tubes. The catalyst is in a continuous bed above the heat exchanger, and tubes for the partially preheated synthesis gas pass up through this bed. The reacting gas flows downward through the bed.

Such a converter contains about 144 cu.ft. of catalyst and produces about 80 lbs. of ammonia per hour per cubic foot of catalyst. (*See* fig. 2.)

In the high-pressure process, hydrogen for the reaction is obtained from steam and natural gas, while the nitrogen comes from the air. The synthesis gas is prepared and then carefully purified and compressed to reaction pressure. Only a part of the hydrogen-

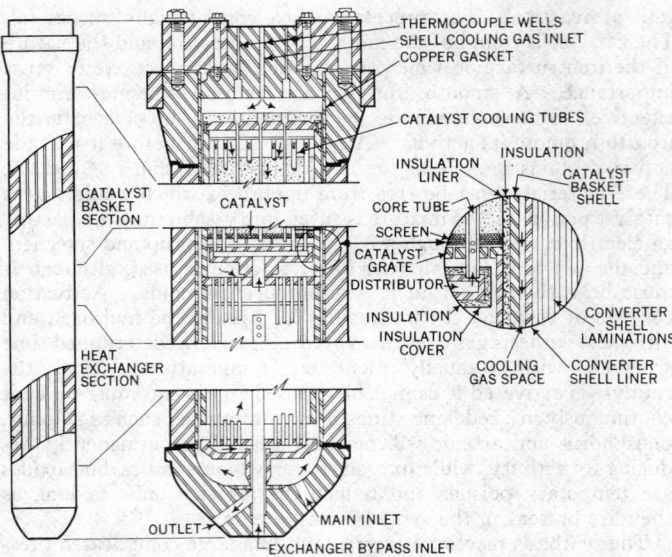

FIG. 2.—AMMONIA SYNTHESIS CONVERTER FOR OPERATION AT 250–300 ATM.
(After A. V. Slack, H. Y. Allgood and H. E. Maune)

nitrogen mixture is converted to ammonia in one pass through a converter. This ammonia is condensed and removed and the remaining gas is passed through a second converter. The unconverted gas is then mixed with make-up gas and recirculated to the first converter.

At 1,000 atm. the conversion per pass through the synthesis reactor is considerably greater than at lower pressures. Approximately one-seventh as much catalyst and converter volume is required to produce the same quantity of ammonia, and about one-fifth as much gas must be pumped and piped on the basis of actual volume at synthesis conditions. Economic factors at each plant location dictate operating conditions.

Other High-Pressure Processes.—The process for synthesizing methanol is in general similar to that for ammonia. The catalyst consists of aluminum oxides, copper and zinc oxide containing chromium. Typical operating conditions are 200 atm. and 750° F. With a similar catalyst, which is made alkaline by the addition of potassium carbonate or chromate, and at temperatures from 750° to 1,000° F. and pressures from 200 to 1,000 atm., higher alcohols are formed.

Fig. 3 shows the manufacture of phenol from chlorobenzene; the raw materials are sodium chloride brine and benzene. The brine is fed to an electrolytic cell and the chlorine produced in this cell is used to chlorinate the benzene. An 18% sodium hydroxide solution derived from the cell is mixed with the chlorobenzene; this mixture is raised to a pressure of 5,000 p.s.i. and passed through a continuous-pipe pressure reactor constructed of 2 in. diameter pipe in long coils in a furnace. This mixture is heated to 360° C.; the pressure maintains a single phase and increases the mutual solubility of the ingredients; the hydrolysis reaction takes place, and sodium phenolate is formed. The sodium phenolate is neutralized with hydrochloric acid, regenerating a salt brine, and

the phenol is distilled from the mixture.

The successful synthesis of diamonds was announced by the General Electric company in 1955. Diamonds are a crystalline form of pure carbon. They are formed when carbon is subjected to extremely high pressure and high temperature with a catalyst for sufficient time. This and other solid state reactions require that pressures of 50,000 to 100,000 atm. and temperatures of 1,500° to 2,500° C. be maintained for hours at a time.

Equipment.—Chemical reactions are carried out in steel or alloy vessels at high pressure. In continuous processes high-pressure tubing, fittings and compressors are required. Closures and fittings are frequently of a special design so that the internal pressure assists in making a tight seal. A large number of designs are available for high-pressure equipment to be used under a variety of special conditions.

A variety of alloys are often used in a single piece of equipment. The wall of an ammonia converter, for example, may be selected to resist the high internal pressure at low temperature, while the liner material may be chosen to resist the corrosive action of the contents. The catalyst tubes may be selected to resist the combined action of high temperature, hydrogen and nitrogen, but not to confine the high pressure.

At high pressure both hydrogen and nitrogen attack steel and certain alloys. Hydrogen apparently is adsorbed on the surface of steel. It ionizes and the protons pass through the openings of the metal lattice. They slowly react with carbon in the steel to form methane, which accumulates at the grain boundaries. The internal pressure built up by the methane forces the grains apart, resulting in such permanent damage as intercrystalline cracking, fissuring, blistering and decarburization.

The introduction of strong carbide-forming elements such as titanium and vanadium has helped materially to reduce the effects of hydrogen. Austenitic stainless steels and beryllium-copper are examples of alloys which do not seem to be subject to hydrogen attack.

BIBLIOGRAPHY.—P. W. Bridgman, *The Physics of High Pressure* (1931); new impression with supplement, (1949); Harold Tongue, *The Design and Construction of High Pressure Chemical Plant* (1934); D. M. Newitt, *The Design of High Pressure Plant and Properties of Fluids at High Pressure* (1940); E. W. Comings, *High Pressure Technology* (1956).   (E. W. C.)

PRESSURE GAUGE can be defined in general terms as an instrument or instrument system for measuring pressures of gases and liquids. Types of pressure gauges include vacuum gauges (*see* VACUUM: *Vacuum Gauges*), barometers, manometers and dead weight piston gauges, as well as the more common Bourdon tube gauges. Also included is equipment for measuring rapidly changing pressures such as engine indicators, or piezoelectric crystal pickups or other pressure transducers, arranged to indicate or record pressure variations by use of an oscillograph, or other means.

Pressure gauges may indicate or record pressure at the location of the pressure-sensing element, or pressure information may be transmitted to a remote point for observation.

Pressure gauges are available for accurate measurement of the minute pressures existing in vacuum systems, to pressures of several hundred thousand pounds per square inch necessary in research and some industrial processes. Various types of instruments are specifically designed for making measurements of pressures over a wide range of pressure rate-of-change, from static or slowly changing pressures, such as atmospheric pressure, to the very rapidly changing pressure transients of explosions. Pressure gauges may be designed for measurement of absolute pressure, gauge pressure or differential pressure as explained below. Pressure measurement is of primary importance in the chemical process industry, in power plants, aeronautics and meteorology.

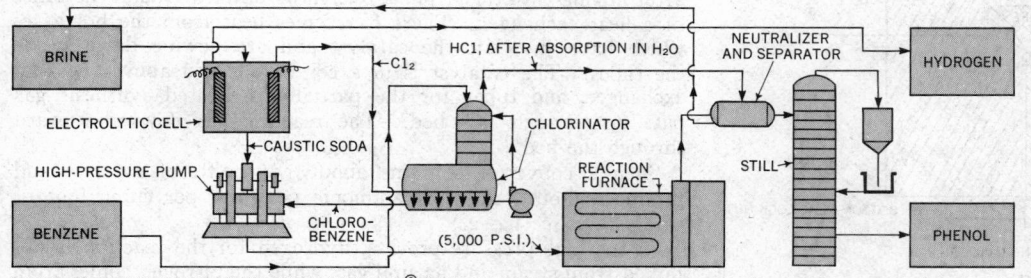

FIG. 3.—FLOW SHEET OF A COMMERCIAL PROCESS FOR MANUFACTURING PHENOL FROM CHLOROBENZENE AT 5,000 LB. PER SQUARE INCH

Industrial Gauges.—The present article is limited primarily to a treatment of pressure gauges used industrially, with only mention of the broader variety of gauges used in scientific research and development.

The pressure element of the majority of mechanical pressure gauges is usually in one of three forms: a Bourdon tube; a corrugated diaphragm or diaphragm capsule; or a bellows. Of these the Bourdon tube type is the most common.

Bourdon Tube.—The Bourdon gauge is one in which the pressure is indicated directly by an attached pointer and scale. The

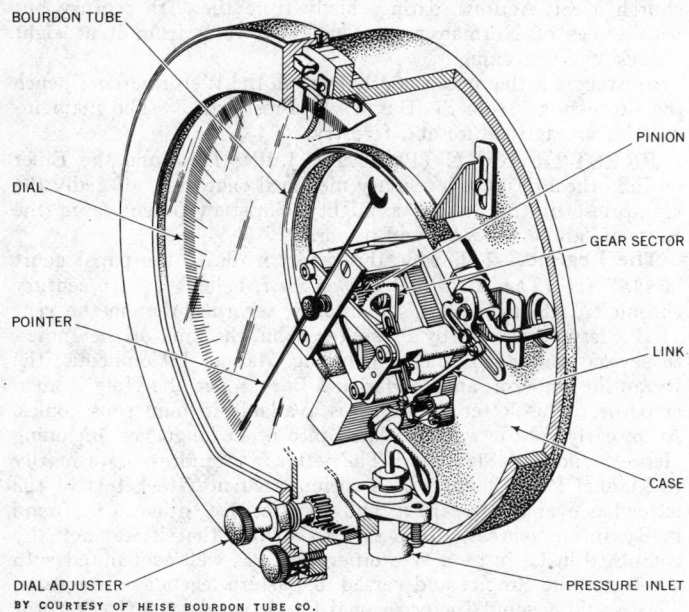

BY COURTESY OF HEISE BOURDON TUBE CO.
FIG. 1.—INTERNAL MECHANISM OF A BOURDON GAUGE

Bourdon tube is elliptical or flattened in cross section and bent into circular form. One end is soldered to a central block through which the fluid enters, and the other end is sealed and coupled by a link to a pivoted quadrant with teeth meshing with those of a pinion on the pointer spindle. Backlash between the teeth is absorbed by a hairspring exerting constant force on the pinion. An increase of pressure within the tube tends to change its cross section from elliptical to circular, and the tube consequently uncoils slightly, thus turning the pointer.

If the case enclosing the gauge is made airtight and the air is exhausted from within the case, the gauge measures absolute pressure (psia or pounds per square inch absolute); if the pressure inlet of such a gauge is then opened to the atmosphere the gauge would read atmospheric pressure, approximately 14.7 psia. If the airtight case is provided with a pressure inlet the gauge may be used to measure differential pressures existing between two sources of pressure connected to the two pressure inlets. Usually the case of the gauge is not airtight and the external surface of the Bourdon tube is thus subjected to ambient atmospheric pressure. Such a gauge measures "gage" pressure (psig or pounds per square inch gauge), *i.e.*, the value of the inlet pressure above atmospheric pressure. This instrument may be used as a vacuum gauge, measuring pressure, below atmospheric pressure; the reduction in pressure causes the Bourdon tube to coil further, and the mechanism must be arranged in reverse fashion to cause the pointer to move clockwise with increasing vacuum. A compound gauge reads for both pressure and vacuum, the dial markings for vacuum being placed to the left of the zero of the pressure scale.

Diaphragm Capsule.—One direct-reading gauge utilizes as the elastic pressure-sensitive element a hollow sealed disk-shaped capsule made from two corrugated metal diaphragms. Changes in pressure cause motion of the centre of the capsule, and this motion is amplified by a mechanical linkage to control movement of the pointer over a calibrated dial. When proper precautions are taken in design to reduce hysteresis, temperature effects and

the like, sustained accuracies on the order of two or three parts in 1,000, or better, are obtainable.

For measurement of absolute pressure, as in the aneroid barometer, the capsule is evacuated, and the varying atmospheric pressure acts on the exterior surface of the capsule. A spring is arranged to supplement the elastic resistance of the capsule to the force of atmospheric pressure, and the motion of the centre of the capsule is transmitted to the indicating pointer by appropriate linkage.

Bellows.—A metal bellows may be used in a pressure gauge designed for pressure ranges of from a few inches of water (*i.e.*, the pressure produced by a column of water a few inches high) to 10 or 15 lb. per square inch. The large deflection of the bellows for small pressure changes provides the high sensitivity needed in gauges for such low-pressure ranges.

Materials.—Bourdon tubes are commonly of phosphor-bronze, beryllium-copper or Monel metal (a nickel-copper alloy), for pressures up to a few hundred pounds per square inch; above this pressure or for elevated temperatures, the tubes are made of steel to obtain a greater elastic range and a smaller change of elasticity with temperature. Diaphragms are most frequently made of phosphor-bronze, beryllium-copper or Ni-Span (a nickel-iron-chromium-titanium alloy). Bellows are usually of brass although bellows of stainless steel and beryllium copper are also available.

Reading Instruments.—All of these gauges are also available in designs to provide a continuous record of pressure. A circular-chart gauge, comprising a Bourdon element of several complete turns, has a pen arranged to trace a record on a circular chart driven by clock work. A microbarograph records absolute atmospheric pressure on a paper strip wound around a drum driven by clockwork. The necessary high sensitivity is obtained by use of an evacuated bellows element whose motion is magnified by the pen linkage. The pressure range of the instrument is generally 28.5 to 31 in. of mercury (about 14 psia to 15.2 psia), for which range the recording pen moves about 6 in.

Remote Indicators.—For remote indication of pressure, or for control purposes, the pressure is often converted into an analogue quantity. This quantity is commonly a direct current voltage or an air pressure. Direct current voltage is used frequently in telemetering systems, and air pressure in industrial recording and control equipment.

One such instrument, designed for use in measuring the pressure at points remote from a pressure recorder, has the elastic motion of a hollow metal cylinder exposed to the pressure arranged to vary the electrical resistance of strain gauges attached to the surface of the cylinder. The strain gauges are connected in a bridge circuit in such a way that the bridge output voltage varies in a linear fashion over the range from zero to perhaps 50 millivolts as the cylinder pressure varies from zero to the rated pressure of the instrument, the rated pressure being from a few hundred psig to 50,000 psig. The output voltage, proportional to the pressure, may be recorded or displayed by use of appropriate electrical instruments. For rapidly changing pressures, to which this instrument will respond, the output voltage is usually recorded by use of an oscillograph.

A common system is that in which the pressure to be measured is converted by use of a force-balance mechanism into an analogue pneumatic pressure in the range 3 to 15 psig. The instrument may be adjusted to have an input pressure range from a small fraction of the analogue pressure range to several times the analogue pressure range. The analogue pressure may be transmitted to a remote location and connected to an indicator, recorder, or used for control purposes. The pressure-sensitive element of the pressure transmitter is a diaphragm acting against a coil spring. Slight motion of the diaphragm due to change in pressure causes a relatively large change in the pneumatic pressure in the force-balance bellows assisting the spring, and the analogue pressure is the pressure in the bellows necessary to maintain the diaphragm near its mid-position. The permitted motion of the force-balance bellows and of the diaphragm and main spring is extremely small, and the system is characterized by high sensitivity and low hysteresis.

Other methods for converting the motion of a mechanical pressure element to an analogue voltage include the use of variable resistors (potentiometers), differential transformers, variable capacitances and variable inductance or variable reluctance devices. In another method the motion of a diaphragm varies the tension, and thus the frequency, of a vibrating wire maintained in motion by a magnetic field acting on an alternating current passing through the wire. The pressure is then represented by an electrical frequency equal to the wire frequency.

Primary Pressure Gauges.—All instruments of the types described above require calibration against known pressures. The two principal instruments used for such calibration are liquid column instruments such as the manometer and barometer (*q.v.*) and dead-weight piston gauges.

A dead-weight piston gauge comprises a vertical cylinder, the

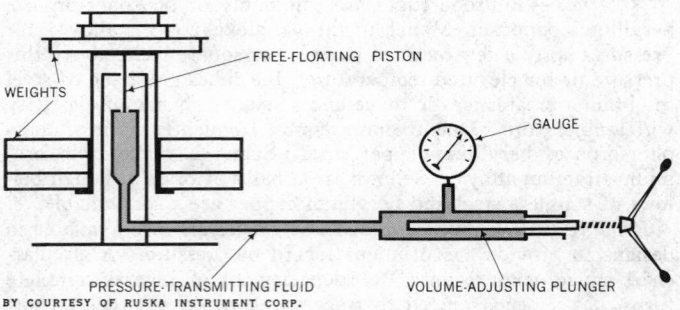

FREE-FLOATING PISTON

WEIGHTS

GAUGE

PRESSURE-TRANSMITTING FLUID

VOLUME-ADJUSTING PLUNGER

BY COURTESY OF RUSKA INSTRUMENT CORP.

FIG. 2.—DEAD-WEIGHT LOADED PISTON GAUGE

upper end of which is closed by a weight-loaded piston. The cylinder is filled with oil, and a pressure connection is provided at the lower end to which an instrument under test may be connected. A pump, operated by a handwheel, is provided to adjust the volume and pressure of the system so that the weight-loaded piston assumes a floating position in the cylinder. The pressure developed by a dead-weight piston gauge is nominally equal to the weight of the piston and its load divided by the cross-sectional area of the piston.

Such instruments are capable of high precision, on the order of one part in 10,000, or better; when precision greater than about one part in 200 is desired corrections must be made including corrections for a number of environmental variables. The following are the most important corrections that must be considered: change in effective piston area due to temperature changes, amounting to 10 to 20 parts per million per degree Centigrade; difference in value of local gravity from standard value of 980.665 cm./sec./sec., amounting to more than one part in 1,000 in some localities; variation in effective area of piston due to elastic distortion of piston and cylinder under pressure, amounting to perhaps 100 parts per million per 1,000 psi in some designs; the buoyancy of the liquid on submerged protuberances of the piston, applicable only for pistons of nonuniform cross-sectional area; the hydrostatic head of liquid between the bottom of the piston and the point of pressure measurement; and the buoyancy of air on the weights, frequently amounting to about one part in 7,000.

For high accuracy at high pressures the controlled clearance piston gauge has been developed, in which a variable hydrostatic pressure is applied to the exterior surface of the cylinder to reduce errors due to elastic distortion.

For pressures below about 50 psig piston gauges are available in which the working fluid is air, and the piston and cylinder operate as an air bearing.

BIBLIOGRAPHY.—W. G. Brombacher and T. W. Lashof, *Bibliography and Index on Dynamic Pressure Measurement,* U.S. National Bureau of Standards Circular 558, 850 references (Washington, 1955); H. Diederichs and W. C. Andrae, "The Measurement of Pressure," *Experimental Mech. Eng.,* ch. iv, vol. i (New York, 1930); R. T. Eckenrode and H. A. Kirshner, "Measurement of Pressure Transients," 112 references, *Rev. of Scientific Instruments,* vol. 25, p. 33–40 (Rochester, N.Y., 1954).   (E. C. Ld.)

PRESTEIGNE, an urban district and the county town of Radnorshire in the Brecon and Radnor parliamentary division of Radnorshire, Wales, 26 mi. (42 km.) NW of Hereford by road and on the Lugg, which there forms the boundary between Wales and England. Pop. (1961) 1,190. The village, lying on the English side of Offa's dyke, was in the lordship of Moelynaidd until the 14th century, when Bishop David Martin of St. David's (1296–1328) conferred market privileges upon his native place. There is an annual May fair.

In 1542 Presteigne was named as the meeting place of the county sessions for Radnorshire in conjunction with New Radnor; a winter and summer assize court is held. It has the fine parish church of St. Andrew, dating chiefly from the 15th century but with traces of Norman work; curfew is rung from it at eight o'clock every evening.

Presteigne is the most easterly spot on the Welsh border; hence the expression "from St. David's to Presteigne." The main industries are agriculture and forestry.

PRESTER JOHN (PRESBYTER JOHN; *i.e.,* John the Elder or John the Priest), a legendary medieval character, allegedly the king-priest of the Indies, a mighty Christian potentate in the East, of fabulous wealth and power.

The Legend.—Following the report made to the papal court in 1145 (see *The Historical Background,* below) a 13th-century chronicler, Alberic de Trois Fontaines, recorded that in the year 1165 a letter was sent by Presbyter John, the king of the Indies, to several European rulers, including Manuel I Comnenus, the Byzantine emperor, and Frederick I Barbarossa, the Holy Roman emperor. This letter, in Latin, is available in numerous copies. At an early date it was translated into other languages, including Hebrew and Old Slavonic. The letter was addressed primarily to Manuel I Comnenus. It is curious that no Greek text of the letter has ever been heard of and no reference to it can be found in Byzantine sources. It is safe to assume that it was actually composed in Latin by a Westerner who was well acquainted with the Byzantine Empire and versed in Eastern legendary literature. This would account for occasional Greek words and Greek turns of phrase in the text.

The letter is an obvious literary fiction. It was circulated mainly in the West and contains several drastic interpolations which prove the great popularity of the document. That it has a strong anti-Byzantine bias is evident from the title: Manuel is addressed as "governor of the Romans." This betrays a Western hand, for people in the West were reluctant to concede any higher title to the Byzantine rulers. On the other hand, John describes himself as "lord of lords," *dominus dominantium,* a highly ambitious title, with an implicit claim to divine authority. He writes to Manuel as to an inferior and invites him to come to his realm in person. There is subtle irony in the question, "does Manuel hold the true faith?" John had heard that "thy little Greeks" (*graeculi*) considered Manuel as divine. For his part, John knew well that he himself was but a mortal.

The land of John, "the three Indies," was indeed a miraculous land: "honey flows in our land, and milk abounds everywhere." Not only did the land abound in natural riches, and in all sorts of fabulous marvels, it was also a land of peace and justice: no vice whatever was known there, no flattery or envy, no avarice, no strife; there were no liars in the land, no robbers or thieves, and also no poor. The splendour of the royal palace was described in glamorous superlatives. Yet, in spite of all this might and glamour, John had, in humility, chosen for himself an inferior rank, that of priest, *presbyteratus nomine.* Too many glorious titles were used at his court: his butler was an archbishop and a king, and even his chief cook was a king and a prior. Accordingly it was not fit for his highness to use any such honorific name for himself. He declared his intention, nevertheless, to come to the Holy Sepulchre with a great army, to fight the enemies of the cross.

The land of John can be identified: his royal throne and palace were at Susa, in Persia. The patriarch of St. Thomas, the bishop of Samarkand, and the protopope of Susa attended his court.

Altogether the letter of Prester John is a curious document, but it had a serious purpose. Prester John posed as an ideal prince. His realm was a kind of earthly paradise, but he wanted to give a lesson in modesty to Western rulers and to rebuke them for their vainglory. The letter belongs to the peculiar branch of medieval lore of which the Alexander Romance (q.v.) is the best-known specimen. It has direct links with the legend of St. Thomas the Apostle and his shrine and with the story of the Three Magi. It may also be compared with other Oriental tales, e.g., with the Arabian story of Sinbad the Sailor in the *Thousand and One Nights* and with the travels of Eldad ha-Dani (q.v.), "the Arabian Nights of the Jews." The name "Presbyter John" itself belongs to an ancient apocryphal tradition. He is an enigmatic person to whom the writings of St. John the Apostle were often attributed. Indeed the name occurs also in the canonical epistles of St. John. It seems that the name itself was the pivot of the whole legend and was not derived from any historic personality.

The descriptive part of the letter—the fabulous picture of India—belongs to the cycle of St. Thomas. On the other hand, the letter also reflects the historical setting in which it was written, i.e., the period of the early Crusades. The image of a powerful Christian monarch, somewhere in the mysterious East, ready to support the Christian cause against the infidel, could not fail to impress the minds of all those who were involved in the crusading enterprise. The land of Prester John was accordingly included in medieval maps, and attempts were made to reach this land of marvels and to establish contact with its glorious ruler. "India" was a vague and comprehensive term in medieval geographical lore, almost coextensive with the East.

The Historical Background.—In 1145 Bishop Hugh of Gebal in Syria (modern Jebeil, Lebanon) came to the papal court at Viterbo and brought a tale concerning Prester John. His story, carefully recorded by Otto of Freising in his chronicle, was that some few years before a certain John, "priest and king," dwelling in the area "beyond Persia and Armenia," a Christian but a Nestorian, defeated in a bloody battle the Samiardi, the kings of the Persians and the Medes, and stormed Ecbatana, their capital. He intended to proceed to Jerusalem, to help the church there, but was unable to cross the Tigris. It was said of him that he was a lineal descendant of the Magi and possessed enormous wealth. The story seems to refer to the victory of Yeh-lü Ta-shih, the founder of the Khara-Khitai Empire in central Asia, over the Seljuk Sultan Sanjar, at Qatwan, near Samarkand, in 1141. It is strange, however, that the Mongol conqueror was mistaken for a Christian king. Obviously, there was a queer admixture of legend in Hugh's story. The mention of the Magi is highly characteristic. Bishop Hugh, an expert diplomat, was but reporting what he had heard in Syria. Yet, there could have been a grain of truth even in these distorted rumours. Nestorian Christians did play some role in the Mongolian realm. The story of Hugh was believed at the papal court.

In 1165 the letter of Prester John arrived. A few years later, in 1177, the pope, Alexander III, dispatched a letter to John, "the illustrious and magnificent king of the Indies and a beloved son in Christ." The pope quoted the information he had received of the king's piety and Christian devotion, both through common report, and especially from his confidant and physician, Philip, who had been in touch with some honourable persons of John's kingdom. It was reported to the pope that John wanted reconciliation with the apostolic see and desired to have a church of his own in Rome and an altar in Jerusalem. The pope was willing to grant these requests if John would specify his wishes and send his envoys with a sealed letter. The pope does not call John "Presbyter" in this letter, but it seems obvious that he was referring to the famous letter of 1165. The letter of the pope was written two months after his reconciliation with Frederick Barbarossa, after years of bitter struggle, while his position was still insecure. He was much interested in the possibility of obtaining allies from the remote East. Nothing is known of the fate of the pope's letter.

In 1221 information came to Rome from two prominent Western churchmen—Jacques de Vitry, bishop of Acre, in Palestine, and Cardinal Pelagius, who was engaged at that time with the crusading army at Damietta—concerning a recent victory of a certain King David of India over the Muslims. David was sup-

posed to be a son or a grandson of Prester John. (Jacques de Vitry says simply: "commonly called Prester John.") Strange as it may seem, the person in question was probably no other than Genghis Khan. It should not be forgotten, however, that these were rumours and there was a great deal of wishful thinking in them. On the one hand, the strength of the Nestorian Church in central Asia and Persia could easily have been exaggerated. On the other hand, certain Mongol rulers at that time were interested in an alliance with the West against the common enemy, the Muslim, in Syria and the Holy Land, and their interests to some extent coincided with those of the crusaders. In the 13th and early 14th centuries direct contact between the West and the Mongols was established by missionaries and by lay travelers, such as Joannes de Plano Carpini, Andrew of Lonjumel, William of Rubruquis, Marco Polo, Giovanni di Monte Corvino (qq.v.) and Oderic of Pordenone. All these were looking for Prester John, and all identified him differently.

A well-known Syriac writer of those times, Bar-Hebraeus (q.v.), told in his history of a Christian tribe, the Keraits, which was ruled over by an Ung Khan (Wang Khan) "who is called King John" (Malik Yuhanna). An Ung Khan was known to Rubruquis and to Marco Polo. A modern theory that "Ung Khan" should be identified as Prester John is, however, hardly tenable and can be discarded on chronological grounds.

After the mid-14th century the search for Prester John was directed toward Ethiopia. This was first suggested by Jordan de Sévérac, a Dominican friar who went to India and failed to find Prester John there. He had no first-hand knowledge of Ethiopia and his description of that country was mainly imaginary. Very soon, however, the identification of Prester John with the negus of Ethiopia was generally accepted. It was popularized by Jesuit missionaries to that country and by Portuguese navigators. Some modern scholars contend that the image of Prester John was originally based on that of the Ethiopian ruler and that the name John is a rendering of *Zan*, the royal title in Ethiopic. This contention cannot be upheld. The title *Zan* was probably not in use before the 16th century. Moreover, the legend and other stories definitely locate Prester John in Asia and in the Nestorian area. Even so, some memories of a Christian king in Ethiopia might be included in the legendary image of Prester John.

BIBLIOGRAPHY.—For a critical edition with text of the letter and commentary see Friedrich Zarncke, *Der Priester Johannes*, 2 vol. (1879–83). See also Vsevolod Slessarev, *Prester John: the Letter and the Legend* (1959). Still valuable is the old monograph of Gustav Oppert, *Der Presbyter Johannes in Sage und Geschichte*, 2nd ed. (1870). See also Leonardo Olschki, "Der Brief des Presbyters Johannes" in *Historische Zeitschrift*, vol. cxliv (1931), *Marco Polo's Precursors* (1943), and *Storia letteraria delle scoperte geografiche* (1937); Constantin Marinescu, "Le Prêtre Jean, son pays, explication de son nom" and "Encore une Fois le problème du prêtre Jean" in *Académie Roumaine* (Bulletin de la Section Historique), vol. x and xxvi (1923 and 1945); C. E. Nowell, "The Historical Prester John" in *Speculum*, xxviii:435–445 (1953); Sir E. Denison Ross, "Prester John and the Empire of Ethiopia" in *Travel and Travellers in the Middle Ages*, ed. by A. P. Newton (1926); Richard Hennig, *Terrae incognitae*, vol. ii, 2nd ed. (1950) and vol. iii, 2nd ed. (1953); Karl F. Helleiner, "Prester John's Letter: a Medieval Utopia" in *Phoenix*, xiii:47–57 (1959). (G. V. F.)

PRESTON, THOMAS (1860–1900), Irish physicist, who made original contributions on heat, magnetism and spectroscopy, and carried out experiments on the influence of magnetic fields on spectral lines, was born in Kilmore, County Armagh, Ire., on May 23, 1860. He studied in Dublin and became professor of natural philosophy in University College, Dublin, in 1891. He was elected a fellow of the Royal Society of London in 1898. The same year Preston discovered an empirical rule concerning types and structures of Zeeman patterns (see ZEEMAN EFFECT). Preston died in Dublin on March 7, 1900. (D. McK.)

PRESTON, a municipal, county and parliamentary borough and port of Lancashire, Eng., 21 mi. (34 km.) S.S.E. of Lancaster. Pop. (1961) 113,341. It is built on a ridge rising above the Ribble where that river is crossed (about 15 mi. [24 km.] above its mouth) by the west coast road and railway to Scotland. It is the administrative centre of the county of Lancashire.

From early days its geographical position made it a trade centre with an agricultural market. Its importance progressively increased after the advent of the cotton industry, to which have been added a wide range of manufactures including engineering, aircraft and vehicles, chemicals and soap, boilers and ships, paper, electrical appliances, textiles and optical goods.

Preston became an independent port in 1843, the corporation acquiring the docks in 1883. The main wet dock is 3,240 ft. (988 m.) long and 600 ft. (183 m.) wide. There is a total quayage of 8,500 ft. (2,591 m.) and the depth of the channel at ordinary spring tides is 22–25 ft. (67–76 m.).

Preston is the chief mart for the produce of the great Fylde agricultural district, with two large covered markets: for general produce (wholesale and retail); and for fish. There are also corn, butter and egg markets and a wholesale fish market at the railway station. The important cattle market holds thrice-weekly sales throughout the year. There are horse sales each month.

The numerous parish churches include that of St. John (1855) which occupies a site that has carried a church from early times. Among several Roman Catholic churches is that of St. Walburge (1854). The town hall was almost destroyed by fire in 1947. The Harris art gallery, library and museum were established by the trustees of E. R. Harris in 1879, and a new building was opened in 1893. This contains William Shepherd's library, the Francis Thompson collection and the Spencer collection of children's books, the Newsham collection of pictures and collections of pottery, glass, costumes, etc. The grammar school, dating from 1550 (Preston had a schoolmaster as early as 1339) is housed in a modern building in Moor park. The parliamentary borough returns two members. The county borough was created in 1889.

History.—Preston, otherwise Prestune, was near the Roman station at Walton-le-Dale, and the great Roman road running from Warrington passed through it. It is mentioned in Domesday Book as one of Earl Tostig's possessions which had fallen to Roger de Poictou, and on his defection it was forfeited to the crown. Henry II (about 1179) granted the burgesses a charter—the first of 14 royal charters granted to Preston (there is evidence of an even earlier charter of 1100–01). Elizabeth I (1566) granted the town its great charter which ratified and extended all previous grants. Charles II (1662 and 1685) granted charters, by which an additional weekly market on Wednesday was conceded and a three-day fair, beginning on March 16. The most important industry used to be woolen weaving. Other early industries were glovemaking and linen weaving. The first cotton-spinning mill was built in 1777 in Moor lane, and in 1791 John Horrocks built the Yellow factory. In 1835 there were 40 factories, chiefly spinning, yielding 70,000 lb. of cotton yarn weekly.

A guild existed perhaps in Saxon times, but the grant of a guild merchant dates from Henry II's charter, about 1179. The first guild of which there was any record was celebrated in 1328, at which time it was decided to hold a guild every 20 years. Up to 1542 they do not appear to have been regularly celebrated, but after that year they were held at regular intervals of 20 years except that the 1942 guild was postponed because of World War II. The mayor elected for the year in which the guild is held is known as the guild mayor. The first mention of a procession at the guild is in 1500. One of the most important items of business was the enrolling of freemen, and the guild rolls are records of the population. The statement that Preston was burned in 1323 by the Scots is probably false. The town suffered severely from the Black Death (1349–50), and again from pestilence in the year Nov. 1630 to Nov. 1631. During the Civil War Preston became the Lancashire royalist headquarters. In Feb. 1643 a parliamentary force marched from Manchester and successfully assaulted it, but in March the earl of Derby recaptured the town. The royalists did not garrison it, but after demolishing the greater part of the works left it unfortified. After the battle of Marston Moor Prince Rupert marched through Preston in Sept. 1644 and carried the mayor and bailiffs prisoners to Skipton castle. On Aug. 17, 1648, the royalist forces under the duke of Hamilton and Gen. Marmaduke Langdale were defeated at Preston by Cromwell. During the rebellion of 1715 the rebel forces entered Preston Nov. 9, and after proclaiming the chevalier de St. George king, remained there

for several days, during which the government forces advanced. The town was assaulted, and Gen. Thomas Forster surrendered his army to the king's forces. In 1745 Prince Charles Edward marched through on the way south and north. The borough returned two members from 1295 to 1331, then ceased to exercise the privilege till 1529, but after that date (except in 1653) it always sent two representatives to parliament. In the 18th century Preston had a high reputation as a centre of fashionable society, and earned the epithet still familiarly associated with it, "proud." Sir Richard Arkwright (1732–92) was born there.

See H. Fishwick, *History of the Parish of Preston* (1900); W. F. Fitzgerald, "The Ribble Basin," *Journ., Manchester Geog. Soc.* (1927).

PRESTONPANS, a small burgh and seaside resort of East Lothian, Scot., on the Firth of Forth, 9 mi. (14 km.) E of Edinburgh by road. Pop. (1961) 3,105. The name refers to the pans, or ponds, in which the monks of Newbattle Abbey (a 12th-century Cistercian foundation now a college for adult education) made salt by evaporation. The chief occupation is coal mining, and there are manufactures of firebricks, tiles, pottery, and soap, besides brewing.

A mile to the east of the village is the site of the Battle of 1745, in which Prince Charles Edward and his Highlanders gained a complete victory over the royal forces under Sir John Cope. Seton Castle, about 1½ mi. NE, was built in 1790 by Robert Adam on the site of Seton Palace to which Mary, queen of Scots, and Lord Darnley rode after David Rizzio's murder in 1566; she visited the castle again, with the earl of Bothwell (James Hepburn), in 1567 just after Darnley's murder. In the castle grounds is the incomplete 15th-century collegiate church of Seton.

PRESTWICH, a municipal borough in the Middleton and Prestwich parliamentary division, Lancashire, Eng., 4 mi. (6 km.) NW of Manchester by road. Pop. (1961) 34,209. It has cotton and rayon mills but is mainly residential. It is contiguous with the cities of Manchester and Salford. It was incorporated in 1939. There are traces of the Roman occupation but the place name is of Anglo-Saxon origin. The present parish church dates from the 15th century.

PRESTWICK, a police burgh of Ayrshire, Scot., on the eastern shore of the Firth of Clyde, 3 mi. (5 km.) N of Ayr and 30 mi. (48 km.) SW of Glasgow by road. Pop. (1961) 12,562. It is a seaside and golfing resort with a broad sandy bathing beach two miles long and a large swimming pool. Besides the Prestwick championship golf links there are two other good courses. The international airport is the most important in Scotland, its development being the result of good climatic conditions. There is a 15th-century Mercat cross (rebuilt 1777), and the ruined church of St. Nicholas is a landmark for shipping. Bruce's Well in Kingcase estate is said to mark the place where Robert I, "the Bruce," was cured of a skin disease. Local industries are coal mining, aircraft construction, and light engineering. Prestwick is thought to have been a burgh since 983 and was granted a royal charter by James VI in 1600. It became a police burgh in 1903.   (A. I.)

PRETORIA, capital city of Transvaal Province and administrative capital of the Republic of S.Af. Pop. (1960) 298,632, including 154,789 Whites, 131,824 Bantu, 7,167 Asians, and 4,852 Coloureds. It lies in a valley between the eastern foothills of the Magaliesberg through which flows the Apies River. The original town was laid out in rectangular blocks around Church Square, which is surrounded by some of the city's most important buildings, including the Raadsaal (old government buildings), formerly the meeting place of the republican *volksraad* (Parliament) and now occupied by the provincial council; the Palace of Justice; the General Post Office; and the headquarters of the South African Reserve Bank. At the centre of the square is the statue of Pres. Paul Kruger; his house, now a national monument, is nearby in Church Street.

Running east-west and north-south from the square are the city's principal streets: Church Street, one of the world's longest straight streets (11.58 mi. [18.64 km.]) and Paul Kruger Street. These and other streets in the central area are flanked by imposing new skyscrapers, erected during the boom period following World War II. The Union buildings, containing most of the cabinet

SATOUR

VOORTREKKER MONUMENT

offices, stand on the slopes of Meintjes' Kop. Erected during 1910–13, they overlook terraced gardens in which is the statue of Gen. Louis Botha, the union's first prime minister.

Pretoria has Anglican and Roman Catholic cathedrals and about 70 Afrikaans and numerous other churches serving various denominations. There are many public and private schools, a technical college, and a teachers' training college. The University of Pretoria was founded in 1930 from the Transvaal University College (1908). It includes the only faculty of veterinary science in South Africa. The headquarters of the University of South Africa are also in Pretoria. The Transvaal Museum is in Paul Kruger Street, and the National Historical Cultural Museum adjoins the National Zoological Gardens. South of the city is the Voortrekker Monument, inaugurated on Dec. 16, 1949, as a tribute to the *voortrekkers* (pioneers), which has a museum.

The city is linked by rail and road with the Witwatersrand and with the rest of the republic and neighbouring countries. Air traffic uses the nearby Jan Smuts International Airport. The South African Iron and Steel Industry (I.S.C.O.R.) was established in 1928; since then, the production of iron and steel and subsidiary undertakings have been the city's most important industries.

Pretoria was founded in 1855 and named after the famous *voortrekker* leader Andries Pretorius. It became capital of the South African Republic (Transvaal) in 1860. During the South African War, after Winston Churchill had been held a prisoner of war there for a short while, it was declared an open town and occupied by British troops on June 5, 1900. The Peace of Vereeniging was signed at Melrose House on May 31, 1902. On the establishment of the Union of South Africa in 1910, Pretoria became its administrative capital. *See* also references under "Pretoria" in the Index.

(H. P. H. B.)

PRETORIUS, the surname of two Boer leaders in the republics established in South Africa during the Great Trek.

Andries Wilhelmus Jacobus Pretorius (1798–1853), commandant general in Natal and subsequently in the Transvaal, achieved fame by leading the Boers to victory over Dingaan's Zulus at the Battle of Blood River on Dec. 16, 1838, and was thereafter until his death the most prominent figure in Boer politics. Born near Graaff-Reinet, Cape Colony, on Nov. 27, 1798, Pretorius left the colony in September 1838 and trekked to Natal, which he had visited previously. He had served as a commandant in the Cape Colony and on his arrival the Natal *volksraad* (elected council) appointed him commandant general (November 1838). Pretorius raised a commando and prepared to move against the Zulus under Dingaan, whose attacks had been endangering the security of the trekkers since the massacre of Piet Retief and his party (February 1838). At Blood River the encamped commando of

nearly 500 Boers withstood the onslaughts of about 10,000 Zulu warriors without loss, while the Zulu dead numbered more than 3,000. When Panda (Mpande) announced his revolt against his brother Dingaan (October 1839), Pretorius decided to assist him and exact from Dingaan reparations outstanding under the peace agreement concluded in May. The combined forces were successful at the Battle of Magongo (January 1840) and in February Pretorius, after receiving a huge number of cattle, returned to Natal in triumph leading his "cattle commando," having established Panda as "ruling Zulu prince."

Inheriting the policy of his more able predecessor, Retief, of uniting the trekker communities in a single republic, Pretorius concluded an agreement with head commandant Andries Potgieter in October 1840, which brought the Potchefstroom and Winburg settlements (*see* Transvaal: *History: The Trekker State*) into a federal union with Natal. Pretorius quarreled frequently with the Natal *volksraad*, which hedged his office with restrictions and even sought to abolish it in peacetime. The *volksraad's* interference explains his failure to prevent a small British force from occupying Durban in May 1842, but Pretorius lost an opportunity of forcing its surrender before commencing a siege. On the arrival of British reinforcements, Pretorius withdrew to Pietermaritzburg and resigned his post of commandant general.

Pretorius accepted the ensuing British annexation of Natal (*see* Natal: *History*) as a *fait accompli* and even took the oath of allegiance to Queen Victoria. Having unsuccessfully urged local British officials to redress the grievances of the Natal Boers, especially those arising from native settlement in locations among the Boer farms, he sought, in October 1847, to interview the Cape governor, Sir Henry Pottinger, who was then in Grahamstown, Cape Colony, on their behalf. Sir Henry refused to see him and Pretorius, after expressing his views in the frontier press, returned to Natal determined to organize a further trek.

The proclamation by Sir Harry Smith, Pottinger's successor, of the Orange River Sovereignty (February 1848), brought British rule up to the Vaal River. Pretorius, believing this to contravene a verbal undertaking given him by Sir Harry, toured the high veld addressing protest meetings before establishing himself in the Magaliesberg, north of the Vaal. In July 1848 he accepted an invitation from the Boers of Winburg in the sovereignty to lead an armed protest against the proclamation. After occupying Bloemfontein, he was defeated by Sir Harry Smith at Boomplaats (August 1848), and withdrew to the Transvaal, outlawed and with a price on his head of £2,000.

Supported by many of his followers from Natal, Pretorius, one of four Transvaal commandants general, became the leader of the Boers of Potchefstroom and Rustenburg, with Potgieter of the Zoutpansberg as his chief rival. Pretorius received appeals from Boer malcontents in the sovereignty and from the Basuto chief Moshesh to help them expel the British (1850–51). Playing upon British fears that he might intervene, Pretorius undertook to support an investigation by two British commissioners into the affairs of the sovereignty, provided that they formally recognized the independence of the Transvaal Boers. As a result, his sentence of outlawry was withdrawn (December 1851) and he met the commissioners near the Sand River, where a convention in this sense was signed (Jan. 17, 1852). After returning to Rustenburg, he crowned his success by persuading Potgieter, who had opposed these negotiations, to approve the convention (March 1852). With the Transvaal independent and more or less united, Pretorius hoped that the British government would now recognize the independence of the sovereignty Boers. This recognition came in the Bloemfontein Convention of Feb. 23, 1854, seven months after his death in the Magaliesberg (July 23, 1853). In 1855 the district and town of Pretoria were established and named in his honour.

Marthinus Wessel Pretorius (1819–1901), eldest son of Andries Wilhelmus Jacobus Pretorius, best known for his unsuccessful efforts to unite the South African Republic and the Orange Free State, is the only man to have been president of both states. Born near Graaff-Reinet, Cape Colony, on Sept. 17, 1819, he succeeded his father as commandant general of Potchefstroom and Rustenburg (1853) and in 1854 led a successful commando against Makapan, a recalcitrant chief in the northern Transvaal.

Pretorius tried to continue his father's policy of uniting the trekker Boers, seeking to establish a unitary state in the Transvaal which could then be united with the newly independent Orange Free State. Less able and diplomatic than his father, he unwisely pursued these aims simultaneously, using high-handed and unconstitutional methods, allowing his personal ambitions considerable rein and provoking much opposition. In December 1856 a *grondwet* (constitution) for the South African Republic, which had been drafted on his initiative in 1855, was confirmed by the Potchefstroom and Rustenburg Boers, who then elected Pretorius as president (January 1857). The Zoutpansberg Boers repudiated these proceedings, while Lydenburg declared its independence.

Ignoring these difficulties, Pretorius turned to the Free State. In April 1857 he arrived in Bloemfontein and, with a few friends, attempted a *coup d'état*. Ignoring the Free State constitution, he claimed the territory in his father's name and invited his Winburg supporters to rebel. After being forced to withdraw by the president of the Free State, J. N. Boshoff, he returned again with a commando, but the calming influence of Paul Kruger, commandant of Rustenburg, prevented a clash and the two presidents recognized each other's independence (June 1857). Pretorius persevered, however, in his scheme to unite the republics and was elected president of the Free State in December 1859.

In the Transvaal the Zoutpansberg and Lydenburg-Utrecht Boers had meanwhile joined the South African Republic and in April 1860 a united *volksraad* ratified the *grondwet* which had been accepted by the Zoutpansberg in 1858. The *volksraad* then charged Pretorius with violating the constitution by accepting office in the Free State and on his arrival from Bloemfontein offered him an honourable discharge (September 1860). Refusing to resign, Pretorius returned to Bloemfontein and the Transvaal plunged into anarchy. Fighting ensued in 1862 between factions supporting the rival claimants, Stephanus Schoeman and W. J. van Rensburg, to the post of acting president. In April 1863 Pretorius resigned the Free State presidency, thus abandoning all hope of uniting the republics, and returned to the Transvaal where, after further fighting, unity was established by his reelection as president. He resumed office in May 1864.

After 1864 Pretorius tried to improve the quality of the Transvaal administration and introduced regular budgets in an unsuccessful attempt to resolve the state's financial difficulties. He issued a proclamation in April 1868, extending the republic's boundaries as far as Lake Ngami, Bechuanaland, in the west and Delagoa Bay in the east, while the Tati goldfield north of the Limpopo River was also included. Portuguese and British protests forced Pretorius to withdraw most of his claims in 1869, in which year he was reelected president; but he maintained a claim to the diamond fields of the lower Vaal. After failing to persuade the African tribes there to place themselves under the republic, Pretorius alienated the diggers by granting a diamond monopoly to three of his friends (June 1870). In 1871, without consulting the *volksraad*, he agreed to refer the boundary question to the arbitration of R. W. Keate, lieutenant governor of Natal. The Keate award went against Boer claims, for which the *volksraad* blamed Pretorius, and he was forced to resign (November 1871).

After the first British annexation of the Transvaal (April 1877), Pretorius acted as chairman of a committee of Boer leaders who pressed in 1879 for the restoration of their independence. Sir Garnet Wolseley, high commissioner for southeast Africa, ordered his arrest on a charge of treason in January 1880, but later released him and offered him a seat on his executive council, which Pretorius declined. When the Boers took up arms in December 1880, and proclaimed the republic, they appointed Kruger, Pretorius, and Piet J. Joubert to govern as a triumvirate. Pretorius was a signatory to the Pretoria Convention (August 1881), but in May 1883, when the triumvirate gave way to the presidency of Kruger, he retired from public life. He died at Potchefstroom on May 19, 1901.

For Andries Pretorius, see G. S. Preller, *Andries Pretorius,* 2nd ed. (1940). For both Pretoriuses see E. A. Walker, *A History of Southern Africa,* 3rd ed. (1957).   (N. G. GA.)

PREVENTIVE MEDICINE. Historically, the prevention of disease is the ideal of medicine. It has two aspects: the preventive medicine of the community—an important part of what is broadly termed public health (*q.v.*); and the prevention of disease or its aftereffects in the individual.

Hippocrates (fl. 400 B.C.) classified causes of disease into those concerned with seasons, climates, and external conditions, and those more personal causes such as irregular food, exercise, and habits of the individual. Through the Middle Ages the principles of preventive medicine were ignored, in spite of the scourges of leprosy and plague. With the Renaissance came the new learning which revolutionized the whole content of medicine. Practitioners began to observe the relation of the seasons, environmental conditions, and personal contact to the incidence of disease.

Concurrent with the growth of medical knowledge there was an empirical movement of practical prevention. For example, in 1388 there was passed the first sanitary act in England, directed to the removal of nuisances; in 1443 came the first plague order recommending quarantine and cleansing; and in 1518 the first rough attempts at notification of epidemic disease and isolation of the patient were made. John Graunt initiated the study of mortality statistics in England in the 17th century. Thomas Sydenham (1624–89) laid the basis of epidemiology by his observation of cases, deduction of laws of prevalence, and hypothesis of "epidemic constitutions." Bernardino Ramazzini, in Italy, published a treatise on occupational disorders in 1700. Richard Mead, an English practitioner in the first half of the 18th century, wrote on poisons, on plague and methods of its prevention, and on smallpox, measles, and scurvy. Edward Jenner introduced vaccination (1798). The early and middle years of the 19th century were notable for discoveries in the transmission of contagious diseases such as typhus (John Howard), cholera (John Snow), typhoid fever (William Budd), and childbed (puerperal) fever (Oliver Wendell Holmes and Ignaz Semmelweis). In the same period increasing attention was given to problems of hygiene and nutrition.

The modern era in preventive medicine opened in the late 19th century with Louis Pasteur's discovery of the role of living microbes as the cause of infections. In 1893 Theobald Smith established the principle of insect-borne transmission of disease. Serological tests were developed, such as the Widal reaction for typhoid fever (1896) and the Wassermann test for syphilis (1906). An understanding of the principles of immunity led to the development of active immunization to specific diseases. Parallel advances in treatment opened other doors for prevention—in diphtheria by antitoxin (Emil von Behring) and in syphilis by Salvarsan (Paul Ehrlich). In 1932 the sulfonamide drugs and later the antibiotics including penicillin, streptomycin, chlortetracycline (Aureomycin) and chloramphenicol (Chloromycetin) afforded new opportunities of prevention and cure.

After 1900 there were many advances in preventive medicine other than those related to infectious diseases. The use of X rays and radioactive substances in the diagnosis and treatment of disease (*e.g.*, tuberculosis and cancer) as well as in fundamental physiological research opened new possibilities. A greater understanding of endocrine functions, with the production of prepared extracts such as insulin (Sir Frederick Banting and Charles Best, 1921), thyroid, pituitary extract, and hormones, led to preventive measures in certain metabolic diseases. The role of nutrition in health and disease and the isolation of many essential food factors illustrated the importance to health of adequate diet. Other 20th-century advances in preventive medicine included a wider recognition of psychological factors in relation to total health, new surgical techniques, new methods of anesthesia, genetics research, and the application of statistical methods to medical problems. *See also* references under "Preventive Medicine" in the Index.

BIBLIOGRAPHY.—Sir William Jameson and G. S. Parkinson, *Synopsis of Hygiene* (1947); J. J. Hanlon, *Principles of Public Health Administration* (1950); M. J. Rosenau, *Preventive Medicine and Public Health,* 8th ed. edited by Kenneth F. Maxcy (1956).   (T. P.; X.)

PREVEZA, a town and *nomos* (department) of western Greece. The town is a small seaport at the entrance to the Gulf

PRÉVOST—PRIAM
485

of Arta, 66 mi. (106 km.) S of Ioannina (Yannina, Janina) by road. Pop. (1961) 11,172. The department, which formerly included the islands of Leukas and Meganisi, is now restricted to the mainland; it has an extent of 423 sq.mi. (1,096 sq.km.) and a population (1961) of 62,523. Though well sheltered, the town is difficult to approach from the open sea, the only entry being through the 21-ft. (6 m.)-deep Khrisanthis Channel. Unloading in the harbour, which has an area of 17 ac. (7 ha.), is usually performed by lighters. There is no railway, but there are road links with Arta and Ioannina. Olives thrive in its vicinity, and these, together with butter, cheese, hides, and wool, account for most of its exports. Founded by Pyrrhus, king of Epirus, about 290 B.C., the place was in later times held and fortified successively by Venetians, French, and Turks. Preveza was seized by Ali (q.v.; the Lion of Janina) in 1798 and recovered by Greece in 1912 during the First Balkan War (the transfer being confirmed by peace treaty in 1913).

(WM. C. B.)

PRÉVOST (D'EXILES), ANTOINE FRANÇOIS, ABBÉ (1697–1763), prolific French novelist whose fame rests entirely on his *Histoire du Chevalier des Grieux et de Manon Lescaut*, which was originally published as the final installment of a seven-volume novel called *Mémoires et aventures d'un homme de qualité qui s'est retiré du monde* (1728–31). This short work, which tells the story of a young man of good family who ruins his life for a courtesan, is a classic example of the 18th-century novel of feeling and the forerunner of the popular romances of later generations. It might in fact be described as a contemporary version of "boy meets girl." Its tranquil underlying assumption that love excuses the betrayal of every principle, its ingenious blend of innocence and depravity, and the skill with which an illicit relationship is invested with an aura of sentiment, explain why it has remained a best seller for over two centuries and why the authorities had it publicly burned as an immoral book when it first appeared in France.

Prévost was born at Hesdin, Artois, on April 1, 1697, of a prosperous middle-class family, and was the second of five sons, several of whom became priests. From an early age he displayed many of the weaknesses which are characteristic of the hero of his most famous work: susceptibility, impetuosity, inconstancy. His mother died when he was 14 and he was sent to the Jesuits' school in his native town. He claims, in the autobiography in the literary periodical he founded, *Pour et contre* (1733–40), that he ran away from school and joined the army before he was 16. After the Peace of Utrecht in 1713 he entered the Jesuit novitiate. He spent another brief period in the army in 1716, reentered the Jesuit novitiate in 1717, but left it again the following year. He was in serious trouble in 1719 and was obliged to ask the Society for sanctuary. He was eventually dismissed for reasons that are not known and in 1721 took his vows as a Benedictine monk at Jumièges. Some of his earlier escapades are believed to have been the result of quarrels with his father over women: in the autobiography he declares that he "buried" himself in the Order owing to the unhappy ending of a love affair. The next seven years were spent teaching, preaching, and studying at different Benedictine houses. He was ordained a priest in 1726 and two years later was at Saint-Germain-des-Prés, Paris, where he assisted with the writing of a historical work called *Gallia christiana*. Four volumes of his first novel, the *Mémoires et aventures*, were published in 1728. The same year he sought permission from Rome to transfer to a less strict branch of the order. Permission was granted, but Prévost was too impatient to wait for the official promulgation and left Saint-Germain without authority. A *lettre de cachet* (November 1728) was issued, and to avoid arrest he fled to England where he soon acquired an extensive knowledge of the language, history, and literature of the country, which was of considerable value to him in his later writings.

He left England abruptly in 1730 on account of another love affair which made it impossible for him to continue his work as tutor to the son of Sir John Eyles, a former governor of the Bank of England and member of parliament for the City of London. He spent the next three years in Holland with a mistress known as Lenki. The last three volumes of *Mémoires et aventures* were published first at The Hague, then in Paris, in 1731. The same year saw the publication at Utrecht of the first four volumes of *Le Philosophe anglais, ou Histoire de Monsieur Cleveland, fils naturel de Cromwell*, in which he drew on his knowledge of England. This was completed in eight volumes in 1739.

During his stay in Holland Prévost was frequently in financial difficulties. In 1735 he and Lenki went to England to escape their creditors. Later that year he was imprisoned for a few days at the Gatehouse for forging the signature of his former pupil on a letter of credit and must be accounted fortunate to have escaped hanging. He returned secretly to France in 1734. Little is known about his religious beliefs during these years, but it has been suggested by C. E. Engel (*Le Véritable abbé Prévost*, 1958) that after leaving the Benedictines he was for a time a Protestant. On his return to France he was reconciled with the church and ordered to undergo a second novitiate, but though he was officially attached to La Grenetière, near Nantes, as Dom Prévost, he was dispensed from residence by becoming chaplain to the Prince de Conti. Although he obtained the living of the priory of Saint-Georges-de-Gesne in 1754, he does not appear to have performed any ecclesiastical functions. He continued his career as a man of letters, producing more novels, translations of Samuel Richardson, and other works.

With the exception of a short period of exile in Brussels and Frankfurt in 1741–42, Prévost spent most of his remaining years at Chantilly, where he died on Nov. 25, 1763.

Prévost's reputation as a one-book man does him less than justice. Although they are little read today, his *Histoire d'une Grecque moderne* (1740), which was based on the famous contemporary love story of the Chevalier d'Aydie and Mlle Aïssé (q.v.), and *Mémoires d'un honnête homme* (1745) are in some respects more mature and more impressive than *Manon Lescaut*.

BIBLIOGRAPHY.—The only collected edition of Prévost's works is the *Oeuvres choisies*, 39 vol. (1783–85). There is an English translation of *Manon Lescaut*, by L. W. Tancock (1949); and a critical edition, for the Textes Littéraires Français, by G. Matoré (1953). *See also* H. Harrisse, *L'Abbé Prévost* (1896); P. Hazard, *Études critiques sur 'Manon Lescaut'* (1929); G. Poulet, *Études sur le temps humain* (1950); H. Roddier, *L'Abbé Prévost, l'homme et l'oeuvre* (1955); M. Turnell, *The Art of French Fiction* (1959). (M. Tu.)

PRÉVOST, (EUGÈNE) MARCEL (1862–1941), French novelist whose gifts of observation and subtle understanding of feminine psychology make his novels a witness to the changes in French bourgeois society between 1890 and 1920. He was born in Paris on May 1, 1862. After an education at Jesuit schools in Bordeaux and Paris and at the École Polytechnique he became a civil engineer in the Administration des Tabacs, but resigned in 1890 after the success of his first two novels, *Le Scorpion* (1887) and *Chonchette* (1888). From then on he gave himself up to the career of a popular novelist, remaining aloof from the literary schools and controversies of his time. Novel followed novel in a steady stream (52 in all); some of these he dramatized and they had a moderate success on the stage. His *Lettres à Françoise* (1902), *Lettres à Françoise mariée* (1908), and *Françoise maman* (1912)—books of wise counsel to young girls—were even more widely read than his novels. He was elected to the Académie Française in 1909. For some years after World War I he was director of the *Revue de Paris* and the *Revue de France*. He died at Vianne on April 8, 1941.

Prévost's first novel revealed the gifts which made him a favourite with a wide public. He was an analyst and realist, an unambiguous painter of the bourgeois life familiar to his readers. His novels were well constructed, skilfully maintaining interest in the development of a plot that was brought to a firm, dramatic conclusion. Their titles indicate their subject: *Confession d'un amant* (1891), *L'automne d'une femme* (1893), *Les Demi-Vierges* (1894; Eng. trans. 1895), *Les Don Juanes* (1922; Eng. trans. 1924), *Sa Maîtresse et moi* (1925; Eng. trans. 1927).

See *M. Prévost et ses contemporains*, 2 vol. (1943). (EM. H.)

PRIAM, in Greek mythology, son of Laomedon and last king of Troy. When Heracles captured Troy and killed Laomedon, Priam, still a boy, was saved. He succeeded his father. As king, he extended his control over the Hellespont. He married first

Arisbe, then Hecuba (*q.v.*), by whom he had many children, including his favourites Hector and Paris. Priam tried to avert the ruinous destiny of Paris (*q.v.*) by exposing the newborn baby; but when he survived his father took him back and thereafter seems to have played a passive role in the irresponsible actions which provoked the Trojan War. Homer describes Priam as an old man, powerless but kindly, not even blaming Helen for all his personal losses (*Iliad* iii, 161 ff.). Indeed, Homer treats Priam less as a king than as a father. In the final year of conflict, Priam sees 13 sons die, of whom Achilles kills Polydorus, Lycaon, and Hector within a day. The death of Hector, which signifies the end of Troy's hopes, also breaks the spirit of the king (*Iliad* xxii, 405 ff.). Priam's paternal love impels him to brave the savage anger of Achilles, to "kiss the hands of the man who killed his sons" and to ransom the corpse of Hector. In his trip to the Greek camp, Hermes guides Priam; Achilles, respecting the old man's feelings and foreseeing his own father's sorrows, ends his wrath by returning the corpse (*Iliad* xxiv, 322 ff.). Arctinus described the death of Priam, now best known from the version of Virgil (*Aeneid* ii, 507 ff.). When Troy falls, Neoptolemus butchers the old king on an altar. Both Priam's death and his ransoming of Hector were favourite themes of ancient art.   (Wm. S. A.)

PRIAPEA, a collection of 85 or 86 short Latin poems in various metres, including hendecasyllables, choliambics and elegiacs, on the subject of the fertility god Priapus, who, with his sickle, protected gardens and vineyards against thieves and from whose axe-hewn image of figwood or willow protruded an erect, red-painted phallus. Though a few of the poems are inoffensive, the majority, despite occasional flashes of humour, are remarkable only for their obscenity. Most appear to belong to the Augustan age or to a date not much later and show evidence of indebtedness to Ovid. They in turn influenced Martial. Some may originally have been the leisure products of aristocratic voluptuaries; others, genuine inscriptions on shrines of Priapus. Donatus says that Virgil wrote some *Priapea,* and the first three poems of the *Catalepton* in the *Appendix Vergiliana* are of this genre; but, though Pliny says that Virgil composed "verses far from staid" (*versiculos severos parum*), there is no proof that these are Virgil's. In *Tibullus,* i, 4, an elegy of 84 lines, Priapus assumes the unique role of a professor of venery (*măgister amoris*) and instructs the poet how best to secure the affection of the boy Marathus. A companion piece to this poem is Horace, *Satires,* i, 8 (50 hexameters), in which Priapus tells how he frightened away two witches from the site of the Esquiline cemetery when his figwood buttocks burst with a disconcerting pop. Martial's *Priapea* include epigrams 16, 49 and 73 in book vi, and 40 in book viii.

See F. Bücheler (ed.), *Petronius,* 6th ed. (1922).   (H. H. Hy.)

PRIAPULIDA (Priapuloidea), a small group of wormlike marine animals formerly included in the obsolete phylum Gephyrea. Of uncertain affinities, they are now generally given phylum rank, though some authorities regard them as a class of the phylum Aschelminthes. There are two genera, *Priapulus* and *Halicryptus,* and at least eight species. They are drab coloured, small- to medium-sized (to about four inches long) cylindrical invertebrates, characterized by a superficially ringed body (not segmented) and a retractile proboscis. Priapulids burrow in the soft mud bottom by extending and retracting the proboscis; they capture and devour worms and other slow-moving prey. Priapulids are found in the cold seas of both northern and southern hemispheres, usually in coastal waters; abyssal specimens have been taken from great depths in both the Atlantic and Pacific oceans.

Structure and Function.—In *Priapulus* the surface of the muscular body wall is provided with rings of spines and papillae, the latter possibly sensory in function. The epidermis secretes a thick cuticle, which is shed at intervals during growth. There are 25 rows of spines on the surface of the proboscis, converging toward the mouth, which is itself surrounded by several five-toothed rings of chitinous teeth, features that gave rise to supposed echinoderm affinities. The mouth leads into a muscular, eversible pharynx, anchored by retractor muscles originating in the trunk. The cuticular lining of the pharynx is provided with

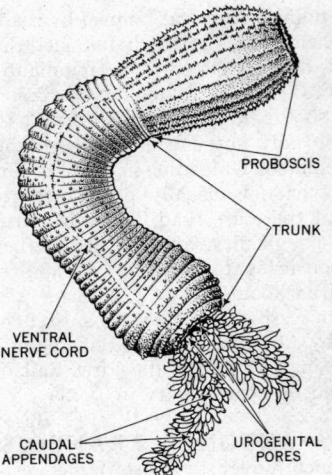

FROM THEEL, "NORTHERN AND ARCTIC INVERTEBRATES"

PRIAPULUS BICAUDATUS, A WORM-LIKE ANIMAL OF THE ARCTIC AND NORTH ATLANTIC SEAS

numerous small projecting teeth. The midgut is straight, and communicates with a short hindgut. The anus is either terminal or opens at the base of the hollow caudal appendages, present in *Priapulus* but not in *Halicryptus.* The body cavity, which in *Priapulus* extends into the ramifications of these gill-like appendages, is probably a true coelom, but its developmental homologies are unknown. There is no vascular system, but red cells containing hemerythrin, the same respiratory pigment as in Sipunculida, flow freely in the body cavity.

The nervous system, consisting of a circumesophageal ring and ventral nerve cord, retains its primitive connection with the ectoderm. There is no evidence of segmental ganglia. A visceral plexus is connected anteriorly with the nerve ring.

The excretory system is protonephric; tufts of flame cells (solenocytes) discharge into the paired urinogenital ducts, which lie suspended in the body cavity and open posteriorly. The sexes are usually separate, but hermaphroditic individuals have been recorded; the gonads develop in the walls of blind evaginations of the urinogenital ducts. Fertilization is external. Segmentation by radial, nonspiral cleavage results in a hollow blastula, and hatching occurs as a solid gastrula in which the outer ectodermal layer encloses an inner multinucleated mass. The eventual loricate larva has a spiny, retractile proboscis and a body protected by chitinous shields; in *Priapulus* larvae there are two pairs of feelers and a forked tail.

Relationships.—Resemblances to the gephyrean groups Sipunculida and Echiurida (*qq.v.*) appear to be of a superficial nature, as are the similarities with sea cucumbers. The larvae have features in common with Rotifera, Kinorhyncha, and Gastrotricha (*qq.v.*). Libbie Hyman placed the class Priapulida in the pseudocoelomate phylum Aschelminthes. K. Lang has suggested a close relationship with the Acanthocephala (*q.v.*), the spiny-headed worms. W. L. Shapeero has concluded that priapulids are true coelomates whose unique morphology qualifies the group for the status of phylum.

Bibliography.—L. H. Hyman, *The Invertebrates,* vol. 3 (1951), vol. 5 (1959); H. L. Sanders and R. R. Hessler, "*Priapulus atlantisi* and *Priapulus profundus.* Two New Species of Priapulids from Bathal and Abyssal Depths of the North Atlantic," *Deep-Sea Research,* 9:125-130 (1962); W. L. Shapeero, "Phylogeny of Priapulida," *Science,* 133:879-880 (1961).   (G. E. P.)

PRIAPUS, a god of animal and vegetable fertility in classical antiquity, whose cult was originally located in the Hellespontine regions, centring especially on Lampsacus, a city of which he was traditionally the chief deity. He was represented in a caricature of the human form, grotesquely misshapen, with an enormous and erect phallus. The ass was sacrificed in his honour. This is without parallel in Greek religious practice and attests the Oriental provenance of the cult, as does the myth that his mother was Aphrodite (doubtless to be equated with the Great Mother Goddess of the East). Ovid explains Priapus' hatred of the ass as being due to its braying when he was preparing to ravish the sleeping nymph Lotis, so that she awoke and escaped. The truth no doubt is that the ass symbolized lecherousness and was associated with the god's sexual potency.

Priapus' worship spread throughout the ancient world in hellenistic times, being popular in the great cities and establishing itself in Italy. This was too sophisticated an age for urban society to take Priapus very seriously and he was regarded rather with ribald amusement. In the country the situation was different; his statue was commonly found in woodlands, vineyards, fields, and especially in gardens, though it was set up less with the idea of promoting the fertility of plants and trees, or of the cattle and bees which were also under Priapus' protection, than as a scare-crow to frighten away thieving birds or men. He was also the patron of seafarers and fishermen, and of others in need of good luck; his presence averted the evil eye. A series of short Latin poems in his honour (*Priapea*) has survived (*see* PRIAPEA).

See H. Herter, *De Priapo* (1932). (D. E. W. W.)

PRIBILOF ISLANDS (FUR SEAL ISLANDS), islands of Alaska, including St. Paul (35 sq.mi. [91 sq.km.]), St. George (27 sq.mi. [70 sq.km.]), and three islets lying in the Bering Sea, about 300 mi. (480 km.) W of the mainland and 180 mi. (290 km.) N of Unalaska. They were first visited in 1786, by the Russian sea captain Gerasim Pribilof, who discovered their famous fur seal rookeries. Control of the islands was transferred from Russia to the United States with the purchase of Alaska in 1867. The population of the islands (1960) is 642 Aleuts and a few government officials. In 1966, the Aleuts, formerly treated as wards by the Fish and Wildlife Service, were granted substantial civil rights by act of Congress.

Fur Industry.—The seals are a distinct species, the northern fur seal (*Callorhinus ursinus*), with fur superior to other species. They visit the Pribilofs from April to November. The older and stronger bulls gather harems; the younger "bachelors" congregate separately. By taking the "bachelors" when ashore, the herd may be conserved. However, sealing at sea (pelagic sealing) permits no selectivity, and half the animals killed are lost.

In 1870 sealing rights were leased to the Alaska Commercial Company. During the 1880s vessels of several nations engaged in pelagic sealing, and the islands' herds were vanishing. In 1886 U.S. vessels began seizing Canadian sealers off the Pribilofs. A tribunal ruled against the United States in 1893. After 1910 the U.S. Bureau of Fisheries had direct supervision of the sealing.

In 1911 the United States, Great Britain (for Canada), Japan, and Russia signed the North Pacific Sealing Convention abolishing pelagic sealing north of latitude 30° N, and providing that each nation should share in the skins collected on the Pribilofs. The treaty was ended by Japan's withdrawal in 1941, on its contention that the seals were despoiling Japanese fisheries.

In 1957 an interim convention on conservation signed by the U.S., Japan, Canada, and the U.S.S.R. created the North Pacific Fur Seal Commission. The herd increased from 125,000 in 1911 to about 1,500,000 in the second half of the 20th century. About 60,000 skins are harvested yearly. (*See also* ALASKA: *History: Diplomacy Involving Alaska*; SEALING; SEA LION.)

Natural History and Climate.—The islands are of volcanic origin. The vegetation is restricted to ferns, mosses, and grasses, creeping willows, and small shrubs. White and blue foxes, gulls, auks, and cormorants abound. The mean annual temperature is about 36° F (about 2° C). The rainfall is about 35 in. annually. Fogs are heavy and frequent. (J. E. CL.)

PRIBRAM, ALFRED FRANCIS (1859–1942), Austrian-Jewish historian who after World War I contributed important knowledge of Austro-Hungarian policy before 1914. Born in London on Sept. 1, 1859, he studied in London and Vienna, and during 1894–1930 was professor of modern history in Vienna. Pribram's first interest was the 17th century; hence his book on Leopold I's diplomat *Franz von Lisola und die Politik seiner Zeit* (1894). After World War I, however, he turned to the period made prominent by the burning issue of war guilt, a subject for which he was well fitted by his natural objectivity and his background. He devoted himself mainly to the publication of state records. His works include *The Secret Treaties of Austria-Hungary 1879–1914* (English, German, French editions, 1919–23), *Austria-Hungary's Foreign Policy 1908–18* (1923), and *England and the International Policy of the European Great Powers 1871–1914* (1931). His lectures abroad also contributed to an understanding of Austrian prewar policy. He died in London on May 7, 1942.

PRICE, RICHARD (1723–1791), British moral philosopher, famous in his own day as a supporter of the American and French Revolutions and as an expert on insurance and finance, was born at Tynton in Glamorgan on Feb. 23, 1723. The son of a dissenting minister, he himself ministered to English Presbyterian congregations in the vicinity of London, notably at Stoke Newington and at Hackney, where he died on April 19, 1791.

Price's *Review of the Principal Questions and Difficulties in Morals* (1758; third edition, enlarged, 1787) criticizes the moral-sense theory of Francis Hutcheson. It is one of the best statements of ethical intuitionism or rationalism, foreshadowing Immanuel Kant's ethics in some respects and 20th-century intuitionism in many (*see* ETHICS, HISTORY OF: *Modern Ethics*). In 1767 Price published *Four Dissertations*, including a reply to David Hume's essay on miracles, and, in consequence, received the degree of D.D. from Marischal College, Aberdeen. Price and Hume met and corresponded with mutual esteem. Another of Price's philosophical opponents, Joseph Priestley, was a close personal friend. They published jointly *A Free Discussion of the Doctrines of Materialism and Philosophical Necessity* (1778), doctrines which Priestley held and Price attacked.

Price was elected a fellow of the Royal Society in 1765 for work on a problem in the theory of probability, which he then applied to actuarial questions. *Observations on Reversionary Payments* (1771) laid the foundations of a scientific system of life insurance and of old-age pensions. It also recommended the reestablishment of the sinking fund to deal with the national debt, a proposal amplified in *An Appeal to the Public on the Subject of the National Debt* (1772). Price's views influenced French governmental policy through Robert Turgot and Jacques Necker and, later, British policy through Lord Shelburne (*see* LANSDOWNE, MARQUESSES OF), an intimate friend, and the younger Pitt.

Price was a friend of Benjamin Franklin and became a leading advocate of American independence. His *Observations on the Nature of Civil Liberty, the Principles of Government, and the Justice and Policy of the War with America* (1776) and *Additional Observations . . .* (1777) had an enormous sale in both England and America. He was given the freedom of the city of London in 1776, was invited by the U.S. Congress in 1778 to advise it on finance and was made LL.D., together with George Washington, by Yale College in 1781. Price welcomed the French Revolution in a celebrated sermon on *The Love of Our Country* (1789), to which Burke's *Reflections on the Revolution in France* was a reply.

BIBLIOGRAPHY.—Price published various other sermons and tracts. For his life and works *see* Roland Thomas, *Richard Price* (1924); and C. B. Cone, *Torchbearer of Freedom* (1952). The *Review of the Principal Questions in Morals* was edited by D. D. Raphael (1948). For discussion of that work *see* J. Martineau, *Types of Ethical Theory*, 3rd ed. (1901); W. H. F. Barnes, in *Philosophy*, vol. xvii (1942); C. D. Broad in *Aristotelian Society: Proceedings*, new series, vol. xlv (1944–45); D. D. Raphael, *The Moral Sense* (1947). (D. D. R.)

PRICE, THOMAS (1852–1909), Australian Labor politician, prime minister of South Australia (1905–09), was born at Brymbo, North Wales, on Jan. 19, 1852, the son of John Price, a stonemason. He was educated at a penny school in Liverpool, and became a stonecutter. Migrating to South Australia for his health in 1883, he again worked as a stonecutter, at one time being employed on the parliament buildings in Adelaide. He was secretary of the Masons' and Bricklayers' Society from 1891 until 1893, when he entered the colony's House of Assembly as Labor member for Sturt. From 1889 he led the Labor Party in Parliament and was premier and minister of education (1905–09) in the first stable Labor administration in Australia. He warmly supported full adult suffrage (including votes for women), the amelioration of factory conditions, and the protection of secondary industry, but his attempts to liberalize the franchise for the legislature's upper house, the Legislative Council, were successful only in part. He had a fervent Methodist belief in the need to regenerate mankind, and was an ardent advocate for temperance and for the diffusion of education. He died at Hawthorn, near Adelaide, on May 31, 1909.

See T. H. Smeaton, *From Stone Cutter to Premier* (c. 1910). (O. M. R.)

PRICE, the measure of value of an article, or conventional unit of commodity or service, that expresses its worth in exchange for other goods. To effect such a measure some common unit of account is necessary. In fact, of course, any standard commodity could be used; for example, if a yard of a given quality of cloth were chosen as the unit of account, the price of a pound of tea could be expressed as equal to, say, 3 yd. of cloth, or the price of a pair of shoes as 12 yd. of cloth. An economist would then say that the cloth price of tea was 3 and that of shoes 12. Alternatively, using tea as the unit of account, the tea price of cloth would be $\frac{1}{3}$ and that of shoes 4. Because of their durability and their value in terms of other goods relative to their bulk and weight, precious metals such as gold and silver have served mankind as standard commodities, as international currencies in effect, for thousands of years.

Today, in all but the most backward areas of the world, prices are expressed in terms of the national currency (U.S. dollars, English pounds, Argentine pesos, or fractions thereof), and the issue of notes and coins of convenient denomination is a government monopoly. The paper or metal itself on which is stamped some amount of the currency may have little material value, yet no creditor can lawfully refuse to accept such currency in full discharge of debts incurred. (See MONEY.)

Though there can, perhaps, be meaningful discussion of ethical rules for determining a socially "just" price, the economist's concern is almost exclusively with the prices that emerge under certain institutions, with special emphasis on their determination in a market economy. His interest ranges from movements in the price of one or two goods to those of virtually every price in the economy during some period, and he is concerned not only with particular prices in the real world but also with prices that exist only in some theoretical model. Again, the economist may be concerned either with the movement of prices relative to each other or with the general tendency of all prices to rise or fall together though in different degrees. Changes in the general price level are measured as movements of an index number, in the formation of which the key problem is that of attributing weights to the movements of the various prices that enter into the index. (See INDEX NUMBERS; PRICES, STATISTICS OF.)

It has been found convenient to separate the study of individual prices from that of the price level, despite their obvious relationship, and this dichotomy of treatment corresponds roughly with what has been called traditionally the theory of value on the one hand and monetary theory on the other. Using modern terminology, however, the determination of prices and quantities of individual goods is deemed the subject matter of microeconomic theory, while macroeconomic theory concerns itself with aggregates such as the levels of prices, output, and employment.

As a rule, microeconomic theory treats of the determination, under given conditions, of the relative prices of a number of goods. If only two goods were being studied, there would be only one relative price, or price ratio (ignoring reciprocals); if three goods, three price ratios; if four goods, six price ratios; and so on. In theories that purport to explain the formation of all prices in the economy—sometimes referred to as general equilibrium systems—the practice has been to minimize the number of price ratios by choosing one good as *numéraire,* its price being, by definition, equal to unity, and expressing the price of each of the other goods as the number of units of the *numéraire* for which it exchanges.

Such prices are sometimes referred to as "real" prices, and they can be translated into a system of money prices by the simple expedient of attributing a money price to the *numéraire.* Though whatever money price is chosen does not, of course, affect the pattern of the real prices, it still cannot be chosen arbitrarily. It must be at a level high enough to make people satisfied to hold the stock of money in existence. (See QUANTITY THEORY OF MONEY.)

Movements of the general level of money prices are of particular interest in connection with theories of inflation and deflation and the study of cycles of prosperity and depression. It is a well-known phenomenon that some groups of prices move faster than others; in a boom, for example, prices of equities rise fastest, followed by wages, salaries, and rents in that order (all these can be regarded as prices; see below).

Price Determination.—The demand price of a good is the maximum price at which, under specified conditions, some particular quantity of it would be bought during a given period. Variation

of this quantity, and also therefore of the corresponding price, generates what is known as the demand schedule or, when constructed diagrammatically, the demand curve (price being measured along the vertical coordinate and quantity along the horizontal coordinate). Alternatively, any point on this curve exhibits the maximum quantity demanded at the corresponding price, this quantity growing, as a rule, as the price declines.

The supply price of a good is the minimum price at which, under specified conditions, some particular quantity of it would be supplied during a given period. Variation of this quantity, and also therefore of the corresponding supply price, generates a supply schedule or, diagrammatically, a supply curve. Such a supply schedule, or supply curve, is commonly defined as the minimum price at which an industry (composed of profit-maximizing firms) would make available to the market a continuous range of quantities of the good in question, either in a short period during which there was no time to alter plant and equipment or in a long period in which there was time enough for all factor prices (see below) to change and for industry to alter fully all its capital equipment. According to the prevailing technical conditions and the given resources of the economy the supply curve can assume a variety of forms. Although in short periods it normally rises as the quantity increases, in periods long enough for full adjustments to be effected it may rise, remain constant, or (especially if there are large economies of scale) decline as output expands.

An "offer curve" is sometimes referred to as a supply curve, though it is concerned not with the cost of production of a good but with the offer from a single person, group, or country of productive services, or of goods from existing stocks or from given inflows, in response to the price. The price-quantity relationship has to be interpreted here as tracing the maximum quantity that would be supplied at any one of a continuous range of prices. (The minimum price definition of the preceding paragraph may, however, be extended to offer curves also, provided the condition is imposed that, in moving along this offer curve, the welfare of each supplier remains unaltered. In general, this definition yields an offer curve somewhat larger than that constructed under the first definition.)

The equilibrium price is the price which, under specified demand and supply conditions, has no tendency to change. An elementary economic proposition lays it down that a necessary condition for an equilibrium price is that it be one at which the respective quantities of the relevant demand and supply schedules are equal. (See SUPPLY AND DEMAND.)

A competitive price is the price ruling in a market in which there is a large number of competing suppliers, and entry into which is unimpeded. The extreme case, or ideal model, of such a market is spoken of as "perfect competition," a market form in which it is supposed that all producers, as well as all consumers, accept the market price as being beyond their resources to influence, since the quantity supplied or demanded by any one person or firm is a negligible proportion of the total. A corollary of such competition is that the market price tends to equal the lowest unit cost of the most efficient producer, as any positive profit (revenue to the firm in excess of payments to the factors of production) attracts new firms into the industry. (See COMPETITION, ECONOMIC.)

A monopoly price is the price set by the sole producer of a good, or by a group of producers of a good acting together. If the monopolist is regarded as producing the output which maximizes his profit, the price corresponding to that output can be shown to exceed his marginal cost (the additional cost of producing an extra unit of output), this excess being greater the fewer the substitutes there are for the monopoly good. A discriminating monopolist can set different prices for markets that are separated by distance or tariff barrier, though obviously such differences cannot exceed the unit cost of transport and duty in sending the goods from one market to another. Acting within this constraint, however, the enterprising monopolist sets the price higher in markets that are less responsive to price changes. (See MONOPOLY.)

Other Prices.—Passenger fares and freight rates are, of course, prices of services rendered. Foreign exchange rates express the prices of foreign currencies in terms of the domestic currency, or vice versa. The spot price of a currency, or spot rate of exchange, refers to the rate of exchange between two currencies for a current transaction. The forward price of a currency, or the forward rate of exchange, is the rate of exchange currently agreed between two parties for the exchange of stated amounts of two different currencies at some designated future date—usually from one to three months, and seldom more than six months, from the current date. Similarly, the price of futures is the current price at which some standard grade of a commodity, such as grain or cotton, may be bought or sold for delivery and payment at some designated future date.

Factor prices are the returns paid for the services of the agents of production classified either narrowly or broadly. In the classical tripartite division of the factors of production, wages are the price of the services of labourers, rent is the price paid for the use of land (or of other resources, or assets, having the essential nondepreciating characteristic of Ricardian land), and interest is the price paid for the services provided by loans. Profits, however, are not regarded as the price of any productive service, or factor, but as a residual after all the firm's contractual payments have been met. They may be justified as the reward of bearing uninsurable risks in business, and are an index of the success of the enterprise in responding to opportunities provided by changing market conditions. See PROFIT; VALUE. See also references under "Prices" in the Index. (E. J. MI.)

PRICE MAINTENANCE, a term applied to the measures taken by individual manufacturers or distributors of specific branded, trademarked goods to protect the retail prices of their products and eliminate price-cutting. The legal status of resale price maintenance varies from one country to another and in the United States from one state to another. See FAIR TRADE LAWS.

PRICES, STATISTICS OF. In the United States, the United Kingdom, and some other countries, price quotations for important commodities are available from early in the 19th century; there are also a few quotations from earlier periods. In general, during these long intervals of time, there have been many changes in the nature and quality of the commodities and in the type of price quotation; sometimes, however, the changes have been small enough to permit the compilation of a continuous series of prices on a reasonably comparable basis. Nevertheless, a few series of prices of single commodities cannot be taken as a description of general movements in prices. What is required for this purpose is a set of indicators showing the general course of prices, in convenient major groups of commodities, over a period of time in a particular country. Such indicators can be constructed only in the form of index numbers (see INDEX NUMBERS), which are generally averages of the changes in prices of certain commodities selected to represent the various groups. The averages can be computed in various ways to give different results. Moreover, the index numbers depend on the accuracy and continuity of the price quotations used, and any one compilation is generally limited to comparisons of prices in a relatively short period, perhaps no more than 10 or 20 years. For longer-run comparisons, different index numbers need to be linked together, and the results are then still more approximate.

The most obvious feature in the general world picture is the effect of major wars on wholesale prices. During the French Revolutionary and Napoleonic Wars (1792–1815) prices rose rapidly and were then maintained at a high level for some years, though with considerable oscillations. Prices fell after Waterloo, but it was not until the 1820s that they had dropped to the level of the years before 1792. The American Civil War (1861–65) gave rise to the second major peak in wholesale prices in the United States, but the effect in the United Kingdom, and in many other countries, was much smaller. World Wars I and II exercised an even sharper effect on prices. Moreover, at least in the United Kingdom and the United States, the course of prices was broadly similar during and immediately after the two wars: an immediate and pronounced rise early in the war, followed by a slower increase as measures of price control became effective, and then another sharp rise after the close of hostilities. The main differences

between the two wars were that price control was effective sooner in World War II and the postwar increase in prices was more protracted.

Between wars the trend of prices was generally downward and, at the outbreak of one war, the level of prices was little different from that immediately before the previous war. Closer inspection, however, reveals major fluctuations in the general course of prices. One cause of disturbance was the discovery of new goldfields or the rapid development of gold production. A growth in the supply of gold coming forward pushes up prices in domestic currencies that are based on gold. The discovery of gold in California and Australia raised wholesale prices after 1850, and prices did not sink below the level of 1849 until about 1890. In the United States the steady decline in prices after the Civil War led to acute agrarian discontent and the demand for increased coinage epitomized by William Jennings Bryan's campaign for the presidency in 1896. The development of the goldfields in Alaska and South Africa was the main influence in the steady rise in prices following the low point reached in 1896, a rise which continued until the outbreak of World War I.

Other major fluctuations, generally working themselves out in a period of less than ten years, are those associated with booms and depressions. The pattern includes four steps: boom, commercial crisis, recession, and recovery. Commercial crises generally appear as peaks in the course of wholesale prices; e.g., those of 1839 and 1847 in the first half of the 19th century and that of 1907 at the beginning of the 20th. No earlier depression, however, had quite the same catastrophic effect as that following the crisis of 1929. Both in the United Kingdom and in the United States wholesale prices in 1929 stood about 35% higher than in 1913; by 1932–33, prices had fallen to nearly 10% below the 1913 level; i.e., a decline of one-third in less than four years.

A remarkable feature of the course of prices in modern times is the broad similarity between the movements in the United Kingdom and the United States (cf. fig. 1 and fig. 2). There are, of course, many factors which exert little more than a local influence. However, major wars, severe commercial crises, and gold discoveries are events which are international in their impact on economic affairs and they affect prices everywhere. For this reason it can be said that there has been a level of world prices, the movements of which can be distinguished in a broad historical survey.

In an index of the general level of wholesale prices, the movements in the prices of commodities of many different kinds are averaged. Individual price quotations are to be expected to show greater fluctuations than the general average, as is well illustrated by the price of English wheat. Until about 1880 imports of wheat into the United Kingdom were small, and the price was largely dependent on the supplies of domestic wheat available and hence on the size of the harvest. The price of wheat showed very large fluctuations, many of which did not correspond at all with movements in the general price level. After 1880, with increasing supplies of wheat arriving from the Western Hemisphere and other overseas areas, the price of English wheat was determined more by world prices than by the British harvest. The results were, first, that the price was reduced in relation to other prices and, second, that there were less violent fluctuations in price. Though still showing wider variations than the general price level, the price of English wheat followed fairly closely the general course of prices. (R. G. D. A.)

UNITED STATES

In the United States, as in other countries, statistics of prices became available in greater quantity and in more varied forms than data reflecting other major aspects of the economy such as production and employment. The quantity of price data was steadily enhanced by the contributions of government departments and private business and research groups, and historical information about prices and price movements was expanded by the painstaking work of individual scholars.

Problems.—Statistics on prices are available in two forms: (1) price quotations for specified commodities, services, or securities;

and (2) index numbers, which usually are designed to summarize the average amount of change in the prices for a specified group of commodities, services, or securities between two or more dates. Despite the careful efforts of price statisticians in business and government who supervise the collection of price data and the compilation of price indexes, the numerous practical and theoretical difficulties involved in their work cannot be completely overcome. Although these problems need not be considered in detail here, some understanding of their general nature is essential to proper interpretation of price data.

The central problem of price collection is to gather a sample of prices representative of the various price quotations for each of the commodities under study. Sampling is almost always necessary because it is not feasible to obtain a record of every single transaction. Price collection must be planned so that observed differences between the prices of any two dates (any two places, when place-to-place rather than time-to-time price differences are being studied) will reflect changes in price and price alone. In order to exclude the influence of variation in quality, commodity prices are frequently collected in accordance with detailed specifications (*i.e.*, descriptions) such as "wheat, no. 2 red winter, bulk, carlots, f.o.b. Chicago, spot market price, average of high and low, per bushel."

When the correct average prices for a commodity for successive dates have been determined, they may be expressed as percentages of the price for a particular date or "base period." These percentages are called "price relatives." The problem of constructing price index numbers is to combine either the prices themselves or the price relatives in such a way that the central tendency of the movement of the whole group of prices from one period to another is accurately described. Although a number of problems are encountered at this stage, the one that is perhaps the most important to an understanding of the limitations of price indexes is the weighting problem. This arises because not all commodities for which prices have been obtained are of equal importance in the price universe under study. The price of wheat, for example, should be given more weight in an index of wholesale prices in the domestic economy than the price of pepper, because wheat is much more important in trade. The difficulty is that the relative importance of commodities changes over time. Furthermore, some commodities drop out of use and new ones appear, and often an item changes so much in composition and design that it is doubtful whether it can properly be considered the same commodity. Under these conditions, the pattern of weights selected can correspond accurately to the relative importance of the various commodities in only one of the periods for which the index numbers have been calculated. The greater the lapse of time between the period of the weighting pattern and other periods, the less relevant the pattern is likely to be for one of the periods, and therefore the less meaningful the price comparisons become. Price indexes thus can give relatively accurate measures of price change only for periods close together in time. F. C. Mills found also that the dispersion of price relatives computed on a given base year tends to increase with time; this means that the price index numbers becomes less representative of the central tendency of the whole distribution of the price relatives for the various commodities.

Sources of Data on Actual Prices.—The most important single source of price statistics in the United States is the Bureau of Labor Statistics (BLS) of the U.S. Department of Labor. In the early 1960s the BLS published monthly prices (at the wholesale level) for about 1,000 different commodities and (at the retail level) for almost 100 foods and for various types of fuels. The prices were generally those prevailing on the Tuesday of the week in which the 15th of the month fell. All the retail prices and the great bulk of the wholesale prices were obtained directly from sellers. Most retail prices were collected during store visits by price agents trained to price goods in accordance with established specifications. A few retail prices, such as those for fuel, were obtained directly from sellers by mail. The other primary market prices were obtained mainly from such recognized trade journals as *Iron Age* and the *Oil, Paint, and Drug Reporter*.

Another important governmental source of price data was the Department of Agriculture, which collected both local market prices and wholesale prices of farm products, the latter referring to prices at central markets. Estimates of Dec. 1 crop prices and Jan. 1 farm values of livestock have been available since 1867; monthly prices of commodities sold by farmers have been available since 1908 or 1910. Prices of articles bought by farmers were published annually from 1910 to 1922 and quarterly (for most items) thereafter. By the 1960s the department was receiving reports on farm product prices from about 9,000 respondents (mostly buyers or dealers) and reports on prices paid by farmers from about 17,000 respondents (mainly independent retailers serving the farm population). The prices thus obtained were made available in the department's publication *Crops and Markets*.

The trade journals were the most readily available nongovernmental sources of commodity price data. Prices for highly standardized commodities traded on organized markets (*e.g.*, wheat, coffee, and sugar) and prices for stocks and bonds were also reported in the financial pages of many metropolitan newspapers.

In 1960 the prices collected by government agencies and the indexes derived from them were subjected to the careful scrutiny of an expert committee headed by George J. Stigler. (*The Price Statistics of the Federal Government*, National Bureau of Economic Research, General Series, Number 73, 1961.) The Stigler committee made some important suggestions for improving the price data collected both by the BLS and the Department of Agriculture. It expressed doubts about the validity of the BLS reliance upon sellers for price information, particularly in connection with wholesale prices, in the following words:

> In summary, the evidence that the BLS company price quotations are not valid transaction prices is highly persuasive. The quotations now collected are at best the initial base for negotiation in many cases, and often represent only the hopes of sellers or the snares of inexperienced buyers.
> We recommend that a major shift be made to the collection of buyers' prices.

These remarks were based largely upon a staff study that showed that actual prices paid by the purchasing departments of government agencies were lower and were characterized by more frequent and wider fluctuations than prices for the same products that were reported to the BLS. However, the long-run movements of prices as revealed by the BLS data were probably less vulnerable to this criticism. The main shortcoming of the Department of Agriculture's price data, in the view of the committee, was that the products for which prices were collected were not narrowly enough defined; the data actually obtained represented the average values of a broad range of qualities rather than the prices of specified qualities. It should be stressed that the Stigler committee's criticisms of the price work of the federal government were based upon a very high professional standard of excellence. In quality as well as in quantity, the U.S. has price statistics that are seldom if ever excelled.

The Consumer Price Index.—The prices from all these sources were used to compute a wide variety of price index numbers. The most generally used index numbers were those computed by the U.S. government, particularly the consumer price index and wholesale price index. The consumer price index prepared by the BLS is probably the one that is best known to the average American. It measures the changes in prices paid by families of wage earners and low-salaried workers living in cities. The average size of the families included was about 3.3 persons in 1953, and the average family income was $4,160 after taxes. (Families with after-tax incomes in excess of $10,000 in 1950 were excluded.) The types of families included represented about 64% of the urban population and about 40% of the total U.S. population. A further revision of the index, effective in January 1964, extended its coverage to include all urban families which derived at least 50% of their total income from wage and clerical occupations (dropping the former overall $10,000 maximum) and to include also single workers living alone.

The quantity of commodities and services purchased by city

wage-earner and clerical-worker families is determined from time to time by sample surveys of their expenditures. In 1950, for example, about 8,000 such families were asked detailed questions about their expenditures for food, clothing, housing, medical care, etc., and another such survey was undertaken in 1961–62. From these surveys, the sample of items and the weights to be assigned to each are chosen. After the 1950 survey the index was computed from the price movements of about 300 items, including 90 foods, 75 articles of apparel, 35 housefurnishings, and 10 fuels. In the 1964 revision the sample of items was extended to 400 items. Prices for each item were collected according to detailed specifications to ensure that price differences between two periods reflected pure price movement and not changes in quality. Prices were collected in a sample of more than 16,000 outlets in 50 representative urban areas. In each community the BLS tried to obtain prices from a sample of stores that would represent the shopping pattern of the families of wage earners and clerical workers. Food prices and the prices of a few other items which change frequently were collected every month in each city, but prices for other commodities and services were collected monthly only in the five largest cities and every three months in the other cities. The prices generally refer to the middle of the month, and most of them are collected by visits of field agents to stores. From these prices two types of indexes are computed, one representing all urban areas of the U.S. and another representing each of 17 large cities. Each index is a weighted average of price changes. Beginning with the January 1962 index number, the base of the consumer price index was shifted from 1947–49 to 1957–59 in accordance with the recommendations of the U.S. Office of Statistical Standards. In addition to the comprehensive index for all items, separate indexes were published for five major categories (food, housing, etc.), for more than a dozen subgroups (dairy products, rent, etc.), and for a large number of minor products. Separate indexes were also available for a number of special groupings (commodities versus services, durable versus nondurable commodities, etc.). The indexes are published in a special monthly release of the Bureau of Labor Statistics; they appear also in the *Monthly Labor Review* and *Survey of Current Business*.

The consumer price index had its origins in World War I, and the official series began with data for 1913. Although historical research has produced consumer price indexes (or cost-of-living indexes, as they used to be called) for the 100 years preceding the beginning of the BLS series, most of these estimates are based mainly on wholesale price changes. Several of these indexes were linked together by the Federal Reserve Bank of New York to form a single series for the period 1820–1913.

A factor that heightens public interest in current index numbers is their use in escalator clauses in labour-management agreements. Such clauses, which covered between 2,000,000 and 4,000,000 employees in the early 1960s, provided for automatic changes in wages when the index moved up or down.

The Stigler committee was concerned lest the important economic interests thus involved in the consumer price index institutionalize the index and hamper improvements in it. The committee felt that use of the index for wage escalation should not be permitted to prevent the development of a broadened consumer price index that would cover the entire population, including persons living in rural areas, single persons, and high-income families in urban areas. Such a comprehensive index is the one that is relevant to the broad analytical uses that the consumer price index should serve—for example, to aid in measuring changes in the national welfare and in measuring inflation (and thus providing guidance for monetary and fiscal policy).

Another problem affecting the preparation of the consumer price index is the treatment of new goods and changes in the quality of old goods. One school of thought, favoured by the government technicians who prepare the consumer price index, is that the index should be primarily a price index measuring the changes in the prices of a fixed "basket" of goods. A second position, held by the Stigler committee, is that the consumer price index should measure the changes in the cost of buying a constant bundle of satisfactions or utilities. Even, for example, if coal remains unchanged in price, the consumer benefits if he can heat his house more cheaply with a newly available supply of natural gas. The BLS price index would show no decline in price as a result of the availability of a cheaper fuel, but an index measuring the cost of a constant bundle of utilities would show a decline reflecting the reduced cost of house heat. Conceptually, there is little doubt that the constant-utility index is superior for virtually all of the analytical purposes for which indexes are used, but there are great difficulties in the path of calculating constant-utility indexes by objective methods that would command wide support and confidence. The practical importance of this issue arises from the fact that the continual improvement in the content and quality of living through the development of new and better products may have led to an overestimation of the extent of price increases and to an underestimation of the extent of the increase in the real volume of production. The two schools of thought tend to differ also upon the quantitative importance they assign to these potential biases.

The Wholesale Price Index.—The wholesale price index, also prepared by the BLS, is less well known to the average person but is more widely used in the business world than is the consumer price index. The BLS official wholesale price index numbers date from 1890. As in the case of the consumer price index, the methods of computation and the commodity composition of the index have changed from time to time, but the revisions were made so as to minimize the adverse effects upon the comparability of the series. The number of commodities included in the index expanded from 250 at the beginning to about 2,200 in the 1960s. The new commodities tended to be more highly fabricated and to have more stable prices, and they therefore tended to dampen the fluctuation in the index. One reason for the expansion of the list of commodities included in the index was a gradual shift in the conception of the function of the index. Originally, the index was regarded as a measure of movements in the general price level, but as other indexes such as the consumer price index and the implicit national income deflators (*see* below) became available, less reliance was placed on the wholesale price index for this purpose. At the same time there was a growing demand for subindexes pertaining to particular classes of products for various business and analytical purposes. Thus the nine major categories for which separate price indexes were originally published (farm products, foods, cloth and clothing, building materials, etc.) were more finely divided. In the middle 1960s monthly price indexes were being published for 15 categories, nearly 100 subgroups (*e.g.,* fresh fruits, grains, etc.), and a large number of product classes (*e.g.,* apples, bananas, barley, corn, etc.). Indexes were also available for the commodities classified according to stage of processing (crude materials, intermediate materials, and finished goods), according to the durability or nondurability of the products (*e.g.,* food versus steel), and according to the economic sector for which goods were intended (*e.g.,* consumers, producers, etc.). In addition, there were more than 50 indexes for special commodity groups, about half of which were for various categories of pharmaceutical preparations. A survey of the users of the wholesale price index indicated that the detailed information about price movements for individual industries, product classes, and commodities was most valued, especially by business firms and trade associations. Of course, the comprehensive monthly index number embracing all commodities is still used as an important indicator of the general movement of prices in the economy, particularly since the implicit deflators of gross national product (which because of their comprehensiveness are conceptually superior for this purpose) are available only on a quarterly basis and then only with a time lag of several months. The utility of the wholesale price index as a general price indicator is enhanced by a weekly index which is intended to provide an estimate of what the monthly index would be if it were computed each week. After 1952, the weekly index was no longer corrected after its issuance to make it conform to the movement shown in the monthly index. The BLS also publishes a daily index of spot market prices, intended to serve as a sensitive gauge of changes in market conditions.

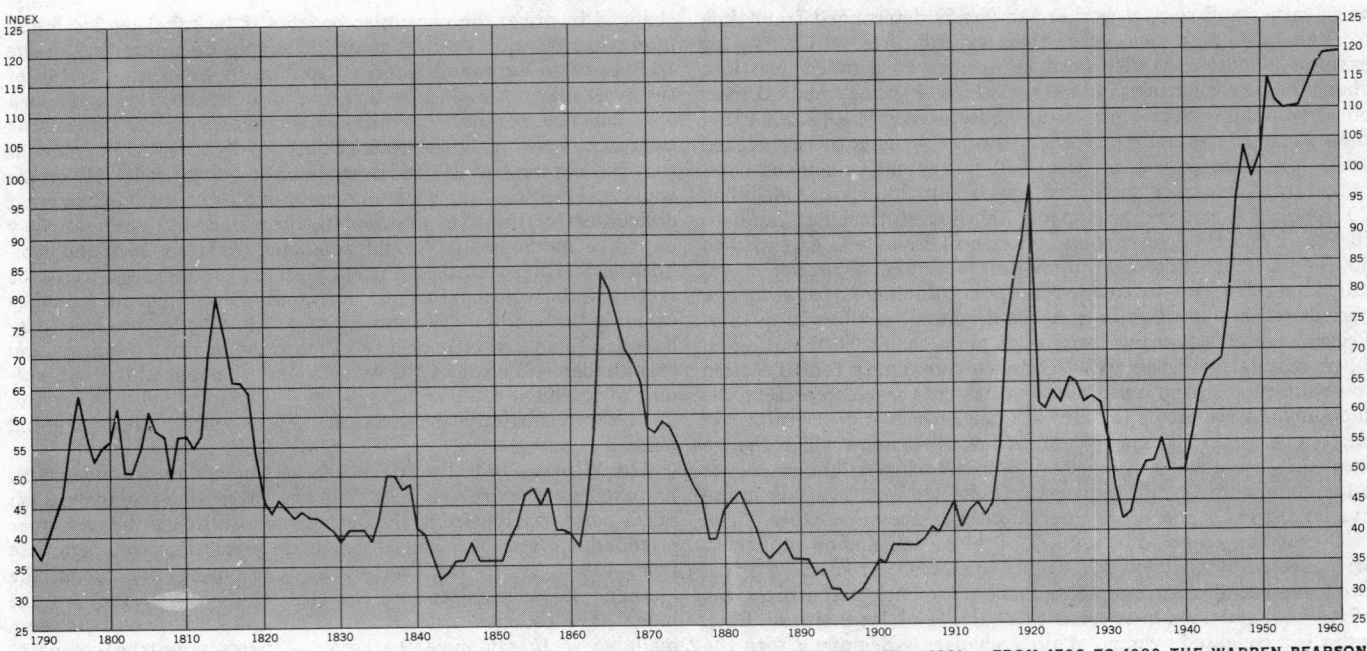

FIG. 1.—MOVEMENTS OF WHOLESALE COMMODITY PRICES IN THE UNITED STATES, 1790–1960 (1947–49 = 100). FROM 1790 TO 1889 THE WARREN-PEARSON-STOKER INDEX (STOKER BEFORE 1797) IS USED; FROM 1890 TO 1960 THE OFFICIAL INDEX OF THE BUREAU OF LABOR STATISTICS IS USED

The wholesale price index represents the price movements of all commodities flowing into primary markets of the U.S.—whether domestically produced or imported. Primary markets are those in which a good in a given stage of fabrication is first sold in substantial quantities. Since the index includes the primary market prices of goods of all degrees of fabrication, the same commodity is often priced at several stages of processing. For example, cotton is priced in the form of raw cotton, cotton yarn, cotton gray goods, cotton piece goods, and cotton clothing.

Each commodity at each stage of production enters into the index with weights corresponding to the value of shipments of the commodity itself plus that of other commodities of a similar character that are not priced but whose prices are known or assumed to move similarly. Usually the weights for unpriced items are assigned—or "imputed"—to commodities with a similar manufacturing process. The BLS makes periodic revisions in weights as new industrial censuses become available. The index is calculated as a weighted average of price changes. Like the consumer price index, it was shifted to a 1957–59 base beginning in January 1962.

The full array of prices and price indexes is published in a monthly publication entitled Wholesale Prices and Price Indexes, but for most users the degree of detail appearing in the Monthly Labor Review and the Survey of Current Business is adequate.

The BLS wholesale price index was extended back to 1801 on the basis of price indexes for 1801–40 computed by A. H. Hansen (Publications of the American Statistical Association, pp. 804–812 [December 1915] and BLS Bulletin No. 367, pp. 235–48) and data for 1841–89 contained in the Aldrich committee's comprehensive report, "Wholesale Prices, Wages and Transportation," Senate Report No. 1394, 52nd Congress, 2nd session, part i, p. 9. Hansen's data were based on prices published in Boston newspapers for the period 1801–25 and for the period 1825–40 on New York prices published in the "Report of the Secretary of the Treasury on the State of Finances" for the year ending June 30, 1863.

The BLS index was also extended back to 1797 by G. F. Warren and F. A. Pearson and to 1720 by H. Stoker. This work was based primarily on New York City prices obtained directly or indirectly from newspaper sources and from the treasury report mentioned above.

Implicit Price Deflators.—The development of statistics of national income and gross national product gave rise to measures of price change—often referred to as implicit price deflators—

that are more comprehensive than either the consumer or the wholesale price index. Once statisticians succeeded in compiling estimates of gross national product in terms of current prices (i.e., the prices prevailing in each year), they turned their attention to estimating these aggregates in terms of constant prices (i.e., estimating the gross national product, for example, for a whole succession of years in terms of the prices of a single year). This step was necessary if the figures were to reveal how much of the observed time-to-time change in gross national product was a real change in physical output and how much represented merely a change in prices. This work was done by expressing each detailed component of gross national product in terms of the prices of the selected base year, a result that was achieved by "deflating" the current value series by some appropriate price index. For the most part, the detailed BLS price series, both consumer and wholesale, were used for this purpose, but a wide variety of other price information was also employed. When these detailed "deflated" components of gross national product are added up, the result is an estimate of gross national product in terms of base period prices. Early in the 1960s, for example, the Department of Commerce, which produces the national income and product statistics, was publishing the data in terms of both current prices and 1954 prices. There is, of course, a comprehensive price index implicit in the comparison of the current and constant-value series. For example, from the fact that the 1961 gross national product was $521.3 billion in current (i.e., 1961) prices and $448.9 billion in 1954 dollars, an implicit price index of 116 can be computed (521.3 divided by 448.9, all multiplied by 100) for 1961 on a 1954 base.

Implicit price deflators provide a generally superior measure of the overall behaviour of prices because they are more comprehensive than either of the major indexes previously discussed and because they refer to a universe that can be more readily defined than that of the wholesale price index. However, they are available only on a quarterly and annual basis, and the other indexes thus are still used as month-to-month indicators of price behaviour.

Implicit price indexes are available for the period since 1946 for 10 categories of consumption, 14 types of construction, and 21 groups of producers of durable equipment. (See U.S. Department of Commerce, U.S. Income and Output, pp. 220–229.) On a current basis they are available in summary form in each issue of the Survey of Current Business and in more detail in the July issue each year. The Department of Commerce has computed implicit deflators in a somewhat lesser degree of detail also for the period

1929–46 (*National Income, 1954 Edition,* pp. 216–217), and Simon Kuznets and others have estimated implicit price indexes back into the 19th century (S. Kuznets, L. Epstein, and E. Jenks, *National Income and Its Composition, 1919–38,* pp. 141 ff., 1941; and S. Kuznets, *Capital in the American Economy,* pp. 511 and 561–566, 1961).

An earlier attempt was made by Carl Snyder to develop an "index of the general price level." Snyder's index was designed to measure changes in the prices of commodities at all levels from primary to retail markets and shifts in the prices of services and property as well as of commodities. The index was extended from 1938 back to 1791. (*Review of Economic Statistics,* February 1934, p. 25 and February 1928, p. 40.)

Indexes of Prices Paid and Received by Farmers.—The indexes of the prices paid by farmers and of the prices received by farmers are unique because they have become so deeply involved in the political processes of federal support for agriculture. Both indexes were first published in the 1920s when a 1909–14 base was logical enough. When the Agricultural Adjustment Act of 1933 was passed, an attempt was made to establish "parity" prices for basic farm products so the farmers' income would have the same purchasing power it had in the 1909–14 base period. At the same time the first steps were taken toward the legislative control of the indexes. Legislation on the books in the 1960s required among other things that the 1909–14 base be retained and that farm-wage rates, farm taxes, and mortgage interest per acre be included in the "prices paid" index. The political importance of the indexes not only solidified practices that were questionable on technical grounds but also inhibited the normal processes of revision and improvement that would otherwise occur.

Export and Import Price Indexes.—With the gold losses that the U.S. suffered in the late 1950s, attention turned to relative price movements as a possible explanation for the continuing deficit in the U.S. balance of payments. Many people were surprised to learn that the U.S. had no real price indexes for exports and imports. The closest approximations were unit value indexes produced by the Bureau of Foreign Commerce in the Department of Commerce. A unit value index differs from a price index in that it measures the changes in the average value per physical unit regardless of whether the change is due to a change in price or to a change in size, quality, or other circumstance. Unit value indexes are relatively easy to compute; the development of true price indexes requires much greater resources of money and personnel.

Unit value indexes are calculated for each of five broad commodity groups of U.S. exports and imports, ranging from crude materials to finished manufactures, and, of course, for total exports and imports. The indexes go back to 1913 and have been available on a monthly basis since 1933. Unlike the BLS indexes discussed above, which have fixed weights, the unit value indexes are constructed by Fisher's ideal index number formula; that is, each index represents the square root of the product of base-year weighted and given-year weighted indexes.

Other Indexes.—Although the steady improvement in the scope and quality of the price work of the U.S. government has brought about a gradual decline in the number of general purpose indexes produced under private auspices, a large number of special-purpose price indexes are still computed for particular firms, especially in connection with their marketing or purchasing activities, and by trade journals. *Iron Age,* for example, publishes an index of finished steel prices, a weighted average of the prices (in cents per pound) of ten major finished steel products.

Aside from the services included in the consumer price index, the most readily available indicators of the changing price of services were indexes of hourly earnings and wage rates. The BLS series on average hourly earnings of production workers in manufacturing industries, available since 1909, was the most general of these series. Indexes of wage rates were restricted to particular groups of workers such as organized workers in the building and printing trades.

A field in which it was necessary to combine wages and commodity prices to derive indexes was construction. These were not price indexes in the strict sense, but construction-cost indexes. A number of these indexes were published in the 1960s by private business groups; in addition, government agencies published index numbers of construction costs in such fields as railroad, highway, and farm construction. Most construction-cost index numbers went back to the 1910–13 period. In addition to the implicit deflators for various types of construction to which reference has already been made, construction-cost indexes were prepared by *Engineering News-Record,* the American Appraisal Co., the Associated General Contractors of America, Inc., and E. H. Boeckh and Associates, Inc.

The last category of price indexes requiring consideration here consists of the indexes of security prices. Among the leading indexes of stock prices in the 1960s were those prepared by the New York Stock Exchange; Moody's Investors Service, Inc.; Standard and Poor's Corp.; and Dow, Jones & Co. The first of these indexes was based on the average price obtained by dividing the market value of all listed stocks at the end of the month by the number of shares. The other indexes were based on a more limited but more constant group of sample stocks selected to represent different groups of stocks. The Dow-Jones averages, for example, were based on 30 industrials, 20 railroads, and 15 utilities; the Standard and Poor's indexes, based on 400 to 500 stocks, were available for a more detailed industrial classification. Indexes of bond prices were also computed by the New York Stock Exchange, Standard and Poor's, and others; such indexes generally derived the bond prices from average yields.

The general user of price indexes may find data for almost all of the price index series mentioned above in *Survey of Current Business,* a monthly publication of the Department of Commerce. An excellent source of information about historical price statistics, going back to the 18th century in some cases, is *Historical Statistics of the United States, Colonial Times to 1957: a Supplement to the Statistical Abstract of the United States.* The biannual publication of the Department of Commerce entitled *Business Statistics* gives the price series currently published in the *Survey of Current Business* for each year of the two most recent decades and for each month of the four most recent years. (I. B. K.)

UNITED KINGDOM

The movement of the general level of wholesale prices in the United Kingdom during the 19th century, between the close of the French Wars and the South African War, can be summarized best by reference to three periods. Between 1820 and 1850 there was a general downward movement, combined with considerable fluctuations, from about 155 in 1820 to about 90 in 1850 (1913 = 100). From 1850 to 1875 the price level was first raised and then maintained, apart from fluctuations, as a result of great economic developments (in industry, transport, etc.) coupled with the new supplies of gold from California and Australia. The earlier downward trend was resumed after 1875, when the level was around 115 (1913 = 100), until a low point of little more than 70 was reached in 1896. Wholesale prices generally fell by half in the 75 years after 1820. (*See* fig. 2.)

From this low point wholesale prices moved upward slowly but fairly steadily until 1914. The immediate effect of the outbreak of World War I was a sharp rise in prices. Control of prices began to moderate the rise toward the end of 1917, and there was even a short-term decline after the Armistice in 1918. The postwar rise of 1919–20 was the most rapid recorded to that date and the reaction of 1920–21 was just as spectacular. Wholesale prices increased by more than 40% in the year ended April 1920 and were then halved by the end of 1921. The subsequent fall until 1929 was the result in part of the restoration of the gold standard in 1925. The depression following the crisis of 1929 was severe, though the effect on wholesale prices was somewhat offset by the abandonment of the gold basis in 1931. By 1938 wholesale prices in general were little more than 5% above the level of 1913.

There were differences of great significance between the movements of wholesale prices of different groups of commodities, and between wholesale prices on the one hand and retail prices

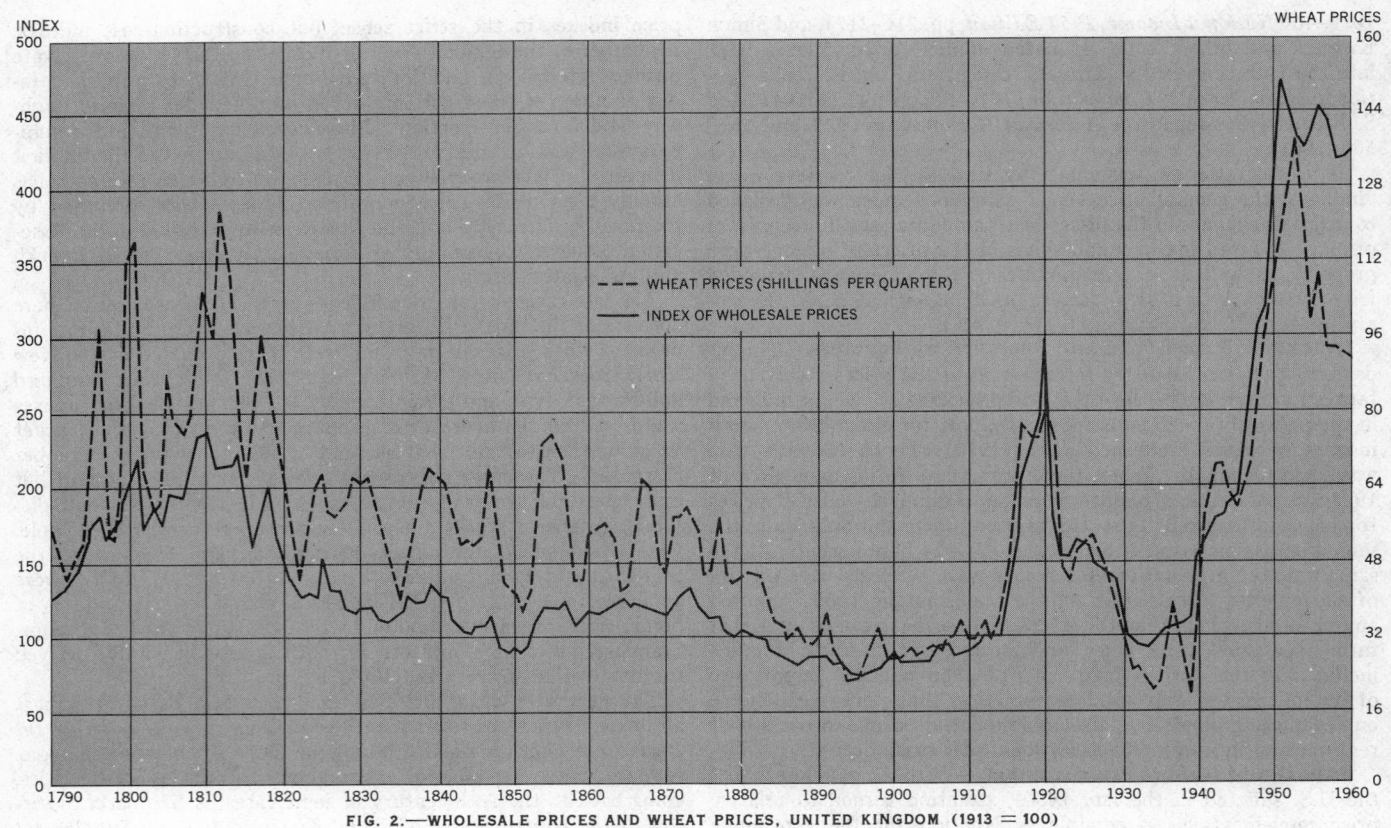

FIG. 2.—WHOLESALE PRICES AND WHEAT PRICES, UNITED KINGDOM (1913 = 100)

of comparable commodities on the other. The broad comparisons of greatest interest are those between the prices of foodstuffs and the prices of textiles and clothing. In a period of booms, depressions, and wars from 1880 to 1938 there is one broad conclusion which stands out—foodstuffs tended to become relatively cheaper, and textiles and clothing relatively dearer. Moreover, this divergence was greater in retail prices than in wholesale prices. Retail and wholesale prices of food (and also of textiles and clothing) marched together quite closely up to 1914, but, in the general decline of prices between 1924 and 1938, wholesale prices fell more rapidly than retail. The increased margin between wholesale and retail prices arose, at least in part, because of the greater importance of distributive and marketing services. In 1938 wholesale prices of textile materials were rather below the level of 1914 but in the same period clothing prices at retail had more than doubled. There were similar, though less pronounced, differentials for wholesale and retail prices of foodstuffs and fuels.

There were rapid increases in prices during the first three years of World War II, amounting to more than 50% at wholesale and nearly 40% at retail by the end of 1942. Price controls then became effective and prices were generally only 5–10% higher at the close of the war in 1945 than in 1942. In comparison with World War I, price controls operated more quickly and efficiently, and there was no repetition after 1945 of the postwar crisis of 1920.

An important feature of price control, during both the late war years and the immediate postwar period, was the widespread use of subsidies paid to farmers or other producers as a means of keeping down prices. Though not by any means confined to foodstuffs, subsidies were particularly effective in restraining the advance of food prices. For a wide range of raw and processed foodstuffs it was estimated that, whereas retail food prices in 1948 were actually only about 50% above those of 1938, they would have been at double the 1938 level in the absence of subsidies.

From about 1948 until the middle of the 1950s the structure of price control was progressively dismantled; the cushion which had previously absorbed much of the pressure on prices was gradually withdrawn. The play of the various factors influencing prices thus became apparent. The devaluation of sterling in 1949 was

followed immediately by rises in the sterling prices of many imported commodities and a little later by increases in domestic prices at wholesale and at retail. From 1948 world prices of basic foods and materials started to fall but the decline was interrupted by the Korean War of 1950–53, which caused worldwide shortages of foodstuffs and raw materials and hence a rapid and fairly general rise in prices. The opposing influences were almost exactly in balance in 1953–54, a period of relatively stable prices in the United Kingdom. By that time retail prices were on average more than 50% higher than at the end of World War II.

The course of prices from 1954 must be interpreted in terms of the contrast between inflationary domestic pressures and the variable movements in prices of imported foods and materials. The period of almost steady prices in 1953–54 was followed by a similar but longer period of relatively stable prices in 1958–60. In both cases the rise in the domestic element in costs, typified by wage rates, was little greater than could be offset by falling prices of imports. When these conditions did not obtain, either because of rising import prices or because of greater inflationary pressures, prices at both wholesale and retail advanced rapidly on a wide front. Thus retail prices rose by 4% annually between 1954 and 1958, and the rise was resumed in the early 1960s.

OTHER COUNTRIES

The course of prices in various countries can only be compared after reference to the rates of exchange between national currencies. A suitable standard of comparison is the course of prices in the United States, and the rates of exchange required are then the rates between various national currencies and the U.S. dollar.

As an illustration of the relevance of rates of exchange, prices in France, expressed in terms of the French franc and related to 1913 as a base year, should be considered. At parity in 1913 the French franc was equivalent to 19.3 U.S. cents. The rate of exchange varied after World War I before settling down, in 1927–31, at the devalued rate of 3.92 cents per franc. Later, on the devaluation of the dollar, the franc appreciated and the rate of exchange in 1934–35 was 6.60 cents per franc. The index number of wholesale prices in the United States varied as follows: 1913,

100; 1929, 137; 1935, 115. If wholesale prices in France had followed the same course, except that they were denominated in French francs instead of U.S. dollars, then the index figure in 1929 would have been nearly five times as great as that for the United States (19.3 divided by 3.92) and in 1935 nearly three times as great (19.3 divided by 6.60). Wholesale price index numbers for France would then have been: 1913, 100; 1929, 675; 1935, 340. The recorded levels of wholesale prices in France (in round figures) were: 1913, 100; 1929, 630; 1935, 340.

There are many factors, such as changes in freight rates, domestic costs, and taxes or subsidies, that operate to make domestic prices diverge from world or import prices. In most important countries, however, wholesale prices are in fact largely determined by world prices, and particularly by prices in the United States, at least during periods of stable rates of exchange. The correspondence between French wholesale prices and U.S. wholesale prices expressed in francs at the current rate of exchange was close in 1929 and 1935, each year being related to 1913.

In the period between World Wars I and II the pound sterling diverged little from parity with the U.S. dollar, except during the period before the restoration of the gold standard in the United Kingdom in 1925, and again briefly about 1932 between the suspension of the gold standard by the United Kingdom and that by the United States. Thus the general movements of prices (e.g., a comparison of prices in 1929 or 1938 with those of 1913) are broadly comparable in the United Kingdom and the United States without modification for changes in the sterling-dollar exchange rates. Similar straightforward comparisons can be made in the case of other countries, such as Canada, South Africa, Denmark, and Sweden, whose currencies were more or less closely related to the U.S. dollar or sterling.

In some countries, however, there were limited depreciations or appreciations of the national currencies in terms of sterling and the U.S. dollar. Australia depreciated the Australian pound in terms of sterling in 1930–31. In any comparison of periods before and after 1930–31, therefore, prices in Australia will be found to have risen more than corresponding prices in the United Kingdom. On the other hand, the Netherlands and Switzerland did not follow the United States off the gold standard in 1933, and, when their currencies were devalued in 1936, the depreciation was less than in the case of the U.S. dollar. After 1933 the Netherlands and Switzerland had currencies which were appreciated relative to sterling and the U.S. dollar, and their price levels were correspondingly lower. There were still other countries in which inflation following World War I proceeded much further than elsewhere. The interwar years in such countries—France and Italy being among the more important—were characterized by periods of instability followed by currency reforms and periods of greater stability. The exchange rate in terms of the U.S. dollar was alternately stable and unstable, but the currency was always much depreciated compared with the rate in 1913. Price fluctuations were similar to those in the United Kingdom and United States but always around much higher levels (as compared with 1913).

There was a general fall in wholesale prices from a peak in 1920, steep at first and then more gradual. In most countries the fall continued slowly until 1929, though there was a subsidiary rise in prices around 1924, followed by a fall in 1926–27. This was, in fact, the broad pattern set by the movement of prices in the United Kingdom and the United States. The closeness of correspondence of price movements was greater for countries on the gold standard and these included, by 1925, the United Kingdom, the British dominions, Sweden, the Netherlands, and Switzerland, in addition to the United States. There were some important deviations from the general pattern. In France and Italy, in particular, depreciation of the currency relative to sterling and the U.S. dollar was resumed in 1922 and continued in the following years; the French franc and Italian lira were not stabilized until 1927–28. The fall in wholesale prices in France and Italy was halted in 1922, and prices then rose rapidly in France, and more moderately in Italy, until 1926, in which year the price level was above that reached immediately after the war. In Japan prices remained high during the whole period from 1921 to 1925

and only began to fall with the stabilization of the currency in 1926.

After the U.S. stock market crash late in 1929, wholesale prices declined everywhere, following to a greater or less extent the rapid fall in prices in the United States. In both the United Kingdom and the United States wholesale prices fell to a low point in 1932–33 when their level was not quite 70% of the 1929 level. The effect of the world-wide depression on prices in other countries was varied but three broad groupings can be distinguished.

In one group are countries which devalued their currencies about the same time as the United Kingdom in 1931. Some of them (e.g., Sweden and Australia) devalued to a greater extent and their currencies remained depreciated in terms of the U.S. dollar, not only during 1931–33, but also after the U.S. devaluation in 1933. This depreciation of national currencies offset to some extent the fall in world prices and, though the low point of wholesale prices was still reached in 1932–33, the level was 75–80% of that in 1929 rather than 70% or less. Japan followed much the same course; but wholesale prices had already fallen to 70% of the 1929 level by 1931 (before devaluation) and then recovered immediately.

In a second group of countries, including Spain, Argentina, and Peru, the national currencies were depreciated in terms of the U.S. dollar almost continuously from 1929 to 1932–33. Thus the offset to the fall in world prices was greater, though the depreciation was in no case quite sufficient to prevent wholesale prices from falling. Low points in the level of wholesale prices were reached, in 1932–33, at about 90–95% of the 1929 figures.

The last group of countries comprises those which did not devalue their currencies with the United Kingdom and the United States during 1931–33. Devaluation was postponed, generally until 1936. The Netherlands, France, Switzerland, and (despite some differences) Italy belong to this group. The governing fact here is that national currencies appreciated in terms of sterling from 1931 and in terms of the U.S. dollar from 1933. Thus the fall in world prices was amplified in translation into wholesale prices in national units. The fall in wholesale prices was greater and more protracted than in the United Kingdom and the United States. Low points were reached generally about 1935 and at levels between about 55% and 65% of 1929.

The recovery in prices from the bottom of the depression was almost as rapid as the preceding fall and in most countries it had come to an end by 1937. In that year wholesale prices in the United Kingdom and the United States stood about 20% above the level of 1913 and a little below the 1929 figures. In some countries, like the Netherlands and Switzerland, whose currencies appreciated in relation to sterling and the U.S. dollar in the 1930s, the 1937 level of wholesale prices was lower—a little above the 1913 level but 20–25% below 1929. On the other hand, in countries like Spain, Argentina, and Peru where the national currency continued to depreciate in the late 1930s, wholesale prices in 1937 stood higher, often at levels about double that of 1913 and well above 1929. The price situation in France, and to a lesser extent in Italy, was exceptional in the years immediately before World War II. As in the Netherlands and Switzerland, the rise in prices began late because of the postponed devaluations of currency. But in France and Italy the devaluation of the currency was much more drastic and the price rise from 1935 was rapid and also continued beyond 1937. By 1939 the level of wholesale prices was above that of 1929, but the process of adjustment was not complete and prices would probably have risen further even if war had not intervened.

Early in World War II most currencies were depreciated and after the war there were further adjustments (mostly downward) in relation to the U.S. dollar. The position in 1948 was that a small group of countries, including Canada, Sweden, and Switzerland, had maintained their currencies at, or restored them to, at least their 1913 par values in terms of the U.S. dollar. Another group, including the Netherlands and Denmark as well as the countries of the sterling area, had devalued moderately in relation to 1913. The difference was larger in Spain and many countries of Latin America, following long periods of almost continuous depreciation in terms of the dollar. The most drastic devaluations of all were in the French franc and Italian lira, occurring for the most part after the war.

Prices rose sharply during the war and early postwar years, the relative levels from one country to another being largely dependent on currency adjustments. By 1948 wholesale prices in the United States were less than double those in 1937. In the United Kingdom the change was somewhat greater, as it was in the British dominions, Denmark, Sweden, and Switzerland, though with some variations; for example, the price increase compared with 1937 in Australia was relatively small and in Switzerland relatively large. In the Netherlands the price level in 1948 was higher, about two and one-half times the 1937 figure, following a rapid rise after liberation of the country. In Spain, and in some Latin American countries for which figures were available, wholesale prices in 1948 were between three and four times the level of 1937, as were prices in Egypt and India. The most striking effects of inflation and currency devaluation are to be seen in price changes in France and Italy. French wholesale prices in 1945 were already more than 4 times those of 1937, but in 1948 they were about 20 times the 1937 figure and still rising. It was not until 1949 that prices in France were brought under control. The inflation was even more rapid in Italy, particularly between 1944 and 1947, and wholesale prices in lire reached a level nearly 60 times that of 1937, before a greater degree of stability was attained in 1948–49.

The countries of the sterling area, following the lead of the United Kingdom, devalued their currencies in terms of the U.S. dollar in September 1949. The currencies of most countries in western Europe were devalued at the same time, although not all to the same extent as sterling. Wholesale prices in these countries rose immediately, reversing a tendency toward lower prices which had become evident throughout the world earlier in 1949.

This downward trend in wholesale prices was generally interrupted by the sharp rise in prices of basic commodities in 1950–51 occasioned by the Korean War. Prices settled down once more between 1952 and 1954 but subsequently there was a quite general upward movement, fairly rapid at first but more uncertain and less widespread after 1957. Where prices did rise at all rapidly in the years around 1960 it was because of further currency depreciations, as in some Latin American countries and in France.

Even when allowance is made for exchange rates, there is much less correspondence between prices at retail in different countries than at wholesale. Many retail prices depend little on world prices of commodities, and some are completely insulated against price changes outside the country concerned. Index numbers of retail prices generally relate to the whole budget of an average working-class family, including rents and other services, and the governing factors are domestic costs, taxation, and subsidies. Nevertheless, a general pattern does emerge. By 1924 retail prices were generally higher relative to 1913–14 than those at wholesale, and the difference was increased during the interwar period. On the other hand, retail prices generally rose less between 1937–39 and 1948 than wholesale prices, largely as a result of price controls and of the subsidies placed on foodstuffs and other commodities purchased by working-class households. In many countries, where wholesale prices in 1948 were about double those in 1937, retail prices had increased by only 50–80% in the same period. This differential was diminished in the years after 1948, as price controls were relaxed and subsidies reduced. There was a general upward movement in retail prices between 1948 and the early 1960s but by no means at a constant rate. There were three short periods of relative price stability in most countries: in 1949–50, in 1953–54, and again in 1958–60.

International comparisons of the purchasing power of national currencies are peculiarly difficult to make. The level of retail prices in one country needs to be compared, with allowance for the exchange rate, with the level of retail prices in another country; it is not sufficient to compare the movements over time in one country with movements in another country. The most complete calculations are those made first by Colin Clark and later by M. Gilbert and I. B. Kravis (see *Bibliography*). (R. G. D. A.)

BIBLIOGRAPHY.—*United States:* U.S. Bureau of Labor Statistics, annual *Bulletins* on wholesale prices; A. H. Cole, *Measures of Business Change* (1951); F. C. Mills, *The Behavior of Prices* (1927), *Price-Quantity Interactions in Business Cycles* (1946); W. C. Mitchell, "The Making and Using of Index Numbers," U.S. Bureau of Labor Statistics *Bulletin 284*, part 1 (reprinted as *Bulletin 656*); A. C. Neal, *Industrial Concentration and Price Inflexibility* (1942); U.S. Department of Commerce, *Historical Statistics of the United States, Colonial Times to 1957* (1960); Price Statistics Review Committee, National Bureau of Economic Research, *The Price Statistics of the Federal Government* (1961). (I. B. K.)

Other Countries: T. Tooke and W. Newmarch, *A History of Prices and of the State of Circulation from 1792 to 1856,* 6 vol. (1838–57; reprint 1928); A. Sauerbeck, *The Course of Average Prices of General Commodities in England, 1818–1907* (1908); W. S. Jevons, *Investigations in Currency and Finance* (1909); A. L. Bowley, *Wages and Income in the United Kingdom since 1860* (1937); W. T. Layton and G. Crowther, *An Introduction to the Study of Prices,* 3rd ed. (1938); M. Gilbert and I. B. Kravis, *An International Comparison of National Products and the Purchasing Power of Currencies* (1954); A. J. Brown, *The Great Inflation, 1939–1951* (1955); Colin Clark, *The Conditions of Economic Progress,* 3rd ed. (1957). (R. G. D. A.)

PRICHARD, HAROLD ARTHUR (1871–1947), a leading member of the Oxford "intuitionist" school of moral philosophers, was born on Oct. 30, 1871, at Willesden, London. He spent most of his life teaching at Oxford, where he was fellow of Hertford College from 1895 to 1898 and of Trinity College from 1898 to 1924, and White's professor of moral philosophy from 1928 to 1937. He died in Oxford on Dec. 29, 1947.

Prichard held that the notion of duty or "ought" is ultimate and irreducible. We become aware of this notion by reflecting on instances of it; in particular circumstances we know directly and immediately, by intuition, that a particular action is our duty, regardless of proof or argument. Moreover, "good" and "ought" are two distinct and mutually irreducible concepts; no proposition about the first can entail a conclusion about the second. Nor can our particular duties be deduced from some more general rule of duty; on the contrary, the ordinary moral rules are themselves generalizations of what we see to be our duty in particular cases.

He also maintained that the rightness of an action does not depend in any way upon its motive; if this precept seems paradoxical, it is because we are liable to confuse motive with intention. With regard to the experience of conflicting obligations, he held that different obligations have different degrees of stringency and that in a particular case we can see which of two conflicting obligations is the more stringent. To account for cases of disagreement about duty, he contended that the capacity of direct moral apprehension may be more fully developed in one man than in another. In his last years Prichard came to think that duty depends not upon the situation as it actually is, but upon what a person believes the situation to be. He also devoted much attention to the concept of promising and concluded that "I promise to do so and so" is not a statement conveying true or false information but that the utterance of these words itself constitutes the act of promising. (*See also* ETHICS, HISTORY OF: *Modern Ethics.*)

Prichard's theory of knowledge was a development of the "realistic" views of Cook Wilson. Knowing, he held, is something ultimate and *sui generis,* which differs in kind from any sort of belief or opinion; it is, as it were, the direct confrontation of mind and reality. But he eventually came to be dissatisfied with the "realistic" theory of sense perception. Instead he held that sense perception is a kind of illusion and that what is called seeing a chair consists of two distinct factors: (1) seeing a colour, whose *esse* is *percipi,* as Berkeley had said; and (2) mistaking this colour for a body of a certain sort. On this view, the material world cannot be known at all, in Prichard's strict sense of the word "know." Nevertheless, by means of a complicated argument from perceptions to their causes, he thought we could find good grounds for *believing* that material objects exist and for believing many detailed propositions about them.

For his arguments see *Kant's Theory of Knowledge* (1909), *Duty and Interest* (1928), *Moral Obligation* (1949), and *Knowledge and Perception* (1950), the latter two edited by Sir W. D. Ross.

See E. F. Carritt, "Professor H. A. Prichard: Personal Recollections," *Mind* (1948); H. H. Price's memorial notice in the *Proceedings of the British Academy* (1947). (H. H. PE.)

PRICHARD, JAMES COWLES (1786–1848), British physician and ethnologist who early assigned all mankind to a single species, was born on Feb. 11, 1786, at Ross, Herefordshire. Prichard also was responsible for the concept of moral insanity (psychopathic personality) as a distinct disease. He received his early education at Bristol, and early acquired knowledge of European and Oriental languages. After attending St. Thomas's Hospital, London, he went to Edinburgh, where he took his M.D. in 1808. Later he spent some time at Cambridge and at Oxford, but in 1810 settled in Bristol. He was appointed physician to St. Peter's Hospital in 1811 and to the Bristol Infirmary in 1814.

His *Researches as to the Physical History of Man* (1813) was expanded into a five-volume work (1836–47). In 1843 appeared his classic *Natural History of Man,* in which he concluded that there was but a single human species. He was also deeply interested in Egyptology and in 1819 traced the early connection between the Hindus and the Egyptians and published a hieroglyphic alphabet. His *Eastern Origin of the Celtic Nations* (1831) established the place of Celtic languages as a branch of Indo-European. Prichard was elected a fellow of the Royal Society in 1827, and at the time of his death was president of the Ethnological Society. In 1845, on being made a commissioner in lunacy, he moved to London, where he died on Dec. 23, 1848. (W. J. Bp.; X.)

PRIDE, THOMAS (d. 1658), English parliamentary soldier during the Civil War, is chiefly remembered for his expulsion of members of Parliament from the House of Commons in 1648, known as Pride's Purge. His early life is obscure. Entering the parliamentary army as a captain, he was a major in 1644 under the earl of Essex and was appointed lieutenant colonel of a regiment of foot in 1645. He commanded the regiment at Naseby (June 14, 1645) and at Bristol (September 1645); during the second phase of the Civil War he served with Oliver Cromwell in Wales and fought at Preston (August 1648). In December he took part in the army's occupation of London which was the first step toward bringing Charles I to trial. Under orders from the army council, on Dec. 6, 1648, Pride took his stand at the entrance to the House of Commons and caused the arrest or exclusion of about 140 Presbyterian members. In January 1649 he was one of the commissioners appointed by the remaining Rump Parliament to try the king and he signed the death warrant. He commanded a brigade under Cromwell at Dunbar (Sept. 3, 1650) and fought at Worcester (Sept. 3, 1651). In 1652 he bought the Great Park and Worcester House which were part of the former royal estate of Nonsuch in Surrey. He was knighted by Cromwell in January 1656.

Though a member of the Parliament of 1656, Pride took little part in politics. After the passing of the Humble Petition and Advice (March 1657) he opposed the proposal to make Cromwell king, but accepted a place in the new House of Lords. He died at Worcester House, Surrey, on Oct. 23, 1658. After the Restoration in 1660, the Commons voted that his body should be exhumed and suspended on the gallows at Tyburn, but there is no evidence that this sentence was carried out.

PRIENE (modern SAMSUN KALE), an ancient city of Ionia near modern Turunçlar on the foothills of Mycale about 6 mi. (10 km.) N of the Maeander (Buyuk Menderes) River, now about 10 mi. inland. According to Strabo, it was founded by Ionians and Boeotians. On its territory was the Panionion, the central shrine of Ionia. Captured by Ardys of Lydia, it enjoyed some prosperity in the earlier 6th century B.C., the period of its "sage," Bias (*q.v.*). Cyrus captured it (*c.* 545), but it sent 12 ships to join the Ionian rebels at Lade (*c.* 494). By 440 it had sunk to being a mere bone of contention between Samos and Miletus. About 350 B.C. it was refounded on the present site, perhaps with outside help. The motive of the refoundation, like the earlier site of the city, remains unknown. The main temple, of Athena Polias, was sufficiently advanced in 334 for Alexander the Great to put his name to it; his dedication stone is now in the British Museum. The whole city seems built to one master plan, and was significantly modified only once—in the later 2nd century B.C. It is tempting to connect this modification with Orophernes, the 2nd-century pretender to the throne of Cappadocia; Priene became his base

and he is known to have restored the temple of Athena Polias. After this the little city (about 4,000 inhabitants) led a quiet life until the 13th century A.D., when it was slowly abandoned. It has now been largely uncovered, first by the Society of Dilettanti, later by the German Institute.

Its remains, which lie on successive terraces between the steep north hill, falsely called the "acropolis," and the plain, present one of the most beautiful examples of Greek town planning. The town wall is 7 ft. thick, with square towers at intervals. The main coastal road traversed Priene from east to west. So all three gates are in the east and west walls, the more southerly of the two east gates giving on to a spring. In the grid plan of the town there are six main streets, about 20 ft. (6 m.) wide, running east and west, and 15 streets, about 10 ft. wide, crossing at right angles, all being evenly spaced; and it was thus divided into about 80 blocks or *insulae*. The normal *insula* was about 150 by 110 ft. (46 by 34 m.). The theatre, the gymnasium, and the agora are the only buildings which really overrun the *insulae*. About 50 *insulae* are devoted to private houses. While the better-class *insulae* had four houses apiece, most were far more subdivided. In and near the agora are Doric stoas, fronting the shops. The hexastyle peripteral temple of Athena Polias is on a commanding knoll which overlooks most of the city; it was by Pythius, perhaps the architect of the Mausoleum. It is the classic example of the pure Ionian style. The great altar to its east, with carved standing female figures, is assigned by A. von Gerkan to Orophernes and to Pergamene artists. But its style seems 4th century.

The agora, originally an open space the size of two *insulae*, was later extended at its northeast corner, at the same time that the whole north stoa was rebuilt. The order (Hellenistic "mixed Doric") dates these alterations to the 2nd century B.C. An arched gate, a simple archivolt in design, marked the new east limit of the agora; while behind the rebuilt north stoa was added an assembly hall (*ekklesiasterion*), remarkable for the large arched entrance in its south wall and for the neatness of its auditorium. These arches at Priene are among the earliest in classical architecture to be used consciously for effect. East of the main agora was the early Hellenistic temple of Asclepius, west of it a small meat market. The theatre is famous for its well-preserved stage buildings, the south gymnasium for yet further instances of decorative arches.

The private houses of Priene, like those of Olynthus and Delos, have each a large room with verandah, facing south across an open yard. But, being smaller, they have to be more oblong in plan.

BIBLIOGRAPHY.—T. Wiegand and H. Schrader, *Priene: Ergebnisse der Ausgrabungen . . .* (1904); M. Schede, *Die Ruinen von Priene* (1934); A. von Gerkan, "Der Altar des Athenatempels in Priene," *Bonner Jahrbücher,* Heft 129, pp. 15 ff. (1924); R. D. Martienssen, *The Idea of Space in Greek Architecture,* esp. pp. 37 ff. (1956); G. E. Bean, *Aegean Turkey,* pp. 197 ff. (1966). (Wi. H. P.)

PRIESTHOOD. The English word priest is the contracted form of presbyter (Greek *presbyteros,* "elder"), also contracted in the form "prester," as in Prester John. The Greek word referred to an office in the early Christian Church already mentioned in the New Testament. English versions of the Bible, however, render *presbyteros* by "elder," a word whose connotation is very different from the meanings normally associated, in current usage, with priestly office and function, reserving the words priest and priesthood for translating the more specifically sacerdotal terminology (Greek *hiereus, hierateuma;* Latin *sacerdos, sacerdotium*) of pre-Christian religions. Hence the etymology of the word priest (and its equivalents in many other European languages) is of no relevance for an understanding of the history, nature, and function of the office it is generally understood to refer to.

Any discussion of priesthood in general, however, assumes that certain types of religious ministry are found in most civilizations, that in spite of their diversity these offices and functions are specific and similar enough to justify comparison, and that the terms indicating them can—with due caution—be considered as analogous or at least comparable. There are, of course, no complete equivalences. Usages and technical designations are not uniform, and not every name covers the whole phenomenon intended. There are transitional forms and many instances of overlapping terms and functions. More precise definitions generally achieve their precision at the price of either excessive concentration on the history and terminology of particular religions and civilizations (*e.g.*, biblical priesthood) or arbitrary emphasis on specific characteristics. Nevertheless, a general phenomenology of priesthood, though necessarily of limited validity, is both possible and legitimate.

This article will deal with priesthood in general and, in view of its importance in Western history, with biblical and Christian priesthood. For priesthood in other religions the reader is referred to the respective entries.

Priestly Functions.—In a very wide sense the adverb "priestly" is applied to any function or activity of a religious, and more particularly of a cultic, character in which certain persons act on behalf of others (individuals, smaller groups, or the community as a whole) vis à vis the supernatural powers, (*e.g.*, gods or ancestor-spirits). In many societies certain forms of social organization (the family, clan, etc.) have a sacral character; hence a priestly quality often attaches to the head of the group (chieftain, king, head of the household, etc.) by virtue of the sacerdotal functions he is required to perform. On the other hand, most civilizations also exhibit a definite tendency toward cultic specialization, and it has, therefore, been suggested that the term priest should be limited to the holder of such special office.

Unlike the Roman paterfamilias, for example, who also performed priestly or semipriestly tasks, the full-fledged priest, as a religious functionary and cultic specialist, is distinct from the *laos*, the ordinary people or "laymen," who require his services and mediation. Specialization, in its turn, leads to social differentiation and to the establishment of a "clergy"—that is, of a priestly class or caste. Obviously such specialization and differentiation could not arise until mankind had sufficiently progressed to be able to exempt some individuals from the common toil for subsistence and to provide for their needs in exchange for their ritual contribution to the welfare of society. Where such institutionalized division of labour does not exist, as in many primitive societies (and probably also with early man), suitably gifted or knowledgeable persons will perform priestly duties in addition to their ordinary social activities.

There are many types of religious functionaries, specialists, sacred persons, and wielders of religious authority, and the corresponding technical vocabulary is accordingly varied. Sociologists of religion distinguish between the types of founder, reformer, prophet, seer, diviner, teacher, saint, and priest as distinct forms of religious authority. Even when restricting discussion to more specifically cultic functionaries, such diverse names as fetish priest, witch doctor, medicine man, diviner, magician, shaman, priest, etc., are found. Frequently functions overlap. Roman Catholic theologians are generally priests; in India only Brahmans were traditionally permitted to study and recite the Vedas; and divination is frequently a priestly function (as, for example, in the case of the college of augurs and the *quindecimviri sacris faciundis* at Rome). The latter institution also shows how sacerdotal mediation operates in two directions: the priest not only does "those things which are ordained to be done toward the gods" (Aristotle, *Politics,* vi, 8) but also acts as the representative or mouthpiece of the godhead vis à vis the community, as in interpreting oracles or in administering sacraments.

The wide spectrum of sacerdotal functions is illustrated by the fact that occasionally the same philological root gives rise to less inclusive and more differentiated meanings in different cultures: the Canaanite word which meant priest in Ugaritic (*khn*) and in Hebrew (*kohen*) signified "inspired soothsayer" (*kahin*) among the ancient Arabs (*see* PROPHET). In many cultures further differentiation occurs within the priestly order and is attested by the existence of different names for different classes of priests as well as by specialized ministries, such as special priesthoods for particular gods (*e.g.*, the Roman *flamines; see* FLAMEN) or for particular functions (*e.g.*, the Roman *pontifices; see* PONTIFEX). Generally speaking, the term priest is best applied to religious functionaries whose activity is concerned less with the purely mechanical techniques of magic than with the right performance

of the ritual acts required by the divine powers and supernatural beings recognized by the group in which the priest exercises his office. As sacrifice (*q.v.*) is one of the most prominent features of man's ritual relations with the world of gods and spirits, it has come to be associated with priesthood as one of its chief functions; *e.g.*, medieval Catholicism owed much of its doctrine of the priesthood to the connection of the latter with the Eucharist conceived as a propitiatory sacrifice.

The specialists leading the group rituals conform most closely to the "ideal" phenomenological concept of priesthood. The ancient Inca, Maya, and Aztec distinguished between priests responsible for the cult of the great national gods and such ritual experts as were resorted to for more specific and individual needs such as divination or curing. Similarly many African societies differentiated between priests responsible for the worship of the tribal ancestors, on the one hand, and witch doctors, etc., on the other.

Priesthood, in its fully developed form, generally implies large societies with centralized authority, a fairly elaborate culture, and the existence of an organized cult with fixed rituals and well-formulated doctrines. However, it would be a mistake to assume that every highly developed religion of necessity possesses a priesthood. Islam is perhaps the best example of a religion without priests, religious authority being defined in other than sacerdotal terms. Buddhist doctrine has no room for sacrificial ritual and priestly intervention, although certain sacrificial aspects are implicit in the Bodhisattva ideal. Yet in actual practice—especially in Mahayana, but to some extent even in Theravada Buddhism—there is little to distinguish a *bhikkhu*, or monk, from a priest. Theravada has never produced a rigid ecclesiastical machinery and hierarchy, but many Mahayana sects have progressed far on the road of hierarchical sacerdotalism. Tibetan Buddhism in particular has produced a type of priesthood whose ritual techniques are indistinguishable from magic.

Many primitive societies exhibit patterns of "priesthood of all believers"; *i.e.*, of all members of the group. Thus the Pueblo Indians in the United States Southwest were organized in religious fraternities, and the highly formalized and elaborate rituals necessary to ensure fertility and the general welfare were performed by these groups and not by priestly functionaries.

Even where individual priests exist, their function is not necessarily one of mediation between men and gods, since prayer, sacrifice, and the administering of oracles do not everywhere require special sacerdotal practitioners. Among the Nuer of the Nilotic Sudan the leopard-skin priest, according to E. E. Evans-Pritchard, "has a central position in the social structure rather than in religious thought." Two social groups may become so violently opposed (*e.g.*, as a result of homicide) that only a person unidentified by lineage attachment to either party can effectively act in the situation and offer sacrifice and administer oaths. Since he has no political authority whatever, it is only in virtue of the sacrosanct quality of his person that the leopard-skin priest can carry out his function—somewhat like a medieval ecclesiastic arranging for a truce of God, precisely because (in theory at least) he stands outside the warring factions.

Popular and State Priesthoods.—The origins of priesthood are largely a matter of conjecture. In some primitive societies, and possibly with early man too, ritual functions (*e.g.*, fertility or hunting magic) are simply performed by such individuals as have shown in practice that they possess more supernatural "power" (*mana; q.v.*) than others—that is, are more successful in curing the sick, controlling the weather, charming deer in the hunting season, detecting sorcerers, etc. Men are distinguished from one another by a variety of gifts, and some, it would appear, possess the gift of mediating between the human and the spirit worlds to a greater degree than others.

As ritual traditions and practices increased in number and complexity, and society evolved forms of specialized division of labour, ritual practitioners arose and were resorted to. Eventually they organized themselves into priesthoods. The Bible still presents Noah, Abraham, Jacob, and other patriarchs as offering sacrifice, but later Old Testament legislation prohibits any sacrifice except that offered in the Temple of the Lord through the priests, "the sons of Aaron" (*see* below, *Semitic and Israelite Priesthood*). Nevertheless a distinction should probably be made between popular priesthoods (the ritual specialists of popular religion) on the one hand and official (state) priesthoods on the other.

The latter appear to have arisen as a result of the centralization of authority in the city-states, and they frequently ousted the earlier popular priesthoods or absorbed them into their ranks. The rise of a state priesthood actually means that the sacerdotal function is conceived as an essential aspect of political authority in general and of kingship in particular. The connection of kingship and priesthood is also implied in G. Dumézil's thesis regarding the tripartite structure of the world of the early Indo-Aryan tribes, according to which the three classes of priests, warriors, and peasants correspond to the three basic social and sacral functions of sovereignty, war, and growth. Most modern accounts of ancient Near Eastern kingship emphasize, to a greater or lesser degree, its sacral and priestly character. The king was, in theory and often also in practice, the chief cultic functionary, though normally his ritual duties were delegated to the priests acting in his behalf. Whereas the popular priesthood is often associated with popular and local shrines, the state priesthood is connected with the temple, which, in its turn, is closely associated, and possibly originally identical, with the royal palace. Even where in actual practice this link no longer exists, traces of it occasionally remain in the royal titles of the highest priestly functionaries; *e.g.*, the archon (*q.v.*) at Athens and the *rex sacrorum* at Rome. (*See* further KING; MESSIAH.)

Recruitment and Training of Priests.—Great variety exists in the forms of recruitment and training for the priesthood. Often a priest is simply chosen and appointed by the traditional owners of a cult. Sometimes a young man (or his family) decides on a sacerdotal career and serves an apprenticeship with an elder priest. Others are called to belong to the god by a personal experience (which may be culturally stereotyped), as by "possession" during an ecstatic trance. With many prospective shamans, signs of a vocation are discernible long before the first possession actually takes place—usually after the shaman has vainly tried to resist the call (*see* SHAMANISM). Sacerdotal appointments, like those of secular magistrates, were often made directly by state authority (as to the Egyptian priesthood during the Old and Middle Kingdoms or to the pontifical colleges of ancient Rome) or subject to its approval.

The sacerdotal office (ownership of a particular cult, the right to serve at a certain shrine or to exercise a specific type of ministry) is frequently inherited, and ritual functionaries tend to form classes in which the priesthood becomes hereditary (as in the New Empire in Egypt). As priestly celibacy is very rare, hereditary priesthood is correspondingly frequent. This can mean that priests must be chosen from certain lineages or that all members of a certain lineage or tribe or caste are *ipso facto* priests. Perhaps the best-known example of a priestly caste is provided by the Brahmans of India (*see* BRAHMAN), who are generally described as possessing an almost complete monopoly on religious affairs: blessing, cursing, sacrificing, administering sacraments, reciting the Vedic scriptures, etc. (In reality, however, matters are more complicated, since certain "priestly" functions, as responsibility for rain and growth, seem to have belonged to the sphere of kingship.) Similarly the Magi (*q.v.*) became a hereditary sacerdotal caste whose presence was indispensable at any Iranian religious ceremony and who eventually completely monopolized the Zoroastrian priesthood. Among the ancient Hebrews, the Levites eventually came to function as the priestly tribe. The leopard-skin priests of the Nuer are members of a particular lineage.

In most civilizations the male sex predominates among ritual functionaries, though female shamans and priestesses (the vestal virgins at Rome, for example) are not uncommon.

Whatever the nature of the priestly "power"—whether the *charisma* of office bestowed through ordination (which may be held to confer an indelible character); or a spiritual or magic power acquired by personal experience (vocation, divine posses-

sion); or the presence of the sacred life force exhibited in mortal combat (as by the priest of Diana at Lake Nemi); or the participation, by reason of birth, in the power of holiness (as the *brahman* of the Indian Brahmans, and possibly the *maga* of the Iranian Magi)—the exercise of the sacerdotal office generally requires preparation and training, both theoretical (myths, traditional lore, cosmology, law, theology, writing) and practical (ritual, divinatory, and other techniques). Even in nonliterate societies the system of training priests occasionally reached high levels of complexity (as in Dahomey) and intellectual sophistication (as in Polynesia). In higher civilizations the priesthoods were the depositaries of literate learning and the guardians of sacred as well as secular lore, including cosmic-astral knowledge and law. Hence also the judicial functions, both divine justice (*e.g.*, by means of the sacred lot or ordeals) and normal jurisprudence, often exercised by the priesthood.

Priestly Castes and Hierarchies.—The consolidation of priestly castes and classes has important religious, social, and political consequences. The special status of priests is frequently indicated by distinctive dress. Even though they may have to observe special restrictions and taboos, they generally have enjoyed considerable privileges and have claimed (often successfully) immunity from temporal law and duties. Priestly monopoly of ritual and the inevitable corruption resulting from the accumulation of power and prestige more than once has provoked or stimulated antisacerdotal reactions both on theological and on social grounds. Priestly establishments tend to develop doctrines extolling their divine nature and function. Even if the well-nigh incredible pretensions sometimes expressed in Brahmanic literature often reflect wishful thinking rather than social reality, the doctrinal tendency is evident: Brahmans are gods. According to the Roman catechism of 1567 priests are fittingly called not only angels but "gods" because *Dei immortalis vim et numen apud nos teneant* ("they are the holders, among us, of the power and the might of the immortal God"); and according to the encyclical *Mediator Dei* of Pius XII the priest *"alter est Christus" cuius personam gerit* ("is 'another Christ,' whose person he represents").

Priesthoods tend to heirarchical organization, and social, cultural, and intellectual differences among the various classes, sections, or subcastes of a priestly order can be very great. Different rules and requirements may be applied to priests of different type or rank. Certain rituals require that the officiating priest be of a specified status: the ancient Jewish ritual of the Day of Atonement had to be performed by the high priest; Christian confirmation and ordination are conferred by a bishop; the priest officiating at a Parsee initiation must have the degree of *mobad*, conferred on the second investiture. As a class with its own interests, values, and loyalties, priesthood has often shown an inclination to exercise direct or indirect political power, thus giving rise to the problem known in Western history as that of church and state (*sacerdotium* and *imperium; see* CHURCH AND STATE) and to such diverse forms of relationship as state control, support, or total suppression of the priesthood, caesaropapism, theocracy, etc. Between the Indian castes of Brahmans and Kshatriyas (the ruling caste) there are indications of an original relationship of both rivalry and complementarity. Even when the priestly hierarchies have made no open bid for seizing direct political control, they often have interfered in political affairs, made and unmade kings, kept armies of their own, and occasionally succeeded in creating a "state within the state" (as, for example, that established during the 21st dynasty in Egypt by the clergy of Amon in Thebes, or the Taoist "papacy" founded by Chang Ling in the 2nd century A.D.). Priestly income consisted of the revenues of the temple at which they served, gifts and sacrificial dues (*e.g.*, tithes), or salaries paid either by the state or by the ecclesiastical organizations.

Semitic and Israelite Priesthood.—The Babylonian and Assyrian priesthoods were associated with an official state cult and organized in specialized priestly guilds (soothsaying, divining, performing the great state rituals); a similar situation probably obtained in the Phoenician and Canaanite city-states. The nomadic and seminomadic Semitic tribes, on the other hand, appear to have had no hierarchical and organized priesthood. There were, of course, local sanctuaries of greater or lesser fame, in the charge of priests, where people would go on pilgrimages or in order to receive an oracle or obtain divine judgment by the sacred lot. Israelite priesthood exhibits the transition from popular to a more fully organized royal priesthood after the establishment of the monarchy by David (10th century B.C.), but its origins and the details of its history are obscure, and reconstruction depends on the interpretation of the literary and other evidence and on the dates ascribed to the biblical documents.

It appears that Hebrew priesthood derives from at least two sources: the tribe of the Levites (*q.v.*) at some time became the hereditary sacerdotal ministers and zealous sponsors of the Mosaic Yahweh religion, whereas the Aaronides (*see* AARON) were the ancient, pagan priesthood of Israel. The biblical account of the institution of Levitical and Aaronide priesthoods compresses a long history of social and religious development and harmonizes the fierce rivalry that must long have existed between the two groups. No doubt the administering of oracles by sacred lot and the ephod (*q.v.*) was one of the main priestly functions at many local shrines; cf. Gen. 25:22, Judg. 17–18, I Sam. 14, Ex. 21:6 and 22:8–9 (reading, with the Revised Standard Version, "God" for "judge," "judges" in the Authorized Version), Ex. 33:7 ff., I Sam. 22:18–23:12. But apart from oracle reading, Israelite priests seem to have performed none of the functions associated with the priestly office among their neighbours. Neither Leviticus nor Deuteronomy suggests that cures, spells, incantations, funerary cults, ecstatic prophecy, mythological recitations, fertility cults, ritual dramas, or the like formed part of the sacerdotal ministry. The view that any of these rituals existed in ancient Israel assumes that many of the relevant facts were concealed by the biblical record but can be inferred from what is known, or thought to be known, about the cultic institutions of the neighbouring societies. In view of the question-begging argument, the case cannot, as yet, be said to be proved.

The Pentateuch presents the priestly cult as being solely concerned with preserving the sanctuary (viz. the "tent of meeting," or tabernacle [*q.v.*], in which the divine presence is thought to be manifest) from ritual defilement. Sacrifice is for purification and atonement. Blessing the people was a marginal rather than a central function (Lev. 9:22; Num. 6:23), though it is the only one which the priests have retained in later Judaism, since the destruction of the Temple (A.D. 70). On the other hand, the priests were in charge of the Torah, Yahweh's laws and statutes (cf. Deut. 33:8; Jer. 2:8) until, in the Second Temple period, this function was assumed by the Pharisaic teachers and rabbis. The priests of the "royal chapel" (*i.e.*, the Temple at Jerusalem), the sons of Zadok appointed by Solomon, gradually gained ascendancy over all other priestly families, especially after the abolition of local sanctuaries and the centralization of worship in Jerusalem.

By the time of the Second Temple (6th century B.C.) the priesthood was considered a hereditary hierarchy officiating by divine right; its prestige as well as its political and social significance in the life of the nation reached unprecedented heights. Politically the priestly class was associated with the Sadducees rather than with the Pharisaic party (*see* JEWISH SECTS DURING THE SECOND COMMONWEALTH), but sectarian groups accorded a major place to the priesthood as such in their theological system, though emphatically repudiating the "usurpers" who actually held priestly office in Jerusalem during the Hasmonaean and Herodian periods.

The doctrine and institution of priesthood play little part in later Jewish theology. When Christianity began to evolve the notion of a sacerdotal ministry, the Temple was no longer in existence; the church was not guided or influenced by any living Jewish example or institution but by its own understanding of the model of priesthood in the Old Testament.

Christian Priesthood.—New Testament usage does not associate any "priestly" notions with the office of presbyter ("elder"; *see* above) and never applies the term priest (*hiereus*) to Christian ministers. On the other hand, the ministry, and more particularly the sacrifice, of Christ were conceived in high-priestly terms (Heb. 5). The sacrifices and priesthood of the Old Testa-

ment were understood as a type or prefiguration of Christ's sacrifice (cf. Rev. 13:8, "the Lamb slain from the foundation of the world") and priesthood (Heb. 5:10), in which they were fulfilled. Christians were held to share in his high priesthood (cf. Eph. 2:18); hence the Christian community as a body could be described as a holy or royal "priesthood" (I Pet. 2:5, 9; cf. also Rev. 5:10).

Nevertheless a Christian ministry of the sacerdotal type soon began to emerge, mainly in connection with the Eucharist. By the 3rd century Cyprian (*Epistles* 66) could declare *episcopum in ecclesia esse et ecclesiam in episcopo* ("the bishop is in the church and the church in the bishop"). In fact, the *sacerdotium* was vested primarily in the bishop, but the "presbyters" shared in it and, in his absence, could exercise certain priestly functions, acting as his delegates. With the spread of Christianity and the establishment of parish churches, the parish priest became the principal celebrant of the Eucharist, and in this capacity, as well as by hearing confession and granting absolution, he eventually assumed the role of the representative of God to the people rather than the other way round. The development of eucharistic theology resulted in a further emphasis of the priest's supernatural powers and qualities in a manner which went far beyond the Old Testament model which was considered to provide the pattern of both priestly mediation and priestly hierarchy.

The Protestant Reformation rejected the doctrine of the sacrifice of the Mass as well as the conception of a "Levitical" priesthood that went with it, and consequently substituted "ministers" for "priests." The English Reformers retained the term priest in the Book of Common Prayer, in order to distinguish priests, who can celebrate Holy Communion, from deacons, who are not entitled to do so. Since the 19th century, theology has witnessed a notable revival of sacerdotalism, accompanied, however, by a renewed emphasis of the priesthood, in Christ, of the whole people of God (*see*, for example, the relevant sections in the encyclical *Mediator Dei* of Pius XII in 1947; Vatican II: *Decree on the Ministry and Life of Priests* [*Presbyterorum Ordinis*], ch. 1, Dec. 7, 1965; and *Decree on the Apostolate of the Laity* [*Apostolicam Actuositatem*], ch. 1, Nov. 18, 1965).

BIBLIOGRAPHY.—E. O. James, *The Nature and Function of Priesthood* (1956); J. Hastings *et al.* (eds.), *Encyclopaedia of Religion and Ethics*, vol. x, pp. 278–336 (1918); T. J. Meek, *Hebrew Origins*, rev. ed., ch. v (1950); A. Michel in *Dictionnaire de Théologie Catholique*, vol. xiii, col. 138–161 (1936); L. Kösters, in *Lexicon für Theologie und Kirche*, vol. viii, col. 462–471 (1936); G. Schrenk in Kittel's *Theologisches Wörterbuch*, vol. iii, col. 257–284 (1938); M. Weber, *Sociology of Religion*, Eng. trans. (1963); G. Dumézil, *L'Idéologie tripartie des Indo-Européens* (1958). (R. J. Z. W.)

PRIESTLEY, JOSEPH (1733–1804), best known for his contributions to the chemistry of gases. A dissenting English minister, he published extensively not only his experimental investigations and the history of science, but also on philosophy, religion, education, and political theory. He is equally well known in his native land and in the United States, where he spent the last ten years of his life. Born at Birstall, near Leeds, on March 13, 1733, the son of strict Calvinists, he soon rejected the authority of the established churches and became a dissenting minister at 22, and five years later a teacher of classics and literature at a dissenting academy in Warrington. While there Priestley wrote essays on education and English grammar, along with a biographical chart, which earned him a doctor of laws degree from the University of Edinburgh.

Experiments and Discoveries.—He began to interest himself in experimental investigations into electricity. His duties at Warrington left him free to visit London for a month each year. He secured an introduction to the London scientist John Canton and through him met Benjamin Franklin, who encouraged him to complete his first major scientific work, *The History and Present State of Electricity* (1767). Meanwhile he had been admitted in 1766 as a fellow of the Royal Society, ostensibly for his biographical chart but with a side-reference to his scientific investigations.

In 1767 he became pastor of Mill Hill chapel, near Leeds. Living next to a brewery, he became interested in the "fixed air" (carbon dioxide) that lay over the liquids in the fermentation vats. On moving to another location he continued his studies with this gas, which he made by pouring acid on chalk. He dissolved the gas in water and obtained "an exceedingly pleasant sparkling water, resembling Seltzer water." For this application, which was his first contribution to the chemistry of gases, the Royal Society awarded him the Copley Medal in 1773. About this time Priestley was fortunate in meeting a fellow sympathizer with the cause of the American colonies, Lord Shelburne (later marquess of Lansdowne). He became librarian to this wealthy nobleman, with enough leisure to indulge in scientific pursuits.

With the aid of a newly acquired burning glass, he obtained on Aug. 1, 1774, a new gas from mercuric oxide that was five or six times as pure as ordinary air. He even foresaw its future uses:

JOSEPH PRIESTLEY, PORTRAIT IN CHALK BY ELLEN SHARPLES, ABOUT 1795

"it may be peculiarly salutary for the lungs in certain cases" and thus anticipated its use in oxygen tents. This discovery, which greatly increased his fame, led to a meeting in Paris with Antoine Lavoisier and other noted scientists to whom he related his findings. Lavoisier at once repeated Priestley's experiments with the new gas, which he named oxygen, from the Greek for "acid-maker," because of its acid-forming properties. It gave Lavoisier the clue to demolish the phlogiston theory of which, nevertheless, Priestley remained a lifelong adherent. Meanwhile, the theological heresies of Priestley so strained his relations with Shelburne that he resigned in 1780 to become minister to a dissenting congregation in Birmingham.

In Birmingham, where Priestley spent the happiest decade of his life, he wrote the final two of his six volumes *On Different Kinds of Air*. An abridged edition in three volumes appeared in 1790. Priestley's nontechnical writings, particularly his *History of the Corruptions of Christianity* (1782), and his espousal of the cause of the American colonists and later of the French Revolution, made him exceedingly unpopular with the public. The smouldering resentment against Priestley and his friends came to a head on the second anniversary (July 14, 1791) of the fall of the Bastille. Mob rule existed in Birmingham for three days. Priestley's church, his house, and his laboratory were burned and he himself escaped in disguise to Worcester. Later he settled in London, where he spent three unhappy years. On April 7, 1794, he left for America to join his three sons who had already found new homes there. Arriving in New York City in June 1794, he was offered a professorship and a ministry, both of which he declined. He built himself a house and laboratory in the town of Northumberland, Pa., and there he died on Feb. 6, 1804.

Priestley's multiplicity of interests has often been commented upon. Trained as a theologian, he was open-minded, fearless and progressive in matters of religion and politics; in science, to which he came later in life, he was orthodox, timid and as he himself stated "not apt to be very confident" about conclusions from his observations. Even so, he had the attributes of a born investigator: an intense curiosity, a passion for "experimental philosophy" and a native honesty and frankness. He was an ingenious manipulator. Being the first to collect gases over mercury, he discovered, in addition to oxygen, several other gases, including nitrogen, ammonia, nitrogen dioxide, nitrous oxide, hydrogen chloride, and sulfur dioxide. Some of these are highly soluble in water and thus had escaped the attention of contemporary chemists. Another significant contribution to chemistry was Priestley's work on "the purification of air by plants and the influence of light on that process," which provided the stimulus for subsequent studies by Jan Ingenhousz, Jean Senebier, and others on respiration and photosynthesis.

The defects in Priestley's work as a chemist derive from his lack of feeling for mathematical relationships, which also adversely affected his *History of the Present State of the Discoveries Relating to Vision, Light and Colours* (1772). The fact remains that, along with the *History of Electricity*, Priestley's *History of Optics*—as it is generally called—was a pioneering work in the history of science, extensively pillaged by later historians. Priestley several times drew attention to phenomena which were subsequently to be rediscovered by later physicists; he himself was not fully aware of their importance, and failed to work them into a general theory.

Philosophy of Education, Government.—As an educator, Priestley was probably the first ever to teach experimental science to school children. His *Essay on a Course of Liberal Education* (1765) is a plea for a curriculum suitable for training men of affairs, emphasizing history and public administration rather than the classics. He introduced the teaching of modern history into the curriculum of the dissenting academies; his *Lectures on History and General Policy* (2 vol., 1788) was a widely used textbook in American colleges and even at Cambridge, England. Emphasizing commerce, law, and administration, Priestley sought to draw the attention of students to the main historical sources rather than to supply them with a ready-made summary of events. The *Rudiments of English Grammar* (1761), many times reprinted, was an even bolder innovation. Instead of, in the traditional manner, attempting to apply classical grammatical classification to English grammar, it set out to describe English usage, as exemplified in the works of the best writers.

In *An Essay on the First Principles of Government* (1768), Priestley defended a laissez-faire theory of government. Legislation should be reduced to a minimum, and in particular there should be no restrictions on civil and religious liberty. In the case of any proposed legislation, the question was whether it would be for the greatest happiness of the greatest number; Bentham admitted that he derived his utilitarian principle from Priestley. Priestley thought it obvious that restrictions on liberty could never be in the interest of the general happiness. Fearful, as a dissenter, of state control, he criticized any sort of social welfare legislation, including proposals for a national system of education.

As a philosopher, Priestley was a staunch defender of determinism and materialism. When a young man, he was profoundly influenced by David Hartley's associationism and Anthony Collins' determinism. His *Disquisitions Relating to Matter and Spirit* (1777) set out to show that materialism was theologically, scientifically, and metaphysically superior to orthodox dualism and in *The Doctrine of Philosophical Necessity* (1777) he argued that the doctrine of free will was theologically objectionable, metaphysically incomprehensible, and morally undesirable.

A dissenting minister from the age of 22, and in charge of a congregation for about 17 years, much of Priestley's time was devoted to a reconstruction of traditional Christian doctrine. This he himself believed to be his most important work.

Starting life as a Calvinist, Priestley's thought led him through Arminianism and Arianism to a Unitarian position. His view that many of the doctrines of orthodox Christianity were mere historical accretions was fully expounded in his *History of the Corruptions of Christianity*. As a materialist, he denied the existence of a human soul separable from the body, attributing Christianity's acceptance of the concept to Neoplatonic and heathen influences. His investigations into the early history of the Christian church led him finally to reject the doctrines of the divinity and pre-existence of Christ, and of the atonement. In his view the mission of Christ was to invite men to virtue by precept and example; by Christ's death and resurrection God demonstrated the certainty of a future life of reward or punishment related to the virtue and penitence, or the vice, characterizing each individual's earthly course. It is hard to escape the conviction that for Priestley, the "end" of Christianity was virtuous living. Indeed, he thought Christianity "less a system of opinions than a rule of life."

See also references under "Priestley, Joseph" in the Index.

BIBLIOGRAPHY.—An excellent account of Priestley's contributions to chemistry is found in J. R. Partington, *A Short History of Chemistry*, 2nd ed. (1948), which contains numerous references. For his electrical discoveries *see* R. E. Schofield's introduction to the 1966 reprint of *The History and Present State of Electricity*. For a popular account of his life and work *see* B. Jaffe, *Crucibles* (1934), and J. G. Gillam, *The Crucible* (1954). His work on oxygen has been republished in *The Alembic Club Reprints*, no. 7 (1901), and in H. M. Leicester and H. S. Klickstein, *A Source Book in Chemistry* (1952). A good account of Priestley's relations with Lavoisier was given by R. E. Oesper in *J. Chem. Educ.*, 13:403 (1936). *J. Chem. Educ.*, 4:145–199 (1927) contains illustrations and details of his life in America. *See* also R. E. Schofield, *Scientific Autobiography of Joseph Priestley* (1966), and for selections with a biographical introduction, J. A. Passmore, *Priestley's Writings on Philosophy, Science, and Politics* (1965).
(H. S. V. K.; Jn. A. P.)

PRIM, JUAN (1814–1870), Spanish general and statesman, a leader of the revolution of 1868, was born at Reus, Catalonia, on Dec. 6, 1814. At the beginning of the First Carlist War (1833–39) he enlisted in the forces supporting Isabella II. His courage, and the fact that he had been in action 35 times, raised him to the rank of colonel by 1839. A liberal by conviction, he entered politics and was elected deputy for Tarragona in 1841. The following year he opposed the regent, Baldomero Espartero, and in 1843 led a rising at Reus which led to Espartero's exile. In the same year Gen. Francisco Serrano y Dominguez appointed Prim military governor at Madrid and later, of Barcelona, where he was responsible for the harsh repression of attempted risings and received the titles of conde de Reus and vizconde del Bruch. He soon became an opponent of the moderates and conspired against the prime minister Ramón Narváez. Captured and condemned, he was later pardoned. He traveled to France and to England, and in 1847 was appointed governor of Puerto Rico. There he repressed disturbances by the slaves and put down banditry.

On his return to Madrid he was given command in 1853 of the Spanish commission attached to the Turkish Army fighting the Russians. He was appointed captain general of Granada in 1856. From there he went in 1859 to Melilla, in Morocco, where he suppressed a rising and was given the titles of marqués de Castillejos and marqués de Wad-Ras (1860). He commanded the English, French, and Spanish expedition to Mexico (1861), and obtained from Pres. Benito Juárez the reparations which the allies had demanded (*see* MEXICO). However, he refused to support the French plan to impose the archduke Maximilian of Austria as emperor of Mexico, and returned to Spain. He then associated with the antidynastic sections of the Progressive Party; he was accused of conspiracy and exiled to Oviedo (1864). From then until 1868 he took part in all the *pronunciamientos* and played a principal part in the successful one of September 1868, which deposed Isabella II.

Prim was made minister of war in October in Serrano's government, and when the latter became regent in 1869, Prim headed the government and acted firmly in suppressing disorder. After considerable difficulty he succeeded in getting Amadeo of Savoy accepted as king of Spain, but on Dec. 27, 1870, Prim was attacked by assassins in Madrid and died there on Dec. 30, the day Amadeo arrived in Spain. (R. S. Ll.)

PRIMARY, a meeting or election at which candidates for office are nominated or at which the first steps are taken toward such nomination. Primaries may be informal gatherings or formal elections held under the same safeguards as final elections. They may be partisan in the sense that participation is limited to persons affiliated with the same party; or nonpartisan. Partisan primaries may be indirect or direct. In the indirect primary, delegates are chosen to nominating conventions which then choose the nominees; in the direct primary party members choose the nominees and the primary becomes a preliminary election.

Historical Development.—The formalized, legally regulated primary election and the direct primary are peculiar to the United States. The earliest method for nominating candidates was the caucus (*q.v.*), adopted in colonial times for local offices and continued into the 19th century for state and national offices. Nominating conventions, instituted by political parties as a means of doing away with the abuses of the caucus system, eventually became subject to abuses which led first to their regulation and

ultimately to their elimination for most offices except president and vice-president (*see* NATIONAL CONVENTION). Observance of early laws relating to selection of delegates was optional, parties being permitted but not required to conform to their provisions, and the laws were limited to certain areas. After 1890 mandatory regulations of a sweeping character transformed the primary into an election conducted by public officers at public expense. Even before these laws were tested a demand arose for making nominations by the voters directly. The direct primary was used by the Democratic Party in Crawford County, Pa., as early as 1842, but it was not until the 20th century, when the Progressive movement tended to divide both parties, that the system came into general use. In 1903 Wisconsin, under the leadership of Gov. Robert M. La Follette, passed the first mandatory, statewide direct primary law. The movement spread so rapidly that by 1917 all but four states had adopted the direct primary for some or all statewide nominations. After the passage of laws in Utah (1937), New Mexico (1938), Rhode Island (1947), and Connecticut (1955), some form of direct primary was used in all states. Primaries in most states are mandatory and cover nominations to all state and county offices, but optional primaries survive in several Southern states, and Michigan, New York, and Indiana are among the states which use conventions for nominations to some state offices. In most states provisions apply only to parties polling a fixed minimum at the last election.

Direct primaries in the states vary widely in detail, and dates of primary elections vary from spring to fall. Various methods are used to place names on the ballot. The simplest is a declaration of candidacy, with or without a filing fee. The more popular method is by petition signed by a certain number of political supporters of the aspirant. In an increasing number of states the primary is preceded by official or unofficial conventions and candidates so designated are listed first on the ballot. Preprimary endorsing conventions are provided by law in Colorado, Connecticut, Idaho, Massachusetts, New Mexico, and Utah. In Rhode Island party committees may endorse candidates and their names appear first on the primary election ballot. On the other hand, California in 1963 prohibited party organizations from officially endorsing candidates and required nominees of unofficial clubs to be labeled "unofficial" on the ballot. In most states an aspirant for nomination may compete only in the primary of the party in which he claims membership, but in a few states it is possible for the candidate to seek the nomination of both parties simultaneously.

"Open" and "Closed" Primaries.—Particularly interesting and important are the variations in qualifications for voting in the primary. Some primaries are "open" in the sense that no declaration of party affiliation is required; the voter may participate in the primary of either party and move from one party to another in successive contests. Sometimes, as in Wisconsin, the participant receives the ballots of all parties and may decide which to use in the privacy of the voting booth, whereas in those states following the Minnesota plan a "blanket" ballot is provided on which the names of all candidates are arranged in party columns. In 1935 Washington adopted a blanket ballot which permitted the voter to cross back and forth between the parties at the same primary; *e.g.*, he might vote for a Republican aspirant for the gubernatorial nomination and at the same time express a choice for a Democrat for the nomination for United States senator. The "closed" primary, used in all but seven states by 1964, limits participation in the primary to party members. Voters are required to enroll as members of a party at the time of registration, to state their party choice at the polling place, or to swear that they meet a specified test of party membership if their right to participate in the primary is challenged. The usual tests are support of the party's candidates at the last general election or the intention to support the candidates of that party at the next general election.

The merits of open and closed primaries have been widely debated. It is argued that the open primary permits participation by independents who are unwilling to declare a party affiliation and that it prevents intimidation of voters. Its opponents say that it destroys party responsibility by permitting those who have no continuing allegiance to the party to control its nominees, and that it permits members of one party to "raid" the primaries of the other party.

Primaries were for many years regarded by the courts as being outside the power of Congress to regulate. Federal corrupt practices acts, for example, were held not to apply to primaries but only to final elections. In Southern states Negroes were barred from voting in Democratic primaries, which were the only elections that really mattered, and the courts held that such action by the Democratic state organizations was not unconstitutional. In the 1940s this interpretation was set aside in several U.S. Supreme Court decisions to the effect that primaries are integral parts of the electoral process, that political parties are not private clubs but state agencies, and that the primaries in which candidates for federal office are chosen are subject to federal regulation.

Other Aspects.—In most states the candidate polling the highest number of votes becomes the nominee, but by the early 1960s most Southern states, in which Democratic nomination was equivalent to election, required a second or "runoff" primary if no candidate received a majority of the votes in the first contest. Preferential voting (*i.e.*, indication of a first, second, and third choice), tried by several states, had been abandoned by all of them.

Studies made in the 1950s and 1960s tended to support the hypothesis that the primaries had altered the character of political competition, at least in the case of nominations for state legislative posts. Even in two-party areas the effective choice had tended to be transferred to the primaries of the majority party, and the vitality of the minority party was weakened.

Attempts have been made to extend the idea of direct nominations to the presidency of the United States. By election of delegates to the nominating conventions, and by preference votes for president, or both, some states have attempted to bring the national conventions within the control of the party membership. The first mandatory presidential primary law was adopted by Wisconsin in 1905, and by 1916 laws varying widely in type and effectiveness were in operation in 24 states. After that the movement lost ground, and in 1964 mandatory laws were in effect in only 16 states and the District of Columbia. Nevertheless, studies published in the 1960s suggested that primary contests affected the action of national nominating conventions and there was a revival of interest in proposals for mandatory national presidential primaries.

Nonpartisan primaries have been widely used for judicial and local offices in the United States and have been extended to members of the state legislature in Minnesota and Nebraska. In reality a double election system in which party labels play no part, nonpartisan elections, and primaries were introduced in an attempt to remove these offices from influence by national party politics. Although nonpartisan in form, they frequently become partisan in fact.

The closest parallel to the U.S. primary has been the "preselection" ballot of the Australian Labor Party, in which candidates in each locality have been selected by party members in that locality from those offering themselves for the preselection vote.

BIBLIOGRAPHY.—C. E. Merriam and L. Overacker, *Primary Elections,* rev. ed. (1928); National Municipal League, *Compilation of 48 State Direct Primary Systems,* 3rd. ed. (1958), and *A Model Direct Primary System* (1951); C. A. Berdahl, "Party Membership in the United States," *American Political Science Review,* vol. xxxvi, pp. 16–50, 241–262 (1942); V. O. Key, *Politics, Parties and Pressure Groups,* 5th ed. (1964), and *American State Politics: an Introduction* (1956); L. C. Rowe, *Preprimary Endorsements in California Politics* (1961).

(L. Or.)

PRIMARY EDUCATION: *see* ELEMENTARY EDUCATION.

PRIMATE (from *prima sedes*, "first see"), an ecclesiastical title used of a bishop who has precedence over a number of other bishops. The term was applied in the 4th and 5th centuries to both secular officials and ecclesiastics; thus the Theodosian code (438) mentions primates of towns, districts, and fortified places (*primates urbium, vicorum, castellorum*), and a pragmatic sanction of Justinian I mentions primates governing a district, *primates*

regionis. During the Middle Ages *primas* also seems to have been used loosely for "head" or "chief," since the word itself means only the one who holds first place.

In the Christian Church primate was one of several titles, others being metropolitan, exarch, and patriarch (*qq.v.*), employed to designate a chief bishop who had certain rights of superintendence over an entire district or area. At the Council of Nicaea (325) the title was assumed to embrace metropolitans, with authority over the bishops of an eparchy or province, and also bishops of high position—especially those later to be called patriarchs (the bishops of Rome, Alexandria, Antioch, and Jerusalem), but also those of "other eparchies" as well (perhaps the bishops of Heraclea, Ephesus, and Caesarea). After the Council of Nicaea the ecclesiastical title of primate came into use, more generally in Africa than in other areas. Then it came to be a formal title conceded by the pope to certain metropolitan bishops who possessed authority over several other metropolitans and were appointed, at the same time, vicars or legates of the Holy See. The False Decretals attempted to strengthen and perpetuate the authority of primates, but the office gradually became more or less honorary.

In the Roman Catholic Church primates are those metropolitan archbishops whose sees, by reason of antiquity or prominence, are the primary sees of a region or nation. Apart from the special case of the pope, who has among his titles that of primate of Italy, primates do not possess any jurisdiction outside their own dioceses but only a limited and honorary right to precedence. An exception to this is the bishop of Esztergom (Gran) who, with rank as primate of Hungary dating back at least to the 14th century, enjoys a measure of true primatial authority.

In the Church of England, the overlapping of the title is illustrated: the archbishop of York still bears the title of primate of England and the archbishop of Canterbury is primate of all England. (F. R. McM.)

PRIMATES, the order of mammals that includes tree shrews, lemurs, tarsiers, monkeys, apes, and men. Linnaeus distinguished the Primates as the highest ranking and most completely developed of all animals. Now, as in Linnaeus' time, this order is regarded with particular interest, for in the study of primate evolution man traces, however haltingly, his own family tree.

Other articles deal with the body systems and natural history of the Primates: see APE; LEMUR; MAMMAL; MAN, EVOLUTION OF; MONKEY; TARSIER. This article, concerned mainly with the relationships, evolution, and behaviour of the Primates, is arranged as follows:

    I. General
        1. Evolutionary Trends
        2. Characteristic Features
    II. Classification and Survey
        A. Primitive Primates (Prosimii)
            1. Tree Shrews
            2. Lemurs
            3. Tarsiers
        B. Higher Primates (Anthropoidea): Monkeys
            1. New World Monkeys (Platyrrhines)
            2. Old World Monkeys (Catarrhines)
        C. Manlike Primates (Hominoidea): Apes and Man
            1. Gibbon
            2. Orangutan
            3. Chimpanzee
            4. Gorilla
            5. Man
    III. Origin and Relationships
    IV. Behaviour of the Primates
            1. Intelligence
            2. Temperament
            3. Socialization

I. GENERAL

1. Evolutionary Trends.—The early Primates lived in an environment in which quick reaction to the ecological factors of arboreal life was essential for survival. When some of the higher Primates were compelled by changing environmental conditions to adapt to life on the ground, the special talents gained during the arboreal phase of their evolution were put to good use. The combination of brain expansion, neuromuscular coordination, and upright posture in the immediate forerunners of man permitted the development of more precise manipulative skills. At the same time, communication by facial expression and vocalization provided the opportunity for a greater degree of social cooperation, and led ultimately to the development of symbolic language. Finally, there appeared the higher faculties of insight, foresight, and reasoning, characteristic of man.

Most orders of mammals can be distinguished by outstanding specialized features. The order of Primates, by contrast, is relatively poor in such specializations: it comprises an evolutionary sequence that was isolated very early from the rest of the mammalian lines by an adaptation to life in the trees. Thus the Primates have tended to preserve a rather more generalized anatomy; they are distinguished from other mammalian orders by a lack of extreme specialization. The arboreal existence effectively removed Primates from the competition of specialization required for survival among the terrestrial animals and provided a wide spectrum of other possible directions of evolution.

One of the notable evolutionary routes explored by Primates has led to an increased perfection of the controlling mechanisms of the brain, which in turn have been conditioned by an elaboration of the sensory pathways to the brain, thus permitting a heightened responsiveness to a great number and variety of environmental situations. It may be said that primate evolution is characterized not so much by a progressive adaptedness to a restricted type of environment as by a progressive adaptability to wider ranges of environment.

Broadly, the Primates may be defined as a natural group of mammals distinguished by the following evolutionary trends: preservation of a generalized structure of the limbs, with a primitive five-digited condition of the extremities; retention of certain basic skeletal elements (*e.g.*, the clavicle); enhancement of the primitive free mobility of all the digits of the hand and foot for grasping purposes—especially that of the thumb and big toe; replacement of sharp claws by flattened nails; abbreviation of the snout or muzzle, leading to a "flattening" of the face; elaboration of the visual apparatus; reduction of the organs of smell (which is of less importance for life in the trees than for ground-living mammals); preservation of a simple cusp pattern of the teeth; and progressive elaboration of the brain, mainly of the cerebral cortex and associated structures.

2. Characteristic Features.

—One of the striking features of the primate order, wherein it differs from other mammalian orders, is that its existing members fall into a graded series, or scale of organization, which (quite apart from the evidence of the fossil record) suggests an actual evolutionary trend leading from the most primitive (tree shrews) to the most advanced (man) within the order. As T. H. Huxley noted: "Perhaps no order of mammals presents us with so extraordinary a series of gradations as this—leading us insensibly from the crown and summit of the animal creation down to creatures from which there is but a step, as it seems, to the lowest, smallest and least intelligent of the placental mammals."

In addition to the principal features of primate anatomy already enumerated, the following are important in identification

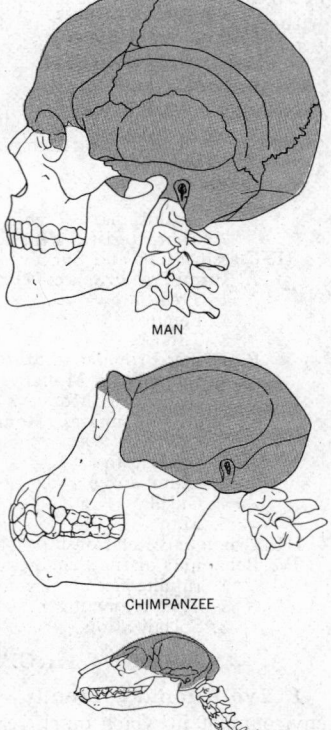

MAN

CHIMPANZEE

LEMUR

FROM M. BOULE AND H. V. VALLOIS, "FOSSIL MEN," 1957

FIG. 1.—COMPARISON OF SKULL CHARACTERS OF SEVERAL PRIMATES. SHADED AREAS INDICATE CEREBRAL PORTION OF THE SKULL. (DRAWN TO PROPORTIONAL SCALE)

and classification of the order. Proceeding up the graded series of modern Primates from tree shrew to man the skull changes considerably. The orbital cavities become relatively large and face forward to varying degrees as well as laterally; the *foramen magnum* (through which the brain connects with the spinal cord) tends to be displaced from the posterior to the basal aspect of the skull; the braincase becomes relatively capacious and globular in form; the cavity of the middle ear becomes enclosed within the petrous bone or in a rounded expansion of this element, the tympanic bulla; the external ear becomes connected with the middle ear by a bony tube called the auditory meatus; the labyrinthine turbinate complex within the nasal cavity undergoes simplification; and the premaxillary element of the upper jaw becomes more or less reduced in proportionate size. In modern Primates the occipital lobes of the brain, which accommodate the visual cortex, are conspicuously developed, the temporal lobes are relatively large, and the cerebral cortex is often richly convoluted.

In the dentition of Primates, the incisor teeth are in almost all cases reduced to two on each side of the upper and lower jaws; the premolar teeth, while preserving a simple structure, are also reduced from the primitive mammalian number of four to three or two; and the crowns of the molar teeth commonly have a tricuspid or quadricuspid pattern. The terminal phalanges are richly innervated, with highly sensitive tactile pads underlying the flattened nails. In the higher Primates the retina of the eye is characterized by the differentiation of a very sensitive central spot, the *macula lutea*, which provides a high degree of visual acuity. The alimentary system in most cases preserves a very simple pattern. The reproductive organs are likewise relatively generalized in their structure: the testes commonly descend permanently into a pendulous scrotal sac; in the higher forms the uterus becomes simplified by the fusion of the uterine horns to form an undivided *corpus uteri*, and there is typically a rhythmic sexual cycle that, in most cases, is not restricted to a limited seasonal period; in passing from the lower to the higher Primates, there is a progressive elaboration of placental structure, which provides ever-improving conditions for the developing embryo. Not all these diagnostic characters of the Primates are developed to the same degree in the different existing members of the order; furthermore, in early fossil primate precursors some of the characters were only incipiently formed. The failure to recognize these temporal and gradational factors in the characters of various groups has led to contradictory views regarding the classification and evolutionary affinities of the Primates.

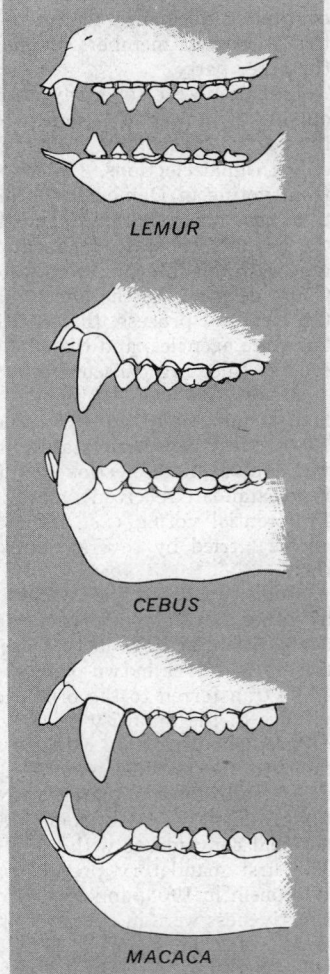

LEMUR

CEBUS

MACACA

FROM J. Z. YOUNG, "LIFE OF THE VERTEBRATES," THE CLARENDON PRESS, OXFORD

FIG. 2.—DENTAL CHARACTERS OF: (TOP TO BOTTOM) LEMUR, COMMON LEMUR; CEBUS, NEW WORLD MONKEY; MACACA, OLD WORLD MONKEY

II. CLASSIFICATION AND SURVEY

The existing Primates may be divided into two suborders: the Prosimii, including the tree shrews, lemurs, and tarsiers; and the Anthropoidea, including the monkeys, apes, and men. Although there is good evidence for including tree shrews in the order Primates (*see* below), some authorities regard this as problematical, for many features link them with the Insectivora (*see* INSECTIVORE for this viewpoint). That Primates stem from insectivore-like mammals is certain; but at what stage in geologic time this offshoot occurred is unknown. The modern tree shrews do show a number of resemblances to the Lemuroidea, but it has been argued that at least some of these are convergent developments resulting from an arboreal mode of life. On the other hand, serological reactions suggest affinities with both the Primates and certain of the modern Insectivora. However, it is generally agreed that the ancestral stock from which the Primates arose must have been much more similar to the tree shrews than to any of the modern Insectivora. Some authorities have referred to the modern tree shrews as "borderline" Primates, and it thus seems reasonable to retain them in the order of the Primates.

The first definite primate types are known to have existed in the Paleocene (58,000,000 to 70,000,000 years ago). These and later prosimians were primitive in the sense that they retained many of the characters of insectivores; *e.g.*, long face, laterally placed eyes, and relatively small brain. The precise time of origin of the higher Primates (monkeys and apes) is doubtful, but fossils of these Primates are first definitely known from the Oligocene beginning about 35,000,000 years ago). The following taxonomic scheme for the Primates may be at least provisionally accepted:

Suborder Prosimii, primitive Primates
  Infraorder Lemuriformes
    Superfamily Tupaioidea, tree shrews
        "   Lemuroidea ⎱
        "   Daubentonioidea ⎰ Madagascan lemurs
  Infraorder Lorisiformes, Asian and tropical African lemurs
    "   Tarsiiformes, tarsiers
    Superfamily Tarsioidea
Suborder Anthropoidea, manlike Primates
  Superfamily Ceboidea, New World monkeys
    "   Cercopithecoidea, Old World monkeys
    "   Hominoidea, anthropoid apes and men

A. Primitive Primates (Prosimii)

1. Tree Shrews.—The tree shrews, which constitute the superfamily Tupaioidea, are exceedingly primitive small mammals of arboreal habitat widely distributed in southeast Asia. The living members of the group differ from other extant Primates in that all the digits of the hand and foot are furnished with sharp claws, and the brain is of relatively simpler construction. They are divided into two subfamilies, the Ptilocercinae and Tupaiinae. The former is represented by one genus only, *Ptilocercus*, the pen-tailed tree shrews, and the latter by a number of genera such as *Tupaia*, *Anathana*, and *Urogale*. The pen-tailed tree shrew is nocturnal, and in many features of its anatomy (particularly the brain) it is more primitive than the other tree shrews. The Tupaiinae are diurnal creatures and vary somewhat in their habits, the larger genera being more frequently found in forest under-

TREE SHREW (TUPAIA), CLOSELY RESEMBLING A SQUIRREL, REGARDED BY SOME AUTHORITIES AS THE MOST PRIMITIVE LIVING PRIMATE

growth than in the higher branches of the trees. Like many tropical squirrels, some Tupaiinae are strikingly coloured, with vivid shoulder stripes and other markings.

The Tupaioidea resemble the other Lemuriformes in the detailed construction of the skull and in certain features of the dentition. In the lower jaw, however, they preserve three incisors, though the third is much reduced, and in the genus *Urogale* it has disappeared (as it has completely in all the higher Primates). The orbital opening is completely encircled by a bony ring; and the tympanic bone, which supports the eardrum, forms a simple ring lying free within a bubble-like bony structure, the bulla. The brain (except in *Ptilocercus*) shows a significant expansion of the

RING-TAILED LEMURS (LEMUR CATTA), ROCK-DWELLING SPECIES OF SOUTH-CENTRAL MADAGASCAR

cerebral hemispheres, the visual area of the cortex having a complexity of structure matched, among mammalian groups, only in the superfamily Lemuroidea. The significance of the structure of the placenta and fetal membranes remains uncertain, but they are more closely similar in this respect to the higher Primates than the lemurs are. The limbs of the tree shrews have a wide range of movement, and the mobility of the thumb and big toe permits grasping by a converging flexion in association with the other digits. The bushy tail of the Tupaiinae gives them a squirrel-like appearance. They, and most lemurs, comb the long hairs of the tail with their procumbent lower incisors.

2. Lemurs.—The term "lemur" is usually taken to include the Lemuriformes, exclusive of the tree shrews, and the Lorisiformes, including the lorises, pottos, and bush babies. In past ages the lemurs were widely distributed over the Northern Hemisphere; the group is now more restricted. The lemuriform lemurs are confined to Madagascar and adjacent islands, while the lorisiform lemurs are widely distributed over the tropical regions of Asia and continental Africa. In general structure the existing lemurs show an obvious approximation to the higher Primates in the degree of development of the brain, in the functional adaptation of the limbs for grasping purposes, in the presence of flattened nails on the digits, and in certain features of the skull and dentition. They also show conspicuous differences and specializations; so much so that some older authorities have even questioned their inclusion among the Primates. Such dissent, however, has found no support among later students of the Primates.

The characteristic features of the modern lemurs include: (1) a curious modification of the lower incisors, which, combined with the procumbent and styliform canines, constitute a fine dental "comb" used to groom the fur; (2) the development of a serrated membrane (sublingua) on the undersurface of the tongue; (3) a pronounced loop in the large intestine; (4) the retention of a modified claw on the second digit of the foot; (5) the presence of a naked area, or rhinarium, around the nostrils, an area that extends down the midline of the upper lip and binds the latter down to the underlying gum; (6) a simple placenta quite unlike that of the higher Primates; and (7) in the lorisiform lemurs, a distinctive pattern of the blood vessels of the limbs in which the main arteries break up into fine vessels forming a complex network. The dental formula of most of the recent lemurs is $\frac{2.1.3.3}{2.1.3.3}$; that is, on each side of the upper and lower jaws are two incisors, one canine, three premolars, and three molars. The molars are of simple construction and possess either three or four cusps. Many lemurs are nocturnal, and have rather large eyes which serve them well for their mode of life.

Lemuriformes.—The lemuriform, or Madagascan, lemurs comprise two superfamilies, Lemuroidea and Daubentonioidea, the former being subdivided into the families Lemuridae and Indriidae. All lemuriforms are characterized by the possession of an intrabullar tympanic ring, and by the forward extension of the palatine bone to form part of the inner wall of the orbital cavity. The Lemuridae have an elongated snout, large and mobile ears, and long furry tails. The ring-tailed lemur (*Lemur catta*), commonly seen in zoological gardens, is conspicuous for its blackish tail ringed with white. The ruffed lemur (*L. variegatus*) is larger, sometimes as large as a mastiff terrier; it has a ruff of long hairs and a variegated coat ranging between dull white and black or sometimes reddish. Other species of the Lemuridae include the black lemur (*L. macaco*), brown lemur (*L. fulvus*), and the mongoose lemur (*L. mongoz*). Much smaller are the dwarf lemurs (*Cheirogaleus*) and mouse lemurs (*Microcebus*); these attractive little creatures are entirely nocturnal. They become inactive and estivate during the dry season, curling up in a nest of leaves and sustaining themselves on fat resources accumulated mainly in the base of the tail. They have large eyes and an abbreviated muzzle.

The Indriidae include the largest of the living lemurs; they are distinguished from the Lemuridae by the loss of the lower canine and one of the upper and lower premolars, their dental formula thus being $\frac{2.1.2.3}{2.0.2.3}$. The hind limbs are long, permitting the animals to leap easily from branch to branch. The tail in some species is rather short, and the external ear tends to be concealed in the long silky hair on the side of the head. In general the Indriidae are thoroughly arboreal. They are exclusively vegetarian, living on the leaves and buds of their native trees; for this reason they are difficult to maintain in captivity and are infrequently seen in zoological gardens.

A remarkable exception to the usual morphology of the Madagascan lemurs is found in the aye-aye (*Daubentonia*), the sole surviving genus of the superfamily Daubentonioidea. This extraordinary creature possesses large rodentlike incisor teeth, while the canines are absent and the postcanine grinding teeth are grossly reduced. It has large ears, a long bushy tail, and well-developed claws on all the digits except the big toe (which is freely opposable and has a flattened nail, as in Primates generally). The

third digit of the hand is curiously elongated and attenuated and is used to extract the animals' principal food, the larvae of woodboring beetles, from crevices in the bark of trees. The brain of the aye-aye is also unusual, differing from all other modern lemurs in the convolutional pattern of the cerebral cortex and in the relatively large size of the olfactory bulbs. Indeed, in their general configuration, the cerebral hemispheres show a surprising resemblance to those of carnivores of the same body size. In one respect, however, the brain does conform with that of prosimians generally—in possessing a distinctive fissure known as the calcarine sulcus, which extends longitudinally through the medial aspect of the visual cortex. The alimentary tract shows the characteristic lemurine loop in the large intestine. Because of its unusual characters the aye-aye has been a subject of considerable discussion, some of the early 19th-century naturalists actually supposing it to be a rodent. It is now classified as a very aberrant lemur, but it is likely that it diverged from the other Lemuriformes at a very early time. For example, in its dentition it has followed a trend quite opposite to that of lemuriform evolution in general. In the Lemuroidea the upper incisors are reduced (together with a corresponding reduction in the premaxillary bone of the upper jaw) and the lower incisors and canines have become procumbent and styliform to form a dental comb; in the aye-aye both the upper and lower incisors are much hypertrophied and there is no dental comb. Unfortunately the fossil evidence for the evolution of the aye-aye is practically unknown, the only available specimen being the Pleistocene form from Madagascar, which was in all respects like the modern genus except for its larger size. Because of its aberrant dental morphology, it has been suggested that *Daubentonia* represents the terminal product of a divergent line of lemuroid evolution that possibly originated at the beginning of the Tertiary Period from a group of an extinct family, the Apatemyidae. The Apatemyidae were also characterized by enlarged first incisor teeth together with a numerical reduction and retrograde changes affecting the rest of the dentition. This conjecture, however, receives no strong support from the fossil record, and there are reasonable arguments against it.

Lorisiformes.—The lorisiform lemurs constitute a single family, Lorisidae, which is subdivided into two subfamilies, Lorisinae and Galaginae. Of the former, two genera, *Loris* and *Nycticebus*, are found in southern Asia and two others, *Perodicticus* and *Arctocebus*, in tropical Africa. They are all arboreal creatures, moving with a slow, delicate crawl. The muzzle is short; the eyes are very large in correlation with their strictly nocturnal habits; and the tail is either reduced in size or absent. *Nycticebus* is the slow loris, and *Loris*, because of its slender elongated limbs, the slender loris. The various species of *Perodicticus* and *Arctocebus* are called pottos and angwantibos. The subfamily Galaginae comprises one genus, *Galago*, the bush baby, which inhabits the equatorial forests of Africa. Bush babies are active creatures with considerably elongated hind limbs used in leaping from branch to branch.

The Lorisiformes differ from the Lemuriformes in certain features of the skull, particularly in the auditory region, for the tympanic ring is not enclosed within a bony bulla but is applied to its outer surface, sometimes being extended into a short tubular channellike auditory meatus. It has commonly been assumed that the intrabullar tympanic ring of the Lemuriformes is a specialized and divergent feature, but it has recently been argued that it is really a primitive feature characteristic of the basal Primates. For one thing, the simple annular form of the tympanic bone is an embryonic character found in all the Primates in the early

(Left) Slow loris (*Nycticebus coucang*), found in southeastern Asia and known for its deliberate and unhurried pace. (Right) Bush baby (*Galago*), a small arboreal lemur inhabiting the equatorial forests of Africa

KINNE—PHOTO RESEARCHERS

stages of fetal development. For another, its intrabullar position is characteristic of the most primitive extant Primates, the tree shrews, and is also present in some of the Early Eocene Primates whose skulls have been preserved.

Thus the Lorisiformes appear to represent a more advanced stage of development than the Lemuriformes. Evidence of the brain supports this conclusion, for in some lorisiform types the convolutional pattern of the cerebral cortex resembles closely that of the monkeys.

3. Tarsiers.—The infraorder Tarsiiformes is represented today by a single genus, *Tarsius*, which inhabits the tropical forests of Borneo, the Philippines, Celebes, and Sumatra, and also some of the lesser islands of the Malay Archipelago. It is a small nocturnal creature about the size of a marmoset, with a somewhat bizarre appearance because of its disproportionately large eyes; prominent, mobile ears; long tail (naked except for a terminal tuft of hair); expanded disc-shaped pads on the terminal digits of the hands and feet; and elongation of the hind limbs for saltatory, or leaping, functions.

Of the modern tarsiers, three different species, each comprising a number of subspecies, are usually recognized, though some authorities have doubted whether these distinctions are really valid. In its general anatomical character the modern tarsier occupies a position somewhat intermediate between the lorisiform lemurs and the New World monkeys. At the same time it presents a remarkable mixture of features: (1) primitive; (2) lemuroid; (3) specialized; and (4) advanced, or monkeylike.

1. Of the primitive characters, those of the dentition are perhaps the most obvious. The dental formula is $\frac{2.1.3.3}{1.1.3.3}$. The incisor teeth are implanted vertically in the upper jaw, and are only slightly procumbent in the lower jaw. The premolars are very simply constructed, being predominantly unicuspid. The molars preserve a generalized pattern, the upper teeth being tritubercular, and the lower having three main cusps in the anterior half and a hollowed-out basin (the talonid basin) in the posterior half. The digits of the hand and the carpal bones of the wrist also preserve a primitive arrangement. The cerebral hemispheres are practically smooth except for a deep calcarine sulcus on the medial aspect of the visual cortex, and the commissure linking the hemispheres across the midline (*corpus callosum*) is short and attenuated, as it is in some insectivores. The cerebellum is extremely simple in its convolutional pattern. The alimentary tract is remarkably generalized, lacking the elaborate colonic loop characteristic of the lemurs. The uterus is bicornuate.

2. The lemuroid features include a sublingua on the under surface of the tongue (but not serrated as it is in modern lemurs); an elongation of the fourth digit of the foot; an opposable big toe; an elongation of the navicular and calcaneal bones of the ankle similar to, but surpassing, that of the bush babies; claws on two of the pedal digits; an expansion of the orbital cavity of the skull; certain details in the pattern of cells of the lower visual centres of the brain; and the conformation of the ossicles of the middle ear.

3. The specialized features of *Tarsius* are the inordinate size of the eyes, which has led to a marked compression of the nasal cavities; the unusually mobile and rather batlike ears; the discoid pads on all the digits, which enhance their grasping power; the excessively elongated calcaneal and navicular bones, which provide leverage for leaping considerable distances; the partial fusion of the tibia and fibula; the mobility of the joints between the skull and the neck vertebrae, which allows the head to be turned through 180°, so that it can face directly backward; and the curious naked tail, sometimes with papillary ridges on its ventral surface, which can be pressed firmly against a vertical branch as a sort of strut to help support the animal when clinging.

4. The advanced, or monkeylike, characters of *Tarsius* include a restriction and simplification of the nasal cavity associated with retrogressive changes in the olfactory parts of the brain; the formation of a well-developed *macula lutea* in the retina, very similar in structure to that of the marmosets; the rounded braincase; the basal position of the *foramen magnum;* the separation

of the orbital cavity from the temporal fossa of the skull by a bony partition (which, however, is incomplete); the formation of a tubular auditory meatus; the extensive area and intrinsic elaboration of the visual cortex; the absence of a naked rhinarium; the mobility of the lips, which permits changes in facial expression; the advanced development of the placenta; and some features of the external genitalia.

Considering this mixed assemblage of anatomical characters, it is not surprising that in the past authorities have expressed contradictory views on the taxonomic position of *Tarsius* among the Primates. Those zoologists who have been most impressed with its monkeylike characters have separated the tarsioids from the lemurs and included them with the higher Primates in a common group, the Haplorhini. Those who have taken fuller account of the lemuroid features of the early fossil tarsiers believe that the line of distinction is not sufficiently abrupt to justify such a taxonomic separation from the lemurs. In the now widely accepted scheme of classification the Tarsiiformes are included with the lemurs and tree shrews in a common suborder, Prosimii, while their distinctive features are recognized by granting them a separate infraordinal status. This classification reverts to the opinion expressed many years ago (1846) by H. Burmeister in his classic monograph on *Tarsius*, in which he postulated that the modern tarsier is probably more closely related to the lemurs than to the higher Primates. In fact, in respect of their dental characters, it is by no means easy to distinguish some of the Eocene tarsioids from the Eocene lemurs (*e.g.*, the genus *Caenopithecus*). It seems probable, therefore, that they originated from a common group of Paleocene prosimians and then became rather rapidly diversified.

The paleontological evidence also demonstrates that some of the extreme tarsioid specializations evolved very early in Tertiary times, and hence it has been surmised that at least some of the simian characters of the modern tarsier may be the result of evolutionary parallelism.

B. Higher Primates (Anthropoidea): Monkeys

The monkeys comprise two main taxonomic groups, the New World or platyrrhine monkeys (superfamily Ceboidea) and the Old World or catarrhine monkeys (superfamily Cercopithecoidea). The terms "platyrrhine" and "catarrhine" refer to the disposition of the nostrils, which in the former case are placed rather wide apart and in the latter close together; this distinction, however, is not always very clear. In spite of their general resemblances, the two groups exhibit certain contrasting features that suggest an early divergence in their evolution. For example, the auditory region of the skull is differently constructed: in the platyrrhines there is a conspicuous swollen auditory bulla with the tympanic bone forming a simple ring applied to its outer surface; in the catarrhines the inflated bulla has disappeared and the tympanic element is produced into an elongated auditory meatus. The pat-

GOLDEN LION MARMOSET (LEONTIDEUS ROSALIA)

tern of the union of skull bones is also different. The more apparent features that distinguish the New World monkeys from the Old World monkeys are: their tendency to develop specialized prehensile tails; their lack of ischial callosities; and their possessing three, instead of two, premolar teeth.

1. New World Monkeys (Platyrrhines).—The ceboid monkeys are confined to South and Central America, reaching as far north as southern Mexico. The group includes two families: Callithricidae (or Hapalidae), the marmosets generally, including the tamarins; and Cebidae, the larger platyrrhines, comprising the subfamilies Cebinae (capuchins and squirrel monkeys), Alouattinae (howlers), Callicebinae (titis), Aotinae (douroucoulis), Pitheciinae (sakis and uakaris), Atelinae (spider monkeys and woolly monkeys).

The Callithricidae contain the smallest and in some respects the most primitive of the extant monkeys, the marmosets; the closely related tamarins include monkeys with long canine teeth. Some authorities have recognized as many as nine different genera of the family.

The Cebidae are all thoroughly arboreal, and many of them have prehensile tails, which they use in hanging or swinging from the branches of trees or even for grasping objects such as food. The thumb is commonly reduced in size and only slightly opposable. Like all monkeys, they are distinguished from the lower Primates by certain features of the skull, in particular the complete separation of the orbital cavity from the temporal fossa by a bony wall. In some genera they have been observed to have a sexual cycle accompanied by a slight menstrual flow.

E. A. BAUMBACH

IMPERIAL TAMARIN (SAGUINUS IMPERATOR)

Marmosets and Tamarins.—All retain sharp, curved claws on all the digits except the big toe, which bears a flattened nail; the thumb is not opposable; and the brain, though relatively large, is covered by a cerebral cortex almost devoid of convolutions. Except for one genus, *Callimico,* marmosets show a specialized loss of the last molar teeth, their dental formula thus being $\frac{2.1.3.2}{2.1.3.2}$, but even in *Callimico,* and indeed in the Cebidae (*see* below), the last molar tooth is much reduced in size and may be absent altogether as an individual variation. The molar teeth preserve a primitive tritubercular pattern.

Marmosets normally give birth to twins, or sometimes triplets; in all other monkeys and higher Primates multiple births occur only occasionally. So far as is known, they have no restricted breeding season and no regular menstrual cycle. They are largely insectivorous but also feed on fruit, seeds, leaves, and shoots. One of the commonest genera, *Callithrix* (or *Hapale*), is characterized by large ears associated with conspicuous tufts of whitish hair and by a tail ringed with black and gray hair.

The tamarins (*Saguinus*) are distinguished by the length of their canine teeth and by the absence of ear tufts. One of them, the lion marmoset, is particularly attractive because of the mane of long orange-coloured fur around the face. In captivity marmosets are delicate and nervous creatures, requiring for their well-being a constant temperature of about 75° F (about 24° C). The genus *Callimico,* a small and rather rare monkey, with a long tail, has been much discussed by taxonomists. As with other marmosets, its digits are furnished with claws, but the possession of a third molar tooth and certain resemblances of the skull to that of the squirrel monkey led to the view that it should be placed with the Cebidae. However, primatologists today regard it as more closely allied to the tamarins, though its unusual features have

HERMES FROM NATIONAL AUDUBON SOCIETY

WHITE-FRONTED CAPUCHIN MONKEY (CEBUS CAPUCINUS)

persuaded some to assign it to a distinct subfamily of the Callithricidae, the Callimiconinae.

Capuchins and Squirrel Monkeys.—The subfamily Cebinae comprises the capuchins (*Cebus*) and the squirrel monkeys (*Saimiri*). The small capuchin monkeys, so named because the peak of hair on the top of the head recalls the peaked hood of Capuchin monks, make attractive and lively pets, and are said to display considerable intelligence. The squirrel monkeys (*Saimiri*) are small creatures characterized by an exceptional elongation of the occipital region of the skull and by a brain which, relatively speaking, appears unusually large. Their long tail is not prehensile.

Howlers and Titis.—The Alouattinae comprise the howler monkeys (*Alouatta*), which have an exaggerated hyoid bone distended in the form of a hollow shell, a condition that greatly amplifies the sound emitted. The vertical ramus of the lower jaw is expanded to cover the enlarged hyoid. The howlers are large animals that range through the forest in bands of a dozen or more; their roaring can be heard for several miles. The males have a conspicuous beard. The long tail is exceptionally prehensile, its tip being provided with a naked surface of skin covered with papillary ridges to give a firm grip.

The Aotinae comprise one diurnal or crepuscular genus, *Callicebus,* the titi (tee-tee) monkeys, small slender creatures with a long bushy tail only moderately prehensile. Titis, mainly found in the forests of Brazil, have been regarded by some as even more primitive than the marmosets. Their dentition certainly presents very generalized characters, the canines being but slightly projecting and the premolar teeth preserving a very simple unicuspid form.

Douroucoulis and Sakis.—The Aotinae also include the night monkeys of Central and South America, from Nicaragua to Paraguay, which are colloquially known as douroucoulis. Because of their exclusively nocturnal habits, unique among monkeys, and because they are not easily kept in captivity, little is known of their behaviour. They possess large eyes with a retina of a nocturnal type, which in its sensory receptors lacks cones and is entirely constructed of rods. The ears are diminutive and partly hidden beneath the thick fur. Because of the superficially

HERMES FROM NATIONAL AUDUBON SOCIETY

SQUIRREL MONKEY (SAIMIRI SCIUREA)

RED UAKARIS, OF THE GENUS CACAJAO, NATIVE TO THE FORESTS OF THE AMAZON

apparent absence of external ears these monkeys have been given the generic name of *Aotus.* A white patch of fur above the eyes, together with the rounded face, gives them a somewhat owllike appearance so that they are also referred to as owl monkeys. The tail is long but not prehensile, and the thumb is quite well developed. They are less vegetarian in their diet than many platyrrhine monkeys, feeding more on insects, eggs, and small birds. Although they possess a retina composed purely of rods, it shows a specialized central spot, the *macula lutea,* and in this respect they parallel the condition in *Tarsius* (*see* above). It is difficult to explain the presence of a macula in these two Primates, for it is assumed to be a device in the higher Primates for accentuating the visual discriminatory functions served by cones. In both cases the macula may perhaps be a vestigial structure that has persisted from evolutionary predecessors of diurnal habits who had a cone retina and the normal type of macula. Certainly this seems the most probable explanation of the macula in *Aotus,* whose cone-free retina is unique among the Anthropoidea and is undoubtedly to be regarded as a secondary adaptation. It now seems clear that the macular formation in the retina first appeared at the tarsioid level of primate evolution, and is thus phylogenetically much more ancient than has been commonly supposed.

The sakis (Pitheciinae) have markedly procumbent lower incisors, widely placed nostrils, a bushy but nonprehensile tail, and a comparatively well-developed thumb. The different genera of this subfamily show considerable variation in coat colour, and in most of them the long hair on the side of the head forms rather conspicuous whiskers.

Spider Monkeys and Woolly Monkeys.—The subfamily Atelinae includes the spider monkeys (*Ateles*), which are the arboreal acrobats par excellence of the New World monkeys. Their long forelimbs are used for swinging from bough to bough—a method of locomotion termed brachiation. While the fingers are long and serve as powerful hooks for suspension from branches, the thumb is small and vestigial. The long tail is marvelously prehensile, and the naked skin on the ventral surface of its tip is employed as a highly sensitive tactile organ. Furthermore, the motor region of the cerebral cortex

has been shown by experimental studies to include an unusually large area for controlling the complex prehensile functions of the tail. The spider monkeys are of particular interest to comparative anatomists because in many details of their limb structure and body proportions they parallel to some degree the gibbons of the Old World (*see* below) which have developed arboreal activities of a similar kind. The resemblance is particularly noticeable in the case of some of the Miocene gibbons, which had not fully achieved the more extreme specializations of the modern gibbons.

Closely allied to *Ateles,* and included in the same subfamily, are the genera *Lagothrix* and *Brachyteles.* *Lagothrix* includes the woolly monkeys, which have a closely set pelage of soft fur and a moderately well-developed thumb. *Brachyteles,* in its general appearance and anatomical structure, represents an intermediate type that links *Ateles* with *Lagothrix.*

2. Old World Monkeys (Catarrhines).—The catarrhine or Old World monkeys constitute the superfamily Cercopithecoidea, which consists of only one family, the Cercopithecidae. The family is further subdivided into two subfamilies, the Cercopithecinae and the Colobinae.

The cercopithecoid monkeys are superficially similar to some of the larger ceboid monkeys, but they are more specialized in certain respects and more advanced in others. The specialized features are exemplified by the development of ischial callosities; by the presence either of cheek pouches or an elaborately constructed stomach; and by the bilophodont character of the dentition (the anterior and posterior paired cusps of bilophodont molars are united by strong transverse crests). The first and second lower molars commonly lack the fifth cusp, called the hypoconulid, while the last molar is usually extended back to form a conspicuous heel, called the talonid. The advanced features are the expansion of the cerebral cortex; the greater opposability of the thumb (in many genera); the more flattened nails on the digits; the more efficient type of placentation; and the regular menstrual rhythm. None of the catarrhines has a prehensile tail and some are not predominantly arboreal in their habits. The similarities between these progressive characters and certain features of the anthropoid apes led some past authorities to place the catarrhines and apes in a common group, a classification that seemed further justified by the fact that certain serological reactions of the blood suggest fairly close affinities. On the other hand, as will be seen, there are marked structural contrasts that most primatologists now consider sufficiently significant to require a taxonomic separation of the catarrhines and the apes. The Old World monkeys have a wide geographical and climatic distribu-

(Left) Spider monkey (*Ateles geoffroyi*), a lanky and agile acrobat. (Right) Woolly monkey (*Lagothrix lagotricha*), distinguished by its dense, close-cropped fur and powerfully prehensile tail

(LEFT) KINNE—PHOTO RESEARCHERS, (RIGHT) HOLTON—PHOTO RESEARCHERS

(LEFT) GUENON (CERCOPITHECUS), TYPICAL OF AFRICAN ARBOREAL MONKEYS. (RIGHT) OLIVE BABOON (PAPIO ANUBIS), FOUND IN WEST, CENTRAL AND EASTERN AFRICA

tion, for while most genera inhabit the tropical regions of Africa and Asia, some reach as far north as Tibet, China, Japan, and the Himalayan Mountains, and (in the case of the baboons) as far south as South Africa. In Pliocene and Pleistocene times some also spread into central and southern Europe.

The subfamily Cercopithecinae are characterized by the consistent presence of cheek pouches for temporary food storage and by well-developed thumbs. They are less arboreal than the Colobinae. The tail varies considerably in its length and may be absent altogether. The stomach is of simple construction.

Macaques.—The various species of the genus *Macaca* (macaque monkeys) are perhaps the most adaptable of the cercopithecines and, although very able climbers, some have become almost entirely terrestrial. They range over southeast Asia from China and Japan to India, also extending into North Africa, where they are found in Algeria and Morocco. A small colony of the North African species, which is sometimes known as the Barbary ape, is still maintained on the Rock of Gibraltar, being fed and cared for by the local populace. Macaques are hardy animals and flourish in captivity. They are mostly omnivorous; one species (*M. irus*), common in Malaya, is colloquially termed the "crab-eating macaque" because it frequents coasts and estuaries, feeding on crustaceans and mollusks that it gathers at low tide. The most well-known macaques are the rhesus monkeys (*M. mulatta*), invaluable subjects in biological and medical research; these monkeys were used in solving the puzzle of blood groups in man and are now being used, among other purposes, in solving some of the problems involved in manned space flights.

Baboons and Mandrills.—The true baboons (*Papio* species) are terrestrial creatures inhabiting open rocky country. They reach a formidable size and have a large projecting muzzle with terminally placed nostrils and (in the males) long ferocious-looking canine teeth. Baboons live in well-established communities and, while predominantly vegetarian, they occasionally attack and eat small mammals. The sacred baboon (*P. hamadryas*) is the species represented in ancient Egyptian sculptures; today it is found in the Sudan, Somaliland, and southwestern Arabia. The males are distinguished by their long mane of hair. The gelada baboon (*Theropithecus*), which inhabits the mountains of Ethiopia, is very baboonlike in general appearance yet differs from the

true baboons in that the nostrils are set back from the end of the muzzle and the latter is not so elongated and pointed. In certain features it shows affinities with the macaques. The mandrills of west Africa resemble the baboons in their body proportions except that they possess only a short and almost rudimentary tail. They are distinguished by their large head and swollen muzzle, the latter marked by conspicuous blue ridges that contrast with the vivid scarlet skin of the nostrils. This remarkable coloration, combined with a white pointed "beard" and long and powerful canines, gives to the animal a particularly striking appearance. The genus *Cynopithecus* inhabits the Celebes and adjacent islands. Although somewhat similar in general structure to the baboons, it is even more macaquelike than *Theropithecus;* its taxonomic affinities still remain rather obscure.

Mangabeys and Guenons.—The mangabey monkeys (*Cercocebus*) are restricted to the tropical forests of Africa. They are more arboreal than the macaques, and, among other features, have long tails and, in most species, conspicuous white upper eyelids. The cercopitheque monkeys (*Cercopithecus*), also called guenons, are the most abundant African types; more than 20 different species are now recognized. Their distribution covers most of the tropical areas of the continent south of the Sahara. They are usually rather small and lightly built animals of arboreal habitat, living mainly on fruit, leaves, and insects. The thumb is somewhat abbreviated, and the tail is always very long. The last molar teeth show some evidence of degenerative changes, and, in the lower dentition, the cusps are reduced to four, or sometimes three. Many of the cercopitheques are conspicuous for their attractive colouring, the coats varying in different species from a gray-black to a sombre green or a ruddy colour, and often contrasted with a white band on the forehead, a white patch on the nose, or ruffs of a white or yellowish colour. Closely related to the genus *Cercopithecus* is *Erythrocebus*, popularly known as Patas monkeys and characterized by their brick–red coloration. They comprise a single species with four subspecies and are widely distributed over the central region of Africa, extending as far north as the Sudan. The main interest of these monkeys is that they are only slightly arboreal in their habits, and are commonly found in open or sparsely wooded country of the savanna type. They move rapidly on the ground. The thumb and big toe are less opposable than in some of the more arboreal cercopitheques.

(LEFT) ROOT–GRZIMEK, FRANKFURT (M)—PUBLIX, (RIGHT) VAN NOSTRAND —PHOTO RESEARCHERS

(Left) Guereza (*Colobus abyssinicus*), African representative of the Colobinae. (Right) Proboscis monkeys (*Nasalis larvatus*), found only in Borneo, are characterized by the long, fleshy nose (upturned and shorter in the females shown here)

GIBBON (HYLOBATES MOLOCH), ONE OF THE MORE AGILE OF ANTHROPOID APES, OF JAVA AND BORNEO

Of all these characters, the expansion of the brain is perhaps the most striking: for example, the brain of the large apes looks like a miniature human brain, and has the same basic pattern of convolutions and a very similar intrinsic structure of the cerebral cortex. Such differences as do exist are quantitative rather than qualitative, and even the quantitative ones dwindle when the endocranial cast of a gorilla is compared with that of extinct early hominids. These casts, which reproduce the cavity of the braincase, indicate the size and proportion of the brain itself because the latter fits the cranial cavity closely. In the Early Pleistocene hominid *Australopithecus*, the brain size approximated closely that of a large gorilla, though it was probably larger in relation to body size. In certain minor characters of the skull and limb skeleton *Australopithecus* is closer to the apes than to modern man, so that the structural contrasts between man and apes become partly obscured when these fossil types are compared. On such evidence as this, taxonomists now generally agree that the Pongidae and Hominidae represent divergent branches of a common ancestral stock, a conclusion reflected in the classification which includes the two families in a single superfamily, Hominoidea. The final justification for this scheme lies in the serological reactions of the blood, which clearly demonstrate that there is a' closer affinity between these two groups than between either of them and the catarrhine monkeys.

Langurs and Allies.—The subfamily Colobinae is composed of the langurs, the proboscis monkey, and the guerezas. They are distinguished by the absence of cheek pouches and the development of a large and elaborately sacculated stomach in association with a strictly vegetarian diet. They are chiefly arboreal, feed largely on leaves and the young shoots of certain plants, and in captivity are much more delicate animals than the Cercopithecinae. The langurs (*Presbytis* and *Rhinopithecus*) range over Malaya, India, and Ceylon, extending up to China and into Kashmir and the southern slopes of the Himalayas. They are lightly built animals with abbreviated muzzles and long slender tails. One of the Himalayan langurs, from its footprints in the snow, may be responsible for the legend of the "Abominable Snowman." The genus *Rhinopithecus* (snub-nosed monkey), characterized by a short projecting nose, inhabits the high forests in the mountains of Tibet and northwest China. Closely related to the true langurs is *Nasalis,* the proboscis monkey, which is found only in Borneo. It is remarkable for its long, fleshy proboscis, which is much larger in the male and gives the animal a most grotesque appearance; in the female the shorter nose is turned up. The functional significance of the proboscis is unknown, but its marked development in the male indicates that it is primarily a sexual character.

The guereza monkeys (*Colobus*) are the only African representatives of the Colobinae; they comprise five or six species and many subspecies. Their arboreal specializations are accompanied by a shortness of the thumb, which may be little more than a rudimentary tubercle or even be absent altogether. Many of the guerezas have a mantle of long silky fur, parti-coloured in black and white. The pelts are prized adornments among local populations, and at one time were exported in large numbers to Europe. (It has been estimated that, toward the end of the last century, as many as 200,000 of these beautiful creatures were being slaughtered annually for commercial purposes; fortunately, the demand for skins no longer exists to any significant degree.)

C. MANLIKE PRIMATES (HOMINOIDEA): APES AND MAN

Extant anthropoid apes approximate much more closely in their anatomical structure to the Hominidae than do the monkeys. They resemble man in the relative size and configuration of the brain; in many details of the skull, dentition, and postcranial skeleton; in the tendency to adopt a semierect, or orthograde, posture (correlated with the shape of the thorax, the orientation of the shoulder girdle, the mode of attachment of the abdominal viscera, and other features); in the possession of a vermiform appendix; in the absence of a tail; and in the more efficient processes by which the embryo is nourished in the uterus.

The modern anthropoid apes constitute the family Pongidae. They are arboreal in varying degree and, in association with their habit of swinging arm over arm among the branches, have developed structural modifications such as the relative lengthening of the forelimb (with atrophy of the thumb) and a relative shortening of the hind limb. The orangutan and gibbon are the most exclusively arboreal and the most extreme brachiators, and in them, therefore, these specializations are most marked.

The subfamily Hylobatinae includes the gibbons; the Ponginae includes the orangutan, chimpanzee, and gorilla. Some taxonomists place the gibbons in a separate family of the anthropoid apes, Hylobatidae, but such a classification has not found complete acceptance.

1. Gibbon.—The Hylobatinae comprise two genera, *Hylobates* and *Symphalangus*. Today gibbons inhabit southeastern Asia from Assam and Formosa to Java, Sumatra, and Borneo. These creatures of slender build and great agility move rapidly through the treetops, swinging along among the higher branches. But, in spite of their skill in arboreal acrobatics, gibbons suffer severe injuries from falls, as is indicated by the frequency of healed fractures observed in gibbons found in the wild. They live in monogamous family groups of up to six individuals.

In some respects gibbons are more like the catarrhine monkeys

Chimpanzee (*Pan troglodytes*), one of the smaller manlike apes inhabiting equatorial Africa

YOUNG ORANGUTAN (PONGO PYGMAEUS) **FOUND IN BORNEO AND SUMATRA**

than are the larger anthropoid apes; for example, they have well-developed ischial callosities and the convolutional pattern of the brain is relatively simple. But in all fundamental characters, such as the cusp pattern of the molar teeth, the proportions of the digits, the presence of a free vermiform appendix, the disposition of the thoracic and abdominal viscera, the absence of a tail, and the orthograde posture of the trunk, they are pongids. In their range of vocalization (they are the most vocal of the anthropoid apes) and in their aptitude for standing and walking on the ground on two feet, they offer points of particular interest in relation to the ultimate origin of the Hominidae.

2. Orangutan.—The orangutan (*Pongo pygmaeus*) is now confined to the forests of Borneo and Sumatra, but in Pleistocene times it extended its range as far north as China. As mentioned above, it is highly specialized for arboreal life, and only rarely descends to the ground. It may reach a height of four to five feet or more and, unlike the active and agile gibbons, usually swings slowly and deliberately from branch to branch. Orangs are fruit eaters, being particularly fond of the durian. They con-

struct sleeping platforms of twigs among the higher branches of the trees.

They have long reddish hair, and are characterized by the pronounced laryngeal sacs in the neck and (in large males) by flanges of dense connective tissue over the cheek region. Orangs contrast with the large African apes in the rounded contour of the cranium and in the absence of projecting brow ridges, but in adult males the cranium is frequently surmounted by a prominent sagittal crest to which are attached the large temporal muscles.

3. Chimpanzee.—Chimpanzees are about the same size as the orang, but they are less specialized. Active climbers, they spend their life in forests and deciduous woodland. They often come to the ground and then usually proceed on all fours, taking their weight on the soles of the feet and the bent knuckles of the fingers. On occasion they stand upright but do not normally walk in this posture. The larger chimpanzees (*Pan troglodytes*) inhabit the forests of equatorial Africa. Over a limited range south of the Congo River is an interesting pygmy chimpanzee (*P. paniscus*). Its teeth are small and delicately constructed, and the skull, preserving infantile proportions, more closely resembles that of hominids than do those of the larger chimpanzees. Chimpanzees move about in small troops made up of a single family, or a group of families, and like the orang they construct crude nests of branches, usually high up in the trees, where they rest during the night. They do well in captivity and can be trained to undertake many complicated tasks, an aptitude that indicates a considerable intelligence. Because of this responsiveness, chimpanzees have made excellent subjects for experimental studies by comparative psychologists.

4. Gorilla.—The gorilla is the largest of the anthropoid apes and shows a marked sexual dimorphism. In adult males the cranium is surmounted by a prominent sagittal crest which, in the living animal, gives a false appearance of a high vaulted skull, while the brow ridges are strongly developed and the canine teeth long and powerful. Males may reach a height, in a vertical position, of over five feet and a weight of 450–600 lb. The females are smaller, with much less exaggerated canine teeth, and only rarely show a sagittal crest on the skull. Like the other apes, gorillas are characterized by the proportionately great length of the arms and the relative shortness of the thumb. However, they are only slightly arboreal in their habits, for they spend much of their daily life wandering about in the undergrowth of the jungle. On the ground they normally adopt a quadrupedal gait, sometimes described as an "obliquely quadrupedal" gait, because of the inordinate length of their powerful arms. Only incidentally, par-

GORILLAS, THE LARGEST OF THE MANLIKE APES
(Left) Mountain gorilla from the mountainous eastern region of the Congo. (Right) A group of immature lowland gorillas inhabiting the rain forests of western Africa

ticularly in attack or defense, do they momentarily rear themselves into an erect posture. The limb proportions indicate that gorillas were originally arboreal brachiating apes which, because of their increasing size, have taken secondarily to a terrestrial habitat, limiting their arboreal activities to the large lower branches of the trees.

Like chimpanzees, gorillas inhabit equatorial Africa but cover a more restricted area. They live in groups of up to 20 or more individuals made up of a few families, and, contrary to travelers' stories which were at one time commonly accepted, they are not aggressive by nature. Indeed, in the wild they appear to be rather shy and docile creatures and are almost entirely vegetarian. The modern gorillas comprise a single species, *Gorilla gorilla,* with two subspecies, the forest (lowland) gorilla, which is commoner, and the mountain gorilla. Some authorities separate the two forms as distinct species, *G. beringei* being set aside for the mountain gorilla. The latter is found in the wooded mountainous country of the eastern Congo. It is said to be more completely adapted for terrestrial life than the forest gorilla, the forelimbs being less elongated, the great toe not so strongly abducted and opposable, and the other toes relatively shorter.

5. Man.—The latest product of the primate evolutionary sequence is the family Hominidae, which includes modern man (*Homo sapiens*) and his extinct precursors. The origin and evolution of the Hominidae, and the physical anthropology of the modern races of mankind, are fully discussed in other articles. However, it is appropriate here to refer briefly to the earliest-known hominids. These form a subfamily called Australopithecinae, and their remains have been found in South Africa and east Africa. Their outstanding characters are a small cranial capacity, which hardly reaches a greater size than that of a large male gorilla; massive jaws; a dentition that conforms in its morphological details to that of *Homo;* and bones of the pelvis and limbs constructed basically on the hominid plan. The lower limbs clearly demonstrate that the australopithecines were bipedal creatures whose erect posture had not reached the degree of perfection found in modern man. The occipital region and the base of the skull also display fundamental hominid characters. The final proof that the Australopithecinae come within the category of the Hominidae has been supplied by the strong circumstantial evidence that they were capable of fabricating crude stone implements. Such implements were first discovered in stalagmitic deposits in South Africa, which also contain australopithecine remains (but no indubitable remains of any more advanced type of hominid). Later, a remarkably complete australopithecine skull was found at Olduvai, in Tanzania, embedded in a layer containing not only stone implements of the Oldowan culture but also fragments that had evidently been struck off in the course of the manufacture of those tools.

The australopithecines date from the Lower Pleistocene, and, since there is evidence that by that time they were already diversified into different varieties or species, it may be inferred that they existed as a group at a still earlier date, at least by the Upper Pliocene. However, there still remains a serious gap in the fossil record between the generalized Miocene and Pliocene apes on the one hand and the earliest hominids on the other. So far as the later history of hominid evolution is concerned, the fossil record is reasonably complete. There is now available an almost continuous graded sequence linking the Australopithecinae through *Pithecanthropus,* or *Homo erectus* (of Middle Pleistocene date), to the more generalized "Neanderthaloids," and finally to *Homo sapiens.*

See further AUSTRALOPITHECINE; NEANDERTHAL MAN; MAN, EVOLUTION OF; RACES OF MANKIND; ANTHROPOLOGY, especially the section *Physical Anthropology.*

III. ORIGIN AND RELATIONSHIPS

During the Paleocene and Eocene ages there existed an exceedingly primitive group of Primates, the Plesiadapidae, which, judging from their morphology, were related to the Eocene lemurs as well as to the tree shrews, thus serving in some measure to link the two groups; it may well be that they were closely related to the ancestors of the tree shrews. The structure of the skull and the postcranial skeleton was of a very generalized type.

In Eocene times an extinct family of Lemuriformes, the Adapidae, extended over Europe and North America. Those found in Europe constitute the subfamily Adapinae, and are mainly represented by the genera *Adapis* and *Pronycticebus.* The former is known from several skulls as well as some limb bones. Its relationship to the modern Lemuriformes is made clear by the construction of the auditory region of the skull and by the orbits' being encircled by a complete bony ring; also the premolars and molars conform to the lemuroid pattern. On the other hand (as might be expected of a lemuriform of some 50,000,000 years ago), *Adapis* shows many exceedingly primitive features. The dental formula is $\frac{2.1.4.3}{2.1.4.3}$, that is, all four premolars of the generalized mammalian dentition were still present. The incisor teeth were not procumbent, the upper and lower canines were stout conical teeth of generalized type, and the dental comb had not yet developed. The *foramen magnum,* instead of slanting somewhat downward as it does in modern lemurs, faced directly backward as in lower mammals generally. The brain, as judged from an endocranial cast of the skull, was far more primitive than that of modern lemurs, being relatively small in size and with large projecting olfactory bulbs. Yet the temporal lobes of the cerebral hemispheres were large and prominent, a characteristic feature of the primate brain that evidently evolved very early in the history of the order. The significance of the expansion of the temporal lobe is probably related to the inference (based on clinical and experimental studies) that this part of the brain constitutes a mechanism for the "storage" of visual memories. Thus, its progressive development in Primates presumably enhanced the ability to profit from experience on the basis of visual cues, an aptitude highly important to arboreal creatures, since they depend far more on their visual than on their olfactory sense for self-preservation. The small size of the brain in *Adapis* is reflected in the small size of the braincase, and this, again, is correlated with a conspicuous development of a sagittal crest which provides attachment for the temporal muscles of the jaw. The Eocene Adapidae of the New World are grouped in a separate subfamily, the Notharctinae, and contain several known genera, including *Pelycodus, Smilodectes,* and *Notharctus. Notharctus* is particularly important in the evidence that it provides from numerous jaws and teeth, and two almost complete skeletons are known. In its cranial characters *Notharctus* is very similar to *Adapis;* it also has the same dental formula, although there is a difference in the construction of the molar teeth. In both the Old World and New World genera, a fourth cusp, the hypocone, has been added to the primitive tritubercular pattern of the upper molars. In *Adapis* this cusp is formed in the more usual manner by an upgrowth from the cingulum encircling the base of the tooth, while in *Notharctus* it apparently arises by fission of one of the other cusps, the protocone. This difference has led to the conjecture that the two genera evolved independently from more primitive lemuroids, a theory that receives some support from various earlier species of *Pelycodus,* from Paleocene and Lower Eocene deposits, which demonstrate the transition from the tritubercular to the quadritubercular molar pattern. One of the interesting features of *Notharctus* is that while the skull, dentition, and cerebral dimensions preserved many primitive features, the limb skeleton approximated closely that of modern lemurs except that it was more robustly constructed. This is an example of "mosaic evolution"; *i.e.,* different anatomical systems developing at different evolutionary rates.

This phenomenon is also seen among other mammal groups where the limbs approached the culmination of their development quite early in evolution. It seems that in such cases the animals first became adapted by their limb structure to one particular type of environment and subsequently perfected their adaptation by further developments of the skull, dentition, and brain.

In Pleistocene times (which began more than 2,000,000 years ago), a variety of unusual types of lemur inhabited Madagascar. One genus, *Megaladapis,* reached considerable size, and in body weight was probably the largest Primate known to have existed. Its skull reached a length of about one foot, the facial skeleton was much elongated, and the limb bones were of massive size. The brain was comparatively small, with poorly developed frontal and occipital lobes and with a projecting olfactory bulb. The molar teeth were large, though constructed on the lemuroid pattern, and the lower incisors and canines were strongly procumbent. So far as can be inferred from the limb bones, the creature may have been preponderantly terrestrial in its habits, but, like the modern gorilla, also capable of moving about among the larger branches of trees. *Megaladapis* may even have survived until comparatively recent times: a French explorer, De Flacourt, who visited Madagascar in 1648, recorded that among the animals peculiar to the island was a large creature the size of a two-year-old calf with a rounded head and humanlike face, both fore- and hind feet like those of a monkey, and ears like those of a man. Other Pleistocene lemurs of Madagascar were astonishingly monkeylike in the facial skeleton, and in the shape and convolutional pattern of the brain. Indeed, the superficially simianlike skull of one genus, *Archaeolemur*, at first led some zoologists to consider it a true monkey. But a detailed study of the skull and teeth revealed specializations peculiar to lemurs. Moreover, it is now known that monkeys came into existence elsewhere at a very much earlier geological date, at least by the Oligocene Period. Still, the development of monkeylike lemurs in Madagascar demonstrates the well-established evolutionary principle that related groups of animals tend to develop similar characters independently (parallel evolution).

There is a serious gap in the fossil record of the lemurs between the Eocene and Miocene periods, but it seems clear that their evolution must have proceeded very rapidly during that time. It is not known when the Lemuriformes reached Madagascar, but the comparative paucity of other mammalian groups on the island no doubt stimulated the wide diversification of the unusual lemuroid types that had evolved there by the Pleistocene Period.

The earliest evidence of lorisiforms comes from Early Miocene deposits (up to about 25,000,000 years old) in east Africa, which have yielded fossilized remains of a genus called *Progalago*, probably a precursor of the modern *Galago*. In the characters of the skull and dentition *Progalago* shows an interesting combination of features, some of which correspond to those of the modern Asiatic lorisiforms. The only trace of a fossil lorisiform in Asia is a single molar tooth from Pliocene deposits (up to about 10,000,000 years old) in India; it was assigned to the genus *Indraloris*.

During the Paleocene and Eocene periods, tarsioids were widely distributed over the world, about 25 genera having been recorded from deposits in Europe, Asia, and North America. Of the European fossils of Eocene date, some quite closely resembled the modern tarsiers, in particular *Pseudoloris*, a genus whose orbital cavities were unusually large and the front part of whose skull is almost identical in its general proportions to modern forms. The dentition also is similar, except that the most anterior tooth of the lower jaw (probably a canine) is greatly enlarged and there is a persistent, but vestigial, first lower premolar. There is some evidence (not conclusive) that in two other genera, *Necrolemur* and *Nannopithex*, the hind-limb skeleton was already specialized to the extent that the tibia and fibula were already fused together in the lower part. This particular character, it should be noted, distinguishes at least some of the tarsioids from all other known Primates, for it does not even occur in the galagos (see *Lorisiformes*, above), whose hind limbs are otherwise specialized in the same way for leaping. A comparison of the modern tarsier with these ancient tarsioids (which existed about 50,000,000 years ago) indicates that the modern tarsier is a "living fossil"—a surviving representative of a group that, in the seclusion of the tropical forests of the Far East, has persisted with little change up to the present day.

The genus *Necrolemur*, grouped together with certain other Eocene types in the subfamily Necrolemurinae, is, in certain features of the skull and dentition, somewhat more generalized than the modern tarsier. However, it displays advanced features that suggest an incipient trend allying it more closely to the higher Primates. For example, the detailed construction of the base of the skull shows certain simian features, as does the extended tubular auditory meatus (even though the tympanic plate is still partly enclosed within the tympanic bulla). Again, the molar teeth have a quadritubercular pattern, which is a conspicuous advance on the primitive tritubercular molars of the modern tarsier.

The fossil tarsioids of North America, so far as they are known, extend from the Paleocene to the early part of the Oligocene. In general they show more aberrant specializations than their Old World relatives, but exceptions are found in a few genera, such as *Omomys* and *Hemiacodon*, in which the dentition remains rather generalized. These types are included in the subfamily Omomyinae, the only subfamily of fossil tarsioids known to have been common to both the Old and New Worlds. A somewhat aberrant genus, *Tetonius*, is known from a fairly complete skull found in Lower Eocene deposits in Wyoming. The base of the skull with its greatly expanded auditory bullae, the large orbital cavities, the globular shape of the braincase, and the much reduced olfactory bulbs are all indicative of tarsioid affinities. The postcanine teeth are also very similar to those of *Tarsius*, but anteriorly the dentition is highly specialized by the loss of at least some of the incisors and the gross hypertrophy (excessive growth) of the lower canine. The last lower premolar is also enlarged and is compressed from the sides. This feature is more exaggerated in another family of American tarsioids, the Carpolestidae, in which the crown of the last premolar forms a sharp, elongated crest with a serrated edge. This may have served to crush or slice into the tough rind of fruit or the hard cuticle of insects. Since the Carpolestidae are known only from fragments of the jaws and teeth, their precise affinities remain uncertain. (Some authorities would even exclude them from the tarsioids.)

Probably the latest known fossil tarsioid is *Macrotarsius*, one of the Omomyinae from the Lower Oligocene of North America. Thereafter the paleontological history of the Tarsiiformes is completely unknown. Evidently most of their early ramifications became extinct without phylogenetic descendants, leaving only the modern genus *Tarsius*. This genus may have migrated to its present habitat from Europe, where, in Eocene times, there existed fossil tarsioids such as *Pseudoloris*, which perhaps included its early ancestors.

The evolutionary origin of the New World monkeys is still obscure. As already noted, they and the Old World monkeys show a degree of structural contrast that suggests the two groups must have diverged quite early in their phylogenetic history. The evidence of paleogeography supports this inference, for it seems that there have probably been no land routes between the Old and New Worlds available to tropical arboreal Primates after Eocene times. Unfortunately, the fossil record of the platyrrhine monkeys is very scanty indeed. Their earliest known representatives are two genera (*Cebupithecia* and *Neosaimiri*) found in Miocene deposits in Colombia, and one genus (*Homunculus*) from the Miocene of Colombia and Patagonia. All are quite similar to some of the modern ceboids. It has been suggested that the platyrrhines are descendants of the New World lemuriform genus *Notharctus*, but, on the basis of the comparative morphology of the different infraorders of the Prosimii, it is more reasonable to suppose that their ancestors were nearer to the Tarsiiformes and that the basal stock from which they have been derived may eventually be found among the diversified groups of extinct tarsioids that populated the American continent up to the early part of the Oligocene.

The origin of the Old World monkeys certainly dates back to the Lower Miocene, for jaws and teeth showing the typical bilophodonty of cercopithecoids have been found in east African deposits of this period. There is also evidence that their precursors were undergoing differentiation even earlier. Two small fragments of jaws from the Eocene of Burma have been regarded by some authorities as the earliest representatives of the Old World monkeys. If this interpretation is correct, one fragment (assigned to the genus *Amphipithecus*) is of particular interest because it still retains a more primitive dental formula, which includes three premolars, though the most anterior of these is rudimentary and apparently in the process of disappearing. Apart from this somewhat equivocal evidence of Eocene monkeys, the earliest indubitable remains of the suborder Anthropoidea have been recovered from Oligocene deposits in Egypt. Of these the most important are small lower jaws with the dentition well preserved, and the frontal part of a skull. This early primate has been given the generic name of *Parapithecus*. The structural details of individual teeth are remarkably primitive, with a formula for the lower dentition of 2.1.3.3, that is to say, the same as the New World monkeys and presumably also characteristic of the ancestral precursors of the present-day Old World monkeys in which one of the premolar teeth has been lost.

Closely allied to *Parapithecus* is the contemporary genus *Apidium* with the same dental formula. Since the molar teeth of these two genera are not bilophodont it has been suggested that they are to be regarded as early representatives of the anthropoid ape sequence of evolution. But it is just as likely that these Oligocene primates belong to the ancestral stock that gave rise to both anthropoid apes and catarrhine monkeys before the bilophodont specialization of the latter had become established. The most ancient of the primates from the Egyptian Oligocene is *Oligopithecus*, probably over 30,000,000 years old; this creature has the same lower dental formula as the modern catarrhine monkeys, 2.1.2.3, but the molar teeth have a primitive structure and show certain resemblances to prosimians. Other fossil primates from the same deposits include *Propliopithecus, Aeolopithecus,* and *Aegyptopithecus*. Of these the first has commonly been regarded as closely related to the ancestors of the gibbons, but some authorities doubt this interpretation and suggest that it may be allied to the ancestors of the Hominidae. On the other hand, *Aeolopithecus,* on the basis of its dental morphology, is regarded as more likely to be an Oligocene representative of the gibbon group of anthropoid apes. *Aegyptopithecus* is of particular importance, for it is represented not only by fossil jaws and teeth but also by an almost complete skull. In general, the skull is similar to that of the Old World monkeys, but the dentition is pongid in character. Moreover, some tail bones found in association with the remains of this extinct primate indicate that, unlike the modern anthropoid apes, it still retained a tail. It has been provisionally suggested that *Aegyptopithecus* may have evolved from a species of *Propliopithecus,* and perhaps gave rise to a group of large apes, *Dryopithecus,* that lived in Miocene and Pliocene times—a group which in turn almost certainly gave rise, by a process of evolutionary diversification, both to the modern pongids and to the earliest Hominidae. The dryopithecine group of apes was fairly widespread in Europe and Asia, extending as far east as China, but over this region, apart from a single humerus and femur, they are only known from jaws and teeth. In the past a number of separate genera of the Dryopithecinae have been described but on such fragmentary evidence that the validity of some of these generic distinctions has now been regarded as very questionable. Of these a type called *Ramapithecus* is of special interest, for the small size of the teeth (particularly the canines), the form of the dental arcade, and the relatively simple construction of the molars suggest that it was not far removed from the transitional phase in which, presumably, the hominid type of dentition was derived from that characteristic of most Pliocene and Miocene apes. Indeed the view has been strongly advocated that *Ramapithecus* is to be regarded as an Early Pliocene hominid rather than an anthropoid ape. The upper jaw of a Pliocene primate found in Kenya has been called *Kenyapithecus,* but its resemblance to *Ramapithecus* is so close that some authorities doubt that it can be distinguished from the latter genus. If further remains of *Ramapithecus* should establish that it is a hominid, this would push back the origin of the human family to between 5,000,000 and 10,000,000 years. Excavations in Miocene deposits of east Africa have demonstrated that many extinct types of apes existed there at that time; they are known not only from jaws and teeth but also from portions of the skull (one almost complete) and a number of limb bones. The smallest of these is a gibbon-like creature to which the generic name *Limnopithecus* has been given, though perhaps it is not distin-

guishable from the previously known genus *Pliopithecus* (*see* below). Its dentition resembles quite closely that of *Hylobates,* while its limb skeleton is more primitive and displays a significant combination of cercopithecoid and pongid features, the latter in certain characters approaching those of the modern gibbons but by no means so specialized for brachiation. The limb bones are remarkably like those of the South American spider monkey in their proportions. Most of the larger apes from the east African Miocene have been attributed to a genus *Proconsul,* but it is doubtful whether it can be differentiated from the dryopithecines known from Miocene and Pliocene deposits of the northern hemisphere. These large east African apes comprise more than one species, ranging in size from that of a pygmy chimpanzee to a creature of gorilloid proportions. Although the dentition is fundamentally pongid, the skull and limb skeleton of the smaller species show cercopithecoid features mingled with traits adumbrating the specialized features of the modern anthropoid apes. They were, it seems, anthropoid apes in the making and, while no doubt predominantly arboreal, were capable of running and leaping in the manner of the quadrupedal monkeys. The endocranial cast of one of the species indicates that the brain was relatively small and very cercopithecoid in its convolutional pattern. During the Miocene period there were gibbon-like apes in Europe, represented by *Pliopithecus*. The greater part of the skull and much of the limb skeleton is known: like other Miocene apes of which the limb bones are known, *Pliopithecus* shows cercopithecoid features making it evident that it was not highly specialized for brachiation.

A cercopithecoid genus of Pliocene date, *Mesopithecus,* is known from unusually well-preserved remains (including an almost complete skeleton) found in Greece, others also being known from Pliocene deposits in Czechoslovakia, southern U.S.S.R., and Iran. This fossil type, quite similar to the modern Colobinae, may have existed still earlier, for the few cercopithecoid jaws and teeth so far recorded from the Lower Miocene of east Africa have been tentatively assigned to the same genus.

The modern genus *Macaca* was well established and widespread by the Pliocene, and during the temperate interglacial phases of the Pleistocene it was a quite common inhabitant of central Europe. The modern colobine genus *Presbytis* has been reported from a Lower Pleistocene stratum in India. A baboonlike cercopithecoid, *Libypithecus,* is known from Pliocene deposits in Egypt, and *Simopithecus* (similar to the modern gelada baboon and in some species reaching a massive size) is found in the Pliocene and Pleistocene of east Africa. Extinct Pleistocene baboons, *Dinopithecus, Gorgopithecus,* and *Parapapio,* existed in south Africa, and remains of modern *Papio* have also been found in Lower Pleistocene strata in northern India, Algeria, and Egypt.

Oreopithecus, of Lower Pliocene antiquity, which is known from fairly abundant remains discovered in lignite mines in Italy, has been the subject of considerable discussion because of its unexpected mixture of anatomical characters. It was usually grouped with the Cercopithecoidea, but the dental morphology has more recently led some authorities to identify it as a generalized type of anthropoid ape. The evidence based on portions of the limb skeleton (unfortunately not very well preserved) lends strong support to this interpretation, but its precise taxonomic position still remains doubtful. It has been assigned to a family of its own, Oreopithecidae, and it may represent a somewhat aberrant offshoot of the basal stock common to the cercopithecoid monkeys and anthropoid apes.

The descent of man and the fossil discoveries that illuminate his origins are treated in detail in the article MAN, EVOLUTION OF.

(W. E. L. G. C.)

IV. BEHAVIOUR OF THE PRIMATES

The close similarity of Primates in their anatomy and physiology is, not surprisingly, paralleled by similarities in basic behaviour, or adaptive responses. Intellectually, man is far superior to apes and monkeys, but there is some overlap in ability between man and the subhuman primates. Primates as a group, excluding the lemurs, are superior to all other mammals; indeed, the differences between monkeys and nonprimate forms may be as great as the differences between monkeys and men. The emotional and social differences that exist between man and the subhuman primates are in large part a consequence of their intellectual differences. It is primarily in the organization of his societies and the learned control of his emotions, and not in the primary physiological and motivational aspects of emotion, that man differs from the subhuman primates.

1. Intelligence.—Man is the only animal that has succeeded in controlling and modifying his environment to meet his own needs. Historical evidence suggests that only in the last several thousand years has man attained sufficient control over his physical and biological world to live more than a simple nomadic or agrarian existence. Subhuman primates remain at the nomadic level, as do some primitive human groups even today. It was only when man achieved social structure that he became free to explore the full intellectual capacities he possessed. His major achievements have been the products of the few among him—those rare individuals with the highest order of intelligence. The vast majority of men are incapable of intellectual creativity, and a not insignificant number are unable even to understand or to apply the accomplishments of the ablest. Thus, man, who as a species has had remarkable intellectual successes, probably has had little more than the minimal intellectual endowment to achieve the civilization that we know today.

There is no scientific evidence to prove that man is superior to other primates or even to other mammals in learning conditioned responses or in solving problems involving orientation in space. In memory tests in which language skills are not necessary (but could be helpful), chimpanzees perform as well as human children and almost as well as adults. But as intellectual tasks grow more complex, man's superiority rapidly becomes evident. Other mammals have at least the rudiments of all aspects of thinking that do not require verbalization. Man's ability to form concepts and to apply them in problem solution—his primary intellectual asset—is also present in apes and monkeys and even rodents, but to a far lesser degree. Rhesus monkeys have been trained, for example, to form concepts of redness and blueness and to apply these concepts. The acquisition of concepts is slow in subhuman animals; in a lifetime they can acquire relatively few. Man, on the other hand, forms thousands of concepts in a lifetime and can transfer them to his fellows who use them to form new and more abstruse concepts.

In laboratory experiments requiring the transfer of learning from problem to problem, chimpanzees and monkeys are the equal of normal young children and superior to severely retarded adolescents. In tasks requiring simple creativity, however, apes and monkeys lag behind normal human children. There are many successful performances of chimpanzees (and of orangutans, gorillas, and cebus monkeys to a lesser extent) in drawing, painting, and tool using, but the predominant behaviour trend is toward destructive rather than constructive use of materials.

The greatest gulf between man and subhuman primates is language. Subhuman primates use sounds and gestures to communicate; these mannerisms suffice for mutual protection and amicable group living. Since they also permit training and discipline of the young, they serve as a limited transfer of concrete culture from generation to generation. Man first verbalized his thoughts and transfered them from generation to generation, then much later he symbolized language, vastly increasing the transfer of knowledge in quantity, complexity, and accuracy through the written word. No ape or monkey shows aptitude for acquiring verbal language, although psychologists have devoted intensive efforts to teaching young apes to talk. Typically, the ape can acquire two or three words after many months of training, but the end results resemble the stage of language of 12–15-month-old human babies who use a few isolated words but cannot put them together to express ideas. Moreover, each newly learned word tends to interfere with the words previously mastered.

The intellectual hierarchy within the primate order has not been fully established beyond placement of man at the top. The most inferior human representatives are inferior to normal apes and to at least some monkeys. Chimpanzees appear to be superior to other apes, although the abilities of orangutans and gorillas have not been as thoroughly explored and may eventually place them on an intellectual level with the chimpanzees. Gibbons appear to be much inferior to other apes and to many monkeys as well. Macaques perform on most laboratory learning tests as well as chimpanzees, but they are inferior to them in the use of tools and in creativity. Spider monkeys appear to be almost as able as macaques on learning tests and to be superior to other South American monkeys. Cebus monkeys, on the other hand, approach chimpanzees in mastery of motor skills and tool using, but are inferior in most learning tests to chimpanzees, macaques, and spider monkeys. Primitive monkeys such as marmosets are clearly inferior to gibbons and to all other monkeys that have been tested. Lemurs appear to have less learning ability than any of the monkeys and apes; furthermore, on many standardized learning tests the lemurs are inferior to cats, dogs, and even pigeons.

2. Temperament.—The basic temperaments of the primates present a paradox both intriguing and bewildering, for in all probability primates as a group are both the most affectionate and the most aggressive of all animals. Their fighting tendencies must have served them well in natural selection, and their strong affectional bonds for members of their species have made them the most effective social animals. Individually, primates are relatively weak and poorly armed, but the bonds that underlie the formation of relatively large, cohesive social groups also facilitate the use of their aggressiveness in cooperative group defense.

It would seem that an extremely aggressive animal is poorly devised to be a highly social animal. The resolution of this paradox, however, is found in the order of development or maturation of the affectional and the aggressive behaviours: habits of affection are firmly established before aggressive tendencies are allowed vigorous expression. Intimate affectional bonds are formed in all the major primate groups within the first weeks or, at most, first months of life, originating in the reciprocal affection of mother and infant.

Primates are relatively immature at birth and have a long infancy. Newborn human beings are almost completely helpless, being unable even to change position or to cling to the mother. Apes are also unable to move about at birth, but within a few days a chimpanzee can cling to its mother for support while she is moving. Gorilla babies either cling less tenaciously or have more cautious mothers, for the mothers move with one arm about the clinging baby during the first few months. Until four months of age, chimpanzees and gorillas never leave their mothers, and then they begin to leave for only a few minutes at a time and for a distance of only several yards. Monkeys are much more mature at birth than human and ape newborn, and they can cling fairly well within only hours after birth. By the second day most monkey mothers need only occasionally to touch the clinging infant while they are moving. Except for langurs, which permit other females to hold their babies, monkey mothers seldom release their babies in the first weeks. Between two and four weeks, monkey babies play between their mother's legs but rarely leave her, and in the second month they may move several feet from her but never stay away for more than a few minutes at a time. Thus the mother-infant relationship in subhuman primates tends to be more intimate and more exclusive than that in human groups.

The mother is the infant's social center for the first one to three years of life, the duration being related to the rate of maturation, the social organization, and, usually, the spacing of births. Japanese and rhesus macaque mothers separate their infants at 10 to 12 months of age, when a new baby generally arrives. Baboons separate their infants at about 10 to 15 months, but usually produce a new baby only every two years. Gorillas and chimpanzees separate their infants at three years, the usual period between births. In all these primates, however, the older offspring retain some physical proximity to their mothers for one to three years after separation, especially when sleeping and when seeking protection in times of danger. Gibbons are an exception in that they live in family groups with as many as four successive young ranging from newborn to young adult.

PRIMATES

515B
During the period of dependency, the mother-infant and infant-mother bonds are the closest of all primate affectional relationships, and the mother, not the infant, takes the initiative in weakening them, usually with great resistance from the infant. In the early months for the monkeys and somewhat longer for the apes, the mother nurses the infant, grooms it, cradles it, comforts it, protects it from threats, and provides its first social training. She sleeps with it in her arms or nestled against her body. She travels with it clinging to her ventral surface at first and on her back later. Her treatment is universally tender, tolerant, and solicitous. In laboratory studies of the rhesus, mothers rarely threatened or punished the infant until it was three months old, and even then the reprimands were mild. Gradually, negative treatment increased in frequency and severity, but even at a year the affectionate responses outweighted the rejecting ones. The primate infant in this same period stays close to the mother and clings to her or leans against her much of the time. It learns early to respond to her sounds and gestures and always returns to her when frightened or when the group is about to move off.

Affectional bonds impart to the infant, through the mother, basic confidence and security, which enable the infant gradually to go forth and explore its physical and social world. The first other living beings it encounters are the members of its own species, and because of the primary affectional bonds already established, it interacts with them in a friendly manner. In all large primate groups there is likely to be a clustering of births, and an exploring infant soon establishes primary contacts with age mates, or, lacking age mates, with young juveniles. Their interaction takes the form of increasingly complex patterns of play out of which develops the age-mate or peer affectional system. Laboratory data on the rhesus monkey indicate that the age-mate affectional system, which persists throughout the individual's life, is probably at least as important as the maternal affectional system in converting the infant primate into a socially mature adolescent and adult. During the first year, monkey and ape babies spend increasing amounts of time with their peers while adults feed or rest. In the second year, monkeys spend most of the day with their peers; chimpanzees and gorillas reach this stage at about three years. As adolescents and young adults, monkeys associate almost exclusively with their age groups, more and more as sex-segregated groups with transient sexual pairing.

3. Socialization.—It is possible to reverse the normal developmental trends of affection and aggression by isolating monkeys in the experimental laboratory and thereby denying them any opportunity to form social bonds at the proper maturational stage. If affection is denied until aggression has matured, the normally social monkey, ape, or man becomes an asocial animal. Researches at the University of Wisconsin Primate Laboratory show that socially isolated male rhesus monkeys never adjust adequately to other rhesus monkeys, showing aggressiveness and failure to understand, utilize, or acquire the gestures and postures normally learned in infancy. The socially isolated female also has difficulty in adjusting. Rhesus females raised with little or no early social experience and impregnated by various techniques frequently ignored their first-born infants in spite of the infants' unending attempts to make maternal contact or treated them cruelly, sometimes to the point of maiming or killing them. Some of these indifferent or brutal mothers produced second babies, however, and all but one were either good or adequate mothers, indicating that they gained socialization experience from the association with their first babies. (Normally, female monkeys are good mothers to their first-born babies and tend to be more lenient with first offspring than with later offspring.)

If primates form affection for their fellows early in life and are not confined in cramped quarters, they adjust to each other with a minimum of quarreling and direct their later-maturing aggressions less to members of their own species and more to intruders from without. Laboratory observations on rhesus monkeys indicate that strong in-group affection is present among infants before the end of the first year, when true aggressive responses begin to appear. Dominance relationships then become more firmly established and, because each member learns its position with respect to its fellows, social order is maintained with a minimum of fighting. Most field observations of monkeys and apes confirm the laboratory studies.

One aspect of the social paradox that has attracted attention is the role of dominant males within monkey or ape societies. Not only do these members defend their group from outsiders, but they accord special protection and special status to mothers with new babies and to all the young. Japanese macaques in some, but not all, troops display especially strong paternal behaviour. The most dominant males adopt infants of about 10 or 12 months of age when the females are delivering new babies, thus providing a transition for the infant between mothering and independent living. Dominant male baboons display very strong interest in new babies and tolerance of all infants up to about two years old, even adopting orphaned infants on occasion. Threat to an infant releases violent aggression in these males. Dominant male gorillas are reported to be especially tolerant and protective of infants. Adult male langurs show little or no interest in infants until they are close to one year of age, when young males establish contact with the dominant males; at that time the males tolerate the youngsters' advances and even embrace them. Male adult rhesus monkeys likewise are tolerant of the young and highly protective.

There is no report of any adult subhuman primate mistreating a youngster under natural circumstances, and there are numerous reports that adult males consistently break up any social situation where an older animal is abusing a younger one, whether it is a female threatening another female's infant or a juvenile or adolescent playing too roughly with smaller members of the group. Thus, the dominant males train younger and less dominant members to respect and protect the young. Among human beings the parental affectional system may break down, as a result of emotional and social disturbance, resulting in child beating or child abandonment; though society disapproves such abuses, privacy may mask them. Among monkeys and apes in the wild, the individual that fails to become socialized is driven from the group or killed before it reaches full maturity. In the laboratory, socially deprived male monkeys, like their female counterparts, show abnormal aggression in their relationships with infants as well as with their peers.

A striking finding in all subhuman primate groups thus far studied is the prevailing peacefulness of interactions within the groups. The emotional tone, however, varies among species, genera, and families. At one extreme among the apes are the mountain gorillas; calm and placid, they show minimal excitement and interaction and maximal group stability. They may be compared to the extreme introverts in human society. In contrast are the chimpanzees of Tanganyika, which show exuberance and joy in their interactions but very low group stability. Friends and acquaintances hoot and embrace warmly when they meet, interact pleasurably while they are together, then often separate to rejoin particular clusters or to join different groups. Their human counterparts are the extreme extroverts. Gibbons live in families with the male-female pair showing equality of dominance and a minimum of friction. The monkeys thus far studied tend toward stable groups dominated by one or more adult males, but the emotional tenor varies from the high excitability of the baboons and rhesus monkeys through the calmness of the Japanese macaques and langurs to the generally more quiescent behaviour of howling monkeys. In all groups, vocalizations and gestures appear to suffice for settling most disputes, and serious injury to other group members is infrequent.

Between groups of the same species, however, there may be a wide range of relations. There may be peaceful intermingling of two gorilla troops, for example, and yet each of these groups may display aggression or withdrawal when it meets still other specific groups. A rhesus troop may withdraw when it meets one troop but force withdrawal of a different group upon encounter. Leaders apparently learn their status among groups just as individuals learn their status within groups, thus minimizing actual destruction of the species. Moreover, ape groups may encounter monkey troops without evidence of aggression, or several species of monkeys may meet without incident and even sleep in the same tree.

There are close parallels between man and the various subhuman primate groups in the basic processes of group organization and interpersonal relationships. Different species vary in the nature of their social relations, suggesting underlying quantitative differences in physiology, which could well have resulted from gradual selection for the physical and biological environment to which the species had to adapt. In different isolated human societies one can approximate the range of group personalities that appear in the subhuman primates. There are some groups almost as placid and calm as the mountain gorilla, and other groups as excitable as baboons and chimpanzees.

Man started with the same basic drives and emotions as other primates and developed his culture to meet his special needs. His greater intelligence and more highly developed system of communication have enabled him to exert subtler controls over the members of his group and to channel responses through more intensive training of the young. Underlying these differences remain the deep-seated primate inclinations to form affectional ties that both satisfy the individual and hold the group together and impulses to aggress against personal interferences to protect the individual and, by extension, the group.

See also Animal Behaviour; Play, Animal; Psychology, Comparative; Sexual Behaviour; Sociology, Animal; and references under "Primates" in the Index.

(H. F. H.; M. K. Ha.)

Bibliography.—*General:* J. R. Napier and P. H. Napier, *A Handbook of Living Primates* (1967); W. E. Le Gros Clark, *History of the Primates,* 7th ed. (1960), *The Antecedents of Man,* 2nd ed. (1962), *The Fossil Evidence for Human Evolution,* 2nd ed. (1964); W. Howells, *Mankind in the Making* (1959); W. C. O. Hill, *Primates,* 5 vol. (1953–62); John Buettner-Janusch (ed.), *Evolutionary and Genetic Biology of Primates,* vol. 1 (1963).
Prosimians: W. E. Le Gros Clark, "On the Anatomy of the Pentailed Tree Shrew," *Proc. Zool. Soc. Lond.* (1926); M. W. Lyon, Tree-Shrews—an Account of the Family Tupaiidae," *Proc. U.S. Mus. Nat. Hist.* (1913); W. K. Gregory, "The Classification and Phylogeny of the Lemuroidea," *Bull. Geol. Soc. Am.,* 26 (1915); W. E. Le Gros Clark and D. Thomas, "The Miocene Lemuroids of East Africa" in *Fossil Mammals of Africa,* no. 5, *Bull. Br. Mus. Nat. Hist.* (1952); G. G. Simpson, "Studies on the Earliest Primates," *Bull. Am. Mus. Nat. Hist.,* 77 (1940). *Tarsiers:* H. H. Woollard, "The Anatomy of *Tarsius spectrum,*" *Proc. Zool. Soc. Lond.* (1925).
Monkeys: C. R. Carpenter, "A Field Study of the Behaviour and Social Relations of Howling Monkeys," *Comp. Psychol. Monogr.,* vol. 10 (1934); W. E. Le Gros Clark, "The Problem of the Claw in Primates," *Proc. Zool. Soc. Lond.* (1936); A. H. Schultz, "The Density of Hair in Primates," *Hum. Biol.,* vol. 3 (1931); J. Beattie, "The Anatomy of the Common Marmoset," *Proc. Zool. Soc. Lond.* (1927); R. Stirton, "Ceboid Monkeys from the Miocene of Colombia," *Bull. Dep. Geol. Univ. Calif.,* 28 (1951); C. G. Hartman and W. L. Straus (eds.), *The Anatomy of the Rhesus Monkey* (1933); R. I. Pocock, "The External Characters of the Catarrhine Monkeys and Apes," *Proc. Zool. Soc. Lond.* (1926); N. C. Tapper, "Problems of Distribution and Adaptation of the African Monkeys," *Cur. Anthrop.,* vol. 1 (1960).
Anthropoid Apes: C. R. Carpenter, "A Field Study in Siam of the Behaviour and Social Relations of the Gibbon," *Comp. Psychol. Monogr.,* vol. 84 (1940); W. Köhler (trans. by E. Winter), *The Mentality of Apes,* 2nd ed. (1925); H. W. Nissen, "A Field Study of the Chimpanzee," *Comp. Psychol. Monogr.,* vol. 8 (1931); G. B. Schaller, *The Mountain Gorilla: Ecology and Behaviour* (1963); H. C. Raven, *The Anatomy of the Gorilla* (1950); R. M. and A. W. Yerkes, *The Great Apes: a Study of Anthropoid Life* (1929); W. E. Le Gros Clark and L. S. B. Leakey, "The Miocene Hominoidea of East Africa," *Fossil Mammals of Africa* no. 1, *Bull. Br. Mus. Nat. Hist.* (1951); W. K. Gregory and M. Hellman, "The Dentition of Dryopithecus and the Origin of Man," *Anthrop. Pap. of Amer. Mus. Nat. Hist.,* vol. 28 (1926); E. L. Simons, "Two New Primate Species from the African Oligocene," *Postilla,* Yale Peabody Museum, no. 64 (1962), "The Early Relatives of Man," *Scient. Am.,* vol. 211, no. 1, pp. 50–62 (July 1964), "The Earliest Apes," *ibid.,* vol. 217, no. 6, pp. 28–35 (Dec. 1967); L. S. B. Leakey, "A New Lower Pliocene Fossil Primate from Kenya," *Ann. Mag. Nat. Hist.,* ser. 13 (1961); E. L. Simons and D. R. Pilbeam, "Preliminary Revision of the Dryopithecinae," *Folia Primatologia,* vol. 3 (1965). (W. E. L. G. C.)
Behaviour: H. F. Harlow, "The Development of Learning in the Rhesus Monkey," *Am. Scient.,* 47:458–479 (Dec. 1959); H. F. Harlow and M. K. Harlow, "Learning to Think," *Scient. Am.,* 181:36–39 (Aug. 1949); "The Affectional Systems," in A. M. Schrier, H. F. Harlow, and F. Stollnitz (eds.), *Behavior of Nonhuman Primates,* vol. ii (1965); H. L. Rheingold (ed.), *Maternal Behavior in Mammals* (1963); C. H. Southwick (ed.), *Primate Social Behavior* (1963).
(H. F. H.; M. K. Ha.)

PRIME MINISTER, the name given to the head of the executive branch of government in countries with a parliamentary system. He serves under the chief of state, except in those rare cases in which the chief of state assumes the functions of prime minister himself. The origin of the title is to be sought in the period of absolute or nonparliamentary regimes when all ministers of government were simply servants of the sovereign and individually responsible to him for the management of their departments. One of them might exercise a predominant influence in fact, but not by any constitutional right. In France, however, with the advance of royal absolutism the cardinal duc de Richelieu was acknowledged in 1624 as *principal* or *premier ministre;* and Cardinal Mazarin succeeded him in this position in 1643. After Mazarin's death (1661), Louis XIV ruled without any chief minister; but the odium that ministerial absolutism had aroused in wide circles both in France and abroad remained long attached to the expression "prime minister," and it was only after an interval that its use in England in the sense with which we are here concerned was revived.

Great Britain.—The preponderance over other ministers of the crown that Cardinal Wolsey or Lord Burghley enjoyed in 16th-century England was short-lived; and in the 17th century, when Gilbert Burnet described the earl of Clarendon as "chief, or the only, minister," he was yet well aware that the style "first minister" was "a title so newly translated out of French into English that it was not enough understood to be liked, and every man would detest it for the burden it was attended with." Even in the 18th century it is more usual to find partnerships of two or three individuals, such as Marlborough and Godolphin, Harley and St. John, Stanhope and Sunderland, or Townshend and Walpole sharing the government. But the place vacated by George I when, from 1717, he ceased to attend Cabinet meetings, had to be filled by a single individual, and this presiding officer developed into a prime minister. Sir Robert Walpole, though he "unequivocally denied" the title, is usually regarded as the first prime minister, and during his long term of office (1721–42) he developed many of the attributes of premiership. He was master of his Cabinet; he insisted that his colleagues subscribe to the principles of his party; he dismissed his opponents; he dispensed the royal patronage; and, with reservations, he may be described as commanding a majority in the House of Commons. How novel, how unpopular, such a position still was may be gathered from the proceedings of both houses in 1741 when an attack was launched against Walpole's government. "According to our constitution," said Samuel Sandys, who led the attack in the Commons, "we can have no sole and prime minister . . . every . . . officer has his own proper department; and no officer ought to meddle in the affairs belonging to the department of another." The minority in the House of Lords which drew up a protest was even more forthright, saying, "We are persuaded that a sole, or even a First Minister is an officer unknown to the law of Britain, and inconsistent with the Constitution of this country and destructive of liberty in any government whatsoever."

On the fall of Walpole in 1742 the further development of the office was checked in the latter half of George II's reign, and in the early part of George III's reign. Thus George Grenville (1763–65) thought that, "Prime Minister is an odious title," and Lord North (1770–82) would not countenance it. It was the younger William Pitt who consolidated the work of Walpole and by his long tenure of power (1783–1801, 1804–06) accustomed the nation to the office, if not to the name. The extent of his achievement can be measured by the terms of his famous interview with Henry Dundas, 1st Viscount Melville, in 1803. Pitt "stated . . . that there should be an avowed and real minister, possessing the chief weight in the council, and the principal place in the confidence of the king. In that respect there can be no rivalry or division of power. That power must rest in the person generally called the first minister, and that minister ought, he thinks, to be the person at the head of the finances." Nevertheless, old prejudices die hard. In 1829 it could still be said in Parliament that "nothing could be more mischievous or unconstitutional than to recognize by act of parliament the existence of such

PRIME MINISTER

an office." Such recognition was not granted until 1905, when by royal warrant the prime minister became known to the law merely as one who had precedence next after the archbishop of York.

The prime minister is appointed by the sovereign. "I offered," said Sir Robert Peel on his resignation of office, "no opinion as to the choice of a successor. That is almost the only act which is the personal act of the sovereign." And, as late as 1894, Queen Victoria could call the earl of Rosebery without consulting the retiring prime minister, William Gladstone, or the wishes of the parliamentary majority. Nevertheless, the crown's freedom of choice became increasingly circumscribed. The "economic" reforms of the marquess of Rockingham's administration (1782), by reducing the royal patronage, made it less easy for the crown to put ready-made majorities at the disposal of whatever minister it might choose, and the Reform Bills of the 19th century made the ministry dependent on Parliament and the electorate instead of on the royal favour. The prime minister is now normally the acknowledged head of the party commanding a majority in the House of Commons, and it is only on occasions when no party commands an absolute majority of the House, or when the majority party has no acknowledged head, that there is room for the exercise of the royal discretion.

An official residence, 10 Downing Street, is assigned to the prime minister and he also has the use of Chequers, a country mansion in Buckinghamshire. But there is no salary attached to the office. The prime minister merely draws the emoluments of whatever other office he may happen to hold. At the close of the 17th century the lord treasurer was already regarded as the most important government official, and the leading minister has normally held the office of first commissioner, or first lord, and it is by virtue of that office that he draws his present salary of £10,000 a year as laid down in the Ministers of the Crown Act (1937). But the earl of Chatham was lord privy seal; the marquess of Salisbury successively foreign secretary and lord privy seal; and Winston Churchill simultaneously first lord of the Treasury and minister of defense. It used to be normal for the prime minister to be the leader of the House of Commons, but increasingly in the 20th century prime ministers have found this burden excessive and transferred it to other shoulders.

In the 18th century, when cabinets were composed almost exclusively of peers, the leading minister, curiously enough, was recruited most of the time from the Commons; in the 19th century, when Commoners came to form the bulk of the Cabinet, the prime minister was, more often than not, a peer. But with the expansion of the franchise and the reduction in the powers of the Lords (notably by the Parliament Act of 1911) it became increasingly difficult for a peer to exercise the premiership effectively from the House of Lords. No peer has been prime minister since Lord Salisbury resigned in 1902 and when Lord Curzon was passed over for the premiership in favour of Stanley Baldwin in 1923 this was generally regarded as a decisive demonstration of the need for a prime minister to be in the Commons. In 1963 when Lord Home was appointed prime minister, he resigned his peerage and was subsequently elected to the House of Commons.

The prime minister, with the sovereign's consent, appoints his fellow ministers to their respective posts. Originally, of course, the sovereign exercised an unfettered choice and even in the 19th century Queen Victoria more than once successfully opposed some ministerial appointments. Today, however, the prime minister can appoint whom he will, though of course he must have regard to political considerations, in particular the need of maintaining the confidence of the House of Commons. Finally, since 1918, it is the prime minister individually and not his Cabinet collectively who advises the sovereign to dissolve Parliament. In the event of a Cabinet dispute this places him in a very strong position, especially since with it is coupled the right of dismissal. However, the responsibility of the Cabinet to the prime minister belongs properly to the history of the Cabinet (q.v.).

The history of the second quarter of the 20th century, with its recurring crises, showed that the position held by the prime minister was still subject to development and was still dependent upon personal factors. In the financial crisis of 1931 George V exercised his prerogative of choosing as leader of a "national" coalition James Ramsay MacDonald, the leader of a minor section in a defeated and divided Labour Party, not Stanley Baldwin, who was leader of the Conservatives, the largest party. For a time the office of prime minister was inevitably weakened. The crisis caused by the abdication of Edward VIII (1936), on the other hand, temporarily gave to the prime minister (Baldwin) the sovereign's prerogative of acting as liaison between the prime ministers of the dominions. The much greater crisis of 1940 produced further drastic changes. When Churchill was appointed he was not the acknowledged leader of any party. The stresses of war and the personal ascendancy of Churchill increased the importance and prestige of the prime minister. He assumed a responsibility for the armed forces and for their direction almost equivalent to the responsibility held by the president of the United States. He became more of an ambassador-at-large than any predecessor. Radio broadcasting put him into an intimate relationship with the whole country, quite without precedent and far transcending his indirect relationship with the electorate through Parliament. The prime minister's position was thus, on the whole, strengthened vis-à-vis his Cabinet colleagues, vis-à-vis Parliament and perhaps vis-à-vis the electorate. The return to peace in 1945 reduced the occasion for such exercise of power, and prime ministers after Churchill were not such commanding figures. The Suez crisis of 1956, however, saw Sir Anthony Eden act with a minimum of Cabinet consultation and was a reminder that, if he has party support, a prime minister can dominate his Cabinet colleagues.

A modern prime minister commands a significantly increased volume of patronage: about 100 ministerial posts alone are his exclusive appointment. In the 19th century Gladstone was thought to be abnormal in having a policy of his own, and most prime ministers before 1914 were, at best, no more than strong chairmen in their Cabinets. Later prime ministers were in this respect far more Gladstonian than Gladstone. This met with criticism, but, by concentrating its attacks upon the central figure, the opposition unwittingly did much to consolidate the prime minister's dominance. Although in 1945 the electorate appeared to be offered a choice between a party program (Labour's) and a party leader (Churchill) and appeared to prefer the program to the personality, in general 20th-century elections were increasingly a choice between rival candidates for the premiership. The use of radio and television contributed powerfully to this trend, as did the whole tendency toward the centralization of politics. (For lists of the prime ministers see MINISTRY, GOVERNMENT.)

Commonwealth Countries.—The British prime minister has become the model for prime ministers in the member states of the Commonwealth and the evolution of the office in the dominions has proceeded along lines similar to those in Great Britain. Thus in Canada it developed *pari passu* with the gradual development of responsible government, so that there is room for dispute about the stage at which a prime minister clearly emerged; though Sir Allan Napier McNab (1854–56) is often regarded as the first, the office was not clearly established until after federation, when John Alexander Macdonald held it from 1867 to 1873. In New Zealand, Henry Sewell, who formed the first responsible ministry in 1856, is sometimes regarded as the earliest prime minister, though his tenure of office was merely 6 days. In Australia the granting of responsible government to the states in the 1850s produced the first crop of initially weak and short-lived ministries, but by the time of federation in 1900 the office of prime minister was fully developed and in 1901 Edmund Barton became the first prime minister of the new Commonwealth of Australia. (The Australians now confine the title "prime minister" to the chief minister of their Commonwealth Cabinets, using the term "premier" for the chief minister of each state.) In South Africa the granting of responsible government to the Cape Colony in 1872 led to the premiership of John Charles Molteno; in Natal, similarly, in 1893 Sir John Robinson became prime minister; the Union of South Africa was established in 1910 with Louis Botha as its first prime minister. In India, elections held in 1937 under the Government of India Act (1935) resulted in the establishment of cabinet government under prime ministers in the 11 provinces and when in

1947 full autonomy was granted Jawaharlal Nehru became first premier of India and Liaquat Ali Khan of Pakistan. Similar developments occurred in other parts of the Commonwealth as they attained self-government.

The constitutional position of these prime ministers is much the same in all Commonwealth countries. In most the tendency has been toward the evolution of strong premierships, and certain figures like William Lyon MacKenzie King in Canada, Nehru in India and Sir Robert Menzies in Australia are notable for long tenure of office. Australia is peculiar in having established a prime minister's department, but this is, in effect, a general Cabinet secretariat. The Australian Labor Party has also adopted a provision unknown elsewhere obliging its leader, on becoming prime minister, to accept for his cabinet those members elected by the party caucus and also to submit his program for caucus approval.

Ireland.—The compelling effect of the British concept of the prime minister's office is well illustrated by its history in Ireland. The constitution of the Irish Free State in 1922 specifically aimed at reducing the prime minister's power. Serving under a popularly elected president, he was to seek the approval of the *dáil éireann* (House of Commons) for the choice of his colleagues, was denied full powers of dissolution in the event of defeat, and was given no option but to resign. So strong, however, were the habits borrowed from Whitehall and Westminster, that these provisions became a dead letter even before the 1937 constitution formally modified them and at the same time, in entitling the prime minister *Taoiseach* (leader), implicitly recognized his command.

France.—Imported into countries in the rest of the world with different traditions of executive leadership, the office of prime minister, or premier, has undergone various modifications. As might be expected, it is in the surviving constitutional monarchies, like those in Scandinavia and the Low Countries, that the British norm is most closely approximated. France, oscillating between the "Napoleonic" and the parliamentary elements in its tradition, has varied the powers of the premier (*président du conseil des ministres*) under its various constitutions. The restoration of Louis XVIII in 1814 brought a measure of representative government and with it the first premiers under a parliamentary system, though their effective powers depended on the monarch they served. Men such as Casimir Périer, Louis Adolphe Thiers, Louis Molé, and François Guizot were, nonetheless, considerable figures. The Second Empire (1852–70), however, represented virtually a return to the sort of uneasy balance of powers between monarch, ministers, and Parliament that had existed in Britain in the 17th century.

The Third Republic (1870–1940) settled down into a system under which a president filled the role of a constitutional monarch and the premier was supposed to discharge the functions of his British counterpart. In fact, with a few notable exceptions, such as Georges Clemenceau, premiers were weak executives, and their terms of office unstable and short-lived (there were more than 50 in the 70 years of the Republic). This was due to the lack of strong parties and the consequent dependence of each ministry upon fluctuating coalitions in the Chamber of Deputies. The premier had no power of dissolution, and no other effective method of disciplining the legislature. The Fourth Republic (1946–58), though it slightly strengthened the premier's hands in forming a government and gave him a very limited power of dissolution, did nothing to increase the stability of governments. The Fifth Republic (1958–   ) represented a swing in the "Napoleonic" direction, strengthening the president, weakening Parliament and placing the premier in an ambiguous position between the two. A "separation of powers" removes him from membership of the National Assembly, though he can appear and speak there; Parliament, dissolvable and restricted in its powers, is less able to control him, though he still needs a majority there. But many of his executive powers, especially over foreign affairs, have passed to the president, whose pale shadow the premier appears to have become. (For lists of premiers *see* FRANCE: *History*.)

Italy.—The European country most closely resembling France in the role of its premier is Italy. Conte Camillo di Cavour became the first Italian premier, but he had been preceded in Piedmont by the marchese D'Azeglio, the first premier under the Piedmontese constitution of 1848. In fact, however, the political backwardness of the country and the fluidity of party groupings in Parliament made premiers more dependent on royal favour than on any other single factor. They were sometimes weak, sometimes dictatorial, and their terms of office always brief. Between 1860 and the coming of Fascism in 1922, Italy had 38 premiers. The new constitution of 1947, however, ushered in a system which, while generally similar to that of the French Fourth Republic, made possible more stable ministries and proportionately stronger premiers. Alcide de Gasperi (1945–53) was an especially notable figure; his successors were less impressive and the presidency tended to grow in power at the expense of the premiership.

Germany.—Germany gives its prime minister the title of chancellor. Under the Empire (1871–1918), even though the chancellor was endowed with explicitly superior powers vis-à-vis the other ministers, he was always (even Otto von Bismarck) dependent on the kaiser. In the Weimar Republic (1919–33) he was a greatly weakened figure; Cabinet decisions were by majority vote and he had to allocate portfolios at the direction of the parties which made up his coalition. The constitution of the German Federal Republic in 1949 explicitly guarded against such weakness by stipulating that the *Bundestag* might "express its lack of confidence in the federal chancellor only by electing a successor with the majority of its members." This, together with the strong personality of the first chancellor, Konrad Adenauer (1949–63), gave the office a strong start. Adenauer interpreted very literally the constitutional clause which asserts that "the federal chancellor determines, and is responsible for, general policy." Creating two "state-secretaries," one for foreign affairs and the other as a kind of chief of staff, both responsible to him personally, he treated his Cabinet as a mere board of experts, discouraging any spirit of collective responsibility. Roughly similar conditions apply to the equivalent office of *minister-president* in the *Land* governments.

Japan.—In Japan, the other state most notably "democratized" after World War II, a somewhat similar situation prevailed. There, by the constitution, the prime minister "exercises control and supervision" over the whole of the executive and his countersignature is required for all laws and Cabinet orders. The ministers are thus very largely merely extensions of his authority. The legislature selects the prime minister from among its own members and normally chooses the leader of the majority party. If the Cabinet loses the confidence of the lower house of the legislature the Cabinet must either resign or dissolve the house.

U.S.S.R.—The post of chairman of the Council of Ministers in the Soviet Union is often identified in English as that of prime minister, though there is little similarity beyond the title. The Council of Ministers is the highest executive organ in the Soviet Union and is answerable only to the Supreme Soviet or to the Presidium. *See* UNION OF SOVIET SOCIALIST REPUBLICS.

BIBLIOGRAPHY.—Sir William Ivor Jennings, *Cabinet Government*, 3rd ed. (1959), and John P. Mackintosh, *The British Cabinet* (1962). For the Commonwealth no adequate comparative treatment exists later than A. B. Keith, *Responsible Government in the Dominions*, 2 vol., 2nd ed. (1928). (H. G. N.)

PRIME NUMBER, a positive integer (whole number) greater than 1 that cannot be expressed as the product of two positive integers neither of which is 1. The first few prime numbers are 2, 3, 5, 7, 11. Every positive integer greater than 1 can be expressed as a product of one or more prime numbers; for example, $2 = 2$, $3 = 3$, $4 = 2 \cdot 2$, $5 = 5$, $6 = 2 \cdot 3$, $7 = 7$, $8 = 2 \cdot 2 \cdot 2$, $9 = 3 \cdot 3$, $10 = 2 \cdot 5$, $11 = 11$, $12 = 2 \cdot 2 \cdot 3$.

In symbols, if p is a prime number and if a and b are positive integers such that $ab = p$, then either $a = p$ or $b = p$. Euclid (*q.v.*, fl. 300 B.C.) proved the stronger assertion (*Elements*, book vii, proposition 30) that if a and b are positive integers such that ab is a multiple of the prime number p, then either a is a multiple of p, or b is a multiple of p. From this follows the so-called fundamental theorem of arithmetic: every positive integer greater than 1 can be expressed as a product of prime numbers in one way only (apart from rearrangement of factors).

Composite Numbers.—A positive integer greater than 1 which is not a prime is said to be a composite number. If n is a composite number, it must be a multiple of some prime number not exceeding

$\sqrt{n}$, since the product of two or more numbers greater than $\sqrt{n}$ must be greater than n. Thus to show that a given positive integer n is a prime number, it need only be shown that it is not a multiple of any positive integer between 2 and $\sqrt{n}$ inclusive.

Sieve of Eratosthenes.—The prime numbers not exceeding any positive integer N can be found by a process known as the sieve of Eratosthenes (*q.v.*): write the positive integers between 2 and N inclusive in numerical order; the first integer 2 is a prime number. Now cross out all the multiples of 2 other than 2 itself; that is, cross out 4 and every second integer, 6, 8, 10, and so on. The smallest integer remaining is 3, the next prime number. Now cross out all the multiples of 3 other than 3 itself; that is, beginning with 6, cross out every third integer. The smallest integer remaining after the deletion of the multiples of 2 and the multiples of 3 is 5, the next prime. Now cross out all the multiples of 5 other than 5 itself; that is, beginning with 10, cross out every fifth integer. The smallest integer remaining after the deletion of the multiples of 2, 3 and 5 is the next prime after 5, namely 7. Continue this sieving process until all the multiples of all primes not exceeding $\sqrt{N}$, other than those primes themselves, have been crossed out. The numbers not crossed out at least once will comprise the set of all primes not exceeding N.

Infinity of Primes.—Euclid (*Elements*, book ix, proposition 20) proved as follows that there are infinitely many prime numbers. Let P denote the product of all numbers in some finite list of prime numbers. Then $P + 1$ is not a multiple of any prime in the list (*i.e.*, division of $P + 1$ by any one of these primes leaves a remainder of 1). Hence, each prime factor of $P + 1$ is a prime number not occurring in the list (meaning just $P + 1$ itself if it is a prime number). Thus, no matter how extensive a finite set of primes is, there must be primes it does not contain.

Dirichlet's Theorem.—No polynomial (*q.v.*) expression in n can take prime values for all positive integral values of n. For example, $n^2 - n + 41$ is a multiple of 43 whenever n is 1 less or 2 greater than a multiple of 43, and $6n + 5$ is a multiple of 11 whenever n is 1 greater than a multiple of 11. However, in 1837 P. G. L. Dirichlet (*q.v.*) proved the theorem that if c and d are positive integers with no prime factors in common, then the expression $cn + d$ takes prime values for infinitely many positive integral values of n. Some of the simpler cases of Dirichlet's theorem can be proved by an elaboration of the argument Euclid used to prove the existence of infinitely many primes. For example, to show that there are infinitely many primes of the form $4n + 1$, merely replace $P + 1$ with $4P^2 + 1$ in Euclid's proof. However, the general proof of Dirichlet's theorem, although simplified since his time, is not easy. No analogous result is known for polynomials of higher degree. For example, it is not known if there are infinitely many primes of the form $n^2 - n + 41$.

Prime-Number Theorem.—The nth prime number is usually denoted by p_n, and the number of primes not exceeding the positive integer N is usually denoted by $\pi(N)$. It is possible to give artificial formulas for p_n and for $\pi(N)$ that amount to giving detailed instructions for the sieve of Eratosthenes, but in neither case is a really simple or natural formula known or to be expected.

The so-called prime-number theorem tells approximately how large p_n and $\pi(N)$ are for given values of n or N. It was conjectured by A. M. Legendre and C. F. Gauss early in the 19th century, but was first proved in 1896 by J. S. Hadamard and by C. J. de la Vallée Poussin, working independently. The prime-number theorem asserts that p_n is roughly $n \ln n$ when n is large, and that $\pi(N)$ is roughly $N/\ln N$ when N is large. Here $\ln n$ denotes the natural or Napierian logarithm of n, which is $2.302585093\ldots$ times the logarithm of n to the base 10 (*see* LOGARITHMS). More precisely, the ratio $p_n/(n \ln n)$ approaches 1 as a limit when n becomes large, and the ratio $\pi(N)/(N/\ln N)$ approaches 1 as a limit when N becomes large. An even better approximation to $\pi(N)$ than $N/\ln N$ is provided by the definite integral $\int_2^N (\ln t)^{-1} dt$, which is essentially the same as the sum of the reciprocals of the natural logarithms of all the positive integers between 2 and N inclusive. While the logical structure of the proof of the prime-number theorem was greatly clarified after 1896, the proof was still difficult in the 1960s.

By counting the number of integers crossed out in performing the sieve of Eratosthenes, it is possible to find the exact number of primes not exceeding a given number N, *i.e.*, $\pi(N)$, without listing all the primes up to N individually. This is an extensive calculation if N is large, but it is much less ambitious than is listing all the primes up to N. The following table gives the results of some calculations of this nature along with corresponding approximations by the prime-number theorem.

N	Integer nearest $N/\ln N$	$\pi(N)$	Integer nearest $\int_2^N (\ln t)^{-1} dt$
10	4	4	5
100	22	25	29
1,000	145	168	177
10,000	1,086	1,229	1,245
100,000	8,686	9,592	9,629
1,000,000	72,382	78,498	78,627
10,000,000	620,421	664,579	664,917
100,000,000	5,428,681	5,761,455	5,762,208
1,000,000,000	48,254,942	50,847,534	50,849,234
10,000,000,000	434,294,482	455,052,511	455,055,614

Distribution of Primes.—Although the prime-number theorem gives a good over-all picture, many questions about how the primes are distributed remain unanswered. For example, in the 1960s it was still not known just how well $\int_2^N (\ln t)^{-1} dt$ approximates $\pi(N)$. Also, relatively little was known about the behaviour of the gaps between consecutive primes. It is clear that arbitrarily large gaps occur, but only crude estimates were known of how far to go in the sequence of prime numbers to find a gap of given size. Whether the gap 2 occurs infinitely often was likewise unknown. *See also* NUMBERS, THEORY OF.

BIBLIOGRAPHY.—For elementary discussions of prime numbers *see* O. Ore, *Number Theory and Its History* (1948); H. Davenport, *The Higher Arithmetic* (1952); H. Rademacher and O. Toeplitz, *The Enjoyment of Mathematics,* Eng. trans. by H. Zuckerman (1957); H. Rademacher, *Lectures on Elementary Number Theory* (1964). For more thorough treatments *see* G. H. Hardy and E. M. Wright, *An Introduction to the Theory of Numbers,* 4th ed. (1960); W. J. LeVeque, *Topics in Number Theory,* 2 vol. (1956); and E. Trost, *Primzahlen* (1953). For advanced monographs *see* A. E. Ingham, *The Distribution of Prime Numbers* (1932); T. Estermann, *Introduction to Modern Prime Number Theory* (1952); K. Prachar, *Primzahlverteilung* (1957); R. Ayoub, *An Introduction to the Analytic Theory of Numbers* (1963).
(P. T. B.)

PRIMITIVE ART is that made and used by members of primitive societies (*see* ART). This discussion deals largely with the visual art of primitive societies. Such art is generally functional to the extent that primitive sculpture, painting, and decoration are usually of religious and social importance; while the meanings and uses of primitive art objects are not always known, it is better to assume them all to be useful, rather than as made for art's sake. The use for which the artist intends his work delineates so-called fine (pure, serious) art from minor (*e.g.*, applied, decorative, industrial, commercial) art. Yet many objects considered to be fine art in modern cultures of European origin were made and first used as religious paraphernalia. An artifact is recognizable as art by the aesthetic organization of its visible form. Order, consistency, rhythm, harmony, and balance of lines, shapes, masses, colours, light values, and textures serve to identify artistic quality in an item of material culture.

Art is one way to present symbols for use in human social life, fixing in visible and enduring form otherwise intangible and transient images, ideas, and events. Barring purposeful destruction, persistence of visual art is limited only by the durability of its materials. But by contrast with everyday experience, the aesthetic characteristics help fix the symbols in human awareness and memory at the moment of presentation. Ceremonial art is a conscious and determined effort to make important symbols visible and permanent. Since aesthetic quality is common to all art, the word primitive refers only to the nature of the society in which the work originates. But authorities may disagree in applying the term. Many (as does this section) have termed primitive those small, isolated, homogeneous, and intimate societies where literacy is absent, where there is informal social control, and where there is strong group solidarity.

On the other hand, if primitive is taken to mean original or first, difficulty arises in applying the term either to contemporary societies or to those of the recent past. The art of the very first human society probably never will be known; however, the term primitive can be used to indicate the relative primacy of a society and its art. The oldest surviving art known is that of the Upper Paleolithic in Europe; but this should not be called the dawn of art, since earlier man may have produced art in Europe, and in other parts of the world as well. The arts of precivilized and non-civilized societies may both be called primitive. The distinction of specific primitive societies hinges in part on judging the origin and rise of civilizations. At any rate, the following distinctions between so-called primitive and civilized peoples should be regarded only as provisional.

In Europe and Asia primitive societies existed prior to the development of civilizations; however, because these civilizations have flourished longer and more widely than those elsewhere, very few primitive societies have persisted. These are the Siberian Eskimo, the Ainu of Japan, and some peoples marginal to the Chinese and Indian civilizations. In Oceania the Indonesian civilization may be thought of as having derived from Asia; however, the aboriginal inhabitants of Malaysia, Australia, Melanesia, Micronesia, and Polynesia fall into a noncivilized (primitive) category. The aboriginal inhabitants of the Americas were members of primitive societies, some of which developed into civilized societies in Andean South America and in Mesoamerica (Valley of Mexico and the Mayan area). Among the intermediate peoples in western Mexico, the Circum-Caribbean, and northwestern South America, evidence in the 1960s failed to clearly separate primitive from nonprimitive societies. Egypt and North Africa are related to Eurasian civilization; but south of the Sahara many aboriginally primitive societies persist. In West Africa there were several indigenous civilized states (Ashanti, Dahomey, Oyo, and Benin); yet their art is often grouped as primitive.

The small size and informal social control of many societies labeled as primitive tend to limit the size of art objects produced; isolation of such societies limits the importation of raw materials. Relatively simple division of labour (by age and sex) tends to limit specialization of artists. Primitive artists, under the necessity of farming, collecting, or hunting for a living, tend to function part-time. The special skills of primitive artists thus tend to have less time to develop than do those of full-time artists in civilized society. This may be why although much primitive art seems relatively vital it sometimes seems crude in technique, compared to some very delicately rendered art objects from civilized societies.

(P. H. L.)

The article contains the following sections:
   I. Prehistoric Europe
  II. Prehistoric Asia
 III. Africa
  IV. Oceania
   V. New World

I. PREHISTORIC EUROPE

The discovery of Ice Age (Pleistocene) art must be linked strictly with E. A. I. H. Lartet (*q.v.*), although a few years earlier the geologist P. A. Brouillet had discovered perforated staffs of bone at the Grotte de Chaffaud near Savigné, Vienne, France, and an Englishman, E. Mayor, had discovered pieces of worked bone near Geneva, Switz. In France, Lartet explored (1862) the caves of Espélugues near Lourdes and carried out excavations in the Les Eyzies district, Dordogne, bringing to light a large number of engraved and sculptured bones and, in the Chaffaud cave, a number of drawings on the cave walls. The case made by Lartet and H. Christy for the high antiquity of these works was strengthened by the discovery in the Grotte de la Madeleine, in an undisturbed Ice Age deposit, of engraved mammoth bone with a representation of this extinct animal.

Between 1860 and 1880, in southern France and on its southeastern frontier, burials of Upper Paleolithic man were found at Laugerie-Basse, in the caves at Grimaldi near Menton, and at Cro-Magnon itself, revealing skeletons, shell ornaments, and flint tools above strata of accumulated Ice-Age artifacts (*see* CRO-MAGNON MAN).

In 1868 in the province of Santander, Spain, the first of the big painted caves (*see* ALTAMIRA CAVE) was found. It seemed to have been closed by a fall of rock at the end of the Ice Age; bone implements lay immediately below the debris. Other Paleolithic paintings were found in France: in Chabot cave, Gard, in 1878 by L. Chiron, and in the cave at Pair-non-Pair, Gironde, in 1883. The Pair-non-Pair pictures were entirely covered by late Aurignacian deposits that permitted accurate assignment. Other caves were opened in rapid succession: Marsoulas, Pyrenees (1897), and Font-de-Gaume and Les Combarelles in the Dordogne. French discoveries in cave painting and minor art were made in 1902 by H. E. P. Breuil (*q.v.*), and in 1912 by Count H. Bégouen. In 1923 N. Casteret discovered Montespan cave and in 1932 that at Labastide, both in the Pyrenees. The most important discovery since has been the Lascaux cave, Dordogne, with excellent frescoes, in 1940.

Meanwhile prehistoric paintings had been discovered in caves in southeast Spain from Lérida to Cádiz, but little was found to help date them.

A number of smaller works of prehistoric art have been found in Germany and the Low Countries. Eastern Europe and the U.S.S.R. are also rich in minor works, few of which approach the high artistic quality of the French finds and some of the Swiss carvings. Britain has produced a few crude engravings on bone, but no evidence of cave art.

Paleolithic Art.—*Carved and Incised Objects.*—Although human beings are rarely represented in the cave art of western Europe, the earliest plastic figures represent mature steatopygous females with pendulant breasts. These figurines show remarkable consistency in style over their total distribution from France to southern U.S.S.R., are carved in bone or schist, once coloured, and are known as Venuses. The earliest examples come from middle Aurignacian contexts, but those from later Aurignacian-Perigordian period are of higher quality. About 130 examples are known, many from the encampment sites of mammoth hunters at Gagarino, Ukraine, U.S.S.R., where special niches to house them were built into the hut walls. One of the most noted examples comes from Willendorf, Aus., while another, the head of such a figure with retted hair and beautifully marked facial features, is the famous Venus from Brassempouy, Landes, France. In the Ukraine and in Moravia, Czech., these figurines become highly schematized, reduced often to pegs of ivory or bone with highly developed buttocks and breasts. Few bodily features are marked, although some examples have extremely thin arms folded over the chest. Moravian examples have incised geometric-spiral designs on the back and buttocks which might represent tattooing. Male statuettes are much rarer and are artistically inferior, but a male head from Dolní Věstonice in Moravia has its features realistically carved.

Larger-scale sculpture is almost entirely confined to France, probably arising from natural rock forms of suggestive shape. A parallel to the Aurignacian Venus figurines is the low relief from Laussel, Dordogne, of a steatopygous female figure holding a "cornucopia." Similar Perigordian reliefs were carved in partly exposed rock shelters at Cap Blanc, Dordogne, and some of ibexes and wild boar were found on the Roc-de-Sers, Charente. High relief animal sculptures at Angles-sur-Anglin, Vienne, are Magdalenian. The only piece of sculpture in the round is the head of a musk ox from Laugerie-Haute, Dordogne, 9 in. high, but Magdalenian sculptures in clay of a bear from the Montespan cave, Garonne, and copulating bison from the Tuc d'Audoubert, Ariège, approach the roundness of sculpture. Some of the stone reliefs are the only art attributable to the ill-defined Solutrean period (*see* ARCHAEOLOGY).

In the Magdalenian period miniature carving of animals predominated particularly in western Europe. Archaeologically stratified ivory carvings have come from Stetten ob Lontal, Württemberg, Ger. (wild horse, panther, mammoth), and from late Aurignacian mammoth-hunting stations in Moravia, where clay models accompanied ivory (mammoth, bear, wild horse, reindeer, owl). In French sites miniature sculptures come mostly from Magdalenian strata. These pieces, particularly those of horse and bison heads, surpass anything in eastern Europe. Particularly

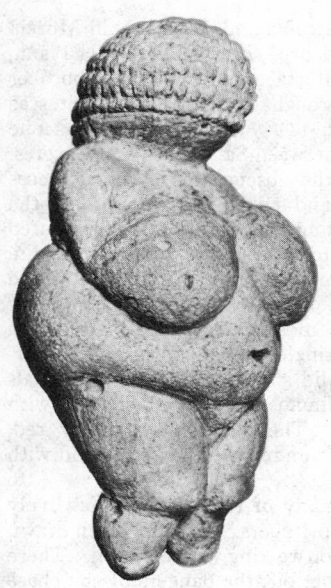

BY COURTESY OF (LEFT) THE PRÄHISTORISCHE ABTEILUNG, NATURHISTORISCHES MUSEUM, VIENNA, (ABOVE) THE HISTORISK MUSEUM, UNIVERSITETET I BERGEN; PHOTOGRAPH, (ABOVE) RAGNAR UTNE

(LEFT) "VENUS OF WILLENDORF," WILLENDORF, AUS. STONE. 4⅛ IN. (ABOVE) ROCK ENGRAVING OF A FISH, SKOGERVEIEN, BUSKERUD, NOR. LENGTH: 8 FT.

fine are a horse's head of reindeer antler from Le Mas d'Azil, Ariège, and a standing horse in ivory from Lourdes. Some have harpoons engraved upon them and must have been used as hunting talismans; some of the best examples are carved on throwing sticks and other hunting implements.

In this category are the carved finials of spear-throwers of Le Mas d'Azil in the form of a chamois or a black cock, handles like one carved in the form of two crouching deer from Bruniquel Tarn-et-Garonne, and another in the form of a single reindeer from Laugerie-Basse. Perforated staves of ivory are sometimes carved with animal terminals; although known as *bâtons de commandement,* they were probably used as arrow-straighteners. These are often covered with designs of deer, horses, birds, and fish.

The vast majority of Magdalenian finds are isolated engravings on bone, flat tines of antler, small slabs of stone or flat pebbles, executed sometimes with surety, sometimes as though they were practice pieces. Notable are Dordogne examples of hairy bisons' heads from Limeuil and Laugerie-Basse on bone and small limestone blocks. From Teyjat come experiments in group drawing: a herd of reindeer with only the outer animals drawn in detail, the herd effect achieved by central multiplication of legs and antlers. A herd of galloping horses is treated less summarily. A more detailed style is seen in antler engravings from Lorthet in the Pyrenees where, on a spear-thrower, reindeer are shown swimming. The hooves and body hairs are drawn with precision, as are details of salmon swimming between the beasts' feet.

Bone engravings of Pyrenean quality are not common elsewhere in Europe, but from the Pekárna cave in Moravia comes a masterly representation of bison in combat. Here too were found perforated staves parallel to the French type, and bone pieces engraved with horse, bison, and chamois. Outline engravings of mammoths have been found at Kostienki I and Maltà, near Lake Baikal, Siberia. In these minor and applied arts of the Magdalenian period no interest is shown in scenic background, or the human figure; the few examples of what appear to be human beings, including an engraved bone from Pin Hole cave, Derbyshire, Eng., are badly executed and difficult to discern. These minor pieces, though scarcely surpassed in treatment and skill, are greatly surpassed in scale by the engravings and paintings in caves.

Cave Engravings and Paintings.—Geographical limitations confine cave art largely to southwest France and northeast Spain, the so-called Franco-Cantabrian province, but isolated finds come from southern Italy, southern Germany, and southern U.S.S.R. In the absence of firm chronology, it is difficult to reconstruct stylistic development, even in France. Cave decoration is either made with stone gravers or with masses of liquid paint. While massive sculpture is usually placed in open rock shelters, paintings and engravings are usually hidden in deep recesses of caves where clay

modeling was also practised. Breuil's lifelong study outlined the evolution of cave art from simple Aurignacian line engraving to late Magdalenian polychrome painting. Incised on hard rock surfaces, painted, or drawn in wet clay with a finger, the lines were originally of uniform thickness, later revised and modulated. The detailed drawing of pelt, muscles, and other anatomy tends to be zonal.

Painting and engraving often appear together in caves and probably came into use simultaneously. Distinctions in style suggest that painters and engravers practised separate crafts. Only one known cave is decorated exclusively with engraved designs: Les Combarelles, Dordogne, has thousands of superimposed engravings from late Aurignacian through middle Magdalenian, suggesting that this cave was the centre of a hunting cult. Bison and reindeer are the main repertoire, but grotesque humans with parts of other animals are perhaps decoys or hunting magicians. Some of the engraved animals are lively, others stiff; chronological distinctions between these styles cannot be accurately made. From stratified caves, however, it appears that Aurignacian style was close-contoured and stiff, and lacked the three-dimensional qualities of the later period. At Altamira, Teyjat (Dordogne), and Font-de-Gaume, engravings accompany Magdalenian wall paintings; it is possible to appreciate the plastic qualities of Magdalenian engraving and efforts to represent dimension, although the positioning of feet (often completely omitted) is embarrassing. Action is depicted at Font-de-Gaume, where a pregnant lioness is engraved ready to spring and horses canter in file. At Altamira leaping hinds and baying stags have lifelike qualities, antlers drawn in fine perspective. These epitomize the extremely flowing style of Magdalenian engraving, seen in plodding mammoths at Font-de-Gaume and some of the bears depicted at Les Combarelles.

At Lascaux, in a ramified cave of passages and chambers on various levels, the best-preserved traditions of later Aurignacian art survive; the Pech-Merle cave, Cabrerets, should be associated with it. Paintings in both caves are executed in thick black outline little refined. The bodies of some of the animals are washed in with red or brown paint, shading off toward the underparts. Horses are painted in solid black silhouette, but some horses, bison and aurochs (*q.v.*) in both caves are painted with an over-all dot pattern. Friezes of horses and bulls traverse the lower edge of the arched roof, while the upper portions are left for depicting larger animals. Although the paintings are superimposed, at Lascaux there seems to have been a consistent attempt to decorate the roof in an orderly fashion. In other caves animals are painted without significant relationships.

Altamira cave remains preeminent in Magdalenian style. The natural bulges of the 7-ft.-high rock roof were painted with standing and squatting bison, thickly outlined in black and filled in with red, producing an effect of unparalleled beauty and realism. About 20 of them cover a distance of about 15 yd. The rock formation was used to give a round effect in the body; the legs were painted from underneath (the alternative in the visual dilemma was to paint the legs from the side) giving the animals a slightly concave appearance countered by the rock surface. Font-de-Gaume cave closely parallels the painted-in technique of Altamira and indeed, in parts, probably represents an earlier late-Aurignacian style, but unfortunately it is badly preserved. The Niaux caves, Ariège, belong to the same black-outline tradition but do not have painted fillings. However, the outlines, painted with thick strokes and adjusted with thin, are more carefully drawn than elsewhere and the perspective of the feet of bison and wild horse is more successfully achieved.

Besides introducing painting as a pictorial technique the primitive art of the Paleolithic begins the expressional and magical use of colour. Black, red, brown, and a dull yellow were chiefly used. Besides animals and anthropoid figures, areas and brush marks of colour and curiously shaped tectiforms (perhaps representing huts) were sometimes painted in, as were colour-blotched outlines of stumpy human hands. Among the pigments at Altamira and Lascaux natural oxides of iron and manganese supplied red and black; iron carbonate gave yellow; at Lascaux blue-black and dark-brown manganese oxides were found; other blacks came from soot. When finely ground these pigments were mixed with water rather than a fatty base, allowing quick application to damp rock. Pigments were stored in such hollow receptacles as bones, stones, and skulls, as at Les Cottés, Vannes. Bone mortars and pestles for grinding paints, and stone lamps for lighting dark recesses have been found. Fingertips, brushes, and daubing pads were used to apply the colour.

The purpose of this art is not clear. Executed far from normal gaze, the work was apparently done in great discomfort. That it was directed at the magical possession of favourable hunting conditions is occasionally indicated. An outline-painted mammoth in the Pindal cave, Asturias, Spain, has a red blotch indicating the position of the heart and a batch of arrows painted in front of it. Outlined bison in the Niaux cave, Pyrenees, have superimposed painted barbs pointing at the heart and midrib and blotches of red (blood?) on the body. Patchwork squares painted in front of such naturally curious animals as oxen and goats at Lascaux might represent pitfalls covered with sheets of skins. In the same cave is a scene in which a man with a broken spear is worsted by a bison. Comblike patterns painted near and on top of some animals might represent fenced enclosures to which they were to be lured. A human-shaped figure (the famous "sorcerer") wearing an antler mask in Les Trois Frères cave, Ariège, might be a decoy or a hunting magician. Hunting rites are evidenced by clay model animals, some with unmistakable signs of use as targets. Other models suggest magical increase of fertility (many painted animals are pregnant and pregnant women are occasionally engraved on bone).

Toward the end of the Magdalenian period naturalistic realism weakened in favour of formalized arrangements of horns, antlers, and fur reduced to a pattern. Schematic female figures have been found from the earlier Paleolithic in Moravia; in the west chamois and reindeer were reduced to formalistic ornaments. In western Europe art was not to achieve such heights of abstraction until the appearance of the formalized Celtic art of La Tène (q.v.).

A branch of Franco-Cantabrian art is represented at the cave of Parpalló, Valencia, where engraved bone pieces are stratified in Gravettian, Solutrean, and Magdalenian contexts; and where stones with animal paintings occur in the Solutrean. At La Pileta cave, Málaga, a peripheral Magdalenian style of painting seems to have been introduced. The animals depicted are, unlike those of France, such forest dwellers as deer, wild boar, the smaller deer and oxen, and not Ice-Age fauna; doubtless the southerly latitude is as much responsible for the difference as is the later date. The art of these two caves is possibly linked with the engraved animals in caves in Liguria, Apulia, and west Sicily and may thus belong to an ill-defined "Mediterranean" province, possibly with African connections, which continued Paleolithic artistic tradition into Mesolithic times.

Epipaleolithic (Mesolithic) Cave Art of Spain.—Another group of cave paintings, while difficult to date, can be largely attributed to the Mesolithic. Found in southeast Spain, they differ sharply in style and content from the paintings of the Franco-Cantabrian province. They incorporate an African style as seen in largely undatable paintings and rock engravings from Algeria, Tunisia, the Atlas Mountains, outer Sahara, and Bushman art in South Africa. These African examples, like those of southeast Spain, are tribal rather than individual; hunting by small family groups in Paleolithic times had been taken over by organized males of the tribe. The Spanish-Levantine painted caves, discovered mostly in the early 20th century, are grouped in Albacete (Alpera

and Minateda caves), in Teruel (Alcañiz and Tormón), in Murcia (Cogul and Yecla), in Valencia (Bicorp), in Castellón de la Plana, and in several shelters in the Valltorta gorge between Albocácer and Tirig. New paintings were brought to light at such sites as the Cueva del Polvorín, Castellón (1947). The group has one outlyer, the cave of Las Batuecas between Salamanca and Cáceres.

Engravings are very rare and the absence of stratified pieces of minor art makes the dating and culture attribution of the paintings difficult, but their beginning is probably to be associated with the Upper Paleolithic Capsian industry of southeast Spain. While large-scale single animals are the rule in Franco-Cantabrian paintings, small-scale compositions of many figures were chosen by the southern Spanish artists. In most of the paintings human groups play a large part, hunting single animals with bow and arrow. All figures are painted in solid silhouette; those of animals are true to nature while those of humans are highly distorted, with elongated bodies and thick legs. The colours are chiefly red, brown, and black, largely derived from manganese and bound with blood, egg, or honey.

With tribalism came war, and many of the scenes depict lively arrow battles or mass execution of prisoners. Women, often drawn in long dresses, are shown dancing or walking with children. There is no evidence of fishing or trapping, but the dangers of the chase are vividly shown in Cueva Remigia paintings where oxen and ibexes turn on fleeing hunters. Little domestic life is shown, but a painting in the Cueva de la Araña, Valencia, depicts a woman gathering wild honey; one in the Gasulla gorge shows a spider surrounded by flies.

Paleolithic and Mesolithic Art of Northern Europe.—A third group of prehistoric art, largely from the northern limits of Europe, while again showing a generic relationship with Ice-Age art of western Europe, cannot be related to an Upper Paleolithic culture. In Finland, northern Norway (Finnmark, Nordland, Troms), central Norway (Tröndelag), and on the upper Yenisei River at Shalobolinsk in western Siberia, the custom arose of engraving scenes of hunting and magic on inaccessible slabs of rock or cliff surfaces. The linear style of arctic reindeer, elk, and bear lacks Magdalenian dimensional qualities, but is very definite and simple. The more naturalistic representations and those with perspective as seen in French Magdalenian art are found only in remotest northern Norway and Siberia. Groups of animals and disguised human decoys are sometimes shown, and great interest in the sea is evidenced by engravings of halibut and seal; and, on the White Sea coast, by boats of a type ancestral to those in Bronze-Age engravings from Scandinavia. Although hunting scenes are not shown, depiction of inner parts of animals strongly indicates that hunting-magic was the primary purpose of these drawings. For decorative purposes, superb small animal models were carved in the Danish Maglemose (Mesolithic) settlements.

Neolithic and Bronze Age Art.—The migration of Neolithic agriculturalists from the Near East to Europe and the rise of European peasant communities brought the beginnings of a folk art expressed chiefly in weaving, basketry, and pottery making. Cave art was now confined to the engraving of simple magico-religious patterns on rocks, as at Newgrange and Lochcrew in Ireland, and standing stones at Morbihan in Brittany. From Anatolia the idea of pottery painting spread into southern and eastern Europe. A variety of techniques of painting and incision are known in the chief areas of Neolithic painted pottery culture at Tripolye, U.S.S.R.; Cucuteni, Rum.; Vučedol, Yugos.; and the Dimini and Sesklo cultures, Greece. In all of these, designs are abstract, often spiriform; the ceramic tradition also includes figurines of women with painted or incised designs indicating elaborately embroidered clothing. Decorations on unpainted pottery from the rest of Europe show the predominant influence of basketry. In perfecting techniques of shaping and polishing stone tools the Neolithic craftsman brought to earlier Stone Age traditions a new combination of utilitarian and aesthetic feeling.

Apart from a few crude anthropomorphic statue menhirs the Bronze Age has no sculpture to show in central Europe, but in Spain rock carvings of weapons are found on the Atlantic seaboard, and at Kivik and Bohuslan in Sweden rock carvings of chariots, plows, and boats continued to the 10th century B.C. and to the beginning of a new artistic tradition in metalwork that spanned central Europe from the Alps to the Baltic. *See* HALLSTATT; VILLANOVANS; FRANCE: *Archaeology;* SPAIN: *History;* EUROPE: *Archaeology.* (WM. C.)

II. PREHISTORIC ASIA

This brief survey is limited to the art of prehistoric China and Japan; *i.e.,* before the use of writing.

China.—As far as archaeological knowledge in the 1960s is concerned, the first truly historic period of early China, that is, the Shang (Yin) dynasty (c. 1523–1027 B.C. according to some authorities), seems to have emerged suddenly with a highly developed civilization. Writing, ceramics, bronze casting, sculpture, and, presumably, painting had attained a very high level under the Shang. This is clearly shown by the great number of materials recovered through numerous excavations since 1928 at the final site of the Shang capital, dating from about 1300–1027 B.C., and located in the northern tip of Honan Province near the present city of Anyang. These materials are not to be considered prehistoric art; however, available prehistoric artifacts include Neolithic pottery collected in abundance, especially in northern China.

After what has been called a Neolithic hiatus, a well-developed Neolithic culture appeared in north China near the end of this period about 4,000 years ago. Best known, perhaps, is the Yangshao culture, named after the type site discovered in Honan Province in 1921. This covers a large area in northwestern China and is characterized by the excellence of its ceramics, which had few equals (if any) for that time. The most spectacular Neolithic ceramics comprise the painted pottery found in many sites in a wide belt across north China. The Yangshao culture had its beginnings about 2500–2000 B.C., and this pottery is associated with burials. In shape and size the painted pottery objects range from a large- and medium-sized amphora type to smaller jars, bowls, and basins. The ware itself is technically excellent, fired at high temperature, and painted with considerable skill. The designs are (generally speaking) geometric, and are based on such elements as the circle, diamond, rhombic checkers, zigzags, triangle and rotary S curves, with a gourd motif, cross-hatching, and the so-called death pattern (a saw-toothed band) as common features. They are painted in black, brown, purple, and similar colours that contrast with the reddish colour of the ware. Of particular interest are those paintings which contain anthropomorphic or zoomorphic designs. In some cases, birds (for example, the whooper swan) are so ingeniously stylized that there is little question about their identity. A few quite naturalistic paintings of human faces and fish have occurred on the Neolithic pottery excavated at the important Pan P'o Ts'un site discovered since the Communist takeover in 1949. Most of this painting was done with a flexible brush, and it may be presumed that paintings, perhaps of a completely different nature, were also being done at this time on perishable materials. One of the most important problems remaining to be solved in this field is that of the origin of this painted pottery. Although there is still no general consensus, and some argue for an independent origin in northwest China, there is much evidence to point to a connection with ceramics from such areas to the west as Tripolye in south U.S.S.R., and even Iran.

A somewhat later wheel-thrown pottery of the Lungshan complex is also noted for its technical excellence. This type was first found at Lungshan in the eastern province of Shantung; later traces of it were found as far south as Hangchow and as far west as Szechwan. This ware is black or brownish, of remarkable eggshell thinness, and so highly burnished that it still retains a mirror-like finish. It is on the whole undecorated, but a few pieces have been found that have simple, incised geometric designs.

While large numbers of carved personal ornaments made from shell, stone, clay, and bone have been discovered, only a very few objects have been found that can be regarded as sculpture in the strictest sense of the word. One of these is a small, highly stylized and unidentifiable animal figure found at the Sha Kuo T'un site in Liaoning, Manchuria. It is carved from marble and the principal features are suggested rather than clearly delineated; in spirit

it is close to some of the cubistic small animal sculpture of the Shang dynasty. Two others, small pottery figurines from Pu Chao Chai in Honan Province, are a crudely made bird and a simple but recognizable human. *See also* CHINA: *History.*

Modern examples of primitive art may be found in the early woodcarving of the aborigines in Formosa (*q.v.*), especially in that of the Paiwan group. Some of the motifs show a relationship to the art of Polynesia, and in one case a close parallel has been found to a motif used in the Dong-son complex of Indochina and southwest China about the third or fourth century B.C. (*see* INDONESIAN ARCHAEOLOGY AND ART).

Japan.—The wholesale Japanese adoption of Chinese Buddhism along with writing, art, and culture in general in the 6th century A.D. marked the end of Japan's scriptless protohistoric period. Before this time, Japan had passed through a still vague Paleolithic phase, a well-defined Neolithic stage, and a Bronze or Bronze-Iron period.

The prehistoric period in Japan is characterized by two principal cultures known as Jōmon and Yayoi (*see also* JAPANESE ARCHITECTURE). The first, literally "rope pattern," is named after a technique in pottery decoration, and the second after a street in Tokyo where this type of pottery was first found. Generally speaking, both types are distributed widely over Japan, but the earlier Jōmon is more common in the north and east while the later Yayoi is more common in the south and west. Jōmon pottery is rich in typology and shows considerable freedom of design. Decoration is accomplished by relief decor, spiral designs, and scraping. Of more artistic interest are peculiar and often grotesque clay figurines that may have been used for totemistic or fertility rites or may have served as penates at different stages in their development. These figurines show a progression from lower animal to human characteristics. In most cases they are skilfully executed, and incised, appliquéd, stamped, and shell- or cord-impressed.

Yayoi pottery seems to have its beginnings in the 3rd century B.C. and is mostly wheel-thrown. It is decorated with painted floral motifs, saw-toothed bands, and rectangular spirals in red and with combed patterns. Some pieces have crude, incised pictures that represent animals of various kinds and other scenes of a very elementary nature. Although there is evidence from certain aspects of decoration and shape to link some of the early Japanese pottery with the Gobi cultures and northeast Asia, it should be noted that there is no trace of influence from the Chinese painted pottery or the black eggshell ware.

Bronze was introduced from China by way of Korea about the first century A.D., but there was hardly a true Bronze Age because the Iron Age almost immediately followed. The most important indigenous Japanese bronze form is the *dōtaku,* a bell-shaped object, ranging from a few inches to almost four feet in height, which often contains cast or incised pictures in panels. The drawing, while very simple, is more advanced than that found on Yayoi pottery and represents animals, buildings, hunting, and domestic scenes. Clay sculpture during the protohistoric period is well known through the figures called *haniwa* which were buried around the perimeter of a tomb, apparently for protection. The earliest, dating from about the 3rd century A.D., were scarcely more than clay cylinders with embellishments of one kind or another. These later developed into human figures: armed guards, dancers, and musicians. Many of them are very finely executed in a realistic style showing much detail in clothing and armour. Many of the faces are painted with definite patterns in red. Other objects represented by *haniwa* are animals (especially horses), and many types of house.

Some actual paintings in the form of tomb murals survive from the protohistoric period. These consist mainly of abstract geometrical designs based on concentric circles, rectangles, diagonal lines, and arcs. Realistic paintings include such objects as horses, boats, quivers, and shields. These decorations are in black, red, blue, and white, and generally are of low quality. (R. C. RU.)

III. AFRICA

Traditional, predominantly tribal arts of subsaharan Africa were nearly unknown elsewhere until studied by 19th-century anthropologists. Popular interest was aroused when early 20th-century European artists found African sculpture worthy of admiration. However, conservatism and commitment were often misread by outsiders as freedom, innovation, and self-expression.

Art may be understood best in the light of its cultural origins. Anthropological studies record the cultural role of the arts, but equally necessary are stylistic analyses, and historical and archaeological investigations.

History.—Much prehistoric art was probably of perishable material, and little is known of the early art of the great empires of Western Sudan or the more modest kingdoms of the forest areas. Yet archaeological discoveries of rock paintings in the Sahara, Nigeria, East and South Africa, as well as clay pieces of the Nok figurine culture of northern Nigeria, hint at a rich art predating Christ. Terra-cotta work of the Sao culture near Lake Chad and bronzes (technically, brasses) from Ife, Benin (*qq.v.*), and elsewhere in Nigeria indicate continuing activity from medieval times.

BY COURTESY OF DEPARTMENT OF ANTIQUITIES, JOS, NIGERIA

TERRA-COTTA HEAD, NOK CULTURE COMPLEX, NORTHERN NIGERIA. 1ST MILLENNIUM B.C. 7 IN.

Rare instances of preserved perishable art (as in a collection in Ulm, Ger., dating to about A.D. 1650) closely resemble much more recent material. Similarly, style continuity (although modified) is apparent in Benin bronze casting over several centuries, in Dogon (*q.v.*) ancestor figures, in the relationship of little steatite Nomori figures of Sierra Leone to modern Mende (*q.v.*) wood carving, and in Kuba (*q.v.*) king figures perhaps extending over three centuries.

Despite its position outside the orbit of medieval Europe, Africa south of the Sahara long has been subject to outside influence. Phoenician traders probably made earliest foreign contact with northwest Africa; and Saharan trade routes have existed for 2,000 years. As early as the 7th century A.D. Islam entered the Sudan with displaced Arabs. After the 11th century the *jihads* (Muslim holy wars) spread the religion throughout Western Sudan. Arab historians and observers followed, some of them associated with the great medieval university and library at Tombouctou (Timbuktu). Likewise, coastal East Africa, as part of the ancient Indian Ocean trade system, has yielded large amounts of Chinese porcelain that have been of help in dating archaeological finds with which they occur. European contact with the west coast dates from the 15th century; significant penetration inland began about four centuries later.

African artistic traditions (including those allied to religion) survived traders, soldiers, scholars, missionaries, empire builders, and holy wars. The Islamic interdiction against imagery was widely resisted, as were early European entrenchments. By the 1960s, however, modern science and technology had undermined much of traditional tribal insularity and disrupted ancient ways. As a result, earlier art forms that reflected the older cultures were rapidly disappearing. Unlike much European and American work, traditional African art neither condemned nor questioned popular cultural values. Reflecting and contributing to the needs of people, art symbolized individual and tribal security, understood in such terms as wealth, prestige, health, children, wives, and crops.

However, there was room in this scheme for the individual skill of the artist. Skill was the basis for a respected and admired specialist group. The artist (usually trained through apprenticeship and working on commission) received rewards as a specialist who contributed to the tribal sense of well-being.

Purely utilitarian objects that are unornamented or undecorated are omitted from this discussion. Relative aesthetic importance among the arts and crafts in Western cultures is not to be taken as indicative of relative prestige in Africa. Bambara (*q.v.*) blacksmiths, for example, have high status as artisans and (probably related to their specialism) as ritual cult leaders. Despite this, few of their products will be considered here. Specialist activities often are limited by sex: pottery is usually produced by women, wood carving by men; blacksmiths are men; women often decorated house exteriors. Widely differing tribal styles are readily distinguishable to experts, as in many instances are styles of individual artists.

Cloth and Clothing.—The simplest clothing consisted of penis sheaths or loincloths for men, bunches of leaves or small aprons for women. Wraparounds of bark cloth or woven cotton were common. Weaving by women was done on broad vertical looms, that by men on narrow horizontal looms. Cotton, raffia, and occasionally wool or imported silk were utilized. Woven patterns were usually stripes, checks, or simple diagonals or zigzags. The Kuba and other Congo tribes are noted for raffia cut-pile "velvets" which carry geometric patterns that have influenced wood carving on boxes, cups, and drums.

Bark cloth and woven materials were coloured with native paints or dyes. Particularly fine printed decorations among the Ashanti (*q.v.*) were applied with small stamps made of calabash. Yoruba (*q.v.*) women produced richly patterned indigo-and-white cloths (*adire*) by tie-and-dye and by a resist method similar to batik but using a starch paste instead of wax; stencils of zinc, tin, or leather were used as well. Some Western Sudanic tribes, particularly the Bambara, produced rich light-on-dark motifs by a discharge method in which dyed cloth was bleached in patterns by special mud and soap.

A number of West African and Congo tribes produced cloth appliqué which in most instances was restricted to royal or ritual use. That produced for royalty by a family guild among the Dahomey (*q.v.*) is among the most impressive.

Embroidery was most probably imported from North Africa along with such typically embroidered clothing types as loose trousers and robes, turbans, and skull caps. Similarly, so-called Moroccan leatherworking may have been imported into the Western Sudan; dyed leather sandals, containers, scabbards, and horse trappings were decorated with patchwork and appliqué designs like those used in embroidery.

Personal Ornamentation.—Palm oil, vegetable butter, and powdered red camwood (*tukula*) were widely used as cosmetics, along with such Islamic imports as kohl and henna (*see* COSMETICS AND COSMETOLOGY). Facial and body scarification, and elaborate coiffures were common, and were accurately depicted in figure carvings. Jewelry was of ostrich eggshell, iron, brass, silver, gold, ivory, glass, and even twisted elephant hairs. Locally manufactured glass was worked into beads and bracelets at Ife and Bida (*q.v.*) in Nigeria. Heavy neck rings, anklets, and bracelets were made of forged iron or cast brass. Amulets were worn less as ornament than as protection or as guarantees of well-being.

Utensils.—Because the potter's wheel was unknown south of the Sahara, pottery was hand-molded. Fired in open pits at a fairly low temperature, it tended to be fragile and crumbly. Domestic ware often had impressed or incised patterns, was burnished, or coloured with vegetable juices or resins after firing. Ritual or prestige ware could be molded or even sculptured; often a mixture of techniques was used on the same vessel.

Utilitarian wood or calabash objects were frequently incised or burned in linear patterns. Wooden stools, headrests, and chairs (the latter influenced by European prototypes) were similarly ornamented, and were also occasionally decorated with carved figures as among the Luba, Chokwe (*qq.v.*), Basonge, and Cameroon Grasslands tribes (where some chief's stools were completely covered with decorative beadwork). The Baule (*q.v.*) are noteworthy for their heddle pulleys (for horizontal looms) topped with animal (including human) head forms; the neighbouring Guro and Senufo (*see* KWENI; SENUFO), and the Yoruba and Dogon also decorated pulleys. Ashanti cast-brass weights (for weighing gold dust) depict humans, other animals, vegetables, and geometric forms. The Nupe (*q.v.*) were excellent metalworkers, manufacturing a variety of vessels decorated with repoussé (hammered or pressed) designs.

Throwing-knives of the Congo, often with punchwork designs, exemplify finely forged, abstract forms of iron weapons. Blacksmiths produced such ritual utensils as single or double gongs, Bambara staffs topped with equestrian figures, and Yoruba and Benin shrine pieces containing mammal and bird forms.

Architecture.—House types ranged from shelters of boughs and leaves, as among nomadic Fulani herdsmen and Congo pygmies, to elaborate mud structures based on North African prototypes. A typical hut consisted of a windowless mud cylinder pierced by a single door, and topped with a conical, thatched roof. One house type (Yoruba) comprised a series of rectangular rooms around an open court or rain-storage area. Families were often found to live in compounds composed of a number of huts surrounded by a mud wall, or mat fence of woven fibre. Carved wooden houseposts, doors, lintels, sills, and jambs were used widely in West Africa. Particularly outstanding architectural sculpture was produced in the Cameroon Grasslands, Nigeria, Ivory Coast, and Western Sudan (*see* DWELLINGS, PRIMITIVE).

Painting.—African painting (and engraving) includes permanent works on rock surfaces, and those that cannot outlast the mud walls which carry them. The latter, essentially architectural decoration, may be figurative (*e.g.*, on Ibo [*q.v.*] houses in Nigeria) or geometric and essentially nonpictorial (*e.g.*, patterns on Mangbetu and Transvaal Ndebele [*qq.v.*] houses). In this category also belong sgraffito designs, and molded and painted mud decorations in low relief.

Main areas of North African prehistoric rock paintings and engravings have been discovered in the Sahara Atlas Mountains, the Ahaggar Mountains and Tassili, and in the hills of the Libyan Desert. Earliest works seem Neolithic and may not predate 4000 B.C. In later examples Egyptian influences are to be noted and some seem to extend into Roman times. Except for extinct buffalo, modern animals (no longer found in the area) are depicted, including lion, elephant, panther, antelope, gazelle, ox (apparently domesticated), ostrich, and (more rarely) giraffe and rhinoceros. The more naturalistic representations seem to be the earliest.

Some human representations resemble the lively silhouette style of Paleolithic eastern Spain but are probably more recent. Others are grotesque roundheaded figures (playfully called Martians by one author) or hourglass figures. North African rock art may link Paleolithic arts of western Europe with Bushman (*q.v.*) art of South Africa, although this was far from settled in the 1960s. Distribution of Bushman art suggests a migration southward; it is found from Tanganyika through Zambia and Rhodesia into South Africa, fanning out south of the Kalahari Desert.

Earliest Bushman works seem to be engraved animals; these and large painted elands precede human representations. Later, hunting, fishing, warfare, and more stylized dancing scenes showing people and other animals were produced by ancestors of contemporary Bushmen. Old paintings were retouched and new ones created until about a century ago; some of the most recent show Europeans in covered wagons, and on horseback.

The tradition of rock painting still existed in the 1960s among the Dogon of Western Sudan; connected with ancestor beliefs, it depicts masked figures that appear in funerary dances. Excessive and dangerous spiritual powers of the masks were thought to be transferred to the paintings, making the masks safe for use.

Sculpture.—Major sculptural traditions existed in tribes of the tropical rain forest (and adjacent savanna) that extends uninterruptedly along the Guinea coast into the Congo River basin.

Most sculpture was of wood (much of it painted) although other materials were utilized. The earliest known sculptures (about 2,000 years old) are of terra cotta, and come from the Nok culture of Northern Nigeria; they represent humans and other animals in a decidedly Negro African style. Other terra-cotta sculptures are from the Sao culture near Lake Chad (dated about A.D. 1200), and Ife in southern Nigeria (about the 15th century). More re-

cent terra-cotta traditions have been reported from the Ivory Coast, Northern Nigeria, Ghana, and elsewhere.

Stone sculpture is quite rare although steatite figures of no great age have been discovered in Sierra Leone, at Esie in Western Nigeria, and in the southern Congo. Older examples have been found at Ife and Zimbabwe, but none seem truly ancient (*see* ZIMBABWE).

Brass, cast by the lost-wax process (*see* SCULPTURE TECHNIQUES: *Bronze Casting*), was usually the prerogative of royalty, as in Dahomey, and at Ife and Benin in Nigeria. Ife castings appear quite naturalistic and are among the finest subsaharan art. First reported by Leo Frobenius (*q.v.*) early in the 20th century, they are mostly hollow-cast heads, possibly used in ancestral rites. Benin "bronzes" were reported as early as the 16th century, but not until the 1890s did they become well known in Europe. Local traditions indicate the technique and the first caster came from Ife, perhaps in the late 13th century. Heads representing deceased Benin kings, often supporting a carved ivory tusk, and plaques used as architectural decoration predominated. Excellent thinly cast pieces, fairly close to the style of Ife, gave way to heavy, crude, overdecorated pieces of the later 19th century.

Precious metals, particularly silver and gold, were usually the prerogative of royalty, as among the Baule and Ashanti. Ivory carving was widespread, with fine pieces coming from Benin and the neighbouring city of Owo, and from a number of tribes in the Congo. Wood was usually carved green; tradition prescribed the choice of wood, the rituals and taboos governing the artist and his tools, and the sacrifices that consecrated the completed object.

Boldly carved masks of human and other animal forms (often combined) were usually worn with elaborate, totally concealing dance costumes. Representing spirit forces, and often manufactured in secret, the masks were used in rituals relating to puberty (Pende and Yaka initiation masks), agriculture (Bambara *Chiwara* masks), policing and judicial functions (Kuba *Shene Malula*, and Bambara *Kono* masks), and ancestor worship (Yoruba *Egungun* masks). Such functions were combined in Poro Society masks of Liberia and western Ivory Coast (*see* MASK).

In figure sculpture, heads tended to be large, legs squat, and torsos and faces generalized (there seems to have been little or no physiognomic portraiture). Although static, and usually frontal and symmetrical, stance was descriptive of normal carriage and gesture. The carvings served for ancestor worship (Dogon and Bambara), dispelling evil (Fang and Kota), fertility (Ashanti *Akuaba* figures), healing (Lower Congo), personal well-being (Ibo *Ikenga* sculpture), secret societies (Lega *Mwami* society), and as commemorative statuary (Baule portraits and Kuba king figures). *See also* AFRICA.   (RY. S.)

IV. OCEANIA

In Oceania four major art styles correspond to the cultures of Australia, Melanesia, Micronesia, and Polynesia. A certain uniformity in style may be observed in Australia and Micronesia; Polynesia and especially Melanesia show regional variations.

Typical of other primitive cultures, this art had religious or social use and was rarely made for its own sake. Magico-religious aspects were especially strong in Australia and Melanesia. In Polynesia and Micronesia, art was also credited with magical power, but it was given most emphasis for social display.

These were originally Stone-Age cultures, and metal tools and weapons appeared after European contact in the 19th century. Consequently even the art of the recent past derived from a Stone-Age technology. With such limitations in tools and techniques, artistic achievements in Oceania seem all the more exceptional.

Knowledge of prehistoric Oceania is limited, but toward the end of the Ice Age there seem to have been three or more migrations out of southeast Asia (*see* OCEANIA). The earliest moved into Melanesia and Australia; later migrations penetrated Melanesia and later Micronesia and Polynesia. Knowledge is so limited that little more can be done than to speculate on the broad pattern of migration. Examples of art from this period are isolated and difficult to relate to other cultural developments. There are remains of stone platforms in Micronesia, the Society Islands, and the Marquesas; handsome sculptured mortars and pestles have been unearthed in New Guinea; petroglyphs, some of which may be ancient, occur throughout Oceania; and design motifs from as far east as the Marquesas resemble some from ancient China. Such motifs may be survivals from a very early period. It may be assumed that there was a great quantity of prehistoric art, little of which has survived. This discussion is concentrated on material produced during the last 150 years and now deposited in the large collections of Europe, America, and Australia.

Australia.—Simple living conditions and few possessions typify the nomadic tribes of Australia, but they show complex social organization and elaborately developed supernatural beliefs (*see* AUSTRALIAN ABORIGINALS). Some of their sacred art is ascribed to all-powerful beings of an ancient, mythical "dreamtime." Although some rock paintings and engravings are secular, those of greatest importance (and probably of greatest age) are held sacred. Several styles in painting range from tiny linear, animated figures to large pictures of the supernatural Wandjina beings (northwest Australia). Found on rock surfaces of shallow caves and shelters, they are sometimes compared in location and technique with rock art in Africa and Spain. However, the so-called X-ray style, in which internal organs are shown in stylized detail, is uniquely Australian. This device is also used in paintings on bark from Arnhem Land (northern Australia) that represent figures, animals, and plant forms in flat areas of massed lines and dots, sometimes spread over the entire surface.

Painting techniques and media of Australia are similar to those throughout Oceania, although allowance should be made for local variations and the recent use of trade colours. The pigments were coloured earths, red and yellow ochres; white came from natural lime deposits and from burned shell; black was charcoal or manganese compounds. Mixed with water, the pigment was applied with the tip of a chewed stem, a feather, or even the finger. It was sometimes mixed with tree sap or oil or treated afterward with fixative made from honey or wax.

Sculptured figures in wood, clay, and wax are rare, but clusters of abstract carved and painted commemorative poles are erected at burial grounds on Melville Island off northern Australia. Carvings on tree trunks and on ground surface at some ceremonial grounds are similar to the highly symbolic totemic designs on spear throwers, shields, and sacred bullroarers and churingas; the designs applied to these are engraved in concentric circles, spirals, loops, and zigzags (*see* BULLROARER).

Melanesia.—In Melanesian art the principal theme is a figure that represented remote mythological beings or images of important ancestor cults. Carving and painting the figures or constructing elaborate ceremonial masks and costumes were important since they were held to maintain contact with the supernatural. Much of the vital and intense Melanesian art seems spectral and fantastic.

New Guinea.—The largest island of Melanesia, New Guinea has been divided into nine roughly distinct style areas: (1) In the northwest coast and Geelvink Bay area art is curvilinear (as throughout New Guinea generally) and uses much open scrollwork, probably influenced from Indonesia. (2) Another curvilinear style combined with rounded sculptural forms occurs in the Humboldt Bay-Lake Sentani district east along the north coast. (3) The most important art style for richness and variety is from the area of the Sepik and Ramu rivers, and adjoining coastal regions. Variations are so highly developed as to represent a cluster of substyles with robust, exuberant application of flowing carved and painted patterns. Some sculpture, figures, and masks show what is termed the "beak style." (4) In the Astrolabe Bay and Huon Gulf area an angular, pointed motif is frequently used in decorating the stiff, static forms of the masks and figures. (5) On the eastern tip of the island and in the Trobriand, D'Entrecasteaux, Woodlark, and Louisiade archipelagos, technique is highly developed but art is conventional. A typical scroll design recalls that of the northwest coast Geelvink Bay region. (6) A colourful, vigorous style is found in the Papuan Gulf area. (7) Small islands between New Guinea and Australia show a distinctive Torres Strait style. (8) Distinguished for fantastic ceremonial art are the Marind-Anim

people along the east coast of Frederik Hendrik Island and the adjacent mainland. (9) The Asmat and Mimika tribes of the southwest coast carve and decorate in an intricate, highly individual openwork, often spectacular. Knowledge of the interior is incomplete and few examples of art are known from that region.

In many areas of New Guinea, art centred on the men's house (in some regions called the *eravo*). In the Papuan Gulf area the 10- to 15-year ceremonial cycles began with the erection of a large *eravo*. Inside, ceremonies were planned in secret, costumes were made, and masked dancers emerged from the house to perform.

As a rule the thatch roof was given prominence in houses; it was pyramidal with a tall spire, or saddleback, or sloped steeply down toward the rear from the high front (which in some examples rose more than 50 ft.). The drop of the roof along each side in many examples (or styles) eliminated side walls, but the front was often covered with painted panels or carving, or decorated with a large house mask. Inside were displayed drums, bullroarers, and carved and painted plaques associated with the ancestor cult.

For ceremonies every effort was made to disguise human aspects of dancers' bodies and to create a supernatural presence. Over a superstructure (in some cases 20 ft. high) a costume was made from a variety of such materials as feathers, fur, shell, teeth, and leaves. The central part of such a construction was a mask (*q.v.*), the image of a mythological or ancestral being. With the exception of the northwest coast Geelvink Bay area, Humboldt Bay-Lake Sentani area, and among the Massim people, masks which varied greatly in form and materials were used in all regions. From the Asmat area come netted fibre masks; some from the Sepik and the Papuan Gulf areas were of wickerwork. Bark cloth stretched over a light framework was made into large masks in the Papuan Gulf area, and turtle-shell plates were fastened together to make them in the Torres Strait islands. The most common forms were carved from wood in the Sepik and Huon Gulf areas, usually polychromed, often decorated with fibre, pig tusks, or encrusted with cowrie shells.

Wood was also carved into such objects as neck rests, hooks, stools, drums, bowls, canoe-prow ornaments, shields, memorial tablets, house posts, commemorative poles, and single figures. Commemorative poles from the Asmat are tall and spectacular; jutting from the top is a pointed wing consisting of a carved openwork panel with figures entwined in vinelike tracery. These carvings like many others in New Guinea are light and open, and whether stiff or sinewy the figures are composed of thin stemlike forms rather than heavy sculptural masses.

In figures from whatever area the head is large and emphatic; in the "beak style" centred in the Sepik area the nose is given great prominence, and may project far below the chin. The importance of the head is also apparent in specially treated and preserved skulls of ancestors and enemies. To control the spirit of the original owner the skull was painted and modeled over with paste; hair, feathers, shell, tusks, or carved eye and nose projections were attached. For preservation and display the decorated skulls were hung from elaborately carved and painted hooks suspended from rafters in the men's house.

Although the human image is the most important subject, fish, snakes, crocodiles, and especially birds are all significant in New Guinea mythology and art.

Most sculpture is polychromed but painting on plane surfaces is rare. In the Humboldt Bay-Lake Sentani area sheets of white bark cloth are painted with dark spidery lines, creating clan emblems of fish or serpents. In the Sepik, flattened Sago palm leaf sheaths cover the front of the men's house. These are painted with human faces and animals in a flowing, curving line that spreads over the entire surface. These painted panels are typical of the curvilinear quality of the art of New Guinea. Combined with the flowing line are concentric circles ringing large dots, and a toothed line and chevron motif used for contrast and variation.

Bismarck Archipelago.—North of New Guinea lie New Britain, New Ireland, and the Admiralty Islands, comprising the Bismarck Archipelago. In the Admiralties masks were not made but figures of crocodiles, fish, and birds (some in large size) were carved and painted in a stiff, rigid style. Probably ancestor images, the figures

Clay funerary urn, Kansu, China, Yangshao period. 11 in. high

Bronze *dōtaku*, Japan. About 28 in. high

Female figurine, possibly a fertility idol, late Jōmon period, Japan.
10 in. high

PREHISTORIC ASIAN ART

Group of clay tomb figurines (*haniwa*) from Kantō, Japan. Seated woman (foreground), possibly a shaman, is 27 in. high

PLATE II   PRIMITIVE ART

Cave painting showing bulls, horses, and deer; Lascaux, Dordogne. France. Photograph covers a span of about 30 ft.

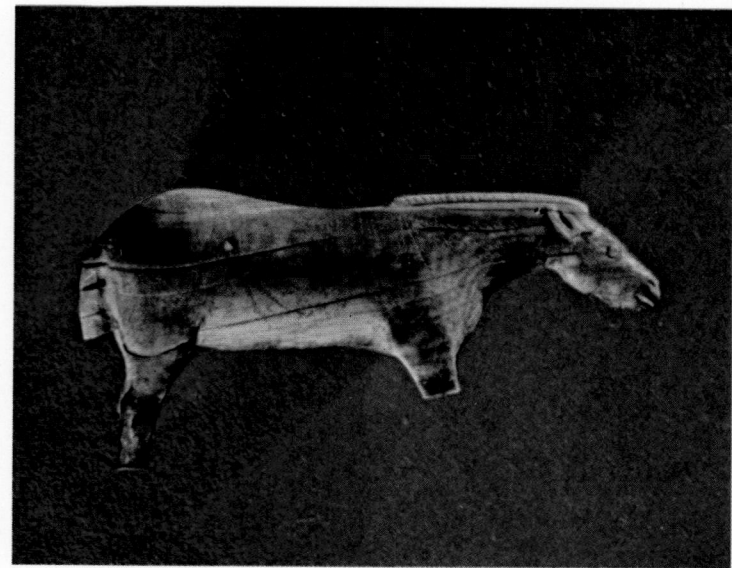

Ivory horse; Espélugues near Lourdes, France.   About 3 in. (actual size)

Views of female head carved in ivory; Brassempouy, Landes, France.
About 1¼ in. high

PRIMITIVE ART

PLATE III

Horse's head carved in reindeer antler; Le Mas d'Azil, Ariège, France. About 2⅝ in. from neck to nose

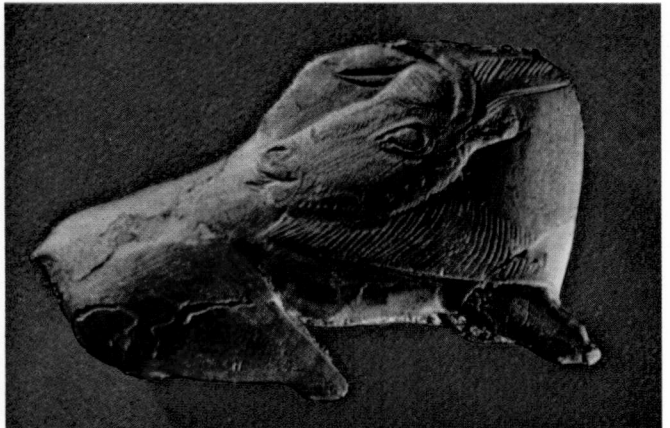

Bison carved in reindeer antler; Grotte de la Madeleine, Dordogne, France. Length 4⅛ in.

Carved relief of a female holding a bison horn; Laussel, Dordogne, France. 15¾ in. high

PREHISTORIC EUROPEAN ART

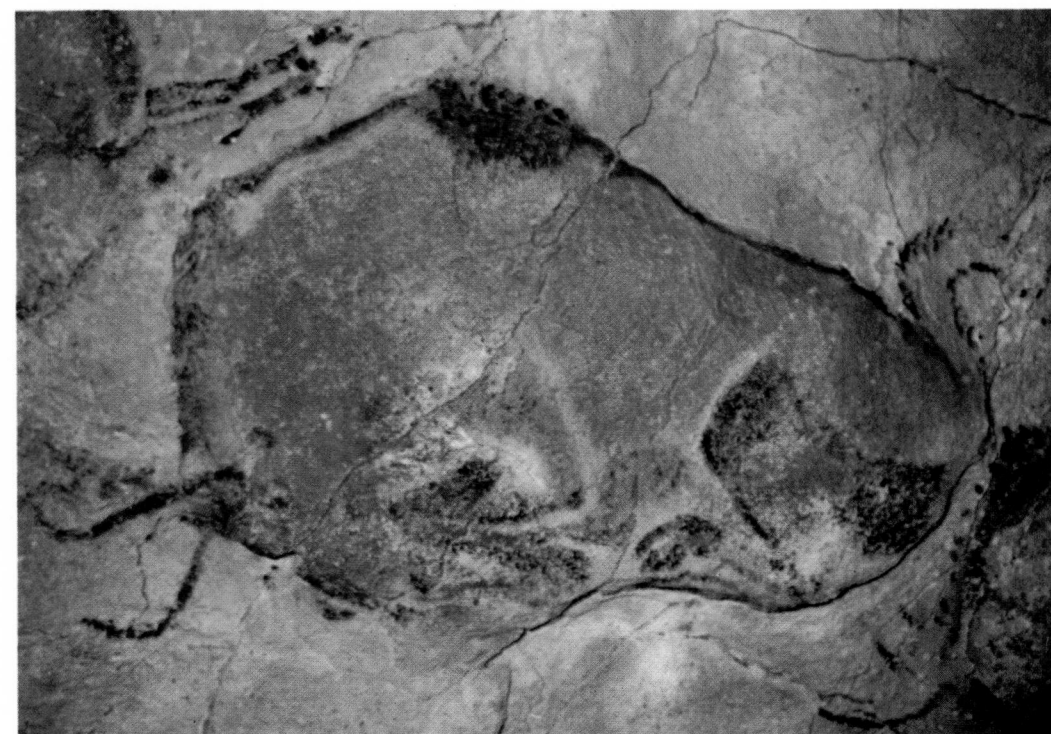

Bison painted over a protuberance on cave roof; Altamira, Spain. About 6 ft. long

BY COURTESY OF (BOTTOM) SPRING BOOKS LTD.; PHOTOGRAPHS, (TOP LEFT, CENTRE LEFT, TOP RIGHT) DMITRI KESSEL, "LIFE," © 1955 TIME INC.

PLATE IV   PRIMITIVE ART

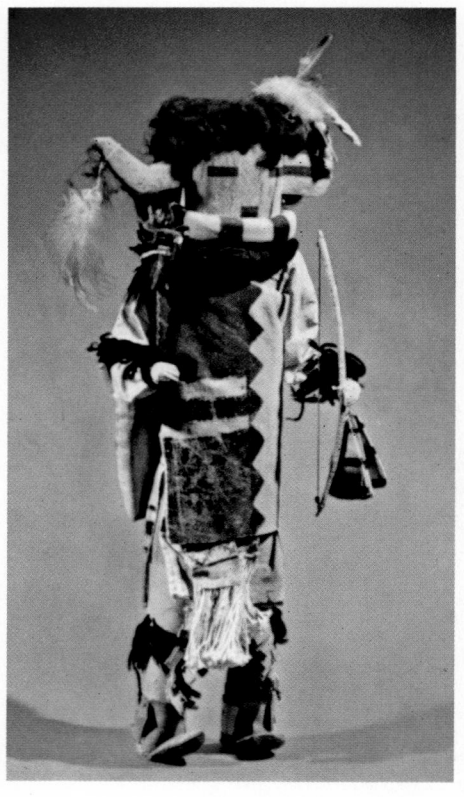

North American artifacts. (Left) Pueblo Indian katcina figure, wooden body dressed in cloth and feathers. About 13 in. (Above) Prehistoric stone pipe, Eastern Woodlands. 3½ in. high. (Right) 20th-century Eskimo carvings, done in the primitive manner. The hunter, about 10 in. high, is stone; the seal is ivory

ART OF THE NEW WORLD

Gold Mixtec deity pendant; Veracruz, Mexico. 4 in. high

Chavín clay pot with characteristic puma-head motif; Peru. About 11 in.

Painted clay effigy vessel, possibly representing a warrior; Colima, Mexico. 14⅜ in.

Painted clay bowl with bizarre monster design; Panama. Diameter about 11 in.

BY COURTESY OF (TOP LEFT, TOP CENTRE) THE BROOKLYN MUSEUM, (BOTTOM LEFT) THE MUSEUM OF PRIMITIVE ART, (CENTRE LEFT) ALBERT SKIRA AND THE NATIONAL MUSEUM OF ANTHROPOLOGY, MEXICO CITY, (BOTTOM RIGHT) ALBERT SKIRA AND THE NATIONAL MUSEUM OF PANAMA; PHOTOGRAPHS, (TOP LEFT, TOP CENTRE) WOLFGANG R. HARTMANN, (TOP RIGHT, CENTRE LEFT, CENTRE RIGHT, BOTTOM RIGHT) LEE BOLTIN, (BOTTOM LEFT) ELISABETH LITTLE

Mayan stone stelae; Copán, Honduras

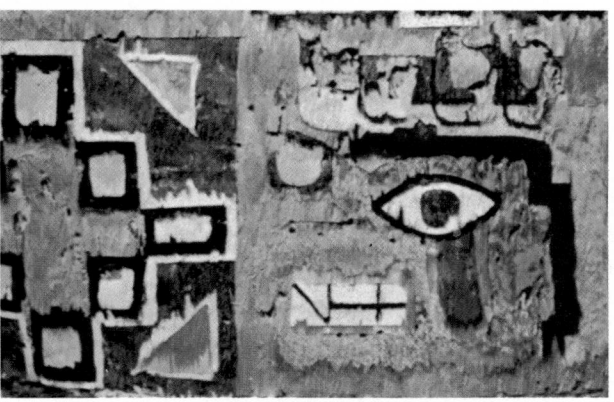

Tiahuanaco featherwork; Peru

Mochica gold earplugs inlaid with turquoise; Peru. Diameter 4 in.

Detail of embroidered Paracas mantle; Peru

Olmec basalt head; Mexico. 8 ft. high

PLATE VI

PRIMITIVE ART

Cult house with carved and painted wood *Malanggan* figures representing mythological scenes,
ancestors, totem birds, and fish; New Ireland.   House is about 8 ft. high

ART OF OCEANIA

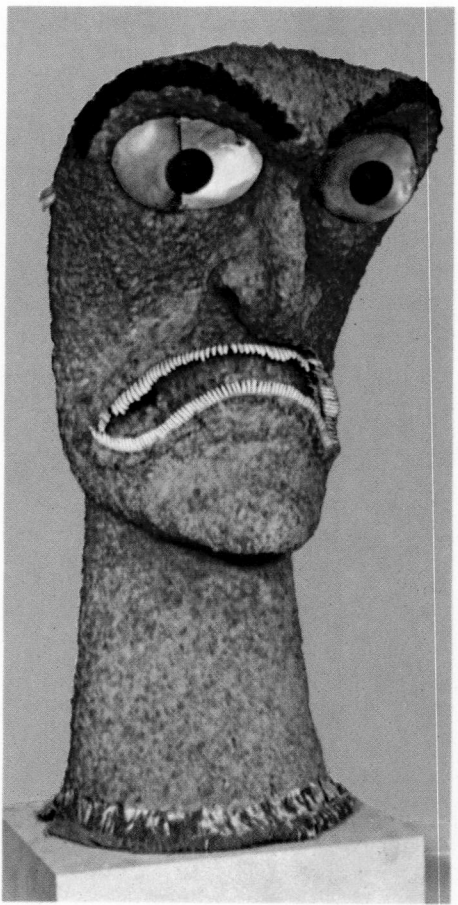

Bird-shaped stone pestle, one of the few Oceanic
artifacts that can be dated to prehistoric times;
New Guinea. 13½ in.

Kukailimoku, war-god of wicker framework covered
with netting and feathers, eyes of shell, mouth rimmed
with dog's teeth; Hawaii. 32 in.

Kukailimoku in wood; Hawaii. 30¼ in.

X-ray style painting of kangaroos, earth colours on eucalyptus bark; Arnhem Land, Australia.   40¾ in. high

Wood image of the god Tangaroa, creating man and lesser gods shown sprouting from his body; Rurutu, Austral Islands.   44 in.

Protective idol, blackened wood inlaid with mother-of-pearl, from prow of a war canoe; New Georgia, Solomon Islands.   7 in. high

Carved wood lintel from Maori council house door; New Zealand.   About 30 in. long

Carved wooden god; Cook Islands. 54 in.

PLATE VIII

PRIMITIVE ART

Thirteenth-century Ife terra-cotta commemorative head; Nigeria.   Life size

Gold Ashanti turtle pendant, Ghana.
3¾ in. long

Gold Baule pendant; Ivory Coast.
About 3 in. long

Wood Ibibio marionette; Nigeria.   28⅜ in.

AFRICAN ART

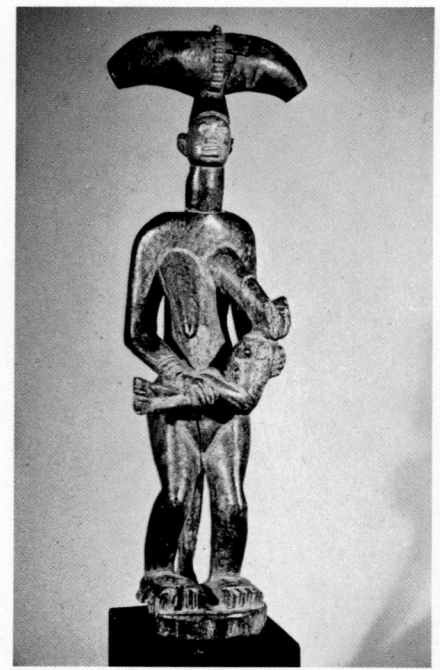

Painted wood Yoruba Shango cult figure; Nigeria.
28½ in.

Painted wood Kurumba antelope headdress; Upper
Volta.   42⅜ in.

Wood Yoruba horse and rider; Nigeria.   About
30 in.

N'gere mask of painted wood, cloth, fibres, cartridge cases; Liberia

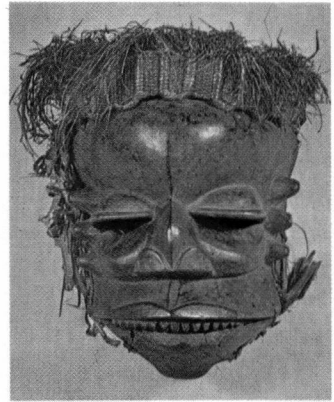

Ibibio Ekpo secret society wood mask with hinged jaw; Nigeria

Wood Dogon granary door; Mali. 36½ in.

Benin artifacts; Nigeria. (Left) Bronze leopard, symbol of royal power. 15¾ in. long. (Above) Ivory pectoral mask. 9⅜ in. (Right) Bronze wall plaque showing a king and attendants. 19½ in. high

BY COURTESY OF (TOP LEFT, TOP RIGHT, BOTTOM LEFT, BOTTOM CENTRE, BOTTOM RIGHT) THE MUSEUM OF PRIMITIVE ART, (CENTRE LEFT) THE LINDENMUSEUM, STUTTGART; PHOTOGRAPHS, (TOP LEFT, TOP RIGHT, BOTTOM CENTRE, BOTTOM RIGHT) ELISABETH LITTLE, (BOTTOM LEFT) LEE BOLTIN

PLATE X

PRIMITIVE ART

Wood Dogon ancestor figures; Sudan. Figure at left 24¾ in.

Painted wood Senufo mask; Ivory Coast. 18 in.

Incised drinking vessel and necklace, both of ostrich shell, Kalahari Bushmen; South West Africa. Vessel is 5⅞ in. high

Painted wood Bobo mask; Upper Volta. 72 in.

Kuba plush fabric and wood carvings; Democratic Republic of the Congo. (Left) Lidded powder jar, 11½ in. high. (Right) Ceremonial palm-wine cup, (right foreground) lidded bowl

Bobo helmet mask; Sudan. 16 in.

Painted wood Pende fertility figure; Democratic Republic of the Congo. 23¼ in.

BY COURTESY OF (TOP LEFT, BOTTOM RIGHT, TWO BACKGROUND PIECES IN PHOTOGRAPH AT BOTTOM LEFT) THE REITBERG MUSEUM, ZÜRICH, VON DER HEYDT COLLECTION, (TOP RIGHT AND PIECE AT RIGHT FOREGROUND OF FIGURE AT BOTTOM LEFT) THE ETHNOLOGICAL COLLECTION, ZÜRICH, (CENTRE) THE MUSEUM OF PRIMITIVE ART, (BOTTOM CENTRE) MR. ELIOT ELISOFON; PHOTOGRAPHS (TOP LEFT, TOP RIGHT, BOTTOM LEFT, BOTTOM RIGHT) "ART OF THE WORLD," HOLLE VERLAG, (TOP CENTRE) LEE BOLTIN, (CENTRE) ELISABETH LITTLE, (BOTTOM CENTRE) ELIOT ELISOFON

were often stereotyped but some of the finest are handsome in stately dignity.

New Ireland art is rich, intricate, and involved. Sculpture showed great virtuosity in carving and in a profusion of applied painted patterns. Birds, fish, snakes, pigs, and such mythological symbols as the sun and moon were interwoven in almost medieval fantasy. In the pole carvings, for example, these and such elements as one animal biting another encircle the human figure to create open cagelike sculpture. The poles, figures, panels, and masks were exhibited in secluded courts as part of the so-called *Malanggan* cycle of ceremonies in commemoration of dead ancestors. Masks were carved and painted in the same complex style, with combs, crests, and large earlike appendages attached to the main carving. The very sacred *uli* figures from central New Ireland with both male and female qualities are in sharp contrast to the extravagant *Malanggan* art. They are monumental, heavy, and aggressive.

There are several distinct styles in New Britain, the largest island of the archipelago. Masks are outstanding; realism is pronounced in two quite different types: one of large massive forms in wood, the other in which the face was made by modeling over the front of a human skull. In strong contrast to these are masks of the Baining and Sulka tribes both living on the Gazelle Peninsula. Those of the Baining that were used in night snake dances are of painted bark cloth stretched over a framework; some are gigantic with long tubular snout and bamboo tail. At the centre, rising from the head of the dancer and expanding like a bellows, are the forehead, nose, lip, and tongue.

Sulka masks were of a conical framework over which long strips of pith were sewed that covered the dancer's upper body. Towering over this was a superstructure (up to nine feet in diameter): an umbrellalike disk, or a carving of a figure or bird. The spectacular effect was enhanced by painting the base bright pink, so unusual a colour in oceanic art.

The Solomons; New Hebrides; New Caledonia.—In the Solomon Islands, the combination of earth reds and yellows with black and white that prevails throughout most of Melanesia is much less frequent than is a polished black surface inlaid with bands of mother-of-pearl pieces. This style is found repeatedly, applied to strong, often elegant shields, clubs, paddles, bowls, canoes, and figures. A limited number of life-size standing figures were made for funerary purposes. More numerous are small, seated, large-headed figures used in initiation rites, to decorate canoe houses, or as guardians lashed to fronts of great canoes. The head is a counterplay of clear-cut planes, convex across the forehead and around the chin, concave in the cheeks and nose. The same approach (though less stylized) may be seen in the modeling of trophy and ancestor skulls, their black-gum surfaces inlaid with mother-of-pearl.

Breast ornaments were made of white disks ground from the giant *Tridacna* clamshell, overlaid with dark turtle shell cut in angular openwork patterns. These and similar pendants from the Admiralties and New Ireland are highly valued by the people of the area.

In the New Hebrides, art is important in ceremonies marking progression in rank among members of men's societies. For each step, large (5- to 12-ft.) images were carved from tree-fern trunks and set up in clusters near the men's house. Deeply undercut grooves defined droll faces with large disk eyes and flaring nostrils. The rough texture of the fern was finished with clay and brightly painted. The same rites employed masks representing mythological beings. A common form, a conical helmet, was modeled with paste over a fibre base with two, four, or even more faces painted in bright reds and blues—probably trade colours. Curved pig tusks that were thought to add to the mask's power and increased its value were inserted around the mouth.

That art remaining from the extinct culture of New Caledonia is limited in variety of form, although it has a distinct style (perhaps lacking in finesse, but vigorous and forceful). Carved wooden masks, some representing a sea spirit, were attached to a fibre base covered with hair and feathers to fit over the upper body. Some had great hook noses and were black-brown, to create a sombre

and grotesque effect. Ancestor images were carved in the round and also in relief. These and family crests were carved on tall, flat spires and doorposts of the large circular houses. The face (often the only recognizable part) was broad and flat with eyes, nose, and mouth completely filling the available shape.

Micronesia.—Material culture in the Mariana, Caroline, Marshall, and Gilbert island groups imposed severe restrictions and Micronesian art is the simplest of Oceania. Sculpture is rare, and masks are all but unknown; decoration is minimal, and basic form stands out clearly and effectively. To realize such sensitive design Micronesian artists developed exceptionally fine craftsmanship, evident in secular, functional work. Such items as coconut-grater stools, wooden bowls, and even outrigger canoes were planned to achieve subtle balance and contour, and to utilize materials fully.

Houses are skilfully made; the fronts of those for young men in Palau (Carolines) show carved or incised, painted representations of mythological or historical events. On Mortlock Island in the Carolines ceremonial house fronts were mounted with large flat masks as protection against typhoons. The few sculptured unornamented cult images were moderate in size, unpainted, and appeared sedate and impersonal.

Polynesia.—Local variations in the culture of Polynesia are not so great as in Melanesia, nor is the art of separate island groups so distinct. In the west, Fiji Islands culture is primarily Melanesian but art is Polynesian. Central Polynesia includes Tonga, Samoa, the Cook, Austral, and Society islands. Along the eastern edge are the Hawaiian Islands, the Marquesas, and Easter Island; far to the south outside the Tropical Zone is New Zealand.

Much Polynesian art is formal, stylized, and created by specialists. As in Micronesia, secular objects were well designed; *e.g.*, wooden oil dishes from Fiji or polished wooden bowls with suave, flowing contour from Hawaii. Wooden bowls in the Marquesas and feather boxes in New Zealand were covered over-all with relief patterns. Such weapons as clubs also were carved in unit motif and inlaid with shell; in some areas they were three-dimensional and sculptural.

In the hands of priestly groups, religion was more formalized than in Melanesia. In some areas ceremonial paddles, adzes, or even fly whisk handles replaced cult images. The finest examples of these carvings show strong, simple contours that served as foils to carved, angular decoration over the full surface.

Most wooden images were unemotional, stylized representations of gods or deified ancestors (as in figures from the Marquesas). Slight swellings indicated parts of the basically columnar body, with low relief for details of hands and face. Figures from Fiji and Central Polynesia differ in detail, but also were stiff and conventionalized.

Not all such representations were so detached in feeling; more intense, stylized expressions are seen in large, menacing Hawaiian war-god figures with oversize crested heads; or in contorted expressions on carvings by the New Zealand Maori. Unusual emaciated images of male ancestors come from Easter Island; stiffness is relieved throughout by curves along rib cage, backbone, hips, chin, and brow.

Stone is used much less often than wood, but some of the largest and most impressive Oceanic sculptures are monumental stone figures from Easter Island (*q.v.*). Carved from volcanic tufa, averaging 12–15 ft. tall, they weigh three to four tons. Set up on mortuary platforms or on hillsides, the figures have sloping facial planes with cheeks, nose, and brow projecting over deep-set eyes.

Pole and thatch houses and temples in Polynesia were well made, but simple and moderate in size; only in New Zealand can they be compared with the large men's houses of New Guinea. The Maori built a great council house in each village, requiring the efforts of a whole community in support of specialized craftsmen. The house was gabled, rectangular in ground plan with a projecting porch at one end; gable, door, and often the entire house front were covered with low relief carvings. Inside, the walls, rafters, and posts were either carved or painted. Small, stilted storehouses were similar in form and even more lavishly decorated with exterior carving around all four sides.

In Maori art the human figure may be carved in the round; more frequently it is in relief as a motif on house fronts and other embellished objects. In low relief as surface decoration it is highly conventionalized; arms and legs are short and often curved; the face is large with heavy brow, spreading open mouth, and protruding tongue. Flowing over the figure itself, and covering the complete surrounding surface, are low ridges in vigorous, curving, spiral patterns. This constitutes a design form that probably originated in Central Polynesia, whence the Maori came, but which has possible affiliations with Melanesia.

Wherever representational art occurs in Oceania it is created by men for religious use. Women are usually excluded from religious activity; their art is most often geometric, and rarely figurative.

Except in Fiji, pottery was not made, but woven mats and baskets were widespread. Outstanding were the twined and netted feather capes from New Zealand; of even greater richness and brilliance were those worn as emblems of rank in Hawaii.

The most important women's art throughout Polynesia (except New Zealand where it was not made) was the making of bark cloth (tapa). Some of the finest tapas are rich in the contrast between pattern textured and painted shapes and achieve an exceptional balance between filled and open space, almost like abstract paintings (see BARK CLOTH).   (WH. H.)

V. NEW WORLD

The European conquest effectively put an end to aboriginal American civilizations, but their splendour survives in a wealth of art forms. (See NORTH AMERICA; SOUTH AMERICA: *Anthropology.*)

Nomadic hunters who first made their way to the Americas perhaps as much as 35,000 years ago contrast sharply with the sophisticated Aztec and Inca empires of their descendants. About 8,000 B.C. the nomads apparently began to shift to a more stable, sedentary existence that favoured artistic development. By the 2nd millennium B.C., at the onset of the so-called Preclassic period in the New World, there were already small farming villages in Middle America and Peru where pottery making and weaving enriched the life of the people. Complex religions and governments later developed in these regions, and for most of the first thousand years A.D., aboriginal American culture flourished in its Classic period. Theocratic realms next were replaced by powerful secular and militaristic Postclassic empires that gave way to the European conquest.

In regions remote from the Peruvian and Middle American centres, cultures never reached similar magnificence and complexity, but what is known of their art and philosophy shows tantalizing promise of what might have been. However, from the 16th century on, aboriginal Indian culture slowly vanished before relentless Euroamerican pressure.

Arctic.—Only a few examples of carved and incised bone, attributed to prehistoric nomadic hunters (and not unlike Late Stone Age European art), have been found in Mexico and the U.S. Southwest. But this early tradition of bone and ivory carving was maintained among hardy Arctic peoples. The oldest of these sculptures come from 2,000-year-old village sites along the Bering and Chukchi seas. Delicately wrought loons' heads, twisted ivory rods and chains, and weird funerary masks were intricately incised with curvilinear patterns. Tiny, centuries-old representations of Arctic fauna differ only slightly from carvings of birds, walrus, and bear made by 19th-century Eskimo (*q.v.*).

Art objects of the Far North from all periods are characteristically small, and consisted earlier of ceremonial pieces, funerary offerings, and carefully decorated useful articles. Recent Eskimo engravings are realistic, narrative, and often gaily humorous; schematic masks of whale bone or painted driftwood, and feather and bone representations of mythological beings are typical. Earliest incised ivory and bone ornaments from the eastern Arctic are simple and unimaginative as compared to ancient Alaskan styles. However, modern eastern Eskimo have revived stone carving, and portray village life with great liveliness.

Northwest Coast.—From the southern tip of Alaska to what are now the states of Washington and Oregon grew a monumental and dramatic art style that was unique in North America (*see* INDIANS, NORTHWEST COAST). The artistic antiquity of the Northwest Coast is evidenced by stone carvings (found principally in the southern area) that date before European contact. However, wood sculpture that flourished before and during the 18th and 19th centuries is most famous and characteristic. The prosperous Tlingit, Tsimshian, Haida, Bella Coola, Kwakiutl, Nootka, and Salishan tribes excelled in carving masks, houseposts, figures, and innumerable other objects. Ivory, copper, fur, stone, and seashell enriched these lavish carvings, or were used alone for jewelry, costume, and ceremonial equipment. Handsome woven textiles depicted the motifs of wood sculpture in sturdy geometrical designs, and baskets were woven in unusual shapes.

Social life revolved around ostentatious display of wealth and rank (*see* POTLATCH) for which great quantities of art objects were produced. A story or myth was connected with each work of art, and the human form, when shown, appears realistically and with remarkable vitality. However, since man and other animals were believed to be intimately related, symbolic and complex depictions of supernatural nonhuman ancestors constituted basic motifs.

Far West.—Aboriginal cultures of the Far West were exceedingly primitive in their way of life. Nevertheless, the early peoples of California and parts of Nevada and Oregon developed a remarkable artistic style and technology. The Pomo, Maidu, Hupa, Paiute (*qq.v.*), and many other tribes inventively utilized natural materials to create an art of great delicacy and vivid colour.

Only stone pipes, vessels, and amulets (usually covered with tiny shell rings) remain from preconquest times in the Far West. In the 19th century the Indians of the Far West were among the world's finest basketmakers; roots and fibres of many colours and textures were twined and coiled into geometrically decorated baskets of numerous shapes and sizes. Many Pomo baskets were covered with vivid feather mosaic and opalescent shell. Feather wands and headdresses, and jewelry of polished stone, shell, and incised bone are marked with the extreme delicacy of this style.

Eastern Woodlands.—Ancient peoples of the Eastern Woodlands were excellent sculptors and created pieces that were small, subtly realistic, sophisticated, and refined. Extending from Canada to Florida, and from the Atlantic Ocean to beyond the Mississippi River, this region was the ancient cultural crossroad of North America. Its art style hints of Middle America, the Far North, even Asiatic influences; but these were integrated in a unique tradition.

Polished, abstract stone ornaments are the earliest evidence of Eastern Woodlands art, beginning a sculptural tradition that reached its height early in the 1st millennium A.D. Effigy pipes and other small carvings have a classic elegance unequalled in North America. Oddly shaped pottery vessels were incised or stamped with decoration; sheets of mica and copper were cut or hammered into silhouettes. These, together with carved wood and painted cloth (of which only rare traces remain), were interred in earthen funeral pyramids or in giant effigy mounds (*see* MOUND BUILDERS).

By about A.D. 800 pyramids no longer served for burial but as bases for temples. Snakes, trophy heads, warriors, and other religious symbols decorated pottery, shell, and copper objects. This religious art died quickly after European settlement, but Woodlands Indians continued to use colour and decoration. Porcupine quills, moose- or elk-hair embroidery, and (later) glass beads were applied to clothing and to articles of birchbark and leather; ribbon mosaics and painted skins also were used for costume. Woven bags and bark articles with scraped designs continued pre-Columbian techniques; however, only grotesque wooden False Face Society masks of the Iroquois (*q.v.*), rare wood effigies, and a few carved wooden utensils remained of the ancient sculptural tradition of the Eastern Woodlands.

Great Plains.—The life of village tribes at the forested edge of the Great Plains was transformed in the 17th century by horses and firearms. Sedentary ways shifted to a nomadic existence on the Plains, sustained by hunting bison. This change remarkably stimulated artistic expression, which benefited (oddly enough) by the coming of Europeans (see PLAINS INDIANS).

Despite the nomadic need for portable and useful objects, the art of the Plains was extremely varied and vital. Hide and leather were primary media for decoration; women painted quivers, parfleches (rawhide articles), and bison robes with traditional geometric motifs. Male ceremonialism involved shamanism (q.v.), spirits, and hallucinations; only men painted magic designs on shields and ritual objects, realistic pictorial narratives of war and hunting on tents and robes, and carved long ceremonial pipes (see CALUMET). Porcupine- or bird-quill embroidery on clothing and utensils later gave way to gaudy European glass beads. Feathers, fur, claws, and skins were fashioned into impressive war and ritual costume.

Southwest.—The break between the ancient and the modern is more difficult to determine in the Southwest than elsewhere in North America. For centuries Indians here have managed to preserve many of their peaceful, ordered ways. The art of pre-Columbian Anasazi, Hohokam, and Mogollon (qq.v.) are reflected in the conservatism and gentle spirituality of Southwestern Indian art in the 1960s.

Ceremonial pottery was abundant; Anasazi (famous for cliff dwellings) maintained a tradition of geometric design. Hohokam (who cultivated the desert using irrigation) cursively painted pottery with scrolls and animated figures. Mogollon briefly drew black-and-white geometry or whimsical naturalistic motifs on their remarkable Mimbres wares.

Baskets were woven from the beige and black fibres of the region, and highly evolved textiles were made with coloured yarns in weaves and openwork similar to ceramic designs. Except for sculptured Hohokam figures and effigy bowls, stone was not commonly used. Pyrite mosaics, turquoise and shell jewelry, however, show ability and dexterity.

Anasazi tradition continued (enlivened and filled with colour) in the arts of the Pueblos (see PUEBLO INDIANS). Ceramic motifs became freer, sometimes naturalistic; images of nature deities, dance masks, and katcina (kachina) figures (see DOLL) appear stylized but vigorously and carefully fashioned.

Apache and Navaho (qq.v.) learned much of their art from the Anasazi; Apache basket designs are abstract but modified with tiny life forms; costumes, robes, hooded masks, and war shields bore magic motifs. The brilliant colour and geometric composition of Navaho blankets and the fine design of their silver and turquoise jewelry are widely admired. Stylized spirit masks and sand painting are the most characteristic Navaho ceremonial art.

Middle America (Mesoamerica).—One of two great centres of American Indian achievement extended from what became Mexico to what is now Nicaragua (see MIDDLE AMERICA). Preclassic agriculturalists made ceramic vessels and effigies, clay masks, and carefully modeled figurines that reflect vigour, imagination, and inventiveness. Olmec architecture (pyramids, and plazas paved with large mosaics of a jaguar deity) and sculpture (colossal heads, figures, and altars depicting dwarfed feline-like creatures) greatly influenced the Classic art that followed.

Flourishing cities and ceremonial centres of the Classic period attracted artists and intellectuals, and encouraged them in the service of religion. Although stylistic influences were readily exchanged throughout Middle America, distinct local forms and character evolved.

In the east, along the Gulf of Mexico and Caribbean coast, the Huastec and Maya Indians (qq.v.) and the peoples of Veracruz created symbolic, subtly realistic, luxuriously baroque art. Ornate pyramids, temples, and palaces held magnificent sculpture and murals that commemorated deities and priests. Carved temple offerings and ornaments were of precious jade, other stone, bone, and shell; ritual costume was of soft textiles and jungle feathers. Pottery vessels were incised with glyphs or abstract motifs, painted with religious scenes, modeled with effigy legs or handles; large and small clay figures were sculpted in abundance.

A contrasting tradition developed in the central Mesoamerican highlands, oriented toward severe geometry and architectural starkness. In Oaxaca and Teotihuacán, immense pyramids and temples dominated the countryside. Monumental sculpture and mural painting reflected this sombre alignment of lines and planes, or was stiffly decorative. Colour of veneered buildings, sculpture, and murals heightened this massive style. Brilliant hues decorated pottery with the same austerity and elegance, despite varied forms and softer naturalistic motifs. Polished greenstone ritual masks and figures were typical of Teotihuacán; in Oaxaca, clay figures and urns in the form of guardian deities were tomb furniture.

Another major tradition along the Mexican Pacific coast often took the prosaic forms of narrative and caricature. These people modeled and painted clay, sometimes humorously, often grotesquely, but always revealingly. Sculpted without molds, hollow, bulky figures of warriors, dwarfs, and entire village scenes were used as funerary offerings. These ceramics show textiles as heavily patterned, and jewelry such as nose rings and earrings as lavish; except for shell and stone ornaments, few examples of these survive.

Before the 10th century A.D. warrior tribes began an era of strife to consolidate vast empires. Their secular outlook is reflected in Postclassic art. Highly decorative, grandiose or too refined, it exhibited great virtuosity in technique.

Toltec, Mixtec, and Aztec (qq.v.) influence penetrated throughout Mesoamerica; Toltec art glorified the military with colossal warrior pillars, serpent columns, and reliefs of fierce jaguars and eagles. Mixtec art served the aristocracy, and produced superb ornaments that today are among the greatest aboriginal American treasures: delicate gold, silver, and copper jewelry, carvings in jade, onyx, obsidian, and crystal, intricately incised bone and shell, turquoise mosaic, and lacquered ceramics of brilliant polychrome. Pictorial Mixtec manuscripts offer a wealth of information on religious beliefs, tribal history, and everyday life.

Aztec art in vast quantities glorified the imperialist state; gods (e.g., of war and death) were terrifyingly symbolized as serpents, monsters, and death's-heads. Mixtec influence is detected in feather and stone mosaic, objects of gold and gems, carved wood, ceremonial armour and weapons, and manuscript painting; while Toltec ideas inspired architectural design.

The conquistadores effectively destroyed this civilization; despite this, Indians of Mexico and Guatemala in the 1960s continued to produce textiles and pottery that show clear evidence of preconquest style, and ancient traces colour the symbols of Christianity in many objects devoted to religious use.

Isthmus.—The ancient peoples of lands that became Costa Rica and Panama depicted fantastic supernatural beings and monster gods. While these Isthmian cultures did not share in all the achievements of the Classic period, influences from north and south were translated into a powerful, unique artistic idiom. Monumental stone carvings of reptile-headed idols, or severely attenuated human figures, incised and relief-sculptured slabs, and ornately carved grinding tables are characteristic.

Isthmian pottery shows the same strange creatures, many modeled in protruding reptile form and painted in brilliant polychrome. Plain wares were appliquéd with tiny figures or were richly textured. Although shell jewelry and jade pendants were magnificent, gold was preferred for personal adornment. Warrior chieftains arrayed themselves in such splendour as golden helmets, breast plates, and nose rings.

Remnants of the once-thriving aboriginal population of the Isthmus are scarce. Modern Panamanian Indians carve rough fetish figures and masks; women's jewelry and blouses, appliquéd with strips of cloth in curvilinear abstractions, are reminiscent of ancient design.

Caribbean.—The islands of the Caribbean have an artistic tradition that flourished during the 1st millennium A.D. and that belonged to the Taino (see CUBA: The People). Ancient Caribbean dance plazas and ceremonial ball courts resemble those of Mesoamerica, incised pottery bespeaks relationships with South America, but the stone carvings are unique. Found chiefly in the Greater Antilles, three curious stone forms, elliptoid (collar), hooked (elbow), and triangular (three-pointed), were polished and carved with masklike, grinning human heads. These and objects of shell, clay, and wood represented supernatural beings from which people (particularly tribal chiefs) were believed to derive their power. This Caribbean art died out under harsh European rule after the 15th century.

South America.—*North.*—In northern South America, tropical forests prevented growth of large populations, great temples and palaces, powerful kings, or elaborate ceremonialism. Nevertheless, Indians of Brazil, parts of Ecuador, Colombia, and Venezuela developed unusual art forms that continue to thrive in the more remote Amazon jungles.

The earliest shell and bone ornaments, and stone carvings of mammals and fish are found along the Atlantic coast. In the interior, particularly along the Amazon River, burial mounds of earth yield giant urns, smaller effigies, and vessels of many unusual shapes. These were modeled with figures and covered with intricate scrollwork painted or cut from the clay surface as in wood carving.

In more recent times wood, bark cloth, feathers, skins, seeds, and iridescent beetle wings were made into tall dance headdresses, grotesque spirit masks, shaman's implements, and personal decorations. Trophy heads, human and other animal skulls, covered with vivid feathers, paint, and fibre, were macabre, colourful ornaments. Undoubtedly, few pre-Columbian objects of such perishable materials survived the humid climate.

The heterogeneous art of Colombia and Ecuador derives from such far-distant styles as that of the Central Andes (a pre-Columbian focal point for aesthetic ideas). There were scores of ceramic styles, clay effigies, and masks that vary from hooknosed, puffy-eyed, amorphous-bodied types in Colombia to stylized, carefully detailed figurines of coastal Ecuador. These peoples (especially some Colombian tribes) produced outstanding goldwork; such intricate techniques as lost-wax casting, gilding (*q.v.*), and filigree were used in ornaments and ceremonial paraphernalia for the aristocracy. In the Colombian highland district of St. Augustine, numbers of massive fanged heads, and human and other animal idols were erected around temples and mounds at very early ceremonial centres. Idols, reliefs, and curved thrones supported by crouching figures exemplify Ecuadorian stone sculpture. Although Spanish chronicles describe large figures of wood, royal featherwork costumes, and painted textiles, these forms have long since perished as has native culture.

The Andes.—Civilization in the Central Andes equalled that of Middle America; reaching a peak in Peru and highland Bolivia, its impact was felt in distant lands. Central Andean art had its inception early in the 1st millennium B.C. with the powerful and inventive Chavín styles (*see* ANDEAN CIVILIZATION). Principal motifs, based on a Chavín cult of a fanged feline deity, were on pottery, in sculpture, and in ornament. For about the next ten centuries three artistic traditions characterize an age comparable to the Classic period of Mesoamerica.

Art styles of the Peruvian north coast tended to be realistic, three-dimensional, and strong in expression rather than in colour. This culminated in the magnificent art of the Mochica; ceremonial ceramics, modeled or finely painted in browns and beiges, depicted everyday life. Gold ornaments inlaid with turquoise, cast copper and silver, and delicate wood carvings attest to Mochica skill. Art was for tombs of the aristocracy or for pageantry around massive pyramids and temples, many of which bore brightly painted murals of priests and gods.

On the south coast a colourful, decorative, two-dimensional art of supernatural beings and symbol was emphasized. Among the Paracas and Nazca peoples a dominant activity was the creation of richly painted ceramics and sumptuous textiles as funerary goods. Designs vary from stylized life forms to depictions of complex deities in a maze of heads and appendages; hammered gold, carved wood, and featherwork also are found among tomb offerings.

A third tradition that centred in the highlands excelled in architecture and stone sculpture; the enigmatic Chavín art bore its greatest fruit in the northern highlands. Centuries later the temples, courts, and gateways of Tiahuanaco, a vast Bolivian ceremonial centre, were the setting for enormous sculptures and reliefs of characteristic angular running figures, puma, and condor-head motifs. Tiahuanaco expanded into an empire and these motifs

spread throughout the Central Andes. They mixed with and engulfed waning Classic styles of the coast to yield the most brilliant of Tiahuanaco textiles and ceramics.

This brief Tiahuanaco imperialism heralded the secular Postclassic period; technically excellent art tended to be decorative and overrefined. The Chimú revived elements of Mochica style in black molded ceramics and elaborate goldwork, but most of their objects are stiff and mass-produced. On the central coast rough black-and-white ceramics and figures were relatively stereotyped, as were textiles, featherwork, and woodcarving. Typical small south-coastal geometric designs are pleasantly decorative but lack the earlier vitality.

The Inca empire represents the last great aboriginal Andean episode; its art emphasized technical mastery and expert craftsmanship. Architecture, ceramics, and textiles derived beauty largely from functional design and skilful construction. Indians in the highlands of Peru and Bolivia still (1960s) wove geometrically patterned textiles not unlike those of the Inca; other crafts such as pottery making survive, but designs are primarily European.

Although the force of Central Andean art penetrated far south, beyond the forbidding Atacama Desert, the simple native cultures of what became Chile and Argentina evolved slowly. Little interest was given to ceremonial and artistic elaboration; instead, these peoples of the Southern Andes buried their dead with handsome useful objects: wooden tubes and palettes (for snuff, and carved with fauna), clay effigy pipes, bone spatulas and flutes, decorated gourds, baskets, textiles, and pottery. Many designs derived from the Tiahuanaco and Inca, but distinctive local forms include burial urns painted and modeled with large stylized human figures. Cast bronze and copper plaques in relief show curious surrealistic faces, figures, or serpents.

After the Conquest the Indian population in Chile and Argentina was drastically reduced. Among the groups remaining in the 1960s, silverwork, basketry, and textiles were still made in limited quantities; in rare instances, shamans still exorcised with magic carved poles and tambourines.

See INDIAN, LATIN-AMERICAN; INDIAN, NORTH AMERICAN. *See* also references under "Primitive Art" in the Index.   (J. P. R.)

BIBLIOGRAPHY.—*General:* L. Adam, *Primitive Art,* 3rd ed. further rev. and enl. (1949); R. Redfield, *The Primitive World and its Transformations* (1953); E. O. Christensen, *Primitive Art* (1955); P. H. Lewis, "A Definition of Primitive Art," *Fieldiana: Anthropology,* Chicago Natural History Museum, vol. 36 (1961); F. Boas, *Primitive Art,* new ed. (1962); P. S. Wingert, *Primitive Art: Its Traditions and Styles* (1962). *Prehistoric Europe:* E. Cartailhac and H. Breuil, *Peintures et gravures murales des cavernes paléolithiques* (1906); J. Cabré Aguiló, *El arte rupestre en España* (1915); A. Lemozi, *La Grotte-temple du Peche-Merle* (1929); J. Bøe, *Felszeichnungen im westlichen Norwegen* (1932); G. Hallström, *Monumental Art of Northern Europe from the Stone Age,* vol. 1 (1939); H. Kühn, *Die Felsbilder Europas* (1949); F. Windels, *The Lascaux Cave Paintings* (1949); H. G. Bandi and J. Maringer, *Art in the Ice Age* (1953); G. Bataille, *Lascaux* (1955); P. Graziosi, *Palaeolithic Art* (1960). *Prehistoric Asia:* T. K. Cheng, *Archaeology in China,* vol. i (1959); J. E. Kidder, *Japan Before Buddhism* (1959); W. Watson, *Archaeology in China* (1960), *Ancient Chinese Bronzes* (1962); K. C. Chang, *The Archaeology of Ancient China* (1963). *Africa:* M. J. Herskovits, *Dahomey* (1938), *The Backgrounds of African Art* (1946); A. H. Brodrick, *Prehistoric Painting* (1948); P. S. Wingert, *The Sculpture of Negro Africa* (1950); L. Underwood, *Bronzes of West Africa* (1949), *Figures in Wood of West Africa* (1947), *Masks of West Africa* (1948); M. Griaule, *Folk Art of Black Africa* (1950); P. Radin (ed.), *African Folktales and Sculpture* (1952); R. S. Rattray, *Religion and Art in Ashanti,* reprinted (1954); W. Schmalenbach, *African Art* (1954); M. Plass, *African Tribal Sculpture* (1956); A. A. Gerbrands, *Art as an Element of Culture, Especially in Negro-Africa* (1957); E. Elisofon and W. Fagg, *The Sculpture of Africa* (1958); W. W. Batiss *et al., The Art of Africa* (1959); E. Leuzinger, *Africa: the Art of the Negro Peoples* (1960); K. M. Trowell, *African Design* (1960). *Oceania:* G. A. Reichard, *Melanesian Design* (1933); F. E. Williams, *Drama of Orokolo* (1940); R. Linton, P. S. Wingert, and R. d'Harnoncourt, *Arts of the South Seas* (1946); A. P. Elkin, C. Berndt, and R. Berndt, *Art in Arnhem Land* (1950); P. S. Wingert, *Art of the South Pacific Islands* (1953); P. H. Buck, *Vikings of the Pacific* (1959); S. Kooijman, *The Art of Lake Sentani* (1959); T. Bodrogi, *Oceanic Art* (1960), *Art in North-east New Guinea* (1961); R. C. Suggs, *The Island Civilizations of Polynesia* (1960); D. Newton, *Art Styles of the Papuan Gulf* (1961); C. A. Schmitz, *Oceanic Sculpture* (1962); A. Bühler, T. Barrow, and C. P. Mountford, *The Art of the South Sea*

Islands (1962); J. Guiart, *The Arts of the South Pacific* (1963); R. Black, *Old and New Australian Aboriginal Art* (1964). *New World:* F. H. Douglas and R. d'Harnoncourt, *Indian Art in the United States* (1958); D. Collier, *Indian Art of the Americas* (1959); F. J. Dockstader, *Indian Art in America* (1961); H. Disselhoff and S. Linne, *The Art of Ancient America* (1961); A. Emmerich, *Art Before Columbus* (1963).

PRIMITIVISM, an outlook on human affairs which sees history as a decline from an erstwhile condition of excellence (chronological primitivism); or, the view that salvation lies in a return to the simple life (cultural primitivism). The term was introduced by A. O. Lovejoy.

Linked with this is the notion of nature and what is natural, as a standard of human values. Nature may mean what is intrinsic, objective, normal, healthy, universally valid. Various senses depend on whether the natural is set over against historical development; against artifact and contrivance; against law, custom, and convention; or against rational mental activity. The first two contrasts belong to chronological, the last two to cultural, primitivism. Sometimes several senses are held at once.

The first great doctrine of primitivism in European literature figures in Hesiod's *Works and Days,* with its myth of the Five Ages. First came "the Golden Age," in which a happy primitive people lived in luxury (their life was far from ascetic) and in perpetual peace; there is a steady decline (except for the intervening Age of Heroes) until the present or Fifth Age, sinking into moral and physical decay. The old legend continued to be popular after Hesiod's time; Empedocles, Aratus, Tibullus, reecho it. This Greco-Roman conception of a Golden Age, later almost a platitude and a topic for satire, was basically a chronological primitivism. Ovid's account in the *Metamorphoses* supplies details missing in the earlier tale; he emphasizes the first age as a reign of justice, when men were good by nature, and therefore had no need of lawyers, judges, or courts. Another version identifies the Golden Age with the reign of Saturn; the most famous text is Virgil's Fourth Eclogue (the Messianic Eclogue), which also describes a future Golden Age. Nonmythological treatments of the idea of human and cosmic decline occur in Lucretius' *De rerum natura,* Dio Chrysostom, Pliny, and Aulus Gellius.

Cultural primitivism comes to the fore in Cynicism, whose doctrine was lived by Antisthenes (a pupil of Socrates and the Sophists) and Diogenes. The philosophical ideal of self-sufficiency, as recast by the Cynics through the notion of nature as a norm, entailed a rejection of luxury, property, rules of social decorum and tact, and all moral rules (including sexual prohibitions). Roman Stoicism derived much from the Cynic teachers and, as through Seneca, greatly influenced primitivism in the 16th and 17th centuries.

Primitivism first enters Jewish and Christian thought through interpretations of the story of the Garden of Eden. The allegorical reading of Genesis by Philo Judaeus (1st century B.C.) shows primitivist notions of Cynic and Stoic origin, and repeats the theory of human decline. At the end of the 2nd century, Theophilus, bishop of Antioch, gave an antiprimitivist interpretation of man's condition in Paradise, as the first stage in a continual advance. Succeeding patristic writers, however, tended to adopt a primitivist view. St. Basil says that the Fall initiated the decline of both man and nature; St. Ambrose went so far as to call the best state that of Adam before the creation of Eve (apparently overlooking Gen. 2:18), and intimates that the first man, if left to himself, would not have fallen. St. Ambrose above all patristic writers echoes the classical tradition of primitivist communism. He describes the child, who is innocent, as following the *lex naturae;* he is like Adam before the Fall. The Marcionites, who made nature a norm of evil, provoked Tertullian to a strong defense of the sensible world ("God has made nothing unworthy of himself"). Lactantius even has a strain of hedonism, against the extreme Marcionite asceticism and contempt for the body and the sensible world derived ultimately from St. Paul. St. Augustine had to adopt the same praise of nature (in the sense of "the whole of things") in arguing against the Manichaean dualism.

The Christian emphasis on poverty, discipline, modesty of dress, moderation of desires, was influenced by the Cynic and Stoic primitivist ideals of a natural life. Some early heretical sects, however, made a different use of nature as a norm. The Carpocratians preached an extreme form of community and equality, both economic and sexual, according to their idea of the state of nature. But the early Christian advocates of asceticism, in rejecting sexuality and even suspecting perfect health, go farther than the Cynics.

Primitivism in the Middle Ages continued to advocate poverty, communism, abstinence, and the simple life, by appeal to the "state of nature" and to the condition of Adam in Eden, as well as to the model of the primitive church of the early Christians. This new retrospective ideal figured decisively in the polemics of the Reformation. Contempt for man, and assertions as to his degeneration, are widespread; the tradition culminates in Pope Innocent III's *De contemptu mundi* with its famous passage on the superiority of even plants to man. However, considering that the fall of man was blamed on his quest for knowledge, and that early Christians had rejected classical rationalist culture and morals, the antiintellectualist tradition of Catholic Europe remained surprisingly weak. Among its few supporters were Pope John XIII and Bernard of Clairvaux.

The idealization of savages is an example of pure cultural primitivism. The Scythians were praised by Euphorion, Strabo, Cicero, Horace, Virgil, and Ovid among others for their vegetarianism, their communism, their justice, and their simple lives. Imaginary primitive groups similarly eulogized include the Cyclops (Homer, Plutarch), the Hyperboreans (Pindar, Herodotus, Diodorus Siculus, Aelian, Pliny, Pausanias), and the Arcadians (Xenophon, Plutarch). The earliest Christian writers abhorred the savage, whose life was not in accordance with Scripture. An exception to this was Salvian, a contemporary of St. Jerome, who declared savages superior to civilized Christians. There is, however, a Christian tradition of an earthly paradise, parallel to the pagan legend of the Island of the Blessed. This tradition begins with Origen, figures in the writings of St. Brendan (a 6th-century Irish monk) and St. Anselm, and reaches a famous expression in the 12th-century legend of the country of Prester John. That the accounts of the 14th-century explorers are written in primitivist language is partly due to this unbroken tradition.

Medieval Christianity also exhibits some views which are chronologically antiprimitivist but culturally primitivist. Foremost among these is the doctrine of the Three Ages, in Joachim of Fiore (c. 1135–1202). According to this, history is a progress from immaturity to maturity, from the Age of the Father to the Age of the Son to the Age of the Holy Spirit. We find the antiintellectualism of cultural primitivism: in the Age of the Holy Spirit rulers will be children; the spiritual man of the Third Age will be full of grace, not knowledge. Similarly, many Christian groups, particularly heretical ones, hold out a perfect future for man, often conceiving it as culturally primitivist. The paintings of Hieronymus Bosch have led critics to regard him as a member of the Adamite sect, who identified Christ with Adam and pursued salvation through ritual nakedness and sexual liberty.

Primitivism played a minor role in Renaissance writing: two notable exceptions are Erasmus' *In Praise of Folly,* which ends with the exaltation of the Christian fool whose folly is wiser than reason, and Montaigne's "Of the Canniballes" (Book I, ch. 30 of the *Essays*). A new crop of primitivist ideas came with the Reformation. Both Lutheranism and Calvinism stress the return to an uncorrupted, and therefore primitive, form of Christianity. The numerous sects which arose at the time (persecuted by Catholic and Protestant authorities alike) generally carried their imitation of early Christianity even further, both in emphasizing the Bible and the experience of conversion, and in distrusting bureaucratic church government and discipline. The most extreme group was the revolutionary community of Anabaptists at Münster (which was destroyed in 1535); there, polygamy was reinstated after the manner of Abraham, Isaac, and Jacob. But the characteristic Anabaptist communities—as well as the Socinians in Poland—repudiated social revolution and the extreme of Münster, preaching instead sobriety, monogamy, poverty, withdrawal from the world, and pacifism. Anabaptist communities, such as the

Mennonites and Hutterites, survive to this day, aloof from bourgeois civilization, in the United States, Canada, and Paraguay. The Diggers and the Levellers in the "left wing" of the Puritan Revolution in England provide another example of the primitivist ethic of Reformation Christianity operating as a social doctrine.

Cultural primitivism was one of the central ideas informing the 18th-century Romantic movement. The Romantic cult of nature and revolt against civilization is stated above all in the works of the marquis de Sade (for whom nature was the ultimate court of appeal) and Jean Jacques Rousseau, following earlier hints in Montesquieu and Diderot. Rousseau's *Émile*, the *Confessions*, and the *Dreams of a Solitary Walker* reject civilization as repressive and enslaving, and equate the primitive, the childlike, and the spontaneous; they suspect the intellect, and praise the noble savage. Many writer-critics of civilization followed, among them Chateaubriand, Théophile Gautier, and Charles Baudelaire.

In Germany, beginning with J. J. Winckelmann's rediscovery of Greek art and architecture in the middle of the 18th century, most writers see the perfect society in that of the ancient Greeks, and some (Winckelmann, Lessing, Herder, Goethe, Schiller, Hölderlin) declare that a new golden age might arise if artists and poets would but imitate the Greeks. The poet Novalis, inspired by a wish to abolish the Christian notions of sin and history, is nostalgic both for the golden age of childhood and for Greek and Oriental antiquity. Similar views figure in the 19th-century poets Kleist and Heine and the philosopher Nietzsche, in the 20th-century poet Stefan George and the novelist Thomas Mann.

Literary primitivism in England and America is mainly cultural. There is less appeal to some ancient or primitive culture, but the same rejection of reason in favor of feeling, the equation of science with disenchantment, and the cult of rural innocence. Wordsworth, Southey, Coleridge, Shelley, and Byron reveal primitivist themes in their work. Wordsworth found his arcadia in the English Lake District, but became progressively disillusioned with primitivist ideals. Coleridge took opium to free his creativity from the bonds of the intellect and dreamed, with Southey, of founding an ideal community in America on the banks of the Susquehanna. The assumptions of cultural primitivism also underlie much of 19th-century American literature up to Henry James.

Primitivism has also left its mark on the social sciences, ever since Rousseau and Herder drew the parallel between the primitive in history and the childlike. Anthropology and the study of primitive religion, which developed in the 19th century (Sir James George Frazer's *The Golden Bough*, J. J. Atkinson, Sir Edward Lubbock, Tylor, Robertson Smith), are evolutionist in temper, but assume the romantic equation of the primitive and the childlike. This same identification influenced the founder of psychoanalysis, Sigmund Freud, who saw neurosis as a form of behaviour similar to that of primitives and children; his technique of treatment cultivates the primitivist value of spontaneity, but his therapeutic goal—an increase in self-consciousness—is antiprimitivist.

A less ambivalent form of cultural primitivism marks much of 20th-century literature, painting, and music. In literature, the works of the Englishman D. H. Lawrence, the American Gertrude Stein, and the Frenchmen Alfred Jarry and Antonin Artaud exalt the primitive and irrational. In painting, the strong influence of African art (reflected in the work of Pablo Picasso, André Derain, and others) was succeeded by an interest in the art of children and the insane (*cf.* Paul Klee, Jean Dubuffet). Similarly, certain compositions of Claude Debussy, Igor Stravinsky, Darius Milhaud, and Heitor Villa-Lobos are influenced by an ideal of the primitive as against the classical.

BIBLIOGRAPHY.—A. O. Lovejoy and George Boas, *Primitivism and Related Ideas in Antiquity* (1965); George Boas, *Essays on Primitivism and Related Ideas in the Middle Ages* (1966); Irving Babbitt, *Rousseau and Romanticism* (1919); A. O. Lovejoy, *Essays in the History of Ideas* (1948); Lois Whitney, *Primitivism and the Idea of Progress in English Popular Literature of the 18th Century* (1934); E. M. Butler, *The Tyranny of Greece over Germany* (1935); Hoxie Neale Fairchild, *The Noble Savage* (1928).   (S. So.)

PRIMO DE RIVERA, JOSÉ ANTONIO, MARQUÉS DE ESTELLA (1903–1936), Spanish political leader, the founder of the Falange, born in Madrid on April 24, 1903, the eldest son of Gen.

Miguel Primo de Rivera (*q.v.*). After a brilliant university course and military service, he began a career as a lawyer in 1925. On Oct. 29, 1933, he launched the Falange Española (*see* FALANGE) as a movement committed to overthrowing the government by violence if an antichristian Popular Front should impose itself in a fashion clearly contrary to "the eternal destinies of Spain." His periodicals, *F. E.* (1934) and *Arriba* (1935), were suppressed after fierce polemics; but he addressed meetings up and down the country and expounded his ideas in notable speeches in the *Cortes,* to which he had been elected in 1933.

Shortly after losing his seat in 1936, José Antonio was arrested. While in prison, he was reelected for Cuenca, but his candidature was annulled by the Popular Front government, which proceeded to dissolve his party. A summary trial ended in a verdict imposed by the government; sentenced to death on Nov. 18, 1936, he was shot in the prison of Alicante on Nov. 20.

In 1939, after Franco's victory, José Antonio's remains were carried shoulder-high across Spain to the Escorial. They were transferred in 1959 to the place of honour in the monument for the dead of the civil war in the Sierra de Guadarrama. His *Obras completas* (articles and speeches) were published in 1944.
                                                                    (T. F. Bu.)

PRIMO DE RIVERA, MIGUEL, MARQUÉS DE ESTELLA (1870–1930), Spanish army officer and statesman, dictator from 1923 to 1930, was born in Cádiz on Jan. 8, 1870. Having been trained in the General Military Academy in Madrid, he served with the army in Morocco, in Cuba, and in the Philippines between 1893 and 1898. A colonel in 1908, he saw further service in Morocco before being appointed military governor of Cádiz in 1915. He

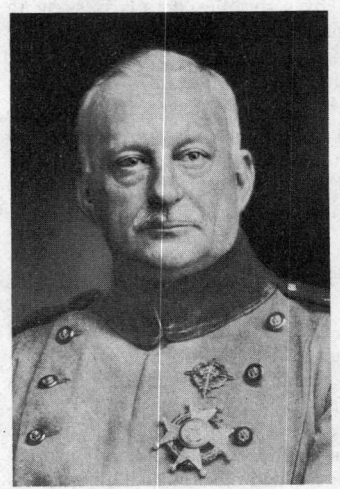

was removed from that office in 1917 (after advocating the exchange of Gibraltar for Ceuta), but was nevertheless promoted lieutenant general in 1919 and appointed captain general of Valencia. For a short period subsequently he was in command of the Madrid infantry division. Next, in 1922, he was appointed captain general of Barcelona, with the task of ending the reign of anarchy in Catalonia. He soon reaped a measure of success; but he saw not only the chaos in Catalonia but also the critical situation of Spain as products of the inefficiency of the parliamentary regime.

MIGUEL PRIMO DE RIVERA

Having already gone to Madrid in an attempt to change the government in June 1923, Primo de Rivera on the following Sept. 13 issued a manifesto proclaiming the suspension of the constitution and the establishment of a provisional military directorate. By accepting the *pronunciamiento* King Alfonso XIII linked the future of the throne with Primo de Rivera's dictatorship, which remained effective after the latter had replaced the directorate with a cabinet mainly composed of civilians under his leadership (Dec. 3, 1925). His subsequent life is part of the history of Spain (*q.v.*) till Jan. 28, 1930, when he resigned power. He then retired to France, where he died, in Paris, on March 16, 1930.

PRIMOGENITURE, a term used to signify the preference in inheritance that is given by law, custom, or usage to the eldest son and his issue, or in exceptional cases to the line of the eldest daughter. In England, primogeniture constituted the rule of intestate succession to land until 1925. *See* INHERITANCE: *Divided or Undivided Inheritance (Primogeniture). See* also references under "Primogeniture" in the Index.   (M. Rn.)

PRIMORSKY KRAY (or MARITIME TERRITORY), of the Russian Soviet Federated Socialist Republic of the U.S.S.R., was created in 1938. Area 64,054 sq.mi. (165,900 sq.km.). Pop. (1970 prelim.) 1,722,000. The *kray* forms the southern part of the Soviet Far East, between the Sea of Japan and Manchuria. The greater part of its area is taken up by the rugged mountains of the Sikhote-Alin, running northeast-southwest along the coast and rising to 6,086 ft. (1,855 m.) in Mt. Oblachnaya. The mountains drop steeply to the sea and in only a few places is the coastal plain well developed. The only important lowland is the Ussuri Valley along the west of the *kray*, the Ussuri River forming the frontier with China. In the upper Ussuri Valley is the large Lake Khanka. The Sikhote-Alin Range is cut up by the valleys of the large tributaries of the Ussuri, the Bikin, Iman, Vaku, Ulakhe, and Daubikhe, and by the shorter streams flowing east to the sea. The climate is of the cold monsoon type, with bitterly cold, dry winters. Vladivostok has a January average temperature of 6° F (−14° C) and farther from the sea conditions are still more severe; *e.g.*, Ussurisk, −3° F (−19° C). Summers, with the onshore monsoon, are wet and cool. Rainfall, about 24 in. (610 mm.) a year in the lowland, rises to over 40 in. (1,020 mm.) on the mountains. Only the sheltered Ussuri Valley is less rigorous. The Sikhote-Alin is covered by dense coniferous forest, chiefly of fir and pine. Below this is a luxuriant deciduous forest, containing numerous tree species, including Mongolian oak and Amur cork, shrubs, and giant vines. In the southern part of the *kray* lotus and giant water lilies are found.

The inhabitants, although predominantly of Russian and Ukrainian settler origin, include small numbers of primitive Tungus-Manchurian tribes: Golds (Nanai), Orochis, Udekheitsy, and Tazy. Of the 1959 population 67% was urban, and this high proportion increased to 73% (1,255,000) in 1970. Growing urbanization is indicated by the presence of only 9 towns but 45 urban districts. The largest towns are the administrative centre of Vladivostok (442,000), Ussurisk (formerly Voroshilov; 128,000), the port of Nakhodka (105,000), and the coal-mining town of Artem ([1967 est.] 65,000). Agriculture is important only in the Ussuri Valley, one of the chief soybean regions of the U.S.S.R. Soybeans occupy over one-fifth of the arable land, while wheat takes another fifth. Oats, maize (corn; chiefly for fodder), barley, rye, and vegetables are also grown. Rice is grown in the south. All around the coasts fishing is a major part of the economy and includes coastal crab fishing, deep-sea fishing, and Antarctic whaling. There are several small coal and lignite fields in the south of the *kray* around Ussurisk and Artem and at Luchegorsk in the Ussuri Valley. In the Tetyukhe region of the Sikhote-Alin, tin, lead, and zinc are mined. The great forest resources are the basis of a rapidly developing timber industry in most of the inland urban centres. Bear, lynx, panther, sable, and squirrel are hunted for furs. (R. A. F.)

PRIMROSE, common name for the genus *Primula*, containing about 500 species distributed throughout the cooler parts of Europe and Asia, and found also on the mountains of Ethiopia and Java; a few are American. They are herbaceous perennials, with a permanent rootstock from which arise tufts of leaves and flower stems, which die down in winter; the new growths formed in autumn remain in a budlike condition ready to develop in spring. They form the typical genus of the primrose family (Primulaceae; *q.v.*), the floral conformation of which is very interesting botanically.

The variation in the length of the stamens and of the style in the flowers of *Primula* has attracted much attention since Charles Darwin investigated them. Some of the flowers have short stamens and a long style, while others have long stamens or stamens inserted so high up that the anthers protrude beyond the corolla tube, and a short style. Gardeners and florists had for centuries been familiar with these variations, calling the flowers from which the anthers protruded "thrum-eyed" and those in which the stigma appeared in the mouth of the tube "pin-eyed."

Darwin showed by experiment that the most perfect degree of fertility, as shown by the greatest number of seeds and the healthiest seedlings, was attained when the pollen from a short-stamened flower was transferred to the stigma of a short-styled flower, or when the pollen from the long stamens was applied to the long style. Since in any given flower the stamens are short (or low down in the flower tube) and the style long, or conversely, it fol-

JOHN MARKHAM

COMMON PRIMROSE (PRIMULA VULGARIS)

lows that to insure a high degree of fertility cross fertilization must occur, and this is effected by the transfer of the pollen from one flower to another by insects. Incomplete fertility arises when the stigma is impregnated by the pollen from the same flower. The size of the pollen grains and the texture of the stigma are different in the two forms of flower.

The best-known species are the common primrose (*Primula vulgaris*), a European perennial with basal, wrinkled leaves and prevailingly yellow flowers—some are purple or blue—but now found in many varietal colours; the cowslip (*P. veris*), also with basal leaves and a long-stalked flower stem bearing a cluster of generally yellow flowers with a dark-coloured eye at the centre and scalelike folds at the mouth; and the oxlip (*P. elatior*), similar to the cowslip, but without the folds at the flower's mouth. All of these are found wild in Great Britain and elsewhere and are widely cultivated, especially in the fine horticultural varieties of polyanthus primroses, which bear profuse clusters of flowers and occur in many colours. The above plants are cool-loving sorts that grow well in heavy soils in slight shade; sloping land (especially an eastern exposure), quite moist in summer but with good drainage, is an ideal situation. In the U.S., about 15 species are native in the region of Oregon and Washington.

The auricula of the garden is derived from *P. auricula*, a yellow-flowered species, native of the Alps and the easiest of all the primroses to grow. The Himalayas are rich in species of primrose, often difficult of determination or limitation, certain forms being peculiar to particular valleys. Of these *P. denticulata, stuarti, sikkimmensis, nivalis* and *floribunda* may be mentioned as frequently cultivated, as well as the lovely rose-coloured species *P. rosea*. The royal cowslip (*P. imperialis*) resembles *P. japonica* (*see* below) but has leaves measuring 18 in. (45.7 cm.) long by 5 in. (12.7 cm.) wide. It grows at an elevation of 9,000 ft. (2,743 m.) in Java and has deep-yellow or orange flowers. Several small-growing hardy species, among which are the choice alpine varieties, afford fine rock garden displays in cool locales; they must be placed where they are secure from excessive dampness during the winter and excessive sunlight in the summer.

One of the most popular of winter and early spring decorative plants is the Chinese primrose (*Primula sinensis*), of which some superb strains have been obtained. *P. japonica*, a bold-growing and very beautiful Japanese plant, is hardy in sheltered positions in England but must be grown in the cool greenhouse over most of the U.S. *Primula cortusoides* of Siberia and *P. sieboldi* of Japan, of which there are many lovely forms, are suitable for outdoor culture and under glass. Many of these are beautiful potted plants of the florist trade. Among the greenhouse primroses, *P. obconica* has hairy leaves which may cause a skin rash in susceptible persons. Two other Chinese species, *P. forresti* and *P.*

bulleyana, orange-yellow flowered, 2½ to 3 ft. (91 cm.) in height, are hardy in favoured spots in the rock garden.

Cultivated primroses may be found in a considerable variety of colours, ranging from the palest yellow to deep crimson and blue. Most hardy sorts may be propagated by seed sown indoors in early spring; seedlings, kept cool and moist in moderate shade, should be transplanted a few times until they are set in the permanent spot in the garden in early autumn. A light mulch will give adequate protection in the winter. Since primroses do not reproduce true to seed, special varieties may be increased by the division of crowns in early autumn.

Evening primrose belongs to the genus *Oenothera* (*q.v.*), of the evening primrose family (Onagraceae). The Cape primrose comprises hybrid forms of *Streptocarpus,* a South African genus belonging to the family Gesneriaceae. The Arabian primrose is *Arnebia cornuta,* of the borage family (Boraginaceae), a garden annual.   (N. Tr.)

PRIMULACEAE, the primrose family of herbaceous plants, belonging to the order Primulales and containing about 800 species in 25 genera (the genus *Primula* has nearly 500 species). The family is cosmopolitan in distribution, but the majority of the species are confined to the temperate and colder parts of the Northern Hemisphere and many are arctic or alpine.

All the members are herbs, sometimes annual, as in scarlet pimpernel (*Anagallis arvensis*), but generally perennial. In *Primula* the plant persists by means of a rhizome and in *Cyclamen* by means of a tuber. The leaves form a basal rosette, as in *Primula* (primrose, cowslip, etc.), or there is a well-developed aerial stem, erect in species of *Lysimachia* (loosestrife), or creeping in *Lysimachia nummularia* (creeping jenny or moneywort). *Hottonia* (water violet) is a floating water plant with submerged leaves cut into fine linear segments.

The leaves are generally simple, often with a toothed margin; their arrangement is mostly opposite or whorled, but may be alternate. The flowers are solitary in the leaf axils, as in scarlet pimpernel, moneywort, etc., or in clusters, as in primrose and cowslip. Each flower is subtended by a bract, and the two first developed sepals stand right and left. The flowers are hermaphrodite, having both stamens and a pistil, and usually have their parts in fives (pentamerous) throughout, though exceptions occur. The sepals are leafy and persistent; the petals are partially joined and form a corolla generally divided into a longer or shorter tube and a limb, which is spreading in primrose, or reflexed in *Cyclamen* and *Dodecatheon;* in *Soldanella* it is bell-shaped; in *Lysimachia* and others the tube is often very short, the petals appearing almost free; in *Coris* and *Omphalogramma* the corolla is irregular; in *Glaux* the petals are absent. The five stamens spring from the corolla tube and are opposite to its lobes; this anomalous position is generally explained by assuming that an outer whorl of stamens opposite the sepals has disappeared, though sometimes represented by scales as in *Samolus* and *Soldanella.* The superior ovary—half-inferior in *Samolus*—bears a simple style ending in a capitate entire stigma, and contains a free-central placenta bearing generally a large number of ovules, which are unusual in having two integuments. The fruit is a capsule, splitting by five, sometimes ten, teeth or valves, or sometimes transversely (a pyxidium) as in *Anagallis.*

Cross-pollination is often favoured by the presence of two structural types of the flower, as shown in species of *Primula.* The two forms have long and short styles respectively, the stamens occupying corresponding positions halfway down or at the mouth of the corolla tube. The pollen grains are also dimorphic and their size corresponds with differences of the stigmatic surfaces of reciprocal flowers (*see* Primrose). Basic to these morphological differences the plants exhibit a certain amount of genetic self-incompatibility.

The family can be divided into five tribes by characters of the corolla, ovary, and capsule, and by the presence or absence of tubers. On the basis of flower and ovary characters, the family is considered to be allied to the pink family (Caryophyllaceae).

The chief British genera are *Primula, Lysimachia* (loosestrifes), and *Anagallis.* The principal American genera are *Primula,*

Samolus (water pimpernels or brookweeds), *Lysimachia,* and *Dodecatheon* (shooting stars or American cowslips). In cultivation the chief genera are *Primula, Cyclamen, Androsace, Omphalogramma,* and *Lysimachia.*

See F. Pax and R. Knuth, "Primulaceae," *Pflanzenreich* 22, iv, 237: I-386 (1905).   (P. S. Gr.; X.)

PRINCE, MORTON (1854–1929), U.S. psychologist and physician, formulated such concepts as neurograms (the neurological record of psychological behaviour) and the coconscious (a parallel, possibly rival, well-organized system of awarenesses comparable with ordinary consciousness). He was born in Boston, Mass., Dec. 21, 1854, and was educated at Harvard University (B.A., 1875; M.D., 1879) with subsequent study at Vienna, Strasbourg, Paris, and Nancy. He recognized motivational forces of emotional conflict but disagreed with Sigmund Freud's insistence on a fundamental underlying theme of sexuality. He was an early user of hypnosis as an exploratory agent and for reeducational therapy.

In addition to studying and teaching abnormal psychology at Harvard, Prince practised medicine, was president of both the American Neurological and the American Psychopathological associations and founded (1906) and edited (1906–29) the *Journal of Abnormal Psychology.* He died Aug. 31, 1929.

He was the author of six books, the best known of which was his study of a multiple personality, *Dissociation of a Personality* (1906). Among others were *The Nature of Mind and Human Automatism* (1885), *The Unconscious* (1913), and *Clinical and Experimental Studies in Personality* (1929).

See H. A. Murray, "Morton Prince," *Journal of Abnormal and Social Psychology,* vol. 52 (May 1956).   (M. H. En.)

PRINCE, a title of rank, the various uses of which have led to much misunderstanding. It may imply (1) complete sovereignty; (2) sovereignty all but complete; (3) membership in a family whose head is a sovereign or formerly sovereign prince; or (4) some noble dignity inferior to that of duke.

The word is derived from Latin *princeps* (plural *principes*), which etymologically means simply "the first" or "the leader." Thus in the Roman Republic the senator whose name stood first on the censor's list was called *princeps Senatus,* or leader of the House; and the young men of noble birth who, apparently, led the Roman cavalry in early times (*see* Equites) were *principes juventutis,* leaders of the youth. By the end of the republic, however, *princeps* had come to mean "the leading man in the state." In this sense it was adopted by Augustus as an unofficial title in preference to the more military *imperator* (*see* Emperor). Hence the Roman imperial regime from Augustus to Diocletian is often called the Principate. The emperor was also in fact *princeps Senatus.* Augustus also revived the ceremonial parade of the *equites,* and his grandsons Gaius and Lucius Caesar were proclaimed *principes juventutis.* Younger relatives of several later emperors received the same title, which virtually designated an intended successor. Even so, *principes* could still mean "leading men" generally.

The ambiguity of the use of the term prince passed from the Western Roman Empire to the states that took its place.

France.—During the Carolingian period feudalism (*q.v.*) in France was gradually changed from a system in which vassals were in fact dependent on the king into one in which their dependence was very often an empty formality. The dukes or counts who profited most from this development sometimes usurped the sovereign's title of prince as well as his prerogatives in matters of government; and the masses of territory over which they established hereditary rule—Normandy, Flanders, Champagne, ducal Burgundy, Toulouse (Languedoc), and Aquitaine, for instance—are conventionally designated as "principalities."

Prince, however, was still not an official title of the nobility, and for centuries the sons of the royal house had it only as a description, being ranked instead among the peers of France (*see* Peerage) with the title of duke or count according to the territories granted to them. In the middle of the 15th century, however, members of the royal house came to be distinguished as "princes of the blood" (*princes du sang*), with precedence over the other peers except at the coronation of the king or in the *parlement*. It was only in 1576 that the princes of the blood who were also peers obtained precedence everywhere over the other peers; and only in 1711 that princes of the blood obtained such precedence absolutely, whether they were peers or not.

By the 16th century the great feudal "principalities" had been broken by the monarchy, and French influence was expanding over territories dependent on the Holy Roman Empire. Members of the ruling dynasties of these territories, for example Lorraine and Savoy, who had peerages in France came to enjoy in France special courtly privileges attached to the rank of *prince étranger,* or "foreign prince." The lords of Monaco had the title of prince from the mid-17th century.

There were also 30 or more "principalities" indistinguishable from petty lordships. In a few cases the king accorded or acknowledged the title without defining the status of a principality in relation to a duchy, a countship or a marquisate. Such princely titles were often borne by the eldest sons of dukes.

Germany.—On the decline of the Carolingian monarchy in Germany the so-called stem duchies or dukedoms of the Saxons, Bavarians, Franconians, Swabians, etc., were the counterpart of the great "principalities" of France insofar as they challenged the royal power. In the 10th–12th centuries, however, a new class of *Fürsten* (singular *Fürst,* prince) arose, consisting of the holders of well-defined territorial lordships in immediate dependence on the king and on the *Reich;* and with the disintegration of the stem duchies an Estate of Princes of the Realm (*Reichsfürstenstand*) came into being from the 1180s. This Estate comprised both secular and ecclesiastical princes: on the one hand dukes, counts palatine, margraves, and landgraves, but not ordinary counts (though from the latter part of the 14th century *gefürstete Grafen,* or "counts ranked as princes," appear); and on the other archbishops, bishops, certain abbots, and the masters of the military-religious orders. New admissions to this Estate required not only the sovereigns' bestowal of the title *Fürst* (lower than that of duke or landgrave) but also the consent of the existing princes. In the *Reichstag* or Diet (*q.v.*) the *Kurfürsten* or electoral princes (*see* ELECTORS) eventually set themselves apart from the others, whose number grew considerably till the dissolution of the Holy Roman Empire. *See* GERMANY: *History,* subsections *Fall of Henry the Lion and the Estate of Princes* and *Emperor and Empire After 1648;* and *The French Revolutionary and Napoleonic Periods* and *The German Confederation, 1815–66,* for the position of the *Reichsfürsten* after 1806. Of the *Fürstentümer,* only ten were not mediatized by 1815—including Liechtenstein, which even survived World Wars I and II. The title of *Fürst* as bestowed by the Prussian monarchy in the 19th–20th centuries was simply honorific.

The German language uses the term *Fürst* for a prince with sovereign or quasi-sovereign rights or for the head of a princely family, but may use *Prinz* for a junior member of a sovereign or princely house. Examples are *Kronprinz,* crown prince; *Kurprinz,* electoral prince, heir to an electorate; *Erbprinz,* hereditary prince, heir to a principality; Prinz von Preussen, heir presumptive to Prussia; Prinz von Battenberg, for descendants of the grand ducal house of Hesse through a morganatic marriage (*q.v.*).

Spain and Portugal.—In Spain counts of Barcelona (*q.v.*) had been regarded as princes of Catalonia in the sense that they were the greatest feudatories of that country; and when Count Ramón Berenguer IV became king-consort of Aragon in 1137 he styled himself príncipe de Aragon instead of king. The sons of Spanish kings, meanwhile, had the style of infante; but the title of príncipe de Asturias was created, in 1388, for the eldest son of John I of Castile, namely the future Henry III of Castile. On the union of the Castilian and Aragonese crowns this title became that of the heir apparent to the whole Spanish monarchy; it long remained the only Spanish princely title. In 1795, however, the title príncipe de la Paz was created for Manuel de Godoy, with higher rank than his duchy of La Alcudia; but it was abolished in 1808. Baldomero Espartero received the title príncipe de Vergara in 1872 for his lifetime only. Outside Spain, on the other hand, the Spanish kings bestowed princely titles with extreme liberality.

In Portugal the heir apparent to the throne had the title of prince royal from the reign of King Edward (Duarte).

Italy.—In southern Italy the Lombard dukes of Benevento became practically sovereign princes after the Frankish annexation of the northern kingdom of Lombardy (774); and successive partitions of their territory, from 847, created three principalities, Benevento, Salerno, and Capua. In the 11th century the latter two fell to the Normans (*see* NAPLES, KINGDOM OF), while Benevento became an exclave of the Papal State. Subsequently, princely titles became very numerous in southern Italy: the Spanish kings conceded at least 120 for Sicily and about as many for Naples. For Italy as a whole the aggregate was increased by Roman principalities created by the papacy and by principalities of the Holy Roman Empire in the north.

Eastern Europe and the Levant.—In Russia and in Poland the title prince (Russian *knyaz,* Polish *książę*) was accorded to descendants of sovereign or formerly sovereign dynasties, whether Russian, Tatar, Lithuanian, or Polish. For grand princes *see* GRAND DUKE. Apart from this use, the title was granted as a high rank of nobility by the Russians from Peter the Great's time. In Poland, where ten princely houses claimed descent from ancient dynasties, there were four more created by the Holy Roman Empire and one created by the Holy See, as well as one created in 1808 by the Russians, but only two created for ordinary nobles by the Polish crown (Poniatowski in 1764, Poninski in 1773).

The Frankish principality of Achaea (Achaia), established in 1205 (*see* GREECE: *History*), disappeared with Turkish conquest in 1456–58; but later the rulers of some Christian countries under the real or nominal suzerainty of the Turkish sultans were styled princes. Such were the rulers of Transylvania in the 16th–17th centuries; those of Moldavia and Walachia under the Phanariote regime (whence some Phanariote families conserve the princely title) and their successors, princes of Rumania, from 1866 to 1881; those of Serbia from 1815 to 1882; those of Bulgaria from 1878 to 1908; and also those of Samos from 1832 to 1913.

The principality of Antioch (*see* CRUSADES) may have been so designated either because of traditions imported by the Normans from southern Italy or because of its controversial relationship to the Byzantine empire, which claimed suzerainty over it.

Great Britain.—In Great Britain the word "prince" can be used in a descriptive way for a sovereign or a magnate (dukes, marquesses, and earls may be so described in their formal style); but as a title of rank it is confined to members of the royal family.

The Anglo-Saxon word *aetheling* survived into the 12th century as a designation of the sons of kings; and Henry III's son was known as simply "the lord Edward" before he became king as Edward I (1272). The indigenous rulers of Wales, however, who had been kings till the 11th century, were thereafter styled princes (*tywysog*); and it was to conciliate the conquered Welsh that Edward I, in 1301, invested his son, the future Edward II, as prince of Wales. From Edward III's time the king's eldest son was usually invested in due course as prince of Wales, but this title had always to be granted anew by the sovereign, who had merged it with the crown on his accession. The king's younger children, meanwhile, were "but gentlemen by birth and called after their names, as Lord Henrie or Lord Edward" (William Harrison, *Description of England,* 1577) till in James I's reign the title "prince" was extended to all sons of the sovereign. As late as Charles II's time the nieces of the king, both of whom later became queens regnant, were called simply the lady Mary and the lady Anne.

From George I's accession (1714) it became settled practice for the sovereign's descendants in the male line (*i.e.,* his children, and the children of his sons) to be styled "prince" and "royal highness"; great-grandchildren in the male line were "prince" and "highness." In 1917 George V limited the title of prince to the sovereign's children and the children of the sovereign's sons; the only extension was for the eldest living son of the eldest son of the prince of Wales. Thus other great-grandchildren in the male line would merely have the courtesy titles of the children of dukes (*see* ADDRESS, FORMS OF), and their children, apart from the eldest son when he inherited the dukedom, would have no title whatsoever. The granting or withholding of a princely title remained, however, a matter of the sovereign's will: Elizabeth II's consort,

Philip, duke of Edinburgh, was expressly created a prince of Great Britain and Northern Ireland in 1957.

PRINCE ALBERT, a city in the province of Saskatchewan, Can., is on the North Saskatchewan river 220 mi. N. of Regina, near the central northern extremity of the settled part of the province. Founded in 1866 as an Anglican mission station, near the site of a fur trade post established in 1776, it became a centre for the lumbering industry in the early 1900s. Now Saskatchewan's northern "capital," it serves a large agricultural and forest region and a vast northern hinterland. It is a northern provincial government headquarters and has good railroad, highway and air services, a television and radio station and a daily newspaper. It is the site of a federal penitentiary. Its industries include an oil refinery, wood preserving plants, a plywood plant, woodworking shops and a packing plant. Pop. (1966) 26,269.   (C. S. Br.)

PRINCE EDWARD ISLAND, in the gulf of St. Lawrence, is the smallest province of Canada. The arc of the crescent-shaped island roughly parallels the curving southern shore of the gulf; it is separated from the mainland by Northumberland strait, which has a maximum width of 25 mi. (40 km.). The province has less than 1% of the population and area of Canada and plays a very minor role in the economy and politics of the country. Yet "the island" is cherished by thousands of its former residents and their families, widely scattered over North America. The almost feudal system in which its lands were held for nearly a century makes its history of unique interest; and L. M. Montgomery's *Anne of Green Gables* made its national park, which enshrines a near replica of "Green Gables," a tourist mecca.

Size, Shape and Location.—The curving island has a maximum length of 145 mi. (233 km.). From a maximum width of 34 mi. (55 km.), it narrows to isthmuses which in two places, northeast of Charlottetown (the capital) and near Summerside (the other town), are less than 3 mi. (5 km.) from tidewater to tidewater. The three lobes thus pinched off roughly correspond to the three counties, from east to west, Kings, Queens and Prince. The land area is 2,184 sq.mi. (5,657 sq.km.).

Physical Geography.—The bedrock, well covered by dune sand on the gulf shore and glacial ground moraine elsewhere, is exposed in low cliffs on the eastern and southern shores. An unusually uniform red sandstone, it does grade off both to sandy siltstones and shales and coarser conglomerates. The age of the formation is thought to be Permian (235,000,000 years). The apparently horizontal strata actually dip toward the northeast and must be younger than similar beds exposed on the mainland to the south. The dip and cliffing suggest the remnants of an old cuesta, elsewhere dismembered or drowned beneath the waters of the gulf. In this soft sandstone block stream erosion has carved a gently rolling plain grading to rougher hills of over 400 ft. (120 m.) elevation west of Charlottetown and to some few stretches really flat to the eye west of Malpeque bay. The intricate serration of the shore line with many deep estuaries brings sea and land into intimate relation; no point of the island is more than 10 mi. (16 km.) from tidewater.

The soils, everywhere developed from the thick mantle of glacial drift, tend to be coarse-textured sandy loams. There are more clayey phases and a good deal of swamp and bog; at the other extreme are the dunes that line much of the northern shore. The soils are strongly acid podsols, rather low in plant nutrients.

As elsewhere in the Atlantic provinces and New England states the weather is markedly variable; the island lies on one of the most heavily traveled storm tracks in North America. There is much sunshine but, on the average, every third day has some precipitation; the annual 40 in. (100 cm.) normally includes 9 or 10 ft. (3 m.) of winter snow. An occasional dry summer month and extremes of open, or deeply snowbound, winters point up the variability. Monthly temperature means lie between February's 17° F (about −8° C) and July figures in the upper 60s (about 20° C); the effect of the sea is seen in a long, laggard, chilly spring and in a late, warm and truly glorious autumn.

When Jacques Cartier visited the island in 1534 it was covered with a dense mixed forest, its trees of both boreal coniferous and northern hardwood types. There is a good deal of tree cover, predominantly spruce, on farm woodlots but the 16th-century forest has disappeared. With it have gone most of the larger animals (bear, moose, caribou, deer, seals, walrus and even beaver) but smaller animals and a wide variety of birds, including migratory ducks and geese, are still plentiful as are the fish and shellfish (cod, hake, halibut, herring, alewife, trout, salmon, eels, lobsters and clams) of its streams, estuaries and offshore coastal banks.

History.—Cartier was the first European of record to visit the island. Afterward it was largely ignored by the French until the 18th century, although, much earlier, it acquired the name Île Saint-Jean (St. John's Island) which it was to retain until 1798, when its present name was chosen (after that duke of Kent whose daughter was to become Queen Victoria).

It received more attention from the French, as an adjunct of Louisburg on Île Royale (Cape Breton) and a refuge for Acadians from the mainland, especially after the treaty of Utrecht, and when Lord Rollo invested it for the British in 1758 it may have held as many as 5,000 settlers, mostly Acadian. Most of these were deported and the island was surveyed and divided into 3 counties, each with a townsite and "royalty," 14 parishes and 67 lots or townships. These were then awarded, by lot, to upward of 100 applicants for royal favour (Scots predominated) under conditions which should have guaranteed rapid settlement. The grantees (proprietors) did little, however, and by 1800 there were scarcely more settlers than in the 1750s. But the few Highland Scots, American Loyalists and remaining Acadians of the turn of the century were soon joined by thousands of others, dominantly Highlanders and southern Irish and, as the tenant farmers slowly won representative and responsible government (the colony was separated from Nova Scotia in 1769), pressure was increased on the often absentee proprietors to open their lands and the freehold was gradually enlarged. By 1873 only the most recalcitrant of the landlords remained to be bought out.

The little colony joined the new dominion six years late and rather reluctantly; it has been said to have been "bought" into confederation by Canada's assumption of its overwhelming railway debt, promises of better communications across the strait and a large subsidy to take care of the extensive land purchases from the proprietors. Since then it has been ever in the forefront of moves by the smaller provinces to obtain a larger share of federal revenues to help them support schools and other local services at levels nearer those prevailing in central Canada.

Government.—The form of government is that defined by the British North America act (*see* CANADA: *History*). The province at first sent 6 members to the Canadian house of commons; it now sends 4 to a house of 265 and 1 of these is occasionally given a cabinet post, usually minor. It has a local assembly of 30 members elected in pairs (a relic of the period of two houses) from 15 constituencies and the government is organized by the majority party in the usual British parliamentary system.

Population.—The population, roughly 30,000 in 1830, reached 80,000 in 1860 and over 110,000 in the 1880s, when immigration

Prince Edward Island: Places of 5,000 or More Population*

Place	Population				
	1966	1961	1951	1941	1921
Total province	108,535	104,629	98,429	95,047	88,615
Charlottetown	18,427	18,318	15,887	14,821	10,814
Summerside	10,042	8,611	6,547	5,034	3,228

*Populations reflect data as each place was constituted at date of each census.

had largely ceased and outflow of population began. The highest total was 109,078 in 1891; by 1921 it was below 90,000 but rose to 99,285 in 1956 and to 108,535 in 1966. The great tide of emigration affected chiefly descendants of Scots and Irish. A population over half Scots and one-fourth Irish (and about 10% Acadian) in the 1860s was, by the 1960s, about 30% each of Scots and English (in claimed ultimate origin), about 20% Irish and something under 20% Acadian. Other elements are negligible; only a few Micmac Indians remain. Population density is over 47 per square mile but more than one-fourth of the people live in Charlottetown and Summerside and the rural population is much denser west of Charlottetown. "Farm" population has declined even more rapidly than "rural"; it numbered 30,841 in 1966.

Education and Religion.—Public, primary and secondary education is available to all citizens. There are some 17 regional high schools. Charlottetown, with a population (1966) of 18,-427, has three primary schools, two junior high schools, one senior high school, and a provincial technical school. There is one secular university, Prince of Wales college (established in 1834), and a Roman Catholic university, St. Dunstan's (established in 1855), each now offering full four-year degree programs.

Roman Catholics comprised the largest single denomination. Estimates as of 1961 suggested that they represented some 46% of the population, divided largely among those of Highland Scots, Irish and Acadian descent. The Protestant majority consisted chiefly of: United Church 26%, Presbyterian 12%, Anglican 6% and Baptist 5%. A major national centre for the graphic and performing arts has been established in Charlottetown.

Production.—In the 1960s about 33% of the population was classed as agricultural and its farms (averaging over 110 ac.) occupied about two-thirds of the surface (much of the rest of which had been farmed in the 19th century). A mixed livestock-and-crop agriculture received most of its revenue from animal products: sales of cattle, swine and dairy products alone yielded half of it. Potatoes (largely seed), which provided about 15% of the total, was the only cash crop of significance. Tobacco growing was introduced in 1960. Most farms were subsistent to a degree, with 17% of all farm production consumed thereon by farmers. More than 19 out of 20 farms were operator-owned. Agriculture accounts for about 33% of the total net value of production.

Fisheries yield about 10% of the total net production. Lobsters, taken in limited seasons, provided two-thirds to three-fourths of that value, cod and related ground fish, herrings, smelts and oysters the rest. Most fishermen and boats were unspecialized; many of the men were part-time farmers.

The island was the birthplace of silver fox farming, for which it was world famous from 1910 to 1940, but after 1950 foxes all but disappeared and the few fur farms left raised chiefly mink. Forest products, derived from indifferently managed farm woodlots, played a steady but minor role in the economy.

The net product of manufacturing industries has comprised about 15% of the total, chiefly from processing industries for agricultural, fishery and forest products; butter and cheese making, meat slaughtering and packing, fish processing and feed milling and mixing predominated. There is an interesting textile industry (bag making for fertilizer and potatoes) and a significant woodworking enterprise although plants are small. The tourist industry, still not strongly developed, offers excellent opportunities if transportation could be improved.

Communications.—The island's railway was begun in 1871 as a narrow-gauge (3 ft. 6 in.) line notable for its curves and grades. The establishment of a car-ferry connection with the mainland (Borden to Cape Tormentine in New Brunswick) during World War I led to a change to standard gauge; by 1960 that service across the strait to and from Charlottetown and Summerside was the chief function it performed. A highway-building program begun in the 1950s greatly increased the mileage of paved roads on the island.

Communication across the strait has been a central problem of island life since the 18th century. Even a supplementary automobile ferry from Wood Islands in the southeast to Caribou (near Pictou) in Nova Scotia has only widened the bottleneck. Good air connections to Summerside and Charlottetown have relieved the situation somewhat. A causeway link is under consideration.

BIBLIOGRAPHY.—A. H. Clark, *Three Centuries and the Island* (1959); D. C. Harvey, *The French Régime in Prince Edward Island* (1926); "Prince Edward Island," *Canadian Geog. Jour.* (May 1938) by F. Walker and (Aug. 1941) by A. McAnn; J. Croteau, *Cradled in the Waves* (1951); Frank Mackinnon, *The Government of Prince Edward Island* (1951). (AN. H. C.)

PRINCE ISLAND (PRÍNCIPE): *see* SÃO TOMÉ E PRÍNCIPE.

PRINCES ISLANDS (Turkish, KIZIL ADALAR), in ancient times Demonesi Insulae, a group of nine islands in the Sea of Marmara about 15 mi. (24 km.) SE of Istanbul forming a district of the province (*il*) of that city. Area 5.4 sq.mi. (14 sq.km.). The smallest, Sedef Adasi (Antirrobinthos or Antirobethos), and the four largest are inhabited, and on Yassi Ada (Plati) there is a branch of the Naval Academy. The four large ones are Buyukada (Prinkipo, ancient Pityoussa); Heybeli Ada (Khalki or Halki, ancient Chalcitis); Burgaz Adasi (Antigoni, ancient Panormos); and Kinali Ada (Proti). Winter population (1965) 15,246; summer population approximately 140,000.

In ancient times copper, known as *demonesios chalkos,* was mined there. The monasteries built during the Byzantine period figured largely as places of exile. The empresses Irene (widow of Leo IV) and the Macedonian Zoe were sent to Prinkipo; the emperors Philippicus Bardanes, Michael I Rangabe, Romanus I Lecapenus, and Romanus IV Diogenes retired to Proti and the anti-iconoclastic patriarch Methodius to Antigoni. The only surviving Byzantine buildings are the chapel of St. John the Baptist on Antigoni, said to have been built by the empress Theodora, part of which dates from the time of Methodius, and the chapel of the Theotokos on Khalki built by Maria Comnena. The monastery of St. John (later of the Theotokos) beside it was rebuilt by her husband John VIII Palaeologus and again rebuilt in about 1680, and in the 18th century by Alexander Ypsilanti, hospodar of Moldavia; it was used after 1831 by the Greek Commercial School and later by the Turkish Naval Academy. Also on Khalki is Hagia Trias, rebuilt in 1844 and housing since then the chief school of theology of the Greek Orthodox Church.

See G. Schlumberger, *Les Îles des Princes,* 2nd ed. (1925). (J. CH.)

PRINCETON, a borough of Mercer county, N.J., U.S., the seat of Princeton university (*q.v.*), is located midway between New York city and Philadelphia. Capt. Henry Greenland established a plantation on the site of the present village in 1681 and 15 years later a number of Quaker families settled in the area. During the colonial period, because of its location, Princeton was the principal luncheon stop for stagecoach passengers traveling between Philadelphia and New York. In the pre-Revolutionary period the College of New Jersey, now Princeton university, became a centre of anti-British feeling; John Witherspoon, its president, Richard Stockton, a resident of the town, and John Hart, from nearby Hopewell, were three of the five New Jersey men to sign the Declaration of Independence. Nassau hall, principal structure of the college, completed in 1756, changed hands three times in the battle of Princeton and it was within its walls that the engagement ended, with Washington's troops defeating the British under Col. Charles Mawhood on Jan. 3, 1777, following the battle of Trenton. The legislature of the state of New Jersey convened in Princeton the following summer and the Continental congress was assembled there from June until Nov. 1783.

Educational institutions in Princeton in addition to the university include the Institute for Advanced Study, established in 1930; Princeton Theological seminary, a Presbyterian seminary established in 1812; Westminster Choir college, a private college established in 1926, and its affiliated Columbus Boychoir school; and several distinguished private schools. The Educational Testing Service, with headquarters there, develops and publishes achievement tests used in schools and colleges throughout the nation. Research laboratories operated by industrial firms and nonprofit organizations have been attracted to Princeton by the presence of the educational facilities.

In addition to a community of scholars who come from many nations, there reside in Princeton business and professional men and women who commute daily to Newark, New York city, Philadelphia and Trenton. Mid-town Palmer square, a business district, is an outstanding example of urban redevelopment emphasizing colonial architecture.

"Morven" in Princeton is the official executive mansion of the governor of New Jersey. The oldest portion was built in 1701 by Richard Stockton, grandfather of the signer of the Declaration of Independence. Walter E. Edge, then governor, purchased it in 1944 and ten years later presented it to the state. The first occupants under its new function, Gov. and Mrs. Robert B. Meyner, moved into it in 1957.

538 PRINCETON UNIVERSITY

For comparative population figures *see* table in NEW JERSEY: *Population*. (E. R. D.)

PRINCETON UNIVERSITY, a privately endowed non-sectarian institution of higher learning for men, at Princeton, N.J., until 1896 called officially the College of New Jersey. Its buildings are grouped in the central portion of a campus of about 2,200 acres. Nassau Hall, the oldest and historically the most interesting building on the campus, was at the time of its completion in 1756 the largest academic building in the American Colonies. Designed by Robert Smith, the architect of Independence Hall in Philadelphia, it was named in honour of William of Nassau, William III of England. There in 1783 George Washington received the formal thanks of the Continental Congress for his conduct of the Revolutionary War.

Characteristic of life at Princeton, in addition to the university's rural location and consequently its active outdoor interests, are the residential dormitory system, the system of elective upper-class eating clubs, and the form of student self-government, illustrated particularly by the honour system, under which undergraduates participate in the administration of university discipline.

The Committee on Admission takes into consideration the entire record of each applicant and endeavours to select those candidates who seem best qualified to gain most from a Princeton education. There are no quotas by schools, or types of schools, or by geographic areas. In the last analysis, admission is based on a comparison of the records of all applicants.

The university offers undergraduate courses in the liberal arts and sciences leading to the degrees of bachelor of arts and bachelor of science in engineering. In addition to the arts and sciences, graduate work leading to the master's and doctor's degrees is also offered in architecture, engineering, and public and international affairs.

Princeton has engaged in a number of pioneering ventures in educational practice, notably the preceptorial method of instruction, introduced in 1905, and the plan of independent study for upperclassmen, introduced in 1923. It has also pioneered in its Woodrow Wilson School of Public and International Affairs in developing men for public life and for professions and businesses related to public affairs, in its School of Engineering and Applied Science in developing engineers who have broad cultural backgrounds as well as technical knowledge, and in its interdepartmental programs of study, a gradual development that culminated in 1953 with the creation of the Council of the Humanities.

Princeton's undergraduate program has as its core an offering of courses in four broad fields of learning—natural science; social science; arts and letters; and history, philosophy, and religion. Such courses are intended to give the student a basic understanding of the discipline of each area. In upper-class years he takes a combination of courses and engages in independent work in a specific field or interdepartmental program.

In assuming the university title in 1896, it was definitely concluded that Princeton's future did not lie in developing professional schools but in upholding pure learning and in devoting itself "to the liberal aspects of those studies which underlie and broaden professional and technical education." The university, therefore, became not a congeries of professional schools overshadowing an undergraduate department but a large, homogeneous, and well-organized body of undergraduate students, with a small, carefully selected graduate school devoted to the liberal arts and sciences.

History.—The university owes its origin to a movement set on foot by the Presbyterian Synod of Philadelphia in 1739 to establish in the middle colonies a college to rank with Harvard and Yale in New England and with William and Mary in Virginia. As a result of dissension in the church, no progress was made until 1746, when the plan was again broached by the Synod of New York, formed by the secession of the presbytery of New York and the presbytery of New Brunswick, radical (New School) presbyteries of the Synod of Philadelphia. Most of the leaders of the presbytery of New Brunswick had been educated at the so-called Log College, a school with restricted curriculum at Neshaminy, Pa., about 20 mi. from Philadelphia, founded in 1726. The opportunity was taken by the Synod of New York to found a larger institution of higher learning, broader in scope and training, and to transfer to the new project the Log College interests. On Oct. 22, 1746, John Hamilton, acting governor of New Jersey, granted a charter for erecting a college in New Jersey, which was opened in May 1747, at Elizabeth, N.J. A second charter was granted by Gov. Jonathan Belcher, who on his arrival in the province in 1747, had at once taken the college under his patronage. The college was removed to Newark, where the first graduation exercises were held in 1748; but the situation was unsuitable, and in 1752 the trustees voted to remove the college to Princeton. While additional funds were being collected in Great Britain, work was begun in Princeton in 1754 on the first college building, Nassau Hall.

John Witherspoon, president during the Revolutionary period, influenced the college strongly by his personality and political prominence, and graduates of his training became leaders in public affairs. The history of the college during the first half of the 19th century was uneventful. Because of its large Southern clientele, it suffered in the U.S. Civil War a blow from which it recovered only under the energetic administration of Pres. James McCosh (1868–88). The undergraduate enrollment was nearly trebled, gifts amounting to more than $2,000,000 were contributed, only half of which sum was for endowment, 14 new buildings were erected, and important changes were made in the curriculum.

Fellowships were established in 1869, a limited elective system was introduced in 1870, the John C. Green School of Science was erected in 1873, the graduate department was systematized in 1877, and the faculty grew from 17 to 40 and the number of volumes in the library from 25,000 to 65,000.

BY COURTESY OF PRINCETON UNIVERSITY

NASSAU HALL AT PRINCETON UNIVERSITY
Originally containing the dormitory, refectory, classrooms and chapel, it has served as an administrative building since the early 19th century

Under Pres. Francis L. Patton (1888–1902) a school of electrical engineering was established, the honour system was instituted, the plan of electing alumni trustees was adopted, 17 buildings were erected, the student body was doubled, and the faculty increased to 100, while the endowment reached $2,500,000. In 1902, Woodrow Wilson, of the class of 1879, was elected president. In his administration the undergraduate curriculum was again revised, the departmental system was organized, and an extensive building program was completed. To obtain the necessary funds, a committee of 50 alumni was formed, later changed into a graduate council. Through their agency in the eight years of President Wilson's administration the university received more than $4,500,000, the faculty was greatly strengthened, and the library increased to 271,000 volumes. A plan for grouping the undergraduate and graduate students into small self-contained residential units on the so-called quad plan was prematurely proposed by the president in 1907 and was withdrawn by the trustees. The Princeton plan of a residential building for graduate students was successfully tested on a small scale, and a bequest in 1908, although inadequate for the full project which included professorships and fellowships, gave the plan its first semblance of permanent realization. Additional funds being conditionally offered in 1909, controversy developed as to the site for the building and finally as to the plan itself, the president no longer favouring it. A further bequest of about $2,000,000 for the project brought matters to a head and the president recommended acceptance of the legacy. In September 1910, having received the Democratic nomination for governor of New Jersey, Wilson resigned the presidency.

John Grier Hibben, of the class of 1882, professor of philosophy in the university, was the 14th president of Princeton, serving from January 1912 to June 1932. His administration was marked by extended administrative reorganization, by large additions to the endowment, and by extensive expansion along material and scholastic lines. Faculty autonomy was made complete: a joint committee of trustees and faculty was organized to consider all matters of educational policy and administration; the faculty was given voice in forming its committees and initiating appointments, promotions, and increases of salary; the rights of the individual in cases of dismissal were safeguarded; faculty retirement allowances and insurance were arranged.

In 1913, the erection of the residential Graduate College rendered permanent what had been an experimental feature of the Princeton Graduate School. The School of Architecture was opened in 1920. The School of Engineering, now the School of Engineering and Applied Science, was reorganized and enlarged in 1921, and the School of Public Affairs, now the Woodrow Wilson School of Public and International Affairs, designed to give its students a broad background for an understanding of and active participation in local, state, national, and international affairs, was founded in 1930. Edward Dickinson Duffield of the class of 1892, a trustee of the university, served as acting president from June 1932 until the election of Harold Willis Dodds, professor of politics, as 15th president in June 1933. His long administration of 24 years saw great expansion of the work and facilities of Princeton University. The university commemorated the academic year 1946–47 as its bicentennial anniversary and in 1949 established ten bicentennial preceptorships at the assistant professor level to encourage scholarship and teaching.

In 1951 Princeton established the James Forrestal Research Center in the former 825-acre plant of the Rockefeller Institute for Medical Research, comprising 15 buildings and laboratories. The centre was established for the immediate purpose of permitting the university to expand its program of basic research for national defense, and for the long-term purpose of providing additional laboratories and facilities to meet the more exacting requirements of modern scientific and engineering research.

The many research programs are concerned with problems in aeronautical engineering, aerospace propulsion sciences, biochemistry, applied nuclear sciences, nuclear chemistry, high energy physics, and auditory research (Department of Psychology). Facilities include a 3-Bev proton accelerator, co-sponsored by the University of Pennsylvania and a plasma physics laboratory.

The University Chapel, its stained-glass windows portraying the life, teaching, and influence of Christ, was dedicated in 1928. The Graduate College, the first residential graduate college in the United States, was dedicated in 1913. A new dormitory quadrangle accommodating 275 unmarried graduate students was completed in 1963. Other buildings include: The Dean's House (1756); Stanhope Hall (1803); Joseph Henry House (1837); McCosh Hall (1907); Palmer Physical Laboratory (1908); Guyot Hall (1909); Holder Hall (1910); Palmer Memorial Stadium (1914); Herbert Lowell Dillon Gymnasium (1947); the Harvey S. Firestone Memorial Library (1948); Edward S. Corwin Hall (1953); George M. Moffett Biology Laboratory (1960); the Engineering Quadrangle (1962); the Charles W. Caldwell Field House, Woolworth Center of Musical Studies, and Architecture Building (1963); the Woodrow Wilson School of Public and International Affairs and the Art Museum (1965).

In 1953 the university reemphasized its long interest in the humanities by the establishment of the Council of the Humanities, which has the function of assisting members of the faculty and graduate and undergraduate students in interdisciplinary studies in the area. The council provides senior and junior fellowships for such study and supervises several special programs of instruction in which the broad range of the humanities and the social sciences is brought to bear upon programs of fundamental value or upon the civilizations of particular areas of the world.

In 1956, in order to provide more effective channels of communication with industrial corporations, a program of conferences was established to cover general and specialized problems of common interest to industry, governmental agencies and the faculty in all areas of the university. The conferences are planned and directed by the various departments and attended by faculty and interested corporation officers and government officials.

On July 1, 1957, on the retirement of President Dodds, Robert Francis Goheen of the department of classics became the 16th president of the university. Developments during the first years of his administration included raising faculty salaries and benefits; the establishment of many cross-departmental programs of study; reorganization of the curriculum of the School of Engineering and Applied Science; the development of a strong graduate program in public and international affairs; a sharp increase in the size of the Graduate School; and provisions for advanced placement and standing for gifted undergraduates. Financial support for present and future developments was provided by the successful conclusion in 1962 of a capital gifts campaign that exceeded the $53,000,000 goal by more than $7,000,000, to which was added an anonymous foundation gift of $35,000,000 for the graduate program of the Woodrow Wilson School.

Princeton University Press.—Organized as a nonprofit association, closely affiliated with, but legally independent of, the university, the Princeton University Press was founded in 1905 and incorporated in 1910. In 1912 it published its first book; approximately 60 new titles are published annually.

The broad aim of the Princeton University Press was defined as "the promotion of education and scholarship," and it serves the university by publication and distribution of its research and offers other services to scholars there and elsewhere.

See also references under "Princeton University" in the Index.

(J. D. Bn.)

PRINCIPAL AND AGENT refers to the law of agency dealing with salesmen, brokers, managers, and other commercial agents having power to make contracts for their employers. This branch of agency came to be treated separately as a result of the great increase in shipping, banking, insurance and other mercantile transactions that occurred during the late 18th and early 19th centuries. *See* AGENCY.

PRINCIPE ISLAND: *see* SÃO TOMÉ E PRÍNCIPE.

PRINGLE, SIR JOHN (1707–1782), British physician, the founder of modern military medicine, was born on April 10, 1707, at Stitchel, Roxburgh, and educated at St. Andrews, at Edinburgh, and at Leiden. He settled in Edinburgh as a physician, but after 1734 also acted as professor of moral philosophy in the university. In 1742 Pringle became physician to the earl of Stair, then commanding the British army in Flanders, and in 1744 was appointed physician general to the forces in the Low Countries. In 1749, having settled in London, he was made physician in ordinary to the duke of Cumberland, and subsequently received other court appointments as physician, being made a baronet in 1766. In November 1772 he was elected president of the Royal Society, but resigned his presidency in 1778. Pringle died on Jan. 18, 1782.

Pringle remedied camp sanitation and the ventilation of hospitals and laid down the principles for preventing dysentery and hospital fever, at the same time showing that the different forms of dysentery were varieties of one disease and that jail fever was the same as hospital fever (*i.e.*, typhus fever). Pringle's chief works are: *Observations on the Nature and Cure of Hospital and Jayl Fevers* (1750); "Experiments on Septic and Antiseptic Substances" in the *Philosophical Transactions* of the Royal Society (1750); and especially the *Observations on the Diseases of the Army* (1752). His *Six Discourses* (1783) contains a biography by A. Kippis.

PRINGSHEIM, NATHANAEL (1823–1894), German botanist, who made outstanding contributions to the study of algae, was born in Upper Silesia on Nov. 30, 1823. He studied at the universities of Breslau, Leipzig, and Berlin; graduated in 1848 as doctor of philosophy with a thesis on the form and development of the thickening layers of plant cells; and rapidly became a leader in the great botanical renaissance of the 19th century. His contributions to scientific algology were of striking interest; together with the French investigators G. Thuret and E. Bornet, he ranks as a founder of the scientific knowledge of the algae. Pringsheim was among the first to demonstrate the occurrence of a sexual process in this class of plants, and he drew from his observations general conclusions as to the nature of sexuality. The conjugation of zoospores, regarded by Pringsheim as the primitive form of sexual reproduction, was a discovery of fundamental importance.

A work (1873) on the course of morphological differentiation in the Sphacelariaceae, a family of marine algae, is of great interest, inasmuch as it treats of evolutionary questions; the author's point of view is that of K. W. von Nägeli rather than that of Darwin. Connected with Pringsheim's algological work was his investigation of the Saprolegniaceae, a family of aquatic algalike fungi. His career as a morphologist reached its peak in 1876 with the publication of a memoir on the alternation of generations in thallophytes and mosses.

From 1874 to the close of his life Pringsheim's activity was chiefly directed to plant physiology. He founded the *Jahrbuch für wissenschaftliche Botanik* and the German Botanical Society. His work was, for the most part, carried on in his private laboratory in Berlin; he held a teaching post of importance for only four years, 1864–68, when he was professor at Jena. Pringsheim died in Berlin on Oct. 6, 1894.

He wrote memoirs on *Vaucheria* (1855); the Oedogoniaceae (1855–58); the Coleochaeteae (1860); *Hydrodictyon* (1861); and *Pandorina* (1869). His complete works were published by his children (*Gesammelte Abhandlungen*, four volumes, 1895–96).

PRINSEP, JAMES (1799–1840), English numismatist and Indologist, whose work on paleography and numismatics shed light on Indian history, was born probably at Troby Priory, Essex, on Aug. 20, 1799. In 1819 he took up an appointment at the Calcutta mint, and was assay master at the Benares mint (1820–30). In 1832 he became assay master and secretary to the mint committee at Calcutta, but ill health forced him to return to England in 1838, and he died in London on April 22, 1840.

As secretary of the Asiatic Society of Bengal (1832–38) and editor of its journal, Prinsep had access to, and developed the study of, the largest collection of Indian coins then existing. His greatest achievement, however, was his brilliant decipherment (1838) of the rock and pillar inscriptions of Asoka (*q.v.*). This placed the chronology of ancient India on a much firmer basis. Originally trained as an architect, at Benares he designed and built an important bridge over the river dividing Benares and Bihar; restored a mosque; improved the design of the new mint and the city's drainage; and conducted a municipal census. At

Calcutta, he completed the construction of an important canal in the Ganges delta, was responsible for the introduction of a uniform coinage (under which the "company's rupee" was substituted in 1835 for the various coins in use), and reformed the Indian system of weights and measures.

See his *Essays on Indian Antiquities, Historic, Numismatic, and Palaeographic*, with a memoir by H. T. Prinsep, collected and ed. with notes, etc., by E. Thomas, 2 vol. (1858). (A. L. Ba.)

PRINTED CIRCUIT, an electrical circuit in which the usual wiring—and, occasionally, resistance elements—is replaced by patterns of conductive material applied on sheets of ceramic, glass, or laminated or solid plastic. The circuit patterns are produced by photographic and mechanical printing procedures much like those used in the graphic arts.

First developed on a large scale after World War II, the techniques for producing printed circuits helped meet the demands of industry for more efficient mass production of electrical equipment. The increasing application of electronic equipment in business and industry during the postwar years created problems of weight, size, reliability and production cost. Most of these problems were solved to a large extent, particularly in the radio and television industries in the United States, by the use of printed circuits.

Of the numerous processes used in the fabrication of printed circuits, the most common were etching, plating, metalizing and printing.

In the photoetching process, a photosensitive film is applied to the copper surface of a copper-clad plastic sheet, and a photographic negative of the circuit pattern is superimposed on the sensitized film. The film is then exposed to ultraviolet light in a manner similar to that used in producing a photographic positive. The exposed film hardens and the unexposed areas dissolve readily in an alcohol solution. The hardened film protects the printed circuit pattern during the subsequent etching process. The exposed copper is dissolved in an acid or ferric chloride etchant bath, leaving the copper circuit pattern.

In stencil etching, a protective film to form the circuit pattern is applied by a printing process such as silk screening, which deposits a film sufficiently thick to protect the copper from the etchant solution. The protective film, an enamel, is dried and the exposed copper is etched as described previously.

In the plating process a plastic laminate is first coated with a material which will conduct electricity. This may be done by forming a .0001-in. silver coating on the surface of the laminate in much the same way that mirrors are silvered. The silver film is then coated with a plating resist, usually an enamel, by a stenciling process, leaving exposed areas to form the circuit pattern. The plating process is similar to the plating of decorative metals. After a sufficient thickness (0.001 in. to 0.005 in.) of copper is deposited,

(LEFT) COMPONENT SIDE AND (RIGHT) ETCHED SIDE OF A PRINTED CIRCUIT BOARD

the plating resist is removed by a solvent. The exposed silver film is removed by acid etching, leaving the much thicker copper plating to form the circuit pattern on the plastic sheet. Another technique, used especially for electronic components (switches, commutators and other low-current-carrying parts), is to evaporate metal such as silver directly on an insulating plate through a stencil.

The printing method of producing circuits uses ceramic or glass as a base material in most cases. A silver paste is applied through a silk screen to form the circuit pattern. After the silver paste has dried, the circuit is fired in a furnace at about 750° F., thus bonding the silver pattern to the base. This process also makes it possible to print resistance elements, composed of various forms of carbon, on the circuit pattern.

Printed circuits assumed an important role in industry because they opened the way to mechanized production of electronic equipment. Mechanized production in turn offered the advantages of lower labour costs and better uniformity and better quality of product.

Printed circuitry also eliminated one major cause of unreliability in electronic equipment, poorly soldered joints between the electronic component and conductor, by permitting the use of the dip soldering process. In dip soldering, the joints between the electronic component and the conductor are exposed to molten solder and joined in one operation.

Printed circuits were used in practically all types of electronic equipment, including radio and television sets, guided missile controls, electronic computers and industrial control equipment.

(L. K. L.; Co. Br.)

In the years after printed circuit boards were first developed, there were many improvements in materials and in the photographic techniques applied to their manufacture, but the basic method remained the same. Improved etchants, such as ammonium persulfate, came into wide use. The type of boards most widely employed consisted of sheets of thin copper foil bonded to a thermosetting reinforced plastic laminate. There was also a trend toward the use of aluminum foil, used extensively in the radio, television and automotive industries.

Higher quality boards made of copper foil bonded to fibre-glass cloth reinforced by laminating with an epoxy resin were used in the electronic circuits required by computer, space and defense industries.

Later improvements on the epoxy resin were Dapon boards of diallyl isophthalate. The overall physical and electrical properties were superior to those of boards employing epoxies, including peel strength, heat stability, dimensional stability, surface resistance and dielectric properties.

Printed circuit boards made of epoxy or Dapon were widely used as baseboards for solid state microelectronic circuits. A large number of microelectronic circuits might be attached to a single board to provide the contacts and conductors for interconnecting the microelectronic circuits.

BIBLIOGRAPHY.—T. D. Schlabach and D. K. Rider, *Printed and Integrated Circuitry* (1963); C. F. Coombs (ed.), *Printed Circuits Handbook* (1967); J. S. Cook, *Printed Circuit Design and Drafting* (1967).
(Co. Br.)

PRINTING is the mechanical multiplication of text, pictures, or designs by putting ink on paper or some other suitably receptive surface. Broadly speaking, printing encompasses all production and use of printed matter.

There are three main methods of printing: letterpress (or relief), in which the image is transferred from a printing surface raised slightly above the body of the type or printing plate; intaglio (gravure), from a design engraved below the surface of the printing plate; and offset lithography (planographic printing), from a flat surface. Letterpress (*see* below), used by the first European printers in the 15th century, remained the commonest method until mid-20th century. The other two methods are described more fully in GRAVURE and LITHOGRAPHY.

Modern printers use techniques and processes that are continually improved through science and engineering, although the basic machines and methods change slowly. Printers choose the printing process best suited for the work to be done, and frequently they use different methods interchangeably or in combination.

This article is divided into the following sections:

I. THE HISTORY OF PRINTING

1. The East.—Although printing as it is known today began in Germany during the mid-15th century, the Chinese, Japanese, and Koreans used printing much earlier. Printing was invented independently in the West and developed along dissimilar lines. The major reason for the separate development is the difference between Asian and European scripts. Mass production of movable letters for the 15th-century European alphabet of 23 letters was a simple affair; for a language demanding thousands of complicated ideographs, it was impossible.

Chinese printing was until modern times achieved mainly from wood blocks engraved in relief, each with one or more pages of text, printed not under pressure but by rubbing the paper against the inked surface with a dry brush or some other rubbing device. As both sides of the thin, porous Chinese sheet cannot be printed, the traditional Chinese accordion book is folded and stitched at the side so blanks do not show. Skilled Chinese craftsmen not only could engrave the blocks rapidly and cheaply but also could duplicate with remarkable fidelity the beauty and delicacy of brush calligraphy, esteemed for aesthetic as well as utilitarian reasons. (*See* CALLIGRAPHY.)

How or when printing was first accomplished in China is not known with certainty. It may have derived from engraved seals, used in China from at least the 3rd century B.C. to make impressions in soft clay. The first-known inked impressions on paper date from the 5th century A.D. Similar stamps, used with a red ink made from cinnabar, are still commonly employed in the East for signatures on documents. In the 6th century A.D. large wooden seals were cut and used for printing Taoist charms.

Another hypothesis is that printing developed from the ancient Chinese practice of making inked rubbings or squeezes from stone inscriptions. About A.D. 165 the standard text of the Confucian classics was cut upon stone to ensure permanence and accurate transmission, and soon thereafter the practice of making copies by means of ink rubbings began. The earliest extant rubbing dates from the 7th century. In the East and later in the West the first great patrons of the printer were officials of church and state, who saw in him a useful ally for maintaining canonical purity of Scripture and law. They recognized the value of printing's ability to transmit an almost exact facsimile, so that once an accurate text was established it was possible to minimize the corruption caused by accretion of scribal errors.

The oldest-known true printed piece is a Sutra printed in Korea in A.D. 750. A Buddhist charm, dating from A.D. 768–770, comes from Japan, where Buddhist missionaries had introduced printing from China during the previous century. It was printed by order of the empress Shōtoku, from wood blocks or thin cast-metal plates, in an edition of 1,000,000 copies. Numerous examples have survived. The oldest printed book in existence also is of Buddhist origin. It is an edition of the *Diamond Sutra* consisting of six sheets of text and one smaller leaf with a woodcut illustration, printed in A.D. 868. The sole known copy, found in a cave in

Turkistan in 1900 and acquired by Sir Aurel Stein in 1907, is now in the British Museum. Religious texts, however, did not constitute the whole of Eastern printing. Textiles, playing cards, and paper money also were printed from blocks.

The Chinese attempted to use typography, as distinguished from block printing, despite the difficulties of trying to cast, compose, and redistribute the thousands of characters required. The first trials are attributed to one Pi Sheng, who made individual characters of thin, fired earthenware for assembly in an iron form. These proved too fragile to be practical. The Chinese later cast letters in tin and cut them from wood, but none of these methods gained wide popularity. A type foundry was established in Korea late in the 14th century, where numerous fonts of type were cast in bronze. Although the use of metal type spread back to China and Japan from Korea, it superseded the use of the wood block as the principal printing method only in the 20th century.

2. The West.—Although any attempt to describe the invention and spread of printing in Europe can be based on somewhat firmer premises than the development in the East, there are still many gaps in our knowledge. The year 1440 has traditionally (and arbitrarily) been chosen as the date of the invention, and Johann Gutenberg (q.v.) is credited with the feat. However, Gutenberg was but one of many seeking to speed book production through mechanization; others were carrying out similar experiments in the Netherlands, France, Germany, Italy, and elsewhere. Gutenberg was the first to assemble the necessary components of the printing process—type production, ink manufacture, the press, paper supply—into a coherent whole. The 15th century was a propitious time for the work. There existed a great market for books among the students of the rapidly expanding universities and the many literate members of the rising middle class, for reading was no longer a clerical monopoly. There was a well-organized book trade to market the sudden explosion of production. Paper, introduced into Europe through Spain and Sicily in the 12th century, was abundant and no longer suspect as impermanent.

As in the Far East, block printing was the predecessor of printing from movable type in Europe. By the early 15th century blocks were being used to print textiles, playing cards, and religious pictures. Block books, which combined pictures with simple texts and were printed by rubbing from inked blocks, made an appearance in the West soon after the first typographic pieces.

Gutenberg possessed two skills essential for successful volume production of individual movable types: metallurgy and engraving. He was able to develop an alloy of lead, tin, and antimony that would cast easily and would be durable. More important, he could engrave single letters on the hardened steel punches used to strike matrices for the casting of type—a technique already in use for the manufacture of coins and medals. Gutenberg's major invention was the mold that could be adjusted to receive matrices of various width (both the letters *i* and *m*, for example, had to be accommodated). The other technical problems of printing could be solved by adaptation of existing materials: presses were commonly used to make wine, oil, paper, etc.; the inks used for writing or block printing could be stiffened to the proper consistency for typographic printing. The best of the incunabula (q.v.; books printed before A.D. 1501) attained a degree of beauty and technical excellence rarely equaled since.

What little is known about Gutenberg and his invention comes from legal records. Unable to finance his work, he had to borrow from a fellow townsman, Johann Fust (q.v.), who became impatient for a return on his investment and in 1455 foreclosed on the inventor. Before then Gutenberg apparently had produced a few small pieces and probably had begun work on the Bible known by his name. Fust employed Peter Schoeffer, later to become his son-in-law, to assist in the new enterprise. Their firm produced many notable books, among them the great Psalter of 1457, the first book to use more than one printed colour and the first to carry a colophon naming its printers and the date and place of publication. The types for these first books copied the hands written at the time, and consequently they contained a great number of ligatures and contractions that were gradually eliminated later, since economy demanded simplicity.

Printing spread with extraordinary rapidity. From Mainz it proceeded throughout Germany in the 1460s, chiefly along the Rhine, the principal trade route. By 1500 there were presses in more than 60 German towns. The first printers in most European countries were itinerant Germans who had been lured by the promise of patronage or forced to emigrate by the intensity of competition at home. The first Italian press was established at Subiaco, near Rome, in 1464; Basel, Switz., had a press in 1465; Paris and Utrecht, Neth., had printers in 1470, Spain and Hungary in 1473, England in 1476, and Sweden in 1483. All Europe except Russia, which had no press until 1563, had printers during the 15th century. By 1500 more than 1,700 presses in almost 300 towns had produced one or more books. It is estimated that almost 40,000 editions were published during the 15th century, comprising somewhere between 15,000,000 and 20,000,000 volumes. These were mainly liturgical, theological, and legal works, but by 1500 many texts of the Greek and Latin classics had appeared, as well as literary works in the various vernaculars. William Caxton (q.v.), the first English printer, published almost every important work of literature written in his native language before his death in 1491.

From Germany the centre of the printing industry moved to Italy during the late 15th century, especially to Venice, then at the height of its political and commercial importance. There Nicolas Jenson (q.v.), a Frenchman, established his press in 1470 and printed some of the noblest early books. His types included a roman face, based upon Italian book hands, that was widely copied and is still used in modern adaptations. Among modern type designers inspired by it were William Morris and Bruce Rogers. The most influential Venetian printer was the scholar-publisher Aldus Manutius, whose output included the first printed editions of many of the Greek and Latin classics. His three chief roman type faces were cut for him by Francesco Griffo of Bologna, who in 1500 was responsible for the first italic type, based on Italian cursive writing. These types, in small sizes, made possible the most important innovation of Aldus—small books that were the prototype of modern pocket-sized editions. (*See also* MANUTIUS.)

Early in the 16th century Italy lost its printing supremacy to France as a result of political and economic upheaval. Lyons and Paris became the great printing centres. French books had at first a distinctly national character, being printed mostly in *bâtarde* and other French Gothic types and illustrated in local style. Then, like architecture and painting, they began to show a strong italianate influence. A series of elegantly designed and printed volumes produced by Geoffroy Tory (q.v.), printer, engraver, and philologist, employed various types, decorative initials, and architectural borders borrowed from Italian sources. These were highly influential in changing the appearance of French books from the Gothic to the Renaissance style. France's greatest contribution was in type design. Early printers had generally cast their own type, but during the first half of the 16th century type manufacture became an independent trade, highly specialized and centralized in cities with a concentration of printers, notably Paris, Frankfurt, and Leipzig. Among the most notable of the early type designers was Claude Garamond (q.v.), who established himself in Paris about 1530 and sold his punches and matrices throughout Europe. His roman, italic, and Greek types, either in their pure form or as adapted by subsequent cutters, dominated type design until the late 18th century and are highly successful in the modern revivals. Robert Granjon (fl. 1560), who worked primarily in Lyons, was another important type cutter; his work included the earliest *caractères de civilité* (a typographic version of the French secretary hand then in use) and flowered ornaments (*fleurons*), which could be combined into innumerable decorative designs.

The wars of religion provided setbacks to the progress of printing in France. Many Huguenot printers emigrated to Switzerland, England, and the Low Countries. Censorship and rigid trade regulations impeded French printing until after 1789. The centre of printing activity moved to the Low Countries, especially to Amsterdam and Antwerp. In Antwerp the establishment of Christophe Plantin (q.v.) became one of the strongest in Europe, with its foundry, bindery, and bookshop. The firm remained in the family's possession until 1876, when the city acquired the premises and established the Plantin-Moretus Museum. A great 16th- and 17th-century printing establishment has been reconstructed in the museum, with cases of type, punches and matrices, and ancient presses.

3. The New World.—The first press in the Western Hemisphere was set up in Mexico City in the 1530s, and in South America at Lima, Peru, in 1584. The first press in what is now the United States was established at Cambridge, Mass., by Stephen Day (*q.v.*) with the help of his son Matthew. Ultimately their press was controlled by Harvard College. Their first two books were the *Freeman's Oath* and *An Almanac for 1639*, no copies of which are known to have survived. The *Bay Psalm Book* (1640) is the earliest colonial book extant. Another Cambridge press, that of Samuel Green and Marmaduke Johnson, printed the first American Bible, an Indian translation by the Rev. John Eliot for his missionary use, in 1663.

As the colonies spread, printing followed. Having started printing in Philadelphia in 1685, William Bradford (*q.v.*) moved to New York and started printing there in 1693. Denied permission to continue printing at Jamestown, Va., after 1682, William Nuthead set up a press in Maryland in 1685. Thomas Short first started printing in Connecticut at New London in 1709, and others began from South Carolina to New Hampshire. Isaiah Thomas, the earliest historian of U.S. printing and a successful printer, said that in the 13 colonies in 1775 there were 50 printers. Of great impetus to the colonial independence movement was the stamp tax on newspapers and advertising. Thus, as the printing press in its earliest days had stimulated the Reformation, the printing of newspapers and pamphlets prepared the colonies for the War of Independence.

4. The 18th Century.—The 18th century was the first in which England developed any strong national typographic style and produced any influential innovators. Two are especially noteworthy: William Caslon (*see* CASLON), a gun engraver turned type founder, whose reworkings of Dutch type faces dominated British and American printing for at least a century and still are widely used; and John Baskerville (*q.v.*), a Birmingham writing master, who used a fortune made as a japanner to finance his unprofitable efforts as a printer and publisher. In his first book, the 1757 *Virgil*, Baskerville used wove paper, the first printer to do so. His sharp, thin types, demonstrating his mastery of calligraphy and letter cutting, were a transition to the "modern" types of the early 19th century; and his severe, unornamented pages anticipated the neoclassic style of the 19th century. His most important influence was on the Continent, where Giambattista Bodoni (*q.v.*) of Parma and the Didots of Paris (*see* DIDOT) admired his work.

The two most important printing developments of the 18th century, however, were not aesthetic but technical. The first of these was the invention of stereotyping—a method of making duplicate printing plates by casting hot metal in a matrix molded from the original type. William Ged, a Scottish goldsmith, invented a method of stereotyping in 1725; it was not commercially successful, mainly because of opposition from the type founders and compositors. The Didots in France and Charles, 3rd Earl Stanhope, in England improved upon the process, and it gained wide acceptance about 60 years later. The other notable 18th-century invention was lithography, the only major printing method whose development can be fully documented. Aloys Senefelder of Munich discovered and introduced the process during 1796–98. Lithography, which depends upon the immiscibility of grease and water, is the basis of all modern methods of offset or planographic printing. (For a detailed account, *see* LITHOGRAPHY.)

The late 18th century saw the beginning of enormous changes in printing, for during the Industrial Revolution printing became one of the first industries to utilize automation. Various problems had to be solved before the partially mechanized handicraft could be transformed into a high-speed factory operation. The most serious of these was shortage of paper, caused by a scarcity of rags. Various 18th-century scientists, particularly the German J. C. Schäffer, proved that paper could be made from the pulp and fibres of many plants, shrubs, and trees. Use of vegetable pulp made practical the development of a machine for making paper

in an endless web. The next requirement was a speed-up of the printing process itself, and this was accomplished primarily through modernization of the printing press.

5. Development of Modern Presses.—In the last quarter of the 18th century the printing press in use was basically the wooden hand press of the 15th century. The development of the high-speed press came in two ways.

For some inventors the problem seemed to be to increase the power, and thus the size, speed, and efficiency of the hand press while maintaining its basic design. Therefore they replaced wood with metal parts designed according to theoretical mechanics. Wilhelm Haas of Basel first introduced metal parts in 1772, but local guilds prevented their use and only in the next century did other inventors, among them Étienne Anison-Duperon of France, Charles, 3rd Earl Stanhope, of England, and George Clymer of the U.S., develop iron presses that were put in use.

Other inventors sought increased efficiency by connecting vertical and horizontal press motion to achieve a complete cycle, an idea first recorded by Leonardo da Vinci in the 16th century. A German, Friedrich König, developed the idea independently and built for the *Times* (London) the first steam-powered, flat-bed cylinder press. The *Times* of Nov. 29, 1814, told its readers that the paper they held was the first thus printed, "the greatest improvement connected with printing since the discovery of the art itself." The press had inking rollers and its capacity was 1,100 impressions an hour, in contrast to the 300-per-hour capacity of the hand-inked press it replaced. In 1848 Augustus Applegath and Edward Cowper constructed for the *Times* a press capable of 8,000 impressions an hour, which was handfed by men at eight stations on a platform above an upright cylinder of cast iron that carried the type. In 1866 in the Walter Press (named for John Walter III, then publisher of the newspaper), the *Times* achieved the prototype of the modern newspaper press—a true rotary press that printed both sides of a continuous web of paper fed from a roll; the rate was 25,000 impressions an hour. In the United States, meanwhile, Richard Hoe (*q.v.*) also developed rotary presses for newspaper work. Most of the changes in press construction since the 1860s have resulted from the demand of periodical publishers for faster, more economical production. (*See* also PRINTING PRESS.)

6. Typesetting.—Once the press had been mechanized printers faced the problem of the supply of type, type composition, and distribution of the individual types after use. Application of a pump to the type mold, which speeded production considerably, was one of a number of advances in hand casting in the early 19th century. Complete mechanization of type founding began with the casting machine of William Church, patented in 1822, which was capable of forming 3,000 sorts (individual pieces of type) per hour.

After the evolution of a number of impractical typesetting machines, the work of many inventors, Ottmar Mergenthaler (*q.v.*) in 1884 patented his Linotype machine, which cast thin slugs of type metal with a printing surface on one edge. Each slug was one line of type, molded from a row of brass matrices assembled by a keyboard operator. After the lines of type were used in printing the metal was melted for re-use. Almost simultaneously (1885) Tolbert Lanston invented the Monotype process, which casts type in individual letters. Both these machines, requiring large numbers of matrices, were made feasible by L. B. Benton's invention of the mechanical punch cutter.

The Linotype, Monotype, and other similar composing machines involve the casting of metal type with the printing image in relief. Tremendous growth in the use of lithography, which does not require a raised surface for printing and which is prepared for the press by photographic processes, has intensified in recent years the search for composition methods that avoid the use of metal type. A number of photocomposition machines have been developed to assemble and transfer letters directly onto a sensitized plate from film matrices. Many typesetting functions have also been accomplished through the use of electronic computers. (*See* further TYPESETTING.)

7. Illustrations.—Acceleration of text printing in the 19th century was accompanied by parallel changes in the printing of illustrations as photography was applied to the making of printing plates. J. N. Niepce produced the first photomechanical plate in 1822 when he etched a reproduction of an engraving of Cardinal d'Amboise upon a sensitized metal plate that was subsequently used for printing. Shortly before his death in 1833 Niepce became associated with L. J. M. Daguerre, who subsequently perfected the first practical method of photography. Many experimenters sought to make line engravings on metal by photographic means, and Firmin Gillot succeeded in 1850. William Henry Fox Talbot, the Englishman who in 1839 introduced the calotype, the forerunner of most modern photographic processes, invented photogravure in 1852; Karl Klič (Klietsch) invented rotogravure in 1890. Other important 19th-century inventors include James Clerk Maxwell and Louis Ducos du Hauron, who during the 1860s established the principle of colour separation with filters to pave the way for colour-separation engravings and colour-process printing, and George Meisenbach and Max Levy, who late in the century perfected the halftone screen, which makes possible printed reproductions of paintings and photographs possessing light and shade. *See* also GRAVURE; PHOTOENGRAVING; PHOTOGRAPHY; ILLUSTRATION, BOOK. (J. M. W.; X.)

II. MODERN PRINTING PROCESSES

The term "printing," once used in the United States only for letterpress printing, today is used generically for all kinds of graphic reproduction. Letterpress was always a fine method for reproducing printed matter but not a good method for reproducing illustrations. Conversely, lithography and gravure were excellent means for reproducing illustrations but not for reading matter. As photoengraving was developed, letterpress became a prime method for printing all kinds of illustration as well as reading matter; and gravure, lithography, and other illustrative methods were made capable of producing reading matter well. Thus the gap narrowed for methods, and the printing industry incorporated everyone who put ink on paper.

All printing processes share four elements: (1) the means of carrying an image, whether type face, printing plate, or gravure cylinder; (2) the press; (3) ink; and (4) paper or other image-bearing material. Printing surface, press, and ink vary for each process. Paper or other material may be common to them, or not. The only process in which metal type can be used on the press is letterpress (typographic or relief printing). It is used in producing books, magazines, newspapers, catalogs, packaging and commercial printing of all kinds (*e.g.*, letterheads and sales forms). (See *Letterpress Printing*, below.)

1. Lithography.—Plates for lithographic printing, also called offset, offset lithography, photolithography, photo-offset, and planography, are mostly made by photographing a print or proof from metal type; a handwritten manuscript or a drawing can also be used. The facsimile reproduction can be enlarged or reduced from the original. Commercial, book, magazine, and newspaper printing use much lithography. If it is desired to reprint a letterpress book after the type is worn, either the proof or the pages from a first edition can be photographed and thus converted to offset method. Offset is particularly suitable for making full-colour reproductions of paintings and colour photographs. (*See* further LITHOGRAPHY.)

2. Dry Offset.—Dry offset, or letterset, combines to some extent both letterpress and photo-offset. (No lithographic principles are involved.) A plate similar to a lithographic plate, but two or three times as thick (0.030 to 0.036 in.), is etched in relief, just as in photoengraving, but to a shallower depth (0.015 in.). When this plate is clamped around the cylinder of an offset press, it prints directly on the blanket, which offsets the image onto paper. Dry offset eliminates the need for the dampening system used in the lithographic process, this being its major advantage.

3. Gravure is a process in which the printing image is formed by wells in the surface of the printing plate. In this intaglio process the depth of the wells controls how much ink transfers to the paper. Gravure includes both sheet-fed gravure printing (used mainly for short-run printing of high-quality work) and rotogravure, the high-speed, web-fed process used for mail-order catalogs, newspaper supplements, packaging materials, and other long-run work. As in lithography, text matter is photographed from type proofs or from films prepared in photocomposition machines, and since both reading matter and illustrations are broken into a screened pattern, fine lines of letters may become weak or ragged. To overcome this a fine screen can be used. (*See* further GRAVURE.)

4. Silk Screen.—Also called screen printing, silk screen (*q.v.*) uses a stencil as the printing-image carrier; it is applied tightly against silk or another fine fabric held tautly on a frame. Although it is the youngest of printing methods, it uses the oldest principle of graphic reproduction of words and designs. Silk-screen printing is preferred when a heavy, opaque layer of ink (or paint) is to be applied to a poster, book cover, or sheet of glass. Fine detail can be reproduced by photographic methods, and halftones of suitable pictures can also be printed.

5. Flexography.—Flexography, originally known as aniline printing, is a form of rotary letterpress printing in which flexible rubber plates and fluid inks are used, mainly for packaging materials. The process originated in Germany in the late 19th century, and at first aniline dyes in alcohol were employed instead of ink. After packaging engineers took the process to the United States in the 1920s, thin inks consisting of finely ground pigments in a vehicle of solvent and resin were developed. Extensive use of cellophane for packaging greatly increased its importance.

6. Other Processes.—Other printing processes include: collotype (*q.v.*), also called the photogelatin process, which is a planographic method of printing continuous-tone images without a screen pattern; steel-die or copper-plate engraving, an intaglio process that produces a raised impression on letterheads and calling cards; and several forms of raised-letter printing ("imitation engraving") called thermography, virkotyping, or process embossing. Using letterpress methods and a slow-drying ink, the printed image is immediately dusted with a resinous powder by hand or machine. When heated, the powder melts and fuses with the ink to produce a slightly raised effect similar to the engraved result, though usually shiny in appearance.

Xerography, sometimes classified under printing processes, is actually a duplicating method often used to prepare a paper-type plate for small offset presses. It is fundamentally electrical rather than chemical or mechanical in nature; through principles of photo-conductivity and electrostatics, xerography transfers the original image (which can be simply a typewritten sheet or a printed proof) to another sheet of paper, or to a paper plate for small offset presses, when a large number of copies are wanted. Fine powder, instead of ink, is electrically deposited on the paper and fused into the surface by heat. This and other duplicating processes related to printing are commonly used in offices. (*See* OFFICE MACHINES AND APPLIANCES.)

7. Colour Printing.—Colour printing can be produced by virtually all of the printing processes. Though each process has a special system of preparing the printing plate itself, the fundamentals of colour printing are the same for each. Except for the use of simple line colour, colour printing usually refers to "four-colour-process" printing, though more or fewer colours may be used, depending upon the quality of the reproduction or the result desired. First steps in all cases require separation negatives made photographically from the original coloured subject, photograph, or painting. As inks used for each of the different plates in process printing are transparent tones of red, blue, yellow (and black for definition), filters are used so that each separation will represent a corresponding portion of the colour spectrum. One separation, usually continuous tone, is made for each of the colours to be used in the printed reproduction. From each separation a screened positive is prepared for the printing plate, each separation having a different screen angle, so that the final halftone will give the illusion of many colours from the intermixed screen pattern. *See* PHOTOENGRAVING.

III. LETTERPRESS PRINTING

The terminology of the graphic arts is not precise. The originally exact names of printing processes have lost their precision as techniques changed or expanded. The terms letterpress and typographic printing refer to a process using movable types, but neither covers the printing of illustrations. A newer term "relief printing" is inclusive of both type and illustration, implying only that the raised surfaces of the image carrier actually print, whether this image is produced by type or illustration. Relief printing refers to many fields, newspaper printing and flexography among them, not ordinarily included in letterpress printing. Hereafter in this article letterpress printing will apply to the range of its applications in the printing of books, magazines, and commercial forms.

1. Typesetting.—There are various typesetting processes. Machines, setting by the line as do the Linotype and Intertype, are used for most book, newspaper, and magazine typesetting. Monotype typesetting involves lines made up of individually set and cast types, and is used where tighter or irregular spacing is advantageous, as in tables or catalogs, though it is also used in book production. Hand composition, the original typesetting method, is produced by a compositor who places individual types in position; such jobs as the setting of display type, as for newspaper headlines and individually designed arrangements for advertising, title pages, and other jobs involving unusual typographic art, are still handset. The Ludlow method combining the handsetting of matrices in a special composing stick is much used in setting display type for advertising. After assembling and spacing the matrices, the compositor casts the line in hot metal. Many printers set their own type, but others buy type composition from special typesetting houses. (*See* also PRINTING TYPE; TYPESETTING.)

2. Photoengraving is a process combining the etching and hand engraving of the image of a photograph onto a relief printing plate, the end result being called a cut, block, or engraving. The original for a photoengraving may be a photograph, a painting, a wash drawing, or any illustration with tonal values reproducible by halftone process; or it may be pen-and-ink, crayon, or pencil-line drawings; a written signature to be reproduced in facsimile; or any similar material that can be rendered in "line cuts" with no tonal values. Such copy is photographed and its image (which may be smaller or larger than the original) transferred to a metal surface by means of photoprinting. After the image has been photoprinted on the metal, the nonprinting areas are removed by etching.

In the 1940s a German manufacturer introduced an automatic electronic halftone engraving machine that scans photographs and controls a stylus to cut, rather than etch, the pattern on the printing plate. This machine has been developed to make colour-printing plates from photographic transparencies and other colour copy.

3. Wraparound Plates for rotary letterpress presses are large photoengravings covering the full printing area of the press. A thin flexible plate is wrapped around the plate cylinder in a manner similar to that used for an offset press. (*See* also PHOTO-ENGRAVING.)

4. Duplicate Printing Plates.—Type and relief engravings are used not only directly on the press as printing surfaces but also as originals in making duplicate printing-image carriers. Short press runs are mostly printed directly if machine-set type is used, but long runs require duplicate plates. Even for short runs in which some or all of the type is foundry type, duplicate plates are preferred in order to prevent wear of the relatively expensive foundry type, which generally is used only for making electrotypes or reproduction proofs. Rotary printing and other specialized branches of relief printing cannot use type or engravings but must have duplicate printing plates.

The advantages of duplicate plates are that they (1) save photoengravings and type; (2) permit longer runs than photoengravings and type without loss of quality; (3) allow the use of both type and engravings on a plate rather than in a form that must be locked; (4) can be curved for use in rotary printing; (5) allow for the printing of many units (multiples) in the same press run; and (6) allow printing of the same subject at different locations, a

necessity for printing regional editions of magazines where advertising varies.

There are peculiar applications for each of the four major kinds of letterpress duplicate plates. Stereotypes are almost universal in newspaper printing, and are common in book and trade-paper advertising; electrotypes are used where there are fine halftones and for non-newspaper rotary colour printing; plastic plates are used in book printing and as intermediaries for machine plates in printing magazine advertising; and rubber plates are used in the printing of continuous forms, of corrugated containers, and for flexographic printing.

At least one intermediary step is required in the preparation of all duplicate plates for letterpress, whether type or photoengravings, or both, are involved. Since the original is in relief, it cannot be duplicated without a mold, or intaglio intermediary, to produce the relief duplicate. The intermediary is made by impressing a hot or cold material against the original. The duplicate plate thus formed is then a relief plate suitable for letterpress printing.

The necessary requirements for duplicating printing plates are to retain the detail of the original, to keep the dimensions exact, and to maintain correct printing height. Retaining detail is particularly important for halftone printing. Several steps are required in the process of making a duplicate. If dimensions are not kept exact, printing will lack register (exact positional conformity), particularly important in colour printing, where one colour overlays another. If printing height is not correct, the plate will not print uniformly over the whole area.

Stereotypes.—Stereotypes for newspaper printing are made routinely in newspaper plants, especially in those using rotary presses where entire pages are cast in stereotypes for mounting on the press. In the making of stereotypes, an imprint of the printing form (type and engravings) is formed mechanically in a matrix or, as it is more commonly called, a mat of papier-mâché or some similar material. This intaglio mat is then filled with hot metal to form the stereotype. Stereotypes are most commonly used for printing type matter, such line drawings as cartoons and trademarks, and coarse halftones.

The first step in matmaking is to assemble the printing form. Thereafter the mat is pressed by one of three methods to produce cold-rolled mats, cold direct-pressure molded mats or baked direct-pressure molded mats. Cold-rolled mats are rolled in a press; a hydraulic press makes the other two, exerting pressure simultaneously over the whole printing form surface. Once a mat is pressed, it is trimmed and prepared to be used as a mold. The stereotypes for newspaper use on rotary presses are cast curved; but those used on flat-bed presses or as part of the printing form for a rotary mat are cast flat. Those for book and publication work are usually used on flat-bed presses and therefore are cast flat. The equipment used to cast curved stereotypes casts and sizes them in one continuous operation so that they are ready for the press. Flat stereotype casting is much less mechanized than the curved casting operation. First, into the nonprinting areas that would otherwise be flattened by the weight of the metal, pieces of stiff paper are placed, a process called backing up. Then, to remove moisture that would convert to steam in the casting process and cause an explosion, the mat is baked or "scorched." Next, the mat is placed in a vertical position in a casting box and cast. Stereotype plates are either cast as a shell for mounting on a base or are cast type-high. After finishing operations, stereotypes are nickel plated whenever they are to be used on long runs where quality is to be maintained.

Electrotypes are duplicate plates combining different kinds of type with photoengravings. Since they keep the detail of the original very well, have excellent dimensional stability, can have adjustment for proper printing height built in (premakeready), and are good for rotary printing, electrotypes are especially desirable for long runs. Thus, while newspaper printing uses stereotypes, printing of magazines, catalogs, and a variety of other matter uses electrotypes. (*See* also ELECTROPLATING; ELECTROTYPING.)

Plastic Plates, which can be made from an original printing-image carrier or from an electrotype, are much used in the printing of books, multiple forms, and newspaper advertising. A pattern plate is first made, and then thermosetting material is used to make an intaglio mold, which can then be used to make any number of plastic relief plates. If the pattern plate is not needed, the thermosetting intaglio mold can be made directly, and the plastic relief plate from it.

Rubber Plates offer the advantage of being able to print on many different kinds of material and are also easily attached to the curved form cylinder. Thus they are good for long runs. While rubber plates are mainly used in flexography, they are also used in letterpress printing; *e.g.,* in the printing of forms, envelopes, and books. They exhibit good printability except for halftone details.

In the making of rubber plates, an original printing-image carrier, whether type, photoengravings, or electrotypes, and a thermosetting mold sheet are both preheated and then put together in a hydraulic press exerting a maximum pressure of 400 lb. per sq.in. for type matter, and 1,000 psi for photoengravings or electrotypes. From 6 to 12 minutes are required for molding. After the thermosetting mold is cured for about 15 minutes with a platen temperature of about 300° F (150° C), the intaglio intermediary and original are separated, and the intermediary is used to make the rubber plate, which is then removed and mounted for printing.

Pressure-sensitive adhesives or double-coated adhesive tape are used to mount the plates, either flat or curved, directly onto impression cylinders or in preposition on heavy paper or light metal that is then mounted on the press cylinder.

5. Presswork transfers the printing image to the stock, most often paper. In this operation four objects must be coordinated: the press (or as it is called in Great Britain, except for proof presses, the printing machine); the printing-image carrier; the ink; and the stock.

There are four parts to the functioning of printing presses: (1) positioning the stock to receive the impression; (2) inking the printing-image carrier; (3) transferring the ink from the image carrier to the stock to make the impression; and (4) removing the printed paper. These four parts of the function are represented by four units of the printing press: (1) the feeding unit; (2) the inking unit; (3) the printing unit; and (4) the delivery unit. Ink is transferred directly to the paper in all letterpress processes but one, dry offset, in which the image is first put on a rubber blanket that then transfers it to the stock.

All four main parts of the printing process—feeding, inking, printing, and removal—were done by hand from the beginning until the early part of the 19th century. Then mechanization began until by modern times all parts were done automatically. Hand presses exist today only in private presses printing limited editions. (*See* also PRINTING PRESS.)

There are many steps in letterpress printing, some executed by the pressman (or machine minder as he is called in Great Britain), some by his assistants, and some by the planning department.

Choice of Press.—The choice of the right press for the job is not always self evident, but may require close analysis and many calculations. The ideal press may not be available at the time it is needed, and the job may need to be handled by a second choice.

Imposition, the layout of the printed sheet showing the location of each page on both the front and back of the sheet, presents another choice. The greatest operating force is the difference in handling the back and front of the sheet. (For imposing, the putting of this plan into effect, *see* below: *Lockup.*) Factors affecting imposition include the detail of the book and its binding.

Preparation for the Press.—With the imposition decided, the printing-image carrier is prepared so that not only is all printed matter correctly positioned but the height of the printing surface is adjusted, if necessary, to assure proper printing quality. (The standardized height of type is 0.9186 in.) Since foundry type, Linotype slugs, and Monotypes are all cast type-high, they merely need leveling. But photoengravings, which are made 0.065-in. high (of 16-gauge metal), must be mounted on blocks to bring them up to type height matching the type. Stereotypes are cast both type-high or 11 point (0.152 in.); electrotypes are all 11 point. The use of only duplicate plates on a flat-bed cylinder press

permits the use on the bed of the press of a metal plate base, called the patent base. The standard plate base height is 0.759 in.; adding on the electrotype brings the height to 0.911 in., leaving 0.0076 to be added in makeready (*see* below). All plate bases come in combination sections; the bases are variously honeycombed or of diagonal or rectangular patterns. The beveled printing plates are fastened to the bases with hooks that grip the edge of the plate.

Lockup of forms made up of type matter and blocked, or mounted, photoengravings is done at a table called the stone because stone was the original material for the table; metal has replaced stone. Here the imposing is done, all being held together by the chase, a rigid metal frame, those for large flat-bed presses being reinforced with movable crossbars. With the imposition determined, printing matter is placed in the chase and wooden or metal blocks, called furniture, are used to fill out empty spaces. Quoins (or coins), expandable lockup devices, tighten up the form. A lockup man "imposing" a form has to inspect it and adjust it to make sure that all the parts are present and that they are type-high. He then places the imposed form on the bed of the press and makes it ready for printing.

Makeready.—Further leveling and adjustment may be required to produce the best print possible. Makeready involves use of three techniques: placing paper of various thickness under the printing element, or underlaying; placing paper between the photoengraving and its mounting, or between the plate base and stereotypes, called interlaying; and adjusting the platen or impression cylinder in order to apply the right printing pressure on the various elements, or overlaying. The last technique involves taking an impression and adjusting the cylinder by gluing on paper of varying thickness on the overlay sheet or reducing its thickness where pressure is too heavy. The packing and tympan of the impression cylinder cover the overlay sheet. Hand-cut overlays for improved halftone reproduction can be supplemented with "chalk" overlays as a faster and better procedure; more recently mechanical devices have been developed to produce halftone overlays for a full press sheet semiautomatically. Great experience is needed for makeready, which for big forms can take much time. Premakeready operations that help to prepare the form for proper printing before it is put on the press can reduce that time.

On the Press.—With the press running, vigilance is still needed. The pressman and one or more assistants check colour and register periodically and keep an eye out for work-ups or press batters, unintentional marks that are caused by loosening of the frame or evidence of wear on the type. New paper must be put in feeding position and the printed sheets removed. Offsetting (unintentional transfer of wet ink from one sheet of paper to another) is controlled by using drying devices on the press, fast-drying inks, or "smut sheets" that are laid between the printed sheets.

See BOOKBINDING; INK; PRINTING TYPE; PUBLISHING; TYPOGRAPHY; *see* also references under "Printing" in the Index.

BIBLIOGRAPHY.—E. C. Bigmore and C. W. H. Wyman, *A Bibliography of Printing,* 3 vol. (1884–86, reprinted 1945); Glen U. Cleeton and Charles W. Pitkin, *General Printing* (1953); Ronald B. McKerrow, *An Introduction to Bibliography* (1951). *History:* Thomas Francis Carter, *The Invention of Printing in China and Its Spread Westward,* 2nd ed. rev. by L. Carrington Goodrich (1955); Theodore L. De Vinne, *The Invention of Printing,* 2nd ed. (1878); H. Barge, *Geschichte der Buchdruckerkunst* (1940); S. H. Steinberg, *Five Hundred Years of Printing* (1959); C. Clair, *A History of Printing in Britain* (1965); P. Butler, *The Origin of Printing in Europe* (1966); J. Carter *et al.* (eds.), *Printing and the Mind of Man* (1967). *United States:* George J. Mills, *Sources of Information in the American Graphic Arts,* Occasional Papers No. 2 (March 1951); Lawrence C. Wroth, *The Colonial Printer,* 2nd ed. (1938); Isaiah Thomas, *The History of Printing in America,* 2 vol., 2nd ed. (1874); H. Lehmann-Haupt (ed.), *The Book in America* (1951). *Plates:* William Blum and George B. Hogaboom, *Principles of Electro-plating and Electroforming (Electrotyping),* 3rd ed. (1949); George A. Kubler, *A New History of Stereotyping* (1941). *Presses:* Lucien Neipp, *Les Machines à Imprimer depuis Gutenberg* (1951); Robert March Hoe, *A Short History of the Printing Press* (1902). *Practice:* Harry A. Groesbeck, *A Primer of Engraving and Printing, Including Composition, Electrotyping, Paper, Presses and Ink* (1950); Marshall Lee, *Bookmaking: the Illustrated Guide to Design and Production* (1965); R. Randolph Karch, *Printing and the Allied Trades,* 3rd ed. (1954); Robert H. Rov, *Management of Printing Production* (1953); S. Morison, *The Typographic Arts* (1949). *Automation:*

T. C. Collins and H. F. Drury, *Computer Applications for Commercial Printing* (1965); L. H. Hattery and G. P. Bush (eds.), *Automation and Electronics in Publishing* (1965).   (K. R. Bu.; X.)

PRINTING PRESS, the machine in which type and illustration images are transferred to paper by means of printing ink. Printing presses can be classified into two major groups—flatbed and rotary—according to whether the form (spelled forme in Great Britain) used for printing has a flat or curved surface. Flatbed presses can be further subdivided as platen or cylinder according to whether a platen (flat plate) or a cylinder is used for impressing the paper against the printing surface. Presses also can be classified in several other ways; *e.g.*, according to the nature of the printing surface: (1) letterpress, in which the image is printed directly from type or other relief surfaces; (2) planographic (*e.g.*, offset lithography), in which the image is printed from a chemically treated surface; (3) intaglio (*e.g.*, gravure), in which the ink is transferred from wells etched or engraved in the printing surface; and (4) silk screen, in which ink is forced through a silk screen to print an image. Presses also can be described by various other features; *e.g.*, according to whether the paper is fed into them in sheets or as a web from a roll; whether the sheets are fed by hand or by automatic devices; and whether one colour, two colours or more than two colours can be printed. In addition, flat-bed presses often are described by the number of revolutions made by the cylinder for each impression or according to whether the type bed is horizontal or vertical. Presses also are sometimes classified according to the size of the impression area or the number of pages, expressed in various standard sizes, that can be printed in one cycle, impression or cylinder revolution. Modern letterpress and offset machines also are classified as oil ink presses if no drying methods are used to set the ink and as heatset ink presses if drying means are used. Heat-set presses usually print on both sides of a web of paper; this process is known as perfecting, or backing up. (*See also* PRINTING; PRINTING TYPE; LITHOGRAPHY; GRAVURE; SILK SCREEN PRINTING.)

Developments Before 1900.—*Early Hand-Operated Presses.* —There is no exact knowledge of the earliest presses although there is no doubt that Johann Gutenberg (*c.* 1398–*c.* 1468) must have used one. The earliest mention of a printing press is in the evidence given at a lawsuit against Gutenberg in Strasbourg in 1439 by Conrad Sahspach, a wood turner who had constructed a press for one of Gutenberg's partners.

A model for the first printing press was available in the heavy wooden presses used in the paper mills of that time; these presses operated on a principle that can be traced to the Roman wine and olive presses described by Pliny the Elder. They consisted of two stout upright pieces of wood joined by two horizontal beams. A screw, working in the upper beam and turned by a long bar, exerted pressure downward upon a wooden plank placed on the paper. Certain modifications had to be made to obtain a quick, precise impression from the type. The pitch of the screw was made

steeper than in the paper press so that the necessary rise and fall was gained within the quarter turn obtainable with a fixed bar. The twisting motion of the turning screw was counteracted by suspending the platen (the wooden plank) from a hollow wooden box (the hose) that slid inside closely fitting guides while the screw turned freely within. The upright beams were frequently braced to the ceiling to keep the press steady. To make the type more accessible for inking, it was drawn on rails from under the platen by a windlass. To the back of the "carriage" which bore the type, a frame tightly covered with parchment (and therefore called the tympan) was hinged. This frame bore the paper, which was attached to it by projecting points and by a light folding frame (the frisket).

Most of these features can be seen in the first-known representation of a printing office, a wood engraving of about 1499, and in the many illustrations of presses used as marks by printers during the 16th century. Many of them are very massive, with thick wooden screws. The introduction of a metal screw is credited to Leonhard Danner (d. 1585), a screw maker of Nürnberg; this innovation greatly reduced friction, making the press easier to operate.

In the first of all printers' manuals, *Mechanick Exercises* (1683), Joseph Moxon recommends an improved Dutch press devised by Willem Janszoon Blaeu. Its only improvement appears to have been the substitution of an iron framework for the hose; it may also have been provided with a brass or iron platen, which seems to have been a common feature of presses in Holland, France, Italy and Germany from the end of the 16th century.

Further improvements were attempted during the 18th century. Printers who prided themselves on "fine" printing, such as J. Baskerville, the Didot family and G. Bodoni, took particular care with the construction of their presses.

The radical defects of the wooden hand press were the lack of stability caused by loosening of the joints and the slowness of operation. The output of a hand press, worked by two pressmen, does not appear to have varied greatly and payment was generally calculated on a rate of 250 sheets an hour printed on one side. Newspapers might have been printed somewhat faster, but careful work required a much slower rate. The stability of hand presses was improved by the substitution of iron for timber. In 1772, Wilhelm Haas, a typefounder at Basel, completed a press with a framework of cast iron and with an iron platen that covered the whole form at once. Local difficulties prevented its development so that it did not gain the immediate recognition and praise accorded the iron press built to the designs of Charles, 3rd Earl Stanhope (1753–1816), by his engineer, Robert Walker. In this press a system of compound levers added to the power of the screw at the moment of impression.

Shortly after the beginning of the 19th century, many lighter and more powerful iron presses that dispensed with the screw were devised. The Columbian press, invented about 1813 by George Clymer of Philadelphia, used a system of compound levers and became popular in Great Britain, France and Germany. Most other iron hand presses incorporated a kind of knuckle joint. The pioneer among these was the press of John I. Wells of Hartford (Connecticut), patented in 1819, which was superseded by the Washington press of Samuel Rust of New York (1821). In Great Britain, the Albion press, devised about 1822 by R. W. Cope, shared, with Clymer's Columbian, the supreme position among iron hand presses throughout the rest of the 19th century. Its robustness and simplicity gave the iron hand press an almost unlimited working life.

The Cylinder Press and the Use of Power.—In 1790 William Nicholson of London patented a printing machine in which the sheet of paper passed between an impression cylinder and a cylindrical printing surface which was inked by a system of rollers. Although this machine was never built because of the difficulty of preparing a cylindrical printing surface, the most important advances of the next century were to be based on it.

The first power-driven printing machine was the work of Friedrich König, born at Eisleben in Saxony, who came to England in 1806. Encouraged by some of the London printers, he patented a

FIG. 1.—ENGRAVING BY ABRAHAM VON WERDT, 1640–80, SHOWING ANCIENT PRINTING SHOP WITH LIGHTLY CONSTRUCTED WOODEN PRESS

machine in 1810 that was, in effect, a steam-driven hand press with automatic inking rollers. The first of these machines was built at the expense of Thomas Bensley, for whom it printed sheet H of the *Annual Register* in 1811 at a speed of 800 copies an hour. König's subsequent experiments, with an impression cylinder in place of the flat platen, led to an order for two machines from the *Times* (London). These were first used to print the edition of Nov. 29, 1814, which proclaimed itself "the first newspaper printed by steam." They printed 1,100 sheets an hour on one side; the speed was later raised to 1,800. König also built a double cylinder machine that produced 750 sheets an hour printed on both sides. In 1817 he returned to Germany, where he set up his own printing machine works. Important improvements to his machines were made by Augustus Applegath and Edward Cowper, appointed engineers to the *Times* in 1818, who in 1827 supplied new machines capable of 4,000 to 5,000 impressions an hour. Among other early cylinder machines, the one built by David Napier in the early 1820s is notable for the introduction of grippers in the cylinder to hold the sheet of paper.

The mechanical advantage of the cylinder made it possible to print larger sheets, but the weight of the heavy type bed and the necessity for reversing directions as it moved rapidly backward and forward under the roller were severe limits on speed.

A machine following Nicholson's design, but with the type attached to the four sides of a revolving prism, was built by Brian Donkin (patented 1813), and in 1816 Cowper patented a means of forcibly curving stereotype plates, which could then be attached to a cylinder.

The Rotary Press.—The first rotary press employed a number of cylinders that rotated in contact with a central cylindrical printing surface. This obviated the need to move the flat beds of type. The first manufacturer to produce a successful rotary machine was Richard M. Hoe (*q.v.*) of New York, whose "type revolving machine" (patented 1845) was installed by the *Philadelphia Public Ledger* in 1847. The type was locked on a large central cylinder by means of wedge-shaped rules, and four impression cylinders were spaced around it, separated by four inking systems. Each

FIG. 2.—TEN-FEEDER "TYPE REVOLVING MACHINE" PATENTED 1845 BY RICHARD M. HOE

impression cylinder was individually fed, so that the 2,000 revolutions an hour of the central cylinder (whose printing surface was in fact polygonal) produced 8,000 sheets printed on one side. Applegath produced a machine incorporating the same principles for the *Times* (patented 1846, erected 1848), with the difference that the axes of the type cylinder and eight impression cylinders were vertical. The Hoe rotary, with an increased number of impression cylinders, was imported into England to print *Lloyd's Weekly Newspaper* and in 1858 was adopted for the *Times*.

Two further developments were required before the rotary machine could be used efficiently: a new method of casting stereotype plates, and a mechanical device for feeding the paper. Following Cowper's experiment with forcibly curving stereotype plates, several attempts were made to cast curved plates. The substitution of papier mâché for the earlier clay or plaster mold (a French patent of 1829) enabled Charles Craske to cast curved plates for

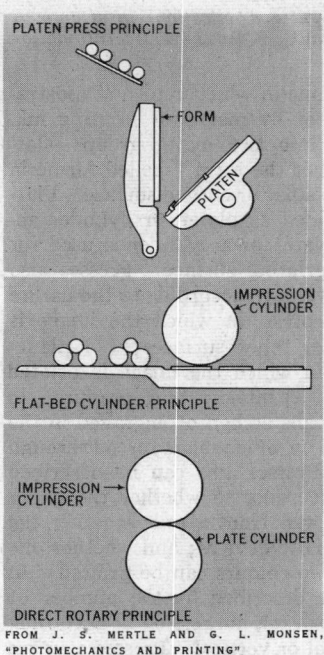

PLATEN PRESS PRINCIPLE

FORM

PLATEN

IMPRESSION CYLINDER

FLAT-BED CYLINDER PRINCIPLE

IMPRESSION CYLINDER

PLATE CYLINDER

DIRECT ROTARY PRINCIPLE

FROM J. S. MERTLE AND G. L. MONSEN, "PHOTOMECHANICS AND PRINTING"

FIG. 3.—PRINCIPAL METHODS OF PRINTING

the *New York Herald* in 1854, and in 1861 Hoe presses were adapted to take such plates. In the early 1860s paper was still being fed to rotary machines by hand in individual sheets, although papermaking machines had been producing it in continuous webs since the first years of the century. In 1835, Rowland Hill produced an experimental type-revolving machine using a web or reel of paper, but the first application to a large rotary machine was made by William Bullock of Philadelphia. His machine (1865) cut the web automatically before it entered the impression cylinders. The *Times*'s engineers had been working on a rotary web press since 1862 and the result, their Walter press (named for J. Walter, then owner of the *Times*), was put into operation in 1866. When automatic folding devices were added to these rotary machines and a printing cylinder was added for each impression cylinder, the full benefits of the rotary principle were obtained. In the United States, the Hoe firm developed the multiple-unit press for the production of large newspapers.

Book and Job Presses.—The rapid pace of development in printing presses during the 19th century was mainly attributable to the demands of newspaper and periodical publishers, but press manufacturers also produced two important types of book-printing machines. In the stop-cylinder machine, the cylinder rotated in gear with the bed of type on its forward journey and remained stationary on the return of the bed. The best known of these was the Wharfedale, which was the outcome of the experiments of William Dawson and David Payne during the 1850s in the Yorkshire town of Otley. In the two-revolution machine, the cylinder turned continuously, making one complete revolution for each traverse of the bed. The impression was made on the bed's forward traverse and the cylinder was lifted clear for the backward traverse. At the same time the principle of the platen was not wholly abandoned; the Napier double-platen machine of 1830, in which two forms moved alternately beneath a central platen worked by a knuckle joint, was valued for the high quality of its output.

The machine that revolutionized job printing (the printing of small posters and handbills, cards and letterheads) was the treadle platen, produced in Boston (Mass.) by Stephen P. Ruggles in 1851 for printing cards. The vertical bed, holding the type, was hinged to the bottom of the platen, on which the paper was placed. This machine was developed by George Phineas Gordon, who used the same principles and the same source of power (a flywheel driven by a treadle) for his Franklin press of 1858; this press was widely known under the name of the inventor and, from that of its first English manufacturer, as the "Cropper." Gordon introduced more powerful machines, known as art platens, capable of printing wood engravings and halftone blocks.   (Js. M.)

20th Century.—The 19th century saw a complete revolution in the mechanical principles of printing; before it was over the foundations of all modern techniques had been firmly established. By contrast, the improvements made in printing in the first six decades of the 20th century, in which so many major advances were made in almost all other branches of technology, were, in the main, relatively insignificant mechanical modifications. In 1900 the standard jobbing letterpress machines were the platen, the stop-cylinder and the two-revolution cylinder press; the rotary principle was employed on a large scale only in the web-fed newspaper field. The rotary offset was already in course of development, and both sheet-fed and web-fed rotary gravure presses were in operation. By 1950 the general situation had altered to the extent that offset lithography had usurped an important part of the letterpress field, but machines were scarcely more advanced technically: letterpress printing was carried out on flat-bed machines very similar to those in operation at the beginning of the century, and, indeed, many presses 50 to 60 years old were still operating and competing successfully with newer machines. Offset lithography presses were substantially identical in design to the first operational models introduced about 1905; and gravure printing had advanced little either in machine construction or in methods for preparing the printing surface. The only major printing process to have developed in the 20th century from the stage of an individual (and very ancient) art to that of a technology was screen printing.

Flat-bed Letterpress Machines.—In the early 1970s the letterpress machine was still, mechanically, the least refined of all printing presses. The flat-bed principle on which the majority of letterpress machines operates is extremely inefficient since it involves reciprocation, either of the type bed or, in the case of some platen presses, of both platen and bed. The reversal of direction creates two problems, one mechanical and one economic: first, considerable energy of momentum must be absorbed rapidly at the end of each movement without causing excessive vibration or heat; second, because the machine does not print on the return stroke, half of the total running time (on most presses) is unproductive.

In cylinder machines efforts have been directed to designing reciprocation systems in which the stopping and reversing part of the movement is speeded up so that it represents only a fraction of the complete printing cycle; as the form on the bed is not under impression during the return stroke it is possible to introduce special gear segments that take over the drive for this part of the cycle only.

BY COURTESY OF CHANDLER AND PRICE CO.

FIG. 4.—MODERN SHEET-FED AUTO-MATIC PLATEN PRESS

Modern platen presses are available in a variety of ranges of size and speed; they are usually especially suited for a particular type of printing job. Most platen presses are used in small print shops for printing letterheads, handbills and similar matter. Their maximum printing areas range from about 7×11 in. to $14\frac{1}{2} \times 22$ in. and their speed ranges from about 2,000 to 5,000 impressions per hour. Most platens are operated by electric motors, are fed sheets automatically and print one colour at a time. Web-fed platens that print up to 6,000 impressions per hour have been developed.

Most modern cylinder presses are designed to print sheets; their printing areas range from about $8\frac{1}{2} \times 11$ in. to $45 \times 68\frac{1}{2}$ in. Hand-fed cylinder presses produce about 2,500 impressions per hour; those with automatic feeding devices can produce up to about 6,500 impressions per hour. Cylinder presses, either sheet- or web-fed, are used to print books, magazines and other matter when good quality of reproduction is desired and when the required quantities call for press runs of up to medium length. These presses are also constructed to print two colours and to print both sides of the sheet.

BY COURTESY OF R. R. DONNELLEY AND SONS COMPANY

FIG. 6.—MODERN ROTARY PRESS

Offset Lithography.—Possibly the most important single contribution of the 19th century to printing-press technology was the development of offset lithography (*see* LITHOGRAPHY: *History*). The great advantage of offset lithography over flat-bed letterpress is the rotary principle. In offset, the printing cylinder (the blanket cylinder carrying the image offset from the plate) runs continuously in one direction while the paper is impressed against it by an impression cylinder. There is no reciprocation, no change of speed, and the fundamental mode of operation remains the same whether the machine is sheet- or web-fed. In addition, offset plates, since they are thin sheets of metal, can be wrapped around the plate cylinder with ease. There is no need to cast or bend thick plates.

Offset presses are built in sizes ranging from that of the smallest platen to that of a medium-size rotary letterpress machine. For web-fed newspaper work, they have a maximum capacity of about 64 standard (or 128 tabloid) pages. These presses are built, as are letterpress rotary units, in four- or eight-page sections that can be arranged to suit the user. Presses such as these can be equipped for printing two or more colours. The top speed of a modern offset newspaper press is 30,000 to 40,000 64-page (standard size) copies per hour. It is possible to equip sheet-fed offset presses to print up to six colours in one run on one side of the sheet.

Rotary Letterpress.—Many difficulties are involved in printing letterpress by rotary means. The most common example of a rotary letterpress machine is the newspaper press, which has a number of inherent disadvantages: the curved or tubular printing plates, cast in stereo metal, require skill, experience and expensive equipment to produce and may crack under stress; the weight of the heavy plates (which can lead to damaging vibration in the axles of the plate cylinders) and unavoidable inaccuracies in their thickness make it necessary to print on a soft stock and against a soft rubber blanket if high press speeds are to be attained. This means that the quality of printing, particularly that of halftones, is not high.

Many nonmetallic materials have been investigated for molding letterpress plates in an attempt to find a surface combining sharpness with sufficient elasticity to give good halftone reproduc-

BY COURTESY OF THE AMERICAN TYPE FOUNDERS COMPANY, INC.

FIG. 5.—MODERN WEB-FED OFFSET LITHOGRAPHIC PRESS

tion: these include rubber, Bakelite, polyvinyl chloride (PVC) and nylon. Apart from molding, letterpress relief plates can also be produced by embossing or etching.

During the 1950s, following the introduction of new techniques for etching letterpress plates, there was a growing interest in the development of etched plates that could be wrapped around the cylinder of a rotary press and in the modifications necessary for this type of press. Within ten years, more than a dozen different models were in production, covering a wide range of sizes. A press using an etched metal plate differs from one using cast stereos in that the increased accuracy of the plate thickness makes great pressure between the impression cylinder and the plate unnecessary, only a "kiss" impression being required. For this reason modified offset machines were found eminently satisfactory in experiments. Modern production models of rotary letterpress machines closely resemble their offset lithography counterparts—indeed, machines adaptable to either process are available, and offset letterpress is also used.

Modern sheet-fed rotary letterpress machines are used mainly for producing catalogues, magazines and similar long-run matter. Sheets ranging from about 21 × 15 in. to 52 × 76 in. can be handled, depending on the press. The number of sheets per hour ranges between 5,000 and 8,000. Up to six colours can be printed in one run. For long runs such machines usually can be adapted to print from a roll.

Modern rotary letterpress machines used in newspaper production are fed by web and are made up of basic 4- or 8-page units arranged to suit special needs. The speed of the newspaper press is limited by several factors; e.g., the resistance of the paper web to breaking, the rate at which the paper absorbs ink, and the speed of the mechanisms that collect and fold the printed paper. The units of the press can be arranged in a straight line on one level or can be stacked in several decks. The total capacity of a press varies according to the size of the paper; for example, in the U.S. the capacity of dailies with 10,000 or less circulation averages about 16 pages, those with 10,000 to 50,000 circulation usually have a capacity of between 24 and 48 pages and those with more than 50,000 circulation may be able to print as many as 128 pages in a run. Extra pages can be inserted into an issue by hand or with special folding machines. Web-fed rotary letterpress newspaper machines can print up to about 60,000 copies of 128 standard-size pages per hour; in the interest of reproduction quality and wear and tear on the press, however, newspaper presses usually are operated at about only three-fourths of their rated top speed. Large daily newspapers may operate as many as ten 128-page press units at one time in order to produce an edition quickly.

Advances in the Printing of Sheets.—Since 1900 the bulk of development in sheet-fed presses, whether printing by letterpress, planographic or intaglio process, has comprised a series of minor mechanical modifications designed to improve the speed of the machines. Stops in sheet-fed presses have been designed that do not cause the sheet to bounce back as it is being fed to the cylinder, and complex mechanical feeders have been devised to work at very high speeds. Swinging grippers take the sheet and accelerate it to the peripheral speed of the cylinder; after the sheet is printed it is taken by other grippers on a continuous chain and delivered printed side up onto a pile; special airblow devices can be employed to slow up the sheet as it is released. To prevent the transfer of wet ink from one printed sheet to the next, a powder or liquid is sprayed on each sheet as it is delivered or the sheet is passed quickly over a small flame or through a heated tunnel to speed drying.

Advances in Web Printing.—In the early 1930s the need for printing mass-circulation magazines at high speed became urgent. To increase the speed of printing on web with the rotary letterpress, methods for drying the printed image to set the ink were introduced. Better plates and paper quickly followed. Automatic paper reels also were introduced; these allowed new rolls of paper to be spliced to old ones without slowing the press.

Other Developments.—Great advances were also made in the design of rotary machines capable of printing on a wide range of packaging materials: plastic film, cellophane, metallic foil,

and laminated surfaces as well as more conventional printing stock. In the 1960s the development of web-fed rotaries for newspaper, book and magazine, and packaging applications went forward hand in hand. The introduction of photoelectric means of controlling colour registration and of instrumentation for control of ink density made high-quality colour printing, by any of the major printing processes, a possibility by the late 1950s. Since that date magazines and catalogues, demanding great accuracy in colour rendition and satisfactory print quality, have been printed on web-fed rotaries.

The range of facilities available to the printer became increasingly wide. At the beginning of the 1970s rotary presses were manufactured capable of speeds in excess of 25,000 copies per hour, and with interchangeable units to print by any process. Some machines printed both sides of the web at the same time; and the number of colours available was in many cases limited only by the number of units possessed by the printer, and web widths up to 88 in. (224 cm.) were possible. In some of the larger presses intended for newspaper production, as many as ten webs could be accommodated; and coupled sheeters, folders, and stitchers could deliver finished work which then required only final trimming.

(B. I.)

BIBLIOGRAPHY.—*Before 1900:* Joseph Moxon, *Mechanick Exercises* (1683), ed. by H. Davis and H. Carter (1958); F. J. F. Wilson and D. Grey, *A Practical Treatise on Modern Printing Machinery and Letterpress Printing* (1888); R. Green, *The Iron Hand Press in America* (1948), *A History of the Platen Jobber* (1953); L. Neipp, *Les Machines à Imprimer depuis Gutenberg* (1951); *The Times Printing Number* (1912); G. A. Isaacs, *The Story of the Newspaper Printing Press* (1931); A. L. Monet, *Les Machines et Appareils Typographiques* (1878); R. Hoe, *A Short History of the Printing Press* (1902); Karl Dietrichs, *Die Buchdruckpresse von Johannes Gutenberg bis Friedrich König* (1930). (Js. M.)
20th Century: E. Kollecker and W. Matuschke, *Der Moderne Druck,* 2nd ed. (1958); J. Bass, *Das Buchdruckerbuch* (1953); *BP Specification Manual of Printing Machinery* (1970). (B. I.)

PRINTING TYPE. This article discusses the design and designing of printing type from its earliest times down to the present. Related material will be found in TYPESETTING; TYPOGRAPHY; PRINTING; PRINTING PRESS.

The Beginnings.—The invention in Europe of printing with movable metal types in the middle of the 15th century introduced the principle of mechanical mass production to a world in which nearly all man-made objects were made one at a time by hand. The earliest designers of printing types were the goldsmiths and other skilled metal workers whose experience with coinage and medal cutting for replica casting enabled them to attack the far more complex task of carving and filing in steel the sets of male dies called *patrones*, or punches; *i.e.*, model letters to be reproduced in quantity as characters on the faces (flat printing surfaces) of a font of type. The cutting of letters on so minute a scale, with strict consistency in the treatment of straight lines and curves throughout an entire alphabet, demanded a degree of manual skill which seems all the more spectacular in contrast with modern methods of cutting punches pantographically by power-driven tools from large mechanical drawings. But in admiring the virtuosity of the early punch cutters it is too easy to

FIG. 1.—ALTERATION OF LETTERS IN SAME BODY SIZE BY CHANGING LETTER WIDTHS AND LENGTHS OF ASCENDERS AND DESCENDERS

overlook their greater role in history; *i.e.*, that of the first practising industrial designers. What they were making by hand was only a means toward what they were actually designing for batch production, namely the appearance of printed words on paper: specifically the ink prints of type in some particular size and style of a face (design) which would indicate, to a predicted class or group of readers, the general nature and purpose of the book at hand.

The pioneer punch cutter, like any other designer for industry, had to take into account successive mechanical processes which might affect the appearance of the multiple end product. Thus the different letters of the alphabet had not only to be consistent in the treatment of stems, curves and serifs (fig. 2) but also had to appear on the printed page in accurate alignment, a matter which would partly depend upon the successful processing of the brass matrices (female dies) that were to be struck from the punches. The types that were to be cast in molten metal from the matrices would have to fit together snugly into whole word shapes with no distracting gaps between the individual letters. Further allowance had to be made for the effect of the printing: the primitive wooden press would be driving an inked form, or forme, of composed type with heavy pressure into damped sheets of handmade paper and the resulting "squash" of viscous ink would leave the printed images of the characters looking considerably thicker and somewhat less sharp in detail than their steel prototypes. The modern type designer faces similar problems, made more complex by the variety of paper surfaces and reproduction processes in use today.

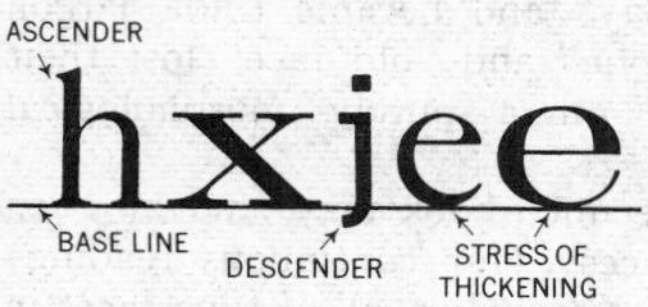

FIG. 2.—TYPE SAMPLES SHOWING DIFFERENT TREATMENTS OF THICKS, THINS AND SERIFS (TERMINAL STROKES)

Above all, the early punch cutter knew that the printed pages would come as bound books into the hands of readers who were accustomed not simply to deciphering the code symbols of the roman alphabet as such but to distinguishing between different kinds of books at first glance by their conventional styles of lettering. What links the modern type draftsman to the Renaissance punch cutter, and labels them both as type designers, is the need to look ahead through a long chain of production stages toward the ultimate object of all typographic design—the conveyance to the reader of meaningful texts through letter images which that reader will accept as appropriate to that particular kind of printed matter.

Printing created its own, entirely new kinds of "matter" (notably the periodical), which in turn had to be envisaged by the type designer as functional problems in legibility. From the early 19th century onward, competitive advertising opened up the distinct field of "display" type design ("jobbing") in which the ruling intention is the very opposite of that which disciplines the designer of type for continuous reading. Letters for a handbill may legitimately imitate any fantasy or distortion of sign writing, for the aim is to arrest and focus attention on a few words. The bold type which appears in various modern works of reference (such as dictionaries and timetables) has the similar purpose of attracting the searching eye quickly to the relevant entry by its abnormal thickness. Type for continuous reading has the contrary aim; it must carry the reader forward through line after line by its self-effacing conformity to whatever norm of legibility the reader counts upon for that particular kind of text. Thus the deliberate exploitation of abnormality in type design is a relatively new development and the inventors of eye-catching advertising types, represented by thousands of different designs since the beginning of the 19th century, seem far closer to sign writers than to the metal cutters of the days when books and booklets constituted almost the whole output of the printing press. Even in the earliest years the designers of type were accepting the principle, already fixed by the medieval scribes, that different sorts of book—liturgical, legal, revived-classical, popular-vernacular—should have different styles of letter.

Fortunately for Johann Gutenberg (*q.v.*) and the goldsmith whose services he used while he was at work on his invention, the northern scribes had evolved a formal script for use in short double-column lines, in which high legibility-for-size was gained by the use of a broad stiff pen that gave maximum thickness to the down strokes. To achieve this blackness with least waste of space, curves were condensed by being broken into angles and straight segments. The resulting textura script offered the metal engraver a model peculiarly suited to his file and burin. The readers of a folio bible in double column expected it to be set forth in this strong angular style of letter; hence the 42-line Bible (Mainz, *c.* 1456) gave them no jar of novelty (fig. 3). The round gothic associated with theological and legal texts in Latin, then the international language of the professional literates of Europe, was also relatively easy to reproduce in metal. It too had been evolved

Quod cū audisset david: descendit in

FIG. 3.—LINE OF TYPE FROM 42-LINE BIBLE, ISSUED AT MAINZ; 1456. ACTUAL SIZE

for use mainly in narrow columns, where the amount of white space between the lines can safely be reduced by shortening the descenders and ascenders and thus increasing the apparent size of the letters. The stubby descenders of the prevailing black letter styles were well adapted to the type cutters' need to strike matrices by hammering the hardened letter punch into a slab of brass. The more informal and free-swinging bastarda style, mainly used for books in the mother tongue, again required little more than simple imitation (fig. 4).

But among a thousand these the one to

FIG. 4.—CAXTON, TYPE NUMBER TWO, FROM DICTES AND SAYENGES OF THE PHYLOSOPHERS, WESTMINSTER; 1477. ACTUAL SIZE

But as printing spread from Germany to the Italian cities, the pioneer punch cutters faced their first insuperable problem: that of reproducing in separate metal letters, and eventually in type prints, the delicate, open-curved, long-descender style of calligraphy with which the humanist scholars and their scribes were optically distinguishing texts in the Latin of classical antiquity—or their own sedulously "Ciceronian" Latin—from those in the modernized Latin of the schoolmen and lawyers. To the humanists, the "language of divine antiquity" was not only to be studied and imitated, it had even to be equipped with its own style of script in which subtlety and elegance, lightness and amplitude would replace the bold simplicities of the styles which were given the contemptuous sobriquet of "gothic." The script revived by the humanists for this purpose was the minuscule standardized by Alcuin under Charlemagne at the beginning of the 9th century. The type cutters never succeeded in producing a plausible imitation of it in metal; but as crude attempts at copying gave way to deliberate paraphrase in terms of metal casting, what emerged was the first new contribution of type design as a creative art; *i.e.*, the kind of letter which is now called roman, or in French *romain.* Today the word is used broadly for "ordinary print" as distinct from anything exotic or attention-catching. But in Germany, where black letter survived as a language-linked style (Fraktur, Schwabacher), roman still bears its historical name of Antiqua.

Nicolas Jenson, formerly master of the royal mint at Tours,

Quare multarum quoq; gentium patrem diu

FIG. 5.—ROMAN TYPE USED BY N. JENSON, USED IN PRAEPARATIO EVANGELICA BY EUSEBIUS OF CAESAREA, PRINTED IN VENICE; 1470. ACTUAL SIZE

cut an admirable roman for the *Praeparatio evangelica* of Eusebius which he printed in Venice in 1470. But it was the famous Venetian printer-publisher Aldus Manutius, directing the skill of the goldsmith Francesco Griffo, who launched the Antiqua

ore fumigantibus : hunc lapi-
ties ambitu angusto circunte-

BY COURTESY OF THE MONOTYPE CORP. LTD.

FIG. 6.—ROMAN TYPE USED BY ALDUS IN DE AETNA BY P. BEMBO; 1495. TWICE ACTUAL SIZE

lower case and its inscriptional style capitals on the rising tide of humanist scholarship by perfecting a type which became the model for the great French type cutters of the next generation, notably Claude Garamond, and so the direct ancestor of a long line of roman fonts, many of which have been revived for present-day use.

Aldus' roman of 1495 appeared in a literary exercise by Pietro Bembo, the humanist poet, later cardinal, who probably took a personal interest in its typography: successive copies show many variants made while the work was on the press.

Aldus' "pocket editions," dating from 1501, made the first use of the kind of type now known as italic; it originated with him as an imitation of the cursive minuscule in chancery style in which scholars had been swiftly copying out coveted texts. Italic was later equipped with its own sloped-roman capitals and adopted as an auxiliary to roman by being cast in alignment with it.

The subsequent history of roman type design falls into four distinct periods. Through the 16th and 17th centuries its treatment by successive engravers varied only in subtle detail, scarcely perceptible to the layman's reading eye, and its debt to the calligrapher remained evident in the angle of thickening or "stress" of the curves and serifs of the lower case. Type founders began, however, to offer alternative fonts of the same body size: one series (of sizes from small to large) for normal bookwork, with the longer descenders that help to create a channel of white space between the lines, and a larger-looking version with short descenders and condensed curves, suitable for narrow columns such as those of the periodical.

Transition and Revival.—The first effort to rethink and rationalize type design came in 1692–93 when Louis XIV commissioned his academicians to devise, and Philippe Grandjean to pro-

e, 25 d'Aouſt, le Gouverneur ſe rendit à l

FIG. 7.—ROMAIN DU ROI. TYPE DESIGNED FOR KING LOUIS XIV BY P. GRANDJEAN. USED IN ROYAL PRINTING OFFICE, PARIS; 1702. ACTUAL SIZE

duce, a new series of roman and italic for the royal printing office. Type cutting entered its "transitional" phase in which sharp thick-thin contrasts brought a new look to the page. In Paris in the middle of the 18th century the learned printer-type founder P. S. Fournier developed the new style in one direction, with ingenious decorative use of *fleurons*, or border units, cast as type. At the same time John Baskerville in Birmingham, Eng., commissioned a rounder and still more sharply cut roman and italic, one which showed off the elegance of his hot-pressed paper and improved ink. Baskerville's chaste neoclassic style had a profound influence on European type cutters.

The transition was in effect from "this style" to **"this style,"** used by G. Bodoni and introduced in France by the Didots shortly before the French Revolution. Here the graver declared its independence from the quill, italic forgot its current script ancestry and the abandonment of the "long s" (ſ) drew the only dividing line in the whole history of roman type that is immediately obvious to the uninstructed reader.

The new short-s style with strong vertical stress and hair-thin horizontals became the prevailing mode for books and periodicals for the first half of the 19th century and the long-s fonts were melted down as antiquities. But just as the humanists had turned from the rigidities of gothic to their "antique" roman, so the Romantic movement in England brought a new appreciation of the "old" (pre-Baskerville) type cut by William Caslon, the first meritorious English punch cutter and letter founder, in 1720. A font preserved by the Caslon type foundry as a museum piece was used as a pastiche type at the Chiswick press from 1840. It found favour among antiquarians and liturgical publishers. In France, the "old" types of the 17th-century Elzevir editions became the inspiration of tentative revivals. The Scottish type foundry of Miller and Richard, sensing a change of taste, brought out in 1860 their historic (to contemporary taste) modification in which for the first time the "old" style reappeared, without its long s, as an alternative to the "modern."

Present Era.—This opened the present era in type design, with the new notion of offering publishers or customers a choice of different styles of roman. At first it meant a costly duplication of

the printer's type storage facilities; but the coming of the hot-metal composing machine reduced the problem to that of a simple change from one set of matrices to another. The term modern lost its meaning of "ruling mode of today" and became trade jargon for the sharper-cut style: "old style" and "old face" lost their antiquarian reference and took on a purely morphological meaning.

A present-day printer's type specimen book may offer an even wider variety of "composition faces" (for continuous reading) than is shown below (fig. 8). These examples, all of type faces in commercial use, are selected to indicate the different historical periods from which designs have been revived (with or without intelligent modifications) to meet the modern publisher's need for variety in taste and also for technical and economic reasons. Type (C), for example, is particularly suitable for printing on coated paper, which requires a very light impression; (E) is broad, (D) relatively condensed, and the difference can either save or bulk out 25 pages in a 248-page novel. (M) is effective in the long line of a book, where the space allowed for its deep descenders leaves a useful channel between the lines, but it is inefficient in narrow columns.

From 1885, Linn B. Benton's punch-cutting machine began to replace the hand craftsmen. New faces could thenceforth be drawn to any scale and cut with microscopic accuracy, in any type size from the same master pattern. The invention had little or no direct, immediate effect upon type design, for 19th-century punch cutters were not employed as creative designers; their pride was in their own manual skill, and there the machine surpassed them. The influence of the Benton machine was first shown in the emergence of the family of different versions (bold, condensed, etc.) of the same basic design—variants easily contrived by alterations to 10-in. drawings. Cheltenham, a roman designed by the U.S. architect B. G. Goodhue in 1905, failed as a book face but became the first runaway success in commercial printing as a family of many variant weights and widths. But meanwhile Benton's invention had made possible the composing machine; this major innovation was indirectly responsible for the emergence of a new class of types—the first bridge ever thrown between the quiet world of "book" faces (for continuous reading) and the restless, occasionally raucous and hitherto completely separate world in which the small jobbing printer's compositor had been confecting auction, theatrical and other "bills," trade cards, etc., from an ever-growing range of poster-like or otherwise attention-catching jobbing types.

Those faces, called in French *lettres de fantaisie,* had throughout the 19th century provided a not unprofitable sideline for the type founders, whose main income depended on the book and periodical printers' demand for ordinary text type in the tonnages required for hand composition. Since no one took advertising seriously to begin with, no self-consciousness inhibited the inventiveness of its type designers and their licence to impudence was exploited with honesty and gusto. Delicate pseudocalligraphic script types had appeared for commercial and society printing before the Industrial Revolution, but now "shock" types offered a new field. Capitals without serifs or thick-thin stress (sans-serif) were in use before 1825; fat black "Egyptians" (slab-serif) multiplied. The lithographic lettering artist's free fancies (*e.g.,* on music title pages) prompted the punch cutters to new feats of skill. Much of the most self-conscious avant-garde typography of the 20th century has drawn upon the early Victorian job printer's repertory; the crude sans-serif called "grotesque" ("grot") has been most often resuscitated for modern experimentalist display.

The new composing machines swept away the type founders' main market and left jobbing types as almost their sole remaining stock in trade. American type founders, banding together under the threat of extinction, began to give serious aesthetic attention to advertising faces. Under the new and respectable name of "publicity types," classic faces of the past were revived primarily for use in brochures and displayed press advertising, which the newly arriving advertising agencies were treating with a solemnity unknown to the old handbill printer. Thus book and display faces drew at least within sight of each other. Today, a fine book face is normally cut in sizes up to an inch high, where abnormality of size is alone enough to make it attention-catching; contrariwise, grotesques and sans-serifs have been used in small reading sizes by designers anxious to devise a "contemporary" style—for reasons more sentimental than rational, since no amount of respect for the machine age will reconcile book readers to alphabets which make it hard to distinguish I and l, or a from o.

(A) Axabcdefghijklmnopqrstuvwxyz1234567MQ

(B) Axabcdefghijklmnopqrstuvwxyz1234MQ

(C) Axabcdefghijklmnopqrstuvwxyz12345MQ

(D) Axabcdefghijklmnopqrstuw1234MQ

(E) Axabcdefghijklmnopqrstuvwxy1234MQ

(F) Axabcdefghijklnopqrstuw1234MQ

(G) Axabcdefghiklmnopqrstuvwxyz1234MQ

(H) Axabcdefghijknopqrstuw1234MQ

(I) *Chancery Italic revived from XVI century Italy. abc*

(J) *'Old style' italic, one of many versions pre-1700*

(K) *'Transitional' italic, English style abcd*

(L) *'Modern' italic, conforming closer to roman*

(M) Axabcdefghijklmnopqrstuvw1234MQ

(N) Axabcdefghijklmnopqrstuw1234MQ

(O) Axabcdefghijklmnopqrstuvwx1234MQ

(P) *Axabcdefghijklmnopqrstuvw1234MQ*

(Q) Axabcdefghijklmnopqrstuvw1234MQ

FIG. 8.—MODERN REVIVALS OF EARLY TYPE FACES AND 20TH-CENTURY DESIGNS

(A) Centaur by B. Rogers, 1914, patterned after N. Jenson's roman, 1470; (B) roman by Aldus Manutius, 1495, prototype old face revived by Monotype Corp. Ltd., 1929; (C) roman by Aldus, 1499, recut in facsimile as Monotype Poliphilus, 1923; (D) roman by P. S. Fournier, revised as Monotype Fournier, 1925; (E) revival of roman by J. Baskerville, 1757; (F) roman by J. Bell, 1788, revived as Monotype Bell, 1930; (G) roman, revived from G. Bodoni, early 19th century; (H) Scotch Roman, 19th-century "modern" face; (I–L) four italic faces showing development of modern style; (M) Perpetua, E. Gill, 1929; (N) Times New Roman, S. Morison, 1931; (O) Gill Sans, E. Gill, 1928; (P) Palace Script, copperplate jobbing face; (Q) Egyptian, slab-serif jobbing face

Sans-serif and other monotone letters have, however, a functional justification in commercial printing, for they can retain their family characteristics through extremes of all-over thickening, condensing, expanding and so on. The sans-serif designed by the English sculptor Eric Gill is a widely used example of the serious treatment of monotone alphabets with care for legibility. Its adoption as a design family for railway printing caused it to proliferate into 25 design variations under the family name of Gill Sans.

The 20th century has seen eclecticism in type choice conquering the earlier concept of one predominant taste in roman type design succeeding another and rendering it obsolete. In the disciplined book type field, where any queerness or romanticism is fatal, modern designers must compete with the greatest masters of past centuries. Very few new claimants to a place in the book printer's repertory have stood up to that rivalry. In 1932 the *Times* (London) commissioned a roman in the general style that the Dutch letter cutters had evolved for periodical work; *i.e.*, large-appearing, relatively narrow and gaining legibility by the tilted stress of the "old" style. Composing machine manufacturers were permitted to market the face commercially, and its world-wide popularity has made it the nearest approach that an eclectic century has to anything that could be called its own characteristic contribution to history. But modern multiplicity of processes, paper surfaces, different uses for print, to say nothing of the advertiser's constant demand for variety, prevent type design from settling back into the succession of ruling styles and fashions which characterized the centuries in which printing was in effect book printing and used one kind of paper (handmade rag) and one process of multiplication (direct letterpress).

The major languages of scholarship (Greek, Hebrew, Arabic) were exercising European punch cutters from the cradle years of printing, and missionary zeal quickly extended their range. Those nearest to the Latin alphabet, *e.g.*, Russian Cyrillic, have undergone parallel changes in style treatment; Arabic remains purely and stubbornly a calligraphic minuscule. No script among the hundreds which western type founders class as "exotics" has achieved the efficiency and adaptability of the roman font with its different member-alphabets—A, a, *A, a,* ᴀ and, where required, "related bold" **A, a.** It will not replace the other great scripts, but as a supranational vehicle of communication it has no rival.

The word "type" is broadly but legitimately used for the printed letters on the page, which are no longer necessarily the prints of metal types; they may be from metal, rubber or plastic plates which, today, need not have been taken from metal printing types; the images may have been photographically composed onto sensitized film. Hence the designers of new faces for filmsetting will still be type designers, subject to the same discipline where continuous reading is concerned and permitted the same licence in the display field, where film offers new possibilities; *e.g.*, novel alphabets can be quickly produced and distorted at will by the camera. Book faces, however, will require extra forethought. The old engravers, who had, of course, to cut a new set of punches for each successive size, subtly altered the proportions and colour value each time for optical consistency. In filmsetting, one set of master letters may have to serve for every size from footnote 6-point upward, and the best designs for filmsetting will be those which best survive arbitrary enlargement and reduction. But film imposes no other mechanical limitation upon the type designer—to his regret, for he would welcome any such technological challenge as stimulating as that which confronted the pioneer punch cutters.

See also biographical articles on outstanding type designers.

BIBLIOGRAPHY.—A. F. Johnson, *Type Designs: Their History and Development* (1959); D. B. Updike, *Printing Types: Their History, Forms and Use,* 2nd ed. (1937); W. T. Berry and A. F. Johnson, *The Encyclopaedia of Type Faces,* 2nd ed. (1958); Cyril Burt, *A Psychological Study of Typography* (1959); Stanley Morison, *Type Designs of the Past and Present* (1926); Nicolette Gray, *Nineteenth Century Ornamented Types and Title Pages* (1938).   (B. L. WA.)

PRINTMAKING. Printmaking is the production of images, normally on paper and exceptionally on fabric, parchment, plastic, or other support by various processes of multiplication. It is here understood as concerning prints made and printed by the hand, or under the supervision of artists. The article is divided into the following sections:

I. ORIGINS

The making of images is one of the earliest activities of man and hand prints are known from Paleolithic times. They could be considered as the voluntary repetitions of involuntary hand prints or footprints observed by man. Even at this stage these could have different functions: either to recall the existence of that object shown, or to convey as sign, gesture, or message the action of making the image. The distinction has persisted to this day.

The earliest examples of true printing may be stones known from the Han period in China (202 B.C.–A.D. 221) on which forms were left in relief on a cutaway background. Such stones are known to have been used later to make patterns on cloth. The cloth was stretched over the stone and rubbed with a cake of hard colour as rubbings from brasses are made today. True printing, however, awaited the invention of paper (also in China) about the 6th century A.D. In these prints ink was laid on the original surface of the block—the spaces between having been hollowed out—and transferred by pressure to paper placed over it by rubbing with some instrument, as the baren still used in Japan. Printing and papermaking did not reach Europe until the late 14th century although no print known can be dated with certainty until the 15th century. In these a drawing was transferred to a wood block (or made directly upon it) and the background cut away by an artisan to leave the line in relief. Printing was done with a crude screw press, possibly derived from a winepress, and not by rubbing (as above) and the imprint was thus slightly indented into the paper surface.

Within the same century another method of printing appeared and is known as intaglio from the fact that printing ink is carried in the incisions made into the plate, generally of metal or stone, and its surface wiped clean; consequently the line on the print is in relief above the sheet. The art of incising lines for decorative or other purposes into metal, known as engraving, is one of the most ancient. Prehistoric man engraved with pointed flints into the soft travertine of cave walls, also into horn and bone; in the book of Exodus engraving is referred to on the Ark of the Covenant. In Europe it was the goldsmiths who were the first to print from engraved plates (generally hardened copper) and their practice of rubbing oily black into the work is said to be the origin of intaglio printing.

Another operation is said to be the origin of plate making by chemical means—armourers from the 12th century onward coated steel with wax, drew designs in it with a point, and corroded the lines with salt soaked in vinegar until of sufficient depth; they were often filled with silver or gold wire. Thus within one generation of the invention of printing from engraved plates, etching on iron was also employed as permitting greater freedom in drawing. In the earlier examples biting was not varied; and although acids for etching copper would have been known to alchemists, it is unlikely that they would be available to artists. Later by exposing different parts, or different stages of work on copper, to acid for longer periods a greater variety of intensity was achieved. A method that originated also in the 15th century is known as drypoint, as no acid is used, and appears similar to engraving. The work generally is carried out on copper and the tool employed is usually a point: steel, diamond, etc.; not the burin (see *Intaglio Printing: Line Engraving,* below). The ink is retained upon the surface of the metal by the flanges or burrs raised by the tool rather than by the incision in the plate, so that in the print some indentation can be seen. Furthermore as the pressure in printing is borne by these fragile burrs the plate loses rapidly in printing.

Another method of producing hollows in a plate for printing either intaglio or relief, known as criblé, consisted of hammering points of different shapes into a metal plate. As no artist of outstanding importance employed this method it had little development.

Engraving was not entirely restricted to the incision of lines in a plate: dotting with short jabs of the burin (making a triangular dot) was used, notably by Giulio Campagnola (*c.* 1482–after 1514), and later became the stipple method of rendering halftone; and, in the crayon method, rough rollers were used to translate the grain of pencil or silverpoint on paper. In the practice of etching also, areas were prepared with a grain laid with resin dust, asphalt, or sand pressed through a ground, in a technique known as aquatint. Although often reported as discovered in the 18th century, it was already used together with engraving by Adriaen van de Velde (1636–72) in the mid-17th century. About the same time Ludwig van Siegen (1609–*c.* 1680), using the roulette (see *Intaglio Printing: Mezzotint,* below) of the crayon method but without removing the burrs this would raise, produced the velvety black surface later known as mezzotint and by working on the surface with scrapers and burnishers produced halftones. Invented in Flanders, the method proved so popular in England that it became known as the *manière anglaise.* A later tool, the rocker, was used to cover plates more rapidly with lines of dots in four or more directions. By inking such plates carrying different colours, multicoloured prints were made from the 18th century. Later, made on steel, they permitted 19th-century mezzotints to be printed in editions of over 1,000 copies instead of the 50 maximum possible from copper.

"ST. JOHN THE BAPTIST," ENGRAVING BY GIULIO CAMPAGNOLA (*c.* 1482–AFTER 1514)

"CALAVERA OF DON QUIXOTE," RELIEF ENGRAVING ON METAL BY J. G. POSADA (1851–1913)

In all these methods, which have given rise to modern mechanical methods of high-speed printing, the pigment is carried either in relief, or within the plate; hence the print shows indentation or relief of ink on its surface. In one very ancient and another recent method, however—known as planigraphic—the ink is not deposited from relief or intaglio. The more ancient method is stencil printing (see *Stencil Printing,* below), definitely known in China as early as the 8th century: a screen printed in this manner is in the William Hayes Fogg Art Museum, Cambridge, Mass. Before their contact with Western civilization, Eskimo in Baffin Island were making stencil prints cut from sealskin. Undoubtedly of Oriental origin, stencil printing has been greatly developed in the United States and Europe in the 20th century.

The other planigraphic technique, lithography, was discovered by A. Senefelder (1771–1834) in 1798 while he was seeking to etch the text of his own plays in relief on stone. Using a grease pencil as a resist, he discovered accidentally that if the stone were wetted, ink would adhere to the wax and be repelled by water. Metal plates, which are generally zinc or aluminum, with a surface roughened to hold water have since been used to replace the stone, which, however, is still preferred for direct work by a great number of artists. As the ink is held on the level surface of stone, there is neither relief above nor indentation below the surface of the printed sheet. Colour prints are made by this method using successive printings from stones or plates in different colours. Another method for printing from lithographic plates, developed in the 20th century, is known as offset, as the ink from a lithographic plate, formed on a roller, is transferred to a rubber surface (offset blanket) on a second roller and from this to the printed sheet. Considered generally as a mechanical reproduction process, offset has exceptionally been used for making original prints. Again the impression on the sheet is neither indented nor in relief.

II. RELIEF PRINTING

1. **Woodcut.**—Woodcut is the conventional term for designs printed from planks of wood cut parallel to the trunk of the tree. Fine-grained woods such as cherry and pear were often used, but in modern times pine and softwoods, which show a strong grain, came also to be employed. The ink, of oil- or water-base pigment, is carried on the original surface of the block and the remaining background then cut away with knives and open gouges as in wood carving. The Western practice is to cut a 45-degree angle around the parts to be printed giving a block with better resistance to pressure in printing, but in the Oriental practice the knife is held vertically since the blocks are not subjected to pressure in printing. Such prints are generally in black line, either drawn on the wood or transferred to it and the background then cut away. Linoleum has been used to replace wood, notably by the German Expressionists of the 1920s and by Pablo Picasso in the 1950s. Permitting greater ease in cutting, it has less resistance in wear and printing. Both wood and linoleum block have been used for colour printing, either by successive impressions from blocks in different colours or by the cutting of blocks into parts coloured differently to produce a mosaic. In one case by A. Derain (1880–1954) elements of colours were separated by grooves in the block and inked through stencils. Metal has also been used to make relief plates; soft type-metal or zinc as used by J. G. Posada (1851–1913) in Mexico and by Pierre Courtin (1921–   ) in France—the latter printed in intaglio. Etched and engraved plates, made by the process described under intaglio (below), are also printed from relief in the same way as a woodcut. Experimental prints have been made in the 20th century from such elements as cardboard and plastic, either mobile or assembled with plastic glue on a support permitting relief to be built up rather than hollowed out, or with wire mounted on blocks or indented into ingrained blocks with pressure (A. Calder, 1898–   ).

2. **Wood Engraving** is understood as designs printed from end-grain wood (box or cherry cut across the trunk), and the tools used are burins or gravers of solid square, lozenge, or oval section, sharpened at a 30-degree angle to the stem. Here the work may be more readily conceived in white line as cut, rather than in black line, which is left. Multiple gravers which are able to cut from two to eight lines at a time (tint tools or "velos") were devised in the 19th century to permit the rendering of halftone. Transparent plastic blocks of the type of lucite or perspex have been used by certain 20th-century engravers to replace end-grain wood, permitting work with the same tools to be executed from drawings seen through the material; Arthur Deshaies (1920–   ) in the United States has used such plates printed either as relief

(LEFT) "THE RIDERS ON THE FOUR HORSES" BY ALBRECHT DÜRER, 1498, FROM HIS "APOCALYPSE" CYCLE OF WOODCUTS. (RIGHT) BUXHEIM "SAINT CHRISTOPHER," 1423, THE EARLIEST DATED WOODCUT

(ABOVE) WOOD ENGRAVING BY WIL-
LIAM BLAKE, 1820–21, FOR R. J.
THORNTON'S "PASTORALS OF VIR-
GIL." (LEFT) "THE TAWNY OWL,"
WOOD ENGRAVING BY THOMAS
BEWICK FROM HIS "HISTORY OF
BRITISH BIRDS," 1826

or intaglio. Exceptionally, intaglio prints have been made
from engraved wood by Eric
Gill (1882–1940) in England
and by Fiorini (1922–) in
France from plywood.

3. History of Woodcut.—
Printing from wood blocks on
textiles in Europe is known from
the early 14th century, but it had little development until paper,
introduced into Spain from the East as early as the 12th century,
was manufactured in France and Germany at the end of the 14th
century. Cuts with heavy outline and little shading, as the
"Christ Before Herod" in the British Museum, may date from
1400, but the earliest dated print of German origin is the Buxheim "Saint Christopher" of 1423. In Bavaria, Austria, and
Bohemia religious images and playing cards were first made from
wood blocks in the early 15th century, and the development of
printing from movable type led to widespread use of woodcut illustrations in the Netherlands and in Italy (*see* ILLUSTRATION,
BOOK: *Early Illustrated Books; The 16th and 17th Centuries*).
With the 16th century, black-line woodcut reached its greatest perfection with Albrecht Dürer (1471–1528) and his followers, Lucas
Cranach (1472–1553) and Hans Holbein (1497–1543). In the
Netherlands Lucas van Leyden (1494–1553) and in Italy Giacopo
de' Barberi (1440–1515) and Domenico Campagnola (*c.* 1484–
after 1563)—like Dürer, engravers on copper—also made woodcuts as did the engravers of Titian. These woodcuts were drawn on
the wood and the cutting done by *Formschneider* (form engraver)
rather than by the artist: in the Basel print cabinet are some of
Dürer's blocks drawn upon and ready for cutting. By the 16th
century woodcut as a medium became less important than line
engraving but Hendrik Goltzius (1558–1617) and Jan Lievens
(1607–74) continued to use it in the 17th century.

As a medium for popular image, woodcut was widely used in the
17th century, but no major artist employed it until Thomas Bewick
(1753–1828) in England used white-line engraving on end-grain
wood. Often credited with the invention of this technique, actually
in use for a century before, Bewick exploited the cut of the tool
as a direct means of expression instead of cutting away from a
black-line drawing, so that most of the drawing appears, when
printed, in white line against a black background. After Bewick
the reproductive wood engraving of the 19th century was developed by his pupils and their followers, among them Luke Clennell
(1781–1840), Charlton Nesbitt (1775–1838), William Harvey
(1796–1866), John Johnson (d. 1797), and Thomas Frazer Ranson
(1784–1828).

In France and Germany it became the most general means of
illustration for books, magazines, and even newspapers. Gustave
Doré (1832–83) in France and Adolf Menzel (1815–1905) in Germany produced enormous quantities of drawings for illustration
engraved by artisans, but nothing was demanded of the engraver
but the most faithful copying, and the original quality of the
wood was suppressed. William Blake (1757–1827) cut few wood
engravings but they are among the finest of this time, as appears
in his small but beautiful illustrations for the *Virgil* of Thornton.
When in the late 19th century photoengraving began to replace
wood for reproduction, the wood-engraving technique ceased to
interest serious artists until the 20th century. In England William
Morris (1834–96) and Eric Gill renewed original wood engraving,
as did Camille Pissarro in France. In Germany and Norway woodcut became an important medium to the Expressionists: Edvard
Munch (1863–1944), Karl Schmidt-Rottluff (1884–   ), Erich
Heckel (1883–1970), Heinrich Campendonk (1889–1957), Ernst
Ludwig Kirchner (1880–1938), and others.

In the United States woodcut began to appear in the 1920s in the
work of Rockwell Kent and to interest artists again in the 1930s.
The Work Projects Administration (WPA) project directed by
Louis Schanker (1903–   ) and the work of Adja Yunkers (1900–
) and Antonio Frasconi (1919–   ) were responsible for a wide
development of colour prints made from wood, often printed wet
on wet to give a result as rich as oil painting. In Italy Tranquilo
Marangoni (1912–   ), in the United States Misch Kohn (1916–
    ), and in Brazil Livio Abramo (1913–   ) found new resources in
wood engraving, while in France Galanis (1882–1966) and Jacques
Boullaire (1893–   ) found new uses for the tint tool. In the mid-
1950s enormous woodcuts, in some cases justifying their scale,
were done by Leonard Baskin (1922–   ) and Carol Summers
(1925–   ). Edmond Casarella (1920–   ) was printing in colour
from mobile elements.

III. INTAGLIO PRINTING

1. Etching.—Etching refers to prints made from plates having
grooves or hollows eaten out with acid in which ink is retained
and transferred by pressure to damp paper or other support. In
the simplest case a clean polished plate of copper or zinc (iron,
magnesium, aluminum, and brass have also been used) is coated
with an acid-resistant ground composed of bitumen, resin, and
beeswax, either melted on or applied in solution. Lines are drawn
through this coating with a point and the plate is exposed to acid
—either in a bath or by acid dropped on it. Differences of size of
line are obtained either by the use of wider points or in the biting;
lines of decreasing force can be added at different stages, or the
completely worked plate progressively covered in part with a stopping varnish. The usual acids are nitric, nitrous, hydrochloric,
with potassium or sodium chlorate, or ferric chloride.

2. Soft Ground.—Where the coating on the plate is mixed with
grease it remains sensitive to pressure. A sheet of drawing paper
laid over a plate so prepared and drawn on will lift the ground
where it adheres to the lines of the drawing and expose metal to
attack by the acid in a trace showing the grain of the paper. The
coating can also be drawn through freely without resistance and
if a texture is applied to this ground with pressure, the threads
or irregularities of the texture again expose the metal to attack
with the acid. This method will permit a collage of texture, by
overlapping in different stages of transparency in depth, or recording stress or torsion in the material. A variant of etching known as
the lift ground or pen method was devised in the 18th century to
avoid the difficulty of etching. On a clean ungrounded plate a
drawing is made with an ink containing sugar, gamboge, gum
arabic, or some other nondrying matter; or such a drawing on
transfer paper is applied with heat to the plate. A resistant ground
covers this and when the plate is immersed in warm water the
ground is lifted wherever this ink is present. Aquatint (*see* below)
is applied where the forms are too wide to hold ink. To transfer an
image to a plate by photographic means the plate is coated with a
solution of potassium bichromate and gelatin. While wet this coating is not sensitive to light; after drying in a dark room it is exposed to intense light through a drawing or other negative and
developed in warm water. This process will remove the coating where unexposed to light. Slow etching with ferric chloride
or Dutch mordant gives an intaglio plate, almost indistin-

(LEFT) "WARRIOR GAGATAI," WOOD ENGRAVING BY MISCH KOHN, 1955, PRINTED ON CHINA PAPER TO GIVE WHITE RELIEF. (ABOVE) "THE KISS," COLOURED WOODCUT BY EDVARD MUNCH, 1902. (BELOW) "HEAD OF A MAN," WOOD ENGRAVING BY LEONARD BASKIN, 1961

guishable from an autographic etching.

3. Aquatint.—Aquatint is a method of printing areas of tone from a plate in which acid has acted through a porous ground. The plate may be prepared by depositing resin or asphalt powder, and then heating the plate to cause the deposit to adhere; or by covering with a solution of resin in alcohol too thin to resist acid; or by pressing a sheet of fine sandpaper into a ground; or by sifting fine salt onto a grounded plate, and then heating the plate. The operation of using texture on soft ground also produces such a porous surface. As with line etching stopping out of whites, then of tones of increasing strength until only blacks are left exposed to acid, may be applied. In the plate, ink will be retained between points representing the resin grain, the original surface being destroyed by acid; the effect is typically opaque and the plate subject to wear in printing. The sand grain or soft ground methods give a plate in which the original surface is intact, the ink being held in small pits within it, so that the effect is typically transparent and the plate is more resistant to wear. However, the transparency is relative and disappears when through successive bitings all of the original surface is destroyed.

4. Deep Etch.—Open areas of plate are removed by the action of the acid. As no texture retains ink in these open areas, they will print in relief on the sheet. A tone that is dependent on the crystallization of the metal or on the bubbling of the acid will appear, surrounded with strong black borders where ink is retained in the margins. Once considered as an error of technique, such methods have been exploited in the 20th century to obtain concrete space effects and separation of colour in simultaneous printing.

5. Drypoint.—Drypoint refers to prints made from direct scratches with a point on a copper, brass, steel, zinc, or other plate without the use of acid. Although drypoint is printed by the same operation as all intaglio plates, the effect is different. The ink is retained on the surface of the plate by the flanges, or burrs, raised by the point rather than held in the slight incisions. Thus in the print it will lie upon, or even be slightly indented into, the sheet of paper and will not be in relief above it. One of the most demanding operations in printmaking, it is seldom well understood by artists. According to the angle of attack by the steel, diamond, or other point in relation to the direction of line, one serrated burr, one razor-edge burr, or two sharp or serrated burrs can be raised. These will have a different effect in the print and will have greater or less resistance to pressure required in printing. As a consequence this method produces fragile and fugitive results and a small number of good prints.

6. Mezzotint.—Mezzotint is a variety of drypoint in which the surface of the plate is roughened mechanically to hold ink between the burrs. The tool used is the rocker—a steel blade with a curved edge, its undersurface grooved with closely set lines and ground off at about 30 degrees. As the rocker is rocked from side to side across a plate it will then produce lines of dots. Dots are also produced with the roulette—a small roller bearing points on its surface. If the burrs are sufficiently close ink is retained between them to print a uniform velvety black. In a variant known as *manière noire* drypoint lines closely set in two or four different directions are used for the same purpose. Another similar effect is produced by planing across the plate in four different directions with a carborundum stone; grinding with carborundum powder and a flatiron has also been used to get such an effect. By the use of scrapers and burnishers the burrs are slowly reduced or removed to regain halftones and whites in printing. Any degree of detail is obtainable in a result that resembles charcoal drawing or even photography. As with other forms of drypoint the plate wears in printing unless steel or steel-faced copper is used, or, exceptionally, the burr removed so that only the holes in the plate print.

7. Sculptural Methods.—From the mid-20th century many artists have developed intaglio printing from plates that function rather as matrices or molds from which reliefs are cast or pressed in printing, than as means to transfer black lines or colour elements to a sheet as drawing or painting. Such plates may be printed white on white or by inking both intaglio and relief, as black on black. The means used for making such plates may be the burins or scrapers as in normal engraving, chemical action as massive biting-out with acid, or combinations of all these methods.

8. Line Engraving.—Line engraving is the process of incising grooves into a metal plate from which a print is made. The tool used, known as a burin or graver, is a steel rod of square or lozenge section on edge, the end of which has been ground to an angle of 45 degrees to the stem and mounted in a handle. Held in the palm of the hand, the stem between the second finger and thumb, the index finger resting lightly on the upper edge, the tool is driven in the direction of the line, which is varied by rotating the plate. The depth of the incision and breadth of the consequent line are controlled by increasing the angle of attack. The tools used must be perfectly sharpened so that the resistance of the metal (preferably hard copper) will not demand excessive force and little burr will be formed except on the outside of curves—the burr formed is usually shaved off with a triangular section scraper before printing. As the ink is held within the grooves in the plate, the lines on the print will stand up in relief corresponding to the depth of the incision.

ETCHINGS AND AQUATINT

(Left) "Woman Washing Her Feet," etching by Urs Graf, 1513. (Centre) "Large Lion Hunt," etching on copper by Rembrandt van Rijn, 1641. (Right) One of the "Carceri" (Prisons) etchings by Giambattista Piranesi, c. 1745. (Below) "Here Comes the Bogie Man," etching and aquatint by Francisco Goya, from the "Caprichos" series published in 1799

Thus a genuine third dimension exists where a deeper cut intersects a finer one, but, as this sculptural space may also be read as inverted, the ambiguity of the space adds a further resource of expression. Since the 1930s work on plates with a round-section tool has been used, either printed black as above, or uninked when a white line in relief will appear across and in front of all other work in the print. Like an object placed before a theatre backdrop this will deepen the apparent space in the image.

9. Printing of Intaglio Plates.—Plates made by all of the foregoing methods are printed by similar means. The design of the roller press used has not changed essentially since the 17th century. It consists of one larger bearing roller; another smaller one driven by bars or gears; a flat parallel bed between them; and woolen blankets to distribute the pressure between the upper roller and the bed. Pressure is controlled by packing above the bearings or by screws. The intaglio plate to be printed is placed on a heated slab and a viscous ink is forced into its crevices with a roller or dabber. Excess ink is wiped away from the surface first with tarlatan, then by hand. The plate is laid upon the bed of the press and paper (which has been dampened many hours before) laid over it, and the closely woven woolen blankets over all. As the upper roller is turned the bed is drawn through: a pressure of several tons transmitted through the blankets molds the wet paper into the ink-filled crevices producing a cast of the plate in ink upon paper. Although such a press can be adapted to relief printing it is usual to employ a screw, platen, or contact press. Printing in varied colours is done either with *poupées* (dolls) using different colours in different parts, or successive printings from separate plates carrying different colours. When successive printings are used, to ensure colour forms falling in place all plates are drilled together with needle holes in the same position and all sheets of paper pricked through with holes in the positions corresponding to these holes. Using two needles passing through the holes in the paper engaging with the holes in the plate, it is then possible for the colour impression to fall in place. Experiments in the United States and in France initiated in Atelier 17 have permitted simultaneous printing in a number of colours from both the intaglio and unworked surface of the same plate in a single operation. The physical properties controlling all printing (except electronic reproductions) are the viscosity of the ink, the surface tension of the layers, and the thickness and adherence of the layers. Thus after a plate is prepared for intaglio printing as above, the unworked surface is free to carry another colour so long as its viscosity is lower than the intaglio ink already present, and the layer of ink is sufficiently thin to permit damp paper to make contact with

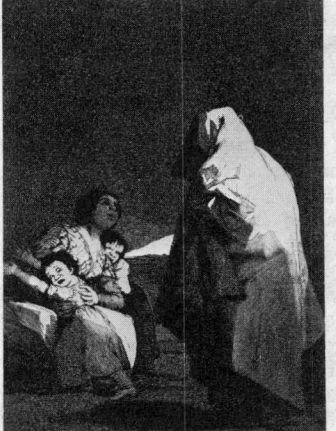

the intaglio ink (*see* above). Using a number of depths of relief and rollers of different hardness and diameter, different colours can be deposited according to the varying depths of penetration of the roller. The colours are separated by a contrast of viscosity, so that a more liquid film rejects a more viscous colour on the roller while a more viscous colour on the plate accepts the more liquid. The most liquid must be above the viscosity of water present in the paper, and the most viscous below the viscosity of the intaglio colour, otherwise the roller will lift the intaglio instead of depositing colour upon it. Thus all the permutations of opaque intaglio and transparent superficial colour can appear on the plate in a single passage through the press.

10. History of Intaglio Printing.—The earliest of European prints known were made in northern Burgundy, Flanders, Germany, and Switzerland. Engravers in the workshops of goldsmiths made playing cards, or rather images, in definite outline distinguished by the manner, broad or fine, in which shading was carried out. Such images were made in Bavaria in the early 15th century by an artist known only as the Master of the Playing Cards. The earliest dated print of an unknown master was made in Germany in 1446 and his work may be contemporary with the Master of the Death of Mary in Flanders or Burgundy. The Master E. S. (active 1440–47) was followed by Martin Schongauer, born in Colmar (c. 1445–94), and the Master of the Hausbuch, not otherwise identified, must have been active at this period. A generation later Albrecht Dürer (1471–1528) in Germany and Lucas van Leyden (1494–1553) were working both in engraving and etching. Engraving in Italy was being done by the Florentine goldsmiths, who were in many cases also sculptors, sometimes painters, and even architects. Maso Finiguerra (1426–64) directed a workshop in which Antonio Pollaiuolo (c. 1430–98) was known to have worked during 12 years making nielli, sculpture, etc., yet only one print of his is known. With Andrea Mantegna (1431–1506) engraving reached a very high point of development. The first known etchings made on iron were the work of Daniel Hopfer

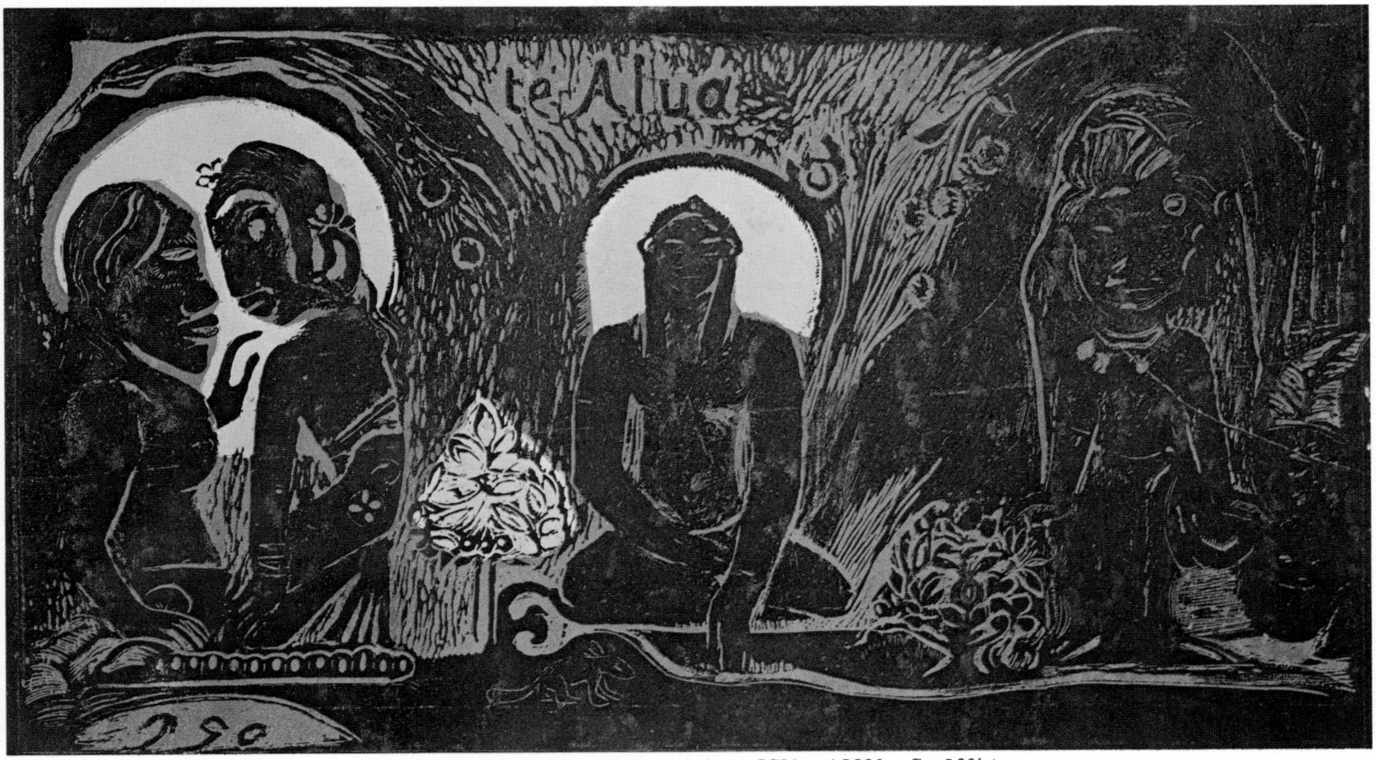

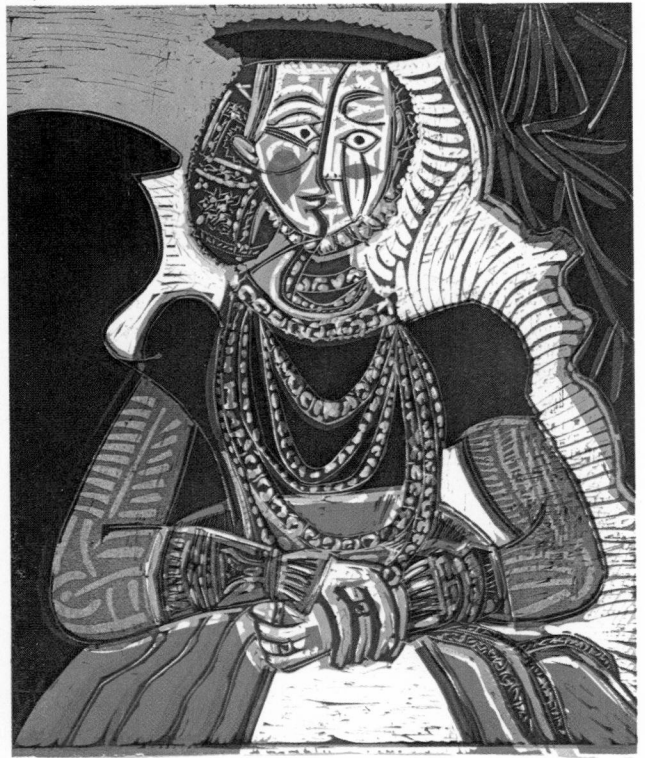

"Te Alua," woodcut by Paul Gauguin, between 1890 and 1903. 8 x 13¾ in.

"Seated Woman (after Cranach)," linoleum cut by Pablo Picasso, 1958. 25⅜ x 21 in.

RELIEF AND STENCIL PRINTS

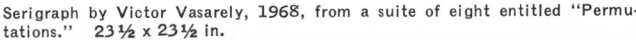

Serigraph by Victor Vasarely, 1968, from a suite of eight entitled "Permutations." 23½ x 23½ in.

BY COURTESY OF (TOP) THE TRUSTEES OF THE BRITISH MUSEUM, (BOTTOM LEFT) THE MUSEUM OF MODERN ART, NEW YORK, GIFT OF DANIEL SAIDENBERG, (BOTTOM RIGHT) DENISE RENÉ, PARIS PHOTOGRAPH, (TOP) JOHN R. FREEMAN

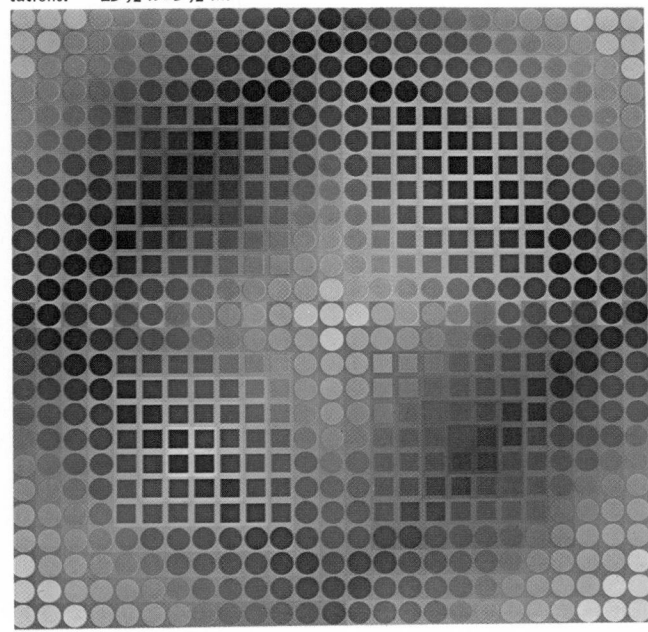

PLATE II   PRINTMAKING

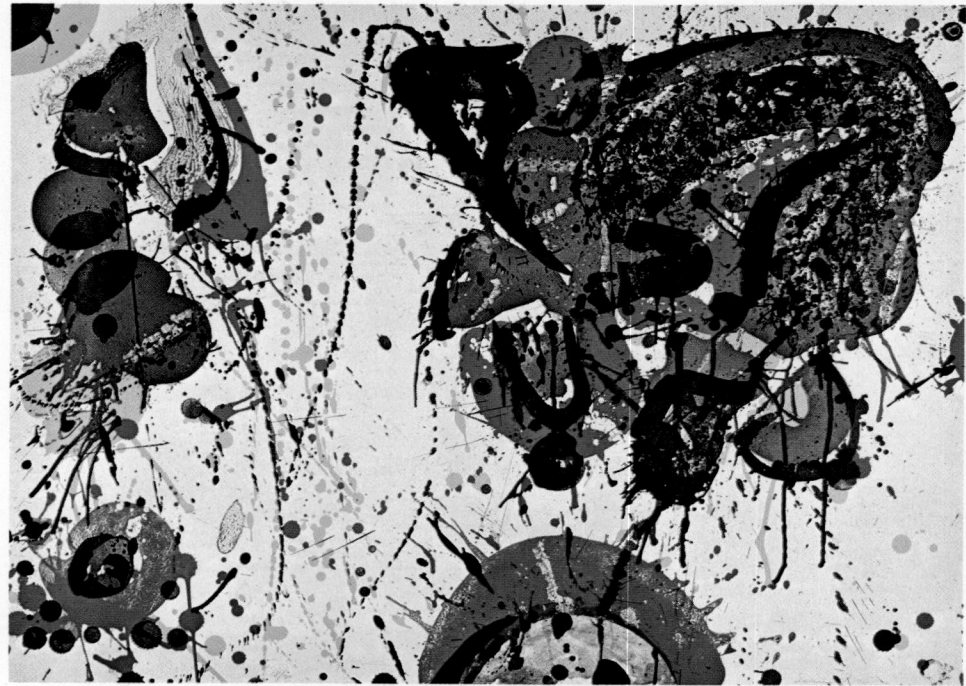

"For Miro II," lithograph by Sam Francis, 1963. 22½ x 30 in.

LITHOGRAPHIC AND INTAGLIO PRINTS

"Papillon," mezzotint by Yozo Hamaguchi, 1967. 4⅝ x 4⅝ in.

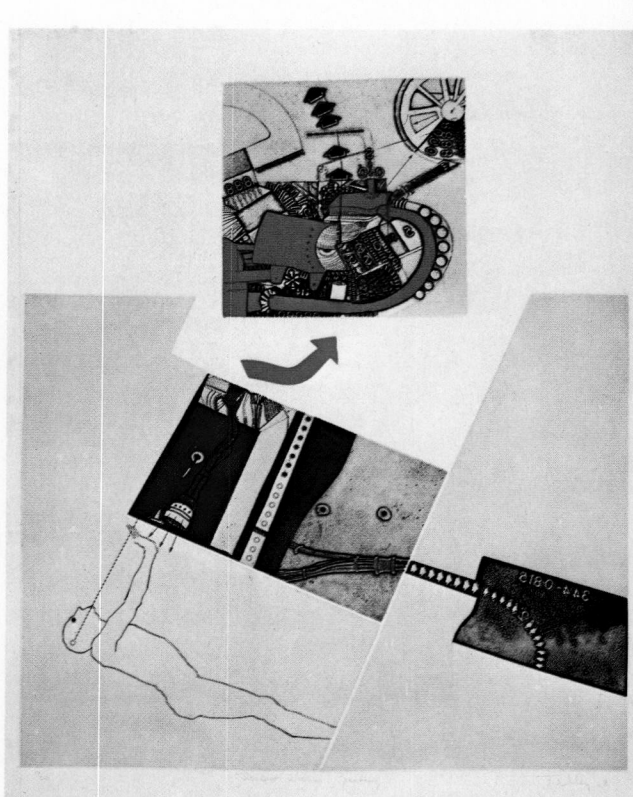

"Norbert Wiener Speaking," engraving and etching by Eugenio Tellez, 1968. 27¾ x 40 in.

(1494–1536) of a family of armourers in Augsburg; Dürer and Lucas van Leyden also made etchings—the latter being the first to use copper. Urs Graf (c. 1485–1527) not only etched but was himself a *landsknecht* (mercenary foot soldier) working in Basel and he made the first dated etching, of 1513. Contemporary with him, Hans Sebald Beham (1500–50), Albrecht Altdorfer (1480–1538) of Ratisbon, and Hirschvogel (1503–53?) made etchings of increasing complexity in which the biting of lines was varied. One of the first engraved portraits was made by Lucas van Leyden in 1521. He was followed by Dirick Vellert (working 1517–44) in Antwerp and Marcus Gheeraerts the Elder (c. 1521–1604) in Bruges who later worked in England where he published the first etching known there.

In Italy Giacopo de' Barberi, Benedetto Montagna (1470–1540), and Giulio Campagnola developed a style in the tradition of Mantegna while Marcantonio Raimondi (c. 1480–c. 1534), from making prints after Dürer and Lucas van Leyden, went in 1510 to Rome where he commenced with others to execute reproduction engravings from the cartoons of Raphael. Thus by the mid-16th century —no more than a century after its inception—engraving became converted from an art of original expression into one of reproduction. In Antwerp Hieronymus Cock (c. 1510–70) engraved after Brueghel (c. 1525–69) and others and functioned also as a publisher. Exceptionally in France Jean Duvet (1485–c. 1561) was still making engravings in which the expression arose from the original cut of the tool and not, as with Hendrik Goltzius, the imitation of the quality of silk and satin. This means that the public of that time preferred the translation by an artisan of the work of a famous artist to prints created by lesser-known artists in the medium. By the 17th century, when the school of the engravers of Rubens (Vorsterman and the van Bolswerts) had followed the school of the engravers of Raphael, the conversion of the art of etching and engraving to reproduction was almost complete. A. Van Dyck (1599–1641) could be considered an exception but his means were those of the reproduction etchers.

In France a school of portrait engravers was developed by Jean Morin (d. 1650), Claude Mellan (1598–1688), Robert Nanteuil (1623/30–78)—the latter working from his own designs—and Antoine Masson (1636–1700). The first English engraver, William Faithorne the Elder (c. 1661–91), working in the tradition of Mellan and Nanteuil, showed less invention and virtuosity. From Prague Wenceslaus Hollar (1607–77) came to England where his popular images were well known. In France Jacques Callot (1592–1635) made the famous series of "Misères de la Guerre" by a very original method of etching, swelled line, while Claude Lorrain (1600–82) etched versions of his painting. Contemporary with these in Holland Rembrandt van Rijn (1606–69), probably the greatest of etchers, was working apparently without any great influence on these other artists. To see his work and that of the great original etchers and engravers in perspective, it must be realized that the operations of etching, engraving, mezzotint, and aquatint had been completely codified as methods of reproduction and were practised by great numbers of highly skilled artisans. Jacques Christophe Le Blon (1667–1741) by successive printing of plates in colour arrived at the most faithful reproduction of paintings, and in colour aquatint it became possible to do this with photographic precision. Against the thousands of such artisans, the work of Rembrandt, of Hercules Seghers (1589/90–c. 1638), Jacques Callot, Giambattista Piranesi (1720–78), F. Goya (1746–1828), and William Blake should be understood as exceptional and the modern revival of original printmaking stems from their example rather than from that of the majority of artisans.

BY COURTESY OF PIERRE COURTIN

"SANS TITRE" BY PIERRE COURTIN, 1956; PRINT FROM HOLLOWED-OUT PLATE IN INTAGLIO

Seghers may well have been attempting to make directly a sort of painting by the methods of etching. Working with grounds of his own invention that disintegrated slowly under the attack of the acids he printed in white and in colour on paper and on fabrics, although it is possible that certain prints may have been retouched with colour after printing. His example had no effect on his time; in fact, he seems to have been appreciated by no one except Rembrandt. Rembrandt, not only a great painter but possibly the greatest master of line, used the free stroke of the point with unequaled intensity; perhaps of less interest, however, were the tonal masses of drypoint carrying out the chiaroscuro of his painting. In Venice G. B. Tiepolo (1696–1770) and Canaletto (1697–1768) projected the matter of their paintings by means of etching, which was not entirely subject to the conventions of reproduction. Piranesi, in his youth, made the famous "Carceri" (prisons) series in which contradictory perspectives create a metaphysical dream space, which has influenced theatre decor to this day. The poet William Blake, trained, like William Hogarth (1697–1764), as a child in the mechanical craft of reproduction engraving, made several attempts to escape from his early conditioning. Unsuccessful in transforming the conventional operations of engraving and etching, he was led to reverse the process by drawing in bitumen on plates etched away to print in relief. Another of the exceptions, Charles Méryon (1821–68) in France, used the language of Rembrandt and Piranesi with brilliant effect to project his magnificent hallucinations. In England, although John Crome (1768–1821) and John Sell Cotman (1782–1842), using soft ground, and J. M. W. Turner (1775–1851), using lift ground, etched reproductions of their paintings, these were frequently completed as aquatints or mezzotints by artisans.

IV. LITHOGRAPHY

Lithography (stone writing) is a method of printing from the smooth surface of limestone, or a metal roughened so that it will hold water on which the image is defined by grease or wax that thus repels water. Lithography is one of the most faithful means of reproduction, printing directly from the touch of the artist. With no wear in printing, almost unlimited copies can be made.

1. Technique.—The stone is ground level and often grained with another stone with wet abrasive between the two stones. Drawing on the stone is then done with wax, grease crayon, or ink (tusche) which contains wax and soap to maintain it in suspension. White elements can be reserved with gum arabic painted on before drawing. Again drawings made with these materials on special paper may be transferred to the stone by pressure avoiding the inversion of the image in the print. The stone is then etched with a solution of gum containing a little nitric acid (other acids such as hydrochloric, acetic, phosphoric are sometimes used on metals) to free the pores of the stone. Washing with turpentine removes colour, soap, and wax from the trace. The stone is then wetted for each printing and a roller carries a sticky ink that adheres only to the worked part of the stone and is repelled by water. A sheet of paper is placed over the stone; the paper covered with blotters and a hard fibre tympan; the whole is then drawn under a yoke that applies pressure. Colour printing is done with a different stone or metal plate for each colour; registration being maintained either with holes as described above (under *Intaglio Printing*), or mechanically from the sheet edge with machine printing. The principle involved, sometimes described as the antipathy of oil for water, is more correctly a phenomenon of viscosity in which water repels ink that is accepted by wax. Machines for printing lithographs from stone or metal sheets were invented in the 1860s and rotary presses in the late 1890s. Prints produced by these means do not have the resources of quality and texture possible in hand prints made from the stone. Offset, in which the lithographic impression is printed onto rubber (offset blanket) on a roller, which then transfers this image to a paper sheet on a third roller, is a commercial process for printing from a lithographic plate at still higher speeds. Exceptionally it has been used for creative works where the plates to be printed in different colours are originated by the artist. It can be used only within the limits of texture and quality appropriate to the medium.

2. History of Lithography.—Although discovered in 1796 lithography was not used by artists for printmaking until the 1820s. In France Théodore Géricault (1791–1824) and Eugène Delacroix (1798–1863) were among the first practitioners but Honoré Daumier (1808–79) was by far the most prolific of them, making nearly 4,000 designs, ranging from newspaper caricatures to major prints. Paul Gavarni (1804–66) and other artists used lithography to illustrate periodicals in the late 19th century. Toward the 1870s Camille Corot (1796–1875), Edgar Degas (1834–1917), and Édouard Manet (1832–83) commenced to work on stone, and Odilon Redon (1840–1916) made it his principal means of expression. In the hands of Henri de Toulouse-Lautrec (1864–1901) colour lithography in the 1890s reached new heights and his example was enthusiastically followed by the Impressionists Paul Gauguin (1848–1903), Auguste Renoir (1841–1919), Pierre Bonnard (1867–1947), and Édouard Vuillard (1868–1940). The technique had been carried to the United States by German lithographers where it was used by Currier and Ives for the production of popular images. In Spain (and later in France) Goya made lithographs of great virtuosity, although his intaglio work in aquatint was more important. In England the formation of the Senefelder Club in 1909 provided facilities for Augustus John (1878–1961), William Rothenstein (1872–1945), and Charles Shannon (1863–1937). However, the greatest appreciation of lithography in the 1920s was among the German Expressionists such as Käthe Kollwitz (1867–1945), Edvard Munch, Franz Marc (1880–1916), Lovis Corinth (1858–1925), Max Slevogt (1868–1932), E. L. Kirchner, Emil Nolde (1867–1956), Ernst Barlach (1870–1938), Max Beckmann (1884–1950), Erich Heckel,

SELF-PORTRAIT LITHOGRAPH BY KÄTHE KOLLWITZ, DRAWN ON PAPER AND TRANSFERRED TO STONE

Oskar Kokoschka (1886–   ), Paul Klee (1879–1940), Lyonel Feininger (1871–1956), and George Grosz (1893–1959). In the U.S. Joseph Pennell (1857–1926), best known for his etchings, promoted lithography through the publication of his book *Lithography and Lithographers* in 1898. He was followed by George Bellows (1882–1925), Arthur B. Davies (1862–1928), Childe Hassam (1859–1935), Rockwell Kent (1882–1971), Max Kahn (1903–   ), Stow Wegenroth (1906–   ), Ben Shahn (1898–1969), Adolf Dehn (1895–1968), Francis Chapin (1899–   ), George Biddle (1885–   ), and John Sloan (1871–1951). The lithographic production of these years shows the concentration of American art of this time on illustration. In Mexico José Clemente Orozco (1883–1949), Diego Rivera (1886–1957), David Alfaro Siqueiros (1896–   ), and later Rufino Tamayo (1899–   ) showed a more vital image, while in England lithography has appealed to Henry Moore (1898–   ), Graham Sutherland (1903–   ), Ceri Richards (1903–   ), Edward Bawden (1903–   ), Edward Ardizzoni (1900–   ), and others. The greatest production of lithography in the 1950s was due to the efforts of dealers handling the works of the École de Paris to circulate colour prints with the aid of the printers Clot, Mourlot, Desjobert, and others. When authentic (and not reproductions) the colour prints of Wassily Kandinsky (1866–1944), Henri Matisse (1869–1954), Pablo Picasso (1881–   ), Joan Miró (1893–   ), Georges Rouault (1871–1958), Fernand Léger (1881–1955), Georges Braque (1882–1963), Marc Chagall (1887–   ), Hans Hartung (1904–   ), Pierre Soulages (1919–   ), Jean Bazaine (1904–   ), Jean Riopelle (1923–   ), and André Masson (1896–   ) are among the most important works of these artists. With the maturity of art in the United States most of the members of the School of New York, or of the Pacific, have made lithographs, as Willem de Kooning (1904–   ), Jackson Pollock (1912–56), Robert Motherwell (1915–   ), Alexander Calder, Saul Steinberg (1914–   ), and Sam Francis (1923–   ). Editions of between 50 and 300 signed copies were made to maintain a certain price per proof. Ambroise Vollard (1865–1939), Daniel Kahnweiler (1886–   ), and Aimé Maeght (1906–   ) are among the best-known publishers of original lithographs.

V. STENCIL PRINTING

1. Early Stencils.—Another very ancient technique in which ink is deposited neither from the relief nor intaglio is by means of stencils. Holes in a mask placed over a sheet permit colour to be deposited with short brushes or dabbers. It was definitely known in China as early as the 8th century and Eskimo in Baffin Island were making prints from stencils cut in sealskin before their contacts with the Western civilization.

2. Serigraphy.—One obvious disadvantage of the method is that although any open form can easily be cut in a stencil, a form enclosing another is impracticable as the middle drops out. This had been dealt with by using two overlapping half forms, but it is clear that if all parts of the stencil are held together with a web of threads greater freedom will result. A silk screen that permits colour to pass except where the screen has been stopped gives this freedom. A screen of silk, or in some cases fine wire, is stretched on a frame that may be hinged to a base to permit register. In one method those parts of the screen that are to be stopped are filled with glue; lines can be reserved in these parts by drawing with lithographic tusche or crayon, which can afterward be washed out of the glue with turpentine. Photographic transfers both in line and in halftone can also be applied to the screen

ENGRAVINGS

(Left) "Saint John the Evangelist on the Isle of Patmos" by the Master E. S. (active 1440–47). (Right) "The Holy Family" by Lucas van Leyden (1494–1533). (Bottom) "Battle of the Nudes" by Antonio Pollaiuolo (c. 1430–98)

 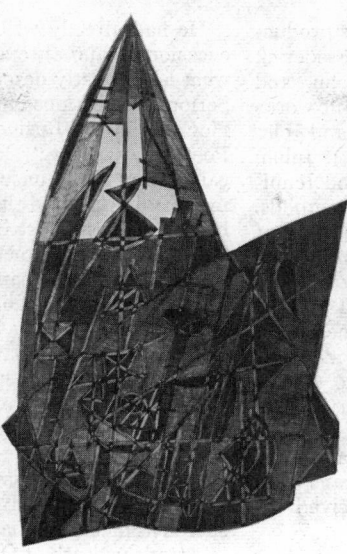 

BY COURTESY OF (TOP LEFT, ABOVE, BOTTOM RIGHT) S. W. HAYTER, (TOP CENTRE) LA HUNE GALERIE, PARIS, (BOTTOM LEFT) ANTHONY GROSS; PHOTOGRAPH, (BOTTOM LEFT) JOHN R. FREEMAN

MODERN INTAGLIO PRINTS

(Top left) "Le Petit Equilibriste" by Jacques Villon, 1914; etching and drypoint on copper. (Top centre) "Penhors Dalles, Sable et eau, No. 5" by Henri-Georges Adam, 1956–57; burin engraving on copper, plate cut away. (Top right) "Tropic of Cancer" by S. W. Hayter, 1949; engraving, soft-ground etching, deep bite on copper. (Bottom left) "Valley No. 2" by Anthony Gross, 1959; etching. (Bottom right) "Child Skipping" by Joan Miró, 1949; etching on copper, printed in relief

1911) that led to the enormous popularity of etching in England in the early 20th century. Inspired by certain Rembrandts, as the engravers of this time were returning to Schongauer and Dürer, and painters to pre-Raphael, they were followed by D. Y. Cameron (1865–1945), Muirhead Bone (1876–1953), William Strang (1859–1921), Frank Brangwyn (1867–1956), and Frank Short (1857–1945). Their work, and that of their followers, based upon Rembrandt, Piranesi, and Méryon, had enormous success up to the 1930s yet the matter of their expression, like that of J. Pennell, D. McLaughlin, and A. Heinzelmann in the United States, has a strange archaic look when it is considered that this was the time of Degas, Cézanne (1839–1906), and G. Seurat (1859–91), to say nothing of Jacques Villon (1875–1963), Picasso, and Matisse. The whole matter and concept of their work ignored the revolution in thinking, in man's concept of his world which had changed.

Contemporary with them and their successors—James McBey (1883–1959), Henry Rushbery (1889–), Gerald Brockhurst (1890–), Jacques Villon, Marcel Duchamp (1887–1968), and Joseph Hecht (1891–1951)—Paul Klee and Picasso, in closer touch with the thought of this time, were finding the graphic means to express it.

Following their example an international group (Atelier 17) was formed in Paris in 1927 by S. W. Hayter (1901–) to encourage experiment in new means of expression in printmaking arising from a different attitude to the operation. This was a new concept of the relation between idea and technique, or even a return to the attitude of the first engravers whose work was originated in the metal and developed by the consequence of action upon it and not a mechanical operation to reconstruct an actual or preconceived original. By extension, technique and expression were understood as interdependent and inseparable—the matter of idea developing through and by means of the operations upon the plate. Thus the final print is the only original, and constitutes an image which could have become visible by no other means. From the 1950s the work of members of this group teaching in the U.S., in Europe, Canada, South America, Australia, Japan, and India, as well as their stu-

as a light-sensitive film, which is exposed to light through a drawing or negative. Printing is done with a liquid ink that is forced through the open screen by the sharp rubber blade of a squeegee, which is drawn across its surface. As most of the inks used for this purpose are opaque the reproduction of gouache is almost perfect; however, transparent colours can be used, as can water-base colours through screens stopped with plastic. Mechanical means for printing from these screens have been devised and it has become a general method for printing on fabric, for posters, or other large surfaces where the number of impressions is not too great. Serigraphy, not only as prints, but on other supports as "multiples," has been enormously developed in France, in the United States, and in England by the Cinetists and artists following V. Vasarely (1908–), Le Parc (1928–), Demarco (1932–), and others; E. Paolozzi (1924–), Jim Dine (1935–), David Hockney (1937–), Bridget Riley (1931–), Peter Sedgely (1930–), and others in England; R. Rauschenberg (1925–), C. Oldenburg (1929–), Andy Warhol (1930–), R. Lichtenstein (1923–), and others in the U.S.

VI. MODERN PRINTMAKING

It was the example of James McNeill Whistler (1834–1903), Sir Francis Seymour Haden (1818–1910), and Alfonse Legros (1837–

dents and again their followers, has provoked an enormous production of original prints. Mauricio Lasansky (1914–), Frederick Becker (1917–), Karl Schrag (1912–), Misch Kohn, and Gabor Peterdi (1915–) have not only produced important works but have formed two generations of printmakers. In England John Buckland Wright (1898–1955), Anthony Gross (1905–), Julian Trevelyan (1910–), Michael Rothenstein (1908–), and Jennifer Dickson (1936–) have taught by experimental methods. Jurgen von Konow (1915–60) propagated modern methods of printmaking in Stockholm, and in France the work of Henri-Georges Adam (1904–68), Roger Vieillard (1907–), and Johnny Friedlaender (1912–) and his group, Pierre Courtin (1921–) with sculpted relief plates printed in intaglio, and Étienne Hajdu (1907–) using uninked embossed relief, have all had wide influence. In France and in the U.S. Sergio Gonzalez-Tornero (1927–), Enrique Zanartu (1921–), and Eugenio Tellez (1939–) have contributed new possibilities to printmaking; Japanese Juichi Saito (1932–), Matsutani (1937–), and Yozo Hamaguchi (1919–)—the latter with mezzotint in colour—have transposed the traditional image. In Japan many artists have revived the *Ukiyo-e* for expression in a modern idiom.

As prints by all these methods, partial reproductions, works done by methods of reproduction by the artist or an artisan, are offered by the same dealer, it is left to the discrimination of the buyer to distinguish between original major works from the artist's hand, minor works of interest only in the context of his work in other fields, and the various categories of reproduction. In the domain of communication by graphic and plastic means from the mid-1950s the Pop movement attempted a reevaluation of the banal image; the Optical or Cinetic group, using light and motion, tended to produce concrete reaction in the eye of the viewer; the Minimal and Environment approach aimed to change the condition of the space relation. In the 20th century an enormous production of prints has taken place with a great variety of techniques from new application of etching, engraving, woodcut, lithography, serigraphy, and photography to xerox or other means of printing from electronically deposited pigment. Clearly the employment of sophisticated photomechanical devices tends to favour ingenuity rather than transposition of idea, so many works of this type depend upon photomontage, "collage," layout, assemblage, and the ideas transmitted may be anything from metaphysical to pornographic. The methods, often borrowed from the arts of publicity, are in fact used by many artists recruited from this field. Printmaking has gone beyond the printed sheet to include indented pattern on metal sheets, progressions, permutations, constructions in folded paper or plastic assembled boxes, impressions on several sheets of transparent plastic, even in motion. It is then left to time and the public to distinguish between momentarily diverting decoration and device and those comparatively few works that can continue to provide solace and delight beyond one generation.

BIBLIOGRAPHY.—J. and E. R. Pennell, *Lithography and Lithographs* (1915); A. M. Hind, *Guide to the Processes and Schools of Engraving* (1933); C. Zigrosser, *The Book of Fine Prints* (1948); J. B. Wright, *Etching and Engraving* (1953); H. Curwen, *Processes of Graphic Reproduction in Printing* (1963); S. W. Hayter, *New Ways of Gravure*, 2nd ed. (1966); S. Jones, *Lithography for Artists* (1967); Museum of Graphic Art, *American Printmaking: the First 150 Years* (1969); W. M. Ivans, *How Prints Look* (1969); R. Marsh, *Silk Screen Printing for the Artist* (1969).   (S. W. HA.)

PRIOR, MATTHEW (1664–1721), English poet and diplomatist, was born in Wimborne, Dorset, July 21, 1664, the son of parents of modest station. His humble origin led to occasional difficulties in his diplomatic career, but did not prevent him from moving in distinguished company all his life. He was educated at Westminster School, where he made friends with Charles Montagu, later earl of Halifax. Both went on to Cambridge, and in 1687 collaborated in a piece of mockery directed at Dryden, *The Hind and the Panther Transvers'd to the Story of the Country Mouse and the Town Mouse*. In 1688 Prior's college, St. John's, elected him to a fellowship, which he retained until his death; but he soon entered diplomacy as secretary to the embassy at The Hague, Netherlands. In 1697 he was made secretary to the plenipotentiaries at the Peace of Rijswijk, and the next year he was transferred to Paris as secretary to the embassy.

He had already written a good deal of verse, both formal and occasional; and throughout his life he maintained his output of what he modestly described as "Public Panegyrics, Amorous Odes, Serious Reflections, and Idle Tales, the Product of his leisure Hours, who had Business enough upon his Hands—and was only a Poet by Accident." His lighter poems were marked by an ease, gaiety, and grace unsurpassed in English literature. It is for his mastery in this field that he will always be most admired, although he could at times strike a more sombre note with telling effect. Perhaps his masterpiece is the poem known as "Jinny the Just," which remained in manuscript until the 20th century.

In 1699 he returned from France and sat in Parliament in 1701 as member for East Grinstead, being also appointed a commissioner of trade and plantations. Soon after the accession of Queen Anne he transferred his support to the Tory Party, and became the trusted confidant of Harley (later earl of Oxford) and St. John (later Viscount Bolingbroke). When the Tories came to power in 1710 his diplomatic talents were again employed. He was concerned in the negotiations which led to the Peace of Utrecht; and from 1712 until 1714 he again resided at Paris, where he served as plenipotentiary.

After the death of Queen Anne he was recalled, and shared in the troubles which awaited the leading Tories; but despite rigorous examinations he refused to disclose the secrets of the fallen ministers who were his friends. During two years of mild confinement he wrote *Alma, or the Progress of the Mind,* a discursive and often subtle exercise in Hudibrastic metaphysics. In 1718 he published a stately folio of his collected poems, including *Alma* and his other long poem, *Solomon on the Vanity of the World,* a didactic work completed at least a decade earlier. He passed his last years mainly with Lord Oxford, by whose family and household he was greatly beloved. Oxford bought for him a small property in Essex, Down Hall, to which he grew much attached. But his health had never been robust; and he died at Oxford's seat, Wimpole in Cambridgeshire, on Sept. 18, 1721.

BIBLIOGRAPHY.—Editions include *The Writings of Matthew Prior,* ed. by A. R. Waller, 2 vol. (1905–07); *The Literary Works of Matthew Prior,* ed. by H. Bunker Wright and M. K. Spears, 2 vol. (1959). See also F. Bickley, *Life of Matthew Prior* (1914); L. G. Wickham Legg, *Matthew Prior: a Study of His Public Career and Correspondence* (1921); C. K. Eves, *Matthew Prior: Poet and Diplomatist* (1939).
(R. W. K.-C.)

PRIPET MARSHES: see POLESYE.

PRISCIAN (PRISCIANUS CAESARIENSIS) (fl. *c.* A.D. 500), the best-known of all the Latin grammarians, author of the *Institutiones grammaticae* which, together with the work of Aelius Donatus, had a profound influence on the teaching of Latin and indeed of grammar generally in Europe. He was born at Caesarea in Mauretania (the modern Cherchel in Algeria), but taught in Constantinople. His minor works include *De nomine, pronomine et verbo* ("On Noun, Pronoun and Verb"), an abridgment of part of the *Institutiones grammaticae; Partitiones xii versuum Aeneidos principalium* ("The Parsing of the First 12 Verses of the *Aeneid*"), for the teaching of grammar in schools; a treatise on weights and measures; a treatise on the metres of Terence; *Praeexercitamina,* an adaptation for Latin readers of some Greek rhetorical exercises; a panegyric in verse on the emperor Anastasius I (*see* E. Bährens, *Poetae Latini minores,* vol. v, 1883); and a verse translation of Dionysius' *Periegesis* (see the critical edition by P. van Woenstijne, 1953). Priscian's *Institutiones grammaticae* ("Grammatical Foundations") is a systematic exposition of Latin grammar. Of the 18 books into which it is divided, the first 16 deal mainly with sounds, word-formation and inflexions; the last 2 (which form nearly one-third of the whole work) with syntax. As far as possible Priscian takes the works of Apollonius Dyscolus on Greek grammar as his guide. He draws illustrative citations from many Latin authors and has thus preserved numerous fragments which would otherwise have been lost (for the text of the grammatical works *see* H. Keil, *Grammatici Latini,* vol. ii and iii, 1855–59).

Priscian's work was quoted by Aldhelm in the 7th century and by Bede and Alcuin in the 8th, and was much used by Rabanus Maurus and by Servatus Lupus of Ferrières in the 9th. Subsequently it became the standard work for the teaching of grammar in the medieval schools; and it provided the background for the rise of speculative grammar (the logic of language) in the 13th and 14th centuries. There are about 1,000 manuscripts extant. Of these, the greater part contain only books i–xvi (called *Priscianus major*); a few contain books xvii and xviii (*Priscianus minor*) and some of the minor works; and a few contain all 18 books of the *Institutiones*. Apart from fragments, the oldest manuscripts are of the 9th century. The first printed edition was that of 1470, at Venice.

BIBLIOGRAPHY.—J. E. Sandys, *History of Classical Scholarship,* vol. i, 3rd ed. (1921); A. Luscher, *De Prisciani studiis Graecis* (1912); R. W. Hunt, "Studies on Priscian in the Eleventh and Twelfth Centuries," *Mediaeval and Renaissance Studies,* vol. 1 and 2 (1943–50).

(R. H. Rs.)

PRISCILLIAN (*c.* 340–385), the first person in the history of the church to suffer death for heresy, was a Hispano-Roman champion of rigorous asceticism and founder of a party in the Spanish Church that persisted into the 6th century. Cultured and wealthy, he acquired a reputation for strictness of life and *c.* 375 began, as a layman, to propagate in and around Mérida and Córdoba a doctrine of absolute renunciation of all sense pleasures. Two bishops, Instantius and Salvian, and numerous other persons joined him and were guided by him, in a sort of secret society, in the search for higher perfection, condemning, *e.g.,* marriage and the use of wine and flesh meats. Before long such groups were found throughout western and southern Spain and in southern Gaul, and the whole Spanish Church was disturbed. The local hierarchy suspected that the new movement was Manichaean in character (*see* MANICHAEISM). Hyginus, bishop of Mérida, and Ithacius, bishop of Ossonoba, were its leading opponents.

The Council of Saragossa (380) condemned certain ideas attributed to Priscillian, who, nonetheless, was elected bishop of Ávila. The emperor Gratian was persuaded by Priscillian's enemies to decree the banishment of all "Manichaeans," whereupon Priscillian, Instantius and Salvian went to Italy, where Salvian died. They were not received by Pope Damasus I or by Ambrose of Milan, but they contrived the revocation of their banishment and were then able to force Ithacius to leave Spain. He went to Trier, seat of the pretorian prefecture in which Spain lay, and when in 383 the usurper Maximus made Trier his capital, Ithacius persuaded him to have Priscillian and Instantius tried. This was done in 384 by a synod at Bordeaux, and they were condemned. Priscillian appealed to Maximus; the latter had him taken to Trier, where, in the criminal courts, he was judged guilty of sorcery and immorality and was executed.

The fall of Maximus in 388 led to a reaction in favour of Priscillianism; Ithacius and some others who had opposed Priscillian were deposed and exiled. The Spanish Church continued to be divided, Galicia and the west being Priscillianist strongholds. In 400 and 447 councils at Toledo condemned certain of Priscillian's doctrines, and in 407–408 the emperor Honorius proscribed them, but the barbarian invasions prevented effective repression. In 561 the Council of Braga renewed the condemnation, and thereafter Priscillianism as an organized cult disappeared.

The question of Priscillian's orthodoxy has been much discussed. G. Schepps discovered and published (1889) 11 treatises which he assigned to Priscillian (though careful study convinced G. Morin in 1913 that their author was really Instantius) and which, though they do not clearly indicate whether the writer held Manichaean views, make plain his unorthodox doctrine of the Trinity, in which the Son differs from the Father only in name. The excitement aroused in Spain and Gaul and the vigorous opposition from outstanding contemporaries are inexplicable if Priscillian was merely an orthodox ascetic resented by worldly prelates.

See A. d'Alès, *Priscillien et l'Espagne chrétienne à la fin du IVe siècle* (1936); Stephen McKenna, *Paganism and Pagan Survivals in Spain up to the Fall of the Visigothic Kingdom,* pp. 50–74 (1938).

(A. G. Bi.)

PRISM, in geometry, a polyhedron (multifaced solid) having two of its faces, known as bases, congruent (identically equal) polygons in parallel planes, and the other faces parallelograms equal in number to the sides of the bases. The faces, excluding

each base, are called the lateral faces, and the intersections of these faces are called the lateral edges, being all equal. The perpendicular distance between the planes of the bases is called the height or altitude of the prism. If the lateral edges are perpendicular to the planes of the bases, the prism is called a right prism;

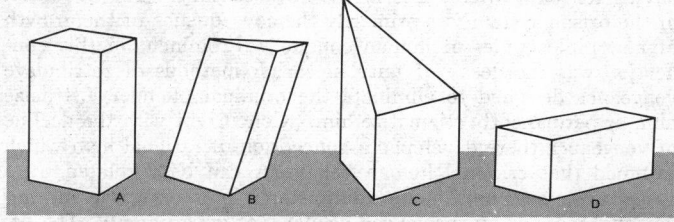

TYPES OF PRISMS: (A) RIGHT; (B) OBLIQUE TRIANGULAR; (C) TRUNCATED; (D) RECTANGULAR PARALLELEPIPED

if they are oblique to these planes, it is called an oblique prism. Prisms are said to be triangular, quadrangular, pentagonal and so on according as their bases are triangles, quadrilaterals, pentagons and so on. A prism having parallelograms for its bases is called a parallelepiped. If the bases and lateral faces are all rectangles, it is called a rectangular parallelepiped. The part of a prism included between the base and a section made by a plane oblique to the base is called a truncated prism.

A geometric solid that has for its bases two polygons in parallel planes, and for its lateral faces triangles or trapezoids (trapezia) with one side in one base and the opposite vertex or side in the other base, is called a prismoid, a prism being a special case. (In optics the word denotes a triangular prism.) The volume of a prism of base B and altitude a is aB; of a prismoid with bases B and B', altitude a and area of a mid-cross section M, is $\frac{1}{6}a(B + B' + 4M)$.

See BINOCULAR INSTRUMENT; CRYSTALLOGRAPHY; REFRACTOMETER; SOLIDS, GEOMETRIC; and references under "Prism" in the Index.

PRISMOID, a solid bounded by any number of planes, two of which are parallel and contain all the vertices. The two parallel faces are called the bases. The volume V of such a solid was found by the self-taught mathematician Thomas Simpson (1710–61) as follows: Let M be a section made by a plane parallel to the bases B and B' and midway between them, and let h be the distance between the bases. Then $V = \frac{1}{6}h(B + B' + 4M)$, a formula frequently used in finding volumes and applicable to most of the elementary geometric solids, and in general to any solid bounded by a ruled surface and two parallel planes. (P. Du V.)

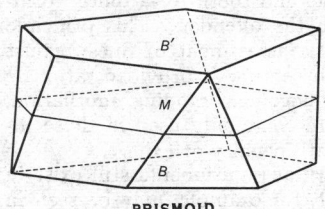

PRISMOID

PRISON. In the United States, where crime rates have long been among the highest observed in modern societies, there are well over 200,000 prisoners confined in more than 200 state and federal prisons and reformatories, with an annual increase in the prisoner population of approximately 4,500. The cost of constructing the required housing for this growing population approaches $45,000,000 per year. Current trends indicate that in the foreseeable future the number of prisoners and the related financial expenditures will continue to increase.

Two-thirds of the criminals committed to penal institutions in the U.S. have prior criminal records. Of all prisoners 98% are returned to civilian life after an average stay in most institutions of well under three years. Evidence from police, court, and parole files suggests that nearly half of the persons discharged from penal institutions return to careers in crime and in most cases within a year after release. Generally, the longer an offender has been confined in prison and the more times he has been committed, the higher the probability of his continued criminality.

The above findings have prompted many criminologists to reexamine the defects and virtues of the prison system in the search for more effective methods of crime control. Prisons, in other words, are now being subjected to the same critical scrutiny that earlier resulted in the substitution of imprisonment for previous methods of crime control.

Few persons realize that the prison system as it operates in nearly all parts of the world is largely an American development having its main origins late in the 18th century. The evolution of the prison system was primarily the consequence of the growth of new philosophies of human conduct. Prominent in this connection was the decay of faith in earlier methods of retributive vengeance designed to eliminate the criminal offender, ostracize him, or permanently stigmatize him. Concurrent with the decline of vengeance there developed a conception of rational man which assumed that criminal human behaviour can be regulated by a system of lesser punishments administered in an objective and impersonal manner by specialized agencies of government. The official punishments now used with greatest frequency are fines and various terms of imprisonment.

Just as expressions of vengeance against the offender have largely given way to a system of punitive confinement, so are current punitive practices gradually being minimized in favour of a new philosophy of therapy and rehabilitation. This shift in emphasis from vengeance to impartial punishment and then to therapy is the general principle that seems to have guided the development of the modern prison system.

MAJOR HISTORICAL DEVELOPMENTS

Prior to the 19th century, basic methods of crime control were designed to exclude the offender from the affairs of the community or to identify him publicly so that other persons could protect themselves in their dealings with him. Major devices used for these purposes were corporal punishment, disfigurement, exile, or execution of the offender. Decreasing use of these measures in the past few centuries is closely associated with the development of the prison system.

Forms of Crime Control.—*Corporal Punishment.*—Early Babylonian law developed the principle of *lex talionis* which asserted that criminals should receive as punishment precisely those injuries and damages they had inflicted upon their victims. Many societies applied the "eye-for-an-eye and tooth-for-a-tooth" principle quite literally in dealing with the offender. This principle still serves as a partial basis for the assessment of fines against minor offenders. Through the 18th century it provided rationale for the corporal punishments, *e.g.*, flogging, branding, mutilation, and the stock and pillory, that were commonly used in those instances that did not call for the death penalty or exile.

Some vestiges of extreme and brutal punishments still exist in some societies. The whipping post, for example, may be seen in the United States, in Delaware, although no floggings have been reported there since 1952. In Scotland, England, and Wales the public whipping of criminals is still prescribed by law, but was greatly limited by the Criminal Justice Act of 1948. Again, Delaware, as late as 1905, also used the pillory (*q.v.*), although England, France, and the U.S. federal government abolished its use before 1840.

Branding of criminals was fairly common in some Oriental societies within the past century and was not finally discontinued in England for army deserters until 1879. Similar penalties were also frequently administered in the American Colonies but were replaced before the American Revolution by badges, such as the "scarlet letter" of the adulteress, which law violators were required to wear. Nazi Germany in the 1940s used both a form of branding with tattoo marks and badges in its persecution of the Jews.

The public demand that physical injury be inflicted upon the criminal has by no means been eliminated and periodic attempts are still made to reinstitute various forms of corporal punishment, especially for juveniles and petty offenders. It nevertheless seems apparent that there has been a drastic reduction in the amount of confidence placed in such methods of retaliation against the criminal and that these devices of social control are progressively being abandoned in most civilized societies. One of the results of this trend has been an increased use of imprisonment.

Transportation.—Another traditional method of crime control now in disfavour in most countries is transportation, a punishment involving the removal of the offender from his own society to a distant penal colony or camp where he is engaged in forced labour. Exile, transportation, and banishment, like corporal punishment, have an ancient origin. They have been observed in certain preliterate societies, sometimes under conditions that made survival of the offender highly problematic. Early Greeks and Romans dispatched their criminals to mines and quarries or put them to sea as galley slaves. The employment of criminals in various kinds of forced labour continued in several countries until modern times. (*See also* DEPORTATION AND EXILE.)

A score of nations in Europe and Latin America transported their criminals to widely scattered penal colonies. However, penal colonies achieved their greatest development among the English, French, and Russians. England, for example, shipped criminals to America until the Revolution and to Australia into the middle of the 19th century. France established penal colonies in Africa, New Caledonia, and French Guiana. Some of the Guiana colonies, including the notorious Devil's Island, were still operating during World War II when they were abolished by the Free French government. The U.S.S.R. maintained penal colonies in Siberia for political criminals and certain other types of offenders. Though initially organized under the tsars, the Siberian colonies reached their greatest expansion from the Revolution through the Stalin era. Most governments have discontinued the large-scale transportation of criminals.

As long as penal colonies were operated at a great distance from the home country, there was relatively little public concern for the standards of health, decency, and welfare that prevailed in these communities of criminals. But the barrier of distance has been continuously reduced by modern communication facilities, making it increasingly difficult for urban industrial nations to maintain isolated colonies. Further, opposition to such colonies has been encouraged by the doctrines of democracy that have become more meaningful in many parts of the world. As a consequence most governments, instead of relying upon physical distance as a means for isolating their convicted criminals, find it advisable to create alternative techniques of crime control. Some of the alternatives used for segregating offenders or for supervising them in the community where their social productivity is usually at a maximum are provided by penal institutions and by the greatly increased use of probation and parole (*qq.v.*).

Capital Punishment.—The third major ancient form of crime control that has shown a steady decline is capital punishment. The execution of a criminal, which a century ago was not an uncommon public spectacle attended by much brutality and torture, has been abolished in many parts of Europe and South America. France (which rarely imposes it) and the United States remain among the chief Western powers that continue the use of the death penalty. Even so, a number of U.S. states have abolished this form of punishment. England, after a 1957 law greatly restricted imposition of the death penalty, abolished it in 1964. (*See also* CAPITAL PUNISHMENT.)

Certain other trends in the use of capital punishment suggest that it will continue to decline. Except for cases of treason and some infractions of military discipline, there has been a marked reduction in the number of offenses that call for the death penalty. In most jurisdictions it can be legally invoked for only a few of the most serious crimes such as murder, kidnapping, and forcible rape, and even in cases involving these offenses there has been a strong tendency toward the elimination of compulsory executions and toward making the punishment subject to the discretion of the court and the jury.

De-emphasis of capital punishment is further reflected in the many legal restrictions that generally prohibit the public from attending executions. Likewise, the earlier gruesome methods of capital punishment have in many places been replaced by less spectacular and comparatively painless methods, including the use of the gas chamber and electrocution.

The above trends mean that capital punishment is very rarely used in any modern society as a device for the control of tradi-

BY COURTESY OF THE ILLINOIS STATE PENITENTIARY

CIRCULAR CELL HOUSE ADAPTED FROM BENTHAM'S "PANOPTICON" AT STATEVILLE PRISON, JOLIET, ILL., PERMITS GUARDS IN THE CENTRAL TOWER TO KEEP WATCH ON EVERY CELL

tional crimes. Execution may be used for political purposes or for ideological reasons, as was the case in the deep South of the U.S. and in the attempted elimination of the Jews by Nazi Germany (*see* LYNCHING AND LYNCH LAW; GENOCIDE). But execution of the criminal has become the exception rather than the rule. In the U.S., for example, few, if any, capital offenders are executed each year although the number of such offenses reported exceeds 10,000. Thus, the abolition of the death penalty would have little effect upon the number of prisoners or the cost of maintaining the prison system.

Development of the Prison System.—Although the decline of ancient methods for handling criminals has no doubt been important, there are other more positive factors that have influenced the rise of the prison system. Some of these factors can be indicated by a brief review of the history of penal institutions in Western culture.

Jails were widely used in 12th-century England as places for the confinement of accused persons until their cases could be tried by the king's court. In 1166 Henry II commanded that every county should establish an institution for this purpose.

Imprisonment gradually came to be accepted not only as a device for holding persons awaiting trial but also as a means of punishing convicted criminals. During the 16th century a number of houses of correction were established in England and on the continent for the reform of minor offenders. In these institutions there was little segregation by age, sex, or other condition. The main emphasis was on strict discipline and hard labour. In England an act of 1711 fixed the maximum term of confinement at three years.

Among the best known of the houses of correction, the immediate forerunners of the prison, were London's Bridewell (*q.v.*) and the Ghent House of Correction, which were established in 1553 and 1775, respectively. Similar institutions were constructed in the American Colonies soon after their settlement.

Although reformation of offenders was intended in the houses of correction, the unsanitary conditions and lack of provisions for the welfare of the inmates soon produced widespread agitation for further changes in methods of handling criminals. Leading agitators included Montesquieu, Voltaire, Thomas Paine, Diderot, Adam Smith, Bentham, Sir Samuel Romilly, John Howard, and Elizabeth Fry. These leaders painstakingly exposed and publicized the conditions of filth and immorality that prevailed in the houses of correction which, they charged, instead of reforming their inmates, actually fostered crime and disease. For example, John Howard (*q.v.*) spent the years 1778–90 traveling throughout Europe in search of more effective correctional practices. He carefully chronicled his experiences and in this way educated the public with respect to the conditions he observed. Several of his observations had great impact upon subsequent developments in the field of correction. He was favourably impressed by the administration and the architecture of the Ghent House of Correction, and by the Papal Hospice of Saint Michael in Rome, an institution that cared for errant boys; founded in 1703 by Pope Clement XI, it may have been the first correctional institution to house inmates in solitary confinement. Both Ghent and Saint Michael segregated several classes of inmates, housed them in separate cells, and provided for their employment at hard labour.

Solitary Confinement.—Solitary confinement of criminals was especially appealing to the rationalists of the 18th century because they believed that solitude would help the offender to become penitent and that penitence would result in reformation. Thus in England in 1779 William Blackstone and William Eden sponsored a law providing for two penitentiaries that would house inmates in solitary confinement at night and congregate them during the day for hard labour. For various reasons this law was never implemented. About 20 years later plans were developed for the construction of a "panopticon" designed by Jeremy Bentham (*q.v.*). The panopticon, a circular, glass roofed, tanklike structure with cells along the external wall facing toward a central rotunda, made it possible for officers stationed in the rotunda to keep all of the inmates under constant surveillance. Although Bentham's novel idea was not incorporated in the plans for penal institutions built at that time, its design had some influence on future construction. For example, a prison incorporating the essential features of Bentham's plan for the panopticon was erected in the United States at Stateville, near Joliet, Ill., nearly 150 years later.

The next important steps in the evolution of prisons occurred in the United States. Pennsylvania's constitution of 1776 embodied certain principles that had been enunciated by William Penn and the Quakers a century earlier. Fines and imprisonment became the major forms of punishment for nearly all offenses, felonies as well as misdemeanours. By 1794 murder remained the state's only capital offense. At about that time, Walnut Street Jail in Philadelphia was converted to become the first state penitentiary; a small number of cells were added to house the most serious offenders and prisoners were segregated by sex and the severity of their offenses. Furthermore, debtors and witnesses were separated from convicted criminals. Hard labour was stressed as a reformative measure, except for the most serious offenders who were kept in complete isolation.

Separate System.—Solitary confinement received far greater emphasis when Eastern State Penitentiary, an institution especially designed for the separate confinement of prisoners, was opened on Cherry Hill in Philadelphia in 1829. Seven blocks of cells radiated like the spokes of a wheel from a central rotunda. The cells were 16 ft. high, nearly 12 ft. long, and 7½ ft. wide. Attached to each cell was an exercise yard, completely enclosed to prevent contact among the prisoners. The prisoner remained in his cell or his yard and saw no one except the officers of the institution and an occasional visitor from outside. Initially, it was planned that the prisoners would have no employment, but this was modified because of the disastrous experience with inmate idleness at Western State Penitentiary, opened three years earlier at Pittsburgh. Under the new plan materials were brought to the cell where the prisoner worked alone at trades such as weaving, tailoring, carpentry, or shoemaking.

This method of prison management, known as the "separate system," became a model for penal institutions constructed in several other states and in various parts of the world. Through much of the 19th century the separate system remained the dominant philosophy of prison management in much of Europe.

Silent System.—Meanwhile, strenuous opposition to the prolonged isolation of prisoners developed very early, especially in the U.S. Even before Eastern State Penitentiary was placed in operation, its critics had been successful in formulating a competing philosophy of prison management, known as the "silent system." A model prison was constructed at Auburn in New York to implement the various features of the new system, which was instituted by 1825. Cells in Auburn Prison were very small compared with those at Eastern State, measuring only 7 ft. long and 3½ ft. wide. Two rows of cells were placed back to back along the center of a long and narrow cellblock, each row being separated from the exterior wall of the building by a corridor used for traffic. Light and air entered through small windows in the cell doors and in the exterior walls of the cellblock.

The main distinguishing feature of the silent system was that prisoners were allowed to work together in the daytime. Silence was strictly enforced at all times, however, and at night the prisoners were confined in individual cells. To and from their workshops the prisoners were required to walk in line and do the lockstep, a slow and rhythmic shuffle in which each person placed one hand on the shoulder of the man in front of him.

Vigorous competition between supporters of the silent system and of the separate system prevailed until about 1850, but by that time the Auburn plan had been victorious in most U.S. states. During this period new developments in Europe and elsewhere were beginning to produce fundamental revisions in both U.S. systems.

Mark System.—The mark system was developed about 1840 by Captain Alexander Maconochie at Norfolk Island, an English penal colony located east of Australia. Instead of serving fixed sentences, prisoners there were required to earn marks or credits proportional to the seriousness of their offenses. Credits were accumulated through good conduct, hard work, and study, and could be denied or subtracted for indolence or misbehaviour. When a prisoner obtained the required number of credits he became eligible for release.

The mark system symbolized the decline of the "let the punishment fit the crime" theory of correction and presaged the use of indeterminate sentences, individualized treatment, and parole. Above all it emphasized training and performance, rather than solitude, as the chief mechanisms of reformation.

Irish System.—Further refinements in the mark system were developed in the middle 1800s by Sir Walter Crofton, director of Irish prisons. Irish inmates progressed through three stages of confinement before they were returned to civilian life. The first portion of the sentence was served in isolation. Then the prisoners were allowed to associate with other inmates in various kinds of work projects. Finally, for six months or more before release, the prisoners were transferred to "intermediate prisons," small portable institutions where inmates were supervised by unarmed guards and given sufficient freedom and responsibility to permit them to demonstrate their fitness for release. In addition, release was conditional upon the continued good conduct of the offender, who could be returned to prison if this seemed advisable.

Reformatory Movement.—*United States.*—Many features of the Irish system were adopted by reformatories constructed in the U.S. in the late 19th century for the treatment of youthful and first offenders. Among the leaders of the reformatory movement was Zebulon Brockway, first superintendent of New York's Elmira Reformatory, opened in 1876. Brockway and his associates advocated classification and segregation of various types of prisoners, individualized treatment emphasizing vocational training and industrial employment, indeterminate sentences and rewards for good behaviour, and parole or conditional release. The reformatory philosophy gradually permeated the entire U.S. prison

system. By the turn of the century isolation and solitary confinement were used primarily as disciplinary actions against recalcitrant prisoners instead of being justified as effecting penitence and reformation.

Europe.—The Irish system and the U.S. innovations had great impact upon European correctional practices. England's famous Borstal System (*q.v.*), for example, was established in 1908 by Evelyn Ruggles-Brise, director of English prisons, after he had studied several U.S. reformatories. The Borstal System is comprised of a variety of institutions, each providing a specified degree of custodial supervision and specializing in a certain kind of training and treatment for young offenders. Individualized treatment also is provided in the period immediately following release. The chief objective is no longer to punish the offender but to develop his capacity to assume full responsibility for his conduct. The use of recreational, employment, and educational resources and facilities in the outside community is an essential feature of the Borstal System (*see* also REFORMATORY).

Trends.—Correctional institutions in a little more than 150 years have almost completely rejected the doctrine of solitude and penitence. Contemporary penal institutions, however, are not guided by any uniform philosophy. Correctional programs in nearly all parts of the world evidence a significant trend toward specialization, diversification, and experimentation. Rapid changes in the design and construction of correctional facilities in their treatment programs and even in their major objectives make it difficult to describe modern institutions in general terms or to anticipate future developments. Certain practices and tendencies may nevertheless be cited as important departures from penal tradition.

Probation and Parole.—Considerable effort, for example, is aimed at the rehabilitation of prisoners and at minimizing their numbers. Minor offenders are sometimes allowed to pay fines in installments, or to serve jail sentences at night or on weekends. The expanding use of probation and parole (*qq.v.*) as rehabilitative procedures also tends to hold down the numbers of inmates in institutions. Other programs include the use of residential community centres, or halfway houses, preceding parole; granting brief leaves, or furloughs, in emergencies or for preparations for release; and work release for private employment or vocational training in the community: in the U.S. these were authorized by the federal Prisoner Rehabilitation act of 1965.

Specialized Treatment.—A second important trend is the substitution of individualized treatment for the earlier doctrine of equal punishments for equal crimes. Indeterminate sentences and segregation of offenders according to their backgrounds and personality characteristics are prevalent in nearly all countries.

ASSOCIATED NEWSPAPERS GROUP, LTD.

A CELL FOR WOMEN PRISONERS IN HOLLOWAY PRISON, ENGLAND, IN THE EARLY 1970S, REFLECTING A TREND TOWARD UPGRADING PRISON CONDITIONS

More reliable methods of diagnosis and classification, largely based on advancements in social and medical sciences, frequently make it feasible to prescribe special treatment relevant to the needs of the individual offender. Increasingly, specialized treatment includes professional counseling and psychotherapy, and various forms of medical care, as well as the more conventional literacy programs and academic and vocational training. The acceptance and use of such treatment programs indicate that social work, psychiatry, and the behavioural sciences will have much greater impact upon the field of correction than they have had in the past.

Specialized treatment programs encourage the diversification of correctional institutions. Ideally, this means each institution should maintain programs specifically designed for certain types of offenders. Some diversification has long been practised, as reflected in the conventional separation of offenders by age and sex. However, current trends are reflected in the establishment of separate institutions for various categories of offenders, such as drug addicts, alcoholics, sex psychopaths, and criminals who are mentally ill. Such diversification is characteristic of the U.S. Federal Bureau of Prisons and the correctional facilities of the state of California. The Scandinavian countries also operate a number of prison hospitals where selected sex offenders may be either castrated or given hormonal treatment. Again, nearly all prison systems provide special facilities for inmates who need either maximal or minimal custodial supervision. Treatment programs in "escape-proof" penitentiaries that house dangerous criminals and habitual offenders (*q.v.*) are vastly different from those in minimum custody farms and camps. Most of the newer facilities have been penal farms, forest camps, and small cottage-style institutions designed to provide individualized treatment for offenders who do not require a high degree of custodial control.

Social Rehabilitation.—The third major trend in prison administration involves an attempt to reduce the social barrier between inmates of the correctional institution and the civilian community. Programs widely used to encourage social participation among inmates and members of their families or groups of citizens who are particularly interested in the field of correction include more liberal policies governing visits, letter-writing privileges, and self-improvement classes. Debating societies, study and discussion groups, and therapeutic agencies such as Alcoholics Anonymous have regular contacts with prison inmates. Sweden and several other European countries have instituted frequent furloughs for home visits and sometimes have provided outside employment for selected prisoners. Soviet Russia has allowed certain offenders to settle with their families in industrial colonies largely populated by convicted criminals. Mexico, Russia, and several other countries have permitted conjugal visits in some of their prisons, a practice intended to alleviate the sexual problem that is universally present in penal institutions.

In addition, other programs are aimed at increasing public interest and participation in prison management. England, for instance, has developed a system of official visits that brings citizens into the institution to assist in the resocialization of the offender and to insure public acceptance of the institution's programs and policies. Similarly, advisory councils of private citizens are widely used for the same purposes in the United States and elsewhere. These councils can provide some of the technical and professional assistance necessary for maintaining adequate standards in prison educational and vocational training programs, industrial operations, recreation, and religious instruction. They also serve as effective instruments for public education regarding prison problems and issues. These developments indicate a growing recognition of the important role played by the civilian community in the rehabilitation of the prison inmate.

Group Therapy in the Prison Community.—A fourth trend is the increasing interest in the possibility that the society formed by the prisoners can be utilized for therapeutic purposes. In the final analysis, the social organization of the prisoners, the prison milieu, may have greater impact upon inmate attitudes and activities than do the various programs previously mentioned. Improved diagnosis and extensive use of small institutions have encouraged the assignment to the inmates themselves of responsi-

bility for their own welfare. Group therapy, it is held, may offer a mechanism by which selected prisoners can be trained to make decisions and accept responsibility for their own conduct.

As practised in the U.S. at Highfields in New Jersey and in the prisons of California, group therapy involves some important differences from the system of inmate self-government that was tried unsuccessfully by Thomas Mott Osborne at Auburn Prison in 1913. It is held that group therapy may give inmates an opportunity to participate more actively in some of the routine affairs of the official prison community instead of being merely passive recipients of rules and regulations. It is believed this may help to develop a greater sense of social responsibility among some of the prisoners. Strict limits are nevertheless placed on the scope of inmate responsibility, and group therapy in no way restricts the authority or responsibility of prison officials. While the preliminary results have appeared to be very promising, the long-run effectiveness of group therapy cannot yet be clearly ascertained.

Professional Personnel.—Finally, the fifth significant trend in correction is the development of prison employment as a career service. Merit systems and civil service have been established in many parts of the United States and in much of Europe. Professional training is required of many prison employees, especially in programs of inmate classification, education, medical care, and therapy. Specialized courses of training are offered by an increasing number of colleges and universities. Criminology (*q.v.*) has for some time been regarded as a specialty within the disciplines of sociology, psychology, or social work, and the University of California has instituted a fully accredited Graduate School of Criminology.

The trend toward professionalization of correctional occupations is still in its infancy, however. As of the 1960s, for example, only a dozen of the U.S. states employed full-time psychiatrists in their prisons and reformatories; and of the total number employed, nearly half were attached to the prison system of the state of California. In other words, there were nearly 6,000 prisoners for every psychiatrist employed in U.S. penal institutions. Further, fewer than 500 social workers and sociologists were employed by state institutions, making an average case load of about 380 prisoners per employee in this essential service. It seems clear that a considerable increase in the number of professional workers is required if the efficacy of techniques of prison therapy is to be established and the achievement of the objectives of such therapy attained. The fact remains that the personnel having the most intimate day-to-day contact with the prisoners, the guards in most prisons, are appointed through the political spoils system rather than through civil service.

An Emerging Philosophy.—The above cursory review of modern correctional history suggests that beliefs concerning the causes of crime and the best methods of crime control are being revolutionized for the third time within the past few centuries. In the late 18th and early 19th centuries the philosophy of rational man resulted in the substitution of imprisonment for the earlier methods of corporal punishment. Then the late 19th and early 20th centuries saw a decline in rationalism and the development of individualized treatment programs based on the assumption that criminals suffered from major mental, emotional, or social deficiencies and emphasizing education, casework, and psychiatry.

Again, an accumulation of evidence contradicted the dominant philosophy of the time: the number of crimes increased at an alarming rate; studies of the effects of individualized treatment were frequently discouraging; law violations came to be recognized as group or gang activities rather than solitary deeds; many law violators revealed few signs of the expected personal inadequacy. It was perhaps inevitable that another new conception of crime and its treatment should come into prominence.

There is some rather convincing evidence that society is in the early stages of a third major revolution in its beliefs concerning crime and correction. The chief feature of the rising philosophy is the idea that society is the patient in need of corrective action if crime control is to become a reality. Various kinds of unconventional behaviour are sometimes richly rewarded. Wealth, power, and prestige are frequently highly regarded irrespective of the means by which they may have been attained. Political corruption and white-collar crime are too often viewed as unavoidable nuisances (see CRIME). Respected and influential citizens may be favourably disposed toward illegitimate activities provided there are sufficient material benefits and good prospects for escaping detection or censure. These are some aspects of crime and deviant behaviour that have recently attracted the systematic attention of correctional experts.

Current explanations of criminal behaviour tend to place more emphasis on the compelling pressures exerted upon any given person by others in his community and the social groups to which he belongs. These pressures reflect a culture that prescribes his goals and his standards of conduct and a society that regulates the various means and mechanisms that are accessible to him in his efforts to achieve his objectives. This does not deny individual differences or a sense of personal responsibility, but it does assert that a given person's behaviour cannot be realistically analyzed or evaluated without taking into account his social and cultural milieu.

This rising philosophy has some important implications for prisons and correctional programs. It maintains that treatment and therapy cannot be foisted upon resistive and suspicious prisoners. Treatment is a dynamic process that requires the cooperation and active participation of the offender if it is to be successful. Therefore the main objective of the prison should be to get the inmates to participate actively in a smoothly functioning organized society, perhaps at first in the prison setting, and then later in the broader community. This, in fact, would seem to be one of the main functions of the correctional program. Illustrations of its application include group therapy as it is practised in prisons and in the supervision of probationers and parolees, milieu therapy in small institutions, inmate advisory councils, home visits, and prisoner furloughs. These approaches are supported by Alcoholics Anonymous and other organizations that appeal to large numbers of former prisoners; halfway houses that help diminish the abrupt shift from prison existence to life in the free community; and the use of citizens' advisory councils and committees in the management of prison programs. All these devices are designed to reduce barriers between the prison and civilian communities and to increase social interaction between inmates and others.

Despite the new attitudes toward crime and correction, the beliefs of the past two centuries have by no means been eliminated. Indeed the most striking characteristic of the typical prisons of today is that they tend to serve as the scene of conflict among the three more or less distinctive philosophies mentioned above. This is the problem to which we now turn.

PRISON ADMINISTRATION AND THE ORGANIZATION OF THE PRISON COMMUNITY

Prison officials carry a public trust. Their duties and responsibilities are defined by the community in terms of conventional beliefs and attitudes. If their policies and objectives deviate very far from those of the broader society, correctional officials encounter serious public opposition. An essential task for the correctional administrator is the assessment of public opinion. To the extent that public beliefs and attitudes are confused or contradictory, it may be expected that prison programs and policies will reflect these discrepancies.

Objectives.—The foremost objective of prison administration is the maintenance of control over the inmates and the prevention of escapes and riots. The most grievous difficulty the prison administrator is likely to face is the breakdown of official authority due to inmate uprising or conspiracy. Other objectives such as therapy, deterrence against potential offenders, and the reinforcement of cultural norms or standards are generally relegated to positions of less importance. Furthermore, the great interest in custodial problems such as escapes and riots means that even those institutions that are oriented toward the treatment of the offender are likely to evaluate their programs in terms of the frequency of custodial incidents. Regardless of the verbal support given to therapy and related functions by correctional administrators, it

is clear that public evaluations of prison administration are still largely determined by matters dealing primarily with custody.

Not only the objectives of correctional institutions but also the policies aimed at their attainment are greatly influenced by conventional beliefs and assumptions. Here again there is conflict between the old and new philosophies. Crime is usually interpreted as deliberate misconduct and prisoners consequently are expected to be belligerent and unruly if they can get away with it. Strict surveillance and punitive actions are generally deemed necessary to show the prisoner that society is stronger than he is, serve as a lesson for potential troublemakers, and promote respect for law and order. It is maintained that prisons should have police powers sufficient to detect and to punish any violations of rules and regulations. Treatment is commonly viewed as the inculcation of useful habits, such as thriftiness and industriousness, and the acquisition of social and occupational skills. Moreover, prison officials are held solely accountable for the attainment of correctional objectives while, according to the usual public view, the inmates are pretty much absolved of any responsibilities.

Maxims such as those mentioned are deeply rooted in contemporary culture. They rationalize and give direction to prison programs and policies and serve as the basic operating assumptions for most prison programs. They also inevitably reflect some of the discrepancies that are inherent in conventional beliefs concerning crime and correction. These maxims hold penal officials responsible for the conduct of their prisoners, for example, while at the same time they encourage the expectation that the prisoners will learn self-reliance and a sense of responsibility. Again, the maxims claim that prisoners are sure to display disobedience, but at the same time they hold officials to be in error if the inmates exhibit nonconformity to prison rules and regulations. Similarly, prisoners may be viewed as sick persons in need of therapy, but it is also demanded that therapy should not interfere with strict surveillance and the maintenance of custodial security. These are some of the dilemmas that confront the prison administrator.

There are some correctional institutions, to be sure, that operate under very different assumptions. In a few institutions inmates are held largely responsible for their own welfare, and attempts are increasingly being made to create a prison milieu in which the expectation of inmate responsibility is the rule rather than the exception. However, these institutions and programs seem to gain widespread public support only if there is firm assurance that more conventional methods of control will be made available for bellicose or belligerent offenders. Consequently, the more advanced methods of treatment tend to be applied chiefly to those inmates who have least need for them. In summary, it seems clear that a systematic and convincing rationale for the use of modern therapy techniques has not yet made its way very effectively into the field of correction. Conflicts between the objectives of therapy and of punitive custody are readily apparent in most penal institutions.

Official Organization.—The official organization of the prison is superimposed upon the goals and operating assumptions mentioned above. At the head of each institution is a warden or superintendent who is in most cases responsible directly to a top-level governmental official. Under the superintendent are division chiefs who manage the programs of custody, classification and treatment, business and budget affairs, industries, and medical care. A separate hierarchy of subordinate officials works under the direction of each of the division chiefs. The custodial staff, for instance, usually includes an assistant superintendent who is generally responsible for the security of the institution, a captain or two, a few lieutenants, a greater number of sergeants, and the guards or custodial officers who comprise the largest segment of the official personnel. Officers of the lowest rank have the greatest amount of contact with the prisoners. They have direct responsibility for enforcing the rules and regulations and otherwise carrying out the policies announced by the head of the institution and his administrative assistants.

Unilateral Authority.—Most prisons operate under a military-style system of authority and communication. Each officer in the staff hierarchy has specified duties and responsibilities and is linked to officers of higher and lower rank through a chain of command and a predetermined channel of communication. At each level in the hierarchy, the officers receive orders from the next higher rank and are held responsible for the performance of the officials in the next lower rank. Thus, everyday observations of inmate behaviour are reported from the lower levels of command up the ladder to the top level. Here the numerous reports are collated and official decisions are made. Then directives and supportive information flow back down the steps of the staff hierarchy from division chief to crew supervisors and to officer or guard. In the typical unilateral sequence of communication and authority, as a consequence, reports of a factual nature move upward in the chain of command, whereas administrative orders and interpretations of factual materials move down the ranks of employees.

Despite its clear logic, however, the unilateral system of authority and communication may have some serious weaknesses. This is especially true in correctional institutions where many discretionary judgments are almost inevitably made by low-ranking officers who have direct contact with the inmates, where different members of the official staff may have varied and sometimes contradictory motives and objectives, and where the society of prisoners is at odds with official policy on some crucial matters.

One problem is that many policy decisions are made by administrators who are far removed from the scene of direct and daily contact with the prisoners where the worthiness of alternative programs and policies can perhaps best be observed. Persons in high authority, dependent as they are upon the reports of lower officers, are sometimes the last to learn about the effects of their decisions. Furthermore, feedback or criticism of top-level decisions is frequently minimized. In many institutions no official procedure for such reverse flow of communication is provided. As a result, the unilateral system of communication and authority may tend to produce a considerable barrier between the officer's world of everyday experience and the picture of that world as it is seen by top-level administrators.

Administrative Communications.—The prison's administrative organization may also tend to create some questions concerning the accuracy and completeness of reports as they move up and down the ranks. For example, the judgments of administrators may be influenced by the distortions of fact likely to occur when reports are repeatedly reviewed and evaluated as they move upward through the ranks of employees. Likewise, administrative directives are inclined to lose some of their content and effectiveness as they are passed down through the ranks. Explanations and elaborations are apt to be deleted from administrative communications as they are passed from higher to lower levels. By the time the directives reach the officers in the lowest rank they are likely to be expressed as bald and unqualified commands. As a result, administrative directives are frequently interpreted in comments and discussions that occur outside the official channels of communication. Thus, the unofficial versions of directives may determine how most officers respond to them. If this is the case, the unilateral organization of the prison, instead of eliminating the influence of hearsay and rumour, may make unofficial messages an essential part of the officer's conception of prison policy.

For many officers in the lower ranks, allegiance to administrative policies may be less important than participation in the unofficial exchange of rumours and messages within the prison community. Lower officers frequently have very little knowledge of the institution's administrative program except for the specific rules and regulations they are expected to enforce. In many cases these officers have no more influence upon the formulation of policies than do the inmates. This lack of information and influence means that officers in the lower ranks are inclined to lose interest in the official program and eventually become alienated from the administration of the institution.

Alienation and disinterest among lower officers encourage departures from administrative policies, criticisms of higher authorities, and fraternization with the inmates. The result that has repeatedly been observed is collusion between certain staff members and inmates in informal but highly standardized procedures for circumventing administrative procedures and regulations. Where such collusion occurs, the effect of prison experience is to give inmates practice in methods of deceit and nonconformity. This is one of the main reasons why prisons have often been called crime schools. It would appear that the unilateral organization that is so characteristic of penal institutions may place severe restrictions upon the possibilities of treatment and may provide an even greater barrier against prisoner rehabilitation than the bars and walls that attract such adverse comment from correctional authorities.

Inmate Organization.—*Prisoner's Code.*—The problems related to administrative policy are not alone responsible for the difficulties encountered in the rehabilitation of prisoners. Prisoners, too, have a code of conduct, and in many instances it calls for behaviour that is directly opposed to the official rules and regulations. The prisoner's code reveals little interest in problems of prison management or programs of therapy. These, prisoners agree, are the responsibility of prison officials, while the main concern of the prisoner is immediate gratification of inmate desires and objectives.

The foremost objective of most inmates is to get out of prison at the earliest possible time. The inmate who views imprisonment as a safe and pleasant substitute for civilian life is rarely found. The basic question is how to get out of prison, and a few prisoners are so intent upon escape that they are willing to assault and if necessary murder anyone who stands in their way. More of them, however, prefer less violent methods, such as digging tunnels under the walls, sawing the bars of their cells, or secreting themselves in prison vehicles that have access to the world outside. But the vast majority of prisoners confine themselves to more legitimate methods for obtaining release. Some prepare writ after writ in an attempt to find technical errors in the indictment, the trial, or the sentence that sent them to prison. Others may work hard, attend school, and participate in treatment programs in an effort to attract favourable attention. The value attached to release from prison is so great, however, that the greatest violation of the prisoner's code is to interfere with another inmate's attempt to gain freedom by any means.

Inmate Society.—Next to getting out of prison, the inmates are interested in good food, comfortable quarters, adequate clothing, a pleasant and interesting or easy work assignment, and recreation and entertainment. Comfort, variety, and individual recognition are as important in the prison community as in the world outside, and, if anything, are enhanced by the restrictions placed upon personal liberty. Most prisoners try to express their individuality by a variety of innovations in the style of their dress, their haircut, or the manner of their speech or conduct. Even more important is the fact that a considerable number of prisoners have deviant habits and unconventional desires that are by no means discouraged by the society of prisoners: the alcoholics are in constant search of intoxicants, and if whiskey cannot be smuggled into the institution, are willing to use antifreeze solution, hair dressing, and numerous other substitutes; the drug addicts make every effort to obtain narcotics; and sex deviants may use force against unwilling partners or sell themselves as male prostitutes. Strong inmates frequently intimidate weak ones, and opportunities abound in most prisons for the enterprising thief, robber, or confidence man. The mere fact of imprisonment does not discourage the inmates from trying to satisfy their illegitimate desires.

Role and Status Assignments.—The prisoner's code is designed to protect the various sub-rosa activities found in most prisons. One means of protection is the informal classification system that helps the inmates make appropriate assignments of prisoner roles and statuses. Prisoners loyal to the official administration must be prevented from becoming involved in confidential inmate activities, while those interested in illicit affairs need to be identified and guided into the social cliques and organizations where their activities are not likely to be discovered.

The process of role assignment commonly proceeds in a standardized fashion within the society of prisoners. Newly committed prisoners are first carefully questioned by inmate leaders to see if their loyalties are directed toward the officials or toward their fellow prisoners. Then the new inmate's knowledge of prisoner society and his skill in handling difficult situations are carefully examined. Finally, the new recruit is confronted by a number of contrived problems that are designed to prove his consistency, reliability, and devotion to the code of the inmates. If he passes these tests, the new inmate is tentatively accepted as a member of the prison community. Within six months or so after he arrives in prison, the new inmate's major roles and statuses are ordinarily pretty well established by his fellow prisoners. His access to different segments of prison society is regulated accordingly.

In addition to exercising great care in the assignment of roles and statuses, inmate society sets up expectations of mutual care and protection among the prisoners. Inmates engaged in any illegitimate enterprise, in order to maintain a climate favourable for its continuation, are expected to support and protect various other forbidden activities. This expectation, of course, contradicts the official rule that inmates are supposed to "do their own time" and avoid involvements with other prisoners. In any case, the expectation of reciprocal loyalties and mutual protection encourages prisoner morale and unites a large number of the prisoners in the pursuit of illicit objectives in the face of persistent staff opposition. The informal rule prohibiting any inmate from acting in a manner that might interfere with the illegitimate activities of others is the second major commandment in the prisoner's code of conduct.

The system of reciprocal loyalties among the inmates, however, is as vulnerable to important sources of outside interference as the official system of unilateral communication and authority. Deviations from the system are as much the rule as the exception. One problem is that inmates striving for power and higher status within the society of prisoners are frequently willing to violate the code. Again, the system is far more vulnerable than the prisoners would care to admit. Officials have easy access to inmate informers who divulge privileged information in return for various rewards that can be granted by the administration. In these cases the secrecy of the reciprocities system actually serves to protect the informers. Finally, many of the inmates are antagonistic toward the society of prisoners. They feel an allegiance to the officials and wish to take their punishment so that they can return promptly to civilian life. All of these factors reduce the efficiency with which the prisoner's code can operate in opposition to administrative policy.

The result is that neither the administrative system nor the society of prisoners can long retain dominance in the prison community. Although the integrity of the two systems may be maintained on the surface, symbiotic relationships between officers and inmates develop in such a way that the behaviour of each in almost any given instance is determined by intersecting influences that cannot be realistically accredited to either system.

Unsolved Problem.—The above discussion indicates why correctional officials are increasingly concerned with the prison milieu as a therapeutic agency. Treatment is not likely to be successful as long as there are significant contradictions between administrative policies and the prisoners' norms of conduct. How to minimize these contradictions is perhaps the greatest unsolved problem in contemporary correction.

Some important initial steps are being taken in this regard. Group therapy and other devices for increasing inmate participation in the routine affairs of prison management are designed to reduce the barrier between the society of prisoners and the dictates of administrative policy. The same general objective is sought by increased use of smaller institutions, reductions in the degree of custodial supervision, prisoner furloughs and home visits, employment of prisoners in the civilian community, and intensive parole supervision after the offender has been released from prison.

Perhaps even more important is the attempt to minimize the discrepancy between public precept and institutional practice through the use of advisory councils and other forms of citizen participation in prison administration. Prison officials are gradually coming to recognize that correctional programs are reflections of public policy, and the public is beginning to assume its share of responsibility for that policy. This, it seems clear, is the most important current development in the prison system.

See also CRIMINOLOGY; CRIME; REFORMATORY, and references under "Prison" in the Index.

BIBLIOGRAPHY.—Donald Cressey, (ed.), *The Prison: Studies in Institutional Organization and Change* (1961); Richard A. Cloward, *et al., Theoretical Studies in Social Organization of the Prison,* Social Science Research Council (1960); Donald Clemmer, *The Prison Community* (1958); *A Manual of Correctional Standards,* American Correctional Association (1959); R. D. Barnes, *et al., Handbook of Correctional Design and Construction,* Federal Bureau of Prisons (1950); Maxwell Jones, *The Therapeutic Community* (1953); Sanford Bates, *Prisons and Beyond* (1936); N. K. Teeters, *Penology from Panama to Cape Horn* (1946); Lloyd E. Ohlin, *Sociology and the Field of Correction,* Russell Sage Foundation (1956); L. Radzinowicz and J. W. C. Turner, *Penal Reform in England* (1946); F. E. Haynes, *The American Prison System* (1939); George Ives, *A History of Penal Methods* (1914); P. W. Tappan, (ed.), *Contemporary Correction* (1951); S. and B. Webb, *English Prisons Under Local Government* (1922); S. Hobhouse and A. F. Brockway, (eds.), *English Prisons To-day* (1922); E. Ruggles-Brise, *Prison Reform at Home and Abroad* (1925); L. W Fox, *The English Prison and Borstal Systems* (1952); H. Mannheim, *The Dilemma of Penal Reform* (1939); M. Grünhut, *The Development of the German Penal System, 1920–1932* (1944); J. T. Sellin, *Recent Penal Legislation in Sweden* (1947); S. Glueck, *Crime and Correction* (1952), *The Problem of Delinquency* (1959); Gresham Sykes, *The Society of Captives* (1958); Terence Morris *et al., Pentonville* (1963); Daniel Glaser, *The Effectiveness of a Prison and Parole System* (1964).
                                                                    (C. C. Sc.)

PRISONERS OF WAR. The term prisoner of war, often abbreviated as PW or POW, is commonly used to mean any person captured or interned by a belligerent power during war. In the strictest sense it is applied only to members of regularly organized armed forces but by broader definition it has also included guerrillas, civilians who take up arms against an enemy openly, or noncombatants associated with a military force.

Historical Background.—In the early history of warfare there was no recognition of a status of prisoner of war, for the defeated enemy was usually promptly destroyed on the battlefield. The women, children and elders of the defeated tribe or nation were frequently disposed of in similar fashion, although occasionally they were enslaved by the victor. The captive, whether or not an active belligerent, was completely at the mercy of his captor, and, if the prisoner survived the battlefield, his existence was dependent upon such factors as the availability of food and his usefulness to his captor. Slaughtering of prisoners was sometimes practised to terrify the enemy or to satisfy sadistic impulses of the conqueror. If permitted to live, the prisoner was considered by his captor to be merely a piece of movable property, a chattel. It is difficult to say which was less humane, immediate slaughter on the battlefield or lifetime enslavement.

Even before the dawn of the Christian era, prisoner exchange and ransom had become common, except when the enemies were barbaric tribes or infidels. Differences in war aims often determined the treatment of captives. During religious wars, for example, it was generally considered a virtue to put nonbelievers to death, but in the time of the Roman conquests of Julius Caesar a captive could, under certain circumstances, become a freedman within the Roman empire.

As warfare changed, so did the treatment afforded captives and members of defeated nations or tribes. Enslavement of enemy soldiers declined during the middle ages but ransoming was widely practised and continued even as late as the 17th century in Europe. A notable example was the ransoming of King Richard the Lion Hearted during the crusades. Civilians in the defeated community were only infrequently taken prisoner, for as captives they were sometimes a burden upon the victor. Further, as they were not combatants it was considered neither just nor necessary to take them prisoner. The development of the use of the mercenary soldier also tended to create a slightly more tolerant climate for a prisoner, for the victor in one battle knew that he might be the vanquished in the next.

In the 16th and early 17th centuries some political and legal philosophers expressed their thoughts about the laws of war generally, and, in an incidental fashion, the amelioration of the effects of capture upon war prisoners. The most famous of these, Hugo

Grotius, stated in his *De jure belli ac pacis* ("On the Law of War and Peace"; 1625) that victors had the right to enslave their enemies but he advocated exchange and ransom instead. The idea was generally taking hold that in war no destruction of life or property beyond that necessary to decide the conflict was sanctioned. The treaty of Westphalia (1648) which released prisoners without ransom is generally taken as marking the end of the era of widespread enslavement of prisoners of war.

In the 18th century a new attitude of morality in the law of nations, or international law, had a profound effect upon the problem of prisoners of war. The French political philosopher Montesquieu in his famous *L'Esprit des lois* (1748) ("Spirit of the Laws"), wrote that the only right in war that the captor had over a prisoner was to prevent him from doing harm. The captive was no longer to be treated as a piece of property to be disposed of at the whim of the victor but was merely to be removed from the fight. Other writers, such as Jean Jacques Rousseau and Emerich de Vattel expanded on the same theme and developed what might be called the quarantine theory for the disposition of prisoners. From this point on the treatment of prisoners generally improved.

During the American Revolution there was no strict observance of any set of rules for the treatment of POWs. The British sometimes applied the kind of harsh punishment customarily meted out during domestic disturbances. At one stage of the conflict Gen. George Washington warned Gen. Thomas Gage that the colonists would regulate their conduct toward British prisoners "exactly by the rule you shall observe toward those of ours now in your custody." This warning illustrated a basic principle that has influenced prisoner of war practice throughout history. Each belligerent tends to treat the prisoners it holds in the same way, be it good or bad, that its own men are treated by the enemy. Shortly after the end of the Revolution the United States entered into a treaty of friendship with Prussia (1785) wherein for the first time in U.S. history regulations for dealing with prisoners were systematically set forth. Similar provisions appeared in U.S. agreements with Tripoli in 1805, Great Britain in 1813 and with Mexico in 1848.

By the middle of the 19th century it was clear that a definite body of principles for the treatment of war prisoners was being generally recognized in the civilized world. Most of these principles were summarized in the famous code prepared in 1863 for the U.S. army in the Civil War by Francis Lieber. But observance of the principles in the Civil War and in the Franco-Prussian War left much to be desired, and numerous attempts were made in the latter half of the century to improve the lot of both wounded soldiers and prisoners, whether wounded or not. In 1874 a conference at Brussels, Belg., prepared a declaration relative to prisoners of war but it was not ratified. In 1899 and again in 1907 international conferences at The Hague, Neth., drew up rules of conduct that gained some recognition in international law. (*See* LAWS OF WAR.) But during World War I when POWs were numbered in the millions, there were many charges on both sides that the rules were not being faithfully observed. Soon after the war the nations of the world gathered at Geneva, Switz., to devise the convention of 1929 which was ratified before the outbreak of World War II by France, Germany, Great Britain, the United States and many other nations, but not by Japan or the Soviet Union.

During World War II millions of persons were taken prisoner under widely varying circumstances and experienced treatment that ranged from excellent to barbaric. In the latter category was the notorious Bataan death march of American prisoners taken by the Japanese early in 1942 in the Philippines. As the Japanese code of military conduct did not condone surrender, the number of Japanese taken prisoner by United Nations forces was limited. On the other side of the world, in Europe and north Africa, treatment of prisoners was generally more nearly in accord with the Geneva convention, though there were some shocking instances of mistreatment. The Soviet Union shrouded its actions in mystery, and many difficult problems of exchange and repatriation developed as the war came to a close. In all theatres, efforts were made through the international Red Cross committee to deliver food parcels and medical supplies to prisoners from their families and friends.

After the war, international war crimes trials were held in Germany and Japan, based on the concept that acts committed in violation of the fundamental principles of the laws of war were punishable as war crimes.

Geneva Convention of 1949.—Soon after the end of World War II the 1929 Geneva convention was revised and set forth in the Geneva convention of 1949. It continued the concept earlier expressed that prisoners were to be removed from the combat zone and be humanely treated without loss of citizenship or of legal identity. The 1949 convention broadened the term prisoner of war to include not only members of the regular armed forces who have fallen into the power of the enemy but also the militia, the volunteers, the irregulars and members of resistance movements if they form a part of the armed forces, and persons who accompany the armed forces without actually being members, such as war correspondents, civilian supply contractors and members of labour service units. Even civilian inhabitants of a country not occupied by the enemy may become prisoners of war if captured when they spontaneously take up arms to resist invasion at the approach of the enemy, provided that the arms are carried openly and the laws and customs of war are respected by them. The protections given prisoners of war under the Geneva convention remain with them throughout their captivity and cannot be taken from them by the captor or given up by the prisoners themselves.

The 1949 convention specifically charged the capturing nation, or detaining power, with responsibility for treatment given prisoners. Physical mutilation and exposure to medical or scientific experiments were expressly forbidden, and the prisoners were to be protected against acts of violence, intimidation, insults and public curiosity. Reprisals against prisoners were prohibited. A prisoner was required when captured to give only his name, date of birth, service number and rank.

During their internment, which was to be in camps or compounds with other prisoners of their own nationality, language and customs, the prisoners were to be quartered, fed and clothed by the captor nation. They were also to be paid a small amount depending in its size upon their grade. Medical inspections were to be held regularly and the prisoners were to have available to them adequate medical facilities. The prisoners were to be allowed to engage in certain religious, intellectual and physical activities. Enlisted prisoners, but not officers, could be required to work for the detaining power but the work was not to be directly connected with the war and the prisoners were to be paid for their work.

Prisoners were made subject to the laws, regulations and orders of the detaining power, but a distinction was made between offenses which might be punished merely by disciplinary action and those punishable by judicial processes, although those judicial processes might be by a military court. As a general rule, a prisoner was not to be sentenced by military authorities to any penalty not provided for members of the armed forces of the detaining power who had committed the same acts. Collective punishments, torture and cruelty were forbidden and a prisoner might not be punished more than once for the same offense. Only disciplinary punishment, which is relatively mild, was permitted for a prisoner captured after an attempted escape, although the prisoner might be punished more severely if in the course of his escape attempt he committed offenses entailing violence against life or limb, or against public property, or involving theft for self-enrichment. If judicial proceedings were initiated the prisoner was entitled to counsel and was to be allowed to call witnesses and have a qualified interpreter. During the conflict prisoners might be repatriated or delivered to a neutral nation for custody. At the end of hostilities all prisoners were to be released and repatriated without delay, except those held for trial or serving sentences imposed by judicial processes.

Korean War and After.—When the Korean war broke out in 1950 neither the U.S., the largest contributor of armed forces on the United Nations side, nor Communist China and North Korea on the other side had formally ratified the Geneva convention of 1949, but early in the conflict each side announced its adherence to the principles of the convention. The communists captured about 7,190 Americans in this war while the United Nations forces captured about 120,000 Chinese and North Korean prisoners.

Treatment of prisoners by the communists was frequently barbaric. Movements from the front lines to prison camps turned into death marches for hundreds of POWs. In the prison camps food was meagre, consisting chiefly of rice. Chinese and North Korean spokesmen pointed out that this diet conformed to the Geneva convention in that it was the same as that eaten by the detaining forces, but for U.S. and British troops it amounted virtually to slow starvation, sickness and death. Many United Nations prisoners were subjected to physical abuse, threats and psychological pressures in an effort to extort information of military value or confessions that UN forces had resorted to germ warfare. When obtained, such confessions were widely used for propaganda purposes. The term brain washing was applied to the coercive methods and indoctrination techniques employed by the communists to induce UN captives to change their political outlook and embrace communism.

The truce agreement that ended the Korean war in 1953 included detailed provisions for repatriation of POWs. The prisoners were given an opportunity to choose to return to their homeland, to remain with their captors or to go to some other country. Under supervision of the Neutral Nations Repatriation commission "explanation sessions" were held during which representatives of the prisoner's own nation were permitted to talk with him and possibly persuade him to return home. Over 21,000 communist troops chose not to return home and 21 American soldiers remained with the communists when the final accounting was made. The entire problem of "forced repatriation" was given much attention at the time by international lawyers, and it became apparent that there still existed considerable disagreement as to whether a prisoner was permitted under the Geneva convention of 1949 the right to elect not to return to his homeland.

The Korean war also illuminated another facet of the problem of handling POWs—the effort to make use of prisoner status to further national war aims. In UN prison compounds POWs often rioted and committed acts of violence upon fellow prisoners and upon guards of the UN forces, apparently in an effort to develop propaganda material for use by the communist forces during the long truce negotiations. UN prisoners in communist compounds were subjected to extensive indoctrination programs designed to furnish the communists either with converts or propaganda statements. The prisoner became an important figure in the Korean war, the object of greater attention by the combatants than in either World War I or II. It appeared that a change in the status of the POW might be taking place with the prisoner being considered still a combatant and the prison compounds mere extensions of the fighting areas. If this apparent trend were to continue it would seriously threaten the improved conditions of prisoners afforded by the Geneva conventions.

U.S. POW Code of Conduct.—Upon return of the surviving U.S. prisoners from Korea—about 4,428 men—the U.S. government undertook a formal study of POW problems, appointing a special committee of military and civilian leaders to consider all aspects of the subject. Some of the specific problems considered were the causes of the apparent defections to the enemy by a few U.S. servicemen, the truth about the so-called brain washing, the propriety of punishing returned POWs for collaboration with the enemy under duress, and the existence or creation of a uniform standard of conduct for servicemen in battle and in captivity.

The report of the committee, made public in July 1955, found proper the action of U.S. authorities in bringing some 14 servicemen to trial by courts-martial for their acts of misconduct while in a prison camp. Brain washing was found to have had little lasting effect upon the prisoners in Korea. To guide U.S. servicemen who might be taken prisoner, the committee formulated a rigorous code of conduct which the president of the United States directed all servicemen to follow.   (G. S. PH.)

Prisoners of War in Vietnam.—The entrance of the United States into the fighting in Vietnam resulted in a considerable escalation of the hostilities and created many new problems, including a number relating to prisoners of war. In June 1965 the International Committee of the Red Cross (ICRC) reacted to this new situation by addressing a letter to the United States, the Republic of Vietnam (South Vietnam) and the Democratic Republic of Vietnam (North Vietnam), all three of which were parties to the 1949 Geneva Prisoner-of-War convention, and to the National Liberation Front (NLF, the political arm of the Viet Cong). This letter reminded them of their obligations under the convention which (1) specifies that it is to be applied in "all cases of declared war or of any other armed conflict . . . even if the state of war is not recognized . . . ," and (2) enumerates certain minimum protections which are to be accorded to captured personnel "in case of armed conflict not of an international character. . . ." The United States and South Vietnam acknowledged their obligation to apply the entire convention. North Vietnam denied that the convention was applicable to the U.S. military personnel it held; and the NLF denied that it was bound by the convention. (The NLF was not, of course, a party to the convention. Any party to an armed conflict, internal or international, however, is obligated to comply with the customary law of war, including that relating to prisoners of war.)

Because of the view originally taken by South Vietnam that captured Viet Cong personnel were traitors not protected by the law of war, and the view of the NLF that it was not bound by the convention, in the early days of the conflict little attention had been paid by either side to the protections to which prisoners of war are entitled. Numerous incidents had been witnessed, and reported by the news media, of South Vietnamese maltreatment of captured personnel. (Similar incidents of Viet Cong maltreatment were reported by U.S. advisers to the South Vietnamese armed forces.) There was considerable criticism of the U.S. because of its apparent failure to prevent the occurrence of these acts by the South Vietnamese armed forces, which it was then advising. By mid-1965, when the ICRC letter was received, the government of South Vietnam had been persuaded to change its position, and it subsequently embarked upon a reasonably successful campaign to instruct the members of its armed forces of their obligations under the convention. While some violations by the South Vietnamese continued to occur, the number of such incidents was materially reduced. Prisoners of war captured by U.S. forces were delivered to South Vietnamese prisoner-of-war camps for internment. The U.S. continued to have a contingent responsibility for the treatment received by these prisoners of war. For this reason, it maintained a small detachment of specially trained personnel at each such camp.

The first question that arises in a situation of guerrilla warfare such as that in Vietnam is, Who is entitled to prisoner-of-war status? The convention covers this subject in considerable detail. Captured members of national armed forces are, of course, entitled to such status. This would include the so-called main force units of the Viet Cong, which were, in effect, their regular units. Also entitled to such status are captured "members of . . . volunteer corps, including those of organized resistance movements. . . ." For the members of units of this nature to qualify for prisoner-of-war status, however, they must fulfill four conditions: have a responsible commander; have a fixed and recognizable distinctive sign; carry arms openly; and conduct operations in accordance with the law of war. Viet Cong "local forces" may, in some instances, have met these conditions. It is doubtful that Viet Cong terrorists could ever have done so. Moreover, should there be a question as to whether a captured individual comes within the provisions of the convention, he must be accorded prisoner-of-war status until a determination is made by a "competent tribunal." The U.S. and South Vietnam established elaborate procedures for such cases. North Vietnam, however, refused to accord prisoner-of-war status to the U.S. airmen shot down over its territory, claiming that they were "war criminals." Under article 85 of the convention, and North Vietnam's reservation to that article, the airmen were nonetheless entitled to full protection as prisoners of war, at least until they had been tried and convicted of the commission of war crimes. No such trials were held, although they were threatened. Comparatively little information is available with respect to the treatment of captured personnel by the Viet Cong. However, it is known that prisoners of war held by them were confined underground for many months, denied adequate food and needed medical care, subjected to violence and even executed without trial. All of these acts are prohibited both by the convention and by the customary law of war.

From time to time each side unilaterally released and repatriated a few selected captured personnel. South Vietnam also embarked upon an extensive "Open Arms" policy, under which North Vietnamese and Viet Cong personnel who would surrender voluntarily were "re-educated" in special camps and then had their choice of enlisting in the South Vietnamese armed forces or of being released into civilian life in South Vietnam. There is a serious question as to whether this procedure, which was followed by the North Koreans during the fighting in Korea in 1950–53, and which is also followed by the Viet Cong, is not a violation of the provision of the convention that prohibits a prisoner of war from renouncing the very rights secured to him by the convention.

Among the other provisions of the convention at issue in Vietnam are those relating to the activities of the ICRC: the obligation to furnish lists of captured personnel; the right of prisoners of war to receive humane treatment and not to be subjected to insults or public curiosity; and their right to correspond with their families and to receive relief packages. The manner in which North Vietnamese and Viet Cong personnel were treated in South Vietnam was fairly well publicized and was under the constant surveillance of the ICRC, which was permitted to visit both prisoner-of-war camps and civilian prisons, and to confer privately with confined personnel. However, the ICRC was not permitted access to North Vietnam or to Viet Cong prisoner-of-war holding areas, and the nature of the treatment received by personnel captured by them is known only through propaganda reports from Hanoi and through statements of persons who have escaped or who have been released. South Vietnam furnished the ICRC with numerous lists of captured personnel interned by it, but no such lists were furnished by either North Vietnam or the Viet Cong. U.S. prisoners of war held by North Vietnam were subjected to insults and public curiosity and, except on rare occasions, such as Christmas 1968, North Vietnam refused to permit captured personnel to correspond with their families or to receive relief packages from home. Each side charged the other with inhumane treatment of captured personnel.

The value of the experience gained from the application of the prisoner-of-war convention in Vietnam is a debatable question. As in Korea, only one side is making any effort to live up to its provisions. In this case, the other side denies its applicability. Were both sides attempting to live under the convention, the prisoners of war held by each side would benefit therefrom, and the lessons learned would benefit personnel captured in future armed conflicts.

See also references under "Prisoners of War" in the Index.

(H. S. Le.)

BIBLIOGRAPHY.—L. F. L. Oppenheim, *International Law,* vol. ii, 7th ed. (1952); W. E. S. Flory, *Prisoners of War: A Study in the Development of International Law* (1942); Herbert C. Fooks, *Prisoners of War* (1924); Julius Stone, *Legal Controls of International Conflicts* (1954); Richard R. Baxter, "So-Called 'Unprivileged Belligerency': Spies, Guerrillas, and Saboteurs," *British Yearbook of International Law,* 28:323 ff. (1951); Morris Greenspan, "International Law and Its Protection for Participants in Unconventional Warfare," *Annals of the American Academy of Political and Social Science,* 341:30 ff. (1962); Howard S. Levie, "Maltreatment of Prisoners of War in Vietnam," *Boston University Law Review,* 48:323 ff. (1968); "The Geneva Convention and the Treatment of Prisoners of War in Vietnam," *Harvard Law Review,* 80:851 ff. (1967); "The International Committee and the Vietnam Conflict," *International Review of the Red Cross,* 6:399 ff. (1966); "The Geneva Conventions of 1949: Application in the Vietnamese Conflict," *Virginia Journal of International Law,* 5:243 ff. (1965).

PRIVATEER, an armed vessel belonging to a private owner and commissioned by a belligerent state to carry on operations of war or reprisals. Since the crew was not paid by the state, privateers were entitled to cruise for their own profit, deductions from the value of prizes taken being made by the admiralty courts in England or their equivalents as prize courts elsewhere, at which all captures had to be condemned as legitimate under the prize laws. This method of commerce destruction was adopted by all nations from the earliest times until the 19th century, but it frequently proved impossible to restrain the activities of privateers within the legitimate bounds laid down in their commissions or letters of marque. Hence in earlier times it was often difficult to distinguish between privateers, pirates, corsairs, or buccaneers, many of whom sailed without genuine commissions. (*See* BUCCANEERS; PIRACY.)

Before regular navies were established, the state relied on the assistance of private ships equipped for war such as, for example, those from the Cinque Ports in England. The earliest mention of letters of marque issued to English ships is in a patent roll of Edward I dated 1293 which ordered a stay of letters of marque previously granted to his subjects in Aquitaine. In the 14th century admiralty courts were instituted in England to administer prize law, and at the beginning of the 15th century the High Court of Admiralty was established. Local vice-admiralty courts were later set up, the earliest being at Jamaica in 1662. Throughout the Tudor period privateers such as Sir Martin Frobisher, Sir Richard Hawkins, and Sir Francis Drake were encouraged or restrained according to prevailing political conditions. At the same period the Dutch Sea Beggars and French Huguenot privateers were active.

This state of affairs continued throughout the next century, English buccaneers in the West Indies such as Sir Henry Morgan or William Dampier sometimes sailing as genuine privateers and sometimes not. From 1690 French privateers from Dunkerque and Saint-Malo were particularly active against English commerce. With the growth of a regular navy the British Admiralty began to discourage privateering, because it was more popular among sailors than serving in the navy, and because it often led to trouble with neutrals, though a declaratory act was always passed at the beginning of a war, laying down the right to capture enemy vessels at sea and to have such captures adjudicated under prize law. Extensive use of privateers was made in France and in New England throughout the 18th century. During the American Revolution the American colonists found it difficult to form a new navy because over 1,000 privateers were licensed. The popularity of privateering continued in the War of 1812 between Great Britain and the United States when, for example, the brig "Yankee" alone seized or destroyed $5,000,000 worth of English property. Meanwhile, the prospects of French privateers had been ruined by the efficiency of frigates and convoy escorts.

Privateering was abolished in 1856 by the Declaration of Paris (*q.v.*), though the United States refused to accede on the grounds that privateering made it possible to economize on the cost of a navy. During the American Civil War the president was authorized to commission privateers, but both sides preferred to arm their own merchantmen as regular warships. The rise of the American navy at the end of the century, and the realization that privateering belonged to an earlier form of warfare, disposed the United States to recognize the necessity of abolishing it. At the Second Hague Conference in 1907 several conventions on naval warfare in respect to merchant vessels at sea were adopted, but the one setting up an international prize court to hear appeals from belligerent prize courts was never ratified. It was then stipulated, and has since become part of international law, that armed merchant ships must be listed as warships, though there have been various interpretations of the word "armed." The ambiguous status of the privateer has ceased to exist, since under the seventh Hague convention the state now assumes full responsibility for all converted ships engaged in military operations; but the right to arm merchant vessels in self-defense was generally admitted in World Wars I and II.

BIBLIOGRAPHY.—R. G. Marsden, *Law and Custom of the Sea,* 2 vol. (1915–16); Sir F. T. Piggott, *The Declaration of Paris, 1856* (1919); E. S. Maclay, *History of American Privateers* (1899); H. Malo, *Les Derniers Corsaires, Dunkerque, 1715–1815* (1925); C. J. Colombos, *The International Law of the Sea,* 5th ed. (1962). (C. C. L.)

PRIVILEGE, in Anglo-American law, has at least two meanings: the first is that of an exceptional power, immunity, or advantage enjoyed by a person or class; the second, in the United States, is analogous to a constitutional right.

Privilege from arrest exempts certain persons from arrest in civil proceedings and, in some cases, on criminal charges. This form of privilege may be permanent, as in the case of a foreign minister and his suite, who may not legally be arrested in any circumstance, or temporary, as in the case of witnesses while a suit is being tried.

Privileged communications are those between persons who have a special duty of fidelity and secrecy toward each other, such as husband and wife. Communications between attorney and client are privileged when made in connection with prospective litigation. The law will not allow such communications to be divulged or inquired into in judicial proceedings without the consent of the person who made them. In a few states of the U.S. this privilege has been extended by statute to other communications, such as those between doctors and patients or confessions to priests. Statements and publications, which otherwise would be libelous or slanderous, may be privileged; this means that a person can make or publish them with immunity if he does so while performing certain political, judicial, social, or personal duties. If absolute, the privilege applies regardless of the speaker's motives or the falsity of his statement, as in the case of statements made in legislative debates. Conditional privilege gives immunity unless the speaker's actual malice and his knowledge of falsity are shown. (See PARLIAMENT: *The Two Houses of Parliament;* DEFAMATION.)

In most countries certain debts are privileged—that is, such debts as funeral expenses or servants' wages must be paid by the executor or trustee in bankruptcy in preference to other debts.

By Art. IV sec. 2 of the United States Constitution, "The Citizens of each State shall be entitled to all Privileges and Immunities of Citizens in the several States." The U.S. Supreme Court has interpreted this as forbidding discrimination by any state against citizens of other states in favour of its own. Discrimination against nonresidents is an infringement, but not reasonable differences of treatment between residents and nonresidents. Thus a state may require residence within its borders for a given time before a person previously a resident of another state may vote; also, discrimination against nonresidents may be reasonable because of considerations of public health, safety, or welfare. Nonresidents, however, must be given access to state courts upon terms that are reasonable and adequate for enforcing their rights, if the terms differ from those for residents. In the exercise of its taxing powers a state may not substantially discriminate between residents and nonresidents, but the test for such an absence of discrimination involves considering the entire state tax system to determine its overall fairness.

The 14th Amendment to the Constitution (sec. 1) provides that "no State shall make or enforce any law which shall abridge the privileges or immunities of citizens of the United States." With regard to this provision, the Supreme Court in 1873 repudiated the idea that, when the amendment was adopted in 1868, it converted the rights of the citizens of each state into privileges and immunities of United States citizenship. The court thereby largely nullified the clause, which had been intended to guarantee the right to vote to Negroes in the South; the court held that the only privileges protected by the amendment were those which owed their existence to the "Federal Government, its National Character, its Constitution, or its laws." (*The Slaughter-House Cases,* 83 U.S. 36, 79.) These privileges existed prior to this amendment and were already protected against state interference under the principle of federal supremacy.

It is a federal crime to conspire to injure, oppress, threaten, or intimidate any citizen in the free exercise and enjoyment of any privilege secured by the Constitution, or under colour of law willfully to deprive any inhabitant of a state of any such privileges or immunities. Civil damage actions may also be brought for deprivation (or a conspiracy for deprivation) of these privileges.

The privilege against self-incrimination is embodied in the Fifth Amendment to the Constitution and in most state constitutions. It forbids compelling any person to be a witness against himself; and it extends to a witness in any type of governmental proceeding when the answer to a question he is legally required to answer might be used against him (but not against others) in a future criminal proceeding by that government.

See IMMUNITY; *see* also references under "Privilege" in the Index. (RT. K.)

PRIVY COUNCIL, theoretically the British sovereign's private council, as distinct from the medieval great council, or council of magnates, and from council in parliament, now called parliament. It ceased to be an active body because (1) it lost most of its judicial functions; (2) the sovereign preferred to use informal meetings of ministers in cabinet; and (3) the sovereign ceased to take responsibility for political decisions. Meetings are held from time to time for the taking of formal decisions (*e.g.,* the making of orders in council), but usually only the quorum of three lords of the council are present and there is no discussion.

There is, however, a privy council office, with the lord president of the council as responsible minister. It is concerned with the making of orders in council and with a wide variety of functions deriving mainly from the power of the sovereign in council to issue royal charters, now used chiefly by municipal corporations and by charitable bodies engaged in education, research, the encouragement of literature, science, art, etc. Among the bodies with which it is concerned are the universities, various research councils (*e.g.,* the agricultural research council, the medical research council and the research council of the department of scientific and industrial research) and the bodies concerned with the maintenance of professional standards (*e.g.,* the general medical council). It bears the main responsibility for scientific research through the department of scientific and industrial research. Usually the privy council functions through committees, some standing and some *ad hoc.* The most famous of its committees is, however, statutory, the judicial committee of the privy council, which hears appeals from ecclesiastical courts, prize courts and courts from all colonies and some independent countries of the commonwealth (*see* PRIVY COUNCIL, JUDICIAL COMMITTEE OF).

History of the Privy Council.—The privy council, like all the British institutions of central government, is descended from the court of the Norman kings. This *curia regis,* composed of the king's tenants in chief, his household officials and anyone else whom the king chose to summon, performed all the functions of central government. According to feudal theory, tenants owed suit to their lord's court; but every great lord had also his household officials to transact his daily business. The *curia regis* expanded or contracted according to the nature of the business under consideration. The ordinary routine would be carried out by the officials, assisted by such barons as happened to be at court; for more important business the king would secure the attendance of a greater number of his tenants in chief; and on really vital matters the household officials would tend to become a numerically insignificant technical element in a large feudal assembly.

As time went by the larger and smaller gatherings came to be distinguished adjectivally; later, these adjectives developed a technical significance, until, although still remaining for a time merely different manifestations of a one and indivisible body, the larger assembly developed into the great council and the parliament, the smaller into the king's council. In early days the presence of many barons at conciliar meetings was the mark of a strong king; later, as the barons came to realize that attendance was not merely a tiresome incident of feudal tenure but a source of political power, that obligation became a privilege. Thus, in the later middle ages there developed a struggle between king and greater barons for the control of the king's council. In the end the barons failed to secure their greater demands—exclusive membership and the control of appointment and dismissal—because, though anxious to control and willing to be appointed, they could never be relied upon for constant attendance. Further, with the passing of the feudal organization of society, baronial counsel ceased to be expert advice on matters of government.

By the time of Henry VII this council had become the instrument of the crown. It was composed of an inner ring of counselors proper, who took an oath and sat at the council board, and of an outer ring of technical experts and dignitaries. Though they might occasionally be called upon for advice, the latter were not members of the board, did not take the conciliar oath, but merely that of their respective offices, and performed the technical and routine work of the central and provincial courts of the council. It was the policy of the Tudors to rule the country paternally by the prerogative exercised through the medium of the council.

This conception of government necessitated precision, subdivision and specialization, and thus the king's council and its functions were divided among the privy council, the courts of Star Chamber, of requests and of high commission (qq.v.), and such local offshoots as the courts and councils of the north, and of Wales and the Marches. A distinction between the council with the king and the council at Westminster had appeared from time to time during the middle ages. It now became "sharper and more permanent." The body following the king was commonly known as the council at court, while the other continued to be called the king's council in the Star Chamber. The former body became the privy council.

This conciliar government was admirably suited to a period of transition. But the need of this somewhat arbitrary, if paternal, government had passed with the Tudors. Moreover, this small but all-powerful bureaucracy depended for its efficiency on a resolute and discriminating sovereign, capable of choosing the right men and of superintending their labours. The Stuarts did not possess these qualifications. The house of commons, hitherto accustomed to follow the leadership of privy councilors, had now, with increased experience of partnership in government, developed a mind and policy of its own. Of the judicial aspect of the council's activities the common lawyers were coming to show an even more threatening jealousy, a jealousy justified by the misguided action of the Stuarts in checking the natural evolution of these courts toward independence of executive control and in using them to enforce, not justice, but policy. No wonder, then, that as religious and constitutional controversies developed between crown and parliament the attention of malcontents became focused on conciliar jurisdiction, nor that, when the parliamentary cause at last triumphed in 1641, the whole system of conciliar government was swept away. Only the privy council was spared. It was never legally abolished. It perished in the interregnum (though the name was resuscitated in 1657) and was restored with the return of Charles II in 1660.

Both in the middle ages and for several centuries later contemporary opinion favoured 20 as about the ideal total of conciliar membership. But seldom did practice conform with theory. When the privy council register begins, in 1540, we do, indeed, find 19 members, but by Henry VIII's death there were 29. In Edward VI's reign the record was 40, in Mary's 44, and, although Elizabeth I reduced the numbers to between 12 and 20, the Stuarts, as usual, were less successful. By 1623 the total had increased to 35, and Charles I's council averaged about the same figure. At the Restoration the problem of numbers became even more acute. Charles II managed to begin with only 28, but the total had reached 47 by 1679. Sir William Temple's abortive attempt at conciliar reform temporarily reduced the figure to 33, but by 1688 it was back again at 48, by 1707 it had reached 60 and, by 1723, 67. In practice, however, Charles II and all later monarchs preferred to have matters of policy discussed privately by their principal advisers in cabinet.

The last serious attempt to restore the privy council to its former influence may be found in the clause of the Act of Settlement (1701), which enacted that, on the Hanoverian accession, "all matters and things relating to the well-governing of the kingdom, which are properly cognizable in the privy council by the laws and customs of this realm, shall be transacted there, and all resolutions taken thereupon shall be signed by such of the privy council as shall advise and consent to the same." But the proposal was by that date impracticable, and the clause was repealed in 1705 before it even came into force. The council board had

been not merely short-circuited by the cabinet, it had even lost the power of debating such measures as came before it. In 1711 a debate on the subject in parliament elicited the remark that "the privy counsellors were such as were thought to know everything and knew nothing. Those of the cabinet council thought nobody knew anything but themselves." And the last occasion on which the council asserted its former rights was when, in 1714, as Queen Anne lay dying, certain Whig lords forced their way in at a meeting of the lords of the committee (see CABINET), claimed their right to be present as counselors of the crown, converted the meeting into a session of the privy council and, reinforced by their conciliar colleagues, ushered in the Hanoverian succession. From the accession of George I the privy council may be described as a purely formal body meeting on purely formal occasions to transact purely formal business. By 1960, there were more than 300 "right honourable lords and others of Her Majesty's Most Honourable Privy Council." They were mostly dignitaries who had held, or held, high political, judicial or ecclesiastical office, though the list occasionally included eminent persons in science or letters. Office lasts for the life of the sovereign and six months after, but a new sovereign may renew the appointment.

See also references under "Privy Council" in the Index.

BIBLIOGRAPHY.—A. V. Dicey, *The Privy Council* (1860); Sir William Anson, *Law and Custom of the Constitution*, vol. ii, 4th ed. (1935); C. L. Scofield, *Court of Star Chamber* (1900); I. S. Leadam, *Select Cases Before the King's Council in the Star Chamber* (1903); Lord E. Percy, *The Privy Council Under the Tudors* (1907); J. F. Baldwin, *The King's Council in England During the Middle Ages* (1913); J. E. A. Jolliffe, *Constitutional History of Mediaeval England* (1937); D. L. Keir, *Constitutional History of Modern Britain* (1938).
(F. L. B.; W. I. J.)

PRIVY COUNCIL, JUDICIAL COMMITTEE OF, a British tribunal composed of certain privy councilors which on petition hears various appeals from the United Kingdom, from British crown colonies, and from those independent members of the Commonwealth which have not abolished this final appeal from their courts.

The tribunal's authority derives from the Judicial Committee Act (1833), but its origins lie deep in English history. From the earliest times the king has been accounted the supreme source of justice and his council has always had judicial as well as advisory functions. In the later Middle Ages, when courts for all ordinary causes were well established, a reserve of residual justice remained with the king and extraordinary justice was done by the king's council. For this purpose councilors worked in committees, which were the origin of some of the prerogative courts. These courts, which came into disrepute under the Stuarts, had all been abolished or had fallen into disuse by 1689. From that time until 1833, appeals to the sovereign, or to the sovereign in council, especially from overseas, were dealt with by a general committee of the Privy Council. In 1833 the Judicial Committee Act created a special judicial tribunal. The rules then laid down with regard to the composition and procedure of the committee and the nature of its jurisdiction continue, with modifications, to determine the committee's form and actions.

The members of the committee are the president of the Privy Council, former presidents of the Privy Council, the lord chancellor, the lords of appeal in ordinary, and any other privy councilors who have in the past held such office. Other members are judges of the Supreme Court of England and Northern Ireland, of the Court of Session in Scotland, and also (by the Judicial Committee Amendment Act, 1895), provided they are privy councilors, judges or former judges of the superior courts of British colonies or of independent Commonwealth countries. The committee sits in the council chamber in Whitehall, where it hears petitions formally addressed to Her Majesty in Council. A quorum of three members is needed for every case, and members cannot attend a hearing unless summoned. The committee can sit in divisions and hear various cases simultaneously. It is in no way bound by previous decisions, and its judgment is made in the form of a report to the sovereign, allowing or disallowing the appeal. Dissenting opinion is not disclosed. The decision may then be implemented by means of an order in council.

Among the independent members of the Commonwealth from whose courts appeal to the judicial committee still lies are Australia, New Zealand, Ceylon, Trinidad and Tobago, Jamaica, and Sierra Leone. Appeals also lie from Jersey, Guernsey, and the Isle of Man. In the case of Malaysia the committee reports not to the queen but to the head of the Federation of Malaysia.

The 1833 act gave to the sovereign the power to refer any question whatsoever to the committee, and such "special references" are still made. One such case was that of the Rev. Godfrey Mac-Manaway, who at the general election of Feb. 1950 was returned to Parliament as member for West Belfast. The judicial committee decided that as an ordained clergyman of the Church of Ireland he was disqualified from sitting in Parliament. Appeals concerning the union of benefices are also referred to the committee under this section of the act. By acts of Parliament passed in 1956 and 1958, doctors, dentists, and opticians may appeal to the committee against the erasure of their names from the registers of their respective professions.

BIBLIOGRAPHY.—N. Bentwich, *The Practice of the Privy Council in Judicial Matters*, 2nd ed. (1926) ; W. R. Anson, *The Law and Custom of the Constitution*, vol. 2, 4th ed. (1935) ; A. B. Keith, *The Dominions as Sovereign States* (1938) ; D. H. Chalmers and O. H. Phillips, *The Constitutional Law of Great Britain and the Commonwealth*, 7th ed., by O. H. Phillips and G. Ellenbogen (1952) ; K. C. Wheare, *The Statute of Westminster and Dominion Status*, 5th ed. (1953).

PRIZE, in law, may be defined as a vessel, aircraft, or goods, acquired through capture by a belligerent state, which is subject to condemnation by a Prize Court (*q.v.*).

Judicial Inquiry.—"Capture" and "prize" are not synonymous terms, and a legal determination that the captured property is good prize, within the accepted definition, is necessary before the captor may exercise any beneficial rights in it. A decree of condemnation declares the prize to be the property of the capturing sovereign and may be accompanied by an order for sale, purchase under which gives an internationally valid title. In the 18th century title to a prize sometimes changed simply by virtue of the capture, but by the modern usage of nations a judicial inquiry must pass upon the case. Within certain undefined limits the nature of the legal process and the definition of condemnable vessels and goods are left by international law to national choice.

Property Subject to Condemnation.—Enemy vessels, enemy goods in enemy or in neutral vessels, neutral goods which are contraband, and neutral vessels which have been captured in the act of running a legal blockade or rendering unneutral service are subject to condemnation. Enemy warships or other public ships are liable to condemnation, but they are seldom the subjects of actual adjudications. During a war enemy states do not appear as claimants before the Prize Court, and after a war rights and liabilities resulting from captures are usually settled as part of the general peace settlement. The enemy character of vessels and goods is determined by the nationality or the domicile of the owner, and evidence both intrinsic and extrinsic to the vessels and its papers may be introduced. Aircraft have been added, by statute, to the subjects of prize law (*see* U.S., act of June 24, 1941, 55 Stat. 261, and U.K., Prize Act, 1939, s. 1 [1], 2 and 3 Geo. VI, c. 65). These statutes provide for the application of the law of prize even when the aircraft is captured on or over land. For England the term "vessels" includes merchantmen, lighters, rafts, tugs, boats, and all other naval craft together with their appointments. For the United States, however, nonseagoing vessels, such as barges propelled by sweeps or by poling, and boats having no means of propulsion are not regarded as maritime prize.

Maritime Capture.—Only "maritime capture" is subject to condemnation under the law of prize. Traditionally, "maritime capture" includes capture by naval forces upon the high seas or in rivers, ports, and harbours. The French Prize Court has held that captures upon inland waters are not liable to condemnation as maritime prize. In Italy prize extends to captures on inland waters; and the German Prize Court Law of 1939 covered captures on land and sea.

Prize Money.—Individuals having some connection with the capture of a prize may share in its value only if the captor state so provides. In the past, prize money or "bounty" has been paid,

partly as a reward for bravery and as a stimulus to exertion and partly as a compensation for the poor rates of pay prevailing in naval services. However, prize bounty was abolished in the United States in 1899 (30 Stat. 1007, sec. 13) and in England in 1948 (Prize Act of 1948, 12 and 13 Geo. VI, c. 9).

BIBLIOGRAPHY.—C. J. Colombos, *A Treatise on the Law of Prize*, 3rd ed. (1949) ; J. W. Garner, *Prize Law During the World War* (1927).
(F. T. v. B.)

PRIZE COURTS AND PRIZE LAW, in naval warfare, are instrumentalities by which the legality of captures of ships and goods at sea and related questions are determined. The establishment of such courts is both a right and duty of belligerents. In a 1916 British case, Lord Parker observed that: "but for the existence of Prize Courts no one aggrieved by the acts of a belligerent power in times of war could obtain redress otherwise than through diplomatic channels and at the risk of disturbing international amity. An appropriate remedy is, however, provided by the fact that according to international law, every belligerent power must appoint and submit to the jurisdiction of a Prize Court to which any person aggrieved by its acts has access, and which administers international as opposed to municipal law—a law which is theoretically the same, whether the court which administers it is constituted under the municipal law of the belligerent power or of the sovereign of the person aggrieved, and is equally binding on both parties to the litigation" (*The Zamora*, 1916, 2 A.C. 77).

The judgment of a prize court is binding upon the parties to proceedings before it, that is, normally the captor and the individual or corporation, neutral or enemy, that challenges the validity of the capture. It is not necessarily binding, however, on the state whose national is involved, whether or not it is binding being dependent upon the conformity of the judgment with international law. In case of inconsistency the state of the captor becomes responsible to the state of the claimant, individual or corporation. As the U.S. commissioner William Pinkney pointed out before the Anglo-American mixed commission, established pursuant to the Jay treaty of Nov. 19, 1794, to determine the legality of the seizure of the American ship "Betsey" by the British captor:

A belligerent has this jurisdiction for its own safety—because it is answerable to other nations for the conduct of its captors. It is allowed exclusive cognizance of the capture for the purpose of ascertaining whether it will confirm it and thus complete its own responsibility, or give to the claimant adequate redress against the captor and thus exonerate itself. . . . The judgment of its prize court in the last resort, in general, perfects or destroys that liability. If it grants adequate redress there is nothing to be answerable for, but if instead of doing so it completes the original injury by rendering it irreparable by any ordinary means, the national responsibility is obviously perfect. The injury becomes its own, and the neutral, from being compelled to ask redress against the captor is now authorized to ask it against his nation. . . .

Claims of belligerents against each other arising from capture are usually settled by the peace treaty. Claims of neutrals against belligerents are settled through diplomatic negotiations or, rarely, international arbitral tribunals. At the second Hague peace conference a proposal was adopted to establish an international prize court to settle disputes between neutrals and belligerents (*see* below).

As the objective of war at sea became increasingly the denial to the enemy of all trade, so prize courts and prize law and particularly the latter were gradually adapted to serve this end. Economic warfare became one of the most significant developments in World Wars I and II. This fact was shown in the expanding and eventually all-embracing concepts of contraband and blockade and the increasing severity of measures taken by belligerents, not merely against enemy, but also against neutral vessels, which came to be regarded by prize courts as permissible.

Prize Courts.—Prize courts are municipal (internal) courts and their character and organization are determined by national tradition and law. It is possible to distinguish two categories: judicial and administrative. English and United States prize courts are purely judicial but the prize courts of other nations are either purely administrative or of a mixed character.

In England, jurisdiction in matters of prize was vested from the 14th century by royal proclamations or commissions in the admiral's court along with jurisdiction over ordinary maritime cases such as collision or salvage. Statutory prize jurisdiction was conferred on the high court of admiralty by the Naval Prize act of 1864 which continued in the second half of the 20th century to be the basic law. It was amended in 1894, 1914, 1918 and 1939. By the High Court of Judicature act of 1891 and the Supreme Court of Judicature (Consolidation) act of 1925 jurisdiction in prize cases was transferred to the high court of justice and exercised by its probate, divorce and admiralty division. The practice continues, though not considered essential since 1864, to issue a royal commission at the beginning of war concerning exercise of jurisdiction in prize cases. Since 1864 appeals have been taken, in prize cases, to the judicial committee of the privy council, whose determinations are final, and in all other cases, to the court of appeal and ultimately the house of lords. The Prize act of 1939 was applicable in the United Kingdom, in the British dominions (but not in Canada and the Union of South Africa), in British protectorates, colonies and territories held under mandate from the League of Nations and in other territories in which the British crown had prize jurisdiction. In these territories prize jurisdiction was conferred upon the appropriate ordinary courts. The act of 1939 applied to ships as well as aircraft.

In the United States, the constitution (art. iii) provides that the jurisdiction of the United States shall extend "to all Cases of admiralty and maritime Jurisdiction." The judicial code (24, par. 3) provides that federal district courts shall have original jurisdiction "of all prizes brought into the United States; and of all proceedings for the condemnation of property taken as prize" (28 U.S.C.A. 41 [3]). Appeals from their decrees in prize cases go directly to the supreme court (Judicial Code 238, 28 U.S.C.A. 345). Bounty and prize moneys were abolished by the act of March 3, 1899, which declared that "all provisions of the law authorizing the distribution among captors of the whole or any portion of the proceeds of, or providing for the payment of bounty for the sinking or destruction of vessels of enemy hereafter occurring in war, are hereby repealed" (30 Stat. 1044, sec. 13). In Britain, the Prize act of 1948 abolished prize money. In France, jurisdiction was exercised by an administrative tribunal composed of a member of the council of state (*conseil d'état*), the highest administrative tribunal in France, six members chosen from the *maîtres des requêtes,* and officials of the ministries of foreign affairs and marine. The *conseil d'état* itself exercised appellate jurisdiction in prize cases. In Belgium prize courts were of a mixed character being composed partly of judges from the court of appeal of whom two were appointed, and four representatives of the navy and commerce. Appeals lie to the regular court of appeal. During World War II no prize court was established in Belgium. In Italy prize courts were partly judicial and partly administrative in composition; limited appeal was permitted to the court of cassation, the highest judicial authority. In Germany the prize courts of both original and appeals jurisdiction were of mixed character, and Chinese and Japanese prize courts followed the same pattern. No prize court was established in the U.S.S.R. during World War II. The difference in the character of prize courts in various countries does not necessarily mean that these countries do not administer justice, but in the fact that whereas in the United States and England prize jurisdiction is exercised by existing ordinary courts, in other countries it is the business of *ad hoc* tribunals.

Prize Law.—The law applied by prize courts is international law, customary and conventional. In England, the United States and other common-law countries the rule prevails that international law is part of the law of the land: "International law is part of our law, and must be ascertained and administered by the courts of justice of appropriate jurisdiction, as often as questions of right depending upon it are duly presented for their determination. For this purpose, where there is no treaty, and no controlling executive or legislative act or judicial decision, resort must be had to the customs and usages of civilized nations" (Justice Horace Gray, *The Paquete Habana,* 1900, 175 U.S. 677). Lord

Parker said: ". . . the law which the Prize Court is to administer is not the national law or, as it sometimes is called, the municipal law, but the law of nations—in other words, international law" (*The Zamora,* 1916, 2 A.C. 77). Similarly Chief Justice John Marshall declared: "The law of nations is the great source from which we derive those rules, respecting belligerent and neutral rights, which are recognized by all civilized and commercial states throughout Europe and America" (*Thirty Hogsheads of Sugar* v. *Boyle,* 1815, 9 Cranch 191).

There is a practice of long standing for belligerents, at the outbreak of war, to enact prize law through statutory legislation dealing with both substantive and procedural law. Thus England promulgated prize court rules in 1939; France the decrees of Sept. 2, 1939, amplified by numerous instructions; Germany the Prize Court law of Aug. 28, 1939, amended on Dec. 13, 1940; and Canada the Prize act of 1945. In the United States, congress enacted the Prize act of June 24, 1941 (55 Stat. 261), extending prize jurisdiction to aircraft. Such enactments are presumed to be declaratory of international law but they are in any event binding upon the courts. "It cannot, of course, be disputed that a prize court, like any other court, is bound by the legislative enactments of its own sovereign state. . . . But it is none the less true that if the . . . legislature passed an act the provisions of which were inconsistent with the law of nations, the prize court in giving effect to such provisions would no longer be administering international law" (Lord Parker, *The Zamora,* 1916, 2 A.C. 77). The same would be true in the United States as indicated by Justice Gray in the *Paquete Habana* (case 9), and in other countries. The difference between the Anglo-American and continental courts is that the latter do not feel free even to examine the consistency between international and municipal law since they are bound to apply the latter in any event. A difference arises in respect of British orders in council and equivalent decrees in other countries. Such orders in council are not binding upon the courts unless based upon statutes for the king in council cannot change the law administered by the courts in England any more than he can prescribe the law to be administered by prize courts. However, the prize court will apply orders in council when "they amount to a mitigation of the crown rights in favour of the enemy or neutral, as the case may be" (Lord Parker, *The Zamora,* 1916, 2 A.C. 77). Equivalent decrees would be given effect in other countries. No problem arises in connection with conventional law as this is applicable in most countries in accordance with national law. In the evolution of prize law in England and the United States precedents played a decisive role as they did in the formation of common law. Precedents do not have a comparable authority on the continent although a court would not easily depart from or overrule them.

With a view to ensuring greater uniformity in the application of law by prize courts, two methods were tried: on the one hand, the adoption of agreed rules by treaties or conventions and on the other the establishment of an international prize court. The most important among the former are: the declaration of Paris, 1856; some of the Hague conventions of 1899 and 1907 (namely the 6th convention relative to the status of enemy ships at outbreak of war, the 7th relative to the conversion of merchant ships into warships, the 11th relative to certain restrictions on the exercise of the right of capture in maritime war, and the 13th relative to the rights and duties of neutral powers in maritime war); the London declaration of 1909; and the London protocol of 1936 regarding action by submarines against merchant ships. The binding force of the Hague conventions was dubious because it depended to some extent on their having been ratified by all belligerents which was not usually the case. The conventions were, however, applied, in principle, by British prize courts in both World Wars I and II. The London declaration never entered into force but its rules were applied to the extent that they were deemed to be declaratory of customary international law. The London protocol of 1936 was largely disregarded in World War II by the major belligerents. This, at any rate, was the opinion of the Nürnberg International Military tribunal for the trial of major German war criminals:

In view of all the facts proved and in particular of an order of the British admiralty announced on May 8, 1940, according to which all vessels should be sunk at sight in the Skagerrak, and the answers to interrogatories by Adm. Chester W. Nimitz stating that unrestricted submarine warfare was carried on in the Pacific ocean by the United States from the first day that nation entered the war, the sentence on Adm. Karl Dönitz is not assessed on the ground of his breaches of the international law of submarine warfare. (Judgment of Oct. 1, 1946. International Military Tribunal, *Trial of the Major War Criminals, Official Documents,* vol. i, p. 313 [1947].)

To ensure greater uniformity in the jurisprudence of prize courts the establishment of an international prize court with jurisdiction on appeals from national prize courts was envisaged at the second Hague conference in 1907. As noted above, judgments of national prize courts, in case of inconsistency with international law, engage the responsibility of the captor states. To provide a judicial method for settling disputes between states in such cases, an international tribunal would be obviously useful. It was also realized that in spite of their professions national prize courts apply international law as interpreted by their governments and they are bound by municipal statutes. However, the Hague convention of 1907 for an international prize court was never ratified.

Task of Prize Courts.—According to the principle "all prizes must be judged," the main question for prize courts is: "prize or no prize." In the past, prize courts, particularly in England and the United States, were also concerned with awarding prize and bounty moneys and allocation of shares between the crown and the admiralty, the so-called droits of the crown and the droits of admiralty. Judgments of prize courts condemning ships or cargoes or both provide a title for the captor which is "good against the world," without prejudice, of course, to the right of the injured state to seek a remedy in accordance with international law. As noted, prize courts were from a functional point of view instruments of economic warfare and continued so to function in World Wars I and II. However, new methods of depriving the enemy of supplies were developed, such as long-distance blockade and various forms of control at the ship's point of departure rather than in the course of its passage on the high seas. In spite of these innovations, which proved very effective, prize courts operated in England, France, Germany and many other countries. However, no prize courts operated in the United States during either World War I or II. In World War I, the president, authorized by the congressional joint resolution of May 12, 1917 (55 Stat. 261), took over about 100 German and Austrian ships lying in U.S. ports. In the Versailles treaty of June 28, 1919, Germany waived all claims arising from requisitioning, loss or damage of German ships. In World War II, the U.S. congress, proceeding in a similar fashion, enacted the Idle Foreign Vessels act (1941), which applied to all enemy and neutral vessels (55 Stat. 242). Some 80 ships, including the French liner "Normandie" were requisitioned pursuant to this act, which also provided for compensation. The U.S. experience has been summarized thus:

The history of the matter shows that the policy of the United States has tended to avoid resort to capture and prize, and to substitute . . . gentler legal devices such as requisition for use or title upon promise or payment of just compensation. It is a fact that from 1899 to 1945, including six years of the two great wars, no prize ship or cargo was brought into a United States prize court for adjudication. Those who guide our policy . . . have employed other methods of bringing about the end result of getting foreign ships and cargoes into the war service of the United States. Thus our country has maintained its position of endeavoring to lead the world towards a general law or rule of immunity from capture or destruction of peaceful merchantmen and cargoes not contraband. (Arnold W. Knauth, "Prize Law Reconsidered," *Columbia Law Review,* p. 69 [1946].)

On the other hand, the policy against enemy merchant ships and cargoes was expressed in the official United States Navy dispatch of Dec. 7, 1941: "Execute unrestricted air and submarine warfare against Japan." It was estimated that more than 2,000 Japanese merchant ships were sunk, of which more than one half were destroyed by submarines. Total war by air and on the sea against enemy shipping and stringent controls at the source of neutral shipping, reinforced by a comprehensive concept of contraband and of enemy destination, it was believed, might well reduce the scope and significance of both prize courts and prize law in a subsequent global conflict.

In a limited conflict, however, prize courts and prize law continued to render the traditional service as was evidenced by the establishment of a prize court in Egypt in 1948 following the outbreak of hostilities in Palestine. On Sept. 25, 1955, the United States chief of naval operations promulgated the *Law of Naval Warfare* as the official United States navy manual on the subject (NWIPIO-2, reproduced as an appendix in the volume by Robert W. Tucker cited in the bibliography).

See also ADMIRALTY, HIGH COURT OF; LAWS OF WAR; VISIT AND SEARCH; ANGARY, RIGHT OF.

BIBLIOGRAPHY.—C. John Colombos, *A Treatise on the Law of Prize,* 3rd ed. (1949); A. P. Higgins and C. John Colombos, *The International Law of the Sea,* 2nd rev. ed. by C. John Colombos (1951); J. W. Garner, *Prize Law During the World War* (1927); Julius Stone, *Legal Controls of International Conflict* (1954); Robert W. Tucker, *The Law of War and Neutrality at Sea,* U.S. Naval War College *International Law Studies* (1955, 1957); S. W. D. Rowson, "Prize Law During the Second World War," *British Year Book of International Law,* pp. 160–216 (1947); Arnold W. Knauth, "Prize Law Reconsidered," *Columbia Law Review,* 46:69–93 (1946); Herbert Arthur Smith, *Law and Custom of the Sea,* 2nd ed. (1950), *The Crisis in the Law of Nations* (1947); Erik Castren, *The Present Law of War and Neutrality* (1954). (L. Gs.)

PROA: see BOAT.
PROBABILISM: see CASUISTRY.
PROBABILITY. Of the precise meaning of probability there are conflicting views among experts (philosophers, mathematicians, statisticians). The reasons for this may be partly grasped from a survey of the various channels through which a scientific concept of probability has emerged.

Commercial insurance against risks was developed in the Italian cities of the early Renaissance. The theoretical foundations of life insurance were laid in the 17th century. John Graunt in 1662 drew attention to the stability of statistical series obtained from registers of deaths. Soon after, the astronomer Edmund Halley (1656–1742) showed how to calculate annuities from mortality tables (*see* ANNUITY).

Another early reason for interest in probability was in connection with the weight of evidence in legal procedure. The theory of judicial evidence occupies a prominent place in probability mathematics up to the mid-19th century.

Mathematical problems relating to games of chance had been considered, though with minor success, by Luca di Paciuolo, Geronimo Cardano (Jerome Cardan), Niccolò Tartaglia, and other mathematicians of the Renaissance. The subject was developed into a "geometry of the die" (*aleae geometria*) by Blaise Pascal, Pierre de Fermat, and Christiaan Huygens in the 17th century. Fermat treated the problems within a general theory of combinations, to become further developed by the Swiss mathematician Jakob Bernoulli. The latter can be regarded as the founder of probability theory as a branch of mathematics: his posthumously published *Ars conjectandi* (Basel, 1713) can be said to aim at a fusion of the a priori methods of combinatory probability and the a posteriori methods of early statistical theory. The research on probability done by 18th-century mathematicians culminated in the immense work of Pierre Simon Laplace, the founder of a tradition that dominated the subject throughout the 19th century.

Laplace advocated a strictly deterministic view of the universe: an omniscient intelligence ("Laplace's demon") would be able to predict the course of nature in minutest detail with infallible accuracy. On this view, probability enters into a science of nature only as a theory of errors; *i.e.,* as a systematic study of the deviations from a mean which appear in repeated measurements of a quantity. This study was developed by Laplace, by A. M. Legendre, and by C. F. Gauss (the normal law of error and the method of least squares). The mathematical calculus of probability soon provided tools for handling statistical material in connection with public finance, health administration, the conduct of elections and other social matters besides insurance. The marquis de Condorcet and later the astronomer Adolphe Quételet were champions of a social science on a statistico-probabilistic basis.

From the middle of the 19th century, probability gradually gained ground as a part of physical theory. It first appeared in the theory of heat. J. C. Maxwell in 1860 deduced the familiar gas laws from underlying probabilities for the distribution of positions and velocities over the molecules. Ludwig Boltzmann (1877) interpreted the irreversibility of thermal processes as a tendency toward a most probable distribution of the energies of the molecules. The rise of quantum mechanics saw the theory of radiation put on a probability basis by Max Planck (1900). With the further development of quantum physics, probability invaded atomic theory. By the middle of the 20th century the deterministic view of nature was thought in some quarters to be in process of being replaced by a probabilistic view. The concept of probability had become one of the fundamental notions of a modern science and philosophy of nature. This gave a new urgency to the need for clarifying the structure and meaning of the idea.

The Abstract Calculus of Probability.—In the course of the development already outlined, several definitions of probability were suggested. Accordingly, alternative methods were devised for basing the edifice of probability mathematics on those definitions. These alternative calculi take different views of the meaning of their fundamental notion, but they agree, by and large, in having a common logical structure.

These observations offer a starting point for attempts to create an abstract calculus of probability. It abstracts from the various interpreted calculi their common structure, the formal properties of which it studies independently of any definition of probability.

In the abstract calculus developed by the Russian mathematician A. N. Kolmogorov (1933), probability figures as a function of sets. This theory, which has found much favour among mathematicians, incorporates probability mathematics within the general theory of measurable sets of points.

Abstract calculi of a type that might be called logistic were constructed by J. M. Keynes (1921), Hans Reichenbach (1932), Harold Jeffreys (1939), and other authors. In these systems probability figures as an undefined logical relation between propositions or attributes (propositional functions, classes, sets).

Let us introduce, following Keynes, the symbol a/h, which can be read as "the probability of a given h." It is often convenient to speak of a as an "event" and of h as some "conditions" or "data" or "evidence." We need not assume that any pair of propositions (or attributes) determines a numerical value of the functor. But if there is a numerical probability, it should, for noncontradictory data, satisfy the following four postulates: (1) $a/h \geqq 0$; (2) $h/h = 1$; (3) $a/h + (\text{not-}a)/h = 1$, the principle of complementarity; and (4) $(a \text{ and } b)/h = a/h \times b/(h \text{ and } a)$, the general multiplication principle. These four postulates suffice, with the aid of a few principles of a subordinate character, for the erection of the whole fabric of probability mathematics.

From the first, second and third postulates it follows that all probability-values are in the interval from 0 to 1 inclusive.

From the third with the aid of the fourth, we can prove the general addition principle: $(a \text{ or } b)/h = a/h + b/h - (a \text{ and } b)/h$.

If a and b are mutually exclusive alternatives, the probability of their joint occurrence is 0. Thus for exclusive a and b we have the equality: $(a \text{ or } b)/h = a/h + b/h$. This is called the special addition principle.

If $a/h = a/(h \text{ and } b)$, we say that a is independent (for probability) of b (in h). The notion of independence is of great importance to the further development of the calculus. It follows from the fourth postulate and the definition of independence that for independent a and b we have the equality: $(a \text{ and } b)/h = a/h \times b/h$. This is called the special multiplication principle.

The Frequency Theory of Probability.—This is the view that, popularly speaking, the probability of a given h means the relative frequency with which the event a takes place when the conditions h are fulfilled. The probability of a given h, in other words, is the proportion of h situations that lead to a events.

The frequency view of probability has a long history. Aristotle defines "a probability" as being "what men know to happen or not to happen, to be or not to be, for the most part thus and thus." A similar opinion was entertained by writers of the 17th and 18th centuries, who were interested in statistics or in a "theory of evidence."

The history of probability mathematics from Jakob Bernoulli

to Laplace and his followers is allied to a different view of the meaning of probability. The rebirth of the frequency theory followed a criticism of the foundations of the Laplacean calculus, particularly of the use of the so-called principle of indifference for the determination of probability values (*see* below). The attack was launched by R. Leslie Ellis, J. Stuart Mill, and A. A. Cournot in publications of the same year 1843. The frequency conception of probability was first worked out into a mathematical theory by John Venn (1866).

Early proponents of the frequency theory spoke of probability as a relative frequency "in the long run." This loose way of speaking is not very satisfactory. Venn was the first to define an event's probability as the limiting value which its relative frequency approaches as the number of occasions is indefinitely increased. An improved version of this frequency-limit theory was presented by Richard von Mises in 1919; another later well-known adherent of the theory is H. Reichenbach.

Von Mises also thought that a probability cannot be simply (the limiting value of) a relative frequency and added the qualification that the event ought to be irregularly or randomly distributed in the series of occasions, relative to which its probability is measured. This demand of randomness he called the principle of excluded gambling systems.

It is a great merit of Von Mises to have stressed the importance of the idea of random distribution to a frequency theory of probability. But with this idea he introduced a considerable difficulty into the theory. How is random distribution to be defined? The definition originally proposed by Von Mises has been accused of inconsistency, but it is doubtful whether any of the alternative definitions proposed by other writers (H. Reichenbach, K. Popper, A. Copeland, A. Wald) can be regarded as satisfactory.

The demand of randomness is relevant to the question of the adequacy of the frequency view as a proposed analysis of the meaning of probability. But it is not relevant to the question of the mathematical correctness of the interpretation of abstract probability in terms of frequencies (either in finite or infinite series). It may easily be verified that a frequency definition satisfies the postulates of the abstract calculus.

Even if we disregard difficulties caused by the notion of randomness, many more objections can be raised against the frequency view. Nevertheless, some form of a frequency theory is thought by many writers to offer the best account (at least for a large category of cases) of the relation between abstract probability and empirical reality.

The Range Theory of Probability.—This theory can, in its simplest form, be explained as follows: We analyze h into a number n of alternative conditions. That h is fulfilled means that either h_1 or . . . or h_n is fulfilled. Some of these alternatives, say m, entail the occurrence of a, the remaining ones entail the occurrence of not-a. Using a traditional terminology, we call the first group of alternatives favourable to a and the second unfavourable to a. The probability of a given h is the ratio $m:n$ of the number of favourable alternatives and the number of all alternatives.

This, if we omit an important qualification to be discussed presently, is substantially the definition of probability that emerged from the mathematical treatment of games of chance and was canonized in the theory of Laplace. We may refer to it as the classical form of the range definition.

It is natural to call the (mutually exclusive) alternatives covered by a proposition (or an attribute) its range. The classical definition given above can be generalized as follows: The probability of a given h is the ratio of the measure of the range of h-and-a and the measure of the range of h alone.

The notion of a range (in German, *Spielraum*) was introduced into probability theory by Johannes von Kries (1886). It was used to define probability as a logical relation between propositions by Ludwig Wittgenstein (1922). Substantially the same definition had been given by Bernard Bolzano as early as 1837. A generalized form of the Bolzano-Wittgenstein definition was suggested by F. Waismann (1929) and was further developed and extensively studied by Rudolf Carnap (1950). The Waismann-Carnap definition is independent of any specific way of measuring the ranges.

The range definition, both in its classical and in its generalized form, satisfies the postulates of abstract probability. The definition, no doubt, is mathematically correct. But does it give an adequate account of the meaning of probability?

The Principle of Indifference.—The main difficulty confronting a range theory of probability concerns the measurement of the ranges. This difficulty is allied to the question of how to analyze propositions (or attributes) into alternatives. Usually there are several possibilities open for the choice of a measure and the analysis of the data into alternatives.

The classics of probability theory were aware of these difficulties and the first one to discuss the matter fully was Jakob Bernoulli. He stressed that the alternatives into which h (of the probability-functor) is analyzed ought to be equally possible; *i.e.,* "each case ought to have the same facility as any other case of coming about." This condition of equipossibility in the cases was usually added to the classical range definition of probability. The condition, it will be noted, is tantamount to a principle of measuring ranges.

But what does equipossibility mean and on what conditions may we rightly pronounce cases equally possible? In answer to the latter question Jakob Bernoulli laid down a rule which has become known under the names of the principle of insufficient reason, the principle of equal distribution of ignorance or the principle of indifference (Keynes). In its classical version this principle states that two cases are equally possible if no reason is known why the one case rather than the other should come about.

Reliance on a principle of indifference for measuring ranges (probabilities) has a certain prima facie plausibility in games of chance, where there usually is complete agreement among experts as regards the right analysis of the situations into alternatives of equal possibility. In cases which present no obvious analogy to games of chance, reliance on the principle becomes dubious. It was the use of it made by Laplace and his followers, particularly for the notorious doctrine of inverse probability (*see* below and also INDUCTION), that, in the middle of the 19th century, provoked criticism of the foundations of the entire classical fabric of probability theory. Among the earlier critics of the principle of indifference mention should be made of R. Leslie Ellis, G. Boole, C. S. Peirce, and J. von Kries.

In modern times J. M. Keynes discussed the principle acutely and in detail. Severely criticizing its unguarded uses, he also attempted to refashion the principle and to make clear its relevance to any philosophy of probability. Warranted use of the principle is tied to the question of symmetry in the unit alternatives under consideration; and the problem of symmetry in its turn is tied to the problem of an ultimate analysis of propositions (attributes) into alternatives. Any judgment of symmetry or ultimacy, as it presupposes that all relevant information about the cases has been taken into account, is, negatively, a judgment of irrelevance or independence for probability among propositions (attributes). Any pronouncement on irrelevance involves, so Keynes thought, an "element of direct judgment or intuition."

The principle of indifference has usually been discussed in connection with the classical range definition, to which it was traditionally regarded as a necessary supplementation. It should, however, be observed that the problems connected with this principle recur, *mutatis mutandis,* within any theory which defines probability in terms of the relative magnitudes of ranges.

The Belief Theory of Probability.—Many authors in the past spoke of probability as a degree of belief or of certainty. F. P. Ramsey (1926) and, somewhat later, B. de Finetti (1937) made a systematic attempt to base the mathematical theory of probability on the notion of partial belief. Both authors take as their point of departure the old idea of measuring a person's belief by proposing a bet and observing the lowest odds that he will accept. It may be shown that a person who distributes his partial beliefs (*i.e.,* subjective assignments of probabilities) contrary to the laws of the calculus could have a so-called Dutch book made against him and would then stand to lose in any event. Because of this, the laws of probability may be called rules for consistent (coherent) sets of degrees of belief.

Ramsey, moreover, made an ingenious effort to generalize the above procedure of measuring beliefs. A bet can be regarded as an option between goods, and accepting lowest odds as a reflection of an attitude of indifference in an option. A distribution of our partial beliefs contrary to the laws of probability, Ramsey says, "would be inconsistent in the sense that it violated the laws of preference between options, such as that preferability is a transitive asymmetrical relation."

The ideas of Ramsey and De Finetti were later taken up by L. J. Savage (1954), who became the founder of a subjectivist or personalist school in modern theory of probability and statistics. The combination of probabilistic ideas with the value-theoretic notions of preference and utility has had fruitful applications to the mathematical study of economic and related forms of human behaviour. Acknowledgment of this fact does not exclude that one may take a somewhat critical view of the epistemological and logical basis of the belief theory of probability.

Is Probability Subjective or Objective?—The subjectivist conception of probability as a degree of belief is often contrasted with the objectivist conception of the notion as either a relative frequency or a ratio of measures of ranges. It is questionable, however, whether one can maintain a sharp contrast between objectivism and subjectivism in the philosophy (epistemology) of probability.

As we have seen, supporters of the frequency view have found it necessary, to reach an adequate analysis of probability, to combine their definition of the concept with the idea of a random distribution of events on a series of occasions. Supporters of a range theory again have, for the same purpose, had recourse to some form of a principle of indifference for the determination of equipossibility in certain unit alternatives. The question may be raised whether randomness and equipossibility can be satisfactorily accounted for independently of reference to a state of knowledge or ignorance. If the answer is negative, we shall have to admit that an adequate account of the meaning of probability cannot be given in purely objectivist terms.

On the other hand, the belief theory does not necessarily entail an identification of probability with belief as a psychological phenomenon. The attitudes in options between goods may be said to reveal subjective estimations of probability. But the derivation of the laws of probability within the belief theory does not confer on them the status of psychological laws of believing. It rather makes them standards of rationality (consistency) in the distribution of beliefs or in preferences. It would therefore be an oversimplification to regard the belief theory as an account of probability in purely subjectivist (that is, psychological) terms.

Bernoulli's Theorem.—Let us assume that the probability for the occurrence of an event a on a certain occasion of h is not affected by its occurrence or nonoccurrence on previous occasions of h. The occurrences of a, in other words, are independent for probability of one another. And let us assume that this probability is p. A simple use of the special multiplication and addition principles can now be made for calculating the probability that the event a will, on n occasions of h, be realized with a relative frequency in the interval $p \pm \epsilon$. From considerations about this second-order probability we can prove that:

1. The most probable value of the event's relative frequency on n occasions is that value which comes nearest to its probability p.

2. The probability that the event's relative frequency on n occasions will deviate from its probability p by less than a given amount ϵ, however small, approaches 1 as a limit when n is indefinitely increased. Thus, popularly speaking, in the long run the event will almost certainly be realized with a relative frequency corresponding to its probability.

An example will illustrate this asymptotic character of the increasing probability. The probability of head and tail in tossing with a normal coin is $\frac{1}{2}$. The results are independent for probability: no combination of head and tail in previous tosses will influence the probability of getting head or of getting tail in the next toss. A simple calculation shows that the probability of getting 49, 50, or 51 heads in 100 tosses is approximately 0.16; the probability of getting between 490 and 510 heads in 1,000 tosses is 0.47; and the probability of getting between 4,900 and 5,100 heads in 10,000 tosses is 0.95. In other words: in 10,000 tosses it is already almost certain that the proportion of heads will deviate by less than 0.01 from its probability ½.

This remarkable theorem is known as Bernoulli's theorem. It is chronologically the first member of a class of propositions called the laws of great numbers. The name was introduced by Siméon Denis Poisson (1837).

Inverse Probability.—In 1763 Thomas Bayes proved that, if $m:n$ is the relative frequency of an event on n independent occasions, then $m:n$ is also the most probable value of the event's probability, provided that any value of this probability is initially (a priori) as probable as any other value. The same theorem was proved independently by Laplace in 1774. Laplace also proved that, on the assumptions mentioned, it will in the long run become almost certain that the probability of the event coincides with its relative frequency.

The Bayes-Laplace theorem is the inversion of Bernoulli's theorem and the cornerstone of the classical doctrine of inverse probability for the estimation of probabilities on the basis of frequencies. The doctrine was developed and put to extensive use by Laplace and his followers. It was thought to be of great relevance to the problem of induction.

The Achilles' heel of inverse probability is its dependence on initial or a priori probabilities. These were in the classical doctrine often established by deplorably uncritical use of the principle of indifference. The doctrine was challenged in the 19th century, particularly by early proponents of the frequency view. The use of inverse probability is still a matter of debate. Some researchers, among them R. A. Fisher, have altogether rejected it.

Asymptotic Probabilities and the Principle of Moral Certitude.—It was often thought in the past that, by virtue of Bernoulli's theorem, events will, in the long run, happen in numbers proportional to the probabilities (A. De Morgan, 1838). But this is a serious mistake. The theorem only says that it becomes increasingly probable that the frequency coincides with the probability. And this, by itself, does not warrant any conclusion about actual frequencies, not even in the long run.

The error latent in the idea that Bernoulli's theorem provides a bridge from a subjectivist conception of probability as a degree of certainty to an objectivist conception in terms of frequencies was first clearly seen and conclusively criticized by R. Leslie Ellis (1843). There were many relapses into the error afterward, but today the correctness of the criticism is universally admitted.

There is, however, another way of using Bernoulli's theorem and other asymptotic principles of probability (laws of great numbers) as a bridge from (uninterpreted) probabilities to statistical frequencies without committing a logical error. It may be briefly indicated as follows:

Let us assume that, either from observations about frequencies or from considerations about ranges or from some other source, we frame a hypothesis about the probability of a given h. From this hypothesis we calculate that it is "almost" or, as Bernoulli would have said it, "morally" certain (say probable to degree 0.95) that in a series of n trials the relative frequency of the event will deviate from its probability by less than a small fraction (say 0.01). In other words, it is "most unlikely" (morally impossible) that the frequency will fall short of the hypothetical probability by more than this fraction. Now we may adopt a maxim that very improbable events are "practically excluded" or that "moral certainty" should be treated as equal to full certainty. Consequently, if the event's frequency nevertheless deviates from the hypothetical value by more than the fraction in question, we say, not that something very improbable has happened, but that our probability hypothesis has to be rejected.

The proposed maxim was in fact suggested already by Bernoulli. It might be called Bernoulli's principle of moral certitude. Its adoption seems to be in good accord with actual use of probability calculations for scientific and applied purposes. And it partially explains why it is possible, without detriment to the applications of probability, to suspend judgment as regards the meaning of this controversial notion. The calculus is a vehicle which takes us from hypothetical probabilities to predicted frequencies. If the

observed frequencies conflict with the principle of moral certitude, the hypotheses are modified or rejected. The boundaries of moral certitude are, of course, elastic; and whether we wish provisionally to fix them at one value rather than at another will depend upon a multitude of circumstances peculiar to each case. Such circumstances are the amount of statistical evidence at hand, the possibilities of repeated trials and the facility with which dependencies between occurrences can be controlled. Among them are also considerations of an ethical nature relating to the gains and losses which we may incur by choosing one probability hypothesis rather than another as a basis of our actions.

Has "Probability" One or Many Meanings?—Compare the following uses of probability: (1) "the probability of a normal six-sided die turning up 'six' is ⅙"; (2) "the probability that Shakespeare wrote the plays commonly attributed to him is overwhelming"; (3) "Fresnel's experiment increased the probability of the undulatory theory of light." Does "probability" mean the same in all the three statements?

According to Hans Reichenbach, one of the chief proponents of the frequency theory in modern times, there is only one (scientific) meaning of probability. A statement of the second type exemplified above, which concerns the probability of an individual event, is literally meaningless, but may be reinterpreted as a statement about that which usually is the case under similar circumstances. Statements of the third type, again, which attribute probability to general propositions (laws of nature, theories, hypotheses) may, according to Reichenbach, be given a frequency interpretation as referring either to a proportion of successful predictions, or to a proportion of true theories within a class.

A unitary view of probability was also taken by J. M. Keynes, though on quite different grounds. According to Keynes, the difficulties presented by cases such as the second and third types exemplified above would indicate that probability is a wider notion than the concept which figures in a frequency theory or even in any theory which requires probability to be a measurable quantity. In its wide sense, probability is a (not necessarily measurable) degree of rational belief.

Those who have advocated a dualistic view of probability have usually wished to contrast cases of the third type, or the probability of laws of nature, with other types of probability. Jakob Friedrich Fries (*System der Logik,* 1811; *Versuch einer Kritik der Principien der Wahrscheinlichkeitsrechnung,* 1842) called the probability of laws "philosophical probability" and contrasted it with "mathematical probability." This distinction was adopted by many logicians and philosophers of the 19th century (E. F. Apelt, A. A. Cournot, M. W. Drobisch). Philosophical probability was thought to be nonnumerical in principle. A similar position found favour with many 20th-century authors: Bertrand Russell (1948) contrasts "credibility" and "mathematical probability"; W. C. Kneale (1949), "acceptability" and "chance"; R. B. Braithwaite (1953), "reasonableness" and "probability."

A dualistic view of a somewhat different nature was developed by Rudolf Carnap (*Logical Foundations of Probability*). Of the two concepts of probability that he distinguishes, the first (which he also calls "degree of confirmation") is probability in the sense of a range theory; the second is probability in the sense of a frequency theory. Carnap tries to reconcile the rival claims of the two theories by assigning to each concept of probability its proper field of application. In view of the difficulties, however, which both theories encounter as proposed analyses of probability, it cannot be taken for granted that this reconciliation is altogether satisfactory. *See also* PROBABILITY, MATHEMATICAL.

BIBLIOGRAPHY.—For a good introduction *see* E. Nagel, *Principles of the Theory of Probability* (1939). For the classical view: Jakob (Jacques) Bernoulli, *Ars conjectandi* (1713), especially book iv; and P. S. de Laplace, *Philosophical Essay on Probabilities* (1952). For modern range theory: W. C. Kneale, *Probability and Induction* (1949), a good introduction to the whole subject; and R. Carnap, *Logical Foundations of Probability,* 2nd ed. (1962). For the frequency view: R. von Mises, *Probability, Statistics and Truth,* Eng. trans. (1939); and H. Reichenbach, *The Theory of Probability,* Eng. trans. (1949). For the subjectivist or personalist view: F. P. Ramsey, "Truth and Probability" in *The Foundations of Mathematics and Other Logical Essays* (1931); and L. J. Savage, *The Foundations of Statistics* (1954). For abstract probability and general questions: H. Reichenbach, *op. cit.*; J. M. Keynes, *A Treatise on Probability* (1921); A. N. Kolmogorov, *Foundations of the Theory of Probability*, Eng. trans. ed. by Nathan Morrison (1950); and G. H. von Wright, *A Treatise on Induction and Probability* (1951).

(G. H. v. W.)

PROBABILITY, MATHEMATICAL. Mathematical probability is an attractive, thriving, and respectable part of mathematics (some say the gateway to its deepest mysteries). It has a well-defined basis in a system of axioms governing the relations of what are called probabilities in a probability algebra or calculus; the probabilities themselves are real numbers between zero and one (inclusive). The most famous axiom system has been formalized by A. N. Kolmogorov, and will be given later. It should be noted that the idea of probability is primitive, beyond definition, distinct from philosophical probability (*see* PROBABILITY), and immune to the controversy that has plagued philosophers. However, there are similarities; probability in its ordinary use is related to uncertainty. In mathematics, the character of the uncertainty is spelled out completely by specifying the alternatives in question, just as any sensible bet specifies exact terms of payoff. In coin tossing, for example, the usual specification is that the coin must fall head or tail; falling on edge, rolling away, and all other bizarre possibilities are ruled out. In mathematical terms, let the event coin-falls-head be labeled E_1 (E for event), the event coin-falls-tails E_2; then the uncertainty only concerns which of the events E_1, E_2 occurs. If it were desired to include bizarre possibilities, corresponding events E_3 (coin falls on edge), E_4 (coin rolls away), and so on, would be required for complete mathematical description. The set of events $\{E_1, E_2, \ldots\}$ is commonly called a sample space, and the events are called points of the space. This terminology seems odd for discrete alternatives (finite sets of events), but it is used for uniformity, to make the theory as general as possible. Although the points of the sample space are called events, they are not necessarily objectively observable events; they also may be imagined (as in so-called conceptual experiments) if this serves a purpose. In either case, the weight or measure assigned to a point of sample space is said to be its probability. Then the axiom system determines the probabilities of all sets of points in the space. Note that the assignment of probabilities to points of the space is under no restraint other than that arising from the axioms. Naturally, simple assignments come first. When the sample space has n discrete points, the simplest assignment is $1/n$ for each of the n points, that is, the outcomes are equally probable; this is a version of what is called the Laplace rule (after Pierre Simon Laplace, whose treatise, *Théorie analytique des probabilités* [1812], is one of the great probability classics). While the direct use of this and similar simple probability models may be hard to justify (*e.g.*, to a philosopher whose job is to look for trouble), there are many indirect uses, including the part the models play in building a coherent body of theory, which commend them to mathematical attention.

To avoid the intricacy and subtleties of measure theory, the exposition below (following the lead of William Feller, whose *Introduction to Probability* . . . is a modern classic) is limited to discrete sample spaces. A sample space is called discrete if it contains a finite or infinite number of points that can be arranged in a simple sequence $E_1, E_2, \ldots$ (that is, are denumerable), with E_j a point of the space. With each point E_j of the sample space, there is associated a real number between zero and 1, inclusive, called the probability of E_j, and denoted by $\Pr(E_j)$, where

$$\Pr(E_1) + \Pr(E_2) + \ldots = 1$$

However there are a few places where results grounded in nondiscrete sample spaces appear; their justification is left to the reader's intuition or background. (*See also* POINT SET.)

Elementary Definitions and Theorems.—For uniform terminology, all points and sets of points of the sample space are called events, in keeping with the notion, given above, of the sample space as a specification of experimental outcomes. If A is an event, its probability is written as $\Pr(A)$; $\Pr(A)$ is the sum of the probabilities of all points in A. The complement of A is the event consisting of all points not contained in A and is denoted by $\bar{A}$, and the complementary probability to $\Pr(A)$ is $\Pr(\bar{A})$,

where $\Pr(A) + \Pr(\bar{A}) = 1$, or $\Pr(\bar{A}) = 1 - \Pr(A)$. This formula expresses the fact that either A or its complement must occur.

With any two events A and B there may be associated two new events: the compound event AB in which both A and B occur, and the union of A and B, denoted by $A \cup B$, in which either A or B or both occur. (The symbol $\cup$ is sometimes called cup, and is used to mean the set consisting of points belonging either to A or B or both; it is generically similar to the plus sign and indeed when A and B have no points in common Kolmogorov replaces $A \cup B$ by $A + B$.) The probabilities of these new sets are denoted by $\Pr(AB)$ and $\Pr(A \cup B)$. Of course these operations may be extended to as many sets as desired; the meaning of the event $ABC \ldots$ is that all $A, B, C, \ldots$ occur, and of $A \cup B \cup C \ldots$ that either A or B or C or . . . or all of $A, B, C, \ldots$ occur. A compound event AB may be regarded as occurring in time sequence: first A, then B; then $\Pr(AB) = \Pr(A)\Pr(B|A)$ serves as a definition of the conditional probability $\Pr(B|A)$, which is read as the probability of B given A. If $\Pr(AB) = \Pr(A)\Pr(B)$, then events A and B are statistically independent (or independent, for short). For n events, Kolmogorov gives $2^n - n - 1$ equations of independence, which may be summarized by saying that every k-combination, $k = 2, 3, \ldots, n$, of the n events must be independent. (A k-combination is an unordered selection of k things.)

With these definitions are associated certain basic theorems. First, the Theorem of Compound Probability (or Multiplication Theorem) is given by

$$\Pr(A_1 A_2 \ldots A_n) = \Pr(A_1)\Pr(A_2 \mid A_1)\Pr(A_3 \mid A_1 A_2) \ldots$$
$$\Pr(A_n \mid A_1 A_2 \ldots A_{n-1})$$

This equation is a generalization of the equation used above to define conditional probability. It provides an easy way to compute compound probabilities when the events may be regarded as occurring in sequence, and the conditional probabilities are easier to compute. Note that the conditional probability of event B when A is known to have happened may be quite different from the unconditional probability $\Pr(B)$. Next if events $A_1, A_2, \ldots, A_n$ are mutually exclusive events that exhaust all possibilities, the Theorem of Total Probability states that for any event X

$$\Pr(X) = \Pr(A_1)\Pr(X \mid A_1) + \Pr(A_2)\Pr(X \mid A_2) + \ldots + \Pr(A_n)\Pr(X \mid A_n)$$

Finally there is Poincaré's formula, a probability version of the Principle of Inclusion and Exclusion (*see* COMBINATORIAL ANALYSIS: *Discordant Permutations*), which applies to compounds of complementary events. For two events A_1 and A_2

$$\Pr(\bar{A}_1 \bar{A}_2) = 1 - \Pr(A_1) - \Pr(A_2) + \Pr(A_1 A_2)$$

The right-hand side may be abbreviated $\Pr[(1 - A_1)(1 - A_2)]$, if it is understood that the internal multiplication is to be performed first, and the terms separated by the rule

$$\Pr(A + B + \ldots) = \Pr(A) + \Pr(B) + \ldots, \text{ while } \Pr(1) = 1.$$

With these conventions, Poincaré's formula for n events may be written in abbreviated notation as

$$\Pr(\bar{A}_1 \bar{A}_2 \ldots \bar{A}_n) = \Pr[(1 - A_1)(1 - A_2) \ldots (1 - A_n)]$$

Note that $\bar{A}_1 \bar{A}_2 \ldots \bar{A}_n$ is the complementary event to $A_1 \cup A_2 \cup \ldots \cup A_n$ so that

$$\Pr(A_1 \cup A_2 \cup \ldots \cup A_n) = 1 - \Pr[(1 - A_1)(1 - A_2) \ldots (1 - A_n)]$$

Simple Illustrative Examples.—*Coin Tossing.*—Consider tosses of two coins. The outcomes may be labeled HH, HT, TH, TT (H for head, T for tail); these are the points E_1, E_2, E_3, E_4 of the sample space. The event two-heads is E_1; its complement less-than-two-heads is the union of E_2, E_3 and E_4; that is, the set $\{E_2, E_3, E_4\}$. The event just-one-head is the set $\{E_2, E_3\}$; its complement no-heads-or-two-heads is the set $\{E_1, E_4\}$. If all four sample points have probability $\frac{1}{4}$, the probabilities of the events just defined are each $\frac{1}{2}$, while the probability of two heads (or two tails) is $\frac{1}{4}$, and the probability of its complement is $\frac{3}{4}$. If all outcomes are regarded as compound events, and are equally probable, then the probability of head equals the probability of tail equals $\frac{1}{2}$; otherwise, if head falls with probability p and tail falls with probability q ($p + q = 1$, necessarily), then the outcomes have respective probabilities (in the order written) p^2, pq, qp, q^2. Note that $p^2 + pq + qp + q^2 = (p + q)^2 = 1$. If the two coins are regarded as tossed successively, so that the outcomes represent sequences in time, another set of events may be considered; these are defined by first-appearance-of-head or number-of-tosses-up-to-first-head (often called a first-crossing or waiting-time problem). Since head may appear first on the first toss, on the second toss, or not at all, the sets of sample points for the three events are, respectively, (E_1, E_2), E_3, and E_4. If the probability of head at each toss is p, the respective probabilities are p, pq, and q^2. Similar results appear in successive tosses of n coins that are alike (or n independent tosses of a single coin), as will appear in the discussion of the negative binomial distribution later.

Arrangements of Distinct Objects.—Consider the six ordered arrangements (permutations) of three objects a, b, and c; namely $abc, acb, bac, bca, cab, cba$. These may be taken as the points $E_1, E_2, E_3, E_4, E_5, E_6$ of the sample space. The event a-in-first-place is the set $\{E_1, E_2\}$. Regarding any arrangement as a displacement of the natural order abc, the event no-object-displaced is the point E_1; the event one-object-displaced contains no points, since a displacement must interchange at least two objects; the event two-objects-displaced is the set $\{E_2, E_3, E_6\}$, and finally the event three-objects-displaced is the set $\{E_4, E_5\}$. The number of points in these successive sets is 1,0,3,2, and these numbers are proportional to probabilities when the points of the sample space are equally probable.

Sampling Surveys.—A sampling survey is a procedure for obtaining statistical information. Suppose the survey is of handedness in people, and each sample has 100 members. Then each sample provides an integral number x (the number of left-handers in the sample, say), where x may be 0, 1, . . . , 100. The sample space consists of 101 points 0, 1, . . . , 100. Presumably if the survey takes sufficiently many samples, many of these points will appear with low frequency, many not at all. The relative frequencies found serve as a guide to the assignment of probabilities of the sample space, for use in other calculations.

Simple Probability Calculations.—Some probability calculations were made in the preceding section; a few more may be helpful.

Card Hands.—An ordinary poker or bridge deck consists of 52 cards, 13 of each suit (two black: clubs, spades; two red: diamonds, hearts) with face values 2, 3, . . . , 10, jack, queen, king, ace. Of the many probability calculations that may be made, consider the following. A bridge hand consists of 13 cards, and the number of different bridge hands is the number of combinations of 52 things taken 13 at a time, that is (*see* COMBINATORIAL ANALYSIS: *Permutations and Combinations*) the binomial coefficient

$$_{52}C_{13} = \binom{52}{13} = \frac{52!}{13! \; 39!} = \frac{52 \cdot 51 \cdot \ldots \cdot 40}{13 \cdot 12 \cdot \ldots \cdot 1}$$

If all hands are equally probable, consider the probability that a hand will contain all face values (not necessarily of the same suit). Since each face value may appear in any of the four suits, there are 4^{13} ways of choosing hands containing all face values and the probability in question is $4^{13}/\binom{52}{13} = 0.0001057 \ldots$ or about 1 in 10,000.

Birthdays.—Birthdays are distributed throughout the year in a nonuniform way, and years themselves are of variable length. Assume equal probability for a birthday each day of a 365-day year, and consider the probability that in a group of r people, all birthdays are different. For r people the total number of possible birthdays (on the equiprobable assumption) is 365^r. Of these, the number in which all are unlike is $365 \cdot 364 \ldots (365 - r + 1)$, since any one can be picked in 365 ways, the next in 364 (it must differ from the first), the third in 363, and finally the rth in $365 - r + 1$. If the expression $n(n - 1) \ldots (n - r + 1)$ is abbreviated to $(n)_r$,

the probability in question is $(365)_r/365^r$ or

$$\left(1 - \frac{1}{365}\right)\left(1 - \frac{2}{365}\right) \cdots \left(1 - \frac{r - 1}{365}\right)$$

Multiplying this out and neglecting cross products leads to the approximation $1 - r(r - 1)/730$. A closer approximation follows from taking natural logarithms (*q.v.*) and using the approximation $\log (1 - x) \approx -x$. Then if the probability is denoted by p, $\log p \approx -r(r-1)/730$. This approximation is particularly apt in answering the question of how large r should be so that p is close to $\frac{1}{2}$. Using the approximation and $\log (\frac{1}{2}) = -\log 2 = -0.69315$ leads to $r(r - 1) = 730 \log 2$; and r is about 22.6. With 22 people the probability that no two have the same birthday is a little larger than $\frac{1}{2}$, (specifically, 0.524), but for 23 people it is smaller (0.493).

Craps.—This is the ordinary dice game, played with two six-faced cubes; one of the dice is called a die. Each throw realizes a number (or "point") between 2 and 12, inclusive. The various ways of obtaining these sums are given in the table below. The table shows, for example, that there is only one way to get the sum 2: both dice must show 1; that is, 1,1. The table also shows that there are two ways to get the point 3, and so on.

2	3	4	5	6	7	8	9	10	11	12
1,1	1,2	1,3	1,4	1,5	1,6	2,6	3,6	4,6	5,6	6,6
	2,1	2,2	2,3	2,4	2,5	3,5	4,5	5,5	6,5	
		3,1	3,2	3,3	3,4	4,4	5,4	6,4		
			4,1	4,2	4,3	5,3	6,3			
				5,1	5,2	6,2				
					6,1					

and the relative numbers of ways for each point are

Point	2	3	4	5	6	7	8	9	10	11	12
Number	1	2	3	4	5	6	5	4	3	2	1

giving a total of 36 possible ways. A player wins if he throws 7 or 11 on the first throw, or, if having thrown one of 4,5,6,8,9,10 on the first throw, he "makes his point," that is, throws the same point before throwing 7. Alternatively, he loses if he makes 2, 3, or 12 on the first throw, or fails to make his point which may be any of 4,5,6,8,9,10. The sample space consists of the 36 pairs of numbers (n,m), $n = 1,2,3,4,5,6$, and m likewise. If each of these has the same probability, the probability of winning may be calculated as follows. First, the probability of throwing 7 or 11 on the first throw is $6/36 + 2/36 = 2/9$. Next the probability of making a point with a probability of $x/36$ (where $x = 3$ for points 4,10; $x = 4$ for points 5,9; $x = 5$ for points 6,8) is

$$\frac{x}{36} \sum_{n=0}^{\infty} \left(1 - \frac{6}{36} - \frac{x}{36}\right)^n \frac{x}{36}$$

The first $x/36$ is the probability of throwing a point with probability $x/36$ on the first throw, the sum following is the probability that the throws intervening between this throw and the last throw give neither 7 nor the point, the last $x/36$ is the probability that the last throw (which may follow arbitrarily many intervening throws) is the same as the first. The sum is that of a geometric series and after simplification becomes $x^2/36(x + 6)$. Hence the probability of making a point is

$$2\left[\frac{9}{36 \cdot 9} + \frac{16}{36 \cdot 10} + \frac{25}{36 \cdot 11}\right] = \frac{134}{495}$$

Adding 2/9 to this makes the probability of winning 244/495 which is about 0.493. The game is not fair in that the probabilities of winning and losing are not equal.

Random Variables, Probability Distributions, and Distribution Functions.—In the framework of the probability theory under description, "random variable" is a misnomer, as is evident in the definition: a function defined on a sample space is called a random variable. Function is used in its mathematical sense, of course, and in the definition simply means that each point of the sample space is assigned a value in accordance with some function. Examples have already appeared; when coin tosses are considered by number of heads, the function assigns the value k to each point of the space that corresponds to k heads; when arrangements are considered by number of elements displaced, the function assigns k to each point of the space having k elements displaced.

Despite this confusing aspect, the term random variable is too firmly entrenched to be changed, and in ordinary usage its definition is as follows: X is a random variable (in a discrete sample space) if it assumes values $x_1, x_2, \ldots$ and to each of these values is assigned a probability: $\Pr(X = x_j) = f(x_j)$. Naturally (by the definition of a discrete sample space), $f(x_j) \geq 0$ and

$$f(x_1) + f(x_2) + \ldots = 1$$

The set of probabilities $\{f(x_1), f(x_2), \ldots\}$ is called a probability distribution. This term must be distinguished from the term distribution function, which is essential in the consideration of non-discrete sample spaces. A distribution function is any nondecreasing function $F(x)$ that tends to zero as x approaches minus infinity

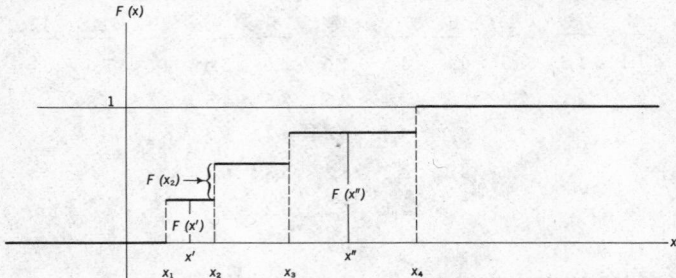

FIG. 1.—DISTRIBUTION FUNCTION FOR DISCRETE SAMPLE SPACES

and to 1 as x approaches plus infinity; the distribution function $F(x)$ of random variable X is $\Pr(X \leq x)$. For a discrete random variable

$$F(x) = \Pr(X \leq x) = \sum_{x_i \leq x} f(x_i)$$

$F(x)$ has the form of a staircase with risers of size $f(x_j)$ at each point x_j; the staircase is entirely included between the lines $F(x) = 0$ and $F(x) = 1$ (see fig. 1). The continuous curves with which engineers and statisticians are more familiar are obtained by increasing the number and density of the points x_j in the way familiar from the limiting procedures of the differential calculus (see fig. 2).

A concept closely associated with probability distribution is its generating function; indeed generating functions were invented by

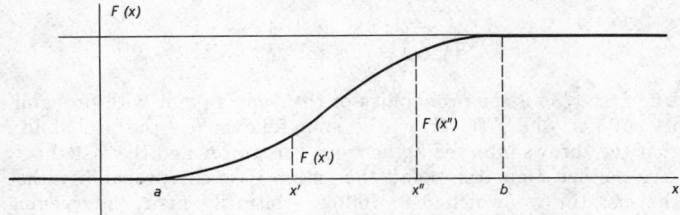

FIG. 2.—CONTINUOUS DISTRIBUTION FUNCTION

Laplace for their service in the probability calculus. The generating function of the discrete distribution given above is written as

$$P(t) = f(x_1)t^{x_1} + f(x_2)t^{x_2} + \ldots + f(x_i)t^{x_i} + \ldots$$

When the x_j are integers $P(t)$ is either a polynomial (q.v.) or a power series in t; it is common to regard t as a real variable with a range such that the sum on the right exists (when the x_j are infinite in number), but for many uses of the generating function in probability and in combinatorial analysis, convergence questions are irrelevant.

Often it is important to know whether or not random variables

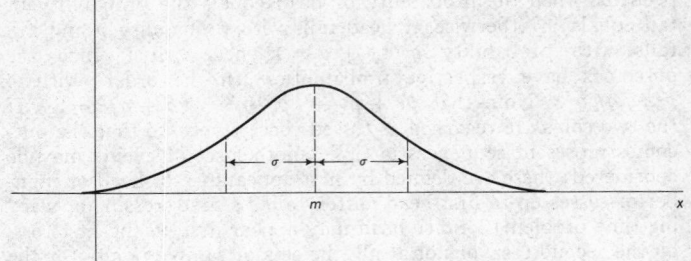

FIG. 3.—NORMAL DENSITY FUNCTION

are independent. The definition of independence is as follows: If n random variables $X_1, \ldots, X_n$ are defined on the same sample space, their joint distribution is given by a system of equations that assigns probabilities to all combinations $X_1 = x_{j_1}, \ldots, X_n = x_{j_n}$ where x_{j_i} ranges over all possible values for X_i. The random variables are mutually independent if for any combination of values $x_{j_1}, \ldots, x_{j_n}$

$$\Pr(X_1 = x_{i_1}, \ldots, X_n = x_{i_n}) = \Pr(X_1 = x_{i_1}) \ldots \Pr(X_n = x_{i_n})$$

Mathematical Expectation, Moments, and Other Properties of Distributions.—For many probability and statistical studies, the knowledge or determination of the full distribution is unnecessary or redundant; it is enough to know a few of its properties. Probably the most commonly used property is the mathematical expectation or mean (average); for the distribution already considered the formula for the expectation of the random variable X is

$$E(X) = x_1 f(x_1) + x_2 f(x_2) + \ldots + x_i f(x_i) + \ldots$$

If there is an infinite number of values x_j, the distribution has finite expectation only if the series on the right converges absolutely; that is, only if the sum $\Sigma |x_j| f(x_j)$, where $|x_j|$ is the absolute value of x_j, converges. Otherwise, random variable X is said to have no finite expectation. More generally the kth moment about the origin is defined by

$$m_k = E(X^k) = \sum x_i^k f(x_i), \quad k = 0, 1, 2, \ldots$$

while the kth moment about the mean has the formula

$$M_k = E(X - E(X))^k = \sum [x_i - E(X)]^k f(x_i), \quad k = 0, 1, 2, \ldots$$

The second moment about the mean ($k = 2$) is called the variance, which is the square of the standard deviation (this is a definition of the latter). Another kind of moment of frequent use is the binomial moment; the kth binomial moment is given by

$$B_k = E\left[\binom{X}{k} \right] = \sum \binom{x_i}{k} f(x_i), \quad k = 0, 1, 2, \ldots$$

in the notation for binomial coefficients used before. Existence conditions for all of these are similar to those for the mean.

Just as the probability distribution is considered as a single entity in a probability-generating function, the moments can be collected together in moment-generating functions, which indeed are related to the former. These relations, for probability distributions with all x_j non-negative integers, are

$$m(t) = m_0 + m_1 t + \ldots + m_k t^k / k! + \ldots = P(e^t)$$
$$M(t) = M_0 + M_1 t + \ldots + M_k t^k / k! + \ldots = \exp(-tm_1)P(e^t)$$
$$B(t) = B_0 + B_1 t + \ldots + B_k t^k + \ldots = P(1 + t)$$

Note that $m_0 = M_0 = B_0 = 1$, $M_1 = 0$, $m_1 = B_1$. Note also that the first two differ from the last, which like $P(t)$ is an ordinary generating function, in that the general term contains $t^k / k!$ rather than t^k; because of this similarity to the exponential function, they are called exponential-generating functions. If $P(t)$ is rewritten as

$$P(t) = p_0 + p_1 t + \ldots + p_k t^k + \ldots$$

$(p_k = f(x_j), \quad x_j = k; \quad p_k = 0,$ otherwise$)$, then the equation $B(t - 1) = P(t)$ is equivalent to the following expression for probabilities in terms of binomial moments

$$p_j = \sum_{k=j}^{\infty} (-1)^{j+k} \binom{k}{j} B_k$$

This is a useful formula when the binomial moments can be determined more easily than the probabilities. Of course the formulas above also supply interrelations of the three kinds of moments. Of these it is sufficient to note that

$$m_2 = 2B_2 + B_1, \quad M_2 = 2B_2 + B_1 - B_1^2 = m_2 - m_1^2$$

Finally notice that if $X_1, X_2, \ldots, X_n$ are random variables with finite means, then the mean of the sum is the sum of the means, that is

$$E(X_1 + X_2 + \ldots + X_n) = E(X_1) + E(X_2) + \ldots + E(X_n)$$

If these variables are mutually independent and the variance of X_k is σ_k^2, then

$$\mathrm{Var}(X_1 + X_2 + \ldots + X_n) = \sigma_1^2 + \sigma_2^2 + \ldots + \sigma_n^2$$

Also, if $X_1, X_2, \ldots, X_n$ are independent random variables with generating functions $P_1(t), P_2(t), \ldots, P_n(t)$, the generating function $P(t; n)$ of the sum $X_1 + X_2 + \ldots + X_n$ is given by

$$P(t; n) = P_1(t) P_2(t) \ldots P_n(t)$$

This formula is especially useful when all random variables have the same distribution and hence the same generating function, say $P(t)$, so that

$$P(t; n) = [P(t)]^n$$

Important Distributions and Their Applications.—*Binomial Distribution.*—Consider a succession of n independent tosses of a coin with probability p for head, $q = 1 - p$ for tail; that is, what are called Bernoulli trials, after Jakob Bernoulli (1654–1705). The generating function for a single toss is $q + pt$, and by the formula just above, the generating function for n independent tosses is $(q + pt)^n$. By the binomial theorem

$$(q + pt)^n = \sum_{k=0}^{n} \binom{n}{k} p^k q^{n-k} t^k$$

Hence the binomial distribution may be written as $\{b(k; n, p), k = 0, 1, \ldots, n\}$ where

$$b(k; n, p) = \binom{n}{k} p^k q^{n-k}$$

For $n = 2$, as already noticed in the coin tossing example, $b(0; 2, p) = q^2$, $b(1; 2, p) = 2pq$, $b(2; 2, p) = p^2$; for $n = 3$, the distribution is summarized in the table

k	0	1	2	3
$b(k; 3, p)$	q^3	$3q^2 p$	$3qp^2$	p^3

The mean for a single toss is $q \cdot 0 + p \cdot 1 = p$; hence the mean for n tosses is np. The binomial moment generating function $B(t; n, p)$ is given by

$$B(t; n, p) = [q + p(1 + t)]^n = (1 + pt)^n$$

$$= \sum_{k=0}^{n} \binom{n}{k} p^k t^k$$

Hence the kth binomial moment, say $B_k(n, p)$, is given by

$$B_k(n, p) = \binom{n}{k} p^k, \quad k = 0, 1, \ldots, n$$

and the variance M_2 is accordingly

$$V(n, p) = M_2(n, p) = 2B_2(n, p) + B_1(n, p) - B_1^2(n, p)$$
$$= npq$$

Since all binomial moments are known, so are all ordinary and central moments, but higher moments are so rarely needed as not to deserve space here. It should be mentioned that the value of k, say m, at which $b(k; n, p)$ reaches its maximum value is given by the inequality $(n + 1)p - 1 < m \le (n + 1)p$.

Lest the reader be bemused by the simplicity of coin tossing into regarding the binomial distribution as a mere mathematical amusement, it may be well to mention two applications:

Given the simplified case of n telephone lines from a central office, each line to a single customer. Suppose that during the busy hour each customer makes one 2-minute call "at random"; more precisely, suppose the probability that he is using his line at any particular time in the busy hour is 1/30. Also suppose customers call independently. Then the probability that k lines are busy simultaneously is the binomial $b(k; n, 1/30)$, a result used in many telephone engineering studies.

In a second application (simplified) suppose there are n power wires supplied by a single electric generator. Each wire runs to a device that uses one ampere of current in a 10-minute interval at random in the busy hour, or at any particular time with probability 1/6. Then the probability that the generator will supply k amperes to the lines is $b(k; n, 1/6)$.

Poisson Distribution.—Though the Poisson distribution is interesting in its own right, it first came to attention as a limit of the binomial distribution, with n increasing, p decreasing, but $np = \lambda$, a fixed number. For this reason it has been called "the law of small numbers," or the "law of rare events," which are now regarded as misnomers. If the binomial moment-generating function of the binomial distribution is rewritten

$$B(t; n, p) = \left(1 + \frac{\lambda t}{n}\right)^n, \quad \lambda = np$$

then it may be expected from the limit formula for the familiar number e that, as n increases,

$$\lim B(t; n, p) = B(t; \lambda) = e^{\lambda t} = \exp(\lambda t)$$

with $B(t; \lambda)$ the binomial moment-generating function for the Poisson distribution, and

$$\exp(x) = 1 + x + \frac{x^2}{2} + \ldots + \frac{x^n}{n!} + \ldots$$

This turns out to be true and the corresponding probability generating function is

$$P(t; \lambda) = B(t - 1; \lambda) = \exp(\lambda t - \lambda) = \sum_{k=0}^{\infty} e^{-\lambda} \frac{\lambda^k}{k!} t^k$$

The Poisson distribution is $\{p_0(\lambda), p_1(\lambda), \ldots, p_k(\lambda), \ldots\}$ with

$$p_k(\lambda) = e^{-\lambda} \lambda^k / k!$$

which is an approximation to $b(k; n, p)$ as n increases, p decreases, while $np = \lambda$. The kth binomial moment is $B_k(\lambda) = \lambda^k / k!$, so the mean is λ and so is the variance.

Negative Binomial Distribution.—Consider, as in the example on coin tossing, the number of tosses up to first appearance of head, in an infinite sequence of tosses. If this number is k, there must be k successive tails followed by a head; the probability of this event is $q^k p$. The corresponding generating function is

$$G(t) = p \sum_{k=0}^{\infty} q^k t^k = p(1 - qt)^{-1}$$

The symbol G in the generating function is a reminder that the probability distribution is the geometric distribution. Consider now the number of tosses up to the rth appearance of head. Noting that the numbers of tails between successive appearances of head all have the same distribution as the number up to the first, this is an example of the sum of r random variables each with the same geometric distribution, and

$$G(t; r) = [G(t)]^r = p^r (1 - qt)^{-r}$$

If

$$G(t; r) = \sum_{k=0}^{} g(k; r, p) t^k$$

then, by the binomial theorem

$$g(k; r,p) = \binom{-r}{k} p^r (-q)^k, \quad k = 0,1,2,\ldots$$

$$= \binom{r+k-1}{k} p^r q^k$$

Note that $g(k; r,p)$ is the probability that the rth appearance of head is at trial $r + k$.

When r is an integer, the distribution is called the Pascal distribution (after Blaise Pascal [1623–1662], commonly regarded as a co-founder with Pierre de Fermat of the theory of mathematical probability); when r is a real number, not necessarily integral, it yields what is called the negative binomial distribution, because r appears with negative sign in the first form of $g(k; r,p)$.

The binomial moment-generating function is

$$B(t; r,p) = p^r(1 - q - qt)^{-r} = (1 - qt/p)^{-r}$$

and so the kth binomial moment is

$$B_k(r,p) = \binom{-r}{k}\left(-\frac{q}{p}\right)^k = \binom{r+k-1}{k}\left(\frac{q}{p}\right)^k$$

The mean is rq/p and the variance is rq/p^2.

Normal Distribution.—The function defined by

$$\phi(x) = \frac{1}{\sqrt{2\pi}} \exp(-\tfrac{1}{2}x^2)$$

is called the normal density function; its integral

$$\Phi(x) = \frac{1}{\sqrt{2\pi}} \int_{-\infty}^{x} \exp(-\tfrac{1}{2}y^2)dy$$

is called the normal distribution function. The term distribution function is used as in a previous section. The graph of $\phi(x)$ is the familiar bell-shaped curve with maximum at $x = 0$ where $\phi(0) = (2\pi)^{-\frac{1}{2}} \approx 0.399$. The area under the curve is unity, as required by $\Phi(\infty) = 1$. The mean is zero (the curve is symmetrical) and the variance is 1. For arbitrary mean m and variance σ^2, a change of scale is required; the normal density function becomes $\sigma^{-1}\phi[(x - m)\sigma^{-1}]$, which is shown as fig. 3, and the distribution function $\Phi[(x - m)\sigma^{-1}]$. Note that $\Phi(-x) = 1 - \Phi(x)$. The value of x such that $\Phi(x) - \Phi(-x) = 0.5$ is $x = 0.6745$; hence 0.6745σ is called in statistics (*q.v.*) the probable error. Also $\Phi(2) - \Phi(-2) = 0.9545$, and the points $m \pm 2\sigma$ are called the 95.5% points; $\Phi(3) - \Phi(-3) = 0.9973$, corresponding to points $m \pm 3\sigma$, usually includes all the curve of interest in statistical work. The ordinary moment-generating function of the normal distribution with mean m and variance σ^2 is defined by

$$m(t) = 1 + mt + m_2 t^2/2! + \ldots + m_k t^k/k! + \ldots$$

$$= \int_{-\infty}^{\infty} e^{tx}\phi\left(\frac{x - m}{\sigma}\right)\frac{dx}{\sigma} = \exp(mt + \sigma^2 t^2/2)$$

Hence the central moment-generating function is

$$M(t) = \exp(-mt)m(t) = \exp(\sigma^2 t^2/2)$$

All odd central moments are zero, and

$$M_{2k} = \frac{(2k)!}{2^k k!}\sigma^{2k} = 1 \cdot 3 \cdot 5 \ldots (2k - 1)\sigma^{2k}$$

As n increases, the binomial distribution $\{b(k; n,p), k = 0,1, \ldots, n\}$ resembles the normal distribution more and more closely. Indeed under conditions spelled out in the De Moivre-Laplace limit theorem (for which the reader may consult the treatise by Feller in the *Bibliography*), the normal distribution is the limit of the binomial distribution.

Central Limit Theorem; Law of Large Numbers.—The Central Limit Theorem (named by George Pólya in 1920) is an outstanding result in probability theory (*see* ERRORS, THEORY OF). It explains the importance and common empirical appearance of the normal distribution, and is stated as follows:

Let $\{X_k\}$ be a sequence of mutually independent random vari-

ables with a common distribution, which has finite mean m and variance σ^2. Let $S_n = X_1 + \ldots + X_n$. Then for every fixed β

$$\Pr\left\{\frac{S_n - nm}{\sigma\sqrt{n}} < \beta\right\} \to \Phi(\beta)$$

The arrow means approaches (for increasing n) and $\Phi(\beta)$ is the normal distribution function. Note that the mean of S_n is nm and the variance of S_n is $n\sigma^2$. The variable

$$S_n^\bullet = [S_n - E(S_n)] / \sqrt{V(S_n)}$$

with $E(S_n)$ the mean and $V(S_n)$ the variance of S_n, is called the normalized form of S_n.

A related limit theorem is the Law of Large Numbers, stated as: Let $\{X_k\}$ be a sequence of mutually independent random variables with a common distribution that has a finite mean m. Then for every $\epsilon > 0$ as $n \to \infty$

$$\Pr\{ \mid S_n n^{-1} - m \mid > \epsilon\} \to 0$$

In ordinary language, this says that the probability that the average S_n/n will differ from m by less than an arbitrarily small positive number ϵ, tends to one. The law furnishes a justification for association of probabilities with frequencies for repeated trials.

While the Central Limit Theorem is a generalization of the De Moivre-Laplace theorem (referred to before as showing that the binomial distribution tends to the normal) it is by no means the most general statement of its kind. For instance its conclusion holds when the variables of the sequence do not necessarily have the same distribution, but the conditions for the validity of the theorem in this case are not easy to state in ordinary language, and in mathematical language would probably be baffling to some.

It should be noted that if X_1 is a random variable with a normal distribution of mean m_1 and variance σ_1^2 and X_2 is independent and similar but with mean m_2, variance σ_2^2, then the sum $S_2 = X_1 + X_2$ is a variable with a normal distribution of mean $m_1 + m_2$, variance $\sigma_1^2 + \sigma_2^2$. Because of this property, the normal distribution is said to be self-reproductive. The Poisson distribution is also self-reproductive, but the binomial and negative binomial distributions are not.

Two or More Random Variables.—A compound event usually needs several random variables for complete description. Consider a compound of two events, say, the outcome of the tossing of two dice numbered 1 and 2; the corresponding random variables are X and Y. Any outcome is associated with a joint probability, say $p_{ij} = \Pr(X = i, Y = j)$ and the totality of outcomes with a joint probability distribution $\{p_{ij}\}$ where i takes on the values $x_1, x_2, \ldots$ of X, and j has the values $y_1, y_2, \ldots$ of Y. Similarly the joint distribution function is

$$F(x,y) = \Pr(X \leq x, Y \leq y) = \Sigma p_{ij}$$

where the sum is taken over all values of i not greater than x and all values of j not greater than y. When y is greater than the largest value of Y (or infinity), the joint distribution function becomes a function of x only and is called the marginal distribution function of X. The marginal distribution of Y is defined similarly. Joint moments also are needed; for moments about the origin these are given by

$$m_{rs} = E(X^r Y^s) = \sum_{i,j} i^r j^s p_{ij}, \quad r,s = 0,1,2,\ldots$$

while joint central and binomial moments are defined by

$$M_{rs} = E[(X - E(X))^r(Y - E(Y))^s]$$

$$= \sum_{i,j} (i - E(X))^r(j - E(Y))^s p_{ij}$$

$$B_{rs} = E\left[\binom{X}{r}\binom{Y}{s}\right] = \sum_{i,j}\binom{i}{r}\binom{j}{s}p_{ij}$$

Of course $E(X) = m_{10}$ and $E(Y) = m_{01}$. The central moment M_{11} is called the covariance and is given by

$$\text{Cov}(X,Y) = E(XY) - E(X)E(Y) = m_{11} - m_{10}m_{01}$$

If X and Y are independent $\text{Cov}(X,Y) = 0$. The ratio of the covariance of X and Y to the product of their standard deviations is called their correlation coefficient and is usually written ρ_{xy}. If $X_1, X_2, \ldots, X_n$ are random variables with finite variances $\sigma_1^2, \sigma_2^2, \ldots, \sigma_n^2$, then

$$\text{Var}(X_1 + \ldots + X_n) = \sigma_1^2 + \ldots + \sigma_n^2 + 2\sum_{i,j} \text{Cov}(X_i, X_j)$$

the sum extending over all $n(n-1)/2$ pairs (X_i, X_j) with $i < j$.

To fix ideas it may be helpful to consider the following simple example.

Correlated Tosses of Two Coins.—Suppose coins are tossed by some device that assures nonindependence, so that sample space points TT, TH, HT, HH have respective probabilities p_{00}, p_{01}, p_{10}, p_{11} (with a sum of unity). The joint probability-generating function is

$$P(t,u) = p_{00} + p_{01}u + p_{10}t + p_{11}tu$$

and the binomial moment-generating function is

$$B(t,u) = 1 + (p_{01} + p_{11})u + (p_{10} + p_{11})t + p_{11}tu$$

The moments are

$$m_{00} = B_{00} = 1; \quad m_{10} = B_{10} = p_{10} + p_{11};$$
$$m_{11} = B_{11} = p_{11}; \quad m_{01} = B_{01} = p_{01} + p_{11}$$

and

$$M_{11} = m_{11} - m_{10}m_{01} = p_{11} - (p_{10} + p_{11})(p_{01} + p_{11})$$
$$= p_{11}(1 - p_{10} - p_{01} - p_{11}) - p_{10}p_{01} = p_{11}p_{00} - p_{10}p_{01}$$

Multinomial Distribution.—This important multivariable distribution is a generalization of the binomial distribution. Instead of two outcomes on a single trial, there are k (as with a k-faced die) and the ith outcome has probability p_i. Associating a variable t_i with the ith outcome, the probability-generating function is

$$P(t_1, \ldots, t_k) = (p_1t_1 + \ldots + p_kt_k)^n$$

where the general term is $[n; x_1, \ldots, x_k] \, (p_1t_1)^{x_1} \ldots (p_kt_k)^{x_k}$, with $[n; x_1, \ldots, x_k]$ the multinomial coefficient $n!/x_1! \ldots x_k!$, and $x_1 + \ldots + x_k = n$.

Multivariable Normal Distribution.—This distribution becomes complicated if stated in more than two variables, but for two variables with means m_1, m_2, variances σ_1^2, σ_2^2, and correlation coefficient ρ_{12}, the two-variable density function may be written as the following equation:

$$f(x,y) = \frac{1}{2\pi\sigma_1\sigma_2\sqrt{1 - \rho_{12}^2}} \exp -\tfrac{1}{2}q(x,y)$$

where

$$q(x,y) = \frac{1}{1 - \rho_{12}^2}\left[\frac{(x - m_1)^2}{\sigma_1^2} + \frac{(y - m_2)^2}{\sigma_2^2} - 2\rho_{12}\frac{(x - m_1)(y - m_2)}{\sigma_1\sigma_2}\right]$$

Kolmogorov System of Axioms.—The simplicity of the Kolmogorov system of axioms may be surprising. Let E be a collection of elements $\{E_1, E_2, \ldots\}$ called elementary events and F a set of subsets of E called random events. The axioms for a finite set E are:

I. F is a field of sets
II. F contains set E
III. A non-negative real number $P(A)$, called the probability of A, is assigned to each set A in F
IV. $P(E)$ equals 1
V. If A and B have no element in common, the number assigned to their union is $P(A + B) = P(A) + P(B)$

Axiom I needs the following explanation. A system of sets is called a field (*see* FIELDS) if the union, product, and difference of any two sets is a set in the field; the product (*i.e.*, intersection) of two sets is the set of elements common to both; the difference of two sets A and B, written $A - B$, is the set of elements of A that are not in B (the difference $E - A$ is the complement of A).

For an infinite set E, the preceding axioms apply, and an axiom of continuity must be added:

VI. For a decreasing sequence of elements of F, that is, $A_1 \supset A_2 \ldots \supset A_n \supset \ldots$ for which $A_1A_2 \ldots A_n \ldots = 0$ the following limit equation holds:

$$\lim_{n \to \infty} P(A_n) = 0$$

The symbol $\supset$ of set inclusion in $A_1 \supset A_2$, for example, means that every element of set A_2 is an element of set A_1.

See also STATISTICS; STATISTICS, MATHEMATICAL.

BIBLIOGRAPHY.—F. N. David and D. E. Barton, *Combinatorial Chance* (1962); W. Feller, *An Introduction to Probability Theory and Its Applications*, 2nd ed. (1957); M. Fisz, *Probability Theory and Mathematical Statistics*, 3rd ed. (1963); T. C. Fry, *Probability and Its Engineering Uses* (1928); M. Kac, *Statistical Independence in Probability, Analysis and Number Theory* (1959); A. N. Kolmogorov, *Foundations of the Theory of Probability* (1950); W. Weaver, *Lady Luck* (1963); W. A. Whitworth, *Choice and Chance,* reprint (1959).

(Jo. RI.)

PROBATE, the judicial proceedings by which it is determined whether or not a paper purporting to be the last will of a deceased person is his legally valid last will. What appears to be a valid will may not be so; it may have been forged, or not executed in the way required by law, or the testator may have signed it while mentally incompetent or under duress, or he may subsequently have revoked it. If the document is held to be genuine and valid, it is admitted to probate; otherwise its admission is refused. Until it has been so admitted it cannot be used for any legal purposes; in particular, the person nominated as executor cannot function, and the court must appoint an administrator of the estate.

The idea that the genuineness and validity of a will should be investigated and determined in special proceedings was developed in England by the ecclesiastical courts, which in the Middle Ages had acquired jurisdiction over succession to personal property. No such idea had been worked out by the secular courts, which had jurisdiction over the descent of real property. In America, secular courts were set up to deal with probate matters, and in the 19th century their jurisdiction was extended to cover the problem of the validity of a will with respect to real property. The same step was taken in England in 1897, after jurisdiction had been transferred in 1857 from the ecclesiastical to the secular courts.

Under the rules developed in the ecclesiastical courts and continued in the English secular courts, probate can be granted simply upon the presentation of an instrument (document) presenting the outward appearance of a will properly executed. Such probate "in the common form" was revocable, however, if within 30 years doubts were raised as to the validity of the instrument. In that case, the person interested in having it admitted to probate had to prove it "in the solemn form." These more elaborate proceedings were also required if an interested person had entered a caveat (asked to have his objections heard) before the probate had been granted. Probate in the solemn form is a regular judicial proceeding in which the facts needed to establish the validity of the instrument must be proved, ordinarily through testimony by witnesses.

In England, probate jurisdiction ordinarily rests with the Probate, Divorce, and Admiralty Division of the High Court, which normally acts through the Principal Registry in London or through its local district registries. Where the gross value of the deceased's property does not exceed £500, application for probate may be made through the local officers of the Board of Custom and Excise. The documents admitted to probate are deposited in the Principal Registry in Somerset House, London, where they are open to public inspection. A certified copy is issued to the executor. When probate is granted, estate duty is payable on the gross value of the personal estate and the real estate owned in England. (*See* ESTATE AND INHERITANCE TAXES.)

In Scots law, proceedings essentially corresponding to probate are called confirmation and are carried out in the Sheriff's Court.

The English pattern is also that of the other common-law parts of the Commonwealth and, basically, also that of the United States. Under the pattern prevailing in most states in the U.S., the document purporting to be a will is admitted to probate in a special court, usually called the Probate Court (Surrogate's Court in New

York, Orphans' Court in New Jersey and Pennsylvania). Proceedings require little proof, but occasionally allow the adjudication of a limited range of objections. But any interested party may have the probate revoked if he prevails in a will contest; this must be raised, usually in a court higher than the probate court, within a short period fixed by statute.

In most states the courts acting in probate matters also supervise the administration and distribution of a deceased's estate by an executor or administrator; in addition, they have jurisdiction over the guardianship of infants and the conservation of the estates of mentally incompetent persons. In Pennsylvania certain probate functions are carried on by an official called prothonotary. In some states, probate matters are handled by the courts of first instance—in California, for example, by the district courts.

Matters of probate belong exclusively to the courts of the several states, federal courts having no jurisdiction. Probate must be obtained in the state of which the deceased was a resident at the time of his death; in addition, ancillary probate must be obtained in every other state in which real property is located and, under certain circumstances, also in every other state in which the deceased had a bank account or other personal property. *See* also
WILL.

BIBLIOGRAPHY.—A. Gibson, *Probate Law,* 15th ed. (1950); L. M. Simes and P. E. Basye, *Problems in Probate Law* (1946); T. E. Atkinson, *Handbook of the Law of Wills and Administration of Decedents' Estates* (1937); M. Rheinstein, *Law of Decedents' Estates,* 2nd ed., pp. 562–621 (1955); G. W. Marshall, *Ancient Courts of Probate* (1895).
(M. Rn.)

PROBATION is a correctional method under which the sentences of selected offenders may be conditionally suspended upon promise of good behaviour and agreement to accept supervision and abide by specified requirements including, usually, reporting to a probation officer or to the court at regular intervals. As distinct from parole (*q.v.*), which involves conditional release from confinement after part of a sentence has already been served, probation permits the offender to retain his freedom and continue to meet his personal, family, and community responsibilities.

Probation Procedure.—*Adult.*—The adult probation process begins with a presentence investigation of the offender after his guilt has been established. The investigation is made by the probation officer and is usually ordered by the court whenever an offender is legally eligible for probation. Statutes commonly exclude from consideration persons convicted of serious offenses (*e.g.,* armed robbery, murder) or those previously convicted of other offenses. The social investigation serves, first, to help the court determine whether the offender is suitable for probation, and, second, to outline a plan of corrective treatment. It is primarily concerned with the offender as an individual, his personality and background, education and employment, and his family and social environment. This information is incorporated and evaluated in a confidential report to the court.

When probation is ordered by the court, the offender is placed under the supervision of a probation officer, or a person appointed by the court, and under conditions specified in the probation order. Typically these require that the probationer conduct himself properly; that he maintain his local residence; report regularly to his probation officer; support his family; pay restitution; avoid criminal associations and disreputable places; and abstain from drinking. In addition he may be ordered to obtain medical or psychiatric care. The status of a probationer may carry other restrictions as to civil rights, freedom to act in certain matters without approval, and access to social or employing organizations.

The duration of probation set by the court generally is limited to some maximum term. Early discharge by the court in recognition of good conduct is a common practice.

The probation officer's fundamental task is to help the probationer become a more responsible and better-adjusted person. The essence of probation is good casework, not mere supervision; and its aim is individual rehabilitation, not the relief of crowded institutions. Individual counseling and available social, occupational, educational, and mental health resources are employed to help the probationer resolve specific problems, conflicts, and attitudes that led to his criminal or delinquent behaviour. As a representative of the court, the probation officer must also enforce the conditions set by the court and be watchful regarding further antisocial activities on the part of the probationer.

If the probationer violates the terms of his probation or commits a further offense during the probation period, he may be brought back before the court for revision or revocation of the original order of probation and may be given some other sentence for the original offence. When the probationer completes his period of probation successfully he is discharged from further obligations to the court. Studies made in several countries show that 70% to 80% of all probationers successfully fulfill the terms of probation and are discharged. Limited evidence suggests that the proportion of former probationers convicted of subsequent offenses is small, probably less than three in ten.

Juvenile.—Probation work among children differs materially from that among adults and is of even greater importance. Juvenile court hearings are characterized by their informal proceedings and discretionary protective treatment. In some jurisdictions the probation officer's investigation is completed and the report submitted prior to the court hearing. Consequently, information in the report may significantly influence the determination of delinquency as well as the disposition of the case. For probation to be effective it is essential that a child offender after being adjudged a ward of the court be given very careful supervision; that his mental, physical, and psychological characteristics and his social situation receive the closest study; and that his probation officer establish and maintain close personal relationships with the child and his home and keep in close touch with his school or work and his free-time activities. Generally, for children and youth under juvenile court jurisdiction, the period of probation is indefinite and dependent upon the individual's attitude and adjustment. (*See* CHILDREN'S COURT; JUVENILE DELINQUENCY.)

Origin and Development.—Probation evolved from Anglo-American judicial practices devised to avoid automatic application of harsh penalties prescribed by the statutory law. These practices originated in the early 1800s in response to humanitarian concern over the harmful effects of imprisonment on the young or first offender. Enlightened English magistrates in such cases imposed only a token sentence, remanding the offender to the custody of his parents or master for more careful supervision. This was a final disposition, however; the court had no power to enforce its order. A remedy was found in the recognizance (*q.v.*), an old measure of preventive justice. Conditional upon his good behaviour, an offender could be released on his acknowledgment of obligation until some later date set by the court for final action. He was often required to post bond or deposit bail to guarantee reappearance.

John Augustus, a Boston bootmaker, initiated the practice he called "probation." In 1841, through his interest in the temperance cause, he appeared in court and posted bail for a man charged with drunkenness. Successful in helping the man get reestablished, he proceeded to assist hundreds of men, women, and children charged with a variety of offenses.

The voluntary work of Augustus and his successors led the Massachusetts legislature to authorize in 1878 the appointment of a paid probation officer to serve the Criminal Court of Boston. Subsequent legislation made probation services mandatory in most Massachusetts courts. Other states were slow to follow the example until the turn of the century, when the children's court (*q.v.*) movement began to sweep the United States. In England the efforts of temperance volunteers in the police courts paralleled the development of probation in the United States. Beginning in 1879, a series of pertinent statutes was enacted culminating in the Probation of Offenders Act of 1907, which established official, salaried probation officers in the criminal courts of the United Kingdom. British criminal courts have general jurisdiction over juveniles as well as adults. In 1948 the Criminal Justice Act added significant improvements in the legal and practical application of the probation system. (*See* also BORSTAL SYSTEM.)

On the continent of Europe, progressive elements had also long supported the mitigation of punishment for juvenile and first offenders. Europeans were primarily interested in a substitute for short-term imprisonment rather than extended probation services. They adopted a procedure whereby sentence was imposed but with provision for suspending execution of the punishment subject to the offender's good behaviour. The measure was considered to be preventive because of the deterrent effect of imminent punishment. First authorized by Belgian law in 1888, the conditional sentence was shortly adopted by France and eventually spread to nearly every European state.

The facilities of the United Nations permitted a comparative view of leading nations with respect to statutory authorization for and administration of probation services in the second half of the 20th century. In the United States and in Canada, the United Kingdom, and other nations of the British Commonwealth, legal provision for probation was nearly universal. Administration of services was predominantly local and subject to close judicial control. The established pattern of service was characterized by public employment of full-time probation officers, but part-time and ex-officio services were relied upon in some localities of the U.S. and in some nations of the Commonwealth.

Of 16 continental European countries, virtually all provided juveniles with services legally and practically comparable to probation. The conditional suspension of sentence for adults was authorized by law in all save one of these countries. In more than half, a supplemental order for personal supervision was legally permitted, but this option was not much employed by the courts. Considerable experimentation was going on with the aim of adapting the probation method to the system of criminal jurisprudence, notably in France, the Federal Republic of Germany, the Netherlands, and the Scandinavian countries.

Most continental European countries have delegated the personal supervision of probationers to social welfare organizations dependent on volunteer services. A general trend toward professional probation services has been exemplified in the Belgian, French, Dutch, and Swedish systems. There, trained probation consultants are responsible for indoctrinating volunteer agents, supervising their work, and in many cases giving direct services to probationers. The move toward professionalization has been accompanied by increased central government responsibility for coordination, regulation, or administration of probation services.

Those metropolitan areas in Latin America, Asia, and Africa where the juvenile court philosophy has been embraced offer probation services largely limited to juveniles. Voluntary welfare organizations usually have provided the necessary supervision and treatment services.

Authorities concerned with the legal and sociological aspects of law enforcement generally agree that probation, rather than institutional confinement, is a more effective and far less expensive program for the rehabilitation of the majority of offenders. By the middle of the 20th century its full potential for successful application had not been realized, even in those countries where it was best developed. Relatively few areas in the world adhered strictly to all of the principles that were considered essential to the proper administration of probation: (1) careful selection of cases amenable to supervision, with consideration given on the basis of the offender's likelihood to improve under treatment, rather than the seriousness of his offense; (2) suspension of sentence for persons so selected; (3) supervision by professionally trained personnel; (4) release of the probationer at the end of a specified period set by the court, provided behaviour has been satisfactory, or revocation of probation if he has committed a new crime or failed to comply with the conditions of his probation.

Among organizations promoting the growth and extension of the probation system throughout the world are the Economic and Social Council of the United Nations; the National Council on Crime and Delinquency, New York; the American Correctional Association, Washington, D.C.; and the National Association of Probation Officers, London.

See also CRIMINOLOGY: *Correction;* PRISON.

BIBLIOGRAPHY.—Charles L. Chute and Marjorie Bell, *Crimes, Courts, and Probation* (1956); David Dressler, *Practice and Theory of Probation and Parole* (1959); Paul W. Keve, *The Probation Officer Investigates: a Guide to the Presentence Report* (1960); Charles L. Newman, *Sourcebook on Probation, Parole and Pardons* (1958); United Nations, *Probation and Related Measures* (1951), *European Seminar on Probation, London, 1952* (1954); Paul W. Tappan, *Crime, Justice and Correction,* ch. 19 (1960); Barbara A. Kay and Clyde B. Vedder (eds.), *Probation and Parole* (1963); Joan F. S. King (ed.), *The Probation Service* (1958); L. Radzinowicz (ed.), *The Results of Probation* (1958); John R. St. John, *Probation—the Second Chance* (1961). (W. C. T.)

PROBOLINGGO, a port of East Java Province, Indonesia, and headquarters of a district of the same name, is situated at the south of the Madura Strait, about 60 mi. (97 km.) SE of Surabaja. Pop. (1961) 68,838, including many Chinese. There is a good harbour for small ships, and the fishing industry is important. Cottage industries include pottery and the manufacture of sarongs. The town is on the rail and road routes from Surabaja to Banjuwangi. The surrounding district grows rice, maize (corn), sugar, and some coffee; its mangoes are renowned for their excellence.

PROBOSCIDEA, an order of mammals that includes the present-day elephants and their fossil relatives, the mastodonts and mammoths. The proboscidean line can be traced back to a tapirlike animal of Upper Eocene Age (about 50,000,000 years ago). The descendants of this modest-sized plant eater became progressively larger during succeeding epochs: the mastodonts (or mastodons), so called because their cheek teeth had teatlike cusps, preceded the elephants proper, including the mammoths.

The body systems of proboscideans generally are those common to other placental mammals (*see* MAMMAL), and the present article is concerned mainly with those special features that characterize the Proboscidea and set it apart from other mammalian orders. A discussion of living elephants precedes a treatment of the phylogenetic relationships of earlier proboscideans.

GENERAL

Elephants are the largest recent land mammals, and may be the largest ever to have existed. They are among the longest-lived mammals, approaching the age of a man. They live in herds now restricted to Africa and tropical Asia. The evolution and spread of the order, the oldest members of which are known from remains in northeastern Egypt, is greatly complicated by the existence of many side branches, some abortive, which migrated into Asia, thence to Europe and, across what is now the Bering Straits, into North America and, near the close of the Ice Age, even into South America.

Common animals of the Ice Age were the woolly mammoths of Europe—whose frozen carcasses have been uncovered in the icebound tundra of Siberia—and, in America, the last of the mastodonts.

The name Proboscidea refers to the elongated snout or proboscis, the trunk; the evolutionary development of this most remarkable feature of living elephants is indicated by a series of fossil skulls. The dentition is also unusual, in many cases involving reduction of the number of teeth in use at one time with corresponding increased complexity of the teeth that gradually erupted during a long period of life. The molars became very effective grinders of plant food; the specialized front teeth were often modified into tusks. *See* ELEPHANT for information of popular interest.

CHARACTERISTIC STRUCTURES

The massive body is supported by pillarlike limbs; the large head is joined to the body by a very short neck. Hair, conspicuous as a body covering in the young, is reduced in the adult to a patch on the forehead and a tuft on the tail.

Soft Parts.—The trunk is a long, flexible, muscular organ that can be turned freely in every direction. It is provided with one or two fingerlike processes at its tip, which can be used to handle articles as small as a penny. Being prehensile, the trunk can be wrapped around large objects; it is capable of considerable precision of movement and is used in feeding.

The trunk represents the whole anterior part of the face, *i.e.,* the nose and also the upper lips, the strip of skin along its ventral surface being essentially a part of the palate. The two nostrils lie at the extremity of the trunk and lead into great canals that perforate the whole of that organ, opening into olfactory chambers at its base. The mouth is short, placed below the trunk, and provided with thick fleshy lower lips that meet anteriorly to form a short spout. The eye is small, laterally directed, and provided with a pair of eyelids often bearing stiff eyelashes. The earflaps are large, largest in certain races of the African elephants. They are usually carried close to the side of the neck but can be erected so as to stand out perhaps a yard from the side of the head.

The anatomy of the soft parts of the elephant presents few features of special interest, except those that result from the modification of the nose and upper lips into the trunk. The animal is peculiar in that there is no pleural cavity. The female bears two teats placed forward just between and behind the forelegs. The fact that the testes are abdominal, the uterus bicornuate, and the placenta zonary and deciduate is of importance because similar conditions occur in the Sirenia (sea cows), which may have sprung from an early Proboscidean stock.

Skull.—The skeleton of an elephant is as peculiar and characteristic as its external appearance. The skull is very short from back to front, deep, and built up of spongy bone full of air spaces. Within the great mass of bone lies the brain cavity; the olfactory chambers form great perforations that, with the nasopharyngeal

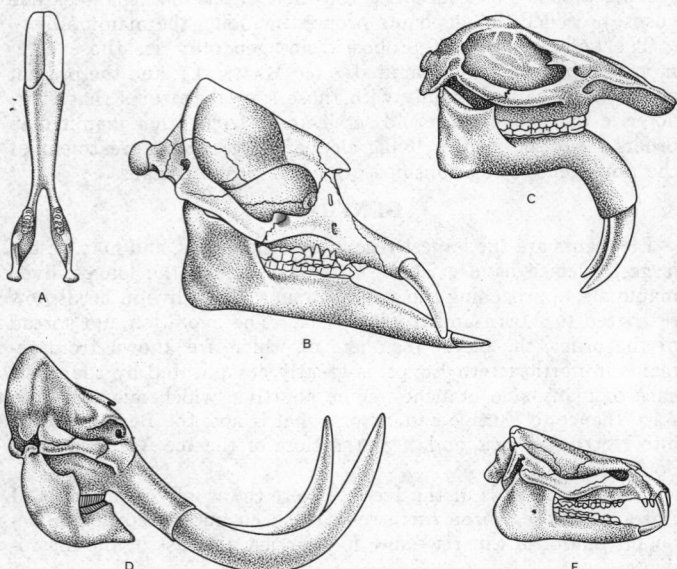

FROM (A, D, E) ALFRED S. ROMER, "VERTEBRATE PALEONTOLOGY," REPRODUCED BY PERMISSION OF THE UNIVERSITY OF CHICAGO PRESS; (B, C) T. J. PARKER AND W. A. HASWELL, "A TEXTBOOK OF ZOOLOGY," VOL. II, REPRODUCED BY PERMISSION OF MACMILLAN & CO., LTD.

SKULL AND JAWS OF EXTINCT PROBOSCIDEANS

(A) Lower jaws of *Amebelodon*, from the Pliocene of North America; (B) *Palaeomastodon*; (C) *Deinotherium*; (D) *Mammuthus*, the woolly mammoth; (E) *Moeritherium*, from the Upper Eocene and Lower Oligocene of Egypt

ducts, penetrate obliquely through the skull and unite posteriorly. The skull of the newborn elephant increases greatly and disproportionately in size, but the brain undergoes much less expansion. Thus during the period of growth of the animal the external surface of the skull, by the development of great air spaces in its middle layer, becomes more and more widely separated from the layer of hard bone that surrounds the brain. The bony layers that separate these air spaces run radially so as to buttress the external surface. The great size of the adult skull is necessary in order to give adequate areas for the attachment of the immense neck muscles, which support and move the very heavy trunk and tusks and take the great strains produced when these structures are used in digging up and tearing down trees.

The jawbones of the elephant and the whole structure of its palate are modified so as to receive, and afford adequate support to, the tusks and cheek teeth. The bony nostrils lie very high up and are overhung by very small nasal bones to which some of the muscles of the base of the trunk are attached. This attachment is brought as far back as possible in order to increase the range of action of the trunk.

Teeth.—The dentition of an adult elephant typically consists

of a single pair of exaggerated incisors, the tusks, and either one or two molars on each side of the upper and lower jaws. The molars are built up of a series of vertical plates, each composed of a core of dentine surrounded by a layer of enamel; the individual plates, joined at their bases, are held together and supported by an infilling of cement. In the elephant the milk incisors, little teeth about two inches in length, are shed and replaced by the permanent tusks, but the milk molars, instead of being pushed out by a permanent premolar that develops underneath them, replace one another from behind as follows.

The new tooth is developed deep down in the posterior part of the jaw and travels obliquely forward and toward the mouth, so that more and more of it erupts from the gum as the preceding tooth is worn down to its root, until finally the latter is shed and its successor is exposed and already partially worn. A living elephant in this way works through six teeth in each side of each jaw during its normal lifetime, wearing down a total thickness of nearly a yard of tooth over an area that increases from about ½ sq.in. to nearly 30 sq.in. on each side of its mouth. This extraordinary dentition is unparalleled in any other animal.

Body Skeleton.—The elephant's backbone consists of a neck of 7 very short vertebrae; a dorsal region of 19 to 21 vertebrae, the anterior ones having long neural spines for the attachment of a ligament that passes forward to the back of the skull; a short lumbar region of 3 or 4 vertebrae; a sacrum composed of 4 fused vertebrae; and a caudal region of about 30 progressively smaller vertebrae extending to the tip of the tail. The ribs are of enormous length surrounding the very capacious thorax. The shoulder girdle consists of a very large triangular scapula placed vertically on each side of the thorax. The upper segment of the forelimb (humerus) is longer than the lower segment so that the elbow of an elephant lies at a point relatively only a little higher than the wrist of a horse. The radius and ulna, in the lower segment, are peculiar in that their surfaces of articulation with the carpus are nearly equal, while the upper end of the radius is relatively small and lies in front of the ulna, the two bones crossing one another as they are traced downward. The carpus of an elephant is unusual in that the bones of the two rows of which it is composed do not alternate but are superimposed on one another. (In this feature the elephants resemble the hyraxes.)

The elephant walks on the extreme tips of his fingers and toes, but the palm of the hand and the sole of the foot are swollen out into great pads of connective tissue and fat, which transmit the weight of the animal to the ground directly and so reduce the load carried by the phalanges. The elephant's pelvis is remarkable for its extraordinary width, the ilia being expanded into transversely placed sheets of bone from whose posterior surface muscles pass down to the hind leg, while their margins give attachment to the muscles of the body wall, which support the weight of the viscera within the abdominal cavity. As in the forelimb, the upper segment of the leg is considerably longer than the lower one, and in the tarsus the astragalus is flattened, as a weight-carrying adaptation, while the calcaneum is produced into a short heel directed backward and downward.

SURVEY AND RELATIONSHIPS

The Proboscidea can be divided into three suborders: Moeritherioidea and Deinotherioidea, each with one genus, and Elephantoidea, which includes the living elephants, the mammoths, and the mastodonts.

MOERITHERIOIDEA

The most primitive and earliest known ancestors of the elephant belong to the genus *Moeritherium* and are found in Upper Eocene deposits in northern Egypt. *Moeritherium* resembled the living tapir in its external appearance and size. The eye was placed far forward and the head was low and elongated; probably the end of the snout was slightly flexible, and it may have been produced into a short proboscis. The legs were considerably more bent than those of modern elephants but are still rather incompletely known. *Moeritherium* possessed three upper and two lower incisors, of which the second pair were enlarged, those in the upper jaw

PROBOSCIDEA

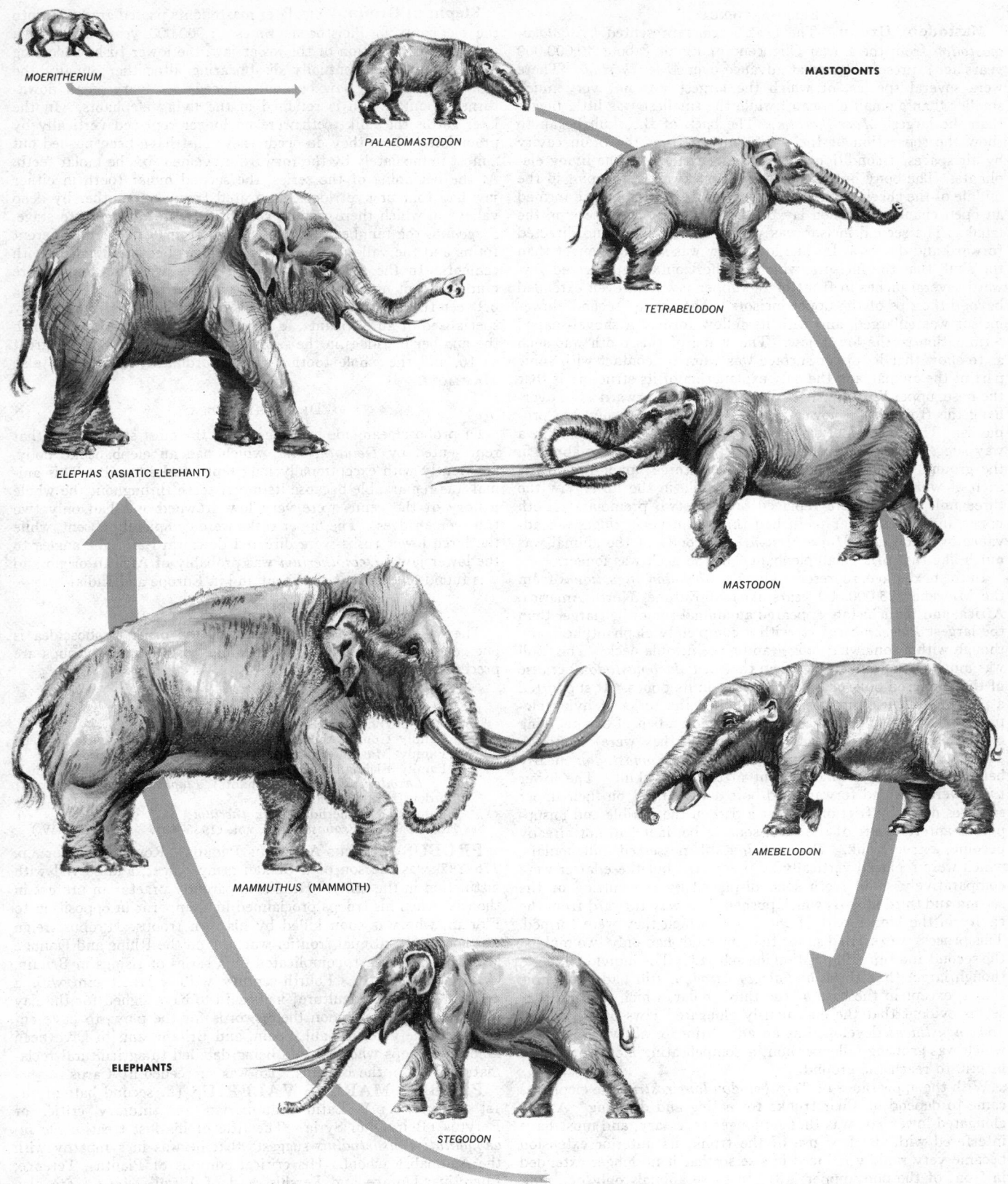

MOERITHERIUM

MASTODONTS

PALAEOMASTODON

TETRABELODON

ELEPHAS (ASIATIC ELEPHANT)

MASTODON

MAMMUTHUS (MAMMOTH)

AMEBELODON

ELEPHANTS

STEGODON

PROBOSCIDEAN EVOLUTION

Some of the more important members of the order (drawn in proportional scale). *Moeritherium*, about 2 ft. tall, was the earliest known proboscidean. The first of the mastodonts, *Palaeomastodon*, had the beginnings of a trunk and two pairs of tusks. *Tetrabelodon* began the trend toward gigantism. *Mastodon* had the longest tusks of any proboscidean (8–10 ft.). *Amebelodon* was a proboscidean experiment with shovellike lower tusks. *Stegodon* was the first of the true elephants. *Mammuthus*, the largest proboscidean, and *Elephas* evolved during the Ice Age.

projecting straight downward, while the lower teeth were directed forward so that their tips bit against those of the upper incisors. There was a small and very reduced canine tooth; three premolars were present in each jaw and there is evidence that each of these vertically replaced a milk tooth. Three permanent molars lay in both upper and lower jaws, each bearing two transverse ridges.

ELEPHANTOIDEA

Mastodont Group.—The next stage, represented by *Palaeomastodon* from the Lower Oligocene of Egypt (about 40,000,000 years ago), presented a great advance over *Moeritherium*. There were several species, of which the largest was not very much smaller than a small elephant, while the smallest was little bigger than the largest *Moeritherium*. The back of the skull began to show the separation of the outer surface from the brain cavity by air spaces, a condition carried to an extreme in the living elephants. The bony nostril was shifted backward to a point in the middle of the cheek teeth, and in front of it the premaxillae formed an open channel in which lay the base of what later became the trunk. The second incisor was very much enlarged and directed forward and downward. The lower jaw was so much longer than the skull that the incisors, which lay horizontally, projected forward several inches in front of the upper jaw, and even extended beyond the tips of the upper incisors. The single "second" lower incisor was enlarged, and with its fellow formed a shovel-shaped termination to the lower jaw. The shape of this tooth was such as to show that its upper surface was worn by contact with some part of the animal, and the only explanation of its structure is that the nose, upper lip, and palate projected so far forward as to overhang the front of the lower jaw and form there a movable proboscis. The lower incisors were, however, worn all round, in a way suggesting that the animal used them for grubbing about in the ground to secure food. There were three upper premolars, each of which replaced a milk tooth, while in the lower jaw the three milk molars were replaced only by two premolars. Both upper and lower molar teeth had three transverse ridges, an advance over those of *Moeritherium*. The body of the animal was much like that of a small elephant, but the neck was longer.

In the next stage, represented by *Tetrabelodon angustidens* from the Miocene (25,000,000 years ago) of Europe, North America, Africa, and Baluchistan, appeared an animal somewhat larger than the largest *Palaeomastodon*, with a completely elephantlike body, though with a somewhat longer and more flexible neck. The skull was much more elephantlike than that of *Palaeomastodon* because of the increased bulk of the air cavities in its bones. It supported a pair of immense incisors, which, unlike the tusks of living elephants, were down turned and provided with a belt of enamel lying on the outer surface of the ivory of which they were composed. The lower jaw was even longer than in *Palaeomastodon*, nearly half its length projecting in front of the bony skull. The lower tusks were directed forward and bore a wear facet on their upper surfaces made by friction against a pad on the flexible and unsupported anterior part of the face, soon to be, if it had not already become, a true trunk. *Tetrabelodon* still possessed milk molars, which were replaced vertically by premolars, but these latter were comparatively small teeth soon displaced by the cutting of the second and third molars, which pushed their way forward from the cavity in the hinder part of the jaw in which they were formed. This process was carried so far that the adult had only two molars, the second and third, in position in each jaw. The individual teeth, though larger than those of *Palaeomastodon*, still had only three ridges, except in the case of the third molar, which had five. It seems evident that the enormously elongated jaws of *Tetrabelodon angustidens* developed as an adaptation to allow the animal, which was growing taller without a compensating increase in neck length, to reach the ground.

With the appearance of *Tetrabelodon longirostris*, the elephants came to depend on their trunks for eating and drinking. As the elongated lower jaw was thus no longer necessary, and must have interfered with the free use of the trunk, its anterior extension became very rapidly reduced in size so that it no longer extended in front of the bony upper jaw. In these animals only one milk molar was replaced by a premolar and the first two molar teeth each had four or five transverse ridges. The lower tusks were short and rounded while the upper tusks became still larger and outwardly directed. In these forms the shortening of the lower jaw allowed the trunk to fall down vertically, as it does in modern elephants, and in external appearance they must have been entirely elephantine. (*See also* MASTODON.)

Elephant Group.—The later mastodonts passed gradually into the elephants in Pleistocene times (1,000,000 years ago) by a still further reduction of the lower jaw, the lower tusks becoming quite small and eventually disappearing altogether; finally the front of the lower jaw became reduced to a very small downturned spout, which is retained in the living elephants. In the later forms the milk teeth were no longer replaced vertically by premolars; where they do occur they must have been pushed out almost immediately by the forward movement of the molar teeth. At the beginning of the series, the second molar tooth in either jaw had four or five ridges, separated from one another by deep valleys in which there was no cement. In an intermediate stage, *Stegodon*, the number of ridges varied from 6 to 12 in different forms and the valleys between these ridges became filled up with cement. In the true elephants the ridges were not only more numerous but much higher, and the cement formed a plate lying between them. Continuation of this process led to the most highly specialized of all elephants, *Mammuthus*, the mammoth, in which the number of ridges in the second molar may have been as great as 16, and the whole tooth was extraordinarily deep. *See also* MAMMOTH.

DEINOTHERIOIDEA

Of proboscidean side branches much the most striking was that represented by *Deinotherium*, which had an elephantlike body, apparently with exceptionally long limbs and a trunk. This animal was remarkable because its molar teeth throughout the whole history of the genus were very low crowned and had only two transverse ridges. The upper tusks were completely absent, while the large lower tusks were directed downward at right angles to the lower jaw. *Deinotherium* was probably of African origin and was found only in that continent and in Europe and India.

CLASSIFICATION

The following taxonomic scheme of the order Proboscidea is one generally subscribed to by mammalogists (extinct groups are preceded by an asterisk):

* Suborder Moeritherioidea
   * Family Moeritheriidae, *Moeritherium*
  Suborder Elephantoidea
   * Family Gomphotheriidae, *Gomphotherium*, *Tetrabelodon*, etc.
   * Family Mastodontidae, *Mastodon* (mastodonts proper)
   Family Elephantidae, *Stegodon, *Mammuthus (mammoths),
     Loxodonta (African elephants), *Elephas* (Asiatic elephants)
* Suborder Deinotherioidea
   * Family Deinotheriidae, *Deinotherium*
See H. F. Osborn, *Proboscidea*, 2 vol. (1936–42). (D. M. S. W.)

PROBUS (MARCUS AURELIUS PROBUS), Roman emperor A.D. 276–282, was the son of a Balkan army officer, and served with distinction in the army. He was apparently praetorian prefect in the east when his troops proclaimed him emperor in opposition to Florian, who was soon killed by his own troops. Probus' reign was spent in continual frontier warfare, on the Rhine and Danube and later in the east, complicated by a series of risings in Britain, Gaul, and the east. Fourth-century writers credit him with a great interest in agriculture; he is said to have sighed for the day when men could abandon their swords for the plow, to have encouraged the vine in Gaul, Spain, and Britain, and to have been killed by troops who resented being detailed to agricultural reclamation work in the Balkans. He was succeeded by Carus.

PROBUS, MARCUS VALERIUS (fl. second half of the 1st century A.D.), Latin grammarian and literary critic, of Berytus (Beirut) in Syria. The title of his lost treatise *De inaequalitate consuetudinis* suggests that he was in sympathy with the Anomalist school. His critical editions of Plautus, Terence, Lucretius, Horace and Persius, and of Virgil's *Aeneid* are also lost; but there is extant a commentary on Virgil's *Eclogues* and *Georgics* under his name. The extant part of *De notis* (probably an excerpt from a larger work), which deals with abbreviations, is printed by H. Keil, *Grammatici Latini*, vol. iv (1864); but other works there ascribed to Probus are not his.

See J. Steup, *De Probis grammaticis* (1871); J. Aistermann, *De M. Valerio Probo Berytio* (1910). (R. H. Rs.)

PROCACCINI, a family of Italian painters of the Bolognese school. ERCOLE THE ELDER (1520?–1591?) was born in Bologna but moved to Milan, where he began a school of painting known as the Academy of the Procaccini, in which many fine painters were trained. He himself was a student of Annibale Carracci, a founder of the eclectic school of painting. His best works are in the churches of Bologna.

CAMILLO (1546–1629?), GIULIO CESARE (1548?–1626), and CARLO ANTONIO (1555–1605?), his three sons, studied with their father; Camillo also studied in Rome. The two elder sons painted principally religious subjects in the tradition of Correggio. Camillo was a more successful colourist than his father, and Giulio Cesare followed the style of Correggio most perfectly of the three. Their paintings are found in the churches of Milan, Bologna, Genoa, and other Italian cities and hang in the galleries of most European capitals. They died in Milan. The youngest and least talented son painted still life and landscapes.

ERCOLE THE YOUNGER (1596–1676) was born and died in Milan. He studied with his uncle Giulio Cesare and was best known for his still-life pictures. On the death of Giulio Cesare, he became director of the academy.

PROCAINE HYDROCHLORIDE, generic name for a synthetically prepared local anesthetic also known by several trade names including Novocain, was introduced by Alfred Einhorn in 1905 as a substitute for cocaine. It is probably the safest local anesthetic agent for injection anesthesia (infiltration, nerve block, and spinal anesthesia). Its penetrating properties are poor, however, and when applied to mucous surfaces it is effective only in dangerously high concentrations. Unlike cocaine, procaine is not a habit forming drug. *See also* ANESTHESIA AND ANESTHETICS.

(F. O. K.)

PROCESSION, in general, an organized body of people advancing in formal or ceremonial manner. The term covers a wide variety of usages, both religious and civil. This article is concerned with the use of the term in the Christian Church, in which public processions seem to have come into vogue soon after the recognition of Christianity as the religion of the empire by Constantine in the 4th century. (For the Procession of the Holy Spirit, *see* HOLY SPIRIT.)

Roman Catholic Church.—Of the vast number of processions that developed during the Middle Ages, the more important and characteristic still have a place in the ritual of the Roman Catholic Church. These liturgical processions, carefully regulated by the church, are governed by rules laid down in the *Rituale Romanum* (Tit. ix) and are classified as ordinary or extraordinary. Ordinary processions are held on certain yearly festivals throughout the universal church and on other days according to the customs of the churches; *e.g.*, in France on the commemoration of the vow of Louis XIII, Aug. 15. Extraordinary processions are those ordered on special occasions—*e.g.*, to pray for rain or fine weather, in time of storm, famine, plague, war, or in any time of trouble, processions of thanksgiving, translation of relics, the dedication of a church or cemetery. There are also processions of honour—for instance, to meet the bishop on his first entry into his diocese.

Other processions characteristic of certain localities, though not regulated so strictly by the church and considered nonliturgical, play an important part in the religious life of the people; *e.g.*, in the United States, May processions in honour of the Virgin Mary.

Antiquity and Provenance.—*Rogation Days.*—It is quite certain that one of the festivals in the pagan calendar of Rome involving a procession was adopted by the Christian Church. The Major Rogation (*litania maior*), an ordinary procession held on April 25, is the equivalent in the Christian Church of the Roman lustration of the crops in spring, the Robigalia, which consisted in a procession leaving Rome by the Flaminian Gate and proceeding by way of the Milvian Bridge to a sanctuary at the fifth milestone of the Via Claudia, where a dog and sheep were sacrificed to avert blight (*robigo*, wheat rust) from the crops. The Christian procession followed the same route as far as the Milvian Bridge, where it turned off and returned to St. Peter's where Mass was celebrated. This festival was already established as an an-

nual event by the year 598, as is shown by a document of Gregory the Great (*Regist.* ii).

The Minor Rogations (*litaniae minores*), held annually on the three days before the Feast of the Ascension, were first introduced in Gaul by Bishop Mamertus of Vienne about the year 470 and were made binding for all Gaul by the first Council of Orléans (511). Later (*c.* 800) these were adopted in Rome by Leo III. It is possible that Mamertus first instituted the Minor Rogations to subrogate three days of pagan crop processions called the Ambarvalia. (*See also* BOUNDS, BEATING THE; LITANY.)

Palm Sunday.—The modern Palm Sunday procession can be traced back to the Christian Church in Jerusalem in the 4th century, whence it spread to the West through the Frankish domains.

Purification.—The procession on the Feast of the Purification (or Candlemas), Feb. 2, might well be another instance of the church's subrogating a pagan lustral procession, for it is known that in pagan times another celebration of the Ambarvalia was held in the beginning of February, and Ildephonsus of Toledo seems to suggest that one was substituted for the other.

Stational.—Among the many types of processions which have fallen into disuse, one of the most important in terms of its splendour and the degree of its influence on subsequent liturgical practice was the papal "stational" procession. At least as early as the 8th century, the pope was accustomed to process with the whole papal court from the Lateran Basilica to a stational church somewhere in Rome. The faithful would arrive at the stational church in seven processions from the seven regions of Rome. The pope would then make a formal entrance into the church. The entrance procession was continued as a custom by the pope and the bishops of the Latin Church till the Middle Ages and still survives on one day a year, Holy Thursday. On special days, *e.g.*, during Lent, the clergy and people would march from a central church with the pope to a stational church. The signs of reverence given to the pope as he entered the church are noteworthy. J. A. Jungmann claims that the thurible and seven torches carried by the acolytes in the pope's honour were marks of reverence to which the Roman emperor and higher state officials had been entitled.

Eucharistic.—The earliest records of the processions that formed part of the Christian ritual of the Eucharist, those of the entrance, the Gospel, and the Communion, date from the 6th century, though they were evidently established at a much earlier date. It is known that the offertory processions were continued, at least on great festivals, until the end of the Middle Ages, but by that time their true meaning had been lost and they were later discontinued. In the 20th century strong efforts have been made by liturgists to reintroduce the offertory and entrance processions.

The eucharistic processions still in use are of late origin: the procession on the Feast of Corpus Christi did not become general until the 14th century, and that in honour of the Blessed Sacrament on Holy Thursday was confirmed and adopted by John XXII (about 1333).

Orthodox Church.—The most noteworthy processions are the two connected with the celebration of the Eucharist. The first is the so-called "little entrance" before the reading of the Gospel in which the Gospel book is carried accompanied by lights and the singing of the *Trisagion* and other hymns. The second is the "great entrance" before the eucharistic prayer, when the offerings of bread and wine are carried in a more splendid procession, accompanied by ministers bearing fans representing angels' wings and the singing of the *Cherubikon*. The people's devotion has tended to centre around these processions because in the Orthodox churches a solid wall (*ikonostasis*) divides the sanctuary from the nave and hides the eucharistic celebration from the people.

Protestant Churches.—The Reformation abolished in all Protestant countries those processions associated with the doctrine of transubstantiation; "the Sacrament of the Lord's Supper," according to the 28th Article of Religion of the Church of England, "was not by Christ's ordinance reserved, carried about, lifted up, or worshipped." It also abolished those associated with the cult of the Blessed Virgin and the saints. The stern simplicity of Calvinism would not tolerate religious processions of any kind, and from the Reformed Churches they vanished altogether. The more conservative temper of the Anglican and Lutheran communions, however, permitted the retention of such processions as did not conflict with the Reformed doctrines. The Lutheran Church in some localities has retained the ancient rogation processions during the week before Whitsunday and, in some cases, during the month of May. In the Anglican churches the funeral procession, the processional litanies, and the solemn entrance of the clergy and choir are still retained. The use of the processional cross, banners, and lights, long abandoned, has been revived.

BIBLIOGRAPHY.—G. Dix, *The Shape of the Liturgy* (1945); L. Duchesne, *Christian Worship* (1912); T. S. Garrett, *Christian Worship* (1961); J. A. Jungmann, *Pastoral Liturgy* (1962), *The Mass of the Roman Rite* (1959), and *The Early Liturgy* (1959); E. B. Koenker, *The Liturgical Renaissance in the Roman Catholic Church* (1954).
                                                                (L. J. MA.)

PROCIDA (Latin PROCHYTA), an island off the coast of Campania, Italy, 2 mi. (3 km.) NE of Ischia and to the west of the Gulf of Naples. Pop. (1961) 9,050. It is about 2 mi. in length and, including the adjacent island of Vivara, is made up of four extinct craters; parts of the margins of all four have been destroyed by the sea. The highest point is only 250 ft. (76 m.) above sea level. The soil is very fertile. The only town, Procida, lies on the east side; its castle is now a prison. The island housed political internees for several years after 1945.   (G. KH.)

PROCLAMATION, a historic form of executive action in England and the United States. In England, while the powers of parliament were evolving, the king in council still asserted and exercised a power to legislate, in the 14th century by ordinance and in the 16th and 17th centuries by proclamation. In 1539 the Statute of Proclamations (31 Henry VIII, c. 8) made a general authorization of legislation by proclamation which should "not be prejudicial to any person's inheritance, offices, liberties, goods, chattels or life" and of its enforcement by forfeitures and imprisonment. This statute was repealed, however, in 1547 by 1 Edward VI, c. 12, s. 5. In 1610 the opinion in the *Case of Proclamations* (12 Coke's Reports 74) declared that the king by his proclamation could not create an offense which was not one before; and this became unquestioned after adoption of the English Bill of Rights (1689). Royal proclamations are still employed in the second half of the 20th century, however, to give wide publicity to actions taken by the king in council, such as dissolving one parliament and summoning the next.

In the U.S. proclamations are issued by governors of states and mayors of cities; but of especial importance are those issued by the president, proclamations and executive orders being, aside from messages to congress, the chief kinds of formal presidential action. In U.S. presidential proclamations the body of the proclamation ("Now, therefore, I . . . ,") is preceded by a preamble ("Whereas . . .") and followed by the formula of attestation, the presidential signature, the seal of the U.S. and the countersignature of the secretary of state. The date is stated, by a tradition going back to President Washington, in terms of the independence of the U.S. as well as the Gregorian calendar.

Some proclamations of the president are merely informative or hortatory, while others are exercises of quasi-legislative authority delegated by statute or inferred from powers vested in the president by the constitution. Two of the most famous are Washington's proclamation of neutrality of April 22, 1793, and Pres. Abraham Lincoln's proclamation of emancipation of Jan. 1, 1863. Careful provision is made by law and executive order for the preparation, clearance and numbering of presidential proclamations and for their publication in the Federal Register. Proclamation of treaties is separately handled.   (J. HT.)

PROCLUS (PROCULUS) (A.D. 410–485), the most important representative of the later Neoplatonism inaugurated by Iamblichus (*q.v.*), was born at Constantinople of Lycian parents and brought up at Xanthus in Lycia. He studied philosophy under Olympiodorus the elder at Alexandria and then under Plutarch and Syrianus, the Platonic *diadochi* ("successors"), at Athens. He eventually became himself *diadochus* (*i.e.*, successor of Plato in the headship of the Platonic Academy at Athens) and held that position until his death in 485. An enthusiastic biography of him by

his successor Marinus is preserved.

Proclus is the most notable figure of the Athenian school of Neoplatonism, which was distinguished by its passionate paganism and by its taste for elaborate metaphysical speculation. He was probably not a very original thinker (we have too little detailed information about the works of his predecessors to be quite sure about the extent of his own contribution). But he was a great systematizer, expositor, and commentator. The type of Neoplatonism that began with Iamblichus reaches its fullest development in the thought of Proclus, and it is through his works that we know it best. His chief importance in the history of philosophy is as one of the principal sources from which Neoplatonic ideas were diffused through the Byzantine and Islamic worlds and the medieval Latin West. He greatly influenced the Pseudo-Dionysius (Dionysius the Areopagite; *q.v.*), whose influence on the Christian thought of both East and West was immense.

Of the Arabic works that transmitted his ideas the most important was the so-called *Liber de causis*, which passed in medieval times as a work of Aristotle, though it is in fact based upon Proclus' *Elements of Theology* (as St. Thomas Aquinas, who knew both works in Latin translations, recognized). The *Liber de causis* and Proclus' own *Elements of Physics* were translated into Latin in the 12th century. Other Latin translations of important works of Proclus, including the *Elements of Theology*, were made in the next century by William of Moerbeke, the translator of Aristotle and friend of St. Thomas Aquinas. These translations, appearing at a time when very little of Plato and nothing of Plotinus was known in the Latin West, became for the later Middle Ages the principal source of their knowledge of Platonism.

The philosophical works of Proclus can be classified as follows: (1) his commentaries on Plato, of which those on the *Republic*, on the *Parmenides*, on the *Timaeus*, and on *Alcibiades I* are extant with excerpts from that on the *Cratylus*; (2) his major exegetical work on Plato, the *Platonic Theology*; (3) two systematic manuals, the *Elements of Physics* and the *Elements of Theology*, the former being based on Aristotle's physical works, the latter, which is considerably more important, being a concise exposition of Neoplatonic metaphysics in 211 propositions; and (4) three occasional essays, the *De decem dubitationibus circa providentiam*, the *De providentia et fato*, and the *De malorum subsistentia*. Of his nonphilosophical writings there survive some astronomical and mathematical works, including the *Hypotyposis* on astronomical positions and a commentary on the first book of Euclid's *Elements*; some grammatical works (the identity of the author of the *Chrestomathia grammatica* with Proclus the philosopher is disputed); seven hymns and two epigrams, one of which (*Greek Anthology*, vii, 341) is an inscription for the common tomb of himself and his master Syrianus; and some fragments on religious-magical themes. *See also* NEOPLATONISM.

BIBLIOGRAPHY.—The best introduction to the thought of Proclus is to be found in the *Elements of Theology,* ed. with Eng. trans. by E. R. Dodds, 2nd ed. (1963). The *Platonic Theology* was edited by A. Portus (1618). A new edition, with French translation, introduction, etc., by H. D. Saffrey and L. G. Westerink was in course of publication in the late 1960s. There is an Italian translation by Enrico Turolla (1957). The Teubner series includes the commentaries on the *Republic,* ed. by W. Kroll, 2 vol. (1899–1901), on the *Timaeus,* ed. by E. Diehl, 3 vol. (1903–06), on the *Cratylus,* ed. by G. Pasquali (1908), and on Euclid, ed. by G. Friedlein (1873); the *Elements of Physics,* ed. with German trans. by A. Ritzenfeld (1912); and the *Hypotyposis,* ed. with German trans. by C. Manitius (1909). The part of the commentary on the *Parmenides* that survives in Greek was edited by V. Cousin (in *Procli opera inedita* [1864; reprinted 1961]). The final section, extant only in the medieval Latin trans. has been edited with Eng. trans. by R. Klibansky, C. Labowsky, and E. Anscombe, *Plato latinus,* vol. iii (1953). The *Commentary on Alcibiades I* has been edited by L. G. Westerink (1954). There is an Eng. trans. by W. O'Neill (1966). There is a French trans. of the *Commentary on the Timaeus,* with notes, by A. M. J. Festugière (1966–69). The medieval Latin trans., with extensive fragments of the original Greek text, of the three essays, has been edited by H. Boese (1960). The *Hieratic Art* was edited with French trans. by J. Bidez in *Catalogue des manuscrits alchimiques grecs VI* (appendix) (1928). The *Eclogae de philosophia Chaldaica* were edited by A. Jahn (1891). The *Hymns* have been edited by E. Vogt (1957). The text of the *Life* by Marinus, ed. by J. Boissonade, is to be found in V. Cousin, *Procli opera inedita* (*see* above). The most important modern work on the thought of Proclus is that of E. R. Dodds (*see above*). *See also* L. J. Rosán, *The Philosophy of Proclus* (1949) with an English version of the *Life* by Marinus and extensive bibliographies, and A. C. Lloyd in the *Cambridge History of Later Greek and Early Medieval Philosophy*, chap. 19 (1967; reprinted 1969).   (A. H. AG.)

PROCOPIUS (fl. first half of 6th century A.D.), Byzantine historian whose works are an indispensable source for his period and contain much geographical information, was born at Caesarea in Palestine, probably between the years 490 and 507. He had a legal training and from 527 to 531 was adviser (*consilarius*) to the military commander Belisarius (*q.v.*) on his first Persian campaign. In 533 and 534 he took part in the expedition against the Vandals and was in Africa until 536 when he joined Belisarius in Sicily. He was in Italy on the Gothic campaign until 540, after which he apparently returned to Constantinople, since he describes the great plague of 542 in the capital. Nothing is known with certainty of his subsequent life. He may have been prefect of Constantinople in 562.

Procopius' writings fall into three divisions: the *Polemon* (*De bellis*; *Wars*, Persian, Vandal, and Gothic), in eight books; *Peri Ktismaton* (*De aedificiis*; *Buildings*), in six books; and the *Anecdota* (*Historia arcana*; *Secret History*), which was only published after the author's death.

The *Wars* consist of: (1) the Persian Wars (two books), on the long struggle of the emperors Justin I and Justinian I against the Persian kings Kavadh and Khosrau I down to 549; (2) the Vandal War (two books), describing the conquest of the Vandal kingdom in Africa and subsequent events from 532 to 548; (3) the Gothic War (three books), describing the war against the Ostrogoths in Sicily and Italy from 536 to 551. The eighth book contains a further summary of events down to 553. These books also refer to certain important internal events, such as the Nika insurrection at Constantinople in 532 and the plague in 542.

The *Buildings* contains an account of the chief public works undertaken during the reign of Justinian down to 560. If not written at the command of Justinian (as some have supposed), it is evidently grounded on official information, and is full of panegyric of the Emperor and the late Empress, but is nevertheless a valuable source of information.

The *Secret History* purports to be a supplement to the *Wars*, containing explanations and additions which the author could not insert into the latter work for fear of Justinian and Theodora. It is a violent invective against these sovereigns, with attacks on Belisarius and his wife Antonina, and on other noted officials. Owing to the ferocity of the attacks upon Justinian, the authenticity of the *Secret History* was questioned, but Procopius' authorship is now generally recognized. In point of style, the *Secret History* is inferior to the *Wars*, and has the air of being unfinished, or at least unrevised.

BIBLIOGRAPHY.—Works in the Bonn *Corpus* ed. by G. Dindorf, 3 vol. (1833–38); critical edition by J. Haury, 3 vol. (1905–13); Haury's text with Eng. trans. by H. B. Dewing and G. Downey, 7 vol. (1914–40) in the Loeb series. *See also* K. Krumbacher, *Geschichte der byzantinischen Litteratur*, pp. 230–237 (1897); G. Ostrogorsky, *History of the Byzantine State*, p. 23 (1956); G. Moravcsik, *Byzantinoturcica*, 2nd ed., vol. 1, pp. 489–500 (1958); J. B. Bury, *History of the Later Roman Empire*, 2nd ed., vol. 2, pp. 417–430 (1923); E. Stein, *Histoire du bas-empire*, vol. 2, pp. 709–723 (1949); P. N. Ure, *Justinian and His Age*, pp. 169–184 (1951).   (J. M. HY.)

PROCRUSTES, also called POLYPEMON or DAMASTES, in Greek legend, a robber dwelling in the neighbourhood of Eleusis, who was slain by Theseus (*q.v.*). He had an iron bed (or according to some accounts, two beds) on which he compelled his victims to lie, stretching or cutting off their legs to make them fit the bed's length. The "bed of Procrustes" has become proverbial for inflexibility.

PROCTOR, a variant of the word procurator, nearly equivalent in meaning to agent; it is now obsolete in English except for certain technical meanings. In law, it was formerly applied to a practitioner in ecclesiastical and admiralty courts, licensed by the archbishop of Canterbury to perform such duties as were performed by solicitors in ordinary courts. With the passing of the Judicature Act, 1873, proctor in this sense became obsolete, the term solicitor being extended to include proctors. (*See* LEGAL PROFESSION: *England and Wales*.) However, the word is still sometimes used in the United States to denote any practitioner in probate and admiralty courts; another trace of it remains in the office of queen's proctor, who represents the crown in British divorce courts and has a duty to expose collusion between the parties.

In the Church of England a proctor is a representative of the clergy in convocation; at certain universities—notably Oxford and Cambridge—a proctor is a university official charged primarily with the enforcement of discipline among undergraduates.

PROCUREMENT, MILITARY. This term denotes the acquisition by a military establishment of goods and services, other than military personnel, whether by purchase, rent, lease, manufacture, or requisition. It includes choice of strategies, determination of requirements, drafting of specifications, selection of sources of supply, determination of contractual terms, inspection of matériel procured, and the payment and audit of accounts.

The importance of military procurement arises from its effects on the nation's economy as well as its effectiveness in supporting military policy. Poor procurement practices may promote social tensions and economic instability, and low civilian standards of living. As the art of warfare has become more complicated in the 20th century, procurement has taken on increased importance. In the United States at the peak of World War II, military requirements absorbed about 44% of the gross national product; in Great Britain and Germany about 50%; in Japan 41%. Even in the peacetime years of the early 1960s military requirements absorbed about 10% of the gross national product in the United States.

Although government arsenals have in the past played a major role in military procurement, today the development and production of advanced weapons systems in the United States and other Western countries depend to a large extent upon private firms under contract with government agencies. Because of the rapid change in modern weapons systems and the desire to move rapidly from design to production, great uncertainties pervade the weapons acquisition process—uncertainties concerning technical capabilities of weapons systems, the time required for development of new systems, and the costs of development and production. In view of the risks involved, the military procurement agencies and private industry have developed new and unique relationships designed to shift the risks to the government and encourage private firms to undertake the development of new systems. It appears that these relations provide strong pressures during the development stage for perfecting better systems in shorter periods, but only weak incentives for minimizing costs.

Choice of Strategies.—The choice between alternative military strategies is, properly conceived, a problem in the efficient use of resources. It is an economic problem, involving the comparison of benefits and costs. But the efficient use of resources for military purposes presents special problems because the market mechanism, which serves as an instrument for solving problems of the efficient allocation and use of resources in the private sector, has limited usefulness in the military sector, particularly in the choice between alternative strategies. This choice requires administrative decisions based on cost-benefit studies involving careful definition of military objectives and alternative military systems, *i.e.*, alternative combinations of weapons, organizational arrangements, and operations for achieving stated objectives.

Requirements.—Making accurate estimates of requirements in the light of strategic plans is essential to effective procurement. This process involves two steps: (1) determination of the requirements for various end products; (2) the conversion of requirements for end products into requirements for labour, material, and productive facilities, and their comparison with available resources in order to determine whether or not strategic plans are feasible. In determining its requirements a country inevitably takes calculated risks and chooses between alternative strategic plans in the light of their costs. Since the impact of procurement on the economy depends upon its timing as well as its magnitude, it is important that requirements be properly phased. Unnecessary strain may be placed on the economy if, for example, contracts for the delivery of ammunition in six months are placed while the weapons that are to use the ammunition will not be ready for two years.

Once requirements are established the objectives of procurement policy are several: (1) fulfillment of requirements in the volume and quantities and at the time and place needed; (2) efficient utilization of resources so that requirements may be fulfilled with minimum impact upon civilian standards of living; (3) budgetary economy; (4) economic stabilization; and (5) sociopolitical objectives, such as elimination of excessive profits, fostering of small business, geographical dispersion of industry, and elimination of discrimination in employment practices. Obviously these various objectives may sometimes conflict, and choices between them will have to be made.

Most governments have reserved the power to requisition goods and services in times of emergency, but in recent times this power has been used cautiously. Countries vary in the extent to which the government itself undertakes the manufacture of military equipment. In the United States, Great Britain, and Germany the military establishments have relied heavily upon purchases from private enterprise.

Purchasing Techniques.—Two principal purchasing techniques are used in military procurement: the system of public advertising for sealed bids; and the negotiated contract. Under the sealed-bid system the contract is normally awarded, after public opening of the bids, to the lowest responsible bidder who meets the advertised specifications. Consequently, once specifications are determined, the purchase function becomes routine and opportunities for favouritism in selecting suppliers are minimized. Moreover, where there is genuine competition the system protects the financial interest of the government.

Often the sealed-bid system is not a useful device and is replaced by the negotiated contract. Since the procurement officer will frequently negotiate with several sources of supply, negotiation does not preclude competition. A conscious policy of promoting competition through the development of alternative sources of supply is often important to efficient procurement policy. Frequently it is desirable to award an unpriced "letter of intent" before specifications can be put in final form and bids sought, so that the supplier may have a head start in tooling up, placing orders for materials, and recruiting a labour force. In other cases national security makes it inadvisable to publicize specifications. In some industries strategic planning requires the maintenance in readiness of several geographically dispersed sources of supply. Often it is desirable to place contracts in the light of the availability of manpower or other scarce resources rather than on the basis of price alone. In the case of research and development contracts, where confidence in a particular supplier is paramount, selection of a supplier on the basis of a low bid may not be practicable. Likewise, where suppliers are few or where costs are uncertain because of rapid change in design or in the rate of output, the sealed-bid system may not be the most efficient way to develop a competitive price. Finally, in situations where military needs can be fulfilled by several products of similar but slightly different specifications, the interest of the government may lie in negotiating on specifications as well as price.

When an economy operates under a general system of price control, the question arises whether such controls should apply to military contracts. In Britain and the United States during World War II, responsibility for the prices of specialized military equipment was generally placed on the procurement agencies while prices on contracts for standard commercial items were subject to the general controls. This practice facilitates the diversion of economic resources to military needs by leaving the military establishment free to attract suppliers by price incentives and relieves price control authorities from possible charges of interfering with the military program.

The system of negotiation permits the tailoring of contract terms to the circumstances of the particular procurement. There are several basic types of contracts in common use. The type selected in a particular case will depend in part on the nature of the procurement, *e.g.*, whether it is for research and development or for production, and in part on the relative emphasis on providing incentives to efficient production in contrast to controlling profits. The simplest type of contract is the fixed price contract. It is the easiest to administer and provides the supplier maximum incentives to control costs. The central problem in the use of this type of contract is arriving at a reasonable price; where there is previous experience in producing similar items under similar conditions or where there are alternative suppliers, it may not be difficult. However, in the absence of good cost estimates, unexpectedly large profits may develop, not because of the effectiveness of the supplier in controlling costs but because of ignorance in estimating costs when the contract is negotiated.

Cost-plus contracts are widely used where there are difficulties in estimating costs. Under such contracts the supplier receives a fee for his services as well as reimbursement for his allowable costs. The earlier practice of calculating the fee as a percentage of actual costs left the supplier with a positive incentive to increase his costs. The cost-plus-fixed-fee contract (CPFF), in which the absolute amount of the fee is predetermined, eliminates the incentives to cost inflation and minimizes the possibilities of excessive profits but provides no financial incentives to cost control. The administrative disadvantages of cost contracts are great, since they require careful audit of the supplier's accounts to verify his costs and frequent inspection of his operations to ensure efficient use of resources.

There are many variations of these two basic types of contracts. Incentive features may be added to cost contracts by providing that the fee shall not be fixed but shall depend upon the extent to which the contractor exceeds or falls short of some target cost. Nonprofit organizations often operate under cost contracts without any fee. Fixed price contracts have been modified in many cases to provide for redetermination of price at some time during the life of the contract on the basis of actual cost experience. A fixed price contract may include an escalator clause providing for change in price in the event of some increase in labour or material costs. Such a clause, by relieving the contractor of risks over which he may have no control, makes it possible to eliminate from the contract price an allowance for contingencies.

In the United States, in particular, there has been considerable concern over the tendency to place military contracts with the larger suppliers, popularly known as "big business." This concern arises in part because of the fear that military procurement will accentuate monopolistic tendencies and in part because of the need during periods of mobilization to use all productive facilities. Consequently, various devices have been adopted for encouraging the dispersing of contracts among small businesses.

Profits.—Control of profits often plays a large part in procurement policy. Because of difficulties in negotiating close prices on many contracts, profits often turn out to be larger than anticipated. Various noncontractual devices have been tried for recouping excessive profits. Many countries at one time or another have enacted excess profits taxes, which usually take normal peacetime rates of profit as a basis for estimating allowable profits during periods of mobilization. Since 1942 the United States has experimented with a system of contract renegotiation designed to recapture excessive profits at the end of the year after review of the supplier's over-all profit-and-loss position on his government business. In determining whether or not a contractor has excessive profits the renegotiation authorities are required by statute to consider various factors, including the contractor's promptness in delivery, the quality of his product, his risk, and his efficiency. The renegotiation procedure establishes a pattern of allowable profits which serves as a guide to suppliers and procurement officers in their negotiations. It also serves to eliminate excessive profits arising from errors in judgment, from deficiencies in contract negotiation, or from the efforts of a willful minority to take advantage of the government. While the elimination of excessive profits serves important social purposes, some students believe that the renegotiation process as practised reduces the incentives for efficiency and is therefore in conflict with the objectives of controlling costs and prices. Whether low profits mean low prices depends on the level of costs.

Another important problem facing procurement officials is the control of prices on subcontracts. This may be achieved in part by direct price controls on many standard items, by requiring that subcontracts be let by competitive bidding, by renegotiation, or by excess profits taxes. Other attempts to control subcontract prices directly have generally met with limited success.

Centralization.—There has been much public discussion in the United States of the relative merits of centralization of procurement in a single agency as against decentralization into various divisions of the armed services. During World War II, each of the armed services was responsible for most of its own procurement, and within each of the services procurement was further decentralized to the technical bureaus or services. Although the Army, Navy, and Air Force have since been absorbed into the Department of Defense and the formulation of procurement policy and the purchase of some items common to the various services have been centralized, the responsibility for the procurement of most specialized military equipment is still decentralized to the component services.

BIBLIOGRAPHY.—John Perry Miller, *Pricing of Military Procurements* (1949); Thomas Blanchard Worsley, *Wartime Economic Stabilization and the Efficiency of Government Procurement* (1949); William Ashworth, *Contracts and Finance* (1953); Charles J. Hitch and Roland N. McKean, *The Economics of Defense in the Nuclear Age* (1960); M. J. Peck and F. M. Scherer, *The Weapons Acquisition Process: an Economic Analysis* (1962); F. M. Scherer, *The Weapons Acquisition Process: Economic Incentives* (1964); J. F. Weston (ed.), *Procurement and Profit Renegotiation* (1960); C. H. Danhof, *Government Contracting and Technological Change* (1968). (J. P. Mɪ.)

PROCYON, the brightest star in the constellation Canis Minor (*see* CANIS MAJOR), hence its Bayer equivalent, α Canis Minoris. It and Sirius (*q.v.*) in Canis Major were called the two dog stars, though Dog Star refers to Sirius, which is the brighter of the two. Procyon is a double star consisting of one bright and one very faint component. Located at a distance of about 11 light-years from the sun it is one of the nearest stars.

PRODIGY, although it may refer to any extraordinary, astonishing person, event or deed, has been particularly applied to children who show early signs of genius or exceptional ability along certain lines. Among these are the arithmetical prodigies; the chess prodigies; and the lightning calculators, who have a remarkable memory for figures and vivid visual or auditory imagery, but often do not excel in other ways. Best known are the musical prodigies—Mozart, Schubert and Mendelssohn, all of whom began to compose before the age of 12; Johann Hummel, Chopin and Yehudi Menuhin, who gave public concerts by 11 years of age; and Ruth Slenczynska, who astounded audiences at 6; Brahms, Dvořák and Richard Strauss all drew musical attention early.

Far less common is precocious ability in acting, writing, drawing and painting, such as that of the famous 19th-century child actor William Betty, popularly known as "the young Roscius"; Minou Drouet, who in 1956 at the age of 8 won fame for poems and letters of doubtful authenticity; and Albrecht Dürer, who painted a self-portrait at 13. Pascal at 11 secretly constructed a geometry of his own; Norbert Wiener and Fred Safier, Jr., read science and literature at 5 years and entered college by the age of 12.

How do children become prodigies? They are both born and made—born with retentive memories and a quality of mind that enables them to relate and organize experiences; made in the sense that they receive opportunities and rewards and special practice, instruction or training. The three prodigies last mentioned had radically different home environments. When Pascal was 11, his father deprived him of mathematical books. In marked contrast, Norbert Wiener was subjected to his father's insistent, severe and often painful demands for precise and ready knowledge. Fred Safier's parents, on the other hand, reported that they never pushed the boy but encouraged him to cultivate varied interests.

Do prodigies fulfill the promise of youth? Few mental prodigies reported in history have met early expectations. (The German prodigy Christian Heinecken [1721–25], said to have learned to speak Latin and French by the age of three, and to be capable of publicly demonstrating knowledge in history, geography and biblical study, died at the age of four.) However, musical prodigies seldom fade into oblivion. Original, creative geniuses who achieve the highest eminence could probably have been identified as extraordinary in early childhood. *See also* GIFTED CHILDREN; GENIUS. (Ru. S.)

PRODROMUS, THEODORE (d. *c.* 1166), sometimes called Ptochoprodromus ("poor Prodromus"), a Byzantine writer, well known for his prose and poetry, some of which is in the vernacular. He wrote many occasional pieces for a widespread circle of patrons at the imperial court. Some of the work attributed to him is unpublished and some of it may be wrongly attributed to him. Even so there does emerge from these writings the figure of an author in reduced circumstances, with a marked propensity for begging, who was in close touch with the court circles during the reigns of John II and Manuel I (1118–80). He was given a prebend by Manuel I, and he ended his life as a monk. Behind panegyric and conventional treatment his writings, often written on the occasion of some public event, provide the historian with vital information on many aspects of contemporary history, both at home and abroad, including details on genealogy, on individual personalities, on everyday social and economic life. There is a strongly satirical vein in his works, which range from epigrams and dialogues to letters and occasional pieces in both prose and verse. He had a biting sense of humour and his comments are shrewd and pithy.

BIBLIOGRAPHY.—Some works in J. P. Migne, *Patrologia Graeca,* vol. 133 (1864), and D. C. Hesseling and H. Pernot, *Poèmes prodromiques en grec vulgaire* (1910); others widely scattered in various publications. *See also* K. Krumbacher, *Geschichte der byzantinischen Litteratur,* 2nd ed., pp. 749–760 and 804–806 (1897); G. Moravcsik, *Byzantinoturcica,* vol. 1, 2nd ed., pp. 522–526 (1958); G. Ostrogorsky, *History of the Byzantine State,* p. 314 (1956); A. A. Vasiliev, *History of the Byzantine Empire,* pp. 500–502 (1952); P. Lamma, *Comneni e Staufer,* 2 vol. (1955–57). (J. M. Hʏ.)

PRODUCTION, CENSUS OF. A census of production is an enumeration of units of production in much the same sense that a population census (*see* CENSUS) is an enumeration of people. However, since the object of the enumeration in a production census is not precisely defined, such censuses are different from population censuses. The latter have in all times and places exhibited similar characteristics because they have been concerned with an easily identified unit of enumeration. Ideas as to which units of production are suitable for enumeration have differed greatly at various times and places; some countries, for example, have used the individual establishment or workshop while others have used the entire enterprise, regardless of the number of establishments it contained. The concept of production itself has also changed from time to time in accordance with prevailing economic ideas. Thus, the French physiocratic school (*q.v.*) in the 18th century held that only agriculture was really production, while in the Soviet Union and other Communist countries in the 20th century, many services are not considered to be part of the production total. In the non-Communist world, however, the terms "economic activity" and "production" are largely synonymous.

Because the term "census" connotes comprehensive coverage of an entire area or country, modern usage would require that the term "census of production" should cover the total production of the country or area, without qualification. Nevertheless, the term "census of production" has been used traditionally in certain countries, notably the United Kingdom, to denote periodic censuses of the output and characteristics of industrial establishments. Other countries use the term "census of manufactures," "census of industry," or "census of industrial production." The tendency in modern practice is to approach the problem of enumerating productive units by means of censuses of agriculture, censuses of manufactures and mining, and censuses of distribution or business which, together, cover the bulk of production as understood by economists in non-Communist countries.

Historical Development in U.S.—The progression of ideas which has led to, and which explains, much of present theory and practice in production censuses is nowhere seen more clearly than in the historical development of the subject in the United States, which was the first country to take a comprehensive approach. In 1810, the U.S. Congress amended the statute governing the population census for that year to instruct U.S. marshals, who were then enumerators for the population census, to "compile an account of the several manufacturing establishments and manufactures within their several districts, territories and divisions." To implement this legislation, a circular was drawn up by Tench Coxe, an assistant to the secretary of the treasury and a remarkable pioneer in the field of official statistics. The circular, which is notable for its foresight as to the kind of data required, set out a sample of the information to be collected:

"George B. Williams, of the township of Northhampton, county of Berkshire, and state of Massachusetts, makes and sells broad cloths at two dollars and one-half, to three dollars per yard; blankets at three to three dollars and one-half each; narrow cloths at one dollar and one-third, to one dollar and one-half per yard; total of goods in a year, 4,231 yards of broad cloth, 7,368 yards narrow cloth, and 413 blankets. Total value, 25,511 dollars and 45 cents.

"The said George Williams employs and moves by water one carding machine and 150 spindles; and by hand four hundred and ten spindles in the woolen manufacture."

Coxe tabulated the information received to show the number of firms in each state and county and the quantities of each commodity produced. The incompleteness and inaccuracies of the census of 1810 were analyzed by Adam Seybert in his *Statistical Annals* (1818); he concluded that the census would be improved by the use of a detailed questionnaire and by giving proper instructions to the enumerators. He recommended a questionnaire which constitutes a model and which, in broad outline, remained unchanged up to modern times. The data to be collected for each establishment consisted of: (1) the county and state in which located, (2) the nature of the manufacturing process, (3) the quantity of each raw material used and the total cost thereof, (4) the number of persons employed and the amount of their wages, (5) the capital invested, (6) contingent expenses, and (7) value of production. These questions, plus a question on machinery employed, were embodied in the questionnaire used in the census of 1820, taken as part of the population census of that year.

The process by which the information given by the individual firms in the census of manufactures is put together to yield information on the entire economy is best seen by consideration of an actual census form. The census form shows the first page of the information given by E. I. du Pont de Nemours in the census of 1820. Only its antiquity and its historic interest permit the reproduction of this material, for information relating to individual firms is kept strictly secret in the production censuses of all countries and is not divulged by the statistical authority even to other departments of government. The forms are first classified according to industries; in this example the data belong to the chemical industry. An important aggregate is obtained by determining the total value of the products of each establishment; in the example this amounts to 606,000 lbs. of gunpowder valued at 17 to 22 cents per lb., or approximately $118,000. This aggregate for all establishments in the country will include not only the value of the production of each establishment, but will contain duplications of products produced in one factory and consumed in another. Consequently, the net contribution of each establishment to production is obtained by deducting the value of materials used from the value of the products. The resulting aggregate is called the value added by, or the net output of, the field covered by the census. In the example shown, since the value of the products was $118,000, and the value of materials $55,670, the net output of that establishment was $62,330. Modern census questions differ from those answered here only in the degree of detail requested and by the addition of questions on capital expenditure, together with certain items necessary to ensure absence of duplication in the calculation of the net output. These questions are relatively easy to answer in countries in the early stages of industrialization, but they become increasingly difficult as the economies develop. Some idea of the complexity of the modern census can be obtained by considering the entries that are required today to show the same data for the establishments which, in the course of time, have grown out of the simple "Gun Powder manufactory on the Brandywine." The current capital value of the Dupont enterprise is measured in billions of dollars and the net

*Completed Census Form**

No. 7
New Castle County, Christiana hundred
State of Delaware.
Gun Powder manufactory on the Brandywine.

Raw materials Employed
1. Salt Petre, Brimstone and charcoal
2. Refined Salt Petre, 454,000 lb.
   Roll brimstone, 70,000 lb.
   Charcoal, 82,000 lb.
3. Cost of raw material, $55,670

Number of Persons Employed
4. Ninety Five men.
5. None
6. None
7. and 8. Six mills and a number of other buildings for manufacturing purposes.

Expenditures
9. Capital Invested $240,000
10. Wages, $36,300
11. The contingent expenses comprehend many different kinds of expenditures, as cooperage, freight, carriage, commission to agents, etc., the amount of which cannot be known—the cost of occasional explosions, which are also a kind of contingent expense peculiar to the manufacture of Gunpowder cannot be easily estimated.

Production
12. Principally fine Gunpowder for shooting, and occasionally common and musket Gunpowder.
13. Market value from 17 to 22 cts per pound.
14. The establishment is composed of two complete Gunpowder manufactories, situated on the Brandywine, the first, the Eleutherian Mills, was erected in 1803 and the other, Hagley, in 1813. The whole amounts

*The first page of the answers made by E. I. du Pont de Nemours to the questions asked by a census enumerator in 1820. The original is among the schedules of the 1820 Census of Manufactures in the National Archives.
Source: National Archives Accessions, No. 54, June 1958.

output alone exceeds $1,000,000,000; the number of separate establishments that produce the output is greater than the number of men employed at the time of the first census and the range of products covers several different industries. For this reason, large enterprises are requested to provide data on each separate establishment, which is then classified into the individual industry which forms the greater part of its activities.

Economic Significance of Data.—The sum of the net outputs of all establishments in an industry, or in all the manufacturing industries of a country, is a most important figure, since it measures, with certain deductions, the contribution of the industries to the national product. Moreover, it provides the basis for many kinds of economic analysis, because it reveals the economic cost of each commodity produced, together with details of the nature of these costs, in terms of labour, material, fuel, and other inputs. The relation between net output and capital invested is used to measure the productivity of capital; the relation between net output and employment is used to measure the productivity of labour. The sum of wages and salaries gives the share of labour in the output of industries; the remainder of the output covers the returns to the other factors of production and the smaller business expenses. Changes in these relationships are of considerable economic significance. The modern census tends to collect more information on plant and equipment because of the importance of plant and equipment as indicators of economic growth. Moreover, to obtain the true net output generated by industry, it is necessary to deduct the value of capital consumed in the process of production. This is done by means of estimates for depreciation and obsolescence of the plant and equipment. Distinction is also made between the activities of the establishment that are directed toward producing goods for current consumption and those that result in the formation of new capital equipment.

Current Census Developments.—It is generally the practice that the unit enumerated is the establishment rather than the enterprise. Some problems arise in defining these terms, but generally an establishment is defined as an individual plant at a single location as distinguished from an enterprise composed of more than one plant, each of which may manufacture different products. In the case of the establishment, it is possible to associate statistics on the goods produced with the geographical location of the plant and with labour and other resources consumed in production. Unless it is a single-establishment enterprise, however, it becomes extremely difficult to associate statistics of plant operations with the financial data, which are normally available only for the enterprise as a whole. For this reason, censuses in highly industrial countries have added a question designed to enable the census authorities to identify the establishments that comprise a single enterprise. By collecting these establishments together, aggregates can be obtained to show the overall production, field of activity, employment, and net output of enterprises. By means of these data, calculations can be made of the degree of concentration of industry by calculating the percentage of employment and the percentage of net output achieved by firms of each size, ranging from small firms to industrial giants. Moreover, the data on enterprises can be associated with the accounting data of the enterprises concerned so that the productive achievement can be associated with the assets, state of indebtedness, and profits and losses of the enterprises.

The census operation involves the enumeration of units at a point in time, but production itself is not measurable at a point in time. Productive instruments, such as installed machinery and equipment, factories, and workshops can be enumerated on a given census date, but the quantity and value of production represent a flow over a period of time. As a result, some countries have concentrated on measuring the flow of production and others on measuring the productive establishments. In the United States and the British Commonwealth the main emphasis has been on the collection of data on the output of goods (*i.e.*, flow data) under the title of Census of Production in the United Kingdom and Census of Manufactures in the United States. In continental Europe, on the other hand, the main emphasis has been laid on the collection of data on the structure and distribution of productive resources under a general heading such as Census of Establishments. These differences in purpose and emphasis are discernible in the information collected and the fields covered. The production approach concentrates on (1) quantity and value of goods produced and materials used up in the process, and (2) the factors of production involved. The Census of Establishments concentrates on (1) the number, nature, location, and size of production units, such as factories, and (2) equipment and employment. Both types of census were originally taken only at infrequent intervals and were usually adjuncts of the population census or closely related to it.

For highly industrialized countries, the census of production is a complex and lengthy operation involving the questioning of each individual establishment, the processing of the returns, and the publication of the final results. While the use of automatic data processing equipment has greatly speeded up the handling of the collected material, there is nevertheless a long interval between the period to which the data relate and the date of their publication. This delay has tended to limit the usefulness of the census for purposes of current economic analysis. In consequence, some countries have adopted methods to speed up the collection, compilation, and publication of results. They mail questionnaires directly to the large producers, omit very small producers (*e.g.*, those employing less than ten workers), and estimate the production of small producers by means of probability samples, in which only a small percentage of producers are questioned by means of a brief questionnaire. An example of these devices was provided by the United Kingdom Census of Production in 1959, which was described as "the first of a new series of simple annual enquiries following the detailed census taken for 1958." (*See* "Census of Production Results for 1959," *Board of Trade Journal*, Dec. 2, 1960.) This inquiry was confined to three items—value of goods sold and work done, stocks and work in progress, and capital expenditure. More important, however, was the fact that instead of using the establishment as the basic statistical unit, the figures collected related to all the business of each firm, company, or group of companies operating in each industry. If the firm was engaged in a number of different activities, separate returns were required for each main activity. The inquiry was confined to firms employing 25 persons or more. Estimates were made for firms employing less than 25; these small firms constituted only 6% of total sales in the more detailed 1958 census.

In a similar development, the Netherlands government made a series of annual inquiries to collect the main data which, in other countries, are collected in infrequent censuses. These developments, designed to yield more up-to-date figures, have occurred in the countries using both the production census approach and the establishment census approach with the consequence that the census proper, as distinct from the more frequent surveys of production that are made annually or at other intervals, has tended to become an operation which provides the basic data necessary for the regular and current series of statistics that provide measurements of a country's production. The census has, therefore, changed from an operation designed to measure production and the production structure at infrequent intervals to one providing the framework and the basic elements for a system of current production statistics.

Current Production Statistics.—Current measures of the level of economic activity, both in the aggregate and for the principal components, are required by all countries and are particularly important in highly developed economies. In these economies, progress in knowledge of the monetary, fiscal, and other measures that can be taken to offset industrial fluctuations in the short term, and to stimulate economic growth in the long run, has brought about a realization of the need for current measures of the main elements of industrial activity. This need has been met in many countries by the development of indexes of industrial production, compiled monthly, quarterly, and annually, on the basis provided by the census data. (*See* ECONOMIC PRODUCTIVITY.) The problem here is to select such elements of the census aggregates as can be conveniently and inexpensively measured in each current period, and which can be compiled quickly into aggregates that will reflect conditions in the entire industry or industries concerned. Thus, from the census data a sample can be drawn of establishments or enterprises or products that will form the basis of monthly or quarterly reports on production and other characteristics. Frequently a separate sample is taken from the large producers, as revealed by the census, since they can report in considerable detail on the basis of up-to-date accounting records. The smaller producers may be required to provide data at less frequent intervals or in less detail. The units thus selected report regularly the quantity and value of goods produced, or even merely the principal items of production. For each branch of industry, or for each product, the quantity of the output in the current period is compared with that of the base period, usually the census year, to obtain the "quantity relative", *i.e.*, the percentage which current output bears to the base output.

The process is simple when homogeneous items are involved, *e.g.*, bicycles, or tons of cement; but when heterogeneous items are involved, such as textiles and clothing, it is frequently necessary to take the value of the products in the current period and deflate it by means of a price index to obtain the value of current production at the prices of the base year. This value, compared with the value of base year production, also yields a quantity relative. In cases where it is not possible to obtain a quantity relative for the outputs, resort is had to a quantity relative of the inputs where it is known that there is a constant relationship between input and output, *e.g.*, steel ingots consumed in the fabrication of structural steel products provide a reliable measure of the output. In other cases resort may be had to the input of operative man-hours as an indication of the output. By such devices a series of quantity relatives is obtained, which gives the relation between production of each item in the current period and production in the base period. These quantity relatives are embodied in a summation in which each of them is weighted by the value added, or net output, of each item as revealed by the census data. The results are then published as the percentage which production in the current period bears to production in the base period.

Production Index Formulas.—The formula used for a production index depends largely on the type of basic data available. The formula usually employed is the aggregate form of the Laspeyres type, viz:

$$Q_{01} = \frac{\Sigma p_0 q_1}{\Sigma p_0 q_0} \qquad (1)$$

where the subscripts 0 and 1 relate to the base period and the current period respectively, p (shorthand for p_i) represents the prices, with the reservation stated below, and q (shorthand for q_i) the quantities, and Σ (shorthand for $\sum_{i=1}^{n}$) indicates the summation over all the items included in the calculation of the index. Substantially the same result is obtained by weighting the quantity relatives for each item by their value in the base year, thus,

$$Q_{01} = \frac{\Sigma p_0 q_0 \left(\dfrac{q_1}{q_0} \right)}{\Sigma p_0 q_0} \qquad (2)$$

In cases where quantity relatives are not available, the value of the items produced in the current period may be converted to base year prices by the following formula:

$$Q_{01} = \frac{\Sigma p_1 q_1 \left(\dfrac{p_0}{p_1} \right)}{\Sigma p_0 q_0} \qquad (3)$$

Each of the formulas above can be changed to the Paasche form by the substitution of prices of the current period in place of the prices of the base period:

$$Q_{01} = \frac{\Sigma p_1 q_1}{\Sigma p_1 q_0} \qquad (4)$$

$$Q_{01} = \frac{\Sigma p_1 q_1}{\Sigma p_1 q_1 \left(\dfrac{q_0}{q_1} \right)} \qquad (5)$$

$$Q_{01} = \frac{\Sigma p_1 q_1}{\Sigma p_0 q_0 \left(\dfrac{p_1}{p_0} \right)} \qquad (6)$$

Furthermore, each of the formulas (1), (2), and (3), which use base prices as weights, can be averaged geometrically with formulas (4), (5), and (6), respectively, which use current weights, in order to yield Fisher's so-called "Ideal" formula.

In the above examples, the letter p has been used to represent prices. It is important to observe that where these prices are the actual commercial or producers' prices of the individual commodities involved, the index that results is a "gross weighted" index. Where the p's represent not prices in the normal sense, but the added value, or net output, per unit, attributable to the item, then the index is a "net weighted" index. The difference between these two types of indexes is important. In general, the production indexes published by the U.S.S.R. and Eastern European countries are gross weighted indexes, while those which are common in Western Europe, the United States, and the Commonwealth are based on the principle of net weights. It should be noted, however, that it is extremely difficult to obtain a complete set of net weights for all items of the production index. This is because the various products issuing from productive establishments can seldom be analyzed in such detail as to establish the value added output content of each item, because many of the costs for raw materials and fuels cannot be apportioned precisely to the individual products but are available only as an aggregate for all the products of the establishment. Consequently, it is common practice to use the relative values of gross output, with or without adjustment, to obtain the weights *within* each industry, or each similar subdivision of the total index (*e.g.*, individual industry or sub-industry). For each industry as a whole, however, and also for certain subdivisions of industries, the census provides the value of the total output and the value of the corresponding input, the difference between the two being the value added as given by the census. Consequently, for each industry (or subdivision) weights can be obtained which are based completely on value added.

The difference between the U.S.S.R. and the Western countries in the construction of index numbers of industrial production is of a conceptual rather than a practical kind. The Western countries seek to obtain a measure of the change in the "work achieved" by the industrial sector of the economy in successive periods of time (monthly, quarterly, annually) and this involves the elimination, from the calculation, of those products or outputs which are consumed (*i.e.*, constitute inputs) within the sector being measured. In the U.S.S.R., while this same concept is used in the national accounts for such aggregates as the "net material product," the concept on which the published index numbers of industrial production are based is that of the "gross value of production" rather than the value added.

It is clear that the gross weighted index will give relatively higher weight to those industries the value of whose products has a relatively low "work" content and a high "material" content— "material" being defined as the input into the industry from other industries. The gross weighted index will also be influenced by the degree of integration of the system of industrial production, *e.g.*, the combination of units into a single unit will eliminate certain products that flowed between the units and will give different weights to the various industries, as where spinning and weaving are combined in a single unit. However, changes in the degree of integration, which distort the index, can be corrected by standardizing the structure, as is done in the U.S.S.R. and Eastern European countries. In these countries the use of the gross weighted index is closely connected with the process of planning and economic control, which requires an indicator of the total flow of products.

It will be seen, from what has been said above, that the indexes of the Western countries, though conceptually weighted by value added, are in practice partly weighted by gross values. A formula which theoretically meets the problem completely, but which poses a number of practical difficulties, is as follows:

$$Q_{01} = \frac{\Sigma P_0 Q_1 - \Sigma \Pi_0 M_1}{\Sigma P_0 Q_0 - \Sigma \Pi_0 M_0} \qquad \text{using base weights}$$

$$Q_{01} = \frac{\Sigma P_1 Q_1 - \Sigma \Pi_1 M_1}{\Sigma P_1 Q_0 - \Sigma \Pi_1 M_0} \qquad \text{using current weights}$$

where P and Q represent prices and quantities of output, while Π and M represent prices and quantities of inputs, and subscripts 0 and 1 represent base and current periods, respectively.

Census of Agriculture.—As in the field of industrial production, the choice of an appropriate unit of enumeration for agricultural production has varied with time and place. The early censuses of agriculture in the United States (beginning in 1840) concentrated on the output of the principal crops, while in France, as early as 1669, a census was taken of wool production. Even as late as 1930, the International Institute of Agriculture, in promoting a world census of agriculture, stated that "perhaps the most important object to be secured by the census is an approximately accurate knowledge of the various products entering into consumption." Here again, however, the nature of production as a flow over a period of time has conflicted with the process of the census as an enumeration at a point in time. In consequence, most countries in recent years have tended to base the unit of enumeration on the productive establishments (*e.g.*, the farm or agricultural holding) rather than on the flow of production (*e.g.*, bushels of wheat or pounds of wool). The recommendations of the Food and Agriculture Organization (FAO) of the United Nations for a world census of agriculture in 1950 stated that the first purpose of the census was to obtain information on the number of agricultural holdings and their principal characteristics. It was assumed that crop production, in most countries, "would be estimated by multiplying the number of producing units by the average yield per unit."

The FAO program for agricultural censuses in or about the year 1960 was similarly based on the holding as the unit of enumeration and provided for the collection of information under the following headings: (1) area of holding; (2) number of separate parcels of land comprising the holding; (3) tenure of the holding; (4) amount of arable land, land under permanent crops, meadows, pastures, woodland, and other land; (5) area devoted to each crop; (6) number of livestock; (7) number of persons engaged on the holding; (8) machinery and equipment employed. These items indicate the general practice in most countries. Over 100 separate countries and territories took censuses of this type in or about 1950. These censuses are in the main decennial censuses. Consequently, separate operations are involved to obtain annual data on the production of the main crops. Thus in the United States annual statistics of crops, livestock, prices, farm employment, and related questions are collected by mailing questionnaires to a large sample of farmers—approximately 750,-000. In addition, samples have been drawn for the purpose of taking actual field measurements. Estimates based on such information are revised periodically on the basis of the data yielded by the census of agriculture. In certain other countries, such as the United Kingdom, all farms above a certain size make an annual report on each crop, thus making it possible to calculate the total of agricultural production.

It may be noted that in agricultural censuses and in current agricultural statistics there is, in most countries, no provision for the reporting of material consumed in the course of production. In consequence, the censuses do not yield a figure of net output or value added by agriculture, such as is available in the case of industry. In the same way index numbers of agricultural production usually reflect the aggregate of the output of the various crops without deduction of the inputs necessary to produce them. In this sense they are gross indexes and require adjustment to yield a figure corresponding to the contribution of the crop, or of the total of agriculture, to the national product. (*See also* AGRICULTURE.)

Census of Distribution.—The division of production into three classes corresponding to agriculture, manufacturing, and trade, is traditional in the United Kingdom and other countries of the Commonwealth, as well as in the United States. As early as 1691, Sir William Petty's celebrated generalization drew attention to the varying productivity of the three classes of production— "There is much more to be gained by Manufacture than Husbandry; and by Merchandise than Manufacture." The measurement of the third category of production, which is variously described as distribution, trade, or business, poses certain problems, and it is only in comparatively recent times that countries have started a series of censuses in the field. In the United States the Census of Business has been taken at intervals since 1929 but since 1948 legislation provides for a quinquennial census. Canada began decennial censuses of distribution in 1921. The United Kingdom took its first full census of distribution in 1950. In Ceylon a similar operation, entitled Census of Merchandising and Services, was taken first in 1952. These various titles all refer to approximately the same sector, namely, the wholesale and retail trade and related service trades. Altogether, more than 40 countries undertake such censuses at fairly regular intervals. In North America and the Commonwealth the censuses are separate operations confined to trade and services, but in continental Europe and Latin America they are frequently part of a larger census covering all productive establishments or non-agricultural establishments. These latter types of censuses concentrate on collecting information on the nature, location, and amount of labour employed for each establishment and have only recently tended to include questions on sales, purchases, inventories, and income generated.

The nature of this type of census is seen most clearly in the recommendations of the United Nations Statistical Commission on the subject. These recommendations state that the area to be covered should include all establishments engaged in wholesale and retail trade, business services (excluding professional consulting, accounting, and bookkeeping), motion pictures and theatres, recreation services, restaurants, cafes, hotels, laundries, barber and beauty shops, commercial photography, and other personal service. The unit of enumeration is the establishment engaged in these activities. The data to be collected include: (1) kind of business,

(2) number of persons engaged, (3) wages and salaries paid, (4) value of sales, (5) value of purchases, (6) value of stocks, (7) expenditure on fixed assets. The information on purchases, sales, and stocks permits the calculation for each kind of business, and for the economy as a whole, of the gross margins, *i.e.*, the difference between the value of the goods and services sold and their gross cost. The gross margin is a basic figure in the calculation of the national income and product generated in the distributive sector. It, of course, exceeds the contribution of distributive establishments to the gross national product by the amount of other business costs, such as transport, advertising, accounting, and the cost of supplies consumed in the course of business.

BIBLIOGRAPHY.—United Nations Statistical Office, *Industrial Censuses and Related Enquiries*, Series F, No. 4, vol. i and ii (1953) contains detailed bibliography of industrial censuses throughout the world; United Nations, *Statistical Yearbook* (annual), *Monthly Bulletin of Statistics, Supplement to the Monthly Bulletin of Statistics* (1959); United Nations, Statistical Office, *Index Numbers of Industrial Production, Studies in Methods*, Series F, No. 1 (1950); M. H. Fishbein, *Early Business Statistical Operations of the Federal Government* National Archives Accessions, No. 54 (June 1958); United Nations, *Growth of World Industry, 1938–1961*, and subsequent volumes in the same series (1963); R. G. Geary, "The Concept of the Net Volume of Output," *Journal of the Royal Statistical Society*, vol. cvii, parts iii and iv (1944). (P. J. L.)

PRODUCTION MANAGEMENT is the process by which the physical output of a business organization is planned and the operations employed to produce the output are directed, coordinated and controlled. As production management has mainly to do with how, when and where products are to be made it is more important in manufacturing firms than in any other business organization. The techniques and methods of production management however are both widely applied. The problem of scheduling machine operations for preparation of customers' statements by a public utility, for example, may be analogous to the problem of scheduling machines for production of an item in a machine shop. The factors considered in an analysis of materials handling are basically similar, whether the site is a shop, a warehouse or an industrial plant. Likewise, choices among alternative sets of equipment for a nonmanufacturing function may be made in much the same way as they would be in the case of production equipment. While the term "production management" may be construed to take in more than "manufacturing management" and cover less than "industrial management," seldom is any clear distinction made among these labels. The following will make evident the objectives and approaches of the branch of management discussed. No particular purpose is served by insisting on one special title and rigid definition. It is convenient to refer to the management principles and practices described in the setting of the manufacturing firm and production-centred activities as production management.

Organizational Arrangements.—Production management is no more confined to a particular organizational segment within a firm than it is restricted to a particular type of firm. Because manufacturing firms frequently have production divisions and because heads of production activities frequently are given the title of production manager, there is a tendency to identify production management either as the management of a production division or as the work done by a production manager. In reality however it is unusual to find the whole of production management being accomplished by a single department; almost invariably persons other than production managers perform functions or make decisions that fall within the scope of production management.

Some management activities involved in planning what to produce and what methods of production to use are "staff" activities conducted in staff departments that are not under the administrative control of the production division. The "line" production organization is primarily concerned with performance and has the responsibility of producing output of acceptable quality, in proper quantity, at the right times and at reasonable levels of cost. Since good organizational practice dictates that authority be commensurate with responsibility, the production organization usually has the final word about the execution of plans. Where production responsibility overlaps another kind of responsibility however an independent organizational unit may be created to handle the problems of coordination and planning that arise; or management may decree that certain decisions affecting production be made outside the division. In many firms, production-planning groups—staff agencies outside the manufacturing division—are expected to reconcile conflicting marketing and production goals such as sales division pressure for small-lot, specially designed items for favoured customers opposed by manufacturing division preference for long runs of standard products. Other specialized organizational subdivisions are frequently found in establishments where the scale and complexity of operations are such that some technical issues can best be handled by experts concentrating their efforts in a narrow field. Organizational arrangements and terminology vary, but separate departments or units may be set up for the performance of any of the following functions: product research, development and design; process development and design; specification and procurement of materials and supplies; standardization; inspection, testing and quality control; cost analysis and control; and study and preparation of work standards and methods. Usually some staff positions are created within the manufacturing division to deal with matters closely connected with its operations; other functional specialties are assigned outside the division.

To secure the advantages derivable from specialization and division of labour, the "line" portion of a manufacturing division is usually divided into departments in a way that reflects the physical organization of production. In small companies having only one plant, the functional form of organization predominates: production processes or manufacturing functions are represented individually by departments or closely related functions are grouped together to compose departments. For example, the line subdivisions in a functionally organized manufacturing division of a metal-working concern might be: (1) shipping, receiving and warehousing; (2) casting and forging; (3) machining; (4) plating and polishing; and (5) assembling and testing.

Although the functional type of organization is also found in large companies, either as the basic organizational form or within plants, some other variant is likely. For multiplant companies, individual plants may be designated as the primary organizational units of the manufacturing division; or, if several production facilities are located together, the geographical area may be made the administrative unit. Large companies with diversified product lines in some instances establish product divisions under which all operations and facilities required for production of a single product type or class of products are grouped. Product line organization is sometimes extended to the company as a whole, with a separate production department (and other line and staff departments as well) in each product division. Some manufacturing firms organize production operations according to the markets for which outputs are destined; e.g., industrial machinery, industrial materials and components, consumer products and military products. Integrated producers who perform all or several of the manufacturing processes entailed in the transformation of raw materials to finished products may organize by production stages, as extraction, transportation, refining and separating, product treatment and packaging.

The representative production organization, then, tends to be built around a line and staff structure containing components to do the staff work of advising, coordinating, controlling and providing services to line executives and departments, in addition to line subdivisions to which responsibility for the conduct of operations is delegated. In small firms, the structure is generally simple and all internal staff services may be provided by one or a few departments; in large firms, intricate administrative structures with numerous levels and a number of superimposed organizational forms can be found. Engineering functions such as product and process design, plant engineering and industrial engineering may be centralized or split among divisions; research may be divorced wholly or in part from production; purchasing and inventory control may be combined or separated, handled as part of production or not. Which production staff services are provided within a manufacturing division and which provided outside it depends on the particular company situation and history.

Functions and Problems.—The management of production may be treated in terms of: (1) the functions normally performed; (2) the problems that must be solved or decisions that must be made; or (3) both the problems encountered and the functions performed in planning, directing and controlling operations. In this discussion, emphasis will be placed on decision making because though essentially the same problems have to be solved in every manufacturing enterprise, there are many ways in which tasks can be combined in jobs, jobs grouped by functions and functions distributed to organizational units.

In the ultimate analysis, production management consists of making choices about the use of money, men, materials and time in production; i.e., production problems are simultaneously human, technological and economic. While one aspect may be dominant in a particular instance, a production decision generally involves selection from the available alternatives of an economical and technologically feasible solution conforming to enterprise objectives and subject to constraints imposed by human factors. Seldom can decisions about production be based on examination of a single factor. What is technically best can be disproportionately expensive. Capabilities of man-machine combinations and not just machines or human skills alone determine performance.

In order to reduce a review of production management problems to reasonable dimensions, some classification is necessary. At the first level a small number of general problems may be distinguished, each of which is resolvable into a series of specific subproblems at the second level of classification. It is helpful to think of production as a system whose over-all function is transformation of sets of inputs into sets of outputs. Two kinds of processes go on in the system: the physical processes of handling and working materials for conversion of material inputs to product outputs; and the decision-making processes that govern operations. When production is viewed in this way, the general problems of production management are discerned as deciding, on the one hand, what the system shall be—what physical equipment shall be employed, what methods of operation shall be followed, what form of organization and channels of communication shall exist and what rules shall be applied for making routine decisions—and deciding, on the other hand, how the system as a whole shall function at any point in time—what the quantity and assortment of output shall be, which production facilities shall be utilized and at what rates and what the composition of inputs shall be. As the solution to each of these general problems is a composite of subproblem solutions and the functions of production management are just the things that are done to arrive at decisions and put them into effect, this discussion may move immediately to specific problems.

Forecasting.—Predictions of what products can be sold and in what quantities they can be marketed usually originate outside the manufacturing organization. Forecasting is nonetheless an important part of the production management process since production programs are shaped by expected general economic conditions, the outlook for the industry and the results of specific product market studies. While accuracy in forecasting is most vital when new products are being introduced, and especially when their introduction accompanies the launching of a new business, it is always a prime determinant of the effectiveness of production planning.

Consideration of production factors begins once existence of demand for a product is demonstrated. After the general prospects for new products are determined and before much time, effort and money are spent in developing detailed sales forecasts and plans based on them, preliminary estimates of production capability should be made: this requires answers to a number of questions. What will production costs be? Are the existing or proposed production facilities suitable for the volume and quality of output involved? What particular production problems will be met; for example, are materials available in dependable supply, are there processing hazards to be guarded against, will the work force have to be expanded or given special training and will the production pattern fit with that of other products? When dealing with established products in going concerns, answers to such questions are more easily available, but the same kinds of factors must be reviewed each time production plans are formulated for an extended period. If it appears that production can be accommodated to fit general product and volume objectives, more refined sales forecasts and plans for financing, staffing, purchasing and marketing can be attacked.

When a sales forecast in its final form is delivered to production executives, its requirements—expressed as product quantities and delivery dates—must be translated into a production program. In firms that manufacture exclusively to customers' orders, forecasts may possess little detail beyond estimates of total volume and general nature of work to be expected for stages following the immediate sales period in which orders in hand are covered. Where manufacturing is performed in anticipation of sales, product characteristics are predetermined and stocks of goods are carried in inventory; sales forecasts and production will usually be in considerable detail. Preparation of the master schedule for production—which takes into account lags between production stages, inventory status in the several product lines, changing sales patterns and availability of various production facilities—by production executives and their staffs is the central planning activity in production management and the point at which the diverse elements in production are finally coordinated.

Production Planning and Control.—The importance and complexity of the task of anticipating and planning for production requirements accounts for the existence of departments of production planning and control as separate entities in manufacturing organizations. These staff groups may be assigned additional functions but their main focus almost invariably is on problems of routing, scheduling, control and dispatching.

Routing.—The routing problem is one of determining for each product to be made the sequence of operations to be performed. Each part must be routed through processes, machines to perform each operation must be chosen and the instructions to operatives of what should be done and how to do it must be written up. In plants of the type called "job-shop" where the production layout groups equipment in departments on the basis of similarity of functions and each product lot may follow a path through the layout that differs from what precedes and follows, rather complete instructions (job orders) relating to tooling, machine operation, product specifications and the like must accompany each individual job released to work. The routing sheet is the form on which most of this information is collected. In plants of the line production type where the production layout has equipment and work centres placed physically in the sequence that successive operations occur on a representative product unit and each product run follows substantially the same path, the routing has been built into the plant arrangement. While doing the original routing and layout design is a complicated job, determination and communication of the order of operations is routine thereafter.

Scheduling.—Scheduling consists of setting the times at which operations will be accomplished. When numerous orders or runs with complex routings requiring many transfers of materials during production are to be in process simultaneously, the task of arranging over-all schedules for products, operating schedules for departments and machines and schedules for supply of materials and parts is formidable. With fluctuating demands for products, it takes considerable skill and intimate knowledge of production to arrive at schedules that are both feasible and economical in view of requirements for overtime work, inventory levels, stable employment and balanced utilization of equipment.

Control.—The problem of control consists in seeing that things get done when and as planned. Quantity, quality, timing and cost are the principal controllable variables dealt with; the control process consists of comparing current progress to planned performance and initiating corrective action as deviations appear. The aspect of control which production planning and control groups are most directly concerned with is control of output through the preparation and enforcement of schedules. However, since it is often convenient to collect data on several dimensions of performance simultaneously, the report forms and procedures handled by the production control staff are likely to be multipurpose, and the

staff itself acts in a coordinating role.

Dispatching.—Dispatching, the function of issuing orders and instructions to the workplace and securing data on performance for transmission to management, is important enough to warrant identification as a separate activity in production planning and control. When only general routings and schedules are set up and some freedom is left dispatchers regarding order of work and assignment to machines and operatives, it is essential that they exercise good judgment, make fast decisions and deal with supervisors and workmen skillfully if the system is to operate satisfactorily.

Inventory Decisions.—Inventory problems are closely connected with operations planning and scheduling and, in consequence, inventory planning and control functions are usually combined with production-planning functions in organizations. Inventories in production are either planned to function as buffers between processing stages to allow their independent operation or appear as unavoidable concomitants of operations.

Inventories of raw materials are maintained to facilitate an even flow to processes as protection against interruptions of supply or because quantity purchases offer economies. The size of work-in-process inventories depends on how production is organized, the size of lots transferred between operations and the way in which schedules are constructed. Finished goods inventories are maintained so that production can be stabilized by building up inventory during slack seasons which is depleted during rush periods and so that various assortments of ordered items can be shipped without delay.

The general inventory problem consists of deciding at what points in the production system stocks shall be held and what their form and size shall be. As some unit costs increase with inventory size—storage, obsolescence, deterioration, insurance, investment, etc.—and other unit costs decrease with inventory size—setup or preparation, shortage, etc.—inventory management in part consists of determining optimal purchase or production lot sizes and base stock levels that balance opposing cost influences. Another part of the general inventory problem is deciding the levels (reorder points) at which orders for replenishment of inventories are to be initiated.

In addition to analytical problems, inventory presents problems of system design. Inventoried items must be identified, coded and catalogued so that they can be located readily when needed. Stock additions and withdrawals must be recorded so that inventory status is readily ascertainable and cost figures are kept current. Provision must be made for physical custody of inventories, storage space arrangements planned and procedures for delivering parts and supplies from stock points to work centres devised.

Facilities Problems.—Attention has thus far been centred mainly on problems of planning operations in a production system, the presence of the physical components of the system being assumed. The capacity and operating characteristics of the system, of course, are set by instrumental decisions on plant and equipment; moreover, such decisions are long-run in nature and normally result in large expenditures: they are crucial for the success of the enterprise. Initial decisions about physical facilities for production, however, are continually modified in the majority of concerns as they grow, as the pattern of output is adapted to altered marketing conditions and as need for replacement of equipment becomes apparent.

In large manufacturing concerns, decisions about the size and location of plants must be made. It is necessary to choose how manufacturing functions will be distributed among decentralized operating units and where plants will be placed in relation to markets and material sources in view of costs of transportation, plant construction and operation and factors such as climate, community attitudes, availability of utilities and presence or absence of competitive or complementary industries. The location of a factory within a selected general area and its siting so as to capture advantages of accessibility, ease of expansion and low construction cost are also significant decisions for the single-unit manufacturing firm as well as the multiplant firm.

Design of the internal arrangement of the plant and choice of the type of construction are further facilities problems to be solved. Analysis of production requirements imposed by the attributes of the products to be manufactured usually precedes selection of a general layout as it indicates what production processes and equipment units must be provided. Limitations on space and physical arrangement are posed by the size and shape of proposed production and materials—handling equipment, the need for access to work and storage spaces and building requirements. Working within these limitations, the planners endeavour to develop a scheme of layout minimizing product flow distances in a logical, orderly, easily maintained and safe arrangement.

Process design and equipment selection normally proceed parallel with layout: the problems are simultaneously technical and economic. The technical problem is determining how desired product attributes can be created in manufacturing processes and what equipment can serve; the economic problem is deciding among process and equipment alternatives on the basis of over-all cost. The same general factors operate both in the case of original equipment selection and replacement of equipment which becomes inefficient or technically obsolete whether production, material handling or other equipment is under examination. High original costs may be justified by correspondingly high durability, increasing quality of output, ease of operation or other operating advantages. Optimal equipage must be determined in light of unit capacity, rate of operation, expected life, maintenance requirements, direct cost of operation, adaptability and versatility and any relevant special considerations.

Analytical Developments.—Because much of production management consists of contending with physical processes and variables with reasonably predictable behaviours, it always has tended to rely heavily on quantitative analysis. Viewed one way, production management is simply an arrangement for solving the classic economic problem of allocating scarce resources to relatively unlimited ends. The conceptual apparatus of economic analysis, as for example its marginal cost-marginal revenue approach, is immediately usable for production decision purposes. Cost minimization models for determining optimum inventory levels and making choices among production methods and equipment alternatives have long been used as a matter of course. Applications of probability theory in sampling inspection and process control are commonplace (see PROBABILITY, MATHEMATICAL). Empirical and computational approaches to scheduling, designing and operating production processes, setting work standards and laying out workplaces are part of the intellectual equipment of every competent production manager.

Developments in the field of operations research or, more broadly, in the management sciences make it possible to push the quantitative emphasis in production management even further. Mathematical programming techniques are applicable to a variety of production allocation and scheduling problems. Queuing theory is being utilized in analysis of production lines and maintenance problems. System simulation, made feasible by stored program electronic computers, is being used to study the characteristics of complex production systems with the aim of improving system designs and decision rules. As automation of production and automatic control technology continue to advance, more reliance on mathematical research can be expected. Substantial contributions to the solution of production problems are still to come from game theory (see GAMES, THEORY OF), organization theory and information theory.

Despite the possibility that production management and other specialized managerial functions may eventually disappear and be replaced by a "universal" management science, no immediate and discontinuous change looms. Analytical methods shown to be helpful in making production decisions will be drawn from varied sources and used; but production management will not soon become a mere package of techniques or management by formula. Production decisions are made by people in human organizations existing in a dynamic environment in which only the fact of change is constant.

See also MANAGEMENT SCIENCES.   (J. D. Rs.)

PROFIT. To the businessman, profit is the monetary expression of a gain in net worth. It may be thought of as the excess of revenue over cost during a specific period of time. Profit is often stated in terms of a percentage of sales, of revenues, or of funds invested.

In accounting for profits, most cost items cause little difficulty because they consist of actual money expenses, such as wages. There are, however, at least three exceptions. The first concerns depreciation of fixed assets, for it has to be decided what part of the original cost of long-lived equipment is to be allocated to each accounting period. The simplest procedure is the "straight-line" method, which assumes equal losses in value over the life of the asset, resulting in equal charges for each year. One doubt about straight-line depreciation is raised by the possibility that depreciation allowances will not suffice to replace old equipment when it wears out, for new equipment may have increased in price. The cost accountant is then faced with the dilemma of choosing between two principles: that of maintaining the productive organization and that of reimbursing historical cost. If he accepts the former, depreciation methods will have to be concerned with replacement problems rather than with past money outlays. Accountants have generally been reluctant to do this, since it introduces a large element of subjective judgment into the measure of profits.

Secondly, accountants face difficulties of definition and measurement with respect to stocks of goods. Large inventories may have been accumulated at different times and at different prices. Preference is often given to the assumption that the units of inventory sold are those which were acquired most recently (the "last in-first out" method), chiefly because the "first in-first out" method would exaggerate profits during periods of rising prices, and losses during periods of declining prices. If the firm's investment plans are made in response to profits, the first in-first out method will stimulate inflation, whereas the alternative method will help to dampen the cycle.

The third problem is that of capital gains. A decision must be made as to how to treat overall increases in the value of the firm's assets. As no actual revenues are derived from such capital gains unless the firm is liquidated and its assets sold, no dividends can be paid from this source. For this reason, accountants have generally chosen to disregard capital gains entirely, though economists have sometimes made much of them for analytical reasons.

Profits: in Economics.—In conventional usage, then, profits are the income of a business firm after deduction of all contractual payments from gross revenues. Closer analysis of this conventional definition raises a number of problems that continue to vex economists. It can be argued both that it includes too much and that it covers too little. It includes too much if, for example, the owner of the firm also provides managerial services, in which case part of the conventionally defined profit should properly be imputed to him as wages for those services. The term "profit" could then be restricted to the return on the capital he has invested in the firm. But, if profit is defined as the return on capital invested in the firm, it is arguable that interest payments, for example, though (unlike dividends) representing a contractual obligation, should be included in a complete measure of "profits."

On the analogy of excluding implicit wages of management from "pure" profits, one might also wish to subtract from the conventional measure implicit rent on land owned by the firm, and implicit interest on the capital invested by the firm's owners. This line of thought leads to the conclusion that in competitive equilibrium profits do not exist. For, should "pure" profits emerge anywhere, capital, land, and labour would be withdrawn from alternative ventures and put to use where their services would yield the most. The demand for all three might increase, raising interest, rents, and wages. Output would rise as a result, and prices would fall until they squeezed out all profits.

However, the real world is never one of complete competitive equilibrium. Deviations from equilibrium can emerge because (1) changing techniques of production alter the relative costs of producing various products, (2) changing consumer tastes alter the equilibrium pattern of output even with fixed techniques, and (3) competition is restricted by elements of monopoly even where tastes and techniques are constant. Each of these disturbances can create "pure" profit.

First, the innovator who introduces a new technique can produce at a cost below the market price to earn "entrepreneurial" profits. These are likely to be temporary, lasting only until other firms adopt the same technique and new firms enter to expand output. Increased output causes prices to fall to the new level of costs. Though temporary, such entrepreneurial gains are thought to provide the incentive for technical progress in free enterprise economies. Joseph Schumpeter was perhaps the most prominent exponent of this view.

Secondly, changes in tastes may cause revenues of some firms to increase, giving rise to what are often called "windfall" profits. Windfall gains—and losses—provide the incentive in free-enterprise economies for an adjustment of the pattern of production to changing consumer preferences. Resources are shifted from industries suffering losses to industries experiencing gains. Output diminishes in the former and increases in the latter, causing prices to rise in the one and fall in the other, until once again prices just cover costs in all markets.

Finally, windfall and entrepreneurial profits can often be prolonged by monopoly control that prevents the entry of new firms into favoured markets. The aim of monopolistic control is to restrict output so as to prevent prices from falling to the level of costs (this is of course possible even in the absence of changes in tastes and techniques). When a firm restricts output, it reduces the supply of its product, contracting at the same time its demand for factors of production. The price of the product rises as a result, while input costs fall. A monopoly will seek to produce at a level that maximizes the margin between factor outlays and product revenues—at a level, therefore, that maximizes "monopoly" profits.

If entrepreneurial, windfall, and monopoly profits represent returns in excess of input costs, the difficult question arises: who appropriates them? Much ingenuity has gone into the quest for a satisfactory answer. F. H. Knight believes that at least an analytical distinction can be made between the owners of the "firm" and the owners of the production factors employed by it, including the owners of capital. If the firm's owners appropriate the pure profit (from which Knight excludes monopoly returns), it must be in return for activities which no one can be hired to perform. The bearing of risks may be such an activity, if risk is defined in a very special sense. It cannot be connected either with chance in gambling or with hazards that can be insured against. Knight settles on risks that produce change or adaptations to change—"entrepreneurial" risks, as he calls them.

Less subtle economists have found it difficult in practice to distinguish between the owners of the firm and the owners of the equity capital invested in it, especially since the returns on risk-bearing are quite commonly appropriated by the investors of that capital. As a result, the existence of monopoly profits, for example, may exert upward pressure on interest rates, at least in the long run. Similarly, should windfall profits persist over a sufficiently wide range to be positive for the economy as a whole, they too would affect interest rates; so would recurring entrepreneurial profits. The conclusion has therefore been drawn that innovations, the degree of monopoly, and changes in tastes are among the determinants of the return on capital, including contractual interest. A satisfactory and complete theory of profits would therefore have to explain the entire return on capital.

The question of what determines this return is an extraordinarily difficult one to answer. Many economists reason as follows: where land and labour are scarce, competition among capitalist employers is likely to bid up payments to landowners and workers, as long as the payment for an additional acre or worker is less than the addition to output and revenue which additional employment creates. Such competition will leave a residual income for the capitalist only if the contribution to output diminishes with each additional acre rented or worker hired. For their wages and rent cannot rise above the output of the marginal acre or worker, even though earlier ("intramarginal") factors produce more. Their excess output is appropriated by the owners of capital. But

not all economists are equally sure that diminishing returns operate with capital. If the doubters are right, another explanation for interest—and for profit—must be found. *See* CAPITAL AND INTEREST; LABOUR; RENT; *see* also references under "Profit" in the Index.

BIBLIOGRAPHY.—D. Ricardo,. *Principles of Political Economy and Taxation* (1817); E. von Boehm-Bawerk, *The Positive Theory of Capital,* Eng. trans. (1891); F. H. Knight, *Risk, Uncertainty and Profit* (1921); W. T. Foster and W. Catchings, *Profits* (1925); R. C. Epstein and F. M. Clark, *Industrial Profits in the United States* (1934); J. A. Schumpeter, *The Theory of Economic Development* (1934); J. Dean, *Managerial Economics* (1951); J. S. Bain, "Relation of Profit Rate to Industry Concentration: American Manufacturing, 1936–1940," *Quarterly Journal of Economics,* vol. lxv (1951); K. H. Marx, *Theories of Surplus Value,* Eng. trans. (1952); M. Kalecki, *Theory of Economic Dynamics* (1954); N. Kaldor, "Alternative Theories of Distribution," *Review of Economic Studies,* vol. xxiii (2) (1955); J. Robinson, *The Accumulation of Capital* (1956); A. K. Sen, "Neo-Classical and Neo-Keynesian Theories of Distribution," *Economic Record* (1963).

(H. O. Sc.)

PROFITEERING, a term that came into use during World War I when it was generally applied to the actions of individuals or firms who made unreasonably large profits during a national emergency. It usually carried the connotation that the recipient of these profits had acted improperly in obtaining them. Although the term has been used most frequently in connection with wartime situations, it is applied during other types of emergencies as well; *e.g.,* excessive inflation. While the word itself is comparatively new, it describes an old phenomenon. During every war, some individuals and firms have made inordinate profits, particularly those producing and selling munitions.

Numerous situations make profiteering possible. For example, an embargo may shut off the supply of certain articles, enabling those who hold supplies of them to sell them at high prices, or the government may suddenly and substantially increase its purchases of scarce materials, bringing about a similar result. The history of profiteering and its sequel, antiprofiteering legislation, discloses continuous public concern with the problem and greater refinements in the devices employed to eliminate it.

United States.—During the American Revolution the continental congress recommended to state legislatures that they regulate the prices of commodities and services in view of the "spirit of sharping and extortion . . . being confined within no bounds." Most of the state legislatures responded with laws that regulated the price of practically every commodity as well as wage rates. One of these laws was directed against the "wicked arts of speculators, forestallers, and engrossers, who infest every corner of the country."

During the Civil War, government suppliers often received higher than market prices for their goods. One supplier might have been preferred over another because he had hired an influential representative to deal with the government. An attempt to prevent such conduct was made by changing the procedures for awarding and checking on contracts. Contracting officials were required to advertise all contracts they proposed to award, where this was practicable, and new criminal statutes to eliminate bribes of public officials were enacted. In addition, a special commission was established to review certain contracts in connection with the awarding of which improper dealing was suspected. This commission had no power to require adjustment of contracts but the publicity given to these transactions persuaded some contract holders to agree voluntarily to accept lower prices than those for which they had originally bargained. No attempt was made during the Civil War, however, to eliminate profiteering which took place outside the area of government contracts or to control prices and the profits received under government contracts.

Before the Spanish-American War, congress for the first time sought to limit the profits of defense suppliers directly when it imposed a maximum price at which armour plate might be purchased by the navy department.

The outbreak of World War I increased the demand for United States goods. When the U.S. entered the war in April 1917, prices had risen 70%; there was also a sharp increase in corporate profits. Before the U.S. entered the war, congress made no serious effort to limit profits, confining itself in this regard to a special tax of

$12\frac{1}{2}\%$ on profits from the production of munitions and an 8% over-all excess-profits tax. After the U.S. entered the war several devices were employed in an attempt to eliminate what was then called profiteering.

First, a new kind of contractual arrangement was evolved. The profits of defense suppliers could not be controlled merely by requiring competitive bidding because as prices of raw material and labour began to rise rapidly contractors refused to take fixed-price contracts. In an effort to protect suppliers against the risks of unanticipated costs and the government against excessive prices, the government began to negotiate contracts under which the supplier was paid his actual costs plus a fixed percentage of such costs. It soon became apparent that this type of arrangement stimulated the supplier to increase rather than decrease his costs of performance and was potentially more costly to the government.

Second, congress and a variety of administrative agencies established maximum prices for certain commodities: basic raw materials and fuels, munitions of war and general consumption necessities. In general, profits were not considered to be sufficiently regulated by this method and a third device, the excess-profits tax, was ultimately relied upon as the principal method of eliminating excessive profits during World War I. The first such tax was imposed in 1916. The rate of tax upon excess profits was increased in subsequent years until it reached 80% in 1918. Although over-all profits of corporations declined in 1918, individual companies, especially those engaged in supplying the government directly, were able to make what were regarded to be abnormal profits despite the measures just described.

While profiteering was doubtless curtailed by the more aggressive controls of World War I, it was by no means entirely eliminated. During the period between World Wars I and II there was a continual outcry against the war profiteering that had taken place. It was even contended that by their desire for profits, munitions makers had helped bring about the war. The American Legion backed various bills to limit war profits and in 1924 the platforms of both the Democratic and Republican parties contained planks for the control of profits from war production.

The first positive action in this area was taken by congress in 1930 when it established a commission to investigate methods of equalizing the burdens of war and determine how war profits could be eliminated: this commission recommended a wartime excess-profits tax of 95%. In 1934 the Nye committee of the senate began hearings to investigate the munitions industry. The committee recommended such measures as the nationalization of the peacetime munitions industry and the imposition of a wartime tax of 99% on personal incomes over $20,000 as well as an excess-profits tax on corporations. Although congress proceeded more moderately, it did take a step in the direction of eliminating large profits from defense contracts when it enacted the Vinson-Trammell act in 1934. This law, as amended and supplemented in the following years, limited the maximum allowable profits of airplane and vessel builders and certain of their suppliers to a percentage of the contract price: the allowed profit was 10% and 12% depending on the type of article involved. This limitation was suspended in 1940 in favor of an excess-profits tax of 90% on all corporations, whether or not they were government suppliers. While this bill was designed primarily to raise revenue, it sought to achieve this by distributing the burden of national defense in a manner calculated to prevent profiteering.

With the entrance of the U.S. into the war in 1941 and the attendant expansion in munitions production, the concern over profiteering mounted. Congress initially used an approach similar to that employed in the suspended Vinson-Trammell act. It considered limiting the profit-cost ratio of munitions makers to 6%. While such an approach doubtless would restrict profits, it discouraged rather than encouraged reduction of costs and production of the most effective munitions in the most economical manner. A far more satisfactory device was the "cost plus a fixed fee" contract employed extensively by the armed services.

Another device—renegotiation—was introduced in World War II to control profiteering. Renegotiation involved an annual review by the government of a supplier's profit after the perform-

ance of his contracts and the refund by him of portions of his profit that the government regarded as excessive under all the circumstances. The advantage of this procedure was that it provided a spur to efficiency since, in theory, the efficient producer might retain more of his profits than the inefficient producer.

Two other devices were employed to eliminate profiteering during the war: one was the excess-profits tax, already discussed; the other was price control. The Office of Price Administration was established in 1941, "to prevent spiraling, rising costs of living, profiteering, and inflation resulting from market conditions." The OPA imposed maximum prices on most commodities and services other than those sold to the military departments.

The activities of the renegotiation and excess-profit authorities suggest in some measure the extent of profiteering that occurred during the war. From defense expenditures of over $190,000,000,-000 that were subject to profit control, renegotiation led to the direct recovery by the government of over $10,000,000,000. Additional amounts estimated at about $4,500,000,000 were refunded through voluntary adjustment of contracts by firms subject to renegotiation. The government also recovered from the defense and nondefense sectors of the economy about $16,000,000,000 in excess-profits taxes.

In 1948, when the nation embarked on unprecedented peacetime expenditures for defense, profit controls in the form of renegotiation were reinstated, principally upon aircraft manufacturers and some of their suppliers. In 1950, after the beginning of the Korean War, profiteering again became a matter of major concern and a series of laws was passed by congress. The Defense Production act of 1950 conferred authority upon the president "to prevent profiteering." A new excess-profits tax law was enacted whose main purpose was the raising of revenue by assessing those "corporations whose profits are higher than they probably would have been in the absence of hostilities and a large military budget." Finally, in March 1951, a new renegotiation act was enacted which applied to most defense contractors and suppliers.

The first two laws ceased to be effective in 1953; as early as 1952 congress directed that price regulations be suspended immediately in cases where no inflationary pressures existed. The excess-profits tax lasted only a short time after the end of hostilities in Korea. Only the Renegotiation act of 1951 which applied solely to profits from defense contracts was continued although its scope was gradually whittled down so that its main impact was on the aircraft and space industries.

Great Britain and Europe.—As in the United States, profiteering in England and on the continent is an old phenomenon; the legislation enacted to combat it is perhaps the best evidence that profiteering existed. Price control laws are found as early as the 4th century in the Roman empire. In 1793, while France was being blockaded by the British fleet, the French government passed the "Law of the Maximum," which fixed prices for grain and other commodities with reference to 1790 prices and set wages at a level of 50% above those of 1790. In England prices and wages were regulated from time to time from the 14th century.

Beginning in the mid-19th century, army purchasing procedures in England were centralized and tightened in an effort to eliminate profiteering; however, these procedures had to be loosened at the beginning of World War I when it became necessary to purchase uncommonly large amounts of supplies within a short time. Among other things, competitive bidding for contracts had to be abandoned.

As soon as purchasing controls were relaxed, much criticism developed concerning speculation and profiteering in war contracts. As a result, the government took over production of many munitions; it also adopted new contracting procedures in connection with the defense production performed by the civilian sector.

Among these was the use of the target cost contract: this prescribed in advance a target cost of production and provided that if the costs actually incurred by the contractor were below this figure, then a share of these savings was to be paid to the contractor along with his actual costs and the profit previously agreed upon. The virtue of this type of contract as compared to the traditional fixed price was that it prevented a defense supplier from profiteering and at the same time gave him an incentive to produce as efficiently as he could.

The British government also began in 1915 to tax excess profits being generated from the war. This form of profit control spread rapidly to other parts of the British empire and all of Europe. In addition to these relatively new devices to combat profiteering the British government employed the old device of price fixing; by 1916 the maximum price of several commodities was being prescribed by the government.

The excess-profits tax was continued in England for a short time after the war; price fixing was not only continued but reinforced by the Profiteering act of 1919. Under this law, which was the first to include the term "profiteering" in its title, the Board of Trade investigated the prices of many commodities and the profits derived from dealing in them: it then issued reports reflecting the results of its investigations. The act lapsed in 1921 before it accomplished a great deal; the problem of profiteering to which it had been addressed ceased to exist as soon as unfavourable economic conditions began to push the price level downward.

The inflation which raged in Germany in 1923 resulted in the establishment of a cartel court which had the responsibility of bringing about reductions in and preventing increases in prices when profiteering seemed to be taking place. During most of the interwar period in Europe profiteering was not a matter of great concern; rather, during the great depression there was the apprehension that profits and prices were not adequate for the proper functioning of the economic system.

As soon as World War II began there was again a preoccupation with profiteering. Germany began the war with a thoroughgoing system of price control which at first sought to hold prices and wages at 1936 levels and which required justification for any price increases or for the maintenance of prices that appeared to be yielding excessive profits.

Bitter memories of World War I and its aftermath reinforced the resolution of the government in Great Britain as well to prevent windfall gains from arising as the result of the war. In 1939 the Price of Goods act was enacted to fix prices at levels designed to freeze sellers' incomes at prewar levels. This act and the Goods and Services act passed in 1941 prevented undue price rises at the retail level but was largely ineffectual at the manufacturer's level. The difficulty was that it was necessary to leave prices high enough to provide an incentive for the production required for the prosecution of the war. This meant that the low-cost producers frequently earned high profits; accordingly, the attack upon profiteering in this area had to be made from another direction.

In general an attempt was made to set firm prices on contracts; however, in order to minimize profiteering the government in many cases postponed the establishment of a firm price until production was well advanced and cost experience had been gained. The objection to this was that, to the extent that the price finally was based upon realized costs, the contractor had no incentive to keep down his costs. An attempt was then made to use target cost contracts as in World War I in order to restore this incentive, but it was usually as difficult to negotiate a realistic target cost in advance as it was to negotiate a fixed price. Ultimately, a choice had to be made in connection with each purchase between the fixed-price contract with its inherent risk that excessive profits would be realized by some contractors and various types of contracts under which the supplier's compensation was determined primarily with reference to actual costs incurred by him.

In general there was no attempt to recapture excessive profits from prime contracts after they were realized, as renegotiation did in the United States; however, an informal procedure resembling renegotiation was instituted with respect mainly to subcontractors. They were required to submit periodic over-all trading reports which disclosed the profits they had made from defense contracts; they were required to refund that portion of their profits considered by the contracting agency to be unreasonable. By 1948 some £57,000,000 had been recovered in this manner from several thousand contractors.

Beyond all this, an excess-profits tax was imposed which, after May 1940, was at the rate of 100% and which was computed with

reference to profits earned from 1935–37. Parliamentary concern with the question was so great that the adoption of this extreme remedy against war profiteering did not result in the discontinuance of the other efforts to prevent excess profits.

After the end of World War II, most of the wartime controls over prices and production were maintained because of shortages. Food rationing did not entirely cease until the summer of 1954 and some price controls lasted longer. Other measures directed against profiteering, however, lapsed at the end of the war.

BIBLIOGRAPHY.—H. S. Hensel and R. G. McClung, "Profit Limitation Controls Prior to the Present War," *Law and Contemporary Problems*, x, 187–215 (1943); W. Ashworth, *Contracts and Finance* (1953); W. K. Hancock and M. M. Gowing, *British War Economy* (1949); H. L. Wilkinson, *State Regulation of Prices in Australia* (1917); E. M. H. Lloyd, *Experiments in State Control* (1924); J. T. Koehler, S. Marcus and P. Nichols, Jr., "Current Renegotiation Problems," *Virginia Law Review*, 45:1–62 (1959); Richard C. Osborn, "Corporate Profits: War and Postwar," *University of Illinois Bulletin*, no. 77 (1954); S. Marcus, "What is Appropriate Public Policy for Profit Renegotiation?" *California Management Review* (Fall 1959). (S. MA.)

PROFIT SHARING, a system by which, in accordance with a scheme defined in advance, employees are paid a share of the profits of the business enterprise in which they are engaged. The way in which profits will be divided between stockholders (shareholders) and employees is prescribed in advance and the amounts distributed vary from year to year according to the profits actually earned.

As far back as 1889 an International Congress on Profit Sharing, held in Paris, defined profit sharing along these lines, specifically stating that payments must be made in accordance with a freely agreed scheme and must consist of a share, determined in advance and not variable year by year at the discretion of the employer, of the profits of an undertaking to a substantial proportion of its ordinary employees. These payments are distinct from and additional to wages, which are generally paid at rates current in the industry and locality. By the requirement that schemes must be defined in advance, profit sharing proper excludes gifts, gratuities, or other payments made by an employer to his employees out of profits at his discretion without being bound to do so. An employer is usually free to terminate a profit-sharing scheme at any time, but until he does so he has bound himself to observe its provisions. The Paris definition excludes schemes in which a share in profits is paid only to a small number of persons in administrative and technical positions and not to manual workers.

Since the payments must be related directly to profits, systems based on production bonuses, individual or group piece rates, or other methods of payment related to output are not profit-sharing systems. Similarly, arrangements by which the total production or gross proceeds of an undertaking are divided in predetermined proportions—for example, by share fishermen, and in some forms of land tenure, as sharecropping or *métayage*—must be excluded, since something other than profits is being shared. On the other hand, if employees are given shares in the capital of the undertaking in which they work, or if such shares can be acquired by them on specially favourable terms, such schemes can be regarded as a form of profit sharing.

Early Examples.—France can claim to have been the pioneer in profit sharing, several plans having been started there before the middle of the 19th century. The earliest known example was that introduced in 1820 by the French National Fire Insurance Company; in 1842 the Paris firm of E. J. Leclaire, house painters and decorators, started a scheme which attracted wide attention in France and abroad. During the next few decades other French firms started profit-sharing plans, some of which were highly successful, as for example, those introduced by Godin of Guise and by the Bon Marché store in Paris.

UNITED KINGDOM

Development of Profit Sharing.—The French schemes attracted considerable interest in England about the middle of the 19th century, and their principles were advocated particularly by the Christian Socialists, who influenced cooperative societies to apply them to their employees. Later the cooperative movement developed along somewhat different lines, and most of the consumers' cooperative societies and cooperative wholesale societies ceased to practise profit sharing, though the system was retained by some cooperative production societies especially in the boot and shoe industry and in clothing, printing, and building.

Outside the cooperative movement the first important scheme was that of Henry Briggs, Son and Co., Ltd., a firm of Yorkshire colliery owners, which introduced profit sharing in 1865. At first the scheme was very successful, but the directors ended it in 1875 because their employees took part in a strike for higher wages. Between 1880 and 1910 about 240 schemes are known to have been started; most of them were straight profit-sharing arrangements, but some took the "co-partnership" form (see below). The rate of growth was much greater between 1910 and 1920 when big wartime and early postwar profits were being earned. More than 200 were started in this decade. After the onset of depression in 1921 fewer schemes were started, but the number was still around 140 in the 10 years to 1930. During the depression years of the 1930s still fewer were started. However, during the interwar years more were soundly based, as there was better knowledge of what was involved. Some of the earlier plans were based on wrong motives and unsound methods, and about 85% of those started before 1900 had been discontinued by 1930, many of them having lasted only from 10 to 20 years. A few, however, were still in operation in the mid-1960s.

On the basis of Ministry of Labour statistics, it is estimated that more than 400 companies in the United Kingdom in the 1950s and early 1960s had profit-sharing schemes on a prearranged basis. The number of participating employees has been about 500,000 or approximately 2% of the total number of persons employed in British industry (excluding those in the nationalized industries, professions, and central and local government services in which profit sharing could not be applied). In addition to these companies, others had arrangements that were broadly profit sharing in practice but paid bonuses arbitrarily in prosperous years instead of on a predetermined basis.

Profit sharing is most widely applied in the chemical industry. In most other industries there are some profit-sharing companies, though they never form more than a small minority. Until after World War II the biggest development was by the gas companies, especially in the London area. This began in 1889 when the South Metropolitan Gas Company introduced a scheme by which employees were paid a cash bonus varying with the profits of the company. After revision the scheme took the form of "co-partnership," half the bonus due to the employees being used to buy for them ordinary shares of the company and the other half accumulating with interest but with the right of withdrawal by the workers in special circumstances. Finally, in 1920, the scheme was made statutory by legislation which provided that surplus profits, after payment of prescribed basic rates of dividend on capital, were to be divided in the proportion of three-quarters for the benefit of consumers by reducing the price of gas, and the remaining quarter in equal parts to the ordinary stockholders by increasing their dividends and to the employee co-partners as a percentage bonus on their salaries and wages. As before, half the bonus was capitalized and the other half invested subject to exceptional rights of withdrawal. Nearly all the leading gas companies and many of the smaller ones introduced similar schemes, which proved highly successful and resulted in large amounts of the capital of the companies being owned by the workers. These schemes, however, were terminated, with compensation, by legislation passed in 1948 to nationalize the gas industry.

In the years of prosperity immediately after the middle of the 20th century, increased interest in profit sharing and co-partnership was shown by certain leading firms, and both the Conservative and Liberal parties favoured the adoption of schemes as a means of promoting better industrial relations. The biggest company to introduce profit sharing during the 1950s was Imperial Chemical Industries, Ltd., which announced in 1954 a plan that by 1957 covered 91,014 out of 115,834 employees. The scheme provides for payment of annual bonuses to adult employees with two and one-half years' service or more. The total amount of the bonus is 22% of the amount paid as interest or dividends to the company's stockholders, but no bonus is paid if the dividend for ordinary shareholders is less than 5%. The bonus money is distributed to eligible employees in proportion to their total annual remuneration. The bonuses are invested in the ordinary stock of the company at the current market price and held by trustees until an employee has a minimum of £40 of stock to his credit, when it is turned over to him without any restriction. The directors have power to amend or terminate the scheme.

Types of Schemes.—Schemes of profit sharing vary widely, since they have mostly been devised on the initiative of individual firms to suit their own conditions. Some undertakings are in process of growth while others have reached stability; some are in industries which experience wide fluctuations in prosperity and need to set aside bigger reserves in good times to meet periods of depression than are required by undertakings in industries which enjoy steadier demand; and some undertakings have much higher labour costs in relation to total cost than others.

Schemes fall into three main categories: (1) profit sharing alone; (2) employee share ownership with participation in management; and (3) shareholding with some form of co-partnership. Some schemes are a combination of the first two kinds or of the first and the last.

Profit Sharing.—Schemes of profit sharing usually provide first for payment of all working expenses, amounts necessary to cover depreciation and reserves, interest on debenture stock and preference shares, and a specified percentage, often 5 or 6%, as dividend to ordinary shareholders. Then employees entitled to participate receive a defined share of any surplus profit. An alternative is to distribute to employees an amount not exceeding a specified sum, say £50,000, the remainder of the surplus being paid in additional dividends to the ordinary shareholders. One variation is for one-half of surplus profits to go to the employees, one-tenth to the management, and two-fifths to holders of ordinary share capital. Where capital costs are high, proportions down to one-tenth of surplus profits may be distributed to the employees.

Most schemes lay down a qualifying period of employment in the firm, often one year, but some require several years and others only three months. Bigger shares are sometimes provided according to length of service. Participation is sometimes restricted to adults in manual and similar grades; in other cases juvenile workers receive lower rates of payment than adults. Some schemes pay higher rates to managerial and other salaried staff than to manual workers, on the ground that salaried staff have a bigger influence on the amount of profit.

Surplus profits are usually divided on the basis of each participant's wage or salary. This ensures that persons will share in profits roughly according to their value to the firm, the skilled workers receiving more than the unskilled. The amount a worker receives varies considerably from industry to industry, from company to company, and from year to year. A frequent rate, however, has been about 6% of earnings (roughly the amount a worker would earn in three weeks).

In more than two-thirds of all British schemes of profit sharing and share ownership the share of profits is paid in cash or is credited in a savings account. Nearly one-sixth of all schemes consist of the issue to employees of shares in the company on specially favourable terms or provide for the payment of dividends varying with profits on deposits made by employees. In a few schemes the amounts due to the workers are paid into a provident or superannuation fund.

Share Ownership.—Employees of a company can buy its shares on the stock exchange, but some firms have made available special shares which can be obtained only by their employees. There is great variety in these schemes, but each is a method of saving and is intended, like profit sharing, to give employees a better understanding of the economic and financial problems of the firm for which they work and to increase their interest in its success. Some schemes combine profit sharing with share ownership by providing that all or part of the amount due to an employee may or shall be invested in the firm's shares. Alternatively, shares in some schemes may be bought by installments paid out of personal savings, often by deductions authorized by the worker from his wages. The shares may be sold to employees at par, at market price, or under market price.

These schemes, which enable employees to accumulate substantial amounts in shares over a period of years, usually last longer than profit-sharing schemes in which only cash bonuses are paid. Dividends on employees' shares are usually at the same rates as on ordinary shares, but some companies issue special preference shares, with a specified rate of interest (*e.g.*, 6%), and these shares may or may not receive additional interest if dividends beyond a given rate are paid to ordinary shareholders.

Restrictions are usually imposed on the holding of special shares, but many companies also provide safeguards to maintain the value of the special shares issued to employees. In many cases the shares must be returned to the company if the employee dies or leaves the company's service. Some companies pay the market value when such shares are returned, but many pay the par value. This protects these savings of employees against loss but reduces the value of the scheme as an education in the risk run by investors. The employee holders' dividends vary with changes in the firm's prosperity, but their capital is safeguarded against the effects of such changes. One argument for such a safeguard is that employees holding special shares are not free, as are ordinary shareholders, to sell their shares whenever they wish and thus cannot exercise their judgment when to sell so as to make a capital profit or avoid a capital loss (*see also* Employee Stock Ownership).

Co-partnership.—Co-partnership between employers and employees implies some participation by the employees in the management of the business. This may range from consultation in works councils or joint production committees to the rights of employee shareholders to attend and vote at annual and other general meetings of shareholders and to elect employee representatives to the board of directors. An increasing number of companies regularly give their employees information about the economic and financial position of the business, its problems, policy, and prospects. In many firms, representatives of the employees take part in the management of welfare and social activities. These methods give employees greater influence on the business in which they work and raise their status.

Only a few schemes provide for employee shareholders to be represented on the board of directors; even then their representatives are in a minority and their influence is usually small because they lack adequate experience of the economic, financial, and technical problems of the business. In these schemes, only those employees who have had considerable service with the firm (*e.g.*, ten years) and who hold a specified minimum number of shares can be nominated for election as directors.

Attitudes of Employers.—The fact that, after a century during the larger part of which there has been active publicity in favour of profit sharing, not more than about 900 British companies have adopted it, and that about half of this small minority of companies discontinued it within two or three decades, is a clear indication that the great majority of employers have not been attracted by profit sharing. Most employers point out that they pay their employees current rates of wages and that in periods of prosperity workers gain higher wages and thus share in prosperity. Profits should, in their opinion, accrue to those who undertake the financial risks of the business. Some argue that if employees share directly in profits they should similarly carry directly a part of the burden in years when losses are incurred. Many do not regard profit sharing as an appreciable incentive to greater effort, especially as those employees who work harder receive only the same share as those who make no greater effort. They claim that there is no satisfactory way of measuring what increase in output results from profit sharing. Against this, however, several hundred employers whose schemes have worked successfully, while not claiming that they can measure results in terms of increased output, are satisfied that profit sharing leads to better relations with their employees, who feel that there is social justice in participating directly in profits to which they have contributed by their labours.

Attitudes of Trade Unions.—Trade unions have been generally hostile to profit sharing and co-partnership, partly because,

in the early days, some employers used them as a weapon against the unions. The workers were told that they would gain more from these schemes than from action by trade unions to raise wages. Also workers in some firms were warned that the profit-sharing schemes would be terminated if they went on strike. Trade unions have feared that profit sharing would strengthen the loyalty of workers to their firm and weaken their interest in the trade-union movement. The policy of trade unions is to gain the best possible general level of wages and working conditions for their members, and the unions have worked to secure standard rates of wages throughout an occupation or industry. With profit sharing the workers' incomes would vary from firm to firm according to the profits of each. British unions are not concerned with special differential advantages for employees who are fortunate enough to be employed by firms here and there which are exceptionally prosperous. Also, as profit-sharing schemes are usually introduced on the initiative of employers, the workers receive benefits which the unions have not won for them. The unions have found no method of regulating profit-sharing schemes by collective bargaining agreements.

However, the former hostility of trade unions changed somewhat in the interwar years and after World War II, the attitude becoming one of indifference or mild acquiescence. This was largely because employers ceased to use profit sharing as a weapon against the trade unions but tended instead to discuss schemes with their employees and often with trade-union representatives before introducing them. The greater strength of the unions would enable them to oppose successfully the misuse of profit sharing by employers.

Value and Limitations.—Those employers who have introduced profit sharing because they believed their workers would be stimulated to greater effort and that output would rise appreciably have been disappointed. This has been largely because profits depend upon many factors in addition to the efforts of the workers; for example, the efficiency of management and the market demand for the product. As an inducement to greater production by the workers, the relationship between effort and reward is not close enough. Profit sharing is much less effective as an incentive than systems of payment by results where remuneration is directly related to the efforts of a worker, and where he receives his reward with little delay instead of having to wait until after the annual general meeting of the company. During periods of depression when profits have been small or nonexistent, schemes have foundered because they ceased to interest either employers or employees. A scheme may be sponsored by an employer who has faith in profit sharing and operates it successfully, but the firm may later come under new management unfavourable to profit sharing and the scheme is terminated. Even the success of some schemes has resulted in their being discontinued; for example, companies with stable profits have frequently distributed amounts which varied so little from year to year that the share in profits has finally been used to increase rates of wages instead.

Profit sharing provides only one among many ways of promoting good relations in industry. The most successful schemes have been those in companies where profit sharing with or without partnership has formed part of a comprehensive program for promoting good will. Applied in this way, profit sharing and co-partnership can strengthen the mutual interest which capital, management, and labour have in the efficient running of the undertaking, ensure a better understanding by the employees of the economic problems of business enterprise, broaden the basis of capital ownership, and raise the status of employees.   (J. H. Rn.)

UNITED STATES

History.—Before 1942 profit sharing did not assume major proportions in the United States. Though experiments with it had begun as early as 1867, only 50 plans were known to exist in 1896 and only 12 of them remained in operation until 1916. C. C. Balderston's study, published in 1937, found only 67 plans in active operation. Labour unions were opposed to profit sharing for several reasons: they were suspicious of the bookkeeping procedures used in determining profits; they looked upon profit sharing as a clever device used by employers to attach employees to their companies and weaken the appeal of unions; they thought that profit sharing would lead to the "speedup" and would be incompatible with collective bargaining. But by the 1960s labour's attitude had changed somewhat and a substantial proportion of the employees covered by profit-sharing plans were in unionized plants. One of the major reasons for this change was the new federal tax policy adopted during World War II. In 1942 the Internal Revenue Code provided that employers' contributions to profit-sharing funds collected and disbursed as specified in the code were deductible expenses for purposes of taxation. With wage and salary rates practically frozen during the war many employers saw in tax-deductible contributions to profit-sharing funds a means of supplementing employees' wages and decreasing labour discontent. For concerns in excess-profit brackets only about 15% of each dollar set aside for profit sharing was a net loss to the company; the other 85% came out of money which would otherwise have been paid as taxes.

In addition to the value of the contributions and the investment earnings of the reserve fund to their credit, employees stood to gain from the fact that when they received the annuities to be paid to them after they retired, they would pay taxes only on the reduced income they would then be receiving. In other words, they would be in a lower income bracket than they were during the years when the fund was being accumulated.

An employer was not permitted by the federal tax code to deposit to the credit of an employee in any year a sum greater than 15% of the employee's wages or salary during that year. Moreover, the employers' contributions had to go into trust funds for deferred benefits. They could not be paid to employees as current cash income. The plan had to be for the exclusive benefit of employees and their beneficiaries, had to be put into written form and its provisions made known to the employees, and, specifically, could not be a device to increase dividends of stockholders or to distribute more of the profits to officers of the company and supervisory employees.

Prevalence of Profit Sharing.—A substantial growth in profit sharing occurred after 1942. The National Industrial Conference Board survey in 1946 revealed that plans were reported by 401 companies out of 3,498 questioned, an increase from only 158 out of 2,700 companies studied in the 1939 survey. The Bureau of Internal Revenue reported that up to Aug. 31, 1946, it had processed 2,508 profit-sharing trust plans for establishments employing 1,312,226 persons (cf. NICB report no. 97, p. 5). How many of these were actually put into effect and how many were actual profit-sharing plans is not clear. Between 1947 and 1951 about 350 concerns joined the Council of Profit Sharing Industries, which had as its objective the promotion of sound, well conceived profit-sharing plans. The idea entered the automobile industry in 1961 when the American Motors Corp., one of the smaller producers, adopted a profit-sharing plan. A survey of a representative sample of small and medium-sized companies published by the Profit Sharing Research Foundation in 1964 concluded that the number of U.S. companies sharing profits with all or some of their employees lay between 85,500 and 145,900.

Cash and Deferred Payment Plans.—Profit sharing may take the form of periodic (usually annual) payments in cash or deferred payments, usually retirement annuities, out of a trust fund accumulated over many years through employer contributions credited to each employee and invested for his benefit by the trust fund. The Profit Sharing Research Foundation reported in 1954 that among 300 companies studied intensively, cash plans predominated among small companies, deferred plans among large companies, and plans that combined cash and deferred methods characterized middle-sized companies. Two factors account for the favour of the deferred plans among large companies. These concerns became more interested, and so did unions, in providing wage earners with lifetime economic security. And they wished to take advantage of the 1942 tax provisions. To do so their profit contributions had to be paid into a trust fund from which their employees would draw annuities in later years. The smaller companies liked plans under which they could pay employees

their shares of profits annually in cash or company stock because it is simpler, and perhaps safer, for them to pay off their obligations annually rather than to handle the complexities of long-lived trust fund retirement plans. Sears, Roebuck and Co., through a deferred payment plan started in 1916, built up a trust fund valued at about $350,000,000. The company contributed 45%; the employees 15%; and interest, dividends, and appreciation in the value of Sears, Roebuck stock contributed the other $118,000,000 to the fund. While the government restrictions were largely removed after the end of the war, interest in such deferred payment plans continued at a high level.

Mortality of Profit-Sharing Plans.—The death rate of profit-sharing plans was high during most of the period after their introduction in the United States. There were many reasons for this state of affairs. Employers, who hoped that profit sharing would keep unions out of their plants or cause employees to be more "loyal" to their employer, that it would make employees work harder, prevent employees from going on strike, or even reduce labour turnover, were often disappointed in their expectations.

Industrial depressions also wrecked many plans. When employees fail to receive benefits to which they have become accustomed, it is hard to convince them that it is because the employer cannot make the payments. Employees' good will, cooperation, or loyalty are not bought by a profit-sharing plan. Experience seems to indicate that where employers have discussed fully and continuingly with their employees the essentials of profitable business operations and have based their profit-sharing plans upon mutually shared understandings and objectives, the plans have been more likely to succeed.

The National Industrial Conference Board reported that of 202 companies which had profit-sharing plans in 1937, 35 or 17.3% had discontinued them by 1947. The board also found that the ratio of discontinuance was ten times as great among the current distribution plans as among the deferred plans. Nearly two-thirds of the plans discontinued had been operating for more than five years.

Leaders in the profit-sharing movement became aware of the fact that the successful management of profit sharing requires as careful attention to principles and techniques as other aspects of business management. The success of profit sharing depends upon such factors as: (1) the skill with which an employer establishes good understanding of the plan among his employees; (2) the amounts and types of employer contributions; (3) the rules governing employee eligibility; (4) whether employees must or may contribute to a deferred plan fund; (5) the method of allocating benefits to employees; (6) whether employees shall have a vested right to the amount of the fund credited to them personally; (7) whether employees shall have a right to withdraw their shares if they take employment with another company; (8) frequency of payment under cash plans; (9) what percent of the company's net profits shall be set aside for stockholders before any of the profits shall be available for profit sharing; (10) how and by whom the plan shall be administered; and (11) how employees' shares shall be computed.   (D. D. L.)

OTHER COUNTRIES

In most of the countries of Western Europe, including France, Germany, Belgium, the Netherlands, Switzerland, and Italy, profit sharing has been adopted by a small number of firms, but relatively fewer than in Great Britain and with fewer participating employees. Among these countries the greatest development is in France, where the biggest application is by insurance companies, some of which have had plans in operation successfully for more than half a century. Among the few plans in Germany which have had a long life, the best known is that of the Zeiss firm of optical glassmakers. In European countries co-partnership is rare, most of the plans providing that the share of profits due to employees shall be paid to them in cash or as credit in a savings fund. There are a few profit-sharing schemes in Australia, and also in New Zealand where the Employee Partnership Institute has undertaken propaganda for co-partnership.

Profit sharing is required by law in Venezuela, and large amounts are paid annually to employees by the bigger firms, including the oil companies. The law provides that specified proportions of profits shall be shared with employees up to a maximum equal to one month's wages in small firms and two months' wages in large firms; the proportion ranges from 2.05% of profits in small firms to 12.45% in large firms. In certain other Latin American countries, including Chile and Peru, laws have been passed making it compulsory for firms to pay a share of profits to employees. In India and Pakistan many companies, particularly expatriate companies, pay substantial annual bonuses more or less related to profits. (J. H. Rn.)

BIBLIOGRAPHY.—*United Kingdom:* Statistical articles on profit sharing and co-partnership published annually, 1922–38, and May 1956, in the *Ministry of Labour Gazette;* G. D. H. Cole, *The Case for Industrial Partnership* (1957); W. Wallace, *Prescription for Partnership* (1959); Industrial Co-partnership Association, *Co-Partnership* (quarterly).
United States: U.S. Bureau of Labor Statistics, *Monthly Labor Review* (April 1923) for bibliography. B. J. Klebaner, "U.S. Labor and Profit Sharing in the Late 1800's," *Monthly Labor Review,* vol. 85, no. 8 (Aug. 1962); P. A. Knowlton, *Profit Sharing Patterns* (1954); Council of Profit Sharing Industries, *Profit Sharing Manual* (1948); F. Beatrice Brower, *Profit Sharing for Workers* (1948); "The Pitfalls of Profit Sharing," *Fortune* (Aug. 1951); Hearings and Report by U.S. Senate Subcommittee on Finance, on "Survey of Experiences in Profit Sharing and Possibilities of Incentive Taxation" (1939); J. S. Lewis, *Partnership for All* (1948); C. C. Balderston, *Profit Sharing for Wage Earners* (1937); B. M. Stewart and W. Couper, *Profit Sharing and Stock Ownership for Wage Earners and Executives* (1945); K. M. Thompson, *Profit Sharing, Democratic Capitalism in American Industries* (1940); B. L. Metzger, *Profit Sharing in Perspective* (1964).

PROGRAMMED LEARNING

PROGRAMMED LEARNING (PROGRAMMED INSTRUCTION) is an educational technique in which the material to be learned is organized and presented in a format permitting self-instruction and self-testing and enabling the student to learn at his own pace with a minimum of formal instruction. The idea behind this technique is that many subjects may be learned best when they are presented in small steps that most students can easily master one at a time in sequence, the successful completion of each step providing its own reward (or incentive) in the form of a sense of accomplishment. It has four important characteristics. First, it recognizes that learning is a form of behaviour. Second, the subject matter, instead of being arranged on the basis of logic, is organized in a psychologically coherent sequence, or program. Third, the student makes an overt response at each step in the program by writing something, pushing a button, moving a lever or performing some other physical act. Fourth, the student immediately knows if his response is correct. The program is broken into items or frames of information comprising a sequence or sequences through which the student works.

Programmed instruction received its major impetus from a paper, "The Science of Learning and the Art of Teaching," published in 1954 by B. F. Skinner in the *Harvard Educational Review.* Programmed instruction is popularly associated with the use of teaching machines, and the first such device was described by S. L. Pressey in 1926. A teaching machine is any device employed to present a self-instructional program. It may consist of a punchboard, or it may be an elaborate electronic device capable of presenting both visual and auditory material. It may be a textbook in which control of the sequence is achieved through the physical arrangement of the material on the printed page.

Techniques.—Several techniques of programming have been developed. The first of these is the linear, or straight-line, program. The logic for the development of this type of program evolved from studies of the differentiation of behaviour in laboratory animals. (For background information on such studies *see* BEHAVIOURISM; CONDITIONING; FEELING, PSYCHOLOGY OF: *Effects of Rewards and Punishments on Behaviour;* LEARNING: *Modes of Acquisition;* PSYCHOLOGY, EXPERIMENTAL.) In linear programming what a student should learn from a program, that is, a terminal behavioural repertory, is set up as the goal. Actions that successively approach the goal, the desired terminal behaviour, are reinforced, or rewarded, as soon as they occur. Responses that do not lead toward the terminal repertory go unreinforced. The result is a shaping of the desired behaviour through differential extinction resulting from the nonreinforcement of undesired behaviour. Specifically, an item of information is given the student, he is required to answer a question or complete a statement and he is then provided with the correct answer for comparison with his own. He then proceeds to the next frame where the process is repeated. The subject is presented one step at a time, building from the simple to the complex. All students work through the same sequence, and a low rate of error is desired to ensure adequate reinforcement of appropriate responses. Initially, stress was placed upon the importance of moving in small steps. It has been recognized, however, that students with various preparations and abilities can progress by different-sized steps.

It is important to note that in the case of programmed learning the primary responsibility for success of an educational technique is placed upon the technique itself rather than upon the student. In constructing a program co-operation is required among a programmer, a subject-matter expert and, most importantly, the students. A properly constructed program is tested out on the students themselves and their responses determine refinements in the order of presentation and other elements of its design. If what the students should learn has been specified clearly and the program adequately revised in response to the needs of individual students, then it will be an effective teaching instrument. The decisions the programmer must make in constructing a program as to the course of the program are influenced by the adequacy of different paths in eliciting or stimulating desired responses, that is, in controlling the student's behaviour. What may appear to be a logical organization of a subject matter may not necessarily be an effective organization from which to teach. For this reason it is said that the sequence developed within a program has psychological rather than logical unity or direction.

A second technique of programming, developed by Norman Crowder, is called branching, or intrinsic, programming. The branching program was initially developed in conjunction with the use of an electronic training device in training military personnel. The branching program emerged in its final form when Crowder introduced the innovation of explaining to the student why a particular choice he made was either right or wrong. The branching program presents the student with a piece of information, provides him with alternative answers and, on the basis of his decision, instructs him to advance to another frame where he is informed whether his choice was correct and, if not, why his choice was incorrect. The student then is either returned to the original frame or routed through a subprogram designed to remedy the deficiency indicated by his choice of a wrong alternative. When he selects the correct alternative, he moves to the next frame in the program. This process is repeated at each step throughout the program. A student may be exposed to differing amounts of material depending upon the errors he makes.

Although the linear and the branching formats do not exhaust all possible techniques of programming they have historic primacy, and the major controversies in the field have centred about the various features of one or both of these types of programming. A number of programs incorporate both linear and branching features. Typically, the linear program employs a constructed response: the student is required to write an answer to a question or to complete a statement for a particular frame. Since it is practically impossible to construct a branching program wherein all possible alternatives are anticipated, the branching program requires a multiple choice or "recognition response."

The relative effectiveness of the two response modes may be questioned but even more general questions may be raised. In teaching mechanical skills, for example, what is the effectiveness of any verbal response as contrasted with behaviour closer to the actual tasks to be performed? Bearing in mind that learning is considered to be a change in behaviour, the nature of the behaviour to be evoked is the final criterion in determining the instrument to be employed for the purpose of conditioning that behaviour. In programs based primarily upon verbal behaviour the question of the most effective mode of presentation has led to the development of the so-called programmed textbook.

Applications.—Proponents have pointed out that programmed instruction releases teachers from many routine tasks so that they may devote more time to creative work in the classroom. From a single program in 1954 the field has seen the development of programs covering such academic subjects as grammar, foreign languages, mathematics, music, science and social studies. Programs have been written and used for levels of instruction ranging from primary through graduate school.

The most effective use of programmed instruction, however, has occurred in industry. The decentralization of educational systems supplemented by the traditional conservatism of professional educators has limited the growth and the application of programmed instruction in formal education. In contrast, industry moved forward both in the application of programmed instruction and in the development of new types of program format and means of presentation. The continuing interest in education on the part of industry and developments in computer technology have given impetus to the educational uses of computers. Where computers are employed in carrying out instruction in specific subjects, the software, or course content, is by definition a form of programmed instruction. Use of the computer can be justified only if large numbers of students have access to it, and if it serves a more significant function than simply turning pages in a book. The capability of high-speed data processing devices to respond selectively to a student's response and to adjust his instruction to match his performance is the basis for much of the interest in the possibilities of computer-assisted instruction.

Because of costs, computer applications in the late 1960s were feasible only in developed countries. Some form of programmed text remains the best method for introducing the new technology into underdeveloped countries. The possible application of programming techniques to improving education in developing countries is obvious. The United Nations Educational, Scientific and Cultural Organization and other world organizations were not only concerning themselves with exploring the theoretical usefulness of programmed instruction in such countries, but they had also sponsored projects to develop programmers and facilities.

Whatever the circumstances of use, programmed instruction is not most effectively employed by simple injection into existing systems. Its logic implies a total break with older philosophies of education. Behavioural engineering as exemplified by programmed instruction will eventually lead to thorough reexamination of educational philosophy and administration, including grading systems and curriculum organization.

BIBLIOGRAPHY.—E. J. Green, *The Learning Process and Programmed Instruction* (1962); National Society for the Study of Education *Yearbook*, "Programmed Instruction," ed. by P. C. Lange (1967); B. F. Skinner, *The Technology of Teaching* (1968).   (E. J. GR.)

PROGRAM MUSIC, the name given to instrumental music that carries with it some extramusical meaning, *i.e.,* some "program" of literary idea, scenic description, personal drama, or national legend. It is contrasted with so-called absolute or abstract music, in which the artistic interest is supposed to be confined to tonal relationships, purely musical arguments, and abstract constructions in sound. Descriptive music is by contrast often regarded as less pure and, by implication, less good. Yet most of the great composers have been unable to resist the pleasure of depicting in music the sort of experiences that graphic artists put into genre painting, portraits, and conversation pieces. William Byrd wrote *The Battell,* a work in 15 sections for virginal; J. S. Bach the *Capriccio on the Departure of a Beloved Brother;* Beethoven *Wellingtons Sieg* and the *Pastoral* Symphony. These (except the symphony) are admittedly not among their composers' best works but they show that the thing can be done: external ideas, natural scenery, solid objects, even a railway engine (Honegger's *Pacific 231*) will go into music and there is really nothing reprehensible in a composer's putting them into music.

Composers of instrumental music explored the possibilities of incorporating an external program at an early period. The *Fitzwilliam Virginal Book* (early 17th century) contains pieces about the weather, hunting, and battle. A little less than a century later Johann Kuhnau wrote six "Biblical Sonatas" in which he indulges in many curious realistic effects in the representation of Saul and David, the healing of Hezekiah, and David and Goliath. In the last named, the flight of the slingstone is a quick upward scale. This sort of realism can be not only naïve but also ridiculous: some of the formulas and clichés used to accompany silent films in the early days of the cinema were of the same order as Victorian descriptions of battles, camels in the desert, and similar absurdities for drawing-room pianists. But with the development of the orchestra the range of experience expressible in music was enormously expanded—although certain specific references in the music could not be immediately identified without verbal clues being given. Controversy about the validity of program music developed into a first-class issue of musical aesthetics in the second half of the 19th century, when the "new music" of Liszt and Wagner was put into the scales against the classicism of Brahms, who never even went so far down the romantic road as to give descriptive names or fancy titles, as Schumann did, to his piano pieces. In the late 20th century the issue was still alive, since Stravinsky went as far as to deny that music needed any expressive powers at all: it was just music. Though there was a truce of live-and-let-live during the 20th century some new arguments were made available, namely symbolism from Freudian psychology and semantics from philosophy, with which to continue the debate.

The Place of Imagery in Music.—Like most other subjects program music can be discussed historically for the facts and critically for the values. Either approach has to deal with one vital fact of the musical imagination: composers have always set words to music, *i.e.,* have gained some sort of conceptual content in music, whose thought is nonconceptual—have illustrated the meaning of the words by the flux and motions of music. They have even gone in for word painting, as in Thomas Weelkes's madrigal "As Vesta was from Latmos' hill descending," where the personages go up and down hill in rising and falling scale passages, two by two in two-part harmony and three by three in three-part harmony, leaving their goddess all alone in a brief soprano solo. Half the business of the accompaniment to a song is to evoke the mood of the poem by suggestion; the other half is to provide the harmonic context and support. Such suggestion operates through images: images of pitch to suggest height, depth, and position, and acuity, stress, or slackness of tension; images of tone-colour to suggest qualities of touch like warmth or hollowness; images of rhythm to suggest any kind of temporal phenomenon, spatial movement, gesture, duration, reiteration, repose, agitation, speed, and so on. These images constitute a language of music that was analyzed with a wealth of illustration in Deryck Cooke's *The Language of Music* (1959). Being images they are the material with which the musical imagination works. Musical imagery of all sorts, amassed by the composer from hearing music already in existence, is employed indifferently in vocal, symphonic, and program music.

Besides these true images, which are capable of taking on further symbolical meanings, there are some sounds in nature which can be imitated in music. Bird song is an obvious example. Olivier Messiaen is the only composer who made a sustained effort to integrate bird calls into serious composition. The cuckoo of course had a long run: L. C. Daquin's harpsichord piece "Le Coucou," Beethoven's *Pastoral* Symphony, and Delius' tone poem *On Hearing the First Cuckoo in Spring* immediately come to mind. Songs about the nightingale usually stylize the bird's performance. More like onomatopoeia are storms, of which opera can provide instances from Rossini's *Il barbiere di Siviglia* to Sir William Walton's *Troilus and Cressida.* Fire in Wagner's hands is presented not only with the crackle of flames but with their visible edges perceptible by means of this mysterious process of the imagination. Water is ubiquitous in music: fresh in Schubert, salt in Debussy—but the sea has many moods: boisterous in the overture to Wagner's *Der fliegende Holländer* (*The Flying Dutchman*); calm and lapping the shore with a phrase in the shape of a wave in Mendelssohn's *Hebrides* overture; or keen in scent, sound, and sight (seagulls, ozone, and shingle) in the first of the interludes in Britten's *Peter Grimes,* where the sea is an arpeggio of superimposed triads, and the dry land a chord of A major. But this is far beyond onomatopoeia, which, however, includes man-made sounds like ships' sirens, steel anvils, church bells, striking clocks, and the rumble of railway trains—all of which can be accommodated in small quantities in, though they invariably stick out of, musical compositions for dramatic or descriptive purposes.

The Problem of Form.—The powers of music to evoke situations in life, as well as to express human feelings, have been recognized by composers from the beginning: after all, imitation is instinctive. Thus vocal music has always used the descriptive devices of musical technique for every kind of expression. Though vocal music is excluded from the definition of program music, its relevance to the aesthetic issue cannot be ignored in quite the airy way that led the combatants in the 19th-century controversy to declare that music presented two separate sets of phenomena and aroused two sorts of emotion. Music is surely one, not two. But without cleaving the art in two it is possible to recognize the difference between a symphony and a symphonic poem. This difference is fundamentally one of logic and form, or perhaps the logic of form.

The ground plan of a symphony is four movements. In Beethoven's Third in E♭ (the *Eroica*), for example, the first movement is in sonata form with its exposition of two groups of themes in different but related keys, its middle section a development of these thematic ideas, and a recapitulation rounded off by a coda. The slow (second) movement is, somewhat exceptionally, a funeral march; the third a scherzo (with trio); and the fourth movement a set of variations. This is a satisfactory scheme for presenting some sort of experience, in this case heroism, in its several aspects, but it is singularly inept for depicting the life history of Napoleon, to whom the symphony was originally dedicated, for the hero is buried in the second movement and is fuller of life than ever in the third. Symphonic order is thus not to be reconciled with chronological order. Furthermore, if in the first movement any indication of the events in Napoleon's career had been the composer's intention he would have found that recapitulation would have made redundant nonsense of what had already been narrated in full. Sonata form is thus not to be reconciled with traditional narrative or drama, which moves on and does not go back. Hence the incongruity of using symphonic movements for ballets with a program, however sketchy, of biographical, historical, or dramatic events. So, when Richard Strauss wants to portray Don Juan's erotic adventures, Don Quixote's chivalric adventures, or (in the *Domestic* Symphony) a day in his family life, he does not employ sonata form, but modifies freely more episodic forms such as the rondo and variation form, or writes in the form of a loose rhapsody held together only by key coherence and the recurrence of themes symbolizing, like Wagner's *Leitmotive,* the persons and events of the story. He writes in fact a symphonic poem. Both the symphonic poem, in which the form is subservient to the subject matter, and the term itself were invented by Liszt, who was thus the cause of all the controversy.

Tchaikovsky's *Hamlet* is a true symphonic poem; however, the story is told in a kind of sonata form, and this is done by dissolving out the chronological element of Shakespeare's play. When Robert Helpmann composed a ballet to it he began with Hamlet's body on a bier and the motto "Our little lives are rounded with a sleep," which fits Tchaikovsky's scheme wonderfully well. For if at the moment of death his past life flitted past Hamlet's eyes it made no difference in what order the gravedigger and Ophelia and the ghost occurred. They were episodes which could be presented in symphonic order with their relationships expounded by themes, rhythms, keys, and orchestration (the oboe for Ophelia, for instance). Once this problem of logical sequence is solved the composer can go ahead and make music out of anything in the world except specific statements such as that the angles at the base of an isosceles triangle are equal, or propositions about monetary theory or the gold standard. Strauss himself did it, saying, in a moment of bravado and in answer to a challenge, that he could set a knife and fork to music. If he did not do that exactly, he bathed his baby, he disturbed a flock of sheep, he hanged a rogue, he produced the smell of ethyl chloride at a death bed, he confounded his critics, and he made love—but then love does not count as program music since it is all-pervasive.

The Romantic and nationalistic movements greatly enlarged the range of subjects that composers desired to express. Literature was well to the fore with *Faust* (Liszt and Wagner), *Romeo and Juliet* (Berlioz and Tchaikovsky), *Falstaff* (Elgar). Then came legend with *The Water Sprite* (Dvorak), *Tamara* (Balakirev), *The Sorcerer's Apprentice* (Dukas), *Scheherazade* (Rimski-Korsakov), and *The Swan of Tuonela* (Sibelius). Geography added a whole gallery of picture postcards: *The Steppes of Central Asia* (Borodin), *Bohemia's Woods and Forests* (Smetana), *The Fountains of Rome* (Respighi), *Paris* (Delius), London (Elgar, under the name *Cockaigne*), *Nights in the Gardens of Spain* (Falla), *Sinfonia Antarctica* (Vaughan Williams), and *El Salón México* (A. Copland). Even philosophy was tried by Strauss in *Also sprach Zarathustra* (after Nietzsche), and pictures by Rachmaninoff in *The Isle of the Dead* (after A. Böcklin) and Liszt in *Hunnenschlacht* ("The Battle of the Huns," after W. Kaulbach). The concert overture form provided a rather shorter medium for program pieces such as Walton's two overtures *Portsmouth Point* (after Rowlandson's picture) and *Scapino* (after the *commedia dell'arte*).

Aesthetic Considerations.—The earlier examples of program music started an aesthetic battle which led Eduard Hanslick, the Viennese critic, to formulate his case against the genre in his book *Vom Musikalisch-Schönen* (1854; Eng. trans., "The Beautiful in Music," 1891). Hanslick argued that the aim of music was not expression but beauty. The conveyance of feeling, which he could not deny in the face of the universal recognition of music's powers in that respect, was incidental and subsidiary to its main purpose. This view was similarly promulgated at the beginning of the 20th century in the field of pictorial art by Clive Bell and Roger Fry, among English critics, who spoke of "significant form" as the element that constituted the artistic excellence of a picture. Likeness, representation, and subject matter, they held, were not only irrelevant to a picture's merits but might be an impediment to its true appreciation. It is a view not easily applied to literature; and in architecture which is not much subject to pressures of content or subject matter, there is function to be accounted for. Although this ruthless emphasis on form, which even consented to the banishment of literature from the realm of art, should have been a warning that there was something wrong with this theory, it found wide acceptance by the best critical minds, and painters themselves developed abstract painting, which corresponds in essentials to Hanslick's ideal music. Later avant-garde musicians of the 20th century claimed that in music sound alone mattered, and how to manipulate it—a doctrine readily understood in an age dominated by technology.

In favour, however, of the traditional view that basically music is expressive and that in this respect there is no difference between any of the kinds of music—vocal, instrumental, abstract, or programmatic—semantics now came to the rescue. Freud accustomed everyone to the pervasiveness of symbolism in thought, action, and art. A symbol is something that stands for something else, but it has a richer, more concentrated content of meaning, and the human mind has an innate tendency to create and use symbols. The symbols might at first be mere signs, like red for danger or a whistle for a summons to attention, but they have a tendency to grow into systems, such as language. Music is like language in being a system of signs and symbols with enormous powers of conveying meaning—especially meaning about states of mind. From this penetrating and fertile idea a whole philosophy of art was constructed by Susanne Langer, the U.S. philosopher, which is crystallized in one of her statements: "Music is 'significant form,' and its significance is that of a symbol, a highly articulated, sensuous object, which by virtue of its dynamic structure can express the forms of vital experience which language is peculiarly unfit to convey. Feeling, life, motion and emotion constitute its import." (Susanne Langer, *Feeling and Form*, p. 32, Routledge & Kegan Paul Ltd. and Charles Scribner's Sons, 1953.)

This doctrine avoids the dichotomy of the pure and the programmatic, for even a symphony can have emotional import. We can allow the title *Eroica* to Beethoven's Third Symphony without blushing and, though we should avoid racking our brains to conjure up novelettish "interpretations" of sonatas, string quartets, and symphonies, we need not fear to read them as documents related to human life, as something more than Hanslick's *arabesques sonores,* more also than contrapuntal algebra. They are documents related to the vital ebb and flow of our consciousness. Strauss, who wrote no symphonies after his Opus 12, recognized no distinction between abstract and program music, but only between good music and bad. It was good if it meant something, bad if it was meaningless. Good music for him was what expressed most. Tchaikovsky and Sibelius recognized that generalized emotion, abstracts of emotional experience, Langer's "pattern of life itself as it is felt and directly known," can be dealt with in symphonies, but that specific feelings arising from specific circumstances are matter for symphonic poems.

The Program Symphony.—Between the symphony and the symphonic poem there is an intermediate stage, the program symphony, illustrated by the *Pastoral* Symphony. Before Beethoven, Haydn had in his humorous way infused an element of external reality in small doses into the *Farewell,* the *Surprise,* and the *Clock* symphonies. But Beethoven in the *Pastoral* Symphony went the whole way and indicated in words what he was depicting: cheerful impressions on arriving in the country, the brook, the peasants, the storm, the shepherds' hymn—though he appeared to have some qualms about it, for he added, quite untruly, that it was more an expression of feeling than painting. From the *Pastoral* stemmed a line of program symphonies, in which the form was musically self-sufficient but the content contained extramusical matter in varying degrees of density: very thick in Berlioz' *Symphonie fantastique,* which purports to depict episodes in the life of an artist, and minimal in Mendelssohn's *Scottish* and *Italian* symphonies. Mendelssohn's *Hebrides* (or *Fingal's Cave*) Overture is probably the most beautifully balanced of such combinations since there is Mendelssohn's own testimony that the programmatic and the thematic idea of it were conceived simultaneously on the spot, at the cave. In Tchaikovsky's Fourth and Fifth symphonies the notion of fate embodied in the motto theme is elaborated to the extent vouched for in Tchaikovsky's own explanation; in his Sixth Symphony the title *Pathétique* is used in a general sense as far as a program permeates the music, at any rate until the extraordinary slow finale which is a clear premonition of death. Similarly in Dvorak's *New World* Symphony there is no detailed program but an allusion to the Negro in the slow movement. Vaughan Williams' *London Symphony* has rather more specific programmatic content in that it incorporates actual sounds from the London scene and employs the unusual combination of nocturne and scherzo, which somehow conveys the animation of London at night. The Soviet composers load their symphonies with significance, or have them loaded for them by commentators: Shostakovich's Seventh (*Leningrad*) Symphony was composed with the events of the defense of that city in mind. But in general the program symphony has grown less programmatic as the symphonic form has grown more ambitious.

Summary.—Program music increased in extent and status within the art through the program symphonies and symphonic poems of the 19th century. At the outbreak of World War I the aesthetic debate as to the propriety of program music had been going on for more than half a century. The swing of the pendulum after each of the world wars was toward neoclassicism, absolute music, sound manipulation, and aural austerity, in reaction to the enormous enrichment of the repertory, the extension of orchestral resources, and the subtlety of music's expressive power during the previous heyday of the symphonic poem. By the second half of the 20th century, as a reaction against the austerities of the neoclassical style, the various literary and pictorial forms of program music were once again in the ascendant.   (F. S. H.)

PROGRESSIVE EDUCATION. Although the sources of progressive education go back to far before the 1850s, the movement sprang into prominence in both the United States and Europe simultaneously but independently at the end of the 19th century. This article traces its origins and European development and then describes its considerable effect on U.S. education and its decline as a separate educational movement.

Origins and European Development.—Modern progressive education has its ancestry in a complex of ideas and practices

which, from the 16th century onward, have been concerned with a reconsideration of the nature of individual man, of the societies in which he lives and of the relationship between them. At different times the emphasis has fallen upon one side of the relationship or upon the other; now on the need to free the individual from social pressures which limit his development, now on the need to provide the kind of social environment which will foster this development. Jean Jacques Rousseau's *Émile* and *Du Contrat social* (1762) are source books for students of progressive education. The roots of the movement, as has been pointed out by W. H. G. Armytage, can be traced back to the utopian tradition which derived from Thomas More and Francis Bacon in the 16th century and embodied the notion that man can, as it were, make a fresh start, *i.e.,* redeem the loss of the fall, by founding a new society or by restructuring an existing one. The implications of this for education are seen in the work of Samuel Hartlib, John Dury and J. A. Comenius; in the communitarian approach of the Quakers to both religion and education; in the work of Robert Owen and in the practical application of Rousseau's ideas by J. B. Basedow, J. H. Pestalozzi, Philipp Emanuel von Fellenberg and Friedrich Froebel.

The link between social reform and education is implicit in the movement which led to the founding of Abbotsholme school for boys, Derbyshire, by Cecil Reddie in 1889. Reddie was a member of the Fellowship of the New Life, founded in 1882. The fellowship promoted the founding of experimental schools, and the utopian tradition is clear in their assertion: "All schools ought to be communities, miniature commonwealths or states, as they were in the Middle Ages."

A secession from Abbotsholme led to the foundation of Bedales at Petersfield, Hampshire (1893); this later became the first coeducational boarding school. Later progressive schools in England were St. Christopher, Letchworth, Hertfordshire, originally intended as one branch of a many-sided community life; Frensham Heights, Farnham, Surrey; King Alfred's, Hampstead; Malting House school, Cambridge; Beacon Hill near Harting, Sussex (founded in 1927 by Bertrand and Dora Russell); Summerhill, in Suffolk, founded by A. S. Neill; and Dartington Hall, Totnes, Devon. Most of these schools are coeducational and stress with varying emphases the freeing of the child from adult pressures and the provision of a rich and varied community life.

Abbotsholme inspired the founding in Germany of the Deutsche Landserziehungsheime (1898) by Hermann Lietz and in France that of L'École des Roches by Edmond Demolins in 1899. In Italy, in 1894, the sisters Agazzi opened a home for preschool children which stressed training in sense perception and play activities in rural surroundings, and this later became the model for preschool education in Italy. In 1907 Maria Montessori began her Children's Houses in Rome, and devised the "didactic apparatus" to enable children to develop their capacities by self-education (*see* MONTESSORI SYSTEM).

Other pioneers of new methods in education were Ovide Decroly in Belgium, Adolphe Ferrière in Geneva, and Elizabeth Rotten in Germany. In 1921 about 150 pioneers from countries throughout Europe met at an international conference in Calais, France, organized by Mrs. Beatrice Ensor who, in 1920, had initiated the *New Era,* a magazine for the exchange of ideas and experience concerning the new education. At this conference the New Education fellowship was formed to link pioneers in different parts of the world. After 1921 the fellowship organized many international conferences; national sections promoted its interests in 11 European countries as well as in Australia, India, Egypt, Pakistan, New Zealand, South Africa and South America. Until 1955 it was linked with the Progressive Education association of the U.S. (called, from 1945 until its end in 1957, the American Education fellowship).

After 1900, the progressive ideas and practices developed in the United States, especially those of John Dewey, flowed back to join with the European progressive tradition. The effect of this was to strengthen the emphasis on social education and the relating of the individual's needs to the needs of a rapidly changing society. The influence on schools within state systems of education was seen in the development of "activity" and "centre of interest" methods in the education of young children, in the use of "projects" and "assignments" with older children, and in general in the greater emphasis on social and emotional education and the modification of the formal and the academic in both content and methods. After 1946 there was a sharpening of the criticism of progressive ideas and methods, with restatements of the traditional aims, and this in turn challenged the progressive movement to redefine its assumptions and objectives.   (J. W. T.)

United States.—In the United States progressive education began during the latter decades of the 19th century as one aspect of that larger program of social reform known as the progressive movement. It was essentially a pluralistic phenomenon, comprehending a remarkable diversity of pedagogical protest and innovation. In the universities it emerged as part of a spirited revolt against formalism in philosophy, psychology and the social sciences. In the cities it was but one facet of a wider program of municipal clean-up and reform. Among farmers it became the crux of a moderate, liberal alternative to radical agrarianism. It was at the same time the "social education" demanded by urban settlement workers, the "schooling for country life" demanded by rural publicists, the vocational training demanded by businessmen's associations and labour unions alike, and the new techniques of instruction demanded by avant-garde pedagogues. It enlisted to its cause parents and teachers, starry-eyed crusaders and hardheaded politicians. And in less than two generations it transformed the character of the U.S. school.

The sources of progressive education lie in part in the stream of pedagogical reform in Europe from the 17th through the 19th century cited above. They lie also in the revolution wrought before the Civil War by Horace Mann and his confreres in convincing Americans of the necessity of universal education in a free society. The very success of this revolution, in bringing into primary and secondary schools a greater diversity of children than ever before, inevitably exerted a transforming influence on the character of the schools themselves. Finally, the sources of progressive education lie in the transformation of society itself under the pervasive influence of industrialism. The advancement of technical and productive processes and the growing complexity of urban life—compounded in the United States by large percentages of non-English-speaking immigrants—led to pressures for the schools to assume educational responsibilities formerly borne by family, shop and neighbourhood.

The first evidence of progressivism in U.S. education appeared as early as the 1870s. Francis W. Parker, later referred to by John Dewey as the father of progressive education, undertook to reform the Quincy, Mass., schools beginning in 1875. He vigorously attacked rote learning and introduced new pedagogical techniques designed to make school subjects more meaningful to children. His reforms attracted national—indeed world-wide—attention as "the Quincy system."

Following upon the revelations of the Russian system of technical instruction at the Philadelphia centennial exhibition of 1876, Pres. John D. Runkle of the Massachusetts Institute of Technology, Calvin Woodward of Washington university, and Col. R. T. Auchmuty, a New York businessman, sharply criticized the narrow intellectual emphases in the secondary school program, demanding a central place for industrial training and vocational education. Throughout the 1870s conventions of the National Grange and other farmer organizations passed resolutions deploring the lack of practical agricultural training in schools and colleges.

Protests like these multiplied during the following decade, and by the 1890s they had assumed all the earmarks of a full-fledged social movement. The themes of this movement were many and various, but they were one in their attack on the narrowness and formalism of traditional education. Businessmen's organizations, and later labour unions as well, contended that under the modern factory system apprenticeship had deteriorated into an exploitive rather than an educative relationship and that because of this, schools would have to assume the classical functions of apprenticeship. Settlement workers, sensitive to the pedagogical vacuums created by broken homes and working parents, and compellingly

aware of the education of the streets, vigorously urged instruction in hygiene, domestic science, manual arts and child care. Likewise, rural educators, deploring the flight from farm to city, argued for a new kind of rural school which would orient young people to the joys and possibilities of country life and equip them technically to realize these possibilities. Finally, university professors and educationists, basing their proposals on the new sciences of psychology, sociology and pedagogy, pressed for revamped school programs which would afford greater importance to scientific studies, tie learning more closely to doing, and educate "whole children"—that is, pay attention to physical and emotional growth as well as to intellectual development.

Outstanding Americans from many walks of life espoused ideas such as these during the quarter-century before World War I, among them Theodore Roosevelt, Jane Addams, Jacob Riis, William James, Charles W. Eliot, Henry Wallace, Walter Hines Page, and James Earl Russell. No one saw the movement whole, though, quite as well as John Dewey, for 50 years the commanding figure among theorists of progressive education. In a series of books, pamphlets and essays, beginning with *The School and Society* (1899) and culminating with *Democracy and Education* (1916), Dewey illuminated the close relationship between progressive education and the larger social transformation being wrought by science, democracy and industrialism. The curse of traditional education, Dewey argued, had been its aristocratic character and its isolation from life. The crux of progressive education was its universality and its closeness to life. Dewey urged that schools be made into "embryonic social communities," active with the occupations and permeated with the values of the surrounding society. "When the school introduces and trains each child of society into membership within such a little community," he wrote, "saturating him with the spirit of service, and providing him with the instruments of effective self-direction, we shall have the deepest and best guarantee of a larger society which is worthy, lovely, and harmonious." (John Dewey, *The School and Society*, p. 44, The University of Chicago Press, 1899.) (*See also* DEWEY, JOHN.)

Progressive education made considerable headway on an experimental basis after 1890. Joseph Mayer Rice found in an 1892 survey that the school systems of Indianapolis and La Porte, Ind., and of Minneapolis and St. Paul, Minn., having freed themselves from undesirable political control, had begun to put teaching on a "scientific basis," to "develop the child in all his faculties instead of simply crowding his mind with facts," to introduce new work in manual and creative arts, and to seek desirable correlation among the several subjects of study. In 1896 John Dewey and his wife founded the Laboratory school in Chicago specifically to test the validity of his pedagogical theories. In 1904 Junius L. Meriam established an experimental school at the University of Missouri, Columbia, and in 1907 Marietta Johnson opened her School of Organic Education at Fairhope, Ala. The following year, William Wirt, school superintendent of the newly created steel town of Gary, Ind., began the sweeping educational innovations which came to be called the "Work-Study-Play" plan. Widely publicized by the progressive press after 1914, the Gary plan represented the best-known effort to apply Dewey's precepts to the public schools of a burgeoning industrial community. Finally, vocational education of every sort advanced rapidly after 1900, and in 1917 congress passed the Smith-Hughes act providing federal aid for trade, agricultural, home economics and distributive instruction in public secondary schools.

The founding of the Progressive Education association in 1919 marks a significant divide in the history of the progressive education movement, since what had formerly been a loosely defined revolt against pedagogical formalism now gained a vigorous organizational voice. Under the initial leadership of Stanwood Cobb and Eugene Randolph Smith, the association quickly gained a notable place in U.S. education. Its membership climbed steadily, passing 5,000 in 1927 and reaching a peak of 10,500 in 1938. Its quarterly, *Progressive Education*, launched in 1924, quickly became a clearinghouse for educational experiments of every conceivable kind. During the 1930s, aided by well over $1,000,000 in foundation money, the association sponsored a number of widely publicized experiments, among them an eight-year study involving 30 secondary schools and over 200 colleges and designed to test the effects of introducing greater flexibility into high school curricula. The results, published in 1942, were taken as decisively in favour of the experimental programs.

Spurred on by the efforts and propaganda of the association, progressive education won ever greater acceptance in school systems across the nation. Success, though, brought ideological schism in its wake; and the quarter-century after 1919 was marked by sharpening conflict over just what progressive education was, and what it meant. One group of educators, epitomized by Marietta Johnson, combined the doctrines of liberty and self-expression into a highly individualistic pedagogy which held that schools in which children are encouraged freely to develop their uniquely creative potentialities are the best guarantee of a larger society devoted to human worth and excellence.

A second group, following the leadership of George S. Counts during the 1930s, sought to tie progressive education much more closely to specific programs of political reconstruction, contending that educators could lead in the building of a new social order. A third group, typified by Elsie Ripley Clapp, saw the crux of progressive education in school activities directed to the social and economic regeneration of local communities. A fourth group, exemplified by Eugene Randolph Smith, concentrated on reorganizing and enlivening the traditional school studies. And finally, there were those like William Heard Kilpatrick, Boyd H. Bode and Dewey himself who continued to regard progressive education as the pedagogical expression of the larger philosophy of experimentalism, with its emphasis on naturalism, scientific method and democratic social planning. Given this conflict over goals, the movement during the later 1930s was increasingly paralyzed by a factionalism which weakened not only its forward thrust but its resistance to outside criticisms as well.

From its earliest days progressive education had elicited sharp and sustained opposition from a variety of sources. Humanists and idealists had vigorously criticized its naturalistic orientation, its Rousseauan emphasis on freedom and interest, and its cavalier treatment of the classics and foreign languages. During the 1930s a group calling themselves the Essentialists had taken progressives sharply to task for failing to pay sufficient attention to the need for disciplined study of systematic knowledge. A number of Christian educators, Roman Catholic and Protestant as well, had accused progressives of materialism and a general denial of supernatural spiritual values; while elements of the patriotic press had been unremitting in their charges of radicalism and "un-Americanism." Criticisms such as these became more insistent after World War II, when progressive doctrines in general seemed eclipsed by a revival of conservatism in U.S. politics and social thought. Unable to meet the challenge, the Progressive Education association disbanded in 1955; and the journal *Progressive Education* ceased publication two years later. For all practical purposes, the movement died in 1957, but not without leaving an indelible impress on U.S. education. (L. A. C.)

BIBLIOGRAPHY.—*Origins and European Development:* Centre National de Documentation Pédagogique, *Éducation nouvelle* (1946); R. Cousinet, *Petite Chronologie de l'éducation nouvelle* (1954); L. B. Pekin, *Progressive Schools* . . . (1934); A. E. Meyer, *The Development of Education in the Twentieth Century,* 2nd ed. (1949); A. Ferrière, *L'École active,* 2 vol. (1922); M. Agosti and V. Chizzolini, *L'Educatore contemporaneo,* 2nd ed. (1950); F. W. Roman, *The New Education in Europe,* 2nd ed. (1930); M. Peers, *Ovide Decroly* (1942); E. M. Standing, *Maria Montessori* (1958); D. E. M. Gardner, *Long Term Results of Infant School Methods* (1950); B. M. Ward, *Reddie of Abbotsholme* (1934); V. Bonham-Carter, *Dartington Hall* (1958); J. H. Badley, *Bedales* . . . , 2nd ed. (1924); A. S. Neill, *The Free Child* (1953); M. A. Bloch, *La Pédagogie des classes nouvelles* (1953); V. Mallinson (ed.), *The Adolescent at School* (1949); W. H. G. Armytage, *The Utopist Tradition in English Education* (1958).

New Education Fellowship Reports: W. Boyd et al. (eds.), *Towards a New Education* (1930); W. Rawson (ed.), *A New World in the Making* (1933), *The Freedom We Seek* (1937); K. S. Cunningham, W. C. Radford et al. (eds.), *Education for Complete Living* (1938).

Periodicals: Education for the New Era (subsequently the *New Era,* 1920–30; *New Era in Home and School,* 1931–); *Pour l'ère nouvelle* (1922–); *Das werdende Zeitalter* (1922–32).

United States: John Dewey, *The School and Society* (1899), *Democracy and Education* (1916), *Experience and Education* (1938); John and Evelyn Dewey, *Schools of To-Morrow* (1915); Eugene Randolph Smith, *Education Moves Ahead* (1924); Agnes de Lima, *Our Enemy the Child* (1926); William Heard Kilpatrick, *Education for a Changing Civilization* (1927), (ed.), *The Educational Frontier* (1933); Harold Rugg and Ann Shumaker, *The Child-Centered School* (1928); Marietta Johnson, *Youth in a World of Men* (1929); George S. Counts, *Dare the School Build a New Social Order?* (1932); Boyd H. Bode, *Progressive Education at the Crossroads* (1938); Elsie Ripley Clapp, *Community Schools in Action* (1939); Harold Rugg, *Foundations for American Education* (1947); Lawrence A. Cremin, "The Progressive Movement in American Education: a Perspective." *Harvard Educational Review,* 27:251–270 (1957); J. M. Rice, *The Public-School System of the United States* (1893); Robert H. Beck, "Progressive Education and American Progessivism," *Teachers College Record,* 60:77–89, 129–137, 198–208 (1958–59). (J. W. T.; L. A. C.)

PROGRESSIVE PARTY, U.S. Three times in the first half of the 20th century a political party with this name took part in U.S. presidential campaigns—in 1912, 1924, and 1948.

The Progressive Party of 1912 began as an insurgent outbreak among Republican members of Congress in 1910 against the speaker of the House of Representatives, Joseph G. Cannon. Opposition to the administration of Pres. William Howard Taft crystallized in 1911 when the National Progressive Republican League was organized by Sen. Robert M. La Follette of Wisconsin. Theodore Roosevelt soon placed himself at the head of that movement. Alleging unfair tactics on the part of the "Old Guard," his followers left the Republican national convention in Chicago, Ill. (June 1912), and Roosevelt was nominated for the presidency by a Progressive national convention, also held in Chicago, early in August. Roosevelt's Progressive Party was popularly known as the Bull Moose Party. With the Republican vote split between Taft and Roosevelt, Woodrow Wilson, the Democratic candidate, carried all but eight states. The electoral vote was 435 for Wilson, 88 for Roosevelt, and 8 for Taft. Of the popular vote, Wilson received 6,293,454, Roosevelt 4,119,538, and Taft 3,484,980. In 1916 harmony was restored in the Republican Party when Roosevelt declined a second Progressive nomination and supported the Republican ticket. During World War I partisanship was in abeyance, but upon its termination the old rift soon reappeared. The administration of Harding encountered dissatisfaction among farmers, as did the Coolidge administration.

In 1924 Wisconsin and other farm states held a conference for progressive political action and launched a new Progressive Party. Senator La Follette was nominated for president and Sen. Burton K. Wheeler of Montana, a Democrat, for vice-president. The party platform promised a "house cleaning" of executive departments, public control of natural resources, public ownership of railways, and tax reduction. Republican strategy in 1924 consisted largely in denouncing the alleged radicalism of the La Follette platform, while ignoring Democratic attacks. Coolidge won easily; La Follette won 4,822,856 votes but carried only Wisconsin, with 13 electoral votes. La Follette's death in 1925 led to the dissolution of the party.

Unlike its predecessors, the Progressive Party founded by Henry A. Wallace in 1947–48 stressed foreign issues in its platform—principally abandonment of the Marshall Plan (*q.v.*) and the Truman Doctrine (see TRUMAN, HARRY S.). This party was formally organized in Philadelphia, Pa., July 22–25, 1948, naming Wallace as its candidate for president and Sen. Glen H. Taylor of Idaho as its vice-presidential candidate. On Aug. 6 the national convention of the Communist Party of the U.S. announced its support of the Wallace-Taylor ticket. In the presidential election of 1948, the party polled only 1,156,103 popular votes and won no electoral votes.

See also references under "Progressive Party, U.S." in the Index.

BIBLIOGRAPHY.—F. E. Haynes, *Social Politics in the United States* (1924); E. E. Robinson, *Evolution of American Political Parties* (1924); H. R. Bruce, *American Parties and Politics* (1927); George E. Mowry, *Theodore Roosevelt and the Progressive Movement* (1946), and *California Progressives* (1951); Russell B. Nye, *Midwestern Progressive Politics* (1951); Robert M. La Follette, *Autobiography* (1913); Belle and Fola La Follette, *Robert M. La Follette,* 2 vol. (1953); Henry L. Stoddard, *As I Knew Them* (1927); Claude G. Bowers, *Beveridge and the Progressive Era* (1932); Matthew Josephson, *The President Makers* (1940). (R. C. B.; R. Tu.; X.)

PROHIBITION, the legal prevention of the manufacture, sale, or transportation of alcoholic beverages. In the United States, nationwide Prohibition was adopted when the 18th Amendment to the Constitution was ratified in January 1919. It was repealed by the 21st Amendment, December 1933.

The adoption and repeal of Prohibition in the United States are best understood in the context of the larger movement of temperance and as part of American social reform. Prohibition and temperance developed, remained, and declined in relation to the general framework of public opinion and social conflict concerning drinking in American culture. While the word "temperance" suggests moderate usage, it became identified with abstinence during the second quarter of the 19th century. In the early development of the antialcohol movement in the United States, the objective was temperate use and not abstinence. While the objective of abstinence became dominant, the name "temperance" remained with organizations and came to be a general label for the antialcohol movement. (*See* further TEMPERANCE.) Prohibition is the form of the movement that seeks abstinence through legal prohibitions.

I. THE PRECURSORS OF NATIONAL PROHIBITION

Temperance Organization in the Early 1800s.—Organized efforts to limit the use of intoxicating beverages did not begin on a large scale in the United States until the 1820s. Under the leadership of Congregationalist and Presbyterian ministers the first national temperance association, the American Society for the Promotion of Temperance, was founded in 1826 in Massachusetts. During the 1830s and 1840s this and other temperance organizations, such as the Sons of Temperance, gained large numbers of adherents. Early support came largely from Eastern states, but nationwide organizations soon developed. The intensive religious revivalism of the 1820s and 1830s stimulated movements toward perfectionism in human beings, including humanitarian doctrines, abolition of slavery, and temperance. It was out of this wave of temperance concern that movements for state and local Prohibition began. The expression "teetotaling" came into being in this period because temperance supporters indicated their total beliefs by a "t" opposite their names on temperance rosters.

Drive for Legislation.—During the 1840s and 1850s temperance people and temperance leaders were linked to a number of movements of a religious and humanitarian nature. Sabbatarianism, home missionary movements, abolitionism, nativistic feeling, and temperance were frequently linked together, many persons adhering to all of them. It was in this period that the temperance movement appeared as an important political link to other strivings. The efforts to legislate abstinence drew support from other movements and issues concerned with religious goals, humanitarian reform, and nativist hostility. The relation between temperance and abolition discredited the movement below the Mason and Dixon's Line; although it had begun well in the South, the temperance movement met with slight appeal in Southern states after 1840.

In 1838 the Massachusetts legislature passed the "15 Gallon Law," the earliest temperance law. It prohibited the sale of ardent spirits in quantities less than 15 gallons, effectively limiting sales to those wealthy enough to make purchases in large quantities. Although repealed two years later, it established the precedent of seeking temperance through law. In 1846 the first state Prohibition law was passed in Maine under the leadership of Neal Dow, mayor of Portland and a prominent temperance advocate. The Maine law, strengthened in 1851, ushered in a wave of state Prohibition legislation before the Civil War. By the 1850s state Prohibition was in effect in 13 states (New England plus Michigan, Minnesota, Iowa, Indiana, Delaware, Nebraska, and New York), although by 1863 only Maine still retained its law.

Temperance Literature and Ritual.—The transition in the temperance movement before the Civil War was one in which the aristocratic leadership gave way to that of the common man. Congregationalist ministers were replaced by more evangelical and revivalistic supporters. Along with this trend went the development of a highly emotional and popular literature appealing to

sentiment and stressing the reform of the drunkard. The development of the Washingtonian movement during the 1840s was in line with this trend. It began in Washington, D.C., and aimed at converting drunkards to total abstinence. This movement was marked by the development of flamboyant oratory and secular leadership, often that of reformed drunkards. These techniques of emotional drama and oratory marked the temperance movement, and Prohibition, throughout its course.

The Post-Civil War Period.—In the decade after the Civil War two major temperance organizations emerged. In 1869 the National Prohibition Party was founded, pledged in the 1872 presidential election to achieve nationwide Prohibition. The platform of 1872, and many others afterward, contained a reformist program expressing many of the same goals as the Grange and, in later years, the Populist Party. In 1874 the Woman's Christian Temperance Union (WCTU) was founded. Under the leadership of Frances Willard (*q.v.*) it was the leading temperance organization of the 1880s and 1890s in the United States. It was also active in a number of other social reforms, including women's rights, the labour movement, and the americanization of immigrants.

Both these organizations may be said to have reflected two major sources of concern. One, manifested to a larger degree in the WCTU, was a concern for the problems brought about by the industrialization of American cities and the arrival of millions of immigrants. The growth of cities with large non-Protestant populations presented the middle-class urban American with a need to assimilate new groups into his culture. The immigration and industrialism of the late 19th century made an appeal to the reformer's sympathies for human perfectionism and threatened the dominance of middle-class Protestant values. In preaching to the working-class and non-Protestant immigrants of the cities, temperance advocates were attempting to provide a similar set of middle-class values and habits that would unite the urban population.

The second source of concern was largely rural. In the Prohibition Party one saw a much stronger representation of the kinds of fears that Midwestern farmers and small-town residents had of the growing power of urban populations. During the 1880s men such as John St. John, Populist governor of Kansas and presidential candidate of the Prohibition Party in 1884, were noted for their combined temperance and Populist support. Both concerns continued to be effective into the 19th century.

These developing activities culminated in the second wave of statewide Prohibition that swept the country between 1880 and 1890. While not as many states passed Prohibition legislation as had during the 1850s, it is still true that more states were actively involved and Prohibition laws appeared before more legislatures than had been true in the earlier wave. By 1890 six states (Maine, Kansas, North Dakota, South Dakota, New Hampshire, and Vermont) had Prohibition laws or constitutional amendments. By the end of the 19th century there were 15 states that had had experience with state Prohibition at some time in their history. Nevertheless, only five states (Maine, Kansas, North Dakota, New Hampshire, and Vermont) still had Prohibition by 1900. Yet in that year approximately 23% of all Americans lived in "dry" areas.

II. 20TH-CENTURY ROOTS OF NATIONAL PROHIBITION

The drive for national Prohibition emerged out of a renewed attack on the sale of liquor in many states after 1906. The 13 years before passage of the 18th Amendment was a period of intensive state and national agitation for Prohibition laws. The dry fight had the support of churches, small towns, Progressivist sentiment, and rural political power. It was led by a new and highly effective organization, the Anti-Saloon League.

Rural-Urban Conflict.—Several underlying forces were at work to support the vigorous drive in the individual states and later at the national level. One of these, and a major force throughout the campaign, was antipathy to the growth of cities. As the United States became a more urbanized society, the industrial culture and the impact of immigration made the rural-urban conflict increasingly important in American politics. That conflict had strong overtones of cultural differences. It was largely in the small towns and agricultural areas of the United States that temperance sentiment had its strongest support. The urban and the eastern industrial areas were the centres of greatest opposition.

Protestant and Nativist Sentiments.—A second major source of Prohibitionist strength lay in the Protestant middle-class segments of the American population, especially the more evangelical ones such as the members of Methodist and Baptist churches. Although there had been some Catholic support for temperance societies, in the main both temperance sentiment and Prohibitionist sentiment stemmed from Protestant sources. A distinctly antialien and anti-Catholic sentiment was evident in much temperance literature of this period.

Rural Power.—Especially in its rural segments the Midwest represented another major source of temperance support. Here again the complex of agriculture, Protestantism, and nativism worked together to develop the drive for Prohibition as an attack on the new industrial and alien cultures that had developed in the big cities of the United States. Urban areas contained many residents whose cultural roots in American middle-class values gave rise to an antipathy to drinking. Political support for Prohibition, however, was heavily rural.

The political power of the rural areas dominated state legislatures. Without it, the enactment of state Prohibition laws and the adoption of the 18th Amendment would have been extremely difficult. In a number of cases, statewide Prohibition came about through state legislative action rather than through statewide referenda. The political power of the rural areas was even stronger in its legislative representation than its numerical majorities within the population.

The Saloon.—The saloon was itself a powerful argument for Prohibition. During the 1890s and early 1900s Americans drank in quantities and in circumstances that have not been equalled since. The liquor and beer industries showed an enormous ineptitude in failing to control the worst features of urban saloons. Many were centres of organized prostitution and political corruption. They became vivid symbols of the manifold evils of urban society and municipal government.

Economic Arguments.—An industrial society found excessive drinking to be a far greater hazard than it was in a simpler agricultural community. The economic argument for Prohibition was aimed at two groups—employers and employees. Industrial employers were concerned with preventing accidents and with increasing the stability, punctuality, and discipline of the workers. In the 1880s and 1890s the Knights of Labor, under Terence Powderly, was openly allied with temperance organizations and waged a campaign to diminish drinking by its members. The American Federation of Labor, however, did not continue this policy. Some industrialists supported Prohibition but many did not. While economic considerations played a role in developing a climate of concern about excessive drinking, they were overshadowed as explanatory factors by religious and cultural elements.

Progressivism and the Populist Movement.—The Progressive movement of the early 20th century, although an urban one, saw in the saloon and in drinking that it fostered sources of the municipal corruption and industrial chaos that the Progressives sought to eliminate. In fighting for Prohibition they saw themselves fighting the organized underworld, the foundation of corrupt politics, and the source of the workers' low standards of living. ·

Populist political sentiments, represented to some degree by William Jennings Bryan in the 1896 presidential election, were expressed in the antiurban quality of the Prohibition movement and in the attack on big business. In the liquor industry Populists saw an enemy, like the railroads and the banks, that put profits above human values.

In the 20th-century movement for Prohibition both the Progressive and Populist strands in American politics came into an alliance for human perfection. The nativist sentiments that bound both of them together contained also the efforts toward the reform of

the immigrant for whom they felt a missionary zeal. They tried to lead the newcomers to perfection through an assimilation of middle-class values.

The Anti-Saloon League.—The Anti-Saloon League, founded in 1895, assumed leadership of the Prohibitionist cause in the state drives of 1906 to 1913. The League adopted a new strategy for temperance organizations and politics. Breaking with the Prohibition Party and its tactics, the League did not put up its own candidates for election. Instead, it operated on the policy of rewarding its friends and punishing its enemies within the two major parties solely for their stand on temperance issues. As a consequence the "drys" assumed a considerable degree of power within both the Democratic and Republican parties, at state and national levels.

The tactics of the Anti-Saloon League were not only those of intensive political pressure on candidates. They generated an intense support through the public opinion of church members. Utilizing the pulpit to spread their message, the ministry as a source of local leadership, and the congregation as a base of financial support, the League became a classic example of the successful American political pressure group. In 1906 only three states (Iowa, Kansas, and Maine), still had Prohibition in force. Between 1906 and 1912 seven states passed Prohibition laws. By 1919, before the passage of the 18th Amendment, an additional 19 states passed restrictive legislation, and more than 50% of the U.S. population lived in dry areas. Most of these shifts into the dry column had occurred by 1917 before adoption of the Amendment seemed highly probable.

By 1913 national Prohibition began to seem at least possible. With passage of the Webb-Kenyon Act (March 1913) forbidding transportation of intoxicating beverages into dry states, the "drys" achieved their first national legislative victory. The liquor and beer industries sensed trouble and made efforts to control saloons, but it was too late. By January 1920 Prohibition was already in effect in 33 states covering 95% of the land area and 63% of the total population of the United States. During World War I a temporary wartime Prohibition Act was passed to save grain for use as food. In 1917 the Hobson resolution for submission of the Prohibition Amendment to the state received the necessary two-thirds vote in Congress; the Amendment was ratified on Jan. 16, 1919, and went into effect on Jan. 16, 1920. The text of the Amendment was as follows:

Section 1. After one year from the ratification of this article the manufacture, sale, or transportation of intoxicating liquors within, the importation thereof into, or the exportation thereof from the United States and all territory subject to the jurisdiction thereof for beverage purposes is hereby prohibited.

Section 2. The Congress and the several States shall have concurrent power to enforce this article by appropriate legislation.

Section 3. This article shall be inoperative unless it shall have been ratified as an amendment to the Constitution by the Legislatures of the several States, as provided in the Constitution, within seven years from the date of the submission hereof to the States by the Congress.

III. THE PROHIBITION ERA

The Enforcement of Prohibition.—It was one thing to have passed the 18th Amendment but quite another to gain compliance with it. Laws that operate against segments of the population with strong countersentiments can seldom expect complete compliance. The Prohibition laws are often viewed as examples of the ways in which a determined population can defeat the intentions of the legislators, but care must be used in making such a judgment. The extent of the enforcement of Prohibition is a matter of considerable debate. What can be said with some certainty is that, especially in urban areas, it was far from universally obeyed, nor was it energetically enforced.

Under the National Prohibition Act, popularly known as the Volstead Act (after Congressman Andrew J. Volstead of Minnesota), the commissioner of internal revenue of the Treasury Department was given the power to detect and suppress violations. In addition, individual states passed further enabling and enforcing legislation. All the states enacted laws to help carry the Volstead Act into effect although Nevada's was later held unconstitutional. Such state laws were repealed in five cases (New York in

1923, Wisconsin, Montana and Nevada in 1929, and Illinois in 1931.)

The support of the federal government to the enforcement of the Prohibition acts varied considerably during the 1920s. New personnel and new methods of Prohibition organization were tried and found wanting. Federal and state legislators did not grant sufficient funds to make possible a large legal and police organization. The salaries of Prohibition agents compared unfavourably with those of other public employees, and the entire staff of the Bureau of Prohibition never exceeded 4,500 men. The first Prohibition commissioner, John F. Kramer, served for a year and a half and was replaced by Roy A. Haines. Under President Coolidge a new head, Gen. Lincoln C. Andrews, was appointed. Andrews resigned in March 1927 and the position was thereafter held for short periods of time by several different people. Only after 1927 were all the employees of the Bureau required to take the civil service examinations. In 1929 the Department of Justice was given the duty of enforcing the 18th Amendment.

Drinking and Bootlegging.—There is considerable debate about the extent of drinking during the period of Prohibition. There is general agreement, however, that illegal manufacture and sales of liquor went on in the United States on a large scale, especially after 1923. In general, Prohibition was enforced wherever the population was sympathetic to it. In the large cities, where sentiment was strongly opposed to Prohibition, enforcement was much weaker than in rural areas and small towns. However, increased price of liquor and beer meant that the working classes probably bore the restrictions of urban Prohibition to a far greater degree than the middle-class or upper-class segments of the population.

Prohibition brought into being a new kind of criminal—the bootlegger. The career of Al Capone was a dramatic instance of the development of bootlegging on a large scale. His annual earnings were estimated at $60,000,000. The rise of the bootlegging gangs led to a succession of gang wars and murders. A notorious incident was the St. Valentine's Day Massacre in Chicago in 1929 when the Capone gang shot to death seven members of the rival "Bugs" Moran gang. Historians of the underworld, however, suggest that by the late 1920s bootlegging was on the verge of semi-monopoly control and that the end of gang wars was approaching.

The Conflict Over Prohibition.—During the 1920s the temperance movement changed radically. The alliance between Progressive and social gospel wings of American Protestantism with the more Populist and Fundamentalist groups was greatly weakened. The increased role and leadership of the Fundamentalist and nativist groups in the temperance movement tended to drive away the less hostile and urban forces, such as those of the Federal Council of Churches of Christ in America. The excessive zeal and political pressure of the Anti-Saloon League and of the Methodist Board of Temperance alienated a number of former supporters. Events came to a focus in 1928 with the nomination of the governor of New York Alfred E. Smith, as the Democratic candidate for the presidency. The Ku Klux Klan aggravated the differences within the Prohibition movement and led to a partial political identification of Prohibition supporters with rural conservatism. The defection of the urban Progressivist wing was a major element in undermining the power and acceptance of Prohibition in American public opinion.

Movement for Repeal.—The opponents of Prohibition began to organize from the moment the law came into effect. The very failure to gain full compliance with the law led to disillusionment among a number of its supporters and to energetic attacks from others. As a consequence, the political power of the so-called "wets" prevented fuller enforcement.

As time went on, some of the major supporters of Prohibition became disenchanted with it. One of the major defections was that of the industrial leader, Pierre Du Pont. From a staunch contributor to Prohibitionist causes, he became one of the major supporters of the Association Against the Prohibition Amendment (AAPA), which became active in 1926. The AAPA borrowed a leaf from the Anti-Saloon League and flooded American magazines and newspapers with literature attacking the virtues of Prohibition

and highlighting the development of the criminal action of the bootlegging industry. The development of the "speakeasy," an illegal saloon, dramatized that decline of morality in many parts of the United States which has been associated with the 1920s. Prohibition was attacked in the name of individual freedom, and drinking was referred to as "striking a blow for liberty." By the middle of the 1920s newspapers and magazines carried numerous articles describing the lack of enforcement of the 18th Amendment. Prohibition leaders such as Wayne Wheeler, Purley A. Baker, and Bishop James Cannon were increasingly criticized.

In the presidential election of 1924 the Prohibition Amendment had not come under intensive consideration; both parties had pledged themselves to its enforcement. In 1928, however, the Democratic candidate repudiated his party's "dry" platform. He opposed Prohibition, and the 18th Amendment became a powerful issue in that campaign. While Smith lost decisively, he carried urban areas of the United States that had never before voted for the Democratic Party. The urbanization of the United States and the increase in the number of persons of voting age in the cities gave promise of an overthrow of the rural power that had been dominant in American politics. While Herbert Hoover gave Prohibition enforcement his support, the turning tides of politics were evident.

Repeal of the 18th Amendment.—By 1929 the demand for some change in Prohibition legislation was considerable although the form and scope of such changes was under considerable debate and discussion. There were those who sought a better and stricter enforcement. There were those who sought a less sweeping indictment of all intoxicating beverages and permission for the sale and manufacture of beer. There were many, however, who sought the complete repeal of the Amendment and the return to the manufacture and sale of liquor, wine, and beer.

As he had promised during the campaign, President Hoover appointed a commission of 11 prominent citizens to make "a thorough inquiry into the problem of the enforcement of Prohibition under the provisions of the 18th Amendment of the Constitution and laws enacted in pursuance thereof, together with the enforcement of other laws." This commission, appointed on May 29, 1929, was headed by George W. Wickersham, former attorney general of the United States. The Wickersham Commission's final report was generally interpreted as critical of the 18th Amendment, although it did not favour repeal. Two of the commissioners favoured repeal; five wanted revision to provide for government monopoly of the liquor traffic; two favoured revision and a further trial of the 18th Amendment; and two supported the existing situation with minor alterations.

The polarization of the two parties in the 1928 election served to identify the Democratic Party as "wet" and the Republican Party as "dry." This was a break with the tactics of the Anti-Saloon League, which had avoided associating any one party with either side of the question. Analysis of votes on the Jones Act (1929) that increased penalties for first offenses against the Prohibition acts shows that the split between the North and the rest of the country on questions of Prohibition was more pronounced than ever. The consequent identification of wet and dry with specific political parties meant that the Democratic victory in the 1930 congressional elections was identified as one favouring the wet cause. In 1932 both parties adopted platforms calling for modification. The Democrats, however, adopted a platform calling for repeal, and the Democratic victory in 1932 was thus considered a mandate for the repeal of the 18th Amendment.

Forces for Repeal.—It is important to recognize the enormous significance of the depression of 1930–33, which affected Prohibition in two ways. First, it strengthened the economic argument for the return of the liquor and beer industries. While labour unions had been cool to the 18th Amendment, after 1930 they were vociferous in demanding repeal as a way of producing jobs in liquor and beer industries. Many businessmen saw in the abolition of the 18th Amendment a return to a source of tax revenue that might ease their own tax burdens. Even such stalwart contributors to the Prohibition cause as John D. Rockefeller, Jr. and S. S. Kresge deserted. A second, and perhaps even more significant

612 PROHIBITION PARTY (U.S.)

effect of depression on repeal, was the shift in attention in American political life to the problem of unemployment. The new urgency of economic issues made Prohibition a relatively minor matter. The polarization of political forces into rural-urban, Protestant versus Catholic, or immigrant versus alien was weakened by economic issues. These tended to make income levels and class differences far more important as political elements and to diminish those social antagonisms from which the Prohibition question drew its strength.

In February 1933 the Senate and House adopted a joint resolution proposing the 21st Amendment to the Constitution repealing the 18th. On Dec. 5, 1933, Utah became the 36th state to ratify the Amendment and repeal was achieved.

Post-Repeal Legislation.—After repeal a few states continued statewide Prohibition, but by 1966 all had abandoned it. The control of liquor and beer in the states in the 1960s varied widely from statewide provisions to systems of local option. In general, there was still a considerable degree of liquor and beer control or outright Prohibition in numerous parts of the country. Despite the passage of time, there was relatively little change in public support for, or opposition to, liquor control. In 1939, 18.3% of the American people lived in locally dry areas. By the 1960s this percentage had only declined very little despite the repeal of state Prohibition in Kansas and Oklahoma. In general, liquor control in the United States came to be determined more and more at local levels. Rural areas and small towns usually demonstrated a much more stringent attitude toward liquor and beer use than did the cities.

American Culture and the Antialcohol Drives.—The United States is relatively unique in the scope and intensity with which it has attempted to legislate against the use of alcoholic beverages. While Aztec society, ancient China, feudal Japan, the Polynesian Islands, Iceland, Finland, Norway, Sweden, Russia, Canada, and India have all attempted some system of Prohibition, only Finland and the United States have ever experimented with national Prohibition. (Finland adopted it in 1919 and repealed it in 1931.) India is the only other country that has attempted a system of Prohibition for any length of time on a fairly large scale.

In the complex of values which has characterized the American Protestant middle classes, self-mastery, industry, thrift, and moral conduct have been signs of the attainment of prized character traits. Self-denial has been viewed as a necessary step to the achievement of social and economic success. Drunkenness and indulgence are signs of unethical conduct because they are signs of a lack of personal control. This ascetic strain in American Protestantism has tended to make for a perfectionist bent in American religion and moral conduct which operates both as a self-oriented set of rules and a disposition to perfect the wayward, the weak, and the alien. The rural, native American Protestant of the 19th century respected temperance ideals. Sobriety was virtuous, and in a community dominated by middle-class Protestantism it was necessary to social acceptance and self-esteem. As American life began to change with the advent of urbanization and the influx of immigrants, these values were called into some doubt. Prohibition demonstrated for a while at least the dominance of that way which was reflected in the ideal of temperance and abstinence. As contemporary America became far more oriented toward values of consumption and toward a more leisurely life such values had less and less resonance in American culture.

Other Countries.—The countries of Northern Europe, especially Finland, Sweden, and the U.S.S.R., have shown a special concern for prevention of alcoholism through liquor control. The absence of ingredients for wine and beer production in these countries has led to frequent use of beverages with high percentages of alcohol. The Finnish experiment with prohibition of sales of spirits was an effort to induce a shift away from such spirits to greater beer consumption. It was unsuccessful and led to a situation of tensions similar to those in the United States. Sweden experimented with systems of rationing liquor use by the individual through a system of national monopolies, which minimized profits,

and a system of liquor ration books, which led chronic drunkards to lose their purchasing privileges. Over the years, however, Sweden moved to greater permissiveness toward drinkers. In these countries, including the U.S.S.R., alcoholism continued to be a great problem.

Amounts and kinds of drinking, as well as systems of control, vary considerably among cultures and societies. The French are heavy users of wines and have the highest alcoholism rate in Europe. The Italians are also heavy wine users but they have one of the lowest alcoholism rates. Neither country has experienced a strong temperance movement. In India, where abstinence is enjoined as a virtue among high-caste Hindus, a strong anti-alcohol movement succeeded in passing prohibitory legislation in many parts of India, especially western India. In 1965 Bombay reversed its legislation and repealed its prohibitions on liquor and beer sales.

Cultures differ both in their attitudes toward drinking and in their systems of control. Studies of American Jews and Italian-Americans have shown high acceptance of drinking as a social custom but a norm directing moderate use. Among the Japanese, drunkenness is accepted and the drunkard simply prevented from harming himself or others. Some societies have attempted to control the drinker, as under the Swedish system, while others, such as the United States, have aimed at the seller. There is little evidence that alcoholism is more or less of a problem under one than another system.

BIBLIOGRAPHY.—Herbert Asbury, *The Great Illusion* (1950); Raymond Calkins, *Substitutes for the Saloon* 2nd rev. ed. (1919); Ernest H. Cherrington, *The Evolution of Prohibition in the United States* (1920); D. Leigh Colvin, *Prohibition in the United States* (1926); Committee of Fifty, *The Liquor Problem* (1905); Virginius Dabney, *Dry Messiah* (1949); Joseph R. Gusfield, *Symbolic Crusade* (1963); John A. Krout, *The Origins of Prohibition* (1925); Raymond McCarthy (ed.), *Drinking and Intoxication* (1959); Charles Merz, *The Dry Decade* (1931); Peter H. Odegaard, *Pressure Politics* (1928); Gilman Ostrander, *The Prohibition Movement in California* (1957); Joseph Rowntree and Arthur Sherwell, *The Temperance Problem and Social Reform* (1901); Andrew Sinclair, *Prohibition: the Era of Excess* (1962); Thomas Justin Steuart, *Wayne Wheeler, Dry Boss* (1928); James Timberlake, *Prohibition and the Progressive Movement, 1900-1920* (1963); Raymond Fosdick and Albert Scott, *Toward Liquor Control* (1933); National Commission on Law Observance and Enforcement, 5 vol. (1931); Irving Fisher, *Prohibition at Its Worst*, 5th rev. ed. (1927); *Prohibition Still at Its Worst* (1928); Herman Feldman, *Prohibition: Its Economic and Industrial Aspects* (1927); Clark Warburton, *Economic Results of Prohibition* (1932); D. Heckman, "Prohibition Passes" (Ohio State Universty Ph. D. Thesis, 1939); James Sellers, *The Prohibition Movement in Alabama* (1943); Daniel Whitener, *Prohibition in North Carolina 1715-1945* (1947); Fletcher Dobyns, *The Amazing Story of Repeal* (1940); David Pittman and Charles Snyder (eds.), *Society, Culture and Drinking Patterns* (1962); J. C. Furnas, *The Life and Times of the Late Demon Rum* (1965); *Quarterly Journal of Studies on Alcohol;* annual reports of Anti-Saloon League, Women's Christian Temperance Union, Assn. Against the Prohibition Amendment, and Distilled Spirits Institute. (J. R. Gu.)

PROHIBITION PARTY (U.S.), a minor political party having as its primary objective the enactment of laws prohibiting the manufacture and sale of intoxicating liquors. Founded in Chicago, Ill., in 1869, the party reached its greatest national strength in the presidential election of 1892 when it obtained 271,000 out of a total of 12,000,000 votes cast. Its candidate that year was Gen. John Bidwell of California, and its platform included woman suffrage, currency reform, and other proposals in addition to prohibition. The party vote declined greatly while the 18th (prohibition) Amendment to the Constitution was in effect, 1919–33; it rose again slightly after the 21st Amendment (repeal of prohibition) was ratified. Although the party has offered presidential and vice-presidential candidates in each national election since its founding, its most effective work has been in local and county elections. The mass of prohibition sentiment has preferred to find expression through other organizations, especially the Anti-Saloon League and the Woman's Christian Temperance Union, rather than through the party. Advocates of prohibition resort to the political campaign primarily to keep the idea of prohibition before the public. Among American third parties, the Prohibition Party remains the oldest. See also PROHIBITION; TEMPERANCE.

(C. F. McI.)

PROJECTION, in geometry, is an operation performed upon points, lines, and planes by which a range of corresponding points or a surface of projection is formed. Let A, B, C, D, etc., represent points of a straight line l and A', B', C', D', etc., points of another straight line l' in the same plane with l. If the straight lines AA', BB', CC', DD', etc., are all perpendicular to the line l', the set of points A', B', C', D', etc., is said to be an orthogonal projection of the set, A, B, C, D, etc. (fig. 1). The correspondence between the two sets of points, by which A corresponds to A', B to B', etc., is called an orthogonal projection. In case the straight lines AA', BB', etc., are all parallel, without being necessarily perpendicular to l', we use the term parallel projection instead of orthogonal projection (fig. 2). In case the lines AA', BB', CC', etc., all meet in a point O we speak similarly of central projection. In all three cases we say that the two sets of points A, B, C, D, etc., and $A', B', C',$ D', etc., are in perspective and that the points of one set are projected into the points of the other set. The point O is called the centre of perspectivity or the centre of projection of the two sets of points as indicated in the accompanying diagram (fig. 3).

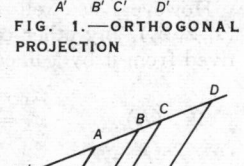

FIG. 1.—ORTHOGONAL PROJECTION

FIG. 2.—PARALLEL PROJECTION

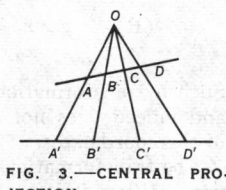

FIG. 3.—CENTRAL PROJECTION

These conceptions have been generalized in various ways. For example, let A, B, C, D, etc., be the points of any figure F in space and A', B', C', D', etc., be corresponding points of a figure in a plane π. If the straight lines AA', BB', CC', etc., are all parallel or all meet in a point O the figure in the plane π is called a projection of the other figure. If the lines AA', BB', etc., are all perpendicular to the plane π, the figure in π is called an orthogonal projection of the other figure.

See also DESCRIPTIVE GEOMETRY; GEOMETRY: *Projective Geometry*; PERSPECTIVE; PROJECTIVE GEOMETRY. (O. V.)

PROJECTIVE GEOMETRY is a branch of pure mathematics that originated in the problems of perspective drawing and the making of optical instruments. These practical applications, however, are now studied under the names of descriptive geometry and optics (*qq.v.*); and the name projective geometry is given to a logical discipline that provides greater abstractness to ordinary geometry and an intimate link between geometry and algebra, this in turn providing the basic ideas for the more recently developed theory known as algebraic geometry (*q.v.*). In this article only a very general introduction to the subject can be attempted; for proofs *see* works in the *Bibliography*.

Perspective Projection.—The distinctive procedure of projective geometry is the representation or mapping of one line l or plane π onto another (l' or π') by perspective projection from any point O not lying in either (*see* PROJECTION). This is essentially what is done when a plane object is drawn or photographed from any viewpoint. The construction whereby the image of any point P of the object π (or l) is obtained as the intersection of π' (or l') with the line OP is not limited (as in drawing a picture) to any finite portion of π (or l).

From the elementary point of view, the object of projective geometry is the study of those properties of figures that are not altered by this mapping; *i.e.*, properties that are the same for the "picture" as for the object, and are not altered by any number of repetitions of the mapping. If, for instance, a plane π is mapped by projection from O_1 onto a plane π_1, this in turn from O_2 onto a plane π_2, and so on, till a mapping on a plane π' is reached, this mapping of π onto π' is called a general projective mapping, and any property of a figure that is unaltered by the first projection will be the same in π' as in π. With certain exceptions, considered in the next paragraph, each point of π has an image point in π', and each line of π is mapped onto a line of π'.

Points at Infinity.—It is familiar that in an ordinary perspective (*q.v.*) drawing of π on π' there are certain points (and one

line) in π' that correspond to nothing in π. That is, the images of a family of parallel lines in π are lines in π' all passing through one point, which is thus not the image of any point of π; and all the points of π' that thus arise from different parallel families in π lie in one line h', the so-called horizon of the picture. Similarly, there is a horizon k in π, that has no image in π'; but all the lines that pass through one point of k have images in π' that are parallel.

This causes confusion, awkward exceptions to otherwise very general theorems, and similar inconveniences. These difficulties are overcome by adding, to each plane, fictitious or ideal points to correspond with those of the other plane that have actually no images. It is agreed conventionally that every line contains just one ideal point, or point postulated as being at infinity, which can be approached (though of course not reached) by traveling very far along the line in either direction; that all lines parallel to one another contain the same point at infinity; that all points at infinity in one plane form a line called the line at infinity; and that all planes parallel to one another contain the same line at infinity. Thus the horizon h' is the image of the line at infinity in π, and similarly the image of the line k is the line at infinity in π'. Finally, all the points and lines at infinity in space form a single plane at infinity.

(It is not suggested, of course, that these ideal points, lines, and planes have any physical existence; but then, neither have any of the pure concepts of geometry, *e.g.*, the point that has position without magnitude; the line that has length without breadth.)

This concept of the ideal not only gives every point and line in π an image in π', and makes every point and line in π' the image of one in π, but also removes troublesome exceptions from many general propositions; *e.g.*, that every two coplanar lines intersect in a point, every two planes intersect in a line, and so on. These, with similar propositions (*e.g.*, that every two points are joined by a line and every two intersecting lines by a plane), are clearly basic to projective geometry, and when the subject is treated axiomatically such are the axioms assumed; they are known as the projective axioms, or axioms of incidence.

Projective Theorems.—Theorems dealing solely with intersections of lines and collinearity of points include the following, which may be cited as playing an important role in any logical development of projective geometry.

Desargues' Theorem.—If ABC, $A'B'C'$ are two triangles, in one plane, such that AA', BB', CC' meet in a point, the intersections of BC with $B'C'$, of CA with $C'A'$ and of AB with $A'B'$ are all in one line (*see* fig. 1).

FIG. 1.—DESARGUES' THEOREM

Pappus' (Pascal's) Theorem.—If A, B, C are in one line, and A', B', C' in another line in the same plane, the intersections of BC' with $B'C$, of CA' with $C'A$, and of AB' with $A'B$ are all in one line (*see* fig. 2). For more details *see* GEOMETRY: *Projective Geometry*.

FIG. 2.—PAPPUS' (PASCAL'S) THEOREM

Duality.—In the plane there is a kind of symmetry between points and lines called duality. In the statement of any proposition or the specification of any figure, if the words point and line, lies in and passes through, intersect in and are joined by, etc., be interchanged throughout, a new proposition or figure is obtained, called the dual of the first. For instance, the axioms, "any two points are joined by a unique line," and "any two lines intersect in a unique point" are dual to each other. It is possible to frame the axioms for a logical treatment of projective geometry in pairs dual to each other; and then if any theorem is true, so is its dual, for the translation indicated above need only be made all through the proof.

Dual to the line, thought of as consisting of all the points in it, is the figure of all lines through a point; say, L. This is called a pencil of lines, and can be denoted by (L). Dual to the mapping of one line l on another l' by projection from a point O, is the mapping of a pencil (L) on another (L'), so that lines $a,b,c,\ldots$ in the one intersect their images $a',b',c',\ldots$ in the other in points all lying in a fixed line o (*see* fig. 3).

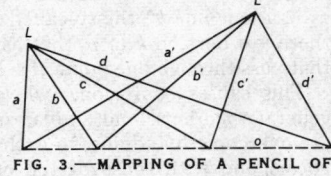

FIG. 3.—MAPPING OF A PENCIL OF LINES

In solid geometry there is the same sort of duality, not between points and lines, but between points and planes, lines being dual to lines. Thus the axioms "any two points are joined by a line" and "any two planes intersect in a line" are dual to each other, as are "any two lines in one plane intersect in a point" and "any two lines through one point are joined by a plane." The dual of a plane, regarded as consisting of all the points and lines in it, is called a star, and consists of all the planes and lines through a point. Geometry in a star is closely similar to that in a plane, lines and planes playing the roles of points and lines respectively. A star can be projectively mapped on another star, or on a plane; for instance the star can be mapped on any plane π not belonging to it, by taking as the image of any line or plane of the star its point or line of intersection with π. The dual of a line of points consists of all the planes through one line, and is called a pencil of planes.

Projectively Generated Loci.—Geometry, of course, contains many figures besides those consisting only of points and lines (and planes, in solid geometry); for example, the circle. If a plane π is mapped projectively on a plane π', the image of a circle is generally not a circle, but a curve called a conic section (*q.v.*), or more briefly a conic; and the image of any conic is likewise a conic. The conic can be defined in projective terms as follows:

If two pencils of lines in one plane be taken, say (O) and (O'), and the one be mapped projectively on the other, in general, *i.e.*, unless the line OO' in (O) has itself as image in (O'), the aggregate of intersections of a line with its image consists precisely of the points of a conic; this is the definition of a conic in projective geometry.

Many other curves and surfaces can be defined similarly. For instance, if two lines l, m are skew (*i.e.*, are not in one plane and do not intersect), and if l is mapped projectively on m, the lines joining each point of l to its image generate a surface (*q.v.*) called a ruled quadric; *i.e.*, the points of the surface are all the points of all the lines. This family of lines is called a regulus; it can also be defined as consisting of all lines that intersect not only l and m but a third line n, skew to both l and m. The important ruled quadric theorem states that any line intersecting three lines of a regulus intersects all of them. Such lines form a second regulus, generating the same surface, of which l,m,n are members.

Again, if a pencil of planes be mapped projectively on two others, the points of intersection of a plane with its two images are in general the points of a curve, called a twisted cubic; and if a star be mapped projectively on two others, the points of intersection of a plane with its two images are the points of what is called a cubic surface.

HOMOGENEOUS COORDINATES

Coordinates (*see* ANALYTIC GEOMETRY) are useful in projective geometry, allowing problems to be formulated as equations and solved by algebraic methods. However, in an ordinary Cartesian coordinate system in the plane, the coordinates (x,y) of a point at infinity are in general both infinite, but have a definite ratio to each other, x/y, depending on the direction of the parallel lines through the point. Calculations with infinite quantities of this kind are confusing, and it is found convenient to represent each point, not by the two numbers (x,y) but by three numbers (x_0, x_1, x_2) such that $x = x_1/x_0$, $y = x_2/x_0$. Obviously, if k is any number except zero, (kx_0, kx_1, kx_2) denote the same point as (x_0, x_1, x_2). If now $x_0 = 0$, then $x = x_1/x_0$ and $y = x_2/x_0$ are infinite, but have the definite ratio $x/y = x_1/x_2$; the numbers $(0, x_1, x_2)$ thus denote a point

at infinity, obviating calculation with infinite coordinates.

Such a method of representing points is called a homogeneous coordinate system, because any equation in (x,y) is equivalent to a homogeneous equation (*i.e.*, one in which all the terms are of the same degree) in (x_0,x_1,x_2); for instance, any line has an equation of the form $a_1x + a_2y + a_0 = 0$, which on substituting x_1/x_0, x_2/x_0 for x,y and multiplying by x_0 becomes $a_0x_0 + a_1x_1 + a_2x_2 = 0$. (The line at infinity, incidentally, has also an equation of this kind, namely $x_0 = 0$.)

However, as well as the homogeneous coordinate system (x_0,x_1,x_2), any other can equally be used, say (x'_0, x'_1, x'_2), derived from it by a linear transformation:

$$\text{(A)} \qquad \begin{aligned} x'_0 &= a_{00}x_0 + a_{01}x_1 + a_{02}x_2 \\ x'_1 &= a_{10}x_0 + a_{11}x_1 + a_{12}x_2 \\ x'_2 &= a_{20}x_0 + a_{21}x_1 + a_{22}x_2 \end{aligned}$$

where the nine coefficients a_{00}, etc., are sufficiently general to let these equations be solved, so as to express (x_0,x_1,x_2) in the similar form

$$\text{(B)} \qquad \begin{aligned} x_0 &= b_{00}x'_0 + b_{01}x'_1 + b_{02}x'_2 \\ x_1 &= b_{10}x'_0 + b_{11}x'_1 + b_{12}x'_2 \\ x_2 &= b_{20}x'_0 + b_{21}x'_1 + b_{22}x'_2 \end{aligned}$$

Such a transformation leaves the equation of a line still linear, and indeed does not alter the degree of any algebraic equation in the coordinates.

The transformation (A) can, however, be thought of in another way. When it is a change of coordinate system, (x_0,x_1,x_2) and (x'_0, x'_1, x'_2) are the coordinates of the same point in two different homogeneous coordinate systems; but they can also be taken as the coordinates of two different points, P,P', in the same system. The equations then define a mapping of the plane onto itself; equations (A) define for every point P a unique image P' and equations (B) show that every point P' is the image of a unique point P. This is in fact the general expression for a projective mapping of the plane onto itself.

In the same way, if (x,y,z) are Cartesian coordinates of a point in space, this can be denoted instead by the homogeneous coordinates (x_0,x_1,x_2,x_3), where $x = x_1/x_0$, $y = x_2/x_0$, $z = x_3/x_0$. Every plane has an equation $a_1x + a_2y + a_3z + a_0 = 0$ in the Cartesian coordinates, and hence $a_0x_0 + a_1x_1 + a_2x_2 + a_3x_3 = 0$ in the homogeneous coordinates; in particular, $x_0 = 0$ is the equation of the plane at infinity. A transformation like (A), but consisting, of course, of four equations each with four terms on the right, can in the same way as equations (A) be used either to define a new homogeneous coordinate system or to specify a mapping of space onto itself, in which the image of any point (x_0,x_1,x_2,x_3) is the point (x'_0, x'_1, x'_2, x'_3). This proceeding maps every plane projectively onto a plane, and every line projectively onto a line, and is called a projective mapping of space.

Duality finds a very simple expression in terms of coordinates. In plane geometry, if the equation of a line l is $a_0x_0 + a_1x_1 + a_2x_2 = 0$, then (a_0,a_1,a_2) are called the homogeneous coordinates of l, and the equation is regarded as the condition for the line (a_0,a_1,a_2) to pass through the point (x_0,x_1,x_2). What is called a dual mapping of the plane onto itself can be defined by taking as the image of every point P the line with coordinates that are the same as those of P; the images of the points in a line l will then be the lines through the point L, with coordinates that are the same as those of l. This dual mapping can be defined in purely geometrical terms, but the definition in terms of coordinates is simpler.

Duality in space can be similarly treated, the homogeneous coordinates of a plane being the coefficients (a_0,a_1,a_2,a_3) in its equation $a_0x_0 + a_1x_1 + a_2x_2 + a_3x_3 = 0$.

Geometry of One Dimension.—Similarly a homogeneous coordinate system (x_0,x_1) can be used in a line, the position of a point in the line being determined by the ratio x_0/x_1, and a linear transformation

$$\text{(C)} \qquad x'_0 = ax_0 + bx_1, \quad x'_1 = cx_0 + dx_1$$

giving either a transformation of coordinates or a projective mapping of the line on itself. As, however, there is only one point at infinity to consider, there is no serious inconvenience in using the single coordinate $z = x_0/x_1$, in terms of which equations (C) become

$$(D) \qquad z' = \frac{az+b}{cz+d}, \qquad z = \frac{dz'-b}{-cz'+a}$$

this is known as a homographic transformation.

If $z = \alpha, z = \beta, z = \gamma, z = \delta$ are the coordinates of four points A,B,C,D of the line, the expression

$$(E) \qquad \frac{(\alpha-\gamma)(\beta-\delta)}{(\alpha-\delta)(\beta-\gamma)}$$

is found to be unaltered by the transformation (D), and thus represents a property of the four points that is independent of the coordinate system and that is unaltered by a projective mapping. This number is called the cross ratio of the four points. If z is a Cartesian coordinate, the differences $\alpha-\gamma$, etc., in expression (E) are proportional to the segments AC, etc.; thus if in any projective mapping of the line on another line or on itself the images of A,B,C,D are A',B',C',D',

$$(F) \qquad \frac{A'C' \cdot B'D'}{A'D' \cdot B'C'} = \frac{AC \cdot BD}{AD \cdot BC}$$

although, of course, neither the length of a segment AC nor the ratio of two segments such as AC/AD will in general be equal to $A'C'$ nor to $A'C'/A'D'$ respectively.

The Fundamental Theorem.—If A,B,C are any three points of one line, and A',B',C' are any three points of either the same or another line, a projective mapping may be constructed in which the images of A,B,C are A',B',C' respectively. This can be done in a great variety of ways; but the fundamental theorem of projective geometry states that the actual mapping will always be the same; *i.e.*, however the construction is made, the image of any fourth point D will be the unique point D' satisfying equation (F). This is closely related to the fact that a transformation of coordinates can be made such that any three chosen points shall have assigned values for their coordinates; in particular, if the values $z = \infty, z = 0, z = 1$ are assigned to A,B,C, the value of z at any other point D will be equal to the cross ratio of the values given for A,B,C,D.

Harmonic Pairs.—Especially important is the case in which the cross ratio has the value -1; *i.e.*, when C and D divide the segment AB internally and externally in the same ratio. In this case C,D are said to separate A,B harmonically. If A,B,C are given in a line, the point D can be constructed, such that C,D separate A,B harmonically by a purely projective construction (fig. 4). Lines are drawn through A,B,C to form a triangle PQR (QR passing through A, RP through B, and PQ through C);

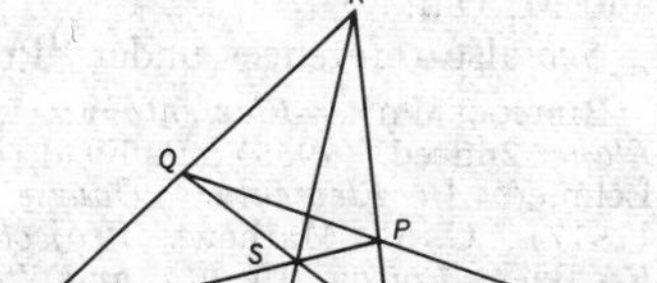

FIG. 4.—PROJECTIVE CONSTRUCTION OF HARMONIC-PAIR DIVISION WITH CROSS RATIO OF -1 (*see* TEXT)

then if S is the intersection of AP with BQ, that of RS with ABC is the required point D.

All these ideas and results can be transferred to the points of a conic or of a twisted cubic curve, or to the lines of a pencil or a regulus, or any other aggregate that can be mapped projectively on a line. Such a mapping is simply taken and each member of the aggregate is given the same coordinate as its image point; four members have the same cross ratio as their image points, two pairs separate each other harmonically if their image points do so, and so forth.

COMPLEX GEOMETRY

There are many geometrical problems which, when attacked algebraically by means of coordinates, require the solution of a quadratic equation; for instance, in the most elementary analytic geometry, that of finding the intersections of a line with a circle, or with any conic. A more important problem is that of finding the fixed points (*i.e.*, those that are their own images) in any

projective mapping of a line onto itself. If $z' = z$ in equations (D), it follows that

$$(G) \qquad cz^2 + (d-a)z - b = 0$$

so that if and only if z satisfies this equation, the point with coordinate z will be its own image in the mapping (D).

As long as operation is confined to real numbers, a quadratic equation may have two solutions, or only one, or none at all. Correspondingly, in the plane of a circle there are lines that meet it in two points (the chords), in one point (the tangents), and not at all (those completely outside the circle). In algebra, however, great simplification is obtained by enlarging the concept of number to include what are called complex numbers (*q.v.*), of the form $a + ib$, where a and b are real numbers and i is an imaginary quantity with its square equal to -1. Every quadratic equation with coefficients that are complex numbers has two solutions that are themselves complex numbers; these may, however, be equal. In particular, if the coefficients are real, either both solutions are real or neither is.

A similar simplification is obtained in geometry by the conventional introduction of complex points, taking in fact any set of three (or, for solid geometry, four) complex numbers to be the homogeneous coordinates of a point. It can then be said, for instance, that in a plane every line meets every conic in two points (which may coincide, the line being then a tangent of the conic). If from the elementary point of view, and as seen in a figure, there are no common points, then the points are imaginary and the equations make it possible to write down definite imaginary values for their coordinates. In the same way, every projective mapping of a line on itself has two fixed points which may coincide.

This conventional extension of complex geometry is logically similar to the addition of points at infinity, and has similar advantages in making it possible to state results in a more general form without the need to enumerate many alternative cases of each theorem.

Metrical Properties.—In plane geometry, a bodily rotation about a fixed centre, whereby each line through the centre is turned through the same angle, is a projective mapping of this pencil of lines on itself. The fixed lines of this are imaginary, and have always the same two directions; *i.e.*, those given in any Cartesian coordinate system by the equations $y = ix, y = -ix$. Lines having either of these directions are called isotropic; they have the paradoxical properties that every isotropic line is perpendicular to itself; and that the distance between any two points joined by an isotropic line is zero.

The points at infinity in these two directions are often called the circular points at infinity, since every circle in the plane cuts the line at infinity in these same two points. In particular, a circle of radius zero (which in Euclidean geometry consists only of its centre) in complex geometry consists of the two isotropic lines through its centre.

The set of all projective mappings of a plane on itself form a group (*see* GROUPS); projective geometry consists of the study of those properties of figures that are unchanged by all the operations in this group. If, however, within this group is considered the smaller group (or subgroup) consisting of only those mappings in which the circular points at infinity are their own or each others' images, then every figure is the same shape as its image; though they may differ in size or scale, as well as in orientation and position. Euclidean geometry, in which the basic measurable quantities are the size of an angle and the ratio of two lengths, thus turns out to be the study of properties of figures that are unchanged by all operations of this smaller group, called the similarity group. All the ordinary properties of a figure can be expressed as its projective relations to the circular points, and to the line at infinity that joins them. In particular the angle between two lines can be expressed in terms of its cross ratio with the two isotropic lines through their intersection, and they are perpendicular if they separate the isotropic lines harmonically.

Intermediate between the similarity group and the full projective group is what is called the affine group, consisting of all mappings in which the line at infinity is its own image. Properties unchanged by these include parallelism and the ratio of parallel segments, but not angles or other length ratios.

If the imaginary circular points be replaced by two real points, the similarity group becomes that of the so-called Lorentz transformations in relativity theory (*see* RELATIVITY); and if instead the mappings in which a particular conic is its own image be considered, non-Euclidean geometry is obtained (*see* GEOMETRY, NON-EUCLIDEAN).

ABSTRACT GEOMETRIES

At this stage, points have little resemblance to the intuitive idea of a point in a drawable figure. They are nothing but sets of numbers (coordinates), and the geometrical theorems about them are only a peculiar way of stating algebraic results about homogeneous equations, especially of the first degree. But algebraically there is no more interest in equations in three variables (plane geometry) or four (solid geometry) than in those in any number. It is therefore agreed to call a set of $n + 1$ numbers $(x_0, x_1, \ldots, x_n)$ a point of n-dimensional space, always with the proviso that if k is not zero, $(x_0, x_1, \ldots, x_n)$ and $(kx_0, kx_1, \ldots, kx_n)$ are the same point. The sets that satisfy r independent linear homogeneous equations are those of an $(n - r)$-dimensional space lying in the whole space. All the propositions about joining spaces and intersections can be summed up in the following intersection theorem: If two spaces of p and q dimensions are joined by an r-dimensional space and intersect in an s-dimensional space, then $r + s = p + q$; if they have no intersection the formula is satisfied by the conventional value $s = -1$.

The idea of projective geometry can be extended by choosing coordinates from a wide variety of algebraic systems. Any set of symbols that can be added, subtracted, multiplied, and divided in the usual way is called a field (*see* FIELDS); for instance, the real numbers are a field and the complex numbers are another field; and we have seen the difference between the geometries obtained by using coordinates from these two fields. Many other kinds of field are possible, however. Some consist of only a finite number of "numbers"; the simplest consists only of 0 and 1, with the relation $1 + 1 = 0$; this being what ordinary arithmetic reduces to if all even numbers are called 0 and all odd numbers are called 1. When coordinates are chosen from this field plane a geometry is obtained consisting of only seven points and seven lines (three points in each line and three lines through each point). Similarly it is possible to construct a solid geometry of 15 points, 35 lines, and 15 planes. (*See* GEOMETRIES, FINITE.)

Algebra also offers systems of symbols, such as quaternions (*q.v.*), that can be added, subtracted, multiplied, and divided nearly in the usual way, but in which a product ab is not necessarily equal to ba. These are called skew fields. Using such a system for coordinates, a geometry can be constructed in which the usual joining and intersecting relations are valid, but in which certain theorems of ordinary geometry, notably that of Pappus, and what have been called the fundamental and ruled quadric theorems, are no longer true.

The topic can be approached from a different point of view by saying that any (finite or infinite) aggregate of things that fall into classes satisfying relations of a certain kind can be regarded as the points of a projective geometry. For instance, if a number of men belong to a number of clubs, and if every two men belong to just one club, and every two of the clubs have just one common member, then the men can be called points, and the clubs can be called lines, to give a projective plane geometry. Seven men A, B, C, D, E, F, G and seven clubs with three members each, say $(ABD), (BCE), (CDF), (DEG), (EFA), (FGB), (GAC)$, form a geometry that is structurally indistinguishable from that constructed from the field consisting of 0, 1 only; in fact, coordinates belonging to this field can be attached to each man so that each club is defined by a linear equation.

Similarly, if there are objects called points, grouped into classes of various sizes called lines, planes, etc., then if these classes satisfy certain relations (of which the chief is what has been called the intersection theorem), this gives a geometry whose number of dimensions depends on the number of different sizes of classes.

Much modern research has been devoted to the classification of all kinds of abstractly possible geometries in this sense, and to the discovery of what groups of theorems are equivalent; *i.e.*, such that in any geometry where one holds, the others hold also. For instance, Pappus' theorem and the ruled quadric and fundamental theorems are equivalent in this sense.

There are three known main categories of projective geometry:

1. Those in which both Desargues' and the Pappus group of theorems hold. These can be of any number of dimensions and can consist of either a finite or an infinite number of points. This class includes the ordinary real and complex geometries. Every geometry of this kind is structurally equivalent to that constructed with some definite field; and its properties completely determine, and are completely determined by, those of the field.

2. Those in which Desargues' theorem holds, but not Pappus' theorem nor those that go with it. These likewise can be of any number of dimensions, and can be similarly constructed from a skew field. They always contain an infinity of points. All geometries of three or more dimensions belong to one of these two classes.

3. However, there can also be plane geometries in which not even Desargues' theorem holds. A good many examples, both finite and infinite, have been constructed; but any general classification of these has proved one of the most intractable problems in modern geometry.

History.—The conception of points at infinity goes back to the 17th-century work of G. Desargues (*q.v.*) and many of the ideas of projective geometry can be traced in antiquity; but projective geometry may be said to appear as a distinct study in 1822 in the work of J. V. Poncelet (*q.v.*). The clear separation of projective from metrical properties dates from the publication of the *Geometrie der Lage* of K. G. Ch. von Staudt in 1847. Most geometers of the 19th century made some contributions to the study, notably L. N. M. Carnot, C. J. Brianchon, M. Chasles, A. F. Möbius, G. Monge, J. Steiner, J. Plücker, L. Cremona, H. J. S. Smith; as well as J. D. Gergonne and H. Wiener. Working out of the relations of metrical properties to the subgroups of the projective group, and of relations between a geometry and its coordinate field or skew field was largely due to F. Klein (*see* KLEIN, (CHRISTIAN) FELIX). The axioms and logical structure of the subject have been studied by many mathematicians, notably M. Pieri and O. Veblen. The possibility of non-Desarguian plane geometry was first demonstrated by H. F. Moulton, and this branch was studied in the 20th century notably by Ruth Moufang and M. Hall.

See also references under "Projective Geometry" in the Index.

BIBLIOGRAPHY.—*Elementary*: H. S. M. Coxeter, *The Real Projective Plane*, 2nd ed. (1955); P. Field, *Projective Geometry* (1923); D. N. Lehmer, *An Elementary Course in Synthetic Projective Geometry* (1917); G. B. Mathews, *Projective Geometry* (1914). *Advanced*: R. Baer, *Linear Algebra and Projective Geometry* (1952); H. F. Baker, *Principles of Geometry*, 2nd ed., 6 vol. (1929–34), *An Introduction to Plane Geometry* (1943); L. Cremona, *Elements of Projective Geometry*, 3rd ed. (1914); W. V. D. Hodge and D. Pedoe, *Methods of Algebraic Geometry*, vol. i, book 2 (1947); G. Pickert, *Projektive Ebenen* (1955); G. de B. Robinson, *The Foundations of Geometry*, 3rd ed. (1952); B. Segre, *Lectures on Modern Geometry* (1961); O. Veblen and J. W. Young, *Projective Geometry*, 2 vol. (1910–18); A. N. Whitehead, *The Axioms of Projective Geometry* (1906).   (P. DuV.)

PROJECTOR, an optical system used to form the image of an illuminated object upon a surface. The essential elements of a projection system include the object to be imaged, a source of light to illuminate the object, an optical system that forms the image, and some surface (usually a screen) to receive the image so that it can be viewed by the observer. All of the elements in the system may assume various forms depending on the nature of the object to be viewed and the purpose for which it is to be projected. For information on motion-picture projectors, *see* MOTION PICTURES: *History: Photography*.

Slide Projector.—One of the most familiar types of projectors is that used for projecting colour slides taken by the amateur photographer. In this the light source is an electric lamp with a concentrated filament. A condensing lens concentrates the light into the projection lens, as shown in fig. 1. The lens, in turn,

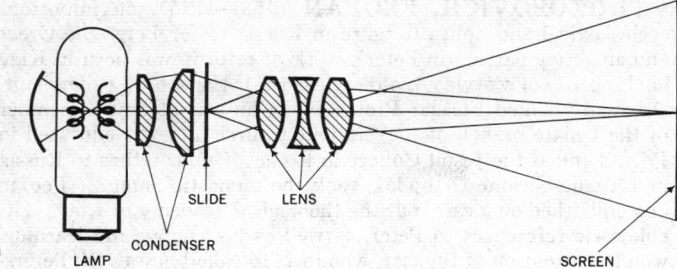

FIG. 1.—SLIDE PROJECTOR

images the slide onto the screen. The small size of the slides makes it possible to use a compact optical system, and since the light can be concentrated through the slide, a great deal of the light may be gathered from the lamp filament and a bright image produced. Common types of amateur slide projectors employ a specially designed 500-w. lamp, a projection lens with a large aperture, and an efficient condenser. Such a projector will provide a bright image for an audience of more than 100 persons.

Larger slide projectors for commercial use accommodate slides $3\frac{1}{4} \times 4$ in.; theatrical slide projectors for very large auditoriums may use carbon-arc lamps with very high light output and slides as large as 5×7 in.

Overhead Projector.—Slides up to 10×10 in. are used with the overhead projector, which has become a popular training aid in both schools and industry. In this projector (fig. 2), the slide

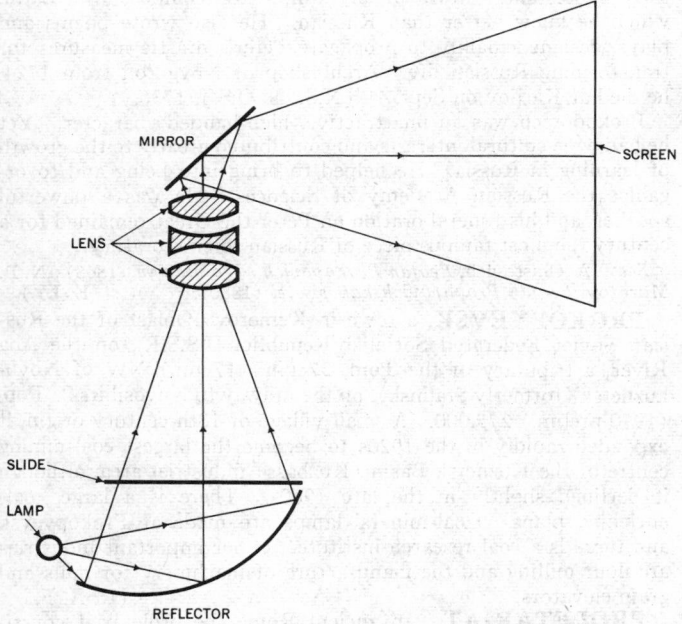

FIG. 2.—OVERHEAD PROJECTOR

rests on a horizontal surface, with the light source beneath and the lens above. A mirror mounted with the lens projects the image to a screen behind the instructor so that he faces the class while projecting the slide. Using a plain piece of plastic and a dark crayon he can also write or sketch as he lectures. The image is projected as it is produced.

Opaque Projector.—Opaque projectors are used to project nontransparent objects (for example, a solid object, a newspaper clipping, or the like). The illumination must be supplied to the object from the side facing the lens. Instead of the light being concentrated through the lens by a condenser, only the light scattered from the object reaches the lens and then the screen. For this reason, even with very high wattage lamps and very fast lenses, it is not possible to produce very bright screen images.

Auxiliary Equipment.—The screen is an important adjunct to a projector. A white matte surface reflects a bright image that can be viewed from any point within a very wide angle. Other types of screens concentrate the light over a narrower angle, thereby providing a brighter image within the angle. Some projection systems employ a translucent screen on which the image is projected from one side, while the audience views it from the other. Typical home screens are either "beaded," consisting of a layer of fine glass beads embedded in a white plastic surface, or "lenticular," having a coating of transparent plastic over a white or aluminum surface. The plastic or lenticular screens are embossed with fine ribs in the form of cylindrical lenses that can be designed to provide nearly any desired distribution of light to the audience.

Microscopes may be equipped with high-intensity light sources and small projection screens so that small objects may be projected at very high magnification. To reduce undesirable heating of biological specimens, the illuminating system must be equipped with filters to remove as much as possible of the infrared light.

Microprojectors equipped with fixed rear-projection screens and object holders that can be moved under the control of very precise measuring screws are widely used in industry for inspecting complex mechanical parts. (M. G. T.)

PROKHOROV, ALEKSANDR MIKHAYLOVICH (1916–), Soviet physicist awarded the 1964 Nobel Prize for Physics, jointly with N. G. Basov and C. H. Townes, for fundamental research in quantum electronics (masers and lasers), was born at Atherton, Queensland, Austr., on July 11, 1916, his father being a Russian revolutionary *émigré*. Taken to the U.S.S.R. after the Revolution of 1917, Prokhorov graduated from Leningrad University in 1939. After army service in World War II (1941 to 1944, when he was wounded and demobilized), he obtained his doctorate (1951) at the P. N. Lebedev Institute of Physics, Moscow, one of the main research institutes of the Academy of Sciences. In 1954 he became head of the institute's Oscillations Laboratory. He is a professor at the Moscow State University. Having worked on masers and lasers since 1950, Prokhorov was awarded a Lenin Prize in 1959, together with Basov, for their joint suggestion of the maser principle in 1953. (D. т. H.)

PROKOFIEV, SERGEI SERGEEVICH (1891–1953), one of 20th-century Russia's most gifted composers, who wrote instrumental music, operas, and ballets. He was born at Sontsovka, in the Ekaterinoslav Government, on April 23 (new style; 11, old style), 1891, began to compose at the age of six, and wrote an opera at nine. After private lessons from Reinhold Glière he entered the St. Petersburg Conservatory, where he studied composition with A. K. Liadov, orchestration with Rimsky-Korsakov, and the piano with A. N. Essipova (1904–14), and won the Rubinstein Prize in 1914 with a performance of his own First Piano Concerto. The concerto had already been performed publicly in 1912, and the Second in 1913; while still at the conservatory Prokofiev was already the young hero of the Russian modernists. In the three years before the Revolution he did much to justify their hopes, producing the First Violin Concerto, the *Classical Symphony*, an opera *The Gambler*, the *Scythian Suite* for orchestra, the Third and Fourth Piano sonatas, and a number of songs and short piano pieces. In the summer of 1918 he left Russia and traveled by way of Japan and Honolulu to the U.S. There he wrote an opera, *The Love for Three Oranges*, for the Chicago Opera Company, which produced it in 1921; and began another, *The Flaming Angel* (the score of which was left in Paris and never performed during the composer's life). In the meantime Sergei Diaghilev had invited him to Europe for the Paris and London productions of his ballet *The Buffoon* (1921). He made his home first at Ettal in Bavaria, then (autumn, 1923) in Paris, working on the *Angel*, a fifth piano sonata, the Third Piano Concerto, and the Second Symphony. In Paris he wrote two more ballets for Diaghilev, *Le Pas d'acier* (produced 1927) and *L'Enfant prodigue* (produced 1929); and one, *Sur le Borysthène* (produced 1932) for the Paris Opéra. The Third and Fourth symphonies were based respectively on material from *The Flaming Angel* and *L'Enfant prodigue*.

In 1927 Prokofiev visited Russia: a number of his works were performed at that time in various cities. He paid another visit in 1929, and at the end of 1932 he returned permanently to his native land. In the music written after his return Prokofiev emphasized the naïve and lyrical aspects of his art and modified the asperities of his harmony, but there is evidence that, in doing so, he was following the curve of his natural development, not merely bowing to the official demand for "socialist realism." The period before World War II was prolific: he wrote the opera *Simeon Kotko* (1940); another ballet, *Romeo and Juliet* (produced 1938); *Zolyushka (Cinderella)* (1945); the Second Violin Concerto (1935), based on film music; the witty orchestral suite *Lieutenant Kizhe* (1934), also drawn from film music; and a quantity of lesser works such as *Peter and the Wolf* (1936), a children's introduction to the instruments of the orchestra. The chief works of the World War II years were the Tolstoyan opera *War and Peace* (first version finished in 1942), the Fifth Symphony (1944), three piano sonatas, and a quantity of chamber music. During the artistically reactionary period after World War II Prokofiev suffered some official rebuffs: his Sixth Symphony (1947) was only half approved, the third violin sonata (unaccompanied, Opus 115) remained unperformed, and the opera *Story of a Real Man* (1948) was suppressed on the eve of production. Bowing to criticism, he produced during his last years "democratically acceptable" works such as the ballet *Tale of the Stone Flower* (produced 1954), the "oratorio" *On Guard for Peace* (1950), the Seventh Symphony (1952), and a revised version of *War and Peace* (1952). He died suddenly in Moscow on March 5, 1953.

Prokofiev's early reputation as an *enfant terrible* was unjust. He was from first to last a creator of vigorous, clean-cut "pure music." Being of his age, he was not a romantic: his marked lyrical gift was never placed at the service of subjective expression. But he commanded a genuine epic power that showed itself first in the *Scythian Suite* and very markedly in the film score *Alexander Nevsky* and other works of his Soviet period. *War and Peace* shows both his lyrical and his epic invention at their best. At the other end of the scale he had wit and simple charm. He showed marked skill in accepting the requirements of "socialist realism" without, except in a very few instances, compromising his artistic integrity.

BIBLIOGRAPHY.—S. Schlifstein (ed.), *S. S. Prokofiev: Materialy-dokumenty-vospominaniya* (1956; Eng. trans. by R. Prokofieva, *S. Prokofiev: Autobiography, Articles, Reminiscences*, 1960); I. V. Nestev, *Prokofiev*, Eng. trans. by F. Jonas (1961); Victor Seroff, *Sergei Prokofiev: a Soviet Tragedy* (1969). (G. Ab.)

PROKOP, the name of two generals of the Hussites (*q.v.*) in Bohemia.

1. PROKOP HOLY (that is, Prokop the Bald or the Shaven) is said to have been the nephew of a Prague merchant. Though he was an Utraquist priest (*i.e.*, administering Holy Communion under the forms of both bread and wine), he became the foremost leader of the Hussite forces, commanding them at their victories at Ústí nad Labem (1426) and at Domazlice (1431) as well as during their frequent incursions into Hungary and Germany. The Bohemian invasion of Saxony (1429) led to Prokop's concluding the Treaty of Kulmbach with Frederick I of Brandenburg (Feb. 6, 1430). Having been one of the leaders of the fruitless Hussite embassy to the Council of Basel in 1433, Prokop on the resumption of hostilities besieged the Romanists in Plzen till indiscipline in his own camp forced him to withdraw to Prague.

When the Bohemian nobles, both Romanists and Utraquists, formed a league against the Taborites, a struggle began in Prague. Prokop tried in vain to defend the more democratic "new town" of Prague against the nobles and the citizens of the old town; then, having called the other Prokop (*see* below) to his aid, the two retreated eastward. At Lipany, between Kourim and Kolin, their forces, mainly Taborites, were defeated by the nobles, and Prokop Holy was killed in battle (May 30, 1434).

2. PROKOP THE LESSER was likewise a priest and a military leader. When Jan Zizka, commander of the moderate Taborites or "Orphans," died (1424), Prokop succeeded him in command of his army. Subsequently he took part in Prokop Holy's campaigns in Germany (*see* above). He continued the siege of Plzen when Prokop Holy had to abandon it. Finally he was recalled to Prokop Holy's side and was sharing the command of the Taborite Army with him when they were both killed at Lipany. (R. R. Bs.)

PROKOPOVICH, FEOFAN (1681–1736), an important ecclesiastical and political figure in Russia under Peter the Great and an active partner in Peter's work of reform, was born in Kiev on June 18 (new style; 8, old style), 1681, the son of a merchant. Originally named Eleazar Prokopovich, he was at first a member of the Uniate branch of the Catholic Church and was educated in Poland and at the Jesuit College in Rome. On his return to Russia in 1702 he became Orthodox, took the monastic name of Feofan and embarked on a career at the theological academy in Kiev. His eulogistic references to Peter, as well as his energy and learning, won the attention of the tsar, who in 1716 called him to St. Petersburg and made him his principal collaborator in the church reforms. It was Prokopovich who drafted the *Dukhovny reglament* ("Spiritual Regulation") of 1721: this abolished the patriarchate and instituted, after the model of Lutheran ecclesiastical administration, the Holy Synod, of which Prokopovich became the first vice-president. The new institution was aimed at making the church an administrative department of the state. Prokopovich went farther than any other Russian prelate in his readiness to support Peter's policy of secularization and westernization and was his most trusted adviser against the opposition of the main body of the church. He also militated against the prevailing Roman Catholic and scholastic tendencies in Russian Orthodox theology.

Prokopovich's other famous work is a political treatise, *Pravda voli monarshei* ("The Truth of the Monarch's Will," 1722). This, as well as his sermons and orations, is Protestant and secular in tone. It is inspired with a cult of enlightened despotism and with a hero-worship of the great tsar which was even more pagan than Protestant. Most of his works are composed in Latin, which he knew better than Russian. He also wrote poems and plays, designed mainly to propagate Peter's drastic measures for transforming Russian life. Archbishop of Novgorod from 1724, he died at Karpov on Sept. 19 (N.S.; 8, O.S.), 1736.

Prokopovich was an unattractive, high-handed character. Yet he had wide cultural interests and contributed greatly to the growth of learning in Russia. He helped to bring into being and to organize the Russian Academy of Sciences. He was a powerful speaker, and his funeral oration on Peter the Great remained for a century the most famous piece of Russian solemn oratory.

See I. A. Chistovich, *Feofan Prokopovich i ego vremya* (1868); N. P. Morozov, *Feofan Prokopovich kak pisatel* (1880). (E. Lt.)

PROKOPYEVSK, a town in Kemerovo Oblast of the Russian Soviet Federated Socialist Republic, U.S.S.R., on the Aba River, a tributary of the Tom, 27 km. (17 mi.) NW of Novokuznetsk (formerly Stalinsk), on the railway to Novosibirsk. Pop. (1970 prelim.) 275,000. A small village of 18th-century origin, it expanded rapidly in the 1920s to become the largest coal-mining centre of the Kuznetsk Basin (Kuzbass) industrial area, although it declined slightly in the late 1960s. There is a large coal-enriching plant. Coal-miners' lamps are made at Prokopyevsk and there is a coal research institute. Other important industries are flour milling and the manufacture of machinery for mills and grain elevators. (R. A. F.)

PROLETARIAT. In ancient Rome the proletariat constituted the body of poor, landless freemen. It included artisans and small tradesmen who had been gradually impoverished by the extension of slavery. The proletariat (literally meaning "producers of offspring") was the lowest rank among Roman citizens; the first recognition of its status was traditionally ascribed to Servius Tullius. Its power resided exclusively in the rights its members enjoyed as Roman citizens. In some periods of Roman history it played an important role, not as an independent force but as a mass following, in the political struggles between the Roman patricians and the wealthy plebeians. Since it had little opportunity for productive work, which was performed in the main by slaves, its existence was largely parasitic on the Roman economy. On occasions it was quieted by doles of bread from the state and diverted by spectacles—"bread and circuses."

Marxian Socialist Theory.—The proletariat, in the restricted usage adopted by Karl Marx (*q.v.*), designates the class of wage workers engaged in industrial production whose chief source of income is derived from the sale of their labour power. As an economic category it is distinguished in Marxian literature from the poor, the working classes and the *Lumpenproletariat*. Because of its subordinate position in a capitalist society and the effects of periodic depressions on wages and employment, the proletariat is described by Marxians as usually living in poverty. But it is not therefore identified with the poor, for some members of the proletariat, the highly skilled or labour aristocracy, are recognized as not poor, and some members of the entrepreneurial class as not wealthy. Despite synonymous use in agitational literature, the term proletariat is distinguished from the working class as a generic term. The former refers to those engaged in industrial production, the latter to all who must work for their living and receive wages or salary, including agricultural labourers, white-collar workers and hired help occupied in the distribution services. The *Lumpenproletariat* consists of marginal and unemployable workers of debased or irregular habits and also includes paupers, beggars and criminals.

The proletariat in this sense appeared comparatively late on the historical scene. Its existence is essentially bound up, according to Marxian analysis, with the development of modern capitalism. Many causes have been assigned for the emergence of the proletariat, the chief of which is the expropriation of the peasants from their individual holdings by the statutory enclosure of commons land, forced sales and bankruptcies, thus compelling them to drift to the cities where they could find a market for their power to work. The proletariat was therefore considered as an urban phenomenon whose size was vastly extended by the Industrial Revolution. Among the contributory factors of the process of proletarianization have been cited the breakup of the medieval guilds, the dispersion of the monasteries, the liberation of the serfs and large increases in the population relative to the possibilities of employment in traditional vocations. The incidence of these factors on the rise of the proletariat varied from country to country.

Capitalist Class as Creator and Enemy of Proletariat.— According to the Marxian analysis, the existence of the proletariat as a definite class presupposes the existence of the capitalist class. Where the capitalist class disappears or becomes subordinate in the control of production to other social groups that abrogate the free market, there is no longer a proletariat. This conclusion, together with the prediction that in the course of its evolution capitalist society necessarily becomes polarized into two classes, was questioned in the light of 20th-century developments in Germany, the U.S.S.R. and the United States. The assumption that in time the proletariat would constitute the overwhelming majority of the population was also challenged on the ground that increasing mechanization and rationalization of production led to a relative decline in the number of unskilled, manual workers and an increase in the numbers of those engaged in managerial functions and distribution services.

More significant in Marxian theory than its meaning as a strictly economic category is the social-psychological conception of the proletariat. Slowly educated by their hardships and their struggles for better conditions and wages, the workers are believed to become conscious of the objective antagonisms that divide them as a class from their employers. The first stage in their awareness is usually marked by the organization of trade unions within the existing framework of society. The second is their acceptance of doctrines which teach either that they cannot permanently improve their human existence in a commodity-producing society because unemployment, crisis and war are endemic to its operation, or that a more just and efficient organization of social relations is possible which would increase their material welfare and remove invidious social distinctions. The third stage is reached in the development of political parties which take on the designation of labour or socialist parties whose ultimate program is directed not to the improvement of the individual lot of the worker or to facilitating social mobility from class to class but to the reconstruction of the whole society which, in abolishing all traditional economic classes, would abolish the proletariat as a class.

Further, by setting up a common faith and objects of ideal allegiance, Marxians seek to unify the diverse ethnic, religious and national differences among the proletariat and to reinforce the sense of solidarity which is presumably born out of consciousness of common material interests. In respect to this function of proletarian ideology, it should be observed that it enjoyed some limited success in overriding ethnic and religious differences among the members of the proletariat, but failed almost completely in transcending consciousness of national differences. In times of national conflict, the proletariat behaved no differently from the *bourgeoisie* of their respective countries.

Marxians seek organizational support for their ideology primarily, but not exclusively, among industrial workers for two reasons. The first is the assumption that whereas the economic grievances of all other working groups, such as the farmers, intellectuals and lower middle classes, can be removed without fundamental social change, the position of the industrial worker is so tied up with the exigencies of capitalist production that he cannot be liberated except by transformation of capitalism itself. The second is the expectation that, in the event of a struggle for power, the industrial workers will be most strategically situated in determining the issue —an expectation also called in question by the development of modern industrial and military technology.

Communist Party the Self-Designated "Vanguard of the Proletarian."—The appeals of proletarian ideologies nevertheless have been addressed to the community at large, to all men of "insight" and "good will," couched in moral terms which try to invoke the ideals of justice, humanity and human freedom. Many elements in the population are won to adherence to proletarian causes whose social antecedents are by no means proletarian. It has been widely observed that many outstanding political leaders of working-class parties in all countries have been drawn from other classes. And since most inspirers of proletarian ideologies have rarely been members of the working class, it has been inferred that the working class, left to itself, is not likely to develop beyond the level of trade unionism. The universalism implicit in the premises of proletarian ideologies led their carriers to proclaim that they represented the best understood interests not only of one class in the community but of the masses of people. In this way the voice of moral prophecy acts to give force and persuasive effect to the analysis of historical destiny. The result, sometimes concealed, sometimes acknowledged, is a broadening of the meaning of proletariat from a term designating a narrow economic class to a term that loosely encompasses all who support the ideology of the class, and ultimately to the masses who are presumed to enjoy its future benefits.

The various ambiguities in the meaning of the term proletariat come to a head in the phrase "the dictatorship of the proletariat." As Marx used it, it denotes the political rule of the proletariat, through representative organs, during a transitional period from capitalism to socialism. It is a dictatorship in that political power is used to abolish the social relations of production which create profit and rent. Since Marx assumed that the proletariat would constitute the overwhelming majority of the population as the polar class to the *bourgeoisie*, the dictatorship of the proletariat was conceived as a form of workers' democracy. It was not conceived as a dictatorship of the minority or of a political party, but of a social class, and emphatically not the dictatorship of a political party over the proletariat. This is evidenced by the language of the *Communist Manifesto* and by Engels' public reference to the Paris Commune as an illustration of a proletarian dictatorship.

After the Russian October Revolution of 1917 the meaning of "the dictatorship of the proletariat" changed. Lenin, Trotski and Stalin declared that it represented substantially the dictatorship of a minority political party. This party consists of the self-denominated vanguard of the proletariat, although its members need not be proletarian in origin. It speaks and acts for the whole of the proletariat and ultimately for the whole working class. The latter, however, cannot freely accept or reject its leadership since no rights of opposition to the ruling party are recognized. To add to this shift in meaning, it should be observed that although the U.S.S.R. was officially proclaimed to be a socialist society without any classes, it continued to be characterized as a dictatorship of the proletariat. Under such circumstances the term proletariat became more of a slogan than a precise designation of a social or economic group. Because of these ambiguities, the term must always be interpreted in relation to the specific historical situation and the concrete social context in which it is employed. *See* Bolsheviks; Communism; Communist Parties; Marxism; Socialism.

Bibliography.—K. Marx and F. Engels, *Manifest der Kommunistischen Partei* (1848); K. Marx, *Das Kapital*, vol. 1 (1867; Eng. trans., 1887); W. Sombart, *Der Moderne Kapitalismus* (1916), *Der Proletarische Sozialismus* (1924); N. Lenin, *State and Revolution* (1917; Eng. trans., 1932); J. Stalin, *Leninism* (1926; Eng. trans., 1928); G. Briefs, *The Proletariat* (1937).   (S. Hk.; X.)

PROLOGUE, a prefatory piece of writing, usually composed to introduce a drama. The Greek *prologos* included the modern meaning, but was of wider significance, embracing any kind of preface. In Greek drama, a character, often a deity, stood forward or appeared from a machine before the action of the play began, and made from the empty stage such statements as it was necessary that the audience should hear. It was the custom to explain everything that had led up to the play, the latter being itself, as a rule, merely the catastrophe following on the facts related in the prologue. The importance, therefore, of the prologue in Greek drama was very great. With Euripides, as has been said, it takes the place of "an explanatory first act." On the Latin stage the prologue was often more elaborately written than in Athens, and in the careful composition of the poems which Plautus prefixes to his plays we see what importance he gave to it; sometimes, as in the preface to the *Rudens*, Plautus rises to the height of his genius. Molière revived the Plautine prologue in the introduction to his *Amphitryon;* Racine introduced Piety as the speaker of a prologue to *Esther.* The tradition of the ancients vividly affected the early English dramatists. Not only were the mystery plays and miracles of the middle ages begun by a homily, but when the modern drama was inaugurated the prologue came with it, directly adapted from the ancient practice. Thomas Sackville prepared a sort of prologue in dumb show for his *Gorboduc* of 1562; and he also wrote a famous *Induction* (practically a prologue) to a miscellany of short romantic epics by diverse hands. In the Elizabethan drama the prologue was very far from being universally employed. In the plays of Shakespeare it is rare. After the Restoration, prologues became obligatory. They were always written in rhymed verse, and were generally spoken by a principal actor or actress. *See also* Epilogue.

(E. G.; E. E. K.; G. W. A.)

PROME, a town and district in the Pegu division of Lower Burma. The district occupies the valley of the Irrawaddy River, between Thayetmyo district on the north and Henzada and Tharrawaddy districts on the south. Area 2,953 sq.mi. (7,648 sq.km.). Pop. (1962 est.) 496,960. There are two mountain ranges, the Arakan Yoma and the Pegu Yoma. The former extends along the western side. The portion of the district on the right bank of the Irrawaddy is broken up by thickly wooded spurs running southeastward. Cultivation is confined to the parts adjacent to the river. On the eastern side lies the Pegu Yoma, and north and northeast of the district its forest-covered spurs form numerous valleys and ravines, the torrents from which unite in one large stream, the Na-win Chaung. The staple crop is rice, but cotton and tobacco are grown, while the custard apples are famous. The forests yield teak and cutch.

Prome town, capital of the district, lies on the Irrawaddy, 161 mi. (259 km.) NNW of Rangoon. Pop. (1953) 36,997. The Burmese refer to Prome as Pyi, which means "the capital," but the actual site of the old city, known as Sri Ksetra ("city of splendour"), is five miles to the southeast of Prome and is now known as Hmawza. Excavations there, started in 1907 by Gen. Léon de Beylié and later by Taw Sein Ko, revealed a Pyu culture quite distinct from both Mon and Burmese. The Pyus were one of the earliest of the Tibeto-Burman stock to come into Burma after the 3rd century. They occupied the Irrawaddy valley from Shwebo to Prome. Sri Ksetra was probably built in A.D. 638 by Hari Vikrama. It was the capital of a new dynasty, the Vikrama, which inaugurated a new era called Sakarac, a term that is still in use. The city was almost circular and its walls enclosed an area of about 18 sq.mi. (46 sq.km.). The northern part seems to have

consisted of paddy fields so that it could withstand a long siege. The city however fell early in the 8th century. The Pyus retreated north and built another city that was destroyed in A.D. 832. The Burmese came into Burma only after this; they learned to respect the Pyu civilization and have continued to call the old Pyu centre Pyi.

See also Burma: *Archaeology.*   (T. Tu.)

PROMETHEUS, in Greek cult "the fire-bearing Titan god" (Sophocles, *Oedipus at Colonus,* 55). The fundamental notion about him is that he stole fire from the gods for the benefit of mankind. Like the Norse Loki, he was a trickster as well as a fire-god, and his intellectual side was emphasized by the apparent meaning of his name, "Forethinker."

In Hesiod's *Works and Days* (700 B.C.?) his story is told to explain why men must toil for their living: the gods have "hidden livelihood" from men because Prometheus deceived Zeus. Zeus did not intend that men should have fire but Prometheus ("Foresight") stole it for them anyway. In return Zeus had the woman Pandora (*q.v.*) created and sent her down to Epimetheus ("Hindsight"), who, though warned by Prometheus, took her in and only afterward realized what woe he had brought upon mankind. Before this, men had lived free from evils and hard work and disease, but Pandora took the great lid off the jar and all these things flew out to wander among mankind. Hope alone stayed within. "So impossible is it to escape the will of Zeus."

The context of this story makes it clear that in Hesiod's mind Prometheus' theft of fire brought with it the working of metals, and metals meant weapons, and weapons meant violence and greed. Though Prometheus' gift brought civilization, it was a "heroic" civilization and Hesiod wanted no part of it. The figure of Pandora, with her jar full of evil and toil and disease, serves to express both the attractiveness and the ultimate hopelessness of civilization. By sending Pandora "as the price of fire" the gods "hid livelihood." As Hesiod saw it, fire and civilization had ended by blighting both men and nature.

In the Hesiodic *Theogony* Prometheus himself is punished. Zeus bound him and set an eagle upon him to devour his immortal liver, constantly replenished. Later he permitted Heracles to kill the eagle, wishing to do his son honour. "Seeking to rival Zeus in counsel," Prometheus had tried to trick him into accepting the bones of sacrifices instead of the meat, which would then be left for men. Zeus saw through the trick, but chose the bones—which became his portion from then on—"because he meditated evil for men." Thereupon he withheld fire, Prometheus stole it, and Pandora was sent to men as in the earlier account, "a bad thing as the price of a good one." "So impossible is it to deceive or circumvent the will of Zeus. Not even the son of Iapetus, kindly Prometheus, escaped his anger, but under Necessity, wise though he is, the mighty bonds restrain him."

In this account the theft of fire is merely one example of Foresight's doomed attempts to have the better of heaven, and Pandora is simply the first woman, expensive, hard to live either with or without, but bringing no jar of evil, toil, and disease. The inner connection between the theft of fire and the coming of Pandora is gone—this poet has no quarrel with technical advances—but all the same, in the bound Prometheus he has, with some help from the *Odyssey* (*cf.* Tityus in Hades), created the great image of human intelligence agonized and helpless in the grip of necessity which has fascinated many poets since.

In working out this theme Aeschylus in *Prometheus Bound* makes Prometheus not only the bringer of fire and civilization to men but their preserver. Zeus had intended to destroy them and create a new race, but Prometheus prevented this and gave men not only the means of survival but all the arts and sciences. For this Zeus has him chained to a crag in Scythia at the ends of the earth. But he knows what Zeus does not, the marriage which will cause Zeus's downfall, and he keeps the secret as the price of his release, though Zeus blasts him down to Tartarus at the end of the play. Though the rest of the trilogy is lost, we know that Prometheus was restored to the upper world still chained, this time with the eagle to torment him, that Heracles came and shot the eagle, and that finally the prisoner was set free, with intelligence and power, human hopes and the will of heaven reconciled at last.

Hesiod and Aeschylus provide the basis for most of the many other treatments of Prometheus. When the gods created men and animals out of earth, according to Plato (*Protagoras*, 320 ff.), Prometheus put into man fire stolen from Athena and Hephaestus to compensate for Epimetheus' having used up the simpler means of survival on the animals. This could account for the tradition, which seems to be later, that Prometheus created man.

See H. J. Rose, *A Handbook of Greek Mythology* (1928).

(G. E. Dk.)

PROMETHIUM is a metallic element of the rare-earth series, symbol Pm, atomic number 61. It is unique in that it is the only rare-earth element that does not occur naturally (except possibly in extremely small traces resulting from the spontaneous fission of uranium in uranium ores). However, fission-product promethium is found in quantities sufficient for identification and study in the residues from nuclear reactors; it is also prepared by slow neutron bombardment of an isotope of neodymium, Nd^{146}. No stable isotope has been found; of the 14 unstable species known, the longest-lived is Pm^{145}, with a half-life of 18 years. Because of the short half-lives of its isotopes, promethium probably does not occur in nature in concentrations which would permit its chemical separation.

The first conclusive chemical proof of the existence of promethium was obtained in 1947 by J. A. Marinsky, L. E. Glendenin, and C. D. Coryell, who isolated the radioisotope Pm^{147} (half-life 2.7 years) from atomic fission products obtained at the Oak Ridge (Tenn.) research site. Identification was firmly established by spectroscopy. The discovery completed the search for missing rare-earth elements. A number of investigators in the past had claimed to have proved the existence of element 61 in naturally occurring rare earths; among the names they applied were illinium and florentium. The name promethium is derived from Prometheus, who in Greek mythology stole fire from heaven and gave it to mankind—an appropriate name, since the element comes from the fierce fires of the atomic furnace.

The properties of promethium appear to be those of a typical rare earth. It is trivalent in its compounds and solutions, most of which are pink or rose in colour. It absorbs ultraviolet and visible light in discrete sharp bands which are useful for quantitative analyses. The ion is paramagnetic due to unpaired electrons. The metal has been prepared by the same methods used for light rare earths (*see* Praseodymium and Neodymium). The metal melts at 1,080° C and resembles the other rare-earth metals both chemically and physically. Though promethium salts have been used for miniature batteries, the main use of the element is in research. *See also* Rare Earths. (Ld. B. A.)

PRONGHORN (Prongbuck, Pronghorned Antelope), the sole living representative of the family Antilocapridae, which earlier evolved numerous and varied forms found as fossils in North America. Called the "American antelope"—though it is not a true antelope (*q.v.*)—the pronghorn (*Antilocapra americana*) stands up to 3 ft. high at the shoulder; it is reddish-brown, with white underparts, white flanks and cheeks, two white bands on the throat, and a large circular white signal patch on the rump. The tail and the short mane on the upper neck are dark brown. The horns are erect and diverging and branch into two prongs, the longer curving backward and inward, the shorter projecting forward; the horny sheaths are shed and renewed annually but the bony cores, on which the front prong is barely represented, are retained. Pronghorns are fleet and inhabit open plains and semideserts; they formerly lived in immense numbers from Alberta to Mexico, at their peak population numbering perhaps more than 40,000,000. After almost having been exterminated in the early 20th century, they have responded well to conservation practices aimed at their recovery.

See A. S. Einarsen, *The Pronghorn Antelope and Its Management* (1948). (L. H. M.)

PRONUNCIATION. In a most inclusive sense pronunciation is the form in which the elementary symbols of language, the segmental phones or speech sounds, appear and are arranged in patterns of pitch, loudness, and duration. In the simplest model

of the communication process in language—ENCODING . . . MESSAGE . . . DECODING—pronunciation is an activity, shaping the output of the encoding stage, and a state, the external appearance of the message and input to the decoding stage. It is what the speaker does, and what the hearer perceives and, so far as evaluation is called for, judges. It is so basic to language that it has to be considered in any general discussion of language or particular discussion of the English language, etc.

In a narrower and more popular use, questions of pronunciation are raised only in connection with value judgments. Orthoepy, correct pronunciation, is parallel to orthography, correct spelling. "How do you pronounce [spell] that word?" is either a request for the correct pronunciation (spelling) by one who is unsure, or a probing for evidence that the respondent does not pronounce (spell) correctly or speaks a different dialect or has an attractive or repulsive idiosyncrasy in his speech. Only mispronunciations are noticeable, therefore distracting; they introduce "noise" into the communication system to reduce its efficiency.

The Act of Pronunciation.—The production of speech is basically the same as the production of any other sound, with an apparatus for setting up vibrations in the air which affect the organs of perception in the ear of the hearer. (*See* Voice.) The sound of speech differs from the sound of a noise- or music-producing instrument because the organs of speech can change the quality of the sound produced as well as alter its pitch, loudness, and duration. It is as though speech were played on a number of instruments, one for *ah*, another for *sh*, etc., each one in operation for only a few hundredths of a second at a time, all smoothed out into a continuous flow.

The term pronunciation is usually restricted to differentiation in the qualities of the speech sounds and in stresses and tones where pertinent. Voice quality, such as nasality or breathy voice, is not included unless it is a differentiating feature of the sounds of the language. The term is only vaguely applied to stretches of speech longer than a word, such as the intonation of sentences, and it may be said that someone has an excellent pronunciation of a language but his tune is all wrong.

The study of the production of speech is phonetics, often defined as the science of pronunciation. (*See* Phonetics.) It is here to be noted only that, whereas adjustments of the organs of speech may be monitored by the speaker's tactile, kinesthetic, and even visual senses, primary monitoring is by ear, and any hearing child learns to speak the language of the group with which he grows up, without any directions as to articulation. For some languages, *e.g.*, English, the consonant articulations are comparatively neat and stable, the vowel articulations less so. For other languages, *e.g.*, Spanish, it is the other way around. For some languages the general pattern of articulation is comparatively precise, for others not so. The pronunciation of English cannot be made better, but only obnoxiously conspicuous, by a precision of articulation which is contrary to the genius of the language.

The System and the Pronunciation.—The systematic function of pronunciation is to make those distinctions among the consonants and vowels in the flow of speech, and, for some languages, among quantities, stresses, and pitches, which have to be made in order to distinguish meanings in sentences. The simplest illustration shows one critical point only in the sentence—*e.g.:* "He's been writing/riding." "Ich will die andere Seite/Seide" ("I want the other page/silk"). "Il est tanné/damné" ("He is tanned/damned"). "No es nata/nada" ("It is not cream/It is nothing"). For the pronunciation to satisfy the ear of the native speaker, however, the way in which the distinctions are made (*i.e.*, the qualities of the consonants and vowels and the way in which they are run into the flow of speech) is fully as important as the fact that the distinctions called for are made. In the terminology of linguistics, the systematic function is said to be phonemic and the qualitative propriety phonetic.

For all examples above the phonemic statement is very simple: $/t/ \neq /d/$; *i.e.*, the distinction between $/t/$ and $/d/$ may be used to mark a distinction in meaning in English, German, French, or Spanish. By other similar operations each $/t/$ and $/d/$ can be shown to be in opposition to all other phonemes in its language. It is

general practice, although not strictly phonemic, to group phonemes into phonetic-named classes and identify as intersections of
classes (*see* below).

The description of the phones, or speech sounds as sounds, is
another matter. These [t]s (*i.e.*, phones rather than phonemes)
are voiceless except that in some varieties of English the [t] in
this environment is voiced. In German it is aspirated, in French
and Spanish not. The [d]s are stops except that the Spanish
phone is a fricative. Both are strictly alveolar in standard English,
dental with the tongue touching the edges of the incisors in Spanish, and differently intermediate for German and French. There
are other small differences in articulation in this environment and
still others in other environments. It is possible to describe pho-
netically close to 90 varieties of [t] for General American English; some of them may be got at only by straining the apparatus
of description, but for most of them any different articulation will
produce a pronunciation not quite right.

Language Systems.—The pronunciations of various languages
may be compared in a general way by noting the inventory of
phonemes by classes.

English has one of the most frequently occurring stop systems,
/p/ /t/ /k/, with an affricate, /č/, *pin, tin, kin, chin.* Other languages have as few as two stops (Hawaiian) to as many as six
(Yuma), with none to three affricates. The English fricative or
spirant system has four, not corresponding, places, /f/ /θ/ /s/ /ʃ/,
fin, thin, sin, shin; Scots has also a /x/, *loch,* as in older English
and present German and Spanish. Some languages have uvulars
or pharyngals. English has a double, tense-lax, system for ob-
struents, /p/ /b/ . . . /ʃ/ /ʒ/, *mop, mob . . . mesher, measure.*
Chinese has an aspirated-unaspirated system for stops, Hindi four
kinds of stops. The English and German nasal systems correspond
to the simple stops, /m/ /n/ /ŋ/, *some, sun, sung.* French and
Spanish have /ɲ/ rather than /ŋ/, *peigne, piña,* other languages
none to four nasals. The *l* and *r* types are not contrasted in
Japanese and furnish two phonemes each in Castilian Spanish.
English /r/ may well be put into the semivowel system, /j/ /r/
/w/ /h/, *yea, ray, weigh, hay.* Russian has a double system of
plain and palatalized consonants, Italian a complete system of
geminates.

Spanish has a five-vowel system, /i/ /e/ /a/ /o/ /u/. Tagalog
has three vowels. The American English system is variously interpreted as 9 simple vowels plus complex vocalic nuclei or as
about 15 vowels plus diphthongs. German and French have front-
rounded and French has nasalized vowels, as English and Spanish
do not. Some languages have long vowels contrasting with short,
as Middle English did—hence the terms "long *a*," "short *a*," etc.,
now quite meaningless.

There are also systems which include types strange to English
and the nearby languages. Burmese has vowels with breathy
voice in contrast to not breathy. Ibo has inspired voiced stops.
Georgian has glottalized stops (air-compressed by raising the
closed glottis). Hottentot has clicks (with mouth-air suction;
see Clicks). There are many tone languages for which the relative pitch level or direction of pitch turn of a syllable is part of
the phonemic system, the pronunciation as distinguished from
the intonation. Chinese is the best-known example. There are
other Far Eastern and many African and American Indian tone
languages. Swedish and Norwegian have limited tone systems.

Dialects and Standards of Pronunciation.—In a technical
sense, without deprecatory or romantic connotations, a dialect is
any form of a language peculiar to any community of speakers of
the language. (*See* also Linguistics: *Linguistics and Other Disciplines.*) Every native speaker speaks a dialect and every native hearer puts the man he hears in a pigeonhole cross-labeled
by region and social class. A language is the sum of its dialects
or a generalization based on them.

For the hundreds of local dialects to be found wherever a language has been spoken by many people over a large area for a
long time, the pronunciation is bound up in a total complex, including also morphology, syntax, and lexicon. The attitude toward
dialect in this sense—avoided as a lower-class marker in Great
Britain, used by many upper-class speakers in Germany in inti-

mate situations—is an attitude toward the dialect as a whole, not
particularly the pronunciation. The emphasis on pronunciation
in dramatic literature, as in Shaw's *Pygmalion* and *My Fair Lady,*
is presumably to suggest the dialect without making it incomprehensible. In the United States, where there are few strictly
English dialects of this sort—as there are, for example, few such
dialects of Spanish in Argentina—the nearest equivalent is the
contamination of English by other languages.

Among regional upper-class dialects of the standard language,
distinctions are made primarily in pronunciation and intonation,
what David Abercrombie calls "accents" rather than "dialects,"
where the morphology and syntax vary almost not at all and the
lexicon not much more. Standard English is differently pronounced
in London and Edinburgh and in Chicago and Sydney, standard
French in Paris and Marseilles and Quebec, standard Spanish in
Madrid and Buenos Aires, standard German in Berlin and Munich.
In some cases the phonemic system varies, as notably among
English, Scots, and American dialects and those of Spain and Central and South America.

There are of course dialects intermediate between strictly local
and strictly regional in the larger sense and between lower-class
and upper-class. Pronunciation is sometimes a more, sometimes a
less, prominent sign. In the United States, where "accent" and
"dialect" are interchangeable terms and "dialect speaker" does
not occur, pronunciation is the primary regional marker, what is
called grammar is the class marker where there is any.

The concept of a standard pronunciation—*i.e.*, of one pronunciation of the standard language with greater prestige than others
and the only proper basis for the concept of correctness—seems
to be common to most cultivated languages. For the French the
standard is said to be "celle de la bonne société parisienne" ("that
of high Parisian society"); for Spanish, "la que se usa corrie-
ntemente en Castilla en la conversación de las personas ilustradas"
("that which is commonly used in the conversation of cultivated
Castilians"). For German the base is a style of speech developed
for the stage, which serves as "ein Ideal, das als Ziel und Maßstab
für alles gebildete Sprechen aufgestellt ist" ("an ideal that is
established as goal and norm for all educated speech"). In all
these cases the standard may be modified in practice; few Germans
outside theatrical circles speak the regionless ideal standard, and
Argentinians are proud of their non-Castilian standard.

The situation is different in Great Britain, where there is now a
nonregional, strictly upper-class dialect of enormous prestige,
Received Pronunciation, spoken by those who learned it at home
and in the public schools. It is said that only an RP speaker
can surely identify RP speech. For those outside the RP circle,
the regional "accents" are a practical standard. In the United
States there can hardly be said to be, and is said not to be, any
definable standard. With J. S. Kenyon's "familiar cultivated colloquial" as a reference, some Americans speak of Eastern, Northern or General, and Southern standards. American English is as
loose a term as British English.

Changes in Pronunciation.—It is accepted as a truism that
pronunciation changes more or less continuously. Since there is
no inheritance of language and every child has to learn from what
he hears about him, it is to be expected that the learning will
not be perfect in every detail. Most individual eccentricities are
discouraged by the conservatism of the community and are not
passed on to the succeeding generation. By and large the language corrects itself. From time to time, however, what might
be called a mistake in pronunciation seems to catch on and a
change gets under way, sometimes so gradual in development as
to be recorded only in retrospect.

A change which affects one phone or a group of related phones
without apparent influence by the environment is known as isolative or independent. Thus the Great Vowel Shift in English
was a gradual change in the pronunciation of all long vowels
wherever they occurred. (*See* English Language: *Modern English: Phonology.*) The only explanation that can be made of this
shift is that it did not materially alter the system, either as to number of phonemes or distribution. The new diphthongal vowels, in
line and *cow,* were not easier to produce than the simple vowels

that were lost, to be reintroduced later in *calm* and *law*. For this and other isolative changes in English and in other languages, it is hard to say why they took place or why they happened when they did.

Changes which affect certain phones or groups of phones in certain environments only are known as combinative or dependent. The general pattern is one of ease of pronunciation, the speaker tending to make the least effort; this tendency is countered by the demand of the hearer for easy intelligibility. Thus the *i*-umlaut or *i*-mutation in English and other languages results when the speaker, anticipating the articulation for a front [i] or [j] in the next syllable (later lost), shifts the articulation of the vowel in question from back to front; thus *fill* (*cf.* Gothic *fulljan*) beside *full*.

The most obvious effort-reducing change is assimilation of consonants. The term is itself an example, from *ad-* "to" + *simil-* "similar," the forms *adsimil-* and *assimil-* both attested in classical Latin. Assimilations may or may not be accepted by the community. Thus [ʃ], representing a reciprocal assimilation of [s] + [j], prevails in *issue* in America but [sj] in England; [č] is usual in *literature* but [tj] occurs, sometimes taken as a sign of affectation; *can't you* may be pronounced with [tj] or [č], the latter subject to social sanctions. Most such assimilations merely shift the distribution of phonemes—more /ʃ/'s and fewer /s/'s, etc. But when [z] + [j] became [ʒ], *vision,* the new phoneme /ʒ/ filled a gap in the English system which John Hart had pointed out half a century earlier.

The change in English which had the greatest effect was the obscuration of vowels in unaccented syllables. As direct consequence the neutral vowel came to be the most frequently occurring syllabic in the language, and as indirect consequence many inflectional endings earlier marked by vowel contrasts became non-discriminating and then were simplified or lost.

The number of reconstructions in the system of English brought about by changes in pronunciation is reported, by C. F. Hockett, as approximately 100.

Graphic Representation of Pronunciation.—The principal way of holding pronunciation still for examination or for transmitting it through time and space is alphabetic, or syllabic, writing. (*See* ALPHABET; WRITING.) The written word is not coordinate with, much less superordinate to, the spoken word. Chinese 石 may correspond in a way to English *stone,* but the one is a first-order symbol, the other a second-order symbolization of the composition of a first-order symbol.

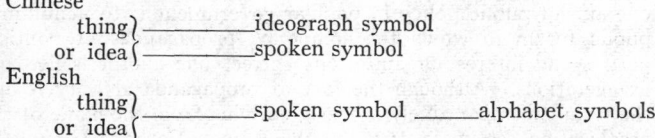

In a way it may be said that any language can be phonemically written with any alphabet and that, as Bloomfield said, "A language is the same no matter what system of writing may be used to record it, just as a person is the same no matter how you take his picture." (Leonard Bloomfield, *Language*, p. 21, Holt, Rinehart and Winston, Inc., New York, N.Y., 1933, © 1961.) But Roman and Cyrillic and Arabic and other alphabets are used for the writing of quite dissimilar languages, and it is not to be expected that they will work equally well for all. Nor does writing often keep up with changes in pronunciation. Thus, although the early writing of English in an augmented Roman alphabet was adequate, most of the later phonemic changes have not been recorded. Moreover useless new spellings were introduced, by Anglo-French scribes, and analogical and etymological spellings—some of the latter encouraging spelling pronunciations. Similarly for other languages, if on a smaller scale, the long-established writing has come to be less than satisfactory. The languages now having adequate phonemic writing are those which have recently adopted a new alphabet or reformed the spelling.

To correct the deficiency, individuals and organizations have developed phonetic alphabets, either for spelling reform, in English

quite unsuccessful, or for special purposes such as language learning. Nonalphabetic systems with symbols descriptive of articulations, such as that of Alexander Melville Bell, have not found favour, although some such symbols are used for teaching the deaf.

Teaching and Learning Pronunciation.—It is only late learning situations that call for comment: the correction of speech defects, the replacement of a class-inferior by a class-superior pronunciation, and the acquisition of a new language. The last may be taken as typical.

The new language learner must use some kind of pronunciation; apparently it is impossible, perhaps with rare exceptions, for one to hold in mind a language form without an aural image of the form as whole, even if his only practical concern is a reading knowledge of the new language. It is only trivially more difficult to use a reasonably good pronunciation of the language being learned than it is to get by, as many have done, with an imagery of pronunciation based on the language of the learner.

When the learner expects to use the language in the ordinary way it is more readily apparent to him that pronunciation is important. The proximity of England to the continent and the use of English in former British colonies undoubtedly accounts for the fact that more apparatus is available for teaching-learning an RP type of pronunciation than for any other standard pronunciation of English. Techniques for teaching the pronunciation of English and many other languages have been enormously developed in the United States since World War II. (*See also* FOREIGN LANGUAGES, TEACHING OF.)

Any plan for teaching pronunciation tends to be dominated by a phonemic approach, primarily concerned with making the distinctions necessary for intelligibility; or a phonetic approach, aiming at a pronunciation that will satisfy the native ear. The difference is more in the materials supplied as teaching aids than in the actual instruction supplied by a master who can fill in the detail for the one plan and the synthesis for the other. Use can be made, especially for unusual languages, of linguistically naïve native informants, the theoretical control being in the hands of a linguist who may have more understanding of the system of the language than skill in speaking it. Phonetic alphabets are in general use, although neither in all cases necessary nor by any means to be taken as having any magic power. For mass instruction, recordings are now generally available, their utility greatly increased when the apparatus provides for recording-playback of the student's imitation for immediate comparison.

Modern Investigation of Pronunciation.—The study of the distribution of linguistic forms over an area is known as linguistic, or dialect, geography. (*See* DIALECT GEOGRAPHY.) The usual systematic technique is direct investigation by trained field workers, who go into selected communities and interview typical informants according to a fixed scheme, recording the findings in phonetic notation. Postal questionnaires may be used rather than, or as supplementary to, direct interviews. Tape recordings are usually made when possible, to serve either as the basis for phonetic interpretation or as a supplementary check. The number of communities investigated, the number of informants used in a community, and the length and coverage of the work sheets vary according to special conditions, especially the number of investigators and amount of funds and time available. Findings are shown on maps or in tables.

Large-scale investigations are rarely limited to data on pronunciation, and the number of strictly phonetic items on a work sheet may be small. But as a rule (*e.g.,* in the *Linguistic Atlas of New England*) the phonetic recording of morphological, syntactical, and lexical data is trustworthy and can be used as data on pronunciation. The European atlases have been primarily concerned with local dialects. American investigations, necessarily concerned more with local variation of the standard language, include some cultured informants.

Some variations on the general plan of investigation are noteworthy. One is the quantitative investigation of a limited number of items with many randomly or systematically selected informants in a community, the results expressed in percentages. Another is the use of a single informant on the basis of whose speech the pattern of pronunciation, the phonemic system, and other features of the dialect or language are described. The last method, particularly useful when informants are hard to come by and more frequently used for individual studies than in large-scale undertakings, has its extreme form in the investigator's use of himself as informant. Another, *Phonometrie,* is the instrumental analysis of field tape recordings and measurement of certain features on the basis of which can be made fine quantitative distinctions quite impossible to ear analysis and useful for marking significant boundaries. *See* also PHONETICS; LINGUISTICS.

BIBLIOGRAPHY.—D. Jones, *Pronunciation of English,* 4th ed. rev. (1956); J. S. Kenyon, *American Pronunciation,* 10th ed. (1958); A. J. Ellis, *On Early English Pronunciation* (1869–89); H. Kökeritz, *Shakespeare's Pronunciation* (1953); M. Grammont, *Traité pratique de prononciation française* (1954); T. Navarro Tomás, *Manual de pronunciación española,* 5th ed. (1957); T. Siebs, *Deutsche Hochsprache; Bühnenaussprache* (1961); A. Camilli, *Pronuncia e grafia dell'italiano,* 2nd ed. rev. (1947). (L. S. H.)

PROOFREADING, the process of correcting for the press printed proofs of articles, books or other matter before publication. That the proofreader's profession goes back to the early days of printing is proved by reference to a corrector of the press in a book printed by R. Pynson in 1530 (the word proofreader seems originally U.S.). A Pynson contract of 1499 also held the author finally responsible for correction of proofs. In modern practice proofs are made first in galley (usually three or four pages unbroken on a long sheet), the first rough proof usually being corrected by the printer before being sent to the publisher and ultimately to the author. Page proofs and galley proofs frequently bear queries that show the proofreader's skill involves not only seeing that there is an exact correspondence between the copy given to the printer and its printed form, but also the catching of errors of fact. Lawsuits between printers and authors, and lists of errata, author's apologies and complaints at not seeing proof in printed books were common through the 15th, 16th, 17th and 18th centuries and are not unknown in modern publication.

Marks commonly used in proofreading follow:

℘	Delete	*em*	Em dash
ℨ	Delete and close up	*en*	En dash
℈	Reverse	;/	Insert semicolon
⌣	Close up	⊙	Insert colon and en quad
#	Insert space	⊙	Insert period and en quad
¶	Paragraph	?/	Insert interrogation point
▢	Indent one em	ⓟ	Query to author
⊏	Move to left	⌢	Use ligature
⊐	Move to right	ⓢⓟ	Spell out
⊔	Lower	*tr*	Transpose
⊓	Elevate	*wf*	Wrong font
∧	Insert marginal addition	*bf*	Set in **bold face** type
⋎	Even space	*rom*	Set in (roman) type
✕	Broken letter	*ital*	Set in *italic* type
↓	Push down space	*caps*	Set in CAPITALS
═	Straighten line	*sc*	Set in SMALL CAPITALS
‖	Align type	*lc*	Set in lower case
⋀	Insert comma	⃫	Lower-case letter
⋎	Insert apostrophe	*stet*	Let it stand
⋎	Insert quotes	*no ¶*	Run in same paragraph
=/	Hyphen	*ld*	Insert lead between lines

BIBLIOGRAPHY.—Percy Simpson, *Proof-reading in the Sixteenth, Seventeenth, and Eighteenth Centuries,* Oxford Books on Bibliography, vol. 1 (1935). R. A. Hewitt, *Style for Print and Proof-correcting* (1957), a practical guide. Other guides include: Oxford University Press, *Rules for Compositors and Readers,* 36th ed. (1952); F. H. Collins, *Authors' and Printers' Dictionary,* 10th ed. (1956); British Standards Institution, *Leaflet 1219* (1958); University of Chicago Press, *A Manual of Style,* 11th ed. (1949); U.S. Government Printing Office, *Style Manual,* rev. ed. (1959).

PROOF SPIRIT, the term applied to those standard mixtures of ethyl alcohol and water that form the basis of customs and excise duties in many parts of the world. The term is variously defined. In the United States proof spirit, by federal regulations, is an alcoholic liquor one-half of whose volume is alcohol of a specific gravity of 0.7939 at 60° F (15.6° C), referred to water at 60° F as unity. At 60° F, proof spirit has a specific gravity of 0.93426 (*in vacuo*); 100 parts by volume of the liquor consists of 50 parts of absolute alcohol and 53.73 parts of water; the difference of the sum of the parts of alcohol and water and the resulting 100 parts of proof spirit is caused by the contraction that takes place when alcohol and water are mixed. The specially designed hydrometers used in determining the alcoholic strength of aqueous solutions read (at 60° F) 0 for water, 100 for proof spirit (also called 100 proof), and 200 for absolute alcohol.

In Great Britain the Spirits Act of 1816 gave for the first time a legal definition of proof spirit as "that which at the temperature of 51° F weighs exactly $\frac{12}{13}$ of an equal measure of distilled water." Subsequently, the temperature of the water was also established at 51° F (10.6° C). Later investigation showed that at 60° F proof spirit has a specific gravity of 0.91976, compared with water at the same temperature, and that it contains 49.28% by weight or 57.10% by volume of ethyl alcohol.

Spirits at strengths other than proof may be described as containing a percentage of proof spirit or as being overproof or underproof. The percentage of proof spirit is the number of volumes of proof spirit that can be obtained from 100 volumes of the mixture. Thus at 50° F, 100 volumes of absolute alcohol if diluted with water to proof strength give 175.35 volumes. It is therefore said to contain 175.35% proof spirit, to be 175.35 proof, or to have a strength of 75.35% overproof. (D. G. Z.; X.)

PROPAGANDA is the dissemination of information—facts, arguments, rumours, half-truths, or lies—to influence public opinion. As a systematic effort to persuade, it is an act of advocacy in mass communication, involving the making of deliberately one-sided statements to a mass audience. In this, it is not necessarily deceptive, although it is well known that one-sided presentations often spread and nourish false images by emphasizing only the good points of one position and the bad points of another. Hence one aim of public policy in popular government is to maintain a public forum in which the competing propagandas of political parties and interest organizations correct one another's lies and exaggerations. Although the fact of propaganda activity is old, the term is comparatively modern, deriving from the name of the organization set up in 1622 by the Roman Catholic Church to carry on missionary work, the Congregation for the Propagation of the Faith (*propaganda fide*).

Propaganda can be distinguished from other acts of mass communication with which it is closely allied. On the approach of a forest fire or a tidal wave, whole communities may dissolve into panic-stricken crowds or mobs whose rumours and cries are collective excitement, not propaganda. In the context of the society in which it occurs, the words reiterating traditional legends in a public ceremonial do not imply advocacy. Similarly, community indoctrination of the young with established beliefs, faiths, and loyalties is not ordinarily thought of as propaganda. However, it is advocacy to editorialize or to select the content of news reports, histories, textbooks, and other channels of communication for the purpose of influencing attitudes on controversial issues. (For some early examples, *see* HISTORY: *Roman Historians.*) When a government distributes a pamphlet on the care and feeding of babies, for example, the act is probably informative and instructive, not propagandistic, unless there is doubt about the authenticity of what is said, or the pamphlet is used for other than instructive ends—as winning goodwill for an official of the government. It is inquiry, not propaganda, to analyze contro-

(RIGHT) CULVER PICTURES, (ABOVE) JOHN R. FREEMAN & CO.

(Right) "Common Sense," published Jan. 10, 1776, by Thomas Paine, decisively influenced revolutionary activity in the colonies. (Above) Three-quarters of a century later, in 1846, a dispute between America and Britain over the boundary of the Oregon territory evoked derisive cartoon in "Punch" captioned, "What? You Young Yankee-Noodle, Strike Your Own Father!"

COMMON SENSE.

Of the Origin and Design of GOVERNMENT *in general, with concise Remarks on the* ENGLISH CONSTITUTION.

SOME writers have so confounded society with government, as to leave little or no distinction between them; whereas, they are not only different, but have different origins. Society is produced by our wants, and government by our wickedness; the former promotes our happiness *positively* by uniting our affections, the latter *negatively* by restraining our vices. The one encourages intercourse, the other creates distinctions. The first is a patron, the last a punisher.

Society in every state is a blessing, but Government even in its best state is but a necessary evil; in its worst state an intolerable one: for when we suffer, or are exposed to the same miseries *by a Government,* which we might expect in a country *without Government,* our calamity is heightened by

B   reflect-

stitutions to moderate innovations or revolutionary change.

In political affairs it has usually been evident to the leaders of revolutions that they can greatly enhance their chances of success, as well as save soldiers and money, by using propaganda to win support for and induce obedience to a new regime. The foundation was laid for large and enduring empires when conquerors learned to convert rather than to exterminate the conquered.

Propaganda, being both elusive and cheap, is a favoured instrument of political oppositionists. The unification of Germany, Italy, and of every modern state was preceded and accompanied by the fervent promotion of national sentiment, often by persecuted minorities. The propagandists of social revolution have developed modern methods of persuasion to the highest pitch, working especially through party and auxiliary organizations.

In communities where the pursuit of knowledge is accepted for its own sake as well as in the service of practical ends, scientists and scholars have organized to win support for programs that combine substantial public and private assistance to research with nonintervention in the conduct of inquiry. Associations that speak in the name of science and learning often try to mobilize sentiment for or against the use of knowledge in military or other operations.

Where the production and distribution of wealth is in the hands of a private sector of society, the use of propaganda by organizations of commerce, industry, agriculture, and labour is a prominent feature of public life. In a dynamic economy the effective rules of the market, including the scope of government regulation and enterprise, are affected by the success or failure of promotional campaigns to influence third parties to give support to particular competitors. (*See also* LOBBYING.)

As interdependence increases with growing industrialization and urbanization, and as the risk rises of accidental death or injury and of infection from polluted air, water, soil, and food, propaganda operations strive to expand the jurisdiction and scale of the welfare state as it touches the safety, health, and comfort of the population.

With the expansion of industry and technology, the number of groups skilled in emerging occupations, the professions, and the arts is greatly multiplied. At the same time they come into conflict with those who have obsolete or obsolescent skills. All these groups rely heavily on propaganda to obtain training facilities, to attract talent, and to achieve favourable opportunities for employment. In these sectors, as elsewhere, conflicting and facilitating propagandas aid in delimiting the role of government in education and the arts.

As the extended-family characteristic of agrarian and folk societies gives way to smaller family units, public policy is affected by propaganda operations for or against the liberalization of divorce, the use of birth control, the protection of children from cruelty and neglect, and other problems of family relations.

In recent times, particularly, propaganda has been employed to upgrade the position of minority groups and depressed castes and classes, and also to exalt the image of particular individuals in public esteem.

At one time the great proselytizing religious sects of Buddhism, Zoroastrianism, Christianity, and Islam sought to expand at one another's expense. (*See* MISSIONS.) More recently, the rise of

versial doctrines for the sake of sharing enlightenment. For an example of such analysis, *see* POLITICAL PHILOSOPHY (*see also* LIBERALISM; CONSERVATISM). Private arguments among intimates are not propaganda unless they are part of a campaign to spread controversial viewpoints, which they often are.

The mass audience with which the propagandist is ultimately concerned is not only characterized by size, but by the impersonality and shallowness of the tie between the communicator and his audience. This is typical of advertising (*q.v.*) as paid publicity. It includes much, though not all, of the field of public relations (*q.v.*), whose aim is to manage the exposures of an individual or a group in order to obtain attitudes of effective support. Advertising, public relations, and propaganda often employ the same techniques and strategies and, operating in closely related fields, may often overlap. Since any act may influence mass opinion, an important part of total policy is calculating and managing the psychological impact of every policy. The most comprehensive term for this frame of reference is "propaganda" or "communication" policy. Directed against an enemy or opponent in wartime, or in cold war, this is "psychological" warfare (for history, examples, and techniques, *see* PSYCHOLOGICAL WARFARE).

The Propaganda Process.—In examining any specific propaganda campaign or describing the total flow of propaganda in any historical or contemporary setting, several questions arise. Who are the individuals or groups who initiate and execute these operations? What objectives are they trying to achieve? What are the boundaries of the situations in which they operate? With what potential assets (and with what constraining liabilities) do they begin? By what strategies are the objectives sought? With what outcomes and effects?

Participants.—In contemporary totalitarian states, the controllers of all permissible communication are governmental officials or the leaders of monopolistic political parties. At the other extreme are the pluralistic states, in which local officials often have great independence of central government, and in which competing political parties are supplemented by diversely controlled media of communication and by a network of pressure organizations recruited in varying degree from all save the least advantaged strata of society.

Objectives.—The objectives sought by the use of the propaganda instrument range from the protection of current values and in-successful secular political movements has inspired attempts to cultivate the ecumenical spirit among believers.

Whatever the objective pursued, no one denies that the success or failure of propaganda initiatives can usually be predicted from the assets at the disposal of the rivals. These assets are not exclusively economic. It counts heavily if the sponsors are politically potent, popular, upright, and respected. The crucial assets may be youth and vigour, especially when joined with an enlightened view of the problems at stake, and skill in communication. Or the crucial asset may be control of the government, or the power of censorship.

Propaganda may pursue distinctive objectives, or serve as an instrument of other policy aims. In foreign policy, for example, a distinctive objective at a given time may be in the field of propaganda policy, such as winning the friendship of the rank and file of the population of a foreign power. Friendship may be sought directly by news and comment, which are the instrumentalities on which propagandists most rely. In addition, cultural, educational, and scientific exchanges, and goodwill tours of outstanding athletes and entertainers may be employed. Other policy means may also be put at the service of the friendship objective. The diplomatic tool may be applied by upgrading a ministry to the status of an embassy. The economic tool may take the form of loans and subsidies. The military instrument may make new weapons available for defense.

Effects.—If a propaganda campaign is to have any chance of success it must at least reach the focus of attention of target audiences. Even under totalitarian conditions audiences are not altogether passive puppets. They may partially frustrate the official line by listening to or viewing official programs in a state of weary detachment, and by inventing or exchanging rumours at variance with the government's view.

Since the impact of propaganda is not necessarily immediate, any serious appraisal must be prepared to examine its middle- and long-range effects on perspective and behaviour. Not the least important impact is on the propagandists themselves. A leader may begin by entertaining private doubts about what he is saying, and end by believing it. This "feedback effect" may undermine his judgment of reality, and culminate in unexpected losses of power.

The Determiners of Propaganda.—Any provisional account of the propaganda process in particular campaigns, or in the aggregate, implies a comprehensive theory of causes and consequences. Systematic scientific studies of propaganda have been

THE GRANGER COLLECTION

THEATRICAL POSTER ADVERTISING A PERFORMANCE OF "UNCLE TOM'S CABIN," 1881, A DRAMATIC ANTISLAVERY WORK THAT BROUGHT TO PUBLIC ATTENTION THE PLIGHT OF THE NEGRO IN THE SOUTH AND THAT IS COUNTED AMONG THE CAUSES OF THE CIVIL WAR

closely identified with research on linguistics and the analysis of nonmaterial culture, the growth of psychoanalysis and other schools of psychology, and the rise of information theory in engineering, neurology, and genetics.

The most general conclusion about propaganda is that it increases whenever the equilibrium of society is threatened or upset, whether by political revolution, technological changes, marked population shifts due to mass emigration or immigration, or by rapidly rising or falling birth or death rates, or by other religious, social, or economic innovations or collapses. And it decreases with the restoration of the imperiled equilibrium or with the emergence of a new level of adjustment. This broad hypothesis can be made more specific in order to account for the use of propaganda, rather than coercion, on those occasions when social equilibrium is in danger. Viewing the available records of human culture it appears that both the practice and the study of propaganda are connected with the rise of urban civilization, notably in the valleys of the Nile, of the Tigris-Euphrates, and of the Indus. With the advent of cities the traditional ties of family and tribe were weakened to the advantage of territorially organized political communities, whether city-states, empires, or nations. The enduring impact of propaganda was increased by the institutionalization of civil government, and by the invention of writing, the making of records, and the growth of scribes in the city environment.

The first surviving studies of propaganda were manuals on state security. The use of mass means of communication for military purposes was advised in *The Art of War* in the 5th century B.C. Sun Tzu wrote that "In night fighting beacons and drums are largely used; in day fighting, a great number of banners and flags, and the enemy's eyes and ears are confounded." In the East Indian classic of statecraft, Kautilya's *Arthaśāstra*, it is noted that "Astrologers and other followers of the King should infuse spirit into the army by pointing out the impregnable nature of the array of his army." Secret agents should circulate among the enemy, spreading rumours of their certain defeat. From Greco-Roman times come handbooks on how to win an argument or even how to win an election. The literature of propaganda includes manuals on converting the heathen, indoctrinating the young, instigating subversion, preventing subversion, obtaining gifts, and making sales. With the expansion of the social and behavioural sciences in comparatively recent times, "how to do it" manuals have been supplemented by scientific researches on the place of mass persuasion in the social process.

Propaganda—"the dissemination of information to influence public opinion," an "act of advocacy in mass communication"— has long (if not always) been used by inspired protagonists of change, from proponents of innovations in religious observances to advocates of lengthening the school day to supporters of public water supplies and sewerage systems, and by their opponents.

FEMALE LOBBYISTS.

THE BETTMANN ARCHIVE

SUFFRAGETTE PROPAGANDISTS IN THE U.S. SENATE LOBBY, c. 1880

More and more it has been used consciously and with planning not only in the cause of revolution but, for example, in the introduction of the comprehensive school in Great Britain; in the American Medical Association's campaign against Medicare in the United States, and organized labour's campaign to support it; and in attempts to stamp out hooliganism in Hungary, Poland, and Czechoslovakia. It has formed the basis of campaigns to abolish capital punishment in the United Kingdom and New Zealand, to enforce traffic regulations in Argentina, and to promote the use of fertilizer in Iran. Fund-raising campaigns for churches and charities, the civil rights movement in the United States, the attempts to defend the Unilateral Declaration of Independence in Southern Rhodesia—all have employed propaganda as part of action for social ends.

In modern history the growth of industrialism has provided one of the greatest incentives to employ propaganda as an instrument with which to defend established patterns of culture or to spread innovation. Advertising, supported by propaganda (advocating, for example, the doctrine of Manifest Destiny [*q.v.*]), fanned the spirit of speculation which fed the reservoirs of capital upon which the expansion of commerce and industry depended. The advantages of large-scale production could be realized by the successful stimulation of consumer demand, and skilful and massive promotion stimulated hundreds of millions of buyers to change their taste in clothes, interior decoration, personal adornment, cooking, and amusement.

Since propaganda depends in part on accessible networks of communication, industrialism also facilitates propaganda by spreading literacy and general education, and by "the communications revolution" in mass media. In free countries the media themselves generate incentives to engage in and to foster propaganda, since some types of controversy stimulate circulation and circulation boosts revenue from the sale of space or time.

Other powerful modern incentives to the employment of propaganda have included the rise of Fascism and Nazism, the rise and spread of Soviet Communism and of Chinese Communism, and, markedly after World War II, the burgeoning nationalism of the newly emerging countries of the world.

The sheer size and heterogeneity of a population is of significance for propaganda. Even in totalitarian states a vast labour of internal persuasion is essential to overcome the bonds of attachment to the old, or the sentiments of fear, hatred, and confusion at the prospect of a new way of life. In Soviet Russia (after 1921) the full orchestra of poster, broadcast, and lecture was mobilized in a series of gigantic campaigns on behalf of literacy, proper care of tractors, and elementary habits of personal hygiene. In the latter 1960s the youth of Communist China were mobilized as the Red Guard in a massive campaign to wipe out all traces of Western influence in a "Great Proletarian Cultural Revolution."

The challenge of a new way of life has faced millions of the earth's population, especially since the end of World War II.

Propaganda has been a principal means of inaugurating new nation-states in the ruins of the colonial empires, of attracting aid from relatively modernized powers for the benefit of the underdeveloped nations, and of creating a sense of nationalism and overcoming internal predispositions unfavourable to nation-building. In many new or reviving countries, the balance has moved precariously between reliance on mass persuasion and resort to coercive means to expel foreign influence from every sector of society, as in Communist China. The revolution of rising expectations has often been exploited by the propaganda of rival groups to create the recurring crises of disappointment which have eventually culminated in take-overs after the model of totalitarian states. Persuasive methods have been best able to survive where traditional institutions, often as modified during the colonial period, have come to include institutions of freedom, whether free government, free market, free education, or free religious proselyting. Contrast, for instance, the early postindependence years of India and of many African states.

Summing up, the direction and volume of propaganda during any period depends upon the changing balance of incentives to influence or manipulate public opinion. Such factors as these are relevant: the intensity of the determination on the part of propagandists to introduce or to discourage change; the availability of mass media and the prevailing level of literacy and general education; the degree of discontent with the old and the difficulty of the new; the number of persons asked to change or to refrain from changing; and the depth of devotion to persuasion in place of coercion. Whatever arouses controversy is likely to foster propaganda until the incentives which sustain it are reduced and the rival methods of social action are tried, or discontent is dissipated without result (that is, catharsis occurs); or a new positive adjustment is made in prevailing social practice.

Strategy.—In view of the importance of strategy and tactics particular attention is given to principles that have been formulated. Proper strategy depends upon the overall frame of policy and the circumstances which favour or stand in the way of success.

When a comprehensive plan of social change is pursued by peaceful means, a major problem of strategic planning is whether to expedite success by making concessions of detail. At one time in China the Jesuits dressed like native scholars as a means of modifying the strangeness of the Christian mode of living. The pope decided to forego immediate advantages and put a stop to those practices. In the absence of unified command, Marxian Socialists split into many branches over the nature and timing of revisions. Leading revisionists softened or abandoned the doctrine of violent class struggle and entered electoral or cabinet coalitions; for example, in Germany and France in the 1920s and 1930s.

A related question of strategy is how far to concentrate upon the teaching and preaching of doctrine, and how far to go in using auxiliary appeals. Lenin insisted upon the necessity of propaganda which he defined as indoctrination, and also of agitation, by which he meant the exploitation of concrete grievances (for a succinct account of the strategy *see* BOLSHEVIKS). In foreign missionary work, auxiliary activities, such as schools and child health clinics, became standard means of providing an indirect approach to prospective converts. Buddhist missions always encouraged charity, but it is reported that in China the translation of the Buddhist canon played a more important part than good works, since the translation aroused the curiosity of the scholar class.

Sometimes the task of propaganda is to prepare the way for

(Above) Vans forming into a file in London for a Conservative political campaign in the provinces, 1907. (Right) Title page of J. K. Hardie's newspaper, the "Labour Leader," during the political campaign of 1895

DAVID LOW, LONDON EVENING STANDARD

DAVID LOW CARTOON OF HITLER AS SANTA CLAUS, PUBLISHED IN THE LON-
DON "EVENING STANDARD" IN 1938, SATIRIZED THE PEACE THAT FOLLOWED
THE MUNICH CONFERENCE BETWEEN HITLER AND PRIME MINISTER NEVILLE
CHAMBERLAIN

activities which, if fully disclosed in advance, would unquestionably fail. Before the seizure of power in Germany, the National
Socialist strategy was to prevent a combination of Socialists, Communists, and conservatives which would have stalled their advance.
Once the National Socialists were in power, the problem was transferred to the arena of world politics and became that of forestalling
joint action by West and East while the country rearmed, occupied
the Rhineland, absorbed Austria, partitioned Czechoslovakia, and
began war against Poland. (For an account of the Nazi's exploitation of propaganda see NATIONAL SOCIALISM, especially the section
Psychological Methods and Theoretical Aims.) Historians of the
American propaganda of secession and independence from Great
Britain, such as Evarts Greene, commented upon the skill of the
leadership in carrying along many moderate persons who, though
not desiring independence, had cooperated with the radicals to
such an extent that they could not effectively withdraw.

The correlation of propaganda inside the frame of totalitarian
policy involves many fundamental and, at first sight, paradoxical
problems. One long-run objective of totalitarian policy is the
substitution of ritual and ceremony for discussion and persuasion,
hence of propaganda. A totalitarian state is a command state that
swallows the whole society. The task of managing the media of
communication under such conditions is to foster a world of fantasy wherein the hero at the top of the pyramid is the champion
of all against the encircling forces of evil which, though powerful,
cannot ultimately prevail. The propagandist does not use current
happenings for news and comment, but for sermons and fables
adorning the dogma as infallibly interpreted by the ruling machine. Only state- or party-controlled newspapers, books, and
periodicals are permitted; all movies, plays, and radio and television broadcasts must support the propaganda message; and participation in parades, mass demonstrations, and political indoctrination sessions is compulsory. (For one sidelight on newspapers
see NEWSPAPER: *Germany: The Hitler-Goebbels Press.*) Since
commands from above allow no answering criticism from beneath,
self-assertion is repressed or turned against the lower strata or
the outside world. In such a garrison-police state leaders live
in perpetual anxiety of losing control and require the reassuring
balm of ritual adulation. All this is in vivid contrast to the operation of a free society which thrives on the clash of news and
views.

Tactics.—The tactical problems of the propagandist are to adapt
to the limits imposed by strategy. This implies that some policies,
persons, groups, and institutions must be presented in a favourable
light, while others are put at a disadvantage. Appropriate audiences and channels must be chosen to obtain the desired effects.
An organization capable of the degree of devotion and expertness
called for by the objectives sought must be assembled. The
choices open to the tactician are ultimately to disseminate, to

withhold, or to modify a statement; to use, omit, or block a channel; to select or reject a person.

In deciding what to disseminate, the perspectives of the audience must be given careful consideration. The significant perspectives include conceptions of the self as identified with particular
cultures, social classes, interest groups, and types of personality. For each component of the self of an individual or a group,
various perspectives express value demands and expectations. In
terms of cultural identity, for example, it is elementary for a
skilful propagandist to show that his client loves and admires
Southerners, for example, if the audience is Southern and that
he is devoted to the Westerners, if the audience is Western. In
addressing any group, the propagandist is fortunate whose principal can be presented as having the same status as the audience.
The widest scope, no doubt, is in the assertion of common interests,
since the network of potential interests cuts across other social
lines. Similarly the propagandist whose principal has highly personal appeal is able to exploit the charismatic predispositions of
the audience. For each group the propagandist can emphasize the
points that put his principal in the best light as a defender or
extender of cherished values. Furthermore, it is possible to
mobilize the expectations of the audience, as did the Spaniard
conquistadors who seemed to fulfill an accepted prophecy when
they appeared in Mexico (*see* MONTEZUMA II; QUETZALCOATL).
The Spaniards were also favoured by a sense of crisis that was
widely shared among the politically important elements of pre-
Columbian society in America.

In deciding what to withhold, as distinguished from what to
disseminate, the perspectives of the audience are crucially relevant
to the tactician. If in a U.S. Information Agency target area the
image of the United States is a nation of millionaires, documentary films of all components of American life may be substituted
for films that depict the wealth of the nation. If the United States
is perceived as materialistic and crude, the propagandists may
play down the technological eminence of the U.S. and send art
exhibits, symphony orchestras, and dance companies to try to
change the image. Developing countries may resent the stereotypes of themselves that they find in industrially advanced societies, where they are often expected to be naked savages who live
in tents or huts. Hence they attempt to reach the audiences of
the industrial world with propaganda that leaves out the traditional
clichés and shows dams under construction for electric power stations, and offices or high rise apartment buildings of glass and concrete.

In deciding whether to remain silent or to reply in response to
an accusation, it is essential for the tactician to bear in mind
that the pattern of conduct deemed appropriate or honourable
varies widely according to the nature and source of the accusation, and the social context in which it is made. In some societies, only statements made by a member of the ruling class are
taken with enough seriousness to warrant reply. Sometimes an
accused leader, if innocent, is expected to display the utmost indignation in denying accusations. Elsewhere the badge of innocence is calmness. In many cases it is difficult to judge how much
influence an adverse whispering campaign may have. When Pres.
Woodrow Wilson was the target of a campaign against his character, he declined to take any notice of it on the ground that it was
false and that all who knew him understood it was false. He
thought that it would give more currency and dignity to the
"smear" if he replied in public than if he kept silent.

So far as facts are concerned, it is generally agreed that some
facts cannot be successfully concealed from an audience. Hence
it does less damage to release bad news promptly than to appear
both unreliable and inefficient. Railroads learned to release news
of accidents and the airlines followed suit. Often there are facts
that are extremely disagreeable to both sides if disclosed. In
bitter controversies it is customary for propagandists to try to
obtain from intelligence services material that can be used privately to intimidate an adversary from spreading material that
stigmatizes one's own candidate or cause.

Innumerable devices are at the command of the working propagandist for nullifying statements. Thus, a Soviet spokesman re-

marked that the Nazis had created a new category of war casualty, the "slightly killed." Wit, humour, calmness, the casting of doubt upon sources, the combining of favourable and unfavourable news, and the playing down of unfavourable statements are standard ways of modifying adverse references. Also there are ample means of inflating favourable statements by emphasis and elaboration.

A continuing tactical problem is how much to praise the self and how much to condemn rivals or enemies. Commercial competitors for the same large market usually refrain from attacking one another on the theory that doubt is cast upon the type as well as the brand of product. Unlike business propaganda, political propaganda tends to present politics as a drama in which the forces of good and evil stand opposed to one another. Revolutionary or urgent reform movements commonly try to induce a sense of guilt among opponents and self-righteousness among adherents, a technique used with marked success by, for example, Thomas Paine during the American Revolution (*see* AMERICAN LITERATURE). This tactic may succeed in provoking conflicts of conscience, since agreed value standards are applied to the disadvantage of the old and the advantage of the new.

In order to reach the mass audience, propagandists rely upon every medium of communication—oral, printed, pictorial, plastic, musical, or dramatic. Every new channel is promptly laid hold of. When the art of printing from movable type appeared in Europe, the printed word began at once to overtake oral media as a principal means of persuasion. In the 20th century the motion picture, radio, and television helped restore the spoken word to its former eminent position. Communication effects are sometimes sought with the aid of physical acts or devices which are not usually employed for the purpose. The act of killing is no ordinary method of communication, yet killing is spoken of as "propaganda of the deed" when political assassinations are carried out as a means of affecting attitudes. The building of the Berlin wall and the staging of marches and demonstrations are acts of propaganda.

In selecting media the propagandist keeps in mind considerations similar to those which apply to the choice of statements. If the problem is to win the support of the rich, powerful, and well-born, favourable mention in organs which they look down upon is no asset. If the aim is to win confidence among the masses, the task is to enlist the leaders and media which they trust. In some nonindustrial societies many members of the upper class may have been educated in other countries—in Japan, Western Europe, the U.S.S.R., or the U.S. They may look down upon the vernacular press and dismiss the authority of those who have not been educated abroad. Hence in the past the communication path of a rising local group in Asia, Africa, or Latin America might lead from Calcutta, Johannesburg, or Lima to London, Paris, or New York, and back to Calcutta, Johannesburg, or Lima.

In the choice of media, time considerations are important since if aims can be accomplished over long periods the more permanent media, such as scholarly books, magazines, and schools, have a significant role. If the goals are short run, the tactician must employ the existing communications network and rely on fast rather than slow media.

The audience of any established channel of communication has selected itself on the basis of predispositions which cannot be disregarded. During World War II, U.S. broadcasters to Germany quickly learned that crisis audiences differ from other kinds. Clandestine listeners who had risked their lives to hear news and comment from the outside world were furious when they tuned in on entertainment. Again, an audience expecting entertainment is irritated if it is given only news (or propaganda).

In the choice of personnel for propaganda work, one factor is emotional involvement. The history of propagandas of religion and revolution make it clear that dangerous propagandas need to be in devoted hands. Where less sacrificial considerations are at stake professional talent can be employed (in the same way that a lawyer takes over the claims of a client, not because the claim is right but because the client has a right to be heard). Political parties and movements have sought to develop or attract personnel that embody both qualifications, often most successfully:

reference has been made to Thomas Paine in the American Revolution; Nazism recruited a dedicated expert in Josef Goebbels (*q.v.*). But more and more frequently, in the United States at least, political parties, like private individuals, corporations, and associations, have employed professional public relations counsels or agencies to plan and direct propaganda and other aspects of their campaigns.

The 20th century has been notable for the rapid application of the social and psychological sciences to the problems of propaganda technique. It is standard operating procedure to pretest posters, labels, slogans, and other details before they are brought to the notice of the eventual audience. A pretest uses a small sample group. Posttests are utilized in the hope of evaluating the effectiveness of propaganda messages or channels. These tests are of the utmost diversity. They may be based on brief or prolonged interviews, upon the participant observation of behaviour, upon the analysis of a wide range of responses such as voting, giving, buying, selling, investing, joining, seceding, boycotting, striking, or attending. Methods have been devised to describe quantitatively the contents of the media of communication. Research is also done upon the control pattern that prevails in different countries, such as the degree of government monopoly or regulation, of private monopoly or competition.

Control.—It is impossible to scan the long history of attempts to control propaganda without being impressed by the power that men attribute to words. The fear of propaganda is fed by apprehension of the magical potency of language for the infliction of harm. These primitive attitudes continue to be an undercurrent in civilizations where the dominant attitude about language is not superstitious, but detached and managerial. The only control problems that disturb a modern totalitarian regime are questions of expediency in the realm of power. In nations where the dignity

"TIME" COVER BY ARTZYBASHEFF, © 1962, TIME INC.

THE COVER OF "TIME", AUG. 31, 1962, EXEMPLIFIES PROPAGANDA AGAINST THE CONSTRUCTION OF THE BERLIN WALL BY EAST GERMANY

WIDE WORLD

BUDDHIST MONK BURNS HIMSELF TO DEATH IN SAIGON (1963) TO PROTEST ALLEGED PERSECUTION OF BUDDHISTS BY NGO DINH DIEM'S GOVERNMENT, AN ULTIMATE ACT OF PROPAGANDA

the end of civil war. The thrust of recent discussions of international law and of treaty agreements has been in the direction of defining permissible limits on the use of managed communications for "aggressive" purposes. Among the classical terror campaigns were the synchronizing of mass media and of fifth column organizations to spread fright, suspicion, and confusion as a prelude to the seizure of power by the Nazis in Vienna and Czechoslovakia on the eve of World War II.

In internal affairs there are differences of opinion about the boundary lines of "incitement." What should public authorities do about statements provocative enough to arouse the anger of members of an audience whose religious, ethnic, or political sentiments are affronted? One view is that restrictions must be imposed when there is "clear and present danger" to public order. A more daring conception is that it is the purpose of a free society to maintain a kind of public order where coercive acts are not permitted in response to words, however offensive.

In time of war, popular governments are compelled to recognize that statements circulated by an enemy are part of the enemy's coercive activities. But what of statements uttered by members of the commonwealth who have no connection with a foreign power? Defenders of freedom assert that repressive measures against domestic propaganda must be kept at a minimum, with reliance for the protection of the body politic put upon the positive advocacy of the majority viewpoint, coupled with the disclosure of parallels, intended or unintended, between domestic propaganda and the line taken by the enemy. It is conceded that, without remarkably successful civic training in self-restraint, the police and the courts, to say nothing of the ordinary citizen, may be unable to tolerate dissent in the midst of crisis.

Experience gained in attempting to understand and in some measure to guide the evolution of modernizing states has drawn renewed attention to the preconditions of a body politic wherein a free forum is protected by lawful coercion. The timing of transitional policies in such a state seems to require that the advantages

of man is upheld, the issues are more complex, since the institutions appropriate to a free society include freedom of information, propaganda, and political decision. Freedom is part of the respect due to the individual and is a condition of enlightenment and democracy. It is intolerable to totalitarianism, under which freedom of speech, freedom of the press, and free assembly are suppressed.

But freedom of utterance is nowhere without qualification. No free society fails to use community coercion against some forms of speech on the ground that the results endanger important values without corresponding gain. In controlling propaganda the aim is to safeguard news and comment without permitting incitement, which is an act of coercion. What shall be prohibited and by whom presents one of the most complicated and vexing problems that face free societies. (See CIVIL RIGHTS AND LIBERTIES.)

A consensus has arisen about the more extreme situations in which words become part of a coercive act. It is incitement when uniformed, armed, and trained formations are organized and begin to act. The appearance of these movements signifies that public order is dissolving and can be restored only by bringing coercion back into the hands of organized government. This may, of course, be deferred until

(LEFT) MARC RIBOUD FROM MAGNUM, (ABOVE) VAN BUCHER FROM PHOTO RESEARCHERS

(Left) Poster glamorizing Mao Tse-tung, the people, and the industrial power of Communist China. (Above) Hong Kong store of the Peace Book Company offers propaganda of Communist China, North Vietnam, and North Korea in a variety of languages

WALLACE DRIVER FROM "BUSINESS WEEK"

RADIO AND TELEVISION ARE OFTEN USED TO DISSEMINATE POLITICAL PROPAGANDA INTO AREAS UNREACHABLE BY PRINTED MEDIA. TWO COMMENTATORS OF THE STAFF OF RADIO FREE EUROPE WITH THE PUBLICATIONS THEY MONITOR FOR MATERIAL FOR BROADCASTS INTO COMMUNIST COUNTRIES

of forsaking the old and adopting the new be prompt and visible. Since propaganda is an instrument of visibility and anticipation it can be effectively used under these circumstances if there is presentation of costs as well as gains, and of risks as well as promises.

The appropriate role of propaganda is becoming more problematic in advanced industrial societies. To an increasing degree the leaders of thought and action in such societies are disturbed by evidence of inner demoralization that cuts across the ideological cleavages of a world permeated by the expectation of violence. The problem is often called the alienation of many members of the younger generations; dissociated from society, they refuse to accept civic responsibility. The question is whether propagandas of "official indoctrination," at one extreme, or of "competitive distraction and anarchy," at the other, can be effectively harmonized with the realities of life in industrial societies in ways that will deter or prevent juvenile crime or self-destructive fads. The "postponement of maturity," which exaggerates the seeming powerlessness and superfluousness of the young, may generate subterranean predispositions and propaganda initiatives that undermine the established order.

To the traditional importance of providing institutional arrangements for the protection of unpopular opinion it may be necessary to add, as an objective of policy, cultivation of incentives for the young to have opinions on any kind of public policy.

One of the greatest dangers arising from the prevalence of propaganda in a free society is that the vigorous prosecution of special interests may prevent the formation of a genuine public will. In times of crisis this may put democratic countries at a disadvantage when totalitarian states institute and maintain strict censorship

and total propaganda. The purpose on the one hand is to insulate the home audience from outside influences, and on the other to obtain maximum access to nontotalitarian audiences.

The very presence of propaganda raises searching problems for the friend of freedom. Does the calculated manipulation of attitudes imply a denial of respect for freedom of opinion? This is true if the forum of communication is not equally accessible to all and if educational opportunities are open only to the privileged. Hence, in countries that aspire toward freedom, stress is laid upon measures designed to achieve genuine equality. Responsible news media and the legislative and judicial institutions of society proceed by the use of discussion and debate in order to subject rival propaganda claims to a common discipline of balanced presentation and of critical evaluation of evidence. Whatever solutions of the control of communication are achieved, the degree of protection received by unpopular opinion and propaganda will continue to be one of the chief working tests of freedom.

See also COMMUNICATION; PUBLIC OPINION; and references under "Propaganda" in the Index.

BIBLIOGRAPHY.—Bruce Lannes Smith, Harold D. Lasswell, and Ralph D. Casey, *Propaganda, Communication, and Public Opinion: a Comprehensive Reference Guide* (1946); Joseph T. Klapper, *The Effects of Mass Communication* (1960); W. Phillips Davison, *International Political Communication* (1965); Lucian W. Pye (ed.), *Communications and Political Development* (1963); John B. Whitton and Arthur Larson, *Propaganda:Towards Disarmament in the War of Words* (1964); Leonard W. Doob, *Public Opinion and Propaganda* (1948); Commission on Freedom of the Press, *A Free and Responsible Press* (1947). (H. D. L.)

PROPAGATION, a term used in physics to denote the transmission or dissemination of energy, as of electrical energy along a conductor or electromagnetic energy through some medium. For example, radio waves that normally travel in a relatively straight line may be propagated over long distances by means of alternate reflections from the ionosphere and the ground or by means of a conducting medium such as a wave guide or coaxial cable. *See* LIGHT: *History: The Dynamical Theories of the 19th Century;* RADIO: *Factors Affecting Radio Performance: Propagation Variables.*

PROPANE, a colourless, gaseous compound of carbon and hydrogen, the third member of the paraffin series following methane and ethane. The formula for propane is C_3H_8. It is separated in large quantities from natural gas, light crude oil and oil refinery gases and is commercially available as liquefied propane or as a major constituent of liquefied petroleum gas (LPG).

As with ethane (*q.v.*) and other paraffin hydrocarbons, propane is an important raw material for the ethylene petrochemical industry. The decomposition of propane in hot tubes to form ethylene also yields another important product, propylene. From propylene organic chemicals like acetone, propylene glycol and many others are derived. The oxidation of propane to such compounds of carbon, hydrogen and oxygen as acetaldehyde is also of commercial interest.

Although a gas at ordinary atmospheric pressure, propane is readily liquefied under elevated pressures. It is therefore transported and handled as a liquid in cylinders or tanks. In this form, alone or mixed with liquid butane, it has great importance as a fuel for domestic and industrial uses and for internal-combustion engines.

In the late 1960s, world reserves were estimated at about 10,000,000,000 tons. The annual production was about 0.3% of this figure. Consumption was about equally distributed among chemical uses, LPG and as an unseparated constituent in natural gas used as fuel. (F. B. B.)

PROPELLANTS, chemical compounds, or other energy-transfer devices, used to: (1) propel rockets or missiles or (2) propel projectiles through the tubes of guns, howitzers, mortars, or other firearms. The basic function of a propellant is to store energy and release it at a controlled rate, thus developing a sustained forward force on the missile or projectile. One important feature of a chemical propellant is that it contains its own oxygen, which is essential, of course, for missiles to continue accelerating in outer space. Chemical systems, solid and liquid, are used almost universally, but nuclear heat-transfer systems are far more efficient energy storage devices, and may be utilized for a few highly specialized space missions.

SOLID PROPELLANTS FOR GUNS

History.—Gunpowder, or black powder, was the original chemical type propellant. It releases its energy by combustion and formation of hot gases. Gunpowder and similar materials were known much earlier than the 14th century, and were used in crude rockets or other mysterious fire-producing devices. Black powder was used as a propellant in guns from the mid-1300s till the late 1800s. (*See* GUNPOWDER.)

But gunpowder has recognized deficiencies. Because it is a mechanical mixture of carbon, sulfur, and potassium or sodium nitrate, its composition and properties are bound to vary. Gunpowder also is far from clean burning, by virtue of the fact that only 44% of it is converted to hot gases, the rest being smoke-producing solids. Other problems were caused by the ingredients, notably the nitrate, absorbing moisture; also there are serious hazards in the manufacture of gunpowder.

The successor to gunpowder as a propellant was a substance called smokeless powder, the term smokeless reflecting the cleaner burning of the nitrocellulose propellant as compared with gunpowder. Thus almost 100% is converted to hot gases, and so the specific chemical energy is double that of gunpowder. Guncotton, the earliest known form of nitrocellulose (more correctly cellulose nitrate) was first described in 1846 by C. F. Schönbein (*q.v.*), who experimented with its explosive nature and suggested its use in firearms.

The first attempts to utilize nitrocellulose as a propellant were unsuccessful, some actually disastrous, for two main reasons: (1) the material was chemically unstable, because of the reactions of the residual acid in the fibres and (2) the raw fibrous nitrocellulose presented an excessive burning area to the flame front. Later the stability problem was solved by a more complete removal of the residual acid from the nitrocellulose fibres and by the addition of chemical stabilizers such as diphenylamine.

Schönbein was the first to treat nitrocellulose with alcohol and ether to form collodion (*q.v.*). It remained for Paul Vieille (1854–1934), a French physicist and chemist, however, to utilize this colloiding action of solvents in moulding the now homogeneous mass into shapes of controlled dimensions and surface areas. This was an extremely important discovery because it laid the groundwork for successful development of colloidal nitrocellulose propellants with improved and controllable ballistic characteristics. The French Army adopted the new and more powerful propellant about 1885 as *poudre B*.

In 1888 Alfred B. Nobel (*q.v.*) discovered the solvent and colloiding actions of nitroglycerin on nitrocellulose and combined them into a more powerful propellant termed ballistite. As it contained both nitroglycerin and nitrocellulose, it was described as a double-base propellant.

About 1889 Frederick A. Abel and James Dewar, British chemists, invented cordite, another double-base propellant consisting of 65% nitrocellulose, 30% nitroglycerin, and 5% mineral jelly. Cordite was made by extruding the colloid into long cords, whereas both Vieille and Nobel had rolled the colloid into sheets and then cut the sheets into flakes of various sizes. Before the end of the 19th century, the U.S. Navy adopted smokeless powder, favouring the single-base type of Vieille and using nitrocellulose of approximately 12.6% nitrogen—it was often called pyrocellulose, or simply pyro. Its complete solubility in an ether-alcohol mixture is an attractive feature.

20th Century.—By 1900 the changeover from black powder to nitrocellulose-based colloidal propellants was well underway, both in military and civilian gun usage. England and some other countries preferred double-base propellants, even though their greater erosive effects on gun tubes had to be endured.

World War I was fought with these two types of propellant, single-base (using pyro) and double-base. Experience in combat indicated serious weaknesses in the pyro-type propellant. Mois-

ture could be absorbed to a degree adversely affecting the muzzle velocity and range from an occasional round; also the intense muzzle flashes from the French 75-mm. gun made men in trenches vulnerable by lighting up the entire front.

TABLE I.—*Data on M1 and M6 Military Propellants*

Ingredients	M1	M6
Nitrocellulose (13.15% nitrogen)	85	87
Dinitrotoluene	10	10
Dibutylphthalate	5	3
Diphenylamine*	1	1
Isochoric flame temperature (°K)	2,433	2,583
Specific energy (ft. lb./lb. X 10⁻³)	1,224	1,272

*Diphenylamine is added and serves as a chemical stabilizer for the nitrocellulose.

The M1 and M6 propellants were developed as nonhygroscopic single-base improvements over pyro, simply by incorporating dinitrotoluene and dibutylphthalate. Muzzle flash can be reduced or eliminated in some weapons by adding a saltlike potassium sulfate, but the smoke is increased in so doing.

In the 1930s Great Britain developed Cordite N, a major improvement over the original cordite. The N denotes nitroguanidine, $NH_2C(NH)NHNO_2$, a crystalline compound containing nearly 55% nitrogen. This high nitrogen content increases the gas volume from a unit weight of propellant and in this way decreases the amount of heat necessary to give the needed ballistic force. Obviously the rate of erosion is reduced and so is the tendency to flash at the muzzle of the weapon.

Following the success of Cordite N, the U.S. developed similar types, M31 and M30 (*see* Table II). Some other countries also have used nitroguanidine-type propellants, notably Canada and Germany.

TABLE II.—*Nominal Formulae and Calculated Properties for Cordite N, M31, and M30 Military Propellants*

Ingredients	N	M31	M30
Nitrocellulose	19.0	20.0	28.0
Nitroglycerin	18.7	19.0	22.5
Nitroguanidine	54.7	54.7	47.7
Dibutylphthalate		4.5	
Diethyl diphenyl urea ("centralite")	7.3		1.5
2-Nitro-diphenylamine		1.5	
Cryolite	0.3	0.3	0.3
Isochoric flame temperature (°K)	2,450	2,599	3,040
Specific Energy (ft. lb./lb. X 10⁻³)	1,280	1,336	1,456

Of the three types of propellant given in Table II, the Cordite N and M31 are designed to be flashless and to produce very little smoke, very valuable attributes for antitank ammunition. The M30 propellant is used with armour-piercing (AP) projectiles of the kinetic energy type, where a premium is placed on high velocities.

To summarize gun propellant military practice in the U.S., single-base types like M1 and M6 are preferred wherever they are adequate ballistically. Triple base (M31 and M30) are needed in some weapons to avoid muzzle flash and smoke, or to give extra velocity at moderate flame temperatures. Double-base types (20% nitroglycerin) are used sparingly, in special purpose weapons such as recoilless rifles and in a few small arms weapons. Smoothbore trench mortars require double-base propellants with as much as 40% nitroglycerin; this type is rolled into sheets or flakes with closely controlled thicknesses.

Small Arms.—The earliest small arms propellant was gunpowder, and many a vivid picture comes to mind of the western U.S. pioneer tamping the powder charge into his muzzle-loader. Actually gunpowder is well suited to this treatment, for it is not very sensitive to variations in packing density.

Even in the much-used shotgun of early days, the excessive flash, smoke, and fouling were troublesome; and for big-game hunting the rifle needed more power and range than was possible with gunpowder.

The first nitrocellulose propellant was made by rolling the soft colloid into thin sheets, then cutting it into square or round flakes. This type of grain worked well and is still used in shotgun and pistol ammunition.

An extruded cylindrical grain with a central perforation (*see* fig. 1) gives improved ballistics for rifles, especially when exposed grain surfaces have been coated with a deterrent material. Such a design became a standard for almost all types of military rifles and for sporting rifles as well; it is well known as Improved Military Rifle (IMR) propellant. Most IMR types are single-base (nitrocellulose). Some double-base compositions are used in both single-perforated and flake form.

Another very useful form of propellant is the spherical or ball shape of grain, developed in the 1930s. The ball type is produced in a unique manner, by dissolving and dispersing the nitrocellulose and other ingredients in a solvent such as ethyl acetate. Upon agitation and the addition of a protective colloid, the lacquer is broken up into small spherical globules.

This process provides an effective means of purifying the nitrocellulose and also lends itself well to making either single-base or double-base propellants. Because of the degressive-burning geometry of the ball grain, an effective deterrent coating is needed. Ball propellant is used extensively in military and sporting ammunition.

Interior Ballistics and Propellant Design.—In a word, a gun or rocket acts as a heat engine, converting the latent energy in the propellant to kinetic energy of motion of the projectile or rocket. The propellant decomposes to form a gas, the chemical energy is converted to heat, and the hot gases exert pressure and accelerate the projectile or rocket (*see* BALLISTICS).

The rate of burning and the accompanying release of energy was expressed by Vieille in 1888 as $r = cP^n$, where r is in inches per second; c is a constant for any given chemical composition; and n is a constant, usually in the range 0.8 to 1.0. Thus, the burning of a propellant is sensitive to the pressure level, P, at any given instant. Also, since burning is strictly a surface reaction, the rate of consumption is directly proportional to the total exposed surface area of the entire charge of propellant.

For maximum effectiveness of propulsion the propellant grain is designed, if possible, so that its actual area increases as burning progresses. Such a design is the multiperforated grain shown in fig. 1. Another device, deterrent coating, slows the initial burning rate, thus promoting faster burning later.

Because consumption rate is so responsive to total surface area and, in turn, to pressure, the propellant grain must be designed carefully and manufactured to close dimensional tolerances. The useful dimension to measure and control is the web, defined as the average thickness between burning surfaces. On the multiperforated grain the web is the average thickness from central perforation to outer perforation and from outer perforation to outer edge.

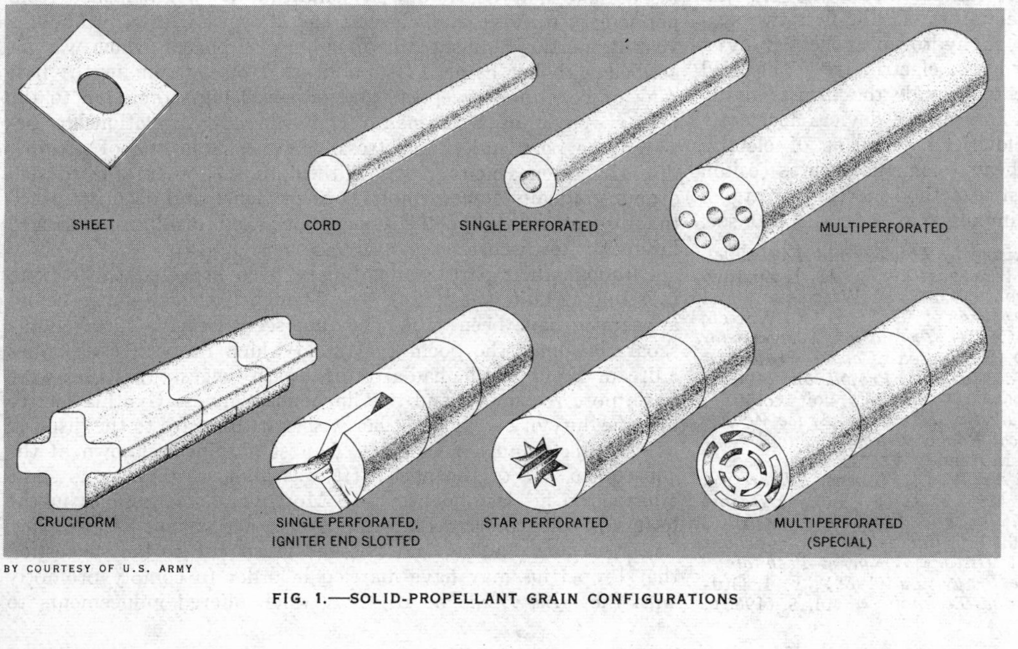

ROCKETS AND MISSILES

The exact origin of the use of rockets is lost in the deep recesses of history but by 1400 they were much in evidence for military purposes. Gunpowder was the very first propellant used. Today a very wide variety of propellant compositions, grain shapes, and burning control devices are in use for the equally diverse list of systems requiring propulsion. (*See* ROCKETS AND GUIDED MISSILES.)

Solid Propellants.—Serious modern solid-propellant experiments began in the late 1930s with the double-base ballistite type, extruded into grains to suit the rocket motor design. As reasonable success was achieved in small rockets, such as the well-known bazooka, larger systems became of interest to the military. Their firepower could supplement the conventional artillery weapons—guns, howitzers, etc.—and by comparison rocket launchers are almost weightless.

The extrusion process, however, has definite limitations as to size and types of compound used in the propellant strand; so various casting and pressing methods were devised to fabricate the large sizes and complex shapes of propellant grains needed. At the same time, the casting technique admitted wide flexibility in the use of compounds needed to secure effective performance. Thus, solid propellant grains contain organic or metallic fuels; oxidizers (nitrates, perchlorates, etc.); binders and other special purpose ingredients such as burning rate strands or accelerators. The casting or pressing may be done in a special mold or an inert plastic container which later acts as an inhibitor and thus restricts burning to an end of the composite mass.

As complexity of charge design increases, however, the greatest care is needed to insure uniform distribution of chemical components and to avoid physical faults such as cracks or air pockets. Also, the smooth and effective action of the ignition system is essential to uniform burning of the propellant charge.

The relative potency of propellants, whether solid or liquid, for rocket or missile application, is gauged by specific impulse (abbreviated I_{sp}). Thus $I_{sp} = Fxt/W$, where F is the average thrust exerted in pounds during time t, and W is the weight in pounds of propellant consumed. Compounds or mixtures which produce a maximum of heat and large amounts of gases of low molecular weight serve to maximize I_{sp}.

In general, for military uses, the comparatively simple double-base propellants (extruded or cast) are favoured for small rockets like the bazooka, and for essentially all the larger rockets used in quantities for artillery types of mission. For more complicated systems and where higher I_{sp} is needed, composites or liquids are chosen.

Liquid Propellants.—Although solid propellants have been the workhorses for many centuries, liquids have gained distinctive roles in modern missile technology. The experiments of Robert H. Goddard (*q.v.*) in the 1920s charted the course; he visualized a system using liquid hydrogen and liquid oxygen as being capable of energizing even an interplanetary rocket. The German V-2 missile of World War II was a milestone in actual application of two liquids, alcohol and liquid oxygen (LOX).

Unlike solids, liquid propellants can be stored on board the missile separate from the combustion chamber, and are forced into the chamber at the desired time and rate. Thus a liquid propellant motor can even be stopped and restarted at will, a factor of extreme importance in maneuvering during space flights. Liquid systems are of two

SHEET   CORD   SINGLE PERFORATED   MULTIPERFORATED

CRUCIFORM   SINGLE PERFORATED, IGNITER END SLOTTED   STAR PERFORATED   MULTIPERFORATED (SPECIAL)

BY COURTESY OF U.S. ARMY

FIG. 1.—SOLID-PROPELLANT GRAIN CONFIGURATIONS

types: monopropellants and bipropellants. A monopropellant may be a single compound such as ethyl nitrate, or a compatible mixture such as hydrazine, hydrazine nitrate, and water. Bipropellants consist of an oxidizer and a fuel; they are kept separate until reaching the combustion chamber, when most combinations ignite on contact.

Table III lists many of the fuel-oxidizer combinations which are used, though some have only an experimental status, e.g., hydrogen and fluorine. A number of other combinations have been tested and utilized in the course of rocket and missile pioneering. The wide range in specific impulse obtainable should be noted, and especially the achievement of values of 350 sec. and more. Oxygen-hydrogen gives 375 sec. and therefore is a favourite for outer-space flights. By comparison solid propellants can develop I_{sp} of little more than 260 sec.

The choice between liquid and solid propellants for a given

TABLE III.—*Theoretical Specific Impulse* (I_{sp})
for Liquid-Propellant Combinations

Oxidizer	Ratio Oxidizer/ Fuel	Fuel	I_{sp} (sec.)
100% HNO₃	4.4	turpentine	221
RFNA	2.5	ethyl alcohol	219
"	3.0	aniline	221
"	2.2	ammonia	225
99% H₂O₂	4.0	ethyl alcohol	230
"	6.5	JP-4	233
Oxygen	1.5	ethyl alcohol	242
"	2.2	JP-4	248
"	4.0	hydrogen	375
70% O₂–30% Ozone	2.3	JP-4	253
100% Ozone	1.9	JP-4	266
"	1.13	ammonia	267
"	0.63	hydrazine	277
"	3.2	hydrogen	369
Fluorine	2.6	JP-4	265
"	2.6	ammonia	288
"	2.37	methyl alcohol	296
"	1.98	hydrazine	298
"	4.5	hydrogen	352

application depends upon many factors in addition to I_{sp}. Some are strictly of a practical nature, perhaps involving ease and even safety of storing the liquids and of loading them into the missile. The major advantage which solids enjoy is their simplicity, and their ability to be stored in a ready condition over long periods of time. These characteristics are desirable and often necessary in strategic missile systems fired from land or submarine.

ADVANCED PROPULSION SYSTEMS

Because of the desire for specific impulses higher than those obtainable from chemical energy, various forms of nuclear powered devices are being investigated. The systems closest at hand are the nuclear heat-transfer type, the electrothermal arc jet, the ion rocket, and the plasma accelerator. In the first two systems listed, a working fluid such as hydrogen is heated by a nuclear reactor directly or by way of an electric arc. The fluid is then expanded through a nozzle to provide the thrust, giving I_{sp} of 1,000 sec. or more. The ion and plasma devices accelerate ions or electrons to very high velocities, by means of electric and magnetic fields. For the ions heavy elements such as cesium or mercury are chosen; for the plasma method mercury or argon. These methods can give specific impulses of 2,500–12,000 sec.

BIBLIOGRAPHY.—T. L. Davis, *Chemistry of Powder and Explosives,* 2 vol. (1941–43); E. Burgess, *Guided Weapons* (1957); M. J. Zucrow, *Aircraft and Missile Propulsion,* 2 vol. (1958); R. W. Bussard and R. D. Delaver, *Nuclear Rocket Propulsion* (1958); F. A. Warren, *Rocket Propellants* (1958); W. R. Corliss, *Propulsion Systems for Space Flight* (1960); B. Kit and D. S. Evered, *Rocket Propellant Handbook* (1960); M. Barrère et al., *Rocket Propulsion* (1960); D. S. Carton et al. (ed.), *Rocket Propulsion Technology,* vol. 1 (1961); H. S. Seifert and K. Brown (eds.), *Ballistic Missile and Space Vehicle Systems* (1961); S. S. Penner, *Chemical Rocket Propulsion and Combustion Research* (1962); R. W. Vance and W. M. Duke (eds.), *Applied Cryogenic Engineering* (1962); R. L. Wilkens, *Theoretical Evaluation of Chemical Propellants* (1963); G. P. Sutton, *Rocket Propulsion Elements* (1963); *Combustion and Propulsion,* AGARD, vol. 6 (1964); B. Siegel and L. Schieler, *Energetics of Propellant Chemistry* (1964); E. M. Emme (ed.), *History of Rocket Technology* (1964); H. F. Crouch, *Nuclear Space Propulsion* (1965); F. I. Ordway III, *Advances in Space Science and Technology,* vol. 8 (1966); W. von Braun and F. I. Ordway III, *History of Rocketry and Space Travel* (1967); E. D. Lowry, *Interior Ballistics* (1968); *Journal of the National Rifle Association of America,* vol. 116, no. 9 (1968).
(B. E. An.; A. E. Th.)

PROPELLER. For a description of the propeller as applied to aircraft *see* AIRCRAFT PROPULSION. For marine propellers, *see* NAVAL ARCHITECTURE: *Resistance and Propulsion.*

PROPERTIUS, SEXTUS (*c.* 50–*c.* 15 B.C.), the greatest of the elegiac poets of Rome, was born of a well-to-do Umbrian family at or near Asisium (Assisi). Ovid says that Propertius was his senior, but also his friend and companion; and that he was third in the sequence of elegiac poets, following Cornelius Gallus, who was born *c.* 70 B.C., and Tibullus, and immediately preceding Ovid himself, who was born in 43 B.C. It may be supposed then that he was born *c.* 50 B.C.

His early life was full of misfortune. He lost his father prematurely; and after the battle of Philippi and the return of Octavian to Rome, Propertius, like Virgil and Horace, was deprived of his estate to provide land for the veterans, but, unlike them, had no patrons at court and was reduced from opulence to comparative indigence. When the widespread expropriations had provoked an insurrection, Propertius lost another of his relatives, who was killed by brigands while making his escape from Perusia (Perugia), the centre of the revolt. The loss of his patrimony, however, did not prevent Propertius from receiving a superior education, thanks no doubt to his mother's providence. Eventually he and she left Umbria for Rome; and there, *c.* 34 B.C., he assumed the dress of adult manhood.

Propertius was urged to take up a pleader's profession; but, like Ovid, he found in letters and gallantry a more congenial pursuit. Soon afterward he made the acquaintance of Lycinna (about whom little is known beyond the fact that she subsequently excited the jealousy of her successor, Cynthia) and was subjected to all her powers of persecution (*vexandi*). This passing fancy was succeeded by a serious attachment, the object of which was the famous "Cynthia." Her real name was Hostia (according to Apuleius, *Apologia,* 10); and she was a courtesan of the superior class, somewhat older than Propertius and, it seems, of singular beauty and varied accomplishments. Her own predilections led her to literature; and in her society Propertius found the intellectual sympathy and encouragement which were essential for the development of his talent. Her character, as depicted in the poems, is not an attractive one; but she seems to have entertained a genuine affection for her lover. Their intimacy lasted from *c.* 29 to 24 B.C. These years must not, however, be supposed to have been a period of unbroken felicity. Apart from minor disagreements an infidelity on Propertius's part excited the deepest resentment in Cynthia; and at some time he was banished from her society for a year. When he had known Cynthia for about a year Propertius published his first book of poems, which was inscribed with her name. Its publication placed him in the first rank of contemporary poets and procured him admission to the literary circle of Maecenas. The subsequent relationship between the poet and his mistress, however, was one of growing disenchantment; neither was faithful to the other; the mutual ardour gradually cooled; motives of prudence and decorum urged the discontinuance of the connection; and disillusion changed insensibly to disgust.

Although their parting might have been expected to be final, it is not certain that it was so. Though Cynthia, whose health appears to have been weak, does not seem to have survived the separation long, the poem (iv, 7) in which Propertius describes a dream of her that he had after her death suggests that they were once more reconciled and that in her last illness Cynthia left to him the duty of carrying out her wishes with regard to the disposal of her effects and her funeral. Almost nothing is known of the subsequent life of the poet. He was alive in 16 B.C., as some allusions in his last book show. Moreover, two passages in the letters of the younger Pliny mention a descendant of the poet, one Passennus Paulus; and this had given rise to the suggestion that Propertius may have married in order to comply promptly with the *leges Juliae* of 18 B.C. (which offered inducements to marriage and imposed disabilities upon the celibate) and had at least one child.

Propertius had a large number of friends and acquaintances, chiefly literary men belonging to the circle of Maecenas. Among them may be mentioned Virgil, an epic poet called Ponticus, a certain Bassus (probably the iambic poet) and at a later period Ovid. He says nothing of Tibullus or of Horace, who also never mentions Propertius. This reciprocal silence may be significant.

In person Propertius was pale and thin, as was to be expected in one of a delicate and even sickly constitution. He was very careful about his personal appearance and paid an almost foppish attention to dress and gait. He was of a somewhat voluptuous and self-indulgent temperament, which shrank from danger and active exertion. He was anxiously sensitive about the opinion of others, eager for their sympathy and regard and, in general, easily influenced by them. His over-emotional nature passed rapidly from one phase of feeling to another; but the more melancholy moods predominated. A vein of sadness runs through his poems, sometimes breaking out into querulous exclamation, but more frequently expressed in gloomy reflections and prognostications. He had fits of superstition, which in healthier moments he despised.

The Poems.—The poems of Propertius, as they have been preserved, consist of four books containing just more than 4,000 lines of elegiac verse. Book i, the *Cynthia* or *Monobiblos,* was published probably in 29 or 28 B.C. As its title indicates, it is concerned almost exclusively with the poet's passion for Cynthia. The arrangement of the poems is, in the Alexandrian manner, one of artful disorder: the phases of the liaison and of Propertius's feelings are described in a series of brilliant isolated impressions, in which a strict chronology is carefully avoided (compare Ovid's *Amores*). This is not the only reason why it is unsafe to draw inferences about Propertius's actual life and loves from his poetry. Throughout, but particularly in the first book, reality and convention, experience and literary artifice, love and learning, are too intimately blended for the reader to be sure of disentangling them. It is important to remember the poet's essentially urban character and the relatively small and highly sophisticated circle of readers to whom his poetry was intended to appeal: for them his mythological allusions, which are frigid and indeed barely intelligible to the modern reader, would be immediately moving and evocative. Books ii and iii, which were published probably *c.* 25 and *c.* 22 B.C. respectively, are of somewhat more varied composition than book i. The poet's love for Cynthia still dominates them, but his tone is more declamatory and less personal, and other themes are heard.

Book iv (*c.* 16 B.C.) offers a remarkable contrast. Propertius had indeed already announced, at the beginning of book iii, that he aspired to follow in the footsteps of Callimachus and Philetas, but there he had been referring only to formal and stylistic obligations, not to subject matter; whereas now (iv, 1, 61–70) he proposed, as the Roman Callimachus, to deal with the history and antiquities of Rome in the manner of the *Aetia.* In fact such themes, which were taken up later by Ovid in the *Fasti,* only occupy five of the poems in the book. The rest, a varied collection, include the poem (3) which seems to have given Ovid the idea for his *Heroides;* a delightfully humorous description of Cynthia's surprising Propertius in the act of being unfaithful to her (8); and the eulogy of the dead Cornelia, which some have thought to be his finest work (11).

The writings of Propertius are noted for their difficulty and their disorder. The workmanship is unequal, curtness alternating with redundancy, and carelessness with elaboration. A desultory sequence of ideas, an excessive vagueness and indirectness of expression, a peculiar and abnormal latinity, a constant tendency to exaggeration and an immoderate indulgence in learned and literary allusions—all these are obstacles lying in the way of a study of Propertius. But those who surmount them will find their trouble well repaid. For power and range of imagination, for freshness and vividness of conception, for truth and originality of presentation, few Roman poets can compare with him when he is at his best; that is, when he is carried out of himself, when the discordant qualities of his genius are, so to say, fused together

by the spark of immediate inspiration. His vanity and egotism are redeemed by his fancy and his humour.

Two of the lasting merits of Propertius seem to have impressed the ancients themselves. The first they called *blanditia,* a vague but expressive word by which they meant softness of outline, warmth of colouring, a fine and almost voluptuous feeling for beauty of every kind and a pleading and melancholy tenderness; this is most obvious in his descriptive passages and in his portrayal of emotion. His second and even more remarkable quality is poetic *facundia,* or command of striking and appropriate language. Not only is his vocabulary extensive but his employment of it is extraordinarily bold and unconventional: poetic and colloquial latinity alternate abruptly, and in his quest for the striking expression he frequently seems to strain the language to breaking point.

Propertius's handling of the elegiac couplet, and particularly of its second line, deserves especial recognition. It is vigorous, varied and even picturesque. In the matter of the rhythms, caesuras and elisions which it allows, the metrical treatment is much more severe than that of Catullus, but noticeably freer than that of Ovid, to whose stricter usage, however, Propertius increasingly tended (particularly in his preference for a disyllabic word at the end of the pentameter). An elaborate symmetry is observable in the construction of many of his elegies, and this has tempted critics to divide a number of them into strophes.

Influence.—As Propertius had borrowed from his predecessors, so his successors, Ovid above all, borrowed from him; and *graffiti* on the walls of Pompeii attest his popularity in the 1st century A.D. In the middle ages he was virtually forgotten; and since the Renaissance he has been studied by professional scholars more than he has been enjoyed by the general public. To the modern reader, acquainted with the psychological discoveries of the 20th century, the self-revelations of his passionate, fitful, brooding spirit are of peculiar interest.

BIBLIOGRAPHY.—For the text of the poems *see* the editions by E. A. Barber (1953) and by M. Schuster, 2nd ed. rev. by F. Dornseiff (1958). For the text with introduction and commentary *see* the edition by H. E. Butler and E. A. Barber (1933); also that of book i only by P. J. Enk, with bibliography (1946). There are English translations in prose by H. E. Butler, with the Latin, in the "Loeb Series" (1912); and in verse by S. G. Treemenheere, 2nd ed. (1932), and by E. H. W. Meyerstein, with bibliography (1935). *See* further F. Plessis, *Études critiques sur Properce et ses élégies* (1884); W. Y. Sellar, *Horace and the Elegiac Poets* (1899); R. Helm, "Propertius," in Pauly-Wissowa, *Real-Encyclopädie,* vol. xxiii (1957). (J. P. P.; E. J. Ky.)

PROPERTY, a term used popularly to refer to a thing owned by a person, but used more accurately in law to refer to a scheme of relationships, recognized or established by government, between individuals with respect to an object. The object may be tangible, such as land, or completely the creature of law, such as a patent or copyright. Since the objects of property and the protected relationships vary among societies and over time, it is difficult to find a least common denominator of property. "My property" probably means at a minimum that government will help me exclude others from the use or enjoyment of an object without my consent, which I may withhold except at a price. Legal relationships with respect to objects are described in the following articles: REAL PROPERTY AND CONVEYANCING, LAWS OF; PERSONAL PROPERTY; LANDLORD AND TENANT; COMMERCIAL PAPER; COPYRIGHT; and PATENT. *See* also references under "Property" in the Index.

(A. DM.)

PROPHET, a Greek word (*prophetes*) denoting one who conveys a divine utterance and thus serves as the "mouthpiece" of a god (*cf.* also Ex. 7:1 and 4:16). In classical Greek the term could signify either the person uttering the oracle (*q.v.*) or (since the utterance would often be unintelligible) the one interpreting it, in which case a distinction would be made between *mantis* (also translated "prophet") and *prophetes.* The Greek version of the Old Testament uses the word *prophetes* to render the Hebrew *nabi* (*see* below, *Israelite Prophecy*), and from there the words prophet, prophecy, prophetic, etc. entered other European languages. Since the prophet's utterance often foretold the future—to warn, to announce the inevitable, or in reply to clients consulting the oracle —prophecy has at times been equated with prediction (*see* DIVINA-

TION). Nevertheless, it has rightly been remarked that prophecy is a matter of "telling forth" rather than "foretelling," although the latter may at times be the more prominent feature.

THE PROPHETIC PHENOMENON

Any attempt at an adequate description of the prophetic phenomenon is brought up against a serious methodological dilemma: The analysis will either refer to one particular culture only, in which case it may be exhaustive but include unessential detail; or else it will embrace many cultures and run the risk of treating the subject in too generalizing a fashion. As a matter of historical fact, the most outstanding and influential prophetic phenomenon, as far as Western culture is concerned, was Israelite prophecy, and most students of the subject have necessarily drawn on the biblical material. Hence some overlap between a general phenomenology of prophecy and the specific analysis of Hebrew prophecy is all but inevitable. However, it is generally agreed that similar phenomena in other cultures and religions, though known by different names and performing somewhat different social functions, may legitimately be discussed under the one heading.

Sources of Prophecy and the Prophetic State.—The prophet differs from other religious functionaries and representatives of religious authority in that he claims no personal part in his utterance. He speaks not his own mind but a revelation "from without." He may be "inspired" with his message (as in Jer. 1:9, "Behold, I have put my words in your mouth") or he may be "possessed" by a spiritual power—a god, a spirit, the Holy Ghost —which uses him as an instrument and speaks through him (as in Aeschylus' description of Cassandra in the *Agamemnon* and of the prophet of Apollo in the *Eumenides*). Plato (*Timaeus* 71b) defined the prophet as one who speaks in ecstasy, and in the Hellenistic period Philo of Alexandria similarly stated that the prophet "speaks nothing of his own" but resembles the lyre on which someone else plays.

Prophecy is, therefore, a "pneumatic" (under the influence of the "spirit") and "enthusiastic" state, ranging from controlled possession or a certain "infused" heightening of natural powers to frenzied ecstasy, convulsive seizures, or catalepsy amounting to a temporary loss of personality. Saul, when the spirit came upon him, was "turned into another man" (I Sam. 10:6), and "he too stripped off his clothes, and he too prophesied before Samuel, and lay naked all that day and all that night" (19:24). The prophetic state may occur spontaneously or it may be induced by a variety of techniques: by meditation, by mystico-magical formulas and gestures (the *mantras* and *mudras* of esoteric Buddhism, for example), by music (II Kings 3:15, "And when the minstrel played, the power of the Lord came upon him"), by drumming, dancing, or the ingestion of intoxicants or narcotics. Prophets very often resist the call (Amos and Jeremiah among the Hebrew prophets; many prospective shamans) until overcome by the superior power that wants to use them as its instrument.

The resultant charismatic (from *charisma*, a divine gift) possession may express itself in acts of physical prowess, as in the case of the Israelite judges (Samson, for example); in (magical) powers of diverse kinds, as the curing in shamanism (*q.v.*); or in inspired speech. The latter may be unintelligible gibberish (*see* Tongues, Gift of), a foreign tongue, or even pseudo-language (xenoglossia), or it may be clear and meaningful speech, uttered in an elevated style and rhythmic diction. It is the intelligible utterance to which the term prophecy is applied more specifically (*cf.* I Cor. 14:29–32). The prophetic state may be accompanied by visions, auditions, and other experiences, as well as by total loss of consciousness.

Prophets and Other Diviners.—Using the criterion of inspired speech, it becomes possible to distinguish the prophet from related types of religious functionaries. Although the prophet often acts as a diviner, he is largely dependent on an outside power, which in some cultures he has at his disposal but in others may not always control Nonprophetic divination uses or manipulates objective techniques or signs; *e.g.*, the ephod, and the Urim and Thummim of the Israelite priests; the spirits of the dead consulted

in necromancy; the animal livers studied by the divining hepatoscopists in Babylonia and elsewhere; the flight of birds observed by the Roman augurs; the animal entrails examined by the Etruscan haruspices. The diviner is consulted by clients, whereas the prophet, impelled by the spirit, may also go out and thrust his message on an unwilling audience. Both prophets and diviners, like priests, are mediators between the ordinary man and the divine powers. The word *kahin*, which in ancient Arabia meant an inspired soothsayer, is derived from the same Semitic root as Hebrew *kohen*, "priest."

Frequently both divination and prophecy are connected with a sanctuary and practised by priestly or semipriestly guilds, or at least are organized or controlled by the priesthood. On the other hand the prophet may be moved to oppose the priestly establishment. But the opposition priest-prophet has, in fact, been somewhat overstressed by some scholars. Even Amos, while emphatically denying any association with prophetic groups (Amos 7:14), uttered his prophecy at the sanctuary of Bethel (7:12–13), the "temple of the kingdom." Divination, like magic, though frequently serving social and collective ends—decisions regarding wars or hunting expeditions, rainmaking, etc.—is more often concerned with private needs and anxieties. In either case it deals with very specific and limited problems. The prophet, impelled by the spirit, may articulate a message of more general and fundamental import, and enunciate principles and norms that are critical of the present, in either a destructive or a reforming sense. He may address his group (tribe, nation) as a whole or may found a new society which will realize his message. The prophetic personality thus frequently becomes a religious founder, reformer, or sectarian leader (Zoroaster, Muhammad, and others). The "ideal-typical" prophet (in Max Weber's sense) is, however, less concerned with founding a new religion or introducing revolutionary reforms than with criticizing his society from the inside, as it were, and in the light of what he believes to be the divinely established norms underlying its existence. If he is a revolutionary, he very frequently does not know it.

The Prophetic Message and Prophetic Religion.—The above characterization has drawn heavily on the classical pattern of apostolic prophecy as exhibited by the Hebrew prophets. It is called apostolic because the prophet—unlike the priest who presides over the ritual, or the teacher who expounds doctrine, or the saintly or ascetic "exemplary" leaders—delivers a message. Discussions of the nature of prophecy therefore vary according to whether they emphasize its formal elements (possession, inspiration, sense of vocation and mission) or the contents of the message (righteousness, purity of heart, universal peace, divine judgment, etc.).

The semantic spectrum of the term prophetic has consequently become rather wide. According to whether the emphasis is on possession and ecstasy, inspired utterance, prediction of the future, visionary experience, ethical fervour, passionate social criticism, sense of absolute commitment, millenarian and apocalyptic expectation, etc., the most diverse phenomena and personalities have been called prophetic: Montanists, Pentecostals, Zoroaster, Muhammad, Joachim of Fiore, Savonarola, Thomas Müntzer, Jakob Böhme, George Fox, Joseph Smith, and many others. The moral seriousness of the ancient Chinese sages and their profound regard for the law of heaven has suggested comparisons with Hebrew prophecy, and the Egyptian text known as the "Peasant's Complaint" has been claimed as a witness for a prophetic movement in ancient Egypt. Even Marxism has at times been qualified as prophetic, both because of its passionate protest against social injustice and because of the eschatological structure of its doctrine.

Disregarding, for our present purpose, this wide and at times merely figurative use of "prophetic," there is little doubt that a distinct prophetic type of religion can be recognized. Its main characteristics are a dynamic conception of the Deity, an emphasis on the will (both of God and of man) as a constitutive of the religious reality, a basic dualism (qualitative gulf between God and man, yet personal and even "dialogual" relationship in faith and obedience), a profound awareness of the seriousness of sin (as distinct from breaking a taboo), a radical ethical outlook based on an unequivocal choice between good and evil, a positive attitude to society and to this world in general, and a relationship to the time process which could crystallize in eschatological and messianic hopes.   (R. J. Z. W.)

PROPHECY IN WORLD RELIGION

ANCIENT NEAR EAST

Prophets were to be found throughout most of the ancient Near Eastern world. Though their activities varied considerably from culture to culture, certain common features are discernible. Because much of their labour centred on advising with regard to future events, the prophets functioned as one kind of diviners at the side of specialists in other divinatory techniques. Inasmuch as the inspired delivery of oracles was part of the rituals of the ancient world, particularly on the occasion of great festivals, prophets were often connected with the temples as regular cultic officials. Prophets also accompanied the kings in battle, giving guidance from the gods.

Some texts suggest that prophets had the freedom to bring their oracles to king and people without having been asked to do so and even if their message expressed criticism of the monarch. Rare though such examples be, they foreshadow the later developments of Israelite prophecy.

Ecstatic prophecy seems to have been rare in Egypt, perhaps because the kings were themselves held to be gods incarnate and hence in a position to provide divine counsel in their own right.

ISRAELITE PROPHECY

The Hebrew noun *nabi* ("prophet," pl. *n^ebi'im*) is probably related etymologically to the Akkadian verb *nabū* ("to call," "to name"). If this derivation is correct, it would suggest either that the prophet was understood as "the one called out" (by the deity, to speak in his name) or that he was understood to be "the caller" (*i.e.*, the spokesman for the deity). Judgments differ as to whether *nabi* should be taken to be a passive or an active form of the noun. Many other etymologies and meanings for the term have also been proposed. The term for prophet in early Israel was, according to I Sam. 9:9, *Ro'eh*, "seer." Another popular designation for the prophet was *hozeh*, "visionary" (Amos 7:12; Isa. 30:10; translated "seer" or "prophet" in English Bibles).

But the origins of what is distinctive of the prophetic tradition in Israel are not traceable by reference to the occurrence of the various names given the prophets. Israelite prophecy is fundamentally rooted in the covenant (*q.v.*) faith of early Israel, which, according to Old Testament tradition, is inseparably connected with the experiences and the work of Moses. Moses is considered by later tradition to be the greatest of the prophets (*e.g.*, Num. 11:29; Deut. 34:10). Events in the life of early Israel and the community's understanding of these events have prepared the soil in which Israelite prophecy is to grow and flourish. The understanding of God as sovereign Lord, redeemer of the oppressed slaves, guide and helper in time of danger, jealous of his prerogatives and demanding unswerving allegiance, engaged in a purpose which includes "all the families of the earth" (Gen. 12:3)—this understanding of the nature and work of God gives the setting and the distinctive stamp to Israelite prophecy.

Origins of the Office of Prophet.—Prophets as a distinct class within Israelite society first appear in the days of Samuel and Saul. During the latter half of the 11th century B.C., bands of prophets were found in several Israelite localities (Gibeah, Ramah); Samuel and Saul were very closely related to them (I Sam. 10:1; 19:18-24). The significance of the ecstatic prophets is not made clear in the texts which speak of them, perhaps because the later Israelite tradition did not wish to associate them too closely with the classical prophets. Yet the movement must have provided much of the impetus which led the Israelite tribes to rally in defense of their land against the Philistines.

These uncontrolled and uncontrollable spokesmen for the God of Israel apparently occupied an ambiguous position within the community. The question "Is Saul also among the prophets?" (I Sam. 10:12; 19:24), and the designation of the prophetic

messenger who came to Jehu as a "madman" (*meshugga;* II Kings 9:11), indicate that they were often held in contempt; yet the same texts reveal that such spokesmen for the deity were feared and that their words and deeds were taken with utmost seriousness. Prophetic bands continued to exist for centuries (I Kings 22:6; II Kings 2:3; Amos 7:14), and from their ranks, it may be inferred, the more individualistic and independent prophetic spokesmen were often drawn.

Early Prophetic Personalities.—Among the many individual prophets named in the traditions covering the 10th and 9th centuries, two stand out in particular: Nathan in the time of David and Solomon, and Elijah (*q.v.*) in the reign of Ahab. Nathan's severe indictment of David for adultery and murder (II Sam. 12) and Elijah's denunciation of Ahab for his theft of Naboth's vineyard (I Kings 21) reveal the prophetic understanding of the sovereign authority of God over the highest human authorities. These denunciations also display another fundamental concern of the prophets: the God of Israel will not tolerate oppression of the weak by the strong. Abuse of power is repugnant to the Lord of Israel; it is at once an attack upon the Lordship of God and a refusal on the part of man to live a responsible and righteous life under God's Lordship. Elijah's assault upon the worship of the Phoenician Baal, which was sponsored in north Israel by Jezebel, also illustrates the prophetic insistence upon the sovereign Lordship of God. If Yahweh is God, he and he alone should be worshiped and served; if Baal is God, then Baal alone deserves worship and allegiance. The people could not, in Elijah's judgment, continue to "go limping with two different opinions" (I Kings 18:21). The issue was decided on Mt. Carmel, when the people cried out, "The Lord, he is God." This practical monotheism was to find even more cogent expression in the subsequent prophetic tradition.

Major Prophetic Collection.—The Old Testament collection entitled the Latter Prophets by the later Jewish community contains a massive body of prophetic literature preserved under the names of 15 individual prophets: Isaiah, Jeremiah, and Ezekiel (the "major" or larger prophetic books; Daniel is placed with these in the English Bible) and Hosea, Joel, Amos, Obadiah, Jonah, Micah, Nahum, Habakkuk, Zephaniah, Haggai, Zechariah, and Malachi (the "minor" or shorter prophetic books; the "Twelve"). The book of Isaiah contains at least 16 chapters (ch. 40–55) which stem from a prophet active among the Judaean exiles in Babylonia *c.* 540 B.C. who is referred to as the Second Isaiah or Deutero-Isaiah (*see* ISAIAH, BOOK OF). All of the prophetic books appear to have undergone a process of editing and arrangement which led, in a number of instances, to the addition of materials. It is probable that "schools" or circles within the Israelite community undertook to preserve and re-present the words and deeds of the major prophetic personalities. In Isa. 8:16–20, reference is made to that prophet's disciples (*limmudim*), to whom are entrusted the "testimony" and "teaching" of Isaiah.

It is not possible, therefore, to recover the exact words of the prophets of Israel. Yet from the circle of disciples has come a collection of materials which undoubtedly bear authentic witness to their words and deeds. It is a tribute to the power of these words and deeds that they should have been remembered, pored over, and recorded definitively for subsequent generations. The total prophetic collection probably assumed its present form no later than 200 B.C.

The prophets were also rather closely related to the Israelite cultic practices. They functioned in connection with the great festivals and ceremonies, particularly the festival at the end of the year when the covenant between Yahweh and Israel was renewed and the king was reinvested with authority under God's sovereignty.

Most probably the prophets served as mediators of the covenant between God and Israel; it would be wrong to dissociate them too sharply from priestly activities and responsibilities. Nonetheless, the prophets of Israel stood over against established religious traditions and customs and brought the divine Word of judgment against all efforts on the part of the community to secure its life by merely external or cultic means. The freedom of

God was to be protected at all costs.

Preexilic Prophets.—During the last half of the 8th century, prophecy in Israel assumed its definitive character. The prophets Amos and Hosea in north Israel, and Isaiah and Micah in Judah, drew with inexorable logic the consequences of belief in the Lordship of God over men and nations. Their messages differ in emphasis, but in all essential respects these prophets bear a common witness. Amos appeared in north Israel just prior to the rise of the Assyrian Empire to new heights under Tiglath-pileser III (745–727). The message of Hosea, Isaiah, and Micah is set in the context of Assyrian domination of Palestine and Syria; never far from view is the menace of this world power to the people of Israel. The word of the prophet is addressed to concrete situations and involves issues of life-or-death significance.

Central to the message of this group of prophets is the theme of divine judgment upon a faithless people. Israel has known God's blessing and protection (Amos 3:2) but has chosen to turn from God. The result must be severe judgment, possibly up to the point of annihilation of the people of God by God himself (Amos 9:8a). Amos pointed specifically to the corruption in public and private life within north Israel as the sign of the people's apostasy. Hosea developed the same theme and also saw in the people's dependence upon godless kings and foreign alliances a mark of their faithlessness to God. Idolatry, not clearly mentioned in Amos (but *see* 5:26), is bitterly attacked by Hosea. Isaiah catalogued the sins mentioned by Amos and Hosea and particularly stressed the sin of rebellion against the sovereign Lord (1:2). Micah's judgment upon Judah is essentially that pronounced by Amos upon north Israel.

God's judgment will be executed by the agency of a foreign invader. Amos does not seek to identify the invader, and the Assyrian Empire was still in a period of decline as the message of Amos was delivered. Hosea can speak of either Egypt or Assyria as the instrument of divine judgment (7:11; 9:6). Isaiah, however, refers to Assyria directly as the "rod" of God's anger (10:5), God's weapon to punish the rebellious people and cause the remnant left from the holocaust to return in faith and obedience to him. In face of such dire consequences, the people are summoned to return to God and be saved. Amos apparently holds out no hope that the people will do so (9:8b–15 are probably from a later hand).

Hosea, though equally pessimistic about the return of Israel to God, speaks of God's continuing love and compassion for the faithless bride (ch. 2) and for the rebellious son (ch. 11). God will not finally destroy his people; his love and mercy are not vitiated by the corruption and perversity of his people. And Isaiah is even more explicit in his hope for the future: from the devastation, a small remnant will be spared (10:22); God will raise up a deliverer from the seed of David who will fulfill the divine purpose for Israel and for the world (9:2–7; 11:1–9; *see* 2:2–4). In the meantime, Israel is to have faith; *i.e.*, she is to trust firmly in the faithfulness of God (7:9; 28:16; 30:15).

These words of hope for the future (the authenticity of which is denied by many scholars) by no means soften the severity of the divine judgment upon Israel. God's Lordship is the fundamental theme of these prophetic texts: God is God, and he will not tolerate perfunctory allegiance to his will. The total life of Israel is to be lived under his authority. God, the determiner of what is good for man, summons the individual and the people as a whole to seek him; to seek God is to seek the good (Amos 5:4, 6, 14). He demonstrates by his own righteousness and mercy the path of goodness and righteousness (Mic. 6:8). He and he alone has the power to save in time of trouble (Isa. 30:1–5; 31:1–3). Yet he calls upon man to seek and to follow the path that leads to peace and safety. He is the Lord of other nations as well as of Israel, whether or not these nations acknowledge his Lordship (Amos 1–2; Isa. 13–23). God has the power to destroy and the power to save. But man cannot presume to exercise the divine power as though it had been entrusted entirely to him. Not even the religious authorities can do so. The attacks of the prophets upon Israelite worship are designed to make this fundamental point clear. No multiplication of sacrifices and offerings can safeguard the lives of a faithless people. Sacrifice and offerings are no substitute for obedience. A "religion" practised in isolation from political, military, economic, and family responsibility is no religion at all. God calls for the loyalty and devotion of the whole man, the whole people.

The words of hope point rather to the prophetic conviction that God's purpose for mankind will triumph, despite the sin of Israel and the nations. In Hos. 11 is depicted a struggle within the "heart" of God himself: how can he bring utter destruction upon a people whom he loves? He is God and not man; God will love his people freely (14:4) and will heal their faithlessness. God remains Lord even over his decision to punish his rebellious sons (Isa. 1:18), whom he summons to repentance and obedience. God judges, but he also forgives.

During the 7th century, the prophetic movement is little in evidence until after the death of the corrupt king of Judah, Manasseh. Under the regency and kingship of Josiah, however, new prophetic voices are heard. Zephaniah (*c.* 630) prophesied the utter destruction of God's people at the hands of a foreign invader and offered hope only that a remnant of the poor and the humble might be spared. Nahum (*c.* 612) prophesied the coming ruin of the hated Assyrian empire and its capital city, Nineveh. And Habakkuk (*c.* 605) pled with God for understanding of the ways of divine judgment: why should God punish his own people at the hands of a people less righteous than they? The answer given is in the spirit of Isaiah: "The just shall live in his faithfulness"; *i.e.*, the righteous man depends upon God's faithfulness even in time of disaster or despair, just as he continues actively to pursue righteousness in his daily life. Faith in God means both confidence in God's own faithfulness to his sovereign purpose and personal obedience to the divine will.

The chief prophet of this period is Jeremiah of Anathoth (*c.* 626 [perhaps 608]–*c.* 586). Jeremiah's message is essentially that of his predecessors Amos, Hosea, and Isaiah: the same denunciation of the sins of Israel appears, as does the same call to radical repentance and return to God (ch. 2–3). Jeremiah's message is distinctive, however, at a number of points. He sees in the rise of the Neo-Babylonian Empire (605 B.C.) the instrument of God's judgment upon Judah, but he does not anticipate, as did Isaiah, that God would send the invader away after he had done his task of devastation (*see* Isa. 37:28–29). Judah must go into exile and there be purged for the day of restoration and return to her own land. All efforts on the part of the Judaean authorities to combat the power of Babylonia are constantly resisted by Jeremiah. On at least one occasion he was very nearly executed as a traitor because of his "weakening the hands" of the people (38:4).

Jeremiah struggled with God over the meaning of the divine message and over the delay in its fulfillment. For many years he prophesied doom—and nothing happened. Jeremiah's prayers, which are scattered throughout the first half of the book, demonstrate clearly the spiritual agony of the prophets of Israel. No other prophet has worked in such isolation from his community, ridiculed, persecuted, and despised. Yet he remained faithful to God through all trials and doubts until the destruction of Jerusalem in 587–586 B.C., when his words of judgment were finally fulfilled.

Jeremiah's hope for Israel is also distinctive. He anticipated the return of the exiles from Babylonia at a future date and the reconstitution of the people in their homeland. For this reason, he urged them to live responsibly in exile and even to pray for the peace of the land of their captivity (ch. 29). A day was to come when God would make a new covenant with his people, write his Law on their hearts, forgive their iniquity and remember their sin no more (31:31–34). Apparently Jeremiah did not share the great cosmic hopes of Isaiah. His more modest picture of the future involves the restoration of God's people upon their own land, but it does not include any restoration of the Temple, the sacrificial system, the old customs and laws. In this respect he differs sharply from Ezekiel as well as from Isaiah. For Jeremiah, Israelite faith is dependent upon no external supports and safeguards. The Temple was destroyed by the very God whose dwelling place it was (*see* ch. 7 and 26). The Law of God was fundamentally an inward reality, not a collection of ordinances to be written down and preserved. Faith was for Jeremiah a matter of communion with the living God. The intimacy of the relationship between God and man has no more explicit depiction than in the Book of Jeremiah (and in the Psalms, where Jeremiah's influence can be observed). Indeed, the entire prophetic movement in Israel is marked by this interior relationship between God and man, a relationship which produces freedom and spontaneity in religious acts and in daily life.

The preexilic prophets received their messages from the deity in some form of immediate experience, according to their testimony. In their conflict with the false prophets, or in defense of the truth of their words before the community at large, they could only say "The Lord sent me" (Jer. 26:12). Other prophets could make the same claim. The criteria of the true prophet were never more than working guides for the community and for the prophets themselves. The test of history was the acid test: did the words spoken by the prophets come true, or did they not (Deut. 18:21–22)? The prophets who prophesied doom rather than peace were also considered to be the more serious and reliable spokesmen for the deity (I Kings 22; Jer. 23:16–17). Yet these criteria would not suffice. In Deut. 13:1–5, appeal is made to tradition: a prophet must speak in line with the fundamental understandings of Israelite faith; if he does not do so, he is to be ignored. Jeremiah's test is finally that of the interior experience of the prophet: the true prophet is one who has sat in the (secret) council of God (23:18, 21–22). No external criteria can finally determine the truth or falsity of the divine Word spoken through the prophet.

Prophets During the Babylonian Exile.—Ezekiel and the anonymous prophet known as Deutero-Isaiah prophesied, respectively, during the early and the closing years of Babylonian exile. Ezekiel was among the captives carried into exile by the forces of Nebuchadrezzar, in 597 (or perhaps 587) B.C. Prior to the fall of Jerusalem in 587, his message was a massive polemic against the corruption of Israelite worship in Jerusalem and Judah. His strange visions and symbolic actions are all designed to express God's wrath over the desecration of Judah's religious traditions; and the prophet's message, like that of Jeremiah, is that God will destroy the defiled Temple; God's glory will depart from it; and the people will be swept off into exile. After the fall of Jerusalem, however, Ezekiel became a pastor to the exiles. His words of encouragement and hope are mixed with denunciations of political and religious corruption, but their chief import is to inspire confidence in God and in his coming deliverance as well as to summon the community and its members to responsible and righteous conduct. The vast program for the reconstitution of the state of Israel (ch. 40–48) was not to be realized; yet this vision probably did much to preserve the exiles as a religious community and hold them in readiness for the deliverance which came some years later.

From the exilic community appeared a prophetic spokesman whose message has no counterpart in the entire prophetic tradition. Deutero-Isaiah composed a prophetic text in the form of a great liturgy which abounds in hope and exultation. The radical and explicit monotheism of this prophet grows out of his conviction that God is bringing to fulfillment his whole purpose for mankind—and the people need to be reminded that God both *can* and *will* accomplish this purpose. God the redeemer is also God the creator; the whole of creation has been for the sake of redemption. With varying themes and an opulent and repetitive style, Deutero-Isaiah displays the imminent deliverance of the exiles, their return across the bleak desert, and their entrance into a restored Zion.

Interwoven with the above materials are four poems (Isa. 42:1–4; 49:1–6; 50:4–9; 52:13–53:12), known as the Servant Songs, in which the most profound hope of the prophet finds expression. Israel, or a chosen representative of Israel (or both), is seen to be God's specific instrument for the redemption of mankind. God's Servant will bring justice to the world (42:1); he will be a light to the nations (49:6), so that God's salvation may reach the ends of the earth. Though faint and despondent, he will be vindicated before his oppressors and adversaries (50:4–9), and on the

day of his exaltation the kings of the earth will discern that he has been wounded for their transgressions, smitten for their iniquities, that they, through his stripes, might be healed (53:5). This Suffering Servant of the Lord represents and embodies the mission of Israel in the world: God's people have been chosen not merely for privilege but above all for service (*see* Amos 3:2); through this representative Israelite, men and nations will come to know the meaning of their own lives and will be drawn to the living God, the only source of life and blessing.

Postexilic Prophets.—During the Babylonian exile, prophets continued to work in the devastated community of Judah. One of these, Obadiah, uttered bitter invectives against the Edomites, who gloated over the fall of Jerusalem and helped the Babylonians to round up fugitives from the besieged city. In 520 two prophets arose who were of great significance in the rebuilding of the Judaean state under Persian rule: Haggai and Zechariah. Although these prophets were particularly concerned with the reconstitution of the Judaean state and the reestablishment of its religious life, they continued to maintain the prophetic judgment upon merely external or half-hearted religious practices. Appeal was made to the "Former Prophets" (Zech. 1:4; 7:7) whose judgments from God had been confirmed in history. The postexilic prophets maintained with rigour the older prophetic insistence upon righteous conduct which shows that God's authority is taken seriously (Zech. 7:9–10; 8:16-17). And they point, in manifold ways, to the coming of God's day of triumph over all forces in opposition to his will (Zech. 9:9–10; Joel 2:28–32; Mal. 4:1–5). The heritage of the prophets is firmly embedded in the main stream of Jewish life and thought; and it also finds its particular expression in the apocalyptic element within Judaism (*see* APOCALYPTIC LITERATURE).

See also articles on the prophetic books; JUDAISM: *Biblical Period: Prophecy.*

POSTBIBLICAL PROPHECY

Early Christian Church.—In the early organization of the Christian communities (Acts 11:27; Eph. 4:11; I Cor. 12:28) prophets are mentioned, ranking next to apostles. Sometimes itinerant, sometimes settled, they were the evangelists of the early Church, credited with a direct spiritual inspiration and gift (*charisma*) for enlightenment and edification. Men can be appointed to a regular office in the Church; they cannot be appointed to prophesy. These prophets were expected to provide intelligible utterances (I Cor. 14:29–32) and were thus differentiated from the ecstatic "speaker in tongues," while they were also distinct from the permanent local officials—catechists, deacons, presbyters, bishops. From the valuable information in the Didache it appears that the high regard felt for them lasted fully a century; yet their position was always precarious. At the end of the 2nd century the wild prophesying in the Montanist Party hastened the end (*see* MONTANISM). Armed with the now-accepted canon of Holy Scripture, the authorities ruled that ecstatic seizure did not emanate from God and that the prophets were not to accept gifts. Soon Christian prophets ceased to exist as a distinct class in the Church's organization.

Yet the prophetic dimension of biblical faith in the Jewish and Christian communities has continued to be a distinctive and dominant element in these communities and in the cultures under their influence. The sovereign Lordship of God, his concern for inwardness of faith and righteous conduct, his power to assess, judge, and recreate even the religious communities which affirm his Lordship—this prophetic theme is a legacy from the prophets of Israel which is vital to any religious community rooted in biblical faith. Prophetic faith always poses issues which are of life-and-death significance; "Seek the Lord and live" (Amos 5:6) is the abiding call of the prophet. (W. HA.)

Later Christianity and Judaism.—In Judaism and Christianity, the ancient prophetic and apocalyptic pattern could always provide a model for either immediate or eschatological realization. Thus the prophetic *charisma* of the primitive Church was claimed also in later periods by various groups and individuals. The Montanists and the "pneumatic" monks (*see* MACEDONIUS) of the first

Christian centuries had their successors in, for example, the vagrant *prophetae* on the eve of the first Crusade and in the children-prophets among the French Camisards (*q.v.*) at the end of the 17th century. The same biblical promises of a large-scale restoration of prophecy (Joel 1–2) which had already inspired the first Christians (Acts 2:16–21) also produced mass prophecy in Jewish messianic movements—*e.g.,* that centred on the person of Sabbatai Zebi (*q.v.*).

In Christian sects the prophetic and the chiliast (millenarian, adventist) elements were always closely intertwined (*see* MILLENNIUM). A less eschatologically oriented view was taken by the medieval Jewish philosophers, among them Maimonides, who held that prophecy was nothing but the illumination of the mind resulting from the perfection of the human intellect; viz., from the contact of the latter with the divine principle known as the "Active Intellect." The prophet was thus the most perfect philosopher. Similar doctrines could also be held with a less philosophical and more gnostic or mystical emphasis (for example, the *Insan al-Kamil,* literally "the Perfect Man," in Islamic mysticism); the prophet is then the perfect man whose soul is united to the Divine Light or Essence. On this view prophecy is a state of mystical and illuminate perfection rather than an individual vocation or a social *charisma.*

ISLAM

In a sense Islam is the prophetic religion *par excellence.* It is the only historical religion, of whose origin we have detailed knowledge, that was founded by a prophet. In a wider sense it belongs to the biblical religions, since Mohammed (Muhammad) knew of the existence of the Old and New Testaments and was profoundly influenced by Jewish and Christian contacts. Zoroaster, too, though he was a priest, seems to have been a definitely prophetic personality, and the religion he founded exhibits a genuinely prophetic structure, but too little is known about his life and ministry to permit positive assertions; some scholars, in fact, describe him as a shaman rather than a prophet.

In the case of Mohammed, however, we possess not only a record which permits a reconstruction of his prophetic experience but also a highly developed theology expounding the nature and calling of the prophet. Whereas the formal characteristics of Mohammad's utterance (style, rhythmic prose, etc.) continue the pre-Islamic tradition of the inspired soothsayer (*kahin*), his religious interpretation of prophecy was determined by Jewish-Christian traditions, including religions influenced by them (*e.g.,* MANICHAEISM; *q.v.*). Whatever the precise identity of the revelatory agent—whether Allah himself (*cf.* Koran, *sura* 75:16 f.) or an angel (Gabriel in *sura* 2:97)—Mohammed experienced an original call (*sura* 96?) and many subsequent revelations. From the Medina period on he described himself as a *nabi,* considering himself as the last in a series of *nabiyun* sent by God (*sura* 6:83–86).

The Koran distinguishes two kinds of prophets: the *nabiyun,* of whom there were many; and the "apostles," of whom, besides Mohammed, there were eight only (including the biblical Noah, Lot, Ishmael, Moses, and Jesus). The apostle (*rasul*) is not merely an inspired speaker but a lawgiver who brings a heavenly book. Muslim doctrine of apostleship is therefore inextricably bound up with the doctrine of Holy Scripture. God sent an apostle to each nation (*umma*); however, Mohammed, who was sent as an apostle to the Arabs, is not only the greatest but also the last (*khatam,* "seal") of the prophets. Hence Islam has no room for subsequent prophecy, unless the term is understood in the wider sense of inspiration and illumination (as in gnostic and mystical circles, particularly in certain Shi'ite sects), or of special and immediate guidance by God (*see* MAHDI).

PRIMITIVE RELIGIONS

Religious leaders or functionaries exhibiting certain prophetic characteristics can be found in most primitive religions. The recognition and description of primitive prophets is largely a matter of definition and of delimitation from the related phenomena of divination, magic, shamanism (*qq.v.*), and augury (*see* AUGUR). Situations of stress have frequently produced leaders showing a certain resemblance to the biblical prophets: an initial spiritual experience or "call," followed by passionate appeals to the prophet's group demanding reform of morals and manners—frequently in terms of a return to the ways of the ancestors—predicting some kind of general catastrophe, and promising a more or less imminent salvation (liberation from white rule, riches and health, return of the ancestors or of a mythical culture-hero, etc.). The emphasis on the two main foci of prophetic preaching, reformation and eschatological preparation, may vary considerably. Most of the prophetic movements that have been studied in detail occurred after contact with whites, and hence many prophets show signs of Christian missionary influence.

In modern ethnological literature millenarian and messianic movements are often called prophetic. Examples from the North American area alone include the prophets Pope, leader of the Pueblo revolt against the Spaniards in 1680; Tenskwatawa and his brother Tecumseh (*q.v.*), leaders of the Shawnee resistance in 1805–13; Smohalla, active 1850–90; the "Prophet Dance" movement which, in its turn, influenced the "Ghost Dance" outbreaks (*see* GHOST DANCE). Whereas the "nativism" of the Ghost Dance prophets was definitely millenarian in character, the "glad tidings" of the Seneca prophet Handsome Lake (active 1799–1815), founder of the Iroquois Long House Religion, was nativistic in a more reformative way. Analogous phenomena have occurred in great numbers in Africa, Oceania, and many other parts of the world. (*See also* CARGO CULTS; NATIVISTIC MOVEMENTS.)

These millenarian prophetisms should be distinguished from sectarian prophetisms. The latter, although they too are often reactions to frustration, oppression, and the "colonial situation," are in many ways similar to revivalist outbreaks in Western Christianity (*see* REVIVALISM). The proliferation of dissident native churches generally takes place under the leadership of prophets who combine Christian ideas concerning the prophetic gift with traditional native patterns of possession, divining, and curing.

OTHER EXAMPLES

Revelations and messages by prophetic founders or reformers, leading to the establishment of new religious groups similar to Christian sects or "dissident churches," occur also outside the Christian orbit. One of the most striking examples in modern history is provided by the remarkable proliferation of religious groups—somewhat ineptly called "New Religions"—in modern Japan (*see* JAPAN: *The People: Religion: New Religious Cults*). Many of these groups, growing from a Buddhist, Shintō, or syncretistic soil, were founded by prophets (or, frequently, prophetesses) who combined some of the ancient shamanistic traditions of Japan with a prophetic sense of mission. This development is particularly interesting in view of the fact that Buddhism has produced many enlightened teachers, masters, and patriarchs but no spiritual leaders of the prophetic type. Perhaps the most outstanding exception to the rule is Nichiren (1222–82; *see* BUDDHISM), whose fanaticism, uncompromising radicalism, sense of mission, and profound conviction of being called to save the Japanese nation give his preaching a prophetic character.

(R. J. Z. W.)

BIBLIOGRAPHY.—A. Guillaume, *Prophecy and Divination Among the Hebrews and Other Semites* (1938); J. Wach, *The Sociology of Religion,* ch. viii (1944); Max Weber, *The Sociology of Religion,* Eng. trans., ch. iv (1963); H. H. Rowley, *Prophecy and Religion in Ancient China and Israel* (1956); G. Lanczkowski, *Altägyptischer Prophetismus* (1960); F. Heiler, *Prayer,* Eng. trans., pp. 135–171 and 227–285 (1958); A. Haldar, *Associations of Cult Prophets Among the Ancient Semites* (1945); W. B. Henning, *Zoroaster: Politician or Witch-Doctor* (1952); K. Rudolph, "Zarathustra—Priester und Prophet," *Numen,* vol. viii, pp. 81–116 (1961); T. Andrae, *Mohammed, the Man and His Faith,* ch. iv, tr. by T. Menzel (1936); E. E. Evans-Pritchard, *Nuer Religion,* pp. 287 ff. (1956); C. G. and B. Z. Seligman, *Pagan Tribes of the Nilotic Sudan,* p. 188 f. (1932); G. Lienhardt, *Divinity and Experience,* pp. 73–80 (1961); K. Schlosser, *Propheten in Africa* (1949); B. Sundkler, *Bantu Prophets in South Africa,* 2nd ed. (1961); H. van Straelen and C. B. Offner, *Modern Japanese Religions* (1963).
Israelite Prophecy: B. D. Napier, "Prophet, Prophetism" in *The Interpreter's Dictionary of the Bible,* vol. iii, pp. 896–919 (1962); Martin Buber, *The Prophetic Faith* (1949); J. Philip Hyatt, *Prophetic Religion* (1947); A. R. Johnson, *The Cultic Prophet in Ancient Israel,*

2nd ed. (1962); Adolphe Lods, *The Prophets and the Rise of Judaism,* tr. by S. H. Hooke (1937); S. Mowinckel, *Prophecy and Tradition* (1946); John Paterson, *The Goodly Fellowship of the Prophets* (1948); H. W. Robinson, "Prophetic Symbolism" in *Old Testament Essays* (1928); R. B. Y. Scott, *The Relevance of the Prophets* (1947); *Studies in Old Testament Prophecy,* ed. by H. Rowley (1950); G. Widengren, *Literary and Psychological Aspects of the Hebrew Prophets* (1948); J. Lindbolm, *Prophecy in Ancient Israel* (1962); A. J. Heschel, *The Prophets* (1963); H. L. Ellison, *Prophets of Israel* (1969); H. M. Orlinsky (ed.), *Interpreting the Prophetic Tradition* (1969).
Christian Prophecy: E. Selwyn, *The Christian Prophets* (1900); H. A. Guy, *New Testament Prophecy: Its Origin and Significance* (1947); M. H. Shepherd, Jr., "Prophet in the New Testament" in *The Interpreter's Dictionary of the Bible,* vol. iii, pp. 919–920 (1962); L. R. Froom, *The Prophetic Faith of Our Fathers* (1946–54); H. Staack, *Prophetic Voices of the Bible* (1968).   (R. J. Z. W.; W. Ha.)

PROPORTIONAL REPRESENTATION (P.R.), the principle that the distribution of seats in a representative assembly reflect as exactly as possible the distribution of the electors' votes among the competing parties (and independents, if any).

To its advocates the case for P.R. is fundamentally the same as that for representative government: *i.e.,* only if the assembly represents the full diversity of opinion within the nation can its decisions be regarded as the decisions of the nation itself. Holding an election is like holding a census of opinions as to how the nation shall be governed.

P.R. is opposed on grounds of both principle and expediency. In principle, its opponents hold that in an election the nation is making a decision, a choice; that the function of the electoral system is to achieve a consensus rather than a census of opinions. To make it possible for small sections of opinion to be represented is to encourage the formation of separate parties, and their mutual bargaining within the assembly leads to a weakening of the government and the processes of government. The electors in these circumstances, in fact, have less direct choice of government. The experiences of the Weimar Republic in Germany (1919–33) and of the Fourth Republic in France (1946–58) are quoted as evidence for the truth of this argument. In order to achieve a system of two parties it is necessary for the electoral system to promote the cohesion of opinions into large forces by devices which reward the stronger parties and penalize the weaker ones. There are various "majority" systems which are intended to achieve these purposes.

Supporters of P.R. reply that the relations between electoral systems, party systems, and the stability and effectiveness of governments are more complex than the opponents of P.R. believe. Belgium, Denmark, Finland, Ireland, Luxembourg, the Netherlands, Norway, and Sweden all apply P.R.; each has only a few parties of real importance and each has usually had stable, durable, and effective governments. On the other hand, countries not applying P.R. have not always had two strong parties; thus the United Kingdom has at times had a complex party system (*e.g.,* 1885–1914 and 1922–31) and precarious governments; in the United States the system of two major parties masks a multiplicity of informal and unstable factions and alliances transcending party divisions in Congress. Moreover, when the electoral system does not provide for proportional representation, an election may result in the majority of seats being won by a party receiving fewer votes than one of its opponents. Thus the Conservatives won more seats but fewer votes than Labour in the British general election of 1951; the Republicans won more seats in the electoral college but fewer popular votes than the Democrats in the U.S. presidential elections of 1876 and 1888 and therefore won the presidency; the parties supporting the Nationalist leader D. F. Malan won more seats but fewer votes than the parties supporting J. C. Smuts in the South African general elections of 1948 and 1953. Advocates of P.R. would argue that results such as these make nonsense of representative government.

The principle of P.R. was first formulated systematically in the middle of the 19th century by C. C. G. Andrae in Denmark and T. Hare and J. S. Mill in Britain. Many electoral systems have been devised to apply it. The one most advocated by the Electoral Reform Society in Britain and the Proportional Representation League in the United States is that of the single transferable vote (S.T.V.) in multimember constituencies, as used in Ireland (since 1922), Tasmania, Malta, and the Australian and South African senates. Voters number the names of the candidates on the ballot paper in order of preference, as for the alternative vote (*see* below). Ballot papers are first counted according to their first preferences. Any candidate who obtains a Droop quota (named after the discoverer of the system, the Belgian H. R. Droop), *i.e.,* $\frac{\text{no. of total valid votes cast}}{\text{no. of seats} + 1} + 1$, of first preferences is declared elected; *e.g.,* in a five-member constituency, one-fifth of the votes is not the smallest number of votes required by a candidate in order to secure a seat; six candidates could each get one-sixth of the total votes, but only five could get more. Any candidate polling even one vote more than one-sixth will be one of the five elected members. Where a quota is exceeded, all the votes of a successful candidate are sorted out for second preference, the total for each other candidate being noted. The number of votes transferred, however, is only that of the surplus over and above the quota; *i.e.,* if a candidate's surplus is one-third of his votes, the number of votes passed on to each other candidate is one-third of the preferences indicated for each of them. Any surplus among subsequently successful candidates is similarly transferred, and so on, if necessary. If any seats are still vacant, the candidate with the least papers is eliminated, and all his papers transferred to second preferences, and so on, if necessary, until all seats are filled by candidates obtaining a quota. In this way the results reflect accurately the preference of the electors and therefore their support both for individuals and for parties.

"List systems" for achieving proportional representation are used extensively on the continent of Europe. In these systems the elector votes for a list of candidates; each list is normally presented by a party organization; each party gets a share of the seats proportionate to its share of the votes. There are various alternative mathematical rules for achieving this. The two principal ones are the largest remainder rule—any seats still remaining after the quota has been filled going to the party with the largest remainder of votes; and the highest average rule, the d'Hondt rule (from its inventor, Victor d'Hondt) where the average number of votes required to win one seat is as nearly as possible the same for each party. The seats a party wins are allocated to its candidates in the order in which they are named in its list; there are various methods of enabling the elector to express preferences between the candidates of the list he supports or even to enable him to split his vote between several lists but none of these has proved as flexible and effective as the S.T.V.

Where the majority representation principle exists, the simplest system is one in which each constituency returns one representative, and the candidate with more votes than any other wins the seat, as in Britain, Canada, New Zealand, and the United States. Multimember constituencies can, however, be used; in these electors may be allowed to vote either for lists of candidates or for individual candidates. The principle is carried to its logical conclusion when the whole country is used as a constituency and the list with most votes gets all the seats, as in the Gabon Republic and Togo in 1961.

Variants of the majority system are intended to ensure some representation for minorities. Provision may be made for two ballots. At the first ballot a candidate (or list) is victorious only if he (or it) has the support of more than half of the electors voting; if an "absolute majority" of this kind is not obtained, then a second ballot is held at which the candidate (or list) with most votes ("a relative majority") is victorious; this system has been much used in France. Competition at the second ballot may be free or restricted to the two leading candidates of those who stood at the first ballot and who still wish to compete (as in France since 1958). Yet the second ballot system is not a means of applying the principle of proportional representation; thus in France in 1958 the Communists' share of the votes was ten times their share of the seats. The single transferable vote in single-member constituencies (usually called the alternative vote) is a more refined and more protracted form of the second ballot; in marking preferences on this ballot paper the elector is in effect voting in successive "second ballots" until one candidate secures an absolute majority. However, as there is only one seat to be filled, the candidate with over half the votes will get it. The limited vote and the cumulative vote are further examples. In the strictest form of the limited vote the elector has only one vote (the single nontransferable vote in multimember constituencies and employing the Droop quota); this system has been used in Japan since 1900, and in the elections when voting has been free the results have been very nearly proportional. In other forms, the elector has fewer votes than there are seats to be filled. In the cumulative vote in multimember constituencies the elector has as many votes as there are seats to be filled, but he can give two or more votes to a candidate instead of only one vote. This is used for the state legislature in Illinois, where it has ensured representation for minorities but does not guarantee that the representation will be proportionate to the parties' shares of the votes.

Some countries have developed mixed systems applying the principles of "majority" and "proportional" representation. Thus in the Federal Republic of Germany since 1949 each elector has had two votes. Half the members in the parliament are elected in the single-member constituencies. The remaining seats are filled proportionately by the list system in multimember constituencies. The number of seats a party gains in the single-member constituencies is deducted from the total number of seats to which it is entitled, so as to obtain the number of seats which will be filled by the party from its lists. This system slightly favours the larger parties but is essentially one providing for proportional representation. In France in 1951 the list system of P.R. used at the previous elections was modified so that in any provincial constituency any party or interparty alliance which secured an absolute majority of the votes would win all the seats; this change was intended to weaken the Communist Party and Gen. Charles de Gaulle's Rassemblement du Peuple Française. In Italy in 1953 the list system of P.R. used at the previous election was modified so that if a party or alliance won an absolute majority of votes in the country as a whole it would get three-fifths of the seats; in fact, no party or alliance succeeded and the P.R. list system was applied as before. *See also* DEMOCRACY; REPRESENTATION.

BIBLIOGRAPHY.—E. Lakeman and J. D. Lambert, *Voting in Democracies* (1959); J. F. S. Ross, *Elections and Electors* (1955); F. A. Hermens, *Democracy or Anarchy? A Study of Proportional Representation* (1941), *Europe Between Democracy and Anarchy* (1951); J. Hogan, *Election and Representation* (1945); W. J. M. Mackenzie, *Free Elections* (1958); M. Duverger, *Political Parties,* 2nd ed. rev. (1959).
(P. W. C.)

PROPOSITION. In scholastic and traditional logic, a proposition was understood as an expression in words having the meaning of an assertion. An example is Petrus Hispanus, c. 1245, "Propositio est oratio verum vel falsum significans indicando" ("A proposition is a statement indicating a true or false meaning"). Thus a proposition is not simply a declarative sentence, in the grammatical sense, but is such a sentence taken together with its meaning. Consequently, propositions may be different even though the sentences are the same (*e.g., I am hungry,* uttered by two different persons), and, although this consequence is less emphasized by traditional writers, propositions are different when the sentences are different and even if the meaning is the same (*e.g., Tempus fugit* and *Time flies*).

The usual scholastic term was the Latin *propositio*—first found in this meaning in the writings of Lucius Apuleius, c. 150, and Manlius Severinus Boethius, c. 500. However, *enuntiatio* (enunciation)—a term taken from Cicero—was also employed, and some of the scholastics used this as the general term, reserving *propositio* for some more special meaning.

This scholastic-traditional notion of a proposition is inconvenient or unsatisfactory in many contexts because of its dependence on the particular form of expression in words, or on a particular language. Hence the different notion of a mental proposition (*propositio mentalis*) came to be introduced, and also, chiefly later, that of a judgment (*iudicium*).

According to William Ockham, and later scholastics who followed him, the mental proposition must be formed internally before a corresponding proposition in words is put forward. It is not of any language. Its parts are mental terms or concepts, which

are analogous to the spoken or written terms and share with them all properties essential to the meaning, but not such purely grammatical properties as having a particular (grammatical) gender or belonging to a particular declension or conjugation.

The notion of a judgment, as the mental act of assent or dissent, has some mention in the writings of various scholastics, and was made an explicit part of the treatment of logic by Petrus Ramus and later by such logicians as Isaac Watts (1725) and Christian Wolff (1728). It was still later that the definition of a proposition as a "judgment expressed in words" became a commonplace.

Immanuel Kant, and many traditional logicians who have followed him, replace the consideration of propositions almost entirely by that of judgments. Thus Kant speaks usually, though not always, of an analytic or synthetic judgment (German, *Urtheil*) rather than proposition (German, *Satz*), of a categorical judgment, etc.

However, the mental proposition and the judgment have a psychological reference which may often be as unsatisfactory as the dependence on a particular language which is involved in the traditional notion of a proposition. For some purposes at least there is needed a more abstract notion, independent alike of any particular expression in words and of any particular psychological act of judgment or conception—not the particular declarative sentence, but the content of meaning which is common to the sentence and its translation into another language—not the particular judgment, but the objective content of the judgment, which is capable of being the common property of many. Such an abstract notion may be seen in the Stoic *Lekta* (*see* LOGIC, HISTORY OF: *Stoics and Megarians*) and the *complexe significabilia* of some 14th and 15th century scholastics, but these ideas fell into oblivion and were reintroduced in different terminology in modern times. By modern logicians the word "proposition" has come to be used for the abstract notion, and we shall therefore here distinguish between *proposition in the traditional sense* and *proposition in the abstract sense*.

Bernard Bolzano attributes the use of *propositio* for proposition in the abstract sense to G. W. von Leibniz in *Dialogus de Connexione inter Res et Verba.* This may be a misunderstanding. But this dialogue does set forth clearly one important ground of the need for the abstract notion. An explicit distinction between the sentence and the proposition (in the abstract sense) which the sentence expresses is made by Bolzano in his *Wissenschaftslehre* of 1837, where *Satz an sich* is used for the latter. Gottlob Frege in 1892 uses *Gedanke* for the sense of a declarative sentence, giving to this German word (as he explains) an objective, rather than its more natural subjective, meaning. *Proposition* is used in the abstract sense by Bertrand Russell in *The Principles of Mathematics* (1903), where Russell recognizes that Frege's *Gedanke* is approximately "what I have called an unasserted proposition," and in *Principia Mathematica* A. N. Whitehead and Russell speak of "what we call a 'proposition' (in the sense in which this is distinguished from the phrase expressing it)." Russell also uses *proposition* in the traditional sense, *e.g.,* in *Introduction to Mathematical Philosophy,* defining a proposition as "a form of words which expresses what is either true or false" (very close to the translation of the Latin of Petrus Hispanus as quoted above); but more recent writers have generally followed him in the abstract usage. *See also* LOGIC. (Ao. C.)

BIBLIOGRAPHY.—R. M. Eaton, *General Logic,* i, 3–5 (1931); Alonzo Church, *Introduction to Mathematical Logic,* sec. 04 (1956); Ludwig Wittgenstein, *Philosophical Investigations,* sec. 134 *et seq.* (1953).

PROPYLAEA, the name given to porches or gatehouses at the entrance of sacred or other enclosures in Greece; propylaea usually consisted, at their simplest, of a porch supported by columns both without and within the actual gate. The name is especially given to the great entrance hall of the Acropolis at Athens, which was begun in 437 B.C. by Pericles. The building was never completed according to plan, but the portion that was built was among the chief glories of Athens and afforded a model to many subsequent imitators. The architect was Mnesicles; the material was Pentelic marble, with Eleusinian blackstone for dadoes and other details.

The plan of the Propylaea consists of a large square hall, from which five steps lead up to a wall pierced by five gateways of graduated sizes, the central one giving passage to a road suitable for beasts or vehicles. On the inner side, facing the Acropolis, this wall is faced with a portico of six Doric columns. At the other end of the great hall is a similar portico facing outward; and between this and the doors the hall is divided into three aisles by rows of Ionic columns. The western or outer front is flanked on each side by a projecting wing, with a row of three smaller Doric columns between antae at right angles to the main portico.

ALISON FRANTZ

EAST FACADE OF THE PROPYLAEA, ON THE ACROPOLIS, ATHENS

The north wing is completed by a square chamber which served as a picture gallery, but the south wing contains no corresponding chamber, and its plan has evidently been curtailed; its front projected beyond its covered area, and it is finished in what was evidently a provisional way on the side of the bastion before the little temple of Athena Nike.

From this and other indications W. Dörpfeld inferred that the original plan of Mnesicles was to complete the south wing on a plan symmetrical with that of the north wing, but opening by a portico on to the bastion to the west; and to add on the inner side of the Propylaea two great halls, faced by porticoes almost in a line with the main portico, but with smaller columns. This would have interfered with sacred objects such as the precinct of Artemis Brauronia and the altar of Nike, and the architect was probably forced to modify his plan even before work on the building stopped. The Propylaea were approached in Greek times by a zigzag path, terraced along the rock; this was superseded in Roman times by a broad flight of steps. In medieval times the Propylaea served as the palace of the dukes of Athens; they were much damaged by the explosion of a powder magazine in 1645. The tower of Frankish or Turkish date that stood on the south wing was pulled down in 1874. (*See* also GREEK ARCHITECTURE.)

The term is also applied to various monumental gateways of modern times, especially in Germany. Examples are the propylaea at Munich (1862) and the Brandenburg Gate in Berlin (1784).

See W. J. Anderson and R. P. Spiers, *The Architecture of Ancient Greece*, rev. by W. B. Dinsmoor, new ed. (1950); D. S. Robertson, *A Handbook of Greek and Roman Architecture*, 2nd ed., corrected (1943). (E. GR.; C. M. RN.)

PROPYL ALCOHOLS. Two compounds, both with the formula C_3H_7OH, are known by this name, and both are widely used.

Normal propyl alcohol, $CH_3 \cdot CH_2 \cdot CH_2 \cdot OH$, is obtainable as a by-product in the synthesis of methyl alcohol by condensing carbon monoxide and hydrogen in the presence of a zinc-chromite or zinc-cobalt-chromite catalyst at 400° C under 200 atm. pressure. It is a colourless, fragrant liquid boiling at 97.4° C and miscible with water in all proportions. It cannot be separated from water by distillation since the two compounds form an azeotropic mixture. *n*-Propyl alcohol, also known as 1-propanol, occurs in fusel oil and may be prepared by any of the synthetic methods applicable to primary alcohols. (*See* ALCOHOL.) It is used in the preparation of lacquers, in organic chemical synthesis, and as a solvent for many materials.

Isopropyl alcohol, $(CH_3)_2CH \cdot OH$, is manufactured on an extensive scale from propylene, $CH_3:CH:CH_2$, obtained by the cracking of petroleum. This olefin is absorbed in sulfuric acid, the liquid is diluted with water, and the mixture is then distilled, with isopropyl alcohol being obtained. It is a colourless, fragrant liquid boiling at 82.7° C. It is used as a solvent, as a deicing and antistall agent in liquid fuels, and as a reagent in organic chemical synthesis. Its alternate name is isopropanol.

PROSE, the plain speech of mankind, when used without reference to the rules of verse (*q.v.*). As a literary term, it is generally opposed to poetry (*q.v.*), but because a definition of poetry involves metaphysical considerations, literary prose may be best defined as including all forms of literary expression not metrically versified. Its derivation from the Latin adjective *prosus* (earlier, *prorsus*), "direct," or "straight," has led at some periods to the theory that prose should be plain and straightforward, and should properly deal with the statement of what is true or provable in fact and reason.

Three main kinds of prose may be distinguished: descriptive (of action, people, places, or things); explanatory or expository; and emotive. In any prose work all may be found; thus a narrative may be primarily descriptive, but may include passages of explanatory and emotive prose. Descriptive prose includes narrative of all kinds: the prose romance (*see* ROMANCE); the novel and short story (*qq.v.*) and their variants (*e.g.*, mystery and detective stories, science fiction, and children's literature, *qq.v.*); autobiography and biography, the essay (*qq.v.*) and the diary, the letter and the memoir, the "character" (*see* ENGLISH LITERATURE: *Early 17th Century*); accounts of travel and exploration; and those writings on scientific subjects that aim at describing, rather than explaining, the natural world. Explanatory or expository prose includes writings on science, law, philosophy, theology, morals, political science, history, and criticism. It may be objective, didactic, or persuasive in character, and may also include descriptive and narrative elements (in historical and scientific works, for example). Although often most nearly approximating to the idea of prose as "plain," explanatory prose may rise to poetic heights. (*See* also HISTORY: *Historiography;* CRITICISM; etc., for some account of writings in this type of prose.)

Emotive prose, aimed at inducing feeling rather than thought, is found in polemical works (*see* PAMPHLET), in oratory (*q.v.*), in the sermon (*see* PREACHING); and also in fictional, historical, scientific, philosophical, and critical writing. Much journalistic prose, though also descriptive and explanatory, is emotive in intention. Much biblical prose is primarily emotive: a fact that has increased the difficulties of translation (*see* BIBLE, TRANSLATIONS OF).

For a historical account of the development of prose in various languages, *see* articles on the national literatures: AMERICAN LITERATURE; ENGLISH LITERATURE; FRENCH LITERATURE; etc. *See* also STYLE, LITERARY; RHETORIC; DRAMA; DRAMATIC CRITICISM; NEWSPAPER; PERIODICAL; SATIRE; and articles on prose works and writers. *See* also the bibliographies to these articles.

PROSECUTION, the procedure by which the law is put in motion to bring to trial a person accused of crime. Constitutionally, maintenance of order is one of the functions of executive government, the whole of which, in the United Kingdom, is carried out in the name of the crown. In this sense the crown can be said to prosecute, and the prosecution is often referred to as "the crown." In theory, the individual who has suffered from the crime is at liberty to conduct the prosecution himself, but rarely does so. In practice, most prosecutions are undertaken by the police, on the basis of complaints made to them. The more serious crimes, such as murder, are prosecuted by a legal officer of the government. The English procedure does not centralize all prosecutions for crime in a public official or department and thus differs from the system employed in Scotland and continental European countries, as well as from the American system.

In the United States, crimes against the federal government are prosecuted by appointed United States attorneys, who act under the supervision of the attorney general. In the states, prosecution is by district or county attorneys. These usually are elected officials and enjoy varying degrees of autonomy from the supervision of the state attorney general; the latter may, however, be empowered on occasion to intervene and conduct a prosecution himself.   (H. L. Pr.)

PROSELYTE, a word that has come to mean a convert to any religious faith but that originally (Greek *proselytos*) meant a convert to Judaism. In Hebrew the verb formed from the noun "stranger" is not "to estrange" but "to disestrange"—that is, to remove a man from stranger's status by converting him into a Jew. In its very morphology the Hebrew language thus records a yearning for converts.

According to the Bible, even proscribed Canaanites lived with their Israelite hosts (I Kings 9:20–21) and apparently accepted at least some precepts of the religion of Israel. On most solemn occasions, such as the final covenant of Moses (Deut. 29:10, "the sojourner who is in your camp") and the reading of the Law on Mt. Gerizim and Mt. Ebal (Josh. 8:33–35), strangers stood alongside native-born Israelites. But it was apparently in the days of Ezra that the rite of formal conversion to Judaism—by baptism, circumcision, and a Temple offering—was developed (Neh. 10:29 and Rashi *ad loc.*). In subsequent centuries, particularly under Rome, there were so many converts to Judaism that Jews came to number almost 10% of the population of the Roman Empire—a percentage which could not have been accounted for solely by natural increase. The Jewish quest for converts is reflected in Jesus' statement that "you traverse sea and land to make a single proselyte" (Matt. 23:15; *cf.* Midrash Genesis Rabba 28:5), as well as in the ascription of proselyte forebears—even wicked forebears like Sisera, Haman, and Nero—to such worthies as Abtalion, Rabbi Akiba, and Rabbi Meïr. The conversion of the royal family of the Kingdom of Adiabene is related by Josephus.

After the Theodosian Code (effective Jan. 1, 439) declared conversion of a Christian to Judaism a capital offense, the quest for converts had to be restrained; and in the course of time what was begun as discretion came to be regarded as policy. Still, throughout the ages individuals, particularly priests and noblemen, converted to Judaism. In modern times even entire communities have become proselytes; in the 1940s the villagers of San Nicandro in southern Italy joined Jewish ranks, and most of them migrated to Israel. Among the mass conversions to Judaism, that of the Khazars in the 8th century is noteworthy (*see* Khazars).

Bibliography.—B. J. Bamberger, *Proselytism in the Talmudic Period* (1939), and "Proselytes" in *The Universal Jewish Encyclopedia*, vol. ix, pp. 1–3 (1943); W. G. Braude, *Jewish Proselyting in the First Five Centuries of the Common Era* (1940); Elena Cassin, *San Nicandro: the Story of a Religious Phenomenon* (1959).   (W. G. Br.)

PROSERPINE, generally accounted the Latin form (*Proserpina*) of Persephone. *See* Persephone.

PROSODY, CLASSICAL. Ancient Greek metre differs fundamentally from modern English metre in that it is based not on stress but on quantity. Greek verses are composed of comparatively complicated and rigid patterns of long and short syllables. Most Latin verse too is composed on a quantitative system in imitation of Greek.

Greek.—The length of a syllable is determined by the length of the vowel sound contained in it: ω, η and diphthongs are long by nature; a, ι, υ may be long by nature (*e.g.*, $\chi\omega\rho\bar{a}$, $\lambda\bar{\upsilon}\omega$, $\bar{\iota}\epsilon\rho o\varsigma$). Vowels with ι subscript or a circumflex accent are long.

A vowel may become long by position when followed by two or more consonants, or by the letters ζ, ξ, ψ; *e.g.*, $\dot{\epsilon}\lambda\pi\iota\zeta\text{'}o\nu$ $\kappa\epsilon\alpha\rho$. But certain combinations of consonants, known as "mute and liquid," do not invariably lengthen the preceding vowel. Such combinations are: $\pi\lambda$, $\phi\lambda$, $\kappa\lambda$, $\chi\lambda$, $\tau\lambda$, $\theta\lambda$, $\kappa\mu$, $\tau\mu$, $\theta\mu$, $\pi\nu$, $\phi\nu$, $\kappa\nu$, $\chi\nu$, $\theta\nu$, $\tau\nu$, $\pi\rho$, $\phi\rho$, $\kappa\rho$, $\tau\rho$, $\theta\rho$. The letters β, γ, δ lengthen the preceding vowel always when followed by μ or ν, usually when followed by λ, but not when followed by ρ. In Sappho and Alcaeus combinations of mute and liquid almost always lengthen the preceding vowel; in Homer, Pindar and Bacchylides more often than not; in Attic drama usually not.

Elision.—When a word ending with a short vowel is followed by a word beginning with a vowel, the final vowel of the first word is

usually omitted, *e.g.*, $\tau\omega\nu\delta$ ' $\dot{a}\pi\alpha\lambda\lambda\alpha\gamma\eta\nu$.

Epic Correction.—In Homer a final long vowel or diphthong may be shortened when the following word begins with a vowel; *e.g.*, $\dot{\epsilon}\gamma\overset{\smile}{\omega}$ $o\dot{\upsilon}$.

Crasis.—Certain short words ending in a vowel may fuse with the initial vowel of the following word; *e.g.*, $\kappa\alpha\iota\,\dot{\epsilon}\mu\epsilon$ becomes $\kappa\dot{a}\mu\epsilon$.

Synezesis.—Certain pairs or groups of vowels other than diphthongs may sometimes be scanned as one syllable; *e.g.*, $\overline{\epsilon\omega}$, $\overline{\mu\eta\,o\dot{\upsilon}}$.

Hiatus.—Where a final vowel is followed by an initial vowel without either vowel being in any way affected, there is said to be "hiatus." In many apparent hiatuses in Homer the consonant "digamma" ($_F$) was originally present, although not written in the manuscripts. The digamma is sometimes present in Pindar.

Greek verse is of two main types: spoken, or "stichic," and sung, or lyric.

Greek Lyric Verse.—Some lyric verse is composed in set stanzas, notably the sapphic and alcaic (*q.v.*), but most is composed in "strophae" stanzas, often long and complicated, composed according to the poet's fancy. These stanzas may be analyzed into verses. The Greek verse is roughly equivalent to the line in English poetry, although one verse is often printed as more than one line in Greek texts. The end of a verse always coincides with the end of a word. When a verse ends with a vowel and the following verse begins with a vowel there is hiatus. The last syllable of a verse is always, in principle, long. If a short syllable occurs at the end of a verse, it is counted as long and called *brevis in longo*.

Each verse consists of one or more "cola" ($\kappa\hat{\omega}\lambda o\nu$ ["limb"]). Some cola are analyzable into "metra" ($\mu\acute{\epsilon}\tau\rho o\nu$ ["measure"]). The elements used in the composition of both metra and cola are: long ($-$), short ($\smile$), anceps ($\overset{\smile}{-}$, meaning that the position may be occupied by either a long or a short syllable), biceps ($\overset{\smile\smile}{-}$ the position may be occupied by either one long syllable or two short ones). Thus $\overset{\smile}{-}-\smile-$ is described verbally as "anceps, long, short, long," and $-\overset{\smile\smile}{-}$ as "long, biceps."

Metra.—Iamb ($\overset{\smile}{-}-\smile-$), trochee ($-\smile-\overset{\smile}{-}$), dactyl ($-\overset{\smile\smile}{-}$), anapaest (basically $\smile\smile-\smile\smile-$, but all four elements are bicipitia), ionic ($\smile\smile--$), cretic ($-\smile-$), choriamb ($-\smile\smile-$). Cola are usually formed of two or more metra of the same type and are named according to the number of metra they contain; *e.g.*, ionic dimeter $\smile\smile--|\smile\smile--$. (*See* Iamb; Ionic Metre; Trochee; Dactyl; Anapaest; Choriambic Verse.)

Catalexis.—Many types of colon may be varied by the omission of one quantity at or near the end. Thus, $\overset{\smile}{-}-\smile-|\smile--$ is a catalectic iambic dimeter; $\smile\smile--|\smile\smile-$ is a catalectic ionic dimeter.

In the following types the cola are not analyzable into metra.

Aeolo-Choriambic.—Basic constituents: anceps, choriamb, $-\smile\smile-\smile-$. Two ancipitia commencing the colon form the "aeolic base." A common aeolo-choriambic colon, the "glyconic" (*q.v.*), consists of base and $-\smile\smile-\smile-$. Longer cola, the so-called "asclepiads," are formed by the addition of one or two choriambs between base and $-\smile\smile-\smile-$ (*see* Choriambic Verse).

Prosodiac-Enoplia.—Cola of this type combine single-short and double-short rhythm. They cannot be analyzed and are perhaps best regarded as prolongations of $-\smile\smile-\smile-$. Examples are:

$$\smile-\smile-\smile--$$
$$\kappa\alpha\rho\delta\iota o\delta\eta\kappa\tau o\nu\ \dot{\epsilon}\mu o\iota\ \kappa\rho\alpha\tau\upsilon\nu\epsilon\iota\varsigma$$

$$\beta\iota o\nu\ \dot{\omega}\ \tau\epsilon\ \delta o\kappa\epsilon\iota\ \psi\epsilon\gamma\omega.$$

Dochmiacs.—The dochmiac may be regarded as an unusually long and variable metron. It consists of anceps, two bicipitia, anceps, biceps. The most common forms are: $\smile\smile-\smile-$, $\smile--\smile-$, $-\smile\smile-\smile-$. Dochmiacs are confined to Attic drama.

Dactylo-Epitrites.—These occur in Attic drama, and about half the extant poems of Pindar are composed in this metre. Its most common constituents are $-\smile\smile-\smile\smile-$ (hemiepes), $-\smile-$ (cretic) and $-\smile\smile-$ (choriamb), which are linked together by ancipitia, usually long, to form compounds like

$$-\ -\smile\smile-\smile\smile-$$
$$\kappa\lambda\epsilon\iota\nu\alpha\nu\ \text{'}A\kappa\rho\alpha\gamma\alpha\nu\tau\alpha\ \gamma\epsilon\rho\alpha\iota\rho\omega\nu\ \epsilon\dot{\upsilon}\chi o\mu\alpha\iota.$$

The link anceps may sometimes be omitted, and verses may begin with acephalous (headless) elements, e.g.:

∪∪–∪|–∪–|∪–∪–|∪–∪–

'Ασιας εὐροχορου τριπολιν νασον πελας.

Several types of metre may be combined in the same stanza. Iambs are found combined with most types of metre. Aeolo-choriambs and prosodiac-enoplia often occur together. Dochmiacs sometimes receive an admixture of iambic. Dactylo-epitrites are rarely mixed with other metres.

Greek Stichic Verse.—This is composed in lines (στίχοι) of the same length and type: dactylic hexameters in Homer, etc., iambic trimeters and trochaic tetrameters in the spoken portions of drama. Stichic lines are always divided by word-end at or near the middle. If this division falls within a metron it is called "caesura" (marked thus: ‖), if at the end of a metron "diaeresis." (For the rules governing caesura and other features of stichic composition see HEXAMETER; IAMB; TROCHEE; ANAPAEST; ELEGY.)

Latin.—The Saturnian, probably the only indigenous type of Latin metre, was employed in the earliest Latin verse: epitaphs, ritual incantations, Livius Andronicus' translation of the *Odyssey* and Naevius' *Bellum Poenicum*. The scansion of the exiguous fragments of Saturnians that survive is disputed, and both accentual and quantitative systems have been proposed. Ancient metricians quote as a perfect Saturnian:

–∪–∪∪|–∪–‖–∪∪–∪–∪

malum dabunt Metelli ‖*Naevio poetae*

which may be scanned quantitatively as catalectic iambic dimetre and ithyphallic (cretic, bacchiac). But few other surviving Saturnians can be scanned so. From the time of Ennius, Saturnians were ousted by metres imitated from Greek.

The length of syllables is determined as follows: Diphthongs are long. A single vowel followed by a single consonant may be long or short by nature; e.g., *mălus* "bad," but *mālus* "mast." A vowel followed by two consonants is long by position. The vowel is not always lengthened if the second of the two consonants is *l* or *r*; e.g., *volŭcri* or *volūcri*. If, however, the first consonant and the following *l* or *r* belong to different words, the preceding vowel is always lengthened; e.g., *arcēbāt longe*. Vowels are always lengthened before *ll* and *rr*.

Elision occurs when a word ending with a vowel or a vowel and *m* is followed by a word commencing with a vowel; e.g., *conticuer(e) omnes, quamqu(am) animus.* The vowel *i* must be distinguished from consonantal *i*, printed in older texts as *j*; e.g., *vitis Iaccho, Coeumqu(e) Iapetum*, but *auxilium iubeat, irĕ iubes.* Initial *h* does not count as a consonant; *i.e.*, it does not lengthen or prevent elision (*e.g., omnis humo, monstr[um] horrendum*). In Latin texts elided syllables are printed, not replaced, as in Greek, by apostrophe.

The principal types of Greek metre used in Latin are dactylic hexameters and elegiacs. Horace uses various lyric metres, notably sapphics and alcaics (*q.v.*), asclepiads, glyconics, etc. (see CHORIAMBIC VERSE and GLYCONIC). Catullus and Martial use the "choliamb" (see IAMB) and the "phalaecian" or "hendecasyllable," an aeolo-choriambic colon composed of base, –∪∪–∪–, bacchiac (∪––):

–∪–∪∪–∪–∪–∪

Cui dono lepidum novum libellum

–∪–∪∪–∪–∪–∪

arida modo pumic(e) expolitum.

Iambic trimeters of Greek type are found in Catullus, Horace and Seneca (*see* IAMB).

The verse of republican comedy differs fundamentally from the metres enumerated above. The lines are analyzable into feet, not metra. The equivalent of the iambic trimeter, the "iambic senarius," consists of six feet, the last of which must be an iamb (∪–). In the other feet a spondee (––), a tribrach (∪∪∪), a dactyl (–∪∪), an anapaest (∪∪–) and even (especially in the first foot) a proceleusmatic (∪∪∪∪) may be substituted. There is usually caesura in the third foot, sometimes in the fourth:

–∪–|–∪–|∪–|–∪–|–|∪–|∪–∪

ego quia non rediit filius quae cogito.

The iambic octonarius (eight feet) and septenarius (seven and a half feet) also occur in comedy.

The "trochaic septenarius" (equivalent of Greek trochaic tetrameter catalectic) is the commonest verse in comedy after the iambic senarius. The seventh foot must be a trochee (–∪). Spondees, dactyls, anapaests and tribrachs may be substituted in the first six feet. There is usually diaeresis after the fourth foot:

∪∪–|–∪|–∪|–|∪∪|–‖––|–|∪∪∪|–∪|–

ubi me dixero dare tanti testis faciet ilico.

In comedy the rules governing the length of syllables differ in some respects from those for other types of classical Latin verse. Syllables which would elsewhere be long must in comedy sometimes be scanned as short. Pronouns especially are often shortened; *e.g., ĭlle, ĭste.* Adjacent vowels are often contracted into one syllable by synezesis, as *fŭisse, seorsum:*

–|–∪–∪|–∪–∪|–|–∪–∪

non fuit necess(e) habere; sed id quod lex iubet.

The reasons for these particularities are much disputed.

Study of Classical Metre.—The most important ancient work on metre which has survived is an abridgment of the treatise of Hephaestion. This work, however, records theories formulated when the principles of classical metre were no longer well understood. His chief mistake was to attempt to analyze all types of Greek metre into short "feet" (*e.g.*, iamb ∪–, as in Latin comedy, instead of ∪–∪–). This system is still found in out-of-date metrical works. His terminology (*e.g.*, names of feet) has been adopted even in English metrical theory, to which it is ill-suited. Since about 1800 classical metricians have discarded much of Hephaestion's theory and terminology, but misleading terminology is still in use, and there are few reliable modern works.

BIBLIOGRAPHY.—U. von Wilamowitz, *Griechische Verskunst* (1921); Paul Maas, *Greek Metre* (1962); A. M. Dale, *The Lyric Metres of Greek Drama* (1948), "The Metrical Units of Greek Lyric Verse," *Classical Quarterly*, vol. 2–3 (1950–51). Useful summaries are: B. Snell, *Griechische Metrik*, 2nd ed. (1957); W. J. W. Koster, *Précis de métrique latine* appended to *Traité de métrique grecque*, 2nd ed. (1953); F. Crusius, *Römische Metrik*, 4th ed. rev. by H. Rubenbauer (1959); J. W. Halporn *et al., The Meters of Greek and Latin Poetry* (1963). For complete scansions of Pindar and Bacchylides *see* B. Snell's editions of those poets in the Teubner series (1953 and 1949). For complete scansions of the lyrics of Greek drama *see* O. Schroeder, *Cantica* (1907–16) in the Teubner series. On the metres of Sappho and Alcaeus *see* D. L. Page, *Sappho and Alcaeus* (1955).

On Saturnian metre *see* J. F. Mountford, "Metre, Latin" in *The Oxford Classical Dictionary* (1949); W. J. W. Koster, "Versus Saturnius," *Mnemosyne*, new series, vol. 56, pp. 267–346 (1929); O. J. Todd, "Servius on the Saturnian Metre," *Classical Quarterly*, vol. 34, pp. 133–145 (1940); W. Beare, *Latin Verse and European Song* (1957).

See also D. S. Raven, *Latin Metre: an Introduction* (1965); K. J. Shapiro and R. Beum, *Prosody Handbook* (1965); G. W. Allen, *American Prosody* (1966). (L. P. E.)

PROSTHETICS is that branch of medical science dealing with artificial organs and parts (prostheses). Though by definition a prosthesis is any artificial organ or part replacing a missing natural one, this article is devoted exclusively to those most commonly called "prostheses"; *i.e.*, those replacing lost arms or legs. Other prosthetic devices are discussed in PROSTHODONTICS (dental prosthetics) and the related article TEETH, ARTIFICIAL; and EYE, HUMAN: *Artificial Eyes*. Devices that assume or augment the functions of diseased organs are discussed in ARTIFICIAL ORGANS (lung, heart, and kidney); EYEGLASSES; and HEARING AID. Braces, which give support or stability to a limb or joint, are not replacement parts, hence are not considered prostheses; instead, they are known as orthotic ("straightening") devices.

History.—Lower-extremity prostheses were used as early as 600 to 500 B.C., but the origin of prosthetics as a science is attributed to the 16th-century French surgeon Ambroise Paré. Later workers developed upper-extremity replacements, including metal hands made either in one piece or with movable parts. The solid metal hand of the 16th and 17th centuries later gave way in great measure to a single hook or a leather-covered, nonfunctioning hand attached to the forearm by a leather or wooden shell. Improvement in the design of prostheses and increased acceptance of their use have paralleled the various major wars. New lightweight materials and better mechanical joints were introduced following World Wars I and II.

The desire to walk causes leg amputees to accept lower-extremity prostheses readily, even if they are not perfectly constructed or fitted. Thus such devices for lost feet and legs are far more advanced than those for hands and arms.

Reasons for Prostheses.—The chief reason for employment of prosthetic devices is surgical removal, or amputation, of a part. Amputation may be a lifesaving measure following severe injuries or crushing fractures; and many diseases affecting muscles or bones require amputation as the only possible treatment. Amputation sometimes is resorted to in cases of severe deformity of an extremity, from either a congenital abnormality or a disease such as poliomyelitis; in these cases the extremity may be not only useless but grotesquely shaped, and amputation and subsequent fitting of a prosthesis gives better function with better appearance. The general rule in all amputation surgery with a view toward the fitting of a prosthesis is to save all the limb length possible.

A less common use of prostheses is to replace arms or legs absent or stunted at birth (phocomelia and similar anomalies: *see* MONSTER). The use of the sedative thalidomide in Europe and elsewhere after 1958 and of other drugs increased the study of drugs in relation to prosthetics.

Wearing a Prosthesis.—The earlier a prosthesis can be provided for an amputee the sooner he will learn its use and the more consistently he will wear it. If he learns to use the amputation stump or to compensate for his loss in some other way, he is likely to reject the prosthesis. The person born without a limb presents a different problem, having always lived without the extremity. This problem is best overcome by providing the prosthesis at the earliest practical age.

The child given a prosthesis before the age of 6 is a better prosthetic wearer than is one to whom the prosthesis is given later in life. A lower-extremity prosthesis should be fitted when the child shows the normal tendency to attempt standing—somewhere between 6 and 15 months of age. Upper-extremity prostheses, being more complicated and requiring more mechanical coordination, are fitted later, the below-elbow type at 18 to 24 months and the above-elbow type at 3 or 4 years.

Lower-Extremity Prostheses.—The leg prosthesis is basically made of willow wood. In the below-knee type the wooden socket is fashioned to fit the stump perfectly. A wood-and-metal foot is attached by a joint so that there is some ankle and toe motion. At the upper end of the prosthesis are metal hinges so that the knee will bend. Attached to the knee hinges is a thigh piece made of heavy leather; this laces in the front and fits the thigh very snugly, so that part of the wearer's weight is supported by the thigh corset and the remainder is supported by the bone below the knee in direct contact with the prosthesis.

A more recent type of below-knee prosthesis is made from plastic and fits the below-knee stump with total contact. This prosthesis is held on either by means of a supracondylar strap, that is, a strap that passes above the kneecap, or the prosthesis may have added to it rigid metal knee hinges with the leather thigh corset described above. Weight bearing is accomplished by having pressure of the prosthesis against the tendon that extends from the kneecap to the tibia (lower legbone). Hence, this type of prosthesis is referred to as the patellar tendon bearing type of prosthesis. It can be used on both children and adults. In addition a new foot piece is commonly used which consists of a solid foot and ankle but with layers of rubber in the heel to give a cushioning effect. This is known as the SACH (solid ankle cushion heel).

The above-knee prosthesis consists of two willow sockets, the below-knee and foot portions being similar to the below-knee type. The above-knee portion is hollowed out to fit the stump, and extends to the pelvis, which bears the body weight. The above-knee and below-knee portions are connected by a mechanical knee joint. The wearer does not have direct control of the knee joint, hence walking requires considerable skill. There are two main types of above-knee prostheses: (1) the prosthesis held on by means of a belt around the pelvis or suspended from the shoulder by straps, and (2) the prosthesis kept in contact with the leg stump by suction, the belt and shoulder straps being eliminated.

The more complicated prosthesis used in cases of amputation through the hip joint or half of the pelvis usually consists of a plastic socket, in which the person virtually sits; a mechanical hip joint of metal; and a leather, plastic, or wooden thigh piece with the mechanical knee, shin portion, and foot as described above.

Upper-Extremity Prostheses.—A great advance in fabrication of functional upper-extremity prostheses followed World War II. Arm prostheses came to be made of plastic, frequently reinforced with glass fibre.

The below-elbow prosthesis consists of a single plastic shell and a metal wrist joint to which is attached a terminal device, either a hook or a hand. The person wears a shoulder harness made of webbing, from which a steel cable extends to the terminal device. When the person shrugs the shoulder, thus tightening the cable, the terminal device opens and closes. In certain cases the biceps muscle may be attached to the prosthesis by a surgical operation known as cineplasty. This procedure dispenses with the shoulder harness and allows finer control of the terminal device.

The above-elbow prosthesis has, in addition to the forearm shell, an upper-arm plastic shell and a mechanical, locking elbow joint. This complicates its use, inasmuch as there must be one cable control for the terminal device and another control to lock and unlock the elbow.

The most complicated upper-extremity prosthesis, that used in cases of amputation through the shoulder, includes a plastic shoulder cap extending over the chest and back. Usually no shoulder rotation is possible, but the mechanical elbow and terminal device function as in other arm prostheses.

A metal hook that opens and closes as two fingers is the most commonly used terminal device and the most efficient, though of somewhat formidable appearance. After World War II the APRL (U.S. Army Prosthetic Research Laboratory) hand was developed. This is a metal mechanical hand covered by a rubber glove of a colour similar to that of the patient's remaining hand. Many attempts were being made both in the United States and abroad to utilize electrical energy as the source of hook or hand control. This is done primarily by having electrodes built into the arm prosthesis which are activated by the patient's own muscle contractions. The electric current generated by these muscle contractions is then amplified by means of electrical components and batteries so that the terminal device, whether hook or hand, will have

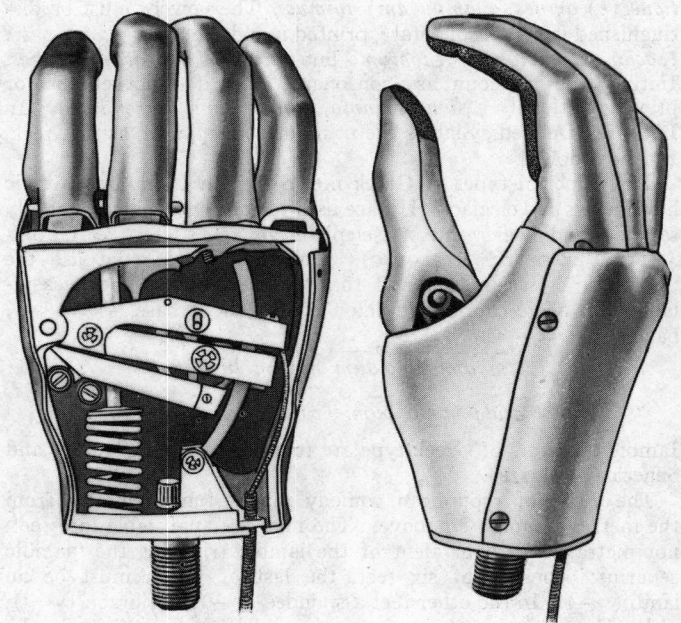

FROM "ORTHOPAEDIC APPLIANCE ATLAS," VOLUME 2

APRL-SIERRA 44C ARTIFICIAL HAND, SHOWN WITHOUT COSMETIC GLOVE WHICH MUST BE USED

Spring and cam mechanism inside the hand (cutaway), operated by a control cable, moves the index and middle fingers toward the thumb. The mechanism is mounted on a steel frame and covered with aluminum. The first two fingers are made of stainless steel and have pads of felt on their inner surfaces. The third and fourth fingers, made of foam rubber, serve only to fill out the glove

this control. Such an arrangement is referred to as the new myo-electrical control system. The batteries used are rechargeable on ordinary house current.

See also ORTHOPEDIC SURGERY. (C. N. L.)

PROSTHODONTICS is the branch of dentistry that deals with the artificial replacement (prosthesis) of natural teeth and associated tissues for the restoration or maintenance of function, appearance, comfort and health. Prosthodontics is divided as follows: (1) fixed partial denture prosthesis; (2) removable partial denture prosthesis; (3) complete denture prosthesis; and (4) maxillofacial (jaw and face) prosthesis.

History.—The earliest prosthodontic devices were banded bridges made by the Etruscans and wired restorations constructed by the Phoenicians. In early history human teeth, animal teeth or teeth carved from wood or ivory were substituted for natural teeth, and complete dentures for either the upper or the lower jaw were sometimes carved from one solid piece of wood or ivory.

Porcelain teeth were introduced during the latter part of the 18th century, and in the 20th plastic teeth came into use. Continued research with both these materials has produced lifelike imitations of teeth to match the large number of variations found in the colours and forms of natural teeth. Gold alloys and chrome alloys possessing the correct amount of rigidity, yet with sufficient flexibility to be suitable for clasps, bars, bases and attachments, have been highly developed. Methods and techniques of manipulating the various materials, and specialized instruments and equipment used in the construction of prosthetic restorations, have kept pace. Crowns, bridges, and partial or complete dentures (*see* below), as well as the several maxillofacial replacements, can be made so realistic in appearance and so functional that they almost defy detection.

Fixed Partial Denture Prosthesis.—This includes the design, construction and maintenance of dental restorations such as crowns and bridges that cannot be readily removed. These types of restorations are rigidly fixed to the natural teeth, which furnish support to them, and may be made of porcelain, plastic or metal. A crown is a replacement used to restore the natural form of an impaired tooth that cannot be preserved by an inlay or other type of restoration. A bridge consists of a span of one or more artificial teeth, with abutment attachments that are cemented to the adjacent natural teeth in the mouth.

Removable Partial Denture Prosthesis.—This includes the construction and maintenance of dental restorations so designed that they can be removed at will by the wearer or dentist. A removable partial denture consists of a base, constructed of plastic material or metal, or a combination of the two, which accurately fits the mouth ridges and tissues and supports the artificial replacement teeth in proper alignment. It is held in position in the mouth by flexible metal bands or clasps encircling adjacent natural teeth, or by other means of attachment to the teeth.

Complete Denture Prosthesis.—This involves the artificial replacement of all the natural teeth and associated tissues, in either the upper or the lower jaw or in both. In this type of prosthodontics, restoration of the functions of mastication, speech and appearance is of the greatest importance. Establishing and maintaining these functions by means of artificial dentures is accomplished by attaching porcelain or plastic teeth to bases (plastic material, metal or a combination of the two) that have been accurately adapted to the soft tissues of the mouth.

Maxillofacial Prosthesis.—This deals with the artificial replacement of tissues in cleft palates and other oral abnormalities. Cleft palates are abnormal openings in the roof of the mouth, usually of congenital origin. Mastication, swallowing and speech are seriously impaired by this type of abnormality. Closure of the opening by inserting a removable prosthesis can greatly improve these functions. Maxillofacial prosthesis has also come to include artificial restorations of some extraoral conditions of the face and head, resulting from injury, disease, or congenital factors.

Prosthodontics as a Specialty.—In the U.S., dentists with the necessary training and experience to deal with all types of dental prostheses are granted certification by the American Board of Prosthodontics (authorized in 1948 by the American Dental Association), designating them as specialists in prosthodontics. Special training in prosthodontics, in addition to that taught at the undergraduate level, can be obtained in many dental schools.

See also TEETH, ARTIFICIAL. (B. L. H.)

PROSTITUTION has been defined often in ambiguous terms and with judgmental adjectives. A precise definition would emphasize two essential elements: (1) the exchange of money or valuable materials in return for sexual activity, and (2) the relatively indiscriminate availability of such a transaction to individuals other than spouses or friends. This definition specifically limits the exchange to money or valuable materials: sexual activity to earn good will or subsequent favours is not properly construed as prostitution. Acceptance of money or gifts in exchange for sexual activity may be found among mistresses, gigolos, friends, and spouses; the economic criterion alone does not suffice. Similarly, sexual activity with strangers or with persons for whom there is no affectional feeling does not in itself constitute prostitution if the economic element is absent. Lastly, sexual activity denotes some physical contact. Sexual gratification solely from visual or auditory stimuli cannot ordinarily be included as prostitution; if it could, a substantial part of the entertainment world would be inadvertently included under the term.

It is most expedient to adopt an operational definition: a prostitute is a person who for immediate payment in money or valuables will engage in sexual activity with any other person, known or unknown, who meets minimal requirements as to gender, age, cleanliness, sobriety, ethnic group, and health.

Even this definition does not wholly suffice, for the concept of prostitution is based on culturally determined values which differ in various societies in the world. Such a definition represents only one end of a continuum ranging from the socially accepted arrangement of marriage wherein one male is morally and legally entitled to sexual gratification in exchange for support to the other extreme where the arrangement is of very brief duration and involves numerous males. Borderline cases are not uncommon. A female who makes herself sexually available only to suitors who bestow gifts is a case in point: how many suitors in what span of time suffice to escalate her status from that of girl friend to mistress to prostitute? The opinion varies according to the attitudes and values of the culture or subculture in which the individuals live. In modern Western society the fact that any sexual relationship generally involves an important economic element is often not faced up to: few females would continue with a male who did not periodically give her gifts of at least some monetary value, but in order to maintain the disguise the male must not proffer cash (unless accompanied by a suitable rationalization) or make the gifts too obviously contingent upon the sexual activity. Gifts must always be seen as symbolic of affection or esteem rather than as payment.

History.—Some primates use sexual behaviour for nonsexual purposes: female chimpanzees and baboons will sometimes present themselves sexually to a male in order to avoid attack or to distract the male while the female purloins his food. It is a small step from such primate behaviour to accepting coitus in exchange for food. Consequently it seems likely that the exchanging of food for coitus began in the transitional period between man and ape, and that with the subsequent development of more elaborate rules of social behaviour, the sexual restrictions of marriage, and the concept of parenthood, prostitution was eventually defined in some form and set apart as an entity to be accepted or condemned.

Prostitution has not, insofar as is known, been a cultural universal. In sexually permissive societies it is often absent because it is unnecessary, while in other societies it has been successfully suppressed. Complete suppression seems virtually impossible in large urban centres where anonymity is easily achieved and where many persons are transients. But in a small community where secrecy is difficult and where life depends on communal cooperation, social sanctions—chiefly in the form of ridicule, economic retribution, pressure from relatives, and ostracism—are extremely effective and inescapable. In such small groups prostitution can be and has been prevented.

Human societies are so labile and diverse that virtually every form of sexual behaviour, even those which are generally assumed to be socially disruptive, has somewhere at some time been either normative behaviour or regarded under some special circumstances as permissible. This is true of prostitution. In addition to the societies where it is absent, there are many (possibly the majority) where it is tolerated, accepted, or encouraged. Toleration with some degree of stigma seems a common societal posture—in such societies prostitution is often the resort of disadvantaged females: slaves, captives, divorcees, widows, outcasts, and the unmarriageable. In brief, it is the solution to the economic problem faced by females without husbands.

Acceptance or encouragement of prostitution under special conditions seems chiefly a matter of economics or religion. In a number of societies girls earn their dowries through prostitution, chiefly away from home, and return enriched and eminently marriageable. This custom occurred in some, but not many, preliterate groups in the New World, among certain ancient Mediterranean cultures such as the Lydians and Cyprians, and within modern times among the Ouled Naïl of Algeria. Sometimes in societies which ordinarily denigrate prostitution and even make some effort to preserve female virginity, it is encouraged when the economic reward is sufficiently great. Thus Marquesan parents may encourage daughters to barter coitus for valuable goods brought by sailors.

Religions have sometimes incorporated prostitution as a transitory rite to be done once or, more commonly, as a continuing religious obligation of a particular class of priestesses. An example of the former is the "Myletta" rite of ancient Babylonia wherein every female was required to sit in the temple of the goddess Ishtar and accept coitus from the first male who threw a silver coin in her lap. Similar rites involving other goddesses are known to have existed elsewhere in the Middle East. Obligatory prostitution by certain priestesses was also a custom in this area, but rare elsewhere, although examples are known in India and West Africa.

In societies of sufficient technological achievement and urbanization to warrant the label "civilizations," there has usually been an attempt to make secular prostitutes identifiable by requiring them to dress in some distinctive manner or live in a restricted area or both. Efforts of this kind were made in ancient Israel, Greece, and Rome, and continued through medieval times into the 20th century. In other areas distinctive garb and locale were typical of prostitutes, but it seems that this was generally a voluntary pattern of behaviour to facilitate the clients' search rather than a regulation imposed by society. It should be noted, however, that informal social pressures have always served the same purpose as codified laws and ordinances: even in modern times prostitutes tolerated in one section of a city find it difficult to establish residence in a "decent" neighbourhood.

Attempts to confine a group as inherently mobile as prostitutes have met with only temporary success. Prostitution always tends to fan out beyond the demarcated borders. The Oriental civilizations were no more successful than those of the West. During the T'ang dynasty in China, prostitutes (as well as merchants) were required to operate in specified areas, but by the Sung dynasty (A.D. 960–1279) cafes employing prostitutes infiltrated other districts and combination entertainment places and brothels known as "Wa-tzu" proliferated; there were over a score in the city of Hangchow alone. It should not surprise readers of modern Western newspapers to learn that prostitutes have been discovered operating from residences in upper middle class neighbourhoods.

Nevertheless sufficient identification and localization was often obtained to make prostitutes liable to the inevitable by-products of civilization: licensing and taxation, which were imposed as early as Roman times. The degree of governmental control of prostitution has varied from nation to nation. Localization of prostitution also rendered it more susceptible to exploitation, often by criminal groups.

Historical data as to classes of prostitutes are scanty, but some hierarchy is inescapable except in small societies. Aside from religious prostitution, prostitutes automatically gradate into classes according to their age, beauty, intelligence, and health, and society treats them accordingly. The independent courtesans who congregated around men of political power, such as the *hetaerae* of ancient Greece; Theodora, who subsequently married the Byzantine emperor Justinian; and certain of the Japanese geisha were accorded considerable respect. Females of lesser wit or beauty who catered to the general public were generally denigrated and ill-treated.

The Industrial Revolution brought with it markedly increased urbanization and economic exploitation of large numbers of persons—both factors conducive to prostitution. At the same time the spread of humanist ideas, concern over public health, and changes in the status of women caused an increasing concern over prostitution, which in Western civilization was identified as a social evil and a problem. Colonization of other parts of the world spread that attitude widely.

Modern Prostitution.—The complexity of modern life, with accelerated cross-cultural diffusion and rapid transportation, makes a brief description of prostitution in any given nation impossible. In an Asian country, for example, there may be villages sharing a few local prostitutes; inland towns with organized brothels staffed by indigenous females; and coastal cities with a potpourri of brothels and independent prostitutes of varying races, nationalities, residential stability, and status. All of these situations are generally subject to rapid change depending upon political change and the establishment or removal of military bases, factories, and other important sources of clients.

Speaking generally, and with special regard for the Western nations, prostitution operates in three guises. First, there is the brothel: an establishment wherein the prostitutes generally reside, supervised usually by an older female who has acquired sufficient money and made enough social contacts to establish a brothel. One or more males may be on the premises to deal with unruly or homosexual clients. Brothels are quite varied, some catering to particular socioeconomic and ethnic groups, but they are generally confined to particular districts in a city or else relegated to its outskirts just beyond municipal authority. In some cities a given area may be almost wholly given over to prostitution, as was the case in Las Vegas, Nev.; the Calle Amistad of Havana, Cuba; and the Herbertstrasse of Hamburg, Ger. In states or nations where prostitution is illegal, brothels tend to be confined to locales where law enforcement is ineffective due to political corruption or to geographic factors such as an adjacent state or national border or an ocean. Since clients prefer novelty, prostitutes not infrequently move from one brothel to another in a different city. The brothel owner or supervisor takes a percentage of the prostitutes' earnings, a percentage which can range from 20% up to a nearly intolerable proportion.

Second, there is the "call girl," a prostitute who has her own residence (sometimes shared with another prostitute). In return for a percentage of her earnings she is notified by the head of the operation where to meet each client, generally the hotel room of the client and less often his home. The "call girl" is ordinarily expected to limit her clientele to persons obtained through the calling system, and is discouraged from developing contacts on her own initiative since she might not share the revenue from these. The "call girl" has a higher status and price than the average brothel inmate, who is known as a "house girl." As there is often some screening of new clients, chiefly through recommendation by known persons, the "call girl" is protected to a considerable degree from undesirable customers and disguised police.

Third, there is the independent prostitute who shares her earnings with no one except hotel employees, taxi drivers, bartenders, her pimp, or others who direct customers to her. For security and companionship, pairs of independent prostitutes sometimes live together. The independent girl is more apt than other prostitutes to pursue this occupation sporadically and in conjunction with some other employment, almost always of low status and pay.

Variations on these three basic forms of prostitution are manifold. A brothel may pass as a massage parlour, a restaurant or bar may have an adjacent room, and escort services and modeling agencies may be disguises. To add to the complexity, there is some specialization among prostitutes in terms of techniques as, for example, those serving sado-masochists. Some prostitutes may largely or wholly avoid coitus: in certain lower class cafes and bars there are females who induce a customer to buy numerous drinks at inflated prices and when he has purchased enough will then lead him to some dimly lit, isolated booth or corner and masturbate him to orgasm. This practice seems commoner in Western Europe than in the United States. A small number of females eschew physical contact entirely, and thereby escape the definition of prostitution, by simply engaging in obscene conversation in exchange for drinks (a percentage of the cost of which reverts to them). On occasion prostitutes may be employed to give exhibitions of sexual activity before audiences. In Latin America and parts of Europe such exhibitions are frequently a standard entertainment in certain taverns and brothels; in the United States they have become much less common and are largely confined to occasional acts for men's organizations.

Entry into a career of prostitution may once have involved parents casting out a seduced daughter or "white slavers" exerting duress upon some hapless girl, but this was no longer true in the second half of the 20th century. Entry has become voluntary and often causes little trauma aside from transient pangs of shame or guilt. Some mentor is almost invariably involved—another girl with experience as a prostitute or a male friend who points out the financial advantages and offers to help the neophyte on her new career if she chooses it. A moment of clearly defined decision is generally lacking and the entry is a transitional phase buffered by rationalizations. A typical example would be that of a girl accustomed to presents from suitors who by degrees comes to accept gifts in the form of cash and whose suitors may become more numerous as they become less known to her. Or another common mode of entry is the financial emergency which can be remedied by "being nice" to someone a friend happens to know, the price being disguised as a gift or loan. Subsequent fiscal emergencies arise and ultimately lead to an acknowledged career of prostitution. In any case, the motivation is financial. Stories of nymphomania giving rise to prostitution belong in the realm of mythology.

Entry into prostitution generally involves entry into the subculture and the neophyte must go through a sometimes stressful period of learning a new set of interpersonal relationships, a new system of patterned behaviour, and a new argot. More importantly, she must develop a new self-image. This change necessarily involves cutting most, if not all, ties with her former life, and the prostitute becomes more exclusively involved with and dependent upon the subculture of prostitution. The term subculture is appropriate since the individuals think of themselves as a group apart from the rest of society, establish their own mores, have their own distinctive linguistic terms, and share similar ideas and values.

While one may find embittered individuals who dislike their work and despise their clients, the majority of prostitutes maintain an attitude similar to that of anyone providing services to a diverse clientele. Some clients prove troublesome and are consequently resented, others may be pleasant or unexpectedly generous and hence engender some regard or even affection, but most are regarded with objectivity and neutrality.

The prostitute often simulates passion and sometimes affection for business reasons, yet in reality she is expected to preserve a rigorous attitude of psychological noninvolvement, precisely such as is required of other professionals who deal with human beings. While the client should be sufficiently pleased to induce him to return, he should be processed efficiently, quickly, and dispassionately. Experiencing sexual arousal or orgasm is regarded not only as unprofessional, but as fatiguing and hence inefficient. Allowing affection to develop for a client is thought of as foolishly making oneself vulnerable to emotional hurt and possible fiscal exploitation.

Having severed her ties with her former life and preserving an emotional aloofness from her clients, the prostitute is prone to be starved for love. This deficiency is remedied by a lover who is frequently also a pimp. The pimp is someone whom she can love and imagine that the love is returned. He gives the sexual pleasure absent in her professional activity. More importantly, the pimp proves that she is needed—if only for mercenary reasons. Many prostitutes take pride in providing well for their "man," whose ostentatious affluence attests to their success. To love, to be loved, and to be needed are psychological necessities for most humans and the pimp provides these for the prostitute. In addition, he has other useful functions: he may find clients, protect her from mistreatment, pay her bail, safeguard her savings, and perhaps even join in her professional work if a client wishes homosexual activity or an exhibition. It is easy to see why the pimp is valued even if he is shared, as is often the case, with several other prostitutes, or even if he is sometimes exploitative or brutal.

The average prostitute is able to successfully compartmentalize her life: in her work she is seldom consciously sexually aroused and seldom or never reaches orgasm, but in her private life she is as responsive as, or perhaps somewhat more so than, the average housewife. The speculations as to prostitutes being either sexually frigid or nymphomaniacs are not supported by scientific evidence. The compartmentalization may extend to sexual techniques and positions, some of these being employed solely in business relationships. This compartmentalization serves a vital buffering protective function and permits the prostitute to keep a tolerable self-image and to engage in the emotional and social relationships which are important to human well-being. The prostitute can say that her work is no measure of herself as a person, that it is a thing apart, simply an economic matter. Nevertheless the defense mechanism cannot wholly negate reality, and the prostitute is to a considerable degree alienated from normal social relationships and functions.

Pregnancy and venereal disease are ordinarily thought of as inescapable occupational hazards for prostitutes. The matter of conception is enormously complicated by varying methods of contraception, the postulated antagonistic effects of one male's semen upon another's, chronic pelvic congestion, consequences of venereal disease, and other factors. It appears, however, that while prostitutes' high coital frequencies do not result in high incidence of pregnancy, neither does it seem that prostitutes are particularly infertile. The majority have been impregnated by boy friends or husbands, but few by clients. On the other hand, venereal disease is an indisputable occupational hazard, and the incidence of having had such a disease at some time or another is far higher among prostitutes than among the general population.

It has been thought that, through overexposure to males and through occasional but repeated unpleasant experiences, the prostitute would turn to other females for affection and sexual gratification. This speculation seems largely unfounded: while prostitutes may be more permissive toward any sexual behaviour and while they may have had some homosexual experience as a part of their work, the incidence of extensive homosexuality does not appear to be substantially greater among prostitutes.

Since the prostitute is somewhat isolated from normal society, confined to her own subculture, and her professional life labeled as criminal in most states and nations, it is not surprising that criminality or, more commonly, affiliation with criminals, often develops. Any lucrative illegal business invites the intrusion of organized crime. This situation is not wholly a case of prostitutes being victimized; it is to a great extent a mutually beneficial arrangement since the criminal organization can provide a greater protection from law and social action than could any individual or small group. In addition, more efficient management is often provided. The price for such benefits is, of course, loss of autonomy and having to adhere at risk of severe punishment to financial agreements which are probably rather onerous.

The prostitute herself is not ordinarily criminal in a narrow sense of the word. Any business operator must maintain a good reputation in order to prosper, and hence only the most desperate or disreputable prostitutes rob or blackmail. The independent lower class prostitute catering to transients is more likely to rob or defraud. The prostitute, is, however, rather prone to be indirectly involved as an accomplice or accessory to a crime simply because her lover, pimp, or management organization is engaged in criminal activity. The police are well aware of this and sometimes attempt to coerce prostitutes into serving as informers.

Exiting from prostitution is, unlike entry, not always voluntary. Loss of physical beauty ultimately forces out of "the life" all those except a few who become administrators or supervisors. The more foresighted prostitutes exit before being compelled to do so, some via marriage (generally to someone who is fully aware of their profession), or the already married may simply become housewives precisely as a conventional woman may give up employment after some years of marriage and devote herself to the home. Others intelligent enough to have saved money may simply buy into some legitimate business. The improvident and less intelligent prostitute faces a grim future since she has neither funds nor skills to save her from eventual unemployment. Such an unfortunate generally ends on public relief or working at the most menial tasks. Actually little is known of the lives of former prostitutes since those who have adequately coped with the transition back into society are anxious to conceal their past; one tends to see the failures rather than the successes, although a few of the latter become famous, most notably Polly Adler and the Everleigh sisters.

The extent of female prostitution is difficult to measure even in those nations which require licensing, but it is no small social phenomenon in all densely populated areas. In the United States the survey data accumulated by Alfred C. Kinsey and his associates indicated that around mid-century roughly one-third of the college educated and three-quarters of the less educated white males eventually had had sexual intercourse with a prostitute. There is, however, evidence that in the second half of the 20th century with the increasing permissiveness toward nonmarital sexual behaviour of women, prostitution was becoming correspondingly less important: the percentage of males with experience with prostitutes seemed to be diminishing and the frequency of contact was markedly lower.

Male Prostitution has been largely disregarded in treatises on prostitution, and the public knows little of it. Heterosexual male prostitution, that is, males hired by or for females, is extremely rare. Almost any female desirous of sexual activity can with little difficulty find a male to oblige her, providing she does not set her standards too high. The gigolo, the male counterpart of the mistress, does not qualify as a prostitute under the definition here employed since the elements of promiscuity and immediate payment are absent.

Homosexual male prostitution, on the other hand, was common in the second half of the 20th century in large cities, and in some cities the male "hustlers" perhaps rivaled the female prostitutes in numbers. Most homosexual male prostitution was of the independent type: "call boy" systems existed, but were not commonplace, and male brothels were extremely rare in the United States and were not usual elsewhere. Some basically heterosexual brothels, however, kept a male around for the convenience of a homosexually inclined client.

In Western civilizations male homosexual prostitution differs radically in many respects from female heterosexual prostitution. There is no pimp, large-scale organization is absent, the price is lower, and the sexual relationship with the client is quite different. In female prostitution the prostitute rarely or never reaches orgasm and the client almost invariably does; in male homosexual prostitution the prostitute almost invariably reaches orgasm, but the client frequently does not. This paradox is the result of a curious mythology which the male "hustler" and his client feel compelled to enact. The homosexual male ideally seeks a masculine appearing heterosexual male, and the prostitute attempts to fit this image. Consequently the prostitute can do little or nothing for or to the homosexual client lest he betray a homosexual inclination of his own and ruin the illusion.

So the prostitute plays an essentially passive role and has orgasm (this is regarded as a necessary part of the bargain), while the client must ordinarily content himself with psychological arousal, self-masturbation, and body contact. This arrangement is reinforced by the male prostitute's protective image of himself as a "real" and heterosexual man who tolerates homosexual activity solely for financial reasons. In actuality, of course, the "hustler" has a substantial homosexual component which is necessary or he could not achieve erection and orgasm, and many of them are predominantly homosexual in orientation although loath to admit it. One might regard this as the reverse of female prostitution—the female simulates a passion she does not feel, while the male prostitute conceals a passion he does feel. There is some evidence that this curious pattern of feigned indifference is gradually breaking down and that more male prostitutes are taking an active role in the sexual relationship while maintaining a masculine image. In societies other than those of Western civilizations the homosexual prostitute does not disguise his interest and is often as active as or even more active than the client.

Social Control.—All human societies exercise varying degrees of control over the sexual behaviour of their members, and in the more urban and technologically advanced cultures prostitution has been subjected to particular control since it embodies two major societal interests: sex and money. Prior to the 19th century the emphasis was upon control or, at least, the localization and identification of the prostitute. The motivation seems to have been partly fiscal (taxes, license fees, graft), and partly moral (to recognize and isolate the sinful). Such isolation served other useful ends; for example, one's favourite prostitute would be unlikely to be admitted to the social groups containing one's wife, fiancee, or employer. Life could be rigorously compartmentalized and the double standard of sexual morality maintained.

In the 19th century the emphasis tended to shift from control to eradication. The previous laws and municipal ordinances concerned with regulation were superseded by statutes prohibiting prostitution. This change seems to have come about through the fusion of several social developments: the emancipation of women, the growth of humanitarian movements involved in social action, and the optimistic rationale that social problems could be cured by suitably worded laws. The League of Nations made prostitution one of its concerns, and attempts at international cooperation in dealing with prostitution survived in the United Nations. The trend toward suppression accelerated after World War II, and in vast areas of former toleration the newly independent nations began to repress or outlaw prostitution. Even France, famous for its tolerance, closed its brothels in 1946. While no federal law prohibited prostitution in the United States, the states and cities did so. Western Germany permitted prostitution, but only under rigorous strictures. The Communist nations usually enacted no laws attempting to regulate or eradicate prostitution since it, according to dogma, is a product of capitalist society and cannot exist in a communist state. Communist control was exerted through generalized statutes or the prostitutes were dealt with in nonlegal fashion.

The results of the attempts to abolish prostitution were predictable. Brothels, especially large or conspicuous ones, became rare or vanished and the prostitutes were forced to operate independently. The "call girl" system, far less vulnerable to police action, developed and flourished. Massage parlours and other disguises were also adopted. Overall, prostitution was decreased, though not drastically, through the loss of the efficient production line activity of the brothel. A more serious blow to prostitution appears to be the growing increase in the number of females willing to engage in sexual intercourse without financial recompense.

Social and Psychological Aspects.—Since prostitution is basically an economic matter it is destined to follow the laws of economics. It will grow or diminish according to the number of individuals who find it difficult or impossible to obtain sexual contact without paying for it. These individuals include not only those with physical or cosmetic handicaps and those few with sexual desires too bizarre to be satisfied by most partners, but also numerous normal persons who experience temporary difficulty in obtaining a sexual relationship. Travelers and military personnel are good examples of the latter group. Added to this are persons who could establish sexual relationships with nonprostitutes, but do not wish to make the effort or do not wish to become emotionally involved. Finally, some individuals seek prostitutes to enjoy sexual techniques their wives or customary partners refuse them—mouth-genital contact being the prime example.

Prostitution is also reinforced by the double standard of sexual morality and by the affiliations with drinking, dancing, and entertainment. These recreational aspects had been, and in many areas of the world continued to be, an important component of prostitution.

This almost inescapable and reasonably steady demand for prostitutes is in many societies complemented by a socioeconomic treatment of females which is conducive to prostitution. If most females are taught to be financially dependent upon males and discriminated against in employment and salary, there will be a substantial number of them who are either economically forced toward prostitution or who turn to it as an easy and more lucrative alternative. Even in a utopian society, however, there would be some individuals whose skills, personality traits, or intelligence would limit their earnings or whose real or imagined needs would exceed the beneficence of the state, and some of these persons would prostitute.

It appears impossible to eradicate prostitution in a complex society, particularly one in which sexual gratification is made difficult by mores and law. Moreover, the trend of legalistic and humanitarian thinking has been toward the idea that what consenting adults do sexually in private should not be subject to law, and that view would presumably include prostitution.

BIBLIOGRAPHY.—Paul Lacroix (trans. S. Putnam), *History of Prostitution Among the Peoples of the World from the Most Remote Antiquity to the Present Day,* 3 vol. (1926); Alfred C. Kinsey, Wardell B. Pomeroy, and Clyde E. Martin, *Sexual Behavior in the Human Male* (1948); Thomas E. James, *Prostitution and the Law* (1951); Polly Adler, *A House Is Not a Home* (1953); British Social Biology Council (C. H. Ralph, ed.), *Women of the Streets: a Sociological Study of the Common Prostitute* (1955); Harold Greenwald, *The Call Girl: a Social and Psychoanalytic Study* (1958); L. Fernando Henriques, *Prostitution and Society, a Survey,* vol. i, *Primitive, Classical and Oriental* (1962), vol. ii, *Prostitution in Europe and the New World* (1963), vol. iii, *Modern Sexuality* (1968); Harry Benjamin and R. E. Masters, *Prostitution and Morality: a Definitive Report* (1964); James H. Bryan, "Apprenticeships in Prostitution," *Social Problems,* vol. 12 (1965); W. B. Pomeroy, "Some Aspects of Prostitution," *Journal of Sex Research,* 1:3 (1965); Paul H. Gebhard, "Misconceptions About Female Prostitutes," *Medical Aspects of Human Sexuality,* 3:3 (1969).

(P. H. G.)

PROTACTINIUM, a chemical element, has the symbol Pa, atomic number 91, and chemical atomic weight 231.05. It is the second member of the rare-earthlike transition series, the actinide series, which includes the elements of atomic numbers 89 to 103 inclusive, and in which an inner electronic shell (the 5f shell) is being filled, but it also resembles tantalum in its chemical properties. The first isotope (mass number 234) was discovered in 1913 by K. Fajans and O. H. Göring, who named it "UX$_2$" or "brevium." The long-lived isotope, Pa^{231}, was discovered by O. Hahn and L. Meitner in 1917, and independently by F. Soddy and J. A. Cranston at about the same time. The name for this isotope, protactinium (progenitor of Ac^{227}), has now been generally adopted for element 91. Over a dozen radioactive isotopes, natural and artificial, are known, of which Pa^{233} is of especial interest as the progenitor of fissionable U^{233} produced by the absorption of neutrons in thorium.

The isotope Pa^{231} (half-life 34,300 years) is a member of the natural ($4n + 3$) radioactive family and exists in uranium ores to the extent of 0.34 parts per 1,000,000 parts of uranium. From this source the first pure protactinium was isolated by A. V. Grosse and others in 1934. Protactinium can also be synthesized in quantity by irradiation of ionium (Th ^{230}) with neutrons from nuclear reactors.

Metallic protactinium is quite electropositive. The element displays the tetrapositive and pentapositive oxidation states with an estimated potential of $+0.1$ volts for the Pa(IV) $\rightarrow$ Pa(V)

couple. The former state behaves like the other tetrapositive actinide elements in aqueous solution and in the solid compounds. The pentapositive state undergoes hydrolysis so readily that it is extremely difficult to keep in acidic solution, and complexing agents such as fluoride ion are often used for this purpose. Included among the identified solid compounds are Pa$_2$O$_5$, PaO$_2$ (and intermediate oxides), PaH$_3$, PaF$_4$, PaCl$_4$, PaOS, and probably PaBr$_4$, PaI$_4$, PaN$_2$, PaF$_5$, PaCl$_5$, PaBr$_5$, and PaI$_5$.

(G. T. Sg.)

PROTAGORAS (c. 490–after 421 B.C.), of Abdera in Thrace, was the first and the most famous of the Greek Sophists. He is a principal character in Plato's *Protagoras.* His work entitled *Truth* began with the statement "Man is the measure of all things," which was probably intended to express the relativity to the individual of all perceptions and, as some hold, of all judgments as well. In *Concerning the Gods* he professed agnosticism as to whether the gods exist or not. Protagoras was perhaps the first to study grammar systematically. He professed to teach the art of politics and, as a friend of Pericles, he had considerable success in Athens, exercising a great influence over contemporary thought on moral and political questions. *See* also SOPHISTS.

For fragments and testimonia *see* H. Diels and W. Kranz, *Fragmente der Vorsokratiker,* vol. ii, 7th ed. (1954). *See* also M. Untersteiner, *The Sophists,* Eng. trans. (1954). (G. B. KD.)

PROTEACEAE, the protea family of plants, about 60 genera and 1,400 species of trees and shrubs confined mainly to the Southern Hemisphere, mostly in Australia (750 species) and South Africa and Madagascar (350 species), but also occurring in Malaysia, southeastern Asia, certain South Pacific islands, and in America from southern Mexico to Tierra del Fuego. In warm regions several species are cultivated as ornamentals, including silver tree (*Leucadendron argenteum*), Australian honeysuckles (*Banksia*), and hakeas (*Hakea*). Silk oak (*Grevillea robusta*), native to Australia, is widely known as a roadside and shade tree in the southern U.S. Queensland nut or macadamia (*Macadamia ternifolia*) is grown for its edible seeds. The family contains several timber trees. The simple or divided leaves are typically spirally arranged. The flowers, uni- or bisexual, have a four-parted perianth and are disposed in often dense and showy clusters. Stamens are four, and the ovary is one-celled. The fruit, containing one to several seeds, may be fleshy or dry.

See articles by C. V. Rao, *Proc. Linn. Soc. N. S. W.,* vol. 82, pp. 257–271 (1957); H. Sleumer, *Flora Malesiana Bull.,* ser. I, vol. 5, pt. 2, pp. 147–206 (1956). (J. W. Tt.)

PROTECTORATE, a term used in international law to describe the relationship between two states, one of which exercises control over the other. The use of the term to designate such a relationship is comparatively modern; it is significant that the word does not occur in Sir George Cornewall Lewis's *Essay on the Government of Dependencies* (1841). Nevertheless the relationship is an ancient one. There have always been states which dominated their neighbours, but which did not think it politic to annex them. Edouard Engelhardt and other writers on the subject have collected a large number of instances in antiquity in which a true protectorate existed, even though such terminology was not used. Thus the hegemony of Athens, as it existed about 467 B.C., was a form of protectorate; although the subject states were called allies, they were, in all important legal matters, obliged to resort to Athens.

In dealing with dependent nations Rome used terms which veiled subjection. Thus the relationship of subject or dependent cities to the dominant power was described as that of *clientes* to *patronus.* Such cities might also be described as *civitates foederatae* (allied communities) or *civitates liberae* (free communities). Another expression of the same fact was that certain communities had come under the power (*in deditionem*) or under the trust (*in fidem*) of the Roman people. The kingdoms of Numidia, Macedonia, Syria and Pergamum were examples of protected states, their rulers being termed *inservientes* (subjects). The Romans drew a distinction between *foedera aequa* and *iniqua* (equal and unequal treaties). The latter created a form of protectorate, the protected state remaining free.

In medieval times this relation existed, and the term protection was in use, but the relationship of subordination of one state to another was invariably expressed in terms of feudal law. One state was deemed the vassal of another, and the ruler of one did homage to the other. In his work *De la République* (1576) Jean Bodin treats of "those who are under protection" or as the Latin text has it, *de patrocinio et clientela*. In Bodin's view such states retain their sovereignty (i, c, 8). Discussing the question, whether a prince who becomes a *cliens* of another loses his *majestas*, he concludes that, unlike the true vassal, the *cliens* is not deprived of sovereignty. Elsewhere he remarks, "the word protection is special and implies no subjection on the part of the party under protection." He distinguishes the relation of *seigneur* and *vassal* from that of *protecteur* and *adherent*. At times letters of protection were granted by a prince to a weak state, as, for example, by Louis XIII in 1641 to the prince of Monaco.

Reverting to the distinction in Roman law, Hugo Grotius and Samuel von Pufendorf, with many others, treat protection as an instance of unequal treaties; that is, "where either the promises are unequal, or when either of the parties is obliged to harder conditions."

In the 16th century, the rise of European national states led to increasing use of the system of protectorates as a prelude to annexation, particularly by France. This use was also developed during the 19th century as a means of colonial expansion. After the Napoleonic Wars, however, establishment of protectorates by the great powers became a means of maintaining the balance of power. Thus, by the treaty of Paris (1815) the Ionian Islands became a protectorate of Great Britain in order to prevent Austria from gaining complete control of the Adriatic. The gradual elimination of the smaller European states by the unification of Italy and Germany, and the strengthening and neutralization of those that remained (*e.g.,* Switzerland and Belgium), brought to an end this development in the use of the protectorate. A curious situation arose, however, with the disintegration of the Ottoman empire. Provinces which owed allegiance to Turkey began to revolt against Turkish rule and, as a stage in their struggle for independence, were sometimes placed under the protection of a foreign power. Thus, Moldavia and Walachia, which became protectorates of Russia in 1829, were placed under international protection in 1856 and in 1878 united to form the independent state of Rumania (*q.v.*).

Definitions.—"The one common element in protectorates is the prohibition of all foreign relations except those permitted by the protecting state. What the idea of protectorate excludes, and the ideas of annexation, on the other hand, would include, is that absolute ownership which was signified by the word *dominium* in Roman law, and which, though not quite satisfactorily, is sometimes described as territorial sovereignty. The protected country remains, in regard to the protecting state, a foreign country; and this being so, the inhabitants of the protectorate, whether native-born or immigrant settlers, do not by virtue of the relationship between the protecting and the protected state become subjects of the protecting state." (Sir William Rann Kennedy, *Rex* v. *Crewe*, 1910, 2 K.B., 576.)

The term protectorate is used loosely to designate a variety of degrees of control of one state by another, from that situation in which it means no more than that the protecting state guarantees and protects the safety of the other, to a situation which is a masked form of annexation, in the manner of the German protectorates established in Czechoslovakia in March 1939. Strictly, it is distinguished from suzerainty, but nevertheless both relationships display the same characteristics of the observance of such ancient forms and traditions in the protected state as are consistent with necessary change, and the reservation of nominal freedom while securing real power to the protecting state. Protectorate is probably best regarded as a form of international guardianship and the modern emphasis is upon the responsibility and duty of the protecting state to the international community as well as to the protected state.

There are two principal classes of protectorates, those exercised over more highly civilized countries having a stable form of government and a historical tradition of their own, and those exercised over underdeveloped peoples, the latter being sometimes called colonial or pseudo-protectorates and being especially common in Africa. Examples of the former exist in Europe in Andorra and San Marino. Strictly, there can be no protectorate over a domain which is uninhabited or ruled by no organized state, but the distinction has not always been maintained.

In its narrowest and strict meaning, the relationship established in a protectorate must be distinguished from the relationship existing between the United States and the states of Central and South America (*see* PAN-AMERICAN CONFERENCES and MONROE DOCTRINE), from the former relationship between Great Britain and the Indian states (*see* INDIA-PAKISTAN, SUBCONTINENT OF) and from so-called spheres of influence (*q.v.*).

Protectorates and International Law.—"The extent of the powers of a protecting state in the territory of a protected state depend, first upon the treaties between the protecting state and the protected state establishing the protectorate, and secondly upon the conditions under which the protectorate has been recognized by third powers as against whom there is an intention to rely on the provisions of these treaties. In spite of common features possessed by protectorates under international law, they have unlimited legal characteristics resulting from the special conditions under which they were created, and the stage of their development." (*Advisory Opinion, The Nationality Decrees in Tunis and Morocco,* "Series B," no. 4, p. 27, 1923.)

The majority of protectorates have been established by treaty by the terms of which the weaker state surrenders the management of all its more important international relations, although some have been imposed by force, *e.g.,* the unilateral declaration by Great Britain concerning Egypt in 1914 (*see* EGYPT). The treaty defines the position of the protected state in the international community, with special reference to its treaty-making powers and its right to diplomatic and consular representation.

There is a conflict of opinion whether or not the protected state loses its sovereignty. Many writers have supported the view that there is no such loss, and have gone so far as to state that the arrangement is *res inter alios acta* ("a thing done between others") and concerns only the parties to it. This is not the modern view, however, and it is now generally accepted that the relationship of protectorate must be recognized by third powers. The right of the protecting state to interfere in all matters of external affairs constitutes a definite loss of sovereignty, and since in orthodox theory sovereignty is one and indivisible, such a situation must imply a loss of sovereignty on the part of the weaker state. Neither position is without its anomalies; for example, it is clear that the sovereign of the weaker state yet has jurisdictional immunity in at least the territory of the protecting state (see *Duff Development Co.* v. *Kelantan* [*Government*] *and A. G.,* 1924 A.C. 797).

On the other hand, it was equally clear that on the assumption of the status of protectorate, the weaker state ceased to qualify for membership in the United Nations.

The relationship does not affect the nationality of the members of the weaker state, although there are frequently facilities for the peoples of the protectorate to become nationals of the protector, and they owe a certain ill-defined allegiance to the protecting state. Thus the British Nationality act, 1948, made provision for the naturalization of British protected persons, the requirements to be fulfilled being less onerous than those imposed upon aliens. Nor, generally speaking, does the territory of the protectorate become part of that of the protecting state, although the applicability of legislation of the dominant state can only be judged from the construction of its terms.

The older view of the position of a protectorate according to international law is contained in the decision of Stephen Lushington in "The Case of the Ionian Ships" (2 Spink 212, 164 E.R. 394 [1855]). The Ionian Islands were at that time subject to the protectorate created by the treaty of Paris, 1815, and it was held that notwithstanding the declaration of war by Great Britain against Russia, the Ionian Islands remained neutral. It was not disputed that as the head of the protecting state the British sovereign had the right to declare war or make peace on behalf of the islands. "Such a right is inseparable from protection." But the intention to involve the protected state in the wars of the protecting power must be clearly expressed, and the state of war does not arise *ex necessitate* on the protecting power's going to war, for there may very well be advantages to one or other of the parties to the protectorate if the protected state is not so involved. It is said that the protected state is only implicated in the wars to which the protecting state is a party where the latter has acquired a right of military occupation of the territory of the former.

See also MANDATE; SUZERAINTY; TRUSTEESHIP SYSTEM. For current data *see* "Protected States, Condominiums, and Trust Territories" in *Britannica Book of the Year,* American edition.
(E. H. LD.)

PROTEINS are highly complex substances that are universally present in living organisms. They are of great nutritional importance, have numerous industrial uses and are directly involved in the chemical processes necessary for the maintenance of life. After water has been removed from the soft tissue of an animal, whether it be the human body or a one-celled animal, the major portion of the solid residue is found to be a mixture of proteins. Proteins make up about 80% of the dry weight of muscle, 70% of the dry weight of skin and 90% of the dry weight of blood. The interior substance of plant cells is also composed largely of proteins.

Biological Function.—Some proteins, such as those of hair, wool, silk and bone, serve an obvious structural function for the organism that has made them. Other proteins, such as those of milk, eggs and seeds, are accumulated as storage depots of food for the young, growing organism. The proteins in the above two categories are extracellular. Another group of proteins present within the living cells participates very directly in the chemical processes essential for the existence of the cell. These proteins serve as specific catalysts, or enzymes (*q.v.*), bringing about and directing the chemical processes of metabolism. It is impossible to describe life processes at a molecular level without taking into consideration the functional role of the enzymes. There appears to be at least one kind of enzyme for each type of chemical reaction that occurs in a cell. Since there are a large number of such reactions, it follows that there are a large number of different enzymes.

The central role of proteins in biochemical processes was recognized by chemists in the early 19th century when they coined the name for these substances from the Greek word, *proteios,* meaning "holding first place."

Proteins in Nutrition.—Green plants and many microorganisms do not require protein food. For man and all animals, however, protein is an essential constituent of the diet. Without it, death is inevitable. Strictly speaking, it is not protein itself that is required, but the building blocks of protein, the amino acids (*see* below). A protein molecule is very large compared to molecules of sugar or salt, and consists of a large number of amino acids joined together to form long chains, much as beads are arranged on a string. In the digestive tract of the animal, enzymes act to degrade the protein of the food by breaking these long chains into shorter chains and free amino acids. The amino acids are absorbed across the walls of the intestinal tract and transported by the blood to the tissues. The cells then assemble their own proteins from these amino acid building blocks. Each species of animal or plant has a unique set of proteins different from those of other species. This difference is the reason that an animal cannot make direct use of the protein of a plant or of another species of animal, without first breaking that protein down to amino acids.

There are about 20 different amino acids that occur naturally in proteins (*see* Table). About half of these can be synthesized from other materials in the cells of the animal body. Eight of these amino acids cannot be synthesized by the human body, however, and must therefore be furnished in the diet (*see* Table). Normally, these essential amino acids are furnished in the form of protein food. The nutritional requirements of an animal for protein can actually be satisfied by feeding a mixture of essential amino acids, but since adequate amounts of such a mixture would be very expensive and not very palatable, there is little likelihood that man will substitute amino acids for good protein food such as meat, milk and eggs. It is striking that the proteins produced in nature for the nourishment of the young (for example, the milk proteins of mammals, the egg proteins of birds and the proteins laid down in seeds by plants) all provide adequate amounts of the essential amino acids. A diet that includes an inadequate supply of one or two essential amino acids, but is otherwise adequate, can be improved by adding the particular amino acids that are in short supply. It is also possible to feed an individual, who may for some reason be unable to ingest food, by intravenous injection of amino acids. The intact protein of ordinary foods cannot be used in this way.

Growth experiments have shown that all of the essential amino acids must be ingested simultaneously if they are to be utilized effectively. If the essential amino acids in the protein of the diet are balanced, then the minimum requirement of a man of average size is about 44 g. of protein a day. In 1943 the United Nations Conference on Food and Agriculture adopted certain dietary allowances that were regarded as the desirable goal for all peoples of the world. These recommendations included the following average values for protein in grams per day: man, 70; woman, 60; woman in the latter half of pregnancy, 85; woman in lactation, 100; girls 16 to 20 years, 75; and boys 16 to 20 years, 100. These goals are based on the assumption that an adequate number of calories and an adequate supply of vitamins are included in the diet. Authorities differ on these values, some setting the requirements appreciably higher.

Metabolism of Protein.—At first thought there may seem to be no reason why an adult should require protein in the diet, since an increase in the mass of body proteins occurs only during growth. Protein is continuously lost from the body, however. The proteins of dying cells, denatured protein and degradation products are broken down into amino acids by enzymes of the tissues. Some of these amino acids find their way back into new proteins. The remainder are degraded further, along with the amino acids that have been taken in the food and which are left over from protein synthesis. All of the amino acids contain nitrogen in the form of an amino group. This nitrogen is converted into urea by the liver, and the urea is excreted as a waste product in the urine. The normal adult excretes between 7 and 15 g. of nitrogen per day. The carbon compounds that remain after the removal of nitrogen are oxidized by the tissues into carbon dioxide and water. In this process the proteins may supply energy to the body. Normally, less than 20% of the energy requirements are supplied by the burning of protein. In the latter stages of starvation, however, large amounts of the tissue proteins are burned away.

The continuous breakdown and synthesis of new protein results in the renewal of all of the proteins in the body. Some tissue proteins are more susceptible to change than others. For example, the proteins of the liver, the blood plasma (but not the red cells) and the lining of the intestine are broken down very rapidly, whereas the proteins of muscle, skin, brain and skeleton are broken down slowly. The average life of the hemoglobin in the red cells is about 120 days, but the serum albumin of the blood is renewed in a few weeks.

Proteins and Immunity.—When a protein of a different species is injected into the blood stream of man or an animal, an immunity to that protein may develop. Antibodies to the foreign protein appear in the blood stream. The antibody is itself a protein that has the ability to combine with the foreign protein eliciting its formation. If the foreign protein has toxic properties, these are thereby neutralized. By this mechanism the animal protects its body from invasion by bacteria. The bacterial proteins induce antibody formation that renders the bacteria harmless and incapable of invading the animal.

Industrial Use of Proteins.—Since animal tissues contain a much higher proportion of protein than plant tissues, most of the proteins of industrial importance are obtained from animal sources. Apart from the food proteins, the proteins which are utilized in the largest quantity are keratin found in wool an

The Naturally Occurring Amino Acids

Name	Formula	Minimum daily nutritional requirement for average man	Name	Formula	Minimum daily nutritional requirement for average man
Glycine	H C—COOH, NH₂	None	Aspartic acid	COOH—CH₂—C—COOH, NH₂	None
Alanine	CH₃C—COOH, NH₂	None	Glutamic acid	COOH—CH₂—CH₂—C—COOH, NH₂	None
Valine	CH₃ CH—C—COOH CH₃ NH₂	0.8 g.	Lysine	H C—CH₂—CH₂—CH₂—C—COOH, NH₂ NH₂	0.8 g.
Leucine	CH₃ CH—CH₂—C—COOH CH₃ NH₂	1.1 g.	Arginine	NH₂—C—N—CH₂—CH₂—CH₂—C—COOH NH H NH₂	None
Isoleucine	C₂H₅ CH—C—COOH CH₃ NH₂	0.7 g.	Phenylalanine	⬡—CH₂—C—COOH, NH₂	1.1 g.
Serine	H H H C—C—COOH OH NH₂	None	Tyrosine	HO—⬡—CH₂—C—COOH, NH₂	None
Threonine	H H CH₃—C—C—COOH OH NH₂	0.5 g.	Histidine	HC═C—CH₂—C—COOH N NH NH₂ C H	None
Cysteine	H HC—C—COOH SH NH₂	None	Tryptophan	⬡ C—CH₂—C—COOH C NH₂ N H	0.25 g.
Methionine	H H H C—CH₂—C—COOH SCH₃ NH₂	1.1 g.	Proline	CH₂——CH₂ CH₂ CH—COOH N H	None

fibroin in silk of the textile industry (*see* WOOL; SILK: *Physical and Chemical Properties of Silk*), and collagen in the processed hides of the leather industry (*see* LEATHER). Glues and sizes are prepared from the casein (*q.v.*) of milk, from the proteins of blood and from the crude gelatin of boiled bones. (*See* ADHESIVES.) Bone protein, called ossein, is similar to collagen. The gelatin (*q.v.*) used as food is obtained from scraps of hide, connective tissue and tendons. Waste proteins, including blood, horn, hooves, bones, etc., are used for plant fertilizer as a source of organic nitrogen.

The plant protein, zein, is a by-product of the starch industry. After starch has been extracted from corn (maize), the protein is separated from the residues by extraction with isopropyl alcohol, in which it is soluble. Zein has industrial uses similar to those of casein. Both proteins have been used to a limited extent in the manufacture of yarns. Seed proteins such as those from the soybean and the peanut have been converted into plastics. Wheat yields a protein, gluten, which is rich in glutamic acid and serves as a source for the condiment monosodium glutamate. Another protein used in cookery is papain from the papaya plant, an enzyme which is applied to meat before cooking in order to make it more tender. Soybean protein is used increasingly in the preparation of synthetic foods. The protein is spun into delicate fibres, which are combined and artificially flavoured and textured to resemble meats and other natural products.

Properties of Proteins.—Proteins vary greatly in their properties. Some, such as the bright red hemoglobin of blood, contain pigments built into the molecule. Other proteins are colourless. Some proteins, such as hair, wool and silk, form long thin fibres completely insoluble in ordinary solvents. Others, for example the albumin of egg white, are very soluble in water but solidify on heating. Muscle cells contain fibres of protein that have the property of contracting and relaxing when the cell is stimulated. All proteins have the common property of being built from the same subunits, the amino acids, according to the same general plan. The amino acids are joined together by primary bonds, called peptide bonds, to form long chains. About 20 dif-

ferent kinds of amino acids are present in one protein molecule, but there may be a hundred or more amino acid subunits in the molecule, some of the amino acids recurring many times along the length of the chain. The sequence of amino acids along the chain is characteristic for each protein. It is clear that the number of possible arrangements of amino acids in the chain is very large, thus explaining why there are such an enormous number of different kinds of proteins.

Proteins, as they are found in nature, are characterized not only by the sequence of amino acids in their chains but also by the three-dimensional configuration of the chains themselves. Certain atomic groupings along the chains are able to form bonds with one another and to stick together. As a result, the chains are held in definite coiled or folded configurations. The properties and biological function of each protein depend upon the maintenance of a specific configuration. Larger aggregates are also formed, composed of several, or even a very large number, of molecules, held together more or less firmly. Since the structure of the native protein molecule is organized in a specific way, it follows from the geometry of these molecules that the structure of the aggregate is also organized into a pattern. Thus the structure of proteins is organized at three levels: (1) the sequence of the amino acids in the chains; (2) the folding of the chains into functional units; and (3) the combination of these units into larger patterns. It is this ability to form organized structures of great complexity and variety, inherent in the chemical nature of proteins, that is the basis for their function in living matter.

Differences in solubility are sometimes used for classifying proteins, but as more is learned, this basis of classification loses its usefulness. Frequently the more soluble fraction of a mixture of proteins is called the albumin fraction, and the less soluble fraction is called the globulin fraction. Albumins are soluble in pure water, whereas true globulins are insoluble in water but are soluble in dilute salt solutions. Proteins insoluble in water or in salt solutions may dissolve in dilute acid or dilute alkali. High concentrations of a salt such as ammonium sulfate will precipitate both albumins and globulins. The chemist makes use of these differences in solubility for the isolation and purification of individual proteins.

Molecular Size.—Many properties of proteins result from their large size. They are very large compared with a molecule of water, which has a molecular weight of about 18 times the weight of a hydrogen atom, or compared with a molecule of cane sugar, which has a molecular weight of about 342. Though some proteins may have a molecular weight as small as 6,000, others have molecular weights greater than 100,000. Some aggregates of protein molecules, uniform in size and composition, are known to have particle weights greater than 1,000,000; *e.g.*, the virus proteins. Since protein molecules are very heavy, they can be caused to fall out of solution in a large centrifugal field. High-speed centrifuges (ultracentrifuges) are used to determine the molecular weight of proteins by measuring how fast they will move to the bottom of a rotating vessel.

Compared with smaller molecules, proteins in solution diffuse very slowly from one place to another in the liquid. Those proteins with the shape of long, thin rods give viscous solutions. The large size of proteins prevents them from diffusing through natural membranes such as the walls of the blood vessels or through synthetic membranes such as cellophane, whereas molecules as small as sugar diffuse freely. As a consequence, proteins are able to produce a permanent osmotic pressure across a membrane. That is, pressure is required to prevent water placed on one side of the membrane from penetrating into the protein solution placed on the other side of the membrane.

Denaturation.—Unlike most simple organic molecules, the physical and chemical properties of a protein are markedly altered when the substance is boiled in water. Similar changes are produced by the following reagents: dilute acid, dilute alkali, alcohol, detergents or concentrated solutions of urea. The process by which these reagents alter the protein is called denaturation. In general, denaturation results in lowered solubility of the protein in neutral solution. In some cases, a gel or coagulum is formed, as when egg white is heated. More significantly, denaturation usually results in the loss of the biological function of the protein. For example, enzymes lose their catalytic powers and hemoglobin loses its capacity to carry oxygen. The changes that accompany denaturation have been shown to result from the destruction of the specific pattern in which the amino acid chains are folded in the native protein. All of the agents able to cause denaturation are able to break the secondary bonds that hold the chains in place. Once these weak bonds are broken, the molecule falls into a disorganized tangle, devoid of biological function.

Conjugated Proteins.—Some proteins contain other chemical groups in addition to amino acids. Such proteins are called conjugated proteins. If the nonprotein portion of the molecule is known to have a biological function, it is referred to as the prosthetic group. A large number of enzymes have prosthetic groups that participate in the catalytic activity. Some of these prosthetic groups are derived from vitamins (*see* VITAMINS; ENZYMES). If the prosthetic group is coloured, the conjugated protein which contains it will also be coloured. For example, hemoglobin, the main constituent of the red cells of blood, consists of the protein globin and a coloured substance called heme. Four heme molecules, each of which contains one iron atom, are firmly attached to each globin molecule. In the lungs, an oxygen molecule is bound to each iron atom and is carried by the blood stream to the outlying tissues. Other proteins are known that contain metal atoms bound to the protein structure. The cerulo-plasmin of blood is a bright blue protein containing copper.

Proteins and Heredity.—The most important conjugated proteins are the nucleoproteins, which consist of proteins combined with nucleic acids (*q.v.*). Nucleoproteins are found not only in the nuclei of cells, but also in extranuclear particles. Chromosomes, viruses and the heads of sperm cells all consist largely of nucleoproteins. These substances serve the mechanism by which hereditary characteristics are transmitted from cell to cell, and are intimately involved in the processes of self-duplication which are basic to life.

Amino Acids.—Proteins may be broken down into their constituent amino acids by prolonged heating with acid, by heating with alkali, or by treatment with certain enzymes which cause a breaking of the bonds between the amino acids. Molecules of the natural amino acids have the common structure shown in the formula:

$$\begin{array}{c} H \\ R-C-COOH \\ NH_2 \end{array}$$

As indicated by the structure, the four covalent bonds of the α-carbon atom are linked to an amino group ($-NH_2$), a carboxylic acid group ($-COOH$), a hydrogen atom ($-H$), and a fourth atomic grouping which is called the side chain ($-R$). As with all organic compounds in which a carbon atom is linked to four different groups, there are two different ways in which the groups may be arranged around the central carbon atom. Only one of these arrangements is found in the amino acids isolated from proteins, and this arrangement is designated by the symbol L. Thus the subunits of proteins are described as L-α-amino acids. The amino acids obtained from proteins are distinguished by their different side chains. The table gives the names of the most important naturally occurring amino acids and their structural formulas, and indicates the importance in nutrition of each substance.

A few additional amino acids occur in proteins only rarely, and so are not listed in the table. An example is thyroxine, an iodine-containing amino acid occurring in the protein of the thyroid gland. One of the compounds listed in the table, proline, is strictly speaking an imino, rather than an amino acid. Aspartic and glutamic acids are frequently classified as acidic amino acids; histidine, lysine and arginine are classified as basic amino acids, and the remaining amino acids are described as neutral. In actual fact, since the carboxyl group is acidic, and the amino group is basic, all amino acids are both acids and bases, but the acidic and basic groups neutralize each other, to give a molecule with the dipole structure shown:

$$\begin{array}{c} H \\ R-C-COO^- \\ NH_3^+ \end{array}$$

The Peptide Bond.—Two amino acids may be joined by condensation between the carboxylic acid group of one molecule and the amino group of the other molecule, with the splitting out of a molecule of water:

$$H_2N.CH(CH_3).COOH + H_2N.CH(CH_2OH).COOH \longrightarrow$$
$$\text{alanine} \qquad \text{serine} \qquad \text{yields}$$
$$H_2N.CH(CH_3).CO.NH.CH(CH_2OH).COOH + H_2O$$
$$\text{alanyl-serine} \qquad \text{water}$$

The bond formed between the carbonyl group ($-CO-$) and the imino group ($-NH-$) is called a peptide bond. A dipeptide is a compound formed by the union of two amino acids through one peptide bond, such as alanyl-serine shown above. A tripeptide is formed from three amino acids joined by two peptide bonds, while a tetrapeptide is formed from four amino acids, etc. When many amino acids are linked into a chain by peptide bonds, the structure is called a polypeptide. Thus proteins may be described as molecules that are composed of polypeptide chains.

When a polypeptide chain is split into the component amino acids by the action of acid, or alkali, or certain enzymes (peptidases), the condensation reaction is reversed. A molecule of water is added to each peptide bond by a process called hydrolysis, and one carboxyl group and one amino group are reformed. If hydrolysis is not complete, the products may consist of di-, tri-, and higher peptides, besides free amino acids. The fact that proteins can be hydrolyzed to amino acids and peptides by the action of certain enzymes which are known to attack the peptide bonds of synthetic peptides provides convincing proof that the peptide bond is the principal means by which amino acids are linked in proteins. A number of simple peptides are found in nature. Among them are the pituitary hormone, oxytocin, and the tripeptide glutathione (*q.v.*). These peptides, and many others resembling them, have been synthesized in the chemical laboratory.

Structure of Protein.—If the structure of a protein is to be completely determined, one of the problems that must be solved is the sequence of the amino acids in the peptide chain. Methods whereby sequence can be determined are known, but the techniques are difficult and laborious. An event that marked a milestone in the advance of knowledge of proteins was the determination by Frederick Sanger (*q.v.*) in the early 1950s of the sequence of amino acids in the polypeptide chains of insulin. This

 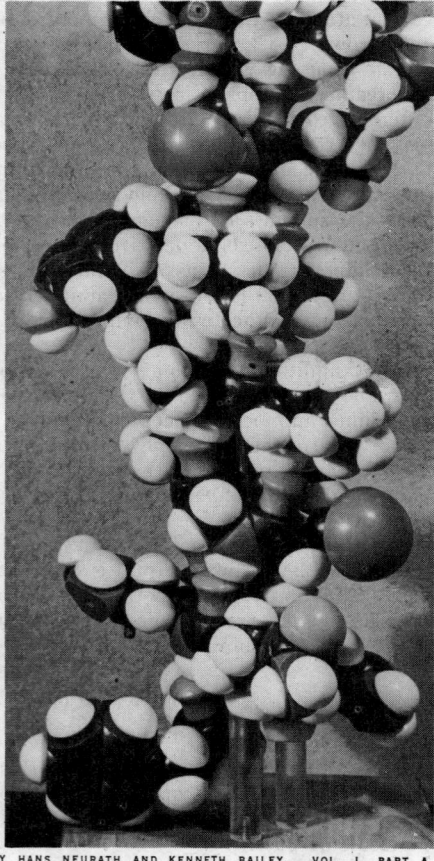

FROM "THE PROTEINS," EDITED BY HANS NEURATH AND KENNETH BAILEY. VOL. I, PART A, 1953, ACADEMIC PRESS, INC., PUBLISHERS; PHOTOGRAPHS BY BARBARA W. LOW

ATOMIC MODELS OF POLYPEPTIDE CHAIN (α-HELIX): (LEFT) THE CORE; (RIGHT) CORE WITH VARIOUS SIDE CHAINS ATTACHED

hormone, which counteracts diabetes, is composed of two different polypeptide chains, one 30 amino acids long and the other 21 amino acids long. Subsequent work by others resulted in the determination by the 1960s of the complete amino acid sequences of the enzyme ribonuclease and the protein subunit of the tobacco mosaic virus.

The polypeptide chains of native proteins are not free to take random configurations. They are fixed by cross-linkages between points on the same chain and between points on different chains. One type of cross-linkage is formed between the sulfur atoms of two molecules of the amino acid cysteine, giving a disulfide ($-S-S-$) bond. Another type of cross-linkage may be formed by phosphorus in the form of phosphoric acid, which may serve to link pairs of side chains.

Another type of bond prevalent in proteins is the so-called hydrogen bond formed between oxygen and nitrogen atoms. A hydrogen atom is found between the two atoms that form such a bond; *e.g.*, $O-H---O$ and $N-H---O$. Although hydrogen bonds are weak compared with primary bonds, the presence of a large number of hydrogen bonds in proteins results in an accumulative effect that contributes significantly to the stability of particular structures. Investigations of proteins by means of X-rays have indicated that hydrogen bonds hold portions of the polypeptide chain in a helical (spiral) configuration. A model of the helical

structure of a polypeptide chain is shown in the accompanying photograph. On the left, the side chains have been removed to show the hydrogen bonds between the carbonyl groups and the imino groups of the peptide linkages. On the right, the side chains are in place. The model demonstrates how the side chains of the different amino acids project out from a roughly cylindrical core within which the hydrogen bonds are buried. Many properties of proteins can be explained by this model.

Electrical Charge.—Although the amino acids have a dipole structure, the peptide bond is relatively uncharged. However, a protein generally contains amino acids with acidic side chains and also amino acids with basic side chains. These groups may carry electrical charges. In acidic solutions most proteins carry a positive electrical charge, while in alkaline solutions they carry a negative charge. An electrical process, called electrophoresis, is used by the chemist to analyze and separate mixtures of proteins according to the electrical charges of the molecules.   (B. V.)

Natural Synthesis of Proteins.—The problem of how the living cell synthesizes protein had been all but completely elucidated by the mid-1960s. Many laboratories had clearly achieved net synthesis of specific proteins in cell-free extracts containing enzymes, nucleic acids and subcellular particles, and the detailed analysis of this interesting and important process was proceeding rapidly.

Amino acids made reactive by combination with adenosine triphosphate (*see* METABOLISM: *Bioenergetics*) become attached to molecules of a low-molecular-weight ribonucleic acid known as transfer RNA. Each amino acid, bound to its transfer RNA, then migrates to one of the subcellular particles, known as ribosomes, where it reacts to form a peptide bond with a lengthening protein chain in a specific sequence determined by a second type of ribonucleic acid, called messenger RNA. This substance originates in the nucleus of the cell where its sequence in turn is determined by that of the genetic material (*see* GENE: *Genes and Development*). Each messenger RNA molecule bears in its sequence specifications for the sequence of amino acids in a protein to be synthesized. In this way amino acids from the transfer RNA are linked together by peptide bonds in specific sequence ultimately determined by the genetic material of the cell. The result is the synthesis of a unique polypeptide structure characteristic of the cell that made it: a protein.

Artificial Synthesis of Proteins.—Although random peptide polymers of amino acids had been created by chemical means, no artificial compound with properties identical to those of a naturally occurring protein had been made in the laboratory until 1964. In that year P. G. Katsoyannis and his collaborators at the University of Pittsburgh reported the synthesis, by purely chemical methods, of the two main chains of the insulin molecule. This was the next-to-last step to complete synthesis, which was achieved in 1966 by a group in China headed by Y. C. Du.

(J. Wy.)

See ALBUMINS; BLOOD; CELL; NUTRITION; PEPSIN; *see* also references under "Proteins" in the Index.

See M. V. Tracy, *Proteins and Life* (1948); H. Neurath and K. Bailey (eds.), *The Proteins*, vol. iA, iB (1953), iiA, iiB (1954); H. Neurath (ed.), *The Proteins*, 2nd ed., vol. 1 (1963), vol. 2 (1964).

PROTESILAUS, Greek mythological hero, son of Iphiclus and Diomedeia (or Astyoche), leader in the Trojan War of the force from Phylace and other Thessalian cities west of the Pagasaean Gulf. Though aware that an oracle had foretold death for the first of the invading Greeks to land at Troy, he was the first ashore and the first to fall. His newly married wife Laodameia was so grief-stricken that the gods granted her request that Protesilaus be allowed to return from the dead for three hours. At the expiration of this time she accompanied him to the underworld, either by immediately taking her own life or by immolating herself in the flames in which her father burned the waxen image of Protesilaus she had been cherishing. The theme is a favourite with Latin erotic poets, whose source is probably Alexandrine. No extant Greek author gives the full story, though Euripides may well have used it as the plot of his lost *Protesilaus*.

(D. E. W. W.)

PROTESTANT, a term applied to those Western Christian communions in separation from the Roman Catholic Church which owe their existence to the Reformation or to later events influenced by the Reformation (*q.v.*). The adherents of those communions are commonly described as Protestants and their teaching as Protestant.

The historical origin of the word is in the second imperial Diet of Speyer (1529), which reversed by a majority vote the decision of the first Diet of Speyer (1526) to allow each prince of the empire to determine the religion of his territory. The minority, consisting of 6 princes and 14 cities, issued a formal *Protestation,* the primary purpose of which was to protest that "in matters which concern God's honour and salvation and the eternal life of our souls, everyone must stand and give account before God for himself." A secondary purpose was to protest against the ban on the expansion of evangelical religion.

The supporters of the Reformation doctrines gradually came to be called Protestants both by their opponents and by themselves, since it was a convenient name to cover the many varieties of Reformed Christianity. It spread from the continent of Europe to England, where, since 1689, the coronation service has contained an oath to defend the "Protestant Reformed Religion by law established." The non-Anglican Reformed churches in Great Britain have accepted the name as a true description of themselves since the 17th century, and this is the case also in America and the other English-speaking countries. But no communion incorporated the word into its title until this was done by the Protestant Episcopal Church of America. The 19th-century Oxford Movement persuaded an increasingly large number of clergy and laity of the Church of England to repudiate the word "Protestant" as a description of their church. The term is officially used on both sides of the Atlantic by a number of societies which propagate the view that the principles of the Reformation are being neglected.

The basic doctrines of Protestantism at the Reformation, in addition to those of the creeds, were: the supremacy of Holy Scripture in matters of faith and order; justification (*q.v.*) by grace alone through faith alone; the priesthood of all believers. There has been variation in sacramental doctrine among Protestants, but the limitation of the number to the two "sacraments of the Gospel," baptism and Holy Communion, has been almost universal. In the 18th century the Enlightenment produced liberal Protestantism, which cast doubt on some doctrines in the creeds and stressed reason, religious experience, and the principle of private judgment in a way that would have been repugnant to the original Reformers. But this form of Protestantism was a spent force by the end of World War I, and by the efforts of thinkers such as Sören Kierkegaard and Karl Barth (*qq.v.*) Protestant theology and devotion have regained their objectivity with, at the same time, a deeper appreciation of the values of pre-Reformation Christianity. Though the doctrine of the verbal inerrancy of Scripture is maintained by several Protestant groups, the supremacy of the biblical revelation usually has been reasserted without it.   (R. E. DA.)

PROTESTANT EPISCOPAL CHURCH. The Protestant Episcopal Church in the U.S. is the denomination which was formed as successor to the Church of England in the American colonies and extended into all of the United States and its territories, with missionary districts in more than a dozen other countries. Associated with other autonomous churches in the Anglican Communion, it has a membership of about 3,500,000 baptized persons (including infants and young children) of whom about 2,500,000 are communicants (registered recipients of Holy Communion, generally 12 years of age or older). Distinctly Protestant in many features of life and doctrine, including its teachings about Scripture, justification, and the priesthood of believers, the church has remained catholic in appreciating the whole Christian heritage and in comprehending a diversity of faith and practice into a unified but not uniform Christian body.

The members are organized into about 7,500 congregations, served by as many clergymen, grouped in approximately 100 jurisdictions called dioceses. The dioceses have federated to form the denomination, whose central administrative body is the Executive Council, with headquarters in New York City.

HISTORY

Origins.—In points of doctrine, worship, and ministerial order the church descended from and has remained affiliated with, and therefore traces its origin to that of, the Church of England, which achieved its distinction from Roman Catholicism under Tudor monarchs in the mid-16th century. (*See* ENGLAND, CHURCH OF.) While doctrine, discipline, and worship were then fully reformed and have remained so, Reformation leaders were careful not to break the line of England's bishops from the traditional episcopal succession of the medieval and patristic periods (*see* EPISCOPACY). Hence the church has claimed connection with the whole of Christian tradition and has cherished the recollection of pre-Reformation episodes in which English rulers and ecclesiastics asserted independence from the papacy.

More particular origins lie in the settlement and activity of the Church of England in the American colonies. Worship services had been conducted in the Colonies by clergy accompanying groups engaged in exploration, but continuous history in the New World began with the Jamestown settlement in 1607. Although it was the established church in the Virginia colony, New World conditions soon produced such innovations as local, lay government through vestries. As colonial policy changed after the accession of William and Mary, church establishment obtained also in Maryland, in five southern counties of New York, in Georgia, and in the Carolinas. The same policy secured for the church the right to exist as Nonconformist under New England's Puritan establishments, and by 1700 it had gained a foothold also in the religiously tolerant middle colonies.

Where local or colonial maintenance was inadequate, growth was fostered by the Society for the Propagation of the Gospel in Foreign Parts. The society was founded through efforts of Thomas Bray, who was superintendent of clergy in Maryland, but whose major work was enlisting public and private support for the church's religious and educational work in the Colonies. All that work was under the absentee jurisdiction of the bishops of London, some of whom appointed commissaries such as Bray in Maryland to act locally in their stead. Existing in every colony by the time of the Revolution, the church was insignificant in only a few.

BY COURTESY OF THE CHURCH HISTORICAL SOCIETY

THOMAS BRAY (1658–1730), FOUNDER OF THE SOCIETY FOR PROMOTING CHRISTIAN KNOWLEDGE (1698) AND THE SOCIETY FOR THE PROPAGATION OF THE GOSPEL (1701)

Both the quest by many colonists for freedom from royal-ecclesiastical control and the difficulties of adapting a royal, episcopal, established church to colonial conditions kept the Church of England from achieving in America the broad membership it enjoyed at home. Having no bishop in the Colonies meant a journey to England for any colonist entering the church's ministry, robbed congregations and clergy of episcopal visitations and supervision, left the rite of confirmation in total neglect, and deprived colonial churchmen of effective channels of appeal to the church at home. Several efforts to obtain bishops for the Colonies failed in the face of steady Puritan protest and of intermittent royal apathy. At the outbreak of the Revolution there were fewer than 300 Church of England congregations in the 13 Colonies. Of the 250 clergymen, half of whom were in Maryland and Virginia, the large majority were faithful to the oath of allegiance to the crown made at the time of ordination. In the South, however, the Revolution enlisted many churchmen into its leadership, and in Virginia two-thirds of the clergy supported independence. As an agency of the crown the church naturally fell under suspicion and attack, especially where its members were royalist, in spite of the fact that two-thirds of the signers of the Declaration of Independence were enrolled as churchmen.

Development in the United States.—Even before the end of the Revolution a prominent clergyman, William White (*q.v.*), chaplain of the Continental Congress, proposed that congregations form themselves into an American church continuing the spiritual legacy of the Church of England but severing jurisdictional connections with that church and the crown. Conventions of clergy and laity were held in various states in the early 1780s both to claim church property where establishment was annulled and to authorize entering into negotiations toward forming a distinct denomination. Interstate conventions in 1784 and 1785 began to draft a constitution and prayer book. Appeals were made to the Church of England to consecrate bishops for the new Protestant Episcopal Church; White was consecrated for Pennsylvania and Samuel Provoost (*q.v.*) for New York on Feb. 4, 1787. Earlier, Connecticut clergy, acting independently, had sought to have a bishop consecrated in England for their congregations; failing that, Samuel Seabury (*q.v.*) was consecrated in Scotland by non-juring bishops, schismatics from the Church of England, on Nov. 14, 1784. When the denomination was formally organized in the General Convention at Philadelphia in 1789, Seabury was recognized by representatives from

BY COURTESY OF THE CHURCH HISTORICAL SOCIETY

WILLIAM WHITE (1748–1836), FIRST PRESIDING BISHOP OF THE PROTESTANT EPISCOPAL CHURCH. ENGRAVING BY T. B. WELCH FROM A DRAWING BY J. B. LONGACRE

other states as a bishop, and New England delegates accepted the revised constitution and prayer book. The following year saw the consecration in England of James Madison for Virginia. All four bishops joined in consecrating Thomas John Claggett for Maryland in 1792, thus making the episcopal order self-sustaining and continuous with that of the mother church.

With its own government, liturgy, and ministry, the church was organized for work. But for a generation it lay dormant. At the General Convention of 1811 only one of the six bishops attended, and there were few more clergy and laymen present than in 1789. A new generation brought vigorous leadership ready and able to adapt the church to the generally American religious impulses of revivalism and denominationalism. John Henry Hobart, who became bishop of New York in 1811, emphasized the peculiar heritage and character of the church in competition with other denominations, enlarging membership, fostering westward expansion, and establishing institutions such as General Theological Seminary in New York. Alexander Viets Griswold became bishop of Massachusetts, Maine, New Hampshire, and Vermont, and increased congregations and membership fivefold through itinerant evangelistic work. In Virginia the evangelical Bishop Richard Channing Moore, by fostering revivals, extraliturgical services, and a theological seminary, reawakened that state's "mother church." High churchmen and evangelicals formed the Domestic and Foreign Missionary Society in 1820 to extend the church westward and abroad. The society, after 1835 the official missionary agency to which all church members belonged, established and staffed missionary districts in all the sparsely settled areas of the growing United States. The energetic work which Philander Chase (*q.v.*) had performed in Ohio and Illinois became the pattern for Bishops Jackson Kemper in the Northwest, Leonidas Polk and James Hervey Otey in the Southwest, and others. In 1853 a bishop was consecrated for California, in 1854 others for Oregon and Iowa, in 1859 one for Minnesota, and so on. In the United States, rapidly becoming more populous through expansion and immigration, the church burgeoned from a proportion of 1 communicant to 400 population in 1830 to 1:107 in 1900. Abroad, an educational mission to Greece began in 1829, followed by the

founding of missions in Liberia in 1835, China in 1840, Japan in 1859.

High and Low Church Divisions.—The Oxford Movement (*q.v.*) of the Church of England became influential during the 1840s, broadening the church's tradition, enriching worship and spiritual discipline, sharpening denominational claims, and exciting espousal among high churchmen and opposition among low churchmen. In 1853 a prominent group of churchmen joined William Augustus Muhlenberg, a New York rector, in pleading that the church rise above partisanship to champion union with

BY COURTESY OF THE CHURCH HISTORICAL SOCIETY

WILLIAM AUGUSTUS MUHLENBERG (1796–1877). ENGRAVING BY JOHN C. MCRAE

other denominations in evangelizing the nation. Too daring for its day, the plea only moderated the churchmanship controversy which by then involved questions not only of sacerdotal authority but also of ritual, ceremonial, sacramental worship, ecclesiology, and doctrine. Interrupted by the Civil War, the controversy raged again, by 1873 with violence that split the church. While some high churchmen championed a view of the intimate kinship of Anglican and Roman Catholic churches, low churchmen were unable to accomplish an official definition of Episcopalianism's Protestant principles and practices. George David Cummins (*q.v.*), then assistant bishop of Kentucky, was attacked for officiating at the united communion service of the sixth General Conference of the Evangelical Alliance in New York, October 1873. Resigning his charge in the Episcopal Church, Cummins, joined by seven clergymen and a score of laymen, organized in December 1873 the Reformed Episcopal Church, rejecting the notion of the episcopacy as an order of ministry while holding it as an office of presidency among equal presbyters.

Later History.—During the Civil War the dioceses of the Protestant Episcopal Church in seceded states judged themselves under necessity to establish a separate church administration, but the church was reunited by 1866. During the war new theological schools were established at Cambridge, Mass., and at Philadelphia, and soon afterward a church-controlled university at Sewanee, Tenn. These schools promoted liberal theology and biblical criticism in the church, forces which along with the social gospel and ecumenical movement have mitigated the internal controversy over churchmanship. The church has participated fully in the affairs of the Anglican Communion since the beginning

GEORGE DAVID CUMMINS (1822–76), FIRST BISHOP OF THE REFORMED EPISCOPAL CHURCH

of decennial Lambeth Conferences (*see* ANGLICAN COMMUNION) of Anglican bishops in 1867. In 1910 the General Convention inaugurated a movement toward ecumenical discussion of faith and order, issuing in the great conferences at Lausanne (1927), Oxford (1937), and Amsterdam (1948), at the last of which this movement became a part of the World Council of Churches.

After World War I the church created a permanent, representative, administrative body known as the National (later Executive) Council, which took over the functions of the Domestic and Foreign Missionary Society as trustees. Foreign missionary work, which had grown especially in Latin America and the Philippines, was consolidated. The council approached domestic missionary work more sociologically than geographically. Social and educational functions of the church were given a concern commensurate with the emphasis laid upon them by the revised prayer book of

1892. A renewed interest in worship which produced that revision was further stimulated by its allowance of liturgical variation and experimentation. Those features and advancement in liturgiological scholarship brought yet another revision in 1928 (*see also* LITURGY, CHRISTIAN). The 1918 hymnal similarly was superseded by the hymnal of 1940. Acknowledging a continual need to modernize and enrich its worship, the church established a standing committee on prayer book revision.

After World War I also was founded the Church Pension Fund for support of retired clergy and families of deceased clergy. Concern for recruiting and training clergymen increased then and again just after World War II. This interest in education led to raising the number and quality of theological seminaries and to the founding of several ministerial training institutes. Postordination training centres and conferences flourished, especially to spread the church's postwar approaches to Christian education of children and adults; approaches which, embodying insights of modern pedagogy, developmental psychology, and group dynamics, prompted the founding of numerous parochial day schools and increased the church's long-standing efforts in the field of preparatory education. Few colleges, however, are sponsored by the Protestant Episcopal Church. The work of Christian education has emphasized lay participation in church affairs. Thousands of men and women have become church school teachers, and the number of lay readers (men licensed to lead certain aspects of public worship) has surpassed the number of clergymen. Women have maintained their traditional support of missionary endeavours, served on altar guilds, directed programs of Christian education; they may enter religious communities or the order of deaconesses but may not be ordained ministers.

POLITY, WORSHIP, AND DOCTRINE

Polity.—As distinguished from church order, which is threefold and episcopally ordained, the church's polity has been basically congregational with admixtures of presbyterial and episcopal elements. Each self-supporting congregation (parish) elects its lay governing board (vestry) for temporal affairs and its clergyman (rector) as spiritual leader. Except in cases requiring episcopal discipline, tenure of the rector is broken by mutual consent of himself and the vestry. Assistant clergymen (curates, assistant rectors, associate rectors) aid larger parishes. Congregations not self-supporting (missions) fall under the bishop, who appoints lay members to oversee temporal affairs and the clergymen (vicars) for spiritual leadership.

In a given area the parishes and missions federate into a diocese; or, where unable to afford diocesan status of self-support, into a missionary district. All clergymen and representatives of all congregations meet annually in convention to adopt budget and program and to set policy. Each diocese is served by a bishop elected by convention to serve until death or retirement, election being subject to approval by a majority of the other dioceses. There may be assistant bishops as coadjutors (with right and duty of succession) or as suffragans (who may be translated to other dioceses or missionary districts). Most episcopal functions are constitutionally limited by an elected standing committee of laymen and clergymen. The bishop acts, however, in his own right and rarely as representing a *collegium episcoporum*.

The dioceses and missionary districts federate into the General Convention meeting triennially. In its House of Bishops sits each bishop, and in the House of Deputies equal numbers of clergy and laymen representing dioceses and missionary districts. Fundamentally a legislative body, requiring concurrence of both houses for action, the General Convention is related to dioceses and districts as a federal, not a national, organ. Its administrative agency, the Executive Council, is headed by the presiding bishop, who also presides over the House of Bishops. That house meets between conventions largely in an advisory capacity.

Worship and Doctrine.—The Protestant Episcopal Church is a liturgical church whose authorized forms of worship are set forth in the Book of Common Prayer adopted by General Convention. The forms of public worship (morning prayer, evening prayer, litany, Holy Communion) are composed very largely of biblical material arranged for much congregational participation. The book also provides forms for ordaining deacons, priests, and bishops; for baptism, catechizing, confirmation, matrimony, churching of women, visitation and communion of the sick, burial of the dead, etc. Usual public worship on Sundays is morning prayer or Holy Communion or both, occasionally litany and evening prayer. Morning prayer consists of call to worship; confession and absolution; canticles, psalms, and lessons; stated and variable prayers. Customarily there are added hymns, sermon, offertory, and closing prayers. Holy Communion consists of preparation; collect, epistle, and gospel; creed and sermon (the latter sometimes omitted); offertory of alms, bread and wine, and prayer; confession and absolution; consecration; administration of communion; closing prayers. Hymns are usually added, and often portions of the service are intoned or sung or accompanied by elaborate ritual. Theologically and literarily, the Holy Communion service blends elements of the Protestant Lord's Supper and of the Roman Mass; rubrical latitude allows for ceremonial variations which in actual practice can give either interpretation to this service. Congregation as well as clergyman is assigned definite parts of each service and thus participates in the leadership of, rather than following or listening to, worship. Appropriate postures are assumed for each type of worship activity: kneeling for prayer, standing for praise, sitting for instruction. At each service is prayed the Lord's Prayer, and, except at the litany, either the Apostles' or the Nicene Creed (*see* CREED) is recited. Scripture readings may be from one of several approved translations and include lessons from the Apocrypha. Public worship is required to be in the vernacular, although its contents are drawn from many eras, languages, and traditions.

The church has inherited its doctrinal formularies from the Church of England but does not apply these statements as rigid confessions. Developing as it did in the context of the Enlightenment's suspicion of strict dogmatism, it has cherished the classic creeds and its changing prayer book as stating its doctrinal position. Baptism and confirmation involve accepting "all the articles of the Christian Faith as contained in the Apostles' Creed." The Nicene Creed is taken to be an adequate summary of belief and thus is recited in public worship, but not, as in the Church of England, the Athanasian Creed. The Thirty-Nine Articles (*q.v.*) of the Church of England, slightly adapted to suit American circumstances, are part of the prayer book and of official doctrine, but formal subscription as such is required neither of clergy nor laity. The prayer book's catechism and offices of instruction are succinct statements of the church's teaching. All these formularies, excepting of course the creeds, bear the unmistakable imprint of the Protestant Reformation. While Scripture is the primary and incontrovertible fountain of doctrine, Anglican tradition appeals also to the early church and to reason. Rather than upon confessions as expressing the whole content of the faith, the church lays emphasis upon not teaching nor believing against Scripture, creeds, and prayer book. Within these limits are held various and often divergent doctrinal and theological opinions both by clergy and laity, some preferring Catholic, some Protestant, some liberal, and some modernist interpretations of the church's basic formularies.

Distinctive Aspects.—Along with other Anglican churches, this church has been distinguished by the richness and dignity of its worship. It has been marked by an ability to hold a full catholic heritage under the control of Reformation principles while opening itself to new intellectual movements, portraying itself as a *via media* between extremes of Roman Catholicism and Protestantism. Engagement in ecumenical discussions has concentrated attention upon the church's preservation of an uninterrupted succession of bishops through the doctrinal and liturgical reform of the 16th century and through subsequent upheavals. From a declaration of the church's General Convention in Chicago in 1886 was formed the "Lambeth Quadrilateral" stating four points upon which Anglicans would enter union negotiations with any Christian body: the Holy Scriptures, the Apostles' and the Nicene Creed, the sacraments of baptism and the Supper of the Lord, and the historic episcopate. The formula has come to be understood as stating th' distinct marks of the church and the communion, but wide acceptance in other communions of the first three points has turned attention to the fourth as a distinctive, but of course not exclusive, possession of this church. Some Episcopalians would insist that no true church exists apart from the historic episcopate in this apostolic succession, while others would hold this feature as a mark of the well-being or fullness, but not of the *esse*, of a true church.

Through membership in the National Council of the Churches of Christ in America and in the World Council of Churches, the Episcopal Church has participated in the movement toward interchurch cooperation and union. Intercommunion with Old Catholics (*q.v.*) has been achieved and has been anxiously sought with Eastern Orthodox and other churches. Unity negotiations with such American denominations as Methodists and Presbyterians have been pursued inconclusively.

See also references under "Protestant Episcopal Church" in the Index.

BIBLIOGRAPHY.—*General Convention Journals* (1785 *et seq.*); *Historical Magazine of the Protestant Episcopal Church* (1932 *et seq.*); W. S. Perry, *The History of the American Episcopal Church, 1587–1883*, 2 vol. (1885); W. W. Manross, *History of the American Episcopal Church* (1935); E. C. Chorley, *Men and Movements in the American Episcopal Church* (1946); J. T. Addison, *The Episcopal Church in the United States, 1789–1931* (1951); C. P. Morehouse (ed.), *Episcopal Church Annual;* J. A. Pike and W. N. Pittenger, *The Faith of the Church* (1951); M. H. Shepherd, *The Worship of the Church* (1952); P. M. Dawley, *The Episcopal Church and Its Work* (1955); R. W. Albright, *A History of the Protestant Episcopal Church* (1964).
(W. A. CL.)

PROTEUS, the prophetic old man of the sea in Greek mythology and shepherd of the sea's flocks (seals, etc.). According to Homer, his dwelling place was the island of Pharos, near the mouth of the Nile; in Virgil his home is the island of Carpathus, between Crete and Rhodes. He knew all things, past, present, and future, but disliked telling what he knew. Those who wished to consult him had first to surprise and bind him during his noonday slumber in a cave by the sea, where he spent his time during the heat of the day surrounded by his seals. Even when caught he would try to escape by assuming all sorts of shapes, that of a lion, a serpent, a leopard, a boar, a tree, fire, water. But if his captor held him fast the god at last returned to his proper shape, gave the wished-for answer and plunged into the sea. He was subject to Poseidon. In post-Homeric times the story (invented by the Greek lyric poet Stesichorus?) ran that Proteus was the son of Poseidon and a king of Egypt, to whose court Helen was taken by Hermes after she had been carried off, Paris being accompanied to Troy by a phantom substituted for her. This is the story followed by Herodotus, who got it from Egyptian priests, and by Euripides in the *Helena*. From his power of assuming whatever shape he pleased, Proteus came to be regarded, especially by the Orphic mystics, as a symbol of the original matter from which the world was created.

PROTEUS (OLM), a blind, aquatic salamander, *Proteus anguinus,* that lives in the dark caves of Yugoslavia and elsewhere in southern Europe. Like its relative the North American mud puppy (*Necturus*), with which it constitutes the family Proteidae, the olm is neotenous; *i.e.,* it is permanently larval and breeds without ever attaining a definite adult stage. The olm attains a length of about a foot; its elongate body is pale except for the carmine red gill plumes (3 pairs). The minute limbs bear three digits on the anterior pair, two on the posterior pair. The head is narrow, with a flat, blunt snout and vestigial eyes covered by opaque skin. Exposure to white light causes the skin to blacken gradually, even over the eyes. *See also* AMPHIBIA.

PROTHESIS, in the liturgy of the Orthodox Eastern Church, the name given to the act of "setting forth" the oblation; *i.e.,* the arranging of the bread on the paten, the signing of the cross on the bread with the sacred spear, the mixing of the chalice and the veiling of the paten and chalice (Gr. *prothesis*, "a setting forth"). In Eastern Orthodoxy the commoner term for the preparation of these elements is "proskomide." The term is used, architecturally, for the place in which this ceremony is enacted, a chamber on the north side of the central apse in a Greek church; the term is also applied to the small table on which it is done.

During the reign of Justin II (565–578) this chamber was located in an apse and another apse was added on the south side for the diaconicon, so that from his time the Greek church was triapsal. In the churches in central Syria both prothesis and diaconia are generally rectangular, and the former constitutes a chamber for the deposit of offerings by the faithful. Consequently it was sometimes placed on the south side, if when so placed it was more accessible to the pilgrims. There is always a much wider doorway to the prothesis than to the diaconicon. There are cases where a side doorway from the central apse leads direct to the diaconicon, but never to the prothesis.

PROTIC, STOJAN (1857–1923), Serbian statesman and first prime minister of the Kingdom of Serbs, Croats, and Slovenes, was born at Krusevac on Jan. 28, 1857. After studying history and philology in Belgrade, he entered government service but resigned in order to devote himself to journalism. As editor of the Radical daily *Samouprava*, he was imprisoned for a press offense. He edited the paper *Odjek* ("Echo"; 1884), in which he advocated a change of the constitution. Elected to parliament in 1887, he became secretary of the Commission for the Drafting of a Constitution. Between 1888 and 1897, being reelected to parliament, he thrice entered government service, but each time he either resigned or was dismissed as a prominent Radical. He founded the monthly *Delo* ("Deed") in 1894 and was its first editor. After an attempt on the life of King Milan (*q.v.*) he was charged with plotting and was sentenced in 1899 to 20 years' hard labour in fetters, but was reprieved in 1900. Appointed keeper of the National Library he reentered parliament in 1901. Between 1903 and 1918 he was four times home secretary and twice minister of finance.

Protic formed the first cabinet of the Kingdom of Serbs, Croats, and Slovenes on Dec. 20, 1918. He resigned on Aug. 16, 1919, but was prime minister again from February to May 1920. Later he was minister in charge of the constituent assembly and the adjustment of laws. He retired from politics in 1923 and died in Belgrade on Oct. 28, 1923.

From 1903, Protic together with Nikola Pasic (*q.v.*) and Lazar Pacu (1855–1915) was a member of the triumvirate which *de facto* ruled the Serbian Radical Party. In June 1914, while Pasic, the prime minister, was canvassing his constituency, Austria-Hungary delivered the ultimatum which was to start World War I. The ultimatum was handed to the senior available minister, Pacu, but Protic drafted the Serbian reply. In the constituent assembly of 1920–21 he disagreed with Pasic and the Radical Party: his constitutional ideas were based on the English concept of home rule and he advocated them in his new daily *Radikal*. He fought his last election (1923) as an Independent Radical, but neither he nor any of his followers was returned. A distinguished writer, he left a number of works on Balkan political questions.   (K. ST. P.)

PROTISTA, a third kingdom of organisms, suggested by the German zoologist Ernst Haeckel in 1866 to provide a convenient taxonomic niche for forms intermediate between the animal and plant kingdoms. Many protists are unicellular (or acellular); those few that have more than one cell lack the tissue differentiation characteristic of higher organisms. Included in this group are both animallike and plantlike forms, which, on the basis of relative biological complexity, are divided into (1) lower protists (sometimes called Monera)—the bacteria and blue-green algae; and (2) the higher protists—the remaining algae, protozoans, and fungi. The concept of the Protista has not met with complete acceptance by biologists because of the general lack of consensus over where the line should be drawn between protists and higher organisms. *See also* ALGAE; BACTERIA; FUNGI; PROTOZOA.

PROTOCOL AND PRECEDENCE, two terms frequently used in diplomacy and public affairs, chiefly in regard to formal ceremonies.

Protocol.—In addition to rules governing diplomatic conduct and ceremonies, this term denotes a variety of written instruments. It is applied to the minutes (*procès-verbaux*) of the several sittings of an international conference or congress; though signed by the plenipotentiaries present, these minutes have only the force of verbal engagements (*see* CONFERENCE, INTERNATIONAL). It is also given to certain diplomatic instruments in which, without the form of a treaty or convention being adopted, are recorded the principles or the matters of detail on which an agreement has been reached; *e.g.*, making special arrangements for carrying out the objects of previous treaties, defining these objects more clearly, or interpreting the exact sense of a doubtful clause in a treaty. Occasionally an agreement between two or more powers takes the form of a protocol, rather than a treaty, when the intention is to proclaim a community of views or aims without binding them to eventual common action in support of those views or aims.

In the other sense of its meaning, "the protocol" (*protocole diplomatique, protocole de chancellerie*) is the body of ceremonial rules to be observed in all written or personal official intercourse between the heads of different states or their ministers. It lays down the styles and titles of states and of their heads and public ministers, and indicates the forms and customary courtesies to be observed in all international acts. "It is," says P. L. E. Pradier-Fodéré, "the code of international politeness."

Precedence.—To a large extent, protocol is based on rules of precedence: who goes first? who follows whom? Priority of place or superiority of rank has appeared in the hierarchical organization of society throughout the world from the earliest times. During the centuries when feudalism flourished in western Europe a complicated system of precedence developed among the families bound to the royal houses through grants of land in exchange for military service. The titles duke, marquess, count, earl, viscount, baron, and knight were military in origin. Knights, at first cavalrymen of the medieval armies, became officers ceremonially created (dubbed), with rank according to the size of their retinue, their prowess, or their membership in one of the religiously inspired orders of chivalry. From the 14th–15th centuries, the kings gradually succeeded in converting them into the modern type of dependent, domesticated nobility, a process made easier by the creation of secular knightly orders constituting an elite of great lustre but without equivalent power. (Some of these orders still survive. *See* KNIGHTHOOD, CHIVALRY AND ORDERS.) The nobility were thus transformed into sophisticated, modish courtiers, holders of rich sinecures and largely preoccupied with gaining or keeping the personal favour of their monarch. Rigid, meticulous, and glittering ceremonial, designed to reflect the glory of the monarch, was instituted at the permanent royal courts which were being established by the mid-16th century. This system reached its apogee at the Versailles of Louis XIV of France, where the greatest nobles deemed it an honour to assist the king at his rising and retiring.

This way of life came to an end with the Revolution. In modern France the former nobility (who may use their titles socially) have no official place. Precedence on ceremonial occasions is accorded, after the president of the republic, to state, academic, municipal, military, commercial, and legal officials according to their rank, a high place being allotted to the chancellors and officers of the Legion of Honour and the Order of Liberation.

Great Britain and Commonwealth.—The British scales of general precedence may be taken as an example of a modern system of precedence in a monarchical state. Its foundation is the Act of 1539 "for the placing of the Lords in Parliament" (31 Hen. VIII c. 10). The elaborate tables for England, Scotland, and Northern Ireland, separate for men and for women, can be found in *Burke's Peerage* (biennial) and *Debrett's Peerage* (annual).

First comes the crown, the fountain of honour, the symbol of continuity behind changes of government and the main link with the older Commonwealth countries. The royal family is followed in the English scale by the archbishop of Canterbury, the lord high chancellor, the archbishop of York, and the prime minister. (Logically, it might be thought that the prime minister, entrusted as he is by the sovereign with the formation of government, should come first after the royal family. In Canada and New Zealand, the prime minister does come first after the governor-general representing the crown; in Australia he comes next after the governors of the separate states, and in India next after the president.) In the Scottish scale, the lord high commissioner to the General Assembly of the Church of Scotland comes next after

the sovereign and the sovereign's consort while the Assembly is in session. The moderator comes immediately before the prime minister. Most of the Commonwealth countries admit to their scales the leaders of all the principal denominations.

In England it is worthy of note that holders of ceremonial offices, such as the lord high treasurer, may precede holders of important government posts, such as the speaker of the House of Commons. Some offices of great importance have a comparatively lowly place in the scale. The chancellor of the exchequer is probably second only to the prime minister in importance in the cabinet; and the lord chief justice is the embodiment of the majesty and power of the law: yet both are ranked after the vice-chamberlain of the household. Among the orders and decorations there are similar anomalies. The highest qualifications are needed for the Order of Merit. Yet it has no place in the scale. The Distinguished Service Order is admitted, but the Victoria Cross, the most highly prized of all military awards, is excluded. Indeed the fighting forces as such have no position in the English scale of general precedence. The anomalous situation with regard to precedence of admirals of the fleet, field marshals, and marshals of the Royal Air Force is concealed by conferring peerages or knighthoods upon the most eminent of them.

The English scale takes no account of local precedence; the lord lieutenant of a county, for example, finds no place. And the precedence of lord mayors and mayors is confined to their cities and boroughs and to their year of office.

The strictly aristocratic and hereditary elements in the scale come in the following order: dukes, marquesses, earls, viscounts, barons; with their wives, sons, daughters, and grandchildren. (*See* also PEERAGE.) It may be important to know, upon ceremonial or social occasions, that the eldest son of an earl comes before the younger son of a marquess. It is all very exact but somewhat remote and antiquated because precedence does not reflect the lords' loss of direct political power or their loss of wealth.

There are also "courtesy" titles, which confer no precedence. They arise because each of the higher peers has one or more subordinate titles lower in degree than that generally used. It is customary to address the eldest son of such a peer by his father's second title; so that the eldest son of the duke of Bedford, for instance, is known as the marquess of Tavistock. But the marquess is not a peer, does not sit in the House of Lords, and takes precedence only derivatively as the son of his father.

The tables of precedence of the older Commonwealth countries, though giving, of course, first place to the representative of the sovereign, follow the U.S. model (*see* below) much more nearly than the British. India, as a federal republic, has a table in which the president is followed by a complex sequence of officials and former officials of the Indian union and states and high-ranking officers of the armed forces.   (X.)

United States.—Precedence at official functions and ceremonies in the United States is based upon official position and custom. The latter, outside of Washington, D.C., reflects the social and economic variables found in state and local communities on official occasions, and these affect strictly official considerations in the order of precedence in terms of religion, wealth, and other factors determining civic status. Political expediency rather than statutes prevails in the determination of the hierarchical order in public ceremonies. The tendency toward informality at state and municipal functions is in sharp contrast with the more ostentatious public affairs of the 19th century.

Washington, D.C.—Precedence in the capital of the U.S. is subject to a combined governmental and diplomatic ranking of which the Department of State is the arbiter. The division of protocol not only rules on official ranking, but informally provides essential guidance for social functions where official status at the national or international level is involved.

Precedence has been established by custom as:

The president; vice-president; speaker of the House of Representatives; chief justice of the United States; former presidents; secretary of state; ambassadors of foreign powers, ranked according to diplomatic rule of seniority by the date of presentation of credentials; widows of former presidents; secretary-general of the United Nations; U.S. representative to the UN; ministers of foreign powers in order of diplomatic seniority; associate justices; president's Cabinet (secretary of state excepted), in order of establishment of their offices: secretary of the treasury, secretary of defense, attorney general, postmaster general, secretaries of the interior, agriculture, commerce, labour, and health, education and welfare; senators; governors of states; former vice-presidents; members of the House of Representatives; chargés d'affaires of foreign powers; undersecretary of state; undersecretaries and deputy secretaries of the executive departments; secretaries of the Army, Navy, and Air Force; director, Bureau of the Budget; chairman, Council of Economic Advisers; chairman, Board of Governors of the Federal Reserve System; chairman, Joint Chiefs of Staff; chief of staff of the Army, chief of naval operations, and chief of staff of the Air Force; generals of the Army and fleet admirals; director, Central Intelligence Agency; director, U.S. Information Agency; administrator, National Aeronautics and Space Administration; and heads of other agencies.

Generally speaking, the states of the union follow a rule-of-thumb order of precedence on official occasions. Reception and seating depend upon the obvious political ranking and the expedient religious, economic, and social considerations in a given situation involving status. This situation has been facilitated by a departure from large, formal state affairs with a trend toward informality in official entertainment.

U.S. cities set up their own protocol for the reception of distinguished visitors. This follows a general political pattern of officials, headed by the mayor or his equivalent in other types of urban government or his representative for the occasion. Precedence again is weighed in terms of religious and civic status; it is flexible in its application in order to permit adjustments suitable for each function.

After World War II the increasing number of foreign visitors to the U.S. with official or quasi-official sponsorship made strategically located cities important points of reception. Chief of these is New York City, where the mayor's office has special machinery for extending such hospitality to visitors. The commissioner of commerce and public events is charged with all arrangements; an officer under him works out the problems of reception and precedence. This official is in contact with the State Department and the visitor's diplomatic mission in Washington or local consular representation; where the visitor's status warrants extensive ceremonies—a chief of state, head of government, etc.—these are planned by close consultation as to details of time, place, and guest list. (Cs. H.)

Communist Countries.—In the U.S.S.R. and other republics of eastern and southeastern Europe, the first secretary of the Communist or Workers' (i.e., ruling) Party takes precedence over all and is followed by the premier. Next comes the chairman of the Presidium of the Supreme Soviet (U.S.S.R.); the chairman of the Council of State (Poland); the president of the Presidential Council (Hungary); etc. (X.)

Diplomatic Corps.—As many ceremonies of state involve the diplomatic corps, diplomats occupy a prominent position in social life. The practice of diplomacy, which had occasioned many unseemly disputes (notably that between the Spanish and French ambassadors in London in 1661) was regularized by the decrees of the congresses of Vienna (1815) and of Aix-la-Chapelle (1818) on an agreed basis.

Four categories of representatives were recognized: (1) ambassadors, legates, or nuncios; (2) envoys extraordinary and ministers plenipotentiary; (3) ministers resident; (4) chargés d'affaires. Precedence within the corps was established on the basis of seniority of appointment, so that the doyen (or dean) of the corps is that ambassador who has been accredited to his post the longest; i.e., from the date of his official arrival and presentation of his letters of credence. In most Roman Catholic countries where the church enjoys a special position, the papal nuncio takes precedence over all his colleagues regardless of the date of his appointment. Even in this case, however, the senior ambassador continues to discharge most of the functions of the doyen. For consular officers (consuls general, consuls, vice-consuls, and consular agents) there is a comparative precedence which equates them with certain ranks of the fighting services. Thus consuls general rank with but after rear admirals, major generals, and air vice-marshals, while consuls rank with but after captains of the Royal Navy, colonels, and group captains of the Royal Air Force. In monarchical countries ambassadors usually have precedence

after members of the reigning family or high dignitaries of church and state. In England they follow the lord privy seal, while ministers come after dukes but before marquesses. In republics, practice varies: thus in France ambassadors come after the presidents of the Senate and of the National Assembly, whereas in the United States they come after the vice-president and before the chief justice. (S. B.-R. P.)

United Nations.—Precedence is a matter wholly determined by the UN itself in governing its procedures, ceremonies, and social functions. Directly under the secretary-general there is a unit at the headquarters to handle problems of precedence similar to that in any foreign office, the chief and assistant chief of protocol. Here all UN precedence, whether procedural, ceremonial, or social, is determined. There are no hard-and-fast rules nor is there an official list. Precedence is a developing process which combines regulations for the functioning of UN bodies, their officials, and representatives of member states with appropriate diplomatic conventions currently prevalent in international intercourse.

Basically, UN precedence rests on function and not upon the personal rank of the person discharging the duty. Hence the president of the General Assembly, irrespective of the delegate's personal rank, is the ranking official of the UN when the assembly is in session. The president of the Security Council, the second most important organ in terms of the Charter, becomes the chief functionary in terms of protocol if the assembly is not in session. However, since the headship of the Security Council rotates each month among the members, the person enjoying this prerogative changes accordingly.

The third post is that of the secretary-general, the executive-administrative officer of the UN who heads the Secretariat. Then follow the presiding officers of the specialized organs of the UN, the Economic and Social Council, the Trusteeship Council, etc., when in session; the heads of the permanent delegations accredited by the member states to the UN of ambassadorial rank; the assistant secretary-general and the undersecretaries; heads of delegations of ministerial rank; the operating heads of the departments into which the secretariat is subdivided.

The diplomatic practice that ambassadors and ministers rank according to the date of their appointment is not followed at the UN; strict observance of the alphabetical order of the countries they represent is the rule in session and elsewhere. In sessions of the UN organs, the actual seating facilities of the chambers used at headquarters, at Geneva, Switz., and elsewhere affect the working out of precedence for those occupying places on the rostrum; the alphabetical order in general seating of delegates on the floor rotates from front to rear so that the position of a member state's spokesman moves progressively, meeting by meeting, and no country enjoys a preferred position by reason of its name. (Cs. H.)

Roman Catholic Church.—The Roman Catholic Church, transcending all national boundaries, has its own hierarchy, or governing body, whose precedence is as follows: the pope; the Sacred College of Cardinals; archbishops and bishops; delegates, vicars, and prefects apostolic; certain abbots and prelates. Lower clergy also are strictly ranked, from provosts and vicars general of dioceses to assistant priests (curates). Precedence within these grades is, generally speaking, by date of election to them.

Normally, secular (i.e., diocesan) clergy have precedence at ceremonial functions over regular clergy (i.e., members of religious orders). However, religious superiors, e.g., fathers general, provincial, etc., are customarily granted special places in accordance with the occasion and circumstances. (X.)

Tendencies of the 20th Century.—As the prevailing policy of the 20th century favours republican forms of government, questions of precedence occupy less attention than heretofore. Even in the few remaining monarchies rank and title possess less significance than before. Thus in Denmark and in Norway all titles have long been abolished. In Japan all titles of nobility were abolished and the house of peers was replaced by a house of councillors in 1945; and the imperial house law of 1947 restricted the emperor's family to his children, his brothers and sisters, and their issue, with the result that 51 princes of 11 princely houses became commoners. Most modern orders (for example the Legion of Honour in France and the 16 orders created in the U.S.S.R.) do not entitle the recipients to any privileges but are simply marks of recognition of merit and service.

The 17th and 18th centuries were the golden age of court ceremonial; *cf.* the *Mémoires* of the duc de Saint-Simon. Since that time the importance of questions of precedence has grown less and less. The emphasis has altered from rank and title to office and position. It is in fact a person's office rather than his personal rank or his relationship to someone else that now tends to be the governing factor in determining his precedence.   (S. B.-R. P.)

BIBLIOGRAPHY.—Viton de Saint-Allais, *Nobiliaire universel* (1814–20); F. Bluche, *Les honneurs de la cour* (1957); F. de Béthencourt, *Historia de la monarquía española, casa real y grandes de España* (1897–*et seq.*); Sir E. M. Satow, *A Guide to Diplomatic Practice,* 4th ed. (1957); *Burke's Peerage* and *Landed Gentry; Debrett's Peerage; Annuario Pontificio;* National Roman Catholic directories.

PROTOGENES, a Greek painter, born in Caunus, on the coast of Caria, but resident in Rhodes during the latter half of the 4th century B.C. He was celebrated for the minute and laborious finish which he bestowed on his pictures, both in drawing and in colour. Apelles, his great rival, standing amazed in the presence of one of these works, could only console himself by saying that it was wanting in charm. On one picture, the "Ialysus," Protogenes spent seven years; on another, the "Satyr," he worked continuously during the siege of Rhodes by Demetrius Poliorcetes (305–304 B.C.), notwithstanding that the garden in which he painted was in the middle of the enemy's camp. Demetrius, unsolicited, took measures for his safety; more than that, when told that the "Ialysus" just mentioned was in a part of the town exposed to assault, Demetrius changed his plan of operations. Ialysus was a local hero, the founder of the town of the same name in the island of Rhodes, and he was probably represented as a huntsman. This picture was still in Rhodes in the time of Cicero, but was afterward removed to Rome, where it perished in the burning of the Temple of Peace.

The picture painted during the siege of Rhodes consisted of a satyr leaning idly against a pillar on which was a figure of a partridge, so lifelike that ordinary spectators saw nothing but it. Enraged on this account, the painter wiped out the partridge. The "Satyr" must have been one of his last works. He would then have been about 70 years of age, and enjoyed for about 20 years a reputation next only to that of Apelles, his friend and benefactor. Both were finished colourists so far as the fresco painting of their day permitted, and both were laborious in the practice of drawing, doubtless with the view to obtaining bold effects of perspective as well as fineness of outline. It was an illustration of this practice when Apelles, finding in the house of Protogenes a large panel already prepared for a picture, drew upon it with a brush a very fine line which he said would tell sufficiently who had called. Protogenes on his return home took a brush with a different colour and drew a still finer line along that of Apelles, dividing it in two. Apelles called again, and thus challenged, drew with a third colour another line within that of Protogenes, who then admitted himself surpassed. This panel was seen by Pliny in Rome, where it was much admired, and where it was destroyed by fire.

In the Propylaea at Athens was a painting by Protogenes representing personifications of the coast of Attica, Paralus, and Hammonias. For the council chamber at Athens he painted figures of the Thesmothetae, but in what form or character is not known. Probably these works were executed in Athens, and it may have been then that he met Aristotle, who recommended him to take for subjects the deeds of Alexander the Great. In his "Alexander and Pan" he may have followed that advice in the idealizing spirit to which he was accustomed. To this spirit must be traced also his "Cydippe" and "Tlepolemus," legendary personages of Rhodes. Among his portraits are mentioned those of the mother of Aristotle, Philiscus, the tragic poet, and King Antigonus. Protogenes was also a sculptor to some extent, and made several bronze statues of athletes, armed figures, huntsmen, and persons in the act of offering sacrifices.

PROTON, a particle which is the nucleus of the hydrogen atom and a constituent of the nuclei of other atoms. It carries a positive electric charge.

Historical Background.—Lord Rutherford, in the course of experiments performed in 1919 during which he bombarded atoms of the lighter gases with alpha particles, found that the atoms disintegrated under the impact, liberating particles that he believed to be hydrogen nuclei. At the Cardiff meeting of the British Association for the Advancement of Science (1920), Rutherford suggested the name proton—Greek for "the first"—for the nucleus of the hydrogen atom, to denote that it is a primary substance. In the same year, in the Bakerian lecture at the Royal Society, he offered the speculation that there might exist yet another particle, this one electrically neutral. This hypothetical particle—the neutron—was brought from the realm of speculation to reality in 1932 by a succession of discoveries by W. Bothe, Frédéric Joliot, and Sir James Chadwick, who made the decisive experiments. The nuclei of all atoms except hydrogen contain neutrons as well as protons. In the case of hydrogen, the atom consists of a single proton as the nucleus, plus a single electron.

Characteristics.—The main properties of the proton are its electric charge, mass, spin, magnetic moment, and statistics. The charge, e, is identical in magnitude to the charge of the electron, 4.80298×10^{-10} esu (electrostatic units), but of opposite sign; and the mass of the proton is 1.6725×10^{-24}g. This is 1,836.1 times as large as the mass of the electron. It is thus apparent that almost the entire mass of an atom is concentrated in the nucleus. The equality in magnitude of the charge of the proton and of the electron is shown by the fact that hydrogen atoms are neutral; hence, in order to know the charge e it makes no difference whether one measures the charge of the proton or of the electron. The latter is perhaps technically easier to measure. The mass of the proton may be determined by mass spectrograph experiments involving the deflection of a beam of protons of known velocity in a known magnetic field. In this way one obtains a measurement of the momentum mv of the proton which, once the velocity v is separately measured, gives the mass m.

In addition to charge and mass, the proton has an intrinsic angular momentum or spin of magnitude $\frac{1}{2}h/2\pi$ where $h = 6.6256 \times 10^{-27}$ erg-sec. (Planck constant). If we visualize a proton as a little sphere of matter, the spin tells us that the proton is rotating around an axis in a way similar to the rotation of the earth around the polar axis. The proton spin is revealed by a detailed study of the hydrogen atom spectrum and by many other phenomena. Connected with the spin there is a magnetic moment $\mu_p = 1.41049 \times 10^{-23}$ erg per gauss. In terms of the natural unit $he/4\pi m_p c$ (where m_p is the mass of the proton and c the velocity of light), this moment has the value 2.79276. This means on our model that the small rotating sphere also has north and south magnetic poles similar to those of the earth. The magnetic moment of the proton, and its spin, can be measured spectroscopically or, with extreme precision, by magnetic methods involving the currents induced by the nuclear magnetic moments of the protons moving in a variable magnetic field. The size of the proton (or its radius, if we consider it as a sphere) is not precisely defined because its value depends on what phenomenon or method we use to measure it. For instance, by bombarding the protons with high-energy electrons (up to 10^{10} ev) one obtains a pattern that reveals the distribution of the electric charge around the centre of the proton (Robert Hofstadter). One thus obtains an average radius of 1.2×10^{-13} cm. There are indications that the proton has a structure consisting of a core surrounded by a cloud of mesons. A similar structure obtains also for the neutron. An important part of the specific nuclear forces originate from an exchange of the pions of the cloud between different nucleons (*i.e.,* neutrons and protons). The radius of the proton can also be investigated by neutron-proton collision at high energy in which only specific nuclear forces are operative. The results resemble those obtained by electron scattering.

In addition to the properties mentioned above, the proton has a very important characteristic which is expressible only in terms of quantum mechanics: it obeys Pauli's exclusion principle. This can be expressed by saying that in a system there cannot be two or more protons with the same quantum numbers, or that the wave function of a system containing several protons must be antisymmetrical with respect to the exchange of any two protons. This property has far reaching consequences in nuclear structure and is one of the most fundamental ones shared by proton, neutron, electron and other particles having spin $\frac{1}{2} h/2\pi$. A nucleus of mass number A having a positive electric charge Ze contains Z protons and has a number of neutrons N given by the number $A - Z$. A is the integer closest to the number expressing the nuclear mass M in units equal to the 12th part of the mass of the carbon nucleus C^{12}.

The Proton in Theoretical and Applied Science.—The proton appears in many different aspects in a variety of chemical and physical phenomena. For example, as the hydrogen ion, it plays a very important role in chemistry, especially in all aqueous solutions (*see* HYDROGEN IONS). In spectroscopy it is the centre around which the electron revolves in the hydrogen atom, giving rise to the hydrogen spectrum, one of the most important subjects in atomic physics. In nuclear physics the proton is commonly used as a projectile to bombard other nuclei in particle accelerators such as the cyclotron or the bevatron.

In nuclear bombardments at relatively low energies, up to a few million electron volts, the general behaviour of the proton is to enter the nucleus, if it has enough energy to overcome the electrostatic repulsion of the target nucleus. Having entered the target nucleus it produces enough excitation to evaporate other particles from it. For instance if it evaporates one neutron, the target nucleus does not change its mass number, but is transformed into an element with the atomic number (Z) one unit larger.

At very high energies the proton gives rise to a host of more complicated effects connected with the structure of the nucleons. Especially relevant to the proton is the existence of excited states of this particle that decompose into a proton in its normal state and a pi-meson (pion). The most prominent of these states has a total energy (including that due to the rest mass) of about 1,238 Mev, and spin $\frac{3}{2}$. It is excited by pion or by other particle bombardments. It is by proton bombardments that mesons, hyperons and antinucleons are most frequently produced in the large accelerators.

The number of protons, plus the number of neutrons involved, remains constant in all nuclear reactions. This principle of the conservation of the nucleons is at present to be considered as an empirical fact still disconnected from the other fundamental principles of physics.

P. A. M. Dirac of England pointed out in 1928 that the phenomena of nature exhibit a special kind of symmetry between the positive and negative electric charge. On this basis he predicted the possible existence of the positive electron (positron), later discovered (1932) by C. D. Anderson. Dirac's theory predicted also the possible existence of a negatively charged proton (antiproton) which was discovered in 1955 by Owen Chamberlain, Emilio Segrè, Clyde Wiegand, and Thomas Ypsilantis. The theory predicted the following properties for this particle: (1) it has the same mass as the proton; (2) it has equal but opposite electric charge; (3) it has the same spin as the proton; (4) it has a magnetic moment opposite to that of the proton; (5) it is stable in the sense that when isolated in a vacuum it does not transform spontaneously into other particles; (6) antiprotons and nucleons annihilate each other in pairs; (7) antiprotons and protons are generated in pairs.

Property (4) means that a proton and an antiproton having their spin equally oriented have opposite magnetic moments, or that if the two small rotating spheres representing them rotate in the same way, their magnetic north and south poles are interchanged.

Properties (6) and (7) are not in contradiction with the principle of conservation of nucleons. On the contrary, if we consider an antiproton as "minus one proton," the condition that generation and annihilation occur only in pairs becomes a direct consequence of the conservation of nucleons. The fact that one antiproton and one proton must be generated together determines

the energy threshold for this process. Thus, for instance, the production by proton-proton collision can occur only at a projectile energy higher than 5.6×10^9 ev (electron volts) in the laboratory system; hence, huge accelerating machines are necessary. Antineutrons are characterized by a set of properties which bear a relation to those of the neutron similar to those listed above for the antiproton in relation to the proton. In particular properties 1, 2, 4, 6, 7 are the same provided the word neutron is substituted for proton and antineutron for antiproton. Neutron and antineutron are both electrically neutral and both spontaneously undergo a beta decay, the neutron emitting electrons, the antineutron positrons.

Antineutrons have been generated from antiprotons by causing the antiproton to collide with a proton. In this process most frequently the proton and antiproton annihilate each other, generating pi-mesons, but in about 1% of the cases they disappear, generating a neutron-antineutron pair. The antineutron is best detected in the subsequent annihilation process with a nucleon.

The symmetry between positive and negative electricity manifested by the electron and positron, and nucleon and antinucleon, opens the possibility of the existence of "antimatter." This would be formed by atoms in which every nucleon is replaced by the corresponding antinucleon and every electron by a positron. In many ways this antimatter would be indistinguishable from ordinary matter. For example, no ordinary astronomical observation, including the study of the spectra and of the Zeeman effect, could distinguish between matter and antimatter in a star. However, a collision of matter and antimatter would result in annihilation with the immediate production of pi-mesons which would in turn decay, leaving as their ultimate residue gamma rays, neutrinos and, if the system is not initially electrically neutral, electrons.

As of the 1960s there was no experimental evidence in favour of or against the existence of antimatter in the cosmos. From a cosmic point of view the existence of antimatter would allow the creation of the universe from energy without the violation of the principle of the conservation of nucleons.

See ACCELERATORS, PARTICLE; ATOM; ELECTRON; NEUTRON; PARTICLES, ELEMENTARY; *see* also references under "Proton" in the Index.

BIBLIOGRAPHY.—E. Segrè, *Nuclei and Particles* (1964); H. Bethe, P. Morrison, *Elementary Nuclear Theory,* 2nd ed. (1956); M. Born, *Atomic Physics,* 6th ed. (1957). (Eo. S.)

PROTOPLASM, the characteristic organized substance on which all activities of living matter are based. The cell is the smallest structural unit of protoplasm that has all the properties essential for its maintenance (irritability, motility, and basic metabolism) and propagation (growth and reproduction).

The physiology of protoplasm is highly complex, and is believed to be largely dependent on the properties of colloidal systems. Physical and cytochemical methods of studying living cells, in conjunction with biochemical studies on isolated protoplasmic structures, have revealed the functions of this vital organization (*see* CELL). Evidently the nucleic acids are ultimately responsible for the pattern of dynamic organization throughout the protoplasm (*see* NUCLEIC ACIDS).

See also references under "Protoplasm" in the Index.
(D. T. H.)

PROTOPOPOV, ALEKSANDR DIMITRIEVICH (1866?–1918), Russian statesman, minister of the interior during the last months of the imperial regime, was a landowner and industrialist who began his political career in the Simbirsk province. He was elected in 1907 to the third duma, where he joined the left wing of the Octobrist Party. In 1914 he became one of the deputy speakers of the fourth duma; and in 1916, during World War I, he led a parliamentary delegation to Great Britain, France, and Italy. On his homeward journey he had talks in Stockholm with a German agent on the prospects of a separate Russo-German peace. The misgivings which this indiscretion aroused among the Russian public were intensified when, through Rasputin (*q.v.*), he was appointed minister of the interior in the reactionary cabinet of B. V. Stürmer (Oct. 1, 1916). His former colleagues in the duma angrily condemned him as a renegade. Protopopov had always been highly strung, and his advent to power seems to have unhinged his mind. Convinced that it was his destiny "to save Russia," he devised schemes for the social and political reconstruction of the country on totalitarian lines, which his cabinet colleagues dismissed as impracticable fantasies. More concretely, Protopopov urged the dissolution, or at least the suspension, of the duma and changes in the supply organization to enhance the powers of his own ministry as against those of the *zemstva* (the elected local councils) and other public bodies. His measures failed to relieve the serious food shortage in Petrograd and other cities; and when he ordered severe police measures as a precaution against possible hunger riots, he was widely suspected of seeking to provoke a popular rising. Yet when this rising occurred, it brought the overthrow of the regime and Protopopov's own downfall: after the revolution of March 1917 he was imprisoned in the Peter and Paul Fortress and in September 1918 he was shot there by order of the Communist *Cheka* (Extraordinary Commission).

(J. L. H. K.)

PROTOZOA, a worldwide phylum of lower animals, most of which are microscopic. Protozoa, almost as ubiquitous as bacteria, are found wherever there is moisture enough for active life. The phylum is abundant in species—more than 30,000; as individuals their numbers far exceed those of any other animal group. The reader should not be dismayed at finding disagreements between classifications of Protozoa, for authorities differ considerably in the disposition of this phylum. A time-honoured scheme divides the group into four subphyla: Mastigophora, the flagellates or whip bearers; Sarcodina, the amoeboid species, with pseudopodia; Sporozoa, the parasitic types that often produce spores; and Ciliophora, the ciliates, equipped with cilia or their derivatives.

This article is divided into the following sections:

I. General Features
II. Natural History
    1. Modes of Living
    2. Nutrition
    3. Food Requirements
    4. Oxygen Requirements
    5. Temperature and Other Relationships
    6. Life Cycles
    7. Species Interaction
III. Structure and Function
    1. Covering and Skeleton
    2. Cytoplasm and Inclusions
    3. Locomotor Organelles
    4. Trichocysts
IV. Reproduction and Development
    1. Asexual Reproduction
    2. Nuclear Changes
    3. Sexual Phenomena
    4. Variation and Heredity
V. Classification and Survey
    A. Mastigophora
      1. Phytomastigophorea
      2. Zoomastigophorea
    B. Sarcodina
      1. Actinopodea
      2. Rhizopodea
    C. Sporozoa
      1. Telosporidea
      2. Cnidosporidea
      3. Acnidosporidea
    D. Ciliophora
      1. Holotricha
      2. Spirotricha

I. GENERAL FEATURES

The variety of form is endless, from the flowing, protean blobs of amoebas to the exquisitely fashioned "sunbursts" of radiolarians and the delicate shells of foraminifers. The range in size is considerable, from the smallest sporozoan blood parasites (*Babesia*) only 2 microns long (a small red blood cell can easily contain a dozen such organisms) to the largest, also a sporozoan (*Porospora gigantea*), which may reach 16 mm. in length (mycetozoan plasmodia, which are multinucleate amoeboid organisms, may measure 30 cm. or more).

Although protozoans are often described as one-celled animals, some protozoologists prefer to think of them as being noncellular,

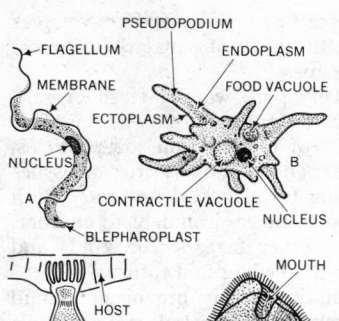
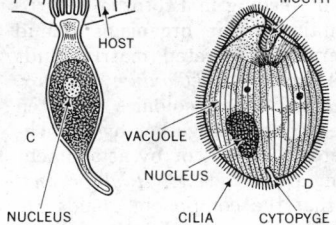

FIG. 1.—REPRESENTATIVES OF THE CLASSES OF PROTOZOA: (A) MASTIGOPHORA; (B) SARCODINA; (C) SPOROZOA; (D) CILIOPHORA

(A,C,D) FROM L. H. HYMAN, "THE INVERTEBRATES," 1940, AND (B) FROM T. I. STORER AND R. L. USINGER, "GENERAL ZOOLOGY," 1957; REPRODUCED BY PERMISSION OF MCGRAW-HILL BOOK CO.

or acellular. The simplest protozoans, comparable in structure to a cell of higher animals, contain only a nucleus and the usual cytoplasmic inclusions (mitochondria, stored food, etc.). More complex species may be equipped with many nuclei, a variety of locomotor and feeding organelles, sometimes with involved fibrillar systems and contractile elements.

Many Protozoa seem to be as closely related to plants as to typical animals. For example, certain phytoflagellates form an apparently continuous series with typical algae. The slime molds are claimed by botanists as well as by zoologists. Accordingly, the protozoologist's concept of the phylum Protozoa is based in part upon arbitrary decisions that may or may not reflect the true relationships of the organisms involved. To this extent, the phylum represents a somewhat artificial assemblage rather than a phylogenetically homogeneous group.

II. NATURAL HISTORY

1. Modes of Living.—Many free-living protozoans are motile; others are sessile or floating. Most species exist as solitary forms, but some form colonies. Parasitic protozoans live in or on a variety of organisms, from plants to a wide range of animals including other protozoans. A number of species serve as decom-

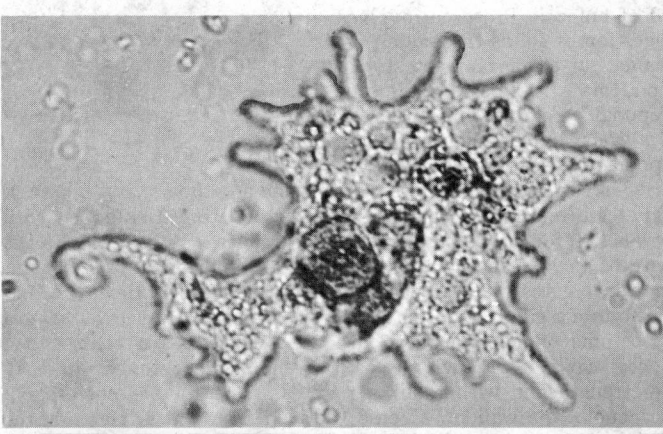
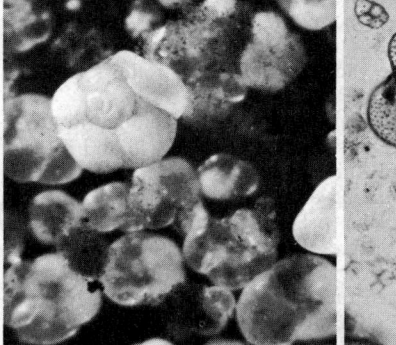
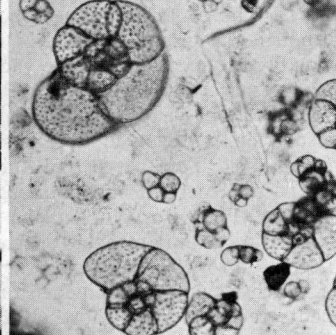

(TOP) HUGH SPENCER; (BOTTOM LEFT AND RIGHT) JOHN J. LEE

VARIETY OF FORM IN PROTOZOA: (TOP) AMOEBA, A CONSTANTLY CHANGING MASS OF PROTOPLASM; (BOTTOM) ROSALINA FLORIDANA, A HIGHLY STRUCTURED FORAMINIFER SEEN UNDER (LEFT) REFLECTED AND (RIGHT) TRANSMITTED LIGHT

posing organisms, hastening the decay of organic matter, whereas several are agents of disease: *e.g.*, those causing malaria, amoebic dysentery, and African sleeping sickness.

Protozoa occur in many relatively pure waters, fresh or salt, containing little organic matter; in waters polluted with material undergoing decomposition; in films of moisture on soil particles, or on particles of sand along beaches; and in body cavities or tissues of their hosts. The species making up a local fauna vary both qualitatively and quantitatively from one environment to another. Such relationships involve, among other factors, the kinds and amounts of food and the methods of feeding in Protozoa.

Protozoan colonies usually contain similar organisms bound together in some particular pattern. A secreted matrix binds the organisms together in various flagellates (*Gonium, Volvox,* etc.) and in such ciliates as *Ophrydium*. These colonies are often spheroid or discoid. Other colonies are held together by branching stalks, by a branching exoskeleton (lorica), or by attachment of individual loricae in a branching pattern (*e.g., Hyalobryon*). The *Volvox* colony is unusual in that the component zooids are differentiated into many somatic and a few reproductive individuals.

Aggregates that are not true colonies occur in certain species in which separation of daughter organisms does not promptly follow fission. Such aggregates include chains (catenoid "colonies") of certain dinoflagellates and ciliates and also palmella stages in certain phytoflagellates, similar to spheroid colonies but with an amorphous matrix and without flagella or specific form and size. The term "gleocystis stage," is sometimes applied to similar groupings with a differentiated layer around each organism.

2. Nutrition.—Protozoan nutrition is of two basic types: holozoic, by active ingestion; and saprozoic, by absorption.

Ingestion.—The feeding method of holozoic Protozoa involves ingestion of solids through a permanent or temporary cytostome. Food may be ingested by pseudopodal engulfment (as in *Amoeba*), by confluence of myxopodia to trap prey outside the

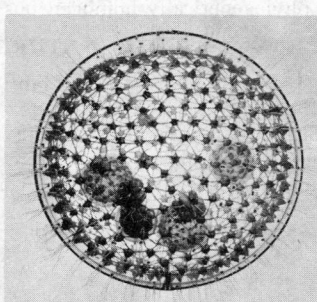

BY COURTESY OF THE AMERICAN MUSEUM OF NATURAL HISTORY
GLASS MODEL OF A VOLVOX COLONY

test (in certain foraminifers), or through a cytopharynx (ciliates). Ciliates often have a buccal cavity (or peristome) equipped with organelles for propelling food to the mouth (cytostome) at the base of the pouch or trough. Such a feeding apparatus is common in ciliates that eat bacteria or other small particles. Many carnivorous ciliates, normally ingesting fairly large prey, have a cytostome opening directly onto the surface rather than into a buccal cavity. In such cases the wall of the cytopharynx may be strengthened with rodlike trichites. The food is enclosed in a vacuole, the wall of which is derived from the surface of the body (*Amoeba*, etc.) or from the lining of the cytopharynx (ciliates). The contents of the food vacuole typically become acid, although the origin of the acid is undetermined. Enzymes presumably are secreted into the vacuole. Digestion follows, and the products are absorbed.

Absorption.—Saprozoic (or osmotrophic) feeding involves absorption of dissolved materials through the pellicle and plasma membrane. To what extent this represents simple diffusion or less passive mechanisms involving enzymatic activity remains uncertain. Pinocytosis, a peculiar process of "drinking," first described in certain amoeboid species, involves ingestion of solutions in gulps through small temporary "gullets," from the inner ends of which vacuoles are pinched off into the cytoplasm. Measurements recorded over short intervals suggest that fluid taken in by an amoeba may amount to at least twice the organism's body volume in a day. In a nutrient-rich medium this could represent a significant contribution to nutrition.

3. Food Requirements.—Since the advent of pure cultures and reasonably pure organic nutrients, it has been possible to

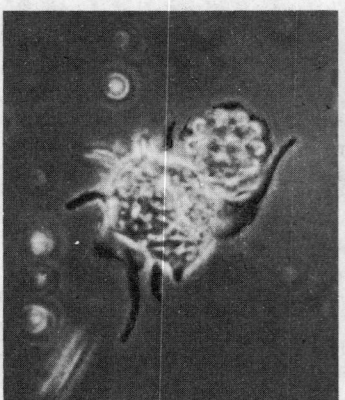
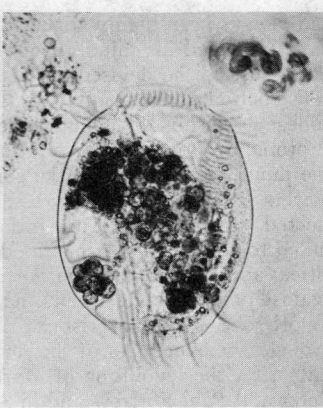

TWO EXAMPLES OF INGESTION IN PROTOZOA: (LEFT) AMOEBA ENGULFING A VOLVOX COLONY; (RIGHT) EUPLOTES DIGESTING ALGAE (MOVEMENT OF CILIA HAS STARTED A WHIRLPOOL OF ALGAE AT RIGHT)

define rather accurately the food requirements of various protozoans.

In flagellates with chromatophores the need for a chemical source of energy (fatty acid, alcohol, carbohydrate, etc.) may be eliminated by photosynthesis. Many photosynthetic flagellates, when exposed to light, can grow in simple media containing inorganic salts and one or two vitamins. A nitrate or an ammonium salt can supply the needed nitrogen, while carbon dioxide provides the necessary carbon. Other needed elements are available in solution in the medium. Although actual requirements are not completely known, elements supposedly needed by one protozoon or another include calcium, cobalt, copper, iron, magnesium, manganese, phosphorus, potassium, sulfur, and zinc. In addition, growth of certain species is stimulated by aluminum, barium, boron, iodine, silicon, sodium, and vanadium. Photosynthetic flagellates can survive in relatively pure waters, their numbers being limited perhaps by available concentrations of minerals and vitamins (*e.g.*, B_{12}, thiamine). Pollution of waters with material containing large amounts of vitamins, stimulatory organic foods, or minerals (*e.g.*, phosphates) may lead to population bursts or "blooms" of phytoflagellates.

Organisms without chromatophores require a chemical source of energy. Some of the colourless phytoflagellates thrive on such energy sources as acetate, pyruvate, or ethanol, but derive little or no benefit from carbohydrates, possibly because these organisms lack a particular enzyme (hexokinase). There are obvious differences in complexity of food requirements. Some of the saprozoic phytoflagellates, except for the energy source, have basal requirements similar to those of related green species. Other groups of saprozoic Protozoa may have food requirements comparable to those of ciliates and other holozoic types. Holozoic organisms apparently can use a wider variety of energy sources than saprozoic types.

Protein Metabolism.—Holozoic Protozoa, under natural conditions, obtain their proteins mostly in the form of other microorganisms. Certain saprozoic Protozoa (*e.g., Leishmania*) apparently produce extracellular protein-splitting (proteolytic) enzymes; the value of proteins as sole nitrogen sources for these organisms is uncertain. *Tetrahymena pyriformis*, a typical holozoic organism, is known to produce two kinds of proteolytic enzymes (proteinases and peptidases). Amino acids, liberated by these enzymes, may be assimilated directly or may be further broken down by other enzymatic mechanisms. In a medium containing 11 essential amino acids *T. pyriformis* assimilates 5 of them and synthesizes at least 7 additional amino acids, using 5 of the original 11 as raw materials as well as "fuel" for the process of assimilation and for the production of proteins. Phytoflagellates may use ammonium salts or, less commonly, nitrates.

The major nitrogenous waste is ammonia, although more complex materials are sometimes eliminated. *Tetrahymena pyriformis* apparently excretes amino acids (glycine, glutamic acid, etc.) as well as ammonia. The occurrence of a urea cycle in *T. pyriformis*, similar to that of mammals, has been disputed.

Carbon Metabolism.—Photosynthetic flagellates may obtain their needed carbon as carbon dioxide. Green flagellates maintained in darkness, as well as all other Protozoa, need one or more organic compounds in addition to carbon dioxide, the organic compound serving as a source of energy and metabolites for synthesis. Radioactive carbon, fed to *Tetrahymena* in carbon dioxide, becomes incorporated in succinic acid and, in lower concentrations, in certain amino acids (alanine, glycine, aspartic, and glutamic acids) and in other metabolites (fumaric, lactic, malic acids, etc.). Under similar conditions, *Euglena gracilis* in darkness produces essentially the same tagged metabolites, with the addition of certain intermediates in carbohydrate metabolism. In addition to utilizing carbon dioxide, Protozoa as a group can use carbon sources ranging from acetic acid to polysaccharides. However, the ability to use particular compounds varies with the species. Cellulase activity has been reported in certain ciliates from the intestinal tract of ruminants and flagellates from termites. Enzymes digesting starch and glycogen to simple sugars also have been demonstrated (*e.g., Trichomonas, Tetrahymena*).

Metabolism of simple sugars follows pathways known in other microorganisms and in higher animals. According to the Meyerhof-Embden scheme of fermentation, glucose and other simple sugars are converted into fructose-diphosphate and eventually broken down, mostly to pyruvic acid, from which Protozoa may produce a variety of materials—carbon dioxide; water; ethanol; acetic, formic, lactic, and succinic acids—depending upon the species. In the phosphogluconic acid route, glucose is phosphorylated to a sugar-monophosphate and then, with a loss of carbon dioxide, converted into a pentose-monophosphate. This pentose may be converted into other pentoses, used in synthesis, or split into products that can be used as energy sources or as intermediates in biosynthesis. In several species (*e.g., Trichomonas vaginalis*) sugar metabolism differs in details. Although extensive information is available for only a few species, it is clear that products of glucose metabolism can vary even among species of a single genus (*e.g., Trypanosoma*). Synthesis of carbohydrates is very common, probably universal in Protozoa. Many species synthesize polysaccharides and store them.

Vitamin Needs.—Most Protozoa need one or more vitamins. Certain green flagellates (*e.g.,* species of *Chlamydomonas* and *Chlorogonium*) require no outside source of vitamins when exposed to light; such species may be considered photoautotrophs in the classical sense—organisms capable of utilizing the energy of sunlight as do green plants. For other green flagellates, one or more vitamins (B_{12}, thiamine, sometimes biotin) must be added to media that are adequate for photoautotrophs. Similar differences are known for colourless phytoflagellates. Certain species of *Polytoma* apparently need no vitamin supplements. Other colourless phytoflagellates, like many of their green relatives, need one to several vitamins. Outside the phytoflagellates, Protozoa have multiple vitamin requirements. Certain strains of *Tetrahymena pyriformis*, for example, must have biotin, folic acid, nicotinic acid, pantothenic acid, pyridoxine, riboflavin, thiamine, and thioctic acid (protogen).

The knowledge of vitamin requirements has made possible the utilization of Protozoa in biological assays. The choice of organisms is determined by such practical matters as rate of growth and suitability for spectrophotometric measurement of growth. Vitamin B_{12} has been assayed, even in body fluids, with *Euglena gracilis* and with *Ochromonas malhamensis*, the former being a very sensitive indicator but slightly less specific than the latter in that it responds to pseudo-B_{12} compounds as well. *Ochromonas malhamensis* also is a sensitive assay organism for thiamine in body fluids, while thioctic acid can be assayed with *Tetrahymena pyriformis*.

4. Oxygen Requirements.—There is a wide range in oxygen needs among Protozoa. Obligate aerobes are limited to habitats with adequate oxygen concentrations; certain aerobes, however, grow best at oxygen tensions below that of the normal atmosphere.

Obligate anaerobes, on the other hand, are restricted to environments lacking oxygen—*e.g.,* natural waters loaded with putrefying material, the lower levels of deep lakes, Imhoff sewage tanks, the intestines of vertebrates, etc.

Typical aerobes utilize the cytochrome system—a terminal oxidative system characteristic of aerobic organisms—in their major oxidative pathway. However, the genus *Trypanosoma* is interesting in that certain species are sensitive to cyanide poisoning, which blocks the cytochrome pathway, while others are rather insensitive. Such data suggest that some oxidative pathway other than the cytochrome route is important in the insensitive species.

5. Temperature and Other Relationships.—The biothermal range varies with the species and, in such cases as *Tetrahymena pyriformis*, with strains of species. Under laboratory conditions, the range for free-living Protozoa usually falls within the limits 7°–40° C (about 45°–104° F), and most species fail to grow above 35° C. In a few instances it has been possible to raise the upper limit by greatly increasing vitamin or amino acid allotments; for example, *Ochromonas malhamensis* can survive at 38° C when given about 3,000 times as much vitamin B_{12} and about 1,000 times as much thiamine as it requires at 34° C.

In general, temperatures near 45° C (113° F) seem to be lethal for active stages, although certain heat-tolerant strains (thermophiles such as amoebas from hot springs of 53° C) are exceptions. Encysted stages of certain species may survive short exposure to temperatures somewhat higher than those lethal for active stages; in rare instances (*e.g., Colpoda*) dried cysts have remained viable for an hour or more at about 100° C (the boiling point for water, at sea level). At sublethal levels, high temperature has caused bleaching of *Euglena gracilis* in darkness. Low temperatures tend to be less harmful to Protozoa than high temperatures; for example, species of *Trypanosoma, Tritrichomonas*, and *Plasmodium* remain viable for weeks at temperatures of −20° to −70° C (−4° to −94° F).

Experiments with freshwater Protozoa have shown that tolerance to increasing salinities varies with the species and even with strains of a single species. In gradually adapted *Tetrahymena pyriformis*, for example, one strain grows well at a salinity higher than that of natural seawater, whereas another strain fails to survive at the salinity equivalent to 80% seawater. Although a few Protozoa (*e.g.,* certain species of *Bodo, Colpoda, Uronema*) survive direct transfer to seawater, such an abrupt transfer is usually lethal. Stepwise transition to seawater is more easily tolerated; *e.g.,* by species of *Amoeba, Cyclidium, Euglena, Euplotes, Lionotus, Paramecium, Phacus, Stylonychia*, and *Tetrahymena*. Several marine amoebas can also be shifted gradually from their normal habitat to fresh water without apparent damage. For such organisms no absolute physiological barrier separates marine and freshwater habitats.

Growth of Protozoa is generally restricted to a pH range from 3 (moderately acidic) to 9 (moderately basic). Certain species can survive for short periods outside this range, within the limits pH 2.5–11. Reported optimal conditions for protozoan growth in laboratory cultures range from about pH 4.5 to 7.5 or higher in different species.

6. Life Cycles.—A life cycle may often be considered a series of changes through which an organism passes in correlation with environmental changes. Completion of a cycle may seem to depend directly upon environmental change. Malarial parasites, for example, must have access to two kinds of hosts at particular periods in the life cycle. At the other extreme, environmental change is not essential for the cyclic changes in reproduction of Suctorida.

The complexity of protozoan life cycles varies considerably. The simplest involve an active trophic stage and an inactive cyst. Modifications include: (1) introduction of more than one trophic stage (dimorphism, polymorphism); (2) production of more than one kind of cyst; and (3) addition of a sexual phase. Life cycles of the simplest type are known in certain intestinal amoebas and flagellates, a few of which seem to have lost even the ability to encyst.

The simplest modification of the basic cycle involves trophic dimorphism. Some of these dimorphic cycles show adult and larval stages, the latter being perhaps the more indicative of ancestral relationships. Other dimorphic cycles include amoeboid and flagellated stages, as seen in certain Mastigophora (*e.g.*, *Tetramitus*) and Sarcodina (*e.g.*, *Naegleria*). Flagellated and non-flagellated trophic stages occur in certain Mastigophora. In addition, amoeboid and plasmodial stages appear in certain Sarcodina (Mycetozoida, Vampyrellidae). More complicated cycles, with asexual and sexual phases, are known in various parasitic Protozoa; in such cases as malarial parasites the asexual phase occurs in one type of host (vertebrate) and the sexual phase in another (mosquito).

The ability to encyst is widespread in Protozoa, though not universal. Cysts vary in both structure and function. Some are primarily protective, enclosing a dedifferentiated (physically simple) "resting" stage. Reproductive cysts serve mainly as containers for reproductive stages and may have little protective value. Protective cysts may be produced by: (1) active stages, which undergo dedifferentiation before completion of the cyst; (2) zygotes, as in gregarines and phytomonad flagellates (*e.g.*, *Volvox*); (3) gametocytes, as in Coccidia that encyst before syngamy; and (4) sporoblasts, division products of the zygote in many Coccidia.

The wall of a protective cyst is typically thick and often compounded of several layers, one is often thicker than the others and mainly responsible for protection. The wall may be mainly protein (ectocyst and mesocyst in many ciliates); keratin-like (certain parasitic amoebas and flagellates); mainly carbohydrate (endocyst of ciliates); mainly cellulose (certain dinoflagellates); siliceous material (chrysomonad flagellates); chitin (*Pelomyxa*); or foreign materials such as sand grains (certain foraminifers). Some cysts (*e.g.*, *Colpoda cucullus*) are quite resistant to desiccation; thoroughly dried encysted *C. cucullus* remain viable for some time at temperatures of 80°–100° C.

Reproductive cysts, with thinner walls, are developed in certain Protozoa prior to fission, budding, or gametogenesis and syngamy. Certain gregarines, for example, pair and secrete a common cyst, within which gametogenesis and syngamy occur. Analogous behaviour is known for certain foraminifers.

Encystment often includes extensive preparatory changes in the organism: food vacuoles tend to disappear; precystic organisms often store food; flagella or cilia are usually resorbed; and the pellicle usually changes its consistency so that the body rounds up. A decrease in volume, perhaps partly from loss of water, is common. Encystment can be induced by various methods in the laboratory, even by vitamin deficiency in certain species, but the primary stimulus—if there is a single one—is still to be identified.

In excystment, the organism must regenerate the locomotor organelles of the trophic stage and escape from the cyst. Rupture of the membranes is effected in some species by absorption of water. Digestion of the endocyst has been reported in ciliates. Emergence through a pore, previously covered by a thin membrane, occurs in certain ciliates (*e.g.*, *Bursaria*) and in some amoebas. Excystment can also be induced by a variety of laboratory methods, ranging, in various species, from immersion of cysts in distilled water to treatment with mixtures of salts, sugars, and vitamins.

7. Species Interaction.—A variety of relationships exist between protozoans and other organisms. On the basis of their relations with the host, dependent types are usually classified as commensals, symbionts, or parasites. A commensal receives food (in excess of the host's needs) and shelter but causes no apparent damage to the host. A symbiont receives the same benefits and also contributes something of value to the host; for example, certain flagellates of wood-eating termites benefit their hosts by digesting wood chips, which cannot be digested by the termites themselves. Likewise, certain intestinal ciliates of ruminants are known to produce cellulose-splitting enzymes not produced by the hosts; in addition, some of the ciliates may serve directly as food, passing from the rumen into the lower digestive tract. Protozoan parasites live on the surface (as ectoparasites) or inside the body (as endoparasites) of a host, another animal

or plant. Parasites that cause appreciable damage to their hosts are called pathogens. Although pathogens form a minority among parasitic Protozoa, some cause diseases of major importance.

Both free-living and parasitic Protozoa may have parasites of their own, the latter combinations representing hyperparasitism. The invaders are sometimes Protozoa—*e.g.*, Dinoflagellida, Suctorida, amoebas, Microsporida. Other parasites of Protozoa include small algae, bacteria, and fungi. The algal partners of *Paramecium bursaria* and similar ciliates are probably symbionts; other dependents of Protozoa may be commensals or pathogens, and supposed bacteria in *Euplotes* have been considered possible symbionts.

In order to maintain themselves, parasitic Protozoa must reach new hosts at intervals. Transfer by vectors, or carriers (mosquito, flea, tick, fly, bug, leech, etc.), is a very important method of dispersal in which the parasite typically passes part of its life cycle in the vector. Malarial parasites complete several stages in the mosquito. Most species of *Trypanosoma* also pass part of the life cycle in a vector (fly, bug, or leech). Infected vectors may inoculate parasites while feeding on a host or, as in *Trypanosoma cruzi*, may void parasites from the hindgut onto the skin of a host, where they may be rubbed into a wound. In so-called mechanical vectors the parasites do not undergo any cyclic development. Flies, for example, may ingest inactive cysts of intestinal amoebas and simply spread them over wide areas, still encysted. Parasites of the digestive tract are usually spread by contamination of food or drink; venereal infection (*e.g.*, *Trichomonas vaginalis*), during

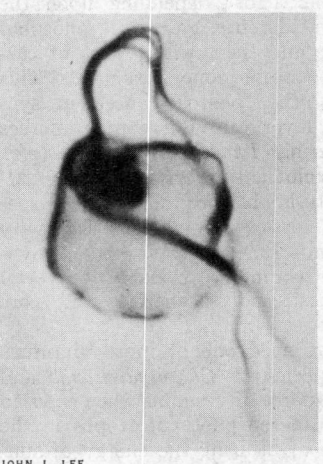

HYPOTRICHOMONAS, **A PARASITE OF THE HUMAN DIGESTIVE TRACT**

coitus; certain parasites of aquatic hosts, by active migration of parasites from old to new hosts. In addition, parasites from a female host may reach a host of the next generation by passage through the placenta (malarial parasites) or by invasion of individual ova before the infected parent lays its eggs (*Babesia bigemina* in tick eggs).

A wide variety of Protozoa may invade a single species of host. Man is a fairly good example. The human mouth is invaded by a flagellate (*Trichomonas tenax*) and an amoeba (*Entamoeba gingivalis*); the small intestine, by a flagellate (*Giardia lamblia*) and a coccidian (*Isospora hominis*); the large intestine, by four flagellates (*Chilomastix mesnili, Pentatrichomonas hominis, Retortomonas intestinalis, Tricercomonas hominis*), five amoebas (*Dientamoeba fragilis, Endolimax nana, Entamoeba coli, E. histolytica, Iodamoeba bütschlii*), and a ciliate (*Balantidium coli*); the urogenital tract, in both male and female, by *Trichomonas vaginalis;* the blood or other tissues, by six flagellates (*Leishmania donovani, L. brasiliensis, L. tropica, Trypanosoma cruzi, T. gambiense, T. rhodesiense*) and four malarial parasites (*Plasmodium falciparum, P. malariae, P. ovale, P. vivax*).

Some of the foregoing organisms are parasites, others probably commensals. The amoeba and flagellate of the mouth, although frequently associated with pyorrhea, are not proven causative agents of the condition. *Giardia lamblia,* although it does not invade the tissues, may be responsible for such disturbances as diarrhea and nausea. *Isospora hominis* cannot complete its life cycle without destroying epithelial cells, and the self-terminating infection usually induces a fairly prolonged attack of diarrhea. The flagellates and the amoebas of the colon (except for *Entamoeba histolytica*) probably approach the status of commensals in most infections, although there may be concomitant digestive disturbances.

Entamoeba histolytica, on the other hand, usually actively invades the tissues, and is the proven causative agent of amoebiasis (see Dysentery: *Amoebic Dysentery*). *Balantidium coli,* which commonly invades the wall of the colon, causes symptoms similar to those of primary amoebiasis, but generally less severe. Invasions outside the digestive tract are unknown in balantidiasis. The malarias, caused by *Plasmodium* species, are always characterized by extensive destruction of red corpuscles, with resulting anemia and paroxysms of alternating fever and chills (see Malaria). Leishmaniasis—visceral, dermal, and mucocutaneous—involves multiplication of certain *Leishmania* species in certain organs or in the skin (see Leishmaniasis). Trypanosomiasis in man is represented by African sleeping sickness and by Chagas' disease in the Western Hemisphere. Sleeping sickness (caused by *Trypanosoma gambiense* and *T. rhodesiense,* both transferred by tsetse flies) is characterized by fever and marked physical weakness. Chagas' disease is caused by *T. cruzi,* and possibly one or two closely related species (see Trypanosomiasis).

III. STRUCTURE AND FUNCTION

The form of Protozoa varies widely—continually changing in active amoeboid species, fairly constant in species with heavy pellicles and tests. The spherical form is common in floating types, whereas sessile species are often conical and radially symmetrical. Swimming types, usually elongate, often show a spiral torsion that tends to mask a tendency toward bilateral symmetry. Even in species that are not amoeboid form may change—*e.g.,* during attainment of maturity; during transformation from one stage to another in dimorphic or polymorphic life cycles; and often following a change of environmental conditions. In species with a relatively constant form, shape may be maintained by secreted coverings (pellicle, theca, test, lorica) or by skeletons.

1. Covering and Skeleton.—The cortex, or outer cytoplasm, is bounded by a plasma membrane, which is covered by the pellicle, ranging from a thin elastic layer (as in *Amoeba proteus*) to a thick and relatively rigid covering (*Phacus, Euplotes*). Even in *Amoeba proteus* the pellicle is not a simple membrane; electron micrographs show delicate fibrils projecting outward to produce a hairy appearance. In *Euglena gracilis* the pellicle (apparently proteinaceous) shows alternating thick ridges and thin flexible strips, structure presumably favouring euglenoid movement (metaboly). The pellicle of *Peranema trichophorum* appears to be a double wall; that of certain gregarines contains three layers. Pores in the pellicle of ciliates and various euglenoids serve for the emergence of cilia, trichocysts, and various secretions.

A cellulose theca, which resembles the cell wall in higher plants, replaces the pellicle in many dinoflagellates (*e.g., Peridinium*) and phytomonad flagellates (*e.g., Chlamydomonas*). The theca may be impregnated with minerals like silica to form a rigid wall. In the armoured dinoflagellates the theca consists of plates, the number and arrangement of which serve as taxonomic criteria.

A secreted test, or "shell," composed mostly of inorganic material, often salts of silicon or calcium, may be present (as in *Arcella, Euglypha,* and many foraminifers). In arenaceous tests (*Centropyxis, Difflugia,* and various foraminifers), sand grains, diatom shells, or similar materials may be cemented together. Reproduction of testate rhizopods may be preceded by secretion and storage of plates, or collection and storage of sand grains to be used in construction of a new test by the daughter organisms. Foraminiferan tests often show several to many chambers produced in succession during growth of the organism.

The lorica, found in certain flagellates and ciliates, is a conical or sometimes tubular covering with an opening through which the anterior part of the body or its appendages may be extended. The wall either is secreted or is built of foreign particles. Lori-

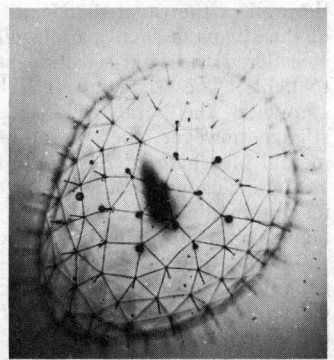

JOHN J. LEE AND HUGO D. FREUDENTHAL
RADIOLARIAN SKELETON SHOWING INTRICATE LATTICEWORK

cate species are sessile, floating, or free-swimming.

Radiolarian skeletons are composed either of silica or mainly of strontium sulfate. In the latter case the basic components are rods that pass through the centre of the organism. Siliceous skeletons, which show great variety, are often complex latticeworks, with one layer or two or more concentric layers.

2. Cytoplasm and Inclusions.—The jellylike colloidal cytoplasm surrounds the all-important nucleus and a number of other inclusions such as vacuoles, mitochondria, pigment bodies, food reserves, etc.

Nucleus.—Protozoa may have one or more nuclei at maturity, depending upon the species; some, in fact, contain hundreds of nuclei. In all Protozoa except the true ciliates and possibly certain foraminifers, multiple nuclei are apparently all alike at any given stage of the life cycle. In the ciliates, however, two types of nuclei, the micronucleus and macronucleus, differ in size, structure, and behaviour. One or more nuclei of each type may be present in different species. The micronucleus takes an active part in conjugation and autogamy, whereas the macronucleus appears to be involved mainly in the usual vegetative nuclear functions.

Nuclei of different species vary in such structural details as amount of chromatin, number and size of chromosomes, and presence or absence of an endosome, or nucleolus. Typical endosomes give negative Feulgen reactions, indicating the absence of chromatin. The endosome of Euglenida is an approximately central body that divides in mitosis; in parasitic amoebas, the endosome disappears early in mitosis.

The appearance of dark-staining chromatin matter in nondividing (interphase) nuclei usually suggests granules on a faintly stained network, an appearance probably produced by coils in the dispersed chromosomes. Electron micrographs indicate that the nuclear membrane is a double wall containing many pores. The macronucleus of ciliates contains many small chromatin granules and a variable number of endosomes. Deoxyribonucleic and ribonucleic acid are both present, the latter being much more abundant. Both form and number of macronuclei vary from species to species. Individual macronuclei are often compact spheroid bodies (as in *Paramecium*), but may be much elongated (as in *Vorticella* and *Euplotes*). The macronuclear apparatus of *Spirostomum* and *Stentor* is represented by a chain of "nodes" joined by filaments.

The significance of nuclear dimorphism in ciliates has remained a puzzle, particularly in view of the fact that both kinds of nuclei are derived from the single zygotic nucleus formed during conjugation. In certain ciliates differentiation of a new macronucleus involves repeated longitudinal splitting of chromosomes to produce polyploidy. Such behaviour is in agreement with the observation that in *Paramecium* the macronucleus contains about 40 times as much deoxyribonucleic acid as the micronucleus. Although usually supposed to be concerned primarily with sexual phenomena and thus essential for conjugation, the micronucleus is not required for fission in certain ciliates since strains lacking it are known in several species. For example, older strains of *Tetrahymena pyriformis,* maintained on artificial culture media, are all amicronucleate; other strains isolated in the laboratory have also lost the micronucleus. The apparent stability of amicronucleate *Tetrahymena* strains over periods of years indicates that the macronucleus has a definite genetic function, at least in these strains. Experiments with fragments have shown also that the macronucleus, or an adequate portion of it, is essential for regeneration, whereas the micronucleus ranges from indispensable (in certain hypotrichous ciliates) to nonessential (in typical heterotrichous ciliates).

Mitochondria vary from small ovoid or spherical bodies to rods or filaments in different species. Available evidence indicates that important respiratory enzymes are associated with protozoan mitochondria, just as with mitochondria of higher organisms. Other cytoplasmic inclusions include: the vacuome, small globules or vacuoles that can be stained with neutral red in the living organism; volutin granules; Golgi material, groups of flattened, closely packed vacuoles similar to the Golgi bodies reported in metazoan cells; and crystals, typically enclosed in vacuoles and possibly representing metabolic wastes.

Vacuoles.—Contractile vacuoles are characteristic of freshwater Protozoa but occur also in certain parasitic ciliates and in many marine ciliates. Contractile vacuoles show cyclic expansion and contraction, the periodicity varying with the species, environmental conditions, and physiological activity. When expansion (diastole) is completed, the contents are discharged abruptly (systole) through a temporary or permanent pore. In many ciliates at least, position of the pore is constant enough to have taxonomic significance.

The major function of the contractile vacuole is elimination of excess water, which enters by osmosis (in freshwater species especially), accompanies ingested food, or accumulates metabolically. Vacuolar activity is influenced by changes in osmotic pressure and temperature and by phagocytic feeding. In some freshwater protozoans, vacuolar activity has been stopped completely by adding sugar to a freshwater medium (*i.e.*, increasing osmotic pressure). Although fluid eliminated by the contractile vacuole may contain some metabolic waste, available data indicate that this excretory function is of minor importance. Furthermore, many Protozoa have no contractile vacuoles.

Digestive vacuoles are typical of holozoic Protozoa. In amoebas, which ingest food at any point on the surface, the lining of the food vacuole is derived from the pellicle or from the plasma membrane. In organisms with a definite "mouth" (cytostome and cytopharynx), the vacuole develops as an outgrowth from the cytopharynx. In suctorian ciliates, food vacuoles are formed in similar fashion at the bases of tentacles. Ingested food may be accompanied by a significant amount of water in organisms ingesting bacteria or other small particles. Fresh food vacuoles in *Amoeba* are surrounded by a thick granular layer, but the granular material disappears during digestion. After ingestion of food, the vacuolar contents usually become slightly acidic, remain at that level for a time, then gradually shift toward the neutral point. Any undigested residues are eventually eliminated, often at a specific point (called cytopyge or cytoproct) in the cortex of organisms that have a highly differentiated body wall, or at any convenient spot in amoeboid organisms.

Certain ciliates (*e.g.*, *Loxodes*, *Blepharoprosthium*) contain one or more peripheral vacuoles in which float small granules (statoliths). On the basis of superficial similarity to certain structures in coelenterates, these vacuoles have been considered statocysts. Another type of vacuole, perhaps containing gas in some species, occurs in the peripheral cytoplasm of floating types, such as radiolarians, and apparently is involved in flotation.

Chromatophores.—Many phytoflagellates possess chromatophores containing chlorophyll and other pigments. In *Chlamydomonas* and related flagellates the chromatophore is often single, fairly large, and cup-shaped, partially surrounding the nucleus. In contrast, euglenoids often have a number of small peripheral chromatophores. In electron micrographs, chromatophores of phytoflagellates show a lamellar organization, opaque layers alternating with electron-transparent layers, the pigments supposedly being localized at the interfaces.

Chlorophyll is the predominant pigment in green flagellates. However, the green colour of chlorophyll may be masked by other pigments to produce greenish-yellow, red, brown, or sometimes bluish chromatophores. Certain of these accessory pigments may be important in absorption of light for photosynthesis. Both accessory pigments and types of chlorophyll may vary from order to order. For example, the euglenoids contain chlorophylls *a* and *b*; the dinoflagellates, chlorophylls *a* and *c*. Lutein, a carotene derivative, occurs in chrysomonads but not in dinoflagellates. Comparable taxonomic differences involve other pigments.

Certain strains of *Euglena* undergo bleaching when grown in darkness for some time or when exposed to high temperature (36° C). Bleaching also has been induced by treating certain strains of *E. gracilis* with streptomycin or the antihistamine drug pyribenzamine. These colourless strains may not regain the ability to produce chromatophores. Such experimental results suggest that the presence or absence of chlorophyll is not in itself a thoroughly reliable taxonomic criterion.

Pyrenoids, apparently homogenous bodies (even in electron micrographs), are often associated with chromatophores in certain orders of phytoflagellates but not in others. Even in orders characterized by pyrenoids, Euglenida for instance, species within a genus may lack them. The function of pyrenoids is uncertain, although they are often assumed to play a part in synthesis of polysaccharides. However, similar polysaccharides are synthesized and stored by related phytoflagellates that do not contain pyrenoids.

Cytoplasmic Pigments.—The cytoplasm of many phytoflagellates and certain other Protozoa contains various pigments (violet, blue, green, yellow, brown, pink, red). The peculiar pink pigment of *Blepharisma undulans* is bleached when the ciliates are exposed to weak light and is regenerated in darkness. In bright light this pigment or some product becomes toxic to *Blepharisma* and may cause lysis of various other Protozoa and small Metazoa. Red pigments and toxins are produced by some phytoflagellates—certain dinoflagellates (*Gonyaulax*). In blooms of dinoflagellates, called "red tides," enough toxin may accumulate to cause death of large numbers of fish. A red pigment in *Euglena rubra* is shifted toward the surface when this flagellate is exposed to high temperatures (35°–45° C) or to bright light.

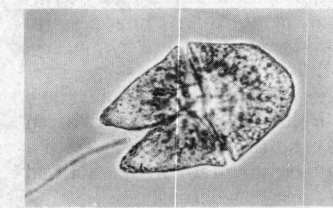

JOHN J. LEE AND HUGO D. FREUDENTHAL

GYMNODINIUM, ONE OF THE DINO-FLAGELLATES RESPONSIBLE FOR THE POISONOUS "RED TIDES" OFF THE FLORIDA COAST

Food Reserves.—Many Protozoa synthesize and store carbohydrates and lipids as food reserves. The type of stored carbohydrate varies with the group—*e.g.*, starches in Phytomonadida, Dinoflagellida, Cryptomonadida; paramylum, another glucose polymer, in Euglenida; leucosin, believed to be a different glucose polymer, in Chrysomonadida; and glycogens, in many other Protozoa. In phytoflagellates especially, these carbohydrates are commonly stored as discrete bodies, such as the paramylum bodies of Euglenida and starch bodies in Cryptomonadida. Glycogens, isolated from a flagellate, *Trichomonas*, and a ciliate, *Tetrahymena*, are chemically similar to, but not identical with, glycogen from mammals. Lipids are stored by many Protozoa, but the amounts apparently vary with the physiological condition of the organism. In pure cultures of flagellates and ciliates, lipids tend to accumulate as the culture grows older, suggesting a qualitative influence of the environment. Less is known about nitrogenous reserves, although chromatoid bodies of parasitic amoebas and volutin granules of many Protozoa may belong in this category. Volutin granules of certain trypanosomes and haemogregarines are destroyed by digestion with ribonuclease and have been presumed to contain ribonucleic acid.

Eyespots.—The light-sensitive stigma, common in chlorophyll-bearing flagellates, but rare in colourless ones, is believed to function in phototaxis, a behavioural response to light. In *Euglena* the stigma is a discoid mass of reddish granules near the wall of the canal that leads from the reservoir. At the level of the stigma, a small paraflagellar body on the flagellum is often considered the light-sensitive structure responsible for reaction to light. The stigma itself is believed to absorb the light that stimulates the paraflagellar body. In many flagellates with a stigma, however, there is no paraflagellar body. After experimental bleaching of *Euglena gracilis*, the stigma may disappear.

An analogous photoreceptor, the ocellus, has been described in certain dinoflagellates (*e.g.*, *Erythropsis*) as a mass of dark pigment partially enclosing a spherical hyaline body.

3. Locomotor Organelles.—These include pseudopodia, flagella, cilia, and certain structures derived from flagella and cilia. Cilia are the only organelles limited to a single group of Protozoa, the Ciliophora, or ciliates.

Pseudopodia.—These temporary protoplasmic extensions are of four main varieties—lobopodia, filopodia, myxopodia (reticulopodia or rhizopodia), and axopodia.

Lobopodia, represented typically in *Amoeba proteus,* are fairly broad extensions with rounded tips. Very small lobopodia may be clear; larger ones usually show a granular core. The outer layer (ectoplasm) appears denser than the inner cytoplasm (endoplasm).

Filopodia are typically slender clear pseudopodia, usually tapering to the tip. They sometimes branch or form simple connections.

Myxopodia are filamentous pseudopodia that branch and connect to form networks in which the outer cytoplasm is obviously more fluid than the inner cytoplasm (when such a core is present). In certain foraminifers the slender myxopodia seem to contain no endoplasm. A striking feature of the network is the flow of granules in individual pseudopodia—toward the organism on one side and away from it on the other. The direction of flow is reversible. The sticky myxopodial net is an efficient food trap. Local fusion of pseudopodia encloses the food. In certain foraminifers (*e.g., Elphidium*) digestion is usually completed outside the test; however, in some species, food may be drawn inside. The myxopodial net may also function in construction of the test during growth, in formation of cysts, and in locomotion.

Axopodia resemble myxopodia in that the outer cytoplasm is the more fluid, as indicated by flowing granules, but the extensions tend to radiate singly from the body without forming complex networks. In typical axopodia the inner cytoplasm forms an axial filament. These pseudopodia, like the myxopodia, are sticky food traps.

Amoeboid movement depends upon protoplasmic flow, and involves gel-sol reversals. In *Amoeba proteus* it usually involves formation of a main pseudopodium into which the rest of the amoeba flows (*see* CELL). In locomotion of testate rhizopods (*Arcella,* etc.) the tip of each pseudopodium sticks to some surface, and contraction of the pseudopodia supposedly pulls the body toward the point of attachment. It is difficult to explain the activity of slender myxopodia in certain foraminifers; protoplasmic flow in different directions is apparent on different sides of pseudopodia in which no endoplasm can be seen.

Flagella.—A flagellum consists of an outer sheath, circular or flattened in cross section, and a central axoneme. The electron microscope shows the typical axoneme to be a bundle of nine pairs of fibrils surrounding two central ones. The bases of the fibrils form the blepharoplast, which appears as a granule when viewed in the ordinary light microscope. The sheath apparently encloses a matrix in which the axoneme is embedded.

In certain Mastigophora, fibrils (mastigonemes) project laterally from the sheath. A flagellum usually extends anteriorly from an anterior blepharoplast. Exceptions include a trailing flagellum, which extends posteriorly from an anterior blepharoplast; a longitudinal flagellum (dinoflagellates), which extends posteriorly from a lateral blepharoplast; a transverse flagellum (dinoflagellates), normally lying in a spiral groove (girdle), which extends partly or completely around the body; and a flagellum forming the margin of the undulating membrane (*Trichomonas, Trypanosoma*). In free-living species there are usually one or two, less commonly three or four; in parasites there are one to many.

Flagellar locomotion involves different mechanisms in different flagellates. For example, the flagellum may trace a spiral from tip to base or from base to tip, or may show planar undulations extending from base to tip or from tip to base, depending upon the species. In some cases a flagellum pushes and in other cases pulls the organism forward. In *Euglena* and various related types, movement of the flagellum causes rotation of the organism on its major axis and gyration about the general path of locomotion. In effect, the body moves through the water somewhat like a screw in such cases.

Cilia.—Cilia are similar to flagella in finer structure but are shorter and usually more numerous. Cilia are usually distributed in meridional or somewhat spiral rows, the pattern being characteristic of the species and thus useful in taxonomy. The axoneme arises from an apparently self-reproducing basal granule, or kinetosome, more accurately a tubular structure representing the ends of outer axoneme fibrils. The basal granules of many species are arranged in a characteristic pattern, corresponding to distribution of ciliary organelles. Since the granules, in contrast

to the cilia, can be demonstrated clearly by silver impregnation, they are useful in identification and in tracing morphological changes during reproduction or in successive stages of a life cycle. In certain ciliates a fibril extends inward from each basal granule to join other fibrils from granules of the same row to form a bundle of filaments, a longitudinal or spiral basal fibril (kinetodesma). These basal fibrils make up a fibrillar system believed by some biologists to facilitate coordination of ciliary activities. This assumption is supported by observations on *Euplotes,* in which destruction of major fibrils eliminates locomotor coordination. In addition to, or sometimes instead of, simple cilia, many species have compound organelles formed by fusion of cilia in rows or in tufts. Membranes are composed of longitudinal rows; membranelles, of short transverse rows; cirri, of tufts.

Myonemes.—Myonemes are superficial contractile fibrils in certain ciliates, gregarines, and flagellates, and presumably are responsible for rapid changes in shape. An example of the action of myonemes is seen in the wavelike constrictions of *Euglena* during euglenoid movement. Analogous fibres occur as "stalk-muscles" in various ciliates (*e.g., Vorticella*).

4. Trichocysts.—These bodies, in the cortex of certain ciliates and flagellates, may be widely distributed over the organism or restricted to certain areas (tentacles, papillae, the area around the mouth). Several types occur in ciliates. Mucoid trichocysts are elongated inclusions that, under artificial stimulation, may be ejected as visible bodies. Apparently similar inclusions occur in such flagellates as euglenoids. Filamentous trichocysts, seen in *Paramecium* and other ciliates, are discharged as filaments composed of a cross-striated shaft and a tip. Toxicysts, in *Dileptus* and certain other carnivorous protozoans, tend to be localized around the mouth. Upon discharge each toxicyst expels a long nonstriated filament with a rodlike tip. These filaments, which paralyze or cause disintegration of other microorganisms, serve in capturing food and presumably in defense. The functional significance of other trichocysts is uncertain, although those of *Paramecium* apparently can be extruded for anchorage during feeding. Cnidocysts of certain dinoflagellates (*e.g., Polykrikos*), similar to nematocysts of coelenterates, develop in the cytoplasm from recognizable precursors; their function is unknown. Filamentous trichocysts, with cross-striated shafts, occur in the flagellate *Oxyrrhis.* The analogous trichocysts of *Chilomonas,* a cryptomonad flagellate, show longitudinal striations.

IV. REPRODUCTION AND DEVELOPMENT

1. Asexual Reproduction.—Protozoa may reproduce asexually, by binary fission, budding, plasmotomy, or schizogony.

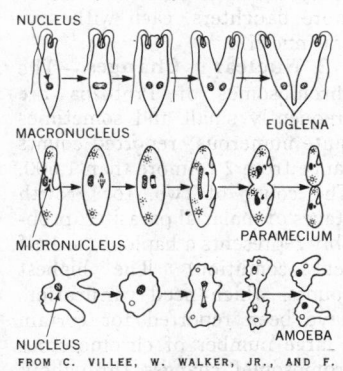

FROM C. VILLEE, W. WALKER, JR., AND F. SMITH, "GENERAL ZOOLOGY," 1963; REPRODUCED BY PERMISSION OF W. B. SAUNDERS CO.

FIG. 2.—ASEXUAL REPRODUCTION IN PROTOZOA

Binary Fission.—Binary fission involves nuclear division, duplication of organelles and approximately equal division of the body. Blepharoplasts, basal granules, and, in certain species, such organelles as chromatophores apparently divide. Various other structures (*e.g.,* parabasal bodies, and locomotor organelles in many ciliates) are usually resorbed so that each daughter organism must produce its own equipment. Some or most of the somatic cilia or cirri may be resorbed during fission. In hypotrichs, for example, new ventral cirri are commonly developed in both daughter organisms. In such cases, however, the basal granules giving rise to such structures seem to have genetic continuity.

Fission in ciliates usually involves extensive dedifferentiation of the parental body, followed by reorganization with two centres of differentiation. In typical transverse division of ciliates, the anterior end of the posterior daughter is differentiated in contact with the posterior end of the anterior daughter. However, *Halteria* and similar ciliates undergo a reversal of polarity in early fission so that the posterior ends of the daughters are in contact.

Development of the new buccal ("mouth") organelles may involve extensive reorganization. The anlage, or beginning, of new buccal ciliature is often recognizable early in fission. The buccal anlage of the posterior daughter in *Tetrahymena* arises by multiplication of basal granules at a particular level in a specific ciliary row. This morphogenetic

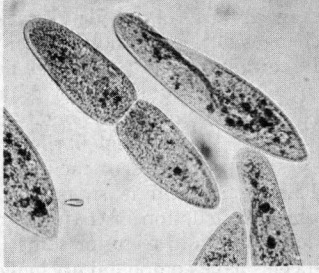

HUGH SPENCER
SIMPLE FISSION IN A PARAMECIUM

specificity is inherited generation after generation. The parental buccal apparatus is retained by the anterior daughter in *Tetrahymena* and comparable ciliates. In various others (*e.g., Bursaria*) the buccal organelles are resorbed and each daughter develops a new set. Sometimes the buccal apparatus (*Paramecium, Vorticella*) is self-reproducing in the sense that the anlage of the new apparatus for one daughter arises as basal granules produced by division of granules in the parental apparatus.

Budding.—Budding involves normal nuclear division but unequal cytoplasmic division. This method, producing either external or internal buds, is characteristic of Suctorida. Internal budding, as in *Tokophrya*, involves formation of a "brood pouch" by invagination of the cortex, or outer layer, of the ciliate. The bud is pinched off inside the pouch and, after development of cilia, is expelled by contractions of the parental body.

Life cycles of Suctorida illustrate clearly the genetic continuity of the basal granules. The nonciliated adult possesses only basal granules. In budding, some of the parental granules migrate into the cortex of the young organism, assume a specific arrangement, and give rise to the cilia of the larval stage. Later on, during metamorphosis into the adult, the external portions of the cilia are resorbed, leaving only the basal granules.

Plasmotomy and Schizogony.—Schizogony, characteristic of many Sporozoa, typically involves a series of nuclear divisions, followed by rapid production of uninucleate buds. In extreme cases many daughter nuclei become located near the surface of the plasmodial stage before the buds are pinched off, often leaving a residual mass of cytoplasm. In plasmotomy an organism with many nuclei divides into two or more daughters, each with several nuclei.

2. Nuclear Changes.—The chromosomes of Protozoa are frequently small and sometimes quite numerous; reported counts range from 2 to more than 1,600. The count of two, for growth stages of malarial parasites, probably represents a haploid (or half set) condition. The highest counts, which need verification, have been reported for certain radiolarians. The small size and large number of chromosomes make it impossible to follow chromosomal changes throughout mitosis in most Protozoa. In *Holomastigotoides tusitala*, however, certain strains have two large chromosomes about 50 microns long (the red blood cell in man is 7.5 microns across).

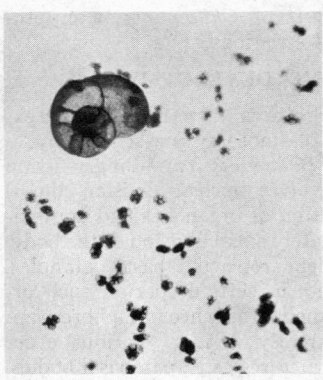

JOHN J. LEE AND HUGO D. FREUDENTHAL
A FORAMINIFER UNDERGOING SCHIZOGONY, A FORM OF ASEXUAL REPRODUCTION

Each chromosome contains a tightly coiled thread, or chromonema, attached at one end to a centromere (a self-reproducing granule attached to a spindle fibre), and forms a series of loose major coils within the chromosomal matrix. In a late stage of cell division (telophase) each matrix disappears, releasing the chromonema. As a result, the major coils loosen and tend to disappear as the chromonemata become untwisted within the nucleus. At this point, the nucleus is in the so-called "resting," or inter-

phase, stage. Each centromere and chromonema next undergoes duplication, the minor coils of the chromonemata being reproduced exactly. The daughter chromonemata now unwind; each acquires a matrix, begins to contract, and develops a series of major coils as the next cycle of cell division begins with the appearance of a prophase chromosome.

Although it may be possible eventually to interpret mitotic behaviour of chromosomes in Protozoa, generally, in terms of the *Holomastigotoides* pattern, there are obvious differences among species in the relation of chromosomes to the spindle—a temporary cell structure closely associated with the movement of chromosomes during cell division. In some cases (*e.g.*, typical micronucleus of ciliates, various flagellates, etc.) the spindle lies within the nuclear membrane. In many other cases the spindle is extranuclear, chromosomal fibrils being attached to centromeres at the nuclear membrane (*e.g., Holomastigotoides*, various other flagellates, and such Sporozoa as *Aggregata*). There is no conclusive evidence that the division of the ciliate macronucleus involves mitosis. Visible details vary with the genus or larger group of ciliates.

The onset of nuclear division in ciliates is correlated with changes in ciliature. In *Stentor coeruleus*, for example, macronuclear condensation normally begins just after a new field of basal granules, the buccal anlage, begins to differentiate. If this anlage is cut out as soon as it is detected, no macronuclear condensation occurs; if it is removed after condensation has begun, there is no further change in the macronucleus. Precocious fission has been induced by grafting a young *Stentor* to a mature specimen about ready to divide; apparently, a stimulus of undetermined nature is transmitted from the dividing ciliate to its immature parabiotic twin.

3. Sexual Phenomena.—The essential feature in sexual activities is the production of haploid gametic nuclei and their subsequent union to form a diploid synkaryon (zygotic nucleus). Reduction division (meiosis), to produce the haploid condition, occurs at different stages in different species. Zygotic meiosis, in phytomonad flagellates and at least certain gregarines and coccidians, ensures that all stages except the zygote are haploid. Gametic meiosis (during formation of gametes) has been described in certain Mastigophora, Sarcodina, and Sporozoa. Gametic meiosis of ciliates is often termed conjugant meiosis. On the basis of superficial features, several varieties of sexual phenomena are recognized: syngamy, autogamy, and conjugation.

Syngamy.—Syngamy, involving fusion of haploid gametes to form a zygote, is found in all major protozoan groups except ciliates. Within each subphylum, however, distribution of syngamy is apparently erratic. Two of the best-known examples of syngamy occur in *Volvox* and the malarial parasites, both of which illustrate anisogamy (gametes obviously different). Superficially apparent isogamy (identical gametes) is known in some species of *Chlamydomonas*, for example, but these gametes are actually of two physiologically different kinds. In homothallic species one population derived from a common ancestor can produce both kinds of gametes; in heterothallic species, each strain produces one kind of gamete.

Autogamy.—This method involves meiosis and subsequent fusion of haploid nuclei within a single organism. The process occurs in a few flagellates (*e.g., Barbulanympha, Rhynchonympha, Urinympha*) parasitic in the wood-roach, and also occurs in certain ciliates. Among the ciliates, autogamy is known in *Paramecium* and in *Tetrahymena*. Autogamy can occur in unpaired ciliates, occasionally in ciliates already paired for conjugation, or in encysted stages (as in *T. rostrata*).

Conjugation.—In conjugation, pairing may be preceded by mating reactions (clumping) of ciliates, as in *Paramecium*. Direct pairing, without such clumping, occurs in many other cases (*e.g., Tetrahymena, Euplotes*). The micronucleus in each conjugant typically undergoes three pregamic divisions, the second of which is usually reductional. If there are several micronuclei, one or more of them may undergo the pregamic divisions, the details varying with, and sometimes within, the species. After nuclear exchange, the migratory gametic nuclei fuse with the

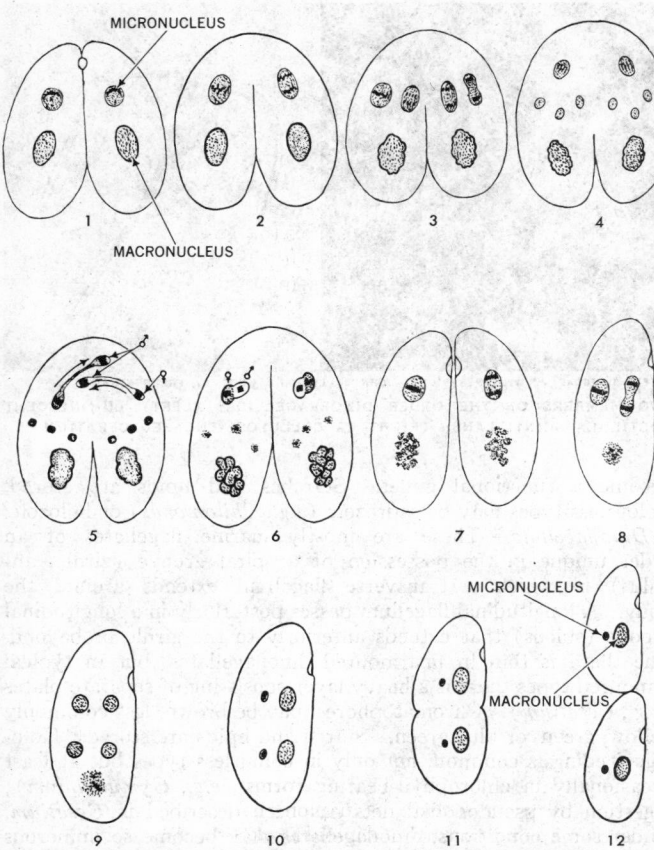

FIG. 3.—GENERAL PLAN OF CONJUGATION IN CILIATES

(1) The paired conjugants; (2) first pregamic division; (3) second pregamic division, reductional in most ciliates; (4) one haploid nucleus in each conjugant is dividing to produce migratory and stationary gametic nuclei; (5) exchange of migratory nuclei; (6) fusion of migratory and stationary gametic nuclei to produce a synkaryon in each conjugant; (7) each synkaryon divides as the conjugants separate; (8), (9) mitotic divisions producing daughter nuclei; (10) differentiation into macronuclei and micronuclei; (11), (12) fissions to restore normal nuclear number

stationary gametic nuclei to produce a synkaryon in each conjugant. In different species, one to four postconjugant nuclear divisions occur and the daughter nuclei differentiate into micronuclei and macronuclei. In production of the latter, there is a tremendous increase in the amount of chromatin. In certain ciliates this differentiation includes chromosomal division, and the mature macronucleus becomes polyploid. According to the number of nuclear divisions, reorganization fissions may be needed to restore the normal nuclear complement. Hence, a pair of conjugants may yield two to eight reorganized ciliates.

As prerequisites for conjugation, Maupas' factors (diverse ancestry, "sexual maturity," and starvation) still seem to be important, even for pure cultures of Tetrahymena. The maturity factor of Maupas seems to be expressed as the inability of appropriate strains to conjugate for some time after the preceding conjugation. This period of "immaturity" varies considerably— from none at all in certain strains of Paramecium aurelia to several weeks or months in some cases. Once suitable strains have reached "sexual maturity," conjugation can be induced readily by rapid starvation. This is effected with Tetrahymena by washing the ciliates and suspending them in distilled water. Maupasian "diverse ancestry" is illustrated by the presence of several mating types, or "sexes," in Paramecium, Euplotes, Oxytricha, and Tetrahymena. A particular species is composed of a number of varieties (syngens), each of which contains 2 or more mating types—e.g., 2 to 11 in Tetrahymena pyriformis; only 2 in Paramecium aurelia and P. caudatum. Normal conjugation occurs between members of different mating types within a single variety. The survivors, if any, of intervarietal matings usually show low

viability so that there may be reproductive isolation of these varieties within the species.

The survival value of sexual phenomena apparently varies with the species. In malarial parasites syngamy is an essential step that initiates the mosquito phase of the life cycle. In the free-living Volvox the zygote encysts to become a dormant resistant stage in which the flagellate can pass the winter. In ciliates, the survival value of conjugation is not so obvious. According to Maupas, strains of ciliates pass through a "cycle" of youth, maturity, and old age, leading to the death of the line. This fate can be prevented by conjugation during sexual maturity. In other words, conjugation rejuvenates the strain, an interpretation challenged by P. Enriques, L. L. Woodruff, and others, but supported by T. M. Sonneborn and his students.

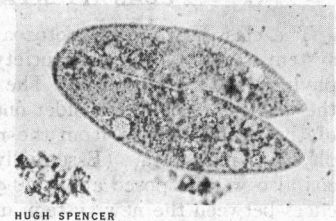

HUGH SPENCER
CONJUGATION OF PARAMECIA

4. Variation and Heredity. —The genetic study of Protozoa involves the inheritance of detectable traits in fission or budding and the inheritance of such traits through syngamy or conjugation. Seemingly heritable changes sometimes occur in "asexual" strains. Examples include spontaneous changes in fission rate in clones of Astasia and the many instances of resistance to drugs developed in free-living and parasitic Protozoa. This resistance to drugs may be inherited over many divisions and over long periods of time after exposure to the inducing drug. The genetic status of such changes is uncertain, especially since syngamy is unknown in some of the species involved. Favourable material for genetic analysis is afforded by species that undergo syngamy or conjugation. In species showing syngamy, the dominant phase may be haploid or diploid, depending upon the type of organism. Ciliates, which undergo conjugation, are normally diploid, although experimentally induced haploid strains have been obtained in Tetrahymena pyriformis. Haploid species, such as typical phytomonad flagellates, offer obvious advantages to the geneticist. The heterozygous, or hybrid, condition exists only in the zygote so that hybrid analysis is much simpler than in ciliates. In these haploid cycles each division product of the zygote may give rise to a clone whose phenotype, or outward appearance, indicates the genotypic, or hereditary, constitution.

In investigations on the haploid Chlamydomonas and Polytoma, Mendelian inheritance has been reported for such traits as size, shape, rate of swimming (normal and "lazy"), photosynthesis (normal and slow), storage of volutin (normal and excessive), etc. Linkage has been established for certain pairs of traits, and crossing-over has been demonstrated in several cases.

Observations on traits inherited through conjugation range from size and fission rate to specific enzyme systems, some of the latter observations involving pure cultures of Tetrahymena pyriformis. For example, the wild strain of T. pyriformis is unable to synthesize serine and must have this amino acid in defined media. The ability to synthesize serine, known in certain mutant strains, seems to be inherited in Mendelian fashion as a recessive to normal (inability to synthesize serine). The status of the pyridoxine requirement in T. pyriformis is similar. Strains that grow without a source of pyridoxine, and synthesize it, appear to be homozygous recessives. When these are mated with the normal type (pyridoxine-requiring), all the progeny require pyridoxine. Mating types in Paramecium, Tetrahymena, and Euplotes also seem to be inherited in Mendelian fashion, although the genetic pattern may vary from one variety to another within a species.

There are indications that macronuclear differentiation during postconjugant fissions may influence determination of mating types in Paramecium aurelia (group A) and Tetrahymena pyriformis (variety 1). Inheritance of antigenic types in P. aurelia is apparently fundamentally Mendelian. The overall pattern shows some similarity to the inheritance of mating types, although antigenic types seem to be somewhat less stable under certain environmental conditions. Also dependent upon genetic composition of the ciliates are the abilities to maintain "infections" with kappa particles ("killer strains" of *P. aurelia*) and with mu particles ("mate-killer" strains of *P. aurelia*). *P. aurelia* that bear the killer trait contain cytoplasmic kappa particles, which secrete killer particles into the surrounding medium. All sensitive strains of paramecia die when they contact killer particles. Kappa particles seem to be self-reproducing but their persistence in individual ciliates is ultimately dependent upon a gene (or genes).

V. CLASSIFICATION AND SURVEY

The classification of Protozoa is not yet stabilized. A newer system, sponsored by the Society of Protozoologists, divides the phylum into five subphyla. The most obvious difference between the new system and the older one followed here is the separation of the Cnidosporidea from the rest of the Sporozoa as the subphylum Cnidospora. (Essentially similar treatment of the Sporozoa also was proposed about 40 years ago.) Less striking differences between the new system and the one followed here involve the taxonomic treatment of certain smaller groups.

A. MASTIGOPHORA

This subphylum consists of organisms flagellated in some stage of the life cycle. Formation of pseudopodia is not uncommon, and amoeboid stages occur in certain species.

1. Phytomastigophorea.—This class comprises the phytoflagellates, or plantlike flagellates, many of which have chromatophores containing chlorophyll. Species without chromatophores are morphologically similar to related chlorophyll-bearing species. Although the chromatophores contain chlorophyll, the colour varies with the kinds and concentrations of accessory pigments. Colourless species may be saprozoic or holozoic, and some of the chlorophyll-bearing forms also can ingest solid food.

Chrysomonadida.—Protozoans of this order may have one, two, or rarely three flagella, the third being a peculiar inactive organelle. Chromatophores, when present, are few, ranging from golden yellow to greenish yellow or brownish green. Holozoic feeding, by means of pseudopodia and without a permanent cytopharynx, is fairly common. Amoeboid and palmella stages occur in some species; occasionally either stage may be the dominant phase in the life cycle. Some colonial and solitary species secrete a lorica. Others secrete a membranous envelope in which siliceous scales or calcareous bits (coccoliths) are embedded. A specialized group of silicoflagellates is characterized by a siliceous skeleton. Stored reserves include leucosin and lipids. The cyst wall, typically siliceous, is formed inside the cytoplasm and has an emergence pore. A few genera develop spheroid or arboroid colonies. Genera include: *Ochromonas, Dinobryon, Synura.*

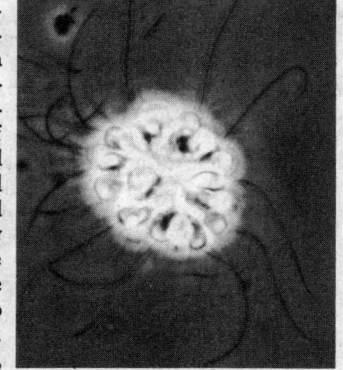
JOHN J. LEE
SYNURA, COLONIAL MARINE PROTOZOAN OF THE ORDER CHRYSOMONADIDA

Heterochlorida.—This order of small flagellates is characterized by flexible bodies, two unequal flagella, and one to several yellow-green chromatophores. Leucosin and lipids are stored. The cyst wall is formed internally as in Chrysomonadida, but shows two valves and lacks a pore. A palmella or a plasmodium is the dominant phase in certain genera. Representatives are *Chloromeson* and *Nephrochloris*.

Cryptomonadida.—The members of this order have two flagella and often one or two chromatophores, rarely more, which may be blue green, brown, red, or occasionally green. The body is typically flattened on one side and convex on the other, and is fairly constant in shape. There is usually a ventral groove, which may be closed ventrally to form an interior pouch (*Cryptomonas*). In the colourless holozoic *Cyathomonas* the pouch has

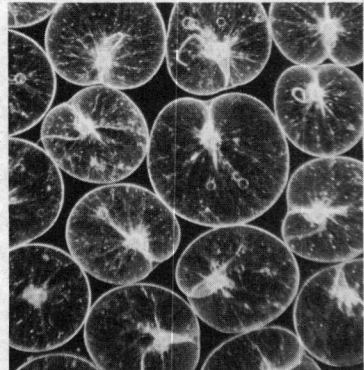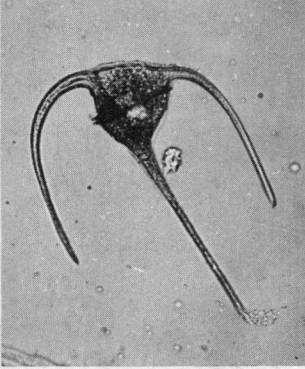
(LEFT) DOUGLAS P. WILSON; (RIGHT) JOHN J. LEE AND HUGO D. FREUDENTHAL
TWO MEMBERS OF THE ORDER DINOFLAGELLIDA: (LEFT) LUMINESCENT NOCTILUCA SCINTILLANS; (RIGHT) A CELLULOSE-ENCASED CERATIUM

become a functional gullet. Starches and lipids are stored. Colourless types may be saprozoic (*e.g., Chilomonas*) or holozoic.

Dinoflagellida.—These are mostly marine flagellates of an order unique in the possession of a spiral groove (girdle, annulus) in which a transverse flagellum extends around the body. A longitudinal flagellum passes posteriorly in a longitudinal groove (sulcus) that extends anteriorly to the girdle or beyond. The theca is thin in unarmoured dinoflagellates, but in typical armoured types there is a heavy layer consisting of separate plates (*e.g., Ceratium*). Chromatophores may be brown, less commonly yellow, green, or blue green. Starch and lipids are stored. Holozoic feeding is common, not only in colourless types but at least occasionally in chlorophyll-bearing forms (*e.g., Gymnodinium*); ingestion by pseudopodial nets has been described in *Ceratium*. Under some conditions, dinoflagellates may become so numerous locally that the water is discoloured—*e.g.,* the "red tides" well known in the Gulf of Mexico and elsewhere. Some dinoflagellates produce a potent toxin (*e.g., Gonyaulax*) that can kill fish. Such a toxin is sometimes accumulated in the tissues of mussels or other shellfish feeding on dinoflagellates. Consumption of these toxic shellfish may lead to occasionally fatal cases of poisoning in man. *Noctiluca* includes large specialized spheroid types up to two millimetres in diameter, widely distributed and responsible for much of the phosphorescence of agitated seawater. Certain dinoflagellates are parasitic in coelenterates and other animals.

Phytomonadida.—This is an order of fairly small (25 microns or less) flagellates, usually ovoid to spherical, but sometimes spindle-shaped or otherwise modified. The theca is usually a moderately firm envelope containing cellulose. The green chromatophore, when present, is usually single and cup-shaped, but two or more smaller chromatophores may be present. The chromatophore usually contains one or more pyrenoids. Some species are colourless saprozoic flagellates. Starch and lipids are stored. In addition, such types as *Haematococcus* may accumulate enough red cytoplasmic pigment to mask the green of the chromatophore; dense populations have been responsible for "red snow." A colonial series ranges from simple types such as *Gonium sociale*, with four zooids, to *Volvox*, species of which may contain 10,000–50,000 component flagellates. Syngamy is known for some species.

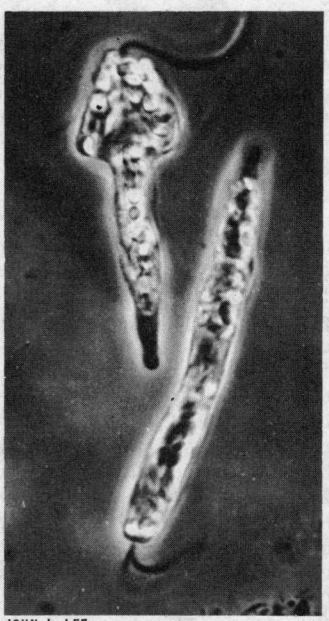
JOHN J. LEE
MARINE EUGLENOIDS IN STAGES OF EUGLENOID MOVEMENT

Euglenida.—The members of this order are chlorophyll-bearing or colourless, with one to three flagella arising near the base of a flask-shaped reservoir (gullet) into which the contractile vacuole empties. The pellicle, if thin enough, permits metaboly, or euglenoid movement, but some genera (*Phacus, Menoidium*, etc.) have a rigid pellicle that prevents metaboly. A hard test (in *Trachelomonas*) or a lorica (in *Klebsiella*) may be present. Green chromatophores, when present, range from one to many, and may or may not be associated with pyrenoids. A stigma is characteristic of the green species, rarely of the colourless types. The major storage product is paramylum, a polysaccharide. Some colourless types (*Heteronema, Peranema*) are holozoic; others (*Astasia, Menoidium*, etc.) are saprozoic. Palmella stages may occur (*e.g., Euglena gracilis*), and cysts are known in several species.

Chloromonadida.—This order of the dorso-ventrally flattened freshwater flagellates is characterized by two flagella, one of them trailing. The numerous chromatophores are bright green. A stigma seems to be absent. Starch has not been reported. Glycogen and lipids are stored in certain species. Representatives are *Gonyostomum* and *Vacuolaria.*

2. Zoomastigophorea. — This is a class of saprozoic or holozoic flagellates, which lack chromatophores. They do not synthesize cellulose, starch, leucosin, or paramylum, although

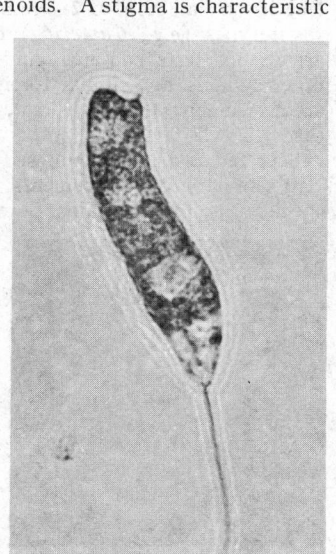

JOHN J. LEE
PERANEMA, A EUGLENOID WITH AN ANTERIOR FLAGELLUM

glycogen is stored by certain species. The flexible pellicle is thin enough in certain genera to permit considerable amoeboid activity. Many are parasites, the class being represented in presumably all vertebrates, many invertebrates, and certain plants.

Rhizomastigida.—This order contains organisms that have one to four flagella but also form pseudopodia (protoplasmic flow is sometimes more important than flagellar activity in locomotion). Representatives are: *Mastigamoeba*, uniflagellate, forming small lobopodia; *Histomonas* (*H. meleagridis* is associated with blackhead disease in young turkeys and other birds); and *Mastigina*, uniflagellate, sluglike.

Protomastigida.—This is an order of small protozoans with one to two flagella and flexible pellicles but not typically amoeboid bodies. Many are holozoic, others saprozoic. Many parasitic species occur in vertebrates, invertebrates, and, occasionally, plants. Certain free-living species are colonial. In choanoflagellates a protoplasmic membrane can be extended to form a conical "collar" around the flagellum. Such flagellates (*e.g., Codonosiga*) resemble the choanocytes of sponges. Important parasitic species belong to the family Trypanosomidae, which includes *Trypanosoma*, parasites of vertebrates and invertebrate vectors; *Leishmania*, commonly represented in vertebrates and sand flies; *Leptomonas, Crithidia, Herpetomonas*, restricted to invertebrates; and *Phytomonas*, in certain plants and sap-sucking insects.

Polymastigida.—This heterogenous order includes uninucleate, binucleate, and, rarely, multinucleate types. The majority are parasites. There are usually three to eight flagella, more in multinucleate species. Representatives are: *Costia*, parasites attacking the skin of fish; *Chilomastix; Giardia;* and several genera (*Dinenympha, Streblomastix, Pyrsonympha*, etc.) that include intestinal parasites of termites or wood-roaches.

Trichomonadida.—This order of uninucleate or multinucleate protozoans is characterized by three or more flagella, one or more parabasal bodies, and one or more axostyles. In multinucleate

types the many flagella occur in groups (mastigonts) associated with blepharoplasts, parabasal body, axostyle, and usually a nucleus; in a sense, they are compound flagellates. *Trichomonas* is represented in many vertebrate hosts; *Coronympha, Snyderella,* and *Stephanonympha* include multinucleate parasites of termites.

Hypermastigida.—The members of this order are uninucleate but multiflagellate parasites of cockroaches, wood-roaches, and termites. Many are holozoic, some ingesting particles of wood swallowed by their termite hosts. The flagella may emerge in anterior tufts, or in spiral or transverse rows covering part or sometimes most of the body. *Lophomonas* is represented in cockroaches; *Rhynchonympha*, in wood-roaches; *Holomastigotoides*, in termites; and *Trichonympha*, in both termites and wood-roaches.

Opalinida.—These opalinid ciliates, of disputed taxonomic position, are here given ordinal rank under the flagellates. The opalinids, never orthodox ciliates, may rest better among the Mastigophora, although their closest flagellate relatives are yet to be identified. These rather uniformly flagellated organisms divide obliquely or almost longitudinally, the plane of fission running parallel to the flagellar rows. Nuclei range from two (*Protoopalina, Zelleriella*) to many (*Cepedea, Opalina*). The bodies are flattened in *Zelleriella* and *Opalina*, rounded in the others. All are saprozoic parasites, most of them in the large intestine of amphibians, a few in snakes and fishes. The life cycles may be fairly complex, and syngamy occurs in the group.

B. SARCODINA

Except for species that develop flagellated stages, this subphylum contains protozoans whose locomotion involves protoplasmic flow, either with or without the formation of pseudopodia.

1. Actinopodea.—These organisms, forming a class, develop slender radiating pseudopodia, usually true axopodia. In some cases the slender pseudopodia apparently lack an axial core but otherwise resemble axopodia.

Helioflagellida.—The members of this order have one or more flagella in some stage of the life cycle and also develop radiating axopodia. In certain genera the axial cores of the pseudopodia converge in a central granule resembling that in certain uninucleate Heliozoida. Representative genera are *Actinomonas, Ciliophrys,* and *Dimorpha.*

Heliozoida.—This order consists of typically spherical, mostly freshwater organisms, floating or stalked, often with a test composed of separate scales or forming a continuous perforated wall. In nontestate genera there are many peripheral vacuoles. Heliozoida usually feed on other microorganisms, occasionally on small Metazoa such as rotifers. Flagellated stages (gametes?) have been described in several genera, and syngamy also is known in a few species. Representatives are: *Actinophrys* (including the "sun animalcule," *A. sol*); *Actinosphaerium*, multinucleate types reaching a diameter of one millimetre; *Acanthocystis*, with a scaly test.

Radiolarida.—In this actinopodian order a central capsule separates the cytoplasm into intracapsular and extracapsular zones. The capsule, sometimes branched or lobed, rather than spherical or ovoid, is composed of chitin, pseudochitin, etc., and

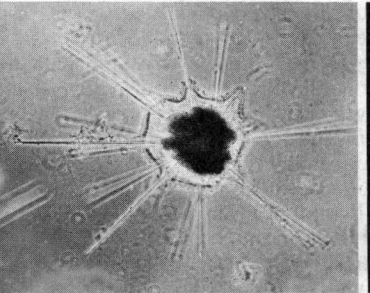
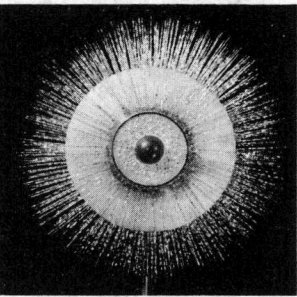

(RIGHT) BY COURTESY OF THE AMERICAN MUSEUM OF NATURAL HISTORY; PHOTOGRAPH, (LEFT) JOHN J. LEE AND HUGO D. FREUDENTHAL

(LEFT) ACANTHARIAN AND (RIGHT) RADIOLARIAN (GLASS MODEL), TWO MEMBERS OF THE CLASS ACTINOPODEA

may be somewhat flexible. The capsule encloses the nucleus, or nuclei. Most species have skeletons. In the Acantharia, or Actipylina, the basic skeletal elements, radially arranged spines containing strontium sulfate, pass through the capsule to converge centrally. These spines show a geometric constancy, polar, equatorial, and tropical spines being recognizable by analogy with the terrestrial sphere. Some species have secondary latticeworks or shells through which the spines pass. In other Radiolarida, skeletons are siliceous and quite varied in structure and complexity. Zooxanthellae, symbiotic dinoflagellates, in some cases live in the intracapsular cytoplasm of many Acantharia but are extracapsular in other Radiolarida. The zooxanthellae of some genera are dinoflagellates showing *Gymnodinium*-like active stages. Reproduction of simple Radiolarida involves fission, with division of the central capsule and distribution of skeletal elements. In other cases plasmotomy results in juvenile organisms that differentiate into the adult form during growth. Flagellated gametes and syngamy have been described. The extracapsular cytoplasm is often highly vacuolated, contributing to buoyancy of these floating organisms. Collapse of the vacuoles, increasing the specific gravity of the organisms and causing them to sink, apparently follows rough wave action. Radiolarida, typically pelagic, are widely distributed in the upper layers of all oceans. The skeletons sink to the bottom and become incorporated in sedimentary rock. Such radiolarian fossils have been recovered from Lower Silurian and later deposits.

2. Rhizopodea.—This class of Sarcodina is characterized by any kind of pseudopodia except axopodia. Many are equipped with tests (Testacida, Foraminiferida); others have only a thin pellicle.

Proteomyxida.—The majority of this order have filopodia or myxopodia, but *Labyrinthula* moves in a gliding manner without obvious pseudopodia or protoplasmic flow. Some Proteomyxida invade algae and Volvocidae; others may be found in eelgrass and hops. Little is known about their life cycles, but the mature stage is a plasmodium in some cases, a uninucleate amoeba in others. *Labyrinthula, Pseudospora, Vampyrella,* and *Leptomyxa* are representative.

Mycetozoida (Mycetozoa).—The slime molds are often considered fungi. The order includes the Acrasina, in which a pseudoplasmodium is developed. *Dictyostelium discoideum* has an unusual life cycle in which uninucleate amoebas form an aggregate (pseudoplasmodium) after responding to a chemical stimulus (acrasin, secreted by certain individuals). In the more typical group, the Myxomycetes, the mature stage is a plasmodium that, in extreme cases, may grow to a length of a foot or more. Representative

ROMAN VISHNIAC
FRUITING BODIES OF PHYSARELLA OBLONGA, ORDER MYCETOZOIDA

genera are *Physarum, Physarella, Fuligo,* and *Ceratiomyxa*. *Plasmodiophora* and its allies invade roots and underground stems of higher plants and lead to the development of galls. (*See* SLIME MOLDS.)

Amoebida.—The members of this rhizopodan order have no test. Movement may involve pseudopodia or merely protoplasmic waves. There are one to many nuclei. Some of the Amoebida are small (*e.g.,* four microns for small specimens of *Dientamoeba*); others, such as *Chaos (Pelomyxa) carolinensis,* may reach a length of four to five millimetres. In one family (Dimastigamoebidae) there are flagellated and amoeboid stages (*Dimastigamoeba, Naegleria*), but this dimorphism is unknown in other families. Other Amoebida include free-living species in fresh and salt water and parasites of many vertebrates and invertebrates.

Testacida.—This order of freshwater rhizopods is characterized by one-chambered tests. These protozoans creep by using pseudopodia that are either filopodia or very slender lobopodia. In a few genera (*e.g., Pamphagus*) the filopodia tend to branch, resembling a very simple myxopodial net. The test is usually

two-layered, the inner one being a chitinous membrane sometimes strengthened with inorganic material. The outer layer may consist of secreted siliceous scales (*Euglypha,* etc.) or of foreign particles such as sand grains (*Difflugia,* etc.) embedded in a "chitinous" cement.

Foraminiferida.—The rhizopods of this order have myxopodia (reticulopodia). The tests, typically covered with cytoplasm, are generally much larger than those of Testacida, often reaching lengths or diameters of 2–5 mm., rarely 40–50 mm. Some of the fossil types (*e.g., Camerina*) exceeded 100 mm. The wall of arenaceous tests contains sand grains, fragments of tests from other animals, and similar foreign material held together by a secreted cement (siliceous, calcareous, or chitinous in different cases).

Secreted tests are composed of calcareous or siliceous materials similar to the cements of arenaceous tests. In many species the test contains pores through which the cytoplasm extends, and usually has an aperture at one end. In more primitive types (*Microgromia, Diplogromia,* etc.) the test has a single chamber. In others there are several to many chambers constructed in series during a growth period of several weeks to six months or longer in different species. The pattern in which the chambers are arranged is an important taxonomic characteristic. Foraminiferida are rarely pelagic, mostly bottom-dwelling animals whose tests, through geological ages, have become incorporated in sedimentary rock, especially limestones, with particular types appearing in specific deposits. For this reason, foraminiferan fossils are useful for identifying strata, especially in drilling for oil. *Globigerina* ooze, formed at certain ocean depths, represents recent deposits containing tests of *Globigerina* and related foraminifers. *See* FORAMINIFERA.

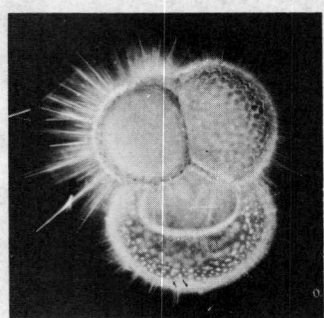

JOHN J. LEE AND HUGO D. FREUDENTHAL
GLOBIGERINA, A RHIZOPOD OF THE ORDER FORAMINIFERIDA

C. SPOROZOA

As often defined, the subphylum Sporozoa includes several groups of parasites not very closely related. Although their name implies that spores are produced, this is true for only some of the Sporozoa. Saprozoic feeding apparently is predominant; however, phagocytic activity is known in malarial parasites and *Nosema,* among others. The subphylum is usually subdivided partly on the basis of structure of spores and timing of sporulation: Telosporidea, sporulation following syngamy; Cnidosporidea, spores with polar filaments, sporulation before syngamy; Acnidosporidea, a probably heterogeneous group producing spores without polar filaments.

1. Telosporidea.—In this class there is typically an alternation of asexual and sexual phases, the latter producing infective stages (sporozoites) in which the parasites are usually transferred to new hosts. Sporozoites initiate the asexual phase, in which the parasites (except for most gregarines) undergo merogony. Sooner or later gametocytes are produced; then gametogenesis and syngamy occur. The zygotes undergo another schizogony (sporogony), which yields sporozoites. In such Telosporidea as malarial parasites, gametocytes are transferred to an invertebrate host (mosquito or other vector) for the sexual phase of the cycle. In other cases (*e.g.,* typical coccidians) both sexual and asexual phases occur in one host.

Gregarinidia.—These sporozoans constitute a subclass of Telosporidea. They are mostly parasites of invertebrates, especially annelids and arthropods, although a few occur in tunicates and hemichordates. Gregarines may be found in such cavities as the digestive tract, seminal vesicles (annelids), Malpighian tubules (certain insects), gonads (mollusks), and the coelom (annelids, echinoderms). The mature gregarine, which may measure two to ten millimetres in extreme cases, is typically elongated, ovoid to spindle-shaped, either flattened or more or less circular in cross section. There is usually a well-developed pellicle. The cortical cytoplasm may be differentiated into two layers, the deeper layer containing myonemes. In certain species both longitudinal and circular myonemes are responsible for changes in shape of the body. In the cephaline gregarines, anterior and posterior portions of the body are marked off by a transverse membrane, a structure lacking in acephaline gregarines. In certain cephaline species the anterior segment bears a struc-

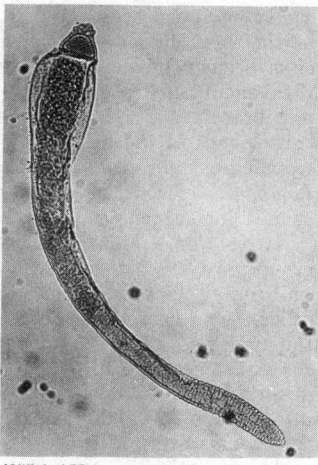

GREGARINA, A SPOROZOAN PARASITE OF THE DIGESTIVE TRACT OF ARTHROPODS

ture that anchors the parasite to some tissue of the host during the growth phase. Although saprozoic nutrition is predominant, ingestion of tissue cells has been reported (e.g., in Monocystis, Apolocystis). Life cycles resemble those of other Telosporidea except that gametocytes (gamonts) of gregarines encyst in pairs. Within this thin-walled gametocyst, oogenesis and syngamy occur. Each zygote secretes an oocyst and divides into sporozoites. The result is a spore, ready for transfer to a new host, in which sporozoites emerge from the cyst. Development of the sporozoite, in many species, begins inside a tissue cell but is completed in some body cavity (digestive tract, coelom, etc.). In the Schizogregarinida (Schizocystis, Ophryocystis, Selenidium, etc.) the mature trophozoite undergoes merogony. Each resulting merozoite may repeat the cycle of growth and merogony until, sooner or later, gametocytes develop to start another sexual phase. In Eugregarinida (Gregarina, Monocystis, Diplocystis, etc.) there is no merogony; each sporozoite reaching a new host grows directly into a mature gregarine. With certain exceptions (e.g., Nematopsis and Porospora, which have two different hosts, a mollusk and a crab or lobster) gregarines complete their life cycles within a single host.

Coccidia.—This subclass of Telosporidea includes parasites of vertebrates and invertebrates. They are primarily intracellular, mostly in epithelial tissues. Merogony occurs in the asexual phase and sporogony in the sexual phase. In certain genera (Adelea, etc.) gametocytes associate in pairs but do not produce a gametocyst. In other Coccidia (Eimeria, Isospora, etc.) the two kinds of gametocytes differentiate independently. Life cycles are usually completed within a single host. However, a two-host cycle occurs in certain genera (Haemogregarina, Hepatozoon, Karyolysus), the sexual phase involving an invertebrate host (leech, tick, mite, tsetse fly, etc.). Certain Coccidia are important as parasites of cattle, sheep, poultry, fox, mink, etc. *Isospora hominis* occurs in man.

Haemosporidia.—In this telosporidean subclass the zygote is extracellular for a time before sporogony begins. No true spores are developed. The sexual phase occurs in an invertebrate host that inoculates naked sporozoites into a vertebrate. In Plasmodiidae (Plasmodium) and Haemoproteidae (Haemoproteus, Leucocytozoon) development of sporozoites occurs in endothelial or related cells of the vertebrate. After exoerythrocytic merogony (one or more cycles) in *Plasmodium*, which includes the agents of malaria, some of the merozoites may invade erythrocytes to initiate a series of erythrocytic reproductive cycles. Others continue the exoerythrocytic cycle. Sooner or later, some of the erythrocytic merozoites become gametocytes, ready for ingestion by a mosquito, in which gametogenesis, syngamy, and sporogony occur. In *Haemoproteus* the stages that appear in circulating erythrocytes are gametocytes; gametogenesis, syngamy, and sporogony occur in bloodsucking flies (e.g., Simulium).

Babesia, Theileria, and related forms, often assigned to the Haemosporidia, show certain differences from typical examples.

However, vertebrate and invertebrate hosts are required, asexual stages of *Babesia* appear in red corpuscles, and a sexual phase occurs in the invertebrate. Although there may be schizogony in the invertebrate host in some cases, the reproductive stages described for *Babesia,* in the vertebrate, suggest fission rather than merogony. *Babesia* and related types are of some importance as parasites of cattle, sheep, goats, horses, and dogs. *Babesia bigemina,* the agent of Texas cattle fever, is of historical interest as the first protozoon shown to be transmitted by a vector (a tick). In their work on *Babesia* in 1893, Theobald Smith and F. L. Kilbourne thus paved the way for later discoveries demonstrating the widespread importance of vectors in the transfer of animal parasites.

2. Cnidosporidea.—This class is characterized by spores that differ from those of Telosporidea in the presence of one to four coiled polar filaments. The spore, its membrane often consisting of two or three valves, contains an infective stage (sporoplasm) analogous to a telosporidian sporozoite. The spore has a "multicellular" origin, in contrast to the spore of Telosporidea. The cells that produce the polar filaments and the spore capsule, and then degenerate, may be considered "somatic" cells with specific functions. The sporoplasm in *Nosema,* according to one account, is attached to a polar filament that, during extrusion from the spore, pulls the sporoplasm with it. Other observations indicate that the polar filament is a hollow tube through which the sporoplasm travels from the spore to a tissue cell of the host. The liberated sporoplasm eventually grows into a plasmodium.

Myxosporida.—This cnidosporidian order features bivalved spores containing one to four polar filaments and one sporoplasm. Most species are parasites of fishes, although a few invade reptiles and amphibians. Infections may involve body cavities (gall bladder, urinary bladder, kidney tubules) or various tissues, according to the species. Heavy infections are frequently fatal. Representative types are *Unicapsula muscularis,* causing "wormy disease" of the muscles in halibut, and *Myxobolus pfeifferi,* causing "boil disease" of barbel.

Actinomyxida.—In this order the spore has three valves, which are sometimes drawn out into spines. There are usually three polar filaments and one to many sporoplasms. Species are known from the coelom and digestive tract of annelids and sipunculids. *Sphaeractinomyxon* and *Triactinomyxon* are representative.

Microsporida.—This is an order of small, usually intracellular parasites that produce small (2–20 microns) spores with membranes not showing distinct valves. There are usually one sporoplasm and one polar filament, rarely two (Telomyxa). Microsporida occur in Myxosporida, flukes, tapeworms, nematodes, frogs, fishes, and arthropods. *Nosema bombycis* causes "pebrine" of silkworms, a disease investigated by Louis Pasteur in 1865. A related species, *N. apis,* was found to cause a serious disease of bees.

3. Acnidosporidea.—This is a heterogeneous class in which spores, if any, lack polar filaments. Organisms often included in the class fall into two distinct groups that may be designated as subclasses.

Sarcosporidia.—In this subclass mature stages (cysts) occur in striated or cardiac muscle in reptiles, birds, and mammals (horse, cattle, sheep, pig, etc.). All these parasites apparently belong to one genus, *Sarcocystis.* Infection leads to the appearance in muscle of characteristic sarcocysts containing many uninucleate "spores," which are not encysted and may be motile. Heavy infections may cause muscular weakness and emaciation.

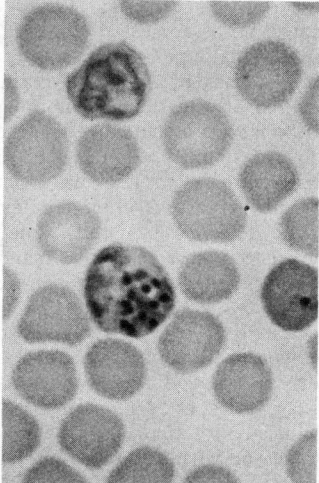

PLASMODIUM IN HUMAN RED BLOOD CELLS: RING STAGE IN UPPER CELL, MEROZOITES IN CENTRE CELL

Production of an endotoxin (sarcocystine), quite toxic for rabbits, has been reported. Infections have been produced experimentally by feeding infected muscle to mice. The life cycle is incompletely known.

Haplosporidia.—This is a subclass in which the infective stage is an amoeboid form transmitted in a cyst (spore) that lacks polar filaments. The spore membrane may be bivalved, operculate, or drawn out into tails or filaments. Species occur in copepods and other crustaceans, insects, lower chordates, fishes, annelids, nemertines, tapeworms, and certain protozoans. Haplosporidia may live in body cavities or may invade epithelia. The trophozoite, upon liberation from the spore, typically develops into a plasmodium. In certain species uninucleate sporoblasts become differentiated within the plasmodium and produce spores. *Haplosporidium*, represented in annelids, tunicates, mollusks, and crustaceans, is the type genus.

D. Ciliophora

This protozoan subphylum contains only one class, Ciliatea, organisms that differ from those of other groups in the possession of cilia or derivative organelles at some stage in the life cycle, in the presence normally of both macronuclei and micronuclei, and in the absence of true syngamy. Two subclasses constitute the class: Holotricha and Spirotricha.

1. Holotricha.—These ciliates lack cirri and the prominent membranelles characteristic of the Spirotricha. Many are uniformly ciliated, but the more specialized show extensive losses of cilia.

Gymnostomatida.—This is a large order in which the ciliation is commonly uniform except in certain genera where enlarged cilia surround the cytostome. There is no well-developed buccal cavity or vestibulum; the apical, anteroventral, or occasionally lateral cytostome opens usually at the surface of the body. The cytopharynx may be surrounded by rodlike trichites (as in *Prorodon*) or by a pharyngeal "basket" in which the skeletal elements are fused together (*Chilodonella*, etc.). The majority, equipped with trichites, are carnivores that can ingest large prey such as other ciliates. Those having a pharyngeal basket are herbivores.

Suctorida.—Members of this order are marine or freshwater forms, sessile or floating, without cilia in adult stages although the basal granules persist. Free-living adults have hollow suctorian tentacles for capture of prey and ingestion of food, which flows down a tentacle and into a food vacuole formed at its base. Reproduction involves budding; in most cases the bud is a ciliated larva that is active only a short period before metamorphosis. The adult stage may change directly into a ciliated stage, which later may turn into a suctorian form or may encyst. Many sessile Suctorida have stalks similar to those of various Peritrichida. *Endosphaera* includes parasites of certain Peritrichida; *Allantosoma* has been reported from the intestine of horses; *Podophrya*, *Tokophrya*, and *Acineta* include free-living types.

Chonotrichida.—Except for a few species of *Spirochona*, the members of this order are marine, and mostly sessile on swimming crustaceans. The adults are somewhat vase-shaped, the free end of the body being modified into a single or double funnel at the base of which lies the cytostome. This funnel has been considered analogous to the vestibulum of various other ciliates. Cilia of the adult stage may be reduced to those on the funnel. Reproduction involves budding; the ciliated larva resembles many Gymnostomatida. *Chilodochona*, *Stylochona*, and *Spirochona* are representative.

Trichostomatida.—These ciliates usually have a well-developed vestibulum leading to a ventral cytostome, but do not have a true buccal cavity. *Balantidium*, formerly considered a heterotrich, is included here. Some of the parasitic types (*Blepharocorys*, *Charon*, *Cyathodinium*) show a reduced somatic ciliature. Reproduction may occur in active stages or within a reproductive cyst by fission (Colpodidae) or budding (*Conidiophrys*). A ciliated larva appears in *Conidiophrys*, sessile ectoparasites of crustaceans.

Hymenostomatida.—The ciliates of this order have a buccal cavity equipped typically (*e.g.*, *Tetrahymena*) with a membrane on the right and a zone of membranelles on the left. In *Paramecium* occur peniculi, bandlike zones of cilia probably homologous with membranelles of other hymenostomes, and a small endoral membrane at the right margin of the buccal cavity, which probably corresponds to the membrane of other genera. Although hypertrophied membranes (*e.g.*, *Pleuronema*) or membranelles (*e.g.*, *Lembadion*) occur in certain genera, these buccal organelles are usually inconspicuous.

Astomatida.—This parasitic order shows no cytostome. The group may be phylogenetically heterogeneous. Most species are uniformly ciliated. Some have spinelike holdfast organelles, others (*e.g.*, *Protoradiophrya*) contain skeletal fibrils of unknown function, and a few (*e.g.*, *Haptophrya*) have an anterior sucker for attachment. Reproduction involves typical binary fission or, in certain genera, repeated fission without prompt separation, producing chains of individuals. Most species occur in annelids; a few in flatworms, crustaceans, and amphibians.

Apostomatida.—This is an order of specialized parasites, mostly in crustaceans, rarely in annelids. Except for such cases as *Cryptocaryum*, there is a small ventral cytostome surrounded by a peculiar rosette containing cilia. The homologies of the rosette, which presumably functions in ingestion, are uncertain. A polymorphic life cycle, including fission in a cyst to produce migratory larvae, is known for several species. *Foettingeria* and *Gymnodinioides* are representative.

Thigmotrichida.—An anterior group of thigmotactic cilia is responsible for the name of this order, although such cilia, serving to attach these parasites to their hosts, are not restricted to Thigmotrichida. The cytostome and buccal ciliature lie in the posterior half of the body, and may even be terminal. A few genera (*e.g.*, *Hypocoma*) have replaced the cytostome with a suctorial tentacle, apparently used for ingestion but perhaps not homologous with suctorian tentacles.

Peritrichida.—This large order contains mostly sessile, more or less conical ciliates, usually with a stalk, the matrix of which is secreted by a scopula, a differentiated area of cytoplasm at the pole opposite the cytostome. In Vorticellidae, the stalk contains a spiral muscle that can coil up, drawing the body down toward the point of attachment. Ciliature of the adult is usually limited to the oral disc—two or three semimembranes (component cilia fused basally) winding counterclockwise toward the cytostome. The outer organelle, becoming a membrane in the buccal cavity (infundibulum), is probably homologous with the buccal membrane of other ciliates. Fission, in sessile species, produces a sessile

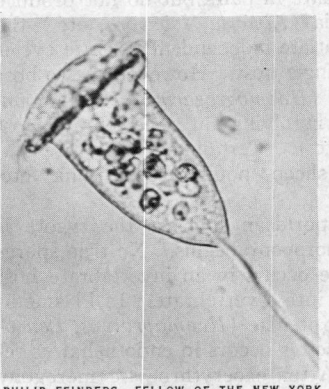

VORTICELLA, A CILIATE WITH A LONG CONTRACTILE STALK

daughter and a telotroch. The latter develops a ciliary girdle before completion of fission and swims for a time before undergoing metamorphosis, during which the locomotor cilia are resorbed. An adult also may develop a ciliary girdle, discard its stalk, and become a telotroch. Peritrichida include solitary (*Vorticella*) or colonial (*Carchesium*, *Epistylis*, *Zoothamnium*) stalked forms; more or less flattened ectoparasites and endoparasites (*Trichodina*, *Urceolaria*); loricate sessile types (*Cothurnia*, *Vaginicola*); swimmers with rudimentary stalks (*Hastatella*); and permanent telotrochs (*Telotrochidium*).

2. Spirotricha.—This subclass is characterized by prominent membranelles extending clockwise toward the cytostome. A buccal membrane may be present. Somatic cilia are often reduced in number and are replaced by cirri in Hypotrichida.

Heterotrichida.—This is an order in which ciliation is commonly uniform, with a tendency toward arrangement in longitudinal rows. Membranelles near the cytostome are well developed, and, in certain genera, a buccal membrane lies at the right of the peristome. Many heterotrichs are large, some reaching a length of two millimetres. *Bursaria, Condylostoma, Spirostomum,* and *Stentor* are representative.

Oligotrichida.—Cilia are greatly reduced in number in members of this order. A series of membranelles is usually found near the cytostome and a spiral band of larger membranelles occurs anteriorly. An equatorial band of course cilia, or bristles, arranged in groups, may also be present. *Halteria* and *Strombilidium* are representative.

Tintinnida.—Mostly pelagic, loricate marine ciliates constitute this order. The more or less conical body is elongated. The zone of membranelles winds down the funnellike peristome, while cilia are sometimes limited to the anterior third of the body. The lorica, mainly organic material to which foreign particles are sometimes added, is an open tube in some species but is more often vase-shaped, closed at the pole opposite the cytostome. *Tintinnus* and *Tintinnopsis* are representative.

Entodiniomorphida.—In this order the ciliature may be reduced to small organelles variously located. These are the rumen ciliates of ruminants and similar ciliates of other herbivores (*e.g.,* horses, elephants). In certain species the internal organization simulates a digestive tract. Certain species digest cellulose. *Diplodinium, Entodinium,* and *Cycloposthium* are representative.

Odontostomatida (= *Ctenostomatida*).—This order comprises small wedge-shaped ciliates with the mouth located on the base of the wedge. The oral (ventral) surface is flat or slightly convex; the dorsal edge approximates a semicircle or smaller arc. The pellicle is differentiated into longitudinal plates. Cilia are reduced to a few incomplete rows, and there are only eight to nine membranelles in the pouchlike buccal cavity. Most are freshwater types that thrive in putrefying material. *Discomorpha* and *Saprodinium* are representative.

Hypotrichida.—Members of this order are dorsoventrally flattened, with a firm pellicle, and with cirri usually limited to the ventral surface. Sensory bristles, perhaps rudimentary cilia, may occur in dorsal rows, less commonly on the ventral surface, adjacent to cirri. The large peristome is triangular and often shows a membrane at the right margin. The zone of membranelles may extend across the anteroventral or anterodorsal surface. *Euplotes, Oxytricha, Uronychia,* and *Gastrostyla* are representative of this order.

See also references under "Protozoa" in the Index.

BIBLIOGRAPHY.—F. J. Cole, *History of Protozoology* (1926); J. O. Corliss, *The Ciliated Protozoa* (1961); P. P. Grassé, *Traité de Zoologie,* vol. 1 (1952); R. P. Hall, *Protozoology* (1953) and *Protozoa* (1964); A. Lwoff (ed.), *Biochemistry and Physiology of the Protozoa,* vol. 1 (1951); S. H. Hutner and A. Lwoff (eds.), *Biochemistry and Physiology of Protozoa,* vol. 2 (1955); L. H. Hyman, *The Invertebrates: Protozoa Through Ctenophora* (1940); T. L. and F. F. Jahn, *How to Know the Protozoa* (1950); R. R. Kudo, *Protozoology* (1954); D. L. Mackinnon and R. S. J. Hawes, *An Introduction to the Study of Protozoa* (1961); R. D. Manwell, *Introduction to Protozoology* (1961).

(R. P. H.)

PROTURA, an order of minute (0.5–1.5 mm. long), pale, wingless, blind insects that live in damp humus and soil and feed on decaying organic matter. The order, which includes about 150 species and is worldwide in distribution, was unknown until 1907. Unlike other insects, proturans lack antennae and possess 12 complete abdominal segments, 3 of which are added postembryonically, one at a time, with nymphal molts. The front legs serve a sensory function, and are carried like antennae. The cone-shaped head carries the suctorial, styletlike mouthparts, largely retracted into it. The abdominal segments 1 to 3 have ventral processes called styli. Some au-

BY COURTESY OF "DISCOVERY," LONDON
PROTURA (ACERENTOMON DODEROI)
MAGNIFIED ABOUT 50 TIMES

thorities do not regard Protura as true insects. *See* APTERYGOTA; INSECT.

(R. L. WL.)

PROUD, JOSEPH (1745–1826), Swedenborgian minister and hymn writer with considerable gifts as a preacher, was born at Beaconsfield, Buckinghamshire, Eng., on March 22, 1745. The son of a General Baptist minister, he served Baptist churches at Knipton, Fleet, and Norwich before in 1788 openly adopting the views of Emanuel Swedenborg. As a minister of the (Swedenborgian) New Church he gathered large congregations in Birmingham, Manchester, and London. His first volume of 300 hymns appeared in 1790 and was several times reprinted. A small book of hymns for children was published in 1810. Many of his compositions are of decided merit and continue to be used in Swedenborgian worship. Proud died at Handsworth on Aug. 3, 1826.

(E. A. PA.)

PROUDHON, PIERRE JOSEPH (1809–1865), French moralist and advocate of social reform, was born on Jan. 15, 1809, at Besançon, in the traditionally rebellious Jura mountain district of France. He came of a poor family and at 19 became a working compositor; later, as a proofreader, he acquired knowl-

ARCHIV FÜR KUNST UND GESCHICHTE, BERLIN
PIERRE PROUDHON, ENGRAVING BY NORDHEIM, AFTER BAZIN

edge of theology, Latin, Greek, and Hebrew. Although he later won academic scholarships, he spurned formal training and remained a self-educated man. His interests turning to economics and politics, he published, in 1840, *Qu'est-ce que la propriété?* His answer, "Property is theft," does not, however, mark him as a socialist. Proudhon voices, instead, the typical middle-class objection to concentrated economic power and the consequent difficulty that small businessmen have long experienced in raising capital even when the security offered was perfectly sound. Far from demanding the abolition of private property in means of production, Proudhon urged that productive property be widely dispersed among owner-producers who would operate as individuals or band together in mutual benefit associations. Proudhon argued that the government should preserve an open door for investment in small businesses locally or mutually owned. To this end the government should establish a semipublic exchange and capital bank to take the place of the Bank of France and the stock exchange. This "people's bank" would furnish currency and credit at a low rate of interest, or none at all, against: (1) written orders for payment drawn by sellers of goods on the purchasers (acceptance bills); (2) payment bills issued to wage-earners by their employers; (3) credit bills presented by buyers of residential housing, industrial or agricultural property, who have been judged eligible for home loans or business loans. Thus Proudhon aimed to universalize the bill of exchange, an instrument of credit whose familiar use was in connection with the shipment of finished goods in commerce rather than in relation to home ownership or business-property transactions. Proudhon wished to divorce money and credit from any basis of gold or specie, so that the economy would constitute a universal credit union, with productivity rather than specie as the basis of credit. Labour and every product of labour would in effect be ready and exchangeable money. Because money in the form of goods or services cannot be hoarded, the aggregate supply of goods and services creates its own sufficient aggregate demand, hence unemployment caused by overproduction would be banished. With money based on productivity rather than specie, market competition would regulate prices so that consumers might buy goods at nearly their real costs of production; prices would not be burdened by surcharges of interest, rents, and capital gains realized by absentee capitalists, landlords, and speculators. Nor can the government create money or manipulate its supply to favour politically powerful special-interest groups. For in Proudhon's scheme, money is only the reflection of productive transactions whose terms are negotiated by private producers without the intervention of government.

Besides his monetary reform proposals, Proudhon projected the concept of associations of owner-producers. Each association was to make its own internal rules; the members were to surrender individual advantages for the common good of the organization. A spirit of give-and-take was to characterize, in Proudhon's vision, the relations among the separate organizations of businessmen, workers and farmers. Thus mutualism within groups would join with mutuality between groups to yield an economy of justice—economic justice not stipulated by the government but justice emanating from the ranks of the producers.

Proudhon's economic reform program was early attacked by Karl Marx (*q.v.*), in 1847, on the ground that finance capitalism, which Proudhon sought to abolish, and industrial capitalism, which Proudhon wished to strengthen, are inextricably intertwined. In the Marxist view, the unplanned nature of capitalist production sets the stage for economic instability under which speculation thrives, as well as for concentration of economic power and exploitation of labour, so that Proudhon's desired working harmony among producers cannot be realized. This controversy—with Proudhon writing *The Philosophy of Misery* and Marx countering with *The Misery of Philosophy*—is of current interest. It exhibits the roots of the continuing difference between middle-class reformers and the would-be socialist transformers of capitalism.

A prolific and passionate writer, Proudhon analyzed in the manner of an unprofessional philosopher, and his writings frequently lapse into merely perceptive journalism, especially those in the field of national and international political affairs. Proudhon portentously combined a rebellious peasant provincialism with a global grandiosity—thus he presaged in his thoughts and deeds the persistently conflicting tendencies of French capitalist democracy, toward anarchy on the one hand and despotism on the other.

Proudhon's works in English translation include: *What Is Property? System of Economic Contradictions: or the Philosophy of Misery; General Idea of Revolution in the Nineteenth Century.* His complete works were published in Paris (1923–52). *See also* ANARCHISM; SOCIALISM.

BIBLIOGRAPHY.—George Woodcock, *Pierre-Joseph Proudhon* (1956); Dudley Dillard, "Keynes and Proudhon," *J. Econ. Hist.* (May 1942); J. Salwyin Shapiro, "Pierre-Joseph Proudhon, Harbinger of Fascism," *Amer. Hist. Rev.* (July 1945).   (G. W. Z.)

PROUST, JOSEPH LOUIS (1754–1826), French chemist, whose great contribution to chemistry was his experimental establishment of the principle of the constant composition of compounds. Born at Angers on Sept. 26, 1754, he was the son of an apothecary. He studied chemistry under the direction of G. F. Rouelle, and became chief apothecary at the Salpêtrière Hospital in Paris. In his lifetime he attained eminence in chemistry in both France and Spain. In France he lectured at the Palais Royal, and in Spain he taught at the Academy of Artillery at Segovia, at the seminary at Vergara, and at the newly established Royal Laboratory at Madrid. The latter had notably excellent facilities, which enabled him to conduct (1799–1806) skilled researches on the composition of many substances, finally proving—beyond doubt that then existed—that pure compounds were strictly definite in composition by elements, no matter what their source. Thus his celebrated controversy with Claude Louis Berthollet (1748–1822) was resolved in Proust's favour. Proust did not formulate the law of definite proportions (John Dalton, 1808), but his work furnished the experimental evidence for its acceptance. After his election in 1816 to the French Academy of Sciences he returned to Angers where he died July 5, 1826.

Proust, a Frenchman, is frequently confused with William Prout (1785–1850), an Englishman. The latter was the proponent of the hypothesis in 1815 that the atomic weights of the elements are exact multiples of the atomic weight of hydrogen.   (R. K. SG.)

PROUST, MARCEL (1871–1922), French novelist whose *À la Recherche du Temps Perdu* (*Remembrance of Things Past*) is one of the supreme imaginative creations of world literature. He was born at Auteuil on July 10, 1871, the son of Adrien Proust, an eminent physician of provincial French Catholic descent, and his wife Jeanne, née Weil, of a wealthy Jewish family. After a first attack in 1880, he suffered from asthma throughout life. His childhood holidays were spent at Illiers and Auteuil, which together became the Combray of his novel, or at seaside resorts in Normandy with his maternal grandmother. At the Lycée Condorcet (1882–89), he wrote for class magazines, fell in love with a little girl named Marie de Benardaky in the Champs-Élysées, made friends whose mothers were society hostesses, and was influenced by his philosophy master Alphonse Darlu. He enjoyed the discipline and comradeship of military service at Orléans (1889–90) and studied at the École des Sciences Politiques under Henri Bergson (his cousin by marriage), Paul Desjardins, and Albert Sorel, taking "licences" in law in 1893 and in literature in 1895. Meanwhile, via the bourgeois salons of Mmes Straus, Arman de Caillavet, Aubernon, and Madeleine Lemaire, he became an observant *habitué* of the most exclusive drawing rooms of the nobility. In 1896 he published *Les Plaisirs et les jours,* a collection of short stories at once precious and profound, most of which had appeared during 1892–93 in the magazines *Le Banquet* and *La Revue Blanche.* From 1895 to 1899 he wrote *Jean Santeuil* (published 1952), an autobiographical novel which, though unfinished and ill-constructed, showed awakening genius and foreshadowed *À la Recherche.* A gradual disengagement from social life coincided with his concern about the Dreyfus affair (1897–99; *see* DREYFUS, ALFRED) and growing ill health. His discovery of Ruskin in 1899 caused him to abandon *Jean Santeuil* and to seek a new revelation in the beauty of nature and in Gothic architecture, considered as symbols of man confronted with eternity: "suddenly," he wrote, "the universe regained in my eyes an immeasurable value." On this quest he visited Venice (with his mother in May 1900), and the churches of France, and translated Ruskin's *Bible of Amiens* (1904) and *Sesame and Lilies* (1906), with prefaces in which the note of his mature prose is first heard.

The death of his father in 1903 and of his mother in 1905 left him grief-stricken and alone, but financially independent and free to attempt his great novel. At least one early version was written in 1905–06. Another, begun in 1907, and interrupted by a series of brilliant parodies of Balzac, Flaubert, Renan, Saint-Simon, and others of his favourite French authors, "L'Affaire Lemoine" (published in *Le Figaro*), through which he endeavoured to purge his style of extraneous influences, was laid aside in October 1908. Then, realizing the need to establish the philosophical basis which his novel had hitherto lacked, he wrote *Contre Sainte-Beuve* (published 1954), attacking the French critic's mandarin view of literature as a pastime of the cultivated intelligence, and putting forward his own, in which the artist's task is to release from the buried world of unconscious memory the ever living reality to which habit makes us blind. In January 1909 occurred the real-life incident of the involuntary revival of a childhood memory through the taste of tea and a rusk (later the famous "madeleine"); in May the characters of his novel invaded his essay; and in July of this crucial year he began *À la Recherche du Temps Perdu.* He thought of marrying "a very young and delightful girl" met at Cabourg, where he spent summer holidays from 1907 to 1914; but instead he retired from the world to write his novel, finishing the first draft in September 1912. After refusals from Fasquelle, the *Nouvelle Revue Française* and Ollendorff, *Du Côté de chez Swann,* the first volume, was published at the author's expense by Grasset in November 1913. Proust then planned only two further volumes, the premature appearance of which was fortunately thwarted by his anguish at the flight and death of his secretary Alfred Agostinelli, and by the outbreak of World War I.

During the war he revised the remainder of his novel, enriching and deepening its feeling, texture, and construction, increasing the realistic and satirical elements, and tripling its length. In this majestic process he transformed a work which in its earlier state was still below the level of his highest powers into one of the profoundest and most perfect achievements of the human imagination. In March 1914, instigated by the repentant Gide, the *Nouvelle Revue Française* had offered to take over his novel, but Proust in turn rejected them. Further negotiations in May–September 1916 were successful, and in June 1919 *À L'Ombre des jeunes filles en fleurs* appeared simultaneously with a reprint of *Swann* and with *Pastiches et mélanges,* a miscellaneous volume containing "L'Affaire Lemoine" and the Ruskin prefaces. In December 1919, through Léon Daudet's recommendation, *À L'Ombre* received the Prix Goncourt and Proust suddenly became world famous. Three more installments appeared in his lifetime, with the benefit of his final revision: *Le Côté de Guermantes,* vol. 1 (October 1920), vol. 2, with *Sodome et Gomorrhe I* (May 1921); and *Sodome et Gomorrhe II* (3 vol., May 1922). He died in Paris on Nov. 18, 1922, of pneumonia, succumbing to the weakness of the lungs which many had mistaken for a form of hypochondria, and struggling to the last with the revision of *La Prisonnière.* The last three parts of *À la Recherche* were published posthumously, in an advanced but not final stage of revision: *La Prisonnière* in 1923, *Albertine disparue* (originally called *La Fugitive,* though the new title may well have had Proust's authority) in 1925, and *Le Temps retrouvé* in 1927.

The Novel: Plot.—*À la Recherche du Temps Perdu* is the story of Proust's own life told as an allegorical search for truth. At first the only childhood memory available to the middle-aged Narrator is the evening of a visit from the family friend Swann, when he forced his mother to give him the goodnight kiss which she had refused. Through the accidental tasting of tea and a madeleine cake he retrieves from unconscious memory the landscape and people of his boyhood holidays in the village of Combray. In an ominous digression on love and jealousy we learn the unhappy passion of Swann, a Jewish dilettante received in high society, for the courtesan Odette, met in the bourgeois salon of the Verdurins during the years before the Narrator's birth. As an adolescent the Narrator falls in love with Swann and Odette's daughter Gilberte in the Champs-Élysées. During a seaside holiday at Balbec he meets the handsome young nobleman Saint-Loup, Saint-Loup's strange uncle the baron de Charlus, and a band of young girls led by Albertine. He falls in love with the duchesse de Guermantes, but after an autumnal visit to Saint-Loup's garrison-town Doncières, is cured when he meets her in society. As he travels through the Guermantes world its apparent poetry and intelligence is dispersed, and its real vanity and sterility revealed. Charlus is discovered to be a homosexual, pursuing the elderly tailor Jupien and the young violinist Morel; and the vices of Sodom and Gomorrah henceforth proliferate through the novel. On a second visit to Balbec the Narrator suspects Albertine of loving women, carries her back to Paris, and keeps her captive. He witnesses the tragic betrayal of Charlus by the Verdurins and Morel, and his own jealous passion is only intensified by the flight and death of Albertine. When he attains oblivion of his love Time is Lost, beauty and meaning have faded from all he ever pursued and won, and he renounces the book he had always hoped to write. A long absence in a sanatorium is interrupted only by a wartime visit to Paris, bombarded like Pompeii or Sodom from the skies. Charlus, disintegrated by his vice, is seen in Jupien's infernal brothel, and Saint-Loup, married to Gilberte and turned homosexual, dies heroically in battle. After the war, at the princesse de Guermantes' afternoon reception, the Narrator becomes aware, through a series of incidents of unconscious memory, that all the beauty he has experienced in the past is eternally alive. Time is Regained, and he sets to work, racing against death, to write the very novel we have just read.

The Novel: Structure, Meaning and Vindications.—Proust's novel has a circular construction, and must be considered in the light of the revelation with which it ends. Throughout a story which ostensibly tells of the irrevocability of Time Lost, the forfeiture of innocence through experience, the emptiness of love and friendship, the vanity of human endeavour, the triumph of sin and despair, the author has in fact reinstated the extratemporal values of Time Regained. Proust's subject is salvation, his message that the life of every day is supremely important, full of

moral joy and beauty which, though we lose them through faults inherent in human nature, are indestructible and recoverable. Other patterns of redemption are shown in counterpoint to the main theme: the Narrator's parents are saved by their natural goodness, great artists (the novelist Bergotte, the painter Elstir, the composer Vinteuil) through the vision of their art, Swann through suffering in love, even Charlus through the Lear-like grandeur of his fall. Proust's novel is, ultimately, both optimistic and set in the context of human religious experience. "I realised that the materials of my work consisted of my own past," says the Narrator at the moment of Time Regained. An important quality in the understanding of *À la Recherche* lies in its meaning for Proust himself as the allegorical story of his own life, from which its events, places, and characters are taken. In his quest for Time Lost he invented nothing, but altered everything, selecting, fusing, and transmuting the facts so that their underlying unity and universal significance should be revealed, working inward to himself and outward to every aspect of the human condition. *À la Recherche* is comparable in this respect not only with other major novels but with such creative and symbolic autobiographies as Goethe's *Dichtung und Wahrheit* and Chateaubriand's *Mémoires d'Outre-Tombe,* both of which influenced Proust.

Proust's projection of his own sexual inversion upon his characters is aesthetically justified by his use of this vice, parallel with snobbism, vanity, and cruelty, as a major symbol of original sin. His insight into women and the love of men for women (which he himself experienced for the many female originals of his heroines) remained unimpaired, and he is among the greatest novelists of both normal and abnormal love. Other frequent charges against Proust are as misleading as those of pessimism, antireligion, or obsession with homosexuality. He has been thought idle, unproductive, weak-willed, corrupted by snobbism, ill-equipped for philosophy, and absorbed in microscopic detail. In fact he worked unceasingly, prolifically, and with iron will from early youth, always in the direction of his great novel. He was an anti-snob with genuine interest in a brilliant and dying culture, a metaphysician with academic training and individual genius, and an impressionist whose detail is an imagery subordinated to the totality of his creation: "my instrument," he said, "is not a microscope, but a telescope directed upon Time." In general, hostile criticism of Proust, being based on a priori assumptions or on misuse of the biographical approach, has tended to reveal deficiencies not in Proust but in the scholarship or sensibility of its exponents.

Proust's Style, Influence, Reputation, Correspondence.—Proust's mature prose style, although the remote inspiration of such varied precursors as La Bruyère, Saint-Simon, Chateaubriand, Balzac, Renan, and Ruskin, and of such contemporaries as Anatole France, Stephane Mallarmé, Anna de Noailles, Francis Jammes, and Robert de Montesquiou is demonstrable, remains unique and self-engendered in its union of speed and protraction, precision and iridescence, force and enchantment, classicism and symbolism. His influence has indirectly affected the whole climate of the 20th-century novel, and is more directly visible in André Gide's *Les Faux-Monnayeurs,* Jacques de Lacretelle's *Silbermann,* Virginia Woolf's *The Waves,* and Anthony Powell's novel sequence *The Music of Time.* His reputation, though still imperfectly liberated from the superficial and semihostile assessments of the first generation of Proustian criticism, has always been safe with the general reader, and continues to rise toward its true level. A new critical tendency, in which Proust's work is considered sympathetically from within and on its own terms (cf. entries under G. Brée, H. Moss, R. Shattuck, and P. A. Spalding in the *Bibliography*), may well predominate in the final judgment.

Proust's enormous correspondence, of which more than 2,000 letters had been printed by 1964 and about twice as many more awaited publication, is remarkable for its elegance and nobility of style and thought, its communication of his living presence, and as one of the most significant exhibitions in all literature of the raw material from which a great artist built his universe.

BIBLIOGRAPHY.—*Editions and Translations.*—The standard text of *À la Recherche* is the Pléiade edition, by P. Clarac and A. Ferré,

680 PROUSTITE—PROVENÇAL LANGUAGE

3 vol. (1954). C. K. Scott-Moncrieff's translation, *Remembrance of Things Past,* 12 vol. (1922–31); vol. 12, *Time Regained,* trans. by S. Hudson [pseudonym of S. Schiff], also in U.S. as *Past Recaptured,* 1932, trans. by F. A. Blossom), is an English classic. Other excellent translations are *Jean Santeuil* (1955) and *Miscellaneous Writings* (1948), by G. Hopkins; *By Way of Sainte-Beuve,* by S. Townsend Warner (1958); *Pleasures and Regrets,* by L. Varèse (1948); *Letters of M. Proust,* by M. Curtiss (1950). Collected articles in *Chroniques* (1927).

Bibliography and Correspondence.—M. Proust, *Lettres à la NRF,* which contains the standard bibliography of Proust's own works (1932); D. W. Alden, *Marcel Proust and His French Critics* (1940), continued for the period after 1940 in D. W. Alden, *Bibliography of Critical and Biographical References for the Study of Contemporary French Literature* (1949–   ); O. Klapp, *Bibliographie der französischer Literaturwissenschaft* (1960–   ). Letters in *Correspondance générale de M. Proust,* 6 vol. (1930–36); also letters to A. Bibesco (1949; trans. 1953), R. de Billy (1930), Lucien Daudet (1929), André Gide (1949), R. Hahn (1956), G. de Lauris (1948; trans. 1949), P. Morand (1949), M. Nordlinger (1942), Mme Proust (1953; trans. 1956), Jacques Rivière (1955); bibliography and chronology of letters in P. Kolb, *Correspondance de M. Proust* (1949).

Biography and Criticism.—A. Maurois, *Quest for Proust* (1950); G. D. Painter, *M. Proust: a Biography,* 2 vol. (1959–65); D. Leon, *Introduction to Proust* (1940); H. March, *Two Worlds of Marcel Proust* (1948); R. H. Barker, *M. Proust* (1959); M. Bibesco, *Marcel Proust at the Ball* (1956); H. Bonnet, *M. Proust de 1907 à 1914* (1959); G. Brée, *M. Proust and Deliverance from Time* (1956); G. Cattaui, *M. Proust: Documents iconographiques* (1957); A. Ferré, *Années de collège de M. Proust* (1959); F. C. Green, *Mind of Proust* (1949); P. H. Johnson, *Six Proust Reconstructions* (1958); P. L. Larcher, *Parfum de Combray* (1945); H. Moss, *The Magic Lantern of M. Proust* (1962); R. Shattuck, *Proust's Binoculars* (1963); P. A. Spalding, *Reader's Handbook to Proust* (1952); W. A. Strauss, *Proust and Literature* (1957). *See* also Edmund Wilson, in *Axel's Castle* (1931). For important articles, including new texts and letters of Proust, *see* the annual *Bulletin de la Société des Amis de M. Proust* (1950–   ).

(G. D. P.)

PROUSTITE, a mineral consisting of silver sulfarsenite, known also as light red silver ore, and an important source of the metal. It is closely allied to the corresponding sulfantimonite, pyrargyrite (*q.v.*), or dark red silver ore, from which it was distinguished by the chemical analyses of J. L. Proust in 1804, after whom the mineral received its name. The composition is Ag_3AsS_3. The colour is scarlet-vermilion and the lustre adamantine; crystals are transparent and very brilliant, but on exposure to light they soon become dull black and opaque. The streak is scarlet, the hardness 2.5, and the specific gravity 5.57.

The mode of occurrence is the same as that of pyrargyrite, although proustite is less common, and the two minerals are sometimes found together. Magnificent groups of large crystals have been found at Chañarcillo in Chile; other localities which have yielded fine specimens are south Lorrain, Ont., and Freiberg and Marienberg in Saxony. It is mined as an ore in Mexico and is found in small amounts in the United States in California, Colorado, Idaho and Nevada.

PROUT, SAMUEL (1783–1852), English water colourist, born at Plymouth, Devon, Sept. 17, 1783, was educated at Plymouth grammar school. He went on sketching expeditions with B. R. Haydon, at whose father's house he met John Britton, publisher of *The Beauties of England and Wales.* He worked for Britton in London, and exhibited at the 1803 Royal Academy. He also painted marine pieces for T. Palser, received pupils, and in 1813 published *The Rudiments of Landscape, With Progressive Studies,* the first of his several handbooks for art students. From 1815 he exhibited regularly at the Water-Colour society, becoming a member four years later. A visit to France in 1819 distinguished him from previous English topographers by his choice of foreign townscapes as subjects, and that same year he attempted the recently discovered process of lithography. His *Illustrations of the Rhine* (1824) comprised the first of many lithographs resulting from frequent visits to France, Germany, the Netherlands and Italy. He died at Camberwell, Feb. 10, 1852. Prout's success was due to his fine draftsmanship, skillful composition and ability to seize upon some strikingly picturesque quality.

See Jane Quigley, *Prout and Roberts* (1926).   (D. L. FR.)

PROVENÇAL LANGUAGE is one of the Romance languages (*q.v.*). In its narrow meaning the term refers to the speech, or the dialects, of the region called Provence. But more

often it is the collective term for all southern dialects of France. Similarly the alternative name *langue d'oc* (*oc* "yes," as compared with northern *oïl,* modern *oui*) refers generally to all idioms of the Midi (the south), although Languedoc as a politico-geographic term signifies only part of the region. In literary history, however, Provençal is the name given to the artificially homogeneous standard language employed by the troubadours (*q.v.*) of the 12th, 13th and 14th centuries.

The boundary separating Provençal (in the widest sense) from northern French runs from the estuary of the Gironde eastward along the northern edge of the Massif Central, crosses the Rhone between Vienne and Valence, and moves toward the Alps; but in the middle ages the frontier lay much farther to the north, being anchored in the west at the mouth of the Loire and in the east in the southern Vosges mountains.

This linguistic boundary, which is so trenchant as to be one between languages rather than dialects, resulted from differing historic and cultural developments. The Midi, or at least part of it, was conquered by the Romans in 122 B.C., about 70 years before the rest of Gaul. A flourishing and rich province, it was quickly and profoundly romanized. Moreover, the Germanic invasions of the middle ages were culturally less effective than they were in the north; even that of the Franks (so decisive elsewhere as to give their name to the whole country) exerted little influence. The southern dialects, in comparison with the northern, are therefore more conservative in their retention of Latin traits and less affected by the Germanic superstratum.

The medieval history of the Midi is that of many small feudal holdings in constant dispute among themselves and with outsiders. The country never attained national independence, but it was officially united with the rest of France in 1486. The greatest single catastrophe to befall the south was the crusade against the Albigenses (*see* CATHARI) early in the 13th century. What began as a religious expedition under the aegis of the church against the Albigensian heresy ended as political suppression of the south and its feudal lords by northern competitors. This calamity brought about the end of the independent flourishing of the Midi's native culture, particularly of its troubadour literature; it was assuredly responsible for the end of Provençal as an interregional standard idiom, for the re-emergence of local dialects, and for the spread, albeit slow, of standard northern French, in particular Francien, the dialect of the Île-de-France, as the literary and official language of the whole region.

Henceforth the southern dialects, bereft of a southern standard language in competition with Francien, sank to the level of patois of strictly local and familiar currency. The present dialects may be classified as follows: (1) Provençal (in the narrow sense as idioms of the Provence proper); (2) Auvergnat and Limousin; (3) Gascon (*see* below). Each of these larger divisions can of course be subdivided into smaller dialects, in the past as much as, or even more than, now.

This dialectal fragmentation of the south raises the question as to which of the southern dialects was employed in troubadour poetry, or which formed the core of their fairly homogeneous language. The main obstacle to a satisfying answer, apart from the insufficient knowledge of the medieval dialects of the Midi, is that Provençal, even in the works of the oldest troubadours (Guil-

Late spoken Latin	Old Provençal	Old French	Modern French
Vowels			
amare	*amar*	*amer*	*aimer*
pede(m)	*pe*	*pie(d)*	*pied*
solu(m)	*sol*	*suel*	*seul*
flore(m)	*flor*	*flour*	*fleur*
fide(m)	*fe*	*fei*	*foi*
auru(m)	*aur*	*or*	*or*
Consonants			
caballu(m)	*caval*	*cheval*	*cheval*
gallina(m)	*galina*	*geline*	*geline*
scribere	*escriure*	*escrire*	*écrire*
castellu(m)	*castels*	*chastels*	*château*
causas	*cauzas*	*choses*	*choses*
securu(m)	*segur*	*seür*	*sûr*
matura(m)	*madura*	*meür*	*mûr*
laudare	*lauzar*	*louer*	*louer*

hem IX, Marcabrun, Cercamon), is already fully developed and standardized, so that the history of its formation escapes linguistic scrutiny. On the whole, it seems to represent a central rather than a peripheral southern speech area. The history of the Provençal language largely deals with the language of the troubadours since little else is known until recent times. It is convenient to compare it with the northern Francien standard in order to show its peculiarities. *See* also FRENCH LANGUAGE and, especially for earliest developments from Latin, ROMANCE LANGUAGES.

Where northern dialects nasalize a vowel before a following *m* or *n*, with eventual absorption of the consonant (*pontem* > *pō*), Provençal may not nasalize at all, or may nasalize the vowel with retention of the consonant (*pontem* > *pon, põn*).

Gascon has certain peculiarities which set it apart from other southern dialects. For example, Latin medial *-ll-* appears as *-r-* (*appellare* > *apera[r]*), final *-l* as *-t* (*bell[um]* > *bet*), initial *r-* as *arr-* (*ramu[m]* > *arram*), initial *f-* as *h-* (*femina* > *hemna, henno*). For these and other reasons some do not include Gascon among the Provençal dialects (in the wider sense). But then the only alternative is to establish it as a separate Romance language, as some linguists do with Catalan or Franco-Provençal or both.

In morphology, the declension of Old Provençal retains, as does Old French, a two-case system, one for the subject and one for the nonsubject case. In the modern dialects, a one-case (that is, no-case) system prevails.

The Provençal verb partakes of all the changes from Latin to Romance in general; but the typically Provençal features relate it more to Ibero-Romance (Spanish, Portuguese, Catalan; *q.v.*) than to French.

A renascence of southern speech ways was unsuccessfully attempted during the 19th century, mainly through the efforts of Frédéric Mistral (*q.v.*), who attempted to create a new literary standard language for the Midi, based chiefly on several patois of the Bouches-du-Rhône district.

BIBLIOGRAPHY.—C. H. Grandgent, *An Outline of Phonology and Morphology of Old Provençal* (1905); D. C. Haskell, *Provençal Language and Literature* (1925); R. T. Hill and T. G. Bergin, *Anthology of Provençal Troubadours* (1941); Frédéric Mistral, *Lou tresor dou Felibrige: Dictionnaire Provençal-Français*, new ed. (1932); J. Ronjat, *Grammaire istorique [sic] des parlers provençaux modernes* (1930–41). (E. PM.)

PROVENÇAL LITERATURE (*i.e.*, the literature written in the Oc-speaking southern France and, for a limited period, in Italian and Spanish cultural dependencies; *see* PROVENÇAL LANGUAGE) can be clearly divided into three periods: the first, a period of unity during which a literary language called "classic Provençal" was universally written, if not spoken (11th–15th century); the second, a period of dispersion in which a variety of provincial dialects were developed (16th–18th century); and the third, a period of partial recovery (19th–20th century).

FIRST PERIOD

Origins.—The new vernacular literature took a poetic form, and its oldest monuments show a virtuosity and a variety that indicate that poetry had already been practised for some time. The oldest piece of Provençal verse extant, a refrain attached to a Latin poem in a Vatican manuscript, is said to belong to the 10th century. More important, however, is a 257-line fragment of didactic verse preserved in an Orléans manuscript and frequently edited since F. J. Raynouard first printed it in his *Choix des poésies originales des troubadours* (1816–21). It is the beginning of an adaptation of Boëthius' treatise *De Consolatione Philosophiae* by an anonymous clerk. The handwriting of the manuscript is that of the period A.D. 1000–50; the language seems to belong most probably to the Limousin or to the Marche. A little later on, at the close of the 11th century, we have the poems of William IX, duke of Aquitaine (Guilhem VII of Poitiers). They consist of 11 very diverse strophic pieces and were meant to be sung. Several are love songs; one relates a *bonne fortune* in very free terms; and the most important of all, of about 1119, expresses in touching and often noble words the writer's regret for the frivolity of his past life and the apprehensions which oppressed him as he bade farewell, perhaps forever, to his country and his young son.

There is no reason to believe that William created the type of poetry of which he is to us the oldest representative: it may have been his high rank that saved some of his work from oblivion while that of his predecessors and contemporaries disappeared. The contrast in form and subject between Boëthius' poem and the stanzas of William IX is an indication that by the 11th century Provençal poetry was being rapidly developed in various directions. Whence came this poetry? How and by whose work was it formed? The view which seems to meet with general acceptance (even if a slight influence from Arabic poetry is admitted) is that Romance poetry sprang out of a popular poetry quietly holding its place from Roman times. Gradually the poets must have found themselves obliged to compound with the refinement of an aristocracy that had become, from century to century, more and more refined.

From what class of persons did this poetry proceed? Latin chroniclers of the middle ages mention *ioculares, ioculatores,* men of a class not very highly esteemed whose profession consisted in amusing their audience either by what we still call jugglers' tricks, by exhibiting performing animals, or by recitation and song. They were called *joglars* in Provençal, *jonglers* or *jongleurs* in French. From among them rose the troubadours (*q.v.*) who originally may have been *joglars* skilled in poetry, thence mere poets staying at a court or riding from castle to castle with a common *joglar* as a performer and companion.

The Provençal love songs reflect the social conditions obtaining in the Midi under feudalism. The daughters of territorial lords, who might well become rich heiresses, were married for political reasons, not to satisfy their own inclinations; but, once married, they seem to have enjoyed a very generous measure of personal liberty. Consequently, they welcomed the attentions of their husbands' dependents, who, as courtiers, would address flattering songs of love to them. As the poets were usually far beneath the ladies in social status, they wrote in a most guarded and respectful style, as though they had very little hope of having their love requited. This profession of "courtly" or "chivalrous" love became a matter of convention (*see* COURTLY LOVE); but it would be a mistake to assume that the real sentiments or experiences were invariably as platonic as the expression given to them.

The Troubadours.—By the end of the 11th century a clear distinction had been drawn between the lower sort of *joglars* and the refined poets; and it is to the poets as such that the name troubadour belongs, comprising as it does not only accomplished poets of the lower ranks of society but also some of the great nobles who wrote poetry. In the Limousin lived a viscount of Ventadour, Eble II, who early in the 12th century seems to have been brought into relation with William IX of Aquitaine and, according to a contemporary historian, Geffrei, prior of Vigeois, *erat valde gratiosus in cantilenis* ("he was a composer of very graceful songs"). We possess none of his compositions; but under his influence Bernart de Ventadour was trained to poetry. Bernart gained the love of the lady of Ventadour and, when on the discovery of their amour he had to depart elsewhere, received a gracious welcome from William IX's granddaughter Eleanor of Aquitaine, consort (from 1152) of Henry II of England. Of Bernart's compositions we possess about 50 songs of elegant simplicity; some of which may be taken as the most perfect specimens of Provençal love poetry. At the same period, or earlier, flourished Cercamon, a Gascon, who composed, says his old biographer, "pastorals according to the ancient custom" (*pastorelas a la uzansa antiga*). Among the earliest troubadours is Marcabrun, a pupil of Cercamon's, from whose pen we have about 40 pieces, those which can be approximately dated ranging from about 1135 to about 1148. His songs, several of which are concerned with contemporary history, are free from the commonplaces of their class, and contain curious strictures on the corruptions of the time. Jaufré Rudel of Blaye, the singer of the *amor de lonh* (far-away love), is scarcely less famous.

Only a few of the troubadours can be cited here. They include Peire d'Alvernhae, Raimbaut III d'Orange, Béatrix de Die, Arnaut Daniel (remarkable for his complicated versification and the inventor of the *sestina*), Arnaut de Mareuil (less famous than

Arnaut Daniel, but surpassing him in elegant simplicity of form and delicacy of sentiment), Bertran de Born (famous for the part he is said to have played both with his sword and his *sirventés* in the struggle between Henry II of England and his rebel sons), Peire Vidal of Toulouse (a poet of varied inspiration who grew rich with gifts bestowed on him by the greatest nobles), Giraut de Borneil, or Guiraut de Bornelh (*lo maestre dels trobadors* and acknowledged master of *trobar clus* or "close" style, though he also composed songs of charming simplicity), Gaucelm Faidit (who wrote a touching lament or *planh* on the death of Richard Coeur de Lion), Folquet de Marseille (who from being a troubadour became first a monk, then an abbot, and finally bishop of Toulouse), the chivalrous Raimbaut de Vaqueyras, the truculent monk of Montaudon, the satirical Peire Cardenal, and "the last troubadour," Guiraut Riquier. Of lesser importance, but still to be remembered among the 460 troubadours whose works exist, are: Peire Rogier, Peire Raimon, Raimon de Miraval, Aimeric de Pegulhan, Rigaut de Barbezieux, Guiraut de Calanson, Uc de Saint-Circ, Peirol, Perdigon, Cadenet, Guilhem Figueira, Montanhagol, Folquet de Lunel, Bertran Carbonel, Elias de Barjols, Bertran de Lamanon, Pons de Chapteuil, Cerveri de Girone, Bonifacio Calvo, Sordello.

The troubadours who were not themselves great feudatories could hardly expect to obtain a livelihood from any quarter other than the generosity of the great. It will consequently be well to mention the most important at least of those princes who are known to have been patrons and some, indeed, themselves poets: in France, Eleanor of Aquitaine, Henry Curtmantle, Richard Coeur de Lion, Ermengarde of Narbonne, Raymond V and Raymond VI of Toulouse, Alfonso II and Raymond Berengar IV, counts of Provence, Barral de Baux, William VIII, lord of Montpellier, Henri I, Hugh IV and Henri II, counts of Rodez; in Spain, Alfonso II and Pedro II, kings of Aragon, Alfonso IX and Alfonso X, kings of Castile; in Italy, Boniface I, marquis of Montferrat, Frederick II, emperor, Azzo VI and Azzo VIII, marquis of Este. These are a few only of the great patrons.

The decline and fall of troubadour poetry was due mainly to political causes. When in the first decades of the 13th century the Albigensian War had ruined a large number of the nobles and reduced to lasting poverty a part of the Midi, the profession of troubadour ceased to be lucrative. It was then that many of these poets went to spend their last days in the north of Spain and Italy, where Provençal poetry had for more than one generation been highly esteemed. Following their example, other poets who were not natives of the Midi began to compose in Provençal; but from the middle of the 13th century, they began to abandon the foreign tongue and took to singing the same airs in the local dialects. About the same time in the Midi itself the flame of poetry had died out save in a few places—Narbonne, Rodez, Foix, and Astarac —where it kept burning feebly for a little longer. In the 14th century composition in the language of the country was still practised; but the productions of this period are mainly works for instruction and edification. The poetry of the troubadours was dead. *See* further TROUBADOURS.

Chansons de Geste and Historical Poems.—Northern France is *par excellence* the country of the *chanson de geste* (*q.v.*); but Provençal literature has some highly important specimens of the class. The first place belongs to *Girart de Roussillon,* a poem of 10,000 lines, which relates the struggles of Charles Martel with his powerful vassal Gerard of Roussillon. The existing recension seems to have originated on the borders of Limousin and Poitou; but it is a recast of an older poem no longer extant, probably either of French or at least Burgundian origin. To Limousin also seems to belong the poem *Aigar e Maurin* (end of the 12th century). Of less heroic character is the poem *Daurel e Beton* (first half of the 13th century).

Midway between legend and history may be classified the Provençal *chanson* on the siege of Antioch, a mere fragment of which, 700 verses in extent, was recovered in Madrid and published in *Archives de l'Orient latin,* vol. ii (1884). This poem (*see* G. Paris, *Romania,* xxii, 358, 1893) is one of the sources of the Spanish compilation *La Gran Conquista de Ultramar.* To history proper

belongs the *chanson* of the crusade against the Albigensians, which, in its present state, is composed of two poems, one tacked to the other: the first, containing the events from the beginning of the crusade till 1213, is the work of a cleric named Guilhem de Tudela, a moderate supporter of the crusades; the second, from 1213 to 1218, is by a vehement opponent of the enterprise. The language and style of the two parts are no less different than the opinions. The second part is certainly one of the masterpieces of Provençal literature. Finally, about 1280, Guilhem Anelier, a native of Toulouse, composed a poem on the war carried on in Navarre by the French in 1276 and 1277, a historical work of little literary merit. All these poems are in the form of *chansons de geste;* that is, in stanzas of indefinite length, with a single rhyme. *Girart de Roussillon, Aigar e Maurin,* and *Daurel e Beton* are in lines of 10, the others in lines of 12, syllables. The peculiarity of the versification in *Girart* is that the pause in the line occurs after the sixth syllable and not, as is usual, after the fourth.

Narrative Poems.—We possess only three Provençal romances of adventure: *Jaufré* (composed in the middle of the 13th century and dedicated to a king of Aragon, possibly James I), *Blandin de Cornoalha* and *Guillem de la Barra.* Connected with the romance of adventure is the novel (in Provençal *novas,* always in the plural), which is originally an account of an event "newly" happened. Some of the extant novels may be ranked with the most graceful works in Provençal literature. Two are from the pen of the Catalan author Ramon Vidal de Besalú: one, the *Castia-gilos,* is an elegant treatment of the story of the husband who disguises himself as his wife's lover in order to trap her and receives with satisfaction blows intended, as he thinks, for him whose part he is playing; the other is the recital of a question of the law of love, departing considerably from the subjects usually treated in the novels. Mention may also be made of *Novas del Papagai* by Arnaut de Carcassès, in which the principal character is an eloquent parrot, who assists the amorous enterprises of his master. Novels came to be extended to the proportions of a long romance. *Flamenca,* which belongs to the novel type, still runs to more than 8,000 lines, though the only manuscript of it has lost some leaves both at the beginning and at the end. This poem, composed in all probability in 1234, is the story of a lady who by very ingenious devices, not unlike those employed in the *Miles gloriosus* of Plautus, eludes the vigilance of her jealous husband. No book in medieval literature betokens so much quickness of intellect or is so instructive in regard to the manners and usages of polite society in the 13th century.

Didactic and Religious Poetry.—The more important works are: the Boëthius poem (unfortunately a mere fragment), already mentioned as one of the oldest documents of the language; an early (12th-century?) metrical translation of the *Disticha de moribus* of Dionysius Cato; Daude de Prades' *Auzels cassadors* (early 13th century), one of the best sources for the study of falconry; and a translation by Raimon d'Avignon (*c.* 1200) of Rogier de Parme's "Surgery." More original are some compositions of an educational character known under the name of *ensenhamenz.* The most interesting are those of Garin le Brun (12th century), Arnaut de Mareuil, Arnaut Guilhem de Marsan, Amanieu de Sescas. Their general object is the education of ladies of rank. Of metrical lives of saints we possess about a dozen, among which two or three deserve particular attention: the life of St. Fides (ed. by A. Thomas and by E. Hoepffner, 1916), written early in the 12th century; the life of St. Enimia (13th century), by Bertran of Marseilles (ed. by C. Brunel, 1916) and that of St. Honorat of Lerins by Raimon Feraut (about 1300), which is distinguished by variety and elegance of versification but is almost entirely a translation from Latin. Lives of saints (St. Andrew, St. Thomas the Apostle, St. John the Evangelist) form a part of a poem, strictly didactic, which stands out by reason of its great extent (nearly 35,000 verses) and the somewhat original conception of its scheme—the *Breviari d'amor,* a vast encyclopaedia on a theological basis, composed *c.* 1288–1300 by the Minorite friar Matfre Ermengaut of Béziers.

Drama.—The dramatic literature of the Midi consists of mysteries and miracle plays seldom exceeding 2,000 or 3,000 lines, which never developed into the enormous dramas of northern France, whose acting required several consecutive days. Generally those plays belong to the 15th century or to the 16th. Still, a few are more ancient and may be ascribed to the 14th century or even to the end of the 13th. The oldest appears to be the *Mystery of St. Agnes* (edited by K. Bartsch, 1869), written in Arles. Somewhat more recent, but not later than the beginning of the 14th century, are a mystery on the Passion of Christ and another on the Marriage of the Virgin; the latter is partly adapted from a French poem of the 13th century. A number of mysteries written in Rouergue, Provence, and Dauphiné, more or less connected with French patterns, are practically void of interest.

Prose.—In the 12th century we find in Languedoc sermons whose importance is more linguistic than literary (*Sermons du XIIe siecle en vieux provençal*, ed. by F. Armitage, 1884). About the same time, in Limousin, were translated ch. xiii–xvii of St. John's Gospel (K. Bartsch, *Chrestomathie provençale*, 1855–1904). Various translations of the New Testament and of some parts of the Old were made in Languedoc and Provence during the 13th and 14th centuries (*see* S. Berger, "Les Bibles provençales et vaudoises," *Romania,* xviii, 353, 1889; and "Nouvelles recherches sur les Bibles provençales et catalanes," *ibid.,* xix, 505, 1890). The Provençal prose rendering of some lives of saints made in the early part of the 13th century (*Revue des langues romanes,* 1890) is also more interesting from a linguistic than from a literary point of view. To the 13th century belong certain lives of the troubadours intended to be prefixed to, and to explain, their poems. Many of them were written before 1250, when the first anthologies of troubadour poetry were compiled; and some are the work of the troubadour Uc de Saint Circ. Some were composed in the north of Italy, at a time when the troubadours found more favour east of the Alps than in their own country. Considered as historical documents these biographies are of a very doubtful value. To the same period must be assigned *Las Razos de trobar* of the troubadour Ramon Vidal de Besalú (an elegant little treatise touching on various points of grammar and the poetic art), the *Donatz proensals* of Uc Faidit and the "life" of St. Douceline, who died in 1274, near Marseilles, and who founded an order of Beguines.

The leading prose work of this period is the treatise on grammar, poetry, and rhetoric known by the name of *Leys d'amors,* composed in Toulouse *c.* 1350. The decay of Provençal literature, caused by political circumstances, arrived too soon to allow of a full development of prose. Nor did anything remain, in the second quarter of the 14th century, of what had been the first Provençal classicism, except in Toulouse. There, the conventional poetry was preserved, from 1324, by the *Consistori del set mantene dors del gay sabor,* the original form of the Collège de Rhétorique, whence developed the Académie des Jeux-Floraux.

SECOND PERIOD

Owing to this, Provençal literature never died out entirely— although its life was not brilliant. The poets crowned by this body up to 1498 stand in the same relation to the troubadours as the *Meistersinger* do to the *Minnesinger* (*qq.v.*): academic correctness takes the place of inspiration. The institution flourished, even to the extent of establishing branches in Catalonia and Majorca; and in 1484, when its prosperity was threatened, a semifabulous person, Clémence Isaure, is said to have brought about a revival by instituting fresh prizes. The town of Toulouse never ceased to supply funds of some kind. In 1513 French poems were first admitted in the competitions, and under Louis XIV (from 1679) these were alone held eligible. This arrangement held good till 1893, when the town very properly transferred its patronage to a new *Escolo moundino;* but it soon restored its support to the older institution, on learning that Provençal poetry was again to be encouraged. In the two centuries that followed the glorious medieval period we have a succession of works, chiefly of a didactic and edifying character, which served to keep alive some kind of literary tradition. Religious mystery plays, which, though dull to us, probably gave keen enjoyment to the people, represent a more popular genre.

In the 16th century there are not only signs of a revival, but a strong movement toward what might be called a Provençal Renaissance. The Gascon Pey de Garros (1525?–85), author of the remarkable *Eglogues,* raised his native dialect to the rank of a literary language with his translation of the Psalms of David (1565) and inserted in his *Poesias gasconas* (1567) a manifesto that might be compared to the Declaration of Font-Ségunge, launched four centuries later by the Felibres (*see* below, *Third Period*). As early as 1579, G. de Salluste du Bartas, in his trilingual *Salut* or *Poème pour l'accueil de la Reine de Navarre,* followed the example of Pey de Garros. The Rabastens wheelwright, Augié Gaillard (1530–92), started the movement in Languedoc, and Louis Bellaud de la Bellaudière (1532–88) in Provence proper.

After Garros, in Gascony, came Guillaume Ader (1578–1638; *Lou Catounet gascoun,* 1612; *Lou Gentilome gascoun,* 1610), Louis Baron (1612–63), who celebrated with great tenderness his native village of Pouyloubrin, Géraud Bedout (1617–93; *Lou Parterre gascoun,* 1642), and J. G. d'Astros who, about the same time, with his remarkable *Trinfe de la lengouo gascouo,* proved a most elegant and witty verse writer. But the most conspicuous among the poets of the Midi between Pey de Garros and Jacques Jasmin is certainly Pierre Goudelin (Goudouli; 1579–1649) of Toulouse, "the Malherbe of Oc," who, had he written in French, would be ranked with the best poets of the period. Nicolas Saboly (1614–75) excelled in the popular form known as the *noël.*

Other 17th-century writers worth mentioning, outside Gascony, are Claude Brueys (1580–1650), remarkable chiefly for comedies dealing with duped husbands (*e.g., Jardin deys Musos Provensalos,* 1628); Gaspar Zerbin (*La Perlo deys Musos et coumedies provensalos,* 1655); Jean Michel de Nîmes, who wrote the picturesque *Embarras de la Fieiro de Beaucaire;* Daniel Sage of Montpellier (*Las Foulies,* 1650); the *avocat* Bonnet, author of the best among the open-air plays that were annually performed at Béziers on Ascension Day (a number of these, dated 1616–57, were subsequently collected, but none can compare with the opening one, Bonnet's *Jugement de Paris*); Nicolas Fizes, of Frontignan, whose vaudeville, the *Opéra de Frontignan* (1679), dealing with a slight love intrigue, and an idyllic poem on the fountain of Frontignan, show a real poetic gift. A number of Toulouse poets, mostly *lauréats* of the academy, may be termed followers of Goudelin: of these, François Boudet, who composed an ode, *Le Trinfe del Moundi* (1678), in honour of his native dialect, deserves mention. The classical revival that may be noted about this time is also generally ascribed to Goudelin's influence. Its most distinguished representative was Jean de Valès, of Montech, who made excellent translations from Virgil and Persius and wrote a brilliant burlesque of the former in the manner of Scarron (*Virgile deguisat,* 1648).

The best of the pastoral poets was François de Cortète (1585/86–1667), of Prades, whose comedies, *Ramounet* and *Miramoundo* (published, unfortunately with alterations, by his son in 1684), are written with such true feeling and in so pure a style that they can still be read with pleasure. Arnaud Daubasse (1664–1727), of Quercy, who belonged to the working classes, was patronized by the nobility in exchange for panegyrics.

In the 18th century the number of authors is much larger, but the bulk of good work produced is not equally great in proportion. The priests are mainly responsible for the literary output of Languedoc. The chief of the band is the abbé J. B. Favre (1727–83), whose *Sermoun de Moussu Sistre,* delivered by a drunken priest against intemperance, is a masterpiece. He also wrote a successful mock-heroic poem (*Lou Siège de Cadaroussa*), travesties of Homer and Virgil, a prose novel depicting the country manners of the time (*Histouèro de Jan-l'an-pres*) and two comedies which give a vivid picture of the village life that he knew so well. Two genuine poets are the brothers Rigaud of Montpellier: Auguste (1760–1835) was the author of a deservedly famous description of a vintage; and Cyrille (1750–1824) produced an equally delightful poem on the *Amours de Mounpëié.* Pierre Hellies of Toulouse (d. 1724), a poet of the people, whose vicious life finds an echo in his works, has a certain rude charm, at times distantly recalling Villon. In Provence, Toussaint Gros (1698–1748), of Lyons, holds undisputed sway. His style and language are admirable, but unfortunately he wasted his gifts largely on trivial *pièces d'occasion*. J. B. Coye's (1711–70) comedy, *Lou Novy para*, is bright and still popular, while J. B. Germain's (d. 1781) description of a visit paid by the ancient gods to Marseilles (*Bourrido dei Dious*, 1768) has considerable humour. In Gascony the greatest poet is Cyrien Despourrins (1698–*c.* 1756).

THIRD PERIOD

The Revolution produced a large body of literature, but nothing of lasting interest. When it was over, scholars like F. J. Raynouard (1761–1836), of Aix, occupied themselves with the brilliant literary traditions of the Middle Ages; newspapers sprang up (the Provençal *Bouil-Abaïsso*, started by Joseph Désanat, and the bilingual *Lou Tambourin et le menestrel*, edited by Pierre Bellot, both in 1841); poets banded together and collected their pieces in volume form (*e.g.*, the nine *troubaire* who published *Lou Bouquet prouvençaou* in 1823). Much has been written about the "forerunners of the Félibrige," and critics are sorely at variance as to the writers that most deserve this appellation. We shall not go far wrong if we include in the list Hyacinthe Morel (1756–1829); Louis Aubanel (1758–1824); Auguste Tandon (1759–1824), "the troubadour of Montpellier"; Antoine Fabre d'Olivet (1767–1825); J. J. M. Diouloufet (1785–1840); Jacques Azaïs (1778–1856); Léon d'Astros (1780–1863); F. H. J. Castil-Blaze (1784–1857); the marquis de la Fare-Alais (1791–1846). While these writers were all more or less academic and appealed to the cultured few, four poets of the people addressed a far wider public: Antoine Verdié (1779–1820), of Bordeaux, who wrote comic and satirical pieces; Jean Reboul (1796–1864), the baker of Nîmes, who never surpassed his first effort, *L'Ange et l'enfant* (1828); Victor Gelu (1806–85), relentless and brutal but undeniably powerful of his kind (*Fenian et Grouman; dix chansons provençales*, 1840); and, greatest of them all, the true and acknowledged forerunner of the Félibres, Jacques Jasmin (*q.v.*).

The Advent of the Félibrige.—In 1845 Joseph Roumanille (1818–91) of Saint-Rémy became usher in a small school of Avignon, which was attended by Frédéric Mistral (*q.v.*). Roumanille had composed some pieces in French; but, finding that his old mother could not understand them, he determined thenceforth to write in his native dialect only. These poems revealed a new world to young Mistral and spurred him on to the resolve that became the one purpose of his life: "to stir this noble race, which Mirabeau in mid-'89 still called the Provençal nation, to a renewed awareness of its glory." There is no doubt that Mistral's is the more powerful personality or that his finest work towers above that of his fellows; but in studying the Provençal renaissance, Roumanille must not be overlooked: his claims, indeed, were put forward with great force by Mistral himself (in the preface of *Lis Isclo d'or*). Roumanille's secular verse (*Li Margarideto*, 1836–47; *Li Sounjarello*, 1852; *Li Flour de Sauvi*, 1850–59, etc.) moves the reader with the sincerity of its poetry, his *noëls* are second only to those of Nicolas Saboly, his prose works (such as *Lou Mege de Cucugnan*, 1863) sparkle with delightful humour. He it was who in 1852 collected and published *Li Prouvençalo*, an anthology in which all the names yet to become famous and most of those famous already (such as Jasmin) are represented. In 1853 he was one of the enthusiastic circle that had gathered round J. B. Gaut at Aix, whose literary output is contained in the *Roumavagi deis troubaires* (1853) and in the shortlived journal *Lou Gay Saber* (1854). At the same time the first attempt at regulating the orthography of Provençal was made by him (in the introduction to his play, *La Part dou bon Dieu*, 1853). In 1854 he was one of the seven poets who, on May 21, foregathered at the castle of Font-Ségugne, near Avignon, and founded the Félibrige. The other six were Mistral, Aubanel, A. Mathieu (a schoolfellow of Mistral's at Avignon), J. Brunet, A. Tavan, and P. Giera (owner of the castle). Of these, Théodore Aubanel (1829–86; of Avignon, son of a printer and following the same calling) alone proved himself worthy to rank with Mistral and Roumanille. "Zani," the girl of his youthful and passionate love, took the veil; and this event cast a shadow over his whole life and determined the character of all his poetry (*La Miougrano entre duberto*, 1860; *Li Fiho*

d'Avignoun, 1885). His is, without a doubt, the deepest nature and temperament among the Félibres, and his lyrics are the most poignant.

The Félibrige After Roumanille, Aubanel, and Mistral.—The Félibrige increased considerably in the period after Mistral. The names of A. B. Crousillat, L. Roumieux, and of the "Muse" Antoinette de Beaucaire should be added to those of the signatories of the Font-Ségugne declaration. In Catalonia, V. Balaguer (*q.v.*) lent his glory to the movement's development, even before he joined it. Among poets of the next generation, the most illustrious is Félix Gras (1844–1901), who, as a young man, settled at Avignon. His rustic epic, *Li Carbounié* (1876), is full of elemental passion, and abounds in fine description. Gascony, which had been less closely associated with the Félibrige, admitted the Landais writer I. Salles (1821–1900) among the heirs of Despourrins and the earlier Xavier Navarrot (1799–1862). Quite independent were Auguste Fourès (1848–91) in Languedoc and Clovis Hugues (1851–1907) and Auguste Marin (1861–1904) at Marseilles. The Latin Félibrean movement developed in Montpellier with A. Roque-Ferrier (1844–1907), and the Federalist movement with F. Amouretti (1863–1903) and Marius André (*La Glòri d'Esclarmoundo*, 1894; *Eme d'arange un cargamen*, 1924). Among the wider heritage of the first Félibres should also be mentioned the Irishman Bonaparte Wyse (1826–92; *Li Piado de la Princesso*, 1882); the popular songwriter Charles Rieu (Charloun; 1845–1924); and, with poets born in Gascony (J. Noulers), Rouergue (J. Bessou), and Languedoc (A. Maffre), the somewhat artificial Joseph Roux (*La Chanson Lemousina*, 1889), and the Auvergnat Arsène Vermenouze, who, with his *Flour de Brousso* (1895) and *Jous la Cluchado* (1908), proved one of the poets most evocative of his homeland. Among those who became famous during the first half of the 20th century should be mentioned Valère Bernard (1860–1936), of Marseilles (*La Legenda d'Esclarmonda*, 1936), Prosper Estieu (1860–1939), Antonin Perbosc (1861–1944), the Languedocian poet of *Lo Got Occitan* (1903), Michel Camélat of Bigorre, Simin Palay of Béarn, and the Pyrenean *trobairitz* Philadelphe de Gerde. Contemporary with them were the *meynadiers* of the Camargue in Provence proper: Joseph d'Arbaud (1872–1950), who is less famous as the poet of *Lou Lausié d'Arle* (1913) than as author of such short stories as *La Bestiou dou Vacarès*, written in an epic vein; Folco de Baroncelli (1869–1943); and Marius Jouveau (1878–1949). A curious case is that of S. A. Peyre (1890–1961), writing in Provençal, in French, and in English. Had Paul Froment (1875–98) not died young, he would probably have been the great poet of Quercy, but this place was taken by the bucolic and religious poet Jules Cubaynes (1894–   ). P. L. Grenier (1879–1954) was a notable artist who revived the classical language of Limousin. J. B. Chèze, in the same region, wrote the delicate *Una princessa dins la Tor* (1932). Albert Pestour (1889–   ), also of Limousin, with a fine command of the vernacular, was the inspired poet of the *Rebats sus l'Autura* and *L'Autura enviblada*. The very considerable number of later authors bear witness to the permanent vitality, throughout every Oc-speaking province, of Occitanian poetry.

BIBLIOGRAPHY.—*General Works:* General bibliography in D. C. Haskell, *Provençal Literature and Language* (1925), a list of references in the New York Public Library; *see also* P.-L. Berthaud and J. Lesoffre, *Guide des études occitanes*, 2nd ed. (1953). On the whole of Provençal literature, *see* C. Camproux, *Histoire de la littérature occitane* (1953); André Berry, *Les Littératures du domaine d'Oc*, in the *Encyclopédie de la Pléiade: Histoire des Littératures*, vol. iii (1958), and *Anthologie de la Poésie Occitane: Choix, traduction et commentaire* (1961).
First Period: On the first and second periods as a whole, *see* A. Jeanroy, *Histoire sommaire de la poésie occitane, des origines à la fin du XVIIIe siècle* (1945). *General Surveys of the First Period* are J. B. de la Curne de Sainte-Palaye, *Histoire littéraire des troubadours*, 3 vol. (1774); A. Restori, *Letteratura provenzale* (1891); J. B. Beck, *Die Melodien der Troubadours* (1908); J. J. Salverda de Graves, *De Troubadours* (1917); J. Anglade, *Pour étudier les troubadours*, 2nd ed. (1930); A. Pillet and H. Carstens, *Bibliographie der Troubadours* (1933); A. Jeanroy, *La Poésie lyrique des troubadours* (1948). *General Surveys With Selections* are F. J. Raynouard, *Choix des poésies originales des troubadours*, 6 vol. (1816–21); K. Bartsch, *Chrestomathie provençale*, 4th ed. (1880); C. Appel, *Provenzalische Chrestomathie*,

3rd ed. (1903); A. Kolsen, *Dichtungen der Trobadors* (1916–19); J. Beck, *Les Chansonniers des troubadours et des trouvères, . . . en facsimilé et . . . en notation moderne* (1927); J. Anglade, *Anthologie des troubadours* (1927); J. Audiau and R. Lavaud, *Nouvelle anthologie . . .* (1929); A. Berry, *Florilège des troubadours* (1930); M. de Riquer, *La Lírica de los trovadores* (1948). *Special Studies and Selections* are Manuel Mila y Fontanals, *Los Trovadores en España*, 2 vol. (1861–89); P. Meyer, *Les Derniers Troubadours de la Provence*, 2 vol. (1869–71); C. Chabaneau, *Poésies inédites des troubadours du Périgord* (1885); F. de la Salle de Rochemaure and R. Lavaud, *Les Troubadours cantaliens* (1910); A. Jeanroy, *Jongleurs et troubadours gascons des XIIᵉ et XIIIᵉ siècles* (1923); H. J. Chaytor, *The Troubadours and England* (1923); J. Audiau, *Les Troubadours et l'Angleterre* (1927); J. Anglade, *Les Troubadours de Toulouse* (1928), and *Actualité des troubadours de l'Aude* (1941); A. Basset, *Les Troubadours limousins* (1949). *Individual troubadours*, see bibliography to TROUBADOURS.

Modern Editions, etc.: Les Chansons de la croisade contre les Albigenses, ed. by Martin-Chabot, 3 vol. (1931–62); *Flamenca*, ed. by P. Meyer, 2nd ed. (1901); *Jaufré, Flamenca*, and *Barlaam et Josaphat*, ed. with trans. by R. Lavaud and R. Nelli, in *Les Troubadours* (1960); on *Flamenca*, see also the study by G. Millardet (1936); *Las Leys d'Amor*, ed. by J. Anglade (1936); *Biographie des Troubadours*, ed. by J. Boutière and A. Schutz (1950). *See also* A. Jeanroy, *Les Joies du Gay Savoir* (1914); J. Anglade, *Les Origines du Gay Savoir* (1919), and *Les Flors del Gay Sabor* (1926).

Second Period: J. B. Noulet, *Essai sur l'histoire littéraire des patois du Midi de la France aux XVIᵉ et XVIIᵉ siècles* (1859), and *Histoire littéraire des patois du Midi de la France au XVIIIᵉ siècle* (1874–77); M. Carrières (ed.), *Pages choisies des écrivains languedociens du XVIIᵉ siècle* (1946).

Third Period: P. Mariéton, *Les Félibres* (1885); G. Jourdanne, *Histoire du Félibrige* (1897); E. Ripert, *La Renaissance provençale, 1800–60* (1918), and *Le Félibrige* (1924, with bibliography); J. Salvat, *Le Félibrige* (1940); I. Caussen, *Paris et le Félibrige* (1954). *Anthologies:* the most important is P. Julian and P. Fontan (eds.), *L'Anthologie du Félibrige provençal*, 3 vol. (1921–24). *See also* R. Nelli, *Jeune Poésie d'Oc* (1944); B. Lesfargues and R. Lafont, *La jeune poésie occitane* (1946); A.-P. Lafont, *Anthologie de la poésie occitane, 1900–60* (1962).

Gascon Literature: See G. Millardet, *Le Domaine Gascon* (1909), for bibliography; also G. Bastid, *La Gascogne littéraire depuis le Moyen-Age jusqu'à nos jours* (1894); J. Michelet, *Les poètes gascons du Oers* (1904); G. Guillaumie, *Anthologie de la littérature et du folklore gascons*, 7 vol. (1941–45); I. Girard, *Anthologie des poètes gascons* (1942); P. L. Berthaud, *La Littérature gasconne de Bordelais* (1953).

(A. A. F. B.)

PROVENCE, a historic country of western Europe, corresponding in general to the southeasternmost part of modern France from the Mediterranean coast northward over the *départements* of Bouches-du-Rhône, Var, Alpes-Maritimes, Basses-Alpes, and Vaucluse (*qq.v.*), with the lower Rhône as its western boundary and the Alps as its eastern (though in the early Middle Ages it was sometimes understood to extend farther northward and westward). In the last centuries of the *ancien régime*, however, the French *gouvernement* of Provence, which was bounded west by Languedoc and Avignon, northwest by the Comtat-Venaissin (with three exclaves beyond it), north by Dauphiné, and east by Savoyard territory, included only a fraction of the area described above, since half of the modern Vaucluse and two-thirds of Alpes-Maritimes did not belong to it.

Greeks and Romans.—Inhabited in prehistoric times by Ligurians, the Mediterranean coast was colonized, about the start of the 6th century B.C., by Ionian Greeks from Phocaea, who made their principal settlement at Massilia (Marseilles) and also founded Antipolis (Antibes) and Nikaia (Nice), as well as places west of the Rhône delta. The colonies flourished as commercial centres and as bases for exploration and did much to civilize the Celts, whose encroachment on the hinterland started in the 4th century B.C.

Early allied with the Romans, the Massiliots appealed to them for help against a coalition of Celts and Ligurians in 125 B.C. The Romans, who founded Aquae Sextiae (Aix-en-Provence), defeated the coalition and remained in occupation of the conquered hinterland as well as of country west of the Rhône, thus establishing the first Roman province in Gallia Transalpina (*see* GAUL)—the *provincia* whence Provence derives its name. Territory subsequently assigned to the Massiliots was taken back by the Romans in 49 B.C., since Massilia had sided with Pompey against Julius Caesar; and *c.* 27 B.C. a single province, Gallia Narbonensis, was constituted, to embrace coast and hinterland from the Alps to the eastern Pyrenees. The Alpine zone, however, became a separate province, Alpes Maritimae, *c.* 14 B.C.

About A.D. 300 the country between the Rhône and Alpes Maritimae was made part of a new province, Viennensis, with Vienne as capital; and in 381 another province, Narbonensis II, with Aquae Sextiae as capital, was carved out between Viennensis and Alpes Maritimae. In the 390s Arelate (Arles), already the area's foremost city commercially and a Christian bishopric, became the seat of the prefecture of all the Gauls.

Goths, Burgundians, and Merovingian Franks.—On the collapse of the Western Roman Empire in 476, the Visigoths (*see* GOTHS), who had been intermittently attacking Arles from the west for the past 50 years, overran all Provence south of the lower Durance River, while the Burgundians (*see* BURGUNDY) moved into the north. After their defeat in 507 by the Franks (*q.v.*), the Visigoths yielded their place in Provence to the Ostrogoths of Italy, who soon began to supplant the Burgundians also. The Frankish conquest of Burgundy (534) and the outbreak of war between the Ostrogoths and the Byzantines (535) led to the annexation of all Provence by the Franks (536 or 537).

In their partitions of their dominions, the Merovingians allotted northern Provence, with Arles, Toulon, and Nice, to their kingdom of Burgundy; but a strip extending from Avignon to Marseilles and thence northward and eastward to the coast south of Nice was sometimes assigned to the kings of Austrasia. For most of the Merovingian period, Provence was economically prosperous, thanks chiefly to the transit trade through Marseilles.

Feebly ruled, the country was not really integrated with France. Arab invaders from Spain, who entered Provence in 732, were well received by some localities, and Charles Martel (*q.v.*), who expelled them in 739, treated Provence almost as an enemy country.

The Carolingians and the Kingdoms of Provence.—Pepin the Short and Charlemagne (*qq.v.*) made Frankish rule effective in Provence, but Arab raids began again in 813. By the Treaty of Verdun (843), between Charlemagne's grandsons, Provence went to the emperor Lothair I as part of the "Middle Realm," which stretched from the Netherlands to central Italy; but on Lothair I's death (855) his third son, Charles, received Provence (with the Viennois) as a separate kingdom. When this Charles died (863) his elder brother, the emperor Louis II, ruler of Italy, took Provence despite the designs of his brother Lothair of Lotharingia and of his uncles Louis the German and the West Frankish king Charles II the Bald (*qq.v.*). Charles the Bald acquired Provence on Louis II's death (875), but died in 877.

In 879 Boso, ruler of the Viennois, brother of Charles the Bald's widow and husband of the emperor Louis II's daughter, was elected king of Burgundy by an assembly at Mantaille. Boso's kingdom, known as that of Lower Burgundy or of Provence (*see* again BURGUNDY), lost territory in the north to the French and German Carolingians before his death (887); but his son Louis was elected king of Provence at Valence in 890. His kingdom included the later Dauphiné (*q.v.*) and also the Vivarais west of the Rhône.

Louis was crowned king of Italy in 900 and emperor, as Louis III (*q.v.*), in 901, but was overthrown and blinded by his rival in Italy in 905. Hugh of Arles, with the title of duke of Provence from 911 or 912, ruled for Louis till the latter's death (928), by which time Hugh had made himself king of Italy (926). Though he acknowledged Rudolf II of Jurane Burgundy as king of Provence in 934, Hugh continued in power *de facto* till his death in 947. Sovereignty over Burgundy-Provence, later known as the Kingdom of Arles (*q.v.*), was transferred by Rudolf II's grandson Rudolf III to the German king Conrad II in 1032. This sovereignty, however, was more theoretical than real.

The Countship-Marquisate.—The task of repelling the Arabs, whose raids penetrated deeper and deeper during the 9th–10th centuries, fell to the local magnates. Boso, count of Arles in 949 (d. *c.* 965), had two sons, Rotbald, count of Arles (d. between 1008 and 1015), and William, count of Avignon (d. 993 or 994). The latter, who appears as count of Provence in 972 and as marquis of Provence in 979, won a decisive victory over the Arabs in 983. Subsequently his male heirs and Rotbald's alike were styled count or marquis, on a basis, eventually, of joint or undivided succession, though the several lines exercised their authority from different seats—at first of course from Arles on the one hand and from Avignon on the other. By 1040, however, Rotbald's male line was extinct, while his heiress Emma was married into the house of Toulouse; and there are grounds for supposing that the Comtat-Venaissin came into being as her sons' share of the Provençal inheritance. On the death (1093 or 1094) of Bertrand of Arles, count-marquis from c. 1065, Boso's house was represented only by females or by claimants through females: (1) Gerberge, Bertrand's sister, heiress of the Arles line; (2) Alix, heiress of the Avignon line and, by marriage, countess of Urgel; and (3) Emma's grandson, Raymond IV (q.v.) of Toulouse.

Catalans and Toulousains.—The countship-marquisate of Provence then underwent a series of partitions. In the first decade of the 12th century the countship of Forcalquier was carved out of the northeast for Alix and her heirs to satisfy their claims against Gerberge. Then Gerberge in 1112 transferred her own rights to her elder daughter Douce or Dulce on the latter's marriage to the Catalan Ramón Berenguer III, count of Barcelona (see BARCELONA, COUNTS OF); and he in 1113 became count-marquis of Provence as Raymond Berengar I, since Douce transferred these rights to him. Raymond Berengar's title, however, was still contested by the house of Toulouse and soon also by that of Les Baux (q.v.; and see ORANGE, HOUSE OF), after Raymond des Baux (d. 1150) had married Douce's younger sister Stephanie. The famous treaty of Sept. 16, 1125, between Raymond Berengar I and Alphonse Jourdain, count of Toulouse (son of Raymond IV), established a frontier on the Durance: Raymond Berengar was to have the country to the south of that river, henceforward specifically called the countship of Provence; Alphonse Jourdain was to have the north, henceforward called the marquisate, as well as the Provençal dependencies west of the Rhône; but Avignon, Sorgues, Caumont, and Le Thor were to remain joint possessions of the two dynasties.

The house of Les Baux fought on for decades against the house of Barcelona; the German kings recognized one claimant after another as their vassal for Provence; and the demarcation between the marquisate and Forcalquier was not settled till c. 1174.

Raymond Berengar I died in 1131, leaving Provence to his second son Berengar Raymond (d. 1144) and Barcelona to his elder son Ramón Berenguer IV (d. 1162). The latter, however, is reckoned as Raymond Berengar II of Provence, also known as the Old, because of his long regency for his nephew Raymond Berengar III the Young. When Raymond Berengar the Young died sonless (1166), Ramón Berenguer IV's son Alfonso II, king of Aragon, took control of the countship of Provence as Alfonso I. Raymond V of Toulouse, marquis of Provence from 1148, then challenged Alfonso, but renounced his claims on the countship in 1176. Alfonso entrusted the government to his brothers Raymond Berengar (sometimes numbered as IV; assassinated 1181) and Sancho (deposed 1185, after renewed warfare with Raymond of Toulouse) and finally to his second son, Alfonso. Married in 1193 to Garsinde, prospective heiress of Forcalquier, this last-named prince became count of Provence as Alfonso II on his father's death (1196), but died in 1209.

An important feature of the 12th century had been the rise of communal regimes, under consular government, in numerous towns of Provence (see COMMUNE [MEDIEVAL]). Arles, Avignon, Nice, Tarascon, Grasse, and Marseilles all came to enjoy this system, usually with the support of the Church and of the local nobility, who clearly profited from the municipality's practical independence with regard to the greater feudatories. These developments coincided with a great revival of commerce. The Arab threat to the ports had practically vanished; the Crusades had opened up the Levant; and fairs in the towns inland enhanced local prosperity.

The union of Forcalquier with Provence, momentarily realized in 1208, was promptly contested by rival heirs. Alfonso II's infant son and successor Raymond Berengar IV (V if his great-uncle the governor is reckoned in the enumeration) was taken into wardship by his uncle Peter II (q.v.) of Aragon, but returned to Provence in 1217 and soon made good the annexation of Forcalquier.

Meanwhile a great French army from the north had set out in 1209 on the "Albigensian Crusade" against the heretical Cathari (q.v.) of Languedoc. The vicissitudes of the next 20 years affected the marquisate of Provence less disastrously than the other dominions of Counts Raymond VI and Raymond VII (qq.v.) of Toulouse, though Avignon, in revolt against the crusaders, was besieged and subdued by Louis VIII of France in 1226. By the Treaty of Meaux, however, in 1229, Raymond VII agreed that his daughter Joan should eventually marry Alphonse (q.v.) of Poitiers, brother of Louis IX of France. As Raymond VII died sonless (1249), the marquisate of Provence passed to Alphonse and Joan with the rest of the Toulousain inheritance; and when they died (1271) it was taken by Philip III of France, who next ceded the Comtat-Venaissin to the Holy See, in accordance with provisions made in 1229.

For the countship, Raymond Berengar IV (V) had notable success in asserting his authority over the communes, though Marseilles did not finally acknowledge him till 1243. Consistently opposed to Raymond VII, Raymond Berengar also became involved in a dispute with his suzerain, the emperor Frederick II, as he frustrated Frederick's attempts to bring Arles under direct imperial control (1239). Peace, however, was made in 1241. Raymond Berengar died in 1245, leaving the countship to his youngest daughter Beatrice.

The First Angevin Countship of Provence.—Beatrice, whose acquisition of the whole Provençal inheritance was resented by her sisters (Margaret, queen-consort of France, Eleanor, queen-consort of England, and Sanchia, wife of Richard, earl of Cornwall), was married in 1246 to Charles of Anjou, later king of Naples and Sicily as Charles I (q.v.); and when she died (1267), he retained Provence for their son, the future Charles II (q.v.) of Naples. Before embarking on his Neapolitan-Sicilian venture, Charles of Anjou engaged in a struggle against the Provençal communes, whose liberties he saw as dangerous to his authority. Arles and Avignon were subdued in 1251 and placed under a *viguier* or vicar nominated by the count, but Marseilles, which came to terms with Charles in 1252, later rebelled against him (1262).

The new dynasty's Italian preoccupations (see NAPLES, KINGDOM OF; SICILIAN VESPERS) had important repercussions on Provence. When Charles of Anjou died (1285), Charles II was a prisoner of the Aragonese, and this situation gave rise to the first recorded meeting of the Estates of Provence (see ESTATES-GENERAL) in 1286 and to a reorganization of the system of audit in 1288, from which the *chambre des comptes* (court of accounts) at Aix grew up. Charles II's later laws showed a concern for the welfare of his subjects as well as for his own authority. Commercially, the ports were more prosperous than ever; banking was growing up; and the reign of Charles II's son Robert (q.v.), king of Naples and count from 1309 to 1343, was notable for the emergence of *syndicats* (municipal councils) in the place of the consuls in many of the towns.

Avignon, which was attached wholly to the countship from 1291 (France losing the half-share inherited from the marquisate), became the seat of the papacy in 1309 and was sold to it in 1348 by Robert's granddaughter Joan I (q.v.) of Naples. Later, however, Joan's inconsequential dispositions and the attendant conflicts over the Neapolitan crown coincided first with the ravages of mercenary bands (let loose in the interruptions of the Anglo-French Hundred Years' War) and finally with the Great Schism of the papacy to plunge Provence into anarchy.

The Second Angevin Countship.—When Joan was murdered (1382), her latest nominee for her succession was Louis, duc d'Anjou, brother of Charles V of France (see LOUIS, kings of Naples); but Aix and other towns formed a union in favour of his rival, Charles III of Naples, and Louis died in 1384. His widow, Marie de Blois, regent for his son Louis II, gradually reduced Provence to obedience, but had to cede Nice and other frontier areas to Savoy (1388). Louis II instituted a *parlement* (q.v.) at Aix in 1415, but his son Louis III (d. 1434), who succeeded to the countship in 1417, replaced it by a *conseil éminent* (supreme council). Meanwhile the wars for Naples dragged on.

Louis III's brother and successor René I (q.v.) spent his last decade in his Provençal castles and palaces (notably at Tarascon). While the Estates, with his consent, reformed the administration of justice, he promoted the economic revival of the country and of its ports and patronized the arts. By his will (1474) he bequeathed Provence, not to his grandson, René II of Lorraine, but to his younger brother's son, the comte du Maine, who succeeded him as Charles III of Provence in July 1480. With French help Charles III overcame René II's partisans, but in December 1481 he died, leaving his countship to Louis XI of France.

Union with France.—The Estates of Provence accepted Louis XI on a basis of personal union between the countship and the French crown (1482), thus intending to safeguard Provençal autonomy; and in 1487 they ratified a declaration in the same sense by Charles VIII of France, whereby the constitutional parity of countship and kingdom was expressly stated. Louis XII, however, established a *parlement* of the French type at Aix in 1501–02; and Francis I, whose wars led to invasions of Provence by the emperor Charles V's forces (1524 and 1536), issued his edict of Joinville in 1535, curtailing the freedom of the Estates, suppressing the *conseil éminent*, and strengthening control by the *parlement* over the local judiciaries—thus in fact reducing Provence more or less to the level of any other French province or *gouvernement*.

Savage repression of Vaudois or Waldensian heretics in Provence in the 1540s preceded the outbreak of the Wars of Religion in the 1560s (*see* FRANCE: *History*). Carcistes (Catholics) and Razats (Huguenots), Ligueurs and Bigarrats (Politiques), disputed the country till Marseilles submitted to Henry IV of France in 1596.

The *parlement* of Aix firmly resisted the edict of 1630 whereby the French government tried to abolish the Estates' control over taxation, and it was only under threat of armed constraint that the Estates in 1631 voted an extraordinary subsidy. After an obstreperous assembly in 1639 the Estates were no longer summoned for nearly a century and a half. The Fronde (*q.v.*) took an eccentric form in Provence, being characterized by hostilities between the *parlement* and the governor (L. E. de Valois-Angoulême, comte d'Alais) before the Sabreurs (adherents of the rebel princes) and the Canivets (royalists) opposed each other in the later stages. Though the Provençal Fronde ended in April 1653, discontent persisted in Marseilles, which rebelled (1659–60) and forfeited its remaining privileges. Subsequently, however, Marseilles and Toulon benefited through development for commercial and naval purposes. Louis XIV in 1673 established the *généralité* of Aix, under an intendant (*q.v.*), whose office was united with the premier presidency of the *parlement* from 1691.

Provence was invaded by Austrians and Savoyards in 1707 and in 1746, during the Wars of the Spanish and of the Austrian Succession. The *parlement*, dissolved in 1771, was reconstituted in 1775. When the French government was trying to solve its problems by provincial assemblies, the Estates of Provence reemerged in 1787–88 and in January 1789.

The *gouvernement* was dissolved into three *départements*, Bouches-du-Rhône, Var, and Basses-Alpes, in 1790. Vaucluse was formed in 1793, after the French annexation of the Comtat-Venaissin (1791). The countship of Nice, annexed to France in 1860, was merged with part of Var to form Alpes-Maritimes.

BIBLIOGRAPHY.—R. Poupardin, *Le Royaume de Provence sous les Carolingiens* (1901) and *Le Royaume de Bourgogne* (1907); G. de Manteyer, *La Provence du Iᵉʳ au XIIᵉ siècle* (1906); R. Busquet and V. L. Bourrilly, *Histoire de la Provence*, 3rd ed. (1957).

PROVERB. The Oxford Dictionary's definition of a proverb as "A short pithy saying in common use . . ." emphasizes that proverbs are part of the spoken language. They belong, in origin, to the same stage of racial history as ballad and folksong, and are related to the fable and riddle. Their literary counterparts are the apothegm, aphorism, maxim, epigram (*q.v.*), and gnome (*see* GNOME AND GNOMIC VERSE); although many proverbs show literary refinement. Thus "God tempers the wind to the shorn lamb," found in Sterne's *Sentimental Journey* (1768), is derived from Latin and was translated from French in George Herbert's *Outlandish Proverbs* (1640) as "To a close-shorn sheep God gives wind by measure."

Distribution and Comparison.—Proverbs are found all over the world, and their comparison provides insight into the effects of cultural conditions, language, and local variations on expression. Thus the biblical "An eye for an eye, a tooth for a tooth," has an equivalent among the Nandi of East Africa: "A goat's hide buys a goat's hide and a gourd a gourd." Both form part of codes of behaviour, and exemplify the proverb's use for transmission of tribal wisdom and rules of conduct. Often, the same proverb may be found in many variants. In Europe this may result from the international currency of Latin proverbs in the Middle Ages. "A bird in the hand is worth two in the bush" originated in the medieval Latin *Plus valet in manibus avis unica fronde duabus*, and is first found in English in the Harleian manuscript (*c.* 1470) as "Betyr ys a byrd in the hond than tweye in the wode." Later English versions are "three" (or "ten") "in the wood," and "One . . . in the net is worth 100 flying." The Rumanian version is "Better a bird in the hand than 1,000 on the house"; the Italian, "Better one in a cage than four in the arbour"; the Portuguese, "Better a sparrow in the hand than two flying"; the Spanish, "A sparrow in the hand is worth a vulture flying"; the German, "A sparrow in the hand is better than a crane on the roof"; and the Icelandic, "Better a hawk in the hand than two in flight."

Content and Style.—Attempts have been made to see in proverbs indications of national characteristics. Certain stylistic similarities are shown by proverbs from the same part of the world. Thus, Arabic and other Middle Eastern proverbs use pictorial forms of expression and hyperbole. Some Arabic proverbs are fables in miniature, or refer to fables; so do classical proverbs (*e.g.*, Seneca's "Every cock crows [crouse = is master of] on his own dunghill"). Hyperbole is exemplified in the Egyptian "Fling him into the Nile, and he will come up with a fish in his mouth" of a lucky man. Dialogue proverbs are popular in Arabic, and in Greek, Ruthenian, Russian, and Polish. Classical proverbs are often terse (*e.g.*, *Praemonitus, praemunitis* = "Forewarned is forearmed"). *Homo proponit, Deus disponit* (derived from the Vulgate version of Prov. 16:9) keeps its style in English and other translations: "Man proposes, God disposes."

Alliteration is found in proverbs of Germanic origin, which also show a liking for personification, as in *"Herr Pfennig geht voran"* ("Mr. Penny heads the procession"). Many languages make use of rhyme and play on words (*e.g.*, the German *"Voll, toll"* = "A drunken man is a mad man"; and the Scots "Many a mickle makes a muckle"; *i.e.*, "Many small things make one big thing").

Proverbs originating among the early Germanic peoples may reflect the heroic spirit. An 8th-century Saxon proverb *"Oft daedlata domae for-eldit gigistha gahwem; swyltit i ana"* ("A coward often misses glory in some high enterprise: therefore he dies alone") illustrates this. Its emergence, by way of the 15th-century "Tarying draweth peril," John Lyly's "Delays breede dangers: nothing so perilous as procrastination" (*Euphues*, 1579) and Shakespeare's "Delays have dangerous ends," as "Delays are dangerous" shows how changing thought and language affect expression.

Folk proverbs use homely imagery—pot and kettle, pig, sheep, horse, cock and hen, cow and bull, dog, the events of everyday life. Some proverbs first found in literary form have been adapted from speech. It is difficult to decide the authorship of a particular proverb. Abraham Lincoln is said to have invented the saying about not changing horses in the middle of the river, but he may only have used a proverb already current. Many biblical proverbs have classical parallels. "A soft answer turneth away wrath" was known to Aeschylus as well as to Solomon. "Physician, heal thyself" (Luke 4:23) is classical in origin, and "It is hard for thee to kick against the pricks [goad]" (Acts 26:14) is used by Aeschylus and Euripides.

Some proverbs refer to historical occasions. "When in Rome do as Rome does" translates St. Ambrose's answer to St. Augustine's mother, who asked whether, when in Milan, she should follow the Roman usage there and keep the Sabbath as a feast day, or that of her home town Tagaste, where it was a fast. Popular usage sometimes creates new proverbs from old ones. Thus some biblical proverbs have acquired new meanings: *e.g.*, "The love of money is the root of all evil" has become "Money is the root of all evil."

Many proverbs are legal in origin, although the laws to which they refer may be obsolete. The allusion in "Possession is nine [or eleven] points of the law" has defied explanation. Some refer to well-known legal principles. "An Englishman's house is his castle" is a reference to the principle by which a man is safe from the bailiffs if he shuts himself up in his own house and denies access.

Proverbs are of interest for their reference to old customs. "Good wine needs no bush" refers to the medieval custom of marking shops by a sign, and "If the cap fits, wear it" to the fool's cap. Proverbs also preserve words in obsolete senses: in "The exception proves the rule," "prove" = "test" (cf. "The proof of the pudding is in the eating"). They also embody superstitions. "Marry in May, repent alway," for example, is recorded by Ovid as a current superstition and refers to the pagan idea that spring, the time of planting, was a critical period when certain tabus should be observed. Weatherlore and medical advice also find their way into proverbs: e.g., "Rain before seven, fine before eleven"; and the early 16th-century "Early to bed, early to rise/ Makes a man healthy, wealthy and wise."

Use of rhyme may show long history. "Who goes a-borrowing, goes a-sorrowing" has its origin in "He that fast spendyth must nede borowe; but whan he schal paye agen, then ys al the sorowe" (c. 1470). Sometimes style shows literary origin: e.g., "Faint heart ne'er won fair lady," of which a version is found in John Gower's *Confessio Amantis* (c. 1390).

Collections and Uses.—Proverbs in the biblical Book of Proverbs, traditionally associated with Solomon, include earlier compilations (*see* PROVERBS; WISDOM LITERATURE). Ancient Egyptian collections include the "Precepts of Ptah-hotep" (c. 2500 B.C.) and the "Teachings of Amen-em-apt" (c. 1000 B.C.). Sumerian inscriptions give grammatical rules in proverbial form. Proverbs were used in ancient China for ethical instruction, and the Vedic writings of India use them to expound philosophical ideas; and although these, like the Greek gnomes, are poetic and literary, they may embody popular sayings. Classical proverbs were collected in the 1st century A.D. In 1500, Erasmus published *Adagia*, a collection of 800 Greek and Latin proverbs. A later edition (1536) contained more than 4,000.

Early English proverb collections include the so-called *Proverbs of Alfred* (c. 1150–80), containing religious and moral precepts; and the more worldly *Proverbs of Hendyng* (c. 1250). Use of proverbs in monasteries to teach novices Latin, in schools of rhetoric, and in sermons, homilies, and didactic works made them widely known and led to their preservation in manuscripts.

The use of proverbs in literature and oratory was at its height in England in the 16th and 17th centuries. John Heywood wrote a dialogue in proverbs (1546, later enlarged) and Drayton a sonnet; and in the 16th century a speech in proverbs was made in the House of Commons. Proverbs were used as titles for plays (e.g., *All's Well That Ends Well*), illustrated in tapestries and paintings, engraved on cutlery, and, from the 16th to the 19th centuries, set as copies for schoolchildren, and for the making of samplers. In North America the best-known use of proverbs is probably in *Poor Richard's Almanac*, published annually between 1732 and 1757 by Benjamin Franklin. Many of "Poor Richard's" sayings were traditional European proverbs reworked by Franklin and given an American context when appropriate. In France proverbs gave rise to the *proverbes dramatiques*, dramatic sketches illustrating a proverb popular in the *salons* in the 17th and 18th centuries, which reached their height with Alfred de Musset (*q.v.*). In the 19th century, they were used in the novel to give a colloquial character to speech or to evoke the atmosphere of the past. The study of folklore (*q.v.*) led to the collection and study of proverbs, and this continued in the 20th century.

BIBLIOGRAPHY.—*Collections:* Burton E. Stevenson, *The Home Book of Proverbs* . . . (1948); S. Gurney Champion (ed.), *Racial Proverbs* (1938); Oscar Konstandt (comp.), *One Hundred Proverbs*, with equivalents in German, French, Italian, and Spanish (1958). *See also* T. Stephens (ed. by W. Bonser), *Proverb Literature: a Bibliography of Works Relating to Proverbs* (1930). *English:* W. G. Smith (ed.), *The Oxford Dictionary of English Proverbs*, rev. ed. (1948). *French:* J. Lebon, *Adages et proverbes de Solon de Voge* (c. 1578) reflects the customs and prejudices of the age; *see also* A. J. V. Le Roux de Lincy, *Le livre des proverbes français*, 2 vol., 2nd ed. (1859). *German:* The first collection was in Plattdeutsch, by J. Agricola of Eisleben, *Drihundert gemene Sprikwörde* (1528). *Spanish:* F. Nuñez de Guzman, *Refranes o proverbes en romance* . . . (1555; ed. by L. de Leon, 4 vol. 1803–04); J. M. Starbi, *El refranero general español* . . . , 10 vol. (1874–78). *Italian:* G. Florio, *Florio, his first fructes* . . . *familiar speeche, merie proverbes* (1578), *Seconde Fructes* (1591); G. Pitre, *Bibliografia delle tradizioni popolario d'Italia* (1894). *Other Languages:* Henry H. Hart, *Seven Hundred Chinese Proverbs* (1937); H. Böhtlingk (ed.), *Indische Sprüche*, 2 vol. (1870–74); R. F. Burton, *Wit and Wisdom from West Africa* (1865); E. Westermarck, *Wit and Wisdom in Morocco* (1930).

Works on Proverbs: R. C. Trench, *Proverbs and Their Lessons* (1905); A. C. Taylor, *The Proverb* (1931); G. Gerber, *Die Sprache als Kunst* (1885); B. J. Whiting, "The Origin of the Proverb," in *Harvard Studies and Notes*, xiii (1931), *Chaucer's Use of Proverbs* (1934); M. P. Tilley, *Elizabethan Proverb Lore* . . . (1926), *A Dictionary of the Proverbs in England in the 16th and 17th Centuries* (1950), with Shakespeare Index; C. G. Smith, *Shakespeare's Proverb Lore* (1963).

PROVERBS, a biblical book also known as PROVERBS OF SOLOMON (MISHLE SHELOMOH), following the Hebrew use of the initial word as title; and as the BOOK OF PROVERBS, corresponding to the Latin title. The book belongs to that section of the Old Testament designated as the Writings (Hagiographa) in contrast to the Law and the Prophets. It is also a part of the literary legacy of the Hebrew Wisdom movement of which King Solomon was the founder and patron; it is, indeed, very probably the oldest extant document of the Wisdom literature (*see* WISDOM LITERATURE). The beginnings of the book, in terms of earlier collections of proverbs that were ultimately absorbed by it, logically go back to the era of Solomon. It was probably completed in its present form in early postexilic times, perhaps in the 6th century B.C. Later books, also products of the Wisdom movement, include Job, Ecclesiastes (Qoheleth), Ecclesiasticus (Sirach), and Wisdom of Solomon. Among these books, Ecclesiasticus shows clear evidence of dependence upon Proverbs, both in form and content.

Contents and Literary History.—As a book, Proverbs is a collection of units originally independent. Thus at 10:1 there occurs the title "The proverbs of Solomon." At 25:1 a special unit is introduced as proverbs of Solomon copied by "the men of Hezekiah." Titles for shorter units occur in 30:1 and 31:1. The title at 1:1, "The proverbs of Solomon . . . ," was probably placed there by the editors who combined the separate units to make a single book and must be understood as applying to the whole work rather than to any part of it. In addition to the sectional titles, changes in literary form and in subject matter help to mark off the limits of the various units. It seems possible to identify at least nine distinct sections, as follows:

1:1–9:18	discourses in praise of wisdom
10:1–22:16	proverbs of Solomon
22:17–24:22	30 sayings
24:23–34	supplement to the 30 sayings
25:1–29:27	Hezekian collection
30:1–14	words of Agur
30:15–33	numerical sayings
31:1–9	instruction of Lemuel
31:10–31	acrostic on the virtuous wife

Discourses in Praise of Wisdom.—The title for this section is given in 1:2–6 as a detailed statement of purpose. This is followed by the motto in 1:7, "The fear of the Lord is the beginning of knowledge," which is a leitmotiv for the entire section. It is the view of virtually all critical analysts of Proverbs that these chapters constitute the youngest unit in the book. This judgment rests on two lines of evidence.

In the first place, the literary form is complex. The independent couplet with its parallel meanings, which is the primary form for proverbs (*see* below), is seldom presented for its own sake, as is the case throughout in 10:1–22:16. For example, the proverb in 1:8, rather than speaking for itself, becomes the occasion for an explanation (v. 9) and an exhortation (vv. 10–19). Paragraphs such as 5:1–6 and 7:1–5 also show how the proverb is being used and absorbed in these chapters by other literary forms.

In the second place, the first nine chapters have a more

speculative quality than the remainder of the book has. The personification of wisdom (1:22 ff.; 7:1 ff.; 9:1-6) is a feature of this section almost without parallel elsewhere (cf. 14:1). Furthermore, unlike the rest of the book, these chapters do not treat wisdom simply as a human quality and achievement or as a cultural legacy imparted by teachers and parents; they present it as a universal and abiding reality, transcending the human scene. Wisdom is the first of God's works and participated with him in the creation of the world (8:22-31).

A constantly debated aspect of this section concerns the identity of "the loose [strange] woman" (2:16-19; 5:1-23; 7:1-27; cf. 9:13-18). Is the author's aim primarily ethical, or is it ideological? Is the evil woman to be taken literally as a social problem threatening the progress and integrity of the young sage? Or is she the symbol of an alien cult or of a wrong view of life? In favour of the former view such passages as 5:15-20 may be cited; and in favour of the latter, the point may be urged that just as Wisdom, the good woman, is the voice and agent of the divine intelligence, so the evil woman is the voice and agent of the satanic powers.

Proverbs of Solomon.—The Hebrew word for proverb, *mashal*, means "comparison" or "parable." The primary form of this "word of the wise" was a parallelistic couplet. This section of Proverbs consists entirely of such two-line units in parallel relation to each other. Each unit is complete in itself and there is rarely a logical continuity of thought holding successive units together. In ch. 10-15 the parallelism of the couplets is overwhelmingly of the antithetic variety in which, in English, the members are held together by the conjunction "but." Thereafter those parallels in which the second line either supplements the first (*e.g.,* 18:7) or is wholly synonymous with it (*e.g.,* 16:16) are more prominent. The motivation of this section, in contrast to the preceding, is strongly practical: wisdom is a human achievement by means of which man's life can be fulfilled. The wise are contrasted with fools and the righteous with the wicked. But it is difficult to establish the nature of the difference, if any, between the wicked and the fool or between the wise and the righteous.

The 30 Sayings.—This section differs from the preceding most obviously by the fact that it consists of longer units or "sayings." These are introduced by a preface (22:17-21) somewhat similar to the title of the first section of Proverbs (1:2-6). The Wisdom movement in Israel was closely related to similar developments in surrounding countries (I Kings 4:29-34). Egyptian sages were especially prolific and the wisdom of Egypt had a continuous history that antedated the rule of King Solomon by at least a millennium and a half. In its outlook on life, in the subjects it treats, and in its literary forms Israel's wisdom corresponds closely to that of Egypt. This section offers most striking illustration of this, for its author used a piece of Egyptian Wisdom writing, "The Instruction of Amen-em-opet," both as a model and as a source. The "thirty sayings" (22:20) of the Israelite work represent an imitation in form of the Egyptian, which consists of 30 "chapters." The Hebrew work can be described as an anthology. The author used "The Instruction of Amen-em-opet" as one of his sources, paraphrasing parts of it. His close dependence upon it extends from 22:17 to 23:11. Thereafter, he may have utilized other sources or done his own composing.

Supplement to the 30 Sayings.—This brief section consists of four "sayings" whose tone and form show that they were intended to continue the wisdom of the preceding 30. Verse 23 emphasizes that they are a supplement to those. Verses 30-34 are a reminder that the Wisdom movement produced the parable, which becomes so prominent in the New Testament. (*Mashal* means both "proverb" and "parable.")

Hezekian Collection.—The spirit and form of this section most closely resemble 10:1-22:16. The main differences are that here quatrains as well as couplets appear and that the antithetic parallelism, so prominent in ch. 10-15, is rare. The superscription in 25:1 serves as a reminder that the polishing of proverbs, both in oral and written form, was a major interest of the movement that produced the Book of Proverbs. In Egypt the education of the young courtiers included the copying of the maxims of the sages.

The Words of Agur.—In spirit and substance this little section differs sharply from the rest of Proverbs; it has much closer affinities with the Book of Job. There is no internal evidence, such as a continuous theme, showing that these 14 verses are a single unit; but in the Septuagint they stand together between the 30 sayings and the supplement. The form is oracular, similar to the oracles of Balaam (*cf.* Num. 24:3 ff., 15 ff.).

Numerical Sayings.—Verses 17, 20, and 32 ff. are alien to the prominent parts of this brief section. The numerical saying has close affinities with the riddle and is common in the Wisdom materials of the ancient Near East.

The Instruction of Lemuel.—Lemuel may be thought of as a tribal chieftain of northwest Arabia, in the region of Edom. The section illustrates the role of the ruler's mother in the society of the biblical world.

An Acrostic on the Virtuous Wife.—In Hebrew this is a poem of 22 lines, each line beginning with a successive letter of the alphabet. The poem ascribes the characteristic virtues of the sages to the wife in her role as "home economist."

Character and Themes.—The Wisdom movement constitutes a very special aspect of the religious and cultural development in ancient Israel. As the primary document of the movement, Proverbs bears a clear impress of this distinctive character, so that in many respects it presents a sharp contrast to the outlook and emphases of Israel's faith as attested in the Hebrew Scriptures generally. This contrast also marks Job and Ecclesiastes, however greatly they may differ from Proverbs in other respects.

Proverbs never refers to Israel's history. In the Old Testament as a whole this history is constantly recalled not so much for social or political reasons as to declare the faith of Israel that in it God had acted to redeem his people and make known to them the character of his rule. The great themes of the promise to the patriarchs, the deliverance from slavery, the making of the covenant at Sinai, the wilderness wandering, and the inheritance of Canaan were celebrated in Israel's worship to tell the story of God's revelation of himself and of his choice of Israel. None of this is alluded to in Proverbs. The implication seems to be that for it God's revelation of himself is given in the universal laws and patterns characteristic of nature, especially human nature, rather than in a special series of historical events. That is, the revelation of God is in the order of creation rather than in the order of redemption. Moreover, the meaning of this revelation is not immediately self-evident but must be discovered by men. This discovery is an educational discipline that trusts human reason, employs research, classifying and interpreting the results and bequeathing them as a legacy to future generations. The wise are those who systematically dedicate themselves to this discovery of the "way" of God.

Unlike Job and Ecclesiastes, Proverbs is optimistic in the sense that it assumes that wisdom is attainable by those who seek and follow it. That is, man can discover enough about the character of God and his law to ensure the fulfillment of his personal life. This character of God is conceived almost entirely in terms of ethical laws. And the rewards for their observance are defined in terms of human values; *e.g.,* health, long life, respect, possessions, security, and self-control. In this respect, the book has affinities with Deuteronomy, though differing with it in respect to the locus and form of God's revelation.

Since God is apprehended in static terms, rather than dynamically as elsewhere in the Bible, the viewpoint of Proverbs is anthropocentric. Man's destiny depends upon his responsible action. There is no appeal to divine mercy, intervention, or forgiveness; and the divine judgment is simply the inexorable operation of the orders of life as God has established them. Implicit in the book is an aristocratic bias. The wise constitute an elite nurtured by inheritance, training, and self-discipline; fools are those who can never catch up, whether because of the determinism of birth or the wasted years of neglect. In its social and cultural attitudes, the book is probably the most conservative in the Bible: wealth and status are most important; obedience to the king and all authorities is inculcated; industry and diligence are fostered, for hunger, poverty, and slavery are the fate of the lazy;

and age and accepted conventions are accorded great respect.
See also BIBLE.

BIBLIOGRAPHY.—W. Baumgartner, "Wisdom Literature," in *Old Testament and Modern Study,* ed. by H. H. Rowley (1951); B. Gemser, *Sprüche Solomos* (1937); O. S. Rankin, *Israel's Wisdom Literature* (1936); Harry Ranston, *Old Testament Wisdom Books and Their Teaching* (1930); J. Coert Rylaarsdam, *Revelation in Jewish Wisdom Literature* (1946); H. Ringgren, *Word and Wisdom* (1947); *Wisdom in Israel and in the Ancient Near East,* Supplement III to "Vetus Testamentum," presented to H. H. Rowley (1955); J. D. Wood, *Wisdom Literature: an Introduction* (1967); E. Beaucamp, *Man's Destiny in the Books of Wisdom* (1970); P. J. Saher, *Eastern Wisdom and Western Thought* (1970).　(J. C. RY.)

PROVIDENCE, the capital of Rhode Island, U.S., is located at the head of Narragansett bay on the Providence river, about 43 mi. S.W. of Boston and 180 mi. N.E. of New York city. It is an active seaport as well as an important industrial and commercial centre.

Providence is built on three hills. College hill, on which Brown university is located, rises most sharply to the east of the central business district; it was at the foot of this rise and on its slope that the first houses and shops were built. The total land area of the city is only 17.9 sq.mi. and the density of population is high (10,011.9 per square mile in 1970). Most of the city is closely built-up with many sections where multiple-dwellings are common. The population remained about 250,000 from 1930 to 1950, declining sharply to 207,498 in 1960 and to 179,213 in 1970. (For comparative population figures *see* table in RHODE ISLAND: *Population.*) In the Providence-Pawtucket standard metropolitan statistical area (SMSA) the population increased 9.3% from 1940 to 1950, 7.4% from 1950 to 1960 and 10.9% from 1960 to 1970, its 1970 population being 910,781. The Rhode Island part of the SMSA consists of six cities (Central Falls, Cranston, East Providence, Pawtucket, Providence, Woonsocket) and seven towns (Burrillville, Cumberland, Johnston, Lincoln, North Providence, North Smithfield, Smithfield) in Providence county; and two towns (Narragansett, North Kingstown) in Washington county. The Massachusetts part of the SMSA consists of one city (Attleboro) and three towns (North Attleboro, Seekonk and Rehoboth) in Bristol county; four towns (Bellingham, Franklin, Plainville, Wrentham) in Norfolk county; and two towns (Blackstone, Millville) in Worcester county. Important manufacturing centres, in addition to Providence, include Pawtucket, Central Falls, Cranston, Bristol, Woonsocket and East Providence.

Among these communities only Woonsocket and Pawtucket have well-developed separate business centres and all are dependent on Providence for many services, retail, wholesale and financial. Local bus lines operate to most of the suburbs and a network of major highways centres on Providence from all directions. Besides the English and the Irish, the major ethnic groups represented are the Italians, followed by Canadians (both English- and French-speaking) and Russians.

History.—After his banishment from Plymouth colony for his unorthodox religious beliefs, Roger Williams made his way slowly to the banks of the Seekonk river and thence by canoe to a point at the foot of what is now known as College hill, where he and his five dissenter companions found a spring with abundant water. On the way he is said to have been hailed by a friendly Indian with the words, "What cheer?"—perpetuated in the names of several businesses. From the Narragansett chieftains Canonicus and Miantonomi, Williams secured a grant of land which he named in gratitude for "God's merciful providence" and which he dedicated as "a shelter for persons distressed for conscience."

The site was a favourable one and the promised freedom of conscience appealed to many. By 1675 about 1,000 persons made up the population. Further growth was only momentarily halted by King Philip's War when 29 homes were burned by the Indians. More important in the long run was the erection of the city's first wharf in 1680 by Pardon Tillinghast; in the years which followed Providence developed into a major commercial centre. Its sailing ships to the West Indies, Africa, India, China and coastal ports carried home molasses, slaves, rum and other items in exchange for colonial exports; this trade was the basis for the development of several wealthy and powerful families whose great mansions filled with expensive furniture and art objects rose along College hill.

Providence took a leading part in the rebellion against Great Britain which led to the colonies' independence. In 1772 a British revenue vessel, the "Gaspee," was burned off Warwick while aground. In 1775 there occurred a Providence Tea Party as an attack upon the idea of taxation without representation. Revolutionary forts were built and manned and French troops were quartered in what is now University hall at Brown university. The city was the scene of the signing of the Rhode Island Independence act on May 4, 1776, two months in advance of the country's Declaration of Independence.

In the post-Revolutionary period, Providence's crippled trade and commerce gradually recovered. The city's prosperity was augmented by new industrial development, starting with the establishment in adjacent Pawtucket in 1790 of Samuel Slater's textile mill, the first in the U.S. The town grew in size and status during the first half of the 19th century, incorporating as a city in 1832. Several notable buildings were erected, including the Arcade, an imposing covered building of many separate shops built in 1828 and designed after an Athenian temple, and the Providence Athenaeum (1836), a private library on College hill.

In the second half of the 19th century the city's industrial activities became of prime importance, supplanting but not diminishing its commerce and trade. The first important industry in Providence was the textile industry, starting with cotton factories and later expanding to include a woolen and worsted industry. Next came the jewelry industry, beginning with the little shop in which Seril Dodge made silver shoe buckles in 1786 and expanding after 1850 into a major industry. By 1880 the state was first in the nation in jewelry manufacture; 142 of its 148 plants were in Providence.

In addition to textiles and jewelry, other industries have developed to places of importance in the city and its metropolitan area, especially the machine tool and metal, rubber and electronics industries. In the second half of the 20th century Providence continued to be of major importance as the centre of the nation's most highly industrialized state.

Historic Sites.—One of the oldest cities in the U.S., Providence contains much of historic interest. The names of many streets are reminders of its trade and commerce and its early search for religious toleration; Benefit, Benevolent, Hope, Friendship, Dubloon, India and Ship streets and many others remain. Other points of historic interest in the city include the First Baptist meetinghouse, oldest of the denomination in the U.S.; First Unitarian church, its bell the largest cast by Paul Revere; the Old State house; the present capitol; and the Rhode Island Historical society, with extensive collections on Rhode Island history. The city contains dozens of old and historic homes and public buildings, many of which are open. The Old Slater mill in adjacent Pawtucket is a museum.

Education and Cultural Activities.—Despite its emphasis on industrial activity, Providence is an educational, cultural and recreational centre. The oldest of its several colleges is Brown university, founded in Warren in 1764 as Rhode Island college (*see* MANNING, JAMES), moved to Providence in 1770 and renamed Brown university in 1804 in honour of Nicholas Brown, a treasurer of the college and a principal benefactor. Its women's college, Pembroke, was organized in 1891.

John Hay library, erected as a memorial to John Hay, secretary of state under Presidents William McKinley and Theodore Roosevelt and a Brown graduate in the class of 1858, and other college libraries contain about 850,000 volumes and many special collections. On the campus are the John Carter Brown library, containing the world's foremost collection of Americana printed prior to 1801, and the Annmary Brown memorial, with a world-famous collection of incunabula from the period 1460 to 1500. Brown's Haffenreffer museum, located at Bristol, has a growing collection of Indian and other anthropological materials.

The Rhode Island School of Design is a private, coeducational college, founded in 1877 and providing four-year degree programs in the fine arts, architecture, design and related fields. The school's museum is notable for its collections of early furniture and early American crafts. There are comprehensive collections of paintings and sculpture of various periods and an oriental collection.

Other institutions of higher learning in Providence include the Rhode Island college, a state college chartered in 1854 and now offering teacher training on a handsome 48-ac. campus opened in 1958; and Providence college, a liberal arts college for men, founded in 1917, Roman Catholic.

The Providence Public library facilities were approximately doubled in 1954 by the opening of a new wing to the main building, erected in 1900. There are several branch libraries and one or more libraries in each of the towns in the metropolitan area.

Recreational Facilities.—The city maintains several parks and playgrounds and a municipal golf course. The largest park is Roger Williams park, with 453 ac. of lakes, flower gardens, walks, animal and bird houses, a museum of natural history, Betsey Williams cottage and a small amusement area for children.

Several state parks and picnic grounds are located in the metropolitan area. Yacht clubs and marinas are found in several waterfront communities and sailing and other forms of boating are common on Narragansett bay and adjacent waters. A ski slope and tow are operated by the state in Cumberland in winter. Dozens of ocean resorts lie just beyond the metropolitan area on the bay and the Atlantic ocean.   (V. H. Wh.)

PROVINCE, ROMAN. The Latin word *provincia* meant originally the sphere of duty assigned to a magistrate; thus civil jurisdiction between citizens was the *provincia* of the urban praetor. When magistrates were assigned the government of dependent territories, the name was applied to these territories.

The Republic.—After the First Punic War Rome acquired western Sicily and Sardinia and Corsica from Carthage. About 20 years later, in 227 B.C., two additional praetors were elected each year to govern them. (*See* PRAETOR.) After the acquisition of the two Spains (Hispania Citerior and Hispania Ulterior) following the Second Punic War, two more praetors were added in 197 B.C. Thereafter, although new provinces were acquired (Africa, Macedonia, Asia, Gallia Narbonensis) no more praetorships were created, and the requisite number of governors was supplied by the prorogation for a year or more of the command of praetors (including the two praetors at Rome, who might serve a second year in a province *pro praetore*). When a serious war broke out in a province it was usually assigned to one of the consuls (whose command might be prorogued *pro consule*). A praetor might also be given *imperium pro consule*, if entrusted with a large army. From the time of Sulla, consuls and praetors rarely governed provinces in their year of office, which they spent at Rome, but usually took a second year *pro consule* or *pro praetore* in the provinces.

In the last years of the republic special provincial commands, sometimes of several provinces and usually for a longer term (five years), were assigned to individuals who were not the consuls or praetors of the year or the preceding year. By a *lex Pompeia* of 52 B.C. Pompey enacted that there should be a five-year interval between a magistracy at Rome and a promagistracy in a province. The provinces to be filled by the consuls and praetors were annually determined by the Senate, which also prorogued the command of the governors who were not to be relieved; the consuls and praetors either drew lots for their provinces or selected them by agreement.

The general who annexed a province laid down a basic statute (*lex provinciae*), usually with the assistance of ten commissioners (*decem legati*) appointed by the Senate. This *lex* established the system of taxation, which sometimes took the form of a fixed *stipendium* levied on each community in the province, sometimes

Roman Provincial Organization at End of 4th Century

Name of province	Date of annexation	Title of governors in the principate*	Equivalent provinces in A.D. 400	Title of governors	Diocese
Achaea	146 B.C. (with Macedonia); separate province from 27 B.C.	proconsul (praet.)	Achaea Thessalia Insulae	proconsul praeses praeses	Macedonia Asiana
Aegyptus	30 B.C.	praefectus	Aegyptus Augustamnica Arcadia Thebais Libya Inferior	praefectus corrector praeses praeses praeses	Aegyptus
Africa	146 B.C.	proconsul (cos.)	Africa Byzacena Tripolitania	proconsul consularis praeses	Africa
Alpes Cottiae	under Augustus	praefectus, later procurator	Alpes Cottiae	praeses	Italia
Alpes Maritimae	14 B.C.	praefectus, later procurator	Alpes Maritimae	praeses	Septem Provinciae
Alpes Poeninae	15 B.C. (with Raetia); separate province from 2nd century	procurator	Alpes Poeninae et Graiae	praeses	Gallia
Aquitania	50 B.C.; separate province from Augustus	legatus Augusti (praet.)	Aquitania I Aquitania II Novempopularis	praeses praeses praeses	Septem Provinciae
Arabia	A.D. 105	legatus Augusti (praet.)	Arabia Palaestina III	praeses praeses	Oriens
Asia	129 B.C.; bequeathed to Rome 133 B.C.; annexed after rebellion	proconsul (cos.)	Asia Hellespontus Lydia Caria Phrygia I Phrygia II	proconsul consularis consularis praeses praeses praeses	Asiana
Baetica	206 B.C.; separate province from Augustus	proconsul (praet.)	Baetica	consularis	Hispania
Belgica	50 B.C.; separate province from Augustus	legatus Augusti (praet.)	Belgica I Belgica II	consularis consularis	Gallia
Bithynia et Pontus	66 B.C.	proconsul (praet.); from Hadrian legatus Augusti (praet.)	Bithynia Honorias Paphlagonia	consularis praeses corrector	Pontica
Britannia	A.D. 43; divided into Superior and Inferior by Septimius Severus	legatus Augusti (cos.)	Britannia I Britannia II Maxima Caesariensis Flavia Caesariensis Valentia	praeses praeses consularis praeses consularis	Britannia
Cappadocia	A.D. 17	procurator; from Vespasian legatus Augusti (cos.)	Cappadocia I Cappadocia II Armenia II	praeses praeses praeses	Pontica
Cilicia	65 B.C. (Earlier "provinces" of Cilicia [the first in 102] were probably military commands against the Cilician pirates.)	legatus Augusti (praet.)	Cilicia I Cilicia II Isauria	consularis praeses comes	Oriens
Creta Cyrenaica	67 B.C. 96 B.C.	proconsul (praet.)	Creta Libya Superior	consularis praeses	Macedonia Aegyptus
Cyprus	58 B.C.; separate province from 22 B.C.	proconsul (praet.)	Cyprus	consularis	Oriens
Dacia	A.D. 107; evacuated by Aurelian c. 270	legatus Augusti (cos.)	—	—	—
Dalmatia	before 59 B.C.	legatus Augusti (cos.)	Dalmatia Praevalitana	praeses praeses	Pannonia Dacia
Egypt: see Aegyptus					
Epirus	146 B.C. (with Macedonia); separate province from Hadrian or Antoninus Pius	procurator	Epirus Vetus	praeses	Macedonia

Roman Provincial Organization at End of 4th Century (Continued)

Name of province	Date of annexation	Title of governors in the principate*	Equivalent provinces in A.D. 400	Title of governors	Diocese
Galatia	25 B.C.	legatus Augusti (praet.)	Galatia I Galatia II Helenopontus Pontus Polemoniacus Armenia I Lycaonia Pisidia	consularis praeses praeses praeses praeses praeses praeses	Pontica Asiana
Gallia Cisalpina	province 81–42 B.C.				
Gallia Narbonensis	121 B.C.	proconsul (praet.)	Narbonensis I Narbonensis II Viennensis	praeses praeses consularis	Septem Provinciae
Gallia Lugdunensis	50 B.C.; separate province from Augustus	legatus Augusti (praet.)	Lugdunensis I Lugdunensis II Lugdunensis III Lugdunensis Senonia	consularis praeses praeses praeses	Gallia
Germania Superior	50 B.C.; separate province from Augustus	legatus Augusti (cos.)	Germania I Sequania	consularis praeses	Gallia
Germania Inferior	50 B.C.; separate province from Augustus	legatus Augusti (cos.)	Germania II	consularis	Gallia
Hispania Citerior (Tarraconensis)	206 B.C.	legatus Augusti (cos.)	Tarraconensis Carthaginiensis Gallaecia Baleares	praeses praeses consularis praeses	Hispania
Hispania Ulterior: *see* Baetica and Lusitania	206 B.C.				
Illyricum: *see* Dalmatia					
Italia	divided into provinces by Diocletian		Venetia et Histria Aemilia Liguria Flaminia Campania Tuscia et Umbria Picenum Samnium Valeria Apulia et Calabria Bruttium et Lucania	consularis consularis consularis consularis consularis consularis consularis praeses praeses corrector corrector	Italia Urbs Roma
Judaea: *see* Palaestina					
Lusitania	206 B.C.; separate province from Augustus	legatus Augusti (praet.)	Lusitania	consularis	Hispania
Lycia et Pamphylia	A.D. 43	legatus Augusti (praet.); from Hadrian proconsul (praet.)	Lycia Pamphylia	praeses consularis	Asiana
Macedonia	146 B.C.	proconsul (praet.)	Macedonia I Macedonia II Epirus Nova	consularis praeses praeses	Macedonia
Mauretania Caesariensis	A.D. 40	procurator	Mauretania Caesariensis Mauretania Sitifensis	praeses praeses	Africa
Mauretania Tingitana	A.D. 40	procurator	Mauretania Tingitana	praeses	Hispania
Mesopotamia	A.D. 199	praefectus	Mesopotamia Osrhoene	praeses praeses	Oriens
Moesia	under Augustus; divided into Superior and Inferior by Domitian	legatus Augusti (cos.)	Moesia I Dacia Ripensis Dacia Mediterranea Dardania Moesia II Scythia	praeses praeses consularis praeses praeses praeses	Dacia Thracia
Noricum	16 B.C.	procurator; from Marcus Aurelius legatus Augusti (praet.)	Noricum Ripense Noricum Mediterraneum	praeses praeses	Pannonia
Numidia	added to Africa in 25 B.C.; separate province from Septimius Severus	legatus Augusti (praet.)	Numidia	consularis	Africa
Palaestina	A.D. 6	procurator; from A.D. 70 legatus Augusti (praet.) from 134 (cos.)	Palaestina I Palaestina II	consularis praeses	Oriens
Pannonia	9 B.C.; divided into Superior and Inferior *c.* A.D. 105	legatus Augusti (cos.)	Pannonia I Pannonia II Valeria Savia	praeses consularis praeses corrector	Pannonia
Raetia	15 B.C.	praefectus, later procurator; from Marcus Aurelius legatus Augusti (praet.)	Raetia I Raetia II	praeses praeses	Italia
Sardinia et Corsica	238 B.C.	proconsul (praet.); from A.D. 6 praefectus or procurator	Sardinia Corsica	praeses praeses	Urbs Roma
Sicilia	241 B.C.	proconsul (praet.)	Sicilia	consularis	Urbs Roma
Spain: *see* Hispania					
Syria	64 B.C.; divided into Coele and Phoenice by Septimius Severus	legatus Augusti (cos.)	Syria I Syria II Euphratensis Phoenice Phoenice Libanensis	consularis praeses praeses consularis praeses	Oriens
Thracia	A.D. 46	procurator; from Trajan legatus Augusti (praet.)	Thracia Europa Haemimontus Rhodope	consularis consularis praeses praeses	Thracia

*The abbreviation "(cos.)" indicates the governor was a former consul, "(praet.)" a former praetor.

was a tithe of the crops and pasture dues, and sometimes included a poll tax. The *lex* also defined the status of the several communities of which the province consisted. The majority were tax-paying subject communities (*civitates stipendiariae*), but some were by grace of the Roman people free and immune from taxation (*civitates liberae et immunes*), while a few had treaties of alliance which guaranteed their rights (*civitates foederatae*). The *lex* also laid down general rules for the self-government of the subject communities (such as age and property qualifications for local office), and often established rules for jurisdiction in cases between citizens of different communities, or between Romans and provincials, or in revenue cases.

The governor was omnicompetent, being responsible for the military protection of the province, the general surveillance of the local government of the communities, and the administration of justice. He was expected to decide, or appoint a judge to decide, all cases involving Romans, and in many provinces could call before himself any case he wished. He issued an edict on entering his province, setting out the rules of law which he intended to follow. He was responsible for taxation in provinces where a fixed *stipendium* was levied or where, as in Sicily, the tithe was farmed locally. (*See* TAXATION: *History.*) In provinces whose tithe was farmed by the censors to *publicani* (*q.v.*) he was concerned only to adjudicate disputes between them and the provincials. He was everywhere entitled to make compulsory purchases of foodstuffs and clothes for his staff and troops and could levy special taxation for local needs, such as maintenance of a fleet. He received a grant from the Senate for his expenses.

The governor was assisted by a quaestor (*q.v.*) to manage his finances; quaestors drew their provinces by lot. He was also assisted by one or more *legati*, appointed by the Senate on his nomination; to them he could delegate military commands or jurisdiction. He chose a *praefectus fabrum* and other *praefecti* and *tribuni*, to whom he could assign lesser military commands or judicial or administrative duties. (*See* PREFECT [PRAEFECTUS].) He was also accompanied by unofficial assistants (*comites*). He was served by an official secretary (*scriba*) and other staff (*apparitores*) including lictors (*q.v.*).

The evidence is overwhelming that the provinces were on the whole badly treated under the republic. The governor, exercising irresponsible power, extorted money from the provincials by a variety of means: judicial corruption, misuse of his rights of requisition, and sundry forms of blackmail. His staff also expected their share of the pickings. Where the taxes were collected by *publicani* they too expected to make additional profits by overassessment of the tax due, and Roman financiers (*negotiatores*) profited from the financial straits of the provincials by lending them money at fantastic rates of interest. Provincial extortion is first heard of in 171 B.C. when the Spaniards petitioned the Senate. In 149 B.C. a special court was established at Rome to deal with extortion (*de rebus repetundis*). The jurors in this court were at first senators, who regarded their colleagues' misdeeds with sympathy. From 122 B.C. they were *equites*, who used their power to protect the interests of the *publicani*, who were members of this order.

The Principate.—In 27 B.C. Augustus was assigned a group of provinces, and henceforth the provinces of the empire were divided into "imperial" (*provinciae Caesaris*) and "senatorial" (*provinciae publicae*). The latter, which were ungarrisoned (save for Africa and Macedonia at first), were governed, as under the late republic (under the *lex Pompeia*), by former consuls and praetors, who were all styled proconsuls, on an annual term. Their number was never increased after 23 B.C. The imperial provinces greatly increased in extent, for all newly annexed areas went to the emperor. They were mostly governed by senators, appointed by the emperor (*legati Augusti pro praetore*), who served during his pleasure; three years became the normal term. Provinces with one legion or none had a legate of praetorian rank, those with two or more legions one of consular rank, who was assisted by the legates of the legions and in some cases by a judicial legate (*legatus juridicus*). Egypt with its three legions (later reduced to two and then to one) was by exception governed by an equestrian prefect, with equestrian prefects of the legions and other equestrian judicial and financial assistants. A number of minor provinces, either turbulent areas like the Alpine districts or annexed kingdoms like Judaea, were governed by equestrian officers known at first as *praefecti*, but from the time of Claudius generally as procurators. In all provinces except those governed by prefects and procurators there was a *procurator Augusti*; in the senatorial provinces he was concerned only with the emperor's private estates, but in the imperial provinces he collected the revenues and paid the troops. The old staff of *apparitores* survived but was increasingly superseded by military clerks; procurators were also served by imperial slaves and freedmen.

Although oppression and extortion were by no means eliminated, in general the condition of the provinces was greatly improved under the principate. In the imperial provinces the governors were selected by the emperor, and in the senatorial he could intervene in virtue of his *imperium maius*. Cases of extortion now came before the Senate, where the emperor could sway the verdict, and appeals to the emperor from the judgments of governors were encouraged. The diet of the province (*concilium provinciae*) came to play an important part in protecting the interests of the provincials. Such diets, consisting of delegates from the several communities, had existed in some provinces under the republic. Under the principate they became universal, and besides celebrating the worship of Rome and Augustus, they passed votes of thanks to popular governors and conducted prosecutions of those who were oppressive or extortionate. They also could make petitions to the emperor and send delegations to him to plead their interests. Provincial taxation was also reformed. For the tithe was substituted a poll tax (*tributum capitis*) and land tax (*tributum soli*)

assessed on the basis of periodic censuses; the *publicani* were eliminated (save for indirect taxes) and the tribute was collected by the provincial communities. Finally the status of the provincials was improved by the grant of Latin right (*see* LATIN RIGHTS) and Roman citizenship in the West, where an increasing number of communities, sometimes whole provinces, such as Spain under Vespasian, were given Latin status, and a large number were made *municipia* or *coloniae civium Romanorum*. In the Greek-speaking provinces of the East, Latin status was not accorded and only a few cities became Roman colonies. All these distinctions were obliterated when, by the Constitutio Antoniniana of A.D. 212, all the inhabitants of the cities became Roman citizens.

Under the principate there were a few provinces which were not groups of self-governing communities but were directly administered on bureaucratic lines. The leading case was Egypt, where the Ptolemaic administrative system was preserved with little change; in some smaller annexed kingdoms, such as Judaea and Cappadocia, a similar system prevailed. The Roman government, however, preferred indirect rule, and Septimius Severus established councils in the capital towns of the nomes (administrative districts) of Egypt and gave them some degree of administrative responsibility.

Diocletian (*q.v.*) approximately doubled the number of provinces, bisecting many and splitting some into four or five; he also divided Italy into provinces. He grouped the provinces into 13 larger circumscriptions called dioceses and governed by *vicarii* of the praetorian prefects. He preserved the proconsuls of Africa and Asia and placed Sicily and the Italian provinces under *correctores* who were usually senators, but elsewhere appointed only equestrian governors, styled *praesides*. Constantine and his successors increased the number of dioceses to 15 and raised the rank of many governors to *consularis*, thus making them senators.

(A. H. M. J.)

PROVINCETOWN, a town of Massachusetts, U.S., situated among extensive sand dunes within a fishhook-shaped harbour at the northern end of Cape Cod, is a noted artists' colony, fishing port and tourist centre. Discovered by explorers Bartholomew Gosnold and Henry Hudson in 1602 and 1609, it was the first landing place of the Pilgrims before they founded Plymouth. The birth of Peregrine White, the first white person born in New England, and the signing of the Mayflower Compact both occurred on shipboard in Provincetown harbour. Settled by lawless traders and fishermen before 1700 on lands owned by the Province of Massachusetts Bay (hence its name), the village was first a precinct of the town of Truro and in 1727 became a separate township. Its exposed position, subject to repeated attacks by sea, forced its abandonment during the French wars and the American Revolution. Its magnificent harbour was used as a naval base by British blockading squadrons in the Revolution and the War of 1812. In the 19th century it was an active maritime and whaling port, and its Portuguese descendants still maintain there the most prosperous fishing industry on Cape Cod. Until 1900 its communications with the mainland were mostly by boat because of the wind-blown loose sand that swept across its highways.

Modern Provincetown was for some time the home of Eugene O'Neill, whose first produced play, *Bound East for Cardiff*, was staged there in 1916 by the Provincetown Players. The top of the great Pilgrim monument, 350 ft. above the sea, affords a superb view of the cape and Massachusetts bay. Drives along the sand dunes, buried forests, and shipwreck-littered beaches of the adjoining Cape Cod National Seashore are popular with tourists as is the old maritime town itself. The resident population (1970) is about 2,900. (H. F. Ho.)

PROVINCETOWN PLAYERS, an experimental theatrical group, was organized in 1915 at Provincetown, an artists' colony in Massachusetts. Its program, the creation of a vital American drama, derived philosophical support from the hypotheses of Jane Ellen Harrison and Gilbert Murray (*qq.v.*). In 1916 they staged *Bound East for Cardiff*, the first of Eugene O'Neill's plays to be produced. That winter they moved to New York's Greenwich Village where, calling themselves the Playwrights' theatre, they encouraged playwrights, actors and stage technicians to "work out their ideas in freedom." The result was to provide an impetus to the individual artists and playwrights (particularly O'Neill), who were responsible for the renaissance of the American theatre after 1920, and to demonstrate to the commercial theatre that its patrons were as ready for provocative treatment of contemporary themes as patrons of museums or novel readers. The group disbanded in 1929.   (A. S. Dr.)

PROVING GROUND, an area set aside and usually specially modified and equipped to "proof test" military devices and military and commercial vehicles. The purpose of such testing is to show up, by excessive or distorted operation, the weaknesses of an item or any of its components; to determine whether the item's operation fits into a standard pattern; or to determine the life expectancy of any product. In many instances, items are tested to destruction; in the case of ammunition the test is actually an expenditure of sample quantities from each lot made. In all cases, data are collected, evaluated, and used in further development or in making engineering or production improvements.

Vehicle proving grounds, whether military or commercial, have a wide variety of roads and road surfaces to cause the vehicle under test to be strained or overworked in one manner or another. Corduroy tracks twist the car frame to determine its stamina; steep slopes show whether the engine can develop sustained power under unusual demand; braking power is tested when a stop is made on the slope. Tires are tested on many types of cobbles and broken stones and in sand and deep mud. Engines and brakes are proof tested by running the vehicle through deep water; brakes and tire traction are put to further test by passing through deep mud.

Military proving grounds also have special facilities and instruments for proofing guns of all sizes, from small arms to the largest cannon. Rifles or machine guns may be fired from stands in indoor ranges to test the gun barrel's resistance to wear when fired at excessive rates, to determine its ability to operate at extreme ranges of temperature or in dust or rain, or to allow studies of bullet flight by flash photography. Some artillery weapons are also fired indoors, but more often the firing is in the open against various types of targets, including different thicknesses of armour plate. Prominent on the artillery test range are tall towers supporting large metal rings. These rings are solenoids (electrical coils affected magnetically by the presence of moving steel objects) through which shells are fired to study their behaviour.

Proving grounds for rockets and guided missiles are distinctive primarily because of the much greater ranges involved. They are usually located in sparsely settled areas where missiles may be fired distances of 100 mi. or more; sometimes they are on coasts so that firing may be out to sea.

Notable proving grounds in the United States are several commercial vehicle test areas maintained by manufacturers of motor vehicles near Detroit, Mich.; the U.S. Army's Aberdeen Proving Ground near Baltimore, Md., for guns, ammunition, and combat and transport vehicles; and the U.S. Army's White Sands Missile Range in New Mexico for rockets and missiles. Aberdeen's area is more than 70,000 ac., but shells may be fired as far as 30 mi. out over Chesapeake Bay. White Sands is a desert valley 40 mi. wide and about 100 mi. long. Very long range missiles for the Army and the Air Force are fired southeastward into the Atlantic Ocean from Cape Kennedy (formerly Cape Canaveral), Fla., and into the Pacific Ocean from Vandenberg Air Force Base in California. These facilities are generally referred to as missile ranges rather than proving grounds.

Germany's great proving ground at Hillersleben before and during World War II resembled Aberdeen Proving Ground in that it permitted the proof testing of many types of weapons and other material at one place. The United Kingdom, however, spread the proof testing or tryout operations to different areas. For example, tanks were tested at Castle Douglas in Scotland; artillery at Holyhead, Anglesey, in Wales and at Lark Hill, Wiltshire, in England; infantry weapons and ammunition at the small arms school at Hythe, Kent, in England. Long-range rockets and missiles developed within the British Commonwealth are tested at the Woomera Range in Australia.   (F. D. McH.)

PROVINS, a town of north-central France, *département* of Seine-et-Marne, lies on the Durteint and Voulzie streams, 52 mi. (83 km.) ESE of Paris by road. Pop. (1962) 7,243. The old town is on a hill, with the new town in the valley below. There are many medieval houses, with narrow cobbled streets, dominated by the Tour de César (the 12th-century castle keep). Churches include St. Quiriace (12th–13th centuries), St. Ayoul (12th–16th), the bell tower of the convent of Notre Dame, and St. Croix (13th–16th). The old town is partly surrounded by medieval ramparts with gateways and towers. Other buildings of interest include the Grange aux Dîmes, a tithe barn (13th century); the Hôtel-Dieu (former palace of the countesses of Blois and Champagne, now a hospital); and the college, on the site of the counts' palace. Provins is on the railway from Esternay to Longueville, both linked with Paris. It lies in the heart of a wheat and sugar-beet region and has important clay pits.

Provins is said to have been named Probinum after the Roman general Probus who was there in A.D. 271. The lower town was founded in the 9th century by religious refugees fleeing from the Normans; they brought with them the remains of the martyr St. Ayoul, and the town became a place of pilgrimage. At this time it belonged to the counts of Vermandois; later it was the residence of the counts of Champagne, under whom it became a prosperous wool centre, with 80,000 inhabitants in the 13th century, and its fairs were attended by merchants from all over Europe (*see* Champagne). After the death of Henry III of Champagne in 1274 its prosperity declined. The name "city of roses" was given to Provins because of its cultivation of the red rose imported from the East by the crusader Thibaut IV of Champagne (d. 1253). Edmund of Lancaster, whose descendants had the red rose as their badge (*see* Roses, Wars of the), married Count Henry III's widow in 1275 and governed Champagne until 1284.   (A. G. Su.)

PROVISION, in ecclesiastical law, signifies the conferring of an office or benefice. With King John's submission to the pope in 1213, presentations of this sort previously made by English patrons were gradually appropriated by Rome to finance the increasingly costly centralized church administration. To secure papal aid in international affairs, English kings tolerated this system, resented by Commons, because so many foreigners were granted English benefices by the pope, until the coincidence of the Hundred Years' War with France and the Avignon papacy led to the enactment of the Statutes of Provisors (1351) and of Praemunire (1353) which outlawed the practice. Nevertheless, despite this and subsequent legislation, papal provision continued, abetted by the king, who eventually managed to secure virtual control over the pope's nominations. Provision was finally eliminated with the death of Mary Tudor. Though papal provision was legally sound, its abuses, condemned alike by satirists and saints, provoked such mass indifference toward the church that it must be considered one of the prime causes of the 16th-century collapse of Catholicism.

See also Benefice; Praemunire.

Bibliography.—H. M. Gwatkin, *Church and State in England to the Death of Queen Anne* (1917); P. Hughes, *A History of the Church,* vol. iii (1947); F. W. Maitland, *Roman Canon Law in the Church of England* (1898); J. R. H. Moorman, *Church Life in England in the Thirteenth Century* (1955).   (P. A. Be.)

PROVISIONAL ORDER: *see* Administrative Law.

PROVO, a city of Utah, U.S., the seat of Utah county, is situated 45 mi. S. of Salt Lake City between Utah lake and Wasatch peaks, at an altitude of 4,549 ft. An amalgam of weathered gray adobes and modern structures of frame or brick set amid trees and gardens, Provo has a dual modern identity as college town and steel centre.

The city takes its name from the Provo river, named for the trapper Étienne Provost (1785–1850), who penetrated to Utah from New Mexico in 1824. Brigham Young sent a Mormon colonizing mission to the site in 1849 and the next year what had been Ft. Utah by legislative fiat became Provo. Incorporated in 1851, Provo was Utah's second city until the Pacific Railroad gave Ogden predominance in 1869.

Decisive in Provo's early fortunes was the founding in 1875 of

Brigham Young academy, a Mormon institution which in 1903 became Brigham Young university. After 1923, steel plants were built in northern and southern suburbs; the Geneva plant, erected during World War II, became the largest integrated steel plant in the western U.S. and Utah's largest single manufacturing enterprise. The city has some other industry and is the trading centre for a rich agricultural area. It has a council-manager form of government, in effect since 1956.

The population of Provo was 53,131 in 1970; that of the Provo-Orem standard metropolitan statistical area (Utah county) was 137,776. For comparative city population figures *see* table in UTAH: *Population*.   (D. L. M.)

PROVOOST, SAMUEL (1742–1815), first bishop of the Protestant Episcopal Church in New York, was born in New York city on Feb. 26, 1742. After graduating from King's college (later Columbia university) in 1758, he went to England for further study, becoming a fellow-commoner of St. Peter's college, Cambridge, in 1761. Though of Reformed background, he united with the Church of England in his college days, if not earlier. He was ordained deacon on Feb. 23, 1766, and priest on March 25, 1766. Returning to America, he was elected assistant minister of Trinity church, New York, in Dec. 1766, resigning in 1771 because of ecclesiastical and political differences with the vestry. Though strongly sympathetic to the American cause in the Revolution, he took no active part in the dispute, living in retirement on a farm in Dutchess county until the end of the war. After the British evacuated New York, the Whig party gained control of the parish of Trinity church and elected Provoost rector. He was appointed a regent of the University of the State of New York in 1784 and served as chaplain to congress in 1785. He took an active part in the organization of the Protestant Episcopal Church after the Revolution and was elected bishop of New York on June 13, 1786. With Bishop William White of Pennsylvania he was consecrated in England on Feb. 4, 1787. They were the first two Americans to be consecrated by English bishops. Provoost was elected chaplain of the U.S. senate in 1789. Ill-health compelled him to retire from all active duty in 1801. He died on Sept. 6, 1815.

      (W. W. Ms.)

PROXY (short for "procuracy"), a term denoting either a person who is authorized to stand in place of another or the legal instrument by which the authority is conferred. Proxies are now principally employed for certain voting purposes. A proxy may in law be either general or special. A general proxy authorizes the person to whom it is entrusted to exercise a general discretion throughout the matter in hand, while a special proxy limits the authority to some special proposal or resolution.

In English and American bankruptcy proceedings creditors may vote by proxy, and every instrument of proxy, which may be either general or special, is issued either by the official receiver or trustee. Under the English Bankruptcy Act of 1914 and the American Bankruptcy Act of 1898, as reenacted in 1938, a creditor may still vote by proxy in the manner prescribed.

The greatest modern importance of proxies is in their use in shareholder voting. The Companies Act (1948) in England and the state statutes in the United States provide that voting by shareholders of limited liability companies and of corporations shall be in person or by proxy.

The separation of share ownership from management, in corporations in which shareholding is widely held by the public, has made the proxy a powerful control weapon, since a majority of shareholders can rarely be assembled in person for meetings at which directors are elected. Because annual shareholders' meetings are usually required by law, the management of such corporations can and normally does solicit the proxies of all shareholders at the company's expense, obtains the proxies of a quorum and majority, and votes the proxies for directors of its choice.

Lack of protection of absent shareholders led to enactment of provisions in the Securities and Exchange Act of 1934 authorizing the Securities and Exchange Commission (SEC) to issue regulations governing proxy solicitations. These regulations apply to proxies in corporations whose shares are traded on stock exchanges and to all other corporations having total assets of $1,000,000 or more and (in 1966) 500 or more shareholders. They require solicitations for proxies to be accompanied by statements informing the shareholder of the measures, so far as known, that will be acted upon at the meeting, and naming and giving detailed information about the directors proposed to be elected or reelected. The proxy itself must show that it is solicited by management, must give the shareholder an opportunity to instruct his proxy how to vote, and must be signed and dated.

These regulations also govern solicitation of proxies by dissident shareholders. They require that management proxy statements include, under certain circumstances, proposals for shareholder action by non-management shareholders, as well as written statements in support of such proposals. Furthermore, the rules sharply restrict the manner of garnering proxy votes by prohibiting the use of statements that have not been approved by the SEC.

These regulations have made it easier for groups of shareholders to contest management control, although in widely held corporations the cost is extremely high. When a contest takes place, the reasonable costs of solicitations, which may include the services of professional soliciting companies that telephone and visit shareholders, may lawfully be charged by successful or unsuccessful management groups, or by successful groups of dissident shareholders, to the company, but the cost to an unsuccessful dissident group falls on its financial backers. The uncertainty of the outcome of such contests is heightened because a proxy is usually revocable until actually voted at the meeting. When a shareholder gives more than one proxy, as often happens, because he is either confused or has changed his mind, only the last-dated proxy counts.

      (G. T. Fr.)

PRUDENTIUS (AURELIUS PRUDENTIUS CLEMENS) (348–after 405), Latin poet who presented Christian doctrines in a form agreeable to those steeped in the old literary tradition. Born in Hispania Tarraconensis, possibly at Caesaraugusta (Saragossa), he studied rhetoric, practised at the bar, held two provincial governorships, and was elevated by the emperor Theodosius to a high, and doubtless honorary, position at court. Tiring of the vanity of life, he devoted himself from about 392 to writing poetry on Christian themes. In 405 he edited a collection of his poems with an autobiographical preface.

The *Cathemerinon liber* comprises 12 lyric poems on various times of the day and on church festivals. The symbolism of light and darkness runs through these, occasionally developing into sustained allegory. The *Peristephanon* consists of 14 lyric poems on martyrs, mainly those of his native Spain, but some were inspired by a visit to Rome in 401–403. In these poems a taste for the gruesome is wedded to a simple piety. In three long didactic poems in hexameters he gives a polemical exposition of Christian doctrine. The *Apotheosis* attacks the views on the Trinity of Patripassianists, Sabellians, Jews, Ebionites, and Manichaeans, and sets forth the Orthodox view. The absence of polemic against Arians and Priscillianists is probably due to caution rather than to ignorance. The *Hamartigenia* refutes dualist views on the origin of sin; though Marcion is often mentioned, Priscillian, and perhaps Pelagius, are the real targets. The *Psychomachia* describes the struggle of Faith, supported by the cardinal Virtues, against Idolatry and the corresponding Vices for the soul of man. The first completely allegorical poem in European literature, it enjoyed immense influence in the Middle Ages. The two *Libri contra Symmachum* were written in reply to a second request that the altar of Victory be restored to the senate house, probably in 402/403. Book i is a critique of pagan polytheism; book ii replies to Symmachus' first request (*relatio*) in 384, developing the arguments then used by Ambrose, bishop of Milan. The *Dittochaeon*, 49 hexameter quatrains, intended as captions for the mural paintings in a basilica in Rome, is of interest mainly to the art historian. In a short lyric epilogue the poet offers his gift of verse to God.

Prudentius gives classical literary form to Christian content without any element of travesty. His poems are full of echoes of Virgil, Horace, Seneca's tragedies, and Lucan. But what he has to say he owes to the Bible (which he knew in a pre-Hieronymian but elegant version), Tertullian, Arnobius, Lactantius, Ambrose, and the Acts of the Martyrs. In vocabulary he uses many neologisms to express Christian concepts, which became part of the common stock of medieval poetry. A tasteful metrician, he not only uses hexameters, iambic trimeters, and many of the lyric metres of Horace, but freely introduces new lyric metres of his own. All the techniques of ancient rhetoric are at his command.

BIBLIOGRAPHY.—Works ed. by J. Bergman in *Corpus scriptorum ecclesiasticorum Latinorum,* vol. 61 (1926); R. J. Deferrari and J. M. Campbell, *A Concordance of Prudentius* (1932). *See also* A. Kurfess in Pauly-Wissowa, *Real-Encyclopädie der classischen Altertumswissenschaft,* vol. 23, col. 1039–71 (1957); A. Salvatore, *Studi prudenziani* (1958); I. Lana, *Due capitoli prudenziani* (1962); H. Woodruff, *The Illustrated Manuscripts of Prudentius* (1930).
(R. BG.)

PRUD'HON, PIERRE PAUL (1758–1823), French artist, was a painter of uneven quality and a draftsman of genius. He was born at Cluny on April 4, 1758, the 13th child of a stonemason. He trained with François Devosge, the director of the art school at Dijon, and then, through the patronage of a local nobleman, the baron de Joursanvault, spent a few years in Paris. In 1784 he was awarded the triennial prize of the Estates of Burgundy, which enabled him to go to Rome for three years. Of his stay in Rome only a few drawings survive, together with a ceiling painting now in the museum at Dijon. It is obvious that he looked at the works of Correggio and Leonardo, and his introduction of softer, more sensual effects into a school of painting dominated by the static and sculptural style of David is his greatest claim to originality.

His early miniature manner, however, persisted for some time after his return to Paris about 1789 (in vignettes designed for stationery used in government departments and book illustrations for the publisher Didot). His manner was broadened and his reputation extended by his decorations for the Hôtel de Lanois in Paris, although these can now be judged only by his preliminary drawings and sketches. Frochot, prefect of the Seine, brought him to the attention of Napoleon, who employed him intermittently as court portraitist and court decorator. His portrait of the empress Jose-

ART REFERENCE BUREAU

DETAIL FROM THE PORTRAIT IN OIL OF EMPRESS JOSEPHINE PAINTED BY PIERRE PRUD'HON IN 1805. IN THE LOUVRE, PARIS

phine of 1805 (Louvre)—Canova crossed with Correggio—is an excellent example of his seductive mildness. Although an exceptionally lazy worker, Prud'hon painted a number of large allegories, of which the best known are "Crime Pursued by Vengeance and Justice" of 1808 (Louvre) and "Venus and Adonis" (Wallace Collection), which was exhibited in the Salon of 1812. Such pictures have now darkened badly owing to Prud'hon's imperfect understanding of the aging of pigment. His drawings, however, have retained their exceptional qualities, as can be seen in his study for

a state portrait of Marie-Louise (Louvre) or his designs for the toilet service which was the wedding present offered to her by the city of Paris. Prud'hon continued to receive government commissions even after the Restoration, and in 1816 he was made a member of the Institute. His last years were shattered by the suicide of his devoted mistress, Constance Mayer, a dramatic episode which was the direct cause of his own death in Paris on Feb. 16, 1823.

See J. Guiffrey, *L'Oeuvre de P.-P. Prud'hon* (1924). (AA. B.)

PRUNE: *see* PLUM.

PRUNING: *see* ARBORICULTURE: *Pruning;* FRUIT FARMING: *Basic Problems and Practices of Fruit Farming: Training and Pruning.*

PRUNUS, a highly important genus of more than 150 species comprising the well-known stone fruits of the Rosaceae family. *See* ALMOND; APRICOT; CHERRY; NECTARINE; PEACH; PLUM.

PRUSSIA, the name given in European history (1) to a tribal country on the southeastern coast of the Baltic Sea; (2) to the territories into which this country was divided between Germans and Poles; (3) to the kingdom which arose from the German territory under the Hohenzollern dynasty; (4) in an extended sense, to the aggregate of Hohenzollern possessions not only in the specifically Prussian country but also throughout Germany; and (5) to the *Land* into which the former Hohenzollern possessions were transformed under the Weimar Republic and which survived as a component of the German *Reich* till its dissolution after World War II.

ANCIENT AND MEDIEVAL PRUSSIA

The Old Prussians.—The original Prussians, in medieval sources variously called Prusi, Pruzzi, Borussi, etc., were a group of tribes inhabiting the country between the Vistula and lower Niemen (Neman; Memel) rivers. They belonged, with their Lithuanian neighbours and with the Latvians, to the Baltic family of the Indo-European peoples (*see* BALTS). The Prussians are described as living dispersed in small clusters in heavily wooded country. They were predominantly hunters, collectors of honey from apiaries, and cattle breeders, but practised some primitive agriculture with wooden tools. Their social organization was loose, but some elements of a stratified society can be traced. They were pagans, having holy groves as their sanctuaries, and adhered tenaciously to their religion.

The German kings of the Saxon dynasty made contact with eastern Europe in the 10th century A.D. (*see* GERMANY: *History*), but the first attempts to convert the Prussians to Christianity ended in failure. The Czech bishop Adalbert (*q.v.*) was killed as a missionary in Prussia in 997; and his disciple Bruno (*q.v.*) of Querfurt died in the same way in 1009. For the next 200 years the Prussians remained pagan in their forests.

The Teutonic Order and the Poles.—The Cistercian monk Christian of Oliva, whom Pope Innocent III consecrated as bishop in 1215, had very little success in his task of converting the Prussians. Then, in 1230, the Polish duke Conrad of Mazovia gave land to the Knights of the Teutonic Order (*q.v.*) for help against Prussian raids on his territory.

The Teutonic Order proceeded to subdue the country along the Baltic coast east of the lower reaches of the Vistula: it built a network of castles, settled German noble families on the conquered lands, and established markets for the control of trade. The peasant population, which under these circumstances appeared to accept Christianity, still consisted of the old Baltic stock. Those members of the indigenous upper class who would acknowledge the new overlords were recognized as landowners.

In 1261 a great rebellion of the Prussians broke out. For ten years the order's rule was in danger of annihilation; and even after this crisis had been overcome there was still violent fighting for another decade. To restore the productivity of the country the order started a systematic settlement of German peasants, who brought with them the iron plow and so could turn the heavy soil of former forests into arable land. That part of the indigenous Prussian population which the order considered loyal was allowed to keep its land and status, and the Old Prussian language did not become wholly extinct till the 17th century; but by the middle of the 14th century the majority of the inhabitants of Prussia were German-speaking. For further details of the organization of Prussia *see* TEUTONIC ORDER, KNIGHTS OF THE.

The latter part of the 14th century was characterized in eastern Europe by a strong reaction among Slavs and Balts against the Germans. Poland and Lithuania formed their first dynastic union in 1386, and the Teutonic Knights were defeated by the Polish-Lithuanian forces in the Battle of Grunwald (*q.v.*), or Tannenberg, in 1410. By the first Peace of Torun (Thorn), in 1411, the Dobrzyn area, on the right bank of the Vistula above Torun, into which the order had infiltrated, was surrendered to Poland; and after renewed warfare the second Peace of Torun was signed in 1466. By this treaty the Polish crown acquired direct sovereignty over the order's former possessions to the west of the lower Vistula, together with the Kulmerland (or Chelmno district) and Ermland (Warmia) to the east; and the eastern part of Prussia was left to the order only on condition that the grand, or high, master should hold it as a fief of the Polish crown. *See* also EAST PRUSSIA.

THE 16TH AND 17TH CENTURIES

Polish Royal Prussia.—The lands on the Vistula, under Polish sovereignty, became known as Royal Prussia. The westernmost area, Pomerelia, in fact the eastern part of Pomorze (*q.v.*), had not come under the order's control till the 14th century and so was less germanized than the country east of the Vistula, to which most of the German peasant colonists were directed. The provincial constitution which was granted to Royal Prussia in 1571 strengthened the links between the local nobility and the Polish. Thus a wedge of predominantly Polish-speaking territory was consolidated between German-speaking East Prussia and the German *Reich*.

Ducal Prussia and Brandenburg.—The Teutonic Order's last grand master in Prussia, Albert (*q.v.*) of Hohenzollern, became a Lutheran and, in 1525, secularized his fief, which he transformed into a duchy for himself. Thenceforward till 1701 this territory was known as Ducal Prussia. When Albert's son and successor Albert Frederick died sonless in 1618, the duchy passed to his eldest daughter's husband, the Hohenzollern elector of Brandenburg, John Sigismund (*see* HOHENZOLLERN: Table III).

The union of Ducal Prussia with Brandenburg (*q.v.*) was fundamental to the rise of the Hohenzollern monarchy to the rank of a great power in Europe. John Sigismund's grandson, Frederick William (*q.v.*) of Brandenburg, "the Great Elector," by military intervention in the Swedish-Polish War of 1655–60 and by diplomacy obtained the ending of Poland's suzerainty over Ducal Prussia at the Peace of Oliva (1660). This made the Hohenzollerns sovereign over Ducal Prussia, whereas Brandenburg and their other German territories were still nominally parts of the *Reich* under the theoretical suzerainty of the Holy Roman emperor. Frederick William was also able to set up a centralized administration in Prussia and to secure control of the duchy's financial resources, thus reducing the power of the Prussian *Landstände* or Estates (*see* ESTATES-GENERAL). These Estates, comprising the landowning nobility and the oligarchies of the towns, among which Königsberg was paramount, had previously run the duchy's affairs. (H. Lz.)

THE KINGDOM OF PRUSSIA, TO 1786

Frederick III and I (1688–1713).—When Frederick III of Brandenburg succeeded his father, the Great Elector, in 1688, Brandenburg-Prussia consisted of four separate groups of lands, scattered across Europe from the lower Rhine in the west to the Memel River in the east and unconnected by any territorial link. The central and largest group comprised Electoral Brandenburg (Old Mark, Middle Mark and New Mark), with the secularized bishoprics of Magdeburg and Halberstadt adjoining it in the southwest and Hinterpommern (central Pomorze) in the northeast; the second group comprised the duchy of Cleves, on the lower Rhine, and the countship of Mark, on the Ruhr River (these two territories were not contiguous); the third group comprised the

countship of Ravensberg and the secularized bishopric of Minden, between the upper Ems and the middle Weser; and finally there was Ducal Prussia in the east, independent of the *Reich*.

The most significant achievement of the Great Elector's son was to secure the royal dignity for himself, as Frederick I (*q.v.*), king in Prussia; he crowned himself at Königsberg on Jan. 18, 1701, after the Holy Roman emperor Leopold I had consented to his assuming this new status in order to ensure his good will in the forthcoming War of the Spanish Succession. Ducal Prussia thus became the basis of his rank as sovereign king; and the other Hohenzollern possessions, though theoretically they remained within the German *Reich* and under the ultimate overlordship of the emperor, soon came to be treated in practice rather as belonging to the Prussian kingdom than as distinct from it. To these possessions Frederick added the countship of Mörs (adjacent to Cleves) and the countship of Lingen (on the Ems) in 1702 and the countship of Tecklenburg (on Lingen's southeastern border) in 1707.

Frederick William I (1713–40).—Frederick I's son Frederick William I began his reign in 1713 shortly before the conclusion of the Treaty of Utrecht, which assigned to him not only the so-called Upper Quarter of Geldern (*see* GELDERLAND), on the Meuse River adjoining Cleves and Mörs, but also the principality of Neuchâtel and Valengin on the border of France and Switzerland. Through participation in the Northern War he further acquired the southern part of Vorpommern (western Pomorze between the Oder and the Peene River, including Stettin) from the Swedes under the Treaty of Stockholm (1720).

It was Frederick William I who endowed the Prussian state with its military and bureaucratic character. He raised the army to 80,000 men (equivalent to 4% of the population) and geared the whole organization of the state to the military machine. One half of his army consisted of hired foreigners, the other half was recruited from the king's own subjects on the basis of the "canton system." This system made all young men of the lower classes—mostly peasants—liable for military service, though after finishing their training they were given leave for ten months of every year so that they could pursue their normal work. While the upper bourgeoisie was exempt from this military service, the nobles were under a moral obligation, which the king repeatedly emphasized, to serve in the officers' corps. If the social structure had not differentiated the classes or estates, it would have been impossible to maintain so great an army without damaging the economy. Economic policy, which was conducted on mercantilist principles, was in fact designed to satisfy the army's constantly expanding requirements.

This close coordination of military, financial, and economic affairs was moreover complemented by Frederick William I's reorganization of the administrative system, which he transformed into something peculiar to Prussia. To resolve the conflict between the administration of the domains, with its predominantly agrarian outlook and the fiscal administration, with its bias in favour of the town's commercial interests, the king in 1723 fused them both into one great central authority, the *Generaldirektorium* (General Directorate). In the separate parts of the monarchy he likewise merged the corresponding lesser authorities into *Kriegs- und Domänenkammern* (War and Domain chambers), to which the *Landräte* (country counselors) in the open country and the *Steuerräte* (tax counselors) in the towns were subordinated.

The *Generaldirektorium* was initially divided into four departments, each of which was headed by a minister and responsible for a number of provinces. Business was handled collegially, by the voting of ministers and counselors, but in all important matters the decision rested with the king himself. Though he was, formally, the president of the *Generaldirektorium*, the king preferred to communicate with his ministers only in writing: it was from the royal cabinet, with the help of his secretaries, that he controlled the whole life of the state. His autocratic temperament and his fanatical addiction to work found expression in complete absolutism. To his son and successor, Frederick II, he left the best-trained army in Europe, a financial reserve of 8,000,000 thalers, productive domains, provinces developed through large-

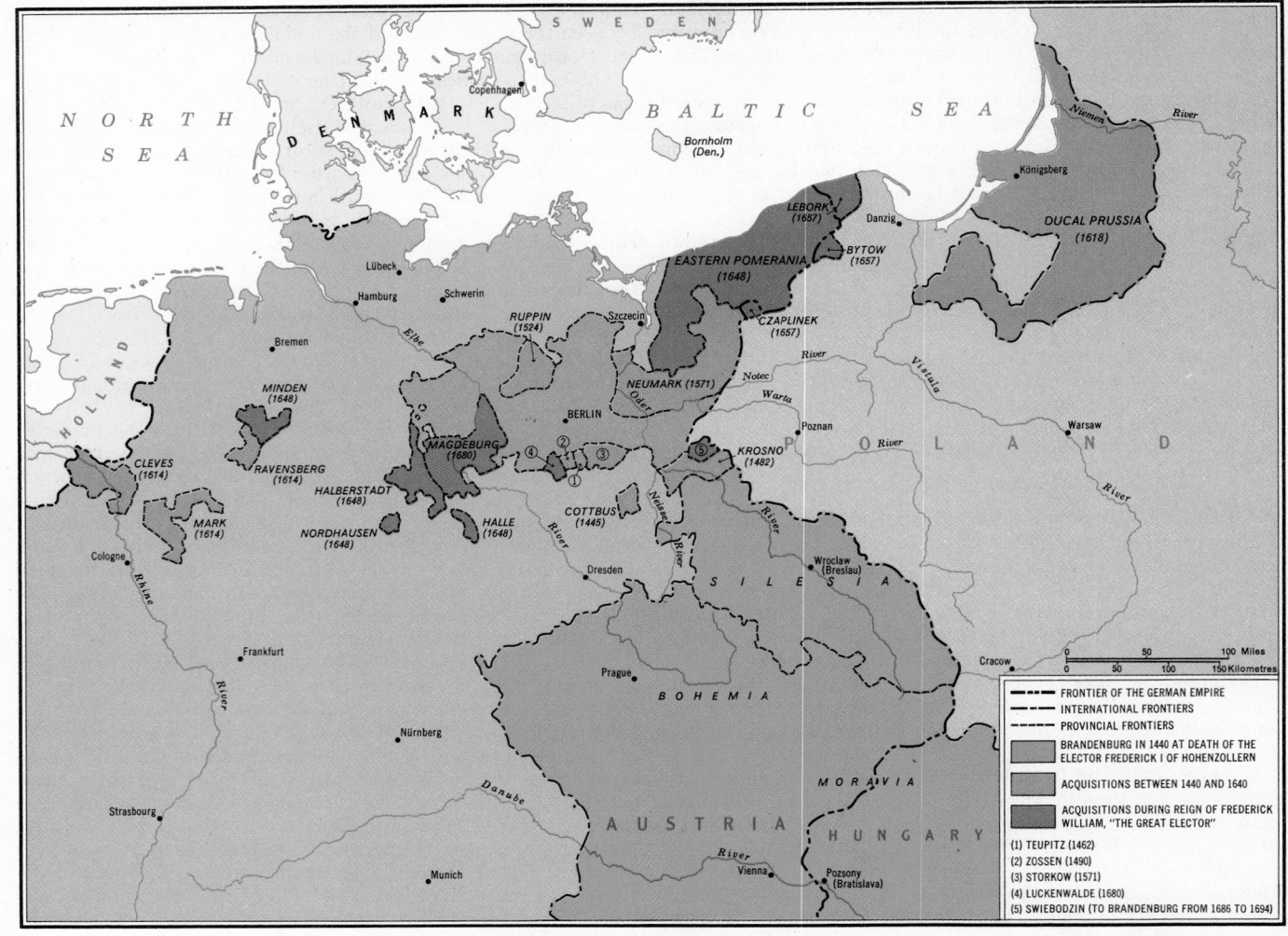

THE RISE OF BRANDENBURG-PRUSSIA (1440–1701)

scale colonization (particularly East Prussia), and a hard-working, thrifty, conscientious bureaucracy.

Frederick the Great (1740–86).—Frederick II (*q.v.*) the Great put the newly realized strength of the Prussian state at the service of an ambitious but risky foreign policy. Hailed by Voltaire as "the philosopher king" personifying the Enlightenment and its ideal of peace, Frederick astonished Europe, within seven months of his accession to the throne, by invading Silesia (December 1740). This bold stroke precipitated the War of the Austrian Succession (*q.v.*); and the Austro-Prussian struggle for Silesia continued, with uneasy intermissions, till the end of the Seven Years' War (*q.v.*) in 1763. Frederick's wars not only established his personal reputation as a military genius but also won recognition for Prussia as one of the Great Powers. Silesia, a rich province of 150 towns and thousands of villages, with an advanced economy and a flourishing culture, was a considerable acquisition for the Prussian monarchy.

Frederick also had incidentally acquired Ostfriesland (East Frisia, on the North Sea coast) in 1744; and later, at the First Partition of Poland in 1772 (*see* POLAND: *History*), he annexed West Prussia, that is, Polish Royal Prussia, thus at last forming a territorial link between his kingdom in the strict sense and the main block of his German possessions.

Frederick made no substantial changes in the administrative system as organized by his father. To the *Generaldirektorium,* however, he added several specialized departments to deal with matters affecting the state as a whole; *e.g.,* the *Fabrikendepartement,* or Factory Department, instituted in 1740 as the supreme organ of his mercantilist economic policy. After the Seven Years' War, moreover, the administration of customs and excise was

transferred from the *Generaldirektorium* to a separate *Regie* organized on French lines. In fact this complex structure of the state produced impressive results, which served primarily to maintain Prussia's new international status and to meet the needs of defense: the strength of the army was raised to 180,000 men; a financial reserve of 55,000,000 thalers was accumulated, and, in the course of the reign, no less than 300,000 settlers were established. In 1775 the Prussian state (excluding West Prussia) had about 4,900,000 inhabitants.

"Enlightened despotism" was well exemplified in the improvement of the judicial and educational systems and in the promotion of the arts and sciences. Certain features of the Enlightenment in Frederick's Prussia were indeed unique in Europe. The church, the bureaucracy, and education in general were pervaded by the state's control over public instruction, which however still allowed a measure of intellectual freedom to the cultured bourgeoisie and, by setting certain moral limits to the state's absolute authority, prevented it from becoming a tyranny. The freedom of conscience which Frederick instituted was the product not merely of his own skeptical indifference to religious questions but also of a deliberate intention to bring the various churches together for the benefit of the state and to allow more scope to the large Catholic minority of his subjects in relation both to the Protestant majority and to the Evangelical establishment.   (S. Sκ.)

THE FRENCH REVOLUTIONARY AND NAPOLEONIC PERIOD

Frederick William II (1786–97).—Frederick William II (*q.v.*) was not nearly so considerable a ruler as his uncle, whom he succeeded. He purchased the margraviates of Ansbach and

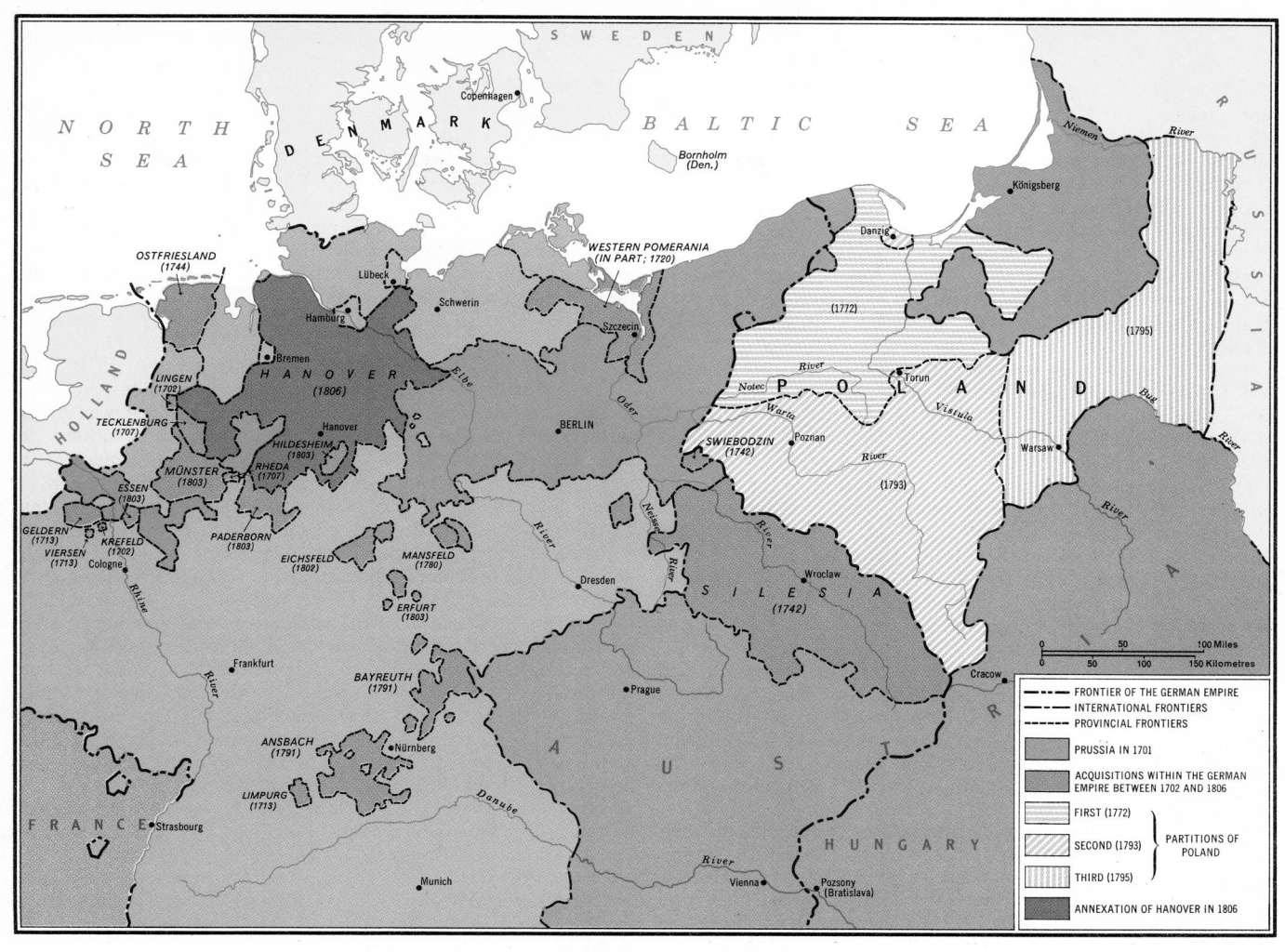

THE RISE OF PRUSSIA (1701–1806)

Bayreuth from the last representative of the Franconian Hohenzollerns in 1791; and he obtained a far larger territory in the east through the Second and Third Partitions of Poland—first Danzig and all the country between West Prussia and Silesia in 1793, and then Warsaw, the whole basin of the Narew River, and all the country west of the middle Niemen in 1795. He had no real success, however, in the War of the First Coalition against Revolutionary France: having entered it at its inception in 1792, he made the separate Peace of Basel in 1795. By this treaty he consented prospectively to France's eventual annexation of the German lands west of the Rhine in return for France's consent to his acquiring, in due course, new lands east of the Rhine in compensation for his losses. (*See* FRENCH REVOLUTIONARY WARS.)

Frederick William's management of the Prussian economy was less prudent than his predecessor's and finally brought the state's finances into disorder. Even so, his reign saw a notable advance by Prussia in the cultural sphere: music and the drama flourished conspicuously in Berlin, where moreover the monumental Brandenburg Gate was built to typify contemporary aspirations in architecture; and Immanuel Kant (*q.v.*) was lecturing in Königsberg. Law was codified in the *Allgemeines Preussisches Landrecht* (1794).

Crisis and Defeat (1797–1807).—Frederick William III (*q.v.*) succeeded his father in 1797. By pursuing the policy of neutrality during the Wars of the Second and the Third Coalitions against France (*see* NAPOLEONIC WARS) he forfeited the respect and the goodwill of the belligerent Powers; and when at last he went to war in 1806 it was too late to avert catastrophe. Meanwhile, however, under the *Reichsdeputationshauptschluss* of 1803 (*see* GERMANY: *History*), Prussia had received the secularized bishop-

rics of Hildesheim and Paderborn, the largest share of that of Münster, two large former dependencies of secularized Mainz (Eichsfeld and Erfurt), and numerous smaller places.

Frederick William III's failure to join Austria, Russia, and Great Britain in their coalition of 1805 was largely due to his hope of annexing Hanover (a kingdom in dynastic union with Great Britain). This hope was momentarily fulfilled in 1806, as a consequence of the unfortunate diplomacy of Christian, Graf von Haugwitz (*q.v.*); but by September of that year Napoleon's duplicity had provoked Prussia into war against France. The overwhelming defeat of the Prussians in the Battles of Jena and Auerstädt (*qq.v.*) was followed by the rapid collapse of the state. By the Treaty of Tilsit (1807) the king had to cede all his possessions west of the Elbe and all that had been gained under the Second and Third Partitions of Poland, together with the southern part of what had been gained under the First, so that the monarchy was reduced to Brandenburg, Silesia, the Pomeranian provinces, northern West Prussia (without Danzig), and East Prussia. Furthermore, the state was required to pay an exorbitant contribution to Napoleon's finances and to accept a French occupation of much of its territory.

Reform and Recovery (1807–15).—The backwardness of Prussia was revealed by the disaster of 1806. Administrative, social, and military reforms were clearly overdue, and the king's chief minister, Karl Stein (*q.v.*), seized the opportunity to introduce them. His basic idea was to evoke a positive consciousness of solidarity with the state by allowing the citizens to take a more active part in public affairs; and this idea underlay the emancipation of the serfs (begun in 1807), the measures for local self-government contained in the *Städteordnung*, or Towns Ordinance

(1808), and the reshaping of the central government.

Though Stein was dismissed from office at Napoleon's behest in November 1808, the work of reform was continued. After the less significant ministry of F. F. A. von Dohna and Karl von Stein zum Altenstein, the king in 1810 took Karl August, Freiherr (later Prince) von Hardenberg (q.v.), as chancellor of state or prime minister. Hardenberg had no particular liking for Stein's idea of self-determination and preferred the absolutist form of governing, though he showed some sympathy for liberal principles in regard to individual branches of enterprise; but for practical purposes at least he was ready to proceed with the reforms. To facilitate the levying of the tribute exacted by France, he made some modest concessions of a constitutional nature: for instance, the summoning of an Assembly of Notables (on French lines) in 1811 and that of a Representative Assembly of the Nation (*Nationalrepräsentation*) in 1812. He also issued ordinances to regulate the accession of the emancipated peasants to the ownership of land (from 1811) and granted equality of civil rights to the Jews (1812). In the economic sphere he introduced freedom to choose one's trade, abolishing the restrictive powers of the guilds.

The Napoleonic domination of Europe, meanwhile, was provoking a great upsurge of national sentiment, which was felt in Prussia no less strongly than in the other German states and was eventually to manifest itself in the War of Liberation (1813–14; *see* GERMANY: *History*). The transformation of the Prussian army from a largely mercenary force into a genuinely national organ was begun by Gerhard von Scharnhorst (q.v.), who thus prepared it for the part that it was to play.

At the same time the Romantic movement in the intellectual and artistic field further stimulated patriotism and the cult of liberty, to the service of which it even brought its interpretation of history. The foundation, in 1809, of the Friedrich Wilhelm University in Berlin, with Wilhelm von Humboldt (q.v.) as its chief promoter, magnificently affirmed Prussia's spirit in the aftermath of defeat.

Hardenberg adroitly steered Prussia through the difficult year 1812, when Prussia and Austria, in enforced alliance with France, had to participate in Napoleon's attack on Russia (*see* again NAPOLEONIC WARS). Napoleon's retreat from Moscow was the signal for a rising against the French. By the Convention of Tauroggen on Dec. 30, 1812, the Prussian general Johann (Hans) Yorck (q.v.) von Wartenburg withdrew his corps from fighting against the Russians; by the Treaty of Kalisz, on Feb. 28, 1813, Prussia's momentary neutrality was replaced by an alliance with Russia; and on Aug. 12, 1813, Austria also declared war on France. The Prussian army, with G. L. von Blücher and A. Neidhardt von Gneisenau (qq.v.) as its leaders, took a major part in the Battle of Leipzig, in the campaign of 1814 in France, and in the Waterloo campaign of 1815.

The Congress of Vienna (1814–15).—The Congress of Vienna (q.v.) did not restore Ostfriesland, Lingen, Hildesheim, Ansbach, or Bayreuth to Prussia; it allowed Neuchâtel to join the Swiss Confederation and to be detached from the Prussian monarchy, though remaining a personal possession of the Prussian king; and Prussia recovered nothing of its gains under the Third Partition of Poland and only Danzig, Posen (Poznan), Gnesen (Gniezno), and Thorn (Torun) of its gains under the Second. But the rest of what Prussia had possessed in 1803 was restored practically entirely by the Congress, with a considerable addition of new territory. This new territory comprised (1) areas taken from the Kingdom of Saxony, which were merged with older Prussian territories on the left bank of the Elbe to form the Province of Saxony (Provinz Sachsen), apart from the Lusatian areas, which were divided between Brandenburg and Silesia; (2) areas west and east of the Rhine, which were merged with older Prussian territories to form the Rhine Province (Rheinprovinz) and the Province of Westphalia (Provinz Westfalen); and (3) the formerly Swedish part of Vorpommern, with Rügen Island, which was merged with the rest of the Pomeranian territory to form the Provinz Pommern. Moreover, by the Peace of Paris (1815), France ceded Saarlouis and Saarbrücken to Prussia, which incorporated them in the Rhine Province.

With its major territorial axis shifted from eastern Europe to western and central Germany, Prussia was henceforth the only Great Power with a predominantly German-speaking population. It was thus Austria's potential rival for hegemony in the German Confederation (*Deutscher Bund*), which the Congress also created. The northeastern provinces of the monarchy, however, namely Prussia proper (subdivided between West Prussia, which included Danzig, and East Prussia, to which Thorn was attached) and Posen (a grand duchy), were kept outside the Confederation's boundaries, as also was Neuchâtel. In foreign policy Prussia adhered, with Austria and Russia, to the Holy Alliance (q.v.); and for internal affairs a conservative and absolutist line was taken in accord with the general spirit of the Restoration.   (E. W. Z.)

THE KINGDOM FROM 1815

The reforming impulse flagged after 1815. Frederick William III promised in May 1815 to introduce a constitution, but failed to carry out his promise; and all that remained of it was an assurance that the state would not contract new loans without the consent of a representative assembly. The army lost much of its new spirit when Hermann von Boyen, minister of war from 1814, resigned in 1819. On the other hand, the educational system remained the best in Europe, the University of Berlin in particular enjoying an unrivaled reputation. The major parts of the kingdom's western provinces, however, had never been Prussian before, and, being mainly Roman Catholic, were alien to Prussia in outlook. This produced a fierce conflict between church and state over mixed marriages in the years 1836–40, with bishops in prison and sees left vacant. Administratively much was done to bind the provinces together. The estates of the individual provinces gradually acquired a Prussian consciousness. The bureaucracy established a high standard of efficiency and honesty, which was at this time unique in Europe. In 1818 a simplified tariff, with moderate customs dues, was introduced for the entire kingdom; and this tariff became the basis for the *Zollverein* (customs union) established in 1834, which by 1852 included all the German states except Austria and Hamburg.

Frederick William IV and the Revolution of 1848.—In 1840 Frederick William IV (q.v.) succeeded to the throne on the death of his father. A product of the Romantic movement, he aspired to revive in Prussia his imaginary conception of the Middle Ages. He called off the conflict with the Roman Church; and in 1844 he actually attended the celebrations which marked the completion, after many centuries, of the Cologne Cathedral—the first king of Prussia to enter a Roman Catholic building. Though opposed to modern constitutionalism, he aspired to create Estates of the Realm on a medieval pattern. Also he wished to raise a loan in order to build the *Ostbahn*, a railway to link Berlin and Königsberg. In 1847 therefore he brought the provincial Diets together at a "United Diet" (*Vereinigter Landtag*) in Berlin. The Diet demanded a promise of regular meetings; and, when this was refused, it refused in turn to endorse the loan for the *Ostbahn*. The Diet was therefore adjourned after barren debates.

In March 1848 revolution broke out in Germany, inspired by the February revolution in France (*see* GERMANY: *History*). On March 16 and 18 there was street fighting in Berlin. Though the army was victorious, the king lost his nerve. He withdrew the army from Berlin on March 19, and for a brief period put himself at the head of the revolution. A liberal government was set up under Ludolf Camphausen and David Hansemann; a Constituent Assembly was summoned. Radicals dominated this assembly; and the king was gradually turned against it by the army officers who surrounded him. The Assembly was moved in October to the provincial town of Brandenburg. Its members called on the citizens of Prussia to refuse to pay taxes, but the call was abortive, the army reoccupied Berlin, and in December the Assembly was dissolved. Meanwhile a conservative ministry under Friedrich Wilhelm, Graf von Brandenburg (a son of King Frederick William II's last morganatic marriage), had replaced the two short-lived ministries which had succeeded Camphausen's. A more moderate Assembly was elected, but this, too, proved obdurate. A third was elected on a more restricted franchise in February 1849.

The Constitution of 1850.—Finally the king imposed a constitution by decree in February 1850. This constitution remained unchanged until 1918. Prussia received a parliament with two chambers. The First or Upper Chamber, officially named the *Herrenhaus* (House of Lords) in 1854, was composed of representatives of the great landed proprietors and of the large towns, and of members nominated by the king, some for life and some with hereditary right. The Second or Lower Chamber was elected by all taxpayers, divided into three classes according to the taxes paid. Though this was a narrow franchise, it was wider than that established in England by the Reform Bill of 1832. The constitution gave the chambers defined rights. Their consent was necessary for legislation; and, though the existing taxes were confirmed in perpetuity, the chambers had to endorse the annual expenditure of money in the budget. The king retained the unrestricted choice of ministers, but it was difficult for them to govern against the express wish of the chambers. The constitution, in fact, corresponded closely to that of England in the 18th century. It appeared inadequate by contemporary liberal standards; but its retention in the years of reaction after 1850 gave Prussia a higher standing than Austria in liberal eyes.

The German Question, 1848–50.—During the revolution of 1848 Frederick William IV aspired to lead the movement for German unification. In March 1848 he declared: "Prussia henceforth merges into Germany"; and he harboured the fantastic idea that all Germany outside Prussia should send representatives to the Prussian Assembly. When this idea miscarried, he regarded the German National Assembly at Frankfurt with suspicion so long as it was under Austrian leadership. But, when Austria forfeited the leadership at Frankfurt by propounding a unitary constitution for the mainly non-German Habsburg empire, Frederick William was tempted to accept the German imperial crown, which was offered to him by a delegation from Frankfurt on April 3, 1849. He was dissuaded with difficulty by his conservative advisers; and grudgingly announced that he could not accept the crown unless it were offered to him by the German princes. He and his friend Joseph Maria von Radowitz (*q.v.*) then tried to build the Erfurt Union on conservative principles and on a "little German" (*kleindeutsch*) basis; *i.e.*, as a union of the German states without Austria. In 1850 Austria challenged this union. Frederick William IV and his conservative ministers shrank from war, and Prussia was obliged to abandon its ambitions by the Convention of Olmütz (Olomouc; Nov. 29, 1850). The old German Confederation was restored; and Otto von Bismarck (*q.v.*) became Prussia's representative at the Frankfurt Assembly. Graf von Brandenburg died during this crisis and was succeeded by Otto, Freiherr von Manteuffel, who ran Prussia on cautious conservative lines for the following eight years.

The "New Era" and the Constitutional Conflict.—Frederick William IV became insane in 1857. His brother took over as regent in 1858 and became king as William I (*q.v.*) on Frederick IV's death in 1861. William I appointed a liberal ministry under Karl Anton, prince of Hohenzollern-Sigmaringen, a Roman Catholic, and for nearly four years Prussia experienced the so-called New Era, during which it was hoped that Prussia would win the leadership of Germany by the force of moral example. But dispute soon arose between the king and the chambers.

William I was a soldier by training. He knew the deficiencies of the Prussian army and wished to remove them. The army establishment had remained unchanged since 1815; the population of Prussia had greatly increased. As a result, a third of the young men escaped military service—in theory universal. Albrecht von Roon (*q.v.*), the minister of war, produced a comprehensive scheme of military reform: artillery and equipment were to be modernized; more barracks were to be built; but at the same time the *Landwehr*, or militia, was to be reduced in importance. The *Landwehr* elected its own officers, who usually did not belong to the hereditary officer class. Roon disliked this democratic principle and wished to make the standing army dominant. The Lower Chamber did not oppose army reform, but wished to preserve the *Landwehr*, which was a symbol both of liberalism and of the struggle for liberation during the Napoleonic Wars. The conflict which

followed was over the character of the army, not over its size or cost.

By the constitution, the taxes were imposed permanently, unless revised. The Lower Chamber therefore could not cut off supplies from the government: it could only refuse to authorize the expenditure of money that had been already collected. In 1860 it authorized additional expenditure on the understanding that no permanent steps, such as the building of new barracks, would be undertaken. Roon disregarded this bargain. In 1861 the Chamber again authorized the additional expenditure, but with an explicit warning that after this it would refuse unless its demands for retaining the *Landwehr* and for reducing the period of military service from three to two years were met. Again Roon disregarded the demands of the Chamber. When it stood firm for its demands in March 1862, it was dissolved, and the New Era ministry resigned; and when the new Chamber still rejected the military budget, William I threatened to abdicate. As his son the crown prince Frederick William (later king as Frederick III) also supported Roon's program, this would have settled nothing. Roon persuaded the king to appoint Otto von Bismarck minister-president (September).

Bismarck devised an ingenious theory. The constitution provided that the budget should be agreed between the two chambers and the king. Bismarck argued that, since the Lower Chamber had failed to agree with the Upper and with the king, there was "a gap in the constitution"; and he claimed that it was the king's duty to spend money without a budget until agreement was reached. This was not much of a theory, and Bismarck himself repudiated it later, but it served its turn. The liberals were helpless. It would have been unconstitutional to refuse the taxes. They could only protest in constitutional form. Bismarck took a middle course. Though he defied the attempt of the Chamber to determine military policy, he also resisted the proposals of Edwin von Manteuffel and others to scrap the constitution altogether.

During the crisis of 1863–64 over the Schleswig-Holstein question (*q.v.*), the Lower Chamber persisted in rejecting the military budget, but this did not prevent Prussia's going to war against Denmark. It was Prussia's Seven Weeks' War (*q.v.*) against Austria in 1866 that ended the constitutional crisis: Bismarck apologized for the illegal expenditure of money; and in September the two chambers passed an Act of Indemnity.

Bismarck's Wars and the Foundation of the Reich.—For Prussia's foreign policy in the 1860s *see*, besides the two articles indicated in the preceding paragraph, BISMARCK, OTTO, PRINCE VON; GERMANY: *History*. The Danish War of 1864 led to an Austro-Prussian condominium over Schleswig-Holstein. The Seven Weeks' War was followed by the annexation not only of Schleswig-Holstein but also of Hanover, Electoral Hesse, Nassau, and Frankfurt am Main to Prussia, which now extended without interruption across Germany and contained two-thirds of Germany's population.

The Franco-German War (*q.v.*) of 1870–71 established Prussia's position as the leading state in the imperial German *Reich*. William I of Prussia became German emperor on Jan. 18, 1871; the Prussian army virtually absorbed the other German armed forces, except the Bavarian army, which remained autonomous in peacetime. Bismarck combined the offices of imperial chancellor and Prussian minister-president, except during an interval in 1872–73 when Roon held the latter post.

Internal Affairs, 1871–1918.—In 1872 the Local Government Act extended to the rural areas the autonomous administration which Stein had in 1808 created for the towns. Prussia was now a predominantly industrial state. The Junker gentry, or landowners, who had a monopoly of public employment at the beginning of the 19th century, held only 17% of the posts at the end, and these only in the provinces east of the Elbe River. (For the anti-Catholic *Kulturkampf*, see again GERMANY: *History*.)

William I died in 1888, and after the short reign of his son Frederick III (*q.v.*; March–June 1888), the latter's eldest son became emperor as William II (*q.v.*). The three-class franchise had become increasingly unrepresentative and aroused much discontent. Bismarck did nothing to change it, though he described

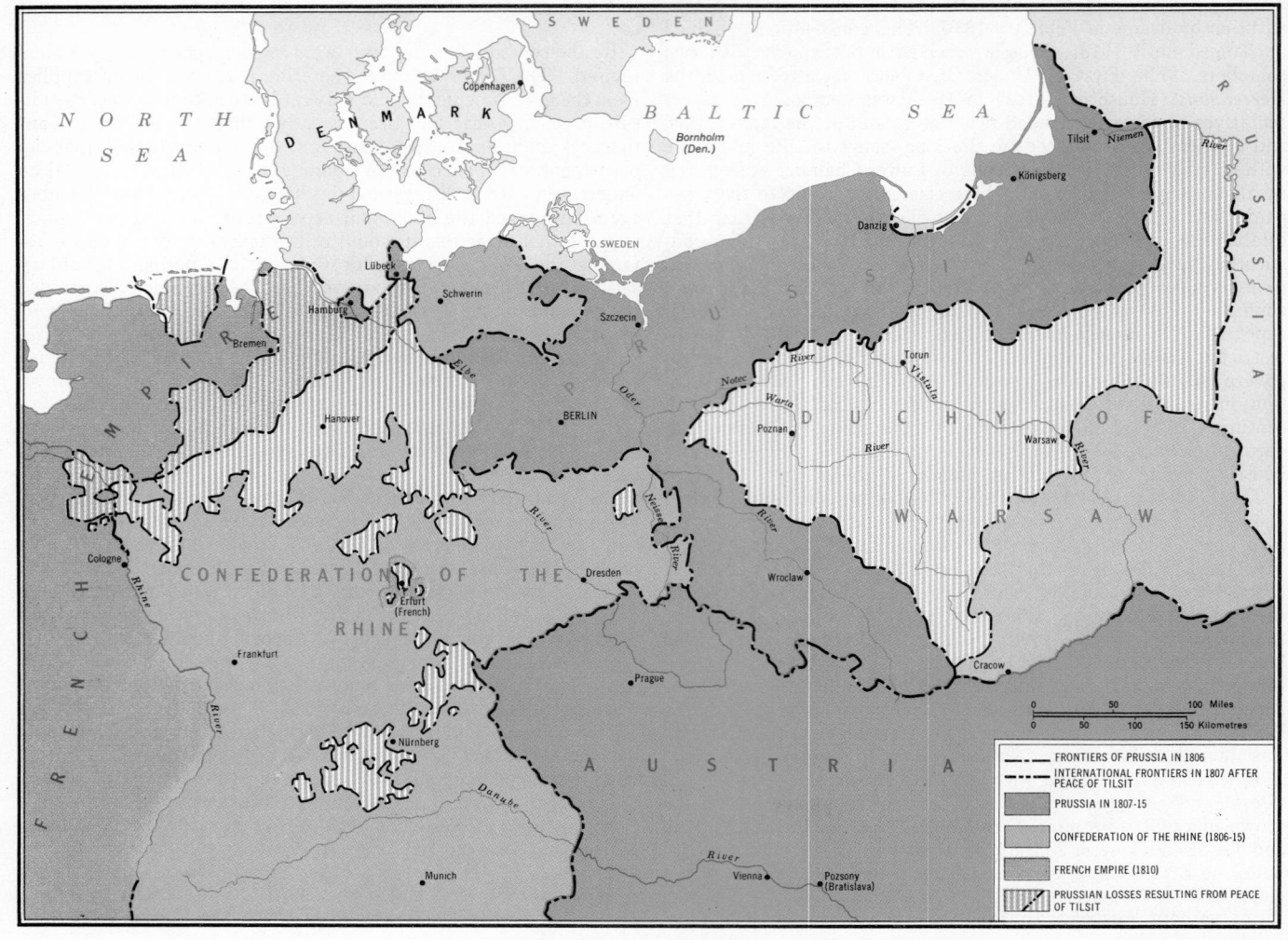

PRUSSIA (1806–15)

Map legend:

- — · — FRONTIERS OF PRUSSIA IN 1806
- — ·· — INTERNATIONAL FRONTIERS IN 1807 AFTER PEACE OF TILSIT

PRUSSIA IN 1807-15

CONFEDERATION OF THE RHINE (1806-15)

FRENCH EMPIRE (1810)

PRUSSIAN LOSSES RESULTING FROM PEACE OF TILSIT

it as "the most miserable franchise in existence." His successor Leo, Graf von Caprivi (*q.v.*), who became chancellor of the *Reich* and Prussian minister-president in 1890, ruled in Germany with the support of a left-wing coalition in the *Reichstag*. In 1892 he relinquished the position of Prussian minister-president, which was taken by Botho, Graf zu Eulenburg. To satisfy his left-wing supporters, Caprivi pressed for a reform of the Prussian franchise. Eulenburg answered by demanding an imperial law against the Social Democrats. Each man was seeking to interfere in the other's sphere. Deadlock was resolved only when William II dismissed both of them (Oct. 28, 1894). Thereafter the office of Prussian minister-president was again combined with that of imperial chancellor.

Johannes von Miquel, the finance minister, introduced important reforms during the 1890s, which made the distribution of taxation more equitable between the richer and poorer classes. Nothing was done to change the three-class franchise; and the Prussian Lower Chamber was now dominated by the conservative landowners. They controlled the government of Prussia, but this control counted for less as the imperial government developed in size and importance. Only the army gave the Prussian Junkers a disproportionate influence in German life.

Reform of the Prussian franchise became a burning question whenever the *Reichstag* had a left-wing majority, as it often had. Chancellor Bernhard von Bülow (*q.v.*) pressed the question ·in 1907, when he appeared to be transforming Germany into a parliamentary state with the support of the "Bülow bloc." His successor, Theobald von Bethmann Hollweg (*q.v.*), also regarded it as the key point in the development of a democratic system. Solemn promises of franchise reform were made on the outbreak

of World War I in 1914; and a reform bill was introduced in the Prussian Chamber in 1917. It was still being discussed when the German revolution of 1918 and the abdication of William II swept away the old order.

THE END OF PRUSSIA

The revolution ended the Prussian monarchy and the three-class franchise. It also ended the connection between the chancellor of the *Reich* and the Prussian minister-president. Prussia, which lost part of Silesia, Posen, West Prussia, Danzig, Memel, northern Schleswig, some small areas on the Belgian frontier, and the Saar district as a result of the Treaty of Versailles or the ensuing plebiscites, became a *Land* under the Weimar Republic, with more restricted powers than before and with little influence on the government of the *Reich*. Its parliament was now elected by universal suffrage; and this always produced a left-wing majority. Between 1918 and 1932 Prussia was ruled by the Social Democrats, sometimes alone, sometimes with the support of the Centre. The outstanding personality was Otto Braun, the Social Democratic prime minister. The *Land* controlled the police force. Hence the Social Democratic government of Prussia was regarded as the essential defense of German democracy.

In April 1932 the coalition of Centre and Social Democrats lost their majority in the Prussian parliament at a general election. Otto Braun resigned; but, as the opposition was divided between Communists and National Socialists, no coalition could be formed to replace that which had been defeated. Franz von Papen (*q.v.*), chancellor of the *Reich* from June 1932, used this situation as an excuse to end Prussian autonomy. He was appointed *Reichskommissar* for Prussia by Pres. Paul von Hindenburg in July.

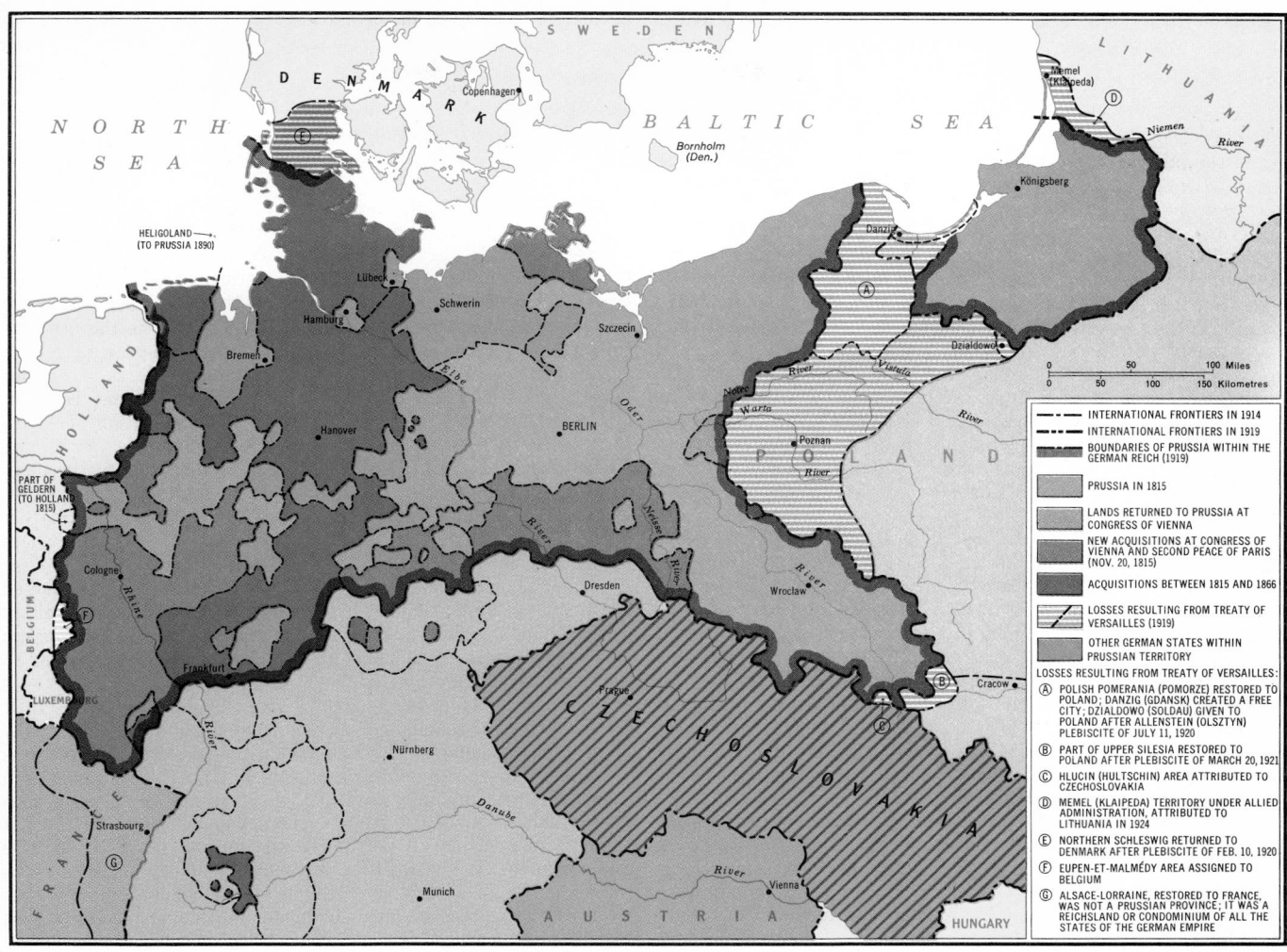

INTERNATIONAL FRONTIERS IN 1914

INTERNATIONAL FRONTIERS IN 1919

BOUNDARIES OF PRUSSIA WITHIN THE GERMAN REICH (1919)

PRUSSIA IN 1815

LANDS RETURNED TO PRUSSIA AT CONGRESS OF VIENNA

NEW ACQUISITIONS AT CONGRESS OF VIENNA AND SECOND PEACE OF PARIS (NOV. 20, 1815)

ACQUISITIONS BETWEEN 1815 AND 1866

LOSSES RESULTING FROM TREATY OF VERSAILLES (1919)

OTHER GERMAN STATES WITHIN PRUSSIAN TERRITORY

LOSSES RESULTING FROM TREATY OF VERSAILLES:

(A) POLISH POMERANIA (POMORZE) RESTORED TO POLAND; DANZIG (GDANSK) CREATED A FREE CITY; DZIALDOWO (SOLDAU) GIVEN TO POLAND AFTER ALLENSTEIN (OLSZTYN) PLEBISCITE OF JULY 11, 1920

(B) PART OF UPPER SILESIA RESTORED TO POLAND AFTER PLEBISCITE OF MARCH 20, 1921

(C) HLUCIN (HULTSCHIN) AREA ATTRIBUTED TO CZECHOSLOVAKIA

(D) MEMEL (KLAIPEDA) TERRITORY UNDER ALLIED ADMINISTRATION, ATTRIBUTED TO LITHUANIA IN 1924

(E) NORTHERN SCHLESWIG RETURNED TO DENMARK AFTER PLEBISCITE OF FEB. 10, 1920

(F) EUPEN-ET-MALMÉDY AREA ASSIGNED TO BELGIUM

(G) ALSACE-LORRAINE, RESTORED TO FRANCE, WAS NOT A PRUSSIAN PROVINCE; IT WAS A REICHSLAND OR CONDOMINIUM OF ALL THE STATES OF THE GERMAN EMPIRE

TERRITORIAL CHANGES IN PRUSSIA (1815–1919)

Otto Braun was absent, ill. Karl Severing, the Prussian minister of the interior, agreed to yield to force and was formally removed from his office by two policemen. The Prussian government appealed to the High Court at Leipzig, which in 1933 ruled that the expulsion had been unconstitutional, but that the constitution provided no remedy by which the illegality could be redressed. Meanwhile Papen, who had temporarily been replaced by Kurt von Schleicher as chancellor, was finally replaced by Adolf Hitler himself, who in April 1933 appointed Hermann Göring (*q.v.*) as minister-president and minister of the interior. In this way control of the Prussian police passed to the Nazis. The Prussian constitution was set aside, and the legislature abolished, though Prussia remained a unit for administrative purposes.

In 1945, after defeat in World War II, Germany came under the four-power control of the victorious allies—Great Britain, the United States, the U.S.S.R., and France. Northern East Prussia was annexed by the Soviet Union; the rest of the *Land* east of the Oder-Neisse line was transferred to Poland; the remainder was divided between the Soviet, British, and French zones of occupation. One of the few acts of the Allied Control Council was formally to abolish Prussia (March 1, 1947).

See also references under "Prussia" in the Index.

(A. J. P. T.)

BIBLIOGRAPHY.—General histories include: J. G. Droysen, *Geschichte der preussischen Politik,* 14 vol. (1855–86; incomplete revision, 4 vol., 1868–72); L. von Ranke, *Zwölf Bücher preussischer Geschichte* (1874–79; new ed. 1930); H. Tuttle, *History of Prussia, 1134–1757,* 4 vol. (1883–96); E. Berner, *Geschichte der preussischen Staates,* 2nd ed. (1896); H. Prutz, *Preussische Geschichte,* 4 vol. (1900–02); R. Koser, *Geschichte der brandenburgisch-preussischen Politik* (1913); G. Schmoller, *Preussische Verfassungs-, Verwaltungs- und Finanzgeschichte* (1921); S. B. Fay, *The Rise of Brandenburg-Prussia, to 1786* (1937); J. A. R. Marriott and C. G. Robertson, *The Evolution of Prussia* (1946). Works on the Teutonic Order particularly relevant to Prussia include H. von Treitschke, *Das deutsche Ordensland Preussen* (1862; Eng. trans., *Origins of Prussianism,* 1942); C. Krollmann, *Politische Geschichte des Deutschen Ordens in Preussen* (1932); K. Forstreuter, *Vom Ordensstaat zum Fürstentum* (1951); F. L. Carsten, *The Origins of Prussia* (1954). For the 17th and 18th centuries and the beginning of the 19th *see* O. Hintze, *Die Hohenzollern und ihr Werk* (1915) and *Geist und Epochen der preussischen Geschichte* (1943); H. Brunschwig, *La Crise de l'état prussien à la fin du XVIIIe siècle et la genèse de la mentalité romantique* (1947); H. W. Rosenberg, *Bureaucracy, Aristocracy and Autocracy: the Prussian Experience 1660–1815* (1958); G. Ritter, *Staatskunst und Kriegshandwerk* (1959). For the period after 1815 *see* general histories of Germany and the biographies of the statesmen mentioned in the text above.

PRUSSIC ACID: *see* HYDROCYANIC ACID.

PRYNNE, WILLIAM (1600–1669), English Puritan pamphleteer, antiquarian, and parliamentarian, whose ears were twice shorn as punishment for his opposition to the religious policy of William Laud, was born at Swainswick near Bath, the son of a farmer, Thomas Prynne. He was educated at Bath Grammar School and at Oriel College, Oxford, and was called to the bar at Lincoln's Inn in 1628. From 1627, when his first pamphlet was published, Prynne emerged as an opponent of Arminianism in church doctrine and of ceremonialism in church services, and thereby attracted the hostility of William Laud (bishop of London, 1628–33, archbishop of Canterbury, 1633–45).

Prynne's famous attack on the theatre and stage plays, *Histriomastix: the Players Scourge or Actors Tragedy* (1632; dated 1633), alleged that plays were evil and corrupted morals. It claimed that kings and emperors who had supported the theatre had met violent deaths, and its vicious denunciation of actresses was assumed to apply also to Queen Henrietta Maria, who at the time of its publication was taking part in a masque. Through Laud's influence Prynne was imprisoned in February 1633 in the Tower of London. On Feb. 17, 1634, he was sentenced by the Star Chamber to be imprisoned for life, fined £5,000, expelled from Lincoln's Inn, degraded from his Oxford University degree, and set in the pillory, where he was to lose both his ears. The latter part of the sentence was carried out on May 7 and 10, when his ears were partly cut off.

Prynne continued his writings while in the Tower, attacking James I's *Book of Sports,* reissued in 1633, which permitted games on Sunday, in *A Divine Tragedie Lately Acted* (1636), and Matthew Wren, bishop of Norwich, and other bishops who supported Laud in *Newes from Ipswich* (1636). On June 14, 1637, Prynne was brought before the Star Chamber with two other puritans, John Bastwick and Henry Burton, and was again sentenced. On June 30 the stumps of his ears were shorn off in the pillory at Westminster and he was branded on the cheeks with the letters S.L., meaning "seditious libeler," though Prynne interpreted them in verse as "Stigmata Laudis" (the marks of Laud). He was later removed to Carnarvon Castle and to Mount Orgueil Castle in Jersey.

When the Long Parliament met in November 1640 it ordered Prynne to be freed and on April 20, 1641, his sentences were declared illegal. He then attacked the Roman Catholics and in 1642 defended Parliament's resort to arms against Charles I. He showed a vindictive energy in the prosecution of Laud, which resulted in the archbishop's execution in January 1645. Having been entrusted (May 1643) with the search of Laud's papers, he published a mutilated edition of his diary, entitled *A Breviate of the Life of William Laud* (1644), and also *Hidden Workes of Darkenes Brought to Publike Light* (1645) to prejudice the case against Laud. Prynne, although opposed to ceremonialism, favoured a national church controlled by the king as head of the state and issued a series of tracts against the Independents. He also violently opposed the Presbyterian system and in his *Foure Serious Questions* (1645) and *A Vindication of Foure Serious Questions* (1645) he denied the right of any church to excommunicate except by leave of the state. He remained throughout an enemy of individual freedom in religion.

Prynne took the side of Parliament against the army in 1647. He was returned as a member for Newport in Cornwall in November 1648. He at once opposed the demand for the execution of Charles I and as a result was among those members excluded by the purge of Col. Thomas Pride on Dec. 6, 1648. Imprisoned for resisting this expulsion, he was released in January 1649 and retired to Swainswick. In June he was assessed for the monthly contribution levied on the country by the Commons to support the army, but refused to pay and published *A Legal Vindication of the Liberties of England* (1649), arguing that no tax could be raised without the consent of the two Houses (the Lords had recently been abolished). As a result, he was imprisoned by the army from June 1650 to February 1653 and on his release renewed his pamphleteering activities. When the Rump Parliament was restored by the army on May 7, 1659, Prynne was refused admittance, but on Feb. 21, 1660, with Gen. George Monck's support, he took his seat. He was returned for Bath to the Convention Parliament (1660), where he supported the restoration of Charles II, and to the Parliament elected in 1661.

Prynne was more notable as an antiquarian than as a politician. His knowledge of the national archives, unrivaled in that age, was acknowledged by his appointment in 1660 as keeper of the records in the Tower. In that office he did much to rescue the documents there from neglect and to secure their proper preservation. His historical writings, though devoid of style and orderly arrangement, have a lasting value because of the original records printed in them. They include *An Exact Chronological Vindication and Historical Demonstration of Our British, Roman, Saxon . . . Kings Supreme Ecclesiastical Jurisdiction, over all Spiritual or Religious Affairs . . . Within Their Realms,* covering the period to the death of Edward I, three volumes (1665–68); *Aurum Reginae, or a Compendious Tractate and Chronological*

Collection of Records in the Tower and Court of Exchequer Concerning Queen-Gold (1668); and *Brief Animadversions on . . . the Fourth Part of the Institutes of the Lawes of England . . . compiled by Sir E. Coke* (1669). Prynne died unmarried on Oct. 24, 1669, at Lincoln's Inn, London.

See E. W. Kirby, *William Prynne* (1931), which contains a bibliography of his writings; W. M. Lamont, *Marginal Prynne, 1600–1669* (1963).

PRYTANEUM, the town hall of a Greek city state. These states normally had a building which housed the chief magistrate (sometimes called prytanis) and the common altar or hearth of the community. There ambassadors, distinguished foreigners, and citizens who had done signal service were entertained. There is evidence for a prytaneum at Sigeum in the Troad in the 6th century B.C., at Dreros in Crete in the 3rd (where an oath by Hestia is taken in the prytaneum), and at many other places at various dates, among them Cyzicus, Erythrae, Priene, Ephesus, Epidamnus, and Rhodes. At Athens one sign of the unification of Attica attributed to Theseus was the creation of a single prytaneum (Thucydides, book ii, 15). This was the ancient seat of the chief archon (*q.v.*) and was situated on the north slope of the Acropolis.

After the Persian invasion administration shifted to the market place (agora), where the council (boule; *q.v.*) then met and where *c.* 470 B.C. a round building, now identified as the Tholos (*see* ATHENS: *Topography and Antiquities: The Agora*), was erected as meeting place and dining hall for the *prytaneis,* the committee of the council. This building was later known as the *prytanikon* and is to be distinguished from the prytaneum, which continued to be used for honorific meals.

Prytaneum was also the name of an Athenian law court. In it sat the "king" (basileus, one of the archons) and the four "tribe kings" (*phylobasileis*). In the 5th century and later it tried cases of homicide due to an unknown person, an animal, or an inanimate object. It was probably the survival of an ancient court set up as the main court of the state at the newly instituted prytaneum after the unification of Attica. In an amnesty law attributed to Solon near the beginning of the 6th century the prytaneum is mentioned as one of a number of courts which had pronounced sentence of exile. It is perhaps significant that court fees at Athens were known as *prytanea.*

BIBLIOGRAPHY.—R. J. Bonner and G. E. Smith, *The Administration of Justice from Homer to Aristotle,* vol. i (1930); I. Thallon Hill, *The Ancient City of Athens* (1953). (A. R. W. H.)

PRZEMYSL, a town in Rzeszow *wojewodztwo* (province), Poland, lies on the San River, near the frontier of the U.S.S.R., and at the border of the Carpathian Mountains and the sub-Carpathian lowlands. Pop. (1960) 47,442. The town began as a fortress on the old route leading south through the Carpathians. It was the object of dispute in the 10th century between Poland and Ruthenia. Occupied at the end of the 11th century by Ruthenian princes, it came into Polish hands in 1340. It acquired city rights in 1389 and numerous privileges, and developed into a large commercial and cultural centre. After the first partition of Poland in 1772 it was taken by Austria, returning to Poland in 1918.

Its long history has left Przemysl many old buildings, including the castle, rebuilt in the 17th century, and the 15th-century cathedral, often rebuilt and enlarged. There are two museums. Industries include metalworking, a knitted-goods factory, and timber working. The town and its surroundings are popular with tourists. (T. K. W.)

PRZEMYSL, SIEGES OF. An Austrian-held fortress town on the San River in modern Poland, Przemysl (*q.v.*) underwent two major sieges in the first year of World War I. Its defense and its attack tied up large numbers of men and huge quantities of matériel, but otherwise they had little effect on the course of the war.

Przemysl was protected by a ring of forts 36 mi. in circumference. Some were of recent construction, but the fortress as a whole was not strictly up to date. To clear the foreground in front of the fortified line no fewer than 18 villages and about five miles of forest were leveled to the ground on mobilization.

During August 1914, the first month of the war, Austrian armies advancing eastward through Galicia had been met and defeated by the Russians at Lemberg (modern Lvov); by mid-September the Austrians had fallen back from the San River line toward Cracow, leaving the garrison at Przemysl to hold as best it could. By Sept. 24 the Russian investment of the fortress was complete, the siege being undertaken by Radko-Dimitriev's 3rd Army. While arrival of Russian siege artillery was delayed by the state of the communications, the Austrians renewed the offensive early in October. In the hope of capturing Przemysl before the progress of the enemy offensive compelled the raising of the siege, Radko-Dimitriev carried out several violent assaults between Oct. 5 and 8; they broke down with heavy loss, and the approach of the Austrian 3rd Army necessitated the withdrawal of the investing forces. The fortress was entered by Austrian infantry of the field armies on Oct. 11, when the Russians retreated east of the San.

During the Austrian attempts to force the San line, which lasted throughout October, the fortress lay in the centre of the battle line, and its garrison took an active part in the operations. Its reserves of supplies and material were largely drawn on by the field armies, from whose operations great results were expected at the time. But when the offensive proved fruitless and Russian pressure necessitated a retirement that would leave the fortress again isolated, special efforts were made hastily to reprovision it. They were so far successful that the fortress, commanded by General Kusmanek, was enabled to hold out for 4½ months in the second siege which began on Nov. 9.

The second siege was undertaken by a specially formed 11th Army under General Selivanov, consisting of four divisions of second-line troops. It had been decided to reduce the fortress by blockade rather than by assault. During November and December such fighting as occurred was initiated rather by the sorties of the garrison than by the attacks of the besiegers. During February and March 1915 the Austrian armies made repeated but unsuccessful efforts to relieve the fortress.

Meanwhile the Russians had gradually closed in and had commenced a systematic bombardment of the fortress. On March 13 they carried the advanced positions on its north front. Kusmanek's situation was now desperate; his supplies and munitions were almost exhausted, and the final effort of the field armies to come to his rescue had been abandoned. He attempted to save a portion of the garrison by a breakthrough to the east, but the effort, made on the morning of the 19th, was soon brought to a standstill. On the morning of March 22 Kusmanek surrendered after destroying the works and military stores as far as possible. The garrison then numbered about 110,000.

The Russians did not hold the fortress for long. At the beginning of May, Field Marshal Mackensen's offensive on the Dunajec broke through the Russian line and drove their armies back to the San. On May 30 the Austrians attacked on the southwest but made little progress; the Germans, attacking with their heavy artillery on the north of the fortress, made short work of the northern group of forts. On the night of June 2 the Russians abandoned the fortress.

Przemysl served no strategic aim commensurate with the efforts expended on its defense and attempted relief. Its resistance during the first siege was of value to the Austrians when their armies again advanced to the San, in assuring to them a bridgehead over the river. But during the second siege Przemysl was an embarrassment rather than a source of strength and led to several ill-considered efforts at relief, which cost the Austrian field armies dearly. The fortress did not control any line of supply vital to the Russian armies operating west of it toward Cracow, since there was a railway available through Jaroslaw. The Russians could therefore afford in the second siege to resort to a simple blockade by second-line troops, so that the fortress did not even weaken their field armies to any appreciable extent.

BIBLIOGRAPHY.—H. Hillger, *Krieg und Sieg, Befreiung vor Przemysl* (1915); E. Ludendorff, *My War Memories* (trans. 1919); E. von Falkenhayn, *General Headquarters, 1914–1916, and its Critical Decisions* (trans. 1919); J. Daniloff, *Russland im Weltkriege, 1914–1915* (1925); A. W. F. Knox, *With the Russian Army, 1914–17* (1921). See also WORLD WARS.   (A. P. W.)

PRZHEVALSKY (PRJEVALSKY), **NIKOLAI MIKHAILOVICH** (1839–1888), Russian traveler, contributed by his explorations and route surveys perhaps more than any other of his generation to the unveiling of central Asia. He was born near Smolensk on March 31, 1839, and was educated at the Smolensk gymnasium. In 1855 he joined an infantry regiment; in 1856 he became an officer. From 1864 to 1886 he taught geography in the military school at Warsaw. The next year he was sent to Irkutsk, and in 1870 he set out from Kyakhta, southeast of Lake Baikal, traveled through Urga (Ulan Bator), and crossed the Gobi Desert to Kalgan (Chang-chia-k'ou), 100 mi. (160 km.) from Peking. He visited Mongolia and then returned to Urga. His second journey began at Kulja in 1876 and took him southeastward across the Tien Shan and Takla Makan, for nearly 200 mi. (320 km.) along the foot of the Astin Tagh, and back by the same route. He set out from Zaisan on his third journey in 1879, crossed Dzungaria and continued southward over the Astin Tagh to within 170 mi. of Lhasa, which he was not allowed to visit. He then turned eastward, partly following the line of the upper Yellow River, and crossed the Gobi to Kyakhta. The fourth journey began at Urga in 1883 and led across the Gobi, south of Koko Nor (Ch'ing-hai) and Tsaidam to the Astin Tagh and Kunlun Mountains and then over the Tien Shan to Issyk-Kul. He had intended to lead another expedition, but died at Issyk-Kul on Nov. 1, 1888. Przhevalsky made valuable collections of the vegetation and animals of the regions he visited and his discoveries include the wild camel and the only known wild horse, named after him Przhevalsky's horse (*Equus przewalskii*).

The accounts of his first two journeys were translated into English: E. M. Morgan, *Mongolia, the Tangut Country, and the Solitudes of Northern Tibet* (1876) and *From Kulja, Across the Tian-Shan to Lop-nor* (1879).

See N. M. Karataev, *Nikolai Mikhailovich Przheval'skii* (1948).   (A. M. F.)

PSALMANAZAR, GEORGE (*c.* 1679–1763), French literary impostor, who published fictitious works on Formosa, was born in the south of France about 1679, of Catholic parents. After his education in Franciscan and Jesuit schools he set out on a wandering life, traveling in Germany and the Low Countries on a forged passport as a native of Japan and under the name by which he was subsequently known. He enlisted in the army of the elector of Cologne and, while still posing as a Japanese, was taken up by an English army chaplain, the Rev. W. Innes, who baptized him, received him into the Church of England, and furthered the imposture by presenting him to Henry Compton, bishop of London. He now posed as a Formosan and translated the Catechism into "Formosan," a language which he himself had invented. He hoodwinked the learned of his time and his *Historical and Geographical Description of Formosa* (1704) and *Dialogue Between a Japanese and a Formosan* (1707) were well received. When doubts of his authenticity arose he attempted to answer objections but soon retired into the obscurity and poverty of a hack writer. In his last years he was a model of rectitude. He died in London on May 3, 1763.

His *Memoirs of . . . Known by the Name of George Psalmanazar* were published in 1764.

See P. W. Sergeant, *Liars and Fakers* (1926).   (H. G. WH.)

PSALMS, BOOK OF (also called PSALTER), a book of the Old Testament. It is entitled in Hebrew TEHILLIM, "Songs of Praise," because it was used from the earliest stages of its present edition as the hymnal of the Second Temple in postexilic Judaism. It belongs to the third canon of the Hebrew Bible known as *Kethubim*, or "Writings" (Hagiographa), together with Job, Proverbs, the Five Scrolls or *Megilloth*, Daniel, Ezra-Nehemiah, and Chronicles.

As all pious Jews in Roman times knew the psalms by heart, Jesus and the early Christians often referred to them. The Psalter became the basis of the Christian as well as Jewish liturgies. No other book of hymnody is common today to all sections of Jewry and Christendom. The psalms are often quoted in the New Testament, usually in the Greek translation of the Septuagint.

The Catholic churches (Greek and Roman), respectively using

the Septuagint and the Vulgate (which follows in this respect the Septuagint), designate the psalms with numbers which differ at times from those of the Hebrew tradition (respected by Jews and Protestants). Modern Roman Catholic scholars, however, are beginning to return to the Hebrew usage. In the Greek-Latin designation, the Hebrew Pss. 9–10 are counted as Ps. 9; Ps. 11 is known as Ps. 10; etc. Other variations are:

Hebrew	*Septuagint-Vulgate*
114–115	113
116:1–9	114
116:10–19	115
117–146	116–145
147:1–11	146
147:12–20	147

In addition, the Septuagint (Greek) Bible adds a Ps. 151, the Hebrew text of which was discovered among the Dead Sea Scrolls.

Division and Superscriptions.—The Hebrew manuscripts of the Book of Psalms include five doxologies which divide it into five sections, perhaps in imitation of the five books of the Pentateuch: (1) Pss. 1–41; (2) Pss. 42–72; (3) Pss. 73–89; (4) Pss. 90–106; (5) Pss. 107–150. This division, however, appears to be artificial. The superscriptions which are found at the head of most of the poems of the Psalter show that there are several collections, which probably represent earlier stages before the final edition of the book. Such collections may have been:

1. Pss. 3–41, which bear the superscription "To David," except for Ps. 10 (which is clearly the second part of Ps. 9, with which it forms an alphabetic acrostic) and Ps. 31 (which however bears the superscription in the Greek).

2. Pss. 51–72, also ascribed "To David," except Ps. 71 (which bears the superscription "To Solomon"). After Ps. 72 comes the marginal comment, "End of the prayers of David the son of Jesse."

3. The Psalms of Asaph (Pss. 50 and 73–83) may well have formed a separate collection, which was closed before the addition of the second group.

4. The Psalms of the Sons of Korah (Pss. 42–49; 84–85; 87–88).

5. The Psalms of Heman (a son of Korah), the Ezrahite (Ps. 88), and of Ethan, also an Ezrahite (Ps. 89).

6. The Psalms of Yahweh-King (Pss. 93–99), which bear no superscription and may have formed at one time a special hymnal, for they present a certain homogeneity of theme and style, and often include the formula "Yahweh has become king."

7. The Halleluja Psalms, which end with the liturgical invitation "Praise the Lord" (*Halleluja*) and sometimes begin with the call to worship, "O give thanks" (*Hodhu*). Such pieces were meant to be chanted antiphonally (Pss. 105–107; Pss. 111–118, except Ps. 115; Pss. 135–136; Pss. 146–150). The Jewish tradition has set apart Pss. 113–118 as "The Egyptian Hallel," or "Praise" in celebration of the exodus from Egypt, and Pss. 118–137 (or Pss. 120–137) as "The Great Hallel" (used in the ceremonies of Passover).

8. The Psalms of Degrees or Songs of Ascents (Pss. 120–134) overlap the preceding classification. A talmudic tradition assigns these 15 pieces to the Feast of Tabernacles and states that they were chanted by Levites at the head of the 15 steps which led from the court of the women to the court of men. These psalms were originally pilgrim songs (*cf.* allusions to travel in Pss. 121, 122, 132, and to Zion in Pss. 126 and 132).

Principles of Classification.—Many attempts have been made to classify the psalms in a systematic, chronological, or thematic order.

Authors.—Some scholars have in the past proposed to group them by authors, and they have taken the superscriptions (*see* above) to designate authorship, thus: Psalms of David, a Psalm of Moses "the man of God" (Ps. 90), two Psalms of Solomon (Pss. 72 and 127); etc. They point out that 13 of the psalms ascribed to David include prefatory notes which relate them to circumstantial events in the life of the king (Pss. 3, 7, 18, 34, 51, 52, 54, 56, 57, 59, 60, 63, 142). Internal analysis of these poems, however, reveals that they are much later than the 10th century B.C., when

David lived. A number of psalms bear more than one superscription; some refer to "the choir master" (Pss. 39, 62, 77). In Roman and New Testament times, Jews and Christians ascribed all 150 psalms to David; the expression "To so-and-so" designated in all probability not authorship but dedication or the name of an early anthology (*cf.* I Kings 16:20; II Kings 15:15).

Chronological Order.—Other scholars have proposed a chronological order, but there has never been any agreement among specialists on the dates of the individual poems. Moreover, some of the psalms combine fragments of different dates (for example, Ps. 24), and most of them have been revised and expanded through the centuries, very much as the hymns of the Christian Church have been (from patristic Greek or medieval Latin to Luther's German and 20th-century American).

Names of Compositions.—Others have suggested that psalms be classified according to the names of compositions which some of them bear in the Hebrew Bible: Pss. 56–59 are called *miktam;* Pss. 52–55 are known as *maskil;* Pss. 62–68 are entitled *mizmor;* still others are merely designated as *shir* (song). Unfortunately, many pieces have no name, and there is no agreement among scholars as to the exact meaning of the name when it appears.

Use and Theme.—Many exegetes of the past generations have grouped the psalms according to their probable use and thematic motifs. It has been recognized, for example, that Pss. 105–106 deal with the history of Israel and that they were used for the celebration of a festival. Thematic motifs, however, are often mixed and sometimes overlapping.

Poetic "Gattung."—Hermann Gunkel was the modern pioneer in the form-critical analysis of the Psalms (1926). From the study of rhythm, strophic structure, chiasmus, key words, and expressions, he has identified five major and seven minor types or genres or *Gattungen* of hymnody:

Major types: (1) hymns, (2) community laments, (3) royal psalms, (4) individual laments, and (5) individual thanksgivings.

Minor types: (1) blessings and curses, (2) pilgrim songs, (3) national thanksgivings, (4) legends, (5) meditations on the Torah, (6) prophetic oracles, (7) wisdom psalms.

In addition, Gunkel showed that most of the psalms fulfill a specific need in the cult, and he sought to determine objective criteria for the reconstruction of this cultic *Sitz-im-Leben* (situation in life). At the same time, Sigmund Mowinckel (1921–24) attempted to relate many hymns and laments to a hypothetical annual Feast of the Enthronement of Yahweh. Later (1949) Artur Weiser sought the cultic milieu of Hebrew psalmody in an equally hypothetical yearly Feast of Covenant Renewal. In all probability, the classification principle enunciated by Gunkel, with some modifications, will stand the test of time.

Classification of Main Psalms.—On the basis of *Gattungkritik* and with due attention paid to thematic motifs and uses, the following classification may be proposed:

1. Hymns of praise: (*a*) praise of the Lord of nature (Pss. 8, 19, 29, 65, 67, 96, 148); (*b*) praise of the Lord of history (Pss. 33, 46, 66, 68, 75, 76, 78, 89, 105, 106, 107, 113, 114, 115, 136, 149); (*c*) praise of the Lord of Zion (Pss. 15, 24, 47, 84, 93, 94, 95, 97, 98, 99, 122, 125, 126, 132, 134, 135, 147, 150).

2. Prayers of crisis: (*a*) national lamentations (Pss. 44, 60, 74, 79, 80, 83, 123, 137); (*b*) personal lamentations (Pss. 5, 6, 7, 9, 10, 22, 51, 69, 77, 88, 130); (*c*) personal supplications (Pss. 3, 4, 13, 35, 38, 39, 41, 42–43, 54, 55, 56, 57, 63, 64, 70, 71, 86, 102, 120, 141, 142, 143).

3. Songs of faith: (*a*) personal thanksgivings (Pss. 18, 30, 32, 34, 40, 118, 144, 145, 146); (*b*) prayers of communion (Pss. 11, 16, 17, 23, 26, 27, 28, 31, 36, 62, 103, 116, 121, 131, 138, 139, 140); (*c*) meditations of Wisdom (Pss. 1, 12, 14 (53), 37, 49, 73, 90, 91, 92, 101, 111, 112, 119, 127, 128, 129).

4. Special psalms: (*a*) royal hymns (Pss. 2, 20, 21, 45, 61, 72, 110); (*b*) prophetic oracles (Pss. 50, 81, 82); (*c*) maledictions (Pss. 52, 58, 59, 109).

Metrical Form.—*Rhythm.*—English versions do not permit the reader to discover the poetic form of the psalms. Ancient Hebrew poetry in general and psalmody in particular followed highly sophisticated rules of rhythmic and strophic structure.

The basic line is made of two or three cola ("limbs"; *see* PROSODY, CLASSICAL), which are symmetrical in the hymns (usually three and three stressed syllables) and asymmetrical in the laments (usually three and two stressed syllables). Lines present various kinds of parallelism of members, as follows:

1. Synonymic, in which the idea is repeated:

   In the law of the Lord is his delight,
   and in his law he meditates day and night. (Ps. 1:2)

2. Antithetic, in which the idea is repeated by antonymy:

   For the Lord knows the way of the righteous,
   but the way of the wicked shall perish. (Ps. 1:6)

3. Synthetic, in which the idea is continued from one colon to the next, as in a comparison:

   As the hart panteth after the water brooks,
   so panteth my soul after thee, O God! (Ps. 42:1)

4. Repetitive-additive (staircase parallelism), in which synonymy and complementariness are combined:

   Ascribe to the Lord, ye sons of the gods,
   Ascribe to the Lord, glory and power!
   Ascribe to the Lord, the glory of his name!
   Worship the Lord in the beauty of holiness! (Ps. 29:1–2)

5. Introverted or chiasmic, in which the first word of the first colon is parallel to the last word of the second colon, and the intermediary expressions form a symmetrical pattern, often in the reverse order:

   O God, break the teeth of their mouths:
   the fangs of the young lions tear out, O Lord! (Ps. 58:6)

6. Mixed, in which any two of the preceding types of parallelism are combined:

   The Lord is my light and my salvation:
   Whom shall I fear?
   The Lord is the strength of my life:
   Of whom shall I be afraid? (Ps. 27:1)

Metre.—In order to determine the intrinsic quality of each line, it is necessary to sense the number of accented syllables in each colon and also to consider syntactic units, with links or separations, pauses, and semipauses. A metrical unit may be: (1) a noun in the construct state and the noun to which it is constructed: "the voice-of-the-*Lord*" (Ps. 29:3); (2) a preposition and a noun: "upon-the-*waters*" (Ps. 29:3a); (3) a noun and its qualifying epithet or apposition: "upon-many-and-deep-*waters*" (Ps. 29:3c); (4) sometimes, a verb, especially in the participle, with its direct object: "breaking-*ce*dars" (Ps. 29:5); (5) sometimes, a verb, especially in the so-called "consecutive imperfect," with its subject: "And-the-Lord-*shat*tereth" (Ps. 29:5b). Cola are made of two, three, and exceptionally four metrical units. Thus, lines may be bicola of 3+3, 3+2, 2+3, 2+2, 4+4; or tricola of 3+3+3, 3+2+3, 3+2+2, etc.

Strophe.—The determination of the strophic structure is complex for it is to a certain extent dependent upon the correct analysis of the metre and of the line. Until the discovery of the Ugaritic literature in 1929 (*see* UGARIT), too many critics imposed a symmetrical pattern, by dividing the text of many psalms in false lines, hence were unable to discern the strophes. The proto-Canaanite poetry of Ugarit revealed sequences of bicola exceptionally interspersed with tricola, and since its recovery the study of the poetic structure has been making progress.

A remarkable example of strophic art appears in one of the most archaic pieces of the Psalter, Ps. 29. A prelude (of two bicola, vv. 1–2) develops the thematic motif of "Glory to God in the highest," while a postlude (of two bicola, vv. 10–11) offers a priestly proclamation (v. 10) and a benediction (v. 11) on the theme "Peace on earth." Between these two elements, three strophes of two bicola or tricola each develop the picture of the thunderstorm: gathering (vv. 3–4); bursting forth (vv. 5–7a); dying away (vv. 8–9). Each of the three strophes, in addition, ends with a key word—"splendour" or "majesty" (v. 4b), "fire" (v. 7a), and "glory" (v. 9c)—leaving no doubt in the mind of the singer that the theological climax does not come with the climactic moment of the natural phenomenon but with the singing of the hymn in the heavenly sanctuary.

Musical Instruments.—Rhythmic and strophic structures are intimately related to the musical aspect of all the psalms, which were originally composed by musicians and were chanted or sung with instrumental accompaniment. At least 17 musical instruments are mentioned in the Old Testament, many of which are also listed in the psalms. They are: (1) idiophones—gold bells on high priest's robe, jingle bells, cymbals, rattler sistrums, gongs or handbells; (2) aerophones or wind instruments—flutes or shepherd's pipes, clarinets or double-pipes, horns (from bulls), short trumpets (ram's horn), the *shophar* (originally, wild ibex horn, often confused with preceding), tubas or long trumpets (made of brass, silver, or gilded silver); (3) membraphones or tuned percussion instruments—drums, tambourines, or tympanons; (4) chordophones or stringed instruments—lyres or ten-stringed instruments, sackbut, trigon, or sambuk (not in the psalms, instruments for music of ill repute), luths or three-stringed instruments, harps or viol or psaltery, perhaps a kind of cithara (guitar) with a box of resonance (of stretched skin on wooden frame).

Modern musicologists are engaged in the difficult task of rediscovering the psalm melodies in Temple and synagogue during biblical times.

Oriental Background.—In both poetic form and musical instrumentation, the Hebrew psalmists inherited skills from the art of their neighbours and predecessors, especially the Egyptians and the Canaanites. The texts of many ancient Near Eastern psalms in Akkadian, Ugaritic, and Egyptian have been discovered, published, and translated. It is now recognized, for example, that Ps. 29 represents a radical adaptation of an Ugaritic (proto-Canaanite) hymn in honour of the storm-god, and that Ps. 104 has been strongly influenced by the Egyptian hymn to the sundeity by Ikhnaton (Amenhotep IV, *c.* 1379–*c.* 1362 B.C.). Differences between the Egyptian prototype and the Hebrew masterpiece, however, reveal the originality of the Hebrew psalmist.

Origins of Hebrew Psalmody.—A rabbinical legend told of King David, roused from his slumbers by the sound of a midnight breeze playing upon his harp; till dawn flushed the eastern skies, David "wedded words to the strains." For centuries both Jews and Christians ascribed the whole Psalter to David. At the end of the 19th century, on the contrary, most critics spoke of a Persian date (538–333 B.C.) and even of the Maccabaean age (165–100 B.C.) for the majority of the psalms. In the 20th century, the Psalter has been considered to be a collection of poems which reflect all periods of Israel's history, from the exodus (13th century B.C.) to the postexilic restoration (*c.* 500 B.C.). Several factors played their part in the origin and growth of the psalms:

Miriam, the sister of Moses and a prophetess, may be credited with having composed the first national hymn of thanksgiving, a paean of praise after the victory over the Egyptian Army at the Sea of Reeds. She shouted forth to the accompaniment of timbrel and of dancing maidens (Ex. 15:20–21).

The ark (*q.v.*) of Yahweh, at first connected with holy war (Num. 10:35–36; *cf.* I Sam. 5–6), was later the cultic sign of real presence in the shrine (II Sam. 6–7), and many hymns were composed for the adoration of Yahweh, present in the sanctuary.

The three seasonal festivals of Unleavened Bread-Passover, Weeks, and Tabernacles (Ex. 34:23) became the occasion for tribal and national gatherings at the shrine, during which elaborate ceremonies of thanksgiving for the fruit of the soil were performed. These included the singing of hymns before, during, and after the performance of the sacred acts, with orchestral music, processions, antiphonal responses, etc.

With the building of the Temple of Solomon in Jerusalem, ceremonial became more and more important in the life of the covenant community. Hymns and laments were composed, edited, and adapted during the whole period of the divided monarchy (10th–8th centuries B.C.) and the last years of the kingdom of Judah.

A few more hymns and national laments were composed during the horrors of the exile in Babylon (587–538 B.C.) and the vicissitudes of the early restoration in postexilic Judaism (from 538 B.C.), and perhaps later (Chronicles, Ezra-Nehemiah).

The influence of the great prophets in the 8th and 7th centuries, together with the crises which led to the destruction of Israel (*c.* 722 B.C.) and Judah (587 B.C.), created classes of economically destitute persons who gravitated around the sanctuary and became "the poor" and "the pious," and sang at the Temple ceremonies. Several of these men are responsible for individual laments and supplications.

The teachers of Wisdom, first recruited among the public servants and the foreign diplomats of Solomon and his successors, especially Hezekiah, reflected upon the commandments of their God and wrote poetic meditations which were later incorporated in the services of public worship.

Members of the royal court composed hymns in honour of a new reign, and their expectations of a righteous king received later on a messianic interpretation (Pss. 2, 110).

Religion of the Psalmists.—It is impossible to think of Hebrew psalmody as a product of literary, artistic, or theological homogeneity. Diversity reigns. The present anthology of the Psalter represents expressions of faith which come from many generations and diverse kinds of men. The religion of the psalmists reflects the theology of the entire Hebrew Bible.

The cult of Israel was unique in the ancient Near East, for the act of adoration brought into the liturgical present both the past and the future. Yahweh (*q.v.*), for the psalmists, was not the personified sun or a deified force of fertility. He transcended absolutely the realm of nature. He was held to be sovereign over both the universe and the history of mankind. Hebrew worshipers in their liturgies hailed the serenity of Yahweh and could even afford to laugh about the reality of cosmic evil: "And that Leviathan, which thou hast made, just to play with!" (Ps. 104:26).

Nations engulfed Israel, but the psalmists lived liturgically at the end of time, when history would be brought to its fulfillment and war would be stilled for ever (Ps. 46). They sacramentally saw all the kings of the earth who would worship Yahweh "as the people of the God of Abraham" (Ps. 47). The psalms, more than the oracles of the prophets, created in Judaism its unique sense of the oneness and purpose of history.

Most of the poets who composed the psalms lived under the protection of the sanctuary, but they almost never spoke of the value of sacrificial worship. When they did, they generally spiritualized the meaning of ritual (Pss. 50, 51, 69). This is one of the reasons, surely, for the popularity of the psalms not only among Catholics but also among Protestants and even Quakers. The psalmists' concern in the affairs of the Temple was ultimately centred upon the presence of God in a psychological mode (Pss. 42–43, 84, 139), and stressed harmony in the brotherhood of the worshipers (Ps. 133).

To be sure, psalmists expressed their love for the Law, but they stressed its moral rather than its sacerdotal aspects (Pss. 15; 24:3–6; 34:13–15). Some of them, disciples of the great prophets, discovered even that the scrupulous observance of the commandments of the Law did not give rise to any claim upon the bounty of God. On the contrary, they sensed that a new kind of inward sinfulness might emerge from their awareness of legal self-righteousness (Ps. 19:13–14).

Certain traits appear also in the psalmists' religion which constitute for the modern mind an element of serious limitation. In a number of prayers of confession, of supplication, and of lamentation there may be detected not only an indulgence toward self-pity but also a spirit of oversimplification which tends to associate the poor with the righteous and the rich with the wicked, yet to apply the dogma of special providence in such a way as to associate prosperity with virtue and misfortune with sinfulness (Ps. 37). A tendency also may be seen to separate the insiders from the outsiders and to prepare the way toward sectarianism, to express an attitude of vindictiveness and to manifest *Schadenfreude* (*i.e.*, a malicious joy at the misfortune of another) against the enemies of Israel (Pss. 58:10; 60:8; etc.).

A few psalmists, on the contrary, influenced both by the prophets' "white-hot" religion (Ps. 51) and the existential agony of the Jobian school (Pss. 73, 139), depicted with sharp lucidity their own spirituality and thus became the models of Jewish and Christian poetry on divine intimacy throughout the ages (Pss. 16, 23, 27, 36; etc.).

It is even possible that this sense of communion was endowed with such a quality of endurance that it presided over the birth of the hope in eternal life (Ps. 73:24b; contrast Ps. 88:5), the overcoming of the fear of alienation (Ps. 22:1), and the expectancy of the heavenly banquet (vv. 25–31). Together with some of the royal psalms (especially Pss. 2 and 110), these songs of faith and communion provided the early church with its first pattern for the needed interpretation of Jesus as the Christ.

See also references under "Psalms, Book of" in the Index.

BIBLIOGRAPHY.—C. A. and E. G. Briggs, *Critical and Exegetical Commentary on the Book of Psalms,* 2 vol. (1906); S. Mowinckel, *Psalmenstudien,* 6 vol. (1921–24); H. Gunkel, *Die Psalmen* (1926); A. C. Welch, *The Psalter in Life, Worship and History* (1926); M. Buttenwieser, *The Psalms* (1938); F. James, *Thirty Psalmists* (1938); W. O. E. Oesterley, *The Psalms,* 2 vol. (1940); E. A. Leslie, *The Psalms* (1949); S. Terrien, *The Psalms and Their Meaning for Today* (1952); H. J. Franken, *The Mystical Communion with JHWH in the Book of Psalms* (1954); W. S. McCullough, "The Book of Psalms," in *The Interpreter's Bible,* vol. iv (1955); A. Weiser, *The Psalms,* Eng. trans. from the 5th Ger. ed. (1962); H. J. Kraus, *Psalmen,* 2 vol. (1960); S. Mowinckel, *The Psalms in Israel's Worship,* Eng. trans., 2 vol. (1963). For Ps. 151, *see* J. A. Sander, "Ps. 151 in 11 QPss," in *Zeitschrift für die alttestamentliche Wissenschaft,* vol. lxxv, pp. 73–85 (1963). For music, *see* E. Werner, *The Sacred Bridge* (1959). For other ancient Near Eastern psalms, *see* J. B. Pritchard (ed.), *Ancient Near Eastern Texts Relating to the Old Testament,* 2nd ed., pp. 365–401 (1955).   (S. Te.)

PSALTERY, a musical instrument related to the dulcimers and zithers, having gut or metal strings stretched over a flat soundbox. Its outline is characteristically trapezoid, often in the Middle Ages with incurving sides. The psaltery was then plucked with the fingers or with a pair of quill plectra. The strings are all open, none being stopped to give different notes as on a true zither. Probably of Near Eastern origin in late classical times (and inheriting the Greek harp name *psalterion*), the psaltery reached its greatest popularity in the West during the 13th to 15th centuries. No medieval specimen survives. The Russian *gusli* and Finnish *kantele* are rudimentary psalteries, played across the knees. The large Egyptian psaltery, *qanun,* is played with two bone plectra worn in rings on the forefingers.

(A. C. Ba.)

PSAMTIK (PSAMMATEK), the name of three pharaohs of the 26th (Saite) Egyptian dynasty (664–525 B.C.). Manetho's Greek transcription of the name, Psammetichos, is often used; Herodotus calls them Psammetichos, Psammis, and Psammenitos respectively. Their predecessors, perhaps of Libyan origin, ruled Sais during the 25th dynasty, first as vassals of the Ethiopian kings of Napata and later, after the Assyrian conquest (671 B.C.), as vassals of Assyria.

PSAMTIK I (Wahibre; 663–610 B.C.) succeeded his father, Necho I, after their victory (663) over Tanutamon, the Napatan, when Necho may have been killed. By *c.* 656 B.C., with the aid of Ionian and Carian mercenaries, Psamtik had subjugated his rivals in the delta, had unified lower Egypt and, with the help of his ally Gyges of Lydia, had expelled the Assyrian garrison. In his ninth year he made himself master of the Thebaid also, installing his daughter as high priestess of Amon at Thebes. During his long reign he restored prosperity to the country, encouraging trade with Greece and reforming the civil and military administration.

PSAMTIK II (Neferibre; 595–589 B.C.), being still troubled by the Napatans, sent a military expedition up the Nile into the Sudan and possibly penetrated far into Cushite territory. On their way back his Greek, Carian, and Phoenician mercenaries left inscriptions in archaic Greek on one of the colossi of Abu Simbel.

PSAMTIK III (Ankhkaenre; 525 B.C.) reigned for a few months only. Defeated by the Persians at the Battle of Pelusium (525 B.C.), he was captured and put to death by Cambyses. *See* also EGYPT: *History: Ancient Period.*

See Sir Alan Gardiner, *Egypt of the Pharaohs* (1961); F. K. Kienitz, *Die politische Geschichte Ägyptens vom 7. bis zum 4. Jahrhundert vor der Zeitwende* (1953).   (M. S. Dr.)

PSELLUS, MICHAEL CONSTANTINE (1018–after 1078), Byzantine author, scholar, and statesman, whose writings are of fundamental importance for the understanding of his period, was born in Constantinople. After an excellent education, he became a civil servant; he then entered the imperial secretariat and under Constantine IX (1042–55) he was prominent at court. He was also distinguished for his scholarship and in 1045 became head of the faculty of philosophy in the reorganized University of Constantinople. After an unsuccessful retreat in 1055 to a monastery on Mt. Olympus in Bithynia, he returned to public life and was exceedingly influential during the years 1056–78, particularly under the regime of his friends the Ducas, the last of whom, Michael VII, had been his pupil.

His *Chronographia*, a lively and highly individual history based on his own experiences, is an invaluable source. The *Chronographia* was edited with French translation in the Budé series by É. Renauld, 2 vol. (1926–28); English translation by E. R. A. Sewter (1953). Other works were edited in J. P. Migne, *Patrologia Graeca*, vol. 122 (1864); K. N. Sathas, *Bibliotheca medii aevi*, vol. 4–5 (1874–76); E. Kurtz and F. Drexl, 2 vol. (1936–41). The extensive corpus of his works (some unedited) ranges from philosophy and theology to letters, orations, poems, and incursions into demonology and Chaldean lore. He has been condemned as a timeserving and unstatesmanlike politician but, apart from the encyclopaedic nature of his knowledge which gained him fame in his own day, he also stands out as a distinguished historian and keen philosopher.

BIBLIOGRAPHY.—G. Moravcsik, *Byzantinoturcica*, 2nd ed., vol. 1, pp. 437–441 (1958); G. Ostrogorsky, *History of the Byzantine State*, pp. 280–281 (1956); É. Renauld, *Étude de la langue et du style de Michel Psellos* (1920); P. Joannou, *Die Illuminationslehre des Michael Psellos und Joannes Italos* (1956); J. M. Hussey, *Church and Learning in the Byzantine Empire, 867–1185* (1937). (J. M. HY.)

PSEUDEPIGRAPHA, literally, books "written under a false name," with the objective of giving them an authority not possessed by the real author or authors, are certain ancient writings, dating from a few centuries before and after the beginning of the Christian era. Among the best known of these are the Books of Enoch, the Assumption of Moses, the Baruch Apocalypses, and the Psalms of Solomon, none of which is included in the Old Testament canon. By convention, books such as Baruch and the Wisdom of Solomon, which are included in the Standard Apocrypha of the Old Testament, are not called pseudepigrapha. *See* APOCRYPHA, OLD TESTAMENT.

PSEUDO-CODINUS: *see* CODINUS, GEORGE.

PSEUDONYM: *see* ANONYMOUS AND PSEUDONYMOUS LITERATURE.

PSICHARI, ERNEST (1883–1914), French writer and soldier who by his life, writings, and death in action symbolized for many the so-called sacrificed generation which inspired France's spiritual regeneration before World War I. Born in Paris on Sept. 27, 1883, the son of a professor of modern Greek and of the daughter of Ernest Renan (*q.v.*), he grew up in an atmosphere of liberal intellectualism. In 1902, however, he abandoned his studies at the Sorbonne, and in November 1903 he joined the army, feeling that, for him, the right course lay in rejecting the freethinking, skeptical dilettantism of his family for a life of disciplined action. This personal reorientation, which followed a period of indecision and acute moral and mental stress, was made partly under the influence of Maurice Barrès (*q.v.*): in the long journey to acceptance of religious faith, of which it proved to be the first step, he was encouraged by his friends, Charles Péguy and Jacques Maritain (*qq.v.*).

In 1906 he joined the Mission Lenfant to the Upper Congo, as a noncommissioned officer. His impressions of the 18 months he spent there, and the meditations inspired by the vastness and solitude of Africa, are recorded in *Terres de soleil et de sommeil* (1908). In 1909 he passed out of the École d'Artillerie with the rank of sublieutenant, and was sent to Mauretania; the discipline of soldiering in the desert acted as a preparation for his later submission to the authority of the Catholic Church. *Les Voix qui crient dans le désert* (1920), begun in 1910, contains the fragmentary notes and sketches, describing both his travels in Africa and his pilgrimage to God, which formed the basis of his autobiographical novel, *Le Voyage du Centurion* (publ. 1920).

His semimystical philosophy of the call to action and to arms finds its fullest expression in the novel *L'Appel des Armes* (1913).

Psichari returned to France in 1912 and on Feb. 8, 1913, in Paris, he was received into the Roman Catholic Church. This acceptance of religious faith was widely regarded as a deliberate rejection of family tradition, and as an act of reparation for his grandfather's apostasy. He intended to become a priest, and, while garrisoned at Cherbourg (1913–14), prepared himself by a life of increasing asceticism, charity, and spiritual self-examination. But the outbreak of war intervened, and on Aug. 22, 1914, he was killed at St. Vincent-Rossignol, Belg. He thus fulfilled his twofold vocation, to God and to his countrymen, and his death, like his life, was a witness to his faith in the church and in France.

BIBLIOGRAPHY.—*Lettres du Centurion*, with preface by Paul Claudel (1933); A. M. Goichon, *E. Psichari d'après des documents inédits* (1921); Henriette Psichari, *E. Psichari, mon frère* (1933); H. Massis, *Notre Ami Psichari* (1936); W. Fowlie, *E. Psichari: a Study in Religious Conversion* (1939). (HE. MA.)

PSILOMELANE, an ore of manganese, is one of a group of hydrated manganese oxide minerals, with very similar appearances and properties, which are difficult to distinguish. They frequently occur in hard black botryoidal or stalactitic masses with a smooth surface, hence the name from the Greek *psilos*, "smooth," and *melanos*, "black." However, they may also be soft and earthy, in which case they are known as wad (*q.v.*). They are distinctly crystalline and not amorphous as once supposed. The name psilomelane was originally applied to material from Schneeberg, Saxony, which has the formula $BaMnMn_8O_{16}(OH)_4$, and should be restricted to this composition. The other manganese minerals of similar appearance are referred to as being of the psilomelane type.

See also PYROLUSITE. (L. S. RL.)

PSILOPSIDA, a class of primitive vascular plants (phylum Tracheophyta) with only two living genera but several extinct members, present as early as the Silurian Period. Psilophytales, the extinct order of the Psilopsida, is academically interesting as the apparent ancestor of the living order Psilotales and is further considered by many botanists to be ancestral to all other vascular plants. The extinct order takes its name from *Psilophyton*, a fossil from Quebec, Canada, described in 1859 by Sir John William Dawson. It was almost 60 years later before the real significance of this plant was understood. At that time extremely well-preserved ancient vascular plants (*Rhynia* and *Asteroxylon*) from deposits of Devonian Age in Scotland were found to resemble *Psilophyton*, and the order Psilophytales was established.

Earlier psilopsids ranged from *Sciadophyton*, a few centimetres tall, and *Rhynia*-like plants, 25–40 cm. tall, to *Asteroxylon* and others, more than a metre high. Unlike the leafy shoot systems of present-day flowering plants, psilopsids had spines instead of true leaves along the stem, and the stems were photosynthetic (based on the presence of stomates and air spaces).

The living genera, *Psilotum* and *Tmesipteris*, are terrestrial or epiphytic. *Psilotum*, an upright, green plant that looks like a leafless shrub about one foot high, is tropical and subtropical in distribution, reaching as far north as Florida and Hawaii; *Tmesipteris*, a pendant green epiphyte, is found in Australia, New Caledonia, New Zealand, the Philippine Islands, and other islands of the South Pacific area. The extinct genera grew in lowlands or were aquatic. *Psilotum* is sometimes grown as a novelty in greenhouses.

Certain features are common to both the living and extinct

D. W. BIERHORST

PSILOTUM NUDUM GAMETOPHYTE SHOWING WHITE GROWING TIPS; TINY WHITE GLOBULES ARE ANTHERIDIA

(LEFT) PENDANT STEMS OF TMESIPTERIS TANNENSIS, WITH FLATTENED LEAVES; (RIGHT) PSILOTUM NUDUM SHOOT BEARING SPORANGIA AND TINY SCALELIKE LEAVES

psilopsids. The conspicuous green plant, the sporophyte, consists of an aerial system and an underground rhizome system, both of which repeatedly fork dichotomously, i.e., into two equal branches. No roots are present, the rhizome performing the functions of a root. In *Psilotum* the "leaves" are very small scales, without vascular tissue. In *Tmesipteris* the "leaves" are larger, flattened structures, each with one unbranched midvein.

All psilopsids have a very simple internal organization. The fossil members had smooth stems or stems with spines or small scales. (These "leaves" of the psilopsids may not have had the same evolutionary development as the leaves of ferns and seed plants.) The spore case (sporangium) is three-lobed in *Psilotum* and two-lobed in *Tmesipteris*. The sporangia appear to be axillary in position in reference to the leaves, but research has shown them to be terminal on short branches, the leaves associated with the sporangia being appendages on the branch. The presence of vascular tissue at the base of a sporangium or even in partitions separating compartments in a sporangium supports the concept of terminality of the sporangium.

The vascular tissue is in the form of a slender cylinder occupying the centre of the stem (protostele) in the rhizomes of both living genera. The protostelic condition is true of the ultimate branches in *Psilotum*, whereas in the lower branches of *Psilotum* and in the stems of *Tmesipteris* the xylem occurs in the form of a cylinder of strands surrounding a pith (siphonostele). The phloem forms a cylinder around the xylem strands. The cells of the outer cortex of the stem contain chloroplasts and in *Psilotum* this region accounts for most of the photosynthesis. One interesting feature of stem anatomy in *Psilotum* is the presence of an endodermis. This is a layer of cells surrounding the vascular cylinder in which each cell has lignin deposited in the form of a band in the cell wall. An endodermis is a characteristic feature of roots in all vascular plants but occurs only rarely in stems of seed plants.

Meiotic divisions occur in the sporangia, with the result that spores are formed that have nuclei with half the number of chromosomes found in nuclei elsewhere in the plant. Only one type of spore is formed; consequently these plants are said to be homosporous. Spores are released by the splitting of sporangia along longitudinal slits.

The released spores germinate to form gamete-bearing plants (gametophytes) or prothallia as they are commonly known. These plants are very small, measuring about one millimetre in diameter and several millimetres in length. The gametophytes may grow on trunks of trees or underground. Like the sporophyte, the

gametophyte branches repeatedly. It is devoid of chlorophyll, however, and lives a saprophytic existence, aided presumably by an endophytic fungus. These plants are so similar to the underground rhizomes that they can be identified only if gamete-producing structures (gametangia) are present on the gametophyte. Two types of gametangia are scattered over the surface and are intermingled. The egg-producing structure, the archegonium, consists of a sterile jacket of four rows of cells enclosing another row of cells, the lowest one of which is the egg. The sperm-producing structure, the antheridium, is globose and emergent on the surface of the gametophyte; it consists of a jacket of sterile cells enclosing many spermatocytes, which upon release become swimming multiflagellated sperms. To effect fertilization a sperm must swim to the archegonium and down a canallike passage to the egg (the passage being created by the disintegration of the cells adjacent to the nonmotile egg). After fertilization the first division of the zygote is transverse (perpendicular to the long axis of the archegonium). The outer cell continues to divide and forms the new sporophytic axis. The inner cell gives rise to a multicellular foot, which is in close contact with the gametophyte and presumably functions in the transfer of nutrients from the gametophyte to the young sporophyte. Frequently the young sporophyte axis branches very early during its existence; one branch may become a green aerial shoot while the other becomes a rhizome. The rhizome continues to branch dichotomously, but any of the underground branches may turn up and develop into a green aerial shoot and form leaves and sporangia.

Unquestionably the extinct order Psilophytales is an ancient and primitive group of vascular plants. The Psilotales also are ancient, but some botanists question the assumption that the two orders have a close linear relationship.

See also PALEOBOTANY: *Appearance of Major Plant Groups: Vascular Plants;* PLANTS AND PLANT SCIENCE: *Classification of Plants* and *Morphology of Plants.* (E. M. GI.)

PSITTACOSIS, an infectious disease of worldwide distribution, is caused by an intracellular bacteriumlike microorganism and is transmitted to man from various birds. The infection has been found in about 70 different species of birds, but parrots and parakeets (Psittacidae, from which the disease is named), pigeons, turkeys, ducks, and geese have been the principal sources of human infection. The disease is also called ornithosis, especially when seen in nonpsittacine birds.

History.—The association between the human disease and sick parrots was first recognized in Europe in 1879, but a thorough study of the disease was not made until 1929–30, when severe outbreaks, attributed to contact with imported parrots, occurred in 12 countries of Europe and America. During the investigations conducted in Germany, England, and the United States, the causative agent was revealed. Strict regulations followed concerning importation of psittacine birds, which doubtlessly reduced the incidence of the disease but did not prevent the intermittent appearance of cases. The infection was later found in domestic stocks of parakeets and pigeons and subsequently in other species. An increase in the number of cases in Great Britain and the U.S. appeared in 1952, following relaxation of regulations concerning commerce in psittacine birds and an increase in the popularity of parakeets as pets. Infected poultry has resulted in many cases in poultry handlers or in workers in processing plants. Contact with turkeys has accounted for such cases in the U.S.; ducks and geese have been mainly responsible in Europe.

The Disease in Man.—Psittacosis is an acute febrile illness, tending to be severe in older persons, in which some degree of inflammation of the lungs (pneumonitis) occurs, sometimes detectable only by X-ray examination. The duration is two to three weeks, and convalescence often is protracted. Before modern chemotherapeutic drugs were available the case fatality rate was approximately 20%, but penicillin and the tetracycline drugs reduced this figure almost to zero. Diagnosis can be rendered more accurate by examination of specimens of the patient's blood serum taken early in the illness and during the second or third week. A rise in antibody content in the later specimens, detected by the complement fixation test in which cultures of the inactivated (noninfectious) microorganism are used, aids in the diagnosis.

The Etiologic Agent.—The infectious particle, or elementary body, is spherical in shape and approximately 0.0003 mm. (0.000012 in.) in diameter, considerably smaller than the typical bacterial cell. Because of its size and obligate intracellular habitat (it will grow only within host cells), this disease agent was formerly regarded as a virus. Investigations showed it resembles a bacterium in the possession of a cell wall and in definite, although limited, metabolic activity. The infectious particles invade tissue cells of a susceptible animal and multiply by binary fission forming an inclusion within the cytoplasm. The cell is damaged or eventually destroyed, and the infectious particles are released to invade other cells of the same or another host. Microorganisms of this general type, in addition to occurring in birds, have been found in mice, hamsters, cats, opossums, sheep, goats, and cattle, but these do not ordinarily infect man. Similar disease agents that are transmitted from man to man directly are those of lymphogranuloma venereum, trachoma, and inclusion conjunctivitis. Several generic names have been suggested for this entire group, *e.g.*, *Miyagawanella, Bedsonia, Chlamydia,* none of which has gained complete acceptance. S. P. Bedson, an English bacteriologist, contributed basic information on the psittacosis virus during the 1930s, and K. F. Meyer in the U.S. made extensive studies over several decades on the epidemiologic aspects of the disease.

Transmission and Control.—Psittacine birds apparently acquire the infection in the nestling stage and may become carriers even though they remain in good health. When such birds are crowded or chilled, as during shipping, or placed under other adverse conditions, the latent infection may be aggravated and become acute. The bird then shows obvious signs of illness and infectious particles are discharged in excess nasal secretions or in a watery diarrhea. After such infectious material is dried, it readily infects other birds or men in the form of an inhaled dust. Psittacosis in poultry plants occurs especially in personnel exposed to dust or feathers. In a few outbreaks transmission from man to man has occurred, but this is exceptional.

Although complete control of psittacosis on a national scale is impossible, some parakeet aviaries have been maintained free of infection by scrupulous care in keeping the birds isolated from disease sources and by practising good housekeeping. Chemotherapeutic measures also offer promise. To protect himself and his household, the individual bird owner should avoid contact with sick birds, purchase birds only from known healthy stock, and strive to keep his pet in sound condition. (F. B. G.)

PSKOV, a town and the administrative centre of Pskov Oblast of the Russian Soviet Federated Socialist Republic, U.S.S.R., stands on the Velikaya River, at its confluence with the small Pskova stream and 9 mi. (14 km.) above its outfall in Lake Pskov. Pop. (1970 prelim.) 127,000. It is one of the oldest and historically most important of Russian towns. It is first mentioned in a chronicle of 903 as Pleskov, but there is archaeological evidence for its existence in the 8th century. It acquired early importance as a centre of trade with the Baltic. On the promontory between the Pskova and Velikaya rivers a kremlin (citadel) known as the Krom was established. The town came under Novgorod as a *prigorod* (suburb) and long continued to have close links with its "elder brother." In 1136–37 Pskov attempted to secede from Novgorod, and autonomous government by the *veche* (town assembly) was granted. The *veche* chose a prince who was responsible for defense. Among the most notable of Pskov's princes was the refugee Lithuanian prince Dovmont, who rebuilt the town's fortifications in 1266. The ruins of his walls still survive. Like Novgorod, Pskov was divided into sectors, or "ends," each with its own local assembly and each having part of the Pskov territories. There were six such "ends." As early as the 12th century, monasteries were established on the left bank of the Velikaya, which grew into a suburb known as Zavelichye. In 1240 the Teutonic Knights captured Pskov, but after their defeat in 1242 on the ice of Lake Peipus by Alexander Nevski, the 13th century saw Pskov at its height. It is estimated that it had a population of 60,000, and during that century 42 churches were built.

In 1348 Pskov achieved full independence as a republic and

entered the Hanseatic League, but in 1510 it was annexed by Moscow and many of its leading citizens were exiled. In 1571 it was sacked by Ivan the Terrible but, despite this, only 10 years later the town survived a 30-week siege by Stephen Báthory, king of Poland. In 1615 it was besieged in vain by Gustavus II Adolphus of Sweden. The fortifications were renewed and strengthened by Peter the Great, but the 18th century saw a steady decline of the town, accelerated by a disastrous fire in 1710. By 1803 there were fewer than 6,000 inhabitants. In World War II Pskov suffered much damage, but a number of churches and other buildings survived. Notable is the magnificent Cathedral of the Trinity in the kremlin. The present 17th-century building is the fourth on the site, the earliest (wooden) cathedral dating from 957. Modern Pskov is an important railway junction, with lines to Leningrad; Dno and Bologoye; Vilnius (Lithuania) and Warsaw (Poland); Riga (Latvia) and Tallinn (Estonia). There is a large linen industry; also leather working (especially footwear), light engineering, brewing, and food processing.

PSKOV OBLAST was established in 1944. Its area is 21,351 sq.mi. (55,300 sq.km.) and its population (1970 prelim.) 876,000. It lies in the lowland basins of the Lovat and Shelon rivers which flow to Lake Ilmen in Novgorod Oblast, and of the Velikaya, flowing into Lake Pskov-Lake Peipus (Chudskoye) in the northwest of Pskov Oblast. Between the two lake basins are the low, morainic Sudoma and Bezhanits uplands. In the extreme south is part of the Valdai Hills. There is everywhere a great deal of surface water in the form of lakes, rivers, and swamps. The climate is continental, much modified by proximity to the Baltic Sea. January average temperatures are about −7° C (19° F) and July averages about 17° C (62° F). Rainfall is about 24 in. (610 mm.) a year, with a summer maximum. The *oblast* lies in the mixed forest zone, and much of it is covered by forest of spruce, pine, oak, and birch. Wide areas are in sphagnum peat bog or reed and grass marsh, and floodplain meadows fringe the many rivers. Soils are usually podzols of low fertility.

Forty-three percent (374,000) of the 1970 population was urban, a figure well below the national average. The 14 towns and 7 urban districts are all small, apart from Pskov and Velikiye Luki (1969 est. 84,000). Velikiye Luki was the centre of a separate *oblast* up to 1957, when most of it was incorporated with Pskov. Industries are principally small-scale food processing or linenmaking from local flax, which is a major crop in this and neighbouring *oblasti*. Rye, oats, fodder crops, and potatoes are also grown. The abundant natural pastures are the basis of well-developed cattle raising and dairying, especially for the Leningrad market. (R. A. F.)

PSOCOPTERA (CORRODENTIA), an order of insects, the best-known of which are book lice, pale flightless insects usually not

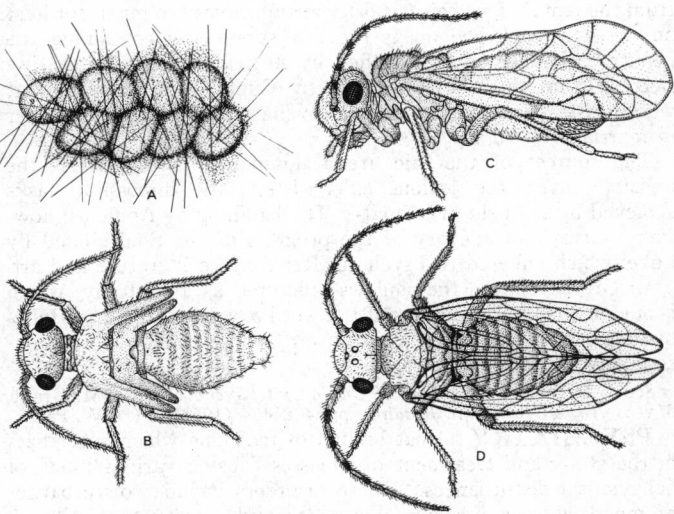

DEVELOPMENTAL STAGES OF A PSOCID (ANOMOPSOCUS AMABILIS): (A) EGG MASS; (B) SIXTH INSTAR (BETWEEN MOLTS); (C) ADULT FEMALE; (D) ADULT MALE

more than one-fourth inch long, found among old papers, on dusty shelves, or in cereals. Outdoor species, called bark lice, are mostly winged and occur on the bark and foliage of trees, sometimes under stones or in ground litter. The outdoor species are not economically important, but book lice often are a considerable nuisance. Psocid is a general term for any member of the order.

Psocoptera are soft-bodied. The wing venation of flying species is distinctive for its simplicity. The lower portion of the leg (tarsus) is two- or three-segmented, and tail filaments (cerci) are absent; mouth parts are for chewing, with part of the upper jaw usually elongate and chisellike. Metamorphosis is gradual, and occasionally the gregarious nymphs of outdoor species form conspicuous clusters on tree trunks. Psocids eat molds, cereals, and organic debris.

About 150 species of psocids have been found in the United States, but neither this figure nor the estimate of 1,250 described world species approaches the total number that exist, because the group, now arranged in over 20 families, has been rather neglected by entomologists.

See also INSECT.

See D. J. Borror and D. M. DeLong, *An Introduction to the Study of Insects,* ch. xiv, pp. 169–179 (1954).   (A. B. Gu.)

PSORIASIS: *see* SKIN, DISEASES OF.

PSYCHE, the Greek word for "soul" (*see* PSYCHOLOGY, HISTORY OF: *Greek Psychology*) and the name of the heroine in the story of Cupid and Psyche told by the Latin author Apuleius in his *Metamorphoses* (*The Golden Ass*).

The outstanding beauty of the princess Psyche arouses the jealousy of Venus, who commands her son Cupid to inspire her with love for the most despicable of men. Instead, Cupid falls in love with her himself, but in order to conceal the affair from his mother he does not reveal his identity to Psyche, whom he places in a remote luxurious palace served by bodiless voices. There he visits her only by night in total darkness, warning her of dire consequences if she ever actually sees him. She is overcome with curiosity, however, after a visit from her jealous elder sisters, who insist, in their dissatisfaction with their own commonplace marriages, that her lover is a hideous monster. So the next night she lights the lamp they have given her and discovers that the figure sleeping at her side is the god of love himself. A drop of oil falls on him from the lamp; he wakes, reproaches her, and flies away. After a vain attempt to drown herself, she wanders over the earth seeking him until she falls into the hands of Venus, who imposes upon her impossible tasks which pitying animals help her to accomplish. The final task is to fetch some beauty from Proserpine in the world below, as Venus' beauty is wasting away through nursing Cupid, wounded by the oil dropped on him from the lamp. Psyche's curiosity again proves too much for her: on the way back she opens the box supposedly containing the beauty and is instantly stupefied by its real contents, a deathly sleep. From this she is rescued by Cupid, now recovered, at whose instigation Jupiter makes Psyche immortal and gives her in marriage to Cupid.

The sources of the tale are a number of folk motifs—the invisible lover, the jealous elder sisters, the impossible tasks achieved by the help of animals. The handling by Apuleius, however, conveys an allegory of the progress of the Soul guided by Love, which adhered to Psyche in Renaissance literature and art.

In Greek folklore the soul was pictured as a butterfly, which is one of the other meanings of the word *psyche.* From the Hellenistic period a young girl with butterfly wings is shown in art accompanying Eros (Cupid).

See J. Ö. Swahn, *The Tale of Cupid and Psyche* (1955); M. Grant, *Myths of the Greeks and Romans,* pp. 408–424 (1962).   (H. W. PA.)

PSYCHIATRY is that branch of medicine which specializes in the study and treatment of illnesses causing various kinds of behavioural disturbances. These disorders include: disturbances of mood, as seen in depressive states and anxiety; excessive or inadequate affective responses or inadequate social control of emotions; conditions characterized by disorganized thinking and perception, such as phobias, obsessions, delusions, hallucinations;

transient as well as irreversible impairments in intellectual activities; and certain physical disturbances which simulate diseases associated with malfunctioning of body organs.

Psychoanalysis, to be distinguished from psychiatry, is both a particular theory of personality development and functioning and a particular method of psychotherapy used in psychiatry. Strictly defined, psychology is the scientific study of the mind; it is not a medical specialty (*see* PSYCHOLOGY).

Questions of symptomatology and diagnosis, and those concerning etiology, treatment and prevention, are the problems of psychiatry. Sometimes the sufferer's condition is manifested in behaviour that is so grossly inappropriate that the existence of an illness is easily recognized. At other times, the difficulty may be known only to the sufferer. Irrational violence or the striking immobility of severely depressed persons are obvious pathological conditions. On the other hand, states of apprehension, obsessive thoughts and unreasonable fears may exist for prolonged periods without recognition. In the latter instance, the conditions become known only through the subjective reports of the ill, or when the symptoms intrude upon ordinary routine activities and force a general awareness of a mental illness.

In explaining the genesis of behavioural disorders, modern psychiatry emphasizes the patient's genetic predisposition; the influence of anatomical, physiological and biochemical processes; and the determining effect upon the nervous system of the recording of the person's ongoing series of life experiences, beginning with the prenatal period and extending through childhood experiences in the family to the environmental and cultural pressures. To the psychiatrist, the sum of these factors determines personality. A human being's personality is recognized as his characteristically recurring patterns of behaviour in response to life experiences, to and with other persons. (*See* PERSONALITY; BEHAVIOUR.)

This article is organized as follows:

I. HISTORY

A. EARLY HISTORY

Many modern scientific concepts regarding psychiatric disorders are derived from the historical past. References to mental disorders in early Egyptian, Indian, Greek and Roman writings show great insight, but for the most part the philosophers, physicians and theologians who contemplated and wrote about the problems of human behaviour regarded psychiatric illnesses as a reflection of the displeasure of the gods or as evidence of demoniac possession. Only a rare few realized that behavioural problems were not separable from physical illnesses and that the sufferers should be treated humanely rather than exorcised, banished or punished. Although progress was slow in banishing the belief in supernatural causes, as early as 860 B.C., some Greek priests supplemented their incantations and exorcisms for the mentally disturbed with recommendations for kindness and physical and recreational activities such as walking, riding and listening to soothing music.

A significant advance toward scientific understanding of mental disorders occurred in the 6th century B.C. when the Greek healers turned to observation and interest in experimentation. At this time, Alcmaeon made the first dissection of the human body and observed the connection of sense organs, such as the eye and the ear, to the brain. Searching for the seat of reason and of the soul, Alcmaeon decided that they were located in the brain.

Shortly after Alcmaeon reported on his experimentation, the problem of mental disorders gained the attention of Greek philosophers. Empedocles spoke about the significance of emotions and the possibility that love and hate were the fundamental sources of change in behaviour. Plato incorporated concepts of Empedocles in his consideration of the role of Eros in the personal and social life of man. This medical and philosophical thought was not recaptured until Sigmund Freud (*q.v.*) presented his theories and clinical studies in the late 19th century (*see below, Modern Schools: Psychoanalytic School*).

Hippocrates (fl. 400 B.C.), a sensitive, perceptive observer of clinical phenomena, described many mental disorders found in modern times, including psychosis after pregnancy, delirious states associated with infections such as tuberculosis and malaria and the acute confusion which follows severe hemorrhage. He flatly rejected the idea that mental disturbances were caused by the intervention of the gods or by possession. He also took an unequivocal position concerning the legal rights and responsibilities of the mentally disturbed. Athenian law recognized the rights of the mentally disturbed in civil affairs, but gave no special consideration to the mentally disturbed when they became involved in capital crimes. Through the vast respect accorded him, Hippocrates was able to provide this consideration. In the Athenian courts, if it could be proved that the person on trial suffered from a condition which Hippocrates designated as paranoia, the court would appoint a guardian for the accused.

Hippocrates classified mental disorders into three categories: mania, melancholia and phrenetis. His descriptions reveal many of the classical symptoms which are recognized in epilepsy, mania, melancholia and paranoia. To Hippocrates, hysteria was a mental disease, but it was limited to women. As he saw it, hysteria was caused by the wandering of the uterus through the body and symbolized the body's pining for the production of a child; he thought that marriage was the best remedy for hysteria.

Hippocrates and his followers were the first group of physicians who approached mental illness scientifically. Their understanding of mental disorders emphasized natural causes, clinical observations and brain pathology. They were the first to describe and examine empirically the clinical materials of psychiatry. In establishing a movement toward the biological study of mental illness, Hippocrates challenged and won people away from the theological interpretations. Many physicians after Hippocrates contributed substantially to psychiatry, notably Asclepiades of Bithynia, Aulus Cornelius Celsus, Aretaeus, and Soranus. Soranus, in his instructions for the treatment of disturbed patients, prescribed the use of tact and discretion; he stated that the patient's attention must be tactfully directed to his difficulties; he advised the physician to observe the mental patient's tolerance to sedation and warned of the need to supervise the patient through his period of convalescence.

The high point in medical thought of this period was reached in the work of the Roman physician Galen (2nd century A.D.), who, through a scientific approach to the study of the anatomy of the nervous system, drew attention to the role of the brain in mental functioning. He discovered that the existence of a symptom did not necessarily mean that the organ or the part of the body which expressed the symptom was the affected portion. As a consequence of his experimental work and his studies of mental disorders, Galen developed a theory of the rational soul as divided into an external and an internal part. The external part consisted of the five senses. The soul's internal functions were imagination, judgment, perception and movement. On the basis of his experimentation, Galen concluded, as Plato had thought and Aristotle had denied, that the brain, not the heart, was the seat of the soul. His observations had shown him that compression of the heart affected only the function of the arteries. Galen rejected the idea that hysteria resulted from the wandering of the uterus about the body, but he considered it to be caused by a local engorgement of the uterus.

In the period following the death of Galen, primitive thinking about mental illness re-emerged. Witchcraft and demonology dominated medical thought of medieval times and continued to exert an influence into the 19th century. However, beginning with the 16th century, signs of scientific questioning began to appear again. Among the physicians who challenged demoniacal explanations of mental disturbances were Paracelsus, Agrippa and Johann Weyer. Beginning with Francis Bacon in the 17th century, a number of philosophers, recognizing that the functions of the mind were a part of their concern with the natural order of the universe, began to exert an effect on medical thought. Notable among those who contributed to the modern science of psychopathology were Descartes, Hobbes, Locke, Condillac and Hume.

B. 19TH CENTURY

1. Humanitarian Movement.—Paralleling the reappearance of scientific questioning and the development of medical science was an improvement in the public attitude toward the mentally ill. These combined factors resulted in the establishment of mental hospitals and in more humane treatment methods. The humanitarian movement received its initial impetus through the efforts of the French physician Philippe Pinel (1745–1826), who after the French Revolution was placed in charge of the Bicêtre, the hospital for the mentally ill in Paris. Under Pinel's supervision, a completely new approach to the handling of mental patients, as well as a new concept of mental hospital operation, was introduced. Chains and shackles were removed from the patients. In place of dungeons, the patients were provided with sunny rooms and permitted to exercise on the hospital grounds. The reforms which Pinel sponsored and their gratifying results placed France in the forefront of psychiatry.

In England, through the efforts of William Tuke and his son Henry, aided by the Society of Friends, York Retreat was opened (1796) for the humane care of the mentally ill. In the United States, an energetic and courageous New England woman, Dorothea Dix (*q.v.*), between 1841 and 1881 carried on a campaign to arouse the people and the legislators to an awareness of the inhumanities which prevailed in all of the country's mental hospitals. Not only was Miss Dix the leading spirit in improving the care of the mentally ill in the United States, but she also helped in promoting the reform movement in Canada and in Scotland. The modern mental hospital in North America and in western Europe aims at providing a friendly, encouraging, therapeutic atmosphere. The hospital staff attempts to provide a variety of activities designed to help the patients regain mental health. While there is still a large gap between practice and theory in many hospitals, the modern mental hospital is moving in the direction of the "open-door" policies initiated in England. The term open-door symbolizes the trend away from the locked ward toward freedom of the patient to move about the hospital and recognition of the therapeutic effects of a sheltered, supportive environment where all the staff help the patients and patients help each other to health. (*See also* MENTAL HEALTH.)

2. Biological Movement.—Along with humanitarian reform in hospital practice and treatment methods during the late 18th and the 19th centuries, there was a resurgence of medical and scientific interest in psychiatric theory and practice. Great strides were made during this period in establishing a scientific basis for the study of mental disorders. A long series of observations by brilliant clinicians in France, Germany and England culminated in 1883 in a classification of mental disorder by Emil Kraepelin (*q.v.*). His integration of a mass of descriptive clinical data into meaningful symptom categories was a major contribution to psychiatry, and his classification system served as the basis of all subsequent nosologies.

Rapid advances in studies of anatomy, psychology, pathology, chemistry and bacteriology led to the expectation of discovering specific brain lesions for the various forms of mental disease. While this search did not attain the results desired, the scientific emphasis was productive in that it did elucidate the gross and microscopic pathology of many brain disorders which produce psychiatric disability. In addition, the research effort illuminated the role of infectious and metabolic disturbances in the production of mental diseases. One of the notable achievements of this period was the discovery of *Treponema pallidum* (*Spirochaeta pallida*), the organism causing syphilis, as the basis of the brain pathology producing general paresis. Other discoveries were the causation of pellagra psychosis in a vitamin deficiency and the recognition of delirious reactions caused by malnutrition and pernicious anemia. Significant observations also were made on the cellular changes in the brain which accompany the presenile and senile psychoses, and a number of pathological conditions associated with mental retardation were identified. The advances made in the 20th century toward establishing the biochemical correlates of mental disturbances and in developing the tranquilizing agents represent the moving fringe of the earlier search for etiological specificity in disordered body organs and systems.

3. Psychological Movement.—Certain of the major psychotic states, notably schizophrenia and manic-depressive reactions, frustrated the effort to find in cellular pathology the principal causative agent of mental disease. Other explanations were needed for the many puzzling aspects of these conditions, and these explanations emerged in a wave of psychological viewpoints, beginning with the study of hypnosis in relation to hysteria. The arrival of Franz Anton Mesmer in Paris in 1778 dated the beginning of broad scientific interest in psychological factors as influencing or altering human behaviour. Advancing the belief that the distribution of a universal magnetic fluid in the body was the basis of health and disease, Mesmer opened a clinic in Paris where he treated all kinds of diseases, including hysterical paralysis (*see* HYSTERIA), in a ceremonial setting in which he "magnetized" the patients by applying·to their bodies iron rods treated with various chemicals. Mesmer's therapy was a group method of treatment; he moved among his patients touching each of them with his hand and waving a wand over them.

Mesmer's own personal success was short-lived, and he was branded a charlatan. His work was studied by a committee of the Academy of Sciences whose members included Jean Sylvain Bailly, Benjamin Franklin, Lavoisier and LeRoi. The committee was unable to find any evidence of animal magnetic fluids, but it was impressed with the results produced by Mesmer's touching of the patients. It advised against the use of mesmerism and warned of potential dangers from harmful imitations. Outside France the recommendations of the academy went unheeded, and mesmerism spread throughout the world. A French magnetizer, Charles Poyen, introduced séances of magnetism in the United States from which the watchmaker P. P. Quimby (*q.v.*) obtained his first conceptions of faith healing and successfully treated Mary Baker Eddy for hysterical paralysis. Use of mesmerism as an anesthetic during surgery was advocated by several physicians, but this practice passed quickly with the introduction of nitrous oxide and chloroform.

The first physician to be attracted by scientific curiosity to the serious study of mesmerism was the English surgeon James Braid (*q.v.*), who showed that the condition resulted solely from suggestion, and introduced the term hypnotism. After Braid, the scientific study of hypnotism lagged until a French country doctor, A. A. Liébault (1823–1904), resumed interest in the subject and learned to use hypnosis for the induction of sleep. Liébault subsequently made wide use of hypnotism in his medical practice, and he also taught the technique to the French physician Hippolyte

Bernheim, the English neurologist J. M. Bramwell and the renowned French neurologist Jean Martin Charcot (1825–1893).

Questioning the view that psychological factors could cause hysteria, Charcot conducted, at the Salpêtrière hospital in Paris, an extensive and detailed study designed to determine the organic factors associated with the condition. On Feb. 13, 1882, Charcot presented a report of his findings to the Academy of Sciences. He convinced the academy members that the phenomena of hypnotism were manifestations of abnormality and that the characteristics of the hypnotic state could be observed only in patients with hysteria. The same academy that earlier had condemned research on animal magnetism was thus won to a new point of view. Charcot's success prepared the way for the harvest of psychological insights that followed. Among his many students was Freud.

Charcot's views were not accepted by all French physicians, however. Bernheim, who was professor of medicine at Nancy, vigorously challenged Charcot's conclusion, maintaining that the phenomena observed at the Salpêtrière took place only when conditions of suggestion were set up by the hypnotist. He stressed the study of the process of suggestion and the characteristics of suggestibility, and rightly claimed that the latter were not restricted to hysterical persons. Bernheim's work, apart from providing a new perspective on hypnosis, had other implications; some psychiatrists have regarded it as the first attempt to evolve a general understanding of human behaviour. Developing out of his studies, for example, were new questions concerning the legal responsibility of criminals and the causes of criminal behaviour; Bernheim, by advancing the belief that mechanisms of suggestion underlay the endless variety of normal and abnormal behaviour, challenged the concept that the will was the agent of crime and evil. Along with Charcot, Bernheim put to final rest the persisting concern with demoniac possession.

Pierre Janet (*q.v.*) also studied hysteria and furthered the acceptance of psychological causation. Recognizing the neurotic components of hysteria (fixed ideas and inner conflict with reality), Janet insisted upon psychological treatment for the condition. His psychotherapy was founded primarily on the use of persuasion and of techniques for altering the patient's environment. The work with hypnotism and hysteria opened the door for further recognition of the psychoneuroses. *See* also HYPNOSIS; FAITH HEALING.

C. MODERN SCHOOLS

Freud took the first steps toward providing the theoretical structure upon which much of modern psychiatry rests. Adolf Meyer (*see* below) had a prominent role in the development of modern psychiatry through his pluralistic and interactional concepts of human behaviour; he drew attention to the multiple biological, psychological and social factors that influence personality. Both Freud and Meyer were greatly aided in the construction of their theories by knowledge of the work of the great English theoretical neurologist John Hughlings Jackson (*q.v.*).

Drawing from the genius of Charles Darwin and Herbert Spencer, Jackson set forth an evolutionary theory to explain the function and development of the nervous system. In the development of his theory, Jackson drew from his extensive and careful clinical observations of epilepsy and other diseases of the brain. He concluded that the functions of the nervous system were integrated at progressively more complex levels, with mentation, the highest level of function, located within the cerebral cortex. Jackson viewed the symptoms accompanying impaired brain function as representing both the disappearance of the most recently acquired functions of the brain, and the reappearance of earlier and more primitive functions that had become submerged during the evolutionary process. According to Jackson, when injury to the brain produced a permanent defect in the functioning of the nervous system, in addition to symptoms caused by loss of function and symptoms representing re-emergence of more primitive functions, the organism also produces another type of symptom to compensate or substitute for the loss. Jackson's theoretical position inherently postulates that the understanding of any behavioural disturbance is dependent upon knowledge of the progressive development of a particular type of behaviour in a given organism as well as knowledge of the presentation of such behaviour in other living species. Such assumptions are basic for both the psychoanalyst and psychobiologist.

1. Psychobiological School.—The psychobiological school of psychiatry, established by Adolf Meyer (*q.v.*), represents in broad outline the theoretical structure of the general field of modern psychiatry. Meyer, who moved to the U.S. in 1892 from Switzerland, received his training in Zürich. He emphasized that the understanding of human processes and the problems of human behaviour lie in the utilization of knowledge from biology, psychology and sociology. The explanation of the total personality requires study of the physical attributes of the individual as well as the many social, cultural and emotional influences to which he has been exposed. Meyer stressed the importance of early parental influences in the development of the personality of the child and conceived of mental disturbances as progressive habit formations. The techniques he developed for psychiatric examination are the basis of all those used in English-speaking countries. Meyer insisted that understanding of maladaptive behaviour required a comprehensive study of the life history of the individual, tracing the development of the personality through each progressive and unfolding stage to the present life situation. To Meyer, the individual was both a product and a victim of his life experiences. Meyer emphasized that each individual personality had its assets and its liabilities. The existence of faulty habit patterns implied possibilities of teaching healthy ones. To the psychiatrist he appealed for careful study of the development of symptoms, and cautioned that symptoms should not be attributed to a specific cause. Meyer's orientation departed markedly from that of theorists and practitioners who explained mental phenomena solely on a physical basis.

The weakness of Meyer's psychiatry lies in its failure to work through the study of intrapsychic processes and their origin in family life; recognition of the importance of these forces represents some of the most significant thought to the psychoanalytic school. The psychobiologists emphasize that psychiatric disabilities are reactions rather than disease processes with established courses.

2. Psychoanalytic School.—The psychoanalytic movement originated in the perceptions and meticulous clinical observations of Freud. After studying with Charcot, Freud returned to Vienna, where he was associated with Josef Breuer (*q.v.*) in studies of neurotic patients under hypnosis. Freud and Breuer observed that their patients tended to relive earlier life experiences, which could be associated with the symptomatic expression of the illness. When the sources of the patients' ideas and impulses were brought into consciousness during the hypnotic state, the patients showed improvement. Although the collaboration was proceeding well, Breuer became disturbed by the responses which the patients made to him (a phenomenon later defined by Freud as the transference relationship) and discontinued the study; Freud pursued it alone.

Observing that most of his patients talked freely without being under hypnosis, Freud evolved the technique of free association of ideas. The patient was encouraged to say anything that came into his mind, without regard to its assumed relevancy or propriety. Noting that patients sometimes had difficulty in making free associations, Freud concluded that certain painful, anxiety-ridden (traumatic) experiences were repressed from conscious awareness. Freud noted that in the majority of the patients seen during his early practice the events most frequently repressed were concerned with disturbing sexual experiences. Thus he hypothesized that anxiety was a consequence of the repressed energy (libido) attached to sexuality; the repressed energy took expression in various symptoms that served as psychological defensive mechanisms.

Freud later modified his concept of anxiety. His new concept regarded anxiety as the emotion generated by the threat of some fearful occurrence or of impending danger. In later years, Karen Horney (*q.v.*) and other psychiatrists extended Freud's concept of a threatening event leading to the arousal of the anxiety. The

more recent theories of anxiety included not merely feelings of fear, guilt and shame consequent to sexual fantasies that the person regards as reprehensible; anxiety is conceived also as resulting from the arousal of fantasies of aggression and hostility and from fear of loneliness caused by separation from a person on whom the sufferer is dependent.

Freud's free-association technique provided him with a tool for studying the meanings of dreams (*see* DREAM AND DREAMING: *Theories of Dreams*), slips of the tongue, forgetfulness and other mistakes and errors in everyday life. From these investigations he was led to a new conception of the structure of personality: the id, ego and superego. (1) The id is the reservoir of drives and impulses derived from the genetic background and concerned with the preservation and propagation of life. Freud regarded the drives resting in the id as the prime sources of the sexuality and aggressive impulses that are needed to perpetuate the race and to satisfy the biological needs for food, water, oxygen and warmth. The impulses of the id are seen as operative beyond conscious awareness. (2) The ego (*q.v.*), in contrast to the id, operates in the conscious and preconscious levels of awareness. It is the portion of the personality concerned with perception, cognition and executive actions. (3) The third portion of the personality structure Freud called the superego. In this rests the individual's accumulated ideals and values and the mores of his family and society; the superego serves as a censor on the ego functions.

In the Freudian framework, conflicts among the three structures of the personality are repressed and lead to the arousal of anxiety. The person is protected from experiencing his anxiety directly by the development of various adaptive psychological patterns known as defense mechanisms (*q.v.*). They are learned through the family and the cultural influences to which the growing child is exposed. They become pathological when they interfere with the capacity of the adult to pursue the satisfactions of living in a society. The existence of these patterns of adaptation or mechanisms of defense are quantitatively but not qualitatively different in the psychotic and neurotic states.

One of Freud's fruitful contributions was his concept of transference. In the course of his work with his patients, Freud became aware of the deep attachments they formed for him. Learning that the patients of other analysts reacted similarly, he concluded that these emotional attachments represented a repetition of the relationship the patient previously had with his parents or their substitutes. The love or hatred which the patient felt for his parents and which he unconsciously projected to the analyst influenced the patient's capacity to make free associations. By objective treatment of these responses and the resistances they evoked, as well as by bringing the patient to analyze the origin of his feelings, Freud concluded that the analysis of the transference and the patient's resistance to its analysis were the keystones of psychoanalytic therapy. Psychoanalytic therapy contrasts with all other forms of psychotherapy in its emphasis on transference. Recognition of the transference relationship has been of major importance to the entire field of psychiatry, however, and to medicine generally.

Freud described the development of personality as a psychosexual evolution that begins at birth and continues through childhood. In the framework of Freud's libido theory, the personality develops through a series of stages: oral, anal, urethral, oedipal and genital. The implication of these stages to personality development is that various body zones have the capacity for pleasurable sensation. As the child grows, the centres of body gratification pass progressively from one area to another. (*See* also PSYCHOANALYSIS.)

3. Interpersonal School.—The U.S. psychoanalyst Harry Stack Sullivan (*q.v.*) stressed the careful study of the interaction between the developing child and his parents and his later relations with others as providing a more significant operational method of understanding human behaviour than that of the libido theory. Sullivan's conceptions, which represent a blend of psychoanalysis and psychobiology, are represented in the interpersonal school of psychiatry.

4. Psychosomatic Medicine.—The term psychosomatic medicine does not properly refer to a school in psychiatry; rather it describes the directed interest of a growing group of psychiatrists who, in close collaboration with other colleagues in medicine, are concerned with the study of reactions to anxiety as expressed through physiologic disturbances. In these instances responses of bodily organs rather than inappropriate symbolic behaviour are the defenses against threat. Psychosomatic disorders comprise not only the "organ neuroses" noted in early psychiatric classifications but also many other physiologic disturbances known to be precipitated by emotional stress. Bodily reactions to stress take expression in cardiovascular disorders; respiratory ailments such as certain forms of asthma and attacks of hyperventilation; gastrointestinal disturbances leading to belching, flatulence, anorexia, obesity, constipation and diarrhea; migraine and tension headaches; pelvic pain; dysmenorrhea; dyspareunia (in women, difficult or painful coitus); and impotence and frigidity. Psychosomaticists also study and treat the stress-induced responses contributing to modifications of the diabetic metabolism, the neurodermatoses, gastric and duodenal ulcers and ulcerative colitis.

Psychosomatic medicine is concerned not only with describing the nature of conflict- or stress-induced physiologic disturbances but also with defining the conditions under which disturbances of internal organs take place. Much emphasis is placed on the fact that emotional problems aggravate all illness and that denial of the existence of an emotional disturbance provokes greater disability.

In determining proper treatment, the psychosomaticist is interested in learning the kinds of situations and thoughts that produce personality disturbances. This knowledge is essential to understanding and preventing many conditions, such as the hallucinations and delusions that some patients have when they are deprived of sight during cataract operations. The gynecologist and obstetrician seek information about the patient's feelings concerning contraceptive practices, artificial insemination, therapeutic abortion and other emotionally laden areas of medicine. The surgeon can be assisted by knowledge of the patient's fears of mutilation or disfigurement; a patient's negative response during convalescence or unwillingness to undertake rehabilitative measures may be a consequence of his emotional attitudes to physical illness. All these conditions, as well as many others, require the attention of either a psychiatrist working in the medical service of a hospital or with a group of physicians who have understanding of psychosomatic interaction.

II. DIAGNOSIS AND CLASSIFICATION OF MENTAL DISORDERS

A. DIAGNOSIS

The psychiatric diagnosis is based on examination of the patient and history of his illness. Information is obtained concerning possible hereditary influences, the patient's physical maturation and his emotional and social development, taking into account experiences in both the family and community environment. Physical as well as neurological examinations are made and, when indicated, are supplemented by psychological tests (see PSYCHOLOGICAL TESTS AND MEASUREMENTS) and other special examinations such as electroencephalographic or biochemical and serological tests. Together these procedures provide data upon which the psychiatrist makes his diagnosis and formulates the determinative factors that explain the reaction patterns of his patient.

1. Symptomatology.—The actions of the mind cannot be isolated and separated into independent functions, such as the senses, memory, imagination, reason, desire or perception. Nor do the symptoms of mental disorders represent disease of a particular area of the brain. Psychiatric symptoms are expressions of loss or impairment of some function or of failure in development of that function. Loss of function may arise from psychological conflict, or it may occur secondary to a structural disturbance of the brain. For example, a defect in memory could be the consequence of an inherited defect; it could result from a blow to the head or from a growing brain tumour; or it could be the expression of a psychological conflict.

For most psychiatrists, anxiety and its control represent the central problem in psychopathology. Although many stressful experiences and conditions give rise to both fear and anxiety, these emotional reactions are usually differentiated. In general, fear is temporary and is directly related to some external event. Anxiety, in contrast, is aroused by any threat to the person's wholeness or his self-concept. It is a pervasive sense of apprehension or tension, the source of which is not consciously recognized. Anxiety has its antecedent in the tensions of early infantile life, and it is aroused in the growing child and in the adult in relation to actual or fantasied interpersonal conflicts.

When fear or anxiety is aroused, the person attempts to adapt and bring about a state of equilibrium or condition without tension. Rightly or wrongly, in actuality or in fantasy, the anxious person expects to receive an unfavourable reaction or estimate of his personal worth or conduct from someone whom he respects or whom he considers to be in authority. Through learning, the expressions of anxiety tend to be disguised or converted into various socially adaptive mechanisms; thus, most people are unaware of anxiety or of the circumstances that provoke it. When the person becomes anxious, however, the anxiety interferes with his capacity to recognize, evaluate and manage properly the situations associated with it. The ability to learn or profit from experience is impaired and capacity to adapt to new situations is limited because only a restricted range of stereotyped and repetitive responses is available.

Hostile and aggressive attitudes, expressed both overtly and covertly, are among the commonest psychiatric symptoms. Such impulses are often repressed in the psychological sense; by reaction formation they may re-emerge as pathologically excessive solicitousness and gentleness. Sometimes the hostile impulses are projected onto other persons; this is a common occurrence with paranoid types, who ascribe their destructive impulses to others. It should be noted that aggressive trends are utilized constructively in certain sports and work.

Pathological disturbances of motility are recognized in the behaviour of hyperactive, nonproductive persons. In these conditions, there may be a tremendous drive to action or to speech, often leading to what is designated as a stream or flight of ideas. Constant repetition of speech or of body movements is an expression of a motility disturbance underlying a compulsive drive. Various mannerisms may occur in which the person grimaces, repeats gestures, shows peculiar types of gait or repeats meaningless words or phrases.

Healthy affect, or the feeling tone of a person's life, is evident in ability to make controlled and variable responses to daily life experiences. Affectivity penetrates and colours the psychological life and influences the thought and action of every person. Disturbances of affect may lead to disturbances of consciousness, motility and intellect. Affective state can modify a person's judgment and ideas to the extent of distorting his capacity to evaluate reality, and thus it may lead to delusional and hallucinatory thinking.

Pathological elation, a condition seen in the manic behaviour of some psychotics, is an affective state of abnormal confidence and enjoyment. It is also recognized with certain brain syndromes such as general paresis, brain tumours and multiple sclerosis. A less frequently observed pleasurable state is that of ecstasy. The opposite of elation and ecstasy is depression, varying from mild downheartedness and indifference to feelings of despair and hopelessness.

Disturbances in perception and thought are seen in hallucinations and illusions, phobias, obsessional thinking and delusions; in apparently disconnected or loose associations; and in unusual retardation or flights of ideas.

(See also DEPRESSION [IN PSYCHIATRY]; HALLUCINATION; MANIA; PARANOID REACTIONS; PHOBIA; SCHIZOPHRENIA.)

2. Predisposing and Precipitating Factors.—Diagnosis of a psychiatric illness requires consideration of the predisposing and precipitating factors. These include a wide range of situations and conditions: hereditary background; effects of previous illnesses; presence of physical defects; use of drugs such as alcohol and narcotics; existence of nutritional and vitamin deficiencies;

vocational, sexual or economic stress; and exposure to particular kinds of privation. Numerous studies have been and are being conducted to determine the precise correlates of mental disorders.

Heredity.—The exact role of heredity in the development of mental and emotional disorders is still a matter of conjecture. Evidence indicates that certain inborn errors of metabolism transmitted through recessive genes underlie some forms of mental retardation. Based on studies of the incidence of schizophrenia among persons with various relationships to a schizophrenic patient, F. J. Kallmann postulated that schizophrenia is transmitted by recessive genes in the form of a predisposition; the schizophrenic reaction develops when a biologically vulnerable person is placed under particular stress. Kallmann reported a concordance rate for schizophrenia of 86% of identical twins and of only 14.5% among fraternal twins and siblings. Criticisms of attributing mental disorders solely to genetic factors rest largely upon the potentiality that parents have for transmitting their emotional difficulties to the next generation through the prolonged social learning that takes place in the course of family living.

Age.—Mental and emotional illnesses tend to make their appearance at certain ages. Adolescence, the middle years and senescence are associated with periods of major physiological changes and psychological stresses involving problems in family, vocational and social roles. During adolescence, the incidence of psychotic reactions rises rapidly. The young person must deal with the stresses arising from sexual maturation, the decisions to be made in the selection of a vocation and the conflicts that ensue in becoming emancipated from parents and assuming independent status. For women, the middle years are particularly critical, as they terminate the opportunity and hope for child bearing. This period also often brings emotional stress with the departure of children from the home and the need for the mother to find satisfactions in new roles and activities. Men at this age often have emotional problems associated with waning sexual energies and failure to attain to aspired goals. In old age, psychiatric disability tends to be precipitated with the mounting limitations of physical incapacities, the loss of satisfactions from work life and the emptiness of the retirement years, the loneliness that comes through the death of old friends and associates and other stresses. (*See* also Gerontology and Geriatrics.)

Sexual Factors.—While sexual behaviour in itself does not appear to be a source of mental disturbance, attitudes toward sexual acts and emotions aroused in relation to sexual strivings contribute to psychiatric illness or influence the content of the illness. No sexual act is in itself a cause of mental illness, but the unremitting anxiety and guilt that some persons experience over such acts may be a cause. (For varying attitudes toward sex practices, *see* Sexual Behaviour: *Human Sexual Behaviour.*)

Married persons appear to be considerably less susceptible to mental disorders than the widowed, single and divorced, but marriage in itself will neither cure nor prevent mental illness. In a marriage from which no sense of security is derived, the emotional disturbance of a partner may be aggravated.

No specific psychiatric disability is aroused by pregnancy or the postpartum period. The mental disturbances which occur sometimes with pregnancy and childbirth arise from the emotional significance these events have to the mother. For a woman who is psychologically unprepared and emotionally immature, the bearing of a child may arouse unconscious and repressed conflicts toward her own parents and siblings. Approximately one-half the psychiatric reactions to pregnancy are schizophrenic; the other half are manic-depressive or psychoneurotic.

Alcohol.—Alcohol plays an important role in producing mental disease; there is a direct correlation between the amount of alcohol consumed in a community and the incidence of observed alcoholic psychoses. Underlying the habituation to alcohol usually is a primary personality disturbance. The same personality defect occurs with narcotic addiction.

Disease and Injury.—In western countries where the diet generally is adequate, cerebral impairment resulting from vitamin and other nutritional deficiencies is seen most often as a second-

ary complication in the elderly or seriously psychotic. However, the longevity achieved in most western populations has greatly heightened the problem of mental debility stemming from the cerebral maladies of old age (*see* below, *Brain Disorders*).

Congenital or acquired physical defects often play an important role in creating personality disturbance. Acceptance of one's body and its acceptance by others represent a nuclear issue in the development of a secure personality. Children born with defects or children whose physical characteristics are unattractive to their parents often develop self-disparaging and self-defeating attitudes. The consequence is frequently a defect in the ability to make social adaptations that may be severe enough to cause psychiatric disability. Adults who suffer a disruption of their body image through injury, surgery or illness also are liable to personality disturbance. Among the commonest precipitants of psychiatric disability are head injuries, which may lead either to organic brain syndromes or to neuroses.

At one time overwork was considered a cause for mental illness. In the modern view the person who works long hours and excessively does so in order to fulfill a personal need—to reduce anxiety or as an outlet for energy or creativity. Work is also a means of maintaining human contacts in an otherwise withdrawn person. When a breakdown does take place in relation to vocation, usually a disruption of some important human relationship is threatened or has taken place. No evidence exists that mental efforts, in the absence of anxiety, produce psychotic or neurotic illness.

B. Classification

Kraepelin's classification system for mental disorders, established in 1883, was in general use until 1917, when the American Psychiatric association introduced the system that became the basis of that recommended in 1948 by the association in the fourth edition of *Standard Nomenclature of Diseases and Operations.* This classification system is more comprehensive and more flexible than the earlier schemes, and it also can be applied to the practice of psychiatry in general hospitals, in out-patient clinics and in private office practice, as well as in mental hospitals. According to this system, mental disturbances may be classified into three general categories representative of physical and psychological pathology: (1) acute and chronic brain disorders caused by or associated with impairments of brain tissue function; (2) mental deficiency; and (3) psychogenic disorders having no clearly defined physical or structural change in the brain. The psychogenic disorders, the major group, comprise the psychoneuroses, the majority of psychotic reactions, psychosomatic disorders and personality disorders.

1. Brain Disorders.—*Acute.*—Acute brain disorders are organic brain syndromes, usually temporary, from which a patient recovers. Although they generally involve reversible impairments in brain function, some of these disturbances may result in permanent changes in brain tissue, which can be detected by modern micropathological techniques. For the most part, they are the result of a serious disruption of the metabolism of the brain, particularly its capacity to metabolize glucose, its basic energy source. The symptoms of these disorders have been known under the general term of delirium (*q.v.*).

Delirious reactions are characterized by varying degrees of disturbances in consciousness and impaired awareness of surroundings. Some persons have the capacity to develop these reactions more readily than others, and the form and content of the delirium tend to be related to the underlying personality and the life experiences. The delirious person may show variable states of cloudiness, bewilderment, periodic somnolence, stupor or, in the deepest stages, coma. Usually, in states of confusion or bewilderment, the sufferer is anxious or apprehensive. Upon being questioned, he shows impairment in his ability to grasp meaning and to comprehend correctly the environment as to place, time or person. He is disoriented. Along with delusions, some persons experience frightening hallucinations.

Deliria are commonly associated with febrile illness, toxic states, metabolic disturbances (such as uremia, pellagra or pernicious anemia), states of cardiac decompensation and trauma following head injury. The best known of the acute brain syndromes is the delirium tremens of the alcoholic.

Chronic.—Chronic brain disorders result from a permanent impairment of cerebral tissue and are characterized particularly by disturbances in memory, judgment and affect (any experience of emotion or feeling). General paresis was once the most prevalent of these conditions, accounting for 8% to 10% of the patients committed to public mental hospitals. The use of penicillin for the treatment of syphilis greatly reduced the incidence of this disease.

At mid-20th century, the most frequently encountered chronic brain disorders are those suffered by large numbers of elderly presenile persons or those that occur as a consequence of cerebral arteriosclerosis in later life. Both these conditions are most prevalent in the U.S. and in western European countries which have expanding aged populations. In the U.S. chronic brain syndromes due to senile and arteriosclerotic psychoses account for approximately 40% of the hospitalized mentally ill. (*See also* DEMENTIA.)

2. Mental Deficiency.—This, the second large category of mental disorders, is defined as an impoverishment in intellectual competency which results either from an innate fault in the individual's developmental potentiality or from arrested development. Thus, the mentally defective person is not equipped with intellectual capacities, judgment, social skills and foresight that are possessed by the average person. (*See* MENTAL DEFICIENCY; RETARDED CHILDREN.)

3. Psychogenic Disorders.—Psychogenic disorders are defined as conditions whose causes or origins are not clearly traceable to a physical cause or to structural damage of the brain and the nervous system. These disorders include the major psychoses, such as the schizophrenic, paranoid, manic-depressive and involutional reactions; psychophysiological (psychosomatic) reactions; psychoneurotic reactions; and personality disorders. They are characterized by varying degrees of personality disturbances, ranging from catastrophic to minor interference in interpersonal relations. Distinctions are easily made between the psychoses and psychoneuroses when the symptoms are well-defined, but these illnesses can be very difficult to differentiate at their early stages or in the borderline states. Symptomatology most commonly is the basis of distinction, but the disorders are also distinguished on legal and social grounds.

Psychosis.—The diagnosis of psychosis usually implies a greater severity of personality disturbance than that occurring in psychoneurosis. In the psychotic person the inner emotions and experience are so disturbing that he is frequently unable to carry on ordinary social functions. The psychotic has a limited capacity for differentiating his own subjective experiences, *i.e.*, describing what he is, has actually observed, tried or known; his capacity to interpret and respond to his environment therefore is gravely impaired. In other terms, he is unable to deal with reality; he creates his own special environment in which his perceptions are distorted or falsified in the form of delusions or hallucinations. The thought processes of the psychotic are often so disorganized that his thinking appears disrupted and irrational. (*See also* PSYCHOSES.)

Psychoneurosis.—Unlike the psychotic, the psychoneurotic presents personality traits which are regarded as a socially acceptable adaptation against anxiety. In psychoneurosis, the inner experiences do not bring about a gross disturbance of external behaviour. The neurotic has the ability to maintain contact and good testing of the external environment. Although his thinking may be restricted or distorted by his overvalued and limited ideas, he does not suffer delusions and hallucinations. Moreover, he is not excessively withdrawn socially, and he usually retains his interest in the people and the world about him.

The question as to whether a neurosis may become a psychosis has been argued for years, but there is no certain or definitive knowledge. Psychiatrists who consider the psychotic reaction as a disease process usually reject the idea that progression can occur. On the other hand, most psychiatrists recognize a large number of borderline states, particularly with schizoid personalities, where the social adaptation of the patient is very precarious.

The multiplicity of neurotic symptoms that certain patients suffer, the ambivalence they demonstrate, their disturbed psychosexual life and their poorly developed self-concept have given rise to the classification by some psychiatrists of "pseudoneurotic schizophrenics." (*See also* NEUROSES.)

Personality Disorders.—Personality disorders are a group of conditions in which there are persisting patterns of inadequate or antisocial behaviour rather than of predominantly psychological or emotional disturbances that cause suffering and a sense of distress. Persons who always react with undue excitability and ineffectiveness in the presence of minor stress or who regularly display judgment that is not dependable are among those classified as having personality disorders. Such persons have little control over their hostile feelings, are fickle in their relations with others and are unable to form enduring or satisfactory relationships. Vocationally and socially these persons do poorly, even though they may be of normal or superior intelligence and physically well-endowed. Also included in the group with personality disorders are persons who exhibit extreme emotional instability characterized by explosive outbursts of rage upon minor provocation. At times, these personalities may be blustering and threatening; at other times they can be despairing and inaccessible. Two other common forms of personality disorder are seen in persons exhibiting either passive dependence reactions or passive aggressive reactions. The former are generally helpless, indecisive and clinging. When faced with minor problems, they show anxious and panic-stricken behaviour. In contrast, the passive aggressive person expresses his hostility in stubbornness, procrastination and inefficiency.

One of the most complex groups of the personality disorders is the category of sociopaths. Persons with sociopathic tendencies act out their hostility on the rest of the world. As a group, they make up the mass of the criminals and delinquent elements of society. Their symptomatology may also include various kinds of pathology expressed in sexual deviations. The commonest expression of this is homosexuality, but there are other forms, such as exhibitionism, voyeurism, masochism and sadism. (*See also* HOMOSEXUALITY; SEXUAL DEVIATIONS.)

Psychophysiologic Disorders.—In the psychophysiologic disorders, also designated psychosomatic conditions, anxiety produces a dysfunction in bodily organs through inappropriate activation of the involuntary nervous system and the glands of internal secretion. Thus the psychosomatic symptom emerges as a physiological concomitant of an emotional state. For example, in a state of rage, the angry man's blood pressure is likely to be elevated and his pulse and respiratory rate to be increased. When the anger passes, the heightened physiologic processes usually subside. However, if the man had a persistent inhibited aggression (chronic rage) which he was unable to express overtly, the emotional state remains unchanged, though unexpressed in the overt behaviour, and the physiological symptoms associated with the angry state persist. With time, such a person becomes aware of the physiological dysfunction. Very often he develops concern over what appears as an inappropriate activation of body organs, but he will deny or be unaware of the emotions which evoke the reactions. *See* above, *History: Modern Schools: Psychosomatic Medicine.*

III. TREATMENT OF MENTAL DISORDERS

1. Psychopharmacology.—One of the most striking advances in the symptomatic treatment of mental illnesses in the middle of the 20th century was the development of the series of pharmacological agents commonly known as tranquilizers. These drugs contrast sharply with the hypnotic and sedative drugs that formerly were in use and that clouded the patient's consciousness and impaired his motor and perceptual abilities. The tranquilizers can allay the symptoms of anxiety and reduce agitation with much less disturbance of consciousness. However, valuable as the tranquilizing substances have been, there is need for further study of their effects alone and in combination with other drugs; also drugs with extended and improved properties should be developed. Occasionally the tranquilizing drugs have toxic side effects, giving rise to such conditions as jaundice or a parkinsonianlike reaction; both these symptoms are reversible upon withdrawal of the drug. The drugs produce other minor symptoms because of their action on the autonomic nervous system.

Tranquilizers are used in treating many different kinds of disturbances but are particularly effective in relieving the symptoms of tension, overactivity, agitation, impulsiveness, explosive outbursts and destructive behaviour. Since they are prescribed for symptoms, they are not specific to the treatment of any diagnostic category. They have been more useful in treating the various psychotic states than in psychoneurotic reactions and personality disorders. The drugs also have been used in the treatment of toxic delirious states resulting from overuse of alcohol and in mental conditions resulting from brain damage.

Because of their ability to modify the behaviour of even the most disturbed patients, these agents have affected greatly the management of the hospitalized mentally ill. They have been responsible for dramatic changes in the behaviour of many psychotic patients. The noisy, untidy, crowded and unpleasant atmosphere that formerly pervaded the wards of many mental hospitals has largely disappeared; in the absence of the destructiveness, apathy and untidiness formerly exhibited by many patients, hospitals can be maintained more attractively. Because of the quieting effects of the tranquilizers, hospital staffs are able to devote more of their attention to other therapeutic efforts, and patients have been given greater freedom to move about and much more rehabilitative assistance. (*See* also NEUROPHARMACOLOGY AND PSYCHOPHARMACOLOGY; TRANQUILIZING DRUGS.)

2. Shock Therapy.—In 1933, Manfred Sakel of Vienna presented the first report of his work with insulin shock. Until the discovery of the superiority of the tranquilizing agents, variations of insulin shock therapy (also called insulin coma therapy) were commonly used in the treatment of schizophrenia and other psychotic conditions. With insulin shock treatment, the patient is given increasingly large doses of insulin which reduce the sugar content of the blood and bring on a state of coma. Usually the comatose condition is allowed to persist for about an hour, at which time it is terminated by administering warm salt solution via stomach tube or by intravenous injection of glucose. Insulin shock had its greatest effectiveness with schizophrenic patients whose illness had lasted less than two years (the rate of spontaneous recovery from schizophrenia also is highest in the first two years of the illness). Insulin shock therapy also had more value in the treatment of paranoid and catatonic schizophrenia than in the hebephrenic types.

Electroconvulsive therapy, introduced in Rome in 1938 by U. Cerletti and L. Bini, has been widely used in treating disturbances in which severe depression is the predominant symptom. It has been particularly recommended for manic-depressive psychoses and other types of depression. The technique is essentially the passage of alternating currents through the head between two electrodes placed over the temples. The passage of the current causes an immediate cessation of consciousness and the induction of a convulsive seizure. In general, electroconvulsive treatments are given three times a week for a period ranging from two to six weeks; some acutely disturbed patients, however, have been given as many as two or three treatments in a single day.

Following a course of treatment there is usually an impairment of memory, varying from a slight tendency to forget names to a severe confusional state. The memory defect diminishes gradually over several months. Electroconvulsive therapy, like insulin shock, declined in use after the tranquilizing drugs were introduced.

3. Psychosurgery.—The first treatment of mental disturbances by means of brain surgery was developed by the Portuguese neurologist António C. Egas Moniz (*q.v.*), the first operation being performed by Egas Moniz' colleague Almeida Lima, in 1935. The operation, called prefrontal lobotomy or leucotomy, was based on experimental studies demonstrating that certain neurotic symptoms induced in chimpanzees could be modified by cutting brain fibres. Egas Moniz' original operation consisted of cutting two openings in the skull, one on each side above the temple, and then severing the nerve fibres connecting the thalamus with the frontal lobes of the brain.

Prefrontal lobotomy has come to be generally regarded as a radical procedure to be followed only after all other forms of treatment have proved ineffective, and since the introduction of the tranquilizing agents the condition of only a very few patients warrants such a drastic measure. Patients selected for this operation usually show chronic agitation and severe distress, persistent depression, emotional aggressiveness and excited and impulsive behaviour. Phobias, obsessions, hallucinations and delusions not of long-standing duration have been relieved by this procedure. On the other hand, psychosurgery has had relatively little effect in modifying behaviour that characteristically expresses cruelty, avoidance of responsibility, excessive use of alcohol or pathological sexuality; it also has proved generally ineffective in the treatment of the chronic and withdrawn psychotic. The procedure tends to accentuate difficult personality traits by lowering inhibitory controls and by leading to development of facetious and tactless social behaviour. Many patients after the operation tend to show increase in self-esteem coupled with lack of self-criticism.

The effect of lobotomy on intellectual functions has been a subject of much controversy. Ordinary psychological tests and observations reveal little change in the patient's psychological functioning in the months immediately following the operation. It is believed, however, that lobotomy results in significant deterioration in intellect over the course of years. Patients who prior to their illness possessed the ability to perform tests requiring a high degree of abstraction showed great impairment in these capacities after lobotomy. Also, close observation of performance of persons with high intellectual capacity indicates a reduction in such capacity after surgery.

4. Psychotherapy.—Psychotherapy is the treatment of personality disturbances by psychological means. The essential factor in the many different techniques of psychotherapy is the establishment of an understanding and accepting relationship between therapist and patient. In this relationship, the therapist does not deprecate, censure or judge the patient, and the patient is encouraged to discover and speak of his emotional life. This is necessary if the aim of treatment is greater insight into the sources of the patient's difficulties and his achievement of greater personal satisfactions. There are many types of psychotherapy, and the indications for their use depend upon a number of variables, including the nature of the illness, age and intellectual capacity of the patient, estimate of his motivation and his capacity to face anxiety. These are discussed in the separate entries PSYCHOTHERAPY; PSYCHOANALYSIS; and PSYCHOLOGY, APPLIED: *Psychology as Applied to Treatment.*

IV. CHILD PSYCHIATRY

The increasing recognition of the crucial influence of parent-child relationships on the child's personality development has provided a strong impetus to the study of psychiatric disorders of childhood. The approach to the diagnosis and treatment of children's mental and emotional disturbances is necessarily different from that with adult patients. The child is living through the most active and critical phases of his development. His personality is constantly being molded and changed as he moves from one developmental stage to another. In assessing the healthy or unhealthy patterns of a child's personality development, the psychiatrist must have extensive knowledge of the ever changing patterns of personality, particularly at the various age levels through adolescence. (*See* further CHILD PSYCHOLOGY; ADOLESCENCE.)

Although many of the general principles relating to therapy of adult psychiatric disorders apply to child psychiatry, a number of special problems arise with children which require special techniques. Usually the parents of the child bring him for treatment, or he is referred to the psychiatrist by a community agency —the school or the juvenile or family court. Because much of the essential information on the child's behaviour and other medical, psychological and social factors must be obtained from the parents, the pediatrician, psychologist, teacher or social workers, child psychiatrists work closely with the parents and other specialists who have been in frequent or close contact with the child. Thus, in the field of child psychiatry, the working relationship between the psychiatrist and the related social and medical disciplines is closer and more essential than it is in adult psychiatry, where the patient usually can provide much of the pertinent and necessary information on his life and his condition.

For the most part, child psychiatry is concerned with the study and treatment of the different neurotic reactions or problems of emotional maladjustment that affect children. The emotional maladjustments of children frequently are manifested in behaviour difficulties, unpleasant character traits or psychosomatic disturbances. Neurotic reactions include habit spasms, stammering, overactivity and phobias. Ticlike movements of the face and other parts of the body are common. Among infants, deprivation of mothering or problems in the infant's relationship with the mother may lead to withdrawn behaviour, continuous crying, inability to eat, insomnia and physical or mental retardation or both. Older children are often seen for such habit disturbances as persistent nail biting, thumbsucking, bedwetting and temper tantrums. Children also are referred for treatment because of conduct problems or propensities for disobedience, lying, stealing, destructiveness, fighting, fire setting, cruelty and running away from home.

As in the treatment of adult patients, psychiatric treatment of children requires determination of any genetic, constitutional or physical factors that have contributed to the disturbance. Also, it is essential that the relationship between the child and the parent be assessed for its contribution to the disturbed behaviour. Where there are disturbing influences that can be associated with parental dissension, alcoholism, hostility, cruelty, neglect, overprotection of the child, excessive ambitions for and expectations of the child, it is common to find behavioural disorders. The existence of neurotic, psychotic or psychopathic illness in the parents also contributes to a faulty parent-child relationship. The parents' unconscious feelings about the child and the kinds of conflicts which disturb the parent-child relationship also must be determined. (It must be recognized that the emotional behaviour of the parents is sometimes the result rather than the cause of the child's misdemeanours.) Another important source of personality problems is the child's relationship with brothers and sisters. In addition, the death or loss of a parent often has a profound and lasting effect, as it reduces the child's opportunity for healthy growth through continuing identification with or differentiation from the absent parent.

School experiences also can create personality problems. Many children exhibit conduct and learning disturbances because they have been unable to cope with modern methods of instruction. Children with perceptual difficulties, for example, may fail to learn to read or may not develop the reading skills appropriate to their age level, because of the scanning method of teaching reading without phonetic sounds or spelling out the letters in a word. As a consequence, they often become anxious over their failure to meet the standards of their family and their class. When these emotions are aroused, conduct disturbances may ensue.

V. PSYCHIATRIC TRAINING AND ORGANIZATION

A. TRAINING

1. United States.—In the United States, to qualify as a specialist in psychiatry, a physician must complete a period of training in an accredited or qualified hospital or other institution. Usually the physician enters a psychiatric residency training program after one year of medical internship, which followed his obtaining the degree of doctor of medicine from an accredited medical school. Residency training in psychiatry provides supervised experience in the diagnosis and treatment of mental and emotional illnesses. It includes opportunities for using all the varieties of treatment in specialized psychiatric hospitals and institutions, out-patient departments, various kinds of children's services and general hospitals. The resident physician in psychiatry also is required to take formal course work in such fields

as psychobiology, psychopathology and psychodynamics, neuroanatomy, neurophysiology and neuropathology. Upon completion of this training, the physician may apply for examination by the American Board of Psychiatry and Neurology. The certificate of the board indicates that the physician has completed his general training; it does not measure his level of competence in the performance of special therapies.

The clinical psychologist, in contradistinction to the specialist in psychiatry, is not trained in medicine. He has the degree of doctor of philosophy in psychology and has been trained in the theory and practice of psychological testing of mental patients. In some institutions he may, under supervision, receive training to do certain forms of psychotherapy. The training of the clinical psychologist, unlike that of the psychiatrist, does not equip him to diagnose, to prescribe drugs and medicine, or to administer shock therapy and other psychiatric diagnostic and treatment procedures.

For the most part, the psychoanalyst in the United States has obtained the degree of doctor in medicine and has completed a residency in psychiatry. In addition, he has completed the requirement of a personal psychoanalysis and has conducted the analysis of several patients under the supervision of a qualified training analyst. Also he has undertaken and completed certain other didactic and clinical training. The majority of qualified psychoanalysts in the United States are members of or candidates for membership in the American Psychoanalytic association.

A small group of clinical psychologists, social workers and others also have been trained to do psychotherapy and psychoanalysis. These persons were trained largely in the past by psychoanalysts in England and other western countries of Europe. The U.S. medical profession generally believes that clinical psychologists, social workers and lay analysts who practise psychotherapy or psychoanalysis should do so in collaboration with a psychiatrist or a physician. This position is based on the belief that proper psychiatric diagnosis requires a physical and neurological examination; only those trained in medicine are able to decide whether the somatic symptoms of an illness are due to an underlying physical process or are representative of an emotional disturbance. On the other hand, psychologists and other nonmedical persons trained in psychoanalysis have made many fundamental and valuable contributions toward the elucidation of the basis of behaviour and the understanding of personality development.

2. Great Britain.—In Great Britain the physician may begin his training for the specialty of psychiatry after he has completed his preregistration appointments and his national service. He then serves on the staff of a mental hospital for a minimum of two years, at which time he may be examined for the diploma in psychological medicine (D.P.M.) by the Conjoint board. The D.P.M. does not qualify the recipient as a consultant in the national health service; such senior appointments are approved by a committee of outstanding specialists, who judge the candidate in competition with others applying for the post.

The teaching program of the Institute of Psychiatry of the British Postgraduate Medical federation conducted at the Maudsley and Bethlem Royal hospitals in London is similar to that of the best residency programs in the United States. In terms of formal scholarship, the British institute is more exacting than any of the American institutes. The British institute awards its own D.P.M., which has higher standards and requires more extensive training than the certificate of the Conjoint board. While the British institute is the only fully developed British university postgraduate centre in psychiatry, Great Britain has other institutes, hospitals and clinics in which special kinds of psychiatric training can be obtained. The Institute of Psychoanalysis in London provides specialized training much like that of the psychoanalytic institutes and training centres in the United States.

3. Other Countries.—In Canada, although each province makes its own arrangements for awarding diplomas in psychiatry, the training of the physician specializing in psychiatry is much like that of the psychiatrist trained in the United States. The training of psychiatrists in Australia and New Zealand is similar to English psychiatric training. South Africa has modeled its training program in psychiatry closely after that of the Netherlands. There, to become registered as a specialist psychiatrist or specialist in mental disorders, the applicant must be qualified as a medical practitioner for at least six years, and must satisfy certain clinical requirements in medicine and surgery as well as in psychiatry. Upon fulfilling these requirements satisfactorily, he obtains a higher degree in his specialty. Several universities in India award a diploma in psychological medicine.

B. Organizations

1. United States.—The American Psychiatric association, oldest national medical association in North America, was founded in 1848, and in the mid-1960s had a membership of more than 10,000 psychiatrists. The organization has an information service, and publishes several journals as well as a biographical directory of its members. Its aims are the improvement of treatment of the mentally ill and the furtherance of psychiatric education and research.

The National Institute of Mental Health of the United States public health service is the major federal government agency concerned with the prevention and treatment of psychiatric disorders. Through the provisions of the National Mental Health act of 1946, the institute makes grants-in-aid to support training, research and community services in the United States. The institute also conducts an extensive research program at the National Institutes of Health in Bethesda, Md.

2. Great Britain.—Under the Mental Health act, 1959, the Board of Control for England was dissolved and mental health was administered by the minister of health advised by a standing mental health committee. The act established a review tribunal for each of 15 regions, under the direction of the lord chancellor. These tribunals were convened at times provided by the act, when certain patients detained against their will could make application to be heard. In Scotland the function of the Board of Mental Welfare (formerly the General Board of Control) is chiefly the control and treatment of patients.

In England, the major professional psychiatric organization is the Royal Medico-Psychological association. Similar professional bodies have been established throughout the British commonwealth. The Canadian Psychiatric association, chartered in 1951 and associated with the Canadian Medical association, has more than 600 members. Since most matters related to the practice of medicine fall within the jurisdiction of the provincial governments in Canada, the Canadian Psychiatric association has been active in developing its relations with these governments.

3. Other Countries.—Psychiatrists of Australia and New Zealand are organized as the Australian Association of Psychiatrists. In India, the psychiatric organization is known as the Indian Psychiatric society. In South Africa the National Group of Neurology, Psychiatry and Neurosurgery represents the aims of the specialty. Each organization supplies information on its aims, its members and the psychiatric facilities of the country. Similar organizations exist in other European and South American countries.

4. International.—International bodies concerned with mental health are discussed in the article Mental Health.

See also Adjustment (in Psychology); Behaviour Disorders; Psychology, Abnormal; and references under "Psychiatry" in the Index.

Bibliography.—E. H. Ackerknecht, *A Short History of Psychiatry* (1959); F. Alexander, *Fundamentals of Psychoanalysis* (1948); Sigmund Freud, *Vorlesungen zur Einführung in die Psychoanalyse* (1916–18), auth. Eng. trans. rev. ed., *General Introduction to Psychoanalysis*, by Joan Riviere, preface by E. Jones and G. Stanley Hall (1920 *et seq.*); E. Jones, *Life and Work of Sigmund Freud*, 3 vol. (1953–57); F. J. Kallmann, *Heredity in Health and Mental Disorder* (1953); Adolf Meyer, *Commonsense Psychiatry*, ed. by A. Lief (1948); "Life Stress and Bodily Disease," *Res. Publ., Assn. Nerv. Ment. Dis.*, vol. xxix (1950); A. P. Noyes and L. C. Kolb, *Modern Clinical Psychiatry*, 6th ed. (1963); H. S. Sullivan, *Interpersonal Theory of Psychiatry*, ed. by H. S. Perry and M. L. Gawel (1953); J. Taylor (ed.), *Selected Writings of John Hughlings Jackson*, 2 vol. (1958); T. A. Ross, *Common Neuroses*, 2nd ed. (1937); L. B. Kalinowsky and P. H. Hoch, *Somatic Treatments in Psychiatry* (1961).　　　(L. C. K.)

PSYCHICAL RESEARCH is the scientific study of such alleged occurrences as thought transference, foretelling the future, hauntings involving appearances of ghosts and movements of objects, and messages received through mediums from the spirits of those who have died. All such alleged events may be included in the class of the paranormal; early subjects of study included hypnotism, which is no longer regarded as paranormal (*see* Hypnosis).

In 1882 the Society for Psychical Research was founded in London, followed six years later by the founding of a similar society in the United States. Such societies were founded later in most European countries, and active work is carried on, particularly in the Netherlands, France, and Italy. Universities have been slower to recognize psychical research as a serious subject for study. The activities of the parapsychological laboratory at Duke University, Durham, N.C., under J. B. Rhine from the 1930s to the 1960s attracted considerable interest. A department of psychical research later was opened at the University of Utrecht under W. H. C. Tenhaeff.

One of the reasons for interest in psychical research in the last half of the 19th century was the rise of the spiritualist movement that grew out of the acceptance of the reality of spirit communication and the use of this as the basis of a new religion. Some of the early psychical researchers were also spiritualists, as, for example, F. W. H. Myers and Sir Oliver Lodge. Other psychical researchers (such as the physiologist C. Richet) accepted paranormal activity as real but rejected the spiritualist explanation, while others were not committed to either view.

Existence After Death.—Advances in psychical research have made the solution of the problem of providing proof of survival after death increasingly difficult. The experimental evidence of the existence of psi cognition (obtaining knowledge by telepathy or clairvoyance) as a paranormal ability among some persons suggests an alternative source of information apparently coming from spirits. For example, some of the early researchers (*e.g.*, Myers and Lodge) left sealed packages with the intention of communicating the contents after their death. In fact, neither experiment was successful, but if they had succeeded their success might have been explained in terms of the clairvoyant powers of the medium. A modification of such an experiment is an attempt by a medium to communicate the message during the lifetime of the person depositing it; failure during his lifetime followed by success after his death would provide at least some evidence that he was communicating after death. No experiment of this type, however, had been completed by the 1960s.

Soon after Myers' death in 1901 an experimental demonstration of survival was arranged ostensibly from the other side of the grave, presumably by Myers himself. Called cross-correspondence, essentially it was communication, through different mediums, of fragments of a message that made a coherent whole only when fitted together. Success in such a task cannot easily be explained by reference to possible paranormal powers of the medium. Its results are not easy to evaluate, but many competent judges are of the opinion that the cross-correspondences provide strong evidence of the survival of the deceased persons who were their ostensible originators.

Evidence along different lines was sought by Whately Carrington, who applied psychological tests to communicators in the attempt to discover whether a single communicator coming through different mediums showed constant measurable characteristics that would indicate that he was one and the same person. Critical examination of Carrington's results shows that he obtained no evidence of the identity of his communicators. The research method was ingenious, however, and the problem remains to be studied further.

Telepathy.—Much better success has attended the experimental investigation of what is called thought-transference or telepathy. The typical form of this experiment is that in which the task is card guessing: an agent turns up and looks at successive cards in a pack of playing cards and a percipient tries to tell him which they are. Promising results were obtained early but critics urged the necessity for further precautions against error before it could be accepted that a thought could pass from one mind to another without use of the ordinary sensory channels of communication. Further experiments with a different type of card were carried out at Duke University (*see* PARAPSYCHOLOGY). They were also carried out with increased precautions against error and a good rate of success by S. G. Soal and K. M. Goldney in Great Britain.

In the meantime, however, Rhine had thrown doubt on the appropriateness of regarding these as tests of telepathy, since he found that equal success could be obtained when no one looked at the cards. The performance would then commonly be called clairvoyance. Extrasensory perception (ESP) is a term commonly used now to cover both telepathy and clairvoyance. The more noncommittal term psi has also been suggested to cover all types of paranormal cognition, and is widely used.

There is, from time to time, an arousal of public interest in telepathy through the appearance on the stage of an entertainer who is supposed to demonstrate telepathy. Less frequently the demonstration is of so-called eyeless sight. The resources of stage telepathy have been enlarged by the development of small wireless receiving sets that can be concealed on the person, although impressive demonstrations were given earlier by the use of codes and other methods. Such trick telepathy has no bearing on the question of whether real extrasensory perception takes place. The experimenter has the task of arranging his conditions so that the experimental subject has no opportunity to trick him. Without such precautions, an experiment is of no value as evidence for the reality of the phenomenon under investigation.

Supernatural Foresight.—A form of paranormal cognition for which there is a long tradition of anecdotal evidence is the foreseeing of the future by dreams and by various devices such as looking at the flight of birds or at the entrails of sacrificial animals, or listening to the wind blowing through leaves (*see* DIVINATION). No important contribution to psychical research has been made by studying any of these devices. On the other hand, experiments have been done in which the percipient's task is to guess the future order of a pack of cards after a process of shuffling and cutting. There seems to be evidence that some subjects can succeed in such a task of precognition, although the level of statistical significance encourages less confidence than that for experimental extrasensory perception.

Physical Manifestations.—Psychical research has also been concerned with such paranormal phenomena as levitation, materialization, and the moving of heavy objects. Sir William Crookes studied both the phenomena of the medium D. D. Home and a materialized figure (Katie King) that developed in the presence of the medium Florence Cook, reporting that he had satisfied himself as to their genuineness. A remarkable medium, an uneducated Italian woman called Eusapia Palladino, exasperated psychical researchers by her crude attempts to cheat if controls were relaxed. A critical experimental study of her, however, by three experienced psychical researchers produced striking physical manifestations under conditions which the experimenters said were such that fraud was impossible.

The most remarkable studies of materializations were made in France by G. Geley and Richet. Wax gloves have been produced that are reported to have been made by spirit hands dipped into molten wax and dematerialized after the wax solidified. There are photographs of ectoplasm, the quasi-material substance that is supposed to be exuded from the medium's body to form the substantial basis for materializations. Many of these photographs show part of the ectoplasmic substance in the shape of human faces or other parts of the human form. These photographs are plainly not in themselves evidence of the reality of ectoplasm, as the wax gloves are not evidence of the reality of materialized hands. In both cases, their weight as evidence depends on the reliability of the persons obtaining them.

Physical manifestations are often lightly dismissed because they can easily be simulated by fraudulent means and are so simulated by dishonest mediums. Their investigation is made difficult by the fact that they are generally produced in darkness or reduced light. At the same time, it should be noticed that those investigators who became convinced of their genuineness were aware of the possibilities of fraud and were satisfied that their precautions to exclude fraud were adequate. Such experienced scientific investigators as Crookes, Lodge, Sir W. Barrett, and Richet are included in this group.

Spontaneous Phenomena.—In addition to these various experimental lines of investigation, a large field of spontaneous phenomena has engaged the attention of psychical researchers. This field includes apparitions of the living and of the dead and also hauntings. An early inquiry into apparitions revealed that these had little of the appearance of the ghost of fiction. They were not vague sheeted figures, but of the form and appearance of living persons, for whom they were often mistaken. It has been argued that there is little reason for regarding them as spirits but rather as hallucinatory perceptual experiences which may originate from a genuinely paranormal process. It was stated that apparitions of persons near the point of death occurred too often for the coincidence between death and the apparition to be entirely a chance coincidence.

Spontaneous reports of hauntings suggest that these are of two main types: that in which an apparition is repeatedly seen in the same place and that in which the main phenomena are noises and displacement of household objects. A good example of the former type is the apparition described by a woman who wrote in the *Proceedings of the Society for Psychical Research* (vol. viii, 1892) under the pseudonym of Miss Morton. This apparition was said to be constant in form, stereotyped in action, seen only occasionally and never when watched for. It was reported as sometimes seen by more than one person at the same time, but also it might be seen by one person and not by another who was also present; it could apparently be seen by domestic animals. The reported visual experiences differed, therefore, from the perception of a physical object and also from an autogenic hallucination. Various theories have been put forward, but the data on hauntings are neither full enough nor sufficiently systematically collected to make it possible to subject alternative theories to critical tests.

Haunting characterized by noise and displacement of objects is commonly called a poltergeist haunting, and cases have been reported for a long time. Epworth rectory, Lincolnshire, the home of Charles Wesley, was the reputed scene of such phenomena, and W. Barrett reported the opportunity of observing and recording similar events at Derrygonnelly farm.

Poltergeist reports at different times and different places show a curious parallelism. One feature that nearly all have in common is that the phenomena occur in the presence of a young person, boy or girl, somewhere between the ages of 12 and 20. This fact led many of the early observers to suppose that all poltergeist phenomena were products of normal mischief. It seems likely that such phenomena result from emotional strain in the young person concerned. Various theories have been put forward to account for poltergeist phenomena, many of which have little evidential support. A fuller understanding must await a closer study of such cases with the use of modern recording devices. Sensational newspaper stories of poltergeist phenomena are not to be regarded as a safe basis for any kind of theory.

See also SPIRITUALISM.

BIBLIOGRAPHY.—C. Richet, *Thirty Years of Psychical Research* (1923); E. Osty, *Supernormal Faculties in Man* (1923); G. Geley, *Clairvoyance and Materialisation* (1927); H. F. Saltmarsh, *Evidence of Personal Survival From Cross Correspondences* (1938); S. G. Soal and F. Bateman, *Modern Experiments in Telepathy* (1954); R. C. Johnson, *Psychical Research* (1955); J. B. Rhine and J. G. Pratt, *Parapsychology* (1958); G. R. Schmeidler and R. A. McConnell, *ESP and Personality Patterns* (1958); R. H. Thouless, *Experimental Psychical Research* (1963); A. R. G. Owen, *Can We Explain the Poltergeist?* (1964).
(R. H. T.)

PSYCHOANALYSIS. The first part of this article, written by Sigmund Freud and lightly revised, appeared in 1926. It describes the development of psychoanalysis and its nature as therapeutic method and psychological theory, and evaluates its status at that date. The latter parts of the article treat of subsequent developments in psychoanalytic theory and practice into the second half of the 20th century, and the influence of psychoanalysis on the arts (especially literature) and social thought.

FUNDAMENTALS

In the years 1880–82 a Viennese physician, Josef Breuer (*q.v.*), discovered a new procedure by means of which he relieved a girl, who was suffering from severe hysteria, of her symptoms. The idea occurred to him that the symptoms were connected with impressions which she had received during a period of excitement while she was nursing her sick father. He therefore induced her, while she was in a state of hypnotic somnambulism, to search for these connections in her memory and to live through the "pathogenic" scenes once again without inhibiting the affects that arose in the process. He found that when she had done this the symptoms disappeared for good.

This was at a date before the investigations of J. M. Charcot and Pierre Janet (*qq.v.*) into the origin of hysterical symptoms, and Breuer's discovery was thus entirely uninfluenced by them. But he did not pursue the matter any further at the time, and it was not until some ten years later that he took it up again in collaboration with Sigmund Freud (*q.v.*). In 1895 they published a book, *Studien über Hysterie*, in which Breuer's discoveries were described and an attempt was made to explain them by the theory of *catharsis*. According to that hypothesis, hysterical symptoms originate through the energy of a mental process being withheld from conscious influence and being diverted into bodily innervation (*conversion*). A hysterical symptom would thus be a substitute for an omitted mental act and a reminiscence of the occasion which should have given rise to that act. And, on this view, recovery would be a result of the liberation of the affect that had gone astray and of its discharge along a normal path (*abreaction*). Cathartic treatment gave excellent therapeutic results, but it was found that they were not permanent and that they were dependent on the personal relation between the patient and the physician. Freud, who later proceeded with these investigations by himself, made an alteration in their technique, by replacing hypnosis by the method of free association. He invented the term *psychoanalysis*, which in the course of time came to have two meanings: (1) a particular method of treating nervous disorders and (2) the science of unconscious mental processes, which has also been appropriately described as "depth psychology."

Subject Matter of Psychoanalysis.—Psychoanalysis finds a constantly increasing amount of support as a therapeutic procedure, because of the fact that it can do more for certain classes of patients than any other method of treatment. The principal field of its application is in the milder neuroses—hysteria, phobias and obsessional states—but in malformations of character and in sexual inhibitions or abnormalities it can also bring about marked improvements or even recoveries. Its influence upon dementia praecox and paranoia is doubtful; on the other hand, in favourable circumstances it can cope with depressive states, even if they are of a severe type. In every instance the treatment makes heavy claims upon both the physician and the patient: the former requires a special training, and must devote a long period of time to exploring the mind of each patient, while the latter must make considerable sacrifices, both material and mental. Nevertheless, all the trouble involved is as a rule rewarded by the results. Psychoanalysis does not act as a convenient panacea (*cito, tute, jucunde*, "quickly, safely, pleasantly") upon all psychological disorders. On the contrary, its application has been instrumental in making clear for the first time the difficulties and limitations in the treatment of such affections.

The therapeutic results of psychoanalysis depend upon the replacement of unconscious mental acts by conscious ones and are operative in so far as that process has significance in relation to the disorder under treatment. The replacement is effected by overcoming internal resistances in the patient's mind. The future will probably attribute far greater importance to psychoanalysis as the science of the unconscious than as a therapeutic procedure.

Depth Psychology.—Psychoanalysis, in its character of depth psychology, considers mental life from three points of view: the dynamic, the economic, and the topographical.

The Dynamic Standpoint.—From the first of these standpoints, the dynamic one, psychoanalysis derives all mental processes (apart from the reception of external stimuli) from the interplay of forces, which assist or inhibit one another, combine with one another, enter into compromises with one another, etc. All of these forces are originally in the nature of *instincts;* that is to say, they have an organic origin. They are characterized by possessing an immense (somatic) persistence and reserve of power (*repetition-compulsion*), and they are represented mentally as images or ideas with an affective charge (*cathexis*). In psychoanalysis, no less than in other sciences, the theory of instincts is an obscure subject. An empirical analysis leads to the formation of two groups of instincts: the so-called ego instincts, which are directed toward self-preservation, and the object instincts, which are concerned with relations to an external object. The social instincts are not regarded as elementary or irreducible. Theoretical speculation leads to the suspicion that there are two fundamental instincts which lie concealed behind the manifest ego instincts and object instincts; namely, (1) Eros, the instinct which strives for ever closer union, and (2) the instinct for destruction, which leads toward the dissolution of what is living. In psychoanalysis the manifestation of the force of Eros is given the name *libido*.

The Economic Standpoint.—From this point of view, psychoanalysis supposes that the mental representations of the instincts have a cathexis of definite quantities of energy, and that it is the purpose of the mental apparatus to hinder any damming up of these energies and to keep as low as possible the total amount of the excitations to which it is subject. The course of mental processes is automatically regulated by the *pleasure-pain principle,* and pain is thus in some way related to an increase of excitation and pleasure to a decrease. In the course of development the original pleasure principle undergoes a modification with reference to the external world, giving place to the *reality principle,* whereby the mental apparatus learns to postpone the pleasure of satisfaction and to tolerate temporarily feelings of pain.

Mental Topography.—Topographically, psychoanalysis regards the mental apparatus as a composite instrument, and endeavours to determine at what points in it the various mental processes take place. According to the most recent psychoanalytic views, the mental apparatus is composed of an *id,* which is the reservoir of the instinctive impulses; of an *ego,* which is the most superficial portion of the id and one which is modified by the influence of the external world; and of a *superego,* which develops out of the id, dominates the ego and represents the inhibitions of instinct characteristic of man. Further, the property of consciousness has a topographical reference; for processes in the id are entirely unconscious, while consciousness is the function of the ego's outermost layer, which is concerned with the perception of the external world.

At this point two observations may be in place. It must not be supposed that these very general ideas are presuppositions upon which the work of psychoanalysis depends. On the contrary, they are its latest conclusions and are in every respect open to revision. Psychoanalysis is founded securely upon the observation of the facts of mental life, and for that very reason its theoretical superstructure is still incomplete and subject to constant alteration. Second, there is no reason for astonishment that psychoanalysis, which was originally no more than an attempt at explaining pathological mental phenomena, should have developed into a psychology of normal mental life. The justification for this arose with the discovery that the dreams and mistakes (*parapraxias,* such as slips of the tongue, etc.) of normal men have the same mechanism as neurotic symptoms.

Theoretical Basis.—The first task of psychoanalysis was the elucidation of nervous disorders. The analytical theory of the neuroses is based upon three ground pillars: the recognition of (1) repression, (2) the importance of the sexual instincts, and (3) transference.

Censorship.—There is a force in the mind which exercises the functions of a censorship, and which excludes from consciousness and from any conscious influence upon action all tendencies which displease it. Such tendencies are described as "repressed." They remain unconscious, and if the physician attempts to bring them into the patient's consciousness he provokes a *resistance.* These repressed instinctual impulses, however, are not always made powerless by this process. In many cases they succeed in making their influence felt by circuitous paths, and it is the indirect or substitutive gratification of repressed impulses that constitutes neurotic symptoms.

Sexual Instincts.—For cultural reasons the most intensive repression falls upon the sexual instincts; but it is precisely in connection with them that repression most easily miscarries, so that neurotic symptoms are found to be substitutive gratifications of repressed sexuality. The belief that in man sexual life begins only at puberty is incorrect. On the contrary, signs of it can be detected from the beginning of extrauterine existence; it reaches a first culminating point at or before the fifth year (early period), after which it is inhibited or interrupted (latency period) until the age of puberty, which is the second climax of its development. This double onset of sexual development seems to be distinctive of the genus *Homo*. All experiences during the first period of childhood are of the greatest importance to the individual, and, in combination with his inherited sexual constitution, form the dispositions for the subsequent development of character or disease. It is a mistaken belief that sexuality coincides with "genitality." The sexual instincts pass through a complicated course of development, and it is only at the end of it that the "primacy of the genital zone" is attained. Before this there are a number of "pregenital organizations" of the libido— points at which it may become "fixated" and to which, in the event of subsequent repression, it will return (*regression*). The infantile fixations of the libido determine the form of neurosis which sets in later. Thus the neuroses are to be regarded as inhibitions in the development of the libido.

The Oedipus Complex.—There are no specific causes of nervous disorders; the question whether a conflict finds a healthy solution or leads to a neurotic inhibition of function depends upon quantitative considerations; that is, upon the relative strength of the forces concerned. The most important conflict with which a small child is faced is his relation to his parents, the *Oedipus complex*; it is in attempting to grapple with this problem that persons destined to suffer from a neurosis habitually fail. The reactions against the instinctual demands of the Oedipus complex are the source of the most precious and socially important achievements of the human mind; and this probably holds true not only in the life of individuals but also in the history of the human species as a whole. The superego, the moral factor which dominates the ego, also has its origin in the process of overcoming the Oedipus complex.

Transference.—By transference is meant a striking peculiarity of neurotics. They develop toward their physician emotional relations, both of an affectionate and hostile character, which are not based upon the actual situation but are derived from their relations toward their parents (the Oedipus complex). Transference is a proof of the fact that adults have not overcome their former childish dependence; it coincides with the force which has been named *suggestion,* and it is only by learning to make use of it that the physician is enabled to induce the patient to overcome his internal resistances and do away with his repressions. Thus psychoanalytic treatment acts as a second education of the adult, as a correction to his education as a child.

Within this narrow compass it has not been possible to mention many matters of the greatest interest, such as the *sublimation* of instincts, the part played by symbolism, the problem of *ambivalence,* etc. Nor has there been space to allude to the applications of psychoanalysis, which originated, as has been seen, in the sphere of medicine, to other departments of knowledge (such as anthropology, the study of religion, literary history, and education) where its influence is constantly increasing. It is enough to say that psychoanalysis, in its character of the psychology of the deepest unconscious mental acts, promises to become the link between psychiatry and all of these other fields of study.

The Psychoanalytic Movement.—The beginnings of psychoanalysis may be marked by two dates: 1895, which saw the publication of Breuer and Freud's *Studien über Hysterie*, and 1900, which saw that of Freud's *Traumdeutung*. At first the new discoveries aroused no interest either in the medical profession or among the general public. In 1907 the Swiss psychiatrists, under the leadership of E. Bleuler and C. G. Jung (*qq.v.*), began to concern themselves in the subject, and in 1908 there took place at Salzburg a first meeting of adherents from a number of different countries. In 1909 Freud and Jung were invited to the United States by G. Stanley Hall to deliver a series of lectures on psychoanalysis at Clark University, Worcester, Mass. From that time forward interest in Europe grew rapidly; it showed itself, however, in a forcible rejection of the new teachings, characterized by an emotional colouring which sometimes bordered upon the unscientific.

The reasons for this hostility are to be found, from the medical point of view, in the fact that psychoanalysis lays stress upon psychical factors, and, from the philosophical point of view, in its assuming as an underlying postulate the concept of unconscious mental activity; but the strongest reason was undoubtedly the general disinclination of mankind to concede to the factor of sexuality such importance as is assigned to it by psychoanalysis. In spite of this widespread opposition, however, the movement in favour of psychoanalysis was not to be checked. Its adherents formed themselves into an international association which survived World War I, and by 1926 there were psychoanalytic societies in Vienna, Berlin, Budapest, London, Switzerland, the Netherlands, Moscow, Calcutta, and two in the United States. There were psychoanalytic polyclinics in Vienna, Berlin, and London, and several training institutes were in process of organization. At that time, too, three journals were the official organs of the societies on the continent and in England: the *International Zeitschrift für Psychoanalyse, Imago* (concerned primarily with applications of psychoanalysis to nonmedical fields), and the *International Journal of Psychoanalysis.*   (S. Fr.)

LATER DEVELOPMENTS

Between 1926 and his death in 1939 Freud made further major contributions to psychoanalytical theory and its applications. His *Inhibitions, Symptoms and Anxiety* (1926; see *bibliography*) gave anxiety a key position in psychopathology, relating it to ego activity and defense against instinct. *The Problem of Lay Analyses* (1926) covers a much wider field than its title suggests; it is in fact a discussion of psychoanalysis in general. In *The Future of an Illusion* (1928) and *Civilization and Its Discontents* (1930) Freud was concerned with the wider application of psychoanalytic knowledge to religion and culture. The *New Introductory Lectures* of 1932 (1933) deal, among other things, with anxiety, dreams, and mental structure. *Analysis Terminable and Interminable* (1937) is concerned with clinical, therapeutic questions. *An Outline of Psychoanalysis* (1938) gives a very succinct, clear account of Freud's final assessment.

In 1954 there was published in English *The Origins of Psycho-Analysis* (1950), consisting of a series of letters and scientific drafts written by Freud to the physician Wilhelm Fliess between 1887 and 1902. This is valuable for understanding the evolution of Freud's theory from a neurophysiological to a purely psychological basis.

Progress of the Psychoanalytic Movement.—The steady growth of the movement, despite opposition, was destined to be interrupted in Europe by political events. Hitler's advent to power in Germany led to the virtual suppression of psychoanalysis there and to the emigration of the great majority of German analysts, most of whom ultimately settled in the United States. In 1938 the Nazis seized Austria, and Vienna, the birthplace of psychoanalysis, had to be abandoned, Freud and his family being brought to England by Ernest Jones. Many of the Viennese analysts finally settled in the United States, but some remained in England with Freud and his daughter Anna. Later, the Hungarian society was affected in a similar way. Thus psychoanalytic activity was almost eliminated from central Europe until a gradual reconstruction of work and training became possible after World War II; although other countries, notably the United States and England, gained many workers through immigration. In the United States, moreover, there was a remarkable expansion largely independent of this. The American Psychoanalytic Association numbered fewer than 200 members before the war, but by the mid-1960s there were about 1,700 members and associates in its various affiliate societies, of whom more than 1,000 were members of the association. The increase was connected with a steady growth in the number and activities of training institutes, a few of which are connected with universities. In the mid-1960s there were 19 training institutes and centres, with about 1,000 students. Psychoanalysis spread rapidly after the war in South America also, especially in Argentina and Brazil. In Great Britain too there was a large increase in membership, from 72 in 1937 to nearly 300 in the 1960s. Other countries with psychoanalytic societies included Canada, Mexico, Austria, Belgium, Denmark, France, Germany, the Netherlands, Italy, Sweden, Switzerland, India, Israel, and Japan. The International Psychoanalytic Association, consisting of these component societies, performed integrating functions. In 1949 it resumed its biennial meetings, interrupted by the war.

During World War II most of the European journals were suppressed or discontinued, but in Great Britain the *International Journal of Psycho-Analysis,* as well as the *British Journal of Medical Psychology,* and in the U.S. the *Psychoanalytic Review* and the *Psychoanalytic Quarterly* continued to appear regularly. After the war some journals, such as the *Revue française de Psychanalyse,* resumed publication, and a number of others appeared for the first time. Such were the Italian *Rivista di Psicoanalisi,* the Argentine *Revista de Psicoanálisis,* the British *Psychoanalytic Study of the Child* and *Psychoanalysis and the Social Sciences,* and the *Journal of the American Psychoanalytic Association.* The *Year-Book of Psychoanalysis* (reprinted articles) had appeared earlier. In the 1950s the *Annual Survey of Psychoanalysis* (a digest and review) and the *Index of Psychoanalytic Writings* began.

Many of the lines along which further theoretical and technical developments were to occur are implicit in the first part of this article, written by Freud himself. It remains true that patients with the milder neuroses are the most likely to benefit from psychoanalytic therapy. However, the types of patients treated have changed with the years; there are increasing numbers in the categories described by Freud as suffering from malformations of character and sexual inhibitions and abnormalities. Psychoanalytic knowledge has also been applied fruitfully in art and literature (*see* below), philosophy, and religion.

Psychoanalysis of Children.—Important developments both of theory and technique took shape in this subject, to which Freud's *Analysis of a Phobia in a Five-Year-Old Boy* (1909) was the first contribution. He left its further development to his daughter Anna, whose *Psycho-Analytic Treatment of Children* appeared in German in 1937. Because the child's nature and circumstances differ so much from the adult's, she held that the technique must be modified in important respects. Melanie Klein, working concurrently along different lines, claimed that all the essential principles of psychoanalytic technique could be applied even to very young children, provided that their spontaneous play activities, utterances, and relationship to the analyst be taken as the material for analysis. The ensuing results, both technical and theoretical, led to one of the major psychoanalytic controversies after 1940. Ernest Jones, much impressed by Mrs. Klein's work, had invited her to leave Berlin and settle in London in 1926. There she gained numerous adherents; and the theories and technique deriving from her work developed so rapidly, and their emphasis appeared in some respects so novel, that they began to meet increasing opposition from those who feared that they represented a serious divergence from Freud.

Freud had regarded the Oedipal phase, from about three to five years of age, as of crucial importance in emotional development, and he worked out its psychology with particular thoroughness. On the basis of Freud's findings, two obvious directions of advance were open. One was to study the consolidation of the ego and of its techniques of controlling instinctual impulse, which occurs between the Oedipal phase and the onset of puberty, as well as the transformations of puberty. The other was to work backward chronologically, studying the antecedents of the Oedipus complex; *i.e.,* the pregenital phases, and especially the oral phase, where the mouth is the chief organ for emotionally charged contact, the mother and her breast the most important external object. The

first direction led to very significant contributions to ego psychology, as by Anna Freud; the second led to various results, among which those of Mrs. Klein and her associates were at once outstanding and controversial.

Developments in Theory.—Freud's tripartite division of the mind into id, ego, and superego remained the essential theoretical model, but it became progressively more elaborate. As regards the id, the fundamental importance of aggressive, destructive impulses gained more and more recognition, and Freud's "theoretical speculation" that the two ultimate instinctual forces are those of Eros and destruction became increasingly convincing to him. Freud supposed that aggression originates from a "death instinct"; *i.e.,* an innate tendency to undo the processes leading to life and to revert to the inorganic state from which life originally arose. Manifestly aggressive activity could then be regarded as a partial turning outward of this destructive death impulse, whereby the self is preserved and the aggression used in support of the life instincts, or Eros. Many analysts, although accepting the fundamental importance of the aggressive impulse, have remained unconvinced by Freud's death instinct theory.

The understanding of anxiety and its effects became a central problem, and its control by various devices was recognized as a major function of the ego. It was seen that the most varied human activities, including sexual ones, may sometimes be a means of coping with anxiety rather than a direct outcome of instinctual drives. The effect on theory was a strong stressing of dynamic factors, the topographical schema gradually dropping into a position of relatively less importance. The superego remained an important concept, describing, as it does, a mode of functioning whereby impulses, especially aggressive ones, are redirected toward the self. The intimate connection of guilt feelings with aggressive impulse became clear, and important precursors, or early stages of the superego, related to the pregenital stages of development, were discovered.

The problems of female sexuality received increasing attention, largely on the initiative of certain women analysts, and Freud found it necessary to modify some of his views; *e.g.,* by recognizing the long period of mother-attachment in girls. He was not prepared, however, to abandon his conviction of the fateful consequences of the anatomical sexual difference (*see* his *New Introductory Lectures*).

Developments in Technique.—These went hand in hand with the changes in theoretical emphasis, and were considerably influenced by the work of child analysts. The full analysis of the patient's behaviour in the analytic situation (the transference) came to be regarded as the most characteristic feature of the psychoanalytic method; the negative or hostile elements in this were recognized as requiring special attention. Much practical importance was attached to the earliest, pregenital stages of personality development. Although the technique of interpretation varied considerably in the hands of different analysts and schools of analysis, the general tendency was in the direction of more active interpretation especially in the sphere of the transference, with emphasis on anxiety, guilt feelings, and defensive maneuvers of the ego.

Developments in Application.—In the clinical field the application of psychoanalysis to children has already been noted. Its application to the treatment of psychoses has followed two main lines. The first is associated with the work of Mrs. Klein, using insights gained from child analysis and from the analysis of early stages of mental development. The second approaches patients from the standpoint of ego psychology, and the failure in psychosis to establish proper ego-boundaries between ego and outer world, etc. Here some kind of reeducation, rather than purely analytic work, is widely considered necessary. The understanding gained from psychoanalytic work has had a profound influence on psychiatry in general, especially in the United States.

Psychoanalytic theory and technique also became applied increasingly to the study of physiology and pathology. These studies of the interrelationship between organic and psychic processes have influenced medical education and the everyday practice of surgery and internal medicine, particularly in the U.S. The study of crime or delinquency too has been enriched by the application of psychoanalytic experience and theory, especially in England and the U.S. Among many extraclinical applications, that to anthropology and sociology has had striking results in the hands of analytically trained field workers and others, such as Géza Róheim, Margaret Mead, Bronislaw Malinowski, Abram Kardiner, and John Dollard. (WI. H. G.)

Areas of Controversy.—Early schisms occurred over such issues as the basic role which Freud ascribed to biological instinctual processes. Jung moved away from this in a direction which was in essence mystical. Otto Rank reverted to an 18th-century facultative will psychology. Alfred Adler placed great emphasis on an artificially isolated power drive. Of necessity these viewpoints entailed a rejection of psychoanalytic technique as well as theory, and the supporters of these psychologies used various names (individual psychology, analytical psychology, etc.) to distinguish their theories from Freud's psychoanalytic psychology.

More recent controversies were over details of Freudian theory or technique and did not lead to a complete departure from the parent stem. The leaders continued to subscribe to the main body of psychoanalytic thought and to look upon themselves as psychoanalysts. Controversies current at mid-20th century focused on such questions as the definition of instincts, details of libido development, and the relative importance of infancy, puberty, and adolescence in the genesis of neurosis; and on such technical issues as the duration and continuity of treatment and the handling of transference phenomena. The controversial issues arising from the work of Melanie Klein (*see* above) touched on all these matters. A significant area of inquiry was developing around the validity of all quantitative metaphors, as these are used not merely to characterize the interplay of psychological processes but as a basis for explaining variations in human behaviour. This development was related to the rapidly evolving changes in current concepts of the way the human brain works. It was expected that these developments would lead in time to important clarifications and simplifications in the conceptual structure of psychoanalysis. It seemed doubtful that any of the issues in dispute at midcentury would lead to the development of new schools or to such schisms as occurred in earlier years. (L. S. K.; B. D. L.)

INFLUENCE ON ART AND THOUGHT

Psychoanalysis has exerted, from the beginning, a profound influence on literature and the other arts and on the whole body of social thought. Freud and Jung, not only in their broad theoretical works but in their speculations directly upon the nature of art and artist, had the greatest impact. Of Freud's works, the most provocative were *The Interpretation of Dreams* (1900), *Three Contributions to the Theory of Sex* (1905), *Beyond the Pleasure Principle* (1920), and a number of the essays and papers in *The Collected Papers of Sigmund Freud* (the English translation published 1924). Conspicuous for their influence on the arts among these last were such essays as "The Dynamics of the Transference" (vol. ii), "Turnings in the Ways of Psychoanalytic Therapy" (vol. ii), "The Moses of Michelangelo" (vol. iv), "The Relation of the Poet to Day-Dreaming" (vol. iv), and "The Unconscious" (vol. iv). The work of Jung best known to modern writers and artists included *Psychology of the Unconscious* (1916), *Psychological Types, or the Psychology of Individuation* (1920), *Modern Man in Search of a Soul* (1931), and several essays which attempted to explain the psychology of art; of these, his "Psychology and Poetry" (which appeared in *Transition*, translated by Eugene Jolas, in 1930) is perhaps best known.

A number of other pioneers in the establishment of psychoanalysis in the 20th century contributed to the very large body of work on psychology and the arts. Most of these followed up suggestions made originally by Freud and Jung, but they also investigated more exhaustively subjects that were for the most part only peripheral to the major interests of the two leading spokesmen for the field. Among these psychoanalysts who were interested in the application of their disciplines to the arts and to criticism were Wilhelm Stekel, Otto Rank, Ernest Jones, and Charles Baudouin. The most important works of these men were Rank's

The Incest-Motive in Poetry and Legend (1912), Jones's *Hamlet and Oedipus* (1910 and 1949), and Baudouin's *Psychoanalysis and Aesthetics* (1924).

The work of many critics was strongly marked by their preoccupation with psychoanalysis and psychiatry: among them the most influential were Herbert Read, Kenneth Burke, Frederick C. Prescott and Maud Bodkin. Psychoanalytic investigations of the lives of writers and artists were responsible for a large body of additional work. Freud himself contributed to this kind of writing in his *Leonardo da Vinci: a Psychosexual Study of an Infantile Reminiscence* (1910) and in his essay "Dostoyevsky and Parricide" (English translation published in *Partisan Review*, fall, 1945). In both cases, Freud attempted to find in the work of the artists evidence that would help toward an understanding of their "psychic life." Biography, following upon the suggestions contained in these contributions and others, as well as the great body of clinical investigation, developed a special approach toward the arts, in which the work of art was related to and explained in terms of the artist's psychological history. Conspicuous examples of this form of psychobiography were René Laforgue's *The Defeat of Baudelaire: a Psycho-Analytical Study of the Neurosis of Charles Baudelaire* (1931), Saul Rosenzweig's "The Ghost of Henry James" (in *Character and Personality*, Dec. 1943), Edmund Wilson's biographical studies of literature (many of them contained in *The Wound and the Bow*, 1941), Joseph Wood Krutch's *Edgar Allan Poe: a Study in Genius* (1926), and Van Wyck Brooks's biographies of Mark Twain (*The Ordeal of Mark Twain*, 1920) and Henry James (*The Pilgrimage of Henry James*, 1925). Clark Griffith's study of Emily Dickinson (*The Long Shadow*, 1964) exemplified a still more mature use of psychoanalysis in literary biography.

Proponents: Thomas Mann and Others.—The question of the influence—of the degree of it and of all the peculiarities of its nature—is as complex as the influence itself is varied and widespread. There were writers and artists who professed to have and sometimes had a great knowledge of psychoanalysis and who worked in terms of a direct recognition of its value for their art. These included most of the surrealists, some of whom (like André Breton) had had actual experience as analysts, and other writers who (like Ludwig Lewisohn, Georg Groddeck, H. R. Lenormand) spoke of psychoanalysis with varying degrees of accuracy and conviction. Of Lenormand's plays, beginning with *Le Mangeur de Rêves* (1922), those which presented tragedy based chiefly on psychoanalytic knowledge of character included *L'Homme et ses Fantômes* (1924), *Asie* (1931), and *Pacifique* (1937); all these works reflect wide and accurate acquaintance with the discipline and the conclusions of psychoanalysis, though Lenormand objected to their being labeled Freudian.

Also included in this first group of writers was Thomas Mann, who not only knew and greatly respected the work of Freud, but was also extremely judicious in his application of this knowledge to his fiction. In an essay on "Freud's Position in the History of Modern Thought" (1928; included in *Past Masters, and Other Papers*, 1933), Mann applauded Freud for his intelligent concern with the psychic life as well as his wish to find new sources of cure and therapy. One of Mann's first uses of his wide acquaintance with psychoanalysis was in the novel *The Magic Mountain* (1924), but here the reference to psychoanalysis is mixed with a generous and eclectic use of many other kinds of knowledge and speculation—notably the philosophies of Arthur Schopenhauer and Friedrich Nietzsche. That he remained objective concerning the advantages of analysis for modern society was abundantly indicated in such remarks from the novel as this made by the character Settembrini: "Analysis as an instrument of enlightenment and civilization is good, in so far as it shatters absurd convictions, acts as a solvent upon natural prejudices, and undermines authority. . . . But it is bad, . . . in so far as it stands in the way of action, cannot shape the vital forces, maims life at its roots. . . ." (*The Magic Mountain*, Thomas Mann, p. 283, Modern Library Edition; A. A. Knopf, Inc., New York, 1927.) In his fictional reconstruction of the biblical story of Joseph, Mann quite deliberately made use of the speculations of both Freud and Jung concerning the value of myth and its symbolic recurrence, through a racial (or "collective") unconscious. Mann's fiction showed the skill of an intellectually disciplined mind whose application of psychoanalysis, as well as of other knowledges, never allowed it to dominate but made it serve the original aesthetic form and subject.

The knowledge of psychoanalysis also led modern novelists to establish the analyst himself as an important fictional personage, sometimes available to satirical observation (as in Waldo Frank's novel *The Bridegroom Cometh*, 1938), sometimes placed in a crucial role as adviser and "physician of the soul" (as in Lewisohn's *The Island Within*, 1928) and sometimes credited with providing the means of a novel's resolution (as in Arthur Koestler's *Arrival and Departure*, 1943). The substance and content of psychoanalytic disclosures (or their equivalents in the artist's imagination) often dominated the content of works of literature. Reliance upon the revelations of the subconscious mind was conspicuous in such works as the fiction of Anaïs Nin; surrealist poetry, prose, and painting; Groddeck's *Der Seelensucher* (1922); F. Scott Fitzgerald's *Tender Is the Night* (1934); Conrad Aiken's *Great Circle* (1933), *King Coffin* (1935), and much of his poetry (particularly *The Coming Forth by Day of Osiris Jones*, 1931); and both the poetry and fiction of Dylan Thomas. Notable for its literary approximation of clinical analysis was the novel by Italo Svevo (Ettore Schmitz), *La Coscienza di Zeno* (1924; translated as *The Confessions of Zeno*, 1930), in which the narrative is presented as a continuous self-analysis by the hero. In musical comedy and the theatre the role of the psychoanalyst was presented in Moss Hart's *Lady in the Dark* (1941) and T. S. Eliot's *The Cocktail Party* (1950).

Antagonists and the "Unlabeled": D. H. Lawrence and Others.—A second group of writers and artists included those who undeniably showed the influence of psychoanalysis but who resisted the labels Freudian and psychoanalytic. These persons gained prominence in literature and art in one of two ways: either they formulated their own theories of the unconscious and other psychoanalytic concerns in an effort to disprove Freud or to discount his values; or their work followed the lines and treated of the material with which psychoanalysis was largely concerned without having derived from a study of it. An important opponent of psychoanalysis was D. H. Lawrence; his novel *Sons and Lovers* (1913) interested psychoanalysts and critics who found a direct influence in its presentation of familial problems. Lawrence's reply was to repudiate psychoanalysis as too narrowly and harmfully scientific; but in the energy of his protest lay an earnest of the contribution made by psychoanalysis to his thinking. In a great number of letters and essays, Lawrence attacked both Freud and Jung, though he gave a qualified approval of another analyst, Trigant Burrow. His principal long attacks on psychoanalysis were *Psychoanalysis and the Unconscious* (1921) and *Fantasia of the Unconscious* (1922). In these works, Lawrence accused psychoanalysis of putting a false and debilitating emphasis upon scientific probing and examination which not only misunderstood the vital sources of human action but helped to defeat human vitality and tended to reduce the "life forces" to objects of intellectual curiosity. These reflections were associated in a large portion of Lawrence's writings of every kind with a general attack upon modern rational and intellectual life, as well as with his repudiation of the mechanistic, life-defeating impact of modern industry upon human vitality.

At the same time, a number of other writers offered in their work tempting opportunities for critics who wished directly to attach the label Freudian to them, but in large part rejected it or confessed to an ignorance of the disciplines that had allegedly influenced them. Among these writers were Sherwood Anderson and Eugene O'Neill; particularly in some of the latter's plays (especially *Mourning Becomes Electra*, 1931) there is abundant evidence of his realization of psychoanalytic techniques and discoveries, though O'Neill himself denied any direct line of influence. Franz Kafka was a special case: many of his writings show a line of relationship to his own familial circumstances, revealed especially in "Letter to My Father"; but, while critics did quite suc-

cessfully exploit that relationship, Kafka's work derived from a complex of other influences which made a too-simple psychoanalytic explanation misleading. (See *The Kafka Problem*, edited by Angel Flores, 1946.) In the 1950s and 1960s, special approaches to psychoanalysis and to sexual problems achieved prominence among young writers. Wilhelm Reich's books, *The Function of the Orgasm* (1942) and *Character Analysis* (1949), were influential. The problems of the homosexual were explored in several novels, including William Burroughs' *Naked Lunch* (1959) and John Rechy's *The City of Night* (1963).

Psychoanalytic Themes.—Another kind of influence concerned the role of psychoanalysis in some of the major preoccupations of literature. Psychoanalysis could rightfully claim a share in the motivating influence upon the release (of literature chiefly, but of the other arts as well) from the restraining and inhibiting cultural and traditional limits of taste and decorum which had fairly well held until the end of World War I. In these circumstances, psychoanalysis may be considered a social instrument, providing a rationalization of social change; but this was not to be its enduring purpose, nor had it been its original or exclusive aim. In many ways, the conjunction of psychoanalysis with social revolt was accidental, and the notoriety hindered the serious progress of the science as much as it helped to popularize it. The clinical studies begun by Freud and revealed in *Three Contributions to the Theory of Sex* and other places had a rather important voice, though by no means an exclusive one; the work of other psychologists, of sociologists and anthropologists was equally important, and the general impact of the war served as a primary cause of the release of inhibitions among artists regarding the treatment of these matters. What psychoanalysis did was immensely to extend and partly to provide phraseology for the discussion of sex matters or for their dramatization in works of literature. The attitude toward psychoanalysis on this level of influence was often largely undiscriminating, amateurish, and ignorant. The principal terms and the popular notions of psychoanalysis were used over and over again in the popular and semipopular literature of the 1920s, as the Marxist and pseudo-Marxist ideas found their way into the work of the 1930s. The catalogue of works which reflected this type of influence is very great; the use of psychoanalysis was sometimes very shrewd, sometimes quite mistaken and misleading, and often merely the result of a desire to be fashionable. In one way or another the work of the following writers showed the widespread impression made by psychoanalysis upon the modern world: Floyd Dell, Max Eastman, Maxwell Bodenheim, Conrad Aiken, Susan Glaspell, Evelyn Scott, Waldo Frank, F. Scott Fitzgerald, Carl Van Vechten, May Sinclair, J. D. Beresford, and Aldous Huxley. In the work of most of these, psychoanalysis was little more than incidentally acknowledged, or was used merely as a form of intellectual small change. By 1940 the relationship of psychoanalysis to social analysis had become much more complex; it was combined with economic determinations of history, with anthropology, and with theology.

However, it must be stressed that in the first half of the 20th century at least, psychoanalytic influence was often haphazard and incidental, and art borrowed from it a means of confusing its terms and its disciplines. Until the time of World War I, the career of psychoanalysis had been largely handicapped by a considerable rejection of it as a valid psychology. The writer or artist, aware of a significant new contribution to human knowledge, even in the early years, was both distrustful and confused concerning its actual value for him. New terms, discoveries, emphases (or extensions of original terms) served to confuse him further. In addition, the sources of information from which the artist was able to draw were often quite remote in both nature and quality of precision from the original; as psychoanalysis became popular, numerous books, essays, editorials, conversations, and amateurish "games" served often to give portions of "information" or vagrant notions of what psychoanalysis was actually doing. This variety of circumstance accounted for the vast majority of errant and erroneous uses of what was, when separated from its accurate source, mostly a fashionable mode of discourse, or a jargon.

The Unconscious.—Serious and accurate considerations of psychoanalysis led to substantial contributions in at least three separate areas of creative work. The first of these was the study of the unconscious itself—often quite aside from the psychoanalytic purpose for making that study. The pioneering influence in this connection was Freud's *The Interpretation of Dreams.* His investigation of the "dream work" had a profound and widespread effect upon the arts, especially as it gradually made available to artists certain information concerning the "behaviour" of the unconscious. The dream not only provided an extension of the uses to which the various languages of the arts might be put; it also suggested a range and a new reordering of symbolism which could be applied in varied ways to literature and art. In literature, the techniques practised in stream-of-consciousness writing were greatly extended through adaptations or applications of Freud's original suggestions. A considerable range of literary styles was made possible as a consequence, as well as new departures in the structure of novels, plays and poems. The popularity of this method was largely the result of the great success of James Joyce's *Ulysses* (1922), imitated in a great number of novels which followed its publication. *Ulysses* was followed by *Finnegans Wake* (first published in part as "Work in Progress" in the magazine *Transition,* 1927–29; as a book, 1939), a much more elaborate and exhaustive exploitation of the literary resources of psychoanalysis, in combination with many other disciplines, knowledges and techniques available to the erudition of its author. The techniques initiated or perfected by Joyce were subsequently taken in other fictions, stylized, and combined with more traditional forms of analysis. The most important contribution made by them lay in the revisions seen of the individual dream consciousness and a world view that was at once anthropological, mythical, and cultural. Other applications of the information about the unconscious made available to the arts included the so-called automatic writing of the surrealists, especially of André Breton, Louis Aragon, Philippe Soupault, René Crevel, and Paul Éluard. These artists, and others, did not confine themselves, however, to a mere simulation of mental disorders in their work; it did remain close to what the founders of surrealism thought were their psychoanalytic origins. Breton's definition of surrealism, given in the *Manifeste du surréalisme* (1924), established both the nature and the limitation of their work: "Pure psychic automatism by which it is intended to express, verbally, in writing, or by other means, the real process of thought. Thought's dictation, in the absence of all control exercised by the reason and outside all aesthetic and moral preoccupations." (André Breton, *Manifeste du surréalisme,* page 46; Éditions du Sagittaire, Paris, 1924.) In its later development, the sponsors of surrealism acknowledged that such work could easily be confined to a too narrow and repetitious form of creation and proposed (in Breton's essays and in those of Nicholas Calas) to free themselves from the limits of psychoanalytic descriptions of the unconscious. This independence of the limits of clinical psychoanalysis was much less true of surrealist painting (Max Ernst, Yves Tanguy, Salvador Dalí and others), which for the most part continued to realize pictorially and without much variation subjects thought to represent the desires embedded in the unconscious.

Motivations.—The second contribution made by psychoanalysis to modern literature and art had chiefly to do with the reexamination and exposition of human behaviour and the motives underlying it. This revision of view, involving as it did much attention to a person's sex life and his relationship to his parents from infancy on, did much to encourage both illuminating and wildly erroneous changes in the explanation of motive. The range of information concerning such mental disorders as were available, to novelists and dramatists especially, increased as the techniques of psychoanalysis expanded and theorists multiplied. Earlier fiction of the 1920s often remained content to speak superficially of "repressions," "neuroses," and "free association" and to narrate visits to psychoanalysts as part of a social fashion. As familiarity with psychoanalysis increased, the use of it became more "professional" in its efforts to achieve clinical exactness. The novels, dramas, and motion pictures of the late 1930s and thereafter demonstrated

much detailed knowledge of psychiatry and a willingness to exploit its opportunities for characterization and melodrama. An early example of such exploitation is Fitzgerald's *Tender Is the Night,* whose major theme depends upon the risk taken by a promising young American psychoanalyst when he marries his patient, and is thus forced to call increasingly upon his reserves of nervous and moral energy until both are completely exhausted. The novel revealed a considerable acquaintance with the terminology, practices, and techniques of the clinic and the sanitarium, and some skill in appropriating them to the problems of a novel's form and structure.

The Mythic Content of Art.—The third contribution is largely the work of Jung. The difference between his influence and Freud's arose chiefly from Jung's explanation of the term "libido." Freud had used this term to designate sexual energy; Jung preferred to expand its definition. Linked with this fundamental difference of interpretation was the much greater emphasis Jung put upon what he called the "collective unconscious," which has been described as "the precipitate of humanity's typical forms of reaction since the earliest beginnings." (J. F. Jacobi, *The Psychology of Jung,* p. 8; Yale University Press, New Haven, Conn., 1943.) The role of the artist became extremely important for Jung; he was considered a form of priest of the "collective unconscious" because he relates the conscious life of his fellows to its archetypes in the unconscious. This view of the unconscious and of its availability to art and literature had no small influence upon 20th-century writers and artists. It was one of several germinal theories which stimulated a great critical interest in myth and mythology. Among the critics whose interpretations of literature showed its influence were Maud Bodkin (*Archetypal Patterns in Poetry,* 1934), Elizabeth Drew (*T. S. Eliot: The Design of His Poetry,* 1949) and P. W. Martin (*Experiment in Depth,* 1955). Jung's influence served in a way to counteract Freud's rather narrow view of the artist and the tendency of his followers to analyze art in terms of the artist's psychic nature. Jung was in a much larger sense concerned with the act of creation and with its significance as a restatement and reshaping of recurrent mythical themes.

At the halfway mark of the 20th century, the usefulness of psychoanalysis for criticism and its influence upon the artist had grown much more complex and varied than at the beginning. New explorations of Freud and Jung continued to appear, as well as a considerable number of studies of the arts by psychoanalysts and by critics of psychoanalysis and psychiatry. In literature especially, the groundwork of psychoanalytic knowledge was accepted as familiar to the majority of both artists and critics.

See also references under "Psychoanalysis" in the Index.

(F. J. HN.)

BIBLIOGRAPHY.—*Freud's Own Works:* Sigmund Freud and J. Breuer, *Studien über Hysterie* (1895; Eng. trans. *Studies in Hysteria,* 1960); Sigmund Freud, *Die Traumdeutung* (1900; Eng. trans. and rev. ed. A. A. Brill, *The Interpretation of Dreams,* 1950), *Zur Psychopathologie des Alltagslebens* (1904; Eng. trans. and ed. A. A. Brill, *Psychopathology of Everyday Life,* 1949), *Drei Abhandlungen zur Sexualtheorie* (1905; Eng. trans. and ed. J. Strachey, *Three Essays on the Theory of Sexuality,* 1962), *Über Psychoanalyse* (1910; the lectures delivered at Worcester, Mass.), *Zur Geschichte der psychoanalytischen Bewegung* (1914; Eng. trans. A. A. Brill, *The History of the Psychoanalytic Movement,* 1917), *Vorlesungen zur Einführung in die Psychoanalyse* (1916; Eng. trans. G. S. Hall, *A General Introduction to Psychoanalysis,* 1920; Eng. trans. Joan Riviere, *Introductory Lectures on Psychoanalysis,* 2nd ed. 1949), "*Selbstdarstellung*" (1925, in *Die Medizin der Gegenwart,* vol. iv; Eng. trans. J. Strachey, *An Autobiographical Study,* 1935), *Hemmung, Symptom und Angst* (1926; Eng. trans. A. Strachey, *Inhibitions, Symptoms and Anxiety,* 1936), *Die Frage der Laienanalyse . . .* (1926; Eng. trans. P. Maerker-Branden, *The Problem of Lay Analyses,* 1927), *Die Zukunft einer Illusion* (Eng. trans. W. D. Robson-Scott, *The Future of an Illusion,* 1928; rev. ed. J. Strachey, 1962), *Das Unbehagen in der Kultur* (Eng. trans. Joan Riviere, *Civilization and Its Discontents,* 1930), *Neue Folge der Vorlesungen zur Einführung in die Psychoanalyse* (Eng. trans. W. J. H. Sprott, *New Introductory Lectures on Psycho-Analysis,* 1933), *Der Mann Moses und die Monotheistische Religion* (Eng. trans. Katherine Jones, *Moses and Monotheism,* 1939), *Aus den Anfängen der Psychoanalyse: Briefe an Wilhelm Fliess, Abhandlungen und Notizen aus den Jahren 1887–1902* (1950; Eng. ed. Marie Bonaparte, Anna Freud, and Ernst Kris, trans. E. Mosbacher and J. Strachey, *The Origins of Psycho-Analysis: Letters to Wilhelm Fliess, Drafts and Notes: 1887–1902,* 1954).

Complete Works: Anna Freud, O. Rank, A. J. Storfer (eds.), *Gesammelte Schriften* (1924 *et seq.*) ; J. Strachey (ed.), *The Standard Edition of the Complete Psychological Works of Sigmund Freud* (1953 *et seq.*). J. Strachey has also listed the English translations of Freud's works (*International Journal of Psycho-Analysis*, 1945, *Psychoanalytic Quarterly*, 1946).

Writings of Other Workers: A. A. Brill, *Psychoanalysis . . .* , 3rd ed. rev. (1922) ; E. Jones, *Papers on Psycho-analysis*, 3rd ed. (1923 ; 5th ed. 1948) ; S. Ferenczi, *Further Contributions to the Theory and Technique of Psycho-analysis* (Eng. trans. Jane Isabel Suttie *et al.*, 1926) ; J. Rickman, *Index Psychoanalyticus, 1893–1926* (1928) ; M. Klein, *Die Psychoanalyse des Kindes* (Eng. trans. Alix Strachey, *The Psycho-Analysis of Children*, 1932), *Contributions to Psycho-Analysis, 1921–1945* (1948) ; Anna Freud, *Das Ich und die Abwehrmechanismen* (1936) ; Eng. trans. C. Baines, *The Ego and the Mechanisms of Defence*, 1937, 1946), *The Psycho-Analytical Treatment of Children* (Eng. trans. Nancy Procter-Gregg, 1946) ; Ives Hendrick, *Facts and Theories of Psychoanalysis*, 2nd ed. (1939 ; 3rd ed. rev., 1958) ; Karen Horney, *New Ways in Psychoanalysis* (1939), *Self-Analysis* (1942) ; E. Glover and M. F. E. Brierley (eds.), *An Investigation of the Technique of Psychoanalysis* (1940) ; O. Fenichel, *The Psychoanalytic Theory of Neurosis* (1945, 1947) ; F. Alexander and T. M. French, *Psychoanalytic Therapy* (4th printing, 1947) ; L. S. Kubie, *Practical and Theoretical Aspects of Psychoanalysis* (1950) ; A. Grinstein (ed.), *Index of Psychoanalytic Writings*, 5 vol. (1956).

Works on Psychosomatic Medicine: E. Weiss and O. S. English, *Psychosomatic Medicine* (1943 ; 2nd ed. 1949) ; Helen Flanders Dunbar, *Emotions and Bodily Changes: a Survey of Literature on Psychosomatic Interrelationships, 1910–33* (1935 ; 4th ed., *Literature 1910–53*, 1954), *Synopsis of Psychosomatic Diagnosis and Treatment* (1948) ; F. Deutsch (ed.), *The Psychosomatic Concept in Psychoanalysis* (1953) ; E. D. Whittkower and R. A. Cleghorn (eds.), *Recent Developments in Psychosomatic Medicine* (1954) ; *Psychosomatic Medicine* and its *Monographs*; *Psychoanalytic Quarterly*.

Works on the Influence of Psychoanalysis on Literature and the Arts: Norman O. Brown, *Life Against Death* (1959) ; Kenneth Burke, *The Philosophy of Literary Form*, see title essay and "Freud—and the Analysis of Poetry" (1941) ; Louis Fraiberg, *Psychoanalysis and American Literary Criticism* (1960) ; Frederick J. Hoffman, *Freudianism and the Literary Mind*, rev. ed. (1957) ; H(ermann) B(oeschenstein), "Psychoanalysis in Modern Literature" in *Columbia Dictionary of Modern European Literature*, ed. by Horatio Smith, pp. 651–657 (1947) ; Stanley E. Hyman, *The Armed Vision*, ch. vi (1948) ; Ernst Kris, *Psychoanalytic Explorations in Art* (1952) ; Patrick Mullahy, *Oedipus: Myth and Complex* (1948) ; Roy P. Basler, *Sex, Symbolism, and Psychology in Literature* (1948) ; Philip Rieff, *Freud: the Mind of the Moralist* (1959) ; Lionel Trilling, "Freud and Literature" in *The Liberal Imagination*, pp. 34–57 (1950), *Freud and the Crisis of Our Culture* (1955) ; W. David Sievers, *Freud on Broadway* (1955).

See also the following journals: *Psychiatry; Psychoanalytic Quarterly; Bulletin of the New York Academy of Medicine; International Journal of Psycho-Analysis; Bulletin of the Menninger Clinic; American Journal of Sociology; Psychoanalytic Review; Psychoanalytic Study of the Child.*

PSYCHOGALVANIC REFLEX.

The term psychogalvanic reflex (PGR) refers to a change in the electrical properties of the body (probably of the skin) following noxious stimulation, stimulation that produces emotional reaction, and, to some extent, stimulation that attracts the subject's attention and leads to an aroused alertness. Galvanic skin response (GSR) and electrodermal response (EDR) are preferable synonyms. Though most of the work on this phenomenon has involved human subjects, it can be demonstrated in other mammals. The PGR can be demonstrated in several ways, but usually with what are essentially modifications and improvements of the method of C. S. Féré (1888).

In these, the response appears as an increase in the electrical conductance of the skin (a decrease in resistance) across the palms of the hands or feet. In the experimental arrangements, the subject forms one arm of a balanced Wheatstone bridge electrical circuit (*see* INSTRUMENTS, ELECTRICAL MEASURING: *Indicating Instruments*). When his resistance to the passage of a weak, impressed electrical current decreases, the bridge is thrown out of balance, as indicated by the deflection of a galvanometer. The amount of change in his resistance can be calculated from the magnitude of this deflection or from the amount of external resistance that must be introduced elsewhere in the bridge to re-balance it. The response appears with a latency of about two seconds after stimulation with a pinprick, threat of injury, etc.; it rises to a maximum after two to ten seconds and subsides at about the same rate.

The PGR is mediated by the sympathetic division of the autonomic nervous system. It is a part of the general arousal or activation pattern of physiological responses that mobilizes and fits the person for effective reaction in an emergency, as described by Cannon (1932). In addition, parts of the premotor cerebral cortex appear to have a role in producing the PGR, and Darrow (1936) suggested that it is an accessory to the activity of the postural mechanisms, for which it could play a preparatory function. The consensus is that the PGR is associated with activation of the sweat glands by the postganglionic sympathetic fibres, but that the perspiration actually secreted does not produce the characteristic decrease in skin resistance by acting as an electrolytic conductor.

A more sensitive indicator of minimal emotional arousal than other physiological responses, the PGR has figured extensively in studies of emotion and emotional learning. It can help to uncover complexes of emotional sensitivities when used with word association tests or interviews; by observing when the response occurs, the skilled worker can deduce which stimuli evoke emotional disturbance. The PGR is involuntary in the sense that subjects cannot suppress it readily, if at all, though it can be produced by voluntary acts such as deep breathing or moving. As a detector of emotion, the response often has served as one of the indicators in the "lie detector," along with blood pressure, pulse, and respiration. If a neutral stimulus such as a light or tone is paired with mild pain, the neutral stimulus acquires the power to evoke the PGR. With such conditioning, the response can become a useful indicator for studying human learning as well as for detecting feigned deafness, blindness, or anesthesia. *See* also EMOTION.

BIBLIOGRAPHY.—D. B. Lindsley, "Emotion" in S. S. Stevens (ed.), *Handbook of Experimental Psychology* (1951) ; R. S. Woodworth and H. Schlosberg, *Experimental Psychology*, rev. ed. (1954) ; E. L. House and B. Pansky, *A Functional Approach to Neuroanatomy* (1960) ; C. H. Wang, *The Neural Control of Sweating* (1964) ; R. A. McCleary and R. Y. Moore, *Subcortical Mechanisms of Behavior* (1965).

(H. F. Ht.)

PSYCHOLOGICAL TESTS AND MEASUREMENTS.

A psychological test may be defined as a standardized procedure for assessing any specific behaviour. Empirical standardization distinguishes a psychological test from an ordinary interview or a typical academic examination.

This article is organized as follows:

I. Historical Development
    1. Earliest Types of Test
    2. General and Special Abilities
    3. Group Tests
    4. Performance Tests
    5. Vocational Testing
    6. Testing Temperamental Characteristics
    7. Recent Research
II. Characteristics Measured, Construction and Uses
    A. Characteristics Measured
        1. Educational and Vocational Attainments
        2. General and Special Abilities
    B. Construction and Standardization
        1. Sampling of Tests and Persons
        2. Reliability
        3. Validity
        4. Types of Measurement
        5. Comparable Scales
    C. Uses of Psychological Tests
        1. Theoretical Value
        2. Practical Value
III. Tests of Personality and Temperament
    A. Early Tests of Personality
        1. Free Association
        2. Questionnaire
        3. Ink Blot
        4. Situational-Observational
    B. Objective or Structured Tests
        1. SVIB
        2. Kuder Preference Record
        3. Minnesota Multiphasic
    C. Study of Values
    D. Factor Analysis
    E. Projective Methods
        1. Theory of Projective Methods
        2. Rorschach Test
        3. Thematic Apperception Test

I. HISTORICAL DEVELOPMENT

1. Earliest Types of Test.—The need for precise techniques to assess mental differences between individuals was first explicitly recognized by Sir Francis Galton (*q.v.*) and formed an essential part of his attempt to transform individual psychology into a genuine science. During the latter half of the 19th century, when psychology was becoming an experimental science, it was found that laboratory measurements displayed marked variations from one person to another. Interest at that time centred chiefly on the general study of conscious activities as such, and these individual variations were consequently treated as errors of measurement, to be eliminated by some method of averaging. Galton noted that many of the differences seemed to be related to the individual's ability and temperamental characteristics as displayed in everyday life, and resolved to study and standardize the procedures from this new point of view.

Of his earlier "mental tests" (as he called them), many were suggested by the experimental techniques already used in laboratory work. In Great Britain the dominant school of psychology at that date held that all conscious processes developed out of the sensory experiences of the individual or the associations formed between them. It seemed to follow that a subject's general efficiency might best be measured by testing his ability to discriminate elementary stimuli. Galton therefore began by devising methods for measuring tactile, visual, auditory, and muscular discrimination. The discrimination of weights had long been employed by E. H. Weber, G. Fechner (*qq.v.*) and their followers to demonstrate the general Weber-Fechner law (*see* PSYCHOPHYSICAL METHODS) and one of Galton's earliest and best-known tests consisted of a calibrated series of weights for measuring the accuracy with which each person could discriminate such differences. These sensory tests were later supplemented by tests for speed and strength of movement, quickness of reaction, and extent of associative memory. Later Galton came to realize that still more complex processes would yield better estimates of general efficiency and accordingly constructed a number of tests for "higher mental processes." No less valuable were the statistical techniques that he devised for validating and standardizing the new procedures—the percentile and the average deviation as metrical units, the scaling methods based on the normal frequency distribution, and above all the coefficient of correlation (*see* STATISTICS).

In the later stages of his work he received active assistance from J. M. Cattell (*q.v.*), a U.S. student who had worked in Wilhelm Wundt's laboratory at Leipzig and acted for a short time as Galton's assistant. In 1890 Galton and Cattell published the program of those tests which, with various other devices, Galton had regularly used in his anthropometric laboratory for studying the characteristics of individuals. On returning to the United States, Cattell and his co-workers started at Columbia University the systematic application of a similar scheme of tests to college students and thus initiated the long series of researches carried out with the aid of these new techniques. The most important was embodied in a large and influential monograph (1901) by C. Wissler (one of Cattell's research students), which reviewed the results obtained and applied for the first time the Galton-Pearson correlation coefficient to measure the relations of the test results with each other and with independent criteria; the correlations of the tests with such criteria as academic performance were disappointingly low.

In 1892 James Sully had opened a department of education at University College, London, where a school for boys happened to be available on the premises. There he and Galton (who had transferred his laboratory to the college) joined in applying tests of physical and mental characteristics to schoolchildren. Sully held that the measurement of attention would provide the best estimates of a child's intelligence; accordingly he devised tests for the "span of prehension" (the maximum number of letters comprehended in a single glance or of digits recalled after a single hearing) and claimed that the differences thus detected varied closely with the child's "general mental capacity."

In 1902 Galton obtained a grant from the British Association for the Advancement of Science for repeating his anthropometric survey of the British Isles, with the inclusion of tests for mental capacities, and a committee was formed to make preliminary inquiries with W. McDougall (head of Sully's laboratory in London) as secretary. It worked in cooperation with a second committee appointed to study psychophysiological factors in education. The outcome was a series of investigations, carried out mainly under McDougall's guidance, by W. Brown, C. Burt, C. Spearman, and others, with a view to constructing intelligence tests for schoolchildren.

2. General and Special Abilities.—Galton, in the course of his investigations, had been led to distinguish between "special aptitudes" (corresponding roughly to the old-fashioned "faculties") and "general ability"—a kind of superfaculty determining mental efficiency in all forms of cognitive activity. In France Alfred Binet (*q.v.*), an admirer of contemporary British psychology and particularly of the views elaborated by Galton, adopted this distinction, but since in French the word "ability" possessed a different meaning he substituted Herbert Spencer's term "intelligence." In 1904 the French ministry of public instruction appointed a commission to study the diagnosis and training of mentally deficient children; and, as a member of the commission, Binet set about compiling standardized scales for measuring not only "pedagogical attainments" but also what he termed "general intelligence" and "partial aptitudes." He determined to discard "the instrumental methods popular in German laboratories" and to compile a series of problems, graded in difficulty and requiring for their solution "little else but pencil, paper, pictures, and a few common objects." The success of his novel procedure as a means of diagnosing subnormal pupils attracted widespread attention, and his age scale of intelligence tests was almost immediately translated and adapted by psychologists in Belgium, Britain, Germany, and the U.S.

3. Group Tests.—All these earlier tests had to be applied individually. For the purpose of large-scale examinations of schoolchildren, however, it was desirable if possible to develop a type of test which could be applied collectively. Accordingly, in London and elsewhere a number of researches were carried out to investigate the possible use of what were subsequently known as group tests. The result was the type of problem commonly used in the so-called 11+ examination, an academic placement instrument administered to English children at about age 11: "analogies," "opposites," "syllogistic reasoning," "code tests," "completion tests" (a device suggested by H. Ebbinghaus) and the like, usually combined into a booklet of half a dozen subtests. Similar principles were adopted for constructing and standardizing tests for the chief subjects of the school curriculum, and in 1913 the London County Council appointed an official psychologist to study and apply such tests, particularly in connection with the examination of children of subnormal and supernormal ability.

4. Performance Tests.—In the United States, in order to test foreign immigrants, special attention was given to performance tests; *i.e.*, tests not entailing a knowledge of some particular language. H. A. Knox developed "construction" and "imitation" tests, S. D. Porteus a series of graded maze tests, H. H. Goddard and W. F. Dearborn form boards, W. Healy a picture-completion test. Finally, R. Pintner and D. G. Paterson combined a carefully chosen selection to form a "performance scale" which was widely used for those handicapped by deafness, lack of schooling, or other disabilities. In the field of education E. L. Thorndike (*q.v.*), who had joined Cattell at Columbia, quickly became the leader of the test movement in the United States and, though at first doubtful about

PSYCHOLOGICAL TESTS AND MEASUREMENTS

the hypothesis of a general ability, was active in producing scientifically standardized tests of scholastic abilities. By the end of the first decade of the 20th century more than 50 well-tried tests for various abilities—sensory discrimination, perception, memory, attention, learning, imagination and the like—were available in standard form and were described in G. M. Whipple's *Manual of Mental and Physical Tests* (1910), with tabulated norms of performances and full instructions for use.

5. Vocational Testing.—Just before the outbreak of World War I, Hugo Münsterberg (*q.v.*) and others in the United States initiated a series of pioneer investigations on adolescents and adults to study the value of psychological tests for purposes of vocational guidance and selection (*see* PSYCHOLOGY, APPLIED). During the war group tests of intelligence were administered to about 1,750,000 recruits for the U.S. Army, and a more limited use was made of aptitude tests for assigning men and women to the most suitable trades in the various fighting services. Similar efforts on a more restricted scale were made in Great Britain. The success of such methods for military purposes resulted after the war in a rapid development of psychological testing for educational and industrial purposes. The experience gained in these two fields during the 20 years of peace proved invaluable in World War II, when both countries made full use of such testing in the various branches of their armed forces.

6. Testing Temperamental Characteristics.—The application of test procedures to what were called affective and conative (as distinct from cognitive) aspects of behaviour developed far more slowly. The emphasis laid by McDougall on emotional tendencies as being the chief determinants of personality and character led several of his research students to apply test procedures to the assessment of temperamental qualities. At first the procedures used were based chiefly on the ordinary laboratory techniques for investigating the physical effects of emotion—changes in blood pressure, the pulse rate, skin temperature, and, most striking of all, the so-called psychogalvanic reflex (a transitory increase in the electrical conductivity of the skin induced by emotional experience). As with intellectual testing, it soon appeared that tests based on these more elementary processes and requiring highly elaborate apparatus were neither the most convenient nor the most effective. Galton had already attempted "psychometric experiments" for the study of associated ideas and had inferred that such devices revealed unconscious interests and motives, particularly early sentiments strongly tinged with emotion, differing widely with different individuals. For stimuli he relied mainly on emotionally suggestive words. Later investigators tried pictures, ink blots (first used by Binet), or ambiguous drawings (a method described by William James) and so developed what British psychologists called apperception tests and U.S. writers call projective tests. The popularization of these procedures and the growing interest in the affective aspects of behaviour (due largely to the influence of the psychoanalytic school) led to numerous researches in the hope of assessing these more hidden constituents of personality.

7. Recent Research.—From about 1930 onward there were no new developments affecting the basic principles or ideas, most of the work being concerned either with improving research techniques already introduced or with devising and applying tests for an ever widening range of abilities, attainments, and other characteristics of individual behaviour. On the theoretical side special attention was paid to the refinement of the statistical procedures used in constructing and evaluating new test batteries, and particularly to such technical questions as scaling, reliability, item analysis, factor analysis, better sampling of test items and test populations and, above all, to improved criteria for validation. On the practical side, the increasing use of tests for educational, commercial, and military purposes, especially by public bodies, led to an attempt to assess not merely theoretical value but also the practical value of large-scale testing: test B may have a much lower theoretical validity than test A and yet, because it adds more to information already available and is at the same time far less expensive, it may have a much higher practical value for the purpose intended. Since financial considerations

are involved, it is desirable to measure the utility of a test by applying the mathematical procedures used in what the economist terms decision theory.

A classified list of tests available for various purposes, with a detailed description and critical evaluation of each, is to be found in the *Mental Measurements Yearbook,* published about every five years by Oscar Buros. The *Sixth Mental Measurements Yearbook* (1965) reported that there were in print 2,171 different tests; the majority are achievement tests, dealing with the chief subjects of the school, college, and university curricula. In these important fields the U.S. Educational Testing Service and College Entrance Examination Board have been particularly active in the 1960s. In Britain similar researches on a far more limited scale have been undertaken by the National Foundation for Educational Research.

Most psychological tests are comparatively short-lived and are quickly replaced in the same way that fashions come and go in women's clothing. A few, however, have proved to be relatively enduring. Of these the best known is the original Binet scale; in Britain one of the London revisions and in the U.S. one of the Terman revisions (the Stanford-Binet) were in regular use in the 1960s, particularly for individual examination of educationally subnormal children. A late version of the latter exists in two forms and contains 62 items grouped into levels of difficulty corresponding to each successive year from infancy to maturity; *e.g.,* for age 5 typical tasks include: defining words by classification or description (two easy words from a standard list of 45), copying a square, repeating a sentence of five monosyllables from memory; for year 10, reading and summarizing a short paragraph, indicating what is absurd in a picture, repeating six digits. For testing adults the Wechsler-Bellevue intelligence scale gained widespread popularity during the 1950s, particularly with clinicians; by the 1960s it was being largely replaced in the U.S. by the Wechsler Adult Intelligence Scale (WAIS). This consists of verbal and performance tests, and, with the aid of a conversion table, the measurements are expressed in terms of a conventional intelligence quotient; a lower-level version (the Wechsler Intelligence Scale for Children: WISC) also was devised for use with children. Other tests are available for infants, for the blind, the deaf, and those otherwise handicapped.

Group tests of intelligence are even more widely used. Under this title the *Yearbook* describes more than 100 U.S. versions, available to the general public, most of them composite instruments based on about half a dozen of the stock types of problem described above. In Britain fresh group tests are prepared every year, but are not published until they are no longer required for official purposes. The name intelligence test is perhaps misleading; most of them are not so much tests of innate general ability as tests for general classification.

Less progress has been made with individual tests for special kinds of ability—observation, memory, imagery, creativity, and the like; but improved apparatus is continually being devised for measuring sensory functions—visual acuity, colour vision, hearing, and so on. So-called multiaptitude batteries have become increasingly popular; these commonly cover such aptitudes as verbal, numerical, and mechanical abilities and, less frequently, speed, accuracy, memory, judgment, reasoning, etc. One of the earliest and best known is L. L. Thurstone's test of primary mental abilities, which largely provided a model for later batteries of this type. There are in addition numerous tests for more complex abilities; *e.g.,* artistic and musical aptitudes, and aptitudes for medicine, law, engineering, teaching, and the clerical professions.

II. CHARACTERISTICS MEASURED, CONSTRUCTION AND USES

A. CHARACTERISTICS MEASURED

As a result of a vast amount of detailed research on the lines of these earlier inquiries, three main types of characteristic can now be measured by means of psychological tests or similar devices with tolerable accuracy. The majority of the tests in regular use can be accordingly classified under three main heads: (1)

tests of attainments (*i.e.*, of achievement: knowledge or skill in various fields); (2) tests of abilities, either intellectual or practical; and (3) tests of other characteristics of personality; *e.g.*, emotional, temperamental, and moral qualities (including interests, attitudes, ideals, and motivational tendencies generally).

1. Educational and Vocational Attainments.—The attainments commonly tested may be subdivided into two broad groups, educational and vocational. Of the educational or scholastic tests the most thoroughly standardized are those designed to measure achievement in the ordinary subjects of the elementary school curriculum—reading, spelling, arithmetic, composition, drawing, handwriting, and handwork. With these the norms usually consist of standard (*i.e.*, average) performances for each sex separately at different ages of school life, together with some indication of the range of individual variation (generally in the form of standard deviations) and of border lines for certain types of child or school; *e.g.*, for mentally deficient children or special schools for the educationally subnormal.

Tests also are available for more advanced subjects in the curriculum, to be used with older children at the secondary school stage; *e.g.*, for foreign languages, both ancient and modern, and for the various branches of mathematics and science. However, because of the difficulty of securing fair samples of pupils at the higher stages, the standardization of such tests is less reliable. Attempts have also been made, particularly in the United States, to develop tests for academic subjects taken at the university—teaching, medicine, dentistry, engineering, accounting, languages, and law.

For occupational guidance and for selection in commerce and industry, vocational psychologists endeavoured to construct tests for assessing the extent to which a given applicant possesses the kinds of knowledge and skill required for this or that specific type of employment. Norms of performance are commonly given for the occupations to which they relate and border lines below which efficient performance is relatively unlikely. Many large firms maintain their own trade-test departments for compiling, standardizing, and administering tests of the proficiency of their own employees.

2. General and Special Abilities.—Tests of ability differ from tests of attainment or achievement in that, while the latter are intended to measure the actual results derived by formal education or occupational training, the former seek to estimate differences in so-called mental ability, regardless of the effects of instruction, training, or experience.

Galton's contention that there were two main types of cognitive function for which tests could be developed—general ability and special aptitudes—met with a double opposition. Spearman and his followers contended that the assumption of a single general factor only would suffice to account for all innate intellectual differences; the hypothesis of special abilities or aptitudes they repudiated as an obsolete relic of the old-fashioned theory of faculties. On the other hand, most U.S. investigators—Thorndike, Thurstone, and their collaborators—accepted the existence of special or primary abilities but were highly skeptical of anything described as general ability or "intelligence." The numerous researches carried out by educational and industrial psychologists leave little doubt about the existence of special abilities, and in his later years even Spearman acknowledged their influence, at least on a limited scale. Most British psychologists accept the hypothesis of general intelligence as well, and the majority of the former critics—Thorndike, Brown, Godfrey Thomson, and Thurstone—retracted or at any rate moderated their earlier objections in varying degrees.

The attempt to identify the precise nature of the various special abilities or aptitudes has formed an important object of later factorial research. Unlike the "faculties" of the older psychologists, the abilities that can most readily be distinguished turn out to be decidedly complex and may themselves be analyzed or subdivided into more elementary types of ability, almost without limit. In fact, there seems to be a hierarchy of abilities: the more general are usually the earliest to mature; but during the course of the child's development, they become progressively differentiated into the more specialized, while the more elementary tend to combine into the more complex.

The special abilities so far established may be conveniently classified according as they arise from differences in the processes involved or in terms of their content. The latter are the easiest to isolate and measure. The more elementary relate to differences in the sensory content: effective tests are available for the visual perception of form and colour, for the discrimination of audible pitch and loudness, and for the discrimination of touch, weight, and muscular movement. Equally well established are the differences between the chief types of conscious imagery, and there are tests and questionnaires intended to discriminate between visualizers, audiles, motiles, and (most common) the various mixtures. From the standpoint of educational and vocational guidance, four content factors are of prime importance, namely, the abilities (or groups of abilities) which underlie (1) the understanding and the use of words (so-called verbal ability), (2) the understanding and use of number and numerical relations (so-called arithmetical ability), (3) the visual and kinesthetic perception of space and (4) the control of coordinated movements such as are involved in mechanical dexterity. Less clearly distinguishable are the factors entering into the understanding and use of relations, especially logical relations, and into aesthetic appreciation in its various forms.

Of factors defined in terms of the processes involved, the most important are those for speed, mechanical memory, productive association (*i.e.*, imagination or, as it is now termed, "creativity"), and certain formal processes underlying rational thinking—abstraction, generalization, and inductive and deductive inference. Since efficiency in tests for all these different activities depends in some degree on general ability or "intelligence," it is essential, when assessing the primary or specific ability in and for itself, to include some test of intelligence as well in order to eliminate its effects by such statistical techniques as partial correlation. On the whole, however, it must be admitted that tests for special abilities can claim neither the high reliability nor the relatively high validity of tests for general intelligence.

With young children it is desirable, as far as possible, to assess innate potentialities—a problem which cannot be solved by tests alone. With adults it is usually sufficient to assess their actual abilities or aptitudes at the time of testing. Accordingly, the earliest vocational tests were commonly based not so much on abstract psychological theory as on a direct study of the work required, often investigated at first hand by a psychologist who himself undertook employment on the job in question. However, the attempt to compile efficient tests for the complex aptitudes required in all the various branches of commerce or industry is a lengthy and circuitous way of tackling the problem. Hence experts in vocational guidance tended more and more to determine the fundamental abilities required for different occupations on the assumption that the same elementary ability may enter (though in varying degrees) into several different occupations. For this purpose the results of theoretical studies, particularly by factorial techniques, have proved of increasing value.

Before turning to the method of assessing temperamental characteristics and what is commonly termed personality, it will be well to consider first of all the various technical devices that were progressively worked out for compiling and calibrating tests of abilities and attainment and then to review the chief uses, both theoretical and practical, to which such tests may be put.

B. Construction and Standardization

1. Sampling of Tests and Persons.—Since psychological measurements are far more liable to be affected by error than bodily or physical measurements, special care has been devoted to ascertaining the most effective methods for constructing and calibrating the procedures used. The first requisite is to define, in precise scientific language and in the light of current psychological theory, the particular characteristic to be measured. Such a definition is needed not merely to select suitable tasks or test material but also to secure an adequate criterion. The abstract definition must be capable of translation into concrete operational terms, so as to indicate what will be the outward and visible signs of the inner postulated trait. The kind of behaviour chosen for observation may consist of answers to oral or printed questions, manipulations of the parts of some piece of apparatus, or relatively complex reactions to some standard situation.

The main part of the psychologist's task, however, is to test the test; *i.e.*, to determine (1) its reliability and (2) its validity. This involves a twofold process of sampling: it is essential (*a*) that the items selected for the test include typical specimens of the activities in question and (*b*) that the persons selected for testing form a typical sample of the population for whom the test is designed. Both items and persons therefore must be chosen to ensure that the samples are genuinely random or at any rate truly representative. As a rule in the trial experiment the number of persons tested will be far smaller than the number to whom the test eventually is to be applied. On the other hand, the number of items should be much larger than the number to be incorporated in the final version. The items selected must be as numerous and as varied as the conditions of the examination permit. Consequently, unlike the question paper set at an ordinary examination which usually requires one full-length essay or about four to eight questions involving fairly long replies, most psychological tests comprise a large number of short problems—often as many as 50 or more to be answered in half an hour. Each is so framed as to reduce to a minimum all irrelevant forms of skill and knowledge (*e.g.*, reading, writing, and cultural information) and to elicit answers that require a minimum of subjective judgment in deciding whether each reply is right or wrong. For example, "Jim is taller than Harry, but shorter than Tom; and Dick is shorter than Harry: which is the tallest of the four—Jim, Tom, Dick, or Harry? (put a line under the right name)." In such a question all the words used can be read by an average child of seven, but the problem in reasoning cannot be solved until a mental age of nearly ten, when practically every child, dull or bright, can read the sentence. For such children, therefore, the ability to find the correct answer depends almost entirely on their ability to reason, and their replies can be marked mechanically by a clerk or even a machine.

2. Reliability.—In administering the preliminary version the first thing is to ascertain whether the results are self-consistent or, as it is usually termed, reliable. When any object or quality is measured more than once, the measurements almost invariably differ in some degree, and with psychological traits the variations may be fairly large. Hence earlier investigators made a practice of applying each test at least twice and calculating the correlation between the two sets of results. Later investigators were more often content with a single application and divided the entire series of items into two equivalent subsections. In this case one procedure is to carry out what is tantamount to calculating the correlation between the two subsections. The correlation computed by one or the other of these methods is known as the reliability coefficient. However, it must be understood that "reliability" estimated from only one administration of a test does not indicate consistency from time to time, and is to be regarded only as a measure of internal consistency.

3. Validity.—The validity of a test is commonly defined as the degree to which it succeeds in measuring the trait that it was intended to measure. For this a criterion is needed. The simplest check is to obtain subjective estimates for the trait drawn up by one or more experienced observers who have known the persons tested for a long period. When the test is to be used as a predictor, it is better to follow up the persons tested during subsequent years and secure new and independent measurements based on their after histories. Occasionally some well-established test of high reliability and validity is deemed a sufficient criterion. In all these cases the validity of the new test is assessed by correlating the test results with those of the criterion, and the index thus obtained is known as the validity coefficient. But, where practicable, by far the safest procedure is to base the criterion not on a single set of assessments derived from direct observation or on a single test but on a wide range of tests and assessments, all assumed to measure the same quality; the criterion will then be the general factor underlying the whole series of assessments, each being duly

weighted. This method involves calibration by means of factor analysis (*see* below). With a composite test, it is also desirable to validate not merely the test as a whole but each component item—a procedure known as item analysis—and those items that show the lowest correlations with the criterion are then eliminated.

4. Types of Measurement.—When an acceptably reliable and valid version has at length been constructed, the final step is to reduce the assessments to terms of a quantitative scale and then compile norms for precisely defined groups of the general population; *e.g.*, in the case of children, average performances for either sex at each successive age. To obtain scaled assessments for different kinds of trait, various types of measurement are available; *e.g.*, (1) classificatory, requiring only the determination of the presence or absence of the class attribute, expressed on a binary scale by 0 or 1; (2) ranking, requiring the determination of more or less, expressed by ordinal numbers; (3) differential, requiring the determination of equal differences or intervals; (4) ratio scales, requiring the determination of equality of ratio; (5) multidimensional scales, expressed by the assignment of a matrix of numbers.

In some instances, as in testing for colour blindness, the assessment is essentially qualitative or classificatory. Modern psychology, however, is skeptical of classification into types: borderline cases and mixed types are nearly always found and are often the most numerous. As a rule, therefore, the assessment is quantitative, and the ultimate aim is to obtain a graded measurement. With many tests (*e.g.*, for drawing or handwriting) the quality assessed exhibits varying degrees of excellence, and these have to be judged by subjective impression. In such a case the nearest approach to a comparable measurement is obtained by simply arranging the individual's performances in an order of merit. Each examinee is then given a rank, stating his position in the whole group, but, since groups differ in size, the ranks are converted to percentile form (*see* PERCENTAGE). However, the intervals between successive ranks and percentiles are far from equal, since persons near the general average are usually far more numerous than those toward either extreme. Hence neither ranks nor percentiles are additive. With the majority of tests it is reasonable to assume that, in a representative sample of the population, the underlying measurements will be distributed approximately in accordance with the normal curve. Accordingly, by using tables for the normal distribution, any percentile can be converted into a multiple of the standard deviation (s.d.). Such measurements are said to be in standard measure or standard score (*see* below).

Often, however, the trait itself by its very nature implies an appropriate quantitative measure. With tests for elementary processes, such as sensory discrimination or speed of reaction, for instance, there are as a rule obvious objective units; *e.g.*, grams for the discrimination of weight, seconds for the measurement of speed. As ordinarily administered, many of the tests for higher mental processes also turn, directly or indirectly, on the measurement of speed. With group tests a limited time is usually imposed, and the raw measurement consists of the number of correct solutions achieved in the time allowed. With individual tests a limited number of problems may be set, each of similar difficulty as the others and all well within the capacity of the examinees; the measurement then consists of the time taken by the person to complete them all. Speed, however, is not always a satisfactory index of ability, and in general it is better to use a series of items, varying in difficulty and arranged in order of increasing complexity, from one so easy that almost all can answer it up to one so hard that almost all will fail; with this modification the actual number correctly solved really depends more on qualitative efficiency than on sheer speed. Tests of the former type are termed uniform tests and tests of the latter type graded tests.

5. Comparable Scales.—*Standard Measure.*—With such varying procedures and different methods of construction the raw measurements, taken as they stand, will seldom be comparable from one test to another. Hence it is usually desirable to convert the measurements as originally obtained to terms of a scale where the zero point and the unit shall always indicate the same amounts. This means a further process of calibration. One device, which is almost always available in a well-planned research, is to treat the average of the entire sample of persons as marking the zero point for the general population; different individuals can then be measured in terms of their deviation about this average, and each deviation can be expressed as a multiple of the standard deviation of the group. Once again, then, the measurements will be in "standard measure." Yet, even here, it is often wiser to deduce each standardized measurement indirectly from the examinee's rank (as described above) instead of directly from the raw measurements themselves. Measurements in terms of the s.d. involve the use of plus and minus signs and of fractions—a type of scaling which has obvious inconveniences in actual practice. Consequently, it is often preferable to substitute an artificial scale in which all the measurements are positive integers—*e.g.*, one with a mean of 50 and an s.d. of 10, or a mean of 100 and an s.d. of 15; the latter has the additional merit of yielding scores that resemble the familiar intelligence quotients.

Intelligence Quotients.—As originally computed the intelligence quotient or mental ratio developed out of a method of standardization popularized by Binet. For the fundamental unit he proposed to take the increment of growth from year to year, with the ability of a newborn infant as the zero point. On this basis characteristics which, like intelligence, mature with increasing age or, like school attainments, accumulate from year to year can be assessed in terms of a mental age. Binet therefore standardized the various problems in his scale according to the age at which the typical child could correctly answer them, the whole series thus forming an age scale measuring intelligence in terms of mental years.

However, unless the children to be compared are all of the same chronological age, this does not yield a satisfactory indication of their basic ability. With many graded tests, including Binet's, the standard deviation for successive age groups increases roughly in proportion to the increase in age. This suggests using the ratio of the child's mental age to his chronological age (usually expressed in percentage form) as an index which may be expected to preserve a fair degree of constancy from year to year up to the time of puberty—a device first proposed by Wilhelm Stern in 1911. With a percentage scale the mean is necessarily 100 and, with the versions of the Binet intelligence scale commonly used in the U.S. and Britain, the standard deviation for complete age groups is approximately 15. However, the underlying assumptions on which the method is based are only broadly true, and "mental ages" and "mental ratios" or "quotients" computed in this way are suited only for rough practical purposes, not for scientific research. In the vast majority of cases the most satisfactory scale is one based on standard measures derived from percentile ranks.

Other methods of scaling, based on more complicated statistical techniques, were put foward from time to time, some of them intended to provide an "absolute scale." Since tested characteristics often consist of patterns of traits rather than of simple graded qualities, one or two statistical writers suggested that the ideal measurement in psychology should take the form not of a single figure but of a "matrix" of elementary assessments, such as will describe a complex structure rather than an isolated tendency and can itself be treated as a unitary system. The easiest way to handle such a matrix is to convert it by statistical transformation into a "factor"—a method developed by British psychologists who adopted Karl Pearson's techniques.

C. Uses of Psychological Tests

1. Theoretical Value.—Psychological tests are widely used both as a research technique for investigating the basic characteristics of human functions and as a practical tool in studying individuals for purposes of educational or vocational guidance. Their adoption for such purposes, however, has not escaped criticism, particularly from psychologists of the Cambridge school such as C. S. Myers and O. L. Zangwill. That their warnings need to be borne in mind is shown by the exaggerated claims of validity often made and by the way in which teachers, school

doctors, and some psychologists and education authorities rely on standardized tests as if they could always be accepted at face value. Nevertheless, such methods can be helpful in the hands of those who have been adequately trained in their use and are aware of their inevitable and substantial limitations.

Contrary to the common notion, such tests were first devised for the solution of theoretical rather than practical problems. Galton and most of his immediate followers were interested primarily in the inheritance of intelligence. To some extent their early inferences were vitiated by the naïve assumption that hereditary characteristics are directly measurable. As far as human beings are concerned, any actual measurement is the product of heredity and environment interacting and, without special mathematical techniques, it is difficult to disentangle their relative influence. However, in spite of persistent skepticism as to the possibility of distinguishing the two components, there has been a fruitful revival of research in psychogenetics, and the substitution of R. A. Fisher's statistical procedures for the cruder methods of Galton and Pearson has yielded trustworthy conclusions in regard to the inheritance of intelligence and other psychological characteristics.

The interest of McDougall and those who worked with him centred rather on what they called the structure of the mind. McDougall himself conceived of hypothetical abilities and emotional propensities as analogous to the hypothetical "forces" of physics. This analogy suggested the adoption of a mode of analysis that would resolve the more complex manifestations of behaviour (the "resultants" of such forces) into elementary "components" in accordance with the so-called parallelogram law of mechanics (*q.v.*). For this purpose Pearson's mathematical formulas for reducing a matrix of correlation coefficients to a set of uncorrelated components seemed to provide the most appropriate working procedure, and, in various simplified forms, it was widely used for determining the "factors of the mind" both on the cognitive (or intellectual) and on the affective and conative (*i.e.*, motivational) aspects. Tests are then constructed for estimating the various "general" and "special" factors; *e.g.*, general intelligence and special or primary abilities on the cognitive side. Here again criticism was active, being directed partly against the type of personality structure conceived by different investigators and partly against the somewhat crude computing methods used by earlier workers. The introduction of electronic means of calculation have made it practicable to adopt more precise and elaborate techniques, which have led to improvements in the test procedures themselves and in the assumptions on which they are based.

2. Practical Value.—From 1910 onward the rapid developments of psychological testing was due to the recognition of its many practical uses. In Britain, particularly in large industrial areas such as London and Liverpool, with their overcrowded slums, the poverty, squalor, and truancy, together with the hostility of many parents to the aims of the schools, prevented many pupils from achieving the full educational progress of which they were in fact capable. Surveys carried out during the earlier decades of the 20th century showed that many children were being certified as mentally deficient who were merely dull or backward, while many who had high ability failed to pass the scholarship examination which entitled them to a free place in a secondary school. The introduction of intelligence tests together with other psychological techniques did much to alleviate these forms of educational injustice.

Where tests are used for selection on an extensive scale, their predictive value is commonly assessed in terms of a correlation coefficient. Thus, to check the efficiency of the so-called 11+ examination carried out annually by most English education authorities (when about 700,000 pupils are examined for admission to a grammar school), representative samples are followed up and reports obtained from the headmasters toward the end of the secondary course. On an average about 20% are selected from the entire age group, and roughly one-fourth of those selected are subsequently reported as unsuitable, while about the same number of those rejected appear to have been rejected wrongly. These proportions are equivalent to a correlation coefficient of nearly .90. The apparent errors have led to complaints that this method of selection is unfair. In defense of the system, however, it has been stated that the pupils who are wrongly selected or wrongly rejected are nearly always borderline cases. Moreover, many of the errors result from inevitable fluctuations in each child's subsequent development and to various accidental conditions, such as ill-health or inadequate motivation at the time of testing.

With adults formal testing is, as a rule, less satisfactory. Nevertheless, it is not without its value in occupational guidance and selection. Here the method of estimating the efficiency of the various procedures has to be modified. The commonest method is to adopt the device of matched groups. One batch of candidates is selected in the ordinary manner and the other on the basis of the test results. The after histories of both are then systematically compared. In the main the data obtained justify the value of scientific testing as an adjunct to other procedures. When tests are used for diagnosing individuals or for predicting their subsequent progress, it is essential that the marks or measurements should not be accepted in isolation from all other information. A single test scale, particularly if obtained during a group examination, may prove a precarious indication of the characteristic the investigator wishes to assess.

Tests used in industrial, educational, and military situations typically show validity coefficients between .30 and .60 in predicting on-the-job performance. This means that such tests account for only about 9%–36% of the variance in performance on any criterion; the margin for error in selection and placement is clearly large. But when interpreted in the light of other data (past history, family records, environmental conditions, observations of general behaviour, etc.) their value is unquestionable.

(Cy. B.)

III. TESTS OF PERSONALITY AND TEMPERAMENT

In personality testing the first major task—shared with all other kinds of psychological testing—is the construction of tests that are valid and reliable and that are addressed to significant aspects of individual behaviour. The second major task is the development of interpreters with sufficient diagnostic and interpretive skill to appraise the individual case. Attainment of the first goal will ordinarily require extensive research and statistical analysis (see *Construction and Standardization*, above). Attainment of the second, however, is more a matter of the intuition and insight of the test interpreter than of the particular tools or techniques of analysis employed. It is for this reason that so much stress is put upon the professional training of the practitioner in the field of personality testing.

An obvious problem in personality testing is the selection of the proper factors for measurement from among the seemingly endless number of traits, attitudes, values, behavioural tendencies, points of view, and other characteristics a person manifests; the next problem is that of organizing them so as to give rise to an integrated and functional view of this person as a distinct individual. The level of understanding desired rests on proper evaluation of three components: (1) the attributes of personality; (2) the structure or dynamic interplay of these attributes; and (3) the behavioural implications of this system of attributes.

G. W. Allport listed about 50 definitions of the term personality, drawn from philosophical, legal, sociological, and theological as well as psychological writings. Many of the definitions stressed the way in which the person is perceived by others. This emphasis, however, seems too restricted, for it neglects the inner, subjective components of personality and their implications for overt behaviour. An adequate view of personality must be broader, incorporating latent traits as well as those more manifest. It should also emphasize the organized pattern of traits and attributes underlying and determining the behaviour of the individual.

From this standpoint, temperament is seen as a factor or component of personality. Specifically, it refers to typical modes of reaction, states of energy, and moods. The descriptive adjective "capable" would refer to personality but not to temperament; the adjective "impulsive" would refer to both. Another broad term

often used in speaking of personality is "character." Following the above, character also is to be seen as an aspect of rather than as a synonym for personality. The emphasis in character is on morally sanctioned and approved attitudes and behaviour. (*See* also PERSONALITY; CHARACTER; TEMPERAMENT.)

The commonest unit of description and measurement of personality is the trait. A trait is an enduring quality showing itself in the typical way a person behaves in many different situations. All trait descriptions imply a basis of comparison with other persons, a dimension of variation. Thus most traits are present to some degree in most persons; the trait becomes salient only if it characterizes a person to a greater or lesser degree than the average. In personality analysis the psychologist looks for these significant departures from the norm; in personality testing one of the tasks is to specify units of variation for a trait and then to locate persons as high, average, or low.

A vexing problem in the psychology of traits is their number. Allport and H. S. Odbert assembled a list of 17,953 English adjectives used to describe specific modes of behaviour and thought. Each of these words represents a potential trait for the personality psychologist. Such a list obviously needs to be reduced in length if economy and efficiency of descriptive language are to be attained. One such attempt was made by R. B. Cattell, using the technique of factor analysis, a method developed first by Thurstone on the basis of work by Spearman. Cattell succeeded in defining what he believed to be the 12 "primary" trait dimensions of personality. These dimensions ranged from cyclothymic (voluble, emotionally expressive) *v.* schizothymic (withdrawn, reserved) through surgency (cheerful, buoyant) *v.* desurgency (listless, phlegmatic) to sophistication (cool, detached, aloof) *v.* simplicity (attentive to people, sentimental).

Another significant attempt to specify the major dimensions of variation in personality was that of H. A. Murray, who defined a set of needs said to have both motivational and orientational implications for individual behaviour. Examples from Murray's list are these: need:achievement, to succeed in something difficult, to rival and excel others; need:infavoidance, to avoid humiliation, to refrain from action through fear of failure; need:sentience, to seek and enjoy sensuous impressions.

Several other bases for the choice of terms to describe and analyze personality warrant citation. The language of diagnostic psychiatry has been a continuously important source of concepts. Personality tests for factors such as hypochondriasis (excessive preoccupation with bodily functions), paranoia (exaggerated and irrational distrust and sensitivity), and hypomania (overexcitability, improvident and unmodulated discharge of energy and impulse) are examples of this tradition. Systematic testing methods also have been based on the typology of personal values developed by E. Spranger, on recurrent and self-revelatory modes of perception (H. Rorschach) and on occupational choices and vocational preferences (E. K. Strong).

In the years since Binet's first test of intelligence was issued there has been a great increase in the numbers and kinds of testing instruments. A bibliography for such testing and rating scales published in 1939 contained 4,279 citations; a supplement published in 1946 contained 5,294. The number of such instruments available in the 1960s is greater than 6,000; it is therefore impossible to discuss any save the most important or most representative examples in this review.

A. EARLY TESTS OF PERSONALITY

1. Free Association.—One of the first methods systematically used as a test of personality was the free-association technique introduced by Galton in his studies at the London anthropometric laboratory which he founded in 1884. The free-association method was later used by the German psychiatrist Emil Kraepelin, who presented a list of words to psychiatric patients, requiring them to give in response the very first word that came to mind for each stimulus. The Swiss psychiatrist C. G. Jung (1910) developed a special stimulus list of 100 words for use in diagnosis of the "complexes" of unconscious conflict envisaged by his theory; various diagnostic indicators of inner conflict were enumerated, such as delay or acceleration of response, inability to respond, facial grimaces, and changes of skin colour. A similar list was prepared by the U.S. investigators Grace Kent and A. J. Rosanoff (1910). Many other lists were later developed, but the two of Jung and Kent-Rosanoff continued to be the most widely used. (*See* also Association, Mental.)

2. Questionnaire.—Galton also can be said to have originated the questionnaire method, although a prominent early practitioner of the technique was G. S. Hall, particularly in his studies of developmental psychology and adolescence (1891, 1904). However, the prototype of the modern personality questionnaire was the Personal Data Sheet developed by R. S. Woodworth (1918) for use as a screening device to detect men psychologically unfit for military service. The Personal Data Sheet included 116 items selected from a much larger number of items on the basis of the correlation between each one and the total score for all the items. This method of inventory construction is called the internal consistency method and, although it provides no evidence of external validity, was widely followed in the development of other tests. The questions in the data sheet covered ten categories of distress, such as physical symptoms, fears, antisocial moods, and compulsions, and included items such as these: "Are you frightened in the middle of the night?" "Do you have continual itching in the face?" and "Does liquor make you quarrelsome?" The score on the test was simply the number of such items answered in the unfavourable or "disturbed" direction. Although at first very widely used, the Personal Data Sheet gradually was displaced by inventories covering more than one category or disposition and including items less obvious and susceptible of direct dissimulation.

One of the personality inventories used in testing of secondary school and university students is the Bell Adjustment Inventory, first published in 1934 by H. M. Bell; the inventory also has a less frequently used adult form. The device contains 140 questions of the "yes," "no," "?" response variety, attempting to assess personal adjustment under four categories (home, health, social, and emotional); it also yields a total score. The adult form includes the above plus 20 additional questions covering occupational adjustment. The inventory is employed as a quick diagnostic indicator of the extent and locus of a subject's problems, but is too transparent and easily falsified for use in settings where "faking" is likely to occur or where significant deficiencies of self-insight are to be expected.

Another questionnaire that has enjoyed wide usage is the Bernreuter Personality Inventory, first published by R. G. Bernreuter in 1931. In its original version this test contained four scales, each in itself the descendant of an earlier and independent test: neuroticism, self-sufficiency, introversion, and dominance. The 125 items in the test were taken from these earlier instruments and resemble those cited above for the Woodworth Personal Data Sheet. Many of the items contributed to the score on more than one of the scales, giving rise to a doubt concerning their statistical independence. A factor analysis of the test by J. C. Flanagan in 1935 suggested the presence of only two discriminable dimensions: self-confidence and sociability. Nonetheless, most users continued to score the test for the original four scales, occasionally using the two factors of Flanagan as additional scores.

Research analyses of the Bernreuter test showed it to have serious weaknesses; for example, its openness to "faking" and its inability to identify psychiatrically disturbed or maladjusted persons who are unaware of their problems or whose modes of self-defense cause them to minimize or deny their doubts and anxieties when asked to report on their well-being.

3. Ink Blot.—Experimentation with ink blots and interpretive responses given to more or less unstructured materials represents another theme in the development of methods for testing personality. Binet, the originator of the intelligence test, also conducted studies in this domain. A number of U.S. investigators at about the start of this century espoused the method, but tended to be more interested in it as a way of studying imagination and the "higher mental processes" than as a technique for personality analysis. Whipple's testing manual (1910) contained a description of ink-blot methods and instructions for their experimental

use. The major impetus to the development of this method, however, came from the Swiss psychiatrist H. Rorschach, who, on the basis of prolonged experimental tryout of various blots and various methods of administering them to subjects, evolved in 1921 a series of ten blots and a technique of administration and analysis that remain the most frequently used procedures in the field. Rorschach stressed the importance of formal and structural elements in response to the blots as well as the content of such responses. Following Rorschach's death shortly after the introduction of his method, the work was carried forward on the continent by his student E. Oberholzer and in the United States largely through the efforts of S. J. Beck and B. Klopfer.

4. Situational-Observational.—In the method of situational testing the subject is asked to carry out some task or to do a certain thing, his behaviour then being observed and rated or measured in some specified way. The performance requested may be one from everyday life (*e.g.*, to participate in an impromptu discussion), or it may be quite alien to the subject's usual experience (*e.g.*, interrogation concerning a make-believe crime by a hostile and disparaging investigator). The first extensive application of situational techniques was found in the work of H. Hartshorne, M. A. May, and their collaborators (1928–30). Their researches, done primarily with school children, attempted to derive quantitative indices of behaviour such as cheating, lying, stealing, cooperativeness, and persistence. Their results were so contradictory to the prevalent belief that conduct is merely the manifest expression of generalized traits (such as honesty, generosity, selfishness, etc.) that for several years other efforts to develop testing methods for these factors were inhibited.

Nonetheless, the situational-observational method began to take root, and a clear statement of its aims and purposes was made in a book published by the United States Office of Strategic Services psychological staff, *Assessment of Men: Selection of Personnel for the Office of Strategic Services* (1948; reissued 1963). The method, involving the intensive observation and study of the person over a two- or three-day period of time and utilizing a wide variety of techniques and testing aids, gradually came to be called that of personality assessment, and in the 1960s this approach was well established as a valuable technique for the appraisal of personality.

B. Objective or Structured Tests

The weaknesses of the Woodworth test and other objective questionnaires are exceedingly difficult to avoid in tests constructed by internal consistency methods. In this approach, the test developer first writes or chooses the items for his test, and also decides how they should be scored so as to indicate "nervousness," "leadership," "occupational dissatisfaction," "poor morale," or whatever the factor is that he intends to appraise. The items are then put into a preliminary test, which is given to a sample of persons and scored. The individual items are next correlated with the total scores, the purpose being to discover any that do not have a significant correlation with the total; such items are eliminated from the test, the justification being that they do not covary with the general tendency being measured by the full set of items. The remaining items—those that correlate highest with each other—are retained for the final version of the test.

This psychometric purification results in a scale or test that represents well the view of the psychological trait that the test developer had in mind when he began his work. The method makes no secure provision, however, for correcting the developer's erroneous preconceptions as to which way items should be answered to indicate abnormality (if this is what he is seeking to measure) and for revealing which items are diagnostically useful. "Nervous" people do not always answer an item in the way one would expect from their symptomatology. For example, more often than not they may answer "false" to the item "Thoughts run through my head so that I cannot get to sleep at night," even though they have insomnia, while well-adjusted people may feel rather free to admit that they have this problem on occasion. Following the method of internal consistency, this item might be keyed "true" because it had a high correlation with total score, whereas a comparison of the answers with a nontest criterion of "nervousness" would reveal that denial of this common experience was the diagnostically more important response.

A contrasting mode of test development is the "known-group" or "empirical" method, in which the responses of externally classified groups (*e.g.*, persons in a certain occupation, students nominated as outstanding leaders, diagnosed patients in a psychiatric hospital) are studied to determine empirically (by observation) which if any questionnaire responses differentiate the group from control or base-line groups. Such a method will automatically reduce the effect of preconceptions held by the test maker; furthermore, if his initial list of items is large and varied, the analysis will almost always uncover several new diagnostic indicators of the trait. The former (elimination of erroneous preconceptions) constitutes a distinct gain for test validity, where validity is taken to be the test's correspondence with the external nontest world; the latter (discovery of new diagnostic indicators) constitutes an equally important advantage.

1. SVIB.—Perhaps the leading example among tests that have used known groups in scale construction is E. K. Strong's Vocational Interest Blank (SVIB), first published in 1927. The inventory was continuously expanded and revised until by the 1960s scores for more than 50 different occupations could be obtained. A parallel Strong Vocational Interest Blank for women was brought out in 1935, this form being scorable for about 25 occupations. The male form of the SVIB contains 400 items, grouped into eight sections. The first five cover the categories of occupations, school subjects, amusements, miscellaneous activities, and peculiarities of people. Preferences are indicated for each item by circling the letter "L," "I," or "D" (for "like," "indifferent," or "dislike"). The last three sections of the device call for ranking of certain activities in order of preference, choosing options in pairs of items and the rating of own abilities and other characteristics.

Scoring keys were developed by studying the responses of persons successfully engaged in a specified occupation and then contrasting their item statistics with those obtained from a sample of men in general. Items that revealed statistically significant differences were selected and marked for scoring to stress the responses actually given by men in the particular occupation.

The test scores of a person who takes the SVIB are entered on a profile sheet that provides letter-grade equivalents ("A," "B," and "C") for each of his scores. An "A" rating signifies a high score, in the range usually observed among persons actually employed in the field; a "B" rating is in a more indeterminate range; and a "C" rating indicates a score significantly lower than those typically found for persons working in the field. These letter ratings, it should be emphasized, are indications of the correspondence between a person's interests and those of persons in the occupational fields; they do not necessarily indicate anything about his aptitudes for work in those fields. The co-variation of scores for the different occupational keys permitted the grouping of scales on the profile sheet into "job families." For example, scores on the keys for lawyer, advertising man, and author-journalist usually vary concurrently and are therefore grouped together into what test interpreters call the verbal-linguistic cluster. These scale clusters on the profile sheet have allowed some users of the Strong test to develop complex forms of profile interpretation and even a form of personality analysis that goes far beyond the simple listing of areas of vocational choice and vocational rejection.

The profile sheet also provides for the listing of several scores besides those directly pertaining to a specific occupation. (1) The occupational-level scale reflects differences between interests of unskilled and semiskilled workers on the one hand and those of business and professional men on the other. (2) the interest-maturity scale was based on a contrast between males of age 15 and those of age 25 (the age at which Strong found a fairly stable crystallization of interest patterns). (3) A specialization-level scale reflects interests characteristic of medical specialists and of research workers in other scientific fields. (4) Finally, a masculinity-femininity scale shows the degree of similarity between the person's interests and those characteristic of men or of women, respectively.

2. Kuder Preference Record.—This test, first begun in 1934 by G. F. Kuder, and issued in various forms since then (1939, 1942, 1948), also yields scores indicative of occupational interests. The vocational form of the test (Form C) includes 168 item triads describing three different activities or interests. The respondent selects in each triad the one he likes most and the one he likes least. On the basis first of logical groupings of the items and later of extensive statistical analysis ten interest scales were developed: outdoor (agricultural, naturalistic), mechanical, computational, scientific, persuasive, artistic, literary, musical, social service, and clerical. A verification scale to detect carelessness and failure to observe instructions is also included. A profile sheet for the record provides for an automatic conversion of raw scores to percentiles, and the profile pattern gives a visual picture of the high, average, and low rankings over the ten categories.

Both the Strong and the Kuder tests are very popular. The Kuder has the advantage of a smaller and simpler set of categories and lends itself to situations where self-interpretation of scores is a necessity. The Strong test, however, contains a greater fund of information and is also supported by a significantly greater amount of validating research literature.

3. Minnesota Multiphasic.—The Minnesota Multiphasic Personality Inventory of S. R. Hathaway and J. C. McKinley, first published in 1943, contains 550 true-false questions, many borrowed from earlier tests such as the Woodworth Personal Data Sheet and the Bernreuter Personality Inventory. It also includes, however, original items more directly pertinent to the areas typically examined by a thorough diagnostic interview in a psychiatric setting; the questions cover 26 such categories.

Fourteen scores are reported on the standard profile for this test. These scales and the diagnostic aim of each are summarized as follows: (1) Cannot say—to identify records rendered invalid by the exclusion of too many items. (2) Lie—items involving improbable claims to moral virtue and rectitude, the answering of which in the scored direction implies an attempt to falsify or the presence of strong repressive-constrictive trends. (3) "K"—reflects the subject's habitual style of verbal behaviour and self-description, ranging from restrictive prudence and inhibition at one end to crudity and lack of restraint at the other; scores on certain of the other scales are adjusted up or down according to the person's score on the "K" scale. (4) "F"—includes highly unusual and atypical response choices, serving to identify records with an undue number of answers of an unusual or infrequent kind whether due to carelessness, deliberate falsification, or distorted thought processes. (5) Hypochondriasis—reflects somatic complaints and preoccupation with bodily functions. (6) Depression—indicative of poor morale, feelings of depression, and worry. (7) Hysteria—reveals tendencies toward repressive, immature emotional life, and bodily expressions of psychological conflict. (8) Psychopathic deviate—identifies persons of disruptive, rebellious temperament who find it hard to accept rules, restraints, and orderly habits of life. (9) Masculinity-femininity—attempts to detect deviations of interests and outlook toward those characteristic of the opposite sex. (10) Paranoia—indicates attitudes of undue or irrational suspiciousness coupled with exaggerated sensitivity. (11) Psychasthenia—a heterogeneous set of obsessions, compulsions, and phobias synthesized as a general index of agitation and perplexity. (12) Schizophrenia—reveals trends toward alienation from self and others, loss of self-direction, and frankly delusional thought content. (13) Hypomania—a gauge of emotional expansiveness, excitability, and accelerated tempo of thought and behaviour. (14) Social introversion—seeks to identify persons of diffident, anxious, and retiring disposition.

These 14 scores are plotted on a profile sheet that provides an automatic conversion of the raw score totals to standard scores that have been statistically adjusted to give a mean score of 50 and standard deviation of 10; this permits direct comparisons among scales. The profile of scale scores for the Minnesota Multiphasic, like that for the SVIB, lends itself to complex configural interpretations; psychologists use the inventory to prepare personality analyses of patients tested in clinics and hospitals. The inventory is principally oriented toward matters of psychopathology and morbidity and has shown its greatest (but limited) validity when applied to clinical and psychiatric problems; it has shown less utility when applied to problems of normal behaviour and everyday life.

Personality inventories more directly concerned with the functioning of normal persons, although later in appearance than those concerned with neuroticism and inner conflicts, were increasing steadily in use during the 1960s. One such instrument is the Edwards Personal Preference Schedule, published in 1954. It seeks to measure variables drawn from Murray's theories (*see* above); *e.g.,* need: nurturance and need: affiliation. A second instrument is the California Psychological Inventory, published in 1956. This inventory is addressed to "folk concepts"; *i.e.,* attributes of personality such as dominance, responsibility, and social presence which arise directly out of social life.

C. Study of Values

The Study of Values was first introduced by Allport and P. E. Vernon in 1931, and then revised in 1951 by Allport, Vernon, and G. Lindzey. The test is derived from a theory of E. Spranger, postulating that in the life of each person a great single unifying theme or value may be discovered. The Study of Values seeks to measure the relative strength of six such values: (1) theoretical—having a dominant interest in the discovery of truth, valuing critical, rational, and logical thinking; (2) economic—primarily interested in utility, in the practicality and efficiency of things; (3) aesthetic—places highest value on form and harmony, seeks out and prefers artistic experience; (4) social—directed toward altruism and philanthropy, values the welfare of others and of mankind; (5) political—is power oriented, seeks esteem and renown, control over others; (5) religious—concerned with unity, the mystic nature of existence and of the cosmos.

The device contains 45 questions presenting either two or four propositions that the subject must rate in order of preference. An example is the following: "In your opinion, can a man who works in business all the week best spend Sunday in: (*a*) trying to educate himself by reading serious books; (*b*) trying to win at golf, or racing; (*c*) going to an orchestral concert; (*d*) hearing a really good sermon." The classification of these options under the value types of theoretical, political, aesthetic, and religious obviously is not difficult, and this very ease reflects one of the limitations of the test—its openness to deliberate dissimulation. Another limitation resides more in the theory than in the test itself; that is, in the restricted applicability of the six value types. Even insofar as the unity thema concept in personality is correct, these particular six values contain an aristocratic bias in that they apply more to persons of intellectual, ratiocinative temperament than to more ordinary individuals.

D. Factor Analysis

The inventories discussed up to this point have dealt with either (1) dimensions of measurement taken directly from the settings in which the test is to be used (*e.g.,* the SVIB) or (2) with dimensions taken from theoretical systems that were offered to explain and account for human behaviour (*e.g.,* the Study of Values). In inventories developed by the technique of factor analysis a markedly different basis of choice is to be seen. In factor-analytic tests the factors to be measured are not necessarily those that seem on the surface most relevant to a particular setting or those that a previous theorist has talked about; on the contrary, the dimensions of choice seem to be those that most economically summarize the variations of response to be found among the components of the testing battery.

The underlying logic of factor analysis is mathematical, and its principle of faith is that mathematically basic test dimensions will also be psychologically basic. Suppose that a number of experimental tests of "personal adjustment" were tried out and then correlations among scores on the experimental tests were computed. Undoubtedly some of the tests would overlap each other, and the full set would contain an unnecessary amount of duplication. The aim of factor analysis in this example would be to specify the extent of such redundancy and then to indicate the minimum number of underlying factors that could be used mathematically to account for all the scores found in the experimental battery. Measurement of these underlying factors could be said to be a more efficient and more valid way of assessing the domain of personal adjustment.

The technical methods of factor analysis are mathematically complex and difficult, but their purpose is simple: to identify the dimensions that will represent most economically the set of interrelationships given by a battery of test scores or test items. At first discovery, the factors may seem strange or different from the usual ways in which the test elements have been discussed, although this is partly a function of the names the analyst chooses to assign to his factors. A second, more significant, difficulty is that the new mathematical factors may have less accuracy as predictors of nontest behaviour than the mathematically impure tests the factors are designed to replace. In such instances the factor analyst seeks an optimum combination of factor-pure tests from which a valid prediction in a specific practical situation can be made.

Perhaps the leading U.S. exponent of factor-analytic methods in personality test development has been J. P. Guilford, whose various inventories are used widely and are among the most important examples of factorially based devices. The Inventory of Factors STDCR (1940) included scales for social introversion, thinking introversion, depression, cycloid disposition, and rhathymia (happy-go-lucky, carefree). The Guilford-Martin Inventory of Factors GAMIN (1943) covered the factors of general activity, ascendance, masculinity, inferiority, and nervousness. A third test, the Guilford-Martin Personnel Inventory (1943), included scales for the factors of objectivity, co-operativeness, and agreeableness. A later test, the Guilford-Zimmerman Temperament Survey (1949), included 300 questions scaled for ten factors: general activity, restraint, ascendance, sociability, emotional stability, objectivity, friendliness, thoughtfulness, personal relations, and masculinity.

Another leading exponent of factorial technique is R. B. Cattell, whose most widely used inventory was the Sixteen Personality Factor Questionnaire (1950). The inventory had two parallel forms, each with 187 items; a third form having 105 items was later added. Several examples from Cattell's designations of the 16 scales can be given: cyclothymia *v.* schizothymia; general intelligence *v.* mental defect; emotional stability *v.* general neuroticism; surgency *v.* desurgency; bohemianism *v.* practical concernedness; sophistication *v.* rough simplicity; and anxious insecurity *v.* placid self-confidence.

E. Projective Methods

Although projective methods for studying personality were used by Galton, Jung, Kent and Rosanoff, and others, as mentioned above, it was not until the appearance of Rorschach's ink-blot technique in 1921 that the approach began its rise to popularity. Even in Rorschach's own work, however, the theoretical implications of the method were little developed, for he saw himself as an empirical scientist engaged in the development of a diagnostic tool having practical objectives. The first significant formulation of the theory and point of view of projective testing was given by L. K. Frank (1939). The fundamental theorem is that when confronted with unstructured stimuli the person will impose structure on them in such a way as to reflect his own needs and impulses; the subject's responses therefore are expected to serve as guides to his private world of fantasy, his attitudes, fears, aspirations, and the like.

1. Theory of Projective Methods.—The word projection in reference to this process and to this category of tests is somewhat equivocal. There has been a tendency to identify the theorem of projective testing with the psychoanalytic (Freudian) concept of projection; *i.e.,* with the mode of ego defense in which unacceptable impulses are externalized and attributed to others or to outside agents (*see* Defense Mechanisms).· However, the projective test responses are by no means delimited to denied and expulsed ("projected") psychological material of this sort, or even primarily focused upon it.

Another meaning of projection is simply that which stands out from its surroundings, that which extends beyond something else. This meaning of the term is somewhat applicable to projective tests insofar as the ambiguity of the stimuli and the freedom of the test situation often do permit the appearance of highly salient mental content, those concerns that are most active and impelling in the mental life of the subject at the time of testing.

However, a third meaning of projective, the geometric or cartographical one, is probably closest to the implications of Frank's thesis. In this meaning the external representation is not considered as merely a general derivative of its originating source, but as a specific point-for-point rendition of it. Thus, a geometric drawing gives an exact representation of the three-dimensional object from which it is made, and a map is intended as a precise guide to a given section of terrain. If to an amorphous ink blot a person replies, "Eyes of bloody fire," and then adds, "but it could be a dear little dancing mouse," the discontinuity is only apparent; each response represents inner experience, and the path from the first to the second (*i.e.*, the relation between them) is as determined and meaningful in the experiential topography as the interval between points A and B in the geographic counterpart. The theoretical aim of the projective test is therefore no less ambitious than this: to chart in a faithful and interpretable way the full range and depth of the inner life of a person.

In practice, the classification of tests as projective or nonprojective has followed lines of custom and convenience not always in accord with consistent interpretation of the theory. Freedom for the subject to respond as he wishes would seem to be an essential element of the projective method if crucial features of the subject's inner life are to have full opportunity to manifest themselves. The instructions in the Rorschach test, where the subject is asked merely to report on what he sees, satisfy this requirement very well; on the other hand, an activity check list where the subject simply marks "like" and "dislike" does not. The Rorschach test is therefore properly classified as a projective test, and the activity check list as nonprojective. However, one of the tests classified by custom as projective, the Szondi test, requires the subject to make this same "like" *v.* "dislike" response to a series of photographs of European mental hospital patients; the Szondi test therefore has no more and no less freedom of response than the nonprojective activity check list.

This logical confusion is seen again in the factor of ambiguity of stimulus materials, held to be an essential condition for projective responses. The ink blots of the Rorschach test are for the most part amorphous and lacking in readily perceived meaning. Yet the geometrical figures that the subject copies in the (projective) Bender Gestalt test are clear and precise, certainly less ambiguous in point of fact than the more difficult items in a (nonprojective) test of spatial visualization. On this particular dimension of stimulus ambiguity, therefore, the nonprojective test of spatial visualization would have to be rated as closer to the projective test ideal than the projective Bender Gestalt.

2. Rorschach Test.—The Rorschach ink-blot test contains ten stimulus cards: five achromatic cards having only shades of gray and black, and five chromatic blots incorporating various colours. The cards are presented to the subject in a standard sequence with brief instructions on the order of: "I am going to show you a series of ink blots, one at a time. The blots do not necessarily represent specific things; different people see different things in them. Would you please look at this blot and tell me what you see, what it makes you think of?" The examiner

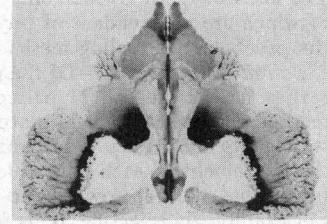
INK BLOT, SIMILAR TO THOSE USED IN RORSCHACH'S TEST

keeps a record from this point on of comments, responses, time consumed, how the cards are held and turned, etc. Questions are answered in noncommittal fashion; *e.g.*, "Whatever comes to your mind," "It's entirely up to you."

Analysis of the test covers four principal categories:

1. The first of these is location, the part or parts of the blot utilized in the response. The main elements in this category are the "whole" response, which involves the complete blot, the large detail, and the small detail. The usual protocol (record of responses) strikes a balance among these three components; emphasis on one or another is seen as evidence for significant modes of personality functioning. For example, concentration on large, common details is held to be characteristic of the mundane, practical, fact-centred personality.

2. The second main scoring category concerns the determinants of the response; *i.e.*, whether form, colour, apparent texture of the surface, shadings, or other factors influenced the perception. Here again a balance among the elements ordinarily prevails, and deviations from the base line are said to hint of salient trends in the personality. An excitable, uninhibited, effervescent person might have many responses in which colour is a vital feature; an aggressive, explosive person might show form elements subordinated to colour in nearly every instance. Where he is doubtful about what qualities in the blot have given rise to a certain response, the examiner makes discreet inquiries. For example, to a certain red-coloured portion of a blot the subject says, "And there I see a bow tie." The examiner, returning to this response after finishing the ten blots, might ask, "Can you tell me why that part is a bow tie?" If the respondent answers, "Why, because it's shaped like one, that's why," the examiner might go on to ask, "Would it still look like a bow tie if it was entirely black?" The form-dominated perceiver would probably now respond "Of course," the colour-dominated, "Certainly not."

3. The third category is that of the content of the response. Here again common clusters appear. Most records contain some references to human beings, to animals, and to natural phenomena of one sort or another. The absence of any of these or overconcentration on a particular one provides a basis for interpretation.

4. A fourth category, more or less included in the interpretations of the first three but still listed as a separate feature in the scoring, has to do with the popularity or originality of each response. For certain blots certain responses are so typically given that they are labeled "populars." Persons whose perceptual habits and reactions are similar to those of others will give an appreciable number of such "popular" replies during the course of the testing. Psychotic or deranged subjects might give very few or none at all. At the other end of the scale are responses that are seldom encountered or that the examiner hears for the first time. Such responses are called "original." A further classification into good quality (O+), average quality (O) or poor quality (O−) is necessary in order to distinguish between creatively original perceptions and those involving distorted or warped conceptions.

On the basis of these and other ancillary scoring procedures the Rorschach analyst attempts to synthesize a model of the functional psychology of the person, one that depicts the formal properties of his personality (*e.g.*, intellectual ability, introversion-extroversion, inhibitions, constraints, level of affective energy, etc.) as well as his particular concerns and problems. The validity of this final formulation is said to rest in large part on the skill and wisdom of the examining psychologist.

However, H. J. Eysenck (University of London), writing in the *Fifth Mental Measurements Yearbook*, concluded that the Rorschach ink-blot test has yet to show ". . . scientific or practical value." And Beck, a leading U.S. exponent of the test's use, wrote in the same volume that any conclusions derived from its use are to be considered ". . . not as facts but as hypotheses." In the 1960s controversy over the trustworthiness of the Rorschach as a test and the competence of its users to draw valid conclusions from the protocols continued to grow.

3. Thematic Apperception Test.—The second most widely used test of the projective group is the Thematic Apperception Test (TAT), first issued in 1935 by Murray and Christiana D. Morgan. In the TAT, pictures are presented on cards to the subject, who is asked to make up a story having an antecedent, a plot, and a resolution. Stress is laid on the concept of "imagination" in instructions, with the offhand comment being made that "imagination is one form of intelligence." There are 31 pictures in

BY COURTESY OF STEPHEN C. CLARK

"SUNLIGHT IN A CAFETERIA" BY EDWARD HOPPER, A PAINTING SIMILAR TO THOSE USED IN THEMATIC APPERCEPTION TESTS (*see* TEXT)

all, these being grouped into special subsets of 20 each for younger and older subjects, male or female. The manual calls for two one-hour testing sessions, ten cards being administered at each. The more unusual and dramatic pictures are reserved for the second sitting, along with one entirely blank card. The subject ordinarily tells his stories aloud, the examiner copying them verbatim. However, all these procedural matters vary widely in practice, depending upon the examiner; the variability in this respect is much greater than for other tests of wide usage.

In the analysis of test results there is also much less standardization in the TAT than in other tests. Some examiners have utilized Murray's "need-press" system of concepts or variations of it; some apply psychoanalytic notions of defense, repression, projection, etc.; others merely attempt a subjective-intuitive résumé of the personality of the storyteller. For special purposes the stories can be scrutinized for particular themes or qualities; one such scoring, for example, is based upon the number of manifestations of the need for achievement; another is based on appraisal of the stories for their level of originality. The test method also has been applied in anthropological field studies to help shed light, for example, on child-rearing attitudes, on moral codes and sanctions, and on philosophical values. Despite these applications, evidence for the validity of the TAT is sparser and more questionable than that for the Rorschach.

F. OTHER METHODS

There are literally hundreds of additional projective methods for the assessment of personality that could be discussed in a complete review of the topic. A few examples are given below, classified by type of task or method of testing.

1. Constitutive Methods.—In these the subject imposes a form or structure upon an amorphous or plastic substance or upon partially structured or semiorganized fields. Examples are the Rorschach test; Hans Zulliger's three-blot ink-blot test modeled after the Rorschach; the sentence-completion method proposed by A. F. Payne in 1928; and finger painting as introduced by Ruth F. Shaw in 1930.

2. Constructive Methods.—In these the subject is asked to build or construct something, the implication being that some of the organizing principles in his own personality will be manifest in his test constructions. M. Lowenfeld's Mosaic Test, introduced in 1929, is an example. The subject is given a set of 465 small wooden blocks of six colours and five shapes and asked to "make anything you like out of the pieces." The mosaics can then be evaluated on some 23 factors, including such characteristics as concreteness *v.* abstraction, over-all harmony of design, simplicity *v.* complexity, and emphasis on form or colour.

3. Interpretive Methods.—In these the subject is asked to tell what a specific stimulus, such as a picture, suggests or means to him. The Thematic Apperception Test provides one example of the type. The Four-Picture Test of the Dutch psychologist

D. J. van Lennep, in which the subject is requested to tell a story incorporating the people and backgrounds shown in four pictures, is another.

4. Cathartic Methods.—In these methods the aim is to release pent-up emotions and feelings in such a way as to permit interpretation and personality diagnosis. An example is the "therapeutic doll" of D. M. Levy, which the subject may dismember, cuddle, maltreat, etc., at will.

5. Refractive Methods.—This category includes the use of any conventionalized mode of communication or expression, verbal or written, as a basis for personality assessment. Handwriting analysis (graphology) is a prominent example (*see* HANDWRITING).

(H. G. G.)

IV. ATTITUDE MEASUREMENT

An attitude may be measured as the degree of positive or negative feeling associated with some psychological object or event (*see* ATTITUDE). The psychological object may be a job, a racial or ethnic group, a governmental policy, or a book title; it may be a person, a thing, an institution, or an idea (*see* PUBLIC OPINION; FLAVOUR: *Flavour Testing;* VOTING BEHAVIOUR; PSYCHOLOGY, SOCIAL).

A. APPROACHES

One possible approach to attitude measurement entails asking respondents direct questions demanding "yes" or "no" answers. This approach often has been used, with varying degrees of success, in the assessment of public opinion to predict, say, voting behaviour. Often it results in a large proportion of "don't know" or "undecided" responses, difficult to evaluate. Not infrequently, particularly on emotionally tinged public issues, respondents either consciously or unconsciously distort their replies, yielding results biased in the direction of the popular or socially approved response. These difficulties have prompted the development of less direct procedures for measuring attitudes.

An attitude schedule is a set of carefully constructed statements about a psychological object, together with some device, such as a rating scale, by which the subjects express their feeling toward each statement. Methods of attitude measurement differ, one from another, primarily in the means for constructing and selecting statements to be included on the schedule. The three main approaches to attitude measurement may be distinguished by noting whether the focus is upon the statements, the subjects, or the responses.

1. Methods Focusing on Statements.—These methods utilize judgments from a group of respondents to scale the attitude statements. Subsequently the scale values of the statements may be used to locate any individual on the attitude continuum on the basis of his responses to the schedule.

Procedures for measuring attitudes were pioneered by Thurstone, through a series of articles and monographs beginning in 1927. Thurstone extended the psychophysical methods (*q.v.*) by proposing a model for scaling psychological magnitudes of stimuli independent of any corresponding physical stimulus magnitudes. The class of methods including those proposed by Thurstone, all of which are independent of physical measurement, are known as the psychological scaling methods.

Paired Comparisons.—Of the psychological scaling methods, the earliest is the method of paired comparisons. In applying this method to the selection of statements for attitude measurement, statements are presented in pairs, with judges instructed to select that statement of each pair which they view as indicating a more favourable attitude toward the psychological object in question. For example, in selecting items for a schedule designed to measure attitude toward public censorship, the following two items might be paired: (1) "to protect the public it sometimes is necessary that censorship be exercised"; (2) "books and plays should be subject to moral censorship." Each respondent would be asked to select statement (1) or (2) as representing a more favourable attitude toward public censorship.

As presented to a sample of judges, each statement is paired with every other statement. Proportions of responses are generated of the form P_{ij}, the proportion of judgments that statement i is more favourable than statement j; these serve as the basic data for application of the method. Data are treated by Thurstone's law of comparative judgment, a theoretical model transforming the proportions and operating on them so as to provide numerical scale values associated with each attitude statement. (In the simplest application of the model, it is assumed that affective values toward each statement have a normal distribution in the population of respondents and that the population variances and covariances of those distributions all are equal.)

Successive Intervals.—A related method for selecting attitude statements is the method of successive intervals, also suggested by Thurstone. Each separate statement is rated by every member of a group of judges to indicate favourability of attitude implied by the statement, the rating being in the form of a check mark in one of several response categories. Categories are defined to extend from "extremely unfavourable" to "extremely favourable," with intermediate categories suggesting more moderate attitudes. A law of categorical judgment here provides the model by which proportions of category ratings are transformed and yield scale values indicating degrees of attitude associated with the statements. Once again it is assumed that in the population attitudes are normally distributed. The method of successive categories has the advantage of providing quantitative estimates of the degree of ambiguity of attitude for each statement (indicated by the variances of distributions of judgments, measured on the attitude continuum). Such estimates are valuable for selecting statements to be included on an attitude schedule. Because of its theoretical advantages, the method of successive intervals has largely replaced the similar method of equal appearing intervals for construction of attitude schedules.

After scale values are assigned for each attitude statement and those to be put on a schedule are selected, the problem remains to estimate the attitude of individual respondents. A simple procedure is to present the schedule to each individual with instructions to check those statements with which he agrees. An average of the scale values for those items checked serves to locate the individual on the attitude continuum.

2. Method Focusing on Subjects.—A method proposed by Rensis Likert treats attitude statements much on the order of objective test items. An attitude schedule is constructed from a group of statements (with unknown scale values) selected to represent either favourable or unfavourable attitudes toward a psychological object or event. For each statement, subjects are instructed to respond by checking one of several possible response categories; *e.g.,* "strongly agree," "agree," "uncertain," "disagree," or "strongly disagree." Likert suggested the arbitrary assignment of weights to these categories: 4, 3, 2, 1, 0, respectively, when statements convey a favourable attitude; 0, 1, 2, 3, 4, respectively, for unfavourable statements. For a given schedule, an attitude score is found for every subject simply by summing the weights associated with the responses of that subject. The approach is aimed at the direct assignment of attitude scores to individual subjects, avoiding the intervening step of assigning scale values to statements.

The Likert method often has been implemented by utilizing techniques of item analysis, borrowed from objective psychological test theory, to select appropriate statements for a refined final form of attitude schedule.

Both the Likert and Thurstone methods have often been used in practical efforts to measure attitudes. The several studies comparing results of the two approaches fail to show marked superiority of either approach over the other. Theory underlying the judgment methods of Thurstone is somewhat more completely defined, and in accordance with the theoretical measurement model, application of the Thurstone methods yields scores with wider general interpretations as numbers (as opposed to numerals representing order relations but not distance along an attitude continuum).

3. Methods Focusing on Responses.—In these methods an attempt is made to assign scale values to both subjects and statements from a single administration of the statements to the sub-

jects. The methods demand a set of attitude statements which vary along a single psychological dimension and assume subjects' responses to depend only upon their positions on this same dimension.

Scalogram Analysis.—One prominent response method is scalogram analysis, proposed by Louis Guttman. In applying scalogram analysis, it is assumed that any subject asked to accept or reject a set of attitude statements will accept all those with scale values at or below that point on the attitude continuum at which the subject is located, rejecting those statements with scale values higher than his own location. Consider the following four statements, listed in the order of increasingly favourable attitude toward cold climate.

    A. I am able to tolerate occasional cold weather.
    B. At times I enjoy cold weather.
    C. I would enjoy living where the climate is one of cold winters.
    D. I revel in cold weather, and would choose to live only in an area with cold climate.

For this set of sentences, anyone accepting the most extremely favourable statement D also would be expected to accept the statements reflecting a more moderate positive attitude toward cold climate, A, B, and C; a person accepting statement C also would be expected to accept A and B; and for someone accepting statement B, acceptance of A also would be anticipated. Conversely, if one rejects statement B, it is typically predicted that he will reject statements C and D. Under these conditions, the statements are said to be scalable. While there are 16 possible response patterns, patterns of acceptance $(+)$ or rejection (0) among four statements, only 5 of these (in general, $n + 1$, where n is the number of statements) are expected to occur for four scalable statements:

	Statement			
Pattern	A	B	C	D
1	0	0	0	0
2	+	0	0	0
3	+	+	0	0
4	+	+	+	0
5	+	+	+	+

Subjects thus are divided, by responses to the four statements, into five groups classified according to favourability of attitude. Statements also become ordered in terms of the attitude variable by the observed response pattern.

Unfolding Technique.—A second response method for attitude measurement, known as the unfolding technique, was proposed by Clyde H. Coombs. Subjects are asked to rank a set of attitude statements according to the extent of their agreement with each. Analysis of such rankings yields information regarding the attitude of the subject relative to the set of statements.

Let the letters A, B, C, and D represent four attitude statements, listed in order from unfavourable to favourable attitude. A given subject S might rank the statements in the order C, D, B, A in terms of his agreement with them. By "unfolding" the rank order, the investigator could achieve a conception of the relative locations of statements and subject on the attitude continuum. The following portrayal is consistent with S's ordering of agreement with the four statements. The line segment represents the attitude continuum, progressing from unfavourable, on the left, to favourable, on the right.

```
                          S
 _____
   A     B        C              D
```

The rank order assigned the statements by a given subject is interpreted as the order of distances between statement and subject on the attitude continuum and thus serves to locate (within a narrow range of values) the affective position of the subject relative to the locations of the statements. Analysis of responses from a group of subjects allows more definite estimates of the locations of statements.

4. Internal Consistency, Reliability, and Validity.—Each of the prominent methods for attitude measurement mentioned above includes means for checking the internal consistency of the method. In addition, reliability of measurement may be determined; numerous applications have verified that consistent (*i.e.*, reliable) measures of attitude may be obtained. A thorny problem, however, is that of determining the validity of attitude measurement. Immediately the investigator is faced with the task of specifying a behavioural criterion against which validity may be assessed. Except for instances in which attitudes are expressed through political action (*e.g.*, voting behaviour), instances of successful specification of such criteria are rare. A few studies indicate that these methods of attitude measurement exhibit at least greater validity than that attending the direct questioning of respondents.

B. Consumer Preference Measurement

Closely related to attitude measurement is the measurement of consumer preference, or acceptance of consumer products. However, the primary aim is somewhat distinct from that of attitude measurement: attention is directed toward the degree of acceptance of a product, judged by numerous consumers, rather than toward the placement of a person along a psychological continuum.

Psychological scaling methods that focus upon stimuli (analogous to statements in attitude measurement) are ideally suited to the aim of consumer preference measurement. These methods yield scale values associated with each stimulus rated or judged by a consumer sample. Stimuli might be food items, items of apparel, or other consumer products. By the method of paired comparison or the method of successive intervals it becomes possible quantitatively to evaluate the relative preferences displayed for a group of such items, and to estimate degree of acceptance of the items by a population of consumers (when the judging group is a random sample from that population).

An interesting application of models for consumer preference measurement allows prediction of consumer choice of competing products on an open market, or even prediction of relative purchase of each of several competing products when these are offered at different (known) costs to the consumer. For the latter problem, there enters the question of (negative) utility of money, which presumably combines with preference for the commodities to dictate proportions of purchase of each. Exploratory research on these problems suggests that the measurement methods are highly reliable and provide a useful quantitative model for estimation of consumer choice behaviour.

1. Multidimensional Scaling.—An extension of the psychological scaling methods not only provides conclusions concerning the distribution of sensory preferences among product samples, but also serves to indicate the (linearly independent) psychological components of the general sensory distinctions. This extension is known as multidimensional scaling, since it yields a solution for the several psychological dimensions responsible for the general differences in preference among stimuli. As an example, consider five distinct samples of coffee, to be evaluated for general flavour characteristics. Preference values could be obtained using the method of paired comparisons, presenting samples in pairs to a group of judges. There are ten pairs of the five samples (in general, $n(n-1)/2$ pairs of n stimuli); for each pair the proportion of judges indicating preferred flavour for each of the two brews of coffee would be determined. Application of the law of comparative judgment would yield solution of general preference scale values for each of the five samples.

Now the coffee samples could be presented again, this time utilizing the method of triads. Samples are presented in groups of three, with judges instructed to determine relative degree of similarity between pairs of samples within the triad. ("Stimulus i is more similar to stimulus j than to stimulus k.") With five stimuli, there are ten triads (in general, $n(n-1)(n-2)/6$ triads for n stimuli), and for each triad, three judgments are required, since each stimulus is compared with the stimuli of every other pair. The result of such an experimental procedure is the generation of n matrices of proportions, one for every stimulus sample, each of order $n \times n$. The elements of the ith matrix take the form $_iP_{jk}$, the proportion of times stimulus i is judged more similar to stimulus j than to stimulus k.

The proportion $_iP_{jk}$ is postulated to depend upon the difference

between distances d_{ij} and d_{ik}, where d_{ij} represents (affective) distance of stimulus i from stimulus j, and d_{ik} represents distance between stimuli i and k. Assuming the distribution of differences in distance, $(d_{ij} - d_{ik})$ to be normal in the population, with equal variances and covariances, a solution is provided for every distance of the form d_{ij}. Once all such distances are computed, imposition of a spatial model (*e.g.*, assuming analogy to Euclidean space) will serve to determine the minimum number of dimensions required to account simultaneously for all empirically derived distances. Analysis of the configuration of interstimulus distances has also become feasible with digital computers without the need for making distributional assumptions.

2. Detection of Sensory Differences in Consumer Products.—In numerous consumer industries, sensory characteristics of the product assume great importance. For manufacturers of processed foods and beverages, perfumes, colour reproductions, to name only a few, the quality of the product depends largely upon its sensory characteristics. Industrial testing for control of sensory characteristics of products has made considerable use of the psychophysical methods, particularly of the constant method.

A typical problem is that of assuring uniformity of the product. Not always does strict uniformity necessarily result from careful control of ingredients; minor variations in climatic conditions, time of preparation, storage conditions, and many other factors as well as quality and quantity of ingredients may affect the product. To assure no major variability in the product as marketed, sensory tests often are conducted. New batches of the product typically are compared with a standard batch, known to be of acceptable quality. In the case of foods and beverages, this constitutes taste testing for flavour characteristics. Samples of the product are judged in pairs, often by expertly trained judges. One member of each pair is the standard, the other is called the variable. The task of the tasters is to judge, for each pair, which is the sweeter, saltier, more pleasant, more bitter, or the like. On the basis of numerous ratings, proportions of such judgments are obtained for each variable as compared with the standard. Statistical procedures are available for guiding the decision concerning acceptability of quality. For example, it might be decided that a batch would be unacceptable if as many as 5% of consumers were to detect a deficiency in the product as compared with the usual standards. Application of the constant method and related statistical tests would serve to yield a decision concerning quality of each batch in terms of such a criterion. A method of analysis nearly identical to that of the constant method of psychophysics is the probit method of biometrics, developed in England by Fisher and D. J. Finney, in the United States by C. I. Bliss.

The psychophysical methods have proved useful not only for quality control of a product; they also are frequently applied to the development of improved consumer items. In this application, detection of a difference in a given direction, that the new product has more desirable characteristics than the old, serves as evidence upon which the new product may be marketed, either replacing the old or competing with it with some assurance that the new product will maintain a favourable competitive position.

See Intelligence; Examinations; Motivation; Differential Psychology; *see* also references under "Psychological Tests and Measurements" in the Index. (L. V. Jo.)

Bibliography.—G. W. Allport, *Personality: a Psychological Interpretation* (1937); Anne Anastasi, *Psychological Testing*, 2nd ed. (1961); O. K. Buros (ed.), *Mental Measurements Yearbook* (1935 et seq.); R. B. Cattell, *The Description and Measurement of Personality* (1946); L. J. Cronbach, *Essentials of Psychological Testing*, 2nd ed. (1960); H. J. Eysenck, *The Scientific Study of Personality* (1952); M. D. Dunnette, *Personnel Selection and Placement* (1966); F. Galton, *Inquiries into Human Faculty and Its Development* (1883); B. Kleinmuntz, *Personality Measurement* (1967); H. A. Murray, *Explorations in Personality* (1938); P. Pichot, *Les Tests Mentaux* (1949); H. Rorschach, *Psychodiagnostics*, Eng. trans., 4th ed. (1949); C. Spearman, *The Abilities of Man* (1927); E. K. Strong, Jr., *Vocational Interests of Men and Women* (1943); D. E. Super and J. O. Crites, *Appraising Vocational Fitness: By Means of Psychological Tests*, rev. ed. (1962); L. M. Terman et al., *Sex and Personality: Studies in Masculinity and Femininity* (1936); L. L. Thurstone, *The Vectors of Mind: Multiple-Factor Analysis for the Isolation of Primary Traits* (1935); P. E. Vernon, *The Measurement of Abilities*, 2nd ed. (1961), *Personality*

PSYCHOLOGICAL WARFARE

Assessment (1964); G. M. Whipple, *Manual of Mental and Physical Tests* (1910); C. Burt, *Mental and Scholastic Tests,* 4th ed. (1962); L. J. Cronbach and G. C. Gleser, *Psychological Tests and Personnel Decisions* (1957). (H. G. G.)

For a general survey of methods of attitude measurement *see* Allen L. Edwards, *Techniques of Attitude Scale Construction* (1957). For a more extensive treatment of psychological scaling and a useful bibliography of the field *see* Warren S. Torgerson, *Theory and Methods of Scaling* (1958); *see also* J. P. Guilford, *Psychometric Methods,* 2nd ed. (1954); R. D. Luce, R. R. Bush, and E. Galanter, *Handbook of Mathematical Psychology,* vol. i (1963); F. T. Juster, *Anticipations and Purchases* (1964); C. R. Wasson, *The Strategy of Marketing Research* (1964). (L. V. Jo.)

PSYCHOLOGICAL WARFARE consists of the use of propaganda against an enemy, together with such military, economic, or political measures as the propaganda may require. Though often looked upon as a modern invention, it is as old as history. The conquests of Genghis Khan were aided by expertly planted rumours about the large numbers of ferocious Mongol horsemen in the khan's army. False though they were, these rumours frightened the enemy. Centuries later, in the American

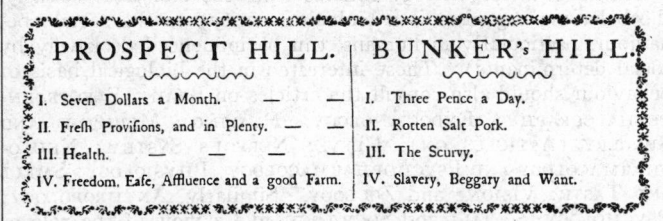

PROSPECT HILL.	BUNKER's HILL.
I. Seven Dollars a Month.	I. Three Pence a Day.
II. Fresh Provisions, and in Plenty.	II. Rotten Salt Pork.
III. Health.	III. The Scurvy.
IV. Freedom, Ease, Affluence and a good Farm.	IV. Slavery, Beggary and Want.

TACTICAL PROPAGANDA ISSUED BY THE COLONIAL COMMAND DURING THE BATTLES FOR BOSTON. LEAFLET IS AN INVITATION TO THE BRITISH TROOPS TO DESERT

Revolution, Thomas Paine's *Common Sense* was but one of many examples of pamphlets and leaflets used to strengthen the colonists' will to fight.

In its modern form, consisting of the application of mass communications techniques to strategy and warfare, psychological warfare differs from the military propaganda of the past in two ways: it is proportionately a larger ingredient of the whole process of war; and modern scientific advances in communications, such as high-speed printing and radio, together with important developments in the fields of public-opinion analysis and the prediction of mass behaviour, make psychological warfare more nearly manageable and predictable than techniques used in the past.

Within armies, psychological warfare includes the training and equipping of specialized units in peacetime armed forces and the application of these skills to military situations when action comes. It is most effective when the entire army knows of its availability and value. The short form of the term, psywar, spread through the U.S. armed forces after the Korean War. The kind of psywar understood by the armed forces is a far narrower and more specialized operation than that to which scholars, journalists, and politicians refer when they say "psychological warfare."

As armies practise it, psywar involves the use of printing presses, radio stations, and air-dropped leaflets in pursuing goals of modern warfare. The term is also used to describe the pseudo-psychiatric twisting of personality by techniques such as "brainwashing" ("thought reconstruction" is the official Chinese Communist term) or the psychopharmaceutical techniques reportedly used in the European Communist countries. In this sense, the United States has not engaged in "psychological warfare." The only U.S. effort in the field has been developing preventives and countermeasures as far as possible. (*See also* BRAINWASHING.)

Finally, psychological warfare is loosely and often improperly used to describe all the forms of power struggle between nations: the "cold war," the "chronic war," "protracted struggle" (in Mao Tse-tung's phrase), "extended strategy," and the like. This is too broad a use for the term to remain meaningful. Marshall Plan expenditures, Mutual Security weapons deliveries, technical-aid programs—all of these have a psychological effect on the many audiences which make up the international scene, but their primary purpose is not the manipulation of opinion.

Modern psychological warfare is neither better nor worse than other forms of struggle. Insofar as it does the least damage to the human body, compared with other weapons, while achieving what may be maximum results in terms of cost, psywar may be regarded as a "better" weapon. A dead enemy is of no use to one's own side or to mankind, and his death may be very costly to achieve, while a live, surrendered enemy is usually useful.

Most psychological warfare material is truthful. Truth is easier to document than falsehood, and it is infinitely superior to lies where consistency is concerned. Lies were used wholesale in World War I; it is a safe guess that they were used less in World War II. Lies continue to be used in military conflict, but they are useful only in exceptional cases. The truth presented in psywar is rarely the whole truth, and the degree of veracity varies with the different countries engaged. During World War II the United States practice of covert psychological warfare, which presumably would be reactivated in the event of future conflict, was the responsibility of the Office of Strategic Services (OSS), while overt psychological warfare was reserved to the Army and Navy and the Office of War Information (OWI).

Overt or white propaganda is that emanating from a known source, while covert or black propaganda is issued from a falsified source. The British "German" transmitter, Gustav Siegfried Eins, which pretended to be inside the Hitlerian *Reich,* is a good example of black propaganda. Many Germans thought for a while that it really was German. In contrast, transmissions of the Domei (Japanese) news service in clear newspaper English to the U.S. during 1941–45 were a good example of white propaganda. Though admittedly Japanese, the dispatches filled a lot of U.S. newspaper space and embarrassed the U.S. war effort.

Strategic and Tactical Levels.—Apart from communications media, psychological warfare is sometimes divided into levels which reflect the frame of space and time in which the military propaganda is expected to operate. Strategic psychological warfare is the term denoting mass communications directed to a very large audience or over a considerable degree of territory. An appeal to the enemy civilian population to hoard food in order to protect their families against privation would be strategic in character. Tactical psychological warfare usually implies a direct connection with combat operations; the most common form is the surrender demand, although on other occasions tactical psywar may merely ask the enemy to retreat, tell individual soldiers to seek cover, warn city populations of bombing raids, or instruct civilians on how to behave if an airborne force suddenly lands among them. Consolidation psywar consists of messages distributed to the rear of one's own advancing forces for the sake of protecting the line of communications, establishing military government and carrying out the governmental tasks of the commanding general.

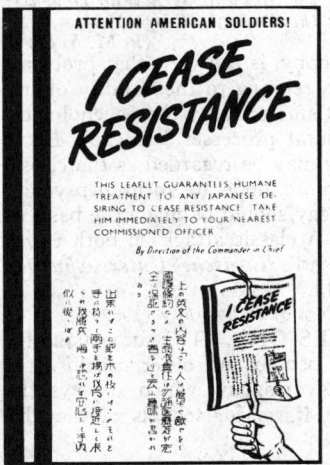

ATTENTION AMERICAN SOLDIERS!

I CEASE RESISTANCE

Surrender leaflet distributed to Japanese troops in the Philippines and other Pacific islands during World War II. The first version of the leaflet carried the words "I surrender," which so shocked the Japanese that they would not use it

The same levels of distinction are sometimes made by use of the criterion of "action response." If an armed force or government uses psywar to prepare an audience for an action to be taken at an indefinite later time, the propaganda is called strategic; if a specific action is called for, it is termed tactical. Continuation of the "cold war" and the threat of "multipolar politics" arising from the admission of a great number of new states to the UN and the community of nations have accented the importance of multinational psychological operations in support of strategic security.

Intelligence Functions.—Two separate but equally important intelligence functions always accompany professionally managed psychological warfare. The first and most obvious intelligence function consists of the analysis of one's own and the competing propagandas, together with the general flow of mass communications through the audience which is addressed. Sometimes particularly important decision-making parts of the audience, termed target groups, will be evaluated in detail. Who is reaching them and through what broadcasts or printed media? What do the audience members prefer? What do they repeat? The amount of communications in an enemy's propaganda to outsiders will often reveal his intentions; an enemy government's home broadcasts almost inevitably show what the enemy leaders think the opinions and problems of their own people are. This is called propaganda analysis; in military form, it is merely an adaptation of civilian methods of public-opinion analysis.

The second form of intelligence is no less important. It consists of audience information for the propagandist. The psywar operator cannot make effective use of persuasion unless he is given concrete details about his audience. In wartime much of this information comes through espionage channels and is therefore difficult to obtain. There is a natural conflict between espionage officials who wish to keep all incoming information secret and psywar officials who wish to use the realistic parts of it to strengthen their messages.

Media.—The communications media most commonly used in psychological warfare are the same as those used in civilian life; radio, newspapers, motion pictures, books, and magazines form a large part of the output. Leaflets are more widely used than they are in civilian life. (The World War II leaflet output of the Western Allies alone, excluding Russia, was at least 8,000,000,000 sheets.) Loud-speakers are often used in the front lines; both sides used them in the Korean fighting. The slow media are those in which a physical object must be transported to effect the communication: magazines, pamphlets, books, lecturers. The fast media are the telegraph and radio. The media used in a war usually reflect the capacity of the civilian economic system of each of the contestants. Whatever the medium, psywar can be successful only if it is credible, simple, and properly timed.

See also PROPAGANDA.

BIBLIOGRAPHY.—W. E. Daugherty and M. Janowitz (comps.), *A Psychological Warfare Casebook* (1958); M. L. De Fleur and O. N. Larsen, *The Flow of Information: an Experiment in Mass Communication* (1958); L. John Martin, *International Propaganda: Its Legal and Diplomatic Control* (1958); J. R. Mock and C. Larson, *Words That Won the War* (1939); P. Davidson, *Propaganda and the American Revolution* (1941); D. Lerner, *Sykewar* (1949), (ed.), *Propaganda in War and Crisis* (1951); C. A. H. Thomson, *Overseas Information Service of the United States Government* (1948); Elizabeth P. MacDonald, *Undercover Girl* (1947); Stewart Alsop and Thomas Braden, *Sub Rosa* (1946); S. K. Padover, *Experiment in Germany* (1946; pub. in England under title *Psychologist in Germany*); E. Hunter, *Brain-washing in Red China* (1951), *Brainwashing: the Story of Men Who Defied It* (1956); Otto Heilbrunn, *Warfare in the Enemy's Rear* (1964).

(P. M. A. L.)

PSYCHOLOGISM, in philosophy, is the view that problems of epistemology (that is, problems relating to the validity of human knowledge) can be solved satisfactorily by the psychological study of the development of mental processes. Locke's *Essay Concerning Human Understanding* may be regarded as the classic of psychologism in this sense. A more moderate form of psychologism maintains only that psychology should be made the basis of other studies, especially of logic. A classic attack on both forms of psychologism is Edmund Husserl's *Logische Untersuchungen* ("Logical Investigations," 1900–01).

See John Passmore, *A Hundred Years of Philosophy* (1957).

PSYCHOLOGY (ARTICLES ON). The subject matter of psychology—the behaviour of people and other organisms— receives a general overview in PSYCHOLOGY, which surveys the scope and methods of the science, its major schools of thought, and fields of specialization.

PSYCHOLOGY, HISTORY OF, traces the evolution of psychological theories beginning with those of the ancient Egyptians. Prior to the 19th century the content of psychology was predominantly philosophical and introspective. The radical shift to the experimental and behaviouristic emphasis of psychology is reflected in articles on BEHAVIOURISM; and PSYCHOLOGY, EXPERIMENTAL.

PSYCHOANALYSIS is devoted primarily to theory; however, the reader who seeks a fuller view of modern psychological theories should consult, in addition, articles on PSYCHOLOGY, ABNORMAL; ANIMAL BEHAVIOUR; EMOTION; GESTALT PSYCHOLOGY; INTELLIGENCE; LEARNING; MOTIVATION; PERCEPTION; PERSONALITY; PSYCHOLOGY, COMPARATIVE; and PSYCHOLOGY, PHYSIOLOGICAL, among others. Much, if not most, of the disagreement among workers in psychology is with respect to theory and interpretation rather than with respect to the facts about behaviour.

Differences in interpretation are greatest in those areas where generally acceptable empirical evidence is limited. For example, active disputes continued in the 1960s concerning the effectiveness of PSYCHOTHERAPY; in this field where rigorous research is difficult, the limited number of empirical studies available indicated that such techniques yield no better results among disturbed people than are observed to occur in the absence of formal treatment. Disagreements continued concerning the validity of reports of paranormal activities as described in PARAPSYCHOLOGY; PSYCHICAL RESEARCH; and SPIRITUALISM.

The range of psychology extends from the biological (clearly, the behaving organism is a biological entity) to the social (behaviour, particularly in humans, can be influenced decisively by social determinants). Those interested in the biological basis of behaviour should also consult the articles on BRAIN; ELECTROENCEPHALOGRAPHY; ENDOCRINOLOGY; HEARING; MEDICINE AND SURGERY (ARTICLES ON); NERVE; NERVOUS SYSTEM; NEUROPHARMACOLOGY AND PSYCHOPHARMACOLOGY; PHYSIOLOGY; SMELL AND TASTE; VISION; and ZOOLOGY. Similarly, ANTHROPOLOGY; PSYCHOLOGY, SOCIAL; and SOCIOLOGY give a view of the role of social factors in behaviour.

Many articles (for example, CHILD PSYCHOLOGY; CONDITIONING; DREAM AND DREAMING; FEELING, PSYCHOLOGY OF; PSYCHIATRY; SEXUAL BEHAVIOUR; THINKING AND PROBLEM SOLVING; UNCONSCIOUS) treat behaviour from both points of view because it is a function of interacting biological and social factors.

From its beginnings, scientific psychology has had strong interests in methodology and has developed a variety of techniques and apparatus for experimentation and analysis—on its own and by borrowing from other sciences. Some of the techniques and devices are primarily for laboratory use; others have been developed for the school situation, the clinic or hospital, and business and industry (EDUCATIONAL PSYCHOLOGY; PSYCHOLOGY, APPLIED; PSYCHOLOGICAL TESTS AND MEASUREMENTS; PSYCHOPHYSICAL METHODS; SPEECH AND LANGUAGE). Applied psychology is growing actively; new applications of basic psychological knowledge emerge continuously as techniques developed for laboratory use demonstrate practical utility (for example, PROGRAMMED LEARNING). The distinction between applied and pure science is often less clear and categorical in psychology than in some other fields. Thus, for example, analogies between electromechanical devices and living organisms as noted in CONTROL SYSTEMS; CYBERNETICS; and SERVOMECHANISM increasingly are attracting both theoretical and practical interest. (C. CE.)

PSYCHOLOGY is a behavioural science that has primary reference to human beings acting alone and in groups. As such it impinges upon several other fields. It is possible to isolate for study living units at the levels of cell, organ, individual, group, and society. Physiology and neurophysiology are concerned with the functioning of cells and organs. Sociology studies the structure and function of groups and societies. Anthropology deals with the multiple cultural adjustments humans make to varied environments. Biology, economics, political science, and, in part, history, philosophy, and theology all focus on problems related to those of psychology. While there are no clear-cut, universally accepted distinctions among the various disciplines, it can be said that the psychologist makes statements that describe behaviour in response to a variety of stimuli, turning to physiology and neurophysiology to demonstrate mechanisms by which the effects are produced. Also he deals with the individual mechanisms that underlie the group and social phenomena studied by the sociologist. In general, the psychologist is interested in the whole individual in his relation to his surroundings and himself. The question of whether psychology is a biological science or a social science has been a point of contention among some scholars. Depending on the major concerns of any given psychologist, the discipline has been classified in either way. In the 1960s, however, it was becoming increasingly common to hear psychology called a behavioural science. Not only are contemporary psychologists concerned with living beings; they also study the behaviour of such nonliving systems as electronic devices.

Because psychology is so inclusive, it necessarily encompasses numerous specialties. This diversity sometimes contributes to an appearance of disunity that is in turn increased by the lack of a theoretical structure acceptable to all psychologists. Thus there are clinical psychologists, experimental psychologists, physiological psychologists, comparative psychologists, industrial psychologists, and social psychologists, all of whom, after undergoing somewhat different training, follow separate specialties. The discipline finds unity, however, in a common interest in highly integrated organisms. It is difficult to discuss sensing without involving perceiving, perceiving separate from learning, learning without reasoning, or any of these processes apart from emotional and motivational aspects of behaviour. And it is difficult to isolate the organism from the external environment, where the immediate situation and past experiences are transparently significant.

Psychology began as a part of philosophy, and it was not until the late 19th century that it became a separate experimental science. A fundamental philosophical question is that of epistemology: What is the relation of experience to reality? The problem, recognized long before Plato, continues to arise in current discussions of consciousness. As their sciences developed, 19th-century physicists and physiologists became interested in whether psychological activities followed laws analogous to those describing, say, the behaviour of gases. Early experiments in psychophysics indicated a link between physiological and psychological activities. (*See* PSYCHOPHYSICAL METHODS; PSYCHOLOGY, HISTORY OF.)

"Pity poor psychology," it has been said. "First it lost its soul, then its mind, then consciousness, and now it's having trouble with behaviour." The lament is a summary statement of the way in which constructs that had served philosophers as explanatory concepts were successively discarded by some scientific psychologists as they moved from attempts to deal with the mind-body question, to consideration of conscious and unconscious processes, and finally to the insistence that behaviour alone is available for study by public science—that such constructs as "mind" either refer to non-existents or are irrelevant. In the second and third decades of the 20th century, behaviourism (*q.v.*) was embraced by many psychologists, especially in the U.S., who believed it would sweep away centuries of speculation and open the way for true science.

Behaviourism was challenged by Gestalt psychology (*q.v.*), a school which began in Austria and Germany and continued in the U.S. after Adolf Hitler rose to power. Gestaltists experimented with perceptual processes and emphasized the importance of the brain in organizing sensory data. They looked upon behaviour as taking place in a field of forces, and held that organized subjective experience is mirrored by a comparable isomorphic process in the brain. Modified forms of behaviouristic stimulus-response and Gestalt field theories still had proponents in the 1960s.

The historic concerns of philosophers with issues of human motivation, emotional behaviour, the bases of aesthetic choice, and ethical aspects of human nature are of major interest in scientific psychology. Sigmund Freud (*q.v.*) was not the first to note that many potent factors in human psychology operate below the level of awareness. (Socrates seems to have felt the same way.) However, Freud substantially influenced psychologists by developing a theory of unconscious determinants of behaviour and applying it to the care of psychologically disturbed people. Since the beginning of the 20th century Freud's work has had great scientific and cultural impact. *See* PSYCHOANALYSIS; UNCONSCIOUS.

THE METHODS OF PSYCHOLOGY

A few of the classical techniques in psychology can be listed here. These methods are in general similar to those of other sci-

ences, and frequently involve variables that are not available for direct manipulation and measurement. However, there are many observable activities that can be used to make inferences about psychological characteristics that defy direct measurement. While there seems to be no such physical entity as intelligence, for example, it is possible to measure the degree to which a person behaves intelligently in solving a number of problems (*see* INTELLIGENCE).

Statistical methods are among the most widely used tools in psychology. They permit masses of behavioural data to be studied efficiently and to be described succinctly. Such descriptive statistics as averages allow convenient comparison of different groups of individuals. Correlational statistics are used to describe relationships among psychological variables, as in assessing the efficiency of vocational interest test scores in predicting occupational success. The probability that psychological changes (*e.g.*, the effect of tranquilizing drugs on anxious patients) are significant rather than mere chance variations can be specified through statistical inference (*see* STATISTICS).

Direct observation with no effort made to control the behaviour under study is the simplest way to gather data. Careful noting of events taking place in a schoolroom, the keeping of a diary describing day-to-day changes in the behaviour of an infant, or the recording of group discussions are examples of this method.

The experimental method adds control over the observations and permits manipulation of behaviour. The method of co-twin control, for example, is used to distinguish genetic from environmental influences: identical twins raised apart may be studied to indicate what effects favourable and unfavourable environments have on measured intelligence. Foster children also have been used to study the problem, by comparing the child's performance on tests with those of his true parents and of the foster parents with whom he was raised. (*See* also PSYCHOLOGY, EXPERIMENTAL.)

Special apparatus is used to teach people or other animals to make discriminations—say between a black and a white card or a right and left turn—by reward or punishment. Variations in performance are produced by the systematic introduction of changes in the experimental situation. Various problem boxes and mazes have been devised for the study of such functions as learning and reasoning.

Some aspects of emotional behaviour can be observed precisely. Facial expressions and gestures can be photographed. The psychogalvanometer (*see* PSYCHOGALVANIC REFLEX) records electrical changes in the body under stress. Breathing rates, blood pressure, pulse rate, and other bodily functions alter with emotional change, and are sometimes used in lie detection (*see* INVESTIGATION, CRIMINAL).

The method of introspection is used to get some idea of the conscious experiences of others. In such studies the subject reports his experience verbally or by pressing a key or performing some other act. Efforts have been made to give some rigour to this method; *e.g.*, by averaging repeated introspective observations to diminish the effects of incidental fluctuations in awareness of stimuli. Questionnaires of various sorts have been used in an introspective approach to the study of attitudes. If the person wants to hide his feelings, he may give inaccurate answers. Or he may be unable to communicate his introspections accurately. His actual behaviour, also, may differ sharply from his indicated attitudes, as is likely to be true in such matters as race relations and family relationships. Despite such difficulties, introspective data are widely and profitably used; without them, the scope of scientific psychology would be sharply curtailed.

Interviews in which the subject is encouraged to talk at length about his attitudes, guided by questions from the interviewer, can yield more detailed information than simple questionnaires and are increasingly used in surveys of public opinion. Unless the sample of people in the survey is representative, serious errors in prediction can arise. Such mistakes, for instance, have been made in election forecasts (*see* PUBLIC OPINION).

The clinical interview is usually designed to learn about the maladjusted person or to help him express his feelings and understand them. Hypnosis (*q.v.*) can help the patient remember forgotten experiences or aid him in overcoming undesirable habits or attitudes. In the techniques of controlled association the patient is asked to say the first thing he thinks of in response to a question or stimulus word, or he may be instructed to say everything that he thinks of (free association) during the interview period.

Psychometric tests sample behaviour to permit comparison of individuals on a relatively standardized basis (see PSYCHOLOGICAL TESTS AND MEASUREMENTS). These may be objectively scored tests, designed to measure specific traits or abilities; or projective tests, consisting of pictures, ink blots, lists of words, sentences, or other stimuli, designed primarily to elicit emotional or attitudinal behaviour that the more restrictive objective tests may miss. These techniques are employed widely in the diagnosis of psychological disorders and as aids in guidance.

Stress interviews and tests employing real-life situations are used in selecting personnel for special military duties or industrial assignments. These techniques are designed to provide sufficient realism and to aid in predicting behaviour under difficult conditions.

Play materials are used with children as projective devices (for instance, to see how the child treats dolls representing family members) or to facilitate expression of emotional behaviour in the treatment of disturbed youngsters. In therapy through role playing patients of all ages play parts along with other actors, usually other patients. Commonly, the action proceeds extemporaneously. See PSYCHOTHERAPY.

THE CONTENT OF PSYCHOLOGY

Input Processes.—The world impinges upon us through such input processes as seeing, hearing, smelling, tasting, touching, and the sensing of vibration and temperature change. Bodily changes are reported by pain, muscle, and joint experiences and what has been called the sense of balance or equilibrium. Of these the earliest to be studied scientifically and the most thoroughly understood are visual processes and hearing. Stimuli reaching the appropriate sense receptors are transmitted by peripheral nerves to the central nervous system. The nature of the receptors and of the neural transmission seems to dictate which sort of energies will be sensed and which will not. Stimuli must be of sufficient intensity to cross the limen or threshold of a sensory system or else people will seem to be unaware of them. Dogs and some other species seem to hear high-pitched sounds beyond the range of human hearing. There is mounting evidence that for normal function, the nervous system needs a constant minimal sensory input; otherwise people will tend to hallucinate and exhibit other abnormal behaviour. (See SENSATION.)

Central Processes.—*The Central Nervous System.*—(See BRAIN; NERVE; NERVOUS SYSTEM; PSYCHOLOGY, COMPARATIVE.) More complex animals tend to have large brains in proportion to body size and show encephalization, a tendency for higher nervous centres to mediate functions controlled by lower centres in less complex species. In humans even those vegetative functions mediated by the spinal cord and more primitive portions of the brain are represented in the cortex. The histology and neuroanatomy of the nervous system have been studied in detail and the activity of many areas is partially understood. The brain is known to be incessantly active throughout life, even in sleep. However, the function of much of the brain, including the frontal lobes, is poorly understood. Studies of other animals as well as brain-injured and surgically treated people have located brain areas whose damage permanently impairs or destroys such processes as seeing or speaking. The neural bases for learning, reasoning, and perceiving are not clear, and the meaning of such factors as attending, willing, and decision-making in terms of brain activity awaits further study. Electronic computers have been viewed as models of brain mechanisms and clearly seem to mimic some brain functions (see CYBERNETICS; SERVOMECHANISM).

In the 1960s split-brain studies were attracting increasing attention. Humans and laboratory animals in whom the nerve fibres that normally connect the two halves of the brain have been severed behave as though they have two brains. The individual seems to learn, perceive, and remember as if he were two independent in-

dividuals that can alternate from moment to moment (depending on which brain hemisphere is being used). In such cases the left hand literally does not appear to know what the right hand is doing.

Perceiving.—The process of meaningfully organizing sense data is called perceiving. Retinal images change shape and size as a stimulus object moves. Colours change with light and shadow as backgrounds alter. The observer, however, perceives that the steadily enlarging image of a car means that it is approaching; that the yellow of a lemon remains the same in sunlight or shadow; that the square has four right angles even though its image on his curved retina has none. He is able to recognize familiar songs in any key (see PERCEPTION).

Learning.—The central process of learning has been a major concern of psychologists since the earliest days of the science. By the 1960s there existed a formidable bulk of experimental data upon which to build theory and to base further research. It continued to grow as rapidly as scientific journals could print papers on the problem. Experiments on memorizing nonsense syllables, published in 1885, were among the earliest of these studies. They demonstrated that such material is acquired in an orderly way that, when plotted graphically, results in regular curves. Learning of meaningful material can produce such curves under certain conditions, but the process is more complex, being affected by the difficulty of the task, familiarity with its content, attitudes toward its meaning, and other factors. Motor habits such as operating a typewriter are learned in similar regular fashion.

Increasingly it has been possible to specify conditions that facilitate or inhibit learning. Active participation of a subject in an experiment, for instance, produces more rapid learning than when he merely listens passively as the material is read to him repeatedly. Motivational factors, such as expectation of reward or fear of punishment, also operate to influence the rate of acquisition of new information. Situations that produce pleasure or prevent pain tend to be learned and retained while those that produce pain or prevent pleasure tend to be forgotten. Up to a point, increasing distraction operates to speed the rate of learning, but beyond that point the process is hampered. The set or attitude of the learner, his emotional reactions to the material, his motivations, social factors such as the presence and reactions of other learners, all affect the process (see LEARNING; CONDITIONING).

In some species a process known as imprinting takes place (see ANIMAL BEHAVIOUR) in which the first experiences have an immediate and lasting effect. It has been shown that a gosling will follow a human being who quacks at him during the first few minutes after hatching if the mother goose does not get there first. Thereafter the gosling will follow the human being in preference to the goose. According to some this effect is permanent, although this has been questioned by others.

In the 1960s it began to appear that in some species the effects of learning could be absorbed through the digestive tract. Untrained cannibalistic flatworms (*Planaria*) seemed to show the effects of training simply as a result of eating trained *Planaria*.

Remembering.—The retention of learned material was regarded classically as the maintenance of associations established in learning. However, as time passes the memory trace is modified. Experimenters have asked subjects to make successive drawings from memory of an outline picture of an owl. Typically such drawings progressively dropped out details, finally losing the characteristics of an owl and ending as the more familiar outline drawing of a cat. Apparently, remembering is subject to change as it is affected by prior experience and by later events. It had been found earlier that forgetting of nonsense syllables, like learning, followed a smooth curve—in this case a decay curve. Much research in remembering actually deals with forgetting. It has been found that to keep a conditioned response lively it must be reinforced from time to time. Also, extinction of the response can be hastened by presenting the conditioned stimulus without reward or punishment.

Events occurring after learning or conditioning can interfere with retention; this is called retroactive inhibition. Remembering is more efficient after sleep than after a comparable waking period, presumably because in sleep there are no interpolated tasks to inhibit remembering retroactively. Proactive inhibition also occurs, whereby later learning is prevented or altered by earlier events.

By hypnosis or free association people are able to remember long-forgotten events. It seems that in some way the brain retains impressions that are not always available to awareness (*see* MEMORY).

Problem-Solving.—Though thinking and reasoning are often held to be particularly characteristic of humans, the body of experimental material on them is relatively small and theory is primitive. About the turn of the 20th century the chief argument in this field centred around the question of whether thinking was characterized by a temporal chain of conscious images or could be carried on without such an association of images ("imageless thought").

Later controversy raged around the insistence that thinking is subvocal speaking; *i.e.*, minimal activity of the laryngeal muscles. Some held that the solution of problems proceeds by random trial and error, the scope of trials becoming more delimited gradually as partial solutions are achieved. Problem-solving by laboratory animals has been studied in various kinds of problem boxes in which the animal receives a reward for completing the task. Multiple-choice apparatus has also been used to observe human problem-solving.

The Gestalt school made other assertions about problem-solving, stressing the instantaneousness of a solution as the conceptual field is restructured. They pointed to the surprise with which subjects suddenly see the answer, calling this the "aha experience." In experiments with difficult problems for which answers were not immediately apparent, solutions were reached by one or more restructurings of the problem.

In ways somewhat similar to the problem-solving process, the central process of decision-making has been increasingly investigated. In some region of the nervous system, many inputs from the environment and from other parts of the body must be resolved in order to give rise to a single output, or a limited number of them. In neurophysiological terms, a final common path must be selected. This is decision-making, and it is being increasingly investigated with the assistance of a special branch of mathematics related to the statistics of probability (*see* GAMES, THEORY OF; THINKING AND PROBLEM SOLVING).

Emotional Activities.—The experiences commonly called fear, rage, sorrow, and love are central reactions that involve visceral and emergency mechanisms of the body (*see* EMOTION). The autonomic nervous system, which controls functions like respiration, digestion, circulation, and glandular secretion, mediates various states of excitement and preparedness for action which characterize emotional behaviour. Digestion may stop, heart and respiration rates increase, adrenaline be excreted into the blood stream, and the blood sugar content be increased. Measures of blood pressure, breathing rate, blood sugar, and the psychogalvanic skin response, among others, have been used in experiments as indicators of emotional states.

Continued emotional stress, conscious or unconscious, is believed to have a role in many psychosomatic diseases, although the mechanisms by which these effects are produced are poorly understood. Disturbances such as schizophrenia have a profound effect not only on cognitive processes but also on the emotional state of the patient, characteristically producing apathy. Manic-depressive psychosis results in either excited or depressed emotional states or cyclical alterations between the two.

Anxiety has been given many definitions and explanations by experimentalists and clinicians. It is most commonly considered a subjective state of apprehension about a potentially harmful input from the environment. Anxiety neuroses are moderately severe emotional disturbances that may be associated with sweating, trembling, palpitation, and other autonomic responses (*see* PSYCHOLOGY, ABNORMAL; PSYCHIATRY).

Personality.—In an effort to unify their findings under a single rubric, many psychologists like to use the word personality. Definitions of personality are legion; however, the fashionable tendency in the 1960s was to consider personality as some sort of unique and relatively enduring organization of an individual's characteristics (*see* PERSONALITY).

Output Processes.—The output of the organism, aside from secretions and excretions, is produced through the effector system of motor nerves and muscles. All responses from the reflex knee jerk to the most complex verbal communication are included. Work output has been investigated experimentally. Time and motion studies, studies of conditions favouring and interfering with working efficiency, studies of optimum length of work periods have become usual in industrial psychology. All concern aspects of motor output. The finger ergograph, a device that records the performance of the finger muscles in pulling a weight, has been used in research on fatigue. Other devices, such as treadmills, have been employed to study larger muscle action. The resulting work curves show a characteristic rise in output as the muscles first warm up and then a decline with fatigue. The effects of rest pauses, interpolated activity, various drugs, and different motivations have been studied by these means. Fatigue in industrial settings, however, depends upon more complex factors than the ability of muscles to do work. Boredom, the feeling of tiredness which may precede real fatigue, variations in motivation, changes in morale—all alter output. Change of task, even though the same muscles are still used, for instance, may result in improved output. The effects of distraction upon work are complicated. Some distracting sound seems to improve performance, but overly intense, prolonged, or unpleasant distraction, noise, or confusion reduces output significantly. (*See* PSYCHOLOGY, APPLIED.)

Speaking is another sort of output. The neural and muscular mechanisms of verbal behaviour, its efficiency, and pathology in such conditions as stuttering and aphasia are being increasingly investigated. Information theory (*q.v.*), derived from physics, is providing concepts and measuring units for research on communication among people and machines. Historically there has been a tendency to minimize the output activity of the organism, with primary emphasis on input and central processes. Much of the work in output processes is recent (*see* COMMUNICATION; SPEECH DISORDERS; PSYCHOLOGY, SOCIAL).

Developmental History.—The study of the development of organisms from the embryo to old age is called the longitudinal approach. Studies of human embryonic and infant motor development indicate that the earliest movements are uncoordinated, involving the whole body. Reflexes such as the sucking response and the Babinski sign (fanning upward of the toes when the sole of the foot is scratched) are present in human infants at birth. Controlled voluntary actions begin to develop within the first weeks of life, as the nervous system matures, proceeding in general from the head downward (*see* CHILD PSYCHOLOGY).

As the number of older people in the population increases, growing interest is being shown by psychologists in the process of aging. Although this surge of interest is a relatively recent development, the effort has begun to bear fruit. For example, reports in the 1960s indicated that ribonucleic acid (RNA), a substance prepared from proteins, acts to ameliorate memory deficit when administered to senile people (*see* GERONTOLOGY AND GERIATRICS).

See also references under "Psychology" in the Index.

BIBLIOGRAPHY.—E. G. Boring (ed.), *The Harvard List of Books in Psychology,* rev. ed. (1955), *Supplement* (1958); E. G. Boring, H. S. Langfeld and H. P. Weld (eds.), *Foundations of Psychology* (1948); L. Festinger and D. Katz (eds.), *Research Methods in the Behavioral Sciences* (1953); D. Krech and R. S. Crutchfield, *Elements of Psychology* (1958); J. B. Best, "Protopsychology," *Scientific American,* vol. 208 (1963); *Annual Review of Psychology* (1950 et seq.); M. S. Gazzaniga, "The Split Brain in Man," *Scientific American,* vol. 217 (Aug. 1967). (JA. G. M.; C. CE.)

PSYCHOLOGY, ABNORMAL, the study of morbid deviations from normal behaviour. Under the term behaviour is included such functions as motivation, perception (*qq.v.*), imagination, thinking, and memory (*q.v.*). Abnormal behaviour is classified under the psychoneuroses, psychoses, and psychosomatic disorders, the personality and sociopathic disorders, and the disturbances occurring in intoxications, brain damage, and brain disease.

The overwhelming and ever increasing evidence for the involvement of physiological factors in the development of abnormal behaviour is considered in many articles including ALCOHOLISM;

Cerebral Palsy; Delirium; Encephalitis; Epilepsy; Heredity; Hydrocephalus; Mental Deficiency; Psychology, Physiological; Speech Disorders; Stroke. The vast majority of psychologists in Great Britain and the United States have no medical training and yield to physicians whenever measures involving physical diagnosis, surgery, or drugs are involved in dealing with these disorders among human beings (*see* Diagnosis; Drug Addiction; Nervous System, Surgery of).

In considering abnormal behaviour among people, psychologists often work in close association with physicians, and tend to limit themselves to so-called psychological methods (*e.g.*, *see* Psychotherapy). In the face of their limitations, some psychologists are especially prone to stress those approaches to abnormal behaviour that require no competence in physical medicine, as do some physicians who are psychiatrists. Thus, much effort among specialists in abnormal psychology is directed toward understanding social-experiential-psychodynamic factors (*e.g.*, *see* Psychoanalysis). These considerations receive primary attention in the discussion to follow.

Certain basic phenomena, not in themselves pathological, are dealt with extensively in abnormal psychology because of the central role they play in abnormal behaviour. Among these are anxiety and the defense mechanisms used to control it; unconscious motivation and drives; conscious, preconscious, and unconscious processes; and the part played by frustration and conflict in precipitating and maintaining abnormal behaviour. In addition, it is customary to include the study of normal dreaming and hypnosis, as well as such normally occurring phenomena as hallucinations and delusions. Much attention has been focused upon the effects of extreme deprivation, found among concentration camp victims and hospitalized infants, and, under experimental conditions, among volunteer subjects isolated from normal sensory stimulation.

This article is organized as follows:

I. NORMAL AND ABNORMAL

A distinction between normal and abnormal behaviour is of considerable practical importance not only in psychology and medicine but in all studies of social interaction among individuals, groups, social classes, communities, and nations. Problems of communication, for example, are fundamental to all social interaction. These problems cannot be met effectively without knowledge of the distortions of perception, interpretation, and decision which personal factors introduce, many of them lying close to or within the borders of the psychopathological. The legal profession is beginning to revise some of its fundamental conceptions of crime,

responsibility, and punishment in the light of modern knowledge of normal and abnormal motivation.

Unfortunately, it is extremely difficult to work out a definition of normal behaviour that is generally acceptable—far more difficult than to define normal business conditions or normal weather. People typically tend to consider themselves as the standard of normality and to regard as signs of abnormality any actions, attitudes, or experiences of other people that differ markedly from their own. Such a criterion, however, is not always acceptable to others. Millions of people who are diagnosed as neurotic and psychotic may consider themselves normal; at any rate, everyone at some time or other acts or thinks a bit strangely.

An alternative is to judge each person's behaviour in relation to that of others in his community who are of the same sex, belong to the same age group, and live under similar socioeconomic conditions. To make such judgments a system of well-defined norms is needed with which any given sample of behaviour may be compared. However, obstacles to the use of rigidly specified behaviour norms include: the heterogeneous composition of contemporary industrial society; the increasing social mobility of individuals and groups, which increases cultural conflict; the rapid changes in accepted standards of behaviour; and the slow rate at which knowledge concerning human motivation has been assimilated into major social institutions.

Because of these difficulties, and the existing limitations in available techniques, a strict differentiation between normal and abnormal remains to be made. A rough working criterion of normality is the relative adequacy of a person's behaviour as judged in comparison with the behaviour of other persons who share his status in his society. Such a criterion is in some degree subjective; indeed, it is not unusual for authorities to disagree in their judgments of normality. However, it faces the fact of a relatively wide range of culturally acceptable behaviour.

It is important to recognize that, in this context, adequacy of behaviour is not necessarily the same as work efficiency or social conformity. Efficient work sometimes involves the compulsive exploitation of oneself or of others, and may stem from a deviant need to display personal power, to punish oneself, or to eliminate irresistible temptation by eliminating one's leisure. Likewise, social conformity is not always a sign of health. Sometimes it expresses extreme social timidity or fear of one's own antisocial impulses. In short, behavioural adequacy as a mark of relative normality must be viewed not only from the point of view of an outside observer but from the point of view of the behaver as well.

With this dual orientation, behaviour may be called abnormal under the following conditions: (1) if a person, otherwise in good health, shows himself incapable of establishing and maintaining mutually satisfying interpersonal relationships; (2) if his behaviour, including perception and thinking, is or becomes strikingly inappropriate in terms of prevailing social norms; (3) if, to carry on ordinary activities, a person is obliged to expend disproportionate effort, in comparison with others of his own age, physique, intelligence, and training; (4) if he is unable to obtain satisfaction from his activities, his memories, and his prospects; (5) if he experiences chronic lack of feeling, sense of isolation, or emotional instability; (6) if he suffers from high levels of tension, anxiety, or conflict for prolonged periods, or must defend against such suffering through pathological symptom formation.

It should be understood that relatively normal people are expected to exhibit some disturbance in sterile or stressful circumstances. For example, a person whose occupation is unchallenging or too demanding is expected to respond with dissatisfaction; refugees among people whose language they cannot speak, or individuals living with others who share few interests or values, typically experience anxiety or a sense of isolation. Thus, any criteria of abnormality (including those given above) must be applied with caution, giving full consideration to the situation in which the person is placed.

II. DEVELOPMENT OF ABNORMAL PSYCHOLOGY

Mankind has shown profound concern over abnormal behaviour from ancient times. Attempts to account for the phenomena of abnormal psychology have varied all the way from ascribing them to demoniac possession and loss of the mind or soul to blaming them upon hereditary taint and organic disease, usually of the brain but by no means invariably so. Galen, for example, ascribed hysteria to malfunction of the ovaries; the medieval philosophers related melancholia to an excess of black bile, which the word actually means.

Treatment through the ages has fluctuated irregularly over a correspondingly wide range, especially with respect to insanity. At one extreme are found drastic medical and surgical interventions; purging and bleeding were extensively used. At the other extreme are found the use of incantation and exhortation, of flogging and cold-water shock, and for centuries the use of capital punishment, as in the worldwide witch prosecutions.

The emotional origins of abnormal behaviour and the crucial part often played by interpersonal relationships have been implicitly or explicitly recognized for millenniums. But it remained for Franz Anton Mesmer (q.v.) to demonstrate, consistently and on a large scale, that emotional crises and pathological symptoms can be deliberately induced and cleared up through the influence of one person upon another. He thus ushered in the modern era of psychopathology.

Because of the tempest of controversy that followed Mesmer's activities, his methods were shunned by reputable persons, and for a long time his positive contributions were overlooked. A gradual revival of mesmerism, renamed hypnotism, developed during the middle third of the 19th century and led to a second public controversy. This time it was between J. M. Charcot (q.v.), the great neurologist in Paris, and H. Bernheim, professor of medicine in Nancy. Charcot maintained that only the potentially hysterical could be successfully hypnotized, while Bernheim insisted that anyone could be. Each was partly right; it is known today that most adults can be hypnotized, and that many hysterical symptoms can be hypnotically induced in apparently normal people. By far the most important outcome of this celebrated quarrel, however, was a greatly increased interest in the origins and characteristics of psychopathology. (See also HYPNOSIS; PSYCHIATRY.)

Pierre Janet (q.v.), who succeeded Charcot, began a series of contributions to abnormal psychology in 1889, devoting his attention first to obsessions and then to hysteria. His early writings have some of the germs of modern psychodynamics and his later clinical descriptions were brilliantly clear. The systems of diagnostic nomenclature used in abnormal psychology and psychiatry in the 1960s stem largely from the work of Emil Kraepelin (q.v.).

Sigmund Freud (q.v.) spent the year 1885 in Charcot's clinic while Janet was there, but he also looked into the other side of the controversy by visiting Bernheim in Nancy for a few months in 1889. He translated the writings of both Charcot and Bernheim into German soon after his visits. Unlike Mesmer, Freud shunned public controversy, worked with the utmost self-critical care, for many years almost in isolation, and met the condemnation of others largely by piling up considerable amounts of clinical evidence. Unlike Janet, he ranged over the whole field of psychopathology and invaded normal psychology as well, and his theoretical contributions were daring and revolutionary. In his *History of Experimental Psychology* (1950), E. G. Boring lists Freud as one of the "four very great men in psychology's history." Certainly no one else has influenced the development of abnormal psychology so profoundly and extensively as Freud. (For an evaluation of the related but divergent views of Alfred Adler, Erich Fromm, Karen Horney, Carl Jung, Otto Rank, and H. S. Sullivan, see R. L. Munroe, *Schools of Psychoanalytic Thought*, 1955.)

III. ORIGINS OF PSYCHOPATHOLOGICAL SYMPTOMS

A. EARLY CHILDHOOD

At birth the infant is separated physiologically from his mother, but for years he remains dependent upon her, or upon her substitute, for his very existence from day to day. His interrelationship with the mother figure is a most important factor in his earliest cycles of need and satisfaction, in his earliest experiences of security and anxiety, in the comforting and disturbing aspects of bodily care, in his development of love and hate, in what he learns to expect from the world around him and how he learns to handle it.

1. The Mother.—Even the child's differentiation of his own body from his surroundings, and of himself from other people, depends upon a healthy maturing of the mother-child relationship. At first the relationship is normally symbiotic, that is, one in which the mother and child form an interdependent unit, each individual being of great importance to the other. There is much clinical and observational evidence to suggest that the infant in a symbiotic relationship does not distinguish between his mother, or her substitute, and himself. He makes such a distinction slowly, over a long period, by means of the normal maturing and use of his equipment for independent action. Under ordinary conditions this process of growing independence and differentiation goes on progressively and at an accelerating rate, especially with the development of walking and talking.

Whatever interferes with the gradual evolution from a symbiotic relationship to one of eventual independence may lay the groundwork for abnormal behaviour later on. An obvious source of difficulty is a mother's inability to give up her child's dependence because of the personal satisfactions she derives from it or because of the anxiety aroused in her by the child's attempts at independent activity.

Such a mother is often called overprotective. Her protection may take the form of overindulgence, which tends to leave a child always infantile in what he expects and demands, even after he grows to adulthood; or it may take the form of domination, which prevents him from developing initiative and enterprise. In either case, he is likely to remain a dependent person, even in adulthood, either expecting privileged treatment without earning it, or looking continually for guidance and approval from everyone. Needless to say, the presence of a strong father and of siblings in the home can offset to a considerable degree the stunting effects of maternal overprotection.

A less obvious but no less fruitful source of difficulty lies in an unsatisfactory symbiotic relationship, particularly one which fails to foster infant trust. This may be the result of maternal coldness or resentment toward the child. It may come from mothering which is carried on with unusual tension and anxiety, or from mothering that is grossly inconsistent and unpredictable. It may also develop because the child has behavioural characteristics, whatever their cause, which make him an unwelcome or uneasy partner for his mother. Apparently if an infant for any reason cannot enjoy a satisfactory symbiotic relationship when he is helpless he may not later develop into a satisfactorily independent person, for if he does not experience a high degree of infant trust he will be less equipped later to experience the basic trust in others which is the foundation of normal emotional relationships. He is likely to grow into a lonely, emotionally withdrawn, or suspicious adult.

2. Identification.—One of the most important means whereby a growing child develops psychologically is called the process of identification. Unlike the simpler forms of learning and problem solving, this process involves idealizing the behaviour of other people on a large scale and becoming in some important respects like them. Early in life identification seems to be relatively massive, rapid, and indiscriminate, but also relatively unstable. It occurs in relation to members of the family with whom the child is in close contact. As time goes on identification grows less complete, slower, and more discriminating, as well as more stable. The child takes over certain aspects of the people around him and ignores or rejects other aspects (partial identifications). Eventually the process of identification leads to a recognizable patterning of child personality, and this patterning influences not only what the child is like but also the direction of his further identifications and therefore of his ultimate character structure.

It is a peculiarity of personality organization that the effects of early processes seem never to be wholly lost. The earliest wholesale identifications may be profoundly modified by later experience; and many shifts in the general direction of identifications may occur during maturation. But in a crisis some of the apparently lost infantile patterns may reappear; this reappearance is what is called regression. This is especially true of the deep and massive regressions seen among psychoses, but it is also responsible for many psychoneurotic symptoms in which regression is more limited in scope and less deep. Failure to establish adequate stable identifications, because of defective parental relationships or the absence of basic security, is held to be especially important in sociopathic personality disturbances.

3. Rivalry.—Rivalry is a very frequent element in family living. Living together means sharing; and sharing means giving something up as well as getting something. The birth of a sibling is an almost unfailing source of rivalry for a first child, and a common source for any child. Not only may it provoke anger and a sense of being unloved in the older one, but it also may lead him to retaliative aggressions which disturb the development of the younger one. Such retaliations at first may be quite open and direct, but in the face of parental disapproval they become disguised and indirect, although still effective. Most children survive the common experiences of rivalry without noticeable harm. The lives of many adults, however, are overshadowed by excessive competition, envy, and jealousy, or by reactive inability to compete and to be envious, which often seem to have their roots in unmastered sibling rivalry.

A small child's rivalry with one parent for the love of the other is potentially the most serious interpersonal conflict in early life. The mere intensity of his own feelings, and the tremendous size and power of his adversary, can conjure up a situation of unreal but frightening danger. And this kind of conflict is further complicated by the fact that, as a rule, the child also loves his rival parent and needs his rival's love. The eventual resolution of this problem is at best slow and painful. Out of it comes the mature form of the normal superego and a newfound freedom for the child to turn with self-confidence to active mastery of the world of people outside the home. Failure to resolve the conflict optimally can be found in a majority of persons showing abnormal behaviour.

4. Maturational Sequence.—A final point of importance is the factor of maturational sequences. Success in any phase of childhood development is in part dependent upon success in preceding phases. A boy, for example, who remains too long in a symbiotic relationship with his mother may lose early opportunities for handling rivalry with his siblings and for resolving rivalry with his father. He begins late, and with less than optimal freedom, to develop initiative in adapting to his environment and mastering its problems.

Moreover, a child who is insufficiently emancipated from close infantile ties with a parent is not free to take advantage of close friendships and group ties as these become available outside the home when he is six or seven. These relationships are critical for his development into a socially adequate person who is capable of mature emotional experience. A child who does not enjoy these maturing relationships will be poorly equipped to enter the turbulent period of adolescence and work out his self-identity in early adulthood. It must be said, however, that a good start does not guarantee freedom from serious difficulty in later emotional maturation; on the other hand, it is possible to overcome the handicaps of a bad start if a later phase of development provides unusually favourable conditions.

B. Development of Ego, Id, and Superego

On the basis of Freud's psychoanalytic theories it has sometimes been assumed that during early childhood certain groupings of psychological functions are differentiated into permanent, organized systems called ego, id, and superego.

1. Ego.—The earliest differentiation is held to be between id and ego. This differentiation begins with the infant's earliest exploration, through which he learns to distinguish between his own body and his surroundings. Ego functions may be considered as those involved in what is called reality contact.

The ego-adaptive functions, which come to include the maturing perceptual, motor, and glandular coordinations, lead to more and more effective performance in relation to the environment. The adaptive ego is said to become organized, during this process, in such a way as to make possible the complex kinds of interpersonal feeling, action, imagination, remembering, and thinking that characterize human beings. Most ego adaptations are held to function automatically and unconsciously in the mature adult. Processes of childhood identification, mentioned above, make indispensable contributions to ego organization. They lay the groundwork for the eventual internalization of culture and for the evolution of social attitudes, value orientations, role taking, and self-identity (*see* Ego).

2. Id.—The id is thought to involve primitive, loosely organized, and potentially disruptive psychological activities. Such impulses push forward constantly for immediate discharge or gratification, without regard for the demands of external reality. Id is completely unconscious in the adult. Its existence and its modes of operation are inferred from certain peculiarities appearing in preconscious and conscious activities, such as the puzzling characteristics of manifest dreams, of slips of the tongue and of wit, the nature of symptom formation in neuroses, and of delusion and hallucination in psychoses. Id activities perpetually tend toward immediate discharge or gratification, even during sleep.

3. Superego.—The superego is said to reach the climax of its differentiation from the ego during the third to fifth year of life. Its familiar conscious form is called conscience. This is experienced as a part of awareness that at times criticizes, reproaches, or condemns us, and at other times seems to approve, justify, or praise us. According to some theorists the personality has a permanent split at unconscious levels into an evaluating system, which praises or blames, comforts or threatens (superego), and an evaluated system which receives the praise, blame, comfort, or threat (ego).

The superego is considered largely unconscious. In normal adults it is held less responsive to current reality factors than is the ego. A great deal of superego activity is primitive and irrational; the system is believed to crystallize during the first three to five years, in relation to powerful infantile emotional conflicts and long before logic or realistic thinking evolve. Evidence of primitive superego magic is said to be seen in obsessive-compulsive symptoms. The clearest evidence for irrational, infantile superego function, however, is said by some theorists to appear in depression and in mania, the one expressing consciously the most cruel and hateful attitudes toward the self and the other expressing extravagantly unrealistic self-adulation and self-will.

The general effect of superego development is to increase psychological stability. In organizing such a system the child acquires his own internal moral control. He can regulate his own behaviour without having to watch his parents continually to see if he is right. He builds up his own standards and ideals which he can carry with him wherever he goes. The superego is also considered a potent source of conflict. Even unconscious fantasies are held to stimulate the superego to arouse unconscious guilt. This is said to be seen in the gnawing sense of inferiority that troubles many neurotics and in the fantasies which make up delusions and hallucinations.

4. Interdependence.—According to psychoanalytic theory impulses and fantasies derived from the id are modified and channeled by ego functions into realistic thought and action, into daydreams, make-believe, and recreation. Interaction with superego functioning is said to provide value orientations and moral qualities for action, thought, daydream, and play. The theory that most of the interaction among these systems is unconscious and preconscious reflects the idea that much human activity cannot be accounted for on the basis of strict conscious rationality, that it has meanings that are not realized at the time.

C. Conscious, Preconscious, and Unconscious

Among many psychologists three levels of activity are distinguished: conscious, preconscious, and unconscious. The conscious level includes whatever a person is aware of at a given moment and is said to constitute only a small fraction of mental activity.

1. Unconscious.—The unconscious theoretically includes all id activity, most of the ego-defensive organization, and the greater part of superego functioning. Its purest form is said to be in id activity; some evidence of unconscious id, ego, and superego functioning comes from the study of manifest dreams, with their related feelings, fantasies, and thoughts, which find expression during free association (*see* ASSOCIATION, MENTAL). Usually the person who is freely associating does not recognize the evidence of unconscious processes in what he is saying, but a person trained in observation often can appear to do so. Psychotic symptoms are sometimes interpreted as reflecting unconscious thinking and feeling more or less unchanged. Neurotic symptoms, on the other hand, are as a rule more realistically adaptive, so that their unconscious origins may be, and remain, obscure for a long time, even during intensive therapy.

2. Preconscious.—The simple form of preconscious consists of all mental activity which is not conscious at a given moment but can easily become conscious by a shift of attention. Its organization is presumably the same while it remains out of conscious awareness as when it becomes conscious. There are said to be other preconscious processes that can become conscious only with considerable effort. These include relatively well-organized daydreams whose material contradicts present reality and manifest dreams which, although they reflect unconscious processes, can be experienced consciously and can be described in words to someone else. It is impossible to make sharp distinctions among conscious, preconscious, and unconscious.

D. NEED, DRIVE, AND MOTIVATION

While it is generally agreed that need is a basic factor in determining behaviour, there is still confusion over the use of the term. Some experts, for example, speak of need and drive as though the two were synonymous, but most show a strong preference for one term and slight or neglect the other. There is actually a difference in emphasis involved. Need stresses what is wanted (*e.g.,* need for food, for love, for mother), whereas drive stresses an internal force or push which seeks an outlet. There is also some lack of agreement as to the number of basic needs or drives, which varies in psychological literature from one to a dozen.

Those who take a psychoanalytic approach to abnormal psychology show a preference for the concept of drive (also called instinct) as the most fundamental. This view may be summarized as follows: there are basic drives, sexual and aggressive, whose derivatives impinge upon the unconscious ego through activities of the id. In controlling, channeling, and discharging these drive derivatives, the ego develops its complex system of defense mechanisms which modify the drive derivatives before these reach the preconscious or emerge in consciousness. The ego at the same time develops adaptive organizations in relation to external reality and, later on, in relation to superego functions also. This ego organization of drives in relation to reality and the superego leads eventually to the formation of complex systems of motivation which have their own hierarchies; *e.g.,* a man's love of country may take precedence over love for his children, whereas a woman's love of her children may reign supreme.

The factor of unconscious motivation is of prime importance in abnormal psychology. As long as life goes reasonably well, it need not be of great significance that a person does not really know why he does many things or has certain fixed attitudes, that he sometimes feels pushed to do unreasonable things and avoids doing reasonable ones, or that his troubles seem always to follow the same general pattern no matter where he is. If, however, life goes badly, if a person's actions grow unmanageable or his satisfactions are overshadowed by anxiety, doubts, or gloom, the unconscious origins of his behaviour can become of major importance. It should be said, however, that contrary to a widely held public opinion, many psychotherapists do not try to make all unconscious motivation conscious to the patient. Often it is best kept unconscious. *See also* INSTINCT.

E. EGO DEFENSE AND ANXIETY

Most ego defenses are seen as related to the control of anxiety, which an adult may experience in two major forms. The more primitive form, called traumatic anxiety, is that of feeling in danger of imminent destruction. The less primitive, called signal anxiety, is in effect an anticipation of such danger, experienced in a much attenuated degree.

1. Traumatic Anxiety.—Traumatic anxiety is what an adult may experience when he is overwhelmed by a sudden catastrophe for which he is wholly unprepared. His response may be panic and headlong flight, a violent reckless assault, or a sudden trance state in which he wanders aimlessly about or becomes paralyzed and mute. Dramatic examples of such responses were reported from the battlefields of many wars; and in civilian life similarly violent and often maladaptive behaviour may be seen, for example, in theatre or school fires. Traumatic anxiety is especially common when flight and attack are both impossible, as when a soldier is isolated and pinned down in extreme danger by enemy fire.

Traumatic anxiety also is experienced when id derivatives break through ego defenses and threaten to disorganize ego function. This occurs in normal and neurotic persons during sleep if for any reason id derivatives threaten a breakthrough and produce a night terror from which the frightened sleeper is glad to awake. It also occurs in psychoses when a defective ego organization proves incapable of coping with direct id derivatives. Acute psychotic episodes sometimes include panic reactions like those seen on the battlefield and in fires.

2. Signal Anxiety.—Signal anxiety is a relatively mild experience of impending danger. If its source seems outside, the anxious person becomes vigilant, cautious, and defensive. If there seems to be no source, he feels uneasy, tense, and anxious without being able to understand why. In most neurotic and psychotic disturbances there is at least some feeling of an external source of anxiety. Much more commonly, however, the basis for the anxiety remains chiefly unconscious, and the threat comes from inner processes. The immediate automatic result is to increase ego defensive action, which also takes place at unconscious levels.

Increases and shifts in ego defense, as a result of signal anxiety, are assumed to occur automatically throughout the 24 hours of every normal person's daily life. What defensive pattern prevails at any moment, and what the commonest changes in ego defense shall be, depends upon the internal economy of the person, upon his personality structure, and upon the nature of the experienced threat. *See* DEFENSE MECHANISMS.

F. FRUSTRATION, REGRESSION, AND SYMPTOM FORMATION

1. Frustration.—Abnormalities of behaviour are usually precipitated by a series of frustrations. Frustration is experience of strong need accompanied by a sense of being prevented from satisfying it. What prevents satisfaction may be (1) an external obstacle—physical, social, or personal; (2) an internal conflict, conscious or unconscious; or (3) the absence of facilities for satisfaction, in the environment or in oneself. These factors of course can be understood only in relation to each individual person. Though some obstacles, conflicts, and lack of facilities affect everyone, even these affect different persons to different degrees. What seems an insuperable and intolerable obstacle to one person does not seem insuperable to another, or else does not seem especially important to him. Conflict and lack of facilities likewise are tolerated differently.

Additional variables are the strength of the drive and the character of the need involved. A frustrated powerful drive, especially one that is not successfully warded off by unconscious defenses, is more likely to precipitate a disturbance than a frustrated weak or well-defended one. Also, a need that involves too much physical, social, or psychological danger is almost sure to be frustrating, because each attempt to satisfy it will arouse intolerable anxiety. The closer one comes to its satisfaction the more intense the anxiety grows, and the less possible it becomes actually to achieve satisfaction.

Two of the commonest normal responses to frustration are aggression and withdrawal; *i.e.,* fight and flight. The aggression may be directed against the frustrating obstacle or it may be directed against a substitute, as when a person shouts at his child after he has been humiliated by his employer, whom he fears. The withdrawal may be in the form of physical retreat or merely of passive withdrawal of interest. This last is the most important in abnormal psychology, because it is the most likely to result in regressive fantasy and symptom formation.

2. Regression.—Passive withdrawal of interest is not in itself pathological. When a normal person is bored, or when he is in a relaxed state before going to sleep, he automatically loses interest and turns to daydreams and fantasies. These imaginings are usually less realistic than are his thoughts about what he plans to do or remembers doing when he is more alert. It is not difficult to demonstrate that unconscious processes play a large part in such normal daydreaming and fantasying. Anyone who examines his thoughts immediately after he has been deeply preoccupied or dozing will find some elements that certainly do not belong to his ordinary logical thinking.

This lowering of the level of functioning, from more to less realistic, is called regression. It is a movement away from logically ordered thought toward more primitive forms. An effective contact with reality and processes of logical thinking tends to prevent the appearance of such primitive functions, although these latter seem always to be potentially present.

During sleep dreams appear which are obviously regressive. They seem unintelligible afterward, and are a reflection of regressive unconscious logic. Wishes, fears, and conflicts that are expressed in dreams often surprise or shock the dreamer when he awakens and make him feel that he has been wandering in strange places with a different kind of reality and different moral codes. Nevertheless, it is usual for manifest dreams to exhibit some degree of superego function and ego defense, as well as to reflect raw id impulses and their fantasy derivatives.

3. Symptom Formation.—Symptom formation in neuroses is held to result from processes much like those resulting in a manifest dream, but the neurotic person withdraws a part of his interest in objective reality to escape frustration while he is awake, and not merely to enable him to go to sleep. In neuroses this withdrawal is never total as it is in sleeping and in some psychoses. A more or less effectual contact with external reality is always maintained. Likewise, regression is neither so sweeping nor so profound as that in normal dreaming and in psychoses. Usually a neurosis is precipitated not by one frustrating experience but by a long series of them, each leading to some withdrawal and partial regression. Eventually the succession of withdrawals and regressions leads to the reactivation of a primitive conflict whose origin lies in early childhood. This reactivated conflict now tends toward becoming conscious.

As in dreaming, so in neurotic symptom formation the superego and the unconscious ego defenses are believed active. The id impulses and derived fantasies, said to help make the reactivated conflict, do not erupt in their naked, primitive forms. They are subjected to defensive transformations more radical than most of those suffered by manifest dreams and, since the adaptive ego is wide awake and most of it attuned to external reality, the erupting impulses are subjected to further transformation until they harmonize more or less with reality. Thus a phobia based on an irrational childhood fear of one's father can be transmuted into an adult fear of dogs which the adult finds easy to rationalize and accept. It is only when, during therapy, a frightening father figure appears in a dream or free association reveals a still more direct relationship that the substitution may be suspected. (*See* also Neuroses.)

Symptom formation in psychoses is held similar to the process in neuroses. A major difference is that ego organization is fundamentally unstable. Defects in ego adaptation are theorized to stem largely from defective early identifications and from early interference with the development of reality testing and initiative. Defects in ego defense consist mainly in the overuse of such primitive defenses as denial, projection, and introjection in situations which normal persons would handle through repression. A succession of frustrations, or sometimes a single severe frustration, leads to massive withdrawal from reality and sweeping regression.

The functioning that emerges in psychosis typically involves delusions and hallucinations that seem to be attempts to rebuild external reality. The reconstructed reality seems made to correspond to primitive id, ego, and superego activities which have become conscious with relatively little defensive and adaptive transformation.

In this may be seen one respect in which a psychotic solution may be quite different from a neurotic one. Whereas the neurotic transforms his emerging conflicts adaptively, to make them conform as much as possible to external reality, the psychotic tends to transform reality, by delusion and hallucination, to make it conform to his emerging conflicts. The relative ineffectuality of ego defense and ego adaptation in psychoses renders it difficult to make an extensive transformation of unconscious material before it erupts into consciousness.

G. Individual Susceptibility

Sex differences, physiological age, and relative biological competence, especially of the brain, may all enter into determination of psychopathology. When it comes to individual differences in susceptibility, these physiological factors seem to be reflected in differences in frustration tolerance, in ego-adaptive and defensive development, in superego maturation, and in the adequacy of object relations and self-representation.

Wide variations in tolerating frustration are to be found not only in comparisons of one individual with others, but also in comparisons of the same person's tolerance level at different times and under varying conditions of stress. Moreover, one person may exhibit low general frustration tolerance (*i.e.*, he reacts maladaptively to almost any frustration) while another may exhibit low specific frustration tolerance (*i.e.*, he reacts maladaptively to some particular kind of precipitating factor but not to others). This multiple variability in frustration tolerance helps account for the great range found in both intensity and variety of precipitating factors in abnormal psychology.

Ego-adaptive and ego-defensive development are directly related to a person's ease of regression under stress, to the completeness of his regression, and to the depth to which his regression goes. In general, the more realistically a person has adapted to his social environment and the richer his psychological resources, the less likely he is to lose his grip on reality when frustration forces him into a withdrawal. The stronger and more mature his ego-defensive organization and the less it is dominated by denial, projection, and introjection, the less likely is regression to bring the sudden eruption of primitive processes. Thus, mildly defective repression and the ready use of projection may result in a neurotic phobia that is not at all disabling, whereas severely defective repression and the ready use of projection may lead to a paranoid psychosis.

Defective superego maturation goes hand in hand with defective ego development, but its effects are sometimes more striking. Thus, susceptibility to severe inferiority feelings, an unfailing indicator of superego pathology, often appears in persons who adapt well to reality in most important respects, even though with greater than average effort. Likewise, susceptibility to psychotic depressions often appears in adults who have managed to handle their lives responsibly and well. It is only when frustration becomes acutely intolerable and such a person grows seriously depressed that one infers how powerful a fixation in primitive superego functioning he has been hiding most of his life.

IV. ABNORMALITIES OF BEHAVIOUR

Abnormalities of behaviour have always been difficult to classify because, no matter how the diagnostic groupings of symptoms are defined, each actual case will exhibit symptoms belonging to more than one diagnostic category. A compulsive person may have a sudden phobia, or a phobic person may show minor compulsive trends. A schizophrenic may be subject to depressions and a depressed person may have brief periods of temporary disorganization. The most common procedure in classification is to determine what seem to be the dominant pathological characteristics, name the disorder accordingly, and bear in mind constantly that such naming is a convenience and not a final judgment.

The current official classifications are oriented primarily toward mental hospital diagnosis and statistical recording. Consequently, they stress heavily the illnesses characteristic of a mental hospital population rather than those most commonly seen in office consultation and therapy. Brain disorders and psychoses, for example, make up 50% of hospitalized illnesses, whereas the psychoneuroses make up less than 10%. In what follows, a few of the most typical varieties of abnormal behaviour encountered in the community outside mental hospitals will be described.

A. Neurotic Reactions

Four of the chief pathological reactions seen in neurosis are discussed fully in the article on neuroses, and hence will not be dealt with here. For anxiety reactions, phobic reactions, conversion reactions, and obsessive-compulsive reactions, *see* Neuroses: *Neurotic Reactions.*

A fifth type of common diagnosis is that of psychosomatic disorders, called also organ neuroses or somatization reactions. What all these names refer to is a variety of disorders in the functions of such body structures as internal organs, blood vessels, and glands. The disorders are either the direct product of continued emotional disturbance or at least an intensification of symptoms by emotional disturbance.

Recognition that internal organs, blood vessels, and glands are affected by strong emotion is by no means new, but the systematic study of their emotional disturbances, the field of psychosomatics, is relatively recent. So is the realization that many chronic organic disorders may have primarily an emotional origin and that structural changes may result from prolonged emotional stress. Among the disorders that have been most emphasized are stomach ulcer, colitis, vascular hypertension, aching in postural muscle systems and joints, allergies, asthma, and skin rashes.

To understand psychosomatic disorders it is necessary to bear in mind three things: (1) that emotional expression normally involves widespread changes in internal organs (*e.g.,* diarrhea or loss of appetite during fear), in blood vessels (*e.g.,* flushed face during anger or love), and in glands (*e.g.,* sweating and urinary hypersecretion in anxiety); (2) that intense emotional expression can continue for long periods of time with little relief; and (3) perhaps most important of all, that a person may be unaware most of the time that he is emotionally disturbed. He is most likely to concentrate on his somatic symptoms and to seek help on this basis; he may resent any mentalistic interpretation of them as an insult. Although dramatic and lasting improvement sometimes follows psychotherapy in psychosomatic disorders, the results may not be so gratifying if the disorder is of long standing. It should be added that sometimes a psychosomatic disorder can be the best defense against other symptomatology (*e.g.,* a stomach ulcer may substitute for a serious depression), and it is sometimes in the patient's best interest to avoid intensive psychotherapy.

There is considerable controversy as to whether or not psychosomatic disorders can be clearly differentiated from anxiety reactions and conversion reactions. A distinction between psychosomatic disorders and anxiety reactions is attempted on the grounds that the former focuses on one organ or one system in any given person, while in the latter most or all visceral systems are involved. As for conversion reactions, some diagnosticians stress perception and voluntary motor functions rather than internal organs, blood vessels, and glands. However, the position of psychosomatic disorders in relation to the psychoneuroses must be regarded as unsettled in the 1960s.

B. Psychoneuroses and Psychoses

Turning to a discussion of the psychoses, the question of their relationship to neuroses (psychoneuroses) arises. In the past this relationship was conceived in different ways. According to one view, psychoses are fundamentally different from psychoneuroses in origin and in dynamics. They are basically manifestations of brain defect or disease, or of disturbances in physiology or biochemistry, whereas psychoneuroses are products of personal stress. According to another view, psychoses are only graver manifestations of the same fundamental mentalistic processes as those underlying psychoneuroses. By the 1960s a growing number of psychologists were interpreting both types of abnormality as arising from the interaction of physiological and experiential elements.

C. Psychotic Reactions

1. Paranoid Reaction.—This illness is characterized by persistent delusions, usually persecutory but sometimes grandiose, without the presence of hallucinations. General behaviour and emotional response are consistent with the patient's ideas, and there is little or no impairment of intelligence aside from the delusions. Paranoia is a rare form of paranoid reaction in which there develops, slowly and progressively, a complex, intricate, and logically elaborated delusional system. The commoner paranoid state is not so highly systematized and elaborate, is sometimes of brief duration, and often ends in symptomatic recovery.

Paranoid states are most likely to arise in tense, insecure persons who are basically mistrustful of others and of themselves and who are ill at ease in interpersonal relationships. The paranoid illness is sometimes precipitated by a person's regressing in the face of serious frustration. Paranoid symptoms may also be seen in such infectious disorders as paresis (*see* Venereal Diseases: *Syphilis*).

In the common persecutory variety, the patient begins to see signs of aggression and evil intent in the actions of people around him. His vigilance grows in such a way that he becomes increasingly alert to further evidence that he is in personal danger. Regression has reduced the effectiveness of his reality testing to a point where he can accept only evidence that confirms his delusional suspicions. His need for an explanation leads him to believe that the signs of hostility he sees are part of a plot of which he is the focus. The more fixed this belief becomes the more difficult the patient is to treat.

The paranoid reaction illustrates clearly two defense mechanisms, denial and projection. When the patient regresses, his already defective repressive defenses become still more ineffectual, and he experiences a breakthrough of id derivatives, especially aggressive ones. To escape ego disintegration he denies and projects the impulses he can no longer repress, and he misperceives in other people (real ones and imagined ones) the aggressive intentions which are actually his own. His persecutory delusion is thus a reconstruction of his human environment in such a way that what actually threatens to destroy him from within seems to threaten him from without. It goes without saying that this achievement neither gets rid of the threat nor leads toward a happy solution. (*See also* Paranoid Reactions.)

2. Schizophrenic Reactions.—Schizophrenia, or dementia praecox, seems to include a number of psychotic disorders which have in common certain basic disturbances in reality relationships, thought processes, and emotional response. Delusions are commonly less well organized and more fantastic than in paranoid reactions, and hallucinations are usually present. Schizophrenic patients show a marked tendency to withdraw from contact with other people, to regress deeply and disorganize.

It is convenient to distinguish four general types of schizophrenia on the basis of symptomatology. (1) If delusions predominate, the condition is called paranoid schizophrenia. The delusions, characteristically vague and fantastic, may be of persecution, grandeur, magical influence, or body change. (2) If, instead, the patient's most prominent symptoms involve motility, the condition is termed catatonic schizophrenia. The catatonic patient postures, gestures, shows great excitement, or grows mute, motionless, and sometimes stuporous. (3) If the patient behaves in a silly, giggling way, with peculiar mannerisms and evidence of hallucination, the disorder is called hebephrenic schizophrenia. (4) If there is an insidious, progressive withdrawal and personality impoverishment, a general deterioration without dramatic symptomatology, the term used is simple schizophrenia. It must be emphasized that patients seldom correspond exclusively to one of these general types. There is much overlapping, and a patient may shift from one type of symptomatology to another.

Controversies over the origin and nature of schizophrenic reactions continued in the 1960s. Aside from evidence of a hereditary basis for these disorders, experiments with mescaline demonstrate that florid hallucinations and weird distortions of the body image resembling those reported by schizophrenics can be produced in normal adults. Lysergic acid and other toxic substances also result in the production of schizophreniclike symptomatology (*see* SCHIZOPHRENIA).

3. Affective Reactions.—This group is characterized primarily by a severe mood disorder, either depressive or elated, with disturbances in thought and general behaviour in keeping with the mood. Psychotic depressions are either agitated, in which case sustained tension, overactivity, despair, and apprehensive delusions predominate, or retarded, in which case the patient is slowed up, his activity is reduced, he is sad and dejected, and he suffers from self-depreciatory and self-condemnatory delusions. Suicidal attempts are common and often successful. Manic excitement is a circumscribed psychotic episode of elation or self-assertive aggression, usually with grandiose delusions.

Although most patients who suffer a depression do not ever develop a frank manic attack, and few with mania ever become frankly depressed, there is a close relationship between the two illnesses. While recovering from a depression, many patients go through a brief period of overoptimism and mild euphoria; and manic patients sometimes have transient episodes of gloom and self-depreciation. A minority of patients actually do pass from a depression into an elation, or vice versa, and some of these go through whole cycles of mania and depression. The current term, manic-depressive psychosis, is derived from *folie maniaco-mélancolique,* introduced in the 17th century.

Statistical studies tend to support the idea of a hereditary predisposition in affective disorders. Some have postulated a large-scale metabolic disturbance to account for the dramatic contrast between a slowed-up, retarded, depressed patient and an excited manic.

Significant environmental precipitating factors can be demonstrated in a great many affective reactions, but not in all. It is believed by some psychoanalytic theorists that a predisposition to affective psychoses lies in abnormal fixations at an immature, dependent level of development. This is thought to leave a person especially vulnerable to deep regression in adulthood, but not to the disorganization characteristic of schizophrenia. The controversy over the origins of affective reactions is far from settled. Its literature is much more sparse than that of schizophrenia.

4. Brain Disorders.—Many diagnosticians include under this head what may also be called toxic and organic psychoses. About 20 different varieties are distinguished. The commonest changes in mental function found in brain disorders are (1) impairment of intellectual abilities, memory, judgment, speech, perception, and orientation; (2) shallowness or instability of emotional response; and (3) alteration in general personality or character.

Brain injury, brain disease, and brain intoxication can result in such changes, either gradually or acutely. So also can general systemic disorders if they interfere with the supply of nourishment and oxygen to the brain or interfere with the removal of waste products. Only one type of brain disorder will be discussed here: that occurring in old age. In old age the brain gradually shrinks in size, certain types of cells disappear and the blood vessels harden. If the blood vessels suffer serious damage, the brain changes may be extensive and may come on suddenly.

Among persons with aging brains will be found all the basic characteristics of brain disorder. The aged person grows forgetful, and he unintentionally distorts what he does recall. He becomes unable to continue at his usual level of work, especially if it involves meeting new situations and making new judgments. He may grow confused about his surroundings, particularly at night and in strange places. He tends to become tearful easily, but he can often be cheered up quickly and even made to laugh through his tears. He may be easily annoyed and he may have temper tantrums. Sometimes striking changes in general character develop. Usually these are only exaggerations of previous personality traits, but occasionally they appear as something new. A kindly, considerate person grows selfish, harsh, and vindictive; a morally strict person becomes involved in antisocial activities; an

honest, reliable person steals, equivocates, or embezzles.

Much remains to be learned about the physiological correlates of abnormal behaviour. Some patients with widespread cellular destruction in the brain show relatively little behavioural deterioration or character change during life. Others with only moderate cellular destruction show considerable behaviour pathology.

In general, old people who live in a peaceful environment, where they experience reasonable satisfaction of their emotional needs, seem to suffer much less deterioration than those whose lives are frustrating, empty, or in turmoil. The patterns of functional change which develop with senility seem usually to correspond to the patient's previous personality, and to the structure of his social environment, as well as to his pattern of senile brain decay. Eventually, however, if the brain grows sufficiently incompetent as an organ, its owner will decline to a vegetative existence no matter what his present situation or his personality structure. (*See* also DEMENTIA.)

See PSYCHOSES; *see* also references under "Psychology, Abnormal" in the Index.

BIBLIOGRAPHY.—J. Hunt (ed.), *Personality and the Behavior Disorders* (1944); R. Grinker and J. Spiegel, *Men Under Stress* (1945); K. Menninger, *Human Mind,* 3rd ed. (1945); R. Hoskins, *Biology of Schizophrenia* (1946); N. Cameron, *Psychology of Behavior Disorders* (1947), *Personality Development and Psychopathology* (1964); G. Murphy, *Personality: a Biosocial Approach to Origins and Structure* (1947); N. Cameron and A. Magaret, *Behavior Pathology* (1951); O. J. Kaplan (ed.), *Mental Disorders in Later Life,* 2nd ed. (1956); S. Brody, *Patterns of Mothering* (1956); H. Selye, *Stress of Life* (1956); R. White, *The Abnormal Personality,* 2nd ed. (1956); J. Dewan and W. Spaulding, *Organic Psychoses* (1958); A. Hollingshead and F. Redlich, *Social Class and Mental Illness* (1958); S. Arieti *et al.* (eds.), *American Handbook of Psychiatry* (1959); W. Mayer-Gross *et al., Clinical Psychiatry,* 2nd ed. (1960); H. J. Eysenck (ed.), *Handbook of Abnormal Psychology* (1960); G. Kisker, *The Disorganized Personality* (1964). (N. A. CN.)

PSYCHOLOGY, APPLIED, describes the use of the findings and methods of scientific psychology in solving practical problems of human behaviour. A more precise definition is impossible because the activities of applied psychology range from laboratory experimentation through field studies of specific utility to direct services to troubled persons. Its practice is not fully controlled by professional or legal methods; there is a zone in which charlatans operate for personal gain. The intelligent layman's major protection against fraudulent practitioners lies in his general knowledge of psychology and in investigating the qualifications of the psychologist whose help he seeks.

This article, which attempts to make reference to all the major areas of applied psychology excluding educational psychology (*q.v.*), is organized as follows:

I. THE FIELD

Psychology deals with the origin, development, and modification of behaviour. The systematic study of psychology includes genetic and physiological bases of behaviour; the social and cultural setting in which behaviour occurs; learning theory and the modification of behaviour via learning; personality theory and the motivational forces producing normal and abnormal behaviour; measurement theory and methods for the quantification of behaviour; experimental and statistical methods for the assessment and prediction of behaviour under defined conditions. The applied psychologist is trained first in these areas of knowledge and in specific techniques; to them is added a period of specialized research or apprenticeship in the area of his particular interest.

A. History

The same intellectual streams whose confluence produced psychology as an independent subject in the latter part of the 19th century led to the later development of an applied psychology. Philosophy, physiology, evolutionary theory, naturalism, and measurement concepts borrowed from the natural sciences contributed to the new discipline. Self-analysis and introspection, as a basis for speculation about human activity, gave way to controlled observation and study. In Germany, England, and France these ideas took shape in laboratories, technical journals, and books. (*See* PSYCHOLOGY, HISTORY OF.)

1. Early History.—Francis Galton's publication in 1883 of *Inquiries Into Human Faculty* foreshadowed the measurement of individual differences. In 1896 Lightner Witmer established at the University of Pennsylvania, Philadelphia, a clinic that was a forerunner of clinical psychology. Intelligence testing began with the work of Alfred Binet and Théodore Simon in the Paris schools; the publication of their classic scale for intelligence in 1905 was followed in 1908 by H. H. Goddard's translation of the French mental age scales and in 1916 by the U.S. standardization of the Stanford-Binet scale by Lewis M. Terman and his associates. In France in 1905 J. M. Lahy was studying the abilities required for typewriting and street-car driving. In Britain work with group tests was started in 1911 by the London County Council Education Authority. *On the Witness Stand* (1908) and *Psychology and Industrial Efficiency* (1913) by Hugo Münsterberg extended psychology into two additional areas of application. Sigmund Freud's writings gave major new insights into human motivation (*see* PSYCHOANALYSIS). William McDougall's ideas about instincts and sentiments aided the understanding of human behaviour. In Britain Cyril Burt, then W. Boyd and J. Drever applied psychology to the problems of delinquency. In 1913–14 E. L. Thorndike published his *Educational Psychology*. At the Carnegie Institute of Technology a division of applied psychology was established as a teaching and research department in 1915 by Walter V. Bingham. The *Journal of Applied Psychology* appeared in 1917 along with the first applied psychology text, by H. L. Hollingsworth and A. T. Poffenberger.

During World War I psychologists in the U.S., Britain, France, Germany, and Italy developed tests for such things as night vision, and for the selection of pilots, drivers, and telegraphers. In the U.S. Army, more than 2,000,000 men were tested and classified for military service by the Army Alpha test battery. In the period 1919 through 1921 four applied psychology organizations independent of universities were established: the Scott Company (U.S.), founded by Walter Dill Scott; the Psychological Corporation (U.S.), founded by J. McKeen Cattell; the National Institute of Industrial Psychology (Great Britain), established by C. S. Myers; and the Personnel Research Federation (U.S.), directed by Bingham.

Between World Wars I and II the basic findings of general psychology and the special techniques of practitioners came to be applied in courts, clinics, and hospitals, classrooms, libraries, and museums, factories and offices, social service agencies, and government bureaus. Even the great depression of the 1930s was a period of expanding activities; vocational counseling was extended to the unemployed, buying habits of the public were analyzed and opinion polling became an aid to government policy formulation.

2. World War II Period.—Many problems related to the war involved the understanding, prediction, and management of human behaviour. To select and assign persons for military duty, psychologists devised or adapted tests to aid in efficient and rapid classification. Since learning time was short, psychologists worked on problems of efficient and rapid learning at all levels of military training. With manpower in short supply, persons judged to be illiterate or undereducated had to be brought to a minimum level of literacy; psychologists worked with such groups. At the point of induction, those whose personalities would probably break under the strain of military service had to be screened out; psychologists worked with medical specialists in devising more effective screening methods.

Polling methods were developed for evaluating the morale and attitudes of military personnel; psychologists were members of research teams working on studies of stress, as in flight, submarine, espionage, and combat operations, to determine which persons might best be assigned to these functions and what stress conditions would create dangerous decrements in human functioning. As new machines of war were developed, psychologists studied man-machine relations to increase speed of training, increase equipment effectiveness, and simplify and improve the design of military equipment.

As the number of physical and psychological casualties of war increased, rehabilitation and reassignment to limited duty became problems to which psychologists—as clinicians, as rehabilitation specialists, and as co-workers with specialists concerned with restoration of lost bodily function—turned their attention. Leadership, group effectiveness, and survival under stress were major concerns, and psychologists conducted field studies of leadership, morale, and combat operations. In cases of military discipline and delinquency, the methods of clinical psychology, counseling, and rehabilitation of offenders were employed in corrective programs.

In civilian life, psychologists concerned themselves with methods for war bond sales; assisted in developing child-care and day-care centres for families temporarily disrupted by civilian employment or military service; helped with the evacuation of children, and studied the effects of air raids; and concerned themselves with spread of rumour, use of propaganda and psychological warfare, and collecting intelligence data. With the end of the war, civilian readjustment and veterans' benefit programs required great increases in clinical and counseling services, and government training programs for specialists in these fields of applied psychology were established. The political climate of the postwar years required continuation of applied psychological research and services and accounted in part for the rapid growth of many fields of psychology. Both in the United States and in Britain, for example, each of the military services maintained specialist groups of psychologists, and each supported both contract and in-service research programs on a wide range of military problems related to human behaviour.

3. After World War II.—Many of the trends in applied psychology were accentuated by the demands of the space age. Educational psychology is applied to the task of early identification and discovery of talented persons as it has become recognized that trained intelligence is an important national resource. Such activities are linked with the work of counseling psychologists, who seek to help persons clarify and attain educational, vocational, and personal goals. Counseling services sponsored by U.S. government agencies, social service organizations, schools and colleges, and offered by private practitioners are available. Concern for the optimum utilization of human resources also has increased the importance of industrial psychology in business and industrial organizations. The aviation industry and the various space agencies and organizations have been important factors in the rapid development of the field of engineering psychology; as machines and engineering systems have grown in complexity it has been necessary to study man-machine relationships. In response to society's concern for treatment of the mentally ill and for preventive measures against mental illness, clinical psychology has shown the greatest absolute growth rate within psychology; it also has produced some of applied psychology's major professional problems, involving as it does relations with older medical specialties. The application of automation is being studied by psychologists, and in the developing countries psychologists are being used to help with the problems of rapid industrialization and manpower planning.

B. Applied Psychology as a Profession

Until about 1940 the majority of psychologists held academic appointments, but after World War II there was a great increase in the number of psychologists engaged in work outside institutions of higher education. Support for such activities, including research, came from the military services, government agencies, and business and industry.

In the United States, where this development was most marked, the American Psychological Association was active in developing a code of ethics for practitioners, examining relationships with other professions, and supporting through consultation the licensing or certification of psychologists in many states. In 1947 the American Board of Examiners in Professional Psychology was independently incorporated to grant diplomas representing special competence to experienced psychologists in the clinical, counseling, and industrial fields; by the 1960s the number of diplomates exceeded 1,600, and continued to grow. Great Britain, with an early emphasis on educational and industrial psychology, was a leader in engineering psychology and in applied social psychology in industry. Australia and New Zealand were particularly active in industrial psychology, as were the Scandinavian countries. Counseling received much attention in India and Japan as well as in France, which was particularly important in the historical development of clinical psychology. Industrial and educational applications were characteristic of German psychology. (A. H. Br.)

II. PSYCHOLOGY AS APPLIED TO TREATMENT

A. Clinical Psychology

Clinical psychology is concerned with the assessment and alleviation of the problems of persons who are defective or emotionally ill. It can be understood properly in any one of three ways: as a type of personal service performed by psychologists; as a professional subgroup of psychologists having commonly recognized and self-imposed standards of training and practice together with sanctions designed to ensure compliance with those standards; or as a special area of scholarship within the main body of psychological knowledge.

1. History.—Clinical psychology emerged at the beginning of the 20th century with the establishment of individualized treatment programs for disturbed or handicapped children. At first the emphasis was upon sensory handicaps and basic defects in muscular skills. The clinic established by Witmer in 1896 had such an emphasis and, moreover, it dealt with children whose problems arose primarily in school.

The practice of clinical psychology in hospitals and in collaboration with physicians dates also from the turn of the century. A psychological "laboratory" was established by Shepherd Ivory Franz at the McLean Hospital in Waverley, Mass., in 1904 and was continued under Frederic Lyman Wells. In 1909 William Healy, a physician, founded the Juvenile Psychopathic Institute—later the Institute for Juvenile Research—in Chicago. At the beginning Healy, a psychiatrist who also had had psychological training under William James at Harvard, and Grace M. Fernald, a psychologist, constituted the entire professional staff. Clinical psychology as

practised in the tradition established by these two ventures has been characterized both by its mutually supportive collaboration with advanced medical practice and by its attention to the so-called dynamic or motivational factors in the human personality.

Another current in the stream of clinical psychology started with the publication of the first successful intelligence scale by Binet and its subsequent adaptations by Goddard and Terman. Through these events the practice of clinical psychology came to be characterized by the use of relatively objective measures of psychological functions with, nonetheless, continued emphasis on dealing with troubled persons one at a time and taking into account those personal factors still requiring, in large measure, the psychologist's judgment.

At the beginning of World War II there were between 400 and 600 trained clinical psychologists in the United States. In other countries, except for the fact that the numbers are disproportionately smaller, the figure is difficult to estimate, primarily because in other countries the clinical psychologist is more difficult to identify. By 1943 the armed services of the United States were employing 1,500 persons as psychologists, a third of them in assignments that might be called clinical; a large proportion of these persons, however, had had inadequate training. At the end of the war the U.S. Veterans Administration adopted a policy of employing clinical psychologists in all its hospitals and clinics; the U.S. Public Health Service and the various state mental health authorities moved in a similar direction; and child guidance clinics, as well as public and private schools, created new positions. By 1964 clinical psychologists in the United States numbered more than 7,000. In Great Britain most clinical psychologists are employed in the National Health Service; in 1964 there were 356 established posts.

In addition to the types of positions mentioned above, there are also places for clinical psychologists in industry, where some specialize in services to emotionally disturbed employees and others in services for managerial officials who need psychological consultation to help them cope with work stresses and interpersonal problems. Other clinical psychologists serve the courts in assessing psychological factors that bear upon judicial decisions; others serve prisons; some are employed by the armed services; and some teach. Many, in all types of positions, are engaged in research. A small proportion are in private practice.

2. Activities.—Clinical psychologists generally classify their essential activities under three headings: psychodiagnosis, psychotherapy, and research. In psychodiagnosis emphasis is placed on skill in the administration and interpretation of psychological tests, particularly those administered to one person at a time. Such tests are described in the article Psychological Tests and Measurements. Less formal diagnostic procedures also are employed, including the psychodiagnostic interview. In psychotherapy a variety of methods is used (see Psychotherapy). Research generally is considered to be a further obligation for the clinical psychologist, but it is often crowded out of his schedule; in some cases, where research is undertaken as a primary service to the client, it continues to be, because of the skills employed, a clinical service.

A considerable number of clinical psychologists perform their services in hospitals and clinics. The patterns of collaboration between clinical psychologists and their colleagues in medicine and social work vary greatly among such institutions. The variations are most marked with respect to psychotherapy; some institutions assign most psychotherapeutic duties, particularly work in behaviour therapy, to clinical psychologists, others to psychiatrists only. Institutional collaboration with pediatricians follows a more regular pattern, the clinical psychologist being more likely to be held responsible for services requiring his clinical skills.

3. Professional Aspects.—Clinical psychology gradually is assuming organized responsibility for its own standards of training and practice. This development was considerably delayed because of the conviction, widespread among psychologists, that the sanctions and restraints of a profession are antithetical to liberal scholarship and that they would impede the advancement of psychology as a science. Because of the threat of restrictions im-

posed from organized psychiatry, however, clinical psychologists were reluctantly joined by their colleagues in an effort to establish standards of training and practice and to provide legal refuge for the continuing development of psychology as a whole. Thus U.S. psychology, and especially clinical psychology, sought to achieve a body that was at once both science and profession.

In Britain the development of clinical psychology is less formal, and this is enabling the psychologist to extend his work to many departments in general hospitals as well as in mental hospitals, especially in the field of rehabilitation.

4. Training.—The pattern of training for clinical psychologists in the United States was established by a committee headed by David Shakow during the 1930s. A broad training in psychology as a science and in related disciplines, as well as demonstration of research competence, was recommended for the doctor of philosophy degree, to which were to be added practicum courses and a fourth year of graduate training to allow time for internship in an interdisciplinary setting.

The American Psychological Association, through its Education and Training Board, annually identifies universities and internship agencies that meet its standards. The American Board of Examiners in Professional Psychology certifies selected advanced specialists in psychological practice, including clinical psychologists, after examination. As a general guide to the practice of professional psychology the association developed a code of ethical standards, which was accepted by its membership and is used as a basis for disciplinary action against those who fail to conform.
(G. A. KE.)

In Great Britain the training of clinical psychologists takes place either in departments of psychology in universities, where diplomas are awarded, usually after two years post-graduate training, or as in-service training for three years in a mental hospital under the direction of a senior psychologist. Regional in-service training schemes have been developed to give trainees experience with different types of patients, problems, and treatments.

B. COUNSELING

In psychological counseling a psychologist participates in interviews with a client for the purpose of increasing the client's level of personal integration. This definition emphasizes (1) that treatment proceeds through communication; (2) that the motives and personality structure of the client are the focus of interest; and (3) that the help offered is nonspecific. This latter means essentially that total personality organization is considered. Such issues as marital, sexual, job, and educational problems and symptoms are not the main concern of the counselor, although they may be resolved as part of the counseling process. Influence rather than guidance is the aim; adjustment of the client, in the sense of fitting in or of conforming to the environment, is not a goal of the counselor.

1. History and Philosophy.—Before 1940 the goal of the counselor would have been to help his client to find some educational or occupational environment conceived to be optimal. The main function of the counselor was to assess personal and environmental possibilities so that the client might make reasonably realistic educational and vocational decisions.

Counseling psychology has its roots in two distinct traditions, both established at the turn of the century. The first is that of mental testing, the second that of vocational guidance (*see* below), as influenced by Frank Parsons and others, with emphasis on matching person and environment. Originally interests, aptitudes, and abilities were given great weight in the counselor assessment of the client. Later, after intelligence tests and personality inventories had been found useful in World War I, the assessment came increasingly to be based upon the results of mental tests and psychometric methods. Since psychometric methods required considerable sophistication in the psychology of individual differences and statistics, the professionalization of counseling began under the influence of the mental test movement.

During the period between World Wars I and II great emphasis was placed upon quantitative assessment of the person and also of his educational and occupational environment. If the client was too maladjusted to discuss and make decisions rationally, he was referred to a psychotherapist; the counselor's client was supposed to have vocational and educational problems only through misinformation or lack of information.

World War II brought to the attention of counselors the notions of personality structure and dynamics. In 1942 Carl R. Rogers published *Counseling and Psychotherapy*, in which he stressed the counseling process rather than diagnosis and assessment; he brought together the traditions of counseling, guidance, and psychotherapy.

2. Activities.—While Rogers' recommendations with regard to treatment deeply influenced professional practice in many ways, his emphasis upon personality development and psychological growth processes was even more influential. The great difference in emphasis can be seen by comparing a textbook such as E. G. Williamson and J. G. Darley's *Student Personnel Work* (1937) with E. S. Bordin's *Psychological Counseling* (1955) or with J. Hadley's *Clinical and Counseling Psychology* (1958). In the first text "psychotherapy" does not appear in the index; in the latter two counseling and psychotherapy are used as virtual synonyms, the distinction being one of degree only. The tendency to identify counseling with psychotherapy, however, is not so significant as the tendency to think of counseling and psychotherapeutic processes in terms of the general psychology of behaviour. Whereas formerly counseling and psychotherapy were discussed in, for example, the specialized terms of individual differences, mental test theory, and psychoanalysis, there has come to be a distinct tendency to relate them to the general psychology of learning, behaviour, and perception.

3. Counseling and Psychotherapy.—In focusing on the modification of personality, the psychological counselor approaches the field of the psychotherapist. Are there useful differentiations to be made between counseling and psychotherapy? With regard to the psychological processes involved the answer is probably no; they are identical. Counseling and psychotherapy are indistinguishable with respect to their primary goal: modification of personal organization in the direction of increased personality integration. Psychological counselors usually assume more of a distributive function. Assessment of aptitudes, abilities, and interests in relation to educational and vocational goals occurs much more often in the counseling than in the psychotherapeutic situation.

Besides the difference in approach, psychotherapists and counselors serve a somewhat different clientele, although there is a very large overlap. Psychiatrists and psychotherapists, by custom and often by law, tend to serve persons whose lack of personal integration is severe enough to be incapacitating or to render them dangerous to themselves or others. Counseling psychologists seldom work with persons so severely ill; when they do so, they conventionally place themselves under medical supervision. In sum, the distinction between counseling and psychotherapy is essentially one of degree, not of kind.

4. Professional Aspects.—In the United States the trends discussed have resulted in an increase in professionalization, and with this has come an increased demand that psychological counselors have the Ph.D. degree and increased emphasis within graduate training programs on the psychotherapeutic aspects of the counseling process and upon mastery of projective psychology and projective tests. In other countries, counseling is yet to be regarded as a distinct profession. However, it is becoming clear that the trends on the American side of the Atlantic are having some effect on the European side. In Japan a deep interest in psychoanalysis, Rogerian psychotherapy, and counseling has developed. The Japanese seem not to make the intellectually arbitrary distinctions forced upon Americans by their history; consequently interaction and mutual influence among counselors, clinical psychologists, and psychotherapists is possible and evident to a degree not realized in the United States and Europe. *See* also PSYCHOTHERAPY.
(J. M. BU.)

III. INDUSTRIAL PSYCHOLOGY

Industrial psychology is concerned with the utilization and conservation of industry's human resources. This is accomplished by the study of people at work and by the development and application of principles designed (1) to increase production; (2) to promote individual satisfaction and adjustment; and (3) to establish a basis for harmonious relations between management and workers.

The application of psychology to occupational problems in the defense services, in prisons, and of school children has encouraged in Great Britain the use of the wider term occupational psychology. The British approach regards occupational psychology as a unity, although it is convenient to subdivide the subject, and this has been shown to be useful in ensuring that mistakes are not made in detecting the causes of manpower difficulties. The distinction is also made in Great Britain between occupational psychology as a science and as a technology. As a science, occupational psychology attempts to provide a precise and comprehensive description and explanation of human behaviour, based where possible on theories; as a technology it is concerned with the effective use of manpower and individual satisfaction with work.

Emphasis on human welfare is to be found in the first detailed program of industrial psychology as formulated in 1913 by Münsterberg, then serving as director of the Psychological Laboratory at Harvard University. In Great Britain the Health of Munition Workers Committee, organized in 1915, and later the National Institute of Industrial Psychology also based research and practice on the view that it is necessary to give the worker greater psychophysical ease at work, as well as to raise output.

A. Vocational Guidance

Vocational guidance is based upon theories and methods derived from the social sciences, mainly psychology, economics, and sociology. It can assist the person (1) to obtain accurate information about his aptitudes, inclinations, and opportunities; (2) to learn about the world of work, kinds of jobs available, training required, and duties, responsibilities, and rewards of jobs; (3) to integrate this information about himself and about available alternatives so that he can arrive at a realistic and reasonable vocational decision; (4) to make sensible educational and vocational plans that eventually will lead to his vocational objective; (5) to acquire the skills and attitudes requisite for success in his chosen occupation; (6) to obtain a position that provides adequate opportunities for the expression and use of the skills he has acquired; and (7) to develop further skills that will lead to advancement and promotion once he has started his career.

1. History and Scope.—Systematic vocational guidance in the United States had its origins in Boston about 1909, in Parsons' book *Choosing a Vocation*. It began under the sponsorship of community agencies, and such organizations have maintained their interest in it. The schools, however, soon began to express interest, and gradually vocational guidance became largely a school function. Research into the effectiveness of vocational guidance was financed by the British government during the 1930s. Most vocational guidance in the United States is provided by school and college counselors trained in adolescent and developmental psychology, psychological testing and measurement, occupational information, and guidance and counseling methods. In addition, vocational counselors in many state employment offices use a comprehensive system of vocational aptitude tests, the General Aptitude Test Battery developed by the United States Employment Service. The U.S. Veterans Administration expanded its vocational rehabilitation program started for disabled veterans of World War I and, in its advisement and guidance program, provided vocational guidance to millions of World War II and Korean War veterans through counseling centres located throughout the country. Most states, in conjunction with the U.S. Office of Vocational Rehabilitation, provide vocational guidance for physically disabled persons.

In Great Britain vocational guidance is provided for the disabled by the Government Industrial Rehabilitation Service. It is obtainable from private organizations such as the National Institute of Industrial Psychology. The government-administered Youth Employment Service provides career advice for those who leave school. In Australia and Canada schools have assumed major responsibility for vocational guidance. Vocational guidance in France was officially made a responsibility of the Ministry of Education in 1922, and since 1928 the national counseling service has been known as the Institut National d'Étude du Travail et d'Orientation Professionnelle; in 1963, about 800 counselors were employed in more than 200 guidance centres in France. The first Belgian vocational guidance centre was established in 1912, and in 1937 a national system of vocational guidance was established under the jurisdiction of the minister of education; in the early 1950s between 50,000 and 60,000 persons were provided with vocational guidance yearly in more than 80 local counseling centres. The first vocational guidance bureau in Japan was opened in 1920, and in that country the program has been sponsored by the Ministry of Education, Ministry of Welfare, Ministry of Labour, and the Japanese Vocational Guidance Association.

2. Methods and Functions.—The instruments used in vocational guidance include biographical questionnaires, tests of intelligence, aptitudes and attainment, vocational interest, and personality inventories. Psychological tests provide information that is sometimes useful in predicting success and satisfaction in various occupations. (*See* also Psychological Tests and Measurements.) The results of these psychological tests are supplemented in interviews by additional information about the person's previous experience and achievement.

Because psychological tests are of limited validity, their use in vocational guidance requires skill and training. In most U.S. states vocational counselors employed in schools must have completed a minimum of a year's work in a graduate school of a university, specializing in guidance, counseling, and psychological measurement.

As important in vocational guidance as test information is occupational information, obtained from such sources as government departments, colleges, universities, professional associations, and commercial firms. Gertrude Forrester's *Occupational Literature*, an annotated bibliography published in 1954, listed approximately 3,200 selected references to occupational literature.

In vocational guidance, relevant occupational information is provided in individual interviews and group meetings. Courses in occupations are taught at the secondary school level, and frequently units in other courses, particularly in the social studies, are devoted to the study of occupations.

Placement, the process of helping persons obtain positions, is another important function of vocational guidance. Persons are taught how to locate positions, write letters of application, behave during employment interviews, and evaluate job alternatives. In a few organizations, counselors and personnel workers are available to assist employed persons in meeting problems encountered on the job. Personnel workers also discuss with employees on-the-job training programs leading to advancement and promotion, relationships with other employees and supervisors, and other matters affecting the worker's vocational adjustment. Thus, vocational guidance is a continuous process.   (R. F. Be.)

B. Personnel Selection, Placement, and Training

1. Selection and Placement.—Application of scientific procedures for matching jobs and workers involves (1) an analysis of the demands of each job in terms of duties, skills, and critical requirements such as causes of difficulty and distaste for the work; and (2) the development of techniques for measuring the aptitudes and inclinations of applicants for employment or transfer to meet these requirements. In the main, such measuring devices take the form of objective psychological tests that are known to have some measure of validity in predicting behaviour on the job. In Great Britain the interview is still the most frequent procedure for assessment.

Many industries have reported striking results from the use of psychological tests, as have the military services. During World War II failures in the U.S. Air Force pilot training program were reduced from 65% to approximately 35% following the introduction of tests for the classification of candidates for pilot training.

Another significant trend is the application of psychological techniques for appraisal and development of supervisory and executive personnel. Not only psychological tests but also rating scales, patterned interviews, and biographical inventories show promise in this area. In fact, such traditional methods, refined and validated, have proved to be more effective in selection for some types of jobs, such as insurance salesmen, than have the tests.

2. Training.—The person who is qualified for a position may become inefficient and even maladjusted without proper training. Principles derived from research on the learning process (*see* LEARNING) are applied to improve quantity and quality of output; to reduce training time; to enhance ease and safety at work. Such research has focused attention on the need for supplementing repetition or routine practice by positive reinforcement. In industry this can be provided most easily and cheaply by giving the trainee immediate and frequent knowledge of results. As an example, in one case a revised program for training radio code operators, in which the correct symbol was given immediately after the trainee had written down each signal as he understood it, reduced by about 25% the time taken by trainees to reach a speed of five groups per minute. The effectiveness of training also can be improved by telling the worker why a job is done in a particular way, as well as how to do it. The psychologist also devises reporting procedures and trains managers and supervisors in their use, so that any training scheme can be followed up systematically to ensure that it is effective. Principles mentioned above and others have been introduced into programs for teaching supervisors to give better instruction on the job. Notable among these is one known as Job Instruction Training (JIT), developed by the U.S. War Manpower Commission, which has been advantageously used in Britain in the Training Within Industry Scheme, and throughout the world.

A highly crucial problem in industry is that of reducing the frequency and severity of accidents. Although some progress has been made, it generally has been found that little benefit has come from tests for measuring accident proneness. On the other hand, training programs in which supervisors make sure that each worker uses only correct methods of work can contribute much to the reduction of accidents (*see* INDUSTRIAL ACCIDENTS).

The application of the techniques of programmed instruction and teaching machines (*see* PROGRAMMED LEARNING) has brought about a major advance in some areas of industrial training. These techniques emphasize the need to state training objectives in detail, to organize learning material into small, meaningful blocks, to present the material so that the trainee obtains immediate knowledge of his performance, and to allow him to learn at his own pace. These programs have encouraged a systematic and empirical approach to industrial training.

C. HOURS OF WORK AND PHYSICAL ENVIRONMENT

1. Fatigue.—One of the significant costs of work is fatigue, which is discussed at length in the separate article FATIGUE. The term fatigue has been used to characterize three interrelated phenomena: (1) a decreased capacity for work, known as work decrement; (2) modifications of the physiological state; and (3) tiredness and related feelings.

2. Hours of Work.—During the 19th century a work schedule including a minimum of ten hours per day and six days per week was predominant in industrialized countries. Opposition to reducing hours of work has been overcome by the discovery that production is not adversely affected, indeed is frequently increased, by shortening the working day and the length of the working week. Output does not necessarily fall off with a shortening of the work week because of a tendency for the human being to adapt his rate of work to the length of time available, and to the amount of work to be done.

3. Scheduled Rest Pauses.—It is advantageous to break up a spell of work by scheduled rest pauses. Rest pauses are desirable in that they may heighten motivation and combat boredom as well as reduce fatigue. Furthermore, they may involve no actual loss of time, since workers tend to take equivalent time off, sometimes surreptitiously, and unauthorized "breathers" do not provide the equivalent of scheduled rest pauses in the way of relaxa-

tion and release from tension. Support for well-controlled coffee breaks, tea breaks, or "elevenses" is found in studies showing that the intake of food during a rest pause contributes to its beneficial effect.

4. Illumination.—Unsuitable lighting accelerates the onset of fatigue, chiefly by increasing muscular fatigue in seeing. A major requirement of good lighting is adequate brightness, associated with intensity of illumination. Low intensity continues to present a problem in many factories and offices, where the level of illumination is lower than 5 foot-candles, as contrasted with the 1,000 to 1,500 foot-candles characteristic of the outdoors even on a cloudy day (*see* PHOTOMETRY). Difficulties in measuring the psychophysiological cost of work under varying levels of illumination and other factors have led to disagreements as to applicable minimum standards for different jobs.

Proper diffusion and distribution of illumination, designed to eliminate glare and undesirable shadow effects, are also necessary to see clearly and easily. Brightness contrast (*i.e.*, the ratio between the brightness of the object and that of the background) must be considered in determining the proper type of illumination. Colour may play a part; it has been shown that it is easier to see when contrasting colours are used on machine tools and that this serves to emphasize danger points on the machine as well as to increase efficiency. (*See* also LIGHTING.)

5. Atmospheric Conditions.—According to a study conducted by the American Society of Heating and Ventilating Engineers, 50% of people engaged in light work in the United States find air temperatures of 63° to 71° F (17.2° to 21.7° C) comfortable in winter, and temperatures of 66° to 75° F (18.9° to 23.9° C) suitable in summer. The same percentage select 30% to 70% as the desirable level of relative humidity. However, people vary widely in their reactions to these atmospheric conditions and also to the rate of air movement, which is another important factor in maintaining efficiency and comfort at work. Much depends also upon the nature of the task.

An index known as Effective Temperature (ET) shows the combined effect of air temperature and humidity on the human experience of warmth or cold for a specified rate of air movement. In general, studies indicate that performance is impaired to a serious degree with effective temperatures in the middle 90s F (middle 30s C) or above, and that incentives do not offset the effects of high temperatures. At temperatures below 50° F (10° C) the precision of hand and finger movements is reduced. There are no materially adverse effects on so-called mental activities even at temperatures below 0° F (−17.8° C), although impairment occurs in the performance of manual tasks. Furthermore, both physical and mental processes suffer and feelings of fatigue are increased under conditions of anoxia, or oxygen deficiency, such as occur moderately at an altitude of 10,000 ft. or less and critically at about 20,000 ft. and above (*see* HYPOXIA).

Careful selection of personnel, provision of protective clothing and oxygen equipment, adjustment of the work period, and so on, can ameliorate the effects of atmospheric conditions characteristic of extreme climates and also of work around blast furnaces, in mines and submarines, in flying, etc. However, atmospheric conditions create negligible human problems in modern, well-ventilated, properly heated, air-conditioned plants. (*See* also HEATING AND VENTILATION.)

6. Noise.—Adaptation takes place in the case of regular exposure to expected and continuous noises of high intensity in the work situation, especially in the presence of high incentives. Prolonged exposure, however, to high noise levels and certain types of noises—as, for example, those experienced by boilermakers and airplane pilots—contributes to hearing loss. On the question of direct fatigue effects there is considerable disagreement among research workers. It is probable that excessive noise acts on the human organism as excessive friction acts on the machine; that it wastes energy (*see* NOISE AND ITS CONTROL).

D. WORK METHODS AND MACHINE DESIGN

1. Methods of Work.—Waste in the use of human resources in industry can be curtailed by the elimination of awkward and unnecessary movements in doing the job. A comprehensive program for doing this, including time and motion study procedures, was developed at the beginning of the 20th century (see INDUSTRIAL ENGINEERING). This and a variety of subsequent programs undertake basically to eliminate unnecessary movements and to combine selected motions into a standard method frequently designated as the one best way of work. The concept of the one best way of work has been a matter of concern to psychologists. Involved, in part, is a question as to whether any single rigid pattern of work is uniformly applicable to all workers, since they differ in psychophysical make-up.

Modern programs designed to improve work methods, generally known as methods engineering or work simplification, reflect these newer outlooks. There is an increasing tendency to make use of general rules of motion economy—dealing with such factors as symmetry, continuity, smoothness, and rhythm of movement—as a substitute for rigid patterning of so-called basic motions. Furthermore, many supervisors and also workers are being taught how to apply these rules. The psychologist's concern is to ensure due regard to the characteristics of workers when developing new work methods.

2. Alleviation of Boredom.—Highly specialized, repetitive work, widespread in modern industry, leads to a feeling of boredom; as indicated by both U.S. and British studies, considerable boredom is experienced by approximately 25% of factory workers. Boredom produces a change in the shape of the daily production curve which, contrary to the situation when fatigue is experienced, tends to fall in the middle and to rise at the end of the work period. Furthermore, employees who experience boredom frequently exhibit low morale.

Efforts to develop tests of susceptibility to boredom and assign to repetitive work only those who are not highly prone to it have not been successful. As a result, attention has been turned increasingly toward modifying the work environment. Research has shown that appropriately spaced rest pauses, freedom to engage in conversation, music, and the social environment of the plant, especially as reflected in the formation of closely knit small work groups, tend to decrease boredom.

A high degree of specialization in work has been favoured in the belief that this tends to increase over-all production. However, it has been shown that redesigning jobs so that the worker can perform a variety of tasks reduces boredom and improves general attitudes without adversely affecting production. Thus job rotation and also job enlargement are being used increasingly. These problems are attracting more interest from psychologists as the use of automation increases (see AUTOMATION).

3. Machine and Instrument Design and Man-Machine Systems.—With the growth of mechanization in industry, it has become increasingly necessary to view man and his machine as an integrated functional unit. There is continuing need to approach the design of machines with full consideration of basic patterns of human perception, communication, and motor response, and also of built-in limitations in the speed, accuracy, and coordination of these and other human functions. Failure to consider the human element in the design of machines has led to the construction of mechanical monstrosities, such as a mine hoist that requires the operator to stand spread-eagled with his weight resting on one foot to read a dial tilted 30° upward and sideward. Many machines and tools tax the capabilities and energy of human operators.

Since the 1940s there has been growing acceptance of the principle that machines should be made for men rather than men forcibly adapted to machines. This view finds expression in specialized research and practice most frequently described as engineering psychology (see *Engineering Psychology*, below).

Visual Indicators.—The widespread use of such instruments as pressure gauges, tachometers, and voltage meters has led to extensive studies of visual indicators. An example of poor design is found in a control panel $17\frac{1}{2}$ ft. in width where all major gauges were 2 to 3 ft. above eye level. Operator complaints of eyestrain and fatigue led to the redesign of the control panel to a width of 6 ft. with better positioning of instruments for seeing.

Poorly designed instruments can cause accidents as well as produce unnecessary fatigue. Thus a survey of 270 pilot errors showed that 13% of aircraft accidents investigated resulted from a misreading of the altimeter by 1,000 ft. There is evidence that the substitution of a numerical counter for the conventional type of altimeter reduces the percentage of errors in reading from 11.7 to 0.4 in the case of experienced pilots. Studies of many kinds of visual indicators have led to the formulation of principles designed to improve both the ease and accuracy of instrument readings, covering such characteristics as intervals between scale markings, size and style of figures, shapes of pointers, and conditions of illumination.

Controls.—The placement, shape, and direction of movement of controls represent important factors in design. Wide separation of controls leads to reduction of output and to increase of effort in the operation of machines; by contrast, major controls placed too close together may produce accidents. The latter has been demonstrated in aircraft accidents where the closeness of the flap control to that used for the landing gear led to accidental operation of the wrong control.

Coding.—Strain can be reduced and safety increased by coding or associating differently shaped controls with distinctive operating functions. Basic principles include the rule that for adjusting a lever or control knob the movement should be in the same direction as the perceived adjustment. Thus toggle switches should move upward for on, go, or increase, and downward for off, stop, and decrease.

E. SOCIAL AND ECONOMIC CONDITIONS

In many instances, hours of work and physical conditions play a less important role than the psychological, social, and economic conditions prevailing in a factory or office in determining the behaviour of the working force. These conditions are largely determined by the personnel practices of the company, and its supervisors and executives.

1. Social Conditions.—*Social Relationships.*—Studies conducted in the Hawthorne, Ill., plant of the Western Electric Company between 1927 and 1932 attracted attention to the significance of social aspects of the work situation. These studies included extensive observations of the effects of changes in number and distribution of hours of work, illumination, rest pauses, wage-payment plans, etc. Such changes were accompanied by increased production, but the upward trend did not disappear when the favourable physical conditions were eliminated. It was concluded that the production increase was the result of a change in the social situation. The conditions of the experiment apparently created a relationship between the employees and their supervisors which did not exist ordinarily. Employee motivation seemed to change in response to increased attention from management. The studies were reported by F. J. Roethlisberger and W. J. Dickson.

Subsequent research by different investigators in many plants has clearly confirmed the view that the way the person acts, the way he feels about his job, the level of his morale—in the sense of willingness to strive for the goals of the company—are very much affected by the sentiments and attitudes of his co-workers. Of particular significance is the influence of the small work group or team to which he is assigned by management, and of the small informal organization which develops spontaneously as a function of the work situation. The influence of the social situation is intensified because the employee is simultaneously a member of many groups, and because some of these (*e.g.,* the company and the union) may be competing for his interest and his loyalty (see PSYCHOLOGY, SOCIAL).

Work Groups.—A study conducted in two British automobile factories showed that higher production and greater satisfaction occur in smaller than in larger work teams. Observation of four gangs engaged in repairing railroad passenger cars in Great Britain showed that, under a group wage incentive, productivity increased at a higher rate in gangs of small size and with a particular pattern of stability than in larger work gangs. These and other studies also yielded evidence of higher levels of satisfaction and morale in smaller work groups.

The explanation of such findings is to be found in the social structure of the groups. Smaller working groups tend to be more cohesive than are larger groups. Under appropriate conditions, especially in the presence of a high quality of leadership, such cohesiveness leads to higher work standards, to acceptance of technological change, and to better achievement of other goals important to management.

A conscious effort to combine in a work team members who like and are friendly toward each other is conducive to the development of such positive attitudes and behaviour. The advantages of using such cohesive work groups are illustrated in an experiment conducted in the construction industry; total production costs were reduced by 5% when carpenters and bricklayers were permitted to select their own workmates instead of being required to work with arbitrarily assigned teammates.

Democratic Leadership.—A number of studies covering many occupations and many countries—ranging from telephone operators in the state of Michigan to textile workers in India—have demonstrated that an atmosphere of democratic leadership, which provides opportunities for employee participation in setting goals and in other aspects of decision making, results in higher production, greater job satisfaction, and improved morale. Evidence of such returns was first demonstrated clearly in a study conducted in a garment-manufacturing plant, where there was considerable resistance by production workers to necessary changes in jobs and work methods. Providing opportunities for the workers to participate in planning the details of the change and in setting production goals led to higher output, decreased turnover, and a more harmonious relationship between workers and supervisors. Such benefits appear not only when small changes are involved but (as was shown in later developments in a garment-manufacturing plant and in the Indian studies) also where a widespread program of modernization or reorganization is required.

In Britain many joint consultation schemes have been established to provide opportunities for fuller expression of opinions and needs among all grades of the workers.

Experience of companies introducing electronic office equipment and other forms of automation shows further that industry can profit from permitting workers to participate in decision making, without any abdication of the responsibility of management for the operation and growth of the business.

Supervision.—Many studies, including that cited above, have demonstrated that the quality of supervision exercises a tremendous influence upon employee motivation and morale. Studies of work groups, including insurance office workers, labourers in railroad gangs, linemen, etc., conducted by the Survey Research Centre of the University of Michigan, showed that employees who perceive their supervisors as "employee centred" have better production records than do groups working under "production centred" supervisors. There is evidence that absence rate is inversely related to quality of supervision.

Other studies show that the quality of supervision is good when workers feel free to discuss their problems with their supervisor; know what he thinks of their work; feel that the supervisor supports them when they have a complaint; when the supervisor uses general rather than close supervision; when the supervisor frequently conducts group meetings where work matters are discussed.

Recognition of the central role of good supervision has led to supervisor selection programs and extended training programs for supervisors.

Communication.—Small groups become cohesive, in part, because in them information can be passed along quickly. Employees look to supervisors for opportunities to discuss their interests. Adverse attitudes toward company plans change for the better when facts concerning them are properly communicated.

The need for adequate communication exists at all levels. Supervisory personnel often complain of the failure of higher management to keep them informed about matters that are of interest to them and their employees. Formal channels of communication following the lines of the organization chart may not be sufficient for full dissemination of information.

Management Procedures.—Basic principles of good supervision require that supervisors at all levels perceive themselves and act as members of the management team. Along with keeping the supervisor informed, it is necessary to define the scope of his responsibility and to delegate to him the authority to use it. One study showed that 79% of foremen with high morale and only 37% of foremen with low morale had a clear understanding of their duties. Similarly, 79% of the former and only 30% of the latter claimed that they had adequate authority to deal with employee and other problems. In addition, the supervisor is at a disadvantage on the job unless his status is made clear by the wage scale and by such physical symbols as desk and office space; and unless he is permitted to play a role appropriate to his rank in policy administration and policy making. Studies of such social factors overlap with those of industrial sociologists. (*See* also INDUSTRIAL RELATIONS.)

2. Economic Conditions.—This emphasis on the social situation should not draw attention from other and even more fundamental motives, associated with basic drives for food, shelter, job security, and self-expression. Research has thrown considerable light on the sources of motivation (*q.v.*)—on the variety and strength of needs that should be gratified in the work situation.

There is evidence that executives and union leaders err in their judgments of workers' needs and the potency of financial incentives. In one survey 75% of executives and of labour leaders and less than 30% of employees included payment among five factors rated as most important to workers. In a later study workers listed "full appreciation of work done" as first and "good wages" as fifth on a list of morale factors. By contrast, supervisors predicted that "good wages" would turn out to be the most important item looked for on the job by the workers, and that "full appreciation of work done" would rate in eighth place.

This does not mean that the pay envelope is unimportant; a low wage scale is a significant source of dissatisfaction and lack of cooperation. Nevertheless, voluntary restriction of output in plants using wage-incentive systems and strikes in plants with high wage scales show that such factors have limited power as incentives. As wages rise above subsistence level, other needs become more influential. Workers seek such returns as the opportunity of doing something worthwhile; the feeling of being recognized as an individual; a sense of belonging; a chance to get ahead; approval of work done; a safe future; guidance in establishing goals and learning how to achieve them; and the opportunity of contributing from their knowledge in dealing with their own problems.

Although the introduction of a new payment system can have an immediate favourable effect on production, in the long term such efforts can only succeed if sufficient prior attention is given to psychological and social conditions at the place of work.

(M. S. VI.)

IV. OTHER AREAS OF APPLIED PSYCHOLOGY

A. ENGINEERING PSYCHOLOGY

Engineering psychology—also called human factors engineering or ergonomics—seeks to ensure that the tools and machines man uses, and the work he performs, are in accordance with his characteristics. Past efforts to achieve them rested chiefly on the ingenuity of inventors and on practical experience rather than on scientific knowledge of human characteristics. The accelerated pace of technology, the increasing complexity of machines, and the trend toward automation have led to increasing emphasis on efficient man-machine systems. This emphasis resulted in the rapid growth of engineering psychology. This growth can be exemplified in Europe by the Ergonomics Research Society that embraces psychologists, physiologists, anatomists, engineers, and other members of industry.

Work in engineering psychology greatly accelerated during World War II, particularly in aviation. Questions concerning design of aircraft instruments for ease of interpretation, design of flight controls for accurate manipulation, and the matching of man's response characteristics to the dynamic characteristics of aircraft were among the critical problems in military aviation. Similar problems arose with other types of military equipment. Some of these problems were solved with data already available from experimental psychology; existing experimental methods were used to solve others. Much basic work has had to be done on the dimensions of the human body and on perceptual functions.

One of the oldest problems is the design of signs and symbols—*e.g.*, alphabetic symbols, the signs used on highways, the codes used in telegraphy, and the symbols used in printing for the blind—to increase speed and accuracy in transmitting information. As new display media, such as radar and television, were developed, new problems of visibility, legibility, and ease of interpretation arose; research on display problems continues to be important.

Another class of problems of historical importance involves the design of tools and various types of controls so that they are adapted to human strength, dexterity, speed, and accuracy of movement. The scope of engineering psychology has broadened to include such questions as "How far is it advisable to go in eliminating people and making manufacturing processes completely automatic?" Answers to such questions obviously should be based on analysis of the relative capabilities of complex machines, such as electronic computers, and of human beings in performing comparable tasks.

Engineering psychology applications thus depend heavily on knowledge of human performance characteristics and on knowledge of individual differences, learning, and motivation, as such variables affect performance in man-machine systems.

(P. M. Fi.)

B. Motivational Research

Motivational (motivation) research is concerned with the motivations of human beings as reflected in mass behaviour relating to sales, advertising, and merchandising. Motivational research resembles—and some of the basic fact-gathering methods it uses are similar to those of—public-opinion polling (*see* Public Opinion). Public-opinion polls, however, are usually based on predetermined statistical samples of people. Motivational research does not normally use such statistical techniques applied to responses to direct questions. Rather it acts on the assumption that many human motives are unconscious or not readily admitted because they are not always socially acceptable.

The methods employed to uncover underlying motives are borrowed from psychiatry, psychoanalysis, and depth psychology (*see* Psychiatry; Psychoanalysis). They include such devices as the depth (nondirective or open-end) interview, projective tests, laboratory experiments, and psychodrama. The depth interview is one in which the subject rarely is asked a direct question; for example, the researcher will not ask him why he bought a particular make of car, but will attempt to infer this from his answers to indirect questions. In using projective tests, it is hoped that inkblots or pictures illustrating specific situations will prompt people to reveal their true motivations (*see* Psychological Tests and Measurements: *Projective Methods*). Laboratory experiments seek to measure responses to specific people and objects—including products, services, and mass media. In psychodrama, people are asked to act out a purchase, interpersonal relations, or emotional problems; in doing so, they may report insights into their own behaviour, and the researcher may feel he gains understanding of their motivations.

Motivational research, since it attempts to change such activities as voting, buying, and attitudes toward national and international issues, raises a question regarding the ethics of using such methods to influence people, often against their will. Some motivational researchers answer that people always have tried to influence each other and that the real issue is one of determination of the morality of the goals. (E. D.)

C. Forensic Psychology

Part of the scientific research on human behaviour carried out by psychologists and other social scientists is pertinent to a wide range of legal problems. Psychologists have also studied detection of guilt and deception, distortions of perception and memory in relation to testimony, the behaviour of juries, problems related to the determination of competence and sanity, personality and motivational factors related to crime, factors influencing success and failure on parole, the sociopsychological organization of prisons, the psychology of drug addiction, and the like. (*See* Investigation, Criminal: *Methods of Investigation: Detection of Deception*.)

In addition, a number have served as clinical psychologists or guidance counselors affiliated with juvenile and criminal courts, prisons and other legal agencies. Further, psychologists sometimes serve as expert witnesses in cases involving determination of mental deficiency, legal insanity, or other problems in which technical psychological knowledge may be of use.

European developments in forensic psychology have drawn heavily on the techniques and findings of experimental psychologists.

See also references under "Psychology, Applied" in the Index.

(X.)

Bibliography.—*The field:* The most extensive references are D. H. Fryer and E. R. Henry (eds.), *Handbook of Applied Psychology*, 2 vol. (1950) and A. Anastasi, *Fields of Applied Psychology* (1964). See also M. Blum, *Industrial Psychology and Its Social Foundations* (1956); H. Hyman, *Survey Design and Analysis* (1955); D. B. Lucas and S. H. Britt, *Advertising Psychology and Research* (1950).
Clinical psychology: American Psychological Association, *Ethical Standards of Psychologists* (1953); E. A. Rubinstein and M. Lorr (eds.), *Survey of Clinical Practice in Psychology* (1954); R. I. Watson, *Psychology as a Profession* (1954); W. A. Hunt, *The Clinical Psychologist* (1956); A. M. Clarke and A. D. B. Clarke (eds.), *Mental Deficiency* (1958); H. Eysenck (ed.), *Handbook of Abnormal Psychology* (1960).
Counseling: E. G. Williamson and J. G. Darley, *Student Personnel Work* (1937); Carl R. Rogers, *Counseling and Psychotherapy* (1942); C. Gilbert Wrenn, *Student Personnel Work in College* (1951); H. B. and P. N. Pepinsky, *Counseling: Theory and Practice* (1954); E. S. Bordin, *Psychological Counseling* (1955); Milton E. Hahn and Malcolm S. MacLean, *Counseling Psychology*, 2nd ed. (1955); J. Hadley, *Clinical and Counseling Psychology* (1958).
Industrial psychology: M. S. Viteles, *Industrial Psychology* (1932), *Science of Work* (1934), *Motivation and Morale in Industry* (1953); F. Roethlisberger and W. Dickson, *Management and the Worker* (1939); H. E. Burtt, *Principles of Employment Psychology* (1942); C. L. Shartle, *Occupational Information*, 2nd ed. (1952); L. E. Tyler, *The Work of the Counselor* (1953); *Personnel and Guidance Journal* (formerly *Occupations*); J. Tiffin and E. J. McCormick, *Industrial Psychology* (1962); H. W. Karn and B. von H. Gilmer (eds.), *Readings in Industrial and Business Psychology* (1962); D. E. Super and J. O. Crites, *Appraising Vocational Fitness*, rev. ed. (1962); T. A. Ryan, *Work and Effort* (1947); W. F. Floyd and A. T. Welford (eds.), *Symposium on Fatigue* (1953), *Symposium on Human Factors in Equipment Design* (1954); G. Friedmann, *Industrial Society* (1955); R. Stagner, *The Psychology of Industrial Conflict* (1956); E. J. McCormick, *Human Engineering* (1957); T. W. Harrell, *Industrial Psychology*, rev. ed. (1958); P. E. Vernon and J. B. Parry, *Personnel Selection in the British Forces* (1949); R. Glaser (ed.), *Training Research and Education* (1962); A. A. Lumsdaine and R. Glaser (eds.), *Teaching Machines and Programmed Learning* (1960); International Labour Office, *Introduction to Work Study* (1957); R. Marriott, *Incentive Payment Systems*, 2nd ed. (1961); A. Chapanis, W. R. Garner and C. T. Morgan, *Applied Experimental Psychology* (1949); C. T. Morgan et al. (eds.), *Human Engineering Guide to Equipment Design* (1963); D. E. Broadbent, *Perception and Communication* (1958); *Journal of Applied Psychology* (U.S.); *Personnel Psychology* (U.S.); *Occupational Psychology* (Great Britain); *Journal of the Institute of Personnel Management* (Great Britain); *Personnel* (U.S.); *Human Relations* (U.S.-Great Britain); *Journal of Personnel Practices* (Australia); *Le Travail Humain* (France); *Ergonomics* (Great Britain). (G. A. R.)

PSYCHOLOGY, COMPARATIVE, the study of similarities and differences in behavioural organization among living beings, from viruses to plants to man. A view of the subject held earlier by W. Wundt and others included human comparisons now generally studied as genetic or child psychology, abnormal psychology, and ethnology or folk psychology. This article is concerned with the psychological nature of man in comparison with other animals.

As animal psychology, comparative psychology centres on discerning qualitative as well as quantitative similarities and differences in animal (including human) behaviour. Similarities by analogy must be distinguished from those based on evolutionary kinship; differences in degree, from those in kind.

Comparative psychology is in itself interesting, and has important applications in fields such as medicine and animal training. With the rise of an experimental comparative psychology in the latter half of the 19th century and its rapid growth during the

20th century, the study of lower animals has cast increasing light on human psychology, in such areas as the development of individual behaviour, motivation, and the nature and methods of learning. Other animals are easier to obtain in numbers and can be better controlled under experimental conditions than human subjects. Much can be learned about man from lower animals; moreover, the discovery of differences illuminates the similarities.

The common-sense tendency to endow lower animals with human capacities always has been strong. People often talk to them as though dealing with human beings. An extreme development of this tendency is the doctrine of metempsychosis (q.v.), holding that after death the human soul may reside in another person or lower animal.

In recorded history two different views have developed concerning man's relation to the lower animals. One, termed for convenience the man-brute view, stresses differences often to denying similarities altogether; the other, the evolutionary view, stresses both similarities and differences. Aristotle formalized the man-brute view, attributing a rational faculty to man alone, lesser faculties to the animals. On the other hand, from the 19th century Darwinism considered man a highly evolved animal, the modern view in science. Scientific evidence indicates that continuity in the evolution of organisms provides a basis for essential psychological similarities and differences among lower and higher animals.

This article is organized as follows:

I. METHODS

1. Gathering Evidence.—Fact gathering requires special training in scientific methods, for which personal feelings are no substitute. All reports, whether anecdotal or arising from laboratory experiments or from studies in natural habitats, must be evaluated for reliability according to what conditions prevailed and what precautions were taken against error in gathering facts.

As in science generally, the soundest method of study at hand is used. An observer of nesting behaviour in birds constructs a hideout or blind to minimize disturbances resulting from his presence. Binoculars, a camera, and special mechanical means for recording the bird's reactions may further increase reliability.

In the laboratory it is possible to regulate general factors such as age and physiological condition of subjects, to exclude disturbances, to change environmental conditions or keep them constant, and to introduce apparatus designed to ensure accuracy. Thus animal psychology has employed the maze method as one means of testing learning, special problem boxes to test intelligent behaviour, and a variety of other techniques to increase the significance of the evidence.

Problems presented by a maze, for example, are not unlike those encountered by an animal finding its way under natural conditions. Such situations, when adequately planned and standardized, can meet the criteria of validity (i.e., relevance to the behavioural variables in question) and reliability (i.e., consistency of results in repetitions).

2. Interpreting Evidence.—Late in the 19th century, in Berlin, Ger., a horse named Hans became renowned for purported mathematical abilities. When a problem was written on a blackboard before him, Hans, by tapping first with right forefoot and then with left, indicated the answer in digits and tens respectively, with such success as seemingly to support the owner's claim for calculations by the horse. Although skepticism was expressed by many, and some alleged trickery, others asserted that the owner must be honest and his claims therefore valid. Scientific surveys of the case, particularly by the psychologist O. Pfungst, supported the following analysis. The horse performed well whether the owner was present or not, apparently ruling out trickery due to the owner's presence. But Hans failed unless the trainer or someone else was present who knew the answers; hence success depended somehow on human influence. The fact that the horse failed when blindfolded excluded telepathy while indicating some other effect from persons present. Observing the audience carefully, the psychologists found that when a problem was written down, someone who knew the answer would bend forward very slowly, whereupon the horse would begin tapping. After the correct number of taps, the person would relax, usually with a little movement, as of the head, and the horse would stop. Slight movements of this kind were known to psychologists as inadvertent activities accompanying acts of close attention. Pfungst concluded that, without the owner's knowing it, the horse had learned to start and stop his taps according to appropriate sensory cues. The horse was equally successful whether the problem was in simple arithmetic or in calculus; also, his responses to easy and to difficult problems alike often were incorrect by only one or two digits, suggesting a direct control of the tapping that could operate now early, now late, rather than mental operations. Hans typically began tapping mechanically when all was ready, without even looking at the figures.

This case brings out some important principles of interpretation in comparative psychology. The investigator selects a likely hypothesis, but considers it tentative until it is supported by experiments in which all factors of possible importance are controlled. (In the Clever Hans case, the roles of sensitivity and habit in the horse, the factors of audience knowledge and of subtle motor aspects of attention, and still others were tested.) After his experiments, the scientist sifts and organizes the available evidence, using mathematical techniques when possible, to find what theory best fits the facts.

These safeguards are essential, whatever the nature of the behaviour problem. Yet Clever Hans mistakes still arise, comparably obscuring the nature of the animal's accomplishment, when bias or preconception blunts the objective planning of research.

3. Anthropomorphism.—People tend to ascribe human attributes to other beings. Thus it is said that moths and other insects fly to the light out of curiosity; the rattlesnake sounds its rattle to warn intruders; pets and domestic animals are noble or sly and deceitful according to conditions; and so on. The practice of interpreting behaviour on the basis of selected stories is called anecdotalism. Thus Plutarch in ancient Rome, Jean de La Fontaine in 17th-century France, and countless other writers have busied themselves in narrating stories about mental feats in lower animals.

Although valuable literary works may be created, such anthropomorphic literature risks fundamental flaws. It typically involves the implicit assumption that any person is likely to be well acquainted with his own behaviour and thoughts (for comparison with those of lower animals). There is, however, much psychological evidence to the contrary. No person, however well intentioned, should rest content with just one or a few outstanding examples as the basis for interpretations of what animals do. A single observation is low in reliability, as is any number influenced by prejudices and preconceived notions.

4. Adaptive Behaviour or Purpose.—Unnecessary complexities often arise because of the interpreter's point of view. Under normal conditions behaviour generally conforms to what might be called "appropriate" or "best" in the given situation. Thus the Venus's-flytrap closes its hinged leaf when a fly alights, but not when stirred by a breeze; the scallop closes its shell as its common enemy, the starfish, approaches; the octopus frequently remains secluded until its prey, the crab, is nearby; the chimpanzee may attain food out of reach by piling boxes. Acts that seem well adapted to particular conditions are often described as purposive. But this generalization of purposiveness in behaviour raises difficulties.

The above cases are typical—what can be said about them? First, these acts occur as described: the reports are reliable. Also, the acts have in common the characteristic of being adaptive. As a result of natural selection, behaviour tends to be adaptive to the typical species environment, promoting individual adjustments to the species habitat and furthering species survival. Although many theorists mean only this when they use the term purposive, a distinction seems desirable between what is adaptive and what is purposive.

H. Driesch and W. McDougall are associated with a view in the nature of teleology (*q.v.*) that all behaviour of the type termed adaptive is endowed with directive forces comparable with human volition. When a man behaves purposively, he strives for an end he anticipates or expects. If all animals actually performed their adaptive behaviour on the basis of such a process, the theoretical problems of comparative psychology would be relatively simple, for the same type of solution would apply to all cases. But the danger exists that the teleological type of explanation may arise from the theorist's preconceived notions rather than from reliable supporting evidence.

5. Morgan's Canon.—A useful rule in scientific interpretation is the principle of parsimony, which may be stated as follows: of alternative explanations for a given phenomenon, choose the simplest, that requiring the fewest assumptions, provided it meets the facts adequately. This principle was stated by C. L. Morgan (*An Introduction to Comparative Psychology,* 1894) as follows: "In no case may we interpret an action as the outcome of the exercise of a higher psychical faculty, if it can be interpreted as the outcome of the exercise of one which stands lower in the psychological scale."

The purposive type of explanation for the above examples would be that the Venus's-flytrap needs food, hence closes when touched by insects but not by inedible objects; the scallop recognizes the starfish as an enemy and closes its valves to avoid destruction; the octopus hides so that its enemies cannot see it and its prey may come close; the chimpanzee stacks boxes in order to obtain suspended food. Although at first sight these purported explanations all may appear simple, actually they are all complex and no one of them should be adopted until alternatives have been considered in the light of Morgan's canon. Each hypothesis assumes that the animal anticipates the consequences of one action or its alternative (*e.g.,* the scallop anticipates death if it does not close) and can weigh the possibilities somewhat as a reasoning man might. Humanlike capacities, such as understanding meanings, anticipating results, and choosing between alternatives, are thereby implied by these purposive explanations. The evidence, however, favours a purposive explanation in only one of the described instances, the case of the box-stacking chimpanzee. W. Köhler and others have shown that this animal seems to anticipate success when jumping from the ground to suspended food, to understand the significance of a box as a means of reaching food, and to solve problems by reasoning. Conversely, to account for the flytrap's reaction, only a simple reflexlike reaction to stimulation need be assumed, for the leaf closes its two hinged halves automatically on any contact sufficient to bend its sensitive trigger hairs at their basal joints. As for the scallop, experiments show that it closes in response to any sufficient chemical effect, as to starfish broth released in the water nearby, but not to a starfish presented behind glass (visual control). In the case of the octopus, an intent to hide is excluded by J. A. Bierens de Haan's finding that the animal slips between plates of glass, where it remains in full sight, as readily as between pieces of slate. The simpler explanation consistent with the data is that the octopus comes to rest when its body touches between surfaces, not because it understands hiding.

These cases illustrate the value of investigation in testing assumptions and reaching an adequate explanation. Too frequently a purposive account merely names the gains of an activity (*e.g.,* protection, food) without clarifying the process involved. But a name alone is no explanation, and may in fact suggest an unwarranted interpretation. Adaptive acts must be explained through evidence from investigation rather than by analogies between lower animals and man, for activities which lead to similar adaptive results (*e.g.,* both the leaf closing of the flytrap and the box stacking of the chimpanzee are food-getting behaviour) may be very different psychologically.

6. Objective Attitude.—Early in the 20th century the view gained ground that careful experimentation on behaviour under controlled conditions should improve psychological theories. A chief contribution of this movement to comparative psychology was its emphasis on objective as against subjective procedures for evaluating and comparing the psychological resources of different animals. To appraise any animal activity, the psychologist must consider its nature and adaptive value, the situation, and what factors in the species' organic makeup and in individual experience may have contributed.

The first task in comparative study is to discover the characteristic behaviour in each animal type; the next is evaluation. It is not sufficient to assign positions in a series, classifying some animals as inferior and others as superior; the presumed inferiority or superiority must be clarified through comparisons. Neither the stability nor the adaptive efficiency of behaviour are as indicative of superior psychological status as are modifications of behaviour to fit new conditions. The principal weakness of a topical study is the implication that functions such as "memory" are much the same wherever found. But any given function, such as learning, overlaps others and may also differ greatly according to the animal involved. Higher animals do not necessarily repeat the lower animals with the addition of certain new abilities. Rather than a recapitulation of the characteristics of lower animals in the higher, research discloses similar properties and others which assume new psychological significance. These matters may be illustrated by some outstanding differences observed among various types of animal.

II. PSYCHOLOGICAL STANDING

1. Psychological Levels.—The earliest formal statement of psychological levels was the scheme of Aristotle, endowing plants with a nutritive faculty alone, the lowest animals with sensory faculties also, higher animals with an appetitive faculty also, and man alone with a rational faculty. Descartes' ideas embodied a simpler scheme: a lower level of animals, viewed as automata, and man as the sole rational being, on a higher level. In 1905 R. M. Yerkes differentiated levels on the basis of functional criteria and experimental evidence: (1) discrimination, a general form of response, shown by lower invertebrates; (2) docility, or modifiable reactions, seen in rodents; and (3) initiative, or response variability, observed in primates.

Such systems are speculative and may restrict the experimenter's viewpoint; they tend to oversimplify and encourage categorical interpretations of animal activities. Distinctions of psychological levels are rejected by those who believe that functions such as perception and learning exist in all animals. Experience, however, favours the concept of psychological levels to represent transitions from lower to higher psychological stages and to summarize knowledge of animal relationships, as long as complete discontinuities from level to level are not assumed.

2. Consciousness.—When we see another individual behaving more or less as we do under comparable conditions, that being (whether man or lower animal) is often assumed to have an experience similar to our own. Thus Montaigne, from occurrences such as the starting and barking of dogs in their sleep, thought that they must have imagination. Late in the 19th century the prominence of introspective methods in psychology encouraged a strong tendency to analogize consciousness. This tendency weakened after the failure of attempts to use consciousness as a criterion of animal mentality. The chief objections were that introspection, considered low in validity for human psychology, could not be valid for lower animals, which lack speech; and that if inferences concerning the subjective aspects of even the simplest mental states in man are held doubtful, little justification exists for applying the method of anthropomorphic analogy to lower animals.

A. CRITICAL POINTS OF CHANGE IN THE ANIMAL SERIES

1. Protozoans and the Concept of Simplicity.—Protozoans frequently are termed the simplest animals. However, H. S. Jennings and F. Alverdes found reactions of the ciliate *Paramecium*, for one, many and varied.

This organism is propelled forward, rotating about its long axis, by the beating of minute, hairlike cilia covering its ovoid body. When stimulated, it pauses momentarily, rotating narrowly or widely before continuing in a new direction, or backs away at an angle varying from acute to obtuse. Specific properties of the stimulus, particularly its intensity, may be critical; for example, weak contact typically elicits slight interruptions of forward movement, strong contact a pronounced backing reaction, and physicochemical properties of stimulation directly influence the extent and the duration of modifications in forward swimming. Although the protoplasmic changes underlying the many variations of ciliary stroke in these different reactions doubtless are biochemically complex, this behaviour is simple in the sense that it can be understood in terms of psychologically simple concepts, for a dictation of response by the physical properties of stimulation is the lowest order of psychological process.

Protozoan behaviour, nevertheless, is adaptive. When Jennings dropped a stream of carmine particles upon the disc of the attached trumpet-shaped ciliate *Stentor*, there occurred a series of reactions from a slight contraction of the oral disc to increasing general contractions which at length broke the animal free from the substratum. Jennings characterized these variable reactions to conditions of repeated stimulation as a series of trials. More objectively considered, such behaviour is the product of protoplasmic changes forced by repetitive stimulation. At first only the funnel end reacts; then as internal excitation spreads, the stalk contracts progressively toward its attached base. Behaviour thus changes successively through a progression of physiological summations producing new results as they reach more remote localities. Although the notion of trials emphasizes the adaptive aspects of these processes, it misrepresents the acts, which are forced by stimulation rather than arising as attempts of the *Stentor* to attain expected results.

This case illustrates how, in the simple psychological system of the protozoan, variable reactions widen an animal's adaptation to surrounding conditions. Jennings demonstrated that paramecia collect around a drop of acid in their medium not through direct approaches to the acid but because they first swim readily into the area, then recoil from the acid-deficient border zone on each encounter. Since, in the ciliates, stimulus changes typically interrupt forward swimming differently according to their intensity and other physicochemical properties, the organisms thereby escape injurious agents in their environment. The adaptability of such reactions in protozoans stems from the persistence of variable swimming until conditions favour normal locomotion.

The status of behaviour changes in protozoans has been much discussed. As examples, amoebae, repeatedly exposed to bright light, put forth fewer pseudopodia before each further reversal of direction; *Paramecium*, introduced successively into a capillary tube from which it can escape only by doubling around, reverses with increasing promptness. Some writers consider such changes equivalent to learning in higher organisms, pointing to graphic records of reduced time or movement in these cases. Others, conversely, stress the limited duration of such changes in protozoans, also that many of them have been duplicated (as by chemical treatment) without putting the organism through trials. Thus, although F. Bramstedt reported that paramecia presented repeatedly with the stimulus pair of light (largely ineffective at first) and heat (generally withdrawn from) later withdrew from light alone, U. Grabowski found the behaviour a function of gaseous changes set up in the water during the trials. J. J. Best demonstrated the specific effect of temperature in sensitizing protoplasm to such agents as light. B. Gelber, however, reported an apparent instrumental conditioning of paramecia to approach an empty needle loaded with bacteria. D. D. Jensen has applied the term pseudolearning to such results, because controlled repetitions of the experiments demonstrate that such uncontrolled environmental factors as chemical traces can account for the changes. (*See also* PROTOZOA.)

2. Psychological Limitations of Lower Invertebrates.—Significant for judging the psychological level of an animal is its behavioural organization. Perhaps least endowed in these respects are low multicellular animals such as adult sponges. The sponge is a bottom-attached organism of the colonial type that feeds by filtering water drawn through chambers in the body wall. The reactions of sponges are simple, local, and sluggish. As G. H. Parker (*The Elementary Nervous System*, 1919) found, sponges lack integration among their parts except that resulting from structural unity and a crude transmission of mechanical impulses through certain primitive cells around the opening to the body cavity, combining sensory and motor properties. Such limitations may have characterized the early ancestors of multicellular animals prior to the appearance of neural tissue.

In the coelenterates a measure of integration exists in activities such as feeding, locomotion, and withdrawal from intense stimulation. This was found by G. J. Romanes and by Parker to be attributable to a nerve net, a continuous conduction network permeating the body wall and transmitting impulses from specialized sensory cells to specialized muscle tissue. Activities here, although far better integrated than in sponges, are still relatively sluggish and considerably below the level of cephalopods, for example. The low-grade centralization of the conduction system, as a major limitation, distinctly handicaps behavioural organization.

Activities are better integrated in echinoderms such as starfish and sea urchins. In normal behaviour, local activities are so effectively combined that J. von Uexküll, who investigated the neurophysiology, was led to characterize the echinoderm in action as a community of reflexes. In a reflex, stimulated sensory cells transmit impulses to association cells in the neural system, which arouse muscular contractions. Thus, the tube feet, small fingerlike muscular structures capable of adhering to the substratum by their terminal sucking discs, when stimulated lightly, bend toward the affected side through one muscular action; when stimulated intensely, they bend away through another action. An appreciable local autonomy is indicated by the fact that the characteristic echinoderm structures, tube feet, pedicillariae (nippers), and spines, when cut from the animal and appropriately mounted, react to stimulation much as before. To be sure, throughout the animal series, reflexlike actions enter into the normal functioning of internal organs (*e.g.*, the vertebrate heartbeat), controlled reflexly in a more or less automatic manner. Even in mammals, reflexes may intervene in general behaviour, as in scratching or sneezing, but with a very different significance than in lower invertebrates. For the latter, the community-of-reflexes concept has some validity for a behaviour in which somewhat autonomous local activities are combined differently according to the conditions of arousal.

Yet the behaviour of lower invertebrates such as coelenterates and echinoderms is more than a chain-reflex combination of functions, as sense organs and motor structures are linked functionally together by the nerve net. Thus, soon after pedicillariae have caught prey, the tube feet extend, attach, and "walk" the object toward the centrally located mouth, which meanwhile everts and folds around the victim. The simplest nerve nets (as in the coelenterate *Hydra*) have a minimal polarization related to the growth gradient, and conduct according to the strength and localization of external stimulation without strict directionality. Such nerve nets exemplify the function of primitive conduction systems, joining local operations without specifying the behaviour pattern. Although in mammals nerve-net functions are visceral and local (as in coordinating intestinal activities in digestion), in the lower invertebrates nerve-net correlation is the main agency unifying behaviour.

Echinoderms advance materially in behavioural organization as compared with coelenterates. A more versatile integration of local function exists in the righting response, aroused when the animal is turned on its back. In the inverted starfish, with previous stimulation and handling equalized, two or three rays twist about, and when the ventral surfaces of these rays touch the ground, tube feet progressively closer to the central disc attach. These rays thereby swing the body of the starfish, overbalance, and right it. For this reaction to occur, it is necessary that the rays of one side become dominant.

A. R. Moore demonstrated that this organization normally depends on impulses through the nerve ring interconnecting the radial nerves of the five arms. When this nerve ring is sectioned, all rays attach, behaviour is uncoordinated, and righting occurs slowly and abnormally. Through nervous impulses, therefore, the normal unitary behaviour of echinoderms involves the temporary subordination of certain local activities to others dominating general action. The studies of J. E. Smith on the starfish nervous system reveal new complexities, including ganglion-cell mechanisms involved with the nerve net, advancing behavioural organization beyond that of the coelenterates.

An improved organization of behaviour thus enters with the subordination of local, reflexlike functions to wider patterns, as when scratching is inhibited as a dog sees food. The local activities themselves are then not only more elaborate and diversified, as in the reflex-cleaning activities of insects, but also better related to other behaviour. Echinoderm behaviour is more than a community of reflexes; sponge behaviour is far less.

Although echinoderm adaptive activities are impressive, they are sluggishly performed and their level of organization should not be overestimated. Jennings endowed the starfish with the ability to learn, on the basis of tests in which individuals shortened the time required to right themselves. One pair of rays was prevented from attaching by a glass rod used to disengage the tube feet from the substratum, and after 180 trials these arms attached less readily than before the trials. Although Jennings interpreted this as habit formation, Moore produced similar results merely by rubbing the tube-foot surfaces of particular rays with a glass rod or treating them with weak acid. He therefore attributed Jennings' results not to learning (*i.e.*, changes in central organization through experience) but to injury of restrained arms through continuous friction with the rod which altered sensory and motor function in further trials. These results are therefore equivalent to the impairment of action through motor fatigue, or its reduction through sensory adaptation or injury, not ordinarily classed as learning in higher animals.

B. Cephalization and Centralized Control

1. Functions of a Simple Brain.—Improvements in both organization and capacities of behaviour appear in worms, mollusks, and particularly insects. Basic advances are illustrated in a simple form in the earthworm. Whereas echinoderms are radially structured, and any of the body sections can lead in locomotion or other activities according to circumstances, worms have an anterior specialized end, which is not only the most sensitive and mobile of all body sections but also the dominant one by virtue of a superior ganglionic centre (brain). Cephalization, or head dominance, improves organization basically, widens the range of environment and action, and carries behavioural organization beyond the conditions prevailing in protozoans, coelenterates, and echinoderms. The significance of specialized head receptors and a brain for efficient behaviour in a marine worm is indicated, after the brain has been destroyed, by irregular crawling about, by turning much more clumsily on contact, and by burrowing less readily than a normal worm. The animal after operation cannot extend from its burrow (on chemical stimulation) and seize prey as does the normal individual. Removal of the worm's brain, although not preventing normal reactions altogether, materially reduces their directness and precision. This is therefore a primitive type of brain, a collector and a transmitter of impulses from the most sensitive parts of the organism, presumably also an amplifier, but not a major organizing centre. The brain of insects, in contrast, is an indispensable organizing centre. Although a bee or ant with its brain destroyed may stagger about for a time before dying, with a degree of locomotor coordination, only scattered reflex acts such as stinging occur and the complex normal repertory (*e.g.*, foraging, building) is gone.

Local functions such as feeding and locomotion in higher invertebrates, as demonstrated particularly in the work of K. Roeder and H. Mittelstaedt with certain orthopterans, have a degree of autonomy and of complexity far above that of corresponding functions in the vertebrates. In cockroaches, for example, after removal of the head, conditioning of isolated ganglia is still possible, modifying control over actions such as leg movements. Comparable alterations in local actions seem unlikely for vertebrates, in which brain and higher centres have a different and more essential role in integration.

2. Advances in Orientation.—Regulation of locomotion and way finding under changing external stimulation improves in worms, mollusks, and arthropods over its status in lower invertebrates. J. Loeb emphasized that the evolution of a specialized anterior and bilateral symmetry opens the way for new patterns of orientation in space. These improvements admit more appropriate changes in adjustment to external stimulation, as when an octopus turns toward the side on which a crab is seen but does not pursue if the object moves too swiftly. At this stage the crude energic properties of stimulation are dominant, as when a worm or snail approaches the source of a weak chemical but withdraws from the source of an intense stimulus, with variable behaviour at intermediate concentrations. The directive effect of stimuli of different intensity acting on receptors of the opposite sides of the body is shown by experiments in which a fly with its right eye covered turns toward the right under strong light but toward the left under weak light.

Progress in the organization and variability of orientation is indicated from the worms to insects, depending on the complexity and specialization not only of receptors but also of the central nervous system. The octopus, for example, has eyes much better fitted than those of marine worms for general vision, with accommodation to distance, and can inhibit its dash at a crab until within range. Social insects such as ants and bees have compound eyes, admitting versatile reactions to visual movements as well as movement with reference to changing visual stimuli. Although the evolution of orientation in space involves receptor specializations, advances in this capacity are especially correlated with the nervous system. Operative longitudinal sectioning of the brain introduces progressive impairments in the orientation of animals from worms to insects. J. Z. Young demonstrated that the octopus, through experience, can master conditioned responses to a crab, or to visual forms experienced with food. In such functions the octopus, far superior to worms, loses correspondingly much more through brain operations. Although in the lower invertebrates quantitative aspects of stimulation such as intensity, size, and rate of change basically control the timing and precision of orientation, in the cephalopods and insects, as compared with the worms, the patterns not only become more complex but also more changeable according to experience.

3. Simple Learned Modifications.—Evidence offered for learning in protozoans (as noted earlier) seems inadequate. The claims of Jennings and others for learned modifications in such invertebrates as coelenterates and echinoderms have been disputed by Parker and others on the grounds that the changes rest on altered peripheral processes (as in sensitivity or in muscular function) rather than on alterations of central neural functions. Results obtained by H. B. Hovey might be taken to suggest that flatworms are the lowest invertebrates capable of conditioned-response learning. Hovey found that, although light ordinarily keeps the marine flatworm *Leptoplana* active, presenting light together with head contact (which stops movement) changed the worm's responses within 20 five-minute periods to a stoppage of movement in light. R. Thompson and J. V. McConnell attempted a correction of Hovey's choice of stimuli in work with the terrestrial flatworm *Dugesia* using four main groups of subjects, with light the conditioned stimulus and shock the unconditioned stimulus. The investigators reported a conditioned reaction to light depending upon its association with shock. E. S. Halas and others, however, could not confirm the results in attempted replications. Jensen has criticized the experiment, centring on the fact that the groups were not adequately compared in terms of the effects of light and shock alone or in combination, suggesting that shock itself may have been the critical factor.

Better evidence for conditioned learning was obtained by M. Copeland, who trained the marine worm *Nereis* to emerge from a tube in response to light or to dark, whichever had been paired with meat juice in training. A more complex habit was acquired by earthworms in Yerkes' experiment, in which turning to the left at a T junction led to electric shock, to the right into a dark box. Within 160 trials some of the worms regularly turned right on reaching the junction. This habit does not depend on specific sensory or muscular changes; when L. Heck reversed the electrodes and dark box after the habit was learned, worms that required more than 120 trials to

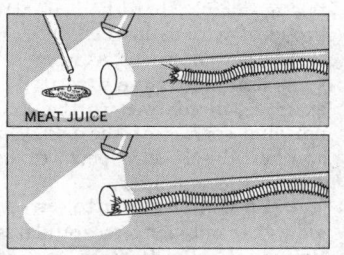

FIG. 1.—COPELAND'S STUDY OF CONDITIONING IN THE MARINE WORM NEREIS

At first, light is ineffective, but after having been combined several times with meat juice, light alone brings the worm from the tube

acquire the right turn now reversed it within 75 trials. Such modifications indicate a basis in central nervous organization rather than in peripheral function. No learning comparable to this adjustment has been demonstrated in coelenterates, echinoderms, or flatworms.

The organization of behaviour is greatly enhanced by a potential for learning. Some worms, through learned changes, can alter their normal activities, though not as much as higher invertebrates. In learning, illustrated by the conditioned response, through experience a specific reaction is given to a stimulus previously incapable of eliciting such behaviour. In Copeland's experiment, light (the conditioned stimulus) initially did not bring the worm from its tube. Meat juice (the unconditioned stimulus) was effective, however, and pairing these two stimuli brought for light a new control over reactions. In the worm's T-maze behaviour, through comparable changes, stimuli near the junction control the right-turning reaction, rendering contact with the electrodes unnecessary. An adequate basis for such changes is afforded by a central nervous system with ganglionic centres and interconnections admitting appropriate new sensory-motor organizations. The mere presence of ganglion cells is not enough, for the starfish despite such equipment seems incapable of such learning. In arthropods, neural evolution

admits further advances in learning capacity. *See* also NEUROLOGY, COMPARATIVE.

III. EVOLUTION OF BEHAVIOUR

1. Behaviour and the Processes of Evolution.—Modern science interprets behavioural differences in animals, from protozoans to man, as the outcome of long and complex evolutionary processes. The role of behaviour in evolution is by no means obvious, however, as inferences from fossils must be validated by evidence on the relationships of structure and behaviour in existing organisms and these, rather than forming a linear series, represent different branches of a complex related system of which many sections have vanished. Also, the relations of structure and behaviour not only resist unraveling but seem to have very different properties in the principal types of existing animals. Despite these and other obstacles, behaviour has clearly evolved.

There is little question that behaviour has played a critical and major role in organic evolution. Efficiency in widely different activities, from foraging to defense and shelter getting, has much bearing on the success of reproductive processes and hence on species survival. In many ways, behaviour must have influenced intimately the selective processes underlying evolution.

The initiatory mechanism for evolutionary change, biologists conclude, involved mutations in the chromosomes, effected through the action of radiation on the organism through chemical, mechanical, or other extrinsic agencies. Mutations (*see* EVOLUTION, ORGANIC) may have involved any aspect of structure in the organism, thereby altering behaviour in diverse ways from the specific to the general. The evolution of mammals must have involved (far more extensively than that of invertebrates) mutations basic to the development of structures capable of complex and plastic relationships with function and behaviour. As new mutations affected existing physical structures, behaviour diverged with increasing frequency from ancestral patterns.

According to conditions, success in behaviour affecting reproduction must depend on what responses are made both in everyday existence and in critical or marginal situations. Because behaviour results from the interactions of functional systems (sensory, neural, secretory, motor, and others), a mutation affecting structure locally can often influence functions in the organism as a whole. For example, a more sensitive eyespot may improve directed responses to light so that orientation and foraging become more efficient, and adding a lens to the system widens the range and efficiency of adaptation still more.

Mutations thereby open the way to specialization in behaviour, favouring the occupancy of species-typical habitats (niches). Within any period, the relative success of behaviour affecting reproduction determines which strains and species can adapt to appropriate niches and survive and which types perish through mutations leading to detrimental or inefficient behaviour. As accumulating mutations favour diversity, successful animal types tend to expand into lineages differing increasingly in their adaptive patterns. The survival of a species then depends on its possessing a set of genes contributing under appropriate conditions to the development of a behaviour pattern adequate to maintain the reproducing population in its species niche.

2. Evolution, Structure, and Behaviour.—Structure, physiology, and behaviour are interrelated, although differently according to phyletic level; hence the role of natural selection may differ from level to level. The progress of evolution is not correctly described as a process adding new properties to the old, but rather as one transforming the old in conjunction with the appearance of new properties in new phyletic settings. The fate of species and species relationships in evolution depends primarily on the relative efficacy of structures rather than on purposive considerations, which involve a basic misconception of species-typical acts and their dependence on structures. Thus a dragonfly that ordinarily lays eggs on water may lay them on a freshly tarred roof, not by mistake, but by responding to the sensory characteristics of a shimmering surface.

At early stages in evolution, structure bears rather directly on behaviour, favouring stereotyped patterns. Invertebrate activities thus are dominated by the functional characteristics of specific sensory, motor, or other equipment or of particular physiological conditions. These relationships can be misunderstood, particularly when they are complex. Thus J. H. Fabre believed in an "inflexibility of instincts" in insects (attributed to inherited nervous patterns), arguing from cases in which performance presumably could occur only once, as he reported the callow mason bee able to escape only once from the paper cell of pupation. But L. Verlaine found that in this case the critical matter was strength of the jaws, for when the cell wall was not too tough, the bee could escape more than once even on the first day. Dependence of behaviour on particular organic conditions is illustrated by the fact that spiders can repair their torn webs or not according to the supply of secretion in their different silk glands. However, structure is much less simply related to behaviour in mammals.

Throughout evolution, and particularly at times of crisis and other turning points, evidently mutations were favoured that increased the complexity of structures basic to functional relationships, promoting more versatile environmental adjustments. Significant sequences thus are indicated, as when local specialization of the skin of early vertebrates added a lens to the primitive eye, increasing the efficiency of space perception, which increased still further when specializations in retina, eye muscles, and brain admitted binocular vision and an augmented depth effect.

New adaptive levels were achieved in evolution not just through added complexity of existing structures affecting function but through qualitative changes as well. In a succession of adaptive radiations from the acellular to the multicellular, and from the primitive vertebrate ancestor to the reptilelike mammalian ancestor, basic changes occurred in the conduction system with important consequences for behavioural organization and for new behaviour. The result presumably was not so much that mechanisms of lower levels were repeated on higher levels as that they were modified in relation to the new context. Accordingly, it is probable that in vertebrate evolution from fish to man the "old brain" was not merely retained in a more complex form, but was progressively repatterned correlatively with increasing cortex. In mammals, as compared with invertebrates, not only are structural mechanisms much more versatile in their functional relationships but limitations of action by specific structures relax increasingly, widening the breadth and plasticity of behaviour in its bearing on species adaptation.

3. Ancestry and Behavioural Resemblance.—In the animal series, behaviour patterns tend to exhibit similarities in proportion to the degree of phylogenetic relationship and dissimilarities in inverse proportion. All animals are similar in the sense that behaviour is adaptive and that each behaves generally to attain beneficial and escape injurious conditions. This similarity depends on the fact that all species have mechanisms favouring approach to stimuli of weak intensity, withdrawal from stimuli of strong intensity. In phyla from protozoa to man, however, these reactions differ in structural bases and in ontogenesis.

In principle, existing animals do not form a linear series but represent the termini of a multibranched system among which exist discontinuities (e.g., insects, birds, mammals) and continuities (e.g., reptiles, birds). Roughly in correspondence with ancestral affinities, increases are found in the degree of structural homology and of similarity in the functions to which structure is basic. An example is seen in the front limbs of vertebrates, all significantly involved in directional control. Superimposed upon such general patterns are disparities among groups that have taken different directions of specialization, as that between fish and birds in the different orientative functions of the pectoral fins of the former and the (homologous) wings of the latter.

Striking differences among the specific adaptive patterns of surviving phyla show that the principle of continuity in evolution must be qualified in view of different branch lines in ancestry. For example, arguments, on grounds of evolutionary continuity, that a learning capacity exists in protozoans analogous to that of mammals oppose the fact that since unicellular and multicellular animals diverged in remote geologic times they have differed progressively, and the advent of mechanisms basic to the learning

abilities of multicellular organisms may well have postdated the common ancestry.

Because structure may influence function very differently on different animal levels, both in the relative directness and in the nature of its effect, the principle of structural homology (i.e., basis in common ancestry) cannot be generalized directly to behaviour. A different reservation concerns resemblances through convergence, or adaptations evolving independently, whereby similar niches are occupied or similar activities arise. Owls and bats, for example, have analogous adaptations for flight and the nocturnal capture of prey; termites and ants have similar patterns in nesting and other social activities.

O. Heinroth, particularly, and later K. Lorenz stressed behavioural characteristics as an additional clue to evolutionary relationships. Thus similar activities in closely related species often exhibit gradations evidently corresponding to the relative recency of the species. For example, in the mating patterns of empid flies prior to coupling, in one species the male presents to the female a freshly killed insect, in another species he presents the booty within a cocoon he has spun, and in still another he presents only an empty cocoon. The last pattern is presumably the most recent.

Striking similarities, not convergences, are often found between related species living in widely separated habitats, as, for example, both English and South American thrushes line their nests with mud. Comparisons are complicated, however, in the similar patterns of related species which are sympatric (i.e., live in the same habitat) by the rise of specialized differences through competitive processes influencing natural selection. Thus two closely related species of doryline ants in the genus *Eciton*, sharing the same New World tropical forest habitat, differ strikingly in the patterns of their predatory raids, with colonies of one species pillaging in large swarms, colonies of the other in complex systems of columns. These species also differ in the booty they capture, with the first taking mainly hard-bodied arthropods, the second, soft-bodied brood of various insects.

At times, however, as when selection pressures are not intensive, sympatric and closely related species may be more alike. For example, in contrast to the *Eciton* species cited, surface-adapted doryline species of the Old World genus *Aenictus* resemble one another closely in aspects of behaviour in which closely related *Eciton* species differ.

4. Phylogeny, Ontogeny, and Instinct.—The traditional view that ontogeny recapitulates phylogeny, questioned for structure by G. R. de Beer and others, is even more doubtful for behaviour. What individuals in each species inherit are their chromosomes, influencing ontogeny in species-characteristic ways provided development occurs under species-typical conditions. Under other extrinsic conditions, different phenotypes (developmental forms) appear, diverging from the species-typical pattern not only structurally but often also behaviourally. Species-typical behaviour patterns, considered in relation to species genetics, constitute the problem of instinctive behaviour.

A useful way of stating this problem is to say that although heredity influences all behaviour in all animals, its influence is more direct in more primitive animals than in the more advanced and seems to be very different on different phyletic levels. This interpretation contradicts the traditional view that the "instinctive" and the "learned" may be clearly distinguished in animal behaviour, with the latter increasingly prominent in higher animals. It is more likely that behaviour evolves through new and increasingly complex reorientations, with the old rebuilt and extended in terms of the new, than through the replacement of the "innate" by the "learned."

On each phyletic level, striking differences appear in the relationships between genes, species-typical structures and physiology, situational conditions at successive developmental stages, and the predominance of species-typical behaviour as against genotypical patterns. In the sense that the activities of invertebrate animals are more directly dominated by structure than are those of mammals, invertebrate behaviour is more instinctive. Accordingly, agencies mediating among genes, organic mechanisms, and behaviour are fewer, with less numerous and less involved interrelationships in protozoans and sponges than in insects, with insects in turn below rodents and rodents below primates. In this succession, the role of heredity in behavioural development is not decreased, but rather becomes increasingly indirect and plastic as further and more diverse intervening variables are added. Consequently, contrasting behaviour patterns arise which are not only increasingly complex but also qualitatively progressive. For understanding these differences, the classical nature-nurture dichotomy is not only too simple but also misleading. Psychological superiority must have emerged in higher animals not through less nature and more nurture but through increasingly complex and qualitatively new properties of nature and nurture, inextricably interrelated in development in ways characteristic of the level.

As an example, function varies strikingly with age both in invertebrates and in mammals. In honeybees, G. Rösch attributed such differences to growth-conditioned organic changes. Young workers just emerged from pupation tend to specialize in feeding larvae, but about the 15th day, when the salivary glands atrophy, they turn mainly to building. This activity falls off about the 25th day, when the wax glands end their active phase, and is replaced by foraging. Such activity successions are not uncommon among social insects. For honeybees, however, E. Lindemann stresses the condition of the colony as a major factor influencing function in workers of all ages. A striking example of functional variations with development is found in such amphibians as frogs and salamanders which change radically in locomotion and other behaviour on leaving the aquatic for the terrestrial stage. In mammals, although ontogenetic changes in function certainly occur on a structural basis, behaviour develops much more subtly and indirectly in relation to structure than in lower animals.

It is therefore probable that the relationship of behaviour to survival, always important in evolution, is very different on various phyletic levels. As it is realized that assumptions of innateness in apposition to the acquired can explain no activity, increasing emphasis is placed upon the need for analytical investigation.

Although geneticists often state that the genes impose species-characteristic limitations on development, even in the 1960s this generalization lacked proof for behaviour. Actually, the influences of the genes are not direct or exclusive in determining behaviour in any animal but are exerted through diverse interrelationships between organism and developmental medium.

In all phyla, the functioning of organic factors underlying the rise of instinctive activities requires a developmental situation typical of the species. Frequently, certain conditions of stimulation (i.e., experiences) can be detected as critical for the development of the species-typical pattern. Thus J. E. Harker found that the normal day-night activity rhythm of the adult May fly does not appear when developing individuals have been subjected to continuous light or darkness but only when eggs or larvae have been exposed to at least one daily light-dark cycle. Comparably, species patterns such as the spinning of characteristic cocoons by caterpillars result from a close relationship between structural growth and features of the developmental situation. G. van der Kloot and C. Williams found that if a *Cecropia* larva cannot attain an upright posture against a support such as a twig, no cocoon is spun. Instead, the arrangement of the thread depends upon prevalent conditions. Thus, if the caterpillar ready to spin is put into a balloon it will line the interior surface with a sheet; if it is tethered to a peg, it will weave a cone around the peg. In the parasitic ichneumon fly *Nemeritis*, responses to the host upon which eggs are laid are influenced by larval experience, as such responses can be modified by changing the type of insect on which the individual feeds as a larva. Indicating the possibility that conditioning influences insect development, although in a secondary and obscure role, is evidence that the act of following odour trails arises in many ants on the basis of individual habituation to nest chemicals beginning as early as the period of larval feeding.

In lower vertebrates, species-typical behaviour such as mating and nesting have the characteristic of stereotypy, as in insects, but with a different aspect relevant to the level. The claim of Lorenz and others that certain critical acts called "instinctive

movements" arise through innate neural patterns determined isomorphically by the genes lacks effective support. Rather, Z. Y. Kuo, from his significant studies on pecking in chicks, concluded that intimate relationships exist between factors in growth and in the extrinsic situation.

Comparably, D. S. Lehrman found that important factors in the reproductive and parental behaviour of ring doves (beyond hormonal processes) are experiences with mates, incubating eggs, and young. E. Klinghammer and E. S. Hess reported that adult ring doves, after experience in incubating eggs, responded to hatchlings with feeding actions whether or not they had ever fed young. Although such patterns are species-typical and genetic, they are not predetermined neurally but result from a development in which organic processes interact intimately with situational factors.

5. Factors in Rhythmic Behaviour.—Behaviour rhythms of animals often parallel such events as the tides, day-night, and seasonal changes. O. Park recognized exogenous rhythms directly controlled by changes in the environment and endogenous rhythms that persist (often for some time) under constant conditions. Examples of the first type are the daily vertical migrations of marine zooplankton and the daily activity-quiescence routine of many grasshoppers, both mainly dependent on changes in light intensity. Examples of the second type are found in the day-night activity rhythms of shore crabs and the rhythmic activities of mussels in opening their valves and feeding at high tide and closing at low tide. The American crayfish *Cambarus*, as J. H. Welsh showed, can maintain such rhythmic actions as pigmentary changes as long as a few months under constant laboratory conditions. Evidence suggests that rhythmic physiological changes in eyestalk pigmentary processes, probably basic to such changes, are regulated by one or more hormonal mechanisms. Such endogenous regulatory processes (called biological clocks) have been demonstrated in animals from invertebrates to mammals; patterns as varied as the daily foraging of honeybees and man's rhythms of activity and sleep may be related to them. C. S. Pittendrigh represents the view that the frequencies of all biological-clock systems are innate, J. Calhoun that they are acquired; J. F. Brown suggests that they may arise through periodic external factors as subtle as changes in the earth's geomagnetic field. Seasonal changes in function and behaviour occur in many birds and mammals (*see* MIGRATION, ANIMAL; MIGRATION, BIRD; REPRODUCTION) and are often referrable to physiological changes paced by such annual variations as daily illumination; puzzling cases include cave-dwelling bats and tropical birds in which an external basis is not apparent.

6. Ontogenesis of Vertebrate Behaviour.—Vertebrate behaviour seems to differ from that of invertebrates by virtue not only of a nervous system with a fundamentally different central pattern but also of organic factors underlying superior processes of perception and motivation. Although such functions as locomotion and equilibrium are well developed even in fish, in mammals the corresponding functions are more complex and more subject to variations according to the conditioning of ontogenesis.

An impressive contrast is that between altricial (blind-born) mammals and the precocial, which have sight soon after birth. The former (the rat is an example) are slower than the latter in structural maturation, and require a much longer time for behavioural development. The latter (illustrated by deer and other ungulates) can move erect soon after birth and show strikingly more rapid perceptual development. Such contrasts raise the question of how species-typical behaviour patterns develop in different vertebrates.

7. Maturation.—The concept of maturation, emphasizing the role in behavioural development of organic changes through growth and differentiation, has been focused by many upon the nervous system. In the study of G. E. Coghill on the salamander *Ambystoma*, successive stages in action were observed with correlated histological changes in the nervous system. In this tailed amphibian, an early nonmotile stage was identified when, with sensory surfaces still unconnected by nerves with muscles, the only action was an anterior bending to the side of direct muscular stimulation. At about 30 hours of age, the head bent away from the stimulated side, paralleling the appearance of crossed nerve connections from the skin of the head to muscles on the opposite side. Then S movements of the body and, later, rapid swimming movements were correlated with further growth changes in the nerve tube. Coghill concluded that in the development of swimming in this vertebrate, the status of neural growth is critical. This conclusion found support in the research of L. Carmichael, who immobilized salamander embryos with Chloretone during the period in which swimming normally appears, yet found that when later released from the drug, these animals apparently swam as well as undrugged normal specimens. The conclusion that organic neural growth alone is sufficient for development of normal swimming in this amphibian is tentative, however, in view of evidence obtained by A. Fromme. His results indicate that opportunities for action and stimulation at certain stages in development also contribute to the swimming pattern, since embryos immobilized at those stages, when later released from the drug, swam less well than normals.

Maturation, as defined, seems basic to the behavioural development of lower vertebrates from fish to birds. The concept needs revision, however, in view of evidence cited below, bearing on the interaction of processes within the developing organism and between organism and external situation, characteristic of growth stage but extending beyond the specific bounds of growth and differentiation.

Although the development of behaviour patterns is often held to depend on an innate central neural control, this question is still controversial. Certainly, neural growth limits behaviour at any stage (e.g., the salamander cannot bend its head until crossed neural connections have grown). Other factors also are involved. The characteristic head lunge of lower vertebrates probably requires sensory maturation as well as neural maturation. Several such mechanisms evidently contribute to the adult lunging response, which, as in many fish, amphibians, and birds, occurs on weak stimulation. Thus the characteristic lunge is elicited by objects below a certain size if these are in motion at not too rapid a rate. Presumably, in lower vertebrates, tissue growth promotes adult patterns such as feeding and mating in discrete ways as through sensory-threshold factors in visual-movement responses. To understand the ontogeny of behaviour, however, the study must be broadened. Although, for example, gonadal hormones are basic to the appearance of mating behaviour in all vertebrates, evidence suggests that they may function in diverse ways beyond their possible neural effects, as by increasing local sensitivity.

8. Factors in Organization.—Against the traditional predeterministic view that instinctive behaviour is organized neurally on a native basis, the alternative epigenetic view holds that such behaviour develops through coordinations of many organic resources in the organism interacting with the developmental medium. Experience, definable as the effect of stimulation on the organism, participates in all development, and in diverse forms, including learning.

From the same genotype (see HEREDITY), variations in the conditions of development may result in phenotypes differing behaviourally as well as organically. Under different temperature conditions in development, M. H. Harnly obtained fruit flies which were flightless, limited and eccentric, or species typical in flight; and K. Moore in a comparable experiment obtained rats differing in both body form and learning ability.

For the organization of instinctive behaviour, evidence for invertebrates and for vertebrates shows that species-typical factors both of maturation and of experience in the standard developmental situation are essential. Certain poecilid fishes, raised apart from species mates in neutral surroundings in which, for example, they never saw their own reflections from the water film or other surfaces, scored much lower than normals in mating tests at maturity. That the role of experience may involve learning in amphibian larvae is suggested by the fact that N. L. Munn found the early swimming stages of certain amphibians capable both of being conditioned and of learning a simple T-maze habit.

Although the roles of maturation and of experience are fused

in all behavioural development and resist experimental separation, certain generalizations are possible. Thus organic factors seem relatively more determinative of behavioural development in lower vertebrates than in mammals. In the former, accordingly, naïve responses to stimulation are less readily modified through experience than in the latter. The lizard Lacerta, studied by E. Ehrenhardt, gave its forward (feeding) lunge most readily to the movement of figures such as circles with even outlines, least readily to figures such as crosses with irregular outlines. When a circle was paired with a quinine-treated mealworm, a cross with an untreated mealworm, initial responses were virtually unmodified within 850 trials. In comparison, mammals such as rats normally change their initial responses readily according to the conditions of training. In lower vertebrates, discrete properties of the stimulus such as movement, size, and brightness characteristically dominate behaviour, evidently as a result particularly of correlated factors in sense organs and nervous system. N. Tinbergen and others use the term releasers for stimuli which typically elicit certain types of response; however, this concept has been criticized as too simple and as obscuring ontogenetic processes. For example, the gaping (mouth-opening) response of nestlings in passerine species such as thrushes is first aroused by mechanical stimulation, as by vibrations of the nest, later by the movement of any object (e.g., a black disk) of sufficient size presented above the nest edge. The facts suggest that, through conditioning, naïve responses (e.g., to nest vibration) become attached to specific features of the external situation, such as first the parent bird's bulk at the nest edge, then the parent's head. The organization of such responses in birds is a complex matter in which experience may figure in various ways.

In this sense, birds have a far more extensive and complex repertory of instinctive, organically determined activities than have mammals. In the organization of activities such as migration, the role of maturation seems predominant, that of experience secondary. The investigations of W. Rowan and others show that the northward spring migration of birds such as juncos is set off through the excitatory effect of internal changes (e.g., pituitary and gonadal secretions) caused by a progressive increase in daily illumination. Evidence suggests that changes in organic condition may influence responses to environmental factors (e.g., temperature gradient, angle of the sun) governing the direction and course of migration.

Organic factors may have a comparable role in such behaviour as homing, as the use of mate and of nest to control direction of flight in homing pigeons attests. G. Kramer and others found that many birds, both in migratory and in homing flights, can maintain a constant or changing course through adjustments to the sun's position; F. Sauer reports similar responses to star patterns; G. V. Matthews and others suggest that for birds such as pigeons an internal time-controlling mechanism is basic to such functions. Much evidence indicates that in many birds homing and, in part, migration depend strongly upon experience with landmarks and topography.

The organization of species-typical activities such as pecking in fowl is known to have a complex individual history, starting in the egg. Kuo showed that, with maturation in neurosensory and muscular tissue, the embryo's head lunge to touch modifies under the influence of self-stimulation through its own actions. Crude conditioning processes are evident before hatching. Shortly after hatching, the significant activities of the head lunge, bill opening and closing, and swallowing are crude and essentially separate. Head lunging occurs, however, on the appearance of small, moving objects and (limited by maturational properties such as muscular strength) within a few days an organized and discriminative pecking at edible objects comes about. Thus it appears that whereas maturation dominates the development of individual components of pecking such as head lunge, experiential factors are required even for the early appearance of these components and are heavily involved in organizing the eventual efficient act. The influence of maturation is emphasized by the fact that, when chicks are kept in the dark and hand-fed for varying times after hatching, the process of improvement leads sooner to efficient pecking than in normal chicks; *i.e.,* experience is more advantageous when strength and other organic factors have advanced. The influence of experience is emphasized by the fact that chicks fed artificially for longer than two weeks after hatching learn only with great difficulty to peck at food, since they have learned to feed otherwise than through pecking. The greater predominance of stereotypy in lower vertebrates than in birds seems attributable to the greater influence of experience in the behavioural development of the latter.

Life activities often are organized with reference to the environment into which the animal first emerged. Solitary wasps tend to establish adult burrows in the localities of their pupation; social insects generally have foraging territories centred on the fixed nest sites in which the workers developed. In invertebrates and lower vertebrates, such territorial attachments have a relatively simple behavioural basis; in mammals the fixation and use of territory in development is progressively more complex. Thus, for many birds such as the common tern and pigeon, A. T. Marshall and others indicate an attachment of the females first to nest site and environs, subsequently and secondarily to eggs and young. In chimpanzees and other subhuman primates, the territorial pattern common to everyday group routines seems often to have a history of many generations, made possible through involved processes of perceptual development and learning in each new generation of young.

9. Nervous Systems and Behaviour.—An important approach to understanding psychological differences between lower animals and mammals is through the role of the nervous system. Although in worms the appearance of a dominant brain permits definite advances over the radial pattern of the starfish, this centre is of a low order, mainly a transmitter rather than an organizer. Insects, much advanced in organization, still reflect a strong influence of sensory and other local components in behaviour.

As comparative neurologists have shown, the brain of lower vertebrates is not only more sparsely supplied with interconnections than is that of mammals, but the brain exerts only rudimentary control over lower centres and is not equipped to influence general behaviour in terms of changing stimuli. The forebrain (dominated by the principal sensory systems) and the midbrain (generally dominated by the visual system) are best equipped for integration of stereotyped behaviour. Such characteristics go far in accounting for the typical shortcomings of these animals in modifying naïve responses based on such stimulus aspects as intensity.

With the appearance of cerebral cortex, correlation among the principal centres of the vertebrate brain improves greatly. Cortex, although restricted in reptiles to a small area in the upper forebrain, and obscure in birds, covers the entire forebrain in mammals. Cortex interconnects the principal centres of the nervous system both directly and indirectly, admitting new types of organization which override specific sensory effects and local activities according to the animal's experience.

The evolution of cerebral cortex, particularly, seems to give mammals their psychological superiority. But, as K. Pribram has concluded, old-brain mechanisms also evolve, permitting an extension of their functions relative to the new brain. Thus, A. Brodal and others have pointed to the significance of the reticular formation, and P. D. MacLean and others to that of the limbic formation in ontogenesis; and D. B. Lindsley has suggested a major limbic role in mammalian perceptual development. The role of such brain-stem mechanisms in promoting plasticity in behavioural development seems to be much greater in higher mammals than in lower mammals and birds, far greater in the latter than in lower vertebrates.

The commissures, connecting the halves of the brain, parallel the cerebral cortex in their appearance and development in mammals. By testing split-brain cases, in which these connections have been cut, R. W. Sperry and collaborators have shown that the specialization of the two hemispheres for separate, complex acts, as well as their degree of integration in complex behaviour, increases in the cat, monkey, and man, in that order.

IV. PSYCHOLOGICAL SUPERIORITY OF MAMMALS

In mammals, from marsupials to man, the psychological limitations of lower animals are overcome progressively. Through more versatile capacities and better organization of behaviour, the world of the individual increases in content and in variety. The general superiority of mammals shows itself particularly in their resources for developing new behaviour. For example, reptiles, although they can be tamed so that they become docile, do not form attachments nor take the initiative in play with people, as do mammals.

A. Development of Behaviour in Mammals

1. Maturation.—Correlated with the longer developmental period typical in mammals, their resources admit a greater weight for experience and a greater variety of behaviour appropriate to changing circumstances than in inframammalian animals. In general, higher mammals require a longer time than lower to develop. Accordingly, whole-body adaptive behaviour appears earlier in lower mammals, which often fend for themselves sooner after birth than the young of higher mammals. For example, the young opossum, just 12–15 days after development begins, crawls from the mother's cloaca over her abdomen to the pouch, moving along by a reflex hair-clutching and forelimb progression. At 60 days it leaves its nipple in the pouch on occasional excursions to the outside, where it runs and climbs about. The young of ungulates, such as the goat, are capable of upright progression shortly after birth; the human infant, in contrast, is incapable of self-progression until it crawls at about eight months of age.

Most mammals are relatively more immature at birth than the young of lower vertebrates, and hence cope less effectively with their environments. Young marine turtles, on emerging from the egg, crawl toward the moonlit sea (in response to reflected light). Newborn kittens and puppies, however, accomplish only a highly variable, nonvisual locomotion to the mother, and in specific activities have little more than crude sucking and righting responses. These mammals improve very slowly from birth in orientation and locomotion. At one week (before vision enters) the kitten returns slowly and inefficiently to the nest when set down nearby, mainly requiring tactual guidance. Although in the appearance of crawling in kittens and walking in human infants maturation is basic, limiting the rate of development somewhat as in lower vertebrates, in mammals the factors of experience have increasing weight.

Man's adult behaviour pattern appears later than that of any other animal and is the least specifically influenced by maturation. When a chimpanzee and a human infant were raised from birth in the same household, with similar treatment, the advantages of more rapid maturation were at first all in the chimpanzee's favour. At five months it exceeded the average one-year performance level of human infants in climbing, manipulating objects, and responding to companions. Although the chimpanzee's motor superiority continued, soon the human infant excelled in other respects. At one year, in acquiring word sounds, object meanings, and social meanings, the human infant far surpassed the chimpanzee. Man's psychological superiority over other animals rests on his greater potential for profiting from experience and not simply on his longer infancy and childhood.

2. Genetics of Behaviour.—Although genetic factors underlie all animal activities, heredity seems to influence behaviour more directly in the lower mammals than in the higher. Sexual patterns, for example, are less stereotyped in chimpanzees than in rats, as a result of evolutionary advances in the primate cortex which admit new relationships between structure and behaviour and make experience and learning more influential.

Correlational study of genetic factors and behaviour, in psychogenetics, offers techniques for comparison. For example, the trait of wildness appears to be dominant in the offspring when the gray Norway rat is crossed with the docile albino rat, and the behaviour of future generations as well as that of backcrosses of the hybrids indicates the opposed influence of different gene combinations (*see* HEREDITY). With this knowledge the organic basis of such behavioural differences can be studied in different strains. The increasing difficulty, as maturity approaches, of taming the young of genetically wild strains of rats, much greater than in domesticated strains, indicates that glandular secretions contribute to strain differences of this type. Supporting evidence is found in the fact that the adrenal glands of wild strains are larger than those of domesticated strains.

3. Influence of Experience.—Traditionally, species-typical activities appearing soon after birth (in isolated animals) have been considered inborn. But experience is not excluded thereby, as conditioned-response learning is demonstrated prior to hatching in certain birds and before birth in certain mammals, including man. Furthermore, under equivalent developmental conditions, experience may influence different individuals similarly and its role therefore may be overlooked. For example, Kuo found that the appearance of mouse-hunting behaviour in kittens depends upon a situation in which organic equipment is utilized. The kitten's first pounce is not hunting, but darting toward a moving object. This response resembles the forward lunge of certain lower vertebrates, except that in the kitten the new stimuli that enter and the patterns that eventuate are largely matters of experience. In the typical feline environment, pouncing soon leads to tasting blood, since the kitten inherits sharp claws capable of piercing the mouse's skin; tasting blood stimulates biting, and with experience the kitten becomes a mouser. Kuo obtained different results by varying developmental conditions. By always shocking kittens with mice present, he displaced pouncing with a fear reaction; by raising kittens with mice, pouncing was inhibited and social companionship developed. Thus, although certain species-typical equipment favours pouncing, drawing blood, and other events essential for mousing, mouse killing as a pattern requires certain interactions of organism and developmental field most likely to occur in the normal species environment.

4. Drive and Motivation.—Certain classes of behaviour once called instincts are related by modern psychology to drives. Drive is a term for physiological processes energizing individual behaviour. Examples are the thirst, sex, and hunger drives. Each of these patterns has its basis in physiological processes; for example, the sex drive emanates from complex conditions centring around glandular secretions, the hunger drive from both gastric processes and changes in blood chemistry. The influencing of changes in general behaviour by internal drive fluctuations has been established experimentally for many different animals. A classical example is G. H. Wang's demonstration of relationship between the ovarian (egg-maturation) cycle and periodic fluctuations of general activity in the female rat. Organic examinations showed that oestrous or heat periods recurred at four- to five-day intervals, and at corresponding times striking increases occurred in the daily amount of activity. Wang concluded that the activity rhythm depended on glandular changes incident to oestrus, as it disappeared in mature females after spaying and during pregnancy and was absent in immature females.

Some broad differences exist in the responses of different types of animals to drives. On maturing sexually, invertebrates and lower vertebrates tend to behave in more stereotyped ways than do higher vertebrates. A female solitary wasp of certain species, fertilized and with mature eggs, stirs about and excitedly stings a spider or other characteristic prey when it is encountered; an egg-laden jewel fish is particularly attracted by objects having certain general properties of movement, coloration and size. The effective stimuli are species typical. In contrast, the incentives or stimuli governing the drive-impelled responses of mammals, increasingly broadened and individually more variable than in lower vertebrates, seem related to superior aptitudes for learning through experience.

A related difference exists between lower and higher mammals in the ability to satisfy or change a drive tension through conditions related only indirectly to the original incentive. Thus a pat on the head stimulates a properly trained dog to intensive efforts but affects a rat much less. Chimpanzees can learn to work for poker chips which are then inserted into a food-delivery slot, whereby an inedible object acquires a measure of drive satisfaction for the animal. A comparable mammalian superiority in motivated behaviour is seen in the individual's ability to initiate

the secondary stimulus, as when a dog "ready for a walk" brings out his leash. Such behaviour has not been established reliably in reptiles or other lower vertebrates. (*See* also INSTINCT; MOTIVATION; PSYCHOLOGY, PHYSIOLOGICAL.)

5. Sensitivity and Perception.—Von Uexküll and others have undertaken to describe the world of lower animals in terms of what is known about sensitivity. Thus one might speculate that for the honeybee in flight a flower patch is a flickering mosaic of colour with a glimmer of ultraviolet here and there; for the bird skimming low the patch has a distinct colour geometry without ultraviolet effects; for the house cat the scene has a washed out, colourless appearance. Such descriptions, from subjective inferences, are in the class of rudimentary speculation.

Only the first step toward understanding an animal's effective environment is accomplished by exploring its sensitivity. The chief problems are: what types of physical effects the animal is equipped to sense; what upper and lower limits (thresholds) hold for the various aspects (*e.g.*, intensity) in vision and other modalities; and what the acuity is in each field. In the sensory properties of animals, striking differences are found. Among the insects, the housefly, honeybee, and others, although blind to the long wavelengths of light seen by man as red, are visually sensitive to very short rays (the ultraviolet band) not seen by most vertebrates including man. Carnivores such as dogs, cats, and rats seem insensitive to wavelength differences in light which man sees as colours; whereas bees, many fish, and most diurnal birds and primates have a distinct wavelength sensitivity. Although these animals may not see hues as does man, they have colour vision, since under experimental conditions they can discriminate between wavelengths and between wavelengths and grays of corresponding brightness.

Important differences also are found in the ranges of corresponding types of sensitivity. Most fish can discriminate among intensities and pitches of sound; many crickets and other insects possess receptors known as chordotonal organs, sensitive to high frequencies of sound; many lower animals react to auditory frequencies above the human limits. The hunter's dog responds to the tone of a whistle near 30,000 cycles per second, soundless to the hunter, whose upper threshold lies below 18,000 cycles.

Striking sensory adaptations, important for orientation, are common. In bats, insect-feeding species and certain others have remarkable aptitudes for flying in the dark, long attributed to tactual sensitivity but found to depend on a keen perception of the bat's own ultrasonic utterances reflected from objects. When D. R. Griffin released bats in a dark room they flew skilfully among wires strung close together, but when hearing was eliminated by plugging the ears, or when the sounds were stopped by fastening shut the mouth, the skill disappeared. Highly delicate auditory reactivity of this type, known as echolocation, has been demonstrated in animals as different as certain shrews and some of the large aquatic mammals (*e.g.*, dolphins). Although echolocation has been found only in mammals, many birds and insects react keenly to high-frequency sounds produced by mates or by other animals (*e.g.*, certain moths move evasively in response to ultrasonic emissions of predatory bats). The work of K. von Frisch suggests that honeybees and other arthropods can orient with reference to the plane of polarization of light, a visual capacity still undemonstrated for any vertebrate animal. In most birds, taste is acute but smell is poor; in honeybees and many other insects, olfaction through antennal reception appears exquisitely acute but taste seems poorer than in man.

An animal's sensory equipment fundamentally influences its way of life. Bats and oilbirds can live in dark caves because of their delicate ultrasonic auditory sensitivity; mammals with keen olfaction can track prey by scent and tend to become night foragers, particularly (as in the cats) when dark adaptation processes favour dim-light vision. In contrast, animals with superior bright-light vision and inferior smell, as the diurnal monkeys, settle into a routine of daytime activity and nighttime sleep. Interesting relationships are often found between the fields of sensitivity and differences in habitat. There are species such as cave fishes living in complete darkness that have poor vision or are blind, with tactual and chemical sensitivity highly developed. Comparable inverse relationships between vision and olfaction prevail in many insects. Most diurnal birds have excellent vision but are poor in olfaction. Sensory equipment basically defines the limits and the nature of an animal's world.

6. Sensing v. Perceiving.—Sensory data, although indispensable for behaviour, are not the best indicators of an animal's psychological standing. Many birds, for example, seem similar to man and are far superior to most lower mammals in visual acuity. Yet, in the critical matter of using sensitivity to master object meanings and their relationships, in which sensory factors are secondary, birds are inferior to man.

An animal's endowment for perception, definable as sensing in terms of meanings, is best judged according to how it deals with objects under varying conditions. The relatively stereotyped responses governing food-getting activities in cold-blooded vertebrates seem best interpreted in terms of relatively direct stimulus-response relationships (*see* ANIMAL BEHAVIOUR). For these vertebrates, object-organism relationships evidently depend mainly on specific characteristics, such as intensity and rate of movement, and not object meanings, and feeding depends essentially on what stimuli are adequate in their physical properties to elicit a reflex-like combination of forward lunge and mouth opening. These animals seem to behave far more in terms of seeing than of perceiving.

Basic in perceptual development may be early experiences, with low-intensity stimulation promoting soothing effects and approach, high-intensity stimulation disturbing effects and withdrawal (T. C. Schneirla). Early object attachments known as imprinting, demonstrated by Heinroth and by Lorenz in birds and later found in mammals, may be established on such a basis. Withdrawal fixations also may arise through stimulus-intensity effects in the early stages of life.

Vertebrate perception from the earliest stages may be influenced by such factors as sensory, neural, and motor thresholds effecting primary approaches or withdrawals. The so-called visual cliff phenomenon may account for apparent fear of heights in the young of many vertebrates. In experiments by R. D. Walk and E. Gibson, young chicks and weanling rats turned toward the seemingly shallow side of a partition on which a checkered pattern was located below glass, but away from the apparently deep side on which the same pattern was located 50 cm. or more below the glass. Chicks one to four days old and one-month-old kittens turned to the shallow side most of the time, but backed up and seemed disturbed when placed on the glass over the deep side. These responses appear in dark-raised animals, suggesting that the underlying factors are the differential effects of visual motion-parallax. That is, the near surface is seen as unchanged, hence is attractive or neutral; but the deep side is seen as in greater visual flux, and hence is disturbing.

7. Simplest Perceptual Relationships.—The organic basis of potentials for response to sensory change and for perceiving is evidenced in the lowest vertebrates. Minnows trained by P. Schiller to snap at the movement of a small bar of light presented with food then reacted to the light when it was presented twice within $\frac{1}{20}$ sec. in closely adjacent positions. The fish evidently perceived a movement, somewhat as would a human subject under comparable conditions. Experiencing apparent movement thus may be present throughout the vertebrate series. Many psychologists, and especially Gestaltists, consider this class of phenomenon an index of ability for distinguishing relationships, basic to perception.

It is probable that such abilities are essential to a meaningful sensing of objects. G. Révész presented chickens with successive pairs of circles, triangles, and arcs differing in size, the smaller one of each pair bearing food, thereby training the bird to peck only at the smaller figure in grain-free test pairs. Then two identical arcs were presented, one directly above the other, both with grain. The trained chickens pecked mainly at the upper figure, apparently seeing it as smaller than the lower arc, thus evidencing an illusion similar to that reported by people under comparable conditions. Correspondingly, chickens trained by Köhler to peck at the brighter member of a training pair pecked mainly at the brighter card in new test pairs of different brightnesses. Similar results were obtained in equivalent tests of a chimpanzee and a human child.

Thus widely different vertebrates have a potential for reacting to successive visual situations as unities in which the members are bound together reciprocally. An organization of this type may be termed a relationship, although in the simplest cases the unity seems due to processes on a primitive level rather than to qualitatively superior intelligence.

8. Contrasts in Perceptual Ability.—Social insects normally accept members of their own colony but attack nestmates bearing the odour of another colony. That the perceptual capacities of lower vertebrates are comparably low is indicated in tests with species mates. Male Siamese fighting fish, for example, respond similarly to females and to artificial objects such as clay plugs, unless size is too great or movement too rapid, whereupon the artifact is attacked as are other males. Hence the male's responses to species mates evidently depend on physical characteristics but not meanings such as "mate" or "enemy." In pigeons, kittiwakes, and numerous other birds, a parent which feeds young regularly on the nest will neglect them when they are off the nest even if close by. Evidently the young have a very simple meaning for the mother bird, rigidly dependent on the nest locus (at least in the early stages of incubation) and much below the level of maternal perception in monkeys, in which mothers feed and protect their young under a variety of conditions.

Sensory Discrimination.—Critical for evaluating perceptual levels is the extent to which experience brings more versatile adjustments to objects under changing conditions. The first step is sensory discrimination, a learning to distinguish sensory differences and respond appropriately. As far as sensitivity permits, stimulative discriminations in every sensory field can be learned with appropriate responses by insects and other higher invertebrates, and by vertebrates from fish to man. The learning is relatively simple for a mammal, which characteristically requires fewer trials than lower vertebrates; the critical matter is whether the animal is sensitive and reactive to stimulative differences under the conditions. Thus dogs discriminate tones more readily than do rats because of better reception as well as superior sound localization and learning capacities. A hunting dog must first discriminate among types of animal scents (*e.g.*, raccoons and rabbits), then he must learn to set himself for the one aspect of scent emphasized by his master.

Complex Discriminations.—The next degree is mastering complex compound stimuli, forming schemata in which successful response under experimental conditions depends on two or more characteristics of the positive pattern (*e.g.*, brightness and size), two or more characteristics of the negative pattern, or on relationships between the positive and negative patterns. Correspondingly, the tracking dog at this stage distinguishes the correct scent from similar false scents depending on different combinations of characteristics.

Conditional Discrimination.—A qualitative advancement is that of conditional discrimination, which demands intelligence well beyond that required for simple discriminations and schemata. This step is not indicated for reptiles and birds, and may exceed the capacities of rodents. Problems requiring conditional discrimination arise when similar schemata are encountered in many situations with important differences in their relevance. For example, not all pet dogs can learn that unless the master also wears his hat he does not necessarily intend to go walking when he holds the leash. When an animal can give the critical response to the essentials of related schemata without mistakes due to conflicting details, he has mastered a set of contingent relationships termed an abstraction. For example, white rats after long training can jump to a triangle, however it stands, rather than to a circle; whereas chickens, having learned to differentiate these two figures in set positions, are lost if the triangle is tilted.

For success in conditional discrimination, aspects such as complexity in the combination of critical details from experience to experience are crucial. Discerning patterns in varying circumstances, in which confusing differences may obscure key details, is an accomplishment in the discrimination of relationships excluded to all but higher mammals. In contrast with the rat, whose limits for abstraction are soon reached, chimpanzees progress well in matching-from-sample tests, as N. Ladygina-Kohts found, and can single out a schema such as a triangle even when it is presented with others matching it in details such as colour and size. Monkeys, although less apt pupils than chimpanzees, can advance, as H. Harlow has shown, to very complex discriminations.

Very different attitudes have been taken in animal psychology toward the subject of perception. Some would use this term for any reaction to sensory effects, others would reserve it (as above) for grasping meaningful patterns through sensitivity. The former practice seems to have its basis in implicit analogies between any animal sensitivity and human consciousness of environment. On this view, the simplest sensory processes indicate perception. Such analogies, however, are vague. Modern experimenters prefer objective methods in which judgments of perceptual abilities depend on data from systematic object-discrimination tests under controlled conditions. The critical matter is not sensitivity alone but how the animal organizes sensory data in adapting to new conditions. For this, resources for learning are critical.

B. Learning Ability

The rich endowment of lower animals in species-typical adaptations related to structural specializations is well balanced in mammals by superior capacities for modifying behaviour. Writers such as E. Hering believe, however, that all organisms have memory, in that the action of a stimulus on protoplasm always leaves traces which influence further responses. In this very general sense, the term learning would be extended to the simplest types of behaviour changes through stimulation, as in plants and protozoans. An alternative view is that such changes should be classed as equivalent to the general kinds of trace effect termed hysteresis (*q.v.*) in physical systems rather than to learning as in higher organisms. For comparative psychology, the primary fact is not just the production of some trace effect through stimulation but what class of trace is involved, and what its relevance to the organization of behaviour may be.

1. Varieties of Learning.—*Adaptation and Fatigue Phenomena.*—The simplest types of trace phenomena are based on processes akin to sensory adaptation or muscular fatigue. A dog or a man in dim light undergoes chemical changes in the retinas to increase sensitivity in the dark. A worm, after circling counterclockwise inside a dish, is likely to turn left when transferred into a T maze; a dog after running all day scratches himself weakly because chemical products have temporarily induced muscular fatigue. Similar instances based on changes in receptors or muscles are common throughout the animal series. They are not classed with learning because they centre on peripheral changes and not directly on central-nervous-system traces altering individual behaviour in persistent ways.

Sensory Integration; Habituation.—Certain classes of experiences may arouse neural trace effects influencing behaviour without altering it specifically. For example, in a phenomenon in mammals termed sensory preadaptation, after different stimuli such as a light and a buzzer are experienced together repeatedly without any specific action being involved, a response then conditioned to one of these stimuli also is elicited by the other without further training. In a similar phenomenon, generally termed habituation, commonly experienced disturbing stimuli lose their initial effect, and may even facilitate ongoing behaviour. Thus snails in an aquarium, bumped and otherwise disturbed for weeks by fish, then carry out their activities without the initial stoppages; a clerk becomes able to work in a noisy office. In such cases, through common experiences, neural traces are set up which influence behaviour in general ways.

Conditioned Responses.—In conditioned-response learning, the gain is a new stimulus-response connection, the nature of which depends on what specific stimuli are experienced together. To take an example from the lowest animal in which learning has been demonstrated, the marine annelid *Nereis* does not extend from its

tube in response to light or dark, but does so in response to meat juice. After the juice and either light or dark have been combined many times, the response is given to the latter alone. Conditioning, therefore, depends on what stimuli are combined under appropriate conditions. With each repetition, an unconditioned stimulus (B) which arouses the critical response (B_R) at the outset is experienced by the animal together with a conditioned stimulus (A) which initially does not arouse this response. Through experiencing the combination, the animal forms both an A-B integration and neural traces permitting A to control the critical response B_R. In the pioneering experiment of I. Pavlov with dogs, A was a bell sound; B, meat powder in the mouth, was a stimulus arousing B_R, a reflex salivation. Through repeated combinations of bell and meat powder, at length A-B_R was accomplished and the bell controlled salivation.

In vertebrates, and in higher invertebrates (*e.g.*, annelids), probably most reflexes and other local reactions may be conditioned if stimuli are appropriately paired. Although at first young dogs scratch only in response to local skin irritation (*e.g.*, flea bites), appropriately pairing this unconditioned stimulus with the smell of flea powder, hearing "Scratch!" or seeing his collar normally conditions the dog to form the corresponding A-B_R pattern. The potentialities of the conditioning principle for practical animal training depend mainly on ingenuity and patience, as is illustrated by a popular Soviet film of the 1950s portraying an enterprise in which dogs run trains, rabbits behave excitedly on missing them, cats punch tickets, and theatrical efforts are also represented convincingly, although evidently without understanding, by the actors.

In the mammals, particularly, aspects of the situation other than the focal stimuli can control behaviour through conditioning, thus serving as secondary conditioned stimuli. In Pavlov's work, stimuli incidentally seen and heard in the test room (*e.g.*, hearing experimenter's movements) at length elicited the critical response in the absence of the experimental stimuli. This enlargement of the habit was indicated also by a reduced responsiveness when the animal was tested in another room or without his harness. In such ways, in laboratory experiments or with pets at home, stimuli considered incidental or even overlooked come to control a habit, as in the Clever Hans case.

Conditioning is not the same in all animals capable of it but varies considerably in its internal pattern and relations to other behaviour. For this fact, differences in neural resources are critical. In invertebrates capable of it, and in lower vertebrates, conditioning is largely restricted to combining simple stimuli with reflex or stereotyped responses, and naïve responses to potent stimuli are reversed only with difficulty if at all. Examples are the difficulty of conditioning an inhibition of the snail's foot retraction to intense contact or the lizard's snapping at figures of complex but not smooth outlines. Mammals can form systems of conditioned responses in which a wider range of responses may be controlled by the same stimuli, the responses themselves varying more than in lower animals. The traditional milkman's horse, starting and stopping skilfully according to combinations of footstep-and-bottle sounds, is an everyday example. The significance of such learning is illustrated by the great variety and flexibility of combinations possible through systematic training in almost any mammal, compared with the limitations of turtles, toads, and fish, increasing in that order.

From the lowest to the highest mammals the ability expands to modify conditioned responses according to prevailing conditions. It is difficult to condition a fish to move one fin alone to a light combined with shock, but with a dog, in time a light paired with shock to one leg controls not only the flexion of that leg, without the shock, but other changes also. Reduced forms of the conditioned stimulus and subtle secondary stimulus effects enter, and the response is curtailed and modified until at length the paw alone moves just enough to avoid the shock. Cases of learning in this class, in which both stimulus and response undergo precise modifications according to motivation and the consequences of action (*e.g.*, obtaining food or evading shock), evidently represent the merging of the conditioning type with the selective type of learning (*see* below). The inferiority of lower vertebrates to mammals in such learning doubtless corresponds to differences in neural equipment. Thus, although normal dogs can be conditioned to withdraw a specific paw skilfully on signal, dogs deprived surgically of cerebral cortex advance little beyond the stage of general excitement and variable responses to the conditioned stimulus. The limitations of dogs without cortex remind the experimenter somewhat of lower vertebrates with their inferior neural equipment. (*See also* CONDITIONING.)

Operant Learning.—Variations of conditioning are possible depending on the animal and technique used. A method known as operant learning approximates conditioning by routinizing stimuli and other conditions, but differs from it in that initiating the response depends specifically on the animal. In the classical experiment of B. F. Skinner, a rat learns to approach and press a bar for a food reward. If the reward is given only in the presence of a signal, say a light, the rat will tend to press the bar during presentation of the light and not in the dark. If his hunger is reduced, he stops pressing, and so on. This method is very useful for research on the properties of sensory discrimination, reaction, and drive; however, it may not be suited to the comparative study of learning. In the operant method, the experimenter plans the situation for the animal so that the successful response is sure to occur. Despite the specific utilities of this method, the fact remains that by selecting what action is to be correct, and by maneuvering the animal's behaviour so that this action occurs, the experimenter substitutes his own role for unexamined selective processes otherwise dependent upon the animal. By this method, therefore, similarities are obtained for pigeons, rats, and men which may be misleading. (*See* LEARNING.)

Trial-and-Error or Selective Learning.—This complex form of learning, not clear below arthropods, reaches its peak in the mammals. It is illustrated by the behaviour of a hungry dog outside a food box that can be opened only by pulling a cord. The first responses of dogs to such problems are highly varied, and include nearly all activities possible under the conditions, from pawing and sniffing at the box and at the floor nearby to running about at intervals and also, finally, sitting and howling. At length the dog, in the course of biting and pawing at objects, happens to pull the cord and enters the door to food. The first trial, particularly, is likely to be very long, but, as E. L. Thorndike found in his pioneering work with cats, random activities decrease and the cord is pulled more and more promptly in further trials. From these characteristics, such learning is called trial and error. Because the animal improves by working more frequently in the correct locus and adapts more efficiently through organizing appropriate responses from initial variable behaviour, the process may be termed selective learning. When D. K. Adams prehabituated animals to the general situation, thereby reducing initial disturbance and emotional excitement, random behaviour decreased and the correct solution was more promptly and efficiently acquired than in naïve animals.

Many kinds of problem situations have been used in studying selective learning, including types in which avoiding shock or getting food depends on pressing a pedal or pulling a string, combinations of these, and other devices. Higher mammals such as the chimpanzee can solve problems involving latch combinations which are difficult for the monkey and insoluble for rats and lower mammals, not merely

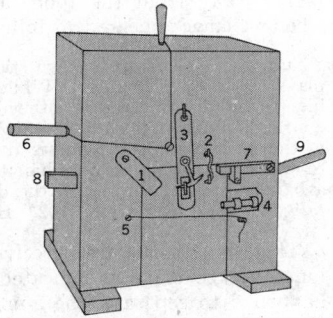

FIG. 2.—COMBINATION PROBLEM BOX USED IN TESTING MONKEYS. TO ENTER THE BOX AND OBTAIN FOOD, THE ANIMAL MUST DEAL WITH THE ITEMS IN THE SEQUENCE INDICATED BY THE NUMBERS

because the chimpanzee excels in manipulative ability but because of his superior capacity for organization in learning. Birds, in contrast to mammals, are limited to easier problems, which they learn more slowly. Sparrows are slow, pigeons much slower, in

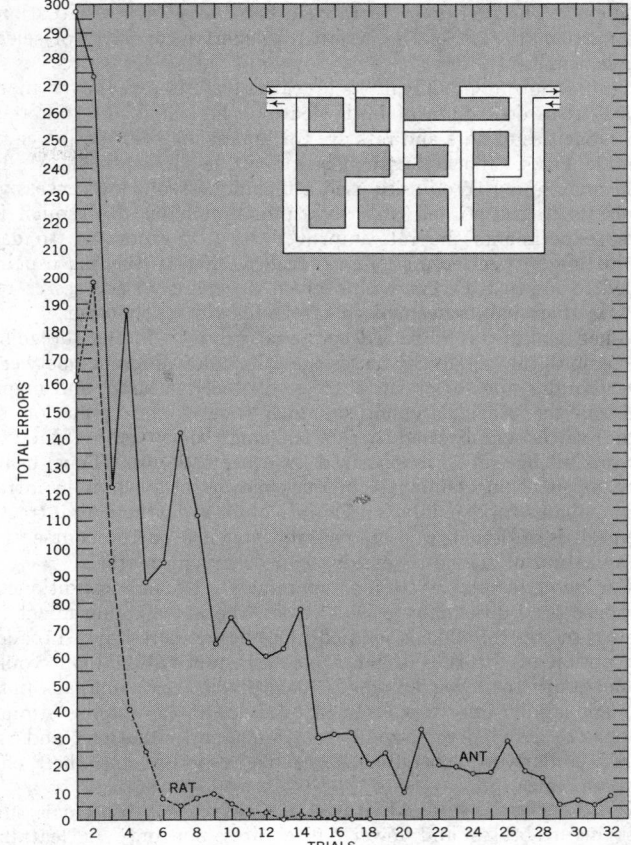

FIG. 3.—SIX-BLIND MAZE PROBLEM USED FOR TESTING BOTH ANTS AND RATS. SOLID LINE INDICATES TOTAL-ERROR SCORES OF EIGHT ANTS, BROKEN LINE, THE TOTAL-ERROR SCORES OF EIGHT RATS

learning to press a string admitting them to a food box, then do not relate the string response to the act of entering the door. The bird's inferior organization of the habit is shown by the fact that, with the habit learned, if the string is moved he tends to work in the habitual place instead of directing his efforts at the shifted string, as most dogs would. The inferiority of lower vertebrates to mammals in problem solving, as W. Fischel has shown, lies especially in their shortcomings for interrelating the critical act (*e.g.,* string pulling), the object acted upon (*e.g.,* the string), and the goal (food).

A method much employed in studying selective learning involves the maze, in which establishing a correct route despite blind alleys makes possible investigating both the elimination of errors and the organization of a complex orientation habit. Animals from earthworm to man have been tested, and striking differences are found. To learn a T maze with only one blind alley the crab *Cambarus* needed more than 60 trials, chimpanzees only a few. In about half the trials needed by the crab for its simple learning, *Formica* ants master mazes containing six blind alleys. Rats, on the other hand, given this pattern used for the ant in an appropriate scale, need only 12 runs or less.

As Schneirla has found, submammalian animals require more trials to learn comparable problems, commit far more errors than mammals, and accomplish an inferior habit in a different and more limited way. The ant, to learn the six-blind maze mentioned, first became habituated, next mastered local difficulties, finally a general organization of the habit, all very gradually. The rat, in contrast, exhibited no distinct stages but mastered local difficulties and organized the general route simultaneously. The superiority of the rat's habit is shown by its facile modification when maze changes shift the correct route through a former blind alley. The rat reverses maze habits readily when required to start at the former exit, whereas for the ant this is a very difficult problem. The ability to reorganize behaviour in new situations is a particular mark of the mammal's superior capacity for selective learning.

Tests requiring modifications in learned habits reveal even more clearly than do studies of initial learning how strikingly different the capacities of ants and rats are for organizing solutions of comparable tasks. To compare fish and rat in this respect, M. E. Bitterman and J. Wodinsky used a technique requiring successive reversals to the stimuli of a discrimination habit. Although in these experiments the rats improved steadily from day to day in shifting between two similar alternative habits, the fish usually failed to improve except within given days, and in successive reversals their habits seemed to interfere with each other.

When learning is reviewed comparatively (as in the foregoing discussion) the possibility arises that the chief difference between invertebrates and lower vertebrates, on the one hand, and mammals on the other may not so much involve the formation of neural traces, emphasized by S-R learning theory, as in capacities for organizing traces, emphasized by other theories. Thus, using food or shock in training techniques may be important in inframammalian forms mainly for the rate of forming the neural traces themselves, although in mammals its influence on the course and organization of selective learning can be much greater.

For good results in training mammals, although conditioned-response procedures may be held basic, the use of punishment or reward to control what is learned must be tempered by a broader conception of the role of incentives and motivation than would be necessary for lower animals. Accordingly, for mammals, punishment is advisedly used only in mild forms (as intense stimuli emphasize avoidance reactions to trainer and situation) and reward, similarly, to encourage desirable responses and their efficient organization.

2. Experience and Abilities in Learning.—Mammals surpass invertebrates and lower vertebrates not only in learning new problems but also in reorganizing habits adaptively. Adapting to this comparison the neurophysiological theory of D. O. Hebb for the ontogenesis of perception, one would say that rodents and higher mammals, with further related experiences, advance much more readily than lower forms from trace effects to linkages to complex neural patterns. Mammalian learning is typically more efficient in familiar situations not only because the animal is less excited and behaves less erratically than under strange conditions but also because mammals can extend habits progressively to better effect than can lower animals.

Virtually any type of problem is mastered more readily by mammals, not only because of their superior organic equipment for original learning but because experience is brought more effectively to bear on further problems. Harlow investigated these matters at length with monkeys given long series of discrimination tests with problems of increasingly difficult natures. Results showed that monkeys master more complex discrimination problems of the same general type with progressive facility. Harlow applied the term "learning sets" to the successive stages of the monkey's progress in learning to learn. He was inclined to emphasize the similarity of learning at successive stages and to doubt that qualitatively new processes enter at the advanced stages. But, as N. R. F. Maier and Schneirla suggested, the discrimination method may not be adequate to reveal qualitative differences in learning. This problem seems to require other methods more appropriate for the investigation of similarities and differences in learning and intelligence at different animal levels.

C. Intelligent Behaviour

1. Criteria.—Intelligence (*q.v.*) is definable as the ability to utilize experience in adapting to new situations. Intelligence is not efficiency in adaptive behaviour, a quality shared by all surviving animals. Furthermore, although intelligence depends to some extent on the organism's aptitude for conditioning, and more so on its aptitudes for selective learning, the crucial matter is how readily the gains of past experience are adapted to new problems.

It is difficult to diagnose any solution correctly without adequate knowledge of the animal's background. Morgan described a case in which, after he had observed a dog in repeated erratic attempts to pull a crooked stick through a paling fence, the animal finally yanked the stick through when the crooked part accidentally broke off. A passer-by, who saw only the last and successful part of the series, remarked, "Clever dog that, sir, he knows where the hitch do lie." Whether success results through accident, a gradual process of selective learning, or an efficient reorganization of experiences appropriate to the problem may depend on (1) species abilities, (2) the abilities and experience of the individual, and (3) the conditions under which the difficulty is encountered.

2. Insight.—Commonly accepted as an index of intelligent behaviour are short-cut solutions known as insight, in which the animal appears suddenly to see the point. Calling such solutions insightful does not of course explain them but may only analogize success with a hypothetical process of seeing into something. The mere rate of accomplishment does not indicate insightful solution, for insects in certain problems occasionally achieve rapid but noninsightful improvements. Insight involves a kind of organizing ability not demonstrated in insects or lower vertebrates, superior to both conditioning and selective learning for overcoming new difficulties.

Pioneer studies by M. Haggerty and others shortly after 1900 revealed that problem solutions by monkeys are often better than would be expected through trial-and-error processes alone. For example, a monkey, after having watched another, in four successive trials, climb the side of a cage and reach into a chute to obtain fruit, when given the problem himself soon solved it by working directly around the chute until he reached the fruit. Later, in the research of Köhler and Yerkes particularly, similar abilities were demonstrated for chimpanzees, superior to those of monkeys.

In these experiments, chimpanzees were presented with problems such as food overhead or behind a fence, unobtainable by direct responses such as reaching or jumping but obtainable only by indirect procedures. Although there were failures and some animals never did well, some of the chimpanzees reached distant food by means such as stacking boxes or raking it in with a stick. One of Köhler's chimpanzees, which had previously used only single sticks as rakes, was shown food beyond reach, requiring a stick longer than any available. First there were actions such as merely reaching out with the arm, or using one bamboo piece alone or to push out another, for getting at the incentive. Even though inappropriately, the animal in such behaviour was using foreign objects as a means to an end—in other words, as crude tools. After an hour, the goal was unattained and the animal sat facing away from the food, idly handling two bamboo sticks. Then a change appeared, as follows:

Sultan . . . picks up the two sticks, sits down again on the box, and plays carelessly with them. While doing this, it happens that he finds himself holding one rod in either hand in such a way that they lie in a straight line; he pushes the thinner one a little way into the opening of the thicker, jumps up and is already on the run toward the railings, to which he has up to now half turned his back, and begins to draw a banana towards him with the double stick. (W. Köhler, *The Mentality of Apes*, Eng. trans., 1925, Harcourt Brace.)

That the sticks were perceived as a useful tool and not combined by accident was indicated by the fact that when the pieces happened to separate, the animal straightway recombined them in a manner seemingly impossible without some understanding of their function together.

3. Relative Aptitude for Indirect Solution.—Solutions of such types resemble the pattern recognizable in mammals as perception of relations. Much evidence indicates that lower mammals are inferior to primates in this respect. Cats and dogs can learn to manipulate levers, but neither can assemble a tool or use it as chimpanzees can in solving problems.

Köhler emphasized the superiority of primates over lower vertebrates in correcting their initial direct responses to the incentive, when necessary, with indirect ones. A hen separated from food by a wire fence persists in zigzag running against the fence, opposite the food, whereas dogs in time abandon direct responses for a detour to the food, and monkeys do so sooner than dogs. Fischel demonstrated that although dogs can respond to one of two incentives with the direct or indirect action that is appropriate, thus solving a task failed by turtles and by birds, they master the critical relationships less effectively than primates do. Chimpanzees clearly surpass monkeys at solving the type of problem requiring the subject to push food away from him around a barrier before raking it in, indicating a superior mastery of the relationship of the subject's position, the barrier, and the goal.

4. Reasoning as Reorganized Learning.—Indirect or insightful solutions are frequently differentiated from patterns acquired directly through selective learning in that the former type of solution often appears suddenly, after a period of apparently fruitless trial and error. Sudden improvements in progress toward or in attaining a new type of solution are notable in the problem-solving behaviour of higher primates such as chimpanzees, less prominent in monkeys, still less in dogs, cats, and rats in that order. This fact does not mean that insightful solutions occur independent of previous learning.

Insightful solutions have not been clearly demonstrated in any inframammalian animal, and various anecdotal claims for such processes, as in insects, seem attributable rather to uncontrolled possibilities for direct responses. What is unique about insightful solutions is that they are attained by reorganizing two or more patterns of response available from experience in similar situations, although previously independent of each other. Thus, perceptual adjustments such as jumping to food and handling a box may exist separately in the animal's repertory until he combines them in solving a new problem. In one of the experiments of Maier, who studied simpler forms of this type of solution in the rat, the subject was first habituated to the elevated pathway shown in fig. 4, passing between each two tables frequently, without receiving food. In the test, the rat was first given food on one of the tables, e.g., no. 3, then was transferred to no. 1, for example. On the basis of his specific habits, the rat in this case would have turned with equal readiness to tables no. 2 and no. 3; the results, however, showed that adult rats were able to return with better than 80% success to the one food table correct in the particular test. Achieving correct solutions when a direct recall of learned responses would have led to chance scores indicates a capacity for combining learned items which had been separate in previous experience.

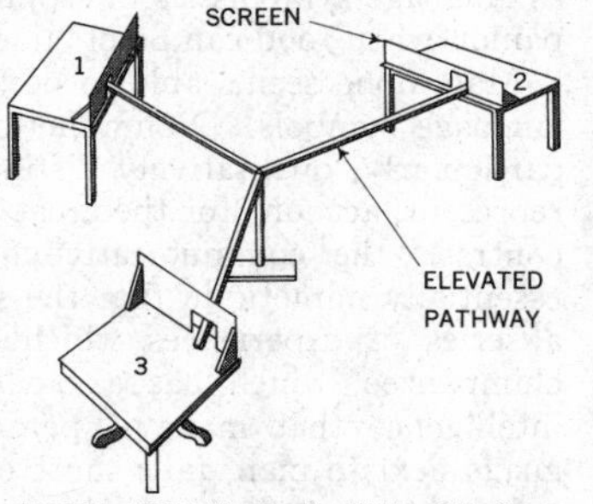

Maier emphasized the qualitative similarity of such solutions to reasoning in man. As an example of a solution by reasoning, not demonstrated in mammals below primates, the joining of short sticks when a longer one is needed has been mentioned. As H. Birch found, however, chimpanzees cannot solve this stick-combination problem by reasoning unless they have previously handled sticks as in play and appropriate unitary perceptual adjustments are thereby made available. The feat then is to combine these elements insightfully in an intelligent adaptation to new difficulties.

5. Relative Independence of Stereotypy.—*Nonsoluble Tests.*—Mammals differ greatly in their freedom from stereotyped behaviour in problem situations, as G. V. Hamilton found. In his nonsoluble test, the subject was presented with four doors, one door unlatched on each trial, but never that unlatched on the preceding trial. This fact was discovered by the human subjects, but not by any lower animal. Next in complexity of response were monkeys, the other primate tested, which often tried all four doors successively and distributed their efforts without trying any

ADAPTED FROM N. R. F. MAIER AND T. C. SCHNEIRLA, "PRINCIPLES OF ANIMAL PSYCHOLOGY"; REPRODUCED BY PERMISSION OF McGRAW-HILL BOOK CO.

FIG. 4.—MAIER THREE-WAY APPARATUS FOR TESTING REASONING IN THE RAT (*see* TEXT)

one door repeatedly on any one trial. Stereotypy of response, or repeating particular reactions frequently, occurred often in dogs and cats and very often in horses. Significantly, the tendency for stereotypy and persistent repetition of errors is marked in the maze learning of rats in which 20% or more of the cerebral cortex has been destroyed. Maier found partially decerebrate rats very inferior to normal subjects on reasoning problems, much as lower mammals are distinctly inferior to primates on such problems. Superior cortical endowment thus inhibits stereotypy in mammals so that new adaptations become possible.

Multiple-Choice Test.—The Hamilton situation was adapted by Yerkes in further studies of plastic behaviour in his multiple-choice test. Here the subject faced nine doors in an arc, with a sequence of five doors unlatched on each trial, but (to eliminate simple position habits) always a different set. Food was to be found behind just one door each time, and the problem was to discover how the correct door was systematically related to the others. Sample problems were: (1) always first at the right; (2) always second from the left; (3) always the middle door. The aim here was to compare the levels of intelligence in different animals. In the above problems (1), presumably the simplest, was solved both by the crow and the rat; they both failed (2). Problem (3) was solved by the monkey but not by the pig. Chimpanzees solved problems more difficult than (3), in which success may have depended on ability to abstract a significant pattern from among complex settings, or on what Yerkes called "ideational processes." To the claim that the multiple-choice method is valid for testing animal intelligence comparatively, critics object that the method affords no basis for clearly appraising such processes; also that it handicaps some animals unduly by admitting irrelevant features such as emotional reactions, which may have caused gorillas to fail problems solved by chimpanzees.

6. Representation as a Secondary Factor in Reasoning.—Attaining solutions by combining previously independent experiences, demonstrated in lower mammals including rodents, represents the reasoning process in simpler outline than in man. Animal psychologists have studied "mental processes" in lower mammals, in comparison with man, to find what other factors are contributive. One interesting method is that of delayed response, an outcome of earlier attempts to test capacities for "ideas." In the form developed by W. S. Hunter, this method involved first training the animal to go through the one of three doors marked by a light; then, in tests, the lamp over one of the doors was first lit briefly and after a given delay the animal had to respond without the light. In modifications of this test by others, the animal was first shown food under one of several cups or saw food buried, and after a delay had to locate it. The general result of such experiments, although specific results differ according to procedure and situation, is that lower mammals require more preparatory training for success and in general rely more on specific bodily orientation during certain types of tests than primates do. In food-concealment tests, monkeys and chimpanzees can delay successfully over intervals of 24 hours or longer. The general interpretation is that success depends on an ability to represent the absent object or the appropriate adjustment to this object as a cue for recalling its location after the delay. Ability to delay the correct act over an interval is often interpreted as centring around an abbreviated form of the actual adjustment; lifting a box, for example, might be represented by a slight tensing of the arm muscles as in raising the box. In comparison with man's great advantage of symbolizing experiences verbally, lower mammals are handicapped by having to represent their adjustments in much less versatile ways.

A related ability indicated in lower primates and certain other mammals is the anticipation of particular absent objects. In one delayed-response experiment with monkeys, in which banana was used in some of the trials and lettuce (less preferred) in others, the subject became disturbed and refused a piece of lettuce surreptitiously substituted for the banana he had seen concealed before the delay. Evidently the animal then specifically anticipated banana, for lettuce was accepted readily in delayed trials preceded by the showing of lettuce.

The ability to represent absent objects and situations may be considered a contributory factor in reasoning. This type of process is suggested by trials in which a chimpanzee, after having worked at suspended food for some time without success, suddenly rushes around the corner for a box previously seen there, then promptly uses this box in a solution. The ability to represent absent objects, although it aids solutions by reasoning, cannot alone account for such solutions, for merely representing an experience without change or recombination would constitute a direct recall rather than a new solution. In the primates, the newness of solutions achieved through reasoning is far more striking than in other mammals.

V. MAN COMPARED WITH THE LOWER ANIMALS

Although man is not the most highly evolved animal in all aspects of structure, he is psychologically the highest. His superiority is not absolute, however, for most of his advantages are also shown, though to lesser extents, by mammalian relatives.

1. **Time, Reasoning, and Foresight.**—Although reasoning seems to be carried on by mammals down to rodents, in the lower orders it is simpler and evidently plays a far smaller part in adaptive behaviour than it does in man.

Man's psychological advantages include foresight and time-binding, or reasoning with reference to problems in the more distant future or past. Time-binding, for lower primates, is largely restricted to the present and is much less extensive and meaningful for the past than it is for man, who thinks in the future as well as in the past and present. The apparent anticipations of lower animals can be conditioned within limits to coming phases of recurrent events, through internal or external stimuli characteristic of given times of day. In rodents, discrimination of short intervals of time in terms of action has been demonstrated; however, their apparent anticipations are held to shorter intervals and simpler processes than in primates. Even in apes, anticipation evidently endures far more briefly than in man, and largely involves more familiar occurrences. The ability to think far forward in time seems to require a wider reorganization of the traces of experience than is found in any lower animal.

Man is capable of systematic sequential reasoning, or planning, organizing into systems the traces of very different experiences with reference to future goals. Foresight in the chimpanzee is typified by his food expectancies, anticipative of specific episodes only a day or two off. If lower primates can reason to obtain goals or forestall hazards expected in the more distant future, these abilities remain undemonstrated.

Planning for future needs requires not only foresight but also reflective thought, or reasoning about one's own condition in relation to the past, present, or future. Differentiating and identifying the self in thinking, marked typically by the first significant use of personal pronouns (e.g., me, I, my) at about two years of age, is a major event in human development. This symbolic accomplishment is far superior to reacting emotionally about one's own behaviour or appearance, as might a monkey observing himself in a mirror, or a growling dog preparing to fight.

Foresight involves taking note of one's own status or condition, in reference to that of other individuals, objects, and situations, to achieve appropriate measures. This type of self-reactive reasoning expresses man's superiority over the lower primates better perhaps than any other aspect of development. The comparison is weakened neither by subnormal human intelligence nor by the fact that any man at times uses his abilities poorly. The best human foresight infinitely surpasses the best in subhuman primates.

2. **Verbal Language and Communication.**—Although language and communication are often confused, the former constitutes a special case of the latter. In communication the behaviour (or related aspects; e.g., odours) of one animal influences the behaviour of others. Thus, odours produced from an excited bee's scent glands mark the food place and attract other foragers; deer and other mammals, by rubbing parts of the body against projections, leave traces as territorial cues to other animals. The flashing of fireflies; the chirping of crickets; and the colour changes, movements, and sounds of mating animals are by-products of excited behaviour frequently crucial to species adaptation. Such behaviour, although significant in communication, does not appear to involve symbolic processes equivalent to human language.

Honeybees, as reported by K. von Frisch, have been accepted by some as using language. Finder bees seem to communicate the location of food sources they have found by performing a kind of dance (see SOCIAL INSECTS: *Social Bees*). However, the dance seems to be a physiological by-product of feeding and flight; its effect on other bees is stereotyped and physiological and many authorities deny that it meets the criteria of language (e.g., it seems to lack conceptual organization).

Communication approaches closer to language when social responses advance through conditioning, as in groups of birds or mammals when the excited cries of one individual throw others into flight. Another advance is made when a general activity is modified through experience into a special device used to influence the behaviour of others, as when barking and biting in a dog change into baring fangs and growling as means of intimidation. When merely beginning the act often causes flight, the abbreviated form is learned as a special social device. Instances of simple, discrete communicative processes of this sort are not uncommon in the everyday life of mammals, as in the "begging" of hungry dogs and the mewing of cats before closed doors. When used with even a limited anticipation of their social effects, such acts approach the stage of language.

Infrahuman primates seem not to develop systems of symbols in the class of language. Yerkes, however, from his extensive experience, indicated in the chimpanzee a variety of sounds and movements which influence other individuals, keeping them in touch with and informed about the presence and attitude of one another as well as about significant features of their environment. To be sure, these sounds and movements of lower primates more often appear as incidental features of the first animal's excitement (e.g., the "hunger cry") than as intentional means of informing others of something. Although proof is lacking that chimpanzees use sounds symbolically, S. Crawford and H. Nissen demonstrated experimentally that these animals can use gestures as language symbols, as in tapping the shoulder of a lagging companion when food can be obtained only with his cooperation.

Man alone seems able to develop and use systematic codes of language symbols. Nonmimetic, conventional types of symbols, particularly, qualitatively distinct from the acts or objects they represent, account for the great efficiency of human language. In contrast, the communicative activities of lower mammals are essentially mimetic in that the sign or signal is a specific part of a series of experiences which represent the whole. Even the chimpanzee, which has a facility for vocal utterances and an intelligence that make it perhaps the best candidate for language next to man, falls short of achieving verbal language symbols. Attempts to teach chimpanzees true words attain only the stage of stereotyped responses given under set stimulus conditions. Parrots can learn to repeat frequently heard sound patterns, which, however, constitute skilled acts largely devoid of any meaningful association with the objects or situations eliciting them and are not manipulated with anticipation of the results; hence, not language.

3. **Conceptualization and Intelligence.**—The psychological deficiencies of chimpanzee as compared with man, and of monkey as compared with chimpanzee, relate significantly to the elaboration of brain cortex. In the mammalian series rat-dog-monkey-chimpanzee-man, there is not only a progressive increase in the proportion of cerebral cortex to body weight but also an increase in the number of cortical cells and the complexity of their interconnections. Such increases parallel improvements in potentials for complex functions centring around learning and its reorganization in perceptual, conceptual, and language processes. This is validated by findings such as K. Lashley's of a high positive correlation in rats between amount of intact cerebral cortex and performance in learning problems, and Maier's that losses exceeding 20% of cortex abruptly reduce to a minimum the scores of rats in reasoning tests. Limitation of symbolic behaviour by

the amount and pattern of cerebral cortex is emphasized for man by the deficiencies of imbeciles and by the degeneration of symbolic functions in step with progressive cortical loss as in tumours. In the final stages of such disorders, the patient may see once familiar objects without being able to name them or recall their meanings.

Mastery of verbal language symbols evidently requires a foundation in object meanings beyond the resources of subhuman intelligence. To be sure, a chimpanzee can be taught human activities such as using utensils, yet the circumstances of training and of use indicate a limited perceptual and conceptual command over the adjustments, and a performance more rigidly bound to specific sensory properties and motor routines than in man. The chimpanzee thus can learn to ride vehicles without forming the abstraction "ride" and using it verbally to initiate the act as does the human child through mastering the common properties of vehicles. Although human infants in their first symbols are bound to particular situations and concrete uses, later they progress steadily with verbal symbols whereas chimpanzees remain in the nonverbal stage.

4. Emotion.—In higher and lower animals alike, a relationship may hold between outer causes and the individual's initial excited, emotionalized responses. Although in the higher mammals these processes progressively involve perceptual states of variable stability and psychological complexity characterized as pleasant or unpleasant, they are grounded in visceral conditions. Primitively, strong stimuli elicit withdrawal and an interruptive visceral condition; weak stimuli, approach and a vegetative visceral condition. What may be called the strong emotions, characterized by interruptive visceral changes such as hampered digestion, quickened heartbeat, secretion of adrenin, and impulsive responses such as flight or fighting, are aroused by intense stimulation. W. Cannon identified equivalent interruptive physiological reactions of these types as accompaniments of strong emotional excitement in both lower mammals and man, "putting the organism on a war footing." Conversely, weak stimulation promotes vegetative changes such as facilitated digestion, and the related overt response is an approach toward the stimulus source, naïvely in mammals a general relaxation and reflex extension of limbs. The interruptive condition seems inherently episodic, the vegetative condition relatively continuous and potentially basic to social life. In mammals, however, with their capacities for psychological plasticity, which of these becomes dominant in personality and society seems increasingly dependent on the prevalent development conditions. Lower mammals and very young children readily tend to perceive objects and situations in terms of their general emotional associations, as conditioned-response learning prevails first. Under severe environmental conditions, with punishment and strong stimulation frequent, interruptive emotional tendencies may become dominant, as in the trembling, cringing, whining behaviour of a frequently punished dog when the whip, his master, or a stranger is encountered. In contrast, an emphasis on approach tendencies and selective learning in development brings intelligence to the fore and contributes to social rather than asocial behaviour.

In man, visceral processes play a far more indirect and delicate role in emotional reactions which are much more influenced by the perceptual significance of the situation than they are in lower mammals. Because man's emotional development is dominated by his perceptual and conceptual processes, according to circumstances, it is unsafe to infer experiences of fear in the human sense in the excited flight of insect or fish from a suddenly moved object or maternal love in the queen ant licking her first brood. That the difference depends particularly on the intimate involvement of cerebral function in man's emotional development is indicated by lapses in emotional specialization and social restraint with cortex-inhibiting agents such as alcohol or more lasting deficits when brain tumours or injuries reduce cortical function. Comparably, in cats and other lower mammals, when the cortex and brain stem are disconnected surgically there are marked increases in activities such as snarling, biting, panting, and other signs of interruptive visceral disturbances normally episodic and associated with high emotional excitement. Man's cortical equipment admits an emotional specialization comparable with his intelligence, and involved with it in an intimacy well beyond the range of lower mammals in general.

The temperamental resemblance of lower primates to man appears much closer than their intellectual resemblance to him. Although well-domesticated dogs are frequently very sensitive to subtle differences in human behaviour, acting almost as members of the family, domesticated chimpanzees seem far more delicately and complexly attuned both to man and to chimpanzee companions. Hebb, by simulating the approach of a timid man and of a bold man in successive tests, obtained significant chimpanzee responses, with one animal friendly in the former situation but aggressive in the latter, two others interested but aggressive and unafraid in both. The first animal may have been hoodwinked by the act, the other two not, as the experimenter was known to them.

Experienced observers report patterns meriting terms such as confidence and discouragement, bluff, suspicion, and others, appearing under comparable conditions in the ape and the human child. These responses involve rough similarities in external signs of emotionality, including facial expressions and general tensional changes, reliably interpreted as indicating emotional attitudes. A common difference is that, in excited emotional responses, overt processes tend to emerge more readily in adult lower primates, with the whole body involved as in stamping and shrieking when rejecting something, and in this sense they are much more dominated emotionally than adult man.

5. Aesthetic Perceiving.—The potential for perceiving objects or situations in emotional terms such as distress or reassurance appears first in mammals. Although in lower vertebrates and some invertebrates stimuli such as body colours or characteristic sounds may be excitatory or calming, repellent or attractive, evidence suggests that specific effects such as intensity (controlling physiological changes), and not their perceptual significance, dominate such responses. Neither simple conditioned responses nor naïve responses to stimuli are truly aesthetic, in that emotional effects accompanying attraction or repulsion reach the level of appreciating object significance, object qualities, and emotional effects as related.

Simple aesthetic perceiving, so defined, is indicated in the subhuman primates. Köhler observed chimpanzees hanging material such as plants or fruit skins about their necks or shoulders, or applying clay or other substances to their bodies or to surrounding objects. Other behaviour was seen which Köhler considered rudimentary dancing, as when animals pranced around a circular path in single file or stood in pairs, one stamping the feet alternately as the other rotated with outstretched arms. Such actions are accepted as primitive types of aesthetic perceiving both because individuals evidently derive an emotional gratification from manipulating object qualities with reference to themselves and because these actions exert an emotional effect on others. D. Morris, from studies of finger painting by chimpanzees in the London Zoo, suggested that free-choice and project methods often reveal indications of aesthetic appreciation in selecting and combining colours, somewhat comparable to the tendencies of human infants. B. Rensch thought that the preferences of *Cebus* monkeys for certain combinations of colours and grays, and certain geometrical patterns, express processes resembling some of the simpler aesthetic tendencies in man.

The potentials of lower primates for aesthetic perceiving are slight in comparison with the potentialities of man, who alone seems able to create systematically visual patterns such as thematic paintings, auditory patterns such as symphonies, or dances worthy of choreography with the expectation of exciting appreciative emotional responses in himself and others. Not only are the chimpanzee patterns vague and lacking in subtlety, but their significance apparently involves only a momentary emotional appreciation, as abilities are lacking for the intellectual synthesis of emotional effects and patterning of material essential for a wider orientation in time. The human artist, with an appreciation of his own relationship to the theme and resources for planning his work to play upon the emotional susceptibilities of others, can treasure and recreate aesthetic experiences. Through his foresight, experiences remote in time and space and with disparate meanings are continued creatively to enrich the environment for himself and others.

6. Personality and Abnormal Behaviour.—Normal behaviour is definable as the developmental pattern characteristic of the given animal group. The major animal forms have been compared here in terms of their normal or typical patterns. Although this is justified, it is also true that every species presents individual differences in all characteristics of behaviour. Individual differences in organic characteristics and in adaptive behaviour constitute an important fact in evolution. Generally such variations are predictable, in that correspondingly fewer individuals deviate from the species norm in more radical ways. Some ants or bees are superior and others inferior to most of their colony mates in orientation, foraging, and nest activities; chimpanzees differ widely in abilities from reaction time to reasoning.

Individual differences that are matters of degree in sensory acuity or in the efficiency of learning may be considered regular or ordinary. Radical psychological deviations from typical species behaviour are uncommon in the lower animals, although special departures may result from extraordinary conditions as in development. Pathological conditions affecting the nervous system can produce behavioural eccentricities. Thus the signs of rabies in dogs and other mammals are extreme emotional excitability with indiscriminate running and biting; brain tumours produce sleepiness, reduced sensitivity, irritability or depression, and other extraordinary signs according to their locus and extent. Man seems to be the animal most frequently plagued by psychological complications arising through disrupted organization of behaviour rather than primarily through nervous system lesions.

Under special stress, lower vertebrates may exhibit emotional disorders resembling those of man. Gun-shy dogs tend to be extremely fearful in specific situations, and perhaps generally, because of emotional conditioning. Disturbances resembling neuroses have been produced in mammals and also birds with Pavlovian conflict technique, in which an animal, trained, for example, to respond to a circle but to inhibit response to an ellipse, is then forced to respond to a figure intermediate between these two. As the animal cannot both respond and inhibit response simultaneously, a conflict condition results, with tension, excitement, and even violent movements, and usually great difficulty in repeating either habit (*see* NEUROSES, EXPERIMENTAL). Under marked frustration in problem situations, with strong hunger but with no response adequate to get food, chimpanzees and other mammals become emotionally disturbed, negativistic, and neurotic. Frequent experiences of this sort cause lower primates and human children alike to exhibit symptoms such as temper tantrums or chronic sulkiness with evasion of or dependence on others rather than attempts at direct solutions. By frustrating chimpanzees from infancy, with frequent stress and blocking of strong motivation (as many human parents treat their children), one may obtain abnormal symptoms resembling human neuroses.

One important reason that types of disorganization common in man are less prominent in his animal relatives centres around the infrahuman deficiencies for redirected motivation, perception, and reasoning, and the consequent lessening of morbid anxieties about unobtainable goals. When a chimpanzee is away from the scene of its frustrations, its limited abilities for symbolism hold down related emotional stress in other situations. The effects of frustration are thereby reduced for the animal and it is freer to recuperate than is a man, who can recreate and enlarge on the situation with its tensions.

Lower animals are not so dominated as man by remote goals or dangers or by attitudes of personal prestige; they are freer to leave the frustrating situation outright. Even so, symptoms frequently arise with some resemblance to human reactions in frustrating situations, as in caged mammals persistently circling their enclosures. Such stereotyped habits tend to reduce tensions from conflicts between escape motivation and the necessity to remain. Such behaviour is adaptive in that it seems to help the animal survive frustration; similarly, in man, delusions and other symptoms may forestall more serious disorganization.

7. Contrasting Social Patterns.—Aggregations are fairly common among all animals. Cells of sponges and other colonial organisms are unified organically, members of general associations remain together temporarily through common responses to the same extraneous stimuli. Social groups as in insects, birds, and men are unified and organized on the basis of interdependence.

Natural selection has placed a premium on mechanisms making for interattraction and grouping of species members. As W. C. Allee demonstrated, even the biochemical products of death facilitate survival of others in various invertebrate associations. In insects and mammals, secretions and other processes have evolved which attract members of the species to one another, facilitating unity in local groups while repelling strangers. In various animals, and particularly birds, specialized visual and auditory mechanisms have a comparable function. Variously, the conditions of development favour the effectiveness of such processes and in many ways grouping contributes to species survival.

Striking similarities in social patterning, as between insects and man, encourage analogies as in A. E. Emerson's stress on the social group as supraorganism and his argument that natural selection affects different animal groups in the same ways. Such views can usefully attract attention to comparable organic factors ensuring social life in very different animals, but they also may obscure major differences. In social insects, cuticular secretions, tactual and other factors promote reciprocal stimulation among workers, queen, and brood, unifying the colony; in mammals, including infrahuman primates, the organic products of parturition promote the female's attention to and licking of young; suckling and approach to the female by neonates strongly promote the development of a parent-young bond basic to individual socialization. Yet Schneirla has emphasized the significance of differences in the socialization process itself on different animal levels, terming the insect patterns biosocial, the mammalian patterns psychosocial. In man, although biological factors are basic, their influence in behaviour is far more indirect and complex than in any lower animal.

Analysis shows that, on different levels, comparable biological factors promoting specialization can differ greatly in their developmental consequences, according to phyletic psychological differences such as those discussed in this article. The abiding characteristic of the biosocial level, as exemplified differently by insects and birds, is that organic processes exert their effects rather directly on group behaviour; that of the psychosocial level is plasticity and diversity of outcome according to conditions in development and in the social situation. Whereas the many types of insect social pattern over the world had reached substantially their present forms by Tertiary times, more than 60,000,000 years ago, man has passed from the Stone Age to produce complex cultural systems, civilizations, science, and recorded knowledge within the past 50,000 years. Insect social evolution was achieved through organic evolution, whereas man has developed socially within a period when his organic makeup, particularly his cerebral cortex, seems not to have changed in any important respect. Insects have fixed communication patterns, men have plastic symbolic languages; insects have structurally canalized caste functions, men are more likely to have those fixed circumstantially, through social heritage or through differences in intelligence; insects have organically stereotyped forms of cooperation but men are capable of intentional forms of concerted goal striving or of competition, according to upbringing and prevalent conditions.

It is not only through his intelligence but also through his emotional potentials that man has succeeded in merging small groups into widespread integrated societies as against the local groups to which all lower animals are held. He has achieved not only vast unitary social organizations, but has become a true international in art, literature, music, and science. Perhaps the most important task of comparative psychology is to show in what respects these achievements are unique and in what respects they are equivalent to the various ways in which lower animals adapt to their worlds. *See* also references under "Psychology, Comparative" in the Index.

BIBLIOGRAPHY.—E. L. Bliss (ed.), *Roots of Behavior* (1962); *Col-*

loque internationale sur l'instinct animale (1956); D. O. Hebb, *The Organization of Behavior* (1949); H. Hediger, *Wild Animals in Captivity* (1950); F. Hempelmann, *Tierpsychologie* (1926); H. S. Jennings, *Behavior of the Lower Organisms* (1906); F. Kaintz, *Die "Sprache" der Tiere* (1961); L. V. Krushinskii, *Animal Behavior: Its Normal and Abnormal Development* (1962); N. R. F. Maier and T. C. Schneirla, *Principles of Animal Psychology* (1935; new ed. 1964); C. L. Morgan, *An Introduction to Comparative Psychology* (1894); A. Roe and G. G. Simpson (eds.), *Behavior and Evolution* (1958); C. P. Stone (ed.), *Comparative Psychology*, 3rd ed. (1951); G. Tembrock, *Verhaltensforschung, eine Einführung in die Tier-Ethologie* (1964); W. H. Thorpe, *Learning and Instinct in Animals*, 2nd ed. (1963); C. J. Warden, T. N. Jenkins, and L. Warner, *Comparative Psychology*, 3 vol. (1935-40); R. H. Waters, D. A. Rethlingshafer and W. E. Caldwell (eds.), *Principles of Comparative Psychology* (1960); J. B. Watson, *Behavior: an Introduction to Comparative Psychology* (1914); H. Werner, *Comparative Psychology of Mental Development* (1940). See also the journals *Animal Behaviour; Behaviour; Journal of Comparative and Physiological Psychology; Journal of Genetic Psychology; Zeitschrift für Tierpsychologie*. See also articles in D. S. Lehrman, R. Hinde, and E. Shaw (eds.), *Advances in the Study of Behavior* (1964 et seq.) and in P. R. Farnsworth, O. McNemar, and Q. McNemar (eds.), *Annual Review of Psychology* (1950 et seq.).
(T. C. S.)

PSYCHOLOGY, EDUCATIONAL: see EDUCATIONAL PSYCHOLOGY.

PSYCHOLOGY, EXPERIMENTAL, is a method of studying psychological problems, but the term generally connotes all areas of psychology that use the experimental method. The experimental method as it applies to psychology is an attempt to account for the activities of living and nonliving systems by manipulating variables that may give rise to behaviour; it may investigate the effects of modifying the organism or device, as well as manipulating external conditions. It is primarily concerned with discovering laws that describe manipulable relationships (see SCIENTIFIC METHOD; PSYCHOLOGY).

The areas of study in psychology that lean heavily on the experimental method include those of sensation and perception, learning and memory, motivation and physiological psychology. However, there are experimental branches of most areas including child psychology, clinical psychology, educational psychology, and social psychology. Usually the experimental psychologist deals with normal, intact organisms, but in physiological psychology, studies are conducted with organisms modified by brain or other nervous system surgery, radiation, drug treatment, induced convulsions, or long-standing deprivations of various kinds. The experimental psychologist often finds that his problems overlap those of physiologists, neurophysiologists, radiologists, biochemists, zoologists, pharmacists, physicists, and geneticists. For example, by the 1970s learning in living beings increasingly was being explained in terms of chemical changes in the nervous system.

EARLY PERIOD

Origins.—Experimental psychology as a systematic study grew out of the work of physicists and physiologists who were compelled to recognize the important part played by the observer in results obtained from experiments. Thus it was at first almost entirely concerned with the measurement of reaction times (*i.e.*, the time elapsing between stimulation and response by the observer) and with a study of the special senses.

Major contributions came from Gustav Theodor Fechner (*q.v.*), appointed professor of physics at Leipzig in 1834, who elaborately sought exact quantitative statements of the relation between the intensity of a stimulus and of the experience it evokes. The methods he initiated were developed to become the foundation of a large part of modern experimental procedure (see PSYCHOPHYSICAL METHODS). In 1885 Hermann Ebbinghaus (*q.v.*) published the results of a long series of experiments he had made upon himself in the memorizing of nonsense syllables. He claimed that this kind of material made it possible for the first time to experiment successfully on so-called higher mental processes. Near the beginning of the 20th century Oswald Külpe initiated researches on judgment and volition, while from Fechner onward, experimental work on feelings and on such psychophysical problems as fatigue was continued (see PSYCHOLOGY, HISTORY OF).

In England from the time of Francis Galton statistics received special attention as a method of dealing with experimental results, and experimental psychology was closely in touch with neurology and medicine.

The experimental study of infrahuman animal behaviour (*q.v.*) is also relatively modern. With a few exceptions, and those for the most part resulting from the interest of comparative anatomists in the localization of bodily functions, the anecdotal method of Aristotle remained predominant in the study of animals till the 19th-century work of Charles Robert Darwin, followed by such investigators as Lloyd Morgan. A flourishing school for the experimental study of animal behaviour arose in the United States, led by Edward L. Thorndike, Robert Yerkes, and John B. Watson.

Soon every important university in the world recognized the usefulness of experimental method in psychology. Most leading universities provided experimental laboratories and professorships in experimental psychology; journals were established for experimental research in psychology. Organizations arose for the application of psychology, particularly to education and industry.

Perceptual Processes.—The earliest psychological experiments were by physicists and physiologists; consequently a great amount of work in the psychological laboratory concerned such senses as touch, temperature, taste, smell, vision, hearing, and kinesthesis. In studying visual function, for example, disks of different colours may be rotated so rapidly that the resulting experiences combine and the effects of mixing colours in varying proportion can be accurately determined. Special apparatus demonstrates the aftereffects of continued light stimulation, and the occurrence of colourblind or colour-weak zones in the normal eye. A darkroom is used to show the differences between vision in daylight and in twilight and to study abnormalities of colour vision and night blindness. There is special apparatus for controlled exposure of objects: stereoscopes and devices for the study of the perception of solidity or of distance, and of the various optical illusions (*see* PERCEPTION; VISION).

Choice and Feeling.—Subjects of psychological experiment are often asked to judge, to choose, to decide; they commonly report accompanying feelings and emotions. The experimentalist brings into play apparatus by which he can record some of the physiological changes that accompany these processes, such as variation in respiration, in pulse rate, or in glandular secretion. At the same time the subject, acting throughout under relatively controlled conditions, gives a verbal report of what seems to him to have led up to the judgment or the choice. The problem situations may be indefinitely varied in complexity, from the simple judgment as to which of two weights is the heavier to decisions upon controversial questions of great difficulty. (*See also* FEELING, PSYCHOLOGY OF.)

To measure the speed at which psychophysiological processes take place the psychologist developed elaborate and delicate reaction-time apparatus to determine accurately the time elapsing between stimulation and response.

Especially interesting questions arise in the investigation of abnormal conditions. What, for instance, are the effects of glare or of flicker in the visual field; of excessive and continued noise or vibration in the auditory and tactual fields; of drugs and fatigue generally? The study of fatigue (*q.v.*) in particular developed a mass of special apparatus and methods, and had an immediate practical application.

Learning and Memory.—After 1920 more experimental psychologists devoted their efforts to studying the intricacies of learning and memory (or retention) than to any other area. The experimental laboratory reflects this interest. For human learning experiments there are tachistoscopes, apparatus for brief visual exposure of verbal or pictorial material, with the length of exposure controlled automatically. There are memory drums for presentation of consecutive learning materials at a fixed, but adjustable, rate. There is a wide range of apparatus for learning motor skills; *e.g.*, the pursuitrotor, complex reaction-time apparatus, a variety of assembly tests, and the two-hand coordinator. In soundproof darkrooms there is highly complex apparatus for conditioning eyeblink response, with both photographic and electronic equipment for continuous recording of the stimulation and responses.

Apparatus for infrahuman learning includes the straightaway maze, a single, straight alley with a starting box at one end and a goal box at the other; other mazes, shaped like T's or Y's, require a single choice of path, while more complex mazes have from 3 to 10 or even 20 sections arranged with cul-de-sacs (blind alleys). Some of these mazes may be immersed in water so that the animal must swim through the pathways to reach the goal. There is jumping apparatus for training animals to discriminate between visual stimuli, the subject being required to jump from a platform at one of two cards. If the animal jumps correctly, the card swings back and the animal drops into a box containing food; if it errs, it hits an unyielding card and drops into a net. There is apparatus for conditioning animals to withdraw a leg to avoid electroshock. There are revolving drums to record activity and shock apparatus for delivering convulsion-inducing electroshocks. There are Skinner boxes, cages containing a lever which, when operated, delivers pellets of food or drops of water. (*See* also LEARNING; MEMORY.)

Social Behaviour.—In one direction in particular experimental psychology advanced rapidly. A great many of the conditions of human behaviour are directly social in character and source. Experiments were arranged to allow observation of at least some of the effects of such socially derived motives as competitiveness, pugnaciousness, assertiveness, submissiveness, friendliness, liability to suggestion, leadership, and cooperation.

The earliest success in the social experimental area was with children in college and university nurseries and elementary schools which, from about 1920, served as extensions of the psychology laboratories. Later, successful research in social relationships was conducted with older subjects.

Microphones and one-way vision windows permit experimental observation without detection. Motion-picture and sound-recording equipment have extensively facilitated collection of data. *See* also PSYCHOLOGY, SOCIAL.

LATER PERIOD

The chief aim of experimental psychology in its early days was a description of experiences as experimentally produced and controlled. Interpretation of results was dominated by theories according to which all complex experiences were made up of unitary sensory elements under the principles of association. Methods were, as nearly as possible, copied from other experimental fields. Particular forms of experience were, as far as possible, studied in isolation; the result was often artificial in the extreme. A need existed to bring the problems of the experimental laboratory much nearer those of real life.

Behaviour.—A powerful influence in bringing about this change was the movement known as behaviourism (*q.v.*). The development of an experimental approach to biology made behaviourism possible. At first, as in the field of general human psychology, experiments with other animals were mainly concerned with the anatomical study of the parts of the central nervous system in which hearing, vision, taste, balance, and the like appear to be mediated.

Then experimenters began to observe how various species of animals learn to discriminate objects or to run a maze. They decided to limit themselves to relating the conditions of their experiments and the behaviour of the animals. It seemed possible to do a great deal without using the notion of consciousness; these experimenters held that to attribute consciousness to an animal is to go beyond directly observable fact. Their success led them to a similar program for experimental work in human psychology.

There was a revived interest in the psychology of the special senses, particularly those of vision and hearing. Memory was investigated less as an isolated type of response and more as falling into place in a whole complex learning process that may continually involve also the activities of judging, choosing, reasoning, and the like. On the side of feeling and emotion increased interest in experiment grew out of work on the effects of the secretions of endocrine glands. Methods of registering emotional expression

through metabolic change were developed. Encephalography was developed in the physiological laboratory and was much exploited by psychologists (*see* ELECTROENCEPHALOGRAPHY).

William McDougall emphasized that purposive or goal-directed behaviour could be studied objectively. John B. Watson stressed the importance of objective measurement in psychology, and his book *Behaviorism* (1925; rev. ed. 1930) had a great influence on subsequent experimentalists. Watson conducted researches on emotional learning in children and maze learning in the rat. He stressed the importance of the biological correlates of behaviour.

By 1920 the research of the Russian physiologist Ivan Pavlov was becoming well known in Europe and the U.S., and his influence was doubtless greater because of Watson. Pavlov showed that learning could be studied objectively in the dog. His concept of the conditioned reflex, or conditioned response, remains a formidable method in psychological research.

Theorists.—*Thorndike.*—Important advances in experimentation and theory were being made by Edward L. Thorndike at the same time Watson and Pavlov were at work. Probably Thorndike's most important contribution was his analysis of the role of motivation in human and infrahuman learning. His work was to have great influence, but his interpretation of learning as the formation of specific bonds or connections represented a position of limited generality.

Tolman.—In 1932 Edward C. Tolman published *Purposive Behavior in Animals and Men*, stressing attitudes that typified experimental psychology in the 1950s. To Tolman, experimental psychology must result from objective measurement and recording. He felt that experimental psychology should seek an understanding of the total, intact organism rather than only the isolated reflexes and underlying neurophysiological processes. He named the total behaviour molar and the underlying psychophysiology molecular. His view that the psychologist's particular domain lay in the study of molar behaviour later received wide acceptance. He emphasized intervening variables: processes which intervene between stimuli and overt responses. Such intervening variables included demand, correlated with some maintenance schedule such as food deprivation; appetite, correlated with appropriateness of the goal object such as a particular food incentive; motor skill, correlated with the type of motor response required; and hypotheses, correlated with the cumulative nature and number of training trials.

Tolman and his co-workers observed sudden changes in learned performance when a preferred reward was substituted for one of lower preference and when an incentive appropriate for a particular drive state, such as food for hunger, was substituted for one inappropriate, such as water. One of his more notable discoveries was that of latent learning, in studies where the animal was allowed to explore a maze in the absence of any extrinsic incentive. When an incentive (*e.g.*, food) was presented at the end of the maze, a sharp improvement in performance was found. Tolman interpreted these data as supporting his position that learning is a process of relating sensory or perceptual processes and that the introduction of an incentive in the latent learning situation does not produce learning but merely provides purpose for performance, the use of previous latent (hidden) learning.

Hull.—Clark Hull beginning in the early 1930s chose physics as a model and developed a theoretical system based on postulates and derived axioms. Unlike Tolman, he did not believe that learning was the result of new stimulus-stimulus connections; rather he conceived of learning as the formation of new stimulus-response connections. Also, contrary to Tolman, he assumed that the operation of incentives and drive states was essential to learning per se and not merely to performance. Indeed, Hull clearly stated that habit strength (*i.e.*, learning) resulted only in the presence of the need reduction which followed reinforcement; reinforcement was defined as the attainment of a reward or the reduction of some deprivation state such as hunger.

In actual operation Hull (as did Tolman) placed great emphasis on intervening variables, and tried to quantify these by determining experimentally the effects of systematic manipulation of the independent variables (*i.e.*, the experimental conditions) on the dependent variables, the directly measured responses. Hull differed from Tolman in that his primary intervening variables represented a chain of symbolic and complex interacting constructs.

Hull's system stimulated a large group of research projects employing both subhuman and human subjects. The subhuman research, mostly conducted with rats, confirmed that it was possible to establish the effect of many variables such as length of deprivation, delay between presentation of the conditioned and unconditioned stimulus, amount of reward and amount of effort required to obtain the reward. Generally, simple response measures were used, such as speed of running down a straight alley or rate of lever pressing in an otherwise barren box. Hull and his followers stated that the results supported his position that learning is fundamentally the formation of new stimulus-response connections arising from need reduction.

Tolman-Hull Controversy.—Because the Tolman and Hull positions appeared to differ drastically, attempts of major historic interest were made to show that one or the other had the greater predictive power. Hullian theory would predict that all learning is gradual and continuous, whereas Tolman had predicted that some learning, at least, was discontinuous, or saltatory. Neither group, however, was able to control adequately the conditions essential for a definitive test.

A second attempt to establish a definitive test centred around the latent learning controversy, because latent learning is similar to sudden saltatory learning, at least as far as performance is concerned. One of Hull's associates, Kenneth Spence, argued that latent learning could not be demonstrated if all experimental controls were adequate. The large number of experiments which resulted from this controversy demonstrated that latent learning phenomena existed under limited and prescribed conditions but were voided in similar test situations by such conditions as those involving intense deprivation. One result of the latent learning controversy was the realization that wandering around a maze might of itself represent some need reduction.

Hullian theory led to a study of the effect of serial position in memorization of nonsense syllables, analysis of the reminiscence effect (improvement in performance after practice has ceased), and the influence of massed and distributed practice on the serial-position effect. In all cases Hull made predictions on the basis of his postulates, and tested the theoretical curves against those obtained empirically. The general similarities indicated that Hull's system, primarily established on the basis of subhuman experimentation, had considerable power in predicting limited but important aspects of human learning. Another application of Hullian theory is the researches by Spence and Janet Taylor on the effect of anxiety on the conditioned eyeblink response. Making the assumption that anxiety, as measured on a paper-and-pencil test, would function to raise drive level, they predicted that high anxiety would improve performance on simple learning tasks and lower performance on more complex learning tasks. Again, the results gave general support to the predictions.

Others.—Edwin R. Guthrie developed a theory of learning based on conditioned-response principles, and though he did not develop the theory to the point at which many specific predictions could be made, the theory did stimulate the collection of experimental data. Kurt Lewin developed a topological theory using geometric models and physical field theory as illustrative and predictive devices; his technique received attention particularly in experimental social and experimental child psychology. Kurt Goldstein, Max Wertheimer, and Norman R. F. Maier independently developed two-factor learning theories that differentiated between so-called conditioned-response type learning and a so-called creative type of learning that has been termed reasoning. Another approach after World War II was the statistical learning theory presented by William Estes and others. By the 1970s, however, the pendulum had swung sharply to such physiological approaches as those of R. W. Sperry and N. E. Miller.

Laboratory Methods.—During the period from 1930 to the 1960s B. F. Skinner and co-workers devised and conducted experiments using a technique in which rate of response is mea-

sured instead of errors or latency. Basically this technique involved use of the Skinner Box, an experimental chamber bare except for a lever (or multiple levers) and an incentive delivery mechanism. After the animal has been trained to depress a lever and receive a reward, it is subjected to various reinforcing schedules. In a fixed- or variable-interval schedule, rewards are given at predetermined periods of time regardless of the number of lever presses. In a fixed- or variable-ratio schedule, rewards are given after a predetermined number of lever presses, regardless of time. The Skinner technique proved useful both in the analysis of the effect of motivational states, such as food or water deprivation, and in the analysis of simple learning phenomena; it was, for example, used extensively by Hull and his associates. In the 1970s studies were being conducted on the ability of subjects to respond to multiple schedules. Although the technique was used primarily in analyzing rat and pigeon behaviour, it was also used with monkeys and chimpanzees.

The breadth of the method was illustrated by the fact that Skinner adapted it for the study of arithmetic instruction among elementary-school children and behavioural analysis of institutionalized mental patients.

The early comparative psychologists studied a wide range of animal species; but a tendency later developed to limit researches to the albino rat. With the establishment of the Anthropoid Experimental Station by Robert Yerkes in 1929 (renamed the Yerkes Laboratories of Psychobiology), there was initiated a series of experiments on the psychobiology of the chimpanzee, including development, sensory function, motives and emotions, social behaviour and learning. Although the Yerkes Laboratories studied other primates only in incidental researches, a beginning was made in the 1930s in the study of other primate species. Carlyle Jacobsen published his ingenious studies on the effect of prefrontal lobectomy on rhesus monkey learning; W. Trendelenberg and W. A. Schmidt, in Germany, studied colour vision in monkeys; in 1933, Heinrich Klüver summarized his work on perception and learning in a wide range of monkey species.

At the same time a primate laboratory was developed at the University of Wisconsin, Madison, under Harry Harlow; by 1945 they had developed standardized techniques for measuring learned behaviour in monkeys. At this laboratory it was found practical to use primates in the same kind of rigidly designed experiments that had been popularized in researches with rats. After 1950 there was an upsurge in the establishment of primate laboratories in the U.S., and psychological research was undertaken at Yale University; Johns Hopkins University, Baltimore, Md.; Emory University, Atlanta, Ga.; the University of Texas, Austin; the University of Oregon, Eugene; the University of Pittsburgh, Pa.; Stanford University, Calif.; the State University of South Dakota, Vermillion; and the National Institutes of Health.

The monkey has a far wider range of trainable behaviour than has the rat. It can solve complex problems on a level of difficulty unapproached by any subprimate form; its speed and proficiency in learning simpler problems make possible far more detailed analysis of the processes underlying learning than is possible with subprimate forms.

Studies at the University of Wisconsin on manipulation motivation and on the rhesus monkey's almost insatiable urge to explore its environment visually made it clear that the monkey's motivational structure is far closer to man's than is that of any other animal except the great apes. This does not imply that other animals lack an exploration drive. Such motives were demonstrated in the rat by David Berlyne in Scotland and by Kay Montgomery in the U.S. The differences between primates and rodents in the form and range of these behaviours is striking, and the limitations of the rat appear to be as pronounced here as they are in the area of learning.

Areas of Interest.—*Learning.*—In the area of human verbal learning there was continuous research on both serial learning, the learning of a series of words or syllables, and paired-associates learning, the learning of pairs of words or syllables. Among the many investigators in this field may be cited the systematic work of Benton Underwood on the effects of distribution of practice.

Underwood found that distribution of practice had a beneficial effect on serial lists of both nonsense syllables and meaningful materials, but that no such effect could be demonstrated for paired associates. Similar research found no evidence for reminiscence with serial lists of nonsense syllables, although this phenomenon had been reported in the past both with serial lists of nonsense syllables and with paired associates.

Thus, the historical inconsistencies from experiment to experiment and from one situation to a similar situation continued to arise. On the basis of a detailed review of the literature, Underwood concluded that there was no single theory such as the reactive-inhibition theory or differential-forgetting theory adequate to account for the existing data. One of the most intriguing contributions in this area in past years was a study by Underwood in which he devised a technique for equating associative strength of both fast and slow learners at the termination of practice. He then tested retention 24 hours later and found no differences between the two groups in terms of response probabilities at recall.

By the 1970s, learning and "thinking" by electronic devices was attracting growing attention (see THINKING AND PROBLEM SOLVING; INFORMATION THEORY).

Motor Skills.—During and after World War II major emphasis was given to the development of motor-skills tests, particularly as devices predictive of pilot proficiency. A large number of specific tasks resulted, such as the pursuitrotor, the two-hand coordinator, reversed alphabet printing, and block turning. Investigators found that there are multiple variables influencing performance on all these tests, but no new integrating approach to these problems was devised.

From the theoretical point of view, most of the work on motor skills revolved around Hull's concepts of reactive inhibition (*i.e.*, inhibition produced by work) and conditioned inhibition, arising from the fact that stimuli associated with the cessation of a response became conditioned or learned inhibitors. A vast array of experiments was conducted dealing with various motor-skills performances under conditions of distributed and massed practice, including the phenomenon of reminiscence. Information on the nervous system locus—peripheral or central—of the inhibitory effects was provided by a number of investigators. Their findings of significant post-rest gain when subjects shift from the active to the passive hand after rest give support to a central locus.

Unlike the results obtained from verbal learning studies, the differences produced by massed and spaced practice on motor skills are enormous, and the phenomenon of reminiscence appears with unfailing regularity. The goal of many investigators was to obtain such precise control over their experimental conditions that they could evaluate precisely the role of reactive inhibition and of conditioned inhibition. Both Underwood and Estes doubted not only the ability of investigators to achieve this, but the theoretical possibility of its being done. Indeed, Underwood expressed skepticism about the existence of the Hullian postulate concerning conditioned inhibition.

Children.—Attention to the experimental study of children, normal and abnormal, was focused during this period on learning studies, and attempts were made to integrate the experimental data uncovered in research on subhuman animals with the developing learning abilities of the child. Most of these studies, such as that of transposition in nursery school children by Margaret Kuenne and the studies by Charles Spiker, emanated from Hull's theory or from Harlow's concept of learning to learn.

Social Psychology.—A renewed interest in experimental social psychology stemmed from the original work of Alex Bavelas, a student of Lewin, on the effects of various communication links on group behaviour. The theory assumes that cooperative action by a group is dependent upon the number and kind of communication links. Various patterns of communication links can be arranged according to definable principles, and their efficiency can be tested on a wide range of task performances by groups of varying size. The effects of different kinds of links on the attitudes of the group members also can be assessed, and the influence of a wide range of conditions, including problem difficulty, distribution of problem-related information, kind of leadership by

selected group members, drug states, and the efficacy of various types of information feedback were investigated. This communication-pattern model became an instrument for the experimental study of the interactions of small- and medium-sized groups.

Perception.—A new approach to the psychology of perception was provided through the researches of Jerome Bruner and co-workers. They were based on the assumption that perception is a selective process and that it will be influenced by the values which the individual places upon selected perceptual objects, whether these values are determined by past affective experiences or by existing internal states. Specific experiments suggested that favourable values accentuate the physical characteristics of objects, such as the size of coins, and that they selectively sensitize the subject's perceptual system and selectively lower his recognition threshold. Unfavourable values, on the other hand, result in perceptual defense, which elevates his perceptual thresholds and increases his latency response. Furthermore, drive conditions (*e.g.*, prolonged periods of food deprivation) may enhance perceptual selectivity. Many of these experiments were subject to criticism on the basis of inadequate experimental controls and failure to control the past experience of the subjects.

In whatever realm and with whatever general background of theory he works, the modern experimental psychologist is definitely committed to a biological method of approach. He regards mental processes as falling into their place in a biological adaptation of the organism to its environment, and his problems are thus becoming more and more an inquiry into the functions which such processes carry out, and less and less merely a description or analysis of the processes themselves (see PSYCHOLOGY, PHYSIOLOGICAL).

Modern Practical Applications.—The possibility of applying experimental psychological methods to the solution of practical problems, especially in education, was early realized. The movement gained momentum and extended into many fields of human achievement during World War I when almost every belligerent country called upon its psychologists for advice in the organization and training of its military. In industry psychologists devised and widely applied special techniques for vocational guidance, selection, and training. Time and motion studies made notable contributions to human productivity and industrial organization. Fatigue, accidents, and the particular effects upon work of special environmental conditions were studied intensively.

In education the intelligence test movement grew to enormous dimensions. Medical applications were everywhere exploited, though they were mainly, in this period, confined to the approach through what were called abnormalities. There was even a beginning of experimental investigation of broad problems of industrial management, and there was a burst of interest in the development of new methods for evaluation of public opinion (*q.v.*).

World War II vastly increased both the amount and the scope of psychological experiment as applied to practical problems. The striking increase of mechanization both in the fighting services and in their attendant industrial processes introduced problems new in magnitude though not in their basic character. In a rapidly increasing number of directions the human operator became an indispensable link in some variety of electrical or mechanical system. By the time of the U.S. involvement in the war in Vietnam and the landing of men on the moon, however, such systems had been devised that required a minimum of human intervention.

Experimental psychology grew in interest to the physicist and engineer. Further, since mechanization at first tended to increase skill requirements, many hitherto unsolved problems concerned with skill training and skill fatigue were effectively studied. With skill training went a development of synthetic trainers; these became obsolescent in the 1970s as machines (*e.g.*, the Unimate) were developed for use as spot welders and other manual labour.

Side by side with all this increased interest in problems of the design and control of machines was an increase of activity and scope in vocational selection as people left industry for service occupations. Even the broader problems of group and individual morale and of the results of the contact of differently organized social groups began to be approached less from the point of view of dogmatic opinion and more from their empirical and sometimes experimental aspects. (*See also* PSYCHOLOGY, APPLIED.)

See PSYCHOLOGICAL TESTS AND MEASUREMENTS; PSYCHOLOGY, COMPARATIVE; see also references under "Psychology, Experimental" in the Index.

BIBLIOGRAPHY.—E. G. Boring, *A History of Experimental Psychology,* 2nd ed. (1950); S. S. Stevens (ed.), *Handbook of Experimental Psychology* (1951); C. E. Osgood, *Method and Theory in Experimental Psychology* (1953); R. S. Woodworth and H. Schlosberg, *Experimental Psychology,* rev. ed. (1955); A. L. Edwards, *Experimental Design in Psychological Research,* rev. ed. (1960); G. H. Zimny, *Method in Experimental Psychology* (1961); F. J. McGuigan, *Experimental Psychology,* 2nd ed. (1968); B. L. Hart, *Experimental Neuropsychology* (1969); S. Bogoch (ed.), *The Future of the Brain Sciences* (1969).

(F. C. Ba.; H. F. H.; X.)

PSYCHOLOGY, HISTORY OF. In psychology, more than any other science, the questions discussed by contemporary writers and the answers they offer cannot be rightly understood without some knowledge of its history. The main problems and the chief types of solution are almost as old as civilization. What has changed are rather the methods of study and the attitudes adopted. Little by little man's thoughts about his nature have developed from the crude speculations of primitive tribes into the traditional myths and dogmas of local theology, then into a topic for critical and philosophical analysis and finally into a systematic branch of natural science, with laboratories, instruments and research techniques of its own. To this progressive evolution almost every civilized nation has made some contribution, varying with race, geography, climate and history.

ORIENTAL PSYCHOLOGY

Early Egyptian Doctrines.—The oldest views about which there are trustworthy documentary records are those of the ancient Egyptians. Their beliefs are of special importance because they exercised a powerful influence on writers of other nationalities who, in their turn, had a more direct effect: history and legend indicate that Moses, Thales, Pythagoras, Socrates, Plato and Herodotus all studied in Egypt. What most impressed those who came into close contact with the Egyptians was their belief in the resurrection of an animated body preserved by mummification. Egyptian religious doctrines, as can be learned from early papyri (*c.* 2300 B.C. onward), were a synthesis of older tribal beliefs and, probably for this reason, their conception of individual personality was peculiarly complex.

Like other primitive thinkers who found it difficult to interpret the concrete in terms of the abstract, they explained the many-sided activities of each human being by referring them, not to distinguishable aspects or components, but to distinct entities, each more or less complete in itself. Physical behaviour was attributed to the material personality, the body or *khat;* this, after mummification, purified by prayer and magical formulae, was transformed into an incorruptible and glorified body, the *sahu.* The conscious activities were referred to the *ba* (or soul), conceived as an invisible and immortal entity, symbolized by a human-headed hawk fluttering from the mouth at death—a pictorial notion doubtless derived from some independent source, since it is hardly consistent with the need for mummification. The man's separable self, the *ka* (his *imago* or double), acted as a kind of protecting genius during life that left him at death but afterward returned: provision for its sustenance had to be made in the tomb. The soul itself was accompanied by a shadow or shade, the *khaibit.* The *khu* (or spirit) was the embodiment of the intellectual attributes. The heart (or rather the *ka* of the heart) was the seat of life and conscience. As the cult of Osiris gained increasing popularity, the belief in a moral judgment after death became more and more prominent: the dead person was conducted to the hall of Osiris, where his heart was weighed against a feather (the symbol of truth); the righteous received rewards, graded according to merit, and the wicked were annihilated. These doctrines with only minor modifications lasted for well over 3,000 years, from the 5th dynasty or before down to Greek and Roman times. And when Alexandria became the world centre for culture and learning they did much to colour the philosophic thought of Hellen-

istic times and of later Christian theology. (*See* EGYPT: *History: Ancient Religion.*)

Hebrew Psychology.—Moses (who bears an Egyptian name) was, it is stated, "learned in all the wisdom of the Egyptians." But the Hebrew conception of human personality found in the older Jewish scriptures was far simpler and more akin to that of the other Semitic peoples of Sumer, Babylon and the Arabian desert. In the pre-exilic writings, man was generally depicted as essentially a material structure of bones, sinews and flesh, covered with skin, into which a principle of life has been implanted. As in most Semitic writings, the name of this animating principle is derived from the verb meaning "breathe" (Hebrew, *nephesh,* commonly translated "soul"; *cf.* Latin *anima*) and conceived as residing in the blood. The words *ruah* ("spirit" or "wind"; *cf.* Gr. *pneuma*) and less frequently *neshamah* were at first used almost as synonyms. As far as there is a difference, *ruah* suggests life in its dynamic or emotional aspect, as given by God, *neshamah* suggests the specific personality and *nephesh* the animated individual being. The heart is regarded as the seat of intelligence. As in the Babylonian cosmology, the dead were vaguely conceived as passing a silent and shadowy existence in the grave (*sheol*) and could be called up by witchcraft to appear, like Samuel, as bodies fully clothed. The notion of a definite resurrection, confined at first to the righteous, did not appear before postexilic times and seems to have been due largely to Persian eschatology; it is essentially a resurrection of the body. The notion that man is a tripartite being consisting of body, soul (the natural life) and spirit (the divine life), which occurs in Pauline writings, was a relatively late rabbinical doctrine, but even here the conception was quasi-materialistic: after death the individual is still a spiritual body, not a bodiless spirit. But the idea of a *resurrectio carnis,* as affirmed in the "Apostles' Creed," would seem to be contradictory to Pauline views. The conception of an immortal soul, capable of existing apart from the body, appeared only in the late Jewish school of Alexandria and was undoubtedly due to Platonic and Neoplatonic influences. For the rest there is no attempt in Hebrew literature to analyze the capacities or faculties of the soul, as there is in Hindu and Greek writings. Such attempts appear first in the philosophic expositions of Philo (*q.v.*), who claimed (with little justification) that the three Hebrew terms cited above refer to the three "parts" of the soul as described by Plato.

Hindu Psychology.—From time to time western thought has been appreciably influenced by the cults and philosophies of India. There are, for example, striking analogies between the Orphic and Eleusinian mysteries (*see* MYSTERY) and the mystical beliefs prevalent at that date in the far east. After the conquests of Alexander, Chaldean astrology, Zoroastrianism, oriental dualism and the religions of India (where Buddhism was becoming supreme) all became familiar to the inquiring mind of the Greeks.

As might be anticipated from their common origin and their common theological and ethical traditions, early Indian psychology shows in its essentials many resemblances to that of the Greeks but, owing largely to geographical and climatic conditions, it tended to become more contemplative and subjective. For this reason the introspective analyses of mental states and processes which it embodies deserve more attention than they usually receive. Almost every variety of theory is to be found, from extreme materialism to extreme idealism and from complete pluralism to complete monism. The most typical doctrines (though not the most orthodox) were those elaborated by the Jainist sages whose teaching goes back at least to the time of the Buddha if not before. Consciousness is regarded as the distinctive characteristic of *jiva,* the "enjoyer" or soul. But the soul is conceived as essentially active, not inactive as in the Sankhya theory. And the doctrine of transmigration, propounded in the Upanishads, fades into the background. Three modes of consciousness are recognized: knowing, feeling and striving (the last two being closely allied). There are five kinds of knowing: (1) direct knowledge, obtained through perception or memory; (2) indirect knowledge, derived from symbols, speech, testimony and the like; (3) knowledge of things at a distance in space or time (*avadhi,* which covers clairvoyance and pre- and post-cognition); (4) direct knowledge of the thoughts of others (*manahparyaya* or telepathy); and (5) omniscience. Buddhist psychology recognizes a subconscious life (*vidhimutta*) distinct from waking consciousness (*vidhicitta*), which is treated as a process disturbing the flow of subconscious existence; the two are separated by a "door (or threshold) of the mind" (*manodvara*). Here, and in the emphasis placed on analyzing dreams and dreamlike states and on the importance of symbolic interpretation, early Hindu psychology displays many anticipations of later psychoanalytic theories. *See* INDIAN PHILOSOPHY.

GREEK PSYCHOLOGY

Pre-Socratics.—In the Homeric poems the soul (*psyche*) is a shadowy but still material duplicate of the individual that survives the death of his body. This materialistic view was retained by the early Ionian scientists (600–500 B.C.). Even Empedocles (*q.v.*; fl. 450 B.C.) regarded man, like everything else in the universe, as made up of four primary elements—fire, air, earth and water—and partaking of their antithetical qualities or states; viz., hot, cold, dry (*i.e.*, solid) and wet (*i.e.*, liquid). In man their presence implies a tension of opposites and the soul is, or should be, a nicely balanced mixture or harmony of the pairs. Perception is also explained in material terms: seeing and hearing, like smell, taste and touch, result from receiving concrete particles given off by the object perceived.

The view that the soul (*psyche*) is a purely immaterial entity emerged first in the doctrines attributed to the Pythagorean brotherhood (*c.* 500 B.C.). They in turn appear to have been influenced by the Orphic and other mystery cults in which the souls of initiates, by virtue of certain purificatory rites, could be fitted for life after death. Pythagoras (*see* PYTHAGORAS AND PYTHAGOREANISM) himself believed in transmigration and held that in this life the soul was entombed in the body and obtained release at death. Empedocles (followed by Aristotle and the Stoics) regarded the heart as the seat of consciousness; Alcmaeon of Crotona (*q.v.*), however, a younger disciple of Pythagoras, contended that the brain was the seat of sensation—a conclusion apparently based on dissection and vivisection, methods that he is said to have used to discover the existence and function of the optic nerves.

Plato.—Greek philosophy took a fresh turn with Socrates (*q.v.*). According to him, virtue depends on knowledge and this doctrine gave Greek psychology a strong intellectualist bias that was retained in nearly all the later schools derived from it. Plato (*q.v.*) was the first to raise the problem of consciousness in explicit form. His main contention may be summarized as follows: "We see not with the eyes but through them; we hear not with the ears but through them; hence there must be a common entity which perceives, combines, recalls, and reflects on these sensations"; this, he says, is the soul, which he defines as "a motion that moves itself"; and he adduces a number of arguments to prove that such a soul must be immortal. The different functions that it performs imply that, although a unity, it comprises different parts or powers. And in the discussions that arise out of the questions thus raised he lays the foundations for a new branch of knowledge—psychology, the study of mental life.

In his view the soul includes three main parts or functions: reason, located in the brain; the nobler emotions or spirit, seated in the chest; and the lower appetites arising in the abdominal viscera. Elsewhere he likens the human personality to a chariot guided by a charioteer (reason) and borne along by a pair of horses (spirit and appetite). There is here a clear distinction between the dynamic or motivational components and the directive or "cybernetic" (Plato's own word). In certain individuals one of the three main elements may be more strongly developed than the others and, as a result, the population can be classified according to innate constitution into three distinct classes or castes. As he puts it in a parable, "Gold was mixed in the composition of the born rulers, silver in that of the auxiliaries, and copper or iron in that of the farmworkers or the artisans."

Aristotle.—In his *De anima* (*On the Soul*) Aristotle (*q.v.*) offered the first systematic treatise on the subject. Because of his

training his standpoint is essentially that of a biologist. The soul is defined as the "form" (*i.e.*, mode of organization) of the body; and by soul he understands, not merely mind, but the principle of life. Every living being is essentially a "besouled body." The fully developed human soul is, as it were, a hierarchical system with three main levels and two main aspects: at the lowest level its functions are purely nutritive, as in plants; at a higher level they are also sensitive, as in nonhuman animals; and at the highest of all it is rational, as in man. In its cognitive aspect the activity of the soul is described as essentially discriminative (dianoetic), whether exercised in simple sensation or in the higher intellectual activities evolved from sensation—imagination, memory and even reason itself; in its appetitive or orectic aspect, its activities include the lowlier functions of moving and desiring, and the higher functions of choosing and willing.

Aristotle's other biological works include an elaborate attempt to interpret both vital and mental processes in terms of what today would be called chemical metabolism, but his chemistry was still based on the Empedoclean theory of four "elements" (*i.e.*, primary principles or states). The qualities of heat and cold were related to active or causal processes and those of dry (solid) and wet (liquid) to relatively passive effects, a distinction that later writers carried over into a doctrine of temperaments. Since the active element in air was believed to be necessary to the production of fire or heat, this aerial or gaseous ingredient, called *pneuma* or spirit (literally "wind"), was held responsible for what Aristotle calls "inborn heat" and thus plays an essential part in the vital processes. Breathing in fact was seen as the typical manifestation of life, while digestion and other vital activities were explained as a kind of internal cookery. The veins were believed to be filled with blood and *pneuma*, and to convey sensations to the heart, which Aristotle regarded as the main sensorium. Since pressing the exposed brains of soldiers wounded in battle produced no conscious effect, consciousness, he argued, could not be located in the brain.

In the psychological theories of the Stoic philosophers (*see* STOICS) the doctrine of "spirit" explains much that was formerly attributed to the soul; it is now conceived, not as something abstract or immaterial, but as a finer kind of gaseous matter. The earlier Stoics described sensation as an impression made by the object on the mind, much as a seal leaves its impression on wax, but the later Stoics maintained that, in vision, the eye emitted "spirits" that, like rays, illuminated the object—a doctrine accepted by many medieval psychologists.

Greek Medicine.—The most important medical school of the Greek period was that at Cos and its most famous representative was Hippocrates, an elder contemporary of Plato (*see* HIPPOCRATES). What is known as the Hippocratic *corpus* was virtually the school's library, copied and preserved by the later librarians of Alexandria. Of the surviving treatises only three or four are as old as Hippocrates and the views put forward are often mutually antagonistic, ranging from the purely empirical to the purely speculative. The best-known formulates the doctrine of humours. In origin this was Empedoclean rather than Hippocratic and was primarily a theory of disease and its treatment: sickness resulted from an excess of cold or heat or dryness or moisture and was to be counteracted by a compensatory regimen aiming at a well-tempered balance of all four.

Herophilus (*q.v.*; fl. 300 B.C.) dissected the parts of the brain and was the first to recognize the functions of the peripheral nerves and distinguish the motor nerves from the sensory. As a result Aristotle's view was corrected and the brain was henceforward acknowledged to be the central organ of the nervous system and the seat of consciousness. Erasistratus made similar studies of the veins and arteries and elaborated the doctrine of vital and animal spirits into a form it retained until the discoveries of William Harvey.

Of later medical writers the most influential was Galen (*q.v.*), court physician to the emperor Marcus Aurelius. A voluminous and eclectic writer, he summarized and synthesized earlier views, giving them a quasi-philosophical as well as an empirical basis. He practised both vivisection and dissection. In contradiction to

Erasistratus, by a method copied by Harvey, he showed that the arteries contained blood and not air; but his most remarkable studies were in the field of neurology. Severing the spinal cord of a monkey at various points, he demonstrated that both movement and sensation were eliminated below the level of the section.

It was Galen who originated the more familiar form of the theory of four "temperaments." Starting from the traditional doctrine of four basic qualities, he regards the individual's constitution as resulting from what in modern terms would be called his "saturations" for two "independent bipolar factors." The outcome is four distinct types: the choleric (hot and dry), the melancholic (cold and dry), the sanguine (warm and moist) and the phlegmatic (cold and moist). They are distinguished physically by body-build and by hair- and skin-colour and psychologically by their emotional characteristics, which are the effects of the dominant "humour" (yellow bile, black bile, blood and phlegm respectively). With varying terminology and interpretations this fourfold hypothesis survived to furnish the basis of the modern theories of temperamental types, such as those of E. Kretschmer and C. G. Jung (qq.v.).

The last of the great pagan thinkers was Plotinus (q.v.; A.D. 205–270) the founder of Neoplatonism. With him, largely in reaction against the materialistic tendencies of the medical schools, psychology at last became a science of consciousness as such, with introspection as its fundamental method, and the conclusions reached were highly subjective. In order to study the religions of the east Plotinus accompanied the emperor Gordian on his expedition against the Persians; in many points his teaching markedly resembled Vedanta philosophy. He vigorously criticized those who had held that the soul is a material substance or the "form" of a material substance; for him the soul is immaterial and eternal, with its own place in the hierarchy of being. It exists before birth; it survives after death; it may be reborn in another body. During terrestrial life, it can "stand out" of the body in a state of "ecstasy" ("standing out"), a condition that Plotinus himself claimed to have experienced. Probably no philosopher of ancient times exercised so powerful an influence on Christian doctrine during its formative years.

MEDIEVAL PSYCHOLOGY

St. Augustine.—Among Roman authors only Cicero has written works of interest to the psychologist. His influence is due, not to any original contributions, but to his skill in adapting or coining Latin words to transmit Greek concepts to the philosophers of later ages. Much present-day terminology is Ciceronian in origin. After the conversion of Constantine to Christianity philosophy became virtually a branch of theology and most philosophers wrote in Latin. Of the earlier Christian writers, St. Augustine (q.v.; A.D. 354–430) was by far the most important. His psychological theories are based on a Platonic or Neoplatonic scheme expressed in Ciceronian terms and his whole doctrine is permeated by a religious mysticism derived partly from the scriptures, partly from Plotinus and partly from personal experience. He reveals exceptional gifts of acute introspection and thus is able to fill in the details of his scheme with firsthand observations. The soul he regards as a simple substance, possessing diverse functions: it is capable of various grades, ranging from the nutritive, sentient, rational, up to the highest of all, a stage of "ecstasy" that yields the fullest form of gnosis or intuitive knowledge of the spiritual world. Its functions are classified on a trinitarian basis into knowing, feeling (or loving) and willing. The cognitive faculties comprise sensation, memory, imagination and understanding; but imagination mediates, not between sensation and memory (as with Aristotle), but between memory and understanding, and is thus given a far more important position than with most other philosophers.

St. Thomas Aquinas.—With the scholastic revival the main task of the leading philosophers was to translate and re-interpret the views of those earlier writers whose teaching could be accommodated to orthodox doctrine. The final synthesis, however, was achieved by St. Thomas Aquinas (q.v.; 1225–74), a Dominican. For him it is Aristotle rather than Plato who is il maestro di

color chi sanno ("the master of those who know"). An extreme dualism was avoided by defining the soul once again as the "form" of the body, but with the additional and (as his critics held) the somewhat inconsistent qualification that it is also substantial. The basic classification of functions is dichotomous and not tripartite. Within each of the two main aspects there is a hierarchy of levels —with the intellectual functions sharply distinguished from the sensory on the cognitive side and the volitional from the impulsive or appetitive on the conative.

RATIONALISM IN EUROPE

Dualism.—Both on the continent of Europe and in Great Britain the scientific movement that followed the Renaissance was characterized by a vigorous revolt against authority. In psychology the chief innovator was René Descartes (1596–1650). His is one of the great names in what A. N. Whitehead called "the century of genius"—the century that opened with Francis Bacon's *Advancement of Learning* and toward its close witnessed the publication of Isaac Newton's *Principia*. In his *Discourse on Method* Descartes explains how he began by doubting everything—even the existence of any real world, which every previous thinker had taken for granted in one sense if not in another; and yet, he argues, no matter how far I carry my doubts, in the very act of doubting I must be thinking: one thing, therefore, remains beyond all doubt —that I think. On this he bases his famous inference: *cogito ergo sum* ("I think; therefore I am"). He makes a complete division between mind on the one hand and matter on the other. Matter is substance that has extension in space, but does not think; mind is substance that thinks, but has no extension in space. How then does Descartes account for the evident relation between mind and body? In the years that preceded his contributions anatomy had made great strides and he himself had undertaken a special study of the nervous system. The brain consists of two hemispheres and most of its structures are consequently paired: in its centre, however, there is embedded a tiny body, the pineal gland, which has no duplicate. This gland, therefore, must represent the point of interaction: "here the soul impels the spirits toward the pores of the brain, which thus discharges them through the nerves upon the various muscles."

The activities of the nervous system itself Descartes endeavoured to explain as far as possible in terms of mechanical analogies. The chief mechanical wonders of that age were the hydraulic machines that pumped water into the fountains in the gardens of the rich and by an ingenious arrangement of pipes caused lay figures to dance, play musical instruments and even make noises resembling speech. He therefore thought the nerves must be hollow tubes that conducted "animal spirits" and so produced bodily movements; by a "reflected undulation" a wave of animal spirits, released by external stimulation, might rebound from the sensory to the motor nerves and so cause automatic muscular contractions. He drew a sharp distinction between animal behaviour and human behaviour. Animals are machines and nothing more. Human actions are sometimes mechanical, but sometimes they are rational —the result of thought.

In order to understand human behaviour more fully, Descartes later undertook a full analysis of the emotions. They are treated as combinations of six elementary passions: love and hate, joy and sadness, wonder and desire. Their operation is treated as quasi-mechanical, due to the motion of the spirits in the brain and other vital organs; their effects, however, are described as if they were intellectual functions—love, for example, being dependent on expected good, hate on expected evil.

Monism.—Among Descartes' immediate successors the most notable was the Dutch Jew, Benedictus de Spinoza (q.v.; 1632– 77). Like Descartes he was impressed by the success of a mathematical approach in dealing with mechanics and astronomy; and his *Ethics* is set forth in the style of Euclid, with definitions, postulates and theorems deductively inferred. Descartes' attempt to explain the interaction between a mental soul and a material body was manifestly unsatisfactory. Spinoza's solution was to regard mind and matter, not as two separate substances but as two aspects of one and the same substance which in itself was neutral. This he termed both Nature and God. For Descartes' psychophysical dualism he thus substitutes a neutral monism. But, he insisted, everything in nature, including a person's own actions, must be ruled by logical necessity; he held that the idea of free will was an illusion resulting from the fact that movement only is perceived, not its cause, and so it is wrongly inferred that the movement must have been self-caused. However, the third part of his book is of greatest interest to psychology. In it he expounded his doctrine of *conatus:* "everything, in so far as it is in itself, strives to persevere in its own being." Self-preservation is the basic motive and the emotions are reduced to a tension of opposing tendencies, with joy and sorrow as the most elementary feelings. The operation of the emotions may thus be both irrational and unconscious, but "a passion which is evil ceases to be a passion as soon as we form a clear and distinct idea." Here there is a remarkable anticipation of the doctrines of a later Jewish psychologist, Sigmund Freud.

Monadism.—To escape from the difficulties raised both by the dualism of Descartes and the monism of Spinoza, G. W. Leibniz (*q.v.;* 1646–1716) suggested that the universe consists of a hierarchy of monads, *i.e.,* units which are essentially psychical but may also possess certain physical properties. The human body, for example, is a system of more or less inferior monads with one dominant monad, corresponding to what would ordinarily be called the soul. There is no real causal interaction: the appearance of causation is due to a "pre-established harmony" or parallelism between the changes in one monad and those in the others—like that of two or more clocks keeping similar time. Even the inferior monads are supposed to be capable of *petites perceptions, i.e.,* unconscious "prehensions" (in Whitehead's phrase); when these become clear and explicit in fully conscious apprehension, the process is described as apperception—a new term that, with varying interpretations, plays an important part in later theories.

With Christian Wolff (*q.v.;* 1679–1754) the rationalist attempt to base psychology on purely deductive arguments reaches its climax. The basic principles were mainly those of Leibniz, but Wolff developed the Aristotelian notion of a scale of faculties into a systematic hierarchical scheme. He began with the double dichotomy of the scholastic philosophers: mental "powers" are divided first vertically (as it were) into cognitive faculties and appetitive (or orectic) propensities; each set is then divided horizontally into lower and higher powers; *i.e.,* into perceptual or conceptual processes on the one hand and into involuntary or voluntary processes on the other. The more specialized functions are then classified under these various heads.

BRITISH EMPIRICISM

The Revival of Materialism.—Throughout the middle ages the atomistic doctrines of Leucippus, Epicurus (*qq.v.*) and their followers were almost wholly neglected because of their antireligious tendencies. In the middle of the 17th century, however, the French mathematician, Pierre Gassendi (*q.v.;* 1592–1655) attacked both Aristotle and Descartes and revived the atomistic theory. In Great Britain a similar materialistic view was adopted by Thomas Hobbes (*q.v.;* 1588–1679), who pushed it to further extremes. A friend and follower of Francis Bacon, he held with Bacon that experience is the only source of knowledge and, in his most famous work, *The Leviathan,* maintained that experience was based on sensation and that sensation, like all other phenomena, was reducible to motion: "'tis but an apparition of that motion which the object worketh in the brain." Hobbes's revolutionary doctrines aroused little interest until the reappearance of materialist theories during the 19th century. Thus the effective founders of British empiricism were the three great writers who followed him, John Locke (1632–1704, an English physician), George Berkeley (1685–1753, an Irish bishop) and David Hume (1711–76, a Scottish man of letters) (*qq.v.*).

Locke's conclusions are always in keeping with those of common sense. In his *Essay Concerning Human Understanding* he borrows from Descartes (whose writings first "gave him a relish of philosophical things") the doctrine that matter and mind are two distinct substances, but he diverges from Descartes in rejecting the

notion of "innate ideas." His method too, unlike that of Descartes, was that of induction (in the Baconian sense) rather than Euclidean deduction; he even, when discussing sensory phenomena, cites the result of an *ad hoc* experiment. In introducing what he calls "the new way of ideas," he starts by urging that the mind should be regarded as being at the outset simply "as it were white paper, void of all characters." Whence then come the materials of reason and knowledge? To this he gives the same answer as Bacon and Hobbes: "in one word from experience." Experience, he holds, is of two kinds: it comes partly from sensation and partly from reflection, which he describes as a kind of "internal sense." Ideas are likewise of two kinds: simple and complex. Simple ideas are thus treated as elementary atoms of consciousness that combine to form more complex states. They may have either primary or secondary qualities, but the former alone reproduce the qualities of external objects. While denying innate ideas, he admits that the mind has innate powers. But these powers must be regarded merely as names for the various ways the mind can act and are not to be treated, in the fashion of the scholastics, as ultimate causes.

Berkeley's earliest work, *An Essay Towards a New Theory of Vision,* studied a specific problem in psychology in and for itself; and his novel conclusion is that the appreciation of distance is not (as had previously been supposed) a direct visual perception, but the effect of earlier associations with experiences of touch and movement. In his *Treatise Concerning the Principles of Human Knowledge* and *Three Dialogues Between Hylas and Philonous* he carries Locke's premises to their logical conclusion, arguing that the primary qualities of sensation are just as subjective as the secondary. There is thus no factual evidence whatever for the existence of material substances such as hitherto had always been postulated as the causes of ideas, but on the other hand, he still assumes the existence of mental substances as the unobservable but logically necessary bases for conscious experience.

Hume's *Treatise of Human Nature,* as its title page explains, is "an endeavour to introduce the experimental method of reasoning into moral subjects": (by "moral" subjects he means "psychological" and by "experimental" reasoning the method of inductive reasoning based on "experience and observation" with a minimum of presuppositions, the method Newton had used in expounding his system of the material universe). And in the principle of association he believed he had found "a kind of attraction in the mental world" that would have the same explanatory possibilities as the principle of gravity in "the natural world." He treats Berkeley much as Berkeley had treated Locke and the arguments that discredit the notion of a "material substance" are turned against the assumption of a "spiritual substance." Book I of the *Treatise* deals with intellectual processes. Mental contents are divided into two main groups: "impressions" and "ideas." Images, it is said, differ from impressions solely by being less vivid. Relations are recognized as a special group of "complex ideas" and a classification of relations is proposed that is a definite improvement on Locke's. The course of thinking is determined by three types of association: by resemblance, by contiguity in space or time, and by cause and effect. Book II discusses "the passions" on somewhat similar lines. Two classes are recognized: (1) the direct affections, which are reduced to terms of three bipolar factors—joy and grief, desire and aversion, hope and fear; and (2) the indirect affections, which involve an associated object as well as a cause, and thus resemble what were later called sentiments.

David Hartley (*q.v.;* 1705–57) in his *Observations of Man* reduced the association of ideas to a purely physiological association. The nerve fibres, he suggests, are not "hollow tubules" but "solid capillaments" and the "vibrations" they conduct can set up permanent connections in the brain between the centres for "ideas." The greater part of his book is an ingenious attempt to explain the whole of mental life in terms of this neurological principle.

In France Voltaire (*q.v.*) did much to popularize the ideas of Newton, Locke and other English writers. A completely mechanistic view of mental life, based on oversimplified sensationalistic and associationistic conceptions, was elaborated by J. O. de Lamettrie (*q.v.*) in *L'homme machine*, by his young contemporary E. Condillac (*q.v.*) and by physiologists like M. F. X. Bichat, P. J. G. Cabanis and P. H. T. d'Holbach. The result was a remarkable anticipation of modern behaviourism.

REALISM, IDEALISM AND ASSOCIATIONISM

Scottish Faculty Psychology.—The reaction against these more extreme types of skepticism and materialism took the form of a return to a common sense realism in Scotland and a transcendental type of idealism in Germany. The first revolt against the mechanistic tendencies of the sensationalist school came from the Scottish universities. In his *Essay on the Intellectual Powers of Man* Thomas Reid (*q.v.*), the founder of the Scottish school, endeavoured to counteract the phenomenalism to which the sensationalist theories were tending by developing a "new realism founded on the common sense of mankind." The result is a revival of a psychophysical dualism; but, in seeking to re-establish the hypothesis of a soul, his arguments are no longer based on the old deductive procedure but on the type of inductive reasoning introduced by the empiricists themselves. In particular, he and his chief expositor, Dugald Stewart (*q.v.*; 1753–1828), revived the traditional doctrine of "mental powers" and produced a classified list of 36 or more, most of which were later taken over by the phrenologists, and so came to furnish a ready-made vocabulary for educational and medical writers and even for biographers and novelists. Thomas Brown (*q.v.*; 1778–1820) incorporated the principle of association by interpreting it not as a physiological mechanism but as a mode of mental activity, which he renamed "suggestion"; his treatment is noteworthy for his detailed formulation of both primary and secondary laws of association and for his theory of "relative suggestion" (the "eduction" of analogies or correlates). Finally, Sir William Hamilton (*q.v.*; 1788–1856), a man of encyclopaedic erudition, went a step further and claimed that all forms of "association" were merely special cases of what he called "redintegration," *i.e.*, reinstating ideas. His main aim, however, was to combine the tenets of the Scottish school with those of the new idealistic movement in Germany.

The Rise of German Psychology.—Immanuel Kant (*q.v.*; 1724–1804), who had been brought up on the Wolffian version of Leibniz' theories, relates how at length a study of Hume "woke him from his dogmatic slumbers," and in the end he evolved a "transcendental" philosophy from a synthesis of Leibniz, Wolff and Hume. His insistence on the "synthetic unity of apperception" struck at the heart of the sensationalist and associationist interpretations; and, by distinguishing the "transcendental ego" from the "empirical or phenomenal self," he relegated empirical psychology to a branch of anthropology. Indeed, it is not so much in his better known *Critiques*, but rather in his *Ethics* and his *Anthropologie in pragmatischer Hinsicht* that his chief contributions to psychology are to be sought. Here he works out the threefold division of mental functions into knowing, feeling and willing, in place of the twofold classification favoured by the faculty psychologists, and sketches a theory of temperamental types. In *Träume eines Geistersehers* ("Dreams of a Spirit-Seer") he had already revealed an interest in paranormal phenomena and an appreciation of the importance of inductive methods in the study of mental life. In the end he concluded that, since all science is essentially mathematical and since mathematical methods could not be applied to the study of mind, psychology could never become a genuine science. As a result the interest of his work for the psychologist lies more in his criticisms than in his discoveries.

The aims of J. F. Herbart (*q.v.*; 1776–1841, Kant's successor at Königsberg) were expressed by the title of his textbook—*Psychologie als Wissenschaft neu gegründet auf Erfahrung, Metaphysik, und Mathematik* ("Psychology as Knowledge Newly Founded on Experience, Metaphysics and Mathematics"). The inclusion of *Mathematik* is Herbart's answer to the challenge of Kant. He rejects the whole concept of faculties, and regards mental life as the manifestation of elementary sensory units or "presentations." These he conceives as mental forces rather than as mere "ideas" in Locke's sense. The study of their interactions gives rise to a statics and dynamics of the mind, to be expressed

in mathematical formulae like those of Newtonian mechanics. Ideas need not be conscious; and they may either combine to produce composite resultants or conflict with each other so that some get temporarily inhibited or repressed "below the threshold of consciousness." An organized but unconscious system of associated ideas forms an "apperception mass": such a system could apperceive a new presentation and thus give it richer meaning. On this basis Herbart later developed a theory of education as a branch of applied psychology and so became the "father of pedagogy."

Associationism.—In England the principles of association outlined by Hume, Hartley and Brown found their most rigorous and complete exposition in the theory developed by James Mill (*q.v.*; 1773–1836). In his *Analysis of the Phenomena of the Human Mind* he describes "sensations" and "ideas" as the two "primary states of consciousness"; these were mechanically linked by association, now reduced to a single principle—"order of occurrence." Its strength is determined by two main conditions—frequency and vividness. To this simple doctrine he added the hedonistic theory of his friend, Jeremy Bentham (*q.v.*): human actions are motivated solely by pleasure and pain. His son, John Stuart Mill (*q.v.*; 1806–73), adopted as his scientific model, not the physics of Newton, but the chemistry of John Dalton. He accordingly modified the mechanical theory proposed by his father, arguing that the "elements" into which consciousness could be analyzed were combined by a kind of "mental chemistry," so that the compound, instead of being just the sum, mixture, or mere resultant of the parts, had novel properties of its own. But the most stimulating of his contributions was his discussion in the closing book of his *System of Logic* of the methodology appropriate to psychology.

RISE OF EXPERIMENTAL PSYCHOLOGY

The Physiology of the Nervous System.—In 1810 F. J. Gall (*q.v.*), a German anatomist, began to issue a lengthy treatise claiming to localize the various faculties of the mind in specific parts of the brain, thus furnishing a diagnostic technique for individual psychology. For various reasons the doctrine became as repugnant to the scientist and the philosopher as it was popular with the general public. Its most effective critic was M. Flourens (*q.v.*), who in 1824 published a series of experimental studies of the brain (chiefly in pigeons) in which he showed by extirpating different parts that each had an *action commune* (a general activity shared by the remaining parts) as well as an *action propre* (a specific action peculiar to itself), the chief emphasis being on the former. In 1825 J. B. Bouillaud, on the basis of clinical evidence, localized a centre for speech in the frontal convolutions of the brain, confirmed by P. Broca's more careful work in 1861. This was followed by the localization of motor and sensory functions by G. T. Fritsch and J. E. Hitzig and others in the second half of the century. In Britain as early as 1811 Sir Charles Bell (*q.v.*) had definitely proved by severing the spinal roots the sharp distinction between the sensory and motor functions of the peripheral nerves; and about 20 years later J. Müller provided experimental evidence for the hypothesis of reflex action and formulated what he called "the law of specific energies" (that each sensory nerve can convey only one sensory quality) (*see* MÜLLER, JOHANNES PETER). During the same period improved microscopical methods had enabled the histologists to demonstrate that the grey matter of the brain and spinal cord alone contained "nerve-cells" while the white matter consisted solely of "nerve-fibres," and that every fibre was connected with a cell—a neural structure that seemed to fit admirably with the requirements of associationist theories.

Alexander Bain (*q.v.*; 1818–1903) was the first to emphasize that "the time had come when the new discoveries of the physiologists should find an appropriate place in the Science of the Mind"; and his two volumes—*The Senses and the Intellect* and *The Emotions and the Will*—provide by far the best survey of mental processes as studied by purely observational methods before psychologists themselves had begun to carry out systematic experiments. The basis of his account is a hypothesis of psychophysiological parallelism, which long remained the most popular solution to the body-mind problem; as he expressed it, "no nerve-currents, no mind." But, unlike earlier associationists, he fully recognized the importance of the innate tendencies (reflexes and instincts) and laid far greater stress on movement and activity.

The Experimental Study of Sensation.—Galileo's discovery of the dependence of audible pitch on the frequency of the vibrations and Newton's discovery of the laws of colour mixture marked the beginnings of a realization that sensory experience is systematically related to the physical characteristics of the stimulus, but little progress was made until the early 19th-century anatomists began to investigate the structure of the various sense organs.

The first step consisted in the collection of factual data by methodical observation. In 1801 Thomas Young (*q.v.;* 1773–1829) published his trichromatic theory of colour vision, which later obtained strong support from the experimental studies of H. L. F. von Helmholtz and W. McDougall (*qq.v.*). An attack on the Newtonian theory by the poet Goethe in his *Zur Farbenlehre* stimulated J. E. Purkinje (1787–1869) to publish two series of observations on colour sensation (particularly under conditions of night vision). A new line was opened up by the experiments of E. H. Weber (*q.v.;* 1795–1878) on touch-sensation, which included the demonstration that the physical intensities of stimuli which are just noticeably different in their perceived intensities bear a constant ratio to each other.

G. T. Fechner (*q.v.;* 1801–87) studied medicine under Weber and, after making his reputation by measuring electrical currents, was appointed professor of physics at Leipzig. Shortly after, in a work entitled *Zend-Avesta* (an attack on materialism) he published his program for psychophysical research; this was based on a philosophical theory (derived in his case from oriental sources) that matter and mind are two complementary aspects of the universe, whose relations can be expressed mathematically by what is known as the Weber-Fechner law. Still more important are his three "psychophysical methods" (1860). In later years he devoted his attention to quantitative studies of artistic appreciation and may thus also be regarded as the founder of experimental aesthetics.

It was, however, Helmholtz (1821–94) who made the most important factual contributions to experimental psychology. He was the first to make experiments on reaction times and determine the rate of conduction in nerves. His hypothesis of "unconscious inference" and his defense of empiricism provided topics of controversy for many years. His four great volumes on physiological optics and tonal sensations and the theory of music formed standard works of reference for more than half a century.

W. Wundt (*q.v.;* 1832–1920) founded the first laboratory of psychology (1879) and the first journal of experimental psychology (1881) and was for 40 years the most influential figure in scientific psychology: his *Grundzüge der physiologischen Psychologie* remained a basic textbook until well into the 20th century. Essentially a systematizer, he brought together a wide array of facts into a more or less coherent scheme: psychology, according to Wundt, shows how experience can be analyzed into specific elements ("sensations," with their various "attributes") and how, by a process of "creative synthesis," they can be combined into "psychic resultants" and what are the laws of combination. This was later supplemented by a tridimensional theory of feelings, with three independent bipolar components combining, like physical forces to yield "resultants."

Evolutionary Psychology.—In his "synthetic philosophy" Herbert Spencer (*q.v.;* 1820–1903), "the last of the associationists and the first of the evolutionists," set out to depict evolution as the key to both inorganic and organic nature. Evolution he conceived as proceeding, by a double movement of analysis and synthesis—of "differentiation" accompanied by "integration," toward an ever-increasing adjustment of the individual organism to its external environment. Biology, as the science of life, applies these principles to the general development of living organisms, and psychology, as the science of mental life, applies them to mind, thus becoming itself a branch of biology rather than a mere branch of philosophy or physiology. These theories formed the basis of his *Principles of Psychology*. Here, adopting the ideas of the neurologist John Hughlings Jackson (*q.v.*), he treats the sensorimotor reflex as exhibiting in its simplest form the general pattern of all mental activity; and, as the nervous system progressively differentiates into a hierarchy of sensorimotor mechanisms of increasing complexity, so the general capacity for adaptation, which Spencer calls "intelligence," was said to differentiate into increasingly complex and specialized capacities for adaptive reaction. In his *Principles of Sociology*, he applied the same interpretative principles to the growth of human societies and laid the foundations for what subsequently became known as "social psychology."

The supreme achievement of Charles Robert Darwin (*q.v.;* 1809–82) was to collect a vast array of factual evidence supporting the hypothesis of "natural selection" as the chief mechanism underlying the process of evolution. His *Origin of Species* thus transformed the idea of evolution from a speculative concept into an established theory. In *The Descent of Man* and *The Expression of Emotions in Man and Animals* he further proved that not only the physical attributes of man but also his "intellectual, emotional and moral faculties" have evolved from those of lower animals and obey the same laws of variation and heredity. His researches on infant development and animal learning paved the way for two further branches of what Spencer had called "comparative psychology"—child and animal psychology.

Sir Francis Galton (*q.v.;* 1822–1911), a half cousin of Darwin, is universally acknowledged as the founder of individual psychology as a genuine branch of science. The phrenologists had raised the problem; but their methods were anything but scientific. Galton introduced a wide variety of techniques: mental tests, psychological questionnaires, anthropometric surveys and the basic methods of statistical analysis. He and his co-worker, Karl Pearson, were the first to apply correlational procedures to the analysis of mental capacities into their elementary components or "factors." It was Galton, too, who led the way in applying Darwin's twofold principles of heredity and variation to the interpretation of individual differences. His work on *Hereditary Genius* established the pedigree method as a useful means of studying mental endowment and his *Inquiries into Human Faculty and its Development* summarized his investigations on mental imagery, free association, the resemblances of twins and his final conclusions on nature, nurture and eugenics.

Neoscholastic Psychology.—In opposition to the materialistic theories of the physiological associationists, who had claimed to reduce consciousness to a mere succession of nerve currents in the brain, there was during the last quarter of the 19th century a new and growing interest in the older "analytic" approach of the medieval philosophers. F. Brentano (*q.v.;* 1838–1917) revived the scholastic doctrines of "intention" and "inexistence," basing them, however, on an empirical study of introspective data rather than on philosophic argument. In his view the distinctive characteristic of a conscious process or act was that it always "intended" (*i.e.,* referred to) an immanent or "inexistent" object beyond itself. The Polish philosopher, K. Twardowski, further distinguished between "content" and "object"; and A. Meinong (1853–1920, Brentano's ablest follower and founder of the first psychological laboratory in Austria) developed the theory that consciousness involves three terms: a process or "act" (*e.g.,* perceiving), a "content" (*e.g.,* a sensum such as "yellow") and an "object," which might be either existent (*e.g.,* a yellow "thing") or subsistent (*e.g.,* a "class," a "relation" or a "fact"). In 1890 C. von Ehrenfels (*q.v.*) published a detailed account of what he called the quality of a shape or form (*Gestaltqualität*), a concept already adumbrated by E. Mach (*q.v.*), the Viennese physicist, who regarded both spatial shape (*e.g.,* a circle) and temporal form (*e.g.,* a melody) as "sense impressions." Such "qualities," it was held, may arise out of relations between "fundaments" but are quite independent of them—an assertion later attacked by C. Spearman. The so-called Austrian school had numerous adherents, highly influential in their day (notably C. Stumpf, who substituted the conception of "function" for that of "act," and T. Lipps whose best known contribution was his theory of "empathy"), and prepared the way for the Würzburg and Gestalt schools of the 20th century.

Functional Psychology.—A similar revolt against the crudities of the materialistic doctrines of their day took place in Great Britain and the U.S. The associationists had approached psychology from an intellectualistic standpoint and were chiefly concerned with analyzing the mind into sensory elements and describing its structure. The theory of evolution led naturally to a study of mind from a more practical standpoint, emphasizing function rather than structure and preaching a dynamic rather than a merely analytic psychology. The leaders of this new movement were William James in the U.S. and James Ward in Britain.

James Ward (1843–1925) opened the attack with his celebrated article on "Psychology" in the 9th edition of the *Encyclopædia Britannica* (1886). Mental activity, he argued, must imply a mental agent. This he termed a "subject" (in the Kantian sense) and, following Kant, he insisted that all mental activity had a threefold aspect, affective and conative as well as cognitive or intellectual. Instead of sensations he preferred to speak of "presentations" (ways in which the cognized object is presented to the subject) and instead of analyzing conscious contents into atomistic elements he maintained that consciousness was essentially unitary and continuous.

James Sully (1842–1923), a lucid exponent with a more eclectic but less original outlook than Ward, sought to amalgamate the new doctrines with what was sound in the old and give the results a more systematic shape, largely with a view to applying them to practical problems such as individual differences, child development, abnormal psychology and education. He had studied under Helmholtz and, impressed with the possibilities of the new experimental techniques, opened at University college, London, the first psychological laboratory in Britain (1896). There he worked in close collaboration with Galton and K. Pearson and established in his education department a kind of child guidance clinic for the study of normal and abnormal children.

His *Outlines of Psychology* and his two volumes on *The Human Mind* became the most popular textbooks of their time. Psychology, he maintains, includes the investigation both of mental functions and of mental elements or contents (the sense data and images mediating between the knowing mind and the object presented or known). Functions and contents imply corresponding potentialities (which he referred to as "factors") varying in strength with different individuals. There are three main functions—cognition, affection and conation—and three main types of content, arranged in developmental levels of increasing specialization and complexity—perceptual, reproductive and conceptual. The basic mental processes—appearing in all functions and at every level—are "discrimination" (mental analysis) and "integration" (mental synthesis), of which association was but one specific form.

G. F. Stout (*q.v.*; 1860–1944) combined the standpoint of Ward with the teaching of Herbart and the Austrian school. His most original and most influential work was his *Analytic Psychology*. Though interested chiefly in problems of cognition, he consistently emphasized the importance of conative activity in all intellectual processes and thus laid the foundations for the more dynamic type of psychology advocated by W. McDougall, R. S. Woodworth and their contemporaries. The distinctive result of mental activity Stout regards as integration or organization into systems ("noetic synthesis" as he preferred to call it): perception, association and the "eduction of relations and correlates" (to use the later description) are merely special manifestations of this more general principle.

William James (*q.v.*; 1842–1910) is generally regarded as having been the greatest U.S. psychologist. His *Principles of Psychology* re-interpreted the facts of physiological and experimental writers in the light of an unceasing insistence on consciousness as something personal, continuous and purposive. In consequence he too became a vigorous critic of the atomism and the mechanical associationism of the older schools, expounding his views with literary brilliance and felicity. He established a laboratory (for demonstration rather than research) almost as early as Wundt. He was an ardent advocate of the interactionist interpretation of the relation between body and mind and by his active interest in unconventional studies, such as hypnosis, religious experiences and

psychical research, did much to render these topics scientifically respectable. In his later years his lively and often paradoxical criticism of contemporary theories laid the foundation for both the "functionalist" and the "neo-realist" schools that developed in the U.S. during the early years of the 20th century. (Cy. B.)

PSYCHOLOGY IN THE 20TH CENTURY

From its earliest days the 20th century held great promise for psychology. Under the impetus of its own achievements in the 19th century, and in partnership with mathematics, medicine and other burgeoning disciplines in the physical and biological sciences, psychology advanced both scientifically and professionally. By the 1960s departments of psychology were firmly established in colleges and universities throughout the world, training scientists and practitioners whose contributions were increasingly in demand by governments, businesses and the general public. This rapid proliferation has been relatively quite recent. In the last half of the 19th century, notwithstanding its increasingly experimental and practical features, psychology was still commonly considered a subdivision of philosophy. Wundt, for example, in order to publish the results of his experiments founded a periodical he apparently was constrained to name *Philosophische Studien;* and, since there was no precedent for a chair of psychology at the University of Leipzig, he carried on officially as professor of philosophy.

The tendency of psychologists to identify themselves with particular systems or schools was passing in the 1960s. Instead, contemporary psychologists are likely to adopt such identifications as learning theorist or clinician or psychophysiologist, stressing a particular problem or area of application. However, the advance of scientific psychology in the early decades of the 20th century was powerfully influenced by three major schools or movements: behaviourism, Gestalt psychology and psychoanalysis, all three flourishing against a background of activity already well in ferment at the turn of the century. For detailed histories of the growth of these movements and of how they contributed to modern psychology *see* BEHAVIOURISM; GESTALT PSYCHOLOGY; PSYCHOANALYSIS.

The emergence of specialized topics in scientific psychology as more or less well-defined subdisciplines with their own corps of investigators, theorists and histories has tended to characterize the period from the 1930s to the 1960s. These developments are traced in such articles as PERCEPTION; EMOTION; MOTIVATION; LEARNING; INTELLIGENCE; PERSONALITY; PSYCHOLOGY, EXPERIMENTAL; THINKING AND PROBLEM SOLVING; PSYCHOLOGY, SOCIAL.

Aside from its considerable progress as a pure science in the 20th century, psychology gave substantial evidence of increasing professional maturity. The professional development of psychology is indicated by its widespread acceptance as an independent science with applications to many aspects of daily living. From the beginning of the century many psychologists began to move toward an interest in problems arising in education, vocational selection and placement, or personal and social interrelations in a wide variety of contexts. As a result, psychology has taken its place among the service professions by developing and employing psychological tests and measurements, counselling and psychotherapeutic techniques and applications to engineering, especially for the purpose of adjusting man-machine relationships in military and industrial settings. The history of such efforts is selectively presented in PSYCHOLOGY, APPLIED; PSYCHOLOGICAL TESTS AND MEASUREMENTS; EDUCATIONAL PSYCHOLOGY; PSYCHIATRY; PSYCHOTHERAPY; PUBLIC OPINION.

See also references under "Psychology, History of" in the Index.

BIBLIOGRAPHY.—J. C. Flügel, *A Hundred Years of Psychology* (1933); E. Heidbreder, *Seven Psychologies* (1933); G. Zilboorg, *A History of Medical Psychology* (1941); E. G. Boring, *Sensation and Perception in the History of Psychology* (1942), *History of Experimental Psychology* (1950); R. E. Brennan, *History of Psychology: From the Standpoint of a Thomist* (1945); B. Russell, *History of Western Philosophy* (1945); H. E. Garrett, *Great Experiments in Psychology* (1951); G. Murphy, *Historical Introduction to Modern Psychology* (1949); G. S. Brett, *History of Psychology* (1953); J. M. Schneck, *History of Psychiatry* (1960); J. P. Chaplin and T. S. Krawiec, *Systems and Theories of Psychology* (1960); J. A. C. Brown, *Freud and the Post-*

Freudians (1961) ; A. A. Roback, *History of Psychology and Psychiatry* (1961) ; J. R. Kantor, *The Scientific Evolution of Psychology* (1963) ; L. S. Hearnshaw, *A Short History of British Psychology* (1964).

PSYCHOLOGY, PHYSIOLOGICAL, is the study of the physical basis of behaviour. Primarily it is concerned with how the brain and the rest of the nervous system function in activities (*e.g.*, thinking and perceiving) recognized as characteristic of man and the other animals. Because the nervous system critically depends upon other organs of the body for its normal function, physiological psychology also is concerned with the mechanisms of metabolism, the elaboration of hormones by the endocrine glands, and other regulations of the internal environment. Furthermore, the structural and functional characteristics of the nervous system, as well as of other organs, are mediated by the mechanisms of heredity and are affected by diet, drugs, and disease. Thus, behaviour may be influenced by all of these things, for the nervous system is the major proximate agent of the behaviour of most animals.

Although the early philosophers did not understand the nervous system very well, they knew that psychological activities were in some way related to the body and its functions. Thus the historic roots of physiological psychology lie in the classical mind-body notions of philosophy (*see* Body and Mind). Aristotle's view of this dispute, known as the double-aspect theory, was that mind and body were different aspects of the same thing, that body was the structure and mind the function. This surprisingly modern view did not entirely satisfy many others, however. René Descartes, for example, was impelled to reserve soul as the realm of the mind of man. He denied mind in animals and viewed their behaviour completely mechanistically, ascribing it entirely to the functioning of the brain and its nerves. For man, however, he argued that while basic reflexes were mechanistically determined, mind was a separate spiritual (immaterial) entity. To explain how mind and body could influence each other he proposed an interaction theory, holding that the site of the interaction between mind and body was the pineal body in the brain.

Even more independence of mind from body was envisaged by G. W. Leibniz in his theory of psychophysical parallelism. Leibniz maintained that mental events and bodily events occurred in two separate realms, entirely independent but nevertheless paralleling each other perfectly, as though in accordance with a predetermined plan.

In modern history, the behaviourists under J. B. Watson tried to carry the solution of the problem one step beyond Descartes by denying the existence of mind in man as well as in animals and by embracing a monistic, deterministic philosophy. They tried to strike all mentalistic terms—mind, consciousness, and feelings—from scientific use and spoke only of observable behaviour, which they believed was the biological outcome of the activity of the nervous system (*see* Behaviourism).

Although mind is still more difficult than overt behaviour to define and specify scientifically, there is actually no need to exclude the term mind when it is useful to designate certain real, if ill-understood, aspects of man and his experience. Scientifically, however, mind cannot be used to refer to the nonphysical (since science is limited to phenomena; *i.e.*, the physical) despite the great emphasis that philosophical and cultural heritage has placed upon the spiritual. Physiological psychology begins, then, with the basic concept that if the word mind is to be used, it is to be understood in such terms as the activities of the nervous system.

Basic Properties of the Nervous System.—The anatomy and physiology of the nervous system are given in detail in the articles Brain; Spinal Cord; Nerve; Nerve Conduction; and Nervous System. Only a brief review will be given here.

Grossly, the nervous system consists of the brain and spinal cord and their nerves. Sensory nerves deliver impulses to the spinal cord; motor nerves leaving the cord go out to the muscles and glands. This provides the basis for reflexes such as the automatic withdrawal of a leg from a painful stimulus (*see* Reflex). In addition, the incoming sensory nerves send impulses up to the brain, and the brain in turn sends motor impulses down to the segments of the spinal cord. At various levels in the brain, the incoming sensory nerves are linked by multitudinous connections to the outgoing motor nerves, making up an infinitely complex mechanism for the integration of behavioural functions, similar in principle to the reflex mechanism.

To understand these connections and their importance in behaviour, it is necessary to appreciate the gross morphology of the brain and its function (*see* fig. 1 and 2). The continuation of the spinal cord into the brain is called the medulla; it contains, in addition to the major sensory and motor pathways and integrating mechanisms, many groupings of nerve cells that mediate such functions as respiration and circulation of blood. Above the medulla is the midbrain, serving in many simple visual and auditory reflexes. Behind the medulla and midbrain lies the cerebellum, concerned primarily with coordination of posture and locomotion. The thalamus, situated above the midbrain, mediates the integration of incoming sensory nerve impulses and relays sensory impulses to the cortex. Below the thalamus is the hypothalamus, concerned with control of the pituitary gland and such complex functions as water balance and thirst, sleep, food ingestion, reproduction, and emotional expression. Above the thalamus are the two cerebral hemispheres so prominent in man. The main mass of these hemispheres consists of white matter entering and leaving the outer mantle of gray matter known as the cerebral cortex. Actually (1) the old cortex, seen in many lower animals as well as in man, seems primarily concerned with vegetative and emotional functions; (2) the new cortex subserves sensory, motor, and associative functions. The new cortex may be subdivided into an occipital lobe in the back of the head, concerned with visual function; a temporal lobe on the lower side of the brain, concerned with auditory and language functions; a parietal lobe with the portion just behind the fissure of Rolando integrating sensory information coming from the skin and muscles; and a frontal lobe, with motor areas (just in front of the fissure of Rolando) controlling discrete movements and postural adjustments; the remainder of the frontal lobe is presumed to serve in complex associative functions, still poorly understood in the 1960s.

In this greatly simplified picture of the nervous system, sensory stimulation typically results in activation of integrative mechanisms at all levels, from the spinal cord to the cortex. The major sensory pathways described so far are quite discrete as to the sensory modality aroused and the part of the body or sensory surface stimulated; this gives the nervous system great discriminative powers. In addition, however, all the sensory pathways contribute branches to a feltwork of nerves lying in the centre of the hindbrain or brain stem (medulla and midbrain), known as the reticular formation. The reticular formation relays nerve impulses to all parts of the brain and serves the important function of activating or arousing the brain generally. It is believed that this arousal function is part of the mechanism of wakefulness, attention, and emotion, and thus it may be thought of as an important mechanism in the preparation of the brain for the reception of impulses arising from stimuli.

The great mass of the nervous system just described consists

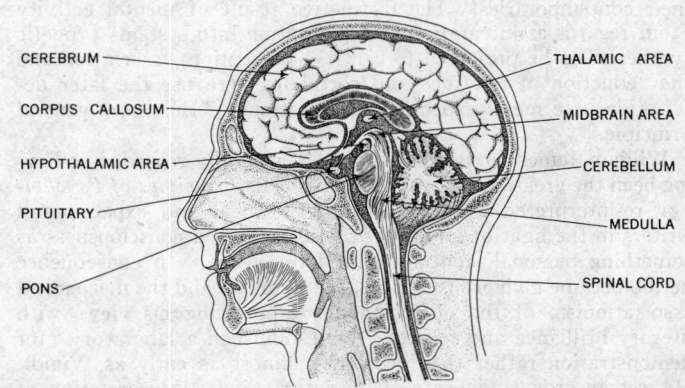

CEREBRUM   THALAMIC AREA

CORPUS CALLOSUM   MIDBRAIN AREA

HYPOTHALAMIC AREA   CEREBELLUM

PITUITARY   MEDULLA

PONS   SPINAL CORD

FIG. 1.—INTERNAL STRUCTURE OF BRAIN

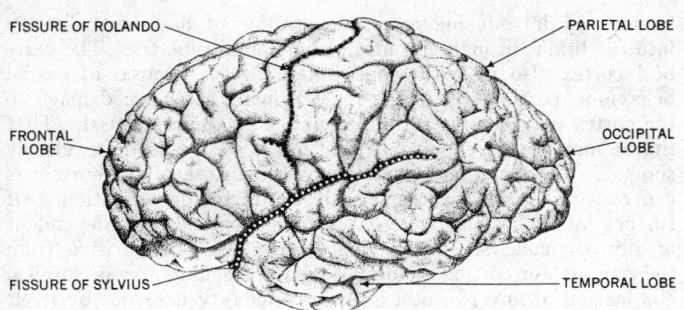

FISSURE OF ROLANDO

PARIETAL LOBE

FRONTAL LOBE

OCCIPITAL LOBE

FISSURE OF SYLVIUS

TEMPORAL LOBE

FROM E. GARDNER, "NEUROLOGY," 1ST ED. (1947), W. B. SAUNDERS COMPANY, PHILADELPHIA

FIG. 2.—SIDE VIEW OF HUMAN BRAIN, SHOWING MAJOR LOBES AND EXTERNAL SURFACE OF CORTEX

of billions of individual nerve cells, some of which send their tiny filaments all the way from the foot to the spinal cord, and some of which are not much longer than they are wide. These individual cells of the nervous system connect with each other across tiny gaps between them, known as synapses. Connections may be such that the activity in one cell will arouse activity in a number of connecting cells; or, conversely, activity in many cells may converge on a small number of cells; or there may be reverberatory loops such that a series of cells is activated in turn until the first cell is aroused again and again by the activity it initiated.

The activity of the nerve cells is detected as the nerve impulse, an electrochemical disturbance that may be propagated as rapidly as 120 m. per second. These disturbances can be recorded electrically with suitable amplification devices; such recording shows that if a nerve cell is to be activated at all, it must be stimulated by a certain minimal threshold energy; once a nerve cell is activated, it discharges fully.

Classically, two major integrative mechanisms have been described in the nervous system. One is excitation, the arousal of a nerve to activity; the other is inhibition, the effect of stopping activity in a group of cells. Excitation and inhibition can be illustrated in spinal reflexes, where painful stimulation leads to excitation of the nerves serving flexor muscles that pull the limb toward the body and to the simultaneous inhibition of the nerves leading to extensor muscles.

Sensation and Perception.—One of the oldest questions in physiological psychology is how information is received from the world outside the body and from within the body as well. For man, this is the problem of the anatomical and physiological basis of sensation and perception (qq.v.).

An early concept concerning sensation and perception is the doctrine of specific nerve energies, first put forward by Johannes Peter Müller in 1826. While the anatomical and physiological details of this conception were inaccurate, the basic notion still seems valid. The doctrine states that sensations or responses to stimulation are determined by events in the nervous system. Thus a finger pressed on the closed eye mechanically produces visual experiences in the absence of the proper visual stimulus, light. Müller argued that people would see thunder and hear lightning if the nerves from the eye and the ear could be interchanged. Many phenomena support Müller's doctrine, but its general validity can be seen most easily in the fact that an electrical stimulus will produce experiences appropriate to the sensory system stimulated, whether it be the eye, the skin, the tongue, or some point within the brain to which impulses from these structures go. Thus the experience or the discriminative response is specifically related to the part of the nervous system that is activated.

To illustrate the point more fully, the case of hearing (q.v.) may be considered. The experience of pitch is determined largely by the vibration frequency of the sound source; the higher the frequency, the higher the pitch. Vibrations are transmitted through the air to the eardrum. The eardrum passes this vibration through tiny bones in the middle ear to vibrate the membrane of the oval window of the cochlea. This vibrates a fluid in the cochlea which, in turn, sets up a standing wave in the basilar membrane, which extends throughout the coiled length of the cochlea. The standing wave has its maximum effect on the basilar membrane at different places, depending upon the frequency of vibration introduced. Low frequencies affect the basilar membrane near the apex of the cochlea, while higher frequencies have their effect near the base. The basilar membrane is lined with the hair cells of the organ of Corti, and as the membrane is moved, the shape of these hairs is distorted. Like crystals that are distorted mechanically, these hairs initiate tiny electrical currents, believed to stimulate the fibres of the auditory nerve that arise from the vicinity of the hairs. In this way, different fibres of the auditory nerve are activated by the different vibrations produced by tones of different frequencies.

More than that, the different auditory nerve fibres are kept distinct from each other in their course into the brain, at each of the relay stations, and at the auditory region of the temporal lobe of the cerebral cortex. Hence it is possible to record electrical activity along different parts of the auditory cortex, representing the different tonal frequencies that stimulate different parts of the basilar membrane. It is even possible (in a cat, for example) to stimulate different parts of the basilar membrane directly with electrical current and find the same array of different places activated in the cerebral cortex. So the experience of pitch seems to depend upon the place in the auditory nervous system that is activated by the stimulus.

The other attributes of sound are mediated by somewhat different mechanisms. Loudness depends on the intensity (i.e., amplitude) of vibration, and it is believed that the experience of loudness is a function of the density of nerve impulses conducted over the nerve fibres serving the specific frequencies associated with pitch experience. Density can be increased by firing individual fibres more rapidly and by the activation of additional fibres of high threshold; i.e., fibres that require a great deal of energy before they will fire.

The temporal pattern of pitches and loudnesses of sounds presumably is given by the temporal pattern of arousal of nerve fibres activated by a frequency- or intensity-patterned stimulus. Finally, the localization of sounds in space depends mainly upon the differences in time of arrival and intensity of vibration from a single source reaching the two ears. These differences show up in electrical recordings from the auditory cortex as appropriate differences in time of arrival and amplitude of nerve impulses on the two sides of the brain.

The same general principles apply to the other senses. Thus there are separate fibres and pathways in the spinal cord bearing nerve impulses produced by stimuli that give rise to experiences of pain, temperature, and pressure in the skin. Different parts of the tongue are activated by sweet, sour, bitter, and salty stimuli; as the tongue is stimulated more intensely, the density of the patterns of impulses increases proportionally. In vision, different parts of the receptor surface of the eye, the retina, are sensitive to the wavelengths of light that induce the experience of different colours. There appear to be different combinations of receptor cells in the retina that are maximally sensitive to different wavelengths in the visible spectrum. (See also VISION; SMELL AND TASTE; TOUCH.)

Physiological approaches to the more complex problems of perception can best be illustrated with some of the phenomena of vision such as the perception of real and apparent movement, the perception of depth, and visual localization. The visual localization of objects in space, for example, depends upon the part of the retina stimulated and the manner in which that localization is preserved in the brain. Philosophical interest in this problem arose when it was learned that the lens of the eye inverts the image of objects on the retina. The question then became: why do we not see the world upside down? This question inspired investigations into the role of early learning as related to the inversion of the visual field.

If the eye of a salamander is rotated 180°, the animal will snap upward at a lure held below it, and to the left at a lure held to its right. Even if the salamander's optic nerve is cut and allowed to grow back, the animal will not reorganize its vision in accordance with its experience, and it will still be 180° out of phase upon recovery. The visual field of man also can be rotated experimentally with reversing lenses. Although there are individual differences, some people seem to adapt to such a visually reversed world, and after a time will say that things look upright again. Thus, although visual localization is largely a function of the central connections of the retina, it seems also to be modified by experience.

The role of the brain in perception has been studied in many animal experiments but is shown perhaps most clearly by the complex effects of brain injury on visual processes in man. In such cases, a man with damage to the area around the visual cortex may fail to recognize familiar objects for what they are (visual agnosia), although he may clearly be able to see them and describe their physical attributes. In other cases, such a brain-injured man may totally ignore all visual events occurring in some part of his visual field, although it can be shown by careful tests that he can actually see in that field; or in certain cases he may be subject to gross distortions in that visual field. Thus the brain, and particularly the cerebral cortex, is concerned with the interpretation of sensory impressions.

Motivated Behaviour and the Emotions.—A second problem of historic interest to physiological psychology concerns the basis of feelings, urges, and emotions—a most difficult area of scientific inquiry.

Behaviouristic analysis divides these complex behaviours into three components: (1) drive; (2) goal-directed behaviour; and (3) satiation. Drive (sometimes called instinct) is the arousal of the organism to intense activity, measured as an increase in general activity or the appearance of a highly specific activity. Thus the hungry animal becomes restless and hyperactive. Typically, however, the drive has a highly specific goal, such as food or a mate; or it might be a bodily expression as in the case of sleep or flight or rage. Upon execution of the behaviour, the organism tends to become satiated; drive is reduced, hyperactivity ceases, and behaviour is no longer directed strongly toward the goal. The clinical case of a three-year-old boy with a history of abnormal craving for salt illustrates the points of this analysis. This boy's history showed that his general appetite was poor and that he was restless and upset in his first years, when fed a normal diet. He strongly preferred salty foods such as bacon and crackers, and these seemed to appease him a great deal, but his great craving did not become apparent until he discovered the saltshaker at the age of 18 months and ate salt by the spoonful. Unfortunately, the case was not understood, and the child was belatedly taken to a hospital for observation and placed on a standard diet; within seven days he died. Autopsy revealed extensive damage to his adrenal glands, leading to a disorder in which the body cannot retain salt normally. Thus the boy had a deficiency which strongly drove him toward the specific goal of salt; when enough salt was ingested, the drive was reduced; it was thus, in repeated cycles of drive and satiation, that the boy managed to stay alive.

There may be two interrelated brain mechanisms, centring in the hypothalamus (q.v.): an excitatory mechanism for the arousal of drive and an inhibitory mechanism for its reduction or for satiation. For example, bilateral destruction of small areas in the ventromedial hypothalamus of the rat, cat, monkey, and possibly also man results in a doubling or tripling of food intake, leading to great obesity; on the other hand, similar destruction of nearby regions of the lateral hypothalamus, on either side of these first areas, results in refusal to eat and starvation in the presence of customary food supplies. That the first areas in the ventromedial hypothalamus are inhibitory is shown by another experiment in which electrodes, insulated except for their tips, are chronically implanted into this part of the brain. Electrical stimulation through these electrodes in the waking, hungry animal results in inhibition or depression of feeding. Conversely, the excitatory nature of the lateral areas is shown by the fact that electrical stimulation of these regions produces increased feeding.

Similar control mechanisms can be found in the hypothalamus in the cases of thirst, sexual behaviour, and sleep. In sexual behaviour it is clear that the hypothalamus also is directly influenced by sex hormones, for it is possible to arouse mating behaviour by introducing minute quantities of hormones directly into the brain through chronically implanted pipettes. The cerebral cortex also makes a contribution to the arousal of sexual behaviour, particularly in the male animal; extensive damage to the cortex may eliminate the possibility of sexual arousal. That the animal is still capable of mating, however, is quite clearly shown by the fact that a massive systemic dose of sex hormones can restore the mating response lost through decortication. Of further interest is the fact that sexual behaviour is independent of any particular sensory modality, including those arising from the genitals, for cutting the nerves from the genital area or surgical elimination of any one other sensory modality does not by itself affect sexual behaviour. In the naïve animal, it takes elimination of no more than two sensory avenues at once to preclude sexual arousal; in the experienced rat, however, sexual behaviour may survive the elimination of three modalities, illustrating the role of learning and experience in the physiological control of sexual behaviour. It is important to point out that the mechanism of sexual behaviour must have gone through marked changes in evolution. Comparing animals from rat to man, it is clear that there is a decreasing dependence on sex hormones and an increasing dependence on sensory stimuli, learning, and the cerebral cortex (see SEXUAL BEHAVIOUR).

Much the same physiological mechanism operates in the case of emotional expression. Cats deprived of the cerebral cortex are easily aroused to apparent rage by almost any mild stimulus, but their response is short-lived and poorly directed. If only the new cortex is removed, cats become placid; if the old cortex is removed alone, they become fierce. Monkeys, on the other hand, become strangely placid in the absence of certain portions of the old cortex, particularly the hippocampus and amygdala. These animals show, in addition to placidity, exaggerated sexuality and markedly increased and indiscriminate oral activity, even to the point of putting a snake or a lighted match into the mouth. Damage to different parts of the hypothalamus can also result in great changes in the expression of emotion. Electrical stimulation of the hypothalamus in people will lead to emotional responses such as weeping and laughter.

Electrical stimulation of the hypothalamus and related structures under somewhat different circumstances illustrates further the physiological mechanisms of motivation and emotion. In this case, an animal is allowed to press a lever which electrically stimulates its brain through chronically implanted electrodes. Such an animal will operate the lever as often as 5,000 times in one hour; under some conditions, pressing the lever is preferred to food, and it has been shown that animals will readily walk through a strongly electrified grid on repeated occasions to depress the lever. Such experiments demonstrate the rewarding nature of this stimulation and point to mechanisms that may mediate all positive emotion and motivation, including the experience called pleasure.

It may be concluded, in general, that the organism is aroused to strong motivated behaviour and emotion as a result of physiological activity in an excitatory neurological mechanism centring in the hypothalamus. Contributing to this are two major influences: (1) sensory stimuli, often as modified by learning; and (2) internal factors such as hormones, blood temperature, osmotic pressure, and salt levels. (See also EMOTION; INSTINCT; MOTIVATION.)

Learning and Intelligence.—While many remarkable adaptations are accomplished through instinct and motivated behaviour, a major factor in the adaptation of the mammal, and especially of man, is the ability to learn. While the mechanism of learning (q.v.) is still poorly understood, learning and memory (q.v.) seem to depend on relatively enduring changes in the nervous system. Classically, two questions have been asked in this connection: (1) where in the nervous system is learning mediated? and (2) what is the nature of the underlying neurological changes?

There are many kinds of learning, but in all of them the organism makes a new response to some specific stimulus or to a general situation. Thus I. P. Pavlov's dog learned to salivate consistently in response to a bell, E. L. Thorndike's cats learned to press a pedal that opened a door when they were locked in a cage and, as is known from common experience, the student of Latin-English vocabulary learns to say table when presented with *mensa*. Describing aspects of the process of learning and resultant memory are the so-called laws of association (*see* ASSOCIATION, MENTAL), some formulated by Aristotle, and others added through subsequent work: (1) contiguity in time and place; (2) repetition; (3) effect or reinforcement; and (4) interference, leading to forgetting or extinction.

Pavlov, for example, found it necessary to present the bell together with meat (a normal stimulus for salivation); this pairing had to be repeated many times before the bell alone would elicit salivation. The meat functioned as a reinforcement of learning in the sense that salivation to the bell lessened each time it was presented without the meat and increased each time the meat was included. The waning of salivation to the bell alone is called extinction and is similar to forgetting. Both extinction and forgetting appear to be the result of responses that interfere with the one that was learned; these interfering responses are favoured when reinforcement is omitted. There is reason to believe that most learning is permanent; most forgetting seems to result from masking by interfering or competitive learning. However, the commonly accepted notion that all experiences are stored permanently in the mind must be regarded with caution. There is growing evidence that specific memories may be permanently abolished through the selective destruction of brain tissue.

Many experiments have been directed toward answering the question of where learning is mediated in the nervous system. Pavlov believed that even simple learning such as conditioning depended upon the cerebral cortex, but it has been amply shown that animals may be conditioned after the cortex has been removed by experimental surgery. K. S. Lashley demonstrated, in a more complex learning situation, that rats surgically deprived of the visual cortex could learn to discriminate between a white square and a black square. But if an animal had learned this discrimination with the visual cortex intact, subsequent lesion of the visual cortex destroyed the discrimination; as would be expected, the discrimination could be relearned without the visual cortex about as rapidly as it was learned originally. This suggested that the memory for the discrimination was lost as a result of surgery but could be relearned with other parts of the brain. On the other hand, it might be that the memory was not lost, but rather that the animal was incapable of responding to the visual details of the black and white cards after operation and had to learn the problem without the benefit of detail vision; *i.e.*, on the basis of ill-defined light and dark areas. That this may be so is suggested by the fact that the rat without its visual cortex cannot learn to discriminate a triangle from a circle where the difference in detail is the only basis for the discrimination. Conversely, if the animal is required to respond only to brightness change in a large area without any dependence on detail, it can retain a brightness discrimination without impairment after brain surgery.

Lashley also studied the role of the rat's cortex in maze learning and found that the larger the area of the cortex destroyed the poorer the learning and the poorer the retention of the maze learned before operation. It did not matter which parts of the cortex were destroyed and which remained intact, the result was the same: the larger the lesion, the greater the impairment. These findings led to the notions of mass action and equipotentiality, according to which maze learning is a function of the amount of cortex available and the various parts of the cortex are equally potential in subserving learning. Again it seems likely that these results can be understood in terms of sensory impairment. It is known from other studies that the more sense organs that are experimentally eliminated in the rat, the poorer the maze learning and retention; furthermore, no one sensory avenue is critical for such learning. Since the rat's cortex is mainly sensory in function, larger and larger cortical lesions would eliminate more and more sensory avenues centrally, and it may be for this reason that larger lesions impair learning and retention more than do smaller ones.

At one time it was thought that the frontal lobes of the brain were critical in the memory processes demanded in the solution of difficult problems. Monkeys without their frontal lobes fail in the delayed reaction test, for example, where they are shown food placed under one of two identical cups and then made to wait for 10–60 seconds before being allowed to uncover the correct cup. Something other than memory is involved in this defect, however, for monkeys without frontal lobes turn out to be quite distractible. If their attention is fixed firmly on the baited cup before the delay, the lobectomized monkeys succeed; if the monkeys are made to keep very still by being put into darkness during the delay period or by being given sedatives, they also perform successfully.

The cortex therefore is important in the performance of a learned task, but probably more because of its importance in perception and attention than in learning per se. On the other hand, some of the difficulty in defining cortical function here may be due to the fact that these studies are based only on the method of experimentally damaging cortical tissue. When W. Penfield studied the temporal lobes of epileptic patients whose brains were exposed for surgery under local anesthesia, he found that electrical stimulation could evoke dreamlike sequences that contained familiar episodes from past life. Furthermore, when the temporal lobes are damaged in man, some curious memory defects do show up. While these patients are able to recall events from past life very well, they typically are unable to remember things they learned or experienced a few hours earlier. Closer examination shows that they actually do remember things they learn quite well if they are tested for memory within about 15 minutes, but beyond that the memory fades and is lost. It is as though there were two memory processes separated by the temporal lobe damage: (1) a temporary memory process capable of very short retention that is spared by the lesion; and (2) a more permanent memory process that is impaired by the lesion.

Support for this notion comes from several rather different experiments. In one performed on the octopus the animal was first presented with a crab, dangled in the far end of its tank, every two hours, six times a day. It quickly learned to venture out and eat the crab. Then, on half the tests, a white card was lowered with the crab, and with this cue the octopus learned not to venture out under penalty of electric shock. Thus a simple discrimination was learned. After removal of the vertical lobe of the brain, the octopus could no longer respond differentially in these tests; it kept emerging when the white card was presented. Even repeated trials every two hours with the white card and electric shock proved ineffective. But if the trials were run closer together, the octopus was able to perform much better; thus if a test came within 15 minutes to an hour after the octopus was shocked upon approaching the white card, it did not venture out toward the crab and white card. Again it appears as though the ability to carry a memory over a long period of time was impaired while very short-term memory was left intact.

In studies in which rats were given electroconvulsive shocks at some interval after each daily learning trial, additional evidence for a two-process memory was found. Here there was very little learning if the convulsive shocks were given within an hour after learning, but if the shocks came beyond an hour after each trial, learning was normal. Thus it seems to take some time for the effects of a learning trial to consolidate in the brain to a point of stability. For an hour after a learning experience, memory can be disrupted by convulsive shock, but after that it is not easily disturbed.

The conclusion from all these studies seems to be that the effects of learning are retained in the brain first by some reversible process, but that after some time (within an hour) some more permanent change takes place within the brain. It is suspected, therefore, that learning is mediated neurologically by at least two types of processes, and the time course of these processes is partly understood. It is still, however, possible only to speculate as to the nature of the change itself. It has been suggested that the first process, temporary and reversible, is a physiological process such as an electrical or chemical change at the synapse or perhaps at a group of synapses, so that a reverberatory loop is activated for some period of time, keeping the memory trace alive. The second, more permanent process has been envisaged by some as an anatomical process consisting of the swelling of nerve terminals or the outgrowth of new terminals over short distances so that synapses are enriched in the number of anatomical contacts they have or that new synapses actually are formed. Another possibility, even more speculative, is that in learning there are changes in the chemical structure of nerves, possibly in the structure of complex protein molecules. Support for this kind of notion comes from the elucidation of mechanisms for coding genetic information in the structural arrangements of the large DNA molecule (see GENE). While there is no proof that learning and memory are coded in a similar fashion, the fact that memory in mice can be obliterated by intracranial injection of a drug (puromycin) that inhibits protein synthesis is highly suggestive.

As to the locus of the change that takes place in learning, there is still no certainty. Many studies show that the cerebral cortex is not essential for many kinds of learning, but they do not offer a positive clue as to where learning might take place outside the cortex. On the other hand, electrical recording studies report that electrical changes take place at many loci in the brain at once during learning. Whether some loci are more important than others, however, still is not known. (For a more detailed discussion of the processes of learning, see LEARNING; see also MEMORY.)

Related to the problem of learning are the even more complex problems of reasoning, problem solution, intelligence, and language. These have been studied primarily in cases of brain damage, particularly in man but to some extent also in animals. First, it should be pointed out that in both man and other animals large amounts of brain tissue may be destroyed without measurable impairment of these complex processes. For example, while removal of one entire cerebral hemisphere results in specific sensory and motor defects, intelligence within the sensory and motor capabilities of the person may be virtually unimpaired. On the other hand, lesions in certain restricted regions of the brain, particularly the cortex, may have devastating effects. Thus following damage in the dorsolateral surface of the frontal cerebral cortex, severe impairment, as measured by intelligence tests in man and tests such as delayed reaction in monkeys, may result. In man, there are also fairly specific speech areas in the lower parts of the sensory-motor area of the cortex in the dominant hemisphere. Damage here results in aphasia, in which there is an inability to name objects properly or to point to objects named by the examiner, even though in both cases the patient can see the object and say what it is used for (see SPEECH DISORDERS). If the lesion is at other temporal, parietal, or occipital loci, there may be difficulty in formulating language, in writing meaningfully (agraphia), or in comprehending written material (alexia).

As mentioned above, lesions in the visual association areas of the occipital lobe produce a visual agnosia in which familiar objects are not recognized even though elementary sensory processes are substantially normal. With parietal lobe lesions, there may be difficulty in recognition of parts of the environmental space, including one's own body, to produce what are called distortions of the body image. Often in such cases skilled acts such as putting on clothes cannot be carried out even though individual movements can be made normally, a disorder called apraxia. In some cases of frontal-lobe damage a patient may not be able to go through the motions of drinking from an empty glass, although he can easily drink from a glass with water in it when he is asked to do so. Disorders such as these are not well understood, but it is clear that in many instances relatively small lesions of the brain can lead to major psychological impairment.

Personality and Its Disorders.—For a long time the dominant thought has been that normal personality, neurosis, and psychosis are purely functional matters, the products of life experiences and life stress. But it has also long been held that personality is partly a matter of inherent physiological processes, some of which may be determined by heredity. Hippocrates, for example, believed that human temperament was largely determined by body fluids (humours). While his view was inaccurate in its details, there are nevertheless many examples in everyday life of the potent role

of body chemistry in personality; consider, for example, the effects of alcohol, mescaline (see PEYOTISM), opium, and nitrous oxide on human behaviour.

These drugs affect the functioning of the nervous system, and so also do many naturally occurring chemicals such as vitamins, hormones, and enzymes. Furthermore, the morphology of the nervous system and the enzymes directing its metabolism, and therefore its function, are functions of heredity. For example, the striking case of feeblemindedness known as phenylpyruvic oligophrenia is mediated by a defective gene that produces a defective enzyme. The resultant inability to metabolize phenylpyruvic acid in some way impairs brain function. F. J. Kallmann's studies of the major psychoses (q.v.) show that heredity is an important factor. When schizophrenia, for example, is diagnosed in one identical twin, it is very likely to occur in the other, even if the two have been reared apart; fraternal twins, having no more similar heredity than siblings, show the same concordance as nontwin members of the same family, typically 10–15%. Quite clearly the genetic factor predisposes the individual to psychosis; life experience, stress, disease, or other factors may, of course, contribute to its precipitation. It is believed that the genetic predisposition is a biochemical defect affecting the nervous system, and the hope in the pharmacological treatment of psychiatric symptoms with tranquilizers and other inhibitors and exciters of brain chemistry is that the defect may be corrected or counteracted to some degree by drugs (see NEUROPHARMACOLOGY AND PSYCHOPHARMACOLOGY).

Neuroses (q.v.) are much harder to understand than psychoses in physiological terms. Here genetic factors are less clear-cut, and the usual defect is not so severe and incapacitating as in the psychoses. The work of H. Selye and others, however, indicates that life stress and anxiety can have widespread correlates in the physiology of the organism, and it may be possible to understand neurosis as partly a matter of an altered physiological state. Experiments have shown that stress activates the pituitary gland, in part through the neurosecretory activity of the hypothalamus. The pituitary, in turn, releases hormones that activate other endocrine glands of the body, particularly the adrenal cortex. Once stressed, this system may become more sensitive to additional stresses, and two kinds of disorders may occur: an early one related to oversecretion of the adrenal gland and possibly contributing to such psychosomatic symptoms as hypertension; and a second one, due to adrenal exhaustion and perhaps contributing to symptoms of rheumatism and arthritis, also believed to be partly of psychosomatic origin. It appears that prolonged emotional stress may affect the physiology of the organism and sensitize it to further emotional disturbances.

See PSYCHOLOGY, EXPERIMENTAL; see also references under "Psychology, Physiological" in the Index.

BIBLIOGRAPHY.—C. T. Morgan, *Physiological Psychology*, 3rd ed. (1965); E. D. Adrian, *The Physical Background of Perception* (1947); S. S. Stevens (ed.), *Handbook of Experimental Psychology* (1951); N. E. Miller, "Experiments in Motivation," *Science*, 126:1271–78 (1957); C. T. Morgan, *Introduction to Psychology*, 2nd ed. (1961); E. Stellar, "The Physiology of Motivation," *Psychol. Rev.*, 61:5–22 (1954), "Physiological Psychology," *Annu. Rev. Psychol.*, 8:415–436 (1957); J. E. Deese, *The Psychology of Learning*, 2nd ed. (1958); D. O. Hebb, *The Organization of Behavior* (1949); F. J. Kallmann, *The Genetics of Schizophrenia* (1938); *Expanding Goals of Genetics in Psychiatry* (1962); H. Selye, *The Physiology and Pathology of Exposure to Stress* (1950); C. M. Child, *Physiological Foundations of Behavior* (1964).   (EL. S.)

PSYCHOLOGY, SOCIAL. Social psychology is the study of individual activity as related to social factors. Although social psychologists may be interested in such topics as the dominance of chickens in pecking one another (see SOCIOLOGY, ANIMAL), or in the dance some bees use to communicate the location of a patch of clover to others in the hive (see SOCIAL INSECTS), human social behaviour has received the bulk of attention. Clearly, the concerns of social psychology have much in common with those of psychology, sociology and social anthropology (qq.v.); and applications are to be found in such aspects of daily life as politics, religion, economics and mental health.

By the 1960s social psychology had produced an impressively

diverse set of empirical findings somewhat loosely bound by ill-fitting patches of theory. In the 19th and early 20th centuries the situation was almost the reverse; there was virtually no experimentation and little careful collection of objective data. It was a period of extremely general theories that have been characterized by G. W. Allport (*q.v.*) as simple sovereign theories. By and large they arose in social philosophy and continually were being modified under the impetus of developments in economics, physical and biological sciences, anthropology, political science and psychoanalysis. This uneasy movement in response to intellectual fashions made it clear that social psychology lacked a solid scientific foundation.

This state of affairs in social psychology was interrupted about 1920 when human instinct theory fell into disfavour. It was at this time that social psychologists seemed to recognize that the search for a touchstone theory, as simple as parts of classical physics, had failed. The wide variety of empirical studies that followed ushered in modern social psychology. Between 1925 and 1945, such research techniques and devices as sociometry, audience reaction measurement, inexpensive recordings for the study of face-to-face interaction, the use of role players as social stimuli, and new modes of attitude assessment made social behaviour more accessible to first-hand study and revealed the value of working with simpler, more readily soluble problems. These new techniques found many applications in World War II and the skills developed in military investigations were subsequently widely applied in U.S., British and Scandinavian universities. These developments are elaborated below. With studies of new problems and smaller segments of earlier problems, there was, however, a growing sense that the complexity of social behaviour may continue to resist synthesis and require the development of many specialties within social psychology.

Early Problems of Social Psychology.—A classic simple sovereign theory involved the psychological hedonism of Jeremy Bentham (1748–1832), who reduced human motives to seeking pleasure and avoiding pain. It was assumed that more stable aspects of human personality were calculated to bring maximum, long-term pleasure to the individual. The same theory had been expressed earlier by Epicurus, Thomas Hobbes and many others; but Bentham elaborated and carefully described different attributes of pleasure and pain. Typical of social theorists, Bentham went beyond pure science, offering his notions in a widely debated ethical theory of utilitarianism (*q.v.*). Herbert Spencer (1820–1903) accepted Bentham's formulations and incorporated into his notions of evolution the idea that organisms most successful in the avoidance of pain survive best.

Later, in an effort to account for such behaviour as seen in trends of fashion, dancing manias and health fads, the term suggestion came into use, particularly for situations in which people accept propositions without logical support. In the writings of J. M. Baldwin (1861–1934) imitation and suggestion were offered as essential processes in early socialization. These nonrationalistic mechanisms were held necessary to start the social process, but were considered something to be outgrown. Writers like G. Le Bon (1841–1931) and S. Sighele (1868–1913) found much evil in these mechanisms. They held man to be unconsciously bestial and criminal; crowds, therefore, were seen as menaces to established institutions: "crowds flourish as civilizations decline." Sighele anticipated later developments by considering two-person (dyadic) relations where one makes suggestions and the other responds without being normally critical. H. Bernheim's (1837–1919) work in hypnosis (*q.v.*) led him into a controversy with J. M. Charcot (1825–93), who taught that only people with hysteria (*q.v.*) could be hypnotized. While time has given more support to Bernheim's position that there is no such discontinuity between normal and abnormal suggestibility, this controversy between French psychiatrists was notable as a historical accident that brought social and abnormal psychology closer together.

William McDougall, in his *Introduction to Social Psychology* (1908), assumed that directly or indirectly men are moved "by a variety of impulses whose nature has been determined through long ages of evolutionary process." For McDougall the fundamental

problem of social psychology was to explain how people become moral and co-operative members of society. In this McDougall anticipated the modern interest of social psychology in the socialization of children. His biological standpoint led him to offer a system of instincts, innate psychophysical dispositions to perceive objects and experience emotions, that lead to action. He posited 13 instincts, including the parental or protective, the instincts of combat, curiosity and gregariousness (in turn built on 6 minor instincts involved with vegetative functions of the body). McDougall's notions became popular objects of derision during the 1920s; but by 1949 G. Murphy was writing "with the passage of the intense wave of anti-McDougall feeling, instinctive mechanisms have come slowly back into place."

Behaviourism (*q.v.*) contributed the theory that human genetic endowments (prepotent reflexes and primary drives) were conditioned into chains of acquired habits seen in mature social behaviour. The position that human nature depends on environmental rewards and thus is alterable, was attractive to many and tended to increase experimentation. Social psychologists familiar with psychological traditions—first in Europe, then in the U.S.—became the important experimenters. In contrast, those recruited from a background of sociological tradition tended to avoid experiment and to concentrate on psychological processes in field situations and institutional contexts.

Simple Group Effects.—Early studies by N. Triplett (1897) showed that people tended to accomplish more in such tasks as spool winding when working in groups than when they worked alone. At first the work increment was attributed to the presence of someone to set the pace. However, later research revealed that the group effect could be produced even if others were not present, provided the subjects believed they were members of groups. This modest research helped to popularize group experimentation and indicated that behaviour may be modified through a desire to conform to what are believed to be group norms.

A classic experiment that followed illustrated that membership in a group can influence the way an individual perceives. In the dark, with no background visible as a frame of reference, a stationary pinpoint of light appears to move. Called the autokinetic effect, this illusion is experienced as movement over distances that vary considerably from observer to observer. M. Sherif demonstrated that people tend to perceive these distances closer to the group average when they report their experiences to each other. He also found that, if initial exposure is in a group, individuals later tend to abide by the group norm when they observe alone. Generally this has been taken to mean that people depend heavily on judgments of others when objective standards are lacking.

Similarly it has been observed that in fashions, attitudes toward racial or religious groups, and similar social behaviour, individuals are apt to respond alone as they have learned to do as members of groups. For example, with individual interviews, Conrad Chyatte, M. Spiaggia and D. Schaefer (1951) found white, non-Jewish children were more likely to verbalize prejudice against Negroes and Jews in Virginia and North Carolina than in New York city. Systematic differences related to the national origin of the child's family were also observed—further evidence that prejudice involves group conformity.

It has been demonstrated that group effects are not limited to subjective judgments. To illustrate this S. E. Asch instructed 11 confederates to report the distinguishably shortest of two lines as being longest. Many individuals, serving as 12th member of the panel, found it difficult to resist the social pressure and give the correct response. However, if even one other group member gave the correct judgment, the effect of the remaining 10 was greatly lessened. This finding has clear implications in the study of decision making by such groups as juries and planning boards.

Such studies, whether in laboratories or in the contexts of society, touch on the individual's search for validation in the responses of others. As one verifies with his own senses what others have told him, he gains confidence in their reports about external objects. He also needs to test his perceptions of himself as a social object. It is interesting that this more difficult subject was thoroughly discussed in the literature of social psychology before the formation of attitudes toward objects other than the self was very extensively analyzed.

The Self and the Primary Group.—G. H. Mead (1922) described personality formation without positing inherited social instincts. In his description the self emerged when the individual perceived himself as a social object. The growing child was seen as duplicating the reactions of others toward him in a process Mead called role-taking.

Roles were described as being highly specific at the outset. For example, a child may assume parental speech and actions toward his toys and real or imaginary playmates, and in fantasy may play many roles. The child talks to himself as he has heard others talk (*see* Child Psychology; Personality).

Yet roles do not remain entirely specific. The repetition of similar drives and situations leads to more general roles. An early general role molded by the individual's status and function in the family is later modified in other primary associations. C. H. Cooley, in *Social Organization* (1909), maintained that primary groups ("characterized by intimate face to face association and cooperation") not only give an individual his earliest experiences of social unity but they form a recurrent source of new relationships. For primary groups to fulfill these functions he anticipated that systematic differentiation in roles must arise and modes of social control must necessarily be created. Cooley's writings stressed that notwithstanding the physical discreteness of individuals, and although the raw material out of which group activity develops is to be found in the activities of individuals, these individual activities are, in a very definite sense, group products.

Communication and Attitude Change.—Attitude and opinion may be technically distinguished: the tendency of an individual to evaluate anything favourably or unfavourably is an attitude, whereas an opinion has sometimes been defined as an overt verbal evaluation. In these terms opinions need not correspond to attitudes, and attitudes may be expressed by actions other than verbal behaviour. Verbal opinion is thus a fallible predictor of action (*see* Attitude).

One of the simpler techniques for changing opinion is to call attention to the individual's group membership; this is intended to prompt people to take group norms into account in response to persuasive communication. Experimentally, communications attributed to sources of low credibility are perceived as biased and unfair while the identical communications, when attributed to more trusted sources, tend to be significantly more persuasive. While these effects tend to disappear after several weeks under the limited conditions of such experiments, they are of great importance in daily life (C. I. Hovland *et al.*, 1951, 1953).

Other studies indicate that, in dealing with hard-to-understand issues, greatest opinion change is effected when the persuader offers a definite conclusion. In more familiar areas, where there is less dependence on experts, it is probably more effective to leave the conclusion to be drawn by the hearer. When alternate sides of a question are presented in such experiments, opinions formed tend to resist change in the face of subsequent efforts (H. C. Kelman, C. I. Hovland, 1952, 1953).

Arguments associated with mistrusted sources sometimes have greater effects in these studies after a lapse in time. This has been interpreted to mean that people tend to forget the association between argument and source and become freer to make evaluations on merit. A most interesting finding from communication research indicates that, if appeals based on fear arouse strong tensions that the persuasive communication fails to relieve, people tend to minimize the threat and to disregard the communication. Fear appeals producing milder tensions are much more effective in motivating experimental subjects to action.

Persons highly motivated to retain membership in a group tend to resist even logical arguments that contradict the norms of the group. Individual response to persuasion is theorized to be a function of the attention given the communication, the comprehension of the message, and the individual's ability to anticipate the relevance of communicated incentives to his own needs. Persuasion is held to become more difficult as the person attempts to appraise the validity of the argument and evaluate the communicator's motives. A most effective experimental technique for changing opinion is to persuade the subject to play the role of an experimenter seeking to persuade others. If his attempts are successful, his own opinions substantially tend to change.

Many aspects of attitude change can be subsumed under a theory popularized by L. Festinger (1957, 1962). Essentially the theory offers the notion that, when faced with discrepancies in what they perceive (cognitive dissonance), people tend to reduce such inconsistencies by shifts in attitude. For example, consider the case of a politically conservative student who discovers an admired teacher to be politically radical. From the theory it would be predicted that in restoring balance to his cognitive field the student either will tend to become less conservative or lose admiration for the teacher.

The same factors seem to operate after difficult choices are made. Suppose a man buys an automobile after considerable debate about the highly attractive merits of another brand. It has been found that such a person will tend to read with renewed interest the advertising that describes the good points of the vehicle he has bought, apparently tending to overcome the cognitive dissonance generated by the tempting brand he failed to buy (D. Ehrlich *et al.*, 1957).

In other experiments opinions about doing unpleasant tasks were found to become less favourable as the reward for the work became increasingly high; and more favourable with relatively modest reward. This apparently paradoxical finding has been interpreted as meaning that high reward is perceived as an adequate reason for doing the work, while modest reward creates cognitive imbalance that is compensated by positive change in attitude. This line of analysis has led to the suggestion that people will tend to be most happy in a job if the rewards are just enough to motivate them to work (L. Festinger and J. Carlsmith, 1959).

One of the most challenging areas of social psychology involves attitudes based on motives that would be unacceptable to an individual if they were consciously expressed. The work of T. W. Adorno *et al.* (1950) has approached the problem, relying heavily on the theories of psychoanalysis (*q.v.*). These authors argue that the authoritarian personality (a person who defers excessively toward strength and status and is aggressive toward weaker people) unconsciously harbours aggressive motives toward his parents (*see* Defense Mechanisms). To cope with such consciously unacceptable feelings the authoritarian personality is held to develop an uncritically favourable attitude toward his parents (reaction formation); to attribute the unacceptable hostility to others (projection); and to redirect the aggression toward weaker persons (displacement). Although it was particularly concerned with explaining the psychological basis of anti-Semitism, the work has been widely cited with regard to other instances of prejudice and hostility.

Socialization and Value Systems.—In considering the development of social behaviour, various cultures have been studied in order to compare the effects of different child-rearing practices. It has been found that practices dealing with feeding, toilet training, dependency, sex and aggressiveness do not appear to be highly correlated. Most of the data obtained thus far do little more than to relate specific ways of treating children to specific larger aspects of particular societies. For example, the practice of feeding infants whenever they are hungry tends to characterize cultures with co-operative economies, and strictly scheduled feeding is used to a greater extent in cultures with competitive economies. These instances must, however, be considered as hypotheses to be validated in other ways, but the case for the interplay between attitudes toward social institutions and child training is becoming increasingly convincing (J. Whiting and I. Child, 1953; Y. A. Cohen, 1953).

It is not clear whether the social institution shapes infancy training or whether the training induces needs that are expressed in institutional and cultural forms. For example, it is believed that funeral ceremonies often have the function of permitting people who may have both loved and hated the deceased to obtain public recognition that they experience sorrow and thereby reduce feelings of guilt. This is a simple instance of a need that may be associated with institutional practice. It is in the explanations of such behaviour that social psychology bridges sociology and social anthropology. One report (J. M. Whiting *et al.*, 1958) indicates that almost all societies with exclusive mother-son sleeping arrangements for the first year of the son's life (during which the mother is prohibited from sexual intercourse) have one of two patterns of behaviour. Either there is a ceremony of initiation into manhood involving such activities as hazing by adult males, acts of endurance and manliness, seclusion from women and painful genital operations, or there is a change of residence that separates the boy from his mother and sisters, commonly placing him under the guidance of an uncle or other males in the community. These measures were interpreted as efforts to overcome emotional dependency, incestuous feelings and hostility toward the father, all held to arise from the practice of sleeping with the mother.

Such inquiries seem remote from the concerns of modern society, but similar ideas have been offered to explain the fact that broken homes are associated with increased delinquency among boys in urban centres. It has been predicted that delinquency will be most likely when the separation of the parents occurs in the child's early infancy, and that a change of residence along with an initiation ceremony and exposure to the authority of responsible adult males may serve to reduce delinquent behaviour.

It is known that people with low social rank doubt the ability of their group to accomplish its goals and are least apt to conform to its norms. D. McClelland *et al.* (1958) have indicated that, where the father dominates in reconciling differences among family members, the adolescent son tends to be reluctant to leave home to strike out on his own and prefers to work in groups rather than assume individual responsibility. Thus, the structure of the primary group, as well as that of the larger society, may be expected to contribute to the shaping of attitudes.

Interacting Groups and Reference Groups.—G. C. Homans (1950), on the basis of studies ranging through primitive people, street-corner gangs and industrial settings, offered such generalizations as: (1) the more frequently persons mutually interact the stronger their friendship is apt to be; (2) the higher a person's rank in a group the more he talks and is talked to; (3) people who talk together frequently resemble each other more in their activities than do persons with whom they talk less frequently; (4) people are more likely to talk together if their social ranks are closer; (5) conformity to group norms increases the degree to which an individual is liked by others in the group; and (6) the closer one comes to realizing the norms of his group, the more he is talked to by others, the higher his rank and the more his behaviour is like that of a leader.

Homans' principles illustrate relationships that tend to hold over a wide range of human group situations. Later investigation showed that when a departure from group norms is essential to the successful adaptation of a group, then the higher-ranking, more secure members of the group are the ones most likely to act at variance to earlier norms. It is to be hoped that such formulations may be incorporated into a more general theory.

The speed with which regularities in group behaviour were being discovered increased greatly after the end of World War II, largely because of the spread of skills required to manage small groups. For example, an experimenter who wishes to increase the cohesiveness of a two-person group may simply tell the pair that they have been selected because they are known to have traits of people likely to be congenial with one another. In contrast with control groups that do not receive these instructions, it has been found that such instructed pairs co-operate much more readily in experiments. Comparable effects may be obtained by telling subjects they are particularly well fitted to do the job together or particularly likely to appreciate the value of belonging to the group (K. Back, 1951). Such experiments demonstrate that cohesiveness (the attractiveness of a group to its members) can be implemented by verbal instructions.

In the analysis of conformity, T. M. Newcomb (1943) studied students from conservative family (reference group) backgrounds at a politically liberal girls' college. He found that those who sought and obtained acceptance and higher rank changed their political attitudes in a liberal direction between their freshman and senior years. Girls who were well accepted despite being conservative were described as active and enthusiastic (presumably in nonpolitical school activities) and tended to refer attitudes toward public issues to their home and family groups. In some cases girls who remained conservative either made the social attitudes of the school a target of negative reference or were found to be docile and much less active.

Considerably greater coercive pressure is brought to bear in brainwashing (*q.v.*) as suffered by prisoners of war. Captors segregate potential leaders, deny informational support by means of censorship, create distrust by suggesting the presence of informers, withdraw group privileges because of resistance by one person, publicize any collaboration, pace demands for conformity so slowly that logically resistance seems unwarranted, maintain deprivation and then give small rewards for conforming. Behind this is the continued threat of physical harm and nonrepatriation.

Investigators also have conducted experiments outside of the laboratory. Boys in cabins at summer camp were made hostile to groups in other cabins as a result of successive competitive activities. It was possible to eliminate the hostility by assigning tasks requiring co-operation among the groups.

Experimental studies of group interaction, the scaling of social attitudes and the highly technical sampling decisions involved in the design of public-opinion surveys require advanced statistical methods. Such techniques are required in other aspects of psychology, social anthropology and sociology; and statistical training was a part of most such programs in British and U.S. universities by the 1960s. However, one demanding skill frequently required of social psychologists for use in the study of group interaction is the scoring of the successive (and sometimes simultaneous) verbalizations of group members. One of the best-known systems (R. F. Bales, 1950) breaks the interaction into units (acts) roughly equivalent to simple declarative sentences and identifies the originator and target of the act. Use of the technique has shown that, as group size increases, the most vocal participant increasingly tends to exceed his pro-rata share of the available time. Dissatisfaction of other group members seeking to be heard may be relieved by such measures as reducing group size and the assignment of roles designed to reduce power and status differences.

Investigators may use interacting groups as analogues for such complicated social situations as those involving the creation of inventions under differing degrees of cultural contact or the behaviour of parties in international political affairs. A. Mintz (1951) applies this approach in making inferences about mobs in panic. His findings cast doubt on the theory that extreme emotional threat is essential for panic at theatre fires and similar crises by showing that groups faced with a task as simple as pulling pegs out of a small-necked bottle will panic (*i.e.*, jam the pegs) when individual rewards for being "first out" are offered. Such exercises suggest that panic arises from a recognition that other group members are quite unlikely to co-operate as required. The attendant emotionality thus may be considered a response to the breakdown in behaviour of fellow members rather than to the intensity of threat.

Collective Behaviour.—Behaviour generally related to panic includes the phenomena of lynchings and riots, and acquisitive jostling and excitement at bargain sales or in anticipation of rationing and shortages. Clearly there is an emergent quality to collective behaviour; people are changed by seeing many others intent on a goal, and there is a loss of some degree of self-consciousness. Tricks of memory and distortions in message reproduction, as they apply to bits of rumour circulated prior to various collective actions, are examples of other psychological processes involved.

Behind the transmission of rumour, for example, is the question of what a person will perceive, remember and tell others. By having experimental subjects recall, after a lapse of time, a dramatic but exotic folktale, it may be shown that these people shorten the story, mainly by omissions; the phraseology becomes more journalistic; and, if the original story was somewhat incoherent, it becomes more coherent. When the story is transmitted along a chain of people (serial reproduction), as much leveling of detail occurs in a few minutes as individual memory accomplishes in weeks. With more realistic stories retelling tends to increase number, size or cost; makes old events more recent; retains and accentuates implications of movement; and tends to add explanations. Once the principal theme has been understood the hearer condenses and changes the story to conform to reality as he understands it. For example, in one study (G. W. Allport and L. J. Postman, 1947), white observers were shown a picture of a Negro standing near a white person who was holding a razor. Half of the serial reproductions initiated after showing the picture resulted in reports that the razor was in the Negro's hand; in some cases the Negro was said to be brandishing the razor or threatening the white man.

In summary, stimuli subject to divergent interpretations initiate a subjective search (by means of leveling of detail, sharpening and assimilation to theme) to reduce the stimulus to a simple structure that is meaningful in the individual's own experience. The more people involved in a serial report, the greater the change is likely to be until the rumour has reached aphoristic brevity and is repeated by rote. In short, topical propositions for belief without supporting evidence (rumours) can be shown to be systematically defective as guides for either belief or action, even though they may fulfill important expressive needs of the persons who transmit and receive them.

The mention of lynching and rumour stresses the ominous side of collective behaviour; but, change in women's fashions is just as properly a collective phenomenon. There is some evidence in contemporary western society for the notion that dress styles percolate down from higher to lower social strata. It is also generally believed that advertising provides a necessary exposure to the new ideas, that salespersons and others seen wearing the styles make a contributory addition, but that in the final analysis information is not enough. People commonly wait for approval of the style change by respected and trusted associates. Thus, advertising informs, but opinion leaders in the local network of interpersonal influence give legitimacy to the innovations.

Greater urgency has been added to the study of consumer decisions by a growing concern over resistance in adopting new products and methods in underdeveloped countries, especially in agriculture in connection with the use of hybrid corn, improved feeds and so on. From an earlier position in which interpersonal relations were viewed simply as intervening in the communication process, social psychology has advanced toward greater specification of the important role they play. For example, it has been found that U.S. physicians in the same local social cliques tend to make their first prescriptions of a new drug at about the same time, and that among these cliques the opinion leaders are characterized by more frequent attendance at medical society meetings as well as broad contacts within their clique. While physicians more isolated from colleagues depend on sales representatives from drug manufacturers, journal reports on drugs are still legitimated in an interpersonal network before they are acted upon (H. Menzel and E. Katz, 1955).

In the great popular fads of the Yo-yo, bobbed hair and the hula hoop, adolescents have been identified as having a conspicuous role as agents of change. And, as the history of bobbed hair well attests, all fads do not have necessarily the steeply rising, quickly falling popularity associated with the great majority; many become relatively permanent parts of the culture.

In the study of the behaviour of audiences listening to speakers, the loss of self-consciousness that attends growing identification with the speaker has been found to involve some of the same structuring tendencies found in rumour studies. Thus, if incongruous elements are introduced into the speaker's message, these are relatively unlikely to be remembered.

Control of group behaviour is frequently attempted through the use of collective images or stereotypes. Antireligious activities, for example, may foster the collective image of a greedy, hypocritical clergy. Pharmaceutical manufacturers, in responding to charges of excess profit-taking coupled with publicity given to

drugs that produce birth deformities, spend considerable sums in an attempt to bolster the collective image of their industry. Mothers, including those who are unworthy, bask in the image of a benign, altruistic collective mother. Collective images can have great influence on the public acceptance of ideas, depending on whether the ideas are associated with trusted or mistrusted images. Control of mass-communication media that foster and perpetuate so many collective images thus looms enormously important in molding public attitudes. However, such efforts may have unanticipated results. For example, if, in a country with commercial television, businessmen compete by praising their own products and politicians compete by denouncing the opposition, the result may be perceived as unopposed praise for business and slander for politics. This may well shape the attractiveness of business and politics as careers.

There is, in the literature on collective behaviour, at least one well-documented instance of a radio audience being moved to panic. *The Invasion From Mars* (1940) by H. Cantril, H. Gaudet and H. Hertzog analyzed the response of thousands of people in the U.S. to a fictional radio drama that realistically described a meteorite supposed to have landed in New Jersey. "It was surrounded by a green gas," "it was not a meteorite but a metal casing," "the top began to unscrew," and the invasion from Mars was on. Listeners who waited for reassurance from the announcer were surprised to hear his voice rising in tremendous emotion as he moved from "This is terrific," to "This is the most terrifying thing I ever witnessed." Throughout the country thousands of people prayed, telephoned warnings, woke children, drove at dangerous speeds or prepared to flee.

There were undoubtedly situational factors that contributed to the panic. The U.S. was still in a prolonged economic depression, and other broadcasts had been interrupted to present legitimate war news—the date of the broadcast was Oct. 30, 1938. Most knew very little about what might be expected from Mars, and most had an unchallenged confidence in what they heard over their radios. Some listeners who attended to evidence given in the broadcast (particularly the speed with which purported scientists and high government officials were contacted) recognized that they were hearing an extremely good piece of fiction. Others, who listened less fully, turned to neighbours who either commonly were uninformed or similarly were in search of confirmation. This added to the anxiety, and frightened listeners continued to take increasingly desperate steps before they met convincing reassurance. However, by midnight of the evening of the broadcast the panic had virtually passed. But thousands had seen in their own reactions the human disposition to turn to the immediate welfare of self and family when faced by incalculable threat.

For additional discussion of topics of interest in social psychology *see* PSYCHOLOGY, APPLIED; CLASS, SOCIAL; PSYCHOLOGY, ABNORMAL; IMITATION; PSYCHOLOGICAL TESTS AND MEASUREMENTS: *Attitude Measurement;* SUGGESTION; PSYCHOTHERAPY; PROPAGANDA; PSYCHIATRY; MOTIVATION; PSYCHOLOGICAL WARFARE; COMMUNICATION; PERCEPTION; PUBLIC OPINION; *see* also references under "Psychology, Social" in the Index.

BIBLIOGRAPHY.—J. Bentham, *An Introduction to the Principles of Morals and Legislation* (1789); J. M. Baldwin, *Social and Ethical Interpretations of Mental Development* (1897); G. Le Bon, *The Crowd: a Study of the Popular Mind* (1895); S. Sighele, *Psychologie des sectes* (1898); S. Freud, *Group Psychology and the Analysis of the Ego* (1922); F. Thrasher, *The Gang* (1927); W. McDougall, *Group Mind* (1920); M. Ginsberg, *Psychology of Society* (1922); F. H. Allport, *Social Psychology* (1924); G. H. Mead, "A Behaviouristic Account of the Significant Symbol," *Journal of Philosophy*, vol. 19 (1922), *Mind, Self and Society* (1934); F. B. Karpf, *American Social Psychology* (1932); K. Lewin, *A Dynamic Theory of Personality* (1935); M. Sherif, *The Psychology of Social Norms* (1936); T. M. Newcomb, *Personality and Social Change* (1943), "Individual Systems of Orientation," in *Psychology: A Study of a Science,* ed. by S. Koch (1959); G. W. Allport and L. J. Postman, *Psychology of Rumor* (1947); G. Murphy, *Historical Introduction to Modern Psychology* (1949); T. W. Adorno *et al., The Authoritarian Personality* (1950); K. Young, *Handbook of Social Psychology* (1946); G. C. Homans, *The Human Group* (1950); R. F. Bales, *Interaction Process Analysis* (1950); D. Krech and R. S. Crutchfield, *Theory and Problems of Social Psychology* (1948); A. Mintz, "Non-adaptive Group Behavior," *J. Abnorm. (Soc.) Psychol.,* vol. xlvi (1951); K. Back, "Influence Through Social Communication,"

J. Abnorm. (Soc.) Psychol., vol. xlvi (1951) ; C. Chyatte, M. M. Spiaggia and D. E. Schaefer, "Prejudice Verbalization Among Children," *J. Educ. Psychol.*, vol. 42 (1951) ; G. W. Allport, *The Nature of Prejudice* (1954) ; G. Lindzey (ed.), *Handbook of Social Psychology* (1954) ; A. P. Hare, E. F. Borgatta and R. F. Bales, *Small Groups* (1955) ; S. E. Asch, *Social Psychology* (1952) ; T. Parsons, R. F. Bales *et al.*, *Family Socialization and the Interaction Process* (1955) ; M. Sherif and C. W. Sherif, *An Outline of Social Psychology* (1956) ; L. Festinger, *A Theory of Cognitive Dissonance* (1957), "Cognitive Dissonance," *Sci. Amer.*, vol. 207 (1962) ; E. E. Maccoby, T. M. Newcomb and E. L. Hartley, *Readings in Social Psychology* (1958) ; D. McClelland, F. Strodtbeck *et al.*, *Talent and Society* (1958) ; J. W. Thibaut and H. H. Kelley, *The Social Psychology of Groups* (1959) ; D. Cartwright and A. Zander, *Group Dynamics*, 2nd ed. (1960) ; F. Kluckhohn, F. Strodtbeck *et al.*, *Variations in Value Orientations* (1961) ; L. Berkowitz (ed.), *Advances in Experimental Social Psychology*, vol. 1 (1964). (F. L. Sт.)

PSYCHOPHYSICAL METHODS. Psychophysics is the science concerned with quantitative relations between psychological events and physical events or, more specifically, with quantitative relations between sensations and the stimuli that produce them. Psychophysical methods are those methods developed for the purpose of specifying and testing such quantitative relations.

Physical science enables us, at least for some of the senses, to measure with accuracy on a physical scale the magnitude of a stimulus. By determining that stimulus magnitude just sufficient to produce a sensation (or a response), it is possible to specify the minimum sensible stimulus or the absolute stimulus threshold (stimulus limen) for the various senses. It is also possible, although practically more difficult, to determine the lowest stimulus magnitude that produces maximal sensation, the terminal threshold; *i.e.*, that point on the physical scale beyond which no increase in stimulus produces any appreciable increase in sensation. Thus are determined limiting stimulus values, between which changes in stimulus intensity are accompanied by changes in sensation. The central inquiry of psychophysics pertains to the search for a lawful quantitative relation between stimulus and sensation for the range of stimuli between these limits (*see* SENSATION).

Psychophysics was established by Gustav Theodor Fechner (*q.v.*), who coined the word, invented the three fundamental methods, conducted elaborate psychophysical experiments and began a line of investigation that still persists in experimental psychology. Fechner's classic book, *Die Elemente der Psychophysik* (1860), may be looked upon as the beginning not only of psychophysics but also of experimental psychology (*see* PSYCHOLOGY, EXPERIMENTAL). Fechner, trained in physics, became interested in his later life in metaphysics and cast about for a way of relating the spiritual to the physical world. He hit upon the notion of measuring sensation in relation to its stimulus. The physiologist Ernst Heinrich Weber (*q.v.*) had discovered that the amount of change in magnitude of a given stimulus necessary to produce a just noticeable change in sensation always bore an approximately constant ratio to the total stimulus magnitude. This fact, properly speaking, is Weber's law: if two weights differ by a just noticeable amount when separated by a given increment, then, when the weights are increased, the increment must be proportionally increased for the difference to remain just noticeable. Fechner chanced upon Weber's law and undertook to use it for the measurement of sensation. If R be the stimulus (*Reiz*), and S be the resultant sensation, and Δ signify an increment of either, then Weber's law becomes $\Delta R/R = $ a constant, for the just noticeable difference. Fechner went further and assumed that all equal increments of sensation must be proportional to the same ratio, $\Delta R/R$, that is to say, $\Delta S = c\Delta R/R$, where c is a constant of proportionality. If this equation is integrated, if R be assigned a value of zero corresponding to the absolute stimulus threshold and if the constant be changed to k for common logarithms, the result is $S = k \log R$.

This particular formula Fechner named Weber's law, although it is really Fechner's law and is thus often called the Fechner-Weber law. It expresses the simple relation that the magnitude of a stimulus must be increased geometrically if the magnitude of sensation is to increase arithmetically. For Fechner it meant that the relation between the spiritual and physical worlds is stable and that there is therefore only one world, the spiritual; but for physiologists and for many philosophers it meant the

measuring of sensation in relation to a measured stimulus and thus the possibility of a scientific quantitative psychology. Fechner got his conception of psychological measurement from J. F. Herbart (*q.v.*), but he was really refuting Herbart in demonstrating that psychology can be experimental.

Fechner's original work stimulated much research and much controversy. It was argued against him that it is introspectively obvious that sensations do not have magnitude (the quantity objection), that "a scarlet is not just so many pinks." This difficulty was met by the Belgian J. R. L. Delboeuf (1831–96), who developed the concept of the sense-distance, holding that sensations, although not complex magnitudes, are separated by variable intervals that can be compared as being greater, equal or less, one to another. In Germany Georg Elias Müller (1850–1934) undertook an elaborate criticism of Fechner and an extension of his work. In the United States E. B. Titchener (*q.v.*) made a historical and practical exposition of psychophysics in the second volume of his *Experimental Psychology* (1905). F. M. Urban, then also in the U.S., improved one of the methods and developed the concept of the psychometric curve or psychometric function. In England William Brown (1881–1952) and Sir Godfrey Thomson (1881–1955) were prominent psychophysicists.

Three Classical Psychophysical Methods.—Among the lasting contributions of Fechner are the three fundamental psychophysical methods he invented. Each method is designed to investigate the nature of relationship between the psychological scale and the physical stimulus scale.

Method of Minimal Changes.—This, also called the method of limits or of just noticeable differences, consists of successively adding small constant increments of intensity to a stimulus until a change is noticed. For example, to determine the absolute stimulus threshold of intensity, imperceptible intensities are presented in increasing order until the stimulus is first sensed; then a descending series from perceptible to imperceptible is observed. The results of many such series are averaged to determine a single reliable estimate of threshold value. To find the difference limen or difference threshold (the difference between two stimuli that marks the boundary between sensed difference and sensed equality) two stimuli always are presented. One, the standard stimulus, is kept constant while the other, the variable, is successively altered by small amounts until a difference between the variable and the standard appears or disappears, according to the direction of change. The difference threshold is the distance from the standard to the average point of change, and there are always both an upper and a lower difference threshold, since change can be noticed on either side of the standard. The method of minimal changes has been used primarily to find intensity thresholds for sounds, odours, tastes, colours, temperature, pain, brightness and tactual stimuli, to name a few.

Method of Average Error.—The method of average error, or method of reproduction, also makes use of two stimuli, a variable and a standard, but in this case the variable is capable of continuous change (in intensity, say) by the turn of a dial. The task of the experimental subject is to adjust the variable stimulus until it is subjectively equal to the standard stimulus. Since subjective equality is not physical equality, the results yield an average error (from physical equality), constant for the subject, and also a variable error about his average. The method of average error has been applied most frequently to the study of visual distance, particularly to determine extent of visual illusions.

Constant Method.—In the constant method the subject is presented, in random order, a predetermined set of stimuli, for each of which he judges presence or absence of a sensation. In the typical application of the method, each selected stimulus is presented a large number of times. As an example from the cutaneous field, consider determination of the two-point tactual threshold. With an esthesiometer two points at graduated distances are simultaneously stimulated on the skin. The subject's task is to distinguish between two points and one. Depending upon the part of the body stimulated, the two-point threshold may vary from approximately 1 mm. (tip of the tongue) to about

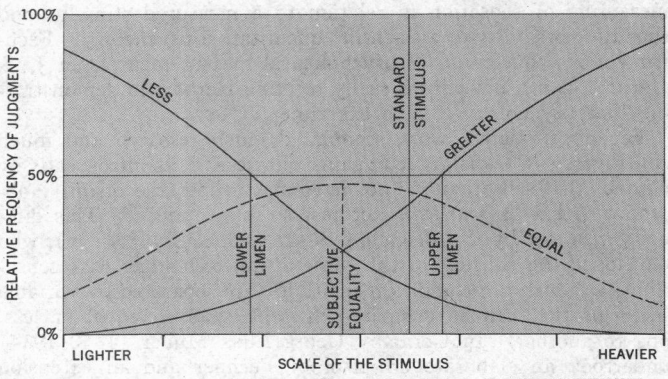

DIAGRAM OF THE CONSTANT METHOD, USING TWO DISTINCT STIMULI

70 mm. (parts of the back, thigh, and upper arm). On the basis of preliminary trials, six or seven distinct distances (stimuli) might be selected so as to include the threshold for a particular subject and a given part of the body. By presenting each stimulus 100 times, a stable estimate for two-point threshold could be obtained. (Due to variability in the conditions of excitation, repeated application of the same stimulus distance is not expected always to yield the same judgment from the subject. However, as the two-point distance increases, the frequency with which the difference is reported increases. The value of that stimulus distance resulting in an equal number of judgments of one point and of two points can be taken as the threshold.)

In a somewhat different application of the constant method, two distinct stimuli are presented, either simultaneously or successively, and the subject is instructed to judge whether stimulus B is greater than, equal to, or less than stimulus A. Stimulus A might be a standard stimulus, presented on each trial; the second stimulus might have any one of six or seven preselected values.

A classic example is that of lifted weights: on each trial a standard weight is compared with a variable weight, and the subject responds with one of three possible judgments. Values for the variable stimulus are selected, some to be heavier and some to be lighter than the standard. Each value of the variable stimulus might be presented with the standard 100 or more times, with order of presentation randomized. Relative frequencies of judgments may be plotted as shown (*see* diagram). It may be seen that as the variable stimulus becomes heavier the frequency with which the variable is judged as less than the standard decreases, the frequency of greater judgments increases, while the judgments of equality become first more, then less frequent, with a maximum near the centre. The lower threshold or limen value L_l of the stimulus is taken as that value where the judgment of less is as likely as it is not; *i.e.*, that point on the stimulus scale corresponding to 50% judgment of less. The upper liminal stimulus L_u is similarly defined, with reference to the distribution of greater judgments (sometimes called the psychometric function for greater judgments). The difference limens are the distances of these liminal values from the standard stimulus S (the distances L_l to S and L_u to S). Subjective equality of variable to standard stimulus is usually taken as the point where judgments of less and greater are equally likely; *i.e.*, where the two psychometric functions intersect. Empirically it has been found for a wide range of situations that the observed relative frequencies for less-than and greater-than judgments can be fitted reasonably well by the ogives of the normal probability integral, in early psychophysical literature sometimes referred to as the phi function of gamma or the phi-gamma function. In current applications, the constant method often is employed using only two categories of judgment, "greater than" and "less than"; more reliable results are obtained when "equal" judgments are disallowed.

The constant method is regarded as the most accurate and general of the psychophysical methods. While its use has been illustrated here primarily for the estimation of threshold values, it is widely used for other problems of sensory psychology. The method has been found particularly useful for industrial research in the quality control of food and beverage products, where sensory characteristics of the product play a large role in consumer acceptance.

Direct Psychological Scaling.—*Method of Paired Comparisons.*—Related to but distinct from the constant method is the method of paired comparisons, developed in 1927 by the U.S. psychologist L. L. Thurstone (*q.v.*). Taken together with Thurstone's law of comparative judgment, the method of paired comparisons provides a model by which sensations may be scaled directly, without reference to corresponding physical measurements of stimuli. In the formulation of Weber ($\Delta R/R = c$), the concern is only with the physical measures of the stimulus R. Fechner's proposal ($S = k \log R$) explicitly introduced a continuum of sensation, and allowed indirect "measurement" of sensation by using a functional relation between sensation and physical measurement. Thurstone's model allows direct measurement of psychological events without having first established an intervening quantitative relation between psychological and physical events. One striking feature of the method, thus, is its applicability to the scaling of human attitudes, consumer preferences, aesthetic values and other psychological variables associated directly with no apparent physical counterparts.

In the method of paired comparisons, each one of a set of stimuli is presented together with every other stimulus in the set. The subject is asked to make one of two possible judgments to each stimulus pair, either that stimulus A exceeds stimulus B or that stimulus B exceeds stimulus A. The word exceeds is specified by the purpose of the study, so that judgments might be heavier, brighter or louder, or could be more valuable, friendlier or the like. Paired stimuli could be presented many times to only one subject or many subjects may judge each stimulus pair just once. In either case the result is a matrix of relative frequency showing the proportion of times each stimulus was judged higher on the scale than every other stimulus.

From these basic data, scaling proceeds by the law of comparative judgment. It is assumed that a subject's response reflects the momentary subjective value associated with the stimulus, and that the probability distribution of these momentary values is Gaussian (normal), either over numerous occasions for one subject or over a population of homogeneous subjects. This is followed by application of the simplest case of the law of comparative judgment: $\mu_i - \mu_j = z_{ij}$, where μ_i and μ_j are the mean psychological values associated with a pair of stimuli i and j, and where z_{ij} is the unit normal deviate associated with p_{ij}, defined as the proportion of judgments that stimulus i is greater than stimulus j. (Note that z_{ij} is uniquely determined from p_{ij} and may be read as an entry in the table of the normal distribution function.) If the numbers z_{ij} are arranged in matrix (tabular) form, the mean values for the columns provide estimates for the n values μ_i. For the case where $n = 4$, the table takes the following form (noting that for z_{ij} may be substituted the quantity $\mu_i - \mu_j$):

$\mu_1 - \mu_1$	$\mu_2 - \mu_1$	$\mu_3 - \mu_1$	$\mu_4 - \mu_1$
$\mu_1 - \mu_2$	$\mu_2 - \mu_2$	$\mu_3 - \mu_2$	$\mu_4 - \mu_2$
$\mu_1 - \mu_3$	$\mu_2 - \mu_3$	$\mu_3 - \mu_3$	$\mu_4 - \mu_3$
$\mu_1 - \mu_4$	$\mu_2 - \mu_4$	$\mu_3 - \mu_4$	$\mu_4 - \mu_4$

Sum: $4\mu_1 - \Sigma\mu_i$ $4\mu_2 - \Sigma\mu_i$ $4\mu_3 - \Sigma\mu_i$ $4\mu_4 - \Sigma\mu_i$
Letting $\Sigma\mu_i = 0$
Mean: μ_1 μ_2 μ_3 μ_4

Since the zero point to this scale is arbitrary, $\Sigma\mu_i = 0$ may be defined as above, and this yields the desired solution.

Psychological scaling methods typically allow measurement on a scale characterized by equality of intervals, but one with only an arbitrary origin or zero point. As upon the Celsius or Fahrenheit scales of temperature, nominal magnitude of zero does not correspond with absolute absence of that which is measured. On such scales ratio comparisons of measures are not valid. (A substance registering a temperature of 40° C., for example, is not twice as hot as a body with measured temperature of 20° C.)

However, the method of paired comparisons has been extended to provide a rational zero point, and thus to allow for meaningful ratio comparisons of psychological magnitudes. On a scale of consumer preference, the psychological zero point is that psychological value which, if assigned to a consumer item, would result in consumer indifference toward that item. An absolute scale is established by first assuming the additivity of psychological magnitudes—that (under specified conditions of independence of stimuli) the subjective value for a combination of two stimuli is equal to the sum of the two values associated with the individual stimulus items. The assumption may be stated $\mu_{ij} = \mu_i + \mu_j$, where μ_{ij} is the mean psychological value associated with a composite stimulus, and μ_i and μ_j are the mean values associated with the two component stimuli. There is one such equation for every composite stimulus included in a particular study, and it becomes a matter for empirical test to determine whether the several equations are consistent with subjects' judgments scaled by the method of paired comparisons.

Method of Successive Categories.—Derived from assumptions similar to those for the method of paired comparisons is the method of successive categories. Subjects are instructed to rate each of a set of stimuli by assigning it to one of a group of ordered categories of judgment (usually between five and ten categories). Ratings are to reflect the subjects' judgments concerning the stimulus and are taken as gross indicants of the underlying psychological values associated with the stimulus. Under the assumption that the ratings represent random variables from a normally distributed population of underlying scale values, it becomes possible to estimate the mean and standard deviation of the underlying distribution of subjective values for each stimulus. The method of successive categories has the advantage of requiring just one rating from each subject for every stimulus, in contrast to the method of paired comparisons which requires $n(n - 1)/2$ judgments for each of n stimuli. Results from the two methods generally have been found to be nearly identical.

An Alternative to the Fechner-Weber Law: the Power Function.—One of the earliest criticisms of Fechner's psychophysical approach was that of the Belgian physicist J. A. F. Plateau (1801–83). Plateau reasoned that, since the apparent relations among different shades of gray remain *sensiblement le même* when the general illumination is changed, the ratios among the sensations produced by the grays must remain fixed. This, he argued, is more rational than Fechner's view that it is the differences that remain fixed. While Fechner's formulation entails a logarithmic relation between sensation and stimulus, Plateau's assumption entails a power function of the form $S = aR^n$, where sensation S is proportional to a constant power n of stimulus magnitude R; a is the proportionality factor.

Since the time of Plateau, the power function alternative to the Fechner-Weber law has been revived on several occasions, but never before with such force as that brought to bear by the U.S. psychologist S. S. Stevens. Stevens vigorously attacked the Fechnerian assumption that the just perceptible stimulus difference may serve as a unit of measurement for sensation. As a result of extensive laboratory investigation, a power function has been found to relate psychological magnitude to stimulus magnitude ($S = aR^n$) for more than a dozen distinct psychological continua. Empirical determination of the exponent n has shown it to vary from about 0.3 (for loudness) through unity (for taste, visual length, visual area) and 1.5 (heaviness) to approximately 2.0 (visual flash rate).

The methods utilized in these studies differ sharply from Fechner's psychophysical methods. In the work of Stevens and his students, subjects are required to make direct quantitative estimates of subjective events. The most prominently used of these methods is that called fractionation. The subject is required to adjust one stimulus so as to produce a sensation half (or some other fractional amount) as great as a given standard stimulus.

It seems highly probable that the distinct psychophysical laws, logarithmic and power function, result from application of different measurement methods. By this view, the power function formulation is not necessarily inconsistent with the Fechner-Weber law. Rather, each is valid, but pertains to a unique definition of psychological magnitude, a definition specified by the psychophysical method employed.

See also PSYCHOLOGICAL TESTS AND MEASUREMENTS.

BIBLIOGRAPHY.—G. T. Fechner, *Elements of Psychophysics*, Eng. trans. (1965). For a detailed summary of 19th-century psychophysics, *see* E. B. Titchener, *Experimental Psychology*, vol. ii, parts i and ii (1905). *See* also F. M. Urban, *Application of Statistical Methods to the Problems of Psychophysics* (1908); W. Brown and G. H. Thomson, *Essentials of Mental Measurement* (1921); L. L. Thurstone, *The Measurement of Values* (1959); S. S. Stevens, "On the Psychophysical Law," *Psychol. Rev.*, 64:153–181 (1957); J. P. Guilford, *Psychometric Methods*, 2nd ed. (1954); W. S. Torgerson, *Theory and Method of Scaling* (1958); R. D. Luce et al. (eds.), *Handbook of Mathematical Psychology*, vol. 1 (1963). (L. V. Jo.)

PSYCHOSES. A psychosis is a mental illness in which the patient fails to discriminate between stimuli arising within himself and stimuli received from the external world. The healthy personality accurately perceives and evaluates the environment. When the stress of conflict between the self and the environment becomes too great, however, the perceptive and evaluative (ego; *q.v.*) functions of the personality may break down. In such situations the person appears to distort his concept of the environment into a form which is more satisfactory for him; he organizes it into a less confusing place in order to protect himself. In the process he loses contact with reality and becomes psychotic.

Psychoses are rare until adolescence, but thereafter continue to increase in incidence with the advance of age. There is an especially sharp rise at the older age levels. The problems and conflicts of phases of development and stress, such as adolescence, marriage, pregnancy, parenthood, the involutional period and senility, tend to disturb psychological integration and may precipitate a psychotic disturbance in vulnerable persons.

Psychoses present symptoms that have multiple causations and multiple meanings. These are indicative of underlying conflict and represent ways of trying to deal with the conflict. Symptoms may represent attempts to adapt through protective and safety devices, or else they may appear when defenses collapse and disintegrate. Psychotic symptomatology is a manifestation of both regressive and restitutional phenomena. Initial symptoms, such as world-destruction fantasies, hypochondriasis and depersonalization, often represent regression to earlier behaviour patterns or renunciation of the objective world. Later symptoms, such as world-saving fantasies, hallucinations and delusions, may be evidence of a swing toward restitution or toward reintegration of the psychotic ego. The psychotic appears to oscillate between an almost complete loss of object relationships and a striving to reembrace them.

Symptoms of Psychosis.—Psychotic symptoms may be considered under the following headings:

1. Disorders of perception. A hallucination (*q.v.*) is a misperception (either auditory, visual, olfactory or, less frequently, gustatory). Something is perceived which has no objective reality; for example, voices may be heard when no sound exists. An illusion is a misinterpreted perception in which a sensory impression is received correctly but then misconstrued so that it takes on an erroneous meaning. For example, the rustling of leaves may be interpreted as whispering reproaches; although the rustling is heard, it is given a specific psychological meaning.

2. Disorders of thinking. In autistic or dereistic thinking the mind appears to operate without regard to reality, building up an unrealistic fantasy life and becoming preoccupied with the fantasy to the exclusion of reality. A "flight of ideas" is characterized by a rapid digression from one thought to another, often expressed as words or clauses run quickly together without an apparent logical connection. Perseverations are repetitive expressions of an idea and include verbigerations, or repetitions of apparently meaningless words or sentences. A delusion is a false belief which is not susceptible to correction by reason or logic. Thus many patients suffering from delusions of persecution may believe there is an international plot directed specifically against them, and they cannot be shaken from this belief. Patients with delusions of grandeur are convinced they are such exalted figures as Napoleon or Jesus Christ.

3. Disturbances of consciousness. A confusional state usually includes bewilderment, perplexity, uncertainty, disorientation and difficulty in grasping the simplest concepts. Stupor is a state of mind manifested by varying degrees of consciousness but always including diminished responsiveness, either through suspension of

thought processes or through intense preoccupation with internal concerns, withdrawal and loss of reality sense. Delirium (q.v.) is characterized by combinations of the above plus illusions, hallucinations and intense fear.

4. Disturbances of affectivity and mood. Affectivity or feeling tone are terms signifying the minute-to-minute variations in the subjective feelings of a person. Mood is a sustained feeling tone over a longer period of time. These emotional states range along a continuum from extreme depression through normal affect to extreme elation. In the most extreme elation reality is completely denied, and attitudes of grandeur and peaceful rapture, detachment and power are assumed. Another dimension of affect includes panic, consisting of marked fear and a tendency toward disorganization of the personality. Characteristic of all these affect states (elation, depression, panic) is their inappropriateness; that is, the feeling tone is not appropriate to the patient's life situation.

5. Disturbances of activity. Marked increases or decreases in the rate of mental and physical activity are common. Hyperactivity includes excessive restlessness, pacing, agitation and excitement. The extreme of diminished activity is called waxy flexibility, in which the limbs are maintained in fixed poses for long periods of time.

Defense Mechanisms.—Although the ego defends itself against overwhelming anxiety with defense mechanisms, the mechanisms themselves may become of pathological degree.

1. Rationalization is a form of self-deception by which a person acclaims in a manner acceptable to himself an act, thought or feeling that in actuality has a different and more unacceptable motive. The real reason thus remains obscure. Although rationalization is commonly used by all people, such self-deception may become a full-fledged delusion if carried to an extreme.

2. Projection is a mental technique whereby a person unconsciously externalizes some of his own thoughts or feelings or inadequacies. He thus defends himself from his unacceptable impulse by attributing it not to himself but to another. Thus a person who cannot face his own hostility may attribute it to another and accuse the other of hostile designs against him. This mechanism characterizes the formation of paranoid reactions (see below).

3. Autism, withdrawal into fantasy and regression (a moving back toward less mature but more comfortable levels of personality development) are protective devices but may lead to psychosis formation.

4. The process of internalization or introjection involves a turning inward upon the self of certain feelings and attitudes that may produce depression. (See also DEFENSE MECHANISMS.)

Causes of Psychosis.—The causes of psychoses appear to be multiple. They include somatic (physical), biological, psychological (intra- and interpersonal) and sociocultural factors, all of which affect attitudes, feelings and behaviours. Studies of psychological causes stress the importance of the mother-infant relationship, inability and/or lack of opportunity for the child to obtain gratification of his basic needs, and defective development of a sense of reality. Extreme maternal deprivation during the first few months of life, caused either by lack of a mothering figure through loss or by an unusually barren mother-infant relationship, generates unbearable tensions. Since deprived children have had no one with whom to relate when relationship was most important, the warmth and security derived from relating to another human being are lacking. Genetic studies indicate that a specific potential for reacting to personality stresses in a specific way can be inherited; that is, it is possible to inherit a constitutional predisposition to psychosis which is then stimulated or extinguished by other etiological factors.

In addition to the basic determinants, there are a variety of factors that may precipitate a psychosis. These may be obvious reproductions or re-enactments of earlier stresses, or they may be less apparent and seemingly irrelevant events whose relationship to previous stress is obscure. Frequently precipitating factors are organic, such as alcohol and other drugs, infectious processes, endocrine and vitamin deficiencies, physical defects and brain injuries. Other precipitating factors appear to be manifestations of stressful times and events of life, as marriage or pregnancy. Overwork has frequently been implicated, but it is a symptom rather than a cause.

Organic Psychoses.—The psychoses are divided into two main categories, organic and psychogenic (for which see below), according to the presence or absence of discernible organic factors. Organic psychoses result primarily from pathological changes in the central nervous system. They are divided into acute and chronic types. The acute group includes those reactions which come on suddenly, last for a limited time and then disappear. The chronic diseases are slower in onset and tend to produce more lasting effects, which do not appear to be reversible but become stationary or gradually progressive.

The brain is particularly susceptible to physiochemical changes. It is dependent on a large flow of well-oxygenated blood, and since its metabolic activity is high, its oxygen consumption is also high. The brain has a small oxygen reserve and cannot withstand oxygen deprivation very long. It can expand little, yet is suspended and quite movable, subject to injury and sensitive to any noxious stimuli. Thus a state of reduced cerebral competence from whatever cause predisposes the individual to the development of an organic psychosis: (1) personality change, defects in judgment and moral code, tendency toward egocentricity; (2) disturbances in memory, especially for recent events, disorientation for time, place and person; (3) emotional instability, irritability and frequent shifts in mood; (4) exaggeration of previous personality problems (persons who have been aggressive tend to become overwhelmingly hyperactive, whereas persons who have been quiet and reserved tend to withdraw even more); (5) diminished tolerance to medications (more severe reactions to sedatives, other drugs).

In addition to acting as a specific cause or precipitating stress for the development of a psychosis, organic brain disease may interfere with and impinge upon the healthy integration of the personality. The result is impaired ego function, and the symptoms are a manifestation of ego disintegration. A less competent ego then permits the release of previously warded-off impulses which overwhelm the ego and lead to a psychosis.

The following are significant clinical entities:

1. Infectious processes. A meningitis (q.v.) may be either intracranial or systemic. Although commonly an acute reaction, some types of meningitis are long-standing, slowly developing diseases. Syphilitic meningoencephalitis, also called general paresis, an infection not only of the meninges but also of the brain itself, may require years to develop (see VENEREAL DISEASES: Syphilis: Neurosyphilis).

2. Intoxications. A variety of drugs or poisons produce acute and chronic symptomatology. Bromides, barbiturates, lead and alcohol taken over a prolonged period of time may lead to psychoses. Profuse and frequent imbibition of alcohol followed by sudden withdrawal and accompanied by a nutritional deficiency leads to a condition known as delirium tremens. Korsakoff's psychosis, associated with alcoholism, is in reality due to a severe vitamin B deficiency and is characterized by amnesia, disorientation for time and place and falsification of memory (see ALCOHOLISM). A detailed discussion of drugs such as LSD and mescaline is found under NEUROPHARMACOLOGY and PSYCHOPHARMACOLOGY.

3. Injuries. Severe head injury may produce an acute syndrome known as traumatic delirium or a chronic personality disturbance such as seen in the prize fighter who is "punch drunk."

4. Metabolic disorders such as hypoglycemia (a deficiency of sugar in the blood) and certain swellings or growths (brain tumours and cysts) may bring about a psychosis.

5. Degenerative diseases. Advanced age may be associated with a degenerative disease of the brain which leads to dementia, a psychotic disturbance characterized by progressive impairment of basic mental capacities. In these cases the brain cells literally "wash away" and disappear (see DEMENTIA).

6. Circulatory disturbances. One of the commonest disease processes expressing itself in both acute and chronic psychotic forms is cerebral arteriosclerosis. In this condition there is

gradual or fairly rapid hardening of the blood vessels of the brain, and deposits of fat in the deteriorating vessel wall tend to narrow or almost obliterate the vessel, thereby obstructing the flow of blood. When less blood is carried to the brain its nutritional status is affected and psychosis appears. There is often a fluctuation in the course of cerebral arteriosclerosis, and the patient often recognizes his decline, in contradistinction to other organic maladies where there is no insight.

The treatment of an organic psychosis depends on its cause, and each is handled individually. Both physiological and psychological therapies are employed, ranging from vitamins, medications and surgical procedures to the establishment of emotional security and an increasing sense of self-esteem.

Psychogenic Psychoses.—Disorders. of psychogenic origin appear to be free of structural, anatomical or physiological changes and are the result of disturbed psychological experience. The six major psychoses of psychogenic origin are divided into two distinct but by no means mutually exclusive types, the affective reactions and the thought disorders. In the former, mood disturbances are dominant; in the latter, there is a predominant disturbance in the capacity to think and judge and the power to reason. The three affective reactions are involutional depression, manic-depressive psychosis and psychotic depressive reaction. The three thought disorders are schizophrenia, paranoia and paranoid state.

Affective Reactions.—An involutional depression is a depression coming on in the so-called involutional period of life (*i.e.,* approximately 40–60 years of age in women, 45–65 in men). It is often accompanied by agitation, usually represents the person's first "breakdown" and occurs in people whose premorbid personalities are characterized as energetic but inhibited, compulsive and over-conscientious, chronically worried, inflexible and sensitive.

A manic-depressive psychosis, as the name suggests, may be made up of both manic (hyperactive, elated) phases and depressive states, alternating with one another or occurring haphazardly without any particular order. Instead of alternating, all episodes may be manic, or all may be depressed. These episodes are usually cyclic in nature and may come on every few months or every few years with reasonable regularity. The disease occurs in young people (early 20s) and may continue intermittently for many years, each attack lasting a few weeks or a few months. The manic phase may represent a defense against a basic depression; certainly the swings from one phase to another give credence to the homogeneity of the two elements. The symptomatology of the manic is characterized by exaltation and excitement, loquaciousness and rapid association of ideas. Psychomotor activity is described as overactive. The depressed phase, on the other hand, is usually characterized by psychomotor retardation; *i.e.,* movement and mental activity are slow and there is an inhibition of the stream of thought.

The prepsychotic personality of the manic-depressive is distinguished by its lability, mood swings and unpredictable oscillations of emotion.

The term psychotic depressive reaction describes a depression of psychotic proportions, arising as a direct result of one or several specific precipitating stresses. It may come at any age, and is often an isolated, single episode in a person's life.

Thought Disorders.—Schizophrenia is a term coined by E. Bleuler in 1911, from two Greek words meaning "splitting of the mind." As with the others, this disorder represents an expression of the total reaction of the person to internal and external stress. There is a breakup in the normal synthesis of thought, and part of the split takes place between the thought process and the affect connected with it. In its most definitive form the schizophrenic syndrome is made up of: (1) a disorder of association— the train of thought that does not seem to follow a usual rational pattern; (2) a disorder of affect—the feeling state is inappropriate to the situation, to the particular thought or idea expressed; (3) autistic thinking—withdrawal into self and a fantasy world; and (4) ambivalence—indecision or complete blocking because of two conflicting feelings or two opposing impulses.

Emerging from these manifestations are a host of varied symptoms and signs including poverty and disharmony of feeling tone, inability to relate to another person and delusional or hallucinatory mental content or both. A schizophrenic person may appear dull and apathetic. He may be catatonic and stay in one position over a long period of time. He may exhibit mutism, impulsive or stereotyped behaviour and occasional phases of stupor or excitement; or he may be preoccupied with delusional thoughts with behaviour corresponding to these thoughts. In general there may be mixtures and combinations of symptoms, attitudes, expressions and patterns, so that it is difficult to classify schizophrenics into subtypes or to place them in various subdivisions (*see* SCHIZO-PHRENIA).

The paranoid psychoses are characterized by delusions of a persecutory or grandiose nature, with varying degrees of ego disintegration. In true paranoia there is usually one basic, well-systematized delusion, while the rest of the ego remains reasonably intact. The true paranoiacs are rarely identified, as they usually manage to conceal their delusions and to function adequately. Paranoid states involve a more elaborate delusional system in which the delusions are less believable and more loosely organized and lead to a more disintegrated ego structure. During the paranoid episode the patient may be obstreperous and hostile (*see* PARANOID REACTIONS).

The bridge between the paranoid psychosis and the schizophrenic psychosis is an entity known as paranoid schizophrenia. In the most serious forms the delusions are poorly organized, bizarre and contradictory, and ego disintegration proceeds at a rapid pace. Paranoid schizophrenics range along a continuum from relatively harmonious ego co-ordination to almost complete ego decomposition and loss of control. The paranoid schizophrenic is potentially dangerous to himself or others because of his feeling that others are against him and because of his bizarre reactions to this thought.

Treatment of the psychogenic psychoses is varied and variable. Several therapies usually are combined in managing a particular syndrome with one or more therapeutic procedures utilized at specific times for specific reasons.

Many patients with psychosis require hospitalization; some do not. Outside a hospital, psychotherapy, environmental manipulation and the administration of drugs are valuable. In a hospital, a program is devised to include individually prescribed activities for the patient and certain helpful attitudes on the part of the ward staff; in addition, somatic therapies such as electroshock and drugs (major and minor tranquilizers) are employed when necessary. The affective psychoses, particularly the involutional depressions, respond more favourably to electroshock than do the thought disorders. In the paranoid conditions sometimes insulin and occasionally lobotomy (surgery on the brain) have been used, and favourable results with drug therapy have been reported. However, the basic treatment in all the psychoses consists of psychotherapy plus the provision of a "therapeutic milieu"—a scientifically manipulated environment within which ego reorganization may take place. Such a milieu encourages creativity and socialization by means of a structured program of activities and the opportunity for the patient to share some of the responsibilities of ward life with the staff. Thus the total experience of living is utilized in the process of getting well.

Childhood Psychosis.—Childhood psychosis is an uncommon but severe form of ego disturbance which becomes apparent in the early years of life (before puberty). Onset may be sudden or insidious. Symptoms include withdrawal, negativism (refusal to do whatever is asked, or doing the opposite of what is expected or desired), anxiety, stereotyped behaviour and a tendency toward an abandonment of reality. In infancy the baby may be apathetic and fail to react emotionally to being approached or when picked up.

Etiologically the lack of an affectional tie between infant and mother appears to be important. Often the mother (or both parents) as well as the child require treatment. Institutional care for the child is sometimes indicated. For other types of mental disorders, *see* NEUROSES. For treatment, *see* PSYCHIATRY; PSYCHOANALYSIS; PSYCHOTHERAPY. *See also* PSYCHOLOGY, AB-

NORMAL; and references under "Psychoses" in the Index.

BIBLIOGRAPHY.—O. Fenichel, *The Psychoanalytic Theory of Neurosis* (1945); H. S. Lippman, *Treatment of the Child in Emotional Conflict* (1956); A. P. Noyes and L. C. Kolb, *Modern Clinical Psychiatry*, 5th ed. (1958); G. Zilboorg and G. W. Henry, *A History of Medical Psychology* (1941); J. and E. Cumming, *Ego and Milieu* (1962).
(P. M. Ma.)

PSYCHOSOMATIC DISORDERS are a class of bodily reactions, *e.g.*, diarrhea, asthma, and rashes, observed in emotional disturbances. *See* PSYCHIATRY: *History: Psychosomatic Medicine*; PSYCHOLOGY, ABNORMAL: *Abnormalities of Behaviour: Neurotic Reactions.*

PSYCHOTHERAPY in its broadest sense is the systematic effort of a person or group to relieve distress or disability by influencing the sufferer's mental state, attitudes and behaviour. Drugs may be used as adjuncts, but the healing influence is exerted primarily by words and actions that are believed by sufferer, therapist and the group to which they both belong to have healing powers and that create an emotionally charged relationship between them. Psychotherapeutic methods are used to treat all forms of suffering in which emotional factors play a part. These include behaviour disorders of children and adults; emotional reactions to the ordinary hardships or crises of life; psychoses, characterized by derangements of thinking and behaviour usually so severe as to require hospitalization; psychoneuroses, which are chronic disorders of personal functioning often accompanied by bodily symptoms of emotional strain; addictions; and psychosomatic illness, such as gastric or duodenal ulcer and certain skin diseases, in which tissue damage is caused or aggravated by emotional components. Since loss of morale contributes significantly to the degree of disablement of all chronically ill or handicapped persons, psychotherapeutic principles are emphasized in rehabilitation programs.

Historical Survey.—Early psychotherapeutic theories and methods were based on either the religio-magical or the naturalistic view of mental illness. The former, originating before recorded history, regarded certain forms of personal suffering, or of alienation from one's fellows, as caused by an evil spirit that gained entrance into the sufferer because he had sinned or through an enemy's curse. The curse could be lifted or the transgression atoned for, leading to expulsion of the evil spirit, by the participation of the victim and his group in suitable rites, under the leadership of a priest-physician, the medicine man or shaman. Thereupon the victim's health was restored and he was once more accepted by his group. The tradition of supernatural healing remained strong and finds its modern expression in, for example, healing shrines and numberless cults led by healers whose claims are accepted only by their devotees.

The naturalistic tradition viewed mental illness as a phenomenon that could be scientifically studied and treated, like other forms of illness. Treatment consisted in measures to promote bodily well-being and mental tranquility. The earliest surviving expression of this concept is in the writings attributed to Hippocrates in the 5th century B.C. Though largely eclipsed in the middle ages, at the turn of the 19th century it again began to come to the fore under the leadership of the great French physician Philippe Pinel. For him, many forms of insanity were the results of excessive exposure to social and psychological stresses, and he tried to help the insane regain their reason through "moral treatment," which included close, friendly contact, intimate discussion of personal difficulties and a planned program of purposeful activities. The popularity of moral treatment depended upon the belief that insanity was curable by psychological influences. As the theory gained ascendance that mental illness was caused primarily by organic disease of the nervous system rather than by the stresses of life, faith in its curability by psychological means declined and, starting in the middle of the 19th century, mental hospitals tended to degenerate into custodial institutions, which most of them continued to be until the mid-20th century.

Psychotherapy of nonhospitalized patients in the naturalistic tradition was not distinguishable from ordinary medical practice until the latter half of the 19th century. The emergence of psychotherapy as a specialized treatment probably is traceable to the dramatic demonstration by Franz Anton Mesmer (*q.v.*) in the late 18th century that many symptoms could be made to disappear by putting a patient into a trance. Although his theories and methods were soon discredited, mesmerism was the precursor of hypnotism, which became a widely used psychotherapeutic method. Through it Josef Breuer and Sigmund Freud (*qq.v.*) made the epochal observations on the relationship to later mental illness of emotionally charged damaging experiences in childhood. From these discoveries grew the theory and practice of psychoanalysis, which, with its many modifications, immensely influenced the subsequent development of psychotherapy.

Despite the widespread recognition that the groups to which a person belongs powerfully affect his attitudes and behaviour, the traditional medical emphasis on the privacy of the doctor-patient relationship slowed general acceptance of group psychotherapy. Though foreshadowed as early as 1905 by Joseph J. Pratt's group treatment of tuberculosis patients, only a few physicians practised group therapy before World War II. The large numbers of soldiers requiring psychotherapy compelled psychiatrists to try to treat them in groups, and the use of group methods proved so effective that they developed rapidly in the postwar years. During this period, two societies and two journals devoted exclusively to group therapy appeared in the United States alone. The professional acceptance of the importance of group influences led to the development of social or milieu treatment for hospitalized patients, recognizing that all aspects of institutional life had therapeutic potential. This gradually began to transform mental hospitals from custodial institutions into therapeutic communities.

The rapid growth of group therapy was one manifestation of a striking upsurge of public interest in mental health, especially in the United States following World War II, leading to a demand for psychotherapy that went far beyond the capacity of the medical profession to meet it. As a result, members of related disciplines, particularly clinical psychology and psychiatric social work, received increasing recognition as competent to treat certain types of sufferers, and programs were developed to train housewives and other non-professionals to conduct simpler forms of psychotherapy under professional supervision.

Psychiatrists continued to have responsibility for treatment of the hospitalized insane and patients in psychiatric clinics. They also enjoyed the highest prestige as private practitioners of psychotherapy. Other physicians continued to practise effective psychotherapy of an informal sort on the large proportion of their patients whose bodily complaints were associated with emotional stress. Clinical psychologists and psychiatric social workers treated patients or their families under psychiatric supervision in mental hospitals and psychiatric clinics for adults and children. In addition, members of each profession used methods analogous to, if not indistinguishable from, psychotherapy in certain institutional settings without medical supervision. The type of person or problem with which psychologists and social workers dealt depended largely on the settings in which they worked. Psychologists in educational institutions counseled children, adolescents and young adults; social workers did casework with clients of social agencies, whose personal difficulties tended to be bound up with environmental stresses. The exact limits of the various fields of competence of these disciplines remained vague and the jurisdictional problem became more acute as psychologists and social workers in the larger cities entered independent private practice in direct competition with psychiatrists.

A significant development during this period was the growing *rapprochement* between naturalistic psychotherapy and religiously oriented psychotherapy in the form of pastoral counseling. As psychotherapy became more popular, certain persons came to seek it as a means of achieving a fuller life and finding personal solutions to the general problems of human existence. Psychotherapists thus were faced with questions that traditionally lay in the province of philosophy and religion. At the same time, parishioners put increasing demands on their ministers for help with personal problems, leading the latter to turn for help to the newer insights of psychotherapy. Both groups saw resemblances between the moral and spiritual conflicts or emotional responses to the crises of life, which were the primary concern of the pastoral counselor, and the issues raised by patients in psychotherapy.

The variety of therapeutic practitioners was paralleled by a wide diversity of theories of mental illness and methods of treatment. The preferred form of psychotherapy in different cultures seemed to accord with the characteristic pattern of social interaction. Psychotherapy in Germany and the U.S.S.R. tended to be directive, while in the United States permissive, democratic methods had a higher prestige. Within a given culture, furthermore, patients of different socioeconomic levels tended to receive the type of psychotherapy that accorded best with their typical views of treatment. One study of patients in psychiatric treatment in New Haven, Conn., in 1951, for example, found that about half the upper- and middle-class neurotics received insight therapy (*see* below) as compared with only 5% of the lower-class neurotics. This seemed related to characteristic differences in the conceptions of these classes as to what constituted treatment.

The existence of so many theories and techniques was an indication of the need for research, which received extensive public and private support following World War II.

Features Common to All Forms of Psychotherapy.—There is no convincing evidence that the results of one form of treatment are better than any other, lending plausibility to the supposition that their underlying similarities might be more significant than their apparent differences. Despite differences in emphasis, most schools of psychotherapy agree that mental illnesses are, at least in part, expressions of chronic states of anxiety and frustration, related to unsolved inner conflicts and unsuccessful ways of dealing with other persons. Though genetically or physiologically caused vulnerabilities might contribute to the difficulties of these patients, unfortunate early experiences with family members and other emotionally significant persons are believed to play a major role.

Chances of successful treatment are generally held to be related to the degree of the patient's emotional involvement in the treatment process. This is influenced by the intensity of his suffering and by his faith in the therapist and the treatment method. The patient's expectancy of help is enhanced by the therapist's ability to convince the patient that he understands him intimately and is dedicated to his welfare. Personal qualities of the therapist seem important in the development of a successful therapeutic relationship.

The close, confiding relationship between patient and therapist, including the shared expectancy that the patient will be helped that is common to all forms of psychotherapy, is probably healing in itself. It tends to allay the patient's anxieties and bolster his morale, resulting in direct relief of bodily symptoms due to emotional tension. In addition, it helps him mobilize the courage necessary to give up habitual but unsatisfactory ways of feeling and behaviour and search for better ones. The search is aided by the fact that the therapist or therapeutic group represent certain values and principles of conduct with which the patient can compare his own and adopt what is helpful to him. This usually occurs not through deliberate choice but more or less unconsciously, just as children take over behaviours and attitudes of their parents, which then become integral parts of their own personalities. Psychotherapy thus is essentially a process of re-education, both emotional and intellectual, through which the patient develops better patterns of adjustment to life.

Major Forms of Psychotherapy.—Psychotherapies differ primarily in the nature of the activity that mediates the therapeutic relationship. The variety of these activities is bewildering, but they may be classed as individual or group, depending on whether or not the therapist treats more than one patient at a time. Both forms can be divided roughly into methods that seek to alleviate the patient's distress or teach him more satisfactory behaviour through direct interventions, and those that try to facilitate his over-all emotional growth and capacity for responsible behaviour. Many psychotherapeutic methods contain an admixture of both, and most psychotherapists emphasize one or the other with different patients, depending on the nature of their difficulties.

Individual Psychotherapies.—Individual psychotherapeutic methods for influencing patients directly include giving advice, persuasion, suggestion, and training in specific curative activities. Such efforts frequently involve the use of hypnosis (*q.v.*) to heighten the therapist's influence over the patient, and often include efforts to change his social environment so as to reduce the stresses it places upon him. Behaviour therapies are aimed at correcting specific pathological emotional states or behaviour patterns by appropriate countermeasures. They are based largely on the conditioned-reflex theory of I. P. Pavlov (*see* CONDITIONING; REFLEX) and on other theories of learning. Irrational fears, for example, may be extinguished by evoking them while the patient is completely relaxed, or a craving for alcoholic beverages may be abolished by making the patient nauseated when he tastes them.

Individual therapies that aim to foster a patient's general personality growth emphasize helping him to gain insight into his feelings and behaviour. They are based on the assumption that, since symptoms of emotional illness are expressions of flaws in the patient's over-all approach to life, permanent relief requires major personality change. To facilitate this they try to create a therapeutic situation that will enable the patient to express himself with complete freedom, while the therapist maintains a consistent, warm, nonjudgmental interest. Feeling himself understood and accepted by someone whom he admires and to whom he feels close, the patient will progressively dare to reveal those shameful or frightening aspects of himself that he has pushed out of awareness. As his self-understanding increases, his self-esteem will grow and he will become more spontaneous, enabling him to relate more flexibly and appropriately to persons important to him. Thus he will derive increasing satisfaction and security and his distress will diminish, leading to further gain in his sense of self-worth. In this way a beneficial circle is set in motion, resulting in increasingly deep and permanent improvement.

Some schools of psychotherapy hold that the consistent, warm "unconditional positive regard" of the therapist for the patient is sufficient to produce these changes. Related to these are "existentialist" schools that view therapy as an encounter between therapist and patient, in which the former's healing power lies in his ability to enter fully into the patient's experience, however painful. This aids the latter to escape from his self-centredness and transform his neurotic guilt into normal guilt. Therapies in the psychoanalytic tradition, while also emphasizing the importance of the therapeutic relationship, try to help the patient understand and master his feelings by labeling and analyzing them. They differ in their concepts and in the relative emphasis placed on different types of material produced by the patient. Traditional psychoanalysis emphasizes the use of dreams as short cuts to the patient's deeper feelings. It also puts great stress on helping the patient to rediscover, re-experience and "work through" the traumatic emotional experiences of early life in which his current difficulties are believed to originate. Hypnosis may be used to facilitate this, although Freud believed free association (*see* ASSOCIATION, MENTAL) to be more effective. Later modifications of psychoanalysis put more emphasis on analysis of the patient's current problems, and some emphasize helping the patient to gain a better philosophy of life. All agree that in an intimate, prolonged relation with the therapist, the patient will eventually experience toward him the feelings that trouble his relationships with persons emotionally close to him in his past and present life. Since both therapist and patient can observe these "transference reactions," as Freud termed them, exploring their inappropriateness is deemed a powerful means of resolving them. At mid-century, the advent of consciousness-altering drugs like *d*-lysergic acid diethylamide (LSD-25) led to widespread experimentation with them, to help patients achieve a fuller, more emotionally charged awareness of their inner experiences, including memories of repressed traumatic childhood events. These drugs also were used to promote rapport with the therapist.

Group and Social Therapies.—Group therapeutic techniques are as varied as those of individual therapy, and similarly tend to stress either alleviation of members' distress by direct measures or creation of a group atmosphere conducive to increased self-understanding and personal maturation. Groups of the first type may have any number of members, up to 50 or more. Some are primarily inspirational in that their chief aim is to raise members' morale and combat feelings of isolation by cultivating a sense of group belongingness through slogans, rituals, testimonials and public recognition of members' progress. Certain of these groups have developed into autonomous movements conducted solely by their members. An outstanding example is Alcoholics Anonymous, organized by chronic alcoholics to help themselves. Two other popular directive methods are didactic group therapy, which seeks, through organized discussions of assigned topics, to stimulate group members intellectually so that they will function more successfully; and therapeutic social clubs, which stress development of social skills through participation in self-organized social activities.

The other class of group methods strives to foster free discussion and uninhibited self-revelation. Most use small face-to-face groups, typically composed of five to eight members. Members are helped to self-understanding and more successful behaviour through mutual examination of their reactions to persons in their daily lives, to each other and to the group leader in an emotionally supportive atmosphere. An influential variety of this approach that utilizes larger groups is the "psychodrama" of J. L. Moreno. In this method patients more or less spontaneously dramatize their personal problems before an audience of fellow patients and therapists, some of whom also participate in the dramatic production itself. The dramatization is followed by discussion between players and audience.

Treatment of the family as a group is based on the view that much of the distress of the mental patient is caused by self-perpetuating and self-defeating ways of communicating with his intimates, in which they are equally involved. The therapeutic focus is on the pathological communication network itself.

Social therapy for institutionalized patients represents at once an extension of group therapeutic principles and a revival of the moral treatment of Pinel. Its aim is to make the mental hospital a therapeutic community, all aspects of which will help to restore the patients' mental health. This involves the creation of a cheerful, homelike atmosphere and a full program of occupational, recreational and social activities. It also involves the development of a flexible, democratic social structure in which all members of the treatment staff work as a co-ordinated team and the patients participate responsibly, to the limits imposed by their disabilities, in all phases of hospital life. Through patient government they help make policy decisions, plan and carry out activities and may even have a voice in the handling of deviant or disturbed behaviour of individual patients.

By heightening the patients' sense of personal worth and instituting social controls of behaviour, social therapy in conjunction with drug therapies may lead to a striking decline in violent or disorganized conduct. This makes possible the reduction or even elimination of physical restraints or locked wards. Social therapy programs lead to a more flexible use of hospital facilities, in that some patients can come to the hospital only during daylight hours, others only to spend the evening and night. In many ways social therapy thus lowers the barrier between mental hospital and community, which improves the morale of hospitalized patients by combating their sense of alienation from the outside world, thereby aiding the recovery process.

Integrated treatment programs finally succeeded in bringing about a progressive decrease in state hospital populations. Though admissions continued to rise, discharges rose even more rapidly. This heartening development enhanced hopes for the increasingly successful treatment of the hospitalized insane.

See PSYCHIATRY; PSYCHOANALYSIS; PSYCHOLOGY, APPLIED: *Psychology as Applied to Treatment; see* also references under "Psychotherapy" in the Index.

BIBLIOGRAPHY.—Lewis R. Wolberg, *The Technique of Psychotherapy* (1954); Milton Greenblatt *et al., From Custodial to Therapeutic Patient Care in Mental Hospitals* (1955); S. R. Slavson (ed.), *The Fields of Group Psychotherapy* (1956); August B. Hollingshead and Frederick C. Redlich, *Social Class and Mental Illness: a Community Study* (1958); H. J. Eysenck (ed.), *Behaviour Therapy and the Neuroses* (1960); Morris I. Stein (ed.), *Contemporary Psychotherapies* (1961). (JE. D. F.)

PSZCZYNA, a town in southern Poland and district chief town of Katowice *wojewodztwo* (province), lies on the Pszczynka River, a tributary of the Vistula, 19 mi. (30 km.) WSW of Oswiecim, and is the junction of secondary railways. Pop. (1962 est.) 15,700. Many old buildings have survived, including the Piast Castle, situated in a park of 78 ha. (193 ac.) and containing a museum. One of Poland's two European bison (*zubr*) reserves, established in 1865, is in the nearby Pszczyna Forest.

A hunting lodge of the prince of Opole stood there in the early 13th century. In 1327 the village, along with the principality of Opole, was pledged to Bohemia. In 1526 the whole of Silesia passed to the Habsburgs and in 1742 to Prussia. In 1847 Graf Bolko von Hochberg bought a huge estate in the district of Pszczyna (renamed Pless) and was later made Fürst von Pless. At the partition of Upper Silesia in 1921, the whole district of Pszczyna, with an overwhelming Polish population, returned to Poland. The princely estate was greatly reduced by the Polish land reform; the remainder was nationalized in 1945.

For the Treaty of Pszczyna (Pless) in 1915 *see* BULGARIA: *History.* (K. M. WI.)

PTA: *see* PARENTS AND TEACHERS, NATIONAL CONGRESS OF.

PTAH, Egyptian god, was originally the local deity of the town of Memphis (*q.v.*), capital of Egypt in the 3rd millennium B.C.; to its political importance was due the expansion of Ptah's cult over the whole of Egypt. The Asiatic origin of Ptah suggested by some scholars is extremely doubtful and the Semitic words from which it has been allegedly derived appear in Egyptian not earlier than the 3rd century B.C. In Egyptian belief, Ptah was the creator of the universe and maker of things, therefore also a patron of craftsmen, especially sculptors; the title of his high priest was "supreme leader of craftsmen." Consequently, the Greeks identified him with their Hephaestus, the divine blacksmith. Ptah was always represented in purely human form. The connection between him and the sacred bull Apis was artificial, but Apis had his stall in the great temple of Ptah at Memphis and was called "intermediary of Ptah," that is, intermediary between men and the god.

See M. Sandman Holmberg, *The God Ptah* (1946). (J. CY.)

PTARMIGAN is the name given to four species of the genus *Lagopus* of the grouse family (Tetraonidae). The rock ptarmigan (*L. mutus*) is slightly larger than a pigeon and exhibits an almost continual change of plumage to match the seasonal change of coloration in its environment. This change has been found to be regulated by hormones under the control of seasonal increase or decrease in the hours of daylight. In spring the mottled plumage is reddish-brown except for the white breast and wings; in autumn brownish-gray; and in winter, white to match the snow. In summer the rock ptarmigan lives in the rocky tundra, feeding on berries and succulent plants. It lays from 6 to 12 eggs, buffy with brown spots, which are incubated by the female but defended by the male. In winter the feet are covered with hairlike feathers that serve as snowshoes for walking over deep snow; in this season the food is tender buds and twigs.

WHITE-TAILED PTARMIGAN (LAGOPUS LEUCURUS) IN SUMMER PLUMAGE

The white-tailed ptarmigan (*L. leucurus*), found in the mountains of Alaska, Canada and in the Rockies of the United States, is a species that has a summer plumage of mottled black and brown with blotches of white. The red grouse (*L. scoticus*) is a larger ptarmigan, confined to Ireland and Scotland, which never becomes white in winter. The circumpolar willow ptarmigan (*L. lagopus*) has a winter-white plumage, almost the only difference between it and the red grouse; indeed, most authorities consider the two forms conspecific. It is migratory and winters as far south as the Canadian provinces. In the mating season the male ptarmigan has a hoarse cry and often battles with rivals.

See also GROUSE. (W. J. BE.)

PTERIA, the ancient capital of the "White Syrians" of northern Cappadocia, in eastern Asia Minor, which Croesus of Lydia is stated by Herodotus to have taken, enslaved, and ruined (547 B.C.), after he had declared war on Persia and crossed the Halys (Kizil Irmak). Pteria, also the name of the land surrounding the capital, is mentioned only by Herodotus (i, 76) and by Stephanus Byzantinus (Pterion) among the ancients.

The identification of Pteria with the ruins near modern Bogazkoy (q.v.), once taken for granted, is still uncertain, for this site, in older times capital of the Hittite Empire, was in the 6th century B.C. of no greater importance than other fortified cities in northern Cappadocia. A position nearer to the Black Sea seems possible. (K. BL.)

PTERIDOPHYTA, in earlier botanical classifications the group of spore-bearing plants, also known as vascular cryptogams, that included the lycopods or club mosses, horsetails, ferns and various fossil groups. In more modern classifications the pteridophytes and spermatophytes (seed-bearing plants) are grouped in the phylum or division Tracheophyta. "Pteridophyte" is still used, but only as a term of convenience. *See* FERN; SPHENOPSIDA; LYCOPODIUM; PALEOBOTANY; PLANTS AND PLANT SCIENCE: *Classification of Plants.*

PTEROPSIDA. Ferns, extinct seed ferns, gymnosperms (conifers and allies), and angiosperms (flowering plants) compose this class of vascular plants (phylum Tracheophyta). It is immediately apparent that there is a broad range in the morphology of the group, differences in vegetative characteristics as well as in reproductive features. The production of unicellular spores by ferns (formed in sporangia found on the lower leaf surface of many ferns) stands in striking contrast with the production of seeds by gymnosperms and angiosperms. In older classifications the ferns were more closely aligned with club mosses and horsetails than with the ferns and seed plants. There are, however, certain basic features that indicate affinity between these seemingly unrelated plants.

The principal unifying characteristic of the Pteropsida is the type of leaf. This is the megaphyll, by definition a leaf with a branched venation system. The megaphyll is correlated with the presence of a siphonostele (vascular cylinder enclosing a pith) in the stem axis (only a few ferns and fewer aquatic angiosperms are exceptions to this generality). Also at the level of leaf attachment (the node) on the stem there is an interruption in the vascular cylinder of the stem above the place at which vascular strands diverge into the leaf. These vascular strands are termed leaf traces and the interruptions leaf gaps. In vascular plants possessing primitive microphylls (leaves with an unbranched midvein) there are no leaf gaps. It is thought that the megaphyll represents a modified branch system from an evolutionary standpoint. Developmentally, there is a close relationship between megaphyll and stem, and this fact tends to strengthen the concept of the branchlike nature of the leaf.

A point of difference between the Lycopsida (club mosses and allies) and the lower Pteropsida is in the position of the spore cases (sporangia). For example, many of the true ferns (Filicales) are characterized by large leaves with numerous sporangia on their undersides, whereas the lycopsids possess small sporophylls, each with one sporangium on the upper side. The underside position of sporangia, although prevalent in ferns, is by no means a constant diagnostic feature of the Pteropsida as a whole. In many gymnosperms the microsporangia, which produce pollen, do occur on the underside of microsporophylls of the male or staminate cone. In angiosperms the microsporangia or pollen sacs, usually four in number, are somewhat embedded in the anther of the stamen of a flower.

Megasporangia or ovules (immature seeds) show an even greater degree of variation in their position on the plant. In some cycads the ovules are attached to sporophylls that are leafy. In the ginkgo or maidenhair tree the ovules appear to be terminal on a modified branch. In many conifers the ovules occur on the upper side of the cone scales (*e.g.*, in pine, fir, spruce). In angiosperms the ovules are enclosed in an ovary in the flower. They become seeds within the mature fruit.

Ferns.—This subclass (Filicinae or Filicinidae) of the Pteropsida comprises both the living and extinct ferns. Four orders are recognized: the Coenopteridales, Ophioglossales, Marattiales, and Filicales. The sporangia of the first three orders differ from those of the Filicales in that the jacket of the sporangium is composed of several layers of cells and in that numerous spores are produced in each sporangium. The Filicales, or true ferns, are characterized by smaller sporangia specialized for spore dissemination. (*See* FERN.)

Gymnosperms.—For many years the members of this subclass (Gymnospermae or Gymnospermidae) have been referred to as "naked seed" plants because their seeds are not enclosed in an ovary as is the case in the angiosperms. Certainly their seeds are protected, if not enclosed, in some cases. Seeds in the cone of a pine tree, for example, are protected during most of their development. In the past the gymnosperms have been looked upon as a natural group, but the evidence from morphology and paleobotany indicates that the orders within the subclass are rather diverse and probably have existed as separate evolutionary lines for a long time, perhaps from their origin. However, the subclass designation Gymnospermae is maintained in conservative systems of classification. There is one reasonably natural group, the cycadophytes, which includes: the extinct seed ferns (Cycadofilicales or Pteridospermae), with seeds borne on large compound leaves; the cycads (Cycadales), with stocky, relatively unbranched trunks and leathery compound leaves with seeds borne on modified leaflike structures; and the Cycadeoidales or Bennettitales, an extinct order having certain features in common with the cycads. Both the cycads and the Cycadeoidales occurred in the Mesozoic Era, which is often referred to as the "Age of Cycads." Only representatives of the Cycadales have survived.

The remaining orders, collectively termed coniferophytes, have characteristics rather different from the cycadophytes. They are extensively branched, with simple leaves that may be scalelike. Abundant secondary vascular tissues are formed and seeds are borne on modified branch systems. The orders Cordaitales and Voltziales are extinct. *Ginkgo biloba*, the only surviving member of the Ginkgoales, is known by its bilobed or notched fan-shaped leaves. It is widely cultivated as a park and street tree in many temperate areas of the world not only for its appearance but also for its resistance to the attacks of insects and fungi (*see* GINKGO). Pines, spruces, firs, and sequoias are familiar trees of the order Coniferales, which reaches its greatest diversity in the Northern Hemisphere, particularly in western North America and eastern and central China (*see* CONIFERS). The order Gnetales is comprised of three rather diverse genera: *Ephedra*, a shrubby plant of the deserts of the world; *Gnetum*, a tropical, vinelike plant with rather large leaves and reticulate venation; and *Welwitschia*, an extremely bizarre plant growing in a desert region of southwest Africa. *Welwitschia* has a large taproot and two continuously lengthening straplike leaves that persist throughout the long life of the plant. (*See* GYMNOSPERMS.)

Angiosperms.—This subclass (Angiospermae or Angiospermidae) comprises the flowering plants, whose seeds are enclosed in an ovary. The major crop plants of the world are included here. Two main subgroups have been recognized for decades: the Dicotyledones and the Monocotyledones. Although there is no clearcut morphological separation between these subgroups, there are certain features that tend to distinguish them. The dicots have two cotyledons in the embryo, leaves with netted venation, and flower parts commonly in multiples of four or five. The monocots have one cotyledon, the major veins of the leaves generally parallel and joined at the tip of the leaf, and the flower parts in multiples of three. Each subgroup is divided into several orders and many families. (*See* ANGIOSPERMS.) *See* also PALEOBOTANY; PLANTS AND PLANT SCIENCE. (E. M. GI.)

PTEROSAUR (PTERODACTYL), terms applied to members of a group of flying reptiles that flourished in the Jurassic and Cretaceous periods, between (approximately) 150,000,000 and 70,000,000 years ago. The order Pterosauria is one component of the major reptile group of the Archosauria or "ruling reptiles," to which dinosaurs and crocodilians (*qq.v.*) also belong and from which birds are descended. Triassic archosaurs tended toward a bipedal gait, thus freeing the "arms" for use in some other fashion; both birds and pterosaurs converted them into wings. In contrast with birds, and as in bats, pterosaurs formed a wing surface by means of a membrane of skin. In bats all the fingers except the thumb support the membrane. In pterosaurs, however, the membrane was attached solely to one elongated finger—the fourth—and extended thence back along the flank to the knee; 'an accessory membrane lay between the neck and the "arm." The first three fingers were slender, clawed, clutching structures. The pterosaur membrane appears to have been well adapted to soaring and gliding, but lacking, in contrast with bat or bird wings, in maneuverability; disadvantageous, too, is the fact that, in contrast with bats, damage to the membrane at any point would affect the entire wing.

The body was compact; the hind legs were long but slender, and their structure suggests that, unlike birds, pterosaurs were little adapted to upright locomotion or perching but rather, like bats, hung suspended by the hind limbs when at rest.

The neck appears to have been held upright in flight, with the head attached to it at right angles and pointing forward. The skull was lightly but strongly built with fusion of most of the component bones; there was a long slender beak. The eyes were large, and the eyeball, as in many birds, was reinforced by a series of bony plates (sclerotic ring) lying in its walls.

Casts of the interior of the braincase show that the brain was large and apparently comparable to that of birds in pattern; as in that group, sight rather than smell appears to have been the dominant sense. Most remains of pterosaurs are found in marine sediments; it is probable that they made their livelihood by diving for fish, like terns and gulls, and it is difficult to understand how they could have risen from land or water after alighting.

Two major groups of pterosaurs are known. *Rhamphorhynchus* of the late Jurassic Solenhofen slates is typical of the more primitive division, although earlier forms are present in the Early Jurassic (Lias).

Characteristics of this group include the presence of a battery of powerful, sharply pointed teeth in the jaws, relative shortness of the bones supporting the fingers (the metacarpals), and the retention of a long tail, which in *Rhamphorhynchus* is known to have had a diamond-shaped rudder at its tip. *Rhamphorhynchus* had a wing spread of about two feet, and members of this group, confined to the Jurassic, were generally of similar size.

A second group of pterosaurs appeared in the late Jurassic and continued on into the Cretaceous. The typical Jurassic form is *Pterodactylus,* of which numerous examples are known from Solenhofen. This was a small reptile, some specimens being no larger than a sparrow. Diagnostic features include the reduction of the

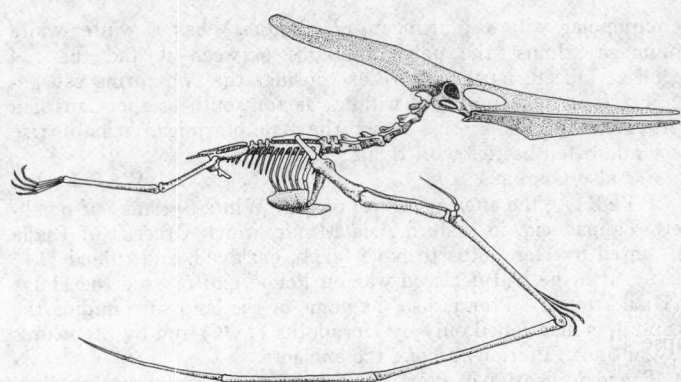

FIG. 2.—SKELETAL RESTORATION OF PTERANODON

dentition to a relatively few small teeth, elongation of the metacarpal bones, and the shortening of the tail to a mere nubbin. Descendants of the pterodactyl type continued on into the Cretaceous, and were generally of much larger size. They are best represented by *Pteranodon* of the Kansas chalk, in which the largest known specimen is estimated to have had a wing spread of 25 ft., making it by far the largest flying animal of which there is knowledge.

The skull was about four feet in length; the long jaws were toothless and presumably covered by a horny bill; a long crest extended back from the point of attachment of skull to body in weather-vane fashion. Despite its great size, the animal was very lightly built; the wing bones consist merely of a thin shell of bone surrounding a central cavity which was presumably air-filled in life.

No pterosaur remains are known beyond the end of the Cretaceous; their place in nature was taken over by their avian cousins.   (A. S. Rr.)

PTOLEMAIC SYSTEM, the name given to the explanation of the apparent motion of the sun, moon, and planets formulated by the Alexandrian astronomer and mathematician Ptolemy (*q.v.; c.* A.D. 150). Ptolemy systematized and synthesized the best of the Greek attempts to account for planetary motions in a treatise known from the title of its Arabic version as the *Almagest,* in which he also suggested hypotheses that were not only elegant but superior to previous ones. The resulting geocentric system was accepted in the Western world for over 1,300 years; *i.e.,* until supplanted by the heliocentric system of Copernicus, which was published in 1543.

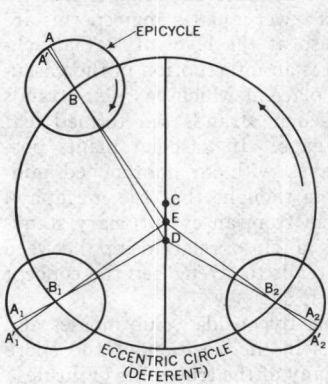

C. A. RONAN

FIG. 1.—PTOLEMY'S LUNAR THEORY

The Ptolemaic system, in which the earth was considered the centre of the universe, utilized devices called the deferent (a large circle) and the epicycle (a small circle) to account with some accuracy for the movements of the planets in terms of uniform circular motion. The motion of the sun was explained by placing it on the circumference of an epicycle, the centre of which moved uniformly around the circumference of the deferent, taking one tropical year (the period of the sun's apparent rotation from an equinox to the same equinox) to complete the circuit. The centre of the deferent coincided with the centre of the earth.

However, in order to explain the observed motion of the moon and planets, the system prescribed deferents for these bodies which were eccentrically situated with respect to the centre of the earth. The centre of the moon's deferent was assumed to lie at a certain distance to one side of the earth. The motion of the centre of the moon's epicycle was uniform with respect to a point situated on the opposite side of the earth at an equal

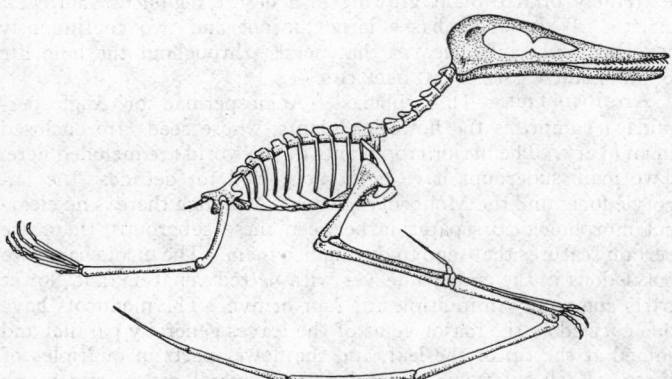

FIG. 1.—SKELETAL RESTORATION OF PTERODACTYLUS

distance from the centre of the moon's deferent. As shown in fig. 1, the moon moved along the circumference of the epicycle, the centre of which (B) moved around the circumference of the eccentric circle. The centre (C) of this eccentric circle moved in a retrograde (*i.e.*, east to west) direction about the centre of the earth (E). In order to account for the irregularities he observed, Ptolemy also proposed that the apse line EBA' (where A' was the apparent apogee) oscillated

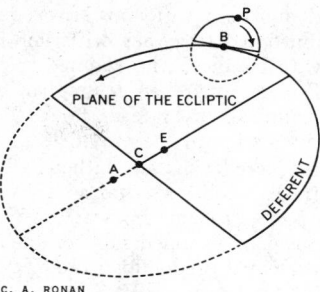

C. A. RONAN

FIG. 2.—PTOLEMY'S PLANETARY THEORY

about a mean apse line, DBA, as the moon rotated about the earth (D being a point on the diameter of the eccentric circle so that CE = ED). This oscillation is shown in positions B_1 and B_2 of the epicycle. The effect of this arrangement was to satisfy the Greek desire to explain the moon's movement by postulating uniform circular motions and, at the same time, to provide for it what was virtually an eccentric orbit with respect to the centre of the earth; it also accounted for its then-known inequalities of motion.

For all of the planets except Mercury, the point about which their uniform angular motion took place was situated on the same side of the earth as the centre of their deferent (fig. 2). This point, known as the equant (A), was so placed that the distance earth-to-centre-of-deferent was equal to the distance centre-of-deferent-to-equant. The planets (P) Mars, Jupiter, and Saturn were taken, with the centres of their epicycles, as moving about C as a centre, but with a line through A and B describing equal angles in equal times. For the planet Venus, Ptolemy found it necessary to assume (1) an oscillation of the plane of the deferent about the plane of the ecliptic and (2) an oscillation of the epicycle.

The planet Mercury presented even more problems, and Ptolemy had to assume the equant (A) to be between the earth (E) and the centre (C) of the deferent (fig. 3); C was supposed to rotate about another point which lay between the equant and the earth; *i.e.*, between A and E.

The planes of the deferents of the planets were believed to be inclined at various small angles to the plane of the ecliptic, while the planes of their epicycles were inclined by equal amounts to those of the deferents; in consequence, the epicycles always lay in planes parallel to the plane of the ecliptic.

Mercury and Venus were treated slightly differently, however. The planes of the deferents

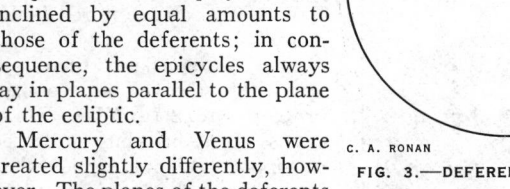

C. A. RONAN

FIG. 3.—DEFERENT OF MERCURY

of these planets were assumed to oscillate above and below the plane of the ecliptic, and likewise the planes of their epicycles were thought to oscillate with respect to the planes of the deferents.

The apparent motions of the stars were accounted for by assuming the existence of two sets of circular motions. The stars were thought of as fixed to a sphere which undertook one component of these motions, while, outside this sphere, yet another sphere was believed to exist. This latter was known as the prime mover because it provided the motive force necessary for the operation of the whole system; it also accounted for the apparent diurnal rotation of the heavens. (CN. A. R.)

PTOLEMAIS, a coastal city of ancient Cyrenaica (the modern TOLMEITA or TULMAYTHAH in Libya). Naturally attractive, with adequate seasonal rainfall and with arable land and some timber in the neighbourhood, the site was also easily defensible and provided the only safe anchorage between Euhesperides-Berenice (modern Bengasi), 66 mi. (106 km.) SSW, and Apollonia

(modern Marsa Susah), 61 mi. (98 km.) ENE. The small settlement that had existed on this site as the harbour for the city of Barce (Al Marj, 15 mi. [24 km.] inland) since the 6th century B.C. was laid out in the early 3rd century B.C. as a city about one mile square, with a gridiron-shaped street plan.

Later in the same century the city received the name Ptolemais from Ptolemy III, who united Cyrenaica with Egypt. It was enclosed with walls and towers ending in an acropolis fort on an adjacent spur of the inland plateau and had five gates. Its economy being based on trade with the interior, the city flourished in Hellenistic times, in the early period of the Roman Empire and again from late in the 3rd century A.D., when Diocletian made it the metropolis of the Roman province of Upper Libya.

From the beginning of the 5th century it suffered greatly from raids of the nomadic inland Austuriani, as recorded in the letters of its best-known historical personage, Bishop Synesius. The Byzantine emperors Arcadius, Anastasius I, and Justinian I attempted to revive it by rebuilding streets, baths, and an aqueduct, using stones of the old city wall to erect forts and blockhouses within. Some occupation continued after the Arab conquest (A.D. 642) to the 11th century. The small modern Arab town occupies the ancient harbour section.

Italian excavations (1935–42) cleared the main gate, foundations of part of the city wall, a church, a large covered reservoir, a theatre, part of a street with remains of a triumphal arch, and an imposing dwelling. American excavations (1956–58) disclosed a villa of the Roman period, a public building, and city baths, all apparently rebuilt in the 5th century A.D.

Other remains, visible but unexcavated, include further large reservoirs, a theatre, a temple, a hippodrome, an amphitheatre, fortresses, and blockhouses. Sculptures, geometric mosaics, remains of wall paintings, inscriptions, and coins were found. *See* also CYRENAICA.

See G. Caputo, "La Protezione dei monumenti di Tolemaide negli anni 1935–42," *Quaderni di archeologia della Libia,* vol. iii (1954); and the report on the American excavations in the series *Oriental Institute Publications.* (C. H. KR.)

PTOLEMIES, a dynasty of Macedonian kings who ruled in Egypt from 323 to 30 B.C.

THE PTOLEMAIC RULERS

PTOLEMY (Greek PTOLEMAIOS) I SOTER (367–283; ruled 323–285), the founder, son of Lagos, a Macedonian nobleman, was one of Alexander the Great's most trusted generals. He played a principal part in Alexander's later campaigns in Asia. Upon Alexander's death he was appointed, in the resettlement of the empire at Babylon, satrap of Egypt (323). He took a firm grip on the province (see EGYPT: *History: Macedonian and Ptolemaic Period*) and subjugated the neighbouring country of Cyrenaica. He contrived to get possession of Alexander's body on its way to burial and placed it temporarily in Memphis. This bold act, which greatly enhanced Ptolemy's prestige in the eyes of the world, led to an open conflict with the regent Perdiccas, who perished in the attempt to invade Egypt (321).

In the long wars between the different Macedonian chiefs which followed (see HELLENISTIC AGE: *Outline of Political History: Struggles of Alexander's Successors, 323–280 B.C.*), Ptolemy's first object was to hold his position in Egypt securely; his second was to possess Cyrenaica, Cyprus, Palestine, and Coele-Syria (Lebanon). In 316 he joined Cassander and Lysimachus in the coalition against Antigonus Monophthalmus (*q.v.*), whose son Demetrius he defeated in the great Battle of Gaza (312). Ptolemy's occupation of Palestine after this victory was, as on earlier occasions, a very short one. After concluding peace with Antigonus in 311 he resumed hostilities in 309 by launching seaborne raids upon the coasts of Lycia and Caria, and in the next year he carried the war across the Aegean to the mainland of Greece, where he seized Corinth, Sicyon, and Megara. By intervening in Greece Ptolemy was encroaching upon territory disputed between Cassander (*q.v.*) and Antigonus. However, he soon afterward abandoned this adventure. In 306 a great fleet under Demetrius attacked Cyprus, which Ptolemy had held since c. 313, and Ptolemy's brother Menelaus was defeated and captured in the decisive Battle of Salamis. Antigonus and Demetrius thereupon assumed the title of kings; Ptolemy, as well as Cassander, Lysimachus, and Seleucus (*q.q.v.*), answered this challenge by doing the same (some scholars believe he did not do so until 305).

In the winter of 306–305, Ptolemy successfully resisted Antigonus' attempt to invade Egypt. The Rhodians, whom he aided in 305–304 when they were besieged by Demetrius, bestowed upon

PTOLEMY I. PORTRAIT ON SILVER TETRADRACHM

him the honorific surname *Soter* ("saviour") by which he was commonly known afterward. When the coalition against Antigonus was renewed in 302, Ptolemy invaded Palestine but evacuated it on hearing a false report that Antigonus had defeated Lysimachus in Asia Minor. When the news of Antigonus' defeat and death at Ipsus (*q.v.*) became known, he reoccupied the country. The other members of the coalition had assigned Palestine and Coele-Syria to Seleucus after what they regarded as Ptolemy's desertion, and for the next hundred years the question of the ownership of these countries became the standing ground of enmity between the Seleucid and Ptolemaic dynasties.

In 285 Ptolemy abdicated in favour of one of his younger sons by Berenice (*q.v.*), Ptolemy II Philadelphus (*see below*). His eldest (legitimate) son, PTOLEMY CERAUNUS—whose mother, Eurydice, daughter of Antipater (*q.v.*), had been repudiated—fled to the court of Lysimachus, later became king of Macedonia after murdering Seleucus I (280), and perished in the Gallic invasion of 279.

Two years after his abdication Ptolemy died (283). Shrewd and cautious, he had a compact and well-ordered realm to bequeath to his heir. He was a ready patron of letters, and the great library at Alexandria owed its inception to him. He himself wrote a history of Alexander's campaigns, distinguished by its straightforward honesty and sobriety, which, now lost, can be largely reconstructed through the extensive use made of it later by the historian Arrian.

PTOLEMY II PHILADELPHUS (b. 308; king 285–246) became involved soon after his accession in wars with the Seleucid king Antiochus I (280–279 and *c.* 276–272). These wars left Egypt the dominant naval power of the eastern Mediterranean with many new possessions (*see below*). A third war with the Seleucid kingdom (involving also war between Egypt and Macedonia) was less successful, but Ptolemy scored a diplomatic success by persuading Antiochus II to make peace and marry (*c.* 252) his daughter Berenice (*q.v.*). Ptolemy's first wife, Arsinoe I (*q.v.*), daughter of Lysimachus, was the mother of his legitimate children. After her repudiation he married his full sister Arsinoe II (*q.v.*), the widow of Lysimachus. He deified his parents as the "saviour gods," and he and his sister-wife were themselves deified as *theoi adelphoi* ("brother gods") before Arsinoe's death (270). The surname Philadelphus ("brother-loving") was used in later years to distinguish Ptolemy II himself, but properly it belongs to Arsinoe alone, not to the king.

The material and literary splendour of the Alexandrian court was at its height under Ptolemy II, as was the general power of the Ptolemaic Empire. Callimachus (*q.v.*), made keeper of the library, Theocritus, and a host of lesser poets glorified the Ptolemaic family. Ptolemy himself was eager to increase the library and aid scientific research. He was the patron equally of Greek and Egyptian religion. State control of Egypt's economy in its fully developed form dates from his reign. In a decree of 258 he forbade the use of foreign money within his kingdom.

PTOLEMY III EUERGETES I (king 246–221), son of Philadelphus and Arsinoe I, reunited Cyrenaica to Egypt at the beginning of his reign (it had been independent since *c.* 258; *see* BERENICE). At the same time he was obliged to open war on the Seleucid king-

dom, where Antiochus II was dead and his sister Berenice had been murdered, together with her infant son, by Antiochus' former wife Laodice, who claimed the kingdom for her son Seleucus II. Ptolemy marched triumphantly into the heart of the Seleucid realm, at any rate as far as Babylonia, and received the formal submission of the provinces of Iran, while his fleets in the Aegean recovered what his father had lost upon the seaboard and made fresh conquests as far as Thrace. This moment marks the zenith of the Ptolemaic power. After Ptolemy returned home, indeed, Seleucus regained northern Syria and the eastern provinces, but the naval predominance of Egypt in the Aegean remained. After his final peace with Seleucus (241), Ptolemy carried on complicated diplomatic intrigues in Greece with the object of disturbing Macedonian power in the country. Egyptian subsidies were given in turn to the Achaean League, Sparta, and Aetolia, but direct intervention was not undertaken.

PTOLEMY IV PHILOPATOR (b. *c.* 238; king 221–*c.* 205), son of Euergetes and Berenice of Cyrene, was a wretched debauchee under whom the decline of the Ptolemaic kingdom began. His reign was inaugurated by the murder of his mother, and he was always under the dominion of favourites, male and female, who indulged his vices and conducted the government as they pleased. Self-interest led his ministers to make serious preparations to meet the attacks of the Seleucid king Antiochus III on Palestine, and the great Egyptian victory of Raphia (217), at which Ptolemy himself was present, secured the province till the next reign. The arming of Egyptians in this campaign had a disturbing effect upon the native population of Egypt, so that rebellions were continuous for the next 30 years.

PTOLEMY V EPIPHANES (b. *c.* 210; king *c.* 205–181), son of Philopator and his sister Arsinoe III, was not more than five years old when he came to the throne, and under a series of regents the kingdom was paralyzed. Antiochus III and Philip V of Macedonia made a compact to divide the Ptolemaic possessions overseas. Philip seized several islands and places in Caria and Thrace, while the Battle of Panium (*c.* 200) definitely transferred Palestine from the Ptolemies to the Seleucids. Antiochus after this concluded peace, giving his own daughter Cleopatra to Epiphanes in marriage (193). Nevertheless, when war broke out between Antiochus and Rome, Egypt ranged itself with the latter power. Epiphanes in manhood was chiefly remarkable as a passionate sportsman; he excelled in athletic exercises and the chase.

PTOLEMY VI PHILOMETOR (king 181–145), the elder of Epiphanes' two sons, succeeded as an infant under the regency of his mother, Cleopatra. Her death was followed by a rupture between the Ptolemaic and Seleucid courts, on the old question of

Palestine. Antiochus IV invaded Egypt (170) and captured Philometor.

The Alexandrians then put upon the throne his younger brother PTOLEMY VIII EUERGETES II. Antiochus professed to support Philometor, but when he withdrew the brothers agreed to be joint kings with their sister Cleopatra II as queen and wife of Philometor. Antiochus again invaded Egypt (168) but was compelled by Roman intervention to retire. The double kingship led to quarrels between the two brothers in which fresh appeals

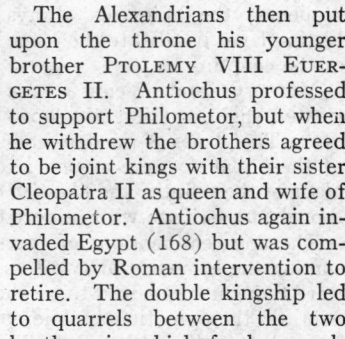

PTOLEMY VI. PORTRAIT ON SILVER TETRADRACHM

were continually made to Rome. In 163 Cyrenaica was assigned under Roman arbitration to Euergetes as a separate kingdom. As he coveted Cyprus as well, the feud still went on, Rome continuing to interfere diplomatically but not effectively. In 154 Euergetes invaded Cyprus but was defeated and captured by Philometor. His brother, however, was willing to pardon him and he was allowed to return as king to Cyrene. In 152 Philometor joined the coalition against the Seleucid king Demetrius I and was the main agent in his destruction. The protege of the coalition, Alexander

Balas (q.v.), married Philometor's daughter Cleopatra Thea and reigned in Syria in virtual subservience to him. But in 147 Philometor broke with him and transferred his support, together with the person of Cleopatra, to Demetrius II, the young son of Demetrius I. He himself at Antioch was entreated by the people to assume the Seleucid diadem, but he declined and installed Demetrius as king. In 145 in a battle near Antioch, in which Alexander Balas was finally defeated, Philometor received a mortal wound. He was perhaps the best of the Ptolemies. Kindly and reasonable, he possessed a good nature that seems sometimes to have verged on indolence, but he took personal part, and that bravely and successfully, in war.

PTOLEMY VII PHILOPATOR NEOS, Philometor's infant son, was proclaimed king in Alexandria under the regency of his mother, Cleopatra II (145). Euergetes, however, swooping from Cyrene, seized the throne and married Cleopatra, making away with his nephew. He soon found a more agreeable wife than Cleopatra in her daughter Cleopatra III, and thenceforth there was chronic antagonism between the two queens, the "sister" and the "wife." In the ancient historians Euergetes (nicknamed *Physcon* because of his corpulence) is portrayed as a cruel and evil tyrant. Massacres inflicted upon the Alexandrians and the expulsion of the representatives of Hellenic culture are laid to his charge. But monuments and papyri show him a liberal patron of the native religion and a considerable administrator, reforming in a series of decrees abuses and weaknesses in the internal government. In fact, while hated by the Greeks, he seems to have had the steady support of the native population. But there are also records which show him, not as an enemy, but, like his ancestors, as a friend to Greek culture.

The old Ptolemaic realm was never again a unity after the death of Euergetes II (116). By his will he left Cyrenaica as a separate kingdom to his illegitimate son PTOLEMY APION (d. 96), while Egypt and Cyprus were bequeathed to Cleopatra III and whichever of his two sons by her, PTOLEMY IX SOTER II (nicknamed *Lathyrus*) and PTOLEMY X ALEXANDER I, she might choose as her associate. The result was, of course, a long period of domestic strife. From 116 to 108 Soter reigned with his mother, and at enmity with her, in Egypt, while her favourite son, Alexander, ruled Cyprus. In 108 Cleopatra called Alexander to Egypt, and Soter, fleeing, took his brother's place on Cyprus and held his own against his mother's forces. Cleopatra died in 101 and from then till 89 Alexander reigned alone in Egypt. In 89 he was expelled by a popular uprising and perished in a sea fight in the following year. Soter was recalled (88) and reigned over Egypt and Cyprus, now reunited. This, his second reign in Egypt (88–80), was marked by a native rebellion which resulted in the destruction of Thebes (85).

PTOLEMY XI ALEXANDER II, son of Alexander I, was killed in 80 by the Alexandrians after a reign of only 20 days. Ptolemy Apion meanwhile, dying in 96, had bequeathed Cyrenaica to Rome.

In Egypt the son of Soter II, PTOLEMY XII PHILOPATOR PHILADELPHUS NEOS DIONYSUS, nicknamed *Auletes* ("flute-player"), became king (80), while his brother PTOLEMY became king of Cyprus until the Roman annexation of the island, when he committed suicide (58). Auletes' position was precarious, for it was claimed in Rome that Alexander II had bequeathed his kingdom to the Roman people. From 58 to 55 Auletes was in exile, driven out by popular hatred. He worked by bribery and murder in Rome to get himself restored. Meanwhile his daughter Berenice (q.v.) ruled in Alexandria. In 55 Auletes was restored by the proconsul of Syria, Aulus Gabinius. He killed Berenice and, dying in 51, bequeathed his kingdom to his eldest son, aged ten years, who was to take as wife his sister Cleopatra VII, aged seventeen.

In the reign of PTOLEMY XIII PHILOPATOR (51–47) and CLEOPATRA VII PHILOPATOR (51–30), Egyptian history coalesces with the general history of the Roman world, owing to the murder of Pompey off Pelusium in 48 and the Alexandrine War of Julius Caesar (48–47). In that war the young king perished and a still younger brother, PTOLEMY XIV PHILOPATOR, was associated as ruler with Cleopatra till 44, when he died, probably by Cleopatra's contriving. From then till her death, her son PTOLEMY XV PHILOPATOR PHILOMETOR CAESAR (who according to her assertion was the child of Julius Caesar) was associated in her rule; he was known popularly as *Caesarion* ("little Caesar"). (For the incidents of Cleopatra's reign see CLEOPATRA; ARSINOE.) After her death in 30 and Caesarion's murder, Egypt was made a Roman province by Octavian (see AUGUSTUS). Cleopatra's daughter by Antony, Cleopatra Selene, was married in 25 to Juba II of Mauretania. Their son, PTOLEMY, who succeeded his father (c. A.D. 24–40), left no issue on his execution by the emperor Caligula (Gaius).

INSTITUTIONS AND ADMINISTRATION OF THE PTOLEMAIC KINGDOM

The Ptolemaic kingdom consisted of Egypt and foreign possessions which varied considerably at different times. The Ptolemaic occupation of Egypt reached, at its limit, to a point south of the Second Cataract of the Nile, while Ptolemaic generals and explorers penetrated as far south along the coast as Somaliland. Several posts established on the western shore of the Red Sea brought Egypt into commercial relationship with Arabia and India, and from the region of Ethiopia elephants were obtained by the early Ptolemies. To the west of Egypt, Cyrenaica constituted part of the kingdom until 96. Cyprus was the principal overseas possession and the last to be relinquished, in 58. Palestine and Coele-Syria were occupied, with brief intervals, till 200. Many of the Aegean Islands were occupied for long periods in the 3rd century, as were cities on the Hellespont and in Thrace. Most of the coastal districts in western Cilicia, Pamphylia, Lycia, Caria, and Ionia were under Ptolemaic control at times during the 3rd century (though always threatened with reoccupation by the Seleucid kings). This overseas empire was the fruit of the domination of the seas by the Egyptian fleet, and with the decline of Egyptian sea power the greater part of these possessions was lost before the end of the 3rd century. Only isolated fragments were retained into the 2nd century, such as Thera, Itanos on Crete, and Methana in the Argolid.

Administration.—The Ptolemaic kingdom was an absolute monarchy of the same general kind as other Hellenistic kingdoms such as the Attalid and Seleucid (see ATTALID DYNASTY; HELLENISTIC AGE; SELEUCID DYNASTY). To the native Egyptians the Ptolemies presented themselves as the legitimate successors of the ancient pharaohs and exercised over them the type of autocratic government traditional in the land. Their Macedonian and Greek subjects, in theory at least, merely acknowledged the king's leadership from free choice. However, the setting up under Ptolemy II of a cult of the living ruler gave the king a claim to universal allegiance. In the court and the army the traditional Macedonian forms were preserved. The other state institutions resembled to a certain degree the usual Hellenistic pattern, but there were features unparalleled elsewhere. Of the royal ministers only one is known with any certainty—the *dioiketes,* specifically the manager of the king's household, which embraced the whole kingdom, for all land outside the Greek cities was treated as forming the royal domain. The competence of this official in both finance and general administration was very wide, if one may judge by the career of Apollonius under Ptolemy II. The titles of a few other departmental officers are known, but almost nothing is known of their functions or comparative importance. On the other hand, the working of the administrative machine in the rural districts of Egypt is well illustrated in the papyrus documents discovered since the end of the 19th century, and from these it has become clear that the system of government was a highly centralized one in which the king and his ministers kept control over every part of the realm.

The administrative division of Egypt was by cantons (*nomoi*) subdivided into districts (*topoi*), each of which comprised so many villages (*komai*). The nomarchs or civil governors of the cantons (about 40 in number) were at first Egyptians, but their authority soon lapsed and their place in the administrative chain was taken by Greek officials with the title of "general" (strategos). The latter had at first a purely military function, but before the end of the 2nd century they had exchanged their original duties for the work of civil administration. They were assisted by finance officers (*oikonomoi*) appointed by the *dioiketes*. Below the nomarchs and generals, there were the native officials of the smaller territorial units—the toparchs and comarchs. All these officials were assisted by secretaries and scribes who through their intimate connection with the control and regulation of taxation and levies played a very influential part in the administration. Thus, for example, the village scribe easily surpassed in importance his nominal superior, the comarch. Government of the foreign territories was regularly by generals or city governors (*epistatai*) assisted by *oikonomoi*.

Economic System.—The chief object of policy in Egypt (and, so far as is known, elsewhere) was to bring about the most effective possible exploitation of the country's resources for the benefit of the king. This was realized by a rigorous implementation of central directives in the villages, which were treated as the basic units of the economy. The peasants, who were compelled by law to remain in their home village, were assigned portions of the royal land to cultivate on lease, seed-grain being provided by the king. As rent they paid to the king's agents the major part of the annual harvest. The threshed grain was then transported by stages to the king's barns in Alexandria whence large quantities were released for export at such times as the market price was favourable for that purpose. Within Egypt the king could use his stores of grain to make payments in kind.

This grain monopoly was the most important feature of the Ptolemaic economic system and the chief source of the king's wealth. As regards other commodities and trades, the royal monopoly was complete in the case of oil (vegetable extract) and partial (in varying degrees) in other cases, such as papyrus, textiles, salt, glass, mining, quarrying, banking, and the rearing of livestock. The object of the monopolies, which affected virtually every form of business, was to fix prices for the benefit of the royal treasury by eliminating or restricting private competition.

Numerous miscellaneous taxes, duties, and imposts (over 200 are known) were also part of the system. In order that the kingdom's resources might be accurately assessed and an appropriate basis determined for taxation, full and continuous records were maintained by the king's officials. The revenue raised by these means was very great, with the result that the kings accumulated a huge treasure, which was still large even after the dynasty's final collapse at the end of a long period of weak government. Moreover, expenditure was heavy. The upkeep of army and fleet, the salaries of the large civil service, the gifts to favourites, the maintenance of religious cults, and many other things had to be provided for. There was also the burden of essential public works, including the repair and improvement of the innumerable irrigation channels along the course of the Nile. This particular work was done by peasants' forced labour.

Hellenization.—The Ptolemies sought to appear as the guardians and upholders of Greek civilization. This policy was carried out for the purpose of increasing their prestige and influence in international affairs and in particular to encourage the entry into Egypt of Greek immigrants. The latter were urgently needed, for the kings at first were not prepared to entrust senior positions in the administration to Egyptians, and as for the army, they believed that it could not be effective unless it contained a large proportion of Greek soldiers. Accordingly they attracted Greek settlers by granting them allotments of land on favourable terms. These allotments were hereditary in return for the settlers' obligation to render military service when required by the king. These settlers (cleruchs) were the counterpart of the military colonists in the Seleucid kingdom. In time of war they filled the ranks of the phalanx, the traditional Macedonian formation of heavy infantry.

To supplement these regular troops the Ptolemies employed mercenary soldiers of various nationalities, willingly paying them at generous rates. The native Egyptians were little used for military purposes until the Battle of Raphia (217), when a critical situation and the lack of sufficient Greek manpower made their employment unavoidable. Thereafter Egyptians were gradually admitted to posts in the administration, and the kings, from neces-

sity, began to make other concessions to their Egyptian subjects. In spite of these changes, the Ptolemies still regarded the small Greek minority as their chief support and continued to foster its interests, even though by the 2nd century Greek immigration had virtually ceased.

Ptolemy I had moved the capital from Memphis to the new coastal city of Alexandria (*q.v.*), one of Alexander the Great's foundations. Under the Ptolemies Alexandria became an international centre of the highest importance. It was only partially Greek in population, and while the Greek citizens enjoyed a privileged status among its inhabitants, they possessed only a limited degree of autonomy. In contrast to the colonizing activity of their rivals, the Seleucid kings, the Ptolemies founded hardly any Greek cities. In Egypt itself there was only one—Ptolemais, near Thebes, in the upper part of the country. The motive for this foundation was doubtless strategic. Ptolemais was a comparatively unimportant place, but it is worth noticing that, unlike Alexandria, it enjoyed the full self-government of the normal type of Greek city. Toward the Greek cities of their overseas possessions the Ptolemies acted in a high-handed fashion; everywhere they installed garrisons, imposed heavy taxes, and disregarded the cities' autonomy. Only the more important Greek cities of Europe and Asia Minor were conceded, as a matter of policy, the status of independent allies.

The Ptolemies manifested their pro-Hellenism principally by a bountiful but carefully controlled patronage of scholars and artists in Alexandria and by following the practice, common among Hellenistic rulers, of endowing new shrines and religious festivals and acting as benefactors of the ancient sanctuaries.

BIBLIOGRAPHY.—A. Bouché-Leclercq, *Histoire des Lagides,* 4 vol. (1903–07); E. R. Bevan, *A History of Egypt Under the Ptolemaic Dynasty* (1927); C. B. Welles, *Royal Correspondence in the Hellenistic Period* (1934); C. Préaux, *L'Économie royale des Lagides* (1939); M. Rostovtzeff, *The Social and Economic History of the Hellenistic World,* 3 vol. (1941); W. W. Tarn and G. T. Griffith, *Hellenistic Civilisation,* 3rd rev. ed., ch. 5 (1961). (R. H. Si.)

PTOLEMY (CLAUDIUS PTOLEMAEUS) (fl. 2nd century A.D.), celebrated astronomer, geographer and mathematician. Virtually nothing is known of his life, but according to Theodorus Meliteniota of Byzantium Ptolemy was born in the Grecian city Ptolemais Hermii. The period during which he flourished is known from the dates of certain astronomical observations which he made. His main work was carried out at Alexandria and while he certainly observed between A.D. 127 and 145, it may well be that he was still at work as late as 151. Arabian traditions claim that Ptolemy died at the age of 78.

Astronomical Work.—Ptolemy's astronomical work, which exerted so profound an influence on subsequent generations and, indeed, for more than 1,200 years after it was completed, was enshrined in his great book *The Mathematical Collection (He Mathematike Syntaxis)*. This became known, in due course, as *The Great Astronomer (Ho megas astronomas)*, to distinguish it from a collection of works of Autolycus, Euclid, Aristarchus, Theodosius, Hypsicles and Menelaus which was known as *The Little Astronomer*. The Arabian astronomers of the 9th century referred to his work by the superlative *Megiste* and from this term, with the definite article *al* prefixed, its title became known as the *Almagest,* the name which is still in use today.

The *Almagest* is divided into 13 books. Book i gives, in broad outline, the geocentric system together with arguments in its favour. Book ii contains a table of chords and what is the equivalent of spherical trigonometry with the theorem of Menelaus (fl. *c.* A.D. 90) as its basis; sample problems are also worked out. Book iii deals with the motion of the sun and the length of the year. Book iv is concerned with the moon's motion and the length of the month and book v deals with the same subjects, as well as discussing the distances of the sun and moon and giving details for the construction of an astrolabe. Eclipses of the sun and moon are dealt with in book vi, as also are planetary conjunctions and oppositions. The next two books, vii and viii, concern the fixed stars, contain a discussion of precession, Ptolemy's star catalogue and a method for constructing a celestial globe. The remaining five books are devoted to the planets and are, in fact, the most original part of the work.

It was, no doubt, the encyclopaedic nature of the work that rendered the *Almagest* so useful to those who followed and gave the views contained in it so profound an influence. In essence, it is a synthesis of the results attained by Greek astronomy and is, of course, our one source of knowledge of the work and hypotheses of Hipparchus (*q.v.*); indeed, it is often difficult to determine which results are due to Ptolemy himself and which to Hipparchus. It is, however, incorrect to assume that Ptolemy himself carried out but few observations, for he extended some of the work of Hipparchus and appears to have used somewhat similar instruments—a type of mural quadrant for determining the altitude of the sun, an armillary sphere (in which the circles were set parallel to their counterparts in the sky and from which, utilizing open sights, celestial latitude and longitude could be read off) and an instrument known as "Ptolemy's rules" which was designed for measuring the altitude of heavenly bodies.

While Hipparchus had carried out much work on the stars and had completed the first star catalogue, Ptolemy extended this work. The catalogue of Hipparchus contains 850 stars and that of Ptolemy lists 1,022. However, Ptolemy used the observations of Hipparchus and, in order to bring them up to date with his own, had to make a correction for precession; unfortunately, he erred in the annual value which he adopted for this correction. Hipparchus had discovered precession and determined the value as 45″ or 46″ per year, but Ptolemy obtained a value of 36″ which is, of course, far too small (present determinations give 50.26″).

On the motions of the sun, moon and planets, Ptolemy followed Hipparchus and took a thoroughgoing geocentric viewpoint, and it was this approach which became dogmatically asserted in western Christendom until, by the 15th century, further detailed observations had made the Ptolemaic system so complex that the validity of such a view became seriously questioned. As is well known, it was Copernicus who took the bold step of proposing a heliocentric system.

Ptolemy considered the earth to be the centre of the universe, and in the *Almagest* he gives various arguments to prove that it must be immovable. Not least, he showed that if the earth moved, as some earlier philosophers had suggested, then certain phenomena should in consequence be observed, and he was able to show that no such observations had ever been obtained.

He accepted the order: earth (centre), moon, Mercury, Venus, sun, Mars, Jupiter and Saturn. He realized, as Hipparchus had done, that the inequalities observed in the motions of these heavenly bodies necessitated a system of deferents and epicycles in order to keep uniform circular motion as the basis. Yet, even so, the observed phenomena could not be fully taken into account. It was here that Ptolemy showed a brilliant ingenuity by introducing the concept of the equant. He supposed that the earth lay a little way from the centre of the deferents for each planet and that the centre of the planet's epicycle described uniform circular motion around the equant which he placed on the diameter of the deferent but at the opposite side of the centre to the earth and at a distance equal to that by which the earth was displaced on the other. He was thus better able to account for the observed planetary phenomena.

Ptolemy also improved substantially the lunar theory of Hipparchus by varying the distance of the centre of the moon's epicycle from the earth. The motion, as with the planetary equant, was uniform, but while the centre of the moon's epicycle rotated around an equant, the position of the latter was on the opposite side of the earth to the centre of the deferent. With this mathematical device he more precisely accounted for the moon's motion and discovered the inequality of the lunar motion known as evection, an inequality which is due to the rotation of the apse line. He then prepared tables of the moon's motion, and these were in use down to the time of Copernicus, 1,400 years later. His value for the evection was close to that accepted today, and although his new theory of lunar motion did not fully account for the observations, Ptolemy made every effort to perfect it. He did not, however, discover any further inequality in the moon's motion, and it was not until the work of Tycho Brahe in the 16th century

that any further development of this kind was made.

Ptolemy realized that the planets were much closer to the earth than the fixed stars, and he seems to have believed in the physical existence of the crystalline spheres to which the heavenly bodies were supposed to be attached. Outside the sphere of the fixed stars, Ptolemy proposed other spheres ending with the *primum mobile* or prime mover, the latter providing the motive power for the remaining spheres which constituted his conception of the universe.

Ptolemy's text was translated into Arabic for the caliph al-Ma'mun in 827, and other Arabic translations followed. The *Almagest* was also the subject of many commentaries. One in Greek and written by Pappus in the 4th century A.D. is still in existence; a commentary by Theon of Alexandria (fl. 4th century A.D.) was published in Basel in 1538 and in the same year the first edition of the Greek text was also published there. The Greek text which has now superseded all others is that edited by J. L. Heiberg, published between 1899 and 1907.

Mathematics.—The mathematical work of Ptolemy was important and he was a geometrician of the first order. He proposed a new proof in place of that of Euclid on parallel lines; he showed in "Ptolemy's theorem" (which concerns a quadrilateral inscribed in a circle) how the formulas $\sin(A \pm B)$, $\cos(A \pm B)$ could be derived and how, with this and a few other simple geometrical theorems, a table of chords could be drawn up. Although it appears that the main theorem was actually due to Hipparchus, Ptolemy deals with the whole matter with a conciseness and elegance which it would be hard to surpass, and was able to calculate a table of chords in increments as small as $\frac{1}{2}°$.

In a work entitled *Analemma*, Ptolemy discussed the details of the orthogonal projection of points on the celestial sphere onto three planes which are mutually at right angles—the horizon, the meridian and the prime vertical. The full Greek text has not survived, but there is a Latin translation made by William of Moerbeke (13th century) from an Arabic original. The *Planisphaerium*, which survives only in a Latin translation from Arabic, is concerned with stereographic projection, and here Ptolemy used the south pole as his centre of projection.

He also prepared a calendar (*Phaseis aplanon asteron*) giving the risings and settings of the stars in morning and evening twilight together with weather indications, and a work in two books entitled *Planetary Hypothesis* (*Hypothesis ton planomenon*) still exists, the first book in Greek but the second in an Arabic translation only.

Early commentators mention two separate geometrical works. One, *On dimension* (*Peri diastaseos*), is concerned with proving that there cannot be more than three dimensions of space; the other contains Ptolemy's alternative proof for Euclid's parallel line postulate. Ptolemy has also been credited by Simplicius (*c.* 6th century) with a mechanical work, *On Balancings* (*Peru ropon*), while Suidas (*c.* 10th century) claims that he wrote three books on mechanics.

The *Optics*, which contains Ptolemy's work on optical phenomena, does not exist in the original Greek but only in a Latin translation made from a 12th-century Arabic copy. It appears that the original was in five books, in the last of which Ptolemy deals with a theory of refraction and discusses the refraction suffered by celestial bodies at various altitudes; this is the first recorded attempt at a solution of this observational problem.

He also wrote a treatise in three books on music. This is known as the *Harmonica* and was edited by John Wallis and published in Latin and Greek in 1682.

Geographical Work.—Ptolemy's reputation as a geographer is mainly due to his *Guide to Geography* (*Geographike Huphegesis*), which, like the *Almagest*, exerted a great influence on future generations. Again, this was due to his scientific approach to his subject and the consequent ease of reference which the book possessed. An eight-book manuscript version was prepared in 1400 and was translated into Latin nine years later. Numerous editions were published in Europe in the 200 years which followed, and the Greek text appeared at Basel in 1533, edited by Erasmus. All these early editions are full of textual errors.

Hipparchus, three centuries earlier, had already pointed out that a map with any pretensions to accuracy could only be prepared by knowing the longitude and latitude of the principal points on its surface. At the time Hipparchus made his suggestions, little information was available and he seems to have contented himself with his method of dividing the then known world into zones, or *klimata* as he termed them. However, Marinus of Tyre (2nd century A.D.), who lived a little before Ptolemy and to whose work Ptolemy refers in his *Guide,* used determinations of position based on itineraries of travelers and other rough methods. In his treatise, which is lost, Marinus discussed the determinations of the authorities he used, but it is not possible now to assess the scientific value of the results he obtained. Ptolemy considered them in general to be satisfactory and used them as a basis for his own work on the Mediterranean countries, although he showed more reserve in accepting them for remoter regions.

Ptolemy's astronomical work and his studies of map projections made him especially fitted for the kind of geographical work he undertook, but his general views were not unlike those of Eratosthenes and Strabo (*qq.v.*). He continued the method, which Hipparchus had originated, of dividing the equator into 360 parts (degrees) and supposing other great circles (meridians) to be drawn through this. His framework consisted also of parallels of latitude. Although Eratosthenes in the 3rd century B.C. had measured the circumference of the earth and had given a value very close to that accepted today, Ptolemy used the later determination of Poseidonius (*c.* 135–50 B.C.) which was nearly 30% smaller, and so his conclusions as to distances were incorrect by this amount. Moreover, as he plotted the positions of many places purely by using measures of distance, many of his values of latitude and longitude were also incorrect. As prime meridian Ptolemy followed Marinus, taking the great circle through what was supposed to be the most western point of Europe, the Isles of the Blest (the Fortunate Islands; corresponding approximately to the Canaries and the Madeira group). He placed the equator too far north and his principal parallel was correct only at Rhodes. In addition, it should be noted that there are some contradictions between the text and the maps in the *Guide.*

In spite of all these faults, Ptolemy's monumental work exerted a great influence. His idea that Asia extended much farther east than is the case strengthened the belief of Columbus that Asia could be reached by traveling westward, and Ptolemy's suggestion that the Indian ocean was bounded by a southern continent was not disproved until the voyages of Captain Cook in 1773. Some of these ideas were probably derived by Ptolemy from Hipparchus.

The *Guide* was divided into seven books. Book i begins with general explanations and there follow corrections made from astronomical observations of some of the results obtained by Marinus. The question of maps and their construction is next discussed, beginning with a conical projection in which the meridians are represented as straight lines all meeting at a certain point (a kind of north pole) and the parallels of latitude (especially that through Rhodes) as circles with the "north" point as centre. Then follows a more elaborate projection, with meridians as actual arcs of a circle. Books ii to vii contain a list of places tabulated according to longitude and latitude. Ptolemy deals here with Europe and the Mediterranean, then Africa, Asia, Palestine, Mesopotamia, Arabia, India, etc. The work is accompanied by maps (usually referred to as book viii).

As a whole, Ptolemy's geographical work cannot be considered "good geography." No mention is made of climate, natural products, inhabitants or peculiar features of the countries with which he deals. Moreover, although Strabo, for example, was well aware of the geographical importance of rivers and mountain ranges, Ptolemy's treatment of these factors is careless and of little real use. However, it is the profound influence which the *Guide* exerted on later generations which makes this work so important from a historical point of view.

See also references under "Ptolemy (Claudius Ptolemaus)" in the Index.

BIBLIOGRAPHY.—Works of Ptolemy ed. by J. L. Heiberg (1898–1907); German trans. of *Almagest* published in *Des Claudius Ptolemaiis Handbuch der Astronomie* (1912–13) by C. Manitius. A photographic reproduction of a manuscript of the *Guide* was published by V. Langlois (1867). A 2-vol. ed. by C. T. Fischer and C. Müller was published between 1883 and 1901. Ptolemy's *Catalogue of Stars,* ed. by F. Baily, was published as a memoir of the Royal Astronomical Society (vol. 13) in 1843, and by E. B. Knobel and C. H. F. Peters in 1915.
(CN. A. R.)

PTOMAINE POISONING: *see* FOOD POISONING, BACTERIOLOGICAL.

PUBLIC ADDRESS SYSTEMS: *see* BROADCASTING: *Broadcasting as a Business.*

PUBLIC ADMINISTRATION

is the application of a policy of a state through its government. Once policy is given general legal formulation in statute law, there then remains the task of defining that law and applying it to specific situations. A statute is the product of a law-making agency that is not always in session and whose members are usually selected to represent general attitudes and opinions rather than to possess expert knowledge. Such legislators may adopt a statute to facilitate traffic and may authorize in general terms the regulation of the movement of motor vehicles by specifying reasonable speeds on public streets and highways with due regard to density of population, location of schools and hospitals, and the existence of intersecting streets. The statute will probably provide also for some agency in continuous operation, and presumably with expert knowledge, experienced personnel, and suitable equipment, to translate the general objectives into specific regulations (*e.g.,* as to coming to a full stop at main arteries or obeying light signals) and to enforce the statute and regulations, with penalties for those who violate them.

Public administration is interrelated with public opinion in that it follows upon the decision of the political leaders to undertake or abandon certain activities; with the legislative process in that effective administration may be rendered difficult or impossible by faulty legislation; and with the judicial process since the action of the administrator may be challenged in the courts by a citizen, and the administrative agency may be required, under the terms of a particular statute, to apply to the courts for judicial action against those presumed by the agency to be violating the law. While there is a theory that administration and policy are two separate processes of government, in fact they are constantly merging. This is because policy-making is inadequate if there is no consideration of the means for making the law effective, and administration of a general objective raises questions of choice, and hence policy, in any specific situation.

Administration and Policy.—The problems of public administration reflect, therefore, these interrelations with opinion, legislation, and adjudication. They also reflect the stage of civilization and the time, place, and environment of the particular political unit. Thus, there should be at the top of the administrative structure an official who can speak for, and to, the dominant political power of the society. This need for making the administrative agency subservient to the original intent for which the activity was authorized explains why the chief of an administrative agency, at least of national agencies, is generally a politician and nonexpert. He is chosen because he must interpret to the experts what the judgment of those in political power is, and to the politicians and the lay public what the more technical considerations that will affect their political objectives are. The greatest quantity of public administration is in the substantive functions of government such as those of public safety and order, public health, public works, education, the development of natural resources, the care of the handicapped, and the regulation of finance, business, and industry. Roads and harbours are built. Social insurance payments are made. Forests are guarded from fire or disease. Each field of activity has its accumulated technical knowledge, personnel, and forms of organization and procedure. For any particular jurisdiction in which several of these functions are administered, the problem of allocating available revenue to each, determining priorities, and coordinating the application by each agency of policies in which account should be taken of what other agencies are doing is one of the most important responsibilities of the highest administrative authority. At this point in the structure and process of government there is a meeting and mingling of political policy, general management, and the conduct of the particular functional departments.

MANAGEMENT

General Staff Work.—The heads of the administration in any jurisdiction have a double responsibility of helping to formulate legislation and of directing and coordinating the administrative agencies. This latter task becomes difficult in those stages of civilization in which many functions are undertaken through government since it includes the proper assignment of activity to organization units, each of which has some necessary share in the activity but each of which is also likely to develop its own personality, attitudes, and jealousies. Hence, the top administrative policy group, in modern times often called a "cabinet," and its chairman or chief—prime (*i.e.,* "first") minister, premier, or president—need to have the problems that are presented to them analyzed by persons of integrity, competence, and experience. This has come to be called "general staff work" from the influential and famous Prussian general staff. Elements of this important step in the administrative process are to be found wherever government has been effectively used. Thus, planning, which is inherent in the process of formulating policy, becomes essential also in its wise application, whether in the conduct of war, the prevention of epidemics, the facilitation of transportation, or the relief of destitution.

Auxiliary Services.—The responsible political chiefs of administration have been found by widespread experience to need other aids to ensure economical and efficient application of policy. These are agents for obtaining and facilitating the best use of personnel, physical materials and equipment, architectural and engineering services, and finances. Since such tools are aids both to general direction and to the operating officials (who are on the front lines in the field, building highways, waging war, or constructing irrigation projects), they are frequently called the auxiliary services or "housekeeping services."

There is inevitably some clash between such auxiliary agencies with their responsibility to the administrative chiefs for over-all policy, and the particular operating agency, which has enthusiasm for and special knowledge of its own field and is often resentful of controls that are called "red tape." To the operating official, there looms the threat of what is termed in the British civil service the "treasury mind"; its cousin is found in all large organizations in all times and places. To the official who is zealous in pressing forward his project, the scrutiny of some part of it by another agency which has no apparent responsibility for its success or failure is irksome. The auxiliary or general staff official, however, is equally impressed with the necessity of relating the single project to the other activities of the government and of bringing the enthusiasm of the official within bounds. Personnel and budget policies illustrate the fact that auxiliary and general staff services (which intermingle through day-to-day activities) are more than narrow technical matters. They are of central importance in the operation of any political system.

Personnel.—Long and varied experience in all parts of the world has demonstrated the necessity, for effective administration, of a reservoir of accumulated knowledge of the administration of a function—a knowledge that can be obtained only from persons of ability and integrity who have been given an opportunity for a career in administration. That is not the only reason why spoils systems, wherever they exist, have been disastrous (except in situations in which they may have served as alternatives to more costly revolutions). Their primary evil is that they undermine any use of parties and legislatures as reasonably accurate instruments of recording political sentiment and ideas, since they replace the relationship of agency for the public by agency for the chief spoilsman and turn responsible public affairs into irresponsible private rackets. Their administrative evil is that they prevent the accumulation of knowledge that only experience can give. No person of ability and integrity would be willing under spoils conditions to seek a satisfying career, and inevitably the agency sinks in effectiveness and in public confidence. Even in revolutionary conditions a new government is generally forced to rely upon such officials as it can find for carrying on those services necessary for the safety and welfare of populations—especially in a society partly urban. The knowledge required here is not only the knowledge of a substantive problem, such as preventive medicine or highway construction, but the more subtle knowledge for which long experience inside the institutions is required. This is the knowledge of who knows what, of how to use procedures and codes to hasten or delay business, of how to avoid arousing group and individual jealousies, of "moving through the correct channels," and of winning the consent of all those whose support is needed. The term "bureaucracy" is sometimes given, often in disparagement, to governments in which the "permanent" or "career" officials exercise or condition power. Such a dependence on officials, however, is inevitable and necessary in governments exercising many and interrelated functions.

The selection and training of civil servants has therefore been an important problem of government since early times. The system of widespread recruitment on the basis of examinations in the classics was a feature of the government of China for hundreds of years. The training of officials for the administrative posts in the mediaeval papacy and empire included courses in such universities as Bologna and Naples. The palace school of the Ottoman empire was the nursery of the civil, military and naval officer classes. The ruling families of the German principalities founded universities in which their civil servants (often jealously opposed by the feudal nobility) were educated. In both 19th-century Germany and France, the rise of a larger and more varied civil service was accompanied by the development of opportunities for secondary, university and specialized education that reflected also the enlargement of the middle class. The École Libre des Sciences Politiques in Paris and the development of careers in municipal administration in Germany illustrate these tendencies. The Trevelyan-Northcote report on the civil service in Great Britain in 1853 was influenced by such educators as Benjamin Jowett of Balliol and John Stuart Mill. The expansion in the functions of government in the United States prior to World War I created an interest in the education of administrators which revived strongly with another expansion in the decade 1930–40.

In general, educational qualifications for administration reflect the general social conditions of the time and place and the classification of the positions to be filled. A more fluid and democratic society opens its opportunities for secondary and higher education widely and this tends to prevent the formation of a special official caste sheltered by inherited privileges. The "single-party" system of government tends to create a new form of special privilege dependent upon party allegiance. But in all systems, a job analysis will reveal the need for continuous education after entrance if there is to be an adequate supply of recruits for the higher directive and technical positions. Hence, the questions of "in-service" training, of educational leave and the recruitment through promotion and from outside the service are as much the subject of discussion and experiment as the older question of "pre-entry" training. At this point the interest of students of public administration turns to developments in education and psychology generally as well as to experience in industry and commerce.

The Budget.—The outstanding instrument whereby the total program of a government for a given period of time is set forth by organization unit, types of expenditure and in other detail is the budget. In most states (notably Great Britain, which contributed most to its development as an important tool of government) the budget originates in the executive departments in the form of estimates of proposed expenditures and the revenues to cover them, is submitted to the legislature for investigation, amendment and legal authorization and is then administered by the budget and other finance agencies. The budget process ends with an audit to determine whether expenditures have been properly based upon the legal authorization—an audit frequently made by an agency of the legislature, or otherwise independent of the administrative chiefs. The budget as authorized by the lawmaking process is thus inevitably the total plan for all the activities of the government for the next fiscal period (generally a year), including the provision for personnel and materials. The long evolution of representative government has centred largely in the development of a good budget system, including "the control of the purse strings" by the elected representatives of the people; that is, the submission to them by the executive (usually in name, at least, by the crown) of the proposals for expenditure. taxation and loans and the scrutiny and amendment, acceptance or rejection of these by the representatives, sometimes with the aim and result of forcing administrative chiefs and policy advisers from office. The cabinet system, whereby the chief executive officials must possess the support of the majority of the legislature, thus had its origins; while the importance of legislative control over expenditure, and of the appropriation process, is illustrated also by provisions concerning them in the constitution of the United States and in the development of government everywhere.

The Planning Process.—The function of cabinets and chief executives as well as the heads of large departments in the preparation of policy for submission to the legislative authority became complex and difficult with the widening and interdependence of the functions of government. Thus, in a metropolitan area the design of streets and highways, water supply, parks and schools is dependent upon population, industrial, commercial and technological trends as well as changes in the ideas held by citizens as to standards of living. As a result, the usual budget processes are sometimes supplemented by special staff agencies for investigation and analysis, or by regular and continuing agencies to which the term planning is applied. Planning as an inherent need in the structure and process of administration was diagnosed and recommended by Frederick W. Taylor in his pioneer work in scientific management, although, as noted above, it has been called into existence in some form, as in military affairs, wherever thought has been applied to the problem of the improved preparation of programs.

The economic policies adopted by the early modern states caused the rise of career civil services and methods of training for them. A similar increase in collective services, whether in the U.S.S.R. with its elaborate central, regional and local programs of state action, or a region of sparse population requiring long-time land policies in the United States, or a great urban agglomeration such as London, Bombay or New York, made desirable and necessary the establishing of planning agencies. Their function is to gather and analyze data concerning the problems of the political organisms they serve and to submit reports on their studies to the political chiefs, the legislatures and the electorate. Sometimes these agencies are also given some operating responsibility and power. Thus, they may be given the enforcement of controls over land use or authority to determine priorities in the allocation of resources to projects. Whether such planning agencies should be exclusively research and advisory in their functions or should have in addition operating functions and powers is a subject of controversy among students of administration. It is agreed, however, that there should be close and sympathetic working relations and an interchange of personnel between them and the budget and other general staff and auxiliary services and the substantive departments.

It may again be stressed that the budget should reflect, as the most comprehensive record of operations proposed for the next fiscal period, the result of the planning process as registered in the working and financial program which the chief executive and his associates are responsibly proposing to the highest lawmaking body of the jurisdiction. Thus, the estimates which are proposed will presumably be supported and justified by the analyzed data. Viewed in this light the planning process in administration is not, as sometimes argued, in opposition to legislative authority but essential to it. A legislature, in fact, may rightly demand that such preliminary collection and analysis of data be undertaken by the executive to ensure a better preparation of proposals placed before it. The use of the fiscal policy of a government to affect general economic conditions by its influence on investment and employment increases the need for careful planning of the estimates.

Internal Operation.—The directive, general staff and auxiliary agencies exist to serve the substantive or operating departments, and it is through them that the functions of a political system are applied. In these basic substantive departments there is a division of labour reflected in an organization of units whose heads are related in some line of responsibility and power. The system may be recorded on organization charts and in standard specifications for every position whereby the duties, qualifications, rates of payment and official titles are set forth. The relation of the different levels, the flow of correspondence, reports, memoranda and dockets of official business and the arrangements for conference between units (bureaus, divisions, sections, branches, regional offices, etc.) may also be guided by written and official codes of procedure. The procedure to be followed in relations with the public generally by correspondence, interview, investigation or inspection, or hearings of an informal or formal type, tends to become standardized and codified. This results in a standardizing of practice that leads to charges of red tape, bureaucracy and the stultifying of initiative. A failure to regularize procedures, however, leads to criticisms of unfairness, capriciousness and abuse of power and an invitation to corruption. The interests affected by the function administered are generally organized in economic or professional associations. Sometimes representatives of these interests are brought into official participation in the administrative process through committees advisory to the agency or committees given some power of administering the program for which the agency is ultimately responsible. At its extreme, such a system might be termed "the corporative state" so much discussed in political theory in recent decades, although never actually embodied in any completeness.

Among the groups involved in the administrative process with some special interest or emphasis of their own are various organizations of the civil servants. Since the number of civil servants in a modern state may be great, collective action in the effort to affect rates of pay and conditions of employment generally developed despite opposition. In some systems, a regular procedure was established (as notably in the "Whitley councils" in the British civil service) for consultation between the directive and personnel officials and the representatives of the civil service organizations.

Thus, the maintenance of some balance in modern administration between the interests and attitudes of legislatures, parties, executive leaders, auxiliary service agencies, interest groups affected and the civil servants themselves is no easy task. The systems appear sprawling, cumbersome and unwieldy and too far removed from the situation from which the call for governmental action originated. Internal operation is complicated further by the relating of decisions taken at the centre to the varied conditions in the field.

The problem of clarifying and explaining the complex task of a department led to increased interest in methods of reporting. Experiments in the use not only of printed and illustrated reports but of the motion picture, the radio, television and direct face-to-face discussion and conference were undertaken. Legislatures are inclined to oppose these on grounds that they may become an alternative to the party system as a means of consulting public opinion and may stimulate public pressure for legislation favourable to the agency employing them.

The problems of internal operation in public administration are in many ways akin to or identical with those in other social institutions, including industry and commerce. The comparative study of institutions, including the relation of individuals in the smaller face-to-face groups, brought scholars and administrators together from many fields to share experience and plan and conduct research. Psychologists, personnel managers, anthropologists, sociologists and many other workers find a common field in what is given various names, such as social relations, human relations or the study of the human group. A special challenge was raised by growth of international programs and agencies in which the problems of a substantive field such as health are complicated by the need for co-operation by peoples of different cultures. The training of administrative personnel for such programs began to reflect the new emphasis on human relations, and also the area or regional studies whose origins may be found long ago in the policies of missionary societies and colonial offices, as well as in World Wars I and II.

DECENTRALIZATION AND DEVOLUTION

Whenever the size in area and population of the jurisdiction served by an administrative system is large, the adjustment of general policies and standards to varied local or otherwise specialized circumstances constitutes a major problem. If too great freedom is given to officials to adjust standards to the particular instance, effective general legislation becomes difficult or impossible, and programs may get distorted and special interests may injure the general good. Partisan, sectional, factional or other special favours and corruption may follow. And yet the particular knowledge of the persons whose life work is in an industry, or is concerned with a commodity or profession, or with a particular region or locality, should be employed if a policy is to be wisely administered. The states of the world have in all times, from ancient China or the Roman empire to the present, attempted to meet this problem either by leaving or giving some measure of local self-government to local areas, or by creating regional units in their central administrative agencies to which some discretionary powers for making decisions within the general rule for problems arising within the area are given.

A variant of the same principle is the assigning of powers for the administration of a statute or general policy of the state to a professional, commercial or industrial association or representatives of such interests. Thus, we may find, as in the Germany of the Weimar republic, not only *Länder* or member states within the Reich but local units within them and also an economic council. Similarly, in Great Britain, which we ordinarily think of as a unitary or relatively centralized state, there are county councils, rural district councils, boroughs and also boards possessing statutory powers in the steel industry or dealing with a commodity such as milk or bacon. In the United States the same problem of relating general policies to the particular situation confronted the constitution makers in 1787, resulting in a federal system, but persists to the present and indeed becomes more complicated as new units such as soil-conservation districts or local housing authorities are created with direct relations with national agencies.

The grant or taking of power by economic groups was advocated perhaps more strongly at about the time of World War I, and a political theory designated "pluralism" or "functionalism" had a period of success. It was indeed supposed to have been reflected in the doctrines of the Russian bolshevists and the fascists in Italy, as well as in the creation of economic councils in France and Germany. Probably local circumstances and situations in the latter two states, just as in the establishment of the National Recovery administration in the United States, with its industrial codes, had a much greater importance, while the Russian and Italian systems quickly revealed themselves as highly centralized single-party controlled governments struggling to secure and retain power and therefore in no position to yield power to regional or commodity or other groups except as forced by circumstances.

The point is, however, that circumstances (*i.e.*, the increasingly complex nature of the activities that go to make up modern economy, the strong pull of neighbourhood and region and all kinds of provincialisms and the necessity to achieve political as well as administrative success for policies) do press for the adjustment of general policies to particular situations and do require the consultation at least by administrators with persons and organizations affected by those policies. It is characteristic of modern legislation affecting industry in some states, for example, that councils on which employers and employees, or members of a profession, are represented, participate in drafting rules and regulations under the act.

Relations of a national or central authority with provincial and local governments are made more complicated by the rise of metropolitan cities that spread over several separate political jurisdictions, the inequality of tax resources of local units, the pressure for national minimum standards of public services and the interdependence of economies. A partial answer to these conditions is found in the grants distributed from national funds to local units on condition of meeting certain required standards, with resulting inspection from the centre, generally entitled "grants-in-aid," and in the employment of officials of one level of government for enforcing the laws of another. The relation of levels of government remains, however, as one of the most difficult and perplexing problems of public administration.

CONTROLS AND STANDARDS

Obviously public administration is certain to be subjected to criticism because the objectives sought are disliked or because the methods employed are viewed as unjust or inefficient or corrupt. Over the centuries various devices for its control have evolved. These efforts are designed to confine it to the political objectives for which a particular administration is established, which we may call political control; to ensure economy and efficiency, which we may call executive control; or to ensure observance of the accepted rules of fair conduct as understood by the particular society to apply to the relation of officials with the public, which we may call judicial control. All these necessarily intermingle, and broadly speaking, with the rise of representative government, a somewhat stronger emphasis inevitably was placed in most states upon political control. This is exercised through making the chiefs of administration politically responsible either to the legislature or to the electorate by some form of popular election.

Probably the most famous example of the evolution of political control is the wresting of power from the king and its allocation to a committee of party leaders representing a majority of the House of Commons in Great Britain. This system, called "cabinet" or "parliamentary" government, served as a model for many other states to follow (with varying degrees of success). The U.S. "presidential" or "congressional" system makes the chief executive responsible to the electorate. Both systems, however, operate through parties; and at times the British prime minister takes on presidential attributes, and the U.S. president similarly at times plays a role in relation to Congress somewhat akin to that of the prime minister in relation to the House of Commons.

The more detailed devices of party and legislative control vary greatly; but most legislatures employ committee investigations of administration, scrutiny of budget estimates, the control over expenditure and audit and frequently the questioning of executive chiefs on the floor as well as in committee. These matters are usually topics of discussion at meetings of the Interparliamentary Union, the conference of delegates from the legislative bodies of the states of the world.

The struggle of legislatures first for independence of the monarchy and later for supremacy is paralleled historically in many states by a similar effort of the courts for independence; and in some states, notably the United States, the system of written constitutions and a federal distribution of powers has been the basis upon which has been constructed the exercise of judicial review not only of the acts of officials but of the constitutionality of the statutes whereby the officials may have justified their actions.

In many states, notably those influenced strongly by the traditions and precedents of the Roman law, a series of special courts evolved in which controversies involving official acts of civil servants are adjudicated, and the resulting case law, as in France, constitutes an important part of the public law. Administrative law is thus everywhere a branch of public and constitutional law that grows in importance as the extent and complexity of the functions of government increase. Questions of the competence of the authority, the adequacy and justice of the procedure, the extent of the grant of discretionary power, the adequacy of the evidence in support of the administrator's action and the finality of the administrative decision are typical issues. The study of comparative government, and in particular of comparative jurisprudence and administration, is resulting in a greater familiarity on the part of scholars and of some practitioners with the similarities between different systems and a tendency to discover devices in one system that may usefully be adopted in another. Many precedents and theories framed long ago during the struggles with monarchy are being reappraised in the light of the contemporary complexities of administration.

While legislative, executive and judicial controls are of basic importance, it should not be forgotten that in the daily life of the administrator his own knowledge, character and sense of personal and professional responsibility, constituting a series of inner standards and checks, are probably more immediately and intimately influential. Hence, the rise of professional organizations, of research, of in-service training, of journals devoted to administrative questions have increasing importance and constitute a professional control which has operated, indeed, at times in all societies.

The increasing participation of citizens in public administration through advisory committees, and their sharing in the exercise of some of the discretionary power in rule making, and the necessity for many types of administration of winning the understanding if not the active support of the citizen, is another less recognized but important control over public administration. Many statutes and programs involve matters touching intimately the lives of great numbers of citizens; it is impossible to enforce them (as, for example, systems of social insurance or of highway safety or disease prevention) without extensive efforts to acquaint citizens with them. But in that process, the official is often educated himself as to attitudes, habits, capacities and problems of those whom he is supposed to serve; he is probably less concerned with possible legislative, judicial or even higher executive action regarding his work than with the people and problems immediately at hand. In this sense, we may consider administration as moving into a stage in which a two-way educative process is discernible; and while it may seem a far cry from the edicts of ancient rulers, one suspects that even they, too, had sometimes to consider how far they could go with subjects unaware of or opposed to their aims and measures.

BIBLIOGRAPHY.—L. D. White, *Introduction to the Study of Public Administration,* 4th ed. (1955), *The Federalists* (1948); John Stuart Mill, *Representative Government,* ch. v, xiv, xv (1910 *et seq.*); C. D. Waldo (ed.), *Ideas and Issues in Public Administration* (1953); P. H. Appleby, *Policy and Administration* (1949); R. K. Merton *et al., Reader In Bureaucracy* (1952); Louis L. Jaffe (ed.), *Administrative Law* (1954); Harold Stein (ed.), *Public Administration and Policy Development* (1952); Solomon Fabricant, *The Trend of Government Activity in the United States Since 1900* (1953); D. K. Price, *Government and Science* (1954); U. S. Commission on Intergovernmental Relations, *Report to the President* (1955); J. M. Pfiffner and R. V. Presthus, *Public Administration,* 4th ed. (1960); M. E. Dimock and G. O. Dimock, *Public Administration,* 3rd ed. (1964); *The Public Administration Review* (quarterly). (J. M. G.)

PUBLICANI, the name given in ancient Rome to public contractors, who either undertook (on receipt of a fixed sum from the treasury) to erect or maintain public buildings or supply armies overseas, or paid a fixed sum to the treasury for the right to exploit state mines, quarries, saltpans, or forests, or to collect certain taxes. The general principle was that only those state assets whose revenue was fluctuating and uncertain were farmed to *publicani;* thus tithes and customs were farmed, but in provinces where the tax was a fixed tribute, it was directly collected from the provincial communities by the quaestors. With the growth of the empire the provincial tithes became the most important contracts undertaken by the *publicani.* The system was well established by the end of the 3rd century B.C. At Rome the contracts were let by auction by the censors, and thus ran for five years; in some provinces, such as Sicily, they were let annually by the praetor. Payment was made in arrears, but the *publicani* had to furnish guarantors (*praedes*) and securities (*praedia*), and since many of the contracts involved very large sums they commonly formed partnerships or companies (*societates publicanorum*). The companies were headed by *magistri* at Rome and *promagistri* in the provinces, and employed large staffs (*operae*), free and slave, as accountants, collectors, etc. They organized their own postal service, which was often used by the provincial governors. They also acted as bankers to the state, making payments in the provinces on behalf of the Roman treasury.

Since senators were legally debarred (probably by the *lex Claudia* of 218 B.C.) from undertaking public contracts, the business fell into the hands of the richest nonsenators, the equestrian

order (*see* EQUITES). Their interests often clashed with those of the state, as represented by the censors and the senate; in 169 B.C., for instance, the censors excluded past holders of contracts from the auction on the ground that they formed a ring to keep the bidding down, and the *publicani* appealed to the tribunes of the plebs, who prosecuted and nearly convicted the censors. From 122 B.C., when equestrians became jurors in the court of extortion, the *publicani* acquired a whip hand over provincial governors, since they could condemn governors who restrained their operations, and most governors found it wise to connive at their malpractices, in which case the jurors would turn a blind eye to the governor's extortion. The provincials suffered as a result, being compelled to accept gross overestimates of the amount of tax due, and to pay extortionate interest on arrears.

Under the early empire the amount of business handled by the *publicani* was greatly reduced, as provincial tithes were abolished and fixed tribute substituted. They continued, however, to exploit mines and collect customs, and were employed to collect the new inheritance tax (*vicesima hereditatum*). They were more closely controlled, being supervised by imperial procurators, and the margin of profit was gradually so reduced that bidders did not come forward.

The government responded by compelling existing contractors to carry on under the same terms—an abuse condemned by Hadrian—or by assigning contracts compulsorily to wealthy men. In many cases the farming system was abandoned, and the tax collected directly by the procurator. Under a law of Constantine the customs were still farmed, but the system was little used in the later empire.

See M. Rostovtzeff, "Geschichte der Staatspacht in der römischen Kaiserzeit bis Diokletian," *Philologus,* Supplementband ix, pp. 329 ff. (1902). (A. H. M. J.)

PUBLIC DOMAIN. Broadly defined, this term denotes the ownership of natural resources by the people of a society generally as distinguished from ownership by particular persons or groups. This broad definition encompasses a wide variety of public ownership possibilities. Thus an Indian tribe that claims exclusive hunting and fishing rights in a particular area, but permits any and all of its own people to hunt and fish therein without restriction, is administering a public domain. So too is a modern Communist state that manages the use of economic resources by means of a centralized planning machinery. And even a feudal society in which all land is held of the king is in effect maintaining its economic organization within a public domain framework. The phrase "in the public domain" is also used to denote literary works or inventions not protected by a copyright or patent.

As the term is most commonly used, it is thought of as referring to the ownership or disposition of natural resources by the government in a society in which private property is also an important institution. Indeed, the concept of public domain could hardly have come to occupy the position it does if it did not suggest a contrast—and perhaps even a conflict—with the concept of private domain. Certainly no experience anywhere in the world illustrates this relationship more concretely than that of the United States.

Several factors have contributed to the sharpness of this contrast in the United States. One is a decision made early in the nation's history that, outside the original 13 colonies, land would be publicly owned before it became privately owned. The converse of this idea was the equally early and definitive policy that public ownership status would, for the most part, be a way station on the road to private ownership. When these two decisions are considered together they largely explain why so much of American history has consisted of a vigorous effort to add to the public domain and an equally vigorous effort to alienate that domain.

It is also necessary to add one more consideration in explaining why the public domain has consistently been a vital dimension of U.S. political life. Because a vast area was originally put into the hands of the federal government (the Floridas and all the territory within what is now the United States that lies west of the Mississippi River, with the single exception of Texas), it was only natural for that government to endeavour to further particular public policies in the process of disposing of these resources. It was only to be expected that, in a private property society, whatever public policies were selected for implementation in this way would encounter some opposition.

When, for example, the central government, immediately after the Constitution was ratified, decided to use the public lands as a source of quick and easy revenue, there were those who bitterly complained that this policy favoured speculators and wealthy farmers at the expense of the landless masses. Later when this policy was reversed during the Civil War, and a Homestead Act passed which gave land to settlers in 160-ac. lots, every conceivable effort was made by larger operators to keep bona fide homesteading to the barest minimum. When simultaneously a broad attempt was made to push railroad expansion by means of a system of land grants, farmers were quick to point out that the railroads were thereby being given much of the most desirable land—that nearest a railroad. And, strange as it may seem, public land policy was for many years closely related to the tariff question because revenue from the sale of public land proportionately weakened the argument for higher import duties.

These instances suggest only a few of the many public policy uses to which the public domain has been put. It has been used to pay men who have served their country by fighting for it—especially after the American Revolution when the soldiers could not have been paid in cash in any event. Even before the advent of the railroads some of the proceeds from the sale of public lands were earmarked for improving the nation's transportation network. And another land grant system was inaugurated to assist the states in developing facilities for higher education. (*See* LAND-GRANT COLLEGES AND UNIVERSITIES.)

More recently the United States has experimented with policies not based on rapid and complete alienation of the public domain. Before the end of the 19th century it was decided that a policy of reserving some mineral rights would be in the public interest. After World War II a retroactive claim on minerals in the fission-fusion family was asserted. Nonalienation has also become a significant element in the government's approach to the remaining public domain. One key instance here is land containing oil. But perhaps the primary reason for nonalienation is conservation of wildlife, of natural beauty, of soil and forests.

BIBLIOGRAPHY.—B. H. Hibbard, *History of Public Land Policies* (1924); Institute for Government Research, *The General Land Office: Its History, Activities, and Organization* (1923); R. M. Robbins, *Our Landed Heritage—The Public Domain, 1776–1936* (1942). (H. R. S.)

PUBLIC ENTERPRISE, an undertaking that is owned by a national, state (or provincial), or local government, supplies services or goods at a price, and is operated on a more or less self-supporting basis. Such enterprises may also be international, interstate, or intermunicipal in character, *i.e.*, owned and operated jointly by two or more national, state, or local governments. They may be operated by a government directly through one of its administrative departments or indirectly through a specially created semiautonomous corporate or other body, or through a company of which the government is the sole or practically the sole shareholder. A company in which the government owns only a portion of the stock, the other portion being owned by private individuals or groups, is generally designated as a "mixed" enterprise, rather than as a public enterprise proper. Social insurance systems and government employee retirement funds are not deemed to be public enterprises, inasmuch as membership in them is generally obligatory and their services are not sold.

Main Characteristics.—Public enterprises have certain characteristics in common with tax-supported administrative services: they are organized and operated for public benefit and they sometimes cater to the same public needs, though in a different manner. Thus, for example, they are often set up for the construction and operation of express highways, bridges, canals, and tunnels which might otherwise have been constructed and operated as free facilities financed from general taxation or tax-supported bond issues. But public enterprises also differ from tax-supported administrative services in several respects. First, they are concerned with the supply of only such services or products as are divisible into specific units for which specific charges can be made to the in-

dividuals wishing to acquire them. Public enterprises can never be set up to supply services or products which confer common benefits for all and are not divisible into such units. Thus, public enterprises can be organized for the supply of postal, telegraph, telephone, broadcasting, railway, seaway, and airway services and for the supply of electricity or gas, but not for the supply of national defense, protection of life, property, and health, social welfare services, and the regulation of business. Secondly, unlike tax-supported administrative services, public enterprises raise their own revenues and sometimes even their own capital funds; they are often allowed to dispose of their funds as they deem best, subject only to the general directives contained in the laws under which they are established or in the broad policy statements enunciated by the government; and their directors, managers, and other personnel are often appointed without regard to either politics or civil service regulations.

On the other hand, public enterprises differ basically from most private enterprises in their motivations and their modes of operation. First of all, they are operated for public benefit rather than private profit. Secondly, in capitalistic or free enterprise economies their prices are generally set at levels merely sufficient to cover their costs of operation, and not, as in private enterprises, high enough to earn a profit. Though their aim most frequently is to furnish services or goods at the lowest possible prices, there may occasionally be involved a subsidiary purpose of earning a profit for the government, thus sparing the necessity for levying additional taxes. Thus, for example, if the services of municipally owned electric light and gas plants are sold not only to the consumers of the owning locality but also to those of neighbouring communities, the locality is able, through the profits earned on such extraterritorial sales, to shift some of the support of its government to the shoulders of the neighbouring communities. In national fiscal monopolies prices are always set considerably above costs in order to earn a net profit for the government. Thus, in various ways public enterprises occupy a midway position between tax-supported public administrative services and private business undertakings, and combine some features of each.

History.—The development of public enterprises during the past three centuries or so can be divided into four periods. The first period began in the middle of the 17th century and extended into the end of the 18th, during which time national public enterprises were generally limited to the operation of the public domain (consisting mainly of state forests), the newly established national postal offices, and one or two fiscal monopolies surviving from the older times, such as the old and rather infamous salt monopolies. Local public enterprises during the period were limited to the operation of municipal markets, docks, and ferries. In general, public enterprises were not clearly differentiated from regular administrative services and were usually administered in about the same manner.

The second period, which began about 1800 and ended with the outbreak of World War I, saw a rapid industrial development and urbanization in the Western world. During that period national and state public enterprises were established for the construction and operation of canals, railroads, telegraph and telephone services, and port facilities, and for the operation of new types of fiscal monopolies, embracing principally the manufacture or distribution of tobacco products and alcoholic beverages. Municipal enterprises were established in the larger cities for the supply of water, gas, and electric light, and for street railway and underground rapid transit services. During this period, too, public enterprises came to be more clearly differentiated from ordinary administrative services and to be organized in a way better suited to their peculiar nature.

The third period began with the outbreak of World War I and ended with the outbreak of World War II. During that period, national and state enterprises multiplied throughout the Western world under the influence of the political, social, and economic forces unleashed by the war and, a decade or so later, by the depressions of the 1930s. The effective prosecution of the war had necessitated in most of the warring countries the nationalization of some of their industries at least for a time, thereby tending for many years to make people regard nationalization with less awe than before. (*See* also NATIONALIZATION.) Moreover, in those countries in which particularly great devastations of industrial plants, homes, and other properties had taken place, the tendency toward nationalization of industry and transport was stimulated because the work of reconstruction required extensive participation by the national government. In many instances the industrial enterprises that had been reestablished by the government were not returned to their former private owners and continued to operate as nationalized enterprises. Moreover, the political and social revolutions which broke out during and after the war in the Soviet Union, Turkey, and Italy and the revolution in Mexico (which started earlier but extended well into the 1920s and 1930s) not only brought about either complete or partial nationalization of industry in these countries but also exerted a powerful influence in the direction of greater extension of public ownership in other countries.

These tendencies toward public ownership were compounded during the world depressions of the 1930s. In the United States, France, and several other countries national governments were compelled to extend various forms of emergency aid to bankrupt business firms, farmers, homeowners, and unemployed workers, and to establish permanent financial institutions and other undertakings to ensure stability and continued growth of the economy.

The fourth period began with the outbreak of World War II and is still continuing. During it public ownership was expanded even more rapidly than before, affecting many more countries and many more industries in each of them. This was a natural consequence of the greater magnitude of World War II and of its far-reaching and lasting political, social, and economic effects. In a number of industrially advanced countries that had been directly involved in the war or otherwise deeply affected by it, some additional industries were nationalized after the war under the pressure of various forces. Moreover, during this period in a number of underdeveloped countries which had become imbued with a desire to achieve rapid industrial development and a higher standard of living for their people, the governments established to that end industrial undertakings, often with the aid of funds borrowed from abroad. Finally, Communism during this period won several more adherents among the nations of the world, resulting in the complete nationalization of their industries.

REASONS FOR ESTABLISHMENT

As the foregoing historical summary indicates, the reasons for the establishment of public enterprises are varied. Some are economic, fiscal, or administrative; others are broadly social, ideological, and political. Economic, fiscal, and administrative considerations were responsible for the establishment of most public enterprises during the 19th century and the beginning of the 20th century; they still play an important role in many countries, including the United States. Public enterprises established for these reasons have not been designed to change the order of society. The second category of reasons, on the other hand, has come to play an important role in the organization of public enterprises since World War I and has tended to transform the capitalist or free enterprise society into either a semi-socialist economy or a completely socialist or communist economy.

Economic.—The economic reasons are generally concrete and deal with specific institutions. If a need has developed in the society for new facilities, services, or products and if private enterprises appear unwilling, or incapable, to undertake to supply these facilities, services, or products, the government has no alternative but to undertake to supply them itself. Similarly, if, after having organized such facilities and operated them for a while, private enterprises appear unable to continue to operate them in a manner satisfactory to the public and profitable to themselves, the government is impelled to purchase or otherwise take over their properties and operate them itself (generally with the hope that by reorganizing and coordinating the facilities it might be able to operate them more efficiently and economically). In the 17th, 18th, and early 19th centuries, for example, the inability of private enterprises to provide satisfactory mail service forced national

governments everywhere to establish them themselves. In many countries the national governments (or their states or provinces) had to construct and operate canals and railways from the very outset or had to take their operation out of private hands at later times. The same thing happened in most countries in the case of telegraph, telephone, and broadcasting services. Even coal mining had to be taken over from private enterprises in many countries in the 20th century because the industry could no longer be operated by private enterprises economically and efficiently and with profit to themselves. In every such instance, the government's entrance into the field was dictated by the economic realities of the situation and not by shifts in ideology or by any play of politics.

Administrative.—Sometimes, however, administrative and public considerations reinforce the economic ones in prompting the establishment of a public enterprise. For example, the construction and operation of railroad lines in some cases was of such strategic importance for national defense, but not likely to be economically profitable, that it had to be undertaken by the national government. In other cases a wholly different set of economic circumstances has impelled the national government to take over a given private enterprise. Thus, for example, when a large private enterprise has developed into a monopoly charging exorbitant prices for its services or products and defying government regulation, its acquisition by the government and its operation as a public enterprise is advocated as one way to deal with the situation. Another way is for the government to establish its own enterprise in competition with the private enterprise, thereby breaking the latter's monopoly and forcing it to cut its prices.

Fiscal.—Fiscal reasons for establishing public enterprises are also specific and concrete. Thus a government may terminate private operation in a certain field of economic activity and establish therein its own enterprise as a monopoly, because that monopoly can then charge high prices for its services and bring in a net revenue larger than any tax imposed by it on the private enterprise operating in that field could possibly bring in. Occasionally, too, a government converts a tax-supported administrative service into a service-charging public enterprise for fiscal reasons. By so doing, it relieves its budget of an additional burden.

Ideological.—Broad ideological, political, and social reasons for establishing public enterprises often involve a desire for the reconstruction of the political, social, and economic order of the society. Sometimes the aim may be to reconstruct it on a supposedly more equalitarian plan; sometimes, conversely, the object may be to reconstruct it along a more authoritarian and militantly nationalistic plan. In other instances, the aim of the political program involving the establishment of some public enterprises is not so much to change the social order as to accelerate the industrial development of the country as a means of quickly improving the economic welfare of the people. In either case, a sweeping and more or less coordinated establishment of public enterprises takes place in the country.

Examples of sweeping nationalizations of industry for broadly ideological, political, and social reasons are afforded by the revolutions of recent decades which have transformed Russia, most of eastern Europe, China, and other countries into communist societies. Examples of politically and ideologically inspired nationalizations tending to transform a national economy into one of semi-socialist or mixed type are found in the programs effectuated in Australia under the influence of the Labor Party in the 1920s and 1930s, in New Zealand under the Labour government (1935–49), in Mexico in the 1920s and 1930s, in France after the end of the German occupation during World War II, in the United Kingdom under the Labour government (1945–50), and in India under Nehru's administration after that country's achievement of political independence. The aims of the nationalization program of the British Labour Party, only part of which was achieved during the foregoing brief period when it was in power, included the removal of the concentration of economic power from private hands in the interest of a more democratic society, increase in the efficiency of industry through better coordination, assurance of greater worker participation in the management of industry, and stabilization of employment.

The sweeping nationalization of finance and industry effected in Italy under Mussolini's Fascist regime, which was designed to achieve economic self-sufficiency for the country and to enhance its military power, was in a class by itself. So, too, was the nationalization of some industries in Germany under Hitler, the aim of which was to mobilize the nation for an aggressive war. Quite different were the attempts made by the Italian government after the liquidation of the Fascist regime to democratize the country's control over the nationalized industries. Finally, the sweeping nationalization of industry in Turkey under Kemal Atatürk in the 1920s and 1930s exemplified an effort to accelerate the country's industrial development rather than to reconstruct its social structure along more equalitarian lines.

Importance.—It is very difficult to measure the relative importance of the public enterprises in various national economies. The proportion of the country's total labour force employed by its public enterprises, even if computed accurately, is not an accurate measure of their relative importance. For one thing, it ignores the qualitative importance of the industries operating under public ownership, and the impact they have on the operations of the whole economy. The proportion of national income or gross national product originating in public enterprises is not an ideal measure of their relative importance. The economic importance of the nationalization of banking, for example, can hardly be measured by the small number of persons employed in banking or by the income produced in banking.

The portion of the labour force employed in public enterprises in the capitalistic or mixed economies is only 9 to 10% in the United Kingdom and France, 6 to 8% in Italy, Australia, New Zealand, and Sweden, and less than 2% in the United States. Such figures are not impressive if taken by themselves. However, when taken in conjunction with a listing of the types of economic activity covered by public enterprises, they become more meaningful.

Among the industrially advanced nations with capitalistic and mixed economies, the widest range of economic activity covered by public enterprise prevails in the United Kingdom, France, Italy, Sweden, Australia, and New Zealand. In addition to the post offices, public enterprises in these countries operate other great utilities such as telegraph, telephone, broadcasting, railway, electric light and power services, large segments of seaway transport, practically all air transport, all coal mining, and substantial segments of financial services. In some of them, public enterprises also operate road haulage, life insurance, some types of housing, some metal mines, steel and iron plants, automobile factories, and shipbuilding. In Sweden even a chain of restaurants is publicly operated. A somewhat narrower range of coverage of both the basic utilities and industries generally prevails in the Federal Republic of Germany, Canada, and Japan. The narrowest is found in the United States where, with a few exceptions such as the Alaskan Railway and the Tennessee Valley Authority, railways, telegraph, telephone, broadcasting, and most of the gas and electric light and power services are still under private ownership and operation.

FORMS OF ORGANIZATION

Centralized or Decentralized Organization.—One of the issues in the organization of public enterprises relates to the extent to which they should be set up as large units owned by the central government and serving the entire nation, or as small units serving regions or local communities and owned by state, provincial, or local governments. To a large extent, this issue takes care of itself through the natural accommodation of the public enterprises to the character of the services in question. Thus, to meet properly the public needs, the public postal, telegraph, telephone, broadcasting, railway, seaway, air transport, and certain types of financial services are generally centralized and operated nationally. Road transport, coal mining, and hydroelectric power development are in some instances organized as national undertakings and in others as regional or local enter-

prises. The supply of strictly urban facilities, such as water, public housing, street railway, bus, and underground rapid transit services are usually municipal undertakings. Harbour and airport facilities are in some countries carried on as national undertakings and in others as nationally subsidized local enterprises.

Degree of Autonomy.—Another important issue in the organization of public enterprises relates to the extent to which, because of their public purposes, they should be controlled by the central government or, because of the business character of their operations, they should be given freedom to make their own decisions and to act upon them. This issue arises in the determination of such matters as the manner in which their chief officers should be appointed and the conditions under which they should hold office; the extent to which they should be required to report to the legislative and executive organs of the government and to take directives from them; and the degree, if any, to which they should depend on the government for the supply of their capital and have their budgets controlled by it, have the right to fix the pay of their personnel, determine charges, and retain and dispose of profits.

The arrangements which may be adopted for the management of public enterprises in these and other respects may range from controls that are almost as tight as those exerted by the government over its regular administrative services to those that are as loose as those applied by it to private businesses. In any event, they are closely interlocked with the type of legal organization under which a public enterprise is set up. There are four main types of such organizations: the administrative department; the so-called trading agency; the company; and the public corporation or "authority." The following paragraphs describe each of them briefly, giving attention to the degree of government control or autonomy generally found with each type.

The Administrative Department.—The earliest public enterprises were organized as regular administrative departments, and many are still so organized in most countries. This is particularly true of the post office and the telegraph and telephone services. Under this type of organization the head of the public enterprise is appointed by the legislature or by the chief executive as is the head of any other administrative department. The budget of the enterprise is often subject to the same control by the treasury or other general budgetary agency of the government as that of any other department. Frequently, no consistent attempt is made under this type of organization to relate closely the charges made by the enterprise for its services to the costs of rendering them and to relate the income of the enterprise to its outgo. Sometimes the receipts of the enterprise from its charges are paid into the general fund and its expenditures are paid out of it without any comparisons being made of the relation of the one to the other. In other cases a contrary arrangement is followed; the receipts are paid into a special fund and the expenditures are made from that fund to the extent that the receipts are sufficient to cover them. If there is an excess of receipts over expenditures it is turned over to the general fund; if expenditures exceed receipts the deficit in the special fund is taken care of by an appropriation from the general fund.

Trading Agency.—The so-called trading agency is a type of public enterprise organization that originated in Sweden. A modification of the administrative department type, it differs from it in two main respects: its heads are nonpolitical persons appointed by the King-in-Council and bearing no ministerial political responsibilities; and it allows the enterprise somewhat greater freedom of operation than is permitted under the other plan. For example, the enterprise may be allowed to retain some of its profits. Its personnel, like that of an administrative department, however, are under civil service. This type of organization is used in Sweden for the management of the largest national enterprises, such as the postal, telegraph, telephone, broadcasting, railway, air transport, electric power services, and forestry.

Company.—The company type of public enterprise organization has its origin in the private companies that used to operate the particular businesses before their stock was purchased by the government. In taking over a given private company the government would retain its legal form, but, through its ownership of all or nearly all the shares and election of all the directors, it would change the internal organization, nature of managerial personnel, policies, and modes of operation. The company type of organization is used also for setting up wholly new undertakings not formerly owned by any private group. Its advantage lies in its flexibility and in the freedom which it affords to the public enterprise to manage its affairs without interference from the treasury or from civil service regulations. It has one major disadvantage, however, from a public point of view: the absence of public accountability. The company type of organization is quite common in France and in Italy. In Sweden it is used mainly for the operation of small public enterprises set up in competition with private enterprises.

Public Corporation.—The public corporation or "authority" is the newest type of organization of public enterprises and, by consensus, appears to be the most satisfactory. (*See* GOVERNMENT CORPORATIONS.) Developed first in the fullest form in England in the case of the Port of London Authority in 1908 and next in the United States in the case of the Port of New York Authority in 1921, it spread rapidly in those two countries and was copied by a great many other countries. The public corporation is set up as a semiautonomous body subject to some degree of public accountability. Its specific features are generally set forth in the special statute which creates it. Each public corporation is supposed to be so organized as to enable it to operate efficiently, economically, and responsibly in the field assigned to it.

William A. Robson in his *Nationalized Industry and Public Ownership* (1960) observed that in Great Britain two factors provided the original impetus for the creation of public corporations; one was the desire to free public enterprises from parliamentary supervision over management and the other was to free them from Treasury control over their personnel and finances. He listed five requisites for the proper organization of a public corporation: freedom from parliamentary or other legislative inquiry into the management of the corporation as distinct from its policy; disinterestedness; operation outside the civil service; independence, *i.e.*, divorcement from the general budget (which does not necessarily exclude the supply of capital funds or operating subsidies to the enterprise from the public treasury); and that the chairman and board members of a corporation be appointed for a fixed term of years, thus ensuring their independence from political control.

In Britain, the public corporation has been represented by such bodies as the Central Electricity Generating Board and Electricity Council (both formed in 1957), Bank of England (1936; reorganized in 1946), National Coal Board (1946), and the Transport Commission (1947). In the United States, it is exemplified by the Tennessee Valley Authority (1933), Export-Import Bank (1934), Port of New York Authority (1921), and the New York State Thruway Authority (1950).

Mixed Private-Public Enterprises.—Mixed enterprises owned partly by the state and partly by private interests are prevalent in France, Italy, Sweden, Brazil, and in some other countries. They have their origin in the acquisition by the state of some or most of the stock of private companies. They retain the legal form of privately owned companies but in their internal organization and in their operations, *i.e.*, in the composition of their boards of directors and in the nature of the policies pursued by them, the mixed corporations reflect to some degree their partial public ownership. Where the proportion of the shares owned in the company by the state is very small (as in the case of the Hispano-Suiza Company in France, where it amounts to only 4%), the enterprise may be deemed to be merely a subsidized private enterprise, rather than a mixed enterprise proper. But where the proportion of the public and private holdings is about evenly divided, the enterprise deserves to be designated a mixed undertaking. There is much controversy regarding the merits and demerits of the mixed type. Criticisms are directed especially against those mixed enterprises in which the state owns a majority of the stock. In analyzing the experience of this type of enterprise in France, Maurice Byé concluded that it differs from genuine governmental undertakings only "by being camouflaged with the trappings of private business, and linked to the state budget by agreements that make the state responsible for unlimited deficits." In the U.S. the establishment of mixed corporations by state and local governments is prohibited in most states by state constitutions. The federal Constitution does not forbid their establishment by the federal government.

Criteria of Soundness and Effectiveness.—The criterion of profitability, by which the soundness of any proposed capital investment and the success of performance generally are judged in private business, plays only a subsidiary role in public enterprises. The main criterion used is the degree to which public good is likely to be served by the proposed capital investment and, similarly, the degree to which public good is advanced by the given operations. At the same time subsidiary consideration is also given to the extent to which the invested capital is likely to return to the enterprise, and also the degree to which a particular operation is likely to help the enterprise to be self-supporting. If the likelihood is slim, the investment or the operation may be avoided or at least only grudgingly made or undertaken. Public enterprises are expected to be self-supporting and to operate more efficiently and economically than private enterprises. If they fail in these respects, their performance is deemed to be disappointing and to call for corrective measures. Comparisons with private operations, however, are possible only if there has been some historical experience with them in the field or if the public enterprises operate in competition with some private ones.

PUBLIC ENTERPRISES IN COMMUNIST ECONOMICS

In a communist society, public enterprises generally cover all industry, mining, transport, communication, construction, major trade, and certain segments of agriculture, leaving to cooperative organizations or to private enterprises only the remainder of agriculture, the trade of artisans, the petty trades, and some professions. In all communist societies, and particularly in the more militant ones, public enterprises are expected not only to produce the assigned quotas of goods (and also quotas of profits for the state) but also to help build socialism and the political, military, and industrial power of the state. Accordingly, factory managers are usually members of the Communist Party and each enterprise usually has within it a communist unit which sees to it that the party's objectives are not neglected. The organization of the public enterprises, however, is not completely uniform in all the communist countries. Particularly great differences exist in their organization in the Soviet Union, Yugoslavia, and China.

U.S.S.R.—In the U.S.S.R. all public enterprises, except such urban services as those of water supply, gas, electricity, street railways, and housing, are controlled by the central government with some help from the constituent republics and regional governments. They are operated under an elaborate hierarchical administrative system and a national long-range economic investment and production plan which is broken down into individual economic plans for the various republics and regions. At the top of the administrative pyramid is the All-Union Council of Ministers assisted by the State Planning Commission (*Gosplan*) and the State Scientific and Technical Committees. Immediately below it are the councils of ministers of the republics, similarly assisted by their two sets of such committees; still further below are the regional economic councils (*sovnarkhom*) likewise assisted by two sets of committees.

Below this administrative, political, and economic hierarchy are the industrial syndicates or combines (*glavki*), below which are the individual enterprises or factories. Each enterprise or factory is managed by a director, who is usually appointed by the regional economic council. He has complete authority to organize the establishment, to hire and fire key personnel, to organize production, and, after consultation with the factory's trade union, to set wage rates. Since the prices of the raw materials which he uses in production as well as the prices and the amounts of capital which he can spend for the improvement of his equipment are largely fixed by superior authority, the only way in which he can fulfill or overfill his assigned quota is by getting more work out of his workers (by offering them bonuses or by organizing brigades of the more able workers who set the pace of work for all the others) or by economizing on the use of raw materials and in this way bringing down the costs of production and maximizing the profits of the enterprise. He gets his rewards for achieving these purposes in the form of bonuses and promotion to the management of a larger enterprise or to a higher position in the administrative hierarchy. Thus, the director of a Soviet enterprise operates somewhat like a capitalistic entrepreneur. The autonomy of the Soviet enterprises is thus limited largely to the organization of production and to the right to retain profits in excess of the assigned quota and to use them for reinvestment, bonuses, or other purposes.

Yugoslavia.—In Yugoslavia, on the other hand, the bulk of the public enterprises are locally controlled. Only the large monopolies, such as the postal, telegraph, telephone, and broadcasting services, railways, and airlines are nationally controlled. Moreover, the enterprises are vested with a large degree of administrative and financial autonomy. Within the general pattern of the economic plan they fix their own production goals and even prices (except for the prices of some raw materials which are generally set by the national government). They raise a large part of their capital themselves through bank loans and from their own profits, although some part, varying in accordance with the nature of the enterprise, is supplied to them from the government budget. Finally, the workers have a large voice in the management of the enterprises through their own workers' councils elected by secret ballot. The director of the enterprise is selected by a specially created local commission consisting of representatives of the Local People's Committee, the trade union, and the workers' council. The selection is made from among the persons who, in response to the advertisement made in the newspapers, have applied for the job. The nomination by the commission is submitted to the workers' council for approval. The directors of the national monopolies are appointed by the government.

Communist China.—In Communist China, public enterprises are managed in an even more authoritarian manner than in the Soviet Union. Their management is almost military in character, but in the mid-1960s information on their organization and operation was scant.

BIBLIOGRAPHY.—W. A. Robson, *Nationalized Industry and Public Ownership* (1960); A. H. Hanson, *Public Enterprise and Economic Development* (1959); A. H. Hanson (ed.), *Public Enterprise* (1955), *Nationalization, a Book of Readings* (1963); W. Friedmann (ed.), *The Public Corporation* (1954); M. Einaudi, M. Byé, and E. Rossi, *Nationalization in France and Italy* (1955); H. McClosky and J. E. Turner, *The Soviet Dictatorship* (1960). (PA. ST.)

PUBLIC HEALTH is defined by the World Health Organization as "the science and art of preventing disease, prolonging life, and promoting health and efficiency through organized community efforts." These efforts are directed toward sanitation of the environment, control of communicable infections, education of the individual in personal hygiene, organization of medical and nursing services for the early diagnosis and preventive treatment of disease, and "the development of social machinery to ensure for every individual a standard of living adequate for the maintenance of health." The broad aim of public health, in the view of WHO, is "to enable every citizen to realize his birthright of health and longevity."

The emphasis in public health practice may be either environmental or personal—with the understanding that one approach complements the other. Environmental public health is concerned with the community's physical surroundings; it consists of epidemic disease control and sanitary hygiene. Personal public health influences the group by applying the principles of hygiene through individuals; it consists of preventive medicine, social hygiene, social medicine, and social insurance. These main orders of public health are by no means clear-cut and the terms themselves are ambiguous: thus environmental public health and preventive medicine are often spoken of as covering virtually all public health, while social medicine and social hygiene are, for

many, little distinguishable. The framework below is offered, therefore, only as a convenient guide, not a rigid plan.

ENVIRONMENTAL PUBLIC HEALTH

Epidemic disease control	*Sanitary hygiene*
Quarantine	Sewage disposal
Epidemiological services	Water supplies
Public Health laboratories	Food hygiene
Contact tracing	Housing
Vector control	Atmospheric pollution
Eradication measures	Radiation hazards
	Light, heat, and noise

PERSONAL PUBLIC HEALTH

Preventive medicine	*Social hygiene*	*Social medicine*
Immunization	Infant health	Hygiene in hospital
Preventive	Child and adolescent	practice
examinations	health	Hygiene of general
Health education	Maternal health	practice
Cancer prevention	Care of the	Rehabilitation of
Nutritional measures	handicapped	the sick
Epidemiological	Care of the neglected	Health centres
studies of	child	
noninfectious	Care of the aged	
diseases	Mental hygiene	*Social insurance*
Social surveys	Tuberculosis control	
Vital and health	Venereal disease	
statistics	control	
	Rehabilitation of	
	social casualties,	
	problem families,	
	and unwed mothers	
	Social welfare	

The above groupings are based on a concept of public health that leaves no room for rivalry between preventive and curative medicine: both hospital and general practice are important. The hospital "should organize itself to serve the community in all aspects of health care.... It should not limit its functions to the restorative sphere" (WHO, 1957); general practitioners "should embrace the work of communal as well as individual medicine" (Dawson Report, 1920). Both hospitals and general practitioners will find themselves involved with the family, which is of paramount importance to the health of the community.

This article recounts the history of public health and describes special aspects of its development in Europe, the United Kingdom and the Commonwealth, the United States, the U.S.S.R., Turkey, Yugoslavia, and other countries. It then examines various types of public health administrative systems, and outlines international cooperative efforts.

For related information *see* HEALTH AND SAFETY LAWS; HEALTH EDUCATION; INDUSTRIAL MEDICINE; MATERNAL AND CHILD HEALTH; MEDICAL CARE, GOVERNMENT; MENTAL HEALTH; PREVENTIVE MEDICINE; and SOCIAL WELFARE.

HISTORY

From Earliest Times to 1500.—Little is known of public health in early civilizations, but all the evidence suggests that, with few exceptions, it was bad. Disease was probably the chief cause of death; in particular, infant and child mortality throughout many thousands of years was very high—in Rome and in Greece it was customary to wait a week before naming babies, for so few survived. Although it is not always easy to identify diseases from the descriptions in ancient writings, enough is known to state with some certainty that all diseases since differentiated have affected man since earliest times. The ultimate effect of so much disease was to check population growth so that the population of the world advanced only slowly, and at different times and places it is known to have declined.

Yet from earliest times some form of public health has existed, as a conscious effort by authority to apply social, scientific, and medical knowledge to the protection of the health of the community. The teachings of the major religions have aided public health by extolling sobriety, cleanliness, the avoidance of excretal pollution, the maintenance of family life, isolation of infectious persons, and the ritual abstention from foods likely to carry parasites. The latrine and flush closet first appeared in Crete about 1000 B.C. Egypt, Greece, and Rome built model towns and had excellent sanitary systems. Greece and Rome developed the hypocaust (*q.v.*) and in Rome public baths (*see* BATH) were available to everyone. Rome also began the isolation of infectious disease by building leprosariums. Both Rome and Greece sought to regulate prostitution. India and China practised inoculation against smallpox some time before the Christian era. The Arabic civilization had health departments with sanitary inspectors, and its food hygiene may have been the best achieved at any time before the 20th century. The Arabs also were the first to build hospitals with differentiation between patients. European towns of the Middle Ages were generally well planned, with water supplies and hospitals: leprosy disappeared following the practice of isolation, and primitive measures were developed to limit epidemic spread.

But there were many deficiencies: crowding and squalor in Rome; epidemic and endemic diseases, such as malaria, which prevailed unchecked; neglect of child life; and an almost brutal misuse of human labour in the early industrial undertakings. Lack of scientific knowledge was a handicap, as seen in the failure to differentiate disease, erroneous theories of the epidemic process, and the stubbornly held theory of derangement of "humours" as the cause of illness. Yet enough was known to make a sound basis for public health action: the connection between malaria and marshy terrain, and the worst effects of industrial processes, had been noted by the ancients; maternal and child health was the subject of Galen's first book on hygiene; the specificity of anthrax, measles, scabies, and smallpox was understood by the Arabs during the Middle Ages; and in the early 16th century it was known how to cure and prevent scurvy and how to treat syphilis with mercury.

That none of this knowledge led to effective public health services was due in large part to social attitudes. Those in authority took little interest in the fate of the masses (except for soldiery), and the learned remained aloof from the ill-educated. Galen said of occupational hazards: "The life of many men is involved in the business of their occupation and it is inevitable that they should be harmed by what they do," adding, "and it is impossible to change it." His treatise on hygiene, *De sanitate tuenda* (A.D. 157), was written for the few, and there was no exception to this outlook until the Renaissance. Sickness and occasional hunger were everywhere considered normal attributes of living. Indeed, the population of the world advanced from about 275,000,000 in A.D. 1000 to only 450,000,000 during the next 500 years.

From 1500 to 1800.—With the Renaissance, ideas about public health began to grow. Sir Thomas More in *Utopia* (1516) described an imaginary country where hygiene protected health, and medicine restored it, and where all that was needed for health was to hand. Other ideas followed, in Daniel Defoe's *Essay upon Projects* (1698), John Bellers' *Essay Towards the Improvement of Physick* (1714), and Lodovico Muratori's *Della publica felicita* (1749). Bernardino Ramazzini's *De morbis artificum diatriba* (1700) was the first full-scale treatise on occupational health. John Pringle wrote *Observations on the Diseases of the Army* (1752) and James Lind *An Essay on the Most Effectual Means of Preserving the Health of Seamen in the Royal Navy* (1757). Richard Mead's *A Short Discourse Concerning Pestilential Contagion* (1722) suggested the need for a central council of health with local public health organization.

Social insurance was encouraged. The more enlightened industrialists sought means to protect their workers from the worst of the poisonings. Attempts were made from about 1600 to establish services of one sort or another; *e.g.*, St. Vincent de Paul began home nursing through his Confraternities of Charity in 1617, while *bureaux de santé* were established in many French towns and municipal doctors were appointed in several European states. Many advances began to be made upon Galenic medicine; *e.g.*, Girolamo Fracastoro (1478–1553) suspected that disease was caused by microorganisms, and Anton van Leeuwenhoek (1632–1723) first observed bacteria. The Greco-Roman theory that epidemics are caused by "miasms," or vapours from the earth, declined although Thomas Sydenham (1624–89) reinterpreted it in terms of atmospheric conditions. The increasing differentia-

tion of disease further weakened the humoral theories. Compulsory parish registration and, in London, the bills of mortality —weekly lists of deaths, compiled by house-to-house visiting— particularized the toll of disease. John Graunt in his *Natural and Political Observations . . . Made upon the Bills of Mortality* (1662) provided one of the earliest classifications of disease.

After 1650, improvements in living conditions had a marked effect, particularly in England. Public health gradually improved in all parts of the world, except perhaps in Africa. Infant and child mortality began to decline and population to advance more sharply, so that by 1798 the world population had doubled to reach 920,000,000. But if industrialization raised general living standards, it also depressed those of the workers in the new slums, and it was this side effect more than anything else that determined the spectacular growth of public health activity after 1750.

From 1800 to Modern Times.—Public health from 1800 on was greatly influenced by general scientific progress. Rapid advances in medical science in the 19th century revolutionized ideas about the basis of health. Physiological chemistry gave rise to the science of nutrition; clinical medicine established the specificity of disease. Most important, the centuries-old erroneous theories of epidemic spread were finally routed. Oliver Wendell Holmes (1809–94) in the United States and I. P. Semmelweis (1818–65) in Vienna added puerperal (childbed) fever to the lengthening list of diseases known to be conveyed by human contact. F. G. J. Henle put forward the hypothesis that the infectious process was biological (1840); Sir John Burdon-Sanderson established it in 1866. John Snow published his pamphlet *On the Mode of Communication of Cholera* (1849) and in 1854 gave convincing evidence of its waterborne spread; William Budd did the same for typhoid (1873). The end of the century was notable for Pasteur's identification of pathogenic bacteria and the final disproof of the theory of spontaneous generation. Robert Koch isolated the tubercle bacillus in 1882 and, in rapid succession, the same was done for many common infectious maladies. An important result of the germ theory of disease was the transformation of hospitals. They took on new meaning when the antisepsis principles of Joseph Lister (1827–1912) were applied, and by the end of the century they began to take the chief position in community health services. During the 20th century science continued, by the discovery of vitamins, antibiotics, and much else, to give public health new weapons. The study of society, particularly by means of the social survey, extended the basic concepts of public health, and the medical officer of health became something of a social scientist as well.

International Public Health.—Public health collaboration among countries originated in the fear of epidemic spread and the inconvenience to trade arising out of the practice of quarantine (*q.v.*). From 1851 a series of International Sanitary Congresses was held in the capitals of Europe and the United States, leading eventually to the formation of the Pan American Sanitary Bureau (1902) with headquarters in Washington, D.C., and L'Office Internationale d'Hygiène Publique (1909) with headquarters in Paris. After World War I the health section of the League of Nations was created (1923) with headquarters at Geneva. It was followed after World War II by the World Health Organization (1948), a specialized agency of the United Nations. WHO, also with headquarters in Geneva, absorbed both the League health office and the Paris office and thus became the sole international health organization, excepting the Pan American Sanitary Bureau, which continued to operate independently but acted also as the WHO regional office for the Americas. Cooperation among the nations has continued in the control of the spread of disease, and has widened into the field of aid in the strengthening of medical services and medical education for the developing countries. *See* WORLD HEALTH ORGANIZATION (WHO).

NATIONAL DEVELOPMENTS

WESTERN EUROPE

The philosophy of public health on the continent was long dominated by the paternalistic concept of absolute rule. The benevolent sovereign devised safeguards for health: he believed that in doing so he was strengthening the state and increasing its riches. Health protection thus became a function of the state and was supervised by officials referred to as "medical police." The German physician J. P. Frank, in *System einer Vollständigen medicinischen Polizey* (1779), discussed every aspect of public health, with the exception of occupational health. Frank's programs were, for the most part, beyond the capacity of the 18th century, and some, such as health education and the prevention of accidents, were only put into operation much later. Each sovereign state tended to develop public health independently: not even Frank's omnibus of social medicine could impose a blueprint. Sweden pioneered vital statistics (1748); Germany made vaccination compulsory within a few years of Edward Jenner's discovery (1796); Denmark set up a system of gratuitous treatment of venereal disease (1790); the Netherlands and Scandinavia trained the midwife in the early part of the 20th century; France pioneered the infant consultation centre. The European pattern spread to colonial territories and, by association with Germany, to Japan.

In France public health was based upon the *département* under the authority of the *préfet*, a nominated state official, and was dependent on directions from a central government agency. French progressives in the 19th century dwelt upon the need for organized medical care. The marquis de Condorcet in *L'Esquisse d'un tableau historique des progrès de l'esprit humain* (1793) asked for a comprehensive system of insurance to eliminate poverty; J. R. Guérin, editor of the Parisian *Gazette Médicale*, urged (1808) that medicines should be dedicated to society; Philippe Buchez (1899) advocated a national health service with a doctor to each 2,000 persons. A. J. P. Parent Duchâtelet (1790–1836) described prostitution in *De la prostitution dans la ville de Paris* (1836); L. R. Villermé (1782–1863) studied differential mortalities in various districts of Paris and surveyed the health of textile workers. The *préfets* received their first national circular about hospitals in 1840 and most European countries began to build state hospitals at about that time. Denmark and Sweden in 1831 had a hospital system financed by taxes. European nations also early evolved extensive systems of social insurance: Germany (under Bismarck) introduced such legislation in 1883, Austria followed in 1888, Hungary in 1891, Luxembourg in 1907, and Norway in 1909. In contrast, sanitary hygiene tended to be neglected.

UNITED KINGDOM AND THE COMMONWEALTH

Public health in the United Kingdom took a different course. Its administrative system, based on local government with a considerable measure of local autonomy, accorded with a dislike of autocratic rule, while its main emphasis was upon environmental hygiene, largely because of the slum living born of the Industrial Revolution. Edwin Chadwick (1800–90) became secretary to the Royal Commission (1832) on the reform of the Poor Law and was largely responsible for its report. The scheme under which the country was divided into unions of parishes, administered by elected boards of guardians, each board having a medical officer responsible for giving medical care to paupers, was essentially Chadwick's, and he himself became secretary to the Poor Law Commission in London (1834). The new system soon acquired public health functions, including vaccination and the registration of births and deaths. Unfortunately the system was based upon the philosophy of "less eligibility" (*i.e.*, that paupers should be accorded less consideration than labourers) and therefore the principles underlying personal public health were mostly denied in practice.

Chadwick came to appreciate that disease causes poverty, and his emphasis on "the pecuniary cost of noxious agencies" led to advances in environmental public health. His views were underscored by the arrival of cholera, which had left India in 1826 to spread relentlessly across Europe. Persons of initiative and public spirit began to see the need for public sanitary measures. Chadwick, marshaling these new forces, was greatly aided by the publication of extracts from the fourth and fifth annual reports of the Poor Law commissioners, *The Sanitary Conditions of the Labouring Population* (1842). Chadwick's campaign culminated

in passage of the Public Health Act of 1848—a landmark in world public health. The act established locally elected boards of health with powers to appoint a medical officer of health, impose a tax, and remedy sanitary defects by recourse to a sanitary code. The act thus embodied Chadwick's belief that public health should be administered locally, to encourage the people to participate in their own protection; and it implemented his pioneering suggestion that such boards employ medical men as specialist advisers.

Another supporter of health reform was William Farr, whose annual reports as compiler of abstracts to the registrar general made vital statistics the basis of constructive thinking, thus dispensing with what he called "vague conjecture" and powerfully stimulating a wide reading public. Among the many who were influenced by his writings was Florence Nightingale, whose *Notes on Nursing* (1860) called attention to the enormous infant and child mortality and discussed the importance of household hygiene. T. Southwood Smith, who worked with Chadwick on the General Board of Health established by the 1848 act, based his *Philosophy of Health* (1835–37) on the new teachings of science.

By 1872 the country was divided into sanitary areas governed by locally elected bodies, with the duty of appointing medical officers of health. Parliament legislated widely to enable local authorities to enforce public health provisions. This legislation was influenced by John Simon, chief medical officer to the central health department (at the Privy Council) 1848–71, who conducted a nationwide series of socio-medical surveys of housing, diet, industrial processes, infant mortality, worm infestations, and hospitals. The Sanitary Act of 1866 saw the beginnings of industrial hygiene. The Public Health Act of 1875 provided a complete sanitary code which, with consolidation and adjustments, remains in force. A succession of housing acts placed increasing responsibility for housing upon the medical officer of health, ensuring that health became the most important consideration in dealing with slums. The diploma in public health, to be registered by the General Medical Council, was made compulsory for senior posts in the public health service.

The local-government system, and the elaboration of the sanitary code under which it worked, was accompanied by growth of a central organization which supervised the work by inspection and was later to regulate it by grants-in-aid. This trend resulted, in 1919, in the formation of the Ministry of Health, which brought together health functions hitherto scattered among government departments; but it left mental health under the board of control and industrial hygiene under the Home Office (later under the Ministry of Labour). The Ministry of Health reintroduced Simon's scientific approach to health problems and gave to medical officers of health a new feeling of being linked sympathetically with the centre. The reports of Sir George Newman, the first chief medical officer to the Ministry of Health, set a new tone and embodied a new spirit of social and preventive medicine.

During the 20th century the emphasis shifted gradually from environmental toward personal public health. A succession of statutes, of which perhaps the Maternity and Child Welfare Act (1918) was the most important, placed responsibility upon county councils and county boroughs for most of this work, leaving the original sanitary areas—urban and rural districts and boroughs—responsible for environmental sanitation. The boards of guardians were abolished in 1929 and their public health functions transferred to the county councils and county boroughs. National health insurance (1911) gave medical, sickness, maternity, disablement, and sanatorium benefits to 16,000,000 workers. This marked the beginning of a process of socialization upon which, after World War II, the National Health Service Act was to build (*see* below). Other social legislation between 1944 and 1948 helped to create the framework within which community health problems were reassessed.

The National Health Service Act (1946) provided a comprehensive cover for most of the health services, including hospitals, general practice, and public health; it included all aspects of mental health but not the industrial medical service of environmental public health. Medical care in the hospital and by the general practitioner became, and largely remained, free. The service was

designed to operate, at the periphery, in three distinct compart
ments: (1) Regional hospital boards, centred upon universities
and covering up to 5,000,000 people, took over the running of
virtually all institutions for medical care. (2) Executive councils
in the areas of counties and county boroughs became responsible
for the general-practitioner service. (3) Local health authorities
(county councils and county boroughs) were made responsible for
many services, including health visiting, home nursing, home helps,
domiciliary midwifery, the prevention of illness and the care and
aftercare of persons suffering from illness or mental deficiency,
and the provision of health centres. Public health under this act
was freed from administrative responsibilities for hospitals, but it
was made part of a wide scheme of socialization in which the
hygiene of both general practice and of hospitals had a new
meaning.

The first 20 years of the National Health Service emphasized
the community as the subject of public health. Though environmental hygiene and the control of communicable disease were together the prime concerns of the medical officer, he was increasingly concerned with the prevention of disease and with the health
and social welfare of the community. Examples of prevention in
the 1960s were a notification scheme for congenital abnormalities
in the newborn and the routine screening of women for the early
detection of cancers of the womb. Similarly, the prevention of
mental illness became associated with the growth of community
social services for the mentally ill and the mentally handicapped.
While the population of hospitals for the mental ill fell, there was
an increasing association of general hospitals with psychiatric
treatment and with community mental health services. Health
education of the community also developed. Thus, dental health
education and informing the public of the relation of cigarette
smoking to lung cancer and bronchitis were major interests of the
Ministry of Health and the Central Council for Health Education.
A few local antismoking clinics were set up.

The organization of the health service moved somewhat toward
the community as the basic unit. Reports of the Ministry of
Health on *Health and Welfare: the Development of Community
Care* (1963) and the *Hospital Plan for England and Wales* (1962),
each with later revisions, formed the basis for policy; but trends
in the 1960s could be seen in the growth of the district hospital
concept, in the setting up of health centres such as those at Peckham (London) and Cleckheaton (Yorkshire), in the attachment
of health visitors to general practices as in Oxford, and in the
growth of continuing medical education for the family doctor.

The Commonwealth.—The influence of the United Kingdom
sanitary movement spread throughout the British Empire. Thus
colonies, dominions, and many other territories which later became independent began to build public health services with
autonomous public health authorities, the medical officer of health,
and the sanitary code as their first considerations. In the absence
of voluntary and other agencies which could shoulder responsibility,
the British pattern of local autonomy had to develop under the
authority of the Colonial Office, centred in London. In the virtual
absence of corps of physicians and in the face of so much sickness, medical relief had from the beginning to be accepted as a
responsibility of government and consequently, as the Bhore Report (1946) said of India, "Medical relief received much more at
tention than the development of those preventive services which
may collectively be termed 'public health activities'." Although
sanitary commissioners were appointed to Indian provinces in the
middle of the 19th century, the establishment of an effective local-
government system for public health did not begin in India and
Ceylon—themselves in advance of other colonial territories—
until the 20th century. The development of public health in any
real sense began in India only in 1921, after the Government of
India Act (1919) had transferred health administration to the
provinces. Ceylon established the first of a series of local health
units, covering 40,000–80,000 population, in 1926 and soon had
virtually complete coverage.

Canada, Australia, New Zealand, and South Africa also developed their public health services much later than did the United
Kingdom. New Zealand established services most closely re-

sembling that of the U.K., with free medical care from the general
practitioner and in the hospital, the chief distinction being the
method of paying the general practitioner by fees for service
rather than by per capita taxation. In Canada and Australia
public health is a state responsibility and the federal government
influences developments by grants-in-aid and consultant advice.
Neither has socialized medicine, but Canada pioneered a scheme
in Saskatchewan for comprehensive care which goes beyond that
of the U.K. in making salaried appointments outside the hospital.
South Africa pioneered "family health care" in the health centre
at Pholela, and the National Health Service Commission (1944)
recommended that the government base a service for the whole
country upon such units, each serving about 25,000 people; but
cost and other considerations, including the pull of curative medicine toward the hospital, prevented this.   (C. F. Bn.)

UNITED STATES

Great epidemics of smallpox raged in North America in the
17th and 18th centuries, and repeated yellow fever epidemics
characterized the 18th century, especially in New York during the
American Revolution. Rigid public health measures were established during these epidemics. Individuals and families, at times
whole communities, were quarantined, and ship quarantine measures attempted to prevent importation of disease. But quarantine
often failed because of misunderstanding of the complex interrelationships among the disease carriers, modes of transmission,
incubation periods, and other epidemiologic factors. Disease
contagion was often attributed to bad odours from decaying animal
or vegetable matter, and the few public health departments in
existence at that time were organized largely for the removal of
community debris.

Municipal health boards were created in Baltimore in 1798, in
Charleston, S.C., in 1815, and in Philadelphia in 1818. In 1850
an epochal report of the Sanitary Commission of Massachusetts
was issued by Lemuel Shattuck and others, and 15 years later a
sanitary survey of New York City was completed by Stephen
Smith. These reports were early charters for broad public health
programs in the U.S. Under their impetus the formation of state
health boards was begun. That of Massachusetts was the first
(1869), and by 1919 all the states had organized health departments. Local health departments, too, began to increase after
1920. Just before World War I the first full-time county health
department was established in Yakima County, Washington.

In 1798 Congress passed an act providing for the medical care
of merchant seamen. This was the first federal health program
—the forerunner of the present U.S. Public Health Service, first
organized in 1870 as a national agency with a central headquarters
and a medical officer in charge.

As early as 1799 Congress had authorized federal officers to
cooperate with state and local authorities in the enforcement of
quarantine laws. Physicians in the marine hospitals also helped
communities curb epidemics of cholera and yellow fever. In 1893
Congress gave full responsibility for foreign and interstate quarantine to the Public Health Service, thereby giving uniformity to
the laws previously administered by the states.

In 1887 the service established a hygienic laboratory in the
marine hospital on Staten Island, N.Y., to apply the new bacteriologic principles to the study of disease in the U.S. This small
beginning eventually resulted in the establishment of the National
Institutes of Health, research arm of the Public Health Service
and the largest supporter of medical research in the country.

The health provisions of the Social Security Act of 1935, which
authorized annual grants to states for general health purposes,
greatly stimulated the development of health services and strengthened federal-state cooperation. The National Cancer Act of 1937,
the Venereal Disease Control Act of 1938, and the Hospital Survey
and Construction Act and the Mental Health Act, both of 1946,
expanded the health work of the federal government.

The Department of Health, Education, and Welfare was created
in 1953, with the Public Health Service as one of its major constituents. Related health agencies, such as the Food and Drug
Administration, the Vocational Rehabilitation Administration, and

the Children's Bureau, were also included in the department.

Voluntary health organizations, supported by publicly contributed funds, have increased greatly in number and strength since the voluntary movement was launched in the late 19th century. The National Tuberculosis Association, the American Heart Association, and the National Society for the Prevention of Blindness are examples of voluntary agencies.

Local Health Services.—Local effort continues to play a primary role in the United States. The size and scope of local programs vary, but the following are some of their typical functions: (1) control of communicable and chronic diseases; (2) operation of clinics for mothers and children and for various preventive and diagnostic services; (3) provision of public health nursing services; (4) environmental health services, including inspection, supervision, and sanitary control of water supplies, sewage disposal facilities, milk production and distribution, and food-handling establishments; (5) public health education and information; (6) collection and analysis of vital statistics; (7) operation of community health centres, hospitals, and other facilities; and (8) community health planning, consultation, and coordination.

A modern local health department consists of a corps of health specialists, such as physicians, nurses, dentists, engineers, sanitarians, and health educators, and supporting technical and administrative personnel. In addition, other local agencies often assume responsibility for certain health services or activities: boards of education may deal with school health programs, departments of public works with construction and maintenance of sanitation facilities, and welfare agencies with provision of medical and hospital care.

State Health Services.—Within a single state, health services may be dispersed among numerous separate agencies of state government. Every state, however, has a specific agency, usually termed the department of health, charged with overall health responsibilities. State health work ranges from regulatory or advisory activities to the operation of certain direct services.

State governments usually carry on five types of health functions: (1) public health and preventive services, such as demonstrations of new techniques and programs, and supervision over utilities of public health importance; (2) medical and custodial care, such as the operation of hospitals for tuberculosis and mental illness; (3) expansion and improvement of hospitals, medical facilities, and public health centres; (4) licensure for health reasons of individuals, agencies, and enterprises serving the public; and (5) provision of financial assistance and technical consultation to local units of government for conducting health programs. In addition, most states maintain regulatory authority over most health matters, and promulgate rules and regulations which are applicable throughout the state.

Federal Health Services.—The Public Health Service of the U.S. Department of Health, Education, and Welfare is the principal federal health agency, but several other departments and independent agencies have specific health interests and responsibilities. Federal health agencies are responsible for identifying and helping to meet national health problems, for helping to improve state and local services, for controlling interstate health hazards, and for working with other countries on international health matters. The federal government also has a number of direct health functions, including: (1) protecting the United States from communicable diseases from abroad; (2) providing medical and hospital care for designated beneficiaries, such as members of the armed services, veterans, merchant seamen, and American Indians: (3) protecting the consumer against impure or misbranded foods, drugs, and cosmetics; and (4) licensing and regulating the production of serums, vaccines, and other biological products. In addition, the federal government spearheads a vast medical research and research training effort. In the 1960s the federal government was supporting more than half of the medical research in the United States, in its own laboratories and through grants to universities and other scientific institutions. Federal agencies provide technical services and grants-in-aid to improve health services and resources throughout the country. For example, federal grants matched by nonfederal funds have helped

to build many new hospitals and related facilities since World War II.

Voluntary Health Agencies.—Voluntary effort is a significant part of health work in the United States. By 1960 there were more than 100,000 voluntary agencies in the health field. Most operated at the city or county level, but nearly 300 had statewide activities and about 30 were national in scope. Supported largely through private sources, voluntary agencies make substantial contributions to public and professional education, research, and programs of medical and hospital care in their respective fields of interest. An agency's interest may centre on a specific disease, such as tuberculosis, cancer, or arthritis; on safeguarding specific bodily functions, such as vision or hearing; or on promoting the health of a special group, such as mothers and children, the aged, or the handicapped. Other nongovernmental groups which contribute to total health services or resources in the U.S. include hospitals, foundations, private laboratories, professional organizations, schools and universities, industrial and labour groups, and civic organizations.

Progress in Public Health.—There is a great variety in the type, content, scope, and quality of performance of health services in the United States. Moreover, these services are provided by a multiplicity of independent agencies; *e.g.*, the three levels of government—federal, state, and local (city or county)—represent distinct and separate entities. In effect, however, they constitute a working partnership for the protection and promotion of human health. Moreover, they work closely with voluntary agencies, professional groups, schools and foundations, management and labour, and families and communities to control disease and improve well-being. The result has been a consistently upward trend in both individual and community health. In 1900 there were 17.2 deaths from all causes per 1,000 population; in 1963 the rate was 9.6. The infant death rate for 1965 was 25.4 per 1,000 live births, compared with a rate of 100 in 1915. In 1935, for each 10,000 live births, 58 mothers died; in 1963 there were 3.7 maternal deaths per 10,000 live births. Since the turn of the century there has been a gain of more than 20 years in life expectancy: from about 47 years to almost 70 years.

Most dramatic has been the continuing success against the infectious diseases which were once the chief causes of death among children. The principal communicable diseases of childhood—diphtheria, whooping cough, measles, and scarlet fever—had a combined death rate of 243 per 100,000 children under 15 years of age in 1900, but they accounted for only about 1 death per 100,000 in this age group in the 1960s. Other infectious diseases, such as smallpox, typhoid fever, pneumonia, gastrointestinal infections, and trachoma, have also been greatly reduced. Tuberculosis mortality fell from a rate of 194 per 100,000 in 1900 to 4.2 in 1965—a drop of nearly 98%. From 1945 to 1951 the average annual decline for this disease rose to 10%, and after 1951 there was an average 21% drop in the death rate each year. The death rate for syphilis fell from 16 deaths per 100,000 in 1938 to 1.5 in 1965.

The chronic diseases constituted the major health problem in the U.S. throughout the 1960s. Cancer and heart diseases together caused more than 70% of all deaths in 1963. These diseases, plus diabetes, arthritis, neurological defects, and mental illness, as well as accidents, accounted for much disability, long-term illness, and hospital care in the U.S. Public health agencies in the U.S. are turning increasingly to the control of these diseases; to the health problems of an aging population; and to the environmental problems associated with a complex industrial and social environment: water and air pollution, unhygienic housing, preventable accidents, the hazards involved in the widespread use of chemicals and ionizing radiation, and emotional stress.   (L. L. Te.)

OTHER COUNTRIES

After World War I the U.S.S.R., Turkey, and Yugoslavia sought to achieve in a few years what Western Europe and the U.S. had accomplished in two centuries. The U.S.S.R. and Yugoslavia had been influenced by European developments in public health—the former had established a form of local government, the zemstvo, employing salaried doctors responsible for both curative and preventive medicine in their districts, and the latter had taken part in Austrian public health developments—but all three were typical underdeveloped countries with high infant and child mortality, low expectation of life, widespread infectious and nutritional diseases, and an almost complete lack of sanitary science.

The principles upon which public health in these countries is based are as follows: complete integration of curative and preventive medicine, medicine as a social service, the predominance of preventive medicine, health centres as the basis of operation, and community participation. These are mainly remarkable for the fact that they were put into operation in the early 1920s, for in themselves they go little beyond the statements made in various white papers which preceded the National Health Service in Britain, or the many national and international reports.

In the U.S.S.R. administration is centralized, with little local autonomy. Standards laid down by the union ministry are administered by the republic through special departments; day-to-day work is conducted by regional and district committees. For many special services, e.g., health education, there are central institutes for research and administrative direction. The chief element in the Soviet system is the polyclinic, a health centre which, in effect, combines the primary and secondary health centres recommended in the Dawson Report. It employs three types of salaried physicians, on a whole-time basis: (1) general practitioners who cover a defined sector; (2) specialists who work in the centre; and (3) public health experts. The centre does most of the work performed in Western Europe and the U.S. in hospital out-patient departments, including preventive examinations by a team of specialists—the method known as dispensarization—and factory health, school health, and maternal and child health work. The training of doctors is designed to use medicine as a social service, and emphasizes the principles of public health; students can specialize in general medicine, sanitary and hygienic work, or pediatrics. The U.S.S.R. system also makes use of soviets; i.e., village or street committees. The 70,000 soviets are responsible for sanitary matters, for seeing that care is given where needed, for work in connection with problem families and marital disharmony, for following up the schoolchildren, for inquiries in relation to surveys, and much else. The social effects of this committee system upon public health work are considerable.

Yugoslavian public health has many of the features seen in the U.S.S.R.: there are health centres and doctors practise largely on salary. But there are many differences, the most striking being an Institute of Hygiene, combining administration and research, in each of the nine republics. After 1948 there was a decentralization of health activities, permitting a considerable measure of local autonomy; town councils, industries, and hospitals, or groups of hospitals, were given powers to manage their own affairs within their respective budgets—hospitals budgeting on the basis of payments for beds from social security funds, industries and town councils on an allocation of industrial profits.

Turkey, with a different political philosophy but an equivalent degree of centralization of powers, took another course. As did the U.S.S.R. and Yugoslavia, it developed the health centre as a focus of preventive and curative work—but in the form of a rural hospital. The Ministry of Health and Social Assistance controls the organization through directors of health in the provinces, the governor of the province being head of the provincial health board, composed of officials. Corresponding district boards exist and a socialized health scheme was being introduced in stages. At the same time new emphasis was being placed on medical and public health education and on the training of health administrators.

After World War II public health advanced notably in Indonesia, Burma, Thailand, the South American states, China, India, and Pakistan. The period was remarkable for the influence of the World Health Organization and of other agencies of the United Nations. The health problems facing these countries were even greater than were those of the U.S.S.R., Turkey, and Yugoslavia in the 1920s: communicable and nutritional diseases abounded; intestinal infections and worms of many kinds were almost universal; special diseases, such as yaws, filariasis, and leprosy, prevailed over wide areas; lack of sanitation caused untold illness; childbirth remained in the hands of village midwives, so that in Indonesia a woman was said to die in childbirth every quarter of an hour and a baby every minute; Indonesia had one doctor to 57,000 people. Moreover, the social framework upon which health services depend had hardly begun to develop in most cases: there was an absence of scientific background, while deeply rooted customs and beliefs made progress difficult.

Success in these circumstances was inevitably limited. Most of these countries had centralized schemes for the eradication of special diseases, often undertaken with the help of international bodies or financed by interested nations. In Brazil there were national services for malaria, leprosy, yellow fever, mental diseases, cancer, plague, and tuberculosis and national agencies for port health, biostatistics, drug control, and health education. Nevertheless large parts of Brazil and of other countries were without local services. Thus in Bolivia, where systematic vaccination began in 1953, the Pan American Sanitary Bureau reported in 1956 that it had been impossible to eradicate smallpox because of the lack of an adequate organization to carry out vaccination on a national scale. Special schemes helped to fill in the gaps: in eight South American countries the reporting of communicable disease was done by "reporting areas."

Perhaps the most important expedient in these countries was the development of the model health unit, in which personnel could be trained and schemes suitable for the country tried out. Such model units, as at Bandung, Java, and Sinpur, Bengal, were the obvious first step at the local level. The training of new types of public health personnel, such as the home visitors in Indonesia, health assistants in Burma, and village workers in India, was important. Most of the countries new to public health also developed health centres. Thus Burma set out in 1941 to establish 800, using health assistants with 21 months' training, and by 1957 there were 300 centres in operation. India implemented the Bhore Report in this and other respects, and in the state of West Bengal there were more than 100 health centres by the 1960s.

Much was accomplished in little time, but it was clear that public health needed to develop a permanent framework, a sound organization at the local level, which could not only begin the services but also maintain them. Many countries, sometimes with the assistance of WHO, have developed national plans for promotion of indigenous medical education and for the increase of community medical services.   (C. F. Bn.)

ADMINISTRATIVE SYSTEMS

The Central Organization.—The forms and functions of central government administration in health matters vary from country to country. There are two main types of central health organization. One is the grouping of major health functions in a separate department; e.g., the Ministry of Health in the United Kingdom and the Commonwealth Department of Health in Australia. The other is the organization of health functions in a department responsible also for closely related functions; e.g., the Department of National Health and Welfare in Canada and the Ministry of Social Affairs and Public Health in the Netherlands. In some countries health functions are organized in the same department with the social insurance program; e.g., the Ministry of Social Security and Health in Ecuador and the Department of Health, Education, and Welfare in the United States.

The official responsible for the administration of national health affairs is, in many countries, a member of the cabinet. His political leadership is of great value in the development of a national program; his cabinet position ensures proper consideration of health problems at the highest level of public policy. The chief executive officer of health is almost universally a physician appointed according to the laws of his country. A minister or a chief executive may change with the party in power, but this lack of continuity in administration is generally overcome by the appointment of a permanent staff of professional and administrative personnel to head and operate the main departments. The United Kingdom is a partial exception to the rule that the executive officer is a physician: full executive power is vested in a permanent secretary; the chief medical officer advises the permanent secretary and himself has a right of approach direct to the minister. In the United States the surgeon general of the Public Health Service is a physician selected from a corps of commissioned medical officers and appointed by the president; this device, provided by law, ensures that the chief executive of the Public Health Service will always be a physician drawn from a group employed permanently in government service. The surgeon general is responsible directly to the secretary of health, education, and welfare.

Advisory councils are employed almost universally in the administration of national health programs. These bodies vary widely in composition, functions, and methods of operation but they invariably bring to bear on national health problems the thought of leading scientists, health personnel, and, in some instances, community leaders. As a rule the functions of councils are limited to giving advice but in some instances the decisions of a council are binding. Most central health departments have one general council whose function is to advise on overall planning, organization, and administration; *e.g.,* the Central Health Service Council in the United Kingdom and the Scientific Medical Council in Hungary. There may be many additional councils or committees dealing with particular programs, as in the U.S. Public Health Service, which has 12 advisory bodies authorized by the Congress and more than 100 *ad hoc* committees.

Few, if any, central departments of health are all-embracing; departments of industry, education, housing, labour, insurance, welfare, and agriculture may operate medical services of one kind or another. No country has concentrated the medical services for its military forces in the central health agency. Even countries with fully socialized health services place important health functions under ministries other than the ministry of health. In Denmark and the U.K. industrial and school medical services are under separate ministries; in the U.S.S.R. the ministries of transportation, river fleet, food industries, social security, and internal affairs have responsibility for specialized health functions. Since unity of control at the centre is virtually impracticable in the ever-broadening field of health, coordination is most important. Advisory councils may play an important role in coordinating activities if their membership includes representatives of other government departments having common interests in health. Planning commissions, interdepartmental councils or committees, and other coordinative devices have been adopted successfully.

Central administration is further complicated in a federal system. In the U.S. there are 50 states, no two of which have the same distribution of health functions in the structure of state government. There is also considerable differentiation in the type of state health organization. In about half of the states a board of health is the governing body, as illustrated in Minnesota, where a body of "nine members, learned in sanitary science . . . shall be appointed by the governor to serve without pay for overlapping three-year terms." The boards vary in number of members and composition, some being composed entirely of medical practitioners. A governing board of health usually has broad authority to adopt regulations which have the force of law, to approve the budget, and to appoint its chief executive officer, with or without the approval of the governor. Other state departments of health have advisory boards or councils, but they vest full administrative authority in a medical officer appointed by and responsible exclusively to the governor. The powers and functions of state health departments, however, are defined by the state legislatures which also appropriate the funds for state services and have exclusive authority over local governments.

To improve coordination between national and state health administrations, the surgeon general of the Public Health Service and the chief of the Children's Bureau (Department of Health, Education, and Welfare) confer annually with the 54 health officers of the states and dependencies of the U.S. The surgeon general also confers with state hospital and mental health authorities. Nine regional offices of the department serve groups of states with consultation on their health and welfare programs. Other federations have adopted effective coordinative devices; *e.g.,* the Central Coun-

cil of Health of India has the union health minister as chairman and the state health ministers as members. It was established "to consider and recommend broad lines of policy with regard to health in all its aspects, including remedial and preventive care, environmental hygiene, nutrition and health education, and the promotion of facilities for training and research." The Dominion Council of Health of Canada meets twice a year under the chairmanship of the deputy minister of national health and welfare. Its membership includes the administrative head of each provincial health department. The council "acts as an agency for promoting joint planning between the federal government and the provinces, and between individual provinces."

Federal grants-in-aid to states or provinces also help to unify health programs in most federations.

The Local Health Unit.—This is the name given to an organization which provides basic community health services under the direction of a medical officer; it is usually governed by a local authority. Its functions include maternal and child health, communicable disease control, environmental sanitation, maintenance of records for statistical purposes, health education of the public, public health nursing, and medical care. Wherever possible school medical services are also included, since these services enable the findings in school to be related more easily to the home, and ensure that the community nurses, or health visitors, are also the school nurses and that the medical officer of health acts as the administrative medical officer.

The local health unit is a suitable administrative device for the development of a much wider range of community health services, particularly for the care of the aged, the physically handicapped, and the chronically ill. Mental health services may be provided through the local unit. Occupational health may be included, as in Yugoslavia, but in many countries, including the U.K., this service has been developed independently. Social welfare service also may be provided by a separate agency; but there are great advantages in amalgamating health and welfare service, since it is not possible to separate the family's health and social problems. In rather more than a third of the local authorities in England and Wales, welfare and public health have been amalgamated; whereas in the U.S. local health and welfare services are almost universally administered by different departments.

In general terms, the population served by a local health unit should not exceed 150,000; but this depends upon many factors, including the size of the territorial area and the location of trade centres, as well as the political jurisdictions involved. In the U.S., for example, a county of 10,000 sq.mi. with a population of 6,000 and a municipality of 300 sq.mi. with a population of 2,000,000 present entirely different administrative problems. The term "local health unit" is often applied only to an organization serving a mixed urban and rural population of 10,000–50,000. Health services in cities and large towns are usually organized in departments comparable with those of state or provincial departments of health. It is possible to overcome the problem of population size by organizing the city health department in districts, each with its medical officer of health responsible to the city health officer. This was done in Toronto, New York City, and Baltimore, as well as in the larger counties (1,000,000–5,000,000) of the United Kingdom.

In the United States increased urbanization since World War II created very large metropolitan areas cutting across county lines and in some instances involving two or even three state jurisdictions. The solution of health problems in these suburban communities and central cities became a major concern of American public health.

The governing body of a local health department may be an *ad hoc* authority which undertakes nothing but health functions, similar to the local boards of health created in England and Wales under Chadwick's act of 1848. In European and most U.S. communities it is generally the town or county council which governs health services together with other community functions, the great advantage of this arrangement being that the medical officer of health can exert a wider influence. Some see in this a good reason for continuing local health administration through town and county councils; others have advocated a system of regional health administration, following the lines of hospital regionalization.

Medical Care in Public Health Administration.—Medical and hospital care is provided as a public service in some degree by most countries. Public medical service may be limited to hospitalization of patients with certain ailments; *e.g.*, mental disease, tuberculosis, chronic illness, and acute infections. Comprehensive health services may be provided for certain population groups, as in Canada and the United States where the federal governments provide such care for Indians and Eskimos. Many countries have compulsory sickness insurance; some combine the socialization of hospitals with sickness insurance covering general medical care, as in Denmark. Full-scale socialization of health services exists in a few countries, including the U.K., the U.S.S.R., and New Zealand.

Some degree of general medical and hospital care is provided as a public service for the needy even in countries that offer a limited range of health services for the civilian population. In federal systems the state or provincial governments are responsible for the development and administration of medical and hospital programs, as well as for public health services, with varying degrees of control and subsidy by the central government. Federal grants-in-aid, consultation, and technical services may be provided for medical care, health programs, and the construction of hospitals and other health facilities. General medical care is almost universally administered by departments of health; however, most states of the U.S. place this responsibility in their welfare agencies.

In countries where voluntary and nonprofit organizations support a considerable share of the health services and operate most of the general hospitals, as in the Netherlands and the U.S., there is bound to be pluralism in health administration. This makes coordination difficult; but strong voluntary effort has the advantages of involving citizens directly in the development of their health services and of infusing the administration with a spirit of experimentation often lacking in governmental services.

All countries experience difficulty in some degree in overcoming the barriers between health personnel with different interests and experience: hospital staffs and practicing physicians are traditionally oriented toward therapy in the acute stages of disease or injury, public health staffs toward preventive measures applied to individuals and community environments. Comprehensive health care aims to apply preventive, curative, and restorative services using all the instrumentalities of modern medicine and environmental science. The objectives are to prevent disease if possible, to give sick people the best available care in all stages of their illness, to rehabilitate the disabled, and to improve the health of the whole community. None of the existing administrative systems was fully achieving those health goals in the second half of the 20th century.

The Place of the Hospital.—Hospitals tended to grow up haphazardly, with little relation to one another and much duplication. General hospitals were located mainly in cities and large towns; outlying districts in consequence were poorly served. Special hospitals for mental disease, chronic illnesses, and infectious diseases often were constructed in isolated places and developed outside the main stream of scientific medicine. Advances in public understanding, medical knowledge, and therapy have been changing this situation: more general hospitals are providing psychiatric and tuberculosis services for diagnosis and intensive therapy, supplemented by community services for home care, follow-up, and rehabilitation.

The growth of the modern general hospital tended to shift the emphasis toward institutional care and away from care of patients in their homes and clinic facilities. In many countries, changes in the patterns of disease and of family life also encouraged hospitalization as the preferred method of receiving and delivering medical services. Hospitals became a first requisite in the development of community health services. In parts of the world where community health services are being provided virtually for the first time, the building of hospitals has priority. In highly developed countries the ratio of hospital beds to population rises as high as 7–10 per 1,000, of which approximately half are in mental

hospitals. In the 1960s many of these countries were attempting to provide adequate community general hospitals in outlying areas, while increased urbanization and deterioration of the older city hospitals were sharpening the demand for expanded hospital facilities in metropolitan areas.

Regional plans for hospital care are based upon a medical centre, usually a university medical school or a teaching hospital, which has facilities and specialists to deal with all types of illness, especially the more complex, and conducts scientific investigations. Intermediate hospitals in the larger communities provide basic medical and surgical services for their own localities and for patients referred from outlying areas of the region. At the periphery there are community and cottage or rural hospitals, the latter often little more than diagnostic or health centres equipped with a few beds for obstetric cases and emergencies. A two-way flow of patients and specialists takes place from periphery to centre and there is integration with public health under a broad overall plan. Regionalization, nowhere fully achieved, is most advanced in Europe and least so in North America, where voluntary hospitals provide most of the short-term general services and retain autonomy in their administration. In Canada and the U.S., however, hospital construction with federal grants is based on regional planning and in some parts of both countries services emanate from certain medical centres.

The Place of the Family Physician and the Health Centre.—There are many reasons to favour the family as the focal point of community health services. The family is the first defense in maintaining health, preventing disease, and caring for the sick; its characteristics largely determine the patterns of health and disease in the community. Logically, therefore, the family should have a physician to care for it as an entity. In the mid-20th century the belief in the family practitioner as the basis of a community health service led to the idea of the health centre. This term is usually limited to the type of institution which brings together into one building: (1) general medical practitioners; (2) nurses, midwives, social workers, and other paramedical workers who serve families in the same localities as the physicians; (3) preventive clinics; (4) diagnostic facilities; and (5) facilities for health education. The health centre was advocated in the Dawson Report (England, 1920), the Bhore Report (India, 1946), the report of the National Health Service Commission (South Africa, 1944), and other national reports, as well as by a committee of the World Health Organization (1952–54).

The health centre is distinct from a hospital although, as in rural health centres in Turkey, it may have a few beds for general nursing and midwifery. There is no reason, however, to exclude a community general hospital as the administrative locus of a health centre, provided that facilities and personnel for the objectives of both institutions are made available. The growth of medical science and the increasing complexity of its techniques in the second half of the 20th century have indicated that administrative integration rather than separation of hospital, medical, and public health services may prove to be the most effective system of the future.

See also CLINIC; HOSPITAL; and references under "Public Health" in the Index.   (C. F. BN.; L. L. TE.; V. J. G.)

BIBLIOGRAPHY.—*General:* S. E. Finer, *The Life and Times of Sir Edwin Chadwick* (1952); R. Sand, *The Advance to Social Medicine,* Eng. trans. from the French by Rita Bradshaw (1952); B. D. Paul and W. B. Miller (eds.), *Health, Culture and Community* (1955); M. J. Rosenau, *Preventive Medicine and Public Health,* ed. by K. F. Maxcy, 8th ed. (1956); G. Rosen, *A History of Public Health* (1958); M. J. Lynch and S. S. Raphael, *Medicine and the State* (1963). *International:* N. M. Goodman, *International Health Organizations and Their Work* (1952); C. F. Brockington, *World Health* (1958); WHO, *The First Ten Years* (1958). *United States:* American Public Health Association, *Medical Care in Transition . . . 1949–57, 1958–62,* 2 vol. (1964). *Great Britain:* W. M. Frazer, *A History of English Public Health, 1834–1939* (1950); J. M. Mackintosh, *Trends of Opinion about the Public Health, 1901–51* (1953); C. F. Brockington, *The Health of the Community . . . ,* 2nd ed. (1960). *U.S.S.R.:* WHO, *Health Services in the U.S.S.R.,* Public Health Papers no. 3 (1960).

PUBLIC OPINION. There is little agreement among political scientists, sociologists, and social psychologists on the exact meaning of this term. It has been loosely used to denote the firmly settled convictions of a group; to denote the process of developing opinions, as distinguished from the product; or to denote statements that are the result of a process of logical reasoning as contrasted with those arrived at by illogical means.

Nineteenth-century commentators stressed the rationality of the opinion process; those of the 20th century do not. In 1828, W. A. Mackinnon declared, "Public opinion may be said to be that sentiment on any given subject which is entertained by the best informed, most intelligent, and most moral persons in the community, which is gradually spread and adopted by nearly all persons of any education or proper feeling in a civilized state." Later, A. L. Lowell wrote that, "An opinion may be defined as the acceptance of one among two or more inconsistent views which are capable of being accepted by the rational mind as true" (A. L. Lowell, *Public Opinion in War and Peace,* Harvard University Press, Cambridge, Mass., 1923). After 1900 the developing science of social psychology increasingly emphasized nonrational factors involved in the opinion process; and the manipulative techniques of the practitioners of publicity, advertising, and propaganda further eroded faith in rationality. Political democracy, however, holds to the principle that the opinions of some men are based on reason and that it is possible to bring popular judgments to positions that are rationally defensible.

According to one definition, relatively stable beliefs should not be considered a part of the opinion process. A state of agreement following an opinion controversy is referred to as a consensus. There is consensus of the type that Montesquieu designated the *esprit général,* that Rousseau spoke of as the *volonté générale,* and that the English theorists called "public will." Wilhelm Bauer wrote of organic opinion as the relatively fixed views as distinguished from transient opinions. But one may consider that public opinion deals with those topics which are controversial and discussible and not with those on which opinions are firmly fixed.

History.—Plato denied the value of any general public opinion. In the main, Roman authors had little respect for mass opinion. It was not until the late 18th century that Alcuin's statement to Charlemagne, *Vox populi, vox Dei* ("The voice of the people is the voice of God"), was quoted approvingly by any substantial group of political theorists. In France, Rousseau and later Necker gave approbation to public opinion and frequently used the term *opinion publique.* In England, in the writings of Jeremy Bentham there was insistence on the significance of public opinion as a basic social control on the excesses of misrule and as a basis for the democratic state.

In the ancient civilizations, public opinion played some part, but the publics were limited in number and size, the mechanisms for expression of opinion were rudimentary and communication was limited. Among the Greeks, public opinion developed to an extent unequaled until modern times; among the adult free citizens who took part in public life argumentative conversation developed and the art of dialectics was codified. The wide-ranging conquests of Rome provided information about many peoples with their values, religions, economic and political systems. Combined with Rome's urban culture, they gave increased scope for the opinion process. There was much to discuss, the culture was dynamic, the opinion process was stimulated and the Romans came to speak of the *vox populi.*

Through the Middle Ages, when people lived in scattered, small groups and agrarian communities and when cultures were blanketed under a common religious ideology there could be little dynamic popular opinion. Rather, there was popular acceptance of the forms of government and submission to the religious hierarchy, not the support of popular opinion.

The opinion process was revived when the Reformation questioned clerical authority and emphasized the individual. Arts, letters, and science began to cast off the bonds of authoritarian revelation. Public opinion began to develop as larger groups became concerned with religious issues, political systems, relative values, and with ideologies in general and the new means of communication, printing, coupled with a slowly growing literacy, distributed the ideas. The Enlightenment of the 17th and 18th centuries marked a further turning from the authority of divine revelation to the authority of reason and human understanding. When "natural reason" was posited, then individual opinions became important, and the theorists turned to an examination of the opinion process.

Modern Public Opinion.—It is evident that the opinions of large publics became increasingly important during the 20th century. Economic groups depended upon influencing large publics by publicity and advertising. Through publicity agents, notable personages attempted to create their own legends in the minds of the general public. Commercial advertising became a partial science and the arts of publicity and propaganda were cultivated. The struggle for power and for the control of opinion was conducted by interest groups implemented with the newer means of communication. Authoritarian states meticulously organized propaganda bureaus, while democracies were reluctantly drawn into political and cultural publicity. The problem became one of values. Was the objective the unity of mass opinion for the furtherance of the purposes of the state and of private interest groups? Or was the preeminent value the integrity of the individual's psychological experience? For both objectives the modern facilities of press, radio, and television provided the channels. Opinions were solicited and expressed upon the widest variety of controversial topics ever presented simultaneously to large publics on matters of morals, religion, education, the details of government, the choice of consumers' goods, and the administration of justice. Advertisers of consumers' goods, politicians, and representatives of interest groups clamored for attention.

Measurement and Polling.—In the democracies, the many interest groups attempting to mold opinion desired an effective check on their results. Though there had long been those who sought to discover public opinion by means of interviews and straw votes, it was not until the emergence of the public opinion polls in the mid-1930s that systematic representative sampling of large publics occurred. Two fundamental problems were involved in the measurement of public opinion:

1. Developing tests sufficiently comprehensive to include at least the more typical opinion positions of most of the individuals of a public. Such tests were conducted by interviews, questionnaires, observations of behaviour, yes-or-no type of questions, multiple-choice tests, rating and ranking tests, and attitude scales, such as those of L. L. Thurstone and Louis Guttman. Motivation research testing for advertising and marketing purposes utilized word tests, picture and cartoon tests, thematic apperception pictures, and Rorschach tests (*see* PSYCHOLOGICAL TESTS AND MEASUREMENTS).

2. Developing adequate methods to report on the opinions of large publics, numbering millions of individuals, by means of the smallest possible representative sample. The representative sampling procedure in public opinion surveying is called polling, and early polls on candidates and issues were referred to as straw polls. The pioneer commercial pollsters, or pollers, in the United States were Elmo Roper and Paul T. Cherington, who established the *Fortune* survey, George H. Gallup, originator of the American Institute of Public Opinion, and Archibald Crossley who originated the Crossley Poll. They used polling in an attempt to predict the results of the national elections of 1936. The pioneer pollers had had previous experience as market research men. In addition to the commercial pollers, various university-sponsored polling organizations, some polls maintained by newspapers, and a few by governmental agencies, both state and national, were established. Similar polling organizations were later set up in more than a score of other countries.

Sampling.—In public opinion measurement, the objective is the selection and polling of a representative sample of the group which constitutes the public under consideration. The public selected for sampling might be the adult inhabitants of a single town, the lawyers of the state of Illinois, the population of the whole United States, or any other of the many thousands of publics. Samples used for the entire population of the United States range from small samples of possibly 2,500 to large samples of 10,000. After the persons to be interviewed are selected (the sample) from the public under consideration (the "universe"), they are questioned by interviewers from the field staff of the polling organization.

Before the use of specially selected samples (made representative by stratified and area-probability sampling), polls were conducted by ballots printed in newspapers or magazines, which could be clipped and returned, by ballots left in stores, by interviews among crowds and on the streets, and by mailed ballots sent to address lists variously obtained. In 1936 the *Literary Digest* mailed over 10,000,000 ballots, received back 2,376,523, and incorrectly predicted the 1936 national election by understating the vote for Pres. Franklin D. Roosevelt by 19.3%. Large numbers alone do not assure representativeness of the sample.

More scientific polling stressed the selection of representative samples of publics. Prior to 1952, most pollers used chiefly the quota sampling methods in which the sample was a small-scale model of the larger universe. For example, a sample of 10,000 individuals to represent the entire voting population of the United States would be selected. The sample would be based on appropriate quotas in proportion to the frequencies in the general population of individuals by age, sex, economic position, community size, past party affiliation, and sometimes a few other criteria. These were the strata. The interviewer would then seek for individuals who would fit the requirements of his assigned interviews. Such stratified sampling permits tailoring the sample to those in the population who are expected to be more significantly involved in the particular opinion topic than the generality. This is an advantage. Moreover, stratified sampling can be carried on in smaller geographic areas than area sampling and is, therefore, much cheaper. Also, it is not necessary to call back again and again to interview the person at a particular address as is true of area sampling. But an objection to the method was that it depended upon the often inexpert judgment of the interviewer in selecting the particular individual to be interviewed and also that the poller could not always be certain as to the frequency and significance of the various factors used as the strata.

Probability, or random, sampling, on the other hand, a more recent and less tested procedure, aimed to choose the sample in such a way that theoretically every individual in the universe would have an equal chance to be included in the sample. Such sampling originated from making selections by random methods from finite, discrete objects. Applied to populations, it would mean selecting every nth person from the total population as recorded in lists of names or other complete censuses. In polling practice the selection is generally made in terms of location of the individuals in space. From the 3,000 counties of the United States a sample would be drawn; from the counties selected, a sample of rural-urban population drawn; and within these areas, households and individuals would be systematically selected. Area sampling is not based on assignment of quotas, thus eliminating interviewer judgment and possible bias. In area sampling, certain areas (block, section, ward divisions of city or town, section, township, or other area of county, county or other division of state) are assigned to the interviewer. Within these areas he interviews every nth individual or member of a family located at an assigned position (the second house from the northeast corner of a block, etc.). The area units are selected randomly in various ways. Due to travel expenses, time consumption for the interviewer in proceeding from one interview to another remote interview and other costs, area sampling is very much more expensive than quota sampling.

The 1944 area sampling procedures of the U.S. Census Bureau provided the first serious use of area sampling. In 1952 area sampling was first seriously used by commercial pollers to supplement quota sampling in the election of that year. Subsequently it was increasingly used by pollers.

Criticism of Opinion Polling Methods.—Possibilities of error exist at every stage of polling. Sample selection, question selection and formulation, the interview with its possible misunderstandings, the coding and interpretation of answers require experienced, skillful, and honest pollers. Prophecy as to future opinion trends, which is involved in election predictions, is an art of a still higher order. In the 1948 presidential election in the

U.S. the leading public opinion polls showed Dewey ahead of Truman, but Truman was the victor on election day. In the 1960 election the major polls showed a very close race with Kennedy the probable winner, which was how it turned out. In 1964 the polls were unanimous in predicting Johnson's landslide victory over Goldwater, giving rise to some criticism that the polls created a "bandwagon effect."

Some political theorists, congressional investigating committees, and social scientists object to widespread use of public opinion polls for such reasons as their alleged employment to force premature executive and legislative decisions, the possibly adverse implications for political parties of election predictions, supposed methodological errors, and an inferred desire for vague, unfathomable public mind-life in preference to attempted exactitudes. The partial failures of the pollers on some election predictions have elated some political theorists who really disapproved of the polls on grounds other than their accuracy (for example, the numerous polls might encourage popular, rather than representative, democracy); have aroused partisan politicians who were fearful of the polls' influence on voters; have given some social scientists an opportunity to criticize polling methods; and have delighted many aesthetes, comedians, and competing prophets. Others vaguely resent public opinion polls as another threat to privacy in an age in which privacy is already grievously assaulted. The polls may, however, be defended as reasonably accurate reporting on both the significant, matured opinions and the ephemeral sentiments of large publics.

See also PROBABILITY; STATISTICS, MATHEMATICAL; PROPAGANDA; PUBLIC RELATIONS; ADVERTISING; PSYCHOLOGY, SOCIAL; PSYCHOLOGICAL WARFARE; VOTING BEHAVIOUR.

BIBLIOGRAPHY.—*General:* W. A. Mackinnon, *On the Rise, Progress, and Present State of Public Opinion in Great Britain* (1828); W. Bagehot, *Physics and Politics,* ch. 5 (1872); G. Tarde, *L'Opinion et la foule* (1910); A. V. Dicey, *Law and Public Opinion in England* (1905); J. B. Bryce, *The American Commonwealth,* 2:261–403 (1889); A. L. Lowell, *Public Opinion and Popular Government,* new ed. (1926), *Public Opinion in War and Peace* (1923); C. L. King, *Public Opinion as Viewed by Eminent Political Theorists* (1916); W. Lippmann, *Public Opinion* (1927); J. Dewey, *The Public and Its Problems* (1927); J. W. Albig, *Modern Public Opinion* (1956); C. Schettler, *Public Opinion in American Society* (1960); F. G. Wilson, *A Theory of Public Opinion* (1962); Angus Campbell *et al., The American Voter* (1960); H. L. Childs, *Public Opinion: Nature, Formation and Role* (1965); B. C. Hennessy, *Public Opinion* (1965); V. O. Key, *Public Opinion and American Democracy* (1961); R. E. Lane and D. O. Sears, *Public Opinion* (1964).

Measurement and Polling: H. Cantril, *Gauging Public Opinion* (1944); G. H. Gallup, *A Guide to Public Opinion Polls* (1948); Lindsay Rogers, *The Pollsters* (1949); M. B. Parten, *Surveys, Polls, and Samples* (1950); H. H. Remmers, *Introduction to Opinion and Attitude Measurement* (1954); J. W. Albig, *Modern Public Opinion,* ch. 9, 10, 11 (1956); J. M. Fenton, *In Your Opinion* (1960).   (JN. W. A.)

PUBLIC RELATIONS, loosely, the activities connected with interpreting and improving the relationships of an organization or an individual with the public.

19th and 20th Centuries.—Although its basic activities are as old as history, the term public relations did not come into general use until after World War I. In the early 19th century, U.S. newspapers frequently granted space in their news columns to publicity stories in return for paid advertisements. Other papers, inadequately staffed, accepted contributions without close scrutiny of the motives of the writers. Shortly after the Civil War, land promoters, railroads, politicians, and financial groups were making systematic use of such opportunities. In 1869 James McHenry, press representative of the Fisk-Gould financial group, obtained wide publication of material in the group's interest. Soon after this, a number of business and political organizations installed publicity departments, under the name of "literary bureaus."

In the early 1900s publicity men were multiplying in New York City, most of them former newspaper reporters. Knowing the ingredients of a lively newspaper story, some of them—particularly theatrical press agents—drew freely on their imaginations. In 1909 the American Newspaper Publishers Association, alarmed at the spread of press-agentry, appointed a Committee on Free Publicity. One bulletin issued by it listed 757 "space grabbers." Nonetheless, most newspapers continued to use a substantial amount of material from publicity sources. A parallel situation occurred later in Britain. *Report on the British Press,* published by Political and Economic Planning in 1938, stated: "Some newspapers are very much opposed to accepting material from press agencies, and not long ago the Home and Southern Counties Newspaper Federation, representing nearly 300 newspapers, made a concerted attempt to eliminate it. Nevertheless, many of these newspapers continued to print such material, the news-value in them proving too strong a bait."

Till the early years of the 20th century, leaders of business and finance had been opposed to any publicity except commercial puffs and had strongly rebuffed newspapermen. The banker George F. Baker told a reporter, "It's none of the public's business what I do." J. P. Morgan said to another reporter, "I owe the public nothing." William H. Vanderbilt, when pressed for a statement about reduction of train schedules on his railroad, exclaimed to a reporter who talked insistently of the public interest, "The public be damned!" While the businessman's belief in his right to secrecy was rooted in a tradition, it was dangerous to rest on real or supposed rights, in view of popular antagonism toward big business, an attitude equally traditional.

A clash between the two traditions was inevitable, and it took place in the "muckraking" era (*see* MUCKRAKERS). A series of harrying congressional investigations of big business accompanied the muckrakers' attacks. "We are passing through a reform—yea, a revolutionary period in business affairs," Henry Clews wrote in 1906. He called on banking and insurance interests to drop their policy of secrecy, which, he said, was "obviously in defiance of public sentiment."

Also in 1906 Ivy L. Lee, a former newspaperman, was appointed publicity adviser to a group of anthracite operators who had aroused the anger of the press by their haughty attitude in labour disputes. Soon after Lee's appointment it was announced that the operators would supply the press with all possible information. Lee then sent to city editors a declaration of his policies, in which he said: "This is not a secret press bureau. All our work is done in the open. . . . If you think any of our matter ought properly to go to your business office, do not use it." Retained by the Pennsylvania Railroad the same year, Lee made information concerning accidents available to the press for the first time. In 1921 his firm issued its bulletin. In 1923 Edward L. Bernays published *Crystallizing Public Opinion.* This book, describing publicity functions and techniques with an emphasis on social responsibility, did much to popularize the term public relations.

Meanwhile, men were being hired in the service of the federal government under such titles as "director of information," "editor," and "supervisor of information research," which evaded a congressional act of 1913 forbidding the spending for "publicity experts" of any funds not specifically designated by Congress for that purpose. In Britain, the Empire Marketing Board began using large-scale publicity for the promotion of trade in 1924. *Report on the British Press* said of the Empire Marketing Board that "before its demise in 1933 it had established the archetype of Government Public Relations Departments." In Britain, as in the United States, appointment of public relations directors by government departments during World War II was the prelude to increased postwar emphasis on public relations. One indication of the greatly heightened interest in the United States was the fact that many colleges were adding courses in public relations to their curriculums. Boston University established the first school of public relations in 1947; in 1964 the name was changed to school of communication.

Philosophy of Public Relations.—Though early parallels can be found for every basic phase of public relations, as an organized activity it represents a major change in the philosophy of business —the recognition of the ultimate authority of public opinion. The basic purposes of a public relations department are the establishment and maintenance of good will. Obviously, the more the organization does to merit this good will, the easier the task of the public relations director will be. When he invites public attention to his company in connection with some attractive phase of its activities, he cannot be sure of limiting the interest of the press

or public to that particular area. The efficient public relations executive therefore works for the elimination of policies he believes to be open to criticism.

The public relations director or consultant frequently needs a high degree of persuasiveness in order to gain a hearing for a long-range point of view in councils concerned with immediate commercial objectives. In order to be an efficient representative of his company he must also be a representative of the interests of its employees, of the local communities in which it has factories, of the retailers who distribute its wares, of the consumers who buy them, and of the public at large. It is not necessary for him to be an altruist in order to do this; he need only realize that it is easier to eliminate sources of irritation than to justify them.

Publicity and Advertising in Public Relations.—When a policy has been set and the public relations representative is seeking publicity for it in news media, he must put his reliance not on techniques of persuasion but on his judgment as to what constitutes an acceptable story. A story with intrinsic news value, simply and clearly presented, usually receives an objective hearing. Public relations departments thus are usually watchful for such publicity opportunities as anniversaries that may be of local or general interest, public events in which an official of the company may logically participate, incidents involving celebrities, and developments susceptible to treatment as human-interest stories. In the handling of adverse news, such as that of accidents, the harm is minimized by candid answers to inquiries.

Creation of news events has become an important factor in the public relations programs of trade groups. For example, a public relations consultant, acting for a group of soap manufacturers anxious to combat a statement by cosmeticians that soap was bad for the skin, advised formation of a cleanliness institute. This was not a dummy organization; it actually conducted a cleanliness campaign, welcomed in public schools, and received widespread publicity. On another occasion a public relations counsel initiated soap sculpture contests on behalf of the industry, a type of oblique publicity found to be of great value. Similarly, when the National Cotton Council was faced with competition from paper bags as feed containers, its public relations department sent representatives to show farm wives how they could convert cotton feed bags into attractive dresses.

As some large corporations became aware of the importance of courting public opinion, they began to supplement their publicity efforts with a new type of advertising—one that was not designed to gain business but to clarify their policies and improve their relationships with their employees, the local community, and the public at large. The Bell Telephone Company was active in this field as early as 1908; after World War II the company, unable to fill the demand for new installations, published a series of advertisements explaining why delays were unavoidable. The flood of complaints subsided to a point below the prewar average.

In public relations advertising by management in connection with labour disputes, a temperate policy, anticipating the day when the strike will be settled, has been found to be wise. During a strike at a General Electric plant in Bridgeport, Conn., in 1946, the company presented the view that wages must be geared to production, but avoided strident controversy; one advertisement was devoted to announcing that the strikers' insurance under the company's employee plan was being kept in force.

Industrial Relations.—Winning the goodwill of its employees is one of the major objectives of every industrial organization. The morale of a factory's workers affects the quantity and quality of production; the company's position in competing for skilled workers; its popularity or unpopularity in the local community, which in turn affects the treatment it receives from the municipal administration; and its reputation as a whole. No public relations technique can offset substandard wages or unsatisfactory working conditions. However, even a policy that is intended to be equitable may run into trouble if administered in impersonal, bureaucratic fashion. Accordingly, an efficient public relations director makes a strong effort to keep management sensitive to human values. Employees are informed of new developments promptly, before rumours have time to spread; they are encouraged to submit complaints as well as suggestions; advance proofs of institutional advertising are posted on factory bulletin boards; facts on the company's earnings and prospects are made available; in some organizations, regular jobholders' meetings, similar to stockholders' meetings, are held; issuance of publications for employees is a standard practice. (*See* further INDUSTRIAL RELATIONS.)

Scope of Public Relations Departments.—Almost every form of the printed and spoken word, and of photography, is used in public relations work. Following are routine public relations responsibilities: issuing news releases to newspapers, radio stations, trade journals, and magazines; arranging press conferences; answering queries from the press and public; preparing text and illustrative matter for public relations advertising, pamphlets, employee magazines, manuals for the training of new employees, reports to stockholders, and form letters; planning documentary motion pictures, recorded television programs, filmstrips, lantern slides, charts, and recorded talks; planning and publicizing exhibitions and "open house" days at factories; and planning research surveys for gauging the opinions of employees, customers, or the general public. In addition, in cases where the product of the company is expensive, such as an automobile, the public relations department may prepare a magazine for distribution to listed customers; some corporations issue special magazines for their stockholders. Public relations directors of trade organizations, long-established companies, and various institutions also have arranged for the publication of books, sometimes by well-known writers, telling the history of the organization or industry; these are usually placed on sale through normal channels but often are subsidized to assure the publisher against loss. Some organizations employ not only a public relations director, with a staff under his supervision, but also a public relations consultant, to provide an outside point of view on questions of policy.

Most public relations work involves a combination of logical and psychological methods. Exaggeration and distortion defeat their own purpose; but often it is possible to switch from an unpopular concept, expressed in a standardized term, to a popular, or at least an acceptable one, without doing violence to truth. An illustration of this is the substitution in public relations advertising by labour unions of the term "union security" for "closed shop." Another is the use by manufacturers of the term "billiards" instead of "pool," which had taken on the connotation of shabby poolrooms.

Much specialization has developed in public relations work in areas such as banking, agriculture, education, philanthropy, etc. Also, many public relations workers specialize in the use of specific media, such as audiovisual materials or stockholder reports.

BIBLIOGRAPHY.—Alfred McClung Lee, *The Daily Newspaper in America* (1937); John William Albig, *Public Opinion* (1939); Francis Williams, *Press, Parliament and People* (1946); Rex F. Harlow and Marvin M. Black, *Practical Public Relations* (1947); Eric F. Goldman, *Two-way Street: the Emergence of the Public Relations Counsel* (1948); E. J. Robinson, *Communication and Public Relations* (1966); R. Simon (ed.), *Perspectives in Public Relations* (1966).   (J. AY.)

PUBLIC UTILITIES, a designation for a diverse group of industries that have certain common characteristics. Originally, from a legal point of view, public utilities supplied necessary services and, hence, were "affected with a public interest." From an economic standpoint, they possessed technological characteristics that almost inevitably resulted in monopoly. In nearly every country, such enterprises are owned and operated by the state (*see* also PUBLIC ENTERPRISE). The significant exception is the United States, where public utility services are supplied, by and large, by private firms subject to government regulation. Both publicly and privately owned utilities, then, sell their services to the general public at prices that are governmentally fixed.

Although economic and technical evolution is continually changing the character of these industries and, in addition, creating new ones, public utilities may be classified according to the generalized function they perform. The main public services supplied through public utilities are: (1) transportation (common carriers), including railroad, highway and local transit, oil and gas pipelines, waterways, and airlines; (2) communications—telephone and telegraph; (3) power, heat, and light—gas and electric; and (4) community

facilities for water, sanitation, and irrigation.

Historical Background.—The furnishing of public utility services was closely associated with developing civilization, supplying wants so fundamental for communal living that government subjected the services to some measure of control. With the growth of trade in ancient empires, facilities providing transport and communication were set up. The governmentally maintained highway system of the Roman Empire and its many aqueduct systems are celebrated ancient public works. In the more populous ancient cities, systems of sanitation also became a necessity. With these needs came the recognition that services used collectively should be supplied by the state. The supply of these services thus began as state functions. By the Middle Ages most of the ancient means of supplying public services had declined or virtually disappeared. By slow stages, upon the manors and in the medieval cities, these public facilities again appeared. Of great importance in British and American legal history is the fact that out of the economic and legal relationships of feudalism there arose the concept of a "common calling" from which the early policy of public-utility regulation developed.

The modern national state gradually supplanted the elements of the feudal system of social control. The expanding domestic system of manufacture was displacing the guild and manorial system of production; foreign trade was growing. National systems of transport involving highways and canals were undertaken and the regulation of these facilities became national rather than local.

The greatest impetus in the expansion of public services came with the Industrial Revolution. Under the stimulus of the factory system, cities grew as never before, creating a need for municipal systems of water supply, sanitation, transport, communication, illumination, and power. But the philosophy of laissez-faire was not fertile ground for the extension of public functions. While the rapid industrial changes intensified needs, the tendency was to give greater scope to private enterprise.

The evils of a system which left the supply of basic economic wants to private industry insufficiently regulated by government, however, became too flagrant to be overlooked. Beginning about 1840 the revolt against laissez-faire doctrines caused an enlargement of the scope of governmental action. The older public services were continued for the most part as public enterprises, while the newer services were supplied by private initiative under some form of public supervision and assistance. Thus emerged the modern notion of a public utility, distinct from strictly governmental services and strictly private business.

Economic Characteristics.—The classic explanation of the need for government enterprise or regulation of public utilities is that such businesses are "natural monopolies." As James R. Nelson has argued, however: " 'natural monopolies' in fact originated in response to a belief that some goal, or goals, of public policy would be advanced by encouraging or permitting a monopoly to be formed, and discouraging or forbidding future competition with this monopoly" ("The Role of Competition in the Regulated Industries," *The Antitrust Bulletin*, xi Jan.–April, 1966). It is more accurate, therefore, to say that the technology of production and transmission almost inevitably leads to a complete or partial monopoly of the market for the services rendered, and that competition in the public utility field is often less effective and desirable than competition in industry in general.

Public utility enterprises are subject to what economists call "economies of scale"; that is, the larger the output of a utility plant, such as a generating station, the lower will be the cost of production and distribution per unit of output. Economies of scale, however, are not unique to public utility enterprises; they are found in virtually every business. What is significant is the fact that a utility's market (in the nontransportation industries) is restricted by the necessarily close connection between the utility plant and the consumers' premises. Further, because storage of a utility's service is limited at best and because a utility must have adequate capacity to meet its customers' peak demand requirements, it tends to have unused or surplus capacity most of the time. Competition only serves to aggravate the situation.

These basic economic characteristics are reinforced by four others. First, utilities require a large investment in a fixed, specialized plant. Electric utilities, for example, must invest about $4.50 to get $1 of annual gross sales, while most manufacturing companies invest about 47 cents to get $1 of sales. This investment, largely bound to its original location, represents a significant percentage of a utility's total cost. Second, utility equipment must be located below, upon, and over public property. (Utilities, in fact, are provided with the governmental power of eminent domain which makes possible the compulsory sale of private property.) While space limitations do not in themselves lead to monopoly, as the number of conduits or mains increases, the streets are torn up more frequently, thereby creating a public nuisance. Moreover, the number of desirable sites also may be limited, such as those for hydroelectric power plants. Third, from the buyer's side, for many types of customers and for many uses, demand is "inelastic"; that is, as the price of a utility's service increases, consumers increase their expenditures rather than decrease their demand. Utilities, to the extent that they are supplying basic necessities, have a significant (but far from absolute) degree of control over the rates they charge consumers. Finally, price differentiation or discrimination is both possible and generally attractive to utility enterprises. Fixed costs represent a significant percentage of total costs; unused capacity exists much of the time; and there are important differences in consumer demands. A utility company often finds that a single rate low enough to maintain full capacity output fails to yield revenues sufficient to cover costs, while one set high enough to cover costs will result in unused capacity. Under these circumstances, discrimination may increase revenues and minimize unused capacity.

While these are the major economic characteristics of public utilities, they do not belong solely to such enterprises. The distinction between utilities and other businesses is one of degree: utilities possess these characteristics to a greater degree than do nonutility industries. For example, economies of scale partly explain the need for large-scale plants in many industries. High fixed costs are characteristic of the concrete and steel industries, among many others. Even though the services of public utilities are considered essential or necessary, society does not regard them as so necessary that they should be provided irrespective of the purchaser's ability to pay for them. And some important manufacturing industries have avoided public utility-type regulation, not because they are more competitive than are the utilities but rather because of the difficulties of extending regulation to the manufacture of commodities.

REGULATION IN THE UNITED STATES

It has long been common to characterize the American economy as a competitive, private-enterprise system. In such a system, the economy is organized on the decentralized lines of private property and private enterprise, and the market is the central institution regulating economic activity. As Adam Smith showed in 1776, in his famous *The Wealth of Nations*, competition among private firms will, as though guided by an "invisible hand," promote the public or social interest. Yet, it has also long been accepted that some industries must be regulated by the government to protect the public interest.

Legal Background.—Beginning with the well-known case of *Munn* v. *Illinois*, 94 U.S. 113 (1877), the Supreme Court attempted to establish a separate category of businesses, known as public utilities, that were affected with a public interest and that required detailed governmental regulation. The *Munn* case involved the validity of an 1871 Illinois statute fixing maximum rates for storing grain in elevators. Munn, who had been engaged in the elevator business since 1862 in Chicago, Ill., was sued for charging rates higher than those prescribed by the act. He was found guilty and fined $100 in the Criminal Court of Cook County but appealed to the Supreme Court largely on the ground that the statute violated the 14th Amendment by depriving him of property without due process of law.

Chief Justice Morrison Waite, in upholding the validity of the statute, noted the importance of the grain trade and the strategic position of the grain elevators ("They stand . . . in the very 'gateway of commerce,' and take toll from all who pass"). Quoting from Lord Chief Justice Sir Matthew Hale's words of nearly two centuries earlier, he held that "when private property is 'affected with a public interest, it ceases to be *juris privati* only.'" Property becomes affected with a public interest "when used in a manner to make it of public consequence, and affect the community at large. When, therefore, one devotes his property to a use in which the public has an interest, he, in effect, grants to the public an interest in that use, and must submit to be controlled by the public for the common good, to the extent of the interest he has thus created. He may withdraw his grant by discontinuing the use; but, so long as he maintains the use, he must submit to the control."

In 1914 the Supreme Court upheld regulation of the fire insurance business (*German Alliance Insurance Co.* v. *Kansas,* 233 U.S. 389). Said Justice Joseph McKenna: insurance "is practically a necessity to business activity and enterprise. It is, therefore, essentially different from ordinary commercial transactions, and . . . is of the greatest public concern." In unanimously holding a state of Kansas statute undertaking extensive control of commodity prices and wage rates unconstitutional (*Wolff Packing Co.* v. *Court of Industrial Relations of Kansas,* 262 U.S. 522 [1923]), the court concluded: "The circumstances which clothe a particular kind of business with a public interest, in the sense of *Munn* v. *Illinois* and the other cases, must be such as to create a peculiarly close relation between the public and those engaged in it, and raise implications of an affirmative obligation on their part to be reasonable in dealing with the public." A majority of the Supreme Court, in 1928, opposed the extension of the public utility concept to employment agencies, holding that the interest of the public in the matter of employment is not "that *public interest* which the law contemplates as the basis for legislative price control." (*Ribnik* v. *McBride,* 277 U.S. 350.) And a year later, the court held unconstitutional a Tennessee statute which sought to fix the prices at which gasoline could be sold within the state (*Williams* v. *Standard Oil Co.,* 278 U.S. 235). The business of dealing in gasoline, said the court, "does not come within the phrase 'affected with a public interest.'"

The Supreme Court's last attempt to clarify the public utility concept came in the 1934 case of *Nebbia* v. *New York,* 291 U.S. 502. In 1933 the New York legislature passed a statute which declared that the milk industry was affected with a public interest. The statute set up a Milk Control Board and provided for control of prices and trade practices of milk producers and distributors. The board proceeded to fix the price of milk at nine cents a quart. A Rochester, N.Y., grocer by the name of Nebbia was promptly sued for selling two quarts of milk plus a five-cent loaf of bread for 18 cents. In upholding the statute, Justice Owen Roberts stated that (1) "the dairy industry is not, in the accepted sense of the phrase, a public utility"; (2) "there is in this case no suggestion of any monopoly or monopolistic practice"; and (3) "those engaged in the business are in no way dependent upon public grants or franchises for the privilege of conducting their activities." He then added:

It is clear that there is no closed class or category of businesses affected with a public interest. . . . The phrase "affected with a public interest" can, in the nature of things, mean no more than that an industry, for adequate reason, is subject to control for the public good. . . . If the law-making body within its sphere of government concludes that the conditions or practices in an industry make unrestricted competition an inadequate safeguard of the consumer's interests, produce waste harmful to the public, threaten ultimately to cut off the supply of a commodity needed by the public, or portend the destruction of the industry itself, appropriate statutes passed in an honest effort to correct the threatened consequences may not be set aside because the regulation adopted fixes prices reasonably deemed by the legislature to be fair to those engaged in the industry and to the consuming public.

It seems clear, then, that the public interest concept is no longer synonymous with the public utility concept; that the latter concept is included within the former. Nevertheless, the essential elements of the public utility concept were succinctly outlined by Judge Frederick Vinson in a 1943 decision (*Davies Warehouse Co.* v. *Brown,* 137 F. 2d 201):

If a business is (1) affected with a public interest, and (2) bears an intimate connection with the processes of transportation and distribution, and (3) is under obligation to afford its facilities to the public generally, upon demand, at fair and non-discriminatory rates, and (4) enjoys in a large measure an independence and freedom from business competition brought about either (a) by its acquisition of a monopolistic status, or (b) by the grant of a franchise or certificate from the state placing it in this position, it is . . . a public utility.

Constitutional Basis.—Federal regulation of business proceeds under Art. I, sec. 8 of the Constitution. The most important clause is that referred to as the interstate commerce clause; the clause that gives Congress power "to regulate Commerce . . . among the several states." After decades of court decisions, the clause has been broadly interpreted, particularly since the late 1930s, and it seems that the clause is unlikely to impose significant limits on federal regulatory powers in the future. As the Supreme Court put it in a 1946 case, federal power to regulate interstate commerce "is as broad as the economic needs of the nation." (*American Power & Light Co.* v. *Securities & Exchange Commission*, 329 U.S. 90.)

The 10th Amendment to the Constitution provides that those powers not delegated to the federal government and not specifically prohibited by it to the states may be exercised by the states. States thus have the broad authority to legislate for protection of the health, safety, morals, and general welfare of their citizens. These are collectively known as the "police powers" of the states and have also been interpreted broadly. Said the Supreme Court in its 1934 *Nebbia* decision: ". . . a state is free to adopt whatever economic policy may reasonably be deemed to promote the public welfare, and to enforce that policy by legislation adapted to its purpose. . . . Price control, like any other form of regulation, is unconstitutional only if arbitrary, discriminatory, or demonstrably irrelevant to the policy which the legislature is free to adopt."

The rights of corporations are protected against invasion by the acts of government in both federal and state constitutions. Corporations, in short, are guaranteed due process of law. Further, under the U.S. constitutional system, all acts of legislatures and administrators are subject to judicial review. The final authority is the Supreme Court of the United States.

Obligations of Public Utilities.—The affirmative obligations upon public utilities arising out of their peculiarly close relation to the public are usually spoken of as that system of rights and duties which constitutes the law of public service undertakings. Briefly, this law places upon a public utility the extraordinary duty to render reasonably adequate service to all who apply. It is required to serve them up to the limit of its capacity, with capacity being defined as the limit of profitableness. It may neither attach unreasonable conditions to contracts for service nor practice undue or unjust discrimination. Finally, a public utility must observe more than ordinary care in the rendition of service in view of the dependence of the public upon such service and the hazards associated therewith. At the same time, the law concedes a public utility the right to collect a reasonable price, to render service subject to reasonable rules and regulations, and to withdraw service under prescribed conditions after giving notice to customers. While customers are given the right to demand that a public utility live up to its duties, they are required to accept reciprocal obligations formally imposed by the regulatory body or implicit in the franchise, such as paying bills on time.

Forms of Regulation.—Modern public utility regulation is largely carried out by administrative commissions or agencies, but such has not always been the case. The earliest form of regulation was judicial; enforcement of the common law duties through lawsuits brought by individuals who thought themselves injured. Legislative regulation gradually supplanted judicial regulation during the second half of the 19th century and by 1898 the function of the judiciary had been restricted to the review of legislative and administrative acts.

Legislative regulation by means of corporate charters or special franchise was the next to be tried. Above all else, such regulation proved to be inflexible. Each change in a charter required a special legislative amendment. But since legislatures were in session only

a small percentage of the time and since they found their attention being claimed by many other matters, the required adjustments were often delayed. Likewise, each change in a franchise provision had to be approved by both parties since the Supreme Court, in an 1819 decision (*Trustees of Dartmouth College* v. *Woodward*, 4 Wheaton 518), held that a franchise had the same status as a contract. Further, it was impossible to pay much attention to financial and accounting control or to service and safety aspects of regulation.

For these and other reasons, all of the early methods of regulation proved defective and, as the demand for more stringent and continuous control arose, "independent" regulatory commissions, operating under general legislative statutes, were created. The first regulatory commissions, generally those created prior to 1870, were largely advisory bodies and their chief concern was with the railroads. They made recommendations to state legislatures and railroad managements, appraised property taken by the railroads under the right of eminent domain, enforced safety standards and, generally, served as fact-finding bodies. However, they had no control over rates. From 1870 to 1907, the first "mandatory" commissions developed as a result of the Granger movement (*see* GRANGE, THE). Illinois, in 1871, passed a statute establishing the initial commission; Minnesota in 1871, Iowa and Wisconsin in 1874, and Georgia in 1879 enacted similar statutes. And in 1887, Congress established the first such federal agency, the Interstate Commerce Commission, to regulate the nation's railroads (*see* INTERSTATE COMMERCE: *Powers of Congress*). Most of these Granger regulatory laws were designed to place a ceiling on railroad rates, either prescribing the maximum rates to be administered by the commissions or leaving their determination to the commissions.

The third or modern period in the development of commission regulation began in 1907 with the creation of two powerful commissions by New York (under the leadership of Gov. Charles Evans Hughes) and Wisconsin (under the urging of Sen. Robert M. La Follette). In both states, the legislatures extended the regulatory powers of the commissions to other utilities: railroad, gas, light, power, telephone, and telegraph companies. Both commissions, moreover, were delegated broad powers, including security regulation, examination of accounts and property, the fixing of rates, the requirement of detailed reports in prescribed form, and the right to prescribe uniform systems of accounts. These two powerful state commissions became models and by 1920 more than two-thirds of the states had regulatory commissions. The state commissions were strengthened, their jurisdictions extended, and their powers further increased after the stock market crash of 1929, and several federal commissions were established to regulate interstate commerce. Today, all 50 states, plus the District of Columbia, have commissions, known as public utility or public service commissions, railroad commissions, corporation commissions or commerce commissions, which regulate the electric, gas, transportation, communications, and other industries.

There are five federal commissions with jurisdiction over the interstate activities of the same industries: (1) the Interstate Commerce Commission, with jurisdiction subsequently extended to cover oil pipelines (1906), motor carriers (1935), interstate and coastal water carriers (1940), and freight forwarders (1942); (2) the Civil Aeronautics Board, created in 1940 (as a reorganization of the Civil Aeronautics Authority of 1938), with jurisdiction over commercial air transportation; (3) the Federal Power Commission, organized as an independent agency in 1930, with regulatory powers over hydroelectric projects and the transportation and sale of electric power (since 1935) and natural gas (since 1938); (4) the Federal Communications Commission, established in 1934 (succeeding the Federal Radio Commission of 1927), with jurisdiction over broadcasting and (by a transfer of powers from the Interstate Commerce Commission) interstate telephone and telegraph services; and (5) the Securities and Exchange Commission, organized in 1934, and given power under the Public Utility Holding Company Act of 1935 to regulate the finances and corporate structures of electric and gas utility holding companies.

The Task of Regulation.—Regulation is concerned with rates, service, safety and, to some extent, the efficiency of management. Rate regulation (*i.e.*, control of the rate level, earnings, and control of the rate structure, rates or prices) has been the major task of the commissions. In order to carry out effective rate regulation, commissions have also been given authority over accounting procedures and other financial matters. Service and safety considerations, moreover, are closely related to rates, since a higher quality of service or more elaborate safety standards may result in higher costs and, hence, require higher rates.

Rate regulation usually involves the determination of allowable operating costs (operating expenses, annual depreciation charges, and operating taxes), the net depreciated value of the tangible and intangible property (known as the rate base), the fair rate of return to allow on the rate base and, finally, the establishment of a structure of rates which will permit the utility to earn the required revenue. Operating costs represent the largest percentage of a firm's total revenue requirement. For a typical electric company, operating expenses average about 44% of revenues, depreciation 11%, and taxes 23%—a total of 78% of revenues. All expenditures that a utility undertakes are subject to review by the relevant commission as to their reasonableness. The value of a utility's tangible property may be measured in two ways: original cost (cost of plant and equipment when built or purchased) or reproduction cost (value of plant and equipment expressed in current dollars). Regardless of the measure used, an appropriate amount of depreciation is subtracted so as to reflect the depreciated value of the property. Other items sometimes included in the rate base are working capital, overhead construction costs, and the value of franchises, water rights, and leaseholds. The fair rate of return is usually expressed as a percentage of the rate base. Thus, a rate base of $200,000,000 combined with an 8% return results in an annual allowance of $16,000,000. To this figure must be added operating costs to determine the utility's total revenue requirement.

After determining the general rate level, a commission must consider what rates (prices) the utility is to be permitted to charge consumers so as to earn the required revenue. Discrimination is permitted, that is, customers are classified into various groups, and the rate charged each group is different. And within each group, rates are generally reduced as the quantity purchased increases, with the result that customers may not pay the same average rate per unit. With respect to reasonable rate structures, there are two general statutory requirements: each specific rate in a tariff must be "just and reasonable," and "undue" or "unjust" discrimination among customers is prohibited.

Service regulation has two aspects: quality and quantity. Quality refers to such matters as methods of billing, accuracy of meters, continuity of service, deposits and repayments, and treatment of complaints. Quantity refers to such matters as entry restrictions, service abandonment, and consolidations, mergers, and acquisitions. For example, entry, including both the certification of a new company and the certification of an existing company to serve a new area or a new route, is rigidly controlled by the commissions. Certificates of public convenience and necessity are required to provide most utility services. Each applicant must show that the proposed service is required by the public and that it is "fit, willing, and able" to perform properly the proposed service and to conform to all relevant regulations. Safety regulation is of particular importance with respect to the transportation industries, and includes such matters as driver or pilot qualifications, air traffic control, inspection and maintenance, and accident reporting and investigations.

If regulation is to be effective, commissions must also concern themselves with accounting and financial control. The commissions have prescribed uniform systems of accounts for the utilities. A majority of the commissions have power to regulate or control the issuance of securities, and a few have authority to regulate dividend payments. And most of the commissions require competitive bidding on new security issues.

Unresolved Problems.—Despite decades of experience with public utility regulation, many unresolved problems remain. Some feel that regulation lacks any guiding philosophy or theory. Some contend that "independent" regulatory commissions are undesirable, that the commissions have been captured by the very interests they were established to regulate, and that the commissions have failed to develop meaningful policy standards. Some maintain that the commissions are smothered in red tape and, hence, are years behind in their decisions.

Similarly, there are countless suggestions for improving the regulatory process. The establishment of the Department of Transportation in 1966 represented a partial attempt to coordinate domestic transportation policy; the Federal Power Commission's *National Power Survey* (1964) represented a similar attempt in the electric power field. Many commissions have tried to streamline their procedures, so as to reduce regulatory delay. Some economists, among others, feel that there is too much regulation; that the forces of competition, particularly in the transportation industries, could be relied upon to a greater extent than at present. But above all, there is general agreement that the basic problem is the development of tools and concepts to regulate industries which are technologically dynamic and increasingly subject to more competitive forces. No implication is intended that regulation has been a failure; the wide variety and high quality of public utility services available suggest that regulation has been successful. Rather, the argument being made is that American public utility regulation, representing a unique attempt to harmonize private and public interests, continues to confront administrators and utilities alike with challenging opportunities.

(M. G. G.; A. D. H. K.; C. F. P.)

REGULATION IN EUROPE

In western Europe many public utilities are nationalized, while some are administered by mixed companies financed with both public and private capital. Nearly all the telephone and telegraph systems are publicly owned and operated, as are most of the railways. Electricity was nationalized in many countries after the development of hydroelectric power; the undertakings were usually brought under the complete control of state, provincial, or municipal authorities, but in some countries they were left partly under private ownership, as in the case of gas. Irrespective of ownership, public utilities are as a rule subject to a measure of public accountability and to statutory control, particularly of standards and prices. With the trend toward larger units of operation, there is a tendency for centralized administration and control to replace the local ownership of utilities.

Great Britain.—In Great Britain before World War II the railways were privately owned though subject to considerable regulatory control, but a great number of other public utilities, including much local road passenger transport, water supplies, and gas and electricity undertakings, were owned and operated by local authorities or by joint public boards. The remainder were privately owned. Many which had been started with private capital were subsequently acquired by the local authorities, but in the case of transport the municipalities were frequently responsible from the start. Thus one-third of the gas, four-fifths of the water supply, and two-thirds of electricity distribution were in the hands of the municipalities, while the wholesale distribution of electricity over the "grid" was the responsibility of a public board. Before the war the municipalities tended to acquire privately owned undertakings, and in most cases those owned by companies were subject to the local authorities' option to purchase on the expiry of the franchise or at fixed dates. Thus the competition resulting from diversified ownership tended to be replaced by local monopolies, and with their establishment came the need for stricter regulation to protect consumers and to maintain standards. Public utilities were exempt from the Companies Acts, which permitted joint stock organization of all concerns complying with the terms of these acts; they had therefore to be established by the lengthy process of private bill legislation, separate acts conferring franchises on a monopoly basis and determining the conditions which were to regulate the operation of each undertaking. Sometimes, however, special legislation to establish each public service undertaking was dispensed with and general powers were granted to enable the appropriate government department to issue provisional orders after due inquiry. Nevertheless, legislative control was retained, for confirmation of the provisional orders had to be obtained from Parliament.

Public and private utilities were both subject to a considerable number of statutory regulations, but the former enjoyed somewhat greater freedom than the latter, particularly with regard to charges. Such regulations fell into three main categories. First, there were safety measures to protect the general public and provisions to safeguard the rights of property owners whose land was compulsorily acquired, as also the rights of the subscribers of capital. Second, minimum standards of quality for the services provided were laid down. Third, there were price controls to protect the consumer against exploitation by monopoly. The British system of regulation was, accordingly, comparable to a certain extent with the system of charter or special franchise prevalent in the United States. Typical laws were the Gas Meters Clauses Act of 1871 and the Gas Regulation Act of 1920, the Electricity (Supply) Acts of 1919, 1922, and 1926, and a whole series of railway acts. The crucial point of all these was the regulation of rates. In the case of private gas companies, for instance, the initial method of control, after a brief period of competition, was the so-called revision system. Maximum rates and maximum dividends were fixed in special acts, but the power to reduce rates was given to the Court of Quarter Sessions. Later, an alternative method, the system of sliding scales, was devised, but its adoption was optional. A standard selling price for gas and a standard maximum rate of dividend having been established, it was provided that the dividend might vary in inverse ratio to the rate of charge. In the case of electricity it was usual to fix maximum prices that could be charged, but rates could be below the ceiling. Railway rates were subject to the authorization of a quasi-judicial body, the Railway Rates Tribunal.

Water was supplied by local boards, municipalities, and private concerns. Here again the trend, even before World War I, was toward larger units. For instance, the Metropolitan Water Board was established in 1903 to take over the eight companies providing London with its water supply.

Both public and private local road passenger transport undertakings, practically all enjoying monopoly of operation in their area, were subject to a licensing system under the Road Traffic Act, 1930. Regional traffic commissioners were appointed and made responsible for licensing public service vehicles within the conditions laid down by this act with a view to regulating competition between road and rail and avoiding the provision of excessive transport facilities. These aims were to be achieved by proportioning the number of vehicles to traffic requirements and by the regulation of fares, services, and frequencies. The safety of passengers was protected by the establishment of standards for the construction, use, and maintenance of vehicles and by the licensing of their crews. Under the Road and Rail Traffic Act, 1933, a licensing system was also introduced to regulate road haulage vehicles operating for hire or reward (but not those carrying the goods of their owners).

In general, communications facilities have been publicly owned since the 17th century, when the postal service became a government monopoly. Telephone and telegraph services were taken over by the state after development by private companies; exceptionally the city of Hull operated its local telephone service. Cable and radio services were merged compulsorily between World Wars I and II, and were finally nationalized after World War II. The British Broadcasting Corporation was established in 1927 as a public corporation under royal charter with a monopoly of sound broadcasting, which it retains. It also pioneered television before World War II but a second public corporation, the Independent Television Authority, was established in 1954, by act of Parliament, to provide commercial television in competition with it, through the medium of private program contractors.

Between World War I and World War II, larger public-utilities units were formed through government-imposed amalgamations. Thus the Railways Act, 1921, compulsorily merged the railways into four main-line companies and fixed their standard earnings,

which the Railway Rates Tribunal was to take into account when authorizing charges. Similarly, the Electricity (Supply) Act, 1919, was intended to bring about mergers and reorganization in the electricity industry in order to facilitate the production of cheaper electricity by larger units. The act established an Electricity Commission of five members appointed by the minister of transport, and to this were transferred many of the regulatory powers previously vested in government departments. Inadequate mandatory powers for the commission, and insufficient cooperation from the electricity undertakings, were largely responsible for the act's failure. Accordingly, the Electricity (Supply) Act, 1926, superseded it, and established the Central Electricity Board, which was charged with constructing a national grid of main transmission lines over which electricity generated at selected power stations could be supplied wholesale to local distributors for retail to consumers. Local distributors remained unchanged until 1948, when, under the Labour government's nationalization program, both generation and distribution of electricity were transferred to public ownership. The British (later Central) Electricity Authority became responsible for generation and the grid, and its 14 (later 12) area boards for local distribution in England and Wales. In Scotland responsibility was transferred to two public boards independent of the central authority. Later legislation was enacted to bring about certain major changes in the administrative and operational structure of the industry. The Central Electricity Authority was abolished and replaced by the Central Electricity Generating Board and the Electricity Council. The board owns and operates the power stations and main transmission lines and is responsible for the provision of bulk supplies to the area boards which own and operate the distribution networks and are responsible for the retail sale of electricity to consumers. The council is a forum for the formulation of general policy, also having certain specific functions in finance, research, and industrial relations. The Atomic Energy Authority had responsibility for the development of nuclear power and established the world's first atomic power project, from which electricity was fed into the grid. The gas industry was nationalized by the Gas Act, 1948, with control of the manufactured gas industry, comprising over 1,000 municipal and private concerns, transferred to the Gas Council and its area boards. The council supervised, the boards being responsible for production and distribution, but new powers and duties were given the council by the Gas Act, 1965, which made it responsible for coordinating and developing the industry nationally. The council was powered to manufacture gas and in order to distribute natural gas from the North Sea fields was given power to acquire gas in bulk and sell it to the area boards or in special circumstances to consumers.

After a government White Paper outlining a national water policy, legislation was enacted to rationalize the industry by regrouping and appointing regional bodies to assist in conservation of resources and joint use of supplies. Nevertheless, water was still supplied by nearly 1,000 separate undertakings, of which about 90% were publicly owned (80% by local authorities and 10% by water boards), the remainder being water companies.

Railways under government control during World War II, were nationalized by the Transport Act, 1947, with ancillary services, including certain road passenger undertakings. Also nationalized were certain docks and harbours, inland waterways, and long-distance commercial road haulage. All were brought within a single undertaking for which the British Transport Commission (BTC) was made responsible as of 1948. Previously most canals had been privately owned, but two in Scotland were already publicly owned and the Manchester Ship Canal was mixed; the BTC did not acquire the latter. Most docks and harbours run either by public boards or by representative trusts, were left untouched. Of the rest, some were operated by the railway companies and some by private companies, and most passed into the hands of the BTC. Long-distance commercial road haulage was in private hands, although there was a considerable railway interest. Local road passenger transport was operated chiefly by municipalities, but a few small companies operated local services, and mergers had created some large companies operating much of the long-distance transport. The railways' considerable holdings in these large companies were acquired by the BTC, which afterward extended its interests. After a committee of inquiry had reported on inland waterways in 1958, an Inland Waterways Redevelopment Advisory Committee was set up to draft plans to dispose of canals no longer used. Under the Transport Act, 1953, a large section of road haulage operating for hire or reward was denationalized, but under the Transport (Disposal of Road Haulage Property) Act, 1956, the commission subsequently retained a substantial proportion, including nationwide trunking and parcels services. Under the Transport Act, 1962, the commission was dissolved, the railways, docks, and waterways became the responsibility of three separate boards, and the road haulage and road passenger undertakings and other ancillaries were transferred to the Transport Holding Company.

In 1967 legislation was before Parliament to organize the British transport industry. The railway freight services, with certain exceptions but including the freight liner services, and the freight road services of the Transport Holding Company were to be transferred to the publicly owned National Freight Corporation; the rest of heavy long-distance road haulage was to be subject to control by a new licensing system. Passenger transport authorities responsible for all forms of passenger transport were to be established, first in the conurbations and later throughout the country and a national bus company was to operate long-distance passenger transport, most of which had been acquired by the Transport Holding Company, whose bus services were to be transferred to the new company. Inland waterways were to be split as between the navigable and other waterways, and the docks were ultimately to be nationalized. Provision was made for various forms of subsidies to assist the transport industry.

Continental Europe.—Before World War II public utilities in continental Europe were mostly publicly owned or operated by mixed companies, although some countries had a number of purely commercial concerns. Thus in France about one-third of the gas output was produced by undertakings owned and operated by the larger city councils, the remainder by commercial companies. But, whatever the ownership, statutory regulations controlled prices and quality and, in some cases, profits. Most railways, e.g., French and Belgian, were run by mixed undertakings, with share capital held both publicly and privately. After World War II a number of concerns were nationalized and the rest increasingly controlled. In France, gas and electricity were nationalized and administered by public corporations supervised by a joint council responsible for coordinating the services. In Italy, in 1953 ENI, the government-owned holding company, took over SNAM, which operated the methane gas pipeline. In 1956 a Ministry of State-Controlled Enterprises was set up which controlled ENI and other state economic enterprises but not the railways, which remained under the Ministry of Transport. By 1960 ENI controlled 10 major gas-distributing companies and 6 nuclear energy corporations.

With the move toward unity in Europe, closer cooperation was established between public utility companies both publicly and privately owned. The European Conference of Ministers of Transport coordinated policies and formulated schemes for cooperation between the railways, while the Economic Commission for Europe was working out a common transport policy for its six member countries. Common policy was also being worked out in regard to production, transport, and distribution of electricity. The exchange of electricity across frontiers was facilitated by international agreement and a link was forged across the English Channel between the nationalized electricity industries in France and Great Britain. In 1957 the European Atomic Energy Community (Euratom) was established to develop atomic energy for peaceful purposes within the European Economic Community and in the early 1960s nearly 1% of community electricity was being produced from nuclear sources. In 1967 three new plants entered into operation: SENA (France/Belgium), EL4 (France) and AVK (West Germany), bringing the total to 15. The protocol of agreement relating to energy problems was adopted by the community in 1964. Similar common policies were being negotiated for the manufactured and natural gas industries. (E. A. J. D.)

BIBLIOGRAPHY.—*United States:* I. R. Barnes, *The Economics of Public Utility Regulation* (1942); C. E. Troxel, *Economics of Public Utilities* (1947), *Economics of Transport* (1955); E. W. Clemens, *Economics and Public Utilities* (1950); M. G. Glaeser, *Public Utilities in American Capitalism* (1957); M. L. Fair and E. W. Williams, Jr., *Economics of Transportation,* rev. ed. (1959); J. R. Meyer *et al., The Economics of Competition in the Transportation Industries* (1959); J. C. Nelson, *Railroad Transportation and Public Policy* (1959); J. C. Bonbright, *Principles of Public Utility Rates* (1961); F. X. Welch, *Cases and Text on Public Utility Regulation* (1961); R. E. Caves, *Air Transport and Its Regulators: an Industry Study* (1962); D. F. Pegrum, *Transportation: Economics and Public Policy* (1963); P. J. Garfield and W. F. Lovejoy, *Public Utility Economics* (1964); C. F. Phillips, Jr., *The Economics of Regulation* (1965); K. M. Ruppenthal (ed.), *Issues in Transportation Economics* (1965); D. P. Locklin, *Economics of Transportation,* 6th ed. (1966); W. G. Shepherd and T. G. Gies (eds.), *Utility Regulation* (1966); M. T. Farris and P. T. McElhiney (eds.), *Modern Transportation: Selected Readings* (1967).
(C. F. P.)

Europe: F. N. Keen, *The Law Relating to Public Service Undertakings* (1925); M. E. Dimock, *British Public Utilities and National Development* (1933); I. R. Barnes, *The Economics of Public Utility Regulation* (1942); E. Davies, *National Enterprise* (1946); H. H. Trachsel, *Public Utility Regulation* (1947); The Twentieth Century Fund, Inc., *The Power Industry and the Public Interest* (1944), *Electric Power and Government Policy* (1948); E. Goodman, *Forms of Public Control and Ownership* (1952); HMSO, *Report of the Committee of Inquiry into the Electricity Supply Industry* (1956), *Report of the Committee of Inquiry into Inland Waterways* (1958); Organization for European Economic Cooperation, *The Electricity Supply Industry in Europe* (1956), *Production, Transmission and Distribution of Electricity in Europe* (1957); W. A. Robson, *Nationalised Industry and Public Ownership* (1960); A. Hanson (ed.), *Nationalization* (1963); Michael Shanks (ed.), *Lessons of Public Enterprise* (1963); F. Ridley and J. Blondel, *Public Administration in France,* ch. 10, "Public Enterprise" (1964); J. C. Adams and P. Barile, *The Government of Republican Italy,* ch. 11 (1961). (E. A. J. D.)

PUBLIC WELFARE. This term has come into use, especially in the United States, to indicate governmental (*i.e.,* public) social welfare programs, as distinguished from similar programs conducted by private, or voluntary, organizations (*see* SOCIAL SECURITY; SOCIAL WELFARE). A further distinction is sometimes made in which "welfare" connotes a program utilizing a needs test, as distinguished from a program of social insurance.

Public welfare programs that developed in colonial America and later in the states evolved from the Elizabethan Poor Law of 1601 (*see* POOR LAW: *United States*). Sole responsibility was placed on local (town or township and county) financing and administration of outdoor relief for the able-bodied poor and custodial care for dependent infants and young children, the handicapped or disabled and the aged in orphanages, almshouses, county homes, or poor farms. State governments did not begin to assume responsibility until the latter part of the 19th century when state agencies, often called departments of charities and corrections, were created. The first board of public welfare was created in Kansas City, Mo., in 1910, and in 1917 North Carolina and Illinois established state departments of public welfare along present-day lines. The movement spread slowly. The great depression of 1929 and the enactment of the Social Security Act in 1935 resulted in the establishment in every state by 1940 of a state welfare department with local units. Both the Congress and the states have made numerous periodic changes in welfare laws. Recent decisions of the U.S. Supreme Court have repealed or modified earlier policies. Congress made important changes in the welfare program in 1971.

Modern public welfare programs include public assistance to the needy, sometimes called "relief" or "welfare"; child welfare services; and services for the aged and other dependent groups. Some programs include aspects of juvenile delinquency or medical care, which in other instances are handled by correction or public health agencies. *See also* PHILANTHROPY; SOCIAL SERVICE.

BIBLIOGRAPHY.—S. P. Breckenridge, *Public Welfare Administration in the U.S.* (1927); Wayne Vasey, *Government and Social Welfare* (1958); William Haber and Wilbur J. Cohen, *Social Security: Programs, Problems, and Policies* (1960); Ellen Winston, "Public Welfare," *Encyclopedia of Social Work* (1965). (WR. J. C.)

PUBLILIUS SYRUS (1st century B.C.), a Latin mime writer contemporary with Cicero, chiefly remembered as the author of a collection of versified aphorisms (*sententiae*) extracted from the mimes probably in the 1st century A.D. Early incorporation of non-Publilian verses and scribal distortions of authentic lines in these *sententiae* have considerably aggravated the labours of the textual critic. Modern editions contain more than 700 verses, alphabetically arranged; most of these are iambic senarii, some trochaic septenarii. Publilius, who went to Rome as a slave from Syria, was soon manumitted. He defeated the veteran mime writer Decimus Laberius (*q.v.*), in a contest held in 45 B.C., when the latter was "invited" by Caesar to perform in one of his own mimes. Though Cicero—no unbiased authority, as Laberius had scored off him—deplored the tedium induced by performances of Laberius and Publilius, Seneca the Elder and Gellius praised him, and St. Jerome quoted a verse remembered from schooldays. Later, he was known to Shakespeare, and the motto of the *Edinburgh Review* (*Judex damnatur cum nocens absolvitur; i.e.,* "The acquittal of the guilty condemns the judge") comes from him.

BIBLIOGRAPHY.—Texts by W. Meyer (1880) and R. A. H. Bickford-Smith (1895); text with Eng. trans. by J. W. and A. M. Duff in *Minor Latin Poets,* Loeb Series (1934); *see also* C. G. Smith, *Shakespeare's Proverb Lore* (1965).   (H. H. Hy.)

PUBLISHING. Publishing is the selection, reproduction, and circulation of written matter. It is older than both printing and paper, though in modern times it has come to depend upon both. Printing from blocks was invented in China some time before the middle of the 9th century; printing from movable type had been invented there by the middle of the 11th century. But at neither time was printing thought of or encouraged other than as an excellent device for avoiding the errors of transcription that often marked the work of even the best manuscript scribes and copyists. In Europe printing from movable type was introduced by the middle of the 15th century. But there, as in China, its major advantage over older methods of reproduction was thought to be the standardization of scripture and official texts. Neither in Asia nor in Europe was printing viewed at first as being useful in the wide dissemination of literature, learning, or political or religious discussion. As an instrument of publishing, printing had to fight its way. Eventually it became a great instrument of spiritual and intellectual development and of theological and scientific discourse. But the earliest reaction, which persisted for centuries, was one of opposition by church, government, university, and other powerful interests (such as the Brahmin caste in India) to its use in giving wide publicity to certain ideas and information. (*See* also PRINTING: *The History of Printing.*)

The Earliest Books.—Before the invention of printing and of paper, publishing was carried on by means of professional scribes or skilled slaves making transcriptions of manuscripts on papyrus or parchment (*qq.v.*). Flourishing industries in Egypt under the Ptolemies and in the major cities of Greece and Rome produced papyrus or parchment rolls for inscribing the classics of ancient literature, religion, and law. Often under the Roman Empire, as under later Western kings, princes, parliaments, and presbyteries, censorship and intimidation controlled or attempted to control publishers' output, thus interrupting the continuous history of commercial publishing for long stretches. Yet these ancient enterprises were authentic prototypes of modern publishing houses. Their work consisted in selecting manuscripts for reproduction in quantity; taking the risks of compensating authors in advance of public sale for rights to their manuscripts; determining the size, price, and format of editions of different titles; and developing markets where such editions could profitably be sold. They were publishers in every modern sense of the word, even though their products had not taken the form of books (*see* BOOK).

Books in the form with which the world has long been familiar (*i.e.*, made up of pages bound together at one side) had a long and obscure development of their own. By the 4th century the bound book had become moderately well known, at least among the jurists and the Christian writers of the later Roman Empire. Its first real vogue, however, was in Ireland two or three centuries later. The climax of the remarkable flowering of intellectual and religious spirit there was the Book of Kells, not infrequently mentioned, according to one authority, as "the most beautiful book in the world" (*see* ILLUMINATED MANUSCRIPTS).

To distinguish it from the old *volumen,* or "roll" (from which

the word "volume," often used interchangeably with "book," is derived), the early bound book was called a codex. The codex became the typical book of the Middle Ages, and theological codices were produced in large quantities especially in the monasteries of various church orders, which were the publishing centres of the day. Codices in law, medicine, rhetoric, and other fields of learning came from the rising universities which, in certain cities, early wrested control of the publishing industries from the church and the state. In such centres the secondhand market was as well known to medieval students as it later became to those of the 20th century. The difference was that the universities, as noncommercial publishers, strove to keep prices down for the students and thus encouraged the use of old copies. This practice also relieved the universities of the need to produce large new editions every year.

The codex, like the papyrus and parchment rolls that it replaced, was written entirely by hand. In the scriptorium or "writery" of the monastery, scribes toiled during the daylight hours (fear of fire from artificial light prevented work on books at night) copying page after page of ancient classics and the Bible, thus laboriously accomplishing the great task of preserving them. The scribe's work was then proofread, and titles and notes were inserted. If illustrations were desired, the book then went to the illuminator, after which it was ready to be bound. This procedure was not very different, in essence, from manuscript preparation in a modern publishing house—except that with modern printing and illustrating methods, these and related publishing tasks are performed only once for an edition of many thousands and not over and over again for every individual codex or book. (*See* BOOK: *Vellum and the Codex; The Medieval Book.*)

Printing and Publishing in Modern Europe.—Though the early history of publishing owes nothing to printing, Johann Gutenberg's invention of printing from movable type gave a great boost to publishing in Europe after the middle of the 15th century. Gutenberg probably was not the first European to use movable letter type successfully. After his epochal achievement, however, Mainz, his home in Germany, became the indisputable publishing centre of the continent, and Germany itself became the source and fount of subsequent printing and publishing developments in the Western world. Before 1500 about 30,000 books were printed in Europe; of these, more than two-thirds came from such great German centres of learning as Leipzig, Cologne, Basel, Nürnberg, Augsburg, and Strasbourg. More important, the German printers trained in these cities about 1460 introduced modern printing and publishing into Italy, where it played an important part in the spread of Renaissance culture and trade. Similarly, the Germans carried the printing industry and modern publishing to France in the early years of the 16th century. (*See* PRINTING: *The History of Printing.*)

It was only then that a broadening of the lay market for books took place. In 1501 Aldo Manuzio designed the first books in small format that eventually replaced the huge, elaborate, and costly codex, just as the codex had replaced the awkward *volumen*. In succeeding decades, especially in France, much attention was given to typography, and names still commonly used for typefaces in the 20th century became well known from the work, for example, of Claude Garamond and Robert Granjon. A customer of both these typographical artists, Christophe Plantin (*q.v.*) was the most famous of the early printers who became publishers. Plantin, who fled from Paris in 1548 to escape religious persecution, settled in Antwerp, where he returned to the good graces of the church and the university, gaining from the Holy See the monopoly of publishing liturgical books for the Spanish Empire and late in life becoming printer to the University of Leiden, a great publishing centre of the time.

Though many early printers remained faithful to the church and to their princes, the publishing of printed works quickly became one of the major means of organizing radical opinion in the late 15th and early 16th centuries. This naturally led to reprisals against the new publishing industry, especially in Germany, and in self-defense the publishers and printers organized into independent corporations and guilds that lasted until the 19th century in many countries. Where printing and publishing was not shut down or forced underground, as was the case in Nürnberg and Augsburg early in the 16th century, it was controlled by other means. Thus in France as early as 1474 the independent printers were brought under the same licensing regulations by which the University of Paris alone had monopolized the work of the old scribes and the publication of their manuscripts. This was indeed a signal recognition of the rapid rise of the printer to publishing eminence; yet it was also an onerous burden to the new publishers who were out of sympathy with officialdom.

Official controls on the one hand and guild restrictions on the other impeded the development of printing and publishing for centuries. On the continent one result was the emigration of printers and publishers to England, where, from 1476 to 1536, it is estimated that two-thirds of all printers, binders, and stationers were aliens. But even in England from 1534, when the Stationers' Company, or guild, was first organized into the monopoly of all English book publishing, to 1709, when the first copyright act was passed in the reign of Queen Anne, there was constant harassment of publishers, which, in due time, was carried across the ocean to America as well. During this epoch, when some freedom of publishing, bitterly won, was challenged by new efforts at control, John Milton wrote his *Areopagitica* in 1644. (*See also* Censorship.)

In France control was more or less thorough until the revolutionary copyright law of 1793 freed publishing and printing from all existing monopolies. This freedom was short-lived, however, ending under Napoleon's First Empire and not restored until the Declaration of the Republic in 1870. French restrictions had a salutary effect on the publishing industries in the Netherlands and Belgium, where during the 17th and 18th centuries large editions of the works of Molière, Boileau, Voltaire, Rousseau, and others were issued clandestinely for the French market.

As is usual with excessively rigorous controls, they often were poorly enforced, and, as is usual with official monopolies, they often bred strong, if sub rosa, competition. Both these situations, whatever the prevailing atmosphere, permitted printed literature and learning to spread rapidly in Europe between the 16th and 20th centuries, and authorship and publishing flourished. The English Copyright Act of 1709 freed the individual author and enterprising publisher from monopolistic printers and recognized the right of both to negotiate for the best royalties and other terms for the publication of literary property. But this right had been recognized as early as Roman times, when publishers of the empire bid competitively for the exclusive privilege (for which they paid fees, not royalties) of duplicating literary creations. What was significantly new about the English act was its recognition of the right of the public to literary property after a specified term. That is the substance of modern publishing copyright; it protects authors in their rights to literary property and publishers in their acquisition of such rights; but more than that, it gives the public freer access to literary property after a limited number of years—under Queen Anne's act the term was 14 years, with the author retaining the privilege of renewing for another 14 years; in the United States it has come to be for 28 years, with the same privilege for another 28 years; in most other countries the term is the remaining years of the author's life plus 20 to 50 years.

The development of copyright practice since the early 18th century is an authentic clue to the growth of professional authorship and commercial publishing, and by the protection of copyright it was a stimulus to both. The limitation in the copyright period, in turn, is an authentic clue to the thirst for learning among the increasingly literate populace. Roman usage and common law had acknowledged the author's right—if he could assert it—to his property in perpetuity. English and later continental statutes freed this property for public use after protecting the author and publisher for specified periods of time. (*See also* Copyright.)

Toward Contemporary Publishing Practice.—Just as the monasteries gradually yielded their monopoly of publishing to the universities, and the universities to the corporations and guilds, and the guilds to the competitive printers, so the printers, under the pressure of this growing market for literary works, gradually

surrendered their dominant position to the booksellers.

None of these transitions took place in a day. Even as early as the 1580s in England the pressure of costs for printing equipment and the like forced printer-publishers to appeal to booksellers for capital and credit. Thus in 1582 Christopher Barker complained to the queen:

> The booksellers being growen the greater and wealthier number have nowe many of the best Copies and keepe no printing howse, neither beare any charge of letter, or other furniture but onlie paye for workmanship . . . [with] the artifice printer growing every daye more and more unable to provide letter and other furniture, requisite for any good worke; or to gyve mayntenaunce to any such learned Correctours as are behovefull. . . .

Yet it was not until the 18th century that the bookseller had his great day as publisher. By then the reading public, especially in England, was growing much faster, and trade in popular new books (as distinct from the earlier staples of the whole industry: Bibles, commentaries, textbooks, dictionaries, and the like) was booming. To meet the new demands circulating libraries were established as early as the 1720s, and new authors were developing sufficiently large popular followings to be able to dispense with their former aristocratic patrons. By the late 18th century booksellers whose names continue to adorn publishing houses—such as Constable and Longmans—had already become kingpins of the publishing industry. Only a few decades later in the New World, Harper, Scribner's, Dutton, and Little, Brown had become well known.

Thus, with the rise of the bookseller contemporary publishing began, and with the rise of the novel and the novelist it flourished, especially in England and the United States. Both developments, reflecting the ascendancy of the middle classes, followed more deliberately on the continent, where literacy was slower to become nationwide and where extremes of wealth and poverty kept the middle-class markets small.

The unity of bookselling and publishing, in turn, persisted far longer in England than in the United States, where the great development of new writers (after piracy of English titles was successfully abated late in the 19th century) gradually stimulated the creation of independent publishing houses which were neither printers nor booksellers. This change brought with it new independent printers, binders, and booksellers: the first two produced, under contract, books arranged for by the new publishers, the third sold those books to the growing public. (*See also* Bookselling.)

By the 1920s still newer publishers appeared in numbers (in England and the United States and in Germany and France on the continent) who were devoted almost exclusively to so-called trade books—that is, books of fiction, popular biography, history, memoirs, inspirational psychology, and books of sentiment and sentimental learning. Many houses among the older group and some among the newer continued to have special departments for Bibles, other religious books, school and college textbooks, medical books, and similar works that once were the foundation of the entire publishing industry. But the newer vogue was the trade publisher as such. The age of specialization had indeed set in, nowhere more strongly than in the United States, where the industry was less encrusted with old traditions and thus afforded the most suitable soil for the new flowerings.

Subscription Books.—One of the widest and most extensively developed methods of distributing books is by subscription: sales are assured by canvassing and pledging subscribers. Today reference works of all kinds—encyclopaedias, sets of children's books, some dictionaries, collections of popular novels—are distributed almost solely by this method.

Sales by subscription, it is believed, began in the 15th century when William Caxton (*q.v.*) is said to have initiated the method to finance the publication of *The Myrrour of the World*. It differed from the traditional practice, of having one sponsor or patron for the book, by enlisting the interest and money of many.

The idea proved attractive to printers and authors, but it was not until the turn of the 17th century that this form of distribution flourished. In most instances the issue remained a single volume, and the cost of production was assured by the persons who promised to buy the book. The method fell into disrepute when some printers, after selling a book in advance of publication, produced trash or no book at all.

In the 18th century larger sets of books were distributed by subscription. *Encyclopædia Britannica* in 1768 was one of the first. In some instances, where the cost of the initial production was excessive, prepublication offers were made, and subsequent sales were continued under installment or, as known in Great Britain, the hire-purchase plan. Mark Twain in the United States adopted this idea for the distribution of Gen. Ulysses S. Grant's *Memoirs*. In his monumental biography of Twain, Albert Bigelow Paine says that Twain was able to present to General Grant the largest single royalty check ($20,000) ever given to an author up to that time, and before the volumes actually were published.

The Age of Specialization.—In the 20th century the number of new titles published each year has grown steadily, except for dips in war years or their immediate aftermaths. In 1963 about 19,000 new titles were published in the United States and over 20,000 in Great Britain. The relative size of the industry in the 20th century can be judged by comparing even its smallest annual volume of titles with that of earlier centuries. In the first half of the 18th century in England, for example, it has been calculated that the average annual number of new titles was about 93. The first quarter of the 19th century saw a jump to an average annual total of about 600. The annual growth of 20th-century totals makes it clear why specialization in publishing could so readily be supported and, indeed, why specialization had to come.

Within trade publishing itself the 20th century saw the development of hard-cover reprinters, paper-cover reprinters, specialized Western-story and detective-story publishers, science-fiction publishers, and others who profited greatly by concentrating on books for special, but sufficiently large, markets. In distribution, moreover, the old-fashioned bookseller—even the one who came to specialize in trade books—was supplemented by book clubs, other types of mail-order houses, and ordinary newsstands. While most regular trade publishers still printed editions ranging from 3,000 to 10,000 copies for most of their titles, for book clubs and paper-cover reprinters editions often ran to more than 100,000 copies and not infrequently to more than 200,000 copies. Clearly the old middle-class market had become a mass market by mid-20th century.

Beginning in the 1950s in the United States a new departure was the publishing of paper-covered books in editions ranging from 5,000 to 25,000 copies at prices that were a mere fraction of those for hard-cover books. These included reprints of great works of scholarship, science, religion, literature, and art. Many had long been out of print; often they had been issued originally by university presses or other specialized publishers with total sales of less than 2,000 copies. The great market for the new editions was found among college students and professors. So successful were these editions that many publishers began reprinting their serious books in paper-cover editions of their own. Some even issued new learned titles in this form for the student market. Specialized reprinters and even publishers of mass editions of detective stories and the like began to seek original manuscripts of a scholarly nature. In the main, however, the book clubs and others selling in mass markets continued to look to the regular publishers for titles to reprint.

To discover manuscripts for the regular publishing industry, two new occupations became prominent after the first quarter of the 20th century. The first was that of the manuscript scout, who often worked for publishers for a fee ranging from 1 to 2% of the retail price of books he might bring in. The second was that of the literary agent, who worked for authors and handled all their business relations with publishers for compensation in the form of 10% of the author's royalties and other income from his literary production. The growth of the agency business reflected further specialization in the publishing industry, whereby the publisher, becoming more a business manager, passed over his editorial functions to others. It also reflected the broadening market for authors, especially authors of fiction. To the magazine and newspaper serial rights were added motion-picture rights, dramatization

rights, radio rights, television rights, digest rights, and a series of others, the sale of which required complicated negotiations and contracts that most authors were incompetent to handle.

In facilitating distribution of books, further specialized agencies appeared in many countries. Advertising agencies sometimes added books to all the other products for which they sought to stimulate demand; others concentrated on books alone. In Germany and England, typically, about 5% of a publisher's net return was spent for advertising and promotion; in the United States the percentage was likely to be twice as high for books of average sales. For books with great sales possibilities much more was often set aside. Spending this money most effectively required skill and experience which the publisher often did not have; thus the advertising agency became involved.

Though trade books and paper-covered reprints grew in popular demand in the 20th century, growth elsewhere also added measurably to the flow of books. So great was the sale of school and college textbooks in the United States in the early 1960s that the securities of textbook publishers enjoyed an unprecedented boom in the stock exchanges. Especially notable too in the United States was the growth of the federal government as publisher—a development that reflected not only the rapidly increasing number of government studies but also the growth of federal services to those not ordinarily reached by regular publishers and regular means of book distribution. Far smaller in volume was the production of the university presses. Their work was largely in books of importance to science and learning which would, without these presses, probably have gone unpublished and thus unknown.

In the 20th century, motion pictures, radio, television, automobiles, massive illustrated magazines, and other vehicles of entertainment and enlightenment competed with the traditional book; but the book publishing industry itself enjoyed the most remarkable growth in its long and troubled history.

See NEWSPAPER; PERIODICAL; *see* also references under "Publishing" in the Index.

BIBLIOGRAPHY.—G. H. Putnam, *Books and Their Makers During the Middle Ages*, 2 vol. (1896–97); O. H. Cheney, *Economic Survey of the Book Industry, 1930–31* (1931); F. G. Kenyon, *Books and Readers in Ancient Greece and Rome* (1932); T. F. Carter, *The Invention of Printing in China and Its Spread Westward*, rev. ed. (1931); D. C. McMurtrie, *The Book: the Story of Printing and Bookmaking*, rev. ed. (1943); S. Unwin, *The Truth About Publishing*, rev. ed. (1946); F. Mumby, *Publishing and Bookselling*, rev. ed., with new and extensive bibliography on the subject in England (1949); W. Miller, *The Book Industry*, selected bibliography (1949); H. Lehmann-Haupt, *The Book in America*, rev. ed., extensive bibliography of the subject in the U.S. (1951); R. L. Duffus, "Printing and Publishing," *Encyclopaedia of the Social Sciences*, vol. xii, bibliography (1948).
(WI. MR.)

PUCCINI, GIACOMO ANTONIO DOMENICO MICHELE SECONDO MARIA (1858–1924), the greatest Italian opera composer of his period. Born at Lucca on Dec. 22, 1858, he represented the fifth (and last) generation of a musical dynasty which dated from the first half of the 18th century. Four of his ancestors held the post of *maestro di cappella* at the Cathedral of S. Martino at Lucca. It was intended that he should follow the family tradition, and he accordingly studied at the Istituto musicale Pacini (now Istituto musicale Luigi Boccherini); but a performance of *Aida*, which he saw at Pisa in 1876, revealed to him that his true vocation was opera. In the autumn of 1880 he entered the Milan Conservatory, where he remained for three years. His principal teachers there were Antonio Bazzini, a composer of symphonic overtures, and Amilcare Ponchielli, the composer of *La Gioconda*. In the summer of 1883 he graduated with an instrumental work, *Capriccio sinfonico*, the success of which attracted the attention of influential musical circles of Milan.

In the same year he entered *Le villi* in a competition for one-act operas. Though it failed to win a prize it was produced with great success in Milan in 1884, and was held to be remarkable for its dramatic power, its operatic melody, and, under the influence of Wagner, the important role played by the orchestra. The publisher Giulio Ricordi at once acquired the work and commissioned him to write another: thus began Puccini's lifelong association with the house of Ricordi, whose head was to become a staunch paternal friend and counselor. While at work on the commissioned opera *Edgar,* based on a verse-drama by Alfred de Musset, Puccini set up home with Elvira Gemignani, the wife of a Lucchese grocer. In 1886 she bore him a son, Antonio; in 1904, after the death of her first husband, her union with Puccini was legalized.

Edgar (Milan, 1889) was a failure; but with *Manon Lescaut* (Turin, 1893), based, like Massenet's *Manon,* on the celebrated 18th-century novel by A. F. Prévost, he achieved his first international success. In 1891 during the composition of *Manon Lescaut* he settled at the simple fishing village of Torre del Lago on the Lake of Massaciuccoli, remaining there until, three years before his death, he moved to Viareggio. *Manon Lescaut* was followed by Puccini's three most popular operas, which established him as the most remarkable Italian opera composer since Verdi. These were *La Bohème* (Turin, 1896), based on the autobiographical novel *Scènes de la vie de Bohème* by Henri Murger;

BY COURTESY OF THE ITALIAN INSTITUTE OF CULTURE, LONDON

GIACOMO PUCCINI

Tosca (Rome, 1900), after Victorien Sardou's five-act drama of that name; and *Madama Butterfly* (first version, Milan, February 1904; second version, Brescia, May 1904), after David Belasco's one-act play. In all three operas the librettists were Luigi Illica and Giuseppe Giacosa, who complemented each other in their work and were also the composer's best collaborators. With *La Fanciulla del West* (*The Girl of the Golden West;* New York City, 1910), also after a Belasco play, Puccini temporarily abandoned his lyrical style for technical experiments in harmony and orchestration under the influence of Debussy and Strauss. His single attempt at operetta, *La Rondine* (Monte Carlo, 1917), was unsuccessful. Then came *Il Trittico* ("Triptych") (New York City, 1918), consisting of three strongly contrasted one-act episodes: the sombre, horrific *Il tabarro,* after Didier Gold's *La Houppelande* (*The Cloak*); the sentimental tragedy *Suor Angelica,* on a libretto by G. Forzano; and the comedy *Gianni Schicchi,* also on a libretto by Forzano derived from Dante's *Inferno.* Puccini's last opera— some consider it his greatest—was *Turandot* (Milan, 1926), based on a play, *Turandotte,* by Carlo Gozzi. He died, before its completion, on Nov. 29, 1924, at Brussels. The last two scenes of the opera were completed from Puccini's sketches by Franco Alfano.

Puccini's approach to dramatic composition is expressed in his own words: "The basis of an opera is its subject and its treatment." The fashioning of a story into a moving drama for the stage claimed his attention in the first place, and he devoted to this part of his work as much labour as to the musical composition itself. The action of his operas is uncomplicated and self-evident, so that the spectator, even if he does not understand the words, readily comprehends what takes place on the stage. The majority of his operas illustrate a theme defined in *Il tabarro:* "Chi ha vissuto per amore, per amore si morì" ("He who has lived for love, has died for love"). This theme is played out in the fate of his heroines—women who are devoted body and soul to their lovers, are tormented by feelings of guilt, and are punished by the infliction of pain until in the end they are destroyed. In his treatment of this theme Puccini combines compassion and pity for his heroines with a strong streak of sadism: hence the strong emotional appeal but also the restricted scope of the Puccinian type of opera.

The main feature of Puccini's musico-dramatic style is his ability to identify himself with his subject: each opera has its distinctive ambience. With an unfailing instinct for balanced dramatic structure, Puccini knew that an opera is not all action, movement, and conflict; it must also contain moments of repose, contemplation, and lyricism. For such moments he invented an original type of melody, passionate and radiant yet marked by an underlying morbidity; examples are the "farewell" and "death" arias that also reflect the persistent melancholy from which he suffered in his personal life.

Puccini's conception of diatonic melody is rooted in the tradition of 19th-century Italian opera, but his harmonic and orchestral style show that he was aware of contemporary developments, notably the work of the Impressionists and of Stravinsky. Though he allowed the orchestra a more active role, he upheld the traditional vocal style of Italian opera, in which the singers carry the burden of the music. In many ways a typical *fin-de-siècle* artist, Puccini nevertheless can be ranked as the greatest exponent of operatic realism.

BIBLIOGRAPHY.—G. Adami (ed.), *Letters of Giacomo Puccini* (1931); M. Carner, *Puccini: a Critical Biography* (1958); G. R. Marek, *Puccini* (1951); V. Seligman, *Puccini Among Friends* (1938).

PUDOVKIN, VSEVOLOD ILLARIONOVICH (1893–1953), Soviet film director, one of the greatest of the era of silent films, was born at Penza, Russia, on Feb. 21, 1893. Wounded and imprisoned for three years in World War I, he returned to the study of chemistry but was attracted to the theatre. D. W. Griffith's film *Intolerance* moved him to apply for admission to the State Institute of Cinematography in Moscow. He worked with Lev Kuleshov in certain early film experiments, directed an educational feature (*Mechanics of the Brain*) and collaborated on a comedy, *Chess Fever.* Pudovkin's best-known theatrical films are *The End of St. Petersburg* (1927), *Storm Over Asia* (1928), and *Mother* (1926), based on Maksim Gorki's novel. He was also occasionally an actor. His sound films included *Deserter* (1933), *General Suvorov* (1941), and *Admiral Nakhimov* (1948). Pudovkin died on June 30, 1953.

In two books, *Film Technique* and *Film Acting,* written for Russian film classes and first published outside Russia in 1929, Pudovkin explained his principles of scenario, directing, acting, and editing. His early films emphasize individuals within the Revolution somewhat more than did Sergei Eisenstein's (*q.v.*), but Pudovkin shared his great contemporary's liking for elaborate crosscutting of images (montage) to represent complex ideas.

(R. D. MacC.)

PUDSEY, a municipal borough (1899) of the West Riding of Yorkshire, Eng., lies between Bradford (4 mi. [6 km.]) and Leeds (6 mi. [10 km.]). Pop. (1961) 34,851. The trade of the town is varied, with woolen textile factories, tanning mills, foundries, crane-making, and light engineering works, together with other light industries. John Tunnicliffe, Herbert Sutcliffe, and Sir Leonard Hutton, eminent cricketers from the borough, played for Yorkshire and England. Pudsey has been in existence since before Saxon times and resisted Roman and Norman invaders and conquests. Fulneck, in the south of the borough, was chosen in 1743 as a Moravian settlement (now with a church and two schools). Farsley and Calverley were added in 1937. All three parts of the borough (Pudsey, Farsley, and Calverley) are mentioned in Domesday Book. (W. R. C.)

PUEBLA, an interior plateau state of Mexico. Pop. (1960) 1,973,837; area, 13,096 sq.mi. (33,919 sq.km.), with its capital at Puebla. On the southeast corner of the Anáhuac Plateau, Puebla varies in elevation (5,000–8,000 ft.), with numerous fertile valleys formed by the Sierra Madre Oriental which runs through the state. Endowed with a temperate, semihumid climate, crossed by main highways running southward from the national capital, and traversed by rail and air lines, Puebla is one of the most densely populated states of Mexico.

Its strategic location and natural endowments in pre-Hispanic times are attested by innumerable archaeological sites and by its many towns and villages, notably Cholula (*q.v.*), Atlixco, and Tehuacán, a noted health resort. Coffee, sugarcane, fibres, maize, and cereals are its main crops. Onyx, gold, and other metals occur in its richly veined mountains. Numerous short, fast rivers provide hydroelectric power.

Its Nahuatl-speaking native peoples were highly developed at the coming of the Spaniards in the 16th century, and the latter founded many estates in this region, a main focus of their religious and economic activities. In the 19th and 20th centuries Puebla developed as an agricultural-industrial area in the important corridor between Mexico City and its main seaport at Veracruz.

(Hd. C.; J. A. Cw.)

PUEBLA (Puebla de Zaragoza), city of Mexico and capital of the state of the same name. Pop. (1969 est.) 383,879. The centre of an important agricultural and industrial region of central Mexico, Puebla is 80 mi. (129 km.) SE of the federal capital and from viceregal days has been considered the military key to the nation. The city was founded as Puebla de los Angeles by the Spaniards in 1532. According to church chronicles, the site was chosen as the result of a dream by Fray Julian Garcés who saw two angels with a line and rod pacing a beautiful plain flanked by tall volcanoes. Puebla is on a broad, healthful plain 7,050 ft. (2,149 m.) above sea level in the foothills of the Sierra Madre Oriental within view of Mexico's three highest snow-topped volcanoes, Citlaltépetl, Popocatépetl, and Ixtacihuatl.

Puebla is characteristically Spanish with noteworthy architecture similar to that of Toledo, Spain's great fortress city. The sumptuous cathedral, whose interior is rich with onyx, marble, and gold, was made a bishopric in 1550 and an archbishopric in 1903. Overshadowing the cathedral is the all-gold-leaf chapel of the Rosary in the church of Santo Domingo. The Casa del Alfeñique, the "almond-cake house" (now a museum), was built in the 17th century of polychrome blue, white, and red tiles with white decorations and black ironwork balconies. The Teatro Principal (1790) was one of the first permanent theatres in the hemisphere. Puebla is the seat of a university, founded 1537.

A conservative, strongly Catholic city, Puebla was often considered politically reactionary in the history of Mexico. U.S. forces under Gen. Winfield Scott occupied the city (1847) during the Mexican War. Most famous of the battles fought in Puebla was the repulse of the French on May 5, 1862. In honour of its defender, Puebla was officially renamed Puebla de Zaragoza after Gen. Ignacio Zaragoza. The French again besieged the city, May 17, 1863, and captured it. Gen. Porfirio Díaz took the city April 2, 1867, and ended the imperialist occupation.

As an industrial centre, Puebla is known for its onyx working, Talavera tiles, cotton and woolen textiles, glass, soap, pottery, leather goods, and other light articles.

(H. R. Hy.)

PUEBLO, a city of Colorado, U.S., situated on the Arkansas River at the mouth of Fountain Creek, 110 mi. (193 km.) SE of Denver, at an elevation of 4,685 ft. (1,428 m.), the seat of Pueblo County. Pop. (1970) city 97,453; standard metropolitan statistical area (Pueblo County) 118,238. (For comparative population figures *see* table in Colorado: *Population.*) Pueblo lies near the great coalfields of the state and is an important manufacturing, retail, and trucking centre. At Minnequa, on the mesa south of the city, is one of the largest steel plants in the U.S. The irrigated region of 50,000 ac. (20,200 ha.) adjacent to Pueblo produces large quantities of small vegetables and garden seeds. The Pueblo Ordnance Depot of the U.S. Army (established in 1942) is on a mesa 14 mi. (23 km.) E of the city. The Colorado State Fair (established in 1886 and provided for by the state legislature since 1907) is held annually in August. The Colorado State Hospital (psychiatric) is in Pueblo. Pueblo Junior College, a public school opened in 1933, became Southern Colorado State College in 1963 and was authorized to grant bachelor's degrees.

The site of Pueblo was visited by Lieut. Zebulon Montgomery Pike, who erected a temporary log breastwork on Nov. 24, 1806. In 1823 John McKnight established a trading post, which was soon wiped out by Comanches. From 1843 to 1854 there was a small settlement of mountain men as well as an adobe fort which was destroyed by Utes. A party of gold seekers located there in 1858. Gen. W. J. Palmer's Denver and Rio Grande Railroad reached Pueblo in 1872 and he organized the Central Colorado Improvement Company with the purpose of creating an industrial city. Reorganized in 1882 and again in 1892, it became the Colorado Fuel and Iron Company and fulfilled the original purpose.

In June 1921 a sudden flood of the Arkansas River struck Pueblo, causing severe property damage and about 200 deaths. A $4,000,-000 flood-control system was immediately built, which effectively prevented any recurrence of the disaster. The headquarters for the Frying Pan-Arkansas Water Diversion Project is located at Pueblo.

The city established a council-manager form of government in 1950.

(Hy. L. C.)

PUEBLO INDIANS, those groups of Southwestern U.S. Indians who live in pueblos (Sp. *pueblo,* "village" or "town"), compact permanent settlements, and who are characterized by intensive agriculture, distinctive arts and crafts (notably pottery and weaving), and complex religion. Up to the time of European arrival, however, they had no metals, and, like other North American Indians, no livestock (the only domestic animals being dogs and turkeys) and no wheeled vehicles. Native crops were corn, squash, beans, and cotton.

History.—The ancestors of the Pueblo Indians occupied the Southwest, as hunters and food-gatherers originally, thousands of years ago. (*See* Indian, North American: *Culture Provinces: The Southwest.*) Cultural advances, with introduction of new traits, primarily from Mexico, formed the developed Pueblo culture during, roughly, the 1st millennium of the Christian era. By the 16th century, when the first Spanish explorers opened the historic period in the Southwest, additional cultural changes had brought the Pueblos to a relatively high level of "Neolithic" culture, with agriculture, architecture, arts, and crafts. By that time, however, large portions of the formerly settled region had been abandoned—especially following the severe drought period in the 13th century—and the area occupied by the Pueblos was broadly similar to the modern distribution. Permanent Spanish occupation of New Mexico, which then included northern Arizona and the Hopi pueblos, began in August 1598. It was interrupted by the successful Pueblo Rebellion of August 1680, and Spanish political control and Catholic missionary effort were not reestablished until the 1690s in the New Mexico pueblos (the Rio Grande area, Acoma, and Zuñi); they were never reestablished among the Hopi. Except among the Hopi (and non-Pueblo, nonsedentary groups such as the Apache, Navaho, and others), the 18th century was a period of quietly firm and successful Spanish control of the Pueblo peoples. (*See* also New Mexico: *History.*)

The Pueblo Peoples.—The modern and historic Pueblo Indians of New Mexico and Arizona include specifically: (1) the Hopi (or Moqui, as the Spanish called them) of northeastern Arizona, including the Tewa village known as Hano on First Mesa (founded about 1700 by refugees from the Rio Grande after the Pueblo Rebellion period); (2) the Zuñi in westernmost New Mexico, since about 1700 in one large town, before the Pueblo Rebellion occupying six pueblos in the same vicinity; (3) the seven Keresan-speaking pueblos of northwest-central New Mexico—the famous pueblo of Acoma the westernmost, then Laguna, a few miles northeast (established only in the 1690s after the Pueblo Rebellion and Spanish reconquest by Keresans and possibly others from various pueblos), and five just above the confluence of the Jemez Creek and the Rio Grande, on both streams (Zia, Santa Ana, San Felipe, Santo Domingo, Cochiti); (4) Jemez, just north and west of the Rio Grande, and formerly Pecos (abandoned in 1838), speaking the same dialect; (5) the five Tewa villages north of Santa Fe—Tesuque, Nambe, San Ildefonso, Santa Clara, and San Juan; (6) the four pueblos which speak Tiwa dialects—Sandia and Isleta south of the Keresans and near Albuquerque, and Picuris and Taos north of the Tewa. Formerly there were other Tiwa pueblos and the related Piros south and east of Isleta.

The Jemez, Tewa, and Tiwa dialects are closely related, forming the Tanoan language family. Tanoan, Zuñi, and Hopi are all distantly related to each other and to languages of western North America in the Azteco-Tanoan stock (including Shoshone-Comanche, Ute-Paiute, Pima-Papago, and various Mexican tongues). Keresan, however, is not known to be related to any other language—in other words, the Keresans have been separated from any linguistic relatives for so long that no connections are recognizable.

Culture.—The distinctive Pueblo culture can be traced from relatively primitive seminomads of several thousand years ago

SAN ILDEFONSO PLAZA

Mexico.

Modern Pueblo social life centres around the village (which is also the political unit) though the pueblos are essentially theocracies. The western pueblos are organized as matrilineal clans and lineages, and households are based on matrilocal (uxorilocal) residence. Secret societies, each owned or controlled by a particular clan, perform calendric rituals for rain and tribal welfare. A tribal-wide katcina (*kachina*) cult is concerned with ancestors, and men's societies are responsible for protection and fertility ritual. In the Rio Grande region there is a dual village division into so-called Summer and Winter people, alternately responsible for pueblo activities; secret societies there deal primarily with curing rituals, and the katcina cult is less developed than it is in the other pueblos.

Native arts and crafts survive primarily among the Hopi, where weaving and basketry are still (1960s) practised and where the Hopi-Tewa revived pottery making in the 1890s. But the most remarkable pottery revival took place at San Ildefonso, where Maria Martinez developed the famous blackware now made by several Tewa pueblos. Silver and turquoise jewelry is currently produced in most pueblos, but silver working is not aboriginal.

who subsisted on wild plants and animals, and who had comparatively few and simple implements of flaked stone, bone, wood, and other plant materials. More advanced traits (mostly from Mexico) developed with appearance of cultivated or semidomesticated corn (maize; *Zea mays*) in southwestern New Mexico more than 4,000 years ago; pottery, first dated in that area to about 2,000 years ago; beans and pumpkins; pithouses (from a northerly source?); polished stone (*e.g.*, ax blades) and, later, stonemasonry and permanent surface structures; cultivation of cotton; domestication of turkeys; the bow and arrow; the hard cradleboard; and many others.

At least a few important religious concepts came from the south—notably the horned or plumed serpent. Basic polytheistic theory, colourful ritual, masked prayer dances, altars and offerings, derived from the south or—perhaps more likely—from the same original matrix as the more complex religion of native

Modern Pueblo Indians have retained the pre-Spanish way of life to a surprising degree. They have added to their material inventory, since 1600, such items as livestock, metal tools, new crops (*e.g.*, wheat, peaches, chili peppers from Mexico), European and, later, modern U.S. clothing, automobiles and radios; after World War II, television aerials appeared on many of the picturesque little adobe houses in the Rio Grande Valley. These changes necessarily have affected ideas, attitudes, and general outlook. But even in the Rio Grande pueblos close to Santa Fe

PUEBLOS AND LINGUISTIC AREAS OF THE PUEBLO INDIANS

and Albuquerque the basic fabric of Pueblo social system, community of organization, and native religion, with modifications only of detail, has fully and successfully survived the blows of drought and arroyo-cutting in the 1200s, incursions and attacks by non-sedentary Indians, Spanish domination after 1600, three and one-half centuries of Christian missionary efforts, and (at least into the 1960s) the impact of modern technology.

See also ACOMA; ANASAZI; HOPI; ZUÑI; and references under "Pueblo Indians" in the Index.

BIBLIOGRAPHY.—F. R. Eggan, *Social Organization of the Western Pueblos* (1950); J. O. Brew, *Archaeology of Alkali Ridge, Southeastern Utah* (1946); J. O. Brew and others, *Franciscan Awatovi* (1946); E. K. Reed, *Excavations in Mancos Canyon, Colorado* (1938); A. V. Kidder, *Introduction to the Study of Southwestern Archaeology* (1924); R. Underhill, *First Penthouse Dwellers of America* (1946); A. Marriott, *Indians of the Four Corners* (1953); H. A. Tyler, *Pueblo Gods and Myths* (1964). (E. K. RE.)

PUERPERAL FEVER (CHILDBED FEVER), a term implying infection of some part of the female reproductive organs following childbirth or abortion. The equivocal term "puerperal pyrexia" covers all cases of fever of 38° C (100.4° F) and over occurring during the first ten days following delivery or miscarriage, but due to either genital or extragenital lesions. Such cases are notifiable to the civil authority in most civilized countries and the notifying physician should clarify the diagnosis later, if possible. Puerperal infection is most commonly of the raw surface of the interior of the uterus after separation of the placenta (afterbirth); but pathogenic organisms may also affect lacerations of any part of the genital tract. By whatever portal, they can invade the blood- and lymph-stream to cause septicemia (blood poisoning), cellulitis (inflammation of cellular tissue), and pelvic or generalized peritonitis (inflammation of the abdominal lining). The severity of the illness depends on the virulence of the infecting organism, the resistance of the invaded tissues, and the general health of the patient.

Illegal abortions performed in unhygienic surroundings commonly result in puerpural fever.

History.—The disease was accurately described in the writings of Hippocrates (5th century B.C.): "If a woman in childbed have erysipelas of the womb she will usually die"—and this held true until 1935 (*see* below). William Harvey was the first to describe (1651) the placental site as "one vast ulcer" in women with childbed fever. Charles White of Manchester identified (1773) puerperal with "surgical" fever, then and later the scourge of hospitals; advised postural drainage of the womb in the lying-in period and, by his insistence on cleanliness in the conduct of deliveries and on isolation of infected patients, made a famous advance in the art of midwifery. Alexander Gordon declared (1795) that puerperal fever was a contagion seizing only such women as were attended by a doctor or midwife in contact with other infected patients. Jean Louis Baudelocque remarked (1789) the greater incidence of fever when hands or instruments had been introduced into the birth canal. I. P. Semmelweis (*q.v.*) rediscovered these facts and demonstrated (1847) that infection was rife among women delivered by doctors and students who dissected cadavers and far less common among women attended only by midwives. He earned tragic unpopularity by advocating washing of the hands in antiseptic solution before attendance on women in labour. Meanwhile in the United States the poet-physician Oliver Wendell Holmes (*q.v.*) had published *The Contagiousness of Puerperal Fever* (1843) and was similarly abused; however, by 1855, when the essay was reprinted with additional evidence, his views had begun to prevail.

Causative Organisms.—"Humours" and "miasmata" were thought to be the causative agents of all fevers until, in 1879, Louis Pasteur isolated a dotlike microorganism, grouped in short chains, from the discharges of a woman with fatal puerperal fever. This, the hemolytic streptococcus, remains the most deadly of all killers. In 1935 Rebecca Lancefield (U.S.) and Ronald Hare (England) identified a single group of these streptococci as the cause of severe puerperal fever, tonsillitis, scarlet fever, and fulminating surgical infections; and Leonard Colebrook showed that these organisms are not normally present in the human

vagina but are conveyed mediately to puerperal patients from the upper respiratory tract of their attendants or contacts.

Other common organisms producing this infection are the staphylococci (casual inhabitants of the skin, of pimples, carbuncles and many other pustular eruptions); the anaerobic streptococci, which flourish in devitalized tissues such as may be present after long and injurious labour and unskilled instrumental delivery; *Escherichia coli* and *Clostridium welchii* (inhabitants of the lower bowel); and, rarely and fatally, the bacillus of tetanus.

Signs and Symptoms.—Fever, sometimes with rigors, usually begins on the third day postpartum; the pulse rate quickens and general prostration develops, as with any acute infection of the body; the uterus remains enlarged and tender, the discharges from it being profuse or scanty, or purulent or malodorous. Danger signs are persistent high fever, repeated rigors, rapid pulse rate, insomnia, diarrhea, and delirium. In favourable cases the infection remains localized to the genital tract or pelvis and recovery is the rule, even without specific medication. Pelvic peritonitis or cellulitis will prolong the illness and may require surgical drainage; invasion of the bloodstream or general peritoneum is of the utmost gravity and in the 1960s accounted for about half of all deaths during the lying-in period. The most serious residue of the illness in all its forms for those who recover is sterility.

Prevention.—The conduct of labour, delivery, and the recovery period must meet the high standards of asepsis and antisepsis essential to modern surgery. It remains true that the more natural the labour and the less the interference, the lower the incidence of sepsis. Conversely, the longer or more traumatic the labour, the higher the morbidity. Accurate antenatal care, prognosis, provision for likely difficulty, skilled attendance, minimizing of fatigue or loss of blood, rigid asepsis and antisepsis, and the greatest gentleness in all maneuvers can prevent the development of very nearly all infections. It is imperative that persons harbouring possibly harmful organisms, especially in the upper respiratory tract, be excluded from attendance at the childbed, and that any such infection in the mother be effectively treated. The antenatal period is devoted to improving the general health of the pregnant woman and detecting and treating any disease.

Curative Treatment.—When symptoms of puerperal fever appear, the patient must be isolated; the nature of the infecting organism determined by culture of swabs from the genital tract; and all contacts examined and made to undergo bacteriological investigation, both to detect the source of the infection and to prevent its spread. While awaiting the results of this, the patient herself and any puerperal contacts should commence a course of sulfonamides or a wide-spectrum antibiotic. The stricken woman is nursed in a semi-upright position to ensure free drainage of discharge, and given blood transfusion if anemia is present.

Until 1935 the treatment of such patients was purely supportive and was successful only if the low invasive power of the infecting organism or the patient's own resistance prevented the development of generalized disease. If septicemia or general peritonitis appeared the morbidity rate was very high indeed. With peritonitis due to the hemolytic streptococcus, recovery was the rare exception. In 1935 the sulfonamides were first used clinically at Queen Charlotte's Isolation Hospital, London, by Colebrook and Meave Kenny, as specific antidotes for severe hemolytic streptococcal infections. Later, pneumococci, gonococci, and *E. coli* yielded to this chemotherapy: there was an immediate and worldwide drop both in the mortality rate of puerperal fever and in its apparent incidence, since the pyrexia could be controlled below notifiable limits within a few hours. Then, in the 1940s, from Alexander Fleming, Howard Florey, and co-workers in England, came penicillin, with its power to check staphylococci as well.

With the discovery of more and more antibiotic drugs, almost every organism associated with puerperal fever has been defeated; severe illness or death from this cause is almost unknown in civilized countries. The mere occurrence of a case was, by the 1960s, an embarrassment to an obstetric unit, for it told of a breakdown in preventive measures which had come to be valued far above cure. Puerperal and neonatal morbidity, when it did occur, was most commonly caused by strains of staphylococci, resistant to various antibiotics, which had become resident in hospitals and among the population. They caused inflammation of the breasts; and eye and skin infections in the newborn. The purely prophylactic use of antibiotics in hospital or their indiscriminate administration in general practice increased this danger of the appearance of resistant strains of organisms. Therefore, the tendency was to limit the haphazard use of these drugs, to choose their type more carefully, and to prefer the sulfonamides when these were equally effective.

BIBLIOGRAPHY.—H. R. Spencer, *The History of British Midwifery from 1650–1800* (1927); Munro Kerr, *Maternal Mortality and Morbidity* (1933); L. Colebrook, "Prevention of Puerperal Sepsis," *J. Obstet. Gynaec. Brit. Emp.*, 43:691 (1936); L. Colebrook and M. Kenny, "Treatment of Human Puerperal Infections and of Experimental Infections in Mice with Prontosil," *Lancet*, 1:1279 (1936).

(M. K.)

PUERTO BARRIOS, the principal port of Guatemala, served chiefly by cargo and passenger ships of the United Fruit Company. Pop. (1964) 32,071 (mun.). Named for Justo Rufino Barrios, president of Guatemala from 1873 to 1885, it was constructed as the Caribbean terminus of the railway, built by foreign contractors from the coast to Guatemala City, which realized a century-old Guatemalan dream of a national commercial outlet through a deep-water Atlantic port. The government became dissatisfied with control of the facilities by foreign interests, however, and constructed a competing port at Santo Tomás (1955) and a highway paralleling the railroad. Puerto Barrios is also connected with the capital by air. (W. J. G.)

PUERTO CABELLO is a city and port of Venezuela in the state of Carabobo. Pop. (1961) 52,493. The mean average temperature of the port is 80° F (26.6° C). Puerto Cabello has a well-protected harbour accessible to the largest vessels calling at Venezuelan ports, with docks, warehouses, a navy yard and dry-dock facilities. The city is connected with Valencia, the capital of the state, by a highway and railway over a 2,000-ft. (610-m.) pass and is considered a natural outlet for the agriculturally rich and commercially important Valencia basin. Commerce dominates the economy of the city, but there are small processing industries. Ten miles from the city, on the Pan-American highway, is a modern petroleum-chemical plant erected by the government. Puerto Cabello was sacked by pirates many times during the colonial period and was a favoured smuggling centre for the Dutch, operating from Curaçao. The city suffered much damage in the Wars of Independence. Simón Bolívar was defeated there in June 1812. Subsequently the port changed hands several times. José Antonio Páez, national hero and long-time president of the republic, led the attack which forced the final Spanish surrender at Puerto Cabello in 1823. The story goes that the waters of the harbour are so smooth that a single hair (*cabello* in Spanish) could moor a vessel to the dock, hence the name Puerto Cabello.

(J. J. J.)

PUERTO DE SANTA MARÍA, EL, a seaport of southern Spain in the province of Cádiz, region of Andalusia, is situated at the mouth of the Guadalete River in the Bay of Cádiz, 9 mi. (15 km.) SW of Jerez de la Frontera by rail (10½ mi. [17 km.] by road). Pop. (1960) 35,505 (mun.). It is an attractive town with many buildings of architectural interest. It competes with Jerez in the production and blending of sherry wines, which are exported. It once housed naval arsenals and shipyards and was an oceanic captaincy general. From it Alonso de Ojeda sailed to the West Indies. (M. B. F.)

PUERTO LA CRUZ, lying in northeastern Venezuela on the Caribbean and in the state of Anzoátegui, is one of the country's outstanding petroleum-handling ports. It is also one of the nation's four leading importing ports, distributing goods mostly in the Barcelona-Guanta-Puerto La Cruz urban complex. Pop. (1961) 59,033.

The eastern llanos presently accounts for more than one-third of the country's petroleum output. The bulk of this comes from the state of Anzoátegui. From Puerto La Cruz petroleum is accessible for industrial and domestic use in the densely populated northern highland region, of which Caracas is the major centre. Pipelines from the eastern llanos oilfields and from smaller fields in the neighbouring states of Guárico and Monagas focus upon Puerto La Cruz. The port is also the site of very large oil storage facilities and refineries (it accounts for about 19% of the oil domestically refined). Until petroleum put its stamp on the eastern llanos and the state of Anzoátegui, Puerto La Cruz was a sleepy fishing village, but has become a busy, thriving, populous port.

There is also considerable industrial concentration in the Barcelona-Guanta-Puerto La Cruz area. (L. WE.)

PUERTO PLATA, a province in northern Dominican Republic. Area 671 sq.mi. (1,739 sq.km.). Pop. (1970 est.) 195,307. Its southern boundary is the Cordillera Septentrional (to 3,993 ft. [1,217 m.]), which is the nation's leading coffee region. Puerto Plata is also one of the leading producers of corn (maize), bananas and tobacco and a significant dairying region. The province was established in 1875. Its capital, San Felipe de Puerto Plata (called Puerto Plata), pop. (1960) 19,073, was founded in 1503 by Columbus. It is the nation's second port and an industrial centre. Thirty miles to the west are the ruins of Isabela (reputed to be the first European town set up in the new world), founded by Columbus in 1493. (D. R. D.)

PUERTO RICO (COMMONWEALTH OF PUERTO RICO, ESTADO LIBRE ASOCIADO DE PUERTO RICO), an island and an autonomous commonwealth voluntarily associated with the United States. It is the smallest and the most easterly of the Greater Antilles, the major island group of the West Indies (*q.v.*), which form the broken northern boundary between the Caribbean sea and the Atlantic ocean. To the west and just out of sight beyond the 70-mi. (113-km.) Mona passage lies the island of Hispaniola. To the east lie the Virgin Islands, one of which, St. Thomas, can be seen on a clear day from the eastern shore. New York, the main U.S. port of departure for Puerto Rico, lies more than 1,500 mi. (2,400 km.) N.W. Directly south, across about 600 mi. (960 km.) of Caribbean sea, is the coast of Venezuela. Puerto Rico is nearly rectangular with a length from east to west of 113 mi. (182 km.) and a width of 41 mi. (66 km.). Its area is 3,349 sq.mi. (8,674 sq.km.) or 3,421 sq.mi. (8,860 sq.km.) including adjacent islands.

This article is divided into the following sections:

I. Physical Geography
    1. Geology and Physiography
    2. Climate
    3. Vegetation
    4. Animal Life
II. Geographical Regions
    1. Lowlands and Coastal Plains
    2. Highlands
    3. Rolling Hill Land
    4. Mona, Culebra and Vieques Islands
III. The People
    1. Racial Characteristics
    2. Language
    3. Religion
    4. Customs and Culture
IV. History
    A. Spanish Rule
        1. Early Settlement
        2. Liberal Reforms
        3. Economic and Political Development
        4. Movements Toward Self-Government and Independence
        5. Spanish-American War
    B. Under the United States
        1. Early Years
        2. Economic and Social Changes
        3. Political Development
        4. Establishment of the Commonwealth
V. Population
VI. Administration and Social Conditions
    1. Government
    2. Taxation
    3. Living Conditions
    4. Welfare Services
    5. Justice
    6. Education
VII. The Economy
    1. Agriculture
    2. Industry
    3. Power

4. Trade
5. Banking and Currency
6. Transport and Communications

I. PHYSICAL GEOGRAPHY

1. Geology and Physiography.—Puerto Rico and the other Greater Antilles are formed by the high parts of a 1,300-mi. (2,100-km.) chain of mountains whose base and bulk are buried beneath the sea. These mountaintop islands are the oldest of all the land masses in the West Indies. In contrast, the Lesser Antilles, which form the eastern boundary of the Caribbean sea, are of more recent formation, and volcanic activity is sometimes still apparent there. Near Puerto Rico the land mass offers its greatest relief contrast in height and depth. To the north of Puerto Rico, running more or less parallel to the island, exists the deep valley in the Atlantic floor known as the Puerto Rico Trench (formerly called the Brownson Deep). The deepest part of this trough lies about 100 mi. (160 km.) to the northwest of Puerto Rico; there the floor of the Atlantic goes down 30,246 ft. (9,220 m.). To the south too the land falls off sharply below sea level. About 55 mi. (89 km.) S.W. of Puerto Rico the Caribbean reaches a depth of more than 17,000 ft. (5,200 m.). If the base of this chain of mountains were elevated to sea level, it would become one of the most imposing land masses in the world. Indeed, the highest point in Puerto Rico, Cerro de Punta, 4,389 ft. (1,338 m.), would attain an altitude greater than that of Mt. Everest.

The island's central mountain chain, the Cordillera Central, rises almost directly out of the sea on the west coast of the island and extends eastward, finally terminating in the Sierra de Luquillo in the northeast and in the Sierra de Cayey in the southeast. While this rugged terrain covers about 70% of the island's area, the fertile coastal plains extend like a fringe between the mountains and the Atlantic on the north and the Caribbean on the south. Geologists agree that while Puerto Rico cannot be considered a volcanic island, in the sense that some of the Lesser Antilles might be so classified, the land mass was formed by early volcanic activity during the upper Cretaceous. In general terms, the Cordillera Central is underlain by lavas and volcanically derived sediments resulting from this igneous activity. In the west a large body of serpentine occurs, and in the central and southeastern areas bodies of coarser plutonic rocks, quartz, diorites and granodiorites are found.

The coastal plain on the south side of the island is not so wide nor so naturally fertile as the northern coastal plain. The north-south drainage divide runs parallel to the Caribbean coast about 10 mi. (16 km.) from the shore line. As would be expected, thus, the southern side of the central mountain chain presents a more precipitous drop to the sea than that found on the north. To the north, most of the principal rivers, such as the Río Grande de Loíza, Río de la Plata or Río Grande de Arecibo, descend to the Atlantic through foothills and slowly declining slopes. The flood plains formed by these rivers are extremely fertile.

2. Climate.—While Puerto Rico lies just within the tropics, its climate is usually agreeable. The average annual temperature is about 76° F. (about 24° C.) and there is no sunshine, on average, for only five days a year. On the coast the winter average is 75° F.; for the summer months it is 80° F. (26° C.). In the interior at an altitude of 1,500 ft. the average winter temperature is 70°; during the summer it is 75°. The absolute minimum temperature recorded in Puerto Rico was 39° F. (4.5° C.) at an altitude of 3,000 ft. Frost may occur at higher altitudes but has never been officially recorded. The maximum recorded temperature in San Juan is 94° F. (34.5° C.). Cool, invigorating sea breezes, constantly brought by the trade winds which bathe the islands of the West Indies, help to soften the effect of the hot sun. During the summer months these winds come directly from the east or slightly southeast. During the winter they shift and come from the northeast. At night, gentle land breezes coming down from the mountainous interior bring cool and refreshing air to the coastal areas, causing a drop of 6° or 7° from the day temperature.

The trade winds also bring abundant rainfall, which for the island averages 74.4 in. (1,890 mm.) annually. It rarely rains for more than a few hours at a time, even during the rainy season, which lasts from May to November. The coastal areas are cooled in the late morning or afternoon by light showers during the warmer months of the year. The variation in rainfall recorded in different parts of the island is much greater than the temperature variation. The rain forest of Sierra de Luquillo, the northeastern branch of the central mountain chain, which receives the trade winds first, recorded an average annual rainfall of 184 in. over a ten-year period. In the southwest corner of Puerto Rico annual rainfall drops to about 30 in. The island is subject to occasional tropical storms. The winds, which reach a velocity of 150–200 m.p.h., are usually accompanied by torrential rains. The storms, which rarely last more than a day, occur from July to October.

3. Vegetation.—The erosive effect of a heavy rainfall on the precipitous slopes of the central mountain range of the island is counteracted by a particularly tenacious soil bound together by clinging and abundant vegetation. The wide variation of rainfall, a fairly rich soil and different altitudes produce a great variety of plant life. Because of the extensive cultivation of the land, the vegetation in a relatively natural state is limited to the insular and national forest reserves located at higher altitudes in the western, central and eastern sections of the island. The tropical rain forest of the Luquillo National Forest reserve, located at the eastern end of the island, is composed of a great variety of trees, clinging and hanging vines and a thick undergrowth of shrubs, ferns and thickets. The junglelike density is almost impenetrable without the aid of a machete, a sharp, long, broad-bladed knife. In this area wild orchids can be found. Trees include bamboo, palm, cedar, ebony, calabash, whitewood, lancewood, boxwood and logwood.

Along the coastal plains, which probably were covered once with a thick forest growth, sugar cane and pineapples are grown. In the northwest corner of the island and in the mountain areas tropical fruits of all varieties are produced. In the western highlands, together with the coffee bush, can be found a great variety of citrus fruits. In addition to the common fruits such as bananas and oranges the island produces papayas, pomegranates, avocados, guavas and mangoes. Spices such as ginger, pepper, vanilla and chicory are also grown.

4. Animal Life.—Physically isolated at an early geological age and densely populated, Puerto Rico has very little wild animal life. Bats, birds, a scarce and harmless species of snake and several varieties of harmless lizards, together with the mongoose and rat, comprise Puerto Rican wildlife. For the patient bird watcher the island offers a wide variety of species of birds, nesting or in transit. About 190 species have been identified, and of these 89 are known to nest. About 36 birds are endemic to Puerto Rico. Thrushes, tanagers, bullfinches, flycatchers, warblers, plovers, terns and sandpipers are the birds most commonly seen.

The waters around the island are excellent for sport fishing. Yellow-fin tuna, white marlin, sailfish, dolphins, kingfish and wahoo are only a few of the commoner varieties which can be found 2 to 5 mi. from the coast. There are fine black bass in the fresh-water reservoirs of the island.

II. GEOGRAPHICAL REGIONS

Puerto Rico may be divided into three geographical regions, using as the principal criteria the contrasting altitudes.

1. Lowlands and Coastal Plains.—Geographers have calculated that 27% of the island's land can be classified as flat or gently rolling lowlands. With one or two minor exceptions offered by small inland valleys, one near Caguas and the other near Cayey, this region is comprised primarily of land along the coastal fringe of the island. Depending upon the availability of water, the flat or rolling coastal lands are the most fertile areas of Puerto Rico. The abundant rainfall on the north coast assures production, but on the south coast, particularly in the southwest corner in the Lajas valley sector, the flat rolling land needs irrigation. In the Lajas valley the insular government built an extensive irrigation project which collects in artificial lakes the heavy rain that falls on the nearby highlands, brings the water down over hydroelectric dams

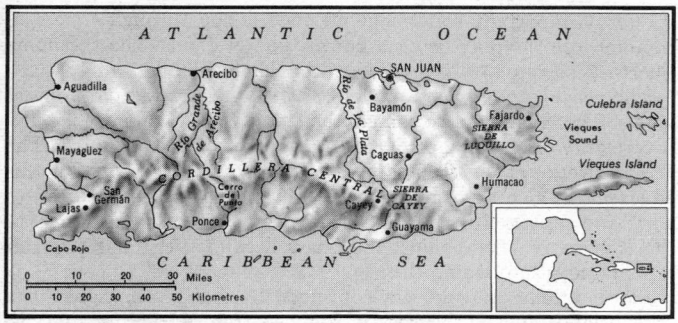

PHYSICAL FEATURES AND MAJOR CITIES OF PUERTO RICO

and channels the distribution into the arid valley.

For the most part the coastal plains produce the bulk of the island's sugar crop. About 16 sugar mills, or *centrales*, located in this region produce more than 90% of the island's sugar. More than 20% of this sugar is produced on the north coast and about 30% is produced on the irrigated plains of the south coast. Some coastal land lacking in rainfall or fertility is used as pasture. Prior to the completion of the irrigation project, the Lajas valley was used primarily in this way. On the north coast about 35 mi. W. of San Juan, near the port of Arecibo, pineapple production has been expanding. The coastal area has some unproductive land in mangrove swamps and in limited areas where sand dunes have moved inland. By far the best of the island's beaches can be found on the sheltered west coast. The north coast also has excellent beaches wherever offshore reefs serve to break the heavy Atlantic surf. The Luquillo beach east of San Juan is perhaps the most popular and widely known.

2. Highlands.—In contrast to the coastal plains is the markedly mountainous terrain of the central part of the island, which accounts for about 36% of the land area. This extensive area is marked by high local relief with little flat land. Most of the slopes range from 30% to over 60% grade. This region, comprised of the Cordillera Central, the Sierra de Cayey and the Sierra de Luquillo, includes the highest peaks of the island drainage divide.

Heavy rainfall and fertile soil permit extensive cultivation of this region in spite of the sharp slopes. Coffee is the main crop in the area which extends from near the west coast to the centre of the island. The shrub which produces the coffee bean is very sensitive to temperature variations and grows best in shaded areas between 1,000-ft. and 3,000-ft. altitude; orange and grapefruit trees and the broad-leaf banana plants are utilized for shade. As a result of the cultivation of coffee in the western mountain area, the impression is given of a cleared, well-gardened forest. Two insular forest reserves, Maricao and Toro Negro, with picnic facilities and lookout towers, can be found in the western and central mountain areas.

The eastern mountainous section, with the exception of the Sierra de Luquillo, receives less rain than the western highlands do, and the vegetation is less thick and the land unprotected by a covering forest. Tobacco is the principal commercial crop. Small farms produce subsistence crops, and extensive pasture areas can be found. The Sierra de Luquillo, where the tropical rain forest is located, has a recreation park with trails, swimming pools and lookout towers.

3. Rolling Hill Land.—The area of the island which lies between the two extremes of the flat coastal plains and the markedly mountain terrain can be described as rolling hill land; it comprises the remaining 37% of the land surface. Foothills adjacent to the central core of mountains are included in this area. In this region the unique limestone belts of the northeastern and north central section of Puerto Rico are found. This area, which is similar to the cockpit area of Jamaica (*q.v.*), is of a more recent geological age than the rest of the island, having been formed during the Tertiary period. The limestone plateau, at one time under the sea, once lifted and exposed to rain and wind erosion, was slowly converted into striking karst topography. The area is characterized by precipitous cliffs, caves and large caverns, deep depres-

sions or sinkholes and undissolved limestone remnants or *mogotes*, which resemble conical haystacks. In this area rivers such as the Tanamá or Camuy disappear suddenly and, running underground, appear just as unexpectedly miles away. In spite of the rugged terrain, the irregular valleys among the *mogotes* and precipices are cultivated with some success by the small farmer. Subsistence crops, vegetables and fruit are the main products.

4. Mona, Culebra and Vieques Islands.—These small islands are politically and culturally linked to Puerto Rico. Fifty miles southwest of the western port of Mayagüez is Mona Island (*q.v.*), consisting of a limestone plateau of about 20 sq.mi. Light rainfall and infertile soil make Mona an island of poor vegetation and no permanent inhabitants. Culebra Island, half the size of Mona, is situated halfway between Fajardo, the east coast port of Puerto Rico, and the port of Charlotte Amalie in St. Thomas, Virgin Islands. Culebra's population of 573 lives mostly in a small town located in the excellent harbour of Puerto Grande. Vieques Island has an area of 52 sq.mi. and is located 10 mi. S.E. of Puerto Rico. While most of the island is used for naval installations by the U.S. government, the small population has struggled to maintain itself by cultivating the sparse soil.

III. THE PEOPLE

1. Racial Characteristics.—Puerto Ricans are mostly descendants of a European stock, specifically Spanish, with an admixture of Negro and some Indian (mainly Arawak or Boriquén) strains. The dominant Spaniards absorbed or eliminated the Indians within a short time after the conquest of Puerto Rico, but physical characteristics of the aboriginal Indian are still evident in dental formation, colour and texture of hair and facial structure, particularly of the people in the mountainous interior.

Negroes were introduced early in the 16th century as slave substitutes for the disappearing Indians. However, under the lenient Spanish treatment many of the slaves earned or were granted freedom. Partly as a result of this attitude the slave population was always smaller than that of free coloured people. In 1846, when Puerto Rico's slave population reached the top figure of 51,265, the number of free Negroes was 175,791 and the combined slave and free coloured population was slightly more than 50% of the total population. As Puerto Rico's population increased during the 19th century, with the slave trade effectively halted and slavery abolished, the percentage of Negroes in the over-all population declined rapidly until by the 1960s less than 20% of the population was classified as nonwhite. However, to be socially considered white, it is not necessary to meet the strict biological requirements of having only white ancestors.

The *jíbaro* is the small isolated independent farmer who has struggled for centuries to sustain himself in the rugged Cordillera Central. Within recent years the *jíbaro* has been converted into an insular cultural, if not political, symbol.

2. Language.—Puerto Rico draws upon a rich Spanish cultural heritage. The Spanish language is spoken everywhere and is used throughout the school system. English is taught as a secondary language, and in the urban areas and particularly in the commercial establishments, English is commonly heard. Rare would be the businessman who could not carry on a limited conversation in English, and many are fluent bilinguists.

3. Religion.—For the almost 400 years of Spanish control over Puerto Rico the Roman Catholic Church occupied an exclusive place as the state-protected religion. Indeed, Puerto Ricans came to look upon the crown and the church as one. Almost every town on the island has, in true Spanish style, a Catholic church located on one side of the central plaza.

After the change of sovereignty in 1898, evangelical sects became active on the island. Most of their followers are drawn from the lower classes and the expanding urban middle class. Approximately 20% of the population is considered to be active in one or another of the evangelical groups. The cost of the insular evangelical work has been sustained by the various missionary boards in the United States, but the local churches have been encouraged to become economically independent.

A growing number of islanders are believers in some form of

spiritualism. These people come from all classes of society but are said to be found most commonly among groups undergoing marked social change.

4. Customs and Culture.—Spanish influence is waning in the social customs of the people of the large towns and cities. The growing industrialization and increasing U.S. influence are converting Puerto Ricans from a two-class, stable, patriarchal, agrarian society to a mobile, three-class, modern, industrial society in which women are achieving a place of equality with men. The rising rate of divorce is an indication of these changing social conditions. Among adolescents of the large cities the chaperon is a thing of the past. Still, in some of the small towns of the interior on Saturday evenings or holidays, the custom of strolling around the plaza, boys in one direction and girls in the other, can be observed. Birthdays, weddings and deaths are occasions for social gatherings. Wakes, *rosarios* (nightly ceremonies in commemoration of a death) and *rogativas* (group supplications) are still observed in rural areas.

In music the fused influence of the African and Latin strains is most notable. Both popular and traditional music have a distinct local flavour. The island has actively cultivated an interest in classical music, and several symphonic groups function, one with the financial backing of the government. A chief contributor to this cultural renaissance was the cellist Pablo Casals.

The island government, concerned at the apparent lack of concerted efforts to preserve the historical and cultural heritage of the island, organized the Institute of Puerto Rican Culture, which, with local branches in all the leading towns, undertook to encourage, through scholarships and prizes, the expression of local artists, musicians and writers. Museums were established, traveling exhibitions were sponsored, drama groups were encouraged, and a series of scholarly publications was initiated, all with the purpose of making Puerto Ricans appreciate their cultural roots.

IV. HISTORY

The first inhabitants of Puerto Rico, originally from the Amazon basin of South America, reached the island by means of the archipelago of the Lesser Antilles about 600 years before the arrival of the Spaniards. These Arawak Indians, living in small villages, were organized in clans and led by a cacique or chief. They were a peaceful people who, with a limited knowledge of agriculture, lived on a variety of domesticated tropical crops such as pineapples, manioc and batatas supplemented by shellfish and other sea food. Anthropologists estimate their numbers to have been between 20,000 and 50,000. On an island naturally fertile, the Arawaks lived an easy life disturbed only by occasional visits from their cannibal Carib neighbours on the islands to the south and east. At the time of discovery, Carib Indians occupied most of the Lesser Antilles, the Virgin Islands and Vieques Island.

In 1493 Christopher Columbus, at the peak of his popularity, left Spain on his second voyage to the Indies with an elaborate expedition of 17 ships and about 1,500 men. At the island of Guadeloupe, the Spaniards rescued several Arawak Indians who had been taken from Boriquén, the Indian name for Puerto Rico, by the Caribs. Columbus agreed to return them to their island, and on Nov. 19, 1493, the expedition anchored in a bay on the west coast of Puerto Rico. Columbus formally took possession of the island in the name of Ferdinand and Isabella, the rulers of Spain, and named it San Juan Bautista. Two days were spent on the island before the ships moved westward to Hispaniola, where the first settlement in the new world was established.

A. Spanish Rule

1. Early Settlement.—For 15 years the island was neglected except for an occasional visit by a ship putting in for supplies. In 1508 Juan Ponce de León (*q.v.*), who previously had accompanied Columbus, was granted permission to explore San Juan Bautista in recognition of his valuable colonizing efforts in eastern Hispaniola. On the north coast, Ponce de León found a well-protected bay which could offer safe harbour for a large number of sailing vessels. The harbour was named Puerto Rico because of its obvious excellent potentialities. In this area was located

the most important settlement on the island; through time and common use the port became known as San Juan while the name Puerto Rico came to be applied to the whole island.

The peaceful and friendly relations with the Arawak did not last long. The Spaniards expected the Indians to acknowledge the sovereignty of the king of Spain by payment of gold tribute. The Indians were to be instructed in Christian ways. In return for this education, which was rarely given, the Arawaks were expected to work and supply either more gold or provisions of food. In 1511 the Indians rebelled against the Spanish, who with their superior arms rapidly subjugated them.

Placer mining of gold was continued by Indians brought from other islands and by Negroes introduced from Africa by some of the early traders. After the 1530s, however, gold production markedly declined, and the Spanish colonists, with slave labour, turned to agriculture. By 1550, with financial aid from Spain, several small sugar mills were in operation on the island.

Puerto Rico did not prosper economically, however. Carib Indians from neighbouring islands made frequent raids, carrying off food and slaves and destroying property. The colony continued to lead a precarious existence, ravaged by plagues and plundered by French, British and Dutch pirates. Repeatedly during the mid-16th century the French burned and sacked San Germán, the second community to be established on the island. Under such adverse conditions people began to leave the island whenever opportunity offered.

In the second half of the 16th century Spain, recognizing the strategic importance of Puerto Rico, undertook to convert San Juan into a military outpost. The fortress El Morro, built with the financial subsidy from the Mexican mines, was well constructed and perfectly located to dominate the narrow entrance to the harbour. Later, a stronger and larger fortress was built to the east and on the Atlantic side of the city. In the early 17th century the city was surrounded by a stone wall, 25 ft. high and 18 ft. thick, two parts of which still stand. These defenses made San Juan almost impregnable.

Sir Francis Drake attacked the town in 1595 but failed to gain the harbour. Three years later George Clifford, 3rd earl of Cumberland, had complete military success but was forced to abandon his conquest owing to an outbreak of plague among his troops. In 1625 a Dutchman, Bowdoin Hendrik, burgomaster of Edam, boldly sailed into the harbour, captured and burned the town, but failed to subdue El Morro.

San Juan, as the most exposed military outpost guarding the heart of Spain's new world empire, received political and economic attention from the mother country. However, the rural inhabitants of the interior of the island were ignored by Spain and scorned by the presidial residents of San Juan. As the French, English, Danish and Dutch fought over and settled the Lesser Antilles during the 17th and 18th centuries, rural Puerto Ricans, ignoring the edicts of Spain, found profit in clandestine trade. Ginger, hides, sugar, tobacco and cattle from the island were in great demand, and while the colonial authorities of San Juan rarely ventured out of their walled defenses for fear of the reprisals of the buccaneers the rural settlers prospered in a modest way through contacts with the non-Spanish European traders. No large plantations were established, and the farmer, with little help, cultivated his own land. Contrary to the fears of Spain, this contact with foreigners did not corrupt the islanders, who remained loyal and were willing to participate in aggressive expeditions.

2. Liberal Reforms.—In 1797 the British Gen. Sir Ralph Abercromby, who had captured Trinidad, unsuccessfully attacked Puerto Rico. The British considered the island—a centre of clandestine trade and of operations for quasi-piratical expeditions, and a refuge for runaway slaves—a weak link in the chain of defense of the Spanish empire. The failure of Abercromby was due in part to the important economic and administrative changes in the Spanish colonial empire which were carried out in the latter half of the 18th century by representatives of the Bourbon rulers of Spain. In the case of Puerto Rico it was hoped that the island might become an economic asset rather than a financial drain on the Spanish crown. Trade relations between the island and Spain were liberalized, agricultural production was stimulated, the island as a whole was integrated into the system of military defense, and, above all, concerted efforts were made to break down the social dichotomy which had developed between the walled city of San Juan and the interior.

The liberal reforms of the enlightened despotism of the Spanish Bourbons coincided with and encouraged rapid population growth, introduction of new products and the beginning of commercial agriculture. Population was estimated in 1765 at 45,000; in 1775 at 70,250; in 1787 at 103,051; and in 1800 at 155,426. By the end of the 18th century there were 34 towns on the island. Immigrants from the Canary Islands, French settlers from Louisiana or Haiti and Spaniards from Santo Domingo, which had been turned over to Napoleon, accounted in part for the increase in population. These newcomers brought with them new ideas and methods of producing marketable crops. Coffee, introduced into the island in 1736, became an important export item by 1776. Sugar production, which had always been small, was undertaken on a large scale by augmented slave labour. From 1765 to 1800 the slave population increased from 5,037 to 13,333.

When Napoleon invaded Spain and placed his brother, Joseph Bonaparte, on the Spanish throne (1808), the colonies of South and Central America asserted their right to govern themselves in the name of the imprisoned Bourbon king, Ferdinand VII. This claim to temporary self-rule eventually evolved into a revolutionary movement for independence. In Puerto Rico, however, for various reasons, the sequence of events and their results were different. The communities of the interior of Puerto Rico, with one exception, offered little objection to the strict rules of Spain's mercantilist policy, which for many decades had ceased to have effect on them. Most of the residents of San Juan, on the other hand, dependent upon administrative and military positions, were most willing to follow the orders of the central government of Spain acting in the absence of the king. Puerto Rico, which had asserted its loyalty by repelling the English, undertook to recapture Santo Domingo from the French.

As the revolutions progressed on the southern and central mainlands, loyal Spaniards reluctant to leave the colonies found refuge in Puerto Rico, which was being used as a supply depot for military movements on the continent. In recognition of its loyalty and in a belated move to liberalize an outmoded colonial system, the Spanish government granted Puerto Rico in 1815 ample economic liberties. The island was opened to all non-Spanish Catholics, the ports were permitted to trade with non-Spanish countries, and free land was granted to the new settlers.

3. Economic and Political Development.—By the end of the 19th century the population had increased to nearly 1,000,000, and the value of foreign trade had increased considerably from an estimated $1,000,000 in the 1820s to $30,000,000 annually. During the 1800s imports from the United States rarely dropped below 20% of the total goods received; exports to the U.S. fluctuated between 50% and 15% depending in part upon U.S. tariff restrictions. By 1899 the United States was buying 61% of Puerto Rican sugar production. The area devoted to sugar had been slowly expanding, and the processing was becoming more centralized. Coffee, in the late 19th century, provided the principal source of income for the island; its production quadrupled between 1862 and 1898.

Political development in Puerto Rico during the 19th century was characterized by periods of liberal advance counteracted by long periods of conservative reaction. In part, this was due to the changes occurring in the Spanish government, and in part due to the antiquated Spanish colonial administrative policy.

During the first half of the 19th century, two short periods of relative political freedom were enjoyed. From 1809 to 1814 and from 1820 to 1823 Puerto Rico was declared an integral part of Spain with the right to elect representatives to the Spanish *Cortes*, or parliament. Ramón Power y Giralt, an able liberal, was selected during the first period and succeeded in revoking the absolute powers of the island's colonial governor. In the latter period Demetrio O'Daly secured the separation of the military authority from the colonial administrator. Freedom of the press

was also permitted. On each occasion moderate colonial rule was thwarted by the return of royal absolutism in Spain.

In 1837, when a fairly permanent constitutional monarchy was established in Spain, Puerto Rico failed to benefit because it was argued that the colonies were not true Spanish provinces and therefore should be governed by special laws. For more than 30 years Puerto Rico waited for special legislation to ease the despotic rule of military colonial governors. During this waiting period, political thought in the island began to crystallize. A liberal current of opinion, remembering the success of previous periods, requested assimilation into the Spanish government and permission to be represented in and governed by the *Cortes*. A bloc of conservative opinion strongly approved of the status quo. A small third group advocated complete independence.

4. Movements Toward Self-Government and Independence.—A local commission was elected in 1865 to draw up a report on the basis of which a governmental reform might be carried out. The majority report, which declared that the abolition of slavery was the *sine qua non* of any political reform, provoked a shocked reaction among the island and peninsular conservatives. The alarmed colonial government took steps to curtail what was feared to be a growing movement of rebellion. Some of the more outspoken and respected islanders were ordered to be arrested and sent to Spain for trial. Thus provoked, a small group of radicals committed to independence attempted an uprising, for which, however, inadequate preparation was made. *El Grito de Lares,* the abortive revolt of Sept. 23, 1868, brought forth severe reprisals on all island liberals. However, the abdication of Queen Isabella II of Spain was forced by a republican government, which pardoned all the political prisoners. The first Spanish republic extended to Puerto Rico its third period of constitutional government, 1868–74, during which slavery was abolished.

During the 1880s a movement for political self-government under Spain led by Román Baldorioty de Castro replaced the sentiment in favour of integrating Puerto Rico into the Spanish government. Again a liberal political movement, this time autonomy, was denounced as disloyal and was violently suppressed in 1887, an infamous year in Puerto Rican history. Such treatment only served to solidify the movement for local self-government, and in 1897 the Partido Unionista (Autonomy party), now guided by Luis Muñoz-Rivera, through co-operation with the Liberal party in Spain, achieved its objective. The autonomous government granted was parliamentary in form but retained the governor general as a representative of the Spanish king. He was empowered to disband the insular parliament and suspend civil rights. The two-chamber parliament was empowered to legislate for the island, create and control an insular tariff and levy local taxes. Puerto Rico's representation in the Spanish *Cortes* was also increased. Any change in the governmental organization had to be first approved by the insular parliament.

5. Spanish-American War.—The Spanish-American War (*q.v.*) prevented the islanders from putting into effect the new government. In May 1898 Adm. W. T. Sampson bombarded San Juan for a short time without serious results. Facing token military resistance and with general popular acceptance, Gen. Nelson A. Miles landed a U.S. force of about 3,500 men in July, and after a short campaign hostilities were ended on Aug. 12.

B. Under the United States

1. Early Years.—On Oct. 18, 1898, the island was turned over to the U.S. forces and Gen. John R. Brooke became military governor. Puerto Rico was ceded to the U.S. by the treaty signed in Paris, Dec. 10, 1898 (ratified by the U.S. senate Feb. 6, 1899). In the work of policing the country, in the accompanying tasks of sanitation, construction of highways and other public works, accounting for the expenditure of public funds and establishing a system of public education, the military control which lasted until May 1, 1900, proved effective in bridging the period of transfer from the control of Spain to the system under the United States civil government. The United States congress passed the Foraker act, under which civil government was instituted in May 1900. Under this act the U.S. element exercised the controlling power;

this, however, having proved distasteful to many Puerto Ricans, the Organic law was subsequently amended to give a wider native participation in the government. The Olmsted act, approved by congress on July 15, 1909, placed the supervision of Puerto Rican affairs in the jurisdiction of an executive department to be designated by the president. The people, however, demanded a larger measure of local control. The majority also asked for U.S. citizenship and many other changes. As a result, congress passed a new Organic act (the Jones act), which came into effect on March 2, 1917. Under its terms Puerto Rico became a territory of the United States "organized but unincorporated," and citizenship of the United States was conferred collectively on Puerto Ricans, allowing the right to retain the old status if preferred. Only 288 persons declared in favour of the latter. The local civil government, however, even with modifications, fell far short of the measure of self-government which Puerto Ricans expected in light of the democratic tradition of the United States. Key officials, including the governor, were presidential appointees and thus beyond local control.

In spite of the legal limitations on political autonomy, a climate of freedom was slowly developed as a result of the change of sovereignty. At first this new order, being abrupt, new and imposed from above in some instances, was sometimes mistrusted, resented and misunderstood, but in the long run it was recognized as beneficial and assimilated by the islanders. For example, labourers were allowed to organize for collective bargaining and to affiliate with labour unions in the United States; the Anglo-Saxon legal procedure of assuming innocence until proved guilty brought slowly a feeling of security and freedom from political persecution; the separation of church from state, resulting in open competition for religious adherence, demonstrated the new climate in a practical way; government programs which dealt directly with the vital needs of the people for education, health and sanitation, regulation of working conditions and public facilities all reflected a change designed to remedy centuries of neglect.

2. Economic and Social Changes.—The economic reorientation of the island as a result of the change in sovereignty had almost an immediate and profound effect on all aspects of life. Included within the U.S. tariff walls, Puerto Rican agricultural products, particularly sugar, had a ready market. Aided by the adoption of U.S. currency and by unobstructed financial movement, Puerto Rico experienced within a short period a large capital investment which revolutionized the production of sugar. Sevenfold acreage expansion (1899 to 1939), new disease-resistant plants, rapid transportation facilities, large and efficient cane-grinding mills and complete corporate management within a generation converted the economy of the island into one in which 75% of the population directly or indirectly was dependent upon sugar. Land which had sustained small farmers producing crops and dairy products for local consumption was absorbed by the sugar corporations.

The island was forced to import its foodstuffs. Coffee was neglected at a time when weather conditions and transportation problems dictated financial and government aid. Only tobacco production experienced growth, which failed to be sustained after the 1920s when United States smokers shifted from cigars to cigarettes.

The shock of these economic changes might have been absorbed in spite of the island's limited resources if at the same time Puerto Rico had not been undergoing a severe social change as a result of the application of modern sanitation means and medical knowledge to a people with a very high death rate. The population was threatening to double its number in two generations. The two counterpressures—expansion of corporate control over the limited productive land and increasing population pressure—reached an explosive stage at the time when the economic depression occupied the attention of government officials in the United States. Recurring hurricanes joined with declining exports to aggravate the economic distress of the island.

3. Political Development.—With one exception, political parties which had developed since the change in sovereignty had centred their attention on modifications in the political relations between the island and the U.S. federal government. The Republican party limited its program to a plea for statehood for the island. The Union party worked for greater autonomy. In the 1920s the Nationalist party rose to affirm the ideal of immediate independence. The one exception was the pro-U.S. Socialist party, led by the highly respected labour leader Santiago Iglesias. This party had expressed since its foundation a concern for the plight of the labouring classes of the island. Nevertheless, its effectiveness had been hampered by insufficient popular support, due primarily to the concentration of attention upon the issue of the political status of the island.

In the mid-1930s, with Pres. Franklin D. Roosevelt's New Deal policies radically enlarging the previously accepted concept of the function of government as that of maintaining order and protecting the citizens, Puerto Rico was not neglected. More important than the much-needed temporary relief were the steps taken by the Puerto Rican Reconstruction administration (P.R.R.A.), designed to readjust the distribution of economic power on the island. A restrictive quota was placed over sugar production. Legal procedures were initiated to enforce a long-neglected law limiting corporate holdings to 500 ac. Thus the process of increasing the sugar acreage was to be reversed and Puerto Ricans were to be returned to their small farms. A model sugar mill was to run on a co-operative basis to compete with the private mills. Coffee and tobacco growers were to receive long overdue attention.

This radical program provoked the open opposition of the sugar interests, locally vocal through the Republican party. The Socialists accepted the program in a tacit fashion. Their reluctance was due to the fact that the young radical wing of the heirs of the Autonomy party, led by Luis Muñoz Marín, the son of Luis Muñoz-Rivera, was recognized in Washington and on the island as the local political proponent of the economic reform.

The success of the New Deal measures was jeopardized by two unconnected factors. Unforeseen administrative and financial problems forced a curtailment of the objectives of the P.R.R.A. No longer was a complete readjustment of the island's economic structure possible; the P.R.R.A. took on a more temporary or experimental nature. The second factor was the interjection of the status issue on the political scene by the U.S. government in answer to Nationalist violence. Taking the form of a vindictive offer of independence under adverse economic conditions, the proposal served to realign again the political parties into pro- and anti-independence groups.

The incipient political movement for economic reform originally fostered by the New Deal and temporarily sidetracked was surprisingly successful in the election of 1940. This new political movement took the form of a political party, led by Muñoz Marín, called the Popular Democratic party. Organized to improve the conditions of the lower classes, particularly the hard-working *jíbaro* of the mountainous interior, the new party's platform was summarized by the slogan "Bread, land and liberty." The island electorate had agreed that the political status was not in issue and that economic and social problems took precedence. Tenuous control over the island legislature and a new-style colonial governor, Rexford Guy Tugwell, allowed the Popular Democratic party to initiate such economic reforms as redistribution of land, enforcement of minimum wage and hour laws, an enforced progressive income tax law and the establishment of an economic development program. In recognition of partial fulfilment of its announced aims the Popular party was overwhelmingly backed by the island electorate in 1944. In 1946 Pres. Harry S. Truman named Jesús T. Piñero, a Puerto Rican, as governor, the first Puerto Rican to occupy that post. In 1947 the U.S. congress amended the Organic act of Puerto Rico to permit election of governors by popular vote. Muñoz Marín was elected Nov. 2, 1948, and took office in Jan. 1949.

For over a generation the Popular Democratic party (PPD), led by Muñoz Marín, governed Puerto Rico. Muñoz served for four terms as governor and was followed by his able administrative assistant, Roberto Sánchez Vilella. In 1968, although the PPD retained control over the insular senate, they lost control over the lower house and the post of governor to the New Progressive party (PNP), when Luis A. Ferré was elected in November. Under the guidance of the PPD, Puerto Rico experienced a remarkable economic recovery which, rather than freeing the island from its economic ties to the United States changed these relations from unrestrained exploitation by absentee sugar corporations to controlled industrial production allowing the islanders to receive greater benefits from the original capital investment. As the island became more industrialized and the people flocked to the cities, where not only better wages but better working conditions and improved social services could be found, Puerto Rico experienced the transition from an agrarian society into a modern industrial society closely patterned after the United States, but with a distinct Latin flavour.

Early in his first term as governor Muñoz Marín turned to the problem of political status. Obviously, any political change would have to take into consideration the economic relationship between the United States and Puerto Rico. The solution was found in the expansion of local political autonomy which did not effect adversely the economy of the island.

4. Establishment of the Commonwealth.—In 1950 the U.S. congress offered to Puerto Rico for its approval or rejection a series of changes in the law which governed the relationship between the federal government and Puerto Rico. These changes if accepted would eliminate all sections dealing with the creation of the local insular government and would turn over to the people of Puerto Rico the power to create their own government under a constitution of their own making. Under the guidance of Governor Muñoz Marín the islanders accepted the offer of congress and drew up a constitution. Duly approved by the people and the congress, Puerto Rico's constitution was proclaimed on July 25, 1952, and the Commonwealth of Puerto Rico came into being. (See *Administration and Social Conditions,* below.) During this period, Puerto Rican extremists dramatized their desire for independence with an attempt to assassinate President Truman on Nov. 1, 1950, in Washington. They attracted world-wide attention on March 1, 1954, when several members of the Nationalist party shot and wounded five congressmen in the house of representatives in the U.S. capitol. Nevertheless, in the judgment of the general assembly of the United Nations, expressed in a resolution of Nov. 27, 1953, Puerto Rico is a self-governing political unit associated voluntarily with the United States and is no longer considered a colonial territory.

In the 1960s, with the admission of Hawaii and Alaska as new states into the United States and the increasing affinity toward the United States of a growing middle class, the Popular party requested a reexamination of the status question and subsequently a United States–Puerto Rican Status commission was named by the president of the United States to explore the range of political statuses open to the people of Puerto Rico. The report of the commission found that commonwealth, statehood, and even independence were theoretically open to Puerto Ricans depending upon their willingness to undergo a prolonged period of economic adjustment should they select a status radically different from that in effect. The commission urged a plebiscite to indicate popular preference for the three principal statuses. In 1967 more than 60% of the voters participated in the plebiscite indicating a preference for commonwealth status; 39% selected statehood. The small vote in favour of independence was due to the boycotting of the plebiscite by those Puerto Ricans who wished to sever their relations with the United States.

Although commonwealth status won impressive support, both the leaders of the PPD and influential members of the U.S. federal government, following the recommendations of the Status commission, recognized that the commonwealth relationship needed to be improved and the degree of self-government broadened even further. Representatives from both governments intended to explore the means of increasing Puerto Rican autonomy, either through statehood or a more ample commonwealth status.

V. POPULATION

The population of Puerto Rico, 2,349,544 in 1960, had more than doubled since 1899, when it was 953,243. The 1950 census gave a population of 2,210,703, of whom about 40% were urban

and 60% rural; 79.7% were classified as white and 20.2% as Negro. This small island, with a population density of over 700 per square mile, is one of the most densely populated areas of the world. One of the principal reasons for the growth was the application of modern medical knowledge to a previously underprivileged island, resulting in a radically declining death rate. From 1901 to 1960 the island's death rate dropped from 36.7 per 1,000 to a subnormal 6.7, a lower figure than that in the United States. The birth rate declined at a much slower rate: from 43.2 in 1947 to 31.5 in 1960. The difference ($+24.8$) between the birth and death rates in 1960 left a high rate of natural increase (a ratio of four births to every death on the average), thus accounting for the high population density. According to demographers, by the mid-1960s the population of Puerto Rico reached an estimated 2,713,000 (1967 est.). The death rate should in time rise automatically to a more normal 12 per 1,000 as the age distribution approximates proportionately the same distribution attained in the U.S. The birth rate in the 1960s dropped markedly to 28 per 1000 as the standard of living rose and the middle class increased.

One factor which allowed Puerto Rico to keep pace economically with the rapidly growing population was emigration to the United States. The difference between the numbers of those leaving and those returning to Puerto Rico in the 1950s resulted in a net exodus of about 50,000 a year. This figure was only slightly under the average yearly natural increase of 60,000 for the same period. For the most part, Puerto Ricans who went to the United States were young persons of working age with an occupation or skill. Those who returned to the island were older people, already past their productive years. In the 1960s the emigration rate declined somewhat and many people returned from the U.S.

The metropolitan areas have absorbed much of the island's population growth. The rural inhabitants, particularly in the western highlands where the coffee haciendas are found, have been migrating to the cities on the north and south coasts. Some indication of this migration can be seen in the growth of San Juan (merged with Río Piedras), which in the 1950s doubled its population to well over 500,000 and which, including suburbs, is expected to reach 750,000 in the 1970s.

VI. ADMINISTRATION AND SOCIAL CONDITIONS

1. Government.—The government of the Commonwealth of Puerto Rico was established by a constitution drawn up by representatives of the Puerto Rican people meeting in a convention; approved by the electorate of the island, March 3, 1952; and ratified by the congress of the United States. This constitution, proclaimed July 25, 1952, provides for an autonomous form of representative government and guarantees the liberties and rights of its citizens through a bill of rights. The people of Puerto Rico are free to modify the constitution as long as such modifications do not conflict with the U.S. constitution or the Puerto Rican Federal Relations act, which, as its title indicates, defines to a limited extent the relations between the commonwealth and the federal government. This act was adopted "in the nature of a compact" by the U.S. congress and the Puerto Rican people. To change this compact the consent of both groups would be required.

The constitution provides for a government whose powers are distributed among the executive, legislative and judicial branches. Franchise is restricted to citizens 21 years of age and over. The governor of Puerto Rico is elected by popular suffrage every four years, and unlimited re-election is permitted. He appoints, with the consent of the commonwealth senate, the heads of departments, who form, with other agency directors selected at the governor's discretion, his advisory council. Aside from the departments such as labour, education and justice, the commonwealth has a department of co-operatives.

The members of the legislative branch, composed of a senate and a house of representatives, are elected for four-year terms. There are eight senatorial (two members each) and 40 representative districts. Eleven senators and eleven representatives are chosen at large. The commonwealth constitution guarantees, by means of automatic appointment based on island-wide voting strength, the representation of minority parties in the legislature.

The island is divided into 77 municipalities, each of which has an elected mayor and assembly whose primary functions are to administer schools, health centres, poor relief and other services of the commonwealth.

The Puerto Rican electorate sends a resident commissioner to the U.S. congress for a term of four years, but he has no congressional vote. Puerto Ricans do not vote in the U.S. presidential elections, but emigrants on the mainland may do so subject to local electoral laws.

2. **Taxation.**—Since the citizens of Puerto Rico (after one year's residence on the island all U.S. citizens fall into this category) are not represented with a vote in the federal congress, they are not subject to federal taxes. The commonwealth government is sustained in part by the local revenue laws, which in general provide for taxes about one-quarter to one-third lower than those of the mainland. A graduated personal and business income tax, an excise tax and a property tax are the main sources of local revenue. The excise tax, which has produced more than half of the commonwealth's locally collected revenue, was used to reduce spending on nonproductive luxury items, the purchase of which tended to drain off potential local capital.

3. **Living Conditions.**—The middle- and upper-class living conditions in Puerto Rico are comparable to those of the United States. The expected difference between rural and urban areas is marked, but the standard of living of the agricultural worker has improved. Federal and commonwealth minimum wage laws cover every important industry and areas of agricultural production. Strict enforcement and periodical revisions ensure a just compensation for the working class. The hourly wage received by labourers is slightly lower than that received by workers in similar industries in the United States, but private professional salaries for the growing middle class are generally on a par with salaries for similar occupations in the United States. Government workers such as teachers, clerks or administrators are not so well paid as private professional workers or federal government employees in the U.S.

The labour force of the island is about 800,000. Unemployment, which fluctuates seasonally, has rarely dropped below 13% of the labouring force.

Since more than half the goods and services which Puerto Rico consumes come from the United States, the general price level fol-

BY COURTESY OF UNIVERSITY OF PUERTO RICO, RIO PIEDRAS CAMPUS

LIBRARY, RÍO PIEDRAS CAMPUS, UNIVERSITY OF PUERTO RICO

lows closely the level on the mainland. Local products are naturally less expensive than imported items, but inability to expand local farm production has caused prices of local goods to be increased at a much faster rate than that of imported goods prices. Large supermarkets, including four large consumer co-operatives, serve the San Juan, Ponce and Mayagüez metropolitan areas.

Faced with the increased migration from the mountains to the cities, particularly to the San Juan area, and a rapidly growing population, the commonwealth government working in close cooperation with the Federal Housing authority was able to undertake during the years after World War II extensive programs of construction of low-cost housing. Although the inadequately serviced housing areas were not eliminated completely, strict enforcement of government laws concerning zoning, new constructions and renovations, coupled with a methodically planned slum-clearing program, improved immeasurably the living conditions of the workers.

4. **Welfare Services.**—In the mid-1960s about 20% (in 1966, $127,000,000; in 1967, $136,300,000) of the total budget of the commonwealth was spent on providing health and public welfare services for the people of the island.

Several hundred public health clinics, functioning under the supervision of doctors and nurses, offered preventive and curative medical services. Six general district hospitals, six general service hospitals and a large psychiatric hospital were run by the commonwealth. The health department offered assistance to the aged, needy families and the handicapped. Almost half of those attending public school received free lunches, milk depots were conducted to supply free milk to preschool-age children, and annually about 80,000 pairs of shoes were distributed free to needy students.

All workers, both industrial and agricultural, are completely covered in case of accidents by a compulsory state insurance fund, which has rendered excellent service for over a generation.

5. **Justice.**—The commonwealth constitution provides for a uniquely unified judicial system consisting of a general court of justice comprised of the supreme court and the court of the first instance. The latter is organized in two divisions, the superior court with 30 judges and the district court with 55 judges. The whole judicial system is administered by the chief justice of the supreme court and his office of court administration. This integrated system permits maximum flexibility. Jurisdiction and venue questions do not prevent a case from being considered. Appeals may be carried to the supreme court in Washington.

6. **Education.**—Compulsory education has been in effect since 1899. To keep pace with the growing population, the commonwealth assigned to education during the 1950s a larger percentage of its budget than did any other Latin-American country, 30%. This percentage was generally maintained through the mid-1960s.

Over 95% of the elementary school-age children are registered and attend classes; about 85% of those eligible attend the secondary schools, and about 50% of those eligible attend high schools. Teaching is in Spanish in the public school system, but special

BY COURTESY OF THE DEPARTMENT OF STATE, COMMONWEALTH OF PUERTO RICO

CULTIVATING TOBACCO ON A STEEP HILLSIDE NEAR TRUJILLO ALTO

emphasis is given to the teaching of English as a second language. In the 1950s, partially as a result of a successful adult education program, the illiteracy rate on the island decreased from 24% to less than 15%, and the decline continued in the 1960s. Special instruction in English for prospective migrant workers was provided.

The land-grant government-financed University of Puerto Rico, near San Juan, which includes a technical campus with a nuclear reactor in Mayagüez, has an international faculty and student body. The other island colleges include the Roman Catholic College of the Sacred Heart in Santurce and the Universidad Católica de Puerto Rico in Ponce, as well as Inter-American university at San Germán, affiliated with the United Presbyterian Church, with campuses in San Germán and San Juan.

VII. THE ECONOMY

The economy of Puerto Rico is closely tied to that of the United States. No trade barriers exist to prevent interchange of goods between the two areas. During the first half of the 20th century Puerto Rico's agrarian-based economy functioned primarily from the sale of sugar and its by-products. After 1956 the economy of the island shifted noticeably from one based on agriculture to one based on manufacturing and industry.

1. Agriculture.—The production of sugar, dairy products, tobacco, coffee, fruits and vegetables annually accounted for about 15%–20% of the island's total net income. Sugar, processed by 16 cane-grinding mills, accounted for about 50% of the agricultural income. This production, subject to a federal quota of 1,125,000 tons annually, supplied about 10% of the sugar consumed in the United States. In recent years, due partly to adverse weather conditions, the island failed to fill its quota, and the island government extended limited aid to sugar growers. The government planned to stabilize the production of sugar at 1,268,000 tons produced on only 300,000 ac. (121,400 ha.) of the most productive flat coastal land.

Coupled with this stabilization is the mechanization of the cane-cutting process. With increasing wages and rural emigration, large cane growers have turned to machines as substitutes for human labour.

Livestock production, second only to that of sugar, contributed about 30% of the agricultural income. Accounting for more than half the livestock income was the sale of milk and its by-products. Eggs, beef, pork, and poultry accounted for the remainder. With 400 dairies and 13 large pasteurizing plants, the commercial dairy industry was well developed, and it was the only phase of agricultural production which showed signs of growth.

Although coffee production declined in the 20th century until it scarcely satisfied local demands, the haciendas in the western mountain area are still numerous. Land dedicated to coffee produced anywhere from 150 to 200 lb. per acre, depending upon varying conditions. In addition, some 35,000 ac. (14,165 ha.) of tobacco, principally in the eastern central part of the island, brought an annual average return of about $8,000,000 to the growers.

2. Industry.—The remarkable industrial development in Puerto Rico was due to the government's economic development program, particularly that phase known as Operation "Bootstrap" which, by the end of the 1960s had established 2,000 new factories on the island. These plants in large part explain why, after the mid-1950s, manufacturing and industrial production surpassed agriculture as a source of wealth. Stimulated by a 10–17 year period of tax alleviation, availability of government-built factories for lease or purchase, and ready access to the United States market, corporations did not hesitate to establish branch centres of production on the island. At first new industries were those which processed local resources such as limestone or clay and agricultural products—e.g., sugar, tobacco, or local fruits. Early in the 1950s new industries were established that hoped to profit from the low labour costs on the island, such as the apparel and textile manufacturers, but assembly plants for the electrical and electronics industry were also established, particularly those producing such lightweight products as electron tubes and microphones. In these industries the employment of women predominated. In the 1960s Puerto Rico greatly increased its number of heavy industries, so classified because of the large capital investment involved in setting them up. The plants can be grouped in two industrial divisions: metallurgical and chemical. Fertilizers, perfumes, detergents, man-made fibres, plastics, ethylene, drugs, paints, and higher alcohols are just some of the products produced by these industries. Three large petroleum refining plants, one on the north coast and two on the south, refine oil from Venezuela and prepare the petrochemical by-products of this modern industry. Large deposits of high-grade copper found in the mountainous area in the west-central part of the island promised to become the basis of another large industrial complex possibly on the north coast near Arecibo. On the south coast near Ponce is one of the world's largest cement factories and there is an ironworks in Santurce, a suburb of San Juan; both industries have played an important part in the construction activity which accounts for one-sixth of the gross insular product. Tourism has become an important industry for Puerto Rico. Over 800,000 tourists visit the island yearly and spend approximately $160,000,000.

3. Power.—The electric power of the island is provided by a government agency, the Puerto Rico Water Resources authority, which came into existence in 1942. As a result of the government's program of rural electrification and a marked increase in industrial demand, the power production of the island by the late 1950s had increased to well over 1,000,000,000 kw.hr. annually. Industrial consumption of power increased 134% between 1942 and the late 1950s. By the mid-1960s total consumption had risen to more than 2,500,000,000 kw.hr. annually.

4. Trade.—Between 80% and 90% of the value of imports comes from the United States. Puerto Rico imports about 50% of its food, and 43% of consumers' expenditure is for food. Rice, lard, pork and dairy products are the most important imports. The island's expanding industrial climate has required the importation of capital equipment for productive uses, and raw or semi-processed goods for further elaboration and sale. About 40% of foreign imports are raw material, including crude oil from Venezuela and the Netherlands Antilles, to be refined and consumed or shipped to the United States.

All but about 5% of the value of Puerto Rican exports is sent to the United States. To the older exports of sugar, molasses and rum have been added electrical appliances, textiles, pharmaceuticals and plastic goods.

The deficit in the balance of trade is in part made up by payments and expenditures of the federal government on the island.

JACK M. HAYNES FROM BLACK STAR

HARVESTING SUGAR CANE NEAR ISABELA, IN NORTHWESTERN PUERTO RICO

About 90% of this is expenditures of the defense department and payments to veterans. Gross fixed domestic investment in Puerto Rico increased to more than $485,000,000 in the mid-1960s. The island continued to develop and expand its profitable tourist business.

5. Banking and Currency.—Since Puerto Rico functions economically as an integral part of the United States, the currency of the island is the same as that of the U.S. The island's banking system is also integrated within the U.S. banking structure. A number of local banks, two Canadian banks and three United States banks operate under the close supervision of the insular government.

Seven of the banks are members of the Federal Deposit Insurance corporation. The branches of the United States banks are indirectly related to the federal reserve system.

6. Transport and Communications.—The island has an extensive system of highways serving every community. In the mid-1960s there were more than 3,000 mi. (4,830 km.) of paved streets and highways and more than 350,000 motor vehicles. No railroads for public use exist on the island; during the cane-cutting season some sugar corporations operate local railroads to bring cane to the *centrales* (grinding mills).

Eleven ports of widely varying importance are open for handling freight and some passenger service. San Juan, Ponce and Mayagüez receive most of the cargo ships. First-class passengers are accepted in limited numbers on the freighters, but no passenger line links the island with the United States. French and Spanish passenger services connect Puerto Rico with the European continent. Most of the Puerto Rican visitors and migrants travel by air. The San Juan International airport, equipped for jet passenger service, is connected with many of the major cities in the U.S. British, French, Dutch, Spanish and Latin-American airlines have frequently scheduled flight services connecting Puerto Rico with other points around the Caribbean and abroad.

The United States postal service offers complete service on the island. Commercial cables extend from Puerto Rico to the mainland and Venezuela. There is a government and commercial wireless service.

The island has about 30 commercial radio stations and 10 commercial television stations, several of which transmit in colour. A satellite communications centre in Cayey permits occasional hook-ups with U.S. networks to transmit important events to or from the island. The government operates an educational radio and television station.

See also references under "Puerto Rico" in the Index.

BIBLIOGRAPHY.—A. Morales Carrión, *Puerto Rico and the Non-Hispanic Caribbean* (1952); J. Steward *et al.*, *The People of Puerto Rico* (1956); C. J. Friedrich, *Puerto Rico: Middle Road to Freedom* (1959); S. W. Mintz, *Worker in the Cane* (1960); E. P. Hansen, *Puerto Rico: Ally for Progress* (1962); G. Lewis, *Puerto Rico: Freedom and Power in the Caribbean* (1963); T. H. Aitken, Jr., *Poet in the Fortress* (1964); R. Picó, *Cartography in Puerto Rico* (1964); R. Anderson, *Party Politics in Puerto Rico* (1965); Oscar Lewis, *La Vida: a Puerto Rican Family in the Culture of Poverty* (1966); T. Mathews, *Luis Muñoz Marín: a Concise Biography* (1967); Governor of Puerto Rico, *Annual Reports;* Puerto Rico Planning Board, Bureau of Economics and Statistics, *Annuario Estadistico Puerto Rico.* Current history and statistics are summarized annually in *Britannica Book of the Year.* (T. G. Ms.)

PUFENDORF, SAMUEL, BARON VON (1632–1694), German publicist and jurist, best known for his treatise on natural law and international law, *De jure naturae et gentium libri octo,* was born near Chemnitz, Saxony, on Jan. 8, 1632, the son of a Lutheran pastor. He commenced theological studies at Leipzig university but soon turned to jurisprudence and studied mathematics and natural law under Erhard Weigel at Jena. Leaving Jena in 1657, Pufendorf took service as a tutor in the household of the Swedish minister at Copenhagen. When Sweden declared war, the whole retinue was imprisoned. Pufendorf occupied his captivity of some eight months reflecting on what he had read in the works of Grotius and Hobbes and mentally constructing a system of universal law. On his release, he went to Leiden where he published in 1661 the fruits of his reflections in the work *Elementa Jurisprudentiae universalis,* in the plan and

structure of which his mathematical training is very evident.

Karl Ludwig, the elector palatine, to whom the work was dedicated, created a chair of the law of nature and nations for Pufendorf at Heidelberg, the first chair of its kind in the world. His next work was written under a pseudonym, Severinus de Monzambano: *De statu imperii germanici ad Laelium, dominum Trezolani, liber unus.* It took the form of a bitter attack, supposedly by a Veronese nobleman, on the constitution of the Holy Roman Empire and the house of Austria, and created a great sensation.

In 1670 Pufendorf left Heidelberg for the University of Lund, Swed., where he produced in 1672 his great work, the *De jure naturae et gentium libri octo,* and, in the following year, the *De officio hominis et civis* which is in the main a résumé of the *De jure naturae.*

Grotius had pointed out the dualism between a natural and a positive law of nations. Where Richard Zouche stressed the precedence of the latter, Pufendorf followed Hobbes in maintaining the priority of the natural law; he differed from Hobbes, however, in proclaiming that the natural state was one of peace, not of war, albeit a precarious peace unless given positive support. For, though originating from God in that God created men as social beings, natural law, for Pufendorf, is concerned with man in this life—as he is, with all his failings—and with external conduct, and it derives from human reason alone: man as a prospective citizen of heaven is the concern of moral theology. This search for natural law in the dictates of human reason understandably enables Pufendorf to maintain that international law is the common link of all men, not merely that of Christendom. In public law, while recognizing the state as a moral person, Pufendorf teaches that the will of the state is but the sum of the individual wills that constitute it, foreshadowing Rousseau and the *Contrat social.*

In 1677 Pufendorf became historiographer royal at Stockholm and thereafter virtually abandoned international and natural law for historical, political and theological studies. To this period belongs (in addition to, *e.g.,* histories of Sweden and the reign of Charles X Gustavus) the *De habitu religionis christianae ad vitam civilem.* This work, in which he traces the limits between ecclesiastical and civil power, was the basis of the *Kollegialsystem* of church government, which, developed by Christoph Pfaff (1686–1760), was the basis of church and state relations in Germany.

This theory makes a fundamental distinction between the supreme jurisdiction in ecclesiastical matters (*Kirchenhoheit* or *ius circa sacra*) which is inherent in the power of the state with respect to every religious communion and the ecclesiastical power (*Kirchengewalt* or *ius in sacra*) which belongs to the church but which is, in some cases, vested in the state by the consent—express or tacit—of the ecclesiastical body. Though naturally not accepted by the Roman Catholic Church, the theory did in fact facilitate a working compromise between the Protestant governments and Rome.

In 1686 Pufendorf went to Berlin as historiographer to the great elector of Brandenburg. He was created a baron and died at Berlin in 1694.

The value of Pufendorf's work was much underestimated by posterity. Responsibility for this rests largely with Leibniz, who would never recognize the greatness of one who was ever his adversary and whom he dismissed as *vir parum jurisconsultus et minime philosophus* ("a man not enough of a lawyer and scarcely a philosopher at all"). Modern scholarship, however, while conceding that he is not a pioneer in the category of Francisco de Vitoria and Grotius, recognizes Pufendorf as a classic writer in the field of international law, and his *Jurisprudence* is the standard one for the 17th and 18th centuries.

BIBLIOGRAPHY.—H. von Treitschke, *Historische und politische Aufsätze,* vol. iv (1897); J. G. Droysen, *Abhandlungen zur neueren Geschichte* (1876); P. Meyer, *Samuel Pufendorf* (1894). *See* also introductions to the translations of *De jure naturae, Elementa Jurisprudentiae* and *De officio* in "Classics of International Law." (J. A. C. T.)

PUFFBALL, the popular name of a group of fungi belonging to the Basidiomycetes (*see* FUNGI), and so called because of the cloud of dark dustlike spores that is emitted when the mature plant bursts or is struck. Puffballs are seldom abundant but are not uncommon in meadows and woods, and when young resemble white balls, sometimes with a short stalk, and are fleshy in texture. While they are white, solid, and fleshy they are edible.

The giant puffball, *Calvatia maxima*, undoubtedly the largest of all fungi, may sometimes attain a weight of 15 lb. or more and measure up to 2 ft. or more in circumference. Such large specimens may produce billions of spores, only a small fraction of which will ever alight on a location that is suitable to germination and growth.

ROCHE
PUFFBALL (LYCOPERDON PERLATUM)

PUFFBIRD, the popular name given to the family Bucconidae, of the order Piciformes, because of the habit these birds have of ruffling the loose plumage of the neck and head while perching. The Piciformes includes also woodpeckers, toucans, jacamars, etc. The Bucconidae are confined to tropical America, from southern Mexico to Argentina. Most dwell in lightly forested areas near water; a few live in deep forest. Puffbirds are plainly coloured, and the majority have a spotted or mottled plumage suggestive of immaturity. They feed on insects that they capture on the wing. The smallest, the lance-billed puffbird (*Micromonacha lanceolata*) of northern South America, is five to six inches long. Most puffbirds are very quiet, and apparently use the same hunting perch for months at a time. The black-collared puffbird (*Bucco capensis*) is one of several similar species that occur in northern South America; they all have a prominent black band encircling the body at chest level.

PUFFER, any of certain chiefly marine fishes belonging to the families Diodontidae and Tetraodontidae, which are able to inflate their bodies by swallowing air or water. The common names puffer, balloonfish, and globefish allude to this ability; the

BY COURTESY OF MARINELAND OF FLORIDA
MARBLED PUFFER (SPHOEROIDES DORSALIS): (LEFT) NORMAL STATE; (RIGHT) DISTENDED STATE

names sea hedgehog, burrfish, and porcupine fish are descriptive of certain spiny members. Puffers are most numerous in the tropics, but occur in all warm seas. The jaws of a puffer resemble the beak of a parrot, the bones and teeth being coalesced into a sharp-edged structure that is used to break off branches of corals, and to masticate other hard food substances. The typical puffer is short, thick, and cylindrical, with weak fins. The body is covered with tough, scaleless skin, but is often provided with prickles or spines.

When frightened, the fish swallows large quantities of water and assumes a globular form, and spines, if present, protrude to form defensive armour. A puffer held out of water will swallow air and then can float belly upward. Although many puffers contain a deadly poison (tetrodotoxin), the Japanese (who call them *fugu*) prize them as food; specially qualified chefs do not always completely remove all the toxic dorsal flesh, and many persons die annually from *fugu* poisoning.   (C. HU.)

PUFFIN, a group of comical-looking birds of the auk family (Alcidae), confined to northern oceans and known also as sea par-

rots, bottlenoses, etc. They have characteristically sharp, compressed, triangular beaks. Colonies occur from Arctic coasts southward to Brittany and Maine. Puffins are noted for the punctuality of their return to breeding sites in successive springs. They nest in large colonies on seaside and island cliffs. Puffins usually lay only one egg. They eat a variety of marine organisms. Naturalists are puzzled by the birds' ability to catch as many as ten small fish in succession and to carry them dangling crosswise in the bill to their nestlings.

The common puffin (*Fratercula arctica*), of the Atlantic, is black above, white below, with gray face plumage, orange-red feet, a blue-gray, yellow and red bill, and plates of coloured horny skin around the beak and on the eyelids. These outgrowths are molted after the breeding season. The horned puffin (*F. corniculata*) is a Pacific relative of the Atlantic species. Of more southerly Pacific distribution is the tufted puffin (*Lunda cirrhata*), which is black, with red bill and legs, a white face and straw-coloured plumes curving backward from behind the pale eyes (*see* also AUK). The generic term *Puffinus* refers to the shear-waters (*q.v.*).   (R. C. MU.)

JOHN MARKHAM
COMMON PUFFIN (FRATERCULA ARCTICA) GATHERING FISH FOR YOUNG

PUGACHEV, EMELYAN IVANOVICH (1742?–1775), famous leader of the greatest Cossack and peasant rebellion in Russian history, was born at Zimoveiskaya Stanitsa on the Don River. The son of a Cossack landowner, he was registered at 17 as a member of the Don *voisko*, or army (*see* COSSACKS), and fought in the final battles of the Seven Years' War (1756–63). In the Russo-Turkish War of 1768–74 Pugachev, then an ensign, was present at the siege and conquest of Bendery (1769–70). Invalided home, for the next three years he led a wandering life, frequenting the monasteries of the Old Believers, who exercised considerable influence over him. When at Mechetnaya Sloboda (later renamed Nikolayevsk and in 1918 Pugachev, Saratov province) he learned about the cruel repression ordered against the Yaik (Ural) Cossack rebellion in 1772. He left for Yaitski (now Uralsk) and discovered among the Cossacks strong anti-government feelings. Arrested as a deserter, he was imprisoned at Kazan and sentenced to be deported to Siberia, but in June 1773 he escaped and in August he appeared in the steppes east of the Volga proclaiming himself to be the emperor Peter III (*q.v.*). Pugachev asserted that he had escaped from his wife who had ordered his assassination, and was resolved to redress people's grievances, restore their freedom to the Cossacks, and put the empress Catherine II in a monastery.

A man of intelligence and great audacity and a good organizer, Pugachev started his campaign in September with a force of 80 Yaik Cossack rebels. He took by storm the small forts along the Yaik river and on Oct. 16 (new style; 5, old style) started storming the fortress of Orenburg. At that time he had under his command 2,500 men and 20 guns; by December his army had grown to 30,000 with 86 guns. His plan was to conquer Orenburg and then march through Kazan and Moscow to St. Petersburg, but Orenburg resisted and Pugachev made a strategic error by committing the bulk of his forces to the siege. This gave the Russian high command time to send a relief army under Gen. A. I. Bibikov. On April 3 (N.S.), 1774, Pugachev was defeated at Tatishchevo, west of Orenburg. The next day he left northward to Bashkiria whose Turkic inhabitants under Salavat Yulaev joined his forces. Turning westward, he stormed Kazan on July 24 (N.S.), but five days later was defeated by another relief Russian army under Gen. I. I. Mikhelson. With a small detachment of 500 men, Pugachev passed to the right bank of the Volga and marched southward with the hope of starting a rebellion among his Don Cossacks. Joined during his progress by new peasant rebels, he stormed Tsivilsk, Kurmysh, Alatyr, Saransk, Penza, Petrovsk and, on Aug. 14 (N.S.), Saratov. Frightened by these successes the

Russian government promised a reward for Pugachev's head and at the same time reinforced the army of Mikhelson that followed the rebels. Pugachev was forced to abandon the siege of Tsaritsyn and on Sept. 3 (N.S.) was finally defeated near Salnikovaya Vataga 47 mi. S of Tsaritsyn. Pugachev crossed the lower Volga with a group of loyal followers, but was betrayed by a few Yaik Cossacks and on Sept. 27 (N.S.) was delivered to Gen. A. V. Suvorov at Yaitski. He was brought in an iron cage to Moscow, where he was executed on Jan. 22 (N.S.), 1775.

BIBLIOGRAPHY.—S. A. Golubtsov (ed.), *Pugachevshchina*, 3 vol. (1926–31); M. N. Martynov, *Vozstanie Emelyana Pugacheva* (1935).

PUGET, PIERRE (1620–1694), most powerful and original of French Baroque sculptors, was also a painter and architect. He was born at or near Marseilles on Oct. 16, 1620, and traveled in Italy as a young man (1640–43), when he was employed by Pietro da Cortona on the ceiling decorations of the Barberini Palace, Rome, and the Pitti Palace, Florence. Between 1643 and 1656 he was active in Marseilles and Toulon chiefly as a painter, but he also carved colossal figureheads for men-of-war. His first important sculpture commission in 1656 was for the doorway of the Town Hall at Toulon; his caryatid figures there, although in the tradition of Roman Baroque, show a strain and an anguish that mark Puget as a type of provençal Michelangelo.

In 1659 Puget was called to Paris, where he attracted the attention of Louis XIV's minister Fouquet. The latter fell from power in 1661 while Puget was in Italy selecting marble for the Hercules commissioned by him (now the "Hercule gaulois" in the Louvre), and Puget remained in Italy for several years, establishing a considerable reputation as a sculptor in Genoa; a St. Sebastian in S. Maria di Carignano is among his best works there.

After 1669 Puget's life was spent mainly in Toulon and Marseilles, where he was engaged on architectural work and the decoration of ships as well as sculpture. His difficult and somewhat arrogant temperament made him unacceptable to Louis XIV's powerful minister Colbert, and it was only late in life that he achieved some degree of court patronage. His "Milo of Crotona" (1671–84) was taken to Versailles in 1683 and the "Perseus and Andromeda" was well received there in 1684 (both now in the Louvre). But Puget was soon the victim of intrigues by his rivals, and his success at court was short-lived. His fine low relief of "Alexander and Diogenes" (1671–93, Louvre) never reached Versailles, and other works planned for Versailles were either refused or frustrated. Embittered by these failures, Puget died at Marseilles on Dec. 2, 1694. *See also* SCULPTURE: *Baroque Sculpture.*

See A. Blunt, *Art and Architecture in France, 1500–1700* (1953).

PUGILISM: *see* BOXING.

PUGIN, AUGUSTUS WELBY NORTHMORE (1812–1852), English architect, designer, author, theorist, antiquarian, and participant in the English Roman Catholic and Gothic revivals, was born in London on March 1, 1812. He was trained by his father, Augustus Charles Pugin, an able architectural illustrator and delineator. After the death of A. C. Pugin in 1832, A. W. N. Pugin began independent professional life by continuing his father's *Examples of Gothic Architecture* (1831–38). The first phase of the younger Pugin's career (1832–36) included intense study of medieval buildings in England, the Low Countries, and France, and the establishment of a place for himself as an expert in medieval art. By 1835 he had attained the confidence of the architects Charles Barry and James Gillespie Graham, both of whom employed Pugin to assist in the preparation of their entries in the competition for the new Palace of Westminster. It was also in these years that Pugin published, with R. Ackermann, the four volumes of plates of Gothic designs for furniture, metalwork, and house details now usually known as *Pugin's Ornaments of the XVth and XVIth Centuries* (1835–36) and that Pugin became a Roman Catholic (June 1835).

His mature professional life began in 1836 when he published *Contrasts* (rev. ed. 1841), which conveyed the argument with which Pugin was throughout his life to be identified, the link between the quality and character of a society with the calibre of its architecture. He contended that decline in the arts was a result of the spiritual decline occasioned by the Reformation.

Between 1837 and 1840 Pugin enjoyed a growing architectural practice. His employment by John Talbot, Earl of Shrewsbury, and other Catholic laymen and clergy resulted in his identification with the leadership of the Roman Catholic revival. St. Chad's Cathedral, Birmingham, and St. George's Cathedral, Southwark, on the plans for which Pugin was at work in 1839, demonstrate both the unsettled condition of his tastes and his imaginativeness and brilliance. The church of St. Oswald, Old Swan, Liverpool (1839; demolished), was the finest of his designs of these years and the one which set the pattern for Gothic revival parish churches in England and abroad.

Pugin was at the crest of his productiveness between 1840 and 1844: his knowledge of his chosen style and his ability as a designer were mature; his theoretical position on the need for a revival of Gothic was refined and relatively free of the religious bias which had earlier dominated it; his literary gifts were equal to his powers as an architectural caricaturist and illustrator; his circle of patrons loyally supported him. From these years come Pugin's splendid drawings for Balliol College, Oxford (1843), which convey the excitement and fervour of the Oxford Movement, the richly brilliant St. Giles, Cheadle, Staffordshire (1841–46), and extensive repairs and additions to Alton Towers, Staffordshire.

Pugin's last major works are his own house, The Grange, and St. Augustine's Church, both at Ramsgate, Kent. The Rolle family chapel at Bicton, Devon, the decorations of the House of Lords, and the chapel at St. Edmund's College, Old Hall Green, Hertfordshire, well represent the elegant, erudite yet original Gothic of which he was capable.

The death of his second wife in 1844 and the recurrence of an old illness cast a shadow over Pugin's last years. His practice declined as other architects emerged to serve Roman Catholic clients. During his last years he worked with Sir Charles Barry on the new Palace of Westminster. Though he married for a third time and remained professionally active despite his ill health, Pugin never regained his emotional and physical balance. On Sept. 14, 1852, seriously mentally ill, he died suddenly.

BIBLIOGRAPHY.—B. Ferrey, *Recollections of A. N. Welby Pugin, and His Father* (1861); H. R. Hitchcock, *Early Victorian Architecture in Britain* (1954); M. Trappes-Lomax, *Pugin: a Mediaeval Victorian* (1932); Peter Ferriday (ed.), *Victorian Architecture* (1963).

(Ph. B. S.)

PUGLIA (or APULIA), a region of southern Italy, extends from the Fortore River in the northwest to Cape Santa Maria di Leuca, the "heel" of the peninsula, in the southeast. It has a total area of 7,470 sq.mi. (19,347 sq.km.), a population (1961) of 3,309,975, and is composed of the provinces of Bari, Brindisi, Foggia, Lecce, and Taranto (*qq.v.*). The northern third of the region is centred on the Foggia Plain, or Tavoliere, flanked by the Gargano massif in the north and the Neapolitan Apennines in the west. The central third is occupied by the low plateau of the Murge, limited in the west by a depression, the "fossa premurgiana," while in the east it slopes gradually to the narrow coastal plains of the Adriatic. The southern third, southeast of the Taranto-Ostuni line, is the Salentine Peninsula, consisting of the lowland of Lecce and the low plateaus east of Taranto and south of Lecce. The predominant rock material of Puglia is limestone, and karst phenomena of underground drainage and large cave formations are present in many areas.

The coastline for the most part is low and sandy, except in the Gargano Peninsula and in the southeasternmost tip of Puglia. The only rivers of significance are the Fortore and the Ofanto, but there are numerous springs, some under the sea near the coastline. Absence of surface water over large areas led to construction of the Apulian Aqueduct, largest of its kind in Italy, that traverses the region as far as Cape Leuca (*see* AQUEDUCT).

Wheat and oats are the principal cereals, raised in the Foggia Plain and in the more fertile parts of the plateaus; olives, grapes, almonds, and figs are grown intensively in the coastal and some inland areas; tobacco is a speciality of the Lecce Plain. The wines of Puglia are among the strongest of Italy and are used to fortify other, lighter varieties. Fishing is carried out in many ports; those of the Gargano, of Barletta, of Monopoli, and of

Taranto are the most important. Salt is produced from seawater at Margherita di Savoia, near Foggia. About 1,000,000 sheep once grazed on the plain but owing to cultivation it only supports half that number today. Bari is the largest city and the leading port, as well as the biggest industrial centre (especially chemicals and petrochemicals); Italy's newest and most modern steel mill was built in the 1960s at Taranto. The largest railroad centre is Foggia, with lines connecting it to Naples-Rome, Bologna-Milan, and Bari-Taranto-Brindisi-Lecce. The so-called "Ionian" railroad follows the Ionian coast from Taranto to Reggio di Calabria. After World War II Puglia became one of the principal areas of Italian land reform, and numerous small farms were created from the old landed estates, new farm houses and rural service centres built, new roads and aqueducts constructed, transforming the face of the land.

The southeastern extremity of Puglia was Roman (not modern) Calabria. For archaeology, Roman and early history *see* APULIA; CALABRIA (ANCIENT). After the tumultuous times following the disintegration of the Roman Empire, Puglia was ruled by the Byzantines for over two centuries, and came to know its greatest glory under the Hohenstaufen emperors. It was a favourite of Frederick II (1220–50) and cathedrals and palaces witness the flowering of Puglia at that time. Thereafter a long period of decline set in, accentuated by neglect by distant rulers (Aragonians, Spaniards, Neapolitans) and by slave raids along the coast. In 1860 Puglia became part of the Italian kingdom. (G. KH.)

PULA (Italian POLA), a seaport of the Socialist Republic of Croatia, Yugos., lies at the southern tip of the Istrian Peninsula at the head of the Bay of Pula, 67 mi. (108 km.) SW of Rijeka by road. Pop. (1961) 37,403 (Croats 63%, total Yugoslavs 79%). The town has a temple of Augustus and Roma and a Byzantine basilica, both restored; also an archaeological museum with Roman and other collections. Pula has a safe, commodious, and almost landlocked harbour and is primarily a naval base. It is the terminus of the railway from Trieste and Ljubljana and linked to these by main roads. It has many industries and shipbuilding yards.

The history of Pula begins with its capture by the Romans in 178–177 B.C., when it was known as Nesakton. It was destroyed by Augustus because of its support of Pompey but later rebuilt as Pietas Julia. In A.D. 198–211 an amphitheatre more than 400 ft. long and 320 ft. wide was built in honour of emperors Septimius Severus and Caracalla. It could accommodate 23,000 spectators; it is well preserved and is used for summer festivals. In the 2nd century Pula became the seat of a Christian bishop. Byzantium occupied it in 539. In 810 it passed to the Franks and in 1148 to the Venetians. In 1379 the Genoese, after defeating the Venetians in a naval battle nearby, took and destroyed Pula, which then disappeared almost completely from history for more than 400 years. In 1797 the Austrians took the town; in 1809–13 Napoleon occupied it, but in 1819 it reverted to Austria and became the main harbour and arsenal of the Austrian Navy. Under the Rapallo Agreement of 1920 it passed to Italy, and in 1947 to Yugoslavia. (V. DE.)

PULASKI, KAZIMIERZ (CASIMIR) (1747–1779), Polish patriot and U.S. army officer, hero of the Polish anti-Russian insurrection of 1768 and of the American Revolution, was born at Winiary in Mazovia, on March 4, 1747, the son of Jozef Pulaski (1704–69), one of the originators of the Confederation of Bar (q.v.). All Jozef's three sons took part in the confederation's military actions: Franciszek (1745–69) was killed in Lithuania; Antoni (1750–1815) was taken prisoner by the Russians; and Kazimierz distinguished himself by his defense of besieged Berdichev in spring 1768 and later by his guerrilla campaign near the Turkish frontier. In 1769 he valiantly defended Zwaniec and Okopy Swietej Trojcy. On Sept. 10, 1770, he occupied the fortified monastery of Czestochowa, which became the base for extensive operations ranging from the Carpathians to Poznan. The defense of Czestochowa against the Russians brought Pulaski fame in Poland and in western Europe. In October 1771 he set out for Warsaw with the aim of kidnapping King Stanislaw II to the camp of the confederates. The attempt failed (Nov. 3, 1771), and

Pulaski was falsely accused of trying to murder the king. In spring 1772, when Prussian and Austrian armies also invaded Poland, the fate of the confederation was sealed; and on May 31 Pulaski left Czestochowa for Saxony, whence he later moved to France. In 1774 he went to Turkey to organize Polish army units there, but Turkey was already on the road to concluding peace with Russia. Returning to France, he lived there in financial straits because of the confiscation of all his estates in Poland.

In December 1776, in Paris, Pulaski was introduced to Benjamin Franklin by Claude de Rulhière; and in June 1777 he landed in America with a letter of recommendation from Franklin to Washington. In Washington's army he served at Brandywine, was made general and chief of cavalry by Congress and fought at Germantown and in the winter campaign of 1777–78. In 1778, as brigadier, he formed a mixed corps, the Pulaski Legion, at the head of which he tried to exploit his experience of guerrilla warfare. In May 1779 he defended Charleston. Wounded at Savannah, Pulaski died on Oct. 11, 1779, aboard the "Wasp" on its way to Charleston.

BIBLIOGRAPHY.—W. Konopczynski, *Kazimierz Pułaski* (1931; Eng. trans. 1947); C. A. Manning, *Soldier of Liberty: Casimir Pulaski* (1945); F. Pulaski (ed.), *Correspondance du général Casimir Pulaski avec Claude de Rulhière* (1948). (EM. R.)

PULCHERIA (399–453), Roman empress, daughter of Arcadius and Eudoxia (q.v.), was born in Constantinople on Jan. 19, 399. Appointed Augusta on July 4, 414, she soon acted as regent for her brother Theodosius II (q.v.), and her court was one of extreme piety and chastity. She quarreled c. 440 with the empress Eudocia (q.v.), her sister-in-law, who left Constantinople forever in 443. When Theodosius II died in July 450, she helped Marcian (q.v.) to succeed him, and she crowned him in the Hebdomon suburb of Constantinople on Aug. 25. She also agreed to become his nominal wife, thus formally preserving the Theodosian dynasty. She was a rigid Catholic and quarreled with the heresiarch Nestorius, who repeatedly insulted her. She attended the Council of Chalcedon on Oct. 25, 451, and was loudly acclaimed by the bishops there. She built several churches in Constantinople before she died in 453, leaving all her possessions to the poor. (E. A. T.)

PULCI, LUIGI (1432–1484), Italian poet whose name is chiefly associated with *Morgante,* one of the outstanding epics of the Renaissance, was born in Florence, Aug. 15, 1432. For many years he lived under the protection of the Medici family, especially Lorenzo il Magnifico, who first introduced him into the circle of poets and artists which was gathering round him and later, after assuming power, entrusted him with various embassies and diplomatic missions. Nevertheless, poverty and other hardships caused him, when about 38–40, to enter the service of a northern *condottiere,* Roberto Sanseverino, with whom he remained until his death at Padua in Nov. 1484.

Pulci's literary output, all in Italian, was very large. Among minor works, his *Lettere* (mod. ed., 1886) and *Sonetti* (mod. ed., 1932) are worthy of mention as revelations of his extravagant character, wide but not always deep cultural interests and biting criticism of contemporary Florentine writers and philosophers. But his masterpiece is the *Morgante* or *Morgante Maggiore,* a chivalrous epic in 23 cantos, later expanded to 28, begun about 1460, of which the earliest surviving complete edition is dated 1483. The plot of the poem is simple. Orlando, the hero, driven from the court of Charlemagne, goes to Pagania, where he meets three giants, two of whom he kills. The third, Morgante, is converted and becomes his faithful squire. Orlando and Morgante are joined by Rinaldo, who has also quarreled with Charlemagne, and the poem then recounts their episodic adventures in Africa and Asia, which continue until Orlando and Rinaldo, hearing that the Saracens have reached the borders of France, hasten to its defense. The story ends with the battle of Ronceveaux and the death of Orlando. The predominantly comic and burlesque tone is varied by a more serious mood in which the author expresses at times deep and sincere feeling, at times a bitter experience of life. Similarly, Pulci's amoral attitude, typical of an age which considered success as the only criterion of salvation, contrasts with his deeply felt religious problems, which constitute a large part of the poem. It is this complexity and richness of feeling which makes the *Morgante* both one of the most original poems in Italian literature, and an essential text for understanding of the Renaissance.

Modern editions of the *Morgante* include those by G. B. Weston (1930), G. Fatini (1948) and F. Ageno (1955).

BIBLIOGRAPHY.—A. Momigliano, *L'indole e il riso di Luigi Pulci* (1907); C. Pellegrini, *Luigi Pulci: l'uomo e l'artista* (1912); A. Sorrentino, *Astarotte e la cultura del Pulci* (1919); G. Getto, *Studio sul Morgante* (1944).   (G. P. G.)

PULITZER, JOSEPH (1847–1911), U.S. editor and newspaper proprietor, was born in Mako, Hungary, April 10, 1847. Educated privately in Budapest he was induced by a U.S. agent to emigrate as a recruit for the Union army. He was discharged from the army on July 7, 1865, and went to St. Louis, where he arrived penniless. In 1868 he became a reporter on the German-language daily newspaper, the *Westliche Post*. He was elected in 1869 to the lower house of the Missouri legislature, where he gained a reputation as a reformer, and in 1871–72 he helped organize the Liberal Republican party in Missouri and was one of the secretaries of the Cincinnati convention that nominated Horace Greeley for president.

THE BETTMANN ARCHIVE, INC.

JOSEPH PULITZER

Pulitzer became a newspaper proprietor in 1871 by buying a share of the *Westliche Post* on liberal terms. This he soon resold for $30,000, using part of the proceeds for an extended tour of Europe. On his return in 1874 he purchased a moribund German daily, the *St. Louis Staats-Zeitung*, and sold its Associated Press franchise to the *Globe* for $20,000. In 1878 he laid the foundation of his fortune by purchasing at auction the dying *St. Louis Dispatch*, and merging it with the *St. Louis Post* as the *Post-Dispatch*, which soon dominated the St. Louis evening field. The paper was independent in politics and devoted to "hard money" and tariff reform. In 1880 Pulitzer became sole owner, but unfortunately in Oct. 1882 his chief editorial aid, Col. John A. Cockerill, shot and killed Col. Alonzo W. Slayback, a lawyer, in a bitter political quarrel. Public reprobation was so great that the *Post-Dispatch* lost revenue and Pulitzer departed for the east in the spring of 1883, where he bought the *New York World* from Jay Gould for $346,000.

Under its new management the *World* won prosperity, its annual earnings by 1886 rising to more than $500,000. In 1887 Pulitzer established the *Evening World*. To the *World,* as to the *Post-Dispatch,* Pulitzer gave a tone of aggressive editorial independence. He supported Grover Cleveland for the presidency in 1884, 1888 and 1892. He was sympathetic to labour; in 1892 he took the side of the striking steel workers at Homestead, Pa. He opposed William Jennings Bryan for the presidency in 1896 and became an advocate of war with Spain.

The *World* was largely responsible for bringing on the New York state legislative investigation of insurance companies in 1905. In 1909 the U.S. government successfully sought an indictment against Pulitzer for criminally libeling Pres. Theodore Roosevelt, J. P. Morgan, Elihu Root and others in connection with allegations about the disposition of the $40,000,000 paid the French Panama Canal Co. The case was never prosecuted.

In his later years Pulitzer's health compelled him to live as an invalid, but he kept in intimate touch with the *World* until within a few weeks of his death in Charleston, S.C., Oct. 29, 1911.

Pulitzer was elected to the U.S. house of representatives from New York in 1885, and served briefly in congress. During his lifetime he endowed the school of journalism of Columbia university, opened in 1912. He also established the Pulitzer prizes, awarded annually for fiction, drama, history, biography, poetry, music and various categories of newspaper work.

BIBLIOGRAPHY.—D. C. Seitz, *Joseph Pulitzer, His Life and Letters* (1924); A. Ireland, *Joseph Pulitzer* (1914); J. W. Barrett, *Joseph Pulitzer and His World* (1941); K. N. Stewart and J. Tebbel, *Makers of Modern Journalism* (1952); J. S. Rammelkamp, *Pulitzer's Post-Dispatch 1878–1883* (1967); G. Juergens, *Joseph Pulitzer and the New York World* (1967).

PULKOVO, a village in Leningrad *oblast* of the Russian Soviet Federated Socialist Republic, U.S.S.R., lies 11 mi. (17 km.) S of Leningrad. The village is notable for the location there of the chief astronomic observatory of the Academy of Sciences of the U.S.S.R. Opened in 1839, it was designed by the architect A. P. Bryullov. It was destroyed in World War II but was afterward rebuilt. Up to the Revolution Russian maps were based on the Pulkovo meridian, 30°19′39″ east of Greenwich.   (R. A. F.)

PULLEY AND BELT, a mechanical arrangement for transmitting torque from one shaft to another. The torque originates at a wheel or drum, called the drive pulley, that applies torque to a continuous, flexible member called the belt. The belt passes around and delivers torque to a second wheel or drum, called the driven pulley. A pulley may be made fast to a shaft by a setscrew or key in the pulley hub, or by a tapered bushing drawn between shaft and hub; or the pulley may turn freely on a shaft as an idler. Pulley rim and hub may be one solid piece connected by a flange, web or tapered arms, depending on the pulley diameter. Pulleys whose peripheral surfaces have circumferential grooves are called sheaves.

Belt drives are used when one or more of the following conditions prevail: (1) Change in rotational speed is great; (2) flexibility is desired to absorb shock; (3) overloads can be absorbed by belt slippage without damaging machine parts; (4) low cost is desired; (5) quietness is desired.

Belts that drive by frictional contact are suitable for approximate velocity ratios only, because overload causes slippage between the surfaces of the belt and each pulley; even when slippage does not occur, some creep takes place. Creep is a small backward movement of the belt relative to the pulley because of belt elasticity. The higher tension of the belt (T_1) reduces to the lower tension (T_2) as the belt travels around the drive pulley (*see* fig. 1), hence the length of belt leaving the pulley is less than the length entering. Creep reduces operating speed about 1%, and slippage causes loss of another 2% or more for leather. Furthermore, excessive slippage causes belt damage.

Both tight (T_1) and slack (T_2) sides of the belt pull on the pulley and result in a net force of their difference ($T_1 - T_2$) act-

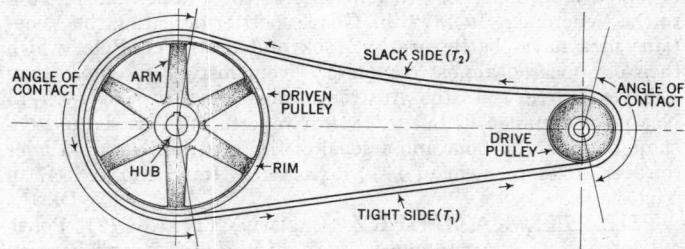

FIG. 1.—BELT ON PULLEYS
Solid pulley (at right) is driving a larger pulley (at left) with rim connected to hub by arms. In arranging pulleys, the slack side of the belt should be on top to increase angles of contact. (See text)

ing at the pulley surface to produce torque. The torque is dependent upon the ratio of effective forces which according to theory is $\dfrac{T_1 - T_c}{T_2 - T_c} = \epsilon^{fa/\sin\theta}$, where T_c is centrifugal force of one foot of belt, $\epsilon = 2.718$, f is the coefficient of friction between surfaces and a is the angle of contact in radians between belt and pulley, and θ is one-half the groove angle. The maximum value of T_1 is limited by the tensile strength of the belt.

Transmissive capacity is dependent upon the effective force ($T_1 - T_2$), hence will be greatest when the ratio of effective tensions, equal to $\epsilon^{fa/\sin\theta}$, is greatest. The frictional resistance to slip depends upon the coefficient of friction, the normal contact force and the angle of contact between belt and pulley. Combinations of materials, form of belt and angle of contact are selected to give the required capacity.

Types of Belts.—Belts are made of any material having suitable strength and flexibility and of any shape resistant to slipping (fig. 2). Combinations of material and cross section used are: flat leather or other material operating on a flat or crowned pulley; round leather wedged in grooves of a sheave; trapezoidal V or narrow V wedge consisting of load-carrying strands of cotton, synthetic, steel, or glass fibres enclosed in a vulcanized rubber trapezoidal body operating on grooved pulley; flat wedge, a flat belt with wedges parallel to the belt edge along the length of belt on inner side operating on grooved pulley; spiral steel spring on a sheave; stranded steel rope resting without wedging in the padded bottom of grooves in a sheave; hemp or Manila rope wedged into sheave grooves. The usual belt speed limitation is about 6,000 feet per minute (fpm)

Leather Belts.—Leather belts of best quality are made of strips from steer hides which are prepared and then tanned in a solution of chromium salts or tannin from oak bark. Chrome tanning gives greater strength, flexibility, and friction as well as resistance to water, steam, and certain chemicals; but it has less lateral stiffness.

Selected pieces are scarfed and cemented together to make a continuous roll of flat belting. Single ply thickness depends upon the hide, usually about $\frac{5}{32}$ in. Double and triple ply for greater loads are available.

Leather is used also for round belts, V-belts, and link belts composed of overlapping links connected by steel pins.

Rubber Belts.—Rubber belts are made of natural and synthetic rubber, generally in combination with a load-carrying core. Flat belts are composed of plies (or layers) of cotton duck impregnated with a slow-aging rubber compound. Most generally used weight is 32 oz. cotton duck. The duck is folded to the desired number of plies and then vulcanized together. The rubberized cords may be left exposed or encased in a protective covering of rubber. Other constructions use load-carrying members of parallel longitudinal cords of fabric or steel within a vulcanized rubber covering. Special construction may allow speeds up to 15,000 fpm.

V-belts of rubber are made of layers of duck or of various combinations of tension cords encased in a rubber body of trapezoidal cross section, the strength of the belt depending upon the fabric rather than upon the belt cross section. The layer type has raw edges; the cord type body is covered with a rubberized fabric.

Because the V-belt is stiff due to its depth, some constructions flute the inner edge to give flexibility without sacrificing contacting surface. Endless V-belts are molded in a press with five standard cross-section sizes available in various lengths. Multiple V-belt drives use a number of parallel belts of the same length running in parallel grooves in the pulley face. The belt does not bottom in the groove. Unreinforced rubber belts of round cross section are used for light loads where considerable elasticity is desired.

Other Types of Belts.—Balata belting is similar in construction to rubber belting. Balata is a gum from the bullet tree (*Manilkara bidentata*) of Guiana and the West Indies. The belting is nonelastic and can be made waterproof.

Polyester and polyamide-film belts are available for precision drives with small pulley and high speeds. Such belts have high strength, very low stretch, good flexibility, and light weight.

Positive-drive, or "timing," belts are used to insure that the surface speed of the driving and driven pulleys is the same. As the forces are transmitted between belt projections and gear-like pulley, the action is no longer dependent on friction and the transmitted torque is equal to T_1 times pulley radius.

Flat belts with steel or glass cords and nylon-coated teeth transmit horsepower at speeds up to 16,000 fpm. A versatile form for milder conditions has a polyurethane body of circular cross section reinforced with prestretched nylon cords. The force-transmitting teeth are transverse cylindrical projections that engage the pulley teeth. Inherent torsional and transverse flexibility allows mesh with pulleys in various planes and guidance through tubes.

Belt Fasteners.—Belt lengths may be connected by the following separate fastenings, accompanied, however, by a reduction in strength as indicated: machine wire lacing, 10%; hand wire lacing, 18%; lacing with rawhide strips, 40%; metal hooks, 65%.

Metal belt loops are bent into the end of each belt, the hooks placed side by side and a pin of leather or steel inserted through the loops to provide a connecting pivot. A stamped sheet may be used instead of separate wires.

The belt must be stretched over the pulleys and made into a continuous strip. The joint may be cemented together in position by stretching with screw clamps and cementing the ends together. Cemented joints develop practically the full strength of the belt.

Construction and Stresses of Pulleys.—Pulleys are usually made in one piece of cast iron. The hub has an outside diameter about twice the bore and is fastened to the shaft by a key, setscrew or compression bushing. The width of the hub is approximately the same as the width of the pulley. The hub is connected to the rim by arms that are elliptical in cross section and tapered from hub to rim. The rim surface is adapted to the form of belt used.

Because of centrifugal force the rim, if free, is subjected to a tensile hoop stress of $\frac{12wv^2}{g}$ where w is the weight of one square inch of section, v is the rim velocity in feet per second, and g is 32.2 ft. per second per second. For cast iron this stress in pounds per square inch is closely $\frac{v^2}{10}$. The rim is partially restrained by the arms and so is subjected to a lesser hoop stress but, consequently, also to a bending stress. The resultant stress is difficult to assess but is greater than the full free hoop stress alone. An unannealed pulley contains shrinkage stresses of unknown amount, so a close calculation of working stress is of little practical use. The arms should be sufficient in number to limit the unsupported length of rim. Four to six arms are sufficient in most instances.

Surface speeds of cast iron pulleys are usually limited to 4,000 ft. per minute. Under favourable conditions webbed cast iron pulleys might be used up to 10,000 ft. per minute. Wooden built-up pulleys of maple have been used for high speeds because wood is lighter for its strength than cast iron. Pressed steel

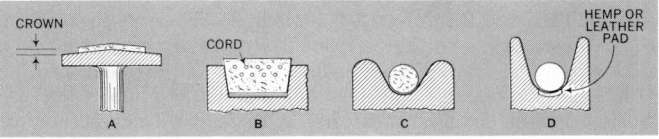

FIG. 2.—BELT AND PULLEY FORMS
(A) flat belt on crowned pulley; (B) V-belt on sheave; (C) round belt on sheave; (D) steel rope on sheave

pulleys are lightweight and have a high strength-weight ratio but are more easily deformed because of the thin sections of which they are made.

Motor pulleys are made of wood, rawhide or pressed paper held between metal end plates. The diameter of a pulley for leather belts is recommended to be not less than 30 times the belt thickness to limit the flexing of the belt as it goes on and off the pulley. The rim of a pulley for a flat belt is made slightly wider than the belt. For cylindrical pulleys in the same plane the belt must be of the same length along each edge and must be mounted on pulleys which are properly aligned. If the pulley centres are not parallel the belt will ride toward the tight side and off the pulley. The belt lies flat on the pulley surface and, because of its lateral stiffness, is tilted toward the high side of the pulley. Thus each successive point of the approaching belt is nearer to the high end of the pulley face. Drive pulleys are crowned by being made with a larger diameter at mid-section; the crown amounts to about $\frac{1}{8}$ in. per foot of width and makes the belt run centrally (fig. 2). Thus the pulley surface is geometrically two slight cones base to base, and the belt rides to the greatest diameter in mid-face. Idler pulleys and pulleys on which the belt is shifted are not crowned.

Belt Arrangements.—An open belt arrangement rotates the driven pulley in the same direction as the driver. Crossed belts cause the driven pulley to rotate opposite to the driver. A crossed belt has considerably greater contact angle than an open belt, hence will transmit greater torque. Such an arrangement is usually avoided, however, because the belt surfaces rub together at the point of crossing and cause wear.

Pulleys with shaft centres in the horizontal plane transmit the greatest torque. As the line between centres departs from the horizontal the transmissive capacity is reduced. The slack side should be on top so that sag in the belt will increase the angle of contact.

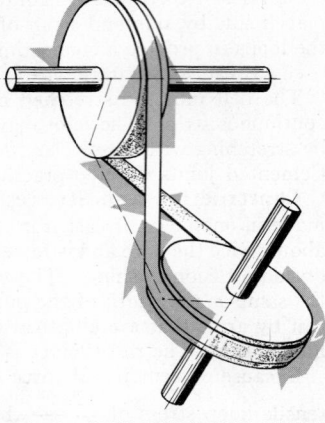

Belts afford a simple means of connecting shafts which are not in the same plane. In order for the belt to stay on the pulleys the centre line of the approaching belt must lie in the centre plane of the approached pulley (*see* fig. 3). Note that if the direction

FIG. 3.—BELT CONNECTING SHAFTS IN DIFFERENT PLANES

of belt travel is reversed the required relationship is no longer satisfied and the belt will run off the pulley.

The addition of an idler pulley in accordance with the above rule would permit travel in either direction.

V-belt sheaves have grooves of the same angle as the belt section used with them. The grooves are deeper than the belt so that it contacts the sides but not the bottom. Wide wedge-shaped belts are used between adjustable sides so that as the sides are moved apart the belt lies lower on the sides and the pitch diameter decreases. As the lie of the belt is lowered, the belt velocity must be increased if the angular velocity of the pulley is to remain the same.

Belt Adjustments.—Short-centre drives are frequently employed when an electric motor is used to drive a machine. The small angle of contact on the smaller pulley caused by the short centre distance of the pulley limits the torque that can be transmitted. The driving motor may be mounted on a base that can be adjusted by a screw so the permanent stretch of the belt may be taken up by separating the pulleys. This adjustment can be made only occasionally and does not maintain tightness because the belt length changes elastically with load. One method of maintaining tightness and increasing the angle of contact is to use a gravity- or spring-loaded idler pulley. Another method is to use a motor base pivoted so the weight of the motor produces balancing tensions on the belt in an amount equal to the desired maximum capacity. The tight side of the belt should be between the pivot and the pulley centre.   (E. S. A.)

PULLMAN, GEORGE MORTIMER (1831–1897), U.S. industrial and inventor of the Pullman car, was born at Brocton, Chautauqua County, N.Y., on March 3, 1831. He moved to Chicago in 1855, accumulated some capital as a contractor, and began to work on his earlier idea of devising a better sleeping car. The first real Pullman car appeared in 1865, embodying Pullman's conviction that if he produced something better than anyone else, regardless of expense, someone would pay the price. He was president of the Pullman Palace Car Company, organized in 1867, which built cars and operated Pullmans under contracts with railroads. His widely discussed social experiment, a paternalistic model town for his workmen, located south of Chicago, came to grief when a strike broke out that precipitated the great Pullman strike of Eugene Debs's American Railway Union in 1894. The state later forced the company to give up control of the town. Pullman died on Oct. 19, 1897.

See A. Lindsey, *The Pullman Strike* (1942), which includes critical appraisals of Pullman and his model town.   (D. L. McM.)

PULP: *see* PAPER MANUFACTURE.

PULQUE, the typical indigenous beer of the peasant and poorer urban classes of the central and northern Mexican high-

lands. For many, it is an important source of carbohydrates, amino acids, and vitamins. For the populations of some arid regions, such as the valley of the Mezquital, it may supply most of the fluid intake in some seasons.

Pulque is the freshly fermented sap of any of ten or more of the larger species of agave or maguey plants, particularly *Agave atrovirens* in the valley of Mexico, which are cultivated in household plantings and large commercial plantations. (*See* AGAVE.) To collect the sap (*agua miel*), a cavity is made in the apex of the short fleshy stem of a four- to six-year-old plant by cutting out the emerging flower shoot. Three or four months later, the cavity walls and surrounding leaf bases are scraped, after which the first sap is drawn. The cavity refills two or three times daily, producing 10 to 15 pints of sap a day until the plant dies.

The sap, which contains about 10% of sugars, is taken to processing centres where, after several days of fermentation, it becomes *pulque*. The fermentation process is usually hastened by adding old *pulque* (*madre pulque*), a starter or inoculum rich in yeasts and lactic acid bacteria. Other additives may be employed to the same end. The result of this accelerated fermentation is *pulque fuerte;* probably most *pulque* is produced in this way. The fresh product is dispensed from barrels in drinking houses or is sold in containers; some is pasteurized and bottled.

The alcohol content varies from less than 1% to 5%; the less alcoholic *pulque* is consumed as a soft drink. A sour buttermilk-like taste is imparted by lactic acid; viscosity results from mucilaginous materials in the *agua miel* and from bacterial action; the whitish appearance is due to suspended yeast and plant cells. *Pulque curado* contains added flavouring; *pulque curado de fresa,* for example, contains strawberry (*fresa*) flavouring.   (L. KA.)

PULVERIZED FUEL: *see* FUELS.

PUMA (*Felis concolor*), which occurs only in the western hemisphere, is exceeded in size among cats of the new world only by the jaguar. Besides the term puma, which is derived from usage by the Incas of South America, it is also known by the following names: cougar, deer tiger, Mexican lion, panther, painter (corruption of panther), mountain lion, and catamount. At least 15 subspecies of the puma are recognized; they range widely, from British Columbia in the north to Patagonia in the south, and formerly ranged coast to coast from the Atlantic to the Pacific. Man has eliminated pumas in many locations; they are now generally restricted to wilderness areas away from dense human populations.

PUMA OR MOUNTAIN LION (FELIS CONCOLOR)

A wide range of coloration exists among puma, from pale buff to reddish brown. The ears and tip of the tail are generally dark, while the rump and the belly, extending to the first hind leg joints, are white. There is no mane. Weights of adult puma range from about 75 to 275 lb.; shoulder height may be 2–2½ ft., the males being larger than the females. From one to six kittens are produced after a gestation period of 90–96 days; they may be born in any month of the year. The young have rows of small, irregular black spots, which disappear at maturity.

The puma exists on a wide range of foods, its favourite, when available, being deer. When killing, the puma brings its victim to the ground with the stunning impact of its entire weight, generally attacking at the throat and breast. *See also* CAT.   (S. P. Y.)

PUMICE, a very porous, frothlike, volcanic glass. Pumice has long been used as an abrasive, in cleaning, polishing and scouring compounds. After 1945 its uses multiplied in applications as railroad ballast and as a lightweight aggregate in precast masonry units, poured concrete, insulation and acoustic tile and plaster.

Pumice is an igneous rock which was almost completely liquid at the moment of effusion and was so rapidly cooled that there was no time for it to crystallize. When it solidified the vapours dissolved in it were suddenly released and the whole mass swelled up into a froth which immediately consolidated. Had it cooled under more pressure it would have formed a solid glass or obsidian (*q.v.*); in fact if fragments of obsidian are heated in a crucible till they fuse they will suddenly change to pumice when their dissolved gases are set free. Hence it can be understood that pumice is found only in recent volcanic countries. Any type of lava, if the conditions are favourable, may assume the pumiceous state; but basalts and andesites do not so often occur in this form as do trachytes and rhyolites.

Pumices are most abundant and most typically developed from acid rocks, for which reason they usually accompany obsidians; in fact, in the Italian island of Lipari and elsewhere the base of a lava flow may be black obsidian while the upper portion is a snow white pumice.

Small crystals of various minerals occur in many pumices; the most common are feldspar, augite, hornblende and zircon. The cavities of pumice are sometimes rounded, and may also be elongated or tubular owing to the flowing movement of the solidifying lava. The glass itself forms threads, fibres and thin partitions between the vesicles. Rhyolite and trachyte pumices are white, contain 60% to 75% of silica and the specific gravity of the glass is 2.3 to 2.4; andesite pumices are often yellow or brown; while pumiceous basalts, such as occur in the Hawaiian Islands, are pitch black when perfectly fresh.

Good pumice is found in Iceland, Hungary, Tenerife Island in the Canaries, New Zealand, Pantelleria Island and the Lipari Islands of Italy, West Germany and Greece. In the United States pumice is mined in the Rocky mountain and Pacific coast states (as Arizona, California, Nevada, New Mexico, Wyoming), and Hawaii. Pumice occurs among the older volcanic rocks, but usually has its cavities filled up by deposits of secondary minerals introduced by percolating water. Pumice, in minute fragments, has been shown to have an exceedingly wide distribution over the earth's surface. It occurs in all the deposits which cover the floor of the deepest portion of the oceans, and is especially abundant in the abysmal red clay. In some measure this pumice has been derived from submarine volcanic eruptions, but its presence is also accounted for by the fact that pumice will float on water for months, and is thus distributed over the sea by winds and currents. After a long time it becomes waterlogged and sinks to the bottom, where it gradually disintegrates and is incorporated in the muds and oozes which are gathering there. After the great eruption of Krakatau (*q.v.*) in 1883, banks of pumice covered the surface of the sea for many miles and rose in some cases for four or five feet above the water level. In addition much finely broken pumice was thrown into the air to a great height and was borne away by the winds, ultimately settling down in the most distant parts of the continents and oceans. *See also* Tuff; Volcano.

(J. S. F.; X.)

PUMP, a device for increasing the pressure of a fluid, usually a liquid. The increase in pressure, or head, is used to move the fluid through some channel or to raise it to a higher level, or both. Pumps are used in many applications: *e.g.,* to deliver water for home and industrial use; to transport oil across the country; to circulate oil, water and fuel in automobiles, airplanes and other vehicles; to lift a barber's chair; and in many industrial plants where fluids are used for power transmission or in manufacturing processes. In a pump, mechanical work is transformed into fluid energy; by contrast, in a turbine, fluid energy is transformed into mechanical work at some rotating shaft.

Pumps may be divided into two main types: the positive-displacement or static type; and the dynamic or kinetic type. In the positive-displacement type the characteristic action is a displace-

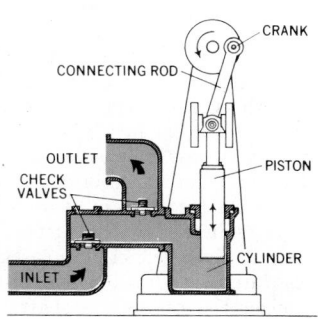

FIG. 1.—RECIPROCATING PUMP

ment by a decrease in volume in the working chamber of the pump. The increase in fluid static pressure is developed by a displacement action rather than by a velocity change or a kinetic energy change. The reciprocating pump, the rotary pump, the gear pump and the vane pump are illustrations of positive-displacement pumps. In the kinetic or dynamic type there is a kinetic or dynamic action between some mechanical element and a fluid; a force acting on the fluid causes a significant velocity change. The centrifugal pump and the jet pump are examples of the dynamic type.

Reciprocating Pumps.—In the common reciprocating pump a piston moves back and forth in a cylinder. An example is the hand bicycle pump, in which, as the hand pushes the piston back and forth, air from the atmosphere enters the cylinder and is pushed out of the cylinder into the tire by the piston action. Suitable valves are necessary to control the flow properly. Fig. 1 illustrates the case in which the piston is moved back and forth in the cylinder by an arrangement of crank and connecting rod. As the piston moves toward the right, the outlet check valve is open, the inlet valve is closed, and the fluid flows from the cylinder through the outlet or discharge pipe. As the piston moves toward the left, the inlet check valve is open, the outlet valve is closed, and fluid enters the cylinder. If leakage past the piston is neglected, then the piston delivers the volume of fluid it displaces in moving through the cylinder; this explains the term positive-displacement.

A single-acting pump, in which fluid is pumped only by one side of the piston is illustrated in fig. 1. This can be turned into a double-acting pump—in which both sides of the piston are in contact with the fluid, and both sides pump—simply by adding inlet and outlet pipes, with suitable valves, at the other end of the cylinder (and, of course, providing a proper seal at the opening where the piston rod enters the cylinder).

For a given volume rate of flow through the pump, the pressure at the pump outlet may be high or low, depending on the pressure necessary to force the fluid through the system connected to the pump; thus the discharge pressure is governed by the load or piping system. The pressure that a reciprocating pump can develop is limited only by the strength of the pump components and the power of the driving unit.

On some reciprocating pumps there is an air chamber on the discharge. The air trapped in the chamber acts as a cushion, making the pump operation smooth and quiet. Generally speaking, reciprocating pumps are best adapted for relatively low rates of flow, high pressures and high suction lifts. They are built of a wide variety of materials and for many different types of service. Reciprocating pumps are not well suited for pumping very dirty or very viscous liquids, because of the possibility of clogging.

Various methods are used for reciprocating the piston, such as different mechanical linkages or a fluid under pressure. For example, steam may be used on one side of the piston to drive it while water or some other liquid is pumped by the other side.

Diaphragm Pumps.—If, instead of the movable piston in fig. 1 a circular diaphragm—of rubber or other flexible material—is fixed at its outer edge to the cylinder, and if the crank and connecting rod linkage is fastened at its centre, the result will be a diaphragm pump. The central portion of the diaphragm is moved back and forth to provide volumetric displacement, and the inlet and outlet valve arrangement is similar to that of the reciprocating pump. Because there is no possibility of liquid bypassing the diaphragm and coming in contact with the connecting rod or other pump parts, diaphragm pumps are used for handling such materials as thick pulps, sewage sludge, acids, alkaline solutions, mine waters and fruit juices.

Rotary Pumps.—The rotary pump is classed as a positive-displacement pump, although its action is one of rotation, not reciprocation. It should not be confused with the centrifugal pump. The gear pump in fig. 2, an example of one type of rotary pump, has a pair of meshed gears in a casing. As the gears rotate, fluid is caught between their teeth and the casing, and is carried from inlet to outlet, the volume of fluid delivered during each revolution depending on the amount of space between the teeth

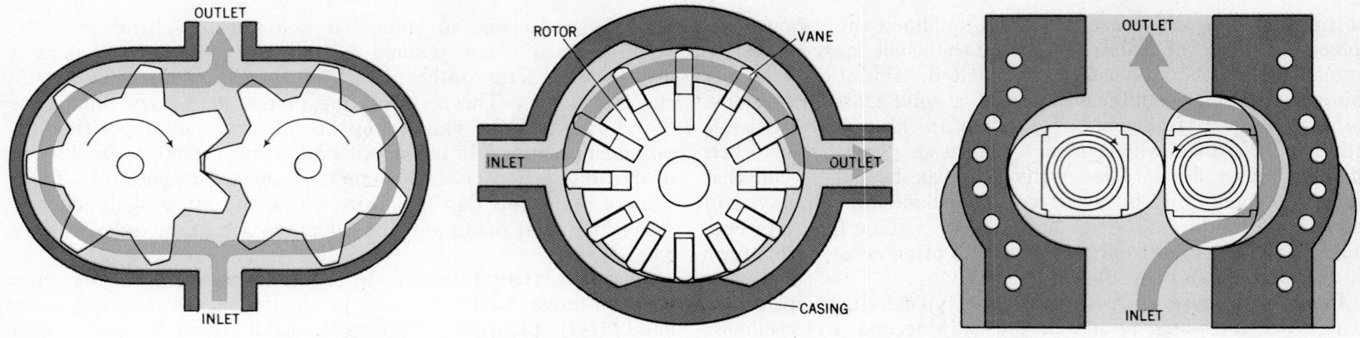

FIG. 2.—SCHEMATIC DIAGRAM OF (A) ROTARY PUMP; (B) HYDRAULIC VANE PUMP OR MOTOR; (C) LOBE PUMP

and the case. Delivery is fairly steady, in contrast to the pulsating delivery of the reciprocating pump.

Rotary pumps are most suitable for applications requiring only low and medium delivery pressure. The absence of valves is an advantage in pumping heavy viscous liquids but because of the close clearances between gears and case, rotary pumps are not suitable for liquids containing any abrasive material that might damage the metal surfaces.

Different types of rotary pumps are available. In some pumps, rotating members with two or more lobes are used instead of gears. In the vane type of pump, there is a rotor set off-center in a casing. The rotor is fitted with vanes which slide in and out radially. The entering liquid is trapped between the vanes, which ride on the inside of the case, and is carried to the outlet.

Centrifugal Pumps.—The essential parts of a centrifugal pump are a rotating member with blades or vanes (the so-called impeller) and a case surrounding it. The action in a centrifugal pump depends upon centrifugal force or a variation of pressure due to rotation.

As shown in fig. 3, fluid is led through the inlet pipe to the centre or "eye" of the rotating impeller; it is thrown out at high velocity through the impeller vanes and into the volute, the spiral casing surrounding the impeller. The volute is designed so that its cross-sectional area increases constantly toward the outlet, and this has the effect of changing the high-velocity, low-pressure stream leaving the impeller into a low-velocity, high-pressure stream at the outlet.

Centrifugal pumps are made with various arrangements of impellers. Fig. 3 shows a so-called "single-suction" pump: fluid enters from only one side of the impeller. Fluid enters both sides of the impeller in a so-called "double-suction" pump. A pump may be in "stages," with several impellers on a single shaft; in a three-stage pump, for example, three impellers are mounted on the same shaft in one casing. The discharge from one impeller enters the inlet of a following impeller. The same weight of fluid per unit time passes through each stage, but each stage increases the pressure. In the radial-flow impeller shown in fig. 3, fluid enters the impeller at the hub and flows radially along the blade to the periphery; in a mixed-flow impeller, fluid flow is along the blade (radial) and across it (parallel to the axis of shaft rotation).

Centrifugal pumps differ from positive-displacement pumps in various ways. As an illustration, the discharge valve of a centrifugal pump can be closed without the pressure rising above a certain value; if the discharge valve of a reciprocating pump is closed, the pump will stall or some part of it will break. The flow from a centrifugal pump is relatively smooth and steady, and these pumps can handle various liquids, sewage and liquids containing sand, gravel and stones of moderate size.

Centrifugal pumps are sometimes classified as volute or diffuser types. Fig. 3 shows a volute type, the fluid being discharged directly from the impeller into the volute. In the diffuser type, there is a series of fixed vanes, surrounding the impeller, that reduce turbulence in the volute by smoothing the flow of fluid and lowering its velocity; there is a decrease in kinetic energy and an increase in static pressure in the vane diffuser.

Axial-flow Pumps.—An axial-flow pump is a dynamic machine which may consist of a single runner in a cylindrical casing or of a runner with one or two sets of fixed guide vanes. In an axial-flow pump the fluid passes through the runner without essentially changing its distance from the axis of rotation (in principle and design, the axial-flow pump is much like a gas turbine). There is practically no centrifugal force effect within the true axial-flow pump. Generally speaking, the centrifugal pump is best suited for producing relatively high pressures and low rates of flow, while the axial-flow pump is best for producing relatively low pressures and high rates of flow.

Deep-Well Pumps.—Various types of pumps have been developed for pumping water or oil from deep wells. One, called the plunger pump, is essentially a reciprocating pump with a long piston rod. In the so-called turbine deep-well pump, a motor at the surface turns a vertical rotating shaft; this shaft drives a multistage centrifugal pump (with impellers rotating in a horizontal plane) which is installed in the well below the surface of the water or oil. For high lifts, the pump may have 20 or more stages.

Fig. 4 illustrates a submersible-motor pump; the motor is mounted below the centrifugal pump. The elongated, small-diameter electric motor operates submerged in the well liquid. The liquid being pumped does not come in contact with the electric parts or motor bearings, because these are enclosed in an oil-filled case which has a mercury seal where the rotating shaft passes through the top to the pump.

The pump and motor form a compact assembly that is fastened to and supported by the outlet pipe. A liquid-tight armoured cable connects the motor leads to the power supply at the surface, and a small copper tube provides a lubrication inlet at the surface for larger models; small models are provided with "permanent" lubrication and require no attention.

Each type of deep-well pump has its advantages. For a specific application in a well of moderate depth, the plunger pump usually is least expensive; and since it is the only one of the three that can be operated directly by a windmill it has often been used in remote locations. As in the case with the turbine pump, the power source is at the surface and readily accessible for maintenance. However, in both cases, trouble with the pumping unit necessitates withdrawing and disconnecting, section by section, the plunger rod or turbine shaft, to raise the pump to the surface; this is true also of the submersible-motor pump.

FIG. 3.—CENTRIFUGAL PUMP

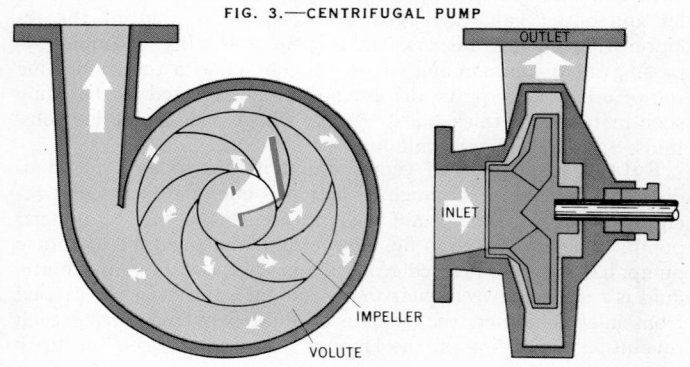

The limit of depth at which the plunger pump will operate economically is reached when the power unit is expending almost as much, or more, energy lifting a long plunger rod than lifting fluid; and this type of pump does not work well except in very straight well bores. The economical limit of the turbine pump is reached when more energy is expended in overcoming bearing friction in the long shaft than in lifting fluid (the shaft must be supported at frequent intervals by "spiders" or frameworks that fit against the sides of the well bore and are fitted with bearings to keep the shaft centred in the bore); the turbine pump will work in an out-of-plumb well, but any deviation from straightness increases frictional losses at the bearings.

The submersible-motor pump overcomes some of these disadvantages (it will work in a very crooked bore, for example, the amount of deviation being limited only by the angle through which the pump unit and outlet pipe can be inserted and withdrawn easily), but it introduces disadvantages of its own. Principal among these is the fact that malfunctioning of either the pump or the motor necessitates withdrawing the entire unit from the well for repair.

Jet Pumps.—In the reciprocating, rotary and centrifugal pumps, there is a moving mechanical part which does work on the moving fluid. However, there is a dynamic type of pump which does not have any moving mechanical parts: it is called variously a jet pump, injector or ejector. In this type of pump the pressure of a fluid is increased as it flows through an arrangement of fixed channels. A "motive fluid" is used to pump, or induce the flow of, some other fluid.

Jet pumps are found in many applications, pumping many different fluids. A common type is one in which water is the motive fluid and water is the fluid being pumped; such pumps are used on domestic water well systems. As illustrated in fig. 5, water passes through the converging nozzle with a high velocity and acts as a motive or driving fluid; at the end of the nozzle the velocity is high and the pressure is low. The mixture of motive fluid and liquid being pumped, or induced, then passes through the diffuser where the velocity is reduced and the pressure is increased.

A number of pumping devices can be explained by reference to the venturi tube. As illustrated in fig. 6, the venturi tube consists of a converging nozzle and a narrow portion or throat. As motive fluid passes through the converging portion, the velocity is increased and the pressure is decreased, and this decrease in pressure can be used to move some other fluid. In the usual aspirator pump, water passes through a venturi channel, and air is drawn into the venturi throat by the low pressure; in the common atomizer, air passing through a venturi tube lifts liquid from the

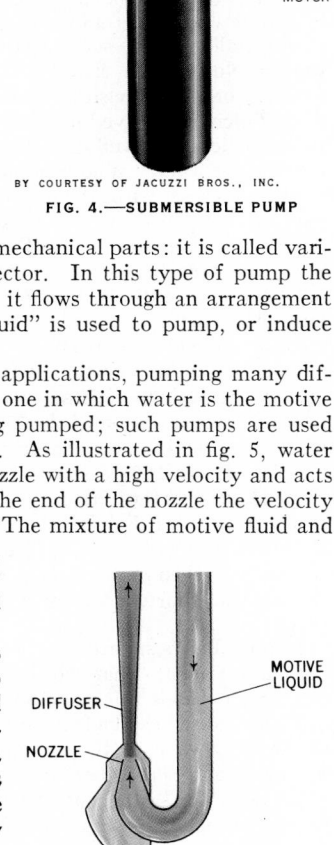

DISCHARGE PIPE
CONNECTION

DISCHARGE
CHECK VALVE

POWER CABLE

THRUST
BEARING

IMPELLER
CASING

PUMP
IMPELLERS

GUIDE
BEARING

INLET
SCREEN

ELECTRIC
MOTOR

BY COURTESY OF JACUZZI BROS., INC.

FIG. 4.—SUBMERSIBLE PUMP

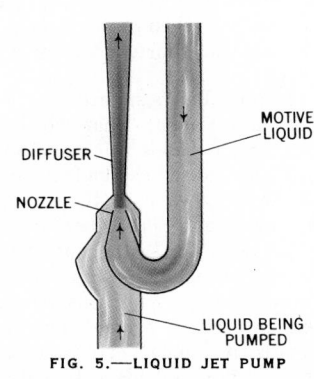

MOTIVE
LIQUID

DIFFUSER

NOZZLE

LIQUID BEING
PUMPED

FIG. 5.—LIQUID JET PUMP

attached container, mixes with the liquid, and ejects it as a fine spray.

Air or Gas Lift Pumps.—In this type of pump there is a vertical lift pipe arranged with its lower end submerged in the liquid to be raised and its upper end connected to a discharge pipe or tank. Air or gas from a compressor is led through a separate pipe to the lower end of the lift pipe, where it bubbles through the liquid to form a gas-liquid mixture that has a lower density (or specific weight) than the surrounding liquid. The resulting buoyant force moves the lighter mixture (of gas and liquid) to the top of the vertical pipe. In this type of pump, air may be used to pump water, or a gas may be used to pump oil. The pumping action depends on the air or gas used, the nature of the liquid, the depth of submersion of the lower end of the lift pipe, and the manner of forming the bubbles.

Vacuum Pumps.—Atmospheric pressure is the force exerted on a unit area due to the weight of the atmosphere. The word "vacuum" is frequently used in referring to pressures below atmospheric. In many cases it is desired to exhaust or evacuate air (or some gas) from a vessel or a piece of equipment. The aspirator pump can be used to develop a partial vacuum; other types, to produce higher degrees of vacuum, are described in the article VACUUM.

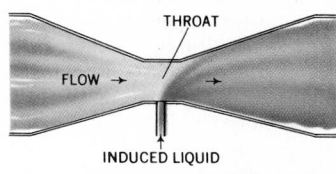

THROAT

FLOW →

INDUCED LIQUID

FIG. 6.—VENTURI PUMPING DEVICE

Magnetic Pumps for Liquid Metals.—Certain characteristics of liquid metals make them attractive as heat-transfer liquids for cooling nuclear reactors. The electromagnetic pump has proved suitable for the circulation of some of these liquid metals. The electromagnetic pump uses the same principle on which the electric motor is based; namely, that a conductor in a magnetic field, carrying a current flowing at right angles to the magnetic field direction, has a force exerted on it in a direction mutually perpendicular to both the field and current. In the electromagnetic pump, the fluid being pumped is the conductor, and the resultant force acts to propel the fluid if suitable arrangements are made. The current and field can be produced in many ways. In one electromagnetic pump, the D.C.-Faraday type, the liquid metal flows through a thin-walled duct of square or rectangular cross-section. A constant magnetic field is passed through the fluid on an axis perpendicular to the flow direction. The magnetic field is developed by windings, carrying direct current, that are mounted on a magnetic core with pole faces that provide a magnetic return path through the fluid metal. Current is passed through the fluid by establishing a voltage drop along the axis of the duct, mutually perpendicular to both the flow direction and the magnetic field direction. In theory, the operation of this pump is similar to that of a direct-current shunt motor.

See also references under "Pump" in the Index.

BIBLIOGRAPHY.—F. A. Kristal and F. A. Annett, *Pumps* (1953); A. J. Stepanoff, *Centrifugal and Axial-Flow Pumps* (1957); R. C. Binder, *Advanced Fluid Mechanics,* vol. i (1958). (R. C. BR.)

PUMPKIN, the fruit of certain varieties of *Cucurbita pepo* or of *C. moschata*, members of the family Cucurbitaceae. The names pumpkin and squash, especially in America, are applied inconsistently to certain varieties of both these species. The quick-growing, small-fruited bush or nontrailing varieties of *C. pepo* (*see* SQUASH) are called squash in America, while the long-season, long-trailing, large-fruited varieties are called pumpkin.

The fruits are large, generally 10–20 lb. or more, yellowish to orange in colour, and vary from oblate through globular to oblong. The rind is smooth and usually lightly furrowed or ribbed; the fruit stem is hard and woody, ridged or angled, and in *C. pepo* not flared at its point of attachment to the fruit. The very largest varieties of "pumpkin" are more properly designated as winter squash, *C. maxima,* and may weigh 75 lb. or more. Varieties cross-pollinate readily within each of the three species, but the species do not cross naturally. A few interspecific crosses have been recorded but the hybrids were highly self-sterile and set no fruit with their own pollen. Neither pumpkins nor squashes will cross with cucumbers or with melons.

The varieties commonly called pumpkin produce very long vines and are usually planted in hills of two to three plants each, about eight by eight feet apart. They are also planted at wide intervals in fields of corn. Pumpkins mature in early fall and can be stored a few months in a dry place well above freezing.

Pumpkins are commonly grown in North America, Great Britain, and Europe for human food and also for livestock feed. The rind is peeled and the flesh is used as a vegetable or for puddings or pies. Pumpkins are used in the U.S. as Halloween decorations, one such being the jack-o'-lantern, in which the seeds and some pulp of the pumpkin are removed and a light inserted to shine through cut-out eyes, nose, and mouth.　　　(V. R. B.)

PUNAN, the name applied to a number of peoples in middle Borneo, all of them, except the Punan Ba (a branch of the Kajang), traditionally forest nomads in the mountainous areas around the upper reaches of the major rivers. The majority are now agricultural. Those still nomadic live in isolated groups averaging about 35 individuals, subsisting on the wild sago palm and on game hunted, until very recently, with blowpipe and spear. Physically and culturally they are very similar to other mongoloid peoples of this part of the island; none of them is Negrito or demonstrably aboriginal in Borneo.

The Punan peoples speak mutually unintelligible languages; and employ various means of exploiting the environment; but they resemble each other in degree of civilization, their general mode of social life, and the egalitarian sharing of foodstuffs.

As a result of the common name applied to these groups, accounts of Punan are confused and misleading. The only nomads who have received attention from ethnographers are those in the Baram area, whose correct name is in fact Penan. These comprise two tribes that have no corporate unity; there is little recognition of common interest beyond directly related groups, and the group has no chief. Their traditional life is simple: they live in flimsy huts, have few belongings, wear only a loincloth, and are almost devoid of ceremony. They differ from the settled peoples mainly in their economy, lack of class stratification, and absence of any trace of a head-hunting cult. About three times a year they descend to fixed points on the rivers to trade with their hereditary overlords in the riverine tribes, exchanging forest products (chiefly dammar resin and wild rubber) for metal tools, cloth, household utensils, and tobacco. Individual groups adopt words and customs from different surrounding settled peoples, whom they tend increasingly to resemble.

The difficulty in obtaining trustworthy population figures for the Punan lay in the transient residence habits and the scattered, isolated status of many Punan groups. During the late 1960s the surveys, more reliable for the Penan subgroups of the Baram region and the Usun Apau Plateau, showed an approximate total of 2.600 Penan. A reasonable estimate of total Punan population in all parts of Borneo (including that of the Penan) was that it probably did not exceed 5,000 people. *See also* BORNEO: *The People.*

BIBLIOGRAPHY.—R. Needham, "Penan and Punan," *J. Malay. Brch R. Asiat. Soc.,* 27:73–83 (1954), "Punan Ba," *ibid.,* 28:24–36 (1955), "More Concerning the Punan of Borneo," *Am. Anthrop.,* 57:131 (1955), "Death-names and Solidarity in Penan Society," *Bijdragen tot de taal-, land- en volkenkunde,* 121:58 (1965); I. A. N. Urquhart, "Some Notes on the Jungle Punans in Kapit District," *Sarawak Mus. J.,* 5:495 (1951); G. Arnold, "Usun Apau Plateau: The Nomadic Penans (Most Primitive of all the Borneo People)," *Geogrl J.,* 123:174 (1957), "Nomadic Penan of the Upper Rejang (Plieran), Sarawak," *J. Malay. Brch R. Asiat. Soc.,* 31:40 (1958); Yap Yoon Keong, "The Punan Corpse that Smells of Durian," *Sarawak Mus. J.,* 11:94 (1963).
　　　　　　　　　　　　　　　　　　　　　(R. NM.; X.)

PUNCH, the abbreviated form of PUNCHINELLO (Italian *Policianelo, Pulcinella;* French, *Polichinelle*), the most popular of the marionettes and glove puppets and the chief figure in the Punch and Judy show. Many modern authorities tend to accept the opinion that the whole family of Italian *maschere* (masked characters of the *commedia dell'arte; e.g.,* Arlecchino and Brighella) are modified survivals of the principal Oscan characters of the *atellanae,* and that Pulcinella is the representative of Maccus, the country bumpkin, or Bucco, the comic servant (*see* ATEL-

ORIGINAL PRINT FROM THE COLLECTION OF GEORGE SPEAIGHT
PUNCH
From a drawing which appeared on a music cover of the mid-19th century

LANA FABULA). But there is a gap of 1,000 years between the last records of the Atellan farces and the first of the *commedia dell'arte,* and it would be ingenuous to follow the antiquaries of the 18th century in accepting a clear connection between the two. At the same time it is interesting to compare a bronze of Maccus with 17th-century pictures of Pulcinella in Italy and France.

It is not certainly known who was the first Pulcinella. Claims have been made on behalf of Silvio Fiorillo and Andrea Calcese, both of whom were performing at the beginning of the 17th century. But some facts of his early history are definite. One of the *zanni,* the comic servants of the company, he was indispensable when the troupe played in Naples but did not always appear in other localities. His characteristics were not clearly marked at first, and the hooked nose, the humped back, the tendency to wife-beating and outrageous lawlessness typical of the English Punch were acquired only gradually. This is clearly seen from the first pictorial representations. The earliest, in which he is called Policianelo, is dated 1618 and is one of a series made from birds' feathers by Dionisio Minaggio, the gardener of the governor of Milan. The second, in 1622, is of Pulliciniello in Jacques Callot's *I Balli di Sfessania.* In both he is depicted as large, shambling and stupid-looking, dressed in a loose white shirt and very full trousers.

The Italian actors soon began to travel abroad. A few of them were in Nottingham, Eng., in 1573. The Gelosi, one of the most famous companies, visited Paris in 1577. It is not known exactly when Pulcinella arrived in these countries, but the French version, Polichinelle, was firmly established in France by the middle of the 17th century. When the actors came from Italy the puppet showmen came with them. By 1649 a showman called Jean Brioché, probably an Italian named Briocci, was displaying a puppet Polichinelle near the Pont Neuf in Paris. The marionette was grotesque, humpbacked and hook-nosed, but its origin may not have been entirely Italian. There was a French tradition of hunchbacked fools, as can be seen from a print of the entertainment at the marriage of Henry IV with Marie de Médicis in 1600, and the popularity of the Polichinelle puppet in France may be due to the fusion of these two traditions.

Similarly a tradition of the humpbacked fool existed in England when the first Italian puppeteers arrived after the restoration of Charles II. In 1662 a showman called Signor Bologna, alias Pollicinella, was performing in London, and by 1667 a more elaborate entertainment of Punchinello was established at Charing Cross by Antonio Devoto. In 1672 the king gave his patronage to this theatre, and then performances with human actors were permitted. Already the shortened form of the name had passed into general usage.

Samuel Pepys mentions (1669) some people who called their fat child Punch, "that word being become a word of common use for all that is thick and short." This general popularity was probably caused by the traveling showmen, who carried puppets to the country wakes in the summer and visited London for the fairs in August and September.

Early in the 18th century Punch became famous in political circles through the use of the name by Martin Powell, a marionette showman, in a scurrilous attack on Robert Harley. This pamphlet, entitled *A Second Tale of a Tub* (1715), furnishes some details of Punch performances and has a frontispiece of Powell with Punch and his wife. But it was in the 1790s that the revival occurred which caused the preservation of Punch and Judy: as the marionettes at the fairs lost their popularity, there was a new interest in the humbler glove puppets, and in this form the

Punch and Judy play became a success. *See also* Commedia dell 'Arte; Puppetry.

Bibliography.—*Punch and Judy*, with illustrations by George Cruikshank and introduction by John Payne Collier (1828); P. J. Stead, *Mr. Punch* (1950); George Speaight, *The History of the English Puppet Theatre* (1955); Vito Pandolfi, *La Commedia dell'Arte*, 6 vol. (1957–61).   (I. K. F.)

PUNCHING AND SHEARING MACHINES: see Machine Tools.

PUNIC WARS, a name specially given to the wars between Rome and Carthage in the 3rd and 2nd centuries B.C. The origin of these conflicts is to be found in the position which Rome acquired, about 275 B.C., as leader and protector of all Italy. The attendant new obligation to safeguard the peninsula against foreign interference made it necessary not to allow the neighbouring island of Sicily to fall into the hands of a strong and expansive power. Carthage, on the other hand, had long been anxious to conquer Sicily and so to complete the chain of island posts by which it controlled the western Mediterranean.

First Punic War (264–241 B.C.).—The proximate cause of the first outbreak was a crisis in the city of Messana (Messina), commanding the straits between Italy and Sicily. A band of Campanian mercenaries, the Mamertini, who had forcibly established themselves within the town and were being hard pressed in 264 by Hieron II of Syracuse, applied for help to both Rome and Carthage. The Carthaginians, arriving first, occupied Messana and effected a reconciliation with Hieron. The Roman commander, nevertheless, persisted in throwing troops into the city, and by seizing the Carthaginian admiral during a parley induced him to withdraw. This aggression involved war with Carthage and Syracuse.

Operations began with a joint attack upon Messana, which the Romans easily repelled. In 263 they advanced with a considerable force into Hieron's territory and induced him to seek peace and alliance with them. In 262 they besieged and captured the enemy's base at Agrigentum. But they made little impression upon the Carthaginian fortresses in the west of the island and upon the towns of the interior.

In 260 the Romans built their first large fleet of standard battleships. At Mylae (Milazzo), off the north Sicilian coast, their admiral Gaius Duilius defeated a Carthaginian squadron of superior maneuvering capacity by grappling and boarding. This left Rome free to land a force on Corsica (259) and expel the Carthaginians, but did not suffice to loosen their grasp on Sicily. A large Roman fleet sailed out in 256, repelled the entire Carthaginian fleet off Cape Ecnomus (near modern Licata) and established a fortified camp on African soil at Clypea (Kelibia in Tunisia). The Carthaginians, whose citizen levy was utterly disorganized, could neither keep the field against the invaders nor prevent their subjects from revolting. After one campaign they were ready to sue for peace, but the terms which the Roman commander M. Atilius Regulus offered were intolerably harsh. Accordingly they equipped a new army in which, by the advice of a Greek captain of mercenaries named Xanthippus, cavalry and elephants formed the strongest arm. In 255, under Xanthippus' command, they offered battle to Regulus, who had taken up position with an inadequate force near Tunis, outmaneuvered him, and destroyed the bulk of his army. A second Roman fleet, which subsequently reached Africa after defeating the full Carthaginian fleet off Cape Hermaeum (Cape Bon), withdrew all the remaining troops.

The Romans now directed their efforts once more against Sicily. In 254 they captured the important fortress of Panormus (Palermo), but when Carthage threw reinforcements into the island the war again came to a standstill. In 251 or 250 the Roman general L. Metellus at last brought about a pitched battle near Panormus in which the enemy's force was effectively crippled. This victory was followed by an investment of the chief Punic base at Lilybaeum (Marsala), together with Drepanum (Trapani), by land and sea. The besiegers met with a gallant resistance, and in 249 were compelled to withdraw by the loss of their fleet in a surprise attack upon Drepanum, in which the admiral P. Claudius Pulcher was repulsed with a loss of 93 ships. This was the

Romans' only naval defeat in the war but their fleet had suffered a series of grievous losses by storm, and now it was so reduced that the attack upon Sicily had to be suspended. At the same time the Carthaginians, who felt no less severely the financial strain of the prolonged struggle, reduced their forces and made no attempt to deliver a counterattack. The only noteworthy feature of the ensuing campaigns is the skilful guerrilla war waged by a new Carthaginian commander, Hamilcar Barca, from his strong positions on Mt. Ercte (247/246–244) and Mt. Eryx (modern Erice) (244–242) in western Sicily, by which he effectually screened Lilybaeum from any attempt on it by the Roman land army.

In 242 Rome resumed operations at sea. By a magnificent effort on the part of private citizens a fleet of 200 warships was equipped and sent out to renew the blockade of Lilybaeum. The Carthaginians hastily collected a relief force, but in a battle fought off the Aegates or Aegusae Islands (Aegadian Is.), west of Drepana, their fleet was caught at a disadvantage and mostly sunk or captured (March 10, 241). This victory, by giving the Romans undisputed command of the sea, rendered certain the ultimate fall of the Punic strongholds in Sicily. The Carthaginians accordingly opened negotiations and consented to a peace by which they ceded Sicily and the Lipari Islands to Rome and paid an indemnity of 3,200 talents.

The Interval Between the First and Second Wars (241–218 B.C.).—The loss of naval supremacy not only deprived the Carthaginians of their predominance in the western Mediterranean, but exposed their overseas empire to disintegration under renewed attacks by Rome. The temper of the Roman people was soon made manifest during a conflict which broke out between the Carthaginians and their discontented mercenaries. A gross breach of the treaty was perpetrated when a Roman force was sent to occupy Sardinia, whose insurgent garrison had offered to surrender the island (238). To the remonstrances of Carthage the Romans replied with a direct declaration of war, and only withheld their attack upon the formal cession of Sardinia and Corsica and the payment of a further indemnity.

From this episode it became clear that Rome intended to use the victory to the utmost. To avoid complete humiliation Carthage had no resource but to humiliate its adversary. The recent complications of foreign and internal strife had indeed so weakened the Punic power that the prospect of renewing the war under favourable circumstances seemed remote enough. But the scheme of preparing for a fresh conflict found a worthy champion in Hamilcar Barca, who sought to compensate for the loss of Sicily by acquiring a dominion in Spain where Carthage might gain new wealth and form a fresh base of operations against Rome. Invested with an unrestricted foreign command, he spent the rest of his life in founding a Spanish empire (237–228). His work was continued by his son-in-law Hasdrubal and his son Hannibal, who was placed at the head of the army in 221. These conquests aroused the suspicions of Rome, which in a treaty with Hasdrubal confined the Carthaginians to the south of the Ebro. At some point also Rome entered into relations with Saguntum (Sagunto), a town on the east coast, south of the Ebro. In 219 Hannibal laid siege to Saguntum and carried the town in spite of a stubborn defense.

It has always been a debatable point whether his attack contravened the new treaty. The Romans certainly took this view and sent to Carthage to demand Hannibal's surrender. But his defiant policy was too popular to be disavowed; the Carthaginian council upheld Hannibal's action, and drew upon itself a declaration of war.

Second Punic War (218–201 B.C.).—It seemed as though the superiority of the Romans at sea must enable them to choose the field of battle. They decided to embark one army for Spain and another for Sicily and Africa. But before their preparations were complete, Hannibal began that series of operations by which he dictated the course of the war for the greater part of its duration. Realizing that so long as the Romans commanded the resources of an undivided Italian confederacy no foreign attack could beat them down beyond recovery, he conceived the plan

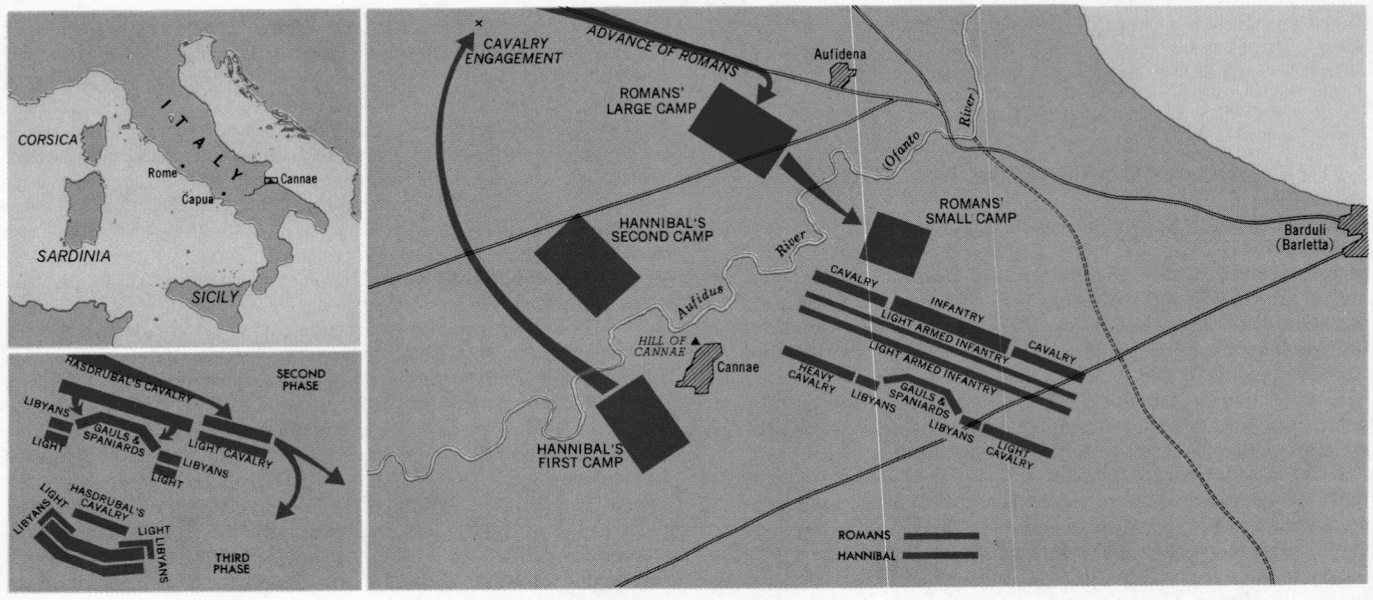

PLAN OF THE BATTLE OF CANNAE, 216 B.C.

A major battle of the Second Punic War (218–201 B.C.) in which Hannibal was victorious over the Romans. Inset at lower left shows the second and third phases of the battle

of cutting off their supply of strength at the source by carrying the war into Italy and causing a disruption of the league. His chances of ever reaching Italy seemed small, for the sea was guarded by the Roman fleets and the land route was long and arduous.

But the very boldness of his enterprise contributed to its success; after a six months' march through Spain and Gaul and over the Alps, which the Romans were nowhere in time to oppose, Hannibal arrived in the plain of the Po with 20,000 foot and 6,000 horse, the pick of his African and Spanish levies (autumn 218: for details *see* HANNIBAL).

His further advance was here disputed by some Roman troops, but the superiority of the Carthaginian cavalry and the spread of insurrection among the Gaulish inhabitants forced the defenders to fall back upon the Apennines. At the end of the year the Roman Army was reinforced by the division from Sicily and led out to battle on the banks of the Trebbia (*q.v.*). Hannibal, by superior tactics, repelled the assailants with heavy loss, and thus made his position in north Italy secure.

In 217 the campaign opened in Etruria, into which the invading army, largely reinforced by Gauls, penetrated by an unguarded pass. A rash pursuit by the Roman field force led to its being entrapped on the shore of Lake Trasimene (Trasimeno, *q.v.*) and destroyed with a loss of at least 15,000 men. This catastrophe left Rome completely uncovered; but Hannibal, having resolved not to attack the capital before he could collect a more overwhelming force, directed his march toward the south of Italy, where he hoped to stir up the peoples who had formerly been Rome's most stubborn enemies. The Italians, however, were everywhere slow to join the Carthaginians, and a new Roman army under the dictator Q. Fabius Maximus ("Cunctator"), which, without ever daring to close with Hannibal, dogged his steps on his forays through Apulia and Campania, prevented his acquiring a permanent base of operations.

The eventful campaign of 216 was begun by a new aggressive move on the part of Rome. An exceptionally strong field army, estimated at 85,000 men, was sent to crush the Carthaginians in open battle. On a level plain near Cannae (*q.v.*) in Apulia, which Hannibal had chosen for his battleground, the Roman legions delivered their attack. Hannibal deliberately allowed his centre to be driven in by their superior numbers, while Hasdrubal's cavalry wheeled round so as to take the enemy in flank and rear. The Romans, surrounded on all sides and so cramped that their superior numbers aggravated their plight, were practically an-

nihilated, and the loss of citizens was perhaps greater than in any other defeat that befell the republic.

The moral effect of the battle was no less momentous. The south Italian peoples at last found courage to secede from Rome, the leaders of the movement being the people of Capua, at the time the second greatest town of Italy. Reinforcements were sent from Carthage, and several neutral powers prepared to throw their weight into the scale on Hannibal's behalf. At first sight it seems strange that the Battle of Cannae did not decide the war. But the great resources of Rome, though terribly reduced in respect to both men and money, were not yet exhausted. In north and central Italy the insurrection spread but little, and could be sufficiently guarded against with small detachments. In the south the Greek towns of the coast remained loyal, and the numerous Latin colonies continued to render important service by interrupting free communication between the rebels and detaining part of their forces.

In Rome itself the quarrels between the nobles and commons, which had previously unsettled Roman policy, gave way to a unanimity unparalleled in the annals of the republic. The guidance of operations was henceforth left to the Senate, which by maintaining a persistent policy until the conflict was brought to a successful end earned its greatest title to fame.

The subsequent campaigns of the war in Italy assume a new character. Though the Romans contrived at times to raise 200,000 men, they could spare only a moderate force for field operations. Their generals, among whom the veterans Fabius and M. Claudius Marcellus frequently held the most important commands, rarely ventured to engage Hannibal in the open and contented themselves with observing him or skirmishing against his detachments. Hannibal, whose recent accessions of strength were largely discounted by the necessity of assigning troops to protect his new allies or secure their wavering loyalty, was still too weak to undertake a vigorous offensive. In the ensuing years the war resolved itself into a multiplicity of minor engagements which need not be followed out in detail. In 216 and 215 the chief seat of war was Campania, where Hannibal, vainly attempting to establish himself on the coast, experienced a severe repulse at Nola.

In 214 the main Carthaginian force was transferred to Apulia in hopes of capturing Tarentum (Taranto). Though Crotona and Locri on the southern coast had fallen into his hands, Hannibal still lacked a suitable harbour by which he might have secured his overseas communications. For two years he watched in vain for an opportunity to surprise the town, while the Romans narrowed down the sphere of revolt in Campania and defeated other Carthaginian commanders.

In 213/212 the greater part of Tarentum and other cities of the southern seaboard at last came into Hannibal's power. But in 212 the Romans found themselves strong enough to place Capua under blockade. They severely defeated a Carthaginian relief force, and could not be permanently dislodged even by Hannibal himself. In 211 Hannibal made a last effort to relieve his allies by a feint upon Rome itself, but the besiegers refused to be drawn away from their entrenchments, and eventually Capua was starved into surrender.

Its fall was a sign that no power could in the long run uphold a rival Italian coalition against Rome. After a year of desultory fighting, the Romans in 209 gained a further important success by recovering Tarentum. Though Hannibal still won isolated engagements, he was slowly being driven back into the extreme south of the peninsula.

In 207 the arrival of a fresh invading force produced a new crisis. Hasdrubal, who in 208–207 had marched overland from Spain, appeared in northern Italy with a force scarcely inferior to the army which his brother had brought in 218. After levying contingents of Gauls and Ligurians, he marched down the east coast with the object of joining his brother in central Italy for a direct attack upon Rome itself. By this time the steady drain of men and money was telling so severely upon the confederacy that some of the most loyal allies protested their inability to render further help. Yet by exerting a supreme effort the Romans raised their war establishment to the highest total yet attained and sent a strong field army against each Carthaginian leader.

The danger to Rome was chiefly averted by the prompt insight and enterprise of the consul Gaius Nero, who commanded the main army in the south. Having discovered that Hannibal would not advance beyond Apulia until his brother had established communications with him, Nero slipped away with part of his troops and arrived in time to reinforce his colleague Livius, whose force had recently got into touch with Hasdrubal near Sena Gallica (Senigallia).

The combined Roman army frustrated an attempt of Hasdrubal to elude it and forced him to fight on the banks of the Metaurus (Metauro). The battle was evenly contested until Nero by a dexterous flanking movement cut the enemy's retreat. Hasdrubal himself fell, and the bulk of his army was destroyed.

The campaign of 207 decided the war in Italy. Though Hannibal still maintained himself for some years in southern Italy, this was chiefly due to the exhaustion of Rome after the prodigious strain of past years and the consequent reduction of Roman forces. In 203 Italy was finally cleared of Carthaginian troops. Hannibal, in accordance with orders received from home, sailed back to Africa, and another expedition under his brother, Mago, which had sailed to Liguria in 205 and endeavoured to rouse the slumbering discontent of the people in Cisalpine Gaul and Etruria, was forced to withdraw.

Campaigns in Sicily and Spain.—Concurrently with the great struggle in Italy the Second Punic War was fought out on several other fields. It will suffice merely to allude to the First Macedonian War (214–205) which King Philip V commenced when the Roman power seemed to be breaking up after Cannae. This compelled the Romans to stretch their already severely strained resources still further by sending troops to Greece, but the diversions which Roman diplomacy provided for Philip in Greece and the maintenance of a patrol squadron in the Adriatic Sea prevented any effective cooperation on his part with Hannibal.

In view of the complete stagnation of agriculture in Italy the Romans had to look to Sardinia and Sicily for their food supply. Sardinia was attacked by Carthaginians in 215, but a small Roman force sufficed to repel the invasion. In Sicily a more serious conflict broke out. Some isolated attacks by Punic squadrons were easily frustrated by the strong Roman fleet. But in 215 internal complications arose. The death of Hieron II, Rome's

steadfast friend, left the kingdom of Syracuse to his inexperienced grandson Hieronymus. Flattered by the promises of Carthaginian emissaries, the young prince abruptly broke with the Romans, but before hostilities commenced he was assassinated. The Syracusan people now repudiated the monarchy and resumed their republican constitution, but, by false threats of terrible punishment at the hands of Rome, they were misled to play into the hands of the Carthaginians.

The attacks of a Roman army and fleet under Marcellus which speedily appeared before the town were completely baffled by the mechanical contrivances of the Syracusan mathematician Archimedes (213). Meantime, the revolt against Rome spread in the interior, and a Carthaginian fleet gained control of towns on the south coast.

In 212 Marcellus at last broke through the defense of Syracuse and in spite of the arrival of a Carthaginian relief force mastered the whole town in 211. A guerrilla warfare followed in which the Carthaginians maintained the upper hand until in 210 they lost their base at Agrigentum. They were dislodged from their remaining positions, and by the end of the year Sicily was wholly under the power of Rome.

The conflict in Spain was second in importance to the Italian war alone. From this country the Carthaginians drew large supplies of troops and money which might serve to reinforce Hannibal; hence it was in the interest of the Romans to challenge their enemy within Spain. Though the force which Rome at first spared for this war was small in numbers and rested entirely upon its own resources, the generals Publius and Gnaeus Scipio by skilful strategy and diplomacy not only won over the peoples north of the Ebro and defeated the Carthaginian leader Hasdrubal Barca in his attempts to restore communication with Italy, but carried their arms along the east coast into the heart of the enemy's domain.

But eventually their successes were nullified by a rash advance. Deserted by their native contingents and cut off by Carthaginian cavalry, among which the Numidian prince Masinissa rendered conspicuous service, the Roman generals were killed and their troops destroyed (211).

Disturbances in Africa prevented the Punic commanders from exploiting their success. Before long the fall of Capua enabled Rome to transfer troops from Italy to Spain, and in 210 the best Roman general of the day, the young son and namesake of P. Scipio, was placed in command. He signalized his arrival by a bold and successful *coup de main* upon the great arsenal of Carthago Nova (Cartagena) in 209. Though after an engagement at Baecula (Bailen; 208) he was unable to prevent Hasdrubal Barca from marching away to Italy, Scipio profited by his departure to push back the remaining hostile forces the more rapidly. A last effort by the Carthaginians to retrieve their losses with a fresh army was frustrated by a great victory at Ilipa (*q.v.*), near Seville, and by the end of the year 206 they had been driven out of Spain.

The War in Africa.—In 205 Scipio, who had returned to Rome to hold the consulship, proposed to follow up his victories by an attack upon the home territory of Carthage. Though the presence of Hannibal in Italy deterred Fabius and other senators from sanctioning this policy, Scipio gradually overbore all resistance. He built up a force which he organized and supplemented in Sicily, and in 204 sailed across to Africa. He was there met by a combined levy of Carthage and King Syphax of Numidia, and for a time penned to the shore near Utica. But in the winter he extricated himself by a surprise attack upon the enemy's camp, which resulted in the total loss of the allied force by sword or fire.

In the campaign of 203 a new Carthaginian force was destroyed by Scipio on the Great Plains 75 miles from Utica, their ally Syphax was captured, and the renegade Masinissa (*q.v.*) reinstated in the kingdom from which Syphax had recently expelled him. These disasters induced the Carthaginians to sue for peace, but before the very moderate terms which Scipio offered could be definitely accepted, a sudden reversal of opinion caused them to recall Hannibal's army for a final trial of war and to break off negotiations. In 202 Hannibal assumed command of a composite force of citizen and mercenary levies stiffened with a corps of his veteran Italian troops.

After an abortive conference with Scipio he prepared for a decisive battle (*see* ZAMA, BATTLE OF). Scipio's force was somewhat smaller in numbers, but well trained throughout and greatly superior in cavalry. His infantry, after evading an attack by the Carthaginian elephants, cut through the first two lines of the enemy, but was unable to break the reserve corps of Hannibal's veterans. The battle was ultimately decided by the cavalry of the Romans and their new ally Masinissa, which by a maneuver recalling the tactics of Cannae took Hannibal's line in the rear and completely destroyed it.

The Carthaginians having thus lost their last army again applied for peace and accepted the terms which Scipio offered. They were compelled to cede Spain and the Mediterranean islands still in their hands, to surrender their warships, to pay an indemnity of 10,000 talents within 50 years, and to forfeit their independence in affairs of war and foreign policy.

The Second Punic War, by far the greatest struggle in which either power engaged, had thus ended in the complete triumph of Rome. This triumph is not to be explained in the main by any faultiness in the Carthaginians' method of attack. The history of the First Punic War, and that of the Second outside of Italy, prove that the Romans were irresistible on neutral or Carthaginian ground. Carthage could only hope to win by invading Italy and using the enemy's home resources against him. The failure of Hannibal's brilliant endeavour to realize these conditions was not due to any strategical mistakes on his part. It was caused by the indomitable strength of will of the Romans, whose character during this period appears at its best, and to the compactness of their Italian confederacy, which no shock of defeat or strain of war could entirely disintegrate.

It is this spectacle of individual genius overborne by corporate and persevering effort which lends to the Second Punic War its peculiar interest.

The Third Punic War (149–146 B.C.).—The political power of Carthage henceforth remained quite insignificant, but its commerce and material resources revived in the 2nd century with such rapidity as to excite the jealousy of the growing mercantile population of Rome and the alarm of its more timid statesmen. Under the influence of these feelings the conviction—sedulously fostered by Cato the Censor—that "Carthage must be destroyed" overbore the scruples of more clear-sighted statesmen. A *casus belli* was readily found in a formal breach of the treaty, committed by the Carthaginians in 150, when they resisted Masinissa's aggressions by force of arms. A Roman army was dispatched to Africa, and although the Carthaginians consented to make reparation by giving hostages and surrendering their arms, they were goaded into revolt by the further stipulation that they must emigrate to some inland site where they would be debarred from commerce.

By a desperate effort they created new war equipment and prepared their city for a siege (149). The Roman attack for two years completely miscarried, until in 147 the command was given to a young officer who had distinguished himself in the early operations of the war—Scipio Aemilianus, the adopted grandson of the former conqueror of Carthage. Scipio made the blockade stringent by walling off the isthmus on which the town lay and by cutting off its sources of supplies from overseas. His main attack was delivered on the harbour side, where he effected an entrance in the face of a determined and ingenious resistance. The struggle did not cease until he had captured house by house the streets that led up to the citadel.

Of a city population perhaps exceeding a quarter of a million, only 50,000 remained at the final surrender. The survivors were sold into slavery; the city was razed to the ground and its site condemned by solemn imprecations to lie desolate for ever. The territory of Carthage, which had recently been much narrowed by Masinissa's encroachments, was converted into a Roman province under the name of "Africa."

See articles on the chief personages (especially HANNIBAL;

SCIPIO; ROMAN HISTORY; CARTHAGE). *See* also references under "Punic Wars" in the Index. (M. C.; H. H. SD.)

BIBLIOGRAPHY.—*Ancient Authorities: First Punic War:* Polybius, book 1 (based chiefly on Fabius Pictor and the pro-Carthaginian historian Philinus). *Second War:* Polybius, book 3 and fragmentary accounts in books 7–15. On Polybius *see* the indispensable work by F. W. Walbank, *Historical Commentary on Polybius,* vol. i (1957). Livy, books 21–30, gives a continuous narrative, derived partly from Polybius and partly from less reliable Roman annalists. *Third War:* Polybius is fragmentary (books 36–38); Appian's account (*Libyca,* 67–135) derives partly from Polybius and partly from inferior annalistic accounts. The subsidiary authorities add little of importance.
Modern Works: G. De Sanctis, *Storia dei Romani,* iii, 1 and 2 (1916–17) and iv, 3 (1964) is fundamental. U. Kahrstedt, *Geschichte der Karthager von 218–146* (1913), provides detailed source-criticism. *Military Aspects:* J. Kromayer and G. Veith, *Antike Schlachtfelder,* iii, iv (1912–31), *Schlachten-Atlas zur antiken Kriegsgeschichte,* römische Abteilung, i, ii (1922). *General Accounts:* Tenney Frank, B. L. Hallward *et al., Cambridge Ancient History,* vol. vii, ch. 21 and vol. viii, ch. 2–5, 15 (1928–30); H. H. Scullard, *History of the Roman World, 753 to 146 B.C.,* 3rd ed. (1961). *See* also S. Gsell, *Histoire ancienne de l'Afrique du Nord,* vol. i–iv, esp. vol. iii (1913–20). *Specialized Works:* J. H. Thiel, *History of Roman Sea-Power Before the Second Punic War* (1954), *Studies on the History of Roman Sea-Power in Republican Times,* ch. 2 for the Second War (1946); H. H. Scullard, *Scipio Africanus in the Second Punic War* (1930); E. Groag, *Hannibal als Politiker* (1929); F. E. Adcock, "Delenda est Carthago," *Cambridge Historical Journal,* vol. viii, no. 3, pp. 117 ff. (1946); J. Baradez, "Nouvelles recherches sur les ports antiques de Carthage," *Karthago,* ix, pp. 47 ff. (publ. 1960), on the final siege of Carthage. (H. H. SD.)

PUNJAB, the traditional name of a large region in the northwest of the India-Pakistan subcontinent and formerly a province of British India. Punjab signifies "five waters" or "five rivers," and refers to the Jhelum, Chenab, Ravi, Beas, and Sutlej (*qq.v.*) rivers, all of which unite to form the Panjnad (Panchnad) which in turn joins the Indus. The name was applied primarily to the triangle of country, mainly alluvial plains, between the Indus and the Sutlej and stretching northward to the base of the Himalayas.

British influence in the Punjab can be traced as far back as 1803. From 1849 to August 1947 the Punjab formed a British Indian province, the boundaries of which were frequently changed. For a long time the province included the greater part of northwestern India beyond the Jumna (Yamuna) River and Delhi. From its territories the North-West Frontier Province was created to the west of the Indus in 1901 and the Delhi Enclave in the southeast in 1912. In 1937 the province was accorded a large measure of autonomy.

With the partition of the Indian subcontinent in 1947, the province also was divided into two parts, the larger West Punjab, with Bahawalpur, falling to Pakistan and the smaller East Punjab, with Patiala and the numerous east Punjab states, to India. The boundary was drawn by Sir Cyril (later Lord) Radcliffe on the basis of Hindu-Muslim majorities and followed no natural features, cut indiscriminately across rail and road networks, and disrupted the irrigation systems on which the country depended.

Later both India and Pakistan changed the names of their provinces to Punjab. At the time of the 1951 census the area of Pakistani Punjab (excluding Bahawalpur) was 62,245 sq.mi. (161,215 sq.km.); pop. 18,828,015. The area of Indian Punjab was 37,378 sq.mi. (96,809 sq.km.); pop. 12,641,205. In October 1955 the provinces of West Pakistan, including the Punjab, were abolished as administrative units. Thus Punjab, in Pakistan, now remains the name of a region only and not of an administrative area. The Indian Punjab, further reduced in size in 1966 by the creation of the new state of Hariana, forms a constituent state of India and is the only remaining political entity bearing this name. (*See* also PUNJAB [India] below.)

The economic history of the region in modern times has been the struggle to control the waters of the great rivers. In the south the land fades into the Thar (Indian) Desert; on the plains in the north parallel to the Himalayan foothills winter rains from temperate cyclones, known as Western disturbances, give better conditions but in many places sudden irregular floods, causing streams draining the Himalayan slopes to burst their banks, formerly resulted in much damage and consequent famine. The gradual development of great perennial irrigation canals using the Jumna and each of the five rivers of the Punjab was one of the great triumphs of the British period of the 19th–20th century. It permitted much expansion of cultivation and many new settlements. (K. S. Ad.; L. D. S.)

History.—The history of the Punjab has been profoundly influenced by the fact that between Peshawar and Dera Ismail Khan the four frontier passes of the Khyber, Kurram, Tochi, and Gumal serve as gateways from Afghanistan to the Punjab Plains. For this reason it is ethnologically more closely related to Central Asia than to India. Until 1922 no structural remains in India could be assigned with certainty to a period earlier than the 3rd century B.C.; later excavations at Harappa, Mohenjo-Daro and Kot Diji unearthed the remains of a civilization 5,000 years old bearing a general resemblance to that of Elam and Mesopotamia (*see* INDUS CIVILIZATION).

The first migration of which there is any evidence, however, is that of the Indo-European (Aryan) peoples who entered the Punjab in prehistoric times. Centuries later, within historical times, successive waves of other invaders swept through the frontier passes; and all these migrations and invasions added to the heterogeneity of the population. (For languages *see* PANJABI LANGUAGE; LAHNDĀ LANGUAGE.)

The exact limits of the Achaemenian Empire of Darius I cannot be determined, but it included the Indus Valley and probably parts of the Punjab (*see* PERSIAN HISTORY). The earliest date known for certain in Indian history is Alexander the Great's invasion of the Punjab in 326 B.C. (*see* ALEXANDER III [the Great]). His invasion was merely a large-scale raid and his death in 323 prevented consolidation of his power in the Punjab and the Indus Valley. The history of northern India proves that the mountain barrier of the northwestern frontier seldom formed a political boundary, for the kingdoms of the Persians, Mauryas, Greco-Bactrians, Sakas, Parthians, Kushans, and Hephthalites extended from Afghanistan to the Punjab Plains.

The first Muslims to penetrate into northern India were the Arabs who, in A.D. 712, extended their power to the Lower Punjab; but the Muslim conquest of the Punjab was the work of Mahmud of Ghazni (*q.v.*, 971–1030). The Punjab remained in Ghaznevid hands until Mahmud's descendants were expelled by Mohammed of Ghor in 1186. It formed part of the sultanate of Delhi from 1206 until Babur's victory at Panipat in 1526 paved the way for the foundation of the Mughal Empire, of which the Punjab remained a part until the first half of the 18th century.

The religious intolerance of the Mughal emperors after the death of Akbar in 1605 led to the growth of Sikh political power in the Punjab and transformed a religious sect, founded by Guru Nanak in the second half of the 15th century, into a military organization animated with undying hatred toward Muslims. The weakness of the emperors after Aurangzeb facilitated the growth of Maratha power. By 1758 Maratha armies had overrun most of northern India as far as Peshawar. They were gradually driven southward by the Afghans under Ahmad Shah Durrani to Panipat, where they were routed with enormous losses on Jan. 14, 1761. After the death of Ahmad Shah the various Sikh groups or *misls* began to consolidate their power in the Punjab. The most important of these *misls* were the Bhangis of Gujrat, Sialkot, Lahore, and Amritsar; the Ahluwalias of Kapurthala, Jullundur, and Hoshiarpur; and the Kanahyas of Gurdaspur.

From 1790 onward, Ranjit Singh, the head of the Sukarchakia *misl*, rose to prominence as leader of the Sikh resistance to the Afghan ruler Zaman Shah. His attempt to establish his authority over his coreligionists, the cis-Sutlejian Sikhs, brought him into contact with the British, and an agreement was formed in 1809 by which the Sikh ruler accepted the Sutlej as his frontier. From that date his power increased rapidly. Between 1813 and 1821 he annexed Attock, Kashmir, Dera Ghazi Khan, and Dera Ismail Khan.

After the death of Ranjit Singh in 1839 the Punjab became the scene of widespread lawlessness, and power passed to the army of the Sikh Khalsa organization. Suspecting the British of contemplating annexation and eager for war, the Sikhs in 1845 in-

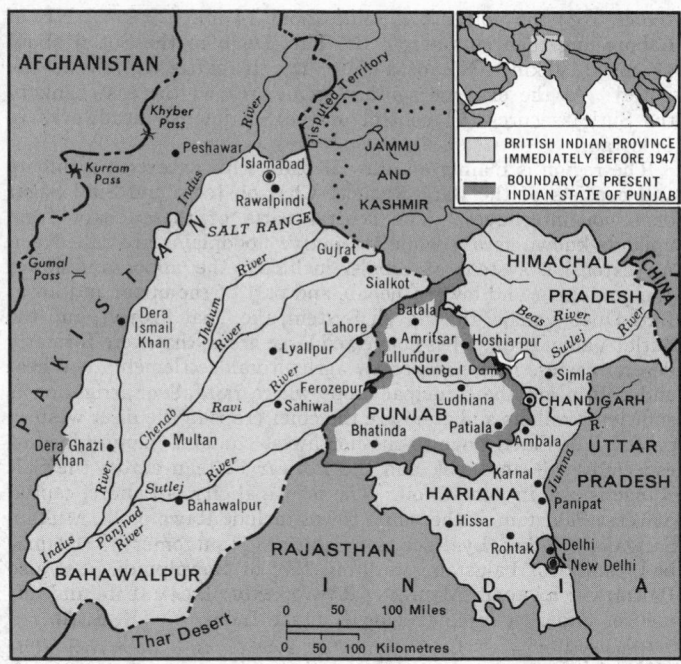

EXTENT OF PUNJAB AREAS OF INDIA AND PAKISTAN

vaded British territory but were defeated in desperate struggles at Mudki (Moodkee), Ferozeshah, Aliwal, and Sobraon. The terms of the treaty of 1846 did not prove acceptable to the Sikhs, and war again broke out in 1848. After the battles of Chillianwala and Gujrat the Punjab was annexed to British India on April 2, 1849. (*See also* SIKH WARS.)

The annexation of the Punjab brought the government of India into closer contact with the Pathan tribes of the northwestern frontier. The tribes remained under the control of the Punjab government until the creation of the North-West Frontier Province in 1901.

After World War I communal relations in the province were embittered, but far more serious than communal strife were the political disturbances culminating in the Jallianwalla Bagh incident of 1919. (For the Punjab Rebellion of 1919 *see* INDIA-PAKISTAN, SUBCONTINENT OF: *History*.)

In 1921 the Punjab was raised to the status of a governor's province. From 1922 until the passing of the Sikh Shrines Act, 1925, the peace was disturbed by the Akali Sikhs who wished to devote the revenues of certain shrines and temples to the spiritual benefit of the Sikh community. Throughout the interwar period the Punjab passed through the same phase of political ferment as the rest of India, with a gradual transfer of power from British hands. It became an autonomous province in 1937. With the partition of the Punjab between India and Pakistan (1947) the boundary was fixed roughly along the line of the Sutlej up to beyond Ferozepur and then due north between Lahore and Amritsar to the boundary of Jammu and Kashmir along the line of the Ravi and the Ujh.

The immediate result was an outbreak of violence with much loss of life followed by a great mass movement of population. Partition also led to a dispute between the two countries over the division of the waters of the Punjab rivers (for the particulars of which *see* PAKISTAN: *History*). The western section of the Punjab was a province of Pakistan until 1955 and was then merged in the newly created province of West Pakistan. For the history of the eastern sector, which, following Sikh agitation, was further partitioned in 1966 into the states Punjab and Hariana, *see* PUNJAB (India); HARIANA. (C. C. D.; X.)

PUNJAB (Pakistan).—This area of West Pakistan is bounded on the north by the outer edge of the Himalayan foothills, northwest by the Northwest Frontier region, southwest by Baluchistan, and south and southeast by Sind and the Indian state of Rajasthan. The boundary with India to the east follows the Ujh and Ravi rivers from the north to a point about 14 mi. (22 km.) NE of Lahore and then cuts across the Bari Doab to the Sutlej about 12 mi. (19 km.) NE of Ferozepur; thereafter it follows the Sutlej. At the extreme south a small area on the east bank of the Sutlej secures the control of the Sulaimanke headworks to Pakistan.

The region is mainly an alluvial plain with an extreme climate and consists of the Bari, Rechna, Chaj or Jech, and Sind Sagar doabs or interfluves. The central parts of these doabs form uplands known as *bar* while the active floodplains are called *bet*. An extensive system of canals, including the upper and lower Jhelum, upper and lower Chenab, and part of the upper and lower Bari Doab Canals, the Haveli System, the Thal Project, and the Sutlej Valley Project has converted large areas, that were formerly desert wastes, into prosperous agricultural settlements. Wheat and cotton are the principal crops where rainfall or irrigation is sufficient; millets and gram are the chief crops in the drier western parts. The Salt Range to the northwest contains many minerals, especially salt and coal, and the Potwar Plateau across the Salt Range is rich in mineral oil. The principal city is Lahore, capital of West Pakistan. Other chief towns include Rawalpindi, Multan, Sargodha, Sialkot, Lyallpur, and Sahiwal (Montgomery). Islamabad, capital of Pakistan, lies 9 mi. NW of Rawalpindi. *See also* PAKISTAN; LAHORE; MULTAN; RAWALPINDI; ISLAMABAD; and references under "Punjab (region)" in the Index. (K. S. AD.)

BIBLIOGRAPHY.—C. L. Chopra, *The Panjab as a Sovereign State* (1928); J. D. Cunningham, *History of the Sikhs*, rev. ed. (1919); M. L. Darling, *The Punjab Peasant in Prosperity and Debt* (1925); C. C. Davies, *The Problem of the North-West Frontier* (1932); H. R. Gupta, *Studies in Later Mughal History of the Punjab, 1707–1793* (1944); H. A. Rose, *A Glossary of the Tribes and Castes of the Punjab and North-West Frontier*, 3 vol. (1911–19); G. S. Chhabra, *The Advanced Study in History of the Punjab*, 2 vol. (1960).

PUNJAB (India), a constituent state of the Republic of India, was formed in 1966 when the former Punjab (India) state was partitioned on a linguistic basis into the two states of Punjab and Hariana, with certain areas of the former state being simultaneously transferred to Himachal Pradesh. The new Punjab state thus formed is a predominantly Panjabi-speaking Sikh area. Hariana is a predominantly Hindi-speaking area (*see* also below). The name Punjab ("five rivers") is now a misnomer; only the Beas (Bias) is wholly in the state together with the upper Sutlej. (*See* also PUNJAB above.) The state has an area of 19,403 sq.mi. (50,255 sq.km.), and though one of the smaller states of India, is densely populated. Pop. (1961) 11,135,100.

It is bordered on the west by West Pakistan, north by Jammu and Kashmir, east by Himachal Pradesh and Hariana, and south by Hariana and Rajasthan. The city of Chandigarh (*q.v.*) was, in the late 1960s, the capital of Punjab and Hariana states and of the Union Territory of Chandigarh.

Physical Features.—Punjab State stretches westward from the Ghaggar (Yamuna) River, which is the boundary with Hariana, across the Sutlej to embrace the doab or land between the Sutlej and Beas rivers (Bist-Jullundur Doab) and part of the Bari Doab between the Beas and Ravi. In the west the boundary with West Pakistan follows the Ravi River to a point above Lahore, then across the open plain southward to Ferozepur on the Sutlej after it has been joined by the Beas.

Because of their distance from the sea and the northerly situation, the plains of Punjab have a markedly continental climate with extremes of heat and cold. From October to March is the cool season, with warm, sunny days and cold nights. Frosts are frequent in January, and from January to March there is a small but useful cyclonic rainfall. From March onward there is a rapid rise in temperature; the atmosphere is dry and afternoon temperatures may reach 52° C (120° F). The rains break toward the end of June and some lowering of temperature results, but amounts of rain are small. The maximum total is reached near the hills (about 50 in. [1,270 mm.]), but on the plains there is only enough for a precarious harvest of millets and other dry-zone crops, except where irrigation water is available.

Little natural vegetation remains—scrub on uncultivated land and the foothills. Shade trees have been encouraged near the canals; these help to break up the otherwise monotonous sweep of the plains and to mitigate the effects of dust storms.

(L. D. S.; X.)

History.—After the partition of the old Punjab province (*see* PUNJAB) in 1947 the resettlement of refugees presented a grave problem: thousands of acres were unirrigated, schools remained closed, communications were disrupted, and there was constant friction along the new frontier. A serious water-supply wrangle and other disputes with Pakistan resulted from the Radcliffe boundary award which, being based inevitably on the preponderance of Hindus or Muslims in the areas concerned, disrupted such unitary services as canal irrigation, electric power transmission, and railways. In May 1948 India decided as a temporary measure to continue the supply of water from its side of the boundary to prevent famine in Western Punjab and Bahawalpur. It was not until February 1963 that the Bhakra Dam on the Sutlej River was completed. (For the Punjab rivers dispute *see* PAKISTAN: *History*.) In 1955 the Sikhs, led by Master Tara Singh, president of the Akali Dal, began to agitate for a Panjabi-speaking state. Tara Singh's activities led to his arrest in May 1960, but in order to promote a peaceful solution he and 6,500 Akali prisoners were released in January 1961. The failure to reach a settlement led Tara Singh in August to begin a fast unto death, which ended when a commission was appointed to inquire into Sikh grievances. The breakdown of negotiations produced fresh agitation, interrupted temporarily because of the Chinese attack in the autumn of 1962. In March 1966 the Congress Party suddenly announced that a separate Panjabi-speaking state would be created in Punjab. The new Punjab State came into existence on Nov. 1, 1966, simultaneously with the new Hariana State. (C. C. D.; X.)

Population, Administration, and Social Conditions.— The population of Punjab according to the 1961 census was 11,135,100. The chief cities and towns with their populations (1961 census) are: Amritsar (384,287); Ludhiana (244,032); Jullundur (265,030); Patiala (125,234); Bhatinda (52,253); Batala (51,300); Hoshiarpur (50,739).

There are 11 districts in the state: Gurdaspur, Amritsar, Bhatinda, Jullundur, Hoshiarpur, Ferozepur, Ludhiana, Kapurthala, Sangrur, Rupar, and Patiala.

The 1961 census recorded about 33% of the male and 14% of the female population as literate. Education is free up to seventh class in all institutions throughout the state, up to eighth class in some districts, and up to ninth class in flood-affected areas; it is compulsory for children aged 6 to 11 in more than 12,043 towns and villages. There are more than 8,720 educational institutions in the state.

Under the government's health program, which aims at providing medical relief for every village within a radius of five miles, health centres which offer institutional domiciliary, maternity, child welfare, and school health services have been established in rural areas. There are many hospitals and dispensaries, and medical care is also provided through panel doctors to factory workers and their families in the industrial centres under the employees' state insurance scheme, which covers the risks of sickness, maternity, and employment injury. Welfare of tribal and other backward classes is provided through scholarships, subsidies for the construction of houses, community centres, technical education, and loans to assist establishment in trades. Welfare centres offer recreational and educational facilities to industrial workers. The state social welfare board provides state homes and district shelters for rescued women and men discharged from noncorrectional institutions, craft-training centres for women, and recreation centres for children. (S. CH.; S. B. L. N.; O. P. B.)

The Economy.—The economy of the state is based on agriculture. So long as the farmers relied on rainfall supplemented by a little irrigation from shallow wells only dry-zone crops—mainly millet—were possible and much fodder had to be grown to keep cattle alive. Good crops were possible only in years of ample rainfall. Irrigation canals were gradually developed during the British period. Main canal systems include the Sirhind Canal and Bhakra Nangal Canal tapping the Sutlej and the Upper Bari Doab Canal leaving the Ravi near Madhopur. Other great systems lie in what is now Pakistan. On the Sutlej the Ferozepur Dam is in India, but much of the land it formerly irrigated is in West Pakistan. Irrigation permitted a great expansion in production of wheat, barley, and oilseeds with some rice and maize (corn) but especially (as a cash crop) of fine-quality cotton (Punjab-American), fodder, and some sugarcane. The state is one of the largest producers of wheat and grain in India; its annual cotton production amounts to one-fifth of the country's output. Since partition India has pushed ahead with river works, notably the Bhakra-Nangal dam system on the Sutlej, the largest multipurpose project in Asia, designed to irrigate 3,600,000 ac. (1,500,000 ha.). The Nangal headworks were completed in 1954. There are no valuable mineral sources and hardly any coal.

The industrial growth of Punjab dates mainly from the early 1950s. Large-scale industries are the manufacture of cotton and woolen textiles, hosiery, bicycles, and sugar refining. Others include the manufacture of agricultural implements, diesel engines, industrial machinery, and the rerolling of ferrous materials.

The state is served by the Northern Railway with headquarters at Delhi, where it is connected with the other lines of the Indian railway system. A section of the line runs north and northwest through Ludhiana and Amritsar and links up with the Pakistan Western Railway of West Pakistan. Amritsar is linked by air with Delhi.

With partition in 1947 the former capital, Lahore, went to Pakistan, so India seized the opportunity of designing and building a new state capital at Chandigarh, on the rail and road route to the old hot-weather capital of India (Simla) and situated on ground high enough to escape the worst heat of summer. It was inaugurated in 1953 and is also the site of Panjab University. With the reorganization of Punjab in November 1966, Chandigarh became a Union Territory but it is still the seat of the Punjab government.

The main towns of Punjab include Amritsar (*q.v.*), sacred city of the Sikhs; Ludhiana (*q.v.*), with hosiery mills; and Patiala, serving the expanding development in the south, the headquarters of Punjabi University (founded 1962).   (L. D. S.; O. P. B.)

PUNO, a southern sierra department of Peru, bounded north by Madre de Dios, west by Cuzco, Arequipa and Moquegua, south by Tacna, and east by Bolivia. Pop. (1961) 727,309. Area 26,-018 sq.mi. (67,387 sq.km.). The northern portion of the department was removed in 1912 to form a section of the department of Madre de Dios. Puno includes most of the shore of Lake Titicaca, the high plateau on which the lake stands, and the mountains surrounding it on the north, east, and west. Vilcanota Knot, on the border of Puno and Cuzco, constitutes the watershed dividing the enclosed lacustrine basin of Titicaca from the Amazon basin. The department is the source of the headwaters of the Amazon, notably the Tambopata and Inambari, affluents of the Madre de Dios.

Crops cultivated in the region are limited to those that mature in a cold climate: chiefly potatoes, barley, and other hardy cereals. Cattle and sheep are bred there; wool, from both sheep and alpaca, is exported. The department contains one of the most important auriferous regions of the world. In addition to silver and gold which have been worked extensively, coal, salt, copper, antimony, cinnabar, arsenic, quicksilver, tin, marble, zinc, cobalt, and petroleum are found. The manufacture of pottery and woolen textiles are also important industries.

The city of Puno, pop. (1961) 24,459, capital of the department and province of Puno, lies at an elevation of more than 12,-600 ft. (3,840 m.) above sea level, on the northwest shore of Lake Titicaca: it is the seat of a bishopric and a superior court. Puno is connected by the Southern Railway with both Cuzco and the Pacific port of Mollendo and with La Paz, Bolivia, by steamer across Titicaca and railway. Motor roads connect with Cuzco, Arequipa, and Guaqui and northeastward to Sandia and Ollachea. Puno is 171 mi. (275 km.) from La Paz, 218 mi. (350 km.) from Arequipa, and 820 mi. (1,320 km.) from Lima.   (J. L. Tr.)

PUNTA ARENAS, with the exception of Ushuaia, Tierra del Fuego, the southernmost city of the world, capital of Magallanes province and department, Chile. Pop. (est. 1966) 67,600. The city, located on the Strait of Magellan, was founded in 1849 by Col. José de los Santos Mardones. Punta Arenas' role as a

port-of-call and coaling station waned after the opening of the Panama Canal and fuel oil became significant in maritime movement; nevertheless, a flourishing export trade in wool and mutton, primarily with the British Isles, continues. Punta Arenas supports slaughterhouses, tallow works and wool exporting houses. The administrative and supply activities of the national petroleum company that operates in oil fields on Tierra del Fuego, the recreation requirements of its employees, the attractions of the free port to Chilean consumers and the maintenance of naval, air, and army garrisons are contributing factors to the city's growth in the 20th century. Frame and corrugated metal construction predominates among the city's buildings. Surface and air communication with the north and Tierra del Fuego is good. Some lignite and placer gold are mined nearby. From 1927 to 1937 the city was called Magallanes. Punta Arenas means "sandy point."   (J. T.)

PUNTA DEL ESTE, a beach resort on the Atlantic coast of Uruguay, about 100 mi. (161 km.) E of Montevideo by road. Its location at the tip of a peninsula provides an ocean surf beach (*playa brava*) on the eastern side and a protected beach (*playa mansa*) on the western side. Its delightfully breezy summers (mean temperature of warmest month, 72° F [22° C]) originally attracted families from Buenos Aires and Montevideo, who built the beach-side chalets that give to Punta del Este its distinctive charm.

Early in World War II a naval engagement took place near the coast of Punta del Este. The German pocket battleship "Admiral Graf Spee" and a British cruiser squadron fought a battle the result of which was the scuttling of the German craft. In recent years new hotels, casinos, and the Cantegril Country Club, scene of international film festivals, have made Punta del Este a leading playground of South America.

The resort achieved international prominence as the locale of the 1961 meeting of the Inter-American Economic and Social Council, which proclaimed the Alliance for Progress; of the 1962 Inter-American Foreign Ministers Conference, which suspended Cuba from membership in the Organization of American States; and of the 1967 meeting of the presidents of the American republics.   (E. M. V.)

PUNTARENAS or Punta Arenas ("sandy point"), a seaport on the Gulf of Nicoya on the Pacific coast of Costa Rica. Pop. (1963) 19,582. In colonial times the city's chief function was to link Costa Rican commerce with Panama and South America. A royal order of 1814 brought the first attempt to improve the harbour facilities: a cart road from San José was opened in the 1840s. Most Costa Rican coffee went to Europe around Cape Horn, and Puntarenas was the shipping centre. Now connected with San José by the Pacific railway, it is an increasingly important port for exporting bananas as well as coffee. There is a considerable coastal trade in rice, corn and beans. Canning and freezing fish and ship repairing are relatively new industries in Puntarenas.

Most imports to Costa Rica from the west coast of the U.S. pass through this city. The city is the capital of Puntarenas province (area 4,247 sq.mi. [11,000 sq.km.]; pop. [1963] 156,508), the largest of Costa Rica's seven provinces. The province skirts the Pacific side of Costa Rica from the Gulf of Nicoya to the Republic of Panama, the two extremes being connected by a long, narrow coastal strip. It includes the Osa Peninsula, the extreme southern tip of the Nicoya Peninsula, and the ports of Quepos and Golfito.

The population of Puntarenas province was the fastest growing in Costa Rica by the 1960s. Much of this was due to greatly increased activity in the banana industry as new areas opened on the Pacific coast.   (T. L. K.)

PUPIENUS MAXIMUS, MARCUS CLODIUS: see Maximus.

PUPIN, MICHAEL IDVORSKY (1858–1935), U.S. physicist, invented devices that are basic in wire communication over long distances (as in telephone and telegraph systems). He was born in Idvor, Banat, Hung. (now in Yugoslavia), Oct. 4, 1858, the son of illiterate parents who took a deep interest in and encouraged his formal education. His early schooling took place in Idvor and at Pancevo, a nearby town where he received his first introduction to the elements of physical science. Pupin emigrated to the United States, arriving in New York, penniless, in March 1874.

He enrolled at Columbia University in 1879, and was graduated in 1883, with an A.B. degree. The first to be awarded the John Tyndall Fellowship (1886–88), he later studied physics and mathematics at Cambridge University and under Hermann von Helmholtz at the University of Berlin (Ph.D., 1889).

In 1890 Pupin returned to Columbia University, having received an appointment as instructor in mathematical physics; he was named adjunct professor of mechanics in 1892, and was made full professor of electromechanics there in 1901; later he was appointed director of the Phoenix Research Laboratories. In 1931 he was retired.

By means of inductance coils placed at predetermined intervals of the transmitting wire, he greatly extended the range of long-distance telephony, particularly over telephone cables. The patent for this invention was acquired in 1901 by the Bell Telephone Company and by German telephone interests. He made several other inventions in electrical wave propagation, electrical resonance and multiplex telegraphy. He discovered secondary X-ray radiation in 1896 and invented in the same year means for short exposure X-ray photography by the interposition of a fluorescent screen.

Pupin wrote the autobiographical *From Immigrant to Inventor* (1923). He died in New York City, March 12, 1935.

See D. Markey, *Explorer of Sound: Michael Pupin* (1964).

PUPPETRY is, broadly, the conveying of a concept to an audience through the manipulation (*i.e.*, movement by hand, directly or indirectly) of inanimate objects. A limited but more common understanding of the term has reference to small models of the human form which are used to present plays. (The word puppet is derived from the Latin *pupa*, is cognate to the French *poupée*, and is the modern variant of the Middle English word poppet—each of which can mean "doll.") Although the limited definition is satisfactory for most forms of puppetry it does not recognize the gloved hands of Yves Joly of France or the 10-to-30-ft. puppets of Remo Bufano of the United States. These variations in size, material, and form suggest that almost anything can be used for puppetry. It is the way the objects are manipulated (usually in a special setting, and commonly with the addition of voices) that makes them lifelike and causes the audience to react.

Following are the principal divisions and subdivisions of this article:

KINDS OF PUPPETS

In their more conventional forms, puppets are operated from above, below, or behind with rods or strings, or by direct hand contact. They are either three-dimensional or two-dimensional and are seen with light directly on them or as shadows. It is these characteristics which divide puppets into various categories.

Hand Puppets.—Hand puppets are the simplest to make and operate. In their basic form they consist of a simple covering for the hand of the operator: two arms and a head. Commonly the index finger extends into the neck and head of the puppet, the thumb into one arm, and the second finger into the other arm. Sometimes the hand covering has accessories; *e.g.*, a ball to represent the head or a handkerchief to provide the body. The covering material may be any fabric, although one which holds the form of the puppet's body without collapsing is usually preferable. The fabric pattern should enhance, not detract from, body form.

Padding may be added to the body and extensions made on the neck and arms to increase the size of the puppet; however, any such gain in size is ultimately limited by the size of the puppeteer's hand. Another variation may be achieved by sewing on arms which appear to be bent, but with the hands positioned at the normal extension of the fingers of the operator; this heightens the illusion of the human form without sacrifice of control such as occurs when cumbersome length is added to the puppet's extremities. Some hand puppeteers add stuffed legs to the stuffed body of the male puppet; the puppet must then be equipped with a sleeve extending below the level of the stage front. These variations, like all features of puppet design, are a matter of the puppeteer's individual opinion as to what is needed for successful performance.

The head of the puppet, as well as the hands, can be carved from wood or a foam plastic such as Styrofoam, cast in plastic wood, fibreglass, Celastic, or papier-mâché, modeled from papier-mâché, clay, or a plastic or sewn from cloth such as felt, muslin, or jersey. The ingenuity of the designer makes almost any material possible. Even the end of a sock may be stuffed, tied off, and painted or embroidered to represent a head. The basic requirements for heads and hands are that they be relatively light and resist damage from rough handling.

While some hand puppets have been constructed with bodily proportions resembling those of human beings, the heads usually are considerably outsize compared with the body and the arms are quite foreshortened. Although a real person reacts with his whole body, in a hand puppet the head necessarily becomes the major indicator and, consequently, is exaggerated. Certain elements—nose, mouth, eyes, or hair—are often abstracted and heightened. Visibility is also a factor in the matter of exaggeration or abstraction. Sometimes the puppeteer may install a movable mouth, eyes that close, or ears that wiggle. While adding the interest of action and close-up expression, the mechanics and synchronization of these elements may also prove distracting and complicating.

Many puppeteers consider the hand puppet to be the ideal form, since the most delicate control can be maintained directly through the hands and fingers. The puppet is exceedingly responsive: unencumbered by levers or strings, it moves either rapidly or slowly, depending on the requirements of the performance. The Punch-and-Judy show, with its swift strikes and slow "sneaking up," suggests the extremes of operation. In addition, the hand puppet can pick up and handle properties, since it has the strength of the hand of the operator. In other puppets, where the puppeteer is at a mechanical remove, such operations are sometimes clumsy, if not impossible.

There are, however, limitations other than the size factor (*see* above). One is the requirement that the hand puppet must almost always have its lower end concealed behind the lower edge of the stage. Another is the limitation on things which can be done on the floor, since, with the exception of the front ledge of the stage, or playboard, there is actually no floor. The essential simplicity of hand puppetry, however, makes it one of the most popular forms of the art.

String Puppets (Marionettes).—Just as hand puppets are usually operated from below, string puppets, or marionettes, are usually operated from above. Thus, while the hand puppet has a space (normally concealed) below it to house the operator, the string puppet needs a space above the stage.

Javanese shadow puppet

Javanese puppet theatre with operator, orchestra and flat, wooden puppets

Production of "Tea and Hashish" by the Braunschweig Marionette theatre; Harro Siegel, director

"The Glowing Bird" by Tatterman Marionettes; puppets by Roy Patton

Chinese shadow puppets

A four-foot Japanese Bunraku puppet operated by Yoshida Bungoro

TRADITIONAL ORIENTAL PUPPETS AND MODERN MARIONETTE PRODUCTIONS

BY COURTESY OF (TOP LEFT, TOP RIGHT, BOTTOM LEFT) MARJORIE B. MCPHARLIN, (CENTRE LEFT) DETROIT INSTITUTE OF ARTS, (CENTRE RIGHT) WILLIAM I. DUNCAN, (BOTTOM RIGHT) KINGSLAND MARIONETTE COLLECTION; PHOTOGRAPHS, (TOP LEFT, BOTTOM LEFT) LAURA GILPIN

PLATE II   PUPPETRY

Harlequin and Columbine by Richard Teschner, Vienna, Aus.

Pathelin from "Pierre Pathelin." Teatro del Nahual, Mexico city; Roberto Lago, director

Sicilian knight in armour from Papa Manteo's company, New York city

Rod puppet serpents from a Hopi Indian snake dance

Victorian English hand puppet theatre of about 1870, with seven characters and many scenes

Scene from "The Man, the Fish and the Spirit" by the Lanchester Marionettes. Carving by Frank Rose

Robinson Crusoe by Tony Sarg

PUPPETS OF EUROPE AND AMERICA

BY COURTESY OF (TOP LEFT, CENTRE RIGHT) DETROIT INSTITUTE OF ARTS, (TOP CENTRE) TEATRO DEL NAHUAL, PHOTO BY RICARDO RAZETTI, (TOP RIGHT) MARJORIE B. MCPHARLIN, (BOTTOM LEFT) LANCHESTER MARIONETTES, (BOTTOM RIGHT) KINGSLAND MARIONETTE COLLECTION

Indian puppet operated by Frank Paris, night club entertainer

Scene from Ralph Chessé's production of "The Emperor Jones." Scenery by Blanding Sloan

Kukla and Ollie from Burr Tillstrom's "Kukla, Fran and Ollie"

Architectural stage used by Marjorie Batchelder in her production of Maeterlinck's "The Death of Tintagiles"

Puppets of Josef Skupa's marionette theatre, Prague, Czech.

"La Misère" by S. Walleshausen. G. Blattner's theatre, Arc-en-Ciel, Paris

Scene from a play by Karel Čapek. Puppets and scenery by Jan Malík, Prague

20TH CENTURY PUPPETS AND PUPPET DRAMAS

PLATE IV

PUPPETRY

Jack Frost from "The Flower Ballet." Hogarth puppets, Eng.

Table puppet made by an 11-year-old boy from wood scraps

Puppets made of roots by Basil Milovsoroff

Children working puppets on a table stage

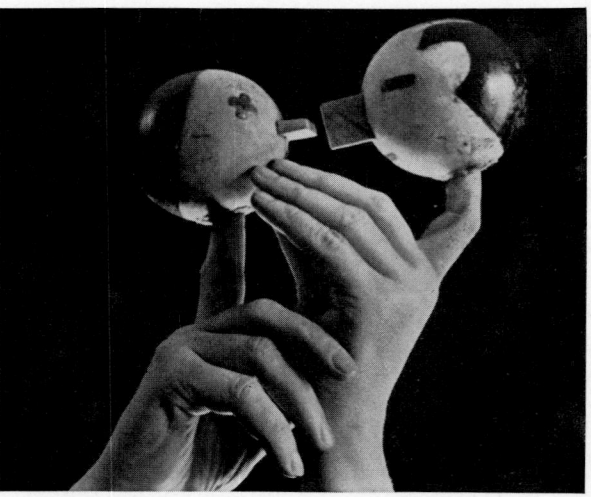

Ball puppets by Sergei Obraztsov. State Central Puppet theatre, Moscow, U.S.S.R.

Scene from "The Tale of Timothy T." Shadows by David Orcutt, Vancouver, B.C.

Space creatures from "The Runaway Rocket." By George Latshaw, Akron, O.

UNUSUAL PUPPETS OF VARIOUS MATERIALS

BY COURTESY OF (TOP LEFT) HOGARTH PUPPETS, (TOP CENTRE) HANK SCHRIEBER, (TOP RIGHT) BASIL MILOVSOROFF, PHOTO BY JOHN A. CLARK, (CENTRE LEFT) HARPER AND BROTHERS; FROM BATCHELDER AND COMER, "PUPPETS AND PLAYS," PHOTO BY LAURA GILPIN, (CENTRE RIGHT) DETROIT INSTITUTE OF ARTS, (BOTTOM LEFT) DAVID ORCUTT, (BOTTOM RIGHT) GEORGE LATSHAW

It is usually thought that a marionette is one thing and a puppet another. Actually, the names are often used interchangeably. In current usage the word marionette indicates a string-operated figure belonging to a subclass of puppets. The origin of the term is just as cloudy as are other aspects of the beginnings of this art. A commonly accepted explanation is that such figures were used in Nativity scenes in churches, the one of Mary being called *maryonete* (Middle French, "little Mary"). Another explanation connects the term with the Italian *morio,* which means "buffoon" or "fool."

While the hand puppet usually uses the operator's hand for the body, the body of the string puppet must be constructed. Customarily it is made of wood with cloth, leather, or pin hinges; but, as with the hand puppet, the materials are limited only by the designer's imagination. Eric Bramall of Wales, for instance, performed a string-puppet ballet with puppets that were chiffon handkerchiefs tied at the corner with a string.

Soft woods such as pine or cedar, any of a number of plastics, or stuffed fabric can be used for making the body of the string puppet. It should be noted that the string puppet's movements are the result of the string acting against the force of gravity. If the materials are either too light or too heavy the resultant action will appear unnatural, at least in the case of puppets designed to represent human beings. As is the case with most constructions which are less than life-size, compensation is made in the costuming to assure freedom of motion; thus, a jersey cloth might be substituted for a heavy damask or a cotton batiste for a broadcloth. Cut of the fabric and means of mounting also affect mobility.

The head, hands, and feet are carved or cast much as for the hand puppet. Although somewhat smaller in proportion to the body than those of the hand puppet, they are nevertheless usually exaggerated.

Stringing the puppet can be as simple or as complex as the designer wishes. One string from the top of the head suffices to keep the puppet upright and allows rather aimless movement. Normal stringing would include one string for each side of the head, one on each shoulder for major support, one for each arm or hand, one for each leg, and one at the middle of the back. Elaborations include strings at the back of the feet, a string between the hands so they may be brought together, double stringing of the lower arm, a string to the centre front, double stringing of the legs, and auxiliary strings for the head if movements of the eyes and mouth are involved. These are for figures that resemble people; other forms require special variations. The string used for puppet manipulation is most often a black fishline, although fine wire, clear nylon filament, or other stranding may be employed. The ultimate intent, as in all of puppetry, is to minimize the intrusion of the operator.

The strings go to an arrangement of sticks, called the controller or control, which is held above the puppet. Its design varies with the number of strings involved, the complexity of action, and the personal preferences of the designer or operator. In the United States a horizontal ("airplane") control is most common; a vertical control is widely used in England. Trick string puppets, which became popular in the 19th century, had elaborate controls which could be moved apart and might require two or three operators. Most marionette controls are in two sections, one being a separable control for the leg strings.

The puppeteer's freedom of action above the stage floor and the almost unlimited size and shape of marionettes are among the advantages of this form. The marionette can seem to defy gravity —which is helpful in creating an airy or supernatural effect. The string puppet can also have legs without a large support. On the other hand, quick and positive action is less easy to accomplish. In downward and horizontal action the string puppet has only its own weight or momentum. While the hand puppet must be operated without a floor, the string puppet must be operated without a ceiling—which makes passing through arches somewhat difficult. Although the string puppet most often appears on a stage above which the operator is concealed, it is not uncommon to see the operator (*e.g.,* a nightclub entertainer) in full view and using very short strings; in these instances he is dressed in subdued colours and depends on the attention-getting power of the puppet to make him "invisible."

Rod Puppets.—Puppets supported on rods are, in effect, marionettes operated from below. As Marjorie Batchelder McPharlin has pointed out, rod puppets permit a degree of control unmatched in other puppets, where the operator is farther removed. Through extension of the rods, larger puppets are possible than is the case with hand puppets, but certain problems of control can develop in the more elaborate versions.

As in hand puppetry the operating space is located below the stage. The bottom of the stage may be completely open, which allows free movement in three dimensions; or it may be constructed with slots, in which case the puppet is equipped with a small disk at its base, which allows the puppet to be left in position without dropping through the slot. On a slotted stage there usually are points where the puppets can be removed from the track, as well as a slot running from front to back down the centre of the stage. Where the audience seating is elevated or numbers of puppets are to remain stationary, this type of construction is almost essential.

Materials for making three-dimensional rod puppets are much the same as for other puppets with the exception of the central supporting member, which is a rod of wood or steel. The rod extends below the performing level and provides a grip for the operator. In southeastern Asia, China, India, and the eastern Mediterranean countries rod puppets are often found in two-dimensional or shadow form. (*See* SHADOW PLAY.) Here the materials may be animal hides which have been elaborately cut and coloured and have supporting members of horn or bamboo. While the problems of production may vary slightly, the movement and operation remains much the same.

With the string puppet, overall support is maintained with the shoulder strings; for the rod puppet this is provided by the central rod. For more elaborate control additional rods are used; *e.g.,* one for each hand and one for the head. Still greater control can be achieved through leg rods and a spring joint with a control rod to allow the puppet to bend at the waist.

A minor variant of the rod puppet is the simple jointed puppet with a rod extending from its back at right angles to the puppet's perpendicular. This puppet can be shown as a shadow or on a stage with the operator in plain view of the audience. The rod merely avoids visual distraction by removing the hand of the operator from the immediate proximity of the puppet.

The so-called paper theatres, popular primarily in England and continental Europe during the 19th and early 20th centuries, utilized a cardboard strip or a rod extending out from the side of the stage. The characters, made of cardboard, could be moved back and forth to act out scenes from plays. The action was, obviously, limited.

Composite Types.—While rod puppets are often found in the "pure" form, they are most often combined with other types to achieve greater flexibility or sensitivity. Or perhaps the other forms adopt the rod for the same reason. This results in hand-and-rod puppets, string-and-rod puppets, or a hand-rod-string combination. For example, to obtain closer control of balance of the rod puppet the central control is shortened so as to place the hand of the operator up inside the body, with fingers extending into the arms. Or one hand grips the central control within the body and the arms are manipulated by rods. In some instances, such as the Japanese *bunraku,* all the rods are shortened and the operator manipulates the rods and strings inside the puppet while he stands in full view of the audience. The 10-ft. puppets of Remo Bufano for the 1932 production of *Oedipus* in New York City were operated with rods supporting the central weight from below while other operators stood above the stage on a scaffold and manipulated the heads and arms by means of strings. The puppets of Liège, Belgium, utilize a single rod from the top of the head; essentially the same form is found in the puppets of Sicily, where another rod is added for the sword arm and a string or rope controls the shield arm. The puppets of the Kungsholm opera theatre in Chicago, as well as those of Richard Teschner of Germany, employ the central control, rods for the arms, and strings inside the puppet for leg and head movement as well as for bending to the front or back. George Latshaw's giant puppets for *Billy the Kid,* performed with the Detroit Symphony in 1959, required one to three persons to control the body, arms, and legs with both internal and external rods; the operators were in full view of the audience.

ILLUSION AND ARTISTRY

Puppets inhabit a wonderful world of their own. Once the performance starts, just as in the theatre of human performers the audience is asked to suspend disbelief. Within this framework the artist performs through the puppet. Normal concepts of space and shape appear to be altered as concentration is fixed upon the puppet. The dancing finger puppets of Herb Scheffel, where the index and middle fingers form the legs, seemingly increased in size even though they were nothing but pieces of fabric and wood fastened to a man's hand. Eighteen-inch marionettes of the Salzburg Marionette Theatre become full-sized performers on an operatic stage. Abstract shapes forming and reforming themselves, animals, flowers, trees, rocks, buildings—all can come to life in a puppet show. The human form can be distorted to suggest personality characteristics in a way that is impossible on the live stage. Music, colour, and special effects can be utilized to inspire, instruct, or amuse. The flexibility of the puppet theatre is almost without limit. The breadth of its possibilities is, however, often ignored and the puppets used only to present things in miniature which could more successfully and easily be done fullscale.

PUPPETRY AROUND THE WORLD

The origins of puppetry, like the beginnings of most of the arts, are prehistoric and are confused in a myriad of conflicting patterns and explanations. There is general agreement among scholars, however, that puppetry, although its origins do not lie exclusively in the Orient, became a highly sophisticated art there at an early period and that the Orient was a source of ideas and techniques for a good deal of the puppetry of the West. The general East-to-West trend discernible in the history of puppetry provides, therefore, the rationale of this section under the headings *The Orient; Europe;* and *The United States.*

THE ORIENT

The earliest recorded material on puppetry in the East is contemporary with that of the West. Although some elements were slow to evolve, many features are today the same as they were three or four hundred years ago.

Japan.—In Japan as in Europe (*see* below) the drama was closely allied with religion, and dolls were used to represent supernatural forces. Elements of both the nō drama and the kabuki theatre (*qq.v.*) are found in the puppet theatre, which reached its zenith in the 17th century in the work of Chikamatsu Monzaemon (*q.v.*) and others and maintained a high technical level for the next two hundred years.

The *bunraku* puppet of Japan (named for the puppetmaster Vemura Bunrakuken [1737–1810]) is approximately two-thirds life-size, with head, hands, and feet somewhat smaller in scale. It is operated by a chief puppeteer who inserts his left hand into the back of the puppet and controls the head by means of a rod to which are attached auxiliary levers for the eyes, mouth, and eyebrows. The right hand of the chief operator controls the right arm of the puppet, which may also be articulated. A second puppeteer controls the left hand and stands somewhat back from the puppet. A third puppeteer operates the feet or, in the case of female puppets, the base of the costume. The stories may be either historical or domestic, but all are highly stylized. The performance takes place on a full-size stage complete with scenery. To the right of the stage are the reciters, who tell the story and speak the lines, and the *samisen* musicians who accompany the action. Besides the *bunraku* puppets, string puppets were also used in Japan.

China and Java.—A somewhat different form of puppetry developed in southeastern Asia (particularly Java) and China. The beginnings may be traced before the 10th century; more specific references are found after the 16th century. The general form of puppetry is called *wayang;* its development falls into three basic categories: *wayang kulit,* a shadow puppet; *wayang klitik,* a shadow puppet with carved relief; and *wayang golek,* a three-dimensional puppet. The evolution of puppetry here seems to have been from the basic shadow puppet of the religious ceremonies to the three-dimensional puppet of the secular dramas. A further advance was transmutation into the dance, which mimics the movement patterns of the puppets and the angular limitations of their jointing.

The shadow puppets are cut from animal hide with horn supports. Elaborate configurations, cut into the hide, serve to define the character. The puppets vary in size from six or eight inches to four or five times that large. Principally, the arms are articulated with two rods for manipulation. Elaborately painted, the puppets perform for a male audience in front of a screen with a light shining on them; on the other side of the screen, women view the performance as a shadow play.

The *wayang klitik* puppets are also shadow puppets but they are of translucent material. Brilliantly coloured, they are often very complicated and are presented in the midst of elaborate scenery and properties. In China the shows do not have the religious connotations of the Javanese performances. Chinese puppets are also to be found in three-dimensional rod form as well as rod-and-string and hand-and-rod forms. As with all other puppets, their origins are lost in antiquity.

Bali and Turkey.—Somewhat akin to the Javanese puppets are the animal-skin shadow puppets of Bali and Turkey. In Bali the puppets often are more complex: strings are used and smaller portions of the puppets are articulated. These puppets also seem to exhibit more humour. The translucent Turkish puppets have the rod inserted at right angles to the puppet in a slot on the puppet's back. The puppet is pressed against the screen, and the light comes from behind the puppeteer. This eliminates the need for supporting pieces fastened to the puppet but poses some difficulties of operation.

India.—The shadow play is well known in India, and there are also string-puppet plays. In spite of the simplicity of their stringing, these puppets are elaborately costumed.

EUROPE

Mediterranean Origins.—Puppetry in the West apparently began in the Mediterranean region. Major evidence is supplied by archaeological remains, folk legends, cognate words, and documents.

Dolls from the Old and Middle Kingdom tombs of Egypt suggest action in both large and small figures, but the seeming articulations may have been a construction feature of figures that never moved. A mask of the dog-headed god Anubis with a movable jaw may be an example of one of the earliest manifestations of puppetry: the use of moving parts in idols to give them a heightened dramatic effect. Made by religious communities from the Greeks onward, figures of this kind were finally banned by the Church of England during the Reformation. Their clockwork brothers, however, remain on the towers of municipal buildings and in other secular settings to this day. (Automata are not considered to be puppets, since they move of themselves.)

From Etruscan tombs and Roman sites come doll-like images with rods protruding from their heads. While some of them are articulated, their use is much debated. There are remnants of Greek and Roman theatres that suggest the origins of the *commedia dell'arte* (16th to 18th centuries), from which may have come the style and, in part, the form of Punch (*see* below, "*Commedia*" *Influence*); but it is to be suspected that over a span of nearly two millennia there was not a single continuous line.

The writings of Herodotus, Plato, Aristotle, and Horace contain seeming references to the art of puppetry; whether there were actual performances is, however, debatable. Until the establishment of municipal records and their preservation, and of more accurate record-keeping of all sorts from the Renaissance forward, the rather ephemeral art of puppetry left little mark. By the very nature of their construction, puppets soon deteriorated, and few permanent structures were built for their performances. While they may have influenced language, social patterns, and religion and did show up occasionally in pictures, puppets were not, apparently, considered worthy of lasting recognition.

Early Developments.—From an early date both live performers and puppets took part in the church's representations of religious stories. There are descriptions of angels ascending and miraculous happenings, in performances within the church edifice and on pageant wagons, which were accomplished with the aid of puppets. Dragons and lions were brought onstage in a very realistic fashion in sacred dramas—an early demonstration that puppetry is most successful when its themes are those which cannot be represented in actuality.

Christmas manger scenes (crèches) in 16th-century France and Italy made use of animated figures, and it was just a short step to other stories and more elaborate action. How much of the action was performed with machines and how much by human manipulation is uncertain; perhaps the human element was a well-kept secret, since the public has always been fascinated by mechanical contrivances and feels cheated if it is revealed that a human being performed some or all of the movements.

"Commedia" Influence.—By the middle of the 16th century the *commedia dell'arte* (*q.v.*) of Italy was flourishing and, seemingly, puppets were firmly mixed with it. The puppets outlasted the living actors, in the form of Pulcinella in Italy, Polichinelle in France, and Punch (*q.v.*) in England. Considerable controversy revolves about the genesis of these terms. Stock characters of the *commedia* also evolved into Kasperle in Germany and Petrouchka in Russia—each an underdog with a well-developed sense of defiance of authority. Guignol of France, which came along two centuries later, has a certain family resemblance.

National Traditions.—*Italy.*—The shadow theatre reached Italy by way of Turkey, and appearances are recorded in the 17th and 18th centuries on the continent and in England. There is some problem of identification here, for puppeteers preferred to keep their methods secret (as is true today).

In southern Italy and in Sicily there is a particular kind of puppet show which, though related to forms of puppetry farther north, in Belgium and France, developed a pattern all its own. Based upon the adventures of Charlemagne and Roland, these tales of Saracens and Christians delighted audiences well into the 20th century. Where these shows began is a matter of conjecture. The puppet versions date from the 11th century and were written down in the 15th century, but each performance is the creation of the puppeteer. Performed by puppets approximately four feet high and weighing 75 to 100 lb., the stories go on almost endlessly. Each evening's performance is liberally punctuated with fierce battles between opposing armies, heroes and monsters, or heroes and witches. Blood flows freely and, as each puppet is killed, the rods supporting him are thrown to the floor. A large supply of puppets is necessary since, once having died, it ill befits a puppet to show up again within that cycle. With changing of folkways these puppet shows are gradually disappearing after centuries of popularity. The remaining puppeteers perform in the evening after making their living at other tasks during the day.

Punch was long active in Italy under any number of names. Just as he varied from country to country, within Italy he was known as Pulcinella in Naples, Rugantino in Rome, Fagiolino in Bologna, Sandrone in Modena, Arlecchino in Venice, Meneghino in Milan, Gianduja in Turin, Virticchio in Palermo, and Gioppino in Bergamo.

France.—Jean Brioché (Giovanni Briocci), an Italian, firmly established puppetry in Paris and performed before the dauphin in 1669. He was followed by a man named LaGrille, who performed with puppets four feet high. At the end of the 17th century a battle between puppetry and live theatre took place in France, with the Opéra, the Comédie Française, and the Comédie-Italienne on one side and various puppet establishments on the other. (A similar rivalry arose in other countries.) Dominique Seraphin was busy with his theatre in Paris starting in 1776; he

used string figures at first but apparently introduced hand puppets later.

England.—In 1573 a letter from the Privy Council to the lord mayor of London authorized some Italians to perform their "motions" within the City. This term is commonly used interchangeably with puppets, and puppeteers were "motion men."

The first recorded performance of *Punch and Judy* on English soil was at Covent Garden in 1661. Prior to this time there were references, possibly to puppets, as in *A Midsummer Night's Dream*:

> Helena: Fie, fie! you counterfeit, you puppet, you!
> Hermia: Puppet! why, so: ay, that way goes the game.
> Now I perceive that she hath made compare
> Between our statures. . .

Shakespeare's reference, as with others earlier, may have been to a doll rather than to figures operated on a stage. There is no doubt, however, about Congreve's reference 100 years later in *The Way of the World*, when Lady Wishfort observes:

> Why dost thou not stir, puppet?
> Thou wooden thing upon wires!

This uncomplimentary view of puppets (latterly given a political meaning) is all too common in English writings. It may have sprung from the running battle between the live stage and the puppet stage, which has been going on for hundreds of years in spite of the many elements they have in common and repeated borrowings from each other.

From the 17th century onward, many English sources tell of puppet shows as entertainment at fairs and in permanent establishments. For instance, one of the offerings of John Harris's booth at Bartholomew Fair in 1650 was *The Court of King Henry II, The Death of Fair Rosamond, with the merry humors of Punchinello and The Lancashire Witches*.

The name of Martin Powell dominates puppetry in 18th-century England. He performed in Covent Garden in London, at Bath, and elsewhere with considerable success. His puppets were operated with strings and wires by his assistants, while Powell himself, a short man with a decided paunch and hump who bore some resemblance to Punch, delivered a prologue and running commentary on the shows from a position in front of the stage. Among his shows on March 18, 1712 (new style; 1711, old style), was *The False Triumph, or The Destruction of Troy,* on other dates he presented *King Bladud, The Beauteous Sacrifice, Heroic Love, or The Death of Hero and Leander,* and *The Vices of the Age Displayed, or Poor Robin's Dream.* His performances were advertised regularly in *The Spectator* (no. 295–550). Other London puppeteers were John Harris, Jean Dumont, Mme de la Nash, and Charlotte Charke. Puppets were also to be seen at Norwich, Kent, and Canterbury. Hand as well as string puppets were used in 18th-century England. The programs varied: there were standard tales, tableaux, social commentary (usually somewhat disguised), and variety turns, with the last-named gaining in popularity toward the end of the century.

The most notable English puppeteer of the 19th century was Thomas Holden. His performances were frequent and elaborate, employing upward of a dozen persons and involving all sorts of trick puppets: singers that turned into balloons, stretching puppets, jugglers and stilt walkers, and seemingly single puppets that turned into many puppets. Throughout the century *Punch and Judy* shows were extremely popular.

Other European Countries.—Both Gluck and Haydn composed operas for the 18th-century puppet theatre of Germany and Austria. In the latter part of the 19th century Maurice Sand was active for more than a quarter of a century doing hand-puppet shows at Nohant, Switz.; in his Theatre des Amis his mother, the writer George Sand, spent much of her time in costuming his puppets.

Early puppetry in Czechoslovakia followed the traditional pattern of string and hand shows. Kaspárek, a Punchlike character presented by Matej Kopecky at the end of the 18th century, was followed by the puppets of Jan Lastovka which voiced the revolutionary sentiments of 1848. Political commentary continued with the puppets of Joseph Skupa in 1917. Annexation by Germany in 1939 caused many puppeteers to leave the country, but Czechoslovakia still has a high ratio of puppet theatre to population.

20th-Century Revival.—By the beginning of the 20th century many European puppet shows were permanently settled in their own theatres, such as those of Munich and Cologne. During the first half of the century a number of persons gave puppetry a new artistic lease on life. Chief among them was Edward Gordon Craig (*q.v.*) of England, who in 1907 suggested that life-size puppets would constitute ideal actors. His use of puppets and interest in them led the puppet revival. Those who took part in Europe and Russia included Richard Teschner in Vienna, Paul Brann in Munich, Ivo Puhonny in Baden-Baden, Nina Effimova in Moscow, and Gera Blattner in Paris. Among the performing groups remaining in the 1960s (some of which were started during the revival) were the Teatro Piccoli of Italy, Anton Aicher's Salzburg Marionettes, the Lalka Theatre of Warsaw, and the State Central Puppet Theatre of Sergei Obraztsov in Moscow. While many of the theatres and troupes on the continent were privately managed, there was a tremendous upsurge in puppetry financed by national governments, particularly in eastern Europe.

THE UNITED STATES

One of the earliest references to puppetry in what is now the United States was the following advertisement in the *Pennsylvania Gazette* of Dec. 30, 1742.

At the sign of the Coach and Horses, against the State House, in Chestnut Street, Philadelphia, every evening at seven a clock [sic] precisely, will be acted, in several scenes, viz. An agreeable comedy or tragedy, by changeable figures of two feet high.
A sight of the sea and ships.
A merry dialogue between Punch and Joan his wife.
With several other pleasing entertainments. The prices, two shillings, eighteen pence and sixpence.

Another picture of puppet entertainment is given in the following notice of Peter Gardiner's troupe from the Williamsburg, Va., *Gazette* of Nov. 19, 1769:

A curious set of figures, richly dressed, four feet high, they are to appear on the stage as if alive, and will perform a tragic performance called *Bateman and his Ghost*. Likewise a set of water works, representing the sea monsters sporting on the waves together with the taking of Havannah, with ships, forts and batteries, continually firing, until victory crowns the conquest; and a magnificent piece of machinery, called *Cupid's Paradise,* representing seventy odd pillars and columns, with the appearance of Neptune and Amphitrite, and music suitable thereto. The whole to conclude with a magnificent set of fireworks, such as Catherine wheels, Italian candles, sea fountains, and sunflowers with the appearance of the sun and moon in their full lustre.

Chinese shadow puppets appeared at the end of the 18th century. Other shadows came from France; *e.g.,* a production of *Don Quixote* in 1812.

If any form may be said to have dominated the American puppet scene in the 19th century it was the variety show with string puppets. This was not, however, to the exclusion of the "story" show. Among the companies active during this period were Alberto Lana's, Bragaldi's, and the Theatre Seraphin, as well as multitudes of *Punch and Judy* operators. The puppets were sometimes called *fantoccini* (Ital., "little puppets") to add a foreign lustre. The puppets of the United States remained primarily touring attractions until the end of the 19th century. The companies, such as Till's Royal Marionettes headed by John Till, the Middleton Marionettes of Harry and George Middleton, and the Deaves Marionettes of Walter and Harry Deaves, presented almost anything that would attract attention, performing for adults as well as children and appearing often in the variety shows latterly known as vaudeville.

Immigrants brought their national puppets with them to the U.S. The technique and stories of German puppetry showed up in Pennsylvania, New York, and the Midwest. The Paladins of Sicily were taken to Boston by Antonio Parisi of Messina; he later moved to New York City, where there were theatres performing the tales of Charlemagne. There were also theatres of this type in Chicago and San Francisco at the turn of the century; the last of these was the Mulberry Street theatre of

Agrippino Manteo in New York City. Greek shadow puppets, bearing a striking similarity to Turkish puppets, could also be seen in coffeehouses and restaurants.

The opening of the 20th century did not suggest anything startling for puppetry in the U.S. The advent of motion pictures was taking away much of the audience—a factor in the decline of puppetry in many countries throughout the world. However, a revival began at the Chicago Little Theatre at the start of World War I. This was closely followed by the first professional show of the English artist-illustrator Tony Sarg in New York City in 1917. (It was with the Sarg company that many puppeteers still active at midcentury received their training.) Sarg productions toured in the 1930s and, by presenting a show with high standards, established a pattern which American amateurs could follow to become the new professionals. He saw puppetry as an integral form of theatrical art. Remo Bufano, another of those who were active early in the revival of puppetry in the U.S., constructed puppets of all shapes and sizes. Among his experiments were the previously mentioned *Oedipus; Master Peter's Puppet Show;* and a 35-ft. figure for Billy Rose's *Jumbo* at the Hippodrome. With Grace Wilder he directed the Federal Theatre Project (*q.v.*) puppet theatre in New York City. In Cleveland, O., Helen Haiman Joseph began puppetry at the Playhouse in 1915. Her *Book of Marionettes,* published in 1920, provided a background against which other work could progress. The company she organized continued to present local productions and touring shows until 1942. Paul McPharlin started in puppetry while at Columbia University in the 1920s. He went to Evanston, Ill., and then to Detroit, Mich., where he established Puppetry Imprints, was instrumental in founding Puppeteers of America, and published *Puppetry,* a yearbook of happenings in the art throughout the world. His collection of books and puppets became the basis for the library and collection of the Detroit Institute of Arts. He wrote *The Puppet Theatre in America* (1949), the first major work on American puppetry. One of the later proponents of puppetry within this period was Marjorie Batchelder McPharlin (Mrs. Paul McPharlin), who wrote extensively about puppets, particularly rod puppets, and traveled throughout the world doing research and teaching.

Several producing companies were formed during the 1920s and 1930s and performed throughout the U.S. One was the Tatterman Marionettes of William Duncan and Edward Mabley, which started in Detroit, later moved to Ohio, and then went to New York. Another, originating near Detroit, was the University of Michigan Puppeteers started by Forman Brown, Harry Burnett, and Richard Brandon. This group toured the Midwest and then went to Yale University, where it acquired the name Yale Puppeteers. After more touring and film work it settled in 1941 at the Turnabout Theatre, Los Angeles, where the puppeteers and live actors performed alternately at opposite ends of the same theatre.

Rufus Rose and Bil Baird, two of the puppeteers with Tony Sarg, continued to be most active. Rose and his wife, Margo, were traditional touring puppeteers known especially for their productions of *Pinocchio* and *Treasure Island.* The Rose Marionettes made one of the early puppet films, *Jerry Pulls the Strings* (1938). For many years Rose was the manipulator in *Howdy Doody,* one of the early puppet successes on television. Bil Baird and his wife, Cora, were among the busiest puppeteers in the country. Active in commercial productions since the Chicago World's Fair (1933), the Bairds presented several full-length television shows, performed at the New York World's Fairs of 1939 and 1965, and made international tours to India and Russia. Others who took part in the U.S. revival of puppetry included Romain and Ellen Proctor of the Proctor Puppets; Pauline Benton of the Red Gate Shadow Players; Ralph Chessé, who produced a puppet version of O'Neill's *Emperor Jones;* Basil Milovsoroff, who used both Russian folk puppets and experimental forms; Martin and Olga Stevens, with their *St. Joan* and *Macbeth;* Frank Paris, originator of *Howdy Doody;* and Paul Walton and Michael O'Rourke of the Olvera Street Puppet Theatre.

Several American museums have collections of puppets, the

most notable being that of the Detroit Institute of Arts; this institution also presents performances by touring puppeteers and has commissioned special productions. The city of New York maintains a large marionette theatre which tours schools and parks, and the Museum of the City of New York presents a regular program of puppet shows.

Except for some nightclub performers, the Kroffts' Les Poupées de Paris, and the Kungsholm theatre of Chicago started by Fredrik Chramer and carried on by William Fosser, puppetry in the U.S. in the 1960s was almost exclusively the province of children. This was in decided contrast with the historical background of puppetry and its practice elsewhere in the world. Puppets were also firmly settled in U.S. television, where they perhaps were seen by more people in a 20-year period than puppetry as a whole had attracted in the previous 2,000 years. Following a decade of work in and around Chicago, Burr Tillstrom and his puppet Kukla first appeared on a daily television show in 1947. In the years that followed, *Kukla, Fran and Ollie* achieved a national following. Other favourite TV puppet characters were Howdy Doody, those of Cosmo Allegretti on *Captain Kangaroo,* Hope and Maury Bunin's Foodini, and Shari Lewis's Lamb Chop and Charlie Horse —all appealing primarily to children. The Muppets of Jim Henson, to some extent Tillstrom's characters, and those of an occasional foreign or domestic guest represented the only puppets performing principally for adult viewers of U.S. television.

LATIN AMERICA

Latin-American puppetry dates from the Cortés expedition to Mexico where, in 1524, one of the personal servants did sleight-of-hand and worked puppets. Since the Spaniards were very fond of puppets in their native land it was inevitable that puppets should be brought to the New World. References are made to performances at Tezcuco, Mex., by Juan de Samora in 1569 and at Lima, Peru, in 1629. As in Europe, the carefree attitude of puppeteers in regard to the licensing laws led to censure as well as to the familiar feuds between live actors and puppets: in Lima in 1787 indignation over puppet performances during Lent resulted in the closing of the theatre.

Leonardo Rosete Aranda, who started performing in 1860 in Mexico, laid the groundwork for companies which were to use his name into the mid-20th century. His plays, done with string figures, centred on folk and religious themes. I. T. Orellana's plays "for children or puppets," published from 1880 on, suggest the folk nature of the puppet theatre of that period. More recently the hand puppeteer Mane Bernardo of Argentina and Roberto Lago with his federally assisted theatre in Mexico have explored new directions for puppetry in Latin America.

MODERN USES OF PUPPETRY

Aside from its entertainment value, puppetry in the mid-20th century was receiving attention as a tool of education and advertising. Puppets can be used to instruct in almost any subject, since they can be made in so many shapes and can portray both abstract and concrete situations. Thus they were used extensively in India to educate the people in such matters as family planning, modern medicine, sanitation, and agriculture. A similar program in Mexico spread health information and improved literacy. In the U.S., puppets were used to promote dental hygiene and in schools and mental institutions to act out problems and find solutions. This also involved, in a therapeutic way, the manual skills needed to construct and present a puppet show. An introduction to puppetry was included in the curricula of many teacher-training colleges. At the University of California at Los Angeles puppetry was offered as a major course in the theatre-arts department.

American industry has made extensive use of puppets for training its personnel, instructing the public, and creating markets. It is perhaps in this field that American puppetry comes closest to the puppetry of eastern Europe: in Poland and Russia, with hundreds on the staffs of the state theatres, the puppet stage concentrates on building attitudes favourable to the government which supports it.

Increasing use of puppetry in education and television suggests an ongoing strength. Like its parent art form, the theatre, puppetry often appears to be the eternal invalid which never dies.

ORGANIZATIONS

The Union Internationale des Marionettes was organized in Prague in 1928 with Jan Malík (later of the National Czechoslovakian Puppet Theatre) as its first secretary. Since World War II it has regularly held international meetings attended mainly by persons from European and Asiatic countries. In North America the Puppeteers of America, organized in 1937, publishes *The Puppetry Journal* and holds an annual festival. Many cities, states, and provinces have their own organizations. The British Puppet and Model Theatre Guild, founded in London in 1926, serves as headquarters for puppetry in England and Wales along with the Educational Puppetry Association. Most of the major countries of Europe have comparable organizations.

BIBLIOGRAPHY.—P. D. Arnott, *Plays Without People* (1964); B. Baird, *The Art of the Puppet* (1965); M. H. Batchelder, *The Puppet Theatre Handbook* (1947) and *Rod-Puppets and the Human Theatre* (1947); C. W. Beaumont, *Puppets and the Puppet Stage* (1938); H. H. Joseph, *Book of Marionettes* (1920); C. Magnin, *Histoire des Marionettes en Europe* (1862); P. McPharlin, *Puppetry* (yearbook, 1930–45) and *The Puppet Theatre in America* (1949); S. Obraztsov, *The Chinese Puppet Theatre* (1961); S. Seyiro et al., *Masterpieces of Japanese Puppetry* (1958); G. Speaight, *The History of the English Puppet Theatre* (1955); D. Keene, *Bunraku: the Art of the Japanese Puppet Theatre* (1965). (A. M. GR.)

PUPPIS, one of the three southern constellations into which the large Ptolemaic constellation Argo was subdivided. The bright new star Nova Puppis was visible during the winter of 1942.

PURĀNAS, ancient Indian compilations in Sanskrit verse on religious and legendary themes, the origin of which is traceable to Vedic times. They share much material with the two great epics, the *Mahābhārata* and *Rāmāyana* (*qq.v.*), and with the law books (*dharma-śāstra*). "Purāna" means "ancient," and, traditionally, a *purāna* treats of the creation of the world, its destruction and renewal, the genealogy of gods and seers, the great ages of mankind, and the history of dynasties. However, of the 18 principal surviving *purānas,* the majority are of sectarian character, concerned with devotion to Śiva or Visnu (Vishnu; *see* HINDUISM). They contain much devotional material (*bhakti*), eulogies on shrines, the duties of the castes, and descriptions of Vedic-brahmanical customs and ceremonies. Recitation and exposition of *purāna* in temples and annually in Brahman households form an important aspect of Hindu devotion. *See* also the article SANSKRIT LITERATURE and its bibliography. (J. E. B. G.)

PURCELL, EDWARD MILLS (1912–   ), U.S. physicist, Nobel Prize winner for research on magnetic resonance, was born in Taylorville, Ill., Aug. 30, 1912. He received his B.S. from Purdue in 1933, and his Ph.D. from Harvard in 1938. During the war he was head of the Advanced Development group on radar problems at the radiation laboratory of the Massachusetts Institute of Technology. He became professor of physics at Harvard in 1949. He was awarded the Nobel Prize in 1952 jointly with Felix Bloch (*q.v.*) for the discovery of nuclear magnetic resonance in solids, a phenomenon observed independently for the first time at Harvard and Stanford. These investigators showed that by the absorption of radio-frequency waves in solids it is possible to detect nuclear magnetic moments. This research opened up a whole new field of physics: magnetic resonance spectroscopy. It yielded information not only on nuclear moments, but also on chemical bonds and atomic binding in liquids and solids, even supplying data on the structure of hydrocarbons useful for the oil industry. Another notable achievement of Purcell was the detection jointly with Harold I. Ewen in 1952 of the 21 cm. line of neutral atomic hydrogen in extraterrestrial radiation. This discovery added a new dimension to radio astronomy by revealing the distribution of hydrogen in galaxies. Purcell was appointed to his second term on the President's Science Advisory Committee in 1962.

See V. Torrey, "Changing Partners in the Atom Dance," *Saturday Review,* 44:68–69 (May 6, 1961). (J. H. V. V.)

PURCELL, HENRY (1659–1695), the most important English composer of his time, was born in the summer or autumn of

1659. His father was a gentleman of the Chapel Royal, where he himself received his earliest education as a chorister, first under Henry Cooke and then under Cooke's son-in-law Pelham Humfrey. When his voice broke in 1673 he was appointed assistant to John Hingston, keeper of the king's instruments, whom he succeeded in 1683. From 1674 to 1678 he tuned the organ at Westminster Abbey and was employed there in 1675–76 to copy organ parts of anthems. In 1677 he succeeded Matthew Locke as composer for Charles II's string orchestra (the "24 violins") and in 1679 was appointed organist of Westminster Abbey in succession to John Blow. A further appointment as one of the three organists of the Chapel Royal followed in 1682. He retained all his official posts through the reigns of James II and of William III and Mary. He married in 1680 or 1681 and had at least six children, three of whom died in infancy. His son Edward (1689–1740) was also a musician, as was Edward's son Edward Henry (b. 1716). Purcell seems to have spent all his life in Westminster; he died there on Nov. 21, 1695, possibly of the aftereffects of malnutrition in his early years. His fatal illness prevented him from finishing the music for *The Indian Queen,*

HENRY PURCELL, PORTRAIT BY J. CLOSTERMAN

which was completed by his brother Daniel (d. 1717). Daniel Purcell was also brought up as a chorister in the Chapel Royal and was organist of Magdalen College, Oxford, from 1688 to 1695. Before his brother's death he was little known as a composer, but from 1695 to 1707 he was in considerable demand for music for stage productions in London, until the advent of Italian opera brought his activities to an end.

Purcell's music covers a wide field: the church, the stage, the court, and private entertainment. In all these branches of composition he showed an obvious admiration for the past combined with a willingness to learn from the present, particularly from his contemporaries in Italy. With alertness of mind went an individual invention which marked him as the most original English composer of his time, and one of the most original in Europe. This originality is found not only in his outstanding gifts as a melodist but also in his capacity for producing unexpected harmonic progressions by means of contrapuntal ingenuity.

To later ages Purcell was best known as a songwriter, because so many of his songs were printed in his lifetime and were reprinted again and again after his death. But the first evidence we have of his mastery is an instrumental work—a series of fantasias (or "fancies") for viols in three, four, five, six, and seven parts. The nine four-part fantasias all bear dates in the summer of 1680, and the others can hardly be later. Purcell was here reviving a form of music which was already out of date, and doing it with the skill of a veteran. It was probably about the same time that he started to work on a more fashionable type of instrumental music—a series of sonatas for two violins, bass viol, and organ (or harpsichord). Twelve of these were published in 1683, with a dedication to Charles II, and a further nine (together with a chaconne for the same combination) were issued by his widow in 1697. The foreword to the 1683 set claimed that the composer had "faithfully endeavour'd a just imitation of the most fam'd Italian Masters"; but side by side with the adoption of an Italianate manner there was a good deal that derived from the English tradition of chamber music.

It is the instrumental movements that are the most striking part of the earliest of Purcell's "Welcome Songs" for Charles II—a series of ceremonial odes which began in 1680. Possibly he lacked experience in writing for voices, at any rate on the scale required for works of this kind; or else he had not yet achieved the art of cloaking insipid words in significant music. By 1683 he had acquired a surer touch, and from that time until 1694, when he

wrote the last of the birthday odes for Queen Mary, he produced a series of compositions for the court in which the vitality of the music makes it easy to ignore the poverty of the words. The same qualities are apparent in the last of his odes for St. Cecilia's Day, written in 1692.

Purcell's genius as a composer for the stage was hampered by the fact that there was no public opera in London during his lifetime. Most of his theatre music consists simply of instrumental music and songs interpolated into spoken drama, though occasionally there were opportunities for more extended musical scenes. His contribution to the stage was in fact very modest until 1689, when he wrote *Dido and Aeneas* for performance at a girls' school in Chelsea; this miniature opera achieves a high degree of dramatic intensity within a narrow framework. From that time until his death he was constantly employed in writing music for the public theatres. These productions included some which gave scope for more than merely incidental music—notably *Dioclesian* (1690), adapted by Thomas Betterton from the tragedy *The Prophetess* by John Fletcher and Philip Massinger; *King Arthur* (1691) by Dryden, designed from the first as an entertainment with music; and *The Fairy Queen* (1692), an anonymous adaptation of Shakespeare's *A Midsummer Night's Dream,* in which the texts set to music are all interpolations. In these works Purcell showed not only a lively sense of comedy but also a gift of passionate expression which is often more exalted than the words. The tendency to identify himself still more closely with the Italian style is very noticeable in the later dramatic works, which often demand considerable agility from the soloists.

Purcell's four-part fantasias, his first court ode, and his first music for the theatre, *Theodosius,* all date from 1680. Some of his church music may be earlier than that, but it is not possible to assign definite dates. So far as is known, most of his anthems, whether for the full choir ("full anthems") or with sections for soloists ("verse anthems"), were written between 1680 and 1685, the year of Charles II's death. The decline of the Chapel Royal during the reigns of James II and of William and Mary may have been responsible for the comparatively few works he produced during that period; or, alternatively, he was so busy with stage music and odes that he had little time or inclination for church music. The style of his full anthems, like that of the fantasias, shows a great respect for older traditions. His verse anthems, on the other hand, were obviously influenced, in the first instance, by Humfrey, who had acquired a knowledge of Continental styles during his travels abroad. The most notable feature of these latter works is the use of expressive vocal declamation which is pathetic without being mawkish. The same characteristics appear in the sacred songs he wrote for private performance. Since composers for the Chapel Royal in Charles II's reign had the string orchestra at their disposal, Purcell took the opportunity to include overtures and ritornellos which are both dignified and lively. The most elaborate of all his compositions for the church are the anthem *My heart is inditing,* performed in Westminster Abbey at the coronation of James II, and the festal *Te Deum and Jubilate,* written for St. Cecilia's Day in 1694. Of these the anthem is the more impressive; the *Te Deum and Jubilate,* though they include sections of a more intimate character, suffer on the whole from a forced brilliance which seems to have faded with the passage of time.

Though the main period of Purcell's creative activity lasted for little more than 15 years, he managed to crowd into it a very large number of compositions, including more than 100 secular songs and about 40 duets, apart from those which he contributed to plays. Many of the songs are quite substantial pieces, incorporating recitative and arias on the lines of the Italian solo cantata. A favourite device which Purcell used widely in his secular music, though rarely in his anthems, was the ground bass (*q.v.*). This can have an invigorating effect in lively pieces, while in laments, such as Dido's farewell, it can intensify the expression of grief. The chaconne in the second set of sonatas uses the same technique with impressive results. Works of this kind represent the composer at the height of his capacity. The numerous catches, on the other hand, though accomplished enough, are little more than an experienced musician's contribution to social merrymaking. Purcell seems to have abandoned instrumental chamber music after his early years. His keyboard music forms an even smaller part of his output: it consists of suites and shorter pieces (many adapted from other works) for harpsichord, and a handful of pieces for organ solo.

Apart from a large number of songs which appeared in vocal collections very little of Purcell's music was published in his lifetime. The principal works were the *Sonnatas of III parts* (1683); *Welcome to all the pleasures*, an ode for St. Cecilia's Day, written in 1683 (published in 1684); and *Dioclesian*, composed in 1690 (1691). After his death his widow published a collection of his harpsichord pieces (1696), instrumental music for the theatre (1697), and the *Te Deum and Jubilate* (1697), and the publisher Henry Playford issued a two-volume collection of songs entitled *Orpheus Britannicus* (1698 and 1702) which went through three editions. A few dramatic works, odes, and anthems were printed in the late 18th and early 19th centuries; but it was not until 1876, when the Purcell Society was founded, that a serious attempt was made to issue all of Purcell's works. The first volume was published in 1878, the second in 1882. From 1889 to 1928 volumes appeared at fairly frequent intervals. After that the scheme was in abeyance until it was revived in 1957 with the publication of a volume of miscellaneous odes and cantatas. It was finally completed in 32 volumes in 1965. Revision of earlier volumes proceeded simultaneously with the issue of later ones, beginning with a revised edition of *Dioclesian* in 1961.

See also OPERA: *England;* SONG.

BIBLIOGRAPHY.—D. Arundell, *Henry Purcell* (1927); H. C. Colles, *Voice and Verse* (1928); E. J. Dent, *Foundations of English Opera* (1928); A. K. Holland, *Henry Purcell: the English Musical Tradition,* 2nd ed. (1949); J. A. Westrup, *Purcell,* 5th ed. (1965); S. Favre-Lingorow, *Der Instrumentalstil von Purcell* (1950); S. Demarquez, *Purcell: la vie, l'oeuvre* (1951); G. van Ravenzwaaij, *Purcell* (1954); R. Sietz, *Henry Purcell: Zeit, Leben, Werk* (1955); H. Wessely-Kropik, "Henry Purcell als Instrumentalkomponist," *Studien zur Musikwissenschaft,* xxii (1955); I. Holst (ed.), *Henry Purcell: Essays on his Music* (1959); R. E. Moore, *Henry Purcell and the Restoration Theatre* (1961); F. B. Zimmerman, *Henry Purcell: an Analytical Catalogue of His Music* (1963). (JA. A. W.)

PURCHAS, SAMUEL (*c.* 1577–1626), English compiler of works on travel and discovery, was born at Thaxted, Essex, and studied at St. John's College, Cambridge, and at Oxford. He was vicar first of a Thames-side parish in Essex and later in London (where he was also chaplain to Archbishop G. Abbot) and met many seafarers. As an editor and compiler he sought to interest the general public of his day. In this he was very successful though his works have been severely criticized by scholars. They are however an indispensable source of information and contain many references to original accounts of voyages. His writings include: *Purchas, His Pilgrimage; or, Relations of the World and the Religions Observed in all Ages* (1613; other editions 1614, 1617, 1626); *Purchas, His Pilgrim. Microcosmus, or the Historie of Man* (1619); and *Hakluytus Posthumus or Purchas His Pilgrimes,* 4 vol. (1625; 20 vol., 1905–07). (A. M. F.)

PURDAH: *see* HAREM.

PURGATORY, according to Roman Catholic faith, is a condition or state of suffering in which the souls of those who have died as friends of God pay the debt of temporal punishment and are purified from all possible stain of venial sin and evil habits. This teaching supposes that before death the sinner has been justified through the all-sufficient merits of Jesus Christ, internally renovated, made an adopted son of God, and freed from the debt of eternal punishment. In baptism the purification of the sinner is complete, every debt of justice satisfied. But if the friend and son of God sins grievously after baptism and is made righteous again in the sacrament of penance, though the eternal punishment is remitted through Christ's infinite merits, there remains as a rule some temporal punishment, a debt of expiation to be paid to God's justice in this life or the next. If the latter, the state of soul ensuing is precisely what the Catholic Church means by purgatory. The suffering of the soul detained therein derives all its expiatory value from the merits of Christ. It may be helped to pay its debt by the suffrages of the living members of Christ's

Body, that is, by their good works offered to God's mercy in Christ's name.

Protestants generally have denied the existence of purgatory consistently with their conception of imputed righteousness through faith in the merits of Jesus Christ. They leave no room or need for any further reparation by the justified sinner. Most Eastern Christians not united with Rome (Armenians, Jacobites, Nestorians, Greeks, Slavs, and others) also reject the doctrine of purgatory. Many Greco-Slav theologians have admitted the existence of a middle state between heaven and hell, but very few have conceded a state of expiatory suffering. Almost universally, however, these Eastern Christians believe that the dead can be helped by the prayers and good works of the living members of the church.

The doctrine is implied in the approval given to the belief and practice of the Jews in II Macc. 12:43–45. Some theologians appeal also to Paul's warning about the purification of apostolic workers after the revelation of their defects by God's judgment (I Cor. 3:10–15). Many places of the Old Testament are cited to justify a belief in temporal punishment to be endured after sin has been forgiven; *e.g.,* God's pardon of the rebellious Israelites and the penalty imposed on them (Num. 14). Paul also seems to imply this truth in the afflictions, at least the untimely death, which he attributes to the unworthy reception of the Eucharist (I Cor. 11:27–32).

The principal argument for temporal punishment and purgatory is the practice of Christians from the early centuries and the teaching of the Fathers of the church concerning the value of penitential works, almsgiving, prayer, and the eucharistic sacrifice, through the merits of Christ, for the expiation of one's own sins, even pardoned sins, and the succoring of the souls of the dead.

Concerning the questions of place, duration, and nature of the pains of purgatory, there is no certain and definitive teaching. The fire of purgatory may possibly be metaphorical, symbolizing the suffering of the soul in its ardent though patient longing for complete purification and admission to the vision of God. With the Last Judgment purgatory will cease to exist.

BIBLIOGRAPHY.—*On Purgatory: Catholic Encyclopedia,* vol. xii; *The New Schaff-Herzog Encyclopedia of Religious Knowledge,* vol. ix; B. Bartmann, *Purgatory* (1936); G. D. Smith (ed.), *The Teaching of the Catholic Church,* vol. ii (1949). *On Prayers for the Dead:* James Hastings (ed.), *Encyclopedia of Religion and Ethics,* vol. x; *Catholic Encyclopedia,* vol. iv. (T. J. Mo.)

PURI, a town and administrative centre of a district of Orissa state, India, is situated on the shore of the Bay of Bengal, 311 mi. (500 km.) SW of Calcutta and 776 mi. (1,249 km.) NE of Madras. Pop. (1961) 60,815. The old name of the town was Purushottam Puri (the city of the Greatest Being), abbreviated to Puri in common usage. William Bruton, the first European to visit the town (1633), called it "the great city of Jaggarnat." As the seat of the well-known shrine of Jagannath (*see* JUGGERNAUT), Puri is one of the most sacred places of pilgrimage for Hindus. The temple of Jagannath was built in the 12th century by Choda Ganga (the greatest of the eastern Ganga kings) and consists of a suite of four chambers, the offering hall, the dancing hall, the audience hall, and the sanctuary with its images. About two miles from the temple is the Garden house (Gundicha ghara), the retreat of Jagannath to which his image, mounted on a huge car or *rath* (preceded by smaller cars of his brother and sister), is pulled by enthusiastic pilgrims during the car festival each summer. The rajas of Khurda, titular descendants of the ancient Hindu monarchs of Orissa, have been in charge of the temple since 1590, but in 1960 the government of Orissa took over its administration. The town contains the summer castle of the state governor, the palace of the raja of Khurda, two colleges, an observatory, and many hotels and hospices (*dharamsalas*). The beach of Puri attracts many tourists.

PURI DISTRICT is a country of alluvial plains with hills and woods in the north and northeast. Pop. (1961) 1,865,439. Area 3,999 sq.mi. (10,357 sq.km.). The main river is the Kuakhai (a branch of the Katjori) which itself divides into two branches, the Daya and the Bhargavi, both flowing into Chilka lake. Chilka is one of the largest lakes in India (length 41 mi. [65 km.]; breadth

13 mi.[20 km.] in the north and 5 mi. [8 km.] in the south). Dotted with islands, it is saline and shallow and most suitable for fish breeding. A large quantity of fish is exported. The district is rich in antiquities. At Dhauli Hill are the rock edicts of Asoka (3rd century B.C.). Sisupalgarh is a fort of 2nd–1st century B.C. and Khandagiri contains the caves and inscriptions of Kharavela (1st century B.C.). Bhubaneswar (q.v.) is a city of temples and at Chandrabhaga is the Konarak (q.v.).

Khurda is the divisional headquarters of Eastern Railway, and has an arts college. There is a science college at Nirakarpur, and Satyabadi (a Brahmin village) is famous for Krishna worship (sakhigopal). This village in modern times was associated with the experiment of an open-air school initiated by Gopabandhu Das. At Atri is a hot sulfur spring around which a big annual fair takes place.

Puri first came under the British in 1803. Later events were the rebellion of the raja of Khurda (1804) and the rising of the paiks (peasant militia) in 1817–18. More than one-third of the population is said to have perished in the Orissa famine of 1866.

(MA. M.; N. K. S.)

PURIFICATION denotes the ritual techniques used in many cultures to protect against what are held to be unclean, sinful, or otherwise undesirable situations. In a society with a strong sense of solidarity, if one man violates a tabu the whole community may feel itself menaced until he is purified.

Childbirth, puberty, marriage, warfare or bloodshed, and death are commonly marked by purifying rites. Contaminating factors may include foods (as the flesh of totem animals), persons (as menstruating women or persons of inferior caste), places, and so on. Rituals of purification may entail the use of water (as in baptism), mutilation (as in circumcision), fasting, prayer, and confession. See also ABLUTION; LUSTRATION; RITES AND CEREMONIES.

See Paul Radin, Primitive Religion (1957); L. H. Gray, J. A. MacCulloch, and G. F. Moore (eds.), The Mythology of All Races, 13 vol. (1964).

PURIM (FEAST OF LOTS): see JEWISH HOLIDAYS.

PURINES. The purines comprise a group of nitrogenous compounds, a few of which are of great importance in living cells. The first purine known was uric acid, which was discovered in human urinary calculi by the Swedish chemist C. Scheele in 1776. The naturally occurring purines include adenine and guanine, two essential building blocks of nucleic acids (q.v.), a group of compounds regarded as carriers of hereditary characteristics. Another well-known purine is caffeine which, along with theobromine and theophylline, gives the stimulating effect to drinks made from coffee beans, tea leaves and cocoa beans.

Chemically, purines are structurally related to the pyrimidines. They are bases because of their nitrogen content. All purines are derived from purine itself, a substance with the empirical formula $C_5H_4N_4$. The structural formula of purine is shown in the accompanying diagram in which each atom is numbered as indicated. The molecule can exist in two forms which are very readily interconvertible, a phenomenon known as tautomerization (see TAUTOMERISM). The change of structure in the tautomerization of purine consists of the migration of a labile hydrogen atom between the nitrogen atoms at position 7 and position 9.

The four hydrogen atoms in purine (at positions 2, 6, 8 and either 7 or 9) may be substituted by other groups, such as hydroxyl (OH), amino (NH_2) or methyl (CH_3) groups. When a hydroxyl group is introduced at position 2, 6 or 8, another type of tautomerization is possible, since the H of the OH group may migrate to a neighbouring nitrogen atom. For instance, uric acid, which is 2:6:8-trihydroxypurine, exists in two tautomeric forms, A and B as shown below.

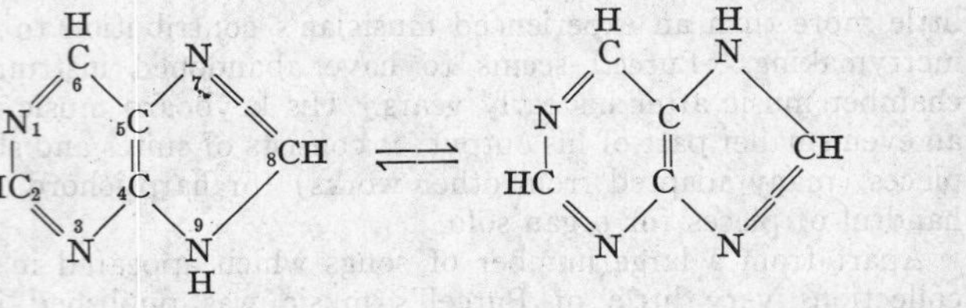

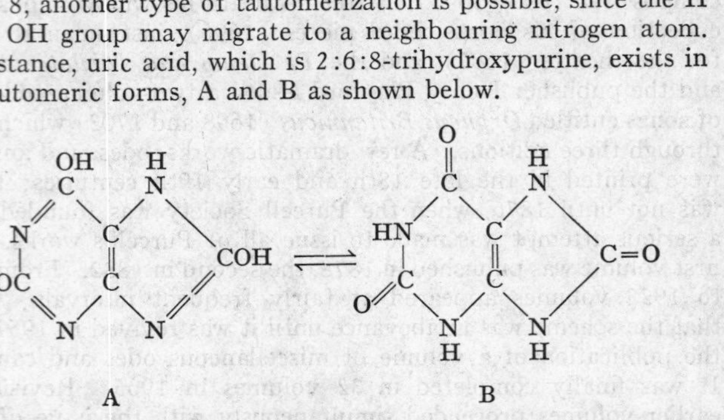

A   B

In form A, uric acid yields salts with metal ions, the hydrogen on oxygen being replaceable and thus making the substance an acid. Form B shows that substitution may occur on the 1 and 3 nitrogen atoms as in the methylated purines such as caffeine.

The following diagram outlines the relationships between the various naturally occurring purines. Starting with purine, and successively substituting hydroxyl groups for the hydrogen atoms attached to carbon, hypoxanthine, xanthine and uric acid are obtained. Most living cells can synthesize the important purines adenine and guanine from simpler precursors. Ingested purines, as well as those formed within the cell, are eventually oxidized to uric acid.

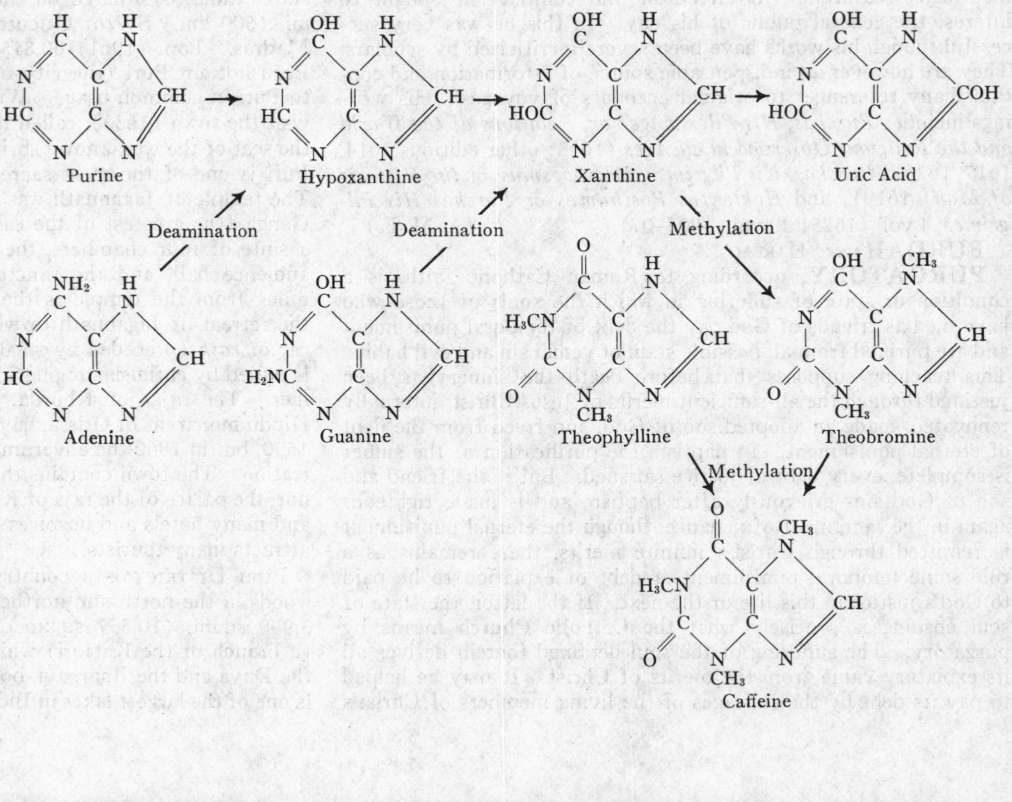

In man, this substance is excreted in the urine as the main end product of purine metabolism. Other mammals excrete allantoin, a degradation product of uric acid. In reptiles and birds, however, uric acid is the main nitrogenous end product of protein as well as of purine metabolism. The excrement of birds and snakes, therefore, consists mainly of uric acid. A rich source of uric acid, guano, the excrement of certain South American sea birds, has been accumulating, with the help of a dry climate, for untold years.

Because uric acid and its monosodium salt are relatively insoluble, they are readily precipitated. Such precipitates constitute the painful nodules characteristic of the disease gout in human beings. The pig is deficient in enzymes which convert guanine to allantoin, and consequently the pig frequently suffers from a form of gout similar in all respects to that in humans, except that the deposit in the joints consists of crystalline guanine instead of acid sodium urate.

Much of the fundamental work on purine chemistry was done by the German chemist Emil Fischer, who coined the name purine from the Latin words *purum* and *uricum*, the latter being chosen because the best-known purine at that time, uric acid, occurs in the urine.

Any modern text book of biochemistry will give further information on this subject. (B. V.)

PURITANISM, the most dynamic form of Protestantism among English-speaking peoples during the 16th and 17th centuries. The age of Puritanism in England may be roughly defined as the century following the Reformation (*q.v.*). It extended from the first years of the reign of Elizabeth I to 1660, when the restoration of the Stuarts brought to an end the attempt to fashion a Puritan state. The Puritan age in New England dated from the first settlement in 1620 to Massachusetts' loss of the old charter and the issuance of a new one in 1691, although there was to be a brief attempt to reconstitute the old order upon a new basis during the 1730s under the leadership of Jonathan Edwards.

The term Puritan was coined as an epithet of contempt during the 1560s, and it was applied to all those persons within the Church of England who sought a more thoroughgoing reformation of the church than had been provided by the Elizabethan religious settlement. It also came to be applied to those who broke away from the Church of England in order to carry out the desired reforms without further delay. The major body of Puritans were Anglicans and remained so until the outbreak of the English Civil War in 1642 (*see* CIVIL WAR, ENGLISH). Most of them were moderate episcopalians in sympathy, although presbyterian and congregationalist sentiment was to be found among them. Even the early Congregationalists of the Massachusetts Bay colony in North America professed themselves to be loyal members of the Church of England. The small non-Anglican wing of Puritanism was composed initially of "separatist" Congregationalists and Baptists, but during the regime of Oliver Cromwell, when religious groups multiplied in a vast profusion, the Society of Friends (Quakers), constituted the extreme left of the Puritan movement.

In North America there was a varying degree of Puritan influence in all the English colonies, but the term tended to be reserved to designate the "separatist" and "nonseparatist" Congregationalists who established the Plymouth and Massachusetts Bay colonies and spread out into the rest of what was to become known as New England.

Nature of Puritanism.—Puritanism arose out of a desire for liturgical reform, being given classic definition at its earliest stage by G. M. Trevelyan: "the religion of all those who wished either to 'purify' the usage of the established church from taint of popery or to worship separately by forms so 'purified'" (*England under the Stuarts,* 16th ed., London, 1933). Questions of polity and theology later were brought into the area of controversy, but the underlying spirit of religious and moral earnestness that had given rise to the initial demand for reform remained the most constant feature of Puritanism. As a consequence, a Puritan became identified quite correctly in the popular mind as one who followed a strict and closely regulated habit of life. Edwards gave expression to this aspect of Puritanism when he described the Christian's "practice of religion" in these words: "It may be said, not only to be his business at certain seasons, the business of Sabbath-days, or certain extraordinary times, or the business of a month, or a

year, or of seven years, or his business under certain circumstances; but *the business of his life*" (*The Works of Jonathan Edwards,* vol. i, p. 314, 10th ed., London, 1865). The Puritan was a spiritual athlete, characterized by an intense zeal for reform, a zeal to order everything—personal life, family life, worship, church, business affairs, political views, even recreation—in the light of God's demand upon him.

The daily routine of the Puritan usually involved private devotions at the hour of rising; family prayers with the reading of Scripture and the catechizing of children and servants; and the keeping of a spiritual diary in which the events of the day were closely scrutinized and an accounting made of moral successes and failures as well as note being taken of the signal evidences of divine grace or displeasure that had been disclosed during the course of the day. The whole thrust of Puritan preaching was designed to reinforce this systematic and carefully controlled pattern of life by sensitizing the conscience to the issues that must be faced from day to day by earnest Christians. A non-Puritan clergyman, Anthony Gilbert, in 1566 put this aspect of Puritanism vividly when he reported that his patron had said that "he could never go to any of these Genevan sermons that he came quiet home, ... there was ever something that pricked his conscience; he always thought that they made their whole sermon against him. But in the reading of Mattins and Evensong at [St.] Paul's, or in my reading of my service in his chapel, he sayeth, he feeleth no such thing, for he is never touched, but goeth merrily to his dinner."

These differing facets of the Puritan's concern make it evident that Puritanism was rooted in a vast sense of dissatisfaction with mediocre and halfhearted endeavour. This dissatisfaction, in turn, was rooted in a deep religious experience of dramatic intensity. The whole object of the Puritan was to experience the miracle of grace himself and to produce it in others. Thus Puritanism falls within the category of a religious revival, and it is analogous in many ways to earlier revivals that sprang from the preaching of the friars and to the later revivals associated with the names of John Wesley, George Whitefield and Gilbert Tennent.

Tudor Puritanism.—Under Henry VIII the authority of the Roman papacy had been formally abolished by a series of parliamentary acts, culminating in the Act of Supremacy of 1534, which declared the king to be "the only supreme head in earth of the Church of England." The few limited reforms of the Henrician period were followed by a rapid Protestant advance under the boy king Edward VI (1547–53). This was followed, in turn, by a restoration of Roman Catholicism under Queen Mary (1553–58). Many of the more prominent Protestant leaders, including the archbishop of Canterbury, were burned at the stake during the Marian regime; the revulsion occasioned by these executions, it has been said, guaranteed that England was to be a Protestant nation in the future. Of greater importance was the fact that the exile on the continent, into which many younger men were forced, proved to be a school for training of men upon whom Elizabeth of necessity was to depend for leadership in the English Church. When Elizabeth I came to the throne late in 1558, she was hailed by the returning exiles as the English Deborah who would restore the Church of England to what they regarded as its pristine purity. She was to frustrate rather than fulfill their hopes.

Elizabeth was committed to the Protestant cause for a variety of reasons, but she detested anything that smacked of Geneva, having been alienated by John Knox's attack upon the right of women to rule and being convinced that the Genevans were "overbold with God Almighty, making too many subtle scannings of his blessed will, as lawyers do with human testaments." It was, she believed, dangerous to royal power to have private men citing Scripture against the government. Elizabeth was determined to exercise power in both state and church as her royal prerogative, and she was especially determined that the religious settlement should follow a middle course. Under pressure from the crown parliament passed an Act of Uniformity which required several observances that most Protestants regarded as popish superstitions. It was at this point, however, that a division occurred.

Some remembered Peter's word that one must obey God rather than men; these were to be the Puritans. Others remembered Paul's counsel that due regard must be given to constituted authority; these were to be the apologists for the Elizabethan settlement who insisted that a godly prince, after the pattern of Israel, must be obeyed in all matters not clearly proscribed in Scripture.

The initial controversy had been foreshadowed in the reign of Edward VI when Knox objected to kneeling as a practice associated with the adoration of the host and indicating a belief in transubstantiation, and when John Hooper objected to a distinctive clerical garb as representing in symbolic form a denial of the priesthood of believers. It was this latter issue that came to the front with the publication of Matthew Parker's *Advertisements* in 1566 as part of the effort to secure uniformity of clerical dress, and resulted in the label of "Puritan" being attached to the dissident party. The Puritans, of course, were seeking to reform the whole liturgy of the church that it might have greater theological integrity; and a rightly ordered worship, they believed, also involved the recovery of gospel discipline within the church. Their program was made explicit in 1572 in *An Admonition to Parliament*, which declared that "we in England are so far off from having a church rightly reformed according to the prescript of God's Word, that as yet we are not come to the outward face of the same." The "outward marks whereby a true Christian church is known," it continued, "are preaching of the Word purely, ministering of the sacraments sincerely, and ecclesiastical discipline which consisteth in admonition and correction of faults severely"; on all three counts the provisions of the Elizabethan settlement were deemed defective.

Puritan sentiment was strong enough in 1563 to come within one vote of adopting a sweeping program of reform in the Convocation of Canterbury, the legislative body for most of the Church of England. Defeated there, the Puritans turned to parliament where they were able to command majority support throughout Elizabeth's reign, but Elizabeth always claimed her prerogative and prevented parliament from dealing with the religious question. Edmund Grindal, archbishop of Canterbury, encouraged the voluntary implementation of a portion of the Puritan program, and this led to his being sequestered from office. While official efforts at reform were rebuffed by the queen, and while she was careful to prevent any widespread organization from being developed, a great deal of latitude and freedom was permitted within the parishes; and it was within the parishes, by virtue of effective preaching and pastoral example, that Puritanism continued to gain strength throughout the Elizabethan period. During this period also there were a few ardent and impetuous spirits who had become impatient with delay and who, adopting as their slogan "reformation without tarrying for any," proceeded to organize "separate" congregations. Ultimately most of these separatists were forced to take refuge in the Netherlands.

Stuart Puritanism.—Puritan confidence in the rightness of their cause may well have been the source of the optimism with which they greeted each new monarch. They were especially hopeful when after Elizabeth's death James I came to the throne in 1603. A dozen years earlier, as James VI of Scotland, he had consented to the establishment of Presbyterianism in his native land. The Puritans believed, therefore, that he might be expected to show some favour to Puritanism in England. With high expectations the Puritans presented the new king with a moderate plea for church reform known as the Millenary petition because it purported to represent the desires of more than 1,000 clergymen. The king promised a conference at Hampton court on the matter. When he met with them in Jan. 1604, he rejected the Puritan plea with scorn. James was an ardent Calvinist, but he was no presbyterian; far from restricting the power of the bishops, his dictum was "No bishop, no king."

One consequence of James's attempted repression of Puritanism was to drive additional Puritans into separatism and exile. Among these groups of exiles was the Gainsborough-Scrooby congregation, one portion of which went to Amsterdam under the leadership of John Smyth, where they became the earliest group of English Baptists. The Scrooby portion under the leadership of John

Robinson went to Leiden, from which in 1620 some of their number departed to establish the colony of Plymouth in the new world. Other Puritans, unwilling to renounce all bonds of fellowship with the Church of England, adopted a middle position which has been called nonseparatist congregationalism. Chiefly under the guidance of Henry Jacob and William Ames, they developed the theory that the Church of England was in essence composed of congregational churches; this fact had been obscured but it had not been obliterated. Thus they were justified in forming independent congregations when necessary and at the same time professing themselves to be loyal members of the Church of England. Nonseparatists of this type established the Massachusetts Bay colony in 1629.

James I, however, was not an effective persecutor, and his policy was moderated by the influence of Archbishop George Abbot, who was sympathetic to the Puritan cause. By virtue of various expedients, many of the clergy were able to retain a measure of freedom in their parishes, and a system of lectureships was developed to provide for those who could not. The lectureships were preaching stations set up voluntarily, and they permitted the occupants to escape from the necessity of reading the required service. Serious trouble developed only after the accession of Charles I in 1625. Under the aegis of William Laud (*q.v.*), archbishop of Canterbury, rigorous measures were adopted to enforce conformity, lectureships were suppressed and when parliament proved to be refractory Charles embarked upon a period of personal rule that lasted through the 1630s.

Puritan Revolution.—As the result of an attempt to impose "Laud's liturgy" on the Scottish Church, Scotland rose in revolt and in 1639 invaded England. Charles was without adequate financial resources to carry on a war and was forced to summon parliament in 1640. Parliament immediately took command of the situation, refusing to grant necessary subsidies until the abuses of Charles's personal rule had been remedied. There was general agreement that the evils of prelacy should be eliminated, but when parliament abolished episcopacy the king was able to rally support; civil war broke out in 1642 (*see* CIVIL WAR, ENGLISH). The Westminster assembly of divines was summoned in 1643 to draft a new religious settlement for the nation, but its essentially presbyterian proposals were unsatisfactory for a variety of reasons to a majority of the people. The more erastian members of parliament did not look with favour upon the establishment of an independent ecclesiastical system. Large segments of the population remained strongly episcopalian in their sympathies. There had also been a vast proliferation of smaller religious groups since the lifting of the restraints of the Laudien regime. Furthermore, the Puritan preachers, who for three generations had been insisting upon the necessity for the Word of God to be freely preached, had cultivated a climate of opinion among many of their followers that was hostile to the placing of new restrictions upon the freedom to preach. Most important of all, widespread sentiment for religious toleration had developed in the parliamentary army. This was "the good old cause" that held the army together in its struggle with the king, and to the army the proposals of the assembly represented the substitution of one repressive ecclesiastical system for another. John Milton spoke for the army when he said: "New presbyter is but old priest writ large."

With parliament becoming increasingly divided and impotent, effective rule shifted to the army under the leadership of Cromwell. The royalists were brought under control in a series of battles, the king was executed and the religious problem was resolved in terms of a voluntary national establishment. Cromwell was less successful in his efforts to shift authority from the army to a stable parliamentary regime. The nation was too divided for any of the expedients he devised to succeed. After his death and the removal of his strong hand, the political situation rapidly deteriorated, and in 1660 the Puritan attempt to fashion a holy commonwealth was brought to an end with the restoration of the monarchy. The religious issue remained troublesome, however, until the adoption of the Act of Toleration in 1689.

American Puritanism.—The term Puritan has been given a much narrower definition in the United States. There was a conspicuous Puritan influence in early Virginia, and the blue laws of that colony have been said to have been even more repressive than those of New England. Moreover a Puritan influence was represented to varying degrees in all the English colonies by Baptists, Quakers and English Presbyterians. Puritanism in America, however, is generally understood to mean the early Congregationalism of New England.

Massachusetts Bay, the strongest of the New England colonies, was founded by a group of nonseparatist Congregationalists who had become convinced—as a result of the dissolution of parliament in 1629 by Charles I and the adoption of the rigorous repressive measures of Laud—that it was no longer possible to reform the Anglican Church in England. Through a defect in the charter they were able to transfer the government of the colony to the new world, and throughout the Laudian decade of the 1630s a large and well-organized migration into the new colony proceeded. No colony in the history of European colonization ranked above Massachusetts Bay in wealth, station, education or capacity. The colonists were a selected people ("sifted grain") with strong clerical leadership, and their purpose was to accomplish in the new world that which they had been prevented from accomplishing at home. Their intention was to create in the American wilderness a new Zion that would become "a city set on a hill" and force by the power of its example the desired reformation in England.

The Massachusetts Bay Puritans established what they believed to be a biblical church order and with it a community that was regulated throughout by divine and natural law. The whole program was outlined in the *Cambridge Platform* of 1648. Church membership was restricted to the regenerate and their children who should "own the covenant," and only church members enjoyed political rights. Religious uniformity was enforced, and dissenters were informed that they had the right to stay away or to cross the river and take up land of their own beyond the boundary of Massachusetts. The restrictions were difficult to maintain; there were demands that the franchise be broadened and religious dissent kept appearing. When Roger Williams was banished, the settlement he established at Providence became a new source of dissidence. The second generation saw a diminution of zeal. The clergy interpreted recurrent misfortunes as signs of God's wrath with the growing laxity, but the adoption of the "halfway covenant" was evidence of clerical inability to halt the trend. The replacement of the charter in 1691 put an end to any real hope they still entertained of maintaining their holy commonwealth in its purity. The story was much the same in the other Puritan colonies of New England. Edwards briefly rallied the waning forces of Puritan zeal, and attenuated Congregational establishments lingered on in Massachusetts, Connecticut and New Hampshire until the 19th century. The Puritan heritage, however, was stamped deep in the character of the New Englanders, and with the great migration westward it became a major factor in the shaping of the American spirit.

Puritan Contributions.—One of the most conspicuous contributions of Puritanism was the sturdiness of character it produced. "The Puritan mind was one of the toughest the world has ever had to deal with. It is inconceivable to conceive of a disillusioned Puritan; no matter what misfortune befell him, no matter how often or how tragically his fellowmen failed him, he would have been prepared for the worst, and would have expected no better" (Perry Miller and T. H. Johnson, *The Puritans*, pp. 59–60, New York, 1938). The Puritan knew that the life of faith is an arduous struggle, that sin is a stubborn fact of human existence and that affliction is frequently the lot of the saints; but he was nerved and strengthened by a great devotion to God and by a great confidence in God's overruling Providence. Later generations were fed again and again from the devotional works the Puritans produced.

Curiously, the Puritans, who began as firm believers in the necessity for religious uniformity, became the architects who fashioned the principles of religious freedom. This was partly the result of the fact that the religious diversity they generated bred of necessity a spirit of toleration, but the necessity was supported by theological convictions whose implications only gradually became fully apparent. They had emphasized the necessity for the Word of God to be freely preached, and they recognized that even the best of men and churches were fallible. Who was to decide who might preach, when God might speak through the humblest of the brethren? Thus the New England Puritans could pursue measures of repression only with a lurking sense of guilt, elaborate apologetics and a tendency to make increasing concessions to dissent. More typical of the logic of Puritanism was Williams' *Bloudy Tenent of Persecution*, which became one of the great Puritan manifestoes in the English civil wars.

Many scholars have noted the contribution of Puritanism to the development of democracy. The army debates, the gathered churches, the demand for liberty and the denunciations of arbitrary power all helped create a climate of opinion favourable to the development of self-government. Even more important was the insistence upon the necessity for checks and balances if the abuse of power was to be prevented. Said John Cotton: "Let all the world learn to give mortal man no greater power than they are content they shall use, for use it they will . . . . It is necessary that all power that is on earth be limited, church power or other. . . . It is counted a matter of danger to the state to limit prerogatives, but it is a further danger not to have them limited" (*An Exposition of the Thirteenth Chapter of Revelation*, p. 72). The relationship that has been suggested between Puritanism and the rise of modern capitalism is more debatable. *See* also references under "Puritanism" in the Index.

BIBLIOGRAPHY.—William Haller, *The Rise of Puritanism* (1938), and *Liberty and Reformation in the Puritan Revolution* (1955) ; I. D. Jones, *The English Revolution* (1931) ; M. M. Knappen, *Tudor Puritanism* (1939) ; Perry Miller, *Orthodoxy in Massachusetts* (1933), *The New England Mind: The Seventeenth Century*, rev. ed. (1954) and *The New England Mind: From Colony to Province* (1953) ; Alan Simpson, *Puritanism in Old and New England* (1955).   (W. S. H.)

PURITY, BRETHREN OF, the usual English designation of the IKHWAN AS-SAFA' (*i.e.*, "Sincere Brethren"), an Arabic secret confraternity who produced, probably in the second half of the 10th century A.D., a philosophical and religious encyclopaedia consisting of 52 "writings" (Arabic *rasa'il;* sing. *risala*) by different authors. The contents of this encyclopaedia appealed to the Ismailian movement, but its authors were not Ismaili themselves. Like all other Islamic philosophers, they attempted to naturalize Greek philosophy in a way of their own, but they differ from other Islamic philosophers in following a more orthodox Neoplatonic line and in admitting Hermetic, Gnostic, astrological and occult sciences on a large scale. According to them, the individual human souls emanate from the universal soul and rejoin it after death; and the universal soul in its turn will be united with God on the day of the Last Judgment.

Rasa'il 1–14 deal with the preparatory sciences such as mathematics, astronomy and astrology, music, geography and the different parts of Aristotelian logic (*risala* 13 was translated into Latin in the middle ages) ; *rasa'il* 15–31 with the natural sciences in the order established by the later Greek commentators of Aristotle and also with man as a microcosm, with the human soul, with the influence of the stars and with the difference of languages (*see* below for *risala* 22) ; *rasa'il* 32–41 with the spiritual world on Neoplatonic lines, with the final destruction of the world, with the longing of the soul for God and its spiritual resurrection, etc.; and *rasa'il* 42–52 with various aspects of the revealed divine law, with the mutual duties of the brethren, with prophetic revelation and with miracles, magic, etc. There is also an important summary of the whole encyclopaedia, *Ar-Risala al-Jami'a. Risala* 22 tells the story of a dispute between animals and men before the king of the genii (in which the animals eventually lose). This story was translated into Catalan by a Franciscan friar, Anselmo de Turmeda, in 1417 (he represented it as his own original work) and into English by way of a Hindustani version, by J. Wall (1863).

Apart from Arabic editions of the whole encyclopaedia, 4 vol. (1888–89), and of the summary, critical ed., 2 vol. (1949–51), there are German translations of several of the *rasa'il* by F. Dieterici (*Die Naturanschauung und Naturphilosophie der Araber*

..., 2 parts, 1876–79; and *Die Abhandlungen der Ichwan es-Safa im Auswahl,* 3 parts, 1883–86). Dieterici, however, was unaware of certain Islamic aspects of the work and overrated its philosophical importance.

BIBLIOGRAPHY.—Adel Arva, *L'Esprit critique des "Frères de la Pureté"* (1948); F. Goldziher, *Richtungen der islamischen Koranauslegung* (1920); C. Brockelmann, *Geschichte der arabischen Litteratur,* i, 2nd ed., pp. 236–237 (1943). (R. R. WR.)

PURKINJE, JOHANNES EVANGELISTA (JAN EVANGELISTA PURKYNE) (1787–1869), Czech physiologist, a pioneer in experimental physiology, histology, and embryology, was born in Libochovice, near Prague, Dec. 17, 1787. He graduated in medicine at Prague in 1819 and in 1823 became professor of physiology and pathology at Breslau University, where he began a course of experimental physiology, established a small laboratory, and created an independent department of physiology (1839), the first of its kind. He established another after becoming professor at Prague University (1850). He died in Prague, July 28, 1869.

Purkinje's scientific work was extremely varied, the most important concerning vision and microscopy. He noticed similar granular formations in different animal tissues and drew attention to the analogy of these animal granules (Ger. *Körnchen*) with plant cells (1837); and he introduced the term protoplasm. Some of his discoveries bear his name: Purkinje's cells in the cerebellar cortex; Purkinje's fibres; the large heart muscle cells beneath the endocardium, forming Purkinje's network; Purkinje's germinal vesicle, the nucleus of the ovum; Purkinje's figure, the shadows of the retinal vessels; Purkinje's images, the reflections on the surfaces of cornea and lens of the eye; Purkinje's phenomenon, the change in the brightness of blue and red in the dark. Publication of Purkinje's *Omnia Opera* began in 1918.

BIBLIOGRAPHY.—R. Heidenhain in *Allgemeine Deutsche Biographie,* 26:717 (1888); V. Robinson, *Pathfinders in Medicine* (1929); H. J. John, *Proc. Roy. Soc. Med.,* 46:933 (1953). (V. O. KR.)

PURNEA, a town and district in the Bhagalpur division of Bihar, India. The town, headquarters of the district, lies near the left bank of the Saura River, a tributary of the Ganges, and 50 mi. (80 km.) NE of Bhagalpur. Pop. (1961) 40,602. It is a nodal town with a brisk trade in rice and raw jute.

PURNEA DISTRICT (area 4,259 sq.mi. [10,372 sq.km.]; pop. [1961] 3,089,128) occupies the eastern part of the north Bihar Plains bordering West Bengal and is traversed by meandering streams and abandoned courses of the Kosi River. The Mahananda is the principal river of the district. Rice and jute are the chief crops; others include tobacco and mustard seeds. Katihar (pop. [1961] 46,837), to the south, is the largest town and an important railway junction and trade centre. Kishanganj, near the Mahananda River, and Forbesganj, near the Nepal frontier, are the other trade centres. The district is served by the North Eastern Railway. (S. P. C.)

PURPLE, a shade varying between crimson and violet. Formerly it was the deep crimson colour called in Latin *purpura,* from the name of the shellfish (*Purpura*) which yielded the famous Tyrian dye. Tyrian purple during many ages was the most celebrated of all dyed colours, and possibly the first to be permanently fixed on wool or linen. Being extremely costly, robes of this colour were worn as a mark of imperial or royal rank, whence the phrase "born in the purple." In the Roman Catholic Church "promotion to the purple" is promotion to the rank of cardinal.

The ancients derived their purple from the mollusks, *Purpura haemastoma,* and *Murex brandaris,* the shells of which have been found adjacent to ancient dyeworks at Athens and Pompeii. The colour-producing secretion is contained in a small cyst adjacent to the head of the animal, and this puslike matter when spread on textile material in presence of sunlight develops a purple-red colour. P. Friedländer showed that the dye developed from the mollusks is 6:6'-dibromoindigotin. (A. G. P.; X.)

PURPURA is the presence of large (ecchymoses) and small (petechiae) hemorrhages in the skin, often associated with bleeding from natural cavities and in tissues. It occurs as a result of failure of hemostasis which, in turn, has five major causes:

1. Damage to the wall of small arterial vessels (vascular purpura), due to vitamin deficiency (scurvy), bacteria, viruses, allergic reactions, etc. A hereditary disease in which the vessels appear normal but cannot contract after injury is known as pseudohemophilia.

2. Deficiency of platelets, small bodies that not only plug leakages in the vessel wall mechanically but also contain many chemicals active in the coagulation of blood. Bleeding occurs when platelets are insufficient in number (thrombocytopenia) either because they are not produced (as a result of destruction of the precursor megakaryocytes in the bone marrow, due to invasion by leukemia or to aplasia induced by drugs or by radiation injury) or because they are too quickly destroyed by an overactive spleen or by antibodies (immunothrombocytopenia). Platelet antibodies develop in the course of other diseases (such as lupus erythematosus) or may be evoked by allergy to viruses, bacteria, or certain drugs. Spleen and antibodies are usually associated in destroying platelets. In one variety of the disease (thrombocytoasthenia) the platelets are normal in number but abnormal in function.

3. Deficiency of clotting factors, either congenital (as in hemophilia, Christmas disease, hypoprothrombinemia, afibrinogenemia, etc.) or acquired in the course of disease (especially of liver), administration of drugs (anticoagulants, etc.).

4. Development of circulating anticoagulants of various types (abnormal proteins, antibodies, etc.) that prevent normal interaction of the various clotting factors and are found in some blood disorders (multiple myeloma, leukemias, etc.), following reactions to drugs, in diseases of the connective tissue, and in radiation injury.

5. Fibrinolysis, due to the activation of a usually dormant system that is able to destroy the blood fibrin clot; this may occur during accidents of pregnancy, delivery, and surgery. A paradoxical type of bleeding is found when tissue materials (as in shock, trauma, burns, etc.) enter the bloodstream and cause clotting within the vessels. As the patient is depleted of clotting factors, he becomes a bleeder. This mechanism is often found behind severe hemorrhage at delivery.

Treatment of purpura depends on the causative mechanism. ACTH and steroid hormones are effective in controlling vascular purpura and the bleeding of thrombocytopenia. Transfusion of platelets may be a useful technique for bleeding emergency, and surgical removal of the spleen is resorted to in thrombocytopenic purpura when other therapy has failed. The administration of either blood or plasma or of the fractions specifically absent (fibrinogen, antihemophilic globulin, etc.) is the basis of the treatment of acute bleeding in disorders of blood coagulation. *See* also BLOOD; BLOOD, DISORDERS OF: *Purpura;* HEMORRHAGE.

See M. Stefanini and W. Dameshek, *Hemorrhagic Disorders* (1955). (M. ST.)

PURSLANE, the common name for certain small fleshy annual plants of the genus *Portulaca,* with prostrate, reddish stems, egg-shaped leaves attached by the narrower end, and small yellow flowers that open in the sunlight. The common purslane (*P. oleracea*), or pusley, is a widespread weed, but is grown to some extent as a potherb, mostly in Europe. All plants of the genus are known for their ability to persist: they grow well even in dry, waste soil and can retain enough moisture to bloom and ripen seeds long after they have been uprooted. The capsules, which open by a lid, scatter many small seeds of great longevity.

The purslane tree (*Portulacaria afra*), native of South Africa, is a fleshy leaved, soft-wooded tree up to 12 ft. high; it is grown in California as a specimen plant for its succulent habit and its tiny pink flowers in clusters.

PURULIA, a town and district in the Burdwan division of West Bengal, India. The town, headquarters of the district, is a straggling settlement, about 1 mi. N of the Kasai River and 135 mi. WNW of Calcutta. Pop. (1961) 48,134. It lies largely to the southwest of the junction of the Asansol–Chandil railway line with the Ranchi–Purulia branch and is a focus of good metaled roads. The town has a radial pattern; there are several tanks (artificial ponds), the largest one (1½ mi. in perimeter) being to the north.

PURULIA DISTRICT has an area of 2,415 sq.mi. (6,285 sq.km.) and a population (1961) of 1,360,016. The present district was formed at the reorganization of states in 1956 from the transferred area of the former Manbhum District of Bihar (with the exception of the thanas [police stations] of Chas, Chandil, Patamda, and Ichagarh, which were retained by Bihar).

Much of the district is an undulating peneplain, 500–1,000 ft. (160–330 m.) above sea level, forming the eastern fringe of the Chota Nagpur Uplands. Toward the west and south are forested scarps overlooking the Subarnarekha Valley. Forests occur in small isolated patches, and the district is dotted with tanks used for irrigation. The flood control and irrigation scheme on the Kasai River consists of a dam, 10 mi. (16 km.) W of the town of Purulia, and a reservoir. The principal crop is rice, which covers 72% of the sown area. Shellac is manufactured in the towns of Purulia, Jhalda, and Balrampur. (E. Ah.)

PURVA MIMAMSA, one of the six schools of thought to which Indian philosophers adhered in the centuries following the Epic period. *See* INDIAN PHILOSOPHY: *Six Systems.*

PURVEYANCE, in England, the compulsory purchase of goods for the king and the compulsory hire of horses and carts to convey the goods, was a standing grievance through the Middle Ages and into the 17th century. Payment was made at "the king's price," a wholesale price less than that current in the local markets. The king's officers exercised this right at the great fairs and took a customary levy of wine coming into the ports. In this way the king's manors were restocked and his castles repaired and provisioned. The first limitation of this prerogative was won in Magna Carta (1215) when the king promised immediate payment for goods taken and that horses and carts should not be seized for carriage duty nor timber for the repair of castles, save with the owner's consent (cap. 28, 30, 31). Although the final version of Magna Carta allowed royal officers to delay payment where there was a royal castle, it exempted the demesne carts of parsons, knights, and ladies from being taken. It was often alleged that the king's officers took more than the king needed and sold the goods for their own profit, and, moreover, did not pay for what they seized. In 1258 the barons complained in their Petition (cap. 23) that because "almost no payment" was made for goods taken, English merchants were impoverished and foreign merchants would not import goods.

Edward I tried to regulate the behaviour of those taking prisages on his behalf in the first Statute of Westminster (1275); but general exactions were made necessary by his campaigns and a long clause dealing with abuses was included in the *Articuli super cartas* (1300). The *Articuli,* however, never became substantive law. The king's obligation to provide hospitality meant that purveyance must be regulated rather than abandoned and it was regulation, not abolition, that was demanded in the 14th century. But the growing complexity of the royal household and the establishment of households for other members of the royal family increased the burden. In the Good Parliament (1376) the Commons petitioned that the justices of the peace should be commissioned to enforce recent statutes against dishonest purveyors, but this was not secured by statute until 1441. By 1600 it was the practice for the justices of the peace to fix with the officers of the Board of Green Cloth (the household accounting office) the price and amount of provisions required; the difference between the agreed and current market prices was raised by county assessments. There were still loopholes for abuse and Sir Francis Bacon spoke against purveyors in the first parliament of James I. Purveyance fell out of use under the Commonwealth and was abolished in 1660 at the Restoration. Even then, the royalist, Fabian Philipps, protested, arguing that purveyance kept taxes and prices down.

BIBLIOGRAPHY.—Fabian Philipps, *Pourveyance for the King* (1663); T. F. Tout, *Chapters in the Administrative History of Medieval England,* 6 vol. (1920–33); B. H. Putnam (ed.), *Proceedings Before the Justices of the Peace in the Fourteenth and Fifteenth Centuries* (1938); W. S. Thomson (ed.), *A Lincolnshire Assize Roll for 1298* (1944); W. Money (ed.), *A Royal Purveyance, 1575* (1901). (D. M. S.)

PURVITS, VILHELMS KARLIS (1872–1945), Latvian landscape painter who introduced Impressionism into northeastern Europe, was born in Zaube rural district on March 3, 1872, and attended a secondary school in Latgale Province. He later abandoned his father's milling business for painting, graduating from St. Petersburg Academy in 1897; awarded a Rome prize, he traveled widely in western Europe. After teaching at Tallinn Cathedral School (1906–09) he directed the Riga State Art School until it was closed in 1916; from 1913, when he was elected academician of St. Petersburg Academy, he was also director of the state museum and professor at Riga University.

Purvits organized the independent Latvian Academy of Arts in 1919 and was its rector and professor until 1934. In 1934–36 he edited a history of art. From Impressionism he developed the Baltic landscape style; later, his methodical compositions became more colourful and expressionistic.

Many of his pictures were destroyed by military action at Jelgava, Latvia, in July 1944; others, evacuated to Bavaria, disappeared. A refugee, Purvits died at Nauheim, Hesse, Ger., on Jan. 18, 1945.

PUSA, a village in Bihar, India, about 40 mi. (64 km.) NE of Patna. In 1796 the government acquired an estate there which was long used as a stud depot and afterward as a tobacco farm. The estate of 1,280 ac. (518 ha.) was made over in 1904 to the Imperial Agricultural Department of the government of India and became its headquarters. In 1905 a research institute was founded with an experimental farm and an agricultural college at which officers were trained for higher posts in the agricultural departments. The institute owed its inception to Lord Curzon, then viceroy, and rendered very useful service to Indian agriculture. A. and G. L. C. Howard produced strains of wheat which gave high yield and were of good milling quality; these strains were rust-resistant and gave good results under diverse conditions of soil and climate.

The Pusa varieties were in their day grown over large tracts of the United Provinces (now Uttar Pradesh), the Punjab, and the former North-West Frontier Province (West Pakistan). E. J. Butler carried out masterly researches there on fungus pests, as did H. M. Lefroy on insect pests troublesome in India. B. P. Pal and other Indian agricultural scientists also did good work. The advantages of selective breeding of cattle were demonstrated; the milk yield of a pure herd was doubled in ten years.

The institute always suffered from its isolated position, and when in 1934 an earthquake destroyed the main block of laboratories it was decided to transfer the work to New Delhi and to found a central research institute there. This plan was duly executed, and the new Indian Agricultural Research Institute was opened on Nov. 7, 1936, by the viceroy, Lord Linlithgow. In 1958 under the Universities Grants' Commission the institute was given the same standing as a university. The road on which the institute buildings stand is called Pusa Road. (E. J. R.)

PUSAN (Japanese FUSAN), a city located along a deep, well-sheltered bay at the southeast tip of Korea, facing the Korean strait. During Japanese control (1910–1945) Pusan became the major Korean port. Ferry services connected it to Shimonoseki, Japan. Rail lines through Korea to Manchuria and China terminated in Pusan. Industries, including shipbuilding, iron and steel, railroad shops and textile manufacturing were developed. Rice milling and salt refining were also carried on.

The beachhead area around Pusan was held by the United Nations forces in 1950, and the city became the temporary capital of the Republic of Korea and a port of supply and disembarkation during the first years of the Korean war. The city was swollen by refugees, whose many temporary shacks covered the hills. Disastrous fires occurred in these areas but the city was rebuilt and more permanent structures established. Industries were redeveloped and the population grew to 1,162,614 (1960 census).

(S. McC.)

PUSEY, EDWARD BOUVERIE (1800–1882), English leader of the Oxford movement, who, though remaining firm in his Anglican beliefs, headed the Catholic revival in the Church of England, was born at Pusey on Aug. 22, 1800. His father was Philip Bouverie, whose ancestor was a Protestant refugee from the Low Countries who reached England in the 16th century. Philip Bouverie took the name of Pusey upon succeeding to the estate of that name in Berkshire. Edward was educated at Eton and Christ Church, Oxford. In 1823 he stood for a fellowship by examination at Oriel college and was elected, thus entering the brilliant common room of which John Keble and J. H. Newman (*qq.v.*) were already members.

From 1825 to 1827 he studied oriental languages and theology in Germany, where the state of German Protestantism, driven to skepticism by the rationalism of the Enlightenment, made a permanent impression upon him by way of reaction.

In 1828 Pusey's reputation as an orientalist caused the duke of Wellington to nominate him to the regius chair of Hebrew in Oxford, which carried with it a canonry of Christ Church. From the year 1833 began his association with the Oxford movement, to which he brought a decisive reinforcement. "He," wrote Newman, "at once gave us a position and a name." He contributed a tract on fasting to the *Tracts for the Times* in 1834 and his most noteworthy work in that series was the extensive tract upon baptism of 1835.

In 1843 Pusey preached his university sermon on "The Holy Eucharist, a Comfort to the Penitent," which asserted the doctrine of the Real Presence. For this he was suspended by the vice-chancellor (without being allowed to speak publicly in his own defense) from preaching before the university for two years, an arbitrary act which, in H. P. Liddon's words, "sealed the doom of the old *régime*—the authority of the Heads and the old ecclesiastical polity of Oxford" and was a factor leading to university reform. Yet, after the ending of the sentence, Pusey preached in 1846 another sermon asserting another principle of the Oxford movement, the right of private confession and the existence of priestly absolution in the Church of England. Newman's secession to the Roman Catholic Church in 1845 was a crushing blow to Pusey.

Pusey's intense industry was devoted to the work of his professorial chair, to learned theological writing, to preaching and to individual spiritual direction. Nor were his activities confined to Oxford. In the cholera epidemic of 1866 he tended the sick in Bethnal Green; he preached in many parts of the country and contributed generously to church purposes, such as building St. Saviour's church, Leeds, at his own expense in 1842–45; and in addition, he was responsible for the revival of the monastic life in the Church of England, encouraging Marian Hughes to take religious vows (the first Anglican to do so since the Reformation) in 1841 and helping, in 1845, to found in London the first Anglican sisterhood.

In matters of biblical criticism Pusey was strictly conservative and to the end of his life combated the newer ideas which were becoming fashionable; his works on *The Minor Prophets, with Commentary* (1860) and *Daniel the Prophet* (1864) show a deep but old-fashioned Hebrew scholarship. Averse to the use of philosophy in theological construction, his doctrinal outlook was marked by a strong attachment to the principle of revelation interpreted by the historic authority of the church. He lacked Newman's speculative brilliance but had the intellectual strength of a well-stored and balanced mind and of a deep reverence for historic truth; he tested all current teaching by its consonance with the Bible and the mind of the early church.

Pusey's private life was marked by severe asceticism, intense personal religion, a capacity for lasting friendship and deep family affection. The death of his wife in 1839, of a daughter in 1844 and of his only son in 1880 were irreparable blows. He died on Sept. 16, 1882, at Ascot priory, the home of a sisterhood with which he was associated; he was buried in Christ Church cathedral.

Two years later his friends founded Pusey house, Oxford, as an institution for theological study and pastoral care in the university. There his library and many personal letters, papers and relics are preserved.

See H. P. Liddon, *Life of Edward Bouverie Pusey*, 4 vol. (1893–94), with a list of Pusey's works; and shorter biographies by G. W. E. Russell (1907) and G. L. Prestige (1933).　　　　(T. M. P.)

PUSHKIN, ALEKSANDR SERGEEVICH (1799–1837), the greatest Russian poet, and the founder of modern Russian literature, was born in Moscow on June 6 (new style; May 26, old style), 1799. His father came of an old boyar family; his mother was the granddaughter of Abram Hannibal who, according to family tradition, was an Abyssinian princeling bought as a slave at Constantinople and adopted by Peter the Great, whose comrade in arms he became. Pushkin immortalized him in the unfinished historical novel *Arap Petra Velikogo* (*The Negro of Peter the Great*).

Early Years.—Like many aristocratic families in early 19th-century Russia, Pushkin's parents adopted French culture, and he and his brother and sister learned to talk and read in French. They were left much to the care of their maternal grandmother, who told Aleksandr, especially, stories in Russian about his ancestors; and from Arina Rodionovna, his old nurse, a freed serf (immortalized as Tatyana's nurse in *Evgeni Onegin*), he heard Russian folktales. During summers at his grandmother's estate near Moscow he talked to the peasants and spent many hours alone, living in the dreamworld of a precocious, imaginative child. He read widely in his father's library, and his wish to write was stimulated by the guests who came to the house—Vasili Pushkin, his father's brother, and himself a minor poet, and members of the literary circle to which he belonged: I. I. Dmitriev, N. M. Karamzin, Vasili Zhukovski, and K. N. Batyushkov—young writers who opposed the prevailing French classicism. (*See* RUSSIAN LITERATURE: *Modern Pre-Revolutionary Literature: The 19th Century.*)

In 1811 Pushkin entered the Imperial Lyceum at Tsarskoe Selo, renamed Pushkin (*q.v.*) in his honour in 1937. While there he began his literary career with publication (1814, in *Vestnik Evropy*, "The Messenger of Europe") of his verse-epistle "To My Friend, the Poet." In his early verse he followed the style of his older contemporaries, the Romantic poets Batyushkov and Zhukovski, and of the French 17th- and 18th-century poets, especially the Vicomte de Parny (1753–1814), with their tradition of Epicurean verse.

St. Petersburg.—In 1817 Pushkin left the Lyceum, and, accepting a position in the foreign office at St. Petersburg, plunged

ALEKSANDR PUSHKIN, AN OIL PAINTING BY V. TROPININ, 1827. IN THE PUSHKIN MUSEUM, LENINGRAD

into social life. He was elected to the exclusive Arzamás, a literary society founded by his uncle's friends; he also became an active member of the "freedom movement" which had begun among progressive members of the aristocracy as a result of the upsurge of patriotism after the Napoleonic invasion of 1812. He joined the "Green Lamp" Association, which, founded in 1819 for the discussion of literature and the theatre, soon became a clandestine branch of a secret society, the Union of Welfare (*see* RUSSIAN HISTORY: *Alexander I: The Revolutionary Movement*). In his political verses and epigrams (widely circulated in manuscript, but unpublished until after his death), especially in the ode to liberty (*Vol'nost'*, written 1817) and *Derevnya* (*The Village*, written 1819), which show the influence of the 18th-century radical thinker and writer, A. N. Radishchev (*q.v.*), he made himself the mouthpiece of the ideas and aspirations of those who were to take part in the Decembrist rising of 1825, and who were to be known as the Decembrists (Dekabrists; *q.v.*).

The most important work of Pushkin's St. Petersburg years was the Romantic narrative poem *Ruslan and Ludmila,* begun when he was first a schoolboy at the Lyceum, abandoned, and finally finished and published in 1820. Though in form and style it follows the mock-heroic epics of Ariosto and Voltaire, its setting is Russian, and it is coloured by elements of folklore and the epic poetry of Kievan Rus (*see* RUSSIAN LITERATURE: *Old Russian*

Literature). Ruslan is modeled on the ideal traditional hero of early folk epic; Ludmila, whom he marries at the beginning of the poem (after a prologue that sets the scene firmly in a Russian landscape, and recalls the heroes and villains of Russian legend and fairy tale), is the daughter of Vladimir, grand prince of Kiev. On her wedding night she is kidnapped by the wicked magician Chernomor, and before he finally rescues her Ruslan encounters the many and varied adventures of such a hero as Ariosto's Orlando, but recalling also the exploits typical of his legendary Russian background.

Because it flouted all the accepted rules of the poetry of the period, and belonged to none of the genres then fashionable, this poem was violently attacked by both the established literary schools of the day, classicism and sentimentalism. But it brought the young poet fame, and Zhukovski presented Pushkin with his portrait, on which was the inscription: "To the victorious pupil from the defeated master."

Exile in the South.—For his political poems, in May 1820 Pushkin, though still in government service, was banished from St. Petersburg to the remote southern province of Moldavia. Sent first to Yekaterinoslav (Dnepropetrovsk), he was taken ill there, and while convalescing, traveled in the northern Caucasus and later to the Crimea with Gen. Rayevski, a hero of 1812, and his family. On return, he was sent to Kishinev, where he remained until 1823, and then to Odessa (1823–24). During this period, he expressed his bitterness at exile in letters to his friends—the first of a correspondence that, when collected, was to take its place as an outstanding and enduring monument of Russian prose.

The "Southern Cycle."—The impressions he gained of the Caucasus and the Crimea, and of Moldavia, provided material for Pushkin's "Southern Cycle" of Romantic narrative poems. Like many writers in Western Europe, he had fallen under the spell of Byron's poetry, and, as he himself said, his southern poems "smack of Byron." They introduced Byronic Romanticism to Russia. But even in the first, *Kavkazski plennik* (written 1820–21, published 1822; *The Prisoner of the Caucasus*), realist tendencies are discernible. Pushkin here creates from his own experience a psychologically truthful portrait of a typical representative of the rising generation in Russia, who, disappointed in love and friendship, and dissatisfied with social life in the capital, seeks freedom in the primitive beauty of the Caucasus and in the simple life of its inhabitants, untainted by "civilization." Taken prisoner by the Circassians, and finally liberated by a Circassian girl who loves him, he is unable to respond to the passion of this "maid of the mountains" because at heart he is cold and prematurely aged; and she, in despair, throws herself into a mountain torrent and is drowned.

In the second poem of the cycle, *Bratya razboiniki* (1821–22, publ. 1827; *The Robber Brothers*), a work permeated with passionate thirst for freedom, and based on an event that took place during Pushkin's stay at Yekaterinoslav, he describes the courageous escape from prison of two brothers, who, although chained and fettered, swam across the Dnieper and got away.

Bakhchisaraiski Fontan (1821–23, publ. 1824; *The Fountain of Bakhchisarai*) is based on a legend. Girei, a warlike Tatar khan of the Crimea, conceives a deep and pure love for his captive, the Polish princess, Maria Potocka: but one of his wives murders her out of jealousy. In her memory Girei erects a fountain (which Pushkin had seen in the khan's palace) surrounded by marble basins into which drops of water fall melodiously like tears.

"Evgeni Onegin."—Although the "Southern Cycle" confirmed the reputation of the author of *Ruslan and Ludmila*, and Pushkin was hailed both as the leading Russian poet and as leader of the Romantic, liberty-loving generation of the 1820s, he himself was dissatisfied with it. In May 1823 he began his masterpiece, the novel in verse *Evgeni Onegin* (publ. 1833), on which he continued to work intermittently until 1831. In it he returned to the idea, which had first found expression in *The Prisoner of the Caucasus*, of presenting a typical figure of his own age, but in a wider setting and by means of new artistic methods and techniques.

Evgeni Onegin unfolds an encyclopaedically broad picture of Russian life in all its actuality. The characters it depicts and immortalizes—the disenchanted skeptic Onegin; the romantic, freedom-loving poet Lenski; and Tatyana, the heroine, a profoundly affectionate and sympathetic study of Russian womanhood: a "precious ideal" in the poet's own words—are typically Russian, and are shown in relationship to the social and environmental forces by which their ways of thought and characters have been, and are being, molded. Although in form the work bears a superficial resemblance to *Don Juan*, Pushkin rejects Byron's subjective, Romanticized treatment for objective description, and shows his hero not in exotic surroundings but at the heart of a Russian way of life. Thus the action begins in St. Petersburg, continues on a provincial private estate, then switches to Moscow, and finally returns to St. Petersburg. This, the first work in Russian literature to take contemporary society as its subject, points the way to the realistic novel of the 19th century.

Exile at Mikhailovskoe.—Though in Kishinev and Odessa Pushkin had devoted much time to writing, he had also lived a full, intense life, straining to be "equal to the age in enlightenment." He was keenly interested in politics, both national and European, and in close contact with the most radical of the southern group of Decembrists. He also shared in the excitements of an isolated "frontier" society: hard drinking, gaming, dueling, amorous intrigue (in a letter to a friend he jokingly described Kishinev as "the Sodom" of Moldavia). His removal from Odessa to exile on his mother's estate of Mikhailovskoe, near Pskov, in the far northwest, in 1824, resulted from an intermingling of these elements. His superior in Odessa, Count Vorontsov, with whose wife Pushkin had fallen passionately in love, began to treat him openly as an enemy, and this provoked the poet to castigate him in a series of biting epigrams. Finally, Vorontsov asked the authorities to have Pushkin removed. Moreover, in a letter to a friend intercepted by the police, Pushkin had stated that he was "taking lessons in pure atheism." Thus he was sent into exile at Mikhailovskoe, as far as possible from "undesirable" political and social contacts.

Although the two years he spent there were unhappy, this was to prove one of Pushkin's most productive periods. Alone and isolated, he embarked on a close study of Russian history. He also got to know the peasants on the estate, and interested himself in noting down from them folktales and folk songs. During this period the specifically Russian features of his poetry became steadily more marked. His ballad *Zhenikh* (1825; *The Bridegroom*), for instance, is based on themes from Russian folklore; and its simple, swift-moving style is very different from the brilliant extravagance of *Ruslan and Ludmila* or the Romantic, melodious music of the "Southern Cycle."

In 1824 he completed *Tsygany* (publ. 1827; *The Gypsies*), begun at Odessa. In this, the most mature of his Romantic narrative poems, he puts into the mouth of an old gypsy, a representative of the people, a condemnation of the typical individualistic Romantic hero, who wants freedom "only for himself." The style is dramatically harsh and spare, and the descriptive passages and dialogue are vigorous and realistic. At Mikhailovskoe, too, he wrote the provincial chapters of *Evgeni Onegin;* the poem *Count Nulin* (1825; publ. 1828), based on the life of the rural gentry; and, finally, the historical tragedy *Boris Godunov* (1824–25; publ. 1831), one of his major works.

"Boris Godunov."—This tragedy marks a break with the neoclassicism of 17th- and 18th-century French drama—the model for Russian playwrights at this period—and is constructed on the "folk principles" of Shakespeare's plays (especially the histories and tragedies), plays written "for the people" in the widest sense, and thus universal in appeal. Written just before the Decembrist rising, it treats the burning question of the relations between the ruling classes, headed by the tsar, and the masses; it is the moral and political significance of the latter, "the judgment of the people," that Pushkin emphasizes. Set in Russia in a period of political and social chaos (c. 1595–1605), its theme is the tragic guilt and inexorable fate of a great hero—Boris Godunov, son-in-law of Malyuta Skuratov, a favourite of Ivan the Terrible, and here presented as the murderer of Ivan's little son, Dmitri. The development of the action on two planes, one political and his-

torical, the other psychological, is masterly; and it is set against a background of turbulent events and ruthless ambitions. The play owes much to Pushkin's reading of early Russian annals and chronicles, as well as to Shakespeare, who, as Pushkin said, was his master in bold, free treatment of character, simplicity, and truth to nature. Although lacking the heightened poetic passion of Shakespeare's tragedies, *Boris* excels in the "convincingness of situation and naturalness of dialogue" at which Pushkin aimed, sometimes using conversational prose, sometimes a five-foot iambic line of great flexibility. The character of the pretender, the False Dmitri, is subtly and sympathetically drawn, and the power of the people, who eventually bring him to the throne, is so emphatically presented that the play's publication was delayed by the censorship. Pushkin's ability to create psychological and dramatic unity, despite the episodic construction, and to heighten the dramatic tension by economy of language, detail, and characterization, makes it one of his outstanding achievements, and a revolutionary event in the history of Russian drama.

Return to Moscow.—After the suppression of the rising of Dec. 14 (O.S.), 1825, the new tsar, Nicholas I, aware of Pushkin's popularity, and that he had taken no part in the Decembrist "conspiracy," in autumn 1826 allowed him to return to Moscow. During a long conversation between them, the tsar met the poet's complaints of censorship with a promise that in the future he himself would be Pushkin's censor; and told him of his plans to introduce from above several pressing reforms, and, in particular, to prepare the way for the liberation of the serfs. The collapse of the rising had been a grievous experience for Pushkin, whose heart was wholly with the "guilty" Decembrists, five of whom had been executed, while others had been sent to forced labour in Siberia. Among them had been his closest friends at the Lyceum, I. I. Pushchin and the poet V. K. Kyuchelbeker (*see* the poem "Arion," and the verse-epistle *Vo glubine sibirskikh rud*, "In the Depths of Siberia's Mines," both written 1827). Thus, when the tsar asked him outright how he would have acted had he been in St. Petersburg on Dec. 14, he answered that he would have joined the ranks of the insurgents.

Pushkin saw, however, that the struggle against autocracy was doomed without the support of the people. He considered that the only possible way of achieving essential reforms was from above, "on the tsar's initiative," as he had written in *Derevnya*. This is the reason for his persistent interest in the age of reforms at the beginning of the 18th century, and in the figure of Peter the Great, the "tsar-educator," whose example he held up to the present tsar in *Stansy* (1826; *Stanzas*); and who is also a central figure of *The Negro of Peter the Great* (1827, publ. 1837), of the historical poem *Poltava* (1828, publ. 1829), and of *Medny Vsadnik* (1833, publ. 1837; *The Bronze Horseman*). In this last poem Pushkin poses the problem of the "little man" whose happiness is destroyed by the great leader by telling a "story of St. Petersburg," set against the background of the flood of 1824, when the river took its revenge against Peter I's achievement in building the city. It describes how the "little hero," Evgeni, driven mad by the drowning of his sweetheart, wanders through the streets, and seeing the bronze statue of Peter I seated on a rearing horse, and realizing that the tsar, here represented triumphing over the waves, is the cause of his grief, threatens him, and, in a climax of growing horror, is pursued through the streets by the Bronze Horseman. Its descriptive and emotional power gives it an unforgettable impact, and makes it one of the greatest poems in Russian literature.

After return from exile Pushkin found himself in a difficult and invidious position. The tsar's censorship proved even more exacting than that of the official censors, and his personal freedom was curtailed. Not only was he put under secret police observation, but he was openly supervised by Count Benkendorff, chief of the police. When in 1829, during the Russo-Turkish War, after his applications to go to Transcaucasia had been refused, he managed to visit the front without permission, he was severely reprimanded by the count. This visit, on which he met several of the exiled Decembrists, is described in *Puteshestvie v Arzrum* (publ. 1836; *A Journey to Erzerum*).

Moreover, the works written at this time met with little comprehension from the critics, and even some of his friends accused him of apostasy, so forcing him to justify his political position in the poem *Druzyam* ("To my Friends," 1828). The anguish of his spiritual isolation is reflected in the cycle of poems about the poet and the mob (1827–30), and in the unfinished novel *Egipetskie nochi* (publ. 1837; *Egyptian Nights*).

Yet it was during this period that Pushkin's genius came to its full flowering. His art acquired new dimensions, and almost every one of his works opened a new chapter in the history of Russian literature. He spent the autumn of 1830 at Boldino, his family's Nizhni-Novgorod (later Gorki) estate; and these months are the most remarkable in the whole of his career. During them he wrote the four *malenkie tragedii* ("little tragedies")—*Skupoi rytsar* (1836; *The Covetous Knight*), *Kamenny gost* (1839; *The Stone Guest*), *Pir vo vrem'a chumy* (1832; *Feast in Time of Plague*), and *Mozart and Salieri* (1831); the five short prose tales collected as *Povesti Belkina* (1831; *Tales . . . by I. P. Belkin*); the comic poem of everyday lower-class life *Domik v Kolomne* (1833; *The Little House at Kolomna*); and many lyrics in widely differing styles, as well as critical and polemical articles.

One of Pushkin's most characteristic features was his wide knowledge of world literature (shown in particular by his interest in English literature, which ranged from Shakespeare to Byron, Scott, and the Lake poets): in Dostoevski's phrase, his "universal sensibility," his ability to re-create the spirit of different races at different historical epochs without ever losing his own individuality. This is particularly marked in the "little tragedies," which are concerned with an analysis of the "evil passions," and which, like *Pikovaya dama* (1834; *The Queen of Spades*), exerted a direct influence on the themes and techniques of the novels of Dostoevski, while his prose style paved the way for the prose of Turgenev, Goncharov, and Tolstoi.

Last Years.—In 1831 Pushkin, after a turbulent courtship and objections from her mother, married Natalya Nikolaevna Goncharova, and settled in St. Petersburg. Once more he entered government service, and was commissioned to write a history of Peter the Great. Three years later he received the rank of *Kammerjunker* (gentleman of the emperor's bedchamber), partly because the tsar wished Natalya to have the entrée to court functions. The social life at court which he was now obliged to lead, and which his wife enjoyed, was ill suited to creative work, but he stubbornly continued to write. Without abandoning poetry altogether (the fairy tales in verse, *Skazki*, belong to this period, as well as *The Bronze Horseman*), he turned increasingly to prose. Alongside the theme of Peter the Great that of a popular peasant rising acquired growing importance in his work, as is shown by the unfinished satirical *Istoriya sela Gory'khina* (1830, publ. 1837; *History of the Village of Gory'khino*); the novel *Dubrovski* (1832–33, publ. 1841); *Stseny iz rytsarskikh vremen* (1835; the dramatic *Scenes from the Age of Chivalry*); and finally, the most important of his prose works, the historical novel of the Pugachev Rebellion, *Kapitanskaya dochka* (1833–36, publ. 1836; *The Captain's Daughter*), which had been preceded by a historical study of the rebellion *Istoriya Pugacheva* (1833; publ. 1835).

Meanwhile, in both his domestic affairs and his official duties, Pushkin's life was becoming increasingly intolerable. In court circles he was regarded with mounting suspicion and resentment, and his repeated petitions to be allowed to resign, retire to the country, and devote himself to writing were all rejected. Finally, on Feb. 8, 1837, in a duel forced on him by influential enemies, in defense of his wife's honour, Pushkin fell, mortally wounded. His adversary, Georges d'Anthès, an officer in the guards, had emigrated from France after the revolution of 1830, and had married Natalya's sister. Pushkin died at St. Petersburg, on Feb. 10 (N.S.; Jan. 29, O.S.), 1837.

Critical Assessment.—Even during his lifetime, Pushkin's importance as a great national poet had been recognized by Gogol (*q.v.*), his pupil and successor; and it was his younger contemporary, the great Russian critic, democrat, and revolutionary, Vissarion Belinski, who produced the fullest and deepest critical study of Pushkin's work, still considerably relevant. To the later classical writers of the 19th century Pushkin, the creator of the Russian literary language, the author of the "standard works" of Russian literature, stands as the cornerstone of Russian literature; in Gorki's words, as "the beginning of beginnings."

Pushkin has become an inseparable part of the cultural and spiritual world of the Russian people and of the other peoples of the former tsarist empire, to whom he bequeathed his work in the poem *Ya pamyatnik vozdrig* (*Exegi monumentum*, 1836). He has exerted, too, a profound influence on other aspects of Russian culture, most notably, on opera.

Today, Pushkin's work, with its nobility of conception and its emphasis on civic responsibility (shown in his command to the poet-prophet to "fire the hearts of men with his words"), its life-affirming vigour, its confidence in the triumph of reason over prejudice, of light over darkness, of human charity over slavery and oppression, has struck an echo worldwide; and his works, translated into all the major languages, are regarded as both the most complete expression of the Russian national consciousness and as transcending national barriers by their power and inspiration.

BIBLIOGRAPHY.—*Editions, etc.:* The best Russian editions of Pushkin's complete works are *Polnoe sobranie sochineni*, 16 vol. (1937–59; reference vol., 1959), and *Polnoe sobranie sochineni*, 10 vol. (1956–58), both edited and published by the Academy of Sciences of the U.S.S.R. Bibliographies include V. I. Mezhov, *Puschkiniana* (1886); A. G. Fomin, *Puschkiniana:* vol. i, *1900–10* (1929), ii, *1911–17* (1937); A. M. Dobrovolski and N. I. Mordovchenko, *Bibliografia proizvedeni Pushkina i literatury o nem, 1918–36* (1952); and bibliographies for *1949* (the 150th anniversary year; publ. 1951), *1950* (1952), and *1954–57* (1958), all by the Academy of Sciences of the U.S.S.R. Editions of separate works include *Boris Godunov*, with Eng. trans. and notes by Philip L. Barbour (1953); *Evgeni Onegin*, with introduction and commentary by D. Čiževsky (1953). *See also* N. L. Brodsky, *Kommentarii k romanu Pushkina "Evgeni Onegin"* (1932); *Pushkin-kritik*, ed. with commentary by N. V. Bogoslovsky (1950); *Pushkin i teatr*, ed. by B. P. Gorodetski (1953); *A. Puschkin in seinen Briefen*, ed. by A. Luther (1927).

Translations: English translations include *Poems*, trans. by M. Baring (1931); *The Captain's Daughter, and Other Tales*, trans. by N. Duddington, Everyman's Library (1933; new ed. 1961); *Complete Prose Tales*, trans. by G. Aitken (1966); *Works*, selected and ed. by A. Yarmolinsky (1936; new ed. 1946), the most comprehensive English edition; *Evgeni Onegin*, trans. by O. Elton (1937; new ed. 1948), by D. P. Radin and G. Z. Patrick (1937), by V. Nabokov, 4 vol. (1964), and by B. Deutsch, Penguin Classics (1964); *The Russian Wonderland*, selected fairy tales trans. by B. L. Brasol (1936); *Verse from Pushkin and Others*, trans. by O. Elton (1935); *Six Poems from the Russian* (including *Ruslan and Ludmila, Poltava*, and *The Prisoner of the Caucasus*), trans. by J. Krup (1936); *Poems*, a selection, trans. by W. Morison (1945); *Two Fairy Tales*, trans. by T. Pantcheff (1947); *The Little Tragedies*, trans. by V. de S. Pinto and W. H. Marshall (1946); *Pushkin*, Russian text with introduction and prose trans. by John Fennell, Penguin Poets (1964); *Letters, Selected Verse*, trans. by J. T. Shaw (1964). *See also* A. Yarmolinsky (ed.), *Pushkin in English* (1937).

Biography and Criticism: For the text of Belinski's essays on Pushkin, *see* the latest edition of Belinski's complete works (*Polnoe sobranie sochineni*, vol. vii, 1955). *See also* N. van Wijk, *De Plaats van Púškin in de letterkunde* (1922); V. M. Zhirmunski, *Bairon i Pushkin* (1924); D. Mirsky, *Pushkin* (1926); V. Bru'sov, *Moi Pushkin* (1929); M. Gofman, *Pouchkine* (1931); N. S. Ashukin, *Zhivoy Pushkin* (1934); B. L. Brasol, in *The Mighty Three* (1934); *Rucoiu Pushkina* (1935); V. Veresayev, *Pushkin v zhizni* (1936); N. L. Brodsky, *Pushkin* (1937); V. F. Khodasievich, *O Pushkine* (1937); W. Lednicki, *Puszkin* (1937); S. H. Cross and E. J. Simmons (eds.), *Centennial Essays for Pushkin* (1937); E. J. Simmons, *Pushkin* (1937); *Pushkin*, a collection of articles and essays (1939); I. M. Nusinov, *Pushkin v mirovoy literature* (1941); V. V. Vinogradov, *Stil Pushkina* (1941); H. Troyat, *Pouchkine*, 2 vol. (1946; abridged Eng. trans. 1951); J. Lavrin, *Pushkin and Russian Literature* (1947); V. V. Ermilov, *Nash Pushkin* (1949); A. Tsyavlovski, *Letopis zhizni i ivorchestva Pushkina* (1951); D. D. Blagoi, *Masterstvo Pushkina* (1955), and *Tvorcheski put Pushkina*, 2 vol. (1950–67); B. V. Tomashevskii, *Pushkin*, 2 vol. (1956–61); G. A. Gukovski, *Pushkin i problemy realisticheskogo stilia* (1957); B. Meilah, *Pushkin i ego epocha* (1958); E. Lo Gatto, *Pùshkin: Storia di un poeta e del suo eroe* (1960); I. Feinberg, *Nezavershennye zaloty Pushkina* (1963); N. L. Stepanov, *Prosa Pushkina* (1962); A. Slonimski, *Masterstvo Pushkina* (1963); *Pushkin. Itogi i problemy izuchenia* (1966); D. Magarshack, *Pushkin* (1963). (D. D. BL.)

PUSHKIN (formerly TSARSKOE SELO), a town of Leningrad Oblast of the Russian Soviet Federated Socialist Republic, U.S.S.R., lies 15 mi. (24 km.) S of Leningrad on the railway to Novgorod. Administratively it is under the Leningrad City Council. Pop. (1969 est.) 73,000. Tsarskoe Selo ("the tsar's village") grew up around one of the main summer palaces of the Russian royal family. The land was given by Peter the Great to the tsaritsa, Catherine I, in the distribution of Ingrian lands after the success of Peter's campaigns of 1702–04. Catherine built first a wooden palace (1712–14) and then a stone palace (1718–24), designed by the architect I. F. Braunshtein. The present palace was designed by V. V. Rastrelli for the tsaritsa Elizabeth and built between 1748 and 1762. The building is imposing and amply proportioned. The superb facade is 220 yd. (200 m.) in length. The palace and its surrounding park, also laid out by Rastrelli, were both considerably embellished under Catherine the Great by the Scots architect Charles Cameron, who redesigned 18 staterooms and constructed a fine gallery overlooking the lake and park. During World War II the palace was deliberately gutted by the Germans, only the Cameron Gallery surviving intact. After the war, restoration was begun and by the early 1960s the fabric and most of the Cameron staterooms had been scrupulously restored. In the magnificent "English" park around the palace is the smaller Alexander Palace, built by Giacomo Quarenghi in 1792–96 for Catherine the Great; it was also gravely damaged but has been restored. In the park also are many pavilions, statues, and monuments, including the Hermitage, designed by Rastrelli, and the Agate Pavilion of Cameron. These two buildings survived the war. Cameron also designed the rococo Chinese village, now mostly in ruins. On the lake side is a neo-Gothic boathouse, known as the Admiralty, and on an island in the lake is the Orlov column, commemorating the victory of Aleksei Orlov over the Turks at Cheshme (Cesme). Immediately adjacent to the main palace is the *Lycée*, now converted to a museum in honour of the Russian poet Aleksandr Pushkin, who studied at the *Lycée* from 1811 to 1817. Also in the poet's honour, the town was renamed in 1937, after having first been renamed Detskoe Selo ("children's village"). The first railway in the Russian Empire was built in 1837 from St. Petersburg (Leningrad) to Tsarskoe Selo. The Leningrad Agricultural Institute is in the modern town.

About 5 mi. (8 km.) S of Pushkin is Pavlovsk, with another royal palace and park, designed by Cameron in 1782. The palace burned in 1803, but was carefully restored. Destroyed once more in World War II, it was again rebuilt. (R. A. F.)

PUT AND CALL: *see* OPTION (STOCK).

PUTA-O, the largest of three districts of the Kachin state (*q.v.*) of the Union of Burma and also the name of its chief centre. The district is in the sparsely inhabited country in the extreme north of Burma and stretches to the borders of India, Tibet, and China. Burmese maps, following Survey of India maps, show most of the basin of the Irrawaddy headwaters within Puta-O and the water parting as the political frontier. The boundary has never been fully demarcated and is not accepted by the Chinese. Virtually the whole district is forested; some shifting cultivation is practised by the Kachins (*see* KACHIN).

Puta-O town, formerly Fort Hertz, is reached by an old mule track from the railhead at Myitkyina to the south. The Stilwell Road, constructed by U.S. forces in World War II, enters Kachin state west of this area, through the Hukawng Valley. (L. D. S.)

PUTEOLI: *see* POZZUOLI.

PUTNAM, RUFUS (1738–1824), American soldier in the Revolutionary War and pioneer settler in Ohio, was born in Sutton, Mass., on April 9, 1738 (old style). He served in the French and Indian War in 1757–60; was a millwright in New Braintree in 1761–68, during which time he studied surveying; and from 1769 until the outbreak of the American Revolution was a farmer and surveyor. He became lieutenant colonel in one of the first regiments raised after the battle of Lexington and served before Boston. In 1777 he served in the Northern army under Gen. Horatio Gates, commanding two regiments in the second battle of Saratoga. In 1778 he laid out fortifications, including Ft. Putnam, at West Point, and in 1779 he served under Gen. Anthony Wayne after the capture of Stony Point.

After the war he returned to Rutland, Mass., where he had bought a confiscated farm in 1780. In March 1786 he founded, with other officers of the American Revolution, the Ohio Company of Associates for the purchase and settlement of western lands (*see* OHIO COMPANY). In Nov. 1787 he was appointed by the company superintendent of its proposed settlement on the Ohio, and in 1788 he led the small party which founded Marietta, Ohio. Putnam was appointed territorial judge, a brigadier general in the regular army and a commissioner to treat with the Indians in 1792–93; was surveyor general of the United States in 1796–1803; and in 1802 was a member of the Ohio state constitutional convention. He died in Marietta, May 4, 1824.

See Rowena Buell (ed.), *The Memoirs of Rufus Putnam* (1903), in which his autobiography, journal and other papers, in the library of Marietta college, are reprinted. His *Journal, 1757–1760,* dealing with his experiences in the French and Indian War, was edited with notes by E. C. Dawes (1886).

PUTNIK, RADOMIR (1847–1917), Serbian army officer, a victorious commander against the Austrians in 1914, was born at Kragujevac on Jan. 24 (new style), 1847, the son of a teacher. Educated at the artillery school, he was commissioned in 1866. He graduated from the staff college in 1889 and rose to be general in 1903. Save for three periods when he was war minister (1904–05, 1906–08, 1912), he served as chief of staff from 1903 to 1916. It was he who was mainly responsible for the professional skill, good equipment, and fighting spirit of the Serbian army.

Putnik headed a brigade in the two wars against Turkey (1876, 1877–78) and the staff of a division in the war against Bulgaria (1885). He was commander in chief in the two Balkan Wars (1912–13), routing the Turks at Kumanovo (October 1912) and—as field marshal—at Monastir (Bitola; November 1912). Largely because of him, the treacherous Bulgarian night attack failed and the Bulgars were defeated at Bregalnica (June–July 1913). When World War I began, Putnik, who was at Gleichenberg in Austria, was escorted to Rumania. In poor health, he resumed the command in chief and routed the overwhelming Austrian forces of Gen. Oskar von Potiorek on Tser Mountain (August 1914; the first Allied victory in the war) and on the Kolubara River (November–December 1914). During the retreat across Albania a year later, Putnik, carried in a sedan chair, shared the fate of his army. After the retreat, he was relieved of his command and withdrew to Nice, where he died on May 17, 1917. (K. ST. P.)

PUTTENHAM, GEORGE (*c.* 1529–1590), English courtier, generally acknowledged as the author of the anonymously published *The Arte of English Poesie* (1589), one of the most important critical works of the Elizabethan age.

Little is definitely known of his early life. His mother was the sister of Sir Thomas Elyot (*q.v.*), his sister married Sir John Throckmorton, and by his own marriage (*c.* 1560) to Lady Elizabeth Windsor he was connected with other wealthy and influential families. Perhaps educated abroad, he visited Flanders and other countries between 1563 and 1578. He had matriculated at Cambridge in 1546 and was admitted to the Inner Temple in 1556. Throckmorton paid his debts, rescued him from prison in 1569 when he was charged with conspiring to murder the Calvinist bishop of London, and in 1570, when he criticized the queen's counselors too freely, and supported him during his long financial wrangle with his wife's family, standing surety for him at its conclusion in 1579. His knowledge of law and public affairs is shown by *A Justificacion of Queen Elizabeth in Relacion to the Affair of Mary Queen of Scottes,* undertaken at the queen's request and anonymously circulated, but attributed to Puttenham in two of eight extant copies of the manuscript (British Museum, Harleian MS. 831; Calthorpe MS.). He was rewarded for "good, true, faithful and acceptable service" to the queen in 1588. He died in London in the autumn of 1590.

George Puttenham's authorship of *The Arte of English Poesie,* early attributed to him but later disputed in favour of his brother, Richard, and of Lord Lumley, is supported by comparison of the style and opinions in it, in *Partheniades* (a collection of poems addressed as a New Year's gift to the queen, probably in 1581–82), and in the *Justificacion;* and also of the known facts of Puttenham's life and abilities with those revealed in the *Arte.*

The *Arte* is divided into three books: I, "Of Poets and Poesy," defending and defining poetry; II, "Of Proportion," dealing mainly with prosody as an indispensable formal element of the art

of poesy; and III, "Of Ornament," defined as all that renders poetic utterance attractive to eye and ear. Its importance lies in its treatment of English poetry as an art, at a period when this was still disputed; in its appeal to "right reason" as the best judge of poetry and the poetic technique; and in its emphasis on the creative, imitative, and "image-forming" faculties of the poet, and on poetry's primary purpose as giving pleasure rather than instruction. In its treatment of English prosody, and of poetic kinds as including those popular in England, and in its critical estimate of English poetry from Chaucer to Wyat and Surrey, it is a pioneer work. It reveals an original, enquiring mind, and a concern to "fashion an art of poesie" which should be perfected by the poets of the future. Its loosely constructed, digressive prose-style is enlivened by anecdote and quotation, for Puttenham wrote for a courtly audience and sought to avoid "scholarly preciosities." His work shows that he had read widely and had interpreted what he read by the critical faculty provided by Nature rather than by the rules of classical rhetoric.

BIBLIOGRAPHY.—*The Arte of English Poesie,* ed. by G. D. Willcock and A. Walker, with introduction on authorship, critical content, etc. (1936); *Partheniades,* ed. by W. R. Morfill in *Ballads from MSS.,* vol. 2, pp. 72–91, Ballad Society Publications (1873); J. W. H. Atkins, *English Literary Criticism: the Renascence* (1947), ch. vi; R. F. Jones, *The Triumph of the English Language* (1953).

PUTTING THE SHOT: *see* SHOT-PUT.

PUTTY, a term that generally means a cement of one of two types: whiting putty or white-lead whiting putty. A high-grade whiting putty consists of 85% to 90% whiting (finely powdered calcium carbonate) blended with 10% to 15% boiled linseed oil. White-lead whiting putty has an admixture of 10% white lead, reducing the amount of whiting proportionately. Prepared putty should roll freely in the hands without exuding oil. It is commonly used to secure sheets of glass in place, to fill nail holes, etc.

The term is also applied to substances resembling putty, for example, iron putty, which is a mixture of ferric oxide and linseed oil, and red-lead putty, which is composed of red and white lead and linseed oil. The term putty is also applied to certain dough-like plastic compounds. Putty is also a shortened name for putty powder (tin oxide), which is used in polishing glass, granite, metal, etc. (E. L. Y.)

PUTUMAYO RIVER, a 980 mi.-long tributary of the Amazon which rises in the Andes mountains of southern Colombia, forms the southern boundary of Colombia with Ecuador and Brazil for almost 800 mi., but for its last 100 mi. before it enters the Solimões or Amazon at Santo Antonio de Içá it flows through Brazilian territory. In Brazil it is known as the Içá river.

The area drained by the Putumayo is a vast zone of tropical rain forest where rainfall ranges upward to 140 in. a year. Except near its headwaters, in the foothills of the Andes, the population along its banks is composed largely of small groups of forest Indians.

A highway built by the Colombian government from Pasto through the Sibundoy valley to Puerto Asís on the upper Putumayo was opening the eastern flanks of the Andes to settlement in the second half of the 20th century. Another road was under construction from Ipiales toward the valley of the Río San Miguel, which is a main affluent of the Putumayo and itself forms the Ecuador-Colombian border near its headwaters. Navigation on the Putumayo is unobstructed by rapids below Puerto Ospina, 80 mi. downstream from Puerto Asís. The only settlement of any size on the Putumayo below Puerto Ospina is Puerto Leguízamo (formerly Caucayá), from which there is a 25 mi. portage road northward to La Tagua on the Caquetá river.

The Putumayo region was the scene of the famous Putumayo rubber scandal during the height of the rubber boom which saw many Indians enslaved and killed by unscrupulous rubber operators. In 1932 there was fighting there between Colombian and Peruvian forces prior to the settlement of the so-called Leticia affair, which gave Colombia a wedge-shaped salient that extends 90 mi. south of the Putumayo to the Amazon port of Leticia. (Js. J. P.)

PUVIS DE CHAVANNES, PIERRE CÉCILE (1824–1898), French painter, was born at Lyons on Dec. 14, 1824. He

GIRAUDON

"THE POOR FISHERMAN" BY PUVIS DE CHAVANNES, 1881. IN THE LUXEMBOURG PALACE, PARIS

occupied a rather unique position in 19th-century painting, for his work was largely independent of the major artistic currents and, perhaps for that very reason, it was approved by representatives of almost all shades of critical opinion. The son of a mining engineer, Pierre Puvis was educated at Lyons and at the Lycée Henri IV in Paris and was intended to follow his father's profession.

Puvis first studied painting under Henri Scheffer, spent some time in Italy and then frequented for a short period the studios of Thomas Couture and Eugène Delacroix. He first exhibited at the Salon in 1850 (a Pietà), but was then consistently rejected until 1858. His work was, however, esteemed by such critics as Théodore de Banville, Théophile Gautier, Charles Baudelaire and Paul de St. Victor. In 1859 he reappeared at the Salon with the "Return from Hunting" (Marseilles), an adaptation of a "Return of the Prodigal Son" executed in 1854 as part of a decorative scheme for his brother's dining room. In 1861, with the production of "War" and "Peace," he began an important series of paintings which were destined to become part of the decorative scheme for the museum at Amiens. The scheme was augmented by various gifts from the artist and finally completed with "Ave Picardia Nutrix" (1865) and the state commission for "Pro Patria Ludus" (1882).

During these years Puvis de Chavannes undertook other decorative work at Lyons, Marseilles, Poitiers and Paris, as well as exhibiting a number of important pictures such as the "Beheading of St. John" (1869), "Hope" (1872), "Family of Fisher-folk" (1875), "Women on the Seashore" (1879) and "The Poor Fisherman" (1881). The work at Lyons includes "Autumn" (Salon of 1864) and the major decorative works "The Sacred Grove," "Vision of the Antique," "The Rhône" and "The Saône" (1884–87).

In the Palais Longchamp at Marseilles are two panels representing "Marseilles as a Greek Colony" and "Marseilles, Gateway to the East" (1868–69) and in the Hôtel de Ville, Poitiers, are two decorative panels of historical subjects, "Radegund" and "Charles Martel" (1872–74). In 1876 Puvis de Chavannes was commissioned to paint a series of panels illustrating the life of St. Geneviève, for the Panthéon; although part of this task was finished and exhibited by 1880, the total scheme was completed only after the death of Puvis in Paris (Oct. 24, 1898) by pupils, under the direction of J. C. Cazin, working from the completed cartoons. Other mural decorations in Paris are those for the Sorbonne (1887–89) and for the Hôtel de Ville, which were completed in 1893. Two other important decorative commissions were those for the museum at Rouen (1890–92) and for the staircase of the public library, Boston (1894–98).

BIBLIOGRAPHY.—M. Vachon, *Puvis de Chavannes* (1895); J. Buisson, *Gazette des Beaux-Arts* (1899); M. Lagaisse, *Puvis de Chavannes*

et la peinture lyonnaise du XIXe siècle (exhibition catalogue, 1937); R. Goldwater, *Art Bulletin* (1946). (R. A. Dy.)

PUY, LE, a town of southern France, *préfecture* of Haute-Loire *département* and former capital of Velay, is situated 56 km. (90 mi.) S.W. of Lyons in the Massif Central at slightly more than 2,000 ft. above sea level. Pop. (1962) 22,396. It lies in the middle of a basin surrounded by basalt plateaus. The basin, crossed by the upper course of the Loire river, has an infilling of soft marls and sands, but is studded with residual volcanic hills (*puys*). In this highland setting it is a relatively rich farming district and was the nucleus of the tribal territory of the Vellaves (whence Velay) in Roman Gaul, although their capital was then at St. Paulien (Revessio) about 8 mi. N. of Le Puy. During the barbarian invasions, about A.D. 500, the capital was shifted to the defensive site that was provided by a steep volcanic hill, the Rocher Corneille (Mont Anis). The bishopric was moved there and a shrine was established to the Virgin. From the 10th century it was an important centre of pilgrimage, known as Podium Sanctae Mariae. The Romanesque cathedral (Basilique de Notre-Dame du Puy), dating from the 12th century and built on a platform beneath the summit of the Rocher Corneille, is reached through the old town, whose narrow, steep streets occupy the mountainside. A great flight of steps leads up to the façade of the cathedral.

Parts of the old town walls are preserved, and beyond the boulevards that mark their line downhill the modern town has grown with squares, wide streets, public buildings and a railway station. On the outskirts another volcanic peak, Rocher d'Aiguilhe, in the form of a natural obelisk is crowned by the 11th-century church of St. Michel d'Aiguilhe, reached by 271 steps. About three miles away, the massive square keep and ruins of the medieval castle of Polignac occupy a tabular fragment of basalt. A magnificent panorama of this bizarre landscape, bristling with volcanic hills, is commanded by the colossal statue (53 ft. high) of Our Lady of France, set up in 1860 on the summit of the Rocher Corneille at Le Puy, more than 300 ft. above the surrounding plain.

The administrative, market, and general service centre of Velay, Le Puy is also closely associated with the rural life of its surrounding district by the lace industry, which grew from the decoration of religious objects and became very prosperous in the 17th and 18th centuries. Changes of fashion have adversely affected the general prosperity of the industry, and handmaking of lace has especially declined. The Crozatier museum at Le Puy houses a notably fine collection of lace. (AR. E. S.)

PUY-DE-DÔME, a *département* of central France formed in 1790 mainly from Auvergne (*q.v.*), with the addition of adjacent districts of Bourbonnais and Lyonnais. It is bounded north by Allier, east by Loire, south by Haute Loire and Cantal, west by Corrèze and Creuse, and consists of very diverse physical regions in the heart of the Massif Central. Area, 3,095 sq.mi. (8,016 sq.km.). Pop. (1962) 505,928.

Puy-de-Dôme is crossed from south to north by the Allier River, which occupies a downfaulted trough, floored with young sediments, between the highlands of Auvergne and Forez. In the south, by Issoire, the plain, known as the Limagne, is narrow and much encumbered with residual hills, but toward Clermont-Ferrand it widens out. To the west a line of young volcanic cones, the Chaîne des Puys, surmounts the edge of the granite plateau of Auvergne and dominates the Limagne above its sharp fault-line margin. Chief among them is the Puy de Dôme (4,806 ft. [1,465 m.]) above Clermont-Ferrand. Farther west the Sioule River drains the granite plateau north toward the Allier. In the southwest part of the *département* the Mont Dore is another volcanic mass, with four major centres of eruption, culminating in the Puy de Sancy (6,188 ft. [1,886 m.]). The volcanoes were active in Quaternary times and fresh volcanic landforms remain, including extensive rocky wildernesses of ash and lava. In the volcanic areas small lakes occupy crater hollows or valleys blocked by lava dams and there are several important thermal springs, notably at Châtel Guyon, Royat, La Bourboule, Mont Dore, and Saint-Nectaire. East of Limagne the granite Forez Highlands, exceeding 5,000 ft. (1,500 m.), separate the basins of the Allier and Loire.

They are cut into by the Dore River, connecting the small, high-lying tectonic basin of Ambert with the Limagne by the gorges of Olliergues.

In contrast with the wet, severe climate of the surrounding highlands, the low-lying and sheltered Limagne is dry and warm, and is occupied by an extension of lowland agriculture. The soils in the west, derived from volcanic rocks, are especially rich, though rather heavy. The damp strip along the Allier, known as Le Marais, especially required costly drainage to realize its present productivity. Farther east the soils derived from the granitic Forez are poorer and gravelly. The plain is predominantly arable and wheat is extensively grown, though grain has lost ground to fodder crops. Hemp, which was once important, has greatly decreased, but potatoes and sugarbeets have become important. The vine has failed to recover much of the area it lost during the phylloxera trouble of the late 19th century. Orchards and market gardens are especially prominent and supply important preserving industries. There is a heavy density of livestock, with pig- and poultry-keeping on small holdings a specially developed feature. There are important lines of villages and market towns at the foot of the bounding highlands, and residual hills in the plain are often crowned by ruins of castles, with villages clustered below.

The flanking highlands are areas of poor farming, largely pastoral, with seasonal use of the highest pastures, which are snow-covered in winter. The pivot of the local economy is the *buron* (dairy), where cheese is made. These districts have suffered severe depopulation since the mid-19th century, as their inhabitants have been drawn away to urban employment at Clermont-Ferrand and farther afield. Clermont, with a great rubber industry, has grown rapidly as an industrial centre. Manufacture of clothing, food preserving, and other industries, *e.g.*, the production of fertilizers, associated with the agriculture of the Limagne, are also important. Clermont is provided with hydroelectric power from the Sioule River and, elsewhere, hydroelectric power has been developed and has replaced the direct use of falling water in the industrial communities on the Dore below Ambert (paper, textiles, rosaries) and at Thiers on the Durolle, where there is a long-established cutlery industry. In the Allier Valley, both in the extreme north and south of the *département*, a little coal is mined at Brassac and Saint-Éloy. There are large quarries in the lava at Volvic, and asphalt is worked at Pont du Château. Among the spa towns, Mont Dore is now developing as a centre of winter sports on the Puy de Sancy.

Clermont-Ferrand (*q.v.*), the regional capital for an extensive area, is the *préfecture* of the *département*, the centre of a bishopric, and the headquarters of educational administration, but the court of appeal remains at the old legal centre of Riom, the scene of trials at the end of World War II. Clermont-Ferrand, Riom, Ambert, Thiers, and Issoire are the centres of the five *arrondissements* into which the *département* is divided. Gergovia, on a basalt table eight miles south of Clermont, was the scene of Vercingetorix' repulse of Julius Caesar during the Roman conquest of Gaul. Among many churches that exemplify the Auvergnat style of Romanesque architecture, those at Issoire, Riom, and Saint-Nectaire deserve special mention.　(Ar. E. S.)

P'U YI, HENRY: *see* Hsüan-T'ung.

PWLLHELI ("salt water pool"), a municipal borough, former seaport, and market town of Caernarvonshire, north Wales, lies 21 mi. SSW of Caernarvon by road on the northern shores of Cardigan Bay. Pop. (1961) 3,642. It consists of an old town (incorporated in 1355 by Edward the Black Prince) and two seaside suburbs known as South Beach and West End. Its economic activities are dependent on its agricultural hinterland and the tourist trade.
　　　　　　　　　　　　　　　　　　(E. G. Bow.).

PYANOPSIA, an ancient festival in honour of Apollo, held at Athens on the 7th of the month Pyanopsion (October). A hodgepodge of pulse was offered to Apollo. Another offering was a branch of olive or laurel, bound with purple or white wool, round which were hung fruits of the season, pastries, and small jars of honey, oil, and wine. Both are old pieces of rustic magic, for which many analogies can be found elsewhere. The offerings were carried in procession to the temple of Apollo where they were suspended

on the gate by a boy whose parents were both alive. The doors of private houses were similarly adorned. The branch was allowed to hang for a year, when it was replaced by a new one, since by that time it was supposed to have lost its virtue. During the procession a chant was sung, the text of which has been preserved in Plutarch's *Theseus*.

Both offerings have been connected with the Cretan expedition of Theseus, who, when driven ashore at Delos, vowed a thank-offering to Apollo if he slew the Minotaur; the offering afterward took the form of the olive or laurel branch and Pyanopsia. His comrades on landing in Attica gathered up the scraps of their provisions which explains the origin of the hodgepodge.

PYAPON, a town and district in the Irrawaddy Delta of Burma. The district, with an area of 2,136 sq.mi. (5,532 sq.km.) and a population (1962 est.) of 518,377, was formed in 1903 when the reclamation of the alluvial marshlands for paddy cultivation had attracted a large number of settlers, both Burmans and Karens. It has no railways and few roads, communication being by water. The district headquarters, Pyapon (pop. [1953] 19,174), lies on the Pyapon River, one of the delta distributaries, 45 mi. (72 km.) SW of Rangoon. It ships rice by delta creeks to Rangoon as do the other centres Kyaiklat and Dedaye. During the Japanese occupation in World War II and subsequent disturbances the paddy trade was disrupted, large areas were abandoned, and cultivators became refugees.　　　　　　　　　　　　　　　(L. D. S.)

PYAT, FÉLIX (1810–1889), French journalist, dramatist, republican deputy, and Communard, was born at Vierzon, Cher, on Oct. 4, 1810. After studying for the bar, he became a journalist and took part in the political struggles of the 1830s. His polemics involved him in many legal actions. Sued by Jules Janin, whom he had ridiculed in a pamphlet (1844), he was imprisoned for six months. He later contributed articles to *Le Siècle*, *Le National*, and *La Réforme*, in which he attacked the Romantic movement as reactionary. He was already writing plays and became a friend of George Sand, through whose influence he was appointed *commissaire-général* of the Cher *département* by A. A. Ledru-Rollin after the Revolution of 1848. After three months in office, he was returned by the Cher to the Constituent Assembly, where he proposed the abolition of the presidency and was a champion of workers' rights. Having inherited a fortune from his father, Pyat was mistrusted by many fellow socialists and fought a duel with Pierre Proudhon, who had called him "l'aristocrate de la démocratie." A member of the Legislative Assembly, he joined Ledru-Rollin in the rising on June 13, 1849. Then he took refuge abroad. He returned to France in 1869, but made further outbursts against the government and had to flee again. The fall of the Second Empire enabled him to return to Paris, where he was imprisoned for a short time after the insurrection of Oct. 31, 1870. His paper, *Le Combat*, was suppressed in January 1871, to be replaced by *Le Vengeur*. Elected to the National Assembly in February 1871, Pyat refused to vote for peace with Germany and was elected to the Commune (*q.v.*) of Paris in March. He managed to escape the repression following the fall of the Commune and fled to England in 1872. Though he had been condemned to death in his absence in 1873, he could return to France after the amnesty of 1880. Elected a deputy for Bouches-du-Rhône in March 1888, Pyat died at Saint-Gratien on Aug. 3, 1889. His publications include: *Une Conjuration d'autrefois* (1833), *Discours aux paysans* (1849), *Lettres d'un proscrit*, two volumes (1851), and *La Folle d'Ostende* (1886).

PYATIGORSK, a town of Stavropol Kray of the Russian Soviet Federated Socialist Republic, U.S.S.R., stands on the Podkumok River, a headstream of the Kuma, in the northern foot-hills of the Caucasus, at the foot of Mt. Mashuk. Pop. (1969 est.) 84,200. The town is the centre of a region of abundant mineral springs and is a popular health resort. The waters of Pyatigorsk contain carbon dioxide, hydrogen sulfide, and radio-active gases, reputedly therapeutic for various ailments. There are sanatoriums and a number of therapeutic baths and physio-therapeutic establishments. The town has many associations with the poet M. Y. Lermontov, who was killed in a duel there in 1841.
　　　　　　　　　　　　　　　　　　(R. A. F.)

PYCNOGONIDA (Sea Spiders) are spiderlike marine animals that occur in all oceans, especially the Arctic and Antarctic, usually as bottom dwellers. Also called Pantopoda, they comprise a subphylum or a class of the phylum Arthropoda (*q.v.*) and resemble spiders (arachnids) in having the first pair of appendages characteristically arachnidlike or chelicerate. In most other respects pycnogonids are distinct from all other arthropods, being characterized by a relatively small body, excessively long legs with a patellar segment, and an additional pair of legs (ovigers) used by the male to carry the eggs about in a compact ball. The ovigers are present in all males except one New Zealand species but are lacking in the females of several genera. In several genera of large, usually deep-water, forms the terminal segments of the oviger are armed with rows of elaborate spines and the segments are held like a shepherd's crook, the oviger being used to keep the surfaces of the long legs clean. The sexes are usually separate, but one hermaphroditic species is known, and a gynandromorph specimen (one side female, the other male) has been described. Most species have eight walking legs, but species with ten legs are not uncommon in Antarctic and Caribbean regions, and there are two 12-legged species in the Antarctic. In addition to the walking legs and ovigers there may be a pair of pincerlike or chelate appendages (chelifores) and sensory palpi; the presence or absence of these appendages constitutes the basis of classification within the group, which includes about 50 genera divided into eight or nine families.

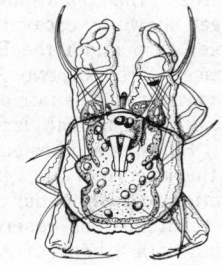

A PROTONYMPHON LARVA

The body of a pycnogonid consists of a cephalic segment or head region, followed by three to five trunk somites, which may be either distinctly segmented or coalesced into a compact disc, and a usually small, fingerlike abdomen with the anus at the tip. The mouth is a triangular opening at the end of an elaborate suctorial appendage (proboscis), which is often much longer and larger than the body. In such pycnogonids as *Nymphon* or *Achelia* the cephalic segment bears three pairs of appendages anterior to and in addition to the first pair of legs, the chelifores, which may or may not be chelate; the palpi usually flank the proboscis; and the ovigers originate on the ventral surface. The extreme of reduction is found in *Pycnogonum*, which lacks both chelifores and palpi and has ovigers only in the males (except one species that has none). There are usually four simple eyes, located in a tubercle or elaborate process on the dorsal surface of the cephalic segment, but eyes are often lacking in deep-sea species. The digestive and reproductory systems have branches into the legs. The genital openings are usually on the ventral surface of the second joints of the last pair of legs but occur on all legs in some genera; the sexual products are stored in the fourth or femoral joints of the legs. The circulatory system is a simple dorsal heart with two or three pairs of lateral slits (ostia). The nervous system is composed of a supra-esophageal brain or ganglion and a chain of five or six ventral ganglia. There is no specialized excretory or respiratory system; secretory or cement glands occur in the males on the legs; and some species have a blood pigment of uncertain nature.

In all species of which the habits are known, the male attaches the eggs to the long joints of his ovigers in masses or clusters as they are extruded from the female and carries them with him till they hatch into larvae. In some species the young larvae become attached to hydroids or polyps, in which they form galls or cysts; others are known to invade the medusa or jellyfish stage. The larval stages of a Japanese species, *Nymphonella tapetis*, are parasitic in the mantle cavity of clams; similar infestation of mussels by a California species has been observed. Others are associated with sea slugs (nudibranchs) and one may live within a sea cucumber (holothurian). Most species, however, are associated with coelenterates. The life cycle of all species of the genus *Colossendeis* is unknown; this genus includes the largest pycnogonids and species are abundant in Antarctic waters and the deep sea.

Pycnogonids occur in all oceans from the littoral zone to depths of more than 3,718 fathoms (22,308 ft. or 6,797 m.). Most species feed on the soft parts and body juices of coelenterates and other defenseless animals, but some live on the floating *Sargassum* in the mid-Atlantic; one, *Pallenopsis calcanea*, is bathypelagic, living at depths of about 4,000–6,500 ft. (1,200–2,000 m.) in the Atlantic and Pacific oceans. Some species ascend to the surface to breed, swimming by treading water with their long legs. In size pycnogonids range from a spread of 3 to 4 mm. in such forms as the littoral *Tanystylum* to about 50 cm. in deep-sea species of *Colossendeis*. While pycnogonids may sometimes occur in massive numbers, they are of no commercial significance.

Pycnogonida are recognized as fossils from the Devonian; ultraviolet light examination of the previously incompletely understood *Palaeoisopus* from the Hunsruck shales indicates that it possesses chelae, palps, ovigers, and a typical pycnogonid eye tubercle. It therefore differs from modern pycnogonids only in having an abdomen of several segments. The Pycnogonida cannot be associated with the Arachnida because the sexual apertures are not restricted to the second abdominal somite (there being no such segment) as in Arachnida; the multiple gonopores are a condition not found in other living arthropods. Nor can they be considered as allied to Crustacea because they do not have antennae or biramous appendages at any stage. The patellar segment of the leg is an arachnid character, and the occurrence of both flexor and extensor muscles in the distal joint of the leg is a character of Crustacea as well as Arachnida. The musculature of the oviger is unique among arthropods: the distal divisions or tarsal segments are individually musculated. The chelate protonymphon larva is unique. The occurrence of supernumerary legs is not comparable with similar phenomena in other groups but seems instead to be a sort of polymorphism, possibly within a species, although the forms have been given generic and specific names.

Bibliography.—J. W. Hedgpeth, "On the Evolutionary Significance of the Pycnogonida," *Smithson. Misc. Collns.*, 106:18 (1947), "On the Phylogeny of the Pycnogonida," *Acta Zool.*, Stockh., 35:193–213 (1954); H. Helfer and E. Schlottke, "Pantopoda," *Bronn's Kl. Ordn. Tierreichs*, vol. 5, sect. iv, bk. 2, i (1935); W. M. Lehmann, "Neue Entdeckungen an *Palaeoisopus*," *Paläont. Z.*, 33:96–103 (1959).

(J. W. Hh.)

PYDNA, BATTLE OF (June 22, 168 b.c.), the engagement that brought victory to Rome in the Third Macedonian War. In 168 the Romans sent out an efficient general, Lucius Aemilius Paulus. Finding Perseus, the Macedonian king, in an impregnable position on the Elpeus (Mavrolongos) River, Paulus sent a detachment round the Olympus Range and forced him to fall back to a weaker position in the plain south of Pydna (modern Kitros). Perseus now faced the risk that Paulus could penetrate into Macedoniā while another Roman army from Illyria might converge from the north. On June 22 the two armies were drawn up for battle on either side of a stream. Perseus, failing to induce the Romans to advance, finally crossed the river. His left wing of Thracians and light troops was defeated by the Roman allies. The Macedonian phalanx in the centre at first advanced but was soon disordered by broken ground. With greater flexibility the legionaries broke through its gaps and round its flanks and won the battle. The Macedonian losses were terrific. Perseus fled and finally was betrayed to the Romans, who ended the centuries-old monarchy and established four republics in Macedonia.   (H. H. Sd.)

PYGMALION, the name of two figures in classical literature and mythology.

1. In Greek mythology, Pygmalion was a king of Cyprus who fell in love with a statue of Aphrodite. Ovid, in the *Metamorphoses*, invents a more sophisticated version: Pygmalion, a sculptor, makes an ivory statue representing his ideal of womanhood, then falls in love with his own creation; Venus brings it to life in answer to his prayer.

Ovid's story was adapted by William S. Gilbert in *Pygmalion and Galatea* (1871). George Bernard Shaw developed ironically the theme of the creative artist in *Pygmalion* (1913), from which was later derived the musical play *My Fair Lady* (1956).

2. In the *Aeneid*, Pygmalion, king of Tyre, was the brother of Dido (*q.v.*) and the murderer of her husband.   (WM. S. A.)

PYGMY, a term used in modern anthropology as a category of size, applied to those human groups whose males are not taller than 59 in. (150 cm.) in average bodily height; a slightly taller group is called pygmoid. Races of true pygmy size have not been discovered in human prehistory.

The best known pygmies are the Bambuti, who inhabit an extended area of tropical Africa. Elsewhere in Africa, some of the Bushmen of the Kalahari Desert also are of pygmy size. All Asian pygmies are known by the generic term Negrito. Each of the several groups of pygmies has its independent biological origin; however, they have in common small bodily height and certain similarities in hair and face.

Culturally, all pygmy peoples remain on the very low level of food-gatherers, neglecting agriculture and stock farming. Nearly all of them maintain close symbiotic relations with culturally advanced tribes in their environment; consequently, in most cases they have lost their indigenous language and adopted that of their hosts.

See further BAMBUTI; BUSHMAN; NEGRITO; and references under "Pygmy" in the index.

See M. J. Gusinde, "Die Kleinwuchsvölker in heutiger Beurteilung," *Saeculum*, 13:211–277 (1962); C. M. Turnbull, "The Lesson of the Pygmies," *Sci. Amer.*, vol. 208 (Jan. 1963).   (M. J. GU.)

PYLE, ERNIE (ERNEST TAYLOR PYLE) (1900–1945), U.S. newspaperman, was one of the most famous war correspondents of World War II. Born near Dana, Ind., on Aug. 3, 1900, he studied journalism at Indiana University and left school a few months before his graduation to become a reporter for a small-town newspaper. Later, after various editorial jobs, he acquired a roving assignment for the Scripps-Howard newspaper chain. His daily experiences furnished him material for a column that eventually appeared in as many as 200 newspapers. His coverage of the campaigns in North Africa, Sicily, Italy, and France brought him a Pulitzer Prize in 1944, as well as several other awards. He was with the U.S. forces in the Pacific on Iwo Jima and Okinawa, during which latter campaign he visited the nearby island of Ie Shima. There, on April 18, 1945, he was killed by Japanese machine-gun fire. Compilations of his columns appeared in book form: *Ernie Pyle in England* (1941); *Here Is Your War* (1943); *Brave Men* (1944); *Last Chapter* (1946).

See Lee Graham Miller, *The Story of Ernie Pyle* (1950).

PYLE, HOWARD (1853–1911), U.S. artist and author, best known for his children's books, was born at Wilmington, Del., on March 5, 1853. He studied at the Art Students' League, New York City, and first attracted attention by his line drawings after the style of Albrecht Dürer. His magazine and book illustrations, particularly his drawings of scenes from American colonial life in New England and New Amsterdam, were of high quality. Some of Pyle's children's stories, illustrated by the author with vividness and historical accuracy, have become classics—most notably, *The Merry Adventures of Robin Hood* (1883); *Otto of the Silver Hand* (1888); and *Jack Ballister's Fortunes* (1894). Later he undertook mural paintings, executing, among others, "The Battle of Nashville" (1907) for the capitol at St. Paul, Minn.

Dissatisfied with his style in painting, he went to Italy for further study but died shortly afterward, on Nov. 9, 1911, in Florence. Pyle had established a free school of art in his home in Wilmington, where many successful American illustrators received their education.

PYLOS. The name of four ancient sites in Greece.

1. PYLOS (or CORYPHASIUM; modern PALAEA-NAVARINO), a town on the west coast of Messenia, noted chiefly for the part it played in the Peloponnesian War (*q.v.*). The Bay of Pylos (modern BAY OF NAVARINO), roughly semicircular, is protected by the island of Sphacteria (modern Sphagia or Sfaktiria), more than 2½ mi. long. To the north lies the lagoon of Osman Aga. North of Sphagia is the rocky headland of ancient Pylos or Coryphasium, called in modern times Palaea-Navarino, or Palaeokastro, from the Venetian ruins on its summit. The modern town of Pilos, alternatively Navarino or Neokastro, is on the southern headland

of the bay. A small island to the south of Sphagia is also called Pilos. Though the identification of Palaea-Navarino with Homeric Pylos (*see* 2, below) cannot be defended, it maintained some kind of settlement during the Bronze Age, for the cave on the north side of Coryphasium, traditionally associated in mythology with the herds of the Neleids and with Hermes' theft of Apollo's cattle, has been shown by excavation to have been at least intermittently occupied throughout the Bronze Age. This is reinforced by the existence nearby of two Mycenaean tholos tombs (*see* AEGEAN CIVILIZATION). The fate of the site between the end of the Bronze Age and the historical classical period is obscure; Thucydides describes Pylos as a deserted headland in 425 B.C. In May of that year, the seventh of the Peloponnesian War, the Athenians sent an expedition to Sicily under command of Eurymedon and Sophocles. With them was the general Demosthenes, who landed at Coryphasium with a body of Athenian troops and hastily fortified it. The Spartans withdrew their army from Attica, which they were then invading, and their fleet from Corcyra, and attacked Pylos vigorously by sea and land, but were repulsed; the Athenians were enabled by the arrival and victory of their fleet to blockade on the island of Sphacteria a body of 420 Spartiates together with their helots. They were overcome by a rear attack directed by a Messenian, who led a body of men by a difficult path along the cliffs on the east, and the 292 survivors including 120 Spartiates laid down their arms 72 days after the beginning of the blockade. This made a deep impression on the whole Greek world, which had learned to regard a Spartan surrender as inconceivable. Though Pylos should have been ceded to Sparta under the Peace of Nicias (421 B.C.), it was retained by the Athenians until the Spartans recaptured it early in 409 B.C.

In the Middle Ages the name Pylos was replaced by that of Avarino or Navarino, derived from a body of Avars who settled there; the derivation from the Navarrese company, who entered Greece in 1381 and built a castle at this spot, cannot now be maintained. From 1498 to 1821 Navarino was in the hands of the Turks, except for two periods (1644–48 and 1686–1715) when it was held by the Venetians. (*See* NAVARINO, BATTLE OF.)

2. HOMERIC PYLOS (modern EPANO ENGLIANOS), an excavated site on a ridge about seven miles north of Coryphasium, three or four miles inland from the sea. Excavation begun there in 1939 and resumed in 1952 under the direction of Professor C. W. Blegen of the University of Cincinnati in collaboration with K. Kourouniotis and S. Marinatos of the Greek Archaeological Service has uncovered a Mycenaean palace and attendant buildings of great importance. Both the evidence of successive building levels within the palace and finds from a number of adjacent cemeteries show that the site was occupied from at least as early as 1700 B.C. It was violently destroyed by fire shortly before 1200 B.C. and never reoccupied. The throne room, the finest feature of the palace, with painted plaster floor and frescoed walls, is closely matched by those at Mycenae and Tiryns. This palace and its despoiled tholos tombs best suit both in dignity and position the requirements of the royal seat of Neleus and king Nestor as described by Homer, and earlier attempts to locate it at the Pylos in Triphylia, or even that in Elis (*see* 3 and 4, below), should be disregarded. Transcending the importance of locating Homeric Pylos was the discovery in the palace ruins of hundreds of inscribed clay tablets, baked hard by the conflagration which destroyed the site, the majority in a single "archive room." These are very closely comparable to the Linear B tablets found earlier in Crete by Sir Arthur Evans in the Palace of Knossos, and those discovered since 1952 in excavations at Mycenae. The Pylos tablets were in use at the time of the destruction, and are thus some 200 years later than the generally accepted date for the majority of the Knossian documents. The decipherment of the Linear B script by Michael Ventris and John Chadwick in 1952 (*see* MINOAN LINEAR SCRIPTS) has shown their language to be an early form of Greek. Their contents, which demonstrate the great importance of Pylos' position as an administrative and military centre, are of a purely business nature; as well as lists of persons and property, they include very detailed records of distributions and dispositions made. The implications of the presence in Crete of documents written in

Greek and the discrepancy in date between Knossos and Pylos are highly controversial.

3. PYLOS IN ELIS, on the Peneus (Pinios) River in the northwestern Peloponnese.

4. PYLOS IN TRIPHYLIA (near Kakovatos). Scholarly dispute over the site of Homeric Pylos began at least as early as the 3rd century B.C. After the German excavation at the beginning of the 20th century of three Mycenaean tholos tombs (belonging to the period c. 1500 B.C.), as well as the remains of a contemporary settlement at Kakovatos, under Mt. Kaipha, Strabo's identification (vii, 348 et seq.) with the Pylos in Triphylia gained widespread acceptance. This lasted until the discovery of the Epano Englianos site. A too-literal interpretation of Homer's account of the journey of Telemachus from Ithaca to Pylos and from Pylos to Sparta lent additional weight to this identification.

BIBLIOGRAPHY.—*Coryphasium* (mod. *Palaea-Navarino*): G. B. Grundy, *Thucydides and the History of His Age*, book ii, pp. 122–133 (1948); A. W. Gomme, *A Historical Commentary on Thucydides*, book iii, pp. 482 ff. (1956).

Homeric Pylos (mod. *Epano Englianos*): *See* interim accounts of the excavations at Epano Englianos published by C. W. Blegen in *American Journal of Archaeology*, vol. xliii, pp. 557 ff. (1939); lvii, 59 ff. (1953); lviii, 27 ff. (1954); lix, 31 ff. (1955); lx, 95 ff. (1956); lxi, 129 ff. (1957); lxii, 175 ff. (1958); lxiii, 121 ff. (1959); lxiv, 153 ff. (1960). The texts of many of the tablets appear in E. L. Bennett (ed.), *The Pylos Tablets* (1955). *See also* L. R. Palmer, *Mycenaeans and Minoans* (1961); C. W. Blegen, *A Guide to the Palace of Nestor* (1962).

Pylos in Triphylia: For excavations at Kakovatos, *see* W. Dörpfeld, *Mitteilungen des Deutschen Archäologischen Instituts,* vol. xxxiii, pp. 295 ff. (1908); xxxiv, 269 ff. (1909); xxxviii, 97 ff. (1913). The problem of the identification has been discussed by W. A. McDonald, *American Journal of Archaeology*, xlvi, pp. 538 ff. (1942), and H. T. Wade-Gery, *ibid.,* lii, pp. 115 ff. (1948). (H. W. C.)

PYM, JOHN (c. 1583–1643), English statesman, and a leader of the parliamentary opposition to Charles I, was the son of Alexander Pym of Brymore, Somerset, a member of a family that had held this seat in direct male descent from the time of Henry III. Pym matriculated as a commoner at Broadgates Hall (now Pembroke College), Oxford, in 1599, and entered the Middle Temple in 1602. Through the interest of Edward Russell, 3rd earl of Bedford—whose agent in the west country was Pym's stepfather, Sir Anthony Rous—Pym became receiver of the king's revenue for Hampshire, Wiltshire, and Gloucestershire.

Growth of Leadership.—As a member for Calne in the 1621 Parliament, Pym delivered a speech on Nov. 28 to "beseech the King that there may be a commission . . . to see the Laws here of England duly executed against Papists." When James I tried to restrict the Commons' freedom of speech, Pym was a promoter of the Protestation (Dec. 18, 1621), which was entered in the Commons' journals, asserting that Parliament's privileges were "the ancient and undoubted birthright and inheritance of the subjects of England." This protest the king tore from the journal. After Parliament's dissolution in January 1622, Pym was ordered to be confined first to his London house and afterward to Brymore, an order which remained in force for more than three months. In the 1624 Parliament Pym sat for Tavistock, which he continued to represent for the remainder of his life. There is no evidence that he took a prominent part in this Parliament or in the first Parliament (1625) of Charles I. In the 1626 Parliament Pym was one of the managers of the impeachment of George Villiers, 1st duke of Buckingham.

The outstanding event of the 1628–29 Parliament was the Petition of Right (1628), of which Pym was a leading supporter. He also spoke at length against Roger Manwaring who had preached the doctrine of nonresistance to a king, deducing that a king could levy taxes without Parliament's consent. Pym was the leader in impeaching Manwaring before the Lords, where he delivered a speech expounding the fundamental principles of government (June 1628).

Between 1629 and 1640, when no Parliament met, Pym's energies were absorbed as treasurer of the Company of Adventurers for the Plantation of the Islands of Providence and Henrietta, in the West Indies, incorporated in December 1630. After struggling for nearly 20 years, the company finally failed. Its importance

was that its members were mostly leading Puritans who had already been associated with Pym in the parliamentary struggle against Charles I and would be associated again when Parliaments were resumed. Hence when the Short Parliament met on April 13, 1640, it included a group of resolute men already accustomed to act together and to recognize Pym as leader. On April 17 Pym spoke for two hours denouncing grievances: "The First, are those Grievances which during these Eleven years interval of Parliaments, are against the Liberties and Privileges of Parliament. The Second, are Innovations in matters of Religion. The Third, Grievances against the Propriety of our goods." "That which marked Pym from henceforth as a leader of men was the moderation combined with the firmness with which every sentence was stamped." (S. R. Gardiner, *History of England,* vol. ix, p. 102.) Pym was concerned in an episode which led to the Parliament's abrupt end: he and others prepared a petition that the king should make terms with the Scots. To forestall this, Charles dissolved Parliament on May 5.

Pym now aimed at compelling Charles to call another Parliament. He drew up the petition (August 1640) which demanded redress of grievances, peace with the Scots, and a new Parliament, and which 12 peers presented to the king. When writs for another Parliament were issued, Pym "rode about the country to promote elections of the puritanical brethren to serve in parliament" (Anthony à Wood, *Athenae Oxoniensis*, vol. iii, p. 73)—the first election campaign in parliamentary history.

The Long Parliament.—Parliament assembled on Nov. 3, 1640. Pym was recognized at once as the leader of the opposition to the court, and his dominance grew. Believing that Thomas Wentworth, earl of Strafford, was set upon accusing the parliamentary leaders of treason for their dealings with the Scots, and that attack was the surest defense, on Nov. 11 Pym, behind closed doors, began his denunciation of him. That same afternoon Pym carried to the Lords his impeachment and a summary of the charges on which the impeachment was based. Between this date and the opening of Strafford's trial (March 22, 1641), attempts were made to win Pym and others over to the king by offering to them ministerial posts. Twice the king interviewed Pym and twice the offer of the office of chancellor of the exchequer was refused, presumably because Charles demanded the dropping of Strafford's impeachment as the price of Pym's appointment. On April 13, 1641, the last day of the impeachment trial, Pym delivered one of his most eloquent speeches, basing his attack less upon Strafford's technical breach of the law of treason than upon his betrayal of trust as the king's adviser. "Shall it be treason," he declaimed, "to embase the King's coin, though but a piece of twelve-pence or sixpence? and must it not needs be the effect of a greater treason, to embase the spirits of his subjects, and to set up a stamp and character of servitude upon them, whereby they shall be disabled to do anything for the service of the King and Commonwealth?" Meantime some of Pym's associates were doubting whether the Lords would convict Strafford of treason on the available evidence. On April 10, therefore, they introduced a bill of attainder. Pym never agreed with this policy, believing that the impeachment should and could be carried. But it was the attainder process which was first completed and by which Strafford was executed on May 12.

Even more important than finance or Strafford to the opposition group was the subject of religion. In this matter Pym's position was different from that of most of his associates in that he was never a Puritan but was a staunch adherent of the orthodox, pre-Laudian church. In his maiden speech (Feb. 16, 1621) he had inveighed against a member named Thomas Shepherd because of his "exasperatinge one partie by that odious and factious name of Puritans." Similarly in the 1628–29 Parliament he condemned Archbishop William Laud's Arminianism because it contravened "the 39 Articles set forth in Queen Elizabeth's time; and . . . the Articles set forth at Lambeth as the doctrine of the Church of England." In December 1640 Pym moved Laud's impeachment, and on Feb. 24, 1641, presented the impeachment articles to the Lords. In February the Puritan members voted that a London petition against episcopacy should be sent to a committee for report, and the Anglican members voted against this; Pym voted with the Puritans, but a fellow member (Edward Bagshaw) wrote: "Mr. *John Pym* . . . spake to this purpose, 'That he thought it was not the intention of the House to abolish either Episcopacy or the Book of Common Prayer, but to reform both, wherein offence was given to the people'." (E. Bagshaw, *A Just Vindication*, 1660.) When, however, Pym became convinced that the bishops were merely the king's nominees to make religious changes and to preach nonresistance, he supported the abolition of episcopacy and in May 1641 voted for the Root and Branch Bill. That this attitude was not due to a change of conviction is shown by his pamphlet *Declaration and Vindication* of March 1643 wherein he averred: "That I am, and ever was, and so will dye a faithfull son of the Protestant Religion, without having the least relation in my beliefe to those grosse errours of Anabaptisme, Brownisme, and the like."

Pym was a leading supporter of the Grand Remonstrance, which listed the grievances that had arisen in Charles's reign, and his speech on Nov. 22, 1641, helped to secure its passing, though by only 11 votes. This small majority was evidence of a reaction in the king's favour. Charles thought to take advantage of it by impeaching a member of the Lords and five members of the Commons, including Pym (Jan. 3, 1642). Next day, Charles went to the Commons to arrest the five members, only to find that "the birds are flown." This breach of privilege turned the tide decisively against Charles and made war inevitable.

The Civil War.—Pym had a large part in the preparations for war. On July 4, 1642, he was appointed one of the 15 members of the Committee of Safety, of whom five had been members of the Providence Company. After the outbreak of war in August 1642 he was the organizer who kept the parliamentary forces in the field, raising taxes and maintaining supplies. He was, in effect, the head of the executive.

At first his aim was to prevent a general war. On Nov. 9, following the Battle of Edgehill, at a conference between the two Houses, he urged a petition to the king for negotiations. The king refused to receive the petition, and Pym appealed to the City of London for its continued support. But a few days later Pym was urging that both sides should disband their armies so that negotiations should not be prejudiced by their existence. When hope of negotiations failed, Pym gave himself entirely to organizing for victory. In March 1643 he proposed an excise on the sale of all goods: though then rejected, the excise was levied four months later. In May he decided to open negotiations with the Scots. In June he reintroduced the idea—rejected the previous October—of a covenant whose signatories should pledge themselves not to lay down arms until the Reformed religion was secure. Meanwhile, negotiations with the Scots were progressing. The final terms (the Solemn League and Covenant) were that the Scots would send an army into England against the king on condition that they were paid £30,000 a month and that Parliament would establish a reformed church after the war. On Sept. 25 Parliament accepted these terms. The Scottish alliance was Pym's last notable contribution to the parliamentary cause. On Nov. 7 Parliament made him master of the ordnance; *i.e.*, of arms stored in the Tower. On Dec. 8, 1643, he died of cancer at Derby House, Westminster, which had been granted to him as a residence. The Commons accorded him a state funeral in Westminster Abbey, where his body was buried on Dec. 13.

Family.—Pym's wife had been Anne Hooke (or Hooker), who had died in 1620. Of their nine children, four were sons. The eldest, Alexander, died unmarried. Charles became a baronet; his title and Pym's male line became extinct in Charles's son (also Charles) in 1688. Anthony emigrated, probably to St. Kitts.

Character.—Moderation of views in both religious and political questions, consistency of principles, and administrative efficiency were Pym's outstanding characteristics, and their combination explains his supremacy in Parliament. His speeches showed a sound political philosophy and logical exposition rather than rousing oratory; but they were evidently impressive and persuasive. Pym's death left a gap in the parliamentary leadership that was never again filled.

BIBLIOGRAPHY.—W. Notestein, F. H. Relf and H. Simpson (eds.), *Commons Debates, 1621* (1935); W. Notestein and F. H. Relf (eds.), *Commons Debates for 1629* (1921); S. R. Gardiner, *History of England 1603–42*, 10 vol. (1883–84); S. R. Brett, *John Pym, 1583–1643* (1940); J. H. Hexter, *The Reign of King Pym* (1941); E. C. W. Stratford, *King Charles and King Pym, 1637–1643* (1949); A. P. Newton, *The Colonising Activities of the English Puritans* (1914).   (S. R. Bт.)

P'YŎNGYANG, capital city of the Democratic People's Republic of Korea, is located northwest along the Taedong River, 30 mi. (48 km.) from the Yellow Sea. The reputed grave of the Chinese sage Kija (1122 B.C.), legendary founder of the city, is north of the city. Artifacts found in graves testify to the high cultural level of the Chinese colony established near P'yŏngyang in 108 B.C. Walls were built to reinforce the natural protection afforded by the two rivers and hills that surround P'yŏngyang. In this well-fortified area, the Koguryo dynasty (*c.* 37 B.C.–A.D. 668) had its capital, until defeated by the combined forces of China and the Silla dynasty in south Korea. Thereafter P'yŏngyang continued to be a political and educational centre for northwestern Korea.

Connected with other parts of Korea by rail, motor road, and air, commercial activities in P'yŏngyang have been of paramount economic importance. Under Japanese control (1910–45) anthracite coal mines and modern industries were developed, mainly to the south of the city where rail lines converged and to the east across the Taedong River. Hydroelectric power was supplied from plants on the Yalu River and its tributaries, and from a thermal plant in the city.

In surrounding areas, heavy industries, such as the iron and steel plant at Kyŏmip'o, cement plants to the east, and chemical plants to the north, were developed. In the city an arsenal was established, and also railroad workshops, and many light industries, such as textiles, rubber shoes, cigarettes, and corn products.

During the Korean War numerous air raids devastated P'yŏngyang. It was captured by UN forces in 1950 but subsequently was lost when Chinese Communist forces entered the war. It was reported that postwar rehabilitation restored many of the industries and that many large new apartments were built.

Pop. (1944) 368,288; (1960 est.) 653,100.   (S. McC.)

PYORRHEA: *see* PERIODONTAL DISEASES.

PYRACANTHA, a genus of evergreen thorny shrubs of the rose family (Rosaceae), commonly known as fire thorn. There are six species native from southeastern Europe to central China. The leathery, alternate leaves are usually minutely toothed. The white flowers are in clusters, followed by red, orange or yellow berrylike fruits. *P. coccinea, P. crenato-serata,* and *P. crenulata* are among the best-known kinds, widely used for foundation plantings and hedges; they are prized for their ornamental foliage and showy fruit. The plants are easily grown in subtropical and temperate regions (*P. coccinea lalandii* is the most hardy form) in areas of full sun or partial shade, and are not particular as to soil type.   (G. H. M. L.)

PYRAMID, in architecture, a monumental structure of stone or brick with a rectangular base and four sloping triangular sides meeting at an apex. Structures of this type were built at various times in Egypt, the Sudan, Ethiopia, western Asia, Greece, Cyprus, Italy, India, Thailand, Mexico, and on some islands of the Pacific Ocean. The most famous, and in many respects most remarkable of them all, are the pyramids of ancient Egypt, with which the present article will deal exclusively.

The ancient Egyptian term for pyramid is *mer*. The English word pyramid comes from the Greek *pyramis*, pl. *pyramides*, a word of doubtful etymology that was thought to have been derived from the ancient Egyptian *per-em-us*, a term used in a mathematical papyrus to denote the vertical height of a pyramid. A purely Greek word *pyramis* means "wheaten cake," and a vague resemblance in shape may have prompted early Greeks to use it as a facetious designation of the celebrated Egyptian monuments.

The pyramids of ancient Egypt were funerary edifices. Chronologically they cover a time span of 2,700 years ranging from the beginning of the Old Kingdom to the close of the Ptolemaic Period; but the time at which pyramid building reached its acme, the pyramid age par excellence, was that commencing with the 3rd dynasty and ending with the 6th (*c.* 2700 to 2300 B.C.). During that 400 years the pyramid was the regular type of royal tomb. It was not, as such, an isolated structure, but was always part of an architectural complex. (*See* EGYPT: *Archaeology; History.*)

The essential components, during the Old Kingdom at any rate, were the pyramid itself, containing or surmounting the grave proper and standing within an enclosure on high desert ground; an adjacent mortuary temple; and a causeway leading down to a pavilion (usually called the valley temple), situated at the edge of the cultivation and probably connected with the Nile by a canal. About 80 royal pyramids have been found in Egypt, many of them, however, reduced to mere mounds of debris and long ago plundered of their treasures.

Early Forms.—The prototype of the pyramid was the mastaba, a form of tomb known in Egypt from the beginning of the dynastic era. It was characterized by a flat-topped rectangular superstructure of mud brick or stone with a shaft descending to the burial chamber far below it. Zoser (Djoser), the second king of the 3rd dynasty, employing Imhotep (*q.v.*) as architect, undertook for the first time the construction of a mastaba entirely of stone; it was 8 m. high and had a square ground plan with sides about 63 m. each. Once completed it was extended on the ground on all four sides, and its height was increased by building rectangular additions of diminishing size superimposed upon its top. Thus Zoser's original mastaba became a terraced structure rising in six unequal stages to a height of 60 m., its base measuring 120 m. by 108 m. This monument, which lies at Saqqarah, is known as the Step Pyramid; it is probably the earliest stone building of importance erected in Egypt. The substructure has an intricate system of underground corridors and rooms, its main feature being a central shaft 25 m. deep and 8 m. wide, at the bottom of which is the sepulchral chamber built of granite from Aswan. Zoser's Step Pyramid rises within a vast walled court 544 m. long and 277 m. wide, in which are the remnants of several other stone edifices built to supply the wants of the king in the hereafter.

A structure of peculiar shape called the Blunted, Bent, False, or Rhomboidal Pyramid, which stands at Dahshur a short distance south of Saqqarah, marks an advance in development toward the strictly pyramidal tomb. Built by Sneferu, of the 4th dynasty, it is 188 m. square at the base and approximately 98 m. high. Peculiar in that it has a double slope, it changes inclination about halfway up, the lower portion being steeper than the upper. It comes nearer than Zoser's terraced tomb to being a true pyramid. A monumental structure at Maydum, also ascribed to King Sneferu, was a true pyramid, though not originally planned as such. It is uncertain whether it was begun as a mastaba, like Zoser's tomb, or as a small step pyramid. The initial structure was gradually enlarged until it became a gigantic eight-terraced mass of masonry; then the steps were filled in with a packing of stone to form a continuous slope. The entire structure was eventually covered with a smooth facing of limestone: a geometrically true pyramid was the final result. In its ruined condition, however, it has the appearance of a three-stepped pyramid rising to a height of about 70 m. The earliest tomb known to have been designed and executed throughout as a true pyramid is the North Stone Pyramid at Dahshur, thought by some to have also been erected by Sneferu. It is about 220 m. wide at the base and 104 m. high; thus it is nearly as large as the celebrated pyramids of Giza.

Pyramids of Giza.—The three great pyramids of Giza stand on a rocky plateau of the desert a few miles southwest of Cairo. They were built by the 4th-dynasty pharaohs Khufu (Cheops), Khafre (Khefren or Chephren), and Menkure (Mycerinus), and came to be numbered among the Seven Wonders of the ancient world.

Khufu.—The largest and oldest of them is that of Khufu, now known as the Great Pyramid and called "Horizon of Khufu" by the ancient Egyptians. Perhaps the greatest single building ever erected by man, the Great Pyramid's almost perfectly square base was, when intact, 230 m. long, thus covering an area of slightly over 13 ac.; it has been calculated that St. Peter's at

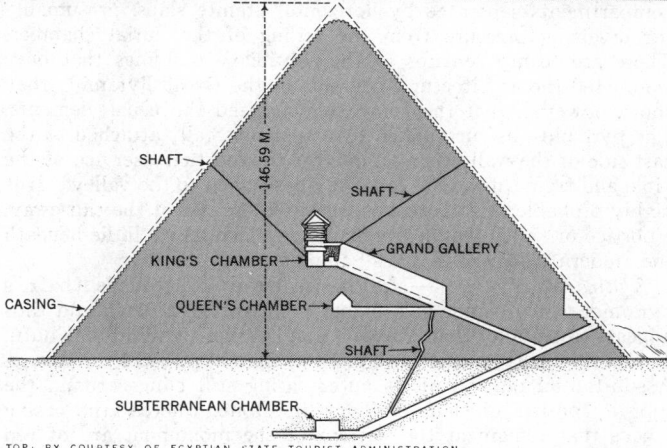

Pyramids of Giza: (Top) Aerial view of the three pyramids; (Bottom) Section through the Great Pyramid of Khufu

Rome, the cathedrals of Florence and Milan, Westminster Abbey, and St. Paul's Cathedral could all be grouped inside that area (E. B. Smith, *Egyptian Architecture as a Cultural Expression*). The original height was 146.59 m., reduced now to 137 m. The sides rise at an angle of 51°52' and are accurately oriented to the four cardinal points. The core is made of yellowish limestone blocks from the nearby Jabal al Moqattam; the outer casing (now mostly gone) and the inner passages are of finer limestone from Jabal Tura, while the burial chamber is built of huge blocks of granite from Aswan. Approximately 2,300,000 blocks of stone went into this stupendous structure, each weighing an average of $2\frac{1}{2}$ tons.

The monument is a masterpiece of technical skill and engineering ability. The geometrical precision of its layout and the accuracy of the stonecutting are truly amazing, particularly when one considers the colossal proportions of the whole and the size and weight of the blocks employed in it. The internal walls as well as the casing stones that still remain *in situ,* some of which weigh as much as 16 tons, show finer joints than any other masonry in Egypt and possibly in the world. The question of how the pyramid was built has not received a wholly satisfactory answer. The most plausible answer is that the Egyptians, who lacked tackle and pulleys for lifting heavy weights, employed a sloping embankment of brick and earth, which was increased in height and in length as the pyramid rose, and on which the stone blocks were hauled by means of sledges, rollers, and levers. According to Herodotus the road for the conveyance of building material from the river to the plateau on which the pyramid stands took 10 years to construct, while the pyramid itself took another 20 years and demanded the labour of 100,000 men. The theories that ascribe prophetic and esoteric meanings to the measurements, angles, and proportions of the Great Pyramid are wholly devoid of scientific foundation.

The entrance to the Great Pyramid is on the north side, about 18 m. above ground level. A sloping corridor descends through the masonry, penetrates the rocky soil and ends in an unfinished underground chamber. From the descending corridor, at a point about 20 m. from the entrance, branches an ascending corridor that leads to a room known as the Queen's Chamber (although there is no evidence that it was designed for her) and to a great slanting gallery 8.50 m. high and 46.50 m. long. At the upper end of this gallery a low and narrow passage gives access to the burial room proper, usually termed the King's Chamber. Entirely lined and roofed with granite, the King's Chamber is 10.43 m. long, 5.21 m. wide and 5.82 m. high and stands at a perpendicular height of 42.28 m. from the ground. From the chamber two narrow shafts run obliquely through the masonry and reach the exterior of the pyramid; it is not known whether they served a religious purpose or were meant for ventilation. The King's Chamber contained only an empty lidless sarcophagus of red granite without ornament or inscription. Above the room are five compartments separated by horizontal granite slabs, presumably for diverting pressure from the ceiling of the burial chamber. There are scanty remains of the subsidiary buildings that once completed the architectural complex of the Great Pyramid; they show, however, that the complex comprised the usual elements. The pyramid was surrounded by a temenos wall; attached to the east side of the wall was a temple for the mortuary service of the king, and from this a long causeway descended to the valley. It is highly probable that there was, at the lower end of the causeway, a portico or valley temple, remnants of which may still lie beneath the modern village of Kafr as Samman.

Khafre and Menkure.—Next in size in the Giza group is Khafre's pyramid, which stands at a higher point of the plateau and thus appears to be taller than the larger and earlier pyramid of Khufu. It was originally 143.50 m. high, and the base 215.25 m. square. A substantial portion of its outer casing still clings around the top; it consists of slabs of Tura limestone, whereas the casing blocks that remain at the bottom of the monument are of red granite. The third Giza pyramid, erected by Menkure, formerly rose to a height of 66.50 m., less than half that of its two towering neighbours.

Other Egyptian Pyramids.—Other noteworthy pyramids belonging to the Pyramid Age are the three built at Abu Sir by kings of the 5th dynasty, of which the largest is that of Neferirkare, originally 106 m. square and 70 m. high. The other two are much smaller, but their adjoining mortuary temples appear to have been magnificent buildings decorated with excellent reliefs, some of a historical nature. The pyramids themselves were poorly constructed, and are now in a state of dilapidation.

Pyramid Texts.—The relatively small pyramids of Unas, the last monarch of the 5th dynasty, of four kings and three queens of the 6th, and of an obscure 7th-dynasty pharaoh named Ibi, all of which are at Saqqarah, are of particular interest because inscribed on the walls of their inner chambers are collections of prayers, hymns, and spells meant to ensure the welfare of the king or queen in the afterlife. These inscriptions, known as the Pyramid Texts, form the world's oldest surviving corpus of religious and funerary writings.

Middle Kingdom.—The pyramids of the Middle Kingdom exhibit some structural innovations. A small pyramid mounted on a high podium surrounded by a terraced structure with a forest of columns was the dominant feature of King Mentuhotep II's tomb-temple at western Thebes. The pyramid was solid throughout, having neither passages nor chambers, and consisted of a rubble core cased with limestone. The core of Sesostris I's pyramid at Lisht consisted of a network of stone cross walls with the interspaces filled in with sand and loose blocks, the whole covered by a casing of dressed limestone blocks. This novel and labour-saving mode of construction was subsequently employed in other 12th-dynasty pyramids at Dahshur, Illahun, and Hawarah, in which, however, mud brick was used for the cross walls of the core, and as filling material as well. A further characteristic of the Middle Kingdom pyramids is the intricate design of the substructures.

No pyramid appears to have been constructed by any of the kings from the 18th dynasty to the 24th, with one exception: the pyramid-cenotaph erected at Abydos for Queen Tetisheri by Ahmose I, founder of the 18th dynasty. Royal tombs of pyramidal form were built once again by the thoroughly egyptianized Ethiopian rulers who held sway over Egypt as kings of the 25th dynasty in the 8th and 7th centuries B.C. They were buried in pyramids which they had erected for themselves in their homeland, at Nuri and Kurru, near the Fourth Cataract, in the northern Sudan.

Tombs of pyramidal design were built for private persons from the Middle Kingdom onward. The earliest have been found at Abydos. They were made of coarse unbaked bricks, coated with mud plaster and whitewashed. The pyramid itself was from 3 to 4 m. high and rested on a shorter rectangular podium. The coffin was deposited in a vaulted chamber which took up most of the interior of the pyramid. In the Theban necropolis, during the New Kingdom, a rather small mud-brick pyramid, sometimes topped with an apex of limestone, was a conspicuous feature of many private tombs.

See EGYPTIAN ARCHITECTURE; *see* also references under "Pyramid (bldg.)" in the Index.

BIBLIOGRAPHY.—I. E. S. Edwards, *The Pyramids of Egypt,* rev. ed. (1961); L. Grinsell, *Egyptian Pyramids* (1947); J. P. Lauer, *Le problème des pyramides d'Égypte* (1948); L. Borchardt, *Die Entstehung der Pyramide an der Baugeschichte der Pyramide bei Mejdum nachgewiesen* (1928); J. Vandier, *Manuel d'archéologie égyptienne,* vol. ii (1954). (R. A. Cs.)

PYRAMID, in geometry, a polyhedron of which one face, called the base, is any polygon and the other faces (the lateral faces) are triangles with one vertex in common. The intersections of the lateral faces are called the lateral edges of the pyramid, and their common vertex is called the vertex of the pyramid. The perpendicular distance from the vertex to the plane of the base is called the height or altitude of the pyramid. If the

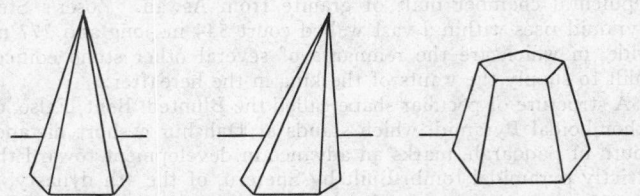

REGULAR PYRAMID, OBLIQUE PYRAMID, AND FRUSTUM OF PYRAMID

base is a regular polygon, the centre of which coincides with the foot of the perpendicular from the vertex to the base, the pyramid is called regular; if the vertex is not over the centre of the base, the pyramid is said to be oblique. As in the case of prisms, pyramids are classified as triangular, quadrangular, pentagonal, and so on, according to their bases. The portion of a pyramid between the base and a plane cutting all the lateral edges is called a truncated pyramid; and if the cutting plane is parallel to the base, the truncated pyramid becomes a frustum of a pyramid. The volume of a pyramid of base area B and altitude a is $\frac{1}{3}aB$. The volume of a frustum of a pyramid with base areas B and B' and altitude a is $\frac{1}{3}a(B + B' + \sqrt{BB'})$. *See* SOLIDS, GEOMETRIC.

PYRAMUS AND THISBE, the hero and heroine of a Babylonian love story told by Ovid in his *Metamorphoses.* Their parents refused to consent to their union, and the lovers used to converse through a chink in the wall separating their houses. At last they resolved to flee together, and agreed to meet under a mulberry tree near the tomb of Ninus. Thisbe was the first to arrive, but, terrified by the roar of a lioness, took to flight. In her haste she dropped her veil, which the lioness tore to pieces with jaws stained with the blood of an ox. Pyramus, believing that she had been devoured by the lioness, stabbed himself. Thisbe returned to the rendezvous, and finding her lover mortally wounded, put an end to her own life. From that time, legend holds, the fruit of the mulberry, previously white, was always black.

PYRARGYRITE, a mineral consisting of silver sulfantimonite, known also as dark red silver ore, is an important source of the metal. It is closely allied to, and isomorphous with, the corresponding sulfarsenite known as proustite (*q.v.*), or light red silver ore. "Ruby silver" or red silver ore (German *Rotgültigerz*) was mentioned by Georgius Agricola in 1546, but the two species were completely distinguished by Joseph Louis Proust in 1804.

The composition of pyrargyrite is Ag_3SbS_3. The colour is usually grayish black and the lustre metallic-adamantine; large crystals are opaque, but small ones and thin splinters are deep ruby red by transmitted light; hence the name, from the Greek words for "fire" and "silver." The streak is purplish red, thus differing markedly from the scarlet streak of proustite and affording a ready means of distinguishing the two minerals. The mineral occurs in metalliferous veins with calcite, argentiferous galena, native silver, native arsenic, etc.

The best crystallized specimens are from St. Andreasberg in the Harz Mountains and Freiberg in Saxony, and Guanajuato, Mex. It is found at Cobalt, Ont., and is not uncommon in silver mines in the United States in Colorado, Nevada, New Mexico and Idaho, but rarely as distinct crystals; and it has been found in Cornish mines.

PYRAZINES (PIAZINES or PARADIAZINES), in organic chemistry, nitrogenous compounds containing a ring composed of four carbon atoms and two nitrogen atoms, the latter being in the 1:4 relationship.

Pyrazine, $C_4H_4N_2$, crystallizes from water in colourless prisms having a heliotrope odour; it melts at 55° C and boils at 115° C. Its structure, which is analogous to that of benzene (*q.v.*), may

be described as a resonance hybrid between I and II (*see* RESONANCE, THEORY OF). As with benzene, the structure is commonly expressed by the conventional symbol III.

Important derivatives of pyrazine include: hexahydropyrazine, or piperazine; the diketopiperazines or amino-acid anhydrides, which are obtained by the elimination of alcohol from the esters of α-amino acids; and the various groups of azine dyes.

(G. W. WD.)

PYRAZOLES are a class of organic compounds containing a doubly unsaturated five-membered ring with three carbon atoms united to two adjacent nitrogen atoms. Some of the pyrazoles have medical and industrial uses. The structure of the parent compound itself, pyrazole, and the numbering system commonly used for derivatives, is shown in formula I. The electron configuration of the pyrazole ring system is related to that of benzene and is responsible for the considerable stability of compounds with this structure. Dihydro- (II) and tetrahydro-pyrazoles (III) are called pyrazolines and pyrazolidines, respectively. While most compounds related to structures I, II, and III are of interest only to the organic chemist, some pyrazole derivatives with an oxygen atom at position 5 (pyrazolin-5-ones) have considerable value as drugs to combat pain and fever, and as dyes.

The discovery of the analgesic and antipyretic properties of antipyrine (2,3-dimethyl-1-phenyl-3-pyrazolin-5-one) (IV) in 1883 by Ludwig Knorr of Germany was the beginning of a systematic search for other pyrazole derivatives with more satisfactory properties. Aminopyrine, the 4-dimethylamino derivative of antipyrine, was the result of these efforts; it has largely replaced antipyrine because of its higher effectiveness and more protracted action. Many 3-pyrazolin-5-ones have been synthesized and tested for activity as antipyretics and analgesics, but only a few have been able to compete with aminopyrine to any extent. Antipyrine, aminopyrine, and related compounds may adversely affect the mucous membranes, skin, and blood; for this reason they are little used in the United States, although world consumption in the 1960s was around 300,000 pounds a year and pyrazolinone analgesics were the drugs of popular choice in Europe, South America, and the Middle East. Phenylbutazone (1,2-diphenyl-4-

butyl-3,5-pyrazolidinedione), a pyrazole derivative with two oxygen atoms, has been found to be useful in the treatment of certain forms of arthritis.

The most important commercial use for pyrazole derivatives is as textile and foodstuff dyes. Most of these dyes are pyrazolin-5-one derivatives containing an arylazo group (two nitrogen atoms attached to an aromatic ring) at position 4. The outstanding features of the pyrazolinone dyes is their excellent fastness to light and severe wet treatments. Complex formation with metal salts is frequently used to upgrade the fastness of the dyes and to obtain more desirable colour shades.

Colour photography makes extensive use of pyrazolinone derivatives as colour couplers, sensitizers, and developing agents.

See T. L. Jacobs, "Pyrazoles and Related Compounds," in *Heterocyclic Compounds*, ed. by R. C. Elderfield (1957); R. H. Wiley and P. F. Wiley, *Pyrazolones, Pyrazolidones and Derivatives* (1964).

(G. L. C.)

PYRENEES, a range of mountains between the Bay of Biscay and the Mediterranean, separating the Iberian Peninsula from France. In general the crest line marks the frontier between France and Spain, though important exceptions are the Valle de Arán, which is Spanish though on the north slope of the Pyrenees, and the whole of the Maladeta Massif, which is in Spain. Another exception is the French area of the Cerdagne, to the south of the main watershed.

The range is about 250 mi. (400 km.) long, has an approximate maximum width of 60 mi. (100 km.), and a steeper northern slope. It can be divided into three geographical regions: the western, central, and eastern Pyrenees. The western Pyrenees, which extend westward from the Col de Somport (Spanish Puerto de Somport), have a generally rounded, subdued relief; their crest line, seldom exceeding 6,500 ft. (2,000 m.), declines gradually to the west. Eastward the high mountains of the central Pyrenees maintain a level exceeding 6,000 ft. (1,800 m.) for over 100 mi. and have areas of permanent snow. The highest peaks are the Pico de Aneto (11,168 ft. [3,404 m.]), highest summit of the Maladeta Massif, the Pico de Posets (11,046 ft. [3,367 m.]), and Mont Perdu (Spanish Monte Perdido; 11,007 ft. [3,355 m.]). The eastern Pyrenees, with their Mediterranean influences, extend eastward from the Col de la Perche. Their decline in height is more sudden than that of the western Pyrenees and longitudinal valleys assume a greater importance in their relief.

In spite of Louis XIV's statement that "the Pyrenees exist no longer," the central mountains are still a barrier to communications, with main road passes closed for more than half the year. The north-south valley routes often end in formidable cirques or cross the frontier ridge as mule tracks. Apart from the important easier routes round the coastal flanks of the range there are eight principal main road passes: Roncesvalles (Ibañeta; 3,468 ft.); Somport (5,354 ft.); Pourtalet (Portalet; 5,880 ft.); the road southward from Viella in the Valle de Arán which tunnels for $3\frac{1}{4}$ mi. beneath the Puerto de Viella; Puerto de la Bonaigua (6,798 ft.); Port d'Envalira (8,022 ft.), the highest pass of the Pyrenees, in Andorra; Col de Puymorens (6,283 ft.); and Col de

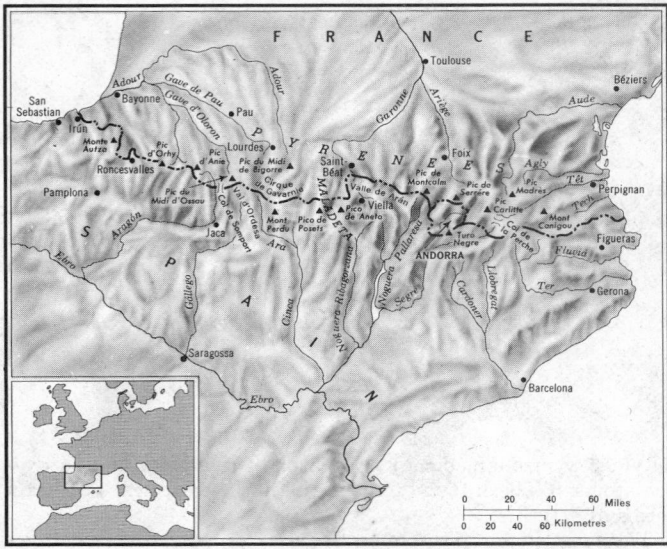

TOPOGRAPHY OF THE PYRENEES MOUNTAINS

la Perche (5,174 ft.). Communication laterally between adjacent north-south valleys remains difficult, though in France the tourist Route des Pyrénées, with such spectacular passes as the Col du Tourmalet (6,939 ft.), south of the Pic du Midi de Bigorre (9,440 ft.), provides a link between valleys in the east. On the Spanish side individual valleys remain single units, with their own local wines and other produce.

Geology.—The geological history of the Pyrenees is epitomized in De Sitter's statement: "In contrast with the Alps, the Pyrenees are more of a rejuvenated Hercynian mountain chain than a Tertiary structure." Between the Aquitaine and Ebro basins to the north and south, the Pyrenean structural belt can be divided into five components: (1) A northern marginal trough with relatively gently folded Upper Cretaceous and Eocene rocks such as the limestones of the Petites Pyrénées; (2) the Ariège zone of folded Mesozoic rocks surrounding minor massifs of Paleozoics, with which they are infolded. A southern boundary for the zone is provided by the important North Pyrenean fault complex; (3) the axial zone with its cleaved and folded Paleozoics and associated igneous rocks, such as the intrusive granites of the Maladeta Massif and the andesite intrusion of the Pic du Midi d'Ossau; (4) the zone of Mont Perdu, a narrow belt of folded Mesozoic rocks, corresponding to zone (2) but of different tectonic form. Here are structures due to gravitational gliding such as the "cascade" of folds in the Upper Cretaceous and Eocene limestones of Mont Perdu and the Val d'Ordesa (a Spanish national park); and (5) a southern marginal trough with thick folded, mainly Eocene, sediments.

Folding in the Pyrenees may be ascribed to three main phases. Precambrian rocks are poorly known but the Lower Paleozoic rocks, such as the graptolitic shales of the Silurian, were cleaved and folded by the first, Hercynian, phase of Upper Devonian and Carboniferous times. Later Devonian and Carboniferous rocks show much lateral variation in response to the active elevations of the time. The Paleozoic rocks of the axial belt are cut by granite and other intrusions following upon the Hercynian movements. The North Pyrenean fault system was initiated during the orogeny; to the north of it folds and faults elevated the minor massifs of the Ariège zone, later to be surrounded by Mesozoic sediments.

Subsequently the axial zone (except for the deposition of continental Triassic rocks) remained essentially geanticlinal. Two phases of Alpine earth movements occurred in late Cretaceous and post-Eocene times. The former accentuated the elevation of the axial zone. In the marginal troughs the marine rocks of the Jurassic and Lower Cretaceous were folded. The post-Eocene movements again affected the marginal troughs and produced the gravitational gliding structures to the south of the axial zone.

Later geological events have been intermittent elevation of the range and the spread of extensive post-Eocene conglomerates and sandstones northward and southward from the mountain belt. This detritus may obscure the earlier fold structures as in the case of the Tertiary fan of Lannemezan, which spreads across the northern marginal trough.

Glaciation.—The present-day permanent glaciers of the central Pyrenees occupy only a few square miles. Individually they are very small, occurring especially on the north-facing summit slopes, the largest group being in the Maladeta Massif. There, to the north of the Pico de Aneto, is the largest individual glacier which is about ¾ mi. long and just over a mile wide. It is not, however, a valley glacier but merely a sheet with an irregular lower edge.

Impressive cirques, such as that of Gavarnie (q.v.) and the Cirque de Troumouse, and pyramidal peaks, such as the Pic du Midi d'Ossau, testify to the greater extent of the Pleistocene glaciation. The north-south valleys have moraines and hanging tributaries and, in France, there is evidence that the ice along them reached as low as just over 1,000 ft. above present sea level.

Drainage.—Viewed from the Boulevard des Pyrénées at Pau the north front of the range appears as a mountain wall, into which penetrate the deep glaciated north-south valleys initiated by consequent streams upon the original axial uplift. These are characterized by "flats" floored by glacial drift, separated by gorges or rapids where there are morainic barriers. Generally, on the French side, there is little longitudinal adaptation to the various rock types. The main rivers, beginning in the west, include the Gave d'Aspe and the Gave d'Ossau, which converge to form the Gave d'Oloron. The Gave de Pau, which rises in the Cirque de Gavarnie, flows northward to Lourdes before turning northwestward through Pau. These *gaves* (a local term for a mountain torrent) are tributaries of the Adour, which forms the next important Pyrenean river. It rises to the east of the Pic du Midi de Bigorre, whence it flows in a generally northerly direction before turning west. The central and much of the eastern Pyrenees are drained by the Garonne, with its tributary the Ariège. The Garonne rises in the Valle de Arán where an east-west longitudinal valley follows the strike of the Paleozoic sediments and in part runs between two igne-

THE GARONNE RIVER AT SAINT-BÉAT IN THE HAUTE-GARONNE REGION OF THE PYRENEES

ous masses. One headstream rises at the eastern end of the valley, the other from a cavern to the west. In the eastern Pyrenees the rivers Agly, Têt, and Tech occupy west-east longitudinal valleys in their courses to the plain of Roussillon. There subsidences associated with the Mediterranean border contribute to the different relief pattern.

On the Spanish side of the Pyrenees is a complex area of sierras and deep valleys drained by the northern tributaries of the Ebro. These, too, cut across the structural grain, but longitudinal elements are stronger. The Aragón, for example, west of Jaca, has an important longitudinal portion of its course. The longitudinal elements of the drainage are separated by strike ridges cut in the extensive Tertiary sediments of the southern marginal trough.

Underground drainage related to the various Paleozoic to Tertiary limestones is significant in the Pyrenees and the French speleologist Norbert Casteret explored many of the underground watercourses and caverns. One of his most important discoveries came after four years' (1928–31) investigation of the supposed connection between the Trou du Toro (6,561 ft.) in the Maladeta Massif, where meltwaters from the local glaciers and snowfields make an impressive disappearance below ground, and the Goueil de Jouéou (4,610 ft.) whence, in the Valle de Arán, the western headwaters of the Garonne appear. Proof of the connection came finally in 1931 when fluorescein thrown into the Trou du Toro coloured the emerging waters of the Garonne.

Economy.—The traditional occupation of pastoral farming, with its associated fodder crop production, still dominates the scene in the Pyrenean valleys. Cattle (for milk, cheese, and meat) and sheep (for wool, meat, and cheese) are both involved in transhumance between the valleys and the high summer pastures. Market gardening takes place in the lower valleys in France.

The woodlands have gradually been felled for timber, for charcoal for local iron forges, and to make clearances for pasture. Garigue and maquis have replaced the trees, but forestry remains important and reafforestation continues. The forest types vary: in the western Pyrenees affected by humid Atlantic winds, ash and chestnut are characteristic; in the central area beech is succeeded at higher levels by conifers; and in the drier east Mediterranean oaks are succeeded by pines. Tree cover is thinner in Spain than France because of the generally drier climate.

The mineral wealth of the Pyrenees is not great, though there are iron deposits and natural gas in France, limestone and talc are quarried, and some coal occurs in Spain. Local industries are expected to thrive when the great potential of hydroelectric power is developed. This potential lies in the deep, steep-sided valleys, the many high-level, rock-basin lakes, and the heavy precipitation. Though installations were small, in the early 1960s the Pyrenees provided about one-sixth of France's hydroelectric power and new developments were occurring also in Spain.

See ANDORRA; ARIÈGE; BASSES-PYRÉNÉES; HAUTES-PYRÉNÉES; HUESCA, province; PYRÉNÉES-ORIENTALES.

BIBLIOGRAPHY.—H. Belloc, *The Pyrenees*, 4th ed. (1928); L. U. de Sitter, *Structural Geology* (1956); N. Casteret, *Ten Years Under the Earth* (1939). (C. H. Ho.)

PYRÉNÉES-ORIENTALES, a frontier *département* of southern France, formed in 1790 from the province of Roussillon (*q.v.*) and the region of Cerdagne (Cerdaña), which had become part of France in 1659, together with small adjacent areas of Languedoc. It is bounded south by Spain, west by the Pyrenean state of Andorra, northwest by the *département* of Ariège, and north by that of Aude, and to the east fronts the Mediterranean Sea from the Étang (Lagoon) de Leucate to the Spanish frontier at Cap Cerbère. Area 1,600 sq.mi. (4,144 sq.km.). Pop. (1962) 251,231. The eastern Pyrenees (Carlitte, 9,583 ft. [2,921 m.]) largely represent the crystalline core of the mountain system and extend right to the Mediterranean as the Albères range. Between the Albères and the crystalline Corbières Massif to the north lies the plain of Roussillon, a downfaulted basin, formerly occupied by a gulf of the sea that has been filled with detritus by the Tech, Têt, and Agly rivers. The western part of the *département* consists of the high mountain valleys of these rivers, between west-east mountain spurs. Cultivation of cereals, potatoes, and fodder

crops is carried on up to about 5,000 ft. (1,500 m.), and a pastoral economy uses summer grazings that are snow-covered for several months. Below the tree line at about 7,000 ft. the forests of the eastern Pyrenees have been ravaged during the centuries by the needs of shipbuilding and iron industries and especially by the uncontrolled grazing of sheep and goats. At higher altitudes are the remains of conifer forests, with hardwoods, especially oaks, below. Altitudinal zoning of vegetation is exceptionally well developed on Canigou (9,137 ft. [2,785 m.]), which dominates the plain of Roussillon. At lower altitudes the mountains are covered with Mediterranean scrub, and the Albères has some cork oak and chestnut woodland.

The plain of Roussillon experiences the characteristically mild winters and dry summers of the Mediterranean climate, the average monthly temperatures at Perpignan ranging from 6° to 22° C (44°–73° F), with an annual rainfall of only 22 in. (560 mm.). The normal mildness encourages the cultivation of delicate and out-of-season crops, but protection needs to be provided against the *tramontane*, a strong, cold wind from the northwest, to which Roussillon is subject. There is a sharp distinction in the cultivated area between (1) the irrigated tracts (*regadiu*), chiefly along the Tech and Têt, watered by channels (*rechs*) from these rivers and devoted to intensive production of peaches and apricots or to a continuous succession of vegetable crops behind the shelter of cypress windbreaks; and (2) the unirrigated cultivation (*aspre*) of gravel terraces and lower hill slopes. There the traditional Mediterranean dry farming, based upon wheat, olive, and vine, has largely been replaced by vineyards. Rivesaltes and Banyuls are well-known wines, the latter being produced from terraced vineyards on the Albères behind its rocky coast. Perpignan has a large distilling industry, and *Byrrh* (a well-known apéritif) is made at Thuir nearby.

The high-grade iron ore of Canigou has long been worked and still supports a local iron industry at Prades and at the modern electric furnaces of Villefranche-de-Conflent. Hydroelectric power has been developed chiefly by stations on the Têt River. Among several notable spa resorts, the chief are Amélie-les-Bains and Vernet. The tourist industry has been greatly stimulated by the construction of motor roads. That from Toulouse over the Col de Puymorens (6,283 ft. [1,915 m.]), skirting Andorra, is joined by a road from Perpignan at the head of the Têt Valley (Conflent) at the frontier post of Bourg-Madame. The lower, historic route farther east by the Col du Perthus (942 ft. [287 m.]), which was used by Hannibal, is open throughout the year. The railway tunnels the ridges of the Albères near the coast, where little coves provide small and picturesque sardine and anchovy fishing ports at Collioure and Port-Vendres.

Perpignan, the historic capital of Roussillon, with the ancient palace of the kings of Majorca embedded within the massive citadel built by Sebastien le Prestre de Vauban, is the largest town and *préfecture* of the *département*. Since 1602 it has replaced Elne as the centre of a bishopric. The *département* comes under Montpellier for the administration both of justice and of education. It is divided into three *arrondissements*, centred upon Perpignan, Prades, and Céret. (AR. E. S.)

PYRETHRUM, the name for certain species of the genus *Chrysanthemum* in which the aromatic flower heads, powdered, constitute the active ingredient in the insecticide commonly called pyrethrum. These plants were formerly considered a separate genus, *Pyrethrum*. The typical species, the perennial *C. coccineum*, is the florists' pyrethrum, commonly called painted lady. Large daisylike flowers—deep rose-coloured petals surrounding the yellow centre or disk—are borne on long simple stems above the crown of finely cut leaves. Modern varieties are remarkable for the colours of their flowers—white, lilac, and shades of red. They are used in flower borders and as cut flowers.

The powdered flower heads of *C. coccineum*, *C. cinerariaefolium*, and *C. marschalli* are chief sources of the insecticide. The active substances in pyrethrum—pyrethrins I and II and cinerins I and II—are contact poisons for insects and cold-blooded vertebrates. The concentrations of pyrethrum powder used in insecticides are nontoxic to plants and higher animals; therefore, these insecticides find wide use in household and livestock sprays as well as in dusts for edible plants.

These highly aromatic plants, native to southwestern Asia, are now widely cultivated as fine hardy perennial garden subjects; they are grown for pyrethrum powder chiefly in Africa, Japan, and India. Seeds sown in the spring in ordinary well-drained garden soil in full sun will produce plants that bloom the following year; plants may be increased by division of the crown after flowering.   (N. Tr.; X.)

PYRIDINE, a colourless, liquid, nitrogenous base with a pungent odour, belongs to the class of heterocyclic aromatic bases and is the most thoroughly investigated member of that class. It may be regarded structurally as a six-membered ring compound similar to benzene in which one hydrogen-carbon (CH) group is replaced by nitrogen (N). Although the pyridine nucleus does not occur so frequently in natural products as the derived condensed systems quinoline (q.v.) and isoquinoline, it is found in the alkaloids of the pomegranate, lobelia, hemlock, areca, and tobacco species and in the B-complex vitamins, nicotinic acid and pyridoxine, compounds of great physiological and pharmaceutical significance. The heterocyclic nature of the ring makes possible the formation of many series of isomeric substituted homologues and derivatives. Best known are the various isomeric mono-, di-, and trimethyl derivatives, the picolines, lutidines, and collidines, found in the light-oil and middle-oil fractions in the distillation of coal tar, and known as the pyridine bases.

These bases were first isolated and characterized by T. Anderson (1846–57) in his investigation of the oil (Dippel's oil) formed in the dry distillation of bones; α-picoline, the first of these bases to be isolated as a pure substance, had been obtained in 1846 from the basic constituents of coal tar. Pyridine and several of its homologues were obtained from bone oil shortly thereafter. Since their formation occurs on dry distillation only if the bones still contain unsaponified fat, the bases are regarded as end products of the interaction of acrolein formed from dehydration of the glycerol from the fat and the ammonia from the decomposition of the nitrogenous constituents. Pyridine was later isolated from coal tar as well as from petroleum, shale oil, peat, crude amyl alcohol, and even from roasted coffee. The modern resolution of coal tar components by vapour phase chromatography provides, in addition to the pyridine bases, the quinolines, isoquinolines, and still more complex ring systems.

In addition to limited supplies from bone oil, pyridine bases have been commercially available from the condensation products of the coking of coal since 1860. With the advent of the successful use of the by-product oven in Germany in 1881 and its introduction later into the United States and the United Kingdom, the coal-tar industry was firmly established, but it was not until spurred by the demands of the growing pharmaceutical industry that, around 1920, the production of pyridine bases from coal tar began to expand rapidly. Of the pyridine and pyridine bases produced in the coking process, part appears in the noncondensed gases and the remainder becomes part of the coal tar formed on condensation. On passage into dilute sulfuric acid the noncondensed gases form a solution of pyridinium and ammonium sulfates known as the "ammonia saturator liquors." These liquors, containing about 60% of the 0.15 lb. of total pyridine and quinoline bases per ton of coal coked, are saturated with ammonia in a continuous neutralizing still and distilled to give crude pyridine bases containing 15–20% water, dried by azeotropic distillation with benzene and fractionated to yield pyridine, α-picoline, a β-picoline fraction, and a mixture of higher alkylated pyridines.

The coal tar is distilled in pipe stills to produce "light-oil" and "middle-oil" fractions with distillation end points around 210° C and 270° C approximately. The light oil is washed free from phenols with caustic soda and then acidified with sulfuric acid to form pyridine base sulfates from which the free bases are "sprung" by treatment with caustic or ammonia. The mother liquors from the distillation of the middle oil, after removal of naphthalene by centrifugation, are extracted with caustic soda, the residual oil distilled, the distillate treated with sulfuric acid,

the acid solution neutralized with ammonia, the crude wet pyridine bases dried by azeotropic distillation with benzene and refined by fractional distillation to give some pyridine and picoline, but mainly the higher alkylated pyridine and quinoline bases.

The amount of coal coked in the United States is limited to supplying coke for steel, and, because between 0.07 and 0.21 lb. of total pyridine and quinoline bases are produced per ton of coal coked, the coking of around 75,000,000 tons of coal per annum in the United States provides a fixed supply of around 5,000,000 lb. of bases per year. Thus no large-scale industrial processing can be based exclusively on the supply of pyridine bases from the coking of coal, and synthetic processes have been developed to meet the ever increasing demands for these products so essential to pharmaceutical and other related industries.

Synthetic Processes.—Since pyrolysis of bones, shale, and coal is actually a synthesis of pyridine bases, various pyrolytic syntheses by the vapour phase reaction of ammonia with acrolein, acetylenes, acetaldehyde, or a mixture of hydrogen and ethanol, by passage of the mixed gases over metal oxide catalyst at 300°–500° C have been developed. The condensation of acetylene (or acetaldehyde), ammonia, and methanol over a fluidized bed of silica-alumina catalyst at 500° C gives a mixture of 35% pyridine and 27% 3-picoline, separated by the fractional distillation of the crude dry basic mixture. Pyrolysis of acetaldehyde and ammonia over silica-alumina-thoria catalyst at 450° C yields 2-picoline and 4-picoline.

The reaction of paraldehyde with aqueous ammonia at 200°–250° C, the so-called Chichibabin synthesis, gives 70–80% yields of 2-methyl-5-ethylpyridine (MEP, aldehyde collidine) with 5–10% of α-picoline as secondary product. MEP is oxidized to the corresponding dicarboxylic acid, which loses carbon dioxide at high temperatures and produces nicotinic acid in 75% yields. Catalytic dehydrogenation of MEP in the presence of an inhibitor gives 2-methyl-5-vinylpyridine (MVP), a valuable monomer for the preparation of synthetic rubbers and acrylonitrile polymers.

Syntheses of pyridine bases and their multifarious derivatives are carried out in ever increasing number on the laboratory and pilot-plant scale. The classical Hantzsch pyridine synthesis (1882) involves the condensation of two molar proportions of acetoacetic ester with one each of an aldehyde and ammonia (β-aminocrotonic esters can substitute for acetoacetic ester and ammonia). The dihydropyridine derivatives thus produced are readily oxidized to a substituted pyridine derivative, or the ester may be hydrolyzed and then decarboxylated to bases such as 2,6-lutidine or collidine. Many modifications of this classical

HANTZSCH PYRIDINE SYNTHESIS

synthesis have been developed: the Knoevenagel-Fries condensation substitutes malonic ester for the acetoacetic ester; the Guareschi-Thorpe modification involves the use of cyanoacetic acid derivatives; and the Gattermann-Skita method employs the reaction of diethyl sodiomalonate with compounds of the type of dichloromethylamine.

The pyridine ring can also be formed by condensation of hydroxylamine with 1,5-diketones. Besides linking up open chain compounds, the pyridine ring may be arrived at by replacement of the ring oxygen atom of pyrones with a nitrogen atom and by expansion of the five-membered ring of pyrroles.

Properties.—Pyridine is a stable, flammable, colourless liquid with a sharp taste and characteristically disagreeable odour, volatile with steam, solidifying at −42° C, bp 115°–116° C, d_4^{25} 0.980, n_D^{20} 1.5102. Its ultraviolet spectrum is similar to that of benzene: λ_{max} 170, 195, 250 mμ. The infrared spectrum exhibits bands at 3070–3020, 1660–1590, 1500, 1200, 750, 710 cm^{-1}. The nuclear magnetic resonance spectrum is that of an AB$_2$X$_2$ system with absorptions for the α, β, and γ protons at τ 14.0, 3.00 and 2.40 ppm, respectively. Pyridine readily absorbs moisture to form an azeotrope corresponding to C$_5$H$_5$N·3H$_2$O, bp 92°–93° C, and may be dried by azeotropic distillation with benzene or over potassium hydroxide or barium oxide. It is an excellent solvent for most organic compounds and gives conducting solutions with silver, copper, lead, mercury and iron halides, nitrates, and acetates. It is a completely soluble weak base (K$_b$ 2.3 × 10^{-9}; pK$_a$ 5.17 in water at 25° C) forming salts with strong acids and complexes at the nitrogen atom with most inorganic salts.

The chemical properties of pyridine may be predicted qualitatively on the basis of molecular orbital calculations of the electron densities around the ring or on resonance theory considerations. According to the latter theory the valence structure of pyridine may be represented as a hybrid of five canonical structures. Based on these theoretical considerations the pyridine ring should be less susceptible to electrophilic attack at carbon and more readily at C-3 and C-5 than at the other carbon atoms. Nucleophilic substitution should occur readily at C-2 and C-4 positions. Upon addition of a strong acid, the pyridinium ion, more resistant to electrophilic attack than is pyridine itself, is formed. With an acid chloride or anhydride, an N-acyl pyridinium salt is formed which is a powerful acylating agent. The higher alkylpyridinium halides such as N-cetylpyridinium chloride are valuable cationic germicides. Pyridine, toxic to humans in doses of 1.8–2.5 cc. per day is detoxified in the dog by conversion to N-methylpyridinium hydroxide.

Like ammonia, pyridine combines with metals of the transitional group of the periodic table to give stable coordination compounds whose study has been important in the development of the coordination theory and of the stereochemistry of metals. Oxidation of quinoline to quinolinic acid, in which the benzene ring is destroyed while the pyridine ring remains intact, shows the extreme stability of the ring to oxidation. Consequently, pyridine can be used as a solvent in oxidation reactions, whereas the pyridine homologues are oxidized to the corresponding carboxylic acids. Degradation of alkaloids containing pyridine, quinoline, and isoquinoline rings by vigorous oxidation often provides valuable structural information. The more important pyridine carboxylic acids are the vitamin nicotinic acid and the isomeric isonicotinic acid, whose hydrazide has found extensive use as an antitubercular agent. On reaction with peroxyacids, pyridine yields an N-oxide, which, in contrast to pyridine, readily undergoes many electrophilic substitutions to yield products having a different orientation from those obtained from pyridine itself.

Pyridine is readily reduced catalytically, electrolytically, or chemically, by sodium in alcohol, to the saturated hexahydro derivative piperidine, C$_6$H$_{11}$N, mp −9° to 17° C, bp 106° C, d$_4^{20}$ 0.8622, K$_b$ 1.6 × 10^{-2}. It is a colourless liquid with a characteristic ammoniacal odour and is miscible with water and most solvents. It forms salts, ring-substituted derivatives, and such well-known N-derivatives as N-acetyl- and N-benzoylpiperidines. Piperidine can be obtained by the hydrolysis of the alkaloid piperine, occurring in various peppers, and is present in coniine, the poisonous principle of hemlock, as its derivative 2-propyl-piperidine. In addition to various synthetic analgesics such as eucaine, prepared from 4-piperidone, the analgesic meperidine hydrochloride is an important derivative of piperidine.

Other important pyridine derivatives of pharmaceutical interest in addition to nicotinic acid, isonicotinic acid hydrazide, pyridoxine, and sulfapyridine are the urogenital analgesic 2,6-diamino-3-phenylazopyridine hydrochloride, the bactericide neotropin, the X-ray contrast materials sodium iodomethamate and iodopyracet, and the antihistaminics pyrilamine and tripelennamine. The most powerful herbicide known at present is the 2-picoline derivative, 4-amino-3,5,6-trichloropicolinic acid. In addition to the above-mentioned MEP and MVP, 2-vinylpyridine used as a monomer for copolymerization with butadiene, styrene, and acetonitrile, and the water-repellent stearamidomethylpyridium chlorides, pro-duced by the reaction of stearamide, formaldehyde, and pyridine hydrochloride in pyridine, are important commercial pyridine base derivatives.

(C. R. Al.)

PYRITE, or IRON PYRITES, also known as fool's gold, is a naturally occurring iron disulfide. This compound is dimorphous, existing both as orthorhombic marcasite (white iron pyrites) and as cubic pyrite (*see* also MARCASITE). The name comes from Greek *pyr,* "fire," since pyrite emits sparks when struck by steel.

Nodules of pyrite have been found in prehistoric burial mounds, suggesting their use as a primitive means of producing fire. Wheel-lock guns, in which a spring-driven serrated wheel rotated against a piece of pyrite, were used before development of the flintlock.

Pure pyrite contains 46.67% iron and 53.33% sulfur. Nickel and cobalt may replace some of the iron, but the frequent presence of gold and copper is probably because of microscopic inclusions of other minerals containing these metals. In some localities auriferous pyrite is an important source of gold, and a considerable quantity of copper is obtained from certain pyrite deposits. Besides the gold and copper which it may contain, the chief commercial use of pyrite is as a source of sulfur and sulfur dioxide (SO$_2$), used for bleaching and in the manufacture of sulfuric acid (*q.v.*).

Unlike most sulfide ores, which have to be roasted to obtain the SO$_2$, pyrite contains such a high percentage of sulfur that when reasonably pure, and in finely divided form, it will sustain its own combustion without the aid of an external source of heat. For the manufacture of sulfuric acid it is desirable that the ore be as free as possible from arsenic. Because of the availability of much better sources of iron (hematite, goethite and magnetite), pyrite is not generally used as an iron ore, although small quantities of sinter, or cinder from the burning of pyrite, may be mixed with the higher-grade ores.

For many years Spain was the largest producer, the large deposits at Ríotinto being important also for copper. Other important producers are Japan, the United States (Tennessee, Virginia, California), Canada, Italy, Norway, Portugal and Czechoslovakia. Beautiful crystals are found in many localities, including Cornwall in England; Westphalia in Germany; St. Gotthard in Switzerland; Elba and Piedmont in Italy; and Colorado, New Jersey, Pennsylvania, Arizona and Utah in the United States. (*See* also NATURAL RESOURCES: *Nonmetallic Minerals*.)

Pyrite crystals are common and sometimes are beautifully developed. The commonest forms are the cube, octahedron and pentagonal dodecahedron (pyritohedron), either separately or in various combinations. The cubes frequently have very characteristic striations parallel to the cube edges. Penetration twins also occur. The hardness of pyrite is 6 to 6.5 and the specific gravity about 5, varying somewhat with composition. A conchoidal fracture is usually conspicuous on crystals and on coarse-grained material. It sometimes has an iridescent tarnish. The lustre is bright metallic and the streak greenish-black. The colour is brass yellow. In comparison marcasite is a paler yellow, while chalcopyrite (copper pyrites) is much deeper yellow as well as softer.

Pyrite weathers rapidly to hydrated iron oxide, goethite or limonite; pseudomorphs of goethite after pyrite are common. They vary from a thin coating of goethite on the pyrite crystals to those which have been completely altered. This weathering produces a characteristic yellow-brown stain or coating, such as is observed on rusty quartz or in the residual iron deposits, or "gossan" capping on exposed sulfide ore bodies.

Pyrite is a mineral of very wide distribution and it occurs under extremely varied conditions of mineral formation; thus it is said to be a "persistent" mineral. It has been reported as resulting from magmatic segregation; it occurs as an accessory mineral in igneous rocks and has been found as a sublimation product at Vesuvius. Especially important are the hydrothermal deposits, from medium- to high-temperature solutions. Pyrite is very common in vein deposits with other sulfide minerals and with quartz. It is common in sedimentary rocks, such as shale, coal and limestone. Pyritized fossils are of frequent occurrence in these rocks.

Pyrite is found in large deposits in contact metamorphic rocks. Deposits of copper-bearing pyrite are widely distributed and often of great size. They usually occur in or near the contact of eruptive rocks with schists or slates, the presence of the igneous rocks probably being connected genetically with the origin of the ore. Well-developed cubes of pyrite occur with magnetite in a chlorite schist at Chester, Conn.

Pyrite Group.—Pyrite has the composition FeS_2 and is the most important member of the pyrite group, an isomorphous series which also includes bravoite $(Ni,Fe)S_2$; laurite, RuS_2; sperrylite, $PtAs_2$; hauerite, MnS_2; and penroseite, $(Ni,Cu,Pb,Co)Se_2$. It is also closely related structurally to the cobaltite group, which consists of cobalt and nickel minerals in which the sulfur pairs (S_2) of pyrite are replaced by arsenic-sulfur (AsS) and antimony-sulfur (SbS), resulting in lower symmetry. (L. S. Rl.)

PYROGALLOL (Pyrogallic Acid), a trihydroxybenzene, $1,2,3-C_6H_3(OH)_3$, is used as a developer in photography, as an antioxidant in lubricating oils, and as an oxygen absorbent in gas analysis. It has antiseptic properties and is employed medicinally in the treatment of psoriasis. It was first prepared by C. W. Scheele in 1786 by heating gallic acid. The process of manufacture is still based on Scheele's procedure. Pyrogallol crystallizes in colourless leaflets or needles, melts at 134° C, and is easily sublimed; it distills at 309° C under ordinary pressure with partial decomposition. It dissolves in $2\frac{1}{4}$ parts of water at 13° C, and its aqueous solution develops a blue colour with ferrous sulfate containing a little ferric salt. Its alkaline solution, when exposed to air, rapidly becomes black because of the absorption of oxygen with the production of complex coloured substances. (G. T. M.)

PYROLUSITE, a mineral composed of manganese dioxide of great importance as an ore of manganese. It is used in the manufacture of steel and manganese bronze, as an oxidizing agent in the manufacture of chlorine and in dry cells, in glass, ceramics, and paint pigments. It is mined in the U.S.S.R., Germany, Brazil, India, the United States (West Virginia, Georgia, Tennessee, the Lake Superior district, and California), Cuba, Morocco, Ghana, and South Africa. This compound, which has the formula MnO_2, is dimorphous, occurring both as an orthorhombic form, ramsdellite, and as the tetragonal form pyrolusite. The latter is isomorphous with rutile and cassiterite, TiO_2 and SnO_2. Crystals are rare and have a hardness of 6 to 6.5, with a specific gravity of about 5, and have been called polianite because of the mistaken belief that they were essentially different from the commoner massive varieties. Pyrolusite is usually fine grained, often fibrous or powdery, and thus appears to be soft, as low as 2, and marks paper. Because of the fine-grained nature it may contain adsorbed water. The fine fibrous masses, sometimes radially arranged, are very characteristic. Ores that are mixtures of pyrolusite and other minerals sometimes are called "soft manganese oxides." The soft powdery material, sometimes called wad (*q.v.*), may or may not be pyrolusite; likewise, harder dense material in crusts or nodules may be pyrolusite or may be one of the psilomelane (*q.v.*) type of minerals. Pyrolusite is formed by the alteration of other manganese ores, such as rhodochrosite and rhodonite, and frequently occurs as a pseudomorph after manganite. Black dendritic growths of manganese dioxide are frequently found in limestones and in moss agate quartz.

See also Manganese. (L. S. Rl.; X.)

PYROMORPHITE, a mineral with the composition of lead chlorophosphate sometimes occurring in sufficient quantities to be mined as an ore of lead. Pyromorphite results from the alteration of galena (*q.v.*) in the oxidized portions of metalliferous veins and is frequently found in the upper levels of lead mines. The name is from the Greek *pyr*, "fire," and *morphē*, "form"; when a fragment is fused the globule assumes a faceted form on solidifying. Crystals are common and have the form of a hexagonal prism terminated by the basal planes, often barrel-shaped and sometimes hollow at the ends; globular and reniform masses are also found. The formula is $Pb_5Cl(PO_4)_3$ and all gradations in composition exist between pyromorphite and the isomorphous lead chloroarsenate, mimetite (*q.v.*). The resemblance in external characteristics is so close that as a rule it is possible to distinguish them only by chemical tests. Likewise, it is closely related to vanadinite, in which the PO_4 is replaced by VO_4. Pyromorphite is usually bright green, yellow or brown, sometimes orange-red

and rarely colourless and transparent. The lustre is resinous to subadamantine.

The hardness is 3.5 to 4 and the specific gravity about 7. (L. S. Rl.)

PYRONES, a term used in organic chemistry to describe a group of six-membered heterocyclic compounds. Pyrones are of two main types derived from 1:2-pyrone (I) or 1:4-pyrone (II);

these two groups are often described as α-pyrones and γ-pyrones respectively.

Pyrones are not in general degraded by acids, but in some cases show quite a strong basic character and yield oxonium salts with acids. Like esters, pyrones are hydrolyzed by alkali and this reaction is frequently of importance in the determination of their structure. They do not usually show ketonic properties, but possess a stability similar to that of aromatic compounds and may be regarded as heterocyclic analogues of benzene.

The main interest in the chemistry of pyrones has developed from the recognition that quite a large number of naturally occurring organic compounds are derivatives of either α- or γ-pyrones. Thus 6-phenyl-1:2-pyrone (III) has been isolated from cotobark and about 70 natural products are known which are derived from 3:4-benz-1:2-pyrone (coumarin) (IV). Coumarin (*q.v.*) itself (IV) occurs in tonka beans, lavender oil and sweet clover and its pleasant fragrant odour has led to its use in perfumery and in foodstuffs. Umbelliferone (7-hydroxycoumarin) is present in many plants and is obtained by the distillation of the resins from various umbelliferae. Umbelliferone absorbs ultraviolet light and is used in some sun-screen lotions and creams.

Derivatives of 1:4- or γ-pyrone occur very widely in plants and to illustrate the variety of structure which is possible, the structures of chelidonic acid (V) from the lily of the valley and the celandine (*Chelidonium majus*), meconic acid (VI) from opium, maltol (VII) from malted barley and kojic acid (VIII) produced by the growth of the mold *Aspergillus niger* may be compared.

In determining the structure of these natural products advantage is often taken of their reaction with aqueous sodium hydroxide. The following example illustrates the general method. The structure of chelidonic acid (V) was indicated by its alkaline cleavage yielding acetone and oxalic acid. This structure was confirmed synthetically by condensing acetone with diethyl oxalate, using sodium ethoxide, and then subjecting the intermediate ester ($EtO_2C.CO.CH_2.CO.CH_2.CO.CO_2Et$) to dehydration and acid hydrolysis.

More complicated derivatives of 1:4-pyrones occur naturally and are probably the most widely occurring oxygen heterocyclic derivatives. They include flavones, e.g., apigenin (IX) from parsley; isoflavones, e.g., irigenin (X) from orrisroot; and xanthones. (W. D. Os.)

PYROPHYLLITE, a mineral species composed of hydrous aluminum silicate. It resembles talc (q.v.) and has long been used in slate pencils and tailor's chalk. It was carved by the Chinese into small images and ornaments; and has been included with talc under the names pagodite and agalmatolite.

The production and uses of pyrophyllite expanded greatly in the second half of the 20th century. Major uses were in the manufacture of insecticides, ceramics, paint, paper, refractories, roofing, rubber, and plaster products.

The most extensive commercial deposits of pyrophyllite are in the United States in the Deep River region of North Carolina, the leading producing state. Pyrophyllite is also mined in California and in Canada. A massive variety produced in South Africa is marketed under the name of "wonderstone." Pyrophyllite occurs in shear zones in highly metamorphosed acid volcanic rocks. Palegreen foliated masses, very like talc in appearance, are found in the Urals, in Switzerland, and in other localities.

Pyrophyllite is one of the silicates having a sheet structure, like the micas and chlorites. The composition is $Al_2(OH)_2Si_4O_{10}$; it is isomorphous with talc, $Mg_3(OH)_2Si_4O_{10}$, and the two minerals have similar properties as well as uses. Both are soft and have a soapy feeling; pyrophyllite occurs in foliated and massive varieties corresponding to foliated talc and soapstone (steatite).

The folia of pyrophyllite have a pronounced pearly lustre and have a perfect cleavage parallel to their surfaces. They are flexible but not elastic and are usually arranged in fanlike or radiating groups. The foliated variety, when heated, exfoliates and swells up to many times its original volume, hence the name pyrophyllite from the Greek pyr, "fire" and phyllon, "leaf." The colour of both varieties is white or pale green, grayish or yellowish. The specific gravity is 2.8 to 2.9. (L. S. Rl.; X.)

PYROTECHNICS: see FIREWORKS.

PYROXENE, in mineralogy, the SiO_3 single-chain, or metasilicate, group of minerals (see SILICON: The Silicates). Pyroxenes form one of the principal minerals in many common rock types, such as gabbro, norite, peridotite, pyroxenite, and basalt, and occur as an accessory mineral in some granites, syenites, diorites, and andesites. The pyroxenes are commonly dark-green to black, but in the absence of iron they can be light-coloured to white. The physical aspects of the pyroxenes are characterized by two planes of well-developed cleavages 87° or 93° apart. Except for the sodium-containing varieties, which are usually needlelike, the pyroxenes usually occur as short, stubby, prismatic crystals or mineral grains. Some crystal faces are usually present so that, as the crystal is viewed parallel to the cleavages, the crystal outline is commonly an octagon.

Species.—Mineral names are given to the ideally pure compounds. The naturally occurring minerals usually are composed of mixtures of two or more of the ideal compounds because of the extensive degree to which different metal ions are accepted into the structure of a single crystal. The pyroxenes are subdivided into two groups according to the symmetry of their crystals. Orthorhombic symmetry characterizes the enstatite ($MgSiO_3$) to orthoferrosilite ($FeSiO_3$) series. Bronzite and hypersthene are mixtures of enstatite and orthoferrosilite. Monoclinic symmetry characterizes all other pyroxenes, of which diopside, $CaMg(SiO_3)_2$; hedenbergite, $CaFe(SiO_3)_2$; jadeite or jade, $NaAl(SiO_3)_2$; acmite (aegirite), $NaFe(SiO_3)_2$; and spodumene, $LiAl(SiO_3)_2$; johannsenite, $CaMn(SiO_3)_2$; and the clinoenstatite ($MgSiO_3$) to clinoferrosilite ($FeSiO_3$) series are representative. The monoclinic pyroxenes augite and pigeonite can be considered as mixtures of the diopside-hedenbergite series with the clinoenstatite-clinoferrosilite series, plus some aluminum.

Spodumene (q.v.), as ceramic material and a source of lithium,

and jadeite, as an ornamental stone (see JADE), are the only economically important pyroxenes. Crystals of diopside sometimes have been cut as gem stones.

Formations.—Most of the pyroxenes can be formed over a wide range of temperatures; e.g., enstatite, $MgSiO_3$, can be formed theoretically by naturally occurring reactions as low as 95° C. ($MgCO_3 + SiO_3 \rightarrow MgSiO_3 + CO_2$ at 1 atm. CO_2 pressure) and by other natural reactions as high as 1,557° C. Diopside, $CaMg(SiO_3)_2$, can be formed theoretically by naturally occurring reactions as low as 135° C. [$CaMg(CO_3)_2 + SiO_2 \rightarrow CaMg(SiO_3)_2 + CO_2$ at 1 atm. CO_2 pressure] and by other natural reactions up to 1,391° C. However, in the high-temperature metamorphic, igneous and volcanic environments the stability fields of the pyroxenes are relatively larger and, therefore, pyroxenes are commoner in these environments and are relatively rare in low-temperature environments.

The formation of pyroxene over a wide range of compositional environments is possible because of its ability to accept a large variety of different metal ions into its structure; it is, therefore, found associated with almost any of the other common silicate minerals. Pyroxenes are found in metamorphic, igneous and volcanic rocks as well as in pegmatites, ore deposits, as in the diamond mines of South Africa (see ECLOGITE), and many meteorites.

Chemical Structures.—In terms of chemistry the pyroxenes are characterized by the structure of the Si-O groups in the crystal. The relative ionic sizes of Si^{4+} and O^{2-} are such that Si^{4+} closely fits in the central space between four O^{2-} ions arranged at the corners of a tetrahedron; thus, silicon always surrounds itself with four oxygen ions. Silicon can furnish only four of the necessary eight electrons needed to satisfy the four oxygen ions, and this results in an excess oxygen problem. The various ways in which this oxygen problem is solved form the basis of subdivision of the silicate group of minerals (see also AMPHIBOLE). The pyroxenes are characterized by the following type of solution: If each silicon ion shares two of its four oxygen ions with two other silicon ions, an endless chain results:

$$\begin{array}{ccccccc} O & & O & & O & & O \\ | & & | & & | & & | \\ O-Si-O-Si-O-Si-O-Si-O \\ | & & | & & | & & | \\ O & & O & & O & & O \end{array}$$

The remaining demands of the unshared oxygen ions for one electron each can be satisfied by the formation of bonds with other electron-donating ions. In this manner parallel Si-O chains are bonded together by rows of metal ions parallel to the chains. Almost any of the two-valent metal ions or mixtures of them, or a combination of a three- and a one-valent metal ion, are able to bind the chains together. The difference in the ionic sizes of the metal ions causes slight angular adjustments in the relative position of one Si-O chain to another which result in the two different symmetry classes for the pyroxene group of minerals. Pure nickel, cobalt, zinc or iron pyroxenes or mixtures of them are not known to form, although these elements can be present in small amounts. The reason for the absence of such pyroxenes is that the pyroxene structure becomes unstable in the presence of large amounts of these high bonding energy ions.

For discussion of mineralogical and crystallographic concepts used in this article see MINERALOGY.

See also GEOCHEMISTRY: Geochemistry of the Lithosphere: Crystallization of Magma; and references under "Pyroxene" in the Index. (G. W. DeV.; X.)

PYROXENITE, a rock consisting essentially of minerals of the pyroxene group, such as augite and diallage (a diopside), hypersthene, bronzite or enstatite. Names have been given to members of this group according to their component minerals; e.g., pyroxenite (augite), diallagite (diallage), hypersthenite (hypersthene), bronzitite (bronzite) and websterite (diallage and hypersthene).

Closely allied to this group are the hornblendites, consisting essentially of hornblende.

PYRRHO OF ELIS (c. 365–275 B.C.), the Greek philosopher from whom Pyrrhonism takes its name. He had as a teacher

Anaxarchus of Abdera, from whom he learned the view—a one-sided development of the system of Democritus—that every perception and judgment of value is relative. He joined the expedition of Alexander the Great and reached India, where he was able to see for himself, in the fakirs, an example of the total indifference to circumstances for which the Greek philosophers often yearned. About 330 B.C. Pyrrho established himself as a teacher in his native Elis. His reputation spread to other parts of Greece, and later skeptics looked to him as their founder. Other philosophers before him had proclaimed that nothing is known with certainty; Pyrrho seemed to have carried doubt to its logical extreme. He wrote nothing, but some impression of his arguments can be gained from the fragments of the poems of Timon of Phlius. The aim of the wise man is to become imperturbable to the changes of fortune; he must utterly abstain from judgment and be prepared to doubt even sense perception, for it is not the infallible test of truth which others have supposed it to be. However, he must equally not distrust perception on principle, for this would imply that it is known or judged to be false. A placid acceptance of things as they appear, fortitude against pain, and indifference to external fortune seem to be the practical consequences. The skeptics of the New Academy (Arcesilaus and Carneades) professed to derive their skepticism not from Pyrrho (*see* ACADEMY, GREEK). *See* also SKEPTICISM.

See L. Robin, *Pyrrhon et le scepticisme grec* (1944).   (D. J. A.)

PYRRHOTITE, a mineral species consisting of iron sulfide. Small amounts of nickel and cobalt are often present; the nickeliferous pyrrhotite of Sudbury, Ont., with its associated pentlandite (*q.v.*), is the most important source of nickel. The name is from the Greek *pyr*, "fire," and *rhotes*, "redness." The formula is $Fe_{1-n}S$, in which *n* may vary from 0 to 0.2. The variety troilite, having a composition near FeS, has been identified as an important constituent of some meteorites (*see* METEORITES: *Mineralogical Composition*). Crystals of pyrrhotite have the form of hexagonal plates bounded at their edges by faces of a hexagonal prism and pyramids, which are deeply striated horizontally. More frequently, however, the mineral is massive, with a granular structure. It is magnetic, sometimes with polarity, and is therefore often called magnetic pyrites. The colour is bronze yellow, the lustre metallic, and the streak grayish black. The hardness is 4 and the specific gravity 4.58–4.64. Pyrrhotite occurs in metalliferous veins and as grains and plates disseminated through various rocks. *See* also NICKEL.

PYRRHUS (319–272 B.C.), king of the Molossians, a people of ancient Epirus, whose costly military successes gave rise to the phrase "Pyrrhic victory." He claimed descent from Pyrrhus or Neoptolemus, the son of Achilles, and was connected with the Macedonian royal house through Olympias, the mother of Alexander the Great. At the age of 12 he became king of Epirus and allied himself with Demetrius I Poliorcetes, who married his sister Deidameia. Dethroned by an Epirote rising in 302, he followed Demetrius to Asia and fought beside him and Antigonus I at the Battle of Ipsus in Phrygia (301). He was then sent to Alexandria as a hostage under the treaty made between Ptolemy I and Demetrius, and there became attached to the king, married his stepdaughter Antigone, and in 297 was by his aid restored to his kingdom; at first he reigned with a kinsman, Neoptolemus II, but soon assassinated him. Pyrrhus now sought to develop his kingdom along Hellenistic lines. In 295 he exploited a dynastic quarrel in Macedonia to obtain the frontier areas of Parauaea and Tymphaea, along with Acarnania, Amphilochia, and Ambracia; and on Antigone's death he married Lanassa, daughter of Agathocles of Syracuse, receiving Corcyra and Leucas as her dowry. He also married Bircenna, daughter of an Illyrian king, Bardylis, and the daughter of Audoleon, king of Paeonia. Soon he became involved in war with Demetrius, now king of Macedonia, and in alliance with Aetolia heavily defeated his general Pantauchus; two invasions of Macedonia left him king of the western half, with Thessaly, and he relieved Athens from Demetrius' siege. In 285, however, Lysimachus shut him up in Edessa, corrupted his men, and drove him back into Epirus.

In 281 Tarentum, in southern Italy, asked his assistance against

Rome; he crossed with about 25,000 men, and in 280 at Heraclea his cavalry and elephants helped him to win a complete, if costly, victory over Publius Valerius Laevinus. He advanced on Rome through Latium, but the towns were all garrisoned, and Appius Claudius persuaded the Senate to dismiss his minister Cineas with a refusal to negotiate so long as Pyrrhus' troops were in Italy.

In 279 Pyrrhus won another victory, costly to both sides, at Ausculum (Ascoli Satriano) in Apulia; he then crossed to Sicily (278) with the idea of expelling the Carthaginians, who had just allied themselves with Rome. As "king of Sicily" he conquered most of the Punic province except Lilybaeum (Marsala), but his despotic methods provoked a Greek revolt, and in 276 (or early 275) he returned to Italy. In 275 he fought a last battle at Beneventum (Benevento) in which the Romans had a slight advantage, though not the overwhelming superiority claimed by Roman tradition. In consequence Pyrrhus retired to Epirus with a third of his force. In 274 he defeated Antigonus II Gonatas, shutting him up in Thessalonica (Salonika); then, abandoning his newly recovered kingdom of Macedonia, he launched an unsuccessful attack on Sparta to restore Cleonymus (272), and perished the same year in a night skirmish in the streets of Argos.

Pyrrhus was a man of lively and volatile intelligence, an adroit tactician and possessed of a dynamic character; his *Memoirs* and books on the art of war are quoted and praised by many writers, including Cicero; the impression he made on his contemporaries is shown in the many legends that attached themselves to him, but he lacked consistency of purpose and failed to draw profit from his victories, so that his career as a whole was a failure.

BIBLIOGRAPHY.—Plutarch, *Pyrrhus;* G. N. Cross, *Epirus* (1932); P. Lévêque, *Pyrrhos* (1957).   (F. W. WA.)

PYRROLE. A colourless oil whose existence in coal tar was surmised by the German chemist F. F. Runge in 1834 but which was first isolated and studied by the Scottish chemist Thomas Anderson in 1857. The name is derived from Greek and Latin roots meaning "fiery oil," from the fiery red colour imparted by pyrrole to a wood splint previously moistened with acid. Pyrrole is of great historical interest because of the fact that one of its derivatives, indole (*q.v.*), is the fundamental building block of the regal dye of the ancients, Tyrian purple, as well as of the most important ancient and medieval dye, indigo. Pyrrole is also the structural unit of chlorophyll, the green portion of the pigment of leaves; of heme, the red portion of the pigment of blood; of the pigments of the bile; and of the pigments of numerous types of bacteria, algae and other living organisms. Pyrrole pigments are found in coal, petroleum and similar substances derived from plant and animal sources.

The colouring matters derived from pyrrole are the objects of extensive scientific investigations because their functions in plants and animals are so critically important to life. Atmospheric carbon dioxide, fixed by photosynthesis involving chlorophyll, is the ultimate source of most of our food and fuel, and the efficiency of transportation of oxygen by the blood pigment hemoglobin is indispensable to the rapid motions of higher animals. In addition, these pyrrole pigments are probably produced by living organisms in greater tonnage than any other class of pigments. Derivatives of pyrrolidine, which is completely reduced pyrrole, occur in alkaloids, such as cocaine and nicotine, and as building blocks of proteins in the form of the amino acids proline, hydroxyproline and tryptophan.

Pyrrole boils at 131° C., is slightly lighter than water (density 0.9669) and has the composition C_4H_5N. It is sparingly soluble in water but dissolves in alcohol, ether and many other solvents. Its structural formula was assigned correctly by the German chemist Adolf von Baeyer in 1870 in the course of his classical investigations on the structure of indigo. It is conventionally represented as in diagram I; diagram II is the formula for pyrrolidine:

Pyrrole is characterized by great chemical reactivity, being slowly destroyed by air with the formation of a brown pigment. It is also destroyed by strong acids, being partially converted into indole, and it enters into combination with a wide variety of chemical reagents. It has been obtained from bone oil and by destructive heating of proteins but is now available commercially from acetylene, formaldehyde and ammonia. Pyrrole is moderately toxic, acting as a nerve poison. Certain of its derivatives have found a limited application in medicine. Their main use is in organic chemical synthesis for the study of the structure and functions of the naturally occurring pigments. The most important pyrrole derivatives are the porphyrins (from the Greek for purple) and the chlorines (from the Greek for yellow-green) and their metallic compounds. A typical iron-porphyrin compound is hemin, the oxidized form of the coloured portion of the blood pigment.

See Hans Fischer and Hans Orth, *Die Chemie des Pyrrols* (1934–40). (A. H. Cn.; X.)

PYRUVIC ACID, $CH_3COCOOH$, is an organic acid that probably occurs in all living cells. It ionizes to give a hydrogen ion and an anion termed pyruvate. Biochemists use the terms pyruvate and pyruvic acid almost interchangeably.

Pyruvic acid is a key product at the crossroads between the catabolism (breaking down) and anabolism (synthesizing) of carbohydrates, fats, and proteins (*see* METABOLISM: *Intermediary Metabolism*). A complex sequence of enzyme reactions leading from sugar (or carbohydrate, in the form of glucose or fructose) to pyruvate is common to five metabolic processes. These are: (1) the fermentation of sugar to ethyl alcohol by yeast; (2) the fermentation of sugar to lactic acid in muscle (for these two processes *see* FERMENTATION: *The Modern Position*); (3) the oxidation of sugar to carbon dioxide and water by way of the Krebs cycle (*q.v.*); (4) the conversion of sugar to fatty acids; and (5) the conversion of sugar to amino acids, such as alanine, which are the building blocks of proteins.

Pyruvic acid, formerly called pyroracemic acid, was first obtained by J. J. Berzelius in 1835 by the dry distillation of tartaric acid. The preparation of pyruvic acid in bulk amounts is similar: tartaric acid is heated with fused potassium hydrogen sulfate at 210°–220° C. The product is purified by fractional distillation under reduced pressure. At room temperature pure pyruvic acid is a colourless liquid with a pungent odour resembling that of acetic acid. On cooling, it forms crystals that melt at 13.6° C. The boiling point is 165° C.

See E. E. Conn and P. K. Stumpf, *Outlines of Biochemistry* (1963); P. Karlson, *Introduction to Modern Biochemistry* (1963). (B. V.)

PYTHAGORAS (fl. 5th century B.C.), a noted Greek sculptor of Rhegium (present Reggio di Calabria), a contemporary of Myron and Polyclitus and their rival in making statues of athletes. One of these, that of the boxer Euthymus of Locri, was erected after the latter's third victory at Olympia in 472 B.C. Pythagoras was born at Samos and migrated in his youth to Rhegium, in Italy. He made a statue of Philoctetes noted for the physical expression of pain, an Apollo shooting the Python at Delphi, and a man singing to the lyre. His technical improvements went far in ending archaic stiffness. No existing work can be certainly attributed to him, and, although his influence must have been widespread, attempts to identify copies of his works remain conjectural.

PYTHAGORAS AND PYTHAGOREANISM.

The Greek philosopher Pythagoras, who was active *c.* 530 B.C. and gave his name to an order of scientific and religious thinkers, was born in Samos. Reputed by legend to have traveled extensively, he was certainly in contact with ideas native to Asia Minor. The historically important part of his career began with his migration to Crotona, a Dorian colony in southern Italy, about the year 529.

According to tradition, Pythagoras was driven from the Aegean island of Samos by the tyranny of Polycrates. At Crotona he became the centre of a widespread organization which was, in its origin, a religious brotherhood or an association for the moral reformation of society rather than a philosophical school. The Pythagorean brotherhood had much in common with the Orphic communities which sought by rites and abstinences to purify the believer's soul and enable it to escape from the "wheel of birth." Although its aims may have been primarily those of a religious order rather than a political league, it actively supported aristocracies. Indeed it gained control over many Western Greek colonies; and it was politics which led in the end to the dismemberment and suppression of the society. The first reaction against the Pythagoreans, led by Cylon, brought about the retirement of Pythagoras to Metapontum, where he remained until his death at the end of the 6th or the beginning of the 5th century.

The order appears to have continued powerful in Magna Graecia until the middle of the 5th century B.C. when it was violently trampled out, its meetinghouses being everywhere sacked and burned. Those Pythagoreans who survived took refuge abroad: Lysis went to Thebes in Boeotia, where he became the instructor of Epaminondas; and Philolaus (*q.v.*), who according to tradition wrote the first exposition of the Pythagorean system, also lived at Thebes at the end of the 5th century. Philolaus, however, and some others were afterward able to return to Italy. Tarentum (Taras) then became the chief seat of the school: Archytas (*q.v.*), the friend of Plato, was prominent there both as a philosopher and as a statesman in the first half of the 4th century B.C. About the middle of that century, however, the Pythagoreans disappeared as a philosophic school.

Philosophical Beliefs.—There seems to have been a split in the school, dating from about the middle of the 5th century B.C. On the one hand, there were "the mathematicians," represented by such names as Archytas and Aristoxenus (*q.v.*), who were interested in scientific studies, particularly in mathematics and in musical theory; on the other, there were the more conservative members of the school, who concentrated on the moral or religious precepts and were called *akousmatikoi* (from *akousmata*, "oral traditions"). It is probable that both the scientific and the religious elements were present from the start in Pythagoreanism. Most of the evidence for the beliefs of Pythagoras himself is doubtful. It was customary for his later disciples to claim the master's authority indiscriminately; and Aristotle speaks only vaguely of "the so-called Pythagoreans," "the Italians," and so on. The doctrines that can reasonably be attributed to Pythagoras may, however, be summarized as follows:

1. First and foremost is Pythagoras' account of the soul. He believed in the transmigration of the individual soul from one body to another, even of a different species. "Do not hit him," he once said to a man who was beating a puppy, "it is the soul of a friend of mine. I recognized it when I heard it cry out." But if a man led a pure life, his soul might be released from all flesh. It is possible that this held good only for the exceptional man, a seer such as Pythagoras himself or Empedocles (*q.v.*). But the view of the body as the tomb or prison of every soul, with philosophy as the meditation of death and the release from the body, seems to be attributed to a Pythagorean in Plato's *Phaedo* (61 D ff.). Its importance in the history of religion need not be underlined. All this must be set in the framework of the belief, brought to the Greeks from Asia Minor, which ascribed to souls a future life in the starry heavens. For nearly all Pythagoreans the actual composition of the soul (*e.g.,* out of fire or air, the warmth or breath of life) gave it a natural affinity with the stars or the sky.

2. The pure life consisted in obeying precepts which are mostly recognizable as primitive taboos; *e.g.,* not to eat beans, not to poke a fire with iron. More strictly moral were the three questions which had to be put to oneself every evening: In what have I failed? What good have I done? What have I not done that I ought to have done? Of external aids to purification one of the most important was music.

3. The fascination of numbers for the school must go back to its founder. Pythagoras' greatest discovery was probably the dependence of the musical intervals on certain arithmetical ratios of lengths of strings at the same tension, 2:1 giving the octave, 3:2 the fifth and 4:3 the fourth. It must have contributed powerfully to the idea that "all things are numbers." Though not necessarily to be attributed to Pythagoras, this idea was the philosophical kernel of Pythagoreanism. Early forms of it probably did not distinguish between things being numbers, having numbers,

and merely resembling them. But in Aristotle's account of it (*Metaphysics*, i, ch. 5 and 8) numbers were the elements of everything, in the way that fire, water, etc., had been for other thinkers.

The whole heaven formed a "musical scale and number"; and even such things as reason, justice and marriage were identified with distinct numbers. The elements of numbers themselves were "the odd" and "the even" or "limit" and "the unlimited," which in Aristotle's view represent a primitive insight into the notions of form and matter. These two pairs headed a list of ten pairs of fundamental "opposites," the remaining eight being "one" and "many," "right" and "left," "male" and "female," "rest" and "motion," "straight" and "curved," "light" and "darkness," "good" and "evil," "square" and "oblong." It was a philosophy of metaphysical and moral dualism: but it came to see the universe as a harmony of opposites, in which "the one" generated the number series, or "limit" successively imposed itself on "the unlimited."

Thus music and the belief in a stellar heaven (especially if this had originally been associated with Babylonian astrology) are two links between the religious content of Pythagoras' outlook and the mathematical and astronomical studies made later by the scientific wing of his school. The first to have made a comprehensive system may have been Philolaus. Thereafter the three doctrines outlined above would have been common to the *akousmatikoi* and to the "mathematicians" alike. Their development by the latter can be seen in what follows. Much of it, as Otto Neugebauer, for instance, points out (*The Exact Sciences in Antiquity*, 1952), had been known to the Babylonians.

Pythagorean Arithmetic.—The unit or 1 (which was not strictly a number) was assigned or equated to the point, 2 to the line, 3 to surface, and 4 to solid. The assertion of J. Burnet and many others, that numbers were regularly held to be spatially extended, is open to question. The normal account seems to have been that the point "flowed into" the line, the line into surface, and so on. But numbers were certainly represented by arrangements of pebbles in triangles, squares, etc.; and the practice assisted the geometrical expression of arithmetical theorems, which was due fundamentally to the existence of both rational and irrational fractions, since these contradicted the strict definition of numbers as magnitudes. The holy tetractys, by which the later Pythagoreans

used to swear, was a figure of this kind   representing the

triangular number 10 and showing at a glance its composition as $1 + 2 + 3 + 4$. To add a row of five dots gives the next triangular number with 5 as the side, and so on, showing that the sum of any number of the series of natural numbers beginning with 1 is a triangular number. The sum of any number of. the series of odd numbers beginning with 1 is similarly seen to be a square; thus

3 and 5 added successively to 1 give figures of the kind

called gnomons. If we take the series of even numbers, we see that the sum of any number of them beginning with 2 makes an

oblong number

The successive odd numbers after 1 were themselves called gnomons because the addition of each to the sum of the preceding ones (beginning with 1) makes a square number into the next larger square. If the gnomon added to a square is itself a square number, there is a square number which is the sum of two squares; thus $1 + 3 + 5 + 7 = 16$ or 4^2, and the addition of 9 ($= 3^2$) gives 25 or 5^2, that is, $3^2 + 4^2 = 5^2$. Pythagoras himself is credited with a general formula for finding two square numbers the sum of which is also a square, namely (if m is any odd number), $m^2 + \{\frac{1}{2}(m^2 - 1)\}^2 = \{\frac{1}{2}(m^2 + 1)\}^2$. This connects itself with the theorem of the square on the hypotenuse of a right-angled triangle, which tradition universally associates with the

name of Pythagoras. In the case of the isosceles right-angled triangle the ratio of the hypotenuse to either of the other sides is what is written as $\sqrt{2}$, which is irrational in the sense that its value cannot be expressed exactly as a ratio between numbers. The Pythagoreans not only perceived the irrationality of $\sqrt{2}$ but also developed the method of finding ever closer approximations to the value of $\sqrt{2}$ by forming the series of the so-called side and diagonal numbers that satisfy one or other of the two equations $2x^2 - y^2 = +1$ and $2x^2 - y^2 = -1$, when x stands for the length of one of the equal sides and y for that of the hypotenuse. The method depends on the proposition $2x^2 - y^2 = (2x + y)^2 - 2(x + y)^2$, whence it follows that, once one set of values for x and for y has been found such that $2x^2 - y^2 = +1$, then $2(x + y)^2 - (2x + y)^2 = -1$, the higher numbers $x + y$ and $2x + y$ in the latter equation taking the place of the x and of the y in the original; then, vice versa, with the higher numbers substituted, we may proceed from $2x^2 - y^2 = -1$ to $2(x + y)^2 - (2x + y)^2 = +1$, where $x + y$ and $2x + y$ stand for a second set of higher numbers; and so *ad infinitum*. Hence is derived the infinite series $\frac{1}{1}, \frac{3}{2}, \frac{7}{5}, \frac{17}{12}, \frac{41}{29} \ldots$ giving progressive approximations to $\sqrt{2}$.

Contributions to Geometry.—Other contributions to geometry were made by the Pythagoreans. In the first place Pythagoras, it is said, himself formulated definitions in geometry. Secondly, the Pythagoreans proved that the sum of the three angles of any triangle is equal to two right angles: there is their proof, which, like Euclid's, uses the property of parallels; hence they knew the theory of parallels. Thirdly, they discovered the powerful method in geometry of the application of areas (*cf.* Eucl. i, 44, 45), including application with excess and defect (*cf.* Eucl. vi, 28, 29), which amounts to the geometrical solution of any quadratic equation in algebra having real roots. Fourthly, they discovered the theory of proportion, together with the arithmetic, the geometric and the harmonic means. The theory and the arithmetic mean appear in the middle terms of the proportion $a: \frac{a + b}{2} = \frac{2ab}{a + b} :b$, a particular case being $12:9 = 8:6$, from the terms of which the three musical intervals can be obtained. The Pythagorean theory of proportion was arithmetical (after the manner of Euclid, book vii) and did not apply to incommensurable magnitudes; it must not therefore be confused with the general theory due to Eudoxus, which is expounded in Euclid v. Fifthly, it was claimed that Pythagoras discovered the construction of the five regular solids. It was more probably Theaetetus who (as we read elsewhere) discovered the octahedron and the icosahedron; but the Pythagoreans were clearly acquainted with the pyramid or tetrahedron and the dodecahedron. The construction of the dodecahedron requires that of a regular pentagon, which again depends (as in Eucl. iv, 10, 11) on the problem of Eucl. ii, 11, about the division of a line in extreme and mean ratio, a particular case of the application of areas. The assumption that the Pythagoreans could construct a regular pentagon is confirmed by the fact that the pentagram, the triple interwoven triangle, or the star-pentagon, was used as a symbol of recognition between the members of the school and was called by them health. Sixthly, the Pythagoreans discovered how to construct a rectilineal figure equal to one and similar to another rectilineal figure.

To sum up, it may be said that Pythagorean geometry covered the bulk of the subject matter of Euclid's books i, ii, iv, vi (and probably iii), with the qualification that the Pythagorean theory of proportion was inadequate in that it did not apply to incommensurable magnitudes.

Pythagorean Astronomy.—Pythagoras was one of the first to hold that the earth and the universe are spherical in shape. He appreciated that the sun, the moon and the planets have a motion of their own independent of the daily rotation and in the opposite sense. It is improbable that Pythagoras himself was responsible for the astronomical system known as Pythagorean, which deposed the earth from its place in the centre and made it a planet like the sun, the moon and the other planets; for Pythagoras apparently the earth was still at the centre.

The later Pythagorean system is attributed alternatively to Philolaus and to Hicetas, a native of Syracuse. The system may be thus described. The universe is spherical in shape and finite in size. Outside it there is infinite void, which enables the universe to breathe, as it were. At the centre is the central fire, wherein is situated the force which directs the movement of the universe. Within the universe bodies revolve around the central fire as follows: nearest to the central fire is the counterearth, which always accompanies the earth; next in order (reckoning from the centre outward) is the earth, then the moon, then the sun, then the five planets and then, last of all, the sphere of the fixed stars. The counterearth, revolving in a smaller orbit than the earth, is not seen by us because the hemisphere in which we live is always turned away from the counterearth. This part of the theory involves the assumption that the earth rotates about its own axis in the same time as it takes to complete its orbit around the central fire; and as the latter revolution was held to produce day and night, it is a fair inference that the earth was thought to revolve around the central fire in a day and a night, or in 24 hr. The counterearth may have been invented to explain the comparative frequency of lunar eclipses. The system amounts to a first step toward an anticipation of the Copernican hypothesis, and Copernicus himself referred to it as such.

Later Pythagoreanism.—A survival of Pythagorean practices and doctrines, particularly that of immortality, is attested in Rome from the 1st century B.C. As a philosophical theory this Neopythagoreanism (q.v.) merged with Platonism. But it was also a kind of cult; and the frescoes in the underground basilica of the Porta Maggiore have been claimed as Pythagorean. In imperial times there were Pythagoreanizing philosophers and mathematicians in Alexandria, in Syria, and elsewhere. Plato's immediate successors had already made a partial return to more purely Pythagorean theory; and Neoplatonists, such as Iamblichus in the 4th century A.D., drew on them as well as on more recent, forged Pythagorean writings (e.g., the Orphic Hymns).

For Christian Fathers, such as Ambrose, Pythagoras was an authoritative figure because he was thought to have been a Jewish intermediary between Moses and Plato. By the 16th century he was liable to be reckoned, and his beliefs cited, according to the interests of the writer, as a poet, as a magician, as the father of the Cabala, as a mathematician, or as a champion of the contemplative life. He is depicted, characteristically an old man, among the philosophers, in Raphael's "School of Athens."

See also references under "Pythagoras and Pythagoreanism" in the Index.

BIBLIOGRAPHY.—Greek texts are given by H. Diels and W. Kranz, Fragmente der Vorsokratiker, vol. i, 7th ed. (1954). See further E. Zeller, History of Greek Philosophy, Eng. trans. by S. F. Alleyne, vol. i (1881); J. Burnet, Early Greek Philosophy, 4th ed. (1930), and Greek Philosophy, part i, Thales to Plato (1914); T. L. Heath, History of Greek Mathematics, vol. i (1921); and, for astronomy, Aristarchus of Samos (1913); B. L. Van der Waerden, Science Awakening, Eng. trans. by A. Dresden (1954); and S. Dill, Roman Society from Nero to Marcus Aurelius (1904); C. J. de Vogel, Pythagoras and Early Pythagoreanism (1966). (T. L. H.; A. C. Ld.)

PYTHEAS OF MASSALIA (Marseilles), Greek explorer and geographer of c. 300 B.C., was the first Greek to visit and describe the Atlantic coast of Europe (including Britain). His main work, On the Ocean, is lost; citations in later authors do not give a coherent picture of it or even show exactly how far he traveled. There is one fragment of a second work, perhaps a complementary description of the Mediterranean coast of Europe. Pytheas' writings were extensively used by later geographers, notably Eratosthenes and Poseidonius; but he was attacked as a Munchhausen by equally eminent men, particularly the historian Polybius (followed by Strabo). Modern scholars have rehabilitated him, often to excess. He certainly visited some northern countries, and his comments on small points, e.g., on the native drinks made from cereals and honey and on the use of threshing barns (contrasted with open-air threshing in the Mediterranean sun), show acute observation. His scientific interests appear from his calculation of the ratio of the hand of a sundial to its shadow at the summer solstice, and from his notes, sometimes rather puzzling, on the length of the longest day as he traveled northward. These ob-

servations were used by his successors (not, it seems, by Pytheas himself) for establishing parallels of latitude. He also noticed that the Pole star is not at the true pole and that the moon affects the tides.

Pytheas is at his worst in giving measurements, whether in days' journeys (five from Cadiz to Cape St. Vincent, three from Ushant to the French coast) or in stadia (40,000, i.e., over 4,000 mi., for the circumference of Britain). His Thule—the northernmost inhabited island, six days' sail from northern Britain and extending at least to the Arctic circle—cannot be identified. It may be Norway (but not Iceland).

Pytheas was too ready to believe what he was told: the story of the Stagnant sea bounding the earth in the far north—a mixture of earth, air and water, like a "sea-lungs" (jellyfish?)—deserves Polybius' ridicule. His work laid a valuable foundation for greater men, though, as Polybius saw, he often misled them.

(E. Ba.)

PYTHIUS (PYTHIOS, PYTHEOS), noted Greek architect of the 4th century B.C. With the architect Satyrus he built the great Mausoleum at Halicarnassus (353 B.C.), one of the seven wonders of the world, ordered by Queen Artemisia as a tomb for her husband, Mausolus. A number of restorations of the mausoleum were made in the 19th century. Pythius cultivated the Ionic style, in which he also constructed the temple of Athena at Priene. The dedicatory inscription, which is in the British museum, records that the founder was Alexander the Great. Pythius is mentioned by Pliny and Vitruvius.

PYTHON, the common name for a subfamily (Pythoninae) of large, nonpoisonous, constricting snakes of the boa family (Boidae). The largest genus, Python, is found throughout the tropics of the Old World. Pythons are sometimes given family rank as the Pythonidae. They are distinguished from the boas, with which they are often confused, in certain skull characteristics (presence of a supraorbital bone) and in the habit of laying eggs instead of bringing forth young alive. As in the boas, vestiges of the hind limbs are present, visible externally as a pair of claws adjacent to the anal cleft. The teeth are strong and adapted for catching and holding prey. There is no venom or venom-conducting apparatus.

Killing of the prey is effected by constriction: one or more coils of the body are thrown around the victim, and pressure is applied by the powerful body muscles. Although the pressure exerted by a large python is considerable, the prey is killed by suffocation rather than by any actual crushing of the ribs. A python, like other constrictors, takes advantage of the struggles of its prey by tightening its coils each time the captive exhales. During the swallowing process much saliva is secreted, and should the prey be disgorged, as may happen if the snake is disturbed, it will be found to be covered with this secretion. This evidently accounts for the fable that pythons cover their prey with saliva before swallowing it.

Large pythons may be strong enough to kill an animal the size of an ox, but stories of their killing and eating cattle and horses are not to be credited. The prey is swallowed whole, and though the mouth is greatly distensible, it cannot be stretched beyond the calibre of a moderate-sized pig. Authentic accounts of attacks on man are extremely few.

Most pythons are partly arboreal and are likely also to be found lying quietly in water. Reproduction is by means of leathery-shelled oval eggs, of which there may be a hundred or more in a clutch. The eggs are laid in a heap and are guarded by the mother, who coils herself around them.

The largest species is the reticulated or regal python (Python reticulatus) of the Malay region, which occasionally reaches a length of 30 ft. The Indian python (P. molurus), up to 25 ft. long, is frequently seen in zoological gardens, as is the African rock python (P. sebae). Other members of the python group include the remarkable arboreal green python of New Guinea (Chondropython viridis) and various other Australasian types. Loxocemus, a genus of smaller snakes of southern Mexico and Central America, is doubtfully placed in the subfamily; some assign these dwarf "pythons" to the family Xenopeltidae. See also SNAKE.

(K. P. S.; X.)

PYTHON, in Greek mythology a huge serpent which was killed by Apollo at Delphi because it would not let him found his oracle, being accustomed itself to give oracles, or, according to another version of the story, because it had persecuted his mother Leto during her pregnancy. In the earliest account (the Homeric Hymn to Apollo) the serpent is nameless and female, but later it is male and named Python (Pytho being the old name for Delphi). Python was generally said to be the child of Gaea (Earth), who traditionally had an oracle at Delphi before Apollo came. The Pythian Games held at Delphi in historic times were supposed to have been instituted by Apollo to celebrate his victory over Python. In Hellenistic Greek the name Python became a common noun meaning the power of divination possessed by certain persons; *e.g.,* by the woman in Acts 16:16. *See* also ORACLE.

See J. Fontenrose, *Python* (1959).

THIS letter corresponds to Semitic ϕ (*koph*), which may derive from an earlier sign representing the eye of a needle, and to Greek ϙ (*koppa*). The form of the majuscule has been practically identical throughout its known history. In the form found on the Moabite stone the vertical stroke extended to the top of the loop, and the same is the case with an early form ϕ from the island of Thera. The Etruscan form was identical with the Greek. The Latin alphabet had two forms, Q and Q.

In the minuscule form the stroke has moved to the right side of the letter owing to the speed of writing. This produced the cursive form ꝗ occurring in the 6th century A.D. Uncial writing also had the form q and the Carolingian form was practically identical.

In Semitic the sound represented by the letter was an unvoiced guttural pronounced farther back than that represented by the letter *kaph*. In Greek the letter was largely redundant, and in the eastern alphabet was entirely superseded by *kappa*. In the Chalcidic alphabet, however, it lingered and spread from there, probably through the Etruscan, into the Latin alphabet, where it was used only with a following *u,* the combination representing the unvoiced labiovelar sound in such words as *quaero.* The combination of these two letters holds to the present day, and in modern English *q* is not used unless followed by *u,* even if, in words such as "oblique," the sound is a simple velar and not a labiovelar. The most usual position of the sound is initial in words such as "queen," "quick." Q is used apart from *u* only very rarely in words of foreign origin, especially to represent a Semitic guttural, as in "Qabala," "Iraq." *See* also ALPHABET.

(B. F. C. A.; J. W. P.)

QADI (KADI, CADI), a judge in a Muslim court where decisions are rendered according to the canon law of Islam (*shari'a*). Theoretically his jurisdiction embraces both civil and criminal matters, but in practice the qadi hears cases that pertain to religion—*e.g.,* those involving inheritance, pious bequests (*awqaf*), marriage and divorce. Usually there have been other courts and officials to deal with the remaining areas of law. Generally the qadi's work was restricted to arbitrating disputes and rendering judgments in matters brought before him and did not include the administrative side of law. Eventually, however, he acquired additional duties such as the management of pious bequests, guardianship of property for orphans, imbeciles and others incapable of overseeing their own interests, and control of marriages for women without guardians. The qadi's decision in all matters was final.

Since the qadi performed an essential function in early Muslim society, requirements for the post were carefully stipulated in Muslim law books. A qadi must be a male of full adult age, a Muslim, who had the status of a free man. Women, minors, slaves and non-Muslims all had an inferior position under the canon law and could not become qadis. Also, he must be a man of good character, possessing a sound knowledge of the canon law. In the first Muslim centuries (7th and 8th centuries A.D.) it was held that the qadi must even be capable of deriving the specific rules of law from their sources in the Koran, the tradition of the prophet and the agreement of the community. In time, however, this view was displaced by another which bound the qadi to accept absolutely the opinions of one of the founders of the four orthodox Muslim law schools. Finally, a qadi must have good vision and hearing and be able to read and write.

The caliph Omar, second in succession to Mohammed, was the first to have appointed a qadi to relieve himself of the necessity of judging every dispute that arose in the community. Thereafter, it was considered a religious duty upon the authorities in every place to provide for the administration of justice through the appointment of qadis. *See* also ISLAM: *Muslim Institutions;* ISLAMIC LAW.

(C. J. A.)

QAIS (JAZIREH-YE QEYS), an island in the Persian Gulf lying about 10 mi. (16 km.) off the mainland of Iran in latitude 26° 32′ N and longitude 54° E, is the site of a trade centre of great importance in former times. Pop. (1954) 1,686. The island, measuring 9 by 5 mi., rises 120 ft. (37 m.) above sea level to a plateau and is bare of vegetation except for small patches of cultivation and a few date groves and stunted herbage. It is surrounded by a reef and pearl banks.

In the early Muslim period Qais formed a part of the province of Fars, but it was only in the later Middle Ages that it attained importance, when a prince of south Arabian origin obtained possession of it, built a fleet there, and gradually extended his power. He captured Siraf (modern Taheri), northwest of Qais on the mainland, which was then the principal market of the Persian-Indian-Chinese trade. In the first half of the 11th century Siraf was gradually deserted, and finally Qais supplanted Siraf.

At its period of greatest power, the dynasty of Qais also ruled over the district of Oman on the opposite Arabian shore. The Rabbi Benjamin of Tudela, Spain, visited Qais between A.D. 1164 and 1173, and noted the rich market of the island whose chief business was the exchange of Persian, Mesopotamian, Arabian, and Indian manufactures and produce. The site of the old city is marked by the ruins known as Harirah on the north coast. Qais in turn lost its importance—for reasons not known—in the 14th century, and its trade passed to Hormuz. (P. Z. C.; H. Bo.)

QAJAR (KAJAR, KADJAR) **DYNASTY,** the ruling dynasty of Persia from 1794 to 1925. Its founder was Agha Mohammed Khan, chief of the Asterabad branch of the Qajars, a powerful tribe of Turkmen origin. Although not crowned until 1796, Agha Mohammed Khan had been in effective control of Persia since the death in 1794 of Lutf Ali Khan, the last of the Zand dynasty. On his assassination in 1797 Agha Mohammed Khan was succeeded by his nephew Fath Ali, to gain whose favour France and Great Britain made strenuous efforts early in his reign. Fath Ali Shah fought two disastrous wars with Russia, losing Georgia, Armenia, and northern Azerbaijan. His grandson Mohammed, who succeeded him in 1834, came much under the influence of Russia. He made two unsuccessful attempts to capture Herat. When he died in 1848 the succession devolved upon his son Nasir ad-Din (*q.v.*), who proved to be the ablest and most accomplished of the Qajar sovereigns. During his reign European science and methods of education were introduced into Persia and one of the factors in the modernization of the country was the introduction of the telegraph in 1859. When Nasir ad-Din Shah was assassinated by a fanatic in 1896, the crown passed to his son Muzaffar ad-Din, the chief feature of whose reign was the granting of a constitution in 1906. Dying early in 1907, he was succeeded by his son Mohammed Ali who attempted, with the aid of Russia, to rescind the constitution and abolish parliamentary government. In so doing he aroused such opposition that he was deposed (1909), his place on the throne being taken by his 11-year-old son Ahmad Mirza. The new monarch proved to be effete, pleasure-loving, and incompetent. On Oct. 31, 1925, while he was absent in Europe, the *majlis* (national consultative assembly) declared that the rule of the Qajar dynasty was terminated. *See* also PERSIAN HISTORY. (L. Lo.)

QALYUBÎYAH, AL, in the United Arab Republic, the smallest of the Egyptian delta *muhafazat* (governorates), immediately north of Cairo and at the apex of the Nile Delta. It is bounded northeast by Ash Sharqiyah *muhafaza,* east by the Arabian (Eastern) desert, and west by the Damietta branch of the Nile after its bifurcation at Al Khayriyah (Delta) barrage. Area 364 sq.mi. (944 sq.km.). Pop. (1960) 988,055. The capital is Banha (*q.v.*) in the northwest between the Nile and the Tawfiqi Canal near the ancient Athribis. There the bridge over the Nile carries the main railway from Cairo to Alexandria.

The *muhafaza* is one of the most heavily populated of the delta (average density 2,060 persons per sq.mi.) with about 60% of the population relying upon agriculture for their livelihood. Farmland is irrigated mainly from the Tawfiqi Canal (paralleling the Nile) and the Ismailia Canal to the east. The principal crops in order of importance are maize (corn), cotton, wheat, and clover. The proximity of the large market centre of Cairo has encouraged the expansion of acreage under market gardening and orchards. There are no mineral resources other than local deposits of basalt at Abu Za'bal on the eastern fringe of the cultivated zone. The principal towns are Banha and Qalyub.   (A. B. M.)

QARO (Caro or Karo), **JOSEPH BEN EPHRAIM** (called Maran, "our master") (1488–1575), codifier of Jewish law (*halakha*), whose code is still authoritative for Orthodox Jewry, was born in Spain. As a child he shared in the expulsion of the Spanish Jews (1492), and migrated from place to place till 1536, when he settled in Safed (Safad), Palestine, then the centre of both talmudic learning and cabalistic mysticism. There he spent the rest of his life.

In learning and critical power, Qaro was second only to Maimonides in the realm of Jewish law. In face of the disintegration in Jewish life caused by the Spanish expulsion, Qaro felt called upon to systematize the laws and customs of Judaism. This he attempted to do in two great works. The earlier and greater of these was in the form of a commentary entitled *Beth Yosef* ("House of Joseph," published 1550–59) on the *Arb a'ah Turim* of Jacob ben Asher (*q.v.*), designed exclusively for specialists. In it Qaro shows an astounding mastery of the Talmud and the legalistic literature of the Middle Ages. But the *Beth Yosef* is by no means systematic. Systematization was effected in Qaro's second work, the *Shulhan 'Arukh* ("The Well-Laid Table"), in its original form an extract from the *Beth Yosef*. Finished in 1555, it was published in four parts at Venice in 1565. The work, which showed a certain prejudice in favour of the Sephardic view, was at first received with some hostility by the Ashkenazic Jews. But after 1578, when it was first published together with Moses Isserles' commentary (*see* Isserles, Moses ben Israel) covering Ashkenazic practice, it gradually became the almost unquestioned authority of the whole Jewish world, and it remained so until the advent of Reform in the 19th century.

The influence of the *Shulhan 'Arukh* was to some extent pernicious. It put Judaism into a straitjacket, inhibiting independence of judgment; the code stood in the way of progressive adaptation of Jewish life to the life of Europe. But its good effects far outweighed the bad. It sanctified the home, it dignified common pursuits. It was a bond of union, a bar to latitudinarianism, an accessible, easily understandable guide to ritual, ethics, and law.

Parts of the *Shulhan 'Arukh* are available in English translation: H. E. Goldin's translation of S. Ganzfried's abridgment, *Code of Jewish Law* (1927); and C. N. Denburg's translation (including Isserles' glosses) of the second and fourth parts, *Code of Hebrew Law*, 2 vol. (1955).

See R. J. Zwi Werblowsky, *Joseph Karo, Lawyer and Mystic* (1962).

QASIM, AL, a district of northern Najd (*q.v.*), Saudi Arabia, lying athwart the middle course of the Wadi ar Rummah (Rimah). It has a settled population of about 200,000; the main centres are Buraydah (*q.v.*) and 'Unayzah. Formerly an area of contention between Ibn Rashid (who had Turkish support) and Ibn Saud, it was recovered by Ibn Saud in 1904 and has remained peaceful. By the 1960s much progress had been made in developing its water resources and agriculture.   (H. St. J. B. P.; X.)

QATAR, a sheikhdom under British protection on the west coast of the Persian Gulf. It occupies a desert peninsula (100 by 50 mi. [160 by 80 km.]) east of Bahrain, and borders on the south Saudi Arabia and Trucial Oman, with both of which its boundaries are disputed but remain *de facto*. Pop. (1964 est.) 60,000. The capital is Ad Dawhah (Dauha, Doha) on the east coast, once a centre of pearling activity, which declined substantially. Oil, discovered at Dukhan on the west coast in 1939, was brought into production in 1946. Output was declining from a peak of nearly 9,000,000 tons a year in the early 1960s and yielding Qatar an income of about £18,500,000. One quarter of the revenue is reserved for the ruler; the rest is used on public development and welfare. Free education and health services and hospitals are provided, the drinking water supply has been doubled, and two power stations

built. In 1960 and 1961 oil was found offshore.

The British political agent and the sheikh's British adviser reside at Ad Dawhah. Various shipping lines visit Musay'id (Umm Sa'id), the oil port on the east coast, and there is regular air service between Ad Dawhah, Sharjah, Bahrain, and Beirut. The population, mainly concentrated in the three centres of Dukhan, Musay'id, and Ad Dawhah, has a sprinkling of Bedouin and semi-Nomadic elements, and Indian and Pakistani nationals.

For long Qatar was under Persian rule, and paid Rs. 3,000 a year to the governor of Bushire for the right to fish for pearls. It became independent of Persia in the 19th century under Thani, the founder of the Al Thani dynasty; he was succeeded by his son Mohammed, who in 1868 signed an agreement with Great Britain. Mohammed's son Qasim died in 1913 at the age of 111 years, and his son 'Abdullah renewed the 1868 agreement with Britain in 1916. He was succeeded in 1949 by 'Ali bin 'Abdullah, who in October 1960 abdicated in favour of his son Sheikh Ahmed bin 'Ali. The sheikh is an absolute monarch.   (H. St. J. B. P.; X.)

QAYEN (Qain), a town and *bakhsh* (subdistrict) in the southern highland (Kuhestan) region of the *ostan* (province) of Khurasan, Iran. Qayen was formerly the chief town of the same region, which was then called Qainat. The whole area consists of a complicated system of hill ranges (reaching more than 9,000 ft. [2,750 m.]) running northwest to southeast and sinking in the south to the Seistan Basin. The rainfall is greater than in most neighbouring areas, and the population depends largely on *deimi* (*i.e.*, non-irrigated) crops. The principal products are grain, saffron, vegetables, and wool; the asafetida plant also grows profusely. Formerly great numbers of camels were reared.

The town of Qayen lies in a broad valley about 200 mi. (320 km.) S of Meshed on the main road to Zahedan. Pop. (1956) 4,414. It is surrounded by a mud wall, which is in a state of disrepair, and the houses of the wealthier inhabitants are outside it. The cultivation of saffron is a speciality of the immediate neighbourhood which supplies nearly the whole of Iran with this commodity. The chief industries are the making of felts and carpets, but the best Qaini carpets are made at Dorokhsh, about 52 mi. SE. The ruins of a fort also lie southeast on the summit of two hills.

Qayen is undoubtedly a place of great antiquity and chequered history. The present town was founded by the Timurid Shahrukh (1405–47) to replace an older town which he is said to have destroyed. Later the Uzbeks took possession of Qayen and held it until Shah Abbas I (1587–1629) expelled them. In the 18th century it fell under the sway of the Afghans and was a dependency of Herat until 1851. *See also* Khurasan.   (H. Bo.)

QENA: *see* Qina.

QESHM (Qishm), sometimes styled by the Arabs Jazirat-at-Tawila (Long Island), is the largest island in the Persian Gulf and belongs to Iran. It lies parallel to the Iranian coast between Lengeh and Bandar Abbas and is separated from the mainland by a channel known to mariners as Clarence Strait (Khuran). It is 68 mi. (109 km.) long and has a very irregular outline, with an average breadth of about 10 mi. although it exceeds 20 mi. abreast of Jazireh-ye Hengam (Henjam Island). The coast is generally rocky but the southeastern and western shores have sandy bays and the northwestern is fringed by mud flats. Irregular table-topped hills almost cover Qeshm; several are more than 900 ft. high and one, Kish Kuh, 18 mi. from Basa'idu (Basidu), the westernmost point, and nearly in the middle of the island, reaches 1,331 ft. The geological formation resembles that of the adjacent coast; upper strata of coarse sandstone grit and conglomerate supported by blue Lias marl interrupted by salt plugs. Salt is mined on the southeastern coast and there are naphtha springs. The island is mostly barren but water from wells is fairly plentiful. Cereals, vegetables, melons, and dates are grown near the villages in the north and around the coasts. The main occupations of the inhabitants are fishing and boatbuilding with some camel breeding, stock raising, and weaving. Wild goats, partridges, and rock pigeons are found in the hills, and some gazelles in the plains. The population in 1956 was about 15,000; more than 5,700 live in Qeshm town on the easternmost extremity of the island. They are mainly of Arab origin and are administered by a sheikh of the

Bani Ma'in tribe on behalf of the Iranian government. Qeshm town and Basa'idu were British naval stations early in the 19th century. (K. C. B.; H. Bo.)

Q FEVER (also known as BALKAN GRIPPE; German QUEENS-LAND FIEBER or Q FIEBER; French FIÈVRE Q or MALADIE DE DERRICK-BURNET; Italian FEBBRE Q) is an acute, self-limited, systemic disease caused by *Coxiella burnetii* (*Rickettsia burneti*), a microorganism of the family Rickettsiaceae. The rickettsiae approximate the smaller bacteria in size and appearance but are obligate intracellular parasites, as are the viruses. Biologically, the rickettsiae occupy a position between the bacteria and the viruses, and *C. burnetii* may be regarded as a bacterium highly adapted to an intracellular life.

History.—Q fever was first recognized as a new disease in 1935 in Queensland, Austr., by E. H. Derrick. According to him, Q stands for "query," an appellation applied because of the many unanswered questions posed by the new disease at the time of its first description. The term "Queensland fever" is therefore un-justified. The causal organism was originally designated *Rickettsia burneti* by Derrick, after F. M. Burnet, who isolated it. It is now generally referred to as *Coxiella burnetii*, after H. R. Cox, who found that Montana ticks were infected by a rickettsia later shown to be indistinguishable from that recovered in Australia, and who uncovered evidence of the possible existence of Q fever in the United States.

The disease, originally encountered almost entirely among abat-toir workers, cattle ranchers, and dairy farmers in Australia, and later among sheep ranchers, was thought for many years to be restricted to that continent. However, several outbreaks of pneu-monitis, later shown to be outbreaks of Q fever, occurred among Axis and Allied troops in the eastern Mediterranean during the winter of 1944–45. These were the first naturally occurring out-breaks of Q fever recognized outside Australia; the disease there-after was reported from various parts of the world.

Transmission.—Q fever is primarily a zoonosis, *i.e.*, an infec-tion of animals transmissible to man. The many species of arthro-pods (ixodid and argasid ticks, lice, mites, parasitic flies) in vari-ous parts of the world found to be naturally infected, together with the variety of naturally infected hosts (mice, rats, rabbits, porcupines, baboons, hyenas, domestic birds, and domestic an-imals [cows, goats, sheep, horses, dogs, swine]), suggests that the infection is maintained in nature by a number of different host-vector associations. The principal animal reservoirs are ungu-lates, rodents, and marsupials, and ticks appear to be the primary vector for transmission of the infection among these species. Man and his domestic livestock, such as cows, goats, and sheep, are, however, not necessary to survival of the rickettsiae in nature and are infected only accidentally.

Tick-transmitted Q fever appears to be rare in man and, in some parts of the world at least, in domestic livestock as well. Since the rickettsiae are excreted in the milk of dairy cows and goats, ingestion of infected dairy products may play a role in the infec-tion of man and livestock. Inhalation of infected material, how-ever, appears to constitute the common mode of infection. The infected animal sheds the rickettsiae through the milk, excreta, and, most importantly, through the placenta and the birth fluids. Con-tamination of the environment leads to airborne dissemination of the rickettsiae and subsequently to infection of persons in close contact with livestock, contaminated clothing, etc.

Symptoms, Treatment, and Prevention.—The incubation period of the disease is from two to four weeks, averaging about 18 to 21 days. The onset of the illness may be gradual but gen-erally is sudden, and the disease is ushered in by fever, chills or chilly sensations, headache, muscle aches, loss of appetite, dis-orientation, and profuse sweating. Symptoms referable to the upper respiratory tract may be present but generally are infre-quent and minimal, and pneumonia, even when relatively exten-sive, may be detectable only by X-ray examination. Although Q fever is, on the whole, a mild disease, it can sometimes result in a severe and protracted illness. Complications are not common, but some may be serious; and it is now recognized that Q fever may take a chronic form involving the cardiovascular system;

subacute endocarditis has been reported and has been uniformly fatal. In general, however, the outlook for recovery in Q fever is excellent; the mortality rate is believed to be less than 1%. Therapy with tetracyclines is highly effective.

Since Q fever in man appears to be, in large part, an infection associated with occupation, control would appear to lie in vaccines prepared from *Coxiella burnetii* although entirely satisfactory vac-cines were not available in the late 1960s. Milk, whether used directly for food or for manufacture of dairy products, should be pasteurized. *See also* RICKETTSIAE. (E. H. LEN.)

QIFT (Arabic KUFT, ancient COPTOS, KOPTOS), a small village in the United Arab Republic (Egypt) on the east bank of the Nile, 25 mi. N of Luxor, known to the ancient Egyptians as Qebti. The town was an early dynastic foundation, the predynastic settle-ments having been at Ombos (ancient Nubyt) on the west bank of the river which the early routes followed. Qebti owed its impor-tance to the gold and porphyry mines in the district; inscriptions there show that they were being worked in the 1st and 2nd dy-nasties. Just outside Qift Flinders Petrie excavated a temple dedi-cated to Min of the Desert Routes and containing three important archaic statues of the god. The town was also associated with Isis, who was said to have found Osiris' body there. By Old Kingdom times Qebti was a place of some importance; both Pepi I and II built and restored temples there, and it was the starting point of expeditions for Punt. By the time of Thutmose III the importance of the city had declined, but it revived in the Ptolemaic period through trade with the East. Queen Arsinoe was banished to Qebti by Ptolemy Philadelphus, and held her court there for some years. A rebellion directed against Diocletian's taxation on the transit trade led to the destruction of the city in A.D. 292, but later it be-came the centre of a thriving Christian community and the Coptic Christians of Egypt derived their name from the town. It retained its influence during the Middle Ages, until replaced as the caravan trade terminal by Kus (Qus). Largely as a result of Petrie's work there, Qift has supplied skilled workers for excavations in Egypt and neighbouring countries. (M. V. S.-W.)

QINA (QENA), a town of Upper Egypt (United Arab Repub-lic) 380 mi. (612 km.) SSE of Cairo by rail and capital of a *muhafaza* (governorate) of the same name. Pop. (1962 est.) 61,000. Qina is built beside a canal 1 mi. E of the Nile at its great bend, about 30 mi. N of Luxor. It was called by the Greeks Caene (New Town) to distinguish it from Coptos (Qift, Quft), 14 mi. S, whose trade it eventually acquired. This early com-merce with Arabia and India, sustained by good caravan routes to the Red Sea, was later reduced to trade with Arabia in dates and grain. Qina's importance revived with World War II as a result of its strategic location at the end of a road through the mountains to Al Qusayr on the coast. Qina manufactures the porous water vessels, made from local Pliocene clays, used throughout Egypt.

QINA *muhafaza* extends about 3–4 mi. each side of the Nile be-tween the Eastern and Western deserts. Essentially it comprises the great bend in the Nile valley. Pop. (1960) 1,351,358. Area 699 sq.mi. (1,811 sq.km.). The Nile bend and the valley to the borders of Aswan *muhafaza* 50 mi. S are the sites of some of Egypt's most famous antiquities, the most celebrated being the ruins at Thebes (*q.v.*) and the Valley of the Kings. Although its soil is fertile, Qina is one of the poorest of Egypt's *muhafazat*, principally because the high density of population (exceeding 1,900 per square mile) is coupled with the fact that much agricultural land is under basin irrigation and therefore yields but one crop a year. Principal crops are sugar (60% of Egypt's production), barley, wheat, and millet. Perennial irrigation water, mainly from the Kelabiya and Asfun canals, is supplied from the Isna barrage. Principal towns are Qina, Luxor, and Isna. (A. B. M.)

QOM (QUM), a city and *shahrestan* (district) in the Central *ostan* (province) of Iran. The town lies on both banks of the Rud-e Qom, 78 mi. (125 km.) S of Teheran, and at the edge of the great salt desert, the Dasht-e Kavir. Pop. (1964 est.) 131,777. The district is irrigated by the Rud-e Qom and Qareh Su and pro-duces grain, fruits, and cotton of a very long staple.

The town is a stronghold of the Shi'ah faith and contains the golden-domed shrine of Fatima, sister of the imam Riza, which is annually visited by many thousands of pilgrims. Besides Fatima, at least 10 kings and about 400 saints are interred in Qom and its neighbourhood. Shah Abbas II, whose piety won him high favour with the religious authorities, is buried in a special mausoleum richly adorned with a set of 14 remarkably fine silk rugs, dated 1666. On the south side of the city is a group of five superb mausoleums, mostly of the 14th century, all distinguished by remarkable polychrome stucco ornaments.

Qom has developed into a lively industrial centre, mainly for textiles; glass, pottery, and shoemaking are traditional industries. In 1956 and 1959 the National Iranian Oil Company discovered oil in the Alborz (Elburz) area to the northeast and in the Sarajeh area to the southeast. In the 1960s several dams were completed or were under construction on the upper reaches of the Rud-e Qom.

The city is an important communications centre where the main highway from Teheran splits into three directions: to Isfahan and Shiraz; to Kashan, Yazd, and Kerman; and southwest via Arak to Iraq. It is on the Trans-Iranian Railway with a branch line to Kashan. (H. Bo.)

QUACKERY, the characteristic practice of quacks or charlatans, who pretend to knowledge and skill that they do not possess, particularly in medicine. The quack makes exaggerated claims as to his power to heal disease, generally for financial gain. The conditions usually treated by quacks are those for which specific methods of treatment, or "cures," have not yet been developed; those particularly feared, such as cancer, venereal diseases and, in the past, tuberculosis; those with frequent remissions and recurrences, such as arthritis, neuritis and migraine; and mental disturbances. People yield to quackery in times of great stress, pain or sorrow. In the absence of exact knowledge, and sometimes even in its presence in the face of insurmountable difficulties, the credulous person craves a miracle. He is ready to be overwhelmed by the personality and the claims of the charlatan.

The typical quack may be a man or a woman, but is likely to be striking in appearance and personality. In the past crippled persons, such as· hunchbacks; rulers, such as high priests and kings; mystics and mentally disturbed persons were believed to possess special powers in healing disease. The modern charlatan in his announcements features an alphabetical appendage, indicating the possession of academic degrees that, however, were not conferred by any recognized scientific organization or university. The charlatan originally may be self-deluded as to his powers, but sooner or later he becomes aware of his failures. He then continues in his practice, consciously deluding those who depend upon him. He is aided by the reluctance of persons who have consulted him with disadvantage to acknowledge the fact, and by magnification of his apparent successes. Advances in psychosomatic medicine have helped to explain some of the healings recorded by quacks.

Techniques.—Whenever a new discovery is made in any field of science, the charlatan may take advantage of public interest and lack of information to utilize it with exaggerated claims. Lack of general knowledge encourages occultism, and the characteristic claim of the quack is the possession of a formula, method, device or product unknown to other physicians or scientists. At the time of the American Revolution, for example, a quack named Elisha Perkins (1741–99), aware of public interest in the recently discovered electricity, invented "metallic tractors" to draw disease out of the body. These were two rods of brass and iron, about three inches long, one of copper, zinc and gold, the other of iron with some other metals; they cost 1s. to manufacture and sold for $5. James Graham (1745–94) in England set up a temple of healing in which he burlesqued the principle of electricity, promising cures and rejuvenation.

Knowledge of powerful drug substances derived from plants (digitalis, belladonna, cascara sagrada, quinine and castor oil) or from metals (mercury, arsenic and particularly gold) led to the development of nostrums that were exploited with false, misleading or exaggerated claims to cure such diseases as tuberculosis, syphilis, cancer, kidney diseases and gynecological, digestive and rheumatic disorders. Sometimes the quack or purveyor of nostrums did not trouble to include a potent drug but merely used any bitter-tasting, dark herb or vegetable with common salt or sulfur. Toward the end of the 19th century alcohol was used as a solvent, and it yielded its typical effects to the satisfaction of the users. Many modern nostrums depend principally on aspirin.

With the discovery of radium, claims were made for mixtures said to contain this substance. In a few instances some radium actually was included, and users died years later from the effects of radium on the bones. Radium was said to be incorporated in magical magnetic belts, and radium plasters with infinitesimal amounts of radioactivity were purveyed.

Increasing knowledge of the glands of internal secretion gave rise to preparations for rejuvenation, beautification and sexual power. Vitamins have been incorporated in preparations for growing hair or preventing grayness, without any real evidence that they could be helpful. Indeed, in the realm of cosmetology, quackery and nostrums seem destined forever to reap a pecuniary harvest.

Because people believe in "nature," uncooked foods, systems of exercise, recital of ritualistic codes, manipulation of bones, muscles and tendons, complicated machines of no particular merit, heat, cold, baths, lights (plain and coloured), static electric currents and even radioactivity have been vaunted as useful in the control of disease and the promotion of health.

With the development of techniques for advertising and promotion, the quacks thrived until legislative controls were brought into action. As early as 1843 a leader in advertising said that pain or the fear of pain attracted the greatest interest in mankind, and that for this reason medical advertising took most of the space available in the press. Vanity had the next strongest appeal. Education of the public in physiology, anatomy and hygiene have not served to dispel gullibility. Quack advertising still relies on blatant exaggeration, use of unusual terms (such as "dyskinesia" for constipation), creation of fear, promise of secrecy and financial saving (actually the employment of nostrums and quackery invariably results in greatly increased and prolonged expense). With the coming of radio, some quacks secured radio stations to sell promised cures, and even television has been so employed.

Legislation.—In the United States, quackery varies from state to state according to the limits permitted by law. In some states it is limited almost entirely to the sale of drugs and herb preparations. In other states institutes or sanatoriums are conducted by quack doctors.

In Great Britain a violator is held liable if he holds himself out as a "listed" or recognized medical practitioner or if a death occurs associated with his ministrations; there the law considers that a person consults a quack at his own risk. The continental European countries have not been successful in curbing quackery. In Germany during World War II the unlicensed healers were actually encouraged and formed an association which received governmental recognition. In Latin America quackery is rampant.

In the United States the Food and Drug act of 1906 eliminated the widely advertised quack cures for cancer, tuberculosis and other serious diseases; thereafter the same preparations were sold as cures for coughs, colds, pains and aches and minor complaints. Labels were required to carry information as to content of certain ingredients, warning as to hazards and, in some instances, references to diseases that would not be helped by the preparation. The Federal Food, Drug and Cosmetic act of 1938 and the Wheeler-Lea act (also 1938) provided a certain amount of governmental control over claims made in advertising, in newspapers and magazines, over radio and television, in circulars and on labels. Such controls are exercised, however, only on products in interstate commerce. Individual states vary in the amount and kind of control they exert. In 1962 the Food, Drug and Cosmetic act was amended to require proof of effectiveness of all drugs introduced for sale, retroactive to 1938, and giving the U.S. Food and Drug administration control over drug advertising. Finally, the post office department has authority to forbid the use of the mails when convinced that they are being used fraudulently.

Organizations concerned with such conditions as cancer and heart disease conduct continuous campaigns of public education, warning against the depredations of medical quackery and the sellers of nostrums, and the United States public health service also has undertaken such activities. The state medical licensing boards, medical societies and Better Business bureaus also are concerned with the protection of the public in these fields.

For these reasons quackery has steadily diminished, and the depredations of quacks have been severely limited. Nevertheless the nature of the human mind is such that charlatans will no doubt continue to appear and wreak damage from time to time until society with a social conscience and legal controls catches up with them. *See* also FRAUD.

See Morris Fishbein, *Fads and Quackery in Healing* (1932); Grete de Francesco, *The Power of the Charlatan* (1939). (M. FI.)

QUACK GRASS

QUACK GRASS (*Agropyron repens*), a perennial grass of the barley tribe (Hordeae), called also couch grass or quitch grass. It is native to Europe, common in northern Europe and widely naturalized in North America. Quack grass has bright-green, smooth, stiffly erect stems, one to four feet high; leaves with flat or inrolled blades; and terminal flowering spikes, two to six inches long, composed of numerous, usually five-flowered spikelets, which often bear short awns. Sometimes it is grown for forage, but it is better known as a troublesome weed in cultivated fields, especially on rich soil, spreading rapidly by its creeping rootstocks, which are ivory coloured and sharp pointed. The best method to eradicate it is to root it out.

QUADRATURE (Lat. *quadratura,* a making square), in astronomy, that aspect of a heavenly body in which it makes a right angle with the direction of the sun. The moon at first or last quarter is said to be at east or west quadrature, respectively. A superior planet (outside the earth's orbit) is at west quadrature when its position is 90° W. of the sun (*see* drawing). It rises around midnight, reaches the south meridian near sunrise and sets near noon. At east quadrature the planet is near the meridian at sunset and sets near midnight. At both quadratures, the planet is at gibbous phase, but only in the case of Mars does it show up conspicuously gibbous.

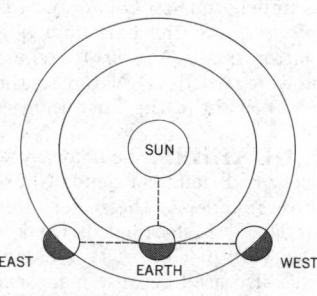

QUADRATURE OF A SUPERIOR PLANET

In mathematics, quadrature is the determination of a square equal to the area of a curve or other figure. Integration by quadratures means calculation by a step-by-step process when no analytical expression for the integral is available. (H. M. Lo.)

QUADRILATERAL, in geometry, a figure formed by four straight lines. It is said to be plane or skew according to whether the four lines do or do not lie in one plane.

Let us consider the plane figure bounded by four lines terminated at the vertices. A line joining a pair of opposite vertices is called a diagonal. The area of such a quadrilateral is half the product of the length of one diagonal by the sum of the perpendiculars drawn to this diagonal from the other two angular points. The sum of the squares of the four sides of such a quadrilateral is equal to the sum of the squares of its diagonals increased by four times the square of the line joining the midpoints of the diagonals. If the vertices of such a quadrilateral lie on a circle, the product of the diagonals is equal to the sum of the products of the opposite sides.

It is in projective geometry that the quadrilateral plays its most interesting role. If A, B, C, D are four points in a plane no three of which are collinear, then the lines AB, BC, CD, DA, each taken to be of indefinite extent, form a quadrilateral (*see* figure). These sides intersect in pairs not only in the four given points (called vertices) but also in a point E on both AB and CD, and in a point F on both BC and AD. The points E and F are also called vertices. Then each side of the quadrilateral contains three vertices. Two vertices

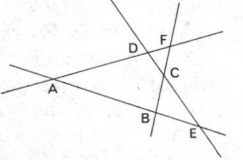

QUADRILATERAL ABCD. ALL LETTERED POINTS ARE VERTICES

not on the same side are called opposite. A line joining two opposite vertices is called a diagonal. The configuration so described is called a complete quadrilateral. The dual figure is called a complete quadrangle. These figures are of fundamental importance in projective geometry (*q.v.*).

QUADRILLE, a lively dance, executed by four couples arranged in a square. A form of *contredanse* known by 1710, the quadrille crystallized about 1815 in the general form popular since then, and consisting of five figures: *le pantalon, l'été, la poule, la pastourelle* or *la trénise,* and the *finale.* The music was often based on operatic melodies; dance patterns were subject to great variation. Although steps and figures have undergone considerable modification, quadrilles such as the lancers are still among the most popular square dances. In theatrical terminology, quadrille has denoted: (1) small groups of dancers in 18th-century ballet; (2) Paris night-club dancers of the 1890s, immortalized by Henri de Toulouse-Lautrec; (3) divisions of ensemble dancers at the Paris opera in the 20th century. (LN. ME.)

QUAESTOR (derived from Latin *quaerere,* "to investigate"), a magistrate usually concerned with finance, in ancient Rome. Tacitus attributed the origin of the quaestorship in Rome to the regal period, but all other evidence refers to the republic. The two *quaestores parricidii,* who were appointed by the consuls and were concerned with capital offenses, are mentioned in the Twelve Tables. The financial quaestors may have arisen from these as assistants of the consuls, but more probably arose independently with the development of a public treasury, and were like the financial officials called *mastroi* in certain Dorian cities of the West. From 447 onward they were elected for annual terms in the *comitia tributa* (*see* COMITIA), with the consul presiding. In 421 the number was raised to four to provide military assistants to the consuls, and opened to plebeians, and after the conquest of Italy was probably raised to eight. L. Cornelius Sulla (dictator 81–79) made it 20 and Julius Caesar 40, but Augustus reduced it to 20, the usual number under the empire. The connection of quaestor with consul, and later with the higher magistrate he assisted, was considered analogous to that between father and son. The office was held after the term of military service, and after Sulla the minimum age was 30, which was reduced to 25 under Augustus. The year of office began on Dec. 5. After Sulla it gave automatic entrance to the Senate, and under the empire remained the first qualifying office in a senatorial career. For insignia the quaestors had a chair (*sella*), and had the fasces (*q.v.*) when they held command in provinces as *quaestores pro praetore.*

Their duties were varied. The two urban quaestors were responsible for the security of the funds, coin and bullion, in the public treasury and for the accounts, as well as for the laws, decrees, and military standards deposited there. They could levy sums owing to the treasury and conduct sales for it. Augustus placed praetors in charge of the treasury, but from A.D. 44 to 56 it returned to quaestors especially selected for three-year terms. The consuls and each of the provincial commanders had a quaestor (the governor of Sicily had two) especially, but not exclusively, concerned with his financial arrangements. The quaestor exercised a delegated jurisdiction, could command troops, and was sometimes left in command when his superior returned. Assignments to provinces were by lot, but a commander's wish might be considered, and the term could be prorogued. Quaestors continued to serve under the empire under proconsuls in senatorial provinces.

In Italy under the republic quaestors collected funds and levied men for the fleet; one, like Saturninus in 104, had the onerous charge of the grain supply at Ostia; one was stationed (still under Tiberius by ancient custom) at Cales in Campania with much of southern Italy in his province; one had the care of water supply in Rome; and one was in Gaul. During the empire their duties passed to imperial appointees, the ones in Gaul and Ostia being given up under Claudius, while special quaestors of the emperor appeared who performed such duties as accompanying him and reading his letters to the Senate. Under Claudius the financial burden of paving roads was changed to the giving of gladiatorial games. The office continued into the 3rd century as a rank and survived into the late empire.

The *quaestor intra Palatium* of the late empire, newly created under Constantine, replaced the praetorian prefect in the internal administration. He headed the *consistorium* (the imperial council), drew up laws and answers to petitions, and was responsible for the list of minor staff officers (*laterculum minus*).

The quaestor in Oscan towns was probably derived from Rome. Quaestors were regularly minor magistrates in colonies and *municipia* with duties similar to those in Rome. Private associations often called their financial officers quaestors.

BIBLIOGRAPHY.—T. Mommsen, *Römisches Staatsrecht,* vol. ii, pp. 523 ff. (1887); A. H. J. Greenidge, *Roman Public Life,* pp. 212 ff., 369 ff. (1901); T. R. S. Broughton, *Magistrates of the Roman Republic,* vol. i–ii (1951–52) for names; K. Latte, "The Origin of the Roman Quaestorship," *Transactions of the American Philological Association,* 67, pp. 24 ff. (1936); E. Stein, *Histoire du Bas-Empire* i, ed. by J. R. Palanque, vol. i (1959).   (T. R. S. B.)

QUAGGA, a zebralike animal (*Equus quagga*) formerly found in vast herds on the great plains of South Africa but now extinct, apparently the last having died in 1872 in the London Zoo. The colour of the head, neck, and upper parts of the body was reddish brown, irregularly banded, and marked with dark-brown stripes, stronger on the head and neck, and gradually becoming fainter until lost behind the shoulder. There was a broad, dark, median dorsal stripe. The undersurface of the body, the legs, and tail were nearly white, without stripes. The crest was high, surmounted by a standing mane, banded brown and white. *See* ZEBRA.

QUAHOG, also spelled QUAHAUG or QUAUHOG, is a corruption of the word *paquahock* used by the New England Indians for the hard-shell clam *Mercenaria mercenaria* in the family Veneridae. The name quahog is used only on the Atlantic seaboard of the United States and particularly in New England. The shell of this clam is large, thick, and solid, marked with concentric growth lines and ridges. It is a dirty gray in colour outside; inside it is often marked with purple, and it was from this that the Indians made their purple wampum. The quahog has short siphons and so does not burrow deeply into the sand; often a portion of the valves is protruding, or the shell may lie on the surface. It ranges from the intertidal zone out to depths of several fathoms and is found on sandy, muddy bottoms. This clam was an important item of food to the Indians and the early settlers and continues to support an important industry on the Atlantic coast from Nova Scotia to Maryland. The young clams, known as cherrystones, are eaten raw; the larger ones are cooked in a variety of ways, though chowder is perhaps the commonest. The black, mahogany, or ocean quahog, *Arctica islandica,* has a heavy dark covering on the outside of the shell. This edible species lives in deeper water and is dredged in quantity off the New England coast. Young of both species are important food for bottom feeding fishes. *Mercenaria campechiensis,* the southern quahog, is also fished commercially. *See also* CLAM.   (R. D. T.)

QUAIL, a game and table bird known throughout Europe, Asia, and Africa. The common quail (*Coturnix coturnix*) varies in colour, but in general is reddish brown above marked with dark brown and buff below, passing into white on the belly. Essentially migratory, the quail nests on the ground, laying 9 to 15 yellowish eggs spotted with dark brown. Immense numbers are netted during the autumn migration in Mediterranean countries. It has been said that the "manna" that came down from the heavens to the Israelites during their wanderings in the desert may have been, in part, a large migration of quail.

Quails are protectively coloured, and are particularly difficult to see when they "freeze"; they tend to remain motionless until pressed closely, then take to sudden, low, erratic flight. Family groups are in the habit of sitting in circles, facing outward. They thus keep warm and at the same time maintain a watch for danger. When approached, the circle of birds "explodes" in all directions, tending to confuse the predator.

The quail is now rare in Great Britain. It feeds largely on weed seeds and insects and is decidedly a beneficial species. Related forms include the rain quail (*C. coromandelica*) of India, the African quail (*C. delegorguei*), and the Australian stubble quail (*C. pectoralis*). The North American quails belong to a

LEONARD LEE RUE III FROM NATIONAL AUDUBON SOCIETY

QUAIL (COTURNIX COTURNIX)

different subfamily of the Phasianidae. They include the bobwhite (*q.v.; Colinus virginianus*), of which some 20 races occur from Mexico and the West Indies to Canada, the California quail (*Lophortyx californicus*), the scaled quail (*Callipepla squamata*), Gambel's quail (*Lophortyx gambelii*), mountain quail (*Oreortyx pictus*), and the harlequin quail (*Cyrtonyx montezumae*). The button quails (*Turnix*), lacking the hind toe in most species, are now regarded as related to the cranes. *Turnix sylvatica* ranges from Spain to the East Indies, with various races.

(K. P. S.; HT. FN.)

QUAKERS, the name by which members of the Religious Society of Friends (Friends Church) are frequently known. George Fox, founder of the society, records that in 1650 "Justice Bennet of Derby first called us Quakers because we bid them tremble at the word of God." It is likely that the name, originally derisive, was also used because many early Friends, like other religious enthusiasts, themselves trembled in their religious meetings and showed other physical manifestations of religious emotion. The term was in fact probably used of other enthusiasts, as in a 1647 reference to "a sect of women (they are at Southwark) come from beyond sea, called Quakers" or a 1646 reference in the parish register of Milford, Hampshire, each predating Friends in the respective localities by more than six years. Despite early derisive use, Friends used the term of themselves in phrases such as "the people of God in scorn called Quakers." No embarrassment is caused by using the term to or of Friends today. *See* FRIENDS, SOCIETY OF.

(E. H. MI.)

QUALITIES. The word "quality" has, both in philosophy and in ordinary speech, a long history. It appeared in English as a translation of the Latin *qualitas,* a word coined by Cicero to translate the Greek *poiotes;* and this Greek word had itself been coined by Plato (*Theaetetus,* 182a), with apology for its barbarous character, and employed as a technical term by Aristotle in his doctrine of categories (*see* CATEGORY). In spite of this highly artificial beginning, the word "quality" soon became acclimatized in ordinary English; in philosophy, however, its uses have been various and somewhat obscure.

The ordinary uses of the word (which cannot here be exhaustively dealt with) may be broadly distinguished under two headings. First, the word is sometimes employed as a synonym of "property" or "characteristic": in this sense it would cover almost anything that might be ascribed to an object for the purpose of describing it—its colour, shape, dimensions and so on. In the same sense honesty, prudence, obstinacy, etc., may be spoken of as "qualities of character." Second, the word is used, perhaps more commonly, in contexts where merit, grade or value is in question. Where, for example, two kinds of cloth are said to differ "in quality," it would usually be meant not merely that they differ but that one kind is better (by the appropriate standards) than the other; it might indeed be said to be of better, or higher, quality. Similarly, when Emerson wrote that "there is more difference in the quality of our pleasures than in the amount," he undoubtedly meant to convey that some of our pleasures are better, more valuable, and not merely more intense or more prolonged than others. It is usually in this way that the word "quality" is to be understood when a contrast is stated or implied with "quantity." The word is also often employed by itself in the sense of "good quality," as in the old phrase "persons of quality" or in such advertisers' phrases as "quality groceries." In view of the existence and, perhaps, prevalence of this second use, it is important to remember that (in the first sense) a "quality of character," for example, is not necessarily good or desirable. Cowardice is as truly a quality of character as bravery.

Qualities and Relations.—The traditional distinction between qualities and relations, so common that it can hardly be regarded as technical or philosophical, has sometimes been attacked as being philosophically unimportant. It cannot be denied, however, that there is such a distinction, or that it is sometimes convenient to employ it. What the distinction is can be roughly indicated by examples. Colour would be said to be a quality, since, in saying of what colour an object is, nothing need be mentioned other than that object to which the colour is ascribed. Proximity, on the other hand, would be said to be a relation, since, in employing the phrase "is close to," two objects must be mentioned, one of which is said to be close to the other. Similarly, a statement of the form "Y is between X and Z" might (rather artificially) be said to assert the relation of intermediacy—a "three-term" relation, since mention must be made in the statement of three things, one being said to be between the other two. A connected and sometimes convenient notion is that of "relational quality." For example, it might be said that being tall is a relational quality since, though it is clearly not a relation (the sentence "Jones is tall" is complete in itself), it could be held that in calling someone tall a comparison is implied between his height and (roughly) that of most other men.

Qualities and Predicates.—The foregoing brief distinction between qualities and relations might suggest the view that, in all subject-predicate (as distinct from relational) statements, the predicate is employed to ascribe a quality to that which the subject-expression is used to designate. It would be usual, however, and seems desirable, not to accept such a general principle without qualification; for there are many expressions, properly used as predicates and not obviously complex, which are yet used so differently from others that it seems inadvisable to regard them all as alike in standing for qualities. It would, for example, be reasonable to deny that the word "real" stands for a quality. For whereas the word "yellow," for instance, is ordinarily (literally) employed in just one way, namely in ascribing a particular colour, and so might be said always to stand for the same quality, the force of the word "real" varies greatly from context to context. It would be most unnatural to insist that a real (as opposed to a pantomime) horse and a real (as opposed to an illusory) advantage share a single quality, reality; the word "real" takes its particular force in each context from the implied contrast, and in this respect, if in no others, the cases differ completely.

Nonnatural Qualities.—An instance which has aroused more controversy, though it is not perhaps of greater importance, is that of the predicate "good." G. E. Moore, in his influential *Principia Ethica* (Cambridge, 1903), launched an attack on what he called the naturalistic fallacy. He distinguished in the course of his argument between the "natural qualities" of objects—for example their colour, shape, texture or weight—and "nonnatural qualities," of which his primary instance was goodness; and the naturalistic fallacy, he claimed, was committed by anyone who sought to define a nonnatural quality in terms of a natural quality or qualities. Doubts were soon expressed, both by Moore himself and by others, about the meaning to be attached to his expressions "natural" and "nonnatural." But other critics were inclined to question whether goodness was a quality at all, of any variety; and some insisted

that it was not. (*Cf.* the symposium "Is Goodness a Quality?" in the Aristotelian society's *Supplementary Volume XI*, London, 1932.)

Now this denial might seem surprising in the light of the ordinary use of the word "quality." For one of its most common uses, as remarked above, is in contexts where merit, goodness or badness, is at issue: good apples are of better quality than bad ones. Moreover, it seems entirely natural to say that goodness of heart is an admirable quality of character. If so, it would seem that there could be no objection to the assertion that goodness is a quality.

The philosophical objections to this assertion are somewhat complex but may be summarized as follows. It has been urged that to classify goodness as a quality reveals, or at least invites, misunderstanding of the distinctive character of value judgments. To say that anything Q is a quality, it is said, is to imply that a statement of the form "X is (or possesses) Q" gives a description of X, or states a fact about X; and it has commonly been held that descriptions or statements of fact, properly so called, must be sharply distinguished from judgments of value (or, that describing an object must be distinguished from expressing commendation or condemnation of it). Hence, Moore's distinction between "yellow" as standing for a natural quality and "good" as standing for a nonnatural quality was held to be inadequate; for it implied that judgments of value were no more than a special kind of statements of fact, or statements of a special kind of facts, thus obscuring the supposedly more fundamental distinction between statements of fact, of whatever sort, and judgments of value. Moore's argument was also held to raise needless apparent problems about the ways in which judgments of value could be supported or attacked, disputed or justified; for it appeared that nothing clear and satisfactory had been said, or could be said, about the way in which the presence or absence of nonnatural qualities could be detected.

However, this criticism of Moore is inconclusive. For it is not in fact the case, as has often been assumed, that descriptions or statements of fact must be evaluatively neutral. It is proper to say that a man may be *described* as dishonest, though thereby his character is condemned; it may be a *fact* that he is dishonest and hence a statement of fact to say so. But if so, to say that goodness is a quality and to concede that the assertion "X is good" may be a statement of fact or a description does not oblige one to misrepresent the peculiar character of value judgments. One may say that, in stating the fact that X is good or in describing X as good, one is necessarily also commending X—that goodness is precisely the quality which commendable things are said to possess. Those philosophers who have distinguished so sharply between "descriptive" and "evaluative" terms might well be held themselves to have misstated the same distinction which Moore was accused of misstating, in his distinction between natural and nonnatural qualities.

A better reason for denying that goodness is a quality might be found in the extreme generality of the word "good" (*cf.* Aristotle, *Nicomachean Ethics*, I, v). It would be unplausible to maintain that the word is actually ambiguous; but if it is not ambiguous and if it stands for a quality, one must hold that, whatever things are called good, the same quality is thereby ascribed to them. But this in its turn seems most unnatural. Can good arguments, good apples, good deeds and good cricketers be plausibly said to share one common quality of goodness? If so, should one not expect a sound judge of cricketers to be thereby equipped to judge apples also, or arguments? But this is obviously contrary to facts. It is noteworthy that the "admirable quality of character" mentioned earlier was not in general goodness but in particular "goodness of heart." It seems that some such particularization of goodness is essential if it is to seem natural to speak of it as a quality. Moore, indeed, when he said that goodness was a nonnatural quality, had restricted his discussion to the alleged special use of "good" in moral contexts. But this restriction seemed somewhat arbitrary, nor is it clear how his argument could be extended if the restriction were dropped. It could not well be held that "good" in other contexts stands simply for natural qualities; but if not, it is not clear how Moore could distinguish between moral and other contexts, nor why he should be at such pains to do so.

Primary and Secondary Qualities.—Locke's celebrated distinction between primary and secondary qualities (*Essay Concerning Human Understanding*, ii, ch. 8), of which some notice must be taken here, in fact exhibits the disconcerting feature that some of those things between which he thus distinguishes would not naturally be regarded as qualities at all. The primary qualities of matter, he says, are "solidity, extension, figure, motion or rest, and number"; the secondary qualities are "colour, sounds, tastes, etc."—the "etc." being evidently designed to cover at least smells and warmth and cold. Of these "motion or rest" would usually be spoken of as states, not qualities—partly at least because an object that was at rest, being set in motion, would not be said itself to undergo alteration, as would be implied by saying that it had lost one quality and acquired another. Number also is not commonly thought of as a quality: yellow flowers are all individually yellow, but ten flowers are not all individually ten. To this it might be replied that the quality of being ten belongs not certainly to the members of a collection of ten things but simply to the collection itself. There are further objections to this reply (*cf*. G. Frege, *Foundations of Arithmetic*, Eng. trans. by J. L. Austin, Oxford and New York, 1950, p. 39e *ff*.); but here it will be sufficient to appeal to the obvious difference between the question "Of what sort? (*qualis?*)" and the question "How many?" as a sufficient reason for refusing to classify number as a quality. From the list of secondary qualities, sounds at least seem to be similarly misclassified. It is clear enough that an actual sound is not a quality of that which makes it, though the capacity, tendency or disposition to make that sort of sound or to be concerned in the making of it might well be so regarded.

Apart from these perhaps minor points, Locke's own account of his important distinction is regrettably confused. He says that our ideas of primary qualities "resemble" those qualities ("their patterns do really exist in the bodies themselves") but that our ideas of secondary qualities are wholly unlike that in objects which causes us to have them. Sometimes, apparently confusing qualities with ideas, he says that secondary qualities, unlike the primary, would not exist at all in the absence of suitably sensitive observers. Sometimes he seems to contend that our ideas of secondary qualities are so various and fluctuating that we cannot say that any such qualities are really "in" objects themselves. He certainly comes very close to saying, and by Berkeley was understood to mean, that our ideas of secondary qualities are only a "false imaginary glare," tempting us to ascribe to objects qualities which really they do not possess at all. It is accordingly necessary to inquire what it was that he was seeking, though unsuccessfully, to convey; and here we must take notice of two different distinctions, with both of which Locke was evidently concerned, though he does not clearly indicate that they are two and different.

First, he was clearly influenced strongly by current scientific accounts of the process of perception. He officially regards the qualities of matter as the causes of our "ideas of sensation" and hence is led to think of matter as really characterized by those qualities required in the current explanatory theory. Now the theory current in Locke's time was a mechanical one, "corpuscles" being supposed to act "by impulse" on the sense organs; it is accordingly not surprising that his list of primary qualities includes all and only those features that are of mechanical importance—solidity, shape, size, motion and number. The secondary qualities, perception of which is accounted for by the action of corpuscles supposed to have primary qualities only, are thus thought of as an almost irrelevant intrusion, making their appearance because and only because the world happens to contain appropriately sensitive organisms.

But, second, Locke also says that primary qualities are those which "the mind finds inseparable from every particle of matter"; and he later suggests that they constitute the "real essence" of matter. Now here his case seems to be founded not on scientific but on logical or conceptual considerations. He seems to say that possession of the primary qualities is, and possession of secondary qualities is not, essential to being "material"—that the concept of

materiality includes the primary qualities but not the secondary. And this view, though baldly stated, seems to be right. It is clear enough that anything that we should regard as a material object must be individually distinguishable from other things (countable); must have some shape and dimensions; must be moving or at rest in space; and must be "solid" (in the sense at least of excluding other things from the volume of space occupied by itself). It is equally clear that a material thing is not logically required to make any sound, or to have any taste or smell. The case of colour is more controversial. For sight is in practice the most important of our senses, and it might be urged that any material object must be at least so far coloured as to be visible, accessible to the important sense of sight.

It appears, however, that visibility is actually less important than this would suggest; there is, for example, no conceptual difficulty in the idea of the Invisible Man. By contrast, an "intangible man" would be thought of not as a genuine though peculiar kind of man but rather as not a man at all—as a ghost, a vision or a hallucination.

Many other questions of intricacy and interest are suggested by Locke's distinction, though not raised by Locke himself—questions, for example, about the importance and limitations of measurement in our dealings with material things and about the relation between actual or conceivable metrical scales and the (usually) rough "qualitative" distinctions marked in everyday speech.

There is also a large family of questions which might be grouped under the heading "appearance and reality." It is, however, impossible to pursue these topics in the present context.

Qualities and Substance.—Something perhaps should be said here of the not wholly obsolete question, whether a material object can be identified with the sum of its qualities, or whether we must (as Locke held) "suppose always something besides" the qualities, in which they inhere or to which they belong—something to which he and others have given the name of substance (*q.v.*). The disagreement on this question appears to be a case of cross-purposes. On the one hand, an object clearly cannot be simply identified with a collection of qualities; for it is an elementary point of logic that qualities must be qualities of something—that there must indeed be something which they qualify. On the other hand, there is no need to reach Locke's conclusion that this is always a "something we know not what," for which "substance" is simply an arbitrary name. For that in which, say, the qualities of a table inhere is of course a table, a something we know quite well. Historically, the controversy on this issue seems to have arisen from a *prima facie* perverse but in fact not unpersuasive tendency to regard the ultimate possessor of qualities as an essentially characterless and hence unperceiveable and indescribable stuff; while the justified opposition to this line of thought expressed itself by reaction in the mistaken form of a denial that anything but qualities need be admitted.

To escape from the dilemma it is necessary to see that, while qualities must certainly inhere in or belong to substances (or at any rate things which are not themselves qualities), there is no need to suppose the existence of a single characterless stuff in which all qualities ultimately inhere. A thorough removal of the difficulty could probably be best secured by an examination of the related but contrasting roles of substantival and adjectival expressions, together with some investigation of such pedestrian expressions as "stuff," "matter" and "something."

Quality of Propositions.—A specialized use of "quality" has long been made by logicians in the Aristotelian tradition. Under this heading propositions are classified as either affirmative or negative. The term "quality" is employed in this way in contrast with a technical use of "quantity"—the three quantities of propositions being "universal," "particular" and "singular." Kant attempted to introduce, symmetrically with the three headings of quantity, a third quality which he called "infinity"; but this alleged further distinction was not well founded and did not find favour.

(G. J. Wk.)

QUANTITY THEORY OF MONEY, a theory concerning the relationship that exists between the quantity of money within an economic system and the purchasing power or value of one unit of money. In its extreme form, the quantity theory states that the price level changes because the quantity of money changes and that the price level moves in the same direction and in the same proportion as the change in the quantity of money. This implies that the total amount of money in an economic system remains constant in value no matter how many units of money there may be.

Equations.—The quantity theory of money may be formulated in one form or another of a quantity equation. Two traditional forms are $MV = PT$ and $N = P(kT)$. The former is the Fisherian equation, named in honour of the U.S. economist Irving Fisher; the latter, the Cambridge equation, developed principally by Alfred Marshall and A. C. Pigou at Cambridge University in England. There are more sophisticated formulations of the quantity theory of money, but these two illustrate the basic concept involved.

M and N in these equations are the supply of money, commonly defined as the sum (expressed in a nation's monetary unit) of coin and paper currency and checking deposits in banks. In both equations P is an average or index of prices for the marketable goods and services that are measured by T. Current usage is to include in T only the goods and services that comprise national product or national income, omitting the stock of existing wealth and all securities. Hence PT is the aggregate market value of goods and services currently produced and exchangeable for money.

V and k are related reciprocally and express the desire of persons and business firms to have money rather than other forms of wealth. The Fisherian equation is relevant to a specific period of time, and its V is the frequency with which the average unit of money is spent during the period. This frequency is low if money users wish to retain a large proportion of their money income for relatively long periods; it is high if they dispose of their money income soon after receiving it. MV represents the spending of money during a period of time and PT is the value of the goods on which it is spent. The Cambridge equation is relevant to a moment of time, and its kT is the real or physical amount of goods which money users do without in order to retain their money.

The derivation statistically of quantity equations is difficult. There is no faultless measurement of the real goods T or of the price level P at which the goods are traded for money. The desire to hold money (represented by k) can be estimated only from the amount of money actually held. Finally, there is disagreement as to whether the money supply M should include all or merely part of coin, currency, and checking deposits, and also whether it should include time and savings deposits in commercial banks and other financial assets.

The theory that price levels vary as a result of, and in proportion to, changes in the supply of money specifies that T and V or k should be stable and should be independent of the supply of money. Otherwise, the effect of, say, an increase of M in inflating P would be either suppressed or magnified by changes in the flow of goods or in the desire of money users to have money rather than the goods and services that money buys.

The theory may be expressed more conservatively, for a context in which T and V or k are independent of the supply of money but variable. Under such circumstances, the theory would hold that prices vary other than proportionally with money—less than proportionally, for example, while T and k rise. Still, with appropriate adjustments for T and k, money is the propellant of change in the price level, and the impact tends to be proportional.

The quantity theory implies a process by which changes in the supply of money can influence the price level. This process is an adjustment of the amount of money demanded by money users to the supply of money. The demand for money may be visualized as $M' = P(kT)$, with desired balances M' responding positively to the other elements of this equation. The supply of money M depends not on money users but on the ability and willingness of the monetary system to provide money. There is equilibrium when $M = M'$. If the equilibrium is disrupted by an increase in M, the excess of money supply over money demanded is spent on goods, services, and securities. If the flow of goods and services is given, and if both old and new money circulate at the same V, commodity prices P must rise until M' is once more equated with M and the excess supply of money is dissipated by price inflation. In the process of adjusting demand to supply, prices have risen less than in proportion to the increment of money, but when the process is completed and a new equilibrium is established the price inflation is proportional.

Relation to Economic Thought.—The quantity theory that proportional changes in price level adjust the demand for money to the supply has been an integral part of some formal systems of economic reasoning. These bodies of doctrine, sometimes brought to bear on economic problems of the 20th century, purport to explain the behaviour of the entire economic system. They assume that V is stable, or very slow to change, reflecting persistent habits of money users in holding money balances and making money payments. They assume, further, that T is determined by such nonmonetary factors as the labour force, labour productivity, the relationship of wage rates to prices of output, and interest rates. The composition of T and the ratios of individual prices to each other reflect comparative costs of different goods and their comparative utilities to buyers. Everything that is real is determinable independently of the demand for and the supply of money. According to quantity-theory reasoning, money merely determines the absolute level at which price relationships are established. In this view, money is a veil which in equilibrium may obscure, but does not affect, real determinants of economic welfare. Moreover, it should be the goal of monetary policy, working primarily through the supply of money, to keep money in this neutral role.

Neutral money, the argument continues, may be distorted by unsound policies. If monetary expansion exceeds growth in demand for money at a stable price level it must lead to consequences that are socially objectionable. The intermediate consequence is an excessive demand for goods and services that will cause inflation of price levels if the excess supply of money is continually replenished. If monetary expansion ceases, the high level of demand for goods and services collapses, and economic recession follows. The outcome of continuous inflation is maldistribution of income and misallocation of productive resources, even a catastrophic paralysis of the economic and social structure. The outcome of a brief period of inflation, with deflation in its wake, is the business cycle, involving waste of scarce resources.

It is concluded that, in the transitional phases of inflation or of cyclical movement, the quantity theory of money does not apply precisely because V and T are subject to change. According to the neutral-money doctrine, the quantity theory does explain differences in price levels between states of general economic equilibrium. Since the quantity of money affects only price levels and not welfare in equilibrium, and since changes in the quantity of money reduce economic welfare in transitional phases, the optimal policy regarding money is to expand it only as kT grows.

Some extremists have contended that, in the interest of monetary stability, "cheap" or "easy" money should be avoided even in recession. However, the predominant quantity-theory view is that money should be expanded to stop recession if only because recessions themselves usually originate in undue restraint on the money supply. Inappropriate changes in the money supply induce business cycles: appropriate changes in the money supply can ameliorate or even prevent cycles.

Historical Influence.—From its primitive antecedents in the economic literature of Greece and Rome to its modern formulations, the quantity theory of money has been an important strand in the development of economic thought. As developed by John Locke in the 17th century, David Hume in the 18th century, and others, it was a weapon against the Mercantilists, who regarded wealth and money as identical. (*See* MERCANTILE SYSTEM.) If the accumulation of money by a nation merely raises prices, the mercantilist goal of export surpluses and imports of monetary metals for enhancement of national wealth must be illusory.

In the 19th century the quantity theory contributed to the gains of free-trade doctrine over protectionism. If the intermediate effect of import duties is to create an export surplus of goods and services, the ultimate effect is that the export surplus stimulates imports of gold, an expansion of the supply of money, and a rise in domestic price levels that nullifies the trade restriction. The duties thus are ultimately self-defeating.

In the 19th and 20th centuries the quantity theory played a part not only in analysis of inflation and business cycles but also in analysis of foreign exchange rates. The doctrine of purchasing-power parity, as developed primarily by Gustav Cassel, emphasizes that monetary expansion within a single country results in domestic price inflation. The inflation of prices, in turn, implies a decline not only in the internal purchasing power of the currency but also in the purchasing power of the inflated currency over money balances of other countries. The corrective for a depreciating exchange rate is stabilization of the supply of money and of the domestic level of prices.

Attacks on the Theory.—As the result of alleged failures of monetary expansion in the 1930s to promote full economic recovery, and also as the result of the doctrines of John Maynard Keynes (*q.v.*), monetary theory deviated sharply from quantity-theory tradition. Into the 1950s the prevalent view among economists was that monetary expansion is ineffective in reversing deflation, and that monetary restraint is effective but inefficient in control of inflation. The quantity theory's proportional relationship between money and the price level was dismissed as a special and improbable case.

During the 1950s the attack on quantity theory was extended. A theory of cost-push inflation evolved; it held that a rise in the price level may occur without monetary cause and that the supply of money must be increased as inflation occurs in order to prevent unemployment and a shrinkage in production of goods and services at the rising prices. A theory of structural inflation took another tangent, that inflation is a necessary aspect of economic growth, especially in some underdeveloped countries, and that money supply must be adapted to the advance in prices. These heresies against quantity-theory tradition attracted a wide following among economists. Dissenting less radically from quantity theory, other economists argued that financial development destabilizes V and k. Their view was that evolution of substitutes for money weakens or breaks the link between money supply and prices in the long run, between money supply and production in shorter intervals.

A reversion to quantity theory became apparent in the 1960s. Experience with postwar inflations, obvious successes of monetary restraint in curbing inflation, and new empirical studies of money and prices restored a degree of quantity theory's lost prestige. Formulation of the theory gained in sophistication with regard both to the supply of and demand for money. Correspondingly there was a revival of faith in monetary policy, as distinct especially from fiscal policy, for regulating aggregate money spending, demand for goods and services, and the levels of employment and prices.

See also CURRENCY; INFLATION AND DEFLATION; MONEY.

BIBLIOGRAPHY.—Committee on the Working of the Monetary System (Radcliffe Committee), *Report* (1959); I. Fisher and H. G. Brown, *The Purchasing Power of Money*, new ed. (1911); M. Friedman (ed.), *Studies in the Quantity Theory of Money* (1956); J. G. Gurley and E. S. Shaw, *Money in a Theory of Finance* (1960); H. G. Johnson, "Monetary Theory and Policy," *The American Economic Review*, vol. lii, no. 3, pp. 335–384 (June 1962); F. A. Lutz and L. M. Mints (eds.), *Readings in Monetary Theory*, American Economic Association (1951, 1952); A. W. Marget, *Theory of Prices*, 2 vol. (1938–42); D. Patinkin, *Money, Interest, and Prices* (1956).   (E. S. S.)

QUANTUM MECHANICS is the mathematical system for describing the behaviour of such aspects of physics as light, molecules, atoms, and subatomic particles; it is the outgrowth of the quantum concept that all forms of energy (*q.v.*) are released in discrete units or bundles called quanta. Although much of this presentation is purely descriptive, certain portions assume some sophistication in such branches of mathematics as differential equations and matrix theory; a thorough understanding of the article MECHANICS is a minimum prerequisite for understanding this discussion in detail. Following are the main sections and divisions of this article:

I. INTRODUCTION

Throughout the 19th century most physicists regarded Newton's dynamical laws as sacrosanct. During the 20th century, however, it became increasingly clear that many phenomena, especially those connected with radiation, defy explanation on Newtonian principles. It is well recognized that two major innovations are essential. One of these is the introduction of the principle of relativity. The relativistic corrections are important only for bodies moving with velocities comparable to that of light, and as a result experimental confirmation is possible only in very special types of laboratory experiments or in the cosmological field. The other innovation is quantum mechanics. Although rather less publicized than relativity, the quantum concepts have equally drastic philosophical implications and furnish richer and more diversified fields for investigation in the laboratory.

Quantum mechanics is the mechanics governing phenomena which are so small-scale that they cannot be described in classical terms. Thus quantum rather than Newtonian dynamics must be used in dealing with the motions of electrons or nuclei inside atoms and molecules. In the equations of quantum mechanics, Max Planck's constant of action $h = 6.625 \times 10^{-27}$ erg sec. plays a central role. This constant, which is one of the most important in all of physics, has the dimensions

$$\text{mass} \times \text{length}^2/\text{time}$$

The term "small-scale" used to delineate the domain of quantum mechanics should not be literally interpreted as relating necessarily to extent in space. A more precise criterion as to whether quantum modifications of the Newtonian laws are of importance is whether or not the phenomenon in question is characterized by an "action" (time integral of the kinetic energy) which is large compared to Planck's constant. Thus, if a great many quanta are involved, the Planck idea that there is a discrete, indivisible quantum unit loses importance, just as to a millionaire it would make little difference whether the smallest unit of currency is the cent or the dollar. This fact explains how the ordinary physical processes appear to be so fully in accord with the laws of Newton. Planck's element of action is, for example, far too fine-grained to have any bearing on the driving of an automobile. Since all matter seems to be built out of atomic or small-scale ingredients, it must be possible to describe the properties of even large-scale bodies by means of quantum mechanics. In other words, Newtonian dynamics must represent a special case of quantum dynamics appropriate to cases where the action is very large compared to the elementary quantum. This indeed seems true; it should be emphasized, however, that quantum mechanics is really an extension of classical statistical mechanics rather than of the deterministic laws of Newton. As a result, one of the most important philosophical implications of quantum mechanics concerns the apparent breakdown of the causality principle in atomic phenomena. (See *Uncertainty Principle,* below.)

The history of quantum mechanics may be divided into three main periods. The first of these began with Planck's theory of black-body radiation in 1900, and may be described as the period in which the validity of Planck's constant of action was demonstrated, but its real meaning was rather obscure. The second period began with the Bohr quantum theory of spectra in 1913. Niels Bohr's ideas gave an accurate formula for the frequency of spectral lines in many cases, and were an enormous help in the codification and understanding of spectra. Still they did not represent a consistent, unified theory, as he himself recognized, but rather a sort of patchwork affair in which classical mechanics was subjected to a rather extraneous set of so-called "quantum conditions," which restrict the constants of integration to certain particular values. The true quantum mechanics appeared in 1926, reaching fruition almost simultaneously in a variety of forms; viz., the matrix theory of Max Born and Werner Heisenberg, the wave mechanics of Louis V. de Broglie and Erwin Schrödinger, and the transformation theory of Paul A. M. Dirac and Pascual Jordan. These different formulations are in no sense alternative theories, but are different aspects of a consistent body of physical law.

Near mid-20th century the status of quantum mechanics was aptly described as follows (from Dirac in *Proceedings of the Royal Society,* A, vol. cxxiii):

The general theory of quantum mechanics is now almost complete, the imperfections that still remain being in connection with the exact fitting in of the theory with relativity ideas. These give rise to difficulties only when high-speed particles are involved, and are therefore of no importance in the consideration of atomic and molecular structure, and ordinary chemical reactions. . . . The underlying laws necessary for the mathematical theory of a large part of physics and the whole of chemistry are thus completely known and the difficulty is only that the exact solution of these laws leads to equations much too complicated to be soluble.

It should be added that conventional quantum mechanics makes no pretense of describing completely what goes on inside the nucleus. In other words, the details of the short-range dynamics of the particles of which the nucleus is composed are not precisely known, although quantum mechanics has been a help in understanding many nuclear phenomena, such as the emission of alpha particles and photodisintegration, and although the rather intricate field theory of quantum mechanics has provided some insight into the properties of mesons, transient particles which are of interest mainly in connection with nuclear phenomena. In short, by the 1960s the theory of nuclear physics was in a more or less embryonic stage comparable, say, with extranuclear quantum theory in its early days.

Thus, quantum mechanics gives appropriate laws of nature down to distances of the order 10^{-10} cm., but the rules are not known in detail below nuclear radii of the order 10^{-12} cm.

II. QUANTUM THEORY PRIOR TO THE BOHR ATOM

First will be described the earlier investigations in quantum theory which anteceded the discovery of the true quantum mechanics in 1926. This procedure is not merely an attempt to preserve historical order, but is also advisable because some of the primitive theories describe some subjects fairly well and help in the visualization of the later, more recondite developments.

1. Black-Body Radiation.—The quantum of action had its birth in the studies of black-body radiation in 1900 by Planck, professor of physics at the University of Berlin. All black (*i.e.,* perfectly absorbing) bodies heated to a given temperature should emit radiation having the same spectrum. The latter can be shown to be identical with the spectral distribution of energy in a so-called *Hohlraum; i.e.,* a cavity whose radiation is in thermal equilibrium with matter. (*See* BLACK BODY.) According to classical physics, the density of radiant energy should be proportional to the square of the frequency, and should increase without limit as the wavelength is made progressively shorter. This prediction is sometimes called the ultraviolet catastrophe, and the corresponding analytical formula for the energy density is called the Rayleigh-Jeans law. It yields the dashed curve of fig. 1. The observed distribution is that indicated by the solid curve, which Planck was able to deduce theoretically by making a quantum hypothesis.

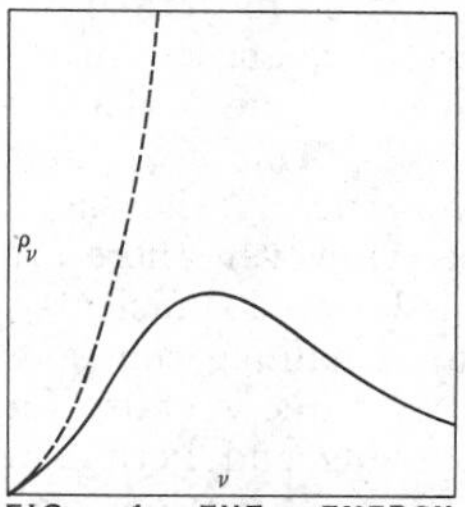

FIG. 1.—THE ENERGY DENSITY (ρ_ν) OF BLACK-BODY RADIATION AS A FUNCTION OF FREQUENCY (ν). CLASSICAL AND QUANTUM THEORIES GIVE RESPECTIVELY THE DASHED AND SOLID CURVES

We shall now indicate how the Rayleigh-Jeans and Planck radiation laws can be derived and shall formulate them mathematically. The method which we sketch is a well-known but rather formal one. It may be characterized as the application of classical equipartition (*see* KINETIC THEORY OF MATTER) or of classical statistics to the degrees of freedom of the ether. It is not presumed that a material ether really exists; this term is used merely to indicate that the standing electromagnetic waves in an enclosure are handled by the same type of statistical procedure as those of a material medium. The first step is the enumeration of the different types of standing waves or modes of vibration of the ether in a rectangular parallelepiped of volume V. Just as a rope with fixed ends can vibrate only in certain ways, represented by the fundamental and the various harmonics, so also in the three-dimensional case only certain modes of oscillation are compatible with the boundary conditions. If the edges of the parallelepiped are large compared to the wavelength, the number of possible vibrations in the frequency interval $(\nu, \nu + d\nu)$ can be shown to be

$$(8\pi\nu^2 V/c^3) \cdot d\nu \tag{1}$$

where c is the velocity of light. Let the mean energy of an oscillation of frequency ν be denoted by ϵ_ν. Then the density of radiant energy in the frequency range $(\nu, \nu + d\nu)$ is $\rho_\nu d\nu$ with

$$\rho_\nu = \epsilon_\nu \cdot (8\pi\nu^2/c^3) \tag{2}$$

It is now necessary to evaluate ϵ_ν. This is done by treating each characteristic mode of vibration as a harmonic oscillator. According to classical statistical mechanics,

$$\epsilon_\nu = kT \tag{3}$$

where k is Boltzmann's constant 1.38×10^{-16} erg/degree. Equation (3) is a direct consequence of the classical theory of equipartition. The latter demands that the mean kinetic energy per degree of freedom be $\frac{1}{2}kT$, and a harmonic oscillator has equal mean kinetic and potential energies, so that the total energy is kT. Substitution of (3) in (2) yields the Rayleigh-Jeans law

$$\rho_\nu = 8\pi\nu^2 kT/c^3 \tag{4}$$

The fact that ρ_ν increases without limit when ν is made arbitrarily large is the ultraviolet catastrophe mentioned above.

In quantum theory, however, the mean energy of a harmonic oscillator is taken to be

$$\epsilon_\nu = \frac{h\nu}{e^{h\nu/kT} - 1} \tag{5}$$

This formula is obtained by assuming that the energy of a harmonic oscillator is restricted to the "quantized" values 0, $h\nu$, $2h\nu$, $3h\nu$, ... The mean energy is calculated by weighting these values in accordance with the usual Boltzmann factor, so that

$$\epsilon_\nu = \frac{h\nu e^{-h\nu/kT} + 2h\nu e^{-2h\nu/kT} + \cdots}{1 + e^{-h\nu/kT} + e^{-2h\nu/kT} + \cdots} \qquad (6)$$

The series in the numerator and denominator of (6) are readily summed, and the result is (5). Substitution of (5) in (2) gives

$$\rho_\nu = \frac{8\pi h\nu^3}{c^3} \cdot \frac{1}{e^{h\nu/kT} - 1} \qquad (7)$$

This is the celebrated Planck radiation formula. This represents essentially one approach used by Planck. He also had other ways of obtaining his formula, but most of these have been discarded. The best present derivation of the Planck radiation formula is probably one made by Albert Einstein in 1916, which is based on so-called detailed balancing for a system of matter and radiation.

2. Specific Heats.—Another early success of quantum theory was in the field of specific heats, where it explained the deviations from the law of P. L. Dulong and A. T. Petit. This law states that the specific heat per gram atom is very nearly the same, about six calories, for many solid elements. However, there are many exceptions. Also, if the temperature is lowered sufficiently, the specific heat approaches zero, instead of remaining constant, as predicted by the law. The behaviour of three metals, for instance, is shown in fig. 2. The law of Dulong and Petit is a direct consequence of the classical theory of equipartition, pro-

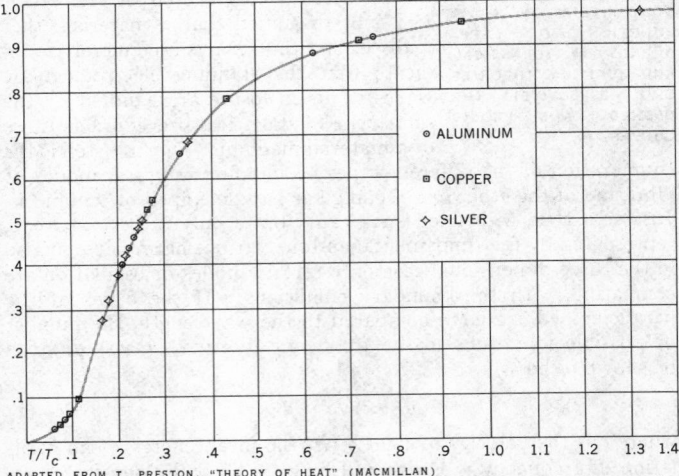

ADAPTED FROM T. PRESTON, "THEORY OF HEAT" (MACMILLAN)

FIG. 2.—SPECIFIC HEAT OF A MONATOMIC SOLID AS A FUNCTION OF TEMPERATURE. THE CURVE IS CALCULATED FROM DEBYE'S QUANTUM THEORY. THE SCALE OF ORDINATES IS SO CHOSEN THAT CLASSICAL THEORY GIVES UNITY

vided the latter is applied to the atom as a whole and no attempt is made arbitrarily to apply classical statistics to the motion of the electrons inside the atom. The specific heat is then independent of temperature, and so in fig. 2 would be represented by a horizontal straight line of unit height in the scale employed there. Debye's quantum model, on the other hand, yields the solid curve, which is in good agreement with experiment. This curve approaches unity if the temperature is raised sufficiently. More generally, all classical and quantum theories of specific heats agree asymptotically at high temperatures. On the other hand, the vanishing of the specific heat at the absolute zero is a characteristic quantum phenomenon.

In the mathematical analysis the difference between the classical and quantum theories of the specific heats of solids parallels closely that between the proofs of the Rayleigh-Jeans and Planck laws for radiation. Instead of considering the electromagnetic vibrations of the ether, it is necessary to deal with the vibrations of the atoms composing the solid with respect to each other. If the forces binding the atoms to their equilibrium positions obey

Hooke's law, the vibrations are simple harmonic. The dynamical system represented by the aggregate of atoms constituting the solid obviously is exceedingly complicated, but, in principle, modes of vibration can be sorted out according to frequency. Let there be $n_\nu d\nu$ such modes in the interval $(\nu, \nu + d\nu)$. Let the mean energy of a harmonic vibration be denoted by ϵ_ν, which, as before, has the value (3) or (5) depending on whether classical or quantum theory is used. The total energy is obtained by integrating over all frequencies, and the specific heat c_V is the temperature derivative of the energy. Hence

$$c_V = \frac{d}{dT}\left[\int_0^\infty n_\nu \epsilon_\nu d\nu \right] \qquad (8)$$

The determination of the factor n_ν specifying the distribution of vibration frequencies represents an exceedingly difficult problem, as n_ν is no longer given by the simple expression (1) which applied in the radiative case. However, if the classical result $\epsilon_\nu = kT$ is employed, it is not necessary to determine n_ν, as kT is merely a constant factor, which can be taken outside the integration. The integral can then be immediately evaluated from the relation

$$\int_0^\infty n_\nu d\nu = 3N \qquad (9)$$

which states that the total number of independent modes of oscillation (i.e., the total number of degrees of freedom) must be three times the total number of atoms N. Hence, according to classical equipartition,

$$c_V = 3Nk \qquad (10)$$

This is essentially the law of Dulong and Petit. If we take an amount of material equal to a gram atom, so that N becomes the Avogadro number, and if we express the specific heat in calories rather than in ergs, then (10) gives a specific heat of 5.96 cal. per degree.

In quantum theory, on the other hand, it is necessary to evaluate n_ν. Peter J. W. Debye assumed a distribution law for n_ν analogous to that (1) for the radiative case, but with allowance for transverse and longitudinal vibrations with different velocities of propagation, which can be calculated from the elastic constants of the material. There is then no limit to the high-frequency end of the spectrum, and the integrals in (8) and (9) diverge. To avoid this difficulty the upper limit in (8) and (9) is rather artificially taken to be ν_c rather than ∞, where ν_c is a cutoff frequency so chosen as to satisfy (9) and thus make the total number of vibrations equal to $3N$. With this model, Debye found $c_V = f(T/T_c)$, where $f(T/T_c)$ is a universal function of a reduced temperature T/T_c, which is the ratio of the ordinary temperature to a so-called characteristic temperature T_c calculable from the elastic properties of the material. This reduced temperature is used for the abscissa in fig. 2. Debye's method for obtaining n_ν originally appeared somewhat artificial, but Born and Theodore von Kármán showed that it had some dynamical basis. The Debye model applies only to simple monatomic solids. When the solid is composed of molecules, it is necessary to consider the vibrations not only of molecules with respect to each other but also the vibrations of atoms inside the molecules. As emphasized by Einstein, the latter effect gives sharp maxima of n_ν at certain frequencies. Improved methods of calculating n_ν have been developed, and the theory correspondingly refined. So far only the solids have been mentioned. There is also considerable literature on the specific heats of gases. Here again, quantum theory explains deviations from the classical theory of equipartition, especially at low temperatures, which are particularly pronounced for hydrogen.

3. Photoelectricity.—Nowhere, perhaps, is the inadequacy of classical theory revealed more strikingly than in the subject of photoelectricity, which is concerned with emission of electrons by an illuminated body. (See PHOTOELECTRICITY.) Photoelectric phenomena exhibit two main features: (1) no emission occurs at all unless the frequency ν of the incident radiation exceeds a certain critical value, called the threshold frequency; and (2) the kinetic energy of the ejected electrons depends on the frequency of this radiation, and not on its intensity. In other words, if a light source is removed farther and farther from the body which it illuminates, the emitted electrons are undiminished in their velocity of escape, but are decreased in number. Such a state of affairs was a complete conundrum at the end of the 19th century, since in classical electromagnetic theory, diminished incident intensity implies a lowering of the energy traversing the absorbing target area, and thus as a result of the lower energy flow, the velocity imparted to the electron should be decreased, contrary to experiment. In 1905 Einstein showed that the observed behaviour could be explained if in the emission of the electron a quantum of energy $h\nu$ is picked up by matter from the radiation, regardless of the latter's intensity. The process merely becomes less likely when the intensity is low. Just how such a corpuscular model was to be reconciled with the undulatory features of light, such as interference, was something not understood for two decades or so, but was finally clarified by the Heisenberg uncertainty principle and by Bohr's theory of complementarity. From the less sophisticated outlook of 1905, Einstein showed that if the conflict with the wave viewpoint was ignored, his picture did indeed account for the salient factors of photoelectricity. The kinetic energy of escape of the electron will not in general be the same as the quantum $h\nu$ absorbed from the radiation inasmuch as part of the energy is consumed in liberating the electron from the metal. This portion is called the thermionic work function, and will be denoted by the letter ϕ. Einstein's equation for determining the velocity of escape v of an electron is thus

$$\tfrac{1}{2}mv^2 = h\nu - \phi \tag{11}$$

Since the kinetic energy $\tfrac{1}{2}mv^2$ is necessarily positive, emission is possible only if $\nu > \phi/h$. Hence ϕ/h is the threshold frequency. Closely related to the photoelectric effect is the Compton effect (q.v.), which also reveals the need of the quantum hypothesis.

III. BOHR ATOM

A signal advance in quantum theory was achieved when the Danish physicist Niels Bohr propounded his theory of the spectrum of hydrogen, in 1913. By that time there was confidence as to the validity of the Rutherford picture of the atom as a miniature solar system, with the nucleus and electrons playing respectively the role of the sun and the planets. (See ATOM.) The number of electrons in the neutral atom is the same as the chemists' atomic number, one for hydrogen, two for helium, etc. Therefore, the dynamics of the orbits of the electrons in the various atoms will be very complex except in the hydrogenic case, for the mathematical difficulties associated with even a three-body problem (e.g., neutral helium, with one nucleus and two valence electrons) are enormous. By a hydrogenic atom is not necessarily meant a hydrogen atom, but any other atom which has been stripped of all but one valence electron as a result of ionization. Examples are singly ionized helium, doubly ionized lithium, etc. Clearly, the study of the spectrum of hydrogen, because of its comparative simplicity, should be the most likely starting point of any attempt to decipher the complexities of atomic spectra.

1. Balmer Formula.—It has long been known that there are some remarkable regularities in the spectrum of hydrogen. As early as 1885, J. J. Balmer showed that the wavelengths λ of many lines are well represented by the empirical formula

$$\frac{1}{\lambda} = RZ^2\left[\frac{1}{n'^2} - \frac{1}{n''^2}\right] \tag{12}$$

in which n', n'' are integers, and R is a constant, the so-called Rydberg constant. If, for instance, one takes $n' = 2$ and $n'' = n' + 1, n' + 2, \ldots$, the expression (12) gives the wavelengths of the lines in what is called the Balmer series. The choices $n' = 1$, 3, 4 and 5 yield respectively the Lyman, Paschen, Brackett and Pfund series, which were discovered later. Since the atomic number Z is unity for hydrogen, the factor Z^2 in (12) is unnecessary for present purposes, but is included to permit later extension to atoms of higher nuclear charge.

2. Postulates of the Bohr Theory.—For many years, the raison d'être for the formula (12) was completely obscure. It is not surprising that the subject of line spectra was a closed book to the classical physicist. As some one has said, the task of constructing a model of the atom merely from knowledge of its spectra radiated under violent electrical or thermal excitation is comparable with trying to learn about a piano merely from the noise emitted when it is dropped downstairs. Bohr, however, showed that the behaviour (12) could be explained by means of two postulates, as follows:

1. The existence of stationary states: In every atom there is a discrete succession of states, in any one of which the electrons can move without appreciable radiation, and which can be identified by a set of integers, usually called quantum numbers. The designation of these states as stationary refers to the absence of radiation from the orbits, in contravention of classical electrodynamics, and does not imply a static atom. Except for omission of the radiation corrections, the motion of the electrons in the stationary states is assumed to conform to the laws of classical mechanics.

2. The Bohr frequency condition: It is assumed that an electron can sometimes pass discontinuously from one allowed orbit to another. In such a transition, the initial and final states will have different amounts of mechanical energy E'' and E'. To secure conservation of energy, the change in the mechanical energy must be counterbalanced by the absorption or emission of a light quantum, whose energy is $h\nu$ if the frequency is ν. This requirement yields the so-called Bohr frequency condition

$$h\nu = E'' - E' \tag{13}$$

The analogy to Einstein's photoelectric equation (11) should be noted.

In connection with the first postulate it is necessary to formulate the quantum conditions which restrict the energies of the atoms to certain particular values. The easiest case to handle is that of a simply periodic system, where the orbit repeats itself after a given interval of time τ. Here the quantization is effected by the relation

$$\overline{T} = \tfrac{1}{2}nh\nu_0 \tag{14}$$

in which n is an integer, $\overline{T}$ is the mean kinetic energy of the system (i.e., the average of the kinetic energy T over a period) and $\nu_0 = 1/\tau$ is the frequency with which the orbit repeats itself. It is to be emphasized that the orbital frequency ν_0 is in general not the same as that ν given by the Bohr frequency condition (13). This nonidentity of the orbital and radiated frequencies is a celebrated paradox of the Bohr atom, as according to classical mechanics or actual observations on large-scale phenomena there is no distinction between the frequencies of motion of a system and those of the waves which it radiates. It should be mentioned, however, that in the Bohr theory there is an asymptotic agreement of the two frequencies for large quantum numbers, which is usually termed the "correspondence principle for frequencies."

3. Derivation of the Balmer Formula From the Bohr Theory.—It will now be shown that the Balmer expression (12) is a consequence of the quantum condition (14) and the Bohr frequency condition. This derivation is such a simple and classic one that it seems worth giving, even though in a sense it is outmoded by later but more intricate calculations by means of wave mechanics, which also yield the result (12) with identically the same value of the Rydberg constant R as that obtained from the Bohr theory.

To simplify the calculations, it will be assumed that the orbit is circular, but it can be shown that the energy levels are no different in the general case of ellipses. Let the mass of the nucleus and electron be denoted by M and m respectively, and let the nuclear and electronic charges be Ze and $-e$. Here e has the value 4.80×10^{-10} in electrostatic units, and Z is the atomic number. The centre of gravity, which may be supposed stationary, divides the line connecting the two particles in the inverse ratio of their masses. Hence, the electron and nucleus revolve around this centre in circles of radii $Ma/(m + M)$ and $ma/(m + M)$ respectively, where a is the distance from the nucleus to the electron. Since the angular velocity is $2\pi\nu_0$, the kinetic energy is

$$T = \tfrac{1}{2}\left[m\left(\frac{M}{m+M}\right)^2 + M\left(\frac{m}{m+M}\right)^2\right](2\pi\nu_0)^2 a^2 \quad (15)$$

This equation can also be written as

$$T = \tfrac{1}{2}\mu(2\pi\nu_0)^2 a^2 \quad (16)$$

where μ is the so-called reduced mass, given by

$$\mu = mM/(m + M) \quad (17)$$

As T is constant in time, there is no distinction between T and $\bar{T}$. Thus application of the quantum condition (14) gives

$$(2\pi\nu_0)\mu a^2 = nh/2\pi \quad (18)$$

In other words, the angular momentum of the system is an integral multiple of $h/2\pi$. The equality between the centrifugal force on the electron and the Coulomb attraction due to the nucleus yields a further relation

$$\mu a(2\pi\nu_0)^2 = Ze^2/a^2 \quad (19)$$

When equations (18) and (19) are solved for a and ν_0, the result is

$$a = n^2 h^2/4\pi^2 Ze^2\mu \qquad \nu_0 = 4\pi^2\mu Z^2 e^4/n^3 h^3 \quad (20)$$

The first relation of (20) shows that the allowed (i.e., quantized) values of the radius of the atom form a progression of the form $a_0, 4a_0, 9a_0, \cdots$, where a_0 is a fundamental unit $h^2/4\pi^2 Ze^2$ called the Bohr radius, and having the numerical value 0.53×10^{-8} cm. if $Z = 1$ (hydrogen). Substitution of (20) in (16) gives

$$T = 2\pi^2\mu Z^2 e^4/n^2 h^2$$

while the potential energy is

$$V = -Ze^2/a = -4\pi^2\mu Z^2 e^4/n^2 h^2$$

Hence the total energy $E = T + V$ is

$$E = -2\pi^2\mu Z^2 e^4/n^2 h^2 \quad (21)$$

When we substitute this value of E in the Bohr frequency condition (13) and remember that $\lambda = c/\nu$, we have indeed the Balmer formula (12), provided the Rydberg constant R has the value

$$R = 2\pi^2\mu e^4/ch^3 \quad (22)$$

The question immediately arises whether (22) yields a value of R in agreement with the optical measurements, when the numerical values of the constants e, h, μ, c are substituted. The answer is that there is certainly agreement within the precision with which these constants are known, for e, h, μ are known only to 1 part in 10,000 or so. On the other hand, since optical wavelengths are known so very accurately, the Rydberg constant R can be determined to within less than 1 part in 1,000,000. A valuable cross-check on the values of the various atomic constants is thus provided: namely, use of (22) along with the spectroscopic determination of R permits determination of one of the four quantities e, h, μ, c if the other three are known. It is thus possible to increase the accuracy with which the value of the particular one of the four constants is known (viz., h) which otherwise cannot be as precisely determined as the other three.

4. Correction for the Motion of the Nucleus, and Spectroscopic Determination of e/m.

If we neglect the motion of the nucleus, or in other words consider the mass M of the nucleus to be infinite, then equation (17) shows that the reduced mass becomes identical with the mass m of the electron. When allowance is made for the finite mass of the nucleus, μ will differ slightly from m. The neutral hydrogen atom and ionized helium atom resemble each other in having only one electron, so that formula (22) should be applicable to either. However, the different masses of the hydrogen and helium nuclei will make the Rydberg constant slightly different for the two. Just this state

of affairs is found experimentally: the best spectroscopic value of the Rydberg constant for hydrogen is $R_H = 109677.58$ cm.$^{-1}$, while that for helium is $R_{He} = 109722.27$ cm.$^{-1}$ (J. W. M. Du Mond and E. R. Cohen). The corresponding value for a hydrogenic atom of infinite nuclear mass is $R_{H\infty} = 109737.31$ cm.$^{-1}$.

Equation (22) shows that the ratio of the Rydberg constants for hydrogen and ionized helium is equal to the ratio of the reduced masses, the other constants canceling out. When (17) is used,

$$\frac{R_{He}}{R_H} = \frac{1 + m/M_H}{1 + m/xM_H} \quad (23)$$

where x is the ratio M_{He}/M_H of the mass of the helium nucleus to that of hydrogen. This ratio can be regarded as known from determinations of atomic weights, since practically all of the atom's mass arises from the nucleus. Hence, by means of (23) and the spectroscopic determinations of R_H, R_{He}, it is possible to evaluate the ratio m/M_H of electronic to protonic mass. Furthermore, it is possible to go a step further and determine e/m spectroscopically, inasmuch as one has $e/m = (e/M_H)(M_H/m)$ and as the value of e/M_H is known from electrolysis; i.e., from the so-called electrochemical equivalent. In this way, the shift between the Rydberg constants for hydrogen and ionized helium furnishes perhaps the most accurate means of determining e/m. In the early 1930s there appeared to be a discrepancy between the values of e/m determined spectroscopically and by more direct deflection methods. This difficulty has disappeared, and the generally accepted value of e/m is 1.759×10^7 e.m.u.

During the first years of Bohr's theory, the only known hydrogenic atoms (i.e., those with one valence electron) were H and He$^+$. Subsequently, X-ray measurements at Uppsala, Swed., revealed lines due to Li^{2+}, Be^{3+}, B^{4+}, and C^{5+}. These lines are particularly useful because they furnish wavelength standards in the X-ray region. Another subsequent development was the discovery of the hydrogen isotope deuterium, which has about double the value of M for ordinary hydrogen and hence a slightly different Rydberg constant. This difference, in fact, historically furnished the first means of demonstrating the existence of deuterium with certainty.

5. Relativity Fine Structure.

A great triumph of the Bohr atom was the theory of the relativity fine structure in hydrogen, which was developed by Arnold Sommerfeld in 1916. In the preceding discussion, the problem was treated by means of Newtonian mechanics. When the relativity corrections are introduced, the orbits cease to be periodic, and the quantization becomes more complicated. It is necessary to introduce two quantum conditions, mathematical details of which will be omitted here except for mentioning that they restrict the values of certain so-called "phase integrals" to integral multiples of Planck's constant. If the nuclear mass is treated as infinite, the formula for the energy can be shown to be

$$E = mc^2\left\{\left[1 + \left(\frac{\alpha Z}{n - k + g}\right)^2\right]^{-\tfrac{1}{2}} - 1\right\} \quad (24)$$

where

$$\alpha = 2\pi e^2/hc \qquad g = (k^2 - Z^2\alpha^2)^{\tfrac{1}{2}} \quad (25)$$

If (24) be expanded as a power series in α^2, and terms beyond α^4 are disregarded, the expression for E takes the form

$$E = -\frac{2\pi^2 m Z^2 e^4}{n^2 h^2}\left[1 + \frac{\alpha^2 Z^2}{n^2}\left(\frac{n}{k} - \frac{3}{4}\right) + \cdots\right] \quad (26)$$

Since $m = \mu$ if $M = \infty$, the first term of (26) is the same as the Newtonian result (21), and involves only the principal quantum number n. The remainder of (26) is due to the relativity corrections, and involves a second quantum number k, which is the so-called azimuthal quantum number. Its physical significance is that the angular momentum is $kh/2\pi$, and the range of values for k is $1, 2, \cdots n$. The dependence of the energy on k is only a minor effect because of the smallness of α ($= 1/137.0$), but it causes lines which would otherwise coincide to be slightly separated so as to form the components of a multiplet. A decomposition is indeed found experimentally, and on the whole the observed spacing of the components agrees well with theory.

6. Stark Effect.—Still another quantitative success of the Bohr theory of the hydrogen spectrum is provided by the Stark effect, or splitting of the energy levels and hence of the spectral lines by means of an electric field. The separation and number of the components accords with theory in a remarkable fashion. The formulas for the displacement in frequency involve Planck's constant h, and so classical theory was powerless to explain any of the features of the Stark effect. On the other hand, in the alternative phenomenon of the Zeeman effect (separation of lines in a magnetic field), Planck's h cancels out of the final formula for the shift in frequency, and so classical and quantum theories give identical results for the normal Zeeman effect (*q.v.*).

7. Moseley's Relation.—In attempting to apply the Bohr concepts to nonhydrogenic atoms, the mathematical complexities are so great that the permitted energy levels or frequencies cannot be exactly determined. Nevertheless, certain successes of the theory should be stressed. One of these is the explanation of Moseley's relation in X-ray spectra, wherein the frequencies of the K lines—*i.e.*, the hardest lines (lines of shortest wavelength or highest frequency)—are proportional approximately to the square of the atomic number. This is simply an expression of the factor Z^2 in (21). The result (21) applies approximately to an interior electron of a nonhydrogenic atom if the screening of the nucleus by the other electrons is so poor that the field is substantially that of the bare nucleus. This approximation will be a good one only for electrons which are deep-seated in the atom, such as are responsible for the emission of X-rays.

8. Relation Between Critical Potentials and Spectral Frequencies.—By electron bombardment it is possible to "excite" an atom from one stationary state, say of energy E', to another of higher energy E''. To be able to do this, the impinging electron must have at least a kinetic energy equal to $E'' - E'$, as otherwise conservation of energy cannot be secured. The energy which an electron acquires in falling through a difference of potential V is Ve. Hence, the minimum or "critical" accelerating potential required for the excitation is given by $Ve = E'' - E'$. Alternatively, the Bohr frequency condition states that $h\nu = E'' - E'$. Thus, $Ve = h\nu$, and this relation holds as a useful consequence of the theory, even though the mechanics of the many-body problem is so intricate that it is not possible to calculate theoretically the energy levels E', E''.

9. Stern-Gerlach Effect.—The application of the quantum conditions to an atom in a magnetic field shows that its component of angular momentum in the direction of the field should be "quantized" and equal to an integral multiple of $h/2\pi$. The corresponding magnetic moment, which is proportional to the angular momentum, should hence likewise acquire only discrete values. Otto Stern and Walther Gerlach verified this prediction by observing the deflections of atoms in an inhomogeneous magnetic field. We cannot overemphasize how beautifully the existence of only certain particular deflections in their experiments offers evidence for the existence of the quantized positions which are the essence of quantum theory. It is clear that the explanation of the precise quantitative values of the deflections found by Stern and Gerlach requires inclusion of electron spin and the refinements of quantum mechanics in certain cases. However, the broad outlines of the phenomenon were sharp even in the days of the Bohr theory, especially the complete contradiction between the classical continuous distribution of orientations and quantum discreteness. The Stern-Gerlach experiment decided unequivocally in favour of the latter.

10. Harmonic Oscillator and Rotator—Molecular Spectra.—There are two very simple schematic models which are particularly easy to quantize and which are rich in physical applications. They are the harmonic oscillator and the rigid rotator or "rotating dumbbell."

For a particle which is harmonically bound (*i.e.*, subject to a linear restoring force) the mean kinetic energy is equal to the mean potential energy. Hence the total energy, which is the sum of the kinetic and potential, is equal to twice the mean kinetic

energy. Furthermore, the frequency ν_0 of a harmonic oscillator is independent of the initial conditions. Therefore, application of (14) immediately yields the result

$$E = nh\nu_0 \tag{27}$$

The quantized values of the energy of a harmonic system given in (27) are the same as those used above in discussing black-body radiation and specific heats.

For a rigid rotator, there is no potential energy, and the kinetic energy has the constant value $\frac{1}{2}I(2\pi\nu_0)^2$, where I is the moment of inertia, and ν_0 is the rotation frequency. The quantum condition (14) yields $2\pi\nu_0 I = nh/2\pi$. The quantization thus consists in equating the angular momentum to an integral multiple of $h/2\pi$. The corresponding quantized value of the energy is, since $E = T$,

$$E = n^2h^2/8\pi^2I \tag{28}$$

These formulas have a direct application to the spectrum of a diatomic molecule such as HCl. As a first approximation, the energy of the molecule can be divided into contributions from (1) the electronic motion relative to the two nuclei regarded as fixed attracting centres, (2) the vibration of the two nuclei along the line connecting them, and (3) "end-over-end" rotation of the molecule as a whole. Effects (2) and (3) are respectively portrayed by the harmonic oscillator and the rotator. The quantum numbers associated with (2) and (3) are not, of course, the same, and so the letters v, J are used for them instead of n. The total energy of the molecule is thus

$$E = E_e + vh\nu_0 + J^2h^2/8\pi^2I \tag{29}$$

The electronic term E_e will be a function of numerous quantum numbers other than v, J, but is too difficult to compute explicitly because of the complexities of the many-body problem. The dependence on the vibrational and rotational quantum numbers v, J predicted by (29) agrees nicely with experiment.

11. Intensities and Transition Probabilities in the Bohr Theory.—The theory so far presented is one-sided, as it tells how to calculate the frequency but nothing about the intensity. In order to have information about the latter, it is necessary to know the transition probability. It is a fundamental concept of the Bohr theory that radiation takes place sporadically and discontinuously, when an electron passes from one stationary state to another, rather than continuously as in classical theory. The transitions between states are governed by the statistics of random processes, like radioactive decay. Thus, if an electron is initially in a state l, there is a certain probability $A_{l \to m}$ that it will pass to another state m. Let us denote by $\nu(lm)$ the frequency associated with this transition, which by (13) is the same as $(E_l - E_m)/h$. Since an amount of energy $h\nu(lm)$ is radiated in each transition, the total rate at which energy is radiated in the frequency $\nu(lm)$ is

$$I_{l \to m} = h\nu(lm)A_{l \to m}N_l \tag{30}$$

where N_l is the number of atoms in the state l.

Part of the contribution to $A_{l \to m}$ in the case of emission, and all in the case of absorption, will come from transitions induced by a radiation field. Even in the absence of the latter, however, there is a certain probability of "spontaneous radiation," provided the energy E_m of the final state is less than that E_l of the initial one. For simplicity, only the spontaneous effect will be considered.

The problem is now to calculate the transition probability in the absence of a radiation field. Here the Bohr theory gave no clear-cut answer. The best that could be done was to make an approximate estimate by means of the so-called correspondence principle, which has been described as a "magic wand which enables one to borrow the results of classical theory for quantum theory." According to classical electrodynamics, an electron moving in a periodic orbit described by Fourier series such as

$$x = \sum_{\tau=-\infty}^{\infty} x_\tau e^{2\pi i \tau \nu_0 t}$$

radiates energy in the harmonic $\tau\nu_0$ at a rate

$$(4e^2/3c^3)(2\pi\tau\nu_0)^4[|x_\tau|^2 + |y_\tau|^2 + |z_\tau|^2]$$

The correspondence principle for frequencies shows that if the difference in quantum number between the initial and final states is τ, the quantum frequency $\nu(lm)$ approaches asymptotically the classical overtone $\tau\nu_0$ if the quantum number is large. Hence, a formula by which the transition probability can be estimated qualitatively or asymptotically is

$$A_{l\rightarrow m} = (4e^2/3hc^3)(2\pi)^4\nu(lm)^3[|x_{l-m}|^2 + |y_{l-m}|^2 + |z_{l-m}|^2] \quad (31)$$

It is to be emphasized that (31) never gives a clear-cut and unambiguous answer, as there is no way of telling whether the Fourier coefficients should be evaluated for the initial or the final orbit of the transition, or should represent some sort of compromise between the two.

IV. ADVENT OF TRUE QUANTUM MECHANICS

Although the Bohr theory had the many triumphs indicated above, still as time progressed, especially in the early 1920s, it became increasingly apparent that it was not adequate. With much labour it was possible to determine the energy levels of the neutral helium atom, a three-body problem, and these did not accord with experiment. Unjustifiable half-quantum numbers (*i.e.*, half rather than whole integers) kept appearing in the empirical description of band spectra. Numerous other difficulties could be recited. It was clear that the trouble was simply that the traditional Bohr quantum theory was a patchwork doctoring of classical mechanics, wherein the quantum conditions were added in a rather artificial way. What was needed was a rational, self-consistent quantum mechanics, which started afresh and evolved a mathematical framework and philosophy all its own. This was discovered in 1926, which was thus an epoch-making year in the history of physics.

This remarkable new mechanics cannot be regarded as the product of any one man, and was instead the result of the impact of thinker on thinker among the leading theoretical physicists of the time. It was developed in a diversity of mathematical forms, which present a rather confusing array to the student beginning the subject. However, these various formulations, though different in superficial mathematical structure, are basically in harmony with each other.

The three main mathematical forms are the following: (1) the matrix theory of Born, Heisenberg and Jordan; (2) Schrödinger's wave mechanics, the outgrowth of De Broglie's concept of "phase waves"; and (3) the so-called transformation theory, based on kinetical indeterminism, developed by Dirac and Jordan, and interpreted by Heisenberg.

A. WAVE MECHANICS

1. Hamiltonian Analogy and De Broglie Waves.—We shall begin with the so-called wave formulation, as this is the version most universally used, and perhaps the easiest to understand. The impetus to the development of this form of quantum mechanics was furnished by De Broglie's interpretation of the classical Hamiltonian analogy between optics and dynamics. This analogy, which is readily demonstrated from Fermat's principle in optics and the principle of least action in mechanics, establishes a formal similarity between the path of the particle in a mechanical system and a hypothetical optical system in which the refractive index is correlated in a rather arbitrary way with the potential energy $V(x, y, z)$ in the mechanical problem. This comparison always seemed highly artificial because the velocity in the optical system was different from that in the mechanical one. However, if somehow it is possible to introduce the concept of wavelength into the analogy, so that it is meaningful to talk about dispersion, then besides the phase velocity there is also a group velocity, which is the velocity with which signals or modulations are propagated.

De Broglie showed that although the velocity of the mechanical particle differed from the phase velocity, it became identical with the group velocity, provided the wavelength has the value

$$\lambda = \frac{h}{\sqrt{2m(E - V)}} = \frac{h}{mv} \quad (32)$$

The second form of (32) is obtained by noting that the energy constant E is the sum of the kinetic energy $\frac{1}{2}mv^2$ and the potential energy $V(x, y, z)$. Formula (32) gives the celebrated De Broglie wavelength which occurs so characteristically in quantum-mechanical diffraction problems. When De Broglie first propounded his ideas in 1925, it was not clear whether they had much physical significance, but only a year or so after his paper, the existence of the De Broglie wavelength was confirmed in a most striking fashion in the experiments of Clinton J. Davisson and Lester H. Germer on the diffraction of electrons by a crystal. They showed that beams of electrons passing through a crystal were diffracted in many ways like X-rays, but with the wavelength given by the formula $\lambda = h/mv$.

2. Schrödinger Wave Equation.—Prior, however, to the Davisson-Germer experiments, Schrödinger recognized the great portent of the De Broglie wavelength, and by means of it was led to the fundamental equation of wave mechanics, usually called the wave equation. Schrödinger conjectured that true quantum mechanics stands in the same relation to ordinary classical mechanics that physical optics does to geometrical optics. Just as the ray-tracing characteristic of the latter fails in explaining the phenomena of diffraction and interference, so, Schrödinger reasoned, ordinary mechanics could not explain atomic phenomena, the reason in each case being that the dimensions are not large compared to the wavelength. Hence he sought to establish a procedure analogous to that used in physical optics, in which the fundamental wave equation is

$$\frac{\partial^2 f}{\partial x^2} + \frac{\partial^2 f}{\partial y^2} + \frac{\partial^2 f}{\partial z^2} = \frac{1}{u^2}\frac{\partial^2 f}{\partial t^2} \quad (33)$$

Here the phase velocity u may be a function of x, y, z. In the monochromatic, or periodic, case, the solutions can be written in the form $f = \psi(x, y, z)e^{2\pi i\nu t}$, where the space factor ψ satisfies the equation

$$\frac{\partial^2 \psi}{\partial x^2} + \frac{\partial^2 \psi}{\partial y^2} + \frac{\partial^2 \psi}{\partial z^2} = \frac{4\pi^2}{\lambda^2}\psi \quad (34)$$

with $\lambda = u/\nu$. For the wavelength λ, Schrödinger inserted the De Broglie value (32). Then (34) becomes

$$\frac{\partial^2 \psi}{\partial x^2} + \frac{\partial^2 \psi}{\partial y^2} + \frac{\partial^2 \psi}{\partial z^2} + \frac{8\pi^2 m}{h^2}(E - V)\psi = 0 \quad (35)$$

This is the Schrödinger wave equation. One immediately wonders how quantized phenomena can be extracted from (35), as a partial differential equation suggests things continuous rather than discrete. The answer is that one must confine one's attention to so-called physically admissible, or, colloquially, "civilized" solutions of (35), which meet certain requirements of continuity, single-valuedness, etc. Solutions which fulfill these demands are called characteristic functions, proper functions or eigenfunctions. The precise conditions that these physically admissible solutions need to meet vary somewhat with the physical nature of the problem. It is usually sufficient that ψ be single-valued, continuous, together with its first derivatives, and finite, except perhaps at a few points at which ψ becomes infinite in such a way that

$$\iiint |\psi|^2 dv \text{ and } \iiint \left\{\left|\frac{\partial\psi}{\partial x}\right|^2 + \left|\frac{\partial\psi}{\partial y}\right|^2 + \left|\frac{\partial\psi}{\partial z}\right|^2\right\} dv$$

exist. Also, ψ must vanish at infinity. Now, to be sure, (35) possesses an infinity of solutions, since the latter involve arbitrary constants of integration and even arbitrary functions. Nevertheless, it often happens that not one of these solutions has the properties demanded of a characteristic function. Instead, an admissible solution is usually obtained only if E is given certain particular values, called characteristic values, proper values or eigenvalues. These values of E are those which are to be substituted into the Bohr frequency condition (13).

3. Rotator and Harmonic Oscillator.—A simple illustration of how the condition that the solution be physically admissible limits the parameter E is provided by the two-dimensional rotator; *i.e.*, the rotating dumbbell whose motion is confined to a plane. Here the wave equation analogous to (35) is given by the expression

$$\frac{\partial^2 \psi}{\partial \varphi^2} + \frac{8\pi^2 I E}{h^2}\psi = 0 \qquad (36)$$

as is seen by specializing (35) to one co-ordinate, with $V = 0$, and noting that in a rotational problem the moment of inertia I and angle φ replace the mass and a linear displacement. The solution of (36) is

$$\psi = A \cos[(8\pi^2 I E/h^2)^{\frac{1}{2}}\varphi - \epsilon] \qquad (37)$$

where A and ϵ are arbitrary constants. The requirement of single-valuedness as a function of position on the circular path of rotation demands that $\psi(\varphi + 2\pi) = \psi(\varphi)$. This is possible only if the coefficient of φ in the argument of the cosine is an integer n. Thus

$$E = n^2 h^2 / 8\pi^2 I \qquad (38)$$

This is exactly the same formula for the energy of a rotator as that (*cf.* equation [28]) obtained with the old quantum theory. It would thus at first appear that the new quantum mechanics did not remove the difficulty that half rather than whole integers are required to obtain agreement with experiment on rotational energy levels. Actually, however, the end-over-end rotation of a molecule should be represented by a rotator not confined to a particular plane, and so associated with a three- rather than two-dimensional space. When this extra degree of freedom is added, it is found that the factor n^2 in (38) is replaced by $(n + \frac{1}{2})^2 - \frac{1}{4}$, so that, apart from an unimportant additive constant, the result is the same as though half quantum numbers were used in the Bohr theory. Details of the analysis are omitted here, but it is essentially the same as that in classical potential theory where it is shown that the characteristic values of the differential equation for surface harmonics are proportional to $n(n + 1)$.

Of course, in most problems the mathematical analysis is more complicated than in this purposely simple illustration of the rotator. When exact, closed expressions are obtained for the characteristic values of a system with one degree of freedom, they are usually derivable by the so-called polynomial method. In this, the solution is expressed as a power series, and it is shown that if the series does not terminate, the solution is not physically admissible. The termination condition then usually restricts the energy parameter E to certain particular or so-called characteristic values.

The polynomial method may be illustrated by the one-dimensional harmonic oscillator. Here the wave equation (35) takes the form

$$\frac{d^2\psi}{dx^2} + \frac{8\pi^2 m}{h^2}(E - \frac{1}{2}ax^2)\psi = 0 \qquad (39)$$

On the introduction of the following abbreviations and changes of variable,

$$A = \frac{4\pi E}{h}\left(\frac{m}{a}\right)^{\frac{1}{2}} \qquad u = \frac{m^{\frac{1}{2}}a^{\frac{1}{2}}(2\pi)^{\frac{1}{2}}}{h^{\frac{1}{2}}}x \qquad \psi = e^{-u^2/2}g \qquad (40)$$

equation (39) becomes

$$\frac{d^2 g}{du^2} - 2u\frac{dg}{du} + (A - 1)g = 0 \qquad (41)$$

A series solution is assumed:

$$g = c_k u^k + c_{k+2}u^{k+2} + c_{k+4}u^{k+4} + \cdots . \qquad (42)$$

After the indicated operations are performed, the entire left side of (41) can be expressed in the form of a series. The coefficient of each power of u in the latter must vanish if (41) is satisfied. The vanishing of the coefficient of the lowest power (viz., u^{k-2}) requires either $k = 0$ or $k = 1$. On equating to zero the coefficient of u^n, one obtains the recurrence formula

$$\frac{c_{n+2}}{c_n} = \frac{2n + 1 - A}{(n + 1)(n + 2)}$$

for determining the ratio c_{n+2}/c_n. The series (42) will terminate at the term $c_n u^n$ if $A = 2n + 1$ or, in other words, by (40) if

$$E = (n + \frac{1}{2})h\nu_0 \quad \text{with} \quad \nu_0 = \frac{1}{2\pi}\left(\frac{a}{m}\right)^{\frac{1}{2}} \qquad (43)$$

It can be shown that if the series does not terminate, then ψ increases without limit as x becomes arbitrarily large, and the solution is not physically admissible. Hence, the only characteristic values of the harmonic oscillator are those given by (43). Comparison with (27) shows that the new quantum mechanics gives the same energy levels for the harmonic oscillator as does the old Bohr theory, except for an additive constant which is equivalent to the use of half quantum numbers in (27). Usually it is unimportant whether the extra term $\frac{1}{2}h\nu_0$ is included, but by study of the shift between the electronic spectra of diatomic molecules differing only in being composed of different isotopes, it is possible to decide experimentally between (27) and (43), and the results unequivocally favour the latter.

4. Hydrogen Atom.—The focal point of the old Bohr theory was its success with the hydrogen atom, and one is naturally anxious to know whether these triumphs are reproduced by wave mechanics. It turns out that the Schrödinger theory usually gives exactly the same energy levels for a hydrogenic atom as did that of Bohr. This remarkable coincidence holds even inclusive of the corrections for the motion of the nucleus, and in the first-order Stark effect. Thus, all the standard achievements of the old Bohr theory regarding the Rydberg constant, hydrogen-helium shift, spectroscopic determination of e/m, etc., are reproduced with wave mechanics. When second powers of the electric field are included in the Stark effect, the results are slightly different with wave mechanics, and the experimental results favour the new formula, though observation of the effect of the second-order corrections requires such high field strengths that precision is difficult. The details of the mathematical analysis will not be given here, but a few salient points will be cited. The calculation for hydrogen is unlike the illustrations of the rotator and oscillator given above, inasmuch as there are three degrees of freedom rather than only one. A problem involving more than one co-ordinate is exactly soluble in wave mechanics as a rule only if the variables are separable; *i.e.*, if co-ordinates can be found such that the wave equation admits a solution which can be resolved into products of factors, each of which involves only one co-ordinate. Fortunately such a decomposition is possible for the hydrogen atom. Variables can be separated by using polar co-ordinates, and the wave function then takes the form

$$\psi = A R_{nl}(r) P_l^{|m_l|}(\cos\theta)e^{im_l\varphi} \qquad (44)$$

Here $P_l^{|m_l|}$ is an associated Legendre function (in which $|m_l|$ is the absolute value of m_l), and R_{nl} is the product of an exponential factor and a polynomial in r (a derivative of the so-called Laguerre polynomial). The constant A is arbitrary, while n, l, m_l are integers. The mathematical problem is very similar to the familiar one of the solution of Laplace's equation in polar co-ordinates, except that the differential equation satisfied by the radial factor is different, no longer admitting a solution in the form of a simple power of r as in the Laplacian case. For the Stark effect, the separation of variables is achieved by using parabolic rather than polar co-ordinates. Both of these types of co-ordinates are special cases of elliptical co-ordinates, and Eisenhart showed generally that if the Schrödinger equation for a single particle admits separation at all, it must be with elliptical co-ordinates.

5. Continuous Spectra.—So far the impression has been given that the characteristic values form a discrete rather than continuous manifold. However, there are certain ranges within which any value of the energy is allowable. The simplest example is furnished by the hydrogen atom. Here, in addition to any of the discrete negative values (21), any positive value of the energy is allowable. The reason for this distinction is the following. The differential equation satisfied by the radial factor of the wave function for the hydrogen atom has two singular points; viz., the origin and the point at infinity. There is always one solution which is regular at the origin, but it will in general increase without limit at infinity if $E < 0$. Only certain special

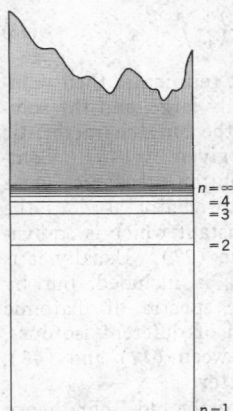

negative values of E avoid this catastrophe, and these are the characteristic values. When, however, the energy constant E is positive, all solutions vanish at infinity, and so the solution which behaves properly at the origin also necessarily does the same at infinity. Hence any positive value of E is a characteristic value. This remark applies even to nonhydrogenic atoms if the origin of the energy is chosen at ionization. The existence of this continuous manifold of positive energy values is reflected experimentally in the continuous absorption beyond the series limit. In fig. 3 the transitions from a fixed lower state to upper states with larger and larger values of n give rise to lines which crowd closer and closer together. Because there can also be transitions to states in the continuum there is a continuous spectrum beyond the limit corresponding to $n = \infty$.

FIG. 3.—DISCRETE AND CONTINUOUS ENERGY LEVELS OF A HYDROGENIC ATOM

There can also be transitions between two values of the energy in the continuous domain, and it is by this mechanism that the continuous X-ray spectrum is emitted from the anode of an X-ray tube.

6. More General Form of the Wave Equation.—So far, in (35), we have given the form of the wave equation for a conservative system consisting of a single particle and having a definite energy. We need a rule for forming the wave equation in other cases, involving either more than one particle or an indefinite energy, or both. In classical theory a conservative system necessarily has a definite, constant energy, but in quantum mechanics this need not be so, as is discussed below more fully in connection with the Heisenberg uncertainty principle. As a result, it is no longer redundant to say that a conservative system has a definite energy. The more general scheme for forming the wave equation given here also applies to the nonconservative case in which the potential energy V contains the time explicitly.

The procedure is as follows. First of all, the Hamiltonian technique is to be used; i.e., the system is to have associated with it a classical Hamiltonian function $H(q_1, \cdots, q_f, p_1, \cdots, p_f, t)$, which is a function of the co-ordinates and momenta. We replace p_k by the operator $\frac{h}{2\pi i} \frac{\partial}{\partial q_k}$, and in this fashion we can form a linear differential equation

$$\left[H\left(q_1, \cdots, q_f, \frac{h}{2\pi i} \frac{\partial}{\partial q_1}, \cdots, \frac{h}{2\pi i} \frac{\partial}{\partial q_f}, t \right) + \frac{h}{2\pi i} \frac{\partial}{\partial t} \right] \Psi = 0 \quad (45)$$

This is the general wave equation. One is led to it primarily by comparison with other forms of quantum mechanics, especially transformation theory, rather than through the De Broglie and Schrödinger interpretation of the Hamiltonian analogy.

In case the system is conservative, so that t does not enter explicitly, (45) will admit a solution of the form

$$\Psi = e^{-2\pi i E_m t/h} \psi_m(q_1, \cdots, q_f) \quad (46)$$

where ψ_m is independent of t and satisfies the equation

$$\left[H\left(q_1, \cdots, q_f, \frac{h}{2\pi i} \frac{\partial}{\partial q_1}, \cdots, \frac{h}{2\pi i} \frac{\partial}{\partial q_f} \right) - E_m \right] \psi_m = 0 \quad (47)$$

However, (46) does not represent the most general solution of (45) for a conservative system, which is

$$\Psi = \sum_m c_m e^{-2\pi i E_m t/h} \psi_m \quad (48)$$

where the summation is over all the characteristic values E_m and where the c_m are arbitrary constants. The expression (46) presupposes that the energy has a definite value, whereas (48) does not involve this restriction.

Equation (47) reduces to (35) for a one-particle system, where the classical Hamiltonian function is $(p_x^2 + p_y^2 + p_z^2)/2m + V$.

To include the correction for the motion of the nucleus, it is necessary to add to this Hamiltonian function an extra term $(p_\xi^2 + p_\eta^2 + p_\zeta^2)/2M$, where M and p_ξ, p_η, p_ζ are respectively the mass and components of momentum of the nucleus. It is, of course, then necessary to use the general equation (47) rather than (35). It can be shown that the variables can be separated by changing them from x, y, z, ξ, η, ζ to X, Y, Z, r, θ, φ where X, Y, Z are the Cartesian co-ordinates of the centre of gravity, and r, θ, φ are polar co-ordinates with origin at the nucleus. The solution of the wave equation takes a form similar to (44) except that there is an extra factor $e^{ik_1 X} e^{ik_2 Y} e^{ik_3 Z}$ which allows for the motion of the centre of gravity of the system, and in which k_1, k_2, k_3 are arbitrary constants. The differential equation satisfied by the "internal" part of the wave function (i.e., the part depending on r, θ, φ) can be shown to be the same as for the one-body problem, in which the nuclear motion is disregarded, except that the reduced mass (17) appears in place of the electronic mass m. The total energy—i.e., the characteristic value of (47)—is the sum of the internal energy given by (21) and an extra term $(k_1^2 + k_2^2 + k_3^2)h^2/8\pi^2(m + M)$ which represents the translational kinetic energy of the centre of gravity of the system. In the discussion of the Bohr theory above, this translational energy was omitted, but its inclusion in the Bohr frequency condition introduces a correction to the frequency which is essentially the quantum analogue of the classical Doppler effect, and yields results substantially equivalent to the latter.

An important property of (47) is that its solutions can be shown to be orthogonal, provided the operator is of the so-called self-adjoint type. This condition is one which can practically always be met. If, in addition, the arbitrary proportionality constants in the wave function are so chosen that they are normalized to unity, one has the relation

$$\int \psi_l^* \psi_m d\tau = \delta_m^l \quad (49)$$

where $d\tau$ is a volume element embracing the co-ordinate space of all the particles (of dimensionality $3n$ if there are n particles), and where the integration is over all the co-ordinates. The expression δ_m^l is the usual Kronecker delta, and has the meaning that $\delta_m^m = 1$ and that $\delta_m^l = 0$ $(l \neq m)$. The asterisk is used here and elsewhere to denote the complex conjugate. It is necessary to distinguish between ψ_m and its conjugate ψ_m^*, because the solutions of the Schrödinger wave equation are not necessarily real. In (49) the case $l \neq m$ expresses the orthogonality, and $l = m$ embodies the normalization.

B. MATRIX FORM OF QUANTUM MECHANICS

A few months prior to Schrödinger's discovery of wave mechanics, another, superficially very different approach to quantum mechanics was developed by Born and Heisenberg. The impetus to this other approach was Born's repeated emphasis to his colleagues at Göttingen that the reason the old quantum theory was then (1925) failing was that it sought to use the same kinematical concepts of space and time within the atom as in ordinary measurable large-scale events. After all, the concepts of space and time have a meaning only when we tell how they can be measured, and obviously at atomic distances we cannot use ordinary measuring rods or clocks. Guided by this philosophy based on the so-called operational viewpoint, Heisenberg discovered his matrix mechanics. He did not originally recognize it as a matrix formulation—Born was the first to see that the equations were best interpreted in the language of matrices.

The basic idea of the matrix mechanics is that the co-ordinates and momenta associated with the electrons in the atom are to be treated as matrices rather than as quantities having a definite numerical value. A matrix is an array of the form

$$a = \left\{ \begin{array}{ccccc} a(11) & a(12) & a(13) & \cdot & \cdot & \cdot \\ a(21) & a(22) & a(23) & \cdot & \cdot & \cdot \\ a(31) & a(32) & a(33) & \cdot & \cdot & \cdot \\ \cdot & \cdot & \cdot & \cdot & & \\ \cdot & \cdot & \cdot & & & a(nn) \end{array} \right\}$$

The matrices involved in quantum mechanics are infinite; i.e., have an infinite number of rows and columns.

The Heisenberg matrix elements are quantities which are intimately connected with the concept of the transition probability in the old quantum theory, and alternatively with Fourier coefficients in classical mechanics. For simplicity consider a system with only one degree of freedom. Then the matrix index can be identified with the quantum number, and a matrix element $a(lm)$ is correlated with a transition between states of quantum numbers l and m. The exact matrix expression replacing (31) is

$$A_{l \to m} = (4e^2/3hc^3) (2\pi)^4 \nu(lm)^3 [|x(lm)|^2 + |y(lm)|^2 + |z(lm)|^2] \quad (50)$$

Here $x(lm)$ refers to an element of the x co-ordinate matrix, etc., and is the quantum analogue of the Fourier coefficient x_{l-m} involved in the rough formula (31) arrived at by means of the correspondence principle. As presented here, and as Heisenberg reasoned historically, (50) is obtained by analogy with classical theory, but it should be mentioned that (50) can also be derived independently from the Dirac radiation theory, which applies quantum mechanics to the degrees of freedom of the ether. By means of (50) the intensity of a line can be calculated if the Heisenberg matrices are known.

In order to compute the matrix elements needed for use in (50), it is necessary to transcribe atomic mechanics into the mysterious matrix language, and for this a matrix algebra and calculus are necessary. The sum of two matrices is formed by adding corresponding elements, so that $(a + b)(lm) = a(lm) + b(lm)$. Matrices are multiplied in the same way as determinants; i.e.,

$$(ab)(lm) = \Sigma_n a(ln) b(nm) \quad (51)$$

There is, however, the difference that whereas a determinant has a numerical value, a numerical meaning is attached only to the individual entries of a matrix and not to its entirety. This loss of numerical value corresponds to the abandonment of ordinary kinematical relationships within the atom. The multiplication is in general noncommutative; i.e., $(ab)(lm) \neq (ba)(lm)$ or more symbolically $ab \neq ba$, if boldface type is used to designate the entire matrix rather than a single entry.

By repeated additions and multiplications it is possible to construct functions of matrices which are in turn matrices, and thus develop a matrix algebra. In order to transcribe atomic mechanics into the mysterious matrix language, it is necessary to have some sort of rule for constructing the derivative of one matrix with respect to another. A consistent mathematical framework is obtained if one defines the derivatives of a function $f(q_1, \ldots, q_f, p_1, \ldots, p_f)$ in the following way:

$$\frac{\partial f}{\partial p_k} = \frac{2\pi i}{h}(fq_k - q_k f), \frac{\partial f}{\partial q_k} = -\frac{2\pi i}{h}(fp_k - p_k f) \quad (52)$$

The special cases $f = p_j$ or q_j yield the so-called quantum conditions

$$p_k q_k - q_k p_k = (h/2\pi)1 \qquad p_k q_j - q_j p_k = 0 \qquad (k \neq j)$$
$$p_k p_j - p_j p_k = 0 \qquad q_k q_j - q_j q_k = 0 \qquad (53)$$

A diagonal matrix is one which has vanishing entries except down the principal diagonal—i.e., $a(lm) = 0$, $l \neq m$—while a unit matrix has the additional property $1(ll) = 1$. A diagonal matrix is the quantum analogue of a Fourier series which contains nothing but a single constant term. Hence, in a conservative system with a definite energy, the energy matrix must be a diagonal one.

It should be stated again that the Heisenberg matrices are infinite arrays in the sense that they involve an infinite number of rows of columns. Namely, each index (number of row or column) is correlated with a stationary state, and there is an infinite number of such states. Furthermore, in connection with fig. 3 we have seen that often the permitted stationary states form a continuous rather than discrete manifold. In the continuous region it is necessary to introduce the rather recondite concept of a matrix with continuously varying indices, so that it cannot then even be tabulated in terms of rows and columns. When there is a continuum, the summation in (51) must be replaced by an integration. Similarly, in the expansion (48) the summations are to be construed as including integrations over the continua when these are present.

1. Relation of Matrix and Wave Theories.—It is possible to work out the energy levels of the harmonic oscillator, rotator, hydrogen atom, etc., by means of pure matrix theory, and the results are always the same as those obtained with wave mechanics. One immediately suspects that the two approaches are interrelated. This is indeed the case. If the Schrödinger wave functions are known, the Heisenberg matrix elements can be computed by a straightforward integration. Suppose that we desire the matrix elements of a function $f(q_1, \ldots, q_f, p_1, \ldots, p_f)$ of the co-ordinates and momenta. Then the appropriate formula is

$$f(lm) = \int \psi_m^* f(q_1, \cdots, q_f, \frac{h}{2\pi i} \frac{\partial}{\partial q_1}, \cdots, \frac{h}{2\pi i} \frac{\partial}{\partial q_f}) \psi_l d\tau \quad (54)$$

where the integrand contains an operator f formed by replacing each p_k by $\frac{h}{2\pi i} \frac{\partial}{\partial q_k}$. We shall not attempt to prove (54) but shall note one or two simple consequences. In the first place, the quantum conditions (53) are satisfied. For instance, if $f = p_k q_k - q_k p_k$, then

$$f\psi_m = \frac{h}{2\pi i} \left[\frac{\partial}{\partial q_k}(q_k \psi_m) - q_k \frac{\partial \psi_m}{\partial q_k} \right] = \frac{h}{2\pi i} \psi_m$$

and except for a factor $h/2\pi i$, the integral (54) becomes identical with (49), so that we have $f(lm) = (h/2\pi i)\delta_m^l$. This result agrees with the first relation of (53), since the elements of a unit matrix are equivalent to a Kronecker delta. The remaining relations of (53) are obviously satisfied. The third relation, for instance, follows since $\partial^2 \psi / \partial q_j \partial q_k = \partial^2 \psi / \partial q_k \partial q_j$.

Satisfaction of the wave equation (47) for a conservative system with definite energy is tantamount to making the energy a diagonal matrix. To see this we note that by (47) the operator H is equivalent to multiplication by a constant E_m. Hence, if f in (54) is taken to be the Hamiltonian operator H, the integral differs from (49) merely by a constant factor and so has the value $E_m \delta_m^l$.

If one is wedded to the extreme matrix viewpoint, one regards the wave functions merely as mathematical auxiliaries used to compute the Heisenberg matrix elements by means of the "matrix computing machine" (54). Such a viewpoint is undoubtedly too one-sided, and is offensive to physicists who take comfort from the parallelism of wave mechanics to classical mathematical physics, and to optics, in particular.

2. Intensities and Polarizations of Spectral Lines.—By combining (54) (as applied to $f = x, y, z$) with (50), it is possible to compute the intensities of spectral lines. Furthermore, by examination of the relative magnitudes and phases of the corresponding x, y, and z components involved in (50), predictions can also be made regarding the polarization behaviour. In this fashion, for example, the intensities in the various components in the Stark effect for hydrogen can be calculated. Also, and even more important, it is possible to derive the various so-called "selection rules," which forbid certain quantum numbers changing except by a specified number of units. It can be demonstrated, for instance, that the quantum number for a harmonic oscillator cannot change by more than one unit. With the restriction $n'' - n' = \pm 1$, the quantum-mechanical frequency ν obtained by substituting (43) in (13) becomes identical with the classical frequency ν_0. Without the restriction, ν could be any multiple of ν_0, a highly unreasonable situation since classically overtones are always absent for a simple harmonic system.

A particularly important case of the selection principle is that for the so-called azimuthal quantum number l, which is involved in the relativistic hydrogen atom and especially in Newtonian nonhydrogenic atoms with one valence electron. By means of (54) it can be proved that l cannot change except by one unit. The quantum number l plays a vital role in interpreting the spectra of alkali atoms. (See SPECTROSCOPY.) An energy level is classified of the s, p, d, f character according as $l = 0, 1, 2, 3$. The selection principle $l' - l'' = \pm 1$ materially limits the "combinations" of the terms; i.e., the possible transitions between the different energy states. The predictions are strikingly confirmed by experiment.

QUANTUM MECHANICS

C. Statistical Significance of Quantum Mechanics

1. Interpretation of the Wave Function.

We have not as yet given sufficient emphasis to the physical meaning of the solution of the Schrödinger wave equation, as distinct from its relation to the matrix formalism. The wave function satisfying the general equation (45) has an important physical interpretation. The square of its modulus is proportional to what may be called a statistical charge density. Let us consider first a system with only one particle. Then the probability that the particle will be in the volume element $dxdydz$ at time t may be taken to be

$$|\Psi|^2 dxdydz \qquad (55)$$

provided the total probability is normalized to unity; i.e,

$$\iiint |\Psi|^2 dxdydz = 1 \qquad (56)$$

This scheme of interpretation is a consistent one, as it can be shown that it is a consequence of the differential equation (45) that the integral on the left-hand side of (56) is independent of time. Otherwise the normalization condition (56) could not be imposed. Similarly, when there are n particles, $|\Psi|^2$ determines the probability in a $3n$ dimensional space whose volume element $d\tau$ is $dx_1, \ldots, dz_n$.

It is to be emphasized that the density given by (55) is inherently statistical in character. We do not say that the particle is in the element $dxdydz$ at time t, but merely that there is a certain probability of the particle being there. In the particular case of a conservative system in a definite stationary state, the relation $|\Psi|^2 = |\psi_m|^2$ is satisfied by virtue of (46), and then the probability becomes independent of time. The places where $|\Psi|$ or $|\psi_m|$ is large are those where the particle is likely to be located, but it is never possible to say when it is there. The situation may be compared to the information obtainable from the time exposure of a firefly on a dark night. Where the photographic plate reveals the most brightness is where the firefly has spent most of the time, but one cannot infer just when the insect was at a particular spot. Similarly in quantum mechanics, the information about particles is inherently restricted because of its statistical nature.

When quantum mechanics was first discovered, there was considerable controversy as to whether it was necessarily statistical in character. For a while many physicists maintained that a deterministic picture was possible, in which the electron was considered to be a fluidlike affair whose density distribution is governed by (55). It is now, however, generally conceded that such attempts are untenable and involve the same fallacy as reasoning from the time exposure of the firefly that the latter is a luminous fluid rather than a discrete insect. It should be regarded as an advantage rather than a drawback that quantum mechanics must be interpreted statistically. When atomic experiments are analyzed from the "operational" viewpoint, it is found that the measurements always involve statistical features inasmuch as some of the parameters are distributed over a range of values and are not determined with complete precision. It is not the co-ordinates alone which must be statistically interpreted, but also various other dynamical quantities, such as energy and momentum.

2. Probability Distribution in Momentum Space.

Again confining attention to one particle, it is possible, for instance, to inquire concerning the probability that its components of momentum fall within a certain range at time t. The symmetrical roles of co-ordinates and momenta in the Hamiltonian technique suggest that there is a function χ such that

$$|\chi(p_x, p_y, p_z, t)|^2 dp_x dp_y dp_z \qquad (57)$$

determines the probability that the momenta are in the element $dp_x dp_y dp_z$ at time t. There is indeed such a function, and the relation between the two functions Ψ, χ is similar to that between a function and its Fourier transform. Namely, it can be shown that

$$\Psi = h^{-3/2} \iiint \chi(p_x,p_y,p_z,t) e^{2\pi i(p_x x + p_y y + p_z z)/h} dp_x dp_y dp_z \qquad (58)$$

$$\chi = h^{-3/2} \iiint \Psi(x,y,z,t) e^{-2\pi i(p_x x + p_y y + p_z z)/h} dxdydz \qquad (59)$$

Equation (58) has intuitively a very reasonable form, as it is natural to regard any disturbance as being built up of a superposition of De Broglie waves, each of the structure $e^{2\pi i px/h}$ in one dimension or $e^{2\pi i(p_x x + p_y y + p_z z)/h}$ in three. In any principle of superposition in physics, the square of the amplitude governs the intensity, and so it is natural to assume that $|\chi|^2$ gives the probability. It can be shown from the mathematical theory of Fourier transforms (Plancherel's theorem) that

$$\iiint |\Psi|^2 dxdydz = \iiint |\chi|^2 dp_x dp_y dp_z \qquad (60)$$

If (60) were not satisfied, the physical interpretation given Ψ, χ would lack consistency, for it is necessary that the total probability for either co-ordinate or momentum distribution be unity; or in other words, the normalization (49) in co-ordinate space must imply a corresponding normalization in momentum space. Another relation which can be established, and which shows the intimate relation between momentum and the operator $\frac{h}{2\pi i}\frac{\partial}{\partial x}$, is

$$\iiint p_x{}^n |\chi|^2 dp_x dp_y dp_z = \iiint \Psi^*\left(\frac{h}{2\pi i}\frac{\partial}{\partial x}\right)^n \Psi dxdydz \qquad (61)$$

where n is an integer. Also there is a symmetrical relation

$$\iiint x^n |\Psi|^2 dxdydz = \iiint \chi^*\left(-\frac{h}{2\pi i}\frac{\partial}{\partial p_x}\right)^n \chi dp_x dp_y dp_z \qquad (62)$$

Clearly (62) and (61) give respectively the mean value of the nth power of the x-component of displacement and of momentum.

3. Interference of Probability Amplitudes.

In ordinary probability theory, probabilities are compounded in accordance with the law

$$P(b) = \int P(b, a)P(a)da \qquad (63)$$

where $P(a)$ is the probability of occurrence of a, and $P(b, a)$ is the probability of occurrence of b when a is given. On the other hand, since $|\Psi|^2$ or $|\chi|^2$ is the density in position or momentum space, the functions involved in the compounding relation (equation 58) are the square roots of probabilities and are spoken of as being probability amplitudes. The function $e^{2\pi i(x p_x + y p_y + z p_z)/h}$ is essentially a De Broglie wave and is called the probability amplitude connecting co-ordinates and momenta. The fact that in quantum mechanics there exists a compounding relation analogous to (63) with $P^{\frac{1}{2}}$ rather than P is sometimes called the phenomenon that involves the interference of probability amplitudes. Although no logical inconsistencies are found to be involved, still this somewhat curious way of associating probabilities leads to many paradoxes which look rather strange from the standpoint of large-scale statistical mechanics. There is a certain amount of parallelism to the unintelligibility of interference phenomena in optics, wherein amplitudes rather than intensities are added, to a person who has been versed only in geometrical optics, ray tracing, and perhaps the corpuscular theory of light. It is now well recognized that radiation has both corpuscular and undulatory aspects. The former, for instance, stands out clearly in the photoelectric effect. As emphasized in Bohr's principle of complementarity, the two aspects are not contradictory but instead play complementary roles. So also, matter has both corpuscular and undulatory features. The type of compounding involved in (58) implies use of the wave amplitude in much the same way as in optics. It is well known that interference phenomena in the latter must be treated by superposing wave amplitudes rather than intensities or the number of corpuscular light quanta.

D. Transformation Theory

1. General.

The general interpretation of quantum mechanics as essentially a theory of probability amplitudes has been developed particularly by Jordan and by Dirac. The details of this so-called transformation theory are much too intricate and abstract to be treated here, but their formulation of quantum mechanics has elegance, generality and a unifying influence on the interpretation of the various other viewpoints. The Schrödinger wave equation, from the standpoint of transformation theory, may be regarded as an equation for finding the probability amplitude for distribution-in-position when the energy is known. One might ask for the probability amplitude for the distribution of other functions than positional co-ordinates—for instance, momenta—and the known quantity might not necessarily be the energy, as certain experiments correspond to fixation of other quantities than the energy. Such more general problems can be solved by means of transformation theory.

2. Uncertainty Principle.—It is to be noticed that in (55) or (57) expressions have been given for the probability of the particle being in an element of volume $dxdydz$ of position space, or in an element of momentum space, but that there is no probability function for a concurrent occurrence of given values of position and momentum associated with a volume element $dxdydzdp_xdp_ydp_z$. This fact takes us to the heart of the Heisenberg uncertainty principle. The latter limits the accuracy with which it is possible to specify simultaneously the values of a co-ordinate and its canonically conjugate momentum. If Δp_x and Δx be the limits of precision within which p_x and x can simultaneously be determined, there exists the inequality

$$\Delta x \Delta p_x \geq h/4\pi \qquad (64)$$

For illustrations of this concept, *see* UNCERTAINTY PRINCIPLE; thus it is meaningless to talk about the probability of a simultaneous occurrence of a given value of a co-ordinate and its conjugate momentum, for by (64) there is infinite uncertainty in a momentum if the position is known with complete precision, or vice versa.

The uncertainty principle should not be regarded as an additional hypothesis artificially injected into quantum mechanics. Instead, it is something which can be proved as a consequence of the latter, along the following lines. By proper choice of the origin for position and velocity, the mean position and velocity can be made zero; in other words, $I_{61}^{(1)} = I_{62}^{(1)} = 0$, where $I_{61}^{(n)}$, $I_{62}^{(n)}$ denote respectively the integrals (61) and (62). The uncertainty in position and momenta can then be regarded as measured by the root mean square displacement and momentum, so that we can take $\Delta p_x^2 = I_{61}^{(2)}$, $\Delta x^2 = I_{62}^{(2)}$ provided Ψ is normalized in accordance with (56). Now it can be shown by pure mathematics, largely by the aid of the so-called Schwarz inequality, that any function Ψ normalized in accordance with (56) and satisfying the requirements of continuity, etc. expected of a physically admissible wave function satisfies the identity $I_{61}^{(2)}I_{62}^{(2)} \geq (h/4\pi)^2$. The uncertainty principle is hence proved for the type of system under consideration. The equality sign in (64) corresponds to the minimum possible value of the product of the two errors, and this is achieved only when the probability functions have a Gaussian distribution.

It can be shown that the time is canonically conjugate to the energy. Hence, if we make an experiment whose span in time is limited, as is always the case, the energy cannot be known with complete precision, and so the appropriate wave function is (48), in which there is a dispersion of energy values, rather than (46), in which it is supposed that the energy is completely determinate. Wave functions of the general form (48), in which a number of stationary states are superposed and thus co-exist, are sometimes spoken of as "wave packets." It is through the construction of the latter that classical and quantum theories merge when the amount of action is large.

V. ELECTRON SPIN

A very important development practically concomitant with the advent of the true quantum mechanics was the discovery of electron spin. The basic idea of the latter is that the electron has an extra degree of freedom which may be likened to the spin of a top about an axis. Or, if the electron moving about the nucleus is compared to the earth in the solar system, then there is an obvious analogy of the spin of the electron to the diurnal rotation of the earth about its own axis. The important features of the spinning electron were first presented by two young Dutch physi-

cists, George E. Uhlenbeck and Samuel A. Goudsmit, in 1925, although some of the earlier literature did contain suggestions of a rotating electron in rather different connections.

The various dilemmas of spectroscopic theory and magnetism which are resolved by the introduction of electron spin are many. One of them is the existence of multiplets in molecular spectra. The simplest and most familiar example of a multiplet is provided by the two components of the D lines of sodium, which arise because the energy level of the upper state is double; *i.e.*, consists really of two stationary states. A single level, however, is obtained if the ordinary theory of a point electron is used. It is hence necessary to introduce a fourth quantum number, whose values subdivide the energy levels more than if only the quantum numbers associated with the external degrees of freedom of the electron were introduced.

If an electron model without spin is used, then there are three quantum numbers per electron. If the force field is dominantly central, as is usually the case even in nonhydrogenic atoms, then these three can be interpreted as the principal quantum number n, the azimuthal quantum number l, and the "magnetic" or "equatorial" quantum number m_l. The range of values of l is $0, \ldots, n-1$, and that of m_l is $-l, \ldots, +l$. The azimuthal quantum number l has the physical significance of specifying the angular momentum of the electron, in multiples of $h/2\pi$, while m_l fixes the component in a particular direction. The mathematical significance in terms of the indices of tesseral harmonics involved in the wave function is that revealed in equation (44).

1. Pauli Exclusion Principle.—Wolfgang Pauli proposed that besides n, l, m_l there be a fourth quantum number, or index m_s, which can take on the values $\pm\frac{1}{2}$. He then (1925) introduced his famous exclusion principle, for which he was awarded the Nobel prize in 1945. This principle states that no two electrons can have all four quantum numbers n, l, m_l, m_s the same. From this, the properties of the chemists' periodic table flow out automatically, including the existence of the "long" periods containing the iron, platinum and palladium groups, and of 14 rare earths. For instance, the choice $n = 1$ for the principal quantum number corresponds to the first or hydrogen-helium period, which has two elements, and $n = 2$ to the second or lithium-neon period. Namely, if $n = 1$, we can have $l = 0$, $m_l = 0$, $m_s = \pm\frac{1}{2}$, two possibilities in all, whereas if $n = 2$, we can have $l = 0$, $m_l = 0$, $m_s = \pm\frac{1}{2}$ and also $l = 1$, $m_l = 1$, $m_s = \pm\frac{1}{2}$; $l = 1$, $m_l = 0$, $m_s = \pm\frac{1}{2}$; $l = 1$, $m_l = -1$, $m_s = \pm\frac{1}{2}$ giving eight possibilities all told. In this general fashion the numbers of elements in the different rows of the periodic table are deduced by a simple enumerative process.

When Pauli published his celebrated paper in 1925, the significance of the fourth quantum number was a complete mystery. The great contribution of the theory of Uhlenbeck and Goudsmit, which appeared less than a year later, was to show how naturally the spinning electron accounts for the Pauli formalism. The two choices $m_s = \pm\frac{1}{2}$ are interpreted as determining the two possible orientations of the spin angular momentum relative to the axis of quantization. In order that there be two choices, and no more, it is necessary to postulate that the electron has a "half quantum" $\frac{1}{2}(h/2\pi)$ of spin angular momentum.

2. Interpretation of the Exclusion Principle in Terms of Antisymmetric Wave Functions.—The spin hypothesis of Uhlenbeck and Goudsmit furnished an explanation of the fourth quantum number. It did not, however, give any indication of why it is that no two electrons have all four quantum numbers the same. Heisenberg was the first to point out that the Pauli exclusion principle has a rudimentary interpretation in terms of the symmetry properties of wave functions. When one solves the wave equation for a system of several like particles, their identity introduces special properties of symmetry, and permits classification of the solution according to symmetry characteristics, the precise codification of which involves complicated group theory. For the very simple special case of only two identical particles, for instance, the solutions are either symmetric or antisymmetric, as regards interchange of the corresponding co-ordinates of the two particles. In other words, the wave function is either invariant or reverses sign when the electrons are permuted. When there are more than two electrons, there are many types of symmetry intermediate between the symmetric and antisymmetric cases, which represent two extremes but which still have a meaning. Furthermore, the antisymmetric solution can never be constructed when the electrons are in identical states (*i.e.*, have all four quantum numbers the same) for then the wave function would have to reverse sign as a result of an operation which does not change the arguments, an apparent impossibility. Hence, the Pauli principle is an automatic consequence of the formalism of quantum mechanics if it is postulated that only those solutions of the Schrödinger equation which are antisymmetric under permutation of the electron co-ordinates are physically realizable. In other words, nature somehow has a penchant for antisymmetric wave functions. In this connection it is to be understood that all four co-ordinates are to be permuted; *i.e.*, the spin co-ordinate as well as the three ordinary orbital ones x, y, z. The spin co-ordinate, unlike the variables x, y, z, which are continuous, assumes only the two values which correspond to the two possible orientations of the spin angular momentum relative to the axis of quantization. The wave function, on the other hand, need not be antisymmetric with respect to permutation of the orbital co-ordinates alone. In fact, no rigorous delineation of symmetry types under purely orbital permutation is possible, although it can be shown that symmetry characteristics associated with the orbital part of the problem determine the multiplicity of a spectral term; *i.e.*, whether it is a singlet, doublet, triplet, etc. The purely orbital forms of the wave equation given in (35) or (45) do not take cognizance of the spin. Inclusion of the latter introduces certain small magnetic interaction terms involving spin operators in the Hamiltonian function, and requires that the arguments of the wave function include spin variables as well as the ordinary orbital co-ordinates $q_1, \ldots, q_f$.

3. Electron Spin and Magnetism.—Electron spin plays a leading role in the theoretical interpretation of magnetic phenomena. A fuller description will be found in the article on MAGNETISM; only two points will be mentioned here. One is that ferromagnetism arises almost entirely from spin rather than from orbital magnetic moment, for in the solid state the crystalline electric fields usually quench the orbital contributions to the magnetic moment. The other is that in the Uhlenbeck-Goudsmit model of electron spin the ratio of magnetic moment to angular momentum is taken to be $-e/mc$, whereas the classical value of the ratio which applies to the orbit is $-e/2mc$. In other words, the so-called gyromagnetic ratio has an anomalous factor 2 when applied to the spin. This anomaly is confirmed not only by measurements on the gyromagnetic effect (rotation of a body by magnetization, or magnetization by rotation), but also by those on the anomalous Zeeman effect. In the latter the so-called Landé g-factor expresses the fact that part of the contribution to the magnetic moment is of the normal orbital type, and part of the anomalous spin variety.

VI. DIRAC ELECTRON

1. General.—In the Uhlenbeck-Goudsmit theory, the half quantum of spin angular momentum and the anomalous factor 2 in the gyromagnetic ratio are introduced in a purely *ad hoc* fashion. Another approach, which avoids this arbitrariness, was developed by Dirac in 1928. In the original Schrödinger theory without spin, the behaviour of an electron was described by a single second-order differential equation. The spin properties assumed by Uhlenbeck and Goudsmit involved two different possible settings of space-quantized spin angular momentum, and were interpreted by means of the matrix theory. Pauli, however, soon showed how the Schrödinger wave theory could be generalized to include the spin, by introducing two wave functions, ψ_1, ψ_2, which satisfy two simultaneous second-order differential equations. Dirac had the revolutionary idea that the electron be described by four wave functions, $\psi_1, \psi_2, \psi_3, \psi_4$, which satisfy four simultaneous first-order differential equations. If the electron is subject to an electrostatic potential $\varphi(x, y, z)$ and vector potential A, these equations are as follows:

$$
\begin{aligned}
(p_0 + mc)\psi_1 + (p_1 - ip_2)\psi_4 + p_3\psi_3 &= 0 \\
(p_0 + mc)\psi_2 + (p_1 + ip_2)\psi_3 - p_3\psi_4 &= 0 \\
(p_0 - mc)\psi_3 + (p_1 - ip_2)\psi_2 + p_3\psi_1 &= 0 \\
(p_0 - mc)\psi_4 + (p_1 + ip_2)\psi_1 - p_3\psi_2 &= 0
\end{aligned}
\tag{65}
$$

where

$$
p_0 = \frac{h}{2\pi ic}\frac{\partial}{\partial t} + \frac{e}{c}\varphi \qquad p_1 = \frac{h}{2\pi i}\frac{\partial}{\partial x} + \frac{e}{c}A_x
$$

$$
p_2 = \frac{h}{2\pi i}\frac{\partial}{\partial y} + \frac{e}{c}A_y \qquad p_3 = \frac{h}{2\pi i}\frac{\partial}{\partial z} + \frac{e}{c}A_z
$$

When first viewed, these equations certainly look arbitrary and artificial. Space will not permit description of how, to the first approximation in the dimensionless constant $(2\pi e^2/hc)^2$, they are equivalent to the more conventional theory based on second-order differential equations. It was this equivalence that first led Dirac to hit upon the equations of the structure (65). If the solutions are normalized to unity in the sense that

$$
\iiint [|\psi_1|^2 + |\psi_2|^2 + |\psi_3|^2 + |\psi_4|^2]dxdydz = 1
$$

then $(|\psi_1|^2+|\psi_3|^2)dxdydz$ and $(|\psi_2|^2+|\psi_4|^2)dxdydz$ are respectively the probabilities that the electron be in the volume element $dxdydz$ with spin parallel or antiparallel to the axis of quantization. It can further be shown that the simultaneous equations (65) have the proper invariance under a Lorentz transformation, so that the requirements of the special theory of relativity are satisfied. This is not true of the simple Schrödinger equation (35), which is essentially Newtonian in character. The relativistic transformation properties of $\psi_1, \psi_2, \psi_3, \psi_4$ are those appropriate to a pair of spinors, each of which has two components. This result is rather surprising, as one's first conjecture would be that the ψ functions would transform like the components of a four-vector.

All the properties of electron spin, including the proper amount of angular momentum, relativistic fine structure and even the gyromagnetic ratio, flow out of the Dirac formalism in an almost miraculous fashion suggestive of a magician's extraction of rabbits from a silk hat. Of course, some mathematical calculation, omitted here, is required to demonstrate that these various properties are indeed implied in (65), but it should be emphasized particularly than when (65) is used, no additional postulates are necessary as in the original theory of Uhlenbeck and Goudsmit. Thus (65) can be regarded as the basis of a relativistic electron, with spin as a by-product. In fact, the discovery of (65) and related methodology must be regarded as one of the most brilliant achievements in the history of mathematical physics.

When the Dirac equations (65) are used, the expressions for the energy levels of a hydrogenic atom have exactly the same form (24) as in the original relativistic Bohr-Sommerfeld theory. This identity of results must be regarded as one of the strangest coincidences in all of physics. In other words, the new quantum mechanics with spin is equivalent to the old theory without spin. Unless the spin is included in some form, either explicitly through the Uhlenbeck-Goudsmit model (which, however, is reliable only to the approximation [26]) or implicitly through the more refined Dirac equations, relativistic wave mechanics gives results different from (24) and not in accord with experiment. There is an important difference between the new and old interpretations of (24). The integer k no longer has the significance of being the azimuthal quantum number, as in the old quantum theory, but rather is equal to $j + \frac{1}{2}$, where j is the so-called inner quantum number which takes on half-integral values. The selection principles allow transitions in which the inner quantum number is unaltered as well as those in which it changes by ± 1, whereas only the ± 1 changes are allowed for the azimuthal quantum number. Hence, even though the energy levels are exactly the same, more spectral lines are allowed in the new than in the old interpretation of the relativistic fine structure. The extra components are confirmed experimentally, although the resolution is usually inadequate to detect them except as satellites of other lines.

Another success of the Dirac model is that it yields the so-called

Klein-Nishina formula for the scattering of X-rays, which, unlike previous expressions, agrees well with experiment.

2. Negative Energy States and the Positron.—To this point, only the triumphs of the Dirac theory have been stressed. Some of its difficulties should also be mentioned. One is that it is uncertain how the relativistic theory should be extended to include the interaction between electrons found in nonhydrogenic atoms. A more serious trouble is the existence of the so-called negative energy states. It is convenient and hence customary in relativity to include, as will be done henceforth, the so-called rest energy mc^2 of the electron in the total energy. This inclusion is equivalent to omitting the term -1 from the brace in (24), and with this modification the energy levels given by (24) are all positive. The dividing line between the discrete and continuous levels in fig. 3 then comes at $E = mc^2$. The equivalence of energy levels in the old and new theories mentioned above applies only as long as attention is confined to states of positive energy. The old quantum theory gave no negative states. However, it can be shown that with the Dirac equations (65) there is a continuum of states of negative energy, filling the entire range of energies below $-mc^2$. The rest energy mc^2 is enormously greater than the binding energy of the hydrogen atom, represented by the span of the discrete levels in fig. 3. The interval between the lowest positive state and the highest negative one is thus very approximately $2mc^2$, or about 1,000,000 ev. To show even the highest negative energy level, it would be necessary to extend fig. 3 about two miles below the bottom of the page, the intervening interval being void, and from there down to minus infinity the figure should be shaded to indicate a continuum. (By contrast it should be noted that the relativity fine structure, first revealed by the second member of the expansion [26] of [24], also cannot be shown in fig. 3, but for a different reason, as on the scale of fig. 3 the splitting would amount to only about a millionth of an inch.)

The states of negative energy are obviously supernumerary and superfluous if viewed in a conventional fashion, and to get a theory that has a meaning, they must somehow be stricken off the books. Dirac suggested that the negative states are to be regarded as filled, each having the one electron allowed by the Pauli exclusion principle. This idea, of course, would not work with conventional Boltzmann statistics without the exclusion principle, as then there would be an overwhelming probability that the electrons be in states of negatively infinite energy. As there is a nondenumerable infinity of negative energy levels, there would be an infinite number of electrons housed in such states, even with the limitations imposed by the Pauli rule. Since the electron has a negative charge, there would hence be an infinite negative charge density. Dirac proposed that the charge is not to be counted in computing the charge density to be used in such relationships as the Poisson law.

According to this apparently fantastic conception, if an electron were somehow taken from one of the normally filled states of negative energy and placed in one of the conventional ones of positive energy, not only would an electron be created, but also a particle of equal mass but positive charge, now called the positron. Namely, a deficit in the full complement of negative charge, carried, so to speak, at zero on the books, is equivalent to a corresponding surplus of positive charge. (Dirac suggested originally that the shortage might correspond to the proton, but this idea is now considered untenable as, for one thing, no explanation is given of the diversity of mass between electron and proton.) Fantasy turned to evidence when Carl D. Anderson obtained cloud chamber photographs showing the existence of positrons; *i.e.*, particles equal to the electron in mass but positively charged. They should not be confused with protons, which are almost 2,000 times heavier. Unlike the protons, which are stable, positrons are extremely short-lived, as there is always the possibility that an electron will be captured out of a state of positive energy and fill the gap in the negative one. Raising of an electron from a negative to a positive level is equivalent to the creation of an electron and a positron, or in other language to pair production. The minimum energy involved in such a transition is very approximately $2mc^2$. Hence, the absorption of gamma rays can give rise to pair pro-

duction if, and only if, their frequency exceeds $2mc^2/h$. In the experimental confirmation of this phenomenon, an apparent difficulty of the Dirac theory is turned into a triumph.

A positron and electron which are near each other move about their common centre of gravity in much the same fashion as do the electron and proton in the hydrogen atom but without the disproportionality in mass between the two constituents. The quasiatom thus formed is called positronium and is highly ephemeral. The existence of positronium was definitely, though rather indirectly, confirmed in the experiments of Martin Deutsch in 1951.

By analogy with antielectrons (*i.e.*, positrons) it was wondered whether antiprotons exist as well. Such particles, which have the same mass as the proton but a charge of opposite sign, and which can be regarded as holes in a continuum of positive charge, were first detected in 1955 by Owen Chamberlain, Emilio Segrè, Clyde E. Wiegand and Thomas Ypsilantis (*see* ANTIMATTER).

VII. QUANTUM ELECTRODYNAMICS

So far the impression has been given that the relativistic fine structure of hydrogen agreed with the Dirac theory within the limits of accuracy of the measurements. Beginning in 1934, however, there was some indication that the separation between the two peaks of the Hα doublet in hydrogen was smaller than predicted by theory. (Each peak of the doublet results from a number of unresolved components, and rather careful analysis is necessary to evaluate properly their combined effect.) Whether there was a real discrepancy was for a number of years a matter of controversy, but painstaking spectroscopic measurements by L. Giulotto and others in 1947–48 made it clear that the discrepancy was real.

At about the same time it occurred to a number of theoretical physicists that an explanation of the discrepancy was that there are corrections because of the interaction of the electron with the electromagnetic field, which is represented in quantum mechanics by a series of quantized oscillators. This is a tricky subject, for the energy associated with this interaction turns out to be infinite, a difficulty which had been appreciated since 1930 and which is known as the divergence in the self-energy of the electron. Nevertheless, by a proper system of bookkeeping, not without elements of arbitrariness and inconsistency, it is possible to compute the differences in the electrodynamic corrections for the various states of the hydrogen atom, and these turn out to be finite. The differential effects agree well with experiment, and so, despite its bothersome divergences, there is more physical reality in the quantum-mechanical formalism of the electromagnetic field than was realized before 1947.

Most of the experimental verification of the quantum electrodynamical theory is concerned with the fine structure of the levels in hydrogen for which the principal quantum number has the value 2. Without the electrodynamical corrections, there are two such levels, given by (24), with $n = 2$ and $k = 1$; or $n = 2$ and $k = 2$. In the uncorrected theory the level $n = 2$, $k = 1$ actually consists of two coincident states, called $2^2S_{\frac{1}{2}}$, $2^2P_{\frac{1}{2}}$ in the terminology of the spectroscopists; while $n = 2$, $k = 2$ is designated as $2^2P_{\frac{3}{2}}$. (The subscript gives the value of J, and the letters S, P mean that the so-called azimuthal quantum number has respectively the values 0, 1.) The electrodynamical corrections prove to be practically the same for the two P levels but differ for the S state. As a result the two coinciding levels $2^2S_{\frac{1}{2}}$, $2^2P_{\frac{1}{2}}$ are split apart, and $2^2S_{\frac{1}{2}}$ is displaced toward $2^2P_{\frac{3}{2}}$, a phenomenon known as the Lamb shift. This decomposition is too small to resolve by conventional optical experiments, but makes the apparent doublet width separating the $J = \frac{3}{2}$ state from the $J = \frac{1}{2}$ state smaller than the difference calculated from (24) with the choices $k = 1$ or $k = 2$. The discrepancy with the best optical measurements is thus explained.

Much more quantitative—in fact, spectacular—tests of the electrodynamic corrections have been made, however, with the microwave and molecular beam techniques, which make possible the direct observation of the small energy differences represented by the transitions $2^2S_{\frac{1}{2}} - 2^2P_{\frac{1}{2}}$ and $2^2S_{\frac{1}{2}} - 2^2P_{\frac{3}{2}}$. With ordinary optical measurements, where the wavelength is of the order

0.0001 rather than 10 cm., these intervals can be observed only as small fine structures or modulations in the Balmer series. The microwave measurements require intricate and difficult detection techniques, which Willis E. Lamb, Jr., and Robert C. Retherford successfully devised and instrumented in 1950.

The Lamb shift for hydrogen, $2^2S\frac{1}{2} - 2^2P\frac{1}{2}$, calculated from the electrodynamical corrections is 0.035292 cm.$^{-1}$ (1057.99 mc.), while in the 1960s the most recent experimental value of Lamb et al. was 0.035285. For deuterium (heavy hydrogen) the corresponding figures are 0.035333 and 0.035326. The large number of significant figures for such small energy differences reveals graphically the high precision of microwave and molecular beam spectroscopy. It is a particular triumph both of theory and experiment that there is such good accord (both 0.000041 cm.$^{-1}$) between the calculated and observed difference in the shift for hydrogen (H^1) and deuterium (H^2), obviously a delicate, high-order correction.

In 1947 Julian Schwinger showed that the electrodynamical corrections make the magnetic moment of the electron somewhat greater than the conventional expression $eh/4\pi mc$. The most accurate theoretical value, inclusive of second order electrodynamical corrections, computed by Charles M. Sommerfield, introduces an extra factor, 1.001159615. Recent electron-beam experiments by D. T. Wilkinson and H. R. Crane give 1.001159622. The difference between the two values is less than either the experimental error or the uncertainty arising from neglect of still higher-order terms in the theory. Earlier molecular beam measurements by Polykarp Kusch and collaborators yielded 1.001146 $\pm$ 0.000012. The work of Lamb and Kusch in confirming quantum electrodynamics won them joint award of the Nobel Prize for Physics in 1955. For theoretical researches in this field, R. P. Feynman, J. Schwinger and S. Tomonaga jointly received this award in 1965.

A field theory analogous with that of quantum electrodynamics is used to describe the properties of mesons, transient particles of intermediate mass used in the mechanics of the interior of the nucleus. (See also NUCLEAR MOMENTS.)

VIII. WHAT QUANTUM MECHANICS HAS ACCOMPLISHED

To summarize, listed are some outstanding contributions quantum mechanics has made to understanding atomic physics.

1. The old Bohr theory owes its success to quantum mechanics. The great triumph of the original Bohr version of quantum theory was its ability to explain the spectral frequencies of hydrogenic atoms; e.g., hydrogen and ionized helium. This is done equally well by wave mechanics—in fact, better in some respects.

2. Quantum mechanics has provided a procedure for calculating the intensities rather than merely the frequencies of spectral lines.

3. Qualitative explanation of the spectra of nonhydrogenic atoms is now possible. The reason that quantitative precision is usually not possible is simply that when there is more than one electron the wave equation becomes too complicated mathematically to solve exactly. In the particular case of the neutral helium atom, which involves a three-body problem, it is possible to calculate the energy levels very accurately after considerable labour. The computed energy of the ground state of the neutral helium atom agrees with the observed energy to within 1 part in 10,000. This atom, on the other hand, was a stumbling block of the old Bohr theory.

4. Electron spin has played an important part in understanding of the phenomena of magnetism.

5. A quantum theory of the chemical bond has been formulated. Although chemical processes are so complicated that one cannot hope to calculate accurately from theory the heats of the reactions, still quantum mechanics does enable one to understand the salient features—how valence rules hold as they do, how there are saturated bonds, and so on. The Pauli exclusion principle is the key to the interpretation. The spin quantum number of an atom is intimately connected with its valence. Atoms with spins other than zero can be regarded as having unsaturated valences. The bonding is not due to any large magnetic coupling between the spins, and usually arises from the so-called exchange energy, which is electrostatic in character but which is correlated with spin alignment because of the constraints imposed by the Pauli exclusion principle. As a rule, the exchange energy is favourable to bonding when the spins are antiparallel. Besides codifying valence numbers, quantum mechanics has furnished a qualitative understanding of the directional valence characteristic of stereochemistry. It has also introduced the concept of resonance energy in chemical bonds. Previously the molecule was thought of as having a fixed structure, but quantum mechanics shows that it can coexist in several states at once, and a lower energy is often obtained if a molecule resonates among a variety of configurations.

6. A quantum theory of the solid state has been formulated. Thanks to quantum mechanics, it can be explained in a general way how atoms are held together in solid bodies. Various properties of solids, such as compressibility, thermal and electrical conductivity, specific heat, etc., also can be explained. Because solids involve more complicated aggregates of atoms than do individual molecules, the difficulties in the way of a strictly rigorous numerical computation are even greater than for the calculation of chemical binding. Nevertheless, semiquantitative as well as qualitative predictions are sometimes possible.

7. Quantum mechanics provides the basis for interpreting of ionization potentials, capture phenomena and especially questions involving the scattering of electrons or such particles as neutrons and protons when they approach atoms or molecules.

8. Numerous phenomena associated with the interaction of radiation with matter were first adequately explained by quantum mechanics, e.g., the Compton effect or the photoelectric effect, and various questions connected with absorption and emission. The so-called Kramers formula gives a far more profound and realistic description of dispersion than does classical theory.

9. Quantum mechanics provides an explanation of the existence of the positron and antiproton.

10. A quantum electrodynamics, describing many phenomena associated with radiation and with the coupling of electrons, has been formulated.

11. Finally, the philosophical implications of quantum mechanics must not be forgotten. The Heisenberg uncertainty principle, which shows that there is a limit to the precision with which nature can be observed, is particularly important in this respect.

See NUCLEUS; RADIOACTIVITY; PARTICLES, ELEMENTARY; see also references under "Quantum Mechanics" in the Index.

BIBLIOGRAPHY.—Relatively elementary: L. C. Pauling and E. B. Wilson, Jr., Introduction to Quantum Mechanics With Applications to Chemistry (1935); V. B. Rojansky, Introductory Quantum Mechanics (1938); W. V. Houston, Principles of Quantum Mechanics (1951); D. Bohm, Quantum Theory (1951); F. Mandl, Quantum Mechanics (1954).
More advanced: P. A. M. Dirac, The Principles of Quantum Mechanics, 4th ed. (1958); E. C. Kemble, The Fundamental Principles of Quantum Mechanics (1937); J. von Neumann, The Mathematical Foundations of Quantum Mechanics, Eng. trans. by R. T. Beyer (1955); L. D. Landau and E. M. Lifshitz, Quantum Mechanics: Non-Relativistic Theory, 2nd ed. (1965); A. Messiah, Quantum Mechanics, 2 vol. (1961).
The following books are concerned with applications of quantum mechanics to particular fields: J. C. Slater, The Quantum Theory of Atomic Structure, 2 vol. (1960); W. Kauzmann, Quantum Chemistry (1957); N. F. Mott and H. S. W. Massey, The Theory of Atomic Collisions, 3rd ed. (1965); R. E. Peierls, Quantum Theory of Solids (1955); W. Heitler, The Quantum Theory of Radiation, 3rd ed. (1954); J. D. Bjorken and S. D. Drell, Relativistic Quantum Mechanics (1964).
(J. H. V. V.)

QUANTZ, JOHANN JOACHIM (1697–1773), German composer who is remembered chiefly as a virtuoso and theorist of the flute, was born at Oberscheden, near Göttingen, on Jan. 30, 1697. As a child he showed musical talent and was taken by his uncle to Merseburg, where he studied several instruments. After the completion of his apprenticeship he obtained posts at Radeberg and later at Dresden, where he studied Vivaldi's violin concertos. In 1717 he took lessons in counterpoint from J. D. Zelenka in Vienna and in 1718 was appointed oboist in the court chapel of the king of Poland. He then took up the practice of the flute, on which instrument he was to become famous. During the years 1723–27 he traveled widely throughout Europe before returning to Dresden. In 1728 he became flute instructor to the crown prince of Prussia (later Frederick the Great) and when the latter succeeded to the throne in 1741 he persuaded Quantz to settle in Berlin. He remained in Berlin as chamber musician and court composer until his death at Potsdam on July 12, 1773.

Quantz composed about 300 concertos for Frederick the Great, very few of which were ever printed. His important book on flute playing, *Versuch einer Anweisung die Flöte traversiere zu spielen*, published in Berlin in 1752, was reprinted many times. He also wrote an autobiography. Some of his sonatas and concertos were published in the 20th century, and a facsimile of the 3rd German edition of the *Versuch* was published in 1953.

See A. Quantz, *J. J. Quantz: Leben und Werke* (1877); A. Yorke-Long, *Music at Court* (1954). (Cs. Ch.)

QUARANTINE AND ISOLATION.
Quarantine is the complete or partial limitation of the freedom of movement of well persons or animals that have been exposed to a communicable disease; its purpose is to prevent further transmission of the disease. Segregation of a sick person or carrier is also commonly called quarantine but is more properly designated isolation.

Venice in 1374 imposed what was probably the first quarantine by banning travelers suspected of having been infected with bubonic plague. In 1377 the Adriatic port of Ragusa (modern Dubrovnik, Yugos.) required all travelers from plague districts to remain for a month at one of two designated points before entering the city. The first quarantine station was erected in 1383 in Marseilles, where all travelers from infected ships were detained for 40 days. It is from this 40-day period of detention that the term quarantine is derived (It. *quaranta*, "forty").

The purpose of isolation is to prevent transmission of the infectious agent from the infected person or animal to a susceptible person by placing the person or animal under such conditions that the possibilities of transmission are minimized. Strict isolation of the patient for the period of communicability (which is determined by experience) is necessary in diseases such as smallpox. In other diseases, such as malaria, the patient need only be protected by screens from the mosquito vector. In still other diseases isolation is not utilized nowadays, either because the method of transmission is not fully understood or because it has been discovered that isolation of the few frank cases of the disease does not prevent further transmission from much larger numbers of mild, unrecognized cases. Modified isolation may be carried on voluntarily by a person's remaining at home when he has a mild infectious disease such as a cold.

While isolation to be effective must be imposed until the end of the period of communicability, the exposed person or animal, called a contact, must not be permitted to expose healthy susceptible persons during the incubation period of the disease. The incubation periods of different diseases or of different cases of the same disease vary in length; but for purposes of quarantine the periods are considered to be the longest usual intervals between first exposure and development of the first signs of infection. Quarantine is often modified so that those contacts who are presumed to be immune because of their ages or histories may be permitted to go about their usual business. Quarantine also is being superseded to some extent by surveillance, the practice of close supervision of contacts so that they may be isolated at the first signs of illness without restricting their freedom prior to that.

Ships usually are no longer quarantined in the earlier manner; the word of the ship's physician is accepted that there are no cases of communicable disease on board. Rapid travel by air, however, has necessitated the institution of new types of quarantine. For example, travelers from an area in which yellow fever is prevalent may be required to remain in quarantine until the end of the incubation period; otherwise they may become sources of infection to the people in the country of their destination.

Quarantine and isolation may be voluntary or official; the latter is enforceable by the government. Official quarantine or isolation is not invoked so often as in the past because in some diseases there are so many unrecognized or missed cases that the identity of the majority of cases and contacts is unknown. When quar-

antine is employed, it usually is enforced to a greater degree against the more susceptible groups in the population or against those who may be dangerous to public health if they become infected; *e.g.*, schoolteachers or food handlers. More efficient methods of controlling communicable disease, such as vaccination (when available) or control of vehicles or vectors of disease, have to a great extent replaced isolation and quarantine.

See American Public Health Association, *Control of Communicable Diseases in Man*, 9th ed. (1960). (H. J. Sy.)

QUARITCH, BERNARD
(1819–1899), English bookseller, who in his time developed the largest antiquarian book trade in the world, was born in Worbis, Germany, on April 23, 1819. His whole life was devoted to books. He was a bookseller's assistant, first in Germany, then, from 1842, under H. G. Bohn in London. He set up his own business in 1847 and about 1858 began to deal in rare books including incunabula, Shakespeareana, Bibles, natural history, and travels. Once he had established himself Quaritch left no important book-sale in the world unattended. He had no interests outside books, and there his interest was concentratedly and ruthlessly technical: he cared nothing for content. Quaritch's catalogues were of great bibliographical interest; the first important one, issued in 1873, was the *Bibliotheca Xylographica, Typographica et Palaeographica*, a remarkable collection of early printed books from many countries. He died in London on Dec. 17, 1899. (M. Kl.)

QUARLES, FRANCIS
(1592–1644), English religious poet remembered for his *Emblemes and Hieroglyphikes*, the most notable emblem book in English. Born at Romford, Essex, he was baptized on May 8, 1592. He was educated "at schoole in the Countrey," at Cambridge, taking his degree from Christ's College in 1609, and at Lincoln's Inn, London. In 1618 he married Ursula Woodgate, and made his home in London. He had private means, and was happiest living in scholarly seclusion. He began his literary career with a series of lugubrious biblical paraphrases, the first, *A Feast for Wormes*, appearing in 1620. These were collected as *Divine Poems* (1630), his most substantial volume. About 1626 Quarles went to Ireland, where he became secretary to Archbishop Ussher. There he completed his first secular work, *Argalus and Parthenia* (1629), a heroic romance based on a story from Sir Philip Sidney's *Arcadia*. By 1633 he had settled in Essex.

With *Emblemes* (1635) Quarles produced a new type of emblem book. Most of the 79 plates for it, and some of his ideas, were borrowed (though he was a devoted member of the Church of England) from two Jesuit manuals. But his characteristic use of conventional material and the merit of his verse gave the emblem book its initial claim to serious consideration as literature. *Emblemes* was so successful that Quarles produced another emblem book, *Hieroglyphikes of the Life of Man* (1638). Printed together in 1639, *Emblemes and Hieroglyphikes* became the most popular book of verse of the 17th century.

The last years of Quarles's life were overshadowed by poverty. Probably for this reason he obtained the post of chronologer to London in 1640, and virtually abandoned poetry to employ his pen more lucratively. His first prose work, *Enchiridion* (1640), became the most popular book of aphorisms of its time.

Civil war found Quarles unhappily conscious of conflicting loyalties, yet a staunch Royalist. He is said to have suffered for his allegiance and for writing *The Loyall Convert* (1644), a pamphlet defending the king's position. Quarles died on Sept. 8, 1644. His wife, with 9 of 18 children who had been born to them, was left in want.

Bibliography.—*Complete Works*, ed. by A. B. Grosart, 3 vol. (1880–81); *Threnodes* and *Hosanna* (omitted by Grosart), ed. by J. Horden (1960); J. Horden, *Quarles: a Bibliography of His Works to the Year 1800* (1953). A primary biographical source is the memoir by Quarles's widow in his *Solomons Recantation* (1645). See also R. Freeman, *English Emblem Books* (1948). (Jn. Hn.)

QUARRYING,
the art of obtaining stone from the earth's crust. Rocks that are quarried for commercial use fall into three great groups: igneous, sedimentary and metamorphic. Granite is the most important of the igneous type. The sedimentary rocks, of which limestones, sandstones and shales are the most important,

WIRE SAWS OPERATING IN A GRANITE QUARRY IN MASSACHUSETTS

are sometimes termed stratified because they have been deposited in successive layers. The third group, metamorphic, contains rocks of both igneous and sedimentary origin that have been changed by tremendous mountain-building forces.

There are two main products of the quarrying industries—dimension stone and crushed and broken stone. The term dimension stone is applied to blocks or slabs of natural stone that are cut to definite shapes and sizes. Crushed and broken stone includes irregular fragments produced by passing the stone through crushers or by grinding the rock to a fine powder.

Dimension Stone.—Although rock deposits are abundant, only in certain places have they the necessary qualities that make them suitable for use as dimension stone. Generally the rock must be uniform in grain size and coloration, and must have attractive colours. Most rock deposits are intersected by natural partings called joints. If the joints are closely spaced the rock is valueless. The most favourable deposits are those in which the joints are vertical, in two more or less parallel systems at right angles to each other and spaced four or more feet apart.

When a rock deposit is located the first step is to clear the surface of soil, gravel or other debris—a process known as stripping.

After the surface of the rock has been cleared, the next step is to separate masses of rock from the parent ledge. It is important in quarrying dimension stone to avoid the use of powerful explosives that would shatter the rock and destroy its usefulness. Blocks must be removed with care to preserve their strength and weather resistance. The first operation is to make a cut or channel which will separate a block from the solid bed. For the softer

rocks such as limestones and sandstones, the channeling machine generally is used. This has a cutting tool consisting of several chisel-edged steel bars clamped together. As the power-driven machine travels back and forth on a track, it cuts a channel 2 to $2\frac{1}{2}$ in. wide and several feet deep.

In the harder rocks such as granites, channeling machines cannot be used. One method of making primary cuts in granite, and sometimes in marble and slate, is to drill a row of closely spaced holes to a depth of eight or ten feet, and to cut the webs or cores between them with a flat broaching tool, thus making a continuous channel. Another method is to use a wire saw. This consists of a three-strand or single-strand wire rope about $\frac{3}{16}$ in. in diameter which runs as a belt, and cuts by abrasion when fed with sand or other hard grains in water.

When the primary cuts have been made, if floor seams are absent, the mass of rock must be separated at the quarry floor. Horizontal holes may be drilled beneath the blocks, and the blocks then can be broken loose by driving wedges in the holes. The masses of rock thus set free may be very large. In limestone they may be 80 or 100 ft. long, 8 or 10 ft. high and 4 ft. wide. These large blocks are subdivided into smaller sizes generally by the plug-and-feather method. The blocks are marked out to desired sizes with square and straightedge. A man with a compressed-air hammer drill then sinks a row of shallow holes along the chalk line. Separation is made by wedging. The so-called feathers are tapered lengths of iron curved on one side to fit the wall of the drill hole and used in pairs, one down each side of a drill hole. The plug is a steel wedge which is driven between each pair of feathers. When the plugs are sledged lightly in succession, the force generated is so great that the rock breaks. The separated blocks are conveyed to mills where they are sawed into slabs, shaped to desired dimensions or turned on lathes into columns. They are then rubbed or polished to give the desired surface finish. Jet-piercing, or channeling, techniques, called "burning," also are used for drilling, cutting, shaping, and finishing (*see* BLASTING: *Drilling*).

The principal uses of dimension stone are for both exterior and interior building construction. Granites and marbles are also used extensively for memorials ranging from simple markers and headstones to elaborate mausoleums. Slate is used for roofing, stair treads, blackboards and many other applications. Sandstones are used as building stone and for abrasive wheels such as grindstones. Quartzites are used chiefly for flagging.

Crushed Stone.—Although the use of stone in fragmentary form is a comparatively recent development, the crushed stone industry has far outstripped the dimension stone industry in tonnage. The chief varieties of rock used are limestone, sandstone, granite and basalt (traprock). As the purpose is to obtain small fragments, explosives are used for shattering.

The first operation is to drill deep holes in rows. The churn drill or well drill is widely used to sink holes 6 in. or more in diameter and 50 or more feet deep. The distance of the row of holes from the quarry face is known as the burden; it is commonly 20 to 30 ft. The distance from one hole to another in the row is known as the spacing and is usually less than the burden. In large quarries a row of 15, 20 or more holes, and two or more rows may be drilled for a single blast. The size of the charge in each hole is calculated according to the toughness of the rock. When the explosive charge is in place the upper part of the hole is tamped with sand or rock dust. The charges are fired simultaneously and a single blast may throw down 20,000 or more tons of broken stone, which is then conveyed to the crushers where it is reduced to a maximum size of about six inches. The fines are separated by screening, and the larger sizes are reduced in smaller secondary crushers (*see* CRUSHING AND GRINDING MACHINES). Crushed stone is used chiefly for road building, concrete aggregate and railroad track ballast. Limestone has special uses such as fluxing stone in blast furnaces and for many chemical applications. *See also* MARBLE; SLATE; etc.

BIBLIOGRAPHY.—Oliver Bowles, *The Stone Industries*, 2nd ed. (1939); *The Quarry Managers' Journal* (monthly); *Pit and Quarry* (monthly); *Rock Products* (monthly). (O. Bs.)

QUARTER DAYS, the days that begin each quarter of the year; in England, March 25 (Lady Day), June 24 (Midsummer Day), Sept. 29 (Michaelmas Day), and Dec. 25 (Christmas Day). Some local variations of these dates are found. They are the days on which it is usually contracted that rents should be paid and houses or lands entered upon or quitted. In Scotland there are two legal terms, May 15 (Whitsunday) and Nov. 11 (Martinmas); these, with the two conventional terms, Feb. 2 (Candlemas) and Aug. 1 (Lammas), make up the Scottish quarter days. In the Scottish burghs, however, the removal terms are May 28 and Nov. 28. In the United States the quarter days are, in law, the 1st of January, April, July, and October.

QUARTERMASTER. In the U.S. army before 1962 this term denoted a member, usually a commissioned officer, of the quartermaster corps, which was responsible for the procurement and supply of food, clothing, fuel, and individual and housekeeping types of equipment (but not weapons), the collection and interment of war dead, and the maintenance of national cemeteries. A sweeping reorganization of the army's headquarters and field establishment in 1962 eliminated most of the technical services, including the quartermaster corps. Most of the corps' supply functions were absorbed by a new army materiel command, while its procurement functions fell largely to an interservice organization, the defense supply agency. The army continued, however, to commission quartermaster branch officers and to employ quartermaster troop units and quartermaster staff officers in the field.

The term quartermaster has a long history in European warfare, dating back at least to the 15th century. In general, quartermasters superintended arrangements for the quartering, and sometimes the subsistence and movement, of troops. In Europe, quartermaster officials on the staffs of higher commanders had evolved by the 18th century into something like the modern chief of staff, or chief of the general staff. In Great Britain and the United States, by contrast, the quartermaster remained a specialized administrative and logistical functionary. (*See* Logistics.)

The U.S. army's quartermaster corps traces its beginnings to June 1775, when the army itself was first established. From the beginning, the basic function of the quartermaster organization was to help plan marches, lay out camps and provide the army's transportation. In 1812 the quartermaster department (as it was then called) acquired broad though ill-defined purchasing responsibilities that conflicted with those assigned to the commissary general of purchases.

By 1842, however, the quartermaster's department was procuring and distributing to the army all its noncombat supplies and equipment except food, which was the responsibility of the subsistence department. During the Civil War the quartermaster general was responsible for all the army's transportation, on water as well as land, and including all its animals with their forage and equipage. He was also responsible for providing clothing; for the operation of utilities at military camps; for military real estate and construction, except fortifications and railway bridges; for operation of military telegraphs; and for interment of war dead. His control of military railroads and military telegraphs was purely nominal, however, as both these services were operated as virtually independent agencies directly under the secretary of war.

On the eve of World War I the quartermaster corps (now so designated) absorbed the functions of the subsistence and pay departments. During the war, all supply and transportation functions were temporarily concentrated in the general staff, but under the National Defense act of 1920 the corps was re-established with most of its old responsibilities (except the pay function). World War II brought a significant reduction in the scope of these responsibilities through creation of a separate transportation corps and assignment of most types of military construction to the corps of engineers. By 1950 the quartermaster corps had thus become essentially a supply service, feeding, clothing and fueling the army and providing much of its noncombat equipment. Under a broadening system of interservice pooling of logistical responsibilities, some of these functions were also performed for the navy and the air force.

The U.S. quartermaster corps has no exact counterpart in the British service. The royal army service corps (R.A.S.C.) stores and issues expendable noncombat supplies such as food, forage and fuel. The R.A.S.C. is also responsible for most transportation except that organic to units. The royal army ordnance corps stores and issues equipment, clothing, ammunition and explosives and certain motor vehicles. The civilian ministry of supply, rather than the military services, handles procurement of supplies. In British army staff organization, the quartermaster general's branch, or "Q" staff, has co-ordinating responsibility for supplying the material needs of troops and for all military movement (except operational, which is controlled by the "G" or general staff branch). Personnel administration is the responsibility of the adjutant general's branch, or "A" staff.

In the naval service, both American and British, quartermasters are petty officers or selected seamen who perform certain navigational and administrative duties under supervision of the captain, navigating officer or officer of the deck, including manning the wheel while at sea.

Bibliography.—Erna Risch, *The Quartermaster Corps: Organization, Supply, and Services,* vol. i (1953); Erna Risch and Chester L. Kieffer, *The Quartermaster Corps: Organization, Supply, and Services,* vol. ii (1955); Erna Risch, *Quartermaster Support of the Army: a History of the Corps, 1775–1939* (1962). (R. M. Ln.)

QUARTER SESSIONS, COURT OF, in English law, the name of the court held in general or quarterly sessions by the justices of the peace for a county (or riding, parts, liberty, or other division of a county); or of the court held, before a recorder, in a borough having a separate court of quarter sessions (*i.e.,* separate from that of the county in which the borough is geographically situated). The borough may be a county borough, a so-called county of a city or county of a town, or simply a municipal borough. The term "general" applied to sessions contrasts historically with "special" or "petty"; the latter is now reserved for sittings of magistrates in courts of summary jurisdiction and the former is virtually obsolete.

The name quarter sessions is derived from a statute of 1388, which required "the justices to keep their sessions in every quarter at the least." By the Criminal Justice Administration Act, 1962 (section 4 [1]), courts of quarter sessions shall be held at such times as directed by the county justices, the recorder or the lord chancellor; but at least four times a year. The intention, in accordance with the Streatfield Report (Report of the Interdepartmental Committee on the Business of the Criminal Courts, Cmnd. 1289, 1961), is to arrange all the sittings of the various courts of quarter sessions in a given county so that there is at least one court sitting every four or six weeks and a speedy trial can be provided for all prisoners. To ensure this the county and borough sessions dovetail their sittings, and the committing justices (by sections 14 and 15 of the above act) have power to commit to any "convenient" court; *i.e.,* a court that will be sitting earlier than the one to which they normally commit.

Every portion of England and Wales is within the jurisdiction of some court of quarter sessions, and justices and recorders may hold additional sessions by adjourning from time to time. If there is no business to transact within five days of the day appointed for holding the sessions (which is not believed to have happened for many years), the court is not held, and jurymen who have been summoned are excused from attendance (Assizes and Quarter Sessions Act, 1908, s. 1 and 2).

A borough recorder is appointed by the crown on the advice of the lord chancellor and must be a barrister of at least five years' standing. Deputy recorders may be appointed if the recorder is unable to attend; and assistant recorders may be appointed in towns of such a size that the business regularly requires two courts. In county sessions the justices may now elect a chairman and as many deputy chairmen as are necessary. Originally the chairman or deputies were elected by the justices from among their own number and did not have to be legally qualified. But it was felt that laymen, however experienced, ought not to preside at trials where difficult issues might have to be explained to a jury or long sentences might have to be passed. By the Administration of Justice (Miscellaneous Provisions) Act, 1938 (s. 1, 2, 4), the county justices were authorized to request the crown to appoint legally qualified chairmen and deputy chairmen, and to pay them out of county funds, sessions held under such chairmen having increased jurisdiction. By the Criminal Justice Administration Act, 1962 (s. 5), all chairmen and deputy chairmen must be legally qualified, and the jurisdiction of county sessions was further enlarged (s. 12). All recorders, their deputies, and assistants are legally qualified, and their courts have the same jurisdiction as county sessions. A recorder sits alone. Normally county justices must form a quorum (at least two and not more than nine); but if other justices cannot attend, the chairman or his deputy may sit alone.

In Greater London and in Lancashire pressure of work led to the appointment from the bar of whole-time, paid, professional judges; other legally qualified chairmen of county sessions retain their practices. Pressure of work also led to changes in Manchester and Liverpool; in those cities the Criminal Justice Administration Act, 1956, created special criminal courts, known as crown courts, the jurisdiction of the courts of quarter sessions being transferred to the new courts, both of which have full-time judges. Quarter sessions for the City of London are nominally held before the lord mayor and aldermen sitting with the recorder of London, but criminal cases are sent to the central criminal court.

Every court of quarter sessions is a court of record and can punish summarily contempts of itself. It is, however, subject to the supervisory jurisdiction of the Queen's Bench Division of the High Court by means of the prerogative orders. Appeal lies to the Court of Criminal Appeal in respect of all decisions in criminal matters and in other matters by way of case stated to the divisional court.

Criminal Jurisdiction.—An order in council dated Feb. 22, 1878, authorized justices to inquire "of all and all manner of crimes, trespasses and all and singular other offences that the justices of our peace may or ought lawfully to inquire . . . ." In fact the jurisdiction is largely statutory. The Quarter Sessions Act, 1842, was the first attempt systematically to regulate (s. 1) the powers of quarter sessions, and it took away their power to try crimes involving a death sentence, long terms of imprisonment, or difficult legal issues.

Thereafter a series of statutes alternately added to and reduced the list of crimes triable in sessions. The Criminal Justice Act, 1925, made a valiant effort to rationalize the position, but the acts of 1938 and 1962 (*see* above) both further enlarged the jurisdiction of sessions. Differences in jurisdiction between various borough quarter sessions were eliminated by legislation in 1956. By the mid-1960s all sessions could try all indictable crimes save treason and kindred offenses; murder; manslaughter; the graver offenses against the person and property and those involving difficult points of law. The list is somewhat piecemeal, arbitrary, and highly technical. Where there is a plea of not guilty the trial is conducted with a jury.

Appellate Jurisdiction.—A recorder can hear appeals from decisions of the borough justices, and county sessions hear appeals from all the petty sessional divisions of the county. Appeals committees, originally created to relieve pressure of work on county sessions, have been abolished, as it was hoped that the more frequent sittings of all sessions would reduce the pressure of work. Such appeals include civil and criminal causes.

Civil Jurisdiction.—Until 1888 the justices in general sessions had wide powers to "conduct the county business," but since then most of their administrative work has been transferred to county councils or other local government bodies, and their civil business now consists of a number of miscellaneous duties that have survived for historical reasons; *e.g.*, the giving of orders relating to the diversion of highways, the appointment of prison visitors, and the hearing of appeals from local justices in civil matters (such as the refusal of a licence for a camping site). As regards the sale of alcoholic liquors, the justices' chief task is to hear appeals from local licensing justices. Their rating functions have been transferred to special tribunals.

United States.—Pennsylvania has courts of quarter session, oyer and terminer, on a county basis; Kentucky has quarterly courts, sharing with city, justice, and police courts jurisdiction over certain classes of cases. Otherwise, courts of other names, differing in the various jurisdictions, perform the functions of the English courts of quarter sessions. *See* also COURT.

(G. A. F.)

QUARTER SQUARES. The product of two numbers is equal to the difference of one fourth the squares of their sum and their difference: $ab = \frac{1}{4}(a + b)^2 - \frac{1}{4}(a - b)^2$. This fact has been used to reduce multiplication to addition with the aid of tables of quarter squares, or using other methods of generating quarter squares. The quarter square of an odd number always has a fractional part $\frac{1}{4}$, which can be ignored in applying the formula. The method is very old and many tables of quarter squares have been prepared, but few are easily available. The most extensive table lists quarter squares of integers not exceeding 200,000. Various mechanical and electrical applications have been suggested. The method is still frequently useful and economical.

See J. Blater, *Tafel der Viertel-Quadrate aller ganzen Zahlen von 1 bis 200,000* (1887). For reference to other tables *see* A. Fletcher, J. C. P. Miller, L. Rosenhead, *An Index of Mathematical Tables* (1946 and later) and mathematical review journals. (C. B. To.)

QUARTON (CHARONTON, CHARRETON), **ENGUERRAND,** French religious painter, famous for his "Coronation of the Virgin," was born in the diocese of Laon, and was active in Provence (1444–66). He adopted the southern form of Quarton for his real Picardian name Charreton (modern Charonton or Charenton). He is one of the best-documented French medieval artists, and details exist of six commissions for important paintings, two of which have survived: the "Virgin of Mercy" (1452, Chantilly), an altarpiece, the predella of which, painted in collaboration with Pierre Villate, is missing; and the "Coronation of the Virgin" (1453–54, Hospice de Villeneuve-les-Avignons), the contract for which is one of the most complete and interesting documents on medieval art, showing that the composition was minutely prescribed. Both paintings reveal a very original style, partly northern (showing affinities with sculptures from Picardy) and partly southern (a sort of "cubist," sharp, sculptural stylization of figures, folds, and rocks). Exactly the same style is to be found in the famous "Avignon Pietà" (shortly before 1457? now in the Louvre), which is most probably the work of Quarton.

Quarton is in the first rank of French painters. He is full of imagination, creating very original types of Virgin and saints; his drawing is precise and graceful, his composition majestic and rich. Like Jean Fouquet, Quarton combines the grandeur of monumental decoration with the subtlety of book illumination.

BIBLIOGRAPHY.—Charles Sterling, *Le Couronnement de la Vierge par E. Quarton* (1939), *Bulletin de la Société Nationale des Antiquaires de France,* pp. 214 ff. (1960); Grete Ring, *A Century of French Painting, 1400–1500* (1949). (C. SG.)

QUARTZ, a widely distributed mineral species, consisting of silicon dioxide, or silica (SiO_2). It is one of the commonest minerals and is found in many varieties and with very diverse modes of occurrence. The various forms of quartz have attracted attention from the earliest times, and the water-clear crystals were known to the Greeks as *crystallos*, "clear ice," being supposed by them to have been formed from water by the intense cold of the Alps; hence the name crystal, or more commonly rock crystal, applied to this variety. The name quartz is an old German word of uncertain origin, first used by Georg Agricola in 1530.

Following a description of the uses, occurrence and general properties of quartz this article deals with its crystallography, the varieties of quartz, electrical properties and optical properties and discusses the changes, known as inversions, quartz undergoes when heated.

Uses.—Quartz is a mineral of great economic importance. Many varieties are in popular use as gem stones, such as agate, amethyst, aventurine, bloodstone, cairngorm or smoky quartz, carnelian, chrysoprase, citrine, onyx (for cameos), rock crystal, rose quartz and tigereye (*see* also GEM). In localities where satisfactory material is available, sandstone, composed mainly of quartz, is an important building stone. Large amounts of sand are used in the manufacture of glass and porcelain. Sand is widely used for foundry molds for casting metals. Quartz is an abrasive, as in sandpaper, sandblasting, millstones and grindstones. Quartz brick is a high-grade refractory (see *Inversion,* below) and is used as a flux in smelting calcareous ores. Both quartz and silica glass transmit ultraviolet light and are used optically for this purpose. Because of the low coefficient of expansion and the refractory nature, tubing and various vessels of fused quartz have important laboratory applications; fibres are used in extremely sensitive weighing devices (*see* BALANCE: *Ultramicrobalance*). Thin plates cut from quartz crystals are used for frequency control in electronic communications equipment (see *Electrical Properties,* below).

Occurrence.—Quartz occurs as a primary and essential constituent of igneous rocks of acidic composition, such as granite, quartz porphyry and rhyolite. It is an abundant mineral in pegmatites, sometimes making up the major part, and often being intergrown with feldspar (graphic granite). It is a common constituent in many gneisses and crystalline schists. By the weathering of silicates, silica passes into solution and is redeposited as quartz in cavities, crevices and along joints of rocks of all types.

Extensive veins of quartz are frequent in schistose rocks. Quartz veins, of economic importance as a matrix of gold, are probably related to igneous action. In mineral veins and lodes, quartz is often the most abundant gangue mineral. Quartz, being a mineral very resistant to weathering, forms the bulk of sands and sandstones, the latter being sand cemented with calcite, gypsum or hematite. A siliceous cement gives an orthoquartzite, while such a rock after being metamorphosed and recrystallized is called metaquartzite. Quartz occurs as pseudomorphs, replacing other minerals, and frequently is the petrifying material in petrified wood.

For ordinary uses, quartz is abundant and cheap. However, lack of adequate supplies of suitable crystals for electrical use has led to many attempts to grow synthetic quartz. Successful methods have been found, and good crystals, free from twinning, have been produced.

General Properties.—Quartz is a hardness standard, being 7 on Mohs' scale; it cannot be scratched with a knife. The specific gravity is 2.65. There is no distinct cleavage, but plunging a heated crystal into cold water may develop planes of separation parallel to the rhombohedral and prism faces. A conchoidal fracture is characteristic of most varieties. Coarse-grained varieties have a vitreous to greasy lustre; fine-grained varieties may be waxy or dull. The mineral is a nonconductor of electricity; it is not attacked by acids, except hydrofluoric, and is only slightly dissolved by solutions of caustic alkalies. It is infusible in the ordinary blowpipe flame, but will fuse in the oxyhydrogen flame to a clear colourless glass.

Crystallography.—Quartz crystallizes in the trigonal trapezohedral class of the hexagonal system. The crystals possess no planes or centre of symmetry, but only axes of symmetry. The vertical (c) axis is a threefold axis, and the three lateral (a) axes are twofold and polar; that is, the opposite ends are not alike. Usually, however, this lower degree of symmetry is not indicated

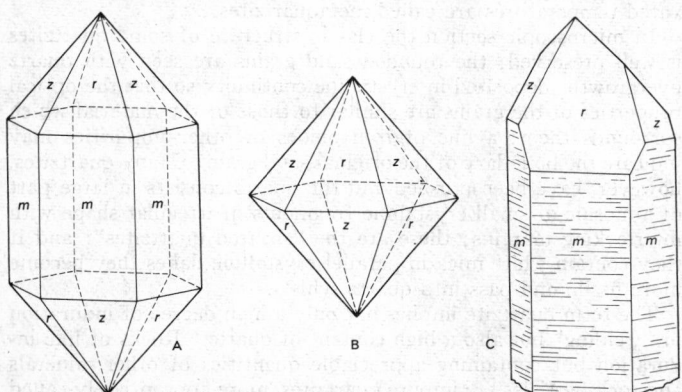

FIG. 1.—QUARTZ CRYSTALS SHOWING RELATIONSHIPS OF FACES AND CHARACTERISTIC STRIATIONS

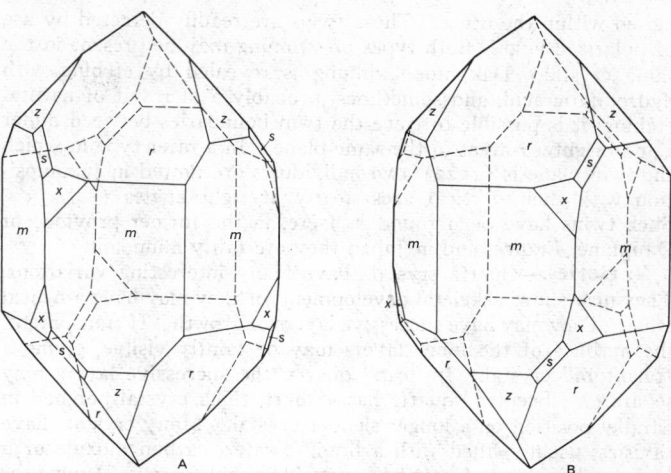

FIG. 2.—LEFT- AND RIGHT-HANDED QUARTZ CRYSTALS ILLUSTRATING MIRROR IMAGE SYMMETRY

by the face development of the crystals. Many crystals are bounded only by the faces of a hexagonal prism m ($10\bar{1}0$) and what appears to be a hexagonal bipyramid (fig. 1A), although sometimes the prism is absent (fig. 1B). Frequently the crystals are distorted (fig. 1C), with similar faces varying in size but still having their proper angular positions. If the distortion is extreme, at first glance the crystals may be difficult to interpret, but they can usually be oriented by aid of the very characteristic horizontal striations on the prism faces. These striations (fig. 1C) are parallel to the edges of intersection between the prism and terminal faces, and are due to the frequent oscillatory combination of these forms. The apparent hexagonal bipyramid is really a combination of two rhombohedrons, one positive, r ($10\bar{1}1$), and the other negative, z ($01\bar{1}1$). Although many exceptions occur, z is usually smaller than r (fig. 2A and B) and sometimes completely absent. The six small faces s ($11\bar{2}1$), situated on alternate corners, are those of a trigonal bipyramid, while the faces x ($51\bar{6}1$) are those of a trigonal trapezohedron. The latter are of comparatively rare occurrence, except on crystals from a few localities. These x faces clearly distinguish between the two types of quartz crystals, left-handed (fig. 2A) and right-handed (fig. 2B). Such crystals are said to be enantiomorphous. They are not superposable, but one is the mirror reflection of the other, like the right and left hands. In some cases the s faces are striated parallel to their intersection with $r;$ this serves to distinguish r and $z,$ and thus show the right- or left-handed character when the x faces are missing. Numerous other faces have been observed on quartz, but they are of rare occurrence. The basal plane, so common on many crystals, is of the greatest rarity on quartz, and when present appears only as a small rough face formed by corrosion of the crystal. Natural etching, or artificial etching by hydrofluoric acid, produces etch figures, which are small pits or depressions of characteristic shape. As would be expected, the etch figures are different on the r and z faces, and on right-handed crystals the etch figures are reversed in position with respect to left-handed, thus clearly revealing the true symmetry and enantiomorphous character. This feature of the crystals is of course related to the internal grouping of the atoms, which actually consists of a spiral arrangement that may be either right- or left-handed.

Twin crystals of quartz are very common; in fact those without twinning are rare. The twinning may not be obvious unless the s or the x faces are present. Penetration twins are the commonest, with the prism planes of both individuals coinciding, and may be of two types. Dauphiné or electrical twins consist of two right-handed or two left-handed crystals intergrown so that the r faces of one coincide with the z faces of the other, which brings the x and s faces on all six corners, both above and below. The contact between the two portions may be very irregular, or there may be a complicated patchwork of the two orientations. Brazil or optical twins are intimate intergrowths of right- and left-handed quartz, laminae or polygonal inclusions of one being enclosed within the other. These twins are readily detected by use of polarized light. Both types of twinning may be present in the same crystal. Dauphiné twinning is revealed by etching with hydrofluoric acid, and sometimes, probably as a result of natural etching, it is possible to trace the twin boundaries between duller z and brighter r areas in the same plane. In a rarer type in which the twin plane is (1122), two individuals are united in juxtaposition with their vertical axes nearly at right angles (84° 33′). Such twins have been found in Isère, in the former province of Dauphiné, France, and in Japan they are fairly abundant.

Varieties.—Quartz crystals have many interesting variations. They may show a skeletal development, or they may have a helical twist. They may have successive layers of growth. If transparent, the outlines of the inner layers may be faintly visible, giving a "phantom" crystal. In "cap" quartz, the successive layers may separate. "Sceptre" quartz has a short, thick crystal perched in parallel position on a longer slender crystal. Many crystals have cavities, usually filled with a liquid (water, carbon dioxide or a hydrocarbon) and containing a movable bubble of gas. Among the many varieties of quartz are amethyst, rose, milky and smoky quartz, which have characteristic colorations. In addition to the pink colour, properly cut rose quartz may show a star-shaped figure (asterism). Citrine is a yellow variety. Some types of quartz contain inclusions of other minerals, such as rutilated quartz, which has long needles of rutile. Aventurine contains glistening scales of mica, hematite or chlorite; moss agate has inclusions of manganese oxide or chlorite. Tigereye is a replacement of asbestos, and retains the fibrous structure; hence it has a beautiful chatoyant (cat's-eye) lustre when cut and polished. There are many fine-grained varieties of quartz. Chalcedony has a waxy lustre, and occurs in botryoidal and stalactitic forms. Agate and onyx are banded, being formed by the successive deposition of very thin layers. Many agates used for ornaments have been artificially coloured. Carnelian is red; chrysoprase and plasma are green; bloodstone is green with red spots. Basanite or touchstone is black, and was formerly used for testing precious alloys by means of the colour of the streak they left when rubbed on the stone. Jasper is impure, and coloured red, brown or yellow by iron oxide. Flint and chert are gray and occur as nodules in chalk and limestone. For particulars concerning the appearance, properties, occurrence, etc., of varieties of quartz see AGATE; AVENTURINE; BLOODSTONE (or heliotrope); CARNELIAN; CAT'S-EYE; CHERT AND FLINT; JASPER; MOCHA STONE (or moss agate); ONYX.

Electrical Properties.—Quartz is piezoelectric; that is, a crystal develops positive and negative charges on alternate prism edges when it is subjected to pressure or tension. The charges are proportional to the change in pressure. The pyroelectric effect supposedly observed on quartz is actually attributable to differential expansion during heating, hence is really a piezoelectric effect. This behaviour is related to the low symmetry, especially to the polar character of the lateral axes. Because of the piezoelectric property, a quartz plate can be used as a pressure gauge, as in depth-sounding apparatus. Moreover, if compression and tension produce opposite charges, the converse effect is that alternating opposite charges will cause alternating expansion and contraction. A section cut from a quartz crystal, with definite orientation and dimensions, has a natural frequency of this expansion and contraction (i.e., vibration) which is very high.

Properly cut plates of quartz may have frequencies measured in millions of vibrations per second, and are used for frequency control in radio and other electronic communications equipment and for crystal-controlled clocks. Quartz plates for this purpose must be from portions of a crystal free from twinning (electronic grade); otherwise the vibrations would be in opposition in the two twin areas.

Optical Properties.—In its optical behaviour, quartz is also of interest, since it shows rotary polarization. This phenomenon is related to the enantiomorphous character of quartz. A ray of plane-polarized light traversing a right-handed crystal in the direction of the vertical axis has the plane of polarization rotated to the right, while a left-handed crystal rotates it to the left. A section one millimetre thick, cut perpendicular to the vertical axis of a quartz crystal, rotates the plane of yellow light (D line) through 22° and of blue light (G line) through 43°. Such a section when examined between crossed nicols with the petrographic microscope shows an interference figure with a coloured centre, there being no black cross inside the innermost ring (this is not shown in very thin sections). Superimposed sections of right- and left-handed quartz, as may be present in twinned crystals, exhibit interference figures with Airy spirals. The indexes of refraction of quartz for yellow light (D) are $o = 1.5442$ and $e = 1.5533$; the optic sign is therefore positive.

See also LIGHT: *Refraction and Double Refraction: Natural Optical Gyration.*

Inversion.—When heated, quartz undergoes a series of remarkable changes. At ordinary temperatures it exists as α-quartz, but at 573° C. it passes over into β-quartz, with a change from trigonal trapezohedral to hexagonal trapezohedral symmetry and an alteration in other properties. At 867° C. this β-quartz changes to β-tridymite, and again at 1,470° C. changes to β-cristobalite. These changes are known as inversions. The inversion from α- to β-quartz is reversible, so that quartz is always the α-form at ordinary temperatures. After β-tridymite or β-cristobalite are formed, they remain as tridymite or cristobalite, but upon cooling they invert to metastable α forms, which may exist for indefinitely long periods. Accordingly, all three α forms are found in nature. The six crystalline modifications have closely related structures, in which each silicon atom is surrounded tetrahedrally by four oxygen atoms. Adjacent tetrahedrons are linked by sharing of oxygen atoms, and the various modifications differ only in the arrangement of these linked tetrahedrons. The change from quartz to tridymite at the inversion temperature is very sluggish. This is of practical importance in the manufacture of silica refractory brick. The original quartz brick must be heated well above the inversion temperature if the inversion is to be completed in a reasonable time. This is necessary before the brick can be used in a furnace lining, since there is about a 15% increase in volume in the inversion from quartz to tridymite. Cristobalite, on the other hand, has nearly the same volume as tridymite, so that it does not matter which is present in the finished brick. For additional information on inversion see SILICA.

For discussion of crystallographic and mineralogical concepts used in this article see also MINERALOGY. See also references under "Quartz" in the Index.   (L. J. S.; L. S. RL.)

QUARTZITE is a sandstone which has been converted into a solid quartz rock. Unlike sandstones, quartzites are free from pores and have a smooth fracture; if struck with a hammer they break through the sand grains, whereas in sandstones the fracture passes through the cementing material and the rounded surfaces of the grains are exposed, giving the broken surface a rough and granular appearance. Conversion of sandstone to quartzite may be accomplished by precipitation of silica from interstitial waters (hydrous metamorphism) at no great depth and under ordinary pressures. In contrast with these rocks, termed orthoquartzites, those produced by recrystallization under high pressure and elevated temperatures are called metaquartzites.

In microscopic section the clastic structure of some quartzites is well preserved; the rounded sand grains are seen with quartz overgrowths deposited in crystalline continuity so that the optical properties of the grains are similar to those of the material which surrounds them: a line of iron oxides or other impurities may indicate the boundary of the original sand grain. Many quartzites, however, have been crushed and the quartz consists in large part of a mosaic of small crystalline fragments of irregular shape with interlocking margins; these are the "sheared quartzites"; and if they contain white mica in parallel crystalline flakes they become more fissile and pass into quartz schists.

The term quartzite implies not only a high degree of induration or "welding" but also a high content of quartz. Rocks of like induration but containing appreciable quantities of other minerals and rock particles are impure quartzites, more appropriately called graywacke, etc. Most quartzites contain 90% or more of quartz, and in some the quartz content exceeds 99%. These constitute the largest and purest concentrations of silica in the earth's crust. Quartzites are snowy white, less often pink or gray; they commonly have a fine angular jointing and break up into rubble under the action of frost. They yield a thin and very barren soil, and because they weather slowly tend to project as hills or as mountain masses. Many of the prominent ridges in the Appalachian mountains are the topographic expression of highly resistant tilted beds of Paleozoic quartzite. The Precambrian rocks of the Lake Huron and Lake Superior regions include thick and very pure quartzites. The Baraboo quartzite in Wisconsin is often deep red in colour. In Scotland, the mountains of Schiehallion in Perth and the Paps of Jura form conspicuous conical mountains of quartzite in the Dalradian system of the highlands and Cambrian quartzites cap mountains in western Sutherland. The pure quartzites are a source of silica for metallurgical purposes and for the manufacture of silica brick. Quartzite is also quarried for paving blocks, riprap, road metal (crushed stone), railroad ballast and roofing granules.

(F. J. P.; X.)

QUARTZ PORPHYRY, in petrology, a group of acidic igneous rocks that are porphyritic, that is, composed of larger crystals in a fine-grained groundmass. They contain visible crystals of quartz in a fine-grained matrix which is usually minutely crystalline in structure. In hand specimens the quartz appears as small, rounded, clear, grayish, vitreous blebs, which are crystals (double hexagonal pyramids) with their edges and corners rounded by resorption or corrosion. Under the microscope rounded enclosures of the groundmass or fluid cavities are often seen; these frequently have regular outlines resembling those of perfect quartz crystals and are known as negative crystals. Many of the quartz crystals contain liquid carbonic acid and a bubble of gas which may exhibit vibration under high magnifying powers. In addition to quartz there are usually prominent crystals (phenocrysts) of feldspar, mostly orthoclase, though a varying amount of plagioclase is often present. The feldspars are usually cloudy from the formation of secondary kaolin and muscovite throughout their substance; their crystals are larger than those of quartz and sometimes attain a length of two inches. It is not uncommon for scales of mica to be visible as hexagonal plates. Other porphyritic minerals are few, but hornblende (an amphibole), and augite and bronzite (pyroxenes) are sometimes found; the augite and hornblende are in most cases green, and are frequently decomposed into chlorite, but even then can usually be identified by their shape. A colourless rhombic pyroxene (enstatite or bronzite) occurs in a limited number of the rocks of this group and readily weathers to bastite. Apatite, magnetite and zircon, all in small but frequently perfect crystals, are almost universal minerals of the quartz porphyries.

Structure.—The groundmass is finely crystalline. To the unaided eye it usually appears dull, resembling common earthenware; it is gray, green, reddish or white. Often it is streaked or banded by fluxion during cooling but as a rule these rocks are not vesicular. Two main types may be recognized by means of the microscope—the felsitic and the microcrystalline. In the former the ingredients are so fine grained that even in the thinnest slices they cannot be identified under the microscope. Some of the rocks show perlitic or spherulitic structure; such were probably originally glassy (obsidians or pitchstones), but by lapse of time have slowly passed into a very finely crystalline state. This change is called devitrification; it is common in glasses, as these are essentially unstable. A large number of the finer quartz porphyries are also in some degree silicified or impregnated by quartz, chalcedony and opal, derived from the silica set free by decomposition (kaolinization) of the original feldspar. This redeposited silica forms veins and patches of indefinite shape or may bodily replace a considerable area of the rock by metasomatic substitution. The opal is amorphous, the chalcedony finely crystalline and often arranged in spherulitic growths which yield an excellent black cross in polarized light.

The microcrystalline groundmasses are those which can be resolved into their component minerals in thin slices by use of the microscope. They prove to consist essentially of quartz and feldspars, which are often in grains of quite irregular shape (microgranitic). In other cases these two minerals are in graphic

intergrowth, often forming radiate growths of spherulites consisting of fibres of extreme slenderness; this type is known as granophyric. There is another group in which the matrix contains small rounded or shapeless patches of quartz in which many rectangular feldspars are embedded; this structure is called micropoikilitic (from the Greek for variegated or mottled), and though often primary is sometimes developed by secondary changes which involve the deposit of new quartz in the groundmass. As a whole those quartz porphyries which have microcrystalline groundmasses are rocks of intrusive origin.

Older Forms.—Many of the older quartz porphyries which occur in Paleozoic and Precambrian rocks have been affected by earth movements and have experienced crushing and shearing. In this way they become schistose, and from their feldspar minute plates of sericitic white mica are developed, giving the rock in some cases very much of the appearance of mica schists. If there have been no phenocrysts in the original rock, very perfect mica schists may be produced, which can hardly be distinguished from sedimentary schists, though chemically somewhat different on account of the larger amounts of alkalis which igneous rocks contain. When phenocrysts were present they often remain, though rounded and dragged apart while the matrix flows around them. The glassy or felsitic enclosures in the quartz are then very suggestive of an igneous origin for the rock. Such porphyry schists have been called porphyroids or porphyroid schists, and in North America the name aporhyolite has been used for them. They are known in parts of the Alps, Westphalia, Charnwood (England) and Pennsylvania. The *hälleflintas* of Sweden are also in part acid igneous rocks with a well-banded schistose or granulitic texture.

The quartz porphyries are distinguished from the rhyolites by being intrusive rocks. *See also* PETROLOGY. (J. S. F.; X.)

QUASIMODO, SALVATORE (1901–1968), Italian poet who received the Nobel Prize for Literature in 1959. He was born at Modica, Sicily, on Aug. 20, 1901, and had a technical education, which may explain the enthusiasm for technological progress of his later poems. After graduating in engineering at the Rome polytechnic, he spent ten years in different parts of Italy in the state engineering service's Department of Geometrical Design, writing poetry in his spare time. In 1935 he went to Milan as professor of Italian literature at the Conservatoire. Later he was drama critic for the Milan *Tempo* and wrote for reviews.

Quasimodo published his first poems in the *avant-garde* review *Solaria*. In the 1930s he became a leader of the *ermetismo*, a school of poetry that derived from the French Symbolistes an experimental attitude to verse form and the theory that words should be used to convey unconscious associations of feeling and thought by being linked in unexpected arrangements. At first a disciple of G. Ungaretti and E. Montale (q.v.), he soon developed a personal style with its own haunting music, introducing to the frigid and calculated skill of his technical innovations a human warmth and a consciousness of the mysterious power of man's ancestral hopes and fears. From *Acque e terre* ("Waters and Land," 1930) to *La terra impareggiabile* ("The Incomparable Earth," 1958) Quasimodo's poetry showed coherent development from a dry, sophisticated perfection of style to understanding of life and a commitment to contemporary struggles, expressed in his statement, "The ultimate conquest of poetry is reality." In his translations, notably *Lirici Greci* (1940), *Il fiore delle Georgiche* (1942), and *La Tempesta* (1952), he combined feeling for the original with modern taste and sensibility. He died June 14, 1968, at Naples. For a portrait of Quasimodo *see* the article ITALIAN LITERATURE.

(F. MI.)

QUASI-STELLAR RADIO SOURCES are bizarre astronomical objects which radiate prodigious amounts of radio and optical energy. First detected in 1961, these sources, hereafter called QSS's, represent one of the fundamental astronomical discoveries of the 20th century. They present a combination of characteristics unlike anything known in the universe and may be the first evidence of a new type of energy source.

The QSS's generate continuous radio power at all the frequencies that can be received on earth. The energy distribution in optical wavelengths shows an abnormal ultraviolet flux compared with other known astronomical bodies. The emission lines in the optical spectra—due to hydrogen, magnesium, and highly ionized neon and oxygen—are all shifted from their laboratory wavelengths toward the red, indicating large velocities of recession, apparently caused by the cosmological expansion of the universe. These red shifts range from $\Delta\lambda/\lambda_0 = 0.158$ for source 3C 273 to $\Delta\lambda/\lambda_0 > 2$ for many sources such as 3C 9. If cosmological in origin, these red shifts indicate that the QSS's are more than 1,000,000,000 light-years distant from our galactic system. These distances, calculated from the velocity-distance relation, when combined with the flux density of radiation measured on earth, show that the power generated by each QSS is about 4×10^{46} ergs per second, which is of the order of 100 times the total power radiated by the largest galaxies known. The diameters of the regions of QSS's which generate the continuum radiation are less than one light-year, which is exceedingly small for objects producing power at the observed rate. Furthermore, the light of many QSS's varies in intensity by ratios ranging up to a factor of 20 over periods of months. How the most powerful sources of energy known can change their power output by such enormous factors in such a short time is not understood.

The mechanism of radio generation is believed to be due to the acceleration of ultra-high-speed electrons in a large-scale magnetic field associated with the QSS's. The origin of the electrons themselves is likely to be connected with a gigantic explosion which transferred energy from the explosive mechanism into the elementary particles created by the catastrophe. The debris of the explosion can be seen optically in the thin, luminous jets which are present in QSS 3C 48, 3C 196, 3C 273, and several others. These jets extend outward to distances of about 300,000 light-years from their parent bodies. These distances indicate that the minimum age of the QSS's is 300,000 years, obtained by assuming that the material comprising the jet escaped from the central object at the speed of light at the time of the explosion. But the true lifetime is likely to be considerably longer because the jets must have traveled more slowly than light.

A minimum value for the energy radiated by the high-speed electrons can be calculated to be 4×10^{59} ergs, obtained by multiplying the radiated power over all wavelengths (4×10^{46} ergs/sec) by the minimum lifetime of the source. The total energy in the system must be greater than that which is in the electrons because only a small fraction of the energy could have been pumped into the electron reservoir. The total energy of a QSS must be about 4×10^{61} ergs if a conversion efficiency of 1% for the energy transferred to the electrons is assumed. This is equivalent to the explosion of 3×10^9 solar masses of hydrogen, the mass of a small galaxy, by thermonuclear processes.

These mass and energy characteristics are so unlike anything previously encountered that some astronomers questioned the distances of the QSS's, which are indicated by the measured red shifts. If the red shifts are not cosmological, the distances could be small and the total energies could be reduced somewhat. But other explanations of the red shifts pose even more baffling problems. The problem was virtually solved in 1967 by noting the observed continuity of properties for QSS and radio galaxies which are known to be at their Hubble distance. The continuity of surface brightness and linear splitting of the radio components shows that the red shifts of QSS are cosmological.

The total number of QSS to optical magnitude B = 19.5 is believed to be at least 100,000, most of which are radio quiet to an apparent flux level of 2×10^{-26} watts per square metre per cycle per second at 178 Mc/sec. Hence, most QSS must be found by optical methods which utilize the excess ultraviolet intensity, the optical variation, and the lack of proper motion.

Bibliography.—T. A. Matthews and A. R. Sandage, "Optical Identification of 3C 48, 3C 196, and 3C 286 with Stellar Objects," Astrophysical Journal, 138:30–56 (July 1, 1963); M. Schmidt, "3C 273: A Star-like Object with Large Red-Shift," Nature, 197:1040 (March 16, 1963). (A. R. Sa.)

QUATERNARY, in geology, is the latest chapter in the earth's history and comprises the time that has elapsed from the end of the Pliocene (q.v.) to the present day. It is the second division of the Cenozoic era (q.v.) as indicated in the accompanying geologic time chart but represents such a short time that some geologists hesitate to give it equal rank and regard it as merely a subdivision of the preceding Tertiary period. Two divisions of the Quaternary period are usually recognized: (1) the Pleistocene, the larger part; (2) and the Holocene or Recent, a short period following the Last Glaciation. For a brief history of the origin and application of the term see GEOLOGY: *Historical Geology: Paleontology and the Scale of Time.*

The Quaternary is characterized by wide climatic fluctuations. Compared with the Tertiary period, the climate was much colder: ice sheets developed in Scandinavia, on the higher mountain ranges of Europe and Asia and in North America. In the southern hemisphere the Antarctic ice, like that of Greenland, was larger and the Andes, Tasmania and New Zealand had important icecaps. Hence the term Ice Age or Glacial period is often used for the Pleistocene, though the Holocene, usually called "postglacial," may still be considered in the Ice Age.

The northern hemisphere probably had four separate ice advances; these ice advances comprise the major divisions of the Pleistocene. Elsewhere, Lower, Middle and Upper Pleistocene are paleontologically distinguished, though strict contemporaneity in different parts of the world has not been established. The Holocene

Geologic Time Chart

System and Period	Series and Epoch	Distinctive Records of Life	Began (Millions of Years Ago)
CENOZOIC ERA			
Quaternary	Recent (last 11,000 years)		
	Pleistocene	Early man	2+
Tertiary	Pliocene	Large carnivores	10
	Miocene	Whales, apes, grazing forms	27
	Oligocene	Large browsing mammals	38
	Eocene	Rise of flowering plants	55
	Paleocene	First placental mammals	65–70
MESOZOIC ERA			
Cretaceous		Extinction of dinosaurs	130
Jurassic		Dinosaurs' zenith, primitive birds, first small mammals	180
Triassic		Appearance of dinosaurs	225
PALEOZOIC ERA			
Permian		Reptiles developed, conifers abundant	260
Carboniferous Upper (Pennsylvanian)		First reptiles, coal forests	300
Lower (Mississippian)		Sharks abundant	340
Devonian		Amphibians appeared, fishes abundant	405
Silurian		Earliest land plants and animals	435
Ordovician		First primitive fishes	480
Cambrian		Marine invertebrates	550–570
PRECAMBRIAN TIME			
		Few fossils	more than 3,490

is subdivided on the basis of its vegetational development.

The beginning of the Quaternary is difficult to define since the transition from the last phase of the Tertiary (the Pliocene) was in every respect gradual. Thus the gradation of animal life is imperceptible from the Late Pliocene into the Lower Pleistocene (Villafranchian). The onset of the First Glaciation is the event most widely accepted as marking the opening of the era. It is, however, being increasingly recognized that the classical Glacial period occupied only about one-third of the 2,000,000 years now to be assigned to the Quaternary.

This article deals with the stratigraphy and climate of the Pleistocene or glacial epoch of the Quaternary in Europe and Great Britain, the pluvial phases to the south of the glaciations and corresponding to them, the chronology, animal life and vegetation of the time up to the Recent or Holocene and briefly discusses the Quaternary as the age of man. For details of the glacial epoch in North America, its correlations with European and other regions and for a more detailed discussion of the extent and effects of glaciation, the glacial and interglacial ages and the life and climate of the epoch, see PLEISTOCENE EPOCH.

Stratigraphy.—A. Penck and E. Brückner in their classical work recognized four Alpine glaciations which they named in alphabetical and chronological order, Günz, Mindel, Riss and Würm. The glaciations were separated by three mild interglacial epochs, Günz-Mindel, Mindel-Riss and Riss-Würm. Of these, the Mindel-Riss or Great Interglacial was the longest: it lasted almost half the total length of the Quaternary. Some geologists subdivide the glaciations: the first three into two and Würm into three phases, the phases being separated by minor mild phases called interstadials. While the interglacial epochs were warmer than the present—the Great Interglacial was warmer by about 2.5° C.—the interstadials remained cold.

A vast Scandinavian ice sheet radiated outward over the Netherlands, against the northern slopes of the Hartz and Sudeten mountains and over the plains of Russia to the Urals and down the valleys of the Don and Dnieper. In Germany three glaciations, Elster, Saale and Weichsel, are recognized. A Warthe stage was intercalated between the Saale and Weichsel; whether it was a separate glaciation, a late phase of the Saale or an early phase of the Weichsel remains undecided. Weichsel is equated with the Alpine Würm, Saale with the Riss and Elster with the Mindel. No northern European equivalent of the Alpine Günz is definitely known, though Germany has indications of an Elbe or Baltic glaciation which preceded the Elster.

Britain was covered with ice as far south as the Bristol channel and the Thames valley; Ireland apparently was completely glaciated. In both countries the ice of the Last Glaciation (Newer drift) was much smaller in extent. The southern quarter of Ireland, parts of Wales, the Midlands, Derbyshire and Lincolnshire were also ice-free, though land ice in the North sea moved southward over Holderness and east Lincolnshire to North Norfolk. East Anglia, the classical region of the British Pleistocene, has the following succession: marine deposits called crags (see *Marine Animal Life,* below); North sea drift (Cromer till and Norwich brick earth); Lowestoft till (Great Chalky boulder clay); Gipping till (Upper Chalky drift); and the Hunstanton boulder clay. The three intervening interglacial horizons are the Cromer Forest Bed, the Hoxne or Great Interglacial and the Ipswich and March Gravels or Eemian.

The North American ice sheet, unlike the ice masses of Europe, was mostly centred on low ground, namely, a Labrador centre east of and a Keewatin centre west of Hudson bay. Only in the west was the Cordilleran ice nurtured on high mountains. These coalescent ice sheets flowed northward to the Arctic ocean and southward across the Canadian boundary, extending as a group of vast lobes over the Great Lakes as far as St. Louis. As in Europe, four glaciations are usually distinguished, the Nebraskan, Kansan, Illinoian and Wisconsin. The Iowan, previously regarded as a separate glaciation or a late Illinoian phase, is now thought to have been the initial phase of the Wisconsin glaciation, corresponding perhaps to the European Warthe. The intervening interglacials are the Aftonian, Yarmouth (Great Interglacial) and Sangamon.

The Alpine Würm, North European Weichsel and British Newer drift are almost certainly contemporaneous. The correlation of the earlier glaciations is less certain; they are usually bracketed as shown in the accompanying table (interglacials in italics).

Alps	North Germany	British Isles	North America
Würm	Weichsel	Newer drift	Wisconsin
Riss-Würm	*Eemian sea*	*Eemian*	*Sangamon*
Riss	Saale	Great Chalky	Illinoian
Mindel-Riss	*Holstein sea*	*Hoxne*	*Yarmouth*
Mindel	Elster	North sea drift	Kansan
Günz-Mindel	*Mauer*	*Cromerian*	*Aftonian*
Günz	Elbe?	Later crags	Nebraskan

Climate.—At the beginning of the Quaternary, the climate of temperate Europe appears to have resembled that of the present day. Considerable cooling took place during the Early Glaciation, sufficient to exterminate many Pliocene types of mammals and to enable arctic species to spread southward. But on the whole, the effect of the first Quaternary Glaciation was slight and in the Antepenultimate Interglacial (that of the Cromer forest bed of East Anglia) decidedly temperate conditions prevailed again. The Antepenultimate Glaciation, however, was more intense and it caused a sharp break in animal life. In a broad zone surrounding the ice sheets (periglacial zone) the climate became cold and pronouncedly continental. Tundra and steppe prevailed; from northern France to southern Russia a broadening belt of loess

(windblown dust) was deposited. Those Pliocene elements in the animal life that had survived into the Antepenultimate Interglacial died out. The following Penultimate or Great Interglacial was a prolonged period of temperate climate, at times apparently milder than the present (*e.g., Rhododendron ponticum* in the Alps). The Penultimate Glaciation, being much the same size as the Antepenultimate, had similar effects on the environment. By this time, however, many animals had adapted themselves to the recurrent phases of rigid climate and they assumed a Pleistocene aspect, with ancestral mammoth, wooly rhinoceros, etc. Man had also adapted his economy to the cold and stayed in the periglacial zone. The Last Interglacial witnessed a repetition of the mild conditions of the Great Interglacial. Fossil soils, animal life and vegetation suggest higher summer temperatures and an absence of frost. The Last Glaciation, though smaller than the preceding two, appears to have had pronounced climatic effects. Its periglacial zone was slightly smaller than that of the two preceding glaciations, but many interglacial mammals which had survived into the Last Interglacial (*e.g.,* straight-tusked elephant, Merck's rhinoceros) became extinct and a most characteristic arctic animal life reigned north of the Alps. A second break in animal life is thus observed in the Quaternary at the beginning of the Last Glaciation. Since the Last Glaciation the climate has returned to the temperate conditions of the present day, with fluctuations for which the vegetation provides evidence.

Pluvials.—In the countries around the Mediterranean basin, including north Africa from Morocco to Egypt, pluvial phases corresponded to the glaciations. The anticyclonic conditions reigning over northern Europe forced more cyclones onto a Mediterranean course than is now the case; lakes were deeper and more widespread; the higher mountains, *e.g.,* the Atlas, were clothed with ice; and the Mediterranean countries were covered with deciduous forests of the temperate type. Pluvial conditions occurred elsewhere on the polar side of the subtropical high pressure zones; *e.g.,* in North America (Great basin), Asia and in the southern hemisphere in the three southern continents. Pluvials and glaciations are generally thought to have been coeval, though those on the equatorial side of the subtropical high-pressure zones may have been in antiphase.

Sea Level.—The formation of large ice sheets, especially in Europe and North America, resulted in the withdrawal of a large amount of water from the oceans. The sea level therefore was low during the glacial and high during the interglacial phases. These fluctuations of the sea level are called eustatic. Evidence for low sea levels is provided by submerged terrestrial deposits (peats, etc.) and drowned river valleys; for high sea levels by traces of ancient shore lines (raised beaches) and terraces in the mouths of rivers. Raised beaches observed on coasts unaffected by tectonic movements or isostasy suggest two Pliocene phases: Calabrian and Sicilian, the latter about 80–100 m. above present sea level; and three interglacial phases: Milazzian (60 m.), Tyrrhenian (32 m.) and Monastirian (18–7.5 m.). The fact that the order in time is one of successively lower levels shows that the eustatic fluctuations are superimposed on a general and persistent drop in sea level which continued from the Tertiary into the Quaternary.

The volume of the Scandinavian icecap of the Last Glaciation has been estimated at 5,000,000 cu.km.; that of the icecap of North America at 21,000,000 cu.km. These masses, by their weight, depressed the ground covered by them. When the ice disappeared and its load was removed, the earth's crust responded elastically by plastic deformation and subcrustal flow and the regions recovered from the depression. This phenomenon is called isostasy. The isostatic rise of Scandinavia was over 300 m. and because of isostatic lag is still taking place at a maximum rate of 1 m. per century. In North America, the uplift was about 1,000 ft. and is also still continuing and tipping the waters of the Great Lakes southward.

Chronology.—Quaternary chronology usually rests on the succession of climatic phases which provide convenient divisions: glaciations, pluviations and phases of high sea level are also used as outlined in the preceding paragraphs. In many parts of the world, however, paleoclimatic evidence is very incomplete and paleontological divisions based on mammals and marine mollusks are used instead. Where prehistoric implements are abundant, chronologies of a more or less local nature have been based on them.

Many attempts have been made to develop an absolute chronology of the Quaternary: several depend upon the time rates of erosion, sedimentation and soil formation. In the Alps, Penck arrived at 600,000 years for the Quaternary; other estimates extend the range to 1,000,000 or 2,000,000 years. A more elaborate time scale correlates the geologically established climatic phases with fluctuations of solar radiation caused by the perturbations of the earth's orbit. This method yields 600,000 years for the Quaternary, 190,000 for the Great Interglacial and 20,000 years for the interval since the Last Glaciation. This astronomical method, which may allow the dating of minor climatic phases, was conceived by J. Adhemar in 1842 and developed by the British scientists J. Croll and Sir Robert Ball in the second half of the 19th century. M. Milankovitch, from 1913 onward, undertook a recalculation of the astronomical tables. His theory, however, is not generally accepted and cannot be regarded as an explanation of the Ice Age as such.

Animal Life.—*Terrestrial Animal Life.*—The land animal assumed its modern character in the course of the Quaternary. This was due to three causes: (1) dying out of Tertiary elements; (2) appearance of new Pleistocene types; and (3) change of Pliocene forms into modern species by gradual evolution. It is noteworthy that in mammals, the lineages of which have been traced from the Villafranchian to the Holocene, the change in specific characters is slight; differences between Pliocene ancestors and Holocene descendants being no greater than differences between existing related species. In the Mollusca, which have been studied equally closely, these phylogenetic changes are even slighter and changes in the composition of the animals are chiefly the result of migration; *e.g.*, the fresh-water shell *Corbicula* in the Pleistocene of Britain, now from Egypt southward.

Characteristic mammals of the European Villafranchian are: monkeys (*Macacus*), a cheetah, sabre-tooth tiger, zebralike horses (*Equus stenonis*), Etruscan rhinoceros, tapir, primitive ox (*Leptobos*), mastodon, southern elephant; of the Lower Pleistocene: the same, except cheetah, tapir and *Leptobos,* but with red deer, elk (*Alces*), roe deer and a giant beaver (*Trogontherium*). Middle Pleistocene animal life is devoid of earlier exotic elements and new types appear which survive into the Upper Pleistocene. In the latter, the warm interglacial animal life and the cold glacial animal life have become more sharply separated. Interglacial species are the brown bear, beaver, Merck's rhinoceros, hippopotamus (west Europe), red deer, etc., straight-tusked elephant; glacial species are the arctic fox, varying hare, susliks (*Citellus*), lemmings, jerboa (loess steppe), true horses, wooly rhinoceros, reindeer, musk ox, mammoth, etc. Some of these became extinct before the Holocene began.

Marine Animal Life.—The marine animal life of the Quaternary shows slight evolution in the species, but there is evidence of much migration caused by climatic changes. The crags of East Anglia, which are Lower Pleistocene beach deposits rich in shells, illustrate this point. In the Sicilian (Mediterranean deposits of the Günz glacial stage), temperate shells like *Cyprina islandica* and the common whelk extended to the Mediterranean. The Tyrrhenian and Monastirian animal life (collectively called Tyrrhenian by paleontologists) is generally warmer than the modern ones, with the west African *Strombus bubonius* in the Mediterranean and *Astralium rugosum* in the Channel Islands.

Vegetation.—The specific composition of the vegetation has changed much less than that of the animal life insofar as it is the result of phylogenetic evolution, though the shifting of vegetational zones in connection with climatic changes is a most characteristic phenomenon. With the growth of the ice sheets, the forest belts moved southward and tundra and cold steppe covered much of the periglacial zone. Each time the ice retreated, the vegetation belts moved northward again, producing a succession of plant associations which have been studied in peat deposits by means of pollen analysis, chiefly for the time since the Last Glaciation. The sub-

divisions of the Holocene make use of these changes in vegetation. Complicated divisions are now used in technical papers, but the classical scheme of Axel Blytt and R. Sernander may, with modifications, still serve in summarizing the major features: (a) Subarctic phase (to *c.* 8,000 B.C.), treeless, with *Dryas octopetala,* dwarf willows and birches, interrupted by the mild Alleröd Oscillation, when Scotch pine and tree birches appeared temporarily; (b) Preboreal (8,000–7,000 B.C.), birch and pine immigrating; (c) Boreal (7,000–5,500 B.C.), with pine and birch dominating and alder, oak, lime and elm as subordinate, but increasing associates—later, hazel woods become prominent, climate continental; (d) Atlantic (5,500–2,000 B.C.), mixed oak forests culminate, hazel reduced to undergrowth, climate oceanic and in part warmer than at the present; (e) Subboreal (2,000–500 B.C.), climate begins to deteriorate, mixed oak forest retreats from the extreme limits reached, pine increases, but beech and hornbeam continue to spread north; (f) Subatlantic, mixed oak forest continues to retreat, beech culminates, present-day conditions.

Man.—The Quaternary is the age of man. The australopithecines appeared in the Lower Pleistocene of East and South Africa and the pithecanthropines (*Pithecanthropus* of Java, *Sinanthropus* of China, *Atlanthropus* of North Africa) in the Middle Pleistocene. The classic Neanderthalers of the first substage of the last glaciation died out and was succeeded by *Homo sapiens fossilis,* who probably descended from the "progressive" Neanderthalers or from the pithecanthropines.

The cultural evolution of man in Quaternary times is evidenced by his implements, mostly of stone. At the beginning of the Pleistocene, very primitive tools (the human origin of which is debated) have been found in East Anglia. In the Antepenultimate Interglacial, the Chellean or Abbevillian hand-ax culture flourished and flake industries of the Clactonian variety appear. By Great Interglacial times, the Chellean had developed into the Acheulian which used the refined "wood technique" in manufacturing implements. The Clactonian persisted, but later the Levalloisian technique of making flakes from specially prepared cores marks another step forward in mental evolution. In the Last Interglacial, the Acheulian develops its final phase, the Micoquian; Levalloisian persists and from the fusion of these the Mousterian results, the culture of Neanderthal man par excellence. All these cultures are grouped together as Lower Palaeolithic. *Homo sapiens* brought with him the Upper Paleolithic culture of blade industries (Aurignacian, Gravettian, Solutrian, Magdalenian) which flourished during the Last Glaciation. When the Holocene began, man had reached the Mesolithic stage; many of his stone tools were now composite, being made up of numerous hafted, small microliths.

In temperate Europe, the Mesolithic was replaced by the Neolithic which introduced agriculture, about 5,000 B.C. *See* ARCHAEOLOGY; MAN, EVOLUTION OF; *see* also references under "Quaternary" in the Index.

BIBLIOGRAPHY.—H. Alimen, *The Prehistory of Africa* (1957); K. W. Butzer, *Environment and Archaeology: an Introduction to Pleistocene Geography* (1965); J. K. Charlesworth, *The Quaternary Era,* 2 vol. (1957); S. Cole, *The Prehistory of East Africa,* 2nd ed. (1964); R. F. Flint, *Glacial and Pleistocene Geology* (1957); H. Godwin, *The History of the British Flora* (1956); R. v. Klebelsberg, *Handbuch der Gletscherkunde und Glazialgeologie,* 2 vol. (1948–49); L. S. B. Leakey et al., *Olduvai Gorge 1951–61* (1965); K. P. Oakley, *Man the Toolmaker,* 5th ed. (1961); A. Penck and E. Brückner, *Die Alpen im Eiszeitalter,* 3 vol. (1909); H. D. Sankalia, *Prehistory and Protohistory in India and Pakistan* (1962); P. Woldstedt, *Das Eiszeitalter,* 2nd ed., 3 vol. (1954, 1958, 1965); H. M. Wormington, *Ancient Man in North America,* 4th ed. (1957); H. E. Wright and D. G. Frey (eds.), *The Quaternary of the United States* (1965); F. E. Zeuner, *The Pleistocene Period* (1959).   (F. E. Z.; J. K. C.)

QUATERNIONS, a linear algebra consisting of four-dimensional vectors whose coordinates are any real numbers. The theory of this algebra was discovered by Sir William Rowan Hamilton in 1843 while he was trying, by analogy with the complex number representation of real two-dimensional vectors, to represent space vectors by the elements of a number system. For the definition of the algebra of quaternions and its place in the theory of algebras, *see* ALGEBRAS (LINEAR). Quaternions were intensively studied during the early part of the 20th century before the general theory of linear algebras came into being. Later, they were usually thought of as a special case of such algebras. Their early importance lay in applications to geometry and mathematical physics. These applications later became a part of vector theory. *See also* VECTOR ANALYSIS; COMPLEX NUMBERS; NUMBER: *Quaternions and-Hypercomplex Numbers;* NUMBERS, THEORY OF: *Algebras, and Their Arithmetics.* (A. A. At.)

QUATORZAIN, the term used in English literature, as opposed to "sonnet," for a poem in 14 rhymed iambic lines closing (as the Italian sonnet never does) with a couplet. The distinction was long neglected, because the English poets of the 16th century had failed to apprehend the true form of the sonnet, and called Petrarch's and other Italian poets' sonnets quatorzains, and their own incorrect quatorzains sonnets. Almost all the so-called sonnets of the Elizabethan cycles, including those of William Shakespeare, Sir Philip Sidney, Edmund Spenser, and Samuel Daniel, are really quatorzains. They consist of three quatrains of alternate rhyme, not repeated in the successive quatrains, and the whole closes with a couplet. *See* SONNET. (G. W. A.)

QUATRAIN, sometimes spelled quartain, a piece of verse complete in four rhymed lines. The length or measure of the line is immaterial. This form has always been popular for use in the composition of epigrams, and may be considered as a modification of the Greek or Latin epigram. The commonest in English poetry is the ballad stanza, an outgrowth of the church hymn, in iambic metre rhyming *abcb,* with alternating four and three stresses to the line. Tennyson in "In Memoriam" used an iambic stanza rhyming *abba.* Though he did not invent it, it is often called the "In Memoriam" stanza. *See* RHYME; VERSE. (G. W. A.)

QUCHAN (KUCHAN), a fertile and populous district of the *ostan* (province) of Khurasan in Iran, is bounded on the north by the Turkmen Soviet Socialist Republic. The population, 169,370 in 1966, is principally composed of the descendants of the tribe of Zafaranlu Kurds which was established there, with a hereditary khan at its head, by Shah Abbas I in the 17th century. Many are still nomads and live in tents in summer. The district produces much grain and there are extensive vineyards. The chief town, renowned for its rugs and metalwork, is Quchan (pop. [1966] 29,133), 80 mi. (129 km.) NW of Meshed. Quchan has suffered severely from repeated earthquakes; in that of 1893, 12,000 people are said to have perished. The present town was rebuilt after 1895 on a site 8 mi. (13 km.) E of the ruined town, 3,770 ft. (1,149 m.) above sea level, and is regularly laid out with broad streets and spacious bazaars. It is on the main road from Meshed to Ashkhabad (Turkmen S.S.R.). On the nearby hill called Nadir-Tepe, Nadir Shah (*q.v.*) was killed in 1747. (P. Z. C.; H. Bo.)

QUEBEC is the largest of Canada's ten provinces. It is bounded on the southwest and west by Ontario, James Bay, and Hudson Bay; on the north by Hudson Strait and Ungava Bay; on the east by the Coast of Labrador (Newfoundland) and the Gulf of St. Lawrence; and on the south by the Bay of Chaleur, New Brunswick, the United States (Maine, New Hampshire, Vermont, and New York), and Ontario. Quebec extends from the U.S. border, about 45°N, to Cape Wolstenholme, about 62°30′ N; and

from Hudson Bay, at a point about 79°30′ W, to Anse Sablon, about 57° W. The total area is 594,860 sq.mi. (1,540,680 sq.km.), about one-sixth the total area of Canada, and includes 71,000 sq.mi. (183,889 sq.km.) of fresh water. Much of the area consists of the territory of Ungava, or New Quebec, whose 351,780 sq.mi. (911,106 sq.km.) were added to the province in 1912. Quebec is slightly larger than Alaska and more than five times the size of Great Britain. The province derives its name from the Indian word *kebek,* meaning strait or narrows, which described the narrowing of the St. Lawrence River at the present site of Quebec City.

PHYSICAL GEOGRAPHY

Quebec falls naturally into three well-defined regions. Over 90% of the province lies within the Canadian Shield, a plateau-like area of crystalline Precambrian rocks whose surface declines northward from its high southern margin overlooking the St. Lawrence lowlands and the Gulf of St. Lawrence. The lowland region occupies a triangular area traversed by the St. Lawrence and Ottawa rivers, lying between the shield to the north and the Appalachian uplands to the southeast. The lowland decreases in width downstream from 70 mi. (113 km.) in the vicinity of Montreal, to about 20 mi. (32 km.) at its apex at the Île d'Orléans below Quebec City. Anticosti Island is geologically part of the same region. The Appalachian uplands include the Eastern Townships of the southeastern part of the province, along the U.S. border, and Gaspé Peninsula, and are part of the belt of Paleozoic fold mountains that extends from Alabama to Newfoundland.

The Canadian Shield.—Geologically, the Canadian Shield is still incompletely known (*see also* PRECAMBRIAN TIME). The Precambrian rocks of which it is formed have been subjected to several periods of mountain building, as a result of which the ancient sedimentary rocks were strongly folded and faulted, intensely metamorphosed, and intruded by masses of igneous rock. The deposition of minerals far below the surface was associated with the orogenies, and the processes of erosion, acting through prolonged periods, have laid bare the deposits, making them accessible for mining. Thus, gold, copper, and zinc are mined in the Noranda and Chibougamau areas. Within the Late Precambrian sediments of the Labrador Trough, extending southwest from Ungava Bay for 600 mi. (966 km.), are extensive bodies of iron ore. (*See also* LABRADOR-UNGAVA.)

A cover of Paleozoic sedimentary rocks formerly extended widely over the shield, and Paleozoic rocks have been preserved in the downfaulted Lake St. John Depression. Most of the sedimentary strata, however, have been stripped away, leaving large areas of monotonous plateau lying between 1,500 and 1,900 ft. (457 and 579 m.) above sea level. The elevation of the plateau declines gently toward James, Hudson, and Ungava bays, but drops to Hudson Strait in cliffs over 1,000 ft. (305 m.) high. Principal mountains of the shield include Mount Tremblant, Mount Ste.-Anne, and Mount Sir Wilfrid. North of the tree line the plateau surface is largely bare of superficial deposits, but toward

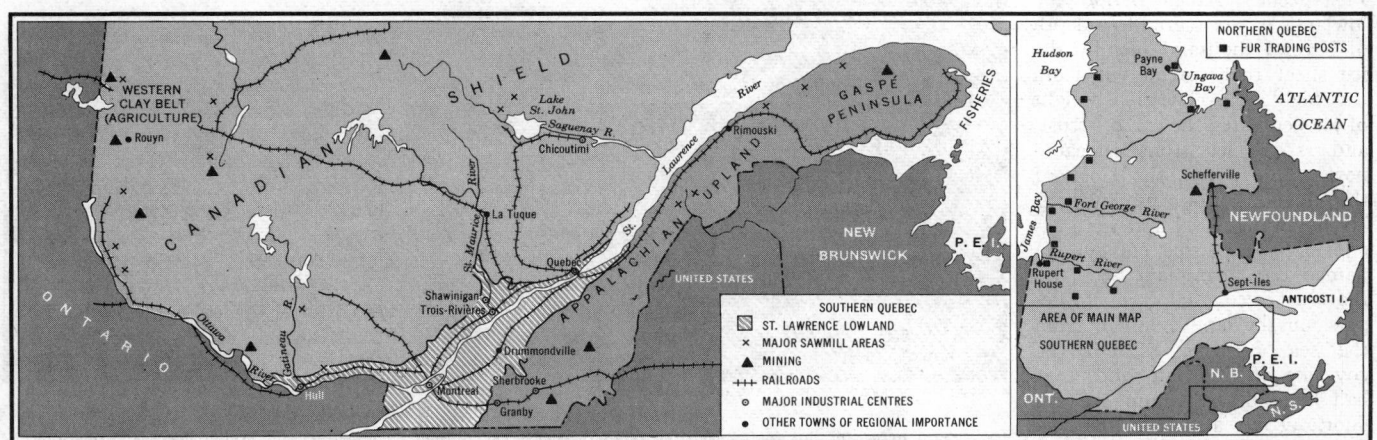

SURFACE FEATURES, LAND USE AND INDUSTRIAL CENTRES OF QUEBEC

the south extensive areas are thickly covered with glacial deposits. Sinuous sandy ridges, or eskers, wind between the low forested morainic hills, and the intervening hollows are occupied by innumerable lakes and bogs. In western Quebec there is a belt of glacial clays, deposited in the Ice Age Lake Barlow-Ojibway, a great freshwater lake impounded by the ice front during its retreat.

The irregular deposition of glacial deposits and the deepening of depressions by the erosive action of the ice served to disrupt the drainage pattern, and many of the rivers of the shield consist of series of lakes connected by falls or rapids, offering great potentialities for the development of hydroelectric power. The power potential of the rivers draining south is especially great, for they plunge from the plateau in deep gorgelike valleys down the dissected fault-line scarps that form the shield's southern margin. The crest of the scarp where it overlooks the estuary of the St. Lawrence lies at elevations of over 3,000 ft. (over 900 m.). The most spectacular break in the shield's rim is formed by the fjord of the Lower Saguenay River, draining from St. John where the great Shipshaw power stations are located. Other rivers with developed or potential hydroelectric capacity include the St. Maurice, the Ottawa and its tributaries, the Peribonca and the Mistassini (tributaries of the Saguenay), the Bersimis, Outardes, and Manicouagan. Rivers that flow into James Bay, Hudson Bay, or Ungava Bay include the Fort George, Nottaway, George, and Whale. Among the major lakes of the shield are the Mistassini, Eau Claire, Minto, St. John, and Bienville.

The St. Lawrence Lowlands.—This region contrasts strongly with the shield, containing the province's richest agricultural land. The bedrock is of sedimentary origin—great thicknesses of limestone, dolomite, and shale of Cambrian, Ordovician, and Silurian ages lying almost horizontally, with occasional faults, upon a basement of crystalline shield rocks. Bedrock is seldom exposed, except in the Monteregian Hills, which are small intrusions of igneous rock of Devonian or later age, aligned eastward from Montreal. Peaks in the Monteregian Hills include Saint-Hilaire Mountain, Yamaska Mountain, and Rougemont. The surrounding strata have been worn down to a gently sloping surface, the Quebec platform, which rises downstream from about 100 ft. (31 m.) at Montreal to 333 ft. (101 m.) at Cape Diamond, where the Quebec citadel was built at the lip of the gorge incised into it by the St. Lawrence River (*q.v.*).

The St. Lawrence is possibly one of the youngest of the major rivers of the world, having occupied its present course for only a few thousand years. During this geologically brief time it has been unable to eliminate the rapids which prevented navigation above Montreal, thus requiring the construction of an elaborate system of canals.

During the Wisconsin (Late Pleistocene) glacial period the lowlands were covered to a depth of several thousand feet by the ice sheet that spread out from the shield area. The great weight of ice depressed the earth's crust, and as the ice front retreated northward toward the close of the glacial period the lowlands lay below sea level and were occupied by a marine embayment named the Champlain Sea. As the crust recovered from its depression the land emerged from the sea, carrying with it the covering of silts and sands that had been deposited on the sea floor. (*See* also PLEISTOCENE EPOCH.)

The Appalachian Uplands.—The southeastern margin of the lowlands is marked by Logan's Line, or fault, a line of faulting that extends from east of Lake Champlain northward to the St. Lawrence River at Quebec City. Beyond Logan's Line lie the folded rocks of the Appalachian region. These range in age from Cambrian to Carboniferous, and consist of great thicknesses of limestone, shale, sandstone, and volcanic rocks that were deposited in a geosyncline and subjected to folding and faulting along the northeast-trending axes in successive Paleozoic orogenies. The asbestos deposits of the Eastern Townships are associated with the intrusions of ultrabasic rock, while granitic intrusions of the Gaspé Peninsula have given rise to deposits of copper. Prolonged erosion has resulted in the reduction of the original mountainous relief in much of the region to a plateau about 1,200 ft. (366 m.) above sea level. In the Eastern Townships three parallel northeast-trending ranges rise above the plateau and include several summits of over 3,000 ft. (914 m.). The highest peak of Quebec province, Mt. Jacques-Cartier, rises to 4,160 ft. (1,268 m.) in the Shickshock Mountains of the Gaspé Peninsula. Other peaks in the Uplands include Mount Richardson, Mount Albert, and Mount Logan.

The bold north coast of the Gaspé Peninsula contrasts with the south coast where the land declines gently beneath the waters of Chaleur Bay. The picturesque inlets and promontories of the tip of the peninsula reflect the structural trend. Glaciation resulted in the deepening of valleys, such as those occupied by Lakes Memphremagog, Témiscouta, and Matapédia, and the mantling of the bedrock by glacial drift. The original forest cover has been cleared from half the area of the Eastern Townships, but from only a narrow coastal strip of the peninsula. The chief rivers of the Appalachian Uplands—the St. Francis, the Nicolet, and the Chaudière—flow northward into the St. Lawrence.

Climate.—The wide spread of latitude and the considerable distance from the Atlantic to the western parts of Quebec produce marked continental characteristics in the climate. At Port Harrison in northern Quebec, the January mean temperature is −13° F (−25° C); in Montreal it is 16° F (−9° C). The July mean temperatures are 48° F (9° C) and 71° F (22° C) respectively. The average number of frost-free days varies from about 180 in Montreal to less than 50 in northern Quebec, and may be further modified by local topography. In July the isotherm of 57° F (14° C)—which determines the northern limit of the growth of crops—runs west-east through James Bay. Hence it is the poor quality of the soil in southern Quebec rather than the temperatures that limits the northern extension of agriculture.

BY COURTESY OF NATIONAL FILM BOARD OF CANADA

NORTHERN COAST OF THE GASPÉ PENINSULA
The rugged nature of this region contributes to its sparse population. Lumbering and fishing are the primary occupations

The outstanding feature of the climate is the constant passage of low-pressure eddies (cyclones) along the St. Lawrence, which results in an almost uniform type of rainfall in the southern part of the province. The weather, however, is quite variable, since the front of such a cyclone gives warm moist winds from the south, while the rear is accompanied by cold dry winds from the north. The annual precipitation increases fairly regularly from 15 in. (380 mm.) in the north to more than 40 in. (1,020 mm.) on the southern boundary of the province. Snowfall is extremely heavy in parts of northern Quebec, often totaling more than 200 in. (508 cm.).

Plant and Animal Life.—The distribution of plant life is controlled largely by climate and may be divided into zones characterized by the arctic tundra north of the tree line; intermingled tundra and northern spruce forest grading into the subarctic lichen and coniferous woodland; the mixed forest of the St. Lawrence lowland; and the mixed and hardwood forest of the Eastern Townships and the Gaspé Peninsula.

The province is rich in wildlife including barren-ground caribou, deer, and beaver, mink, and other fur-bearing animals. Birds are varied and numerous and game fish include trout, arctic char, bass, pickerel, and salmon. For additional details on plant and animal life see LABRADOR-UNGAVA.

HISTORY

17th and 18th Centuries.—History has a vital importance for the French Canadian people of Quebec. The great majority of the population are descended from the 10,000 immigrants who came to New France in the 17th and early 18th centuries. The 65,000 French Canadians who remained in Quebec after the conquest of 1763 formed a closely knit, homogeneous group, determined to resist outside influences. Although Lord Durham was later to refer to them as "a people with no history," the opposite is far more correct; the provincial motto, Je me Souviens ("I remember"), provides a key to understanding the people of Quebec.

France's interest in the New World began in the days of Jacques Cartier who made three voyages to the area and wintered at the Indian village of Stadacona (near the present site of Quebec City) in 1535. After the failure of a small colony in 1541, no permanent settlement was established until Samuel de Champlain founded the *Habitation* at Quebec in 1608. In the interim, however, French fishermen and whalers had come into contact with the Indians who lived around the Gulf of St. Lawrence and had initiated the first commerce between the two groups. At first the population was sparse and the life of New France was attuned to the interests and activities of the trading companies (such as the Company of One Hundred Associates), who were given exclusive charters by the French monarchy to exploit the new lands. By 1640 the population was still less than 400.

In 1663, however, New France was placed under direct royal control and a highly paternalistic, if sometimes neglectful, type of rule began. Louis XIV and his vigorous minister Jean Baptiste Colbert took a personal interest in the welfare of the colony and dispatched the Carignan-Salières regiment to repel the Iroquois menace. Immigration and settlement were officially encouraged, so that the population increased almost fourfold in the 20 years following 1665. Although royal interest in the colony declined after 1672, by the turn of the century New France was firmly implanted in the New World.

An analysis of French Canadian society in the 18th century emphasizes the colony's distinctiveness. The nonconformist ideology of English-speaking North America had little place in New France. Those who came to live there were loyal, orthodox, and exclusively Catholic Frenchmen. They were ruled by a governor and intendant appointed by the king; institutions of self-government were of minimal importance. Furthermore, New France was guided by a potentially powerful ecclesiastical authority represented by the Bishop of Quebec and the religious orders, especially the Jesuits, who also carried out extensive missionary activity. The colony's system of land tenure was based on the quasi-feudal seigneurial system of France, modified to take into account the conditions of life in North America, where land was

usually quite inexpensive. Moreover, social stratification was much less rigid and onerous than in France. The seigneurs, whose holdings were divided into long strips of land, each with a narrow frontage on the St. Lawrence, bore little resemblance to the nobility of the mother country. The economy was organized along mercantilist lines and trading activity was rigidly controlled, forcing many adventurous young men to seek their fortune as *coureurs de bois*. Life was rarely peaceful; war with the Iroquois and the English colonies to the south was frequent, especially after 1715, when France committed herself to maintaining a series of outposts stretching from New Orleans to the Ottawa River. Nevertheless, the colony grew steadily until the British conquest during the French and Indian War (q.v.). The fortress of Quebec fell to Gen. James Wolfe in 1759 and by the Treaty of Paris, 1763, New France was ceded to Great Britain.

British Rule.—The full significance of the conquest is still a matter of debate among historians, since it is difficult to determine how many of the characteristics of post-conquest society were a simple prolongation of earlier tendencies and how many were distortions induced by the trauma of defeat and alien rule. But there is little disagreement as to the broad features of Quebec life as it evolved in the late 18th and 19th centuries. French Canadians became firmly attached to an agrarian way of life, centred around the parish, with leadership coming from the clergy and seigneurial classes. The latter gradually gave way to members of the liberal professions, especially notaries and lawyers, but no strong commercial middle class emerged to challenge the English and Scottish merchants who controlled both external, and to a lesser extent, internal trade. The conservative mood was well established in French Canada by the end of the 18th century. The overriding collective goal could not be progress or expansion; it was survival. The preservation of the French language, the Roman Catholic religion, and traditional ways of life (particularly Quebec's system of civil law) absorbed the attention and energies of the people and their leaders. After some hesitation, the English came to recognize Quebec's special place in the Empire. The Quebec Act (q.v.) of 1774 guaranteed the French civil code and the status of the Catholic religion, thereby weighting the scales heavily in favour of survival. In addition, the early British governors supported the seigneurial and clerical leaders against the Montreal merchants and were thus able to conciliate a majority of the French Canadian population. As a result, the American Revolution evoked little response along the St. Lawrence Valley. The French Revolution created even less of a ripple as its radical and anticlerical character made it anathema to the key elements of French Canadian society. The majority of French Canadians, influenced by the tales of a handful of *émigré* priests, henceforth regarded their ancestral home with dismay and suspicion and turned inward, relying even more resolutely on their own resources.

Representative government, which finally came to Quebec in 1791, was not the result of agitation on the part of the colony's French Canadian majority, who had little enthusiasm for an elective assembly. Rather, the Constitutional Act of 1791, which authorized an elected lower house in a bicameral legislature, was a concession to the many Loyalists who settled in the upper St. Lawrence Valley and the eastern Great Lakes area following the American Revolution. These settlers were accustomed to self-government and could not long be satisfied with rule by a governor and appointed council. The Constitutional Act thus divided the St. Lawrence Valley settlements into two units—Upper Canada (the future Ontario) and Lower Canada (the future Quebec) and established parallel forms of government in each. (See CONSTITUTIONAL ACT, CANADIAN.) The English and Scottish merchants of Lower Canada who had for years demanded representative government were thus recognized, but under different circumstances than they had imagined. Lower Canada's assembly was to be elected by both Protestants and Catholics; as a result it would inevitably be dominated by a vocal and opinionated French Canadian majority.

The legislative assembly became the focal point of French Canada's struggle to assure its future and as far as possible control its own destiny. The new secular elite of lawyers, notaries, and other middle-class professionals came to the fore within it, led by men such as Pierre Bédard, John Neilson, and Louis Joseph Papineau (*q.v.*). Opposing them was the "Chateau Clique" of English administrators, merchants and land speculators, Church of England clergy, and French office holders that gathered around the British governor. The two groups clashed frequently, if indecisively, throughout the first three and a half decades of the 19th century. A comparable battle was being waged against the family compact in Upper Canada, but there the ethnic differences which complicated the situation in Lower Canada were absent, and a more clear-cut goal—responsible government, *i.e.,* an executive responsible to the majority in the elected assembly—was apparent.

In both colonies armed rebellion flared up in 1837, but the causes and aims of the *patriotes* were not identical with those of the Upper Canadian reformers. Lord Durham, the governor sent out to cope with the aftermath of the rebellions, may have underestimated the strength of social and political radicalism among the *patriotes,* but his famous comment on the situation in Lower Canada contained a large element of truth: "I expected to find a contest between a government and a people: I found two nations warring in the bosom of a single state: I found a struggle, not of principles, but of races."

Lord Durham's epochal report proposed two main solutions to the difficulties in Canada: first, the union of Upper and Lower Canada in order to place the French Canadians in a minority position from which defense against assimilation would be difficult; and second, the granting of responsible government to the new union regime. Only the former recommendation, however, was acted upon immediately; another decade of struggle was necessary to achieve responsible government. The moderate reformers of Canada West (as Upper Canada became known) under the leadership of Robert Baldwin (*q.v.*) joined the French Canadian majority of Canada East (Lower Canada) led by Louis Hippolyte Lafontaine (*q.v.*) in a coalition whose avowed purpose was the introduction of responsible government. But after the achievement of responsible government in 1848 and the resignation of the Baldwin-Lafontaine ministry three years later, the underlying differences between the two groups became increasingly apparent. The French Canadians became more and more conservative, concerned with the preservation of their traditional rights and prerogatives. The English Protestant majority of Canada West demanded representation by population in the union legislature and resented attempts to extend educational privileges to the Catholic minority in Canada West. Chronic political instability characterized the 1850s and 1860s.

Confederation.—The confederation of the British North American colonies (Canada East and Canada West, Nova Scotia, and New Brunswick) in 1867 brought an end to the union regime. The chief attraction of the newly formed Dominion of Canada to French Canadians was that it gave them control of a territorial unit, the province of Quebec, in which they had an assured majority and could elect a government with a defined autonomous jurisdiction. To some extent they shared the English

Canadian vision of a new nation stretching from the Atlantic to the Pacific, with a growing internal market and ample room for expansion. But a central concern was undoubtedly to assure cultural survival both by securing Quebec's right to control its own education, property, civil rights, and local affairs and by obtaining guarantees for the existing educational rights of Roman Catholics in other parts of Canada.

In the years that followed confederation, Quebec came to play an important role in Canadian life. For 20 years federal politics in Quebec were dominated by the Conservative party, or *parti bleu,* under the successive leadership of Sir Georges Étienne Cartier, Sir Hector Langevin, and J. A. Chapleau. The Liberal Party, or *parti rouge,* faced with determined clerical opposition because of its alleged radical tendencies, was unable to gain substantial support in the province. However, the *parti bleu* itself was weakened by the presence within its ranks of a reactionary ultramontane faction known as the *castors.*

In provincial politics, the Conservatives similarly held sway until 1886. In that year the aftermath of the Riel affair (*see* RIEL, LOUIS) led to the election of Honoré Mercier, leader of the *parti national.* Although the Conservatives returned to office in 1891, they were unable to consolidate their power; beginning in 1897 the Liberal Party completely dominated Quebec provincial politics under the leadership of Sir Lomer Gouin and L. Alexandre Taschereau. Federally, the Liberals gained power in the election of 1896, with Wilfred Laurier assuming office as the Dominion's first French-Canadian prime minister. From then on, Quebec was a Liberal stronghold in federal as well as provincial affairs.

Despite this pattern of one-party dominance, however, issues arose throughout the late 19th and 20th centuries which accentuated the divisions in outlook between the English Protestant majority and the French Catholic minority of Canada as a whole. As a result, French Canadians attached great importance to the only province in which they had a consistent majority, regarding it as their special homeland. Three main sources of tension are worth noting. First there was the schools question, which concerned the right of French Catholics outside Quebec to secure the education they desired. Crises occurred in Manitoba in 1890

VIEW FROM THE NORTH OF QUEBEC CITY, CAPITAL OF THE PROVINCE OF QUEBEC
In the foreground is the Anglo-Canadian Paper company. In the upper centre is the Château Frontenac, a historic landmark of the upper town

and Ontario in 1912 when those provincial governments attempted to curtail the activities of Catholic separate schools. A second question on which Quebec had a special viewpoint was the imperial relationship between Canada and Great Britain. French Canadians opposed schemes aimed at imperial federation and were reluctant to participate in overseas wars. The conscription crisis of 1917 created great animosity between French and English and threatened to permanently divide the country along ethnic lines. Third, Quebec was consistent in its desire to maintain provincial rights in Canada's federal system. These and other questions emphasized the province's unique position in confederation.

At the same time, important social and economic developments were shaping the destiny of French Canada. By the middle of the 19th century, the limited agricultural resources of Quebec were no longer able to support the province's growing population. Thereafter, industrialization encouraged the migration of large numbers of workers from rural and semirural areas to the developing urban centres. Half a million French Canadians left Canada altogether, establishing themselves in the mill towns of New England. Although Quebec apparently lacked a significant measure of exploitable iron and coal resources, the province could provide cheap labour for English and other investors. Protected industries such as clothing and textiles grew rapidly during the last decades of the 19th century.

20th Century.—Industrialization and urbanization proceeded apace during the 20th century, stimulated by the frantic economic expansion of World War I. By 1921, 56% of the province's population of 2,360,510 lived in urban areas. In the 1920s and 1930s, light processing industries gradually gave way to those based on the exploitation of Quebec's abundant natural resources—hydroelectric power, pulp and paper, and minerals. Although largely excluded from economic decision-making in their own province, few French Canadians were yet able to articulate a social philosophy adequate to 20th century needs.

Political life, however, still remained the domain of French Canadians. In 1936 a new political party, the Union Nationale, came to power under the forceful leadership of Maurice Duplessis (1890–1959) and remained in office, with the exception of a single five-year interval, until 1960. Although the Union Nationale had originally been elected on promises to eliminate corruption and political control by corporations and trusts, it quickly established a potent machine with close relations to the U.S. and English-Canadian business interests it had denounced. After its first election, its popular appeal was based on a strenuous defense of provincial rights, the commanding personality of its leader, and the support of the Roman Catholic hierarchy.

After World War II, continued industrialization and urbanization created a desire in some circles for more dynamic social and economic policies at the provincial level. Such feelings were largely pent up during the Union Nationale era. Duplessis' death in 1959 and the subsequent defeat of his party by the Liberals in June 1960 released a variety of forces for change. Pressures for educational reform and a greater role for the laity in schools and social institutions; for civil service reform; for the elimination of political corruption; for French Canadian control of industry through public ownership if necessary; for a redefinition of Quebec's status in the Canadian federal system, including a bigger share of total tax revenues—all these and more combined to create a dynamism that was unmistakable and that continued largely undiminished under the reformed Union Nationale which, led by Daniel Johnson, upset Premier Jean Lesage's Liberal Party and returned to power in 1966. After Premier Johnson's death in 1968, he was succeeded in office by Jean Jacques Bertrand. At the same time as these momentous developments were taking place, strongly nationalist groups, such as the Parti Québecois of René Lévesque, advocated that Quebec separate entirely from Canada and establish an independent republic. Regardless of the outcome of such controversies, it became clearer than ever before that Quebec's French Canadian majority expected the provincial government to play a vital role in shaping its social and economic future. *See also* CANADA: *History,* especially the section *National Sovereignty and Unity.*

Prime Ministers of Quebec since Confederation

Pierre J. O. Chauveau	Conservative	1867–73
Gédéon Ouimet	Conservative	1873–74
Charles Boucher de Boucherville	Conservative	1874–78
Henri C. Joly	Liberal	1878–79
J. Adolphe Chapleau	Conservative	1879–82
J. Alfred Mousseau	Conservative	1882–84
John Jones Ross	Conservative	1884–87
L. Olivier Taillon	Conservative	1887
Honoré Mercier	Liberal	1887–91
Charles Boucher de Boucherville	Conservative	1891–92
L. Olivier Taillon	Conservative	1892–96
Edmund J. Flynn	Conservative	1896–97
F. Gabriel Marchand	Liberal	1897–1900
S. Napoléon Parent	Liberal	1900–05
Sir Lomer Gouin	Liberal	1905–20
L. Alexandre Taschereau	Liberal	1920–36
Adélard Godbout	Liberal	1936
Maurice Duplessis	Union Nationale	1936–39
Adélard Godbout	Liberal	1939–44
Maurice Duplessis	Union Nationale	1944–59
Jean Paul Sauvé	Union Nationale	1959–60
Antonio Barrette	Union Nationale	1960
Jean Lesage	Liberal	1960–66
Daniel Johnson	Union Nationale	1966–68
Jean Jacques Bertrand	Union Nationale	1968–

GOVERNMENT

Political institutions in Quebec, as in the rest of Canada, follow the parliamentary model. Executive authority is theoretically vested in the lieutenant governor, who is appointed by the federal government to act as the sovereign's representative. Although contemporary Quebec is not noted for its enthusiasm for Canada's monarchial forms, it retains a lieutenant governor, whose position is protected by the British North America Act (*q.v.*). He leads an unobtrusive existence and is largely preoccupied with formalities. Actual government is carried on in his name by a prime minister and cabinet who are responsible to an elected legislature.

The legislature is composed of 108 members elected on the basis of universal suffrage from single-member constituencies. In 1968 the name of this body was changed from the Legislative Assembly to the National Assembly of Quebec. At the same time, the 24-member Legislative Council, the only remaining provincial upper house in Canada, was abolished. The maximum life of the National Assembly is five years, although dissolution and a general election usually comes after four years. While procedures are broadly similar to those in other Canadian legislatures, special practices (*e.g.,* in the use of public and private bills committees) have developed over the years. The National Assembly also has complete power to amend the provincial constitution, except as regards the office of lieutenant governor. The capital is Quebec City.

Public administration in Quebec long followed a North American tradition involving a high degree of patronage and an arbitrary and often corrupt handling of public and party funds. Following the change of government in 1960, however, an extensive reform of the provincial civil service was undertaken, culminating in the Public Service Act of 1965, which set up a commission charged with the selection, classification, indemnification, etc., of provincial government employees. Departmental employment in the late 1960s numbered 47,000. The government contains 20 ministries and more than 50 agencies, commissions, and crown corporations.

Municipal divisions in Quebec embrace the more thickly settled areas comprising about one-third of the province, with the remainder being governed as territories. The organized area is divided into 74 counties. Quebec contains 66 cities, 174 towns, 315 villages, and 1,096 townships and parishes.

Provincial government finance is the responsibility of the minister of finance, an office sometimes held directly by the premier. In the mid-1960s, Quebec's ordinary annual revenue totaled nearly $1,900,000,000, derived chiefly from personal income tax (24.7%), the retail sales tax (17.7%), gasoline tax (10.6%), federal equalization payments (8.2%), and corporation profits tax (7.9%). Ordinary annual expenditure totaled more than $1,800,000,000 spent on education (25.6%), health (24.6%), transportation and communications (13.9%), and social welfare (10.9%). Capital expenditures annually were more than $250,000,000. The net funded debt of Quebec was more than $1,000,000,000.

Criminal law in Canada is the exclusive responsibility of the federal government while civil laws fall under provincial jurisdiction. Although the federal government appoints the justices of the superior courts, the administration of justice rests with the province. The Court of Queen's Bench, composed of a chief justice and 11 associate justices, has original jurisdiction in indictable criminal matters and appellate jurisdiction in both criminal and civil matters. The Superior Court consists of a chief justice, an associate chief justice, and 75 associate justices with original civil jurisdiction. The Provincial Court has jurisdiction in civil cases of less than $1,000. Other courts include the Court of Sessions, municipal courts, and social welfare courts.

EDUCATION AND CULTURE

Primary and Secondary.—Quebec's complex educational system is divided along both religious and linguistic lines. Sect. 93 of the British North America Act gives jurisdiction over education to the provinces but provides protection for denominational schools established prior to confederation. Accordingly, Quebec has parallel Catholic and Protestant school systems at both the primary and secondary level. Students not affiliated with either religion generally attend Protestant schools. The language of instruction in most Catholic schools is French and in most Protestant schools English, with separate provisions made for English-speaking Catholics and, on a much smaller scale, for French-speaking Protestants.

Originally, Quebec's educational system did not operate under the overall control of a ministry of education, as in other Canadian provinces. In 1964, however, such a ministry was set up, following the recommendations of the Parent Royal Commission on Education. Its authority is limited by a complex advisory and administrative structure. The 24-member Superior Council of Education, named after consultation with religious authorities and organizations representing parents, teachers, school administrators, and socioeconomic groups, can exert considerable influence. Two committees of the Council, one Catholic and one Protestant, must approve texts and curricula for use in the denominational structure. The minister of education has under him not only a deputy-minister but also two associate deputy-ministers, one of whom is named after consultation with the Catholic committee, the other after consultation with the Protestant committee. At the local level, boards of school commissioners or trustees have certain financial and administrative responsibilities. In the mid-1960s there were 55 Catholic and 9 Protestant regional school boards, in addition to more than 3,000 local or independent boards. Complete gratuity was granted to students at the elementary and secondary levels in 1961. Total annual expenditure on education in Quebec in the mid-1960s was more than $860,000,000, of which 51% was provided by the provincial government, 33% by school taxes, 9% by school fees, and 4% by the federal government. Enrollment in elementary and general secondary education totaled more than 1,500,000 students, nine-tenths of whom attended Catholic schools. The teaching staff comprised over 75,000 persons. (*See* CANADA: *Education;* and SCHOOL ADMINISTRATION: *Sectarian Systems: Canada.*)

Higher Education.—French language higher education in Quebec was traditionally dominated by private, Roman Catholic institutions known as classical colleges (*collèges classiques*). These colleges offered an eight-year program of study, four years of which were at the secondary level and four at the college level. With few exceptions they were run and largely staffed by the clergy, and constituted the faculty of arts of Laval University (founded 1852) in Quebec City or the University of Montreal (1876). Beginning in 1967, they were largely replaced by public, free, nondenominational, and coeducational general and vocational colleges known as CEGEPs (*collèges d'enseignement général et professionnel*). These institutions offer two to three year programs in a variety of subjects and are designed to prepare the student for either university studies or for entering the labour force. The first English language CEGEP opened in 1969 and others were planned for the future. The province's other French language university is the University of Sherbrooke (1954) at Sherbrooke in the Eastern Townships. The province's three English-language universities, Bishop's (Anglican, 1843) at Lennoxville and McGill (1821) and Sir George Williams (1929) in Montreal, are similar in organization to U.S. universities. Future expansion in university education will be provided for by the University of Quebec, established by the provincial government in 1968. In the mid-1960s enrollment in Quebec's universities and colleges reached 75,000. There are also opportunities for vocational and adult education through both public and private agencies.

Culture.—Quebec has a rich cultural and artistic heritage. Well-known French Canadian artists include Antoine Plamondon (1804–95), Henri Julien (1854–1908), Marc Aurèle de Foy Suzor-Coté (1869–1937), Clarence Gagnon (1881–1942), Paul Émile Borduas (1905–60), Alfred Pellan (1906–), and Jean Paul Riopelle (1923–). Poets such as Octave Crémazie (1827–79), Alfred Garneau (1836–1904), Pamphile Lemay (1837–1918), Louis Fréchette (1839–1908), Émile Nelligan (1879–1941), St. Denys Garneau (1912–43), and Anne Hébert (1916–), and novelists such as Antoine Gérin-Lajoie (1824–82), Philippe Pan-

THE INDUSTRIAL CITY OF SHAWINIGAN FALLS ON THE ST. MAURICE RIVER. IN THE FOREGROUND ARE THE ST. MAURICE POWER PLANTS

neton (pseudonym Ringuet, 1895–1960), Félix Antoine Savard (1896–   ), Gabrielle Roy (1909–   ), and Roger Lemelin (1919–   ) have made important contributions to literature. Leading scholars and historians include Jean Baptiste Antoine Ferland (1805–65), François Xavier Garneau (1809–66), Henri Raymond Casgrain (1831–1904), Thomas Chapais (1858–1946), Lionel Groulx (1878–1967), Marcel Trudel (1917–   ), and Guy Frégault (1918–   ). The Provincial Museum in Quebec City and the Château de Ramezay in Montreal display items of artistic and cultural interest.

Concern for the expansion of cultural activity and for the survival and development of French culture in particular led to the creation in 1961 of a Ministry of Cultural Affairs, which includes a special bureau for the French language. Quebec Houses have been established abroad, notably in Paris, to strengthen the province's ties with Europe. A provincial Arts Council distributes grants and literature is encouraged by government guarantees to book publishers. A Quebec Film Office assists in the production of motion pictures. *See also* CANADIAN LITERATURE (FRENCH).

HEALTH AND WELFARE

Health.—The Quebec Department of Health was organized in 1936 succeeding the provincial Health Service established in 1922. Its main divisions include a system of county health units and divisions concerned with tuberculosis, epidemiology, laboratories, venereal diseases, sanitary engineering, mental health, occupational health, nutrition and child care, and health education. Hospital insurance became effective in January 1961. In the late 1960s Quebec also planned to participate with the federal government in a shared-cost program providing universal medical care insurance. In the mid-1960s the province had 130 public general hospitals with more than 25,000 beds and almost 100 allied special hospitals, both public and private, totaling more than 8,000 beds. Twenty-eight public mental hospitals provided more than 18,000 beds. In all, there are over 300 hospitals of all kinds in Quebec totaling more than 57,000 beds, or 9.9 per 1,000 population. The province had 7,000 physicians, one for every 820 citizens.

Public Welfare and Social Security programs come under the jurisdiction of the Department of Family and Social Welfare, established in 1961; government involvement in these activities, however, dates from the Public Assistance Act of 1921. The functions of the department are grouped in four directorates: administration, social assistance, services to youth and children, and services to the aged and other adults. The Quebec Social Allowances Commission, created in 1951, supervises assistance to widows and spinsters, needy mothers, invalids, and the blind, and is also responsible for student allowances. In 1967 Quebec introduced a family allowance program, supplementing the federal plan in existence since 1944. Since 1951, the federal government has also provided a universal old age pension, payable (from 1970 on) at age 65. Unemployment assistance is provided jointly by the two governments. In January 1967 the Quebec Pension Plan paid its first benefits in the form of retirement pensions. This contributory, funded pension scheme, substantially the same as the Canada Pension Plan which operates in the other nine provinces, represents a milestone in the social development of Quebec.

In the mid-1960s 276,000 old age pensioners in Quebec received a total of nearly $230,000,000; family allowances totaling more than $165,000,000 were paid to more than 2,000,000 children in the province. Some 161,000 students received allowances amounting to more than $18,000,000 from the provincial government. In April 1965 Quebec withdrew from federally administered programs providing supplementary old age assistance and allowances for blind and disabled persons.

POPULATION

At the 1966 census the population of Quebec was 5,780,845, representing an increase of 9.9% since 1961, nine-tenths accounted for by natural increase. The population was 78.3% urban and 21.7% rural; only 8.5% lived on farms, while 61.9% lived in 18 urban centres of 30,000 or more population. Almost half the population were centred in the metropolitan areas of Montreal and Quebec City. By ethnic origin in 1961, 80.6% of the population were French, 10.8% were British, 2.1% were Italian, 1.4% Jewish, and 5.1% other. Of the total population 61.9% spoke only French, 11.6% only English, and 25.5% were bilingual. English speaking people live mainly in the large cities, especially Montreal, and in Pontiac, Brome, Huntingdon, Argenteuil, Gatineau, and Chambly counties. The Roman Catholic religion predominates (88.1%), followed by Anglican (3.7%), United Church (2.9%), Jewish (2.0%), and others (3.3%). In 1967, 46,000 immigrants to Canada gave Quebec as their destination, the third largest number in 50 years. The 1966 provincial birth rate was 19.0 per 1,000 population, down from 37.6 in 1921 and 29.7 in 1957. The death rate was 6.7 per 1,000 population compared with 14.2 in 1921. The resulting rate of natural increase was 12.3 per 1,000 population, a sharp decline from the 1957 figure of 22.1.

Quebec: Incorporated Places of 30,000 or more Population

Place	Population				
	1966	1961	1951	1941	1921
Total province . .	5,780,845	5,259,211	4,055,681	3,331,882	2,360,510
Montreal . . .	1,222,255	1,191,062	1,021,520	903,007	618,506
Metropolitan area	2,436,817	2,110,679	—	—	—
Laval* . . .	196,088	124,741	37,843	—	—
Quebec . . .	166,984	171,979	164,016	150,757	95,193
Metropolitan area	413,397	357,568	—	—	—
Verdun . . .	76,832	78,317	77,391	67,349	25,001
Sherbrooke . . .	75,690	66,554	50,543	35,965	23,515
St.-Michel† . .	71,446	55,978	10,539	2,956	493
Montreal North .	67,806	48,433	14,081	6,152	1,360
Hull . . .	60,176	56,929	43,483	32,947	24,117
St.-Laurent . .	59,479	49,805	20,426	6,242	3,232
Trois-Rivières . .	57,540	53,477	46,074	42,007	22,367
Jacques-Cartier .	52,527	40,807	22,450	—	—
LaSalle . . .	48,322	30,904	11,633	4,651	726
Sainte-Foy . .	48,298	29,716	5,236	2,682	1,473
Lachine . . .	43,155	38,630	27,773	20,051	15,404
Granby . . .	34,349	31,463	21,989	14,197	6,785
Chicoutimi . .	32,526	31,657	23,111	16,040	8,937
Outremont . .	30,881	30,753	30,057	30,751	13,249
Shawinigan . .	30,777	32,169	26,903	20,325	10,625

*All municipalities on Île-Jésus merged to form Ville de Laval in 1965.
†Annexed to Montreal in 1968.

THE ECONOMY

The economy of Quebec has been radically transformed in the century since confederation. In 1867 agriculture dominated all other activities and occupied the great majority of the province's labour force. One hundred years later agriculture accounted for less than 5% of total production, while manufacturing represented almost 70%. In the mid-1960s the annual gross provincial product in Quebec was more than $15,850,000,000 with an increase of 8% over the preceding year. Annual personal income totaled more than $12,140,000,000, one-quarter of the Canadian total. However, *per capita* income was only slightly over $2,000, 11% less than the Canadian average and 22% below that of Ontario.

For many years the economy of Quebec was subject to little regulation by the provincial government. The dominant laissez-faire economic philosophy allowed English and American investors free rein, resulting in what one authority later described as "a 19th-century capitalist's dream." After 1960, however, the government of Quebec was far more ready to intervene in the economy on the public behalf. Organizations such as the Quebec Economic Advisory Council and the General Investment Corporation assist in provincial economic planning.

Agriculture.—The concentration of population in the southern part of Quebec developed historically in response to the possibilities for agriculture afforded by the fine level soils of the lowlands and the undulating moraine-covered plateaus of the Appalachian region. At the 1966 census there were 80,000 farms in Quebec of which 42,000 were classified as commercial farms with sales of $2,500 or more. Approximately two-thirds of these were dairy farms. Seventy percent of the province's commercial farms registered sales of less than $7,500 while less than 10% had sales of more than $15,000. Quebec had 7,629,000 ac. (3,087,456 ha.) of improved farmland including 5,166,000 ac.

BY COURTESY OF THE CONSULATE GENERAL OF CANADA

ST. LAMBERT LOCK, PART OF THE ST. LAWRENCE SEAWAY, WITH THE CITY OF MONTREAL IN THE BACKGROUND

(2,090,680 ha.) under crops and 2,121,000 ac. (858,369 ha.) of improved pastures. Annual cash receipts from farming operations totaled nearly $590,700,000; net income was more than $190,265,000.

The lowlands are used largely for animal feed, particularly hay, for dairy cattle. Tobacco is grown on the sandy soils of the Joliette area, vegetables in the area of muck soil south of Montreal, and apples on the slopes of the Monteregian Hills. The Eastern Townships are another dairying centre, although only half the land in the area is cleared. Maple sugar and maple syrup provide additional income. The Gaspé Peninsula and the shield region, with the exception of the western clay belt and the Lake St. John Depression, provide only limited opportunities for agriculture.

The two most important trends in Quebec agriculture after World War I were the increasing degree of mechanization and the gradual elimination and consolidation of small farm units. The federal Department of Agriculture and the provincial Department of Agriculture and Colonization provide farm credit and a variety of subsidies and deficiency payments, as well as offering informational and educational services. The leading farm products in the mid-1960s were: dairy products (more than $203,500,000); hogs (nearly $95,250,000); cattle and calves (more than $75,300,000); poultry (more than $70,000,000); eggs (more than $31,700,000); forest and maple products (nearly $23,000,000); vegetables (nearly $16,000,000); fruits (more than $12,350,000); and potatoes (more than $9,800,000).

Furs and Fisheries.—The fur trade has played a part in the economy of Quebec since the beginning of the French regime, and is still important today in Ungava. In the mid-1960s Quebec produced as many as 450,000 pelts in one year valued in excess of $4,000,000 dollars; about one-half of these came from the province's 141 fur farms. Mink easily ranks first in production while other species include beaver, fox, lynx, otter, and chinchilla. The gross value of production of the fur industry was $43,000,000, two-thirds of the Canadian total.

Maritime fisheries are important in the Gaspé Peninsula, the north shore, and the Magdalen Islands. The Quebec Department of Industry and Commerce operates a network of 58 cold-storage plants. Principal species include cod, lobster, and rosefish. The total annual value of the catch in the 1960s was $7,000,000.

Forestry.—Quebec contains 378,000 sq.mi. (979,016 sq.km.) of forest land, equal to 64% of the province's total land area. Of this amount, 221,000 sq.mi. (572,387 sq.km.) are classed as productive forest land. Provincial crown land leased to private companies accounts for three-quarters of the 100,000 sq.mi. (258,999 sq.km.) actually occupied. Reserves of merchantable standing timbers are estimated at 108,000,000,000 cu.ft. The volume of wood cut in the mid-1960s was as high as 933,000,000 cu.ft. in one year. Varieties include spruce, fur, pine, hemlock, cedar, birch, maple, elm, and oak. Administration of the province's forests is the responsibility of the Department of Lands and Forests. Pulp and paper is the province's largest industry; the selling value of factory shipments in the mid-1960s was as high as $776,000,000 in one year.

Manufactures.—Quebec accounts for approximately 30% of the value of manufactured goods produced in Canada, ranking second only to Ontario. In the mid-1960s the province had almost 11,000 manufacturing establishments employing approximately 500,000 persons; the value added was approximately $4,500,000,-000. Quebec's leading industries are pulp and paper, tobacco products, cotton yarn and cloth, miscellaneous machinery and equipment, synthetic textiles, and petroleum products. Textile industries account for the largest employment, almost one-fifth of the total in manufacturing. The average manufacturing establishment has approximately 40 employees.

Three factors—abundant hydroelectric power, the mineral and forest resources of the shield, and the presence of the navigable channel of the St. Lawrence—have contributed to the development of manufacturing in Quebec. Industrial activity is strongly concentrated in the Montreal metropolitan area which accounts for 55% of the province's total manufacturing output. The next most favoured region is the natural plain bordering on Montreal along the Richelieu River and to the north and south. The city of St. Jean contains establishments in metal working and textiles while Ste. Thérèse boasts an automobile plant. Sherbrooke, the principal city of the Eastern Townships produces textiles and rubber goods; and Three Rivers specializes in newsprint, aluminum, and chemical products. In the Saguenay-Lake St. John area, industrial employment centres on the aluminum plant at Arvida and on numerous pulp and paper mills. Little manufacturing activity is found in the rest of the province, especially in the Gaspé Peninsula.

Hydroelectric power has played a vital role in Quebec's economic development. In the mid-1960s installed generating capacity was 10,746,000 kw., 47% of the Canadian total. By the mid-1970s total capacity was expected to surpass 16,000,000 kw. Large installations include the Beauharnois plant on the St. Lawrence and the Shipshaw plant on the Saguenay. One of North America's most spectacular engineering projects is the construction of seven hydroelectric plants to harness the power potential of the Manicouagan and Outardes rivers. When completed in the mid-1970s the project will provide in excess of 5,500,000 kw. of new generating capacity. Completion of Quebec's first nuclear generating plant, the 250,000-kw. Gentilly Station, was scheduled for 1971. The Quebec Hydro-Electric Commission (Hydro-Québec) is responsible for plants totaling almost 8,000,000 kw. In 1963 it assumed control of eight privately owned power corporations.

Mining.—Quebec ranks third to Ontario in annual total value of mineral production (excluding fuels), accounting for almost 20% of the Canadian total of $4,000,000,000 in the mid-1960s. Quebec's leading mineral products were copper (more than $154,-450,000), asbestos (more than $138,500,000), iron ore (nearly $130,350,000), zinc (more than $88,500,000), gold (more than $35,275,000), and titanium (more than $20,500,000). Quebec is Canada's largest producer of zinc and asbestos, and is second only to Newfoundland in the production of iron ore. Apart from the asbestos deposits at Thetford Mines and Asbestos in the Eastern Townships, which date from 1877, most of the province's minerals are obtained from the Precambrian rocks of the shield. The mining centres of the Noranda area, which date from the

1920s, produce gold, copper, and zinc, as do the Chibougamau Mines to the east developed later. Copper is also found at Murdochville in the Gaspé Peninsula. In 1954 production of iron ore from the vast Labrador-Ungava fields began, following capital expenditures of $250,000,000 and the completion of a 360-mi. (579 km.) railway from Schefferville to the port of Sept-Iles on the St. Lawrence. (*See* LABRADOR-UNGAVA: *Economy; see also* CANADA: *The Economy: Mining and Minerals.*)

Tourism.—Tourism is an increasingly important economic activity in Quebec. The province has seven provincial parks, 12 fish and game reserves (occupying more than 43,000 sq.mi. [111,370 sq.km.]), and 20 camping areas. The main provincial parks are La Vérendrye Park (4,953 sq.mi. [12,828 sq.km.]), 140 mi. (225 km.) NW of Montreal; Laurentide (3,613 sq.mi. [9,358 sq.km.]), 30 mi. (48 km.) N of Quebec City; Mont Tremblant (920 sq.mi. [2,383 sq.km.]), 80 mi. (129 km.) N of Montreal and a well known year-around resort area; and Gaspésian Park (514 sq.mi. [1,331 sq.km.]) on the Gaspé Peninsula. Excellent fishing is found in all but two of the seven parks. National historic parks in Quebec are Fort Chambly at Chambly, and Fort Lennox at Île aux Nois, near St. Johns. In 1967 Montreal was the site of Expo 67, a universal and international exhibition celebrating the centennial of Canadian confederation. Held on partly man-made islands and a peninsula in the St. Lawrence, it attracted a total attendance of over 50,000,000 visitors in six months. (*See* EXHIBITIONS AND FAIRS: *Montreal.*)

Transportation and Communication.—Quebec has an extensive, 5,000 mi. (8,050 km.) railway system that carried 62,000,000 tons of freight in 1966. Most of the lines are operated by the Canadian National Railway or the Canadian Pacific Railway. The province has 56,000 mi. (34,800 km.) of roads, 83% of which are surfaced. The Laurentian and Eastern Townships autoroutes carry some of Quebec's 1,600,000 registered vehicles to and from the Montreal metropolitan region. In the late 1960s the three levels of government spent $400,000,000 annually on highway construction, maintenance, and administration. The St. Lawrence Seaway, opened in 1959, links the ports of Quebec with the Great Lakes and the Atlantic. In the mid-1960s, 87,500,000 tons of cargo were loaded and unloaded annually at these ports; Montreal, Sept-Iles-Pointe Noire, and Port Cartier accounted for almost 60% of this total. The province of Quebec is served by Air Canada, the nation's largest airline, and by Quebecair, founded in 1953. Quebec has 64 private and public licensed airports.

The province had 2,163,000 telephones in the mid-1960s, or 37 per 100 population. There are 60 radio and 13 television stations in Quebec. Radio-Québec, an agency of the provincial government, provides educational broadcasting in both French and English. Quebec has 4 English-language daily newspapers with a circulation of 340,000 and 10 French-language dailies with a circulation of 692,000. There are also 174 weekly newspapers scattered throughout the province.

Labour.—The provincial labour force in the mid-1960s was estimated at 2,200,000 persons. Unemployment has traditionally been high in Quebec, especially in comparison with Ontario, and is a particular problem outside the Montreal metropolitan region. The average rate of unemployment in Quebec was 5.3% compared with the national average of 4.1% and 3.1% in Ontario.

In the mid-1960s, 49% of the labour force had completed elementary schooling or less; 21% had some high school education; and 30% had completed high school or more. Primary industry accounts for 14% of the male labour force, while secondary industry (37%) and tertiary industry (46%) make up the remainder. Quebec's average weekly wage in the late 1960s was $101.13. Unions are usually affiliated with either the Quebec-based Confederation of National Trade Unions (CNTU) or the nationwide Canadian Labour Congress (CLC–AFL-CIO). In one year in the mid-1960s there were 137 strikes and lockouts in Quebec involving 91,000 workers; a record of 1,900,000 workdays were lost. Unemployment insurance is provided by the federal government.

Trade and Commerce.—The provincial Department of Industry and Commerce, created in 1943, encourages industrial and com-

mercial development in Quebec, in cooperation with the federal government. Its services include the Office for Economic Research and the Quebec Bureau of Statistics. In the mid-1960s annual retail trade in Quebec totaled nearly $6,100,000,000; 25% of this from grocery stores. Annual sales of alcoholic beverages were valued at $300,000,000. The Quebec Liquor Board, a provincial government agency, controls the sale of all wines and spirits. In the late 1960s there were 1,600 branches of Canadian chartered banks in the province, including over 900 branches of two predominantly French Canadian banks. A feature of particular interest is the presence of over 1,300 credit union institutions, known as Caisses Populaires, with assets in the late 1960s totaling almost $1,700,000,000.

BIBLIOGRAPHY.—Census of Canada (decennial); *Canada Year Book;* provincial annual reports of departments; *Quebec Yearbook. General Works:* M. Wade, *The French Canadians, 1760–1967,* 2 vol. (1968); A. L. Burt, *The Old Province of Quebec* (1933); F. Ouellet, *Histoire économique et sociale du Québec, 1760–1850* (1966); R. Rumilly, *Histoire de la province de Québec* (1940–); H. T. Manning, *The Revolt of French Canada, 1800–1835* (1962); R. Cook, *Canada and the French-Canadian Question* (1966); J. C. Falardeau (ed.), *Essais sur le Québec contemporain* (1953); M. Wade (ed.), *Canadian Dualism* (1960); E. C. Hughes, *French Canada in Transition* (1943; paperback, 1963); D. F. Putnam (ed.), *Canadian Regions* (1952); Economic Research Corporation, *The Economy of Quebec* (1960); P.-A. Crépeau and C. B. MacPherson (eds.), *The Future of Canadian Federalism* (1965); R. I. Cohen, *Quebec Votes* (1965); F. R. Scott and M. Oliver (eds.), *Quebec States Her Case* (1964); M. Chapin, *Quebec Now* (1965); E. M. Corbett, *Quebec Confronts Canada* (1967); H. F. Quinn, *The Union Nationale: a Study in Quebec Nationalism* (1963); P. Garigue, *Bibliographie du Québec, 1955–1965* (1967).   (M. K. O.)

QUEBEC, the oldest city of Canada and the capital of Quebec province, is situated on the north bank of the St. Lawrence river at its junction with the St. Charles, about 400 mi. (644 km.) from the Atlantic ocean and 180 mi. (290 km.) by river northeast of Montreal. It consists of an upper and a lower town. The upper town is built on the northern extremity of an elevated tableland which forms the left bank of the St. Lawrence for a distance of 8 mi. (13 km.). The highest part of the headland is Cape Diamond, 333 ft. (101 m.) above sea level, and crowned by the Citadel; toward the St. Lawrence it presents a bold and precipitous front, while on the landward side and toward the St. Charles the declivity is more gradual. The lower town is built all around the tableland, at the foot of the cliffs and in the basin of the St. Charles river, and expands on the Beauport coast. Steep, winding streets and an inclined elevator connect the two towns.

The climate of Quebec is severe but bracing, the mean temperature in winter being 12° F (about −11° C) and in summer 68° F (20° C). The city returns four members to the provincial house of assembly and three to the house of commons.

History.—The first known white man to visit Quebec was Jacques Cartier, the French navigator who, in 1535, found on the site a large Indian village called Stadacona. In July 1608, the present city was founded and named by Samuel de Champlain. The origin of the name Quebec has been much disputed, but it is apparently the Algonkian word for a sudden narrowing, a strait, such as the case opposite Cape Diamond where the St. Lawrence narrows to 1,314 yd. (1,202 m.).

The most westward French settlement in America, Quebec was captured in 1629 by the English under Sir David Kirke. They held it until the treaty of St. Germain-en-Laye of 1632, when it was restored to the French. When the colony of New France was made a royal province in 1663 Quebec became the capital and the centre of French operations in North America for a century. In 1690, Sir William Phips, governor of Massachusetts, attempted to reconquer it with a fleet and army but was defeated by the French governor, the comte de Frontenac. In 1711 a great British expedition sent against Quebec under Sir Hovenden Walker was shipwrecked in the Gulf of St. Lawrence, and the French held possession until the French and Indian War. In 1759, a young British general, James Wolfe (*q.v.*), was given the command of an expedition against Quebec from the lower St. Lawrence, while Lord Jeffrey Amherst led a force from New England by Lake Champlain on Montreal. With 8,000 men convoyed by a powerful fleet,

Wolfe tried unsuccessfully to disembark at Beauport and Montmorency below the city; seizing Point Lévis, he bombarded Quebec from there. Many weeks later he decided to land at the Foulon cove above Quebec, and move the main body of his troops to the top of the cliffs on the heights of Abraham. There he was able to fight and defeat the French army commanded by the marquis de Montcalm. Both Wolfe and Montcalm were killed. Quebec surrendered on Sept. 18, five days after the battle. New France was ceded to Great Britain by the treaty ending the war in 1763.

In the winter of 1775–76 American forces under Richard Montgomery and Benedict Arnold attacked the city, but Montgomery was killed (Dec. 31, 1775) and Arnold was compelled to retreat in the following spring. Quebec was the capital of the province of Quebec (1763–91) as then existing; the capital of Lower Canada (1791–1841); the capital of the United Province of Canada, 1851–55 and again in 1859–67; and from 1867 the capital of the province of Quebec. During World War II Pres. Franklin D. Roosevelt and Prime Minister Winston Churchill held a conference at the Citadel in 1943, known as the Quebec conference, that prepared for the invasion of Europe by Allied forces.

Urban Characteristics.—The most notable feature of Quebec is the city within the walls, the only remaining enclosed city in North America. The present walls and the Citadel that crowns Cape Diamond cover an area of about 40 ac. (16 ha.); they were built in 1823–32. Since then several of the gates have been destroyed and others rebuilt; among the best-known are St. Jean and St. Louis gates. Between 1865 and 1871 three forts were built on the Lévis side of the river but these were neither manned nor armed.

In the city, with its narrow and irregular streets, the visitor will discover the old world character of Quebec. Several houses built during the French regime are still occupied. Among the famous buildings located in this part of Quebec are the Château Frontenac, a large hotel erected by the Canadian Pacific railway; the Anglican cathedral, built in 1804; the Roman Catholic basilica, founded in 1647, enlarged at various times, destroyed by fire in 1922 and rebuilt on the original site; the old Roman Catholic seminary, founded in 1663; Laval university; and the Ursulines

DUFFERIN TERRACE OVERLOOKING THE ST. LAWRENCE RIVER. TO THE RIGHT IS A MONUMENT OF SAMUEL DE CHAMPLAIN

convent. The Dufferin terrace is a magnificent 1,400-ft. (427 m.)-long promenade overlooking the St. Lawrence, 200 ft. (61 m.) above the level of the river. During the winter, the terrace is a favourite winter sport centre for skating and toboggan rides. The lower town (*basseville*) is a mixture of old buildings such as the Notre Dame des Victoires church (erected in 1688, but so named in memory of the defeats of Phips in 1690 and Walker in 1711), old houses and new warehouses and other commercial buildings. It is the financial and wholesale district of Quebec.

In the upper town, beyond the walls, are the historic Plains of Abraham, a national battlefield park and site of the museum of the province of Quebec; the parliament buildings of French Renaissance style, built in 1878–92; and the Bois de Coulonge residence, seat of the lieutenant governor of the province.

Churches and Institutions.—The numerous spires and towers of buildings are another distinctive feature of Quebec. The city is 90% Roman Catholic and 92% French Canadian; many religious orders and congregations have established their mother houses there. Laval university, named after the first bishop of Quebec, was founded in 1852 by royal charter from Queen Victoria and in 1876 received a charter from Pope Pius IX. It includes faculties of theology, philosophy, law, medicine, sciences, arts, letters, forestry and commerce, a library, a museum and a picture gallery. In 1952 the university began its move to a new campus in the suburb of Sainte-Foy. The principal benevolent institutions of Quebec are also administered by religious congregations. The Hôtel Dieu, one of the largest hospitals of the city, was founded in 1639 by the duchess of Aiguillon and has continuously served the public. Under the dual system of education in the province (French and English), there are two separate groups of primary and secondary schools and colleges. A number of government buildings are scattered over the city and in some of the suburbs.

Commerce, Industries and Transportation.—Quebec was long the chief port of Canada and one of the most important wooden shipbuilding and repair centres on the continent. With the deepening of the St. Lawrence channel upstream in the second half of the 19th century, Montreal became the great shipping port of Canada and Quebec suffered a serious economic setback. Later, with the construction of railway lines in all directions from the old capital, the building of new harbour facilities, the abundant services of hydroelectric power and the availability of skilled labour, an important industrial development followed. The chief industries are shipyards and shipbuilding, pulp and paper, shoe and leather, textiles, clothing, mechanical industries, gunpowder, ropes, and food and beverages. Quebec is the main trade and commercial centre of the eastern part of the province. The principal commodities handled in the port are grain, coal, petroleum products, asbestos, steel, cement, pulp and paper, newsprint and general cargo. The port, formerly icebound between Christmas and the end of March, is now open to winter navigation. Quebec harbour is the seat of the regional administrator of the federal department of transport for marine operations, who is responsible for the maintenance of the St. Lawrence waterway from the ocean to Quebec. From the Dufferin terrace one can see the Queen's wharf at the bottom, where arctic supply ships are loaded, buoys manufactured and repaired, maintenance barges and ships loaded or unloaded and icebreakers assigned to special duties in the winter.

The Quebec bridge across the St. Lawrence, 7 mi. (11 km.) above the city, was completed in 1917, after ten years of work and two serious accidents to the structure (on both occasions one of the sections fell into the river). It is used by railway and vehicular traffic. Construction of another bridge a few hundred yards away was begun in the late 1960s. Quebec is a major railroad centre, the terminal of the transcontinental line from Prince Rupert (British Columbia), the Lake St. John-Saguenay line and the North Shore line to Murray Bay (La Malbaie). These lines and the modern freight yard of Charny are operated by the Canadian National railway. Quebec is also the terminal of the Montreal-Quebec line of the Canadian Pacific railway and is linked with major Canadian and U.S. cities by bus and truck transport service. The Quebec airport is located at Ancienne-Lorette, 10 mi. (16 km.) W. of the city, and is served by Trans-Canada air lines and Quebecair, with several daily flights to Montreal, Chicoutimi, the iron ore district of Sept-Îles-Schefferville and other Canadian metropolitan districts.

The Quebec metropolitan area has a population (1966) of 413,397 (Quebec city proper, 166,984) and comprises 30 municipalities; several of these municipalities are located on the south shore, Lévis and Lauzon being the most important ones. Sainte-Foy and Sillery are two residential suburbs in the upper town. There is a Huron Indian reservation near Loretteville.

See also references under "Quebec" in the Index.

BIBLIOGRAPHY.—Sir G. Parker and C. G. Bryan, *Old Quebec* (1903); B. Sulte, *History of Quebec* (1908); *The King's Book of Quebec*, 2 vol. (1911); J. C. Sutherland, *The Province of Quebec* (1922); M. J. Pelton, *Natural Resources of Quebec* (1923); Willa Cather, *Shadows on the Rock* (1931); M. de la Roche, *Quebec, Historic Seaport* (1944); C. M. Barbeau, *J'ai vu Quebec* (1957).   (P. Ca.)

QUEBEC ACT, an act of Parliament assented to on June 22, 1774, that vested the government of Quebec in a governor and council and preserved the French Civil Code and the Roman Catholic religion. The act was an attempt to deal with major questions that had arisen during the attempt to make the French colony of Canada a province of the British Empire in North America. Among these were whether an assembly should be summoned, when nearly all the inhabitants of the Province of Quebec, being Roman Catholics, would, because of the Test Acts (*q.v.*), be unable to be representatives; whether the exercise of the Roman Catholic religion should be allowed to continue, and on what conditions; and whether French or English law was to be used in the courts of justice.

The act, declaring it inexpedient to call an assembly, put the power to legislate in the hands of the governor and his council. The exercise of the Roman Catholic religion was allowed, and the church was authorized to continue to collect the tithe. The Test Act was waived and an oath of allegiance substituted so as to allow Roman Catholics to hold office. French civil law continued, but the criminal law was to be English. Because of these provisions the act has been called a generous and statesmanlike attempt to deal with the peculiar conditions of the province.

At the last moment additions were made to the bill by which the boundaries given the province by the Proclamation of 1763 were extended. This was done because no satisfactory means had been found to regulate Indian affairs and to govern the French settlers on the Ohio and Mississippi rivers. It was decided, therefore, to put the territory between the Ohio and the Mississippi under the governor of Quebec, and the boundaries of Quebec were extended southward to the junction of the Ohio and the Mississippi and northward to the height of land between the Great Lakes and Hudson Bay.

This provision of the act, together with the recognition of the Roman Catholic religion, was seen to threaten the unity and security of British America by in effect reviving the old French Empire destroyed in 1763. The American colonists viewed the act as a measure of coercion. The act was thus a major cause of the American Revolution, and provoked an invasion of Quebec by the armies of the revolting colonies in the winter of 1775–76. (*See* AMERICAN REVOLUTION.) Its provisions, on the other hand, did little at the time to win French support of British rule in Quebec and, except for the clergy and seigneurs, most of the French remained neutral. The act eventually became important to French Canadians as the basis of their religious and legal rights.

See also CANADA: *History: Canada as Quebec;* QUEBEC: *History.*   (W. L. Mo.)

QUEDLINBURG, a town of East Germany in the *Bezirk* (district) of Halle, German Democratic Republic. It is situated on the Bode, 48 mi. (77 km.) SW of Magdeburg by road in the fertile northern foothills of the lower Harz Mountains. Pop. (1964) 30,820. Quedlinburg has town walls and towers and many half-timbered buildings, the oldest dating from the 10th century. The town is dominated by the castle, now a museum, and the abbey church of St. Servatius (now Protestant), a Romanesque basilica. Paints, precision instruments, engineering products, wagons, chemical and pharmaceutical goods, and jewelry are produced and it is an important seed-growing centre, the Institute for Plant Research being situated there. The town is said to have been founded by a certain Quitilo in the 5th century. Henry I built the castle and is buried in the abbey church. In the 10th and 11th centuries Quedlinburg was an important intellectual centre and was often the residence of the Saxon German emperors. Until 1477 it was part of the Hanseatic League, and then came under the protection of the elector of Saxony. In 1698 it passed to the elector of Brandenburg. The poet Friedrich Gottlieb Klopstock (1724–1803) was born in Quedlinburg.

QUEEN ANNE'S BOUNTY: *see* CHURCH COMMISSIONERS.

QUEENBOROUGH, a former municipal borough in the Faversham parliamentary division of Kent, Eng., in the Isle of Sheppey near the junction of the Medway and Swale rivers, 3 mi. (5 km.) S of Sheerness. In 1968 Queenborough was incorporated with Sheerness and Sheppey to form the new municipal borough of Queenborough-in-Sheppey. Pop. (1970 est.) 28,860. In 1339 the marshes were drained and the town's foundations laid. In 1361 Edward III replaced a nearby Saxon fortress by the castle, designed by his chancellor William of Wykeham. From 1582 until demolished by Cromwell this was the official residence of the lord warden of the Cinque Ports. Edward III named the town Regina Burgia when he stayed there with Philippa, his queen, in 1366, granted it a charter, and built the parish church. The guildhall contains valuable old regalia. Queenborough was a wool staple town in Tudor times and in 1579 Matthias Falconer started manufacturing chemicals. This industry still goes on; others include glassmaking, iron-founding, the production of sanitary pottery, and the importation and distribution of coal.

QUEEN CHARLOTTE ISLANDS, a compact group lying off the northern part of the coast of British Columbia, form part of that province of Canada. Pop. (1966) 2,222 (excluding about 950 persons living on Indian reserves). Land area 3,705 sq.mi. (9,596 sq.km.). The islands were named after his ship by Capt. George Dixon who, in 1787, sailed through Hecate Strait, which separates them from the mainland. The islands contain resources of minerals (coal, gold, iron, and copper) and softwood timber. The surrounding waters support prolific fisheries (chiefly salmon, halibut, herring, crabs, and clams), but comparatively little settlement has occurred. The largest community, Queen Charlotte, had less than 500 inhabitants in 1960. Logging and fishing are the main occupations, most of the output going to processing plants on the mainland. There are scheduled air and marine transport connections with Prince Rupert but bad weather often disrupts the service, especially in winter. The native Haida Indians possessed one of the highest cultures and art forms found among aboriginal peoples of northwestern America.   (A. L. Fy.)

QUEEN ELIZABETH ISLANDS, the name given in 1953 to the groups of islands of the Canadian Arctic archipelago north of latitude 74° 30′ N in honour of Queen Elizabeth II. The islands are the most northerly land area of North America and are almost completely uninhabited. Total area 134,920 sq.mi. (349,-443 sq.km.). Pop. (1961) 310. The largest is Ellesmere (*q.v.;* 82,119 sq.mi. [212,688 sq.km.]); ranking next in size are Devon (20,861 sq.mi. [54,030 sq.km.]); Melville (16,369 sq.mi. [42,396 sq.km.]); and Axel Heiberg (15,779 sq.mi. [40,866 sq.km.]). Administratively, the islands are a part of Franklin District of the Northwest Territories (*q.v.*). For their geology, exploration, and the like, *see* ARCTIC, THE.

QUEENS, one of the five boroughs of the city of New York, U.S. Located on western Long Island, it extends across the island from the junction of the East River and Long Island Sound to the Atlantic Ocean; Queens County is conterminous with the borough. In the early Colonial period the area was part of New Netherland and the first settlement was made by the Dutch in 1636 near Flushing Bay. Gradually towns were organized, including Newtown in 1642, Far Rockaway in 1644, Flushing in 1645, and Jamaica in 1656. These settlements along with the rest of New Netherland came under English control in 1664 when Peter Stuyvesant surrendered to an English force acting for the duke of York. In 1683 the English established Queens County as one of the 12 counties of the province of New York. It was named for Catherine of Braganza, queen consort of Charles II.

During the American Revolution the residents of Queens County were divided in their allegiance; when the English captured Long Island in 1776 many of the patriots fled, and at the conclusion of the struggle a group of the Tories migrated to Newfoundland.

Throughout the 19th century Queens continued to be primarily a rural community with a few small trading centres. Some of the shore communities began to attract large numbers of summer vacationists and such popular resorts as the Rockaways became well known. In 1898 Queens borough was formed as a part of greater New York and at the same time assumed its present size (126.6 sq.mi.) when the three eastern towns of Hempstead, North Hempstead, and Oyster Bay opposed joining New York City and were chartered as Nassau County. Pop. (1970) 1,973,708.

Queens experienced rapid development after the opening of the Queensboro Bridge in 1909 and the Long Island Railroad tunnel the next year. This development continued and Queens became the fastest growing borough of the city, still retaining for the most part its residential character. *See also* LONG ISLAND; NEW YORK (CITY). (D. L. D.)

QUEEN'S (KING'S) **BENCH, COURT OF,** in England, was descended from the court held *coram rege* ("before the monarch") when it was part of that undifferentiated *curia regis* (*see* HOUSEHOLD, ROYAL) which was still performing legislative and executive as well as judicial functions. It was a court to hear cases which concerned the sovereign, or cases affecting great persons privileged to be tried only before him. If he was absent abroad, such cases were heard *coram consilio nostro* ("before our council"). It was also a court to correct the errors and defaults of all other courts, and after the close of the civil wars of Henry III's reign was mainly occupied with the trial of criminal or quasi-criminal cases. In 1268 it obtained a chief justice of its own, but only very gradually did it become a separate court of common law. Thus it was not until a century after the Court of Common Pleas (*q.v.*) had become a distinct court of common law that the Court of King's Bench attained a similar position.

It exercised a supreme and general jurisdiction, which comprised (1) criminal jurisdiction; (2) civil jurisdiction; and (3) jurisdiction over the errors of inferior courts including those of the Court of Common Pleas, until by the act of 1830 the Court of Exchequer Chamber became a court of appeal intermediate between the three common law courts and Parliament. It also heard appeals from the Court of King's Bench in Ireland until 1783, and exercised jurisdiction over officials and others by means of the prerogative writs; *e.g.*, habeas corpus, certiorari, prohibition, mandamus, quo warranto, and ne exeat regno.

By the Judicature Act, 1873, the court was merged in the Supreme Court of Judicature, while its name survived in, and its functions largely devolved upon, the Queen's Bench Division of the High Court of Justice. It consists of a chief justice—the lord chief justice of England—and 38 of the total of 70 judges of the High Court authorized by the Administration of Justice Act, 1968. Appeals from inferior courts come before a divisional court, composed of two or three judges of the division. *See also* COURT; PRACTICE AND PROCEDURE. (H. H. L. B.; W. T. Ws.)

QUEENSBERRY, EARLS, MARQUESSES, AND DUKES OF. The Queensberry title, one of the many associated with the Scottish house of Douglas (*q.v.*), originated when SIR WILLIAM DOUGLAS (d. 1640) was created earl of Queensberry in 1633. He was a direct descendant of Sir William Douglas (d. *c.* 1421), illegitimate son of James (d. 1388), 2nd earl of Douglas, who received from his father a grant of the lands of Drumlanrig in Dumfriesshire.

Sir William's grandson, WILLIAM (1637–1695), was created marquess of Queensberry in 1682, and in 1684, as a reward for his services in helping suppress the Scottish covenanters, duke of Queensberry. From 1682 to 1686 as lord high treasurer of Scotland he wielded great power. He supported the revolution of 1688, taking the oath of allegiance to William and Mary in April 1690. His son JAMES (1672–1711), 2nd duke, also supported the revolution. He held many offices in Scotland and was created (1701) a Knight of the Garter for his services as commissioner to the Scottish Parliament. Deprived of many of his offices in 1704 as a result of his association with the Jacobite intriguer Simon Fraser, Baron Lovat (*q.v.*), he was restored in 1705, and in 1706 was commissioner for effecting the union between Scotland and England. In 1708 he was created duke of Dover and marquess of Beverley, both in the peerage of Great Britain.

The 2nd duke's eldest son died in infancy and his second son JAMES (1697–1715) was an idiot. In 1706 the 2nd duke resigned the dukedom of Queensberry and certain other of his titles and

obtained a novodamus (regrant) by which he was able to arrange that they should pass on his death to his third son CHARLES (1698–1778). The titles of marquess and earl of Queensberry, not being mentioned in the novodamus, are presumed to have belonged *de jure* to James, between 1711 and 1715, although he was never so styled. His brother Charles was, therefore, after 1711, 3rd duke, and after 1715, since James died unmarried, 4th marquess and 6th earl of Queensberry. The 3rd duke was keeper of the great seal of Scotland from 1761 to 1763, and lord justice general in Scotland from 1763 until his death.

Charles's two sons predeceased him, and on his death the dukedom of Dover (of which he had had special remainder by the creation of 1708) and the marquessate of Beverley became extinct. His Scottish titles descended to a cousin, WILLIAM DOUGLAS (1725–1810), 3rd earl of March, grandson of William, 1st Douglas earl of March, younger brother of James, 2nd duke of Queensberry. He was lord of the bedchamber to George III from 1760 to 1789, when he was dismissed for having opposed the government on the regency question (1788). A notable personality in the racing world, the 4th duke was often known as "Old Q" or "the star of Piccadilly." He died unmarried and the earldom of March passed to a distant cousin, Francis Charteris (afterward earl of Wemyss). Because of the 1706 novodamus, the dukedom of Queensberry again became separated from the marquessate and the earldom. The former, with the Drumlanrig lands, went to the 2nd duke's second cousin once removed, HENRY SCOTT (1746–1812), 3rd duke of Buccleuch, and is presently held by his direct descendant SIR WALTER JOHN MONTAGU-DOUGLAS-SCOTT (1894–   ), 8th duke of Buccleuch and 10th duke of Queensberry. The marquessate and earldom passed to SIR CHARLES DOUGLAS (1777–1837), 5th baronet, a descendant of William, 1st earl of Queensberry.

Charles died without male issue and the dignities passed to his brother JOHN (1779–1856) and to John's heirs. JOHN SHOLTO DOUGLAS (1844–1900), the 9th marquess, was a boxing enthusiast and the Queensberry rules, which govern the sport in Britain, were drawn up under his auspices. DAVID HARRINGTON ANGUS DOUGLAS (1929–   ) is 12th marquess.

QUEENSLAND, a state of Australia in the northeast of the continent occupying 667,000 sq.mi. (1,727,532 sq.km.), or about one-fifth of the total area. A coastline of 3,236 mi. (5,208 km.)—after that of Western Australia the longest of any individual state—bounds it on the north from the Gulf of Carpentaria and on the northeast and east from the Coral Sea and the Pacific Ocean respectively, the 480-mi. (772-km.)-long Cape York Peninsula forming the only major irregularity in the coastal plan. In the west the boundary runs successively with that of Northern Territory along longitude 138° E and with that of South Australia along latitude 26° S and longitude 141° E to the northwest corner of New South Wales. In the south the boundary marches with that of New South Wales along latitude 29° S, the Barwon-Macintyre-Dumaresq rivers and the crest lines of the McPherson Range to Point Danger. The waters and islands of Torres Strait nearly to New Guinea, as well as the Great Barrier Reef, are included within the political boundaries. Maximum length (north-south) is 1,238 mi. (1,992 km.) and maximum breadth (east-west at latitude 26° S) is 945 mi. (1,521 km.). The capital is Brisbane (*q.v.*).

PHYSICAL GEOGRAPHY

Physical Features.—Queensland is characteristically an area of subdued relief. Great plains extend over wide areas of the state, and, although they merge into higher country of sharper relief both to the east and the northwest, there are relatively small tracts of country that are mountainous.

The Eastern Range, Plateau, and Lowland Region.—This area occupies the eastern quarter of the state between the Main Divide (as the western continuation of the Eastern Highlands is called in Queensland) and the Pacific coast. In the north, however, its western limits extend beyond the Main Divide. It is underlain mainly by Paleozoic rocks, folded into complex structures and invaded by widespread igneous intrusions between Devonian and Permian times, with a superposition of Mesozoic sediments in

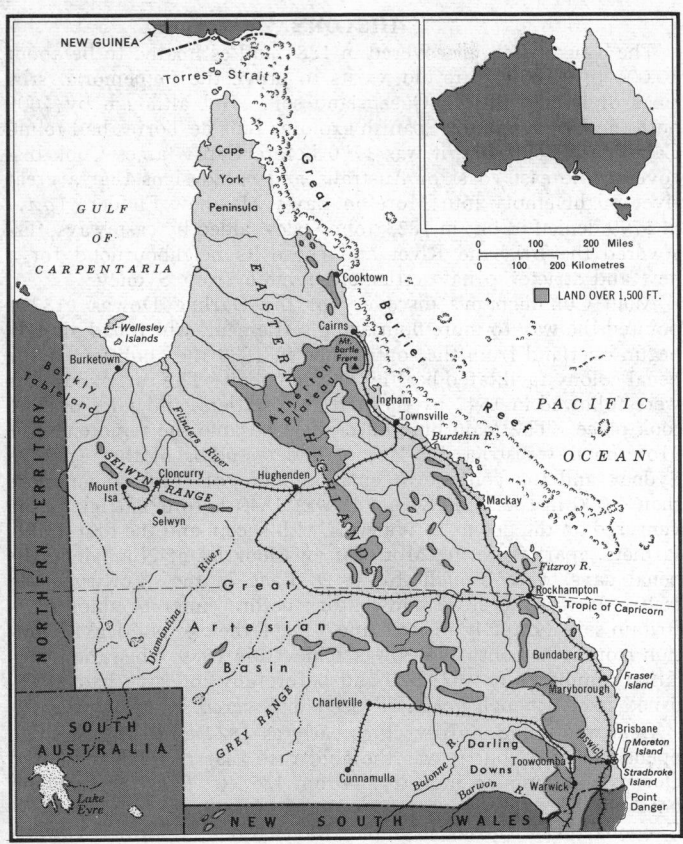

PHYSICAL FEATURES, MAJOR CITIES, AND RAILROADS OF QUEENSLAND, AUSTRALIA

some central and southern basins and with Tertiary basalt-flow residuals capping many of the higher areas. The two main components in the surface configuration pattern are the coastal ranges —a discontinuous and much-denuded series of low ranges and plateaus, often with cores of granitic rocks and flanks of metamorphics—and the present Main Divide which follows generally the upwarped eastern rim of the Mesozoic rocks of the Great Artesian Basin. Between these two structural swells is a series of extensive, shallow, interior basins and narrow, near-coastal lowland corridors separated by ranges and plateaus.

The Main Divide follows a course that is convex to the southwest, so that the region has its greatest width (about 300 mi. [488 km.]) near the Tropic of Capricorn. In this central area, too, elevations are lowest, the great interior catchment basins of the Fitzroy and Burdekin river systems (occupying about 54,500 and 53,500 sq.mi. [141,000 and 138,500 sq.km.] respectively) with their markedly convergent tributary patterns being mostly undulating lowland westward of the coastal ranges. The dominant structural feature of this central area is the huge Bowen syncline, a downwarp including the most extensive bituminous coal measures in Queensland.

Northward and southward from the tropic, the coastal and Main Divide ranges become more conspicuous and continuous and converge to form the most striking ranges and highest plateaus in the state. In the far north the Atherton Plateau of about 12,000 sq.mi. (31,000 sq.km.) everywhere exceeds 2,000 ft. (600 m.) and rises irregularly southward to more than 3,000 ft. (900 m.). Pliocene basalt, weathering into rich red soils, covers much of its area, and the Bellenden Ker Range with Queensland's highest peak, Mt. Bartle Frere (5,287 ft. [1,612 m.]), bounds it on the east. In the far south, the rugged McPherson Range (Mt. Barney, 4,449 ft. [1,356 m.]) lies astride the state border inland from Tugun beach for 60 mi. (100 km.), merging thence into the highest part of the Queensland Main Divide (Mt. Superbus, 4,525 ft. [1,379 m.]) which there presents a steep face to the east but a slighter and more gentle descent westward toward the Darling Downs. The

rivers in these mountainous areas have a more uniform flow than those of east-central Queensland. The latter are classed as perennial, but considerable stretches of their courses dry out in winter.

The Pacific coastline cuts transversely across the structural grain and is characterized by an alternation of rocky, north-facing promontories, sheltering picturesque inlets and gently curving sandy beaches, often backed by sand dunes and salt marsh. The rivers generally flow to the sea across deltaic plains, those of the Burdekin and Fitzroy being of considerable size. The long, narrow islands close off the southern coast (Fraser, Bribie, Moreton, and Stradbroke) are composed of sand dunes which are among the highest in the world. The string of reefs and cays, collectively known as the Great Barrier Reef, that stretches for more than 1,100 mi. (1,770 km.) from Torres Strait to latitude 24° S, lies along the seaward margin of the continental shelf. (*See* BARRIER REEF.) The coast along the Gulf of Carpentaria is low lying and mangrove lined.

The Western Plains.—These plains occupy more than half the area of Queensland and form a great tract of lowland extending continuously from the Gulf coast to the southern border but constricted to a width of 280 mi. (450 km.) in the low Kynuna watershed (latitude 21° S), an upwarped structural and surface swell (600–1,200 ft. [180–370 m.] generally rising eastward) with occasional low ridges. Northward and southward from this swell and westward from the hill country flanking the western side of the Main Divide there is a very gentle overall slope northwestward toward the Gulf of Carpentaria and southwestward toward the Lake Eyre region, corresponding with two great shallow sags in the thick Cretaceous sandstones and shales that underlie the plains. These slopes are closely followed by the watercourses which form three systems converging respectively toward the Darling in the south, the Lake Eyre flats of South Australia in the southwest, and the Gulf of Carpentaria in the northwest. Some of these watercourses are of considerable length but most flow only for short periods each year following the summer rains. In floodtime the Channel country of the far southwest is widely inundated, but with the loss of water by evaporation and seepage the waters rarely reach Lake Eyre.

West of the Channel country and astride the southwestern boundary of the state is a tract of fixed and partly vegetated sand dunes aligned generally along north-northwest axes.

The extent of the western plains coincides fairly closely with

DOUGLASS BAGLIN

DIVIDING RANGE IN THE EASTERN HIGHLANDS NEAR HUGHENDEN, QUEENSLAND

that of the Queensland part of the Great Artesian Basin with its underlying strata of water-bearing rocks.

The Northwest Uplands.—In the far northwest of Queensland is an outlier of the Precambrian rocks of the Australian shield trending north-northwest for 300 mi. (480 km.) from near Selwyn and Dajarra to the state border west of Burketown. Especially in the south, the rocks are closely folded, intimately penetrated by igneous intrusions, and locally mineralized. Dissected hill country with steep-sided rocky valleys characterizes this area. The Georgina Plains west of Mount Isa are floored by Cambrian limestones and rise gently northward to the Barkly tableland.

Climate.—Queensland is divided into almost equal parts by the Tropic of Capricorn and includes comparatively little high country, so that hot summers and mild winters are characteristic of the state. The rainfall shows a well-marked summer maximum and varies widely. The heaviest rains occur in the northeast coastlands between Cooktown and Ingham and on the mountain slopes immediately to the west (Tully, 178.06 in. [4522.7 mm.]). The heaviest and most prolonged falls are from December to March.

(R. H. G.)

Vegetation.—Rain forest with strong Papuan floristic affinities occurs in the higher rainfall districts, reaching its best development along the eastern coast in scattered areas with an annual rainfall of about 60 in. (1,520 mm.) or more. Inland, with a decreasing annual rainfall and a marked dry season, it passes gradually into monsoon forest and farther west, in the areas of less than 30 in. (760 mm.) of rainfall, it disappears as a vegetation unit. The predominant vegetation type in a belt about 250 mi. (400 km.) wide along the eastern coast is eucalyptus forest, interspersed with extensive grasslands. The eucalyptus forests are the source of valuable hardwoods and the rain forests provide many important cabinet timbers. With increasing aridity the eucalyptus forests thin out, and the great pastoral areas stretch to the edge of the desert in the extreme west of the state. Extensive mangrove forests occur in the estuaries and on tidal mud flats, especially in the tropical north.

Animal Life.—Terrestrial mammals native to Queensland include the 2 monotremes (echidna and platypus), more than 50 species of marsupials, and more than 50 of placental mammals. The echidna is common, and the platypus is more abundant in the southern part of the state than in the far north. Marsupials range in size from the great gray kangaroo to a two-inch broad-footed pouched "mouse." Numbers of some species such as the koala have been greatly reduced as the result of settlement. Some, however, have adapted themselves to urban conditions, notably the brush-tailed opossum and the short-nosed bandicoot. Two species of tree-climbing kangaroo and two of the cuscuses in the north are examples of links with the marsupial fauna of New Guinea. Destructive carnivorous marsupials are few, the native "cat" (*Dasyurus*) being the largest. Among placental mammals are the dingo, bats (including some destructive fruit-eating species, the flying foxes), and rodents. Of the snakes the largest authentic specimen is of *Python amethystinus*, 12½ ft. long, from north Queensland. Lizards are common and among the turtles is the edible green turtle. Notable among the birds are the emu, cassowary, and several kinds of birds of paradise and bowerbirds.

Marine fish species are numerous and of the freshwater species the lungfish (*Neoceratodus forsteri*) is of special interest. The corals and other marine life of the Great Barrier Reef are of extraordinary richness, and there is a marine biological research station at Heron Island in the Capricorn group.

National Parks.—About 100,100 ac. (40,500 ha.) of national parks have been permanently reserved under the protection and administration of the Forestry Department. They vary from a few acres to whole mountain ranges such as in the Carnarvon National Park of 66,480 ac. (26,900 ha.). Essentially they are natural reserves maintained in their original state except for access paths and, where necessary, accommodation areas for visitors. Designed to preserve a full range of habitats of Queensland plants and animals against the encroachment of settlement they range from coral islands to mainland forests.   (D. A. Hт.)

HISTORY

The Talgai skull, discovered in 1884 and estimated to be about 10,000 to 25,000 years old, exists to prove the immemorial stirrings of human life on Queensland soil. But although by 1606 both the Dutch and the Spanish explorer Luis de Torres had found Cape York Peninsula, it was 1770 before Capt. James Cook discovered the east coast of Australia and noted signs that a great river might empty into Moreton Bay. Matthew Flinders (*q.v.*) in 1799 denied it, but in 1823 John Oxley, aided by castaways, discovered the Brisbane River and chose its neighbourhood for a new and stricter penal settlement remote from Sydney.

Allan Cunningham's discovery of the Darling Downs (1827) pointed the way to more flourishing settlement, which had already begun overland from the south when in 1839 the abolition of the penal colony facilitated healthy development. The early squatters were followed in 1842 by the first free settlers, and sales of land took place. The main hindrances then became the remoteness of Moreton Bay district, the lack of understanding of the region in Sydney and the consequent small number of settlers—no more than 2,000 in the mid-1840s. It was 1840 before Patrick Leslie ventured on the downs at Warwick with sheep, and the first arable farmers, apart from the Moravian missionaries at Nundah in the penal days, were brought by J. D. Lang in the "Fortitude" in 1849. It was therefore mid-century before emigrant ships from Britain sailed directly to Brisbane. Nevertheless, political separation from New South Wales was achieved in 1859, when the population numbered only 23,520 and before any industry had established itself, though gold had been discovered in 1858.

Coal was found at Ipswich as early as 1827 and the first mine opened in 1846, but it was the gold rush that really inaugurated Queensland's mining industry. From 1858 to 1873 the east and north of the state were invaded and opened up by diggers at Canoona, Peak Downs, Gympie, Ravenswood, Charters Towers, and Palmer River. Within a few months isolated spots in the bush became townships of 10,000 people. There some of the beginnings of the "White Australia" policy may be seen in the discrimination by act of Parliament against Chinese and other Asian speculators (1877). By 1867 the population of the state had grown to 100,000. Even where the gold failed, as at Canoona, a town such as Rockhampton could rise from the ruins. In 1882 came the discovery of a mountain of gold and copper, Mt. Morgan, near Rockhampton.

In the 1860s westward migration was very rapid wherever there was water, and the movement was encouraged in 1869 by an act of Parliament which granted 21-year leases to those who had 25 sheep or 5 cattle to the square mile. Many of the early pastoralists failed. Wool had to be transported in drays by long trains of bullocks and markets were far away and uncertain. But by 1873 Victorian prosperity (in gold) began to be invested in Queensland. Sheep studs were improved, and fences replaced the shepherd. The first railways, from Ipswich to Dalby and Warwick, were operating by 1870. In the 1880s attempts were made, not always successfully, to end the bitter struggle between grazier (livestock rancher) and squatter by a succession of acts of Parliament. Artesian boring was introduced in 1881 and was energetically developed after the bad years of drought and depression between 1890 and 1902, which wiped out flocks and herds. In addition, after 1894 cattle suffered the onslaught of the cattle tick from northern Queensland, and an industry which had been stimulated by the advent of refrigeration and which had made its mark on Australian life in the tradition of droving over huge distances saw its 7,000,000 cattle halved by 1902.

There was similar strife between the early arable farmer and the grazier who had come before him. Hewing out his farm by clearing the bush, attempting crops where none had ever been cultivated, the farmer won the contemptuous name of "cockatoo farmer." But, supporting himself, he advanced from maize (corn) and pumpkins to lucerne and sorghum; his livestock increased; and the plow, reaper, and farmhouse replaced the hoe, scythe and sickle, and bark hut. By 1900 the government had recovered much pastoral land for the arable farmer, and by the mid-20th century land which had originally belonged to graziers had become renowned for wheat, sugarcane, and bacon.

Dairying did not flourish till the 20th century, when there were sufficiently populous towns to give it encouragement. Until 1888 Queensland imported much of its butter from the south, but by 1895 it had become self-sufficient in dairy products.

Between 1860 and 1904 Queensland was closely involved in the long dispute over the employment of South Sea islanders (Kanakas) as cheap labour. The recruiting of Kanakas (often against their will) began with the introduction of cotton cultivation during the American Civil War. After cotton failed at the end of the war, recruiting continued with growth of the sugarcane industry. The replacement of the hoe by the plow and the greater productiveness of the white man lessened the usefulness of the Kanakas; by an act of 1904 the new federal government ended the importing of coloured labour and agreed to support sugar financially, when necessary, in the interests of the "White Australia" policy.

The Kanaka problem influenced the separatist movement in northern Queensland (where both sugarcane and the goldfields were), but whereas the planters wanted separation the miners did not, fearing that the planters would impose a policy of continued importation of coloured labour.

Toward the end of the 19th century the increase in population, the advance of social legislation in Europe, the socialist idealism of William Lane, and the depression of the 1890s encouraged the growth of trade unionism and led to the emergence of a Labour Party with well-defined policies. The most notable event in Queensland at this period was the shearers' strike in 1891. It was broken, but subsequent legislation providing for shorter working hours, improved conditions of work, and the encouragement of the smaller settler showed clearly the trend of the times. In 1899 Queensland had Australia's first Labour government, though a minority one, but Labour's position rapidly became so strong that after World War I it was almost continuously in office. In 1922 it abolished the upper house of Parliament. Among its most successful measures were the handling of agriculture through local producer cooperative boards, the free hospital services from 1946, the irrigation schemes on the Burdekin and Dawson rivers, followed by the Tully Falls hydroelectric scheme and the Mareeba-Dimbulah project (near Cairns) still developing in the late 1960s. A split between the parliamentary party and the Queensland Central Executive resulted in the fall of Labour in 1956, and thereafter coalition governments encouraged industry, overseas investment, and tourism.

In the 20th century improved farming methods, irrigation, insecticides, communications, and new markets at home and in Japan greatly strengthened primary production. In 1923 vast silver-lead-zinc deposits were found at Mt. Isa, and in 1969 further vast

OPENCUT URANIUM MINE AT MARY KATHLEEN

deposits were found. Uranium was discovered and mined at Mary Kathleen from 1950 to 1963, and bauxite was found in great quantity at Weipa. In the 1960s have come the Mooni oil field, the natural-gas field at Roma (piped to Brisbane), and the huge development of the mining port of Gladstone.　　　　(J. M. Cr.)

POPULATION, ADMINISTRATION, AND SOCIAL CONDITIONS

Population.—At the 1966 census, the population of Queensland was 1,663,685 (excluding 10,201 full-blood aboriginals). The Brisbane statistical division, covering an area containing the cities of Brisbane (656,222), Ipswich (54,531), Redcliffe (27,327), and parts of a number of contiguous shires, had a total population of 777,674. Provincial cities, the largest of which are coastal or near-coastal in location, had the following populations: Townsville, 58,847; Toowoomba, 55,799; Gold Coast, 49,481; Rockhampton, 46,083; Cairns, 26,696; Bundaberg, 25,402; Maryborough, 19,659; and Mackay, 18,640. The greater part of the remaining urban and rural population is concentrated in the coastal and southeastern areas of the state.

The Aboriginals.—In December 1966 the number of persons descended fully or in part from the non-European indigenous population was officially estimated at 49,700. These were made up from two ethnic groups: (1) 41,700 aboriginals of the Australoid group and (2) 8,000 Torres Straits islanders, ethnically and linguistically related to the nearby mainland Melanesians of Papua. The 1966 federal census counted 10,201 persons half to fully descended from aboriginal stock, the remainder having less than half descent.

The Department of Aboriginal and Island Affairs of the Queensland government has as its particular concern about 11,000 aboriginals and 5,000 Torres Straits islanders. These live in communities supported and run by various Christian missions or by the department itself. The remainder, including many of full descent, live without special legislative welfare provisions. They have a wide variety of occupations and increasingly live in the towns and cities, mainly in the tropical part of Queensland. Many are employed as stockmen on cattle stations.

Many Torres Straits islanders work on the mainland. Those who live on the islands are mainly engaged in fishing, pearl-shell gathering, and in the artificial pearl industry. Normal or special schooling is provided for all aboriginal and islander children. Virtually all children and young adults speak English, but some older adults still speak their original languages.

Administration.—The government consists of the governor, the Executive Council (*i.e.*, the governor and the ministers in office), and the Legislative Assembly of 78 members elected by adult suffrage for a period of three years. There are three electoral zones subdivided into electoral districts, each for the election of one member as follows: (1) metropolitan (28 districts of between 10,000 and 18,000 electors); (2) eight provincial cities with 12 districts, of between 10,000 and 16,000 electors obtained by dividing each of the cities of Ipswich, Rockhampton, Toowoomba, and Townsville into two electorates, and constituting the cities of Bundaberg, Cairns, Mackay, and Maryborough each as one electorate; and (3) 38 country electorates of between 7,000 and 14,000 electors. Voting at elections is by secret ballot and is compulsory, as is electoral enrollment for all British subjects by birth or naturalization who have lived in Australia for six months and in the electoral district for three.

Local authority councils are elected by adult suffrage every three years for 14 cities, 2 towns of more than 7,000 persons, 3 other towns, and 112 shires; they administer such services as public health and sanitation, roads, water, parks, amenities, and sometimes electricity and transportation.

Health and Welfare.—In the mid-1960s there were 143 public hospitals and sanatoriums supplying free consultation and treatment, 123 public maternity hospitals, 270 maternal and child welfare centres, 3 dental hospitals, and 40 branch clinics for free dental treatment. The Royal Flying Doctor Service of Australia provides medical and dental services to white and aboriginal persons in isolated areas and operates from three air bases. Maternal, child endowment, and widows' pensions are financed by the federal government.

Education.—The State Education acts (1875–1964) established free and compulsory primary education from the ages of 6 to 15 years. In the mid-1960s, there were more than 1,200 state primary schools with an enrollment of more than 190,000;

while more than 1,750 pupils attended special schools for handicapped children. Primary pupils numbering over 3,000 in outlying parts of the state were receiving education by correspondence. Teachers in state schools numbered (primary) more than 6,000 full-time, 560 part-time; and (secondary) 3,250 full-time, 100 part-time. There are seven years of primary schooling, followed by five years of secondary schooling. The junior examination at the end of three years' secondary schooling qualifies pupils for assistance during a further two years at the end of which they may sit for an examination which is accepted as an entrance standard for public service employment and for university matriculation purposes. The secondary course accommodated more than 73,750 children in over 90 state high schools and 150 secondary departments of primary schools. Private grammar and denominational schools accommodated over 85,500 (including more than 29,700 secondary) scholars with teaching staffs totaling over 2,600 full-time and 560 part-time. Fourteen technical colleges provided trade apprentice training for full-time, part-time, and correspondence students. There were also two teachers' training colleges, three institutes of technology, an agricultural college, a rural training school, and a conservatorium of music. The University of Queensland, situated in Brisbane, also has a college in Townsville and offers degree courses within the faculties of arts, science, engineering, commerce, economics, agriculture, law, dentistry, veterinary science, medicine, education, and architecture. (F. J. SL.)

THE ECONOMY

Agriculture.—*Pastoral Industries.*—Livestock raising has played a fundamental part in the economic development of Queensland, and the net annual value of pastoral production in the mid-1960s was about A$335,000,000 (including dairy products), considerably greater than that of agriculture (A$272,000,000), but less than that of manufacturing industries (A$434,000,000). The relative importance of pastoral as compared with agricultural production is largely a reflection of the low and unreliable rainfall over a large part of the state and the concentration of rainfall mainly within four summer months.

Although sheep and cattle are raised together on many proper-

BY COURTESY OF AGRICULTURE AND STOCK, BRISBANE

HERDING CATTLE IN QUEENSLAND

ties, a belt of central Queensland extending from the southern border northward for 600 mi. (970 km.) through Charleville and Longreach to the Hughenden-Cloncurry downlands is used mainly for the raising of sheep and carries nearly all the sheep grazed in Queensland. This corresponds with the plains country, receiving between about 10 and 20 in. of rainfall and lying south of latitude 20° S. Almost all the animals are Australian merinos bred for their fine wool. Numbers fluctuate from year to year in relation to variations in rainfall and pasture growth. Stock losses because of drought can be severe. In the mid-1960s flocks totaled about

BY COURTESY OF AUSTRALIAN NEWS AND INFORMATION BUREAU

SUGARCANE GROWING AT NORTH JOHNSTONE, INNISFAIL

24,000,000 (about 14% of Australian sheep). The annual wool clip was about 247,000,000 lb. (greasy), valued at about A$124,-000,000 (about 14% of Australian production).

Queensland is the leading Australian beef-producing state, carrying nearly 6,000,000 cattle (about 45% of the national total) and producing about a third of Australia's output of beef and veal. The raising of cattle for beef takes place under a wide variety of conditions and over a much greater total area of Queensland than that of sheep. Cattle ranches are generally larger than those carrying sheep, about two-fifths of the stock being on holdings of 100,-000 ac. (40,500 ha.) or more. Properties of 1,500 sq.mi. (3,900 sq.km.) are not unusual in the remote north and west. Zebu crossbreds, more tolerant of dry feed, water shortages, and the cattle tick, have been introduced on a number of ranches. Slaughtering and freezing works at the ports of Brisbane, Rockhampton, Bowen, Townsville, and Cairns handle the bulk of the exported beef, the balance passing through Sydney, Melbourne, and Adelaide.

Dairy Production.—Dairying is a major industry in three high-rainfall areas—the southeast coastlands as far north as Rockhampton, the Darling Downs, and the Atherton Plateau. In the mid-1960s the annual production of milk was about 230,000,000 gal., butter about 75,000,000 lb. (16% of Australian production), and cheese about 19,000,000 lb. (14%). Pig raising is closely associated with dairy farming in the south. In the mid-1960s there were about 400,000 pigs (25%).

Crops.—The cultivation of crops is of major importance in the high-rainfall areas of the tropical east coast (sugar and fruit) and the Atherton Plateau (maize [corn] and peanuts), on the rich, moisture-holding soils of the Darling Downs and south and central Burnett areas (wheat, lucerne, sorghum, maize, cotton, and peanuts), and on the alluvial, volcanic, and red-earth residual soils of the southeast coastal region (maize, lucerne, fruit, and vegetables). The total area under crops in the mid-1960s was 3,700,000 ac. (1,497,300 ha.).

Sugarcane is the leading crop in terms of value of production. In the mid-1960s about 12,600,000 tons (valued at about A$137,-000,000) were cut annually, yielding about 1,760,000 tons of raw sugar (96% of Australian production). Refineries at Brisbane and Bundaberg meet the needs of Queensland consumers, the remaining sugar being exported—both to other states and overseas—mainly in its less perishable raw state.

In respect of acreage under cultivation, wheat is Queensland's leading crop (about 960,000 ac. in the mid-1960s) though the value of the crop (about A$30,500,000) was much less than that of sugarcane. Production of wheat has increased markedly through the more widespread use of drought-resistant varieties giving higher yields and a significant increase in area of cultivation. Production is concentrated mainly on the black soils of the Darling

Downs (Warwick-Toowoomba-Dalby) and the chocolate soils of the South Burnett region, but an increasing amount derives from the central highlands astride the tropic region. Cultivation and harvesting are highly mechanized.

Maize is grown on many of the mixed farms of southeastern Queensland to provide supplementary feed for stock, and it is also the main crop of the Atherton Plateau. Total annual production in the mid-1960s was more than 4,800,000 bu. (valued at A$6,460,000). Grain sorghums are also important as feed for livestock and during the same period total annual production was nearly 7,000,000 bu. (valued at A$7,500,000). Peanuts are an important crop in the South Burnett region and on the Atherton Plateau. Production of other oil crops such as linseed and sunflowers is steadily increasing, but cotton growing fluctuates as a result of unfavourable seasons (dry farming methods are used), labour shortages, and comparatively low profit margins. Tobacco growing is firmly established in the Border rivers, Mareeba Tableland, and Burdekin Delta districts, and rice production has been established near Ayr.

A variety of tropical and subtropical fruits and vegetables is grown on small holdings and mixed farms in coastal and near-coastal areas, the bulk of the production being within 100 mi. (160 km.) of Brisbane. Pineapples superseded bananas after 1940 as the chief fruit crop, the gross annual value of the pineapple crop in the mid-1960s being about A$5,200,000. A substantial proportion is canned for sale in southern and overseas markets. Papaws and mangoes are grown in coastal areas; citrus fruits are concentrated mainly in the Gayndah, Maryborough, and Nambour areas of the southeast. The elevated "granite belt" around Stanthorpe, near the New South Wales border, is the only part of the state where apples, peaches, and plums are grown commercially, and this is also the chief grape-producing area.

Forestry.—Queensland forests are of three main types: the tropical rain forest (known locally as scrub or jungle) of the northeastern coastlands and ranges; the rain forests of the southeast; and the open forest covering much of the remainder of the eastern half of the state. Considerable areas of the tropical rain forest have been cleared for farming, but limited reserves of silky oak, red cedar, Queensland maple, and Queensland walnut remain. The southeastern forests provide a higher proportion of native pinewood, especially hoop and bunya pine, and the state government plantations of Caribbean and Mexican pine and the native hoop pine are now being commercially used. The open forest of eucalypt hardwoods is a major source of the state's building and constructional timber. About 220,000,000 sq.ft. (20,439,000 sq.m.) of sawn timber and 180,000,000 sq.ft. (16,723,000 sq.m.) of veneers worth A$30,000,000 are produced annually.

Mining.—The metalliferous areas of Queensland are concentrated in the metamorphosed zones of the Precambrian rocks of the northwest and the Paleozoic rocks of the northeast and southeast. With the gold rushes of the 1860s and 1880s gold production rose steadily from 2,738 fine oz. (worth £12,000) in 1860 to 676,027 fine oz. (£2,872,000) in 1900, but subsequent production declined. Production in the mid-1960s was about 80,000 fine oz., valued at about A$3,000,000, mainly from Mt. Morgan and Cracow. The state's most extensive mineral workings are in the far northwest at Mt. Isa (copper, lead, silver, zinc), at Weipa in the Cape York Peninsula (bauxite), and at Mt. Morgan, 26 mi. (42 km.) southwest of Rockhampton (auriferous blister copper). In the mid-1960s the average annual production was: copper 70,000 tons, lead 60,000 tons, zinc 37,000 tons, silver 5,500,000 fine oz. Production of bauxite at Weipa increased from 10,000 tons in 1961 to 973,250 tons in 1966 and the capacity of the treatment plant in the late 1960s was 3,000,000 tons annually. The Gladstone alumina refinery, completed in 1967, had an initial capacity of 600,000 tons per annum. The total value of mineral production in the mid-1960s was about A$80,000,000. Values of production for copper, lead, zinc, and silver were, however, difficult to specify as a large proportion of the metals was shipped from Queensland to other Australian states or overseas in the form of complex concentrates. Coal production increased from 2,000,000 tons per annum in 1949 to 2,800,000 in 1962 and to 4,660,000 tons in 1966 (value A$25,-

000,000) by the development of large opencut workings in east-central Queensland (Callide and Kianga-Moura). Contracts current in the late 1960s demanded the export of 7,000,000 tons of Queensland coal by 1970, primarily to Japan.

Manufacturing Industries.—Manufacturing expanded considerably after World War II, the number of factories increasing from just under 3,000 in the mid-1940s to nearly 6,000 in the mid-1960s, and the net value of production from about A$58,000,000 to about A$460,000,000. The two major groups of factory industries are metalworking engineering and food processing. A little more than half of the total production came from factories in metropolitan Brisbane, where industries range from shipbuilding (naval craft and cargo ships up to 10,000 tons), motor-vehicle assembly, and furniture manufacture to sugar refining, fruit canning, and brewing. Two provincial cities are primarily industrial in function: Ipswich, with railway engineering and woolen mills; and Maryborough, with railway engineering, factories making mining machinery, and a small shipyard. Railway workshops are also maintained at Rockhampton and Townsville, and Toowoomba and Dalby manufacture agricultural machinery and implements. Forty-eight power stations (mainly thermal) generate 3,520,000,-000 kw-hr. of electricity annually.

External Trade.—In the mid-1960s the total value of Queensland's exports was about A$780,000,000, of which about A$300,-000,000 went to other Australian states. The chief items of overseas exports were: wool, sugar, beef and veal, canned meat, wheat, titanium and zircon concentrates, lead and silver-lead ores and bullion, copper ores and concentrates, coal, bauxite, and butter. Imports received directly from overseas consist largely of manufactured goods, the main items being motor vehicles and parts, machinery, hardware and metal manufactures, and oil.

State Finance.—As the federal government has the exclusive right to customs and excise duties and collects income taxation on behalf of the states, a substantial portion of the Queensland government's revenue is made up of payments by the commonwealth government. These amounted in the mid-1960s to about A$140,-000,000 annually, of which A$25,000,000 was specifically provided for highway construction and maintenance and A$5,000,000 for university requirements. Additional revenue amounted to about A$350,000,000, including approximately A$80,000,000 from the state railways and $A60,000,000 from state taxes and duties. State expenditure amounted to about A$500,000,000 annually, including approximately A$90,000,000 for the state railways and A$50,-000,000 for education. Other major items of expenditure were roads and bridges, public health, the State Insurance Organization, housing development, and law and order.

Transport and Communications.—With a comparatively small population dispersed over a wide area and with a large volume of primary commodities needing transport over great distances, the provision of adequate public transport facilities (rail, road, and air) has involved a high capital outlay in relation to returns. Standardization of the 3 ft. 6 in. gauge by the State Railway Department enabled maximum railway mileage to be constructed and operated at minimum cost; by 1924, when the Brisbane–Cairns coastal line was completed (1,043 mi. [1,678 km.]), the present system was substantially in operation, though the 80 mi. of standard-gauge (4 ft. 8½ in.) line from Brisbane to Kyogle was not completed until 1930. In the late 1960s rail mileage was about 5,700. Air-conditioned trains with diesel-electric power serve the four main lines: the Brisbane–Cairns ("Sunlander"); Brisbane–Cunnamulla ("Westlander"); Rockhampton–Winton ("Midlander"); and Townsville–Mount Isa ("Inlander") lines.

There is a network of interstate and internal air services, operated by the commonwealth government's Trans-Australia Airlines, by Ansett-ANA Airways Pty., Ltd., and by several smaller concerns. Regular services are operated to New Guinea and New Caledonia, and Brisbane is a port of call on regular international air services. Flying doctor aircraft are based at Charleville, Mt. Isa, and Charters Towers.

There are about 121,000 mi. (194,700 km.) of roads in the state, including 6,300 mi. (10,138 km.) of state highways and 5,200 mi.

(8,368 km.) of main roads. Passenger and cargo ships maintain regular services along the Queensland coast and to southern states, Thursday Island, and New Guinea; and Queensland ports are also served by overseas shipping lines.   (R. H. G.)

BIBLIOGRAPHY.—Australian and New Zealand Association for the Advancement of Science, *Introducing Queensland* (1961); *Queensland Yearbook, Queensland Chamber of Manufactures Yearbook,* and *Australian Sugar Yearbook* (published annually); D. Hill and A. K. Denmead (eds.), *The Geology of Queensland* (1960); Sir Raphael Cilento and C. Lack (eds.), *Triumph in the Tropics* (1959); Government of Queensland publication, *Our First Half-Century* (1909); C. Lack (ed.), *Queensland: Daughter of the Sun* (1959); J. M. Holmes, *Australia's Open North* (1963); R. H. Greenwood, *Queensland: City, Coast and Country* (1959); W. Beatty, *The Awakening Giant* (1961); A. M. Duncan-Kemp, *Our Channel Country* (1961); F. M. Bailey, *The Queensland Flora,* 6 vol. (1899–1902); W. D. Francis, *Australian Rain-Forest Trees,* 2nd ed. (1951); K. Gillett, *The Great Barrier Reef and Adjacent Isles* (1959); M. Gough and others, *Queensland, Industrial Enigma* (1964). *See* also such periodicals as *The Australian Journal of Politics and History, Economic Record, Australian Geographical Studies, Proceedings of the Royal Society of Queensland, Queensland Government Mining Journal, Queensland Journal of Agriculture,* and *University of Queensland Research Papers.*

QUENTAL, ANTERO TARQUÍNIO DE (1842–1891),

Portuguese poet and essayist, who played a prominent, enthusiastic, and lifelong part in the struggle to create a new outlook in literature and society, and to organize the working classes. His activities were interrupted by fits of acute depression arising from personal anxieties, or from intellectual and ideological crises, and in his poetry, especially in the sonnets, he gives outstanding aesthetic expression to both personal problems and philosophic themes. In the 109 sonnets of *Os Sonetos completos* (1886) the reader can follow Quental's spiritual evolution.

He was born on April 18, 1842, at Ponta Delgada in the Azores, of an aristocratic and illustrious family; among his forebears were writers and mystics, and he was brought up as a practising Catholic. While studying law at the University of Coimbra (1858–64) he was profoundly influenced by the new literary and ideological movements which were at that time gaining ground in intellectual circles. His romantic early poems, *Raios de extinta luz* (written 1859–63) and the delicate lyrics (written 1861–64) published as *Primaveras românticas* (1875), were soon replaced by the poems of *Odes modernas* (1865), which gave expression to the problems agitating him and his contemporaries. Their publication won him a remarkable intellectual and moral ascendancy among his fellow students. This prestige was shown, for example, on the occasion of the visit to Coimbra of Prince Umberto of Savoy (Humbert I of Italy) in October 1862, when Quental addressed him on behalf of the undergraduates with a political audaciousness also revealed in the *Odes modernas.* He was prominently involved, too, in the famous literary polemic, known as the "Coimbra Question," which was started by his pamphlet, *Bom senso e bom gosto* ("Good Sense and Good Taste," 1865), in which he attacked the hidebound formalism of Portuguese writing as exemplified especially in the work of the poet António Feliciano de Castilho. His later pamphlet, *A dignidade das letras e as literaturas oficiais,* proclaimed his mission to create a new poetry which would be "the voice of the Revolution."

After graduation, and a visit to the Azores, Quental settled in Lisbon, and looked for employment in accord with his social ideals. He tried a job as a typographer, first in Lisbon and then (1867) in Paris, thus gaining firsthand acquaintance with working-class life. Six months of this experience, however, awakened him from his dream of becoming a modern social apostle, and disillusionment and ill-health forced him to return to Portugal. After a trip to the United States and Canada (1869), he went back to Lisbon, where he again tried to realize his ideals, taking an active part in propaganda on behalf of the workers and also working to reawaken Portuguese cultural life. In 1870, with his friend J. P. Oliveira Martins (*q.v.*), he founded a republican journal, *A República,* and also organized a group of writers, *O Cenáculo,* which prepared a famous and provocative series of lectures, the *Conferências democráticas do Casino,* given in 1871, aiming to make known in Portugal the main trends of modern thought. Influenced by the Socialist theories of Proudhon, he collaborated in

the attempt to organize the First International in Portugal, and edited the Socialist journal, *O Pensamento Social* (1872).

But, amid all this activity, Quental was troubled by increasing discontent. He felt within himself a struggle between two opposing forces, thought and will. The resultant spiritual anguish is splendidly expressed in some of his sonnets, which also reflect his reading of the German philosophers, especially Schopenhauer and Edouard von Hartmann. At this stage, he abandoned many cherished projects, and tore up his early poems and other writings. His health declined further, and, his illness proving difficult to diagnose, in 1877 he went to Paris to consult the neurologist, Jean Martin Charcot. Treatment gave temporary relief and during a period of renewed calm he wrote some of his last and finest sonnets.

In 1882 he retired to Vila do Conde, near Oporto, to supervise the upbringing of two orphan girls whom he had adopted. He continued to watch political developments, however, following with interest the experiments in government of Oliveira Martins. The crisis provoked by the British ultimatum of 1890 (*see* PORTUGAL: *History*) brought him back into politics, and he accepted the chairmanship of the *Liga Patriótica do Norte,* but resigned a few weeks later when the league broke up under the pressure of the rival political factions of which it was composed.

In 1891, Quental left Vila do Conde to visit his relations and properties in Ponta Delgada, but his contacts with his family proved strained. His nervous condition was thereby aggravated, and on Sept. 11, 1891, he shot himself.

As a philosopher, Quental opposed positivism, and moved, by way of Hegelian idealism, to acceptance of Schopenhauer's view of the universe, and of man's only possible escape from irrational suffering as being through quietism. He avoided Schopenhauer's pessimistic conclusion by stressing the importance of the individual conscience, and finally, he approached independently the position of Kierkegaard (whose work was unknown to him), and came to believe that by exploration of his own ego, man can attain union with God, who is the Ego of his ego, the Spirit of his spirit. Progress, he concluded, evolves not only through history, but through the individual, irrespective of material circumstances. The thoughts behind his struggle to find a solution to these problems were expressed in many of his sonnets and in his most important philosophical study, *Tendências gerais da filosofia na segunda metade do século XIX* (1889).

As a poet, Quental made few formal innovations, and his use of the sonnet, a classic form in Portuguese poetry, is traditional in imagery and vocabulary. Yet these formal limitations did not prevent him from giving direct, dramatic, and universal expression to the anxieties arising from the crisis in late 19th-century Western thought.

BIBLIOGRAPHY.—*Editions, Correspondence, Translations: Raios de extinta luz, Poesias inéditas,* ed. by T. Braga (1892); *Odes modernas* (1st ed. 1865; 2nd ed. 1875); *Os Sonetos completos,* ed., with preface and some trans. into German, French, Spanish, and Italian, by J. P. Oliveira Martins (1886); *Primaveras românticas,* critical ed. by A. Sérgio (1943); *Sonetos completos,* critical ed. with valuable commentaries by A. Sérgio (1943, 1962); *Prosas,* 3 vol. (1923–31); *Cartas,* ed. by E. do Canto (1915); *Cartas a Oliveira Martins,* ed. by F. de Oliveira Martins, with preface by J. de Carvalho (1931); *Cartas a W. Storck,* ed. by H. Maier (1931); *Cartas a António de Azevedo Castelo Branco,* ed. by A. Casais Monteiro (1942); *A. de Quental: Sixty-Four Sonnets,* trans. by E. Prestage (1894); *Sonnets and Poems by A. de Quental,* trans. by S. G. Morley (1922); *Ausgewählte Sonnette von Anthero de Quental,* trans. by W. Storck (1877).

Biography and Critical Studies: J. B. Carreiro, *A. de Quental, Subsídios para a sua biografia,* 2 vol. (1948), a well-documented biographical work; A. Sérgio, *Ensaios,* vol. iv (1934), v (1936), vi (1946), vii (1954) includes important studies on Quental; J. de Carvalho, *A evolução espiritual de Antero* (1929); F. de Figueiredo, *Antero, quatro conferências* (1942); Sant' Anna Dionisio, *A sinceridade politica de A. do Quental* (1949); A. de Quental, *In Memoriam,* a collection of studies and essays by friends and admirers (1896).

(F. DE D. C.)

QUERCIA, JACOPO DELLA (*c.* 1374–1438), one of the

most original Italian sculptors of the early 15th century, was born, probably at Siena, between 1370 and 1374. In *c.* 1406 he carved the tomb of Ilaria del Carretto in the cathedral of Lucca, a town with which his father, the goldsmith and sculptor Pietro d'Angelo, had long been associated. The effigy and sarcophagus from this tomb alone survive. In 1408 Quercia was employed at Ferrara on a statue of the Virgin and Child which still exists in the Museo dell' Opera del Duomo, and a year later he received the commission for the celebrated Fonte Gaia in the Campo at Siena (now replaced by a copy, original in the loggia of the Palazzo Pubblico). The scheme of this highly individual fountain was repeatedly modified, and effective work upon it seems to have been confined to the years 1414–19. Concurrently with the Fonte Gaia, Quercia was engaged on commissions at Lucca which included a statue of an apostle for the exterior of the cathedral (1413), the tomb slabs of Lorenzo Trenta and his wife in S. Frediano (1416) and the Trenta altar in the same church (1416–22). These are strongly northern in character. In 1417 Quercia agreed to undertake two gilt bronze reliefs for the baptismal font in S. Giovanni in Siena; the contract for one of these was later transferred to Donatello, but the second, "Zacharias in the Temple," was completed in 1430 and is still on the font. Between 1427 and 1430 he also designed the hexagonal tabernacle in the centre of the font and carved the reliefs of prophets in the niches with which five sides of it are filled. In 1425 he had signed a contract for the central doorway of S. Petronio at Bologna: work on this occupied him until his death on Oct. 20, 1438. In its present form the doorway consists of ten scenes from Genesis set in the pilasters at the sides, five scenes from the early life of Christ across the architrave and a lunette surrounded by reliefs of prophets containing statues of the Virgin and Child and SS. Petronius and Ambrose (the latter an addition by Domenico da Varignana). The Genesis scenes are Quercia's most inspired and expressive works. In 1435 Quercia was appointed superintending architect of Siena cathedral for which he was employed on the decoration (unfinished) of the Cappella Casini. To the same late phase belongs the Vari-Bentivoglio monument in S. Giacomo Maggiore, Bologna (after 1433). Quercia also carved in wood, notably an Annunciation group in the Collegiata at San Gimignano (1421). Though his work is exceptionally fully documented, Quercia is a mysterious artist and his ambivalent style fits less easily than that of his more conventional contemporary Ghiberti into the context of Tuscan early Renaissance sculpture.

ALINARI

"THE VIRGIN AND INFANT JESUS" BY JACOPO DELLA QUERCIA. IN THE LOUVRE, PARIS

BIBLIOGRAPHY.—P. Bacci, *Jacopo della Quercia. Nuovi documenti e commenti* (1929); G. Nicco, *Jacopo della Quercia* (1934); L. Biagi, *Jacopo della Quercia* (1946). (J. W. P.-H.)

QUERCITRON BARK is the inner bark of *Quercus velutina*, the black oak, a native of the middle and southern United States. The exterior bark is removed from the tree by shaving and the inner portion, which contains a colouring matter, is detached and ground. The colouring matter of quercitron bark is quercitrin, $C_{21}H_{22}O_{12},H_2O$, a glycoside which by hydrolysis with acid yields quercetin, $C_{15}H_{10}O_7$, and the sugar rhamnose, $C_6H_{12}O_5$. When quercitron bark is exhausted with hot water under pressure, the extract deposits a crude quercitrin which is known commercially as yellow flavine. A second variety known as red flavine, prepared by digesting an extract of the bark at the boil with dilute acid, is in reality a crude quercetin. These products dye wool mordanted with aluminum and tin bright yellow and orange shades; they were at one time used with cochineal for obtaining especially vivid scarlets. (A. G. P.)

QUERCY, an ancient *pays* or district of southwestern France, corresponding, in terms of modern *départements*, to the greater part of Lot and part of Tarn-et-Garonne (*qq.v.*). Cahors (*q.v.*) and Figeac were the chief towns of Haut or Upper Quercy, Montauban (*q.v.*) and Moissac those of Bas or Lower Quercy.

In Gallo-Roman times the district was organized as the *civitas* or community of the Cadurci, a Celtic people whose name is reflected in those of Cahors and Quercy alike. Occupied by the Visigoths in the 5th century A.D., Quercy was taken by the Franks in the 6th. It was part of Carolingian Aquitaine in the first half of the 9th century, but soon came into the possession of the counts of Toulouse. Louis VIII of France, however, accepted homage for northern Quercy from the bishop of Cahors, Guillaume de Cardaillac, in 1223; and the south was included in the possessions of Alphonse of Poitiers and Toulouse. The Anglo-French Treaty of Paris (1259), which accorded to the English king some ill-specified rights within the diocese of Cahors and a conditional claim on the western areas of Alphonse's territory, made Quercy a subject of dispute, first diplomatic and then military, between France and England (*see also* GUIENNE). By the Treaty of Brétigny in 1360 France ceded Quercy to the English, but they were finally expelled in 1443, during the last phase of the Hundred Years' War. Quercy was subsequently made part of the French *gouvernement* of Guienne.

In the 16th-century Wars of Religion, Quercy was savagely contested between Catholics and Huguenots; and in the 1620s Montauban was a major centre of Huguenot resistance. The *généralité* of Montauban, under an intendant (*q.v.*), was instituted in 1635.

QUERÉTARO, a central plateau state of Mexico. Pop. (1960) 355,045; area 4,544 sq.mi. (11,769 sq.km.). On the semiarid mesa and traversed at the north by a spur of the Sierra Madre known as the Sierra Gorda, Querétaro is about evenly divided between mountainous mineralized areas and the rolling plains and fertile valleys of the south which form part of Mexico's granary or *bajío*. The state has good air connections and is traversed in a southeasterly direction by the trunk highway from Nogales to Mexico City and the National Railways of Mexico. The climate is generally dry and temperate except in the northwest portion which is hot. Rainfall is moderate and frosts are few and light.

With soil 10 to 15 ft. (3 to 5 m.) deep in the southern lowlands, the state produces a large variety of crops: fruits, grain, medicinal plants, and a notable sweet potato or *camote*. Though deposits of gold, copper, lead, tin, and other metals occur, the chief products are opals and mercury, especially in a compound (sulfoselenide of mercury) known as onofrite, from Cerro San Onofre. The breeding of fighting bulls is also an important activity.

The area was inhabited by the Otomí-Chichimec Indians who were conquered by the Spaniards in 1531. Colonization took place in the 1550s and Querétaro was administered with Guanajuato before it became a state in 1824. (J. A. Cw.)

QUERÉTARO, a city of Mexico and the capital of the state of Querétaro, is 167 mi. (269 km.) by rail and 162 mi. (261 km.) by highway NW of Mexico City, and located at the foot of the Cerro de las Campanas. Elevation 6,168 ft. (1,880 m.); pop. (1960) 67,674. Querétaro is considered an excellent example of a Spanish colonial city. It was founded by the Otomí Indians and was incorporated into the Aztec empire in 1446 and henceforth served as an outpost against the warlike tribes to the north until it was brought under Spanish control in 1531. Throughout most of the colonial period Querétaro was important primarily as a way station and supply centre serving the rich mining districts of Guanajuato and Zacatecas. Colonial buildings include the cathedral (restored several times), the federal palace and the churches of Santa Rosa, Santa Clara, and San Augustín. Water is brought to the city by an aqueduct (built 1726–38) approximately 5 mi. (8 km.) long, with 74 arches, 50 ft. (15 m.) high and upborne by piers 46 ft. (14 m.) thick. The main products are textiles, pottery, and agricultural produce. The city has one of the largest and oldest cotton factories in Mexico.

Querétaro has witnessed many fundamental changes in the evolution of modern Mexico. In 1810 it was the scene of a plot against Spain which led to the uprising headed by Miguel Hidalgo y Costilla in September of that year. In 1848 the Treaty of Guadalupe

Hidalgo terminating the U.S.-Mexican War was signed there. The forces of Benito Juárez defeated those of Emperor Maximilian at Querétaro in 1867; and on a nearby hill Maximilian and his generals Miguel Miramón and Tomás Mejía faced the firing squads. The Mexican constitution of 1917 was written in Querétaro which was also the birthplace of the National Revolutionary Party of Mexico (1929), the dominant political force in the republic.

(J. J. J.)

QUESNAY, FRANÇOIS (1694–1774), French economist and leader of the first systematic school of political economy (*see* PHYSIOCRATIC SCHOOL), was born, perhaps at Méré, near Paris, on June 4, 1694. He studied surgery, graduated as a doctor of medicine (1744) and eventually became consulting physician to Louis XV. He did not publish anything on economics until the age of 60 and then mainly anonymous articles. But at Versailles, where he enjoyed the support of Mme de Pompadour, there gathered around him and Jean C. M. V. de Gournay (1712–59) the *secte des économistes,* notably Victor Riqueti de Mirabeau, Nicolas Baudeau, P. P. le Mercier de la Rivière, G. F. le Trosne, and P. S. du Pont de Nemours, who looked to Quesnay as their leader and enthusiastically propagated his doctrines. A. R. J. Turgot was also associated with the group; Adam Smith got to know Quesnay and had a great respect for his ideas. Quesnay died at Versailles on Dec. 16, 1774.

Quesnay's peculiarities of expression and his extreme emphasis on agriculture as the sole economically productive activity yielding a *produit net,* as contrasted with the "sterility" of industry and commerce, should not be allowed to conceal the great importance of his contributions to economic thought. He contributed, above all, to that systematization of economic analysis which introduced the classical period in Britain and France; only Richard Cantillon, who published *Essai sur la nature du commerce* in 1755, preceded him in this. Quesnay's system was summed up in his *Tableau économique* (1758), which displayed diagrammatically the interdependence of the different economic classes and sectors and the flow of payments among them. In his *Tableau* Quesnay developed the assumption of a state of stationary economic equilibrium, a fundamental simplifying concept from which so much subsequent economic analysis departed. The general equilibrium analysis of Léon Walras and the input-output analysis of modern economics developed by W. W. Leontief are descendants of Quesnay's *Tableau.* Especially important was his analysis of capital as *avances,* or a stock of wealth which had to be accumulated in advance of production, and his classification of these *avances* in a manner which developed the distinction between fixed and circulating capital. Quesnay's analysis of savings as possibly harmful in that uninvested savings may disturb the equilibrium of the flow of payments is similar to that of J. M. Keynes. However, Quesnay's ideas on saving were supplanted in orthodox economic thought for a century or more by the theory of Turgot and Smith, according to which saving is unconditionally beneficial.

The methodology of Quesnay's system and his principles of policy started from an extreme form of the doctrine of natural law which led him to proclaim that *laissez faire* in economics—plus the single tax on net income from land—represented the divinely appointed economic order. Quesnay, in fact, was one of the originators of 19th-century doctrines of the harmony of class interests and of the related doctrine that the maximum social satisfaction occurs under free competition. He also developed the a priori method, often employed subsequently, of attempting to demonstrate these doctrines. In their day his principles of policy represented an active campaign against monopolies and privilege, requiring a strong government based, as Quesnay advocated, on a powerful monarchy.

Quesnay's *Oeuvres économiques et philosophiques* were edited by A. Oncken (1888).

See M. Beer, *An Inquiry Into Physiocracy* (1939); J. A. Schumpeter, *History of Economic Analysis,* pp. 223–243 (1954). (T. W. H.)

QUESNEL, PASQUIER (1634–1719), French Jansenist theologian and author of the *Réflexions morales,* leader of the Jansenist party after the death of Antoine Arnauld, was born in Paris on July 14, 1634, and joined the French Oratory in 1657.

His Jansenist sympathies led to his banishment from Paris in 1681, and three years later he was expelled from the Oratory. Fearing further measures of persecution, he fled to Brussels where he lived with Arnauld. In 1703 he was arrested, but soon escaped to Amsterdam, where he lived until his death on Dec. 2, 1719.

Quesnel's *Nouveau Testament en français avec des réflexions morales* (1692) played almost as large a part in the literature of Jansenism as Jansen's *Augustinus.* The bull *Unigenitus* (1713) condemned 101 sentences from the *Réflexions morales.* Quesnel, who had never admitted that his opinions were heretical, received the last sacrament on his deathbed. *See also* JANSENISM.

See A. Le Roy's edition of Quesnel's correspondence, 2 vol. (1900); A. Vacant, *Dictionnaire de théologie catholique,* vol. xiii, col. 1460–1535 (1937). (N. J. A.)

QUÉTELET, (LAMBERT) ADOLPHE (JACQUES) (1796–1874), Belgian mathematician, astronomer, and statistician, known for his work on census taking and the application of statistics and the theory of probability to social phenomena, was born in Ghent on Feb. 22, 1796. He studied astronomy at the Paris Observatory and the theory of probability under Pierre Simon Laplace. He lectured at the Brussels athenaeum, military college, and museum; became head and founder in 1828 of the Royal Observatory; and perpetual secretary (1834–74) of the Royal Academy. He made important contributions to the study of meteoric showers.

Quételet was a prime mover in the development of methods for simultaneous observations of astronomical, meteorological, and geodetic phenomena at scattered points throughout Europe. His outstanding contributions to statistical organization and practice included many aspects of governmental statistics, notably census taking; organization of the first international statistical conference; the development of uniformity and comparability in international statistics; and the application of probability theory to anthropology and sociology. His *Sur l'homme* (1835) developed the concept of the "average man" as the central value about which measurements of a human trait are grouped according to the normal probability curve. His studies of the numerical constancy of such voluntary acts as crimes stimulated extensive studies in "moral statistics" and wide discussion of free will versus social determinism in human behaviour. He died on Feb. 17, 1874, in Brussels. (F. H. Hs.)

QUETTA, a city in West Pakistan, formerly capital of Baluchistan (*q.v.*), now the headquarters of the Quetta-Pishin District and of Quetta Division, lies 536 mi. (863 km.) N of Karachi by rail. Pop. (1961) 106,633, including the cantonment. It rose to prominence in 1876, when Sir Robert Sandeman founded a residency there. The name Quetta (Kawatah) is a variation of the word *kwatkot,* signifying a fortress, and the town is still locally known by its ancient name of Shal or Shalkot. The cantonment and civil station of Quetta stand in an open plain about 5,500 ft. (1,676 m.) above sea level, within a ring of mountains (such as Takatu, Murdar Ghar, and Chiltan), which overlook it from a height of more than 11,000 ft. (about 3,400 m.). North of Quetta is the open plain leading to Pishin. The defensive works, stretching from the base of Takatu to the foot of the Mashelakh Range on the west, bar the way to advance from the Khojak Pass, which leads through the Bolan Pass to Sibi. During the last quarter of the 19th century Quetta grew from a dilapidated group of mud buildings, with an inferior bazaar and a few scattered remnants of neglected orchard cultivation, into a well-laid-out and widespread town and cantonment and a strongly garrisoned army station. The Staff College was opened there in 1907. Jinnah Road is the principal bazaar. There are two government colleges and a technical school. Sandeman Library has existed since 1885 and a geophysical institute was established in the early 1960s.

Quetta is a market for western Afghanistan, eastern Iran, and much of central Asia, and its population had grown to 83,892 by 1951, despite a disastrous earthquake which practically destroyed the city on May 31, 1935, with the loss of between 20,000 and 40,000 lives. Its importance as a summer resort increased after the establishment of Pakistan.

Quetta is the southernmost point in the line of frontier posts and in the system of strategic railways on the northwest frontier of West Pakistan. The railway was built in 1879, with a view to its continuance to Kandahar, but its terminus is at Chaman on the Afghan border. A branch line to Nushki was completed in 1905 and carried on to Zahedan in Iran during World War I. Roads link Quetta city with Peshawar, Multan, Karachi, and southeastern Iran. The city is also linked by air with Karachi and Lahore.

QUETTA-PISHIN DISTRICT has an area of 5,314 sq.mi. (13,763 sq.km.) and had a population (1961) of 267,400. It consists of a series of valleys of considerable length but medium width at a height usually of 4,500–5,500 ft. (about 1,400–1,800 m.) above sea level, enclosed on all sides by the Toba Kakar and Central Brahui ranges. Except for a small northern part, the drainage of the district is carried off to the southwest through these valleys by the Pishin Lora River and its tributaries. All the valleys show similar features, a flat plain of alluvial soil in the centre with a pebbly slope or *daman* of varying length on either side to the surrounding mountains. Two different systems of the hill ranges meet in the neighbourhood of Quetta giving rise to a complicated geological structure.

The climate is generally dry and on the whole temperate. Snow lies for a considerable period in the mountains. Piercingly cold winds blow off the hills in winter. The climate of the valleys is suitable for growing fruit, including grapes, peaches, apples, pears, apricots, almonds, and pomegranates. The sweet melons produced, *sarda* (in the cold season) and *garma* (in the hot season), are well known. Wheat and barley are the chief crops. Quetta, Pishin, and Chaman are the only towns in the district.

QUETTA DIVISION as formed in 1954 consisted of the district of Quetta-Pishin and the agencies of Zhob, Loralai, and Sibi, which were subsequently formed into districts. In 1960 Chagai District was added. Area 53,115 sq.mi. (137,567 sq.km.). The population of the division in 1961 was 630,118, the majority of which is Pathan (*q.v.*). The division is mostly mountainous, lying across the great belt of ranges connecting the Safed Koh with the hill system of southern Iran. The Sulaiman Range bounds it on the east and the Toba Kakar Range separates it from Afghanistan. South of Chaman (near the Afghan border) are the Khawaja Amran and Sarl Ath ranges. Across the Khawaja Amran lies the famous Khojak Pass with the Shelabagh railway tunnel piercing 2½ mi. of hard rock. From Nushki (75 mi. [121 km.] SW of Quetta city) to Dalbandin (110 mi. [177 km.] SW of Nushki) the division consists of a level plain, covered with sand dunes, and farther west, beyond Dalbandin, Chagai District is mainly a sandy desert. The Zhob and Pishin Lora are the chief rivers, and there are numerous small streams cutting through the ranges in gorges and frequently disappearing in the pebbly beds. These are quite shallow for the greater part of the year, but after the rains they turn into raging torrents. Within the mountains are glens fringed in early summer by carefully terraced fields. The climate varies in proportion to local elevation above sea level and the rainfall is scanty and irregular and mostly in winter. Cultivation depends mainly on irrigation which is from *karezes* (underground channels) in the submontane area, springs and streams in the highlands, and wells in parts of Sibi Plain. The cultivable land is therefore divided into three classes: *khuskaba*, depending upon rainfall or snowfall; *sailaba*, subject to flood cultivation; and *abi*, having permanent means of irrigation. Wheat is the most important *rabi*, or spring crop, while jowar is the chief *kharif*, or autumn crop, in the plains and maize (corn) in the highlands. Coal is mined at Khost, Shahrig, and Harnai (Sibi), from the Sor Range near Quetta city, and at Mach (Bolan Pass). There is natural gas at Sui (*q.v.*). Chromite is mined at Hindubagh (Zhob) and sulfur at Koh-i-Sultan (Chagai District). (K. S. AD.)

QUETZAL, a Central American bird, *Pharomachrus mocinno*, of the trogon family. *See* TROGON.

QUETZALCOATL ("Plumed Serpent"), first worshiped in central Mexico possibly starting with the pre-Classical period (before *c.* A.D. 300), was god of the wind and of the dawn, identified with the planet Venus, the light, and the colour white. He symbolized wisdom and knowledge, and he was regarded as god of life and fertility, inventor of agricultural processes, patron of arts and

industries, and originator of the calendar. He was thus the god of civilization, of the priests, and of learning, who presided over the education of the young.

In the Aztec pantheon Quetzalcoatl ranked as one of the great gods, together with Huitzilopochtli (*q.v.*), the war-god; Tezcatlipoca ("Smoking Mirror"), who often appears in the mythology as the enemy and opponent of Quetzalcoatl; and Tlaloc, the rain-god. Although not completely without sanguinary aspects, the cult of Quetzalcoatl apparently involved considerably less of the bloodshed and human sacrifice that played such an important part in the worship of the other major Aztec deities. In addition to his guise as the plumed serpent, Quetzalcoatl was often represented by artists as a man with a beard; as Ehecatl, the wind-god, he was shown with a projecting mask.

A confusing circumstance is that a great Toltec king (Ce Acatl Topiltzin), who founded the city of Tula (*c.* A.D. 925–950) and led his people to civilization, was a high priest of Quetzalcoatl and therefore called by that name. Physically, this king was described as being fair-skinned and bearded. According to legend, the partisans of the more warlike god Tezcatlipoca drove Ce Acatl Topiltzin into exile. He left, sailing eastward, and prophesied his return in the year of "One Reed" (Ce Acatl), which occurred once during the Aztec cycle of 52 years. The year of "One Reed" coincided with the landing of Hernán Cortés in Mexico, and the Aztec ruler Montezuma and many other Indians thought that Cortés was the returned god-king; among their gifts to him were various objects appropriate to the god, including a turquoise mask and feather mantle. Welcoming Cortés with honour, they facilitated his conquest of Mexico. Some early Catholic missionaries attempted to identify Quetzalcoatl with St. Thomas the apostle.

(M. D. BE.; X.)

QUEVEDO Y VILLEGAS, FRANCISCO GÓMEZ DE (1580–1645), one of the greatest Spanish poets and prose writers. Born in Madrid on Sept. 17, 1580, he studied arts and theology at the universities of Alcalá and Valladolid from 1596 to 1606. In 1613 he became a counselor of the duke of Osuna, viceroy of Sicily and later of Naples, who entrusted him with diplomatic missions in Italy and Spain. Accused by the Venetian government of being one of the ringleaders of the conspiracy of 1618, he is said to have escaped from the city disguised as a beggar. Compromised by the fall of Osuna, Quevedo was imprisoned in 1620 but released in the following year. After refusing the post of ambassador in Genoa, he was given the honorary title of king's secretary in 1632. In 1639 he was arrested and confined in the monastery of San Marcos at León. This downfall has been traditionally attributed to a poem denouncing the political conduct of affairs, which was placed upon the king's table, but the incident may be apocryphal and Quevedo's authorship of the poem is not certain. He was released from the monastery in 1643 and died at Villanueva de los Infantes on Sept. 8, 1645.

Quevedo is an outstanding figure in the European literature of his age. Of brilliant intellect and strong passions, he reveals his complex personality in the extreme variety of tone in his life and work. His learning and wide culture impelled him to write works of high moral seriousness; but he shows familiarity with low life and he kept a mistress by whom he had several children. The enormous range of his work, from the obscene to the devout, shows a capacity to live intensely on every level of experience but not to unify its extremes. The tension underlying his work reveals pent-up bitterness, traceable to sincere self-reproach. His humour is never far from the sardonic. By itself much of his satire would seem splenetic, but in association with his serious poetry and prose treatises it discloses anguish at his failure to reconcile the defects of the world and of himself within it with the standards set by his own intelligence and conscience.

As a poet, Quevedo is supreme. His large output ranges from verse in the cant of the underworld through lampoons and parodies to meditative poems on time and death. His love poetry includes both poems showing an obsession akin to disgust with the crudely physical, and sonnets that transform the conventional Petrarchan tradition by their intensity of feeling. The keynote is his feeling that the divine calls the mind to a love which is torture to the

QUEZALTENANGO—QUIBERON BAY

body, that passion shows the light of life while consuming itself in darkness. There is no sensuous prettiness or emotional softness in Quevedo's poetry: his intense feeling is conveyed with dignity of expression and intellectual strength.

Though an opponent of the Latinizing innovations introduced by Luis de Góngora, whom he parodied unmercifully, Quevedo was adept in the new Baroque style. The greatest exponent of *conceptismo* (*see* SPANISH LITERATURE), he shows as masterly a use of the metaphysical conceit as does John Donne. In his satires his linguistic ingenuity and audacity are unbounded, and as a virtuoso of language he is unequaled in Spanish literature. The *Sueños* (1627), mostly visions of hell written at intervals from 1606 to 1622, show his development in the technique of satire: the conceits grow from mere puns into scintillating images that transpose the identities of objects and invert their functions. This culminates in his masterpiece, *La hora de todos* (written 1635–36). Here transposition and inversion produce a picture of a world where commercialism, imperialism, racialism, slavery and international politics have turned values inside out. No less masterly is the picaresque novel, *La vida del Buscón* (1626). Its verbal wit and often grotesque exaggeration have tended to obscure the acuteness of its psychological insight: the son of disreputable parents, the protagonist carries a burden of shame and guilt from which he seeks escape in illusory fantasies that lead to a life of roguery and deception.

In his nonsatirical work, Quevedo's *conceptismo* produces a terse and dignified style. His precision in the association of disparate concepts gives, in such works as *La política de Dios* (I, 1626; II, written 1634–35) and *La providencia de Dios* (written 1641), an original and powerful expression to a thought that is mainly conservative and traditional. His *Marco Bruto* (1644) is an interesting defense of monarchy against democracy. For Quevedo social and political issues resolve themselves into questions of personal morality. This made him promulgate in Spain the Stoic doctrines which Justus Lipsius had popularized throughout Europe. He translated Phocylides, Epictetus and Seneca and wrote Stoic treatises of his own of which the chief are *La cuna y la sepultura* (1634) and *Virtud militante* (written 1634–36). Their originality consists in presenting the subject in terms of the 17th-century preoccupation with the paradoxes of human nature and life. Quevedo's Stoicism is neither priggishness nor indifference, but a concern for one's own integrity that does not exclude compassion for one's neighbour, but does exclude the desire to judge, rebuke and punish him.

BIBLIOGRAPHY.—*Obras Completas*, ed. by F. Buendía (vol. i, *Prosa*, 1958; vol. ii, *Verso*, 1960); *Poesía Original*, ed. by J. M. Blecua (1963); *Epistolario*, ed. by L. Astrana Marín (1946). *See also* A. Papell, *Quevedo: Su tiempo, su vida, su obra* (1947); D. Alonso, *Poesía española*, pp. 531–618 (1950); A. Mas, *La Caricature de la femme, du mariage et de l'amour dans l'oeuvre de Quevedo* (1957); R. Lida, *Letras hispánicas* (1958); A. A. Parker, *Literature and the Delinquent: the Picaresque Novel in Spain and Europe, 1599–1753*, pp. 56–73 (1967).
(A. A. P.)

QUEZALTENANGO is a department in western Guatemala. Its surface elevations range from near sea level to more than 12,000 ft. (3,658 m.) at the peak of the volcano Santa María; its mountain valleys lie at altitudes of about 8,000 ft. (2,438 m.). It has some industry and a diversified agricultural production which includes grains, coffee, bananas, and livestock. Area 753 sq.mi. (1,950 sq.km.). Pop. (1964) 271,184, chiefly Indian or mestizo descendants of pre-Conquest Quiché stock.

The capital city Quezaltenango (pop. [1964] 56,921 [mun.]), the second city of the republic, is connected with Guatemala city by paved highway and air transportation. It stands at the foot of the volcano Santa María near the site of the battle in which the Spaniards under Pedro de Alvarado and their Indian allies from Mexico decisively defeated the native Quichés in 1524. Before the conquest it had been the capital of a Quiché kingdom known as Xelajú. It is a marketing and processing centre important for textile factories, mills, and breweries, and the seat of two university faculties.

An electrified railway, built in 1930 to connect with the coastal line, ceased operation in 1933 after extensive flood damage, but

the Santa María hydroelectric plant continued to operate and in the early 1960s was capable of supplying power in excess of demand.

The name Quezaltenango means "palace of the quetzal," a native bird which had great symbolic importance among the Mayas and is now the national symbol of Guatemala. (W. J. G.)

QUEZON, a long, narrow coastal province of Luzon, Republic of the Philippines, is 270 mi. (435 km.) long and varies from 5 to 35 mi. (8 to 56 km.) in width. Area 4,612 sq.mi. (11,946 sq.km.). Formerly called Tayabas, the name was changed in 1946 in memory of Pres. Manuel Luis Quezon y Molina. The northern two-thirds of the province is mountainous and sparsely inhabited, but excellent cabinet and plywood timber is produced near Infanta and Baler. Southern Quezon contains some of the largest coconut plantations in the world. Provincial population (1970 est.) 916,-000. Lucena, on Tayabas Bay, is the capital and major copra centre; Tayabas, 8 mi. (13 km.) N of Lucena, is also a trading and copra centre. (R. E. HE.)

QUEZON CITY, capital of the Republic of the Philippines, named for Pres. Manuel Luis Quezon y Molina, is immediately east of Manila on Luzon. Pop. (1970 est.) 585,100. Much of the city lies at an elevation about 100 ft. (30 m.) above downtown Manila, which is slightly above sea level. Temperatures are lower than in Manila; because Quezon City is farther from the bay, humidity is lower.

Quezon City officially replaced Manila as the Philippine capital in 1948, and construction of government buildings was begun. Most functions of the national government, however, remained in Manila. The University of the Philippines is located in Quezon City, as well as Ateneo de Manila and a veterans' hospital. The city is bisected by the Circumferential Highway, along which light industry began to develop.

San Francisco del Monte and Kamuning were among the first residential areas to be developed, while the Cubao section is an important transportation junction and bazaar area.
(R. E. HE.)

QUEZON Y MOLINA, MANUEL LUIS (1878–1944), one of the leaders of the Philippine independence movement and first president of the Philippine Commonwealth, was born Aug. 19, 1878, at Baler, Tayabas Province (renamed Quezon Province in 1946), on the island of Luzon. He joined the insurrectionist movement of Emilio Aguinaldo (*q.v.*) but later swore allegiance to the territorial administration. He was a member of the Philippine Assembly (1907–09), resident commissioner to the United States (1909–16), and president of the Philippine Senate (1916–35). As a fiery nationalist leader, he worked for the passage of the Philippine Commonwealth and Independence Act (Tydings-McDuffie Act) in 1934, and he was elected the first president of the Philippine Commonwealth in 1935. In that office he launched his program for "social justice" in the interest of the peasants and the urban labourers, promoted commerce and industry, undertook a new defense program for the Philippines, and began the construction of a new national capital in Quezon City in the suburbs of Manila. After Japan attacked and occupied the Philippines, Quezon went to the United States. On behalf of the Philippines he signed the Declaration of the United Nations against the fascist nations and became a member of the Pacific War Council in 1942. He worked on plans for rehabilitation of the Philippines and wrote his autobiography entitled *The Good Fight*. Quezon died of tuberculosis at Saranac Lake, N.Y., on Aug. 1, 1944. (C. A. B.)

QUIBERON BAY, BATTLE OF, was fought between an English and a French fleet on Nov. 20, 1759, in Quiberon Bay, south of Lorient, France, during the Seven Years' War. The English victory put an end to French plans to invade Great Britain. In 1759 the duc de Choiseul ordered concentrations of troops in Flanders and Brittany and the conjunction of the Brest and Toulon fleets to cover their passage. On Aug. 5, 1759, the Toulon fleet under Adm. de la Clue slipped out of port but was caught by Adm. Edward Boscawen off Lagos, Port., and defeated on Aug. 18–19.

Adm. Sir Edward Hawke (*q.v.*) had meanwhile maintained a close blockade on Brest and on the French transport ships in the Morbihan, the landlocked waters of Quiberon Bay, but on Nov. 9

bad weather forced him to run into Torbay, Devon. He was able to leave port again on Nov. 14, and on the same day the Brest fleet under the comte de Conflans put to sea, having learned of Hawke's withdrawal. Conflans headed south for Quiberon Bay, followed by Hawke. At dawn on Nov. 20 both fleets were about 30 mi. west of Belle-Île, opposite the bay, though still out of sight of each other. Conflans stood in close to attack a British squadron of frigates under Commodore Robert Duff, which was blockading Quiberon, but on sighting Hawke to the northwest, Conflans ordered his fleet to close up and run into the bay. He hoped that the shoals, lack of pilots, and a northwesterly gale blowing on a lee shore would discourage Hawke's pursuit. Conflans had 21 ships of the line and Hawke 23, with Duff's squadron of frigates.

At 9:45 A.M. on Nov. 20, receiving confirmation that it was the French fleet, Hawke ordered a "general chase." At 2:30 P.M. the British van engaged the French rear to the south of Belle-Île and soon afterward the fleets swept between the Cardinal rocks and the Four sandbank into Quiberon Bay. A fierce battle followed before nightfall at 5:30 P.M., by which time two French ships had struck their colours and two others had been sunk. During the night nine French ships escaped south to Rochefort, one sinking on the way. On Nov. 21, two ran ashore and were burned the next day, and the remaining seven escaped across the bar of the Vilaine River, where four broke their backs. The British lost two ships which ran aground and were burned. The battle, one of the decisive naval battles of the century, inspired David Garrick's song "Hearts of Oak."

See J. Corbett, *England in the Seven Years' War,* vol. ii (1907); G. Marcus, *Quiberon Bay* (1960).

QUICHÉ is a Mayan language spoken in the 1960s by about 275,000 Indians in the western highlands departments of Quiché, Quezaltenango, Totonicapán, Retalhuleu, and Sacatepéquez of Guatemala. Quiché, Cakchiquel (*q.v.*), and Tzutuhil (or Zutuhil; *q.v.*) make up the Quichean family of languages, all of which are confined to Guatemala.

The Quiché-speaking Indians live in villages, each having its own blend of the broadly similar culture and social organization common to highland Indians. The culture is a mixture of pre-Conquest, Spanish colonial, and modern elements, worked into a local variety by each community. Each has its own hierarchy of civil and religious officials, its own patron saint, and an economic specialty. Details of costume, speech, and custom vary from one community to another, but all depend primarily on small-plot agriculture, carried on without draft animals, plows, or the wheel. Most communities have supplementary occupations: in Totonicapán they are potters and woodworkers; those of Chichicastenango are lumber producers; in Cantel many work in a modern cotton mill; and near coffee plantations many work as field peons. The communities vary in size from a few hundred up to the largest, Chichicastenango, with a population of 30,000.

When the territory was conquered in 1524 by Pedro de Alvarado, the people apparently were more highly integrated politically than they are now. Alvarado defeated a large army of Quiché and other Indian allies on the plains of Xelajú, just outside modern Quezaltenango, in a battle so sanguinary that the river running through the plains is still called the "river of blood." Today, in many communities, masked dancers reenact in a *baile de conquista* the battle and the death of their leader, Tecum Uman.

Archaeological remains in Quiché territory show large population centres before the Conquest and indicate several social classes. The ruins do not approach those of the Northern Maya in artistic achievement, but these Southern Maya had achieved higher levels of political organization. With the Conquest the Quiché class system was eliminated. Present-day communities are the result of regrouping under Spanish conquerors and under Guatemalan national programs. They show no recall of ancient glories or pre-Conquest times, nor do they exhibit pan-Quiché feeling.

History and legend are preserved in the *Popol Vuh*, written shortly after the Conquest; it relates legendary magical beginnings and wanderings that led the Quiché to Guatemala. It is a chronicle of kings and of wars they fought among themselves or with neighbouring principalities. The pre-Conquest Quiché shared in the development of an intricate and accurate Mayan calendar marking the changing disposition of heavenly forces toward human beings. Pre-Conquest life was oriented to religion and politics and attained little technological development.

Present-day Quiché loyalties tend to be local rather than national. Though legally Guatemalan citizens, they participate little in national life and, along with other Indians of the highlands, form the poorest segment of society there. All the Indians are nominal Christians, mostly Catholic, with some Protestant converts. Each community is built around a central plaza on which face the church, the city hall, and the school.

Like other Guatemalan highlands Indians, Quiché-speakers have shown a steady increase in population; the rate of absorption into Guatemalan society is more than offset by local birthrate. *See* also MAYA INDIANS.

BIBLIOGRAPHY.—A. Recinos, *The Popol Vuh* (1947); L. Schultz-Jena, *La Vida y Las Creencias de los Indigenos Quiches de Guatemala,* Spanish trans., in "Instituto Indigenista de Guatemala Series" (1946); R. Bunzel, *Chichicastenango* (1952); M. Nash, *Machine Age Maya* (1958); B. Saler, "Nagual, Witch, and Sorcerer in a Quiché Village," *Ethnology,* vol. iii (July 1964). (M. Na.)

QUICHERAT, JULES ÉTIENNE JOSEPH (1814–1882), French historian and archaeologist, whose work was an important contribution to medieval studies in the 19th century, was born in Paris on Oct. 13, 1814. He was educated at the Collège of Ste. Barbe and completed his studies at the École des Chartes in 1835. After a period at the Bibliothèque Royale he was appointed professor at the École des Chartes in 1849 and later became its director. He died in Paris on April 8, 1882.

His first published study was *Recherches sur le chroniqueur Jean Castel* (1840), but it was his *Procès de condamnation et de réhabilitation de Jeanne d'Arc*, five volumes (1841–49), followed by *Aperçus nouveaux sur l'histoire de Jeanne d'Arc* (1850), which drew attention to his skilful marshaling of his original research. This was followed by a study and an edition of the writings of Thomas Basin, bishop of Lisieux (five volumes; 1855–60). Quicherat published many essays in contemporary reviews and the posthumous publication of *Mélanges d'archéologie et d'histoire* (two volumes; 1855–60) was a memorial to his wide and painstaking erudition. (H. G. Wh.)

QUICKSAND, a state in which saturated sand loses its supporting capacity and acquires the character of a liquid. Once considered, especially by construction men, to be a special type of sand, quicksand is now recognized as a condition that may be assumed by any sand if its effective weight is temporarily or permanently carried by interstitial water. Some natural sands are in a condition so loose that minor disturbances caused by a footstep may collapse the loose structure and produce a "quick" condition. Under these circumstances a person may become engulfed as in a fluid, but since the density of the sand-water suspension exceeds that of the human body, the body cannot sink. Struggling may lead to loss of balance and drowning. This possibility has no doubt led to the superstition, prevalent in literature, that quicksand has the ability to draw a person to his death. *See* SOIL MECHANICS. (R. B. P.)

QUIETISM, a doctrine of Christian perfection which disturbed the Roman Catholic Church, particularly in Italy and France, in the 17th century and was condemned as a heresy. Quietism, in general, holds that perfection consists in passivity (quiet) of the soul, in the suppression of human effort so that divine action may have full play. Quietistic elements have been discerned in Buddhism, Gnosticism, Manichaeism, in the teachings of the medieval Brethren of the Free Spirit, in the Spanish Alumbrados, and even in certain doctrines of Martin Luther. But Quietism is, strictly speaking, the doctrine of Miguel de Molinos (*q.v.*), according to whom the way of Christian perfection is the interior way of contemplation to which anyone with divine assistance can attain and which can last for years, even for a lifetime.

Contemplation for Molinos was a vague, undetermined view of God which inhibits man's interior powers. The soul remains in dark faith, excludes all definite thought, and abstains from all interior action. To wish to act is an offense against God, who desires to do everything in us. Inactivity brings the soul back to its principle, the divine being, into which it is transformed. God, the sole reality, lives and reigns in the souls of those who have undergone this mystic death. They can will only what God wills, because their own wills have been taken away. They should not be concerned about salvation, perfection, or anything else, but must leave all to God. It is not necessary for them to perform the ordinary exercises of piety. Since they worship God in spirit and in truth, they must exclude the use of all pictures and images. In temptation the contemplative should remain passive. He neither consents nor, by making acts of virtue, resists. The devil, indeed, can make himself master of the contemplative's body and force him to perform acts which seem exteriorly to be sins. But they are not. Indeed, this violence of the devil is an efficacious means of attaining to humility and contempt of self.

Molinos went to Rome in 1663 and soon won a reputation as a spiritual director of unusual ability: lay men and women, religious women, priests, even prelates were greatly impressed by his teaching. In 1675 he published his *Guía Espiritual,* which was approved by leading theologians and soon translated into a number of languages. When some priests who considered the *Spiritual Guide* a dangerous book wrote against it, their works were forbidden by the authorities. Soon, however, pernicious consequences of Molinos' doctrine began to manifest themselves, and in 1685 he was arrested by the papal police. Some 20,000 of his letters were examined. He himself and numerous other witnesses were interrogated with the result that 68 propositions embodying his system were condemned by Innocent XI in the bull *Coelestis Pastor* of Nov. 19, 1687. Molinos, who renounced his errors, was sentenced to life imprisonment. Cardinal Pier Matteo Petrucci, who had defended him, was obliged to recant.

Quietism was perhaps paralleled among Protestants by some of the tenets of the Pietists and Quakers (*see* PIETISM; FRIENDS, SOCIETY OF). It is certain, at any rate, that after the condemnation of Molinos a milder form of Quietism appeared in France, propagated by Mme Guyon (*see* GUYON, JEANNE MARIE BOUVIER DE LA MOTTE). She was influenced by the priest François Lacombe and in turn influenced him. When he was imprisoned in 1687 under suspicion of Quietism, Mme Guyon won the sympathy of Mme de Maintenon, the favourite of Louis XIV, and of François de Salignac de la Mothe Fénelon (*q.v.*), archbishop of Cambrai. The latter developed a doctrine of pure love sometimes called Semi-Quietism, which was condemned by Innocent XII in 1699. Both Fénelon and Mme Guyon submitted. This condemnation has often been looked upon as a blow at true as well as false mysticism and has been attributed to the narrow-mindedness of J. B. Bossuet.

See R. A. Knox, *Enthusiasm,* pp. 231–255 (1950). (E. A. R.)

QUILLER-COUCH, SIR ARTHUR THOMAS (1863–1944), English writer (pseudonym "Q"), best remembered for his anthology *The Oxford Book of English Verse,* was born at Bodmin, Cornwall, on Nov. 21, 1863. He was educated at Newton Abbot College, Clifton College, and Trinity College, Oxford, where he was afterward appointed lecturer in classics (1886–87). *Dead Man's Rock* (1887), a romance in the style of R. L. Stevenson, was the first of a score of novels from only a few of which Cornwall and the sea are absent. From 1887 to 1892 he worked in London for a publishing firm and as assistant editor of *The Speaker.* A number of short stories which he contributed to this were reprinted in book form as *Noughts and Crosses* (1898), the first and best of a dozen similar volumes. In

1892 he settled at Fowey, the small Cornish port which appears in his stories as "Troy Town." Here he continued to write fiction and other prose, and also compiled several anthologies, such as *The Oxford Book of English Verse 1250–1900* (1900, revised 1939) and *The Oxford Book of Ballads* (1910). He was knighted in 1910 and in 1912 was appointed King Edward VII Professor of English Literature at Cambridge and also elected a fellow of Jesus College. His highly popular lectures were published in book form as *On the Art of Writing* (1916), *Shakespeare's Workmanship* (1918), *Studies in Literature* (3 series: 1918, 1922, 1929), *On the Art of Reading* (1920), *Charles Dickens and Other Victorians* (1925), and *The Poet as Citizen and Other Papers* (1934). Most of his serious verse is collected in *Poems* (1930) and his light verse in *Green Bays* (1930). He died at Fowey on May 12, 1944.

One of the most versatile and prolific writers of his time, "Q" was essentially a romantic. His chief contribution to letters was his clear and apparently effortless style. It reflects the personality of its author—neat, thorough, colourful, unhurried, hospitable, humorous, and chivalrous.

See *Memories and Opinions, an Unfinished Autobiography,* by "Q" (1944); F. Brittain, *Arthur Quiller-Couch* (1947). (FK. BN.)

QUILLWORK, embroidery work done with quills of the porcupine or, sometimes, those of bird feathers. This type of

QUILLED BUCKSKIN, ABOUT 17 IN. WIDE, USED AS ORNAMENTATION FOR A BABY CARRIER

decoration was used by American Indians from Maine to Virginia and westward to the Rocky Mountains. For all practical purposes the art has died out. Quills seem to have been an article of barter; hence their use was not confined to the natural habitat of porcupines. Quills were used on tobacco and tinder bags, workbags, knife and paintstick cases, cradles, amulets, burden straps, tunics, shirts, leggings, belts, moccasins, arm and leg bands, robes, horse trappings, and birchbark containers.

The gathering of raw materials—the hunting of porcupines or birds—was the duty of the men, who in some tribes also prepared the dyes. Sorting and colouring the quills, tracing the design on dressed skin or birchbark, and the embroidering were the work of women.

Dyes were compounded of roots, whole plants, and buds and bark of trees. The natural colour of quills was white, with red, yellow, green, blue, and black being produced by steeping in solutions of the plant materials. No variegated hues were made and rarely more than one shade of a colour. Patterns were stenciled or drawn with a bone paintbrush, stick, or dull knife, on the skin or bark that was to be worked. Although a cut stencil was usually used, a woman who was adept at drawing might copy a design free hand, making just a few measurements beforehand. Some even composed designs, both in form and colour, and worked them out as they embroidered. All designs were made up of wide or narrow lines, each composed of a series of close stitches. The decorations put on men's garb were generally related to their work, hunting, and war, while figures worked on children's garments were usually symbolic and expressed prayers for safety, long life, and prosperity. There was considerable borrowing of designs, and figures that were sacred symbols in some tribes came to be purely ornamental in others. (A. S. LI.)

QUILMES, Argentine city and suburb of greater Buenos Aires, 12 mi. (19 km.) SE of the federal district on the estuary of the Río de la Plata. Pop. (1960) 318,144. The Indians who gave the city its name were subdued and settled in the area by the Spanish in 1666. During the early 19th century it was twice the scene of hostilities: in 1806 when the first English invasion landed on its shores, and in 1827 when Argentine forces defeated the Brazilian fleet in the estuary. Quilmes is one of the important industrial centres of Buenos Aires and the location of large breweries and distilleries. (Js. R. S.)

QUILON, a town and district of Kerala, India. The town, headquarters of the district, lies 471 mi. (760 km.) S of Madras and 45 mi. (72 km.) N of Trivandrum. Pop. (1961) 91,018. It is one of the oldest ports of the Malabar Coast (*q.v.*) and variously known as the Elancon of the early travelers, Kaulam Mall of the Arabs, and Coilum of Marco Polo. It stands on Ashtamudi Lake, a backwater with eight creeks. Its site, commanding the navigation of the large backwater system, made it commercially important; the Portuguese had a factory there, which was captured by the Dutch in 1662 and later passed to the British. The Thevally Palace of the former maharaja of Travancore, with an array of leaning coconut palms, is a notable beauty spot.

The spinning and weaving of coir and cotton, the manufacture of tiles, and the hulling of cashew nuts (mainly imported from East Africa) are the chief industries. The town is a large educational centre with three colleges, one of which is managed by the Roman Catholics and the other two by a trust of the Ezhava sect, all affiliated with Kerala University. A metre-gauge railway links it northward with Ernakulam, and another route southward with Trivandrum and eastward with Shencottah.

QUILON DISTRICT has an area of 1,944 sq.mi. (5,035 sq.km.) and a population (1961) of 1,941,228. (G. KN.)

QUILTING, the process of stitching together several layers of fabric, usually with some soft, thick substance placed between them. The layer of wool, cotton, or other stuffing provides insulation; the stitching keeps the stuffing evenly distributed and also provides opportunity for artistic expression in both design and execution. Quilting has long been used for clothing and other purposes in many parts of the world, especially in the Far East, India, Iran, the Middle East, and in the Muslim regions of Africa. It was also used for military doublets worn under armour, and quilted articles sometimes provided a less expensive substitute for armour (*see* ARMOUR, BODY). Quilting, particularly of bedcovers (quilts), reached the status of a minor art in Europe in the 14th century and from there was carried to North America, where it reached its greatest development in the period from the middle of the 18th to about the middle of the 19th century.

Although references and inventory records attest to the popularity of quilted articles, few surviving pieces predate the 17th century. One of the earliest is the Sicilian quilt, dating from about 1400, with scenes portraying the early life of Tristan. Part of this quilt is in the Victoria and

Albert Museum, London, and part in the Bargello at Florence. It is made of linen and quilted with linen thread, using both the back stitch and the darning stitch. The age, the fine craftsmanship of the stitching, the design, and the detail of the figures make this an excellent example of the quilting art.

By the 17th century quilting in Europe and in England began to reach a high degree of popularity that was to last about two centuries. Three fine examples from this period are preserved in the Victoria and Albert Museum. The first is a cotton bedcover quilted in Portugal, measuring 8 × 5 ft. 11 in., with a well-executed design of alternating single and double bird motifs. The other pieces are costume items of white satin stitched with white silk, the one a jacket and the other a doublet. Many examples of fine 18th-century English and European quilting remain as evidence of its wide and continued use.

In America the technique of quilting moved west with the early settlers. The most popular items were petticoats and quilts. Those produced in the early 18th century imitated English and Dutch designs, but by the end of the century the American quilt took on many new and distinctive features. First from necessity and later from choice, quilt tops were made of coloured fabrics appliquéd to a white muslin ground or joined together as patchwork; in some instances the two techniques were combined in one quilt. The design was completed by the quilting itself, which often picked up and echoed the shape of the patchwork or appliqué pattern. Although a few examples can be found in other countries, this style is of American origin and was used more extensively there than elsewhere.

A popular late-18th-century design was the appliquéd tree of life, adapted from the painted cotton bedcovers then being imported from India. As styles changed, the tree of life was gradually decreased until it became merely a centre motif enclosed by frames of pieced chintz. From this the frames evolved as the more important design feature and the framed medallion became a second important pattern. Single-unit designs remained in vogue throughout the 18th century. Sometimes these were made of hundreds of small pieces stitched together—an effective way of

EXAMPLES OF QUILTING

Details of (top left) Sicilian quilt, about 1400, showing Tristan wounding Merold; (top centre) Portuguese quilt, 17th century; (top right) English linen quilt, 1703; (bottom left) "Fairground near Russellville, Kentucky, 1856," an example of stuffed work; (bottom right) pieced quilt, Indiana, 1866

utilizing every available scrap of fabric. As the patchwork and appliqué became more dominant, the quilting frequently reverted to its original utilitarian purpose of holding the stuffing in position.

By the 19th century the quilt designs evolved into multiple units or repeated designs, either pieced or appliquéd. The patterns were of infinite variety and many were traditional. Another favourite was the one-patch, in which the entire quilt was made up of pieces cut in the same size and shape, the diamond and the hexagon being the two favourites.

The work of quilting a large bedcover, which might measure as much as 10 ft. square, was usually done on a frame, which could be as simple as two smooth poles or long bars of wood set on four chairs. Each sidebar of the quilting frame was covered with fabric to which the edges of the quilt lining were sewn, one side to each bar. The cotton or wool fibres used for the stuffing or filling were spread smoothly and evenly on the stretched lining. Then the top was placed in position and its edge was pinned or basted to the edge of the lining, drawing it tightly over the fibre filling. The quilting pattern was marked on the top with a tracing wheel and chalk, by pencil, or by pressure of the needle marking an indentation around a rigid pattern of wood. The running stitch was most commonly used for the quilting, but even this simple stitch was difficult through three layers of textile. Some of the fine 19th-century quilts have heavily stuffed or padded areas that enhance and emphasize the design. In these, the quilts were first stitched in the normal manner. Then the quilts were turned wrong side up, small holes were made in the lining, and considerably more fibre was forced into the desired area. A heavily padded effect took much painstaking work but produced beautiful "stuffed work" quilts.

The invention of the sewing machine in the mid-19th century was quickly followed by a series of attachments for machine-stitched quilting. Utilitarian items were quilted in this manner, but stitching by machine did not lend itself to artistic work. The creative impulse in quilt design also diminished. Although fine quilts were made after the mid-19th century, they usually copied or adapted earlier styles.

BIBLIOGRAPHY.—William Rush Dunton, Jr., *Old Quilts* (1946); Ruth E. Finley, *Old Patchwork Quilts and the Women Who Made Them* (1929); Ruby Short McKim, *One Hundred and One Patchwork Patterns* (1931); Florence Peto, *Historic Quilts* (1939); Marie D. Webster, *Quilts: Their Story and How to Make Them* (1926); and two pamphlets published by the Victoria and Albert Museum, London: "Notes on Quilting" (1949) and "Notes on Applied Work and Patchwork" (1949).
(G. R. Co.)

QUIMBY, PHINEAS PARKHURST (1802–1866), U.S. pioneer in the field of mental healing and generally regarded as the father of the New Thought movement, was born in Lebanon, N.H., on Feb. 16, 1802. His active career was spent largely in Belfast and Portland, Me., and he died at Belfast on Jan. 16, 1866.

Professionally interested in hypnosis (*q.v.*), Quimby employed it for a time as a means of healing, but later discovered that he was quite as able to heal by suggestion. He came to believe that illness resulted from the patient's mistaken beliefs, and that its cure lay in discovering the truth. Not primarily religious in the orthodox sense, he believed that he had rediscovered the secret of Jesus' healing ministry. He wrote down his philosophy in the so-called Quimby manuscripts. Quimby became a controversial figure because Mary Baker Eddy (*q.v.*), who sought healing at his hands, and was at first a disciple and warm admirer, later denied, as it was thought by many, that she had been influenced by him. It is the official belief that her discovery of Christian Science (*q.v.*), a divine revelation, depended in no sense on Quimby.

The best source is *The Quimby Manuscripts,* edited by H. W. Dresser (1921), the first edition of which contains a number of letters of Mrs. Eddy to Quimby and others not found in later editions. *See* also NEW THOUGHT. (C. S. B.)

QUIMPER (from the Breton *kemper,* a "confluence"), the chief town of Finistère *département,* Brittany, France, and the seat of a bishopric, stands at the confluence of the Odet and Stéïr rivers, 127 mi. (205 km.) W of Rennes by road. Pop. (1962) 40,223. Most of the town is on the right bank of the Odet, lying among seven hills. On the left bank of the Odet are the wooded slopes of Frugy Hill below which is the site of the Roman Locmaria, with a Romanesque church, partly of the 11th century. The cathedral of Saint-Corentin, in the heart of Quimper, is a fine Gothic building of the 13th–16th centuries. There are two museums. An annual festival is held in July at which all the costumes of Brittany are displayed.

Quimper is linked by rail and road with Brest, Nantes, and Rennes, and has an airport (4½ mi. [7 km.]) with internal and external air services. It is the tourist centre for south Brittany. The traditional craft of faience has long been carried on at Quimper, and there are large potteries on the left bank. There are also some metal and other industries.

After Roman times Quimper became the capital of the *comté* (county) of Cornouaille (Cornwall, the name brought from Britain), and the first bishop, at the end of the 5th century, was St. Corentin. The *comté* was united with the duchy of Brittany in the 11th century, but the town suffered in the local wars of succession and in 1344 was sacked by Charles of Blois. The duchy returned to the Montforts (John V), however, after the defeat of Charles at Auray in 1364.

Notable people born at Quimper include Élie Catherine Fréron (1718–76), the polemical writer and opponent of Voltaire; Yves Joseph de Kerguélen-Trémarec (1734–97), the navigator whose discoveries included the Kerguélen Islands in the southern seas; and René Théophile Hyacinthe Laënnec (1781–1826), the inventor of the stethoscope. (SE. C.)

QUIN, JAMES (1693–1766), a leading English actor of his day, was born in London on Feb. 24, 1693. He made his first stage appearance at the Smock Alley theatre, Dublin, as Abel in Sir Robert Howard's *The Committee* in 1712. Engaged at Drury Lane theatre for small parts, his remarkable memory enabled him to deputize at short notice as Bajazet in *Tamerlane* with great success. Quin then went to Lincoln's Inn theatre and remained there for 14 years. A noted swordsman, he was convicted of manslaughter for killing another actor in a duel, and at Lincoln's Inn he defended the stage with his sword against rioters. He went to Covent Garden theatre in 1732 and became a leader of the stage, returning to Drury Lane from 1734 to 1741. His style was declamatory, very slow but impressive, and he always wore the same costume. In 1746 his supremacy was challenged by David Garrick (*q.v.*), the exponent of a new type of acting, and when the two played together in *The Fair Penitent* at Covent Garden, Garrick triumphed. Quin bore him no ill will; they became friends and acted together at Drury Lane. Quin was one of the finest Falstaffs the stage ever knew. He retired to Bath in 1757 and died there on Jan. 21, 1766, being buried in the abbey church with an epitaph by Garrick. Although of poor education, Quin had great wit and warmhearted generosity. He was also a great epicure, his appetite being as prodigious as his memory.

See *Life of Mr. James Quin, Comedian,* anon., 2nd ed. (1887). (W. J. M.-P.)

QUINCE, a fruit tree classified by some botanists as a distinct genus, *Cydonia,* and by others as a section of the genus *Pyrus* (family Rosaceae; *q.v.*).

The name *Cydonia oblonga* is to be preferred to *Pyrus cydonia.* Bailey gives five varieties of *C. oblonga;* namely, varieties *lusitanica, maliformis, pyriformis, marmorata,* and *pyramidalis.* The quinces are much-branched shrubs or small trees with entire leaves, small stipules, large solitary white or pink flowers like those of the pear or apple, but with leafy calyx lobes and a many-celled ovary, in each cell of which are numerous horizontal ovules. The fruits may be round and flattened or somewhat pear-shaped, with large leafy calyx persisting on the mature fruit.

The common quince is a native of Iran and Anatolia, and perhaps also of Greece and the Crimea. By Franchet and Savatier *C. oblonga* is given as a native of Japan, with the native name "maroumerou." It is certain that the Greeks knew a common variety upon which they grafted scions of a better variety from Cydon in Crete, whence it was obtained and from which the later names have been derived. The fragrance and astringency of the fruit of the quince are well known, and the seeds formerly were used medicinally for the sake of the mucilage they yield when soaked in water. The quince is but little cultivated in Great Britain; in Scotland it seldom approaches maturity, unless favoured by a wall. The fruit has a strong aroma and in the raw state is astringent; but it makes an excellent preserve, and is often used to give flavour and sharpness to stewed or baked apples.

The Japanese quince, formerly considered in the genus *Cydonia* but now known as *Chaenomeles lagenaria,* has been widely used as an ornamental plant in gardens as a shrub, particularly because of the beauty of its flowers that appear on the stems before the leaves open fully in late winter and early spring months. Some of the small shrubs bear large green fragrant fruits that are quite inedible in the fresh state but have been used in making preserves.

ROCHE
QUINCE (CYDONIA OBLONGA) BLOSSOMS

The quince was formerly grown in home fruit gardens and commercial plantings in the northeastern United States but later became the least esteemed of all tree fruits for orchards in that area. The fruit is almost inedible in the uncooked state, and other fruits are preferred in the fresh state for the diet. It thrives under the same systems of cultivation as do apples and pears and does fairly well along fencerows, where it may be given little care. The quince is susceptible to a bacterial disease called fire blight, which is also a serious hazard to pear growing in the United States. Trees that are not forced into strong vegetable growth by pruning and fertilization are less susceptible to the fire blight disease. The trees are subject to the same scale insects that attack apples and pears and should receive the same dormant spray treatment for the control of these pests. The fruits are golden yellow in colour and the flesh takes on a pink colour when cooked, giving an attractive colour to jellies and conserves made from this fruit. Orange and Champion are the more commonly grown varieties. Quince stocks are used on which to graft the pear to dwarf the tree and hasten early bearing. The Angers variety, imported from France, is the most important stock used for dwarfing pears. (F. P. C.)

BIBLIOGRAPHY.—W. W. Robbins, *Botany of Crop Plants* (1924); L. H. Bailey, *Standard Cyclopedia of Horticulture* (1914–27) and *Manual of Cultivated Plants* (1924).

QUINCY, a city of Illinois, U.S., on the Mississippi River, 110 mi. NW of St. Louis. First settled in 1822, it became the seat of Adams County, March 4, 1825, the day Pres. John Quincy Adams was inaugurated, and was named in his honour. Incorporated as a village in 1834 and chartered as a city in 1839, Quincy had a population of about 7,000 and was second in size to Chicago when the sixth Lincoln-Douglas debate was held there in John's Square (now Washington Park), Oct. 13, 1858. A prosperous river town, Quincy declined with the passing of the steamboat era in the latter part of the 19th century but after 1920, with the development of industry, population again increased. Among the manufactures are agricultural and industrial machinery, automotive parts, clothing and footwear, food products, chemicals, office supplies, paper products, and heating equipment.

Most of the city occupies the upland about 150 ft. above the valley floor where the Mississippi River flows against its steep left bank. A navigational dam and lock impound the water in Quincy Bay. Riverview, Sunset, and Gardner parks north of the business section and Indian Mounds and South parks to the south line the river bluffs. Quincy, a Roman Catholic coeducational college established in 1860, is in the residential part of the city. Illinois Soldiers and Sailors Home (founded 1887) occupies more than 200 ac. at the northern city limits.

Pop. (1970) 45,288. For comparative population figures *see* table in ILLINOIS: *Population.* (J. H. GD.)

QUINCY, a city of Norfolk County, Mass., U.S., located on Boston Harbor, about 8 mi. SE of Boston. A part of the Boston standard metropolitan statistical area, it is a manufacturing city and a centre of retail trade. Pop. (1970) 87,966. (For comparative population figures *see* table in MASSACHUSETTS: *Population.*) Manufacturing is diversified (gears, detergents, electronic tubes, machinery for riveting, packaging and materials handling) but it is dominated by shipbuilding; the shipyards are among the most important in the country. The city was formerly famed for its granite quarries, which supplied granite for King's Chapel and the Bunker Hill Monument in Boston. Retail sales per capita are substantially above the average for the Boston metropolitan area and for the state, with sales of lumber, building materials, hardware, and farm equipment constituting nearly 10% of the total. A community junior college was established in 1958. Quincy's residents are distinguished by the high proportion with origins in Scotland, Sweden, and Finland and by the predominance of craftsmen, foremen, and clerical workers in the labour force. Prior to 1792, when Quincy was incorporated as a town, the area was part of the town of Braintree. It became a city in 1888. The birthplaces of two presidents, John Adams and John Quincy Adams, are preserved in Quincy. The two buildings, as well as the Quincy Homestead (built about 1636) and the Adams National Historic Site, are open to visitors. (E. E. M.)

QUINDÍO, a department of Colombia, situated in the west-central part of the nation. Area 705 sq.mi. (1,825 sq.km.); pop. (1964) 305,745. It formed the southernmost section of the department of Caldas (*q.v.*) until 1966 when it became a separate department. The capital city is Armenia (pop. [1964] 125,022). Although three-fourths of the inhabitants of Quindío are classified as urban, the only other sizable urban centre is Calarcá (est. pop. [1967] 54,834). The department, named for a traditional alternate term for the great Cordillera Central of the Andes ("the Quindío"), lies mainly on the western slopes of that range, and most of its area enjoys a temperate climate. It is one of the chief coffee producing departments of Colombia despite the fact that there is only one annual planting and harvesting. Plantains and other fruits are produced, and industries, centred mainly in the capital, were increasing in the 1960s. Armenia is on the main highway connecting the national capital, Bogotá, with the Pacific coast, and the department is serviced by air and rail lines. Quindío has suffered from the sporadic bloody violence experienced in parts of Colombia in recent decades (*see* COLOMBIA: *History: The 20th Century*). (T. E. N.)

QUINET, EDGAR (1803–1875), French patriot, poet, and philosopher, made a significant contribution to the developing tradition of French liberalism. He was born at Bourg-en-Bresse, Ain, on Feb. 17, 1803. Moving to Paris in 1820, he forsook the faith of his Protestant mother, became greatly attracted to German philosophy, and published in 1827–28, as his first major work, a translation of Herder's *Ideen zur Philosophie der Geschichte der Menschheit.* Soon, however, despite lengthy visits to Germany, he became disillusioned with German philosophy and alarmed by the aggressive nature of Prussian nationalism. His literary reputation was increased by the publication of his epic prose poem *Ahasvérus* (1833). In *Le Génie des religions* (1842) he expressed sympathy for all religions while committing himself to none, but shortly afterward his increasingly radical views alienated him finally from Catholicism.

It was not until 1842 that he obtained what he had really wanted —a professorship in Paris. There he joined his friends Jules Michelet and Adam Mickiewicz (*qq.v.*) at the Collège de France. His lectures attacked Catholicism, exalted the French Revolution, offered support for the oppressed nationalities of Europe, and promoted the theory that religions were the determining force in society. Because his treatment of these topics aroused heated controversy, the government intervened in 1846 and, to the satisfaction of the clergy and dismay of the students, he lost his chair.

Quinet hailed the revolution of February 1848, but, with Louis Napoleon's *coup d'état* of December 1851, was forced to flee first to Brussels (1851–58), and thence to Veytaux, near Montreux, Switzerland (1858–70). His faith in humanity shaken, Quinet's optimism failed him for a while, and in *La Révolution religieuse au XIXe siècle* (1857) and *La Révolution* (1865), he sympathized with the use of force against an all-powerful church, and even wistfully hoped that France might yet embrace Protestantism. In his last years the conquests of science fascinated him and restored his faith in the progress of humanity (*La Création*, 1870; *L'Esprit nouveau*, 1874). He returned to Paris on the fall of the Empire in 1870, and was elected to the National Assembly in the following year, but exercised little influence over his fellow deputies. He died at Versailles on March 27, 1875.

Although Quinet was never insensitive to popular acclaim, he lived mainly in the world of ideas. His interests ranged widely, and frequently he allowed his imagination to outstrip his sense of academic caution. His histories, political essays, and works on the history of religion, though little read today, remain full of suggestive theories. His style inclined to the vague and the abstract, for which he has wrongly been credited with mystical tendencies. It is in the educational reforms of the Third Republic, including the banishing of religious instruction from the schools, that his most lasting influence is seen. Yet, because the schools failed to provide their own moral instruction, the results were far from what Quinet would have wished.

BIBLIOGRAPHY.—*Oeuvres complètes*, in 26 vol. (1877–82); and in 30 vol. [1885–95]; A. Valès, *Edgar Quinet, sa vie et son oeuvre* (1936); R. H. Powers, *Edgar Quinet, a Study in French Patriotism* (1957); M. du Pasquier, *Edgar Quinet en Suisse* (1959).   (A. H. V.)

QUININE is the most important alkaloid of cinchona bark; its chief use is in the treatment of malaria. In the 300 years between its introduction into western medicine and World War I, quinine was the only effective remedy for malaria. As a specific for this disease, quinine benefited more people than any drug ever used for the treatment of infectious diseases. The treatment of malaria with quinine marked the first successful use of a chemical compound in combating an infectious disease.

Like the other cinchona alkaloids, quinine is a large and complex molecule, and its total laboratory synthesis by Robert B. Woodward and William von E. Doering in 1945 is one of the classical achievements of synthetic organic chemistry. However, commercial synthesis of quinine is not economically feasible.

Quinine

Cinchonine, $C_{19}H_{22}N_2O$, the desmethoxy derivative of quinine, is one-fifth as active as quinine.

Quinine acts by interfering with the growth and reproduction of the malarial parasites inhabiting the red cells of the blood, probably by preventing them from oxidizing glucose, their chief source of energy. Administration of quinine dramatically improves the condition of a person suffering from malaria; the parasites promptly disappear from the blood, and the symptoms of the disease are quickly alleviated. However, when quinine treatment is terminated, many recovered patients suffer another attack of malaria several weeks later. This is because quinine does not kill the malarial parasites living in cells of the body other than the red blood cells. These parasites persist and, after a time, reinvade the red blood cells and precipitate the second malarial attack, or relapse.

Because quinine fails to produce a complete cure in malaria, better antimalarial drugs were long sought for. At the beginning of World War II, two new synthetic antimalarial drugs, pamaquine naphthoate (Plasmochin) and quinacrine hydrochloride (Atabrine), had already been developed in Germany. They were defi-

nitely effective but not clearly superior to quinine. When the Allies' supply of East Indian quinine was cut off by the entrance of Japan into World War II, the search for new and more effective antimalarial drugs was greatly intensified. Although Atabrine remained the mainstay of Allied forces throughout the war, wartime research produced a number of antimalarial drugs that later almost completely replaced quinine. Some of them, such as chloroquine and chlorguanide, are more effective than quinine in suppressing the growth of the blood forms of the malaria parasite; while others, such as primaquine and pyrimethamine, act upon both the blood and tissue stages of the parasite, thus producing complete cures and preventing relapses. All the newer antimalarials, unlike quinine, may be completely synthesized in the chemical laboratory on a commercial scale.

During the 1960s several strains of the malaria parasite *Plasmodium falciparum* developed resistance to the synthetic drugs, particularly the highly valued chloroquine. The parasite remained sensitive, however, to quinine, which had to be reinstated in various parts of the world as the drug of choice in spite of the side effects (*see* below) which sometimes occur when the necessarily massive doses of quinine are given.

In addition to its specific use in malaria, quinine is sometimes used as a nonspecific remedy for fever and pain. It probably reduces fever by dilating the small vessels of the skin, while its analgesic effect may result from depression of certain centres in the central nervous system. Prolonged administration of quinine may produce toxic symptoms such as deafness, disturbances in vision, skin rashes, and digestive upsets; and, in the opinion of some experts, patients who undergo quinine treatment may be predisposed to develop blackwater fever, a little-understood complication of malaria marked by rapid and severe anemia and the appearance of hemoglobin in the urine.

See also CINCHONA; CINCHONA BARK, ALKALOIDS OF; MALARIA; and references under "Quinine" in the Index.   (J. W. MR.; X.)

QUINOLINE is an organic compound of formula C_9H_7N which in general chemical behaviour resembles pyridine (*q.v.*) very closely. It is, in fact, a benzopyridine, bearing the same relation to pyridine as naphthalene does to benzene. The benzene and pyridine rings are fused together in the 2,3 position, the other possibility, fusion in the 3,4 position, giving isoquinoline which is discussed below.

Quinoline   Isoquinoline

The positions of substituents in derivatives of the two compounds are indicated by numbers as shown above. The prefixes N, α, β and γ were also used formerly for the pyridine ring of quinoline.

Quinoline itself was first isolated from coal tar by F. F. Runge in 1834. The modern commercial product is obtained from that source or is made synthetically. It also occurs in bone oil. C. F. Gerhardt in 1842 obtained quinoline by heating the alkaloid cinchonine with potassium hydroxide and this was the first evidence of the occurrence of the quinoline nucleus in certain of the natural alkaloids; quinine similarly heated gives 6-methoxyquinoline.

The first synthesis of quinoline was achieved by W. Koenigs in 1879 by passing the vapour of allylaniline over hot lead oxide. A large number of further synthetical methods are available for the preparation of quinoline and its derivatives. Of these, the best known is probably the Skraup reaction (1880), which is of exceedingly wide application; it is employed for the formation of quinoline itself and for that of the derivatives substituted in the benzene ring. A primary aromatic amine is heated with glycerol, sulfuric acid and a mild oxidizing agent, nitrobenzene or arsenic acid being often used. Aniline is converted into quinoline in good yield by this method which can also be applied to practically all aromatic amines.

As was mentioned above, the natural alkaloid quinine contains the quinoline nucleus. Several synthetic antimalarial drugs, which are like quinine in being derivatives of 4-aminoquinoline, have also been prepared; of these, quinacrine (Atabrine) has found the widest use. (*See* MALARIA.)

Quinoline is a colourless, highly refractive oil boiling at 239° C. and with a characteristic smell. It is almost insoluble in water but miscible with organic solvents, and it behaves as a weak monoacidic base. Its salts are readily soluble in water except the bichromate which is sparingly soluble in the cold and can be used for the purification of quinoline. Since the pyridine ring is deactivated by the presence of the nitrogen atom, a substituting reagent such as nitric acid attacks the benzene ring and gives a mixture of the 5- and 8-substituted compounds. Further nitration gives the 5,7- and 6,8-dinitro derivatives.

These nitro compounds can be reduced to amines which behave as true aromatic amines and can be diazotized and converted into other derivatives. Anionoid substituting reagents, such as sodamide, react with the pyridine nucleus in the 2 and 4 positions, and 2-aminoquinoline can be obtained directly by the action of sodamide.

Quinoline and its homologues are tertiary bases and thus react with alkyl halides to give quaternary ammonium salts which show the normal behaviour of strong electrolytes. The quaternary hydroxides derived from these salts are not stable and tend to pass more or less completely into un-ionized forms, as with many other cyclic bases. The reactivity of these compounds is the basis for the preparation of dyestuffs of the cyanine class (isocyanines, pseudocyanines and carbocyanines) which are of great value as sensitizers of the photographic emulsion to wavelengths in the red and infrared.

Isoquinoline is found in coal tar and crude quinoline from that source contains about 4% of isoquinoline. It is a solid melting at 24° C. and boiling at 240° C. and with a smell quite different from that of quinoline. It is more strongly basic than the latter, since the nitrogen atom is not directly attached to the benzene ring, and its sulfate is not very soluble in cold water; separation from quinoline is based on these facts.

The isoquinoline nucleus is found in a number of important alkaloids; *e.g.*, papaverine, berberine, hydrastine and narcotine. A valuable reaction for synthesizing this nucleus is that of A. Bischler and B. Napieralski (1893). Acyl derivatives of β-phenylethylamines when heated with powerful dehydrating agents in boiling xylene or tetralin give 3,4-dihydroisoquinolines which can be dehydrogenated to isoquinolines with permanganate or catalytically with palladium. Many of the isoquinoline alkaloids have been synthesized by means of this reaction.　　(T. W. J. T.)

QUINONES, a group of coloured cyclic organic compounds containing two carbonyl groups, C = O (*see* ALDEHYDES AND KETONES), either adjacent (orthoquinone, I) or separated by a vinyl group, C = C, (paraquinone, II) in a usually six-membered unsaturated ring. All quinones have these features except a few in which the carbonyl groups are located in different rings: *e.g.*, amphinaphthoquinone, III. The term quinone usually refers to the specific compound parabenzoquinone (*p*-benzoquinone), II, but it may also apply to any other compound having the required structural features.

A similar ambiguity exists also for the terms hydroquinone and quinhydrone (*see* below). The general reactions of quinones are entirely analogous to the specific reactions of *p*-benzoquinone.

By a variety of reducing agents, *p*-benzoquinone is easily and quantitatively reduced to its corresponding hydroquinone, IV. This change is readily reversed by oxidizing agents:

$$C_6H_4O_2 + 2H^+ + 2e \rightleftharpoons C_6H_6O_2 \text{ where } e \text{ is an electron.}$$
p-Benzoquinone　　　　　　*p*-Benzohydroquinone

Photographic development is largely a reflection of this oxidation process. Most general-purpose developers are a mixture of hydroquinone and Metol, Elon, or a similar *p*-aminophenol derivative. Contact of the silver salt in the photographic emulsion with the hydroquinone causes reduction of the salt to metallic silver, while the dissolved hydroquinone is oxidized to quinone. This reaction tends to be very sluggish at temperatures below 50° F (10° C),

I

II

III

IV

so that for ordinary purposes warmer solutions must be used.

If a platinum electrode is put into a solution which contains equivalent amounts of some quinone and its hydroquinone, and which is saturated with respect to the addition compound of the two (the so-called quinhydrone), an electric potential is produced which is dependent on the hydrogen ion concentration. By making connection through a suitable conducting solution with a reference half cell, this potential can be measured. A device called the quinhydrone electrode was developed to make use of the above principle in measuring the hydrogen ion concentration of an unknown solution.

The ring of atoms in a quinone is said still to have a quinonoid (or quinoid) character if one of the sets of doubly bonded carbon and oxygen atoms is replaced by another doubly bonded atom pair, or even if both of those sets are so replaced. Quinonoid structures are important in theories concerning the relationship of chemical constitution to colour. Many quinones, among which one of the most important is anthraquinone (*see* ANTHRAQUINONE), are used as dyestuff intermediates. All vat dyes have quinonoid structures. An important feature in the use of vat dyes is the fact that the dye is placed on the cloth while in the hydroquinone state, and the oxidation to the quinone state takes place on exposure to air. (*See* DYES AND DYEING.)

Many quinones occur in natural products. One of the most important of these is vitamin K_1, which possesses the structure V and is the antihemorrhagic agent found in certain green plants. (*See* VITAMINS: *Vitamin K.*) Synthetic quinones, in particular 2-methyl-1,4-naphthoquinone, VI, have similar properties and are used in medical practice.

V

VI

A number of interesting naturally occurring quinones are described in *Advanced Organic Chemistry* by L. F. Fieser and M. A. P. Fieser, pp. 845–875 (1961).　　(M. S. N.; X.)

QUINTANA, MANUEL JOSÉ (1772–1857), Spanish patriot and poet, was born in Madrid, April 11, 1772. A typical Spanish neoclassic, he wrote tragedies (*El Pelayo*), eloquent organ-voiced odes on large humanitarian themes, dared comparison with Plutarch—*Vidas de españoles célebres* (1807–33)—and wrote the best literary criticism of the century in his anthologies *Colección de poesías castellanas* and *Musa épica*. The national respect he earned for his clarion calls for unity against the French invaders never waned (Queen Isabel crowned him national poet in

1855), though his liberalism excluded romanticism and his pen was silent for half a century before his death in Madrid, March 11, 1857.   (R. F. B.)

QUINTANA ROO, a federal territory of Mexico on the eastern side of the Yucatán peninsula, bounded by British Honduras and Guatemala. Pop. (1950) 26,967; (1960) 50,169; area, 16,228 sq.mi. (42,031 sq.km.); formed in 1902 from parts of the states of Yucatán and Campeche. The territory is hot, humid, and heavily forested, with 50 to 60 in. (127 to 152 cm.) of rain annually. Like the rest of the peninsula, Quintana Roo is a level, porous limestone plain through which water percolates to form underground grottoes, caverns, and wells.

The area is populated chiefly by descendants of Maya Indians who in 1847 rebelled in Yucatán and were eventually driven into these fastnesses by continuous military campaigns. Distrustful of Yucatecan Mexicans, they carry on sporadic trade in chicle with British Honduras. Their main contacts with the outside world lie along the narrow-gauge railway that connects Felipe Carrillo Puerto (Santa Cruz de Bravo) to Vigía Chico on Ascensión Bay. Another penetration from the coast inland is by a rail line in the northern section from Leona Vicario (Santa María) to Puerto Morelos. Air strips at various points, and regular service to Belize, British Honduras, and Mérida lessened some of the characteristic isolation of the territory, which for many years was used as a dumping ground for political prisoners.

Chicle and a small amount of copra, produced on the coast near Cozumel Island, are the main products. There are valuable stands of mahogany and other hardwoods which are largely unexploited. Sponge and turtle fishing is significant along the coast. The small Mayan hamlets are nearly self-sufficient.

The capital is Chetumal. The territory contains numerous important archaeological remains of the earlier pre-Spanish Mayan Empire, notably those at Tulum.

In 1517 the first Spanish landing in Mexico was made at Cape Catoche. Hernán Cortés in 1519 landed first on the island of Cozumel alongside Quintana Roo. An airline links the island, now a tourist resort, with Mérida.   (J. A. Cw.)

QUINTESSENCE, according to some Renaissance philosophers (Paracelsus, Heinrich Cornelius Agrippa, Rudolf Goclen), was the purest and most intimate nature of created things. Earlier the Latin term *quinta essentia*, "fifth essence" (equivalent to the Greek *pempte ousia*, which occurs in John Philoponus), was used to denote the thinnest and most divine material element surrounding the world of the four Empedoclean elements (fire, air, water, and earth); the Pythagorean Philolaus (*q.v.*) spoke of a *pempton soma* or "fifth body"; and Aristotle described the ether as a primary substance distinct from the other four.   (L. M.-Po.)

QUINTILIAN (MARCUS FABIUS QUINTILIANUS) (*c.* A.D. 35–*c.* 100), Roman writer whose work on rhetoric is one of the most valuable contributions of the ancient world to educational theory and to literary criticism, was born at Calagurris in Spain (the modern Calahorra in the Logroño province). He received at least part of his education in Rome; the orator Domitius Afer had a share in his training. He went back to Spain (not before A.D. 57), then returned to Rome in the retinue of Galba (68). There he taught rhetoric and was subsequently (*c.* 71?) appointed a public professor of that subject by Vespasian. The younger Pliny was among his pupils. At the same time he was a successful pleader in the law courts. After 20 years spent in these activities he retired (*c.* 90) and devoted himself to writing; it took two years to compose his great work, the *Institutio oratoria* ("The Training of an Orator"), which was published *c.* 95. He achieved fame and wealth; ultimately Domitian made him tutor of his two grandnephews, prospective heirs to the throne, and awarded him the consular insignia. The preface to book vi of the *Institutio* expresses in tenderest terms his grief for the loss of his young wife (when she was 19) and of both his very young sons.

The *Institutio oratoria* was written at a time when, political life being no longer free, eloquence had lost its former power. But it had not lost its prestige. Rhetoric dominated education—in the form essentially of a training in liberal culture. The *Institutio*, in 12 books, provides a comprehensive course of in-

struction taking the student from infancy to the time when he has become a complete orator. Book i deals with the training prior to the study of rhetoric, book ii with the first rhetorical exercises and with declamation, and also with the nature and end of oratory. These two books contain the best Roman thought on education, much of it of enduring value for its practical good sense, sympathetic personal quality and insight into human nature. "Grammar" is considered in its two departments, the art of speaking correctly and the interpretation of literature. Books iii–xi are concerned with the five departments of rhetoric: books iii–vi with "invention" (iii discusses also the origin of rhetoric, and its kinds—of these the judicial receives most attention in the *Institutio* as a whole; in iv–vi invention is applied to the formal parts of a discourse; and vi includes a lively chapter on the arousing of laughter); book vii with arrangement; books viii–x with style (in viii and ix the elements of a good style are treated, and in x various practical methods of assuring command over them).

Book x contains the much-praised survey of Greek and Latin authors recommended to the orator for study, with neat summaries of their outstanding qualities. Often Quintilian gives us the established opinions of his time, but sometimes again he is independent, especially with respect to Roman writers; and his exposition is felicitous and interesting. He reproves certain stylistic abuses of his day (and the influence of Seneca) and would effect a return to the classical tradition of the Golden Age (his greatest admiration is for Cicero), but with concessions to the demands of changed conditions. The subjects of book xi are memory and delivery.

Quintilian's aim was to mold the character as well as to train the intellect (iv, preface, 3); and book xii delineates the ideal orator—taking the elder Cato's definition, "a good man skilled in speaking"—and offers advice for the employment of his gifts in public life. Since eloquence serves the public welfare, it must be fused with virtue; and philosophy is a component part of the rhetorical training. The moral power of this book makes it especially impressive and induces one to overlook the author's occasional lapses, as when he asserts with worldly wisdom that "Sometimes the public interest requires that the speaker defend what is not true" (ii, 17, 36) or accords fulsome praise to Domitian (iv, preface, 3–5).

Quintilian reviews and studies the principles of rhetoric in their fullest scope and variety, preserving what is valuable in the Greek and Roman tradition, but without slavish adherence to any one school; he applies discriminating judgment where the doctrines of his predecessors are contradictory, rejects them when they are absurd. He scorns superstitious conformity to rules as though they were immutable laws and particularly to such as are laid down without experience of actual battle in the courts. The work is everywhere marked by learning, wisdom and taste; and the engaging personality of the author, combining kindliness, sincerity and high principle, shines through it.

Quintilian's style exhibits some of the characteristics of the silver Latin, such as point, the use of rare and poetic words, and occasional looseness of structure, but no writer of his time departs less widely from the best models of the late republican period. The language is on the whole clear, unlaboured, energetic and dignified.

The *Institutio* exerted its greatest influence during the Renaissance and Reformation, after the discovery of a complete text by Poggio at St. Gall (Sankt Gallen) in 1416.

For the text of the *Institutio oratoria* see the edition by L. Radermacher, 2 vol. (1907–35); for the text with Eng. trans., that by H. E. Butler in the "Loeb Series," 4 vol. (1921–22). For commentary *see* Jean Cousin, *Études sur Quintilien* (1936), and the separate editions of book i by F. H. Colson (1924), of book x by W. Peterson (1891; new ed., 1903) and of book xii by R. G. Austin (1948). The text of *Declamationes majores* is ed. by G. Lehnert (1905), that of *Declamationes minores* by C. Ritter (1884).

Quintilian published one other rhetorical work, *De causis corruptae eloquentiae*, which has not survived; it probably dealt with the technical and educational aspects of the decline of oratory rather than the political and social. Of his speeches he published only one (now also lost), in defense of Naevius Arpinianus, accused of killing his wife. The other speeches that once circulated under his name he repudiated as having been corrupted by careless stenographers bent on profit (vii, 2, 24). He disowned also two books on rhetoric which kindly intentioned pupils had published from lecture notes without his authorization (i, preface, 7). Neither of the two extant collections of declamations ascribed to him (*Declamationes majores,* 19 in number; and *Declamationes minores,* 145 from a collection originally numbering 388) is regarded as genuine; both are of uncertain date.

(HY. CN.)

QUINTILLUS (MARCUS AURELIUS CLAUDIUS QUINTILLUS), Roman emperor A.D. 270, was the brother of the emperor Claudius Gothicus, on whose death he was proclaimed emperor at Aquileia. He died or was killed a few weeks later. (JN. R. M.)

QUINTUS SMYRNAEUS (fl. *c.* A.D. 375), Greek epic poet, author of a hexameter poem in 14 books, narrating events at Troy from the funeral of Hector to the departure of the Achaeans after sacking the city (and hence called *Ta met' Homeron* or *Posthomerica*). Quintus claims that the Muses inspired him when, still a beardless lad, he kept sheep near the temple of Artemis (xii, 308–313). His style is monotonous, and his vocabulary and metrics are alike traditional, but his very unoriginality makes his work a valuable guide to the content of the lost epics (*Aethiopis, Little Iliad, Iliupersis*) which had provided men of the classical period with their information about the last days of Troy.

BIBLIOGRAPHY.—Edition with English verse trans. by A. S. Way in the Loeb series (1913, reprinted 1943). *See also* F. Vian, *Recherches sur les Posthomerica de Quintus de Smyrne* (1959). For Quintus' relations with earlier epic *see* W. Kullmann, *Die Quellen der Ilias* (1960), and R. Heinze, *Virgils epische Technik,* 3rd ed. (1915, reprinted 1957). C. A. Sainte-Beuve, *Étude sur . . . Quinte de Smyrne,* 3rd ed. (1878), is still worth reading. (JN. A. D.)

QUIPU, a knotted cord used by the Incas of ancient Peru and other Indians of the central Andes as a mnemonic aid and recording device. Many quipus were found in Inca graves and have been acquired by museums. They were still (1960s) in limited use as simple recording devices in the central Andes. The Inca type consisted of a heavy, central cord from which 1 to 100 variously coloured strings were suspended. A single knot or loop in a pendant string represented a number from 1 to 9, depending on the distance of the loop from the central cord. There also were positions for tens, hundreds, thousands, and ten thousands. Various meanings have been suggested for the different colours used, such as: white for silver, yellow for gold, black for elapsed time (nights), red for soldiers or warfare. Different types of knots were employed, lumped together or spaced in certain ways.

Quipus were used to record statistical information, such as census reports, numbers of livestock, and production figures; probably they were used also in recording and reciting genealogies, in narrating legends, and for recalling the proper order of complex ceremonial events. As time went on, historical events, laws, and edicts may have been communicated by means of quipus. Apparently the quipu was not a calculating device, since the Incas seem to have used a pebble-type abacus for that purpose. In the Guianas, knotted strings were used as timekeepers for ceremonial events; and similar mnemonic devices were used in the Old World. *See also* MESSAGE STICK.

See J. H. Steward (ed.), *Handbook of South American Indians,* vol. 5, pp. 616–619, with bibliography (1949); J. H. Steward and L. C. Faron, *Native Peoples of South America* (1959). (L. C. FA.)

QUIRINO, ELPIDIO (1890–1956), second president of the Republic of the Philippines, was born Nov. 16, 1890, in Vigan, in Ilocos Sur Province, on the island of Luzon. He attended high school in Manila and took his law degree at the University of the Philippines. Quirino served in the Philippine House of Representatives (1919–25) and in the Senate (1925–31). He was a member of the Philippine independence mission which helped to obtain the passage in the U.S. Congress in 1934 of the Tydings-McDuffie Act under which the Philippines achieved independence on July 4, 1946. Also in 1934 he was elected to the Constitutional Convention. Thereafter he served as secretary of finance and later as

secretary of the interior in the Commonwealth government (1935–38). He was elected to the Senate in 1941 and stayed in the Philippines during the Japanese occupation. After the war, Quirino again became secretary of finance in May 1946. As the candidate of the newly formed Liberal Party, he became vice-president and secretary of foreign affairs of the new republic in July 1946. He succeeded to the presidency on the death of Pres. Manuel Roxas in 1948 and was elected president in 1949. During his term of office an intensive program of economic development was initiated with the assistance of the United States, the treaty of peace was signed with Japan, and a new mutual defense treaty was concluded with the United States in 1951. The Hukbalahaps, or social dissidents in Luzon, were pacified primarily because of the efforts of his secretary of defense, Ramón Magsaysay. After being defeated for reelection in 1953 by Magsaysay he retired to private life and died on Feb. 28, 1956.

Quirino's six years as president were marked by notable post-World War II reconstruction progress and by general economic gains, although members of his administration were accused of corruption in office—which contributed to his 1953 defeat despite his vigorous campaigning in the midst of serious illness. *See also* PHILIPPINES: *History.* (C. A. B.)

QUIRINUS, a major Roman deity ranking close to Jupiter and Mars (*qq.v.*). Their *flamines* constituted the three major priests at Rome. His name is in adjectival form and would seem to mean "he of the *quirium,*" a word generally taken to signify the very ancient Sabine settlement which united with the Palatine community to form the original Rome. It has also been derived, however, from *covirium,* meaning "assembly of men." That the Quirinal, traditional site of Sabine settlement, was the seat of his cult there is no doubt, and the Sabine origin of the god is reflected in Ovid (*Fasti* II, 475). In spite of his importance rather little is known about Quirinus. He bears a similarity to Mars, and some believe that he is only another form of that deity. By the late republic he is identified completely with Romulus, a confusion perhaps originally suggested by Quirites (*q.v.*). (*See* also ROMULUS AND REMUS.) He had a festival, the Quirinalia, on Feb. 17; his temple on the Quirinal was one of the oldest in Rome. A cult partner Hora is spoken of, also minor deities, the Virites Quirini, of whom nothing else is known. Janus (*q.v.*) appears with the epithet Quirinus, but the relationship between the two is a matter of conjecture.

BIBLIOGRAPHY.—W. W. Fowler, *Roman Festivals,* pp. 322–324 (1899); G. Wissowa, *Religion und Kultus,* 2nd ed., pp. 153 ff. (1912); F. Altheim, *History of Roman Religion,* pp. 138 ff. (1938). (R. B. LD.)

QUIRITES, an early term, of uncertain derivation, for the citizens of Rome. Ancient scholars associated the word with Sabine *Cures* as typifying the Sabine element in Rome, with the Sabine deity Quirinus and the Quirina tribe. In the phrase "populus Romanus Quiritium" it denoted the individual citizen as contrasted with the community, and *ius Quiritium* in Roman law denoted the full body of rights of Roman citizenship. Any military connotations were soon lost, so the term refers to citizens as civilians. Julius Caesar, it is said, quelled a mutiny among his soldiers by addressing them as "Quirites." (T. R. S. B.)

QUIROGA, HORACIO (1878–1937), Uruguayan short-story writer, became famous for his ability to portray man's futile struggle against the tropical jungle in the Argentine territory of Misiones. Born Dec. 31, 1878, in Salto, he spent a good part of his life in Argentina, taking frequent trips from Buenos Aires to San Ignacio in the jungle province of Misiones. This primitive environment as well as his many personal experiences in the jungle furnished material for most of his *cuentos.*

His early period of literary apprenticeship, marked by his tendency to emulate the modernistic fashion, is reflected in his first book, *Los arrecifes de coral* (1901), a collection of prose and verse; he soon realized, however, that his talent was better suited to short stories. Some of his finest compositions, *Cuentos de la selva* (1918), *El salvaje* (1920), *Anaconda* (1921), *El desierto* (1924), *Los desterrados* (1926), and others, belong to this genre. *Más allá* (1935) reflects the depressed mood of his later years when he suffered from ill health and other misfortunes. He took his own life in a charity hospital in Buenos Aires, Feb. 19, 1937.

(H. Co.)

QUISLING, VIDKUN ABRAHAM LAURITZ JONSSON (1887–1945), Norwegian fascist whose name became synonymous with "traitor." An army officer, he served as military attaché in Petrograd (later Leningrad) and Helsinki and later assisted Fridtjof Nansen in Russian relief. From 1927 to 1929 he represented British interests at the Norwegian legation in Moscow. He became Norwegian minister of defense in the Agrarian government, 1931–33. Resigning, he founded the fascist Nasjonal Samling (National Union) Party, but never won a seat in the *storting*. Friendly to the Nazis, he visited Hitler in December 1939 and collaborated in the German invasion of Norway in April 1940. The new regime proclaimed by him so incensed the Norwegians that it collapsed within a week, but he continued to lead Nasjonal Samling, the only party permitted by the Germans. On Feb. 1, 1942, Reichskommissar Joseph Terboven named him "minister president." Quisling's attempts to nazify the Norwegian Church, schools, and youth aroused bitter opposition. He persecuted the Jews, sending almost 1,000 to death in concentration camps. Despite difficulties with his party and the Germans, he held office until Norway was liberated in May 1945. Arrested, tried, and found guilty of treason and other crimes, he was executed on Oct. 24, 1945.   (HD. LN.)

QUITO, the capital of Ecuador and of the province of Pichincha, is situated about 114 mi. (183 km.) from the Pacific in a narrow Andean valley. Pop. (1962) 354,746; (1968 est.) 483,847. It was already an ancient city when the Spaniards arrived there in the 16th century, since the Incas had established an empire there in 1487. Between that date and the year 1000 it was ruled by the Shyris, sovereigns of the Caras, who are said to have come "by way of the sea." Prior to the Caras, it was the seat of the kingdom of the Quitus, the largest unit of an Indian tribal confederation that left no recorded history. Sebastián de Belalcázar, one of Pizarro's lieutenants, occupied it on Dec. 6, 1534. In the presence of his soldiers and 206 native inhabitants, he set up a municipal council (*cabildo*) and declared it in operation. He planned Quito as a typical Spanish city with streets running north and south, east and west from the central square, or *plaza mayor*.

Quito lies on the lower slopes of the Pichincha (15,700 ft. [4,785 m.]), a volcano that last erupted in 1666. The central plaza, bounded by the cathedral, the palaces of the president and the archbishop, and the municipal building, is only 15 mi. (24 km.) south of the equator, but because of its altitude of 9,350 ft. (2,850 m.) Quito enjoys a stimulating climate, the mean temperature at noon being 70° F (21° C). Carved by two ravines spanned by masonry bridges, the city, oldest of all South American capitals, preserves much of its ancient atmosphere. The towers of numerous churches outlined against a circle of volcanoes, peaceful squares, fountains, balconied houses, steep streets, iron-grilled doorways, and secluded gardens mark it as a place of charm.

Quito of the Spaniards was not a year old when the Franciscans established an art school, the first of its kind in South America. Thus began a celebrated religious art movement that flourished throughout the colonial period, leaving a wealth of polychrome sculpture in wood, and paintings without equal in the New World. Indian artists made of the churches, cloisters, and old mansions of Quito veritable museums. The names of the sculptor Manuel Chili (Caspicara), and the painters Adrián Sánchez Galque, Miguel de Santiago, and Gorívar González, among others, are noteworthy. Among the most admired Quiteño churches and convents are La Compañía (Jesuit), whose baroque columns, ceilings, and massive altars are covered with gold leaf; San Francisco, with its magnificent cloister; Carmen Alto, where the native Saint Mariana de Jesús lived and died; San Agustín, famous for carved ceilings, and Santo Domingo, noted for a handsome façade; the Sagrario, where Ecuadorean independence was declared in 1809; and the 17th-century cathedral, burial place of the hero of independence, Antonio José de Sucre. Also worth mentioning is the church of the Merced convent, decorated in the Quiteño style by the contemporary Ecuadorean artist Víctor Mideros.

LA COMPAÑÍA CHURCH, QUITO, CONSIDERED ONE OF THE FINEST IN SOUTH AMERICA, IS RENOWNED FOR THE GOLD LEAF THAT COVERS MUCH OF ITS INTERIOR

Although the city's convents and monasteries and its museum of colonial art indicate the deeply religious and contemplative character of its life, Quito is no longer an isolated capital, as in the past. There is a modern and busy airport meeting all international standards, including a 9,000-ft. (2,743-m.) runway required at that altitude. Quito has several daily newspapers and broadcasting stations, new housing projects for workers, and athletic fields. Factories produce everything from textiles and soap to matches, shoes, hats, soft drinks, cosmetics, ready-to-wear apparel, and pharmaceutical products. There are two institutions of higher learning, Central University founded in 1787 and the new Catholic University, offering facilities for the study of all the liberal and technical professions; also a technological institute, national library, astronomical observatory, and conservatory of music. The city has several hospitals and a nursing school, two schools of social work, an American grade and high school, many modern residential developments, and good public utilities. The city is governed by a municipal council of 11 councilmen, headed by the mayor of the city. The council is elected by popular vote every four years.

Ecuadoreans are proud of the *Casa de la Cultura*, a cultural centre created in 1943 and financed with a share of the export duties. It acts as publisher and distributor of the works of Ecuadorean writers and organizes concerts, lectures, art exhibits, and theatrical performances. In addition, it awards prizes for scientific research, and literary and artistic excellence.

Among the characteristic sights of Quito are several outdoor markets or fairs operating once a week in different quarters of the city. Equally typical are the countless diminutive shops where native craftsmen make silver jewelry, religious figurines, rugs, shoes, men's suits, furniture, and other items. Although Quito is predominantly Roman Catholic there are a number of Protestant churches and a Jewish synagogue.   (C. R. J.; P. DE S.)

QUOITS: *see* Horseshoe Pitching.

QUORUM, the number of members whose presence is required before a meeting can legally take action. The quorum refers to the number present, not to the number voting. The presiding officer, in determining the presence of a quorum, counts all members visible, whether voting or not; he is not required to announce the names of members so counted. A quorum is a majority unless the law, charter, constitution, by-laws, or articles creating the body fixes it at a different figure or proportion.

The term quorum came into use in the commission formerly issued to justices of the peace in England. In a day when legal scholarship on the local bench was the exception rather than the rule, it was necessary in commissioning the members of the court to add "of whom" one or two or three should be men of sufficient learning and experience to discharge the technical duties of the tribunal. These became known as the quorum, without whom the court did not sit.

The presence of a quorum is required for the transaction of all business. In the absence of a quorum, pending business is suspended and no business, however highly privileged, may be transacted even by unanimous consent. The minutes of the previous meeting cannot be read or approved without a quorum, and the point of "no quorum" may be made at any time before the reading is completed. However, prayer by a chaplain of a legislative assembly does not require a quorum, and the chair declines to entertain a point of "no quorum" before prayer is offered.

A quorum is necessary even for debate. Any member may raise the question of "no quorum" and the chair is constrained to recognize for that purpose even though another member has the floor. The absence of a quorum invalidates proceedings in which the question of a quorum was raised, and pending business retains the exact status it occupied at that time. However, if proceedings have been completed, it is too late to make the point of order that a quorum was not present.

In the absence of a quorum the meeting must either adjourn or secure a quorum. The only motions admissible are those to fix the time at which to adjourn, to adjourn, to recess, or to further the effort to secure a quorum. The previous question may be ordered on a motion incidental to securing a quorum, and an appeal from the decision of the chair is in order in that connection. A quorum is not necessary in order to adjourn, but the point of "no quorum" is in order on a negative vote on adjournment.

When a quorum is obviously present, the chair may decline to entertain a point of "no quorum" as dilatory.

As in the parent body, a majority of a standing committee is a quorum and is essential to the transaction of business. Boards of directors or trustees fall into this category. No report of a standing committee is valid unless authorized by a majority vote taken at a formal meeting of the committee with a quorum present, but it is too late to raise the question after the report has been received and taken up for consideration. Furthermore, a report adopted by a majority vote, with a quorum present, at a duly authorized meeting, is binding even though the number subsequently signing minority views outnumber those who voted for the report.

A session of a standing committee, having adjourned without securing a quorum, is *dies non* and may not be counted in determining the admissibility of a motion to reconsider. When the committee adjourns on a stated day of meeting for lack of a quorum, subsequent sessions on the same day, even when attended by a quorum, are not competent for the transaction of business.

A point of "no quorum" may be withdrawn at any time prior to ascertainment and pronouncement by the chair, but not after absence of a quorum has been determined and announced.

If it has been erroneously announced that a quorum has voted when the roll later discloses the absence of a quorum on the vote, the chair declares subsequent proceedings void.

See also Rules of Order. (C. Ca.)

QUOTAS, IMPORT AND EXPORT, are measures that directly limit the quantity or, in exceptional cases, the value of goods or services that may be exported or imported. They stand in contrast to controls that operate by making imports or exports more expensive but without fixing a limit on the quantity; of these latter, tariffs, which put a special tax on exports or imports, are the main type.

The principal quantitative trade controls are the quota, payments restrictions (exchange controls), licensing, and monopoly systems. Under the monopoly system a governmental agency has an exclusive monopoly for the import or export of the restricted commodities. The distinction between the quota, exchange control, and licensing system is not so clear-cut. By exchange control is meant the complex of measures controlling and regulating international payments which enable a country to maintain the international value of its currency at a higher level than it would have in the absence of these controls. One of the most important of this complex of measures is the quantitative restriction of imports by quotas and licences. There is a tendency to speak of quotas when the quantities are determined in advance and the rules for the distribution of the quota among countries of origin and traders are more or less clearly formulated; and of a licence system when the granting of import licences is left to the discretion of the administrative organs. This article refers chiefly to quotas, but much of what is said holds of exchange control and licensing and monopoly systems as well.

Some quotas are fixed by autonomous action of one country while others are fixed by two or more countries operating in agreement. Another distinction is between import quotas and tariff quotas. A tariff quota is a regulation that permits the import of a certain quantity (quota) of a commodity duty free (or at a specially low duty), while quantities exceeding the quota are subjected to a (higher) duty. An absolute or import quota restricts imports absolutely. Another type is the milling or mixing quota; this is a rule requiring that imports of, say, barley must be milled or mixed in a certain proportion with home-grown grain. In the following, reference will be made chiefly to absolute import quotas.

Throughout the last quarter of the 19th century and up to 1914 the predominant method of trade control was the tariff. In the 20th century quantitative restrictions on trade were first imposed on a large scale during and immediately after World War I. During 1914 to 1918 such controls were an integral part of war economics, and for Great Britain they were imperative because of the acute shortage of shipping. After the Armistice, quotas were fairly rapidly abolished except in central and eastern Europe. There the dislocations produced by the war were much more serious than elsewhere. Trade was resumed, first, on the basis of intergovernmental barter and then on that of general prohibitions modified by licences. During the 1920s quotas were progressively abolished and replaced by tariff protection. The next great wave of quota protection of trade came with the great depression in the early 1930s. Especially after 1931 one country after another introduced quantitative restrictions, first on cereals and certain other foodstuffs and then on a great variety of agricultural and industrial products. France was the first large country to introduce a comprehensive quota system (1931), but it was followed by practically all European countries. In 1935 and 1936 there was a slight relaxation, but this movement toward somewhat freer trade soon came to an end. Everywhere economies were being geared for the approaching war; and a tightly controlled trade is an integral part of a war economy. The United States was the only important country that made very little use of quotas during the 1930s. The only significant U.S. quota was on sugar.

After the end of World War II quotas and other quantitative restrictions on imports and exports were widely used at first to meet pressing needs of physical and currency shortages and later to maintain equilibrium in the balance of payments. In the U.S. they were used more than before the war for the purpose of restricting imports of agricultural products, especially those supported by the agricultural parity price program.

After 1955 the rapid recovery of the industrial countries of Western Europe, the restoration of confidence in their currencies, and the disappearance of the dollar shortage brought about a gradual dismantling of quantitative import restrictions by those countries. In the United States, on the other hand, somewhat more use was made of quotas for the restriction of imports (*e.g.,* crude petroleum, lead, zinc). Textile imports from Hong Kong and

Japan were restricted on a quota basis by "voluntary" agreements with those countries. Quantitative restrictions are widely used by many underdeveloped countries where open or repressed inflation prevailed. The General Agreement on Tariffs and Trade (GATT) in Geneva tried with little success to discourage the use of quantitative restrictions and to enforce an orderly, nonarbitrary and nondiscriminatory administration of quantitative restrictions.

Why did quotas become so popular and how does quota protection differ from tariff protection? The increasing use made of quantitative trade controls is a phase in the trend toward autarky and protection observable from about 1878. Tariffs went higher and higher, the last free-trade countries (Great Britain, the Netherlands, Denmark) introduced protective measures, and eventually quantitative restrictions were piled on top of tariffs. But quotas are a much more effective device for restricting trade than tariffs and much more disturbing to the international trade mechanism. Under the tariff system, volume and value of trade, although restricted, are still flexible. The flow of goods changes according to changes in demand and supply at home and abroad. Despite an import duty, imports can rise if cost of production and prices fall abroad or rise at home. Thus the effect of a tariff can be offset by a depreciation of the foreign currency or by an export subsidy but a quota constitutes a rigid bar to imports. This is one of the main reasons why during the great depression of the 1930s one country after the other switched from tariffs to quotas. Tariffs were no longer regarded as sufficient protection in the face of violently changing prices, unstable currencies, and extensive utilization of export subsidies. Another related reason was that tariffs could in many cases not be increased at short notice without violating international treaties, while such treaties did not mention, and therefore were thought not to prohibit, the imposition of quotas. Quotas are a more powerful weapon of discrimination between individual countries and traders. This makes them popular with economic nationalists and protectionists in all countries. In fact, it has been practically impossible to find a method of quota allocation which could be called nondiscriminatory and in accordance with the most-favoured-nation principle, while under the tariff system nondiscrimination has a precise, generally accepted meaning. During the post-World War II period the principal motive for the use of quotas and other quantitative import restrictions was the balance of payments difficulties (dollar shortage) experienced by many countries. These problems stemmed from inflation and overvaluation of currencies.

An important characteristic of the mode of operation of quotas differentiates them sharply from tariffs. If a quota is effective, *i.e.*, if it is smaller than the quantity which would be imported in the absence of the quota, it creates a price differential between the importing and exporting country which is not covered by transportation cost plus duty. Under the tariff system, too, the price of the taxed commodity will be higher in the importing than in the exporting country, but (except if the tariff becomes prohibitive and imports cease altogether) the price difference tends to be equal to transportation cost plus duty; if it were greater, imports would increase; if it were smaller, imports would fall until the price differential was again equal to transportation cost plus tax. Under the quota system this mechanism is eliminated. It follows that the importation of the quota-restricted commodities becomes a very lucrative business. Under the tariff system the price difference flows into the coffers of the government; under the quota system it flows into private pockets, and in all countries with extensive quota systems fortunes have been made by importers. The consequence is that the government is forced to distribute the quota among individual traders.

When quotas were first introduced in 1931, many countries made the mistake of fixing only global quotas and of letting everybody import until the quota was exhausted. Naturally every trader tried to import at once as much as possible, and the quota was exhausted within the first few days of the period (usually a month or a quarter of a year) for which it was fixed. Distribution of the licences to import within the quota must be made according to some prin-

ciple. It should be remembered that the granting of an import licence under the quota system is equivalent to the granting of an unearned income. While under the tariff system the selection of the actual importers is left to the automatic mechanism of the market and is no concern of the government, under the quota system the authorities have to decide how much each trader is allowed to import. The import function ceases to be a business activity where success depends on commercial efficiency and imagination, but becomes a sinecure handed out by government agencies. In the 1930s, the usual procedure was to distribute quotas among countries of origin and individual traders (usually importers but sometimes also foreign exporters) in proportion to the imports from the respective countries effected by the individual traders in some base period which was considered as "normal." It is easy to see that this is not a satisfactory solution and that it becomes less and less satisfactory as time goes on and the underlying situation changes. But the fact that quotas give rise to large profits, made in connection with imports and exports, has made the system popular with importers and exporters. This popularity is enhanced by the fact that quota restriction, much more than tariffs, facilitates monopolistic price policies by domestic producers. All these unavoidable abuses, inefficiencies, and inconveniences made it unlikely and undesirable that the quota system would replace the tariff system. *See* MOST-FAVOURED-NATION TREATMENT; TARIFFS.

BIBLIOGRAPHY.—F. A. Haight, *French Import Quotas* (1935); C. R. Whittlesey, "Import Quotas in the United States," *Quarterly Journal of Economics*, vol. 52, pp. 37–65 (Nov. 1937); H. Heuser, *Control of International Trade* (1939); M. S. Gordon, *Barriers to World Trade* (1941); *Trade Regulations of Commercial Policy of the United Kingdom*, National Institute of Economic and Social Research (1943); G. Haberler and M. Hill, *Quantitative Trade Controls—Their Causes and Nature*, League of Nations publication (1943); J. Viner, *Trade Relations Between Free-Market and Controlled Economies*, League of Nations publication (1943); W. Diebold, *New Directions in Our Trade Policy* (1941); C. Wilcox, *A Charter for World Trade* (1949); W. A. Brown, *The United States and the Restoration of World Trade* (1950); Henry Chalmers, *World Trade Policies* (1953); Annual Reports of Secretariat of General Agreement on Tariffs and Trade (1951 *et seq.*); J. E. Meade, *Trade and Welfare* (1955).   (G. HL.)

QUTB UD-DIN AIBAK (d. 1210), general of Mohammed of Ghor (*q.v.*) and a founder of Muslim rule in India, was brought in childhood from Turkistan to be sold as a slave. Qutb ud-Din was brought up at Nishapur by Qazi Fakhr ud-Din Kufi before coming into the possession of Mohammed of Ghor who promoted him to be *amir-i-akhur* in charge of the royal stables. Eventually he was appointed to the military command of Kuhram (in the former Patiala state) captured from the Chauhans after their defeat at the second battle of Tara'in in 1192. During Mohammed of Ghor's absences, Qutb ud-Din acted as the principal Ghorid commander in Hindustan. Establishing his headquarters at Delhi about 1193, Qutb ud-Din subjugated areas between the Ganges and the Jumna before joining Mohammed of Ghor in defeating the Gahadavala ruler, Jaichand, at Chandawar in 1194. Despite this important victory, Rajput opposition to the Turks was far from overawed and campaigns followed in swift succession against Ajmer (1195), Anhilwara (1197), Bada'un (1197–98), Kannauj (1198–99) and Kalinjar (1202–03). After the assassination of Mohammed of Ghor in 1206, Qutb ud-Din moved to Lahore and assumed power there. He was not, as is sometimes stated, the founder of an independent Delhi sultanate. Surviving inscriptions describe him as no more than *malik* or *sipahsalar*. Until his death in 1210 from injuries received in a game of *chaugan* (a kind of polo), he kept his headquarters at Lahore. In 1208, he occupied Ghazni, only to be expelled by a rival, Yilduz. Although Qutb ud-Din apparently made no attempt between 1206 and 1210 to consolidate and extend the earlier Ghorid conquests in Hindustan proper, it was his leadership, generalship and loyal service to Mohammed of Ghor that made it possible for Iltutmish to establish the independent sultanate of Delhi (*q.v.*).

See A. B. M. Habibullah, *The Foundation of Muslim Rule in India*, 2nd rev. ed. (1961).   (P. H.)

THE letter corresponding to modern R in the ancient Semitic alphabet was 𐤓 (*resh*), perhaps deriving from an earlier sign representing a head. Greek *rho* is found in a form practically unchanged in the early inscriptions from the island of Thera. The same form also occurs in early inscriptions from Attica and Corinth and in the Chalcidic alphabet. The most usual Greek form was rounded P; this is the form in which the letter occurs in the Lydian alphabet. A form D in which the loop is extended to the bottom of the vertical stroke also occurs in both the eastern and western alphabets. This was the form of the letter in the Umbrian and Oscan alphabets of Italy, while Etruscan had a form in which the loop reached nearly to the bottom. In the Chalcidic alphabet a form ʀ with an additional oblique stroke occurred, and this must be the ultimate source of the Latin form, in which the oblique stroke was exaggerated.

The minuscule form has been subject to many variations. In cursive Latin of the 6th century occurred a form ⋀ in which the loop has disappeared, the three right-hand oblique strokes, or the loop and oblique stroke, being reduced to a single stroke. The Irish form in the 7th century was ⋂ in which a similar process had taken place, but the remnants of the loop and oblique stroke had become extended in a horizontal direction. On the basis of this was formed the Carolingian ⲅ, in which the vertical stroke was not extended below the line. The Carolingian form is the minuscule ꞃ of modern printing, but in handwriting it still contends with the form ⋌, resembling the Latin cursive tradition.

The sound represented by the letter has been in general the liquid formed by contact between the tip of the tongue and the palate, but its precise quality differs considerably from one language or dialect to another. The trilled *r* produced by rolling the tip of the tongue, is found not only in several continental languages but in certain dialects of English as well. The back or uvular *r* is characteristic of standard French and is current in many parts of Germany. In southern England and the eastern United States the *r* is feebly pronounced and in final position is often dropped altogether. The spelling with initial *rh* is practically limited to words of Greek origin (*e.g.*, rhetoric), where it represents the classical Greek writing of *rho* with a rough breathing (ῥ-) to indicate an unvoiced pronunciation. It has intruded itself incorrectly in "rhyme" (for "rime") and in "Rhegium," "Rhaetic." (B. F. C. A.; J. W. P.)

RAABE, WILHELM (1831–1910), German novelist, an important representative of middle-class realism in the second half of the 19th century, was born on Sept. 8, 1831, in Eschershausen, near the Weser, in Lower Saxony, the son of a lawyer. After four years' apprenticeship to a bookseller in Magdeburg, he studied at Berlin university for two years (1854–56). It was as a student that he became conscious of his gift for writing and from that time he lived as an independent writer in Wolfenbüttel, Stuttgart (1862–70) and finally in Brunswick, where he spent the last 40 years of his life and where he died on Nov. 15, 1910.

Raabe's philosophical and artistic development was as complicated as, externally, his life was unremarkable. His early writings show traces of classical and romantic influence and are sentimentally idealistic. They include *Die Chronik der Sperlingsgasse* (1857), the historical novel *Unseres Herrgotts Kanzlei* (1862) and two novels showing the evolution of character, *Die Leute aus dem Walde* (1863) and *Der Hungerpastor* (1864; Eng. trans. 1885). His book *Drei Federn* (1865) was the beginning of a new creative period which reached its peak in the great contemporary novels *Abu Telfan* (1868; Eng. trans. 1881) and *Der Schüdderump* (1870). In the novels of this period Raabe's realistic, often satirical, attitude was an attack on the illusions with which the middle classes glossed over the questions of human existence and of the contemporary social order. The human situation then appeared to him as basically tragic, and he approached, independently, the pessimism of Schopenhauer, without, however, sharing his skepticism.

In his third period, which began in the middle of the 1870s, Raabe found the strength to accept human existence in spite of its unsatisfactoriness. This position grew out of ethical conviction, sustained by sympathy and helpfulness, and expressed itself in the creation of figures representative of fundamental human potentialities. This reconciliation with the world found its happiest expression, from the literary point of view, in humour. Formally speaking, the once prominent realism of his writing deepened to a symbolic realism through an illumination of the essential. Notable works of this last period are *Horacker* (1876), *Alte Nester* (1880), *Das Horn von Wanza* (1881), *Unruhige Gäste* (1886), *Das Odfeld* (1889), *Stopfkuchen* (1891), *Die Akten des Vogelsangs* (1896) and *Hastenbeck* (1899).

BIBLIOGRAPHY.—*Sämtliche Werke*, historical and critical ed. by K. Hoppe, 21 vol. (1951 *et seq.*); F. Meyen, *Raabe-Bibliographie* (1955; supplementary vol. 1 of above ed.); *Werke*, ed. by K. Hoppe with notes and biography, 4 vol. (1961–63). *See also* W. Fehse, *W. Raabe, Leben und Werke* (1937); H. Pongs, *W. Raabe, Leben und Werk* (1958); G. Mayer, *Die geistige Entwicklung W. Raabes* (1960); B. Fairley, *W. Raabe: an Introduction to His Novels* (1961; Ger. trans. 1961); *Jahrbuch der Raabe-Gesellschaft* (1960 *et seq.*). (K. HE.)

RAB (Ital. ARBE), an island in the Adriatic Sea forming the northernmost point of Dalmatia, Yugos. Pop. (1961) 8,369. Rab is 13.3 mi. (21.4 km.) long; its greatest breadth is 6.8 mi. (10.9 km.). The capital of the same name is one of the best-known Yugoslav seaside resorts, a walled town of rare charm on the steep ridge of the west coast. At the seaward end is the 13th-century cathedral in Romanesque style, behind which the belfries of four churches rise in a row along the crest of the ridge. Behind these again are the castle and a background of desolate hills. The island also has six villages. Agriculture and fishing are the main occupations. Rab was the birthplace of Marco Antonio de Dominis (d. 1624), the Italian theologian. (V. DE.)

RABAH ZUBAYR (ZOBEIR) (d. 1900), the conqueror of Bornu (an ancient sultanate on the western shores of Lake Chad, included since 1890 in Nigeria), was a half-Arab, half-Negro chief-

NAME OF FORM	APPROXIMATE DATE	FORM OF LETTER
PHOENICIAN	1200 B.C.	𐤓
CRETAN	600	𐤓
THERAEAN	700-600	𐤓
ARCHAIC LATIN	700-500	P
ATTIC	600	𐤓
CORINTHIAN	600	𐤓
CHALCIDIAN	600	P
IONIC	403	ᑫ
ROMAN COLONIAL	PRECLASSICAL AND CLASSICAL TIMES	ꝶ ʀ ʀ ʀ
URBAN ROMAN		R
FALISCAN		ʀ ᴙ ꝶ
OSCAN		◁ D D
UMBRIAN		D D
CLASSICAL LATIN AND ONWARD		R

DEVELOPMENT OF LETTER "R" FROM EARLIEST TIMES TO THE PRESENT

tain and originally a slave or follower of Zubayr Pasha Rahma Mansur. In 1879, Zubayr being in Egypt, his son Suleiman and Rabah were in command of Zubayr's forces in the Bahr el Ghazal. They persisted in slave raiding, and denied the khedive's authority. Col. (later Gen.) C. G. Gordon, governor general of the Sudan, therefore sent against them Romolo Gessi Pasha. Gessi captured Suleiman and routed Rabah, who in July 1879 fled westward with some 700 Bazingirs (black slave soldiers).

He made himself master of Kreich and Dar Banda, countries to the south and southwest of Wadai. He finally established himself in Baguirmi, a state southeast of Lake Chad. In 1893 Rabah overthrew the sultan of Bornu. In his administration of the country he showed considerable ability and a sense of public needs. To the British, represented by the Royal Niger Company, Rabah gave comparatively little trouble. Early in 1897 he began an advance in the direction of Kano, the most important city in the Fulani Empire. The news of the crushing defeat by Sir George Goldie of the Fulani at Bida induced Rabah to return to Bornu. He now turned his attention to the French. Émile Gentil had in this same year (1897) reached Lake Chad, via the Congo and Baguirmi, and had installed a French resident with the sultan of Baguirmi. As soon as Gentil had withdrawn, Rabah again fell upon Baguirmi and forced sultan and resident to flee. In 1899 the French sent an expedition to reconquer the country, but it was only after a third encounter (April 22, 1900) that Rabah was slain and his host defeated. The chieftain's head was cut off and taken to the French camp.

The French continued the campaign against Rabah's sons, two of whom were killed. Rabah had left instructions that if his army was finally defeated by the French, his successor should return to Bornu and make friends with the British. Rabah's third son, Fader-Allah, accordingly threw himself entirely upon British protection. But in the later part of 1901 Fader-Allah, who had 2,500 riflemen, again made aggressive movements against the French. In retaliation, French forces pursued him into British territory. A battle was fought at Gujba, Fader-Allah being defeated. He fled mortally wounded and died the same night.

RABANUS (HRABANUS) **MAURUS, MAGNENTIUS** (780–856), abbot of Fulda and archbishop of Mainz, one of the leading teachers of the Carolingian period, was born at Mainz in 780. From the school at Fulda he went to study at Tours under Alcuin, who called him Maurus after St. Benedict's favourite disciple. His passion was the accumulation of knowledge, and he became the head of the school at Fulda, where he greatly increased the library. He was made abbot in 822, but resigned in 842 for personal and political reasons, only to become in 847 archbishop of Mainz, where he died on Feb. 4, 856.

In all his numerous writings Rabanus did not attempt to be original but was content from his great range of reading to use the work of others. So his encyclopaedic *De naturis rerum* owes almost everything to Isidore of Seville, and his massive commentaries for students and teachers on various books of the Bible are based on material taken from the Church Fathers. The same is true of his collection of homilies, his influential educational work *De institutione clericorum* and his verse as a whole. His *De laudibus sanctae crucis* contains a number of ingenious *carmina figurata* (verse in which the lines are superimposed on a drawing so that the individual letters along the outline of the drawing can be read to form further words or sentences). Rabanus' one poem not in quantitative metre incorporates, with adaptations, Columba's *Altus prosator*. There is no evidence for attributing the hymn *Veni, creator spiritus* to Rabanus. Rabanus' importance rests on his merits as a teacher and on his encouragement of the study of the ancient authors, though always for Christian ends. He was deservedly called *praeceptor Germaniae,* for under him Fulda became a rival of Tours.

BIBLIOGRAPHY.—Works in J. P. Migne, *Patrologia Latina,* vol. 107–112 (1851–52); poems ed. by E. Dümmler in *Monumenta Germaniae historica. Poetae Latini aevi Carolini,* vol. 2, pp. 159–258 (1884); *De institutione clericorum,* ed. by A. Koepfler (1901). See also M. Manitius, *Geschichte der lateinischen Literatur des Mittelalters,* vol. 1, pp. 288–302 (1911); P. Lehmann, *Erforschung des Mittelalters,* vol. 3 (1960).   (F. J. E. R.)

RABAT, the political capital of the kingdom of Morocco, North Africa, lies on the Atlantic coast, at the mouth of the Bou Regreg, 57 mi. (92 km.) NE of Casablanca and 174 mi. (280 km.) SW of Tangier by road. Rabat, on the south bank, is separated by the Bou Regreg from the town of Salé (Sla) opposite. Pop. (1960) 227,445; of whom 182,295 were Muslim, 11,008 Jewish, and 34,142 non-Moroccan.

The old town, still surrounded by ramparts, lies near the coast, from which it is separated by a hill covered with extensive cemeteries. Within the ramparts are the *medina,* or ancient Muslim town, and the *mellah,* or Jewish quarter. To the north stands an ancient fortress, the Kasbah des Oudaya (Oudaia), on a cliff above the mouth of the Bou Regreg; it is entered by a splendid 12th-century gateway built during the dynasty of the Almohads (*q.v.*). The Kasbah has a charming Andalusian garden and the adjoining medersa (college) houses a museum of Moroccan art. Southeast of the old town, dominating the valley, is the 12th-century Hassan Tower, a magnificent minaret of the Almohad period, at the foot of which are the ruins of the mosque of Al-Mansur. Intended to be the biggest in the world, it was never completed.

The modern quarter of Rabat is partly enclosed within a great fortified wall which still stands along the greater part of its perimeter. In the south, the fortifications surround the Dar Al Makhzen, or Sultan's palace, in front of which is the *Mechouar,* an immense walled courtyard, once bare, but laid out at the end of the 19th century with lawns. It was there that the sovereign received homage from his subjects. Various administrative buildings, among them the supreme court of justice, are in this part of the town, and nearby is Bab Ar Rouah, or the gate of the winds, a beautiful Almohad gateway. A summer palace, the Dar As Salam, was built 4 mi. (6 km.) S of Rabat by Mohammed V in the 1950s.

Most of the government buildings are situated on the slopes of a hill around the former residency general, which is now the French embassy. The residential districts of Orangers and Aguedal, consisting of villas surrounded by gardens, extend far beyond the Almohad walls.

The port was never busy because its approach was obstructed by the sandbar outside and by the constant silting up of the channel. The harbour has been abandoned and a bridge, completed in 1957, links Rabat with Salé, making it impossible for ships to enter. Rabat has a modern textile industry and is noted for its carpets and *hanbels* (blankets). Vegetables and fruits are preserved for export, and there are factories producing bricks, asbestos, and fish cakes.

History.—The town's history is inseparable from that of Salé. The first settlement was the Roman town of Sala Colonia, the remains of which were excavated in 1930 near Chella to the south of the city. These ruins adjoin the tombs of the Marinid (Banu Marin) dynasty (14th century). The present town of Salé was established between the 10th and 11th centuries and was founded by the Zenata Berbers, who were orthodox Muslims, to house the heretical Berghouata Berbers, whose domain stretched from the Bou Regreg west to the Oum Ar Rebia during the 10th and 11th centuries. The Kasbah, later called "des Oudaya," was in the first place a bridgehead on the south bank for the occupants of Salé, and was for a long time called Salé-le-Neuf.

In the 12th century the first Almohad sultan, Abd-al-Mumin, built a *ribāt* (camp), where he concentrated troops for his religious war in Spain. His second successor, Yakub al-Mansur, called it *Ribāt al-Fath,* "the camp of victory," from which the town of Rabat takes its name. He erected the great fortified wall, within which the modern town has developed, as well as the tower of Hassan. In the 17th century numbers of Moors driven from Spain (the *Hornacheros*) settled in Rabat, which became with Salé a Corsair republic. These "Sallee-rovers" preyed initially on Spanish shipping but ultimately terrorized the Atlantic seaboard. (*See* BARBARY PIRATES.)

The Filali (Alaouite) sultans, who stopped in Rabat on their way from Fès to Marrakesh, had a palace built there in the 17th century. Under the French protectorate (1912–56), Rabat was made the capital of the country. Following Moroccan independence, Rabat was one of two cities to be created independent prefectures (the other being Casablanca).

Rabat province (pop. [1960] 1,156,555) mainly occupies the Al Gharb coastal plain and the western foothills of the central plateau. Salé (pop. 75,779) is the administrative capital.

See H. Terrasse, *Villes impériales du Maroc* (1937); R. Coindreau, *Les Corsaires de Salé* (1948); J. Caillé, *La Ville de Rabat jusqu'au Protectorat français,* 3 vol. (1949).   (A. Am.)

RABAT SKULL, belonging to Rabat man, a North African pre-Neanderthal, was discovered in 1933 in a quarry in a suburb of Rabat, Mor. Recalling Neanderthal man (*q.v.*) by certain traits, *Sinanthropus* (*q.v.*) by others, it was found in the upper part of a thick layer of sandstone, which contained also *Elephas atlanticus;* Chelleo-Acheulean stone tools were found in another part of the pit. These Rabat sandstones are considered as dating from the third or perhaps even the second interglacial epoch; the age of the skull could therefore be about 200,000 years. The skull, broken before its discovery and very incomplete, is represented by the anteroinferior part of the face. It has a very high and remarkably wide palate and a very robust jaw with no chin. The very large teeth have a great many primitive characteristics, the most important being the presence of a basal bulging, or cingulum, on the molars and premolars.

The paleoanthropological discoveries later made in the same region, at Sidi Abderrahman and Temara, have brought new arguments in favour of the existence of this human fossil group, which seems to have evolved independently of its European contemporaries. *See also* MAN, EVOLUTION OF.

See M. Boule and H. V. Vallois, *Fossil Men* (1957).   (H. V. V.)

RABAUT, PAUL (1718–1794), French Protestant minister who succeeded Antoine Court as leader of the "church of the desert" (*see* HUGUENOTS: *18th Century*), was born at Bédarieux, Hérault, Jan. 29, 1718. In youth he acted as a guide to the ministers who held secret meetings in the Cévennes. In 1738 he became an exhorter at Nîmes and married there. He studied theology at the college founded by Court at Lausanne and returned as minister to Nîmes, about 1743, becoming vice-president of the general synod of the Reformed Church in 1744. But the *dragonnades* (*see* HUGUENOTS: *17th Century*) recommenced after the end of the War of the Austrian Succession, and Rabaut went into hiding under various disguises and aliases with a price on his head. He sustained the Protestants, conducted a vast correspondence (preserved in the National Library at Geneva and only partially published) and, like Court, sought to prevent armed rebellion by the Protestants. The government tried to persuade Rabaut to leave France, but he refused, seeking, through his influence with high officials, to reduce persecution. The Calas affair and its consequences brought alleviation of the Huguenots' suffering (*see* CALAS, JEAN), and in November 1787 Louis XVI signed an edict of toleration. Rabaut crowned his efforts by dedicating the new church at Nîmes in 1792. His eldest son, Jean Paul Rabaut-St. Étienne (1743–93), president of the revolutionary National Assembly (1790), was killed in the Terror, and Rabaut himself died on Sept. 25, 1794, at Nîmes after a brief imprisonment.   (B. H.)

RABBI (Hebrew "my master" or "my teacher"), RABBAN or RABBENU ("our master" or "our teacher") and RĀB ("master" or "teacher") are titles applied to Jewish scholars or teachers. The title rabbi first came into general use toward the end of the 1st century A.D., although the heads of the Sanhedrin (*q.v.*) had borne the title rabban since the time of Gamaliel I. Scholars who received their ordination in Palestine were called rabbi, while the Babylonian scholars who were not ordained in Palestine were called rab.

The title rabbenu was applied to Judah the Prince, the codifier of the Mishna (2nd–3rd century A.D.), and since then it has been a title designating the outstanding scholars of every generation.

There is no sharp distinction in religious status between the rabbi and the layman in Judaism. The rabbi is simply a layman specially learned in the Scriptures and the Talmud. To be recognized as a rabbi, however, a talmudic student has to be ordained. The custom of ordination is very old.

Joshua was ordained by Moses, the ceremony being as follows: Moses placed Joshua before Eleazar and the congregation and laid his hands upon him while giving him instructions. Symbolically, a portion of the spirit of Moses was transferred to Joshua through Moses' hands.

Moses also ordained the 70 elders who assisted him in governing the people. According to tradition the elders ordained their successors, who in turn ordained others, so that there existed an unbroken chain of ordination down to the time of the Second Temple.

The practice of ordination in its Mosaic form ceased in Palestine in the second half of the 4th century when the Judaean academies were closed. (In the 16th century an attempt was made in Palestine to revive the ancient ordination, as well as the Sanhedrin, with all the power and authority that it possessed, but this attempt resulted in failure.) Down to the end of the 14th century, rabbinic ordination was purely a verbal ceremony. Later a new procedure was introduced whereby ordination was conferred upon a candidate in the form of a written statement awarded by a well-known and recognized scholar. Traditionally, the authority to act as a rabbi may be conferred by any other rabbi, but it is usual for students in theological academies to receive this authority from their teachers. In America the best-known rabbinical schools that ordain graduates are: the Hebrew Theological college, Skokie, Ill. (Orthodox); the Hebrew Union College-Jewish Institute of Religion, Cincinnati-New York city (Reform); the Jewish Theological Seminary of America, New York city (Conservative); and the Rabbi Elchanan Theological seminary, New York city (Orthodox). The main associations of U.S. rabbis are the Central Conference of American Rabbis (Reform), the Rabbinical Assembly of America (Conservative) and the Rabbinical Council of America (Orthodox).

In the middle ages there was strong opposition toward the chief rabbis, who usually were government appointees rather than persons chosen by the Jewish communities. The office of the chief rabbi exists today in some western European countries and in Israel. In England the chief rabbi of the United Hebrew Congregations of the British Commonwealth of Nations is elected by representatives of the congregations in Great Britain and the British dominions. He is thus recognized as the spiritual head of the majority of Jews in the British Commonwealth. The first chief rabbi of England was Rabbi David Tebele Schiff (1765–92).

In France the office of the chief rabbi goes back to the Napoleonic consistorial system of 1808.

In Israel the chief rabbinate is based on the Religious Community ordinance of 1926, which conferred religious authority upon the rabbinical council headed by two chief rabbis, one belonging to the Sephardic, the other to the Ashkenazic section of the Jewish community.

See Louis Finkelstein, *The Beliefs and Practices of Judaism,* rev. ed. (1952).   (J. M. Rl.)

RABBIT, any member of the mammalian family Leporidae (order Lagomorpha) whose young are born naked, blind, and helpless in a furlined nest. They are generally smaller than hares, although some rabbits, especially of the many domestic breeds, are very large. Collectively, rabbits are not sharply separated from the hares structurally, but in any given region local species of the two groups may differ significantly. (*See* HARE for points of difference.)

The typical rabbit is the European *Oryctolagus cuniculus,* the so-called Belgian hare or domestic rabbit. Seemingly in early times this species occurred over central Europe north of the Mediterranean region, from Ireland to western Russia, and in north Africa. It has been raised domestically for centuries, however, and has been introduced and established in many parts of the world. It is an exceedingly prolific animal, having no fixed periodicity to the breeding cycle. Females, or does, begin breeding when about eight months old. Gestation lasts about 30 days, and the female may breed again very shortly after producing a litter. The number of young varies with the breed and age of the female, but six to nine kittens or bunnies to a litter is about average. Ovulation is caused by coitus; when coitus does not result in pregnancy, a pseudopregnancy ensues, at which time the mammary glands are in condition for lactation and the doe constructs a nest. The doe cares for the young, the buck offering no assistance.

In the wild the European rabbit inhabits brushy fence rows and thickets from which it ventures into the fields to feed in the evening and night. It is a social animal, living usually in colonies but evincing only a weakly developed social system. It possesses a placid and timid temperament. As is true of many other kinds of small mammals, the density of rabbit populations undergoes extreme cyclical fluctuations.

The common North American rabbits, which belong to the genus *Sylvilagus,* are generally called cottontail rabbits. The marsh cottontail (*S. palustris*) and the swamp cottontail (*S. aquaticus*) occur in swampy areas in the southeastern United States. Both have short, thin hair. The eastern cottontail (*S. floridanus*) ranges over the United States east of the Rockies and southward to Costa Rica; occupying a wide variety of habitats and a large geographic range, it is a highly variable animal. Nuttall's cottontail (*S. nuttallii*) replaces the eastern cottontail in western North America, and extends from southern Canada to central Arizona. Audubon's cottontail (*S. audubonii*) is another western species, extending from Montana to central Mexico. Other rabbits occupy generally more restricted areas and some extend into South America, where the large Patagonian rabbit is found. Rabbits of several species are also found in Asia, South Africa and on some islands.

Rabbits are of considerable economic importance. They are important as buffer species and form the bulk of the diet of many predators. They act as reservoirs and hosts of pathogenic organisms such as those causing tularemia (*q.v.*), which can be transmitted to man. In some areas they become serious pests because of their depredations on cultivated crops or grazing lands. Australia is a notable example. After several attempts at introduction, man successfully established rabbits in the late 1800s, but the animals bred prodigiously and soon overran the continent despite costly control measures. The successful establishment of the virus disease myxomatosis in Australia in the early 1950s acted as a great brake on the rabbit population; however, the appearance of rabbits resistant to the disease raised doubts of the continued effectiveness of the virus in controlling their increase. Australia is still a principal source of the rabbit fur used commercially.

Rabbits are the most widely hunted small game animal wherever they occur. Hunters usually use small dogs such as beagles to find and flush the rabbits from cover. In Europe ferrets are trained to drive the rabbits from their burrows. Rabbits are most

LEONARD LEE RUE—ANNAN PHOTO FEATURES
VARYING HARE (LEPUS OTHUS)

often hunted in the colder seasons. Rabbit fur (sometimes called lapin) is used in great quantities in the fur industry although the pelts are fragile. The soft, delicate fur is plucked, trimmed and dyed to simulate more valuable furs, frequently seal and chinchilla. Many unusual varieties of the European rabbit have arisen during domestication by man. Among the popular kinds as pets and as fur bearers are the Flemish giant, New Zealand white, silver gray, chinchilla, Havana, American blue, Dutch belted and Angora. The silky, white hairs of the Angora rabbit (so named for the resemblance of its pelt to that of the Angora goat) often measure seven inches long and are used in fine, fluffy woolen yarns. The fur of other rabbits is the main source of felt, and the delicately flavoured flesh is excellent to eat. Because of the ease with which they are reared in captivity, rabbits are important as laboratory animals, both in experimental work and in certain diagnostic medical tests.

See also references under "Rabbit" in the Index.   (K. R. Kn.)

RABBULA (d. A.D. 435), bishop of Edessa (411–435), was a leading figure in the Syrian Church. At first a follower of Antiochene theology, in 432 he became an ardent supporter of Cyril of Alexandria, whose *De recta fide* he translated into Syriac. He initiated aggressive action against the representatives of Antiochene theology in the school of Edessa. His canons made an important contribution to ecclesiastical legislation. He also wrote a homily against Nestorius, and of his letters one to Andrew of Samosata and excerpts of those to Cyril and to Gemellinus of Perrhae have survived. The hymns attributed to him are of dubious authenticity. The surviving remains of the biblical text of Old Syriac provenance which Rabbula employed prove that he was not the author of the Peshitta as has been generally thought. He died in Edessa on Aug. 7, 435. *See* also EDESSA: *Edessene Christianity;* SYRIAC LITERATURE.

BIBLIOGRAPHY.—W. Wright, *A Short History of Syriac Literature* (1894); P. Peeters, "La Vie de Rabboula," *Recherches de science religieuse,* vol. xviii, pp. 170–204 (1928); A. Vööbus, *Investigations into the Text of the New Testament Used by Rabbula* (1947); *Syriac and Arabic Documents* (1960; Syriac text of the canons with Eng. trans.); "Solution du problème de l'auteur de la 'Lettre à Gemellinos',"

JOHN H. GERARD
EASTERN COTTONTAIL (SYLVILAGUS FLORIDANUS)

L'Orient syrien, vol. vii, pp. 297–306 (1962); *Die syrischen Kanones-sammlungen,* vol. i (1965).

(Ar. Vö.)

RABELAIS, FRANÇOIS (*c.* 1494–1553), French writer, who for his contemporaries was an eminent physician and humanist, and for his posterity is the author of a comic and satirical master-piece, *Gargantua et Pantagruel,* which sought to liberate the late Middle Ages from the shams and superstitions that imprisoned the natural man.

Life and the Genesis of His Work.—The date of his birth is uncertain; tradition and the scholars who have worked on the problem place it as either 1483, 1490 or 1494. A manuscript epitaph in the church of St. Paúl, Paris, dates his death as April 9, 1553, at the age of 70; if, as is probable, this date is exact it would indicate that he was born in 1483. But various indications in his work, in his life and above all his use of the term "adolescent" in a letter of 1521 to Guillaume Budé, do not allow that the date of birth should be placed before 1494. He was born at La Devinière, a farm in the parish of Seuilly not far from Chinon in the province of Touraine. This is based on a local tradition unearthed in 1699 by a scholar named Roger de Gaignières, a tradition verified by modern scholarship and from scattered allusions in *Gargantua et Pantagruel* itself. His father, Antoine Rabelais, bachelor of law and advocate at the royal court of justice at Chinon, owned a town house as well as La Devinière and other country properties; this house (the present no. 15, Rue de Lamproie) became a tavern about 1590, whence the legend, later put in circulation, that Rabelais was the son of an innkeeper. An unverifiable tradition claims that he was sent as a child to the convent of Seuilly; at an unknown date tradition takes him to the convent school of La Baumette near Angers—but in all this nothing is certain. He certainly entered the Franciscan friary of Fontenay-le-Comte, and he must have been there during the last six months of 1520, because during the month of October in that year he had written, on the advice of his companion in study, the friar-minor Pierre Amy, a letter (now lost) to the famous scholar Guillaume Budé.

FRANÇOIS RABELAIS, LATE 17TH-CENTURY PORTRAIT BY AN UNKNOWN ARTIST: IN THE MUSÉE DE VERSAILLES

Rabelais wrote a second letter to Budé, dated March 4, 1521, persuaded, as he says, that Budé would interest himself in an "adolescent" who, however unknown, was passionately devoted to literature; the autograph of this letter is extant, perhaps the only one certainly in his own hand. He was also in communication with Amaury Bouchard, president of Saintes, and he frequented the learned circle which met at the house of the lawyer André Tiraqueau. Toward the end of 1524, or at the beginning of 1525, Rabelais, who had made up his mind to devote his life to study and writing, petitioned Pope Clement VII to grant him leave to be transferred to the Benedictines, which he obtained. He then became secretary to Geoffroy d'Estissac, abbot and bishop of Maillezais, and perhaps tutor to his nephew Louis also; he remained in this post until 1527. Geoffroy d'Estissac resided in his see, either at the priory of Ligugé or at Coulonges-les-Royaux, but for the most part he traveled about his diocese and visited his abbeys in Poitou and Périgord. Rabelais accompanied him on these journeys, and, curious about all he saw, was an amused observer of village and peasant life; he began to collect the legends, proverbs, and rustic words that give such a tang to his writings. At the same period he allied himself in friendship with the *rhétoriqueur* Jean Bouchet of Poitiers and Antoine Ardillon, abbot of Fontaine-le-Comte; doubtless he was already interesting himself in medicine. But even this studious existence based on Maillezais did not satisfy him. About 1528, after visiting Bordeaux, Agen, Toulouse, Bourges, and Orléans, he went to Paris where he was lodged at the Hôtel

Saint-Denis, a house of study belonging to the Benedictines. In 1530 he cast aside his monk's habit without leave of his superiors and, as a secular priest, entered in the faculty of medicine at Montpellier on Sept. 17; so high was the opinion of his attainments that he became bachelor on Dec. 1. Early in 1531 he gave public lectures on Galen and Hippocrates. After a short stay in Poitou (probably the autumn and winter of 1531–32) he went to Lyons in June 1532. Sometime before the beginning of winter he was appointed physician to the Hôtel Dieu in Lyons, with a salary of 40 livres per annum, and lectured on anatomy with demonstrations from the human subject. In the same year (1532) he edited for Sebastian Gryphius the medical *Epistles* of Giovanni Manardi, the *Aphorisms* of Hippocrates, with the *Ars Parva* of Galen, and an edition of two Latin documents which, however, turned out to be forgeries.

At this time Lyons was the centre of an unusually enlightened society which welcomed Rabelais as an intimate. A manuscript distich of Jean de Boyssonné (in the library of Toulouse) mentions the death of an infant named Théodule, whose native place was Lyons and whose father's name was Rabelais, but nothing more is known of this matter. Rabelais had had two other children by an unknown woman while in Paris between 1528 and 1530; they were named François and Junie, and a petition for their legitimacy was presented to Pope Paul III on Jan. 9, 1540.

What makes the Lyons sojourn of the greatest importance is that at this time probably appeared the beginnings of the work which was to make Rabelais immortal. In 1532, perhaps at the beginning of August, a book called *Les Grandes et inestimables chroniques du grand et énorme géant Gargantua* made its appearance at Lyons. This is a short book (of which there are several versions) having similarities to the later burlesques and romances of the Round Table. Arthur and Merlin appear with Grandgosier, as he is here spelled, Galemelle (*i.e.,* Gargamelle), Gargantua himself, and the terrible mare. But as yet there is no trace of the action or other characters of the *Gargantua* that was to come, nor is it the style in the least worthy of Rabelais.

The popular tales in this chapbook of 1532 that recounted the deeds of "the enormous giant Gargantua" are probably anterior to the period when they were written down, and thus belong to oral tradition. Countless place-names in France refer to the name of Gargantua, the voracious giant to whom are ascribed the various Gargans or Garganos, cult-centres of St. Michael, as well as the Spanish and Languedocian *garganta* (throat) and *gargantuan* (glutton). The only written and dated evidence of the name before Rabelais' time is to be found in the account books of the bishop of Limoges at St. Léonard in 1471, in which a certain Gargantua is mentioned, a friend of the prelate—and this is clearly a nickname. These popular stories served as nothing more than an outline for Rabelais, and he used them with complete freedom. The first book of *Pantagruel* (the second of the whole work) was composed with the chapbook of 1532 in mind and not in relation to the existing first book of *Gargantua* which was written subsequently, after Rabelais had discovered the popularity of his work and felt that it ought to have some worthier starting point than the *Grandes Chroniques.* Pantagruel, in popular tradition, is an imp whose name can be found in many *mystères* of the period, among others the *Mystère des Actes des Apôtres* of Simon Gréban. The imp's particular role was to make men thirsty and force them to drink. There must often have been allusions to him in the torrid summer of 1532—one of the most terrible ever to have been endured, according to contemporary chroniclers: "Pantagruel," people said, "has us by the throat." The earliest edition of *Pantagruel* appeared in the first days of November 1532, and of *Gargantua* in 1534, but this would not of itself be conclusive; the definite description of Gargantua in the title as *Père de Pantagruel,* the omission of the words *"second livre"* in the title of the first book of *Pantagruel* while the second and third are duly entitled *"tiers"* and *"quart,"* the remarkable fact that one of the important personages, Friar John, is absent from Book II, *i.e.,* the first book of *Pantagruel,* though he appears in Book I (*Gargantua*), and many other proofs show the order of publication clearly enough. It is also significant that in 1533 there was published an almanac, the first of a long series which exists only in titles and fragments, and the amusing *Pantagrueline Prognostication* (still, it is to be observed, Pantagrueline, not Gargantuine), republished in 1535. Both this and *Pantagruel* itself were published under the anagrammatic pseudonym of "Alcofribas Nasier," shortened to the first word only in the case of the *Prognostication*.

On Oct. 23, 1533, *Pantagruel* was condemned by the Sorbonne as obscene, and in January 1534 Jean du Bellay (*q.v.*), passing through Lyons on an embassy to Rome, engaged Rabelais as physician. This visit did not last long (Feb. 2–April 1), but it left literary results in an edition of a description of Rome by Bartolomeo Marliani which Rabelais published in September 1534. However the "affair of the *placards*" against the Mass, which occurred in Paris on the night of Oct. 17–18, provoked severe measures against those suspected of Lutheranism. Rabelais judged it prudent to leave Lyons for an unknown destination (Grenoble or Poitou) on Feb. 13, 1535, without announcing the fact.

On March 5, 1535, the authorities of the Lyons hospital, considering that Rabelais had twice absented himself without leave, elected Pierre de Castel in his place; but the documents do not imply any blame and the appointment of his successor was at one time definitely postponed in case he should return. In July 1535 Rabelais once more accompanied Jean du Bellay, now a cardinal, to Rome, passing through Ferrara where he met Clément Marot (*q.v.*); he remained at Rome until April 11, 1536. To this period belong letters to Geoffroy d'Estissac and a *Supplicatio pro Apostasia* (Dec. 10, 1535) and the Bull of Absolution which was the reply to it. This bull freed Rabelais from ecclesiastical censure and gave him the right to return to the Order of St. Benedict when he chose, and to practise medicine. He took advantage of the bull and became a canon of Saint-Maur, of which Jean du Bellay was the dean. It was not long before he began his wandering life once again, going to Montpellier where he received his licentiate (April 1537) and doctorate (May 22, 1537); he practised at Narbonne and Lyons and delivered a course of lectures at Montpellier on the Greek text of the *Prognostica* of Hippocrates from Oct. 18, 1537, to April 14, 1538. On July 14, 1538, he was present at the conference between Francis I and Charles V at Aigues-Mortes. He went to Italy for a third time in 1540, on this occasion in the service of Guillaume du Bellay (*q.v.*), elder brother of Jean, who was governor of Piedmont; according to the letters of Pellicier, bishop of Montpellier and ambassador to Venice, Rabelais was then employed by him to collect manuscripts for the king's library. In the autumn of 1540 he was compelled to clear himself of the charge of having revealed diplomatic secrets, but he remained at Turin in the service of Guillaume du Bellay until the latter died on Jan. 9, 1543. Rabelais wrote a panegyrical memoir of Guillaume, which is lost. In the previous year an edition in which *Gargantua* and the first book of *Pantagruel* formed a single volume (both had been repeatedly reprinted separately) was published, and in this edition certain dangerous expressions were excised. Nothing at all is known of Rabelais' life, whereabouts, or occupations from 1543 until the publication of Book III which appeared in 1546 *avec privilège du roi* (granted in September 1545).

Up to this time Rabelais, despite the condemnation of the Sorbonne, had experienced no persecution or trouble. Even the action of Étienne Dolet (*q.v.*), who in 1542 reprinted the earlier form of the books which Rabelais had recently modified, seems to have done him no harm.

But religious intolerance, which toward the end of the reign of Francis I was fatal to Dolet himself and to Bonaventure Des Périers (*q.v.*), while it exiled and virtually killed Marot, also threatened Rabelais. It is certain that he passed nearly the whole of 1546 and part of 1547 at Metz in Lorraine as physician to the town at a salary of 120 livres, and John Sturm, the educational reformer, speaks of him in a contemporary letter (dated March 28, but no year given) as having been "cast out of France by the times"; he himself in another letter gives a doleful account of his pecuniary affairs and asks for assistance. On the death of Francis I on March 31, 1547, Du Bellay went to Rome and at some date

not recorded Rabelais joined him. He was certainly there before June 1548, and remained there until September 1549; he dates from Du Bellay's palace a little account of the festivals given at Rome (March 14, 1549) to celebrate the birth of the second son of Henry II and Catherine de Médicis. This account, the *Sciomachie* as it is called, is extant. In the same year a monk of Fontevrault, Gabriel du Puits-Herbault, made in a book called *Theotimus* the first of the many attacks on Rabelais. It is, however, as vague as it is violent, and it does not seem to have had any effect. Rabelais had again made for himself protectors whom no clerical or Sorbonnist jealousy could touch. The *Sciomachie* was written for the cardinal of Guise, whose family was all-powerful at court, and Rabelais dedicated his next book (*Le Quart Livre*) to Odet de Châtillon, afterward cardinal. Thus Rabelais was able to return to France, and in January 1551 was presented to the livings of Meudon and Saint-Christophe du Jambet. There is very little ground for believing that the "*curé* of Meudon" ever officiated or resided there. He certainly held the living for less than two years, resigning it on Jan. 9, 1553, with his other benefice, and at the episcopal visitation of 1551 he was not present.

Some chapters of Book IV had been published in 1548, but the whole of it did not appear until 1552. The Sorbonne censured it and the *parlement* suspended the sale, taking advantage of the king's absence from Paris; the suspension was soon removed. Rabelais died, it is said, on April 9, 1553, in Paris. The legends of his deathbed utterances—"La farce est jouée," "Je vais chercher un grand peut-être," etc.—are entirely apocryphal.

Ten years after the publication of Book IV and nine after the supposed date of the author's death there appeared at Lyons 16 chapters entitled *L'Ile sonnante par ·maître François Rabelais* (1562); two years later the entire Book V was printed as such. In 1567 it took its place with the others and has ever since appeared with them, though from the beginning of the 17th century there have been disbelievers in its authenticity. It is possible, and indeed almost certain, that it was prepared from his papers by the hand of a Protestant, after the Massacre of Vassy (March 1, 1562).

(G. Sa.; Je. Po.)

The Nature of the Work.—Rabelais' purpose was to entertain the cultivated reader at the expense of the follies and exaggerations of his times. If he points lessons, it is because his life has taught him something about the evils of comatose monasticism, the trickery of lawyers, the pig-headed persistence of litigants, and the ignorance of grasping physicians. He was a friar with unhappy memories of his monastery; his father had wasted his money on lengthy litigation with a neighbour over some trivial water rights; and he was himself earning his living by medicine in an age when the distinction between physician and quack was needle-fine. Though it is an entertainment, therefore, his book is also serious. Its principal narrative is devoted to a voyage of discovery which, though it parodies the travelers' tales current in Rabelais' day, has something of the imaginative intensity of Don Quixote's three expeditions. Like Cervantes, Rabelais begins lightheartedly. His travelers merely set out to discover whether Panurge will be cuckolded if he marries. A dozen oracles have already hinted at his inevitable fate, yet each time he has reasoned their verdict away; and the voyage has provided a number of more amusing incidents. Yet, like Quixote's, it is a fundamentally serious quest directed toward a true goal, the discovery of the secret of life, for "men are searchers and discoverers," as Rabelais tells us in his final chapter.

The oracle of the *"Dive Bouteille"* (sacred bottle), when it is spoken in the fifth book (to which Rabelais did not give final form), is delivered in an atmosphere of hocus-pocus. Yet its monosyllabic *Trink* is completely serious. Rabelais is not recommending intoxication with wine. Yet intoxication—with life, with learning, with the use and abuse of words—is the prevailing mood of the book. It is true that there are great scenes of drunkenness, as on the occasion of Gargantua's birth. But elsewhere Rabelais scolds the monks for their boozing, and there is no room in his model and secular abbey of Thélème for drunkenness, only for the conviviality of friendship and good living.

Rabelais himself provides the model of the intoxicated man,

the exuberant creator. Words fly to his head. His five books provide a cunning mosaic of scholarly, literary, and scientific parody. One finds it in its simplest form in the catalogue of the library of St. Victor, in the list of preposterous substantives or attributes in which Rabelais delights, and in the inquiry by means of Virgilian lots into the question of Panurge's eventual cuckoldom. But at other times the humour is more complicated, and works on several levels. Gargantua's campaign against King Picrochole (Book I), for instance, contains personal, historical, moral, and classical points closely interwoven. The battles are fought in Rabelais' home country, in which each hamlet is magnified into a fortified city. Moreover they refer also to the feud between Rabelais the elder and his neighbour. They also have historical connotations, however, and comment on Charles VIII's campaigns in Brittany and Charles V's imprisonment of Francis I after the Battle of Pavia. They could even be read as propaganda against war, or at least in favour of the more humane conduct of hostilities. On yet another level, Rabelais' account of this imaginary warfare can be taken as mockery of the classical historians. Gargantua's speech to his defeated enemy (Book I chapter 50) echoes one put into the mouth of the emperor Trajan by Pliny the Younger.

Rabelais' readers no doubt missed many of the references that have been tracked down by scholars. They no doubt saw that he was laughing at Livy or Cicero or Pliny, but could not have guessed at the parallel between these battles and a local quarrel in his boyhood. But Rabelais was not a consequent or self-conscious writer; he made his book out of the disorderly contents of his mind. It is ill-constructed; the same thoughts are repeated in *Gargantua* that he had already set down in *Pantagruel*. The nature of an ideal education, for example, is examined in both books. Moreover, the main action of the story, which arises from the question of Panurge's intended marriage, only begins in the third book. The first, *Gargantua*, throws up the enormous contradiction which has made the interpretation of Rabelais' own standpoint almost impossible. On the one hand we have the rumbustious festivities that celebrate the giant's peculiarly miraculous birth and the "Rabelaisian" account of his childish habits; and on the other a plea for an enlightened education, like that subsequently devised for Montaigne by his father. Again, the brutal slaughter of the Picrocholine wars, in which Rabelais obviously delights and in which the most jovially barbaric slaughterer is the beloved Friar John of the Hashes, is followed by the utopian description of Thélème, the Renaissance ideal of a civilized community. *Pantagruel* follows the same pattern with variations, introducing Panurge but omitting Friar John, and putting Pantagruel in the place of his father. In fact the characters are not strongly individualized. They exist only in what they say, being so many voices through whom the author speaks. Panurge, for instance, has no consistent nature. A resourceful and intelligent poor scholar in *Pantagruel,* he becomes a credulous buffoon in the third book and an arrant coward when he lies blubbering during the storm in the fourth. So little did Rabelais care for character that he lifted four of Pantagruel's companions from the poem *Baldus* by Teofilo Folengo (*q.v.*), who wrote under the name of Merlin Cocai. Indeed, Panurge himself, in his later existence, seems to be modeled on Cocai's buffoon Cingar.

The third, fourth, and fifth books pursue the story of the inquiry and voyage, borrowing from time to time from Lucian, the classical writer to whom Rabelais is most akin. But at least in the third and fourth, Rabelais' invention is at its height. The early books contain incidents close in feeling to the medieval *fabliaux* (*q.v.*); the later are rich in a new, learned humour. Rabelais can be compared with James Joyce as a writer molded by one tradition, the medieval-Catholic, whose sympathies are to a greater extent with another, the Renaissance or classical. Yet when he writes in praise of the new ideal, in the chapters on education, on the foundation of Thélème, on the mysterious herb Pantagruelion—which appears to be hemp and to symbolize the virtues of hard work—or in praise of drinking from the sacred bottle—of learning or enlightenment—he easily becomes sententious. His head is for the new learning; his flesh and heart belong to the old. It is in his absurd, earthy, and exuberant inventions,

which are medieval in spirit even when they mock at medieval acceptances, that Rabelais is a great, entertaining, and worldly-wise writer. Here too he is like Joyce, and the comparison goes further. Like Joyce, Rabelais is a master of language. He uses and misuses words, making them mean what he will. To define the spirit of Pantagruelism is impossible. To recognize it and enjoy it, one has only to take a swig at the sacred bottle of his book.

(Jo. M. C.)

BIBLIOGRAPHY.—*Editions, etc.:* The first complete edition of Rabelais was published by Jean Martin (Lyons, 1567). By 1600 about 60 editions had been published (*see* P. P. Plan, *Bibliographie rabelaisienne, 1532–1711,* 1904). The first important critical edition was that of Le Duchat (Amsterdam, 1711). Eloi Johanneau published an elaborate edition in 9 vol. (1823–26). Later editions include those by Charles Marty-Laveaux, 6 vol. (1868–1903); Abel Lefranc, 6 vol. (1912–55); Jean Plattard, 5 vol. (1929); and J. Boulenger, 1 vol. (Pléiade, 1959); and P. Jourda, 2 vol. (1962). There have been many commentaries on Rabelais, beginning with that of Jean Bernier in 1697. A complete and exhaustive bibliography has been supplied by A. Cioranesco, *Bibliographie de la littérature française du XVIᵉ siècle* (1959), no. 17,934–18,789.

Translations: Sir Thomas Urquhart translated the first two books of Rabelais into English in 1653; his work reproduced the spirit of the original with remarkable felicity and was recognized by many as a masterpiece of translation. In 1693 Pierre Motteux republished Urquhart with a long commentary and added the third book which Urquhart had not completed. Later Motteux translated the last two books. W. F. Smith made a new translation of the five books and minor writings in 1893 and a second edition of this appeared in 1934. Other English translations are those by S. Putnam, 3 vol. (1928); J. Le Clercq, 5 vol. (1942); and J. M. Cohen (1955).

Biography and Criticism: A. Mayrargues, *Rabelais* (1868); E. Noel, *Rabelais et son oeuvre* (1870); J. Fleury, *Rabelais et ses oeuvres,* 2 vol. (1877); P. Stapfer, *Rabelais, sa personne, son génie et son oeuvre* (1889); L. Sainéan, *La Langue de Rabelais,* 2 vol. (1922–23); H. Hatzfield, *François Rabelais* (1923); P. Villey, *Marot et Rabelais* (1923); A. F. Chapell, *The Enigma of Rabelais: an Essay in Interpretation* (1924); J. Boulenger, *Rabelais à travers les âges* (1925); W. Nicati, *Rabelais notre maître: son oeuvre, son doctrine, le Pantagruelisme* (1926); N. H. Clember, *The Influence of the Arthurian Romances on the Five Books of Rabelais* (1926); J. Plattard, *La Vie de F. Rabelais* (1928), *François Rabelais* (1932), and *La Vie et l'oeuvre de Rabelais* (1939); A. J. Nock and C. R. Wilson, *Francis Rabelais: the Man and his Work* (1929); S. Putnam, *François Rabelais: Man of the Renaissance* (1928); J. Porcher (ed.), *Rabelais. Exposition organisée à l'occasion du quatrième centenaire . . .* (Bibliothèque Nationale, 1933); H. Brown, *Rabelais in English Literature* (1933); G. Lote, *La Vie et l'oeuvre de Fr. Rabelais* (1938); L. Febvre, *Le Problème de l'incroyance au XVIᵉ siècle: La religion de Rabelais* (1942); P. Jourda, *Le Gargantua de Rabelais* (1948); J. C. Powys, *Rabelais* (1948); M. P. Willcocks, *Laughing Philosopher* (1951); V. L. Saulnier, *Le Dessin de Rabelais* (1957); D. B. Wyndham Lewis, *Doctor Rabelais* (1957). For Book V, *see* J. Porcher, *Les Songes drolatiques de Pantagruel et l'imagerie en France au XVIᵉ siècle,* in *Les Songes drolatiques de Pantagruel, facsimilé intégral* (1959).

(JE. Po.)

RABI, ISIDOR ISAAC (1898–   ), U.S. physicist, invented in 1937 the atomic and molecular beam magnetic resonance method for observing atomic spectra in the radio-frequency range. Subsequent development of several spectroscopic methods over a wide frequency range depended greatly on Rabi's pioneering work, for which he was awarded the Nobel Prize in 1944. The importance of the work lies in the fact that a number of fixed mechanical and magnetic properties and the shape of a nucleus in an atom or molecule may be deduced from the observations of radio-frequency spectroscopy (*q.v.*). The observations also yield detailed information about the structure of atoms and molecules.

Born in Rymanow, Aus., on July 29, 1898, and raised in the United States, Rabi received a Ph.D. degree from Columbia University in 1927, joined its faculty in 1929 and became professor of physics in 1937. After he spent the year 1928 in Germany in the laboratory of Otto Stern, who had done important work with atomic beams, Rabi's continuing work in this field brought refinements in experimental technique and increasing insights into atomic phenomena. After 1940 he was active in research administration, and dealt with the relationships of scientific inquiry and its technological consequences to national and international affairs. From 1940 to 1945 he was associate director of the Radiation Laboratory of the Massachusetts Institute of Technology, Cambridge, Mass., for the development of microwave radar. After World War II Rabi served on various government scientific committees, including the general advisory committee of the U.S. Atomic Energy Commission. He was also a U.S. representative to

UNESCO and was instrumental in arranging the 1955 Geneva conference on the peaceful uses of atomic energy. In 1962 Rabi was appointed to the general advisory committee for the U.S. Arms Control and Disarmament Agency. (P. KH.)

RABIES (HYDROPHOBIA) is an acute, ordinarily fatal, infectious disease of the central nervous system caused by a virus and is, as a rule, propagated in domestic dogs and wild carnivorous animals such as the wolf, jackal, coyote, fox, mongoose and skunk. Rabies is propagated by vampire bats and insectivorous bats in some regions. Man and all warm-blooded animals are susceptible to infection with rabies.

History.—Rabies has been known in Europe and Asia since ancient times. The people of ancient Egypt, Greece and Rome ascribed rabies to evil spirits because ordinarily docile and friendly animals developing this disease became suddenly vicious and aggressive without evident cause and, after a period of maniacal behaviour, developed paralysis and died. Celsus (1st century A.D.) recognized the relationship of hydrophobia in man to rabies in animals and recommended cauterization of wounds produced by rabid dogs.

The transmission of rabies from a rabid dog to a normal dog by the inoculation of saliva was accomplished by Zinke (1804), by Grüner and by Salm-Reifferscheidt (1813). These experimental studies showed that the disease was infectious, and on the basis of this evidence it was assumed that destruction of stray ownerless dogs and quarantine of other domestic dogs would eliminate the disease. Sanitary measures including these provisions were adopted in Norway, Sweden and Denmark, and by 1826 these countries were free from rabies and remained so. Rabies was eliminated from some urban centres in continental Europe during the 19th century, but after a few years they often became reinfected, since rabies was established among wild animals.

Nature of the Disease.—The disease often begins with such symptoms of excitation of the central nervous system as irritability and viciousness. During the early stages of the disease a rabid animal is most dangerous because it appears to be healthy and may seem friendly but will bite at the slightest provocation. Wild animals which appear to be tame and approach man or human habitation in daytime should be suspected of having rabies. The virus is often present in the salivary glands of rabid animals and is excreted in the saliva, so that the bite of the infected animal introduces the virus into a fresh wound. Under favourable conditions, the virus becomes established in the central nervous system by propagation along nerve tissue from the wound to the brain. When infection occurs, the disease develops most often between four and six weeks after exposure, but the incubation period may vary from ten days to at least eight months.

Bat Rabies.—A variety of rabies propagated by the vampire bat, *Desmodus rotundus murinus*, is known as paralytic rabies, paresian rabies, *mal de caderas* and *derriengue*. Although the disease symptoms produced by this virus differ from those of rabies contracted from dog bite, they are varieties of the same disease. One vaccine will protect against all types of rabies. In the vampire bat the rabies infection sometimes is limited to the salivary glands so that the animal can transmit rabies by bite for a period of several months without exhibiting symptoms of illness. This animal lives on blood alone and feeds by biting and lapping up the blood after inflicting a craterlike wound with its sharp incisor teeth. Therefore it does not need to become vicious in order to transmit rabies. Vampire bats are found only in Mexico, Central America and South America. The occurrence of epizootics of cattle rabies in Brazil, Trinidad and Mexico, in regions where dog rabies was rare or unknown, stimulated research on rabies during the period 1931-44 which resulted in the discovery that rabies exists as an enzootic disease of vampire bats in these countries. Rabies is found also in fruit-eating and insect-eating bats. Bats found flying in daytime or which try to attack and bite are likely to be infected with rabies. There is experimental evidence to indicate that both man and other susceptible animals can acquire bat rabies by inhaling virus particles from the concentrated aerosol produced in certain caves heavily populated by bats.

Dog Rabies.—Dog rabies is commonly classified as furious rabies or dumb rabies, depending on the signs shown by the animal. In the former type the excitation phase is prolonged, while in the latter the paralytic phase is present from the beginning or develops early. Most infected dogs show some manifestations of each type, that is, a short excitation phase characterized by restlessness, nervousness, irritability and viciousness, followed by depression and paralysis. Sudden death from rabies, without recognizable signs of illness, is not uncommon. Dogs that develop the predominantly excited type of rabies invariably die of the infection, usually within three to five days after the onset of symptoms. Dogs developing the paralytic type of rabies without any evidence of excitation or viciousness may in rare instances recover from the infection. The symptom of hydrophobia or fear of water does not occur in dogs, but difficulty in swallowing is a common symptom of dog rabies. The paralysis of the muscles of phonation in rabid dogs often produces a characteristic change in the bark. There is no characteristic seasonal incidence of dog rabies.

Hydrophobia or Human Rabies.—Rabies in man is similar to the disease in animals. The excitation phase may continue until death occurs during a convulsive seizure. More often, symptoms of depression of the central nervous system develop before death. The hydrophobia symptom consists of repeated episodes of painful contraction of the muscles of the throat on attempting to swallow. This symptom may be elicited by the sight of water because of the association of water with the act of swallowing, hence the fear of water or hydrophobia. Rabies in man is uniformly fatal when associated with excitation of the nervous system and the hydrophobia symptom. Death ordinarily occurs within three to five days after the onset of symptoms. Abnormal sensations about the site of exposure are a common early symptom of rabies. Sometimes the disease is characterized by paralysis without any evidence of excitation of the nervous system. In such cases the disease may be prolonged to a week or more and recovery does occur on rare occasions. Human rabies contracted from the bite of vampire bats is uniformly of the paralytic type and the hydrophobia symptom does not occur. Rabies virus is often present in the saliva in human rabies and saliva specimens are examined for rabies virus by the mouse inoculation test.

Diagnosis.—Inclusion bodies, first described by A. Negri (1903), are found in the nerve cells of the brain of animals that die of rabies. They are not always present but a prompt diagnosis of rabies can be made in about 90% of the cases of furious rabies in dogs by demonstration of Negri bodies in the brain tissue after the animal dies. Negri bodies are found more frequently in those animals that show symptoms of viciousness for several days before they die of rabies. They are a specific reaction product and not a visible form or conglomerate of virus particles. Negri bodies are not found in the brains of animals infected with fixed varieties of rabies virus (*see* below).

The mouse test for rabies virus consists of intracerebral inoculation of mice with aqueous extracts prepared from brain tissue, salivary gland tissue or diluted saliva from cases of suspected rabies. Mice are uniformly susceptible to infection with rabies virus when thus inoculated and ordinarily sicken and die about one week after inoculation. The fluorescent rabies antibody (FRA) test has supplanted the Negri body test for the diagnosis of rabies. It is a highly specific and accurate test for the presence of rabies virus in brain specimens.

Treatment.—*Investigation by Pasteur.*—The discovery by Louis Pasteur (1881) that the infective agent of rabies could be recovered in a relatively pure state from the brain of an animal that died of the disease opened the way for an extensive study of rabies. Since the infective agent as obtained from brains of rabid animals could not be identified by microscopic examination and could not be cultivated in nutrient mediums used for the growth of ordinary bacteria, it was called virus, from the Latin word for poison. The ultramicroscopic nature of some disease-producing organisms was first postulated by Pasteur. He was also the first to modify the pathogenicity of a virus for its natural host by serial intracerebral passage in another host. In an attempt to develop a variety of rabies virus which could be used safely for vaccination, he passaged the virus of rabies intracerebrally in rabbits. This resulted in the development of an infection characterized by a short, fixed incubation period; this modified virus was called fixed, to distinguish it from the natural, or so-called street virus. After 100 passages in rabbits, the fixed virus had little capacity to infect dogs when given by subcutaneous inoculation. By means of a series of ten daily subcutaneous injections of fixed virus, graded from no infectivity to maximum infectivity by drying infected rabbit spinal cord tissue at room temperature for various time periods, dogs were made resistant to experimental infection with the natural street virus. During 1885, a peasant boy who had been severely bitten by a rabid dog was taken to Pasteur, and, in view of the serious nature of the exposure and the plea that something be done, the boy was vaccinated in a manner similar to that used for immunization of dogs, the theory being that, if dogs could be immunized in a two-week period so that they would resist infection with the natural virus, the long incubation period of rabies in human beings would allow the development of a high grade of immunity before the potential onset of the disease. The treatment appeared to be without ill effect and the boy remained well. This became known and other persons were taken to Pasteur for treatment; soon the vaccine treatment for rabies was adopted as a routine procedure in medical centres throughout the world. The mortality from rabies was reduced from about 9% for all types of bites by rabid dogs to less than 0.5%. In rare instances the vaccine treatment will not prevent the onset of rabies, because the virus produces the disease before an adequate immunity is achieved by vaccination. (*See also* PASTEUR, LOUIS.)

Vaccine Treatment (Active Immunization).—There have been many modifications of the Pasteur method of vaccination with live fixed virus vaccine. C. Fermi (1908) was the first to use chemical treatment—with phenol—of the fixed virus in the preparation of the vaccine. Later D. Semple (1919) showed that by incubation of the phenol-treated fixed virus at 37° C. it could be killed and still retain its capacity to immunize. A variety of chemical and physical methods have been used for inactivating fixed virus for the preparation of rabies vaccine. The commonly employed vaccines are the live fixed virus (Pasteur strain), the killed-virus vaccines of the Semple type and the U.V. (ultraviolet light treated) type. The vaccine treatment consists of 7 or 14 daily injections, depending on the severity of the exposure to rabies.

Serum Treatment (Passive Immunization).—V. Babès and Lepp (1889) introduced the serum treatment whereby animals are immunized with fixed rabies virus and the blood serum of these animals is injected into exposed persons to give them temporary immunity to rabies. This treatment is most effective if given within 24 hours after exposure. It has little value, if any, when given three or more days after exposure to rabies. A combination of serum and vaccine treatment is given in cases of severe exposure to rabies. Immediate treatment of animal bite wounds by cleansing with soap and water is important because much, if not all, of the virus can be removed thus. Chemical treatment is to be avoided before the wound is seen by a physician.

Control of Dog Rabies.—Dog rabies can be eliminated by enforcement of quarantine regulations for dogs, except in those regions where rabies is present in wild animals. Rabies has been kept out of Australia, Great Britain, Denmark, Norway, Sweden and the Hawaiian Islands by enforcement of quarantine regulations for imported dogs. The fact that dogs have developed rabies while under quarantine in these countries, and the development of rabies in dogs eight months after their arrival in Great Britain, makes it certain that the virus can remain latent in an exposed dog for at least this period of time. The eradication of rabies from Great Britain (1903) was accomplished with great difficulty and with much opposition from the dog-owning public because the quarantine regulations for dogs had to be maintained for several years before the disease disappeared. The vaccination of dogs, when combined with the collection of ownerless dogs, will eliminate dog rabies. The single-dose vaccination for dogs with Semple-type vaccine combines in one dose the amount of killed fixed virus ordinarily given in a complete course of vaccine treatment for

persons bitten by rabid animals. The avianized live virus vaccine (Flury strain) is a fixed virus modified by serial intracerebral passage in one-day-old chickens and by prolonged cultivation in chicken embryos. This live virus vaccine is used for immunization of dogs and a single injection of the vaccine will produce good immunity for at least three years following vaccination.

See also references under "Rabies" in the Index.

BIBLIOGRAPHY.—Harald N. Johnson, "Rabies," in *Viral and Rickettsial Infections of Man,* 2nd ed., ed. by Thomas M. Rivers, pp. 267–299 (1952); "Rabies," *Bulletin,* World Health Organization, 10:703–866 (1954); WHO Expert Committee on Rabies, *Second Report,* World Health Organization: Technical Report Series, 82 (1954). (H. N. J.)

RACAN, HONORAT DE BUEIL, SEIGNEUR DE (1589–1670), French poet, and one of the earliest members (1635) of the Académie Française. His celebrated *Stances sur la Retraite* (c. 1618) are as much a witness to his good-natured indolence as to the poetic discipline of his master, François de Malherbe (*q.v.*), whose life he wrote. He was born at Champmarin (on the borders of Maine and Anjou) on Feb. 5, 1589, became a page at the court of Henry IV, served in the army, and in 1639 retired to his country seat in Touraine. His best-known work is a pastoral drama, *Les Bergeries,* performed at the Hôtel de Bourgogne in about 1620 and published in 1625. (*See* PASTORAL.)

His other poems are mainly bucolic and religious. His verse paraphrases of the Psalms, to which he devoted his retirement, are marked by sincerity and more feeling for the beauties of the original than was usual at the time. He died in Paris on Jan. 21, 1670.

BIBLIOGRAPHY.—*Oeuvres complètes,* ed. by Tenant de la Tour, 2 vol. (1857); *Poésies* and *Les Bergeries,* ed. by L. Arnould, 2 vol. (1930–37). See also L. Arnould, *Un Gentilhomme de lettres au XVIIᵉ siècle: Honorat de Bueil, Seigneur de Racan* (1901); V. Larbaud, "Notes sur Racan," in *Ce vice impuni, la lecture: Domaine français* (1941).
(R. A. SA.)

RACCOON, a common name for several carnivorous mammals of the family Procyonidae. The typical North American raccoon, or coon (*Procyon lotor*), with a stout body, short legs, bushy tail, and small, erect ears, measures 2½ to 3 ft. long, including the 10-in. tail, and weighs about 20 lb. (however, a very large male may weigh 50 lb.). The fur is shaggy and coarse, iron gray to blackish with brown overtones; the face displays a conspicuous black mask; the tail is ringed with five to seven black bands. The feet are small; the forefeet especially resemble delicate, slender human hands, and are used almost as such.

Raccoons prefer the vicinity of water in woods but are not restricted thereto. They eat a variety of arthropods, rodents,

WILLIS PETERSON
RACCOON (PROCYON LOTOR)

birds and their eggs, frogs, berries, fruit, and other vegetative materials. Their fondness for eggs, nestlings, corn, and melons makes them a nuisance in local areas. If water is available, they "wash" their food even though they may have just captured it from the water by probing beneath underwater rocks with their sensitive "hands." They climb trees readily, principally for refuge rather than for food. The preferred den site is a large hollow branch of a tree, where the three to six young are born after a gestation of 63 days. Raccoons are selectively polygamous, breeding in midwinter in cooler climates and around the year in warm climates. The female is highly solicitous of her young and cares for them for about a year, even though the young begin hunting food and are weaned when two months old.

Raccoons are seldom abroad in daylight. In very cold weather they sleep for extended periods but do not hibernate in the sense of becoming torpid. They are hunted and trapped extensively for their fur and tasty flesh. Most commonly they are hunted at night by trained hounds; when hard pressed they "tree" and can be shot easily. A much-hunted old raccoon becomes as wily and elusive as the cleverest fox.

Raccoons are inquisitive, methodical, and intelligent, and when young make agreeable pets; older animals tend to become irascible. Full-grown raccoons are preyed upon by few animals. When cornered they are savage fighters, ripping and slashing with claws and teeth; few dogs can successfully attack an adult. Especially in water, where he is very much at home, a raccoon often will drown his adversary. Raccoons adapt to man's presence exceptionally well, and are not uncommon even close to metropolitan areas, provided food and den sites are available. Although raccoons thrive in captivity, raising them is not profitable because of their large appetites and the low value of their pelts.

P. lotor and its closely related species occur from northern Alberta, over the United States, excluding the High Plains and Great Basin regions, and southward into South America. One species (*P. maynardi*) is known only from the Bahama Islands, and two other species from Barbados and Guadeloupe islands in the Lesser Antilles. A related species, the large crab-eating raccoon (*P. cancrivorus*), inhabits much of South America as far south as northern Argentina. *See also* CARNIVORE. (K. R. KN.)

RACE RELATIONS: *see* INTERRACIAL RELATIONS; ACCULTURATION; APARTHEID; CAPE COLOUREDS; CIVIL RIGHTS AND LIBERTIES; MARRIAGE, LAW OF: *United States: Impediments to Marriage;* MIGRATION; NATIVISTIC MOVEMENTS; NEGRO, AMERICAN; PSYCHOLOGY, SOCIAL: *Simple Group Effects;* SEGREGATION, RACIAL; SOUTH, THE.

RACES OF MANKIND. Race as a biological concept in man and other animals refers to the taxonomic (classificatory) unit immediately below the species. Biologically, a race is a population or a group of populations distinct by virtue of genetic isolation and natural selection; in these terms a race is neither an artificial construct, a collection of individuals arbitrarily selected from a population, nor a religious grouping, linguistic division, or nationality. In man, in which only one species (*Homo sapiens*) survives, race serves as a major basis for distinguishing one person from another. Investigation in anthropology is concerned with the origin (phylogeny) of races, their classification and relationships, and the documentation of evolutionary mechanisms involved in racial differentiation.

Satisfactory explanations for the many differences among races were difficult to formulate until after the advent of evolutionary genetics (*see* MAN, EVOLUTION OF). Tradition favoured an oversimplified phylogeny, a three-race theory, and admixture to account for all living races of mankind. Modern research clearly documents the role of local environments in bringing about genetic differences among races.

Geographical, Local, and Micro-Races.—The term race alone is, however, inadequate to describe the larger and smaller natural units that can be distinguished. In Africa south of the Sahara, for example, all native peoples are obviously related and quite distinct from the populations of Europe or Asia; nevertheless, within Africa there are numerous local populations such as the Bushmen and Hottentots, or the pygmies of the rain forest, that are clearly distinct. The peoples of West Africa, in Ghana and Ivory Coast, are demonstrably different from those of East Africa and the Sudan. Such larger geographical groupings and smaller local groupings are more easily described by reference to geographical races (the larger group) and local races (the smaller group).

There are relatively few geographical races, and these coincide fairly well with the major continents or great island chains. In all, nine geographical races may be defined as follows: American Indian, Polynesian, Micronesian, Melanesian-Papuan, Australian, Asian, Indian, European, and African. This system of geographical races accounts for the vast majority of the world's population, excluding only a few groupings, such as the Ainu of northern Japan, and some of the aboriginal tribes of Formosa (Taiwan) and southwest China. It is a convenient system, referring in general to collections of populations that have long been isolated from each other and that have developed many distinctive features.

Nevertheless, geographical races as units do not lend themselves to direct investigation. It would be a formidable task

to study Africans, for instance, or American Indians, or Australians as independent groupings. Actual studies of races involve the far smaller, often clearly delimited local races, examples of which include the Lapps of Scandinavia, the Ituri forest pygmies of Africa, or the Alacaluf of Patagonia. There are in fact hundreds of local races, some of them relatively isolated for thousands of years (as the Andamanese) and others of recent development (as the Neo-Hawaiian and American Negro). Most commonly, it is such local races as these that are studied.

In more densely populated places, however, such as Western Europe, Southeast Asia, or West Africa, it is difficult to find local races as neatly delimited as Lapps, Ainu, Apache, or Bushmen. Nevertheless, genetic makeup differs from locality to locality, as can be documented by blood-group frequencies, taste acuity, palm-print patterns, and frequencies of many other genetically determined traits. The term micro-race conveniently describes such smaller divisions, which are most conveniently studied by physical anthropologists and geneticists.

Race Differences.—Races differ considerably in size and shape, in pigmentation and blood-group frequencies, in dress, and in behaviour. Leaving out such obviously learned differences as costume or gesture, and differences due to the way of life or availability of food, characteristics of most value to the scientific study of race are hereditary (*see* HEREDITY).

Such genetic differences include size, shape, and cusp number

TABLE I.—*Some Morphological Differences Among Races and Populations*

Trait	Comments
Bone density	Higher in American Negroes than in American whites
Suture bones on the back of the skull .	Common in many American Indian populations and in Asians
Shovel-shaped incisors . . .	Especially common in American Indians of the Southwest
Agenesis of third molars	Common in American Indians, rare in Africans
"Peppercorn" or spiral tuft hair form .	Limited to Africa, south of the Sahara, especially well developed in Bushmen
Internal or Mongoloid eyefold . .	Limited to Asia, the Pacific Islands, and the Americas
Male pattern baldness	Especially common in Europeans, rare in American Indians and many Asians

of teeth; proportions and even densities of the various bones; and configurations of the skull and face. They include the form and abundance of head and body hair, the tendency toward male pattern baldness, and the number of sweat and sebaceous glands. Racial differences are obvious in palm prints and fingerprints; in the form of the eyelids, eyebrows, and nasal tip; in the thickness of the lips; and in the amount of pigmentation of the gums. The tendency to form raised scars (keloids), the ability to fold the tongue and to taste phenylthiocarbamide (PTC) and thiouracil also vary with race. Racial differences also exist in the frequencies of the various blood groups, in the haptoglobins, in the abnormal hemoglobins, in sensitivity to numerous antimalarial drugs, and in resistance to various infectious and parasitic diseases, especially malaria.

However, such racial differences are rarely absolute. While many American Indians exhibit shovel-shaped incisors, not all of them do. It is the relative frequency of the B blood type that distinguishes Asians from Europeans; and the same is true of other blood groups, such as Kell, Kidd, or Lutheran. Moreover, races do not differ to the same extent in all trait frequencies or gene frequencies. Asians are markedly different from Europeans in the frequency of the Diego-positive blood type but not in the MN frequencies. American Indians and Australian Aboriginals are vastly different in MN frequencies but similarly low in the frequency of blood type B. (*See* BLOOD: *Individuality of Human Blood;* BLOOD GROUPS.)

Furthermore, contiguous races may be quite unalike in the frequency of a particular hereditary trait. American Eskimos differ from both American Indians and Asians in the frequency of the Diego-positive blood type and in the proportion of PTC taste-blind individuals, though resembling both Asians and American Indians in many other respects.

Thus, while races differ from each other in a great many gene-determined traits, these differences are best expressed as trait, or gene, frequencies. A major racial difference in one respect may be associated with a minor difference in another. And, while geographically remote races, because of long isolation from each other, tend to differ most widely, they may be closer to one another in particular respects than they are to contiguous local races.

Blood Group Differences.—From data on blood groups that have been accumulated since 1900, it is now possible to generalize about many racial differences. Blood group B, for example, is virtually absent from the aboriginal peoples of the Americas and Australia and is found in about 12% of Europeans and in about 25% of Africans and Asian Indians. In some parts of Asia, however, B may be found in as much as 40% of the population. Furthermore, while blood type A is found in all geographical races, the A_2 subtype is uniquely European.

The Rh-negative blood type is peculiarly European. Approximately 15% of Europeans are Rh-negative (the frequency is far higher in the Basques), but Rh-negative individuals are extremely rare among Asians, Africans, and American Indians. In Africa, however, the Rh_o subtype is especially common. In the MN series, M and N are equally common over most of the world; American Indians and Australians are extremes, being largely M and N respectively.

Differences among local races are especially apparent in the Diego system. Commonly, American Indians and Asians are Diego-positive. However, in some American Indian groups the frequency of Diego-positive individuals is near zero, especially among the northern tribes, and in fact among those geographically nearest Asia.

Racial differences also exist in the frequencies of the Kell, Kidd, Lutheran, and Duffy blood group systems; *e.g.*, a vast majority of Indians and American Indians and 65% of Europeans are Duffy-positive, compared with less than 10% in Africa.

Such differences, as with the MN system, make it clear that a simple picture of three "original" races fails to account for the distribution of blood groups in the world. The fact that each blood group system has its own unique distribution indicates the paramount importance of local environmental factors in mediating racial differences.

Other Biochemical Differences.—A particularly well-known biochemical difference among races is the tendency to excrete β-amino isobutyric acid (βAIB). European and African adults rarely excrete βAIB, but it is commonly observed among Micronesians, Asians, and American Indians. Among the hemoglobin-fixing haptoglobins, the haptoglobin type Hp^1 is commoner in Europeans and the Hp^2 type is commoner in Africans. Racial differ-

TABLE II.—*Biochemical Differences Among Races and Populations*

Trait	Frequencies in different populations
Haptoglobins	Hp^1 in over 60% of Africans, over 40% of Europeans, and under 20% of Asian Indians
βAIB excretion	Extremely rare in adult Europeans, common in American Indians and Asians, and absent in Eskimos
Taste "blindness" to PTC, thiouracil .	Under 5% in most American Indians and Africans, 20–30% in Europeans, and over 40% in western India
Drug sensitivity (glucose 6-phosphate dehydrogenase deficiency) . . .	Low in northern Europeans, up to 20% in Mediterranean, up to 30% in Africa, and up to 15% in lowland South American Indians

ences also exist in the frequency of the abnormal hemoglobins C, D, E, and S, and in blood glutathione instability.

Race and Disease.—Since races are natural units, reproductively isolated and adapted to particular local environments, it is not surprising that there are racial differences in the frequency of various genetically determined diseases. A record example is kuru, a hereditary, progressive neurological disorder so far known only in the Fore peoples of eastern New Guinea. In the Mediterranean area is found a hereditary blood disorder, thalassemia, with a minor and a major form. A similar but genetically independent condition is the so-called sickling trait and the severe sickle-cell anemia that is found in much of Africa south of the Sahara and in a smaller proportion of American Negroes. Abnormal hemoglobins characteristic of thalassemia and sickle-cell anemia are also found in a broad belt stretching to India and Indonesia. (*See also* ANEMIA.) Some persons of Mediterranean origin and many from Africa have a hereditary red blood cell glutathione instability, which renders them sensitive to certain substances, among them the fava or broad bean (*Vicia faba*), many antimalarial drugs, and some sulfa drugs. Affected persons may suffer red blood cell destruction by eating a plate of fava beans, or even by walking through a field of beans in flower. These beans were a prohibited food in ancient Egypt, apparently in recognition of their potential threat to susceptible persons.

Yet thalassemia, sickling trait, and hereditary drug sensitivities are not without their compensations. Persons with thalassemia minor or with the sickle-cell trait are to some extent protected against malaria, as, apparently, are drug-sensitive persons and those who suffer from favism. The striking coincidence of the distributions of abnormal hemoglobins, glutathione instability, and malaria is interpreted as indicating the selection pressure that malaria exerts in favour of thalassemia minor and sickle-cell trait and the sensitivity to certain drugs.

Race and Climate.—The fact that different races inhabit climatic zones ranging from Arctic to tropical suggests some degree of genetic adaptation, and there is indeed indirect evidence of climatic adaptations. The people of Tierra del Fuego and some Australian Aboriginals sleep almost nude at near-freezing temperatures. American Negro troops experienced more cold injuries than did white during the Korean War, and there is evidence that they withstand humid heat better. Texans of European ancestry tend to develop skin cancer in outdoor occupations. Eskimos retain the finer motor skills even when their hands are exposed to severe cold. Experimental studies bear out some of these suggestions: Eskimo peripheral skin temperatures remain higher than normal in the cold; Negro-white differences in sweating capacity and heat tolerance have been confirmed; Australian Aboriginals endure moderate night cold because their skin temperatures and metabolic rates are lowered.

Such differences, however, point to the importance of local races and local environmental factors. Australians of the tropical zone are not cold-adapted; northern Europeans appear to adapt to cold more easily than southern Europeans do. While the Congolese may be adapted genetically to humid heat, Bushmen seem to be better fitted for drier and cooler conditions.

Origin of Races.—Individual races arise from evolutionary mechanisms working on isolated populations. A race long resident in a particular environment encompasses a series of genetic adaptations to that environment. By whittling away less adaptive traits and favouring those more adaptive under the particular circumstances, an optimum genotype results: that is, a genetic constitution best fitted to the circumstances.

Numerous evolutionary mechanisms are involved in race formation. In small populations genetic drift (random changes in gene frequencies) is at work. Race mixture inevitably results in new genotypic combinations, some deleterious, others superior to either parental group. Mutations add new genes to be acted upon by natural selection. Inevitably and always there is the screening effect of environment and of natural selection—the major evolutionary mechanism responsible for the differences among races (*see* SELECTION).

All human races, geographical and local, past and present, seem to derive from a relatively small group of early *sapiens* hominids originating perhaps half a million years ago. As this small but variable group increased in number, and segments moved into different climatic and geographical zones, genetic isolation and differential selection apparently led to the formation of numerous race populations. These, in turn, probably gave rise to further races down to the present. With this continual change, it is obvious that no contemporary population resembles the original *sapiens* progenitors of mankind, nor can it be said that particular races are "purer" or less changed than others. Likewise, it is impossible to guess, from examination of living races, what the pigmentation, facial features, or blood groups of the earliest races of man might have been.

Population Size of Individual Races.—Populations of individual races vary from less than a hundred people for some, to thousands for others, to hundreds of millions for yet others. The number of Bushmen is minuscule compared to the southeast Asian local race, and the size of the American Negro population is 10,000 times that of the Ainu.

The populations of a few geographical races, as the aboriginal Australians, have decreased markedly in the last few centuries. Some American Indian groups have gone to extinction; on the island of Umnak, in the Aleutians, the number of Aleuts has decreased from 25,000 to less than 100. Other American Indian groups have increased in size, and certain European and Asian populations have multiplied fourfold in less than a century. In mid-19th century the increase in numbers of the Bantu-speaking peoples set them on a path of expansion and conquest to the southern tip of Africa.

Five thousand years ago there were probably more Australian Aboriginals than northern Europeans. The population of Italy 2,000 years ago exceeded that of England, Ireland, Germany, and the Low Countries. Clearly, the modern size of particular racial populations is no indication of their past magnitude or of their future numbers.

Generally speaking, races that developed sedentary agriculture, with its greater assurance of food supply, far outstripped races dependent upon hunting and gathering. Increased numbers led to security and further population expansion, until balanced by disease attrition. Sanitation, public health, and regular medical care (plus organized attention to poverty) further led to population expansion in the technologically and socially most advanced races. With better medical care and food supply, the relative sizes of different races and populations are again changing. Antibiotics, infant care programs, and improved nutrition have, in a short span of years, as much influence on the relative sizes of races as all the technological advances since the introduction of agriculture.

Future of Races.—In the history of a species, any race is transitory, forming, expanding, then dying out or being absorbed by other races. Since the earliest man there have been thousands of different races, some now known only as fossils, others from historical records, and still others so recently extinct that photographs and plaster masks of the last survivors are available. Some local races, like the Ainu, seem doomed to extinction within the next century, while many American Indian local races are being incorporated into the larger community.

As populations increase and spread, the smaller local races lose separate identity, though leaving their traces in characteristic local differences in gene frequencies. Admixture, long an important race-forming mechanism, increases as distances are nullified by rapid transportation; and the races of today will not continue, since they are contributing to new races in process of formation.

Moreover, individual races undergo continual change, even when isolated. Changing environments, including the disease and food environments, mean corresponding changes in the genetic makeup of race populations. As malaria ceases to be a major health problem, through insect control and antimalarial drugs, the abnormal hemoglobins will probably decrease in frequency until ultimately they will be as rare in Sardinia, about Lake Victoria, or in Indonesia as they now are in northern Europe. On the other hand, increasing medical care and control of metabolic diseases, leading to survival and perhaps reproduction of persons who formerly would have died young, will probably—in favoured populations—result in an increased gene frequency for such conditions.

There will continue to be human races, though not necessarily the same races known today. Even in isolated areas with an unbroken line of continuity, races of the future will not be identical with those of today. Local races are the units of evolutionary change. While such change may be minimized through isolation or maximized through admixture, there is no way known to prevent changes in the genetic makeup of individual races or in the total number of races.

See also ANTHROPOLOGY: *Physical Anthropology: The Rationale of Race Formation and Classification;* and references under "Races of Mankind" in the Index.

BIBLIOGRAPHY.—S. M. Garn (ed.), *Readings on Race* (1960), *Human Races* (1965), (ed.), *Culture and the Direction of Human Evolution* (1964); E. W. Count (ed.), *This Is Race* (1950); G. W. Lasker (ed.), *The Processes of Ongoing Evolution* (1960); R. R. Race and R. Sanger, *Blood Groups in Man,* 4th ed. (1962); G. A. Harrison *et al.,* *Human Biology* (1964); A. G. Motulsky, "Metabolic Polymorphisms and the Role of Infectious Diseases in Human Evolution," *Hum. Biol.,* vol. 32 (1960). (S. M. G.)

RACHEL, MLLE (ÉLISA FÉLIX) (1820–1858), a leading French classical tragedienne, was born at Mumpf, Switz., Feb. 28, 1820, the child of wandering peddlers. She sang on the streets of Lyons and Paris, where her acting ability was quickly discovered by Isidore Samson, who taught her all the technique he had learned from Talma. Rachel studied classical statuary for posture, practised vocal intonations and gestures, performed in many academy plays and at 17 made her debut at the Comédie Française as Camille in Corneille's *Horace*. Press and public acclaimed the new star, who, although thin and less than five feet tall, dominated the stage with her regal bearing, fiery glances and intense concentration.

Rachel was admired for her pantomime, the feverish excitement she brought to climactic scenes and the evil fascination of some of her characterizations. For 17 years she dictated the policy and program of the Comédie Française, bending its facilities and personnel to her will. Knowing that her genius and drawing power lay in classical plays, Rachel appeared in five by Corneille and seven by Racine, finding her greatest triumph in Racine's *Phèdre*. She was persuaded to join the popular romantic movement and appeared in plays by Hugo, Dumas *père* and De Musset, but of these only *Adrienne Lecouvreur* by Scribe and Legouvé was successfully received.

Rachel toured the provinces regularly and traveled to England, Austria, Russia, Italy, Germany and Belgium. Her United States trip in 1855 failed. Weakened from the constant struggle to maintain her artistic and social eminence, the strenuous touring and the vicissitudes of her notorious private life, Rachel died of tuberculosis on Jan. 3, 1858, and was buried at Père Lachaise in Paris.

BIBLIOGRAPHY.—Joanna Richardson, *Rachel* (1956); Bernard Falk, *Rachel the Immortal* (1936); James Agate, *Rachel* (1928). (E. P. K.)

RACHMANINOFF (RAKHMANINOV), **SERGEI VASILIEVICH** (1873–1943), Russian piano virtuoso and composer of piano and orchestral music and songs, was born at Onega in the Novgorod Government on April 1 (new style; March 20, old style), 1873. After a period of unsuccessful study at the St. Petersburg Conservatory (1882–85), he was sent to Moscow where he studied the piano with N. S. Zverev and Aleksandr Siloti and composition with A. S. Taneev and A. S. Arenski. He completed his piano course in 1891 and his composition course the following year, winning a gold medal with his one-act opera *Aleko*. His First Piano Concerto dates from the same period. During the next two or three years he produced piano pieces and songs, an Elegiac Trio in memory of Tchaikovsky, an orchestral fantasia *The Rock*, and a symphony in D minor. The disastrous first and only performance of this First Symphony in St. Petersburg in March 1897 caused him to suffer a nervous collapse; he composed nothing more until 1900. From 1896 to 1898 his only musical occupations were as second conductor of the Mamontov Opera in Moscow and piano teacher in a girls' school. The popular Second Piano Concerto, in C minor, originally performed in 1900 without the first move-

THE BETTMANN ARCHIVE INC.
SERGEI RACHMANINOFF

ment (written in 1901), marked the resumption of Rachmaninoff's creative career. The concerto was soon followed by a cello sonata, the cantata *The Spring,* and more songs and piano pieces. A brief appointment as conductor of the Bolshoi Theatre in Moscow (1904–06) led to the composition of two short operas, *The Miserly Knight* and *Francesca da Rimini.*

From the autumn of 1906 to the summer of 1908 Rachmaninoff, with his family, lived in Dresden where he wrote four major works: the Second Symphony, in E minor (1907), a piano sonata in D minor (1907), the symphonic poem *The Isle of the Dead* (suggested by Böcklin's painting), and the Third Piano Concerto, in D minor (1909). This last was specially composed for a concert tour of the U.S. in the autumn of 1909, in which he appeared as composer, pianist, and conductor. (London had heard him in all three roles as early as 1899.) From 1910 to the Revolution Rachmaninoff again made his home in Moscow, appearing as conductor (*e.g.,* of the Philharmonic concerts from 1911 to 1913) more often than as pianist. His compositions of that period include the *Liturgy of St. John Chrysostom* (1910), a choral symphony based on K. D. Balmont's translation of Poe's "The Bells" (1913), the Second Piano Sonata (1913), and the *Vesper Mass* (1915). At the end of 1917 Rachmaninoff left Russia for Scandinavia; in 1918 he went to the U.S. where he made his principal home for the rest of his life, though from 1931 to 1939 he spent his summers on a small estate on Lake Lucerne. After 1917 he devoted himself mainly to the career of piano virtuoso, appearing all over America and Europe (except Russia); but the Fourth Piano Concerto, in G minor, was written in 1927, and during the 1930s he found the leisure to compose *Variations on a Theme by Corelli* for piano (1932), *Rhapsody on a Theme by Paganini* for piano and orchestra (1934), the Third Symphony (1936), and three *Symphonic Dances* (first performed 1941). He died on March 28, 1943.

Rachmaninoff was a superb pianist, and all his most characteristic works—the concertos and the *Paganini* rhapsody, the solo preludes and *Études-Tableaux* (1916–17), and the songs—are marked by rich, euphonious, and highly effective piano-writing. He had a modest but real gift for somewhat elegiac melody but no great creative range, and he never made any serious attempt to develop the harmonic idiom of his youth.

BIBLIOGRAPHY.—J. Culshaw, *Sergei Rachmaninov* (1949); O. von Riesemann, *Rachmaninoff's Recollections* (1934); V. I. Seroff, *Rachmaninoff* (1950); S. Bertensson and J. Leyda, *Sergei Rachmaninoff* (1965). (G. Ab.)

RACIBORZ (German RATIBOR), a town in the Opole *wojewodztwo* (province), Poland, lies on the upper Oder River near the Czechoslovak frontier. Pop. (1960) 32,523. It is a railway junction on the ancient trade route leading through the Moravian Gate into Czechoslovakia. The town's fine old buildings suffered damage in World War II. Raciborz has rail and road links with Wroclaw, Cracow (Kraków), Katowice, and Ostrava, Czech. Its varied industries include the production of machinery, cosmetics, building materials, sugar, and tobacco; and there is flour milling and tanning. Mentioned in documents in the 12th century and chartered in 1235, Raciborz later became capital of an independent principality. In 1327 the principality became tributary to Bohemia. Both passed to the Habsburgs in the 16th century. In 1742 the town was seized by Prussia. At the partition of Upper Silesia in 1921, Raciborz was retained by the Germans. It returned to Poland in 1945, two-thirds of the town having been destroyed.

(T. K. W.)

RACINE, JEAN (1639–1699), the younger rival of Pierre Corneille (*q.v.*), and the master of French tragedy in the so-called classical period, was born in December 1639 at La Ferté-Milon, near Soissons. He was the first child of Jean Racine, a local official, and his wife, Jeanne Sconin, who died 13 months later in giving birth to a daughter. In 1642 his father married again, but died within 12 months. The paternal and maternal grandparents took charge of the son and daughter respectively; and when Jean's grandmother lost her husband—before Jean was 10—she withdrew to the convent of Port Royal des Champs, where her daughter Agnès had become postulant. Agnès took vows in 1648 and in 1689 became abbess.

Racine thus came early into the world of Port Royal (*q.v.*). He attended the famous "*Petites Écoles*" from the age of 10, probably at Paris and other centres as well as at the École des Granges, near the convent, and received instruction from Claude Lancelot, Pierre Nicole (*qq.v.*), and Antoine Le Maître (*see* ARNAULD). He spent two years at the Collège de Beauvais, itself strongly marked by Jansenist doctrines, and then returned to Port Royal des Champs. He spent three further years of free study there, in touch with his masters, now dispersed by persecution, and with his kinsman, Nicolas Vitart, steward to the Jansenist and Cartesian duc de Luynes, whose château (Vaumurier) provided a refuge for Jansenist *solitaires*. In 1658 he went to Paris to study at the Collège d'Harcourt, also known for its links with Port Royal. Racine, who had responded to the unique opportunities his Port Royal education provided, did not relish his philosophy classes at the Collège d'Harcourt. He had already written some Latin and French verses; and in Paris he developed his powers in French verse, and made literary and social contacts through his connection with the Vitarts, with whom he went to live, in their quarters at the Hôtel de Luynes, in 1659. He made several friends, among them the young literary abbé, François Le Vasseur, and Jean de La Fontaine (*q.v.*). Aided by Jean Chapelain and Charles Perrault, in 1660 he published an ode, *La Nymphe de la Seine,* celebrating Louis XIV's marriage. He also composed a play—*Amasie* —with the encouragement of an actress of the Théâtre du Marais; but this was refused and has not survived. For another lost play, *Les Amours d'Ovide,* he had the advice of Mlle de Beauchâteau, a leading actress of the Hôtel de Bourgogne.

His close relations with the theatrical world were bound to cause concern to those closest to him at Port Royal; and in the autumn of 1661 he was sent to the cathedral town of Uzès in the south of France, where his maternal uncle was vicar-general. He was to take orders and obtain a benefice. He pursued side by side his theological studies and his literary occupations—reading, for example, Ariosto, extensively, and showing in his letters that he had no idea of renouncing the world nor his literary ambition. The benefice did not materialize and he returned to Paris some time between August 1662 and June 1663. A second ode, *Sur la Convalescence du Roi,* was printed in July, and a third, *La Renommée aux Muses,* in November 1663.

Dramatic Career.—Racine's dramatic ambitions had already been realized that summer when Molière (*q.v.*) put on his *La Thébaïde* at the Palais-Royal (June 20, 1664). The subject— which Racine knew from Euripides, Statius, Seneca, and from the *Antigone* (1638) by Jean de Rotrou (*q.v.*)—was that of the hostile twin sons of Oedipus who slay one another in single combat, one defending, the other attacking, his native Thebes. It is not a great play, but it has great moments and deserves attention for Racine's ruthless compression of the two plots presented so diffusely by Rotrou, and for the powerful expression he gives to the brothers' hatred.

His next tragedy, *Alexandre* (based on Quintus Curtius), also first played at the Palais-Royal (Dec. 4, 1665), reveals a greater desire to be in the fashion, and an advance in style. It shows Racine concerned to compete with Corneille on his own ground. Though it lacks the power of *La Thébaïde,* the magnanimity of Alexander and the nobility of Porus, the lofty sentiments of the rival princesses, are skilfully presented. When Racine published it (1666) he dedicated it to the king—the "Alexander" of that age. In the meantime, however, soon after its performance at the Palais-Royal, the tragedy was given privately by the actors of the Hôtel de Bourgogne, with Floridor (*q.v.*), the greatest tragic actor of his day, in the title role. It was transferred to their theatre on Dec. 18, 1665. Racine has often been criticized, no doubt justly, for a step which suggests ingratitude toward the great actor-manager-playwright who had given him his first chance, but it is recognized that Molière's company was considered inferior in tragedy to the older troupe. However much Racine may have concurred in Molière's satire of the "grand manner" in his *Critique de l'École des Femmes,* he disliked the diction of Molière's troupe, and he gave to the *Comédiens du Roy,* as the troupe of the Hôtel de Bourgogne were called, all his subsequent tragedies. He humanized the "grand manner," and made of the rhymed Alexandrine an instrument capable of expressing the most subtle human nuances and the most violent passions, and of touching the heart.

Racine had "arrived" with *Alexandre*—but only in the face of "excommunications upon excommunications" from his aunt at Port Royal. One of these missives, probably of 1663, survives. She denounces his associations with people of the theatre and begs him to think of his soul. And now, after he had succeeded with *La Thébaïde* and triumphed with *Alexandre*, there appeared in the press a series of *Lettres sur l'Hérésie imaginaire*, of which the last two, *Les Visionnaires*, were directed by Racine's old master, Nicole, against Jean Desmarets de Saint-Sorlin, a leading writer hostile to Port Royal. In the first (December 1665) Nicole ventures the generalization that "a novelist and a dramatic poet is a public poisoner, not of the bodies but of the souls of the faithful. . . ." Though Racine had no need to take this attack as directed against himself, the malicious anonymous reply (*Lettre à l'Auteur des Hérésies imaginaires et des Deux Visionnaires*, 1666), which he subsequently avowed, could indeed be explained by the hypersensitiveness of a young poet rushing almost quixotically into the lists. But the evidence also suggests another motive: readiness to curry favour with the public enemies of Port Royal at a time when Port Royal was under attack. According to his son, Louis, Racine refrained, on Boileau's advice, from publishing further venomous contributions to a controversy which continued well into 1667. He probably knew, from a letter to Vitart from Lancelot (May 18), how critical the latter was of "faults of judgment" in the works he had published. He knew that his only self-defense in terms of his humanistic education was to reply in kind; and when, having in the course of the next ten years produced his seven masterpieces from *Andromaque* to *Phèdre*, he comes again, in his preface to the latter play (1677), publicly to address the former teachers whom he had so cruelly attacked, it is with the plea that he has shown in *Phèdre* that tragedy can still be, as it had been with the Ancients, a school of virtue.

Andromaque was presented before the king and queen in the queen's apartments on Nov. 17, 1667. The title role was played by Thérèse Du Parc, who had been the most beautiful actress of Molière's troupe and whom Racine seems to have enticed to join the *Comédiens du Roy* at Easter 1667. She continued to interpret his leading roles until her death in 1668. Opinion viewed them as lovers, and the evidence that he was present at her death and was deeply shaken by it, seems conclusive. That she was poisoned is less sure, and it is still less sure that they were secretly married (these assertions were made by the famous poisoner, "La Voisin," at her trial in 1679; *see* POISONS, AFFAIR OF THE); but there is evidence that they had a daughter who died at about the age of eight.

In *Andromaque*, developing a theme indicated in Virgil, drawing upon plays of Euripides and Seneca, and influenced also by Corneille's *Pertharite* (1652), Racine presents Oreste in love with Hermione, Hermione with Pyrrhus, and Pyrrhus with Andromaque, his captive, Hector's widow. Pyrrhus threatens that if she persists in refusing him he will hand over her son, Astyanax, to Oreste, who in the name of the Greeks has come to demand his surrender. Andromaque, torn between fidelity to her dead hero and the wish to save her child, finally accepts Pyrrhus' offer, secretly resolving to kill herself at the altar once the marriage vows have been exchanged. Hermione, driven by jealous rage, sends Oreste to kill the faithless Pyrrhus as proof of his own (Oreste's) love for her. The reluctant deed done, she turns on him, disclaims responsibility, and rushes out to slay herself on the dead body of Pyrrhus, while Oreste becomes a prey to the Furies. In this play Racine presents the passion of love carrying all before it and destroying its victims. To the ability already revealed in *La Thébaïde* to contrive a strong plot and to give powerful expression to the passions, and to the verbal facility shown in *Alexandre*, Racine here adds an ability to interpret and express the deepest feelings of the heart. His Andromaque, in her fervent and single-minded devotion to the dead Hector, is as moving as his fierce Hermione, whose successive pleas and reproaches to Pyrrhus (Act IV) and denunciation of Oreste (Act V) are among the great things in dramatic literature. The play enjoyed a success comparable to that of Corneille's *Le Cid* 30 years before.

Racine's next play was a three-act verse comedy, *Les Plaideurs*, given in the latter part of 1668 and published in December. He first planned to write for the Italian actors (who shared the stage of the Palais-Royal with Molière's company) a skit in the manner of Aristophanes' *Wasps*. When the famous Scaramouche (Tiberio Fiorelli) left Paris, he adapted his scheme to the French stage. He claimed that the idea came to him from an obscure lawsuit concerning a benefice in which he was involved. Aristophanes' attack on the Dicasts inspired him to give expression to his own irritation at the pedantries of the law. But his Dandin—corresponding to the Greek Philocleon and also owing something to Rabelais— stands in his own right as one of the permanent comic types of French comedy: the judge so intent on judging that he gets up in the middle of the night to judge and has to be kept in his home by his son and the porter. The final scene in which he presides at the trial of the dog which has run off with a capon is the *reductio ad absurdum* of Dandin's profession. Among the characters Racine introduced into this Aristophanic situation are the comtesse de Pimbesche, the incorrigible *plaideuse* (litigant); the incorrigible *plaideur*, Chicanneau, with whom she vies; and the young couple who, duping their elders, bring this brilliant trifle to a conventionally happy conclusion. In this, his only comedy, Racine showed a wide variety of comic gifts and adapted the Alexandrine to comic uses in masterly fashion. The king's enjoyment of the play turned opinion in its favour; and it has held the boards of the Comédie Française ever since.

Racine had already challenged Corneille with *Alexandre*, only to be reprimanded by Saint-Évremond (*q.v.*) for lack of a sense of history. In returning to tragedy with *Britannicus* (performed Dec. 13, 1669; published January 1670), he meets Corneille more directly and advisedly on the consecrated ground of Roman history. Taking his subject from Tacitus, he gives a masterly picture of the imperial despotism at the moment in history when Nero cunningly and ruthlessly frees himself from the tutelage of his dominating mother, the dowager empress Agrippina, by contriving the death by poisoning of his rival Britannicus. His tragedy, Racine explains, is at once the fall of Britannicus and the disgrace of Agrippina; and he intensifies the conflict by making Nero and Britannicus rivals for a Junie whose innocence shares no trait with her supposed Roman prototypes. While Nero is only shown as the "*monstre naissant*," Narcisse is presented as the wholly evil counselor of his imperial master. Burrhus represents the stoic virtues in a setting in which they fail to restrain the violence of Nero, even if they give it momentary pause. With its careful study of the imperial despotism and its verse of bronze—nowhere more impressive than in the great speech in which Agrippina momentarily resumes her authority over her son—*Britannicus* has for long been recognized as "*la pièce des connaisseurs*" (Voltaire). If *Andromaque* presented in all their terrible beauty the passions of tragic love, *Britannicus*, while giving these full poignancy, presents a study of evil in a setting close enough to the realities of the French court to make eloquent sense.

Though the play did not enjoy the success of *Andromaque*, it has gradually imposed itself as Racine's great Roman tragedy. Racine again treated a Roman subject with *Bérénice* (Hôtel de Bourgogne, Nov. 21, 1670), though the theme is a very different one—a poignant parting of lovers: Titus, though he loves, and is loved by, the Palestinian Queen Berenice, sends her away when he becomes emperor. Racine refers to Suetonius as the source of this, the simplest of his tragedies. Racine's intermediary between the new emperor and Berenice, Antiochus, king of Commagene, has himself long cherished an unanswered passion for the queen. With these three characters, supported by their confidants, Racine builds up a tragic tension—each character in turn threatening suicide if the other makes away with him or herself—finally resolved by Berenice herself in a speech of renunciation which is one of the most moving and beautiful things in all tragedy. A story neither disproved nor finally confirmed was put about by Boileau in his latter years, that Henrietta of England (Henriette d'Angleterre), duchesse d'Orléans, invited Racine to treat this subject, no doubt because of the parallels with the relationship of Louis XIV and several great ladies, particularly Henrietta herself and Marie Mancini, Mazarin's niece. Evidence does not bear out Fontenelle's addition—that Henrietta invited Corneille as well as Racine (each without the other's knowledge), to treat the same theme; but it seems likely that Corneille's *Tite et Bérénice, comédie héroïque*, performed by Molière's troupe on Nov. 28, 1670, was composed with knowledge of Racine's text and in rivalry with it.

With *Bajazet*, performed early in January 1672, Racine broke new ground with a subject drawn from recent Ottoman history. The young prince, Bajazet, and the innocent Atalide, a young Ottoman princess, are presented as the victims of the jealousy of the ferocious sultana, Roxane, and of the intrigues and ambitions of Acomat, the grand vizier. In contrast with those of *Bérénice*, all three characters of *Bajazet* suffer violent death. Roxane's violent and purely possessive love is depicted with the overtones of Oriental passion; and the despotism of the seraglio, with its mutes, its slaves, its stranglings, is powerfully suggested; but the idiom and vocabulary of the classical Alexandrine remain the same. Distance in time, which made heroes drawn from antiquity acceptable, is here replaced by distance in space. The tragedy was played in costumes and décor "*à la turque.*"

With *Mithridate* (January 1673), Racine again openly vies with Corneille in presenting a subject of epic dimensions: the resistance to Rome and the heroic death of one of Rome's greatest opponents, Mithradates VI. Mithradates, emerging powerfully from utter defeat, plans to lead his resurgent forces across more than half the known world to strike at the heart of the oppressive republic. Racine presents this Oriental despot as the rival with his sons for the Greek princess Monime, the noblest and the most touching of his creations. In his old man's jealousy Mithradates resorts to ruthless trickery and reveals all the symptoms of a man carried away by passion. After fighting the Romans to the last, he turns his sword upon himself, and, knowing that he is dying, gives Monime to Xipharès, the son who had remained true and withstood the Romans—the only example in Racine of a hero rising above himself in the Cornelian manner, even if only *in extremis*. It is not surprising that this was the one of Racine's tragedies which Louis XIV most admired.

Racine had been elected to the Académie Française on Dec. 5, 1672, and his reception by it on Jan. 12, 1673, at the time of the triumph of *Mithridate*, marks the height of his fortunes as a successful dramatic poet enjoying royal favour. In October 1674 he was awarded a lucrative sinecure as "*trésorier de France*," an office which conferred nobility.

He seems at about this time to have resumed intensive study of the Greek tragic poets, especially Sophocles. *Mithridate*, in several of its moments and in the touching and serene figure of Monime, provides evidence of this. For his next subjects, Iphigeneia and Phaedra, though not without debts to contemporary or earlier French dramatists, he went back to Euripides.

His *Iphigénie en Aulide* was acted on Aug. 18, 1674, in the park of Versailles. As is known from a surviving prose fragment, Racine was first attracted by the theme of *Iphigeneia in Taurus* but abandoned it for a free adaptation of the other Euripidean tragedy of *Iphigeneia in Aulis*, in which Agamemnon is presented as conniving, against his own fatherly affections, in the sacrifice of his daughter, so that Calchas' prophecy may be fulfilled and the ships sail for Troy. Racine presents with power and poignancy the conflict which first opposes Agamemnon and Clytemnestra; Achilles appears in character fierce, relentless, ready to oppose his Agamemnon in arms; while Iphigénie is touchingly depicted as the affectionate daughter. But Racine avoids either shocking his audience or provoking their incredulity by introducing another "Iphigénie," Ériphile, an unsuccessful rival for Achilles' affections. Her jealousy, envy, and violence make us accept the application to herself of the words of the oracle and her self-immolation as a sacrificial victim.

Iphigénie was another triumph for Racine. He had now to contend, however, not only with the aging followers of Corneille, but with several younger rival dramatists and the spreading cult of

opera. This transpires from the polemical part of his preface to the published play. While all his prefaces are, indeed, in part polemical, the earlier ones—particularly those of *Britannicus* and *Bérénice*—had already shown his positive concern with tragic doctrine. And now his ideas found a champion in Boileau's *L'Art poétique* (1674). Boileau had become a treasured literary counselor; and there is evidence that Racine when composing his next play also submitted it to the other leading critics of the day: the *pères* Rapin and Bouhours.

This play, at first entitled *Phèdre et Hippolyte*, and acted on Jan. 1, 1677, goes back to the Hippolytus of Euripides, but also draws substantially upon Seneca's play on the same subject and has smaller debts to modern dramatists—two of whom, Gilbert and Bidar, had, unlike Euripides and Seneca, made their Hippolytus susceptible to love. Racine presents Phèdre (Phaedra) as dying of a hidden passion for her stepson, which she confesses to her nurse Oenone. Following the report of the death of her husband Thésée (Theseus), she finally declares her love to the horrified Hippolyte. When news comes that Thésée is not dead and is returning, Phèdre acquiesces in Oenone's calumniation of Hippolyte; and Thésée, in his fury, calls upon Neptune to avenge him. Phèdre is about to exculpate Hippolyte when she learns that he has defended himself by confessing his love for Aricie, a daughter of a hostile race. Thésée has refused credence; but Phèdre knows in her heart that Hippolyte's avowal must be true and gives herself up to jealousy and despair: hell gapes and she has a vision of her father Minos sitting in judgment in the Underworld. Hope has been raised that Hippolyte and Aricie may escape the wrath that threatens them but Hippolyte has been dragged to his death by his own chariot horses startled by a monster sent from the sea in response to Thésée's prayer. Phèdre, who has taken poison, confesses her guilt and dies on the stage; and Thésée proclaims his adoption of Aricie. Though characters and plot are carefully balanced, Phèdre holds the attention and stirs the emotions from the outset. She is, as much as Hermione or Roxane, a prey to overwhelming passion; but is at the same time pitiless in her self-condemnation, and sublimely alive to the better course which she cannot follow. Racine has succeeded in engaging us in her fate despite her guilt and in stirring all our pity as well as our fear. Phèdre comes to us, like Oedipus or Lear, a sacrificial victim representing the human condition in all its awareness and helplessness.

Racine's "Retraite."—Though Racine's genius surpassed itself in *Phèdre*, the play encountered opposition. The duchesse de Bouillon's faction had engaged a young dramatist, Nicolas Pradon, to treat the same subject in a play, *Phèdre et Hippolyte*, produced two days later than Racine's at the Théâtre Guénégaud. Boileau stood by his friend, and, in his seventh verse epistle, lauded the qualities he had displayed as a tragic poet and stressed the astringent value of hostile criticism. But the violent conflict and threats only served to bring out Racine's dependence as a tragic poet upon the vicissitudes of theatrical life. After the death of La Du Parc, his name had been linked with that of a second, even more noted, actress, "La Champmeslé," who had joined the Hôtel de Bourgogne in the spring of 1670 and had thereafter created Racine's leading female roles. Racine tutored her in her parts, which she is reported to have spoken and played divinely. Plausible gossip makes her share her favours between a more than complacent husband, Racine, and a variety of other lovers, several of them noblemen of high rank.

There is no evidence that Racine's debt to La Champmeslé was greater or less in *Phèdre* than in his other plays since *Bérénice;* but the preface which accompanied the play when it was published on March 15, 1677, strikes a new note. In no work of his, he declares, has virtue been given more emphasis than in this. The slightest faults are punished and vice is painted in all its horror. Such had been the aim of the first tragic poets; and Racine concludes his preface with the gesture of conciliation to Port Royal mentioned above.

Though the nomination of Boileau and Racine as historians of the great reign, which they owed to Mme de Montespan, was not known until autumn 1677, it seems likely that it was provisionally decided early in the year, and the acceptance of such duties involved Racine's abandonment of direct connection with the theatre. His carefully prepared marriage with Catherine de Romanet, a good *partie* of a family of La Ferté-Milon, took place on June 1, 1677. She had never read any of his plays and, to the end of her life, "did not know what verse was." His life was thereafter divided between his duties at court and his Paris home, where between 1678 and 1692 he became the father of two sons and five daughters. The youngest, Louis Racine (1692–1763), was the author of two didactic poems notable for their clarity and Jansenist piety: *La Grâce* (1720) and *La Religion* (1742). The latter, a verse apologia based on Pascal's *Pensées*, was particularly successful, being classed by La Harpe with Pope's *Essay on Man*. He also wrote *Mémoires sur la Vie de Jean Racine* (1747; prefacing an edition of his father's works), containing valuable information, as well as much hearsay, mainly derived from Boileau. They must be read with caution because of his wish to whitewash his father. His *Remarques* (1752) on his father's tragedies paid attention to their classical sources.

Much discussion has taken place regarding Jean Racine's so-called *retraite* which (as Mme de la Fayette wrote in her *Mémoires*) withdrew the "best poet of his age from his poetry, in which he was inimitable, to make of him . . . a very imitable historian." His duties involved following the king in his campaigns. He was also required, as member of the Académie des Inscriptions, to choose the themes and Latin legends for the "Histoire métallique," a commemoration in medals of the great reign. He was nearly involved in composing with Boileau—at Mme de Montespan's behest—a libretto for an opera on the fall of Phaëton; and he wrote words for an *Idylle sur la Paix*, set to music by Lully and performed on July 16, 1685, before the king at Sceaux.

He returned unexpectedly to dramatic poetry, if not to the stage, with *Esther* and *Athalie*—both based on biblical material and written at the request of the king's new consort, Mme de Maintenon, for performance by pupils of the school she had founded for daughters of the poorer nobility at Saint-Cyr; and he took the opportunity to reintroduce the chorus into tragedy. *Esther*, produced at Saint-Cyr in January and February 1689, presents in three acts the story of the Jewish wife of the Persian King Ahasuerus, who, exhorted by her uncle Mardochée (Mordecai), a powerful prophet-figure, succeeds in confounding in the royal presence the wicked Haman who has sought to have her people massacred. Her triumph is celebrated by rapturous chants of thanksgiving sung by the chorus of Israelite maidens.

Racine's dramatic ambitions were rekindled by the triumph of this pious play at a court where religious devotion had become fashionable, and the outcome was *Athalie*. It presents an earlier biblical story: the restoration of Joash to the throne of David and the destruction of Athaliah, the impious daughter of Jezebel. Racine's Athalie—in whom some of the traits of Agrippina and Phèdre, with echoes of the Clytemnestra of Sophocles' *Electra*, come together with great effect—is a figure so arresting that she gave her name to a play which should properly have been entitled "Joas Reconnu et mis sur le trône" (Racine's preface). God's instrument in the restoration of Joas is the high priest Joad (Jehoida), perhaps the most powerful of all Racine's creations. Though responses to this great play have varied somewhat as political or religious sympathies dictated, Racine succeeded in building up a poignant interest in the fate of the young king and in his relationship with his foster-parents—the high priest and his wife, Josabeth, who, in a situation fraught with political and transcendental tensions, movingly and beautifully embodies maternal solicitude. At the very centre of this play, the setting of which is the Temple of Jerusalem, he puts into the mouth of his fighting high priest a prophecy of the birth of the Messiah, thus emphasizing the religious character of a work which has been felt to be closer in spirit than any other of modern times to ancient tragedy despite its Judaeo-Christian inspiration.

Owing to clerical intervention *Athalie*, unlike *Esther*, was performed without *décor* or costumes, before a limited audience in a classroom of Saint-Cyr in January 1691; and though it received a more spectacular performance at court, it was never, during Racine's lifetime, represented as he had intended. The lyrical beauty of the choruses, based upon the Psalms and passages from the Prophets, and the spectacular conclusion, made such a realization the more difficult.

His last poetical works, the four *Cantiques spirituels*, also based on biblical texts, were set to music (three by Jean-Baptiste Moreau, composer of the music of *Esther* and *Athalie*; one by Michel de Lalande) and performed in the royal presence (1694).

The history of the reign upon which he and Boileau were engaged was destroyed in a fire which burned down the house of his friend Valincour, who succeeded him as academician and historiographer; but his work as historian is shown in the incomplete and very different *Abrégé de l'Histoire de Port Royal* (published 1767), a secretly and objectively composed apologia of an institution the interests of which he used his good offices at court to defend in his latter years. He had received further advancement when he became *gentilhomme ordinaire* (December 1690), and early in 1696 he was nominated one of the 50 *conseillers secrétaires du Roi*. He was in frequent touch with the king and was called upon to read to him in periods of illness and sleeplessness. The charge of Jansenism seems to have underlain an eclipse of royal favour in 1698. His biographers agree as to the genuine humility with which he faced this and the illness of his last two years. He died in Paris on April 21, 1699. In his will he asked to be buried at Port Royal des Champs. When Port Royal was destroyed by royal decree (1710), his remains were taken to Paris and reinterred at Saint-Étienne du Mont.

Character, Reputation, and Poetic Genius.—All the evidence points to Racine's paramount desire to succeed at all costs as a tragic poet in an age when patronage was all-important. An exact contemporary of Louis XIV, and gifted with all the social graces, he chose, when private problems and professional rivalry counseled abstention, to consolidate his position at court and to renounce the tragic theatre, of which he had become the acknowledged master.

Already recognized as a classic in his own age, Racine came in the 18th century to replace Corneille as the leading representative of French tragedy. Voltaire, who claimed to be his successor, acknowledged his supremacy. But for Schlegel, and still more for Stendhal, he primarily represented the *ancien régime* and its religious, political, social, and literary conventions, to which he had given perfect expression. No major dramatist has indeed since then sought to revive the French classical convention. But, despite the Romantic explosion, and the wide variety of works seen in Paris, French and foreign, past and present, it is Racine's tragedies from *Andromaque* onward, and the four most notable of Corneille's, which still constitute the core of the tragic repertory of the Comédie Française, a company which can claim to be the direct inheritors of the tradition of the *Comédiens du Roy* who first acted Racine's masterpieces under his direction.

Racine entered the lists at a time when Corneille had written his masterpieces, and had, in his *Discours* on dramatic art (1660) and his *Examens* (which he attached to each of his dramas written up to that time), reconsidered his own practice in the light of an ideal of regularity which found its strictest expression in the abbé d'Aubignac's *La Pratique du Théâtre* (1657), with its rigorous formulation of the three unities of space, time, and action. Gradually refining upon the accepted pattern in the light of his own experience of the theatre, his knowledge of ancient poetry and theory, and his growing responsiveness to human passions and situations, and gradually reducing to a minimum the contemporary "precious" elements of social convention, Racine produced a series of tragedies unique for their range, power, concentration, expressiveness, and strictness of form—and for a felicity of style on occasion so exquisite as to have become associated in our time with a conception of "pure poetry" quite dissociated from the dramatic and tragic purposes its author intended. It is as a great tragic poet that he claims to be judged—and as one whose high dramatic qualities are inseparable from the language in which they find unique expression.

BIBLIOGRAPHY.—*Editions, etc.:* The first collected edition of Racine's works appeared in 1675–76, and the last revised by him in 1697. A new collected, annotated edition was published by his son Louis in 1747.

The first complete critical edition (with critical life, and L. Racine's *Mémoires*) was that by P. Mesnard in *Collection des Grands Écrivains de la France*, 8 vol., with supplements (1865–70; 2nd ed., 1885–88). A new critical edition of the *Oeuvres complètes* (also with the *Mémoires*) by R. Picard appeared in the Pléiade series, 2 vol. (1950–52); Picard also published *Corpus Racinianum*, a collection of contemporary documents concerning Racine (1956; *Supplément*, 1961). Both the Mesnard and Picard editions contain the posthumous writings, correspondence, and notes on Homer, the Greek tragic poets, and other, mainly ancient, writers. Useful collected editions of the plays include those by A. Debidour (1948) and P. Mélèse, 5 vol. (1951). Notable editions of separate plays are *Bérénice* by W. S. Maguiness (1929); *Bajazet* by C. M. Girdlestone (1955); *Mithridate* by G. Rudler (1943); and *Phèdre* by R. C. Knight (1943). *See also* the *Mise en Scène* with text of *Phèdre*, by J.-L. Barrault (1946).

General Histories and Studies: H. C. Lancaster, *A History of French Dramatic Literature in the 17th Century*, iv and v (1942); J. Schérer, *La Dramaturgie classique en France* (1950); A. Adam, *Histoire de la littérature française au XVIIᵉ Siècle*, vol. iv (1954), v (1956).

General Studies on Racine: C. A. Sainte-Beuve, in *Histoire de Port-Royal*, vol. vi (1867), and elsewhere; J. Lemaître, *Racine* (1908); G. Lanson, *Racine* (1908); L. Strachey in *Books and Characters* (1922); F. Mauriac, *La Vie de Racine* (1928); J. Giraudoux, *Racine* (1930; Eng. trans. 1938); H. Bremond, *Racine et Valéry* (1930); G. Truc, *Le Cas Racine* (1921) and *J. Racine, l'artiste, l'homme et le temps* (1926); K. Vossler, *J. Racine* (1926; new ed. 1948); A. F. B. Clark, *J. Racine* (1939); P. Moreau, *Racine, l'homme et l'oeuvre*, rev. ed. (1956); G. Brereton, *J. Racine, a Critical Biography* (1951).

Particular Aspects: Sister Mary Philip Haley, *Racine and the 'Art Poétique' of Boileau* (1938); J. G. Cahen, *Le Vocabulaire de Racine* (1946); G. May, *Tragédie cornélienne: Tragédie racinienne* (1948), and *D'Ovide à Racine* (1949); J. Orcibal, *La Genèse d'Esther et d'Athalie* (1950); R. C. Knight, *Racine et la Grèce* (1950); E. Vinaver, *Racine et la poésie tragique* (1951; Eng. trans., *Racine and Poetic Tragedy*, 1955); J. Pommier, *Aspects de Racine* (1954); J. Lapp, *Aspects of Racinian Tragedy* (1955); L. Goldmann, *Le Dieu caché* ... (1955; Eng. trans. 1964); R. Picard, *La Carrière de J. Racine* (1956); K. Wheatley, *Racine and English Classicism* (1956); J. D. Hubert, *Essai d'exégèse racinienne* (1956); R. Jasinski, *Vers le vrai Racine*, 2 vol. (1958); P. Butler, *Classicisme et baroque dans l'oeuvre de Racine* (1959); W. Stewart, "Le Tragique et le Sacré Chez Racine," in *Le Théâtre tragique*, ed. by Jacquot (1960); B. Weinberg, *The Art of J. Racine* (1963).

Bibliography and Documentation: H. Peyre, *Racine et la critique contemporaine* (1930); E. E. Williams, *Racine depuis 1885: bibliographie raisonnée* (1940); Frantz Calot, *Les Portraits de Racine* (1941); *Cahiers raciniens*, ed. by L. Vaunois, Société racinienne (1958–); *Jeunesse de Racine* (1958–), and *Actes du Iᵉʳ Congrès international racinien* (1962), both ed. by J. Dubu.

Translations: There are acceptable modern blank verse versions by R. Henderson and P. Landrin (1931, new ed. 1959; *Andromache, Britannicus, Phaedra, Athaliah*); by Kenneth Muir (1960; as above, with *Berenice*); and by J. Cairncross (1964; *Iphigenia, Phaedra, and Athaliah*). The most successful modern rhymed versions, in heroic verse, are Harold Bowen's *Britannicus* (1948) and Robert Lowell's *Phaedra* (1963). (W. McC. S.)

RACINE, a city of southeastern Wisconsin, U.S., situated on Lake Michigan at the mouth of the Root River, 25 mi. (40 km.) S of Milwaukee and 65 mi. (105 km.) N of Chicago. It was founded in 1834 by a lake captain, Gilbert Knapp, and quickly obtained settlers in the first important American population movement into southeastern Wisconsin in the late 1830s. At first it was called Port Gilbert after its founder but in 1837 it adopted the French name of the river on which it stands and in 1848 it was incorporated as a city. Pop. (1970) city 95,162, of which about 10% was foreign-born white (mainly from Denmark, Germany, Czechoslovakia, Italy, Russia, Poland, and Lithuania). The standard metropolitan statistical area (Racine County) had a population of 170,838. (For comparative city population figures *see* table in WISCONSIN: *Population*.) Industry began to develop shortly before the American Civil War and Racine became an important centre for farm machinery at an early date. Its industrial development received a considerable impetus from World War II and was exceedingly diversified. Among its more important industrial products are tractors and farm machinery, automobile accessories, power tools, iron and steel castings, electrical products, floor wax, malted milk, household appliances, and printing. The city serves as an extension division of the University of Wisconsin, which provides two years of accredited college work; Parkside, a four-year campus of the university between Racine and Kenosha, was opened in 1969. Racine possesses an extensive park system including recreational areas and Zoo Park. (RE. H.)

RACKETS (RACQUETS) and SQUASH RACKETS are games played in an enclosed court with a ball and a racket. Rackets, the older game, is played in a large court with a hard ball and squash rackets in a smaller court with a soft ball.

Introduction.—Attempts have been made to trace rackets, like tennis, to an ancient origin; but the game as now known can hardly be said to have existed before the 19th century. In England, the first school that took to rackets was Harrow in the 1820s. In the middle of the 19th century the game achieved standing in England, but by the 1930s the expense involved reduced the amount of play outside British public schools, and many courts were converted into squash courts. As rackets declined, squash rackets, much cheaper to play, caught on. Curiously, squash started at Harrow some years later as a soft-ball game of rackets. It was not until after World War I that squash achieved popularity beyond the public schools and country houses and came to be recognized as an excellent game (because of the maximum exercise it afforded in the minimum time) to help maintain physical fitness.

Rackets was first played on the North American continent in Canada, being well established in the second quarter of the 19th century. The first court known was built in Montreal in 1836. The first definitely recorded court in the United States was built in New York in 1850. The game was played in a few clubs in a half-dozen cities and the Racquet and Tennis Club of New York was the game's stronghold. But here again the number of courts and players dwindled because of the expense and because of the popularity of squash.

RACKETS

In rackets the racket, for which no specific dimensions are laid down, is about 2½ ft. (about 76 cm.) long and the head, strung with catgut, 7 or 8 in. (about 178–203 mm.) in diameter. Made of ash, its average weight is about 9 oz. (about 255 g.). The ball, which has a renewable covering of adhesive tape, is 1 in. (2.54 cm.) in diameter and weighs 1 oz. (28.35 g.).

The Court.—Most courts are about 60 ft. (18 m.) long by 30 ft. (9 m.) wide and accommodate both the single and double, or four-handed game. Courts have four walls. The roof, where skylights or other lighting is placed, is out-of-bounds for play; in India courts were left unroofed. The cement floor and walls must be perfectly smooth and very hard since the faster the ball travels the better the game. Front and side walls are about 30 ft. (9 m.) high, the back wall being about half that height with a spectators' gallery (containing the marker's box) above it. The court is entered by a door in the centre of and flush with the back wall. On the front wall is fixed a wooden board, the upper edge of which, 27 in. (.68 m.) from the floor, constitutes the play line; 9 ft. 7½ in. (2.93 m.) from the floor a second line called the cut line or service line is marked. On the floor, 35 ft. 10 in. (10.92 m.) from the front wall and parallel to it the short line runs from wall to wall. From the centre of the short line to the centre of the back wall, the fault line divides the space between the back wall and the short line. These latter rectangles are the service courts. Against the side walls and separated from the service courts by the short line are the service boxes.

The Game.—Rackets is played by two persons (singles) or four persons playing two against two (doubles). The object of the players is to return the ball either before it reaches the ground or on its first bound so that it strikes the front wall above the play line (or service line in the case of a serve) and returns into the court, and to continue to do so alternately (either player of each in doubles) until one player fails to make a valid return and loses the stroke. The ball must not go out of court (into the gallery or roof of the court) or touch the players' clothing or person. Hard, low hitting close along the side wall is the essence of the game, with cutting, volleying, half-volleying, drop shots, and angled shots also in the repertory. In the four-handed game one of each set of partners takes the right-hand side of the court and his partner the left. The game consists of 15 points called aces. Aces can be scored only by the hand-in (the player, or side, having the service) and the hand-out (receiving service) must therefore win a stroke or strokes to obtain service before he or they can score an ace. In doubles each of the partners serves in turn; both must therefore be ousted before handout obtains the service; except that in the first hand of each game only one partner has service.

The server, with at least one foot inside the service box, serves the ball as in tennis, but directly to the front wall above the service line so that it rebounds and hits the floor within the service court on the opposite side, permissibly striking the side wall, back wall, or both before or after touching the floor. The serve is a fault if the ball (1) strikes the front wall below the service line; (2) touches the floor on the first bounce in front of the short line; or (3) touches the floor, on its first bounce, in the wrong court. If the hand-out player chooses to take a faulty first serve, play proceeds as if the serve had been good; otherwise the server must serve again; if he serves a second fault he loses his hand or innings and his partner or opponent, as the case may be, takes his place. In the United States and Canada only one serve is permitted. A serve that makes the ball strike the board, or the floor before reaching the front wall, or that sends it out of court, counts the same as two consecutive faults: it costs the server his innings.

Skill in service is most important. A combination of cut (making the ball spin so that it rebounds at varying angles) and pace can make the service very difficult to return, and service aces are more frequent in rackets than in squash rackets. Rackets courts vary in pace, and this too influences service.

The server may begin in either of the service boxes and proceeds alternately from one to the other until put out. The other side may then also begin in either box. In doubles the serve is taken alternately by the two hand-out players who permanently occupy the right- and left-hand courts, being allowed to change the order in which they receive the service at the end of any game or rubber.

If hand-out succeeds in returning the serve, the rally proceeds. If hand-out fails in the rally (or in receiving service), hand-in scores an ace and the side that first scores 15 aces wins the game. When, however, the score reaches 13-all, hand-out may, before the next serve is delivered, declare that he elects to set the game either to 5 or 3, making the game 18 or 16 points, whichever he prefers; and similarly when the score stands at 14-all, hand-out may set the game to 3 (game 17).

It is the player's first duty to give the opponent full room for his stroke, but it is not always easy and sometimes, especially in doubles, absolutely impossible not to obstruct him. The rules, therefore, carefully provide for "lets." When in matches a let is claimed by any one of the players and allowed by the referee, the service or rally counts for nothing and the server serves again from the same service box. The server in possession at the end of a game continues to serve in the new game, subject as before to the rule limiting the first innings of a doubles game to a single hand.

The usual number of games in matches is five for singles and seven for doubles. In matches where there is a referee, there is an appeal to him from the marker's decision but no appeal is allowed if a foot fault is called.

SQUASH RACKETS

Squash rackets, often called squash, is played on exactly the same principle as rackets, by two players only. The rules are in most particulars similar, but the scoring is different. In England, hand-in only can win an ace. A game consists of 9 points; if, however, the score becomes 8-all, hand-out has the option of a set to two—making the game 10 points. In the U.S. a game consists of 15 points, and an ace is scored for each rally irrespective of which player is serving; at 13-all, hand-out may set to 5 points (game 18), to 3 points (game 16), or no set (game 15). Doubles games are also played in the U.S. and Canada. In both countries a rubber consists of the best three out of five games. The squash racket is similar to that used in rackets, but the handle is shorter, and the U.S. racket is heavier than the British. The ball is of rubber or rubber and butyl composition and is larger in the U.S. than in England.

The Court.—The standard British court has four walls, which are of wood or composition, and can either be covered or uncovered. The dimensions and markings of the British court are shown in the accompanying diagram. The board, or telltale, is a strip of sheet metal or other resonant material that produces a clearly different sound when the part of the front wall "in play" or "out-of-play" is hit. The standard U.S. court is considerably narrower than the English, being 32 ft. by 18 ft. 6 in. (5.64 m.). The playing area of the front wall is 16 ft. (4.9 m.) high and the side walls are 16 ft. (4.9 m.), extending back 22 ft. (6.7 m.), from which point they may be 12 ft. (3.7 m.) high. The playing area

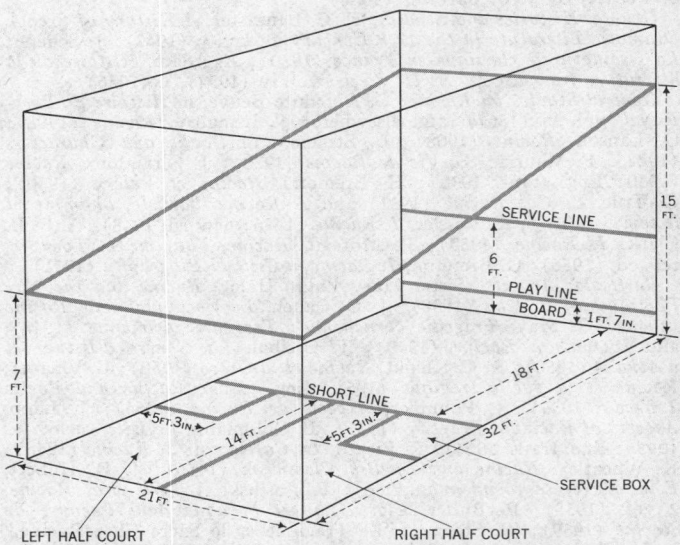

DIMENSIONS AND MARKINGS OF A BRITISH INDOOR SQUASH RACKETS COURT

of the back wall is 6 ft. 6 in. (2 m.) high. The top of the play line and top edge of the telltale is 17 in. (43 cm.) and of the service line 6 ft. 6 in. (2 m.) from the floor. The short line, or service court line, is 10 ft. (3 m.) from the back wall, and the service boxes are in the shape of a quarter circle, of 4 ft. 6 in. (1.4 m.) radius, from the intersection of the short line and the side wall on each side. Doubles courts are 45 ft. (13.7 m.) by 25 ft. (7.6 m.); front walls are 20 ft. (6.1 m.) high; side walls 20 ft. for 31 ft. (9.4 m.) and 15 ft. (4.6 m.); back walls 7 ft. (2.1 m.); and service lines 8 ft. 2 in. (2.5 m.); and service court lines are 15 ft. (4.6 m.) from the back walls.

Competitions.—*Great Britain.*—Open competition in squash rackets started after World War I, the Amateur Championship (1922), the Professional Championship of the British Isles (1920), and the Open Championship of the British Isles (1930) being the most important. Players from South Africa, Egypt, Australia, and Pakistan have generally dominated championship play, but a British player, J. P. Barrington, won both the Open and Amateur championships in 1966. During November–April many tournaments take place, including county and intercounty championships, and the Bath Club Cup and the Cumberland Cup in the London area. International matches are played between the countries of the British Isles, and between Great Britain, Australia, and South Africa, in addition to the International championships of the International Squash Rackets Federation. The British Women's Championship, in London, attracts a large entry and since 1962 has been won by Australian players. There are tournaments held for juniors culminating every April in the Drysdale Cup, the unofficial junior championship, whose entry includes players from India, Denmark, and the Netherlands.

United States.—The first courts constructed in the United States, as far as is known, were at St. Paul's School in Concord, N.H., in the early 1880s. The development of the game was more rapid in the United States than in England, and it achieved great popularity in the late 1920s and 1930s. Many courts were built in the large cities, particularly in New York, Boston, and Philadelphia. The game is also played in Canada. British teams visited America after 1924, and U.S. teams also toured in England, but competition between the two countries is hampered by the considerable differences in the rules.

In 1933 a biennial international team match for the Wolfe-Noel Cup was started between British and U.S. women.

Other Countries.—Since World War II the game has made tremendous strides in several countries, particularly in Australia, where in Sydney alone there were more than 400 courts. In South Africa the game is also growing. In the 1960s clubs and national associations in 35 different countries of the world were affiliated with the Squash Rackets Association.

In Europe the game is not played as much as it is elsewhere, but national championships are held in Belgium, Denmark, Greece, the Netherlands, and Sweden. In 1966 an International Squash Federation was formed by Great Britain, Australia, India, New Zealand, Pakistan, South Africa, and the U.A.R. to promote the game and to coordinate tours and championships between nations. For champions *see* SPORTING RECORD: *Squash Rackets*.

Squash Tennis.—Another game of squash, known as squash tennis, is played in the United States. It had a bigger following than squash rackets until the rise in popularity of the latter game in the late 1920s, after which, since squash tennis is not played at the colleges, the number of players dwindled. By the 1960s it was largely extinct, being kept alive by only a comparative handful of players at a few university clubs in New York City.

Squash tennis is played in the same court as is squash rackets, a combination court for the two games having been adopted in the 1930s; there are minor differences, including service-line markings. In squash tennis a modified lawn tennis racket is used and the ball is inflated, traveling with great speed around the walls, at times rebounding from the front wall to the rear wall and even to the front wall again.

BIBLIOGRAPHY.—E. B. Noel and C. N. Bruce, *First Steps to Rackets* (1925); A. Danzig, *The Racquet Game* (1930); Lord Aberdare (ed.), *Rackets, Squash Rackets, Tennis, Fives and Badminton* (1934); Walter Debany, *Squash Racquets* (1950); D. G. Butcher, *Introducing Squash* (1948); Gerald Pawle, *Squash Rackets* (1951); B. C. Phillips, *Tackle Squash Rackets This Way* (1960); R. B. Hawkey, *New Angles on Squash* (1963); A. M. Potter, *Squash Racquets* (1957); John Skillman, *Squash Racquets*, 2nd ed. (1964); Sports Illustrated, *Book of Squash* (1963). *See* also U.S. Squash Racquets Association *Official Yearbook* (annual); U.S. Women's Squash Racquets Association *Handbook* (quadrennial). (E. B. N.; A. DA.; J. H. Ho.)

RADAR is an electronic device which provides man with the ability to detect and locate objects of a certain sort at distances and under conditions of lighting or obscuration which would render the unaided eye quite useless. Further, radar affords a means for extremely precise measurement of the range, or distance, to each of the objects it detects and locates—or "sees." It can also measure the speed of such an object toward or away from the observing station in a simple and natural way.

Radar is superior to the eye because it can "see" regardless of visibility conditions and because it affords an easy and accurate means for measuring target range and its rate of change. Largely because of the lack of detail in radar vision, the class of objects usefully seen by radar is smaller than the class distinguishable by the eye. Radar deals best with isolated targets in a relatively featureless background: aircraft in flight, ships on the open sea, islands and coast lines, and the like.

This article is divided as follows:

I. INTRODUCTION

How Radar Works.—Radar is an acronym derived from the initial letters of the phrase "radio detecting and ranging." Radio waves sent out from the powerful radar transmitter are reflected by objects within range of the set. A tiny fraction of the outgoing energy returns as an echo to the radar receiver, which is usually located at the same place as the transmitter. The properties of the received echo are used to form a picture or to determine certain properties of the object which caused the echo. As we shall see later on, there are several different forms of radar systems, making use of different properties of the received echo and involving different sorts of radio transmissions from the radar transmitter. The form employed in the majority of the sets is pulse radar. When the word "radar" is used without qualification in this article, pulse radar will be meant.

Pulse radar is so called because the transmitter is keyed to send out short, very intense bursts or pulses of energy with a relatively long interval between pulses. The receiver receives echoes from the nearest objects soon after the transmission of the pulse, from objects at intermediate range later on and from the most distant objects near the end of the interpulse interval. When sufficient time has elapsed to permit the reception of echoes from the most distant objects of interest, the transmitter sends another short pulse, and the cycle repeats.

The delay between the transmission of the pulse and the reception of the echo is due to the fact that the radio waves used travel with the great but finite speed of light. In the units convenient in radar, the speed of light (about 186,000 miles per second) is 328 yd.[1] per millionth of a second, or microsecond. Since the radio energy from the radar transmitter must travel the distance from the radar to the target twice, once out and once back as an echo, each microsecond of delay between the transmission of a pulse and the reception of an echo corresponds to 164 yd. of range between radar set and target. If the delay corresponding to target range R is called T_R, it will be given by

$$T_R = \frac{2R}{c} \tag{1}$$

where c is the velocity of light.

This is the clue to the accuracy with which range can be measured by radar. Range measurement is reduced to the measurement of time, which can be performed more accurately than the measurement of any other basic quantity of physics. Very short intervals must be timed to get absolute precision in range, of course; if an error in range of only five yards can be tolerated, time intervals must be measured with an accuracy of one-thirtieth of a microsecond. Electronic timing and display techniques developed during World War II enabled such measurements to be made with great ease and convenience.

In 1945, for example, a serious map error was discovered by the use of bombing radar. This equipment enabled a bombing plane to find its position accurately by measuring the ranges to two fixed ground stations at which radar beacons (*see* below) were located. One beacon station was on the island of Corsica. A miss of about 1,000 yd., nearly 50 times the error expected, was scored on the first bombing mission carried out in Italy with this system. After an investigation of all possible sources of error, it was suggested that the reputed position of Corsica might be wrong. A correction of about 1,000 yd. in the position of the island was used on the next bombing run. The results, and those of later missions that used the corrected position of the island,

---

[1] This is about 1,000 ft. (984) in one microsecond.

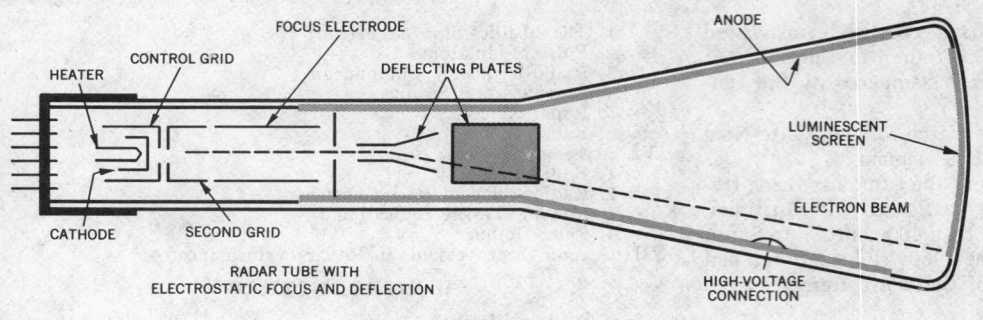

RADAR TUBE WITH
ELECTROSTATIC FOCUS AND DEFLECTION

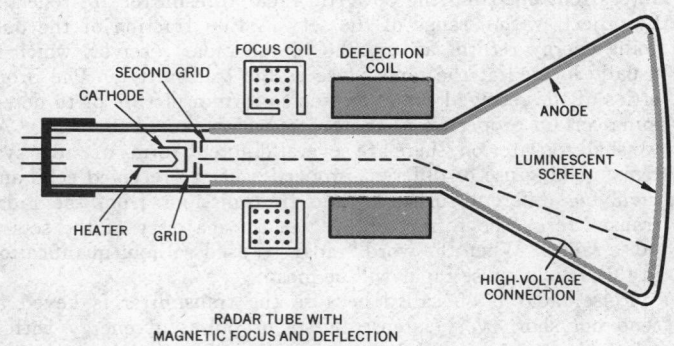

RADAR TUBE WITH
MAGNETIC FOCUS AND DEFLECTION

FROM RADIATION LABORATORY SERIES, McGRAW-HILL BOOK COMPANY, INC.

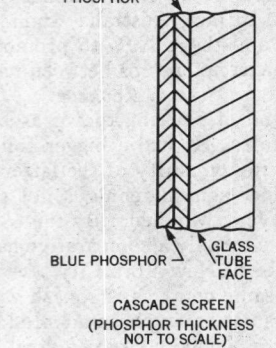

CASCADE SCREEN
(PHOSPHOR THICKNESS
NOT TO SCALE)

FIG. 1.—ELEMENTS OF A CATHODE-RAY TUBE

appears as an upward deflection of the trace. To make sure that the weakest signals that are detectable at all are not missed, the over-all amplification of the receiver is great enough so that random electrical disturbances, called "noise," originating in the receiver, can be seen on the display. For example, in successful attempts to receive a radar echo from the moon, time exposures were taken of the CRT screen. The photograph showed the entire path traced by the spot of light on the CRT face, in this case, in $2\frac{1}{2}$ sec.

On the left could be seen the "tail" of the transmitted pulse leaking into the receiver, and, on the right, the echo signals from the target. The distance of the echo signals from the left side of the CRT screen gave the distance of the target, the moon, as about 250,000 mi.

The type of indicator just described has come to be called an A-scope. Besides being simple, it affords an easy and straightforward way of measuring range. It makes no use of alterations in the intensity of the CRT spot.

were indistinguishable from those of optical bombing.

A cathode-ray tube (CRT) is almost always used for the display of radar signals. This device, shown schematically in fig. 1, has an "electron gun" at the base of its glass envelope, deflection plates or coils in the neck of the tube and a luminescent screen on the inside of the large, nearly flat face of the tube. The electron gun produces a narrow, accurately focused beam of electrons which is aimed toward the centre of the screen. This pencil of electrons can be deflected in its flight from gun to screen either by electric fields produced by voltages applied to deflection plates, or by magnetic fields produced by electric currents passing through deflection coils.

Means are almost always provided for producing two independent deflections of the beam at right angles to one another. When the beam of electrons strikes the screen covering the inner face of the tube, the impact of the electrons excites the luminescent material there and causes it to emit light.

Thus the CRT screen instantaneously displays a single small spot of light whose position depends on the deflecting voltages or currents effective at that instant. Because of the very small mass of an electron and the consequent small inertia of the electron beam, the spot can be deflected at very great rates of speed. "Writing speeds" (that is, speeds of CRT spot motion) of as much as 200 in. per microsecond were used in laboratory test equipment during World War II. Writing speeds of 1/10 in. per microsecond were common in service radar equipment. Not only the position of the spot but also its intensity can be controlled electrically.

The voltage applied to a "control grid" in the electron gun determines the electron beam current to which the light intensity produced at the screen is proportional.

A simple way to display radar signals is in the form of a "one-dimensional" display. The signal beam of the CRT is swept across the face of the tube from left to right at a uniform rate of speed, beginning at the instant a pulse is sent out from the radar transmitter. Thus the distance the beam has traveled to the right from its initial position is a measure of the time that has elapsed after the transmission of the pulse, and the distance of an echo signal from the left end of the sweep is proportional to the range of the target causing the echo. The output signals of the radar receiver are applied to deflect the beam vertically, so that an echo

In addition to finding target range, it is usually necessary to determine also the direction in which each target lies as viewed from the radar station. This could be done, in principle, by triangulation, using two or more simultaneous range readings on the same target as seen from separate radar stations. From the standpoint of simplicity, it is far preferable to measure both range and direction from a single radar station.

This is possible if the radio energy sent out from the radar can be confined to a narrow beam, like that of a searchlight. Echoes will then be received only from targets which lie in the direction in which the beam is pointing. If the radar beam is swept or scanned around the horizon, the strongest echo will be received from each target when the beam is pointing directly toward it, weaker echoes when the beam points a little to one side or the other of the target and no echo at all when the beam points in other directions. The bearing of a target can thus be determined by noting the direction in which the radar beam must be pointed to give the strongest signals from that target.

This can be done in several ways, some of which are highly precise. None is more graphic than the radar display called PPI, for plan position indicator. The PPI shows the range and angular disposition of all targets seen by a radar set which is scanning the horizon. In the PPI, the radar echo signals from the receiver are applied to the control grid of the CRT indicator tube in such a way that the screen will be dark in the absence of a signal, and a bright spot will appear when a signal is received.

The electron beam executes a sweep of uniform speed beginning at the instant each pulse is transmitted, just as in the A-scope, but in the PPI each of these sweeps commences at the centre of the tube and goes radially outward. Target bearing is indicated on the PPI by making the direction of each radial sweep on the indicator correspond to the geographical direction in which the antenna (and hence the radar beam) is pointing at that moment. North can be chosen to be at the top of the tube, for example; when the radar beam is pointing north, the radial sweep is executed from the centre upward. When the antenna has swung around to point east, the sweep on the PPI will take place from the centre to the right, and so on. The result is a map, on which the direction of each luminous spot marking a radar echo, measured from the centre of the tube, shows the bearing of the target causing the echo, and the distance of the spot from the centre of the tube face shows the target range.

In addition to the A-scope and the PPI, many other forms of radar indicator have been devised for special purposes; some of these will be referred to later.

The Basic Radar Set.—A radar set is shown schematically in fig. 2, separated into the major components fundamental to its action. The operation of these components is as follows.

A cycle of operation is begun by the modulator, which applies a high-power, high-voltage pulse to the magnetron, a type of transmitting tube developed specifically for radar use. For the brief duration of the modulator pulse, which may typically be one microsecond, the magnetron oscillates at a frequency of several thousand megaHertz (MHz; millions of cycles per second)[1], transforming the D.C. power applied to it by the modulator into RF (radio frequency) power

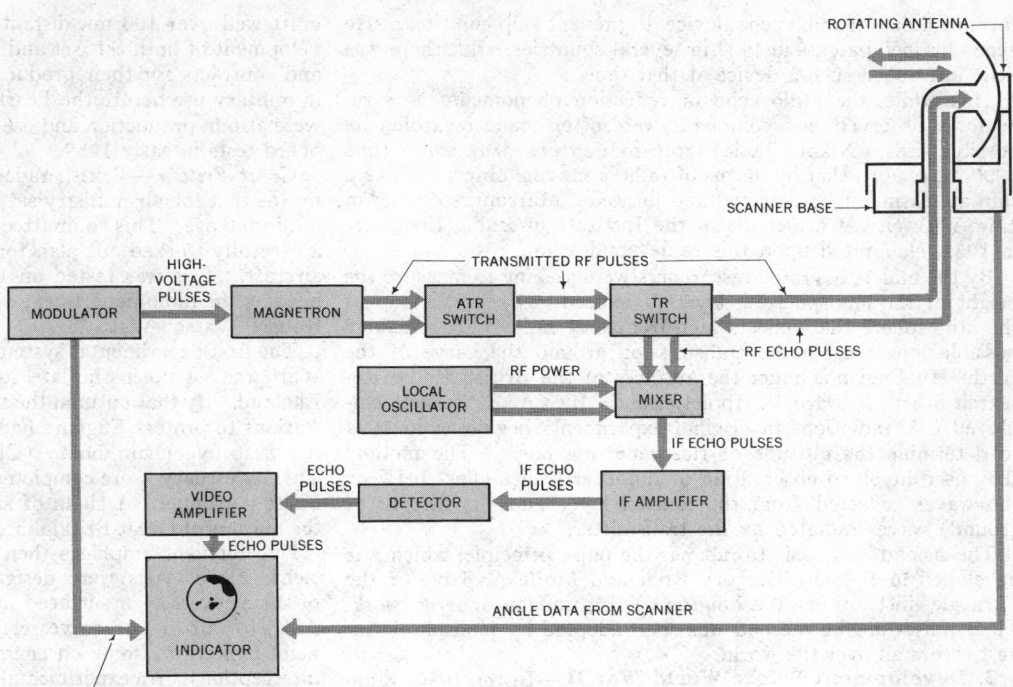

FIG. 2.—BLOCK DIAGRAM SHOWING COMPONENTS OF A SIMPLE RADAR SET

with an efficiency usually larger than 50%. The RF pulse thus produced travels down the RF transmission line shown by double lines in fig. 2, and passes through the two switches marked TR and ATR. These are gas-discharge devices in which the discharge is initiated and maintained by the high-power RF pulse produced by the magnetron. During this time, the TR (transmit-receive) switch connects the transmitter RF line to the antenna, and disconnects the mixer and the rest of the receiver, in order to prevent damage to these sensitive circuits by the high outgoing power. The ATR (anti-TR) switch, when operated, simply permits the RF pulse from the magnetron to pass through it with negligible loss. Between pulses, when these gas-discharge switches are in a quiescent state, the TR switch connects the mixer to the antenna, and the ATR disconnects the magnetron to prevent any of the feeble received signals from being lost.

The RF pulse, after passing through these two switches, travels down the RF line to the antenna, where it is radiated. As is usual in radar, a single antenna is indicated in fig. 2 as being used both for transmitting and receiving; this requirement gives rise to the need for the duplexing arrangements involving the TR and ATR switches. The antenna design depends on the shape of radar beam required to meet the functional demands placed on the radar. It is almost always mounted on a scanner arranged to sweep the beam through space in the manner desired; simple azimuth rotation is indicated in fig. 2.

After the pulse has been transmitted, the discharges in the TR and ATR switches cease and the system is ready to receive echoes. These are picked up by the antenna and sent down the RF line to the mixer. The mixer shown is identical with the usual mixer of a superheterodyne radio receiver; it is a non-linear device which, in addition to receiving the signals from the antenna, receives power from a CW (continuous-wave) local oscillator operating at a frequency only a few tens of megaHertz away from the frequency of the radar transmitter. The difference frequency that results from mixing the echoes with the local oscillator signals contains the same intelligence as did the original echoes, but it is at a sufficiently low frequency (typically 30 MHz)

[1]The electromagnetic waves used in radar, like light and radio waves, can be characterized either by their wave length, λ, or by their frequency, ν. These two quantities are related, since their product is the velocity of propagation of light, c,

$$\lambda\nu = c$$

Numerically, a wave length of 10 cm. corresponds to a frequency of about 3×10^9 cycles per second (Hz), or 3,000 MHz.

to be amplified by more or less conventional techniques in the intermediate frequency (IF) amplifier shown. Output signals from the IF amplifier are demodulated by a detector, and the resulting unipolar signals, still containing the echo intelligence, are further amplified by a video-frequency amplifier similar to those familiar in television receiver technique.

Output video signals are passed to the indicator for display. The indicator shown is a PPI which must, in addition to receiving echo signals from the indicator, receive a timing pulse from the modulator to indicate the instant for the start of each sweep. It must also receive information from the scanner on the direction in which the antenna is pointing, in order that the radial range sweep be executed in the proper direction from the centre of the tube. The necessary connections are indicated in fig. 2.

Each of the components shown in fig. 2 presented a series of difficult new problems of design during the period of radar development in the years 1935–45. Broad problems of component design are treated later in this article.

II. THE DEVELOPMENT OF RADAR

1. Early History.—Radar was developed independently and nearly at the same time in the United States, England, Germany and France during the 1930s under various names, such as radio detection or radio location. In 1942 the U.S. Navy coined the term radar which became universal in all later applications.

The independent occurrence of almost simultaneous and very similar radar developments in all these countries should not be surprising. The ideas basic to radar principles had been repeatedly presented for many years preceding the development of radar. It is perhaps more surprising that practical radar systems were not evolved at an earlier date.

Of the two ideas basic to pulse radar, the echo principle and the pulse principle, the former dates from the pioneer work of Heinrich R. Hertz in electromagnetic waves. This German physicist in the 1880s, seeking demonstrable proof of theories on the nature of light and radiation that the English mathematician James C. Maxwell had published in the 1870s, produced radio waves in the laboratory. Hertz also demonstrated that these radiations could be reflected by metallic objects, as light is reflected by a mirror.

While Marchese Guglielmo Marconi and others at once pursued the radio communications possibilities that Hertz had opened up, a German engineer, Christian Hülsmeyer, developed a simple form of radar, or radio echo device, to prevent ship collisions. He even obtained patents in 1904 in several countries. But there was little interest in such a device at that time.

Meanwhile, the radio echo or reflection phenomenon was repeatedly observed, and comments were often made regarding its possible uses. Nikola Tesla wrote in *Century Magazine* (June 1900, lx, p. 208) that by means of radio a moving object such as a ship at sea might be detected and located. Marconi, speaking in New York city at a meeting of the Institute of Radio Engineers in 1922, elaborated upon this same application.

By the mid-1920s radio researchers were seeking to measure the height of the ionosphere, a layer of ionized gas near the top of the atmosphere that reflects high-frequency radio waves, making possible long-range radio transmission around the curve of the earth. In England, under the auspices of the British Radio Research board, Edward V. Appleton and Miles A. F. Barnett employed CW radiations in original experiments beginning in 1924 to determine the altitude of this reflecting layer. The method they used involved observation of the interference effect between the waves reflected from the ionized layer and the direct (or ground) waves radiated by the transmitter.

The second idea basic to radar is the pulse principle, which was developed in 1925 by Gregory Breit and Merle A. Tuve of the Carnegie institution, Washington, D.C., in ionospheric work. Their pulse-ranging method was soon adopted by ionospheric investigators all over the world.

2. Development Before World War II.—In the 1930s radio detection research began to receive earnest attention in a number of countries, largely under military supervision and in secret, because of the urgent need to detect and locate enemy warplanes at night or in cloud.

Germany.—German scientists, having begun development of a ship detector for the navy as early as 1933, soon concentrated their efforts on aircraft detectors. By Sept. 1939 a German ground set, the Freya, for early warning of approaching airplanes, was in production. The ship detector Seetakt went into production soon after. An especially excellent radar, the Würzburg, its medium-length waves of 50 cm. (at 600 MHz) giving sufficient accuracy to direct effective antiaircraft fire against unseen planes, began to be employed in mid-1940 before any comparable precision position finder or gun layer (GL) radar had been developed by the Allies.

France.—The French, who had developed a simple obstacle warning set (an iceberg detector) for use aboard the ocean liner "Normandie" in the mid-1930s, also devised an aircraft warning system just before World War II. This was an interference-type radar using long waves (at 30 MHz) and requiring wide separation of the transmitter and receiver. The system was developed by Pierre David, chief engineer of the National Radio laboratories, who worked in great secrecy with army officers and civilian technicians. Not until about the time of an exchange of radar information with the British in 1939 did the French begin serious work on high-power pulse radar.

United States.—Scientists under A. Hoyt Taylor and Leo C. Young in the Naval Research laboratory and under Col. William R. Blair in the Army's Signal Corps laboratories made early progress in radio detection. Navy workers had devised an interference type of radio detector by 1930. Army scientists first worked on microwave radar types in the early 1930s, but the sets were failures militarily because they could not attain sufficient range. The output power of microwave oscillator tubes at that time was too weak.

Success came by 1936 when both the army and navy developed pulse radars on longer wave lengths generated by special high-power tubes. The signal corps demonstrated a model of the army's first radar, a searchlight control (SLC) set, in May 1937. This set was developed for the coast artillery corps to locate in darkness any airplane within searchlight range so that gun crews could trap the plane in searchlight beams and direct visual fire upon it.

The army air corps at once put in a priority request for a long-range aircraft detector for early warning (EW). This led to the development of a mobile set capable of detecting and locating aircraft well over 100 mi. distant. The signal corps completed development of both this set and a fixed version by the end of 1939, and contracts for their production were let by 1940. Both were in military use before the Pearl Harbor attack. U.S. navy radars were also in production and use by then, following successful shipboard tests in early 1939.

Great Britain.—British radar grew from the efforts of a committee that the air ministry set up in 1934 for the scientific survey of air defense. This committee received, among other suggestions, a carefully worked out plan for the radio pulse-echo detection of aircraft. This was tested on Feb. 26, 1935, by a physicist then heading the radio department of the National Physical laboratory, Robert Watson-Watt.

The first experimental system of the type proposed by Watson-Watt was set up in the late spring of 1935 on the east coast of England. By that autumn the main features of a chain of warning stations to protect England had been worked out. By early 1938 the first five chain home (CH) stations, which protected the Thames estuary, were completed and in operation under Royal Air Force personnel. A chain of similar stations was erected around the borders of Great Britain in succeeding years.

Development emphasis then shifted to air-borne radar equipment. Two types were designed: (1) a set for the detection of surface vessels or surfaced submarines by patrol aircraft (called ASV, for air-to-surface vessel), and (2) an equipment to enable night fighters to home on enemy aircraft (called AI, for aircraft interception). An experimental ASV system was successfully demonstrated during British fleet maneuvers in Sept. 1938. Experimental AI equipment was demonstrated to the chief of R.A.F. fighter command in Aug. 1939.

The focusing of radar energy into sharp beams is especially important in the case of air-borne radar; for energy reflected when the radar beam strikes the ground or sea beneath the plane can mask entirely the much weaker echoes of the targets sought. Sharp beams can be obtained by the use of either very large antennas or very short radio wave lengths. Since large antennas cannot be carried in aircraft, short wave lengths are essential. The early British interest in military air-borne radar led to an intensive search for a type of radio transmitter which could give very high-power pulses at wave lengths of a few centimetres.

By early 1940, British researchers succeeded in developing just such a transmitting tube, the revolutionary multicavity magnetron, which gave about ten kilowatts of pulse power. The invention of this tube made microwave radar practical for the first time, and the history of modern radar can be said to date from the introduction of this device.

3. World War II Radar Development.—By the end of 1940 U.S. and British radar work was being carried out on a basis of full mutual exchange of information. A British technical mission, headed by Sir Henry T. Tizard, visited the U.S. in September and October of 1940, bringing complete information on British radar developments and samples of the cavity magnetron. Arrangements were made for continuing exchange of technical information and for co-ordinating the development work of both nations.

In discussions with the microwave committee of the U.S. National Defense Research committee (NDRC), which had been set up a few months before, members of the British mission proposed that the U.S. undertake two specific microwave developments: a microwave AI radar and a microwave position finder or gun layer (GL), for antiaircraft fire control. To implement these proposals, the microwave committee arranged to create a radar development laboratory staffed principally by university physicists in a pattern originated by the British several years earlier.

United States.—The Radiation laboratory, as the new NDRC establishment was named, opened its doors at the Massachusetts Institute of Technology, Cambridge, Mass., early in Nov. 1940. Its director throughout its 62 months of life was Lee A. DuBridge, on leave from the University of Rochester, later president of California Institute of Technology, Pasadena, Calif. The U.S. army and navy looked to the new Radiation laboratory for the development of microwave radar. Their own development agencies were already fully occupied with the many problems connected with getting the long-wave radar, already developed, through manufacture and into service use. At the end of 1940, the usefulness of microwave radar seemed highly speculative, and the army and navy laboratories quite properly felt it more important to concentrate their effort on radar techniques which had already been worked out.

During 1941, though not a single microwave radar unit was delivered for service use, development work at the Radiation laboratory broadened far beyond the two specific projects which had been suggested by the British mission. Microwave equipment was showing great promise for many different wartime uses, and a considerable amount of army and navy interest was developing.

The tremendous expansion of the radar development program during the war years can be measured by the personnel figures of the various laboratories. The total personnel of the Radiation laboratory was about 40 at the beginning of 1941; by the middle of 1945 it had risen to its peak of nearly 4,000. The radar section of the Naval Research laboratory increased its personnel to about 600 in the same period. The radar section of the Signal Corps laboratories grew into the Evans Signal laboratory, with a peak personnel of more than 3,000. A similar growth took place at the Aircraft Radio laboratory at Wright field, Dayton, Ohio.

Great Britain.—British research and production experience during World War II set a precedent for wartime radar development in the U.S. The Telecommunications Research establishment (TRE), located during the last years of the war at Malvern college, Eng., pioneered the path followed by the Radiation laboratory in the U.S. TRE originated five years earlier than its American counterpart, having begun with a nucleus of dedicated physicists and technicians who built the first CH station on the shore of the North sea in 1935.

By 1945 TRE personnel grew to number about 3,000. Throughout these years British government and military officials co-operated closely with university scientists and industrial engineers, providing funds and facilities while permitting great latitude and free play of imagination to the end that complex but workable equipment might be devised and quickly brought to combat use. A new pattern of military-civilian co-operation and a spirited partnership of civilian scientists and military users was created with marked success, first in England and then in the U.S., bringing revolutionary concepts and weapons to bear upon the enemy with devastating effectiveness and crucial timeliness. Experimental radar devices, hand-built at the laboratories, were often used in combat missions, the equipment being installed and maintained by civilian technicians who sometimes operated it as well.

The British and U.S. radar efforts together brought against the enemy increasing quantities of superior microwave radar. Notable examples were the precision position finders or GL sets that, by 1944, surpassed the German Würzburg radars. Such too were the efficient air-borne microwave radars whose shorter wave lengths permitted use of smaller antennas and gave greater detail (higher resolution) of target reflections. The first of these was the British H₂S (wave length 9 to 10 cm.), used in 1943 in such effective raids as those on Hamburg. Next was the improved H₂X which employed still shorter waves (about 3 cm. long).

Increasing use of these and other microwave radars replacing long-wave sets such as the enemy continued to employ (for want of efficient microwave generators like the cavity magnetron) gave the Allies through the last two years of the war an overwhelming radar superiority. In particular, the Allies developed jamming devices that blinded all German radars, both ground and air-borne types, that were operating on medium or long waves. Meanwhile, the Allies freely employed their superior microwave sets (unaffected by medium- or long-wave jamming) to direct attacks upon enemy targets at sea, on land and in the air.

Germany.—German radar development during the war was much retarded, as compared with the Allied effort, by over-confidence at first and throughout by poor management and defective co-operation between the military services and civilian scientists. Particularly harmful was a cutback in research that Hitler ordered in 1940. But as Allied air attacks increased, German radar production was stepped up.

More than 2,000 Freyas were built during the war and thousands

of other sets as well. Improved Würzburgs and other types were developed and organized into effective systems of early warning, target tracking, and fire control or gun laying. An effective AI set, the Lichtenstein, was hastily devised and placed in night fighters. All these efforts enabled the Germans to take an increasing toll of Allied aircraft over western Europe until a turning point in the radar war came in mid-1943.

When in Feb. 1943 the Germans salvaged an H₂S radar and its magnetron from a plane wreck near Rotterdam, they first learned that the Allies had developed microwave sets. (By the end of 1943 they learned of the still better 3-cm. radar when an H₂X set was recovered from a U.S. bomber that also crashed in Holland.) Desperately, the Germans hastened to set up the Rotterdam commission to develop cavity magnetrons and microwave radars, but only toward the very end of the war did they begin to produce the Berlin series of microwave sets, and these were too late to be of any help.

Japan.—Such radar as the Japanese had developed before World War II was of the continuous-wave type, utilizing interference or Doppler techniques. Not until 1940 did work begin on pulse-type radar.

Some types were strongly influenced by foreign radar design. For example, a Japanese version of the Würzburg was developed by 1945, based on plans the Germans had sent via submarine. The army's Taichi-6 resembled a U.S. army set, and a type of naval ground-based radar for antiaircraft fire control, the S-3, was based upon another U.S. set, a number of which had been captured in the Philippines in 1942. More than a thousand sets of an ASV type, the Taki-1, were produced. Using waves a metre and a half long, at 200 MHz, the set was mounted in Japanese bombers that carried the necessarily large antennas mounted on the exteriors of their fuselages.

The Japanese also developed a 10-cm. magnetron. One of their best shipboard radars employed this type of tube. They did not, however, develop in World War II any radar comparable to the Allied microwave SCR-584 or the MEW (microwave early warning) radar set.

4. Use of Radar in World War II.—The brilliant success of the early British chain home stations in countering the threat of the *Luftwaffe* demonstrated the usefulness of radar in its original military role—the detection and location of aircraft at ranges and under conditions of visibility that precluded locating planes in any other way. As the war continued, many other uses for radar were developed. The most important are described below.

Aircraft Warning.—The earliest sets used were those of the British home chain. These large installations used radio waves about ten metres in length, and gave their display on an A-scope. Target bearing was found by comparing the intensity of the target signal received on one fixed receiving array with the intensity of the echo from the same target received on another fixed array aimed in a different direction; the elevation angle of a target, and thus its altitude, was measured in a similar way. These CH radar stations, as they were called, remained the principal reliance of the British radar defense throughout the war, and were used in 1944 and 1945 for the detection of German V-2 rockets aimed at England.

Later aircraft warning sets used shorter radio wave lengths, usually about 1.5 to 3 metres. At this wave length, a relatively narrow beam can be produced by an antenna array small enough for installation on shipboard, or for use in a transportable ground equipment. At the same time, the use of a radar beam requires continuous scanning in azimuth in order to cover all directions from the station.

In early 1944, there was introduced a microwave early-warning radar, operating on a wave length of 10 cm., which was highly successful. The radar beam produced by this set was only 1° wide in azimuth; in consequence, the ability of the set to resolve closely spaced targets on its PPI display was very much better than that of earlier equipment having broader beams. In large R.A.F. raids, often comprised of more than 500 individual aircraft, most of the bombers could be seen separately by MEW radar.

In situations of heavy air traffic, or under conditions where precise control of aircraft is important, such high radar resolution is extremely valuable.

Identification Equipment.—When a radar indicator shows echoes from dozens, or even hundreds, of aircraft, it becomes important to know which of these aircraft are friendly and which hostile. This requirement was recognized by the British early in their work on radar, and they devised an identification system, called IFF (identification as friend or foe), which was adopted by the Allied forces during World War II.

All friendly aircraft were equipped with a transponder—a radar beacon (*see* below) which gave a coded response when the aircraft carrying it was in the beam of a radar set. Arrangements were made to display this response on a scope which was either that used by the challenging radar set, or a special scope associated with the radar. Aircraft showing an IFF response were taken to be definitely friendly; aircraft not showing such a response were doubtful. Either they were hostile, or they were friendly planes whose transponders were out of order or not turned on.

While IFF was extremely useful in the early days of the war when aircraft density was still low, it failed operationally in the enormously high aircraft densities of the latter years of the war. A means for rapid and secure identification was, therefore, one of the unsolved operational problems of radar at the end of World War II.

IFF equipment of the standard type was also used by Allied naval vessels in order to identify friendly ships both to aircraft and to other surface vessels. In this use, of course, the problem of high density seldom arose, and maintenance of transponders was easier than it was in aircraft. IFF in ships was, therefore, considerably more reliable than it was in aircraft.

Control of Aircraft Interception.—The observation was early made by the British that, since both a hostile plane and a friendly fighter can be seen on the indicator of a single radar, it might be possible for a ground controller, viewing the radar scope, to coach the fighter into position to make an interception. The development of the plan position indicator greatly facilitated such ground control of interception.

Special radar equipment, called GCI, was designed for this purpose in the earliest days of the war, and proved to be quite successful.

When the Germans abandoned daytime attacks on England at the end of 1940, the technique of ground control became much more exacting. It was no longer sufficient to bring the defensive fighters into the general vicinity of the enemy aircraft and then to rely on the pilot's vision to complete the interception. A skilful ground controller could, under favourable circumstances, bring a fighter close enough to his target to enable a visual contact to be made even at night; but this was so difficult that further radar aids to the interception were clearly needed.

AI Radar.—It was this reasoning which led to the development of radar for aircraft interception. Night fighters were provided with air-borne radar sets with a range of a few miles against other aircraft. The ground controller coached the night fighter into a position a mile or two behind the hostile plane, a little below and on the same course. He then instructed the radar observer in the night fighter to turn on his AI equipment. If the early phases of the interception had been successfully carried out, the hostile aircraft gave a signal on the AI radar, and the combat was joined on the basis of homing information made available by the night fighter's own radar.

By the time reliable microwave AI equipment had been developed by the Allies in World War II, they enjoyed such thorough air superiority that it did not play a major tactical role. The early British 1.5 metre AI equipment used in 1940 and 1941 had many drawbacks, but it was sufficiently effective to enable the R.A.F. to master the night-bombing campaign of the *Luftwaffe*.

Antiaircraft Position Finders or Gun Layers (GL).—The earliest radar set developed by the U.S. army signal corps was the searchlight control set, mentioned above, for determining azimuth, elevation and range of aircraft targets at night in order to direct searchlight beams upon them. These sets also were employed for control and direction of gunfire under conditions preventing visual tracking—at night or in cloud—although the set had not been designed for GL use. Such use of radar for fire control became a most important application in World War II, but neither early British nor U.S. sets, working at wave lengths of a metre or more, had sufficient accuracy to direct very effective blind gunfire.

The introduction of microwave sets, however, enabled the design of radar position finders whose accuracy was good enough to permit blind fire that was as effective as visually controlled fire. The most successful of all Allied types of such equipment was the SCR-584. This U.S. radar measured the azimuth and elevation angles of a target with an error of less than one-twentieth degree, and range with an error less than 25 yd. It was the first radar equipment which incorporated automatic tracking; when the SCR-584 was pointed at a target, it could be "locked on" in such a way that servomechanisms actuated by the radar kept its antenna pointing continuously at that target.

Naval antiaircraft fire was controlled by radar of a similar sort, although no navy, Allied or Axis, had equipment for the purpose that was as effective or as satisfactory as the U.S. army's SCR-584.

Close Control of Aircraft.—The GCI techniques which were referred to above had as their aim the location of a friendly fighter in such a position that he could attack a hostile bomber, usually with the help of an AI radar carried by the night fighter. Minor errors in positioning the friendly plane were usually relatively unimportant, and the target with respect to which the friendly plane was being positioned was an aircraft moving with a speed comparable with that of the plane under radar control. Both these facts simplified the GCI problem.

As the position-finding precision of radar grew, it began to be clear that a ground controller could direct aircraft accurately into a desired position with relation to ground targets. Two principal problems presented themselves during the war, one of which is important in peacetime air operations.

First, the tactical air commands that accompanied the U.S. armies on the continent of Europe were composed, for the most part, of fighter bombers. These single-seat aircraft were much too small to carry radar equipment, and the pilot of such a plane was much too busy to interpret its readings even if he had had radar. Nevertheless, the TAC aircraft had to operate often in conditions of greatly restricted visibility. Controllers located at ground radar sets had considerable success in guiding TAC fighter bombers to their targets by radiotelephone instructions. Even entirely blind bombing was done by such aircraft, altogether on the basis of course and release-time instructions received from a controller at a ground radar. The SCR-584, suitably modified, was used for this work.

The second application of close aircraft control from the ground is that of coaching a plane in to a landing under poor visibility conditions. A special high-precision radar set, called GCA (ground controlled approach), was designed at the Radiation laboratory for this purpose. Though it emerged from production rather late in World War II, it was used quite successfully both in Europe and in the Pacific. Its use had become common by the 1960s in both civil and military air operations.

Surface Search and Fire Control.—In addition to locating aircraft and directing fire against them, radar was used during the war to locate and direct fire against surface vessels, both from other ships and from coastal defense stations. As will be seen in the next section, microwaves enjoy a great superiority in search for targets near the surface of the sea, so that it often happened that the same radar was used for search and for fire control against surface vessels.

Such radar could also locate precisely the splashes caused by the fall of shot, thus permitting the spot correction of unseen fire. In naval engagements in the Pacific, on several occasions, ships of the U.S. fleet engaged and sank Japanese vessels without ever seeing them visually.

ASV Radar.—Of the several types of air-borne radar equipment used in the war, that employed by patrol aircraft for searching out and attacking surface vessels was one of the most common.

A ship on the open sea is an ideal radar target, and even quite primitive equipment suffices to home on such an object. As the art of radar design advanced, ASV equipment developed from a heavy, bulky installation to a compact and effective unit.

ASV radar was most effective in the antisubmarine campaign. During much of 1943, German submarines were sunk at a rate not far from one per day, two-thirds of them by aircraft attack. Almost all of the aircraft attacks developed from radar sightings.

Means were also developed for bombing ship targets accurately on the basis of the radar display. In a single month, a single squadron of the U.S. 14th air force sank 110,000 tons of Japanese shipping in the China sea, entirely at night and entirely by radar.

Air-borne Radar for Navigation and Bombing.—During trials of AI and ASV radar, it was found that microwave equipment, with its narrow beams, could give a sufficiently good picture of the terrain beneath an aircraft to enable navigation by pilotage. Cities and built-up areas returned much stronger signals than open country, and hills, rivers and coast lines were especially well defined.

The British R.A.F. bomber command pioneered in using such radar to guide its pathfinder aircraft. These planes, manned by specially chosen personnel, dropped flares on the target at which the main force aimed by ordinary optical means. The U.S. strategic air forces, committed to daytime bombing, found by experience that target visibility was often so poor that in order to maintain full operation they also needed such radar aids.

Even on occasions when target visibility was good, the radar was useful in permitting the bombers to line up correctly on their approach to the bombing run. A medium-sized city is visible for about 50 miles on radar of wartime performance; it can rarely be seen as far as this with the eye. Of the 400,000 tons of bombs dropped by the 8th air force after Nov. 1943, when this equipment (called "Mickey" or "H$_2$S") was introduced, more than half was aimed entirely by radar.

Beacon Bombing Systems.—Mention has already been made of the use of radar beacons for identification. Since these beacons give an immediate response to a radar challenge, they provide an excellent means for measuring the range to a point whose nature is known. Two such measurements based on a single point enable the exact position of such a point to be found by triangulation. Since range can be measured so conveniently and so accurately by pulse-timing methods, every precise position can be determined.

Two different bombing systems were based on this principle during World War II. In one of them, called "Oboe," the aircraft carried a radar beacon. The beacon was challenged by two ground stations, and the range of the aircraft from each station measured. Signals were sent to the plane by radio to keep it on a circular course of constant range from one station, called the "cat." The other station, called the "mouse," sent signals to the aircraft indicating the exact moment of bomb release necessary to hit the previously chosen target.

The Oboe system was highly accurate; with good ground and air crews the operational errors were less than 250 yd. from an altitude of 30,000 ft. Its limitations were that, since it depended on the ability of ground stations to see the signals from a beacon in the bombing aircraft, it would not work over the optical horizon (about 250 mi. for an altitude of 30,000 ft.); and that it demanded a high degree of co-ordination between two widely separated ground stations. Even with this co-ordination, it could handle only one aircraft at a time.

Despite the limitations of the Oboe system, the British used it quite successfully to guide the pathfinder aircraft of R.A.F. bomber command. The devastation of the Ruhr, which was just within Oboe range from the United Kingdom, was carried out almost entirely with the help of Oboe.

In the other type of beacon bombing system, called "H" by the British, beacons were placed on the ground at accurately located spots, and the interrogation and display equipment was carried in the bombing aircraft. A U.S. system based on this principle, called Shoran (for short range navigation), was highly successful during World War II.

Although Shoran was subject to the same horizon limitation as that affecting Oboe, it did not suffer from as severe a limitation in traffic-handling capacity. Each aircraft could challenge the ground beacons independently of all the other planes that might be doing so at the same time. It was with Shoran that the error in the map position of Corsica, already mentioned, was discovered.

Electronic Navigation Systems.—The beacon bombing systems and the air-borne radar for navigation that have just been described will be recognized as navigational equipment. They were rather specialized in nature, being designed for the exacting use of leading a bomber to its target. No such accuracy is needed to facilitate the ordinary navigation of aircraft from base to base. Radio-beam navigational aids to such navigation had been in use for years, but the development of pulse-timing methods for radar led to the development of navigational aids based on the pulse-ranging principle. Among the more important systems of this sort are the British Gee and the U.S. Loran.

Air-borne Range-finding and Gun-laying Radar.—The vigorous opposition of German fighters to Allied bombing in the early days of World War II led to the U.S. development of light, compact radar to aid in air-to-air gunnery, intended principally to contribute to bomber defense. One type was an automatic radar range finder for optically aimed fire by daylight. Another provided complete position-finding to protect bombers against night fighters under conditions precluding optical sighting. Both of these radars became available during World War II, but at such a late date that their operational usefulness was small. In the Korean War, however, they and successor equipment proved indispensable aids to air-to-air gunnery in jet aircraft combat.

Radar Countermeasures.—Use of radar by the Germans and the Japanese led to a considerable Allied effort in the field of countermeasures designed to mislead enemy radar or to render it ineffective. A similar effort was mounted by the Germans and the Japanese. These countermeasures took two forms: they consisted either of electronic "jamming" or "spoofing" of enemy radar by the transmission of suitably timed signals on the appropriate frequency; or, alternatively, they involved the dispersal of material which gave confusing radar reflections and thus hid attacking aircraft.

The second type of radar countermeasure was the most important single means of confusing enemy radar. Aluminum foil, cut into strips about a half wave length long at the enemy radar frequency, was the most commonly used form of material dispersed from aircraft to give false echoes. Such material was called "window" by the British, "chaff" by the U.S. army air force, and *Dueppel* by the Germans. Long-wave radar, with its broad beams, was the most readily confused by this means. The appearance on the scope of an Allied 10-cm. radar of "window" cut to confuse the German 60-cm. radar showed false echoes which were prominent but not hopelessly confusing. German radar, however, could see the aircraft targets under these conditions only with the greatest difficulty.

For about 18 months, both the Germans and the British refrained from using this deceptive trick, on the theory that the other side was ignorant of the possibility of doing it. Once it was introduced, however, the R.A.F. bomber command dispensed in the form of window, on each full-scale raid, a weight of aluminum sufficient to construct three heavy bombers. Loss figures showed that the protection afforded by this amount of window saved, on the average, seven bombers per raid.

5. Military Development After World War II.—At the close of World War II the main outlines of radar system design had been reasonably well defined, and many of the operational applications had been completed. In the following years radar development included improvements of components and circuitry, electronic processing of received data, increasing use of solid-state transistors and masers, introduction of genuinely new components such as ferrite duplexers and new scanning methods, both mentioned below, and many new applications.

In U.S. military uses, remarkable attainments in transmitters of ever higher power and in receivers of greater sensitivity led to extremely long-range radars for early warning of ballistic missiles. Pulse-Doppler (PD) methods, utilizing such refinements as data processing and "memory" circuits, enabled the development of supersensitive radars for use in ground surveillance and personnel detection.

Military radar equipment, as such, underwent little improvement in the period between the end of World War II and the beginning of hostilities in Korea in 1950. The Korean conflict made greatly increased military budgets available, but even then only detailed improvements in radar performance took place, resulting mainly from the development of improved components. This is well illustrated by the fact that radar sets differing only slightly from the SCR-584 (development of which was undertaken in 1941 with field use beginning in early 1944) were built for equipping the NATO military forces in the mid-1950s.

The most prominent postwar trend in the design of military radar systems was toward the elimination of human beings as links between a radar indicator and the controls of a weapon system. This general development was forced on military technologists by the astounding increase in aircraft performance, the development of nuclear weapons, the appearance of successful guided missiles and by the growth of commercial aviation.

In the years following World War II, the development of jet engines tripled the speeds of relatively conventional aircraft, thus putting unprecedented demands on air warning and control organizations and on air defense generally. The leisurely human plotting-and-telling organizations of World War II clearly had to be replaced by something faster and less fallible. If antiaircraft guns were to be useful at all, they would clearly have to be controlled entirely automatically to engage such high-speed targets. The performance of fighter interceptors had increased to the point where the reflexes of a human pilot were barely adequate to control an attack; a high degree of automatic control extending from the AI radar to the final weapon—gun or rocket—was clearly required for the best results.

In the case of guided missiles, the situation was even plainer. An interceptor missile is a fighter aircraft without a human pilot. There can be no debate about the requirement for automatic control. The same is true of long-range missiles intended for a strategic bombing role, and indeed for missiles in general. In all these cases, radar is an important part of the system as a whole.

In addition, the development of nuclear weapons, to the point at which a single well-executed air raid might utterly destroy the capability of a great country to wage war, made it imperative to have an air-defense system that would be continuously alert and effective against a single unexpected raid. At the same time, the vast growth of civil aviation translated this requirement into the need for developing a system which could keep current track of thousands of aircraft, so that potentially hostile aircraft could be distinguished and investigated (counterattacked, if necessary) before they had an opportunity to attack. Any such system obviously would require a degree of automatic operation not dreamed of during World War II.

Fortunately, the development of high-speed digital computers, begun in the late years of the war, provided the basic techniques which made it possible to mechanize the use of radar data. The most ambitious undertaking of this sort in the 1950s was the development of the semiautomatic ground environment (Sage) system, designed to control weapons defending the continental United States against air raids.

In the Sage system, high-performance ground radar sets were placed in the U.S. and Canada at locations that gave reasonably continuous coverage of aircraft, except those at very low altitude. Signals from these radars were transmitted to central control stations, each equipped with a vast computer capable of establishing and maintaining aircraft flight paths from the intermittent radar data, performing partial identification of aircraft from flight-plan information filed by friendly aircraft before take-off, assisting in the assignment of defensive fighters to investigate unknown aircraft, and doing the GCI job for fighters and interceptor missiles ordered to the attack. In addition, such defense

organizations as naval units and the antiaircraft missile batteries guarding important targets could be alerted and given information on the tracks of incoming hostile aircraft.

To increase the time available to ready defenses, long-range radar installations (the distant-early-warning, or DEW, line of radars) were constructed in the far north of the North American continent. Man-made islands (Texas towers) were built on the eastern continental shelf as far out as 200 mi. into the Atlantic. Ultra-long-range aircraft equipped with high-performance radar were flown as air-borne pickets as far out as 1,000 mi. at sea.

The DEW line was designed to detect and locate aircraft while they were yet a considerable flight time distant, even at supersonic speeds. But against much swifter long-range ballistic missiles, which began to present a threat by the mid-1950s, another radar system had to be developed. Called the ballistic missile early warning system, or BMEWS, this comprised two stations in North America and one in northern England.

The first BMEWS station, which began operation in Oct. 1960 at Thule, Greenland, under U.S. air force direction, cost nearly $500,000,000. Four antenna arrays, each standing 165 ft. high and 400 ft. long, were designed to emit the highest power radiations employed up to that time in military radar. The immensely powerful transmitters, generating several million watts at peak pulse, projected two fanlike beams over the north pole and far beyond, capable of detecting a missile 3,000 mi. distant when it attained an altitude of 600 mi. Two sets of echo data, which would be received as the missile passed first through the lower beam and then through the upper one, would enable electronic calculators at Thule to predict within moments the missile's course and impact area. Thus about 15 or 20 minutes could be provided for warning and countermissile action.

During the late 1950s there were many military applications of radar besides the advanced warning and interception efforts described above. Marked progress was made in radar range and accuracy. A variety of new applications appeared. Unprecedented demands for both offense and defense uses arose from the needs of military technology in support of radically new concepts of modern armed forces in the atomic and missile era. The needs and the applications involved navigation, meteorology, bombing, mapping, missile tracking and guidance, reconnaissance and surveillance.

Combat surveillance, to illustrate only one application, resulted in U.S. army requirements for radar able to detect and locate such moving targets as a creeping soldier at short ranges and moving vehicles and troops at longer distances. The need for such "intrusion detectors" led to radar systems that combined certain characteristics of both pulse and CW techniques. The consequence became a type of radar system called pulse-Doppler, or PD, discussed near the end of this article.

Several types of PD radar, for detection and location of moving targets only, were developed for sensory and surveillance uses by ground troops. A small portable set called the "silent sentry," which used transistors instead of electron tubes and could therefore be readily powered by batteries, was able to detect moving tanks, trucks or troops up to 3 mi. distant, converting the pulse-Doppler echoes into audible sounds in the earphones of the radar operator. Differences in the sound made it possible to distinguish a walking from a running man up to a half mile away. Target location could be determined with an error of less than 25 yd.

A larger medium-range system indicated moving echoes, both audibly in headphones and visually on an oscilloscope, with a sensitivity so great that the audible signals differed recognizably for tanks, trucks or troops up to 10 mi. distant, and for a creeping man up to 2 mi. away.

Military needs for detailed surveillance of large areas of enemy terrain under conditions of cloud or night (preventing normal photography) and at considerable distances from one side (safely within friendly territory) led to a remarkable air and ground radar system developed by University of Michigan scientists and the U.S. army signal corps. The echo signals of the air-borne radar are recorded on film during the surveillance flight. This film is developed after the plane lands and is then processed by an analogue computer. The process yields a detailed presentation of the scanned area, which appears as if it had been viewed directly beneath the airplane, although actually it lay miles to one side. The entire system thus departs radically in its signal storage and delayed output aspects from radars that give an instant visual or aural indication of targets. The system also embodies a major innovation in its unique antenna treatment. Fine radar focusing and resolution, revealing great detail at long distances as well as in the foreground, would ordinarily require an immensely wide antenna, obviously impossible to mount in an airplane.

Yet the superior effects of such a huge antenna array are attained with a 5-ft. antenna (the size that is actually employed) by coupling its action to the forward flight of the plane. The forward motion, combined with the recorded reception of echo pulses and subsequent treatment in a computer, permits a scanning and focusing effect as though the short antenna were extended many times the length of the airplane. This circumstance requires exact navigation and automatic correction of inevitable flight aberrations. Therefore, a flight navigation system, including an automatic pilot, is included in the system design. As a result the radar is kept in accurate focus throughout the surveillance flight and is focused simultaneously at all ranges. The printed product turned out by the computer resembles a photographic map with better detail at greater ranges than previously possible—revealing, for example, the individual poles of a telephone line seen almost lengthwise many miles away.

6. Civil Development After World War II.—In civil uses commercial aviation and marine vessels increasingly employed radar aids to navigation. Highway police used a simple form of CW for the detection of speeding vehicles, the Doppler shift of the reflections from moving cars enabling instant and direct measurement of their speed. Astronomers and space researchers found that radar could help map the moon and could yield usable echoes from the sun and planets.

Marine Radar Developments.—Immediately after World War II several manufacturers in Great Britain and the U.S. offered simple radar equipment suitable for coastwise navigation. Shipborne sets generally employ microwaves in the X band (3 cm.) in order to keep the antenna size small. The rotating antenna presents upon a PPI scope the echoes from the coast lines, obstacles and other ships. Shipboard radars steadily increased in number, coming into use even in small fishing and pleasure craft.

(L. N. R.; G. R. T.)

The radar indicator on a ship conventionally shows motion of fixed and moving targets in a manner that is relative to the movement of its own ship. This calls for a considerable degree of interpretation based upon experience and special training. Misinterpretations are easy. In true-motion radar, interpretation of the traffic pattern is simplified.

True-motion radar depicts the radar scene as though viewed from a stationary overhead point apart from the ship. Both the base ship and other targets having motion are shown moving along their true headings, and fixed targets such as buoys, anchored ships and landmarks are shown as stationary. The display of true motion is achieved by feeding speed and heading information continuously into vector resolver circuits which control the position of the electrical centre of the PPI. Thus, the centre moves across the screen in accordance with ship movements and can be manually set to any position. As the centre spot approaches the edge it must be reset to another point of beginning.

Through use of an indicator tube having long persistence or a memory storage tube (see *General Improvements in Radar Performance,* below), all moving targets show trails depicting true heading and an indication of speed. The effects of wind and current may be detected by noting apparent motion of known fixed targets and corrections made therefor by trimming the input levels to the speed and heading vector resolvers, thus converting the display to ground reference.

The U.S. Maritime administration has successfully tested an automatic data computer that accepts input information consisting of ships' speed, heading and bearing rate. Additionally, up to 10 radar targets are automatically tracked. The computer output of this equipment is displayed on a special indicator and in numerical readouts showing bearings, range, speed, closest point and time of approach, and safe course and speed.

The following recommendations for minimum performance standards have been prepared by the U.S. Radio Technical Commission for Marine Services (RTCM) and offered for use by administering government agencies. The work is in response to the recommendation of the International Convention for the Safety of Life at Sea (SOLAS) of 1960 concerning the carrying of radar. Subsequently the Inter-Governmental Maritime Consultative organization (IMCO) has been moving to propose that radar be mandatory on oceangoing ships of 1,600 tons gross or over, and that each member government develop its own specifications.

The recommendations of the RTCM are here condensed and reproduced in part.

Range (for an antenna height of 50 ft. above sea level):
  200 ft. coastline, 20 nautical mi.
  20 ft. coastline, 7 nautical mi.
  Surface object, 7 nautical mi.
  Standard target of 100 sq.ft. effective with centre 3.3 ft. high, 2 nautical mi. (50% of scans)
  Minimum range 50 yd.
Range accuracy.—1.5% of the maximum range of the fixed scale rings in use, or 75 yd., whichever is greater; or 2.5% of the maximum range of a variable marker.
Range discrimination.—50 yd. at 1 nautical mi., target area 10 sq.m.
Bearing accuracy.—± 1°, target area 10 sq.m.
Bearing discrimination:
  Main beam: S band, ± 2° at 3 decibels down
                      ± 5° at 20 decibels down
             X band, ± 1° at 3 decibels down
                      ± 2.5° at 20 decibels down
  Side lobes, ± 10° at 26–30 decibels down
  Discriminate between two 10-sq.m. targets 1 nautical mi. distant, 4° or less on S band and 2° or less on X band
  Vertical beam, 3 decibels down at ± 10°
Scan.—Target data at least each 6 sec. Wind velocity 80 knots operation, 150 knots damage.
Display:
  7.5 in. diameter, PPI area; 14 in. diameter preferred
  Scales, 6 scales ½ or ¾ to 32 nautical mi.
  Heading indicator, accurate to 1°
  Azimuth stabilizer, 0.5°
Power supply.—A.C., −10% to +20% voltage; D.C., 110/220 v., −20% to +10% voltage.
Interference, climatic and environmental specifications.—Typical for high-reliability electronic equipment.   (F. B. D.)

In some ports large radar surveillance sets have been installed ashore overlooking the harbour and approach waters in order to assist shipping when visibility is bad. The radar operator observing ship movements in the confined waters advises pilots of harbour traffic conditions from moment to moment by means of radiotelephone. A notable system at Liverpool, Eng., installed in 1948, guided ships through the narrow approach waters under adverse conditions of visibility. The system utilized six PPI scopes to cover in detail (discriminating within 40 yd.) the 14 mi. of the Mersey river channel and harbour front that are kept under constant surveillance.

Aeronautic Developments.—Proposals were also made soon after World War II for the installation of radar navigational equipment in commercial airliners and for the establishment of ground radar stations along commercial airways and at airports. The U.S. Civil Aeronautics administration, which became the Federal Aviation agency (FAA) in 1958, promoted installation at major airports of GCA radar systems by means of which traffic controllers could observe airliners approaching in bad visibility or at night, guide them by means of radio-telephone and "talk" the pilots safely down to the field. GCA had not been provided at all airports in the early 1960s, partly because pilots preferred the instrument landing system, or ILS, a radio navigation and landing aid that has long been standard equipment at many airports over the world.

GCA in this application requires two types of radar. Airport surveillance radar (ASR) scans a circle 30 mi. or more in radius around the field and displays upon a PPI scope in the control tower all aircraft within range up to within about 5 mi. Within this smaller inner circle a precision approach radar (PAR) takes over, using a limited-angle PPI or B-scope and a range-height indicator. Airport surveillance sets employ pulse modulation, and all recent types also include MTI so that operators can switch to the MTI technique if necessary in order to distinguish moving echoes (airplanes) from fixed reflections in the area being scanned.

More GCA radar of an improved type was coming into use by the early 1960s as the FAA carried out a program of installing sets with longer range and greater refinement. A high-definition radar, known as airport surface detection equipment (ASDE), that gives almost photographic clarity (using very short 1-cm. waves) in distinguishing planes and motor trucks on the field, began to be used in 1960. The first two installations were made at the Kennedy, N.Y., and Newark, N.J., airports.

Meanwhile, air-borne radars, using wave lengths of about 5 cm., were being installed in increasing numbers of large modern air transports, primarily for storm detection, enabling pilots to fly evasive courses around dangerous turbulence. Frequencies corresponding to the wave lengths of about 5 cm. were found to be best for echo reflection from storm clouds.

Astronomical Developments.—Radar astronomy, the study (by means of radio reflection) of the moon and other bodies in the solar system, became possible with increased transmitter power, greater receiver sensitivity and the uses of electronic computers to discriminate the extremely weak echo signals from the stronger interfering signals of inevitable noise. The radar technique enables more accurate measurement of distance than optical methods permit, and it enables study of surface structure of bodies in the solar system. Radar astronomy is closely related to radio astronomy (*q.v.*), since the supersensitive radar receiver can be used alone to listen to the many active emitters of radio waves, such as those from heat and gaseous sources within the solar system and from innumerable other sources both in our galaxy and beyond it.

The first radar contact with the moon, about 250,000 mi. away, was made by the U.S. army signal corps in Jan. 1946, using a modified SCR-271 radar. This initial success was followed in 1958 with radar reflections from Venus, some 28,000,000 mi. distant, and in 1959 by radar contact with the sun, nearly four times as far.

Both the Venus contacts (by the Lincoln laboratory of the Massachusetts Institute of Technology) and the echoes from the sun (accomplished by researchers at Stanford university) required computer techniques for study of the echo patterns. The echoes, returning minutes after the transmission because of the enormous distances involved, were so weak that they could not be immediately distinguished from the radio noises, both those received from without and those generated within the receiver circuits. But by recording the received signals and processing them with an electronic computer, researchers were able to separate out the echo pattern. From it they could determine something of the nature and characteristics of the reflecting body. With improved equipment and techniques radar astronomers expected to be able to map the planets in considerable detail.

III. FACTORS AFFECTING RADAR PERFORMANCE

1. The Free-space Radar Equation.—A radar set must detect the weak signal returned from a distant reflecting object. The radar equation is important because it connects the various quantities that govern the strength of the signal so received. This relation will not serve to determine the maximum range at which the radar can detect a target unless the minimum power which gives a detectable radar signal, S_{min}, is known. The value of this latter important quantity will be found to depend on many factors, not all of which are accessible to measurement.

In discussing the radar equation, we first assume the very simple case of free-space propagation of the radio waves used in radar. This corresponds to a situation in which (1) no large obstacles intervene between the radar antenna and the target, along the optical line of sight; (2) no alternate transmission path, via a reflecting surface, exists for the radio energy; (3) the intervening atmosphere which must be traversed by the radio energy is homogeneous with respect to index of refraction at the frequency used; and (4) no appreciable absorption occurs in the atmosphere.

These conditions restrict our attention to radar targets within the optical horizon, and in fact to targets high enough above the horizon to avoid important effects (*see* below) which arise from the reflection of an appreciable amount of energy from the surface of the land or sea. If the conditions of free-space propagation apply, the transmitted radio wave has spherical wave fronts (limited in extent by the directional properties of the antenna) which spread out in such a way that the intensity of the radio wave changes with the inverse square of the distance from the radar antenna.

If the transmitting antenna radiated energy uniformly in all directions, the power flow through unit area at a distance R from the antenna would be the transmitted power, P, divided by $4\pi R^2$. Most radar antennas are directive, however, and concentrate the energy in certain directions, so that the power flow observed at some distant point will differ by a factor G from that which would be produced by an antenna radiating uniformly the same total power. The quantity G is called the gain of the antenna in the direction in question. Its average taken over a complete sphere surrounding the antenna must clearly be unity. As radar antennas are ordinarily highly directive, we shall usually be interested in the maximum value of G, which we call G_o. When the radiating system, or antenna, can be regarded as an aperture of large area (measured in square wave lengths), over which a substantially plane wave is excited, we can write a useful expression for the maximum antenna gain, G_o. The maximum antenna gain is related to the antenna area A and the wave length λ by the following relation:

$$G_o = \frac{4\pi A d}{\lambda^2} \qquad (2)$$

For actual antennas, the dimensionless factor d is usually about 0.6.

A second important property of an antenna is its effective receiving cross section. This quantity, whose dimensions are those of area, yields the total signal power available at the terminals of an antenna when an incident plane wave of unit power per unit area falls upon it. Effective receiving cross section is related to antenna gain as follows:

$$A_r = \frac{G\lambda^2}{4\pi} \qquad (3)$$

In this equation, G has been written instead of G_o to emphasize that the applicability of eq. (3) is not limited to the direction of maximum gain or to beams of special shape. Once the gain of an antenna in a particular direction has been specified, its effective receiving cross section for plane waves incident from that direction is fixed.

To obtain a measure of the amount of power reflected by the target, we define the radar cross section of the target, σ, as follows: σ is to be 4π times the ratio of the power per unit solid angle scattered back toward the transmitter, to the power per unit area in the wave falling on the target. In other words, if the power falling on an area σ located at the target position were to be scattered uniformly in all directions, the power received at the radar would be just the same as it is in the case of the actual target. Ordinarily, σ must be inferred by measurements on actual targets, since it depends in a complicated way on the wave length and on the angle at which a target is viewed.

We are now ready to formulate the radar equation. If S is the signal power received, P the transmitted power, G the antenna gain, λ the wave length, σ the radar cross section of the target, and R the range, or distance between radar and target,

$$S = \left(\frac{PG}{4\pi R^2}\right)\left(\frac{\sigma}{4\pi R^2}\right)\left(\frac{G\lambda^2}{4\pi}\right) \qquad (4)$$

The quantity in the first parentheses gives the power density at the target; when we multiply by the second parentheses we obtain the power which returns to the radar antenna; the last factor is the receiving cross section of the antenna. Rearranging,

$$S = P\frac{G^2\lambda^2\sigma}{(4\pi)^3 R^4} \qquad (5)$$

This equation contains G, not G_o, and is thus valid for any direction. Usually we are interested in the return signal when the target lies somewhere along the direction the radar beam is pointing; G should then be replaced by G_o. If we then write G_o in terms of A, according to eq. (2), we obtain

$$S = \frac{P\sigma A^2 d^2}{4\pi R^4 \lambda^2} \qquad (6)$$

The received signal power is proportional to the power of the transmitted signals, to the radar cross section of the target and to the square of the antenna area. It is inversely proportional to the wave length squared, and to the fourth power of the range. If the minimum signal power required for detection, S_{min}, is known, we can rearrange eq. (6) to give the maximum range of detection, R_{max}, for a target of given cross section, σ:

$$R_{max} = \sqrt[4]{\frac{P\sigma A^2 d^2}{4\pi S_{min}\lambda^2}} \qquad (7)$$

To help fix ideas, it will be useful to give a numerical example of the use of this equation, with values for the quantities involved which were not unusual in wartime pulse radar practice. Let $\lambda = 0.10$ ft. ($= 3.0$ cm.), $P = 10^5$ watts, $A = 10$ ft.^{2}, $d = 0.6$, $\sigma = 100$ ft.^{2} (the radar cross section of a small aircraft) and $S_{min} = 5 \times 10^{-12}$ watts. We then obtain $R_{max} = 155,000$ ft. or 29 statute miles.

A sixteenfold increase in transmitted power is required to double the maximum range. It would appear that R_{max} could be doubled by doubling the linear dimensions of the antenna. However, this change cannot be discussed so simply, as the decrease in radar beam width resulting from making the antenna larger indirectly affects S_{min}. A change in wave length is also difficult to discuss, since it produces changes in S_{min}, P and possibly σ as well.

2. The Minimum Detectable Signal.—The reason that S_{min} has a finite value, and cannot be made indefinitely small, is that an amplifier intended to increase the power of a feeble electrical signal always produces random electrical fluctuations, called "noise." As the true signal entering any receiver is made weaker and weaker, it subsides eventually into the fluctuating background of noise and is no longer discernible.

The limit of sensitivity of an ordinary low-frequency radio receiver is set, not by internal noise, but by similar random disturbances which originate outside the receiver. These disturbances enter the receiver by means of the antenna, so that the effectiveness of a desired signal in competition with such interference is the ratio of signal to the interference power at the antenna terminals. The absolute level of interference power throughout the conventional radio bands (down to a few metres wave length) is so high that internal noise in a reasonably well-designed radio receiver is negligible by comparison.

The situation is different in the microwave region, where external noise interference is almost wholly negligible. Great effort has, therefore, been put on reducing the inherent noise of microwave receivers.

Quite general theoretical considerations give the result that the mean square noise voltage unavoidably generated in a receiver is proportional to the width of the band of frequencies amplified by the receiver. This band width will be denoted by B. The excellence of a receiver in respect to its noise output is usually specified in terms of an over-all noise figure, N. This quantity is more or less arbitrarily defined as the ratio to the quantity kTB of the signal power at the antenna necessary to make the output signal power equal to the mean noise power. In this definition, k is Boltzmann's constant (1.38×10^{-23} joules/degree), and the temperature T is taken as $291°$ K.

Over-all noise figures of 10 were not uncommon for the best postwar microwave receivers. A noise figure of 10, at a bandwidth of 3 MHz, means that an input signal of 1.2×10^{-13} watts is sufficient to increase the receiver output by an amount equal to the average noise output.

When a receiver is designed to detect pulses of duration τ seconds, there will be a best choice for the band width B. As already remarked, the average noise power increases in proportion to B. However, this does not mean that B should be made as small as possible, for when B becomes much less than $1/\tau$, the output signal power resulting from each pulse will be proportional to B^2. Experiment has shown that the best value of B is about $B = 1.2/\tau$, but it can be changed by small amounts from this best value without any serious effect on the performance. In the mid-1950s, a value of B near $2/\tau$ was typical of pulse radar practice.

What has just been said does not yet constitute a specification for S_{min}, the minimum detectable signal. The noise with which a signal must compete for recognition is statistical in character; that is, while the likelihood of large noise peaks is small, such large peaks do occur. For example, in the output of a receiver whose band width is 2 MHz, there is better than an even chance that one noise peak having more than 20 times the power of the average will be seen in an hour's observation. About 100 noise peaks greater than 10 times the average will be observed each second. This random character of the magnitude of noise peaks makes signal detection largely a game of chance. It is a game of chance in which several factors favour an actual signal, however. A true radar echo is repeated at the same point on the indicator for each successive sweep, while noise peaks occur at random locations. This important difference between a signal and noise can either be used by the indicator directly—if the indicator screen shows a stronger signal for repeated excitation in the same place—or by the eye and mind of the observer. The latter means is astonishingly effective, as has been shown by experiment. The practical effect of this phenomenon of integration, whether it occurs in the indicator or in the mind of the observer, is to make S_{min} depend upon the pulse repetition frequency, n, of a radar approximately in proportion to $1/\sqrt{n}$.

The problem of actual signal detectability is much more complicated than has been indicated here. It should be noted, however, that the very strong dependence of signal power on range shown by eq. (6) illustrates the fact that most signals which are at all detectable will be very strong.

3. Propagation of Short Radio Waves.—We shall now examine the principal ways in which propagation conditions near the surface of the earth and through the atmosphere introduce effects which are not included in the free-space radar equation, eq. (6). This is a vast subject, and only a few of the basic considerations can be mentioned here.

Effect of a Reflecting Surface.—If the transmission path between radar and target lies near a reflecting surface, energy may be able to reach the target (and scattered energy to return to the radar) by way of reflection from the surface, as well as directly (fig. 3). In the case of a flat, perfectly reflecting surface, the ratio, W, between the actual power at the point B of fig. 3 and the power which would have been observed at B for free-

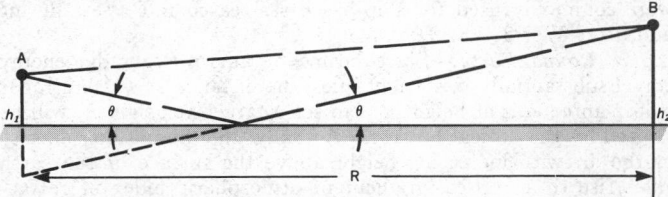

FIG. 3.—WAVE PROPAGATION OVER A FLAT REFLECTING SURFACE. RADAR ANTENNA AT A, TARGET AT B

space conditions, can be readily computed. It depends on (among other things) the phase change produced in the reflected wave by the process of reflection. This phase change depends on the angle of incidence, θ, on the state of polarization of the incident wave and on the electrical properties of the reflecting surface. In radar, only grazing angles of incidence are practically important, and only the surface of the sea is sufficiently smooth to be an adequate reflector for microwaves. Under these circumstances, the ratio of the power actually reaching B to that which would reach it under free-space conditions is given by

$$W = 4 \sin^2 \left(\frac{2\pi h_1 h_2}{\lambda R} \right) \qquad (8)$$

This ratio, as shown by eq. (8), varies between 0 and 4; the latter value being attained when the direct and reflected waves arrive at the target exactly in phase, as they will do when $4h_1 h_2 / \lambda R$ is equal to an odd integer. As the geometry of the problem is not affected by interchanging source and target, the reflection must affect the return of the radar echo to the same degree as it affects the pulse transmission. Therefore the required modification of the radar equation is obtained by multiplying the radar equation for free-space propagation by W^2, giving

$$S = P \frac{G^2 \lambda^2 \sigma}{(4\pi)^3 R^4} \cdot 16 \sin^4 \left(\frac{2\pi h_1 h_2}{\lambda R} \right) \qquad (9)$$

The effect of this modification is to introduce a strong dependence upon target height into the expression for the signal returned by a target to a radar which looks out over the surface of the sea. This is important for ship-based and coastal radar sets. Radar coverage under such circumstances shows a strong "lobe" pattern like that of fig. 4. At the maxima of the lobes, the received signal shows an increase by a factor of 16, leading to a doubling of the maximum radar range against a given target. An aircraft flying high enough to be well above the lowest lobe shown in fig. 4 will give a signal which flashes up and disappears repeatedly as the plane flies in toward the radar at constant altitude. Target height can be estimated by noting the ranges at which signal "fades" occur.

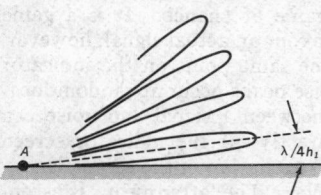

FIG. 4.—LOBES OF SIGNAL-STRENGTH PATTERN RESULTING FROM INTERFERENCE OF DIRECT AND REFLECTED WAVES

For targets at low angles (i.e., in the region where $\frac{2h_1 h_2}{R\lambda} < 1$) we can replace the sine in eq. (9) by its argument, obtaining

$$S = 4\pi P \frac{G^2 \sigma (h_1 h_2)^4}{\lambda^2 R^8} \qquad (10)$$

In this region of angles, the signal strength falls off as the inverse eighth power of the range, rather than as the inverse fourth power, if all other factors are held constant. Since the range at which this eighth-power dependence begins varies as the reciprocal of the radar wave length for fixed heights of radar antenna and target, the shortest radar wave lengths have a very considerable practical advantage when the primary task of radar is to search the sea for low-lying targets, the radar antenna itself being mounted at no great height.

Experiments have borne out this conclusion, and microwaves were commonly used for ship-based sea-search radar sets during and after World War II.

The Round Earth.—Since beams of microwave radio energy travel substantially in straight lines, the distance at which a radar whose antenna is at height h_1 can see a target at height h_2 will be limited by the optical horizon. Actually, the diminishing density of the air with increasing height above the surface of the earth gives rise to a vertical gradient of atmospheric index of refraction, with the result that a slight downward curvature is introduced into all rays. The effect of this curvature is to extend slightly the practical horizon for microwaves. Due to a chance numerical relation between units, the following easily remembered formula gives R_h, the range to the horizon under "standard" conditions, for a height h above the surface of the earth:

$$R_h(\text{statute miles}) = \sqrt{2h(\text{feet})} \qquad (11)$$

If we desire to find the greatest range at which a radar whose antenna is at height h_1 can see a target at height h_2, we must add the corresponding horizon distances, obtaining

$$R = R_{h1} + R_{h2} = \sqrt{2h_1} + \sqrt{2h_2} \qquad (12)$$

Radio waves in the ordinary communication bands (down to a few metres wave length) are propagated over the horizon by either of two effects. At the longest wave lengths, the energy is bent over the horizon by the phenomenon of diffraction; but energy can also travel around the curve of the earth, far beyond the horizon, because of the reflection of radio waves from the ionosphere, the ionized layer in the upper atmosphere. At radio frequencies around 100 MHz there is little reflection from the ionosphere; in the microwave region, from about 1,000 MHz up to higher frequencies, the ionosphere is transparent to radio waves. Thus neither diffraction effects nor ionospheric reflection can enable microwave radar to detect targets over the horizon, but there is some extension of range due to refraction in the lower atmosphere.

Within the horizon, the curvature of the earth complicates somewhat the geometry of the interference problem involving reflection. Eq. (9) and (10) are not strictly applicable, for they were derived on the assumption of a flat reflecting surface. The result of taking the earth's curvature into account can be shown by means of a coverage diagram (fig. 5). The curves of fig. 5 are contours of constant field strength, which means that the signal received from a given target will be the same no matter where it is located along a given contour.

Superrefraction.—It has already been mentioned that the atmosphere normally shows a vertical gradient of refractive index that results in a slight downward bending of rays of light or microwaves. Were this curvature only a few times greater, it would equal the curvature of the earth; under such conditions the "horizon" would vanish and a ray would bend around the earth without leaving the surface. Refractive index gradients of the magnitude necessary to produce such curvature amount to about five parts in 10^8 per ft. Under some conditions such gradients can be produced by temperature gradients alone, or, more commonly, by a vertical gradient in the concentration of water vapour in the atmosphere. Over the surface of the sea, the effects of evaporation of water into the air immediately above the surface and the diffusion of water vapour into still higher layers of air lead sometimes to the creation of a relatively shallow layer just above the water within which the vertical gradient of refractive index is negative and exceeds the critical value of five parts in 10^8 per ft. In such circumstances, superrefraction takes place,

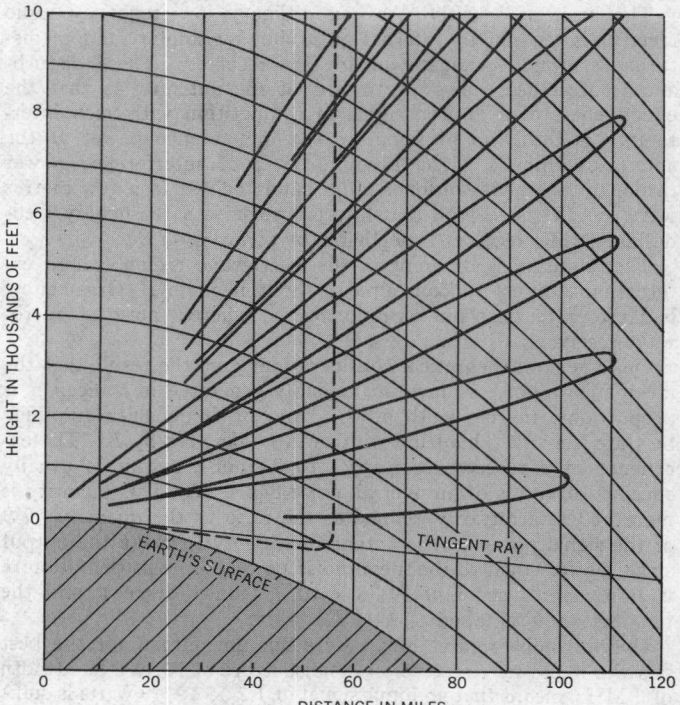

FIG. 5.—COVERAGE DIAGRAM FOR 2,600 MHz RADAR WITH OMNIDIRECTIONAL ANTENNA AT HEIGHT OF 120 FT. SOLID CURVE FOR TOTALLY-REFLECTING EARTH, DOTTED CURVE FOR NONREFLECTING EARTH

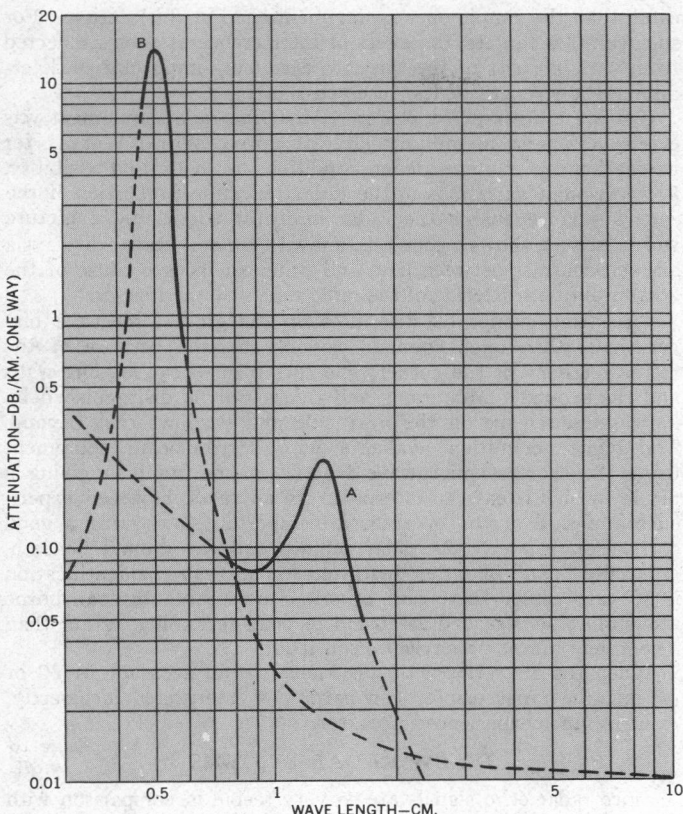

FIG. 6.—ATTENUATION CAUSED BY WATER VAPOUR (CURVE A) AND BY OXYGEN (CURVE B) AS A FUNCTION OF WAVE LENGTH. CURVE A APPLIES TO AN ATMOSPHERE CONTAINING 10 G. OF WATER VAPOUR PER CUBIC METRE. CURVE B APPLIES TO AN ATMOSPHERE WHICH IS 20% OXYGEN AND HAS A TOTAL PRESSURE OF 76 CM. OF MERCURY

and it is possible for microwaves to be propagated to distances many times the usual horizon distance. This phenomenon is specially common in certain parts of the world where climatic conditions favour its occurrence.

Atmospheric Attenuation.—At the shortest microwave lengths, the earth's atmosphere is not entirely transparent, as it is for all practical purposes to waves of frequency lower than about 1,000 MHz. The loss of energy, or attenuation, of a radar beam traveling through the atmosphere may be due to: (1) direct absorption of energy in the gases of the atmosphere; or (2) absorption and scattering of energy by condensed matter such as raindrops. All such processes lead to an exponential decrease of energy in the beam with increasing distance from the source.

This exponential decrease is superimposed on the inverse-square decrease in energy with increasing range that was used in formulating the radar equation. Of the atmospheric gases, oxygen and water vapour absorb microwave energy in the frequency range experimentally used for radar. This absorption is due to the production thereby of a transition of the molecule of water vapour or of oxygen between two definite energy states. The observed absorption is thus characterized by "lines," such as those found in more familiar regions of the electromagnetic spectrum. Experimental results (solid lines) and their theoretical extension (dotted lines) are shown in fig. 6.

Energy is also absorbed and scattered by particles of solid and liquid in the atmosphere. Droplets of water, present as fog, cloud or rain, are practically the most important particles of this sort. The attenuation by water droplets is of little practical consequence at wave lengths of 10 cm. or more, although sufficient energy is scattered from storm areas to give echoes at all microwave lengths. At wave lengths shorter than 10 cm., increasing attenuation is observed. Experimental results are given in fig. 7.

4. Target Properties.—Some useful things can be said about the radar cross section, σ, of various targets. In the case of the simplest single targets, σ can be calculated by electromagnetic theory; for other simple cases an approximate calculation will yield good results. Values of radar cross section of typical simple targets may be computed as follows:

(1) Dielectric sphere of radius small compared with wave length. Sphere radius a, dielectric constant ϵ, wave length λ.

$$\sigma = 4\pi \left(\frac{2\pi}{\lambda}\right)^4 \left|\frac{\epsilon - 1}{\epsilon + 2}\right|^2 a^6 \qquad (13)$$

(2) Metal sphere of radius small compared with wave length.

$$\sigma = 9\left(\frac{2\pi a}{\lambda}\right)^4 a^2 \qquad (14)$$

(3) Flat metal sheet of area A placed perpendicular to radar beam. Dimensions of plate large compared with wave length.

$$\sigma = \frac{4\pi A^2}{\lambda^2} \qquad (15)$$

(4) Cylinder of radius R and length l, both large compared with wave length. Cylinder is viewed perpendicular to axis.

$$\sigma = 2\pi \frac{R l^2}{\lambda} \qquad (16)$$

(5) Segment of spherical surface of radius R, viewed either on concave or convex side. Diameter of segment, perpendicular to the incident beam, must be greater than λ.

$$\sigma = \pi R^2 \qquad (17)$$

Eq. (17) is also valid for a nonspherical curved surface, if the geometric mean of the two principal radii of curvature is used for R.

An important type of simple target is the corner reflector. This is used when a compact radar target with a large cross section in any direction of observation is desired. It consists of an arrangement of three planes intersecting at right angles. The law of optical reflection yields the result that a ray directed into the corner formed by three such planes will undergo triple reflection and be sent back in the direction from which it came (*see* fig. 8).

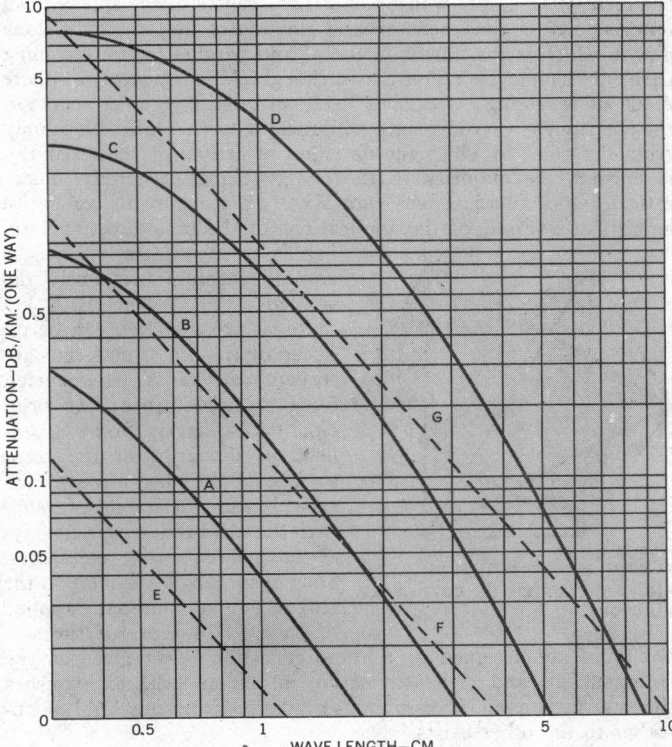

FIG. 7.—ATTENUATION OF SHORT RADIO WAVES IN RAIN (SOLID CURVES) AND FOG OR CLOUD (DOTTED CURVES). CURVE A, DRIZZLE (0.25 MM./HR.). CURVE B, LIGHT RAIN (1.0 MM./HR.). CURVE C, MODERATE RAIN (4 MM./HR.). CURVE D, HEAVY RAIN (16 MM./HR.). CURVE E, FOR VISIBILITY ABOUT 2,000 FT. (0.032 G. OF WATER PER CU. METRE). CURVE F FOR VISIBILITY ABOUT 400 FT. (0.32 G. OF WATER PER CU. METRE). CURVE G FOR VISIBILITY ABOUT 100 FT. (2.3 G. OF WATER PER CU. METRE)

The maximum radar scattering cross section of such a corner, which it exhibits when viewed along the axis of symmetry of a single corner, is

$$\sigma_{max} = \frac{4\pi a^4}{3\lambda^2} \qquad (18)$$

where a is the length of an edge of the corner and λ the radar wave length. The cross section remains large over most of the octant for which a single corner is effective; all directions can be covered by making a cluster of eight such corners (fig. 9).

(L. N. R.; G. R. T.)

The Luneberg lens overcomes the angular sector limitation of a single corner reflector to a considerable degree. This device utilizes the refractive property of a radio path having a varying dielectric constant. In the form of a sphere made of concentric layers of dielectric material, the lens focuses the radar rays upon a reflecting surface on the side opposite from the direction of arrival and reflects them back toward the point of origin. The area covered by the necessary reflector is approximately a hemisphere and the useful sector of the lens-reflector is somewhat less than a hemisphere. In designing a modified form of the Luneberg lens, E. M. Lipsey has eliminated the reflector and thereby the feature which prohibits omnidirectivity, since the rays cannot enter the sphere through the reflector. This is accomplished by causing the dielectric constants of the concentric layers of the sphere's material to increase toward the centre in such fashion as to cause the rays to bend in the form of an ellipse whose focus is the centre of the sphere. An entering ray is thus bent around the centre and emerges along a path which is the mirror image of and parallel to the incoming path. It should be noted that although the surface of a sphere made of reflecting material is itself an omnidirectional reflector, the efficiency is very low since reciprocal reflection takes place only from the point to which the direction of arrival of the radar ray is normal, the majority of the energy being scattered. Theoretically the spherical lens target has an aperture of an entire hemisphere. Some of the applications of the omnidirectional reflector are the same as for the corner reflectors previously described. (F. B. D.)

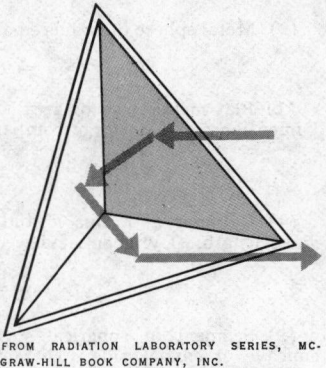

FIG. 8.—PRINCIPLE OF THE CORNER REFLECTOR

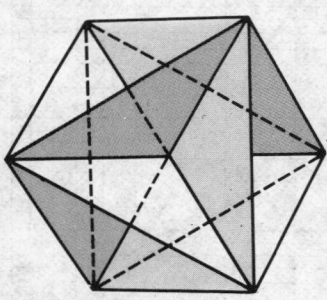

FIG. 9.—CLUSTER OF CORNER REFLECTORS

Radar cross section can be reduced by the use of materials absorbent at radar frequencies. Such materials are of two principal types. In the first kind, reflections occurring at the front surface of the absorber are canceled by destructive interference with the wave that enters the layer and subsequently re-emerges. Such absorbers are similar to the anti-reflection coatings applied to glass. Absorbers of the second kind are designed so that no reflection takes place at the front surface and high attenuation in the material extinguishes the entering wave. A continuous gradation from one kind of absorber to the other exists.

During World War II, the Germans produced a material of the first kind which was used for the camouflage of U-boats, to lessen the likelihood of radar detection of a surfaced submarine. An absorber of the second kind, which was never actually used, was also produced by the Germans. Its absorption was excellent over the wave length range from 4 to 13 cm.

Complex Targets.—Most radar targets are much more complicated than the simple ones so far mentioned in this section. For such complex targets, the effect of interference of waves reflected from various parts of the target is extremely important in determining the strength of the received signal.

Ground "Painting" by Radar.—Air-borne radar equipment was extensively used in military aircraft during World War II for navigation by pilotage under conditions of restricted visibility. Point-to-point variations in the radar reflection properties of the earth's surface enable the radar indicator to display a picture which, at best, shows a good relation with a map. Radar displays a marked contrast between land and water surfaces because of the greater diffuse scattering of the radio waves by the former.

Cities and groups of structures on the ground return a bigger signal than open country, possibly in part because of the retrodirectivity of the corner reflectors formed by building walls and the ground. Mountains and ridges can be distinguished by increased intensity on the near side and shadows cast beyond. The higher definition available with narrow-beam equipment using the shortest microwave lengths is important in giving a display which is easy to interpret. In all cases, however, experience and skill of the operator are important in making a good correlation between the radar picture and the ground beneath, especially inland in rather featureless country. Misidentification is so easy under these and other circumstances that air-borne radar must be regarded as an aid to dead reckoning, rather than a complete means of navigation in itself.

When the aircraft position is known to an accuracy of 20 or 30 mi., the radar display can hardly be interpreted incorrectly, even by an inexperienced operator.

IV. CW RADAR SYSTEMS

Since radar echo signals are so very feeble in comparison with the transmitted energy, they must be detected by some property which differentiates them from the transmitted signal in a readily measurable way. In pulse radar, this is done by turning off the transmitter for most of the time, so that signals received during the "off" time of the transmitter can be identified as echoes. It is possible to recognize echoes, however, even while the transmitter is working, on any of several schemes. Radio detection devices that involve a transmitter duty ratio of as much as 10% (in pulse radar this duty ratio is typically 0.1%) will be lumped here under the name CW radar. Devices of this sort have found important practical applications. (*See* NAVIGATION.)

If the targets of principal interest all have a radial motion relative to the radar, their echo signals can be distinguished by the frequency shift which is a consequence of the reflection of waves from a moving mirror. This frequency shift, f_d, is given by $(2v_r/c)f$, where v_r is the radial velocity, c the velocity of light and f the unmodified radar frequency. Numerically, with v_r in statute miles per hour and f defined by a wave length λ in cm. (equal to c/f), the frequency shift, which is called the "Doppler frequency," is given by

$$f_d = 89.4 \frac{v_r}{\lambda} \qquad (19)$$

Thus at 10-cm. wave length, v_r amounts to about 9 c.p.s./m.p.h.

The Doppler-shifted return signal, when added to the transmitter voltage and rectified, gives rise to a voltage with small pulsations recurring at the Doppler frequency. The steady component can be removed by a high-pass filter (which may be simply a transformer or a series condenser) and the fluctuations then amplified and used to actuate an indicator. If the output signal is fed to ordinary telephone receivers, the ear can detect signals denoting the presence of a moving target over the range of World War II aircraft speeds, if the radar works at 10-cm. wave length.

CW radar systems of the type just described, with suitable technical modifications that do not affect the principle of operation, were built during World War II. Although they were not used in actual combat, they proved most useful in making precise measurements of the velocities of projectiles.

The system just described, though measuring the radial velocity of a target in a simple and accurate way, affords no information regarding target range. To measure range, the outgoing wave must be marked or modulated in some way, and the time required for the marks on the wave train to return as an echo must be measured. Either amplitude modulation (AM), or frequency modulation (FM), of the outgoing wave can be used.

The most familiar way of employing AM is that of pulse radar to determine the time delay between the transmission and reception of a pulse. However, we can also measure range by the use of two separate CW radar systems like the one described above, the transmitter frequencies of the two differing by an amount f_r. Let f_o be the frequency of one transmitter and $f_o + f_r$ that of the other. The Doppler frequencies developed by the two systems when they look at a single target moving radially will differ, since these Doppler frequencies involve the transmitter frequency, as eq. (19) shows.

If the target is very close to the system, the number of wave lengths in the distance from transmitter to target and back is very nearly the same for the two systems, since their frequencies differ only slightly. Thus the transmitter signal and the target signal will be in phase or out of phase with one another at the two receivers simultaneously, and the two Doppler outputs will be in phase for very short range. As the target gets farther away, one Doppler signal shifts phase more rapidly than the other, so that a phase difference between the Doppler outputs of the two systems is developed. When the target is far enough away so that the number of wave lengths to the target and back is one greater for $f_o + f_r$ than it is for f_o, the phase difference in the outputs is 2π. This phase difference, which is given by

$$\phi = \frac{4\pi f_r}{c} r \qquad (20)$$

where ϕ is the phase shift, r the range, and c the velocity of light, is a linear function of range and can be used as a measure of range. It becomes ambiguous for targets so far away that the phase shift is greater than 2π.

1. Range Measurement by FM.—One of the most important applications of CW radar systems during World War II was their use for the measurement of the altitude of aircraft with reference to the earth or sea below. A system employing frequency modulation of the transmitted signal was developed for this purpose in the U.S., and independently a very similar system was worked out in Germany.

A schematic diagram of the system components is shown in fig. 10; the operating principle of the system is illustrated by the curves of fig. 11. The transmitter frequency varies linearly with time in the fashion shown. Energy arrives at the receiver both directly from the transmitter and by reflection from the target. Since the trip to the target and back takes time, the received frequency (indicated by the dotted line) is displaced along the time axis relative to the transmitter frequency. The two frequencies combine in the mixer to give a beat of constant frequency (except during the short crossover intervals when the sign of the FM is changing). The greater the target distance, the greater this beat frequency; its magnitude is a direct measure of the range. The beat signal between transmitter signal and echo is therefore amplified, and its frequency measured by a direct-reading frequency meter which can be calibrated in terms of range.

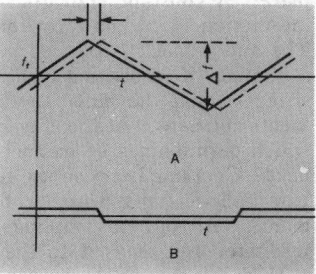

FIG. 11.—PRINCIPLE OF FM RADAR ALTIMETER

If it is desired to use this same principle for radar search several targets may give return signals simultaneously. The receiver output will then contain several signals at different frequencies. These can be individually detected either by a frequency meter which will respond to and indicate several signals simultaneously, or by scanning a single-frequency meter over the frequency range corresponding to the target distances which must be covered. The vibrating-reed frequency meter will serve as an example of the first technique. In the second method, for example, a variable frequency can be added to the output signal and observations made when the beat frequency between the two signals falls in the pass band of a resonant circuit. Scanning devices are usually objectionable because they increase the time necessary to make an observation.

In addition to the CW radar systems whose operating principles have been sketched, there are many other types that involve different schemes of modulation of the transmitted signal and different techniques for handling the received echo. Though the amount of wartime development work which went into such CW systems was only a very tiny fraction of that expended on pulse radar, there are various applications for which CW radar is markedly superior.

For example, in accurate measurement of ranges as small as ten feet, a CW system is simpler than pulse radar. A system making use of the Doppler shift in frequency will measure the speed of a bullet in an easy and direct way and to any desired degree of accuracy. Or again, simple equipment may be desired, as in the familiar speed-detector radar employed in policing highway traffic, involving operation at short ranges (using microwaves of about 1 cm. in length).

V. RADAR COMPONENTS

1. The Multicavity Magnetron.—Beginning about 1938, the British made strenuous efforts to develop sources of high-power pulses at microwave frequencies, because of the importance of narrow radar beams in the air-borne equipment they were then attempting to develop. The modification of conventional tube types offered little promise since to a first approximation the electronic characteristics of a low-frequency tube are maintained at high frequency only if all tube dimensions are scaled in proportion to the wave length, λ. Near 1,000 MHz, the practical consequences of this reduction in tube dimensions become serious. Electrode clearances become so small they are hard to maintain, while the reduction in cathode and plate areas (proportional to λ^2) rapidly reduces peak emission and plate power dissipation.

An entirely new type of tube, the multicavity magnetron, was invented to serve the new requirement. By the 1950s, magnetrons had produced pulse powers as high as 10,000,000 watts at frequencies near 3,000 MHz, and hundreds of kilowatts even at 24,000 MHz. Klystrons are useful sources of continuous RF power at frequencies as high as 24,000 MHz and can also be designed to give high pulse power.

The magnetron is a self-excited oscillator capable of converting D.C. power into RF power with high efficiency. The main features of the design of a typical magnetron are shown in fig. 12.

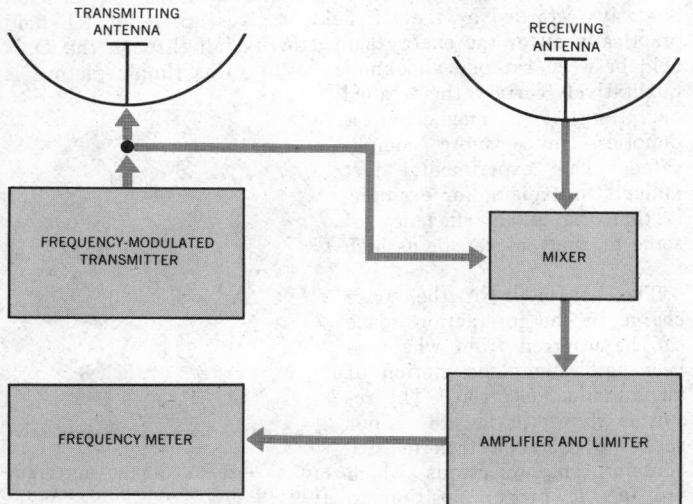

FIG. 10.—SIMPLIFIED BLOCK DIAGRAM OF FREQUENCY-MODULATED CW RADAR SYSTEM FOR MEASURING RANGE

Between the indirectly heated cylindrical cathode and the anode block is an interaction space in which the conversion takes place. A constant, uniform, magnetic field is maintained in this interaction space in a direction parallel to the axis of the cathode. The anode block is pierced in a direction parallel to the field by a number of resonating cavities, which open into the interaction space so that the inner anode surface consists of alternate segments and gaps. At the ends of the cavities are open "end spaces" which permit lines of magnetic flux to link one resonator to the next. Coupling between the resonators is increased by conducting bars called straps, which connect together alternate anode segments. An output coupling loop extracts RF power from one resonator and feeds it to the output circuit.

Each of the eight resonant cavities shown in fig. 12 can be thought of as a simple oscillating circuit consisting of lumped inductance L_o and capacity C_o. When the magnetron is oscillating in the desired way, the capacities of the individual cavities are connected in parallel, and so are their individual inductances. The frequency of the magnetron as a whole is then about the same as that of an individual cavity, since the frequency is proportional in either case to the product of inductance and capacity. The impedance of the oscillators, however, depends on L_o/C_o, and magnetrons of the same frequency but different impedance can be constructed by changing the shape of the individual resonators to keep L_oC_o constant while altering L_o/C_o.

Like all systems of coupled individual oscillators, the resonant systems of a magnetron can oscillate in different modes; in general these modes will have different frequencies. One of these modes has been found to be by far the most desirable from the standpoint of reliable operation, and much attention has been paid to the problem of making the frequency of the desired mode sufficiently different from that of any other to encourage the magnetron to oscillate in the desired mode. The straps shown in fig. 12 are primarily for this purpose of accomplishing mode separation in frequency; another way of achieving such separa-

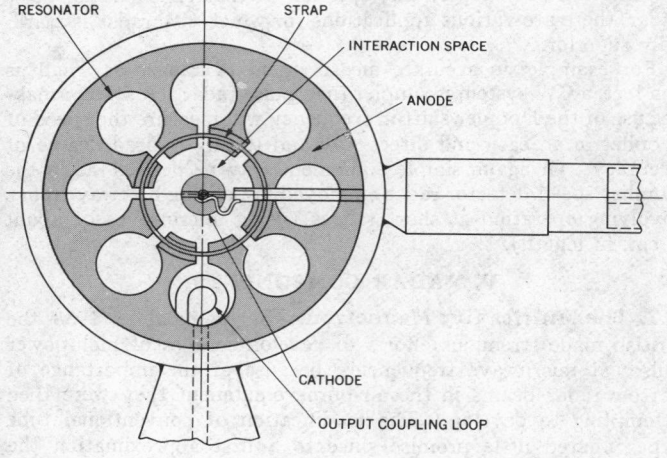

RESONATOR   STRAP
INTERACTION SPACE
ANODE
CATHODE
OUTPUT COUPLING LOOP

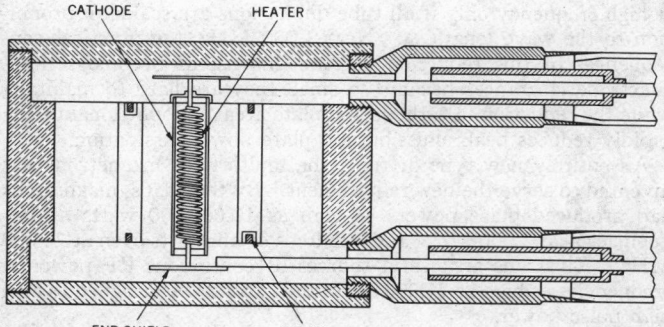

CATHODE   HEATER
END SHIELD   STRAP

FROM RADIATION LABORATORY SERIES, MCGRAW-HILL BOOK COMPANY, INC.

FIG. 12.—CROSS SECTIONS OF A TYPICAL CAVITY MAGNETRON. MAGNETIC FIELD PERPENDICULAR TO UPPER FIGURE: VERTICAL IN LOWER FIGURE

tion is to make the alternate individual resonators of different natural frequencies.

Instead of a tube such as that of fig. 12, intended to be put between the poles of an electromagnet or a permanent magnet, a tube can be built in which the magnet pole tips are actually part of the construction of the magnetron proper. In this way, the air gap over which the magnetic field must be maintained is cut down, and as a result the required magnetomotive force (and the physical size of the magnet) can be greatly reduced. Permanent magnets are usually employed with magnetrons.

An electron in the interaction space is acted on by a constant magnetic field parallel to the cathode axis, a constant radial electric field resulting from the D.C. voltage applied between anode and cathode, and the rapidly varying electric field extending into the interaction space from charges momentarily concentrated near the ends of anode segments. Such an electron is also part of a space charge subject to extreme variations in density. The very complex problem of the resulting electron motion has not been solved in detail, but a qualitative idea of the major processes responsible for magnetron behaviour can be given.

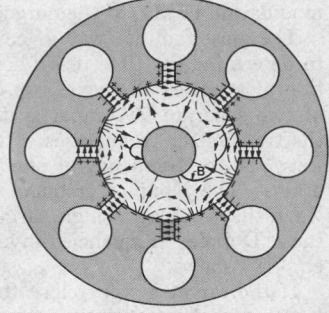

FROM RADIATION LABORATORY SERIES, MCGRAW-HILL BOOK COMPANY, INC.

FIG. 13.—PATHS OF ELECTRONS IN THE INTERACTION SPACE WHEN MAGNETRON IS OSCILLATING. ELECTRON AT A WOULD TAKE ENERGY FROM RF FIELD, BUT HITS CATHODE AS A RESULT OF SPEEDING UP, AND IS THUS REMOVED FROM SPACE CHARGE. ELECTRON AT B CONTRIBUTES ENERGY TO RF FIELD, THUS SUSTAINING OSCILLATIONS

A simplified picture of the motion of individual electrons is offered in fig. 13. The distribution of charges shown on the anode segments is that appropriate to the desired mode of magnetron operation. The dotted lines with arrows show the resultant electric field. An electron located at point A at the instant shown will be speeded up by the RF field. The result of an increase in the tangential velocity of an electron is, under the field conditions obtaining in the magnetron, to increase the curvature of the electron's path. The electron thus moves along the path shown, strikes the cathode, and plays no further role in the operation of the magnetron.

An electron at point B, however, is in a decelerating RF field; the curvature of its path will thus be decreased. If the frequency of oscillation is appropriate to the motion of the electron, this electron will always be in a decelerating field as it passes before successive anode segments. It will then follow a path of the sort shown, and eventually strike the anode. Since the electron is always retarded by the RF field, it gives up to the RF field practically all of the energy gained in its fall through the D.C. field between cathode and anode. While this simple picture is qualitatively correct, the detailed operation of a magnetron is doubtless much more complicated. One experimental fact difficult to explain, for example, is that the anode efficiency of some magnetrons can be as high as 85%.

The behaviour of the space charge in the interaction space can be inferred from what has been said about the motion of an individual electron. The result is shown in fig. 14. Four spokes of high electron density contain those electrons which are in the proper position to be decelerated by the RF field. This configuration rotates about the cathode with an angular

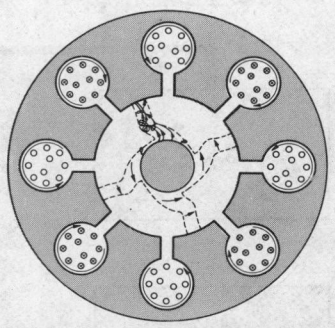

FROM RADIATION LABORATORY SERIES, MCGRAW-HILL BOOK COMPANY, INC.

FIG. 14.—SPACE-CHARGE DISTRIBUTION IN AN OSCILLATING MAGNETRON. INSTANT SHOWN IS THAT OF ZERO RF ELECTRIC FIELD. LINES OF RF MAGNETIC FIELD ARE INDICATED WITHIN CAVITY RESONATORS

velocity which keeps it in step with the alternating RF charges on the anode segments. The RF current flowing in the oscillators is principally a displacement current produced by this rotating space charge. Fig. 14 shows the space charge at an instant when the RF electric field is zero; the lines of magnetic field in the resonators are shown.

The behaviour of a magnetron with changes of anode current and of pulse voltage can be displayed on a performance chart, which shows how these parameters affect frequency, power, magnetic field and efficiency under conditions of constant RF load.

The magnetron as it has so far been described is a fixed-frequency device. However, several different schemes have been worked out for tuning cavity magnetrons. In one way or another, each of these schemes involves loading the resonators so as to change their natural frequency of oscillation.

2. Pulse Modulators.—The modulator, or pulser, of a radar set is a somewhat unusual electrical device. It must supply, in the form of electrical pulses whose duration is in the range from 1/10 to 5 μ sec., currents of some tens of amperes at voltages as high as 50 or 60 kv. These pulses must be generated with a recurrence frequency of a few hundred to a few thousand per second, usually must be accurately spaced relative to one another and, since the magnetron is such a highly nonlinear load, they must be "flat" on top to better than 5% of the rated pulse voltage. In a typical case, a variation in pulse voltage of only 3 kv., will produce, in a magnetron operating at 25 kv. and 13.5 amp., a drop in anode current of 7 amp., which practically stops the oscillation of the magnetron.

In all pulsers, electrical energy stored in some circuit element is released rapidly during the pulse, and replenished during the interval between pulses. Energy can be stored either in the electrostatic field of a condenser or in the magnetic field of an inductance carrying a current. Pulsers employing electrostatic energy storage are far more common than those using an inductance as the storage element, largely because power losses in the latter type of pulser are ordinarily much greater for the same useful pulse output.

The following discussion refers to pulsers using electrostatic energy storage.

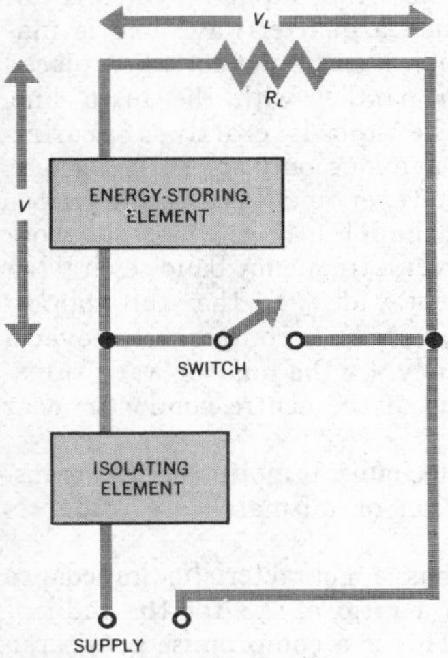

The basic circuit of a pulser is shown in fig. 15. If the energy-storage element is a condenser of capacity C, charged to a voltage V, the stored energy is $\frac{1}{2}CV^2$. At $t = o$ the switch S is closed, and the condenser begins to discharge exponentially through the load resistance. If S is now opened suddenly at a time τ small compared with the time constant $R_L C$ of the circuit, the voltage appearing across the load while the current is flowing is given by

$$V_L(t) = V\left(I - \frac{t}{R_L C}\right), \qquad 0 \geqq t \geqq \tau \qquad (21)$$

which is constant within a few per cent if $\tau < R_L C$.

In practice, vacuum tubes are the only switches that can be used to open the load circuit suddenly while it is still carrying a large current. The plate resistance of such tubes is always rather large, resulting in a high voltage drop across the switch during the pulse, and a corresponding loss in pulser efficiency. It would be desirable to use a very low-resistance switch, such as a spark or gaseous discharge, to eliminate this difficulty. However, all such devices have the property that the current flow through them, once started, cannot be interrupted until the voltage across the switch has fallen to an extremely low value. Thus,

FIG. 15.—BASIC CIRCUIT OF A PULSER EMPLOYING ELECTROSTATIC ENERGY STORAGE

if such a low-resistance switch were used with a pulser having a simple condenser for an energy-storage element, the condenser would have to be completely discharged at each pulse. This is unsatisfactory, since the wave shape of the output pulse would then be exponential instead of being substantially rectangular, as desired.

If, however, a transmission line is used as an energy-storage element instead of a condenser, its discharge properties under the appropriate load conditions are such that it will supply energy at constant current until it is completely discharged. This is exactly what is wanted for the generation of rectangular pulses. Elementary transmission-line theory shows that if a line of inductance L and capacity C per unit length is charged to a voltage V and then suddenly connected across a resistance R_L, a discontinuous current of magnitude $V/(Z_o + R_L)$ will flow for a time $2t$, where Z_o is the characteristic impedance of the line ($= \sqrt{L/C}$) and t is its one-way transmission time. If $R_L = Z_o$, no current flows after a time $2t$, and a genuinely rectangular pulse has been generated. The time t is given by $l\sqrt{LC}$, where l is the physical length of the line.

Since the pulse durations desired in radar are usually a micro-

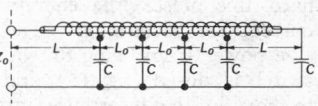

FIG. 16.—SCHEMATIC DIAGRAM OF A PULSE-FORMING NETWORK. NUMBER OF MESHES REQUIRED DEPENDS ON DURATION OF PULSE

TABLE I.—*Comparison of the Two Pulser Types*

Characteristics	Hard-tube pulser	Network pulser
Efficiency	Lower; more power required for auxiliary circuits and for dissipation in switch tube	High, particularly when pulse-power output is high
Pulse shape	Better rectangular pulses	Poorer rectangular pulse, particularly through pulse transformer
Impedance matching to load	Wide range of mismatch permissible	Smaller range of mismatch permissible (± 20–30%). Pulse transformer will match any load, but power input to nonlinear load cannot be varied over a wide range
Interpulse interval	May be very short; as for coding beacons (*i.e.*, 1 μ sec.)	Must be several times the deionization time of discharge tube (*i.e.*, 100 μ sec.)
Voltage supply	High-voltage supply usually necessary	Low-voltage supply, particularly with inductance as isolating element
Change of pulse duration	Easy; switching in low voltage circuit	Requires high-voltage switching to new network
Circuit complexity	Greater, leading to greater difficulty in servicing	Less, permitting smaller size and weight

second or more, it is ordinarily impracticable to use actual transmission lines or cables in pulsers; a cable to supply a 1-μ sec. pulse would be about 500 ft. long. Instead, an "artificial line" (fig. 16) made up of properly chosen inductances and condensers is used. Such an artificial line is sometimes called a "pulse-forming network." A pulser employing a network as storage element is less flexible than one which uses a condenser and hard-tube switch, since the properties of the network itself fix the pulse duration and the load impedance. Components available for network construction make it desirable to give the network a low impedance; 50 ohms is typical. The magnetron load usually has a much higher impedance, in the neighbourhood of 500 ohms. Specially designed "pulse transformers" are used to match the load impedance to that of the network.

Devices used as the low-impedance gas-discharge switch in a network pulser include rotary spark gaps, fixed spark gaps in series, fixed gaps with an auxiliary electrode for triggering (called "trigatrons"), and thyratrons using either mercury or hydrogen as the filling gas. Hydrogen thyratrons were developed specifically for radar pulsers, and have the advantage over heavy-gas thyratrons in that they can pulse at much higher frequencies, because of the higher ion mobility in hydrogen.

The charging circuit used with either type of pulser so far

considered—the "hard-tube" pulser which uses a single condenser as storage element, or the "network" pulser which uses a low-voltage switch—is an important part of the circuit. In the hard-tube pulser, the energy source must clearly supply direct current for recharging. The isolating element prevents excessive power from being drawn out of the energy source when the switch is closed (fig. 15), and must also permit sufficient energy to flow in the interpulse interval to replace that used during the pulse. In the hard-tube pulser, it can be either a high resistance, an inductance or a series combination of resistance and inductance.

In the case of the network pulser, on the other hand, the full energy of the charged network must be supplied by the recharging circuit after each pulse. This means that a resistance is a very inefficient isolating element, for as much energy will be dissipated in it, each time the network is recharged, as is usefully stored in the network. Accordingly, an inductance is almost always used as an isolating element. Further, the network can be recharged from an alternating-current source, provided the pulse repetition frequency is a multiple of one-half the A.C. supply frequency. An extremely simple high-power pulser can be made by mounting a rotary spark gap switch directly on the shaft of the A.C. machine supplying the recharging current for the network. The hard-tube and the network types of pulser have different fields of usefulness. A comparison of their properties is shown in Table I.

3. Radio-frequency Components.—A considerable body of new theory and technique grew up during the development of microwave radar because of the necessity of handling power at frequencies so high that the wave length of the RF energy is of the same order as the physical size of the circuit elements. The length of a microwave transmission line may be, and usually is, several wave lengths. For a fuller description of RF techniques at microwave frequencies, reference should be made to the works quoted in the bibliography.

Coaxial Line.—A transmission line is characterized, as already remarked, by a characteristic impedance which depends upon the inductance and capacity per unit length of line, and is thus a function of the geometry of the insulators and conductors of which the line is made. In a coaxial line, a type frequently used for the transmission of high-frequency energy (fig. 17), the characteristic impedance, Z_o, is given by

$$Z_o = \frac{138}{k} \log_{10}(r_2/r_1) \ ohms \qquad (22)$$

where k is the dielectric constant of the material in the annular space between the conductors, r_2 is the inner radius of the outer conductor, and r_1 is the outer radius of the inner conductor.

A uniform line terminated at any point in a load duplicating its characteristic impedance behaves as if it were infinitely long; there is no reflection of energy from the termination. However, any impedance changes along the line (such as those introduced by dents, bends or obstacles in the line), or any departure of the load from the characteristic impedance of the line, will cause the reflection of energy. The reflected wave, which travels back toward the power source, interferes with the outgoing wave to produce standing waves in the line. These can be detected and measured by exploring the voltage along the line with a small movable probe, such as that shown in fig. 17. There will

be voltage maxima spaced at half-wave length intervals with minima halfway between them. A line which is properly terminated and uniform, so that it exhibits no standing waves, is said to be "matched."

When a lossless transmission line a quarter-wave length long and of characteristic impedance Z_o is terminated in an impedance Z_t, the input impedance of the line is

$$Z_i = Z_o^2/Z_t \qquad (23)$$

This property enables two transmission lines of different impedance to be matched to each other by joining them through a quarter-wave line whose characteristic impedance is the geometric mean of the impedances of the two lines. Such a quarter-wave section is called a "matching transformer." If a quarter-wave line is terminated by a short circuit, its input impedance is infinite; conversely, an open-circuited quarter-wave line appears at the input terminal to be a short circuit.

For a lossless line a half-wave length long,

$$Z_i = Z_t \qquad (24)$$

irrespective of the characteristic impedance of the line.

At microwave frequencies, the losses in the solid dielectrics used to insulate the inner from the outer conductor in a coaxial line are prohibitive at the power levels usually encountered. "Stub-supported" lines have therefore been developed (fig. 18), in

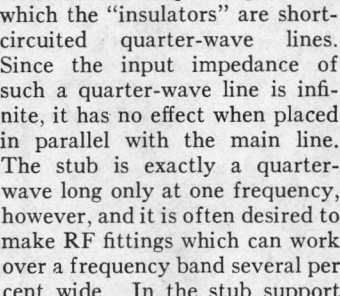

FIG. 18.—BROAD-BAND STUB SUPPORT FOR CENTRE CONDUCTOR OF COAXIAL LINE

which the "insulators" are short-circuited quarter-wave lines. Since the input impedance of such a quarter-wave line is infinite, it has no effect when placed in parallel with the main line. The stub is exactly a quarter-wave long only at one frequency, however, and it is often desired to make RF fittings which can work over a frequency band several per cent wide. In the stub support

shown in fig. 18, this frequency sensitivity is compensated, over a band of ±15% of the base frequency, by the quarter-wave transformers formed by the fat sections of the centre conductor near the stub support.

Rotary joints which permit mechanical motion while transmitting RF power without reflection or mismatch are often required.

Standard coaxial line usually has a characteristic impedance of 50 ohms, this corresponding to a ratio of 2.3 for the radii of the outer and inner conductors. This is a compromise between a ratio of 3.6 (77 ohms) which, for a given outer diameter, gives the lowest attenuation due to conductor losses, and a ratio of 1.65 (30 ohms) which enables the maximum power to be carried at a given breakdown voltage gradient across the dielectric.

The size of a coaxial line is limited by the wave length of the radiation transmitted. The electric fields within a coaxial line have axial symmetry if the line is small enough. If, however, the mean circumference of the annular dielectric space between the conductors exceeds one wave length, a second "mode" of propagation of the RF energy can be excited. In this second mode, the field distribution has diametral symmetry. Since serious design complications arise if it is possible for two modes of propagation to be excited simultaneously in an RF line, the overall size of coaxial line is always kept so small that only the axially symmetric mode of propagation can exist. The resulting limitation on power-handling capacity has restricted the use of coaxial lines to wave lengths of 8 cm. and more.

Wave Guide.—At shorter wave lengths, and for handling the highest powers even in the 10-cm. band, a wave guide is used. Though a metallic pipe of almost any shape will transmit or guide electromagnetic waves whose wave length is short enough, rectangular tubing whose internal dimensions have a ratio between 2.0 and 2.5 is ordinarily used to transfer microwave energy. Though a detailed understanding of the propagation of RF energy in wave guide demands the solution of Maxwell's equations with

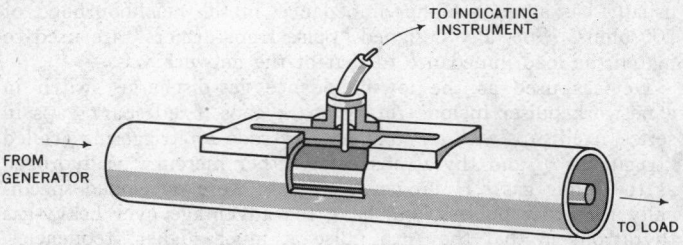

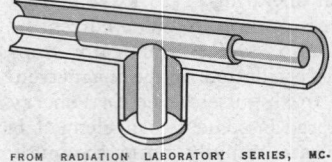

TO INDICATING INSTRUMENT

FROM GENERATOR

TO LOAD

FIG. 17.—SLOTTED SECTION OF COAXIAL LINE WITH PROBE FOR MEASURING STANDING WAVES

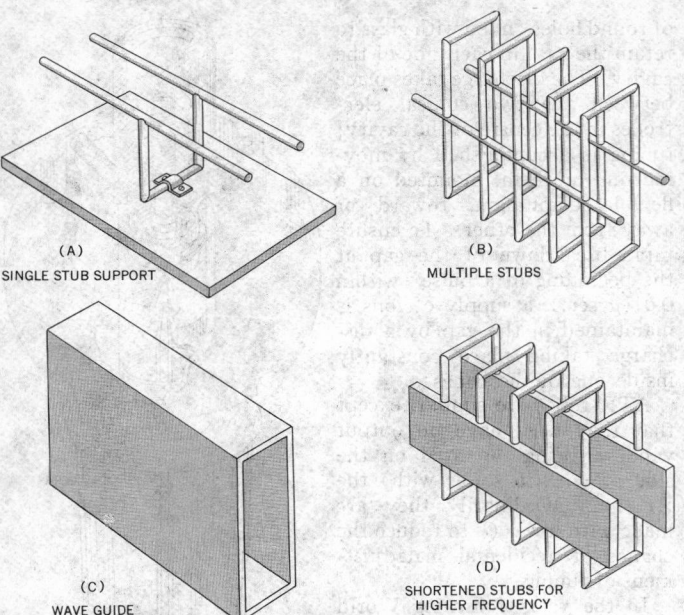

FIG. 19.—TRANSITION FROM STUB-SUPPORTED TWO-WIRE TRANSMISSION LINE TO WAVE GUIDE

(A) SINGLE STUB SUPPORT

(B) MULTIPLE STUBS

(C) WAVE GUIDE

(D) SHORTENED STUBS FOR HIGHER FREQUENCY

the appropriate boundary conditions, we can get a picture of the mechanism of this propagation by considering the resemblance between a rectangular wave guide and a two-wire transmission line.

Fig. 19(A) shows a two-wire line with a single short-circuited stub support, analogous to the coaxial quarter-wave stub support already described. At the proper frequency, the input impedance of the stub is very high and the stub has no effect on the propagation of the wave on the line. In fig. 19(B) a great many stubs, extending both ways from the two-wire line, have been added, still without affecting the propagation of the frequency in question. In fig. 19(C) the stubs have been coalesced into a rectangular tube which looks like a wave guide. For a single stub, a slight correction to the length must be made to compensate for the inductance of the crosspiece, but when the stubs become a solid tube, no lines of force can link the narrow side, and the quarter-wave distance becomes exact. This also shows why the length of the narrow side of the rectangular tube is not critical.

All frequencies higher (wave lengths shorter) than that for which the quarter-wave stubs of our model were designed can be transmitted by wave guide. In such a case (fig. 19 [D]) the two wires become broad bus bars with only as much of the wide side given over to stubs as is required by the now shorter wave length. Wave lengths greater than twice the broad dimension of the guide

cannot be propagated because then the stubs become less than a quarter-wave long and shunt the line with a rather low inductive impedance which would extinguish the wave.

Fig. 20 shows an instantaneous picture of the electric and magnetic fields in a rectangular wave guide whose wide dimension is slightly more than half the free-space wave length of the radiation being transmitted. Lines of current-flow in the walls are also shown. As the dimensions of the wave guide increase relative to the wave length of the radiation being transmitted, modes of propagation different from that illustrated (i.e., having different space distributions of electric and magnetic field) can be excited.

As in the case of coaxial line, this is almost always objectionable, and the maximum size of the broad dimension of a rectangular guide is usually chosen to be less than 0.95 of the free-space wave length of the radiation to be transmitted.

Each type of wave guide has a cutoff frequency for propagation in the lowest mode. Waves of higher frequency are transmitted; those of lower frequency are rapidly attenuated. The wave length of the radiation inside the guide is longer than the free-space wave length and is given by

$$\text{Guide wave length} = \lambda_g = \frac{\lambda}{\sqrt{1 - \left(\frac{\lambda}{\lambda_c}\right)^2}} \tag{25}$$

where λ is the free-space wave length and λ_c is the cutoff wave length. For the lowest mode in rectangular guide, as we have seen, the wave length corresponding to the cutoff frequency is twice the broad dimension. This sets a lower limit to the practical size of wave guide. Its broad dimension is usually chosen to be greater than 0.6 times the free-space wave length, because of design complications that ensue if the cutoff value of 0.5λ is approached too closely.

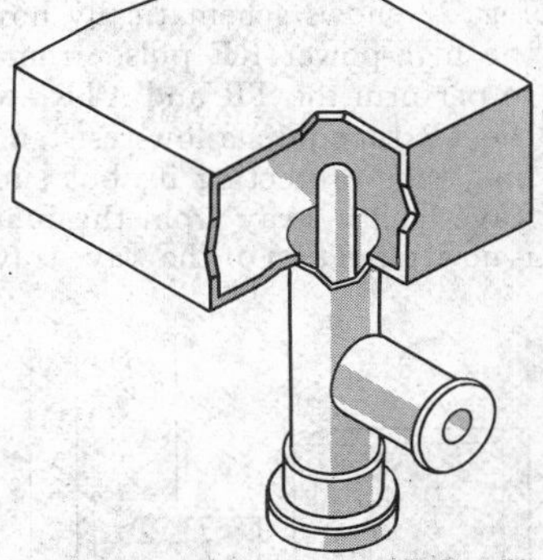

The narrow dimension of rectangular guide is chosen as large as possible to raise the breakdown field strength (the electric field being across this narrow dimension); but it must be less than half a free-space wave length of the radiation to be transmitted, so that there is no possibility of transmitting a wave polarized at right angles to that shown in fig. 20.

Transitions between wave guide and coaxial lines usually take the form of a quarter-wave stub antenna on the coaxial line projecting into the wave guide at the proper distance from a reflecting end plate, as shown in fig. 21. Rotary joints make use of quarter-wave choke sections. The power-handling capacity of wave guide is more than double that which can be realized by the largest coaxial line it is practical to use; the attenuation in a given length of wave guide is about half that encountered in coaxial line. Mechanically, wave guide is superior, since it is both easier to fabricate and more difficult to damage in use.

FIG. 21.—TRANSITION FROM CO-AXIAL LINE TO WAVE GUIDE

Resonant Cavities.—If both ends of a wave guide are closed by short-circuiting plates, and energy is introduced by a probe or through a hole so small that the properties of the enclosure are not affected, the resulting box is called a resonant cavity. When

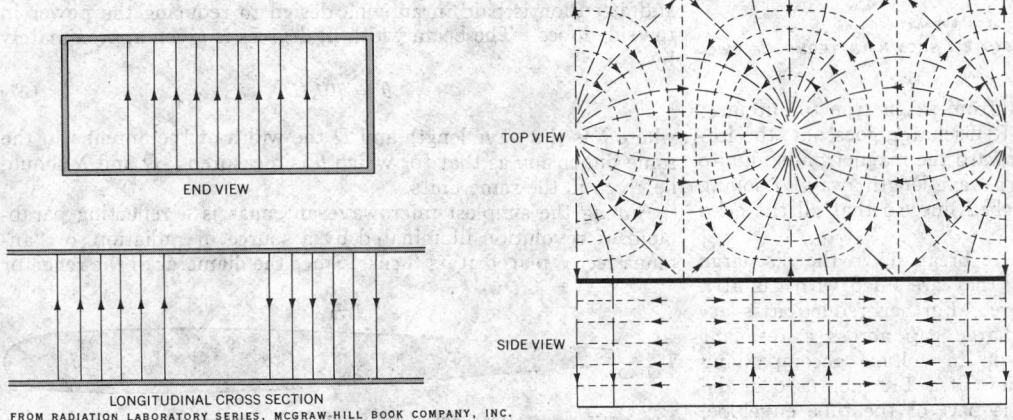

END VIEW

TOP VIEW

SIDE VIEW

LONGITUDINAL CROSS SECTION

FIG. 20.—FUNDAMENTAL MODE OF WAVE PROPAGATION IN A RECTANGULAR GUIDE. SOLID LINES ARE THOSE OF ELECTRIC FIELD; DASHED LINES SHOW CURRENT FLOW IN WALLS; DOTTED LINES SHOW MAGNETIC FIELD

its length is an integral number of half-wave lengths of the radiation in the guide, the reflections from the end plates will reinforce one another and cause a resonant build-up of the energy in the cavity. Because the wave length in the guide differs from that in free space, as shown by eq. (25), the shortest resonant piece of a wave guide whose broad dimension is $1/\sqrt{2}$ free-space wave lengths is also $1/\sqrt{2}$ free-space wave lengths long. The narrow dimension of the cavity does not affect the resonant wave length, though it should be less than $\lambda/2$ to avoid the possibility of exciting the cavity in a mode polarized at right angles to the one desired.

The sharpness of resonance exhibited by a resonant cavity at microwave frequencies is very great. It is usually measured by a number called the Q of the cavity. If f_o is the resonant frequency and f_1 and f_2 are the two frequencies, one above resonance and one below, at which the voltage in the cavity is 0.707 that at resonance, then

$$Q = \frac{f_0}{f_1 - f_2} \qquad (26)$$

The Q of a 10-cm. cavity made of copper is typically as great as 15,000. This is much higher than the Q of resonant circuits made of coil-and-condenser combinations, for use at lower frequencies, because of the great effectiveness of a resonant cavity as a device for the storage of energy.

TR and ATR Switches.—Resonant cavities are used in the construction of the TR and ATR switches needed to permit duplex operation of a radar transmitter and receiver on a single antenna. Fig. 22 shows schematically how gas-discharge switches, fired by the high-power RF pulse from the magnetron, can be mounted to perform the TR and ATR switching functions. Breakdown of the TR tube puts a low-resistance short circuit across the receiver line, thus protecting it; but since this short circuit is a quarter-wave length away from the junction with the antenna line, there is no attenuation of the wave traveling toward the antenna. Break-

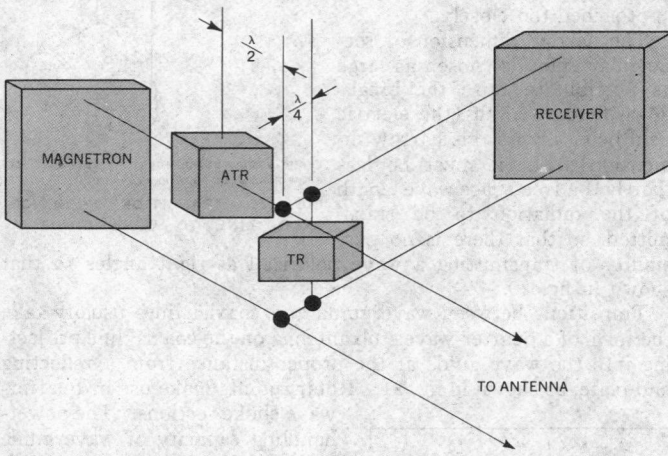

FIG. 22.—PRINCIPLE OF A DUPLEXING SYSTEM SHOWN IN TERMS OF TWO-WIRE RF TRANSMISSION LINE

down of the ATR closes the circuit from magnetron to antenna; when the pulse is over and the ATR discharge goes out, the impedance at the T junction looking toward the magnetron is infinite because there is an open circuit half a wave length away. Looking toward the receiver, there is a matched line, so that all the echo power goes into the receiver.

To reduce the voltage necessary to break down the discharge gaps of the TR and ATR switches, they are filled with gas at a pressure of about 1/200 atmosphere. Further reduction is accomplished by mounting the discharge gap across a resonant cavity, to make use of the build-up in voltage accompanying resonance. Fig. 23 is a cutaway view of a TR tube used in the 3-cm. band. The resonant cavity is part of the tube envelope, and is made to be bolted between standard wave guide coupling flanges. Energy is coupled into and out of the cavity by means

of round holes (filled with glass to retain the gas) in each side of the cavity. The discharge takes place between the two conical electrodes in the centre of the cavity; tuning is accomplished by moving one of them, mounted on a flexible diaphragm, toward or away from the other. To ensure rapid breakdown of the gap at the beginning of a pulse (within 0.01 μ sec.), a supply of ions is maintained in the gap by a discharge taking place constantly inside one of the cones.

ATR tubes are similar, except that they need have no output window, being mounted on the side of (*i.e.*, in series with) the RF line. Ordinarily they are made with lower Q, to reduce the chance of accidental maladjustment of tuning.

In the years following World War II, use of the newly developed ferrite materials, which exhibit a very pronounced Faraday effect at microwave frequencies, permitted the construction of circuit elements which were highly nonlinear, in the sense that they

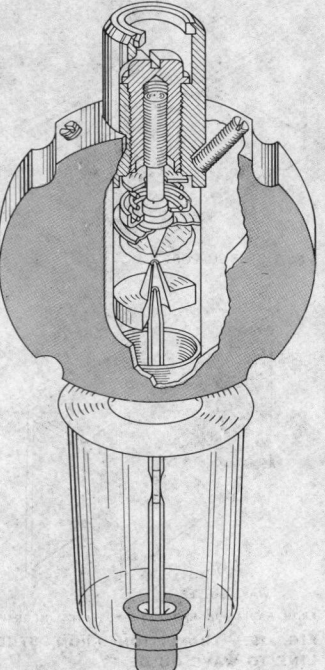

FIG. 23.—CUT-AWAY VIEW OF 1B24 3-CM. TR SWITCH

behaved differently for microwave energy traveling in opposite directions. This made possible the design of duplexing and isolating elements less complicated and more effective than the gas-discharge devices of wartime radar.

4. Antennas and Scanners.—The antenna of a radar set must radiate into space the energy fed to it as RF pulses, and must gather in the echo signals and send them down the RF line to the receiver. A good transmitting antenna is also a good receiving antenna; thus only the former function need be considered. Sharp beams are needed to make radar direction-finding possible, and a great deal of attention has been paid to the design of highly directional antennas that are capable of producing beams of the desired shape and dimensions. The nature of the beam wanted depends, of course, on the radar application.

Antenna Design.—The beam width, θ, produced by an antenna is directly proportional to the wave length of the radiation used, and inversely proportional to the width of the antenna. Beam width as usually defined is the full angular interval between the points at which the power radiated from the antenna has fallen to half its maximum value (fig. 24). Fig. 24 shows also the "side lobes," small subsidiary maxima unavoidably produced by a directional antenna. Their effects are usually objectionable, and attention is paid in antenna design to reducing the power in the side lobes. The beam width in degrees is given approximately by

$$\theta = 70\lambda/D \qquad (27)$$

where λ is the wave length and D the width of the antenna in the same dimension as that for which θ is measured. D and λ should be given in the same units.

Among the simplest microwave antennas is a reflecting paraboloid of revolution illuminated by a source of radiation, or "antenna feed," placed at its focus. Since the diameter of the reflector

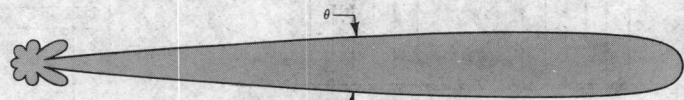

FIG. 24.—A TYPICAL ANTENNA PATTERN. MAIN LOBE HAS BEAM WIDTH θ. SIDE LOBES ARE SHOWN

is several wave lengths, this antenna can be regarded from the standpoint of ray optics (fig. 25). Fig. 25 does not explain the side lobes or the beam width, but it does emphasize that the feed for such an antenna must itself be directive.

In accordance with eq. (27), a paraboloid whose top and bottom have been cut off to leave a reflector wider than it is high will produce a fan-shaped beam whose vertical beam width is larger than its beam width measured horizontally. A "beaver-tail" beam wider in the horizontal than in the vertical direction can be produced by cutting off the sides of a paraboloid to leave a tall, narrow reflector. Further adjustment of the energy in the beam can be accomplished by altering the shape of the reflector without changing its over-all dimensions. Instead of a paraboloidal reflector with a feed at its point focus, a parabolic cylinder with a linear feed located along its line focus can be used as an antenna.

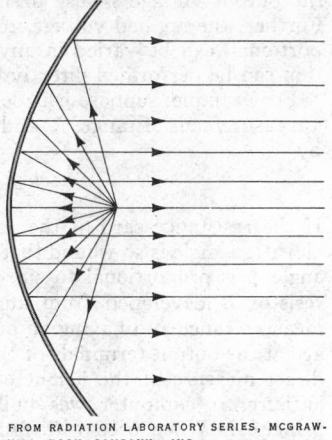

FROM RADIATION LABORATORY SERIES, MCGRAW-HILL BOOK COMPANY, INC.

FIG. 25.—RAY DIAGRAM OF A PARABOLOID ANTENNA

Mechanical Scanning.—In order to cover the necessary volume of space with the narrow beam produced by a directional antenna, the beam must be swung around, or scanned. In most cases, the permissible rates of beam motion, fixed as they are by the desirability of receiving several echo pulses from each target per scan, are so low that scanning can be accomplished by mechanical motion of the antenna array. The assembly of an antenna on its supporting structure, or pedestal, is called an antenna mount, or scanner. (L. N. R.; G. R. T.)

Electronic Scanning.—Early methods of shifting a beam from a planar surface or within a parabolic reflector involved mechanical motion of radiating or illuminating elements. When the beam was required to scan relatively large horizontal and vertical sectors the entire array or reflector was moved in an oscillatory fashion. This required rapid oscillations when searching for fast-moving targets such as aircraft. Not only was the oscillation rate limited but the mechanical design and construction problems were severe.

The development of simple electronically controlled microwave phase shifters made possible the evolution of phased arrays having great functional flexibility. Various functions can be activated simultaneously or interlaced in time. The net result is that not only are several simple radars effectively combined into one but also the performance of the several radars is done with far greater agility.

Phased arrays are typically mounted upon a planar surface whose dimensions are inversely proportional to the product of frequency and beam width. The beam is a narrow pencil, nominally 1° to 3° in width. A large number, 1,000 to 10,000, of radiating (and reciprocally receiving) elements such as dipoles or slots are arranged in a rectangular or triangular grid. Each element, or group of elements, is equipped with its own phase shifter that is controlled electronically in accordance with the desired function and programming. The energy radiated by the elements adds in one direction and almost cancels in another, forming the beam. The beam direction is instantaneously shifted by changing the phase relationship between elements. The width of the scanned sector may extend up to 120° with some widening of the beam and reduction of array power gain away from the perpendicular. For complete azimuthal coverage, there are required three or four arrays depending upon the degree of beam width and gain degradation to be tolerated. Alternately, a single array along with its functional control unit may be rotated as desired. Circular arrays also have been designed. Large fixed arrays lend themselves to rugged construction.

The electronically controlled phased array is capable of operating simultaneously in various modes such as target search with broad beam and narrow beam, multitarget acquisition and tracking, automatic search for lost targets and monitoring. The absence of large masses in slewing operations makes for high agility in all operations. Because many of the operations are automatic the application of computer control and data processing is particularly suitable. Still another advantage is the ability to operate upon different radiated frequencies at the same time as dictated by interference and countermeasures situations.

As has been stated before, the electronically operated phase shifter is the device that has made possible the development of the multifunctional scanning phased array. The two types of phase shifters are electronically controlled ferrites and solid state diodes. The choice of type is influenced by the insertion loss, which is lower at high frequencies for ferrites and at low frequencies for diodes.

In application the ferrite rod is inserted into a wave guide and becomes a part of the path for the wave energy. Its electrical length is varied by magnetizing with the control pulse by means of a wire running through the rod.

There are two general types of flux control. In the "latch" method several lengths of ferrite rods are selectively driven to magnetic saturation; and in the flux-drive method a single length capable of giving 360° phase shift is appropriately magnetized for the desired shift. Generally, ferrite devices provide nonreciprocal path directions so that the polarity of the control pulse must be reversed between transmitting and receiving. The latch method lends itself well to the equal amplitude positive-negative pulses from a digital generator since the remanent of flux saturation is the only condition of magnetization. The flux-drive method first requires saturation as a reference, followed by the discrete time-current corresponding to the desired phase shift. Since discrete time-current is adjustable, compensation is available for spurious phase shifts in temperature-sensitive ferrite materials.

Diodes whose forward and reverse directions can be controlled—such as, for example, semiconductor p-i-n diodes—are used to vary relative phase between radiating elements by switching, in and out, portions of a transmission line circuit, thus effectively changing its over-all effective length, producing a phase shift.

Where the operational criteria consist of a designated maximum range, scan sector width, wide band width—short pulse and/or multifrequency—and minimum beam side lobes, a design technique is used in which a number of optimum-dimension arrays are grouped into several subarrays. The subarrays are integrated into the over-all system by inserting true-time delays or phase shifters into their feeders. The time delays may consist of switching lengths of coaxial cable or other methods.

Phased-array feeders systems consist of either illuminating the front of the array made of dipole elements with a space horn or lens feed, or series-feeding dipoles or other type elements from the rear of the array. In either case the phase shifters are connected in series with the elements. The space feeder may be offset to minimize obstruction to the re-radiated energy from the array. Whatever feed system is used will entail phase or true-time difference compensations for differences in physical or electrical distances introduced by unavoidable departures from identity of energy flow to the elements.

The extreme degree of redundancy inherent in the multi-element array favours reliability. Individual failure of elements and their individual accessories produces only gradual degradation and the chance of complete failure is minimized. Mechanical breakdowns, a major consideration of pre-phased-array radar, particularly on mobile equipment, are practically absent.

Phased-array radar opens the way for very high-power radiating capability. Although the energy radiated from each element may be relatively small the coherent energy in space from the large number of elements can exceed that of radars of earlier design and similar size.

High-power phased-array radars are largely solid state except for the transmitter. Cost, initially high in any new complex device, can be expected to decrease with further development and production organization.

An example of the predecessor of the scanned phased array is the slot antenna which is fixed in phase. The properties of radiation from a slot cut in a wave guide, or other shape of conducting surface, are utilized in the construction of radar antennas. The design is treated in the manner of a fix-phased-array antenna where the parameters are dimension and orientation of elements, spacing of elements, number of elements and phase-feeding. Feeding of a slot array is usually accomplished through wave guides. The thin slots are resonant—cut to one-half wave length. Spacing between slots is made greater or less than one-half wave length in order to achieve large band width. The slotted antenna can handle high power at normal atmospheric pressures. Polarization may be controlled by the orientation of the slots, the electric field being perpendicular to the long dimension. (F. B. D.)

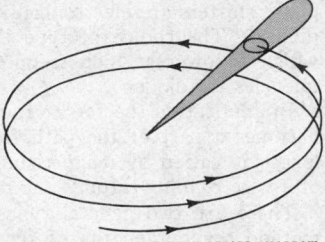

FROM RADIATION LABORATORY SERIES, MCGRAW-HILL BOOK COMPANY, INC.

FIG. 26.—HELICAL SCANNING PATTERN

Types of Radar Scanners.—Radar scanners are of many different sorts, the detailed design being dictated principally by the size of the antenna (this being determined by the wave length used and the beam width desired), and by the scanning pattern used to cover the volume being searched. A few simple scanning patterns are:

(1) *Azimuth scan.*—The beam is swung around the horizon at a uniform rate. The desired vertical coverage is obtained by fanning the beam in the vertical direction.

(2) *Helical scan.*—If information on the elevation angle of targets is wanted, a pencil beam can be used, uniform azimuth rotation employed and the elevation angle of the beam altered constantly at a slow uniform rate (fig. 26). When the full elevation-angle range of interest has been covered, the motion in elevation angle is reversed.

(3) *Conical scan.*—For accurate direction-finding on a single target, a pencil beam can be rotated rapidly in a cone whose angular opening is smaller than the beam width. Only when the axis of the cone is directly pointed at the target will the signals received in various phases of the rotation of the beam have constant intensity. A change in signal strength will accompany conical scan when the axis of the cone is not quite on the target. The magnitude and phase of this change in signal strength as the beam rotates indicates the direction and the magnitude of the pointing error. The direction of the cone axis is changed to make the "error signal" zero. By the use of this scheme, radar direction-finding can be given a precision of about one-fiftieth of a beam width; this is far greater precision than can be obtained by noting the direction of maximum signal return when a beam is swept over a target.

(4) *Spiral scan.*—If a rapid axial rotation of a pencil beam, like that used in conical scanning, is combined with a slow change in the cone opening, a spiral scan (fig. 27) results. This permits rapid coverage of a fairly large area, with facilities for determining roughly both the azimuth and the elevation of targets.

Data Transmission.—In order to make use at the radar indicator of the directional information afforded by scanning, means must be provided for transmitting to the indicator a knowledge of the scanner position in all important co-ordinates. Only azimuth must be transmitted for an azimuth scan, azimuth and elevation for a helical scan, and azimuth, elevation and phase of rotation for a conical or a spiral scan.

This "data transmission," as it is called, is almost always accomplished electrically. The flexibility of mechanical means of

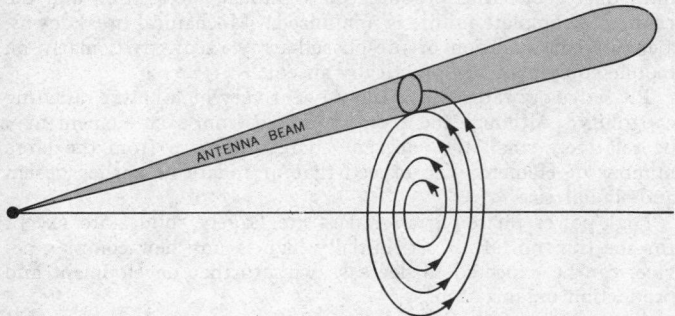

ANTENNA BEAM

FROM RADIATION LABORATORY SERIES, MCGRAW-HILL BOOK COMPANY, INC.

FIG. 27.—SPIRAL SCAN

data transmission is not sufficient to meet radar requirements. Self-synchronous generators and motors of the type used in other applications for transmitting position information are frequently employed. So are precision adjustable resistors. The latter have the advantage that they can be wound in such a way that the output voltage is any desired function of angle of rotation. Further, the applied voltage, to which the output voltage is proportional, can be varied in any fashion desired. Thus computation can be performed directly by the data transmission device.

For example, suppose it is desired to find target height, *h*, from a measurement of range, *R*, and elevation angle, ϕ; it will be given by

$$h = R \sin \phi \qquad (28)$$

If the resistance card of the adjustable resistor used to measure elevation angle is so wound that its output voltage for an elevation angle ϕ is proportional to $\sin \phi$, and the voltage applied to this resistor is developed from another adjustable resistor used to measure range and having an output linear with R, then the voltage at the output terminals of the elevation-angle resistor will be a direct measure of the height of the target. A highly successful antiaircraft computer was built during World War II on this principle. When used with radar, the data-transmission units of the radar actually formed part of the computing mechanism.

Rapid Scanning.—In some radar applications, such rapid scanning is desired that mechanical motion of a large antenna mount is not feasible. A number of devices have been developed to permit rapid scanning in one dimension by relatively subtle mechanical motions of parts of the antenna. These devices are sometimes referred to as "electrical" scanners, although rapid mechanical motion is almost always fundamental to the scanning.

Stabilization.—When a radar scanner is mounted on an unstable platform, such as a ship or an aircraft, readings of azimuth and elevation relative to the platform must be converted into readings of these angles with respect to a stable set of reference axes. Compasses, directional gyros, and gyro stable verticals are commonly used as reference devices, and the stabilization of the radar data, as this conversion process is called, can be performed in a variety of ways.

5. Radar Receivers.—Under the term "receiver" is classed that part of the radar equipment which accepts the feeble echo pulses from the RF line, amplifies them, rectifies them and delivers to the terminals of the indicator or display equipment unipolar pulse signals at a level usually of several volts.

Most radar receivers are of the superheterodyne type, in which a local oscillator supplies CW signals at a low level to a mixer, where the echo signal and the local oscillator signal beat to give a signal at a frequency (called the intermediate frequency) equal to the difference between the frequencies of the signals mixed. This beat signal is modulated with the same intelligence as that conveyed by the RF echoes, and its frequency is chosen to permit fairly standard techniques to be used in the IF amplifier.

The IF amplifier is normally tuned to a fixed frequency, and the receiver tuning is changed by altering the frequency of the local oscillator. Arrangements, called AFC (for automatic frequency control), are incorporated in most radar receivers for keeping the local oscillator properly tuned with respect to the radar transmitter. Demodulation of the amplified IF signal is accomplished by a second detector followed by a filter for the intermediate-frequency signal. The resulting signals, called "video signals" because their frequency range is about that of television video signals, are further amplified and sent to the indicator. (L. N. R.; G. R. T.)

Low-Noise Amplifiers.—In the radar receiver two of the most rewarding spots open for improvement have always been the RF amplifier and the first-stage IF amplifier. One noise generator is the crystal mixer which typically is the first stage in the receiver. Thus it is important that the incoming signal level be amplified with a large ratio of signal to noise. There is always the opportunity of trading transmitter power and antenna gain for receiver sensitivity in any type of radar. Some principal developments of this and other applications during the 1960s follow.

Transistor amplifier. The transistor has replaced the thermionic tube almost universally in electronic equipment where high power and high voltages are not required. One of the reasons for this popularity is the low-noise characteristic of the better transistors; another is the low cost. As high-frequency and microwave transistors became available the transistor was applied to RF and IF amplification in the radar receiver.

Microwave transistor amplifiers typically have characteristics as follows: frequency, 0.1 to 8 gigaHertz (GHz); band width (above 300 MHz), 4 to 80%; gain, 5 to 8 db.; noise figure (2 to 8 GHz), 4.5 to 25 db.

Tunnel diode amplifier. A heavily doped p-n junction diode in which electrons are biased from passing over the barrier exhibits the phenomenon that the electrons tunnel under the barrier at an accelerated speed. This presents a negative resistance from which amplification results. The tunnel diode is particularly useful where low-noise wideband characteristics are required. Useful gains over octave band widths are obtained. Because phase linearity with respect to frequency is typically a benefit derived from wideband devices, the tunnel diode is of particular value as a component of wideband phased radar arrays. It is further characterized by extreme insensitivity to temperature variations, operating from liquid helium to 600° F. Some characteristics of tunnel diode amplifiers are: frequency, 0.25 to 19 GHz; band width, 3.5 to 18%; gain, 12 to 20 db.; noise figure, 3 to 7 db.

Parametric amplifier. By the 1960s the long-known principle of parametric excitation and amplification had found practical application by achieving greatly increased sensitivity in UHF and microwave receivers. The development of the varactor, a microwave p-n junction semiconductor diode, inherently low in noise contribution, made the low-noise parametric amplifier (termed paramp) practical. The parametric amplifier is principally applied to long-range ground-to-air surveillance and traffic control systems, ballistic-missile early-warning radar, ground-based space radars and radar astronomy; also in communications and telemetry. The sensitivity of the parametric amplifier can be further increased by cooling with liquid nitrogen or liquid helium whereby thermal noise is minimized and the door opened for reduction of remanent circuit noise.

The usual parametric amplifier employing a varactor operates because of the nonlinear relationship between the capacity of the varactor and the applied voltage; that is, the capacity varies as the voltage. An uncommensurate higher frequency whose voltage is greater than the signal voltage supplies the energy or pump action to the varactor. The amplified same-frequency output appears at the input terminals of the amplifier and must be separated from the input by a non-reciprocal device such as a ferrite circulator or hybrid circuit. The lower sideband, termed the idler frequency, generated between the signal and the pump frequency, although necessary for amplifier performance, is filtered from the output. Band width is usually increased by multiple tuning. Characteristics of parametric amplifiers follow: frequency, 0.3 to 35 GHz; band width, 0.5 to 7%; gain, 10 to 20 db.; pump frequency, 7.5 to 50 GHz; noise figure (0.3 to 35 GHz range): uncooled, 0.4 to 25 db.; cooled to 77° K, 0.1 to 1 db.; cooled to 20° K, 0.04 to 0.4 db.; cooled to 7° K, 0.02 to 0.2 db.

Traveling-wave maser amplifier. This device is unchallenged for its low noise properties at room temperatures and champions the continuation of competition of tubes with solid state developments. Other characteristics are extremely large band width, high gain and large dynamic range with quick recovery. Its versatility also includes operational design either as a low-noise or power amplifier. In a traveling-wave tube a velocity-retarded RF wave traveling along a helix is velocity-modulated by a magnetically focused electron beam concentric to the helix. Amplification is accomplished by extraction of energy from the beam. Some characteristics of the traveling-wave maser amplifier are as follows: frequency, 0.25 to 100 GHz; band width, 36 to 67%; gain, 25 to 35 db.; noise figure: 3 to 7 GHz, 3 to 7 db.; 7 to 18 GHz, 7 to 11 db.; 20 to 100 GHz, 11 to 20 db.

Microwave Mixers.—Somewhat removing the requirement for low-noise RF amplifiers in medium-performance radars has been

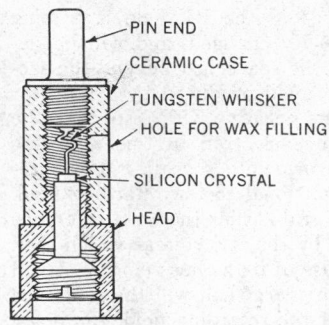

FROM RADIATION LABORATORY SERIES, MC-GRAW-HILL BOOK COMPANY, INC.

FIG. 28.—STANDARD MICROWAVE MIXER CRYSTAL

the development of low-noise mixers and associated local oscillators, still employing solid state devices. Silicon Schottky Barrier type mixers have noise figures as low as 6 db. at 10 GHz.

(F. B. D.)

Conversion to intermediate frequency in the mixer at the low level of received signal power requires that the nonlinear element used in the mixer be as efficient as possible and introduce a minimum amount of random noise. The most satisfactory element was the rectifying contact between a metallic point and a silicon crystal. The whole assembly was sealed up in a cartridge, referred to as a "crystal," for protection and stability. One standard form for this cartridge is shown in fig. 28.

The contact area between the metal and the silicon is only about 10^{-6} cm². High current densities are therefore produced even by low currents, and a crystal can readily be burned out, especially by a pulse so rapid that heat cannot be conducted away from the contact.

The RF circuit in which the crystal is installed is called the "mixer." It has input terminals for the signal and for the power from the local oscillator. Its output terminals are connected to the first stage of the IF amplifier. Care is taken in mixer design to make the crystal appear as a matched load to the incoming signal; to prevent, as far as possible, loss of echo-signal power into the local-oscillator input line; and to provide a reasonably good match looking into the mixer from the local oscillator.

Local Oscillators.—The magnetron, although a very efficient source of high pulse powers, was not employed in wartime radar as a source of the low-level CW signal required from the local oscillator of a superheterodyne receiver. Quite satisfactory tubes of other types were developed for this purpose.

Some World War II radar sets used a special triode, called a "lighthouse" tube because of its construction, as a local oscillator. The lighthouse tube is designed with planar electrodes and extremely small interelectrode spacing to reduce electron transit time. External connections to its electrodes are provided in the form of disks and cylinders (fig. 29), so that a cylindrical RF circuit can be built directly around the tube. An average power output of a few watts can be obtained from a lighthouse tube, and the tube can also be pulsed to give peak power of about 1 kw. It has been used as a transmitter in some low-power radar sets.

Most radar sets used a reflex klystron as a local oscillator. Fig. 30 is a schematic diagram of such a tube. Integral with the tube structure is a doughnut-shaped resonant cavity with grids across its central portion. An "electron gun" focuses a stream of electrons through the grids. Upon arrival at the first grid, the electrons have a velocity corresponding to the 300 volts applied to accelerate them. If oscillations exist in the cavity, electrons will either be accelerated or decelerated by the RF field which they encounter as they pass through the space between the cavity grids.

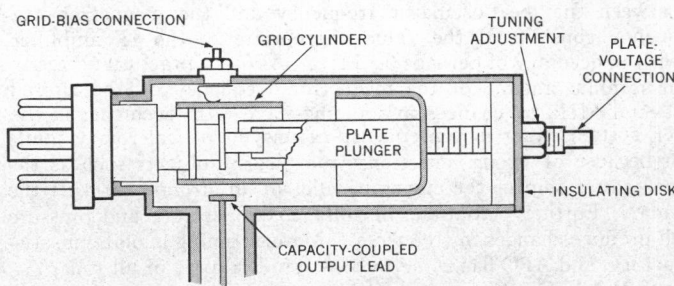

FROM RADIATION LABORATORY SERIES, MCGRAW-HILL BOOK COMPANY, INC.

FIG. 29.—LIGHTHOUSE TUBE MOUNTED IN A COAXIAL CIRCUIT

An electron which goes through just as the RF field is passing through zero will not have its velocity changed, and will be described as a reference electron. In the space just beyond the second grid there is a strong retarding field produced by a reflector electrode maintained about 100 volts negative with respect to the cathode. The path of the reference electron in this retarding field is similar to that of a ball thrown into the air. It will return to the grids after a time proportional to the retarding field. An electron that leaves the second grid earlier than the reference electron will have been accelerated by the RF voltage which then existed across the cavity, and, because of its higher velocity, it will spend a longer time in the reflection space than will the reference electron. By proper adjustment of the retarding field, the delay can be made to compensate for its earlier departure, so that it arrives back at the grids at the same time as the reference electron.

Similarly, an electron leaving later than the reference electron has been decelerated by the RF field, has a lower velocity, and thus catches up with the reference electron because it spends less time in the reflection space. The net effect is that the electrons gather in a bunch which is formed about the reference electron. At certain reflector voltages, the bunch will return through the cavity grids in such a phase that the RF field retards the electrons, and thus receives from them energy to sustain the oscillations in the cavity. Oscillation is observed for more than one reflector voltage, since drift times differing by a whole RF period still produce satisfactory bunching.

The net energy given to the electrons during their first passage through the cavity is negligible when averaged over a whole RF cycle, being balanced between acceleration and deceleration.

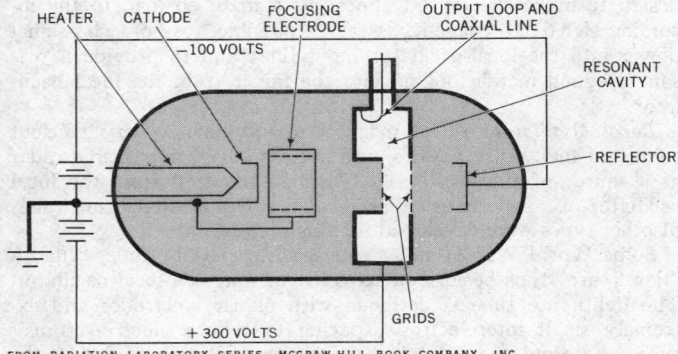

FROM RADIATION LABORATORY SERIES, MCGRAW-HILL BOOK COMPANY, INC.

FIG. 30.—SCHEMATIC DIAGRAM OF REFLEX KLYSTRON OSCILLATOR

On the return passage, most of the electrons go through in a bunch at the most favourable phase to aid the oscillation. Very few electrons pass through on the return trip half a cycle later, when they would absorb energy from the RF field. Power is coupled out of the cavity through a loop feeding into a coaxial line. Power outputs in the range from 20 to 50 mw. and efficiencies of about 1% were typical of such tubes produced in the postwar years.

Tuning over a wide range is accomplished by changing the size of the cavity mechanically; a small amount of tuning can be done by varying the reflector voltage.

Automatic Frequency Control.—The problem of keeping a radar set properly in tune consists in maintaining the difference between the local-oscillator frequency and the magnetron frequency constant at the value appropriate to the IF amplifier, with an accuracy of perhaps 0.5 MHz. AFC is a practical necessity in scanning radar, for the magnetron frequency can be altered several MHz by changes in standing-wave ratio occurring in the RF system either in consequence of unsymmetrical rotary joints or because of strong reflections from nearby objects such as the masts of a ship or the engine nacelles of an aircraft carrying the radar. Further, variations in voltage, temperature and pressure all produce changes in frequency. Manual tuning is quite unsatisfactory, and AFC has come to be a standard part of all radar.

In the AFC system, part of the local-oscillator power is mixed, in a crystal, with a small fraction of the magnetron power drawn out during transmission of the pulse. The resulting signal at the difference frequency is applied to a discriminator circuit similar to those used in a frequency-modulation receiver. The crossover or no-output frequency of the discriminator is set at the intermediate frequency of the radar. The pulses which come from the discriminator are integrated to produce a voltage that is applied to the reflector of the local oscillator in the proper sense to change the frequency toward that value which will bring the discriminator output to zero. It is desirable to use an AFC mixer which is separate from the signal mixer, but it is possible to make an AFC system which obtains its information from the leakage power which inevitably reaches the signal mixer during the transmission of an RF pulse from the magnetron.

The IF Amplifier.—Because of the low power level of the input signal to a radar IF amplifier, the greatest attention must be paid to minimizing the inherent noise of the amplifier itself. Further, since strong pulses several hundreds of μ sec. in length may be followed immediately by weak signals which must not be missed, the transient response of the IF amplifier must be excellent. The amplifiers which resulted during World War II from attention to these requirements were rather different from anything which had previously existed.

The intermediate frequency is usually chosen in the range from 15 to 60 MHz. The over-all gain of the IF amplifier is usually around 120 db. or 1,000,000 times in voltage. The desired over-all band width of the amplifier is ordinarily about 2 MHz. Since the cascading of amplifier stages results in an over-all band width much less than the band width of an individual stage, it is very important to attain the highest possible product of gain and band width in the individual stages.

The design of the interstage coupling circuit used in an IF amplifier has an important effect on the gain-band-width product that can be achieved with given tubes. The characteristics of the tubes themselves are also of the greatest importance, the leading property being the ratio of transconductance to input and output capacity.

It is important that regenerative feedback of signals does not take place from later stages to earlier stages of the IF amplifier, or from plate to grid circuit in a single stage. Circuit layout and shielding must be carefully planned to avoid regeneration.

Second Detector.—The second detector produces a rectified voltage proportional to the amplitude of the IF waves. In most radio receivers it is important that this proportionality be exact; in a radar receiver the response of the second detector may be proportional to a higher power of the IF amplitude, so long as reasonable efficiency is maintained. Either a thermionic diode or a rectifying metal semiconductor contact ("crystal") is used as the nonlinear rectifying element. Second-detector crystals usually employ germanium, instead of silicon, as the semiconductor, since germanium crystals can be made to stand a somewhat higher reverse voltage.

Video Amplifier.—The unipolar signals from the second detector, usually at a level of a few volts, are further amplified by a wide band resistance-capacitance-coupled amplifier called the video amplifier, because of its similarity to the video amplifiers used in television.

When the line from the radar proper to the indicator must be long, it is economical to drive the line at a low video-signal level and provide video amplification at each indicator. Since the standard dielectric-filled coaxial cable ordinarily used for the transmission of video signals has a low impedance—in the neighbourhood of 75 to 100 ohms—a "cathode follower" stage is frequently used to drive the line.

6. Radar Indicators.—The device which presents radar data in observable form is called the indicator. It is almost always a cathode-ray tube (CRT). The CRT presents a representation of electrical phenomena in terms of a picture painted on a phosphorescent screen by a sharply-focused beam of electrons controlled in position and intensity by electrical signals. The CRT is capable of using and displaying many millions of separate data per second, and the geometrical expression which it gives to radar data is particularly appropriate, since a geometrical situation involving the various radar targets is usually precisely what must be represented.

CRT Screens.—Both magnetic and electrostatic CRT types are used, the terms referring to the means of deflecting the stream of electrons (fig. 1). The properties of the materials (phosphors) making up the luminous screen are of particular importance to the performance of the tube. If, as is usually the case, the scanning of the radar antenna interrupts the display in a given sector of the screen for longer than the retentivity time of the eye, it is desirable to introduce persistence into the screen—that is, to use a phosphor which will glow for some time after having been excited.

If little or no persistence is needed, the green willemite phosphor used in ordinary oscilloscope tubes and known as type P-1 is satisfactory. This material is extremely efficient in converting the energy of the electrons which strike it into luminous energy; it has an exponential decay with a time constant of a few milliseconds. If a rather short persistence is needed, a zinc-magnesium fluoride phosphor designated as P-12 is used.

Most radar applications demand even a longer persistence. This can be achieved by a "cascade" screen consisting of two layers of different phosphors. The electrons strike and excite an inner layer of silver-activated zinc sulphide, which glows with a blue light. This blue light excites a layer of persistent phosphor, usually copper-activated zinc-cadmium sulphide. The zinc-to-cadmium ratio determines the decay characteristics.

Because the long-persistence phosphor emits a predominantly yellow or orange light, an orange filter is used to remove the blue "flash" of the inner phosphor, which is annoying to the observer.

Radar Displays.—Because of the many special purposes that radar can serve, a considerable variety of different forms of

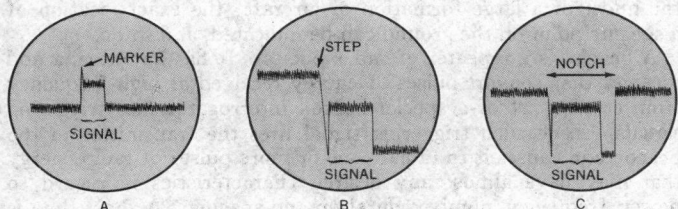

FROM RADIATION LABORATORY SERIES, MCGRAW-HILL BOOK COMPANY, INC.

FIG. 31.—RANGE SCOPES: (A) PIP MARKER; (B) STEP MARKER; (C) NOTCH MARKER

display have been developed and used. The A-scope and the PPI have already been mentioned. These are typical of two general classes in which the radar echo signals are used either (1) to deflect the CRT electron beam, or (2) to alter its intensity. Displays of the first type (deflection-modulated displays) are useful for giving precise information on the strength and character of the signals delivered by the receiver, but leave only one dimension of the tube face free to represent a geometrical quantity. Displays of the second type (intensity-modulated displays) permit the presentation of a two-dimensional figure on which the signals appear as bright spots or patches, but the intensity response of CRT electron guns is so nonlinear that the brightness of each patch offers only qualitative information about signal intensity.

When a three-dimensional picture must be presented on the two-dimensional face of a CRT indicator, either more than one display must be used, or a formalized way of presenting the third dimension in an understandable, though unnatural, fashion must be devised.

The vast majority of radar displays use as one co-ordinate the value of slant range to the target. Range is displayed by causing the electron beam of the CRT to sweep across the tube at a uniform rate starting from a given point or line at a definite time in each pulse cycle. Distances on the tube face from the starting point are then proportional to increments of range.

The angle at which the scanner is pointing, either in azimuth or elevation, may enter the display (1) directly as a polar angle, (2) directly as a Cartesian co-ordinate, or (3) as the basis for resolving a range sweep in a particular direction.

Usually markers are employed to assist in making measure-

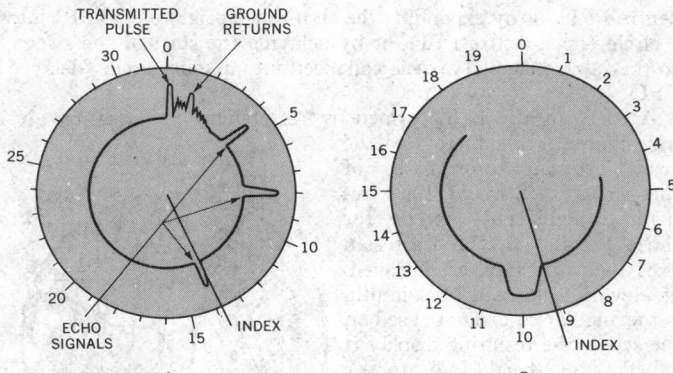

FROM RADIATION LABORATORY SERIES, MCGRAW-HILL BOOK COMPANY, INC.

FIG. 32.—J-SCOPE, ANOTHER TYPE OF RANGE SCOPE SHOWING READING IN (A) THOUSANDS OF YARDS; (B) HUNDREDS OF YARDS

ments of range or angle on a radar indicator. These may be "electronic" markers introduced into the signal channel as artificial video signals generated by a precision timing circuit (for range markers) or an angle-measuring circuit (for angle markers). Alternatively, they may be mechanical grids or markers placed over the face of the CRT.

A few of the most important radar displays are catalogued below, according to the spatial geometry represented.

One-dimensional Deflection-modulated Displays.—The simplest display of this type is the A-scope described earlier. Range is invariably the spatial co-ordinate presented on a display in this class. If it is desired to do accurate range-finding with the help of an indicator in this category, arrangements are made to delay the start of the range sweep by any desired amount, so that the interval displayed will include the target of interest. The sweep speed is then greatly increased to give higher resolution in range. Usually a movable electronic marker is provided for the precise measurement of range. Such a display is called an R- (range) scope. Fig. 31 shows R-scope displays with various types of movable range markers.

Greater sweep length can be obtained by bending the range sweep into a circle on the face of the tube, and using the radar echo signals to deflect the beam radially from the centre of the CRT. Fig. 32 shows such a display called a J-scope.

Simple deflection-modulated range displays can be used for comparing the signal strength from two antennas whose patterns make a small angle with one another, or from a conically scanning antenna in two positions 180° apart. The K-scope is so arranged that the range sweeps to be compared start from different origins, so that the echoes to be compared are side by side. In the L-scope, signals from the two antennas produce deflections of opposite sign, the range origin being common (fig. 33).

Two-dimensional Intensity-modulated Displays.—The PPI is the most generally useful of the indicators in this category. For certain purposes, it is altered by moving the range origin (off-

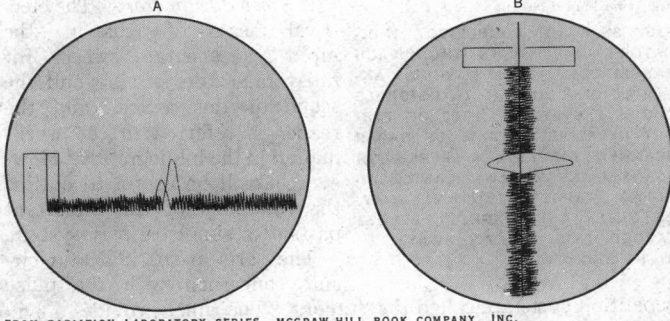

FROM RADIATION LABORATORY SERIES, MCGRAW-HILL BOOK COMPANY, INC.

FIG. 33.—DISPLAYS PERMITTING COMPARISON OF STRENGTH OF ECHO FROM A GIVEN TARGET ON TWO ANTENNAS, OR IN TWO POSITIONS OF A CONICAL SCAN. (A) SIDE-BY-SIDE PRESENTATION (K-SCOPE). (B) BACK-TO-BACK PRESENTATION (L-SCOPE)

centre PPI), or by expanding the zero-range origin of the PPI into a circle (open-centre PPI), or by delaying the start of the sweep, so that a ring-shaped area is collapsed into a solid circle (delayed PPI).

A PPI can also be deformed by "stretching"; that is, by giving different scale factors to the two Cartesian co-ordinates of the display. Straight lines remain straight but, except for those parallel to the Cartesian axes, their directions are changed. If elevation, instead of azimuth, is the angular co-ordinate used on the scope, the resulting display is called a range-height indicator, or RHI. Lines of constant target height are horizontal and equally spaced. (*See* fig. 34.)

A plane surface can also be represented in a deformed manner useful for certain radar applications by presenting range and angle in Cartesian rather than in polar co-ordinates. This is accomplished by moving a range sweep laterally across the tube face in synchronism with the scanner motion so that the range origin is stretched out into a line. If the angular field shown by such a display is small enough, it

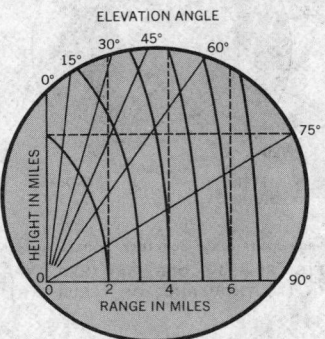

FROM RADIATION LABORATORY SERIES, MCGRAW-HILL BOOK COMPANY, INC.

FIG. 34.—THE RANGE-HEIGHT IN-DICATOR (RHI). THIS IS A POLAR DISPLAY WITH DIFFERENT SCALE FACTORS ALONG THE TWO CARTE-SIAN CO-ORDINATES. THE VERTICAL STRETCHING IS SHOWN BY THE TWO-MILE GRID SHOWN DOTTED IN THE DIAGRAM. LINES OF CONSTANT HEIGHT ARE STRAIGHT AND HORI-ZONTAL ON THIS DISPLAY

can be "normalized" to reduce the distortion to modest limits. Normalization is performed by keeping the angular dispersion proportional to the range to the centre of the display.

Three-dimensional Displays.—As already remarked, no real three-dimensional display can be presented on the two-dimensional face of a CRT. However, certain formalized ways have been developed for indicating target elevation on a display which already shows target range and bearing. An example of this type is the "double-dot" display. On alternate range sweeps the origin of this modified Type-B indicator is moved to the right and left sides by a fixed amount. On the sweeps occurring in the right-hand pattern the origin is simultaneously shifted vertically by an amount proportional to the sine of the elevation angle.

Any single echo then appears in two neighbouring positions, and the slope of the line joining the two dots is a rough measure of elevation angle, accurate to two or three degrees under the usual circumstances of use. (*See* fig. 35.)

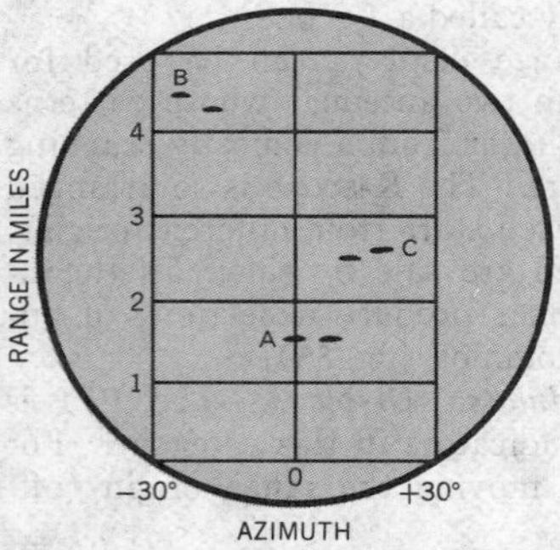

A Simple Indicator.—The electrical means of achieving the rapid and accurate sweeps for radar indicators are beyond the scope of this article, and the reader is referred to the works quoted in the bibliography. However, it will be useful to outline the functions of the important parts of a simple display system.

The parts of the indicator circuit concerned with the pulse repetition cycle are called the "timer." The timer provides a synchronization with the modulator, sweeps and markers for the display and measurement of range, blanking of the CRT during unused parts of the pulse cycle, and other related operations.

In some cases, the timer exerts control of the firing time of

FROM RADIATION LABORATORY SERIES, MCGRAW-HILL BOOK COMPANY, INC.

FIG. 35.—THE DOUBLE-DOT INDI-CATOR, A B-SCOPE IN WHICH EACH TARGET ECHO APPEARS TWICE. AN-GLE OF LINE JOINING TWO SIGNALS SHOWS ELEVATION ANGLE OF TAR-GET RELATIVE TO AXIS OF RADAR SCANNER. TARGET A IS LEVEL WITH SCANNER, 1.5 MI. AWAY, AND DEAD AHEAD. TARGET B IS 4.5 MI. AWAY, 25° LEFT AND SLIGHTLY BELOW. TARGET C IS 2.5 MI. AWAY, 12° RIGHT AND ABOVE

the modulator by sending it a trigger pulse; in others it responds to a trigger from the modulator. The latter type of system is shown in fig. 36. The square wave is used to turn the CRT on during the useful display cycle. The linearly increasing (or saw-tooth) waveform is used to provide the uniform range sweep for the indicator.

Timing of this wave is controlled by the square wave. Electronic range markers are also generated by the timer and mixed with the radar video signals before they are sent to the CRT.

For illustrative purposes, fig. 36 shows provisions for either an A-scope or a B-scope display. For the former presentation, the range-sweep voltage is applied to one pair of deflecting plates and the mixed signal and range-mark voltages to the other pair. The square wave controlling the CRT intensity is applied to the cathode in the proper polarity to brighten the tube during the range sweep.

In the Type-B display, the range sweep is applied to one pair of deflection plates, as before. Signal modulation is applied to the control grid, and the second set of deflection plates receives a voltage which produces the azimuthal deflection. This voltage may be furnished, for example, by a linear potentiometer geared to the axis of rotation of the scanner.

The arrangement shown is equally applicable to a magnetic CRT, the only changes being in the deflection amplifiers.

VI. ACCESSORY DEVICES

1. Radar Beacons.—In nearly all cases where it would be advantageous if a particular radar echo could be made much stronger or more readily distinguishable from other confusing echoes, a radar beacon is indicated. By the use of a beacon, particular aircraft can be identified among heavy ground echo signals, or in the midst of a large formation of aircraft; the exact location of a specific point on the ground can be indicated, and so on.

A beacon is a repeater of radar pulses. It has an antenna and receiver that convert pulses of energy received at high frequency from a radar set or a special beacon interrogator into triggering signals. Each such triggering signal fires the transmitter in the beacon and causes it to radiate one or more pulses of radio energy that may have almost any desired characteristics in regard to power, frequency, number, duration and spacing. A short time is required for the beacon to reply to an incoming pulse, so that the first reply pulse is slightly delayed beyond the radar echo which would be received from an object at the beacon location. This delay can be made as small as a few tenths of a microsecond (a few tens of yards in range); if this small delay is still not negligible, it can be made extremely constant and allowed for in interpreting the beacon signals.

To permit the display of beacon signals alone, without radar echoes, the beacon transmitter frequency is ordinarily chosen to be different from the radar frequency. Beacon signals can be received at a radar set either by retuning the receiver to the beacon reply frequency, or by providing an extra independent receiver tuned to the beacon. Since the power of the beacon transmitter can be made as great as desired, there is no limit to the strength of the beacon reply. The range at which a beacon can be seen will then be limited only by the power of the radar transmitter and the sensitivity of the beacon receiver, which together determine whether the beacon will be triggered or not.

Since the beacon interrogation and reply links are independent, instead of being two paths for the same energy (as in the case of radar echoes), the range at which beacons can be challenged and their replies received is usually very great, and ordinarily limited only by the optical horizon. The interrogation signal at the beacon falls off as the inverse square of the range to the challenging radar; the reply of the beacon has a power at the radar which is the same function of range.

Beacons of the synchronous sort just described are variously called radar beacons, responder beacons, racons or transponders, there being no important distinction among these terms. Free-running beacons that are not triggered by a pulse challenge are seldom used in conjunction with radar sets, since from them only the bearing of the beacon can be determined, and not its range.

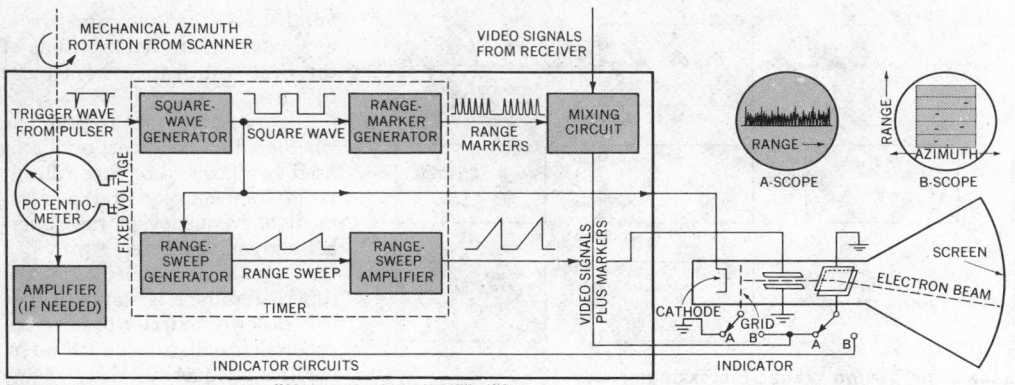

FROM RADIATION LABORATORY SERIES, MCGRAW-HILL BOOK COMPANY, INC.

FIG. 36.—BLOCK DIAGRAM OF A SIMPLE INDICATOR SYSTEM PROVIDING FOR EITHER A-SCOPE OR B-SCOPE DISPLAY

Range is so useful a part of the data supplied by radar that beacons which enable its measurement are far preferable to those that do not.

In order to avoid overloading a beacon located where there are many radar sets, it is usually desirable to provide an interrogation coding arrangement whose purpose is to limit the beacon responses to only those interrogation pulses specifically intended to elicit such a response. The decoder is intended to serve this purpose. In the case of ground beacons serving as navigation check points for air-borne radar, it is customary to use pulse-width discrimination in the decoder. The usual radar pulses of an airborne set are one microsecond or less in duration; the beacon decoder is arranged to produce a trigger for the beacon transmitter only if it receives a pulse whose duration is two microseconds or more.

The air-borne radar is then fitted with a control which lengthens the transmitter pulses and simultaneously retunes the receiver to the beacon reply frequency when it is desired to look at beacon signals instead of at radar echoes.

Reply coding is intended to identify the particular beacon whose response is seen. In the case of microwave radar beacons, this reply coding is usually "range coding," involving the transmission of a closely-spaced series of short pulses from the beacon transmitter.

Other possibilities for coding both interrogation and reply are numerous. Distinct frequencies can be chosen. Simultaneous challenge on two or more frequencies may be necessary to unlock the beacon and elicit a reply. Combinations of properly timed multiple pulses can be used. The beacon reply may be keyed on-and-off to send letters in Morse code. The particular coding system chosen will depend on the application.

Sometimes it is desirable to use, as the device intended to trigger a beacon and to display its replies, instead of a radar set, a much lower-powered device intended only to work with beacons. Such an equipment is called an interrogator-responsor. It is a radar set in all respects except that its transmitter power is so low that radar echoes cannot be obtained at useful ranges. This reduction in power output enables the equipment to be made much lighter and simpler than a radar set at the same frequency.

The interrogator-responsor can be especially small and light if only range information is wanted from the beacons, so that a scanner is not necessary and fixed antennas can be used. By providing two sets of fixed antennas aimed in slightly different directions, homing on a beacon can be done by turning the aircraft or ship carrying the interrogator-responsor until equal beacon responses are received on the two antennas. By altering the interrogation and reply coding of a beacon so that it corresponds with intelligence which it is desired to transmit, two-way communication using a radar-beacon link is feasible and has been accomplished.

2. Radio Relay of Radar Displays.—It frequently happens that the best site for a radar equipment is not the best location for the organization which is to make use of the information provided by the radar. For example, in the World War II organization

for fighter defense of the British Isles against hostile air attack, the operating centre was maintained at Stanmore, north of London; information was sent there from radar sets located all around the coasts.

During World War II it was customary to transmit radar information from one point to another by "plotting and telling." The radar echoes seen were entered at the proper range and bearing on a map with a superimposed rectangular grid; this was plotting.

The letters and numbers comprising the grid reference for the location of the plot were "told" vocally over telephone lines or radio circuits to the control centre, where the targets were replotted.

This particular type of system has several drawbacks. Not only are there many chances for the introduction of errors in the target position, but also the speed and traffic-handling capacity of the system are severely limited. It has already been remarked that a radar indicator presents several million units of data per second. By no means are all of these significant, but in a situation involving hundreds of targets, which may not be at all uncommon, it is clearly impossible for even many tellers to give as useful a picture of the air situation as is available at the radar set.

For these reasons, methods were worked out during the war for transmitting, by a radio link, radar video information, synchronizing signals and signals giving the direction in which the radar scanner was pointing at any instant. At the receiving station, these data could be used to construct a radar indication whose quality was just as good as that of the indicators located at the radar set itself.

The problems are mainly those of any wide-band radio link, complicated by the fact that both pulses and long blocks of video signals must be transmitted and received. The elements of a system for accomplishing radar relay are shown schematically in fig. 37. Radar data are delivered to a "synchronizer" which arranges them in proper form to modulate the transmitter. At the receiving station, the receiver amplifies and demodulates the incoming signals and delivers its output to an "analyzer." The latter sorts out separately video signals, trigger pulse and scanner data. The video signals and the trigger are delivered immediately to the display system.

The scanner data must usually be modified in a "scan con-

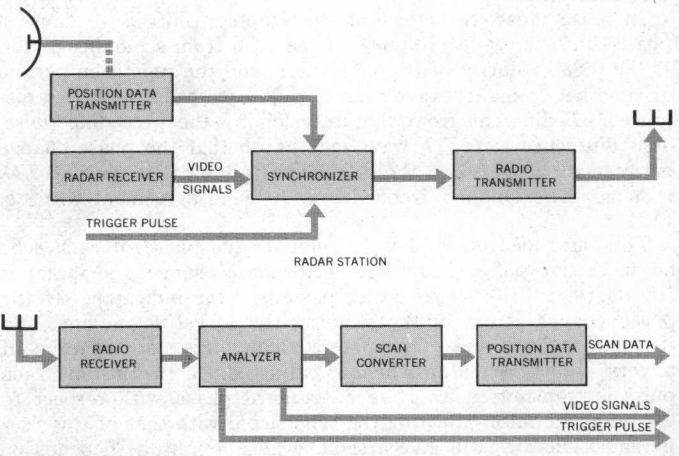

FROM RADIATION LABORATORY SERIES, MCGRAW-HILL BOOK COMPANY, INC.

FIG. 37.—ELEMENTS OF A SIMPLE RADAR RELAY SYSTEM FOR THE DIRECT TRANSMISSION OF RADAR INDICATIONS TO A REMOTE POINT BY RADIO MEANS

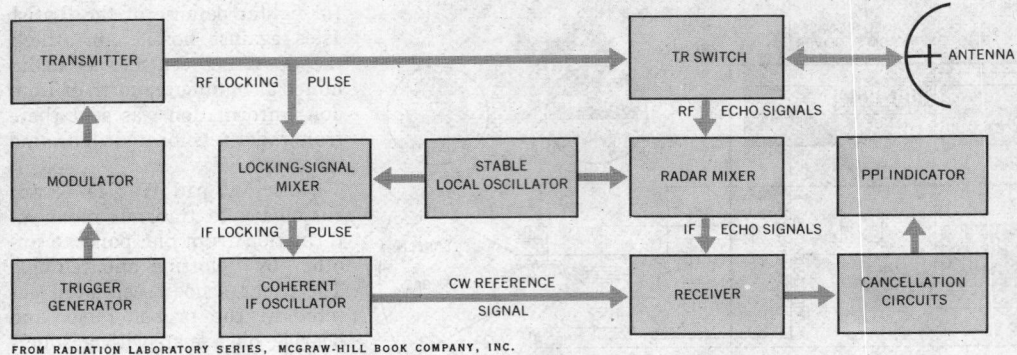

FIG. 38.—SCHEMATIC DIAGRAM OF MOVING TARGET INDICATION (MTI)

verter" before being used in display synthesis, because a code is ordinarily used for the transmission of scanner angle. The scan converter uses the coded data to construct a duplicate of the scanner motion that can be used to drive a position-data transmitter connected to the indicators. The over-all requirements of the system are quite similar to those of television, since the band of frequencies which must be transmitted is about the same.

Comparative PPI photographs may be taken simultaneously at a transmitter and receiver several miles apart.

The direct relay of radar video signals is preferable to televising an indicator at the radar station and transmitting the information by television means, for the following reasons: (1) Persistent indicators do not televise well; their light is too far toward the red end of the spectrum. This leads to a loss in signal-to-noise ratio and in definition; (2) the display available at the receiving end must be identical with that scanned by the television camera at the transmitting end. If video signals are transmitted directly, any desired type of indication can be synthesized at the receiver. The first, but not the second, of these objections can be removed by storing the radar information on an orthicon or other television pick-up tube directly, instead of viewing a CRT with a television pick-up.

3. Moving Target Indication.

—"Ground clutter," the system of strong permanent radar echoes returned by hills and buildings in the vicinity of a radar set, is often a limiting factor on the performance of radar, especially in mountainous terrain. Similarly, the echo signals returned by waves to a radar set carried on a ship or located on the shore ("sea clutter") can be most troublesome. CW radar often makes use of the Doppler shift in frequency of the signal returned from a target in radial motion relative to the radar, and thus responds only to moving targets. This same property can be conferred on pulse radar by special techniques, which will be described below, called MTI (moving target indication).

In pulse radar, the effect of the Doppler shift is to cause a phase shift from pulse to pulse of the echo from a moving target. If the radial velocity of the target is v, and the repetition period, or time between successive pulses, is T, each pulse travels a distance $2vT$ different from that traveled by the preceding pulse. This difference is $2vT/\lambda$ wave lengths, so that the phase change between each pulse and the one which follows it is $2\pi \times 2vT/\lambda$ radians. The Doppler frequency is $2v/\lambda$, in agreement with eq. (19).

The basic idea of MTI is to compare the phase of each echo on successive pulses. If there is no phase change, the target is stationary, and its signal is not passed to the indicator. If the phase changes from pulse to pulse, the target is moving, and its signal is displayed. The phase comparison is made in terms of a very stable oscillator which is adjusted, at the instant each pulse is transmitted, to have a standard phase with respect to the outgoing pulse. Beating the echo signal with that of this "coherent oscillator" will give a signal whose amplitude depends on the relative phase of the echo and the output of the coherent oscillator. If the echo comes from a stationary target, the amplitude of the signal which results from beating the echo with the coherent oscillator output will not change from one pulse to

another. If the echo comes from a moving target, the amplitude of the beat will change from pulse to pulse.

It is not important in principle whether the coherent oscillator used as a phase reference runs at radio frequency or at the intermediate frequency of the superheterodyne receiver, provided that the local oscillator of the superheterodyne is stable. Since it is easier practically to have the coherent oscillator run at intermediate frequency, this scheme has been used. A schematic diagram of a practical MTI system is shown in fig. 38.

A stable local oscillator supplies a signal to two mixers, one of which provides a "locking signal" for adjusting the phase of the coherent oscillator to its standard value with reference to the outgoing RF pulse. The other mixer is the signal mixer of the receiver. When the IF echo signals and the IF reference signal beat against one another, the phase of the receiver output signal depends on the number of cycles executed by the local oscillator and by the coherent oscillator during the out-and-back time of travel of the pulse. The result is shown in fig. 39(A). Four successive sweeps of an A-scope are shown, corresponding to four successive pulses.

It will be seen that four of the five echo signals seen on each trace are of constant amplitude from pulse to pulse, and thus correspond to stationary targets. The other echo signal shows a changing amplitude from pulse to pulse; this corresponds to a changing echo-signal phase, and indicates radial target motion.

The way in which stationary targets can be cancelled is shown in fig. 39(B). If the signals from successive pulse cycles are subtracted from one another, echoes of constant amplitude vanish, while echoes of changing amplitude do not.

The actual subtraction is performed by sending the receiver output to a "subtraction circuit" both directly and through a delay line which introduces an amount of delay exactly equal to the interpulse interval. Thus the subtraction circuit receives and compares echo signals from the immediately preceding pulse (direct from the receiver) and from the next earlier pulse (through the delay line).

The length of the usual interpulse interval is so long—some hundreds of microseconds—that electrical delay networks are impracticable for use in MTI. Instead, an ultrasonic delay device is often employed. Signals from the receiver output are turned into sound waves in a liquid or solid by a piezoelectric transducer, allowed to travel through the liquid or solid medium as ultrasonic waves for the distance necessary to introduce the required delay, and turned back into electrical signals by a transducer at the end of the medium.

The velocity of sound waves in such a medium as mercury permits the necessary delays to be produced by sonic paths of reasonable length ($17.6\ \mu$ sec./in.). Alternatively, an electronic "storage tube," which works in a manner related to that of a television iconoscope can be used as a delay element.

As the applications of MTI (and subsequent pulse-Doppler radar) came into wider use in postwar years, many advances were made. For example, mercury delay lines were replaced by quartz types that have a better signal-to-noise characteristic, entail smaller losses per unit of delay time and are more stable than the mercury lines they replace.

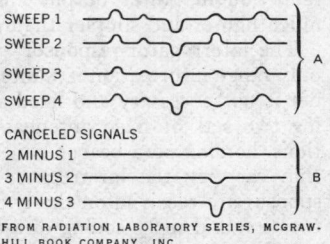

FIG. 39.—PULSE-TO-PULSE CANCELLATION OF ECHO SIGNALS HAVING CONSTANT PHASE. (A) FOUR SUCCESSIVE SWEEPS OF AN A-SCOPE. (B) THE RESULT OF SUBTRACTING EACH SIGNAL FROM THE CORRESPONDING ONE ON THE SUCCEEDING PULSE

4. Pulse-Doppler.—The development of pulse-doppler (PD) radar types in the 1950s for specific military needs (*e.g.*, ground surveillance) also made it possible to locate moving targets (distinguishing them from innumerable fixed objects on the ground and the resultant radar clutter) and to determine their range. CW emission is theoretically best for the discrimination of moving targets because of the frequency change, or Doppler effect, which is imparted to the reflected signals by the radial velocity of the target relative to the radar set. But since CW generators at centimetre wave lengths tend to lack adequate power output, and since CW does not of itself enable range measurement to be made (unless frequency-modulated, as in the radio altimeter), PD radar employs powerful pulse transmission that also effectively measures the distance to the target.

The PD system employs the Doppler shift phenomenon that occurs within the pulse reflected from a moving object and enables the moving object to be detected in a background of fixed echoes.

The Doppler shift that denotes target motion can be detected in either of two ways. One method, called coherent MTI (described above), involves maintaining a stable reference frequency at the transmitter-receiver set to beat with the Doppler-shifted frequency of echoes received from targets in motion. The other method, termed noncoherent MTI, is used in military surveillance radars. It depends upon the presence of echoes from fixed objects in the same vicinity as the moving target under search. In this case the unchanged frequency of pulse-echo return from the fixed objects beats with the Doppler-shifted echo from the moving target to produce an aural or visual radar indication. (L. N. R.; G. R. T.)

VII. GENERAL IMPROVEMENTS IN RADAR PERFORMANCE

Response to operational requirement for increased radar range has taken the form of larger arrays, phased arrays, low-noise receiving amplifiers and mixers, high-power magnetrons, high-power amplifiers such as the amplitron and other devices and techniques.

The addition of the amplitron having a peak power of 3 megawatts, and a 1-μsec. pulse, to air traffic control radars has resulted in a nominal increase in range of from 200 mi. to 350 mi. on passive aircraft targets. The amplitron is further characterized by light weight (10 lb.), a power gain of 14, broad frequency response with rapid tuning and an efficiency of 80%. The amplitron is suitable at lower power outputs for small radars such as used on small boats, aircraft and portable units reducing equipment weight accompanied by the probability of better performance.

Some long-range surveillance radars achieve target detection at distances up to 3,000 mi. by employing the various appropriate techniques. Magnetrons used in such installations typically produce peak powers of 800 kw. to 5 megawatts with long pulse lengths—up to 10 μsec. on 750 MHz and 5 μsec. on 1,500 MHz.

Some magnetrons are tunable against a crystal frequency source or are directly crystal controlled, simplifying moving-target indicator radars and assisting in the avoidance of interference between different radar signals.

For the removal of dissipated heat in high-power transmitters, vapour cooling is used in some equipment in lieu of high-maintenance water-cooling systems. Other developments have brought the use of high frequencies—up to 80 GHz with power up to 5 kw. and with nanosecond (10^{-9} sec.) pulses for very high resolution and definition; also general improvements in longer life, reliability, stability and quick warm-up. Because the greatest general use of radar is in the X band—10 MHz—the main improvement activity is with respect to that band.

An interesting technique used in air surveillance and traffic-control radars is pulse-rate staggering. A synchronous situation may occur with a fast-moving azimuthal target which can cause the target to be located between the incrementally positioned radiated beams for a greater number of times if the repetition rate is periodic than if it is staggered. The amount of stagger is very small, so range information is not seriously affected.

Frequency correlation techniques are used to improve target visibility by generating a local display pulse which, when coherent with the target pulse, enhances the display on the oscilloscope indicator screen. Memory storage display tubes are used to enhance the display by virtue of long retention and integrated buildup of the display. When the screen becomes cluttered because of this retention it can be erased, after which a new display builds up. A moving target shows as a streak, shaped similar to a comet, that reveals direction of motion and a general indication of speed. Memory storage tubes are bright in display and can be used in ordinary ambient lighting.

The application of modular construction whereby a complete circuit function such as an IF amplifier series or two or more functions such as the IF amplifier and video amplifier—or various pulse-generating, gating and delay circuits—are contained in one package that can be easily and quickly replaced, has done much to facilitate the maintenance of radar and other electronic equipments. Printed wiring cards, when they are not direct replacements themselves, and integrated circuit cards serve as modular sub-units.

The development and use of solid state devices have been largely responsible for modular construction. They are inherently reliable, long-lived, low in power needs and heat dissipation, very small in space requirements and electronically fast.

Printed wiring connects discrete units of transistors, diodes, resistors, capacitors, etc. In the integrated circuit the entire device is constructed of slices and various chemical and alloy forms of solid state and other materials, all effectively welded into many integrated circuit functions.

See ELECTRON TUBE; ELECTROMAGNETIC WAVES; NAVIGATION; RADIO; *see* also references under "Radar" in the Index.

(F. B. D.)

BIBLIOGRAPHY.—*Historical:* Sir E. V. Appleton, "Radiolocation: An Account of its Development," *Electronic Engineering* (Sept. 1945), pp. 679 ff.; Sir R. Watson-Watt, "Radar in War and Peace," *Nature* (Sept. 15, 1945), pp. 319 ff., (*see* also Watson-Watt, *Three Steps to Victory* [1957], and a less complete version entitled *The Pulse of Radar* [1959]); H. E. Guerlac, "The Radio Background of Radar," *Journal of the Franklin Institute* (Oct. 1950), pp. 28 ff.; *see* also Guerlac's thorough and detailed manuscript history "Radar," available in the Library of Congress; R. I. Wilkinson, "Short Survey of Japanese Radar," two parts, *Electrical Engineering* (Aug.–Sept. 1946), pp. 370 ff. (part i), and (Oct. 1946), pp. 455 ff. (part ii); L. Brandt, "German Radiolocation in Retrospect," *Interavia* (1950), pp. 315 ff.; A. E. Hoffman-Heyden, same title and same journal (1951), pp. 623 ff.; A. P. Rowe, *One Story of Radar* (1948); C. Bekker (pen name of H. D. Berenbrok), *Radar-Duell im Dunkel* (1958); D. Terrett, *The Signal Corps: The Emergency* (1956); R. M. Page, *The Origin of Radar* (1962).

General and Technical: L. N. Ridenour (ed.) and various authors, Massachusetts Institute of Technology Radiation Laboratory series, 28 vols. (1942–1953) (the Index volume is especially useful); J. F. Reintjes and G. T. Coate, *Principles of Radar*, 3rd ed. (1952); H. E. Penrose and R. S. H. Boulding, *Principles and Practice of Radar,* 6th ed. (1959); J. McQuay, "Principles of Modern Radar," two parts, *Radio-Electronics* (June 1960), pp. 42 ff. (part i), and (July 1960), pp. 34 ff. (part ii); I. Ritow, "Radar Fundamentals," *Electro-Technology* (Nov. 1960), pp. 107 ff.; *J. Instn. Elect. Engrs.*, vol. 93 (1946) part iii A (Radiolocation) no. 1–10 (over 200 papers on all aspects of radar); E. G. Bowen (ed.), *A Textbook of Radar*, 2nd ed. (1954); D. Taylor and C. H. Westcott, *Principles of Radar* (1948); L. G. H. Huxley, *A Survey of the Principles and Practice of Wave Guides* (1947); S. S. Attwood and C. R. Burrows (eds.), *Radio Wave Propagation* (1949); L. A. Moxon, *Recent Advances in Radio Receivers* (1949); R. A. Smith, *Radio Aids to Navigation* (1947); F. J. Wylie (ed.), *The Use of Radar at Sea* (1952); Institute of Electrical and Electronics Engineers, *Proceedings* (Nov. 1968; March 1969); T. C. Cheston, "Phased Arrays for Radars," *IEEE Spectrum*, vol. 5 (Nov. 1968); A. C. Schell *et al.,* "Electronic Scanning," *Electro-Technology*, vol. 82 (Nov. 1968); C. Kurz, *Evaluation and Critique of Radar Data Computer*, (1966); H. Jasik (ed.), *Antenna Engineering Handbook* (1961); L. P. Hunter, *Handbook of Semiconductor Electronics*, rev. ed. (1962); H. A. Watson (ed.), *Microwave Semiconductor Devices and Their Circuit Applications* (1969); "Syllabus on Low-Noise Microwave Devices," *Microwave Journal*, pp. 59–69 (July 1969); International Association of Lighthouse Authorities, Rome Conference Reports (1965), Bull. no. 1, suppl. 1 on radar reflectors (May 1966).

(L. N. R.; G. R. T.; F. B. D.)

RADAR METEOROLOGY generally signifies the use of radar to observe and study the state of the atmosphere. It may be considered a division of radio meteorology, which also includes the study of the effects of the atmosphere on radio and radar propagation; *i.e.*, bending and attenuation of electromagnetic waves. Radar meteorology comprises the study of radar echoes received from natural reflecting sources within the atmosphere and the relation of the echo characteristics to the nature of the atmospheric processes influencing the reflecting mediums. Some natural reflecting sources are: (1) hydrometeors (raindrops, cloud droplets, ice crystals, and snowflakes); (2) regions of highly perturbed refractive index (temperature or moisture fluctuations) both in the clear air (fronts, inversions, thermals) and at cloud boundaries; and (3) the highly ionized paths of lightning discharges. Echoes from invisible targets such as (2) above are known as "angels" and include those from birds and insects. Not until the mid-1960s were methods devised to distinguish the latter from true meteorological echoes. While such echoes are of interest mainly to ornithologists and entomologists, the meteorologist may also use them to infer information about the atmosphere. The field logically includes the use of optical radar or lidar (LIght Detection And Ranging) for studying the echoes from atmospheric aerosols, dust, and molecules.

History.—The first verified report of a precipitation echo occurred on Feb. 20, 1941, when a 10-cm. wavelength, 3,000-megaHertz (MHz; millions of cycles per second) frequency, radar tracked a shower to a distance of seven miles off the English coast. Prior to that time the unavailability of the microwave magnetron restricted radar equipment to relatively low transmitted powers at the longer wavelengths. Under these conditions the relatively small precipitation particles could not be detected, although weak echoes were thought to be associated with storms as early as 1938 in England. The first detection of what are now believed to have been clear air echoes from the lower atmosphere was made by R. A. Watson-Watt, A. F. Wilkins, and E. G. Bowen in England in 1935, using a 50-m. wavelength pulsed system intended to explore the ionosphere. The earliest documented observation of lightning echoes was made by M. G. H. Ligda with a 10-cm. radar on July 20, 1949, in Cambridge, Mass. With the development of shorter wavelength (1.25 cm.) radars toward the end of World War II, it became possible to detect some of the larger particles in nearby nonprecipitating clouds, while the increasing use of radar throughout the world brought with it the more widespread detection of both clear air echoes and lightning discharges. While Doppler radar had been in use since World War II for the measurement of target velocities, its use in meteorology was initiated only in 1960 by E. H. Boyenval and R. M. Lhermitte. The advent of the laser as a source of intense coherent optical radiation in 1960 opened the way for atmospheric probing by lidar. In 1963 G. Fiocco and L. D. Smullin first used lidar to detect echoes from the atmosphere up to heights of 140 km. while M. Ligda used it to explore the lower atmosphere.

Theory.—The radar transmits extremely short pulses of electromagnetic energy in a well-defined beam which is aimed by a parabolic reflector or the like. When the beam is directed toward precipitation, a small fraction of the energy is scattered, a small fraction is absorbed, and the remainder is transmitted through to be scattered and absorbed by particles deeper in the storm. The portion of the energy which is scattered or reflected back to the radar is amplified and displayed on an indicator in a position relative to the origin. This position depends upon the time taken for the energy to travel the round-trip path between radar and target at the speed of light. If the beam is held in a fixed direction, the echoes are usually displayed on an A-scope (see RADAR: *How Radar Works*) which shows their amplitude or intensity versus distance. If the beam is made to rotate in azimuth around a vertical axis, the echoes brighten a spot on a cathode-ray tube at a distance out from the centre (radar position) depending on the target range and at a direction determined by the direction of the beam. This display is known as the PPI scope or plan position indicator. Since energy is usually reflected from the entire depth of the storm, the geographical position and extent of precipitation may be mapped accurately on the PPI scope to ranges limited mainly by the earth's curvature. For example, a storm at a range of 200 mi. must extend above 20,000 ft. to be detectable above the radar horizon. With this restriction, the PPI display enables the meteorologist to watch the motion and development of precipitation areas. When the beam is made to scan in a vertical plane, the echoes are displayed on the range height indicator or RHI scope showing a vertical cross section of the storm. On this scope, the meteorologist determines the height and growth rate of the storm, and its physical nature such as snow or rain, in addition to other storm features.

When the wavelength of the electromagnetic radiation is large with respect to the size of the scattering particle, the energy returned to the radar is given by the Rayleigh scattering law and is proportional to the 6th power of the particle diameter; *i.e.*, doubling the diameter of a drop increases the echo by a factor of 64. In addition, the echo power is inversely proportional to the 4th power of the wavelength; *i.e.*, doubling the wavelength decreases the echo by a factor of 16. Since a raindrop is roughly 100 times as large as a cloud droplet, its echo is about 1,000,000 times as strong as that from a cloud droplet. However, since there may be 1,000 times as many cloud drops as raindrops, the total rain echo is about 1,000 times as strong as that from a water droplet cloud. Cloud radars operate at wavelengths near 1 cm. while precipitation radars operate between 3 and 23 cm. Clouds comprised of ice crystals are more readily detected because the crystals are usually much larger than the cloud droplets.

Of course, at any instant the radar receives the energy scattered back from a large number of particles confined within a volume defined by the beam width and half the pulse length in space. This is called the pulse volume. A 1 μ sec. pulse intercepts a 492-ft. depth of precipitation while a 1° beam intercepts a width of about 9,200 ft. at a range of 100 mi. Since there are roughly 100 raindrops per cubic foot of air, an individual echo from such a range may include the energy scattered from about 4,000,000,-000,000 (4×10^{12}) raindrops. At a particular instant, the drops may be so distributed as to cause their individual echoes to reinforce each other; at another time, their individual echoes may cancel each other. Because the drops change position with respect to each other as a result of wind shear and turbulence, the total echo received from such a group of particles fluctuates rapidly from one pulse to the next. However, since the drops are randomly distributed within the pulse volume, the average echo intensity over a number of pulses is the sum of those from the individual particles; *i.e.*, it is proportional to the sum of the 6th powers of the particle diameters. This quantity summed over a representative unit volume of space within the pulse volume has been designated by the symbol Z, the reflectivity factor.

For a small target such as an airplane, the incident and reflected energy both spread out and decrease in intensity as the square of the target range. Thus, the echo from such a target decreases as the 4th power of the range. However, a storm usually intercepts the entire area of the radar beam so that the total energy incident on it does not depend on its range; it is only the reflected power which decreases with distance. For this reason, the average echo intensity from a storm decreases only as the square of its range, provided its reflectivity or Z remains constant.

Water drops scatter microwave radiation about five times as well as ice particles of the same mass because of their higher index of refraction. Therefore, when snowflakes begin to melt as they fall into warm air with temperature above 32° F, their echo suddenly increases by a factor of 5 over that of the dry snow above. When the particles melt completely, however, the resulting raindrops quickly begin to fall at an average of about five times as fast as the original snowflakes, decreasing the number of particles per unit volume and the echo intensity proportionally. This causes the echo from the melting particles to be about five times as strong as that from both the dry snow above and the completely melted raindrops below. The exact variation of echo intensity through the melting zone depends on a number of other factors. In any case, the echo intensification in that layer makes it appear as a horizontal "bright band" on the RHI scope. Such "bright bands" are characteristic of most widespread precipitation in temperate latitudes and indicates that the rain originates in the form of ice crystals aloft. In active thunderstorms intense updrafts may carry raindrops and water-coated hailstones to heights considerably above the melting level without freezing. Thus the "bright band" does not appear until the decaying stages of such storms.

When hydrometeors have diameters equal to or greater than a third of the radar wavelength ($D \gtreqqless 0.3 \lambda$), a variety of complex phenomena may occur depending upon size, shape, and composition. Among other things, when $D \gtreqqless 0.8 \lambda$ dry hailstones scatter about one order of magnitude better than water-coated ice or water spheres of equal size. Also spongy hail (a mixture of ice and water) with $D \simeq 0.3 \lambda$ scatters several times better than equal size ice or water spheres. The latter effect is believed to be responsible for the reflectivity of hailstorms reaching a maximum value at altitudes of 15,000 to 20,000 ft. when observed by 3-cm. radar.

The storm reflectivity factor or Z has also been found to be related to the precipitation rate, R, in both snow and rain, and to the water content per unit volume in clouds. Although the exact relation between Z and R depends on the nature of the particle size distribution, and it is possible to have equal rainfall intensities comprised of a large number of small drops with small Z or a few large drops with large Z, under average conditions the storm Z as measured by the echo intensity can provide an estimate of the precipitation rate within a factor of about 2. If the echo intensity is averaged over long periods, the estimates of total rainfall can be made with greater accuracy. Since a calibrated radar can measure the average rainfall over an area approximately 50 mi. in radius (about 7,500 sq.mi.) with an accuracy comparable to that from a network of several hundred rain gauges, and can secure these data quickly, it has great value for flood warning purposes.

One of the facts which limits the use of radar for the quantitative measurement of distant rainfall is the attenuation of the radar energy by scattering and absorption in intervening rain. Attenuation reduces the echo power by an amount which is unknown or difficult to determine; the echo may then be a useless measure of rainfall. At wavelengths of 10 cm. and larger, the attenuation in normal rains is negligible, and such wavelengths are therefore preferable for quantitative measurements. As the wavelength decreases below 10 cm., the losses due to both scattering and absorption increase so that 1-cm. wavelength radars can only penetrate a few miles into moderately intense rains. Even at 3 cm., only the front edge of an intense rainstorm may be seen on the radar scope. Attenuation in snow is due only to the scattering and is generally negligible except at the very short wavelengths and in the most intense snowstorms.

Echoes are also detected from regions of highly disturbed refractive index in the clear atmosphere and at cloud boundaries by radars of high sensitivity or at very short range by less powerful radars. The reflectivity of such a region is dependent upon the mean square refractive index fluctuation at a scale equal to $\lambda/2$. This is to say that only the changes in refractivity over distances equal to half the radar wavelength contribute to the echo; all other scales are ignored. Considering the way in which the turbulent refractivity perturbations in the so-called "inertial sub-range" vary with scale, it has been found theoretically and confirmed experimentally that the reflectivity of a clear air turbulent region decreases inversely as the cube root of the radar wavelength ($\lambda^{-1/3}$). This very weak wavelength dependence contrasts sharply with the λ^{-4} dependence for small (Rayleigh) scatterers and suggests that the echoes from particulates and those from inhomogeneous refractivity may be distinguished from one another by reflectivity measurements at two or more wavelengths. This has, in fact, been done.

Echoes due to refractivity perturbations have been associated with pre-squall gust fronts and sea breeze fronts, with thermals below clouds and with cloud boundaries, and with inversions (i.e., layers in which temperature increases with altitude). The sharp vertical gradient in moisture (and thus in refractivity) at an inversion is conducive to the establishment of refractivity perturbations which are detectable by sufficiently sensitive radars. As a consequence, a sharp inversion appears as a fine horizontal line on the RHI scope. Powerful radars have also detected the inversion at the tropopause, the base of the stratosphere, and the re-fractivity perturbations associated with a number of confirmed cases of high altitude clear air turbulence.

The simultaneous use of ultrasensitive radars at three wavelengths (beginning in 1964) has also permitted the resolution of the long-standing controversy as to whether "dot-angels"—echoes from invisible point targets—are due to insects and birds or to atmospheric structures such as the caps of convective thermals or sheaths of sharp temperature and moisture transition. The finding that the cross-sections of most "dot-angels" decreased approximately as λ^{-4}, and that the echo signatures closely resemble those of individual known insects released and tracked by radar, proves that most of these angel echoes are indeed due to insects. Birds too are responsible for many angel reports; these are readily distinguished from insects by their relatively large radar cross-sections. Most small birds also have maximum cross-sections at a wavelength of 10 cm.

During the warmer seasons insects have been detected in concentrations up to about 1 per 10,000 cu.yd. at altitudes up to 7,000 ft. and for periods exceeding 60 hours. Their average velocities as measured by Doppler radar agree remarkably well with those of the winds at their altitude; accordingly, insect echoes provide a very useful measure of the winds.

Since 1960, Doppler radars have come into increasingly more effective use for studying the velocities of hydrometeors and the air motions with which they are carried. Doppler radars measure the shift in frequency of the received signal from that transmitted. This frequency shift is given by $f = 2\ v/\lambda$ where v is the radial component of the target velocity; velocities toward the radar produce positive Doppler shifts and vice versa. At 10-cm. wavelength a velocity of 10 m. per sec. (i.e., 20 knots) produces a 200 Hz shift. While this is only $\frac{1}{15,000,000}$ of the transmitted frequency, it is readily measured. Thus target velocities are measurable with great precision.

When the radar beam is pointed vertically in widespread rainfall, the Doppler radar senses the velocities of all the drops within the pulse volume. The associated Doppler "spectrum"—the distribution of returned echo power with velocity—can then be translated into the corresponding size distribution of the raindrops. On the other hand, in thunderstorms the entire Doppler spectrum of particle fall velocities may be shifted by an amount equal to the updraft or downdraft velocity. The amount of the shift is then a measure of the draft velocity. This method of deducing draft velocities is subject to errors of a few metres per second because the displacement of the Doppler spectrum must be estimated relative to some assumed position. Nevertheless, the resulting measurements of draft velocity have provided the first views of the overall field of motion within thunderstorms.

When the radar beam is tilted at a substantial angle from the vertical, the Doppler shift has components due to the particle fall speed and the wind. If the beam is then scanned in a complete azimuthal circle, the component due to the wind varies in a sinusoidal fashion with a maximum in the upwind direction, a minimum in the downwind direction, and zeros in the two crosswind directions. Assuming that the mean particle fall velocity is constant over the scanned circle, a reasonable assumption in widespread snow or rain, it is then possible to separate the fall speed and wind components. In this way, Doppler radars have provided almost instantaneous soundings of the wind up to heights in excess of 20,000 ft. during storm conditions and to heights of 7,000 ft. using insects as tracers. Clearly, Doppler radars also have important applications in the measurement of atmospheric turbulence, in the detection of tornadoes, and in mapping the winds in hurricanes. While only one tornado had been observed by Doppler radar in the late 1960s, it was confidently expected that tornadoes would produce a unique Doppler signature because of the extremely large circulatory velocities of the debris within and near the funnel cloud.

While conventional non-Doppler radars do not provide a measure of the mean velocity of the scatterers, their relative motions cause the individual signals from the various scatterers to interfere with one another, and so the net echo intensity fluctuates from pulse to pulse. The greater the relative velocities within the pulse volume the more rapid the pulse-to-pulse fluctuation rate. Thus the echo fluctuation rate provides a measure of the breadth of the velocity spectrum of the scatterers and is of some use in estimating turbulence and wind shear within the pulse volume.

At wavelengths of 10 cm. and longer, the highly ionized columns produced by lightning discharges may also be detected. However, since the ionized path dissipates rapidly, the radar beam must be directed at the lightning region just at the discharge time. Cloud-to-cloud lightning is more readily discernible because of its greater horizontal extent than the cloud-to-ground variety; also it tends to occur in the upper and weaker snow regions of the storm so that its echo is not easily obscured by the more intense rain echoes. Lightning echoes as long as 100 mi. have been observed.

Radar in Observation and Forecasting.—The greatest use of weather radar is in the observation of the geometric structure and motion of clouds and storms.. Widespread precipitation such as that associated with warm fronts in middle latitudes is generally seen on the PPI scope as a fairly uniform echo mass covering large areas of the scope. On the RHI, the advance deck of alto-stratus clouds and evaporating precipitation lowers slowly as the storm centre approaches until snow or rain finally starts at the ground. On the PPI, some pattern may usually be discerned within the larger echo masses associated with trails of ice crystals released from occasional discrete cloud cells; these trails twist and turn as the ice crystals fall into layers of different wind velocity. On the RHI scope, the trails frequently take the form of hooklike cirrus clouds such as may be seen visually in the sky on a clear day. Their slope on the RHI and pattern on the PPI are helpful in determining the variation of winds with height.

While individual trails or small precipitation areas move with the winds at the heights of the cloud cells from which the precipitation is released, the entire region of precipitation echo moves with the velocity of the large-scale pressure pattern or storm system.

The precipitation echoes associated with a cold front most frequently take the form of lines of shower or thunderstorm cells several hundred miles long oriented along the front. Individual cells tend to move with the mean winds or those near the 10,000-ft. level, and may be less than 10 mi. in diameter, although some lines fail to show any separation. On the RHI, the echoes appear as tall vertical columns with sharply defined edges and tops which may become diffuse as the water particles are transformed to ice crystals and form the anvils of cumulonimbus clouds. Such storms do not display the "bright band" except in their decaying stages. Similar echoes are associated with isolated showers and thunderstorms on hot days when the atmosphere is unstable. Their severity may be indicated on the radar by their height, sometimes exceeding 50,000 ft., their rate of growth which may exceed 2,000 ft. per min., their strong echo intensity caused by large raindrops and hailstones, and an attenuation shadow cast on other storms behind (at the shorter wavelengths). Tornadoes have occasionally been identified by a figure-6-shaped tail extending out from the edge of a larger thunderstorm echo.

The PPI pattern of a hurricane shows a number of spiral bands each perhaps several hundred miles long and 20 mi. wide which spiral into the vicinity of the hurricane eye or pressure and wind minima. The centre of spiral is readily identified making it possible to pinpoint and track the "eye" by radar with an accuracy of about ± 7 mi. In the tropics where the storms generally move slowly, the spiral bands may be more like complete concentric rings; however, as they move into middle latitudes the major precipitation tends to occur in the forward right sector. The outer bands are comprised of individual shower cells, while the inner bands are more continuous and display the "bright band" near the melting level.

Prior to the development of meteorological satellites, simultaneous PPI scope photos from an array of radars distributed over the eastern portion of the U.S. were pieced together to show the fascinating large scale storm systems which are now seen more readily and dramatically in the satellite cloud photos. Even today, however, the radar data are helpful in distinguishing those cloud regions which are producing rain and snow from nonprecipitating clouds.

In the U.S., the operational weather radar network comprises some 150 radars. Other extensive networks are found in Australia, England, France, Germany, Italy, India, and Japan, and elsewhere around the world. Airborne weather radars for storm avoidance are also in common use in virtually all large airliners.

Detecting clear air turbulence (CAT) was a problem that was being actively investigated in the late 1960's. Investigations included the use of long-wave VHF airborne radar, ground-based ultra-sensitive radar, and infrared techniques. While CAT has been detected by powerful ground-based radars, these were much too large for aircraft installation; they were also too costly if used in sufficient numbers on the ground to provide reliable coverage. Therefore, the use of radar chaff (slow falling reflecting filaments) as a means of marking turbulent air for detection by airborne weather radar was being studied.

For more information on radar theory, terminology and equipment, *see* RADAR.

BIBLIOGRAPHY.—R. Wexler and D. M. Swingle, "Radar Storm Detection," *Bull. Amer. Meteor. Soc.,* 28:159-167 (1947); M. G. H. Ligda, "Radar Storm Observation" in *Compendium of Meteorology,* ed. by T. F. Malone, pp. 1265–82 (1951), "The Radar Observation of Lightning," *J. Atmos. and Terr. Phys.,* 9:329–346 (1956); J. S. Marshall, W. Hitschfeld and K. L. S. Gunn, "Advances in Radar Weather" in *Advances in Geophysics,* ed. by H. E. Landsberg, vol. ii (1955); E. Kessler and D. Atlas, "Radar-Synoptic Analysis of Hurricane Edna," U.S. Air Force, Defense Department, *Geophysical Research Papers 50* (1956); V. G. Plank, "A Meteorological Study of Radar Angels," U.S. Air Force, Defense Department, *Geophysical Research Papers 52* (1956); J. S. Marshall and W. E. Gordon, "Radio Meteorology" in *Meteorological Research Reviews,* ed. by A. K. Blackadar (1957); E. H. Boyenval, "Echoes from Precipitation Using Pulse Doppler Radar," *Proceedings Eighth Weather Radar Conference,* American Meteorological Society, pp. 57–64 (1960); R. M. Lhermitte,. "The Use of a Special Pulse Doppler Radar in Measurements of Particle Fall Velocities," *Proceedings Eighth Weather Radar Conference,* American Meteorological Society, pp. 269–275 (1960); G. Fiocco and L. D. Smullin, "Detection of Scattering Layers in the Upper Atmosphere," *Nature,* 199:1275 (1963); M. G. H. Ligda, "Meteorological Observations with Pulsed Laser Radar," *Proceedings 1st Conference on Laser Technology,* U. S. Navy, p. 63 (1963); D. Atlas, "Advances in Radar Meteorology" in *Advances in Geophysics,* 10:317–478 (1964); K. R. Hardy, D. Atlas, and K. M. Glover, "Multiwavelength Backscatter from the Clear Atmosphere," *J. Geophys. Res.,* 71:1537–1552 (1966). (Dd. A.)

RADCLIFFE, ANN (née WARD) (1764–1823), was the chief exponent in England of the Gothic novel, a kind of fiction extremely popular in the late 18th and early 19th centuries, which, rejecting the restraint of the classical tradition, indulged the imagination and the emotions with fearful happenings, and characteristically exploited the effects of crumbling buildings, the mysterious past, foreign settings, and the apparent or actual supernatural.

She was born in London on July 9, 1764. In 1787 she married William Radcliffe, a journalist and, later, proprietor of the *Morning Chronicle,* who encouraged her literary pursuits. Mrs. Radcliffe led a retired life, and the descriptions of French and Italian landscapes in her novels were based primarily on books and paintings. Her only journey abroad, to Holland and Germany, is described in *A Journey Made in the Summer of 1794* (1795).

Her first novels, *The Castles of Athlin and Dunbayne* (1789) and *A Sicilian Romance* (1790), were published anonymously. She achieved fame with *The Romance of the Forest* (1791). *The Mysteries of Udolpho* (1794), by which she became the most popular novelist in England, tells how the orphaned Emily St. Aubert is subjected to the cruelties of her aunt Mme Cheron and of Montoni, who marries Mme Cheron. Emily is separated from Valancourt, her lover, and, in an attempt to make her relinquish her fortune, is imprisoned first in Château-le-Blanc in Languedoc and then in the Castle of Udolpho in the Apennines. Strange and fearful occurrences take place in these castles which are all, however, ultimately explained. Emily escapes, and is finally reunited with Valancourt.

In *The Italian* (1797), Mrs. Radcliffe shows improved techniques of dialogue and characterization, and the plot is more tightly constructed. Vivaldi, a young Venetian nobleman, falls in love with Ellena de Rosalba, who is considered an unworthy match for him, and his mother conspires with Schedoni, a monk of massive physique and sinister disposition, to keep the lovers apart. Schedoni's personality overshadows the whole story. (His character influenced, among others, Byron in his concept of his heroes.) After various fearful adventures, Schedoni, about to murder Ellena, is led to believe from a locket round her neck that she is his daughter. Schedoni himself is revealed as a fratricide by the Inquisition, to which he has consigned Vivaldi, and the lovers are reunited. Mrs. Radcliffe's poems (1816) and her posthumous novel, *Gaston de Blondeville* (1826), were comparatively unsuccessful. She died in London on Feb. 7, 1823.

In spite of their reputation as "tales of terror," there is little physical horror in Mrs. Radcliffe's novels, and, except in *Gaston de Blondeville,* the apparently supernatural elements are finally explained away. Her characterization is usually weak, her historical insight almost nonexistent, and her plots abound in impossibilities. Her undoubted powers are revealed in her ability to create a limited but poetically intense world, seen through the sensibility of her heroines. She excels at intimating evil, maintaining suspense, evoking atmosphere, and varying her mood effects. It is this reliance on atmosphere rather than incident that distinguishes her from "Monk" Lewis, although he was influenced by *The Mysteries of Udolpho.* The Gothic interest in ancient, decaying buildings informs her imaginative world, as do romanticized views of nature, in particular of woods, mountains, and lakes. She describes these in word pictures that reflect her delight in Romantic painting, and in that of Guido Reni. Her heroines, too, gain a spiritual consolation from nature that reminds one of Rousseau. Scott called Mrs. Radcliffe "the first poetess of romantic fiction," and her many admirers included Coleridge and Christina Rossetti. Writing in the tradition of the novel of sensibility, she boldly focused the themes of nascent Romanticism in her stories, and paved the way for the greater talents of Scott and of the Romantic poets.

BIBLIOGRAPHY.—C. F. McIntyre, *Ann Radcliffe in Relation to Her Time* (1920); J. M. S. Tompkins, *The Popular Novel in England, 1770–1800* (1932); A. Grant, *Ann Radcliffe* (1951). (W. L. G. Ja.)

RADCLIFFE-BROWN, ALFRED REGINALD (1881–1955), British social anthropologist, whose major contribution was his systematic framework of concepts and generalizations relating to the social structures of simple societies, was born on Jan. 17, 1881, in Birmingham. After being educated at Trinity College, Cambridge, he took up the study of anthropology. In 1906 he went to the Andaman Islands, where his field work later won him a fellowship at Trinity College. In 1910 he carried out a second field expedition to Western Australia, concentrating on kinship and family organization. In 1916 he became director of education in the kingdom of Tonga and in 1921 took the chair of social anthropology at the University of Cape Town. In 1925 he accepted the chair of anthropology at Sydney University, where he built up a vigorous department for teaching, and for research in both theoretical and applied anthropology. A brilliant lecturer and conversationalist, he became a well-known personality in Australian intellectual circles in spite of a somewhat aloof and critical temperament. Between 1931 and 1937 he was professor of anthropology at the University of Chicago, after which he held the chair of social anthropology at Oxford until his retirement in 1946. He received many academic honours. He died in London on Oct. 24, 1955.

Among his works are *The Andaman Islanders* (1922; new ed., 1948); *Social Organisation of Australian Tribes* (1931); *Structure and Function in Primitive Society* (1952); *A Natural Science of Society* (1957); *Method in Social Anthropology* (1958). See also ANTHROPOLOGY: *Analysis of Culture and Society.*

See M. Fortes (ed.), *Social Structure: Studies Presented to A. R. Radcliffe-Brown* (1949); memoir in *Man,* vol. lvi (1956). (M. Fs.)

RADEK, KARL (1885–1939?), Soviet propagandist, and a notable victim of Stalin's purges, was born in Lwow (Lvov) in Galicia, of a Jewish family named Sobelsohn. Educated at the universities of Cracow and Bern, he became a member of the Social Democratic Party of Poland and Lithuania in 1901. Arrested during the revolution of 1905, he spent a year in a Russian prison. Subsequently he worked on the editorial staffs of left-wing Social Democratic newspapers in Poland and later in Germany. During World War I, after some months of illegal antimilitarist activity in Germany, he established himself in Switzerland, where he wrote for the *Bern Tageblatt.* He took part in the Zimmerwald and Kienthal conferences (*see* INTERNATIONAL, THE) in September 1915 and April 1916. After the Russian Revolution of March 1917, he crossed Germany with Lenin on the way to Russia, but broke his journey in Sweden and stayed at Stockholm to issue a weekly bulletin on the Russian Revolution, in French and German, on behalf of the Russian Communist Party. After the revolution of November 1917, he joined the Communist Party and took part in the Brest-Litovsk peace negotiations. When the German revolution broke out in 1918 he made his way illegally to Germany. There, as a representative of the central committee of the Russian Communist Party, he was active in reorganizing the German Communist Party, working in its central committee after the murders of Karl Liebknecht and Rosa Luxemburg, but was imprisoned from February to December 1919. On his release he returned to Russia to become a leading member of the presidium of the Communist International. He returned illegally to Germany, however, and helped to organize the joint congress of German Communists and Left Independents. He was made a scapegoat for the German Communists' failure to seize power in autumn 1923; and, because of his support of the "right" groups of the German Communists, he lost his authority in the Communist International and his place in the Soviet Communist Party's central committee (1924). Expelled from the Communist Party as a Trotskyist in 1927, he was readmitted in 1930, and was a member of the editorial board of *Izvestia* from 1931 until 1936, when he was once again expelled from the party. In January 1937, Stalin had him tried with 16 others on a trumped-up charge of treason and sentenced to ten years' imprisonment. Radek must be presumed to have died in captivity.

(L. B. Sc.)

RADETZKY, JOSEPH, GRAF (full surname RADETZKY VON RADETZ) (1766–1858), Austrian army officer, a military reformer whose victorious campaigns made him a national hero, was born at Trebnice, near Tabor, in Bohemia, on Nov. 2, 1766, of an old family of Hungarian extraction. Joining the Austrian Army in 1784, Radetzky became a first lieutenant in 1787. He served in the Turkish War of 1787–91 and later in the Low Countries in the first years of the French Revolutionáry Wars (*q.v.*). From the first his courage and enterprise were conspicuous and, among other ventures, he led a successful cavalry raid near Fleurus, which penetrated behind the French lines. During the Italian campaigns of 1796–97 he took part under J. P. de Beaulieu and later under D. S. von Wurmser in operations against Napoleon Bonaparte. In 1805, with the rank of major general, he was given a command in Italy under the archduke Charles; and in 1809 he was fighting at Wagram with the rank of lieutenant field marshal. (*See* NAPOLEONIC WARS.)

JOSEPH RADETZKY PHOTOGRAPHED ABOUT 1855

In 1809 Radetzky became chief of the Austrian Army general staff and thus entered the field of politics and military policy. His efforts to remodel the Austrian forces on more efficient lines were frustrated by lack of funds, but nevertheless he succeeded in carrying out some essential measures of reorganization and in modernizing the tactical doctrine. In 1813, however, he left Vienna and went to the new army that was being formed in Bohemia, as chief of staff to Karl Philipp zu Schwarzenberg (*q.v.*). As such he had considerable influence in the councils of the Allies opposing Napoleon, particularly in planning the Leipzig campaign. He entered Paris with the Allied sovereigns and notábles in March

1814 and accompanied them later to the Congress of Vienna. Returning to the army general staff, he tried for a time to reform the army further, but had no more success than before, and eventually resumed ordinary military duties. In 1829, by way of retirement, he was given the sinecure of governor of the fortress of Olmütz (Olomouc).

In 1831 Radetzky was again recalled to active service in Italy, at first nominally under J. P. von Frimont, but from December in supreme command himself. In 1836 he was made a field marshal.

The European revolutionary upheaval of 1848 found Austria unprepared, chiefly because Radetzky's advice had been neglected. Recalled for the last time, at the age of 82, he conducted the operations which ended in the victory of Novara on March 23, 1849 (see ITALIAN INDEPENDENCE, WARS OF). He was governor of Lombardy-Venetia from 1850 to 1857.

Radetzky was one of the most efficient and remarkable of the galaxy of central European professional soldiers of the troubled 18th and early 19th centuries. War was his only interest, and he had the attribute, not very common among Austrian generals, of being idolized by the rank and file; he was affectionately known as "Vater Radetzky." He died in Milan on Jan. 5, 1858.

See E. Schmahl, *Radetzky* (1938). (C. N. B.)

RADHAKRISHNAN, SARVEPALLI (1888–   ), Indian scholar and statesman, president of India 1962–67, was born of Telugu Brahman parents in Tiruttani, Chittoor district, Madras presidency (later in Andhra Pradesh), on Sept. 5, 1888. After being educated at the Madras Christian College, Radhakrishnan had a most distinguished scholastic career. His appointments included the professorship of philosophy at Mysore University (1918–21); the King George V professorship of philosophy at Calcutta University (1921–31 and 1937–41); the vice-chancellorship of Andhra University (1931–36); the Spalding professorship of eastern religions and ethics at Oxford University (1936–52); and the vice-chancellorship of Benares Hindu University (1939–48). From 1953 to 1962 he was chancellor of Delhi University. He delivered the Upton lectures at Oxford in 1926 and the Upton and Hibbert lectures in 1929. He also lectured extensively in the United States and China.

Radhakrishnan's written works include *Indian Philosophy*, two volumes (1923–27); *The Philosophy of the Upanishads* (1924); *An Idealist View of Life* (1932); *Eastern Religions and Western Thought* (1939); *East and West: Some Reflections* (1955). In both his lectures and his written works he has performed a notable service in interpreting Indian thought to the West.

From 1946 to 1952 Radhakrishnan was leader of the Indian delegation to the United Nations Educational, Scientific and Cultural Organization, being elected chairman of UNESCO's executive board for 1948–49. From 1949 to 1952 he served as Indian ambassador to the U.S.S.R. On his return in 1952 he took up his appointment as vice-president of the Republic of India. On May 11, 1962, he was elected president, succeeding Rajendra Prasad; in 1967 Radhakrishnan retired from politics, Zakir Husain succeeding. In his speeches, both as vice-president and as president, Radhakrishnan stressed the importance of creating a casteless and classless society in India, urging his countrymen to purge all thoughts of caste distinction from their minds.

See S. J. Samartha, *Introduction to Radhakrishnan: the Man and His Thought* (1964).

RADIAN MEASURE, a method for specifying the lengths of circular arcs. The circumference of a circle (*q.v.*) may be divided into 360 equal parts (degrees) and the length of an arc may be given by the number of degrees it contains; or the arc may be measured in units of length, for example inches; or, if different arcs of the same circle are involved, the radius may be used as unit of length. An arc with length equal to the circle radius is called the radian. The ratio of circle circumference to diameter (approximately 3.14) is denoted by π. Thus the circumference is 2π radii; *i.e.*, 360° equals 2π radians. One degree is $\frac{\pi}{180}$ radians and one radian is $\frac{180}{\pi}$ degrees (slightly more than 57°).

To every angle formed by two radii of a circle there is a corresponding arc; and the ratio of such angles is the same as the ratio of corresponding arcs. It follows that arcs may be used to represent angles, and that angles may be measured in radians as well as degrees. Often radian measure is preferable to degree measure. For instance, the ratio of a leg of a right triangle to the hypotenuse (the cosine of the angle adjacent to the leg) is approximately given by the expression $1 - \alpha^2/2$, where α is the radian measure of the angle; for an angle less than 30° the error is less than 1 in 375. A related advantage of radian measure is that it is the unique measure of angle such that the derivative (*see* CALCULUS, DIFFERENTIAL AND INTEGRAL) of the sine is the cosine. See also ANGLE; TRIGONOMETRY. (G. Y. R.)

RADIATION: BIOLOGICAL EFFECTS. All life is constantly being bombarded with various kinds of radiation—visible light, infrared, ultraviolet, radio waves, X rays (from cosmic and terrestrial sources)—all of which are manifestations of energy transfer from one place to another. In a wide sense any consequence of the transfer of radiation energy to a living organism is a biological effect of radiation. This definition includes both the normal effects on many life processes (*e.g.,* photosynthesis in plants and vision in animals) and the abnormal or injurious effects resulting from the exposure of life to unusual types of radiation or to increased amounts of the radiations commonly encountered in nature. This article, devoted chiefly to the discussion of the deleterious effects of radiation, is divided into the following sections:

I. Definitions and Concepts
   A. Types and Measurement of Radiation
      1. Electromagnetic Waves
      2. Particulate or Corpuscular Radiations
      3. Measurement of Radiation
   B. Mode of Action
      1. Mechanisms of Energy Transfer
      2. Ionization and Penetrating Power
      3. Mechanisms of Biological Action
II. General Biological Effects
   A. Genetic Effects
      1. Gene Mutations
      2. Chromosome Mutations
   B. Bodily (Somatic) Effects
      1. Long-Term Effects
      2. Short-Term Effects
III. Radiation and Human Health
   A. Man's Radiation Burden
      1. Natural Sources
      2. Artificial Sources
   B. Injury from Ionizing Radiations
      1. Historical Background
      2. Radiation Effects on Cells
      3. Radiation Effects on Tissues and Organ Systems
      4. Acute Lethal Effects
      5. Prenatal Exposure and Exposure of Children to Radiation
      6. Protection Against External Radiation
      7. Long-Term Effects, Somatic and Genetic
      8. Radioisotopes and Fallout
      9. Cancer and Radiation
      10. Chromosome Aberrations and Radiation
   C. Effects of Hertzian Waves and Infrared Rays
      1. Hertzian Waves
      2. Infrared Rays
   D. Effects of Visible and Ultraviolet Light
      1. Intrinsic Action
      2. Photodynamic Action
      3. Effects on Development and Biological Rhythms
      4. Effects on the Eyes
   E. Effects of Lasers

I. DEFINITIONS AND CONCEPTS

For a better understanding of the later sections of this article a review of the two main types of radiation—electromagnetic waves and moving atomic particles—their measurement, sources, and mechanisms, is in order.

A. TYPES AND MEASUREMENT OF RADIATION

1. Electromagnetic Waves.—Energy can be transferred through matter or through space by means of oscillatory variations in electric and magnetic fields originating at various sources. Electromagnetic wave radiation is classified into several types, depending on frequency and wavelength. The various types (in order of decreasing wavelength and increasing frequency) and their

TABLE I.—*Electromagnetic Waves*

Wave type	Sources
Hertzian (Radio waves and Microwaves)	Radio transmitters
Infrared	Hot bodies
Visible	Hot bodies
Ultraviolet	Hot bodies; excited gases
X-rays and gamma rays* . . .	Atoms struck by high-energy particles; radioactive materials; cosmic sources

*Similar to X rays but emitted from the nuclei of some radioactive atoms.

sources are summarized in Table I.

2. Particulate or Corpuscular Radiations.—Simply speaking, an atom consists of a nucleus (composed chiefly of neutrons and protons) surrounded by a cloud of electrons; in addition there are other special particles. When separated, either by natural radioactive disintegration or by artificial means (as in a cyclotron, for example), these particles, charged or uncharged, are capable of transferring their energy, wholly or in part, to any substance through which they pass. Streams of such particles constitute particulate radiations. The more important types of particle, the magnitudes and signs of their charges (relative to that of an electron, defined as the unit negative charge), their masses (relative to the mass of a hydrogen nucleus, defined as the unit mass), and their main sources are summarized in Table II. The rate of transfer of energy by a particulate radiation depends on the mass of the particle, its velocity, and, if charged, the magnitude of its charge.

TABLE II.—*Particulate Radiations*

Particle type	Charge	Mass	Sources
Electron*	−1	1/1843	Accelerating machines, radioactive materials
Proton†	1	1	Accelerating machines
Alpha (α) particle‡ . . .	2	4	Radioactive materials
Neutron	0	1	Nuclear reactors, accelerating machines

*Electrons emitted by radioactive nuclei are called beta (β) particles.
†Protons are the nuclei of hydrogen atoms.
‡Alpha (α) particles are the nuclei of helium atoms.

3. Measurement of Radiation.—Radiation is detected and measured by various methods that rely on the property of the radiation to cause ionization in gases or emission of light from sensitive materials, or blackening of a photographic emulsion. Among the instruments used are the ionization chamber, the geiger counter, and the scintillation counter.

Roentgen Unit.—The original biological unit of X- (or gamma) ray exposure, the roentgen unit (r), is defined as that quantity of radiation that produces a given number of charged ions in a given quantity of air under standard conditions.

Rad.—A more general and more accurately defined measure of local exposure to all types of radiation is the rad, the radiation dose absorbed in tissue itself. It is equal to 100 ergs per gram.

Rem.—The same dose in rad from different radiations may produce different degrees of biological effect. The dose in rem is the product of the dose in rad and a factor called the relative biological effectiveness (RBE) of the radiation used. The rem is taken to be that dose from any radiation that produces biological effects in man equivalent to 1 rad of X rays.

For more technical definitions *see* RADIOLOGY; *see* also RADIOACTIVITY.

B. MODE OF ACTION

1. Mechanisms of Energy Transfer.—There are several mechanisms by which energy is transferred from radiations to biological materials. Wave radiations yield up their energy through resonance. In general, the smaller a body, the higher its resonant frequency and therefore the higher the frequency of the radiation from which it will absorb energy. The energy of infrared and visible radiation is absorbed mainly by whole molecules and atoms and therefore appears mainly as heat. The energy of ultraviolet radiation is absorbed partly by the planetary electrons of atoms; an electron jumps to a higher-energy orbit, thereby bringing the atom into a state of excitation, in which it is chemically reactive. The energy of X rays is also absorbed mainly by the planetary electrons of atoms, but the amount absorbed is usually great enough

to produce ionization; *i.e.*, to induce an electron (or electrons) to escape altogether from the atom, thereby ionizing the atom; an ionized atom is highly reactive, even more so than one in a state of excitation.

Particulate radiations yield up their energy through collision with the planetary electrons or atomic nuclei of the material through which they pass. Charged particles usually react with the planetary electrons and therefore leave the atom in an excited or, more commonly, ionized state. Neutrons, being uncharged, are able to pass through the orbits of the planetary electrons and collide with the nucleus of an atom. The nucleus may then recoil, or it may capture the neutron. In biological material neutrons yield up most of their energy through collision with hydrogen nuclei, which recoil as hydrogen ions (*i.e.*, protons). The neutron is eventually captured by some nucleus, and capture is usually followed by the ejection of one or more charged particles, often accompanied by a gamma ray.

2. Ionization and Penetrating Power.—Although all higher-energy radiations (*i.e.*, X rays and particulate radiations) produce ionization in biological material, the spatial distribution of the ionization depends on the type and penetrating power of the radiation, the nature of the material irradiated, and the spatial distribution of the radiation source or sources. High-energy X rays produce ionization that is rather sparsely but uniformly distributed along the track of the radiation; alpha particles cause intense ionization along their tracks; in between these come neutrons, protons, and beta particles. In general, the lower the speed of a particle, the denser the ionization along its track, so that all particles tend to be more densely ionizing toward the ends of their tracks. High-energy X rays penetrate deeply (X rays commonly used in medicine are less penetrating), but most beta particles penetrate only a few millimetres in biological tissues and alpha particles only a small fraction of a millimetre. Animal tissues such as bone and teeth that contain elements of fairly high atomic weight, such as calcium, absorb much more energy from a given radiation than do soft tissues, which are composed mainly of elements of low atomic weight. Ultraviolet radiation is of very low penetrating power.

3. Mechanisms of Biological Action.—The biological effects of the higher-energy electromagnetic radiations and of all the particulate radiations are mediated through the ionization (and, to a lesser extent, the excitation) that they produce in biological tissue. Thus all ionizing radiations have broadly similar biological effects; such differences as are found are the result of differences in the spatial distribution of the ionization. Ionization in biological tissues is largely intracellular. Therefore, an explanation of its mode of action must be sought at the cellular level; effects on the whole organism are likely to be secondary. Two main types of intracellular action have been distinguished: first, direct action through ionization of biological structures along the ionized track; and, second, indirect action through the formation of reactive chemical fragments (free radicals) that diffuse away from the ionized track and subsequently undergo further reaction elsewhere.

Direct Action.—Direct biological actions were studied in great detail in the period between 1927 and 1947. The leaders in this work included H. J. Muller in the U.S., N. Timofeeff-Ressovsky and K. G. Zimmer in Germany, and D. E. Lea in Great Britain. A detailed quantitative theory was elaborated, the target theory or *Treffertheorie*, whereby a tissue undergoing irradiation was likened to a field traversed by the fire of a machine gun. It was supposed that to produce a given effect there must be one or more hits by an ionized track on a sensitive target, so that the probability of obtaining the effect was dependent on the probability of obtaining the requisite number of hits on the appropriate target. This theory was very successful in giving a quantitative treatment of many of the biological effects of radiations, particularly in the field of genetics.

Indirect Action.—In the field of radiation chemistry, where free radicals produced by radiation play a vital role as intermediates in chemical reactions, the target theory had little application, and from about 1940 the interest of radiation biologists tended to shift toward the indirect actions of radiations. This shift was given impetus by the discovery in 1947, by J. M. Thoday and J. Read, that the induction of chromosome breakage, which had until then been viewed as a target-theory effect par excellence, was enhanced if the tension of oxygen was increased in the material irradiated. Similar effects are known in radiation chemistry in which oxygenated solutions can lead to more extensive radiation damage to solute molecules than do oxygen-free solutions. Highly active molecular particles called free radicals are known to be mainly responsible for the changes produced in these cases. Substances were then sought that have a high reactivity toward free radicals in order to reduce the biological effects of radiation exposure. Z. Q. Bacq (Belg.) and H. M. Patt (U.S.) were leaders in the search for protective agents. Two such substances are cysteamine and cysteine. Unfortunately, these compounds can themselves cause adverse biological effects.

II. GENERAL BIOLOGICAL EFFECTS

The biological effects of radiations may conveniently be subdivided into somatic effects—short-term somatic effects (*i.e.*, short-term effects on the body of the individual) and long-term somatic effects—and genetic effects. Historically, they were discovered in that order. But, as the genetic effects are nearest to the cellular level and the short-term somatic effects farthest from it, it is more convenient to consider them in the reverse order.

A. GENETIC EFFECTS

The genetic effects of radiations arise through damage to those intracellular bodies in the germ cells that are the material basis of heredity (*q.v.*). These are the chromosomes, with their constituent genes (*see* GENE). Genetic effects therefore occur only if the radiation reaches the germ cells. Thus in those animals (man is one) and plants in which the germ cells are fairly well covered by tissue, radiations of low penetrating power, such as ultraviolet light and alpha and beta particles, cannot produce genetic changes; however, radiations of high penetrating power, such as X rays and gamma radiation, can induce genetic effects.

Radiation-induced genetic effects on animals and plants are probably not qualitatively different if consideration is given to the physiological variations between these two kinds of life. For obvious reasons, more research has been done on the changes induced in the genetic material of animals. Mutations induced by irradiation of seeds are of interest to plant breeders because of the possibility of producing new varieties. Differences have been found in the mutagenic effect of radiations on plants which appear to depend upon the density of ionization produced. Fast neutrons were found to be 10 to 100 times more mutagenic than X rays. Radioactive elements taken up by plants can also be strongly mutagenic. In choosing a suitable dose for the production of mutations a compromise has to be reached between the mutagenic and damaging effect on the plants of the radiation. As the number of mutations increase so also does the extent of damage to the plant. A critical dose is defined as that allowing 40% survival. In the irradiation of dry seeds by X rays, doses of 10,000 to 20,000 r are usually given. Mutants can be produced by radiation that effects such properties as early ripening, resistance to disease, etc. Much of the work on the radiation breeding of plants has been carried out in Sweden and the U.S.S.R., and economically important varieties of various species have been produced.

In plants and animals genetic changes of two sorts are induced, namely, gene mutations and chromosome mutations. They differ in important respects and will be considered separately.

1. Gene Mutations.—Radiation-induced gene mutations were first demonstrated by H. J. Muller in 1927. They are all of the same types that occur spontaneously in nature. Most gene mutations, whether spontaneous or radiation-induced, are harmful. They reduce the fitness of the organism in the sense that an individual carrying a mutated gene is less capable of surviving and leaving descendants than is an individual carrying the gene in its unmutated form. This is an empirical observation, but it may also be expected on theoretical grounds: any advantageous mutation that could occur spontaneously would probably have occurred at some time in the past and, being advantageous, would have

BY COURTESY OF BROOKHAVEN NATIONAL LABORATORY
GENETIC MUTATIONS IN FRUIT FLIES
These flies with abnormal wings are offspring of males that received internal radiation from radioactive phosphorus

spread through the species, thereby coming to represent the normal form of the gene; any mutation away from the normal form would therefore be a mutation to a less advantageous form.

Although the mutations induced by radiations are all of types that occur spontaneously, the relative frequencies with which any two particular genes mutate under irradiation may not be the same as the frequencies with which they mutate spontaneously; however, if whole classes of genes are considered, the mutational idiosyncrasies of particular genes are lost, and the overall picture shows that exposure to radiation causes a proportionate increase in the mutation frequency of all classes of genes.

Experiments with animals and plants, notably by Muller and Timofeeff-Ressovsky and their co-workers, in the period between 1927 and 1935 established a number of factors influencing the induction of mutation by radiations. The yield of mutation is directly proportional to the amount of energy absorbed in the germ cells; *i.e.*, to the radiation dose. This linear dependence of mutation on dose, which is to be expected on target-theory considerations if gene mutation is the result of a single hit by an ionized track, has been demonstrated experimentally for doses down to a few r and is believed to be valid for all doses, though for statistical reasons it would be difficult to obtain experimental verification at doses much lower than this. The implication is that there is no threshold dose for the induction of gene mutation; *i.e.*, any dose, no matter how small, will induce some mutation.

Radiation intensity was originally thought to have no importance, the total amount of mutation induced being dependent only on the total accumulated dose. However, in 1958 it was shown that this does not hold good for mutation induced in immature germ cells (spermatogonia and oöcytes) of the mouse, the amount of mutation induced by a dose accumulated at a rate of about 1 r per day being only about a third of that induced by the same dose accumulated at about 100 r per minute. If this is true of mammalian spermatogonia and oöcytes generally, it holds important implications for man, whose germ cells are present mainly in the form of spermatogonia in the male and oöcytes in the female.

The amount of mutation induced by radiation is usually expressed in terms of the mutation-rate-doubling dose, which is the dose that induces as much mutation as occurs spontaneously in each generation. This is merely a mathematically convenient way of relating the amount of induced mutation to that arising spontaneously; there is no special biological significance in a mutation rate twice the spontaneous rate. The more sensitive the genes to radiation, the lower the doubling dose. Doubling doses for high-intensity exposure of several different organisms have been found experimentally to lie between about 30 r and 150 r; for seven specific genes in spermatogonia of the mouse the doubling dose is about 30 r for high-intensity exposure and about 100 r for low-intensity exposure. Very little is known about the doubling dose for human genes: studies of the children of survivors of the atomic bomb explosions at Hiroshima and Nagasaki indicate that it must be higher than 10 r, but how much higher is not known; most geneticists assume that it is about the same as the doubling dose for the mouse.

The existence of a linear law relating induced gene mutation to radiation dose holds an important implication for populations: it implies that very small doses of radiation given to very large numbers of individuals may introduce into the population as many mutant genes as would be introduced through large doses to small numbers of individuals. Furthermore, it is necessary to take into consideration the probability that an exposed individual will contribute to the next generation at some time after exposure. It follows that exposure of individuals below reproductive age (including unborn fetuses) is genetically of the greatest importance, and exposure of those above reproductive age is of no importance.

The effect on a population of a rise in its mutation rate depends on the role played by mutation in determining the characteristics of the population. Deleterious genes enter the population through mutation but, because they reduce the fitness of their carriers, they tend to die out; thus a genetic equilibrium is set up at a point where the flow of deleterious genes into the population through mutation is counterbalanced by the loss through reduction in fitness. At equilibrium a constant fraction of the population will be handicapped by deleterious genes. Increasing the mutation rate would increase the gene-handicapped fraction proportionately. However, the full increase would not be manifest immediately; this would occur only when genetic equilibrium had again been established, which would probably require several generations.

2. Chromosome Mutations.—Ionizing radiations not only cause genes to mutate but also may break the chromosomes in which the genes are carried. Chromosome breaks often heal spontaneously, in which case no damage becomes apparent. If a break fails to heal, a germ cell may be formed that lacks an essential part of the gene complement; such a germ cell may be capable of taking part in the fertilization process, but the ensuing zygote is usually incapable of full development and dies in an embryonic state. When two chromosomes in the same nucleus are broken, it sometimes happens that the broken ends join together, but in such a way that the order of the genes in the chromosomes is changed; for example, part of chromosome A may join onto part of chromosome B and vice versa. A germ cell carrying such a chromosome structural change may be capable of giving rise to a zygote that may develop into an adult individual, but the germ cells produced by the latter include many that lack the normal chromosome complement and so give rise to zygotes that are incapable of full development. An individual of this sort is called semisterile, and the number of his descendants is correspondingly lower than normal. Chromosome structural changes, therefore, usually die out of a population; for this reason they are of little importance in human populations. In some species, however, there are mechanisms that reduce the loss of fertility usually associated with chromosomal changes, and in them such changes may be present in the majority of individuals. They include the evening primrose, *Oenothera,* and some species of the fruit fly *Drosophila.* As would be expected from target-theory considerations, the induction of two-break chromosome changes is not dependent on radiation dose in a simple linear fashion. High doses, and doses given at high intensities, induce proportionately more changes of this sort.

B. Bodily (Somatic) Effects

Somatic effects due to radiation include all the injuries, long-term and short-term, to all the cells of the body of an organism—plant or animal.

1. Long-Term Effects.—Long-term somatic effects include damage to cells that are continually proliferating, so that the injury is passed on to succeeding cell generations. Such cells are found in embryonic tissues and in those tissues of the adult in which cell division normally continues throughout life; in vertebrates these include the blood-forming tissues, the basal layer of the skin, the intestinal mucosa, and, in the male, the germ cells. Furthermore, the radiation may affect the rate of cell division: the cells may be killed or otherwise rendered incapable of further division; division may be slowed down; or, conversely, tissues in which cell division normally ceases in the adult may escape their normal biological control and cell division may continue. Mosaic sectors have been observed in many organisms exposed to radiations during embryonic development. They include humans who have been exposed *in utero* during diagnostic examination of the mother; in some fetuses there was a brown sector in the otherwise blue iris of an eye; in others there was a black patch in an otherwise blond head of hair. Unilateral and nonheritable expression of a congenital defect of a type that is normally bilateral and heritable is also believed to arise sometimes through somatic mutation. Sometimes the mutant region includes some of the germ cells, and the genetically mutant nature of the mosaicism can then be confirmed by a breeding test.

Slowing down or suppression of cell division, including radiation-induced cell death, may have important end results where embryonic tissues are exposed. This is because the rate of cell division is not uniform throughout an embryo; at any one stage of development the cells in some parts will be dividing rapidly, while in other parts there will be relatively little cell division. Exposure to radiation will affect the rapidly dividing tissues more strongly than the others, with the result that the pattern of development will be distorted and the individual, when adult, will have disproportionate parts. This phenomenon, which is well known in experimental plants and animals, is also known in man. (Among the persons exposed as early embryos to the atomic bomb radiations in Japan were a number with abnormally small heads and mental defect. Such children have also occurred following exposure *in utero* to medical X rays.)

Radiation exposure of the blood-forming tissues leads to a reduction of cell division and therefore to a reduction in the blood-cell count which may, if sufficiently great, amount to clinically recognizable anemia (for this reason regular blood-cell counts used to be carried out on all radiation workers). Radiation exposure of the germinal tissues likewise leads to a reduction of cell division, which may be sufficient, if the dose is large enough, to induce

BY COURTESY OF BROOKHAVEN NATIONAL LABORATORY

SOMATIC MUTATION IN A DAHLIA
White petals on a normally red flower caused by daily exposure to gamma radiation

sterility; a dose of 200 r to the gonads of the human male induces temporary sterility, lasting a few months; a gonad dose of about 500 r to either sex induces permanent sterility. Opacity of the lens of the eye, which may develop into a full cataract, has been observed after exposure to ionizing radiation, especially neutrons.

A further long-term effect of radiation exposure is a general shortening of the life span, not associated with death attributable to any specific cause. It is a phenomenon well established in laboratory animals, but evidence about its extent in humans is conflicting; the mechanism, whether through gene mutation in somatic cells, a reduction of cell division, or some other cause, has not been established.

Loss of biological control over cell division, i.e., the induction of cancer in animals and distortion of parts in plants, is one of the more serious long-term somatic effects of excessive radiation exposure. It may occur in any tissue. Cancer of the skin was the first long-term effect to be observed; it may result from exposure to ultraviolet as well as to ionizing radiation.

The nature of the dependence of the long-term effects of radiation on radiation dose, type, and intensity is not yet established with certainty. Many authorities assume that the relationship is of a nonthreshold type, meaning that any additional exposure increases the probability of long-term effects occurring. It is a characteristic of the induction of cancer that there may be a long period of time between the causal exposure and the appearance of the effect: for some skin cancers in man induction periods of 40 years have been recorded.

2. Short-Term Effects.—A sufficiently large dose of radiation will kill any organism, but the dose required varies greatly from species to species; mammals are killed by less than 1,000 r, but fruit flies may survive 100,000 r and many bacteria and viruses even higher doses.

This lethal action of radiation can be used as an alternative to heat treatment for sterilizing materials such as surgical sutures. It has found little application in the sterilization of foodstuffs, mainly because the high doses required induce chemical changes in the food that render it unpalatable. (T. C. CA.; Jo. C. O.)

III. RADIATION AND HUMAN HEALTH
A. MAN'S RADIATION BURDEN

1. Natural Sources.—Throughout the ages man has been exposed to what is called natural background radiation. This includes radiation from cosmic as well as terrestrial sources. It has probably played the major role in the evolution of life.

TABLE III.—*Cosmic Radiation Exposure*

Location	Mean dose in rads* per year
Sea level, temperate zone	0.020–0.040
5,000 ft.	0.040–0.060
10,000 ft.	0.080–0.120
40,000 ft.	2.8
30 km.–600 km.	7–15
Interplanetary space	13–25
Van Allen radiation belt (protons)	<1,500
Single solar flare (protons and helium)	<1,000

*Rad is the unit of radiation dose; it corresponds to 100 ergs energy transferred to one gram tissue.

Cosmic rays (q.v.) rain down incessantly on the Earth's atmosphere. The primary particles, protons, helium ions, heavier nuclei, and some electrons interact with atoms of the air and cause secondary radiations—chiefly electrons, gamma rays, and mesons (a class of atomic particles)—by the time they reach the Earth. There is considerable variation in the intensity of cosmic radiation, both geographically and temporally, since sunspots and solar flares influence the primary intensity. For about every 5,000 ft. of altitude, the intensity approximately doubles (see Table III). One of the hazards of space travel is a belt of "trapped" radiation that surrounds the Earth at a height of several thousand miles (see VAN ALLEN RADIATION BELTS).

Variations of cosmic-ray dose have occurred during the geological history of the Earth by the reversals of the geomagnetic field, which acts as a protective shield at present. Appearance of a supernova near the solar system could cause a sudden rise in cosmic-ray intensity several hundredfold.

Man also receives external and internal radiation from natural radioisotopes, particularly radium and its daughters, members of the thorium series, potassium-40, carbon-14, and hydrogen-3 (tritium). The last two are produced by cosmic rays, whereas the former are due to decay of radioisotopes believed to have been present when the Earth was formed. The greater part of external radiation comes from the radioactivity of minerals, whereas radioactive contamination of drinking water and food plays an integral part internally. Drinking waters vary by a factor of 10,000 in their radioactivity content. Among the foods, radium content of nuts and cereals is higher than that of milk or meat. Internal doses in normal persons from natural radioactivity are listed in Table IV.

TABLE IV.—*Internal Dose Due to Natural Radioactivity*

Isotope	Radioactivity in curies*	Radiation	Dose in rads per year	Critical organ
Carbon-14	9 X 10⁻⁸ per g.	beta rays	0.0016	gonads
Potassium-40	10.4 X 10⁻⁸ per g.	beta rays	0.0165	gonads
Potassium-40	1.15 X 10⁻⁸ per g.	gamma rays	0.0023	gonads
Radium and daughters	1 X 10⁻¹⁰ in body	alpha, beta, gamma rays	0.0380	bones

*Curie is the unit of radioactivity; one curie corresponds to 37,000,000,000 disintegrations per second.

There are certain localities with relatively high background due to the presence of radioactive minerals near the soil surface. Such areas occur in Brazil, Sweden, and France. The state of Kerala in India is rich in monazite sands, with considerable natural radioactivity. External doses due to natural radioactivity from sources such as these are shown in Table V.

TABLE V.—*External Dose Due to Natural Radioactivity*

Source	Dose in rads per year
Ordinary regions	0.025–0.160
Active regions	
Granite in France	0.180–0.350
Houses in Sweden (alum shale)	0.158–0.220
Monazite alluvial deposits in Brazil	mean 0.500; max. 1.0
Monazite sands, Kerala, India	0.37–2.8

2. Artificial Sources.—Since the discovery of radioactivity, man has substantially added to his natural radiation load. Medical X rays and radioisotopes often are necessary for the diagnosis or treatment of disease. In some countries almost the entire population is exposed to periodic diagnostic X rays and a significant fraction to therapeutic doses. Therapeutic doses vary widely depending on, among other things, the disease being treated. Routine diagnostic doses, though they may vary somewhat depending on the apparatus, usually falls within certain limits (see Table VI).

TABLE VI.—*Typical Doses Received in Routine X-Ray Diagnosis*

Examination	Dose per exposure
X-ray photograph	
Chest X ray	0.04–1 rad
Gastrointestinal X ray	1 rad
Extremities	0.25–1 rad
Fluoroscopy	10–20 rads per minute
X-ray movie	25 rads per examination

High-voltage power supplies for radar or television, dental X rays, luminous-dial watches, phonograph static eliminators, and television sets give significant doses of radiation, sometimes more than is warranted. The yearly dose from diagnostic X rays has become comparable to the dose received from cosmic rays. Further man-made sources causing concern are fallout from nuclear weapons testing (Table VII) and radioactivity from reactors.

TABLE VII.—*Worldwide Dose Commitment from Nuclear Tests Prior to 1970*

(North Temperate zones; doses calculated for bone surface)

Source	Isotope	Half-life	Dose to bone surfaces, mrad
External radiation	short-lived (e.g., iodine-131)	8 days	36
	longer-lived (cesium-137)	30 years	36
Internal radiation	strontium-89	50 days	1
	strontium-90	28 years	130
	cesium-137	30 years	21
	carbon-14*	5,730 years	16
Total			240

*Calculated to year 2000 only.

Most of the radioactivity produced in power reactors is safely contained. A small percentage escapes as stack gas or liquid effluent and eventually may contaminate the atmosphere and water supplies. Similar problems exist in nuclear fuel reprocessing plants. Peaceful uses of atomic explosions in digging harbours or in mining minerals far underground also produce radioisotopes. While atomic plants promise to be abundant and clean sources of energy, they may eventually contribute considerably to world-wide radiation background (Table VIII).

TABLE VIII.—*Estimate of Long-Lived Radioactive Gases Released in Air and Water by Power Reactors and Fuel Reprocessing Plants, Global Scale**

Isotope	1970	1980	2000
Curies, released/year krypton-85 equivalent†	17,000,000	200,000,000	1,900,000,000
Curies, released/year hydrogen-3	340,000	4,000,000	37,000,000
Curies, hydrogen-3‡ accumulated in air and water	1,000,000	62,000,000	590,000,000
Curies, hydrogen-3 in air due to cosmic rays	40,000,000–80,000,000		
Curies, krypton-85 accumulated in air	50,000,000	3,000,000,000	25,000,000,000

*Courtesy of Thomas Pigford, University of California, Berkeley.
†In units of krypton-85 equivalent, maximum permissible concentration 0.0003 microcurie/litre air. ‡Maximum permissible concentration 3 microcuries/litre air.
Amounts shown are much smaller than the permissible concentration if one assumes uniform distribution in atmosphere. In 1971 maximum permissible emissions from power reactors were lowered by a factor of 100; the estimates given here may be high.

Coal power plants also produce undesirable atmospheric contaminants. Besides chemical pollutants, the stack gases contain radioactive products of radium. Portable atomic batteries contain large amounts of dangerous radioisotopes, *e.g.*, polonium or plutonium, safely sealed. Atomic power rockets will be available soon for interplanetary travel. These will produce some radioactive contamination (*e.g.*, hydrogen-3) in interplanetary space.

It appears from the tables that, if the current trends are maintained, by the end of the 20th century the entire human population may be exposed to twice the radiation level from natural sources. It is important to study and understand the possible consequences of these changes in radiation level.

B. INJURY FROM IONIZING RADIATIONS

Although all forms of radiation, if intense enough, may produce some adverse effects on man, the "hard" or penetrating ionizing rays, including X rays and moving atomic particles, present the greatest hazard. Paradoxically, these same ionizing rays, when judiciously used in medicine, constitute a formidable weapon against cancer and an invaluable aid in diagnosis (*see* RADIOLOGY).

The concept of maximum permissible exposure to radiation is a much-debated point, subject to change as more information accumulates. Although the body may not be noticeably affected, genetic damage may occur and pass unnoticed for several generations, as was mentioned earlier. Maximum permissible exposures are proposed for persons who, by the nature of their work, are exposed to amounts of radiation beyond that to which the general population is exposed. (Recommendations vary somewhat in different countries; those given in Table IX are for the U.S.)

TABLE IX.—*Maximum Permissible Exposures to Ionizing Radiations for Professional Radiation Workers*

Organ exposed	Exposure in rem*
Whole body	3 rem in 13 weeks
Professional emergency dose (once in life)	25 rem
Accumulated dose under 18 years	No professional exposure permitted
Accumulated dose over 18 years	Average of 5 rem per year less than 15 rem in any single year
Skin	8–10 rem in 13 weeks or 30 rem per year
Gonads	5 rem per year
Bone	10 rem in 13 weeks or 30 rem per year

*One rem denotes the dose of radiation of various kinds that cause effects equivalent to one rad of X rays.

The limiting factor for persons in the general population is based on the genetic hazard. The greater worldwide concern for heritable, nonthreshold types of radiation damage is expressed in the recommendation of the International Commission on Radiological Protection: for individuals not engaged in radiation work the exposure to ionizing radiation should not exceed five rem in a lifetime, in addition to natural background radiation and to the lowest practical dosages from medical exposure. The permissible exposure levels are being constantly reviewed and adjusted as new evidence becomes available on biological effects.

1. Historical Background.—In December 1895 the German physicist Wilhelm Conrad Röntgen demonstrated the first X-ray pictures, among them that of the left hand of Mrs. Röntgen. Within a few weeks the news of the discovery spread throughout the world, and the penetrating properties of the rays were soon exploited for medical diagnosis without immediate realization of possible deleterious effects. The first reports of X-ray injury to various human tissues and to vision came in 1896. In that same year Elihu Thomson, the physicist, deliberately exposed one of his fingers to X rays and provided accurate scientific observations on the development of roentgen-ray burns.

Also in 1896 Thomas Alva Edison discovered "fluoroscopy"; he was engaged in developing a fluorescent roentgen-ray lamp when he noticed that his assistant, Clarence Dally, was so "poisonously affected" by the new rays that his hair fell out and his scalp became inflamed and ulcerated. By 1904 Dally developed severe ulcers on both hands and arms; these lesions, which soon afterward became cancerous, caused his early death. During the next few decades many investigators and medical doctors developed radiation burns and cancer, and more than 100 persons died, presumably as a result of their exposure to X rays. These sad early experiences eventually led to an awareness of radiation hazards for professional workers and stimulated development of a new branch of science—radiobiology.

Radiations from radioactive materials were not immediately recognized as being related to X rays. In 1906 A. H. Becquerel, the French physicist and discoverer of radioactivity (1896), accidentally burned himself by carrying radioactive material in his pocket. Noting this, Pierre Curie, the co-discoverer of radium, deliberately produced a similar burn on himself. A few months later it was found that radium could be useful in medicine; this discovery led to the founding of the Radium Hospital (Institut du radium et de la fondation Curie) in Paris in 1906. It was also soon recognized that radium could be very toxic. Beginning about 1925 a number of women in the painting industry who were exposed to luminescent paint containing radium became ill with anemia and lesions of the jawbones and mouth; some of these persons later developed bone cancer. The same symptoms appeared in some patients who had received radium internally to relieve arthritis and other diseases. In the 1930s attention was called to these radium hazards and the practices were stopped.

In 1933 Ernest Lawrence and his collaborators completed the first full-scale cyclotron at the University of California at Berkeley. This machine was a copious source of the neutron rays that had at that time just been discovered by Sir James Chadwick in England. This time, however, human guinea pigs were spared. Ernest, his brother John, and Paul Aebersold exposed rats to the beam of the cyclotron; they found that fast neutron radiation was about $2\frac{1}{2}$ times more effective in killing power than were X rays. These facts indicated the need for protection for investigators engaged in research with the cyclotron; thus a form of shielding was devised for the machine. When the first atomic reactor, built in Chicago, proved Enrico Fermi's principle of self-sustaining fission chain reactions (1942), considerable knowledge of the biological effects of neutrons was already available. Atomic reactors are now rapidly becoming a prime source of power for the world.

Modern accelerators produce a wealth of different types of radiations, including leptons (electrons, positrons, muons, and neutrinos) and hadrons. There are more than 100 known baryons and about 60 known mesons, each with different interaction properties. In addition, since the advent of space flight, the effects of certain space radiations on man became of interest. Protons in the Van Allen radiation belts and protons and heavier ions in solar flares and near the top of the atmosphere are of particular importance. To meet the problems presented by these advances, health physics has become an elaborate discipline.

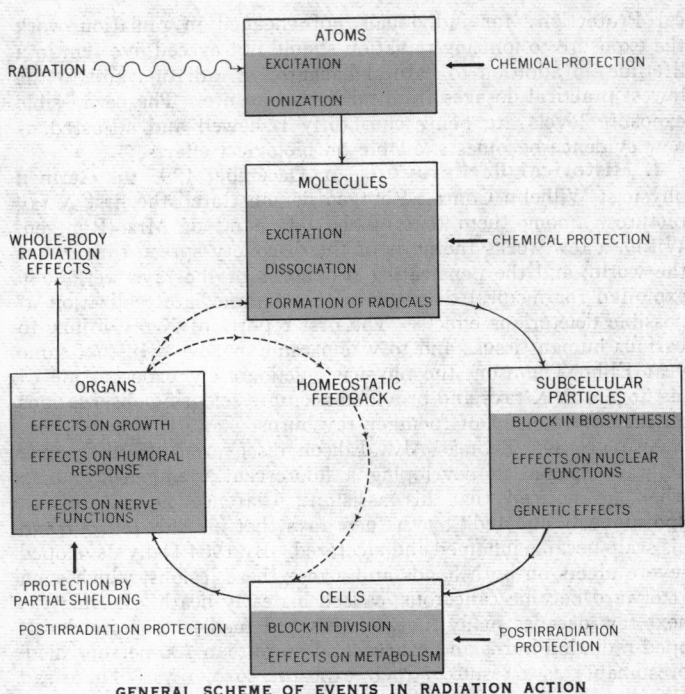

GENERAL SCHEME OF EVENTS IN RADIATION ACTION

Radiation acts on atoms, which in turn cause modification in molecules, cells, and organs as shown. The existence of homeostatic regulation in the human body causes highly complex "feedback" interactions. The levels at which various protective agents act are also shown

2. Radiation Effects on Cells.—To understand radiation effects it is necessary to study the cellular and subcellular events that succeed a radiation insult and that give rise to gross effects. The work done in this area has already contributed a great deal to the understanding of normal and diseased states. How radiation may inflict biological damage is shown in the accompanying diagram.

The radiosensitivity of individual human cells in laboratory cultures was first measured by T. T. Puck, an American biophysicist, in the 1950s. He used the progeny of human cervical cancer cells (of the strain named HeLa) kept alive in tissue culture. An amazing aspect of radiation effects is that the actual energy needed for producing changes or mutations in genes is exceedingly small—often 1,000 times smaller than chemical or heat energy needed to produce similar changes. HeLa and other available human cells are so sensitive to radiation that half of them are killed by doses of 80 to 300 rem. The killing effect manifests itself primarily when the cells attempt to divide but cannot do so since their chromosomes are broken and abnormally jointed as a result of radiation. Neuroblasts (nerve cell initials) and cells of the intestinal epithelium, of mucous membrane, and of blood-forming organs exhibit the greatest sensitivity. Rapidly proliferating tissues of the reproductive system are particularly sensitive to radiation. It was demonstrated that spermatozoa in the mouse can be killed by a few roentgens. Given time, however, reproductive organs recover fully from sublethal doses of radiation. Most resistant are adult nerve cells, which owe their resistance to the fact that they do not normally divide; specialized nerve endings and synapses (*e.g.*, in the retina), however, may exhibit great radiosensitivity. At sublethal doses human cells exhibit delay of cell division following radiation, perhaps as a consequence of a block in the synthesis of new genetic material (deoxyribonucleic acid, or DNA), while the synthesis of proteins goes on. Such cells frequently turn into "giants," having several hundred times normal volume. Late effects, *e.g.*, the initiation of cancerous growth, may have their origin in sublethally injured cells and are in part due to genetic and chromosomal alterations.

Cellular radiation effects are the complex result of breakage and rejoining of chromosomes and of direct genetic damage of a more subtle nature. The synthesis of new DNA is also usually markedly affected. Effects on other cell constituents appear to be of secondary importance. In bacterial viruses it is known that X rays cause the breakage of both strands of the DNA molecule in order to cause lethal effect. Many single strand breaks also occur, but most of these are reparable by enzymes in the cell. Chromosome breakage may be followed by normal or abnormal rejoining of the broken ends. There are mechanisms available in mammalian cells that can repair sublethal injury. Thus, the final effect is dose-rate dependent and is less at low dose rates.

3. Radiation Effects on Tissues and Organ Systems.—Since tissues are composed of cells, tissue effects reflect the lethal and sublethal changes in the cells. These initiate a complex defense pattern: cells injured by radiation may release toxic substances; *e.g.*, proteolytic enzymes and nucleases that are able to inflict further injury. The injury is often followed by a regeneration accomplished by increased rate of cell division: the sick cells are often lysed and removed and, if recovery is not complete, scar tissue may form.

Inhibition of epithelial tissues with cellular breakdown and increased permeability leads to invasion by pathogens, inflammation, ulceration, loss of fluids, nausea, and diarrhea.

Inhibition of blood formation leads, in the course of days or weeks, to leukopenia (reduction of the number of white cells), which lessens defense against infection; anemia (reduction in the number of red cells), which results in defective oxygen transport; lassitude; anoxia (reduction of oxygen in tissue); bleeding, due to a failure of platelet synthesis; and some loss of immunity. None of these effects is as yet completely understood by medical science.

It is known that, because of the varied cellular effects of radiation, the function of individual organs can become imbalanced. Since the body has widespread humoral and neuronal interconnections, irradiation of a single organ can modify the functions of the rest of the body. For example, George de Hevesy demonstrated in 1945 that radiation of the spleen and liver causes retardation of nucleic acid synthesis elsewhere in the body. Another example of this effect is given by irradiation studies on the pituitary of animals and humans, as shown by C. A. Tobias and others. Pituitary irradiation can arrest the growth of a young animal and can affect his sexual development and metabolism. In humans irradiation of the pituitary can arrest proliferation of certain hormone-dependent cancer cells, thereby causing regression of this type of cancer wherever it may be located in the body.

Radiation effects due to whole-body radiation can be lessened by the shielding of particular parts of the body. L. O. Jacobson and others demonstrated in mice that shielding of part of the blood-forming system, *e.g.*, the spleen, increases the radiation tolerance by a factor close to two. Shielding of other parts of the body also protects, but to a lesser extent. Least protection is afforded by head shielding.

Some investigators claim a chronic deterioration of the central nervous system from moderate dose levels (although others have shown in experiments with monkeys that radiation doses up to lethal levels do not impair learning ability).

Generally speaking, man does not sense a moderate radiation field, though very low doses of radiation, less than one rad, can produce "phosphene," a light sensation on the dark-adapted retina. In some food preference tests, rats, when given a choice, will avoid radiation fields of even a few roentgens. Three roentgens, probably acting on the olfactory system, are sufficient to arouse a slumbering rat, and a few roentgens can accelerate seizures in mice genetically susceptible to these.

In man and other mammals the retina and smooth muscle respond to intense pulses of radiation; the cornea and peripheral nerves require much higher dose rates to respond.

4. Acute Lethal Effects.—Prior to Aug. 6, 1945, there was no known case of widespread loss of human life due to penetrating radiation. On that day the first atomic bomb used in warfare was exploded over Hiroshima, Japan, causing the death of about 75,000 persons, many of whom died of the effects of radiation. In persons exposed to very large doses of radiation, painful, ugly, and repulsive symptoms occur prior to a delayed death. During the years since World War II, man has learned to make atomic weapons of more than a thousandfold the power of the Hiroshima bomb, and arsenals of hundreds of such bombs are available in various countries. A study by the UN has shown that if atomic war were to be unleashed in full fury, the effects of the blast, heat, radiation, and fission product isotopes could kill millions of persons and drastically alter plant and animal populations. This might mean the end of civilization as it is known.

In the lethal radiation syndrome the greater the dose given, the sooner and more profound the radiation effects. Following a single dose of 400–800 rem to the whole body, survival is improbable. Very high doses, 5,000 rem or more, cause immediate and discernible effects on the central nervous system. States of intermittent stupor and incoherence vary with hyperexcitability resembling epileptic seizures. Death is certain within several days. This syndrome has been carefully studied in animals; a human case was described in 1959 by S. G. Wilson of the U.S. School of Aerospace Medicine.

When the dose is between 600 and 1,000 rem, the earliest symptoms are loss of appetite, nausea, and vomiting, followed by prostration, watery and bloody diarrhea, abhorrence of food, and fever. The blood-forming tissues are profoundly affected, and in 15 to 30 days the white blood cell count may decrease from about 8,000 per mm.^{3} to as low as 200 per mm.^{3} The body loses its defenses against microbial infection, and inflammation of mucous membranes and of intestinal lining may occur. As a result of the reduction in blood platelets, the blood loses its ability to clot and spontaneous internal or external bleeding may result. Return of the early symptoms, often accompanied by delirium or coma, presages death. There can be great individual variation in the symptoms. At lower doses they may be delayed for a few days. Complete loss of hair within ten days has been taken as an indication of the lethal severity of the exposure.

In the dose range 150 to 600 rem, survival is possible (though in the upper range improbable), and the symptoms appear as above, but in milder form and generally following some delay. Nausea, vomiting, and malaise may begin on the first day, then disappear, and a latent period of relative well-being follow. Anemia and leukopenia set in gradually. After three weeks internal hemorrhages may occur in almost any part of the body, but particularly in mucous membranes. Susceptibility to infection remains a very great hazard and some loss of hair occurs. Weight loss, lassitude, emaciation, and fever may last for many weeks before either recovery or death occurs.

Moderate doses of radiation can interfere seriously with the immunity mechanism. In animals this manifests itself in enhanced sensitivity to bacterial toxins, greatly decreased fixation of antigens, and reduced efficiency of formation of antibodies. Furthermore, antibiotics, unfortunately, appear to have reduced effectiveness in combating post-irradiation infections. In the 1960s plastic isolators became available that allow antiseptic isolation of a person from his environment and thus may protect him from infection from external sources during the period critical for his recovery.

Man is generally able to survive a single dose of less than 150 rem. The symptoms are similar to those already described, but milder and delayed. In doses under 100 rem the discernible radiation effects may be so slight that the exposed person is able to continue his normal occupation though there is measurable depression of his bone marrow and some persons suffer subjective discomfort from doses as low as 30 rem. Sublethal doses may have chronic effects many years later.

5. Prenatal Exposure and Exposure of Children to Radiation.—During embryonic and fetal development the human organism is extraordinarily sensitive to changes in the environment that may affect the offspring in spite of the protective mediation of the mother's body. Exposure of the mother to significant doses of radiation may result in chronically expressed injury to her offspring.

Most of the information on the effects of radiation during pregnancy is based on studies with animals. Increased sensitivity is apparent in the period following fertilization. Radiation effects strongly depend on the stage of development of embryo and fetus at the time of exposure. For example, congenital malformations are caused in rats and mice when exposure occurs during periods of initial formation of the organs. Exposure of the rat embryo to 200 rads during early embryonic life is more likely to kill the embryo than to cause congenital malformations, whereas irradiation in late pregnancy is more likely to produce functional abnormalities in the offspring than lethal effects or malformations.

A wide variety of radiation-induced malformations have been observed in small rodents. Many of these are malformations of the nervous system, and include microcephaly (reduced size of brain), exencephaly (part of the brain outside the skull), hydrocephaly (enlargement of the head due to excessive fluid), and anophtalmia (failure of the eyes to develop). Such effects follow doses of 100–200 rads at the appropriate time period. At a dose of 25 rads, only eye anomalies are seen; 20–50 rads in late pregnancy causes disorganization in the microscopic structure of rat brain; 10 rads causes some retardation and alteration in the rate of development of the cortex. Functional abnormalities seen in animals after prenatal radiation include abnormal reflexes, restlessness and hyperactivity, impaired learning ability, and susceptibility to externally induced seizures. The malformations induced by radiation are similar to those that can be caused by specific virus infection and certain types of neurotropic drugs, pesticides, and mutagens.

In human populations 1–2% are born with malfunctions of the nervous system. Several studies have established that children born to mothers who received radiation to the pelvic region have much higher incidence of anomalies, particularly of the microcephalic type. A study was conducted among several hundred pregnant women who survived the Hiroshima or Nagasaki atomic explosions. Their children were medically observed for more than 20 years. At the higher dose levels many of these children developed smaller-than-normal head size and among these there was a significant increase in the incidence of mental retardation (10% at 100-rad dose). The greatest sensitivity for such effects occurs between the second and sixth months of pregnancy. There is an increased risk of leukemia and of malignancies for children who were exposed to radiation while *in utero*. This risk is greater when radiation exposure is prolonged over several weeks: for single doses, the risk of mental retardation is greater.

Radiation exposure of children during the first few years of life causes somewhat similar effects as irradiation of the fetus during late pregnancy. The major source of information is from studies of cases treated for tumours and conditions of the scalp. Therapeutic doses can lead to the induction of tumours, particularly those of the thyroid and of the nervous system, to leukemia, and to retarded mental development.

It is clear from the above that the exposure of pregnant mothers to excess radiation entails risks for their offspring. It is prudent to avoid extensive pelvic X-ray diagnosis or therapy unless the mother's health warrants it. At the same time one should not construe radiation as a major current cause of developmental abnormalities or of mental retardation. The latter condition is clearly related to other causes: malnutrition of the mother and of the newborn, often related to poverty, and genetic factors are responsible for the great majority of cases.

6. Protection Against External Radiation.—Great efforts have been made by scientists of many countries to find agents that will increase radioresistance of the body.

Findings in 1933 that living systems deprived of oxygen are more radioresistant, and in 1942 that newborn rats kept in carbon dioxide atmospheres were twice as resistant as their litter mates kept in air, went largely unnoticed until 1950. In that year it was demonstrated that large doses of the amino acid cysteine given prior to irradiation provided substantial protection against radiation effect. Following this discovery many substances were found with some protective action. Although the matter is still under debate, it appears that many of these substances act by producing anoxia or by competing for oxygen with normal cell constituents and radiation-produced radicals. Since anoxia is in itself a highly hazardous physiological state and all protective compounds tried thus far are toxic, it cannot be said that protection of humans by these drugs prior to radiation exposure is a practical matter.

TABLE X.—*Some Chemical Protectors Effective in Mice or Rats*

Class	Specific chemical	Effective dose milligram/kilogram tissue
Sulfur compounds . .	glutathione	1,000
	cysteine	1,000
	cysteamine	150
	AET*	350
Hormones	estradiolbenzoate	12
	ACTH	25 for 7 days
Enzyme inhibitors . .	sodium cyanide	5
	carbon monoxide	by inhalation
	mercaptoethylamine (MEA)	235
	para-aminopropio- phenone (PAPP)	30
Metabolites . . .	formic acid	90
Vasoconstrictors . . .	serotonin	50
Nervous system drugs .	amphetamine	1
	chlorpromazine	20

*Aminoethylisothiuronium bromide hydrobromide.

Beginning in 1961 some diurnal changes in the radiosensitivity of rodents were reported—an indication that the complex humoral factors responsible for daily rhythms also alter the response of tissues to radiation. On the other hand, a few classes of substances are known that render animals more sensitive to acute radiation effects. Compounds that sensitize mice or rats to radiation include: thyroxine, methylandrostenediol, Synkayvite, porphyrins, beta-homocysteine, thioethanolamine, 3,4-benzopyrene, and monoiodoacetic acid. Perhaps the most interesting of these is the hormone thyroxine, a normal secretion of the body. A large class of sensitizers at the cellular level include nucleic acid analogs (*e.g.*, 5-fluoro-uracil).

It may appear from the foregoing that acute radiation syndrome in mammals is the result of complex interaction from many affected organ systems. Nevertheless, it was shown in the early 1960s that there is some genetic control of radiosensitivity, since susceptible and resistant mouse strains were developed. Inability of recovery of the hemopoietic (blood-forming) system appears to be linked with high radiation sensitivity.

Beginning with the 1950s the Lobund laboratories of Notre Dame University, which pioneered in the study of germfree animals, has shown that germfree mice that spend their entire lives in a sterile environment exhibit greater resistance to radiation than do animals in a normal environment, no doubt due in part to elimination of the hazards of infection.

For many years it was held that cure of radiation disease was hopeless since events were thought to be irreversible once a person had received a lethal dose. It was historically important, therefore, when it was demonstrated in mice that ground substance of embryo, spleen, or bone marrow administered following irradiation allowed the animals to survive what would otherwise be a lethal dose of X rays. It is hoped that detailed study of this finding will lead to the understanding of various physiological processes.

It has been shown that most of the effect of transfused bone marrow depends on the provision of intact, living cells, which then migrate to the marrow of the irradiated host and proliferate there, repopulating the host's marrow with cells characteristic of the donor. Bone marrow transfusion between animals of different strains is successful in these cases because the irradiated animal loses its ability to develop antibodies against the injected "foreign" tissue. If the injected bone marrow proliferates rapidly enough, it may save the host from acute lethal effects of radiation.

Mammals that carry successful grafts of bone marrow become "chimeras," *i.e.*, organisms producing cells of more than one genotype. Several months later the transplanted tissue may develop a disease sometimes called "wasting disease" (or homologous disease). This is an immune reaction between the proliferating donor cells and the irradiated host and is often rapidly fatal.

If bone marrow could be taken with ease (as blood is taken) from normal human volunteers, and then cultured and preserved under refrigeration and injected only into immunologically compatible individuals, it might prove to be a powerful therapeutic agent against radiation disease. Transfusion of fresh, normal human bone marrow has already demonstrated some worth in alleviating radiation effects. In 1958 an unfortunate accident occurred at a nuclear reactor in Yugoslavia in which five persons were exposed to near-lethal doses of mixed neutron and gamma radiation. They were flown to the Radium Hospital in Paris, where four of them received human bone marrow transfusions. As judged by their recovery, several of these men were considerably benefited. In time it will be feasible to culture cells in the laboratory for transplanting into a victim of radiation sickness. At the present state of the art, however, cultured cells are not yet suitable for the therapy of radiation disease by transfusion.

Bone marrow transfusion, as well as transplantation of other organs, may be of importance in future control of various seemingly incurable conditions; *e.g.*, leukemia and some types of anemia. The clue to successful bone marrow transplantation is the complete understanding of the genetic and biochemical aspects of immunological compatibility. Only when this knowledge is attained will transplantation of bone marrow (and also of essential organs such as heart, pancreas, or kidney) become established as a safe and feasible medical practice.

7. Long-Term Effects, Somatic and Genetic.—Much of man's radiation exposure is at very low levels. There are some components of natural and man-made radiation (*see* below) to which persons may be exposed continuously or intermittently through most of their lives. Usually the effects of such low-level radiations are so minute that often even the most refined methods fail to demonstrate immediate functional effects or late deleterious effects that can be unequivocally assigned as the effects of radiation on the individual. Instead, long-term effects must be studied on a statistical basis in a population of individuals, and they are usually described as altered statistical risks for the populations. These risks are: lower average life expectancy, reduction in fertility, acceleration of the rate of mutations, and increase in the occurrence of chronic diseases such as cancer and cataracts. While these effects may be brought about by radiation, they are also affected by a host of environmental and hereditary factors.

Significant doses of radiation delivered daily (*e.g.*, 0.5 rad/day or more) cause rats and mice to become "physiologically" older than their actual age would indicate, with subsequent shortening of life span. Some experiments with mice, however, showed a life span lengthening for 0.1 rad daily dose. It is exceedingly difficult to make valid deductions from animal data to human beings. Data for radiologists, whose radiation exposure is assumed to be greater than that of other segments of the population, provide some information on radiation effects in man. A study of British radiologists showed that their mortality generally was lower than that of other doctors, whereas the mortality of American radiologists was found higher than that of their colleagues in ophthamology and otolaryngology. A sample of nearly 100,000 survivors of Hiroshima and Nagasaki yielded the anomalous result that groups exposed to doses between 11 and 120 rads actually had a lower death rate in the ensuing 15 years than those receiving a lesser dose. Results such as these point to the fact that there are great variations in life span due to many factors. Despite conflicting data, for the sake of health protection estimates, the life shortening effect of 1 rad on man may be assumed to lie between 2 and 15 days.

There are several concepts of the nature of radiation-induced aging. One theory maintains that all disease experiences from early childhood, as well as toxic factors in the environment, act together to determine the physiological age of an individual. According to this model, the fallout radiation hazard currently is much less of an aging factor than cigarette smoking, lack of exercise, obesity, or childhood diseases. Another concept, one more specific to radiation injury, states: the aging effect produced by radiation is due to the number of irreversible chromosome aberrations produced in the somatic (tissue) cells of mammals. Many of the chromosome aberrations can be demonstrated in blood cells or in liver cells several months following exposure to radiation, and chromosome aberrations have generally been associated with impaired cellular function. Neither of these theories has thus far been able to account fully for the modifying effects of the homeostatic system controlled by organs regulating the elaboration of hormones.

A dose of a few hundred rem is believed unlikely to impair the fertility of normally fertile women, and it is believed that up to 15 rem yearly will not impair the fertility of normally fertile men. The doses that cause genetic effects to the population are delivered in the years prior to conception of children. Although there are many genetic data for mice, it is difficult to arrive at reliable genetic estimates for man since genetic effects occur at the chromosome as well as the gene level. H. J. Muller, the discoverer of mutation induction by radiation, suggested that recessive lethal mutations constitute the greatest genetic hazard; they can penetrate the population in the course of many successive generations and exert their toll, mainly when they appear in individuals born to parents who both carry the recessive lethal gene. Furthermore, certain chromosome mutations (e.g., when chromosomes are present in abnormal numbers) also represent important genetic risks. In any case, it appears that lethal mutations exert their greatest effect in the first generation born subsequent to radiation exposure but that in subsequent generations more lethals will appear due to the same recessive genes. In a population of 1,000,000 individuals who have been exposed to an average dose of 1 rem, about 2,000 lethals will be observed in the course of 10 successive generations. This is, however, less than 0.1% of the lethals that will occur in the same population in the same time due to the normally present "genetic load" of lethal genes in the population. The normal lethal "genetic load" will approximately double when a population is exposed to a dose of 60 rem. Such estimates usually are made by assuming that all radiation doses are strictly additive and that the effect is proportional to the total dose. Evidence has been mounting, however, that genetic radiation damage is almost completely repaired in the female reproductive system at low dose rates of X or gamma rays. The effect on the male reproductive system may be less than previously assumed due to the fact that normal sperm has better viability and motility than sperm carrying radiation-induced damage. Genetic effects from neutrons have been reported to repair less than effects from gamma rays; neutrons also are responsible for many more chromosome aberrations.

It is generally believed that most of the radiation-induced mutations are "bad" in the sense that they are lethal or usually impair some property. It is also known, however, that a fraction of induced mutations are "good," and that mutations are essential to maintain a steady rate of evolutionary change. Evolutionary changes occur at random and tend to better adapt the species to its environment. Some data on populations of fruit flies indicate that radiation can be useful in accelerating the rate of evolution when the population faces an environmental crisis.

8. Radioisotopes and Fallout.—Radioactive isotopes usually emit electrons or positrons, alpha particles and/or gamma rays, or even characteristic X rays. The exposure may be external, in which case penetration is an important factor. Alpha particles do not penetrate deeply enough in the skin to cause damage. Beta particles or X rays over 30 kv. can be hazardous to the skin, causing redness, loss of hair, or ulceration. Large doses may cause skin cancer.

Isotopes can also enter the body by ingestion, inhalation, or injection. Their radiation effects then depend on their internal distribution, duration of retention in the body, energies, and rate of radioactive decay (half-life or half-value period). The problem is enormously complicated since isotopes have different and sometimes elaborate distribution patterns.

The definition "critical organ" has been assigned to that part of the body that is most vulnerable to a given isotope. The critical organ for plutonium, radium, strontium, and many other fission products is bone and the adjacent bone marrow. For soluble fission products (and also some forms of uranium), which will distribute in the entire body, the critical organs are the gonads, or sometimes the kidneys. For iodine the critical organ is the

TABLE XI.—*Maximum Permissible Concentration (MPC) of Some Radioisotopes*

Isotope	Chemical form	Critical organ	Microcuries in body
Tritium (Hydrogen-3)	water		2,000
Carbon-14	carbon dioxide		400
*Strontium-90	water soluble salt		40
		bone	4
Iodine-131	water soluble		50
		thyroid	0.7
Cesium-137	water soluble		30
†Radon-222	gas		
‡Radium-226	water soluble		0.2
		bone	0.1
Uranium	water soluble		0.2
		kidney	0.005
Plutonium-239	water soluble		0.4
		bone	0.04

*MPC in drinking water: 0.001 microcurie/litre.
†MPC in air: 0.00001 microcurie/litre.
‡MPC in drinking water: 0.0001 microcurie/litre.

thyroid gland. Insoluble airborne radioactive dust often deposits in the alveoli of lungs, while colloidal particles of very small size can reach the bone marrow, liver, or spleen. Table XI is an abbreviated list of the maximum permissible concentrations (U.S. recommendations) for man of some radioisotopes. (Maximum permissible concentration is the greatest amount of a radioisotope that can be accumulated in the body without producing noticeable damaging effects; compare with maximum permissible dose, which is applicable to radiation received from external sources.)

Since isotopes continuously deliver radiations to the surrounding tissue, one must distinguish between the effect of protracted exposure and single acute or periodically repeated exposures. For beta, gamma, and X radiations, utilizing split dose delivery, it has been found that up to about 60% of an acute radiation effect "disappears" within several hours; the body, therefore, is able to tolerate a greater total dose when the dose is protracted or when part of it is given at later times. For neutron and alpha radiation the recovery is less. (Neutrons are generally more effective than X rays: for acute effects, by a factor of 1 to 8; for long-term effects of chronic radiation, by a factor up to 35.) Studies of such repair processes are complicated by the fact that there is some dependence of the effects on the age of the individuals exposed.

Fallout is the deposition of airborne radioactive contamination on Earth. Radioisotopes may be produced naturally in the air by cosmic radiation or may enter the air from stack gases of atomic reactors following industrial accidents or from bombs or bomb tests. After 1954 bomb tests carried out by several nations produced fallout measurable on the surface of the entire world, arousing great attention and controversy with respect to its health and genetic effects. It is within the realm of practical feasibility to cover a significant portion of the Earth's surface with fallout in time of war. While much of the bomb hazard is due to blast waves and heat, the radiation dose from fission products could be so intense that only persons remaining in underground shelters for some weeks could hope to survive such an attack. Usually the most prominent isotopes in fallout are fission products; however, all materials exposed to nuclear blasts may become radioactive. A list of exposures to fallout isotopes is given in Table VII.

Several of the radioisotopes contained in fallout are especially hazardous because they remain radioactive for relatively long periods (have long half-lives). Cesium-137, strontium-90, and plutonium may be most important (see FALLOUT). On the ground, fallout material can cover external surfaces and foliage and later be washed into the soil, where plants incorporate strontium-90 along with the chemically similar calcium, and cesium-137 with potassium. Humans obtain these radioactive materials mostly from drinking water and from plant and animal foods, including milk. In the sea much of these materials can eventually lodge in the bodies or skeletons of fish and in plants near the coast.

Strontium-90 becomes concentrated in bone and remains there in steadily decreasing amounts for almost 30 years, producing local irradiation. Its actual concentration within the body is difficult to measure because of the softness of its rays. There is generally lower concentration of strontium-90 in man than in other animals or in plants or soil. Newborn babies, who have actively growing

BY COURTESY OF ARGONNE NATIONAL LABORATORY

WHOLE BODY COUNTING ROOM (THICK METAL WALL BETWEEN SUBJECT AND RECORDING APPARATUS CUT AWAY)

The scanning head (cylinder above model) can distinguish the whole spectrum of gamma-ray emitting radioisotopes to determine the radioisotopic content of the subject's body

bones, retain relatively greater amounts of strontium-90 than do older persons.

The most easily detectable fallout product in animals and in man is iodine-131; this isotope emits beta and gamma rays and is enriched about 100 times in the thyroid gland through selective accumulation. Because of its relatively short half-life (8 days), iodine-131 is probably not the most hazardous fallout isotope. If a large population, however, is affected by excessive amounts, radiations from this isotope could lead to metabolic disturbances and increased thyroid cancer incidence, especially in children.

Atomic power reactors discharge a mixture of radioactive gases into the atmosphere. Reactors are placed at sites where the atmospheric mixing and transport are such that the short-lived gases decay and are diluted before they can be inhaled in appreciable amounts by the population. The long-lived gaseous products are usually quoted in units of krypton-equivalent. When inhaled, krypton-85, a radioisotope of 10 years half-life (half the radioactivity will disappear in 10 years), is preferentially deposited in body fat. Projected krypton-equivalent concentrations from power reactors for the end of this century appear high, suggesting better containment of the gaseous products of reactors in the future (Table VIII).

Many fallout isotopes that reach the sea and inland waterways eventually end up in concentrated form in the bodies of waterborne animals and plants and become a source for concern when they are part of the food chain for man. Radioactive iodine, for example, has shown up in many fish and shellfish.

Methods that have been developed for biological protection from fallout extend from efforts for keeping isotopes out of the body to biochemical means for rapid elimination of isotopes from tissues. At times of atomic emergencies, airborne radioactive particles may be kept from the lungs by masks having suitable filters. Ingested isotopes may be prevented from being absorbed in the intestinal tract by certain mucoprotein substances that show great surface affinity for adsorption of strontium and other substances. In 1964 Canadian investigators demonstrated that sodium alginate prepared from the brown seaweed kelp is particularly useful in this regard. It is possible to remove virtually all radioactive strontium from cow's milk without affecting the essential nutritive components. Certain chelates, for example EDTA (ethylenediaminetetraacetic acid), will react with strontium and "cover" this atom. As a result, when EDTA is present in the blood, dep-

osition of strontium in bones is reduced (elimination of already deposited isotopes also is somewhat accelerated). Most chelating agents are not specific for strontium; unfortunately, they also chelate the closely related and important element calcium, an undesirable feature.

9. Cancer and Radiation.—The role of large doses of radiation in increasing the incidence of cancer and leukemia cannot be questioned—it has been demonstrated in all animal species tested thus far. Studies on animal populations have indicated that the onset of cancer can be delayed by many years following radiation exposure and that protracted radiation exposure is more carcinogenetic than single exposures. Initially, radiation may produce precancerous lesions in the cells of the body, but it may take some additional factors to turn those lesions into malignant tumours.

It is interesting to note that radiation-induced leukemia in certain strains of mice can later be propagated to other members of the mouse population by a virus factor. It appears that the role of radiation in this instance might be to activate a leukemia virus already present in mice.

Generally speaking, the increased cancer incidence in irradiated populations parallels radiation-induced aging and may be a manifestation of the older physiological age of the irradiated individuals. Studies of the origin of cancer point to a number of factors, including genetic, hormonal, and injurious factors (chemical, radiation, or virus), that usually act together to produce cancer. The great majority of cancer and leukemia cases in the Earth's population is probably not caused by radiation but by other agents.

There are some thousands of chemicals that can induce tumours, and even "inert" plastics, when imbedded in tissue, can cause cancer. Nevertheless, the following generalizations are true in most instances:

1. There is often a long delay between radiation exposure and the appearance of tumours (in human beings the delay may be many years).

2. Higher radiation doses usually lead to more tumours, and sooner, than do lower doses.

3. Tumours often arise from precancerous groups of cells, not necessarily from a single cell.

4. Densely ionizing radiation (*e.g.*, neutrons, alpha particles) are more effective in inducing cancer than lightly ionizing X or gamma rays.

The relationship of radiation to human cancer has been studied almost exclusively in persons who are exposed to high radiation doses. Cancer induction from radiation below the "permissible" exposure levels has not been identified. It is the task of health protection experts and special government agencies (*e.g.*, the U.S. Federal Radiation Council) to set the permissible radiation levels so that the risk for cancer induction is either negligible compared to other risks or at least tolerable in view of the beneficial effects of radiation to humanity.

The role of induction of leukemia in man at doses higher than 50 rads appears proportional to dose. Only acute leukemia and chronic myeloid leukemia seem to be induced. A number of such leukemias appeared among the survivors of Hiroshima and Nagasaki and in a special group of British patients who received large doses of radiation for the rheumatic condition of ankylosing spondylitis. From these data it appears that 1 rad induces 1.5 cases of leukemia per million individuals per year, or a total of 20 cases per rad per million. The incidence in children, exposed under 10 years of age, is about twice as high; the induction of acute lymphatic leukemia is particularly age dependent.

In addition to leukemia, other malignancies also are induced. After large doses of radiation the number of all induced cases combined appears to be about twice the number of leukemias. There are many questions to be settled in connection with these figures; among these are the problem of additivity of low daily doses, and whether or not cancers that have a high spontaneous incidence are also more prone to be induced by radiation.

The yield of thyroid carcinoma after external radiation is somewhat lower per rad than the yield of leukemia; and children are more sensitive than adults. When radiation is delivered by the radioactive isotope iodine-131, fewer carcinomas result than from external radiation. Radioiodine is an abundant fission product and is often used in medical diagnosis.

The human population carries a body burden of about 0.0001 microcurie of radium and has a natural incidence of four to seven bone sarcomas per million individuals per year. Radium, an alpha particle emitter, has somewhat similar chemical properties as calcium and it remains deposited in bone for many years. Some hundreds of individuals exist who have several microcuries in their bodies; these were radium-dial painters, or individuals who may have received radioactivity as a therapeutic measure (in the 1930s) for arthritis and other conditions. The incidence of bone tumours in this population appears to be higher when the body burden is more than 0.5 microcurie.

It has been known for some time that radium and uranium miners have a high incidence of lung tumours. Radioactivity can find its way to the lungs by inhalation of gas (radon) or of radioactive dust particles that may become lodged in the lungs. Since a single dust particle can give off significant local radiation, the radioactive dust content of the mines must be kept at a safe level. In the initiation of lung tumours, several factors interact: nonradioactive dust can cause silicosis and perhaps some cancer. Smoking and radioactive mine exposure cause more lung cancer than either of these factors singly.

10. Chromosome Aberrations and Radiation.—It has long been known that a major expression of radiation effect occurs in the form of chromosome aberrations. These have been studied in human cell cultures prepared from a variety of organs, and in leucocytes, or white blood cells. Chromosome aberrations at the rate of a few cases per thousand cells can be found in human blood from very low doses of radiation of only a few rads, and some of these aberrations persist in the body for several years. With the establishment of accurate dose effect relationships, the frequency of certain types of aberrations can give information on the degree of radiation exposure of individuals.

In addition to causing chromosome breaks and rejoinings, radiation can also produce aneuploidy (abnormal number of chromosomes in cells) and polyploidy (multiple chromosome numbers).

Tumour cells in many forms of cancer also carry chromosome aberrations, and in advanced forms of cancer there is often extensive fragmentation and regrouping of chromosomes. Whether radiation-induced chromosome breaks cause cancer or are a consequence of cancer is not known with certainty.

There is only one type of human neoplasm, chronic granulocytic leukemia, where a specific chromosome abnormality is seen in over half of the cases. Chromosome no. 21, the "Philadelphia" chromosome, named after the city where it was discovered, lacks about one-half of its longer arm. Other conditions where specific chromosome abnormalities are seen include Waldenström's macroglobulinemia, Burkitt's lymphoma, and multiple myeloma. The study of chromosome aberrations in human cells and tissues is extremely tedious because of the smallness of chromosomes and the need to carefully observe several thousand in each individual case. The use of computers may help to differentiate normal from abnormal patterns.

C. Effects of Hertzian Waves, Infrared Rays

1. Hertzian Waves.—The effects of Hertzian waves (electromagnetic waves, radio waves, and microwaves or radar waves) and of infrared rays usually are regarded as equivalent to the effect produced by heating. The longer radio waves induce chiefly thermal agitation of molecules and excitation of molecular rotations, while infrared rays excite vibrational modes of large molecules and release fluorescent emission as well as heat. Both types of radiation are preferentially absorbed by fats containing unsaturated carbon chains.

Nikola Tesla in 1891 was the first to record the fact that heat production resulted from bombardment of tissue with high-frequency alternating current (wavelengths somewhat longer than the longest radio waves) and to point out the possibility of its utilization for medical purposes. At the same time, J. A. d'Arsonval, the French physicist, using the same current, began to experiment on animals and human beings. In 1898 high-frequency current to produce heat within the organism was used. To this form of treatment K. F. Nagelschmidt, a German physician, in 1909 applied the term "diathermy." This method of internal heating is beneficial for relieving muscle soreness and sprain. Diathermy can be harmful, however, if so much internal heat is given that the normal cells of the body suffer irreversible damage. Since man has heat receptors primarily in his skin, he cannot be forewarned by pain when he gets a deep burn from diathermy. Sensitive regions easily damaged by diathermy are those having reduced blood circulation; e.g., bone or the lens of the eye. Cataracts of the eye lens have been produced in animals by microwave radiation applied in sufficient intensity to cause thermal denaturation of the lens protein.

Recently, microwave ovens have found widespread use in commercial kitchens and some homes. These can heat and cook very rapidly and if used properly constitute no hazard to operators. In the radio-television industry and in the radar division of the military, persons are sometimes exposed to high densities of microwave radiation. The hazard is particularly pronounced with exposure to masers, capable of generating very high intensities of microwaves (e.g., carbon dioxide masers). The biological effects depend on the absorbency of tissues. At frequencies higher than 150 megahertz significant absorption takes place. The lens of the human eye is most susceptible to frequencies around 3,000 megahertz, which can produce cataracts. At still higher frequencies, microwaves interact with superficial tissues and skin, in much the same manner as infrared rays.

Acute effects of microwaves become significant if a considerable temperature rise occurs. Cells and tissues eventually die at temperatures of about 43° C (109° F). Microwave heating is minimized if the heat that results from energy absorption is dissipated by radiation, evaporation, and heat conduction. Normally one-hundredth of a watt (10 milliwatts) can be so dissipated, and this power limit generally has been set as the permissible dose. Studies with animals have indicated that, below the permissible levels, there are negligible effects to various organ systems. Microwaves or heat applied to testes decrease the viability of sperm. This effect, however, is not significant at the "safe" levels.

Some investigators in the Soviet Union have documented a variety of "nonthermal" effects of microwaves and recommend about 1,000 times lower safe occupational dose levels than are in force in the United States. Most prominent among the nonthermal effects appears to be those on the nervous system. These have resulted in untimely tiring, excitability, and insomnia registered by persons handling high-frequency radio equipment. Nonthermal effects have been observed on the electroencephalogram of rabbits. These may be due to changes in the properties of neural membranes, or to denaturation of macromolecules.

The heating effect of high-frequency waves and currents has had some use in surgery. The first surgical use of short waves (8 megacycles) was made in destroying a patient's tonsils without the necessity of giving an anesthetic. This procedure produces cutting by heat coagulation of tissue without producing bleeding. It has been used to cut certain structures (e.g., the dura membranes) in brain surgery and in minor skin operations. Higher-frequency electromagnetic waves (about 10 megahertz) are also used in brain surgery for producing "heat lesions" in the treatment of Parkinson's disease and cerebral palsy. Such heat lesions produced in certain parts of the brain may temporarily relieve the tremors accompanying these diseases. (For laser therapy, see below.)

2. Infrared Rays.—An important part of solar energy reaches the Earth in the form of infrared rays. Absorption and emission by the human body of these rays plays an important part in temperature exchange and regulation of the human body. Principles of infrared emission and absorption must be considered in the design of air conditioning and of clothing.

Overdosage of infrared radiation, usually resulting from direct exposure to a hot object (including heating lamps) or flame, can cause severe burns ("flame burns"). While infrared exposure is a hazard near any fire, it is particularly dangerous in the course of atomic chain reactions. In the course of an atomic detonation a brief but very intense emission of infrared occurs, together with visible and ultraviolet light emitted from the fireball ("flash burns"). Of the total energy of nuclear explosion, as much as one-third may be in the form of thermal radiation, moving with the velocity of light (186,000 mi. per sec.). The rays will arrive almost instantaneously at regions removed from the source by only a few miles. Smoke or fog can effectively scatter or absorb the infrared components, and even thin clothing can greatly reduce the severity of burn effects. *See also* BURNS.

D. EFFECTS OF VISIBLE AND ULTRAVIOLET LIGHT

Life could not exist on Earth without light from the sun. Plants utilize the energy of the sun's rays in the process of photosynthesis to produce carbohydrates and proteins, which serve as basic organic sources of food and energy for animals. Light is a powerful regulating influence on many biological systems (*see* ANIMAL BEHAVIOUR: *Sensory Capacities of Animals;* PLANTS AND PLANT SCIENCE: *Plant Movements: Tropisms;* PHOTOPERIODISM; PHOTOSYNTHESIS). Most of the strong ultraviolet rays of the sun, which are hazardous, are effectively absorbed by the upper atmosphere. At high altitudes and near the Equator the ultraviolet intensity is greater than at sea level or at northern latitudes.

Very-short-wave ultraviolet light, below 2,200 angstroms (Å; 1 Å = 1/10,000,000 mm.), is highly toxic for cells; in the intermediate range the greatest killing effectiveness on cells is at about 2,600 Å. The nucleic acids of the cell, of which the genetic material is composed, strongly absorb rays in this region. This wavelength, easily available in mercury vapour, xenon, or hydrogen arc lamps, has great effectiveness for germicidal purification of the air.

Since penetration of visible and ultraviolet light in body tissues is small, only the effects of light on skin and on the visual apparatus are of consequence. When incident light exerts its action on the skin without additional external predisposing factors, scientists speak of intrinsic action. In contrast, a number of chemical or biological agents may condition the skin for action of light; these latter phenomena are grouped under photodynamic action. Visible light, when administered following lethal doses of ultraviolet, is capable of causing recovery of the cells exposed. This phenomenon, termed "photorecovery," has led to the discovery of enzyme systems capable of restoring damaged nucleic acids in genes to their normal form. It is probable that photorecovery mechanisms are continually operative in some plants exposed to direct action of sunlight.

The surface of the Earth is protected from the lethal ultraviolet rays of the sun by the top layers of the atmosphere, which absorb far ultraviolet, and by ozone molecules at the stratosphere, which absorb most of the near ultraviolet. Even so, it is believed that an enzymatic mechanism operating in the skin cells of individuals continually repairs the damage caused by ultraviolet to the nucleic acids of the genes.

There is some evidence to indicate that not only overall light intensity but spectral compositions also have differential effects on organisms. For example, in pumpkins red light favours the production of pistillate flowers and blue light leads to development of staminate flowers. The ratio of females to males in guppies is increased by red light. Red light also appears to accelerate the rate of proliferation of some tumours in special strains of mice. The intensity of incident light has an influence on the development of light-sensing organs: the eyes of primates reared in complete darkness are much retarded in development.

1. Intrinsic Action.—Light is essential to man because of its biosynthetic action. Ultraviolet light induces the conversion of ergosterol and other vitamin precursors present in normal skin to vitamin D, an essential factor for normal calcium deposition in growing bones. While some ultraviolet light appears desirable for formation of vitamin D, an excess amount is deleterious. Man has a delicate adaptive mechanism that regulates light exposure of the more sensitive deeper layers of his skin. The transmission of light depends on the thickness of the upper layers of the skin and on the degree of skin pigmentation. All persons except albinos are born with varying amounts of melanin pigment in their skins. Exposure to light further enhances the pigmentation already present and can induce production of new pigment granules. N. R. Finsen of Denmark around 1900 realized the therapeutic possibilities of sunlight and ultraviolet light. He was an exponent of the idea that exposure of the whole body to sunlight promotes health.

The French physician J. M. Charcot in 1858 was the first to recognize that large doses of ultraviolet radiation caused "sunburn." The wavelength of about 2,800 Å is most effective. It induces reddening and swelling of the skin (due to dilation of the blood vessels), usually accompanied by pain. In the course of recovery, epidermal cells are proliferated, melanin is secreted, and the outer corneal layer of dead cells is thickened.

In 1928 it was first shown clearly that prolonged or repeated exposure to ultraviolet light leads to the delayed development of skin cancer. The fact that ultraviolet light, like X radiation, is mutagenic (induces mutations) may explain its ability to cause skin cancer, but the detailed mechanism of cancer induction is not yet completely understood. There seems very little doubt, however, that skin cancer in man is in some cases correlated with prolonged exposure to large doses of sunlight. Among dark-skinned persons who are protected by rich melanin formation and thickened corneal structure of the skin, skin cancer is several times less frequent than it is among whites living at the same latitude.

2. Photodynamic Action.—There are a number of diseases in man and animals in which light sensitivity is involved; for example, hydroa, which manifests itself in blisters on parts of the body exposed to sunlight. It has been suggested that this disease is due to a light-sensitive porphyrin compound found in the blood.

Actually there are many organic substances and various materials of biological origin that make cells sensitive to light. When eosin is added to a suspension of human red blood corpuscles exposed to light, the red corpuscles will break up in a process named hemolysis. Other typical photodynamic substances are rose bengal, hematoporphyrin, and phyllo-erythrin—all are dyes capable of fluorescence. Their toxicity manifests itself only in the presence of light and oxygen.

Some diseases in domestic animals result from ingestion of plants having photodynamic pigments. For example, St. Johnswort's disease is caused by the plant *Hypericum*. Fagopyrism results from eating buckwheat. In geeldikopp (yellow thick head) the photodynamic agent is produced in the animal's own intestinal tract from chlorophyll derived from plants. In humans the heritable condition of porphyria frequently is associated with light sensitivity, as are a number of somewhat ill-defined dermatological conditions that result from exposure to sunlight. The recessively inherited rare disease xeroderma pigmentosum also is associated with light exposure; it usually results in death at an early age from tumours of the skin that develop on exposed areas. The cells of such individuals possess a serious genetic defect: they lack the ability to repair nucleic acid lesions caused by ultraviolet light. Certain drugs (*e.g.*, sulfanilamide) sensitize some persons to sunlight. Many cases are known in which ingestion of or skin contact with a photodynamic substance was followed by increased light sensitivity.

3. Effects on Development and Biological Rhythms.—In addition to its photosynthetic effect, light exerts an influence on growth and spatial orientation of plants. This phototropism is associated with yellow pigments and is particularly marked in blue light. The presence of illumination is a profound modifier of the cellular activities in plants as well. For example, while some species of blue-green algae carry out photosynthesis in the presence of light, they do not undergo cell division.

Diffuse sensitivity to light exists also in several phyla of animals. Many protozoans react to light. Chameleons, frogs, and octopuses change colour under the influence of light. Such changes are ascribed to special organs known as chromatophores, which are under the influence of the nervous system or endocrine system. The breeding habits and migration of some birds are set in motion by small consecutive changes in the daily cycle of light.

Light is an important controlling agent of recurrent daily physiological alterations (circadian rhythms) in many animals and probably man (see RHYTHMS, BIOLOGICAL). Lighting cycles have been shown to be important in regulating several types of endocrine function: the daily variation in light intensity keeps the secretion of adrenal steroids in synchrony; the annual breeding cycles in many mammals and birds appears to be regulated by light. Ambient light somehow influences the secretions of a tiny gland, the pineal body, located near the cerebellum. The pineal body, under the action of enzymes, produces melanotonin, which in higher concentrations slows down the estrus cycle; low levels of melanotonin, caused by exposure of animals to light, accelerates estrus. It is believed that light stimulates the retina and information is then transmitted by sympathetic nerves to the pineal body.

4. Effects on the Eyes.—The wavelength of light that produces sunburn can also cause inflammation of the cornea of the eye. This is what occurs in "snow blindness" or after exposure to strong ultraviolet light sources. Unusual sensitivities have been reported. Ultraviolet light, like infrared or penetrating radiations, can also cause cataract of the eye lens, a condition characterized by denatured protein in the fibrous cells forming the lens. The retina usually is not reached by ultraviolet light, but large doses of visible and infrared can irreversibly bleach the visual pigments, as in "sun blindness." Numerous pathological conditions of the eye are accompanied by abnormal light sensitivity and pain, photophobia. The pain appears to be associated with reflex movements of the iris and reflex dilation of the blood vessels of the conjunctiva. Workers exposed to ultraviolet light sources or to atomic flashes should wear protective glasses.

E. EFFECTS OF LASERS

Masers and lasers are devices capable of generating exceedingly intense microwave and light beams that travel in narrow beams. These devices have made many applications possible. Laser beams can carry radio broadcasts, and made possible the refined studies of the surface of the moon. They also have potentially useful applications in biology and medicine. Table XII gives some pertinent properties.

TABLE XII.—*Selected Properties of Some Lasers*

	Type	Mode	Wavelength*
Solid state	ruby (chromium doped)	pulsed	6,943 Å red
	neodymium (glass)	pulsed	10,600 Å infrared
Gas	argon	continuous	4,545 to 5,145 Å yellow-green
	helium-neon	continuous	6,328 Å red
	carbon dioxide	continuous	106 microns microwave
	nitrogen	pulsed	2,300 to 4,000 Å ultraviolet

*In Angstrom (Å) units.

The highly intense laser beam can instantly vaporize the surface of a target. This has led to its application in research as well as to surgery. The laser microprobe is used for microanalysis of surface composition. Laser beams have been found to have a selective effect on cellular organelles: those that absorb light of the wavelength of the beam are destroyed, whereas transparent parts of the cells remain unaffected. Organelles such as mitochondria, responsible for cell respiration, or chloroplasts, involved in plant-cell photosynthesis, can thus be separately studied. The use of special dyes can alter laser action. The availability of high pulse intensity laser beams is also revolutionizing medical photography and microscopy. It is becoming possible to photograph microaction in a very small fraction of a second and to use the relatively new technique of holography for image synthesis.

It was found that, at the appropriate intensity, initial local thermal effects of a laser beam are followed by formation of scar tissue. This property is used in microsurgery of the eye, particularly for treating retinal detachment. Since light can be focused to a small spot on the retina, damage to lens and cornea can often be avoided; vascular tumours and retinoblastomas also have been treated. In such procedures care must be taken to avoid hemorrhage; the nature and extent of scars and the hazard for developing cataract must also be considered.

Lasers have been used in investigative therapy for a number of conditions of the skin, including hemangiomas and various types of skin cancer. The cells of malignant melanoma tumours carry a dark pigment, which it is believed might selectively absorb laser wavelength and thereby destroy the cell. Nerve cells are more sensitive to laser beams than are a variety of the supporting cells, suggesting neurosurgical applications. Laser treatment of the surface of teeth may have an eventual role in the control of caries.

See also references under "Radiation: Biological Effects" in the Index.

BIBLIOGRAPHY.—*Ionizing Radiation:* O. Glasser, *Wilhelm Conrad Röntgen and the Early History of the Roentgen Rays* (1934); P. Brown, *American Martyrs to Science Through the Roentgen Rays* (1936); D. E. Lea, *Actions of Radiations on Living Cells* (1947); A. Hollaender (ed.), *Radiation Biology,* 3 vol. (1954–56); M. Errera and A. Forssberg (eds.), *Mechanisms in Radiobiology,* vol. i and ii (1961); S. Glasstone (ed.), *The Effects of Nuclear Weapons,* U.S. Atomic Energy Commission (1957); K. Z. Morgan, "Permissible Exposure to Ionizing Radiation," *Science,* 139:565–571 (1963); W. D. Claus (ed.), *Radiation Biology and Medicine* (1958); E. Teller and A. L. Latter, *Our Nuclear Future* (1958); Hearings of the Joint Committee on Atomic Energy, U.S. Congress (1957 and 1969); N. N. Klemparskaya et al., *Problems of Infection, Immunity and Allergy in Acute Radiation Diseases,* trans. by Lydia Venters (1961); C. A. Leone (ed.), *International Symposium on the Effects of Ionizing Radiations on Immune Processes* (1962); *Report of the United Nations Scientific Committee on the Effects of Atomic Radiation,* UN General Assembly Official Records, 13th session, suppl. no. 17 (1958), and 24th session, suppl. no. 13 (1969); U.S. Department of Commerce, "Safety Regulations by the National Committee of Radiation Protection," National Bureau of Standards Handbooks 41, 47–61, 63, 69; *Atoms for Peace Manual,* presented by Alexander Wiley in U.S. Senate (1955); C. W. Shilling (ed.), *Atomic Energy Encyclopedia in the Life Sciences* (1964); J. F. Loutit, *Irradiation of Mice and Men* (1962); E. Cronkite and V. Bond, *Radiation Injury in Man* (1960); B. Wallace and T. Dobzhansky, *Radiations, Genes, and Man* (1959); World Health Organization, *Effect of Radiation on Human Heredity* (1957); H. Blatz (ed.), *Radiation Hygiene Handbook* (1959); E. L. Saenger (ed.), *Medical Aspects of Radiation Accidents,* U.S. Atomic Energy Commission (1963); T. J. Haley and R. S. Snider (eds.), *Response of the Nervous System to Ionizing Radiation* (1962 and 1964); J. F. Thomson, *Radiation Protection in Mammals* (1962); J. M. Fowler, *Fallout* (1960); F. McLean and A. M. Budy, *Radiation, Isotopes, and Bone* (1964); W. and L. Taliaferro and B. N. Jaroslow, *Radiation and Immune Mechanisms* (1964); G. Tievsky, *Ionizing Radiation* (1962); J. H. Lawrence, B. Manowitz, and B. Loeb, *Radioisotopes and Radiation* (1964); J. C. Bugher, J. Coursaget, and J. F. Loutit (eds.), *Biological Sciences,* vol. i, *Progress in Nuclear Energy* (1956–); D. S. Grosch, *Biological Effects of Radiations* (1965); L. H. Lanzl, J. H. Pingel, and J. H. Rust (eds.), *Radiation Accidents and Emergencies in Medicine, Research, and Industry* (1965); L. G. Augenstein, R. Mason, and H. Quastler (eds.), *Advances in Radiation Biology,* vol. i (1964–); U.S. Department of Health, Education, and Welfare, *Radiological Health Data and Reports* (1969); *Reports* of the International Commission on Radiological Protection (1969); F. E. Lundin, *et al.,* "Mortality of Uranium Miners," *Health Physics,* 16:571 (1969); "Population Dose from X-Rays, U.S. 1964," U.S. Public Health Service Publication no. 2001 (1969); H. Blatz, *Introduction to Radiological Health* (1964); A. C. Upton, *Radiation Injury* (1969); D. J. Kimeldorf and E. L. Hunt, *Ionizing Radiation, Neural Function and Behavior* (1965); D. W. Bekkum, *Radiation Immunology* (1967).

Hertzian Waves, Infrared Rays, and Visible and Ultraviolet Light: H. P. Schwan and K. Li, "Hazards Due to Total Body Irradiation by Radar," *Proc. of I. R. E.,* 44:1572–81 (1956); E. L. Dobson and S. F. Warner, "Factors Concerned in the Early Stages of Thermal Shock," *Circulation Research,* 5:69–74 (1957); A. Hollaender (ed.), *Radiation Biology,* vol. ii, *Ultraviolet and Related Radiations,* vol. iii, *Visible and Near Visible Light* (1956); H. F. Blum, "The Physiological Effects of Sunlight on Man," *Physiol. Rev.,* 25:483–530 (1945), and *Photodynamic Action and Diseases Caused by Light* (1941); A. C. Giese, *Photophysiology,* vol. i and ii (1964); H. Whipple, "Photoneuro Endocrine Effects in Circadian Systems," *Ann. N.Y. Acad. Sci.,* vol. 117 (1964); S. Fine and E. Klein, "Biological Effects of Laser Radiations," *Advances Biol. Med. Phys.,* vol. 10 (1965); L. Goldman, *Biomedical Aspects of the Laser* (1967). (C. A. T.)

RADIATION BALANCE OF THE EARTH: *see* METEOROLOGY: *Solar and Terrestrial Radiation: Heat-Balance and the Field of Temperature of the Atmosphere.*

RADIC, STJEPAN (1871–1928), Croatian peasant leader and a firm advocate of self-government for his country, was born on July 11, 1871, at Trebarjevo. Impulsive and dynamic, he was in trouble for his nationalist outbursts while still a student at Zagreb. After travels in Bohemia and Russia and studies in political science in Paris, he worked as a journalist and became editor of the Zagreb newspaper *Hrvatska Misao* in 1902. With his brother Ante, he organized the Croatian Peasant Party in 1904. This party advocated Slav solidarity and the predominance of the peasantry in Croatian politics, claiming that the peasantry preserved the national individuality through its numerical and economic strength and its cultural and moral values.

In March 1918, having ceased to believe in a federalist reorganization of Austro-Hungary, Radic began to cooperate actively with the National Council in Zagreb for the establishment of a Yugoslav union (*see* YUGOSLAVIA: *History*). Yet he was against hasty unification and demanded equal rights for Croats and Serbs and the recognition of Croatia's traditional autonomy. Disagreement with the Belgrade regime led to his imprisonment in 1919–20. In the general election of 1920 the majority of the Croats voted for his party, but the only result for him was a long period of sterile opposition, during which his party's boycott of parliamentary proceedings enabled Nikola Pasic in 1921 to give the first Yugoslav constitution a centralist and unitary character. In July 1923 Radic went to Paris, London, and Moscow to seek support for a Croatian peasant republic. Greatly disappointed by the indifference of the Western powers, he returned to Zagreb in August 1924 and was imprisoned. In March 1925, however, his nephew Pavle Radic effected a reconciliation with the government; and Radic himself was released in July. Accepting the constitution, he entered the government as minister of education in November 1925, but returned to opposition in 1927. Then, with Svetozar Pribicevic, a Serbian Democratic leader, he formed the peasant-democratic alliance which demanded a federalist reorganization of Yugoslavia. During a heated debate in the national assembly on June 20, 1928, the Serbian deputy Punisa Racic shot Radic and several of his political friends. Radic died of his wounds on Aug. 8, 1928.   (A. S. Pa.)

RADICAL, one who desires extreme change of part or all of the social order. The word (Lat. *radix,* "root") was first used in a political sense in England, and its introduction is generally ascribed to Charles James Fox, who in 1797 declared for a "radical reform" consisting of a drastic expansion of the franchise to the point of universal manhood suffrage. The term radical thereafter began to be used as a general term covering all those who supported the movement for parliamentary reform. After the passage of the Reform Act of 1832, which extended the suffrage only to part of the middle class, a group of Radicals allied with the Whig faction in Parliament continued to press for an extension of the vote to include even the working class. When the Reform Act of 1867 further widened suffrage, the Radicals, notably in London and Birmingham, took the lead in organizing the new voters, helping to transform the Whig parliamentary faction into the Liberal Party of the later Victorian era. Because of their efforts on behalf of the working-class vote the Radicals earned the loyalty of the trade unions; from 1874 to 1892 every trade unionist who sat in Parliament regarded himself as a Radical.

In France before 1848, the term radical designated a republican or supporter of universal manhood suffrage; the open advocacy of republicanism being technically illegal, republicans usually called themselves radicals. After 1869, a self-styled Radical faction led by Georges Clemenceau began to drift away from the moderate democratic-republicanism of Léon Gambetta. These Radicals regarded themselves as the true heirs of the French Revolutionary tradition. In 1881 at Montmartre they adopted a platform calling for a wide range of social reforms, and at the turn of the century the Radical-Socialist Party (*q.v.*) was formed.

The English Radicals of the 19th century were influenced by philosophical ideas assuming that men are able to control their social environment by collective action, a position held by the so-called philosophical radicals. These assumptions also underlying Marxist theories of social reform, in time the label "radical" was affixed to Marxists and other advocates of violent social change, thus becoming inapplicable to the gradualist reformers.

In the United States, although the term is usually one of opprobrium, this was not always true in the postdepression years of the 1930s; and it is generally not true in less stable, less prosperous societies. In popular U.S. usage, radicalism stands for political extremism of any variety, of the left or right; Communism serves as an example of the former, Fascism of the latter. The term has more commonly been applied to the left, but the expression "the radical right" came to be used commonly in the U.S. Various youth movements in the U.S., widely labeled as radical, were associated with denunciation of basic social and political values. *See* also LIBERALISM; MARXISM; NIHILISM; SOCIALISM; ANARCHISM; COMMUNISM; CONSERVATISM.

For a discussion of philosophical radicalism *see* Elie Halévy, *La Formation du radicalisme philosophique,* 3 vol. (1900–03; Eng. trans., *The Growth of Philosophical Radicalism,* 1928).   (S. Mr.; H. M. S.)

RADICAL-SOCIALIST PARTY (PARTI RÉPUBLICAIN RADICAL ET RADICAL-SOCIALISTE; commonly called the RADICALS), one of the major political parties of modern France. The party's title is misleading, because there never was anything socialist in its program, and its radicalism revealed itself only in its struggle against the Roman Catholic Church; nevertheless, in the peculiar atmosphere of French politics, this label was electorally useful. Founded in 1901 on the reunion of the Radical-Socialists with the Radicals from whom they had broken away, this party dominated the Third Republic in the 20th century as the old Radicals had done in the 19th (*see* FRANCE: *History*). The party was loosely organized and drew its funds from a small number of subscriptions, being primarily representative of sectional interests. Its power was founded on the influence of local personalities (mayors and departmental councilors), of various committees (notably those of Freemasonry), and of provincial newspapers with large circulations. Its supporters were mainly people of the urban middle class (*petit bourgeois* rather than business magnates), professional men (lawyers, doctors, and teachers), farmers, and craftsmen. It was strongest around Lyons and in the south of France.

Radical ideology comprised (1) loyalty to the principles of the Revolution of 1789, with ready use of Jacobin slogans; (2) rationalism and anticlericalism; and (3) the systematic protection of group interests, particularly those of small tradesmen, small businesses, people with small private incomes, and the lower ranks of the civil service. Albert Thibaudet makes a distinction between the authoritarian, patriotic radicalism of such men as Clemenceau and the individualist radicalism of "the citizen against the ruling powers"—as propounded, for instance, in Alain's *Éléments d'une doctrine radicale.*

Men of the centre, between the right and the Socialists, the Radicals were essentially the governing party of the Third Republic. A Radical, Édouard Daladier, was premier at the time of the Munich Agreement (1938) and at the outbreak of World War II (1939). Immediately after that war the party seemed just a relic of a past age; and in the elections of October 1945, under a form of proportional representation, the Radicals won only 6.8% of the votes and 35 seats, whereas in 1936, under a single-member majority system of election, they had won 14.6% and 116.

During the next 15 years the party's influence rose temporarily and then fell. Its opposition to "three-party rule" by Communists, Socialists, and Christian Democrats (MRP) and, after the Communists had left the government in 1947, its holding of the balance between the parties enabled it to restore its fortunes (1945–53). The party itself was reconstituted, its newspaper propaganda revived, and public confidence in it recovered. Several coalition governments were formed under Radical leaders (René Mayer, Henri Queuille, André Marie); and in the elections of 1951 the Radicals won 72 seats. Next followed the attempt (1953–56) by Pierre Mendès-France to consolidate the party, to attract more youth into it, and to make its propaganda more cogent (*e.g.,* in the newspaper *L'Express*), identifying it moreover with a progressive economic policy and with a liberal attitude toward the countries of the French union. Mendès-France, however, was only partially successful in the elections of January 1956 and was very adversely criticized by other Radicals, so that he had eventually to retire from leadership of the party. The parliamentary group splintered, and divisions within the party became more acute than ever before. Under the constitution of the Fifth Republic (1958) this once-powerful party was overshadowed by the Gaullists. *See* FRANCE: *Administration and Social Conditions.*   (J. Td.)

RADIN, PAUL (1883–1959), U.S.-Canadian anthropologist who contributed influential ethnohistorical analyses in several fields, was born April 2, 1883, in Poland and was taken to the

U.S. as an infant. He was significantly influenced during his university years by James Harvey Robinson and Franz Boas. After work at the College of the City of New York, he received the Ph.D. in anthropology at Columbia University.

Radin was primarily interested in the folklore, religion, and language of primitive peoples, contributing such works as *The Winnebago Tribe* (1915–16) and *Primitive Man as Philosopher* (1927). His view of anthropology as a branch of history and his emphasis on primary documentation are reflected in *The Road of Life and Death* (1945), *Culture of the Winnebago: as Described by Themselves* (1949), as well as in his major critical-theoretical work, *Method and Theory of Ethnology* (1933). Radin pioneered in what later became important fields of anthropology (culture-personality studies, cultural contact) and in the use of autobiographical documents; see, *e.g.*, *The Autobiography of a Winnebago Indian* (1920), republished as *Crashing Thunder* (1926). From the 1930s on, a growing interest in Marxian sociology led him to a reinterpretation of some of his earlier formulations; see *Primitive Religion* (1937; reprinted 1964).

Though not primarily active as a teacher, Radin at various times taught at the University of California, the University of Chicago, Cambridge University, Kenyon College, Gambier, O., and Brandeis University, Waltham, Mass. For many years he was field ethnologist for the geological survey of Canada. Radin died Feb. 21, 1959. (A. M. H.)

RADIO, the radiation and detection of signals propagated through space as electromagnetic waves to convey information. Radio is one of the chief branches of telecommunication. It embraces telegraphy, telephony, and television without wires, and radar.

Wireless was the original term for radio and is still widely used in Great Britain. The word radiotelegraphy was substituted generally for wireless telegraphy (and similar terms in other languages) following international conferences on radio communication held in Berlin, Ger., in 1903 and 1906.

This article, in the sections outlined below, describes the historical development of radio technology and the theories of radio wave propagation. Basic material on the nature and behaviour of radio waves may be found in ELECTROMAGNETIC WAVES. The growth of the industry that produces scheduled programs of entertainment, news, and educational material is traced in BROADCASTING, while the article TELEVISION describes the technical aspects of that subject as well as the production of programs. Additional material on telecommunication may be found in the articles RADIO RECEIVER; TELEGRAPH; TELEPHONE; and FACSIMILE TRANSMISSION. Examples of radio aids to navigation are given in the article NAVIGATION. The following article is divided into these sections:

I. Forms of Radio Communication
II. Early History
  1. Experiments by Hertz
  2. The Coherer-Decoherer
  3. Guglielmo Marconi
III. Maritime Wireless and the Vacuum Tube
  1. Maritime Wireless
  2. Spread of Commercial Wireless Telegraphy
  3. Transoceanic Operation
  4. Improvements in Transmitters
  5. Improvements in Receivers
  6. The Electron Tube
  7. Developments During World War I
  8. Radiotelephony
IV. The Rise of Broadcasting
  1. Improvements in Transmitters
  2. Amateur Radio
  3. Commercial Shortwave Radio
V. Spectrum Expansion and Electronics
  1. Electronics
  2. Marine Radiotelephony
  3. Commercial Radiotelephony
  4. Aviation Radio
  5. Mobile Radio
  6. Advances in Techniques
VI. Pulse Techniques and Television
  1. Modulation
  2. Television

VII. Microwaves and Remote Control
  1. Microwaves
  2. Extremely High Frequencies (EHF)
  3. Radiotelemetry for Missiles, Satellites, and Space Vehicles
VIII. Factors Affecting Radio Performance
  1. Mechanism of Propagation
  2. Propagation Variables
  3. Interference
  4. Signal-to-Noise Relationships
  5. Radio Noise
IX. Use of the Radio-Frequency Spectrum
  1. Frequency Sharing
  2. Modulations, Bandwidths, and Tolerances
  3. Division of the Spectrum
  4. Radio Spectrum Management

I. FORMS OF RADIO COMMUNICATION

Any form of telecommunication by radio requires a transmitter to furnish the energy for transmission; an antenna or aerial from which the energy may be propagated; the medium of propagation, which is the same as that pervading free space outside the earth's atmosphere, although its electrical transmission properties are modified by the atmosphere and the proximity and character of the earth's surface; and, finally, the receiver. In the receiver, the weak signal is resonated (tuned), amplified, and demodulated (detected) to recover the original signal, which is reproduced by a teletype printer, loudspeaker, or television picture tube. The highest rate of information reproduction is about 10 bits per second for high-speed code, 10,000 bits for high-fidelity sound, and 10,000,000 bits for high-definition television. (A bit, or binary digit, is the binary unit of information, capable of expressing such quantities as 0, 1; yes, no; off, on; etc. *See* INFORMATION THEORY.)

These basic requirements are essentially the same for both radiotelegraphy and radiotelephony. The various forms of telecommunication are distinguished by the way that the continuous radio-frequency power generated in the transmitter (usually called the carrier wave) is interrupted or varied (that is, modulated) from moment to moment. In radiotelephony the primary controls to modulate the carrier in the transmitter are directly responsive to the human voice or to music and other sounds. In radiotelegraphy the elemental modulation is led to the transmitter in the form of a signal unit, or pulse of power, successive combinations of which, in various time patterns and usually in opposite senses (such as on-off, present-absent, plus-minus, high-low, mark-space), are given either arbitrary language code meanings or various functions in the remote interconnection of machines. In television two simultaneous (multiplexed) modulations are employed. One modulation is radiotelephonic (audio) and the other consists of signals (video) representing a range of light values of successive elemental areas into which a scene can be divided by a process called scanning. In basic radar the transmitter is pulse-modulated in a continuous manner, but without information. The informational content of radar is supplied as modulation en route at a point or points of reflection.

The modern concept of radiotelegraphy does not confine it to the system of reducing messages to Morse code signals for the purpose of transmitting and transcribing them for delivery as telegrams, or even to the system of accomplishing the same end by use of remotely actuated printing telegraph machines, important though both systems are to the worldwide radiotelegraph business. In modern usage, all information to be conveyed—words to be typed, a speech to be reproduced, a song to be sung, a switch to be operated, a card to be punched, a piece of Linotype text to be set, a television scene to be displayed, or a calculating machine to be operated—can be reduced to a stream or succession of elemental units in a time domain. Radio telecommunication concerns itself with the collecting and processing of such information, if necessary its compression through codification, its propagation without wires, its detection, reexpansion, or decodification, and, finally, its dissemination and utilization for purposes of intelligence or control. Radiotelegraphy concerns itself with that portion of the radio telecommunication product which is a matter of record (hence often called record communication) or control, as distinguished from radiotelephony, radio broadcasting, and television, in all of which the information is only momentarily made audible or visible. Generally speaking, the pulse-transmission techniques associated with radiolocation (radar), radio navigation (loran), and radio direction-finding are considered specialized branches of radiotelegraphy.

II. EARLY HISTORY

James Clerk Maxwell was the first scientist to foresee the propagation in space of electromagnetic energy from waves originating in wires and the first to show mathematically the laws of the transfer of such energy through space at the speed of light. Maxwell built upon and united the expressions of earlier mathematicians and physicists in his own equations expressing the relationship of electromagnetic forces within, and at the boundaries between, conductors and dielectrics.

In 1845 Michael Faraday was first to bridge the existing gap between light and electricity by observing the phenomenon of magnetic gyration. When he passed a beam of polarized light through transparent glass, application of a strong magnetic field was capable of rotating the axis of polarization of the light. Faraday's experiment led him to conclude, with Thomas Young, that light waves represent transverse vibrations.

Maxwell's equations are given with their derivatives and implications and discussed at length in the articles ELECTRICITY: *Electromagnetic Waves*; ELECTROMAGNETIC WAVES: *Maxwell's Field Theory*; LIGHT: *History*. Published in 1864 and 1873, they remain a working tool of radio and telecommunication research despite the questions raised by the relativity, electron, and quantum theories, and the wave-corpuscular controversy.

1. Experiments by Hertz.—Radio is a superb example of a phenomenon whose principles were known to mathematicians some time before they were demonstrated practically. Maxwell made no attempt to prove physically his thesis of the identity of light and electricity, and his writings were known only by other mathematicians. Among these was H. L. F. von Helmholtz, who held the chair of physics in Berlin and whose best-known work was on the resonance of sound (1862). However, his other work in electrical oscillations and electrodynamics involved his theories in controversy with Maxwell's (1874). Among Helmholtz's pupils was Heinrich Hertz, who in 1886–88 brought into electrical resonance, at a wavelength of approximately 4 m. (or at a frequency of about 75,000,000 cycles per second [cps]), a pair of plates radiating electrical energy and a detecting loop of wire some feet away. A micrometer gap in the loop, by producing sparks that could be seen in the dark, revealed a transfer of energy as predicted by Maxwell (fig. 1).

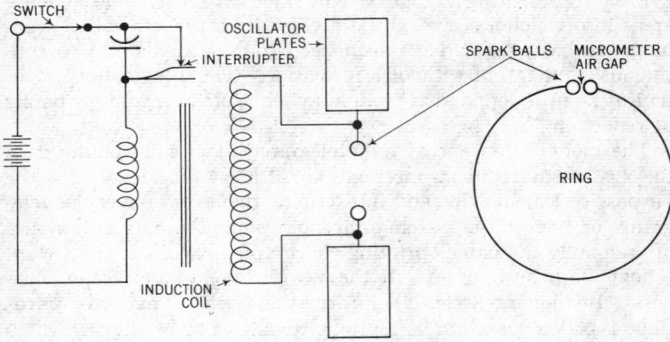

FIG. 1.—HERTZ OSCILLATOR, 1887

2. The Coherer-Decoherer.—The coherence of dust particles in air when electrified was discovered by Pierre Guitard of France in 1850. In 1879 D. E. Hughes, an Anglo-American electrician, while investigating the resistance of loose contacts between carbon granules in his microphone transmitter, discovered the phenomenon on which the action of coherers depends. The coherence when electrostatically charged, and a resulting decrease in the resistance of loose brass and copper filings to the flow of a current, were noted by C. Onesti of Italy in 1884. E. Branly, a French physicist, published in 1890 his discovery that the resistance between loose iron filings in a glass tube decreases with the impact

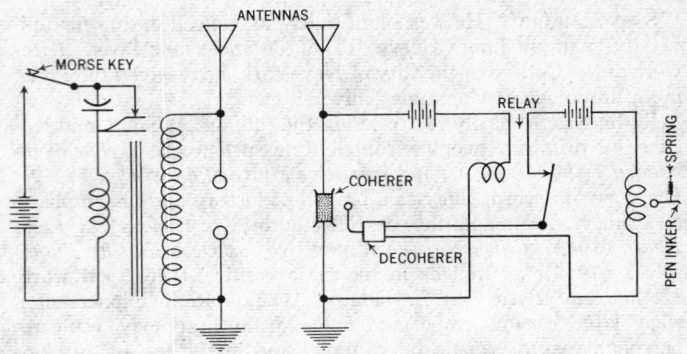

FIG. 2.—MARCONI-LODGE APPARATUS, 1896

of radiated electric waves. Branly did not apply his coherer to the reception of electromagnetic waves as communication signals, but he found it necessary to tap the cohering filings mechanically to make them "decohere." Sir Oliver Lodge, an English physicist, demonstrated improvements in Branly's coherer in 1894. He used the device, in place of a Hertz loop, for the detection and pen recording of Morse signals transmitted in a laboratory by radio. Included in the inker circuit was Lodge's "trembler" or decoherer, which automatically shook the filings to restore their high resistance, thus making the device responsive to no-current as well as to marking-current conditions in the dipole radio-frequency receiving circuit (*see* fig. 2). In 1895 A. S. Popov, a Russian physicist, in his study of distant lightning flashes, used Lodge's receiver with two improvements. One was the use of choke coils to nullify the effect of local sparking at the inker-decoherer circuit relay contacts; more important was the use of an external insulated wire and a ground (earth) connection, between which the coherer was inserted. He sent Hertzian signals into his receiver over a distance of 300 yd. in 1896. Further improvements in the coherer were made by Marconi.

3. Guglielmo Marconi was a native of Italy, but from 1896 was identified quite as much with England. He was the pupil of Augusto Righi, professor of physics at the University of Bologna, who was working with waves 2.5 to 20 cm. in length and had invented an early quenched-spark emitter. Unlike his predecessors, Marconi was not a laboratory scientist but an entrepreneur with a driving purpose—to find the way to unguided electrical communication through space. He dedicated his life to translating radio from the laboratory to the marketplace, always looking for the slightest advance in reliability of wireless equipment and in the distances over which it would work. Marconi saw the commercial usefulness of a method of electrical transmission that, because it was not restricted by wires or cables, could reach an unlimited number of receivers anywhere at the same time.

Marconi was first to transmit and receive signals by Hertzian waves purposefully directed but without wires (1895). He used an induction coil with a telegraph key in the primary circuit. Across the secondary circuit was an untuned spark gap. Marconi did not terminate the gap in a dipole, as had Hertz and Lodge, but in a ground plate for one pole and in an elevated metal cylinder for the other. For a receiver he used a simple coherer with improvements in sensitivity. By the end of the year he had increased the transmitting range to more than a mile.

In 1896 Marconi went to London, secured patents on his system, and interested government officials in it. Ranges of 2 to 9 mi. obtained that year were gradually increased to 200 mi. by 1901.

III. MARITIME WIRELESS AND THE VACUUM TUBE

Marconi set the pace for widening the transmission range of wireless. In 1897 he established the station at Needles, on the Isle of Wight, that took part in several records in wireless: 1897 —first maritime use of wireless in England, to a tugboat 18 mi. away; 1898—first paid-for wireless telegram; 1899—first newspaper published aboard ship using press matter sent by wireless, 56 mi.; 1901—first 200-mi. communication. Marconi also was the first to bridge the English Channel by wireless, in 1899.

1. Maritime Wireless.—The fact that radiated waves carried well over water led to the entrance of commercial wireless into the maritime field, where it filled a need not served at all by wire telegraphs. Apart from its obvious usefulness to ship owners in communicating with ship captains and pursers during the course of a voyage, it was quickly put to use by the press, by the military, and in sea rescues.

By 1904 the role of wireless in summoning help to ships was so important that adoption of a universal code call of distress was in order. Addition of the letter D (for danger) to the "all stations" collective call CQ gave the CQD signal, eventually replaced by the Morse mnemonic SOS. When radiotelephones became common, especially on aircraft, the voice of distress, "May Day" (from the French *m'aidez*, "help me"), was added.

2. Spread of Commercial Wireless Telegraphy.—Marconi's influence rapidly spread to other countries. A. K. H. Slaby saw Marconi's apparatus in England and introduced it into Germany in 1897, and the first German commercial wireless station was established on Borkum Island in 1900. Pioneer wireless work in Germany was also done by K. F. Braun, G. W. A. von Arco, Alexander Meissner, and the firm of Siemens and Halske. Out of an amalgamation of these interests the Telefunken company was created in 1903.

Two outstanding names appear in the early wireless annals of the U.S.—those of R. A. Fessenden, physicist, and Lee De Forest. Fessenden lectured on Hertzian waves and experimented with them prior to 1900, when he was engaged by the U.S. Weather Bureau to develop wireless as a weather forecasting aid. He became a prolific producer of wireless inventions. De Forest, while a student in 1898, was attracted by demonstrations of the Hertz experiments. He set out to produce a better detector of waves than the coherer, and he produced several inventions of great importance.

3. Transoceanic Operation.—In 1900 Marconi built a station at Poldhu, Cornwall, Eng., that established a number of records, and in 1907 he built another station in Clifden, County Connemara, Ire. The Federal Telegraph Company opened a radio-telegraph service between San Francisco, Calif., and Honolulu, Hawaii, in 1912. The American Marconi Company opened a similar circuit in 1914 and extended service across the Pacific to Japan by manual relaying in Hawaii during the next year.

4. Improvements in Transmitters.—The improvements in transmitter equipment and antennas in the first quarter of the century greatly extended the range and reliability of long-wave and medium-wave radiotelegraphy. Until the introduction of the vacuum tube, spark gaps, arcs, and alternators took many forms during the 20-year period beginning around 1903.

Rotary Spark Gap.—Invented by Fessenden, the rotary spark gap consisted of a toothed or spiked wheel turning between two electrodes. A whistlelike note could be produced to any desired audible pitch by proper selection of wheel speed and number of teeth. Self-cooling, the gap could be decreased to any minimum length desired. The rotary spark gap was widely used in the 1906–20 period.

Quenched Sparks.—As the power supplied to ordinary open spark gaps and their associated oscillatory circuits was increased over the years, it was found that the sparking rate could be increased if ionization of the gas between the electrodes could be prevented. A technique was discovered by the German physicist, Max Wien, in 1906, wherein sparks—which in that day were thin and often several inches in length—were increased in volume but reduced to a fraction of a millimetre in length. This resulted in an abrupt decay (or quenching) of the oscillation produced by the spark. The frequency emitted was therefore that of the circuit coupled with the antenna, excited by rapid, successive impacts from the quenched gap. Arc-over was prevented by using large electrode areas cooled by circulating air or water. For very rapid sparking rates a high-voltage direct current could be used, with an oscillating circuit in series with the quenched gap. As installed by the German Telefunken organization for telegraph use in 1909–15, the quenched gap was fed from alternators producing 500 to 1,000 cps (now referred to as 1,000 Hertz).

Rotary gaps and quenched gaps made the emitted telegraph signals more distinctive and more easily identifiable by the receiving operator, who often had to read them through the interference of static and other transmitter signals. Rotary and quenched gaps produced tones more or less unique to each station. Despite such advances, it was clear that the intervals of no power, between bursts of rapidly decaying ether disturbances caused by discrete sparks, could not be reduced so long as sparks were employed; consequently, some source of continuous-wave production had to be found.

Arc Oscillators.—W. B. Duddell, an English engineer, discovered in 1900 that an arc lamp could be made to "sing" a musical note if it was placed in a direct-current circuit containing an inductance and a capacitance. V. Poulsen of Denmark, by cooling the lamp electrodes and enclosing the arc in an atmosphere of hydrogen, raised Duddell's limit of 10 kiloHertz (kHz) to 100 kHz; and, when coupled to an antenna, the arc generated and emitted the first pure continuous waves in the low-frequency wireless field. However, Poulsen's arc was not tested successfully until 1908, when it worked over a distance of 150 mi. Meanwhile, in 1906, the German Telefunken arc appeared; by 1913 Telefunken's Nauen station used it over a range of 1,550 mi. In 1910 the Federal Telegraph Company brought the Poulsen arc to the United States. It was installed as standard equipment by the U.S. Navy in 1912 and continued in use through World War I.

High-Frequency Alternator.—Fessenden applied in 1901 for a U.S. patent on a high-frequency alternator for the generation of continuous waves that would make possible the transmission of the human voice by wireless telephony. To Fessenden's specifications, E. F. W. Alexanderson, a pupil of Slaby working in the U.S., built in 1903 a 10,000-Hz alternator. Later he built one of 80,-000 cycles, with which, at Brant Rock, Mass., Fessenden was the first to broadcast music and speech (1906). Alexanderson's problem was the design of multipolar machines (*e.g.*, 300 poles mounted on the stator) with rotor speeds of about 20,000 rpm and air-gap clearances of about 0.015 in. Such a machine, developing 100,000 Hz, was built by Alexanderson in 1909 for radiotelegraph use.

Resonance and Tuning.—Lodge patented in England, in 1898, the use of adjustable inductance in the transmitter, antenna, and receiving circuits of wireless systems. Lodge called this syntonic tuning (*see* fig. 3). While the patent was in conflict with some

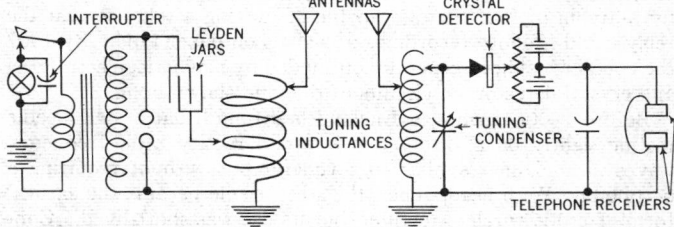

FIG. 3.—TUNED CIRCUITS AND CRYSTAL DETECTOR, ABOUT 1903

of Marconi's claims, Lodge had an influence on early tuning theory and the adaptation of antenna sizes and configurations to the frequencies being emitted and detected. John S. Stone applied for four-circuit tuning patents in 1900 and was the first in the U.S. to assert that antenna circuits and spark and detector circuits could be independently tuned and loosely coupled together, thus increasing selectivity (*see* fig. 4). Stone also studied the tuning

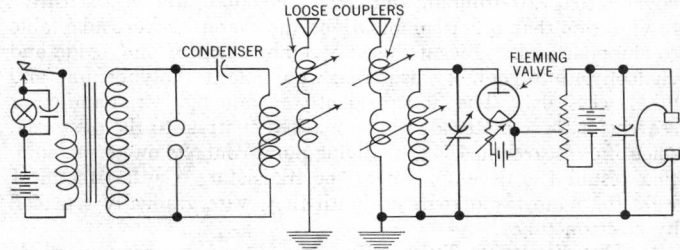

FIG. 4.—LOOSE COUPLING AND FLEMING VALVE, ABOUT 1907

of telephone wires and their adaptation to the guidance of electromagnetic waves.

In wireless, as in wire telephony, a parallel attack on the problems of resonance had been made.

Antennas.—Antennas were found to have a natural resonance period important to the tuning of a circuit consisting of antenna, ground, and coupling inductance. Marconi and his organization, Lodge, Fessenden, and many others developed formulas for antennas of various virtual heights, for optimum ratios of antenna lengths to wave lengths, and for various configurations—notably the vertical antenna and the flat-top antenna supported between towers and between ships' masts. Alexanderson invented the multiple-tuned panel transmitting antenna. It divided a directionally pointed, horizontal, tower-supported antenna into sections connected through down leads and tuning inductances to ground at various points throughout its length of approximately 900 ft. Alexanderson and his assistant, Harold Henry Beverage, developed a "barrage receiver" that incorporated directional discrimination and required long horizontal antennas (1916). In 1921 Beverage patented the "wave antenna" that became standard for long-wave reception throughout the world. It consisted of a wire supported on a straight-pole line of the length of one wave (approximately nine miles in practice) and oriented to the direction of arrival of the wave. It had the useful property of rejecting static that came from any other direction.

5. Improvements in Receivers.—The counterpart of increased power in transmitters was increased sensitivity in receivers. The single step of most significance was the substitution of a pair of head telephone receivers or headphones for the early pen inker as the receiving device used by the operator. Headphones were sensitive enough to work directly in a rectifying receiving circuit when a series potentiometer and a shunt-blocking condenser were added (*see* fig. 3). Between about 1903 and 1916 the standard method of telegraphing by wireless was headphone reception of hand-keyed Morse code (ship-to-shore) or slow-speed automatic Wheatstone (transoceanic) transmission.

As in the case of spark gaps in transmitters, many improvements were made in the rectifier element (detector) of receivers. These improvements served a vital purpose in the interval 1902–20, before the De Forest three-element vacuum-tube circuit became available for general use after World War I. In Marconi service the coherer was replaced by the magnetic detector. As developed by Marconi in 1902, it was capable of moving a relay so that the relay could produce recordings of signals on paper tape. By 1907 the coherer had been generally outmoded by magnetic, electrolytic, and crystal detectors in circuits of the kind shown in fig. 3.

Before 1900, Hughes in England had found that a steel needle resting lightly on a carbon block would rectify radio-frequency waves in a manner similar to a coherer but without requiring a decoherer. With headphones, the steel needle became the earliest form of crude wireless rectifier, but its use was short-lived. Contemporary with the magnetic detector was the electrolytic detector, an invention of Fessenden in 1902, consisting of platinum wire dipped in nitric acid. Beginning in 1903 G. W. Pickard, an American engineer, began experimenting with the rectifying properties of magnetite and other crystals that had surface spots sensitive to radio signals upon contact with wire probes called "cat whiskers."

In 1906 Pickard discovered a superior crystal in silicon, and in that same year Gen. H. C. Dunwoody of the U.S. Army discovered that carborundum and carbon in contact were less sensitive to vibration than other combinations and therefore were adaptable to shipboard use. Pickard used a combination of zinc oxide and chalcopyrite in contact; also tried were galena, molybdenum, and other crystals. The independently conducted, trial-and-error search for these materials was in marked contrast to the organized scientific research in 1948, involving point contacts on germanium, that resulted in development of the transistor. Crystal rectifiers were the mainstay of wireless until they were gradually replaced by electron tubes.

6. The Electron Tube.—Sir John Fleming's vacuum diode valve of 1904, based upon his discovery that the "Edison effect"

(*see* THERMIONICS) could be applied in a wireless receiver circuit for the detection of incoming waves, was a rectifier. It fulfilled the function of a crystal as a detector of high frequencies (*see* fig. 4). It was the first of a long series of electron tubes that had a heated source of a stream of electrons (cathode) and a collector plate, both in a partially exhausted glass housing with external electrical connections. The development of the electron tube is traced in the article ELECTRON TUBE: *History*. The De Forest triode audion of 1907 was the most important of the electron tube series. It contained two features absent in Fleming's valve: an external local battery, connected between plate and cathode, from which the tube derived its power to amplify weak input signals; and a third electrode, the grid, interposed in the electron stream and capable of controlling the plate current in accordance with incoming radio-frequency signals. Under optimum conditions, De Forest's triode displayed high amplification characteristics as a detector, although Fleming's valve had not.

However, it was not until 1912 that the triode's amplification was stabilized and its versatility became clear. In that year H. D. Arnold and Irving Langmuir independently found that the triode amplifier could be stabilized if pumped to high vacuum, and De Forest increased amplification by operating his tubes in cascade—the plate output of one tube fed into the grid input of a second tube, etc. De Forest discovered that the audion could be made to oscillate, in suitable circuits, so as to generate radio frequencies. This meant that the vacuum tube could be used for transmission as well as reception. E. H. Armstrong in 1913 and De Forest in 1914 filed conflicting patent applications on the feedback circuit (*see* RADIO RECEIVER: *History*). The feedback circuit led a portion of the amplified plate current back into the grid of the same tube, greatly increasing its sensitivity by regenerating weak signals.

7. Developments During World War I.—Maritime wireless telegraphy was generally in use on ships and between ships and shore stations by the outbreak of the war. Arc transmitters up to 500 kw. in capacity had been installed at naval stations in the United States, and the Marconi timed-spark system linked units of the British Commonwealth. New German Telefunken stations erected in the U.S. were among those that warned German ships, upon the declaration of war, to make for neutral ports. The British fleet was recalled by radio. During this period very long-wave transoceanic radiotelegraphy became well established for military purposes, using arcs and alternators for transmitting and triode tubes for receiving. In 1918 the U.S. Army erected its Lafayette station at Crois d'Hins near Bordeaux, France, for transatlantic communication. It achieved world ranges on a wavelength of 20,000 m. The original plant comprised two Poulsen-Federal arcs rated at 1,000 kw.

The Heterodyne Principle.—Radio frequencies generated by arc and alternator were above the range of audibility in a telephone receiver, so that they had to be modulated at a steady audible tone before being turned on and off with a telegraph key. This modulation was accomplished at either the transmitter or receiver. The German inventors modulated their alternators by means of a tone wheel. Poulsen tone-modulated his arc with an interrupter. Fessenden invented a method of tone-modulating a circuit at the receiver instead of at the transmitter by generating at the receiving station another high frequency that differed from the transmitter frequency by a value within the audible range. The device that produced this steady interference pattern was called a heterodyne apparatus (1902). Fessenden used the heterodyne principle at his Brant Rock station in 1904, and it was necessary to generate the beat frequency by a ponderous local arc. Nevertheless, U.S. Navy experiments in 1913 demonstrated the superiority of this method for radiotelegraphy. With the introduction of the vacuum tube as an oscillator in 1912, a simple receiving circuit component became available to generate a heterodyne beat-note audible in headphones.

To solve a military problem with the U.S. Army Signal Corps in Europe in 1918, Maj. E. H. Armstrong converted a received radio-frequency signal into an intermediate, supra-audio frequency by beating it with the output of a local oscillator, detecting signals twice before giving them audio amplification. He called this the superheterodyne method and patented it in 1919–20. It possessed advantages of stability over other methods of amplifying signals above the audio range. With the advent of the screen-grid tetrode in 1927, the superheterodyne became the most widely used receiver circuit.

Radio Direction-finding.—Direction-finding, or radiolocation, began in wireless telegraphy as a specialty of wave-direction measurement. In modern aviation and in some marine work direction-finding is an auxiliary function of radiotelephony. The original work on direction-finding was performed by Stone in 1904 and by E. Bellini and A. Tosi in 1906. The patents of the Bellini-Tosi system were acquired by Marconi in 1912, and in that year the first English merchant vessel was equipped with a direction-finder. Credit for major improvements thereafter is shared by an American, F. A. Kolster (1913); Marconi's assistant, Capt. H. J. Round, whose devices tracked down the German fleet in the battle of Jutland (1916); and R. L. Smith-Rose, a British physicist. Because of its usefulness in World War I, direction-finding equipment did not find full commercial use until the period 1921–25, by which time it employed vacuum-tube circuits. By 1925 the radio compass had come into widespread shipboard use.

8. Radiotelephony.—The technique of radiotelephony represents the combination of two developments: high-powered radiotelegraphy and weak-current wire telephony. From the time of Alexander Graham Bell and Hertz until 1906, the two modes of communication had been separated in orders of magnitude of power and frequency, even though they derived from a common theoretical source in Maxwell's equations. As early as 1896, Stone and M. I. Pupin were involved in a patent controversy in applying telephony to Hertzian waves.

Poulsen used his hydrogen-arc generator of continuous wireless telegraph waves in 1904 to transmit voice over short distances. In Germany H. T. Simon and M. Reich (1903) and O. Nussbaumer (1904) suggested the application of high-frequency alternating currents to the purposes of wireless telephony. In 1906 the Telefunken arc of Von Arco was voice-modulated, making it possible to talk by wireless over a span of 25 mi., and in the same year Fessenden staged the first demonstration of the broadcasting of music and voice by radio, using a water-cooled microphone and an Alexanderson 80,000-cycle alternator at Brant Rock. Reception was reported by radio operators aboard many ships at sea. De Forest demonstrated an arc radiotelephone in 1907 in tests between a ferryboat on the Hudson River and its terminals in New York and New Jersey. Using a liquid microphone to modulate an arc, F. Majorana in 1908 telephoned from Rome to Sicily, Italy, a distance of 300 mi. and in 1910 H. P. Dwyer used a Poulsen arc to telephone from San Francisco to Los Angeles, Calif. (490 mi.). In 1911 Alexanderson built a high-frequency alternator with a laminated-iron field, designed to act as a self-contained magnetic amplifier. Its input was a microphone and its output a varying field flux that amplitude-modulated the generated continuous waves. In 1914 Marconi long-wave radiotelephone signals originating at Clifden, Ire., were received aboard two Italian war vessels off the coast of Sicily, 1,750 mi. away. In 1915 radiotelephone signals were successfully transmitted across the ocean for the first time, using a long-wave transmitter powered by a bank of some 500 telephone repeater type vacuum tubes in parallel and sending from the Navy station at Arlington, Va., to the Eiffel Tower in Paris and to Honolulu.

IV. THE RISE OF BROADCASTING

Medium-frequency telephone broadcasting and shortwave telecommunication dominated the decade 1920–30. The radiotelephone, useful for private conversations, became most valuable in public mass communication and entertainment. Public demand for broadcasting service and equipment caused manufacturers to demand new electronic devices, circuits, and equipment. Broadcasting studios, feeder networks, and overseas remote pickups became commonplace. Early radio by-products, including public-address systems and telephotography, presaged the decade of electronics that was to follow. Short-wave transmission also came into its own during the 1920s.

1. Improvements in Transmitters.—Better performance in transmitters stemmed in part from transmitting tubes of larger size and greater efficiency. Two important improvements were the copper-to-glass seal and the water-cooled tube (1922). Broadcasting transmitters, which in 1922 operated at outputs of less than 500 w., were increased in power; 50-kw. stations were common in 1928, and by the early 1960s outputs had reached 500 kw. Efficient use of power by the transmitter was found to be economically important, and efficiencies were increased by such advances as the constant-current system of modulation of R. A. Heising (1921), the class C amplifier (1932), and W. H. Doherty's linear radio-frequency power amplifier (1936).

Jacques and Pierre Curie discovered the piezoelectric effect in 1880, and they later found that if a high-frequency field is applied to a crystal held under pressure, and if the applied frequency exactly coincides with the natural period of vibration of the crystal, the crystal will oscillate and produce useful alternating voltages between its surfaces. This property proved invaluable in preventing radio transmitters from wandering off assigned frequencies. G. W. Pierce found that the resonance of a crystal is very sharp. He was issued several patents on applications (1924 to 1931) for vacuum-tube circuits containing quartz crystals as oscillating-circuit stabilizers. The first use of crystal-controlled master oscillators took place in 1923.

There are other less precise but effective ways of accomplishing frequency control. Pierce investigated magnetostriction effects in nickel, while W. H. Eccles, of the Marconi staff, used tuning forks as early as 1901 to keep stations on frequency. Identically-ground crystals were employed on a wide scale during World War II in transmitters and receivers, and the practical subdivision of the radio-frequency spectrum among thousands of users in the middle of the 20th century was made possible only by crystal frequency controls.

2. Amateur Radio.—Young men had turned to wireless telegraphy as a hobby in the period 1903–12 in the same spirit that their fathers had strung rooftop wire telegraphs between houses. Thousands of the long-wave transmitters shown in fig. 3 and 4 (but without receiving tubes) were installed. Unfortunately amateurs increasingly interfered with commercial and government wireless, and in 1911–12 they became subject to licence restrictions. During World War I amateur sets were sealed; however, the operators' talents proved so valuable in military service that they were encouraged to resume amateur operations after the war. Amateurs adopted vacuum tubes when these became available around 1919, and they became an important source of listening material for the many thousands of people who bought broadcast receivers in the years following 1920.

In resuming operations in 1919, the amateurs had been crowded into a medium-frequency band that was not broad enough to accommodate them. They had also been assigned a medium-high-frequency portion of the spectrum believed unsuitable for long-distance operation. The good use to which they put these bands in 1920–21 was their most valuable contribution to the development of radio. In 1921 a U.S. amateur, P. F. Godley, with the cooperation of British amateurs and the Post Office, set up a receiver in Ardrossan, Scot., through which he received from a group of six American amateurs at Greenwich, Conn., a 12-word message in radiotelegraphic signals. The distance was 3,200 mi., the power 1 kw., and the wavelength 230 m. (1,300 kc.). Soon American, British, French, and other European amateurs by the hundreds were in frequent communication at low power in this band as well as on 180 m. In 1923 amateurs used low-power, 100-m. waves to talk between New York and California.

3. Commercial Shortwave Radio.—Commercial interests were caught off guard by the amateurs' successful exploitation of the upper medium-frequency (MF) and the lower high-frequency (HF) bands. Marconi had never lost faith in the possibilities of short waves, but he had dropped the investigation of them in the 1890s in favour of long waves that were yielding him quicker results. He had taken out a patent on "beamed transmission" in 1905, and in 1916 assigned C. S. Franklin to investigate short waves. Franklin's results, published in 1922, indicated that short waves, 15 to 100 m. in length, were suitable only for distances less than 200 mi. This conclusion was controverted by the experience of the amateurs, whose records spurred more experimentation by Marconi, the Radio Corporation of America, and the American Telephone and Telegraph Company. The first commercial long-distance radiotelegram dispatch by short waves was sent from Belfast, Me., to Buenos Aires, Arg., in 1923. In the same year Marconi dispatched his yacht "Elletra" to test 100-m. short waves at sea as received from Poldhu, Eng., using reflectors designed by Franklin to concentrate the transmitted energy in a beam. The signals from Poldhu were heard 1,200 nautical miles in the daytime and double that distance at night. In 1926 beam transmission was considered practical for commercial use, and by 1928 Marconi stations had been erected in England, Canada, Australia, South Africa, and elsewhere throughout the British Empire. The Radio Corporation of America had abandoned its ambitious plans for a long-wave radio central station and was installing shortwave equipment. By 1930 the American Telephone and Telegraph Company had made an almost complete transition to shortwave.

Opening up of the extensive shortwave portion of the radio spectrum made room for thousands of long-distance and other services that could not have been accommodated on longer waves. Antennas became smaller and less expensive to build, had increased radiation efficiency, and had substantial portions of their energy directed toward desired reception points. Directivity of antennas reduced the interference between stations and permitted worldwide sharing of channels. Interference by static caused by distant thunderstorms was less. Because of these advances, transmitter power could be reduced or the existing power could be used to make transmissions more reliable. Shortwave radio was adapted to long-distance telephony and to high-speed, multichannel telegraph operations. After 1927 virtually no new long-wave radio circuits were established, and most of those in use at that time were gradually abandoned. The long-wave spectrum is still useful, to a limited extent, for specialized military radiotelegraph services and for navigation.

The Kennelly-Heaviside Layers.—In 1902, long before short waves were being used, A. E. Kennelly of Harvard University and the British mathematician Sir Oliver Heaviside independently reasoned that a stratified layer must exist in the upper atmosphere; between that layer and the surface of the earth the long waves of wireless must be contained, and this fact accounts for the waves not leaving the earth tangentially at the horizon as light waves do. With the beginning of shortwave investigations, this theory was rapidly expanded. A. H. Taylor accounted for the ground- and sky-wave components of short waves; L. W. Austin reasoned that sky waves underwent refraction rather than reflection; and Ernest Rutherford attributed refraction to the presence of free electrons in the layer. Frank Conrad developed the "multihop" theory of repeated refractions in the layer and reflections from the earth's surface. The height of the layer was measured by Sir Edward Victor Appleton in England, by triangulation, and by George Breit and Merle A. Tuve in America, who measured the echo of a transmitted pulse. The latter method eventually revealed the existence of several concentric layers rather than one. (*See* IONOSPHERE.)

Diversity Reception.—H. H. Beverage and H. O. Peterson, observing transoceanic shortwave signals in 1925, found that fading does not occur simultaneously in two receivers working on antennas spaced a short distance apart. This led to the development of space-diversity reception, in which the combined (or overriding) signals from two or more receivers, working off carefully placed, separate antennas, govern the operation of a receiving relay, which automatically selects the strongest available signal.

V. SPECTRUM EXPANSION AND ELECTRONICS

Continued progress in broadcasting, and a new probing of the ionosphere by short waves, tied the decade 1930–40 to its predecessor. In the period between 1933 and 1937, improved designs for broadcast antennas made possible higher efficiencies and better control of directional effects, thus further reducing interference between stations. Continuing research in the high-frequency portion of the spectrum led inevitably to exploitation of the shortwave

band for international broadcasting. By 1932 broadcast transmitters were operating with sidebands 8,000 Hz in width, making it possible to transmit undistorted voice and music tones as high in pitch as 8,000 Hz; this meant better fidelity in reproduction (FM broadcasting almost doubled this tonal range two decades later), but unfortunately the quality of the receivers then in use was not equal to that of the transmitters.

1. Electronics.—A widespread movement to apply radio theory and apparatus to other fields began in the middle 1930s. The radio industry contributed the electron tube, the photoelectric cell, the oscilloscope, electronic amplifiers, the principle of feedback for automatic control, and techniques for utilizing both audio and radio frequencies in many ways. The term electronics came into use in the mid-1920s to designate all of the theoretical and applied work involving the movement of electrons in a vacuum. About 1928 electronics began to be used as a collective term for all the applications of the electron tube and its associated circuitry to purposes not directly associated with radio emissions, and, after invention of the transistor, to similar applications involving solid-state devices.

2. Marine Radiotelephony.—The earliest demonstration of two-way marine telephony was aboard the USS "New Hampshire" in 1916. In World War I the long-wave radiotelephone was used to communicate with submarine chasers and other small vessels and aircraft. Ship-to-shore radiotelephony was tested in 1920 on low-power long waves, and commercial radiotelephone service between land and steamships began in 1929 with the installation of radiotelephone equipment on the "Leviathan." By 1933 long-distance, shortwave, ship-to-shore radiotelephony was common on the North Atlantic. Extensive use was made after 1934 of medium- and high-frequency radio in commercial telephone service to small craft in coastal waters, as well as to private aircraft.

3. Commercial Radiotelephony.—The first commercial radiotelephone circuit was established in 1920 between Long Beach, Calif., and Catalina Island, a distance of 30 mi., using a frequency of 1,000 kiloHertz (kHz). Commercial transoceanic radiotelephone communication began in 1927, using single-sideband transmission on a frequency of 60 kHz; shortwave transoceanic radiotelephony came in 1929. The multiple-unit, steerable receiving antenna was first used commercially in 1939. Independent double-sideband transmission on a common carrier frequency originated on the Netherlands-Java shortwave circuit in 1937, and by that year the principal countries of the world were interconnected by 92 groups of radiotelephone circuits, making it possible to talk between any of about 93% of the world's telephones.

4. Aviation Radio.—Radio serves aircraft not only as a means of communication but as a navigational aid. The problems of designing aviation radio equipment are similar to those encountered in marine equipment, but they are aggravated by restricted space for equipment and antennas, as well as by interference from other electrical equipment, by unusual types of static, and by a varying power supply. Also, in order to maintain continuous communication and navigation facilities, it is necessary to work several channels independently and simultaneously, and two or more transmitters and receivers therefore are required.

In the United States, the first navigational aids to aviation appeared in 1920, when the Post Office Department established ground stations for the airmail service. By 1930 a radio-range beacon system had been developed for universal application to airways, and in 1931 a radio beacon system had been devised for the "blind" landing of aircraft, although it was not officially adopted until later. In Europe and the United States very short waves (above 30 mc.) were being used in instrument-landing systems in 1935. A rotating radio compass, making possible automatic direction-finding for airplanes, was developed in 1936. It worked as a homing device in connection with radio beacons. Radio altimeters, working on the principles of the marine depth-finder, became available in 1938. The first U.S. blind-landing system, in which a definite radio slope of descent could be followed by a pilot, was installed at Indianapolis, Ind., in 1940. (*See* AIRCRAFT INSTRUMENTS.)

5. Mobile Radio.—The Detroit, Mich., police department in

1928 became the first to dispatch police squads by radio, and by 1935 about 400 cities in the U.S. had police radio service, some in the 30- to 40-mc. bands. Widespread two-way operation from police cars and private vehicles came with the opening of the ultra-high-frequency (UHF) spectrum after World War II.

Broadcast receivers for automobiles were introduced in 1932, and within a year they were in wide use.

6. Advances in Techniques.—The principles of negative feedback, set forth by Stuart Ballantine in 1923, were spectacularly applied by H. S. Black in 1934 to produce wide-band, noise-free amplifiers having marked stability of operation. These amplifiers also were capable of a high degree of linearity (the ability to produce an amplified output signal with a wave form as similar as possible to that of the input signal over a wide range of frequencies); thus they could reproduce a much wider range of modulations without distortion.

In 1930 a widely published graph of the radio spectrum showed all waves shorter than 10 m. (30 mc.) as "not now useful." Yet there was general agreement that radio would have to expand into the higher frequency bands. Marconi's 1896 patent had contemplated using waves having a minimum length of about 25 cm. (10 in.); *i.e.*, a maximum frequency of about 1,200 mc. When tubes capable of generating such ultrahigh frequencies did become available, no time was lost. Report was made of experiments with 3-m. very-high-frequency (VHF) waves in 1930, and in the period 1930–35 there were many more reports, covering UHF as well as VHF. The first important microwave telephone circuit was established across the English Channel (Dover-Calais) in 1931, using an 18-cm. wave (UHF). The first multichannel telephone microwave circuit joined Belfast, N.Ire., with Stranraer, Scot., in 1937, on 3 to 6 m. (VHF). Transmission of superhigh-frequency (SHF) electromagnetic waves in hollow wave guides was reported by W. L. Barrow in 1936 and by G. C. Southworth in 1937.

John Bardeen and W. H. Brattain introduced a semiconductor device in 1947 that became known as the transistor (*q.v.*). They discovered that a metal point resting on a germanium crystal, when emitting a forward current into the crystal, would influence the reverse current in a nearby metal collector point. W. B. Shockley, an associate of Bardeen and Brattain, developed the theory and distinguished the different types of transistor junctions. The 1956 Nobel Prize for Physics was awarded to Bardeen, Brattain, and Shockley for their work in this field. The transistor and other devices evolving from it have revolutionized the electronics industry and replaced the vacuum tube for many purposes.

VI. PULSE TECHNIQUES AND TELEVISION

During World War II radio development was cloaked in military secrecy, but the easing of restrictions in 1946 disclosed as many accomplishments as in any previous decade. The most important advance had been radar, not alone because of its military successes but because radar theory and the electronic apparatus and techniques that arose from it were basic to the further utilization of the highest-frequency reaches of the radio spectrum. Out of military research, too, came such new concepts as printed circuits, modular construction, and miniaturization. The end of the war also permitted resumption of work on television, which rapidly began to overtake radio as the most important entertainment medium in many countries.

1. Modulation.—The continuous wave of power (the carrier) delivered into an antenna by an oscillating electron tube may be varied or modulated, in its strength or amplitude, by voice signals from a microphone. The process is called amplitude modulation (AM). As an extreme example, amplitude may be varied suddenly between zero and full strength by working a telegraph key, thus either interrupting a steady musical tone that modulates the carrier or interrupting the carrier itself; wireless began by using such coded interruptions of a train of sparks. The process of amplitude modulation, as used in standard radio broadcasting, consists in varying the amplitude of the carrier wave at a rate identical to the frequency of the sound to be transmitted; *e.g.*, if a tone with a frequency of 1,000 Hz is to be broadcast, the strength of the transmitter carrier is varied 1,000 times per second. Fre-

quency modulation (FM), as its name suggests, consists in varying the frequency of the transmitter carrier wave (while its strength remains constant) at a rate identical to the frequency of the sound to be transmitted. The outstanding advantage of FM is its freedom from interference by atmospheric and man-made electrical noises. These unwanted noises are of an amplitude-modulated nature and hence are not detected by circuits in FM receivers.

It also is possible to transmit signals by other types of modulation, some of which are important to radiotelephony, radiotelegraphy, picture transmission, television, and radar. In FM telegraphy, for example, two tones, differing in pitch, convey the dots and dashes of the code signals; this was done with Poulsen arcs in the period 1912–22. Alternatively, the carrier itself may be varied in frequency by changing certain circuit constants; this is called frequency-shift keying and was developed during World War I. FM was applied generally to telegraph carrier transmission over wires in the U.S. during and after 1937. In 1945 it was applied to microwave radio for public telegraph service. Frequency modulation also is used to transmit the sound for television.

Pulse Modulation.—An electron tube can be overloaded drastically but safely if the overloads are of extremely short duration and are interspersed with relatively long periods of inactivity. One electron tube especially designed for this type of service is the magnetron, a two-plate version of which was described by A. W. Hull in 1921. A water-cooled magnetron was available in 1930 having an output of 5 kw. at 20 mc. and 1 kw. at 85 mc. (in the HF and VHF frequency ranges). However, successful ultrahigh-frequency radar had to await development of the British 10-kw. multicavity magnetron tube (1940), public announcement of which was withheld, for security reasons, until 1946.

The signals sent by radar and other pulse methods may be likened to a line of poles along a roadway. So long as the poles are equally spaced and of equal height they convey no information. It is possible, however, to convey information in any of three ways: (1) by varying the height of the poles (pulse-amplitude modulation—PAM); (2) by moving individual poles a short distance one way or the other from their normal, equally spaced positions (called both pulse-position and pulse-time modulation—PPM or PTM—developed in 1944); or (3) having grouped the poles into sets of five, for example, by omitting certain poles in accordance with a prearranged code (pulse-code modulation—PCM—developed in 1947). Pulse-modulation methods were adapted to multichannel telegraphy and eight-channel telephony, and pulsing was found particularly adaptable to microwave relay transmission in the superhigh frequencies. Because of steepness of the wave fronts of the pulses and because the signals could be completely regenerated (*i.e.*, rejuvenated) at each repeater point, they were singularly free of noise, approaching the reliability and continuity of a wire line.

Single-Sideband Techniques.—Single-sideband (SSB) operation had been applied to low frequencies in 1927 and to high frequencies in 1937. Before the advent of SSB, it was necessary to transmit both the upper and lower sidebands of speech, each the mirror image of the other; one sideband is the sum of, the other is the difference between, the carrier radio-frequency and the voice-modulation band of frequencies. In single-sideband operation, one sideband (*e.g.*, the lower) is suppressed, leaving only the upper, with its carrier. A second voice modulation, consisting of a lower sideband whose upper-sideband image has been suppressed, can "ride" the same carrier, and the carrier is thus doing double duty. This type of operation saves frequency space, reduces power requirements; and, by limiting the bandwidth of each voice signal, reduces the noise. Any voice channel may be further broken down into radiotelegraph channels, like teeth in a finer comb.

2. Television.—Television is an outgrowth of the techniques developed in (1) the transmission by wire of graphic material; (2) the utilization of the cathode-ray tube; (3) the perfection of the motion picture with its synchronized sound track; and (4) radio broadcasting. The period of early television development from 1924 to 1939 was interrupted by World War II, and when work in the U.S. was resumed in 1946, transmission was in the VHF band that had been opened during the war. Coaxial cables were first used for intercity network television in 1946, and microwave radio transmission, using relay towers, began that same year. The first coast-to-coast television broadcast over a nationwide system of microwave radio relay took place in 1951. Attempts were made, with better technical than commercial success, to introduce television into the UHF band in 1950. *See* TELEVISION: *History of Television.*

VII. MICROWAVES AND REMOTE CONTROL

The introduction of microwave radio relay systems on a large scale after 1950 to supplement wires and cable for general intercity communications ranks high among the important developments in radio technology. While conventional microwave systems operate at low power over line-of-sight paths, propagation studies indicated that these frequencies could also be employed over greater distances by making use of higher power and transmission phenomena dependent on dissimilarities in the troposphere and ionosphere, and even on meteor trails. Discoveries in solid-state physics resulted in a number of important developments applicable to radio through the use of semiconductors, ceramics, phosphors, and crystals. An outstanding example is the transistor, which has replaced the electron tube in many of its applications and supplemented it in others. Radio communication took new forms, and nonlanguage data transmission became important in the control of machines, missiles, and space vehicles. Techniques for detecting and amplifying very weak signals for space communication were advanced to the point where the receiver's first circuit thermal noise was of the same order as the thermal noise of the atmosphere itself; and the use of the "noise figure" of a receiver as a measure of its noise generating characteristic has given way to the more convenient and meaningful use of the effective noise temperature in degrees Kelvin (K). Thus the noise temperature of the sky, the antenna, and the waveguide can be added to the first circuit noise temperature in the receiver to get the overall effective noise temperature.

1. Microwaves.—Microwave experimentation was carried on in both Europe and the U.S. in the 1930s. During World War II, microwave installations were used by military signal units in Europe, and in the United States the first practical SHF microwave radio system for transmitting commercial telegrams was placed in operation in 1945. In 1946 the first radio relay system for long-distance telephone service was reported. After six months of experimental operation, the Boston-New York microwave system was placed in commercial service in May 1948. Microwave radio techniques were applied in 1950 in France and Germany to public telephone service and in the U.S. to pipeline and railway communication and dispatching. Wave-guide techniques already had been used for antenna feeders and other SHF purposes. Coaxial cables had been tested comparatively with microwave radio relay systems in the U.S. for intercity telephone and television transmission and while both were technically suitable, it appeared that radio might be lower in first cost, though not necessarily in annual charges. The decision was made by the American Telephone and Telegraph Co. in the late 1940s to proceed with development of a new and improved microwave system based on experience with the New York-Boston experimental system. In order to provide the necessary bandwidth and operating stability, the design made use of a new triode vacuum tube with very close spaced elements capable of producing $\frac{1}{2}$ w. output power (subsequently increased to 5 w.) at frequencies in the 3,700–4,200 megaHertz (MHz) band, instead of the klystrons used in the experimental system. The initial installation was made on the route from New York City to Chicago which was placed in service on Sept. 1, 1950. With subsequent improvements the system proved so successful that it found widespread application on routes throughout the U.S.

The principle of operation of a microwave system can be best understood by following a signal through such a system. The input normally consists of either a television signal or the signal from a multiplex terminal in which hundreds of telephone circuits are stacked one above another in frequency, each occupying a separate assignment about 4 kHz wide; the total bandwidth for such a system handling 1,200 circuits would be about 5 MHz.

This input to the microwave system is first converted to a frequency modulated signal with a carrier of 70 MHz. After amplification this 70-MHz signal is converted up to a transmitting frequency in the 4,000-MHz band where it is further amplified in the close spaced triode referred to earlier. It is then fed through waveguide networks to combine it with the outputs of other similar transmitters, each operating in a discrete portion or channel of the 4,000-MHz band. Thence the signal travels through a waveguide to a highly directional antenna which focuses the major part of the output power in a beam about 2.5° in width directed at a distant repeater station antenna 20–40 mi. away over a direct line-of-sight path. At the repeater station the signal in each broad-band channel is separated from the others by means of waveguide networks and fed through a down converter to a 70-MHz amplifier. The 70-MHz amplified signal is then converted upward in frequency to a different 4,000-MHz channel than the received one, amplified again in the triode transmitting amplifier, passed through a series of waveguide combining networks to the outgoing antenna, and sent on to the next repeater. This process is repeated over and over again, the radio transmitting signal occupying the same two microwave frequency channels alternately, from one station to the next, until it reaches the terminal station where, after amplification at 70 MHz, the frequency modulated signal is demodulated to reproduce the original input. If the channel is handling a television signal it is connected to the television broadcast studio or other designated location, but if the output carries telephone or telegraph circuits it must be fed through a multiplex receiving terminal which demodulates the "stacked" circuits to recover the individual baseband telephone signals for connection to the customer's premises.

The foregoing outlines the process for one-way transmission only. Separate channels must be provided in the reverse direction, and in the system described, the same two 4,000-MHz frequencies or channels are reused, a given repeater station transmitting in both directions on the same channel. Separate antennas are used for transmitting and receiving, thus requiring four antennas at a repeater station if there are no branching routes. Some lightly loaded microwave systems utilize a single antenna in each direction, the transmitting and receiving signals, which are usually on widely separated frequencies, being separated by means of waveguide filter networks.

A broad-band channel such as that described, if routed from Boston to Los Angeles over the original transcontinental route, would pass through 140 repeater stations requiring a very high level of equipment performance for satisfactory commercial service. For reasons of economy repeater stations are unattended, troubles being automatically detected at distant maintenance centres by an elaborate alarm and remote-control system. The microwave equipment is usually operated from storage batteries

TYPICAL HEAVY ROUTE MICROWAVE REPEATER STATION

charged from commercial power lines backed up by automatic start diesel generators to protect against possible power failure. To further protect against equipment failure, separate broad-band channels are provided along each route which are automatically and instantaneously substituted for a working channel which fails or experiences a deep fade in signal level. Some microwave systems utilize space diversity reception with duplicate antennas at different elevations on the tower to protect against fading and standby radio equipment for instant switch-over in case of equipment failure.

The original system described here was designed to handle five broad-band working channels and one protection channel in each direction of transmission along a route, each pair of working channels (one each way) being capable of handling two television signals or up to 480 telephone conversations (or other usual types of communication signals including data, telegraph, and facsimile). Since the initial installation, numerous improvements have been made including the doubling of the number of broad-band channels which can be operated in the 3,700–4,200-MHz band (ten working, two protection in each direction, adjacent channels being cross-polarized) and increasing to 1,200 the telephone circuit capacity of each pair of channels. The efficiency of utilization of this portion of the radio frequency spectrum measured in terms of the telephone circuit handling capacity has thus increased fivefold and at the same time the performance has been improved by reducing circuit noise. On heavily loaded routes the antennas have been arranged to simultaneously handle signals in the three principal microwave bands, 3,700–4,200, 5,925–6,425, and 10,700–11,700 MHz. Equipment has been developed and is used extensively in all these bands. A fully loaded route with all three systems can handle as many as 24,600 telephone circuits.

While the above relates to a particular system in the U.S., expansion in the use of microwave radio has been worldwide, and significant developments have originated in various countries. One such development widely used in microwave systems starting in the late 1950s was the traveling-wave amplifier, a special type of vacuum tube invented by R. Kompfner, an Austrian by birth. In this tube the signal passes through a spiral conductor in the presence of a strong electron stream directed along the axis of the spiral. Energy from the electron stream combines with the signal to increase its amplitude much as the wind blowing over the surface of the sea increases the size of the waves. The Japanese made practical application of these tubes in their microwave system in the late 1950s and in the U.S. a heavy route microwave system operating in the 6,000 MHz band and initially placed in service on the Denver-Salt Lake City route in March 1961 made use of traveling-wave tubes of 5-w. power output.

Antennas and Arrays.—The antennas most widely used for microwave services include the parabolic dish reflectors and the parabolic horn reflectors or "jack-in-the-pulpit" type so commonly seen on microwave towers and telephone buildings throughout the U.S. The latter type is not frequency-sensitive, permitting operation throughout the microwave bands without changing the feed mechanism. The parabolic dishes are frequently mounted at the foot of the radio towers and aimed upward at flat or slightly concave reflectors at the top to redirect the signal to the next repeater station. The size of an efficient antenna depends upon the wavelength it is designed to transmit or receive; thus, as higher frequencies came into use, the size of antennas decreased. A familiar contrast is the 500-ft. broadcasting tower and the SHF "whip" antenna for police patrol cars.

Arrays of antennas may be so arranged and fed by transmission lines that they produce strongly directional signal patterns. In the 1960s there was increased use of pedestal-mounted, servo-operated, steerable paraboloid (dish) antennas. Another type was a stationary array of phased elements disposed in the form of crossed combs. The length, spacing, and configuration of the "teeth" determined the pattern of the transmitted beam.

Ionospheric and Tropospheric Scatter Propagation.—Thomas L. Eckersley reported in 1932 that cloudlike ionization concentrations in the Kennelly-Heaviside layers might be used to propagate VHF signals beyond horizon distances. D. K. Bailey, of the U.S. National Bureau of Standards, and several associates reported in 1952 that such propagation was observable over long distances. By 1955 Bailey and his associates reported transmissions of VHF signals through the ionosphere, using radar superpower pulsing techniques.

Henry G. Booker and others developed the hypothesis in 1950 that heterogeneity of turbulent volumes of the troposphere also propagates VHF radio waves beyond the horizon. Thus, it became possible to employ scatter techniques in inaccessible terrain, on sea routes, and in the Arctic where other radio systems meet unstable refraction conditions. By 1958 a dependable range of 650 mi. had been achieved by tropospheric scatter, using a power of 50 kw. in the UHF spectrum and single sidebands carrying a 24-channel telephone-teleprinter traffic load. Commercial scatter systems for combined telephony and television were inaugurated in 1957.

Meteor-Burst Communication.—Unseen meteors and meteoric dust particles bombard the earth's atmosphere day and night, often in quantities sufficient to support a type of sporadic radio communication that takes advantage of the propagation scattering effect of a trail of free electrons left in the upper atmosphere by each meteor. Since meteor bursts last only a matter of seconds, messages must be prepared in advance and high-speed data handling systems must be provided. The reflection paths of contact are automatically established by the occurrence of a meteor burst, resulting first in an instantaneous exchange of "trigger" signals between the two stations involved, followed by transmission of the message. When the signal strength falls below a predetermined level, communication is positively terminated so that no message material is lost, and transmission is resumed automatically upon the occurrence of a subsequent burst. Measurements of radar-type signals reflected by meteoric ionization were reported as early as 1948. The technique of applying such reflections to point-to-point radio was considered in Canada, Australia, and the United States in 1952 in connection with other types of forward-scatter transmission, and two-way communication of this kind was first achieved in Canada in 1953.

Satellite Communications.—With the increasing demand for communication services in the period following World War II it soon became evident that improved means of handling large volumes of overseas traffic would be necessary. The high frequency spectrum was overcrowded and radio interference as well as the vagaries of HF transmission made it difficult to maintain good service. Conventional microwave systems could not be used because the curvature of the earth blocked line-of-sight transmission across the long over-ocean paths. The problem was finally solved in two ways—by the use of undersea broad-band coaxial cables and by microwave radio satellite systems.

The use of man-made satellites for communication purposes was first suggested in an article published in England in 1945 by Arthur C. Clarke. In 1946 radar signals reflected from the surface of the moon were successfully detected and by 1958 the use of the moon for narrow-band communication between widely separated points on earth had been demonstrated. However, the moon is not an ideal reflector and its rotation around the earth results in long periods when it is not visible for use between any two fixed points. In 1955 J. R. Pierce in the U.S. made detailed technical studies which indicated that man-made satellites might prove useful for long-range multichannel microwave communications. The orbiting of the Russian Sputnik 1 satellite in 1957 and the U.S. Explorer 1 in 1958 gave impetus to such use and these events were soon followed by the launching in a low level elliptical orbit of the U.S. Army communication satellite Score (Signal Communication by Orbiting Relay Equipment). This was the first communication satellite of record. It carried an active battery-powered repeater equipped to handle a single voice or teletype transmission in real time or by tape recording in the satellite for delayed transmission to any of the four earth stations spread across the U.S. Reception from ground was on 150 MHz and transmission from the satellite on 132 MHz with a power of 8 w. While tests were carried out over a period of only 12 days before battery failure, it demonstrated that communication via active satellites was practicable.

In August 1960 the U.S. National Aeronautics and Space Administration (NASA) launched into an orbit approximately 1,000 mi. above the earth a 100-ft. aluminized Mylar sphere, Echo 1, for tests of long-range communication by reflection from the satellite surface. Extensive tests were made between earth stations of the Jet Propulsion Laboratories at Goldstone Lake, Calif., the Bell Telephone Laboratories at Holmdel, N.J., and the Naval Research Laboratory at Stump Neck, Md. Powerful transmitters and large size steerable antennas with means of keeping them accurately pointed at the satellite in its passage across the sky were used. While the test results fully confirmed the theoretical studies indicating the practicability of long-distance communication via passive satellites it was recognized that the provision of high-quality broad-band television and multichannel telephone service could be more readily achieved by the use of active satellites carrying microwave repeaters.

The first broad-band active satellite of this kind was Telstar 1, which was designed and constructed by the Bell Telephone Laboratories and launched by NASA on July 10, 1962, into an elliptical orbit ranging from 593 to 3,502 mi. above the earth. It carried a microwave repeater similar to those used in terrestrial systems, receiving in the 6,000-MHz band and transmitting in the 4,000-MHz band with an output power of 2.25 w. The antennas consisted of cavities around the periphery of the $34\frac{1}{2}$-in. diameter satellite producing a nearly isotropic radiation pattern. Power for operation of the satellite was derived from 3,600 solar cells which charged a nickel-cadmium battery.

Specially designed earth terminals were constructed at Andover, Me., Pleumeur-Bodou, France, Goonhilly Downs, Eng., and near Rome, Italy. In order to keep things as simple as possible in the satellite, it was necessary to use powerful transmitters, large antennas, and sensitive receivers at these earth stations. At Andover, for example, a 2-kw. transmitter was employed with a steerable horn reflector antenna (multiplexed for simultaneous transmitting and receiving) having an aperture of 3,600 sq.ft. and a beamwidth of only 0.12° at 6,000 MHz. Elaborate equipment was also provided at each station for tracking the satellite and steering the antennas.

INTELSAT SATELLITE GROUND STATION AT GOONHILLY DOWNS, CORNWALL, ENG.

During the seven-month period over which Telstar 1 operated before its radio equipment failed, more than 300 technical tests and 400 demonstrations were performed. These tests as well as tests with other satellites (Courier, Relay, Telstar 2, Syncom 2 and 3, and Early Bird) proved the practicability of utilizing active satellites for communications of all types, including multichannel telephony, telegraphy, data, telephoto, and television (both black and white and colour). In order to provide service continuity with satellites such as Telstar and Relay traveling at random in low-level orbits, large numbers of satellites must be used so that at least one will be in operating range between desired earth terminals at all times. Thus 30 satellites in random polar orbits at 3,000 mi. above the earth were estimated to be required to provide service 99% of the time from New York to Paris, though the same satellites could also be used to serve other points as well. Detailed records would be required of predicted satellite orbits as well as means for switching communications from one satellite to another. On the other hand, a satellite flying eastward in an equatorial orbit 22,300 mi. above the earth will make one revolution around the earth in 24 hours and when viewed from a point on earth will appear to be stationary in space. Three active satellites properly spaced in such a synchronous orbit would suffice to provide coverage of the major portions of the globe, assuming they could be held on station. Such a system would avoid many of the problems inherent in low-level satellite systems.

To test the practicability of such satellites NASA built and placed in orbit the first near-synchronous satellite, Syncom 2, on July 26, 1963. Syncom, which weighed only 86 lb., had a power output of 2 w., an antenna gain of 5 db. at the transmitting frequency of 1,815 MHz (it received at 7,360 MHz), and provided a single two-way voice circuit. The satellite was equipped with gas jets remotely controlled from earth for station keeping. Syncom was stationed at 75° E longitude and was tested initially with an earth station aboard the USS "Kingsport," and a portable earth station at Lakehurst, N.J. These and subsequent tests and observations confirmed the practicability of using satellites in synchronous orbit for communication purposes.

Meanwhile, the Communications Satellite Corporation (COMSAT) was organized under the provisions of the U.S. Communications Satellite Act of 1962 and through its efforts the International Telecommunications Satellite Consortium (Intelsat), a partnership of nations to establish a global commercial communications satellite system, was formed in 1964 with COMSAT as the U.S. participant and manager of the consortium. Intelsat owns the satellites and the ground control equipment as contrasted to the earth station communication terminals which are owned individually by the telecommunications entities in the countries where they are located.

On April 6, 1965, the COMSAT satellite Early Bird, the world's first satellite to be used in commercial service, was launched and was soon stabilized in synchronous equatorial orbit. It had a capacity of 240 two-way telephone circuits or one television signal. Subsequently, additional satellites of this same general type and of an improved type known as the Intelsat III series were orbited to provide essentially worldwide coverage and to handle the increasing traffic loads. Each Intelsat III satellite is capable of handling a load of 1,200 two-way telephone circuits or four television signals through two repeaters, each designed for simultaneous communications between several pairs of earth stations. The repeaters which receive in the 6,000-MHz and transmit in the 4,000-MHz bands employ traveling-wave tube amplifiers connected to a directive antenna to provide an effective radiated power of 160 w. The antenna is a conical horn mounted on top of the cylindrical satellite. As the spacecraft spins clockwise for stability, the antenna spins counterclockwise at precisely the same rate so it can be pointed and held in a fixed direction. The beam centre is aimed into the earth's equatorial plane by spacecraft earth sensors or in response to command signals from ground. The satellite command subsystem provides control of the operating modes, the gas jets used for station keeping, and various other functions. Microwave telemetering-beacon signals are radiated continuously from the two amplifiers providing data channels indicating the status of operations. Power for the operation of the satellite is derived from an array of 10,720 solar cells mounted on the outside of the cylindrical satellite which is 41 in. tall and 56 in. in diameter, the antenna protruding another 37 in. above the top.

Intelsat provides interconnection between earth terminals throughout the world, bringing distant places within vocal and visual range. Most of these terminals employ large parabolic antennas of 40–105 ft. in diameter with means of aiming them accurately toward any of the satellites with which they wish to communicate.

BY COURTESY OF AMERICAN TELEPHONE AND TELEGRAPH COMPANY

TELSTAR COMMUNICATIONS SATELLITE LAUNCHED IN JULY 1962

Although the active satellites in synchronous equatorial orbit have proved most useful for commercial service, the U.S. Army Satellite Communications Agency has developed a system known as the Initial Defense Communications Satellite Project utilizing some 25 repeater type satellites (the number may vary from time to time) moving randomly in a near-synchronous equatorial orbit about 21,000 mi. above the earth. The first of these satellites was launched in June 1966. The satellites are spin stabilized and carry simple state of the art repeaters utilizing traveling-wave tube amplifiers providing an effective radiated power of 5 w. with omnidirectional antennas. Frequencies in the 8,000-MHz range are used for transmission to the satellite and in the 7,000-MHz range from satellite to earth. For simplicity and as a protection against enemy jamming, no command system is used. Power is supplied by solar cells arranged over the polyhedral surface of the satellite. Operation is carried on through various types of earth stations located at military bases throughout the world and including fixed terminals at Fort Dix, N.J., and Camp Roberts, Calif., with their 60-ft. steerable antennas and 20-kw. transmitters. Transportable terminals use 18- or 40-ft. antennas and 5–10-kw. power.

The U.S. Army is also carrying on an experimental tactical satellite communication test project in cooperation with the Lincoln Laboratories utilizing two satellites, one in synchronous orbit and one in slightly subsynchronous orbit, to demonstrate the feasibility of this type of operation for combat forces. Frequencies in the UHF band are employed with a power of 50 w. in the satellite. Portable earth terminals with yagi and helix antennas and powers of 100 w. to 1 kw. are used to provide one or two voice or teletype circuits.

The Soviet Union launched its first communication satellite, Molniya, in April 1965 and in the next few years added a number of additional satellites to the system which is used to provide television transmission between Moscow, Vladivostok, and Paris and to serve a number of receiving-only earth terminals located throughout the U.S.S.R. The system is also understood to be used for telephone service. The satellites are in a 65° inclined orbit ranging from about 300 to 25,000 mi. above the earth. The apogee is over the U.S.S.R. so that the satellites are visible from both Moscow and Vladivostok for reasonably long periods during their 12-hour flight around the earth. The satellite repeaters operate in the UHF band with a power of 40 w.

The remarkable development of microwave satellite communication systems could hardly have been so successful without improved methods of detecting and amplifying the very weak signals received from the satellites in the presence of receiver thermal noise. While a number of devices for reducing thermal noise have been invented, two deserve particular mention—the maser amplifier and the cooled parametric amplifier, both of which were developed in 1957. The maser makes use of the different energy levels of electrons in a selected material such as ruby with a small amount of impurity added. By raising some of the electrons from the lower level to create an excess at a higher level,

some of the excess energy can be siphoned off and made to amplify an incoming signal. For this purpose a pump frequency of much higher order than the signal to be amplified is fed into a cavity or a waveguide containing the ruby material in the presence of a strong magnetic field and the desired signal. Photons released when the excess electrons at the higher stages in the ruby fall back to the lower stages combine with the desired signal to amplify it. Unfortunately, in order to make the ruby amplify it must be cooled to low temperatures by liquid helium (see LOW-TEMPERATURE PHYSICS). The cooled parametric amplifier usually employs a variable-capacitance diode or varactor. A pumping frequency connected across the strongly biased varactor causes its capacity to fluctuate at a rate which results in transfer of energy to the signal which is also connected to the varactor. Thermal noise is generated in the circuit resistances in the parametric amplifier in direct proportion to its physical temperature. For best results, therefore, the amplifier must be operated at very low temperatures by use of a suitable refrigerant.

2. Extremely High Frequencies (EHF).—Millimetre and submillimetre waves (4 mm. and less) have been undergoing experimentation since the late 1950s, with prospects of great advantages for long-distance communication through multimode wave guides. Dielectric wave guides, containing no metal, were investigated in Germany before 1920, and in Great Britain, the United States, and Italy between 1936 and 1948.

At extremely high frequencies the thermal noise inherent in a vacuum tube severely limits the amplification of a very weak signal, and both the parametric amplifier and the maser amplifier were used to solve this problem.

The invention of the laser (*q.v.*) provided a means for generating coherent light; *i.e.*, electromagnetic waves of essentially single frequency purity in the visual portion of the spectrum. This has stimulated work on use of these frequencies for communication, particularly in waveguides where the environment can be controlled and for space exploration in regions free from atmospheric absorption problems. By the use of harmonics of oscillators and techniques for mixing frequencies to derive sum and difference products, experimenters are able to produce essentially any frequency in the EHF band up through the visual portion of the spectrum. Because of absorption and stability problems, however, not much practical use is being made of radio at frequencies above 35 to 50 gigahertz (GHz).

3. Radiotelemetry for Missiles, Satellites, and Space Vehicles.—With the age of rockets and missiles and the increasing use of satellites and space vehicles for many purposes such as communication; weather observations; measurements of temperatures, solar radiation, magnetic fields, and solar wind; and ionosphere soundings and exploratory flights to the vicinity of the moon, the planets, and the sun, the requirements for transmitting the results to earth have greatly increased. The process of encoding instrument readings, transmitting them on multichannel radio circuits, and recording the data at ground stations has developed into a special engineering field called telemetry. Telephoto and television signals are also used for sending information back from space. The fact that these transmissions have been performed reliably, even though they sometimes take place over astronomical distances, such as the 10,000,000-mi. circuit from Mariner 2 when operating in the vicinity of Venus, is a tribute to present-day engineering skill.

See also SPACE EXPLORATION.

VIII. FACTORS AFFECTING RADIO PERFORMANCE

1. Mechanism of Propagation.—When a charge of electrons is guided along a wire in response to the application of an electromotive force to one of its ends, a concentric electromagnetic field (which takes a form roughly analogous to parallels of latitude about the earth's axis) is formed about it, in a direction determined by the familiar righthand screw analogy of electric current. At the same time an electrostatic field is produced whose lines of force (again roughly by analogy like the earth's great circles of longitude) are everywhere at right angles to the electromagnetic field. This twofold field is formed outwardly to great distances from the wire, the wave front of the disturbance, involving collision of electrons in space, moving forward at the velocity of light. In this field is stored the energy of the electric charge on the wire. The combined field should not be thought of as having been established in a static manner. Because the electron flow along the wire takes the form of a wave, there is a building up of potential, a transformation of energy, and a reflection from the wire's open end after the manner of a sound wave in an open organ pipe; possibly a second reflection from the opposite end; and so on until the wire is charged and the energy of the charge is completely stored in a steady field.

At this stage, removal of the electromotive force from the end of the wire causes collapse of the field and return of the energy to the wire. In an electromagnet the wire is wound in a coil about an iron core for the purpose of confining the field to a small area. The collapse of the field when the circuit is broken and the oscillating nature of the return of energy to it are made evident by the spark which occurs at the open contacts. In this case the inductive component of the collapsing field is high, the radiation component low. In the antithetical case of a straight antenna wire, the induction field is low and the radiation field is purposely made high. Radiation is promoted—indeed it is made possible—by applying to the antenna continuously reversing polarities of electromotive force, created by an alternator or more often by vacuum tubes or valves oscillating in tuned inductance-capacitance circuits in the transmitter, at radio frequencies (10,000 Hz or more). The rapidity of reversals results in the forming of successive oppositely poled fields before the initial ones have had time to restore, to the antenna to which they were bound, the energy due to the initial fields' collapse. Thus the initial fields are detached and set free to continue onward and outward at the velocity of light in air. At frequencies lower than those used in radio, such detachments of energy are entirely insignificant. Even at radio frequencies there is little radiation from a transmission line electrically balanced with respect to the earth, consisting of a pair of parallel wires, closely spaced, fed simultaneously with opposite polarities; such low-loss transmission lines are often used to conduct power from transmitters to certain types of antenna proper. Radiation does occur when the parallel wires are moved apart or to an angle with each other; maximum radiation occurs under conditions of maximum unbalance, which is the general condition of an aerial or antenna wire in vertical relationship to the horizontal plane of the earth's surface. Another condition of unbalance is represented by the doublet, or dipole, consisting of a straight wire or rod fed from a discontinuity at its middle. In both these cases, controlled unbalance may be said to have produced effective coupling of guided power in the transmitter and antenna to the medium of propagation —that is, the transformation to radiated power is efficient. Receiving antennas and receivers are also effectively coupled to the medium of propagation by the same considerations of design. In fact, except for complications of economics, site limitations, the direction of arrival and polarization of the wave front, and the necessity to discriminate between the wanted signal and interfering signals, sending and receiving antennas are alike in form and purpose and by the theorem of reciprocity are interchangeable.

The respective functions of transmitters and receivers is to emit and extract power to and from the medium of propagation. At the point of reception, the transverse wave associated with each ray of propagation may be represented by electrostatic and electromagnetic vectors lying at right angles in a plane normal to the ray, the electrostatic field being measurable in terms of potential gradient (microvolts) per unit of wave-front length (the metre), as applied against the effective height of the receiving antenna. In free space, away from complications resulting from proximity to the earth and from the constitution of the earth's atmosphere, the receiving field intensity can be calculated in terms of the current in the transmitting antenna, the frequency or wavelength of the electromagnetic disturbance, and the distance between transmitter and receiver. In the case of low frequencies at all distances, mathematical calculations can give useful figures of field intensity as foundation for further consideration of the variables of the transmitting medium.

Sky Waves.—Much effort has been expended by researchers in theoretically establishing, examining, and measuring the now well-understood complexities of the propagating medium. The original Kennelly-Heaviside concept of stratified ionization of the upper atmosphere has been expanded to account for the observed and measured behaviour of radio sky waves. When solar radiation impinges upon the atmosphere from above, it is absorbed unequally at various levels, giving rise to the formation of layers with differing refractive (hence reflecting) properties. In the process of absorbing solar radiation, electrons are detached from gas molecules. The density of the electrons during the daytime and the rate of their recombination with the ionized particles at night determine the changing usefulness of the layers to return radio waves to the earth. Several successive layers are postulated, each characterized by partial inversion of the vertical gradient of ionization density, with the highest value in the midposition of each layer. The layers have been given designations and their approximate virtual daytime elevations above the earth's surface have been determined as follows: D, 50–90 km. (30–55 mi.); E, 110 km. (70 mi.); F_1, 175–200 km. (110–125 mi.); F_2, 250–400 km. (155–250 mi.). Ionization density is greatest in the outer F_2 and least in the inner D layer. At night the D layer disappears and F_1 loses its identity by combining with F_2 at 300 km. (185 mi.). Sunset and sunrise produce diurnally unstable conditions, as the layers rise and fall. Ionization and height vary also with the seasons and with latitude, in accordance with the altitude of the sun and duration of the hours of daylight. While all layers absorb some energy of the wave front by electron collision in the process of refraction, the air density in the D layer produces absorption with little refraction. In the other layers, propagation is best at night, and attenuation of high-frequency signals by absorption in the daytime increases sharply as the frequency used is lowered.

Double Refraction.—Because of magnetoionic interaction between the earth's magnetic field and the free electrons whose progressively increasing density refracts radio waves, the latter undergo double refraction and are split into two elliptically polarized components. The refraction indices and the absorption of the medium are both different for the two, so that a somewhat unstable, emergent resultant wave exhibits elliptical polarization. This has negligible effect upon the handling of message traffic, but does adversely affect the degree to which direction finders yield correct bearings for navigational purposes.

Critical Frequencies.—Important to the course which radio waves take through the refractive layers is the discrimination offered to their transit by virtue of their frequency. As frequencies are increased, experimental waves directed straight up toward the zenith have been found to require ever higher electron densities if they are to be reflected downward. There is a critical frequency, f_c, higher than which the waves will pass on through the layer and not be returned. This property of frequency discrimination is still effective when the angle of incidence, Θ_0, is changed from the experimental $0°$ at vertical incidence to its practical value, Θ, shown in fig. 5. Here the wave passes from point of transmission T to point of reception R through refraction along the arc BAC within a layer having an effective height of FE. The highest frequency which will travel the course TBACR has been called MUF, the maximum usable frequency for distance TR, height FE, and the electron density in the layer. The MUF bears to f_c the relationship: $\text{MUF} = f_c \times \text{secant } \Theta$. Government laboratories make available to radio station technicians graphs and nomograms predicting what MUF will be under given circumstances, taking into account f_c, the time of day at longitude of FE, the latitude of FE, the season of year, conditions related to the 11-year cycle of sunspot maximum, the electron density, and distances approximating TR and height FE. Transmitting station T will use if available an optimum working frequency of about 85% only of the MUF to afford leeway for approximations used in the predictions and for propagation abnormalities. It is evident that if the frequency used exceeds MUF, the signal will follow the straight line TBF and be lost to R, instead of taking the trajectory TBACR. On the other hand, if the working frequency is reduced too much, the layer will absorb too much of its energy; signal strength at R will

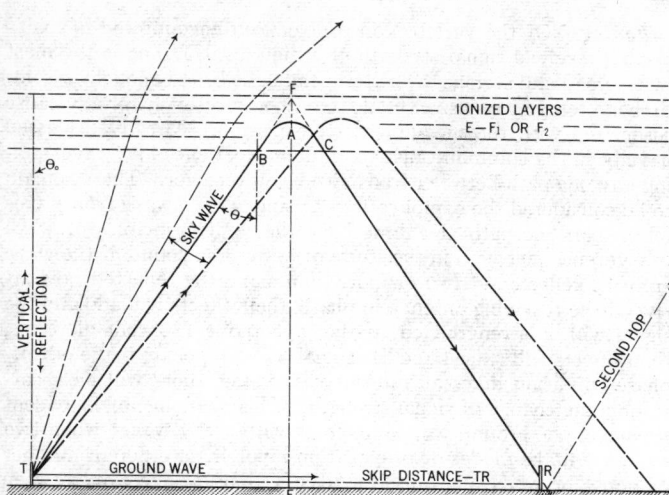

FIG. 5.—RADIO WAVES, SKY PROPAGATION (*see* TEXT)

be too low, or an uneconomical power level will be required at T. The lowest useful high frequency, called LUHF, is roughly half the MUF; its calculation is complicated by variables connected with receiving conditions.

Modes of Transmission.—Fig. 5 depicts what is known as "one-hop" transmission from T to R. If R were twice as far removed from T, the same frequency could be used in two-hop propagation. As a matter of practice, two-hop and three-hop propagations are common and offer no difficulties compared with single hops so long as conditions in the reflecting layer are uniform. Along great circles of the earth, like meridians, which do not cut through the ionospheric transitional effects of sunrise and sunset, multihop transmissions girdle the globe, not only once but several times, and have required that special precautions be taken to prevent unwanted "echo" signals.

Skip Distance.—Assume that in fig. 5 the transmitter is emitting the MUF but that the wave, as is ordinarily the case, is not the single ray TB but a rather wide solid cone of rays with apex at T, fanning out a few degrees with TB as an axis. Confining attention to the plane of the paper, all the rays in the cone to the right of TB will be reflected and fall at points to the right of R. All the rays to the left of TB (by definition of MUF) will pass through the layer unreflected. No signals will reach the ground between T and R from the sky. TR is the skip distance. If the antenna at T is omnidirectional, TR defines the radius of a ground circle about T lying within the skip distance associated with the MUF used.

2. Propagation Variables.—In relation to its medium of propagation, telecommunication has to concern itself not only with the fairly stable complexities which have been described but also with instabilities. For at times the refracting ceilings which the layers present to radio waves from below are almost mirrorlike and still, at other times they undulate, giving rise to shifting transmission paths that change phase interference relationships and polarization of wave fronts at points of reception. Again, especially in the auroral regions, extending 23° in radius about the earth's geomagnetic poles, and particularly around times of the equinox, ionization, also giving rise to aurora polaris, causes severe turbulences and abnormal absorption in the ionosphere. The earth's magnetic field converges on the Arctic regions, leading charged particles from the sun to bombard them. The F_2 layer, especially, is adversely influenced during periods of abnormal earth currents. A statistical correlation has been observed between high sunspot numbers, the location of spots on the sun's limbs, the period of rotation of the sun on its axis, and poor sky-wave propagation due to effects of extraordinary ultraviolet radiation into the upper atmosphere. A more recent theory identifies sunspots, earth currents, aurora, and ionospheric turbulence as concurrent effects that find a common cause in critical juxtapositions of planets in the solar system. Sudden solar flares or eruptions, accompanied by direct ultraviolet radiation which reaches down into the low D

layer on the light side of the earth, result in abnormally high absorption in that layer, whose normal characteristic is to absorb, rather than to refract, wave-front energy. The result is radio blackout, lasting minutes to hours, to which the names Dellinger effect and SID (sudden ionospheric disturbance) have been applied. Radio communication using sky-wave propagation is stopped for the duration of SID because of the inability of radio waves to reach the E and F layers.

Sunspots rotate with the surface of the sun and thus exhibit a periodicity of 27 days in repeating their influence upon radio transmission. The number of sunspots varies over an uneven 11-year period.

Sporadic Transmission.—Not all the variables of the atmosphere are adverse to the propagation of radio waves. Some of them make possible transmissions which otherwise would not occur. One has been given the name Sporadic E, to designate what behaves like a cloud stratum of ionization, E_s, with a "blobby" subsurface from which propagation is neither by refraction nor by reflection but is the summation of contributions of scattering, by secondary emission, from a multiplicity of sources closely spaced. Because they are integrated, such sources may give reliable transmission of very high frequencies below 150 mc. if the beam is aimed nearly tangential to the earth's surface. These transmissions are at frequencies exceeding the MUF of the E layer. They are at a maximum in summer and in zones of visible aurora. Unlike refraction, the mechanism of scattering transmits in all directions from the ionized layer. This may cause direction-finder inaccuracies if, unknown to the manipulator taking a bearing, he happens to be standing within the skip zone of the transmitter. In that event he will be receiving the transmitter's signal not upon the observed bearing of a primary source but upon that of a secondary, scattering source located at some point in the E_s zone having no valid geographical relationship to the point of primary signal emission. The error may amount to 180°.

In the heterogeneous troposphere there exist, as a result of air turbulence, eddies demonstrating deviations from mean dielectric constants (and hence refractive indices) with which they are surrounded. These discontinuities produce scattering effects that at times cause abnormally strong signals, at others abnormally strong interference. In the troposphere, also, where the very high frequencies are transmitted, the air may stratify as to its quasi-optical refractive index, under meteorological influences, in such a way that radio waves are either led along a plane of maximum index between layers of lower index, or are confined between a layer and the earth. In either event, being trapped as though in a duct or wave guide leading over the horizon to distances beyond line of sight, attainable distances of communication are increased. Some observed instances have proved amenable to wave-guide analysis.

Diffraction.—Somewhat akin to scattering is diffraction, the bending of superhigh-frequency waves around an obstacle, building, or the protuberance of the horizon, thus increasing the service range of a transmitter. The intersection of the beam with the horizon defines a point above which the atmosphere may be thought of as a radiator of secondary emissions. In microwave beam practice, passive reflectors are sometimes employed to make definitive the jumping of an obstruction in lieu of diffraction.

3. Interference.—Proper reception of radio signals depends upon ability to receive wanted signals that are stronger than unwanted signals and accompanying noise. Another station using the same frequency in a different part of the world is an example of an unwanted signal. Another instance is a station whose frequency has been assigned so closely to that of the wanted signal that the harmonic content of the unwanted signal overrides or beats with the wanted wave. If the interference is caused by the interfering station's exceeding its authorized tolerance for frequency drift, the remedy lies in having the offending station put back on its assignment. Assuming the interfering station to be on its proper frequency, unless the situation can be cured by use of directive receiving antennas, relief must be sought from the authorities who made the assignments. Regulatory authorities have adopted and enforced standards of frequency departure tolerances, maximum harmonic content of emitted waves, and authorized maximum power to be employed, in order to keep interfering signals within practical control. Based upon these factors, with additional allowances for filter inefficiencies and frequency drift inherent in receivers, the widths of bands for all types of emission and modulation rates have been specified on a worldwide pattern.

Among the types of interference sometimes encountered for which there is no ready remedy at the receiver is cross modulation. When a powerful transmitter's wave strikes the ionosphere, the free electrons, which determine the dielectric constant and therefore the effect of refraction, are agitated to collide with ionized molecules at rates varying from high to low in accord with the wave's modulation. The wave front from another transmitter, striking the agitated layer at that point and at that time with a modulation pattern of its own, will be subjected to cross modulation from the more powerful wave.

4. Signal-to-Noise Relationships.—If a received signal is clear of interference from unwanted signals, its field strength can be amplified to any degree permitted by the thermal noise and vacuum tube shot effects in the initial stage of the receiver. These place a final limitation upon amplification, but serve to limit it only in the very-high-frequency and superhigh-frequency bands where other forms of interference are absent. All efforts at the receiver are therefore bent upon improving signal-to-noise-level ratio, S/N. The three avenues of approach are to improve S, to mitigate N, or to introduce some distinguishing characteristic into S at the transmitter (frequency or phase modulation, for example) so that the receiver will be more responsive to S than to N.

Improvement of the signal may be achieved by increasing power at the transmitter, by choosing a type of modulation such as pulse-position modulation in which bursts of high power are obtainable without overloading vacuum tubes, by adopting directive antenna arrays, or by frequency-diversity transmission. At the receiver many manipulations are possible, including choice of suitable space-diversity antennas, crystal-driven stabilizers, and filters designed to accept all possible power of the carrier and its necessary sidebands and harmonics and to reject all other signals.

Antenna Gain.—Modern antennas for nonmobile use are designed to favour concentration in azimuth, or direction toward the correspondent station, of as much as possible of the transmitter's power. They are of two general classes: antenna arrays and wave antennas. Arrays take advantage of interference between two, three, or more like antenna structures so placed with respect to wavelength and the line of desired propagation that their power adds in the forward direction and cancels toward back and sides. In a receiving array this results in desirable discrimination between a wanted signal and an interfering disturbance or signal arriving from a different direction. The power advantage which an array or other form of directive antenna achieves is called the antenna's gain. It is greatest for multielement VHF arrays and SHF reflectors. A wave antenna is generally less effective in concentrating its beam than an array, but in the larger forms associated with the lower frequencies it has economic advantages and will effectively handle a 2:1 ratio of frequencies. Some large wave antennas are steerable in range. Such a steerable antenna is in the shape of a rhombus or diamond floating on pulleys attached to four poles and so arranged that if the short diagonal is purposely altered in length by force applied through the pulleys, a counterweight will correspondingly adjust the length of the long diagonal, keeping the antenna taut. The antenna wires at one end of the long diagonal are connected to the station feeder; wires at the opposite end terminate in resistors. When the long diagonal is altered, the angle which the sky wave, emitted from it, makes with the earth plane is modified. By manipulation of antenna configuration, therefore, the vertical angle of the wave's departure can be aimed at the point of reflection in the ionosphere. If the long diagonal was put in proper azimuth when the supporting poles were set, the beam will fall directly upon the point of reception. There an array of similar rhombic antennas a mile long may be lined up along the path of propagation for phasing and integration of their outputs, some having been steered low on the horizon to receive the one-hop mode of propagation and others steered higher to respond to other modes.

Fading.—Of the variables in propagation encountered in maintaining received signal strength at a high level, fading is the most widespread and serious. The term fading is broad enough to comprehend temporary loss of field strength at a receiver for any cause associated with the medium of transmission. Already discussed have been the common causes of fading experienced by waves taking any one path between transmitter and receiver. There remain to be considered the complications arising when a wave front takes more than one path at a time. By the same principles of wave interference met with in the study of optics and sound, if the wave front be reflected at two or more points and the reflected rays arrive at the receiving antenna in phase, their effects will add and the signal will be strengthened; if the rays arrive 180° out of phase, their effects will cancel and the signal will disappear; if the out-of-phase condition takes an intermediate value, there will be a corresponding change of signal strength. This phenomenon is evident whenever the ground wave interferes with a sky wave; when two sky waves take modes of propagation involving a different number of hops; or when one of the modes is along a layer, or between two layers; when, in communication between two airplanes in flight or between two beam radio towers, a direct wave beats with another reflected from the ground or from air-layer interfaces caused by temperature-density inversion; or when the arrival waves have taken different routes in the horizontal plane; or one in the horizontal, the other in the vertical; or when polarization rotation occurs in a different manner or to different degree over two routes, or is caused by double refraction. Fading of all these types is called multipath interference. It is rare at very low frequencies. At other parts of the spectrum the fading occurs in cycles whose rapidity increases from around 60 times an hour at 1,000 kc. up to millions of times a second in the SHF and EHF bands. This rapid increase in the fading rate as transmitted frequencies are raised explains the occurrence of selective fading within sidebands so wide that the effects at the top of the sideband do not coincide with those at the bottom. The discovery that fading of a received signal does not occur simultaneously at two points that are three to ten wavelengths apart led to the invention of space-diversity systems of reception. The outputs of separated antenna-receiver systems, equipped with independent automatic volume controls and tuned to the incoming wave, are fed into a common mixing and limiting system that delivers a substantially constant signal to the terminal apparatus, even during periods when the fading is severe.

5. Radio Noise.—*Industrial Noise.*—Upon the assumption that in achieving the best possible signal-to-noise (S/N) ratio everything has been done to favour S, the qualities of N remain to be examined. Noise may be divided into two categories, man-made and natural. Man-made or industrial noise is greatest in the cities, least in rural or isolated localities. The latter are therefore preferred for receiving sites. The chief cause of man-made noise is electrical circuit transients which cause radiation from portions of circuits where sparks occur. Switches, motors, ignition systems are offenders; so are X-ray apparatus, diathermy machines, and industrial precipitators, high-frequency heating, and other equipment employing radio frequencies. Mitigation at the receiver is difficult. The use of directive antennas, wave traps, and narrowband receiver filters is sometimes effective. Usually the correction of industrial noise conditions is sought at their sources, by shielding or isolating radio-frequency circuits.

Atmospherics.—Noise from natural sources, entering the receiver by way of the antenna and affecting the receiver output in the same way as amplitude-modulated signals, takes two forms: atmospheric and extraterrestrial. The superhigh-frequency band (centimetre waves) is the only one free from both forms of extraneous noise; so that in that band, receiver thermal (or resistance) noise alone limits the amplification level. Atmospheric noise, or static, is the characteristic natural interference which has to be dealt with in radio. At point of reception it represents the integration of the field strengths there apparent from nearby and distant thunderstorms going on within signaling distances, transmitted by means of ground wave and sky waves of all modes in accordance with the same laws which govern signal propagation. Atmospherics are at a maximum at night on account of sky-wave transmission from great distances. They are stronger in summer than in winter, weaker in high latitudes than in the tropics. Their sources are concentrated somewhat in geographical areas like the eastern Caribbean Sea, where median values of field strength are shown by measurement to be high. Directive antennas are frequently oriented to discriminate between direction of arrival of atmospherics and the wanted signal.

Since natural atmospherics, like man-made disturbances, contain random frequencies over a wide band, filters are introduced into receivers to reject sharply all noise except the components necessarily admitted with the signal sidebands. Amplitude limiters are also used.

Extraterrestrial Noise.—Extraterrestrial noise interferes with radio telecommunication in the very-high-frequency band (metric wave lengths) and down to 20 mc. There its strength is, roughly, 20 times the thermal noise in the receiver. It is attributable to influences classified as galactic (stellar or cosmic), solar, and meteoric. Galactic noise is at a maximum from the direction of the region of Scorpio and Sagittarius, in the galactic centre of the Milky Way.

Solar noise is of lower field strength than galactic noise at frequencies below 30 mc. but is appreciable at 100 mc. and more. Like cosmic noise it is of random nature, fairly constant in amplitude except at times of abnormal solar disturbances. At such times its strength, at 100 mc., may exceed galactic noise. Solar noise increases are often concurrent with other effects of solar eruptions already mentioned—the influence of ultraviolet light in increasing D-layer absorption of radio-wave energy, and turbulences in the E and F layers which make them temporarily incapable of refraction and reflection. *See* RADIO ASTRONOMY.

IX. USE OF THE RADIO-FREQUENCY SPECTRUM

The value of the radio spectrum depends upon the skilful management of this natural resource. Radio waves recognize no political boundaries and therefore hold the threat, unless controlled, of interfering with radio operations in neighbouring and even far distant countries. Governments enforce within their own territories agreements upon such matters as call signs for identification; allotment of frequencies to specified services; limitations upon the type of emissions (modulations), bandwidths, and power which may be employed; and specifications leading to full occupancy of each band.

1. Frequency Sharing.—Congestion makes it necessary to adopt expedients for making maximal use of the various available frequency channels by assigning a single frequency to simultaneous use in different parts of the world, and by requiring stations to share their frequencies with others, to take advantage of differences in time zones or paucity of traffic to be handled. The urge to conserve spectrum space is made evident, in large transoceanic radiotelegraph operations, by the practice of assigning a single transmitter to cover the requirements of more than one circuit. Such forked use of a transmitter will cover from 1.5 to 2.0 channels of communication. On the most important circuits two transmitters are often allotted for dual operation, so that if transmission on one fails, service will not thereby be interrupted. Pairs of frequencies in a station's complement are also involved in dual emission on most circuits during twice-daily periods of transition between optimum uses of either wave.

2. Modulations, Bandwidths, and Tolerances.—The bandwidth occupied in the spectrum by any emission depends upon the type of modulation, being narrow for hand-keyed Morse telegraphy, considerably wider for voice broadcasting, and very wide for television. Bandwidths are therefore specified in accordance with emission types. A bandwidth may be considered the minimum safe separation between adjacent carriers so modulated. It includes the "guard-band" protection necessary to prevent overlap of its fundamental and harmonics with those of adjacent channels, if frequency deviations are held within specified tolerances. Except for single-sideband (SSB) operation, the band is considered as bisected by the assigned frequency of its carrier.

Radio transmitters must maintain assigned frequencies within narrow limits. For broadcast stations the deviation or drift toler-

ance is 10 Hz, which is 0.001% at 1,000 kc.—a narrow tolerance. In general, a powerful broadcast station is allowed a tolerance only half that of a weaker station; a ship working in the HF band, four times the tolerance of a coastal station; and a fixed station working in the congested international shortwave band (0.0015%), less tolerance than a long-wave station (0.02%). Lifeboats, ships' emergency transmitters, and survival craft have the widest latitudes (0.5%). Drift tolerances have narrowed as pressure for spectrum space brought improved means for controlling frequencies.

The types of emissions permitted and bandwidths specified in the international regulations annexed to the Buenos Aires convention of 1952 are shown in Table I.

TABLE I.—*Radio Emissions and Their Bandwidths*

Purpose and modulation	Emission type	Typical bandwidths (kc.)
Amplitude Modulation		
Telegraphy, hand-keying	A 1	.06–0.1
Telegraphy, four-channel multiplex	A 1	.85
Telegraphy, audio-tone	A 2	2.1
Telephone, double-sideband (DSB)	A 3	6–8
Telephone, single-sideband (SSB)	A 3	3–4
Broadcasting, clear-channel	A 3	10
Broadcasting (depending upon quality)	A 3	8–20
Facsimile	A 4	5
Television	A 5	4,000–9,000
Frequency Modulation		
Telegraphy, Frequency shift	F 1	1.4–1.7
Telephone and broadcasting	F 3	36
Facsimile	F 4	25
Pulse Modulation		
Radar	P 0	40,000

3. Division of the Spectrum.—Table II indicates the useful range of communication in various parts of the radio spectrum, a

TABLE II.—*Uses and Ranges of Assignments*

Frequency	Principal media	Principal uses	Most useful ranges
10-500 kHz low frequencies	Ground wave D layer E layer	Maritime Navigational Military	More than 1,000 mi.
500–3,000 kHz medium frequencies	Ground wave E layer F layers	Broadcasting Navigational	0–1,000 mi.
3–30 MHz high frequencies	F layers	All uses	All distances
30–1,000 MHz ultraionospheric	Ground wave Troposphere	Television Aviation Mobile	Over horizon
More than 1,000 MHz microwave	Troposphere	Broad band Radar	Quasi-optical

list of uses to which the parts are assigned, and the Kennelly-Heaviside layers involved in propagation.

The radio spectrum was arbitrarily divided as shown in Table III by the Geneva Administrative Radio Conference of the International Telecommunication Union (1959) in order to facilitate orderly consideration of its parts. The transmission properties of these groups differ widely. The table shows the active radio spectrum subdivided into nine groups. The first three—VLF, LF, and MF—were used before 1925, the HF band before 1939.

Low Frequencies.—Groups 1 and 2 in Table III, the VLF and LF or ground-wave ranges, alone are capable of following the

TABLE III.—*Subdivisions of the Radio Spectrum*

Group	Frequency denomination	Abbreviation	Frequency range (MHz)	Wavelength denomination	Wavelength range
1	Very low	VLF	Below .03	Myriametric	Above 10 km.
2	Low	LF	.03–.3	Kilometric	1–10 km.
3	Medium	MF	.3–3	Hectometric	100–1,000 m.
4	High	HF	3–30	Decametric	10–100 m.
5	Very high	VHF	30–300	Metric	1–10 m.
6	Ultrahigh	UHF	300–3,000	Decimetric	10–100 cm.
7	Superhigh	SHF	3,000–30,000	Centimetric	1–10 cm.
8	Extremely high	EHF	30,000–300,000	Millimetric	0.1–1 cm.
9	—		Above 300,000	Decimillimetric	Below 0.1 cm.

curvature of the earth. These ranges, called collectively terrestrial radio, are therefore used for long-distance communications as well as for navigational radio.

In the absence of any available alternative, VLF and LF radiotelegraphy was the favoured method for transoceanic use prior to 1927. After that year it rapidly gave ground to transmission on higher frequencies, but served as standby to protect shortwave circuits, especially where routes cut the auroral zones that exist around the earth's geomagnetic poles. Even this utility largely disappeared when, around 1946, electrical relay points located in or near the tropics were found capable of dividing east-west circuits between terminals into two coupled links, the one availing itself of relatively dependable north-south transmission, the other conducting the east-west circuit components through the tropical belt where auroral zones could be bypassed.

The longer VLF and LF waves interested Marconi and other early workers in transoceanic wireless telegraphy because of the results, measured in working mileages, that they yielded. Transmission is dominated by a ground wave propagated to distances up to about 1,000 mi., plus a relatively stable mode of multiple mirrorlike reflections between the two concentric spheres consisting of the earth's or sea's surface and the troposphere and low ionosphere. These act as an effective and efficient wave guide. The rate of decay of the ground wave depends upon the conductivity and dielectric constant of the ground; except for the very lowest frequencies and extreme distances the decay rate is less over water than over land. The wave-guide effect tends to conserve signal strength over global distances. Except for sunrise and sunset effects, fading of signals is not a factor with long waves. The three chief drawbacks to long-wave operation are: the prevalence of noise and static (lightning disturbances are also propagated to global distances by the wave-guide mode of transmission); the requirements of large amounts of power to radiate from an antenna at the very low frequencies and to override the static; and the necessity for building large, high, and consequently expensive antenna structures. VLF waves are generally not suitable for telephony because of the low ratio of the modulation to the carrier frequency.

Medium and High Frequencies.—MF transmission, Group 3 of Table III, occupies a midposition between ground-wave and sky-wave propagation and is best understood by reference to conditions in adjacent bands. The lower part of the band found early use in ship-to-shore wireless telegraphy. Antenna sizes and power requirements are adapted for marine work; distances workable, however, are shorter than for high frequencies. The middle part of Group 3 is reserved for broadcasting. Its characteristics are well known to the public, a ground-wave service area of greater or less extent depending upon power assigned and a night area served by sky-waves subject to fading. Static conditions are moderate. Beaming of antennas and sharing of hours of operation among stations are practices that prevent mutual interference and increase public service.

Group 4, the high frequencies or shortwaves, are transmitted over global distances by multiple-hop refractions through the ionosphere. The HF band is one of the most crowded portions of the spectrum. While ionospheric transmission can be used at frequencies up to 60 mc. or so during high sunspot years, its principal use is at frequencies below 30 mc.

Higher Frequencies.—Groups 5 and 6 of Table III, VHF and UHF, the metre and decimetre waves, were extensively investigated during World War II. VHF transmission is primarily limited to line of sight, but it is stable and suitable for such uses as television broadcasting. With the advent of UHF transmitters of very high power, a new type of UHF transmission called UHF scatter propagation was discovered. This effect was largely attributed to wave refractions in the troposphere (altitudes below 10 mi.). UHF scatter permitted the reception of weak but stable signals far below the horizon. Television transmission over several hundred miles by means of scatter propagation was accomplished in 1953.

Superhigh Frequencies.—Group 7 (centimetre) frequencies are often referred to as microwaves. While Groups 6 to 8 are all quasi-optical, Group 7, SHF, is particularly adaptable to quasi-optical devices such as focusing antennas using parabolic reflectors, dielectric lenses, and horns for concentrating and directing narrow beams of communication power. Expansion of use of this band for terrestrial microwave relay systems was a spectacular development of the 1950s and for satellite relay systems during the 1960s (*see* above). Because of their extremely high carrier frequencies,

microwaves furnish an ideal medium for such high-speed communication as multiplex telegraphy and telephony and television relays.

Frequencies in this band below about 8,000 MHz are not seriously attenuated by hail, raindrops, or snow; but at higher frequencies attenuation due to rain becomes increasingly important. Added absorption due to water-vapour resonance effects occurs in the neighbourhood of 20 GHz. These frequencies are not low enough to be affected by atmospheric or industrial noise. The limiting transmission factors are the thermal agitation and vacuum tube shot effects in the first stages of the receiver, made troublesome because they are amplified along with the received signals.

When communication satellites first became feasible following the launching of the Sputnik 1 satellite, no frequency allocations existed for such services other than a few inadequate assignments for experimental services. Because of the urgency of this matter an Extraordinary Administrative Radio Conference of the International Telecommunication Union was called to meet at Geneva in 1963. This conference allocated a number of broad-frequency bands for space radio communication services as well as frequencies for astronomy and space research. Most of these bands are shared with allocations for terrestrial microwave systems and so the conference placed limitations on the power of terrestrial stations in these bands. Limits were also placed on the field strength at the earth's surface due to transmissions from the satellites. While this was not a perfect arrangement, it did provide frequencies in the crowded spectrum for development of satellite communications, without dislodging existing services.

Extremely High Frequencies.—The EHF or millimetre waves were at the forefront of radio research in the 1960s, and EHF held great promise for long-distance communications. Millimetre waves can propagate with low loss per mile through straight, hollow pipelines, if the so-called circular-electric mode is set up in the lines. In this mode, the lines of the electric field close upon themselves without touching the wall of the guide. In this way, wall currents in the guide are avoided and losses actually decrease with increasing frequency. The use of these frequencies for radio transmission in the earth's atmosphere is difficult because of high rain attenuation, oxygen absorption bands in the vicinity of 60 and 120 GHz, and a water-vapour absorption band above 150 GHz.

4. Radio Spectrum Management.—International agreements on radio take the form of conventions and annexed regulations. Like other treaties under international law they are, in general, binding only upon the ratifying states. Nations are not bound to attend the conferences. Delegations are not bound to sign. In signing they may take reservations that release them from particular provisions. Sovereign states may refuse to ratify, or in ratifying may also take reservations. Nevertheless, so greatly does national advantage lie in international cooperation in the radio field, and so unlikely is it that any other method will prevent chaotic conditions in the radio spectrum, that refusals to sign or ratify are rare. By ratifying, a state agrees to pass laws to enforce the provisions of the treaty, subject to its reservations.

International Telecommunication Treaties.—The first radiotelegraph conference of an international nature was called by invitation of the German government in Berlin in 1903, seven years after Marconi's successful demonstration of wireless. This preliminary conference produced the initial draft of an international convention, which was considered, revised, and signed by delegates of 27 nations, together with its annexed Radio Regulations, at the Berlin Radiotelegraph Conference of 1906. At that time the Radiotelegraph Union was formed, a governing body modeled after the International Telegraph Union, which since its formation at Paris in 1865 had been responsible for the Telegraph Convention and the International Telegraph Regulations. The London conference of 1912 revised the convention and the regulations. The Washington Radio Conference of 1927 inaugurated the subsidiary International Radio Consultative Committee (CCIR), to take its place beside the already functioning consultative and exploratory technical committees on telegraph (CCIT) and telephone (CCIF); it also initiated an action, supplementing that of the International Telegraph Union (Paris, 1925), to amalgamate the Radiotelegraph and Telegraph conventions. This objective was accomplished through creation of the International Telecommunication Union at Madrid, Spain, in 1932, which codified and combined the 1875 Telegraph and the 1927 Radiotelegraph conventions. The regulations that were annexed to the Telecommunication Convention were drawn up separately by a telegraph-telephone conference and by a radio conference at Madrid, as they were again at Cairo, Egy., in 1938.

The Madrid convention and the Cairo Radio Regulations were revised at Atlantic City, N.J., in 1947, at Buenos Aires, Arg., in 1952, and at Paris in 1959; the Cairo Telegraph Regulations were revised at Paris in 1949, with the United States a signatory to telegraph regulations for the first time, and again at Paris in 1958. The Radio Regulations were again revised at Geneva in 1959, and in part by the Extraordinary Administrative Radio Conference to Allocate Frequency Bands for Space Radiocommunication Purposes at Geneva in 1963 and the World Administrative Radio Conference to Deal With Matters Relating to the Maritime Mobile Service at Geneva in 1967.

Agreements on Frequency Spectrum.—The history of the radio and telecommunication conferences after 1927 traces the shifting emphasis from marine radiotelegraphy to the later wide diversity of telecommunication. The complexity of making frequency allocations to users increased exponentially over the years despite the expansion of the usable spectrum into the upper frequencies.

The Washington conference was the first to produce a comprehensive frequency allocation table covering services other than marine. Its work was carried on at the Madrid, Cairo, Atlantic City, and Geneva conferences. As a result of work at Madrid, an official list of frequencies was produced, showing, among other things, the date of notification to the bureau of the ITU at Bern, Switz., of each use of each frequency, and the date each service commenced, as a basis of establishing priority rights to such use. At Atlantic City in 1947 the delegates were faced with the de facto aftermath of World War II, during which the use of radio had expanded at an unprecedented rate under circumstances of enforced inactivity of the Bern bureau.

International Organization.—By the early 1960s there were about 100 member states in the International Telecommunication Union. Headquarters had been with the United Nations at Geneva, Switz., from 1948, when the former headquarters arrangement at Bern with the government of Switzerland was terminated. The ITU became a specialized agency of the United Nations by resolution of the UN General Assembly, Nov. 15, 1947.

The International Scientific Radio Union, with headquarters in Brussels, Belg., is a member of the International Council of Scientific Unions (ICSU), a nonpolitical world organization of scientists maintaining relationships with the United Nations and its specialized agencies, particularly UNESCO. ICSU embraces several fields of science, including radio.

Domestic Regulation.—In accordance with the international conventions, every important country enacted domestic legislation to enable the international provisions to be enforced. In Great Britain and Northern Ireland, control was in the hands of the postmaster general, by virtue of the Wireless Telegraphy Act of 1904, subsequently renewed each year. The application of the act to shipping is regulated under the Merchant Shipping (Wireless Telegraphy) Act, 1919, and the rules made by the Board of Trade under this act. In January 1947 the British government, in harmony with other nationalization programs, purchased the assets of the British company which from 1929 had represented the merged international telegraph interests of cable and wireless; in the self-governing dominions similar action was taken. The government-owned operating company continued in control of operating the worldwide network until April 1950, when operations and assets in the United Kingdom were transferred to the British Post Office. In 1952 the Post Office put its international telecommunications under an external telecommunications executive.

In the United States, commercial radio services are operated by private enterprise, regulated by the Federal Communications Act of 1934, as amended in 1943. The law is administered by an appointive group of seven members constituting the Federal Communications Commission. Among the features regulated by licences or rules of the commission are: assigned frequencies of transmission, tolerances of departure from assigned frequency, types of emission, transmitter power, specifications of performance relating to distortion and interference, hours of operation, and qualification of operators and technicians.

See also references under "Radio" in the Index.

BIBLIOGRAPHY.—*General:* G. L. Archer, *History of Radio* (1938); W. R. Maclaurin, *Invention and Innovation in the Radio Industry* (1949); H. Pratt, "The First 50 Years of International Radio Communication," *Communication and Electronics,* no. 3, p. 371 (1952); O. E. Dunlap, *Radio's 100 Men of Science* (1944); J. M. Herring and G. C. Gross, *Telecommunications* (1936); G. A. Codding, Jr., *The International Telecommunication Union* (1952); P. Richard, "The Problems of Frequency Assignment in the Fixed Service Bands," *Telecommunication Jour.,* vol. 17, pp. 158–370 (1950); President's Communications Policy Board, *Telecommunications—a Program for Progress* (1951); Joint Technical Advisory Committee, *Radio Spectrum Conservation* (1964); J. Laffay, "The State of International Telegraphy," *Telecommunication Jour.,* vol. 20, p. 72 (1953); J. A. Smale, "Some Developments in Commercial Point-to-Point Radiotelegraphy," *Jour. Inst. El. Eng.,* vol. 94, part iii-A, p. 345 (1947), "Commonwealth Telecommunications," *Proc. Inst. El. Eng.,* vol. 100 (1953); S. Sparks, "International Radiotelegraph Communications," *Am. Inst. El. Eng. Paper 48–131* (1948); J. A. Krcek, "Aspects of Naval Communication Systems," *Trans. Inst. Radio Eng.,* vol. CS–1, p. 54 (1953); J. C. Walter, "A Million-Watt Naval Communication Transmitter," *Communication and Electronics,* no. 8, p. 369 (1953); E. Barnouw, *Tower in Babel: a History of Broadcasting in the U.S.,* vol. 1 (1966); A. Briggs, *History of Broadcasting in the United Kingdom,* vol. 1, *Birth of Broadcasting* (1961), vol. 2, *Golden Age of Wireless* (1965); I. Settel, *Pictorial History of Radio* (1967); S. J. Slate and J. Cook, *It Sounds Impossible* (1963); P. Tyler (ed.), *Television and Radio* (1961); G. C. Southworth, *Forty Years of Radio Research* (1962); J. D. Kraus, *Radio Astronomy* (1966); J. R. Pierce, *Beginnings of Satellite Communications* (1968); D. Sarnoff, *Looking Ahead: the Papers of David Sarnoff* (1968); R. Kompfner, "Electron Devices in Science and Technology," *IEEE Spectrum,* 4:47–52 (September 1967); R. I. Colin, "Otto Scheller and Invention and Applications of Radio-Range Principle," *Elecl. Commun.,* 3: 359–68 (1965); J. H. Hammond and E. S. Purington, "A History of Some Foundations of Modern Radio-Electronic Technology," *Proc. IRE,* 45:1191–1208 (September 1957); "Electronics" (50th Anniv. Issue), *Proc. IRE,* 50:529–1420 (May 1962); G. Marconi, "Radio Telegraphy," *Proc. IRE,* 50:1748–57 (August 1962); C. Susskind, "Popov and the Beginnings of Radio-Telegraphy," *Proc. IRE,* 50:2036–47 (October 1962); J. Blanchard, "A Pioneering Attempt at Multiplex Telephony," *Proc. IRE,* 51:1706–09 (December 1963); E. H. Colpitts and O. B. Blackwell, "Carrier Current Telephony and Telegraphy," *Proc. IEEE,* 52:340–59 (April 1964).

Handbooks: A. T. Starr, *Radio and Radar Technique* (1953); K. Henney (ed.), *The Radio Engineering Handbook,* 5th ed. (1959); H. Pender and K. McIlwain (eds.), *Electrical Engineers' Handbook,* 4th ed., vol. 2, *Electric Communication and Electronics* (1950); F. E. Terman, *Radio Engineers' Handbook* (1943); Federal Telephone and Radio Corporation, *Reference Data for Radio Engineers* (1956).

Periodicals: Institute of Electrical and Electronics Engineers, *IEEE Spectrum, Proceedings, Transactions, International Convention Record;* Institution of Electrical Engineers, *Proceedings; Proceedings of the National Electronics Conference;* International Telecommunication Union, *Telecommunication Journal;* Armed Forces Communications Association, *Signal;* American Radio Relay League, *Q. S. T.; Electronic Engineering; Wireless World; Electronic and Radio Engineer; Electronics; Bell System Technical Journal; Bell Laboratories Record; Electrical Communication; RCA Review; Western Union Technical Review; Post Office Electrical Engineers Journal.*

(I. S. C.; R. D. C.)

RADIOACTIVITY, the property exhibited by certain types of matter of emitting energy spontaneously, was first reported in 1896 for a double salt of uranium and potassium. Very soon it was found that all uranium compounds, and the metal itself, were similarly radioactive. Intensity of activity was proportional to the amount of uranium present (chemical combination being of no consequence) so the effect was attributed to the individual atoms of that element. In 1898 thorium was found to be radioactive in a similar sense: all compounds studied exhibited the property in proportion to their thorium content.

Before these discoveries the position of thorium and uranium in the periodic table of the elements had been strangely anomalous (*see* PERIODIC LAW). The table had listed in almost regular sequence about 75 elements from hydrogen (atomic weight 1) to bismuth (atomic weight 209); beyond bismuth the sequence had been broken and, after a gap of six or seven places, the list had ended abruptly with thorium (atomic weight 232) and uranium (atomic weight 238). Prior to these discoveries there seemed to be no common property by which these two elements could be distinguished from the rest. When uranium and thorium, out of all the known elements, were found to be radioactive, a significant distinction appeared possible for the first time. By 1914 the gap between bismuth and thorium had largely been filled with newly discovered elements polonium, radon, radium, and actinium, also radioactive, and four vacant places at the head of the table had been filled. Understandably, opinion was growing that radioactivity was peculiar to the elements of very great atomic weight. Apart from trivial exceptions, nothing was reported until the 1930s to contradict this view. Up to that time studies in radioactivity involved the heavy elements almost exclusively.

The early study of the radioactivity of the heavy elements led to revolutionary changes in ideas of the structure of matter. At the beginning of the 20th century the theory that matter is constituted of atoms was generally accepted by men of science; notions of the inner structure of atoms were entirely speculative. The study of radioactive processes and radiations led, by 1903, to the realization that atoms are not necessarily permanently stable. By 1911 the conclusion emerged that (as far as mass is concerned) the atom is mostly emptiness, almost all of the mass being concentrated in a nucleus occupying roughly $\frac{1}{1,000,000,000,000}$ (10^{-12}) of the total volume. Next came the important concept of isotopes (1913); and in 1919 transmutation, the modification of an atomic nucleus, was achieved in a laboratory experiment. Finally, the neutron (q.v.) was identified as a product of transmutation (1932). With this last discovery, the science of nuclear physics entered its so-called modern phase; acceptable theories of nuclear structure became possible, and the large-scale release of nuclear energy was achieved (1942). By the 1960s practical exploitation of the discovery of the neutron had effected greater changes in world affairs than had been wrought over more than twice as many years by the only other comparable exploitation— that of the discovery of the electron (q.v.; 1897).

Early in 1934, it was discovered that radioactivity could be induced in ordinary matter by transmutation in a man-contrived arrangement. In these first experiments radioactive varieties of nitrogen, aluminum, and phosphorus were identified; within a few months it had been shown that neutrons could effect transmutation, and the list of newly discovered radioactive species covered the whole range of known elements, from hydrogen to uranium. At this early stage (1934) there were indications that radioactive isotopes of transuranium elements (those of atomic number greater than that of uranium) might be obtained through transmutation, but it was not until 1940 that the first clear identification of such an element (neptunium) was made. Between 1940 and 1961 more than 80 isotopes of 10 more transuranium elements were produced and characterized, and at the latter date more than 1,000 man-made radioactive species were known.

Of the various processes leading to production of radioactive species, neutron-induced fission of the heavy elements has been the most fruitful; this process was first identified in 1939. In 1940 it was discovered that fission may also occur spontaneously, disclosing a new type of radioactivity. The discoveries of 1934 had put an end to the belief that the types of radioactivity as then known were peculiar to elements of very great atomic weight, but in the 1960s it appeared that a similar belief was justified in relation to radioactive fission; for all practical purposes, as far as was known, spontaneous fission must be unobservable with any element below thorium (atomic number 90) in the periodic table. Moreover it was very probable that the ultimate limit in the direction of greater atomic numbers is set by the same process. By 1965 estimates were that, for atomic numbers greater than about 112, every hypothetical nucleus would be so unstable in terms of spontaneous fission that it would never be formed as an identifiable entity. Of the known transuranium elements, that of greatest atomic number (103) is lawrencium. (See TRANSURANIUM ELEMENTS.)

The history of radioactivity divides (as has been shown) with the year 1934. In the following 20 years it was customary to accept this division, and to treat the subject formally under two heads; it was so treated in earlier editions of *Encyclopædia Britannica*. One article (on so-called natural radioactivity) dealt with the phenomenon as exhibited by uranium, thorium, their congeners, and to a very feeble degree by a few other radioactive elements occurring in the earth's crust. The other article (on so-called artificial radioactivity) discussed the much larger number of radioactive species that had been man-made. Although there were historical reasons for this distinction, it was never justified in terms of the principles of physics.

The historical distinction between natural and artificial radioactivity is based on the relation of the lifetime of a radioactive species to the age of the earth. Each radioactive species has a characteristic lifetime (half-value period, or half-life). The half-life is defined as that period in which the rate of radioactive emission by a pure sample falls by a factor of two. In 10 half-value periods it falls by a factor of about 1,000; in 20 half-value periods by a factor of about 1,000,000, and so on indefinitely. For most practical purposes, after 20 half-value periods any radioactive source may be regarded as "dead." Among known species, half-lives range from 10^{-7} sec. to 10^{16} yr. By comparison, the age of the earth as a planet is estimated at about 5×10^9 yr. The only radioactive species with lifetimes within a factor of three of the age of the earth are the common isotopes of uranium and thorium (and two rare isotopes of potassium and lanthanum). By and large these are the species responsible for so-called natural radioactivity. Species of much shorter lifetime (most of those known) must have "died" long ago, even if they had been present in considerable amounts on earth when it was formed. To obtain knowledge of the thousand or more radioactive substances with effective lifetimes that are much less than the age of the earth, it has been necessary to produce these species in the laboratory; their natural breeding place is believed to be in the stars (see COSMOGONY: *Origin of Chemical Elements*).

It has been said by way of definition that radioactive substances emit energy spontaneously. More particularly, this energy is emitted in the form of ionizing radiations; *i.e.*, radiations that dissipate their energy in passing through matter by producing ionization (whereby gases may temporarily be put into a state of electrical conductivity) and other effects. The radiated energy is either kinetic energy of particles or quantum energy of photons; these are eventually degraded into heat. If the radioactive source is a compact portion of matter, some of the energy of its radiations is dissipated in the source itself; the source then tends to maintain a temperature higher than that of its surroundings. The emission is spontaneous in that it is uncontrollable by external agency; its rate is uninfluenced by all changes of pressure and temperature available to laboratory study. But it is not inexhaustible; there is no failure of the law of conservation of energy. For each source the rate of emission of energy continually decreases, as measured by its half-life. Over an infinite time the total amount emitted would be strictly finite.

It has also been said that radioactivity is an attribute of the individual atom (q.v.). More particularly, it is an attribute of the individual atomic nucleus. In radioactive matter the nuclei of the atoms emit energy spontaneously, and thereby tend to change their chemical character. Historically, the hypothesis of the spontaneous radioactive disintegration of atoms was put forward (and accepted as the only satisfactory account of the phenomenon) about eight years (1903) before the hypothesis of the nuclear structure of atoms was introduced (1911).

Many statements have been made without a full definition of terms thus far. The subject will now be followed more systematically, to justify and expand this introduction and summary. The detailed account that follows is organized according to this outline:

I. DISCOVERY OF RADIOACTIVITY

The discovery of radioactivity in February 1896 was an indirect consequence of the discovery of X rays by W. C. Röntgen (*see* X Rays). Production of X rays in a vacuum tube is accompanied by a strong phosphorescence of the glass, and it occurred to several investigators that ordinary substances made phosphorescent by visible light might emit a penetrating radiation similar to X rays. Following this idea, A. H. Becquerel placed a phosphorescent compound (uranium potassium sulfate) on a photographic plate enveloped in black paper. The weak photographic effect obtained was shown to arise from radiation that can penetrate sheets of matter opaque to ordinary light. Photographic action was later found for uranium metal and all its compounds tested, and had nothing to do with phosphorescence. Uranium showed equal activity whether kept in darkness or in the light. Becquerel showed that uranium radiations (like X rays) could discharge positively or negatively electrified objects. A uranium compound brought close to the charged plate of a gold-leaf electroscope caused a rapid collapse of the gold leaves.

E. Rutherford (1899) showed that the effect arose from the production of charged carriers (ions) in the gas through which the radiations pass. In an electric field the positive ions travel to the negative electrode (cathode) and vice versa to discharge the electrified body. If the gas is contained in an ionization chamber and a sufficiently strong field is applied, the ions are all swept to the electrodes before appreciable loss of their number can occur by recombination. The ionization current then reaches a steady maximum value that is not altered by a large increase in voltage. The maximum current through the gas is called the saturation current; its value is proportional to the intensity of incident radiation. Rutherford showed that ions produced in a gas by radiation from such substances as uranium are identical with those produced by X rays, and that the mechanism of conductivity of the gas is the same in both cases.

Marie Curie (1898) used the electric method to test a large number of chemical elements and their compounds for radioactive properties. Only thorium was found to show this effect to a degree comparable with that of uranium—a result independently established by G. C. Schmidt (*see* Thorium; Uranium). Mme Curie also found that the radioactivity of compounds of uranium was proportional to the amount of uranium present, independent of its combination with other substances. This led to the conclusion that radioactivity is an atomic property. With uranium-bearing minerals, however, Mme Curie found that the activity was always four or five times as great as that to be expected from their uranium content. If radioactivity were an atomic phenomenon, this could be explained only by the presence in these minerals of an unknown substance more active than uranium itself. Relying on this hypothesis, she made a chemical study of uranium minerals to try to separate this new radioactive substance. For these experiments the Austrian government generously provided a ton of the residues from the state manufactory of uranium at Joachimsthal (Jachymov), Bohemia. From these residues, which were three to five times as radioactive (weight for weight) as uranium, Mme Curie separated a far more radioactive substance which she called polonium in honour of the country of her birth. Further examination (P. Curie, M. Curie, and G. Bémont, 1898) revealed a second radioactive substance that separated with the barium in the mineral, to which the name radium (*q.v.*) was given. Through successive fractionations of the chloride, the radium was gradually concentrated until it had a specific activity (activity per unit mass) more than a million times greater than that of uranium. The atomic weight was determined (1902) as about 225, and a characteristic spark spectrum of bright lines was observed, similar to the spectra of the alkaline earths. Radium had all the characteristics of a new

chemical element; it had a definite atomic weight, a well-marked and characteristic spectrum, and distinct chemical properties. Its comparative ease of separation and great activity attracted much attention at the time. F. O. Giesel was the first to place preparations of a pure radium salt on the market. He found that the separation of radium from barium by fractional crystallization proceeded much more rapidly with the bromides than with the chlorides, and it was in the form of radium bromide that his preparations were marketed.

While these early chemical discoveries were being made in Paris, Rutherford, in Cambridge, Eng., reported the remarkable observation (1899) that, with a very thin layer of uranium oxide placed inside an ionization chamber, the ionization current (already of necessity very small) was reduced by a factor of about 20 when an aluminum foil 0.002 cm. thick was placed over the preparation. This simple observation indicated that the original discovery by Becquerel depended on only a very small fraction of the (ionizing) energy emitted by the uranium preparation (separated by thick black paper from the photographic detector); it also suggested to Rutherford that two distinct types of radiation were involved. With the assurance of youth (he was 27 years old) Rutherford proposed names for these hypothetical radiations. He called the easily absorbed energy alpha radiation, and the more penetrating type, beta radiation. This daring hypothesis, a characteristically inspired guess, was to be fully confirmed in a few years.

Rutherford had moved from Cambridge to Montreal, Que., in the autumn of 1898, and repeating with thorium compounds the experiments he had performed with uranium, he found that the ionization current was diminished when a slow stream of gas was passed over the preparation. When this gas was collected in a previously evacuated ionization chamber, an ionization current could be obtained in the chamber. When the chamber was sealed, the ionization current slowly decreased to zero, falling to half value in about one minute, to quarter value in two minutes, and so on. He concluded (1900) "thorium compounds continuously emit radioactive particles of some kind which retain their radioactive powers for several minutes." Later, in the same year, E. Dorn observed a similar "radioactive emanation" from a preparation of radium.

Rutherford and the Curies independently discovered the phenomenon of excited radioactivity. Rutherford described the effect with thorium as follows (1900): "thorium compounds under certain circumstances possess the property of producing temporary radioactivity in all solid substances in their neighbourhood. The substance made radioactive behaves . . . as if it were covered by a thin layer of radioactive substance." The Curies had described a similar effect with radium compounds a few months previously.

In 1901 Rutherford and F. Soddy began a long series of experiments on the emanation and excited radioactivity produced from thorium. Rutherford had already shown (1900) that the decay of the excited radioactivity in this case followed the same general (exponential) law as the decay of activity of the emanation, but that the half-life was about 11 hr. rather than 1 min. Rutherford and Soddy demonstrated (1902) that the emanation is a true molecular gas (and very probably "a chemically inert gas analogous in nature to the members of the argon family"); that it is not formed directly from thorium but from a substance "present in minute quantity" and which, when chemically separated from thorium, loses its radioactivity and potency as a source of the emanation exponentially with half-life of about 4 days. They showed that the excited radioactivity arises by deposition from the emanation of an "active deposit," as Rutherford had earlier postulated, and that the radiations from the active deposit comprise the previously recognized alpha and beta radiations.

Rutherford and Soddy then proceeded to study the emanation and excited radioactivity (active deposit) produced from radium. They found (1903) these two substances to be related in precisely the same way as those from thorium, but the half-lives they determined for the radium products were about 3.7 days (for the emanation) and less than 1 hr. (for the active deposit)—values widely different from those characterizing the corresponding products from thorium.

Rutherford and Soddy were not the only early investigators to consider the variation of radioactivity with time, but only they succeeded in bringing order to the findings. In 1899 Giesel had observed spontaneous increase of activity of radium preparations during the first few weeks after their purification, as well as gradual decrease in activity of preparations of polonium. These observations had been confirmed and extended by the Curies in the following year, but none of them had been able to formulate any simple law of time dependence.

In 1900 Sir William Crookes, while attempting to free uranium preparations from any thorium or similar impurity, found that the impurity fraction carried all of the (photographic) activity of the original preparation. He gave the name uranium X to the (then unidentified) substance, chemically different from uranium, which was thus shown to emit the beta radiation of the parent material. Becquerel independently observed a similar effect in the same year. In 1901 he was surprised to discover that his chemically purified uranium salts slowly regained photographic activity with the passage of time, and that samples of separated uranium X gradually lost their initial activity. In 1902 Rutherford and A. G. Grier showed that chemical purification did not appreciably diminish the intensity of the easily absorbed (alpha) radiation from uranium preparations. By contrast, preparations of uranium X emitted very little alpha radiation indeed. It could reasonably be concluded that alpha radiation was specific to uranium itself, and that beta radiation was specific to the "non-uranium type of matter uranium X." Rutherford and Soddy showed (1903) that the decay of activity of uranium X followed an exponential law, with a half-life of about 22 days, and that, as the uranium X lost its activity, the uranium from which it had been separated regained activity of equal amount. At any stage in that renewal of activity more uranium X could be separated from the uranium, thereby again removing from the original source the (newly formed) material responsible for its renewed activity. They speculated "that each type of radioactive matter when got by itself, free from the matter which produced it on the one hand and the products of its further change on the other, gives rise to homogeneous rays . . . either alpha radiation exclusively, or beta radiation exclusively."

By this stage (April 1903), then, radioactivity and its evident complexity had been fully recognized. Criteria had been suggested for distinguishing a single radioactive substance from a mixture of such substances: its time-decay of activity shall follow an exponential law; it shall emit alpha or beta radiation exclusively. However, no one had yet been able to detect diminution with time of the activity specific to uranium or thorium, the only radioactive substances known as chemical elements prior to 1896.

II. THE DISINTEGRATION HYPOTHESIS

Rutherford and Soddy gave a final definitive account of their theory of spontaneous atomic disintegration in "Radioactive Change" (*Philosophical Magazine*, May 1903). This startling hypothesis, designed to explain the manifold phenomena observed, had gradually taken shape over the previous two years. The last sentence of a short paper by Rutherford and H. T. Brooks, read before the Royal Society of Canada on May 23, 1901, had posed the problem clearly in terms of one particular case: "The radium emanation not only continues for long intervals to be a source of radiation . . . but in some ways manufactures from itself a . . . substance, which . . . becomes a source of secondary radioactivity." The important insight here is in the phrase "manufactures from itself"; there were two basic phenomena to be explained: the emission of ionizing radiations and the concomitant production of new types of matter. This point was stressed with greater insistence, and for the first time the notion of subatomic change was canvassed in print, in a paper by Rutherford and Soddy in July 1902: "The position is thus reached that radioactivity is at once an atomic phenomenon and the accompaniment of a chemical change in which new kinds of matter are produced. The two considerations force us to the conclusion that radioactivity is a manifestation of sub-atomic chemical change."

Rutherford and Soddy referred again to the problem in two papers published in September and November 1902. In the first they wrote that the essential features of radioactivity "in all manifestations" are "the production of radioactive material" and "the dissipation of its available energy by radiation." Implicit in this statement was their assumption that the process of dissipation is never very slow by human standards. They imagined at that time that the seemingly constant activities that appeared to be specific to uranium and thorium would be found to arise from separable substances of "normal" lifetime. In the November paper the unnecessary complication of this view was recognized. "A slightly different view is at least open to consideration and is in some ways preferable. Radioactivity might be an *accompaniment* of the change. . . . On this view the non-separable activities of thorium and uranium would be caused by the primary change. . . ."

This modified view became the central feature of the definitive theory. In the paper of May 1903 Rutherford and Soddy stated categorically "it is not possible to regard radioactivity as a consequence of changes that have already taken place. The rays emitted must be an accompaniment of the change. . . . Apparent constancy [of radioactivity] is merely the expression of the slow rate of change of the radioelement. . . . Over sufficiently long periods its radioactivity must also decay according to the law of radioactive change, for otherwise it would be necessary to look upon radioactive change as involving the creation of matter."

Further brief quotation is probably the best way of summarizing this classical paper:

"The complexity of the phenomena of radioactivity is due to the existence as a general rule of several different types of matter changing at the same time into one another. . . ."

"In all cases . . . the law of radioactive change . . . may be expressed in one statement—the proportional amount of radioactive matter that changes in unit time is a constant . . . the constant . . . possesses for each type of active matter a fixed and characteristic value."

"The law of radioactive change . . . is also the law of monomolecular chemical reaction. Radioactive change, therefore, must be of such a kind as to involve one system only . . . the changing system must be the chemical atom . . . in radioactive change the chemical atom must suffer disintegration."

It was not necessary in the 1960s to affirm that the disintegration hypothesis of Rutherford and Soddy has long been accorded universal acceptance; never since its formulation has any alternative even been offered for serious consideration. But it is worthwhile to examine the last three quotations, for the logical connections among them are not as simple as might appear.

The first statement is descriptive of the physical situation as it was appreciated at the time; its content, however, is not fundamental. All that it involves of novelty is the empirical fact that new types of matter are formed in radioactive change. It is rather in the relation of the second and third quotations that the difficulty lies. The second quotation appears to state a general law, the third to exhibit a deduction from that law embodying the minimum of ancillary assumption. That this is assuredly not the case in no way discredits the disintegration hypothesis—every successful hypothesis in physics has involved an intuitive step beyond what was securely known, and the disintegration hypothesis is no exception.

What was known in this case was simply that the ionization current due to the radiations from a pure sample of radioactive material, in an arbitrary arrangement, decreases exponentially with the passage of time:

$$I = I_0 e^{-\lambda t},$$

where I is the intensity of the radiation at any time t, I_0 is the initial intensity, e is the base for natural logarithms, and λ is a constant. No progress beyond such a statement is possible unless notions of quantity and quality of the radiations are introduced. If it is assumed that quality remains constant, then the mathematical expression relates to the quantities: $n = n_0 e^{-\lambda t}$ (n is now the "number of rays passing through the ionization chamber in unit time"). But this statement leads nowhere without a further assumption. The flux of rays must be related to the processes taking place in the radioactive source if anything more is to be said. Assume that each atom makes only one contribution to the flux of rays in an act of radioactive change. If N is the number of unchanged atoms present in the source, the flux of rays is proportional to $-\dfrac{dN}{dt}$. On this assumption

$$-\frac{dN}{dt} = A_0 e^{-\lambda t}$$

where A_0 is a constant; in consequence

$$N = N_0 e^{-\lambda t}$$

(if all the N_0 atoms initially present in the source eventually undergo the same change). From this last equation

$$-\frac{1}{N}\frac{dN}{dt} = \lambda \qquad (1)$$

Logically, there is no shorter way from the experimental results of Rutherford and Soddy to the "law of radioactive change"—and the basic assumptions of the disintegration hypothesis, and others, have already been freely used on the way.

In the mathematical development of the law of radioactive change that has just been given (essentially as Rutherford and Soddy presented it), λ is the characteristic radioactive constant of the second quotation. It is deduced empirically from the ionization current measurements (when the logarithm of the current is plotted against time). The half-life has a simple relationship to λ: when $I = I_0/2$, then $t = \log_e 2/\lambda$. Representing the half-life by T, then $T = 0.693/\lambda$.

In equation (1), the mathematical paraphrase of the statement that the "proportional amount of radioactive matter that changes in unit time is a constant," the symbol N (representing a number of atoms) should strictly take only integral values. The equation itself embodies no such restriction, and to that extent it is unrealistic. Arguments along these lines were first made explicit by E. von Schweidler (1905). Von Schweidler interpreted equation (1), in relation to the individual (unchanged) atom in the radioactive source, by recognizing that λdt represents the probability that such an atom will in fact disintegrate in any arbitrary short interval of time dt. On this basis, $e^{-\lambda t}$ is the probability that the atom will still remain unchanged after a finite time t (reckoned from any instant at which it is known that the atom is still unchanged), and $(1 - e^{-\lambda t})$ is the probability that it will in fact have disintegrated during that time. In this interpretation the disintegration constant λ, defined empirically in relation to the large-scale behaviour of a radioactive source, is identified as a probability constant characterizing the individual atoms constituting the source. In equation (1) it will then be seen that λN does not give the unique, completely predictable disintegration rate at time t, when there are precisely N atoms left unchanged in the source (a situation that could not in any case be identified in practice), but instead gives some kind of average rate, or expectation value of that rate. Since the disintegration process is spontaneous, emission from a collection of similar atoms is random in time: in successive equal intervals the number of disintegrations (even in a source that is effectively constant during the time of observation) must vary around the expectation value according to simple probability theory. According to that theory these variations are relatively more important when the expectation value is small. These are the conclusions of Von Schweidler. They were first put to the test by K. W. F. Kohlrausch (1906) by the relatively insensitive method of balancing the ionization currents from two sources of alpha radiation against one another; they were first thoroughly investigated and confirmed by Rutherford, H. Geiger, and H. Bateman (1910) soon after Geiger's introduction of the first successful electrical counter of individual alpha rays (see NUCLEAR INSTRUMENTS).

Accepting the disintegration hypothesis, it is instructive to recognize the different connotations of the adjective "radioactive" as applied to bulk matter and to single atoms. When a chemical preparation is called radioactive, it is implied that an effectively steady (if diminishing) effect is produced over an extended time. For the individual atom radioactivity is a potential for change that

cannot be gauged by any test, and which is realized in a unique (unpredictable) act of disintegration in a moment of time. Radioactive atoms are in every particular indistinguishable from nonradioactive atoms, except at the instant of disintegration.

The statement of Rutherford and Soddy that "Apparent constancy [of radioactivity] is merely the expression of the slow rate of change of the radioelement" was not nearly so arbitrary in its context as it appears in isolation. Rutherford and Soddy had in fact concluded on very reasonable assumptions, "we obtain the number 6×10^{-10} as a maximum estimate for the proportionate amount of uranium or thorium undergoing change per year." On the basis of that estimate the half-life could not be less than 10^9 yr. for either substance. It is now known that the half-life of uranium-238 is 4.5×10^9 yr., and that of thorium-232 is about 1.4×10^{10} yr., so that the estimate was well founded.

III. THE NATURE OF RADIOACTIVE RADIATIONS

The preceding account of the disintegration hypothesis advisedly makes no specific reference to the nature of the radioactive radiations, save for the statement that to suppose that the radioactivity of uranium and thorium did not decay in time would be "to look upon radioactive change as involving the creation of matter." Thereby, Rutherford and Soddy implied that the radiations were material in character (i.e., particles). Indeed, it had been known since 1899 that beta radiation was deviated in a magnetic field in the same sense as cathode rays (q.v.), and the measurements of the electric and magnetic deviations by Becquerel (1900) had left little doubt of the particulate nature of the radiation and the identity of the beta particles with negative electrons. Further confirmation was provided by more sophisticated experiments by W. Kaufmann in 1902. These experiments, in particular, demonstrated the very high velocities (within a few parts percent of the velocity of light) with which beta particles are emitted in some cases. However, in 1902 the situation had not been so clear-cut in respect of the alpha radiation; many investigators used the purely descriptive term "nondeviable" because of their failure to detect the deviation of alpha radiation with the magnetic fields and radioactive sources then available. It required a long series of experiments (extending over six or seven years) to settle the question of the nature of this radiation. From these experiments, as side issues, emerged the first tolerably accurate direct determination of the magnitude of the elementary electric charge, and the most convincing verification of a basic assumption of the kinetic theory of gases that has ever been achieved.

As long as alpha radiation was thought to be magnetically nondeviable, many workers regarded it as a type of easily absorbed X radiation. As late as September 1902 Rutherford and Soddy appeared to incline to this view. Describing the then recent discovery of beta radiation from thorium products, they wrote: "It has recently been found . . . that thorium compounds, in addition to a type of easily absorbed Röntgen rays . . . emit also rays of a very penetrating character deviable in the magnetic field." But by January 1903, Rutherford had entirely revised this opinion. He wrote, "I have recently been led, by a mass of indirect evidence, to the view that the α-rays are in reality charged bodies projected with great velocity." In May 1903 Rutherford and Soddy were in no further doubt: "In the light of this evidence there is every reason to suppose, not merely that the expulsion of a charged particle accompanies the change, but that this expulsion actually is the change."

The crucial evidence on which this revision of view was based was Rutherford's observation of the magnetic and electric deviation of alpha rays (February 1903). From measurements made with the simplest apparatus (a gold-leaf electroscope as detector, and a thin layer of radium bromide as alpha-ray source), he concluded that the easily absorbed radiation from such a source consists of positively charged particles, of mass comparable with that of the hydrogen or helium atom, projected with velocities of the order of one-tenth the velocity of light.

In the 1960s it seemed almost incredible that Rutherford should have been able to deduce such precise information from so crude an experiment. He had, in fact, estimated the specific charge (see

ELECTRON: *Specific Charge [e/m] for Free Electrons*) of the particles to within 20% of its accurately determined value. A few months previously (November 1902) he had remarked on the fact that the apparently inert gas helium (then recently discovered in terrestrial sources) is found on earth only in minerals that have uranium or thorium as an important constituent, and he had written, "the speculation naturally arises whether the presence of helium . . . may not be connected with their radioactivity." By May 1903 this speculation had hardened into personal conviction: helium was an end product of radioactivity; indeed, alpha particles and helium were merely active and passive phases of the same ultimate product; in fact, alpha particles were charged atoms of helium. That, it is clear from the evidence, was Rutherford's personal conviction at the time; but he was still a long way from proving it to others' satisfaction.

By 1906 stronger sources of radiation had become generally available, and Rutherford was able to examine alpha radiation under experimental conditions more precise than any previously contrived. He showed that, besides being the same from whatever source the alpha particles were obtained, the specific charge (e/m) was almost exactly one-half of that of hydrogen ions in electrolytes. Thus the particles could be singly charged particles of mass 2, doubly charged particles of mass 4 (helium), particles with three charges and mass 6; Rutherford did not consider that they could be heavier than this. Clearly, it was necessary to determine the charge e, if the mass m were to be known directly.

In 1907 Rutherford moved to Manchester, and in the following year he and Geiger determined the charge on the alpha particle experimentally through three distinct series of measurements: the rate of emission of alpha particles from a weak source; the rate of transport of charge by alpha particles from a very much stronger source; and the comparison of the radioactive strengths of these sources. The value obtained for the charge was 9.3×10^{-10} electrostatic units (esu). Determinations of the electronic (ionic) charge available for comparison ranged from 3.1×10^{-10} to 4.06×10^{-10} esu. There was an obvious temptation to conclude that the alpha particle carried three unit charges—but Rutherford suggested that the magnitude of the elementary charge should be revised to 4.65×10^{-10} esu. His intuition was later verified (the accurately measured unit charge is 4.80×10^{-10} esu), but he had still to convince his colleagues in other laboratories.

In 1909 Rutherford and J. T. Royds performed the crucial experiment. They introduced an intense source of radium emanation into a capillary tube, the walls of which were thin enough to allow alpha particles to pass through. In one arrangement the tube was fitted with a lead sheath, and was surrounded by an evacuated vessel. After some days, when the lead sheath was removed, and melted in a vacuum, it was established spectroscopically that helium gas was released from the lead. Control experiments showed that there had been no helium in the lead previously, and that the thin capillary tube was impervious to ordinary helium under considerable pressure. By this essentially simple experiment Rutherford reached his long-foreseen goal in a single step: "dead" alpha particles are atoms of helium gas. Harking back to the results of the previous year's determination of the charge carried by the alpha particle, Rutherford could assert that "live" alpha particles are fast-moving atoms of helium (mass 4) carrying two positive charges. In this way his earlier suggestion regarding the magnitude of the elementary electronic charge was also verified.

It should be recorded that Rutherford's speculation concerning the intimate connection between helium production and radioactive disintegration (1902) had been shown to be valid at a much earlier stage. In 1903 Sir William Ramsay and Soddy had observed production of helium by radium, and by radium emanation. In 1908 Sir James Dewar determined the rate of production quantitatively, and the experiment was repeated by B. B. Boltwood and Rutherford in 1911. Under steady conditions in a sealed container helium accumulates at a rate of 172 mm³ (at standard temperature and pressure) per year, per gram of radium enclosed.

Recall that Rutherford and Geiger had already (1908) determined the rate of emission of alpha particles from a known quantity of radium. When this value was combined with the determination of the rate of (volumetric) accumulation of helium by Boltwood and Rutherford, what had effectively been achieved was a direct evaluation of the number of molecules of an ideal gas contained in unit volume at standard temperature and pressure. This constant of the kinetic theory of gases is Loschmidt's number, and the agreement between the value of the constant obtained from such experiments in radioactivity, and that deduced by earlier (less direct) methods, provided convincing support for the theory (*see* ATOM: *Size and Mass of Atoms*).

The earliest investigations (1899) of the penetrating power of beta radiation from uranium had shown that its intensity (estimated by ionization or photographic effect) was reduced to half value in about 0.5 mm. of aluminum or 0.15 mm. of copper, and that the law of absorption was approximately exponential. In 1900 P. Villard reported that a photographic effect could still be detected with radium preparations through 20 cm. of iron or several centimetres of lead; moreover, the radiation responsible for this effect was not deviable by a magnetic field. It appeared that a third type of radioactive radiation had been discovered. Becquerel confirmed Villard's observations, and in 1902 Rutherford showed that the radiations in question originated in the active deposit of radium and that very similar radiations were emitted by the active deposit of thorium. But he did not immediately accept the view that these very penetrating radiations were different in character from beta rays (electrons with velocities very close to the velocity of light would be effectively nondeviable magnetically). In the paper "Radioactive Change" (May 1903) there is, in a footnote, the first indication of such acceptance: "These rays have not yet been sufficiently examined to make any discussion possible of the part they play in radioactive processes." Then, for the first time, in June 1903, Rutherford referred to the very penetrating radiation by a distinctive name—the obvious designation, "gamma rays": "There are three distinct types of radiation spontaneously emitted from radioactive bodies, which may be called the α, β and γ rays . . . . The γ rays are probably like Röntgen rays . . . ." Others had made this last suggestion earlier, but it was not until the following year that Rutherford was really satisfied with it. Following an investigation by A. S. Eve (1904), he wrote: "All the experimental evidence so far obtained is now in agreement with the view that the γ rays are very penetrating Röntgen rays which have their source in the atom of the radio-active substance at the moment of expulsion of the β or kathodic particle . . . it is to be expected that Röntgen rays would be set up at the sudden starting as well as at the sudden stopping of the electron or β particle."

The conclusions that gamma rays are the same as X rays, and that in general their emission in radioactive disintegration is a secondary process associated with particle emission, have both stood the test of time, but the precise nature of the relationship suggested by Rutherford in 1904 has not. A secondary radiation related to beta radiation in very much the same way as Rutherford suggested that gamma rays were related was discovered (1927) as a very feeble accompaniment in all beta disintegration processes. This secondary radiation (bremsstrahlung) has since been the object of many investigations.

IV. RADIOACTIVE SERIES AND ISOTOPES

The idea of a series of successive radioactive disintegrations is explicit in the writings of Rutherford and Soddy quoted earlier (*e.g.*, "each type of radioactive matter when got by itself, free from the matter which produced it on the one hand and the products of its further change on the other . . ."). The working out of this idea proceeded rapidly in the years that followed. In May 1904 Rutherford gave a detailed mathematical discussion of its implications in a Bakerian lecture before the Royal Society of London. Before he submitted the lecture for publication in August 1904, much new material had been included, and more was added when he received the proofs for correction. At that stage four fragmentary disintegration series had been recognized, with uranium, thorium, radium, and actinium as effective parent bodies (actinium was identified and named in 1899 by A. Debierne), though it was clear that radium could not be the original parent of the third of these series, and unlikely that actinium could be the initial parent of the fourth. In estimating the half-lives of uranium and thorium as greater than 10^9 yr. Rutherford and Soddy had also concluded that the half-life of radium could not be more than a few thousand years, "so that it appears certain that the radium present in a mineral has not been in existence as long as the mineral itself, but is being continually produced by radioactive change."

The ratio of the amount of radium to the amount of uranium in geologically old minerals that had lain undisturbed for very long periods was investigated by Boltwood, R. J. Strutt (later Lord Rayleigh), and H. N. McCoy in 1904–06. Their conclusion that this ratio is effectively constant has been amply confirmed. Unchanged uranium minerals more than a few million years old always have been found to contain about 3.43 parts of radium by weight to 10^7 parts of uranium. This is what would be expected if radium were a direct descendant of uranium in the disintegration series, and if none of the hypothetical intermediate products had a half-life longer than about 5×10^5 yr. In such circumstances there would be so-called radioactive equilibrium in the mineral, each of the daughter products being present in such amount that its rate of disappearance through disintegration counterbalanced its rate of production from the immediately preceding product in the series. Disintegration rates, in these circumstances, would be the same for all members of the series, and equilibrium concentrations by weight (more precisely, by number of atoms) of the members of the series would be in the same proportion as the half-lives (T).

Boltwood (1908) was first to try chemically separating the daughter products of uranium from an unchanged uranium mineral in the expectation of finding that their (alpha-particle) activities would be the same, as indicated above. He had already (1906) discovered a product (to which he later gave the name ionium), which he precipitated with thorium as oxalate salts, and which he showed to produce radium at a constant rate (in preliminary experiments over a period of 16 months). But when he carried out the quantitative separation, and compared the alpha activities of the products, he found the results to be less simple than had been foreseen. The activities of the ionium and radium fractions were essentially the same, but the activity of the uranium fraction was at least twice as great as either of the other two. Apart from this seeming anomaly, the total alpha activity of the untreated mineral agreed very closely with expectation, assuming that (in equilibrium with longer-lived products) the mineral must contain appropriate amounts of radium emanation and three other alpha-emitting substances of the active deposit. This double activity of uranium, and certain aspects of the chemical behaviour of ionium, may now be seen as the first of a series of puzzling facts that tended to confuse the understanding of radioactive disintegration series, until the matter was clarified by the introduction of the concept of isotopes by Soddy in 1913 (see Isotope).

When the double activity of uranium was first discovered, there was no known theory to dispute the naive assumption that each disintegrating uranium atom emits two alpha particles simultaneously, whereas the atoms of all the other products each emit only one such particle. This assumption was put to the test by E. Marsden and T. Barratt (1911), who used the method of coincidences, employing two scintillation screens as particle detectors (as Geiger and Marsden had first done in the previous year). No time-coincident pairs of scintillations beyond chance expectation were found. The naive assumption was therefore negated, and it had to be concluded (Rutherford, 1912) that ordinary uranium "is a complex substance and must contain at least two components uranium I and uranium II which emit α rays ... and are chemically so allied that none of the ordinary chemical methods are effective in separating them."

Recall that Boltwood had first separated ionium from uranium minerals by coprecipitation with thorium. By 1909 he had convinced himself (the same conclusion had been reached independently by B. Keetman) that no subsequent chemical treatment availed to separate these two substances, once mixed in aqueous solution. Moreover, he found that any method of separating ionium from a uranium mineral invariably separated the uranium

X as well. It seemed as if thorium, ionium, and uranium X (so different in radioactive properties) were indistinguishable in chemical behaviour. A similar situation developed for products that O. Hahn had been finding in the thorium series: he identified radiothorium in 1905, and mesothorium in 1907. Although it appeared that mesothorium was formed directly from the long-lived parent, thorium, and was the parent of radiothorium, it also seemed that radiothorium (half-life T about 2 yr.) was inseparable chemically from thorium itself. Thus in 1909 four products (distinct in origin and radioactive properties) were known that would unhesitatingly be labeled as thorium on the basis of standard qualitative chemical analysis. There were similar cases: mesothorium had proved chemically inseparable from radium, and radium D (the longest-lived of the products in the active deposit of radium) was inseparable from ordinary lead.

The challenge of these confusing results led to detailed studies of the chemical properties of radioactive substances in many laboratories in the years 1910–13. K. Fajans, G. de Hevesy, A. S. Russell, and Soddy and A. Fleck contributed notably. The outcome was the important displacement law announced independently by Russell, Fajans, and Soddy almost simultaneously in 1913. This states that the daughter product in alpha disintegration has a place in the periodic table two lower than that of the parent, and that the daughter product in beta disintegration holds a place one higher than that of the parent. It follows that if two products in the same disintegration series are to take the same place in the periodic table (that is, to have the same chemical properties) the simplest requirement is that there shall be two other products of the series intermediate between the first and the second of these chemically indistinguishable products, and that (overall) one alpha disintegration and two beta disintegrations shall intervene.

The displacement law very soon received a simple explanation. The nuclear atom model (see Nucleus) had been introduced by Rutherford in 1911, and the work of H. G.-J. Moseley (1914) was interpreted in terms of the quantitative theory of N. H. D. Bohr (1913) by the statement that the elements in the periodic table are arranged in order of increasing nuclear charge, the atomic number (taken from the table) and the nuclear charge number being identical. On this basis the displacement law follows immediately if the alpha particle carries a positive charge of two units, the beta particle has a negative charge of one unit, and if disintegration in both types of radioactive change involves the ejection of the disintegration particle from the nucleus itself. (By the Rutherford-Bohr theory the alpha particle, at least, could have no other origin.) Note that identification of atomic number with nuclear charge number indicates that the nuclear charge number of helium is 2. The whole picture, therefore, fits together; alpha disintegration involves emission from the nucleus of the radioactive atom of a helium nucleus (doubly charged alpha particle), leaving a daughter nucleus with mass number diminished by four units, and charge number appropriate to an element two places lower in the periodic table than its parent. Similarly, beta disintegration (at least in the context of classical radioactivity) involves emission of a negative electron from the nucleus, leaving the (integral) nuclear mass number unchanged, and charge number appropriate to an element one place higher in the periodic table than its parent.

According to the displacement law there should be two intermediate products of predictable behaviour between the two chemically inseparable members of each of the three pairs of genetically related products thorium-radiothorium, uranium X-ionium, uranium I-uranium II. Because thorium and uranium I are alpha emitters, the intermediate products belonging to the first and the third pairs should all be beta emitters; because uranium X is a beta emitter, the products between it and ionium should be one alpha emitter and one beta emitter. When the law was originally put forward as an empirical generalization the position was still uncertain for all these cases.

Progress toward clarification was first made for uranium I-uranium II. Fajans (1913) showed that the intermediate product uranium X was in fact a complex of two successive products (both beta emitters), the second very short-lived (half-life $T = 1.17$

min.) compared with the first ($T = 24.1$ days). These two products subsequently became known as uranium X_1 and uranium X_2. Fajans' discovery effectively verified prediction in this particular case, but because of the great disparity in half-lives it was not until 1931 that it was shown by direct experiment that uranium II is in fact produced as daughter product in the disintegration of uranium X_2 (C. H. Collie). Thereafter, it was tacitly accepted that the sequence of disintegrations at the head of the uranium series is given as

$$\text{uranium I} \xrightarrow{\alpha} \text{uranium X}_1 \xrightarrow{\beta} \text{uranium X}_2 \xrightarrow{\beta} \text{uranium II} \xrightarrow{\alpha} \text{ionium} \xrightarrow{\alpha}$$

though no one was then able to demonstrate the experimental production of ionium from pure uranium II. At the time no method was available for the separation of this product in the necessary amount. On the other hand, the accepted scheme satisfied the requirements of the displacement law for the chemical inseparability of uranium X_1 and ionium (the second of such pairs of products mentioned above), and its validity was not questioned.

For the third pair of chemically inseparable products (thorium and radiothorium) in 1908 it already was known that there were two intermediate products. Hahn had shown that the product he had named mesothorium in the previous year was a complex of two chemically separable successive products. In the nomenclature of the time these two products were designated mesothorium 1 ($T = 6.7$ yr.) and mesothorium 2 ($T = 6.13$ hr.). However, when mesothorium 2 was separated chemically from mesothorium 1 (as far as could then be ascertained) it took with it all the beta activity of the original preparation. For some years, therefore, until the displacement law was thoroughly verified, it was customary to refer to mesothorium 1 as a "rayless" product. Later investigators generally adopted the assumption that it was a beta emitter as the law required, but this was not verified by direct experiment until the 1960s (J. Tousset, 1960; Tousset and A. Moussa, 1961). The difficulty resides in the very low energy of the beta particles, the relatively long lifetime of the product, the rapid growth of its daughter mesothorium 2, and the unfeasibility of removing such radium contamination as the source very likely contains.

Implicit in the displacement law is the concept of isotopes. Empirically, isotopes are atomic species with chemical properties that put them in the same place in the periodic table; formally they are atomic species that differ in nuclear mass number A, though the nuclear charge number Z is the same. Because the only known disintegration process that involves a change in mass number (at least with the heavy elements) is alpha disintegration, mass numbers of the isotopes of any element represented by more than one member in any one disintegration series must differ by four units (or a multiple thereof). Thus if the mass number of uranium I is 238, that of uranium II is 234. In taking the various series together there is no such restriction. In the thorium series, thorium and radiothorium have mass numbers 232 and 228, but the thorium isotopes uranium X_1 and ionium occur in the uranium series with mass numbers 234 and 230, respectively.

A high-resolution mass-spectrometric analysis of natural uranium was first successfully performed by A. O. Nier in 1939 (*see* MASS SPECTROSCOPY). Three isotopes were found ($A = 238, 235, 234$); the first and last are the genetically related uranium I and uranium II. Their relative abundance (approximately 17,000:1) gave the first close estimate of the half-life of the lighter species (*see* Table I). The isotope of mass number 235 is the parent of the actinium series; its existence was postulated in this connection (1929) on the basis of F. W. Aston's mass analysis of uranium lead (*see* below). It was first detected by A. J. Dempster in 1935.

By 1914, apart from two places in the periodic table ($Z = 85, 87$), every value of Z for the heavy radioactive elements up to and including 92 had been found to be represented, in most cases by several isotopes. It also had become clear that (in addition to their stable isotopes) bismuth (83), lead (82), and thallium (81) had radioactive isotopes that belonged to the three disintegration series. It remained to identify the stable end product of each series, for there was no evidence of alpha activity in any species with $Z < 83$, or beta activity in any species with $Z < 81$.

As early as 1905 Rutherford had concluded that polonium (radium F) was the last radioactive constituent of the active deposit of radium (thus the last member of the uranium series). Knowing the atomic weight of radium, the sequence of alpha disintegrations from radium to polonium, and assuming the identity of alpha particles and helium ions (based then on circumstantial evidence only), he deduced that the atomic weight of the stable end product, the daughter of polonium, was approximately 205. Noting that this value approaches that of lead (207.19), and that old uranium minerals invariably contain lead, he suggested that the lead in the mineral is the stable end product of the disintegration series. Rutherford made this suggestion even though it had been shown (K. A. Hofmann, 1901) that lead from uranium minerals is radioactive; by 1905 he had already given good reasons for supposing that this activity is to be ascribed to radium D, the grandparent of polonium. According to this view, the (temporary) radioactivity of uranium lead is no argument against the hypothesis that a variety of lead is a stable end product of the series; it is an (early) instance of the kind of chemical-identity situation that the displacement law and the concept of isotopes were later to clarify.

The suggestion that lead is an end product of radioactive transformation was made independently by Boltwood in 1905, substantiated by his chemical analysis showing that the amount of lead in uranium minerals increased with the sample's geological age.

With the acceptance of the displacement law it could be predicted that the end products of the uranium and thorium series were the lead isotopes of mass numbers 206 and 208, respectively. Determinations were made of the atomic weight of lead from primary uranium minerals (O. Hönigschmid, T. W. Richards, Maurice Curie), and a preliminary value was obtained by Soddy (1914) for the lead from a Japanese thorite (*q.v.*). These determinations strongly supported the predictions and were reinforced by subsequent similar determinations. However, definite identification of the end products (including the end product of the actinium series, the mass number of which then could not be predicted for lack of atomic weight data) came through the mass spectrograph. Aston found in common lead this isotopic mixture: Pb^{204} 1.5%, Pb^{206} 23.6%, Pb^{207} 22.6%, Pb^{208} 52.3%. With a thorium lead from Brevik, Nor., he found Pb^{206} 4.6%, Pb^{207} 1.3%, Pb^{208} 94.1%; with a uranium lead from Morogoro, Tanganyika (Tanzania), Pb^{206} 93.1%, Pb^{207} 6.9%. The complete absence of Pb^{208} in the latter case correlated well with the absence of thorium in the mineral; the Pb^{206} in the former correlated with the presence of uranium (as is almost universal). More significantly, the Pb^{207} in the uranium lead could not be explained as a chance admixture with ordinary lead, since Pb^{208} was absent; its only obvious correlation was with the actinium products that invariably occur with the products of the uranium-radium series in mineral deposits. It was concluded that Pb^{207} must be the end product of the actinium series; the later discovery of the uranium isotope U^{235} revealed the parent of that series.

By 1935 the three classical disintegration series had been fully delineated with the mass spectrograph. Reflecting the restriction in mass number in any one series, they are characterized as the $4n$ (thorium), $4n + 2$ (uranium), and $4n + 3$ (actinium) series; n may have appropriate integral values to specify the mass numbers of the products of each series.

In this section it has been tacit that the sequence in any radioactive series is unique; for example, that each atom of uranium-238 eventually undergoes precisely predetermined transformations to produce an atom of the stable isotope of lead Pb^{206}. This is an oversimplification: formally, the stability of a particular atom in relation to alpha or beta distintegration depends on whether its mass is less or greater than the sum of the masses of the disintegration particle and the product atom. Frequently, both types of disintegration are energetically possible. Atoms for which beta disintegration is least likely on energetic grounds are those of even atomic number Z, particularly those with mass numbers A that are also even. Most of the alpha emitters of the uranium and thorium series have even values for Z and A, and invariability of sequence is a marked feature of these two series. However, as early as 1906, evidence was found that could not easily be reconciled with the assumption of sequence invariability for the products of the active deposit of thorium. Hahn found that two groups of alpha particles of very different ranges (8.6 cm. and 4.7 cm. in air at standard temperature and pressure) are emitted from these products in equilibrium, the disintegration rates appropriate to the two groups being approximately in the ratio 2:1. Such a ratio could not be understood in terms of an invariable sequence in which one alpha emitter was the daughter (or grand-

daughter) of the other. The situation was clarified by Marsden, C. G. Darwin, and R. H. Wilson (1912, 1913). They showed that the product thorium C ($A = 212$, $Z = 83$) breaks up in two distinct ways. In 65% of cases the thorium C atom emits a beta particle, in 35% of cases an alpha particle (of range 4.7 cm.). The daughter products subsequently produce a common granddaughter, thorium D (Pb[208]); in the 65% mode from thorium C′ by alpha disintegration, in the 35% mode from thorium C″ by beta disintegration. Formally, this behaviour of thorium C requires for its description two partial disintegration constants λ_α, λ_β specifying the (mutually exclusive) probabilities that (per unit time) the atom will disintegrate by the one mode or the other. In this case, equation (1) becomes

$$-\frac{1}{N}\frac{dN}{dt} = \lambda_\alpha + \lambda_\beta \qquad (2)$$

representing the simultaneous decay of alpha and beta activities of a pure source of this product with half-life $T = \log_e 2/(\lambda_\alpha + \lambda_\beta)$.

Radioactive branching, as the phenomenon of alternative modes of particle disintegration traditionally has been called, is now known to occur with all the radioactive isotopes of bismuth ($Z = 83$) belonging to the three classical disintegration series. Apart from thorium C, the other three species in this group, with the corresponding branching ratios (alpha mode:beta mode), are as follows: radium C ($1:5 \times 10^3$), radium E ($1:8 \times 10^6$), actinium C (370:1). With radium C and actinium C the phenomenon was recognized early (1912, 1914), but it was not until 1947 that the rare mode of alpha disintegration of radium E was detected by E. Broda and N. Feather. Meanwhile, an alpha mode of about 1% intensity had been established with actinium (M. Perey, 1939), and rare modes of beta disintegration had been found with radium A and actinium A (B. Karlik and T. Bernert, 1944). Then it was shown that actinium K, the daughter of the alpha mode of actinium, itself exhibits a rare alpha mode (E. K. Hyde and A. Ghiorso, 1953). Careful searches for possible alpha modes with meso-

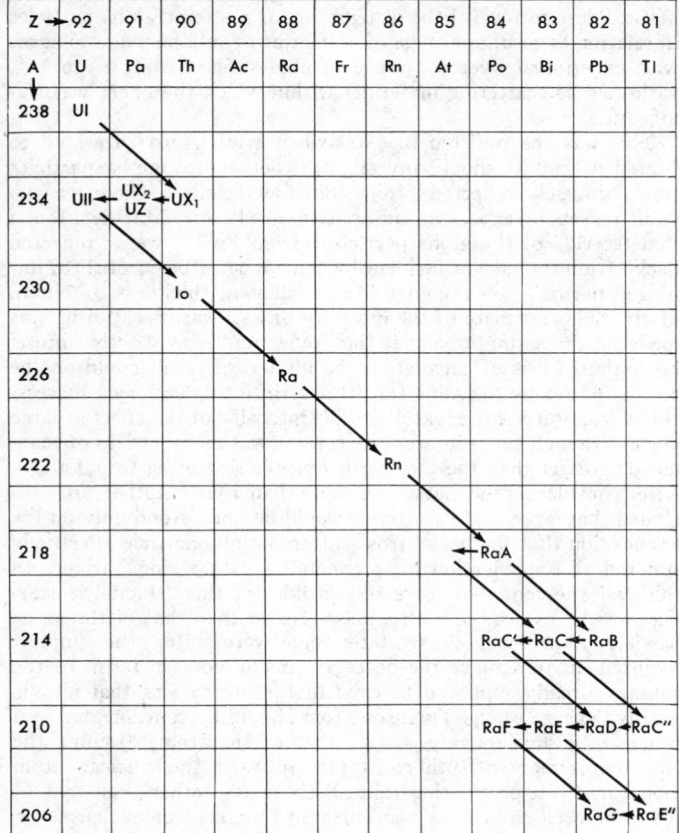

FIG. 1–3.—RADIOACTIVE SERIES SHOWING ATOMIC NUMBER Z AND MASS NUMBER A. THE THREE SERIES ARE REMARKABLY SIMILAR AFTER ATOMIC NUMBER 90, VIZ., IONIUM (Io), RADIOTHORIUM (RdTh), AND RADIOACTINIUM (RdAc)

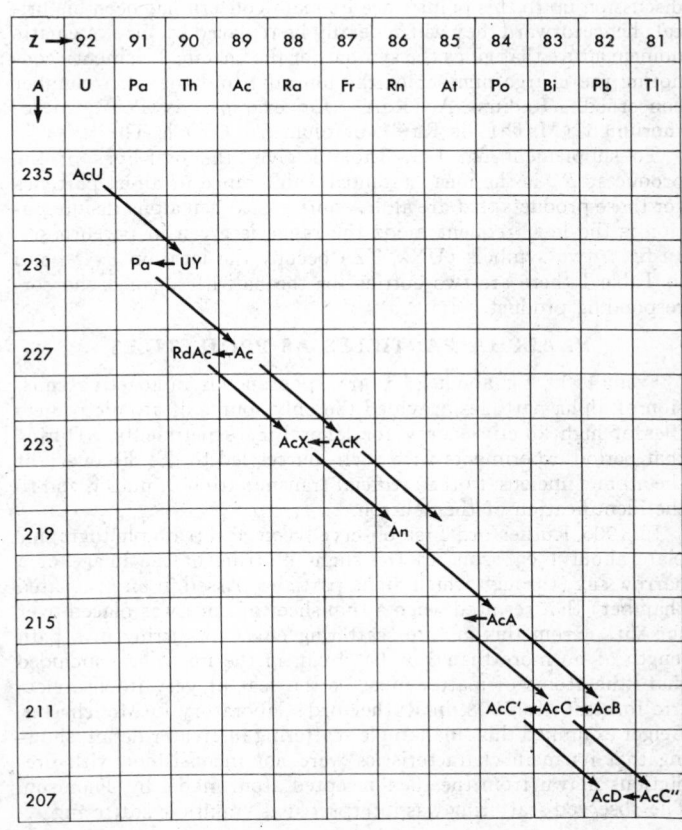

Table I.—*Naturally Occurring Radioactive Species*

Product	Half-life	$R\alpha$(cm.)	Product	Half-life	$R\alpha$(cm.)
			Ra^{224}	3.64 days	4.28
	(See fig. 1)		Rn^{220}	54.5 sec.	5.00
U^{238}	4.51×10^9 yr.	2.69	Po^{216}	0.158 sec.	5.64
Th^{234}	24.1 days	–	Pb^{212}	10.6 hr.	–
Pa^{234}	1.17 min. (6.7 hr.)	–	Bi^{212}	60.5 min.	(4.73)
U^{234}	2.50×10^5 yr.	3.26	Po^{212}	3.0×10^{-7} sec.	8.56
Th^{230}	8.0×10^4 yr.	3.16	Tl^{208}	3.1 min.	–
Ra^{226}	1,620 yr.	3.29			
Rn^{222}	3.825 days	4.05		*(See fig. 3)*	
Po^{218}	3.05 min.	4.66	U^{235}	7.13×10^8 yr.	2.90
Pb^{214}	26.8 min.	–	Th^{231}	25.6 hr.	–
Bi^{214}	19.7 min.	(4.08)	Pa^{231}	3.43×10^4 yr.	3.52
Po^{214}	1.64×10^{-4} sec.	6.91	Ac^{227}	22 yr.	(3.4)
Tl^{210}	1.32 min.	–	Fr^{223}	21 min.	(c. 4.0)
Pb^{210}	21 yr.	–	Th^{227}	18.6 days	4.71
Bi^{210}	5.02 days	–	Ra^{223}	11.4 days	4.32
Po^{210}	138.3 days	3.84	Rn^{219}	3.92 sec.	5.69
Tl^{206}	4.2 min.	–	Po^{215}	1.83×10^{-3} sec.	6.46
			Pb^{211}	36.1 min.	–
	(See fig. 2)		Bi^{211}	2.16 min.	5.43
Th^{232}	1.39×10^{10} yr.	2.49	Po^{211}	0.52 sec.	6.56
Ra^{228}	6.7 yr.	–	Tl^{207}	4.79 min.	–
Ac^{228}	6.13 hr.	–			
Th^{228}	1.90 yr.	3.96			

thorium 2 (Hahn and O. Erbacher, 1926) and mesothorium 1 (Feather, N. Miller, and S. W. Peat, 1957) set upper limits of $1:6 \times 10^6$ and $1:5 \times 10^7$ in these cases.

One further aspect of branching is of interest: actinium K, formed from actinium by alpha disintegration, is an isotope of francium ($Z = 87$); the two daughter products of the rare beta modes of radium A and actinium A are isotopes of astatine ($Z = 85$). These are the only two elements within the range $83 < Z < 93$ that remained to be identified in 1914. The discoveries of 1939 and 1944 showed that these elements exist (albeit in minute quantities) in the radioactive deposits of earth's crust.

Figures 1–3 summarize the data discussed in this section through schematic representations of the successive disintegrations in the uranium, thorium, and actino-uranium (actinium) series, respectively. In these diagrams atomic number Z is plotted as the abscissa, and mass number A as the ordinate. Immediately below the atomic numbers are the symbols of the chemical elements to which they refer. Symbols given for the radioactive products are those derived from names assigned at the time of discovery (or within a few years thereafter). These names have been used in the discussion up to this point since its main concern has been historical; henceforward they will generally be replaced by the systematic nomenclature that gives the symbol for the chemical element (connoting the charge number of the nucleus) and the mass number concerned. Radium A (RaA), for example, is Po^{218}, mesothorium 1 (MsTh1) is Ra^{228}, uranium Y (UY) is Th^{231}.

To supplement fig. 1–3, Table I gives the half-lives of the products; R_α is the mean (standard air) range of alpha particles for those products that are alpha emitters. When alpha disintegration is the less frequent mode the range is given in parentheses. In fig. 1 two symbols (UX_2, UZ) occupy the location Pa^{234}, and in Table I there are two entries for the half-life against the corresponding product.

V. ALPHA PARTICLES AS PROJECTILES

From 1906, for about 25 years, spontaneous radioactive emission of alpha particles provided the only source of atomic projectiles of high kinetic energy for laboratory experiments. During that period experiments with such sources led to the discovery of the atomic nucleus, to the artificial transmutation of nuclei, and to the identification of the neutron.

In 1906 Rutherford first observed (on a slip of photographic plate about 1 cm. square) the slight blurring of the image of a narrow slit (through which alpha particles passed in an evacuated chamber) that resulted when a thin sheet of mica was placed over the slit. From this minute scattering effect, occurring in a path length of no more than 3×10^{-3} cm. in the mica, he concluded that "the atoms of matter must be the seat of very intense electric forces." In 1908, in Rutherford's laboratory in Manchester, Geiger examined this small-angle scattering in greater detail, showing that its main characteristics were not inconsistent with predictions drawn from the then-accepted atom model by Thomson. The observed scattering was interpreted as "multiple scattering"—

the resultant of the many small deflections of the alpha particle as it passed through successive atoms in the scattering foil. In the Thomson model the whole volume of the atom was assumed to be occupied by a uniform distribution of positive electrification, somehow carrying the mass of the atom, yet if alpha particles passed through atoms it was necessary to regard the volume occupied by this positive charge as entirely transparent. The interpretation was not in every respect convincing, but the resulting mathematical description (of the distribution of scattered alpha particles in relation to resultant angle of scattering) could be made to agree with experiment over the range of angles (say, from 0° to 15°, with gold as scattering material) within which the effect was significant.

This was the position in 1909 when Rutherford suggested to Marsden that he should investigate whether any alpha particles were "diffusely reflected" from thin metal foils. There was no valid reason to expect an affirmative result, but Marsden found that 0.005% of the alpha particles (from Po^{214}) were "reflected back" from the face of incidence when a narrow beam of them impinged normally on a gold foil equivalent in thickness to 2 mm. of air. This estimate of the intensity of backwards scattering was made on the assumption that the "reflection" was strictly diffuse, but on any basis of calculation the numerical result could not be accounted for by the same formal description as had been successful in describing earlier results. The intensity of the effect at large angles (though small in absolute terms) was many orders of magnitude greater than the theory of multiple scattering would allow. After considering the matter for more than a year Rutherford concluded that large-angle scattering could be understood only on the assumption that the backwards-scattered alpha particle effectively suffered all its deflection in an encounter with a single atom. In this case the centre of force responsible for this "single" scattering must be associated with a mass greater than that of the alpha particle; if ordinary electrostatic force were acting, the simplest requirement to achieve the necessary magnitude (in terms of the charges already supposed to exist in the atom) was that all the positive charge of the Thomson atom should be concentrated in a sphere of radius roughly $\frac{1}{10,000}$ that of the atom. Joining the two requirements, Rutherford put forward the nuclear atom model in 1911, postulating that all the mass (other than that of the atomic electrons) be concentrated in a central nucleus. On the basis of this model he worked out precise predictions regarding the distribution in angle of alpha particles that are singly scattered in passing through a thin foil; over the following two years Geiger and Marsden put these predictions to exhaustive test. Agreement between experiment and theory was startlingly good over a wide range of angle, alpha-particle velocity, and thickness of foil, and the nuclear hypothesis was verified.

In 1920 J. Chadwick used thin foils of copper, silver, and platinum to determine the absolute probability of scattering under well-defined conditions of angle and alpha-particle velocity; on the basis of Rutherford's scattering formula he deduced the magnitude of the (integral) nuclear charge numbers of these elements as 29, 47, and 78, respectively. The agreement of these numbers with the atomic numbers of the elements in question put the seal of numerical test on the whole general theory. Meanwhile the development of the expansion cloud chamber (C. T. R. Wilson, 1912, 1923) whereby tracks of individual alpha and beta particles in moist gases could be seen and photographed, provided striking visual evidence of the single scattering that Rutherford had postulated (*see* CLOUD CHAMBERS).

As seen in the Wilson cloud chamber (and as required by the conservation laws of classical mechanics) the large-angle scattering of an alpha particle in a close encounter with an atomic nucleus involves transfer of energy to the scattering atom. This transfer generally becomes greater as the difference in mass between target nucleus and alpha particle grows smaller. If an alpha particle were to collide directly with the nucleus of a helium atom, the atom ideally would acquire all the kinetic energy of the alpha particle, and the event would pass undetected in a cloud-chamber photograph, since the recoiling nucleus would assume all the kinetic properties of the alpha particle. It would travel the same distance in the gas (before losing its energy through ionization) as the alpha particle would have done if it had not suffered collision. In a head-on collision with the nucleus of a hydrogen atom, an alpha particle ideally would lose only $\frac{16}{25}$ of its original energy; but the recoiling nucleus would then travel farther than the alpha particle would have done, since it has only one unit of charge rather than the two units of charge of the alpha particle (rate of loss of energy by ionization, other things being equal, being proportional to the square of the charge of the moving particle).

These considerations were first given theoretical form by Darwin in 1914; in the same year Marsden first observed the "knock-on" hydrogen nuclei (first in hydrogen gas, and then projected from thin films of paraffin wax, under alpha bombardment), determining the maximum range of the projected particles as about four times the range of the alpha particles that produced them. During the later years of World War I, Rutherford continued Marsden's investigation, and throughout 1917 paid particular attention to "an anomalous effect in nitrogen," an account of which was published with other results (*Philosophical Magazine,* June 1919). What Rutherford had observed in nitrogen—but not in helium, carbon dioxide, or oxygen—was the appearance of a few particles of range in the forwards direction about seven times greater than that of the alpha particles producing them. By simple comparative experiments he decided they were very energetic "atoms of hydrogen, or atoms of mass 2." He wrote, "If this be the case we must conclude that the nitrogen atom is disintegrated under the intense forces developed in a close collision with a swift α-particle, and that the hydrogen atom which is liberated formed a constituent part of the nitrogen nucleus."

Rutherford moved from Manchester to Cambridge in the summer of 1919, and did no further experiments on the nitrogen anomaly for some time. However, at the meeting of the British Association for the Advancement of Science in the following year, he suggested that the name "proton" should be used to denote a hydrogen nucleus with independent existence. What was to prove to be one of the primary constituent particles of the nucleus was provided with an identity (*see* PARTICLES, ELEMENTARY).

During 1921–24 Rutherford and Chadwick confirmed and extended the earlier observations with nitrogen, and found that, of the light elements of atomic number greater than 4 and less than 20, only carbon and oxygen did not give rise to disintegration protons when bombarded by alpha particles of Po^{214}. (It is interesting that Rutherford had chosen carbon and oxygen, along with helium, as controls in his original experiments with nitrogen in 1917.) In 1925 P. M. S. Blackett published cloud-chamber photographs showing disintegration events in nitrogen gas. From these photographs it became clear that the alpha particle was captured in the process of transmutation, and that no significant momentum was transported from the scene of collision by any particle that had failed to produce a detectable track in the chamber. On this basis the "anomalous effect in nitrogen" was described in traditional symbols as

$$N^{14} + He^4 \rightarrow O^{17} + H^1$$

Artificially produced nuclear transmutation of nitrogen, and of most of the elements in the periodic table up to and including potassium, became accepted fact. In order of magnitude the effect was minute: with nitrogen, about one disintegration per 10^5 alpha particles of Po^{214} completely absorbed in the gas; with potassium, at least ten times smaller—at the limit of confident detection with equipment then available.

Identification of the neutron, a third fundamental advance made through using alpha particles as projectiles, was merely an episode (albeit most important) in the study of artificial transmutation. By 1930 it had been found (W. Bothe and H. Becker) that penetrating gamma rays, as well as protons, are produced by alpha bombardment of boron, magnesium, and aluminum. These observations helped explain an otherwise perplexing result obtained the previous year: Rutherford and Chadwick found that the energies of protons produced in aluminum by alpha particles of well-determined energy were not themselves well determined. In the absence of other radiation it would have been concluded that the

balance of energy in the disintegration was an indeterminate quantity. With the discovery of gamma rays it was possible to suppose (as later confirmed by more sophisticated experiments) that, when a proton of less than the maximum energy is emitted, energy balance is subsequently restored by emission of a quantum of electromagnetic radiation. However Bothe and Becker also found gamma radiation with beryllium and lithium under alpha bombardment, and these elements did not appear to give rise to protons. Indeed, the gamma radiation with beryllium was considerably more intense than with any other element investigated. Early in 1932 Irène Curie and F. Joliot observed the surprising result that the penetrating radiation from beryllium, in passing through hydrogenous materials, projected protons with energies up to 4 Mev by some process that could only be of the nature of an elastic collision. Theoretically this was not inconceivable for gamma radiation, but their effort to interpret their results in this way involved serious difficulties regarding both the quantum energy (55 Mev) and the intensity (of the order of one quantum per alpha particle incident on the beryllium) of the hypothetical radiation.

In February 1932 Chadwick showed that the beryllium radiation produced recoil particles not only in hydrogen, but in all light elements, by elastic collision. By determining the maximum transfer of energy in a number of cases, he was able to show that the hypothesis of a quantum radiation was untenable, and that the radiation "particle" should have a mass very much the same as that of the proton. Because the radiation was highly penetrating, the constituent particles clearly were devoid of charge; Chadwick concluded that the particles were neutrons. The idea of a neutron (mass number 1 and charge number 0) as a constituent particle of nuclear structure had been suggested by Rutherford in a Bakerian lecture in 1920.

Identification of the neutron n^1 having been accepted, the primary disintegration process in alpha bombardment of beryllium was written

$$Be^9 + He^4 \rightarrow C^{12} + n^1$$

Subsequent investigation showed that the kinetic energies of neutrons produced by bombarding beryllium with alpha particles of a definite energy are not all the same; that, as in proton disintegration, gamma-ray emission is necessary if the balance of energy is to be constant. Later appraisal of the experiments of Bothe and Becker made it clear (considering the methods of detection employed) that what they observed in 1930 was predominantly the balancing gamma radiation, as they had supposed. Penetrating radiation observed when beryllium is bombarded with alpha particles is a mixture of gamma rays and neutrons.

VI. MAN-MADE RADIOACTIVITY

When interpretation of the "anomalous effect in nitrogen" was essentially complete in 1925, the species O^{17} (assumed to arise in nuclear transmutation of nitrogen) was unknown as a stable entity. In 1929 W. F. Giauque and H. L. Johnston postulated that this species occurs in small concentration in the oxygen of the air (along with O^{18}). They observed that certain faint bands in the absorption spectrum of atmospheric oxygen could most reasonably be explained in terms of the heavier isotopes, and estimated the concentration of O^{17} as about 0.01% of the total oxygen. In 1932 Aston observed the lines due to the molecular ions $(O^{16} O^{17})^+$ and $(O^{16} O^{18})^+$ in a mass spectrograph; determination of relative intensities by Nier (1950) gave O^{17} as 0.0374% of the total. The hypothetical transmutation product (O^{17}) of the alpha particle-proton (α,p) reaction in N^{14} was seen to be a stable species.

Even before 1929 it had been possible to adopt a similar conclusion concerning every other α,p transmutation process then observed. This conclusion was inevitable for products from the "pure" target elements fluorine, sodium, aluminum, and phosphorus. From the "mixed" elements boron, neon, magnesium, silicon, sulfur, chlorine, argon, and potassium, by a plausible assumption regarding the isotope involved in the transmutation, it could be assumed that the product species was likewise stable.

In the early 1920s, when details of the transmutation process were not yet clear, two experiments in Rutherford's laboratory (by N. Ahmad and A. G. Shenstone) dealt with the possibility that the product nucleus might not be stable. In association with the primary transmutation, no significant emission of heavy charged particles (protons or alpha particles) was observed within the first minute or two after intense alpha bombardment of nitrogen, nor within the first few ten-thousandths of a second after similar bombardment of aluminum. No systematic attempt seems to have been made to look for beta-particle emission. It was not entirely a question of lack of facilities; the cloud chamber, which Blackett was to use in 1925 to study artificial transmutation in nitrogen, could have been used even more simply to detect any electrons emitted from the products of alpha bombardment. But not until the neutron had been discovered (1932) was the stability of products of artificial transmutation again seriously discussed in Rutherford's laboratory. Then it was realized by Chadwick (1933) that the fact that a single nucleus (e.g., F^{19} or Al^{27}) might emit either a proton or a neutron (on capture of an alpha particle) raised a serious problem concerning the stability of one or the other of the nuclei that are alternative products of the transmutation. Arguing from known regularities in mass and charge numbers (A and Z) of stable nuclei, Chadwick and Feather independently pointed out that if neutrons were obtained on alpha bombardment from a target species for which $A < 2Z + 1$, then the product nucleus would not satisfy one of the normal conditions for stability ($A \geq 2Z$). B^{10} (from which positron-active N^{13} was later obtained in this way) was recognized as one such target species, and Chadwick suggested (1933) that in some cases the product might pass to stability through K-electron capture (see below). That year in Chicago, W. D. Harkins, D. M. Gans, and H. W. Newson, having evidence that N^{16} results from neutron irradiation of fluorine, suggested that this species might transform into the stable O^{16} by emitting a negative electron. These speculations, however, were unconvincing and man-made radioactivity continued to await empirical recognition.

Man-made radioactivity was discovered by Irène Curie and Joliot in 1934. In the previous year (with a cloud chamber operated in a magnetic field as detector) they had observed emission of positive and negative electrons from target materials bombarded by alpha particles from Po^{210}. First they were inclined to think that the positrons they observed with aluminum and boron were emitted along with neutrons known to originate in alpha-induced transformations of these elements. (Arguing from assumptions later shown to be invalid, Bothe had suggested [1931] that negative electrons might be emitted along with the protons produced from boron under alpha bombardment.) Later they found that the positron activity of the target was much lower in earlier stages of irradiation than at the end, and that the activity persisted (in steadily decreasing degree) for some time after the alpha source was removed. In that way, the nature of the phenomenon became apparent.

Curie and Joliot showed that the positron-active substance produced from boron had the chemical properties of nitrogen, and that it decayed exponentially (half-life about 14 min.); similarly, the positron-active substance from aluminum had the chemical properties of phosphorus, and a half-life of $3\frac{1}{4}$ min. Finally they identified a negative-electron-active substance from magnesium, with a half-life of $2\frac{1}{2}$ min., which they concluded to be an isotope of aluminum. The conclusions can be stated more precisely

$$B^{10} + He^4 \rightarrow N^{13} + n^1; N^{13} \xrightarrow{\beta+} C^{13}$$

$$Al^{27} + He^4 \rightarrow P^{30} + n^1; P^{30} \xrightarrow{\beta+} Si^{30}$$

$$Mg^{25} + He^4 \rightarrow Al^{28} + H^1; Al^{28} \xrightarrow{\beta-} Si^{28}$$

Note that the final products of radioactive decay (C^{13}, Si^{30}, Si^{28}) are all stable.

Recall that two of the first three examples of man-made radioactive species in 1934 were positron active. The positive electron had been identified only two years earlier by C. D. Anderson as a component of cosmic rays (q.v.) at sea level. Anderson, and

Chadwick, Blackett, and G. P. S. Occhialini (1933, 1934) independently observed positron production in the laboratory when high-energy gamma radiation was absorbed in matter. Anderson and his colleagues showed that positrons are also produced (much more rarely) as a result of the close collisions of negative electrons with nuclei. In all these cases it appeared that positive and negative electrons (of comparable energy) were produced in pairs.

These findings fitted remarkably with P. A. M. Dirac's (1928) relativistic wave-mechanical theory of the electron (see QUANTUM MECHANICS: *Dirac Electron*). This theory had considerable success in explaining the spin properties of the electron without extraneous assumptions, but could not avoid the concept of negative energy states. Serious consideration had to be given to the physical interpretation of these states. As long as a vacancy in a state of negative energy existed in any region occupied by matter, an ordinary negative electron in a state of positive energy should "fall" (in energy) into the vacancy, losing kinetic energy (and positive mass) by radiation. On this basis Dirac assumed that normally all states of negative energy must be "fully occupied"— and he showed that such a system of "completely filled" states would be unobservable. Next, physical meaning was given to the reverse transition (from a stable to an unstable configuration) in which an electron from a negative energy state is raised through absorption of energy to a state of positive energy. Assuming all the other negative energy states to be occupied, Dirac showed that this occurrence would be observed as the creation of two electrons of opposite charge, but both of positive kinetic energy. The positive electron (positron) was indeed discovered in circumstances in which the production, not of individual positrons, but of positron-electron pairs was involved.

By contrast, spontaneous emission of positrons from nuclei in beta disintegration first appeared to be a process of "creation" of a different character. However, G. C. Wick noted (1934) no necessity for this crudely empirical view. In terms of Dirac's theory the process consists in the capture (by the nucleus) of a negative electron from a state of negative energy. When the process is complete, all that is observable is the vacancy ("hole") in the otherwise fully occupied continuum of negative energy states —which "hole" is the free positron. The process involves the expenditure of energy overall, but the energy is available in the (unstable) nucleus from the beginning. Before discovery of the positron G. Gamow (1931) suggested that some atomic species might be unstable (and so be recorded as "missing" in a list of stable isotopes), suffering spontaneous transformation through nuclear capture of an extranuclear electron (probably from the K-electron shell). The suggestions of Gamow and Wick are basically the same (H. Yukawa and S. Sakata, 1935), though different amounts of "ionization" energy are involved. K-electron capture was not recognized experimentally for another seven years.

Once some of the products of transmutation under alpha bombardment were found to be radioactive, similar results were produced with other projectiles: high-energy protons and deuterons, and neutrons. The original observations, all within a period of a few weeks, were by J. D. Cockcroft, C. W. Gilbert, and E. T. S. Walton (protons); C. C. Lauritsen, H. R. Crane, and W. W. Harper (deuterons); and E. Fermi (neutrons). Before the end of 1934 many others had contributed. By the end of 1935 about 100 man-made radioactive species were known.

The first example of transmutation by gamma rays (from thorium active deposit) was observed by Chadwick and M. Goldhaber in 1934. In 1937 Bothe and W. Gentner made many substances radioactive by irradiation with the gamma rays of 17-Mev quantum energy from lithium under proton bombardment. Electron accelerators (the betatron of D. W. Kerst [1940] was first to operate successfully) provided more intense sources of high-energy quantum radiation, and greatly increased the flexibility of this method in studying nuclear transformations (see ACCELERATORS, PARTICLE).

In the first experimental recognition of spontaneous transformation by extranuclear electron capture (1938), L. W. Alvarez showed that Ga^{67} (formed by bombarding zinc with protons, deuterons, or alpha particles) preponderantly emitted a quantum radiation with all the properties of the characteristic K-shell X rays of zinc. Since there is a difference of 1 in the atomic numbers of zinc (30) and gallium (31), and since no positrons or protons appeared to be emitted, Alvarez concluded that transformation by K-electron capture produced the effects. This conclusion received strong support from the discovery of similar effects with many other man-made species, and within a year or two, transformation by orbital-electron capture was accepted as a well-authenticated mode of radioactive decay.

By far the largest single extension of knowledge of man-made radioactive species followed the discovery of neutron-induced fission of uranium by Hahn and F. Strassmann in 1939. By the 1960s considerably more than 200 beta-active species of atomic number between 30 and 63 had been identified among the products of this reaction alone. Since 1945 atomic reactors have produced neutrons of total intensity enormously greater than that of any source of charged high-energy particles, and it is of academic interest only that uranium fission may be brought about by proton and deuteron bombardment, as also by irradiation with gamma rays, in each case at energies less than 10 Mev. But the more recent use of charged particles of very high energy (100 Mev and more) for bombardment has opened a new field of investigation. The distribution of fission products from uranium is quite different with very high-energy charged particles than with neutrons of low or moderate energy; at sufficiently high energies (as I. Perlman, D. H. Templeton, and J. J. Howland first showed in 1947) ordinary stable elements from bismuth ($Z = 83$) to tantalum ($Z = 73$) undergo fission, producing radioactive species in great variety. At these very high energies, spallation (G. T. Seaborg and Perlman, 1947), in which lighter atomic particles are ejected under bombardment, yields radioactive products not produced in fission (see ATOMIC ENERGY; NUCLEAR ENGINEERING).

Since 1940 man-made radioactive species with atomic numbers higher than that of uranium ($Z = 92$) have been produced and studied in detail. By 1958, 88 such species were listed, together with another 143 species with atomic numbers from 81 to 92, many of them formed from transuranium parents by normal disintegration. As early as June 1934 Fermi and his collaborators had obtained negative-electron activities by irradiating uranium and thorium with neutrons. As with similar results with many other elements (from the lightest to the heaviest), these activities were ascribed to new isotopes of the elements irradiated; thus the daughter product in the case of the uranium activity was posited as an isotope of the hitherto unknown element 93. However, not until 1940 was Fermi's hypothetical daughter product identified as neptunium-239, the first recognized isotope of a transuranium element (E. M. McMillan and P. H. Abelson). In 1941 the alpha particles of plutonium-239 ($Z = 94$) were detected for the first time in an "old" preparation of Np^{239}; in that way one small portion of the disintegration scheme of the new elements was in principle determined. The relevant production and disintegration processes may be represented

$$U^{238} + n^1 \rightarrow U^{239}$$

$$U^{239} \xrightarrow{\beta-} Np^{239} \xrightarrow{\beta-} Pu^{239} \xrightarrow{\alpha} U^{235} \xrightarrow{\alpha} \ldots$$

The daughter of Pu^{239} is naturally occurring actino-uranium, parent of the actinium series; thus all of this "natural" series may be said to be produced from uranium under neutron irradiation.

After 1945, Pu^{239} became available in considerable quantity as a possible target material for further irradiation, and techniques of producing multiply charged heavy ions and accelerating them to high energies developed. In that way it became possible to produce isotopes of elements beyond plutonium in the periodic table. Their discovery greatly widened application of the concept of the disintegration series. From experimental data of classical radioactivity, three such series had been identified, with parent species Th^{232}, U^{238}, and U^{235}, and as stable end products three isotopes of lead, Pb^{208}, Pb^{206}, and Pb^{207}, respectively. It is now clear that each series is part of an extensive system of interconnecting collateral decay chains (the species Fm^{254}, for example,

produces U^{238} through four successive alpha disintegrations). A fourth series has come to light (of mass type $4n + 1$, with Bi^{209} as its end product) that is not represented in earth's crust because its longest-lived member (Np^{237}) has a half-life of no more than 2.2×10^6 yr.

Disintegration series for the heaviest elements are most obviously regarded as sequences of alpha disintegrations, interrupted from time to time by single beta disintegrations, or by pairs of beta disintegrations. Among the radioactive products of fission, a different type of series exclusively with beta disintegrations is found in abundance. This difference is simply understood. Radioactive disintegration generally involves the transformation of an unstable species to a more stable species. Among the stable species the ratio A/Z generally increases regularly from a value 2.00 at $A = 40$ to 2.54 at $A = 208$ (and it remains almost constant about this value for the most stable species $82 < Z < 102$). When $A/Z > 2$, alpha disintegration has the effect of increasing this parameter slightly; negative beta disintegration always has the effect of reducing it more significantly. Over a range of Z within which the value of A/Z for the most stable species changes very little, therefore, many alpha disintegrations are possible in sequence before the overall trend from stability requires compensatory beta disintegration. On the other hand, since primary fragments in fission have values of A/Z very close to that appropriate to the fissioning nucleus, they are necessarily very far from stability in relation to the mass (or charge) with which they are formed. For most of these fragments (A/Z being considerably greater than the stability value for the relevant A) a sequence of several negative beta disintegrations has to occur before stability is reached. In view of these considerations it is not surprising that there has been no report of the production of any positron-active species in the low-energy fission of heavy elements.

Since the first observation of so-called stars (see COSMIC RAYS: *Methods of Detection*) in photographic emulsions by M. Blau and H. Wambacher (1937) it has been evident that nuclear transmutations of great complexity may be produced by the high-energy particles of cosmic radiation: neutrons, protons, heavier nuclei in much smaller numbers; also mesons, and other particles of transient existence. Long before all these particles had been identified, certain features of the transmutations had been studied in some detail. It would have been very surprising if the end products had been stable nuclei in every instance, and as early as 1948 the observation of characteristic "hammer" tracks (C. Franzinetti and R. M. Payne) was taken as evidence for the production of the beta-active Li^8 in certain events. It can now be assumed that there is nothing unusual in this particular case, though recognition is especially easy when the characteristic breakup of Be^8 into two alpha particles marks the occurrence:

$$Li^8 \xrightarrow{\beta-} Be^8$$

$$Be^8 \rightarrow He^4 + He^4$$

and there can be little doubt that many "artificially" radioactive species are continually being formed "naturally" in minute amounts in the atmosphere and in the outer layers of earth's crust by the penetrating radiation from outer space. Indeed, maintenance of an effectively steady concentration of beta-active C^{14} (combined as carbon dioxide) in the atmosphere by the action of low-energy cosmic-ray neutrons on nitrogen is well established (E. C. Anderson and W. F. Libby, 1951). It is the basis of one method of estimating the age of archaeological materials (see RADIOCARBON DATING; GEOCHRONOLOGY). The transmutation reaction in this case is

$$N^{14} + n^1 \rightarrow C^{14} + H^1$$

Thus the distinction between natural and artificial radioactivity has become completely blurred.

VII. CONCENTRATION AND CHEMICAL IDENTIFICATION OF RADIOACTIVE PRODUCTS

Radioactive products almost invariably are found in minute concentration, and must be separated from other material to allow careful study. Early studies were complicated by chemically impure radioactive parent materials containing numerous daughter products. Later work done by irradiating pure elementary substances with particles of a single kind simplified the situation. When full-scale investigation of fission products began, chemical complications increased.

In irradiating pure elements, products may be obtained that are isotopes of the target material, as well as those that are not. Of the two, the isotopes are the most difficult to concentrate. If the radioactive product is not an isotope of the target element, the safest procedure is to dissolve the irradiated material, add a small quantity of a so-called carrier substance containing the natural element with which the product is isotopic, and separate the active isotope with it (e.g., by precipitation). Addition of the carrier guards against the likelihood that the original concentration of the transmutation product is so small that its chemical behaviour would be atypical on that account alone. When the mass of the target material is of the order of grams, it is very rarely necessary to add more than a milligram of carrier for successful separation.

Sometimes a transmutation product that is not isotopic with the target element may be separated by older methods without a carrier. For example, in 1935 M. Haïssinsky separated pure Cu^{64} (produced by neutron bombardment of zinc) by electrochemical deposition on lead; as early as 1902 W. Marckwald had obtained polonium on bismuth by this method. J. Steigman (1938) separated Cu^{64} from zinc by electrolysis; F. von Lerch had already made electrolytic separations of the active isotopes of lead and bismuth from the active deposit of thorium in 1903. D. C. Graham and Seaborg (1938) used the partition between ether and 6N hydrochloric acid to separate pure Ga^{67} from irradiated zinc, as well as Mn^{54} and Co^{57} from irradiated iron; the method was used by Crookes to separate Th^{234} from uranium in 1900. Crookes found that, if uranyl nitrate is dissolved in ether, an aqueous layer separates (derived from the water of crystallization of the salt) in which the Th^{234} is concentrated. E. Segrè showed that the Na^{22} (formed from magnesium by deuteron bombardment) could be dissolved out of the hydroxide quantitatively by treating it with water; as early as 1902 Rutherford and Soddy partially extracted Ra^{224} from thorium by shaking the oxide with the same solvent. Alvarez, A. C. Helmholz, and E. Nelson (1940) obtained practically pure Cd^{107} by condensing the vapour given off by deuteron-irradiated silver that was heated to its melting point. Although the process was not understood even in its simplest aspects until 1912 (Russell, and others), the volatilization of the active deposit of radium was first observed in 1903 by F. C. Gates; differences in volatility of the constituent products were already providing methods of separation in 1905 (W. Duane).

When the transmutation product forms an extremely insoluble compound, it may be separated by precipitation even though no carrier is added. Although the precipitate is so scant as to be invisible, it may be collected by centrifuging. In this way highly active preparations of artificially produced isotopes of titanium, scandium, yttrium, zirconium, and the rare earths have been obtained (e.g., J. D. Kurbatov, M. L. Pool, and H. B. Law, 1941). The method was used successfully by C. Chamié and M. Guillot (1930) with hydroxides of the elements of the active deposit of radium. Bi^{210} and Po^{210} may be obtained carrier-free by centrifuging water in which radium emanation has been allowed to decay even though, strictly in terms of solubility, products in this case should not precipitate.

Straightforward chemical methods of separation cannot be used when the transmutation product is isotopic with the target element. L. Szilard and T. A. Chalmers (1934) were first to devise a successful (essentially chemical) method applicable in some cases. To a large amount of neutron-irradiated ethyl iodide, they added a small quantity of free iodine which (after reduction) was precipitated as silver iodide. They found that almost all the I^{128} formed in the reaction I^{127} (n,γ) I^{128} was contained in the precipitate. For this method of concentration to be successful, the transmuted target atom (a) must be removed from the molecule in which it was originally bound, and (b) must not be recaptured into a similar molecule through isotope exchange. The first condition is satisfied in most cases of simple neutron capture. Neglecting any momentum the captured neutron may impart to the target nucleus, if a gamma-ray quantum of W Mev is emitted in capture, the nucleus (of mass number A) will recoil with energy $540\,W^2/A$ ev. A recoil energy of a few electron volts is generally sufficient to free the radioactive atom from the chemical bond in the molecule, and on the average a total of about 8 Mev of energy is available for emission as gamma rays when a neutron is captured. Thus, for any possible value of A it is likely that the first condition will be satisfied. The second condition is more difficult to satisfy; it is more likely if the target material is an organic compound in which there is no ionic dissociation.

In principle the Szilard-Chalmers method of concentration also can be applied in transmutations of the class in which Z does not change (if the two conditions just mentioned are met). These conditions are generally fulfilled for radioactive chlorine, bromine, and iodine, formed in organic compounds or in the inorganic halogenates. Similarly, manganese dioxide precipitated from an irradiated permanganate is found to carry most of the radioactive manganese under certain conditions.

Radioactive halogens chemically permit many other methods of concentration when they are produced by neutron irradiation of organic halides. Erbacher and K. Philipp (1936) employed adsorption on active charcoal, and S. Roginski and N. Gopstein (1935) used both aluminum oxide and active charcoal as adsorbents. V. Majer (1937) used a trace of colloidal gold in a similar way to supply condensation nuclei for the deposition of Au^{198} atoms formed in a neutron-irradiated alkaline solution of gold chloride.

When irradiation results in a radioactive species isomeric with the isotope of the original target element, the Szilard-Chalmers method may still be used for its concentration if the necessary conditions can be met. Sometimes a product, though not isomeric with a stable isotope (of the target element or any other), is formed as two isomers, or in one form from which a second is produced by isomeric transition. Br^{80} is produced in two forms in the reaction Br^{79} (n,γ) Br^{80}; the shorter-lived isomer ($T = 18$ min.) is produced from the longer-lived ($T = 4.4$ hr.) by isomeric transition. Segrè, R. S. Halford, and Seaborg (1939) modified the Szilard-Chalmers method to separate the daughter isomer from the parent. A sample of tertiary butyl bromide was prepared containing the parent isomer; subsequent extraction as hydrobromic acid carried the daughter isomer produced in the sample. D. de Vault and Libby (1940) effected the same separation by precipitating silver bromide from an ammoniacal solution containing the parent isomer as bromate; J. L. le Roux, and C. S. Lu and S. Sugden used the same precipitation from ethylene dibromide and n-butyl bromide. The principle has since been employed in many other separations of daughter isomers from their parents.

Under such requirements as those of the Szilard-Chalmers method (that the newly formed radioactive atom be liberated from molecular combination and be unable to return to its original state of binding) recoil of the atom on emission of the capture gamma-ray quantum may ionize the product if sufficient energy is available. (Atomic ionization energies are of the order of 5 ev to 25 ev for the loss of one electron.) If the ionized atom is not easily neutralized, it may be possible to collect the radioactive product by applying an electric field during the course of irradiation (if the target material is liquid or gaseous). Used by Fermi and associates (1935), by F. A. Paneth and J. W. Fay (1935), and by J. Govaerts (1938), the method may be applied whether or not the product is isotopic with the target element if the necessary conditions are fulfilled.

When very thin targets are employed in reactions other than those of pure neutron or proton capture, the method of recoil permits continuous collection of products during irradiation. The method was originally used for products of natural alpha disintegration by Hahn and L. Meitner (1909), following an observation by Brooks (1904). In slow-neutron-induced fission the recoil fragments have energies ranging from 40 Mev to 100 Mev. Joliot (1939) was first to use this fact, showing that radioactive fission products could be collected on a solid surface placed some distance away from a thin layer of neutron-irradiated uranium. In the same year McMillan found what later proved to be the beta activity of Np^{239} in a thin layer of irradiated uranium from which most of the fission products had escaped by recoil. The heaviest of the transuranium elements were identified (1958, 1961) in samples containing only a few atoms, collected by recoil from heavy-ion bombardment in experiments of considerable sophistication.

Chemical separation of rare-earth elements (long a problem, and most acute for the rare-earth fraction of radioactive fission products) was virtually solved with ion-exchange resins (see ION EXCHANGE). These resins commonly are organic polymers, such as polythene, carrying functional groups that make hydrogen or hydroxyl ions easily available by ionization. In a cation-exchange resin these groups may be sulfonic or carboxylic acid groups or a phenolic hydroxide; in anion-exchange resins they may be a quaternary amine or an ethanol group. The method was introduced by G. E. Boyd, F. H. Spedding, and W. E. Cohn, and their co-workers (1947). A long column is packed with the appropriate resin; the material to be separated is shaken up for adsorption with a sample of the resin under controlled acidity, the mixture is placed at the top of the column, and a suitable eluting agent is allowed to flow slowly through. Lanthanide rare earths are separated with a cation-exchange resin; 0.25 molar citric acid (brought to pH 3.05 with ammonia) is a satisfactory eluent (G. Wilkinson and H. G. Hicks, 1947) at a rate of flow of 0.03 milli-litre/cm² min. In such an arrangement the rare earths appear in the reverse sequence of atomic numbers as elution proceeds: Lu, Yb, Tm, Er, . . . (see RARE EARTHS). It was early suspected and later established that a second series of rare-earthlike elements has actinium as its first member. All known transuranium elements belong to this actinide series. The ion-exchange column enormously aided study of these elements; since about 1950 all separations of the higher transuranium elements have been made this way. Generally, tracer amounts of almost any two ionic species may be separated by ion exchange if appropriate conditions are established; by suitable increase in column size, macroscopic amounts of material may be handled with equal success.

This section has dealt chiefly with the concentration of known radioactive products of transmutation. Obviously when the species is not known, chemical and other methods of separation greatly assist in identification.

VIII. MATHEMATICAL THEORY OF SUCCESSIVE TRANSFORMATIONS

It has been shown how Rutherford and Soddy developed the law of radioactive change from experimental data. Their first-order differential equation

$$\frac{dN}{dt} = -\lambda N$$

was interpreted as giving the expectation value of the disintegration rate of a pure radioactive sample at the instant when N atoms of the original material remain unchanged; λ is the empirically determined disintegration constant of the material. Generally (though not invariably) N is a very large number; and λN quite frequently represents a high rate of disintegration, so that fluctuation effects are relatively unimportant. In view of this it should be stressed that the mathematical theory to follow considers no such fluctuations, treating a random phenomenon as if it were causally determined, and taking no account of restriction of N to integral values. This imposes a formal restriction on the relevance of the theory (in some circumstances a more sophisticated approach may be necessary), but it is entirely adequate for most experimental purposes.

Rutherford (1904) was first to formulate and solve differential equations representing successive disintegrations of specific parent substances to stable end products. A more general treatment was first given by Bateman (1910).

If $N_1, N_2, \ldots, N_k, \ldots, N_r$ represent numbers of atoms of the products (N_1 parent atoms . . . N_r atoms of stable end product)

of a single-chain disintegration series in a given sample at any time t, the appropriate differential equations are

$$\frac{dN_1}{dt} = -\lambda_1 N_1$$

$$\frac{dN_2}{dt} = \lambda_1 N_1 - \lambda_2 N_2$$

$$\cdots$$

$$\frac{dN_k}{dt} = \lambda_{k-1} N_{k-1} - \lambda_k N_k \tag{3}$$

$$\cdots$$

$$\frac{dN_r}{dt} = \lambda_{r-1} N_{r-1}$$

where $\lambda_1, \lambda_2, \ldots, \lambda_k, \ldots, \lambda_{r-1}$ are disintegration constants appropriate to each product. The general solution of this set of equations may be written

$$N_1 = {}_0N_1 e^{-\lambda_1 t}$$

$$1 < k < r, \quad N_k = {}_0A_k + \sum_{i=1}^{k} {}_iA_k e^{-\lambda_i t} \tag{4}$$

$$\sum_1^r N_k = \sum_1^r {}_0N_k$$

Here ${}_0N_k$ is the number of atoms of the kth product present in the sample at $t = 0$; the constants ${}_jA_k$ depend on these initial values and on the magnitudes of the disintegration constants concerned.

Equations (4) may seem too complicated for easy application, but they may be considerably simplified without loss of generality. Since this spontaneous process proceeds so that the disintegration of any atom is totally uninfluenced by that of its neighbours, solution for any set of initial conditions (values of ${}_0N_k$ different from zero for all values of k from 1 to r) may be obtained by superposition of simpler solutions in which each product in turn is regarded as the only one present in the original sample. It is then sufficient to solve for the case in which only atoms of the parent species are present initially (in number ${}_0N_1$), and then apply this solution to the other products in turn (their initial amounts being specified), merely adding the resulting expressions. When only the original parent is present at $t = 0$, values of the constants ${}_jA_k$ of equations (4) are given explicitly as follows ($1 < k < r$, $0 < j < k + 1$):

$$_0A_k = 0$$

$$_jA_k = \frac{{}_0N_1\lambda_1\lambda_2 \ldots \lambda_{k-1}}{(\lambda_1 - \lambda_j)(\lambda_2 - \lambda_j) \ldots (\lambda_{j-1} - \lambda_j)(\lambda_{j+1} - \lambda_j) \ldots (\lambda_k - \lambda_j)} \tag{5}$$

Consider the general solution represented by equations (4) and (5) when the parent has a half-life significantly longer than that of any of its daughters. In that case λ_1 is the smallest of the disintegration constants involved, and (if λ_j is next smallest) then at times considerably greater than $1/\lambda_j$ only one term in any of the expressions in (4) remains significantly different from zero. This is the term involving $e^{-\lambda_1 t}$; i.e., the first term in each expression. After a certain time, therefore, all the products effectively decay together, with the half-life of the parent, and the relative amounts of the products still present in the sample remain constant with time. In such case the successive products are said to be in radioactive equilibrium with the parent, under which

$$\frac{N_k}{N_1} = \frac{{}_1A_k}{{}_0N_1} = \frac{\lambda_1}{\lambda_k - \lambda_1} \left[\frac{\lambda_2}{\lambda_2 - \lambda_1} \cdots \frac{\lambda_{k-1}}{\lambda_{k-1} - \lambda_1} \right] \tag{6}$$

When the disparity between the half-life of the parent and that of the next longest-lived product is very great ($\lambda_1 << \lambda_j$), to a very close approximation equation (6) may be written

$$\lambda_1 N_1 = \lambda_2 N_2 = \ldots = \lambda_{r-1} N_{r-1} \tag{7}$$

When equation (7) applies without significant error (as in the case of an old and unaltered uranium [or thorium] mineral) the radioactive state is called secular equilibrium; when equation (6) must be used, the equilibrium is said to be transient. Disintegration rates at any time in secular equilibrium are essentially the same for all members of the genetically related series; in transient equilibrium, according to equation (6)

$$\lambda_1 N_1 < \lambda_2 N_2 < \ldots < \lambda_{r-1} N_{r-1}$$

and disintegration rates increase progressively from one product to the next throughout the series.

When Rutherford first solved equations (3) for his experimental data (1904), direct determination of disintegration rates was not a practical possibility. All that was measured was an ionization current proportional to the disintegration rate for a pure source, with an unknown constant of proportionality, and differing considerably from one pure source to another. For a given disintegration rate the ionization current would almost certainly be greater (by an order of magnitude or more) for an alpha-emitting source than for a beta emitter; such complications now generally can be avoided. However, Rutherford encountered one situation of special interest, whatever experimental techniques are available. It occurs when $r = 3$ in equations (3), and when the parent and radioactive daughter emit radiations of different types, one much more easily detectable than the other. Investigators will first tend to use the easily detectable radiation. If a source originally contains only the parent substance it may be found that the easily detectable activity decreases exponentially with time; in which case the radiation belongs to the parent, and its half-life may be determined directly. If the radiation belongs to the daughter its intensity will vary with time in proportion to $\lambda_2 N_2$ where, from equations (4) and (5)

$$N_2 = {}_0N_1\left(\frac{\lambda_1}{\lambda_2 - \lambda_1}e^{-\lambda_1 t} + \frac{\lambda_1}{\lambda_1 - \lambda_2}e^{-\lambda_2 t}\right) \qquad (8)$$

Values of λ_1 and λ_2 may be deduced from experiment, but the symmetry of the situation is such that it cannot be decided (on this evidence alone) which value refers to the parent and which to the daughter. According to equation (8) $\lambda_2 N_2$ varies with time in precisely the same manner whether the smaller of the two constants refers to the parent or to the daughter.

This discussion has been confined to single-chain disintegration series for simplicity. Series branching involves no new principles; only added complexity in mathematical formulation. The basic expression for the law of radioactive change in branching disintegration has been given as equation (2). All that is needed is appropriately to introduce an expression of this type in equations (3), and to represent disintegration side-chains separately to arrive at the set of simultaneous differential equations for the more general case.

No new mathematical approach is involved when radioactive substances are produced from stable species by controlled irradiation. Equations (3), with their solutions given in equations (4) and (5), provide a complete description of an ideal situation of this class through a simple reinterpretation of the symbolism. Description of an actual situation may then be derived by suitable superposition of partial solutions and adjustment of parameters.

The ideal situation to which equations (3), (4), and (5) immediately apply is that in which ${}_0N_1$ atoms of a single kind are placed in a uniform field of irradiation of constant intensity at time $t = 0$, and when only one type of transmutation is possible. If the transmutation gives rise to a radioactive product, N_2 in equations (3) represents the number of atoms of this product (of disintegration constant λ_2) present after irradiation duration t, and N_1 gives the number of parent atoms still unchanged. The remaining symbols $N_3, N_4, \ldots, N_{r-1}$ allow for the possibility of intermediate products before a stable end product is reached; N_r denotes the number of end-product atoms present at t.

The symbol λ_1 in the equations is interpreted in terms of flux density of bombarding radiation (in particles or quanta per unit area per unit time) and the cross section of the target nucleus for the relevant transmutation (as an area per nucleus) under the conditions of irradiation obtaining. If ϕ represents this flux density and σ this nuclear cross section, then $\phi\sigma$ gives the prob-

ability per unit time that any atom of the target species remaining unchanged will suffer transmutation. Expressed this way, the significance of $\phi\sigma$ is precisely that of a disintegration constant in a spontaneous process; the required interpretation is: $\lambda_1 = \phi\sigma$.

Values of ϕ and σ vary considerably from one practical situation to another. In nuclear reactors the flux density of slow neutrons may reach 10^{14} (or in extreme cases 10^{15})/cm^2 sec., and (depending on the target material) σ may have any value up to about 10^{-20} cm^2 per nucleus under these conditions. In fast-neutron reactions, and those produced by high-energy charged particles (generally in light nuclei) σ will more usually be 10^{-28} to 10^{-24} cm^2 per nucleus, but radiation flux densities tend to be smaller. A beam current of singly charged particles of 1 microampere focused on an area of 1 cm^2 corresponds to a mean ϕ value of 6×10^{12}/cm^2 sec.; however, in accelerators producing particle energies of a few hundred million electron volts, average beam currents are more likely to be of the order of 1 millimicroampere. Values of $\phi\sigma$ then range from about 10^{-5}/sec. to 10^{-18}/sec. in practical situations, and the effective half-life T_1 of the target material in such transmutation will range, accordingly, from about 1 day to 10^{10} yr. Very much more frequently than not, T_1 will be considerably longer than the total time of irradiation in laboratory experiments.

Equation (8) provides an expression that can be interpreted in relation to the production of radioactivity by controlled irradiation. With $\lambda_1 << \lambda_2$, $t << T_1$, the equation becomes

$$\lambda_2 N_2 = \phi\sigma_0 N_1(1 - e^{-\lambda_2 t}) \qquad (9)$$

In this form it gives the activity of the directly produced radioactive product (in all but the most extreme circumstances; see above) as a function of irradiation time. According to equation (9) the activity of the first product eventually reaches a saturation value $\phi\sigma_0 N_1$, and its atomic concentration in the target material reaches a value of $\phi\sigma/\lambda_2$. This concentration, which cannot be exceeded under the given conditions of irradiation, may also be expressed as the ratio T_2/T_1, where T_1 is the characteristic time defined in the last paragraph, and T_2 is the half-life of the transmutation product concerned. If a target material with nuclear cross section 10^{-24} cm^2 for thermal neutron capture that gives rise in this way to a product of half-life 2 hr. is irradiated in a nuclear reactor at flux density 10^{12}/cm^2 sec., it will develop at saturation a concentration of roughly one atom in 10^8 of the product. This arbitrary example (typical of practical experience) emphasizes the magnitude of the problem of separating or concentrating the active material in the short time before it loses its activity.

IX. RADIOACTIVITY AS A PROPERTY OF THE ATOMIC NUCLEUS

It was recognized early, in the context of the nuclear atom model, that so-called natural radioactivity is essentially a property of the atom nucleus; that an alpha particle (helium nucleus) or a beta particle (negative electron) is emitted spontaneously from an intrinsically unstable nucleus. A similar interpretation was later applied to radioactivity produced in man-contrived experiments. Positron emission and orbital-electron capture (empirically unknown before 1934) were accepted from the outset as nuclear processes.

In 1965 there were about 270 species listed as stable isotopes. To be so listed, a species had to have been detected in mass analysis of terrestrial material, and could not have been shown to be radioactive. Improved sensitivity of mass spectrometers may tend to add to the list by revealing species present in samples in previously undetectable amount; but improvements in the sensitivity of particle counters may show feeble radioactivity of species thought to be stable. On the basis of present knowledge such improvements are most likely to reduce the number of species accepted as stable. In a two-dimensional diagram with mass numbers represented along one side of a rectangular grid and charge numbers along the other, each grid point represents a possible nuclear species. Points representing accepted stable species form a well-defined band across such a diagram, and the much more numerous points representing man-made radioactive species encompass this band on either side and fill in the gaps in its structure; there were (1965) very few unfilled points within the band of conceivable stability.

Nuclear stability can be considered in relation to heavy-particle (*e.g.*, alpha-particle) emission, and in relation to electron emission (or capture). In some respects the second is more fundamental, yielding a very simple generalization that has no counterpart in the case of heavy particles. This generalization states that it is overwhelmingly unlikely that two isobaric species (socalled because they have the same mass number) can both be stable if their nuclear charge numbers differ only by one unit.

Consider two such neighbouring isobars (A, Z) and $(A, Z + 1)$; it is a truism that the exact masses of the two neutral atoms cannot be precisely the same. If the neutral atom (A, Z) has the greater mass, then mass-energy is available for emission of a negative electron from the nucleus. For, if this electron were taken up in the extranuclear electron cloud, it would produce the neutral atom $(A, Z + 1)$. If the neutral atom $(A, Z + 1)$ has the greater mass, then capture of one of its outer electrons by the nucleus is energetically possible, producing the neutral atom (A, Z). Either case rests on the assumption that the nuclear process is completely described; but, apart from this, the statement is precise. One or the other of a pair of neighbouring isobars is intrinsically unstable in relation to an electron-involved process (either emission or capture of a negative electron). It was satisfactory to find that in the 1960s there remained no more than a single case of neighbouring isobars in the accepted list of stable species.

The concept of stability against electron processes can be applied to nuclei for which Z exceeds 83 in precisely the same way as it has just been applied to nuclei of smaller Z. For $Z > 83$ it is currently supposed that all nuclei are intrinsically unstable in relation to alpha disintegration (*see* below), but the problem of beta stability is a separate issue. By extending the argument of the last paragraph very slightly it may be concluded that all species of any given mass number A (and $Z > 83$) are intrinsically unstable in a single sense (all capture-active or all negative-electron-active, except the end product having $Z = 0$ or $Z = A$, as the case may be), or else that at least one such species is stable against both types of (electron-involved) transformation. Of these alternatives, only the second conclusion makes sense physically; the other implies a degree of discontinuity in the general properties of nuclei at $Z = 83$ that is quite contrary to experience. Precise measurements of disintegration energies for the 200 or more species known to belong to the disintegration series of the four mass types discussed in section VI permit calculation (by the method of closed decay cycles) of the energies available for electron-involved disintegration in cases in which such disintegrations have not hitherto been observed. In this way it has been shown that beta-stable species do indeed occur with $Z > 83$ (L. A. Turner, 1940), as the general argument would indicate. A list of these species is given in Table II.

Table II.—Beta-stable Species with $Z > 83$

Z	A
84	210, 211, 212, 213, 214, 216
85	215(?)
86	214(?), 215(?), 216, 217, 218, 220, 222
87	219
88	220, 221, 222, 223, 224, 226
89	225
90	224, 226, 227, 228, 229, 230, 232
91	231
92	230, 232, 233, 234, 235, 236, 238
93	237
94	236, 238, 239, 240, 242, 244
95	241, 243
96	242, 244, 245, 246, 247, 248, 250(?)
97	–
98	246, 248, 249, 250, 251, 252, 254
99	253
100	252, 254, 255, 256

The table shows that the distribution in A and Z for these alpha-unstable but beta-stable species has the same character as that for species normally regarded as both alpha- and beta-stable in the range of smaller $Z (< 84)$. In this connection the main feature to be noted is the different incidence of odd and even values of

A and Z in either distribution. No odd value of A is given with confidence more than once in Table II; no value of Z is associated with more than two odd values of A; no odd value of Z is associated with any even value of A. These rules apply (with negligible exceptions) throughout the whole range of Z as well as to the restricted range covered by the table. This serves to justify the earlier statement that in some respects the question of beta stability is more fundamental than that of alpha stability.

For all species (with $Z > 82$) identified as alpha emitters, disintegration energy empirically exceeds 4 Mev. Beta emitters, on the other hand, include radioactive species with disintegration energy as low as a few thousand electron volts. Note that within any small range of Z, the half-life of an alpha emitter increases very rapidly indeed as disintegration energy decreases. In summary, absence of experimentally detectable beta radiation is a relatively trustworthy indication of a product's absolute beta stability; the absence of detectable alpha radiation would be a much less reliable indication of absolute alpha stability in comparable circumstances. If the product were of large Z, all that could reasonably be deduced from such a negative experiment might be that the energy available for alpha disintegration must be less than 4 Mev in that case. The conclusion from known facts is that the energy available for alpha disintegration decreases abruptly as Z decreases below 83; but it would be rash to conclude that all species of smaller Z are alpha-stable in the absolute sense.

In current theory the nuclear constituent particles (nucleons) are protons and neutrons. A nucleus of mass number A and charge number Z is assumed to contain Z protons and $A - Z$ neutrons. On this basis an alpha particle comprises two protons and two neutrons; this system is relatively the most tightly bound (stable) of all possible nucleon combinations. In terms of available energy this is the reason that alpha-particle emission (rather than emission of protons or any other charged composite particles) occurs at all significantly in nature.

The energy available for alpha emission can be expressed in terms of the energies binding nucleons. It is supposed that two protons and two neutrons are removed one by one (it does not matter in what order) from the original nucleus. At each removal the binding energy of the appropriate nucleon must be supplied from outside. When the four particles have been removed in this way let them combine to form an alpha particle. In this process the total energy binding the alpha particle is released. The energy Q_α available for alpha disintegration of the original nucleus is the excess of this liberated energy over that supplied from outside. Let B represent binding energy, p proton, and n neutron; then

$$\begin{aligned} Q_\alpha(A, Z) &= B(4, 2) - B_p(A, Z) - B_p(A - 1, Z - 1) - \\ &\quad B_n(A - 2, Z - 2) - B_n(A - 3, Z - 2) \\ &= B(4, 2) - B_n(A, Z) - B_n(A - 1, Z) - \\ &\quad B_p(A - 2, Z) - B_p(A - 3, Z - 1) \end{aligned}$$

Two variants (not shown) represent the other possible sequences of removal of the four particles concerned.

Recall that it has been concluded from experimental data that energy available for alpha disintegration decreases abruptly as Z decreases below 83. From the analysis just given, this implies that the binding energies of the last added protons or neutrons (or both) must increase abruptly as Z decreases through this value. This is one of the many generalizations from experimental results which are regularized in the shell model of the nucleus (M. G. Mayer, J. H. D. Jensen, *et al.*, 1949). According to that model (*see* NUCLEUS: *Nuclear Structure and Nuclear Forces*), as nuclei are built up by successive addition of nucleons, the binding energy of the last added particle varies in a periodic manner. There is an odd-even variation whereby the binding energy is less, when an odd-numbered particle is added, than when the next (even-numbered) nucleon of the same kind is added. (This consideration is basic for understanding the systematic characteristics of beta-stable nuclei discussed earlier.) There is also a variation with longer periods, within each of which the binding energy rises progressively to a peak value at the end of the period. These periods end at the proton (or neutron) numbers 2, 8, 20, 50, 82, and

126. On the basis of this model, the cutoff in relation to alpha-disintegration energy for $Z < 83$ is particularly sharp because two of these so-called magic numbers are involved in this range of Z; the stable end product of the thorium series is the doubly magic species Pb^{208} ($Z = 82$, $A - Z = 126$). Pb^{208} is the daughter of alpha-active Po^{212}, and it is consistent with the shell model that the value of Q_α in this case is greater than that for any other isotope of polonium (84) or bismuth (83). The entries in Table III substantiate this, and also give alpha-disintegration energies of the isotopes of astatine (85) for comparison.

Table III. Values of $Q\alpha$ (Mev) for the Isotopes of Astatine, Polonium, and Bismuth

Z \ N	126	127	128	129	130	131	132	133	134
85	5.98		9.4	8.95	8.15	7.94	7.18	6.75	6.39
84	5.40	7.59	8.95	8.51	7.83	7.50	6.90	6.66	6.11
83	3.2	5.04	6.75	6.21	5.97	5.61			

Table III shows proton number Z along one axis, and neutron number N ($= A - Z$) along the other. Variation of Q_α with N, for constant Z, shows a pronounced maximum at $N = 128$ for each Z value; for N constant, the increase in Q_α between $Z = 83$ and $Z = 84$ is in general greater by a factor of about 5 than it is between $Z = 84$ and $Z = 85$. (For higher Z values not shown in Table III the rate of Q_α increase with Z, at constant N, continues quite small.) Thus the phenomenon of alpha disintegration emerges suddenly, being empirically unobservable ($Q_\alpha < 4$ Mev) when $Z < 83$ and $N < 127$, and highly energetic when $Z > 83$ and $N > 127$.

The entry $Q_\alpha = 3.2$ (for $Z = 83$, $N = 126$) in Table III refers to the nominally stable species Bi^{209}; it reflects the repeated report (*e.g.*, W. Porschen and W. Riezler, 1956) of detecting very feeble alpha activity with ordinary bismuth. The estimated half-life is 2×10^{17} yr., and the observed disintegration energy is what might be expected on the basis of the shell model. The observation seems valid, though avoidance of background effects at this level of activity is almost impossible; it emphasizes the need for the caution already expressed, that the absolute and empirical limits of alpha stability (on the A/Z diagram) are far from the same. After 1956 definite evidence was found for weak alpha activity with hafnium and platinum as well. Experiments with sources of enriched isotopes have made it possible to attribute these activities to the rare isotopes Hf^{174} and Pt^{190} (0.18% and 0.012%, respectively, of the normal element), and to determine the respective disintegration energies and half-lives as 2.56 Mev and 3.18 Mev, and 2×10^{15} yr. and 7×10^{11} yr. (R. D. Macfarlane and T. P. Kohman, 1961; K. A. Petrzhak and M. I. Yakunin, 1962).

The first alpha activity observed with an element of $Z < 83$ was that of ordinary samarium (62) (De Hevesy and M. Pahl, 1932); it was unambiguously attributed to Sm^{147} (B. Weaver, 1950) by isotope separation. The disintegration energy is 2.29 Mev, and the half-life is 1.4×10^{11} yr. (*See* SAMARIUM.) Even before the isotopic attribution of its alpha activity had been settled, samarium had been recognized as unique in another respect among the "stable" elements of even Z. For all other such elements the mass spectrum of the isotopes of even A is of the same general type: a compact group of lines with no missing member. With samarium the inner line of Sm^{146} is missing. The shell model indicates that alpha activity is most likely to appear (if at all) with the medium-heavy nuclei, among those with neutron number 84 or slightly greater; for Sm^{146} $N = 84$, and for Sm^{147} $N = 85$. This conformity with prediction spurred the production of such species by man-made transmutation (S. G. Thompson, J. O. Rasmussen, and Seaborg, 1949; Rasmussen, Thompson, and Ghiorso, 1953; D. C. Dunlavey and Seaborg, 1953). In this way Sm^{146}, Eu^{147}, Gd^{148}, Gd^{149}, Gd^{150}, Tb^{149}, Tb^{151}, Dy^{152}, Dy^{153}, and Dy^{154} were shown to be alpha emitters. It was also shown that Nd^{144} (23.9% in ordinary Nd) is alpha active, with half-life the order of 10^{16} yr. (E. C. Waldron, V. A. Schultz, and Kohman, 1954; Porschen and Riezler, 1954). Alpha activity of the rare isotope Gd^{152} (0.2% in ordinary Gd) was

established (Macfarlane and Kohman) in 1961.

Table IV shows values of alpha-disintegration energies for this group of species. The same general features appear as in Table III: for constant Z, Q_α passes through a maximum as N increases (the maximum occurring when N is two units greater than the magic number, in this case 82); for constant N, Q_α increases slowly with Z (there is no magic proton number involved in this case). The empirical limit of alpha stability now occurs ($Z \sim 60$) at about $Q_\alpha = 2$ Mev, rather than at about 4 Mev as when $Z \sim 80$. All except three of the cells in Table IV represent man-made species that are unstable in terms of electron capture. In these circumstances alpha disintegration is merely a rare mode in a fairly short-lived activity, so its detection presents experimental difficulties.

Enough is known about the exact masses of nuclei, on the basis of reaction energies characteristic of transmutations with a variety of projectiles (L. A. König, J. H. E. Mattauch, and A. H. Wapstra, 1962), to predict values of Q_α with fair accuracy for a great many species. Through application of semiempirical mass laws (P. A. Seeger, 1961) these predictions may be extrapolated to all species at all likely to be produced. The chance of obtaining experimental evidence of alpha activity associated with values of N or Z just greater than the magic number 50 is extremely

Table IV.—Values of $Q\alpha$ (Mev) for the Alpha-active Isotopes of Neodymium, Samarium, Europium, Gadolinium, Terbium, and Dysprosium
(bracketed values represent uncertain attributions)

N \ Z	60	61	62	63	64	65	66
88					2.20		3.46
87							3.57
86					2.8	3.53	3.76
85			2.29		3.1		(4.17)
84	1.88		2.62	2.96	3.25	4.06	(4.31)

remote. In low-energy fission of heavy elements certain species are produced in small yield (as primary fission fragments) that would appear in Table IV if it were extended to smaller Z values. Predictions are that Q_α is positive for some of these species (in particular for La^{141}, Ce^{143}, Ce^{144}, Pr^{145}, Nd^{148}, and Nd^{149}). This may have some bearing on the emission of alpha particles in fission (Feather, 1964).

X. BETA DISINTEGRATION AND ELECTRON CAPTURE

Even if it had not marked discovery of man-made radioactivity and the associated process of spontaneous positron emission, 1934 would represent a turning point in the study of beta disintegration. The main features of negative beta disintegration had been laboriously learned from naturally radioactive species, the proton-neutron model of the nucleus (W. Heisenberg, 1932) had come to be accepted, and the neutrino hypothesis (*see* below) had been suggested by W. Pauli (1931). Remarkably, all these developments were compounded in 1934 in Fermi's coherent theoretical account of disintegration. Formulated in general terms, the theory later was used to describe positron emission and orbital-electron capture with equal success; in 1965 (some of its ambiguities having been resolved) it remained the accepted general theory of electron-involved nuclear processes.

The crucial observations prompting the theory were made largely with naturally radioactive Bi^{210} (radium E) in the 1920s. This body is particularly suitable for such experiments since it has no significant gamma radiation to complicate observation; it has a single longer-lived alpha-active daughter (Po^{210}); its half-life (5 days) is convenient for laboratory work. The daughter provided an independent monitor of disintegration rate, and a comparison unit of energy (the known kinetic energy of the alpha particles of Po^{210}).

When the experiments with Bi^{210} were planned, the main problem had already been identified. Chadwick had shown (1914) with electrical recording methods that the magnetic spectrum of electrons emitted by sources of radium active deposit (Pb^{214}, Bi^{214}) consisted of a continuous distribution and a series of spectral lines. The lines had been the subject of much study through photographic recording (*e.g.*, Rutherford and H. R. Robinson, 1913), but the continuous spectrum had not yet been accurately observed. The total intensity of the lines was low compared with that of the continuum, and Chadwick deduced that the disintegration electrons must belong to the latter, the electrons of the lines being of secondary origin. Rutherford, Robinson, and W. F. Rawlinson (1914) independently concluded that the electrons of the line spectrum were secondary, in the sense that they obtained very similar groups of electrons by passing the gamma rays of the source through thin metal foils. The immediate problem was whether the continuous spectrum was a feature of all beta disintegrations, even the simplest; and, if so, how to reconcile this apparent variation of energy with the conservation law. A basic question was whether the continuous spectrum represented one electron per disintegrating atom, or more.

In 1924, K. G. Emeléus used the disintegration rate of the daughter Po^{210} as monitor to show that the average number of electrons detectable for each disintegration of Bi^{210} is very close to one. In 1927, E. Madgwick found the magnetic spectrum of these electrons to be continuous. In the same year C. D. Ellis and W. A. Wooster determined (in terms of the energy of the alpha particles of Po^{210}) the average energy per disintegration appearing as heat when radiations of Bi^{210} were absorbed in the metal walls of a microcalorimeter. The first two experiments showed the continuous spectrum to be characteristic of the disintegration electrons; at least these electrons did not seem to dissipate energy significantly by sharing it with other electrons through some preferential interaction within the disintegrating atom. The experiment of Ellis and Wooster showed that the heating effect corresponded to the average energy of the continuous spectrum, rather than the maximum energy, so that no other (easily absorbed) secondary radiation could be made responsible for any hypothetical dissipation. The overall conclusion in the simplest case was that electrons are emitted from the nucleus (in beta disintegration of a single species) with energies having all values from zero up to a characteristic maximum for the species. This was in strongest contrast with the situation in alpha disintegration. At that time it was believed that alpha particles for a given species are emitted with precisely the same energy from all disintegrating nuclei. In terms of experimental evidence the principle of energy conservation seemed in doubt for beta disintegration.

During the period 1927–31 data were accumulating on the rotational attributes of nuclei. Concepts of intrinsic nuclear angular momentum and magnetic moment had been validated in terms of the detailed optical features of atomic and molecular spectra (*see* NUCLEAR MOMENTS). The generalization emerged that the quantum number specifying the resultant angular momentum of a nucleus is integral or half-integral as the mass number of the nucleus is even or odd. The spin quantum number of the electron had already been accepted as $\frac{1}{2}$, supported by Dirac's theory of 1928. Angular momentum (as well as energy) empirically appeared not to be conserved in beta disintegration; nuclear mass number does not change in this process, so the change in angular momentum quantum number must be integral—but for the emitted electron the angular momentum quantum number is half-integral.

Pauli's neutrino hypothesis was an attempt to salvage the challenged conservation laws. He suggested (1931) that beta disintegration involved the simultaneous emission of an electron and an uncharged particle of small mass (possibly zero) and half-integral spin. In the simplest case (*e.g.*, Bi^{210}), a perfectly definite amount of energy would be shared by these two particles. The name neutrino was introduced by Fermi when he began to incorporate Pauli's idea into a thoroughgoing theory of the process.

Fermi's theory (1934) stems from the assumption that negative beta disintegration consists in the transformation of a neutron into a proton within a nucleus. A negative electron and a neutrino are created in this elementary process "much as a quantum of light is created at the moment of emission from an excited atom." (The simile had been used before the neutrino hypothesis by V.

Ambarzumian and D. Iwanenko, 1930.) Fermi showed how to calculate the relative probabilities of the sharing of a constant amount of energy between the two disintegration particles (giving effectively the form of the continuous energy spectrum of the disintegration electrons), and how to relate the absolute probability of disintegration per unit time (the disintegration constant) to the total disintegration energy and other parameters. Predictions from the theory conformed with experiment; in particular, the many-valued relation between disintegration constant and available energy (many-valued, depending on the change of nuclear angular momentum involved) accorded well with the empirical generalization of B. W. Sargent (1933) relating these quantities for natural beta emitters.

Discovery of positron emission and orbital-electron capture added support for the general validity of Fermi's theory. It was possible to describe both processes, and to evaluate their relative probabilities when they were in competition, by regarding each as involving the transformation of a nuclear proton into a neutron; the former by capture of a negative electron from a state of negative energy and emission of a neutrino, and the latter by capture of an electron from an extranuclear bound state with neutrino emission.

For twenty years after publication of Fermi's theory the free neutrino remained undetected. In 1935 the experiments of M. E. Nahmias suggested that the range of a 1-Mev neutrino in lead is greater than 10^6 km. if energy loss is by ionization only. From 1942 on, experiments reviewed by O. Kofoed-Hansen (1955) showed that linear momentum is not conserved in electron-involved nuclear processes unless neutrino emission be postulated. These results merely brought to focus the apparent nonconservation that led to Pauli's hypothesis; they were hardly convincing empirical evidence of the neutrino. Experimentalists were thrown back on the early suggestion that a neutrino might interact only with an atomic nucleus in the direct reverse of beta disintegration. Such reverse beta disintegration is highly improbable since it requires simultaneous nuclear capture of an electron and a neutrino. Also, conditions under which it might occur depend on whether the particle-antiparticle distinction applies to the neutrino (*see* ANTIMATTER). If the distinction is relevant, then the neutrino from negative beta disintegration will be captured only along with a negative electron (or only when a positron is emitted); the neutrino emitted in positron disintegration (or in electron capture) will be captured only when a negative electron is simultaneously emitted.

Development of nuclear reactors promised intense sources of (hypothetical) neutrinos from negative beta disintegration, opening the possibility of investigating nuclear capture of free neutrinos. A reactor at a steady power of 1 megawatt yields about 2×10^{17} negative beta disintegrations per second; F. Reines and C. L. Cowan used such a source finally to demonstrate neutrino capture in hydrogen (1954). They recognized this process by recording (in correct time sequence) the annihilation quanta resulting from final disappearance of the positron, and the quanta resulting from ultimate capture of the neutron, produced in the process. About a ton of water provided the hydrogen target for neutrino radiation, and a cadmium salt dissolved in the water served for neutron capture. These investigators failed earlier to find evidence of production of Ar^{37} from Cl^{37} under pile-neutrino irradiation. For this to have occurred a neutrino from negative beta disintegration would have had to condition the emission of a negative electron in the act of capture by a chlorine nucleus. This earlier negative result coupled with the later positive evidence of neutrino capture strongly supported the idea of a significant distinction between neutrino and antineutrino.

As soon as it was established (Chadwick and Goldhaber, 1935) that the neutron mass is greater than that of the neutral hydrogen atom, it was a corollary that the neutron itself is beta active. Not until intense sources (nuclear reactors) became available, however, was direct evidence possible; even then, experimental difficulties were considerable.

J. M. Robson (1951, 1958) detected protons recoiling from beta disintegrations taking place in a beam of thermal neutrons traversing an observation chamber; in terms of the flux of neutrons, their known velocity distribution, and length of path under observation, he determined the half-life as 12.8 ± 2.5 min. He determined the energy spectrum of observed beta particles coincident in time with the recoiling protons, showing that it was continuous, of normal type, and of maximum energy 782 ± 13 kev (thousand electron volts). Robson later investigated the angular correlation between the directions of electron and proton emission. Beta disintegration of the neutron being the prototype of all such disintegrations, the first test of relevant theory is that it should describe the process in full detail; but even the results of 1958 were neither sufficient nor precise enough to remove all ambiguities in the basic theory.

Hitherto, beta disintegration has been discussed only in the simplest case in which no gamma radiation is emitted; however, beta-active species devoid of gamma radiation are only a small fraction of known beta emitters. When gamma radiation is emitted the electron spectrum of the beta-active source in general contains groups of lines indicating electrons of well-defined energies. Rutherford, Robinson, and Rawlinson (1914) already had made it appear very likely that these electrons originated in the absorption (within the atom of origin) of the energy of gamma-ray quanta. When, as was generally more probable, the quanta escaped from the disintegrating atom, they gave rise (by absorption in surrounding atoms) to photoelectrons with a very similar spectrum of isolated lines. Thus the line spectrum was interpreted as indicating internal photoelectric absorption of the gamma radiation in the radioactive atom.

These interpretations were confirmed. In a many-lined spectrum such as that from radium active deposit, Ellis (1921) detected a repeating pattern with constant energy difference between pairs of lines, the intensities of which showed an apparently constant ratio. He identified this difference as characterizing the ionization energies of the electrons of the K and L shells of the emitting atom, concluding that these line pairs represented photoelectrons ejected by monochromatic gamma rays from the two most tightly bound atomic shells. Consistent with this, he identified the lines corresponding to internal absorption in the less tightly bound M,N, . . . shells in certain cases.

Ellis and Wooster (1925) verified this interpretation by showing that the values of characteristic ionization energies (W_K, W_L, . . .) were those appropriate to the daughter, rather than the parent atom, for the beta disintegration concerned. In this way it was concluded that the emission-and-internal-absorption of the gamma-ray quantum occurs after the disintegration electron has left the nucleus.

Although the basically valid notion of internal photoelectric absorption of gamma radiation had been widely accepted in 1920, there was less unanimity regarding where the gamma rays originate within the atom. Ellis (1922), and later he and H. W. B. Skinner (1924), provided the first circumstantial evidence. Calculating the quantum energies E_γ of the gamma rays, from the electron energies E_e, using the general expression

$$E_\gamma = E_e + W_{K,L} . . .$$

Ellis and Skinner showed that the gamma-ray energies themselves provided several examples of the simple Ritz combination rule: $E_{\gamma 1} = E_{\gamma 2} + E_{\gamma 3}$. From this they concluded that the emitting system must be characterized by well-defined energy states; and, since the excitation energies of states so revealed were entirely different from those known for extranuclear states of the atom, they were interpreted as quantum states of the nucleus. The view was never seriously contested; in the 1960s the view was that whenever beta and gamma radiation originate in the same pure source, then the daughter nuclei from primary disintegration are left in one or more states of excitation (possibly in the ground state also) from which they eventually revert to ground state by emitting gamma-ray quanta (or by transferring the energy to internal-conversion electrons). When gamma rays are emitted by positron-active or by capture-active species, similar statements are appropriate.

The primary process in the general case of beta disintegration is now seen to be of some complexity. The initial nuclei are all in the same energy state, but many energy states of the final nucleus have to be considered. The partial processes by which particular final states are produced are mutually exclusive competing modes of disintegration of the parent species. The available energies Q_0, Q_1, Q_2, . . . are different, and each mode is independently characterized by a partial disintegration constant λ_0, λ_1, λ_2, ... The empirical (total) disintegration constant for the species is given by the sum of these partial disintegration constants (compare equation [2]), and the overall energy spectrum of the disintegration electrons is compounded of the partial continuous spectra appropriate to the individual modes. This view was first explicitly given by Ellis and N. F. Mott in 1933; in such a case Fermi's theory is concerned with the values of λ_r and Q_r (and other parameters specifying the transition) when each mode is considered independently.

Unraveling the complex continuous spectrum in the general case may call for quite sophisticated methods of experimentation. Gamma-ray processes for partial disintegration modes that populate all final states except the ground state are generally rapid in relation to the resolving times of particle-detector electrical circuits. Genuine prompt coincidences are to be expected between pulses in one detector that records gamma-ray quanta of given energy (or the corresponding internal conversion electrons), and another that detects disintegration electrons, only when the latter electrons belong to the partial spectrum or spectra associated with the gamma rays under observation. Developments of older coincidence methods on this basis (Bothe and others, 1935, 1937; Feather, 1940) have greatly increased the possible range of experiment. More recent improvements in electronic techniques permit direct determination of gamma-ray lifetimes (of the order of 10^{-10} sec.) by the method of delayed coincidences, in suitable cases.

Experimentally (though not theoretically) orbital-electron capture poses problems very different from those of beta disintegration. In the general case the most easily observed emissions from a capture-active body are likely to be gamma radiations corresponding to partial modes in which the daughter nucleus is left with energy of excitation. In the simplest case, when there is no gamma radiation, there are only fluorescent X rays, Auger electrons (alternatively emitted through partial internal conversion of the energy of inner-shell excitation into electron energy; see PHOTOELECTRICITY), inner bremsstrahlung (see below), the recoiling atom of the daughter product, and the neutrino (emission of which is mainly responsible for that recoil). None of these emissions is easy to detect with species of small Z; they have been mentioned here in approximate order of increasing difficulty of detection, whatever the value of Z.

Experimental observations establishing occurrence of capture should be distinguished from observations through which values of disintegration energy may be deduced. Detection of fluorescent X rays or Auger electrons provides no information about disintegration energies; to that extent the less difficult observations are also the less informative.

A brief history of improvements in fluorescent X-ray detection (and energy measurement) can be given in a few examples. In 1939 H. Walke, E. J. Williams, and G. R. Evans detected K-shell X rays resulting from electron capture in V^{49} ($T = 330$ days) in a Wilson cloud chamber and showed that the rapid absorption of this radiation in the chamber gas was consistent with its assumed quantum energy (4.5 kev). In 1949 B. Pontecorvo, D. H. W. Kirkwood, and G. C. Hanna detected and identified in terms of their energy (250 ev) the L-shell X rays resulting from electron capture in Ar^{37} ($T = 34$ days) in a proportional counter. They established (by comparative experiments using counters containing argon and xenon, respectively) that this L radiation is both primary and secondary in origin. The secondary component is the result of atomic rearrangement that takes place after K radiation has been emitted; they saw the primary component as resulting from L-electron capture operating as an independent nuclear process competing with the (more probable) capture of an electron from the K shell. In 1957 J. Scobie and G. M. Lewis pushed the limit toward lower energies, detecting the K radiation of boron emitted as a result of electron capture in C^{11} ($T = 20.4$ min.). They were able to introduce the radioactive material into their proportional counter as a gas, as in the other case cited, but their detection problem was more difficult because 99.8% of disintegrations of C^{11} proceed by positron emission. An anticoincidence arrangement, discriminating against the much more numerous positrons, had to be used.

In respect of the inner bremsstrahlung, P. Morrison and L. Schiff (1940) noted that the sudden redistribution of electric charge in an atom in which electron capture occurs should lead (with small probability) to emission of a quantum of radiation, the energy of which is thus not available to the emitted neutrino. The corresponding effect in beta disintegration had been discussed theoretically by J. K. Knipp and G. E. Uhlenbeck (1936). Inner bremsstrahlung associated with electron capture (in Fe^{55}) was first observed by H. Bradt and collaborators in 1946. Its intensity was estimated as about 3×10^{-5} quantum of 70 kev average energy per disintegration. The first rough spectral analysis of the Fe^{55} radiation was made by scintillation spectrometer (D. Maeder and P. Preiswerk, 1951); the observed spectrum was continuous, as predicted. Quantum intensity per unit energy interval theoretically should increase in a roughly parabolic way as the energy falls below a limiting value equal to total disintegration energy. Thus disintegration energy should be derivable by a linear plot of the high-energy end of the bremsstrahlung spectrum. Maeder and Preiswerk deduced a value of 206 ± 20 kev for the capture disintegration energy of Fe^{55} in this way; a more precise value (217 ± 10 kev) was obtained by P. R. Bell, J. Jauch, and J. M. Cassidy (1952) by the same method. Scintillation spectrometers have since been applied to the spectral analysis of inner bremsstrahlung from many other capture-active bodies. This method (difficult in that intensity of effect is so low) becomes more difficult when capture transformation also involves emission of nuclear gamma rays; in certain cases even this has been overcome (e.g., R. G. Jung and Pool, 1956).

Most of the disintegration energy released in electron capture is carried away by the emitted neutrino. If transformation occurs between well-defined nuclear states, the kinetic energy of the neutrino should be single valued for any particular mode, apart from such trivial secondary effects as inner bremsstrahlung. Correspondingly, when the final nucleus is left in the ground state the recoil energy of the daughter atom should also be single valued. (When the final nucleus is left in an excited state it suffers successive recoil from neutrino and gamma-ray emission.) The earliest investigations of recoil (J. S. Allen, 1942) were primarily to study the overall balance of linear momentum; with the neutrino no longer hypothetical, more precise determination of recoil energy can be taken as determining the neutrino energy (or the disintegration energy) in suitable cases. Assuming the rest mass of the neutrino is zero, a nucleus of mass number A emitting a neutrino of kinetic energy T (Mev) must recoil with energy $540 \, T^2/A$ (ev). In 1952 G. W. Rodeback and Allen used a time-of-flight method to determine the velocity of recoil of Cl^{37} produced in the capture disintegration of Ar^{37} in a gaseous source. On the above assumption they obtained $T = 0.8 \pm 0.1$ Mev in this case. Two years later accuracy was increased by more than an order of magnitude; Kofoed-Hansen ingeniously crossed electric and magnetic fields in a double guard-ring condenser to obtain $T = 806 \pm 8$ kev for the same disintegration. This value shows excellent agreement with that calculated (816 ± 4 kev) from the energy balance of the production reaction $Cl^{37}(p,n)$ Ar^{37}.

As has been implied, the overall probability of capture disintegration involves contributions corresponding to capture of electrons from the K, L, M, . . . shells. If any of these electrons suffers rearrangement (as in chemical combination) its contribution to the overall probability of capture must change. The effect must be small even when atomic number is small, but it has been experimentally detected for Be^7. Showing results of earlier investigators to have been inconclusive, J. J. Kraushaar, E. D. Wilson, and K. T. Bainbridge (1953) carefully compared the decay of Be^7 sources in the form of metal, oxide, and fluoride, combining these in their three possible pairs. Taking the disintegration constant determined for the metallic sample as standard, they found that of the beryllium fluoride sample to be less by 7.4 ± 0.5 parts in 10^4, and that of the beryllium oxide sample to be less by 1.3 ± 0.5 parts in 10^4. In agreement with these results the directly determined disintegration constant of the oxide was 6.1 ± 0.6 parts in 10^4 greater than that of the fluoride. The effect is in the direction anticipated from considerations of molecular structure; the more completely the two valence (q.v.) electrons are removed from the beryllium atom the smaller the overall probability of electron capture by the nucleus. These experiments were the first to exhibit limitations of the classical dictum that radioactivity is entirely uninfluenced by chemical combination; on the other hand they demonstrate how nearly accurate this categorical statement is, even in the most extreme situations encountered in the laboratory. Quite another order of disturbance of "normal" conditions has to be envisaged for the interiors of stars; in such circumstances (chemical combination being now irrelevant) an altogether greater effect is to be anticipated.

To consider the origin of this effect in quantitative terms, suppose that a nucleus of charge number Z is transformed by an electron-involved process into a nucleus of charge number $Z + 1$, or $Z - 1$. In either case the strength of binding of the extranuclear electrons changes (the original system being assumed to be a neutral atom with its full complement of electrons). In the $Z + 1$ case the energy of binding increases, in the $Z - 1$ case it decreases. Thus, in the former case energy must be liberated, in the latter energy must be absorbed by the extranuclear electron system. The amount of this energy is approximately $150 \, Z$ (ev) (G. Allard, 1948; L. L. Foldy, 1951)—more than 12 kev when $Z > 80$. When energy must be absorbed by the extranuclear system (the case in positron emission and electron capture), that the process takes place spontaneously at all indicates that energy is supplied at the expense of the products of disintegration (essentially, at the expense of the kinetic energy of the neutrino).

Conversely, energy liberated by the change in binding (as it must be in negative beta disintegration) should become available for the nuclear process. There are at least two beta-active species (Pb^{210} and Ra^{228}) among the natural radioelements for which the energy of negative beta disintegration in the most probable mode (under laboratory conditions) is of the same order as $150 \, Z$ (ev). If atoms of these species existed in the body of a bright star, they would be almost completely ionized. The half-life for beta disintegration of the bare nucleus then would be many orders of magnitude greater than that of the neutral atom; indeed, the bare nucleus might be beta stable (knowledge of the energies involved was not sufficient to state this with certainty in 1965). That would be an extreme consequence of an absolute kind.

XI. ALPHA DISINTEGRATION

Compared with beta disintegration, alpha disintegration is relatively simple. For more than 25 years after the first magnetic and electric deflections were made of alpha particles, no observations contradicted the conviction that alpha particles from disintegration of a pure species are all emitted with the same velocity. Admittedly, velocity often had to be estimated from the measured range of the particles in air under standard conditions, but when more powerful methods could be used the generalization still seemed to hold. On this view, the only measurable quantities for any alpha emitter were the range of the particles (or velocity, or disintegration energy) and the disintegration constant (or half-life). Having considerably improved the measurement of range, in 1911 Geiger and J. M. Nuttall produced convincing evidence that these two quantities are significantly related. In terms of disintegration energy Q_α, the relation stated by Geiger and Nuttall can be written

$$\log \lambda = A + B \log Q_\alpha \qquad (10)$$

where the empirical value of B is about 80.

At face value, equation (10) suggests a power-law dependence of λ on Q_α, with an exponent of about 80. The Sargent relation that connects observed values of λ and Q_β, when expressed in the same form, suggests a power-law dependence with exponent of roughly 5 or 7, according to type of beta disintegration. The contrast is striking in practice or theory. In the latter connection the significant power laws in physics (1960s) almost universally involve rational powers of the independent variable not many times greater than one: a 5th-power law is a rarity, an 80th-power law almost absurd. But these considerations did not figure conspicuously in the 1920s. With no satisfactory theory of alpha disintegration the original form of the empirical regularity commonly was accepted without question. R. Swinne (1912, 1913) suggested the fundamentally less objectionable form

$$\log \lambda = C + DQ_\alpha^{\frac{1}{2}} \tag{11}$$

but without theoretical justification.

By 1930 theoretical and experimental aspects of alpha disintegration had been revolutionized. In 1928 Gamow and, independently, R. W. Gurney and E. U. Condon provided the basis of an acceptable theory; in 1929 S. Rosenblum obtained the first evidence contradicting the over-simple experimental picture.

The difficulty besetting any theory of alpha disintegration in terms of classical mechanics (q.v.) is illustrated in experiments on scattering and disintegration involving uranium and plutonium. Pu^{239} emits alpha particles of 5.15 Mev maximum energy, the daughter being U^{235}. At the instant it is just breaking from the nucleus the alpha particle (in classical mechanics) cannot have kinetic energy less than zero. As the alpha particle recedes, its kinetic energy should increase under repulsion between its own positive charge and the charge on the residual nucleus U^{235}. The experimental result implies, however, that the increment in energy derived in this way cannot be greater than 5.15 Mev, and, if the field is a coulomb force (see ELECTRICITY: Coulomb's Law) over the whole range involved, that the separation of the centres of alpha particle and residual nucleus at the instant of release cannot be less than 5.14×10^{-12} cm. Experiments on the scattering of alpha particles by uranium were carried out by Rutherford and Chadwick in 1925. If these can be regarded as referring to U^{235}, as is certainly the case, they show that the repulsive field is indeed coulombian, but from 3.02×10^{-12} cm. outward (alpha particles of Po^{212} of 8.78 Mev energy were employed). The scattering experiments show all of the region beyond 3×10^{-12} cm. from the centre of the U^{235} nucleus is devoid of nuclear matter; in escaping from the Pu^{239} nucleus the alpha particle must pass through this region, yet on emerging it is found paradoxically to have much less energy than expected. The paradox may be posed as a question: if an alpha particle with nearly 9 Mev of kinetic energy is turned back in the repulsive field so that it is unable to enter a U^{235} nucleus at which it is directly fired, how can an alpha particle ever escape that nucleus when little more than 5 Mev of energy is available for disintegration? Within the original nucleus it must be held in an essentially attractive field; more than the total available energy must be required to overcome that attraction before the alpha particle reaches the region of repulsive field through which it can escape.

This paradox was seen by Gamow, Gurney, and Condon to characterize a general situation for which wave mechanics gave formal results that differed fundamentally from those according to classical mechanics (see QUANTUM MECHANICS). Classically, a region in which the total energy of a particle is less than its potential energy in the field is forbidden; according to wave mechanics this prohibition is never absolute. If the classically forbidden region is not too large in extent, and if the energy deficit is not too great within the region, the particle wave will leak through. This idea had already been applied earlier in 1928 to the problem of the field emission of electrons from metals by L. Nordheim and J. R. Oppenheimer; the problem in relation to alpha disintegration was seen to be essentially similar. Alpha disintegration, then, is basically a nonclassical process; calculation of the disintegration constant in any case is primarily a matter of de-

termining the penetrability of the potential barrier that by classical mechanics should confine the alpha particle within the nuclear system indefinitely. In its simplest form the result of these calculations was not unlike equation (11) with the important conclusion that the parameter D in that equation is proportional to the charge number of the residual nucleus.

Rosenblum (1929) was first to apply magnetic focusing to the examination of alpha-particle spectra. For lack of sufficiently intense magnetic fields of large enough spatial extent, earlier investigators had been restricted to the much less powerful direct deviation method. Having an opportunity to work with a large general-purpose electromagnet at Bellevue (Paris), Rosenblum quickly discovered a previously unsuspected fine structure in the alpha-particle spectrum of Bi^{212} (ThC). Instead of a single sharp line, there appeared to be at least four lines attributable to this species. This precipitated attacks on the problem elsewhere, particularly in Cambridge, Eng., where equipment was developed specifically for this purpose. The differential ionization chamber (Rutherford, F. A. B. Ward, and W. B. Lewis, 1931) provided a high-resolution device for the measurement of particle ranges, and a specially designed semicircular focusing magnet (Rutherford, C. E. Wynn-Williams, Lewis, and B. V. Bowden, 1933) more than matched in performance the much larger instrument in Bellevue. Very soon it was established that the alpha disintegration of many of the naturally radioactive species is complex. By the 1960s the gridded pulse ionization chamber and the semiconductor total ionization counter had largely superseded earlier energy spectrometers for man-made species of large Z; their use merely reinforced the conclusion (already forming in 1940) that it is the exception rather than the rule for the radiation from a pure alpha-active species to consist of particles of single energy only.

Explanation of complex alpha disintegration was first given by Gamow in 1930; previously, not much attention had been paid to the generally feeble gamma radiation observed with some alpha emitters. Compared with that associated with beta disintegration, this gamma radiation was not only of low intensity in most cases but it was also of low quantum energy. Only Meitner and her collaborators (1924-28) had investigated this field systematically. Gamow offered the view that gamma rays should be associated with all alpha disintegrations for which the energy spectrum is complex. He ascribed the line of maximum energy in any complex spectrum to the alpha particles of the partial disintegration mode in which the daughter nucleus is produced in the ground state; the other lines he regarded as evidence for partial modes giving rise to excited states of the product—and so to gamma rays. (This was the forerunner of a similar suggestion Ellis and Mott made three years later in relation to complex beta disintegration.)

Gamow supported his suggestion by examples of numerical agreement between observed values of gamma-ray quantum energies and differences in observed particle-disintegration energies; more substantial support came from experiments by Ellis (1932) with Bi^{212}. Thereafter, the basic notion of competing partial modes of disintegration was accepted. To interpret the many complex alpha disintegrations that have since been found, Gamow's original description had to be generalized only in one respect. In a small minority of cases it appears that the ground state of the daughter nucleus is not significantly populated by any one of the primary modes of particle disintegration that occurs. In such cases the emission of a gamma-ray quantum (or a corresponding internal conversion electron) follows emission of the alpha particle in every instance.

The fact that complex alpha-particle spectra show fine structure (i.e., particle-disintegration energies for the partial modes of a given species are not very different—perhaps varying within a 10% range) is a consequence of the rapid variation of disintegration probability with energy to which equation (10) first drew attention. But it is also a fact that in any one fine-structure spectrum the intensities of the lines and their energies may exhibit no obvious correlation; thus, as Gamow pointed out, some parameter besides the energy must determine disintegration probability.

That the change in angular momentum between initial and final nuclear states should be one such parameter was at once accepted (the disintegration probability being less, the more angular momentum the alpha particle has to carry away). However, this does not seem to be the only additional parameter. Reference has been made to the almost complete suppression of the energetically most favoured modes in certain cases; such an extreme effect could not result from unfavourable spin change alone. Alpha disintegration is empirically simpler than beta disintegration, in that discrete energies are observed; it is theoretically simpler in that only heavy particles are involved; but, it is far from simple in detail. A heavy nucleus is a complex system of many particles, and it is unrealistic to suppose that its behaviour can be fully described in simple terms.

The statement that all species with $Z > 83$ are intrinsically alpha unstable refers to nuclei in the ground state. Energy available for alpha emission from an excited state of a heavy nucleus is necessarily greater than from ground state, perhaps enough for alpha emission to compete significantly with normal deexcitation (gamma-ray quantum emission). These considerations underlie the interpretation (Feather, 1929) of long-range alpha particles, a rare disintegration effect first reported with thorium active deposit by Rutherford and A. B. Wood in 1916. A similar effect was found with the active deposit of radium a few years later; in 1965 these remained the only well-attested examples. The nuclei Po^{212} (ThC′) and Po^{214} (RaC′) in ground state have more energy available for alpha disintegration than any other naturally radioactive nuclei; as a result of the preceding (beta) disintegrations, they are sometimes left in states of considerable excitation (particularly RaC′). Competition between alpha and gamma emission from these states is such that about 220 long-range alpha particles are observed overall per million normal (ground-state) alpha particles from ThC′, and about 30 long-range per million normal from RaC′. Three separate groups of particles were found with ThC′, and 12 with RaC′ (Rutherford, Lewis, and Bowden, 1933); critical examination of relevant gamma-ray spectra (Ellis, 1934) verified the interpretation given.

XII. SPONTANEOUS FISSION

The distinction between absolute and empirical stability limits has been stressed for alpha disintegration. An obvious limit occurs between $Z = 82$ and $Z = 83$: with very few exceptions, naturally occurring nuclei with $Z < 83$ are alpha stable; in an absolute sense, however, very many with Z from 60 to 82 are alpha unstable.

All heavy nuclei are unstable in an absolute sense for other processes that are not observed. For example, U^{234} emits five alpha particles in succession in producing Pb^{214}; 26.2 Mev of energy are set free in these disintegrations. Five alpha particles go to make up the nucleus Ne^{20} which, if formed by such alpha-particle aggregation, would liberate an additional 19.3 Mev. Altogether then, 45.5 Mev are available for $U^{234} \rightarrow Pb^{214} + Ne^{20}$, yet this process is not observed.

There is nothing fundamentally mysterious about this result: calculation of potential-barrier penetration probabilities on the basis of any reasonable assumption shows the improbability, to the point of inconsequence, even of $U^{234} \rightarrow Ra^{226} + Be^8$ (for which 9.5 Mev of energy are available) compared with normal alpha disintegration of U^{234} (for which only 4.86 Mev are available).

It is unlikely that such considerations were seriously entertained before 1940, although all the needed numerical evidence (alpha-particle energies and nuclear masses) had been accumulated with enough accuracy for predictions to be made. When neutron-induced fission was discovered in 1939, it came as something of a shock to most physicists to recollect that the heaviest nuclei are absolutely unstable (to the extent of nearly 200 Mev) in respect of division into two roughly equal fragments. The newly discovered fact was that this process of division becomes "instantaneous" (with the compound nucleus U^{236}) when no more than about 6.4 Mev (the energy of binding of the last-added neutron) is given to the system. This, indeed, was the important result.

Perhaps physicists were not so entirely forgetful of the extent of the absolute instability of the heaviest nuclei in respect of this hypothetical process; what they had no means of knowing was that the height of the potential-energy barrier opposing the process was so little greater than the available energy. As soon as this fact was given by experiment Bohr and J. A. Wheeler (1939) pointed out that spontaneous fission was to be reckoned with experimentally. It was first detected in natural uranium by Petrzhak and G. N. Flerov in the following year.

In 1965 spontaneous fission had been established as a partial disintegration mode for about 35 species with $Z > 90$. For a few species it appears to be the predominant mode. Spontaneous fission generally is more probable by a factor of about 10^4 for species of even A and even Z than for neighbouring species of odd A, or even A and odd Z. According to the simplest theoretical model of the process the probability should depend on the value of the fissionability parameter Z^2/A; however, for even A and constant (even) Z, the facts do not bear out this prediction. For each such value of Z the partial disintegration constant for spontaneous fission shows roughly parabolic variation with A, passing through a minimum when the number of excess neutrons $(A - 2Z)$ is 52. On the other hand, if attention is concentrated on the behaviour of the species of maximum beta stability, for each value of Z, a monotonic variation of partial disintegration constant with Z^2/A is obtained (Feather, 1964). Empirically for such species

$$\log \lambda = E + FZ^2/A \qquad (12)$$

These results can be extrapolated only tentatively beyond the observational range from which they were drawn. On the basis of equation (12), with constants E and F taken from experiment, $Z^2/A = 41.65$ when $\lambda = 10^9/\text{sec.}$; $Z^2/A = 43.5$ when $\lambda = 10^{20}/$ sec. These values of λ correspond approximately to the limits of possible experimental detection and absolute instability, respectively. With $A = 3Z - 48$ (roughly appropriate for species of maximum beta stability in this range of Z) the limiting values of Z become 106 and 112. On this basis, if the extrapolation were accepted, it would be concluded that even-even species of maximum beta stability would be too short-lived in respect of spontaneous fission to be identifiable experimentally when $Z > 106$, or to be considered capable of independent existence at all when $Z > 112$. It should be repeated that neighbouring species of odd A would tend to be significantly more stable— and that for a given (even) Z there would also tend to be other species of even (and smaller) A somewhat more stable in respect of spontaneous fission—than the representative species of maximum beta-stability to which the empirical equation (12) has been assumed to apply. Such considerations represent the most that could be said in the 1960s regarding the problem of the natural number of the elements that was first posed by Turner in 1940.

Spontaneous fission has been most widely studied with Cf^{252}; this beta-stable body of half-life 2.2 yr. exhibits a 3% spontaneous fission mode in competition with alpha disintegration. Details of the process are very similar to those of thermal-neutron-induced fission of U^{235} and Pu^{239}. The mass-yield curve for the fission fragments shows the same double-peaked structure as in the more familiar case (with the valley between the peaks somewhat more pronounced); there are secondary neutrons and long-range alpha particles characterized by energy spectra almost indistinguishable from those applicable in low-energy induced fission (though with absolute intensities somewhat greater for $Z = 98$, than for $Z = 92$ or 94). Studies with other species emphasize this similarity.

Spontaneous fission is theoretically a barrier-penetration process, but the significant details of the barrier are not so easily specified as in alpha disintegration. Nor is the broadly satisfactory approximation for alpha decay, that the structure of the residual nucleus is unimportant, permissible in fission where disintegration particle and residual nucleus cannot be sharply distinguished. In fission, too, the saddle-point configuration (that of maximum potential energy) is definitely one of less than final distortion; actual scission occurs later in the process. This last makes it possible to imagine the distribution of mass and charge between the fragments as being determined (statistically) after fission has become "inevitable" for any particular nucleus. Thus the disintegration constant for spontaneous fission is not expressed as the sum of many terms (representing partial mass-modes), but as the sum of very few terms that correspond to possible fission channels effective through the saddle point. What happens once the saddle point is passed (e.g., what fragments are formed, their energy of excitation, number of neutrons emitted from each, what gamma rays) is a matter for description in other terms.

Two species for which spontaneous fission is the only observed disintegration mode are Cf^{254} ($T = 61$ days) and Fm^{256} ($T = 2.7$ hr.). Spontaneous liberation of energy by the latter amounts to about 5 megawatts per gram of the pure species; at 1.5×10^{-7} molar concentration (aqueous) its energy of decay would evaporate the solution to dryness. These figures indicate the great difficulties involved in collecting such species in weighable or visible amount.

In the stars the situation is different; L. B. Borst suggested (1950) that a peculiar feature of the light curve of type I supernovas (see NOVA AND SUPERNOVA) required identification of a radioactive decay with half-life about 55 days that might be effective on a large scale in the exploding star. The peculiar feature is that, from about 100 days after the initial outburst, light emission from these stars falls off exponentially with about that period (W. Baade, 1945, 1956). In 1956 G. R. Burbidge, E. M. Burbidge, et al., offered spontaneous fission of Cf^{254} as a plausible explanation. They conjectured that the supernova was a relatively cold star that had collapsed, transforming gravitational into thermal energy; that multiple neutron capture had then produced a sudden buildup of heavy elements; and after a time the dominant (temporary) source of energy was the Cf^{254} that remained. This is an attractive suggestion, even though it requires the production of about 10^{29} grams of Cf^{254} in each stellar outburst (E. Anders, 1959; P. Fong, 1960).

XIII. DECAY OF LONG-LIVED EXCITED STATES OF NUCLEI

Species distinct in radioactive properties but with the same mass and charge numbers are called nuclear isomers. The phenomenon was envisaged as a possibility by Soddy in 1917, and first observed by Hahn in 1921. Elucidation of the main disintegration sequence

$$U^{238} \xrightarrow{\alpha} Th^{234}(UX_1) \xrightarrow{\beta} Pa^{234}(UX_2) \xrightarrow{\beta} U^{234} \xrightarrow{\alpha}$$

by Fajans (1913) has been described earlier. In 1921 Hahn found a second beta-active daughter of UX_1, considerably longer-lived ($T = 6.7$ hr.) than UX_2, and of much lower activity when in equilibrium with its parent. This product (which he named uranium Z) was chemically inseparable from UX_2, and Hahn concluded that both were the same protactinium isotope Pa^{234}— only that the same constituent particles of each nucleus were differently organized. Although Hahn's observation was of a previously unrecognized phenomenon, it aroused little interest until many more examples of isomeric pairs were found among the products of man-contrived transmutation.

The first case of man-made nuclear isomerism identified was with an isotope of bromine. Common bromine has two stable isotopes of mass numbers 79 and 81. Slow-neutron bombardment produced three activities of half-lives 18 min., 4.4 hr., and 36 hr. (Fermi and B. Kurtchatov, and their respective collaborators, 1935); gamma irradiation also yielded three activities of half-lives 6.4 min., 18 min., and 4.4 hr. (Bothe and Gentner, 1937). Slow-neutron bombardment of medium-Z elements normally results exclusively in (n, γ) processes, low-energy gamma irradiation giving (γ, n) transformations. Therefore the activities of half-lives 18 min. and 4.4 hr. were both ascribed to Br^{80}; subsequent investigation substantiated this conclusion. In 1965 about 200 isomeric pairs were known—though the precise total turns on a convention of definition (see below).

Nuclear isomers justify their name in that the same numbers of neutrons and protons are held to be differently arranged in two nuclei that are isomeric. The two configurations can be regarded as two energy states of the nuclear system; one is usually the ground state. The other configuration differs only in lifetime (longer than normal) from any other excited state of the given nucleons. Experiment has thoroughly vindicated C. F. von Weizsäcker's suggestion (1936) that the long lifetime results because the ground state and its isomeric state differ in angular momentum by more than two quantum units. Then, if there is no state of intermediate energy through which more rapid cascade deexcitation is possible, and particularly if the excitation energy of the upper isomeric state is small, that state will be metastable in relation to gamma-ray emission.

Empirically, isomeric pairs may be classified according to whether the ground-state isomer is stable or unstable; and according to whether the upper-state isomer transforms predominantly by particle emission, or reverts to a lower state by isomeric transition. Since isomeric-state excitation energies generally are small when the ground-state isomer is stable, isomeric transition is usually the only possible transformation mode for the upper state of the pair. (Exceptionally, the isomer of naturally occurring Cd^{113} is beta active; but it is almost certain that empirically stable Cd^{113} is beta unstable in absolute terms.) When the ground-state isomer is unstable, enough energy is available for an upper-state isomer to transform by particle emission also; then, the relative probability of this mode (as against isomeric transition) depends on the details of the situation.

Both members transform predominantly by particle emission in the classical Pa^{234} isomeric pair UX_2 and UZ. Many investigations have been made of these bodies since 1936—without fully resolving all the problems that have arisen! Feather and E. Bretscher (1938) showed that the total disintegration energies are approximately the same, but very differently distributed (hardly any gamma rays from UX_2; more than twice as much energy in gamma rays as in beta particles from UZ); that the equilibrium activities are roughly as 99.85% to 0.15%; and that UX_2 is very probably the upper-state isomer. These conclusions were later confirmed and extended. It became clear that the ground-state isomer (UZ) is not formed significantly as a result of the beta disintegration of UX_1, but that the UX_2 state is produced almost exclusively. This state then suffers branching disintegration, the major mode being the normal beta disintegration (of UX_2), the minor mode (0.18%, according to G. R. Martin and collaborators, 1960) the isomeric transition producing UZ. The energy of the isomeric transition was estimated as about 60 kev (S. Bjornholm and O. B. Nielsen, 1962), and the large change of angular momentum associated with it is seen as responsible for the great difference in beta-disintegration modes of the isomers (for which the various final states of the product nucleus are very differently available because of angular momentum selection rules). The UX_2 beta disintegrations proceed largely to the low-lying states of the product U^{234}, the UZ beta disintegrations to states of high excitation (for which the corresponding spin change is more favourable). From these states of high excitation the gamma rays of UZ are emitted in cascade.

When "isomeric" transition (to a stable or unstable ground state) is predominant, the decision that the case actually qualifies as one of isomerism is a matter of convention. It is a question of the relation between the lifetime of the gamma-ray transition involved and the resolution-in-time of the apparatus employed for its investigation. In the end the decision turns on the investigator's ability to recognize the difference in radioactive properties of the two states concerned. Lifetimes of excited states of nuclei vary from 10^{-12} sec. upwards (some are even shorter), and much can be learned from their measurement throughout the range; but empirically it appears desirable to restrict the term isomeric to transitions with a range of lifetimes much narrower than the measurable. Internal conversion empirically becomes considerably more prominent in relation to gamma-ray emission as the difference in angular momentum between nuclear levels increases. The larger this difference, the more completely does the radiation emitted in an isomeric transition consist of electrons, and the more comparable the case is with that of a beta emitter, except that the spectrum energy of the electrons is a line spectrum rather than a continuum. In the recognition of distinctive radioactive properties, therefore, it is most realistic to make the comparison between an isomeric transition and a beta disintegration, and to limit the range of the former (as the latter is limited naturally) to processes of lifetime longer than about 0.01 sec. This would automatically rule out a considerable number of the roughly 200 known isomeric pairs.

Nuclear isomerism generally shows more regularity among species of odd A than among those of even A. In the former group, whether the neutron number N or the proton number Z is odd, isomerism seems likely when the odd nucleon number is just less than one of the shell-closure numbers 50, 82, and 126 (if applicable); and much less likely when the odd nucleon number is just greater than one of these numbers (Goldhaber and R. D. Hill, 1952; Goldhaber and A. W. Sunyar, 1955).

XIV. APPLIED RADIOACTIVITY

There is hardly any pure or applied science that has not advanced since 1945 through the use of man-made radioactive bodies; these bodies also find wide application in industry.

Noteworthy application of naturally radioactive bodies is made in therapy, particularly for cancer (*see* CANCER: *Treatment*). In 1938 all radium used in the hospitals of the world probably was no more than 1,000 curies. By the 1960s there were 160 therapy units, of 1,000 curies of Co^{60} each, in the U.S. alone; units using 10^5 or 10^6 curies each were predicted within a few years. The half-life of Co^{60} is 5.23 yr.; and its gamma-ray spectrum is much simpler than that of radium and its products, consisting of two basic components (1.17 Mev and 1.33 Mev) of about the same intensity. Absence of gamma rays of smaller quantum energy is an advantage for deep therapy. Million-curie single units were also predicted in the 1960s for Cs^{137}. The gamma radiation from this body is effectively monochromatic (0.66 Mev); its half-life is about 27 yr. These high-intensity gamma-ray sources of long lifetime were almost certain to replace X-ray tubes in the near future for many nonmedical applications also. Cautious advances in therapy with shorter-lived radioactive bodies that are taken up preferentially in certain organs (as iodine is concentrated in the thyroid gland) continued to be made (*see* THYROID GLAND, DISEASES OF).

Radioactive isotopes as tracers of the reaction paths of the stable elements to which they belong were exploited with naturally radioactive lead and bismuth in the 1920s. Success of the method depends upon the fact that (until radioactive nuclear change takes place) the chemical behaviour of the radioactive atom is commonly the same as that of a stable atom of the same nuclear charge. The effect of the radioactivity of the unstable isotope is entirely unspecific and negligible in all but extreme situations; a like effect would be produced if the system were irradiated by an external source of X rays or gamma radiation of proper intensity.

In fundamental chemistry the most extensive application of radioactive tracers has been in the study of exchange reactions. Such a reaction may occur when two compounds with one component atom in common are in the same aqueous solution. If initially only one compound contains a tracer isotope of the common element, then separation of the two compounds from solution will permit determination (in terms of radioactivity associated with each) of the amount of exchange. It has been shown that chlorine exchanges between chloride and chlorate ions, lead between lead nitrate and lead chloride, and that free iodine exchanges with iodide ion. Phosphorus does not exchange between phosphate and phosphite ions, nor sulfur between sulfate and sulfite, nor free sulfur with carbon disulfide, nor iodine between iodoform and iodide ion. This has been widely used to provide information almost impossible to obtain otherwise.

The impact of radioactivity on chemistry has been spectacular in relation to the periodic table, as in the production of transuranium elements. In 1934 atomic numbers 43, 61, 85, and 87 were conspicuous gaps in the list of known species. For element

43, the most likely mass numbers of stable isotopes were 97 and 99, but the occurrence of $_{42}Mo^{97}$ and $_{44}Ru^{99}$ in nature made it unlikely that either of the former species would in fact be stable. For element 61, mass numbers 147 and 149 (or 145) might conceivably have belonged to stable species, but for the existence of the beta-stable isobars $_{62}Sm^{147}$ and $_{62}Sm^{149}$ (or, alternatively, $_{60}Nd^{145}$). In 1937 C. Perrier and Segrè first produced radioactive isotopes of element 43 by deuteron bombardment of molybdenum. They used this material for tracer study of the chemical properties of the new element, and suggested the name technetium. Technetium is chemically more akin to rhenium than to manganese, its congeners in group VIIa of the periodic table. Three of the isotopes, Tc^{97}, Tc^{98}, and Tc^{99}, are long-lived. Tc^{99} (half-life 2.2×10^5 yr.) is obtained in relatively high yield in uranium fission. In this way it has been prepared chemically pure in gram amounts. Radioactive isotopes of element 61 were first identified by J. A. Marinsky, L. E. Glendenin, and C. D. Coryell in 1947; the element was named promethium on their suggestion. The longest-lived isotope is Pm^{145} ($T = 18$ yr.); the 2.6-yr. beta-active Pm^{147} is separable in weighable amounts by ion exchange from the products of fission. D. R. Corson, K. R. MacKenzie, and Segrè produced the first recognized isotope of element 85 by the bombardment of bismuth with alpha particles in 1940. They suggested the name astatine, and showed that this last member of group VIIb (halogens) exhibits the general behaviour of a metal. The isotope they had produced was At^{211}; it has a half-life of 7.2 hr., and transforms 41% by alpha emission and 59% by electron capture. The first isotope of element 87 (francium) to be identified was the Fr^{223} Perey recognized in 1939 as a daughter of actinium. Francium behaves as an alkali metal; the perchlorate, the picrate, and certain complex salts coprecipitate with corresponding salts of cesium.

In the application of tracer methods in biology, C^{14} and H^3 have a great number of uses. For many years before its radioactivity was detected (first by S. Ruben and M. D. Kamen, 1940) it was known that C^{14} is produced by the (n,p) reaction in nitrogen. Radioactivity of the product was difficult to detect since its half-life is long (5,568 yr.) and the maximum energy of the emitted beta particles is low (155 kev). Though the half-life of H^3 (tritium) is considerably shorter (12.26 yr.), the maximum energy of the beta particles is very much lower (18.1 kev). Production of H^3 by the (d,p) reaction in deuterium had been established in 1934; its radioactivity was not detected until 1939 (Alvarez and R. Cornog). Tritium may be produced in weighable amounts by the reaction $Li^6(n,\alpha)H^3$ in a nuclear reactor (*see* DEUTERIUM AND TRITIUM). Long-lived radioactive isotopes of carbon and hydrogen being thus available in quantity, the way is open to an unlimited variety of tracer studies in organic chemistry, in biochemistry, and in the biological sciences generally. There are difficulties in working with C^{14} and H^3, particularly with the latter because its radiations are so easily absorbed (in a few millimetres of standard air equivalent thickness). But this may also be put to good advantage; uptake of H^3-labeled material in tissue may be localized to within correspondingly fine limits (about 1 micron) by autoradiography. One complication remains in all tracer work with this isotope; hydrogen presents the extreme case in which the ratios of the masses of the individual isotopes differ widely from 1. Therefore the chemical indistinguishability of the isotopes (particularly of H^1 and H^3) cannot be taken for granted without further inquiry.

BIBLIOGRAPHY.—E. Rutherford, J. Chadwick, and C. D. Ellis, *Radiations from Radioactive Substances* (1930); Marie Curie, *Radioactivité* (1935); G. von Hevesy and F. A. Paneth, *A Manual of Radioactivity* (1938); Irène Joliot-Curie, *Les Radioéléments naturels* (1946); J. Chadwick (ed.), *The Collected Papers of Lord Rutherford of Nelson*, vol. 1–3 (1962–66); K. Siegbahn (ed.), *Alpha-, Beta- and Gamma-Ray Spectroscopy* (1965); E. K. Hyde, I. Perlman, and G. T. Seaborg, *The Nuclear Properties of the Heavy Elements*, 3 vol. (1964); O. Hahn, *Applied Radiochemistry* (1936), *New Atoms* (1950); G. Friedlander and J. W. Kennedy, *Nuclear and Radiochemistry* (1955); K. W. Bagnall, *Chemistry of the Rare Radioelements* (1957); J. J. Katz and G. T. Seaborg, *The Chemistry of the Actinide Elements* (1957); E. Broda and T. Schönfeld, *Die Technischen Anwendungen der Radioaktivität* (1956); W. E. Burcham, *Nuclear Physics* (1963).

(N. FR.)

RADIO ASTRONOMY, a branch of astronomical science, has contributed fundamental information on a variety of classical astronomical problems: the statistics of meteors, the distance of the sun from the earth, the surface temperatures of planets, the structure of the outer envelope of the quiet sun, and the spiral structure of our galaxy. It has also given insight into phenomena such as solar bursts and flares and their relation to such terrestrial phenomena as auroral and geomagnetic activity. Radio astronomy has provided clues to the origin of cosmic rays possibly in old supernovae. These are identified with pulsars, which are tentatively interpreted as neutron stars. Pulsars and quasars, sources of vast amounts of energy, were discovered by radio astronomy techniques. The astrophysical importance of nonthermal processes in nature and the apparent omnipresence of large-scale magnetic fields have been recognized for the first time. From a study of the 3° K background radiation in the universe, radio astronomy may help solve fundamental cosmological problems.

History.—In 1931 a U.S. engineer, Karl G. Jansky, was investigating atmospheric radio-frequency disturbances that might hinder transoceanic telephone service. Although some were caused by local or even remote thunderstorms, there was a third, apparently of extraterrestrial origin. Jansky showed that this radiation resembled noise generated in metallic conductors and attributed this cosmic "static" to interaction between electrons and ions in interstellar space. Also in the U.S., Grote Reber, with the aid of modest equipment, demonstrated that the origin of cosmic radio-frequency radiation was not confined to the region of the galactic centre but was spread along the galactic plane with a strong secondary maximum in the constellation Cygnus. Radio observations of the sun and of its transient phenomena were started in the early 1940s.

After 1945 a combination of technological advances, ingenious ideas, and adequate support led to spectacular developments. Large antennae, both fixed and movable, and interferometers enabled fainter sources to be observed and with higher resolution. The sensitivities of receivers were improved enormously with the development of masers (q.v.) and parametric amplifiers. Modern data-processing techniques permitted rapid assessment of observations. See further TELESCOPE, RADIO.

Advantages and Limitations of Radio-Frequency Studies.—Besides the obvious advantage of examining celestial objects in an entirely different frequency range, radio astronomy offers other opportunities. Radio waves penetrate the smog and dust of interstellar space and also the clouds of a planetary atmosphere. Thus, astronomers can obtain a view of the central regions of our galaxy unhindered by the obscuring clouds of small particles that restrict optical observations. Likewise, they can study the surface of Venus either by the thermal radiation it emits or from the reflection of radar waves.

There is, however, one basic limitation in much radio-frequency work which somewhat limits its usefulness for certain problems: the lack of angular resolution. Whereas the wavelength of visible light is very small compared with the aperture of the telescope, the wavelength of the radio-frequency radiation is often comparable to or even larger than the aperture of the radio telescope. The resolving power, i.e., the ability to distinguish two objects separated by a small angular distance d, depends on the ratio of the wavelength λ to the aperture D ($d = 1.2\lambda/D$). For a 60-in. telescope and a wavelength of 5×10^{-5} cm. (an average for visible light), $d = 4 \times 10^{-7}$ radians or 0.08 sec.

With a 60-ft. dish and 21-cm. radiation, the angular resolution is 1.38×10^{-2} radians or about 0.8°; i.e., somewhat larger than the angular diameter of the moon or sun. With the wavelengths ordinarily employed, most radio telescopes have resolving powers considerably less than that of the human eye. Accordingly, interferometric techniques are applied much oftener than in optical astronomy. In particular, the long base-line interferometer permits very high angular resolution to be achieved. Likewise, very high resolution in frequency can be obtained. The profile of the 21-cm. line of neutral hydrogen gas can be studied to yield important information on the motion of the gas and its temperature.

The range of wavelength over which observations can be secured also must be considered. The long wavelength limit is between 15 and 30 m. It is fixed by the degree of ionization of the ionosphere. The upper limit of the wavelength is fixed by the condition that a radio wave can travel through an ionized gas only as long as its frequency is greater than a critical frequency v_c, in megacycles (Mc.) per second, given by

$$v_c^2 = 8.06 \times 10^{-5} N_E \qquad (1)$$

where N_E is the number of electrons per cubic centimetre. Radio waves of frequencies less than v_c are reflected by the ionosphere. Since the degree of ionospheric ionization, i.e., the number of electrons per cubic centimetre, depends on the solar radiation in the far ultraviolet, v_c will vary from time to time. The atmosphere is opaque for wavelengths shorter than 1.5 mm. There are strong absorptions at 2.5 mm., 5 mm., and 1.34 cm. The transparency at 8.5 mm. is better than the sky in the optical regions. At the high-frequency end of the spectrum the radio astronomer is hampered by nuisances, such as rain, that also plague optical astronomers. Low-frequency cosmic radio radiation, which is extinguished in the earth's ionosphere, can be studied with detectors carried by rockets or satellites. High-frequency radiation between the far infrared and the microwave region can be studied only from space.

Sources of Radio-Frequency Radiation.—Three important types of cosmic radiation are studied by the radio astronomer: (1) thermal radiation; (2) discrete spectral line radiation; and (3) nonthermal radiation. Each of these types has its own distinctive characteristics; by studying radiation from a source at different frequencies it is possible to distinguish between types (1) and (3).

Thermal radiation in the radio-frequency region is emitted by any heated body in accordance with the usual laws for the emission of radiation. (See HEAT: *Radiation.*) The surface brightness of a source (not necessarily a thermal emitter) can be expressed in terms of the temperature T of a black body (q.v.) that would give the same intensity of thermal radio noise. Also a black-body source can be used to calibrate the receiver.

Radio-frequency radiation received from extraterrestrial sources has the character of random noise superposed on the background of thermal radiation from the surroundings. It is as though an ordinary telescope, its dome, and all terrestrial surroundings glowed brightly so that the astronomer had to measure sun and stars which appeared as objects only slightly brighter than their background. Hence the radio-frequency detection equipment has to discriminate between objects with radio-frequency surface brightness only slightly greater than those of their surroundings.

Differences corresponding to 0.05° K are measurable. If the angular size of the source is smaller than the "beam width" or resolution of the antenna, the measured "brightness temperature" T_b will be less than its true temperature (unless the object is superposed on a hotter source). Since the surface brightness declines as the wavelength increases, thermal sources can be measured best at high frequencies.

An incandescent gas in interstellar space is fully ionized; i.e., the individual atoms are broken down into ions and electrons. Such a "plasma" may emit thermal radiation by the mechanism of what is called free-free emission. An electron (which is negatively charged) moving in the neighbourhood of a positive ion becomes accelerated, and as the electron speeds up it radiates energy. The electron remains free; i.e., it is not captured by the ion. The amount of energy radiated depends on the temperature, frequency, and density of the gas. Such emission is observed in our galaxy from large, glowing clouds of hydrogen such as the Orion nebula.

Spectral Line Radiation.—The first spectral line emission to be discovered was the 21-cm. radiation which is produced by neutral hydrogen atoms. The proton and electron are held together by strong electrostatic forces. Both particles spin, and since they are electrically charged they behave like tiny magnets, so that in addition to electrostatic forces there are weak magnetic forces. When the atom is in its normal condition with the electron moving in the smallest orbit, two different energy states are possible: these correspond to the spinning electron and proton being lined up parallel, or antiparallel, to one another. A jump from the lower to the higher energy state may be produced when radio-frequency corresponding to a wavelength of 21 cm. impinges on the atom. Conversely, a "flip" of the electron spin, corresponding to a change from the higher to the lower energy state, causes the emission of 21-cm. radiation. In the early 1940s H. C. van de Hulst predicted this radiation should be emitted by cold hydrogen clouds. E. M. Purcell and H. I. Ewen in 1951, at Harvard, actually detected the line.

The 21-cm. line is intrinsically "infinitely" sharp; the width of the line as observed in clouds of cold hydrogen in the Milky Way arises from the motions in the line of sight. Part of the widening is due to motions of individual radiating atoms, but most of it comes from large-scale differential motions of gas clouds caused by galactic rotation, "turbulence," and hydrodynamical streaming. Special multichannel receivers have been devised for 21-cm. work so that when a radio telescope is pointed to a hydrogen cloud the entire line profile can be observed at once. In addition to the 21-cm. line there are also lines arising from transition between very high levels (involving states with principal quantum numbers 100 or more). These emissions appear in the ionized hydrogen or HII regions. Line radiation due to the hydroxyl radical OH, and molecules of water, ammonia (NH_3), and formaldehyde (H_2CO) have also been found.

Nonthermal radiation, which is of great importance in the radio-frequency range, is believed to originate mostly in two types of mechanism: plasma oscillations and synchrotron emission.

If the charges of opposite sign in an ionized gas are displaced with respect to one another, they will oscillate back and forth with a frequency given by equation (1) (see *Advantages and Limitations of Radio-Frequency Studies,* above). Thus the forced period of oscillation, or "plasma frequency," is determined entirely by the density of the ions in the gas.

Electrons accelerated to very high velocities (almost that of light) and placed in a magnetic field will emit polarized electromagnetic radiation in the same direction as they are moving. If a host of electrons of different energies are simultaneously thus accelerated, they will emit a continuous spectrum of radio-frequency radiation and even visible light if they are moving fast enough. Such radiation was first observed in a synchrotron and thus is called synchrotron radiation.

Finally, there is an omnipresent background radiation corresponding to 3° K; it is believed to correspond to the residual glow of the primeval fireball, produced by the expansion of the universe.

Radar Astronomy.—Most radio astronomy work is of the "passive" type, concerning itself with measuring the intensity and polarization of radiation emitted by a distant source. In this respect it resembles optical astronomy. To nearby objects, such as meteors, the moon, and terrestrial planets, however, it is possible to direct radar signals and obtain a reflection.

An important early application of radar was to the study of meteors. As a meteor passes through the rarefied upper atmosphere of the earth it ionizes a column of gas. A radio wave may be reflected from this column. From the intensity and time dependence of the reflected beam, it is possible to obtain the direction and velocity of the meteor. Radar technique possesses one important advantage. Since radar reflection depends only on the ionization of the air by a meteor, it can be applied during the day as well as during the night. Thus it has been possible to identify several daytime meteor streams that had not been previously observed. Extensive radar observations also substantiated the more reliable optical observations in showing that the orbits of meteors are elliptical, rather than hyperbolic; *i.e.,* meteors belong to the solar system. (*See* METEOR.)

Radar reflections from Venus and other planets provide a precise method for establishing the scale of distances in the solar system and even tests of the theory of general relativity. Orbit theory gives the relative positions and distances of all bodies in the solar system, but the scale can be fixed only when one particular distance (*e.g.,* the distance from the earth to Venus at a known time instant) is found. The problem is beset with great technical difficulties, not the least of which is that the strength of radar

echoes decreases with the fourth power of the distance instead of with the square of the distance. Nevertheless, radar reflections from planets and returned signals from spacecraft give us our most accurate measurement of the astronomical unit (semimajor axis of the earth's orbit), or, more loosely, the distance from the earth to the sun. The chief limitation is the uncertainty in the speed of light. For most practical purposes we can take the astronomical unit as 149,600,000 km.

Radar techniques yield other valuable dividends. They indicate that Venus is rotating slowly but apparently in such a way as to present the same face to the earth at each inferior conjunction. The reflection characteristics of the surface correspond to substances such as rocks or sand and not to water. Reflections from Mars suggest that the dark areas are probably tilted with respect to the red areas and are certainly at a different elevation. Jupiter yields no reflection; the radar signal is simply extinguished in its vast dense atmosphere.

Observations of Planets and the Moon.—Radio-frequency emission and radar reflections from the moon confirmed the conclusion that the moon's surface layers have good thermal insulating properties. Only a few inches beneath the surface the extremes of heat and cold between the lunar day and night are "smoothed" out and the temperature remains constant. The reflective properties resemble those of sand.

The sunward side of Mercury has a temperature of about 600° K (620° F), while Venus appears to have a similar surface temperature in spite of the fact that it is almost twice as far from the sun. Presumably, the atmosphere of Venus acts as a heat trap; both sunlit and dark sides are extremely hot. Although the planet's surface is hidden by clouds and optical measurements therefore could only apply to high levels in the atmosphere, radio observations apparently give an accurate surface temperature which seem substantiated by the Russian Zond measurements.

Radio observations of Mars show that the average temperature of its surface layers is about 190° K, *i.e.,* about 83° C below the melting point of ice. This observation supports the conclusion that the Martian polar caps are frozen carbon dioxide. The planet may contain vast areas of permafrost. Jupiter emits three types of radio-frequency radiation. The first is the thermal radiation corresponding to the temperature of its thick atmosphere which is heated by the sun. The planet also emits a steady, continuous, nonthermal radiation often attributed to synchrotron emission from an extensive magnetosphere encircling the planet. Finally there are bursts of low-frequency (decameter) radiation connected with the position of the innermost large Jovian satellite, Io. Possibly this emission is due to high-energy particles that have been trapped in the planet's magnetosphere and occasionally leak to the atmosphere.

Solar Radio Observations.—Radio-frequency observations have contributed greatly to gaining an understanding of the outer envelopes of the sun. These are called the photosphere, chromosphere, and corona. The photosphere of the sun is the bright surface seen in white light, where radiation corresponds to a temperature of about 5,800° K. Its average density is low—less than 0.01 that of the sea-level atmosphere. Above this lies a very nonhomogeneous filamentary structure called the chromosphere; during eclipses it appears as a bright red ring surrounding the moon. The outermost envelope, the corona, is about 1,000,000 times fainter than the sun and consists of gases with a temperature of about 1,000,000° K as measured by the speeds of ions and electrons. Optically, the corona can be studied only with great difficulty except during an eclipse, but in the radio-frequency region it can be studied at all times.

The equation for critical frequency shows that at the lower frequencies (longer wavelengths) radiation is obtained only from an attenuated gas, whose density corresponds to that of the outer corona. As the receiver is tuned to higher frequencies it is possible to penetrate deeper into the corona and finally into the chromosphere. At the shortest wavelengths it is possible to reach to the optical photosphere itself. Interferometers provide fairly high angular resolution and by combining observations from several days one may eliminate any effects caused by disturbed areas (which may occur even at times of sunspot minimum).

The radio emission from the quiet sun is of thermal origin; its intensity depends on the temperature of the radiating gas and on the total amount of material along the ray. By combining optical and radio data it is possible to construct a useful model of the chromosphere and corona. Difficulties arise from the extremely nonhomogeneous nature of the chromosphere and the fact that the emitting gases are far from thermal equilibrium. Furthermore, the radio waves suffer pronounced refraction effects and the observations suffer from effects of low spatial resolution. Observations of the occultation of the Crab Nebula show that the outer corona has a nonuniform structure. As the sun passes in front of this strong radio-frequency source, the latter's signal shows irregular fluctuations.

It is in studies of transient solar phenomena, particularly those connected with sunspots and flares, that radio astronomy has made its most dramatic contributions. Because the radio emission is produced in the solar corona in regions that cannot be observed in optical frequencies, radio-frequency data provide indispensable information on solar phenomena. Earlier work was done with receivers operating at single frequencies and antennas with low angular resolution. Outstanding "bursts" were often observed at times of solar flares but not until J. P. Wild's invention of the radio spectrograph were solar radio-frequency observations obtained in a form that permitted meaningful interpretations.

A radio spectrograph contains a tunable, narrow band-pass receiver capable of detecting signals over a broad frequency range. A tuning device causes the detection frequency to sweep over its entire range twice per second. The signal is displayed on a cathode-ray tube, displacement being proportional to frequency, and intensity to signal strength. This tube is monitored with a motion-picture camera so that the record gives intensity as a function of frequency and time. The resultant display is called a dynamic spectrum.

Of the five types of bursts that are generally classified, four, which are associated with flares, are of particular interest. Types III and V appear to be associated; type IV is always connected with type II but the converse is not true.

In the "slow" drift type II bursts, the frequency slowly decreases with time. A fundamental and a first harmonic exist; furthermore, the emission is often doubled. Type II bursts have been interpreted as plasma oscillations. It is supposed that at the time of the flare a strong shock wave or hydromagnetic wave leaves the spot region and rushes into the corona where it produces oscillations. As the disturbance rises higher it excites oscillations in a gas of steadily declining density. Therefore, the frequency decreases. If a model of the corona (which gives electron density and temperature as a function of height) is available, it is possible to relate frequency and height and thus obtain the velocity of the disturbance. In this way velocities of the order of 500 km/sec were obtained if average coronal densities were assumed, an interpretation confirmed by Wild and his associates by an interferometer technique.

Type II bursts are sometimes followed by type IV bursts, which display a continuous spectrum covering a wide range in frequency. The broad range in frequencies of large angular size and long duration of the type IV bursts suggests synchrotron radiation. Apparently what happens is that at the time of certain unusual flares, a "blast" generates a shock wave or hydromagnetic wave which travels through the corona and excites the plasma oscillations that generate the type II bursts. The plasma carried behind the shock front conveys a magnetic field with it, and charged particles, becoming accelerated to high energies in the twisted and warped field, produce synchrotron radiations.

All flares that produced cosmic rays and high-energy protons had type II bursts followed by type IV events. Likewise, auroras and geomagnetic storms tend to be associated with type II plus type IV bursts. Evidently large pockets of ionized plasma carrying magnetic fields with them may be "blown" from the sun and engulf the earth.

The types III and V bursts somewhat resemble the II and IV bursts, respectively, except that type III bursts are characterized by short duration and a drift in frequency 200 times faster than that of type II bursts. The type III bursts are produced by a disturbance which moves out at about half the speed of light and produces plasma oscillations. Behind the shock front are more electrons which become accelerated in magnetic fields up to energies as high as 2 Mev or more and produce synchrotron radiation over a large radiating volume. These are the type V bursts.

The entire phenomena may be summarized somewhat as follows. Sunspots and associated magnetic regions are manifestations of the hydromagnetic phenomena in the sun. The coolness of the spot and the transient phenomena that occur in or near it all result from the existence of strong magnetic fields in the solar photosphere. The most spectacular of these phenomena are the flares that may be produced when magnetic energy is suddenly liberated. At such a time there occurs something akin to an explosion low in the solar atmosphere. Optically, this is seen as a sudden brightening of the red line of hydrogen. Blobs of fast electrons with velocities approaching that of light escape suddenly from the sun and cause type III and type V bursts. Also material is ejected at a slower velocity, carrying with it a magnetic field. These produce the types II and IV bursts and ultimately geomagnetic storms or even cosmic-ray enhancements.

With Wild's radioheliograph, which consists of 96 parabolic aerials equally spaced around the rim of a circle of 3 km., it is possible to obtain high-resolution moving pictures of the sun at a frequency of 80 Mc/sec and to observe transient effects in the corona, i.e., sudden bursts and brightenings of 1/sec or even less duration.

Radio astronomy has provided valuable clues concerning the structure of the outer solar envelopes and the nature of transient phenomena such as flares. The importance of nonthermal radiation has been clearly demonstrated, and challenging theoretical problems have been proposed.

Cosmic Radio Noise.—The first cosmic radio source detected was the central bulge of our galaxy. After developments of interferometers permitted a great improvement in resolution and as the sensitivity of receivers was improved, the amorphous galactic mass was resolved into a "fine structure" of smaller sources; likewise, a number of discrete sources distributed over the entire sky were recognized and catalogued.

At the highest frequencies, thermal sources are relatively brighter. These sources are clouds of ionized hydrogen (diffuse nebulae), and the emission is produced by the interaction of electrons and ions (free-free transitions). The dependence of emission on frequency is in agreement with theoretical predictions. The positions of many of them agree with diffuse nebulae observed in the optical region of the spectrum; others would be visible as diffuse nebulae were there no obscuring clouds to hide them. At the lowest frequencies, e.g., 20 Mc/sec, these ionized hydrogen regions appear in absorption against a bright background. At intermediate frequencies, e.g., 120 Mc/sec, they are lost in the background. The Milky Way contains many nonthermal sources in addition to the thermal ones.

It is a point of considerable interest that the central bulge of the galaxy, the nonthermal galactic sources, and the discrete sources far from the galactic plane all show roughly the same type of radio spectrum—dependence of intensity on frequency. It is tempting to suggest that all these nonthermal sources are dependent on the same mechanism; i.e., synchrotron radiation.

Discrete sources were first regarded as radio "stars," but as the resolution of radio telescopes improved and the source positions could be accurately determined, it became evident that they could not be identified with optical stars and that many showed finite angular sizes. Such bright nonthermal sources that could be identified with optical objects turned out to be rather unusual nebulae. At the position of the bright Cassiopeia source, filaments of nebulosity in very rapid motion were found. These were interpreted as remnants of a supernova, largely dimmed by intervening clouds of absorbing material. Tycho Brahe's and Johannes Kepler's supernovae of 1572 and 1604, respectively, have now been identified by their radio-frequency emissions.

The radio source Taurus A was identified with the Crab Nebula, which had been a supernova in 1054. Optically, this remarkable object shows an amorphous mass which emits a bright-line spectrum. Furthermore, the light of the amorphous mass is polarized, suggesting that it is produced by electrons moving with such high energy that they radiate in the visible as well as in the radio-frequency ranges. The enormous energies involved during the 900-year lifetime of this object present one of the most challenging problems for theoretical astrophysics.

Other optically identified galactic nonthermal discrete sources, such as IC 443 and the network nebula in Cygnus, appear to be defunct supernovae; it is generally believed that most of the discrete sources in the galaxy are of this type. A diffuse background radiation, presumably also of nonthermal origin, is attributed to synchrotron radiation emitted in large regions of our galaxy. Some radiation may come from external galaxies.

External galaxies fall into two classes: the normal type, in which the ratio of radio emission to optical brightness is roughly constant, and the abnormal type, which are strong radio emitters, called radio galaxies. Some elliptical galaxies are powerful radio emitters. For example, the giant elliptical M87 in Virgo radiates a thousand times as much radio-frequency energy as does our galaxy. This particular system contains a peculiar "jet," the like of which has not been found in any other galaxy. Other radio galaxies require a different interpretation.

Interferometer measurements show that for certain optically identified radio galaxies the source of radio emission was centred not on the optical image but was located in two invisible "blobs" on either side of it, separated by hundreds of thousands of light years. In yet other systems, the central bulge seems to be a region of great turbulence and violent motions as well as a strong radio-frequency source.

The most dramatic phenomena discovered by radio astronomy are the quasi-stellar objects, starlike optical and radio-frequency emitters at enormous distances from the earth, and the pulsars which are believed to be neutron stars. (*See* QUASI-STELLAR RADIO SOURCES.)

The 21-cm. Radiation.—The 21-cm. line has proved to be one of the most useful tools for studying spiral structure and the distribution and mass of cold hydrogen in this and nearby galaxies. From the peak intensity of the 21-cm. profile it is possible to deduce the temperature of the hydrogen, normally about 20° K in cold dense blobs and several thousand degrees in the surrounding medium.

From the shape of the profile and the displacement from its zero-velocity position the motions in the line of sight may be determined. By observing profiles in different galactic longitudes and by making the assumption that the gas is moving in circular orbits, one can attempt to derive the positions of the spiral arms. The analysis is difficult because the material is not uniformly spread along the spiral arms, appears to have "turbulent" motions of its own, and may be moving outward along the arms, at least near the centre. Since the distance of any particular cloud of neutral hydrogen cannot be ascertained from radio data (only its line-of-sight velocity can be measured), interpretations are often difficult. Observations of other spiral systems, notably M31, are helpful in suggesting clues. The total mass of neutral hydrogen can be measured roughly as a function of distance from the galactic centre. It is found, for example, that in great nebulous complexes such as Orion or 30 Doradus, the luminous nebula contains but a small fraction of the total mass. The rest resides in vast surrounding clouds of cold hydrogen. The Orion complex is estimated to contain 50,000 solar masses; that of 30 Doradus is even more extensive.

The OH molecule emits several observable lines whose relative intensities cannot be interpreted in terms of simple thermal emission of a hot gas. Rather, there is indication of some kind of a maser action (*see* MASER). Angular diameters of OH sources and quasars have been measured by very long base-line radio interferometers. Two widely separated antennas, *e.g.*, in North America and Australia, are used to observe the same source. The phase relationship between the two signals received at the two sites is obtained by comparing each set of observations with its own rubidium frequency standard (atomic clock). When the two sets of signals are compared, interference fringes are obtained; these change as the earth rotates and the path difference between the two stations changes (*see* INTERFEROMETER). In this way it was found that a small OH emission knot in IC 1795 in Cassiopeia has a diameter of 0.0045″, which corresponds to a linear diameter of about three times the earth's orbit if this source is at a distance of 5,500 light years. The knots fill only a tiny fraction of the total region occupied by OH emission, which in turn is small compared with the HII region in which it is embedded. The H_2O (steam) emission tends to occur in OH regions and shows rapid changes in intensity. Formaldehyde likewise has been found only in OH condensations. It is possible that these are the first stages of star formation and the building of complex molecules.

Interstellar Magnetic Fields.—Two techniques have been applied to measure the interstellar magnetic field. One is to look for the Zeeman splitting in the 21-cm. absorption line observed against a strong background emission. In this way, Gerrit Verschuur obtained a negligible magnetic field in the local (Orion) arm, a field of 20 microgauss (about 0.00002 the magnetic field of the earth) in the Perseus arm, and about three microgauss in the direction of the Crab Nebula.

A second method is to use Faraday rotation of the polarization vector of radiation received from distant sources. If plane-polarized radio waves pass through an ionized gas which is placed in a magnetic field, the plane of polarization will rotate by an amount proportional to the square of the wavelength, the magnetic field in the line of sight, and the product of electron density and path length. By measuring the time retardation of each pulsar "beep" as a function of frequency one can obtain the electron density times the path length. Then, by measuring the angle of polarization of the polarized pulsar signal as a function of wavelength, we can get the magnetic field. In this way it is established that the magnetic field in the direction of the spiral arm is about 1 microgauss. Over long distances the method fails because if the magnetic field is directed toward the observer in one region and away from the observer in another, the two effects tend to cancel.

The problem of the origin of cosmic rays appeared to be approaching solution in the late 1960s. If interpretations of pulsars as neutron stars were correct, these objects may serve as sources of very high-energy particles. Subsequently, these particles may be accelerated to higher energies by collisions with nonuniform magnetic fields in the galaxy (Fermi mechanism). (*See* COSMIC RAYS.)

Future Outlook.—Impressive contributions by radio astronomy have wrought profound changes in our understanding of solar phenomena, the galaxy, and physical processes in interstellar space. The most impressive discoveries—pulsars, quasars, and properties of the interstellar medium—were made by a judicious combination of optical and radio techniques. However, correlation of optical and radio cosmic phenomena, interpretation of diffuse nebulae, etc. have been retarded because of inadequate support for ground-based optical astronomy.

A serious menace to radio astronomy looms ahead. As communications satellites are developed, less and less of the radio-frequency spectrum will be available for astronomical research. Just as many optical observatories have been "submerged" below the illuminated sky of a growing metropolis, so may all radio observatories be made useless by a sky filled with communications satellites, reflecting needles, etc., jamming so many frequencies with sidebands and harmonics that little cosmic radio noise will be able to get through.

See also references under "Radio Astronomy" in the Index.

BIBLIOGRAPHY.—F. G. Smith, *Radio Astronomy* (1960); R. Hanbury Brown and A. C. B. Lovell, *The Exploration of Space by Radio* (1957); I. S. Shklovskii, *Cosmic Radio Waves* (1951; Eng. trans. by R. B. Rodman and C. Varsavsky, 1960); J. L. Pawsey and R. N. Bracewell, *Radio Astronomy* (1955); R. N. Bracewell (ed.), *Paris Symposium on Radio Astronomy* (1959); J. D. Kraus, *Radio Astronomy* (1966). For experimental techniques, *see* W. N. Christiansen and J. A. Högbom, *Radiotelescopes* (1969). (L. H. A.)

RADIOCARBON DATING. Radiocarbon age dating, developed in the late 1940s at the University of Chicago, is an example of the application of one of the newest sciences (atomic energy) to one of the oldest (archaeology). The technique involves measuring the relative activities of radioactive carbon (C^{14}) in (1) present-day living organic matter and (2) the sample under investigation, and multiplying the logarithm of this ratio by the rate at which the activity of C^{14} decays with time. Careful measurements have shown that the activity of any given preparation of carbon-14 is reduced by exactly one-half during each interval of 5.730 ± 40 years. This value is called the half-life of C^{14}. Actually all dates are reported on the earlier value of 5,568 and require correction by a factor of 1.03. The earlier half-life is used to avoid confusion.

Radiocarbon is produced in nature by an indirect process involving the interaction of cosmic rays from outer space with the nitrogen in the earth's atmosphere. The competing processes of formation and of decay of C^{14} have been going on for so long that the equilibrium has been established, and the world inventory of C^{14} is estimated at about 70 metric tons. Radiocarbon therefore has been introduced into the biosphere, and all living matter contains a small quantity of radiocarbon which averages 15.3 ± 0.1 disintegrations per minute per gram of contained carbon. This activity remains constant throughout the life of the organic matter because of the above-mentioned equilibrium processes.

However, at death the introduction of radiocarbon into the specimen ceases, while the normal decay of the contained radiocarbon continues according to the half-life mentioned above. Therefore an archaeological specimen (for example, a mummy or a tree) which yields 7.65 disintegrations per minute per gram of carbon instead of 15.3 is judged to be 5.730 ± 40 years old. If the material shows only one-fourth the radiocarbon content of living matter, the age of the specimen is 11.460 ± 80 years, etc.

Refinements in the technique of measurement have been made

by reducing, as far as possible, the effects of spurious radiation, including background activity due to cosmic radiation, and radioactive impurities in the shielding of counters and in the materials of construction of the counter itself. These refinements permit the extension of radiocarbon dating to samples which could be as much as 50,000 years old.

See Willard F. Libby, *Radiocarbon Dating,* 2nd ed. (1955); F. Rainey and E. K. Ralph, "Archeology and Its New Technology," *Science,* vol. 153, no. 3743 (1966). (W. F. LI.)

RADIOLOGY is the branch of medicine that deals with the employment of X rays and isotopes in the diagnosis of disease and the use of X rays, gamma rays, and other forms of ionizing radiation in the treatment of disease. For details of the physical nature, method of production, and technical and industrial applications of the various components of the electromagnetic spectrum, *see* RADIOACTIVITY and X RAYS.

This article is divided into the following parts and sections:

Note: The energy of the gamma radiation released by disintegration of isotopes is expressed as ev (electron volts), kev (thousand electron volts), or Mev (million electron volts). By currently accepted standards X-ray energies are expressed in vp (peak volts) if generated by pulsating currents and in v. (volts) if the generating current is non-pulsating. In this article we omit the "peak" terminology in describing the energy of diagnostic and therapeutic X rays, believing that to retain it would confuse rather than clarify.

I. DIAGNOSTIC RADIOLOGY

A. APPARATUS

1. Quality and Intensity of Radiation.—Concern with the various implications of thermonuclear weapons stirred up exaggerated fears of the radiation risks involved in X-ray diagnosis. It is unwise to employ diagnostic radiology (or, for that matter, drugs or surgery), of course, unless there is real need for it. When there is such need, X-ray examinations conducted by qualified ra-

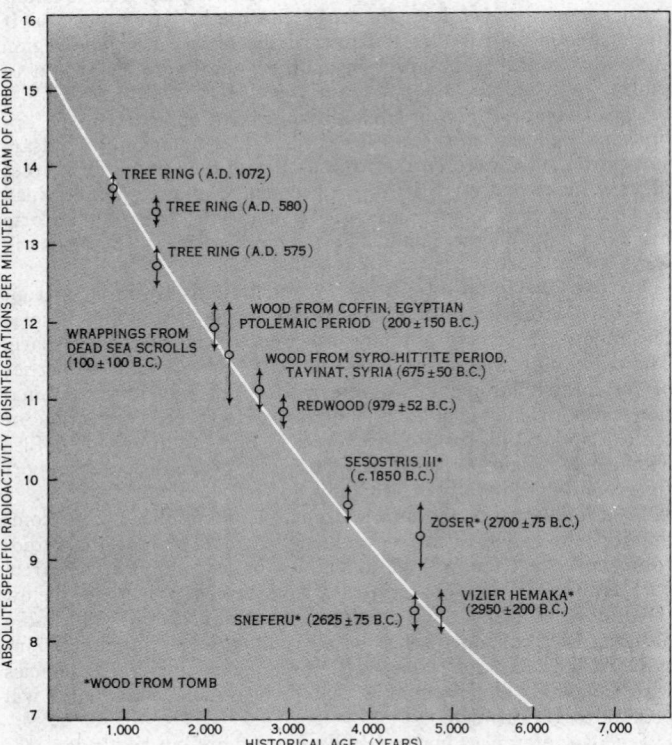

SAMPLES OF OBJECTS OF KNOWN AGE DATED BY RADIOCARBON METHOD

The curve is calculated from the assay for modern wood and the laboratory measurement of the half-life of radiocarbon ($5,568 \pm 30$ years). The individual points show the specific radioactivities of the various samples of known age (the latter given in parentheses). The age of the sample as estimated by the radiocarbon method is shown by the point on the curve corresponding to the indicated specific radioactivity. The range in specific radioactivity for a given sample is the standard deviation based solely on the number of counts taken; it does not include other errors, such as those arising from contamination.

diologists involve risks smaller than those encountered every day at home, at work, and on the street, it may be argued, and smaller than the risk of getting along without examinations, which might have revealed remediable disease.

In X-ray diagnosis it is the practice to indicate radiation quality and intensity by stating the voltage and current applied to the tube, the current being expressed in milliamperes, abbreviated ma. (1 ma. = 0.001 amp.), and the voltage in peak kilovolts, abbreviated kv. Current is measured by means of a milliammeter inserted between the two halves of the secondary winding of the X-ray transformer at a point where the potential is close to zero; and tube voltage is measured by means of a kilovoltmeter wired across the primary of the X-ray transformer.

For fluoroscopy and the making of X-ray films, tube current may be as low as 3 ma. or as high as 1,000 ma., and voltage usually ranges from 45 kv. to 90 kv. or even up to 130 kv. The magnitude of the voltage applied to an X-ray tube determines the wavelength composition of the beam and therefore its penetrating ability, and in addition affects the intensity of all beam components exponentially. For example, a tube voltage of 45 kv. will produce radiation having a maximum shortness of approximately 0.274 angstroms (Å) (0.274×10^{-8} cm.), radiation so feebly penetrating that it is unsuitable for the fluoroscopy or filming of heavy body parts. Doubling voltage to 90 kv. brings the maximum shortness of the beam down to 0.137 Å, thus providing penetration adequate for the thickest anatomical parts, and quadrupling the intensity of all the components of the beam.

Over a considerable range, these factors—voltage, current, and exposure time—may be juggled almost at will, provided only that the time-intensity product of the radiation reaching the film approaches a constant that has been determined empirically as adequate for recording the tissue densities of the body part that is being examined.

2. X-Ray Generators.—In their simplest form the X-ray generators used in diagnosis consist of a hot-cathode X-ray tube, a controllable means of heating the cathode, a source of single-phase 60-cycle alternating current, and a means of regulating the voltage of that current. Circuits of this sort are known as self-rectified because the X-ray tube itself acts as a rectifier, passing one and suppressing the other half cycle of the high-voltage alternating current supplied by the transformer. Thousands of sets of this design are in use throughout the world, as dental X-ray machines, portable, and bedside X-ray machines. They are adequate where the service is intermittent and the loads are not greater than 10 to 15 ma. at 70 to 80 kv., but for heavy work full-wave rectification is preferable.

In theory, full-wave-rectified generators differ from the self-rectified sets described above merely by the insertion of electronic or solid-state rectifiers between the high-voltage terminals of the transformer and the X-ray tube. In practice, they are much more complex, including voltage stabilizers for the filament of the X-ray tube, voltage regulators for the primary windings of the high-voltage transformer and the X-ray filament transformer, devices for the automatic selection and limitation of tube voltage and current, circuits for energizing the rotors of rotating anode tubes, meters, fuses, circuit breakers, and some means for the precise timing of both short and long exposures. Modern generators are completely insulated or "shockproof," regardless of whether they are of the self-rectified or the valve-tube-rectified type.

Small to moderate size full wave-generators are designed for operation on single phase power, but for the heaviest loads and for rapidly repeated short exposures, three-phase generators are preferred. Such machines are expensive and complicated but the best of them provide a practically "ripple-free" high-voltage output, which makes for X-ray beams of maximum intensity for a given degree of punishment of the target of an X-ray tube.

3. X-Ray Tubes.—The tubes used in X-ray diagnosis consist of a well-exhausted glass-enveloped diode surrounded by a metallic housing lined with lead except at a small port through which the useful beam of X rays emerges. The space between glass insert and housing is filled with insulating oil. In the simplest and smallest sets the tube housing is integral with the transformer housing,

but in larger machines the two usually are separate, tube and transformer being connected by means of flexible, shielded cables. In these modern descendants of William David Coolidge's hot-cathode tube, the cathode stream is focused as a ribbon on a steeply inclined target so that the heat of impact is distributed as widely as possible and yet the optically effective source of rays approaches a point. Frequently two filaments are provided: one focusing the electrons sharply for use when great detail is required and small currents are allowable, the other distributing the electrons over a larger target area when heavier currents must be employed. Targets are of two general types: those that are stationary and those that rotate during operation. In stationary-anode tubes, the target is of tungsten embedded in a massive copper anode, which extends out through the glass envelope to conduct the heat of electron bombardment into the insulating oil surrounding the tube.

Rotating anodes turn on precision bearings mounted within the exhausted glass envelope and therefore devoid of ordinary lubricants. The stator lies outside the envelope, its lines of force passing through the glass to operate the rotor attached to the anode stem. Sometimes the anode disk is of massive copper with an embedded belt of tungsten to receive the electron bombardment, but more commonly it is of solid tungsten or tungsten alloy capable of withstanding a cherry-red heat during heavy loading.

4. Films, Screens, and Cassettes.—X-ray films consist of a sheet plastic base coated on both sides with an emulsion of silver halide and gelatin. Since most X-ray films are used in conjunction with calcium tungstate intensifying screens, emulsions are given maximum sensitivity to the fluorescence of calcium tungstate rather than to X rays themselves. For the examination of certain parts, such as the teeth, fingers, and toes, plain film without screens ordinarily is the film used, and in such applications it suffices to enclose it in black paper or cardboard. For the filming of heavier parts, however, exposure time can be reduced and the contrast in the image enhanced if films pressed between two intensifying screens are used instead of plain films. These screens must be in intimate contact with the emulsions if sharp detail is to be recorded, such contact being provided by rigid lightproof containers known as cassettes. The fronts of cassettes are made of bakelite or magnesium to exclude light but admit X rays, and when phototiming is employed the backs also must be reasonably radiolucent.

In the making of a film of the chest, for example, the patient stands facing a 14 × 17-in. duplitized X-ray film (emulsion on both sides of base) contained in a double-screen cassette of the sort described above, the X-ray tube being arranged so that its beam of radiation passes through the patient's back in a direction perpendicular to the surface of the film. The X rays induce a fluorescent image of the lungs, ribs, heart, etc., on the front screen, a slight photographic effect directly on the front and rear layers of film emulsion, and finally a fluorescent image on the rear screen. The light from the two fluorescent images photographs itself onto the emulsion along with the two direct X-ray images, and in the completed film all four images, being superimposed, appear as one.

5. Grids.—From their point of origin X rays are propagated in straight lines in all directions; but most of them are absorbed in the lead lining of the tube housing, and the cone of useful radiation that emerges through the port has an apex angle of only approximately 15°. Except under especially arranged conditions X rays are not reflected or refracted by the substances they encounter on their straight-line course to the X-ray film, but some of them do become scattered. For small, thin parts, scattering is negligible, but for heavy parts, such as the skull and trunk of an adult, radiation scattered in the patient's body fogs the image formed by the straight-line or primary radiation to such a degree that finer details become indistinguishable.

Before 1917 good X-ray plates of the skull, spine, hip, etc., required that the primary beam be narrowed to a very small diameter to reduce scatter, and 14 by 17-in. plates of the entire pelvis of a heavy subject were so badly fogged by scattered radiation as to have little clinical usefulness (glass plates were used in those days rather than films). In 1912 Gustav Bucky in Germany had laid the groundwork for overcoming this difficulty, and by the early 1920s there became available, first in the U.S. and later in Europe, moving grids designed by the U.S. radiologist Hollis Potter. These instruments, known as Potter-Bucky grids or, less properly, as Potter-Bucky diaphragms, became an indispensable part of the equipment of all diagnostic radiologists. Such grids, consisting of an assembly of lead strips interspaced with strips of wood, plastic, or other radiotranslucent material, are interposed between patient and film and are kept in motion while the exposure is being made. The lead strips are aligned as radii of a segment of a theoretical cylinder that has a diameter equal to twice the target-film distance. A small portion of the primary or unscattered radiation that emerges from the patient's body is lost by impingement on the thin edges of the lead strips, but most of it passes through the interstices between the strips and thus to the film. The scattered radiation, on the other hand, not being aligned with the translucent interstices, impinges for the most part on the broad sides of the lead strips, where it is absorbed.

Bucky's original grids were stationary and cast disturbing patterns on the film. Potter's contribution was to conceive and build grids that could be moved during exposure, thus obliterating the pattern of their grid members but not interfering with their ability to absorb scattered radiation. Modern moving grids are flat rather than curved; they are built to extremely precise dimensional tolerances, have great ability to absorb scattered radiation, and reciprocate throughout the exposure instead of starting before exposure begins and continuing to move in the same direction until it has been completed. In their original form stationary grids were virtually useless except as precursors to a great idea, but after the Swedish radiologist Eric Lysholm revived interest in them, excellent European and U.S. units became available. Unlike moving grids, the stationary ones inevitably leave their own images on films along with the images of the body parts that are being examined. In modern stationary grids, however, these superimposed patterns are regular and faint, detracting little from appearance and nothing from clinical usefulness.

6. Fluoroscope.—The fluoroscope is an apparatus for direct observation of body tissues by means of X rays. In its simplest form it consists of a fluoroscopic screen supported in front of the port of an X-ray tube so that a patient may be interposed between screen and X-ray source. The fluoroscopic screen is made up of a thin sheet of cardboard or plastic coated with zinc cadmium sulfide and covered with lead-bearing glass impervious to X rays but transparent to the greenish light given off by zinc cadmium sulfide when X rays impinge on it. In the hands of a skilled examiner, with eyes well accommodated to darkness, working in a thoroughly darkened room, and employing a small screen of the best quality and a closely collimated X-ray beam, the direct fluoroscope was a useful instrument involving only slightly greater radiation doses to patient and examiner than those required in the best of modern instruments. Unfortunately such ideal conditions seldom obtained and most fluoroscopy involved far more than the theoretically necessary radiation exposure to patient and examiner. The direct fluoroscope was abandoned in favour of the intensifier or preferably the video fluoroscope, both of which employ Coltman-type X-ray image intensifier tubes. Such image intensifiers convert a visible fluoroscopic image into an electron image and then electronically accelerate and focus the electrons, delivering them to a secondary screen where they produce a small but very bright visible image. In the intensifier type of fluoroscope the examiner views the output phosphor of the Coltman tube by means of mirrors and lenses; in the video fluoroscope viewing by means of a closed circuit television camera that displays a still further intensified image on one or more monitors located at convenient points in the fluoroscopic room.

In direct fluoroscopy even though one kept the intensity of the X-ray beam as low as possible, the point was not quite reached where statistical fluctuation in the X-ray photons rather than screen brilliance was the limiting factor. In the newer type fluoroscopes the reverse is true. Screen brilliance can be maintained even in the face of very marked reduction in X-ray intensity, but if such reduction is of more than modest amount statistical fluctuation of X-ray photons deteriorates the fluoroscopic image regardless of its degree of brilliance. In spite of this unavoidable limitation the newer fluoroscopes, by making it possible for the examiner to see well even without accommodating his eyes to darkness, not only have improved the clinical quality of fluoroscopy but also have made significant reductions in the X-ray doses delivered under practical working conditions.

B. Technique

1. Timing the Exposure.—When the intensity of the X-ray beam is low and exposure time of the order of seconds, simple spring-driven time switches are adequate; but for tube currents of from 100 to 1,000 ma. and exposure times of the order of $\frac{1}{120}$ sec., precise timing becomes important and difficult, much of the difficulty being inherent in the pulsating nature of the current applied to the X-ray tube. When single phase 60-cycle current is employed, X rays are emitted by the target in brief bursts starting from zero, rising to full intensity, and returning to zero every $\frac{1}{120}$ sec. (each half cycle). Brief exposures therefore must be measured in half cycles, beginning and terminating approximately at zero points on the voltage wave. The delivering of very brief high-current X-ray exposures has been rendered more precise by the use of three-phase rather than single-phase machines and the employment of solid-state timers and contactors.

In the early 1940s it became possible to time X-ray exposures automatically by means of light-sensitive cells scanning fluorescent screens that received radiation which had passed through patient and film; but for reasons having to do with marketing rather than with engineering or medicine, application progressed slowly in radiology during a period when the principle became almost universal in ordinary photography.

2. Processing X-Ray Films.—By the mid-1940s automatic processors had begun to supplant the hand processing of X-ray films and by the late 1960s replacement was almost complete. Exposed films are fed directly into processors and one and a half minutes later are delivered: developed, fixed, washed and dried, ready for examination. Needed but not available were processors that require no dark room, receiving exposed films in cassettes and delivering processed film together with cassettes loaded with fresh film.

3. Stereoscopic X-Ray Filming.—Three-dimensional vision is helpful in the radiography of any part of the body and almost essential in examinations of the skull and trunk. Two films are required, made with the film and body part in identical spatial relationship for each but with the X-ray tube shifted slightly between the two exposures.

Even without the aid of instruments some workers are able to view one of the films with one eye, the other with the other eye, fusing these two slightly dissimilar, real, flat images into a single, virtual, three-dimensional image. It is more convenient, however, and for some persons essential, to employ a special viewing apparatus.

4. Tomography.—In certain special situations images of one body level are best distinguished from those of overlying or underlying structures by means of a device known as a tomograph. The anatomical level of interest is brought to the level of the fulcrum of a tomograph and films are made with the tube moving in one direction and the film in the opposite direction relative to fulcrum and part. Using massive, well-constructed apparatus in which extraneous motion is

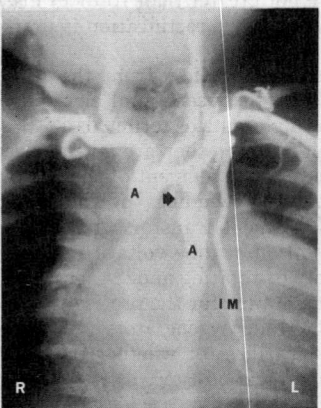

FROM L. P. ELLIOTT AND G. L. SCHIEBLER, "X-RAY DIAGNOSIS OF CONGENITAL CARDIAC DISEASE"; REPRODUCED BY PERMISSION OF CHARLES C. THOMAS PRESS, SPRINGFIELD, ILL.

FIG. 1.—CONGENITAL COARCTATION OF AORTA IN A CHILD

The proximal aorta (A) is congenitally narrowed high in its course through the thorax (arrow) with resulting increased blood pressure above and lowered pressure below the point of narrowing. Vessels such as the internal mammary (IM) dilate and provide life-saving pathways for blood to the abdomen and lower extremities (R is right; L is left)

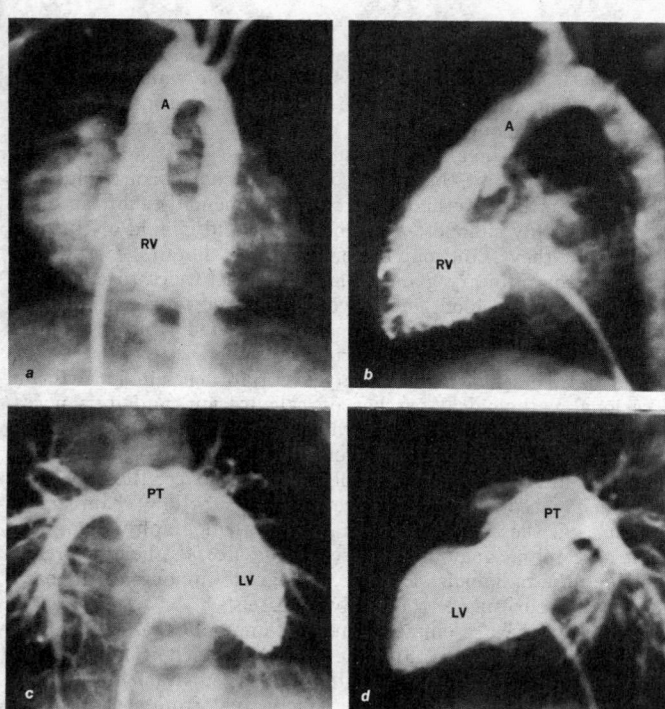

FIG. 2.—TRANSPOSITION OF GREAT VESSELS

In this seemingly hopeless congenital abnormality (seen here from four different angles) the right ventricle (RV) delivers its blood to the body's main artery, the aorta (A) and it is the left ventricle (LV) which sends blood to the lungs by way of the pulmonary artery (Pulmonary Trunk, PT). It is not practical to attempt to establish normal artery-heart relationships, but surgical rerouting of venous blood within the thorax is proving to be a reasonable substitute

negligible, the resulting films provide reasonably sharp images at the level of the fulcrum, with those above and below blurred to the point of obliteration, such films being referred to as "cuts." Cuts are thick when the angular displacement about the fulcrum (blurring angle) is small and thin when it is large. The method finds its greatest usefulness in examination of the skull, particularly the small structures of the ear.

5. Contrast Media.—The lungs show in X-ray films and in fluoroscopic images because of the difference between the X-ray absorbing power of air and that of pulmonary tissue. The heart contrasts strongly with air-filled lungs adjacent to it but scarcely at all with the liver beneath; bones are distinguished from surrounding muscle and the various parts of bone from one another by virtue of the calcium phosphate they contain. To a considerable extent, however, X-ray examination depends on the employment of artificial contrast media. The medium most extensively used is barium sulfate. Stirred into water thickened with powdered resins, it is employed for examination of the esophagus, stomach, small bowel, and colon. Iodized organic compounds are used for examination of the gallbladder, urinary tract, blood vessels, spleen, liver, and bile ducts. X-ray visualization of the bronchi is made possible by the introduction into the bronchial tree of unsaturated vegetable oil partially saturated with iodine. An emulsion of ethyl iodophenylundecylate is used in the examination of the spinal canal (myelography).

6. Photofluorography.—From the earliest days of radiology, attempts were made to make permanent records of fluoroscopic images by photographing them, but until the late 1930s the maneuver had little practical application. The advantage of photofluorography lay in its ability to employ small, inexpensive, and easily processed photographic roll film instead of large, costly, individual sheets of X-ray film; its disadvantage lay in the fact that fluoroscopic images were faint and the camera lenses available for recording them slow. As far as the chest is concerned, the disadvantages finally were overcome by developing faster film emulsions and more brilliant photofluorographic screens and the substi-

tution of large-aperture reflector lens systems for refractors, but in other body parts even this was not enough to keep radiation dosage within allowable limits.

7. Fluorography.—A special form of photofluorography (technically "fluorography") consists in having the 70-mm. camera photograph the output phosphor of an image intensifier. During video fluoroscopy all the light from that phosphor goes to the television camera, but at intervals the radiologist interrupts his viewing to divert most of the light to the 70-mm. camera reserving for television only enough to allow him to "monitor" the position of parts and timing of events. By the late 1960s 70-mm. fluorography had developed to the point where it was beginning to supplant direct "spot-filming" in such examinations as those of the stomach, colon, bronchovascular system, and urinary tract. Important among these developments were improved lenses, easy-loading cameras, multiple film-receiving magazines capable of removal and replacement at the end of each examination, and film that could be processed in whatever automatic processors that were standard for the department, including the 90-sec. variety.

8. X-Ray Motion Pictures.—Within a year following the discovery of X rays, attempts were made to produce X-ray motion pictures; but until the 1960s, such large tissue doses were required that cineradiography was impractical except for acute experiments on animals. The development of image intensifiers coupled to television rekindled the hope that motion pictures of the television screen would become practical. Modern X-ray motion pictures almost invariably are made from the output phosphor of an image intensifier. With 16-mm. and particularly with 35-mm. film, the images are of excellent quality and for certain specific purposes, notably the examination of coronary vessels, they are important diagnostic aids. With any considerable length of run, however, the loading of generator and tube and the radiation dose to the patient are considerable.

9. X-Ray Videotape.—Magnetic tape recordings of the electronic output of the television camera are as useful to radiologists as "instant replay" tapes are to sports announcers. Requiring no increase in radiation dose, they may be set to monitor everything seen by the radiologist during the day's work, or more commonly may be turned on and off as he observes something worthy of recording. In subsequent viewing when the tape is stopped at some particular moment, the detail of such a "still" is poor but during motion the picture becomes as good as the original monitor image. Complicated and expensive "central station" equipment is required if edited tape is to be recorded on 16-mm. film, but the tape itself can be stored and replayed indefinitely and when its usefulness has passed it can be erased and reused.

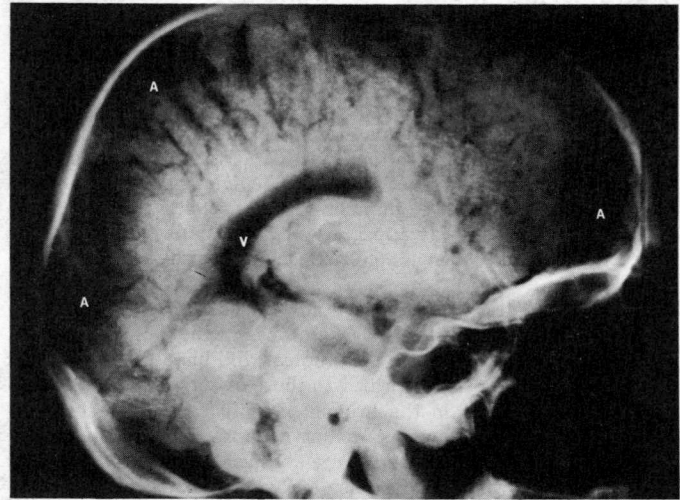

FIG. 3.—PNEUMOENCEPHALOGRAM

Child with cerebral atrophy. Air has collected in large amounts in the subarachnoid space over the entire surface of the brain (A). In a normal child the cortex is much thicker and the subarachnoid space correspondingly thinner. The lateral ventricles (V) are of normal size

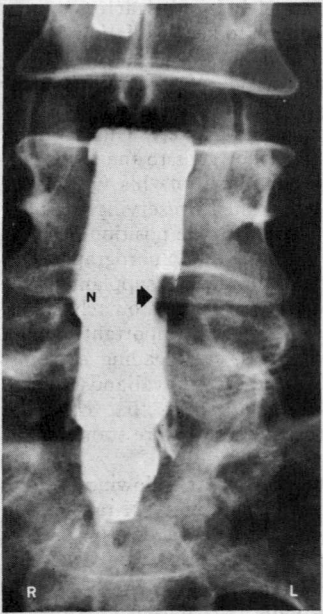
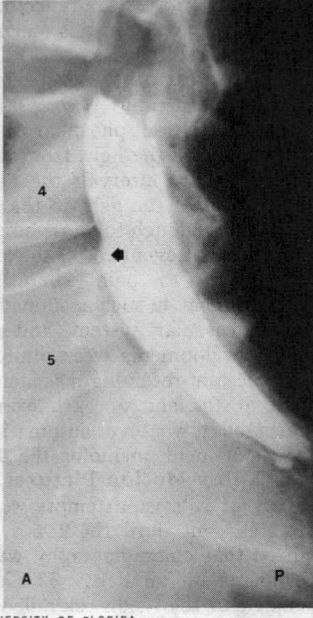

FIG. 4.—MYELOGRAM SHOWING HERNIATION OF INTERVERTEBRAL DISC

(Left) Frontal view of spinal canal following injection of organic iodine contrast into subarachnoid space. Contrast surrounds and therefore demonstrates the cauda equina in the lower spinal canal. On the right (R) a nerve sheath (N) is filled normally but on the left is "amputated" (arrow) by pressure from a herniated intervertebral disc. (Right) Lateral view: Backward herniation of the disc between the bodies of lumbar vertebrae 4 and 5 indents the anterior (A) surface of the sacral sac (arrow)

C. CLINICAL APPLICATIONS

1. Teeth.—Intraoral films are used for detecting abscesses about the apexes of the teeth, unerupted or impacted teeth, retained broken tooth roots, small cavities at abutting surfaces, poorly fitting fillings and inlays, recession of the bone from the necks of the teeth and, most important of all, subgingival deposits of salivary calculus.

2. Bones.—For the first few years following their discovery, it seemed that clinical use of X rays might be limited to the diagnosis and reduction of fractures, but today the usefulness of X rays is far more extensive. In normal bone the cortex shows as a dense amorphous shell and the spongy portion as a honeycombed structure. Disuse of living bone causes a generalized loss of density known as osteoporosis, but when portions of bone are killed by disease or injury before osteoporosis has occurred, they retain their original density for long periods of time. Some tumours and infections cause localized destruction and others cause bone to become denser than normal.

Marrow, periosteum, and articular cartilage, though they are not discernible, when diseased may produce subtle changes in bone adjacent to them, leading to their own detection. Rickets, scurvy, syphilis, tuberculosis, Paget's disease, benign and malignant tumours, and a considerable number of other skeletal diseases produce changes in the X-ray appearance of bones almost always easy to see and frequently so characteristic as to warrant a specific diagnosis.

3. Chest and Heart.—Active fibrocaseous tuberculosis produces rather characteristic dense splotches in the lung apexes, but at certain stages some of the pneumonias and histoplasmosis show X-ray patterns almost identical with those of tuberculosis. Malignant tumours arising in the bronchi usually cause bronchial obstruction with resulting areas of lung collapse. Foreign bodies in the trachea or bronchi frequently are dense enough to show directly in X-ray films; when such bodies are radiotranslucent they may be detectable by virtue of changes they produce in the air patterns of the lung.

Radiology may be employed to determine the size and shape of the heart and great vessels, and, with the aid of opaque media, it provides detailed information about the chambers and valves of the heart and pulmonary vessels, particularly in children suffering from congenital defects.

4. Skull, Brain, and Spinal Cord.—In the vault of the skull, fractures, tumours, and infection usually are reasonably evident, but in the face bones where the cortex may be as thin as paper, such lesions may be almost invisible.

Because of the air that they contain, the normal mastoids and the sinuses (frontal, ethmoid, maxillary, sphenoid) show as black shadows sharply silhouetted against bone; and if fluid or tumours are present they stand out in contrast with the air. Certain tumours of the pituitary gland cause the sella turcica to enlarge in a characteristic fashion, and in young children long-continued increase in intracranial pressure may be inferred from a resulting separation of the bones of the skull.

The brain itself is radiolucent except for certain normal and occasional pathological patches of calcification, and it is necessary to employ contrast media when the brain is to be examined, the medium of choice being oxygen or carbon dioxide. When such gases are introduced into the subarachnoid space, the procedure is termed encephalography; when into the hollow chambers of ventricles at the centre of the brain, ventriculography. Development of cerebral angiography (see *Blood Vessels*, below) greatly expanded the radiologist's ability to diagnose tumours of the brain and small aneurysms of the cerebral vessels.

Opaque media are employed more commonly than gas for examining the spinal cord and the canal in which it lies. Under fluoroscopic control, contrast material in the subarachnoid space is maneuvered into all parts of the spinal canal from the tip of the caudal sac in the lumbosacral region up to (but not into) the cisterna at the base of the brain. Films made at all levels and in several positions show the cord as a translucent or negative shadow with the surrounding subdural space dense by virtue of the opaque medium it contains. Protruding knobs of intervertebral cartilage, spikes, or ridges of arthritic osteophytes, tumours of bone, cord, or meninges are among the abnormalities that may be detected by myelography; but normal variation is great and differentiation difficult even when the examination is conducted by teams of specially trained neurosurgeons and radiologists.

5. Gallbladder and Bile Ducts.—In 1923 E. A. Graham introduced the method for the X-ray examination of the gallbladder, known as cholecystography. An iodized organic contrast medium given by mouth in tablet form is absorbed from the gastrointestinal tract into the blood and then removed from the blood by the liver and combined with the bile. A normal gallbladder, receiving

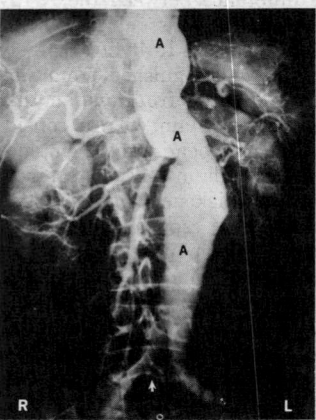

FIG. 5.—ANEURYSM OF THORACIC AND ABDOMINAL AORTA

A catheter was introduced and advanced until its tip lay in the lower thoracic aorta. Contrast was injected into the left axillary artery and four seconds after the onset of injection this film was made. It shows widening of the aorta (A) from the upper limit of visibility down almost to its bifurcation (arrow) into the two common iliac arteries (L is left, R is right)

through its cystic duct weakly iodized bile, concentrates it until it becomes thick and its iodine content high. In X-ray films made 10 to 15 hours following administration of the opaque medium, the normal gallbladder casts a dense shadow and cholesterol stones if present stand out as negative shadows. If the gallbladder is seriously diseased or its cystic duct occluded, bile will fail to reach the gallbladder or, reaching there, will fail of concentration, either event resulting in nonvisualization.

Cholangiography, or examination of the bile ducts, usually is conducted in conjunction with surgery to assure that stones or a tumour obstructing the ducts have not been overlooked. A contrast medium is injected either through a T tube tied into one of the bile ducts or by means of a hypodermic needle introduced through the wall of a duct or of the gallbladder itself.

6. Urinary Tract.

6. Urinary Tract.—Pyelograms are X-ray films of the urinary tract made following the introduction of an opaque medium. In the retrograde method, the contrast is injected through ureteral catheters introduced with the aid of a cystoscope. In the excretion or intravenous method, it is injected intravenously followed by filming at intervals of 5 to 15 min., or, under certain circumstances, several hours.

Most tumours lying in the fleshy part of the kidney outside its collecting system compress, stretch, and otherwise distort the calyces and pelves. Tuberculous abscesses are prone to break through into the calyces, allowing contrast to extravasate into diseased tissue, and the infrequent kidney stones that are radiotranslucent may be rendered visible by the opaque medium. Cystograms are films of the urinary bladder made after the direct or excretory filling of that organ with contrast. Bladder tumours, diverticula, and urethral obstruction produce rather characteristic alterations in the appearance of cystograms. By means of serial 70-mm. fluorograms or full-size films made during the voiding of opacified urine, one may examine the urethra and determine the presence or absence of reflux from the bladder into the ureters.

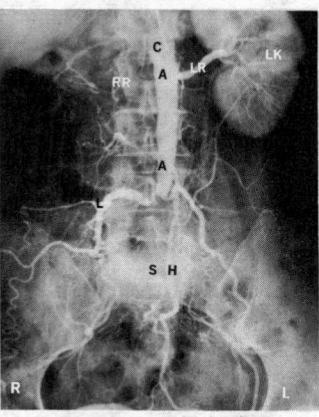

BY COURTESY OF DEPARTMENT OF RADIOLOGY, UNIVERSITY OF FLORIDA

FIG. 6.—ARTERIOSCLEROTIC OBSTRUCTION OF LOWER ABDOMINAL AORTA

Catheter introduced through left axillary artery lies with tip (C) in upper abdominal aorta. Contrast injected through catheter fills upper part of abdominal aorta (A) and left renal artery (LR). The right renal artery (RR) is occluded as well as the lower aorta and its bifurcation into common iliacs. The left kidney (LK) has a normal blood supply and the lower extremities continue to receive blood through a dilated superior hemorrhoidal (SH) and right and left lumbar arteries (L)

7. Female Reproductive Tract.—Sterility of the human female results from numerous causes, one of which is occlusion of the fallopian tubes. Such occlusions may be demonstrated by making X-ray films following the injection of iodized oil into the uterus. In the normal subject, oil passes out through both fallopian tubes to spill into the peritoneal cavity, where, 24 hours later, it becomes smeared over the serous surfaces of loops of bowel and appears by X ray as a slightly opaque, crumpled veil. When no connection exists between the uterine cavity and the peritoneal cavity, perito-

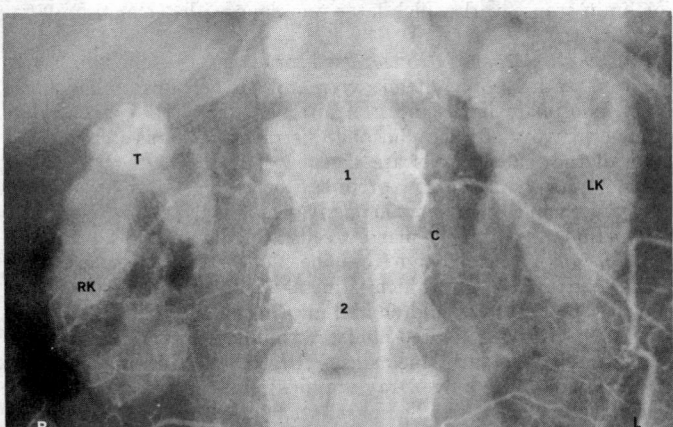

BY COURTESY OF DEPARTMENT OF RADIOLOGY, UNIVERSITY OF FLORIDA

FIG. 7.—CANCER OF THE KIDNEY DEMONSTRATED BY ANGIOGRAPHY

A catheter (C) has been introduced into the abdominal aorta through one of the femoral arteries and lies with its tip at the level of the disc between the first (1) and second (2) lumbar vertebrae. Contrast was injected through the catheter and earlier films of the series showed filling of aorta, renal and other large arteries. When this film was made most of the arteries had emptied except for the abnormal "tumour vessels" in a 3 cm. spherical cancer (T) in the upper pole of the right kidney (RK) (L is left, R is right)

neal spread of oil does not occur, and when occlusion is due to sac-like adhesions about the outer ends of the fallopian tubes, the oil breaks up into droplets retained in the watery fluid that fills the sacs. While the purpose of the injection is diagnostic, it is believed that it may sometimes be therapeutic as well, breaking up adhesions if they are not too tough and developing communication where none existed before.

When a pregnant woman is known to have an obstetrically adequate pelvis and a presumably normal fetus, pelvic X-ray examination should not be done; but if circumstances require quantitative knowledge as to the dimensions of the birth passages, X-ray examination provides by far the best means of measuring them.

X rays diverge from their point of origin and the X-ray images of anatomical parts that are parallel with the plane of the film are always somewhat larger than the parts themselves. If the parts are oblique to the film, that too causes distortion of the image. With the aid of some special equipment and the application of simple geometry it is possible to compensate for both types of distortion and translate measurements of film images into the actual dimensions of the maternal or fetal parts they portray, the procedure being known as pelvimetry or fetometry.

8. Blood Vessels.—Opacification of blood vessels in anatomical material was an early development and for many years there has been limited application in living subjects. Widespread clinical employment has had to wait, however, for the synthesis of iodated organic substances combining ability to opacify effectively with an acceptable degree of physiological tolerance. Important among such substances are sodium or methylglucamine salts of various iodine-containing organic acids. Because individual products vary from one another in viscosity, iodine content, and tolerance by particular body tissues, selection of a particular material depends largely on the particular part of the cardiovascular system that is to be examined. Several films must be made in rapid succession, each exposure being brief, the first in the series phased carefully with the beginning of the injection.

In the 1960s radiologists and surgeons throughout the world regularly investigated and frequently solved vascular-tract problems, some of which would have been unsuspected, much less capable of solution, a decade earlier. These included obstruction or dilatation of blood vessels in all parts of the body, including those of the brain and of the lungs. Workers of many nationalities laid the groundwork for modern vascular radiology, those in Sweden playing a particularly important role.

9. Stomach and Intestine.—X-ray examination has become an indispensable agent in the diagnosis of gastric and duodenal ulcer; benign and malignant tumours of the esophagus, stomach, and bowel; diverticulosis and diverticulitis; ulcerative colitis; regional ileitis; and several other diseases. Barium sulfate is the contrast medium almost invariably employed, and video fluoroscopy plus 70-mm. fluorography (*see* above) have largely replaced ordinary fluoroscopy and "spot-filming" with full-size films.

Ulcers deform the outline of the stomach or duodenal bulb and, in addition, frequently excavate craters which, when filled with barium, are highly diagnostic. Cancers appear as soft tissue masses protruding into the lumen of the stomach or bowel and distorting the appearance of the gastric or intestinal mucosa. (P. C. H.)

II. NUCLEAR MEDICINE

The discovery that elements have more than one stable atomic form laid the groundwork for nuclear medicine. (*See* ISOTOPE.)

1. Radioisotopes.—The first isotopes (as such variant atomic forms were called) to be recognized were naturally occurring, unstable and, therefore, radioactive. Naturally occurring isotopes are used as tracers in various branches of science, but most of those which are radioactive have such long half-lives that they are not safe for ingestion or for injection into the blood streams of patients. To be clinically useful an isotope, in minute amounts, located deep in a patient's body must emit gamma radiation powerful enough to affect recording devices outside his body, but have such a short half-life that irradiation of the patient's tissues continues for only a brief time after recording has been completed. Radioisotopes with precisely such characteristics can be produced artificially by neutron bombardment in a nuclear reactor, by physical or chemical separation from by-products of fission of uranium-235, or by bombardment in a cyclotron or other type of particle accelerator. (For an understanding of how such isotopes are produced and how subsequent rearrangement of their nucleons releases gamma and other forms of radiation, *see* RADIOACTIVITY.)

Cobalt-60 applicators are of major importance in radiation therapy, but the employment of various other radioisotopes has been disappointing except for a few specific situations such as the treatment of hyperthyroidism with iodine-131 and of polycythemia vera with phosphorus-32. It is as diagnostic tools that radioisotopes have large and growing importance in medicine, such employment constituting the principal activity of the specialty known as nuclear medicine. Of the more than 1,000 radioisotopes discovered by the early 1960s only a few dozen were used clinically. Among them interest centres on a rather small number (see *Uses*, below).

2. Uses.—Some isotopes are employed in ionic form as salts, others as radioactive tags for specific organic compounds. Tagging, or labeling, is accomplished by various means. For example, iodine-131 may be used to tag albumin by causing the iodine to react chemically with tyrosine radicals in the albumin molecule. Vitamin B_{12} may be labeled with cobalt-57 by adding the latter to the culture medium in which have been grown bacteria capable of synthesizing B_{12}. When chromium-51 in the form of sodium chromate is added to red blood cells in vitro which are then incubated for specific times at specific temperatures such cells become radioactive.

Cobalt-57-tagged vitamin B_{12} ingested in very small amounts is useful in confirming a suspected diagnosis of pernicious anemia and differentiating that condition from malabsorption defects. Despite the fact that the substance emits both beta and gamma radiation and has a half-life of 270 days, it may be used safely because the amounts needed are so extremely small.

Chromium-51-tagged red blood cells when returned to the blood stream behave like any other red blood cells and their passage through vessels, lodgment in tissues, and eventual destruction can be followed by radiation detectors. In the form of chromium chloride, chromium-51 may be used to tag blood plasma to determine plasma volume. The rather long half-life (28 days) is not a drawback because of the small amounts needed and the total absence of beta particles.

Gold-198 in colloidal form when injected intravenously is selectively picked up by the reticuloendothelial cells, most of which are normally in the liver, thus making it useful for liver scanning. Isotopes which do not involve such large tissue doses were replacing Au[198] in the late 1960s.

Iodine-125 is not employed intravenously but is useful for in vitro determination of thyroid-binding globulin. The blood serum of a patient with a normal thyroid has a certain ability to bind added thyroxin, the ability falling in those who have hyperthyroidism and rising in those with hypothyroidism. The material triiodothyronine acts like thyroxin and when it is tagged with I[125] and added to serum in vitro it may be used as a test for thyroid function. Numerous factors, for example liver deficiency and pregnancy, increase or decrease uptake by serum; but when care is taken to exclude such factors the test is of great clinical importance.

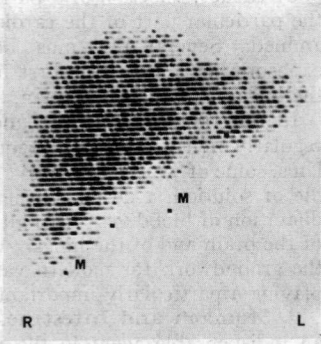

BY COURTESY OF DEPARTMENT OF RADIOLOGY, UNIVERSITY OF FLORIDA

FIG. 8.—RECTILINEAR SCAN OF NORMAL LIVER

Colloidal gold-198, injected intravenously, has been concentrated in the reticuloendothelial cells of the liver. As motors drove a detector probe back and forth over the upper right quadrant of the patient's body a flashing light on an arm attached to the probe made this film recording of the liver. Radioactive markers (M), attached to the skin, define the location of the lower edge of the rib cage relative to the liver (R is right, L is left)

Iodine-131-tagged albumin is used for the determination of plasma volume, the detection of pericardial effusion, and in other examinations of blood circulation. Under the influence of heat and acid, such tagged albumin aggregates into particles of from 20 to 50 microns in diameter and, injected intravenously, is employed for lung scans. The dye Rose Bengal is a complex organic molecule which, following intravenous injection, is picked up selectively by the parenchymal cells of the liver. When the dye is tagged with I[131], it is useful in functional and morphological examinations of the liver. For example, in an infant with suspected biliary tract atresia, the amount of radioactivity in the stool after intravenous injection may indicate whether or not the biliary tract has sufficient patency to warrant surgical intervention. Following the injection of I[131]-tagged Rose Bengal, liver scans will show the presence of neoplastic and other masses in the liver if they have reached considerable size. I[131] is used to tag hippuric acid for functional and morphological examinations of the kidney and in its ionic form, as sodium iodide, for examinations of the function and morphology of the thyroid gland.

Iron-59, in spite of its half-life of 45 days, is of great importance in experimental studies of iron metabolism. Clinical applications are not common, but they are very useful when needed.

Indium-113m, a daughter product of tin-113, was introduced in the late 1960s as a substitute for technetium-99m in some examinations (*see* below). Tin-113, which has a half-life of 118 days, decays into an intermediate material, indium-113m, which in turn decays into stable indium-113. In the terminology of quantum mechanics, indium-113m is in a metastable state, the "m" symbolizing "metastable." Prepared in nuclear reactors by thermal neutron bombardment of tin, the tin nuclide is dispensed to users adsorbed on ion exchange resin enclosed in a lead-shielded generator. Indium-113m is eluted from the resin column with hydrochloric acid, the "milking" being done as the isotope is needed at daily intervals.

The long half-life of the parent material on the column of the generator is of great practical importance, and the short half-life (1.7 hr.) of the eluted isotope adds another advantage. The gamma radiation, which is much more energetic than that of technetium-99m, involves the use of somewhat heavier lead collimators in scanning devices used for indium-113m. The isotope is used principally for lung and liver scans.

Mercury-197-tagged chlormerodrin is used for kidney scans, its short half-life of 2.7 days making it preferable, in most cases, to the older mercury-203-tagged material with a half-life of 48 days. In the late 1960s, however, the geographic location of a patient relative to isotope supply occasionally required that mercury-203 be employed. Formerly mercury-tagged chlormerodrin was used for brain scans, work which later was done with technetium-99m. (*See* below.)

Phosphorus-32 was no longer used for diagnosis in the late 1960s, but for treating polycythemia vera and some forms of leukemia. When phosphate ion is injected intravenously it is concentrated in bone marrow. If the phosphate is radioactive, as it is in P[32], some of the marrow cells are destroyed by the beta radiation it emits. When bone marrow produces too many red blood cells, as in polycythemia vera, or too many white cells, as in leukemia, destruction of part of the marrow cells is of therapeutic advantage.

Strontium-85 is removed from the blood stream selectively by bone, particularly bone which is metabolically active, such as the growing epiphyses of children and in primary and metastatic bone neoplasm. It has a limited clinical usefulness in diagnosing bone neoplasms, particularly metastases, before they have reached a size that is detectable by X-ray examination. The 65-day half-life is disadvantageous, but the substitution of strontium-87m (half-life 2.8 hr.) involves other problems which limit its clinical employment.

Technetium-99m in the form of pertechnetate ion is used principally for brain scans. Normal brain tissue is protected from many of the substances present in the blood stream by a mechanism known as the blood-brain barrier. When technetium-99m is injected intravenously that barrier excludes it from normal brain tissue. When in scans made after the injection of technetium-99m one sees evidence that the isotope has accumulated in brain tissue that fact is evidence of brain damage, for example infarction.

Under certain circumstances Tc^{99m} is substituted for iodine-131 in thyroid scanning and occasionally for scanning the pregnant abdomen in cases of suspected placenta previa. The short half-life (6 hr.), which is clinically advantageous, makes it difficult for manufacturers to supply the radionuclide itself; but the difficulty has been overcome by the development of generators containing the parent material molybdenum-99 (half-life 66 hr.). The parent is adsorbed on an aluminum oxide column sealed in a glass envelope with rubber ends. After sterilization the envelope is placed in a thick-walled lead cylinder, measuring about 3 by 4 in. and weighing about 10 lb., which is shipped by air express from manufacturer to user. The daughter nuclide, technetium-99m, accumulates steadily on the column and is eluted as needed by injecting sodium chloride solution through the upper rubber diaphragm. The eluate is collected by another needle inserted through the lower diaphragm. Such so-called "milking" may be done daily or, if necessary, at six-hour intervals for periods of approximately one week, by which time the old generator is usually discarded and a fresh one substituted. Assaying the eluate for radiation intensity is done in "well" counters. Instruments have been developed to perform the necessary weighing, recording, and computing automatically so that the nuclear technician has merely to administer an indicated number of cubic centimetres in order to assure a stipulated dose.

3. Detecting and Recording Devices.—When by accident or design considerable amounts of a radioisotope are lodged in such tissue as bone, the presence, distribution, and to some degree the amount of the radioisotope may be determined by autoradiography. Thin slices of the tissue are placed in intimate contact with the emulsion of special photographic films and left there for hours or even days. On development such films show images of tissues containing the isotope, and it is possible to arrange conditions of exposure time and film processing so that the degree of blackness of the image is an indication of the amount of activity producing it.

Autoradiography has extensive applications in science but cannot be employed in clinical nuclear medicine. For one thing, the amounts of radioisotope that are safe for a patient are far too small to register on films within practical exposure times. Furthermore, the geometry involved in detecting, for example, technetium-99m in a lesion deep in the brain of a living patient is vastly more involved than in the autoradiography of thin slices of tissue lying in contact with the film.

The difficulty of the low intensity of emitted radiation is met by having the radiation fall on a sodium iodide crystal where, on absorption, it generates light. That light, falling on the cathodes of photomultipliers generates a flow of electrons which, after being augmented by suitable electronic circuits, operates recording devices. Other electronic circuits and certain mechanical linkages solve the problems of geometry mentioned above.

Well Detectors are used for determining the amount of radioactivity in fluid samples such as blood drawn from a patient's veins or technetium-99m eluted from a molybdenum-99 generator. A hole or well is excavated in a large sodium iodide crystal one face of which is in intimate contact with the window of a photomultiplier tube, the hole being shielded from radiation other than that emitted by a sample lowered into the well. Individual flashes of light within the crystal (scintillations) are converted into pulses of electrons from the phototube which activate various types of digital recorders. When such instruments have been calibrated empirically against radiation sources of known activity they constitute useful secondary standards.

Flat-Field Probes consist of a cylindrical crystal, approximately 2 in. in diameter, mounted with its upper face in intimate contact with the window of a photomultiplier tube, its lower surface looking downward through a thick-walled rectangular-sided lead funnel which is continuous above with the lead shield about the crystal and phototube and open below. The size of the open end of the funnel varies with particular applications. For renograms, for example, it measures about 2 by 5 in., and two probes are employed, one for

either kidney. The rectangular openings of the heavy lead funnels are pressed against the skin of the prone patient's back at points which are believed to lie directly over the kidneys. Iodine-131-labeled hippuran is injected intravenously, and as the material is eliminated by the kidneys the outputs of the two photomultipliers are fed to writers which record graphically time-intensity relationships. The resulting traces, known as renograms, provide no information as to the point of origin of scintillations (as in scans), merely minute to minute values of the intensity of radiation emitted by the entire kidney.

Rectilinear Scanners portray anatomical structures in which injected or ingested radionuclides are being concentrated or from which they are being excluded. They employ crystals and photomultipliers of the sort used with flat field detectors but, unlike them, are able to deal with complicated problems in "geometry." They are made up of a probe and circuits for translating crystal scintillations into flashes of light for recording on film or into episodes of pressure or electric current flow for recording on paper. Motors drive probe and recorder over the anatomical part and film in a pattern (called boustrophedon) which has been likened to the passage of a plow across a field, first in one direction, then, after dropping down one "furrow," back in the opposite direction.

The collimator and certain of the electronic circuits of a scanner probe are quite unlike those of a flat-field probe. The collimator is a lead block pierced by a system of tapered holes which fan out above to cover the surface of the crystal but converge below so that their projected axes come to a point. The arrangement acts something like the lens of a camera, increasing light-gathering power but keeping "in focus" point sources of radiation in tissue perpendicularly beneath the probe. The electronic circuits are able to discriminate between scintillations produced by gamma radiation and those produced by scatter, and by certain other phenomena associated with absorption of gamma photons in the crystal.

When the apex of the collimator passes over tissues heavily loaded with the radionuclide, flashes of the recorder occur so rapidly that a solid black band is produced on the film; when the probe point passes beyond the patient's body there are only a few light flashes and little film blackening occurs. In regions of moderate radiation activity the probe and recorder move a few millimetres during the time required for electronic signal to build up to a critical level and as a result film blackening occurs as series of gaps and dots. (*See* fig. 9.)

Stationary Detectors (Scintillation Cameras), introduced by Hal O. Anger in 1953, were developed by the late 1960s to the point where they were of great and increasing importance in nuclear medicine. One surface of a circular sodium iodide crystal 11 in. in diameter and $\frac{1}{2}$ in. thick faces a multiaperture lead collimator; the other surface faces a plastic disk which serves as a light pipe

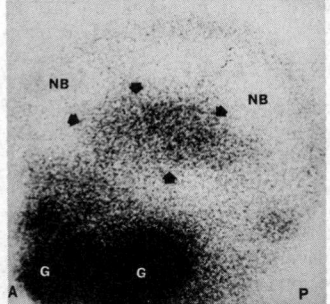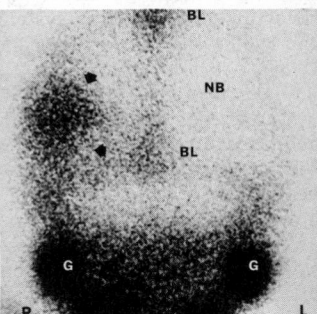

FIG. 9.—ANGER CAMERA BRAIN SCAN OF CHILD WITH INFARCT IN LEFT CEREBRAL HEMISPHERE

Many substances when introduced into the blood stream are largely excluded from normal brain tissue by a mechanism known as the blood-brain barrier. Dead or badly damaged brain tissue is not able to exclude such material and that fact has been put to diagnostic use in this case. (Left) is a lateral and (right) an occipital scintillation camera scan of the head of a child suffering from obstruction of the left middle cerebral artery. A large infarcted area (arrows) in the left cerebral hemisphere takes up much radionuclide whereas normal brain tissue (NB) contains little. Concentration of activity in the blood (BL) of lateral and transverse sinuses and scalp and in the parotid and submaxillary glands (G) is a normal occurrence (A is anterior, P is posterior, R is right, L is left)

to conduct the light from crystal scintillations to the windows of an array of 19 photomultiplier tubes. One type of collimator consists of a lead disk $1\frac{3}{4}$ in. thick pierced by 4,000 square holes, each 2.5 mm. in diameter. These rectangular ducts are straight-sided and have their axes perpendicular to the face of the crystal. Practically speaking the only radiation able to enter the portion of the crystal directly above a particular hole is that which originates in tissue perpendicularly below that hole, but the resulting scintillations are received by all the photomultipliers, the strength of their resulting signals depending on their nearness to or remoteness from the location of a scintillation event. The 19 signals flow to a resistor network which in computer fashion determines the exact points on the crystal where scintillations originated, in mathematical language, their X–Y coordinates. The signals are fed also to summing and analyzing circuits which select only those representing genuine gamma emission from a particular radionuclide. The outputs of these circuits are connected to the cathode grid and the deflection plates of a five-in. cathode-ray tube which has a fast decay phosphor.

For every particular scintillation identified as originating in the radionuclide the cathode beam is directed to corresponding X–Y coordinates on the display screen and the grid triggered to produce a flash of light at that point. All these electronic phenomena develop and collapse in times of the order of one-millionth of a second, whereas gamma photons are emitted from the tissue being examined at intervals of thousandths of a second. Usually, therefore, the system has to deal with but a single scintillation at a time. Photographs of the display screen made with exposure times several minutes in length record tissues containing radionuclide as clusters of dots similar to the stippling of a pen and ink drawing.

In earlier models photographing was done on polaroid image-reversing paper on which bright points on the display screen show as white dots. Later film cameras became available. Unlike the polaroid camera, which minifies the image on the 5-in. display screen, the film camera enlarges it to the full 11-in. diameter of the crystal and records bright points as black dots.

The statistical probability that gamma photons emitted at a particular point in a patient's body will pass through collimator holes and produce scintillations in the crystal becomes greater when emission rate is high and smaller when it is low. Closely packed film dots, therefore, represent tissue areas emitting gamma photons vigorously and widely spaced dots indicate a low rate of emission. (*See* fig. 8.)

Stationary detector cameras are more rapid than single probe scanners and more adaptable to positions other than straight frontals and straight laterals, but they are expensive. Multiple probe rectilinear scanners overcome the limitation of slowness but not of positional inflexibility and they too are costly. Many other detecting and recording systems were under investigation late in the 1960s.   (P. C. H.; C. M. Wɪ.)

III. RADIATION THERAPY

One of the most remarkable attributes of the X rays that Röntgen discovered in 1895 was the seemingly innocuous way in which they penetrated human tissue without causing pain, a feeling of heat, or any other immediate sensation. It did not take long, however, for experimenters to learn that in spite of the absence of immediate effect, large doses led presently to redness of the skin, blistering, and ulceration. Even small doses, if repeated often enough, were followed by serious skin lesions that showed up only after a considerable lapse of time. Of course, an agent capable of damaging normal tissue was bound to be considered for employment therapeutically if some means could be found to direct its damaging effects specifically against diseased parts.

The energy of the radiation employed in therapy ranges from 100 kv. to 40 Mv. X rays and from 0.55 to 1.65 Mev gamma rays from isotopes. It has become traditional (but not strictly correct) to refer to "low voltage," "medium voltage," and "super voltage" radiation therapy, including in the latter category therapy with the output of cobalt-60 applicators. The dose of radiation is expressed in roentgen units (R) (see *Radiation Physics* below)

and ranges from fractions of one R to several R in diagnosis and from 500 to 8,000 R or more in radiation therapy.

1. Low-Voltage Therapy (Energy 20 to 100 kv.).—The apparatus consists of transformers and X-ray tubes similar to those employed in diagnosis, which produce radiation of such low energy that most of it is absorbed by tissues near the surface of a patient's body. The usefulness of such radiation is limited to superficial conditions such as skin cancer. In the past a number of benign skin diseases were irradiated with low energy X rays, but with the availability of new drugs this mode of therapy had virtually disappeared by the late 1960s.

2. Medium-Voltage Therapy (Energy 100 to 500 kv.).—By 1915, German scientists had learned three concepts and a group of associated techniques which became basic to the radiation therapy of deep-lying lesions. These concepts were: the role of voltage, filtration, and the geometry of patient and X-ray beam in determining the dose delivered to deep-lying tissues. The techniques were Walter Friedrich's thimble ionization chamber for measuring the dose in air, body cavities, wax, water, etc., and Friedrich Dessauer's 200-kv. X-ray generators, isodose charts, and employment of wax, water bags, and similar material to reduce the patient's body to a straight-sided geometric form to which his isodose charts could be applied. In succeeding decades knowledge and experience advanced enormously; but Dessauer's paper, presented in 1921 to the American Roentgen Ray Society, lacked little that is really fundamental to an understanding of medium-voltage X-ray therapy as it came to be practised.

The X-ray tubes had to be much larger than those used for diagnosis and required special facilities for removing the large amount of heat developed in their targets. Transformers and rectifiers sometimes were simply larger varieties of those used in diagnosis, but, particularly at voltages above 200 kv., voltage doubling circuits or resonating systems were employed.

Increasing the voltage to 200 kv. made it possible to treat deep-seated lesions, most of which had been inaccessible before; but raising it another 50 kv. did not prove to be essential. Increasing the voltage still further to 400 kv. brought some advantages, but most workers agreed they were more than offset by reduced flexibility and greater cost. Numerous contributions to the treatment of cancer by X ray were made during the medium-voltage era. Techniques were standardized on an empirical basis and guides to safe dose schedules were established for most clinical situations.

Two characteristics of medium energy X rays limit their clinical usefulness. (1) The intensity of the tissue effect inevitably is greatest at the surface of the body, falling off as the radiation penetrates to deeper tissues. (2) Bone and cartilage absorb more radiation than neighbouring soft tissues, in the case of bone from two to six times as much. As a result, when one delivers an adequate dose to a deep-seated cancer, it may be impossible to avoid damaging overlying skin or injuring neighbouring bone to the extent of producing necrosis and fracture.

3. Supervoltage Therapy (Energy 1 to 40 Mv.).—The supervoltage era, which began about 1941, brought about dramatic changes in radiation therapy. The first generators employed X-ray tubes capable of operation at 1 Mv., to be followed shortly by 2 Mv. tubes. In 1951, tele-applicators containing the artificially produced radioisotope cobalt-60 began to be employed clinically and soon became the "workhorses" in hundreds of cancer therapy centres.

Cobalt-60 Applicators.—Formerly cobalt-60 was used to some extent in needles and ampules placed in contact with the patient's tissues, and, to distinguish such "short distance" applicators from the more common "distant" sources, the latter were called tele-applicators. Needles and capsules were gradually abandoned, and by the late 1960s the cobalt-60 applicator was usually the distant type, and the prefix "tele" was disappearing from radiological terminology.

Cobalt-60 is prepared by subjecting cobalt-59 to neutron bombardment in a nuclear reactor, the degree of radioactivity depending on the strength of the neutron flux and the duration of bombardment. The first high-intensity cobalt-60 "sources" were turned out in the summer of 1951 by the heavy water pile at Chalk

River, Ont., and each had an intensity of approximately 1,000 curies. Thereafter many other reactors produced them as well and intensities ranged as high as 10,000 curies. Sources follow a standardized design consisting of cobalt-60 pellets sealed in stainless steel cylinders having a volume of approximately $3\frac{3}{4}$ cu.in. These cylinders are mounted near the centre of massive spherical or cylindrical shields jacketed with sheet steel and carried on various types of arms or cranes for convenient alignment of the radiation beam relative to patients. The beam (energy about 1.25 Mev) can escape from the shield only when a remotely controlled device moves the source into the "open port" position. Shields commonly are made of lead and tungsten, but in a few instances depleted uranium is employed instead to reduce shield dimensions.

The initial cost of cobalt-60 applicators is lower than that for most other generators of radiation having the same energy, but upkeep is high because of the necessity of replacing the source at intervals of from three to five years at costs of from $25,000 to $52,000 for each replacement.

Cesium-137 Applicators.—Cesium-137, which can be recovered from the waste products of nuclear fission, has a half-life of 30 years and an energy of 662 kev. The relatively low energy simplifies construction of primary and secondary barriers, and long half-life is an asset, particularly in parts of the world where replacement of the source is difficult. The principal disadvantage lies in the fact that it is impractical to construct sources having intensities much in excess of 3,000 curies; hence treatments must be administered at undesirably short source–patient distance or prolonged to the point of sharply reducing the number of patients who can be treated each working day.

Betatron.—R. J. Van de Graaff's belt static machine, invented in 1933, later was developed as a clinical instrument for producing high energy X rays. Several particle accelerators introduced for work in nuclear physics were similarly adapted to radiation therapy, notably the betatron, invented in 1941 by D. W. Kerst. A doughnut-shaped vacuum chamber of glass or ceramic lies between the pole faces of a powerful electromagnet, which operates on alternating current. If electrons introduced into the chamber were allowed to do so they would be impelled by the magnetic field to travel, first in one direction then in the other, in circular paths around the centre of the doughnut. Instead, toward the end of the first quarter cycle, after they have traveled hundreds of thousands of times around the centre of the doughnut in one direction and have attained almost the speed of light, they are made to spiral out toward the periphery. There they encounter a gold or tungsten target, and their energy is converted into X-ray photons which pass through the target to emerge from the doughnut as an extremely high energy X-ray beam. Unlike the situation with electrons moving at slower speeds, these high speed electrons produce X rays so efficiently that little energy is wasted as heat and no provision need be made for cooling the target. In some models the spiraling electrons penetrate a thin metallic window instead of a target and escape from the betatron as an electron rather than as an X-ray beam.

Effectiveness of Supervoltage Therapy.—As so frequently happens in medical advances, early workers with supervoltage radiation hoped it might possess specific advantages making possible the cure of cancers not amenable to older methods. Those high hopes fell short of the mark, but there were solid accomplishments. In the case of advanced-stage cancer of the uterine cervix, G. H. Fletcher reported modest gains in five-year survivals when supervoltage was substituted for medium-voltage therapy. (Medium voltage 1944–54 five-year survivals were 59%; supervoltage 1954–59 five-year survivals were 64%.) Improvement in response when supervoltage radiation is substituted for medium voltage was noted also in selected cases of cancer of the urinary bladder and of the tonsil and the pharyngeal wall. The response of cancers in other locations was under investigation late in the 1960s.

In addition to minor gains in survival rates, two secondary advantages proved to be of great practical importance. First in importance is the fact that for a given dose at a depth, the dose to overlying skin is significantly lower than with medium energy radiation, the so-called skin sparing effect. Second, with super-

voltage the radiation absorption in bone and cartilage is no greater than that in soft tissues. Application of these facts reduced damage to skin, bone, and cartilage; and the resulting reduction in patient discomfort increased acceptance of therapeutic radiation by patients and their referring physicians.

4. Radium and Other Isotopes.—Opinion as to the clinical importance of radium fluctuated widely after the discovery of that element was announced by Pierre and Marie Curie (*qq.v.*) in 1898. In 1901 Henri Becquerel accidentally discovered its biological action when he carried a glass tube of radium salt in his vest pocket and found that it burned the skin of his abdomen. Pierre Curie deliberately produced a similar burn on his own arm, and this led to a series of animal experiments and clinical trials. (*See* RADIUM.)

Administered internally, radium is a slow but lethal poison devoid of any therapeutic value; but confined in airtight needles or capsules, sheathed with a filtering layer of 0.5 mm. or more of platinum, it, together with its daughter products, constitutes a gamma-ray emitter of established clinical importance.

The alpha and beta rays of radium and its daughter products are screened out by the platinum walls of radium needles and capsules, leaving only gamma radiation. The spectrum of radium is complicated but according to Harold E. Johns may be looked on as a mixture of energies 0.55 and 1.65 Mev which makes it quite similar to cobalt-60 (1.25 Mev).

Radium needles and tubes, ranging in length from about 1 cm. to 6 cm., are used principally by insertion into relatively small cancerous lesions of the tongue, face, or neck, or by introduction (in special applicators) into the vagina and uterus. The usefulness of such needles and applicators lies in the fact that the effect of the gamma rays is principally limited to tissue close to the radium with sparing of tissue farther away from the source. In view of the penetrating nature of gamma rays this seems paradoxical. The explanation lies in the geometry of the situation. Like the X rays formed at the target of an X-ray tube, the gamma rays emitted from radium needles and capsules fall off in intensity as the square of the distance from the source. With small needles and capsules the source can be brought into close proximity with the tissue that is being treated, thus making it possible to give large doses to that tissue without delivering much radiation to tissue a short distance away.

5. Tele-Radium Applicators.—In a few instances large amounts of radium (4 to 10 grams) were concentrated in heavily shielded containers that could be located 5 to 10 cm. distant from the patient's body. These so-called radium bombs, forerunners of tele-cobalt applicators, did possess the skin-, cartilage-, and bone-sparing features subsequently made widely available by cobalt-60; but they were extremely costly (about $20,000 per gram) and aside from cost there were problems of geometry which made it impractical to build applicators having great enough activity to allow delivering therapeutic doses in reasonable lengths of time.

6. Artificial Isotopes in Needles and Capsules.—Radioactive cobalt, gold, tantalum, iridium, and many other artificial radioisotopes have been used as substitutes for intra-cavitary and interstitial radium, but the latter retained its popularity partly because of its very long half-life (1,600 years) and even more because of the backlog of clinical experience which accumulated from its use.

7. Biological Effect of Radiation.—The tissues of the body are unaffected by radiation which merely passes through them; it is only absorbed radiation that produces an effect. When there is an effect, it is invariably cell injury; and the direct agency in this injury appears to be the ionization associated with absorption. The relationship between the degree of ionization and the magnitude of the biological response is fairly constant throughout the low- and medium-voltage range. In the supervoltage range, however, because of a decrease in linear ion density, the dose must be increased by from 10 to 15% to produce the same degree of biological damage that is produced with low- and medium-voltage radiation.

Radiation does not selectively destroy malignant cells; it damages all cells, normal and malignant, in which it is absorbed. Its effectiveness against cancer depends therefore on a favourable differential between cancer tissue and normal tissue in sensitivity to radiation or in ability to regenerate following radiation injury. Of these two, repair appears to be the more important factor, particularly in cancers of slight to low radiosensitivity.

8. Radiosensitivity.—The susceptibility of tissue cells to damage by radiation may be expressed as the dose in Roentgens required to kill all or a stipulated fraction of such cells in a given amount of tissue. For many years it was believed that cancer cells were more sensitive to radiation than were the normal cells of the tissue from which they originated, but later work cast doubt on this belief and indicated that cancer cells and the normal tissue from which they arise have similar, perhaps identical sensitivity. For example, approximately identical amounts of radiation are required to destroy epidermoid cancer of the skin and the superficial cells of normal skin from which this cancer arises. Arranged in order of decreasing sensitivity to radiation, normal tissue cells and their malignant counterparts fall into the following approximate sequence: (1) lymphocytes; (2) granulocytes; (3) epithelial cells—(a) basal cells of secretory glands, (b) basal cells of testes and ovaries, (c) basal cells of skin and intestinal tract, (d) alveolar cells of lungs, (e) tubules of kidneys; (4) endothelial cells; (5) connective tissue cells; (6) muscle cells; (7) bone cells; (8) nerve cells.

While sensitivity to radiation depends largely on cell type, other factors play a modifying role, for example oxygen tension. The dose of radiation required to produce a stipulated amount of damage in tissue that is largely or completely devoid of oxygen may be two or three times as great as the dose required when the tissue is in its normal state of oxygenation. Numerous factors may reduce radiosensitivity by reducing oxygenation: for example, anemia, infection and necrosis, preexisting surgery or irradiation, or cardiac or pulmonary disease. Hormones, temperature changes, and many chemical substances have been found to modify radiation response, but unfortunately these are unselective, modifying normal and cancer tissues equally.

9. Radiocurability.—The susceptibility of a cancer to cure by irradiation is not solely dependent on its cell type. For the most favourable results cancers should be well localized to keep at a minimum the total mass of tissue (cancerous plus normal) which must be irradiated. Treatment becomes difficult and even impossible when cancer cells are widely distributed in the body, as in lymphatic leukemia. Its malignant cells, derived from lymphocytes, are exquisitely radiosensitive, but because they are distributed throughout the body, a dose large enough to destroy all of them would destroy the patient.

On the other hand, epidermoid cancer of the uterine cervix, if it is treated during the stage when it is localized to the pelvis, can be cured in spite of the fact that its cells are only moderately radiosensitive, because one can administer up to 20,000 R or more to the cervix, which has a rich blood supply and remarkable healing power.

Even in those cancers which are localized, curability is greater in those which are small and diminishes with increase in size. There are several reasons for this. One explanation lies in a fact demonstrated in 1956 by Theodore Puck and Philip Marcus, that in tissue cultures of mammalian cells a particular dose will kill a particular percentage of the total number of cells present. Since in radiation therapy the aim is to kill all the cells in a cancer, it follows that the larger the cancer the larger will be the required dose. Herman D. Suit, extending the ideas of Puck and Marcus to cancer-bearing animals, demonstrated that the magnitude of the radiation dose required to sterilize a cancer is a direct function of its size, and his clinical observations indicate that the same holds true for human cancer.

At least two other factors operate to reduce the curability of larger cancers. First, with increasing size the total mass of tissue (normal plus cancerous) that must be irradiated increases with resulting increased damage to the patient as a whole. Second, as neoplasms enlarge they tend to develop areas of necrosis with resulting lowered oxygen tension which, as has been seen, itself causes a decrease in radiosensitivity.

10. Time-Dose-Volume Relationships.—C. Regaud and other early radiation therapists found that their cancer patients responded better when the radiation was spread out over a considerable period of time. Such fractionation came to be widely employed, a common regimen being 6,000 R divided into five daily treatments a week for six consecutive weeks. As will be seen, there is theory to support such fractionation, but the details are the result of empirical trial and error carried out over many years by many different workers. The development of variations in timing and total dosage is necessarily slow because failures and complications may not show up until two years after treatment has been completed, and "cures" cannot be claimed until the lapse of at least five years.

Research in radiation therapy began early in the 20th century and later reached vast proportions, but many of the basic questions remain unanswered, and some of the answers formerly accepted as fact were in doubt in the late 1960s. It is questionable whether individual cancer cells differ from individual normal tissue cells in radiosensitivity, but the total response of a cancerous mass differs significantly from that of the normal tissue in which it lies. If the irradiated field includes all of the cancer (as it should), there are no non-irradiated cancer cells to migrate in and "repopulate" the tumour, but the reverse is true in normal tissue; and repopulation plays an important role in the host defense against cancer.

There is experimental evidence that repopulation is most effective following small doses; this fact presumably explains the advantage of fractionating the dose. When treatment is divided over several weeks to take advantage of improved repopulation, the total amount delivered must be large, because the effect on the cancer is the algebraic sum of the damage produced by individual doses and of the partial recovery that occurs in the intervals between them.

11. Radiation Therapy of Nonmalignant Conditions.—Opinions differ as to whether radiation should be used to treat such nonmalignant conditions as arthritis, bursitis, and hypertrophic lymphoid tissue. The earlier view—that such therapy, though possibly ineffective, certainly was innocuous—was later challenged. Physicians increasingly believed that X-ray treatment of benign lesions should be confined to a very few specific conditions. Since radiation-induced cancer may follow from 5 to 30 years after the administration of even small doses of radiation, though the likelihood of such a sequela admittedly is slight, the risk is unwarranted when the condition being treated is nonmalignant, nonlethal, and amenable to other forms of therapy.

12. Palliative Radiation Therapy.—From the standpoint of numbers of patients concerned, the most extensive use of radiation therapy is as a palliative for those in whom, for various reasons, cancers no longer are curable. Small doses are employed and frequently they accomplish restraint of cancer growth with relief of pain, hemorrhage, and obstruction. Occasionally, radiation applied as a palliative may have the gratifying and unanticipated effect of causing dramatic clinical improvement leading to the prolongation of a patient's useful life by months or even by years.

13. Radiation Physics.—The work of calibrating X-ray machines, mapping the dosage of the radiation that is purposely delivered to the tissues of a patient's body, and protecting patients and radiation workers from unwanted radiation, is a subspecialty within the specialty of radiation therapy. Modern treatment centres require the full-time services of considerable numbers of specially trained graduate physicists.

It is the responsibility of the radiologist to judge as closely as possible the size and location of the lesion, the amount and delivery rate of radiation most likely to be effective, and the tolerance of neighbouring uninvolved tissues. When this has been done the physicist determines the energy, intensity, geometry, and aiming of the single or multiple beams best suited to place the radiation in the amounts and at the points stipulated, following which the technician administers the treatment as directed.

Employing slide rule, graphs, and tables, the skilled radiation physicist frequently required hours of painstaking work to plan the geometry and determine the technical factors required to deliver doses of desired magnitude to tissues of stipulated dimensions at stipulated distances beneath the surface. Properly programmed computers, however, can perform such tasks in minutes. The usefulness of the physician-radiologist is enlarged greatly by such assistance from physicists and technicians, but it is necessary that he be competent in their fields as well as his own; legally as well as morally he must be responsible for the whole.

14. Dosage.—*Measurement of Dose.*—The dose employed in X-ray therapy cannot be defined merely by stating the voltage and current at which the X-ray tube is operated. Numerous other factors are involved, including diameter and filtration of the X-ray beam, target–skin distance, and the size and location of the lesion being irradiated. The need of dependable dosage guides was recognized more or less clearly from the outset, but their development proved difficult. Tried and found wanting were measurement of the heat produced by the absorption of X rays; intensity of fluorescence; colour changes in several different combinations of chemicals; blackening of silver bromide paper; liberation of iodine from a solution of iodoform in chloroform; and increase in the electrical conductivity of selenium under the action of X rays.

Ionization Methods.—Röntgen's original papers described the ability of X rays to ionize air, and in 1896 J. J. Thomson independently discovered the effect and suggested its use by physicians as a means of measuring X-ray intensity. P. Villard in 1908 advocated ionization for measuring the clinical dose, but his idea was not practical at that time because the large, delicate ionization chambers that were serving physicists so well were not suitable for clinical work, and no others were available. Gradually, small rugged chambers were developed, and in 1928, at the second International Congress of Radiology in Stockholm, there was adopted the "roentgen unit," which became the standard throughout the world. The symbol for roentgen units changed from "R" to "r" but in the late 1960s was back again to "R."

Roentgen Unit.—The roentgen unit was defined in Stockholm as: "The unit of dose is that quantity of roentgen radiation which, when the secondary electrons are fully utilized and the wall effect of the chamber is avoided, produces in 1 cc. of atmospheric air at 0° C and 760 mm. mercury pressure such a degree of conductivity that one electrostatic unit of charge is measured under saturation conditions."

This definition sufficed as long as the X rays to be measured were produced at voltages up to 200 kv., but as R meters began to be employed in the 1,000-kv. range and for the gamma rays of radium, the following definition was substituted: "The roentgen shall be the quantity of X or gamma radiation such that the associated corpuscular emission per 0.001293 g. of air produces, in air, ions carrying 1 esu of quantity of electricity of either sign. (The mass of 1 cc. of dry atmospheric air at 0° C and 760 mm. of mercury pressure is 0.001293 g.)"

Rad.—When the absorbed dose is the chief matter of interest, the roentgen unit has the disadvantage that the energy absorption in air is independent over a considerable wavelength range, whereas in water-containing tissues energy absorption per gram increases from approximately 84 ergs for long-wavelength (low-energy) radiation to about 93 ergs per gram for short-wavelength (high-energy) radiation. The unit of absorbed dose is the rad, representing the amount of radiation which delivers energy equivalent to 100 ergs to a gram of irradiated matter.

Roentgen (R) Meters.—Condenser-type R meters consist of two parts, a chamber-condenser unit and a charging-measuring unit. Three sizes of chambers usually are supplied: a large one that measures up to 25 R; an intermediate size measuring up to 100 R; and a small chamber for measurements up to 250 R. The electrometer that measures the charge has three corresponding scales calibrated from 0 on the left to 25 R, 100 R, or 250 R, respectively, on the right.

Chamber-Condenser Unit.—In the 100 R unit the chamber is a small plastic thimble that contains one cubic centimetre of air at room temperature and pressure. The inside of the wall of the chamber, which has been rendered conductive by a thin coating of carbon or graphite, constitutes one electrode and is connected to the metal sheathing that forms one of the plates of a condenser. The second electrode is a carbon-coated plastic rod mounted in a block of high-impedence material with its tip protruding into the air in the chamber, its base in electrical contact with the insulated plate of the condenser. Care is taken to exclude air from all parts of the system except the space inside the chamber itself.

Charging and Measuring Unit.—This consists of a quartz-fibre electroscope calibrated in roentgen units and a means of charging the condenser. Formerly the charge was supplied by rotating a plastic disk against a leather pad, but in later versions a small power pack was used. The condenser-chamber assembly is plugged into the charging unit, and when the power pack is activated the condenser becomes fully charged so that the fibre of the electroscope stands at 0. The charged condenser is then disconnected from the electroscope and placed for a measured period of time with its chamber in the beam that is to be measured. X rays ionize the air in the chamber, causing it to become an electrical conductor, and this in turn allows the charge on the central plate of the condenser to leak to the wall of the chamber and thence to the outer plate of the condenser. When the partially discharged condenser is reconnected to the electroscope, the fibre moves from the fully charged 0 position on the left toward the discharged 100 R position on the right, the precise amount of loss of charge being read directly in roentgens without computations of any sort.

Roentgen meters of this sort are secondary standards requiring initial checking against large standard chambers and occasional subsequent rechecking; but when they are carefully built and properly calibrated, their accuracy is well within the limits necessary for radiation therapy. (P. C. H.; R. R. Mɪ.)

Bɪʙʟɪᴏɢʀᴀᴘʜʏ.—B. Krönig and W. Friedrich, *Physikalische und biologische Grundlagen der Strahlentherapie* (1918); G. W. C. Kaye, *X-Rays,* 4th ed. (1923); P. C. Hodges, D. B. Phemister, and A. Brunschwig, *Roentgen-Ray Diagnosis of the Diseases of Bones and Joints,* (1938); W. E. Chamberlain, "Fluoroscopes and Fluoroscopy," *Radiology,* 38:383 (1942); O. Glasser *et al., Physical Foundations of Radiology* (1944), (eds.), *Medical Physics* (1944); J. W. Coltman, "Fluoroscopic Image Brightening by Electronic Means," *Radiology,* 51:359 (1948); R. Paterson, *The Treatment of Malignant Disease by Radium and X-rays* (1948); R. E. Sturm and R. H. Morgan, "Screen Intensification Systems and Their Limitations," *American Journal of Roentgenology,* 62:617 (1949); U. V. Portmann (ed.), *Clinical Therapeutic Radiology* (1950); H. E. Johns, *The Physics of Radiology,* 2nd ed. (1964); R. D. Moseley, Jr., and J. H. Rust (eds.), *The Reduction of Patient Dose by Diagnostic Radiologic Instrumentation* (1964); W. S. MacComb and G. H. Fletcher, *Cancer of the Head and Neck* (1967); Michel M. Ter-Pogossian, *The Physical Aspects of Diagnostic Radiology* (1967); H. N. Wagner, Jr. (ed.), *Principles of Nuclear Medicine* (1968); P. Rubin and G. W. Casarett, *Clinical Radiation Pathology* (1968).
(P. C. H.; C. M. Wɪ.; R. R. Mɪ.)

RADIOMETER, an instrument for measuring the intensity of radiant energy. The term is applied most often to instruments of the vane type described below, but it can also be applied to the bolometer, pyrheliometer, thermopile and radio balance. For information on these instruments *see* Hᴇᴀᴛ: *Radiation.*

It was noticed by A. J. Fresnel that a body delicately suspended *in vacuo* is apparently repelled by radiation. Using this principle, Sir William Crookes constructed an instrument, which he called a radiometer, by pivoting a vertical axle carrying vertical vanes inside an exhausted bulb; one side of each vane was blackened and the other side bright, the black sides all facing the same way round the axle. When rays from the sun or other light source or dark radiation from a warm body fall on the vane, the black sides are repelled more than the bright sides, and the vanes are set into rotation. The more intense the radiation the more rapidly do the vanes rotate. It was Crookes's idea that the instrument might be used to measure the intensity of radiation.

Instead of allowing free rotation of the vane system on a pivot, it may be suspended by a quartz fibre. Radiation falling on the black face of the vane will then cause the system to turn round until the restoring couple, because of the torsion of the suspension, balances the deflecting couple due to the radiometer action. A small mirror, attached to the vane system and reflecting a beam of light on to a scale, permits very small deflections to be observed. Ernst Pringsheim constructed such an instrument in 1883 and used it for spectrographic investigations in the infrared. In 1893 E. F. Nichols improved the radiometer by using mica vanes, one at each end of a horizontal arm suspended on a quartz fibre and each blackened on its front surface. Radiation falling on both vanes would tend to turn them in opposite directions, and if they were correctly adjusted the system would not move under the influence of general stray radiation. The radiation to be measured was allowed to fall on one only of the vanes, and the resulting deflection of a spot of light was observed. With such a radiometer Nichols was able to measure the radiation from individual stars. The radiometer has been applied to measurements of ultraviolet radiation and to that of short Hertzian waves (wave length one to two millimetres).

The explanation of the radiometric action has presented a problem of considerable interest. The question arises whether the rotation of the vanes may be caused by the direct impact of the radiation, somewhat as the rotation of a cup anemometer is caused by the wind. This explanation has been disproved in several ways. If, for example, the vanes are made of transparent material and blackened on the back face, they move toward the direction from which the light comes. The ordinary radiometer effect appears to be caused, therefore, by stresses set up in the gas. As the pressure of the gas is reduced, the rotation increases to a maximum and then decreases. Even in a very high vacuum, however, a small effect persists, directed away from the light. The magnitude of this residual effect agrees with the value as calculated from the electromagnetic theory of light, which predicts a small pressure because of incident radiation.

The ordinary radiometric action in the presence of gas has been rather definitely shown to be a consequence of the creep of the gas over the unequally heated surface of the vanes near their edges, as was suggested by J. C. Maxwell in 1879. The gas creeps toward the more heated part of the vane's surface and produces there a slight condensation of the gas and an increase in its pressure; the inequalities of pressure thus created give rise to a reverse flow in the surrounding gas, but this flow is hindered by viscosity, so that some inequality of pressure persists and forces the vane back. This phenomenon of gas behaviour, known in other occurrences as thermal transpiration (with "transpiration" used in the pure sense of leaking), is discussed in E. H. Kennard, *Kinetic Theory of Gases*, 1st ed., pp. 333–37 (1938).

BIBLIOGRAPHY.—J. Strong and others, *Procedures in Experimental Physics* (1938); E. Fredlund, *Absolute Measurement of Radiometric Action in Gases* (1940); B. G. Tunmore, *A Simple Low-Temperature Radiometer for Heating Research* (1963).   (E. H. KD.)

RADIO RECEIVER. The two principal parts of a radio system are the transmitter and receiver. The waves radiated from transmitting antennas set up voltages in a receiving antenna, so that the first function of a receiving set is to select the signal desired. This must then be amplified and further modified so that a faithful reproduction of a program can be produced by the loud-speaker. Although a modern broadcast transmitter may have an output of 50 kw., often only a few microwatts from distant stations are available at the receiving antenna, principally because of the spreading out of the radio waves as they are propagated through space. A large amount of amplification is thus required in order to obtain a sound output of one watt, for example.

History.—The first demonstration of the production and reception of radio waves was made by Heinrich Hertz in Germany in 1887. His receiver consisted of an open wire loop with spheres attached to the ends to form a gap. The presence of the waves was "detected" by observing a spark set up in the sphere gap. Hertz was interested only in studying the properties of the waves and expressed no thought of practical application. It remained for Oliver Lodge to develop a system of wireless communication in England in 1894. The receiver included an antenna, tuned circuit, a detector consisting of a glass tube filled with metal filings called a "coherer" and a relay-controlled inker for recording Morse code. Lodge subsequently received several patents on radio apparatus—two of the better-known covering tuned circuits and loop antennas.

There was much activity in wireless telegraphy following Lodge's initial disclosures. Many new and improved types of detectors or "cymoscopes" were invented. These included magnetic types by Guglielmo Marconi, Ernest Rutherford and others; electrolytic by F. K. Vreeland, R. A. Fessenden and Lee De Forest; and a wide variety of crystal detectors using carborundum, galena and iron pyrites.

The first electronic device to appear in radio receivers was the Zehnder trigger tube cymoscope in Germany in 1892. This was a glow tube in which the potential difference between anode and cathode was set to a value of several hundred volts. A discharge could then be initiated by impressing a radio signal between the pair of trigger electrodes with which the tube was provided.

The first thermionic electron tube for radio use was patented by J. A. Fleming in England in 1904. This was a vacuum diode detector tube, known as the Fleming oscillation valve. Its apparent advantage over other types of detectors was the ability to undergo mechanical shocks and static surges without "jarring out." Its inherent insensitivity to weak signals, together with the primitive status of manufacturing, limited its application.

The three-element vacuum tube was invented by De Forest in 1906. A receiver using an audion, as it was called, could deliver more power to an output device than was received from the antenna, so that it was operating in the dual capacity of detector and amplifier. Subsequent work showed that it could be used simply as a radio-frequency (R.F.) or audio-frequency (A.F.) amplifier, or even as a modulator. De Forest manufactured radio sets equipped with audions for several years. The audion was greatly improved by others during World War I and was manufactured in large quantities.

One of the most remarkable applications of the audion was to the feedback, or regenerative, circuit. In this, coupling was introduced between the plate and grid circuits such as to produce an appreciable increase in both the selectivity and sensitivity of the circuit. By providing adequate coupling, such a circuit could be made to oscillate continuously without benefit of external grid signal.

It is difficult to place proper priority for the invention of the feedback circuit. In 1913 Alexander Meissner was granted a patent on an oscillator in Germany and E. H. Armstrong presented a paper describing regenerative circuits. Other names associated with contemporary work were those of C. S. Franklin and H. J. Round in England and De Forest and Irving Langmuir in the United States. A four-way litigation initiated by Meissner, Armstrong, De Forest and Langmuir was decided finally in favour of De Forest by the supreme court of the United States in 1928, and it reaffirmed its action in 1934.

Considerable progress was made in the theory, construction and applications of vacuum tubes and their circuits between 1910 and 1920, much of it in connection with the World War I efforts and long-line carrier-current telephony. The greatest single impetus to be noted in radio history, however, was the introduction of radio broadcasting in 1921. This created a tremendous demand for receivers as transmitters were established throughout the world. The vacuum-tube receiving circuits were battery operated for the first few years, but rectifier-type power packs soon appeared for plate and grid supplies. These were followed almost immediately by the self-contained alternating-current sets, which were made possible by the development of tubes whose cathodes could be operated on alternating current without introducing excessive hum in the output.

The first broadcast signals were amplitude modulated (AM) exclusively, and many types of receiving sets were in use. Some of the commonest were: regenerative, superregenerative, reflex, tuned radio frequency, neutrodyne and superheterodyne. The superheterodyne came to be used almost exclusively for broadcast reception, although a few portable models employ tuned-radio-frequency circuits.

The difficulties of static elimination inherent in AM operation led Armstrong to develop frequency modulation (FM). Although he began work on the problem in 1914, his system was not perfected until 1933 and several more years elapsed before much use was made of it.

Modulated Waves.—It is impractical to transmit audible signals by wireless because the radiated output of an antenna depends upon its size expressed in terms of the wave length of the signal to be transmitted. Since the wave-length range is 3,720 to 37.2 mi. for the ordinary broadcast audio-frequency range of 50 to 5,000 cycles per second, it is only too obvious that not only would the necessary audio-frequency antennas be prohibitively large but there would also be the possibility of a 10,000 to 1, or 40 db., variation in the output over this 100-to-1 frequency range. Furthermore, only one station could be on the air at once in any given locality, since it would be impossible to tune out the unwanted signals. Thus, it is practical to transmit wireless signals only at the high frequencies known as radio frequencies.

The problem was easily solved in radiotelegraphy by the comparatively simple process of keying, or turning on and off, a high-frequency signal. However, it was necessary to devise a different method to transmit a "message" in the form of articulate speech or music. Such a method was found in the utilization of a high-frequency wave as a vehicle, or carrier, for the comparatively low-frequency message. The exact mechanism consists of modifying, or modulating, the carrier signal in some manner by the audio signal, the resultant radiated signal being known as a modulated wave.

Any high-frequency electromotive force, of a form denoted by the formula $e = E \cos (\omega t + \theta)$, is completely specified if the amplitude E, angular frequency ω and phase angle θ are given. An audio-frequency signal to be transmitted can be introduced into the given radio signal by causing it to modify any one of these functions, the three methods being known as amplitude, frequency and phase modulation, respectively. A fourth possible method involves breaking up the signal into pulses. However, this discussion will be limited to amplitude and frequency modulation since they are the most commonly used.

Amplitude Modulation.—If, in the general equation above, E is set equal to $E_c + E_m \cos \omega_m t$, the result is

$$e = (E_c + E_m \cos \omega_m t) \cos \omega_c t = E_c (1 + m_a \cos \omega_m t) \cos \omega_c t$$

in which E_c is the amplitude of the unmodulated carrier voltage; E_m is the amplitude of the modulating signal voltage; ω_m is the angular frequency of the modulating signal; ω_c is the angular frequency of the carrier voltage; and m_a is the amplitude modulation index (E_m/E_c). Applying a trigonometric identity now gives

$$e = E_c \cos \omega_c t + E_s \cos (\omega_c + \omega_m)t + E_s \cos (\omega_c - \omega_m)$$

in which E_s is the amplitude of the side bands $(m_a E_c/2)$, where $(\omega_c + \omega_m)$ is the angular frequency of the upper side band and $(\omega_c - \omega_m)$ is the angular frequency of the lower side band.

This is the equation commonly used for an amplitude-modulated signal, which consists of a carrier term together with upper and lower side bands for each component of the modulating signal. In order to transmit, at a carrier frequency of 1,000 kc., music of regular broadcast quality covering a frequency range up to 5 kc., a band width of 10 kc., or 995 to 1,005 kc., is required. Since this involves a maximum frequency variation of only 0.5% on either side of the carrier frequency, no special difficulty is involved in the design of the equipment.

The process of removing the original signal from the modulated one at the receiver is known as demodulation. As an illustration of this, assume the response curve of some nonlinear device, such as a crystal or vacuum tube operating over the curved portion of its characteristic, to be given by

$$i = a_1 e + a_2 e^2$$

Substitution in the equation for an amplitude-modulated signal and application of trigonometric identities yields, in addition to radio-frequency terms, an audio-frequency response given by

$$2a_2 E_c E_s \cos \omega_m t = a_2 m_a E_c^2 \cos \omega_m t$$

and

$$a_2 E_s^2 \cos 2\omega_m t = \frac{a_2 m_a^2}{4} E_c^2 \cos 2\omega_m t$$

The former corresponds to the original signal to be transmitted; the latter to second harmonic distortion.

Frequency Modulation.—This is accomplished by introducing into the frequency of the signal to be radiated a variation about the carrier frequency that is proportional to the modulating signal. This gives, after some manipulation, for the general equation for a frequency modulated voltage,

$$e = E_c \sin (\omega_c t + k_f \frac{E_m}{\omega_m} \sin \omega_m t)$$

in which k_f is the ratio of the maximum variation in frequency to the maximum strength of the modulating signal.

This can be expanded to yield a carrier and an infinite number of pairs of side bands whose amplitudes are expressed in terms of Bessel functions (*see* FUNCTIONS, SPECIAL). Although from a practical standpoint it is only necessary to pass a limited number of side bands, the required band width is much greater than that for the AM signal, which requires only one pair of side bands for each component of the modulating signal.

In particular, it has been found possible to transmit a maximum audio frequency of 7.5 kc. within a band width of 200 kc., which shows that FM transmission is not practical in the regular band of 550 to 1,500 kc. allocated for AM broadcast. A special band of 88 to 108 mc. is used for the stations being spaced 200 kc. apart.

TYPES OF RADIO RECEIVERS

Regenerative Receivers.—One of the first circuits in common usage is shown in fig. 1. In this the single tube acted as both radio-frequency amplifier and detector. The input circuit was tuned by means of the variable air condenser and taps on the vario-

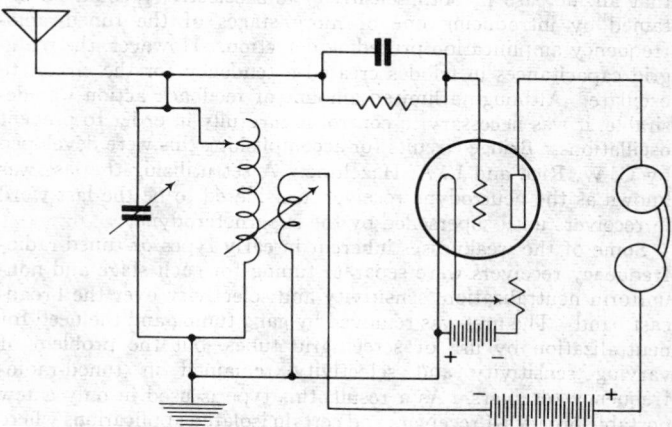

FIG. 1.—SINGLE-CIRCUIT REGENERATIVE RECEIVER

coupler tuning coil, and the amount of feedback was controlled by rotating the tickler coil. This circuit was especially common in home-built sets, principally because of its simplicity. Other types of regenerative receivers were the two- and three-circuit, tuned plate, Cockaday, etc. Most of them had a tendency to oscillate and to act as a radio transmitter while being tuned. The radiated output would combine with other signals present to produce obnoxious squeals and whistles in neighbouring sets. This, together with a demand for more selective receivers as the number of broadcast transmitters with closer frequency allocations increased, eventually limited the regenerative receiver to long-wave and marine use.

Superregenerative Receiver.—The selectivity and sensitivity of a regenerative receiver increases rapidly with the coupling and resulting approach to the condition for sustained oscillation. Armstrong in 1922 first described a circuit for taking advantage of this by superimposing a supersonic signal upon the received signal in a manner such as to prevent the circuit from oscillating at a high frequency. This principle is used in the superregenerative receiver, which is characterized by extremely high sensitivity. Because of poor quality of output, its use is limited principally to short-wave reception in police and radio amateur sets.

Reflex Receiver.—Reflex action consists of feedback action

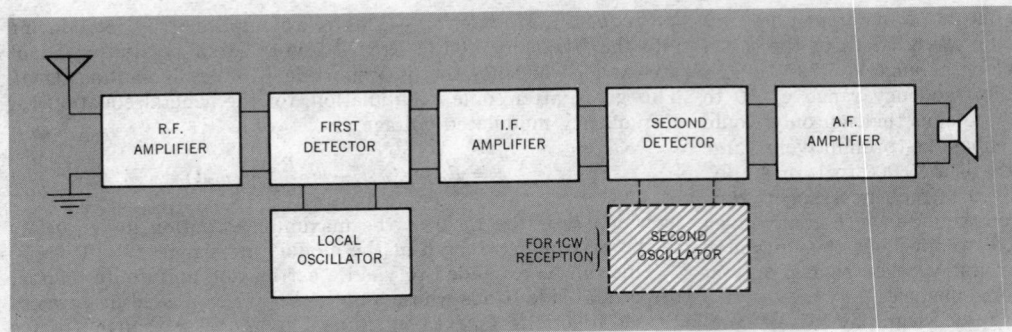

FIG. 2.—BLOCK DIAGRAM FOR SUPERHETERODYNE RECEIVER

ceived station is equal to the intermediate frequency. Since the major part of the amplification is in the intermediate-frequency amplifier, both the selectivity and sensitivity of the set are essentially independent of the original station frequency. The advantages of the superheterodyne receiver were quickly recognized, but since the early sets required eight or ten expensive battery-operated tubes its use was limited to the more expensive models. Within 20 years, however, it had almost completely supplanted other types of broadcast receivers.

between the plate circuit of one tube and the grid circuit of the preceding tube. In the reflex receiver, the antenna signal was first amplified by one stage of tuned radio frequency (T.R.F.) and then applied to the grid of the detector tube. The audio-frequency output of the latter was then fed back to the grid of the first tube by means of an audio-frequency transformer, the headset or loud-speaker being connected in the plate circuit of that tube. Thus, the first tube acted simultaneously as a radio-frequency and audio-frequency amplifier, to give sufficient output to operate a small loud-speaker upon occasion. This was an important consideration in the days of high-priced tubes, parts and batteries. Poor selectivity was the principle factor which brought about an early obsolescence.

Tuned-Radio-Frequency (T.R.F.) Receiver.—It was found that an increase in both sensitivity and selectivity could be obtained by introducing one or more stages of the tuned-radio-frequency amplification preceding detection. However, the plate-grid capacitances in triodes created a tendency for the circuit to oscillate. Although a limited amount of feedback action was desirable, it was necessary to control it carefully in order to prevent oscillations. Bridge circuits for accomplishing this were developed by C. W. Rice and L. A. Hazeltine. A set utilizing the last was known as the neutrodyne receiver, considered to be the last word in receivers until superseded by the superheterodyne.

Some of the weaknesses inherent in early types of tuned-radio-frequency receivers were separate tuning for each stage and non-uniform neutralization, sensitivity and selectivity over the broadcast band. The first was removed by gang tuning and the need for neutralization by use of screen-grid tubes, but the problem of varying sensitivity and selectivity remained in tuned-radio-frequency receivers. As a result, this type is used in only a few portable broadcast receivers and certain isolated applications where the selectivity requirements are not too stringent.

Superheterodyne Receiver.—A circuit which gave uniform performance over a wide range of station frequencies was developed by Armstrong while working in France during World War I. This made use of the heterodyne principle, which consists of combining two frequencies to give a different frequency. It had been introduced by Fessenden of the University of Pittsburgh in 1913, to convert radio-telegraph signals into interrupted audio-frequency code signals.

In the Armstrong superheterodyne receiver, or supersonic heterodyne receiver as it was called first in England, the incoming signal is combined with the output of an oscillator to produce a given supersonic frequency, called the intermediate frequency (I.F.). The latter is then amplified by means of one or more tuned stages, demodulated to give the required audio-frequency signal, amplified and finally fed into a loud-speaker. The selection of the particular station to be received is accomplished by adjusting the oscillator frequency so that the difference between it and the carrier frequency of the re-

The accompanying block diagrams show the principal features of typical modern receivers. Starting at the input terminals, the signal is first amplified with one stage of tuned radio frequency in order to provide initial selectivity and thus to reduce so-called image and cross-modulation effects and mixer tube noise. The tuned-radio-frequency amplifier and local oscillator circuits are gang-tuned with a single control.

The mixer, converter or first detector tube, as it is called, changes the carrier frequency of the signal to the intermediate-frequency value. This was originally taken as 50 kc., but was later increased to 130–175 kc. Later it was further increased to 450–480 kc., with a tendency to standardize at 455 kc. in order to accommodate multiband receivers.

The intermediate-frequency amplifier usually consists of one or two transformer-coupled stages. The primaries and secondaries are permanently tuned, aside from small "trimmers" which are used for alignment purposes. The major portion of the high-frequency gain occurs in the intermediate-frequency amplifier. Remote cutoff pentodes are used to permit automatic gain control.

The function of the second detector is to convert the modulated intermediate-frequency signal into audio frequency. Square-law detection by means of a triode was used originally. This is preferable for weak signals, but since the percentage of second harmonic distortion increases rapidly with signal strength and percentage modulation, linear detection came to be used.

Among the advantages of high-level linear detection are the elimination of one stage of audio-frequency amplification, low harmonic distortion, reduction in tube noise and a lowering in cost of power pack filter because of the higher permissible hum.

The process of linear detection is essentially one of rectification and can be accomplished with either diodes or suitably biased grid-control tubes. Duplex tubes are often used, one part feeding into the audio-frequency amplifier, the other into the automatic volume-control system.

The audio-frequency amplifier may consist of one stage of voltage amplification and a power stage which utilizes two power pentodes in push-pull, when considerable output is demanded.

Automatic volume, or gain, control (AVC) was one of the most important developments in radio receivers. Its principal purpose is to maintain constant detector input. In this way the output of the receiver is unaffected by the strength of incoming signals. In brief, automatic volume control is accomplished by introducing an extra bias in the remote-cutoff tubes in the tuned-radio-

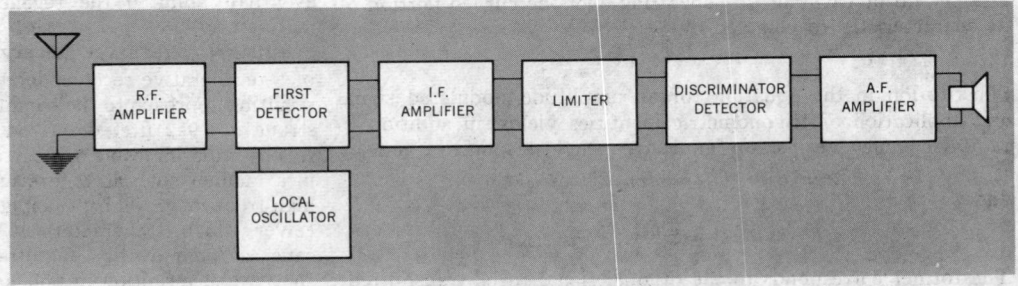

FIG. 3.—BLOCK DIAGRAM FOR FM BROADCAST RECEIVER

frequency and intermediate-frequency stages, which increases with the carrier input to the second detector. This automatically adjusts the gain of those stages so as to maintain nearly constant detector input as long as the incoming antenna signal exceeds a minimum threshold value.

The output of a receiving set is adjusted to suit the listener by means of a volume control, consisting of a potentiometer in the audio-frequency amplifier.

Since the sensitivity of the ear varies with frequency, some volume controls also include fixed coils or condensers such that the quality of the loud-speaker output will appear to be independent of intensity.

The purpose of the tone control is to allow the listener to vary the relative intensity of the high and low tones. The circuit for doing this often consists of a variable resistance connected in series with a fixed capacitor, its effect being to emphasize the bass notes by de-emphasizing the treble.

Receivers for FM Reception.—The block diagram in fig. 3 is schematic for a typical receiver designed for use in the 88- to 108-mc. FM broadcast band. In commercial sets, however, a converter stage replaces the local oscillator and the first detector mixer. Except that the intermediate frequency is 10.7 mc. instead of 455 kc., a change made necessary by the greater band-width requirements of FM, the functioning of the set is similar for receiving both AM and FM up to and including the I.F. amplifier. The output of the I.F. amplifier, however, instead of feeding into the detector as for AM, first goes through a limiter which levels off

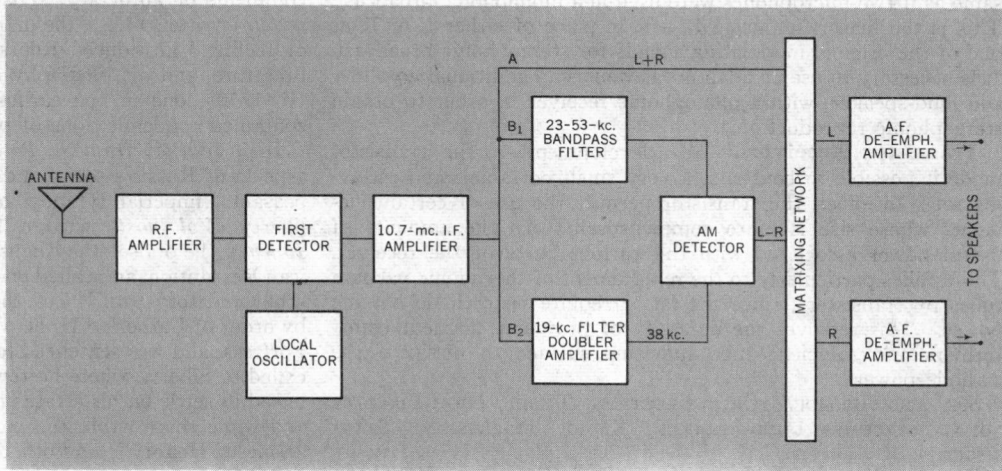

FIG. 5.—FUNCTIONAL DIAGRAM FOR STEREOPHONIC RECEIVER

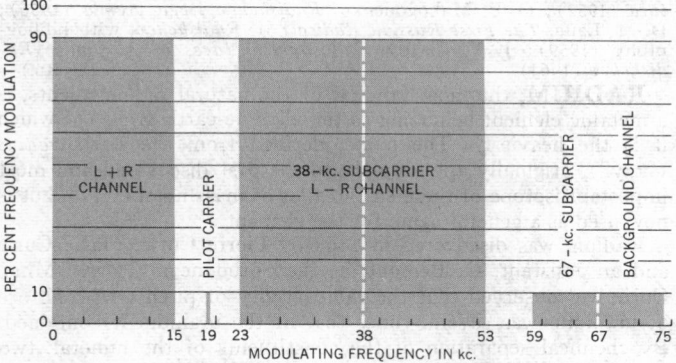

FIG. 4.—FREQUENCY SPECTRUM FOR FM STEREOPHONIC BROADCAST

the signal to a fixed amplitude of a few volts. This is very effective in eliminating interference as well as noise due to static, ignition systems, etc., since it is estimated that only about 3% of such disturbances are of a frequency-modulation character. This results in a possible gain in the signal-to-noise ratio of as much as 30 db. by the use of FM.

The first step in the demodulation process is to convert the output of the I.F. amplifier into an AM signal. This is done with a frequency-sensitive circuit called the discriminator. A typical arrangement consists essentially of a coupling transformer with tuned primary and secondary. The desired shape of its frequency response curve is obtained by using coupling slightly less than critical. The output of the discriminator is fed into a detector and the resulting audio signal is further amplified and fed into a loud-speaker as in AM reception.

Receivers for Stereophonic Reception.—The U.S. Federal Communications commission on April 19, 1961, approved a multiplex system for broadcasting stereophonic programs in a single band in the regular 88 to 108 mc. FM broadcast spectrum. The

approval became effective June 1, 1961. Previously, FM multiplexing had been utilized for several years by at least 200 stations in the U.S. as a means of broadcasting background music on a rental basis to factories, restaurants and other commercial establishments. The approved system for stereophonic broadcast made provision for continuing this special service, although—as in the case of monophonic broadcasting—background music signals are filtered out in home receivers.

The specified FM spectrum for stereophonic broadcasting, including the optional band for transmitting background music, is shown in fig. 4. With appropriate changes in the co-ordinates, this diagram also can be used to represent the upper sideband halves of both the radiated and received signals or, by omitting the background music portion, it can be used to portray the output of the FM limiter-detector stage in a stereophonic home receiver.

The transmitted signal consists of a main carrier that has been frequency-modulated as follows: (1) up to 90% (75 kc. constitute 100% modulation in FM broadcast) by $L + R$, the sum of the left- and right-hand audio signals; (2) 8% to 10% by a 19-kc. pilot carrier; (3) up to 90% by a 38-kc. subcarrier which has been amplitude-modulated, with carrier suppressed, by $L - R$, the difference between the left- and right-hand audio signals; and optionally, (4) up to 10% by a 67-kc. subcarrier amplitude-modulated by background music whose upper limit has been set at 8 kc. The standards of performance are the same as for monophonic FM broadcasting.

The principal functions that must be performed by a stereophonic home receiver are portrayed in fig. 5. The first four sections in this are essentially the same as would be found in a similar diagram for a monophonic receiver, including 10.7 mc. for I.F. amplification. It is principally in the I.F. amplifier that background-music signals are filtered out in both monophonic and stereophonic home receivers; a specially adjusted receiver must be used to detect and amplify the background-music signal.

Starting with the output of the I.F. amplifier in fig. 5, channel A accepts and transmits $L + R$ to the matrixing network, a network whose output is a linear combination of two or more input signals. Channel B_1 accepts the 38-kc. subcarrier that is amplitude-modulated by $L - R$. Channel B_2 accepts the 19-kc. pilot carrier, doubles its frequency and amplifies it so that it can replace the 38-kc. subcarrier that was suppressed in the transmitter. The outputs of B_1 and B_2 are then applied to an AM detector which delivers $L - R$ to the matrixing network.

The output of the matrixing network consists of the sum and difference of its two inputs, to give $(L + R) + (L - R) = 2L$, and $(L + R) - (L - R) = 2R$, respectively. After de-emphasis and amplification, these are fed into two loud-speakers so arranged as to give the proper stereophonic effect.

A stereophonic receiver can ordinarily be used for monophonic FM reception, although some interference may be heard if the received signal happens to include a background-music subcarrier that is at some point in the range of 20–53 kc. If a stereophonic signal is picked up by a monophonic receiver, a true monophonic reproduction, consisting of L + R, will be heard; the effect is the same as if two microphones were used in a monophonic broadcast. This is the reason for using L + R in place of either L or R as one of the original modulating signals for stereophonic broadcast. It is necessary to use an adaptor, as well as an additional amplifier and loud-speaker, with a monophonic receiver in order to obtain stereophonic reproduction.

Transistor Receivers.—The development of the transistor made it possible to construct a very small portable radio receiving set. In effect, the transistor permits the use of certain elements whose size is more commensurate with the amounts of useful power associated with the various parts of the receiver. This applies particularly to the replacement of thermionic vacuum tubes by transistors, since the latter require no cathode heating power. This removes the necessity of providing filament transformers and sufficient tube radiating surface to dissipate the cathode power.

See also Broadcasting; Electron Tube; High-Fidelity Sound Systems; Loud-Speaker; Radio; Television; Transistor.

Bibliography.—Keith Henney (ed.), *Radio Engineering Handbook,* 5th ed. (1959); W. R. Maclaurin, *Invention & Innovation in the Radio Industry* (1949); William Marcus and Alex Levy, *Practical Radio Servicing* (1955); K. R. Sturley, *Radio Receiver Design* (1943–45); F. E. Terman *et al., Electronic and Radio Engineering,* 4th ed. (1955); S. W. Amos and F. W. Kellaway, *Radio Receivers and Transmitters* (1948); J. A. Fleming, *The Principles of Electric Wave Telegraphy and Telephony,* 4th ed. (1919); J. H. Morecraft *et al., Principles of Radio Communication,* 2nd ed. (1927); D. R. von Recklinghausen, "Stereophonic FM Multiplex System," *Electronics World* (July 1961).
(C. S. Rs.)

RADIOSONDE, an instrument sent aloft, attached to a freely rising balloon, for the purpose of obtaining information on the temperature, humidity and other properties of the upper atmosphere. It includes a radio transmitter which sends down signals representing the numerical values of these properties. *See* Upper Air Soundings.   (W. E. K. M.)

RADISH, *Raphanus sativus* (family Cruciferae), an annual or biennial grown for its large, succulent root. The edible part of the root, together with some hypocotyl, form a structure varying in shape, among varieties, from spherical through oblong to long cylindrical or tapered. The outside colour of the root varies from white through pink to red, purple and black; the size of the edible part varies from a few grams in the most popular early American and European varieties to two pounds or more in the late Japanese field type of radish, or daikon. As generally grown, flower stalks form the first season, bearing white or lilac-veined flowers. The seeds are borne in a spongy, nondehiscent, beaked pod called a silicle.

The small, quick-growing spring varieties have a mild, crisp, moderately firm flesh, and are quite perishable. The large, slow-growing summer and winter types have pungent, firm flesh. Winter varieties can be stored through the winter. The common radish is probably of Oriental origin. *R. raphanistrum* is a wild radish found along the Mediterranean. The rat-tailed radish (*R. sativus,* var. *caudatus*) has no enlarged root, but bears enormous seed pods 8–12 in. long which are eaten fresh or pickled. *R. sativus* (var. *longipinnatus*) produces deeply pinnate leaves up to two feet long; the roots are large, firm and are grown as a winter radish. This type is much grown in the Orient and is generally known as Chinese radish.   (V. R. B.)

RADISHCHEV, ALEKSANDR NIKOLAEVICH (1749–1802), Russian author, whose *Puteshestvie iz Peterburga v Moskvu* (1790; *A Journey from St. Petersburg to Moscow*) founded the revolutionary tradition in Russian literature and thought. The son of a nobleman, he was born on Aug. 31 (new style; 20, old style), 1749, in Moscow, and brought up at Ablyazovo, Saratov Province. Educated in Moscow (1756–66), at the St. Petersburg Corps of Pages, and at Leipzig, where he studied law (1766–71), he served under the minister of justice, as military procurator at the war office (1773–75), and at the Imperial College of Commerce (1776–90).

In 1773 he translated the abbé Mably's *Observations sur l'histoire de la Grèce* (1766), and, in a footnote to Mably's attack on Alexander the Great as a dynastic conqueror, made sharply critical comments on autocracy. His first original work, *Dnevnik odnoy nedeli* (written 1773), the diary of one week in the life of a "man of feeling," introduced Rousseau's cult of sentiment to Russian literature, and his biography of a college friend, Fedor Ushakov (d. 1770), one of the earliest intimate biographies in Russian, contained condemnations of political tyranny.

In *A Journey from St. Petersburg to Moscow,* he attacked all aspects of Russia's social and political order: the serfdom of the peasants, imperial tyranny, and the censorship. In an ode to liberty (*Vol 'nost',* written 1781–83; partially included in the *Journey*) he praised the English Revolution of 1688 and the American Revolution, and called on his countrymen to take arms against "the predatory wolf" (*i.e.,* the tsar). Arrested (June 30, 1790) by order of Catherine II, he was imprisoned in the Peter and Paul Fortress, and was sentenced to death, but was later reprieved and exiled to Siberia, where he remained until 1797. He was then allowed to settle on his estate at Nemtsovo, near Malo-Yaroslavets, and while there wrote the mock-heroic ballad, *Bova;* a pathetic "Song of History"; and other poems. Pardoned by Alexander I, in 1801 he became a member of the legislative commission under Count Zavadovsky, and as well as helping to draft several liberalizing social and constitutional statutes, set forth his own plans for reform in memoranda on legislation and the civil code. Opposition, even from his friends, to his radical views on the freedom of the individual and free speech, and realization that the promised liberal reforms were not being achieved, led to increasing despondency, and on Sept. 23, 1802, he took poison, dying at 1 A.M. on Sept. 24 (N.S.; 12, O.S.).

Bibliography.—*A Journey from St. Petersburg to Moscow* (ed. with introduction by A. Herzen, London, 1858; new translation, 1958) was first republished in Russia in 1905, in a collected edition of Radishchev's works, 2 vol. (1905–07). His complete works were ed. by the Academy of Sciences of the U.S.S.R., 3 vol. (1938–52). *See also* A. S. Pushkin, *A. Radishchev* (1836); V. P. Semennikov, *Radishchev* (1923); D. D. Blagoi, *Radishchev* (1939); V. Orlov, *Radishchev i russkaia literatura* (1952); G. P. Makogonenko, *Radishchev i ego vrem'a* (1956); D. M. Lang, *The First Russian Radical: A. Radishchev,* with bibliography (1959); J. V. Clardy, *Philosophical Ideas of Alexander Radishchev* (1964).
(D. D. Bl.)

RADIUM, the most familiar of the natural radioelements, is a metallic element belonging to the alkaline-earth group, of which it is the heaviest. The name, derived from the Latin *radius* ("ray"), originally applied only to the first discovered and most important isotope of the element, that of mass number 226, but is now used as a general name for the element.

Radium was discovered in 1898 by Pierre Curie, Marie Curie and an assistant, G. Bémont, at the Sorbonne in Paris. Mme. Curie had observed that the radioactivity of pitchblende, an ore of uranium, was several times that of the uranium it contained. By chemical separation of the constituents of the mineral, two highly radioactive elements—polonium and radium—were discovered. Prior to this discovery, it had been customary to discard the residue of pitchblende after extraction of uranium.

Radium was found to adhere closely to the common element barium, which it followed in the chemical treatment of the ore, indicating a very close chemical relationship of the two elements. Only after developing a complicated fractional precipitation procedure could the two elements be separated. Then, in 1902, Mme. Curie was able to prepare a pure salt of radium by working up several tons of pitchblende residues. The same general method of extracting radium is used commercially, a tribute to the genius of this pioneer in radiochemistry.

The pure element was first prepared in 1910 by Mme. Curie and A. Debierne; it is a shiny white metal.

The symbol of radium is Ra; atomic number 88; atomic weight 226.

Isotopes and Radioactive Properties.—Several isotopes of radium, all radioactive, are known. Only Ra^{226} is stable enough to permit its isolation in visible and weighable amounts, and the name "radium" often refers simply to this isotope. Its half life is approximately 1,620 years, and it disintegrates with the emission of alpha particles. It is a member of the uranium, or radium, family of natural radioelements, following ionium in the series. Its immediate transformation product is radon, a rare gas of 3.825-day half life, which in turn changes into a series of shorter-lived radioelements, radium A, B, C, C′ and C″. It is rarely encountered in a radioactively pure form, for immediately after purification from its disintegration products they rapidly grow in again. Radium C emits penetrating gamma rays, so that, although radium itself emits only small numbers of gamma rays of low penetrability, a sample which has been sealed up to prevent loss of the gaseous radon is a source of strong gamma radiation. About a month is required for the gamma activity to reach its maximum, or equilibrium, intensity. The end product of the short-lived descendants of radium is radium D, which is also radioactive, and from this grow radium E and polonium, or radium F. Since the half life of radium D is 20 years it comes to equilibrium slowly in radium preparations.

The half life of radium is so great that it cannot be determined by directly observing the decay, and recourse must be had to indirect methods. Most of these involve the determination of the specific activity, or the number of disintegrations per unit weight in unit time. This can be done by counting the alpha particles emitted in a measured interval by a sample of known weight. The first measurements were done by visual counting of the scintillations produced by the impact of the particles on a zinc sulfide screen, while later experimenters have used electrical detection and counting instruments. Since alpha particles are helium nuclei, measurement of the rate of helium generation by radium provides another means of determining the specific activity. The half life also can be calculated from the rate of growth of radium in a sample of purified ionium relative to the amount in equilibrium with the same quantity of ionium in ancient and intact uranium minerals. Finally, from the equilibrium ratio of radium and uranium in such minerals the half life of radium can be calculated if that of uranium is known independently. The specific activity is close to 3.61×10^{10} alpha disintegrations per second per gram, whence the half life is 1,620 years. The disintegration rate of radium formed the basis of a standard unit of radioactivity, the curie, originally a rate of disintegration equal to that of a gram of radium. Now, a curie of any radioelement is by definition that amount undergoing 3.7×10^{10} disintegrations per second.

In the thorium series of radioelements occur two radium isotopes, mesothorium I (Ra^{228}) and thorium X (Ra^{224}), the former a beta emitter of 6.7-year half life and the latter an alpha emitter of 3.64-day half life. One of their descendants, ThC″, emits gamma radiation even more penetrating than that of RaC, and as a result of the complex sequence of half lives the gamma activity of freshly purified mesothorium increases for about four years and then decays steadily. A fourth isotope, actinium X (Ra^{223}), occurs in the actinium series and is an alpha emitter of 11.7-day half life. (*See* RADIOACTIVITY.)

Several artificial radioactive isotopes of radium are also known. (*See* NUCLEUS.)

Natural Occurrence.—Although the half life of radium, 1,620 years, is long with respect to human experience, it is infinitesimal in the geological time scale, and any radium present at the time of the formation of the earth has by now completely disappeared. It is only because a new supply of the element is continually being generated by the disintegration of uranium that any is found at the present time, and its distribution in nature is practically identical with that of uranium. There is a constant ratio between radium and uranium, 0.00000034, in all sufficiently old minerals in which radioactive equilibrium has not been disturbed by weathering or leaching. In altered minerals the radium is generally relatively lower because of the greater solubility of its oxide. Springs, rivers, sea water and the ocean sediments contain small amounts of radium. Uranium, and consequently radium, are widely distributed in minute traces in nearly all common rocks, both igneous and sedimentary, the average concentration of radium in the earth's crust being about 1 part per 1,000,000,000,000. The bulk of the earth's radium is so accounted for; but in this form it is, of course, commercially unavailable. Only in uranium minerals is

radium present in high enough concentrations to make its extraction feasible, and even the richest ores contain only about $\frac{1}{4}$ g. of radium per ton. Most deposits contain smaller amounts; and some which contain as low as 1% of uranium, or 1 g. of radium in 300 tons, have been exploited for the latter.

Radium was discovered in the mineral pitchblende, an oxide of uranium, which had been mined since about 1840 at Joachimsthal, Czech., for its uranium content. More extensive pitchblende deposits were later found at Katanga in the Belgian Congo and at Great Bear lake and Beaverlodge lake in Canada. Second in importance as a radium source is carnotite, a double vanadate of uranium and potassium found principally as a yellowish impregnation of sandstone in the western United States. Altogether several dozen different radium-containing minerals are known, and deposits of varying extent are found in many other places; some of these have been worked from time to time for radium. The increased importance of uranium, as a source of atomic energy, has resulted in intensive prospecting and the discovery of many more such deposits. (*See* URANIUM.)

Mesothorium is obtained principally from monazite, a mixed phosphate of thorium and rare earths occurring frequently in alluvial sands. (*See* THORIUM.) Thorium X and actinium X occur naturally in thorium and uranium minerals, respectively, but are usually obtained from their parents rather than from natural sources.

Industrial Production.—For a number of years following its discovery the only important source of radium was the Joachimsthal mines, operated by the Czechoslovakian government. Later some radium was produced in other European countries. The United States became the first major producer and from 1913 to 1923 was the chief world supplier, with carnotite from the western states being extracted principally at Denver, Colo., and Pittsburgh, Pa. The rich Belgian Congo pitchblende deposits were discovered in 1913; and the refinery at Oolen, Belg., began production in 1922, immediately dominating the world market. The extensive Canadian deposits were discovered in 1930; and the refinery at Port Hope, Ont., started producing radium in 1933. In the late 1930s the world market was divided between the Belgian and Canadian producers on a 60:40 basis by a cartel agreement. After Belgium fell to the German army in 1940, the Congo ores were shipped to the United States and Canada for refining. Following World War II, radium-bearing residues from these ores were shipped to Oolen for extraction of radium.

The following is a typical procedure for the commercial production of radium from pitchblende. The ground ore is digested with a mixture of nitric and sulfuric acids to which a little barium is added to act as a carrier for the radium. The uranium dissolves, and an insoluble residue of radium, barium and lead sulfates and siliceous gangue remains. This is separated by filtration and boiled with sodium hydroxide solution to leach out the lead sulfate and some of the silica. The residue is then autoclaved with sodium carbonate solution to convert the barium and radium sulfates to carbonates, which are dissolved in hydrochloric acid. After filtering off the remaining silica, the barium and radium are again precipitated as sulfates and converted to carbonates to effect a purification. The carbonates are now dissolved in hydrobromic acid and the bromides subjected to an involved fractional crystallization process. Since radium bromide is somewhat less soluble than barium bromide, the crystals are enriched in radium. After ten recrystallizations the ratio of radium to barium in the head crystals is changed from a few parts per 1,000,000 to a few parts per 1,000. At this stage, the bromides from several batches are accumulated, purified again and subjected to further crystallizations until radium of the desired purity, usually 95% or 99%, is obtained. This is sealed into small glass tubes to be measured and sold.

Variations in this process are dictated by differences in the nature and quality of the ores found in different locations. Canadian pitchblende contains considerable native silver, which is recovered by roasting the ore with sodium chloride to convert the silver to its chloride and subsequently leaching the latter out of the sulfate residue with sodium thiosulfate solution. With carnotite, the treatment can be altered by leaching the ground ore with hydrochloric acid to dissolve the radium, uranium and vanadium away from the siliceous matter before adding sulfuric acid. The sulfate precipitate can alternatively be heated with charcoal to reduce the sulfates to sulfides, which dissolve readily in hydrochloric acid. In the fractional crystallization the chlorides are often used instead of the bromides.

Newly developed methods for separating radium from barium involve cation exchange resins and precipitation from homogeneous solution.

Radium was originally interchanged freely among scientific and medical investigators, but when it became an item of commerce it became extremely expensive. However, as new and richer sources have become available, the price has steadily fallen. Typical market prices per gram were $10,000 in 1904, $80,000 in 1912, $120,000 in 1915, $135,000 in 1918, $90,000 in 1920, $70,000 in 1923, $50,000 in 1929, $25,000 in 1936, $20,000 in 1941, $25,000 in 1946, $20,000 in 1950, $16,000 in 1953 and $15,000 in 1957. The total world production in grams was approximately 50 by 1916, 300 by 1925 and 1,000 by 1940. Production was greatly accelerated during and shortly after World War II, but was declining in the 1960s because of the competition of substitutes.

Chemical Properties.—Of the 88 electrons of the radium atom, the first 86 are strongly bound, whereas the outer two are readily lost leaving a divalent cation of noble gas structure. This property classifies it among the alkaline-earth elements, which include, in order, magnesium, calcium, strontium, barium and radium. There is a general gradation of properties in going from the lighter to the heavier members of the group, and radium continues this trend. It is very similar to barium, all of its known compounds being isomorphous with the corresponding barium compounds and differing so little in properties as to make the separation of the two elements a matter of great difficulty. The chemistry of radium, is, therefore, well understood.

Radium is divalent in all of its compounds. The sulfate, $RaSO_4$, is the most insoluble sulfate known and for this reason is important in the separation of the element from its ores. However, it is only because lead sulfate is also precipitated from the solution of the ore that quantitative precipitation of radium is obtained, for the amount of radium sulfate present is far too low to precipitate by itself. This principle, whereby an element present in quantity too small to permit manipulation by itself is caused to undergo certain chemical reactions by the presence of a larger quantity of a similarly behaving element, is called "carrying" and is important both in the isolation and in the chemical study of radium. The nitrate, $Ra(NO_3)_2$, chloride, $RaCl_2$, and bromide, $RaBr_2$, are soluble in water but highly insoluble in concentrated solutions of the corresponding acids, and are consequently of use in the purification of radium, including its separation from the last traces of barium. The chloride and bromide crystallize as hydrates, $RaCl_2 \cdot 2H_2O$ and $RaBr_2 \cdot 2H_2O$, but form the anhydrous salts on heating. The hydroxide, $Ra(OH)_2$, is the most soluble of the alkaline-earth hydroxides. The carbonate, $RaCO_3$, is insoluble in water but soluble in acids and the sulfide, RaS, is soluble in water.

Metallic radium melts at approximately 700° C. and has high chemical reactivity. It dissolves in water with vigorous evolution of hydrogen and darkens in air with the formation of the nitride. It is prepared by electrolysis from an aqueous solution of the chloride into a cathode of mercury, followed by volatilization of the mercury in a stream of hydrogen.

The optical spectrum of radium is similar to that of the other alkaline-earth elements, consisting of comparatively few relatively strong lines. The ordinary compounds of radium are all colourless but become coloured upon standing as a result of the continual bombardment by radioactive particles. Glass containers of considerable quantities of radium also become coloured, and sizable preparations can be seen to glow in the dark. Those properties are not peculiar to radium but are common to all strongly radioactive substances.

Analytical Methods.—The assay of radium is generally made not by the usual chemical procedures, such as weighing, but by methods based on its radioactivity. Strong samples, such as those for medical and radiographical use, are assayed by their gamma radiation by means of an ionization chamber and electrometer. The sample must be sealed for at least a month before the measurement so that the equilibrium quantity of radium C is present. For calibration of the measuring apparatus, standard preparations of radium have been made. The primary international standard was prepared by Mme. Curie by precise weighing and has been preserved at Sèvres, France. Secondary standards, carefully checked against the international standard, are kept in the capitals of the principal nations. In using these standards allowance must be made for their decay, which amounts to 0.043% per year. Another assay method is the emanation technique, in which the gaseous radon generated by the radium sample in a measured time is collected in an ionization chamber and the intensity of its radiations measured. This method can be made extremely sensitive by electrically counting the individual alpha particles, and as little as 10^{-14} grams of radium can be so detected.

Uses.—The uses of radium all result from its radiations. The most important of these have been in medicine, principally for the treatment of cancer. For this purpose the element may be used directly, sealed in a tube, or the accumulated radon may be drawn off and compressed into a small capsule which may be used until it has decayed to a low intensity. (*See* RADIOLOGY.) Large amounts of radium have been employed for industrial radiography, particularly for the inspection of metal castings. Radium is mixed, in small concentrations, with a paste of zinc sulfide to make a luminescent paint for watch, clock and meter dials and signs which must be read in the dark. An intimate mixture of radium with beryllium is a moderately intense source of neutrons. Such neutron sources have been used extensively in scientific work and have found practical applications in well logging in geophysical prospecting for petroleum. Radium-bearing slime from uranium processing is used as a marking compound in oil-well casings.

Mention should be made of the hazards of handling radium, which result from the physiological effects of its radiations and which are enhanced by the gaseous nature of its decay product, radon. Before the dangers were recognized and adequate precautions taken a number of radium workers suffered serious injury or death. For physiological effects of radioactive substances *see* RADIOLOGY.

Mesothorium can be used in a manner similar to radium for all the purposes mentioned, but its greater expense and shorter lifetime limit its applications. It is superior to radium as a luminous paint activator because the intensity of its radiations increases for several years and thus compensates for the fatigue of the zinc sulfide. Except for scientific purposes, the other radium isotopes have no practical value.

For all the uses of radium, substitutes have become available. Artificial radioelements and high-voltage X-ray generators are supplanting radium in radiotherapy and radiography. Fluorescent paints activated by ultraviolet radiation are replacing radium paints in airplane panel meters. Cyclotrons and nuclear chain reactors provide much more intense neutron sources. Nevertheless, the use of radium is still important because of its special properties and its availability as a by-product of uranium.

See also references under "Radium" in the Index.

BIBLIOGRAPHY.—M. Curie, *Recherches sur les substances radioactives* (1904) and *Radioactivité* (1935); S. Meyer and E. Schweidler, *Radioaktivität* (1927); E. Rutherford, J. Chadwick and C. D. Ellis, *Radiations From Radioactive Substances* (1930); L. Gmelin, *Gmelin und Krauts Handbuch der anorganischen Chemie*, 8th ed., "Syst.-Nr. 1" (1926) and "Syst.-Nr. 31" (1928); U.S. Bureau of Mines, *Minerals Yearbook* (annual volumes). (T. P. K.)

RADNORSHIRE (SIR FAESYFED), an inland county of Wales, is bounded on the east by Shropshire and Herefordshire and on the west and north by Brecknockshire and Montgomeryshire. Its area is 470.7 sq.mi. (1,219.1 sq.km.).

Physical Features.—Most of the county exceeds 600 ft. (about 200 m.) above sea level, and half of it is more than 1,000 ft. (328 m.), reaching 2,166 ft. (711 m.) centrally in Radnor Forest. Only in the lower Wye Valley is there a small area below 300 ft. (about 100 m.). Because the general trend of relief is from northeast to southwest, the rivers Wye and Teme flow southeast in deep valleys. The Lugg and Arrow flow east from Radnor Forest, while the Ithon drains the centre of the county south and then southwest to the Wye.

Geologically, the county is largely composed of Ordovician and Silurian rocks with igneous intrusions between Llandegley and Llanelwedd. Old Red Sandstone occurs in the east and south only. Recent alluvium lies in the lower river valleys; glacial drift is widespread.

Radnorshire has cool, damp summers and mild, wet winters, but relief creates surprising contrasts; the lower Wye Valley at 300 ft. can be 6° F (3.3° C) warmer than Radnor Forest at 2,166 ft., while rainfall averages 80 in. (2,032 mm.) annually in the high western hills compared with only 35 in. (889 mm.) in the low eastern valleys. The west of the county has poor, acid soils, peat soils developing on the wet, badly drained hilltops. On the Old Red Sandstone and alluvium soils are more fertile.

The original deciduous forests of the valleys have disappeared except from the hedges and steep river banks, and from the private and public parks and woods. The high hills are covered with rough fescue pastures, grading upward into heather moor or *Molinia-Nardus* moor. Below 1,000 ft. are mainly enclosed fields of grass, generally of *Agrostis* with rushes on fields which are difficult to drain. Only in the more fertile eastern valleys and in the Llandrindod and Llanelwedd areas is there better *Agrostis*-rye grass pasture. The only large areas of woodland are coniferous, planted in the Elan Valley by the Birmingham Corporation, and planted by the Forestry Commission on the northeastern slopes of Radnor Forest, in Coed Sarnau northeast of Rhayader, and (on a smaller scale) in the Edw Valley, totaling 20,000 acres.

History.—No archaeological finds proving permanent settlements by Stone or Bronze Age man have yet been made in Radnorshire, but burial mounds and finds of stone and metal artifacts prove their presence, at least, in the county. Later, iron-using Celts built simple hill forts on the lower hill slopes. Their descendants, the Ordovices, were subdued by the Romans between A.D. 50 and 100 and held in subjection for 300 years from forts linked by roads. One road is presumed to have crossed the country from south to north, and on it, *c.* A.D. 80, was built Castell Collen Fort near Llandrindod; another that followed the lower Wye Valley was guarded by the Gaer Fort near Hay. The Roman legions used these roads and forts to keep peace among the Ordovices and to carry metals to their ports and towns of south Wales. When the Romans withdrew late in the 4th century the Welsh tribes continued their pastoral life, but intertribal warfare made Radnorshire (then called Rhwng Gwy a Hafren, "the land between Wye and Severn") a cockpit between the rival princes of Powys and Brycheiniog for six centuries. Meanwhile, the Anglo-Saxons had crossed England, and late in the 8th century King Offa halted the Mercian struggle with the Welsh by building the boundary dike, which is still a conspicuous feature of the county between Knighton and Burfa.

The beginnings of Christianity in southeast Wales died after the Roman withdrawal, but the faith soon reentered southwest Wales by sea from western Gaul, which still remained in touch with Rome. Along the ancient tracks and the disintegrating Roman roads, Irish and Gallic immigrants carried the cults of SS. David, Teilo, and Padarn inland and eventually into Radnorshire where Glascwm became a "mother church" of David. Dedications to SS. Michael, Mary, and Bride, common in the area, only came with the Normans who, after the victory at Hastings in 1066, swept to the Welsh border and by 1100 had a castle at New Radnor. For a century the local Welsh fought the barons Mortimer and de Braose, who built many castles to help their campaigns. Already the Welsh Church was being organized on Latin lines, and Radnorshire became part of St. David's diocese and was divided into rural deaneries. Houses of almost all the monastic orders were then founded in Wales, and these included the Cistercian abbey of Cwmhir, reputed burial place of the last Llewelyn in 1282.

The conquest of Wales in 1283 by Edward I left Radnorshire as marcher land, and another 250 years of fighting was only ended by Henry VIII's acts of union in 1536 and 1542, joining the Mortimer and Warwick lordships to form the modern shire of

Radnor. The county's boundary has changed little since, and the Tudor hundreds are basically the five modern rural districts of Colwyn, Knighton, New Radnor, Painscastle, and Rhayader.

Apart from the Civil War, when the county took the Royalist side, religious and economic strife has most upset local peace since Tudor times. Nonconformity dates from the Commonwealth; Maesyronen Baptist Chapel was built in 1696, and the Quaker Meeting House at Llandegley is even older. Methodism, too, was established early in the 18th century. In the 1840s grievances over turnpike tolls caused the Rebecca Riots (*q.v.*), and the local fondness for poaching led to serious affrays starting in 1856 and ending only in 1907. Poverty and retaliation against enclosures explain these savage outbursts. The Rev. Francis Kilvert (*q.v.*) began his *Diary* while curate of Clyro (a village near the borders of Brecknockshire and Herefordshire) from 1865 to 1872.

Population and Administration.—The administrative area is 470.7 sq.mi. and Radnorshire (pop. [1961] 18,431) is the most thinly populated county in England and Wales. Nearly one-third of the total live in the three urban districts of Llandrindod Wells, Knighton, and Presteigne; the rest live in the five rural districts. There are also 23 parishes. The county's population in 1801 was 19,135, rising to a maximum of 25,458 in 1841, since when there has been a slow decline, the result of agricultural depression and mechanization and migration to the coal fields and large towns.

Though Presteigne (*q.v.*) is still the county town holding the courts of quarter sessions, the administrative centre since 1889 has been Llandrindod Wells (*q.v.*) where the county council meets. Radnor is joined with the county of Brecknock for parliamentary purposes and returns one member.

The Economy.—Public administration, distributive trades, transport, building, and contracting employ the bulk of the workers of the county, which has no mines and has fewer than 100 quarrymen producing granite, gritstone, and limestone. The Forestry Commission employs a small number in planting conifers on poor land up to 2,000 ft. Farming is widespread, and by reason of the height of the land, its climate and comparative isolation, the breeding of sheep and store cattle is paramount. About two-thirds of the land is under grass and less than 10% under the plow. Many thousands of Welsh, Kerry, and Clun sheep (pure and crossbred) and large numbers of Hereford cattle are sold annually, especially at autumn sales inside and outside the county. Radnorshire is completely devoid of large-scale manufacturing, although each town has one or two small factories which help slightly to check rural depopulation, endemic in the county.

Tourism is of increasing importance, based on the beauty and solitude of the county and the fame of its streams among fishermen. The reservoirs in the Elan and Claerwen valleys, which supply water to Birmingham, are a great attraction for visitors. Birmingham Corporation owns more than 30 sq.mi. (78 sq.km.) of land from which water drains to the reservoirs. Llandrindod Wells, a spa and conference centre, and Knighton, a market town, lie on the Shrewsbury to Llanelly railway which crosses the county. Rhayader, a small resort and fishing centre, is on the trunk road from Worcester to Aberystwyth, and Presteigne is an old border town within easy reach of the Midlands.

BIBLIOGRAPHY.—Jonathan Williams, *History of the County of Radnor* (1905); Lewis Davies, *Radnorshire* (1912); W. H. Howse, *Radnorshire* (1949); Land Utilisation Survey of Britain, *The Land of Britain*, pt. 35, *Radnor* by L. K. Redford (1941); *Radnorshire; County Handbook* (1960); *Radnorshire Society Transactions* (annually, 1931—); *Mid Wales Investigation Report* (HMSO, 1955); *British Regional Geology; South Wales* (HMSO, 1948); *British Regional Geology; Welsh Borderland* (HMSO, 1948); *Report on Welsh Holiday Industry* (HMSO, 1963); *Report and Proposals for Wales* (HMSO, 1962); *Wales 1964* (HMSO, 1965). (R. C. B. O.)

RADOM, a town in the Kielce *wojewodztwo* (province) of Poland, lies about 64 mi. (103 km.) S of Warsaw by road. Pop. (1960) 130,116. Radom is first mentioned in the 12th century. In the 14th century the town was walled and obtained market privileges. After the third partition of Poland in 1795 it was seized by Austria. Under the Duchy of Warsaw, from 1809 to 1815, Radom was the capital of a department. After incorporation in 1815 into the Polish kingdom, dependent on Russia, it became capital of a *guberniya* (Russian province). It returned to independent Poland in 1918.

Because of frequent war damage Radom has few old buildings, but both the old town and the 14th-century town are apparent from its street layout. It has a museum and theatre. Radom is on the Warsaw–Cracow road and railway and is a rail junction for Deblin on the Warsaw–Lublin line. It is an important industrial centre, whose manufactures include tanning and producing leather, tobacco, chemicals, glass, timber and paper, clothing, and food.

(T. K. W.)

RADON is the heaviest element of the noble gas group and is an important radioelement. Its atomic weight is 222, its chemical symbol is Rn and its atomic number is 86. The name radon is used either for the most important isotope, that of mass 222, or for the element as a whole, although for the latter purpose the name emanation (symbol Em) is sometimes preferred. Other isotopes are thoron (Tn, mass number 220) and actinon (An, 219). Thoron was discovered in 1899 by R. B. Owens and E. Rutherford, who observed that some of the radioactivity of thorium preparations can be swept away by a current of gas. Radon was similarly discovered in radium samples by F. E. Dorn in 1900, and actinon was found associated with actinium in 1904 by F. O. Giesel and A. Debierne.

Radon is the immediate product of the decay of radium and undergoes alpha disintegration with a half life of 3.825 days. It yields several short-lived radioelements called the active deposit because of their tendency to adhere to solid objects. Thoron and actinon have similar properties, but because of their short half-life periods, 51.5 and 3.92 seconds respectively, they are of less importance than radon. (*See* RADIOACTIVITY; RADIUM.)

Because of its transient existence, radon is found only in conjunction with a source of radium. The atmosphere contains traces of radon near the ground as a result of seepage from soil and rocks, all of which contain minute quantities of radium. For preparing intense samples a supply of radium is kept in a glass vessel in aqueous solution or in the form of a porous solid from which the radon can readily effuse. At intervals of a few days the accumulated radon is pumped off, purified and compressed into a small tube, which is then sealed and removed.

Radium C rapidly grows into equilibrium with the radon and, since the former is the source of the intensely penetrating gamma rays, the gamma activity is in effect transferred from the radium sample to the tube by this process. The radon can then be used for radiotherapy, radiography or other purposes until its strength decays to too low a value. "Dead" radon tubes are often saved for the extraction of radium D and polonium.

Radon possesses a particularly stable electronic configuration that gives it a chemical inactivity that is characteristic of the noble gas elements. Chemical compounds of radon and fluorine have been synthesized. They are analogous to the xenon fluorides but are less volatile and more stable chemically than the corresponding xenon compounds. Radon fluorides can be distilled under vacuum at a temperature of 250° C.

The radioactivity of radon makes the study of radon compounds by conventional chemical procedures difficult. The physical properties of radon are similar to those expected by extrapolation from the other noble gas elements, helium, neon, argon, krypton, and xenon. It is the most easily condensed and solidified of the group, the boiling point being −62° C and the freezing point −71° C. It dissolves more readily in water than the other noble gases and is very soluble in a number of organic liquids.

See also references under "Radon" in the Index.

See C. L. Chernick *et al.*, "Fluorine Compounds of Xenon and Radon," *Science*, 138:75 (Oct. 12, 1962); P. R. Fields *et al.*, "Radon Fluoride," *J. Am. Chem. Soc.*, 84:4164–65 (Nov. 5, 1962). For additional bibliographical reference *see* RADIUM. (T. P. K.; R. N. CL.)

RADOWITZ, JOSEPH MARIA VON (1797–1853), the first statesman to attempt the unification of Germany under Prussian military leadership, was born at Blankenburg in the Harz Mountains on Feb. 6, 1797. A Roman Catholic who combined romantic conservatism with a strong will for military efficiency, he entered the Prussian service in 1823, became an artillery expert,

and won the friendship of the crown prince, who in 1840 succeeded to the Prussian throne as Frederick William IV. Since it was then thought that France was likely to attack the territory of the German Confederation, Radowitz began to preach the doctrine of German military union under Prussia, with the emperor of Austria enjoying only a titular supremacy. Yet Radowitz was an isolated figure at the Prussian court and could rely only on personal influence with the king. He occupied only minor posts before the Revolution of 1848.

In 1848 Radowitz sat in the Frankfurt Parliament (*see* GERMANY: *History*), where his combination of military knowledge and strict religious views earned him the name of "the Warlike Monk." In April 1849, however, Frederick William refused the imperial crown offered by the liberals of Frankfurt. Radowitz then proposed to win that crown for Prussia by conservative methods, that is, by agreement with the German princes instead of the people. Still without an official position, he became the principal director of Prussian policy and proceeded to organize a union of German states willing to accept Prussia's leadership instead of Austria's. When the Parliament of this union met at Erfurt in March 1850, Radowitz was the chief figure present. He failed, however, to conciliate the other European powers, as he hated the French Republic and was determined to exclude Russia from the Balkans and from the Near East. Furthermore, the Prussian Junkers themselves disliked the policy of adventure into which he was leading them. Radowitz thus could rely only on the hesitant Frederick William, and Prussia was diplomatically isolated.

Against the Erfurt Parliament, Austria revived the old Diet of the Confederation at Frankfurt. Then, in autumn 1850, revolution in Hesse-Kassel (*see* HESSE) precipitated a crisis between Austria and Prussia. The appointment of Radowitz as Prussian minister of foreign affairs in the last week of September seemed to be the prelude to war; but the other Prussian ministers resisted his policy, the Russian emperor Nicholas I exerted his influence on Austria's side, and Frederick William finally yielded to the pressure for a compromise. Radowitz resigned on Nov. 3 and was sent to London in a vain attempt to secure an alliance with Great Britain in exchange for tariff concessions. By the Austro-Prussian Convention of Olmütz (Nov. 29, 1850) the policy of Radowitz was completely discarded. Thenceforward Radowitz had no influence on Prussian affairs, though he retained the king's personal friendship. He died in Berlin, on Dec. 25, 1853, a disappointed man. He had prematurely anticipated the policy that Bismarck was to carry to success in the Seven Weeks' War of 1866.

RADZIWILL, a princely family of Lithuanian origin, conspicuous in Polish history. Its earliest known ancestor was Syrpuc, prince of Kiernow in 1280. Fourth in descent from him was Ostik (Krystian), who had a son Radvila, in Polish called Radziwill Ostikowicz (d. 1477). The latter's grandson MIKOLAJ I (d. 1509) was palatine of Wilno and chancellor of Lithuania from 1492.

MIKOLAJ II (1470–1522) succeeded his father Mikolaj I as palatine of Wilno and chancellor. In 1518 he led an embassy to the emperor Maximilian I, who on Feb. 25 made him a prince of the Holy Roman Empire, hoping that he would cease to support the transformation of the Polish-Lithuanian union from a personal into a real one. This Mikolaj had three brothers: JAN MIKOLAJ (d. 1522), castellan of Troki; WOJCIECH (1478–1519), bishop of Wilno; and JERZY (1480–1541), hetman of Lithuania in 1531 and commander in the wars against the Tatars, Muscovy, and the Teutonic Order.

Jerzy's daughter BARBARA (1520–1551) was first married to Stanislaw Gasztold, but after his death (1542) she became the mistress and then, secretly, the wife (1547) of the heir apparent to Poland and Lithuania, Sigismund Augustus. When he came to the throne (1548), his mother, Bona Sforza, and the Polish Senate demanded an annulment of the marriage, but he had Barbara crowned in 1550. The Radziwills became the virtual rulers of Lithuania.

MIKOLAJ the Black (1515–1565), Jan Mikolaj's son, marshal of Lithuania in 1544, chancellor from 1550 and palatine of Wilno from 1551, was an opponent of union with Poland. As Mikolaj I's children left no issue, the emperor Charles V on Dec. 10, 1547, transferred the imperial title of prince to him. Becoming a Calvinist, Mikolaj the Black promoted the Reformation in Lithuania and published the first Polish translation of the Bible (1563).

MIKOLAJ the Red (1512–1584), Barbara's brother, became a Calvinist in 1564 and was the leader of the non-Catholics in Lithuania after the death of Mikolaj the Black, whom he succeeded as palatine of Wilno and chancellor in 1566. Twice appointed hetman of Lithuania (1553 and 1576), he fought well in the wars against Muscovy. His son KRZYSZTOF MIKOLAJ (1547–1603), palatine of Wilno from 1584 and hetman of Lithuania from 1589, distinguished himself likewise against the Muscovites and also against the Swedes. Wanting to promote collaboration between the Protestants and the Orthodox Eastern Christians, he objected to the rapprochement of the latter with the Catholics in the Uniate Church.

Mikolaj the Black's sons, who returned to Catholicism and supported King Sigismund III's Counter-Reformation policy, were: MIKOLAJ KRZYSZTOF (1549–1616), marshal of Lithuania in 1579, a founder of monasteries, a patron of science, and the author of the vivid *Hierosolymitana peregrinatio* (1601; the narrative of a pilgrimage that he had made to Palestine); JERZY (1556–1600), bishop of Wilno and later of Cracow, a cardinal from 1584; ALBRYCHT (1558–1592), marshal in 1586; and STANISLAW the Pious (1559–99), marshal in 1592, but also a theologian. Stanislaw's son ALBRYCHT STANISLAW (1595–1656), chancellor of Lithuania from 1623, was a notable diplomat, published several works on religion, and left valuable memoirs (printed in 1839).

Krzysztof Mikolaj's sons JANUSZ (1579–1620) and KRZYSZTOF (1585–1640) maintained the Calvinist tradition. Janusz took part in Mikolaj Zebrzydowski's rebellion of 1606–07 against Sigismund III and inaugurated the Radziwills' links with the Hohenzollern dynasty by his marriage (1613) to Elizabeth Sophia, daughter of the elector John George of Brandenburg. Krzysztof, hetman of Lithuania in 1633, campaigned against the Swedes and Muscovites.

Krzysztof's son JANUSZ (1612–1655), leader of the Calvinists, ruled Lithuania almost as a sovereign. Palatine of Wilno (1653) and hetman of Lithuania (1654), he put the country under Swedish protection by an act signed at Kiejdany when Charles X Gustavus of Sweden invaded Poland (1655). His first cousin BOGUSLAW (1620–1669), son of the elder Janusz and last of the Calvinists, served Sweden and then Brandenburg (1656) against the Poles and made plans with Bohdan Chmielnicki and György Rákóczy II (*qq.v.*) for a partition of Poland. Frederick William of Brandenburg made him governor general of Ducal Prussia (1657).

Leadership of the family next passed to the Radziwills of the Nieswiez line, descendants of Mikolaj the Black's son Mikolaj Krzysztof. The latter's grandson MICHAL KAZIMIERZ (1625–1680), who married Katarzyna Sobieska, sister of the future king John III (*q.v.*), in 1658 and became palatine of Wilno in 1667 and hetman and vice-chancellor of Lithuania in 1668, was active in the military and diplomatic struggle against the Turks. His son KAROL STANISLAW (1669–1719), chancellor of Lithuania from 1698, took the Saxon side in the Northern War (*q.v.*). Karol Stanislaw's son MICHAL KAZIMIERZ (1702–62), whose immense wealth and popularity among the nobles greatly helped the Saxon dynasty in the War of the Polish Succession (*q.v.*), became palatine of Wilno and hetman in 1744; his first wife, née Urszula Wisniowecka (1705–53), was a prolific dramatist and the first in Poland to imitate Molière. Their son KAROL STANISLAW (1734–1790), who in 1762 succeeded to the palatinate of Wilno, was an enemy of the house of Czartoryski (*q.v.*) and led a private army to oppose the election of Stanislaw August Poniatowski as king of Poland (Stanislaw II) in 1764. Driven into exile, he reappeared in 1767 at the head of the Russian-sponsored Confederation of Radom, hoping that it would lead to a restoration of the Saxon dynasty. Disillusioned, he next joined the patriotic Confederation of Bar (*q.v.*), but soon had to emigrate again. He recovered his lands in 1776.

After the partitions of Poland ANTONI HENRYK (1775–1833), of the fifth generation from the first Michal Kazimierz's brother Dominik Mikolaj, was married in 1796 to Louisa Frederica of Prussia. In the Napoleonic Wars he twice tried to detach the Poles from the French (1806–07 and 1813), with the idea of a restored Poland under Prussian protection. He was lieutenant governor of Prussian Poznania from 1815 to 1831 and was also a composer of music. His sons WILHELM (1797–1870) and BOGUSLAW (1809–1873) were members of the Prussian *Herrenhaus.* Boguslaw's son FERDYNAND (1834–1926) sat in the German *Reichstag* from 1879 to 1918 and was for many years chairman of the Polish party in it.

In Poland after World War I, Ferdynand's son JANUSZ KSAWERY (1880–1967) led the Conservatives and contributed to their rapprochement with Jozef Pilsudski. His son STANISLAW (1914–) was married in 1959 to Caroline Lee Bouvier, sister-in-law of the future U.S. president John F. Kennedy.   (EM. R.)

RAE, JOHN (1813–1893), Scottish Arctic explorer who surveyed and mapped new coast lines of Arctic Canada, was born on Sept. 30, 1813, in the Orkney Islands. He studied medicine at Edinburgh University and was for 10 years resident surgeon at the Hudson's Bay Company's station at Moose Factory. In 1846 he voyaged to Repulse Bay, and the next spring surveyed 700 mi. of new coast line connecting the earlier surveys of J. C. Ross and W. E. Parry. He then joined Sir John Richardson's expedition in search of Sir John Franklin. During 1851 he traveled about 5,300 mi. and explored and mapped 700 mi. of new coast on the south side of Wollaston and Victoria Lands, a feat which gained him the gold medal of the Royal Geographical Society. In 1853 he commanded another expedition which proved King William Land to be an island and elicited the first definite information as to the fate of Franklin. Subsequently he traveled across Iceland, and in Greenland and northern America. He died July 22, 1893, in London. He wrote *A Narrative of an Expedition to the Shores of the Arctic Sea in 1846 and 1847* (1850).   (H. G. KG.)

RAE BARELI, a municipal town and district in the Lucknow division of Uttar Pradesh, India. The town, headquarters of the district, lies on the Sai River, 45 mi. (72 km.) SSE of Lucknow. Pop. (1961) 29,940. It has many architectural features, chief of which is a large brick fort built by Ibrahim Shah in the 15th century. Among other ancient monuments are the palace and tomb of Nawab Jahan Khan, governor under Shah Jahan, and four fine mosques including the Jamma Masjid and the mosque without domes which is a copy of the Ka'ba in Mecca. The town is at the junction of several metaled roads and is an important station on the main railway from Amritsar to Mughal Sarai. It is a trade centre for agricultural products and is well known for its handloom cloth and muslins.

RAE BARELI DISTRICT (area 1,758 sq.mi. [4,553 sq.km.]; pop. [1961] 1,314,949) is slightly undulating and well wooded. The soil is remarkably fertile and the cultivation of a high order, the main crops being rice, pulses, wheat, barley, and millet. The principal rivers are the Ganges (Ganga) and the Sai.   (B. Si.)

RAEBURN, SIR HENRY (1756–1823), the leading Scottish portrait painter after Allan Ramsay, was born at Stockbridge,

SIR HENRY RAEBURN, A SELF-PORTRAIT. IN THE NATIONAL GALLERIES OF SCOTLAND

near Edinburgh, on March 4, 1756. He became a scholar of Heriot's Hospital and in about 1771 was apprenticed to the goldsmith James Gilliland. He is said to have met the seal-engraver David Deuchar in 1773, and the leading Edinburgh portrait painter David Martin in 1775, but for the most part he was self-taught, progressing from miniature painting to full-scale portraiture. A full-length presentation portrait of George Chalmers of 1776 (Dunfermline Town Council) is Raeburn's earliest known portrait, and its faulty drawing and incorrect perspective suggest the artist's lack of formal training. By his marriage to Ann Edgar, a rich widow, early in 1780 he achieved financial security and during the next four years considerably improved his artistic skill. In London in 1785 he met Sir Joshua Reynolds, whose works were already familiar to him from Scottish collections and engravings, en route for a prolonged tour of Italy whence he returned to Edinburgh in 1787.

His reappearance was opportune; the rising professional classes of Edinburgh could support a gifted portrait painter and these, with members of the old Highland families, provided him enough sitters. Unlike Ramsay, he never needed to go south in search of patronage. The portrait of "The Archers" (trustees of the late Viscount Novar), of Robert and Ronald Ferguson of Raith, was probably painted soon after his return, and is an ingeniously composed group already showing something of the broad, assured style of his maturity. This concern with elaborate composition was afterward to give place to greater simplicity and directness of presentation. By about 1790 he had painted the outstanding portrait of his wife (Countess Mountbatten collection), a finely characterized work of expressive simplicity, and the double portrait of Sir John and Lady Clerk (Sir Alfred Beit collection), in which the artist experimented with an unusual lighting from behind the sitters' heads (they are in an evening landscape setting) to bring out the character of their faces.

During the years 1790–1800 Raeburn produced some of his most brilliant portraits, such as the dramatic full-length "Sir John Sinclair" (c. 1794–95, Viscount Thurso), a romantic composition of a uniformed Highland laird seen against a mountainous landscape background. This foreshadowed the famous "The MacNab" (c. 1803–13, John Dewar and Sons, Ltd.), in which the tonalities became darker and the lighting even more contrasted. It is significant that no drawings by Raeburn survive; he was essentially a painter rather than a draughtsman. This accounts for the weak drawing of the hands in several of his portraits; he is said to have begun his portraits with the brush, without any preliminary drawing on the canvas. After 1800, he concentrated upon the heads and hands of his sitters, reducing to the absolute minimum all accessories and preferring a dark background to set off his subjects. His technique broadened and he used a vigorous, square brushstroke with which boldly to model in the features of his sitters. Although this was often extremely effective, as in the "Lord Newton" (1806–11, earl of Rosebery collection) or "Mrs. James Campbell" (c. 1805–12, Colonel Thomas, Glasgow), in his less successful works it became brash and vulgar. Some softening of his brushwork appeared in the last ten years of his career.

In 1810, after the death of John Hoppner, he revisited London with the intention of seeing whether he could establish himself there, but did not pursue this plan. Two years later he was elected president of the Edinburgh Society of Artists, becoming a Royal Academician in 1815. Knighted in 1822, he was appointed His Majesty's limner for Scotland. He died at Edinburgh on July 8, 1823. In many ways Raeburn fulfilled in Scotland the position Reynolds had earlier achieved in London. A popular member of the new cultured Edinburgh society, he rarely associated with fellow artists; he was a man of many interests and a good conversationalist.

BIBLIOGRAPHY.—William Raeburn Andrew, *Life of Sir Henry Raeburn, R. A.,* 2nd ed. (1894); Sir Walter Armstrong, *Sir Henry Raeburn,* etc. (1907) with catalogue; J. Greig, *Sir Henry Raeburn,* etc. (1911); *Ramsay, Raeburn and Wilkie,* exhibition catalogue, Scottish National Gallery (1951); *Raeburn: Bicentenary Exhibition* catalogue, Scottish National Gallery (1956).　　(D. L. Fr.)

RAEDWALD (REDWALD) (d. between 616 and 628), king of the East Angles, was son of Tyttla and grandson of Wuffa. He became a Christian during a visit to the court of his overlord, Aethelberht of Kent, but reverted to paganism on his return, contenting himself with placing an altar to Christ in the same temple as one for the sacrifice to idols. Before Aethelberht's death in 616, Raedwald began to wrest from him the supremacy over the lands south of the Humber and is counted among the Bretwaldas. By his wife's advice he refused to surrender or kill at the request of Aethelfrith of Northumbria the heir to the throne of Deira, Edwin, who had entered his service when in exile. With his support Edwin defeated and killed Aethelfrith at the battle by the River Idle (Nottinghamshire) in 616. Raedwald's son Raegenhere was also

killed. Another son, Eorpwald, succeeded him, not later than 628.

See Bede, *Historia Ecclesiastica,* bk. ii, ch. 5, 12, 15; F. M. Stenton, *Anglo-Saxon England,* 2nd ed. (1947).　　(D. Wk.)

RAEMAEKERS, LOUIS (1869–1956), Dutch cartoonist who gained international fame by his anti-German cartoons during World War I, was born at Roermond on April 6, 1869. He at first painted landscapes and portraits. His first political cartoons appeared in 1907 and he joined the *Amsterdam Telegraaf* in 1909. The sincerity and vigour of his wartime cartoons roused enthusiasm in England, France, and the United States and after 1916 he lived for some years in England to supply the Allied Press more easily. He was also a cartoonist during World War II. He died at Scheveningen near The Hague on July 26, 1956.

RAETIA (so always on inscriptions; in classical manuscripts usually RHAETIA) was a Roman province comprising Vorarlberg and Tirol in modern Austria, the eastern cantons of Switzerland, and parts of Bavaria and Württemberg in Germany. The tradition (*see* Livy, v, 33) that the Raeti were Etruscan can be disregarded, except that there were Etruscan elements in their language: the primitive inhabitants were Illyrian, but Celtic elements predominated early. Roman conquest was carried out in 15 B.C. by Augustus' stepsons Tiberius and Drusus (*qq.v.*), the former operating from Lake of Constance, the latter from the Resia Pass; and the country's subjection was quickly made decisive by road building. Initially there were possibly two legions at Oberhausen near Augsburg, and consequently a senatorial governor. But these troops were withdrawn, probably when advance in Germany was abandoned in A.D. 9, and the province was administered by a Roman knight (called at first *praefectus* and later *procurator*), with a garrison (including native levies) totaling perhaps 9,000 men. With Raetia was coupled Vindelicia (*q.v.*), and the Vallis Poenina (modern Valais) was for about a century under the Raetian governor's control.

The southern boundary of the territory was the Alpine summit, leaving Tridentum (Trento) in Italy; on the east was Noricum (*q.v.*); on the west the frontier with Gallia Belgica ran west of Lake of Constance. Under the Flavians the northern frontier, till then on the Danube, was pushed forward to join the new line of fortifications on the Neckar River, and in Hadrian's time the perfected *limes Raeticus* (*see* LIMES) ran in a convex formation of forts to near Castra Regina (Regensburg). Under Marcus Aurelius, who was faced with new barbarian threats, a legion (*legio III Italica*) was stationed at Regensburg, and its senatorial commander became governor of the province. The 3rd-century invasions pressed heavily on Raetia. As early as 234 the Alamanni were attacking the *limes;* and its western sector was withdrawn south of Lake of Constance about 260 and possibly never restored to its old line, though Castra Regina was maintained. For a generation after this there was almost constant fighting in northern Raetia. In the 4th century the province (divided into two by Diocletian) was firmly held, but by 450 the whole country down to the Alps had passed into barbarian possession.

The Roman roads of Raetia illustrate its importance for communications between Italy and the Danube and between Gaul and the Balkans. In 47 Claudius as emperor completed the Via Claudia Augusta along the route of his father's conquest, up the Adige Valley and across the Resia to Augsburg and the Danube; and under Septimius Severus a road was carried across the Brenner Pass. Another great highway from Brigantium (Bregenz) to Curia Raetorum (Chur) was continued over the Splügen Pass to Mediolanum (Milan), though its date of construction is unknown. For its culture Raetia looked more to Gaul and the Rhineland than to the other Danubian provinces. The northern area (including that between Danube and *limes*) was rich in timber, pitch, and iron; but the economic value of the province as a whole was small, and its romanization went much less deep than that of the neighbouring province of Noricum.

BIBLIOGRAPHY.—J. Whatmough, *The Foundations of Roman Italy,* ch. 7 (1937); F. Stähelin, *Die Schweiz in römischer Zeit,* 3rd ed. (1948); W. W. Hyde, *Roman Alpine Routes* (1935). (G. E. F. C.)

RAETO-ROMANCE DIALECTS are spoken by about 450,000 persons in the Alpine regions of southeastern Switzerland and northern Italy, including the Friuli region. They do not cover a contiguous area; they do not now and never did belong to a single cultural, administrative or linguistic unit; and they are not written in any single standard language. They are also not founded upon the same pre-Latin linguistic substratum, nor do they have the same linguistic superstratum. Apart from being all Romance, that is, Neo-Latin dialects, they owe their being classified together under one name not so much to their similarities, which merely suffice to set them off from all other Romance dialects, as to their geographic location. The term Raeto-Romance (RR) has, therefore, been contested on various grounds; for example: it had little to do with the Latin province called Raetia, which covered a larger surface, though not so dispersed; it had even less to do with a pre-Roman population called Raeti, whose dialect, imperfectly known, forms the substratum of only a small part of RR; all dialects concerned should be called Ladin in order to avoid Raetic connotations, and RR should be restricted to the dialects of Switzerland; the term RR should be abandoned altogether because all dialects concerned are really Italian: the western of the Lombard group and the eastern of the Venetian group. All these terminological disagreements bedevil the linguistic literature, which must, therefore, be used with proper caution. National animosities and disputes, many still alive, have penetrated (linguistic) research, particularly regarding the districts of northeastern Italy: the Alto Adige (the former Austrian South Tirol) and Friuli.

The RR dialects are spoken in three major areas: (1) In Friuli, the region between the Alps and the head of the Adriatic sea, with the capital at Udine. This idiom is called Friulian. It accounts for over 90% of the total number of speakers of RR. (2) In some valleys of the Alto Adige region, east and west of the city of Bolzano, and in some parts of the Dolomites. This idiom may be called Ladin. (3) In parts of the Swiss canton Grisons (Graubünden), in particular in the valleys of the two confluents of the Rhine (the Vorderrhein and the Hinterrhein), and of the Inn (the Engadine, Upper and Lower), approximately as far as the Austrian border. These dialects are called Romansh (or, in the native tongue, Grishun) and may be subdivided into Surselvan (Vorderrhein), Sutselvan (Hinterrhein) and Engadinian (Inn).

There is no doubt that at one time the area of RR was much larger. But owing to the absence of documentation it is difficult to learn when a given district changed to another type of speech, Italian or German. In many areas, however, the switch is relatively recent. For example, the Inn valley between Finstermünz, Switz., and Imst, Aus., from the Swiss border halfway to Innsbruck, spoke RR until the 16th century; there were Romance minorities in the Vintschgau as late as the 18th century and in some villages into the 19th; Innsbruck did not become wholly German-speaking until the 13th century, and Vorarlberg, Aus., even later, especially the Montafon (valley of the Ill river); the Rhine valley past Liechtenstein, and the Wallensee area west of it, were Romance until the 11th century; Chur, the capital of the Grisons, was prevalently of Romance speech until the beginning of the 15th century.

The retreat of RR before Italian and German continues under the impact of the national languages which have greater prestige and currency. Friulian will probably cede to standard Italian, as will all dialects of the state of Italy; whether Ladin will be replaced by German or Italian is not certain: it is spoken within the Italian state, but its nearest and most influential neighbouring language is German (Austrian-Bavarian) of Bolzano-Merano. Romansh of Switzerland is in a slightly more favourable situation; it is spoken in a country where local dialects, both Germanic (Alamannic) and Romance, are not considered socially inferior but cultivated and cherished. Romansh has also been best described of all the RR dialects, has been codified in dictionaries and grammars, has a literature (including a translation of the New Testament of 1560) and has in fact been the fourth official language of Switzerland since 1938.

Ethnically the area of RR has been mixed and unstable from prehistoric times. Because of its passes it has always served as the crossroads between east and west, and north and south; and because of its inaccessible valleys and heights it has likewise served as a refuge for populations driven in war from more hospitable surrounding regions. Preceding its Latinization it was most likely of Celtic and Raetic speech in its western parts, of Italic (Venetic) speech in its eastern parts. But it is impossible to draw sure boundaries for these linguistic substrata or to give dates for their Latinization. The political conquest of the district of Friulian, a part of Gallia Cisalpina, occurred around 220 B.C., but the Alpine area of Ladin and Romansh was not conquered until 15 B.C., when it became in part the province of Raetia.

All these beautiful but poor mountainous tracts, Raetia, Noricum, Vindelicia, seem to have interested the Romans mainly for logistic reasons, in order to keep open communications with Gallia Transalpina and other northern and western possessions. Hence these regions were neither as intensively nor as extensively Romanized in culture and speech as other parts of the Roman empire which are now Romance-speaking. Furthermore, the Alpine provinces were the first to fall before the onslaught of the Germanic tribes which invaded Roman soil in the 5th century: the Alamanni pushed south across Switzerland about the end of the 5th century; the Baiuwarii crossed the Brenner pass, reaching the upper Isarco valley about 600 and the Bolzano-Merano district around 765. Friuli was the territory through which the invading Ostrogoths and Visigoths moved into Italy; it became eventually a Langobardic possession, but it was no more Germanized by these German tribes than was the rest of Italy. If the Germans had been better organized and if they had pursued a common goal, such as a Germanic state on the soil of the Roman empire, the entire RR area, if not, indeed, large portions of Italy, might have become Germanic in speech. Or if the speakers of the different RR districts had formed a coherent political whole, the various RR idioms might eventually have brought forth a separate standard Romance language. In view of the extremely checkered history of the area throughout the middle ages and into the modern era, the linguistic situation has become difficult to analyze.

The few linguistic traits common to all RR languages are archaisms rather than common innovations. This testifies to a lack of communication among them and the absence of a common culture. The greatest amount of agreement is to be found in the vocabularies of the various dialects; but this is not very significant, since they are all of Latin origin. In phonology the retention of Latin final -s over large areas is important both phonemically and morphemically. In the latter respect it causes plural formations with -s, thus connecting RR with the western, Gallo-Romance languages. Otherwise the retention of pl-, kl- (cl-) and bl- (rather than palatalization, as prevails in Italian and Rumanian), the palatalization of ka- (ca-) and ga-, and the diphthongization of vowels in free (that is, syllable-final) position are widespread but far from ubiquitous. Of all the Romance idioms, the RR languages have been least studied because of the scarcity of records of the medieval and even modern period and the absence of any standard literary language or languages. Outside of Switzerland all RR speech is considered mere patois. The description of contemporary speech awaits modern scientific treatment; but it will have to be undertaken soon, lest RR go the way of other now extinct Romance speech forms.

BIBLIOGRAPHY.—G. I. Ascoli, "Saggi ladini," *Archivio glottologico italiano,* vol. i, pp. 1–326 (1873); C. Battisti, *Popoli e lingue dell'Alto Adige* (1931), *Storia della questione ladina* (1937); R. Brandstetter, *Rätoromanische Forschungen* (1905); B. Gerola, *Correnti linguistiche e dialetti neolatini nell'area retica* (1939); G. Marchetti, *Lineamenti di grammatica friulana* (1952); R. von Planta, *Dicziunari Rumantsch Grischun* (1938), "Ueber Ortsnamen, Sprach- und Landesgeschichte von Graubünden," *Revue de linguistique romane,* vol. 7, pp. 80–100 (1931); G. A. Stampa, *Der Dialekt von Bergell* (1934). (E. Pm.)

RAFF, (JOSEPH) JOACHIM (1822–1882), Swiss composer who wrote in the style of Mendelssohn and Liszt, wrote over 300 works including 11 symphonies, chamber music, and choral works, and many piano pieces. He was long known for his "Cavatina" for the violin. Born on May 27, 1822, at Lachen, Lake of Zürich, Raff became a schoolteacher at Rapperswill in 1840 and taught himself the piano, violin, and composition. In 1844 he went to Zürich where he devoted himself to composition and teaching.

In 1848 the pianist Hans von Bülow played Raff's *Concertstück* at Stuttgart. In 1850 Raff went to Weimar where his opera *König Alfred* was given the following year. Between 1856 and 1877 he was a piano teacher at Wiesbaden, producing during this period seven symphonies and his comic opera *Dame Kobold*. In 1877 he was appointed director of the Konservatorium at Frankfurt am Main and died there on the night of June 24–25, 1882.

See Helene Raff, *Joachim Raff* (1925).

RAFFI (pseudonym of HAKOB MELIQ-HAKOBIAN) (1835–1888), the most celebrated Armenian novelist, was born in Phayajuk, in Iranian Azerbaijan, the eldest son of a merchant. After his father's bankruptcy in 1868, he worked as a schoolmaster and a journalist, collaborating with the Russian-Armenian paper *Mshak* from 1872 to 1884. He died in Tiflis, where he is buried. His principal novels are *Jalaleddin* (1878), *The Fool* (1880; Eng. trans. 1950), *David Bek* (1880), *The Golden Cockerel* (1882), *Sparks* (1883–1890), and *Samuel* (1885). He wrote also a number of short stories and historical articles.

An ardent nationalist, he was preoccupied with the lot of his fellow Armenians in Persia and Turkey, and his interest in history was that of a writer of the Romantic school. He had a fertile imagination and narrative skill, but the psychology of his characters tends to be shallow, and the construction and style of his work uneven.   (C. J. F. D.)

RAFFIA, a fibrous product obtained from the palm *Raphia pedunculata* of Madagascar. It is prepared from the leaves of the palm, which are cut before they begin to curl. The underpart is removed in strips and dried, after which the strips can be split easily from end to end in any desired width.

Raffia is used in connection with the tongue grafting method of tree or shrub propagation. A tongue cut on the face of the scion (cion) is fitted into a matching notch on the parent stock, and scion and stock are securely bound together with raffia.

Raffia is also widely used in basketry, particularly in the sewing of coiled reed or plaited rush baskets. It may also be woven in the conventional manner by passing it under and over warp strings on a loom.

Raffia can be satisfactorily dyed with vegetable colourings, such as those derived from barks, leaves, berries, and flower petals.
                                                                         (E. L. Y.)

RAFFLES, SIR THOMAS STAMFORD (1781–1826), British colonial governor and founder of Singapore, was born on board his father's merchantman, off Port Morant, Jamaica, on July 6, 1781. Educated at the Mansion House Boarding School, Hammersmith, London, he entered the service of the East India Company in 1795, was appointed a permanent clerk in 1800, and, five years later, was posted as assistant secretary to the presidency government of Prince of Wales Island (Penang, Malaya).

He arrived there on Sept. 19, 1805, and became secretary to the government 18 months later. His heavy official duties soon undermined his health, but during a period of recuperative leave at Malacca between August and October 1808, he prepared a long report which argued so convincingly against the company's proposal to abandon the settlement that orders for the evacuation were countermanded.

The report on Malacca brought Raffles under the notice of the Bengal authorities, and in June 1810 he visited Calcutta, where he was received cordially by the governor-general, Lord Minto. In October, Britain being at war with France, which had occupied the Netherlands, he was appointed agent with the Malay States to prepare the way for the British invasion of Java.

The British expeditionary force under Sir Samuel Auchmuty, and accompanied by Lord Minto, consisted of about 11,000 troops, transported in 57 ships. On Raffles' recommendation the fleet sailed by the direct passage through the Karimata Strait and arrived safely off Java in July 1811. Batavia (Jakarta) was occupied without opposition, and the combined Dutch-French forces under Jan Willem Janssens, the governor-general, were defeated at Meester Cornelis on Aug. 26.

Lord Minto's instructions were to withdraw the British forces from Java after its reduction, but, as he felt repugnance at leaving unarmed Dutch colonists at the mercy of the Indonesians, he established a provisional British administration with Raffles as lieutenant governor. Thereafter, until his departure in March 1816, Raffles' energies were devoted to the task of reforming the Dutch colonial system. This system, which aimed at the collection of tropical produce by means of forced deliveries and contingents, was closely geared to the Indonesian economic and social organization; it appeared to Raffles, however, to be based upon forced labour and compulsion, so he attempted to substitute in its place a land rent system, founded on principles of free cultivation. The new system was designed not only to supply the treasury with much needed funds, but, by establishing a money economy, to throw open Java to British manufacturers. In both objectives it failed during the short-lived British administration, but the system was important in giving direction for future colonial reform under the Dutch, who returned to Indonesia in 1816.

Raffles arrived back in England in July 1816 and was elected a fellow of the Royal Society in March 1817. His book, *The History of Java*, was published in May 1817, and he was knighted shortly afterward. In November he sailed to take up his appointment as lieutenant governor of Ft. Marlborough (Bengkulu, Sumatra).

During his Sumatran administration, Raffles attempted to reform the system of forced pepper cultivation in the company's districts, and at the same time made a number of unsuccessful efforts to prevent the restoration of the Dutch to Padang and elsewhere in the island. In the belief that British influence should be extended in southeast Asia, he sailed for Bengal in September 1818 in order to draw the attention of the governor-general, Lord Hastings, to the aggressive nature of Dutch policy in the region. He quickly gained Hastings' confidence and was instructed to establish a settlement at the southern entrance to the Malacca Strait. There, on Feb. 6, 1819, he raised the British flag on the island of Singapore (*q.v.*). After a brief period of absence at Benkoelen, he returned to Singapore in October 1822, when he organized the various branches of the administration. He left the East for England in April 1824, secure in the knowledge that Singapore was a flourishing free-trade port.

Raffles died at his country house at Highwood, near Barnet, on July 5, 1826. Before his death he helped to found the London Zoological Society, of which he was the first president.

BIBLIOGRAPHY.—Lady Sophia Raffles, *Memoir of the Life and Public Services of Sir T. S. Raffles* (1830); D. C. Boulger, *The Life of Sir Stamford Raffles* (1897); C. E. Wurtzburg, *Raffles of the Eastern Isles* (1954); J. Bastin, *The Native Policies of Sir Stamford Raffles in Java and Sumatra* (1957).   (J. S. BN.)

RAFFLESIA, a genus of six species of plants native to the forested mountains of Malaya. They are of interest for their bizarre flowers, the largest known in the world. The plants, having no green parts, are parasitic on species of *Tetrastigma*, mammoth woody vines belonging to the grape family. The sticky seeds of *Rafflesia* germinate in the rough bark of the basal stems of *Tetrastigma*, which lie on the ground. Each seed produces threadlike strands that penetrate the stem and absorb nourishment. The new plant produces a small flower bud soon after the seed germinates, but forms no stem, leaves, or true roots. About nine months later the fully opened flower is 15–28 in. across (some reports give 3 ft.) and weighs 12–24 lb.; it remains open for five to seven days. Each flower, either male or female, has five limp, fleshy, petallike segments, coloured reddish- or purplish-brown and sometimes mottled. The sex organs are inside a partially covered central cup, coloured fiery red. The flowers emit a fetid odour of rotting meat. Pollination is believed to be effected by carrion-feeding flies attracted by the odour, and seed dissemination is thought to be accomplished by fruit-eating rodents.

                                                                         (G. H. M. L.)

RAFINESQUE, CONSTANTINE SAMUEL (1783–1840), a naturalist and early theorizer about the evolution of species, was born of French-German parents at Galata (Constantinople) on Oct. 22, 1783. He lived in Marseilles and after 1792 in Italy, studying in Leghorn, Genoa, and Padua. In 1802 he went with his brother to the United States. He worked in Philadelphia and Germantown, Pa., visited Pres. Thomas Jefferson at Washington, and made many trips in search of natural history specimens.

In 1805 he returned to Europe, spending the next ten years in Palermo, Sicily. In 1815 he returned to the United States, where he taught and made botanical collections. In 1819 he became professor of botany, materia medica, and modern languages at the Transylvania University, Lexington, Ky., where he founded a botanical garden in 1825. In 1826 he moved to Philadelphia where he lectured at the Franklin Institute. He died in poverty in Philadelphia on Sept. 18, 1840.

Rafinesque was a controversial figure in the history of U.S. botany. He was severely criticized by such an authority as Asa Gray (*q.v.*) for careless work and his passion for establishing new genera and species. On the other hand, he was lauded as a genius who had a definite idea about the theory of evolution long before Charles Darwin.

His publications numbered more than 950; the most important among his botanical works are: *Autikon botanikon* (1815–40, facs. ed., 1942); *Florula ludoviciana* (1817); *Medical Flora,* 2 vol. (1828–30); *New Flora and Botany of North America,* 4 pt. (1836–38); *Flora telluriana,* 4 vol. (1837–38); *American Manual of the Mulberry Trees* (1839) and *Sylva telluriana* (1838, facs. ed., 1942). He also wrote *A Life of Travels and Researches* (1836, facs. ed. 1943).

See T. J. Fitzpatrick, *Rafinesque, a Sketch of his Life with Bibliography* (1911) and F. W. Pennell, *The Life and Work of Rafinesque* (1942). (V. C. As.)

RAGES: *see* RAY.

RAGLAN, FITZROY JAMES HENRY SOMERSET,

1ST BARON (1788–1855), British field marshal, commander in chief of British troops during the Crimean War, was born at Badminton, Gloucestershire, on Sept. 30, 1788, the youngest son of Henry, 5th duke of Beaufort. He was first commissioned in 1804 and at the outbreak of the Peninsular War in 1808 went to Portugal as aide-de-camp to Sir Arthur Wellesley (afterward 1st duke of Wellington) with whom he remained closely associated for much of his military service. Somerset was wounded at Bussaco (1810) and distinguished himself at the storming of Badajoz (1812); in the Waterloo campaign (1815) he received a wound which necessitated the amputation of his right arm. He had been military secretary to Wellington from 1810 to 1814 and served him again in this capacity when the duke became master general of the ordnance in 1818, retaining the position in 1827 when Wellington became commander in chief. His tact, urbanity, punctuality, and accuracy made him invaluable to the duke. When Wellington died in September 1852, Somerset became master general of the ordnance and in October was raised to the peerage as Baron Raglan of Raglan. In 1854 he was appointed commander in chief of the British expeditionary force sent to Turkey and to the Crimea.

In his conduct of the campaign in the Crimea, which has always been much criticized, he was severely hampered by the neglect of successive British governments to equip the army for long and arduous military service, and by the necessity of cooperating with intransigent allied commanders. It was against his judgment that the British, French, and Turkish forces were sent to the Crimea in September 1854 to attack the strong naval fortress of Sevastopol. After the victory at the Alma (Sept. 20) he was opposed to the march around Sevastopol to besiege the city from the south, favouring instead an immediate assault from the north, but for the sake of allied unity and cooperation he agreed to the views of the French military commanders on this and later occasions.

After the battles of Balaklava (Oct. 25, 1854) and Inkerman (Nov. 5), in the second of which Raglan showed great personal courage and leadership, he was made a field marshal. His troops had then to endure a fierce winter without proper clothing, supplies, or accommodation, all of which it was the government's responsibility to supply. Although Raglan was made the target of much ill-informed and partisan criticism, he refused to justify himself at the expense of his staff or the government in England. With the advent of better weather early in 1855, the siege of Sevastopol was more vigorously pressed, but a combined assault on June 18 by the allied armies was repulsed with heavy loss. Raglan was then gravely ill and this failure so aggravated his weakness that

he died in the camp before Sevastopol on June 28, 1855, "the victim," wrote Gen. Sir Evelyn Wood, "of England's unreadiness for war." He was buried on July 26, 1855, at Badminton.

See C. Hibbert, *The Destruction of Lord Raglan* (1961). (E. W. SH.)

RAGNAR LODBROK (fl. 9th century A.D.), a Viking hero, appears first as a purely genealogical figure. In the English *Annals of St. Neots* (early 12th century) he is the father of Inwaer (Ivar the Boneless) and Hubba (Ubbe), Scandinavian brothers who attacked England in the 9th century. Slightly earlier, the German historian Adam of Bremen (*c.* 1075) made him father of Inwaer, and William of Jumièges (*Gesta Normannorum ducum, c.* 1070) thought him father of a Viking, Berno (Bjorn), who appears in continental annals in 855 and 858. Modern authorities have added to Ragnar's sons Sigefridus, who figures in continental annals from 873 onward, and some have attempted to give Ragnar further historicity by identifying him with Reginherus, a Viking who invaded France in 845.

In history, therefore, Ragnar is little more than a genealogical figure. Later sources, however, surround his name with legend to a remarkable degree. So, in the *Gesta Danorum* (*c.* 1185) of Saxo Grammaticus (*q.v.*), he is a 9th-century Danish king, whose wars and expeditions are detailed at great length and include a clash with Charlemagne. Ragnar was ultimately captured by the Anglo-Saxon king Aella of Northumbria and cast into a snake pit to perish. His sons later avenged him. This story also appears in the Icelandic version of Ragnar's legendary history, given in the very late works *Ragnarssaga* and *Tháttr af Ragnarssonum.* These works retail a version of the legend generally agreeing with that upon which the violent 12th-century poem *Krákumál* is based. In this version Ragnar links history with legend by marrying a daughter of Sigurd (Siegfried) and Brynhild (Brunhild).

Ragnar may be the Lodbrok mentioned in a runic inscription found in the Orkneys, apparently claiming that a how (barrow) was built to commemorate him.

BIBLIOGRAPHY.—A. Mawer, "Ragnar Lothbrók and His Sons," and A. H. Smith, "The Sons of Ragnar Lothbrok, *Saga Book of the Viking Society,* vol. vi (1908–09) and xi, part ii (1935); J. de Vries, "Die historischen Grundlagen der Ragnarssaga Lothbrókar," *Arkiv för nordisk Filologi,* vol. xxxix (1923); *The Saga of the Volsungs: the Saga of Ragnar Lodbrok together with The Lay of Kraka,* Eng. trans. by M. Schlauch (1930). (AL. C.)

RAGNARÖK, in Scandinavian mythology, the name for the end of the world of gods and men. The word means literally "Doom of Gods." A later form, *Ragnarökkr,* meaning "Dusk [Twilight] of Gods," was adopted by Richard Wagner for his opera *Götterdämmerung.*

The Ragnarök is fully described only in the Icelandic poem *Völuspá* ("Sibyl's Prophecy"), probably of the late 10th century (*see* ICELANDIC LITERATURE: *Mythological Lays*); and in the 13th-century *Prose Edda* (*see* EDDA) of Snorri Sturluson (d. 1241), which largely follows the *Völuspá.* It will be preceded by cruel winters and moral chaos. Giants and demons approaching from all points of the compass will attack the gods, who will meet them and face death like heroes. The sun will be darkened, the stars vanish, and the earth sink into the sea. Afterward earth will rise again; the innocent Baldr (*see* BALDER) will return, and the hosts of the just will live in a hall roofed with gold. (*See* also GERMANIC MYTHOLOGY AND HEROIC LEGENDS.)

Disjointed allusions to the Ragnarök, found in many other sources, show that conceptions of it varied. According to one poem two human beings, Líf and Lífthrasir ("Life" and "Life-holding"), will survive it and repeople the earth. It is widely held that Scandinavian conceptions of the Ragnarök were influenced by Christian and Oriental conceptions of the Day of Doom. (G. T.-P.)

RAGUSA, a town and capital of Ragusa Province, Sicily, stands in the Iblei (Hyblaei) Hills above the gorge of the Irminio River in the southeastern tip of the island, 69 mi. (111 km.) WSW of Syracuse by rail and 54 mi. (87 km.) by road. Pop. (1961) 57,260 (commune). The upper (modern) town is separated from the lower town (on the site of the ancient Hybla Heraea) by a declivity. After an earthquake in 1693 had destroyed most of the old town a new town was built to the west, the two communes created after the earthquake being united in 1926. Handsome Baroque buildings include the cathedral (1706–60) and the Basilica of S. Giorgio (1738–75). Some 15th-century fragments survive in Sta. Maria delle Scale and the portal of S. Giorgio Vecchio. Already noted for its nearby asphalt mines, Ragusa's petroleum wells made it the principal Italian oil-bearing zone by the end of the 1960s. Cement is also manufactured. The town, formerly an agricultural centre, has asphalt products and a polythene plant.

RAGUSA PROVINCE comprises the western half of the southeastern tip of Sicily. Area 623 sq.mi. (1,614 sq.km.). Pop. (1961) 248,585. (M. T. A. N.)

RAGWEED, any North American plant of the genus *Ambrosia* (family Compositae). The ragweeds are chiefly coarse annuals, with rough hairy stems, mostly lobed or divided leaves, and inconspicuous greenish flowers borne in small heads, the male in terminal spikes and the female in the upper axils of the leaves. The common ragweed (*A. artemisiifolia*), called also Roman wormwood, hogweed, and bitterweed, found across the continent, grows from one to seven feet high, with thin, alternate or opposite, much-divided leaves. The great ragweed (*A. trifida*), called also bitterweed and horse cane, native from Quebec to British Columbia and southward to Florida, Arkansas, and California, grows from 3 to 17 ft. tall, with opposite, entire, or palmately three- to five-lobed leaves. Both the foregoing are annuals and often become pernicious weeds; their pollen, which is shed in great abundance in late summer, is a prolific source of hay fever (*q.v.*). Since these species are annuals, their eradication is easy if they are mowed well before they shed their copious seed. The western ragweed (*A. psilostachya*), found from Illinois to Alberta and southward to California, Texas, and Mexico, is similar to the common ragweed, but is a shorter plant, perennial, and with thicker leaves. All the ragweeds can be killed with 2,4-D. (N. TR.)

RAIKES, ROBERT (1736–1811), English philanthropist and pioneer of the Sunday school movement, was born at Gloucester on Sept. 4, 1736. His philanthropic work started with the prisoners in the local jail. Later, the lawless behaviour of Gloucester children on Sundays led him to experiment with a Sunday school in Sooty Alley, where he engaged a number of paid women teachers to give instruction in reading and the church catechism. The experiment was so successful that in his newspaper, the *Gloucester Journal* (Nov. 3, 1783), he was able to record that the district had become "quite a heaven upon Sundays, compared with what it used to be." The Sunday school movement spread to all parts of the country with great rapidity. In 1785, the Sunday School Society was formed, and four years later Sunday schools were established in Wales. The Sunday School Union (1803) was a direct result of Raikes's work. He died at Gloucester on April 5, 1811.

BIBLIOGRAPHY.—A. Gregory, *Robert Raikes* (1877); J. H. Harris, *Robert Raikes, the Man and his Work* (1899); G. Kendall, *Robert Raikes* (1939). (S. J. C.)

RAIL, the common name for marsh birds comprising the family Rallidae, of which there are more than 130 species recognized, worldwide in distribution except in high latitudes. They are somewhat chicken-shaped, with short rounded wings and large feet with long toes. Rails are secretive in habit and infrequently seen; their loud, harsh calls, however, give away their presence in dense vegetation. Many are excellent game birds; when flushed, they take wing reluctantly, flying a short distance and then dropping to the ground.

In the United States the king rail (*Rallus elegans*), a reddish-brown bird the size of a small chicken; clapper rail (*R. longirostris*), a grayer form; and the Virginia rail (*R. limicola*), reddish brown and about 10 in. in length, are hunted as game, as is the Carolina rail, or sora (*Porzana carolina*). The little yellow rail (*Coturnicops noveboracensis*) and the six-inch-long black rail (*Laterallus jamaicensis*) are too scarce and small to be of interest to the hunter.

The land rail, or corn crake (*Crex crex*), is found throughout Europe and western Asia and is a summer visitor to England. Brownish above and yellowish white below, it is inconspicuous except in flight, when it is recognized by its chestnut wings, barred flank, and dangling legs. It nests on the ground and forages for food, chiefly insects, in long grasses. Eight to ten eggs are laid, of a cream colour blotched with red-brown. The young hatchlings are covered with black down. Less abundant but more widely distributed (extending to northern Africa) is the water rail (*Rallus aquaticus*). This is a slender bird of much the same habits as the corn crake. It is distinguished by darker plumage and a long, reddish bill.

HUGH M. HALLIDAY FROM NATIONAL AUDUBON SOCIETY

VIRGINIA RAIL (RALLUS LIMICOLA)

The rail family includes coots and gallinules (*qq.v.*). In the latter group is *Notornis* (*q.v.*), the large flightless takahe of New Zealand, rediscovered in 1948. Flightless rails of several genera are found on remote oceanic islands. (HT. FN.)

RAILWAY, a mode of land transportation in which freight and passenger carrying vehicles, or cars, with flanged wheels, move over two parallel steel rails. The guideway, or track, consists of the parallel rails laid on crossties, or sleepers, and anchored in a bed of crushed rock or other ballast. The cars usually are pulled or pushed by a locomotive, although they may be self-propelled. The track gauge (distance between inside faces of the rails) varies from country to country; however, most railways use standard gauge, which measures 4 ft. 8½ in.

TABLE I.—*U.S.-British Railway Terms*

United States	Britain
Baggage car	Luggage van
Boxcar	Goods van or box van
Classification yard	Marshaling yard
Caboose	Brake van
Crosstie or tie	Sleeper
Diaphragm (car)	Corridor connection
Dining car	Restaurant car
Engineer; engineman	Engine driver
Freight car	Goods wagon
Grade crossing	Level crossing
Gondola car	Open wagon
Interlocking plant	Signal box
Journal box	Axle box
Joint bars (rail)	Fishplates
Passenger car	Passenger carriage
Self-propelled car	Rail car
Self-propelled-car train	Train set
Signal tower	Signal cabin
Switching (of cars)	Shunting
Switcher (locomotive)	Shunting engine
Switch or turnout	Points
Tie plate	Baseplate
Truck, swivel car	Bogie

The development of railways is one of the great landmarks in the progress of human civilization. Coming early in the 19th century, railways provided an element that was essential to full realization of the promise of the surging Industrial Revolution—namely, a reliable, low-cost, high-volume system of land transportation.

It is the principle of flanged steel wheels rolling on steel rails that gives the railway its preeminence for heavy-duty transportation. The flanges guide the wheels of locomotives and cars, causing them to follow the line of the rails, and the rolling friction of the wheels on the rails is extremely low. In fact, if a 40-ton railway freight car of the type common in the United States were set rolling on level track at 60 mph, it would travel five miles or more before coming to a stop. In contrast, a highway truck of similar weight set free on level road at the same speed would roll only about one mile.

Because of this self-guiding characteristic and the low rolling friction, a locomotive of relatively modest horsepower can pull a long train of cars. This, basically, is the reason for the economy of railway transportation, an economy that is clearly evident in terms of manpower and fuel consumption. In 1952, for example, all other forms of transport in the United States used 11 times as much fuel as did the railways—yet the latter produced more than half the total gross ton-miles of transportation. In 1955 U.S. railways produced five times as much transportation per employee as did the intercity trucklines, despite the fact that the railways build and maintain their own roadways, which the highway carriers do not. This article is divided as follows:

Information on the economic aspects of railway operation may be found in the article INTERSTATE COMMERCE, while a general survey, from a historical viewpoint, of all forms of transport is presented in the article TRANSPORTATION. Forms of urban and interurban rail transport are described in ELECTRIC TRACTION and SUBWAY (UNDERGROUND RAILWAY).

I. HISTORICAL DEVELOPMENT

The railway as we know it originated in England, but the use of wheeled vehicles on rail lines came many years before the advent of mechanical traction. There is a reference to a railway in Europe as early as 1550. Before the end of the 16th century, mining railways were introduced in Britain, particularly in the northeastern coal-mining area. In the 18th century horse-drawn railways of this kind were to be found not only in England but also in Wales and Scotland. Their application was increased with the introduction of cast iron for wheels and for the plateways over which the wagons ran. The earliest atmospheric steam engines, however, were too bulky and heavy for traction purposes.

In 1797 Richard Trevithick made three models, one of which may have represented a proposal for a self-propelled steam engine or locomotive. In February 1804 a locomotive built by Trevithick ran on a tramroad in Wales, but these and subsequent experiments were unsuccessful, probably because the weight of the locomotive broke the rails. In 1808 Trevithick exhibited a locomotive and carriage on a circular track in London, but it was regarded as an amusement and not taken seriously.

Following Trevithick's pioneering, the first practical and successful locomotive was built in 1812 to the instructions of John Blenkinsop, an inspector at Middleton colliery near Leeds. It ran on cast-iron rails and had two vertical cylinders driving two shafts geared to a toothed wheel which engaged a rack rail. Three further locomotives were built in 1812 and 1813 and used between the colliery and Leeds, a distance of three and one-half miles.

In 1813 William Hedley built "Puffing Billy," a simple adhesion locomotive (i.e., one that relied on friction between wheels and rails, dispensing with the toothed rack rail). It was used for hauling coal trucks between Wylam colliery and the wharves at Lemington-on-Tyne, a distance of about five miles. In the following year George Stephenson, pioneer railway and locomotive builder, completed his first engine, the "Blücher." It was put to work at Killingworth colliery.

In 1823 Stephenson was invited by Edward Pease to build and equip a railway from Stockton to Darlington. This was completed in 1825 and ceremonially opened on Sept. 27 of that year. It was the first public railway in the world that employed locomotive traction and that was intended to carry both freight and passengers, and as such it marked the birth of the public service railway. It was not the first public railway, this honour going to the Surrey Iron Railway Company, which was created through an act of Parliament passed in 1801; it was opened in 1803 between Wandsworth and Croydon, using horses. In 1804 the Oystermouth Railway was incorporated and this became the first railway to carry fare-paying passengers (March 1807), horse traction being used.

During the first two years of its existence, steam traction proved unreliable and expensive to maintain on the Stockton and Darlington Railway. The first locomotive was "Locomotion" (now preserved at Bank Top Station, Darlington). This and similar machines were suitable only for hauling low-speed mineral trains, and their tractive effort and weight were limited by the comparatively weak track. At times the railway reverted to horses, but the situation was improved with the introduction in 1827 of the "Royal George," a six-coupled locomotive designed by Timothy Hackworth. This and other locomotives eliminated the use of horses in rail freight service by 1833.

In 1829 the Liverpool and Manchester Railway held a contest to decide upon the best kind of traction to use and it was won by Stephenson's "Rocket" (now preserved at the Science Museum, London). The success of the "Rocket" was due principally to the use of a multiple fire-tube boiler in place of the single-flue boilers previously used. The Liverpool and Manchester Railway was opened on Sept. 15, 1830, and became the first public railway on which all traffic was hauled by steam locomotives. At this time another great stride was made in track construction by Blenkinsop's patent for fish-bellied, rolled-iron edge rails (1829). These were much stronger than cast-iron rails and enabled heavier locomotives to be used.

A. Railways in the United States

Paralleling this early English development, interest in railways began to develop in the United States, as well as in other countries. One of several horse-drawn tramways built early in the 19th century was Gridley Bryant's Granite Railway in Quincy, Mass. Horses supplied power for this 3-mi., broad-gauge line, which carried the granite used in building the Bunker Hill monument.

By 1813 the inventor Oliver Evans was proposing a railway between New York and Philadelphia. Two years later, John Stevens received from the New Jersey legislature the first charter for a railway ever granted in America. However, Stevens was ahead of his time: the chartered line, between the Delaware and Raritan rivers, was never built. But in 1825 he built and operated the first locomotive to run on rails in America. It ran on a half-mile circle of track at Stevens' home in Hoboken, N.J.

This was the year that the Stockton and Darlington line opened in England; the success of that pioneering enterprise helped overcome the opposition and apathy toward railways in the United States. On Feb. 28, 1827, the Baltimore and Ohio Railroad Company (B & O) was chartered (in the following, abbreviations or names in parentheses are those by which U.S. lines are commonly known). The line began carrying revenue traffic Jan. 7, 1830, and the first 13 mi. of line, from Baltimore to Ellicott's Mills (now Ellicott City) opened on May 24, 1830.

The B & O was the first railway in the United States to be chartered as a common carrier of freight and passengers. Moreover, its promoters looked beyond purely local needs. They envisaged a line going all the way to the Ohio River to channel the commerce of the growing Middle West through the port of Baltimore. By 1834 the B & O had built to Harpers Ferry, Va. (now W.Va.), and on Dec. 24, 1852, it reached the Ohio River at Wheeling. Subsequently the B & O expanded, both through new construction and by acquiring other railways, until it reached Chicago, St. Louis, and the Great Lakes. (Today, the B & O is a controlled affiliate of the Chesapeake & Ohio Railway.)

Almost simultaneously, several other railways came into being. Construction of the 5-ft.-gauge line from Charleston to Hamburg, S.C., by the South Carolina Canal and Rail Road Company began in February 1829. On Dec. 25, 1830, this line became the first in the United States to start scheduled passenger operations using a steam locomotive. When the entire line to Hamburg was completed in 1833, it was the longest (136 mi.) then operating in the U.S. Ultimately, the original Charleston–Hamburg route became one segment of the 10,000-mi. Southern Railway system.

Still other railway systems that later grew into giants of the U.S. railway industry had their beginnings in the decade of the 1830s. The Mohawk and Hudson, first predecessor of the New York Central System (now Penn Central), operated its first train between Albany and Schenectady, N.Y., on Aug. 9, 1831. Predecessors of both the Boston and Maine Railroad and the New York, New Haven and Hartford Railroad Company (now a division of Penn Central) started regular service in the summer of 1835. Three local lines chartered in Virginia evolved into major rail systems. The Richmond and Petersburg, chartered in 1836, and the Portsmouth & Roanoke, dating from 1832, were the first segments of what is today the Seaboard Coast Line Railroad (SCL). The Chesapeake & Ohio Railway Company (C & O) had its beginning in the little Louisa Railway, chartered in 1836.

The Richmond, Fredericksburg & Potomac Railroad Company, which operates between Richmond, Va., and Washington, D.C., was incorporated Feb. 25, 1834. It is the oldest American railway that has continued to exist since the beginning under its original name, and without reorganization.

By 1840 there were 2,800 mi. of line in the United States, and the country had entered its first great era of railway building. Twenty years later, on the eve of the American Civil War, the country had more than 30,000 route miles of track.

With but few exceptions (such as the B & O), early railways were purely local in character. They were designed to promote the commercial interest of local communities or areas. As growth progressed, however, many of the small roads were consolidated, forming through routes that served fairly large territories, and new railway projects became more ambitious. The Pennsylvania Railroad Company completed its line from Philadelphia to Pittsburgh in December 1852, using ten inclined planes to climb over the Allegheny Mountains. A little more than a year later, it completed an all-rail route.

1. The Westward Movement.—By the 1850s U.S. railways were taking on their historic role as civilizers of the western frontiers. The first locomotive in Chicago, the "Pioneer" of the Galena and Chicago Union, now the Chicago and North Western Railway (North Western), made its initial run on Oct. 25, 1848—and Chicago was on the way to its ultimate destiny as the nation's largest rail centre.

Soon railways were pushing west from Chicago. The Chicago and Rock Island, now the Chicago, Rock Island and Pacific Railroad Company (Rock Island), was the first railway to link Chicago with the Mississippi River (1854). It also built the first railway bridge across that river in 1856. Other pioneer lines built west from the Mississippi. The first locomotive to operate west of the river made a 5-mi. run from St. Louis in December 1852. This was on a short railway that became part of the Missouri Pacific Railroad Company. The Hannibal and St. Joseph, which became part of the Chicago, Burlington and Quincy Railroad (now Burlington Northern), reached the Missouri River in 1859.

The Civil War slowed, but did not stop, the headlong growth of railways in the United States. After the close of that conflict, another era of intensive railway building began and continued into the early years of the 20th century. It reached its high point during the decade of the 1880s, when some 70,000 route miles were laid. In 1882, the greatest single year of railway building in the United States, 11,569 mi. of track were completed.

Highlighting this era was the completion of several lines—the transcontinentals—which, more than any other factor, helped make the United States a truly united nation. On May 10, 1869, the first transcontinental route was created when the Union Pacific Railroad Company, building west from Omaha, Neb., met the Central Pacific, now part of Southern Pacific (SP), which was built east from Sacramento, Calif. In 1881 the Atchison, Topeka and Santa Fe Railway (Santa Fe) joined rail with the SP at Deming, N.M., to form the second transcontinental route. Ultimately, there were about nine major routes leading from the Middle West or South to the West Coast. From Chicago, the Santa Fe, the Chicago, Milwaukee, St. Paul and Pacific (Milwaukee Road), and the Burlington Northern (BN) run all the way to the West Coast over their own rails. The SP has its own trackage from New Orleans, La., to Los Angeles, Calif., and on up the coast to Portland, Ore.

2. Land Grants.—A feature of the post-Civil War railway-building era was government aid to a number of lines through land grants, loans, and other types of assistance. About 131,000,000 ac. of public land were granted to 29 railways for about 18,000 mi. of line. These grants (about 8% of the total U.S. railway mileage) made it possible for the railways to push their lines across prairies and mountains that were then almost entirely undeveloped.

Railway aid was, on balance, a profitable activity for the U.S. government. For instance, the government received about $167,-000,000 in principal and interest from the $65,000,000 it loaned to six pioneer Western railways. The original value of the land grants was about $130,000,000, but in return the railways agreed to carry government traffic at reduced rates. By the time this agreement was abrogated in 1946, the railways had paid back to the government, through these reductions, more than $1,000,000,000.

3. Railway Regulation.—For almost 50 years after their beginnings, railways in the United States were subject to little governmental regulation. After the Civil War, however, abuses such as rate wars, rate discrimination, and financial piracy became more widespread. In these things railways were probably no worse offenders than many other businesses of that era, but since they had by then attained almost a monopoly over domestic transportation, the public could not tolerate these abuses.

Regulation at first was largely at the state level, but public sentiment resulted in the passage, in 1887, of the Interstate Commerce Act, which placed the railways under federal regulation. Later, other acts broadened and extended the areas of federal regulation so that the railways finally had to clear through the Interstate Commerce Commission (ICC) almost all proposals for changes in such matters as financing, equipment standards, signaling, and rates.

Although rate and other economic regulation remains with the ICC, regulation of railway safety standards is under the Federal Railroad Administration (FRA), a bureau of the U.S. Department of Transportation. The FRA was greatly strengthened by the Railroad Safety Act of 1970; it also is charged with the development and promotion of more efficient rail transportation.

4. Labour Relations.—One of the first U.S. industries in which employees were unionized was the railway industry. In the late 1960s there were 19 "standard railroad labour organizations" which represented employees in various classes or crafts. In 1888 the U.S. Congress passed legislation providing, among other things, for special presidential emergency boards to investigate disputes. Through the years, other legislation was added. Labour-management negotiations are conducted under the complex provisions of the Railway Labor Act. Enacted in 1926 and subsequently amended, it provides a national mediation board that has power to mediate disputes, and a national railway adjustment board, composed of management and union representatives, which considers grievances, interpretations, and applications of the complicated labour-management working agreements.

Over the years, relations between railway labour and management in the U.S. have been marked with few industry-wide work stoppages—although there were violent and bloody strikes in 1877 and 1894. A brief nationwide strike also tied up U.S. railway lines in 1946. During the 1960s there were a number of strikes involving one or several lines; in 1963 Congress passed a special act providing compulsory arbitration of a dispute involving the number of men to be used in train crews. By 1970, increasingly frequent strikes and threats of strikes had triggered several proposals for revision of the Railway Labor Act. (*See* also LABOUR LAW.)

5. Developments to World War II.—By the early years of the 20th century, railway building had slowed in the United States, and the network had reached about its fullest extent. This was a period of improvement in railway plant and equipment; emphasis was on standardization of equipment and operating techniques. After a brief period of government control during World War I, the railways entered an era of further operating refinements but of few spectacular advances, although several technological developments that later had vast impact, among them the diesel locomotive, were being tried. The first inroads of highway competition were being felt. The economic depression, beginning in 1930, dealt the railways a disastrous blow, and many companies went through bankruptcy proceedings. Emerging from this depression decade, U.S. railways faced their supreme challenge, the years of World War II.

6. Wartime Role.—Almost from the first, some military men recognized the value of railways. An early proposal called for a network of railways to be built in the United States primarily for military purposes. In many other countries, some or all of the railways originally were constructed strictly for military reasons.

The American Civil War was really the first "railway war," although some use was made of railways in the Crimean and Mexican wars. Since then, nations in every major war have depended on railways as basic transportation.

Experience has shown that railways can move huge quantities of supplies and troops overland with a tremendous economy of fuel and manpower—a vital advantage, of course, during a war

emergency. Moreover, railways, while seemingly vulnerable to enemy action, can be more quickly restored to full-capacity operation than any other form of land transport. This was amply demonstrated in World War II and in the Korean War of 1950–53.

At the very beginning of the Civil War, railways played a key role. The Confederate victory at the first Battle of Bull Run (Manassas) was due in considerable measure to the Manassas Gap Railway, which was able to deliver a number of reinforcements to the battlefield just in time to turn the tide. Throughout the war, the Confederacy was able to use its railways to concentrate troops where needed and thus help to overcome its numerical disadvantage. However, the Confederacy was not able to exercise effective organized control of its railways so they could operate to best military advantage. On the other hand, the Union side was able to organize its military railway operations more effectively. This, along with its better-developed railway network and the fact that most of the locomotive and car-building plants were in Union territory, played an important part in the final outcome of that conflict.

One of the important lessons learned in the Civil War was that railway cars must be used only for the movement of troops and supplies—not for storage. By World War I this lesson had been forgotten, however. Cars were loaded and sent on their way with no place to unload them. As a result of this practice, congestion approaching paralysis hit the railway system in 1917. In order to unravel the tie-up, the U.S. government took over the operation of the railways on Dec. 28, 1917. The lines were restored to private operation March 1, 1920.

No such problem arose in World War II, when the railways demonstrated how efficiently a well-run system can operate to handle extraordinary traffic movements. In the war year of 1944, freight ton-miles were two and one-half times the level of 1938; passenger-miles had increased fourfold. This tremendous traffic was handled with relatively modest increases in the supply of locomotives and cars. Moreover, this wartime job was done at a time when the railways had supplied about 40,000 officers and men for Army transportation corps units and another 300,000 employees were in other branches of the armed services.

During the World War II period, U.S. railways carried almost 98% of all military personnel moving in organized groups and more than 90% of all military freight handled by inland transportation. In the Korean War the railways performed a similar job on a smaller scale while at the same time handling normal civilian transport requirements.

In the Korean War, too, the flexibility of railways under front-line conditions was reaffirmed. Neither the UN nor Communist forces could permanently disable the other side's strategic rail lines even under the impact of heavy air strikes.

B. RAILWAY GROWTH IN CANADA

The growth of Canadian railways paralleled somewhat that of the United States. Construction of the first line, between Laprairie and St. John, Que., began in 1835; its first train operated on July 21, 1836.

By 1860 there were about 2,000 mi. of railway line in Canada. One of the terms on which British Columbia entered the confederation in 1871 was the construction of a transcontinental route. This line, the Canadian Pacific (CP Rail), was completed in 1885. It is literally the tie that bound Canada into a unified nation.

Two other transcontinental lines reached the Pacific Coast in 1914 and 1915. They were the Grand Trunk Pacific, which reached Prince Rupert, B.C., in 1914; and the Canadian Northern, built into Vancouver in 1915. Both of these lines were built with government assistance.

The dislocations of World War I dashed the hopes of internal development that had sparked the construction of these two transcontinentals. They required further government financial help and were finally taken over by the dominion government. In 1923 both the Grand Trunk and the Canadian Northern, along with other railways always owned by the dominion, were unified, forming the Canadian National Railways (CN).

In normal years the CP Rail operates at a profit; the CN, which has many lines serving as yet sparsely settled areas, usually records a deficit. The latter also serves as an agency of national policy. As a result it has built a number of lines to open up new territory during the years since World War II. One of the more important of these is the Great Slave Lake Railway, running 432 mi. from Peace River, Alta., to Hay River and Pine Point, N.W.T.

Other Canadian railways were being built or extended as the dominion entered a period of rapid economic growth. The Quebec, North Shore and Labrador, a 320-mi. ore-carrying line from the iron-ore deposits near Schefferville, Que., to the St. Lawrence River at Sept-Iles, was opened in 1954. In 1958 the Pacific Great Eastern Railway (PGE) completed its line all the way from Vancouver, B.C., to Dawson Creek and Fort St. John, B.C. By the early 1970s it expected to complete a further 250-mi. extension to Fort Nelson, B.C.

C. U.S. and Canadian Railways After World War II

For about a century, railways were the dominant form of intercity transportation in the United States and Canada. Indeed, their monopoly was almost complete, with the exception of a fair volume of water transport, including river, Great Lakes, and intercoastal. But the development of the internal-combustion engine and its application to highway vehicles (starting about the beginning of the 20th century) and the invention of the airplane were to have far-reaching effects on railway transportation. In the period between the two world wars, highway transportation of goods by motor truck and of people in buses and private automobiles was already seriously cutting into railway business.

The demands of war hastened the technological development of these new forms of transportation, and by the late 1950s their inroads had reached critical proportions from the railway point of view. Despite the dropoff in passenger revenue, railways held their own during most of the 1960s; but competitors again appeared to be gaining as the decade ended. This loss of traffic to newer competitors was especially pronounced in the United States.

The U.S. railways (with limited exceptions) no longer carry significant numbers of intercity passengers; but they finally began to fight back with considerable success against their freight competitors. In the late 1960s, U.S. railway freight volume set new records, surpassing even the peak years of World War II. This was due primarily to adoption of the "marketing approach," wherein railways closely tailored their rates, services, and equipment to the needs of specific shippers. Typical are the "unit trains" operated for shippers of bulk commodities such as coal, ores, or grain. Composed of large, modern cars designed for the commodity to be carried, unit trains operate on fast schedules between one origin and one destination, bypassing all intermediate yards and terminals en route. With faster operation and larger cars, these trains permit the railways to offer greatly reduced rates. By 1969 more than 80% of all coal shipped by rail was moving under unit-train rates. In 1968 the Illinois Central Railroad (IC) introduced "rent-a-train," wherein the shipper rents a train (minus locomotive) for a fixed annual fee (plus certain per-mile operating charges) and may use it as he sees fit.

As part of their new approach to marketing freight service, railways also offered their shippers many special types of freight cars designed to load particular commodities quickly and at minimum expense. The trilevel rack car, for instance, has revolutionized the shipping of autos from assembly plants to distribution points. Other new types include 10,000-cu.ft. boxcars for carrying automobile parts; 100-ton covered hopper cars for bulk commodities; and 100-ton gondola or open hopper cars for coal and ore.

By 1969 most U.S. railways had discontinued the handling of small-lot (less-than-carload, or LCL) shipments. A few, however, were moving LCL shipments in highway trucks that were often carried "piggyback" on flatcars between major rail terminals.

1. "Piggyback" and Container Systems.—As early as the 1920s, a U.S. railway was carrying loaded highway trucks on flatcars (although the idea dates back to the 19th century). Piggyback combines the flexibility of truck pickup and delivery with the economy of rail movement between cities. It did not begin to grow rapidly until the later years of the 1950s, but some authorities estimated that piggyback traffic might eventually amount to one-half the total volume of railway traffic.

Along with piggyback, there was increasing interest among railways and other modes of transport in "container" systems. Clearly, the trend was toward a system of freight transport in which merchandise could be loaded into standard containers or boxes, which then would move via highway on a truck chassis, via rail on special container cars, in ships especially equipped to handle them, or even by air. A single shipment might use two or more modes of transport in the course of its trip. Railways in the United States had used containers on a small scale in the 1920s, but not until the late 1960s did the technique begin to meet with widespread acceptance, primarily for import-export traffic.

2. Passenger Service.—By the late 1960s long-haul railway passenger service seemed about to disappear in the United States. To maintain "essential" medium and long-distance passenger services, Congress in 1970 set up a quasi-governmental corporation (initially called Railpax and changed to Amtrak), which in May 1971 took over and operated a limited network of such trains. In the densely populated "corridor" extending between Boston and Washington, however, increasing congestion of highways and airways led to renewed interest in high-speed intercity trains. The U.S. Department of Transportation and the Penn Central were experimenting with ultramodern, high-speed trains capable of top speeds of 150 mph. If these proved successful it seemed likely that similar services would develop in other heavily populated areas.

In Canada, the CN for several years tried a "market-oriented" service concept plus heavy promotion. This greatly increased the patronage of its intercity passenger services; however, these trains still operated at a large financial loss.

3. Mergers.—Beginning in the late 1960s, a trend toward consolidation of U.S. railways developed. The object was to preserve the profitability of the companies in the face of increased operating costs and the intensifying competition from other modes. Well-conceived mergers promised to reduce the number of parallel rail lines in certain areas and to concentrate the available freight traffic on the most efficient and fastest routes. Further advantages were improved service to railway freight customers and more efficient use of locomotives and cars.

By 1971 it appeared likely that the U.S. railway industry would ultimately evolve into a small number—perhaps six or fewer—of very large companies. The growing financial pinch also raised the possibility that at least some would require government support, if not outright government operation, in order to maintain essential services.

The complex regulatory laws under which U.S. railways operate make the merging of lines a slow and difficult process. Thus, it required about nine years after formal application to the Interstate Commerce Commission before the Burlington Northern merger (Great Northern, Northern Pacific, Chicago, Burlington & Quincy, and Spokane, Portland & Seattle) could be accomplished in 1970. Other mergers included Erie-Lackawanna (Erie Railroad and Delaware, Lackawanna & Western); Norfolk & Western (Norfolk & Western with the Virginian Railway and later with the Nickel Plate Road and the Wabash Railroad); and Penn Central (New York Central, Pennsylvania, and New Haven).

D. Mexican and Central American Railways

The railway systems of Mexico and Central and South American countries are less advanced than those in the United States and Canada. Most countries (except Mexico) have a predominance of narrow-gauge lines of relatively light construction.

The Mexican railways, almost all of which are owned by the federal government, have a route mileage of approximately 12,200. Of this, approximately 8,600 mi. are operated by the Ferrocarriles Nacionales de México (N. de M.; National Railways of Mexico). The N. de M. was acquired both by purchase and expropriation, beginning in 1937. Prior to that time much of the railway development in Mexico had been by private interests.

Most of the Mexican railway mileage is standard gauge, and there are interchange connections with U.S. railways at several points. As a result, the Mexican railway network may be said to be integrated with those of the U.S. and Canada to a considerable extent. Since World War II a vigorous modernization program has been under way.

The railways of Central America are all narrow gauge and of light construction. Some are government owned and some are privately owned.

E. South American Railways

South America has about 66,000 route miles of railroad, of which about 62% is narrow gauge. The rest is either standard or wide gauge. Although early development of South American railways, beginning in the middle of the 19th century, was largely by private enterprise, there later was a trend toward government ownership and operation. This was particularly marked in Argentina, where in 1945 only about 31% of the trackage was state owned; by the 1960s Argentina's 27,600 mi. of line were all under the jurisdiction of the Argentine State Railways.

Brazil is second to Argentina in total track miles. Of its 19,847 track miles, virtually all are owned by state or federal governments.

There is little integration of railways in the South American countries. This is due partly to the rugged terrain over which many of them operate but even more to the diversity of gauges, as well as of equipment standards. Many early South American railways were built by British, French, U.S., and German concerns and this resulted in considerable variation in the types of equipment, methods of operation, and even terminology.

Nearly all South American railway systems had improvement programs planned or under way in the 1960s, but most were handicapped by lack of funds.

F. European and Asian Railways

1. Great Britain.—The success of the Stockton and Darlington and the Liverpool and Manchester lines touched off widespread railway construction in Britain. In 1836 the opening of the London and Greenwich Railway brought the first public passenger service to London. In 1838 the London and Birmingham Railway was opened throughout its length and in 1840 the line from London to Southampton was completed. The Great Western Railway's 7-ft. broad-gauge line from London to Bristol was opened to traffic in 1841; the railway later converted to standard gauge.

Between 1844 and 1846 Parliament authorized the construction of over 400 railways. This represented the height of what was known as the railway mania, and there followed a period of slower development and a growing number of consolidations. Early in the 1900s some systems realized that mergers could create a stronger economic position for them, but because of monopoly fears, acts sanctioning such moves were not passed by Parliament.

Amalgamation of Lines.—Following World War I, it was evident that large-scale consolidation was a financial necessity, and the government decided upon compulsory amalgamation. As a result of the Railways Act of 1921, about 123 separate railway companies amalgamated into four main groups on Jan. 1, 1923. The four systems were the London, Midland and Scottish Railway; London and North Eastern Railway (LNER); Great Western Railway; and Southern Railway. Certain minor railways and London's Underground retained their separate existence. The latter were amalgamated with London area bus and tramway systems in 1933 under authority of the London Passenger Transport Board, a public body constituted by act of Parliament.

The object of creating four large railway systems was to consolidate control and obtain more economical methods of operation. The consolidation also allowed the introduction of a new classification of rates and charges designed to enable the railways to earn a standard revenue.

During the 1920s the railways began to suffer from increased highway competition. To combat this, various new services were introduced. In 1928, an act of Parliament authorized the railways to operate both passenger and freight road services, and they acquired extensive financial interests in existing undertakings, principally bus companies.

Despite competition and the general economic depression of the 1930s, the four railway companies were responsible for some remarkable achievements between 1925 and 1939. In 1928 the LNER began the nonstop running of its principal express train between London and Edinburgh, a distance of 392¾ mi. The high-speed running of streamlined passenger trains began in 1935 with the introduction of the "Silver Jubilee" between London and Newcastle. It was followed in 1937 with the "Coronation" (London–Edinburgh) and the "Coronation Scot" (London–Glasgow).

At the outbreak of World War II in 1939, the railways were placed under government control. Coordination and direction were through the Railway Executive Committee, appointed by the Ministry of Transport. During the period 1939–45 the railways operated 260,000 special troop trains and 280,000 matériel trains for the armed services. Over 9,000 incidents of enemy action were recorded on the railways and nearly 400 railway men were killed and 2,444 injured by enemy action. At the end of the war the state of the railways had deteriorated considerably due to lack of maintenance, abnormal wear and tear, shortage of personnel, and damage through enemy action.

Railway Nationalization.—In 1946 a bill was introduced in Parliament for setting up a publicly owned inland transport system. Under the Transport Act, which became law on Aug. 6, 1947, the British Transport Commission (BTC) was established as the body responsible for taking over the railways, the railway-owned docks, road haulage contractors, many road passenger undertakings, and the inland waterways. On Jan. 1, 1948, the nationalization of the railways took effect and they became the British Railways. The Railway Executive Committee became the body responsible to the Railway Commission for the management and coordination of British Railways. The latter were divided, on a geographical basis, into six regions: Eastern, Northeastern, Western, Southern, London Midland, and Scottish. Later the Eastern and Northeastern were merged into one region.

A transport bill which became law on May 6, 1953, provided for greater decentralization of the railways. The Railway Executive Committee was abolished and the chief regional managers were made responsible to the commission.

On Jan. 24, 1955, the BTC announced an extensive and ambitious modernization and reequipment plan. The plan aimed at producing a really modern system that would be able to meet both current traffic requirements and those of the foreseeable future. It was intended that the main features of the plan would be started within 5 years and completed within 15 years. The plan began to show concrete results in 1958, although no large-scale improvements had been completed by that time. In 1959 there was a reappraisal of the plan, aimed at accelerating certain portions of it. In 1958 there was a total deficit for the year of £89,-000,000, covering all the commission's activities. To meet the situation the government agreed to increase the limit of deficit borrowing from £250,000,000 to £400,000,000, as well as to increase the general borrowing powers. By the early 1960s the total deficit for the British Railways had reached about £160,000,000.

An act of Parliament in 1962 dissolved the British Transport Commission and replaced it with the British Railways Board, which took over Jan. 1, 1963. Later in that year the board proposed measures to bring the railway system into line with present and future requirements. The main features of the proposals were:

The closing of many branch lines and a reduction in the number of passenger stops.
A reduction in the number of freight depots, those remaining to be linked by express freight services.
Development of a network of high-speed, "containerized" freight services, called Liner Trains, between key centres.
Movement of the bulk of coal and mineral traffic in block trains (called unit trains in the U.S.), each of which would carry only one type of material.
Reduction in the freight and passenger car fleets.
Replacement of the remaining steam locomotives by diesels.

The board announced that the original modernization plan would continue, but with modifications to adapt it to the new program.

In 1957 the BTC (railway merchandise) Charges Scheme came into force, allowing freight charges to be varied below the permitted maximum. This enabled the railway to charge on the basis of loadability, except for consignments of 100 tons or more, for which charges had to be reasonable.

Further extensive changes were incorporated in the Transport Act of 1968, which was based on three main proposals by the government:

To redefine the size and shape of the system so that it would accord more closely with the country's commercial and social needs. Commercially viable services were expected to pay their way but the government would assume financial responsibility for losses incurred on services offered for social reasons.

A National Freight Corporation would be responsible for all freight traffic originating by road: parcels, sundries, Freightliner (express container) services, road vehicles, containers, depots and warehouses, and British Road Services and services previously under the Transport Holding Company. Traffic would still be carried by rail; in fact British Rail would have a 49% interest in the Freightliner Company. This would enable an integrated road-rail service to be offered.

An examination of key aspects of railway operation.

One result of this act was that the former proposals for a contraction of the system would, to some extent, be reversed. This would result in a network of about 11,000 route miles in place of the previously planned total of 8,000 route miles.

Passenger Service.—Passenger train developments included widespread introduction of diesel-powered trains and railcars. In 1960 a number of luxury diesel Pullman trains were introduced. Passenger schedules were accelerated; in 1968 nearly 1,400 services were being operated at 60 mph or over. The speed limit was raised to 100 mph over a growing number of sections. Fast intercity services, designed especially for businessmen, were introduced.

In 1955 a new type of service aimed at the motorist had been initiated. Called the "Car-Sleeper Limited," it carried automobiles in specially designed cars, their drivers and passengers traveling in sleeping cars. Following the success of the first route, a complete network of services was established under the name of Motorail. In 1966, 100,000 passengers and 45,000 autos were carried on these trains.

In 1968 British Rail received approval to design and construct an advanced passenger train capable of a speed of 150 mph and using electric motors or gas turbines for propulsion.

Electric Traction.—Direct-current electric traction is used extensively in southern England. Current collection is via a third rail mounted alongside the running rail. In 1967 this system was extended to Southampton and Bournemouth; it is also used on certain lines around London, Manchester, and Liverpool. Electrification of the line connecting Manchester, Sheffield, and Wath had been completed in 1954. This uses the 1,500-v. DC overhead conductor wire system. The same system was employed for the electrification of the London–Shenfield line, which was completed in 1949 and extended to Southend in 1956 (this, however, was later converted to AC to bring it into conformity with later electrification projects in the same area). In 1956 it was announced that future electrification would be on the 25-kv., 50-cycle AC system. The first application of this form of electric traction was on the Colchester–Clacton–Walton line, about 24½ route miles (inaugurated in 1959). The first trunk route using 25-kv. power was completed in 1966 between London, Manchester, and Liverpool. This was later extended to embrace the London, Coventry, and Birmingham route. There is also 25-kv. electrification in the Glasgow area.

In 1968 steam locomotives were completely withdrawn from all standard-gauge British Rail lines.

2. China.—Following creation of the People's Republic of China in 1949, an intensive program of rehabilitating war-damaged lines and constructing new ones was started. Among the new lines were the Ch'eng-tu–Chungking railway, opened in 1952, and one connecting Mongolia and China, opened in 1955. There were some 5-ft.-gauge lines adjoining Russian territories and also some narrow-gauge mileage; however, the majority of the system was standard gauge. Through-passenger train services were being operated between Peking and Moscow; Peking and Ulan Bator; and Peking and Hanoi.

3. France.—The first railway in France, from St. Étienne to Andrézieux, was officially opened on Oct. 1, 1828, although it was in unofficial use the year before. At first only freight was carried, passenger traffic commencing in 1832. Horse traction was employed until the adoption of steam locomotives in 1832. In 1830 the first section (between Givors and Rive-de-Gier) of the St. Étienne–Lyons Railway was opened, and the line was completed in 1832. Both steam and horse traction were used, steam taking over completely in 1844. The first international line from Strasbourg to Basel, Switz., was completed in 1841, by which time France had 350 mi. of railways.

In the 1850s railway construction was at its height and there emerged six principal companies: Nord, Est, Paris–Orléans, Paris–Lyons–Méditerranée, Midi, and Ouest. In 1878 the state took over a group of small companies in western France, thus creating the État System. By 1902 the railway network had grown to 28,400 mi.

The Ouest Railway became state owned in 1908, and after World War I the Alsace–Lorraine railways also became government property. On Jan. 1, 1938, the five remaining privately owned railways were taken over by the government. They—and the existing État System—formed the Société Nationale des Chemins de Fer Français (SNCF; French National Railways), a joint stock company with 51% of its capital held by the government.

During World War II the SNCF suffered extensive damage and by 1944 about 82% of the motive power, 80% of the coaches, and 64% of the freight cars had been damaged or destroyed. Extensive damage had been wrought on many other installations, but by mid-1946 nearly all track was restored to use and by mid-1948, 2,491 bridges and viaducts had been rebuilt.

Following the immediate postwar restoration of basic facilities, the SNCF embarked on the modernization of its system. Initial recovery was aided by the supply of 1,340 steam locomotives from the United States and Canada and 48,000 freight cars from the United States, Canada, and Britain.

The principal features in the modernization of the system were the steady abandonment of steam traction, increased use of diesel power, and large-scale electrification. Extensive improvements also were made to track and signaling, and large quantities of new rolling stock were introduced.

The initial postwar project was to electrify the main line from Paris to Lyons, and this was completed in 1952. The prewar 1,500-v. DC system was adopted. This was later extended all the way to Nice, via Lyons and Marseilles. SNCF also uses electrification at 25 kv., 50 cycles (commercial frequency) AC on many lines in the north and east of France. In 1968 electric traction moved 74% of all traffic. SNCF progressively increased the speed of its passenger trains; in 1969 the "Capitole" was allowed a maximum of 125 mph over certain sections between Paris and Toulouse. The SNCF also expected to introduce gas-turbine-powered trains on selected nonelectrified routes.

4. Germany.—The use of the steam locomotive in Germany began on Dec. 7, 1835, with the opening of a railway between Nürnberg and Fürth. Both private companies and states built railways, but after 1876 the privately owned systems were gradually absorbed by the states. By 1909 the total route mileage was 35,625. In 1920 there was a further change in ownership when the state systems were unified as the German State Railways. Their status was changed in 1924 to that of a publicly owned company, but a few years later they again reverted to government ownership.

Following World War II and the partition of Germany, two railway systems emerged. In the Federal Republic of Germany (West Germany) there emerged the German Federal Railway (Deutsche Bundesbahn or DB), while in the German Democratic Republic (East Germany) the title of German State Railway (Deutsche Reichbahn or DR) was retained. In West Germany, apart from the DB, there were about 250 public railways owned by commercial concerns, municipalities, and provincial governments.

After World War II a great deal of reconstruction was necessary and the opportunity was taken to introduce new equipment. There were improvements in track, signaling, communications, locomotives, and rolling stock, and steam traction was being replaced by diesel locomotives and electrification. These more modern forms of traction—especially electrification—enabled train speeds to be raised; in 1968 a series of express services were introduced over selected routes under the title of Inter City.

5. India.—The most complex railway network in Asia, and also the oldest, exists in what was the dominion of India, subsequently split into the republics of India and Pakistan. In 1849 the East Indian Railway Company registered, and the first line to be opened was between Bombay and Thana in 1853. This was due to British influence, and the various networks gradually extended and increased in size and scope.

The control of the Indian systems comes under the Ministry of Railways at New Delhi. There are eight railways, which serve different areas of the country: Central, Eastern, Northern, North Eastern, Northeast Frontier, Southern, South Eastern, and Western. The Central Railway is principally 5-ft. 6-in. gauge, and the Eastern Railway is entirely 5-ft. 6-in. gauge, except for 17 mi. of 2-ft. 6-in. gauge. The Northeast Frontier Railway is mainly metre gauge, and the North Eastern Railway is entirely of this gauge. The Northern Railway is largely 5-ft. 6-in. gauge, as is the South Eastern Railway. The Southern Railway is mainly metre gauge, and the Western Railway has a majority of metre-gauge mileage, with some 5-ft. 6-in., 2-ft. 6-in., and 2-ft. gauges. The total mileages for the various gauges of the entire network are: 5 ft. 6 in., 16,246; metre, 15,480; and 2 ft. 6 in. and 2 ft., 2,735.

6. Ireland.—The first railway in Ireland was opened Dec. 17, 1834, between Dublin and Kingstown (now Dun Laoghaire). It was originally constructed to the 4-ft. 8½-in. gauge but was converted to the principal Irish gauge of 5 ft. 3 in. in 1857. The first line to be opened in Northern Ireland was the Ulster Railway, between Belfast and Lisburn in 1839, originally built to a gauge of 6 ft. 2 in. and converted in 1847 to 5 ft. 3 in.

On Jan. 1, 1925, the majority of all lines wholly within the Irish Free State were combined into the Great Southern Railway, and on Jan. 1, 1945, this system and the Dublin United Transport Company were merged into the Irish Transport Board (Córas Iompair Eireann or CIE). The Great Northern Railway Board's facilities in the Republic of Ireland were merged with CIE in 1958.

Under the 1948 Transport Act (Northern Ireland), the Irish Road Transport Board, the Belfast and County Down Railway, and the Northern Counties Committee were acquired by the Ulster Transport Authority (UTA), and in 1958 the portion of the Great Northern Railway Board in Northern Ireland was merged with the UTA.

7. Italy.—The first railway in Italy was between Naples and Portici, opened in 1839. Railway construction in other parts of the country followed, but it was not until the union of the states took place in 1861 that the idea of a national rail network could be put into practice. In 1885 the major systems were merged into three railways and in 1905–07 these networks, and other smaller lines, were taken over by the state.

During World War II the system suffered considerable damage and extensive reconstruction was necessary. The electrified network, which dates back to 1901, was restored and greatly extended. The majority of the electrification was 3,000-v. DC, but there was some 3,600-v., 16⅔-cycle AC. Conversion of the latter to DC was scheduled for completion in 1971. About 4,900 route miles of the system are electrified.

8. Japan.—Japan's first railway was projected in 1869, but construction did not start until 1870 and the first section, between Shimbashi (Tokyo) and Yokohama was not opened until 1872. The years 1885 to 1895 saw the rapid growth of privately built lines in various parts of the country. In 1906 and 1907, under the Railway Nationalization Law, the government acquired 17 of the major private lines, boosting the proportion of government-owned mileage from 32% to 91%.

In 1949 the government railways were reorganized into a public corporation, the Japanese National Railways (JNR), which in the 1960s operated about 12,600 route miles of line, most of it 3-ft. 6-in. gauge. There were still about 4,600 mi. of private railways, most of them short, but some carrying heavy traffic.

Japan's railways, largely built to high standards, carry a very heavy traffic. JNR's Tokyo–Ōsaka route (the Tōkaidō line) in the early 1960s carried the heaviest traffic density on the system (about 60 to 80 passenger trains and 50 to 60 freight trains each way daily). However, the capacity of the double-track, electrified 3-ft. 6-in. gauge line had almost been reached. In 1964 a new double-track, standard-gauge line was opened between Tokyo and Ōsaka, a line that had no grade crossings and was built to permit a top speed of 150 mph. This New Tōkaidō line, which carries only passenger trains, proved outstandingly successful and highly profitable. By 1970 it was averaging 240,000 passengers daily in 192 trains (96 each way).

9. Norway.—Norway's first railway was completed in 1854 between Oslo (then Christiania) and Eidsvoll. Railway construction has always been difficult because of the mountainous nature of the country, the rigorous climate, and the relatively small population. Main lines radiate from Oslo to Bergen, Trondheim, the Swedish frontier, and Stavanger. A completely isolated section of the system is the electrified Ofoten Railway from the Swedish frontier at Riksgränsen to Narvik; this carries a heavy iron-ore traffic. Some other lines are also electrified, the longest running from Oslo to Stavanger (370 mi.) and the total electrified mileage in 1968 was 1,313.

10. Pakistan.—The partition of India and Pakistan resulted in the latter having two territories, separated by the widest part of India. As a result Pakistan has two distinct railway systems. East Pakistan is served by the Pakistan Eastern Railway, which has its headquarters at Chittagong. The majority of its route mileage is metre gauge, with some 5-ft. 6-in. gauge and 2-ft. 6-in. gauge. West Pakistan is served by the Pakistan Western Railway, which has its headquarters at Lahore. It is largely 5-ft. 6-in. gauge, with some metre gauge and 2-ft. 6-in. gauge. There is no electrification in Pakistan, but the use of diesel traction was growing in the 1960s.

11. Spain.—The first railway in Spain was the Barcelona–Mataró line, opened Oct. 28, 1848. The topography of the country made subsequent construction slow and expensive. From the many companies in existence there emerged, through a series of consolidations, four major systems. During the civil war of 1936–39, all the railways suffered damage and their position after hostilities ceased was so difficult that the Spanish National Railways (Red Nacional de los Ferrocarriles Españoles) was formed in 1941, taking control of 7,580 mi. of 5-ft. 6-in. gauge lines in 1943. There is also an extensive mileage of narrow-gauge track in the country, operated by about 50 privately owned systems.

12. Sweden.—The railways of Sweden were built partly by private companies and partly by the state. The first standard-gauge line was opened in 1856 and the first trunk line from Stockholm to Göteborg was inaugurated in 1862. As early as 1879 the state began taking over private companies and, in 1939, the Swedish Parliament decided that the majority of lines still privately owned should be taken over by the Swedish State Railways. As a result about 95% of the railway network had come under state control by the 1960s. One of the most important aspects of the system is the heavy traffic in iron ore between mines in Lapland and the ports of Narvik, Norway, and Lulea.

13. U.S.S.R.—A gauge of 6 ft. was selected for the first public railway in Russia, which was opened—with horse traction—in 1836. In the following year, steam traction was introduced, with locomotives supplied from Britain. The first line of any length was from Warsaw to the Austrian frontier, opened in 1848, followed by the 400-mi. Moscow–St. Petersburg (now Leningrad) line, opened in 1851; this was of the 5-ft. gauge, which became the standard in Russia. The network spread somewhat slowly at first, gathering momentum from the 1860s onward, until in 1900 there were about 33,000 mi. of line. At the time of the Russian Revolution, route length was 43,800 mi. and there were 25 state-owned and 13 privately owned systems.

Following the Revolution, the railways were nationalized and by a series of five-year plans the system was rehabilitated and modernized. World War II resulted in the railways being worked to capacity and, in many areas, being extensively damaged. Postwar reconstruction and modernization included diesel traction, electrification, improved signaling and train control apparatus, and new rolling stock. The railway is the principal form of transportation in the U.S.S.R. and handles approximately 80% of all freight traffic.

The network is split up into 45 railways controlled by railway boards, which, in turn, are under the supervision of the Ministry of Transport and Communication.

An important development after World War II was the introduction of dual-gauge passenger coaches which can have the trucks of one gauge exchanged for those of another, using special lifting installations at the break-of-gauge point. This permits the through running of coaches between the Soviet Union and East and West Europe.

One of the most notable lines is the Trans-Siberian Railway, 5,787 mi. long, which links Moscow and Vladivostok. Construction commenced in 1891, the work starting simultaneously from the east and west terminals. Originally, passengers could not make the entire journey by rail but had to travel by boat (or, in winter, by sleigh) across Lake Baikal. However, by 1916 a line had been laid around the lake, allowing the entire journey to be made without changing cars. In the late 1960s the "Russia" express left Moscow daily, requiring eight days to reach Vladivostok. There was also a through train twice weekly between Moscow and Peking (one service via the Trans-Siberian Railway and the other via Ulan Bator).

G. African Railways

Construction of the first railway on the African continent was started in 1852 in Egypt. It was the Alexandria–Cairo line, the first section of which was opened in 1854. It was followed by the opening, in 1860, of a line between Durban and the Point in South Africa. Development of railway mileage in Africa as a whole was slow until the turn of the century, when a number of construction schemes were started. Some other early railway building took place in Tunisia (first line planned in 1875); the Sudan (first tracks of a military line laid in 1897–98); former French Equatorial Africa (construction started in 1880); and Tanganyika (now Tanzania [construction started in 1891]).

1. Republic of South Africa.—In South Africa, the discovery of diamonds at the Cape gave considerable impetus to railway construction. By the time the Union was founded in 1910, about 7,570 mi. of track had been laid, of which the majority was state owned. There were three systems, the Central South African Railways, the Cape Government Railways, and the Natal Government Railways, all of which were merged in 1916. By the 1960s, the South African Railways and Harbours Administration had the most extensive network on the African continent. Apart from the operation of the railroads, the administration operates road services, the principal harbours, and the South African airways.

2. Central Africa.—The East African Railways and Harbours system was formed in 1948 by the amalgamation of the Kenya and Uganda Railways and Harbours and the Tanganyika Railways and Ports services. Construction of the original Uganda Railway was begun at Mombasa in 1895; the site of the present city of Nairobi was reached in 1899 and Kisumu, on Lake Victoria, in 1901. Kampala, the commercial centre of Uganda, was linked with the coast (871 mi.) in 1931 following the completion of a line around the north shore of Lake Victoria and the bridging of the Nile at Jinja. Subsequently, extensions were made to Mityana (1953), Kabagole (1955), Kasese (1956), Gulu (1963), and Mnyusi to Ruvu (1963).

The first line in the Tanganyikan section was completed in 1911, between Tanga and Moshi. The Dar es Salaam line was constructed between 1905 and 1914. A branch from Tabora and Mwanza, on Lake Victoria, was built between 1925 and 1928, after the country came under British mandate. Steam traction predominates, although some diesel locomotives have been introduced.

In 1947 the Southern Rhodesian government purchased the railroad systems in Northern and Southern Rhodesia (now Zambia and Rhodesia) and the Bechuanaland Protectorate (now Botswana). There are connections with the Congo Railway, the Beira

Railway (Mozambique), and the South African Railways. The railway was making growing use of centralized traffic control and it also operated 2,000-hp. diesel locomotives, some of the most powerful units ever built for 3-ft. 6-in. gauge tracks.

In the Democratic Republic of the Congo the principal lines were operated by the Nouvelle Cie du Chemin de Fer du Bas-Congo au Katanga (BCK). The first lines to be built were from Sakania to Bukama (1910 to 1918) and Port Francqui (now Ilebo) to Bukama (1923–28). The Tenke-Dilolo line was started in 1928 and completed in 1931. Another line from Kamina to Kabongo links the BCK with the Société Congolaise des Chemins de Fer du Grand Lac (formerly CFL). The former CFL has 596 route miles of 3-ft. 6-in. gauge track from Kalemi to Kabalo and Kabongo and from Kabalo to Kindu-Port-Empain. A separate 78-mi. metre-gauge line runs from Ubundi to Kisangani.

Other 3-ft. 6-in. gauge systems are found in Nigeria, Malawi, Sudan, Republic of Congo, Ghana, and Angola. The majority of the remaining systems are of metre gauge. In former French West Africa ([1] Senegal to Mali; [2] Guinea; [3] Ivory Coast; and [4] Dahomey) there are four lines of this gauge, totaling 2,542 mi., all operated entirely with diesel traction. The railway system in Ethiopia is also metre gauge. The building of the main line from Djibouti on the coast of French Somaliland (now Afars and Issas) began in 1897 and reached Addis Ababa in 1917.

3. Northern Africa.—Egypt, the scene of the first railroad in Africa, by the 1960s had an extensive standard-gauge system extending to 2,967 mi., with some narrow-gauge mileage as well. There was also a considerable amount of standard-gauge mileage in northern Africa. Post-World War II developments included extensive modernization and the virtual replacement of steam traction by diesel and electric power. There were also other lines of narrower gauges, some of which were being converted to standard gauge.

H. Australasian Railways

1. Australia.—The first railway to be operated by steam traction in Australasia was a 2-mi. line from Flinders Street, Melbourne, to Sandridge (now Port Melbourne). It was built by the Melbourne and Hobson's Bay Railway Company and opened on Sept. 12, 1854. In the following year a second line was opened in New South Wales. Construction was originally in the hands of two private companies, but when they experienced financial difficulties they were bought out by the New South Wales government. The first steam railway in South Australia was opened in 1856. It was 7½ mi. long, of 5-ft. 3-in. gauge, and ran between Adelaide and Port Adelaide. Other parts of Australia did not have the benefits of rail transportation until later.

Unfortunately, in the early days of development each state laid down tracks in whatever gauge it considered most suitable to its needs and finances. Only one state, New South Wales, chose the standard 4-ft. 8½-in. gauge. Victoria and South Australia selected a broad gauge of 5 ft. 3 in. and Queensland and Western Australia chose the narrow 3-ft. 6-in. gauge. This meant that freight often had to be transshipped and passengers transferred from a train of one gauge to that of another.

In later years the Commonwealth Government Railways built several standard-gauge lines, the longest being the Trans-Australian Railway from Port Pirie, South Australia, to Kalgoorlie, Western Australia, a distance of 1,108 mi. A feature of this line is one track length of 300 mi. without a curve, said to be unique in the world. In 1963 a standard-gauge line was opened between Melbourne and Albury that provided, for the first time, through running between Melbourne, Sydney, and Brisbane.

After World War II, efforts were made to standardize gauges, but progress was slow. Adding to the gauge problems were problems of long distances, sparse population, and large concentrations of population in a few large cities.

By 1963, all the principal railway systems were state or government owned.

The Commonwealth Government Railways was unusual in Australia in that it was operating profitably, largely because of the adoption of diesel traction. Piggyback transport (road trailers and semitrailers carried on flat wagons) and container traffic also were introduced on the Trans-Australian route to overcome break-of-gauge delays.

With the completion of the New South Wales System between Broken Hill and Parkes, one of the major problems of the different gauges was ironed out. Uniform width rails (except for a 6-mi. stretch) connect Perth with Sydney and Brisbane. Another standard gauge branch line traverses New South Wales and links up with the Victorian line to Melbourne.

2. New Zealand.—In New Zealand the first railway to be operated with steam traction was opened on Dec. 1, 1863, between Christchurch and Ferrymead. It had a gauge of 5 ft. 3 in.

Following the start of this line, numerous others were built by the different provincial governments. These were of various gauges, but in 1870 an act of the general government stated that all future construction should be of 3-ft. 6-in. gauge. In 1876 the provincial governments were abolished and their railways were taken over by the general government and the lines gradually converted to a uniform 3-ft. 6-in. gauge. Between 1885 and 1908 various private railways also were taken over.

The system was faced with strong competition from air and road transport, but in 1968 it operated at a small profit. In the 1960s emphasis was on increased use of diesel power, the installation of long welded rail, increased use of centralized traffic control, and the completion (in 1955) of the 5¼-mi. Rimutaka tunnel. An unusual operation was the rail-air freight service between the two islands.

The general trend in Australasia was toward the adoption of more modern equipment (particularly diesel traction), electrification where traffic justified it, and improved passenger and freight rolling stock.

II. TRACK AND ROADWAY

1. Railway Location.—Ideally, a railway should be built in a straight line, over level ground, between large centres of trade and travel. In practice, this ideal is rarely approached. In planning, the location engineer must balance the cost of construction against annual maintenance and operating costs, as well as against the probable tonnage to be carried and the revenue it will produce.

Thus, railways in areas of dense population and heavy industrial activity generally have been built for heavy duty—with minimum grades and curvature, heavy bridges and perhaps multiple tracks. This was so in the case of most of the main-line railways of Britain and continental Europe. In sparsely settled country, as in much of the United States during the 19th century, as well as in Canada and South America, railways were built to minimize initial construction costs. As a result, the lines had sharper grades and curves, and were generally of lighter construction. As traffic grew, the main routes were improved to increase their capacity and reduce operating costs.

2. Gauge.—One of the main cost determinants is the gauge, or distance between the inside faces of the running rails. Generally, the narrower the gauge the less costly is the line to construct and equip. This explains why many of the railways in underdeveloped, sparsely settled countries have been built to narrow gauges. On a narrow-gauge line, curvature can be more severe, less space is required and overall construction can be lighter. Disadvantages are the limitation of speed because of reduced lateral stability and limitations in the size of locomotives and rolling stock.

Track gauges vary throughout the world from less than 2 ft. to 5 ft. 6 in., and in the past have been as wide as 7 ft.

About 60% of the world's railway mileage is of so-called standard gauge, which measures 4 ft. 8½ in. It is not clear how this odd width originated. One of many suggested possibilities is that it evolved from the wheel spacing of vehicles used on early English wagonways or tramways, which were the predecessors of the modern railway.

Standard gauge got its foothold in North America through the English locomotives imported for some of the earliest U.S. lines. Today, nearly all the railway mileage in North America is standard gauge, although in the early years many lines were built in both wider and narrower sizes.

In Central and South America are to be found extremes ranging from 1 ft. 11⅝ in. to 5 ft. 6 in. The majority is narrow gauge, although many countries have systems in different gauges—a legacy of uncoordinated development. Standard gauge, or a width so nearly identical as to allow the through running of vehicles, is found in most of Europe, excepting Finland and the Soviet Union (5 ft.), Ireland (5 ft. 3 in.) and Spain and Portugal (5 ft. 6 in.). A considerable mileage of narrow gauges—including metre (39.37 in.), 2 ft. 6 in., and 1 ft. 11⅝ in.—also exists on the continent of Europe, particularly in Germany, Austria, Spain, and Switzerland.

In Africa the principal gauges are 3 ft. 6 in. and 1 m. India and Pakistan both have extensive 5-ft. 6-in. broad-gauge systems, together with a large metre-gauge mileage and narrow-gauge lines of 2 ft. and 2 ft. 6 in. The lines of the Japanese National Railways are of 3-ft. 6-in. gauge, except for the standard-gauge New Tōkaidō (Tokyo–Ōsaka) line. Japan also has a number of short, privately owned railways, some of which are standard gauge, as well as 3 ft. 6 in. The railways of mainland China, on the other hand, are laid largely to standard gauge, although there is some 5 ft. and narrow gauge as well. New Zealand employs a gauge of 3 ft. 6 in., but Australia has major networks in three different gauges: 3 ft. 6 in., 4 ft. 8½ in., and 5 ft. 3 in.

The benefits of a uniform gauge were recognized early. It permits free interchange of cars between various railway lines, thus speeding the flow of commerce and, of course, greatly reducing the overall cost of transporting goods and people. Only because of this virtual uniformity of railway gauge in North America was the railway able to play the dominant role in the settling and development of that continent. Conversely, in areas where uniformity of gauge has not been achieved, such as South America and Australia, development of the railways—and consequently the economic growth of the countries they serve—has been correspondingly slowed.

TABLE II.—*Railway Systems of Selected Countries*

Country	Service commenced	Ownership*	Gauge†	Mileage‡
Argentina	1857	state	5′ 6″	25,560
			metre	
Australia	1854	state	standard	8,397
			5′ 3″	5,667
			3′ 6″	11,746
Austria		state	standard	4,084
Belgium	1835	state	standard	2,695
Brazil	1854	state	metre	19,847
Bulgaria	1866	state	standard	2,329
Burma	1877	state	metre	1,925
Canada	1836	state	standard	41,481
Ceylon	1865	state	5′ 6″	939
China	1881	state	standard	23,900
Czechoslovakia		state	standard	8,284
Denmark	1847	state	standard	2,198
Egypt	1854	state	standard	2,802
Finland	1862	state	5′	3,465
France	1828	state	standard	23,275
Germany	1835	state	standard	28,418
Greece		state	standard	1,598
Hungary	1846	state	standard	6,256
India	1853	state	5′ 6″	17,768
			metre	15,867
			2′ 6″; 2′	2,693
Indonesia		state	3′ 6″	3,788
Ireland	1834	state	5′ 3″	1,537
Italy	1839	state	standard	10,078
Japan	1872	state	3′ 6″	13,200
		private	3′ 6″	3,500
Mexico	1850	state	standard	12,261
Netherlands	1839	state	standard	2,005
New Zealand	1863	state	3′ 6″	3,140
Norway	1854	state	standard	2,642
Pakistan		state	5′ 6″	5,191
			metre	1,457
			2′ 6″	400
Poland	1845	state	standard	16,553
Portugal	1856	state	5′ 6″	2,238
South Africa	1860	state	3′ 6″	13,701
Spain	1848	state	5′ 6″	11,429
Sweden	1856	state	standard	8,020
Switzerland	1844	state	standard	1,765
		private	narrow	1,192
Taiwan	1891	state	3′ 6″	609
Thailand	1893	state	metre	2,339
Turkey		state	standard	4,976
U.S.S.R.	1837	state	5′	82,828
United Kingdom	1825	state	standard	13,559
United States	1830	private	standard	210,500
Yugoslavia		state	standard	7,053

*Predominant ownership is given; most countries have both private- and state-owned lines.
†Gauge of the principal mileage; most countries have lines of several gauges.
‡Data are for the late 1960s.

The principal gauges in use in major countries are shown in Table II. The total route length of all railways throughout the world is 781,000 mi., divided approximately as follows: North America, 36%; Europe, 34%; Asia, 12%; Central and South America, 8%; Africa, 6%; Australia and New Zealand, 4%.

3. Rail.—Railway track as we know it originated in the plateways used in English coal mines, consisting of squared timbers on top of which iron plates were fastened. The earliest examples of iron rail were L-shaped, the upright portion keeping the flangeless wagon wheels running on the flat baseplate. From this developed the I-shaped rail, which was carried in pedestals or chairs, these in turn being secured to stone blocks or, later, wooden sleepers or crossties. The rails were retained in position in the chairs with the aid of oak keys.

The I-shaped rail led to the bullhead rail, in which the head was of greater area than the foot. The use of this rail in conjunction with chairs attached to wooden ties became the standard for the British railway systems until 1949; the weight of rail for main lines was 95 lb. per yard and the length 60 ft. After 1949, British railways were converting to a standard flat-bottomed rail weighing 109 lb. per yard.

In the 1830s a French engineer, Charles Vignoles, invented the flat-bottomed rail, which was like an inverted T. It was spiked direct to the tie, which made for simple and inexpensive construction. A further refinement was the introduction, in 1847, of the fishplate, which joined the ends of the rails together. This kept the ends of adjoining rails in alignment.

The majority of continental railways and those in other areas adopted the flat-bottomed rail from the beginning. The standard rail length in Europe is 30 m. (98 ft. 5 in.) and the weight, for main line use, is 118.8 lb. per metre, or about 109 lb. per yard.

Some of the earliest U.S. railways used iron rails shaped like an inverted U, but, since iron had to be imported from England, it was very costly. A more common and much less expensive type of construction consisted of iron straps fastened to the tops of longitudinal wooden stringers. The main problem with these iron straps was their often disastrous tendency to break loose and slash up through the floors of passing cars.

The modern type of track, using the flat-bottomed T rail on wooden crossties or sleepers, was tried in the United States as early as 1831. The Camden and Amboy Railroad and Transportation Company used iron T rails designed by its president, Robert L. Stevens. At first they were attached, with spikes much like those used today, into wooden plugs inserted in stone blocks. Later, during a shortage of the stone blocks, the rails were spiked directly to wooden ties in order to keep the construction going. The emergency wooden ties proved far superior. The track was more flexible; it held up better, gave a smoother ride, and was much easier on the rolling stock.

It was not long before most of the railways in the United States began using this type of construction, although it did not become standard until about 1850 (as late as 1848 the Galena and Chicago Union Railroad laid some strap-iron track). Iron rails were used in the United States until 1865, when rails of Bessemer steel made their appearance. By the early 1900s U.S. railways were using open-hearth steel rails, which soon largely supplanted Bessemer steel.

Although present-day rail is, in appearance, similar to the early designs of Stevens and Vignoles, it is actually a highly refined product in terms of both engineering and metallurgy. Much study and research have produced rail designs that minimize internal stresses under the weight of traffic, and thus prolong rail life. Sometimes the rail surface is hardened to reduce the wear of the rail under extremely heavy cars or on sharp curves. After they have been rolled at the steel mills, rails are allowed to cool slowly in special cooling boxes. This controlled cooling minimizes internal shatter cracks which at one time were a major cause of broken rails in track.

Hundreds of different rail cross sections were designed for U.S. and Canadian railways, and most of the larger lines used sections of their own design. Many of these rail sections are still in use, but there developed a strong trend toward standardizing on a few

sections. The bulk of the new rail being purchased in the 1960s in North America was of sections weighing 115, 132, or 136 lb. per yard. The standard U.S. rail length is 39 ft.

In general, lighter rail sections are used in countries other than the United States and Canada. This is partly because most use lighter rolling stock; in some it is also due to traffic conditions or the need for economy in building the railways. Rail sections varying from 36 to 75 lb. per yard are common in South America. In Japan, 110-lb. rail, or heavier, is used on dense traffic lines, but there is much mileage of lighter rails in service.

Rail Fittings.—As rolling stock became heavier, railways found that under heavy traffic the rails tended to dig into the crossties, thus shortening the life of ties and making it difficult to maintain proper gauge and track alignment. To overcome this difficulty, tie plates are used between the base of the rail and the top of the tie. These plates (they may be up to 14 to 16 in. long on U.S. heavy-traffic lines) distribute the load over more of the tie area. In some cases a resilient tie pad of rubber or a similar material is used between the tie plate and the tie.

The standard spike, with offset head, is still the most used fastening. It is driven through holes in the tie plates. In some cases railways have used special types of fastenings, including screw spikes and compression clips. These do an excellent job for critical locations, as on sharp curves or bridges, but they are considered too expensive for general use in the United States. Bolts or clips are used extensively in Europe.

Welded Rail.—One of the most important developments was the welding of rail into long lengths. This continuous welded rail increases travel comfort and saves maintenance. The rail is usually welded into lengths of up to a half-mile. In some cases these lengths have, in turn, been welded together to produce rails several miles long without a break.

Welded rail was tried for the first time anywhere in 1933 by the Delaware and Hudson Railroad in the United States. This line had laid 30-odd miles of continuous rail by 1939. It was not until the decade of the 1950s, however, that U.S. railways began to turn to welded rail in earnest. By 1969 nearly all the rail being laid in the United States was in welded lengths; and 10% of the country's route mileage consisted of long rails. Welded rail was also standard practice or extensively used in many other countries, including Japan, Canada, Germany, France, and Britain. In France, SNCF alone laid more than 6,000 mi. of long welded track between 1951 and 1966.

Controlling the temperature expansion of long welded rails proved not so difficult as was first thought. It was found that the problem could be minimized by extensive anchorage of the rails against the ties to prevent them from moving when the temperature changes, and by laying the rails when the ambient temperature is close to the mean temperature prevailing in the particular locality. In France and some other countries, beveled expansion joints, in appearance somewhat like switch points, are sometimes provided at the ends of long welded rails.

4. Crossties (Sleepers).—Although timber is still the commonest tie material, both steel and concrete also are used. Steel ties are common in certain European countries, notably Switzerland, and they have also been adopted by a number of African and Asian systems. Concrete ties gained in popularity after initial stressing problems were overcome. Both prestressed and poststressed types are in use, as well as concrete ties and concrete blocks joined by metal spacing bars. A combination of concrete ties and long welded rail is said to produce an especially solid form of track.

With concrete ties, the resilience of wood is, of course, lost. To avoid excessive pounding of both the tie and rolling stock, some form of cushioning pad, of rubber or similar material, is always used between the tie plate and the concrete ties. Bolts or clips are used to fasten the rail to the tie.

Methods of treating wooden ties with preservative chemicals (usually creosote) were improved to a degree that the average life of crossties in the United States increased to more than 30 years. Nevertheless, the cost of wooden ties rose steadily, thus creating some interest in ties made of substitute materials. By 1969 a number of U.S. railways were using concrete ties to a limited extent. One, the St. Louis-San Francisco (Frisco), had built a new 33-mi. branch line entirely with concrete ties. The Florida East Coast Railway was using concrete ties regularly in main-line renewals.

5. Roadbed.—Early U.S. railways often were constructed as cheaply as possible. This meant that they usually followed the contour of the ground; earth cuts and fills, where required, were minimized. Railways built in this way often have steep grades and sharp curves, features that greatly increase operating costs and restrict train length and speed. With the advent of modern high-capacity earth-moving machinery (developed primarily for highway construction) in many cases railways were able to eliminate the old adverse grades and curves through line changes. Graders, bulldozers, and similar equipment make it practicable to dig deeper cuts through hillsides and to make higher fills where necessary in order to smooth out the profile of the track, and to do this at a reasonable cost.

Modern equipment also helped railways improve their existing roadbeds, even where major changes were not required. For instance, a number of railways carried out ditching programs in which the drainage ditches on each side of the right-of-way were deepened, thus improving drainage and increasing the stability of the roadbed. Where roadbed conditions are unstable, railways often find it pays to remove the unstable material and replace it with filler material from another location. Stabilizing of the subgrade by injecting concrete grout under pressure is another widely used technique. In planning roadbed improvements, as well as in new construction, railways turned to modern soil engineering techniques (*see* SOIL MECHANICS).

The first step in building a new railway line, after the route has been surveyed and cleared of brush and trees, is to grade the right-of-way, much as is done in building a highway. Next, the ties are distributed and the rails laid and spiked. Then, ballast (usually crushed rock, slag, or volcanic ash) is applied. Finally, the track is aligned in both the horizontal and vertical planes and the ballast is tamped or compacted around and under the ties.

In Canada, where much new railway mileage was built in the years following World War II, track-laying machines often were used. A track-laying machine, mounted on railcars, feeds ties and rails ahead of the working crew, moving forward over the new track as soon as it is spiked down.

6. Track Maintenance.—Until after World War II, the system of section maintenance—descended from the early days of railways—remained standard in the United States and Canada. The typical section was only a few miles in length. It was under the supervision of a section foreman and a gang which might vary in size from 4 to 12 men. They had only a few hand tools. However, because of rapidly rising labour costs, the pressure to develop more economical track maintenance methods became intense.

With modern techniques, a small mechanized force of men can maintain a long stretch of track to high standards. Machines are available to do all the necesary track and maintenance jobs: removing and inserting ties, tamping ballast, spiking rail, tightening joint-bar bolts, and leveling and aligning the track. Mechanized forces also can renew rail, either in conventional bolted lengths or with continuous welded lengths; they use cranes to remove the old rail and lay the new. Gauging, spiking, and bolt-tightening devices complete the installation.

Ballast-cleaning machines pick up old ballast, sift it, reject oversize or undersize stones, and replace it. Tamping machines consolidate ballast beneath the ties, thus improving running conditions. Scarifiers break up hard, compressed ballast. Complete sections of track—rails and crossties—may be prefabricated at a central shop and then laid on the site by mechanical means.

Rail-grinding machines are used to even out irregularities that occur on the running surface of rails. For checking any irregularities in track alignment, other machines are capable of testing for gauge, curvature, etc., while in motion, the results being recorded on moving charts. So-called detector cars, equipped with electronic inspection apparatus, move over main-line tracks periodically to locate any internal flaws in the rails that might cause them to break under the stress of traffic.

Mechanization reduced the number of track and roadway maintenance workers in the United States by more than one-half in the years following World War II. It constituted a major technological revolution. Improved and more automatic maintenance machines were constantly being developed, and U.S. railways were adopting new construction techniques that promised to reduce the amount of maintenance the track structure requires. The trend to mechanization of track and roadway work was evident also in many other countries, but, in most, mechanization was less advanced, largely because labour costs were not so high as in the United States.

III. LOCOMOTIVES

Although some of the earliest railways used horses for motive power, it was only after the development of practical locomotives that railways became efficient arteries of volume transportation.

Normally the term locomotive refers to a separate unit incorporating nothing more than the machinery to generate (or, in the case of an electric locomotive, to convert) power. However, motive power also can be incorporated in a vehicle equipped with passenger or baggage accommodations, or both. Broadly speaking, there are three sources of power for a locomotive: steam, oil, and electricity. Steam, the earliest form of propulsion, was in universal use for over 100 years, but after World War II the popularity of the steam locomotive dwindled in favour of diesel and electric traction, which are more efficient.

The steam locomotive is a self-sufficient unit, carrying its own water supply for steam generation and either coal, oil, or wood for heating the boiler. The diesel locomotive also carries its own fuel oil supply, but because of the characteristics of the diesel engine, direct drive to the wheels is not employed. Instead, mechanical, hydraulic, or electric transmission is used; with the last, the diesel engine drives a generator to produce electric power and this, in turn, is fed to traction motors that propel the vehicle.

With electric traction the locomotive normally is not self-sufficient. As the locomotive moves along the track, electric current is picked up from either an overhead conductor wire or a third rail mounted alongside the running rails. The only self-sufficient examples are battery-driven electric locomotives and railcars, which are not widely used. The only other category of motive power is the turbine locomotive—either the turbo-diesel or the gas turbine. Both use oil fuel and have electric, hydraulic, or mechanical transmission.

A. STEAM LOCOMOTIVES

It was George Stephenson's "Rocket"—winner of the Liverpool and Manchester Railway's competition of 1829—that ensured a place for the steam locomotive as a means of propulsion and the railway as a means of transport. The success of the "Rocket" was attributed to its multitube boiler and its more efficient system for exhausting the steam and creating a draft in the firebox, basic features that continued to be used in the steam locomotive. The principal characteristics of the "Rocket" were a boiler pressure of 50 pounds per square inch (psi); cylinders $8 \times 16\frac{1}{2}$ in.; one pair of driving wheels, 4 ft. $8\frac{1}{2}$ in. in diameter; and a total weight of about 9,500 lb.

The number of coupled drive wheels soon increased. After the "Rocket," with its single pair of driving wheels, came the four-coupled locomotive, followed by the six-coupled. The number of coupled wheels grew to a maximum of 14. Additional wheels of smaller diameter are often provided ahead of and behind the coupled wheels. The pilot wheels ahead of the coupled wheels fulfill various functions, the principal one being to assist in guiding the coupled wheels around curves. The pilot wheels usually consist of two on a single axle or four on two axles. Those to the rear of the coupled wheels normally support the weight of the firebox, enabling it to be larger than if it had to be accommodated between the last pair of coupled wheels. (Common wheel arrangements, and methods of designating them, are shown in Table III.)

Steam locomotive driving wheels are of various diameters, usually larger on passenger locomotives and smaller on freight locomotives. In Europe the average is between 66 and 78 in. for

TABLE III.—*Designations of Wheel Arrangements of Steam Locomotives*

Symbol			Wheel Arrangement (Front to Back)	Type name
U.S.-British	French	German		
0-6-0	0-3-0	C	○○○	Six-wheel switcher, Bourbonnais
0-8-0	0-4-0	D	○○○○	Eight-wheel switcher
2-6-0	1-3-0	1C	○○○○	Mogul
2-6-2	1-3-1	1C1	○○○○○	Prairie
2-8-0	1-4-0	1D	○○○○○	Consolidation
2-8-2	1-4-1	1D1	○○○○○○	Mikado
2-8-4	1-4-2	1D2	○○○○○○○	Berkshire
2-10-0	1-5-0	1E	○○○○○○	Decapod
2-10-2	1-5-1	1E1	○○○○○○○	Santa Fe
2-10-4	1-5-2	1E2	○○○○○○○○	Texas
4-4-0	2-2-0	2B	○○○○	American
4-4-2	2-2-1	2B1	○○○○○	Atlantic
4-6-0	2-3-0	2C	○○○○○	Ten-wheeler
4-6-2	2-3-1	2C1	○○○○○○	Pacific
4-6-4	2-3-2	2C2	○○○○○○○	Hudson, Baltic
4-8-2	2-4-1	2D1	○○○○○○○	Mountain, Mohawk
4-8-4	2-4-2	2D2	○○○○○○○○	Northern, Niagara, Pocono
4-8-8-4	2-4-4-2	2D-D2	○○○○○○○○○○○○	Union Pacific "Big Boy"

express passenger engines and 54 and 66 in. for freight or mixed-traffic types. Typical locomotives built in the United States just before the end of the steam era had drivers ranging from 60 to 84 in. in diameter. At one time it was thought that locomotives with small coupled wheels could not be operated at high speeds, but this later was disproved; for example, 2-10-0's with 5-ft. diameter wheels have been run at 90 mph.

Supplies of coal and water can be carried on the locomotive frame itself (in which case it is called a tank engine) or can be carried in a separate vehicle (the tender) attached to the locomotive; the latter arrangement allows far greater supplies of fuel to be carried. The average capacity of a tender of a European main-line locomotive is 10 tons of coal and 8,000 gal. of water. In the U.S.S.R. and on some African, Asian, and Australian systems, higher capacities are common. The tender for a typical large U.S. steam locomotive of the World War II period was carried on 14 wheels and had a capacity of 28 tons of coal and 25,000 gal. of water.

1. U.S. Locomotives.—In relatively short order, the steam locomotive in the United States evolved to the general type that became known as the American Standard. It had a horizontal fire-tube boiler, a four-wheel pilot truck to steady and guide the front of the locomotive, and four coupled driving wheels. This 4-4-0 type was used for all kinds of services; it dominated United States railroading until well after the Civil War period. In fact, many 4-4-0's were still in service in the early years of the 20th century.

Nevertheless, to meet the needs of heavy freight traffic, other types of locomotives with more (and usually smaller) drive wheels were developed. Common were the Mogul (2-6-0), the Consolidation (2-8-0), and the Mikado (2-8-2). The Union Pacific used a three-cylinder 4-12-2, which had 12 coupled driving wheels. In the late years of steam locomotive development, still greater tractive effort was obtained by using two separate engine units under a common boiler. These articulated locomotives culminated in the Union Pacific's famous "Big Boy," said to be the largest steam locomotive ever built. Used in mountain freight service, "Big Boy" was an articulated 4-8-8-4 type that weighed nearly 600 tons. It could exert 135,375 lb. of tractive force and developed over 6,000 hp. at 75 mph.

2. Articulated Locomotives.—Articulated designs also have been produced in other countries. One of the best known is the Beyer-Garratt, in which there are two frames, each having its own driving wheels and cylinders, surmounted by water tanks. Separating the two chassis is another frame carrying the boiler, cab, and coal or fuel-oil supplies. This type of locomotive is of particular value on tracks that permit only light-axle loads, as the weight is spread over a considerable distance. Also, the Beyer-Garratt can negotiate sharp curves. It is widely used in Africa.

Another form of articulation is the Mallet, in which there is a long, rigid frame, below which are two sets of driving wheels, each with its own set of cylinders. The rear driving wheels are frame mounted, but the leading ones are pivoted. The name is taken from the Swiss engineer Anatole Mallet, who devised the layout for use with compound propulsion.

Simple-expansion steam locomotives can be equipped with two or more cylinders and, especially in Britain, three- and four-cylinder locomotives were common. For double expansion or compounding, more than two cylinders are mandatory. In this system, steam goes first to one or two small cylinders and then to two larger cylinders before being exhausted into the atmosphere; thus it is expanded or used twice, resulting in greater thermal efficiency. In Europe, compound locomotives were most popular in France, where for many years the majority of the designs were of this type.

3. Modern Types.—Steam locomotives are still used to a limited extent in some European countries, but they are rare in main-line service. Typical of the modern continental locomotive is the French railways' 2-4-1 P class (4-8-2), a four-cylinder compound engine with 79½-in. drivers, a boiler pressure of 250 psi and tractive effort of 45,084 lb. A typical British postwar design was the "West Country" class Pacific (4-6-2) with three cylinders, 74-in. driving wheels and a tractive effort of 27,720 lb. The South African Railways class 25 (4-8-4) has two cylinders, 60-in. driving wheels, and develops 51,400 lb. of tractive effort. The Indian Government Railways class WG (2-8-2) has 61½-in. driving wheels and develops 38,890 lb. of tractive effort.

Typical of latter-day U.S. steam passenger locomotives were the Pacific (4-6-2) and the Hudson or Baltic (4-6-4), which could haul heavy trains at high speeds. The Mountain (4-8-2) and Northern (4-8-4) types were logical further developments in passenger train power. The New York Central's Niagara 4-8-4 represented perhaps the highest stage of development in passenger locomotives; also used in high-speed freight service, it had a tractive force of 61,500 lb. and developed 4,850 hp. at 65 mph.

Various refinements gradually improved the reciprocating steam locomotive. Some included higher boiler pressures (up to 290 psi in France and up to 310 psi for some of the last U.S. locomotives), superheating, feed-water preheating, roller bearings, and the use of poppet valves instead of the sliding piston valve. Nevertheless, the thermal efficiency of even the best modern steam locomotives seldom exceeds about 6%. Incomplete combustion, heat losses from the firebox, stack, boiler and cylinders, and other losses dissipate most of the energy of the fuel burned. In terms of modern technology, the reciprocating steam locomotive is obsolete. Yet it had its good points, not the least of which were its simplicity and ability to withstand abuse. (*See* also STEAM.)

B. ELECTRIC LOCOMOTIVES

The first challenge to the supremacy of steam came from the electric locomotive. Although efforts to propel railway vehicles using batteries date back to 1835, the first successful application of electric traction was in 1879, when a locomotive designed by Werner von Siemens was operated at an exhibition in Berlin. In 1881 the first public electric railway commenced operation at Lichterfelde, near Berlin; in 1883 the first part of Magnus Volk's electric railway at Brighton, Eng., was opened. Another early electric line was the City and South London Railway between King William Street and Stockwell. This was opened in 1890 and was the first electric underground railway. The initial applications of electric traction were for suburban or metropolitan railways such as those in Berlin, Budapest, Paris, and London (*see* ELECTRIC TRACTION). In 1895 the B & O electrified a stretch of track in Baltimore to avoid smoke and noise problems in a tunnel, marking the first use of electrification by a steam railway in the United States.

One of the first countries to use electric traction for main-line purposes was Italy, where a three-phase, 3,000-v. system was inaugurated in 1902. In the same year, some remarkable experiments were carried out on an experimental line near Berlin, where an electric train achieved a speed of 130.4 mph.

By 1906, a number of electrified lines were operating all over Europe and a start had been made on major electrification schemes. Of these, the most extensive was in Switzerland, where large-scale electrification started at the end of World War I. Other countries that began extensive electrification in the 1920s were Sweden, Germany, and Austria. All of these, together with Norway, made use of the same system: 15,000-v., 16⅔-cycle, single-phase AC. In other countries, direct current was preferred, although Italy electrified a considerable mileage with 3,700-v., 16⅔-cycle, three-phase AC. The use of the overhead conductor wire was almost universal, except for suburban lines and the Southern Railway in Britain. By the end of the 1920s nearly every European country had at least a small percentage of electrified track. Electric traction was also introduced in Australia (1919), New Zealand (1923), India (1925), Indonesia (1925), and South Africa (1926).

Following the pioneer B & O tunnel electrification, a number of other terminals in the United States (such as the New York Central's Grand Central terminal in New York City) and difficult mountain segments of main lines were electrified. Some of these relatively small electrifications were later removed with the advent of the diesel locomotive.

In the late 1960s, the only major line-of-road electrifications in the United States were on the Penn Central (about 750 route miles between New Haven, Conn., and the New York-Philadelphia-Harrisburg-Washington areas) and on the Milwaukee Road in Montana, Idaho, and Washington (about 660 mi.).

The suburban passenger services of several U.S. and Canadian railways were electrified, including the Canadian National at Montreal, the Long Island, Erie-Lackawanna, and Penn Central railways around New York City, the Penn Central and Reading lines around Philadelphia, and the Illinois Central at Chicago. Several South American countries (notably Brazil) have small mileages of electrified track. About 22% of the route mileage of the Japanese National Railways is electrified.

Following World War II, electrification was greatly extended in Europe in a comparatively few years, and there was also expansion in Africa, Asia, and Australasia.

1. Advantages and Disadvantages.—Electric traction is generally accepted as the most economical and efficient means of operating a railway, provided the traffic justifies the capital expenditure and cheap electricity is available.

Being simply power-converting, rather than power-generating, devices, electric locomotives have several very real advantages. Since they draw on the resources of the central power plant, they can develop power greatly in excess of their nominal ratings to start a heavy train or surmount a steep grade. A typical modern electric locomotive rated at 4,000 hp. has been observed to develop as much as 10,000 hp. for a short period under these conditions. Moreover, electric locomotives are quieter in operation than other types, produce no smoke or fumes, accelerate rapidly, and are completely predictable in performance. Electric locomotives have a high availability factor (that is, they require little time in the shop for maintenance) and, because of their relatively simple construction, the maintenance costs are low. It also appears that electric locomotives have a longer economic life than diesels.

The greatest drawback to electrified operation is the high capital investment and maintenance expense of the fixed plant—the trolley wires and structures, power substations, and associated equipment. A less important disadvantage is the lack of flexibility of electric motive power: it cannot operate where there are no trolley wires.

Electric operation is most suited to railway systems carrying very dense traffic; this is the basic reason why it made rapid headway in many European countries. In Japan, too, further electrification was undertaken as a means of more economically handling the extremely heavy traffic that characterizes its railways.

2. Types of Systems.—Electric traction systems can be broadly divided into those using alternating current (AC) and those using direct current (DC). With DC, the most popular line voltages are 1,500 and 3,000, although there is a large mileage in southeastern England of 600-v. and several systems in the 600–700-v. range around New York City. The disadvantages of DC are that

expensive substations are required at frequent intervals and the overhead wire or third rail must be relatively large and heavy. Thus, a very high density of traffic is necessary to justify the cost of this form of electrification.

However, the low-voltage, series-wound DC motor is well suited to traction purposes, being simple to construct and easily controlled. Typical of modern locomotives for DC operation is the French railways' 1,500-v. 9200 series, weighing 82 tons and developing 5,200 hp. It was on a line equipped with the 1,500-v. DC system that, in March 1955, two different types of French locomotives achieved a speed of 205 mph.

Single-phase AC at 16⅔ cycles per second (cps) also is widely used by a number of European systems. With this system, substations need not be so numerous nor does the power transmission equipment need to be so substantial. Its application has been bound up with the lengthy development of the AC commutator motor. Initial AC electrification was on the three-phase system and the first practical application was on the Burgdorf-Thun Railway in Switzerland in 1899, using a line voltage of 750. The first trial with a single-phase supply was on the Seebach-Wettingen line in Switzerland in 1907. The Bern-Lötschberg-Simplon, another Swiss system, was the first railway to be operated on single-phase, 16⅔-cycle AC, at a line voltage of 15,000, throughout its length (1910–13) and this type of power was subquently adopted by the Swiss Federal Railways. In the United States, single-phase AC at 25 cycles was used on a number of main-line electrifications. Most of the Penn Central system is of this type.

Quite early in the development of electric traction the question of using AC at the industrial or commercial frequency (50 cps in Europe, 60 in the U.S.) was considered. Use of commercial-frequency AC means that current can be obtained from the commercial supply network, eliminating the need for the railways to generate and distribute their own power. The overhead contact wire can be much lighter, far fewer substations are necessary, and, therefore, lines with a lower density of traffic can be electrified on a profitable basis. Initial experiments with 50-cycle AC were carried out in Hungary in 1933, using a line voltage of 16,000. In the same year the German State Railways decided to experiment on the Höllental branch with this form of electrification, using a line voltage of 20,000.

In 1945 Louis Armand, former president of French Railways, set up a commission to study 50-cycle operation on the Höllental line. As a result, French Railways pressed forward with the further development of 50-cycle electrification, converting a line between Aix-les-Bains and La Roche-sur-Foron for their first practical experiments. This was so successful that in 1952 it was decided to electrify a network of lines in northeastern France using 25,000-v., 50-cycle, single-phase AC. Subsequently, a number of other countries adopted 50-cycle electrification, including Britain, Turkey, Portugal, the Soviet Union, India, mainland China, Japan, and Argentina.

With the commercial-frequency AC system, there are three ways of taking power to the driving wheels: (1) a rotary converter or static rectifier to convert the AC supply to DC to drive DC traction motors; (2) a phase converter to produce three-phase, variable-frequency current to drive AC motors; (3) direct use of AC traction motors. The first method, using mercury-arc, germanium, or silicon rectifiers, is the most popular.

The problem of international operation of electric locomotives in Europe was increased by the variety of electrification systems. It was partially overcome by the construction of multivoltage and multifrequency locomotives. A similar problem exists in New York City, where trains of the former New Haven Railroad operate into Grand Central terminal over a 660-v. DC system. Equipment on this line can operate on either 660-v. DC or 11,000-v., 25-cycle AC. This line also operates unique electric-diesel electrics. When in the terminal these locomotives operate from the 660-v. third rail; at all other times their traction motors are supplied from a standard diesel-electric engine-generator set carried on the locomotive.

Although electrification had made little headway in the United States up to mid-20th century, several factors were at work that showed promise of resulting in further electrification. These included the demand for faster freight trains, the rising costs of diesel fuel, and a trend toward mergers that would tend to increase traffic density on the surviving lines. There was also the possibility of reducing fixed-plant costs through the use of the high-voltage, commercial-frequency system that has proved so successful in Europe and Japan.

C. DIESEL-ELECTRIC LOCOMOTIVES

By the end of the 1960s the diesel-electric locomotive (or simply, the diesel) had almost completely superseded the steam locomotive as the standard railway motive power in North America, as well as in many other parts of the world. During the 25 years ending in 1960 U.S. railways had completely replaced the steam locomotive—which had been standard for 100 years—with the diesel. Actually, most of this change was accomplished in an even shorter period: as late as 1951 U.S. railways had had more steam locomotives than diesels in service.

TABLE IV.—*Designations of Wheel Arrangements of Electric and Diesel-Electric Locomotives*

Symbol	Wheel Arrangement (front to back)	Description
A1A-A1A	○○○–○○○	Single-unit locomotive with two six-wheel trucks, each with centre idler axle.
B-B	○○–○○	Single-unit locomotive with two four-wheel trucks, all axles driven.
C-C	○○○–○○○	Single-unit locomotive with two six-wheel trucks, all axles driven.
2+(B–B)	○○–○○ + ○○–○○	Two-unit locomotive, each with two four-wheel trucks, all axles driven, units joined with articulated connection.
2-C+C-2	○○○○○ + ○○○○○	Electric locomotive with four-wheel leading and trailing (idler) trucks; six driven axles in two frames with articulated connection between frames.

What caused the diesel to supersede the faithful steam locomotive so rapidly? Briefly, the pressure of competition from other modes of transport and the continuing rise in wage costs forced the railways to improve their services and adopt every possible measure to increase operating efficiency. Compared with the steam locomotive, the diesel has a number of major advantages. For instance:

It can operate for long periods with relatively little down time for maintenance. This high availability makes it possible for diesels to operate through on a run 2,000 mi. or more in length and then, after brief servicing, to start the return trip. Steam locomotives must be serviced after only a few hours in operation and thus are limited to relatively short runs.

It uses less fuel than a steam locomotive (its thermal efficiency is about four times as great).

It can accelerate a train more rapidly and run at higher sustained speeds with less damage to the track structure.

These are the major points at which the diesel excels. It is also superior to the steam locomotive because of its smoother acceleration, greater cleanliness, standardized repair parts, and operating flexibility (a number of diesel units can be combined and run by one man under multiple-unit [MU] control). With diesels, too, there is no problem of supplying large quantities of boiler feed water; there is no loss of power capability in cold weather; and there is less stand-by cost, since the locomotive can be completely shut down when not in use.

Because of advantages such as these, most U.S. railways found that diesel locomotives quickly paid for themselves, despite their relatively high initial cost. It is no exaggeration to say that without the diesel locomotive the U.S. railways could not have continued solvent under private operation.

1. Early Diesel Development.—The earliest patent for an oil-engine using the compression-ignition principle was granted in 1890 to a British pioneer, Akroyd Stuart. A small locomotive incorporating an engine of Stuart's design was built by Hornsby and Sons in 1896. The first patent for a compression-ignition engine was granted to the German engineer Rudolf Diesel in 1894, and the first engine to be built in accordance with his designs was completed in 1897 (*see* DIESEL ENGINE). The pioneer diesel-engine locomotive of any size was a 1,000-hp. unit built by the Diesel-Klose-Sulzer Company in 1912. It had a four-cylinder, two-stroke engine directly coupled to the driving wheels. This was followed in 1913 by the first diesel-electric railcar to operate in regular service, a Swedish design powered by a 75-hp. engine coupled to a DC generator.

Gasoline-engine vehicles were in existence as early as the first compression-ignition engines. In 1891 two German firms jointly produced a small industrial locomotive with a 4-hp. gasoline engine, and numerous other examples of gasoline-engine vehicles were produced in several countries following the turn of the century. Railcars of various kinds with gasoline engines continued to be used up to the 1930s. In Europe, however, gasoline was too expensive to use for traction purposes, and its flammability was a source of danger in the event of an accident.

The earliest ancestors of the modern diesel locomotive in the United States were the gasoline-driven railcars used by the Union Pacific and other railways on branch-line passenger runs beginning early in the 20th century. The engines used in these cars were neither powerful nor reliable, nor were their mechanical transmissions suitable for such severe service. Next, gasoline-electric railcars were developed, using larger engines and electric, rather than mechanical, transmissions. These proved more satisfactory, but they still did not fully solve the problem of branch-line passenger service.

After World War I, increased highway competition made the problem of money-losing branch lines even more critical in the United States and led to renewed interest in gas-electric cars. The Electro-Motive Company was formed in 1922 to build gas-electric cars, using engines supplied by the Winton Engine Company and electrical equipment by the General Electric Company. Meanwhile, the American Locomotive Company (Alco) had been experimenting with diesel engines and in 1925 produced the first commercially successful diesel-electric switching locomotive. This 300-hp., 60-ton unit was sold to the Central Railroad of New Jersey for service at its Bronx terminal in New York City. The locomotive went to work in October 1925 and served continuously until its retirement in 1957 (it is now preserved at the B & O transportation museum in Baltimore).

A little-remembered next step in North American diesel locomotive development was the delivery, in 1928, of "road" type locomotives to the Canadian National and New York Central railways. The CN's locomotive, a 2,660-hp., two-unit affair, was built by Canadian Locomotive Company. Two smaller single-unit locomotives—one freight, one passenger—were delivered to the New York Central by Alco and General Electric in the same year. These were not especially successful, but the CN's two units were separated and continued in service, one until 1939 and the other until after World War II.

Diesel development continued in Europe during this period, also. There were railcar applications in several countries, as well as many examples of higher powered locomotives, notably in Germany and Italy. A Russian engineer, G. V. Lomonosoff, had been pressing the claims of diesel traction since 1910. The Russian government finally agreed to let him put his ideas into practice and in 1925, in conjunction with the German railways, a 1,200-hp. diesel locomotive was completed. This was followed by a similar unit equipped with mechanical transmission.

Much European development work in the 1920s centred on the transmission of power. Because of its characteristics, the diesel engine is very limited when equipped with direct drive because it cannot rapidly adapt to variable load requirements. Also, it cannot start from rest under load. Experiments were carried out with mechanical, hydraulic, pneumatic, compressed gas, compressed steam, and electric transmissions. Gradually it was found that mechanical, hydraulic, and electric transmissions were the most satisfactory. In 1928 a diesel-electric train was tested in Britain, and a diesel-hydraulic railcar was placed in service in Northern Ireland in 1933. However, it was in 1932 in Germany that the first really striking results with diesel traction were obtained. A two-car, streamlined diesel-electric train, equipped with two 400-hp. engines, commenced operation between Berlin and Hamburg. This train, the "Flederhamburger," was soon on a 77-mph average speed schedule that called for the regular attainment of 100 mph. Other units were built and a network of fast services was introduced all over Germany. In the 1930s diesel railcars and diesel-engine multicar train sets were brought into use in most European countries.

A turning point in U.S. diesel development came in 1930 when Electro-Motive and Winton Engine were acquired by General Motors. This merger led to the development of a lightweight, two-stroke-cycle diesel engine suitable for general railway application. This was the engine used in the "Pioneer Zephyr" of the Chicago, Burlington and Quincy Railway. Delivered in April 1934, this was the first train in the United States to use diesel-electric power successfully in main-line service. Together with the Union Pacific's "M-10000," later renamed the "City of Salina," the "Pioneer Zephyr" also inaugurated the era of streamlined, light-weight passenger trains. The "Pioneer Zephyr" remained in service for more than 25 years and then was preserved in the Museum of Science and Industry, Chicago.

The "Pioneer Zephyr," the "M-10000" (which used gasoline as fuel) and a few other early diesel-powered passenger trains were actually modernized versions of the old gas-electric cars. They were articulated trains in which a single truck supported the adjacent ends of adjoining cars. Cars could not be added or removed easily to meet traffic demands. In most cases the new trains were so popular that the traffic soon outgrew them, and eventually most of them had to be relegated to lighter-traffic runs.

Logically, the next step was to build a nonarticulated diesel locomotive that could be used to pull any train. In 1935 Electro-Motive division delivered one 1,800-hp. unit to the B & O and two to the Santa Fe. The latter two units, operated as a single 3,600-hp. locomotive, were used to begin the first high-speed passenger service between Chicago and Los Angeles, May 12, 1936. They covered the 2,226-mi. run, pulling the "Super Chief," in 39¾ hr.

After 1935 the diesel began to play an increasingly important role in passenger-train operations in the United States, as well as in yard switching work, but it was not until 1939 that the first road freight diesel, a four-unit Electro-Motive demonstrator, was built. This 5,400-hp. locomotive could be split and operated as two 2,700-hp. locomotives. The original demonstrator eventually was sold to the Southern Railway. (It is now preserved in the Museum of Transport, St. Louis.) Meanwhile, the Santa Fe, in 1940, had become the first railway to operate diesel locomotives in regular freight service.

By the end of World War II the diesel locomotive had become a proven, standardized type of motive power, and it rapidly began to supersede the steam locomotive in North America. In 1943 there were nearly 40,000 steam locomotives and only 2,100 diesel units in service in the United States. Twenty-five years later there were but a handful of operating steam locomotives (mostly on short "tourist attraction" railroads) and about 27,000 diesel units. Because of its greater efficiency, this smaller number of units proved fully capable of performing more transportation work than the larger steam locomotive fleet it replaced.

After World War II, the use of diesel traction greatly increased in all other parts of the world as well. In Britain steam-locomotive operation ended in 1968; in most other large countries steam power had been largely superseded by diesels or by a combination of diesels and electrification.

2. Elements of the Diesel Locomotive.—Although the diesel engine has been vastly improved in power and performance, the basic principles remain the same: drawing air into the cylinder, compressing it so that its temperature is raised and then injecting a small quantity of oil into the cylinder. The oil ignites without a spark because of the high temperature. The diesel engine may operate on the two-stroke or four-stroke cycle and may have cylinders arranged in line, in V formation, horizontally opposed, or in vertical formation. Rated operating speeds are from 350 to 2,000 rpm and rated output may be from 10 to 3,600 hp.

In the United States, early road units, and most yard switchers, use diesels ranging from 600 to 1,500 hp. Road units commonly use engines ranging from 2,000 to 3,600 hp. Most builders use V-type engines, although the in-line type is used on smaller locomotives (up to 1,200 hp.).

Electric transmission is the most popular and is nearly universal in North America. With electric transmission, the diesel engine is directly connected to a main generator that converts the mechanical energy produced by the engine into electrical energy. Through the appropriate control equipment, this in turn is used to drive the traction motors. The traction electrical system operates at a nominal 600 v., but there is great variation in the voltage under operating conditions. The traction motors are of the series-wound type, each geared to the axle it drives. Most locomotives have a traction motor on each axle, although some passenger locomotives or units designed for light branch-line service may have six-wheel trucks with the centre axle an idler.

Hydraulic transmission employs the principle of a centrifugal pump or impeller driving a turbine in a chamber filled with oil or a similar fluid. The pump, driven by the diesel engine, converts the engine power to kinetic energy in the oil impinging on the turbine blades. The faster the blades move, the less the relative impinging speed of the oil and the faster the locomotive moves.

Mechanical transmission is the simplest type and is mainly employed in the lower power range. Basically it is a clutch and gearbox similar to those used in automobiles. A hydraulic coupling, in some cases, is used in place of a friction clutch.

3. Types of Diesel Motive Power.—There are four broad classes of equipment using diesel prime movers:

The light railcar or rail bus (up to 180 hp.) usually is four-wheeled and employs mechanical transmission; it often is powered by a standard motorbus engine or a horizontal or pancake engine. The vehicle may haul a light trailer car.

The railcar in the low-horsepower range (up to 1,000 hp.) usually is equipped with mechanical transmission; higher powered versions may have hydraulic or electric transmission. Nearly all railcars are capable of hauling trailer vehicles, while the most powerful types are designed essentially for hauling additional vehicles, although they also have passenger or baggage space.

Train sets (500 to 2,000 hp.) are formations of more than one vehicle, usually designed to be worked from a single set of controls. They include one or more powered vehicles in their formation and usually have hydraulic or electric transmission.

Locomotives (10 to 6,600 hp.) may have mechanical, hydraulic, or electric transmission, depending on power output and purpose. They frequently are designed to work in MU formations. In the lower power range (to 600 hp.) the usual duties are switching and light freight traffic. Medium-power locomotives (600–1,200 hp.) may be used for freight haulage, passenger work, or heavy switching purposes. Locomotives over 1,200 hp. are normally required for main-line duties in Europe and North America. The 1,500–2,000 hp. range is the most popular class for express-train haulage in Europe. In North America, road freight units may range as high as 6,600 hp., and several units totaling as much as 15,000 hp. may be used in multiple on heavy, fast trains.

4. Diesel Operations in North America.—In North America diesel locomotives are built in three distinct types designed for switching, freight, and passenger service. Freight and passenger types are very similar in appearance, but passenger units usually are geared to a higher top speed and are equipped with an automatic steam boiler for train heating.

Road locomotives may be of either the streamlined or cab type, an outgrowth of the early streamlined articulated train designs, or of the purely functional hood type. In the former the body conforms closely to the cross-sectional dimensions of modern passenger cars. In hood units the covering for the engine, generator, and other components is smaller and is not streamlined. Yard engines are always of the hood type in the United States and Canada (with the exception of a few early box cab yard switchers).

The so-called road-switcher or general-purpose diesel became the most popular in the United States and Canada. This hood-type unit is usually geared for medium top speeds and has an offset cab located between a short hood (which may contain a steam generator) and a longer hood covering the diesel engine, generator, and control equipment. The road-switcher can be used in either passenger or freight service interchangeably, and it can also be assigned to yard switching service as needed.

In the 1960s, the growing size and speed of freight trains sparked a trend to higher-horsepower diesels and a "horsepower race" developed among locomotive builders. The standard road unit became first 2,250 hp., then 2,500, 3,000, and 3,300 hp. on four axles; and 3,000, 3,300, and then 3,600 on six axles. A few locomotives with two diesel engines were rated as high as 6,600 hp. by 1969; similar locomotives of more than 7,000 hp. were expected by the early 1970s.

5. Operating Methods.—It has become almost universal practice in North America to equip diesels for MU control. This permits setting up a "building block" system in which two or more units can be combined and operated as a single locomotive from one control cab. This can be done on short notice to cope with, for example, fluctuations in traffic or to obtain extra power for a mountain grade. The electrical systems of the different locomotives are sufficiently standardized so that it is possible to operate units of mixed makes together in a locomotive "consist."

A number of U.S. and Canadian railways also use so-called slave locomotives, which are spotted in the middle of a freight train and controlled automatically by radio from the locomotive cab at the front end of the train. Radio-controlled slave locomotives permit easier and more efficient control of very long freight trains—125 to as many as 250 cars in regular operations.

In the early days of dieselization, railways tended to emulate the operating methods they had used with steam locomotives, but to take advantage of the diesel's special characteristics they soon found it necessary to change their techniques, and often their physical facilities. For one thing, the diesel closed many division-point roundhouses, since it could run across a whole continent, if necessary, without requiring any maintenance attention.

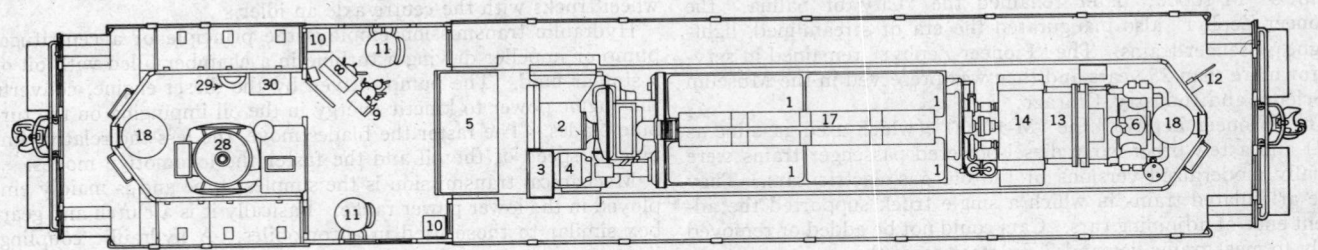

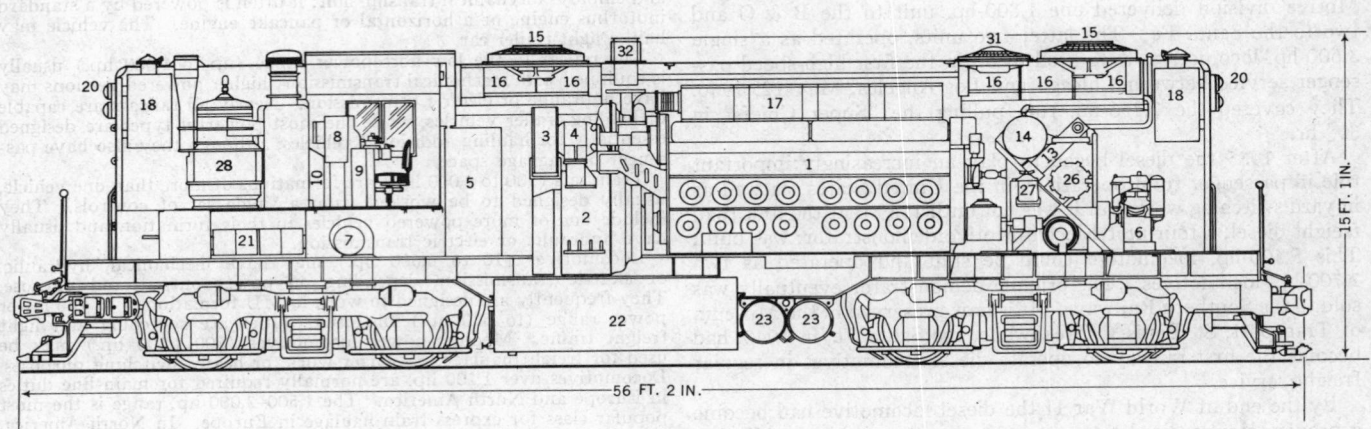

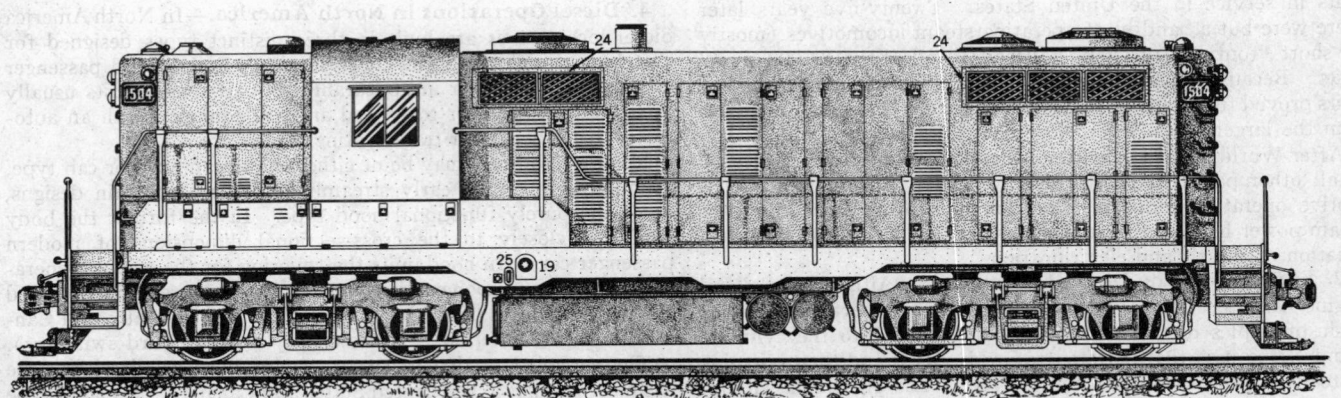

FIG. 1.—ROAD-SWITCHER (GENERAL-PURPOSE) LOCOMOTIVE, 2,000 HP.

(1) Engine; (2) main generator and alternator; (3) generator blower; (4) auxiliary generator; (5) control cabinet; (6) air compressor; (7) traction motor blower; (8) engineer's control stand; (9) air-brake valve; (10) cab heater; (11) seat; (12) hand brake; (13) lubricating oil cooler; (14) engine water tank; (15) ventilating fan; (16) radiator; (17) exhaust manifold; (18) sandbox; (19) fuel filler; (20) headlight; (21) batteries; (22) fuel tank; (23) main air reservoir; (24) air intake and shutters; (25) fuel tank gauge; (26) lubricating oil filter; (27) fuel filter; (28) steam generator; (29) lavatory; (30) clothes locker; (31) ventilating fan; (32) turbocharger exhaust stack

Moreover, many railways found it necessary to pay increased attention to the scheduling of motive-power operations. It became common practice to have all locomotive runs assigned by a central office connected to the outlying locomotive terminals by telephone. Electronic computers often aid the motive-power controllers in making the best possible "match" of available locomotive units with the freight tonnage to be moved.

D. Special Locomotive Types

Although the diesel locomotive with electric drive is the standard type in North America and over much of the rest of the world, railways are constantly experimenting with other types of locomotives. For example, on several occasions experiments have been made to adapt the steam turbine for rail-traction purposes. One of the first examples was built in Sweden in 1921. Other prototypes followed in Europe and there were also experimental turbine-electric locomotives, none of which met with success.

The first gas-turbine locomotive was developed in Switzerland and completed in 1941. Another Swiss-built gas-turbine locomotive developing 2,500 hp. was supplied to British railways in 1949. The first British-built gas-turbine locomotive developed 3,500 hp. and was completed in 1951 (it was later converted to 25,000-v., 50-cycle AC operation).

Shortly after World War II the Union Pacific Railroad (UP) acquired 25 gas-turbine electric locomotives of 4,500 hp. each, and later another 30 rated at 8,500 hp. They were used in main-line, heavy-duty freight service between Omaha, Neb., and Ogden, Utah. By 1970, however, they had been superseded by high-powered diesel-electric locomotives. UP also experimented with a coal-fired gas-turbine electric locomotive. However, the problem of excessive wear on the turbine blades, caused by the fly-ash in the coal, was never satisfactorily solved.

In 1969 high-speed passenger train sets powered by aircraft-type turbines were placed in service between Montreal and Toronto by CN; and between New York and Boston by Penn Central and the U.S. Department of Transportation. Built by United Aircraft Corporation, these trains have a power unit at each end and use mechanical transmissions.

In Europe the French railways tested a two-car gas-turbine-powered passenger train set at speeds up to 142 mph. SNCF introduced such trains in regular service on certain routes in 1969–70. British Rail was also studying gas turbines for advanced passenger trains to operate at 150 mph. The German Federal Railway used a small gas turbine as a "booster" in one class of diesel-hydraulic locomotive.

Also employing a turbine is the turbo-diesel or free-piston gasifier locomotive. In this design the turbine is driven by power gas from a free-piston diesel compressor. Pioneer work with this type of engine for rail traction purposes commenced in Sweden in 1933. A 1955 Swedish example had a power-gas producer that worked on a two-stroke-cycle diesel principle (the power gas is exhaust gas leaving the producer under high pressure at a temperature of 900° F [482° C]). The locomotive was driven, via a reduction gear, by the turbine, fed by the power gas.

E. Self-Propelled Railcars

Although the gas-electric and gas-mechanical cars of the 1920s and earlier evolved into the diesel-electric locomotive, they were not too successful in their intended role. In the United States, especially, there was still a need for a self-propelled railcar that could be used on light-traffic lines.

In 1949 the Budd Company introduced a modern self-propelled coach that it called the rail diesel car (RDC). The 85-ft. stainless-steel car was powered by a pair of 300-hp., 6-cylinder in-line diesels, each of which drove one axle through a torque converter. The engines were mounted under the floor, leaving almost the entire car body available as revenue space. The car had a control compartment at each end, could be operated in MU trains with other RDC's, and was air-conditioned. The RDC found favour with many railways in the United States and other countries. The Commonwealth Railways in Australia began using these self-propelled diesel cars on long-distance runs.

Self-propelled cars have been widely used for many years for electrified commuter service serving larger cities, as well as on local subway and rapid-transit systems. Modern MU cars, as they are called, can accelerate and decelerate rapidly because of their lightweight construction and improved motors and control equipment. (See ELECTRIC TRACTION.)

The Chicago and North Western Railway (and later several other U.S. railways and the CPR) began using nonpowered cars equipped with MU control equipment and a control cab in conjunction with standard diesel-electric locomotives. By having one of these control cars at the rear of a train, it is possible to operate the train in either direction at normal speed without turning the locomotive or cars at either end of a run.

IV. RAILWAY CARS

The ancestors of modern freight and passenger cars were the wagons and stagecoaches of the early 19th century. Some of the earliest railway cars were, indeed, merely road vehicles fitted with flanged wheels.

After the first crude beginnings, railway car design took diverging courses in North America and Europe, partly because of differing economic conditions and partly because of differing technological developments. Early railway cars on both continents were largely of two-axle design, but passenger-car builders soon began constructing cars with three and then four axles, the latter arranged in two four-wheel swivel trucks or bogies. Swivel trucks produce smoother riding qualities and allow the weight of heavy cars to be distributed over more axles—an important consideration, especially on some of the early, lightly built rail lines.

In North America, the two-truck design soon became the standard for freight as well as passenger cars. Over the years, American freight cars have become much larger than their European counterparts. A typical modern American boxcar is about 50½ ft. long, weighs 53,000 lb. empty, and has a capacity of 100,000 lb. of lading and a cubic capacity of 4,860 cu.ft.

To a remarkable extent, the characteristics of rolling stock reflect the background of the early railway builders in each country. Thus, the cars used in Africa and most Asian countries reflect European origins; South American equipment favours North American or European practice, depending on who built the first lines.

In Japan most freight cars are of the four-wheel type, but in Australia eight-wheel truck-type cars are more common. After World War II, there was a trend in European countries toward larger eight-wheeled freight cars, and the present trend is toward bigger capacity eight-wheeled vehicles capable of higher speeds than previously.

A. Freight Cars

Three basic types of freight cars have developed: the open-top car, the boxcar, and the flatcar. Apart from these examples, many additional designs have been introduced to suit particular types of freight. In Europe, the freight vehicle usually runs on four wheels. Capacity varies: British cars are the smallest, having an average capacity of 12 long tons, but many newer British cars are of 16, 20, or 24½ long tons. On the Continent, capacities vary from 16 to 30 metric tons. However, the Soviet railways generally use much larger two-truck vehicles with capacities of up to 90 metric tons. There is also a growing trend toward higher capacity four-axle vehicles in Britain and on the Continent, capable of carrying loads up to 80 or 90 tons. Two-truck freight cars also are used to a great extent in Africa, Australia, and most Asian countries.

After World War II a number of new freight-car designs evolved in Europe. These included double-deck vehicles for transporting automobiles; open cars with sliding roofs; pressurized tank cars for the transport of dry solids in bulk; boxcars with wide side doors for easy movement of loads packed on pallets; and hydraulically operated tipping cars. European railways also made great strides in the use of demountable containers carried on flatcars. These were first introduced in the 1920s to enable the railways to offer a door-to-door service and there came to be many examples in service for the transport of all kinds of merchandise from liquids to highly perishable commodities such as frozen food.

The high-capacity flatcar for carrying containers of the accepted international dimensions (20, 30, or 40 ft. long by 8 ft. wide by 8 ft. high) is another development, pioneered in Europe by British Rail's Freightliner vehicles.

Of the approximately 2,500,000 freight cars operating on U.S., Canadian, and Mexican railways, about 800,000 are boxcars—the standard house car with closed sides, a roof, and sliding doors on each side. Cars of 40- and 50-ft. lengths are common, but the trend is to larger units. American railways use an equally large number of open-top cars—so-called gondola and hopper cars, the latter having hoppers with doors for unloading through the bottom. Other common American freight-car types include flatcars, tank cars, and refrigerator and livestock cars.

Many thousands of cars are equipped with special internal fittings designed to accommodate specific products without the need for dunnage (i.e., bracing or blocking of the load). Typical of these are the automobile-parts cars, which are often designed to carry a certain automobile component, such as bodies, frames, or engines, of just a single manufacturer. The internal loading equipment in these cars must be changed whenever the automobile manufacturer changes the design of his product.

Among other special types of cars are those with "long-travel" cushioned draft gear to prevent damage to fragile commodities; heated cars to protect commodities such as potatoes during winter; extra-long flatcars with two- or three-deck automobile racks, and so on.

During the 1960s, still other types of specialized freight cars were becoming more and more important. Especially notable was the growing use of piggyback cars designed for efficient loading and hauling of highway trailers and containers. Other new types included 100- and even 125-ton covered hoppers for dry bulk commodities, 100-ton gondolas for unit-train coal service, and 89-ft.-long, 10,000-cu.ft. boxcars for light but bulky automobile parts.

For the railways, the growing variety of specialized freight cars complicated the problem of keeping all shippers supplied with cars of the proper types. On the other hand, specialized cars usually ran more miles and earned more revenue than standard cars and thus were a worthwhile investment. To supply special freight cars more efficiently, the private car companies played an increasing role. These companies buy the equipment and either operate it or lease it to shippers and often to the railroads themselves, a practice that has long been followed in the United States with tank and refrigerator cars.

B. Passenger Cars

Cars with two four-wheel trucks were used in the United States almost from the beginning, but the two-truck coach was not introduced into Britain until 1874 and on the European continent until 1880. At about the same time the flexible gangway or corridor connection was adopted for main-line cars, enabling passengers to have access to any part of a moving train. Early U.S. cars had open platforms at each end; it was not until around 1900 that closed-vestibule cars came into general use.

Sleeping cars were operated in the United States as early as 1837, and the first Pullman sleeper was placed in service in 1859; sleeping cars were introduced in Britain in 1879.

In Europe there was a gradual trend toward longer and lighter passenger vehicles. The standard British coach measures 67 ft. in length, while continental designs are up to 86 ft. 6 in. long. The introduction of steel, first for coach frames and later for frames and bodies, added to the weight of vehicles. An all-steel continental coach might weigh up to 45 metric tons, or 55 metric tons for a sleeping car. However, it was found possible to reduce these weights without loss of strength by using lightweight steels, stainless steels, and light alloys. For example, a modern lightweight steel coach of the Swiss Federal Railways is 73 ft. long, seats 80 passengers, and has a tare weight of only 26 metric tons. In contrast, typical U.S. passenger cars weigh about 60 to 80 short tons, or even more.

Experiments have been carried out with ultra-lightweight trains. The Spanish National Railways operate a number of lightweight sets, called Talgo trains, consisting of several short coach units, each resting at one end on a single axle. At the other end, the weight is carried on a pivot that forms part of the next vehicle, and the leading coach is supported on the diesel locomotive. The train is thus made up of a series of jointed units and, having a very low centre of gravity, it can traverse curves at high speed. The turbine trains introduced in 1969 on CN and PC are of similar design.

The interior accommodations of passenger cars vary widely. In Europe the six- or eight-seat compartment with the corridor along one side of the coach is still favoured, although the use of coaches with a centre aisle has increased, particularly for suburban service. Reclining coach seats were adopted by a number of systems for long journeys.

U.S. passenger cars use the centre-aisle arrangement almost exclusively, except for some sleeping cars. Besides the coach, with its two rows of seats, a "deluxe" U.S. passenger train often includes several types of sleeping cars for overnight travel, a dining car, and a lounge or observation car. In addition, "head-end" cars—for mail, express, and baggage—are operated in most U.S. and Canadian passenger trains.

A typical modern sleeping car has six bedrooms (each with two beds) in the centre of the car, with six roomettes (each with a single bed) at each end. Thus the total capacity of the car is about 24 persons. This relatively low capacity produces low revenue, making necessary rather high fares to cover the cost of operating the car. The high fares, in turn, discourage patronage in competition with the much faster airlines. This is a basic problem of sleeping-car service under modern conditions.

As one answer to this problem, the Budd Company in the United States developed the "slumbercoach," a sleeping car similar to the roomette but with smaller rooms. It has 8 small double rooms and 24 single rooms. The total capacity of 40 makes possible rates only slightly above the standard coach fare.

The dome car, developed in the United States after World War II, enables passengers to ride under a raised, glassed-in roof section from which they have a wide-range view of the countryside. Below the dome section may be sleeping rooms, a lounge section, or coach seats. Although costly to build and operate, dome cars without doubt helped attract patronage. They became widely used on railways having scenic routes in the western U.S. and Canada. The same type of car is used in other countries as well, notably France, Italy, and Germany.

With growing industrialization many countries began building their own rolling stock, whereas previously they had obtained their cars from European or American builders. Many of the cars in service have been designed to suit climatic and other special conditions of the countries in which they operate.

The narrow-gauge railways also impose restrictions as to weight and size. Even so, a 3-ft. 6-in.-gauge coach of the South African Railways, for example, may be up to 63 ft. 5 in. long and weigh up to 43¾ long tons. In Australia the trend has been to longer coaches, many of which follow the American pattern in design and appearance.

C. Dual-Gauge Vehicles

Vehicles capable of running on more than one gauge are in use in Europe. The Spanish Transfesa Company operates freight cars that can be used on the 5-ft. 6-in. broad gauge of Spain and on the standard 4-ft. 8½-in. gauge of other European countries. Special apparatus at frontier yards enables wheel sets of one gauge to be exchanged quickly for those of the other. Similar arrangements, on a larger scale, are to be found at certain Soviet frontier stations, so that through passenger coaches can operate between points on the 5-ft.-gauge Soviet system and the standard-gauge tracks of other European countries. In 1969 new trains were introduced that could run through between France and Spain (which has 5-ft. 6-in. gauge). Trucks of the sleeping cars are changed at the frontier; but the coaches are equipped with adjustable axles.

In some countries special cars are used to carry cars of a different gauge in piggyback fashion. In Australia, for example, complete trains of specially adapted flatcars are in use to carry, in turn, entire trains of a narrower gauge, thus obviating the need for transshipment of freight.

D. STANDARDIZATION OF RUNNING GEAR

Although U.S. and Canadian railways build many different types of cars to suit their own needs or whims, most of the cars can operate interchangeably among railways. Through the work of the mechanical division of the Association of American Railroads (and its predecessors) the elements of the running gear—wheels, trucks, draft gear, couplers, and brakes—have been standardized. Not only does this permit most cars to operate over almost any railway in North America but it also allows any railway to repair or maintain any car it is using, regardless of who owns the car.

This mechanical standardization was an important factor in the growth of the North American railway industry, yet it does impose some problems. Any improved type of coupler or brake, for example, must be compatible with existing older equipment if it is to be used on cars operated in interchange service. Despite this limitation, mechanical progress has been steady. Roller bearings replaced the traditional plain journal bearings on all new cars and locomotives. Several improved types of couplers were adopted; an improved freight air brake, the type AB, became universal, and wheels were constantly being improved. Truck or bogie spring systems were made more effective against vertical shocks and oscillations in moving cars, and the draft gear used in freight cars was refined to provide more cushioning against longitudinal jolts. As a result of these changes, the mechanical standards of freight cars approached more and more those of passenger cars. This was a necessity because longer trains were being operated at higher speeds, and it became even more urgently necessary to prevent damage to merchandise in transit.

1. Couplers.—European couplers originally consisted of nothing more than chains linking the vehicles, with solid buffers to help absorb the shock when one vehicle came in contact with another. Later, spring buffers were introduced, along with screw couplings that permit two vehicles to be brought together so that buffer faces are just touching; this helps ensure smooth starting and stopping.

During their first half-century, U.S. railways used a crude link-and-pin coupler that was extremely dangerous to employees who had to couple cars. Beginning in 1882, North American railways began to convert to the knuckle-type automatic coupler. This basic design, built heavier for today's larger cars and much improved in detail, is still the North American standard. Knuckle couplers also are used in many other countries, notably Japan, the U.S.S.R., and Australia. In fact, the majority of non-European railways use automatic couplers of one pattern or another. A type of automatic coupler compatible with that in use in the Soviet Union is under development in Europe.

In Britain, automatic centre couplings were tried out on the Great Northern Railway in 1898. Later, automatic couplings were used on the main-line passenger coaches of the London and North Eastern and the Southern railways. In 1948 British Railways adopted this type of coupler for all their main-line coaches, and experiments later began on an automatic coupler for freight cars.

Multiple-connection automatic couplings have been adopted by a number of railways, principally for diesel railcar trains or MU electric trains. This type of coupling incorporates connections for the continuous brakes, heating and electrical controls, as well as joining the vehicles together.

Instead of buffers, U.S. cars have a draft gear, directly behind and attached to the couplers, which may employ spring, friction, rubber, or hydraulic elements to help absorb coupling and operating jolts. The standard draft gear is mounted in a pocket 24 or 36 in. long, but a number of long-travel draft gears and cushioned centre sills have been developed to give greater protection to fragile commodities.

2. Brakes.—Two continuous braking systems are in general use—the vacuum brake and the compressed-air brake. Of the two,

the more popular is the air brake, patented in 1869 by George Westinghouse and made compulsory in the United States by the Railroad Safety Appliance Act of 1893. The vacuum brake is used principally in Britain, where continuous brakes have been compulsory on passenger vehicles since 1889. With either system, every vehicle is connected by a brake pipe; therefore, application of the brake on the locomotive applies brakes throughout the train.

Although virtually all passenger rolling stock throughout the world is equipped with continuous brakes, this is not the case with freight cars.

The brake itself takes the form of a single or double shoe that presses against the wheel tread. The disk brake has been widely used on U.S. and Canadian passenger trains, and is also being applied in Europe to cars used in high-speed freight services (*see* also BRAKE).

V. CAR AND LOCOMOTIVE MAINTENANCE

The design, construction, and maintenance of rolling stock is a responsibility of a railway's mechanical department. In steam locomotive days, some of the larger railways built their own locomotives, as well as many of their own cars. U.S. railways, however, did not build new diesel locomotives, although some continued to assemble cars in railway shops rather than have them built by the commercial car manufacturers.

In terms of money spent for wages, materials, and the operation of shops, rolling-stock maintenance is a vast operation. In normal years U.S. railways, for example, spend about 18% of their income for this purpose.

Railway shops perform all the operations and contain much of the machinery common to a heavy manufacturing industry. Moreover, much railway production is organized around assembly-line techniques, just as in other industries.

1. Locomotive Shops.—In contrast to the steam-locomotive back shops that railways formerly required on each operating division, the dieselized railway usually needs only one heavy repair shop. There the locomotives are more or less completely dismantled and their major components—engines, electrical equipment, running gear—are either completely overhauled or renewed. Under normal conditions, a diesel locomotive is given heavy repairs or rebuilding only after a period of perhaps five to seven years. Between these major overhaulings, certain routine maintenance and inspection is performed at specific mileage or time intervals (in the United States certain inspection and maintenance work is prescribed by the Federal Railroad Administration of the Department of Transportation).

In addition, locomotives are given certain routine inspections at the end of each run. Although some railways still use converted roundhouses for diesel maintenance, most have found that specially built diesel shops are more efficient.

2. Car Shops.—Freight car maintenance may be classified as running repairs, intermediate repairs, and heavy repairs or rebuilding (the exact definition of each varies among railways). As trains enter terminal yards they are inspected for running gear or other defects. Cars requiring attention are switched out of the train and sent to the "rip track," a shop equipped to do light repair work such as wheel changing, air-brake repairs, and minor repairs to the car bodies.

If a car has been severely damaged, it may be sent to a heavy repair shop. Railroads often rebuild an entire series of cars. This is most likely to occur after the cars have seen 15 to 20 years of service. The rebuilt cars may be equipped with entirely new bodies and emerge from the assembly-line shop virtually equivalent to new cars.

VI. BRIDGES, BUILDINGS, AND TUNNELS

The fixed plant of a railway consists of much more than just the track itself. In the United States alone, about 4,000 mi. of line are on bridges. In mountainous country, tunnels must be built to avoid excessive grades or excessively roundabout routes. Where mountain railways are not in tunnels they must sometimes be protected against drifting and avalanches by snow sheds. In addition, railway engineering departments are concerned with constructing and maintaining thousands of buildings ranging from small watchman's shanties to huge passenger terminals.

1. Bridges.—The designer of a railway bridge faces challenging problems. He must allow for the forces that result from the concentrated impact as a train moves onto the bridge, the pounding of wheels, the sidesway of the train, and the drag or push effect as a train is braked or started on the bridge. These factors mean that a railway or rail-highway bridge must be designed more stringently than a highway bridge. The heavier construction of a railway bridge designed for main-line traffic, as compared with a highway bridge of similar length, is usually quite evident even to a casual observer.

As trains and locomotives became heavier, bridges had to be strengthened accordingly. In the past, heavier steam locomotives usually caused the need for stronger bridges, but modern diesel-electric locomotives are less damaging to bridges than large steam locomotives. However, as freight loads became heavier and train speeds higher, railways still had to design and build their bridges to high standards.

Besides the need to strengthen bridges, there was another major objective in much modern railway bridge construction: reduction of maintenance costs. This became evident in the widespread trend toward replacing timber trestles with concrete-slab structures or with concrete or steel-pipe culverts. Prestressed-concrete-slab bridges came into use on an increasing scale. All-welded steel bridges became more common, as did the use of high-strength bolts rather than rivets for field assembly of bridge spans.

Under the spur of rising labour costs, U.S. railways sought ways to mechanize the maintenance of bridges and other structures. Typical of solutions to the problem were the bridge sprayer machines used to apply protective coatings, as well as special types of derrick equipment for replacing bridge ties and stringers. (*See* also BRIDGES.)

2. Buildings.—Railway buildings in the 20th century have become fewer and more functional. The newer types of motive power, for instance, require only a few maintenance shops. Car shops, too, were being consolidated into fewer but usually more modern structures. In the United States, the declining importance of intercity passenger traffic resulted in the elimination of many passenger stations, and some local freight stations were removed, too, since with paved highways almost everywhere, it became more economical to concentrate freight terminal operations at a few large stations.

Only a few really modern passenger stations have ever been built in the United States. One is the Los Angeles Union Passenger Terminal; one of the latest is the New Orleans Union Passenger Terminal, completed in 1954. Grand Central Terminal in New York City, completed in 1913, is perhaps the best-known railway station in the world: approximately 120,000 passengers use it daily. In contrast, however, approximately 1,250,000 use the main Tokyo station of the Japanese National Railways daily.

Europe, however, has a number of large, modern passenger stations. One of the most striking is Rome Termini, the construction of which started in 1938, although it was not completed until 1951. Of prewar construction is the Central Station, Milan, one of the largest in Europe. Opened in 1931, it has 22 platforms, of which 18 are 1,051 ft. long. A new Euston Station was opened in London in 1968.

3. Tunnels.—Although it is a highly expensive form of construction, tunneling provides the most economical means for railways to traverse mountainous terrain and to gain access to the heart of a crowded city. However, railway tunnels confront the construction engineer with some unique problems, particularly in matters of ventilation on nonelectrified lines.

Some examples of famous tunnels and methods of construction may be found in the articles TUNNEL and SUBWAY (UNDERGROUND RAILWAY).

VII. COMMUNICATIONS AND SIGNALING

A. COMMUNICATIONS

Railways have operating and service problems as complex as those of a major manufacturing concern—in some respects even more so. The railway's plant and its operations may be spread out over thousands of miles of line serving hundreds of communities. Quick communication between stations is usually essential in the operation of trains. It is also required in order to give service information to the public and to carry on the vast amount of routine correspondence and accounting data that a railway enterprise generates.

1. Telegraph and Telephone.—Railways were among the first to adopt the electric telegraph and the telephone. The railway telegraph dates back to 1837, when it was tried on the London and Birmingham line. In the United States, the telegraph was first used for dispatching trains in 1851; the telephone was first tested in 1877.

Modern railways are among the larger operators of electrical and electronic communications facilities. For example, the dial-telephone network of the SP system covers the entire western area of the United States. It allows personnel anywhere on the railway and its affiliates to dial direct to offices anywhere on the 14,000-mi. rail system serving 12 states. Other railways have similarly extensive telephone systems.

The Morse telegraph, originally used in North America for all railway business messages as well as for train dispatching, eventually was superseded by use of the telephone, radio, and teleprinter systems.

2. Computers.—The railways were leaders in adopting punched-card and other advanced techniques of data processing. In the late 1960s there was a strong trend toward "total information" systems built around large-scale electronic computers. Each field reporting point—usually a yard office or station—is equipped with a computer input device that allows full information about every car movement taking place at that point to be placed directly into the central computer, usually located at company headquarters. The computer is programmed to produce, from this basic information, a variety of outputs. These may include train consist reports for the next terminal to be reached by the train; car location reports for the railway's customer service offices; car movement information for the car records department; revenue information for the accounting department; as well as traffic flow and commodity statistics useful in market research and data on the freight car needs at each location to aid in distributing empty cars for loading.

Other pertinent data may also be integrated into the system so that the railway's managers have a complete, up-to-the-minute picture of almost every phase of its operations. Such comprehensive information and control systems promised to be a powerful tool for optimizing railway operations and producing better service.

In 1967 U.S. and Canadian railways agreed to standardize a system of automatic car identification (ACI). Each freight car is equipped with a coded light-reflective label, which can be read by a trackside scanner and the data (car owner, number, and type) automatically placed into a computer, either at the scanning point or at company headquarters. ACI promised to be another aid to quicker, more accurate reporting of freight car movements and more efficient distribution of empty cars.

Centralized computer information and control systems vastly increased the demand for communication circuits. Many railways turned to broad-band radio beams (microwave) to supply needed data transmission circuits as well as the circuits needed for direct-dial telephone systems.

3. Radio.—In 1959 the Pacific Great Eastern Railway, between Vancouver and Dawson Creek-Fort St. John, B.C., became the first railway to use microwave radio for all line-side communications, doing away almost entirely with line wires. Other major North American carriers, notably the Santa Fe, SP, UP, Southern, CN, and CPR also installed extensive microwave systems. Microwave has the additional advantage of minimizing communication failures in areas subject to heavy sleet and snowfalls, which might bring down conventional open-line wires.

American railways also began to use very high-frequency (VHF) radio on a large scale after World War II. In freight operations VHF permits communication between the locomotive and caboose of a long train, between two trains, and between the train dispatcher and wayside stations and trains.

In terminals, radio greatly speeds yard switching work, because it allows the yardmaster to keep in close touch with the yard engines. Through VHF radio, too, widely separated elements of mechanized track maintenance crews can maintain contact with each other and with oncoming trains. Supervisory personnel use radio in their automobiles to keep in touch with activities under their jurisdiction.

To some extent, train radio took over some of the communication functions formerly reserved for the locomotive whistle. Enginemen commonly use standard combinations of long and short whistle sounds to communicate with the rest of the train crew and with wayside stations. On U.S. passenger trains, an intra-train air whistle system allows the conductor or trainmen to signal the engineman.

B. Signals

Railway signals are a form of communication designed to inform the train crew (in particular, the engine crew) of track conditions ahead and to instruct it in the operation of the train.

The earliest form of signaling consisted of a lamp by night or a flag during daylight. The first movable signal was a revolving board, introduced in the 1830s and followed in 1841 with the semaphore signal, which provided "stop," "proceed with caution," and "all clear" indications. Among the widely used early types of signals in the United States was the highball signal, consisting of a large ball hoisted to the top of a pole, to inform the engineman that the train might proceed. The first attempts at interlocking switches and signals were made in France in 1855 and in Britain in 1856. Interlocking at crossings and junctions prevents the signalman from displaying a clear signal for one route when clearance has already been given for a conflicting route.

Another forward step was the introduction of train operation on the distance interval or block system. The electric tablet machine (1878) for the safe operation of traffic over a single track was another noteworthy development.

The next major step forward was the application of power to signaling. Experience gained with large power interlocking frames having mechanical interlocking between levers led to the development of all-electric interlocking. This, in turn, led to relay interlocking in which interlocking and controls are effected by electrical relays.

A development in the design of the signal itself was the introduction of the colour-light type in addition to the semaphore pattern. The colour-light signal uses a separate bulb and lens for each aspect. By the 1960s it was being generally superseded in the United States by the searchlight type, which uses only a single lens and bulb, the different colours being displayed by means of roundels or colour filters that are rotated in front of the lamp. Two other types of signals are used in the United States: the position light, in which rows of yellow lights duplicate the positions of semaphore arms, and the colour-

position signal, which uses coloured lights arranged in rows.

Most lines in Europe are controlled from wayside signal towers, or cabins at stations, in conjunction with fixed signals. Block signaling is usual, the track being divided into sections, and a train is not permitted to enter a section until the train ahead has left it. This manual block system was once much used in the United States also, and is still found there on some lines. Electric interlocking improves this system by making it impossible for the "line clear" indication to be given for a section already occupied by a train.

Of more recent introduction is automatic block signaling. This uses track circuits that are short-circuited by the axles of a train, putting the signals in the rear of the train (and, on single track, in front of it as well) at the danger aspect. A track circuit is made by the two rails of a section of track, insulated at their ends. Electric current, fed into the section at one end, flows to a relay at the opposite end and the wheels of any vehicle will then short-circuit the current supply and de-energize the relay.

Signaling on African, Asian, and Australian systems usually follows European practice in areas of heavy traffic. On lines of lighter traffic, control is often via the telegraph or telephone.

In the early years of U.S. railways, it was common to program operations on the basis of a strict timetable, which set up all the places where trains were to meet. If one train was delayed, others also would be held up, since it was impossible to change the meeting points.

By using the telegraph it became possible for the dispatcher to issue orders to keep trains moving in unusual circumstances, or to operate extra trains when required. This "timetable-train order" system is still used on about 100,000 mi. of lighter-traffic line in the United States and on much Canadian mileage. It is

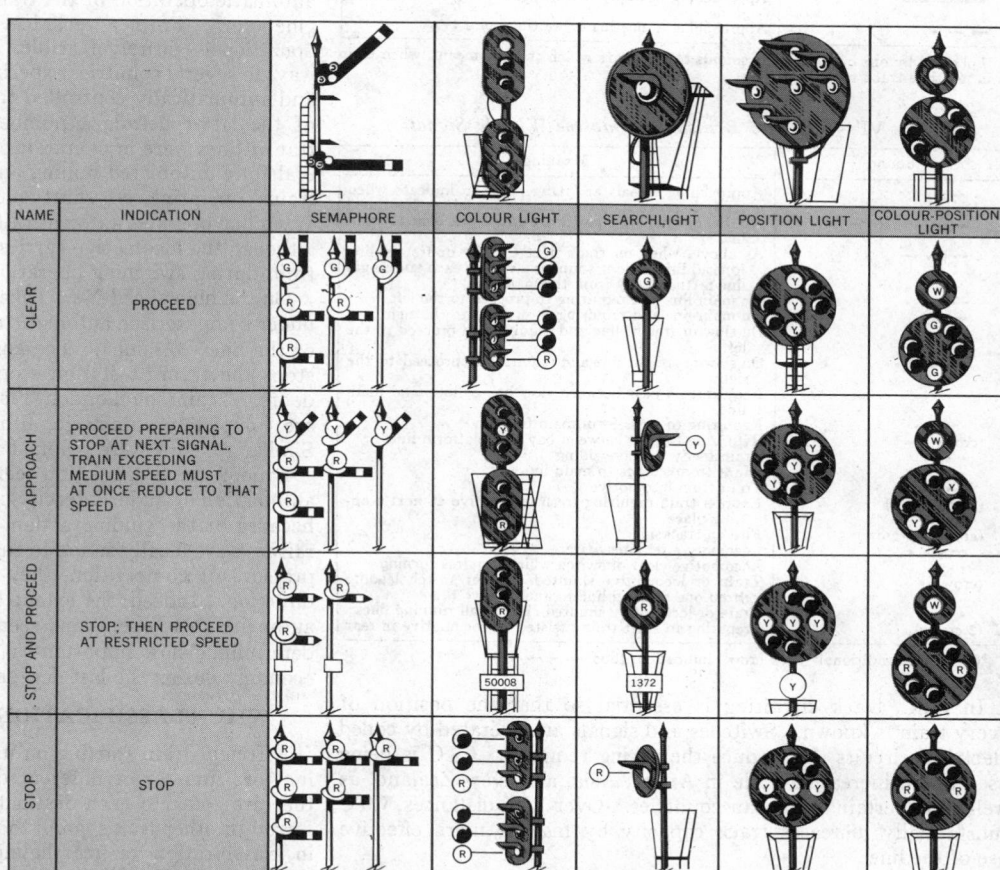

NAME	INDICATION	SEMAPHORE	COLOUR LIGHT	SEARCHLIGHT	POSITION LIGHT	COLOUR-POSITION LIGHT
CLEAR	PROCEED					
APPROACH	PROCEED PREPARING TO STOP AT NEXT SIGNAL. TRAIN EXCEEDING MEDIUM SPEED MUST AT ONCE REDUCE TO THAT SPEED					
STOP AND PROCEED	STOP; THEN PROCEED AT RESTRICTED SPEED					
STOP	STOP					

FIG. 2.—STANDARD NORTH AMERICAN SIGNAL INDICATIONS AND ASPECTS

Lamp colours: G, green; Y, yellow; R, red; W, white. The three columns under "Semaphore" show how the same indication may be given with one, two, or three signal heads on the same mast (any of the other types of signal may also be combined in the same fashion); two- and three-head signals ordinarily are used at junctions, passing sidings, etc. A stop-and-proceed signal is designated by a number plate on the mast below the signal head, by a marker light, by a pointed semaphore blade, or by a combination of these features widely supplemented by automatic block signals, which provide an additional safety factor.

The earliest function of signaling was to advise the engineman when it was unsafe to proceed and to indicate where a train should stop. In contrast, the aim of modern signaling is to keep trains running to the best advantage. Route-setting is one of the developments that helps accomplish this. With it, a complete route can be set up by operating push buttons on an electrical control panel. Equipment of this kind allows a large area to be controlled from one point, thus reducing the number of signal towers and personnel required.

1. Centralized Traffic Control.—A logical extension of the route interlocking principle is centralized traffic control (CTC), a system in which trains are operated from a central point entirely through remote control of the switches and signals. The operator sees the track layout in miniature on his control panel, and directs the movement of trains over distances from a few miles to several hundred miles. Lights on the panel show the location and progress of all trains at all times.

TABLE V.—*Standard U.S. Locomotive Whistle Signals*

Sound	Meaning
•	Apply brakes; stop
— • • •	Release brakes; proceed
	Flagman protect rear of train
— — — —	Flagman return from west or south*
— — — — —	Flagman return from east or north*
• •	Engineman's answer to any signal not otherwise provided for
• • •	When standing: will back up. When running: will stop at next passenger station
• • • •	Call for signals (usually to request towerman or operator to clear a signal so train can proceed)
	Another section of this train is following
— — — —	Approaching public crossing at grade
— — •	Approaching station, junction, or railway crossing at grade
— — •	Approaching a meeting or waiting point

*Followed by one or more short sounds to designate which track is meant, when train is in multiple-track territory

TABLE VI.—*Standard British Locomotive Whistle Signals*

Sound	Meaning
—	Approaching signals at "danger" or to indicate when ready to proceed on same track (on main or fast lines)
— —	As above, when on slow, or freight, track next to main line
— — —	As above, when on track next to slow or freight line (one additional long sound is given for each additional line farther away from the main line)
— •	On main line and requiring to proceed to the left
— — •	On main line and requiring to proceed to the right
— • •	On slow or freight line and requiring to proceed to the left
— — • •	On slow or freight line and requiring to proceed to the right
— — • •	Requiring to pass between slow line or loop and main line
• • • •	Requiring to cross from main to main
(crow)* —	Requiring to pass between bay and platform lines
• • •	Train ready to leave siding
• • • •	Shunt from sidings to main line
(three crows)	To or from locomotive
(crow) — (crow)	Express train requiring fresh locomotive at next stopping place
— • • •	Fire on trackside
	Locomotive requires water
(crow) •	Locomotive clear of switch which requires turning
	Train or locomotive shunted clear of switch leading from one running line to another
• • •	Train or locomotive shunted clear of all running lines
(2 crows)	Preparing to start train assisted by locomotive in rear

*Crow: the traditional "cock crow" indication, thus: — • — •

In CTC, track circuiting is essential so that the position of every train is known. Switches and signals are operated by coded electrical circuits that reduce the wiring required. CTC is being used on an increasing scale in Africa, Asia, and New Zealand, as well as in certain European countries. Over long distances, CTC substantially increases track capacity by making more effective use of the line.

Since CTC eliminates any need for written train orders or manual operation of block signals, it permits closing of telegraph or signal stations—another major economy. On lines of light traffic, most of the benefits of CTC can be obtained at less cost by having the signals controlled from the central office and the switch points operated manually by the train crews.

2. Recent Developments in Signaling.—Completely automatic signaling, activated by electronic program machines, had been introduced by the 1960s on some of London Transport's subway lines. The program machine has a plastic band incorporating a complete timetable translated into a series of punched holes. The line of holes is positioned for each train by a photoelectric cell. A comb with steel "feelers" scans the line of holes, causing a series of electrical contacts to be closed; these in turn carry out all signal, switch, and interlocking movements.

In Germany, experiments were being conducted with train control by radio signals to the enginemen, instead of by fixed wayside signals. Signal indications are given on a panel in the self-propelled car or locomotive and are accompanied by tone signals. Orders are acknowledged by a train recognition signal and the position of the train on the line is visually presented to the control operator on a track panel. In addition, all locomotives and self-propelled cars are linked to the controller by radio telephones.

3. Automatic Train Control.—Automatic train control (ATC) provides the engineman in the locomotive cab with audible (and sometimes visual) information on track conditions. Should a restrictive indication be ignored, the brakes are applied automatically to stop the train. Several railways in the United States use automatic speed control, a refined form of ATC. A miniature signal in the cab repeats the wayside signal aspects (or it may take the place of wayside signals). Should train speed exceed that indicated by the aspect being displayed, the brakes are automatically applied to reduce the speed below the permissible level.

4. Automation of Train Operations.—Only a slight further extension of the above type of control is needed to permit fully automatic operation of the train—dispensing entirely with the engine crew. From a technical standpoint, fully automatic train operation is entirely feasible. During the 1950s and 1960s railways in several countries experimented with both remote-controlled and automatically controlled trains and locomotives. By the end of the latter decade a number of automated railways and rail transit lines were in operation. In North America there were several fully automated mining and industrial railways with crewless trains operating on short shuttle runs. A mining railway in Wyoming operates automatically over a distance of nearly 100 mi., although the locomotive carries an engineman who can control the train during switching operations and in emergencies.

On the high-speed New Tōkaidō line in Japan, all trains operate under computerized automatic control throughout the entire length of the line (325 mi.). The engineman, however, starts the train, stops the train at station stops, and opens and closes the train doors. Trains on London Transport's new Victoria line subway are completely automatic, although one crewman is still carried. Similar systems were planned for other rail transit systems.

Labour union opposition seemed likely to delay any widespread automation of major intercity common carrier railways. However, because of the guiding action of the flanged wheels on the rails, railways are ideally suited to fully automatic operation. Under the pressure of competition, they may be expected to move in this direction. Indeed, the extent to which railways would be able to automate their operations seemed likely to be a major factor in determining how important a role they would play in the world economy during the last decades of the 20th century.

VIII. CLASSIFICATION (MARSHALING) YARDS

A freight train starting on its run usually consists of cars moving to a number of different destinations. Somewhere en route, the cars going to each destination must be sorted out and transferred to other trains going to the proper terminals. This is done in classification or marshaling yards. In the years following World War II, railways made much progress in improving the efficiency of these yards—mainly through the use of automatic equipment.

Most large classification yards have a hump over which cars are pushed. The cars then roll down the hump by gravity and each is routed into a classification track corresponding to its destination.

The "Rocket," built by George Stephenson. It was the winner of the 1829 trials by the Liverpool and Manchester railway, England

Richard Trevithick's "New Castle," 1803, the first locomotive in the world to do actual work

The "Stourbridge Lion," built in England and shipped to the U.S. where it was placed in operation in 1829

The "Best Friend of Charleston," first locomotive built in the U.S. for regular service on a railway. It began scheduled passenger service in 1830 from Charleston, S.C., over a route which eventually became part of the Southern Railway system

HISTORIC LOCOMOTIVES OF ENGLAND AND THE U.S.

The "General," active during the American Civil War. This locomotive was the basic type of the American class (4-4-0 wheel arrangement), a design which continued in service until the 20th century

Engine 999 of the Empire State Express, New York Central railroad, a somewhat later version of the 4-4-0 type. It set a speed record of 112.5 m.p.h. in 1893

PLATE II   RAILWAY

Mikado (wheel arrangement 2-8-2), a heavy-duty freight locomotive of the U.S.

Decapod class (2-10-0) locomotive of Germany, a typical freight engine widely used in Europe

Beyer-Garratt articulated type (4-8-2-2-8-4), a unique design with its weight spread over considerable length and also capable of operating over railroads with sharp curves. Used in Africa, Asia and Australasia

Hudson or Baltic type (4-6-4), used extensively on U.S. lines for high-speed, heavy-duty passenger hauling during the steam locomotive era

Pacific (4-6-2) of the French railways, typical locomotive of the years between World War I and World War II

Another Pacific, the British "Britannia" class, a standard type used after World War II

A U.S. "streamliner," a modification of the Northern or Niagara (4-8-4), a final stage of development of steam locomotives for passenger service

The "Big Boy" (4-8-8-4) of the Union Pacific railroad (U.S.), considered to be the largest steam locomotive ever built. Used for hauling freight in mountainous areas

STEAM LOCOMOTIVES

BY COURTESY OF (TOP ROW LEFT) LOUISIANA & ARKANSAS FROM ASSOCIATION OF AMERICAN RAILROADS, (TOP ROW RIGHT) GERMAN FEDERAL RAILROAD, (SECOND ROW) EAST AFRICAN RAILWAYS & HARBOURS, (THIRD ROW LEFT) NEW YORK CENTRAL RAILROAD, (THIRD ROW RIGHT) NORD FROM FRENCH NATIONAL RAILROADS, (FOURTH ROW LEFT) BRITISH RAILWAYS, (FOURTH ROW RIGHT) NORFOLK & WESTERN RAILWAY FROM ASSOCIATION OF AMERICAN RAILROADS, (BOTTOM) UNION PACIFIC RAILROAD

Rectifier locomotive of the Pennsylvania railroad (U.S.), a large, post-World War II model of the C-C type

Dual-frequency switching engine of the Swiss Federal railways. Operates on either 15,000-v., 16 ⅔-cycle or 25,000-v., 50-cycle A.C.

Dual voltage "Benelux," a passenger train operating in Belgium and the Netherlands

Class T type of electric locomotive of the New York Central railroad

Pennsylvania railroad (U.S.) GG-1, a 2-C+C-2 electric used for high-speed passenger and freight operations

French C-C type which operates on 1,500-v. D.C. Set a world speed record of 205 m.p.h. in 1955

E-10 locomotive of the German Federal railroad serving on international routes. Operates on 15,000 v., 16 ⅔-cycle A.C.

Japanese B-B unit which can operate from commercial-frequency A.C. (50 c.p.s.) or 1,500-v. D.C.

ELECTRIC LOCOMOTIVES

PLATE IV　　　　　　　　RAILWAY

Three DL-600 locomotives, 2,400-h.p. modern diesel-electric units powered by 16-cylinder engines. Santa Fe, U.S.

Diesel-hydraulic type, the V200, a 2,000-h.p. locomotive of the German Federal railroad

TE-3, part of a twin-unit diesel-electric of the Soviet railways. Each of the C-C type articulated units is equipped with a 2,000-h.p. engine

Gas-turbine locomotive of the Union Pacific railroad, an 8,500-h.p. unit which can develop high speeds with heavy trains such as the long freight shown in the photograph

Diesel locomotive unit of a Trans-Europ express (T.E.E.) train. T.E.E. trains serve eight nations on international runs. They are operated jointly by the Dutch, Swiss, German, French and Italian railways

Diesel rail car of the French railways, a self-propelled passenger unit equipped with a domed observation section

Self-propelled rail diesel car (R.D.C.) powered by a pair of 300-h.p., 6-cylinder diesels. Individual units can be joined to make up longer trains

DIESEL, GAS TURBINE AND OTHER SELF-PROPELLED UNITS

BY COURTESY OF (TOP LEFT) ALCO PRODUCTS, INC., (TOP RIGHT, CENTRE RIGHT BELOW) GERMAN FEDERAL RAILROAD, (CENTRE LEFT) UNION PACIFIC RAILROAD, (BOTTOM RIGHT) NEW HAVEN RAILROAD FROM ASSOCIATION OF AMERICAN RAILROADS; PHOTOGRAPHS, (CENTRE RIGHT ABOVE) SOVFOTO, (BOTTOM LEFT) AUTHENTICATED NEWS

Sliding-roof boxcar permitting loading and unloading from both the top and the sides. German Federal railroad

"Big John," 97-ton capacity aluminum hopper car, used by the Southern railway for carrying bulk commodities. Left, a conventional 70-ton capacity covered hopper car

A 30,000-gal. capacity tank car designed to carry a variety of liquids such as chemicals, acids, vegetable oils, and petroleum products

Flatcars in the "piggyback" service of the Santa Fe railway. Each flatcar is carrying two 40-ft. truck trailers

Gondola car owned by the French National railroads, but operated as a unit in the Europ freight car pool, co-operative plan of the International Union of Railways

Specialized flatcar with low central section designed to carry electric power transformers and maintain clearance in tunnels and under low bridges. The car is also unusual in its arrangement of eight axles

Modern automobile carrier of the U.S. railways, a flatcar equipped with two extra decks to accommodate a total of 12 automobiles

German automobile carrier, a two-decked, five-axle type which will hold 10 compact cars

FREIGHT EQUIPMENT

BY COURTESY OF (TOP ROW LEFT) "MODERN RAILROADS," (TOP ROW RIGHT, SECOND ROW LEFT) TIMKEN ROLLER BEARING CO., (SECOND ROW RIGHT) SANTA FE RAILWAY, (THIRD ROW LEFT) FRENCH NATIONAL RAILROADS, (BOTTOM LEFT) PULLMAN-STANDARD, (BOTTOM RIGHT) GERMAN FEDERAL RAILROAD; PHOTOGRAPHS, (THIRD ROW RIGHT) UNITED PRESS INTERNATIONAL

PLATE VI　　　　　　　　　RAILWAY

First Pullman sleeping car, a converted day coach which went into service in Sept. 1859

Interior of the "North Coast Limited," a luxury train of 1900, Northern Pacific railway. It was the first electric-lighted train of the U.S. northwest

ETR 300 "Settebello," a high-speed electric passenger train of the Italian State railways. Unique design provides passengers with an observation area in the first car while the engineer operates the train in a "blister" cabin above

Interior of an air-conditioned dining car of the Swedish national railways

First-class compartment, express train of the German Federal railroad

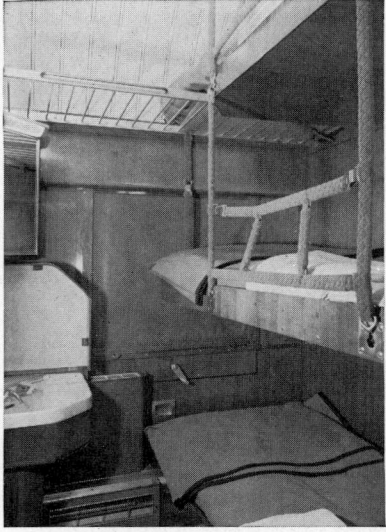

Three-bed sleeping compartment, tourist class, of the Wagon-Lits company which operates passenger equipment on railways of Europe, Africa and the middle east

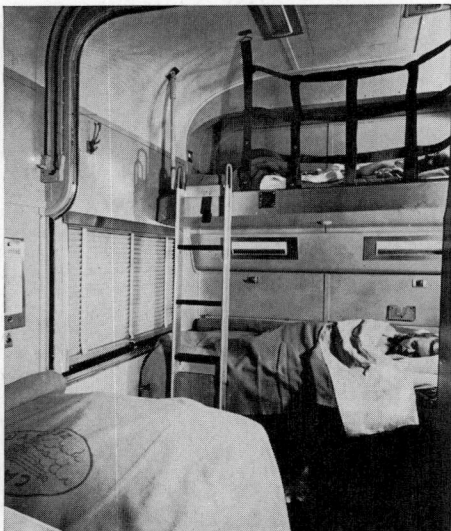

Master bedroom of the "California Zephyr" of the Chicago, Burlington and Quincy railroad. It accommodated six passengers by day and had four beds (one not shown)

PASSENGER SERVICE, EARLY AND RECENT

BY COURTESY OF (TOP LEFT, TOP RIGHT) ASSOCIATION OF AMERICAN RAILROADS, (CENTRE LEFT) ITALIAN STATE RAILWAYS, (CENTRE RIGHT) KUNGL JARNVAGSSTYRELSEN, (BOTTOM CENTRE) FRENCH NATIONAL RAILROADS, (BOTTOM RIGHT) CHICAGO, BURLINGTON & QUINCY RAILROAD COMPANY FROM ASSOCIATION OF AMERICAN RAILROADS; PHOTOGRAPH, (BOTTOM LEFT) AUTHENTICATED NEWS

Lounge car equipped with a full-length observation dome. In service on the "Empire Builder," Burlington Northern (U.S.)

Modern passenger station at Rotterdam, the Netherlands

Auto transporters used by Canadian National railways enable passengers to travel by rail and have their own cars available at destination

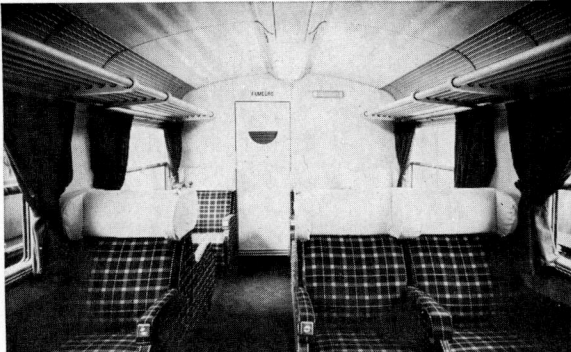

Reclining seats in a first-class coach of the French National railroads

Double-deck coach for commuters on suburban divisions of the Chicago and North Western railway. Locomotive (out of sight at right) can be operated either from its own cab or from auxiliary control cab (upper left) in last passenger coach, permitting service in either direction without turnaround

The "Canadian," a high-speed transcontinental passenger train equipped with two domed observation cars. Canadian Pacific railway

PASSENGER SERVICES

BY COURTESY OF (TOP LEFT) BURLINGTON NORTHERN, (TOP RIGHT) FRENCH NATIONAL RAILROADS, (CENTRE LEFT) N.V. NEDERLANDSCHE SPOORWEGEN, (BOTTOM LEFT) CANADIAN NATIONAL RAILWAYS, (BOTTOM RIGHT) CANADIAN PACIFIC; PHOTOGRAPH, (CENTRE RIGHT) UNITED PRESS INTERNATIONAL

PLATE VIII   RAILWAY

Adzing machines, which cut a uniform seat for tie plates before new rail is laid

Rail inspection car equipped with electronic devices which detect the presence of flaws in rails. Rubber tires permit car to be driven off the rails onto highways

Track maintenance machines which tamp crushed rock roadbed ballast

Dual rail-laying equipment unloading continuous welded rail sections from flatcars onto cradles. Follow-up crews remove old rails and properly position new rails

Lightweight wiring of 50-cycle, commercial-frequency electrification of French National railroads

Installing an overhead electrical system on a division of the British railways

A modern roadbed: long welded rails set into concrete and steel crossties (sleepers)

TRACK MAINTENANCE AND ELECTRIFICATION

Fueling and sanding centre for diesel locomotives on Southern Pacific railroad at Taylor Yard, Los Angeles

Diesel shop for light and heavy repairs. Work pits and platforms at three levels provide easy access to all parts of the locomotive

Assembly-line maintenance of diesels at the Cumberland, Md., shops of the Baltimore and Ohio railroad

Car repair shop where all types of freight rolling stock are refurbished or rebuilt and modernized

Assembling passenger cars at Madras, India. The coach shell is shown being lowered onto the wheel trucks or bogies

LOCOMOTIVE AND CAR MAINTENANCE

BY COURTESY OF (TOP) "MODERN RAILROADS," (CENTRE LEFT) CHICAGO, ROCK ISLAND AND PACIFIC RAILROAD FROM ASSOCIATION OF AMERICAN RAILROADS, (CENTRE RIGHT) BALTIMORE AND OHIO RAILROAD, (BOTTOM LEFT) GREAT NORTHERN RAILWAY FROM ASSOCIATION OF AMERICAN RAILROADS; PHOTOGRAPH, (BOTTOM RIGHT) AUTHENTICATED NEWS

PLATE X   RAILWAY

Electronic program machine, York, Eng., signal station. Trains passing through the more than 30 mi. covered by this station are controlled by signal and switch changes dictated by electronic scanning of a punched plastic tape

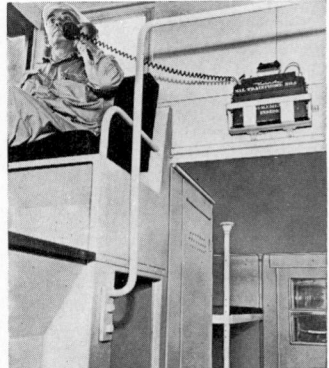

Two-way radio installed in the caboose of a freight train enables the conductor to communicate with the engineer or with operators of other passing trains

Train dispatcher at the console of a centralized traffic control (C.T.C.) board of the Penn Central railroad at Rochester, N.Y. The dispatcher controls the movement of all mainline traffic between East Rochester and Syracuse Junction (about 50 mi.) with buttons and levers that activate signals and switches on the right of way

Control tower in the Markham, Ill., yard of the Illinois Central railroad. As freight cars roll down a hill, operator punches buttons to direct each car or group of cars to its appropriate classification track. Electronically controlled retarders regulate speed of the rolling cars

Four-aspect colour light with double junction indicator, a modern trackside signal of the British railways for block traffic control

TRAIN OPERATION AND CONTROL

BY COURTESY OF (TOP, BOTTOM RIGHT) BRITISH RAILWAYS, (CENTRE LEFT) SEABOARD AIR LINE RAILROAD FROM ASSOCIATION OF AMERICAN RAILROADS, (CENTRE RIGHT) PENN CENTRAL RAILROAD; PHOTOGRAPH, (BOTTOM LEFT) HEDRICH-BLESSING

The principle is similar to that of sorting letters into pigeonholes at a post office. The speed of a car rolling down the hump siding can be controlled by retarders—electric or electropneumatic clamps that grip the wheels of the car as it passes over them. The degree of retardation can be controlled automatically by an electronic computer which takes into account such factors as the weight, speed, and rolling friction of the car. Equipment of this kind enables more cars to be handled, reduces human error, lessens the risk of damage to cars and their loads, and reduces delays.

Modern improvements, however, involve more than just the automatic humping of cars. The electronic yard is usually blanketed with a local radio network, as well as telephone, tele-printer, and pneumatic-tube communication circuits. Television or ACI may be used to scan trains entering or leaving the yard. Infrared detectors scan the wheels of incoming trains to pick out any journal bearing that may be overheated. Repair shops adjacent to the yard are mechanized to speed the repair of cars found to be in bad order as they move over the hump. Every phase of the yard's operation can be monitored and recorded by the railway's centralized management information and control system.

Because modern classification yards can sort cars with such efficiency, they eliminate the need to do this work at other, smaller, intermediate yards. Thus, the establishment of one hump yard may permit the curtailing or closing of a dozen or more other yards. Most of the modern yards built in North America have paid for themselves in operating savings in three or four years, and this takes no account of the benefits of improved service to shippers.

IX. COOPERATION AMONG RAILWAYS

In both North America and Europe, close working relations among different (and often competing) railway systems developed almost from the earliest years. It was found desirable, for in-stance, that connecting railways agree on such basic elements as the gauge of track and the type of couplings to be used on cars.

This was done to such an extent that a shipper can send a car-load of goods from almost any railway point in North America to any other point; and a passenger may buy, at his local rail-way agency, a ticket for a trip covering thousands of miles in the cars of many different railways.

1. Western Hemisphere Organizations.—The principal ele-ment for coordination among North American lines is the Associa-tion of American Railroads (AAR), with headquarters in Wash-ington, D.C. Members of the AAR include about 150 of the principal railways in the U.S., Canada, and Mexico. The Ameri-can Short Line Railroad Association is a similar organization, serving 200 smaller lines.

In addition, railways and the companies that supply them with materials and equipment work together through numerous regional groups and trade associations.

Through its several divisions and their numerous working com-mittees, the AAR coordinates the operations of the individual companies that make up the North American rail network. Among results of this joint activity (by the AAR and its various prede-cessor groups) are standard items of car equipment, such as cou-plers, brakes, and safety appliances; standard time; standard train operating rules; standard rules governing the interchange of cars among railways; and rules covering the collection and divi-sion of revenues for interline movements of freight and pas-sengers.

Through its research centre at Chicago, the AAR also carries on technological research and testing; this is in addition to testing and research work by some individual railway companies. The AAR also represents the U.S. railway industry in connection with legislative proposals in Congress that may affect the rail-ways, and it carries on a public relations program for the industry as a whole.

The Pullman Company, jointly owned by the principal railways, formerly operated most of the sleeping cars on U.S. lines. How-ever, with the decline in intercity passenger traffic, Pullman ceased

(as of January 1969) to be an operating company; the few sleep-ing cars still running were operated and maintained by the indi-vidual railways.

A number of companies also own large fleets of freight cars but do not actually operate any railway line. These so-called private car lines usually were formed to meet the need for specialized types of equipment that could be better supplied in this way than by the individual railways.

Railways also cooperate throughout the Western hemisphere through the Pan American Railway Congress Association, which has its headquarters at Buenos Aires, Arg. It operates much like the International Railway Congress Association (which has world-wide membership), that is, through the exchange of technical information among railways in the different North and South American countries.

2. European Organizations.—In Europe, too, the gradual spread of railway routes led to the need for some form of co-operation and uniform regulations relating to the movement of equipment. From this need came the Convention Internationale sur le Transport des Marchandises (CIM), or International Con-vention for the Transport of Freight, which was established in 1890.

Later came the Convention Internationale sur le Transport des Voyageurs (CIV), or International Convention for the Trans-port of Passengers. These were followed by the Regolamento Internazionale Veicoli (RIV) or International Wagon Union, and Regolamento Internazionale Carrozzi (RIC) or International Carriage and Brake Van Union. They succeeded earlier ar-rangements concerning the international movement and inter-change of passenger and freight vehicles. From these arrange-ments also came annual passenger and freight train timetable conferences.

In 1885 the International Railway Congress Association was formed for the purpose of exchanging technical information be-tween administrations, and in 1922 the Union Internationale des Chemins de Fer (UIC), or International Union of Railways was created. Its original aim was to improve international serv-ices. During the interwar years it was also concerned with tech-nical measures and joint regulations for improving international traffic.

After World War II, European railway cooperation made great strides in many different spheres, and, in particular, the scope of the UIC was considerably enlarged. From the UIC sprang a num-ber of other organizations that made important contributions to the economy and progress of the European railway systems.

The freight car pool known as Europ came into being in 1953. Previously, freight cars entering another country had to be re-turned to the owning system as quickly as possible after unloading, subject to efforts being made to find a return load. Europ cars are not bound by this requirement, which saves millions of empty car miles a year.

Interfrigo was created in 1949 with the object of developing the international transport of perishable traffic at controlled tempera-tures. It is owned jointly by 11 railway systems, and there are agreements with nonmember administrations. Interfrigo has a fleet of 900 vehicles and, in addition, operates in international traffic about 10,000 refrigerated vehicles belonging to members and their subsidiaries. Eleven European railway systems are also members of Intercontainer, a body formed in 1967 to organize the international rail movement of containers.

The Office for Research and Experiments (ORE) was created by the UIC in 1949. Its purpose is to conduct research and tests for the benefit of members. Unlike the Association of Ameri-can Railroads, ORE does not have its own research establish-ment. Instead, it uses the laboratories and testing plants of its members. Financing is handled by a common fund, the cost being divided among the 29 members in proportion to the operated track mileage of each.

Eurofima is a financing company that was established in 1955 with about 16 administrations as members. It finances the pur-chase of locomotives and rolling stock.

Trans-Europ Express (TEE) services are operated jointly by

the Dutch, Swiss, German, French, and Italian railways. They consist of a network of international express trains linking important cities in eight countries. Operations commenced in 1956. The trains are owned by the different administrations but must conform to accepted standards of comfort, speed, etc. The first trains were all diesel-powered, permanently coupled sets, but the majority of the trains are now locomotive hauled. This follows the spread of electrification and also allows greater flexibility in train makeup. In addition, some TEE trains operate wholly within the boundaries of one country (e.g., the Paris–Nice "Mistral").

Although it is a private company, the Compagnie Internationale des Wagon-Lits (CIWL) occupies a unique position in the field of international passenger services in Europe. It has been engaged in the operation of sleeping cars on international services since 1876. It also operates dining cars, Pullman cars, buffet and light refreshment facilities, restaurants at stations and airports, a motel, and restaurant and cabin facilities on river steamers. The company is registered in Brussels and has its operational and administrative headquarters in Paris. Its activities, although concerned principally with Europe, also extend to Africa and the Middle East.

X. CONCLUSION

The railways can look back over a proud history. They were a vital element in the Industrial Revolution. They helped make Britain an industrial power, played similar roles in countries such as France and Germany, and went on to do much the same in Russia. Railways essentially built the United States and Canada, and they remained the economic backbone of most of the major world powers.

But the railways in a number of countries—especially in Britain and the United States—were in serious trouble by the 1960s: they were steadily losing traffic to other modes of transport. In most countries, the railways had long since come under state control, and the remaining privately owned lines were finding it difficult to operate at a profit. Railway mileage was shrinking in many countries. Did this foretell the end of this great form of transportation?

Technology was evolving so rapidly that it was probably unwise to say that this could not happen. However, as of the late 1960s, it seemed unlikely. No other form of transportation had yet been developed to the point where it could challenge the railway as an all-around carrier.

Railways still offer two major advantages: (1) At distances of more than 100 or 200 mi., they can haul any kind of freight, and in some cases passengers, at a true cost lower than any other form of transportation on land or air; (2) they are all-purpose land carriers. Pipelines may carry liquids and some solids economically; airplanes may produce savings on very high-value commodities; trucks offer speed and flexibility for relatively short hauls; overland conveyer belts may prove of value for certain bulk commodities. But only railways can carry anything, almost anywhere—and do it with little regard for weather conditions.

In sum, the railway is one of the earliest and greatest material achievements of the industrial era. It seemed likely to continue serving man's evolving civilization.

See also references under "Railway" in the Index.

BIBLIOGRAPHY.—General: Jane's World Railways (at intervals); Overseas Railways (annually); Directory of Railway Officials & Yearbook (annually).
United States: T. W. van Metre, Trains, Tracks & Travel, 8th ed. (1950); R. S. Henry, Trains (1954); Moody's Transportation Manual (annually); S. H. Holbrook, The Story of American Railroads (1947); W. W. Hay, Railroad Engineering (1953), An Introduction to Transportation Engineering (1961); F. H. Hubbard, Railroad Avenue (1945); B. A. Botkin and A. F. Harlow (eds.), A Treasury of Railroad Folklore (1953); G. E. Turner, Victory Rode the Rails (1953); A. W. Bruce, The Steam Locomotive in America (1952); Modern Railroads (monthly); Railway Age (semimonthly); Trains (monthly). Association of American Railroads, Railroad Facts (annually); Interstate Commerce Commission, Annual Reports, Statistics of Railways in the United States (annually); Association of American Railroads, Quiz on Railroads and Railroading (at intervals), A Review of Railway Operations (annually).
Canada: Canadian Transport Commission, Annual Reports; Canadian Transportation (monthly).
Latin America: National Railways of Mexico, Ferronales (monthly);
Pan American Railway Congress Association, Bulletin (monthly).
Great Britain: British Railways Board, Annual Report; R. Bell, History of British Railways During the War, 1939–45 (1946); Concise Encyclopaedia of World Railway Locomotives (1959); E. A. Binney, Electric Traction Engineering (1955); Railway Gazette International (monthly); Journal of the Institute of Transport (bimonthly); Railway Magazine (monthly); Modern Railways (monthly).
Europe: Rail International (monthly); Revue Générale des Chemins de Fer (monthly); Ingegneria Ferroviaria (monthly); Jahrbuch des Eisenbahnwesens (annually); European Railways (quarterly); Railway Electrification in Switzerland (1954); International Railway Journal (monthly).
South Africa: Railway Engineering (bimonthly); J. R. Day, Railways of Southern Africa (1963).
Japan: Japanese National Railways, Facts and Figures (annually); Japanese National Railways at a Glance (JNR); Japanese Railway Engineering (quarterly).
Australasia: Railway Transportation (monthly).

(TH. C. S.; R. B. S.)

RAIMONDI, MARCANTONIO (called MARCANTONIO) (c. 1480–c. 1534), Italian engraver, outstanding Italian master of engraving of the Renaissance and the first who practised it to reproduce designs of other artists rather than his own. He received his training in the workshop of the famous goldsmith and painter Francesco Raibolini, called Francia. There, according to Vasari, "he made waist buckles and many other things in niello . . . being in truth most excellent in that craft."

The real fame of Raimondi was to be founded on his attainments in that particular development of the goldsmith's art which consists of engraving designs on metal plates for printing. About 80 engravings can be attributed to the first six years of his career (1505–11). They include many subjects from mythology and some of religious character. Figures, drapery and composition bespeak the influence of Francia, but the landscape backgrounds and the expression of form by light and shadow indicate German traditions as well. Perhaps for commercial reasons or to improve his style, he produced a series of counterfeits of copper engravings from Albrecht Dürer's woodcuts. There are 69 of these: 17 from the "Life of the Virgin," 37 of the woodcut "Little Passion" and a few others. The "Life of the Virgin" was copied in 1506 and signed with Dürer's signature. Dürer, traveling in Italy in the same year, complained to the Venetian senate and Raimondi added his own signature to the copies he subsequently completed in 1510 of Dürer's "Little Passion." Raimondi profited greatly by these studies of Dürer's energetic line and his use of crosshatching in modeling. He was to make brilliant use of these under another influence. Until this time he had lived only in Bologna, with the exception of a visit or visits to Venice.

Soon he was attracted to the circle that surrounded Raphael in Rome. Where or when he met Raphael is uncertain. His passage to Rome by way of Florence was supposedly marked by an engraving (1510) known as "The Climbers" (Les Grimpeurs), in which he reproduced part of the design of Michelangelo's cartoon of soldiers surprised while bathing, he added behind the figures a landscape imitated from the young Dutch engraver Lucas van Leyden. The piece in which he is recorded to have first tried his hand after a work of Raphael is the "Lucretia." Raimondi was almost exclusively engaged in engraving the designs of Raphael or of his immediate pupils. Raphael, the story goes, was so delighted with the print of the "Lucretia" that he later personally trained and helped Raimondi.

A printing establishment was set up under the charge of Raphael's colour grinder, Baviera, and profits in its early days were shared by the engraver and the printer. The sale soon became very great; pupils gathered about Raimondi, of whom the two most distinguished were Marco Dente, known as Marco da Ravenna, and Agostino De Musis, known as Agostino Veneziano. During the last 10 years of Raphael's life and for several years following his death, the group produced a great number of engravings after the master's works. They did not usually copy his finished paintings, but worked up (with the addition of simple backgrounds and accessories) his sketches, which often gave the composition in a different form from the finished work, and are all the more interesting on that account.

Raimondi's best engravings (e.g., "Massacre of the Innocents") were done during the first years after he had attached himself to Raphael. In them he entered into the genius of his master and lost little of the chastened science and rhythmical purity of Raphael's contours. In the parts where he was left to himself (the rounding and shading, the background and landscape) he managed his burin with all the skill and freedom he had gained by the imitation of northern models, while dispensing with the northern emphasis and redundance of detail. Raimondi's engravings after the works of Raphael's later years were colder and more ostentatious. Still more so, as is natural, were those which he and his pupils produced after the designs of the followers of Raphael and Michelangelo, such as Giulio Romano, Polidoro Baccio or Bandinelli.

Raimondi's association with Giulio Romano (*q.v.*), was the cause of his first great disaster in life. He engraved a series of obscene designs by that painter in illustration of the *Sonnetti lussoriosi* of Pietro Aretino which caused his arrest. Marcantonio's ruin was completed by the calamities attendant on the sack of Rome, by the German troops of the emperor Charles V of Spain in 1527. He had to pay a heavy ransom to escape the Spaniards, and fled, to quote Vasari, "all but a beggar." It is said he took refuge in his native city of Bologna, but he never again emerged from obscurity. All that is known with certainty is that in 1534 he was dead.

BIBLIOGRAPHY.—H. Delaborde, *Marc-Antoine Raimondi* (1887); A. M. Hind, *Great Engravers* (1911) and *A Short History of Engraving and Etching* (1923). (H. Es.)

RAIMUNDO, DON (d. 1152), archbishop of Toledo from 1125 to 1152, was one of the many French monks who went to Spain with Bernard of Périgord (archbishop of Toledo, 1085–1124) in the time of Alfonso VI. He was appointed bishop of Osma (1109), but was dispossessed and imprisoned (1111) by Alfonso VI's successor Alfonso I of Aragon, for opposing the marriage of Alfonso I with Alfonso VI's daughter Urraca. This persecution commended him to Alfonso VII, whose chancellor he became. On Bernard's death he was appointed to succeed him as archbishop of Toledo and primate. Raimundo's main importance is in the history of medieval learning; it was under his patronage—and probably as a result of his encouragement—that the famous Toledan school of translators came into existence. Already some effort to make available to Christians the learning of the Spanish Arabs had begun, notably under the aegis of Miguel, bishop of Tarazona (1119–51). Raimundo was, however, made aware that there were still in Toledo not only a great many Arabic and Jewish works on science, mathematics, and philosophy unknown to Christian scholars but also learned Jews, Mozarabs, and Muslims able to read them. The archbishop—who was without his predecessor's fanaticism—either saw for himself, or was persuaded of, their importance. He, therefore, encouraged Spanish scholars, especially converted Jews, to translate them into Latin; soon foreign scholars arrived in Toledo to commission translations or investigate the material available there and in Spain generally. Raimundo's patronage was sometimes acknowledged in the dedications of their translations. One of the earliest Toledan translators, Johannes Hispanus, was as much interested in astronomy and astrology as in Arabic and Jewish philosophy, but Raimundo's own patronage was especially reserved for philosophical translations such as that of the *Fons Vitae* of Ibn Gabirol and Neoplatonic works generally. The Toledan translators, subsequently associated with a flourishing cathedral school, went on working for three centuries.

See Ángel González Palencia, *El arzobispo don Raimundo de Toledo* (1942). (P. E. R.)

RAIN: *see* METEOROLOGY; RAINFALL.

RAINALD OF DASSEL (*c.* 1118 or 1120–1167), German statesman and military leader, chancellor of the Holy Roman Empire and archbishop of Cologne, was the second son of Count Rainald I of Dassel. After attending the school at Hildesheim, he studied at Paris, probably *c.* 1140–46 and under the English dialectician Adam du Petit-Pont. In the following years he became provost of four churches, including two in Hildesheim, and in 1153 he refused an offer of the bishopric. Apparently his ambitions were already fixed on the imperial court, to which he had been intro-duced by the statesman and diplomat Wibald of Stablo. By the end of 1154 he was prominent in the entourage of the emperor Frederick I (*q.v.*), and in May 1156 he was appointed imperial chancellor. From then until his death he played a leading part in the formation and execution of imperial policy.

At the Diet of Besançon (October 1157) Rainald "exposed" and "interpreted" the letter in which Pope Adrian IV referred to the empire as a *beneficium* conferred by the pope; and he then directed a dashing propaganda campaign on behalf of the empire. Between 1158 and 1164 he several times led troops to Italy and negotiated with towns on Frederick's behalf. In 1159 he was elected archbishop of Cologne. In the same year Pope Adrian IV died, and Rainald championed the emperor's antipope Victor IV against Alexander III, going on missions to the kings of France and England in 1160, 1162, and 1165, and asserting that the bishop of Rome was in the same relationship to the emperor as any French bishop to the French king. Excommunicated by Alexander III in 1163, he ensured the continuance of the schism by rushing through, on his own responsibility, the election of a new antipope on the death of Victor IV. It was he also who secured the canonization of Charlemagne in 1165. On May 29, 1167, he won, with a small force, a decisive victory over the Romans; but on reaching Rome he was afflicted, like most of the imperial army, with malaria, and he died on Aug. 14, 1167. He was buried in Cologne Cathedral, to which he had given the relics of the Magi (received by him as part of the loot of Milan). He had been the mainspring of Frederick I's imperial policy in Italy.

BIBLIOGRAPHY.—J. Ficker, *Rainald von Dassel* (1850), to be used with caution; R. Knipping, *Regesten der Erzbischöfe von Köln*, ii (1901); W. Föhl, articles in *Jahrbuch des Kölnischen Geschichtsvereins*, xvii and xx (1935, 1938). (R. H. C. D.)

RAINALDI, CARLO (1611–1691), Roman Baroque architect, noted particularly for his works of the 1660s, was born in Rome in 1611 and died there in 1691. He collaborated with his father, Girolamo Rainaldi (1577–1655), a distinguished architect who transplanted to Rome the north Italian Mannerist tradition of Pellegrino Tibaldi. After his father's death, Rainaldi evolved a monumental grand manner, without entirely discarding his paternal heritage. The final building of his masterpiece, Sta. Maria in Campitelli (1663–67), showed a north Italian rather than a Roman pedigree. The use of many freestanding columns gave the building a scenographic quality which had neither past nor future in Rome but influenced late Baroque north Italian church design. Nor was the facade, closely set with columns, rooted in the Roman tradition. Again, its basic motif—two enormous aediculae, one set into the other—was current in northern Italy.

Rainaldi's last important work was the grand facade uniting the old apse of Sta. Maria Maggiore with the chapels of Sixtus V and Paul V (1673). Thenceforth his practice was confined to a number of smaller enterprises. (Rf. W.)

RAINBOROW (RAINBOROWE or RAINSBOROUGH), **THOMAS** (d. 1648), English soldier and republican who fought for Parliament during the Civil War, spent his youth as a sailor and after the outbreak of war commanded the "Swallow" in the parliamentary fleet in 1643. He was soon transferred to the land forces and became a colonel first in Lord Fairfax's army and then under the earl of Manchester. In 1645 he commanded a regiment in the New Model Army and fought at Naseby (June 14, 1645) and at the siege of Bristol. He became M.P. for Droitwich in 1646. Rainborow took a prominent part in the debates in the army council (October–November 1647) concerning the army's negotiations with Charles I and was a leader of the republican officers and a supporter of the Agreement of the People, which called for manhood suffrage and religious toleration. This caused a rift between Rainborow and the army commanders, but in December 1647 he was reconciled with Oliver Cromwell. In January 1648 he returned to sea as vice-admiral, but failing to gain the goodwill of his officers he returned to the army after five months. Appointed commander for the siege of Pontefract Castle, he was mortally wounded when royalists tried to capture him at Doncaster on Oct. 29, 1648.

See H. R. Williamson, *Four Stuart Portraits* (1949). (S. R. Bt.)

RAINBOW, a name for a set of coloured arcs seen against the sky whenever falling water droplets (from a rain cloud or in a spray of a waterfall or fountain) are illuminated by a strong light source (the sun or the moon).

The bows appear as concentric arcs, with the common centre on the line connecting the eye of the observer and the light source. Most frequently only one bow is clearly visible. It appears on the opposite side from the source; its angular radius of the red border is about 42°. Other colours of the spectrum can be seen inside of this border, ending with the violet. Occasionally another, secondary rainbow is observed above the primary rainbow. Its angular radius is about 54°, and the sequence of the colours is reversed: the red is inside and the violet on the outer border of the bow. The space between these two bows seems to be relatively dark. The centre of these bows is, angularly, as far below the horizon as the source (the sun) is above. Hence, usually less than a semicircle of these coloured arcs is visible. However, if the droplets are illuminated by a reflected source from a large water surface, the rainbow will appear as arcs of circles, with the centre above the horizon. Such a reflected rainbow will intersect the ordinary rainbow at the horizon.

Inside of the outer border of the primary rainbow, additional coloured bows can be sometimes seen, called (improperly) supernumerary bows. The appearance of these bows depends primarily upon the size of the droplets; thus it varies quite considerably. When superposed on the ordinary rainbow, these supernumerary bows cause eventually a broadening or disappearance of any particular colour in the rainbow, which then results in a great variety in the brightness and purity, as well as in the angular width of coloured bows. In particular, if the water droplets are very small (of a diameter of 0.1 mm. or less), the superposition of the ordinary and supernumerary bows leads to an almost white rainbow, sometimes known as Ulloa's ring or a fogbow.

The rainbow was first correctly explained by M. A. de Dominis in 1611. The primary bow is formed by two refractions and one internal reflection in the water droplets, the secondary bow by one more additional internal reflection. This explanation was further developed and experimentally confirmed by Descartes (1637). The explanation of the colours in the rainbow was given later by Sir Isaac Newton. The supernumerary rainbows were explained much later by Thomas Young (1803) as the interference effect of two ray systems in the inner space of the bows; the mathematical theory was given by Sir George Biddell Airy (1838).

The original explanation of the rainbow by De Dominis and by Descartes is based on tracing the path of a light ray falling on

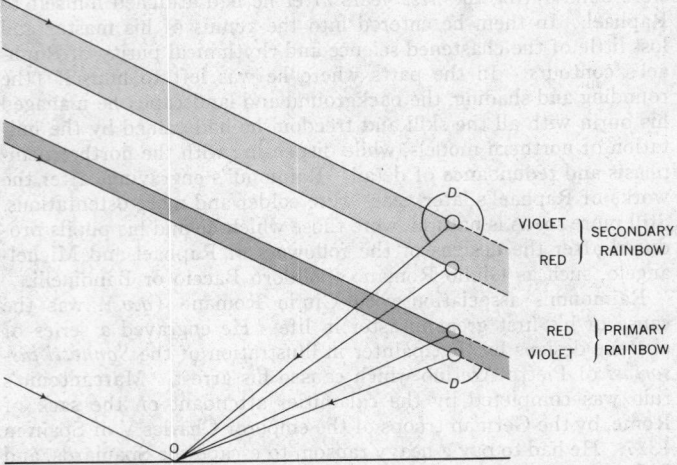

SCHEMATIC DIAGRAM OF THE ORIGIN OF THE PRIMARY AND SECONDARY RAINBOW. D IS THE ANGLE OF MINIMUM DEVIATION OF EMERGING RAYS

n	Minimum deviation (D)	
	Red (.656μ)*	Violet (.397μ)
Primary rainbow . . .	137°6 ($\pi - 42°4$)†	139°4 ($\pi - 40°6$)
Secondary rainbow . . .	230°4 ($\pi + 50°4$)	233°6 ($\pi + 53°6$)
Tertiary rainbow . . .	317°5 ($2\pi - 42°5$)	322°1 ($2\pi - 37°9$)
Quaternary rainbow . . .	402°8 ($2\pi + 42°8$)	408°6 ($2\pi + 48°6$)

*$\mu = 10^{-4}$ cm.   †$\pi = 180°$.

a transparent sphere with the use of the laws of geometrical optics. From the law of refraction and reflection it is easy to determine the deviation of the emerging ray from its original direction of incidence.

The angle of this deviation depends upon the angle of incidence, the number of internal reflections n and the index of refraction of the medium inside the sphere. For a particular angle of incidence the deviation has a minimum, given in the table.

The light emerging from the sphere reaches a high intensity around the direction of minimum deviation; the intensity then gradually decreases as the deviation increases. There are, however, no rays, hence no intensity on the other side of this direction (for smaller deviations). The observer will then see the highest intensity looking against the rays having minimum deviation, called sometimes Descartes rays. The Descartes rays from all individual droplets will form a cone with the vertex in the observer's eye and with the axis in the direction from or toward the source—the sun.

The light emerging from the droplets after one internal reflection will have the greatest intensity in the directions forming such a cone with the angle of 42°.4 in the red and of 40°.6 in the violet. The observer will see bright arcs of all spectral colours from the red over yellow, green, blue to violet. Since the angle for the red is greater, the red arcs will form the outer border, the violet arcs the inner one. The display fits the description of a primary rainbow. Similarly the secondary rainbow can be explained as consisting of Descartes rays from two internal reflections; the angle between the axis of the corresponding cones and the rays is 50°.4 for the red and 53°.6 for the violet. The secondary bows appear above the primary, and the sequence of the colours is reversed. (See fig.) The rays from the droplets above the primary and below the secondary bow would have to have the deviations smaller than the corresponding Descartes rays if they were to reach the observer's eye. This explains the dark space between these two bows. The tertiary and quaternary bows are quite faint and thus difficult to see against the bright sky in the vicinity of the sun.

The rays incident on the sphere on either side of the Descartes rays emerge only on one side of the minimum deviation. In this region the two systems of rays are crossing each other. Their superposition leads necessarily to interference patterns, with alternative maxima and minima of intensity in different directions. For a particular colour the positions of these maxima and minima are strongly dependent upon the size of the sphere, being closer for larger diameters of the sphere. The main maximum is usually close to the primary rainbow.

The superposition of the secondary maxima and minima is responsible for the great variation in the brightness and in the width of individual coloured arcs in the rainbow. If, for example, the secondary maximum in the red falls in the direction of the green arc in the primary rainbow, the mixture of these two colours produces an additional yellow arc; in the rainbow the yellow arc has enlarged width compared to that of other colours. For smaller droplets the secondary maximum in the red may be shifted beyond the blue or violet of the primary rainbow, thus giving rise to a supernumerary bow.

BIBLIOGRAPHY.—More detailed description and the theory of rainbow can be found in J. M. Pernter and F. M. Exner, *Meteorologische Optik*, 2nd ed. (1910); W. J. Humphreys, *Physics of the Air*, 3rd ed. (1940); H. C. van de Hulst, *Light Scattering by Small Particles* (1957).

(Z. S.)

RAINFALL or snowfall usually occurs from fairly thick cloud systems fed by ascending moist air. In its ascent the air expands as a result of the decreasing pressure with height and cools adiabatically (*see* ADIABATIC PROCESSES IN ATMOSPHERE). Water-vapour saturation is reached and maintained, accompanied by the production of great quantities of liquid water droplets or ice crystals.

In such active clouds the physical processes required for growth of the cloud droplets or crystals to raindrops or snowflakes are accomplished easily. Meteorological evidence indicates that the ascending motion is far more important than the minutia of precipitation physics in determining when and where the precipitation will occur. Radiation, conduction and mixing are relatively inefficient atmospheric cooling processes, producing the less spectacular forms of condensation, such as dew, frost, fog and drizzle. Air cooled by lifting may be internally stable and require forced lifting, such as produced by mountains, or it may be potentially unstable and require only an initial impulse to establish free convection.

Raindrops have limited fall velocities and may be deposited some distance downwind from their point of formation, but, in general, rates of precipitation are closely related to rates of ascent. Rapid and extensive lifting by free convection in unstable air masses produces the intense rainfalls associated with showers and, in the warmer, more humid air masses, thundershowers.

Lifting processes are represented by air gliding upward over mountain slopes or over wedges of cooler air, free convection, underrunning by cooler wedges of air and large-scale net horizontal inflow of air at lower levels. The last is the most effective natural lifting process, since large masses of air are forced upward. Any or all of the lifting processes may operate on stable or unstable air within the life cycle of one major rainstorm. Orographic lifting of stable air gliding upward over gently sloping cooler wedges of air produces the typical winter rains, which are uniformly light, steady and extensive. The flash floods of the southern United States represent the other extreme, in that highly unstable and very moist maritime air is lifted by the combined effects of horizontal convergence, upglide over cooler continental air and orographic lifting.

Forced lifting of maritime westerlies produces more than 100 in. of rainfall a year on many windward points on western mountain ranges, leaving some leeward continental areas with ten inches or less per year. Rainfall is greatest on windward coastal slopes, near warm tropical waters and in areas of marked cyclonic activity. Rainfall is least near the centre of continents, in colder higher latitudes, leeward of mountain ranges and within areas of persistent anticyclonic activity.

Mt. Waialeale, Hawaii, with a 20-year average of 460 in. from tropical easterlies, is the wettest known point. The nearest competitor is Cherrapunji, Assam, with an annual average of 450 in. from the moist tropical monsoon. Less than 10 in. and more than 60 in. per year represent approximate extremes of rainfall for all of the continents. Rainfall is slight in the central regions of the subtropical anticyclones, which are therefore the desert regions of the earth. In parts of the desert no appreciable rain has ever been observed.

Over most of Europe, South America, eastern North America and central Africa the annual rainfall exceeds 20 in., while over most of Asia, excluding India, Tibet and China, the annual rainfall is less than 20 in., being less than 10 in. in a long tongue extending from Arabia across to northeast Mongolia. The central regions of Australia, most of northern and a part of southwest Africa, portions of the intermontane area of the United States, portions of the west central coast and southern east coast of South America also have less than ten inches of rain in the year. Portions of the west coast of Africa, between the equator and 10° N., a strip of the west coast of India, parts of Assam, a coastal strip of Burma, windward mountain slopes in the temperate latitudes of North and South America and many isolated tropical stations average more than 100 in. of rain in the year. Rainfall intensities greater than 1 in. in five minutes, 4 in. in one hour or 20 in. per day are quite rare, but these intensities on occasion have been more than doubled for the respective durations.

The measurement of rainfall over an area by means of a network of rain gauges is often unsatisfactory because large variations in the amount of rainfall occur between adjacent gauges. This defect can be partly remedied by the use of a 3 to 10 cm. radar, which can give an areal picture of relative rainfall intensities at any moment as far as 200 mi. away. This is possible because the amount of radar reflection from raindrops is very sensitive to

Average Rainfall and Melted Snow Water
(in inches)

	London	Paris	Berlin	Rome	Moscow	Tokyo	Bombay	New York	Cape Town	Sydney
Jan.	1.9	1.5	1.9	3.6	1.6	2.3	0.1	3.5	0.7	3.9
Feb.	1.6	1.2	1.3	2.7	1.4	3.0	0.1	3.1	0.6	3.2
March	1.6	1.6	1.5	3.1	1.4	4.3	0.0	3.6	0.8	4.4
April	1.6	1.7	1.6	3.1	1.4	5.3	0.0	3.2	1.9	5.6
May	1.8	2.1	1.9	2.4	1.9	5.9	0.6	3.5	3.7	5.0
June	2.0	2.3	2.3	1.8	2.5	6.8	19.8	3.7	4.4	3.7
July	2.2	2.2	3.2	0.8	3.1	5.6	23.9	4.2	3.6	4.9
Aug.	2.2	2.2	2.2	1.0	2.8	7.1	14.1	4.3	3.3	2.4
Sept.	1.9	2.0	1.9	3.0	2.4	10.1	10.6	3.7	2.3	2.8
Oct.	2.6	2.3	1.7	5.3	2.5	7.9	2.1	3.0	1.6	2.8
Nov.	2.3	1.8	1.7	4.5	1.8	3.5	0.5	3.1	1.0	2.5
Dec.	2.3	1.7	1.9	4.1	1.6	2.2	0.1	3.1	0.8	3.6
Year	24.0	22.6	23.1	35.4	24.4	64.0	71.9	42.0	24.7	44.8
Days of rain	164	173	171	106	184	148	75	126	97	143
Days of snow	13	12	32	2	91	16	0	16	0	0

their size and number. (*See* Radar Meteorology.)

Average annual rainfall plus melted snow water is given in the table for some of the chief cities of the world. Data for other places will be found in standard textbooks on climatology. Detailed rainfall data for specific areas is best obtained by inquiry directed to any of the more prominent national meteorological services.

See also references under "Rainfall" in the Index.

Bibliography.—W. G. Kendrew, *Climates of the Continents*, 5th ed. (1961); U.S. Department of Agriculture, *Climate and Man* (1941); U.S. Department of Commerce, Weather Bureau, *World Weather Records 1941–1950* (1959); H. M. Conway (ed.), *The Weather Handbook* (1963).
(A. K. S.; E. M. Bs.)

RAIN FOREST, commonly, the luxurious evergreen forest typical of wet tropical lowlands. Some authors have chosen to broaden the term to include certain forest types found in subtropical and temperate climates. Factors favourable to the development of the true tropical rain forest are annual rainfall amounts in excess of 80 in. (2,032 mm.) (with no pronounced dry season) and mean temperatures between 68° and 85° F (20° and 30° C). Rain forests are evergreen, with the dense canopy at least 98 ft. (30 m.) high, but usually much taller, and are rich in thick-stemmed lianas and in woody as well as herbaceous epiphytes.

A characteristic feature of the climax tropical rain forest is the storied or stratified layering of the dense tree canopy. The crowns of the trees usually form three distinguishable stories, but occasionally they form only two. The trees themselves are remarkably uniform in general appearance even though the number of separate species may be large (often as many as 100 distinct species of trees per acre); trunks are usually straight and slender, bases often flanged by plank buttresses; foliage consists most frequently of large, leathery, dark-green leaves with entire or nearly entire margins; flowers are usually inconspicuous. As P. W. Richards stated, "So uniform is the foliage that the non-botanical observer might easily be excused for supposing that the forest was predominantly composed of species of laurel" (P. W. Richards, *The Tropical Rain Forest,* Cambridge University Press, 1952).

Contrary to popular belief, the tropical rain forest is not an impenetrable jungle of undergrowth, creepers, and rotted vegetation. Such a description applies only along edges of clearings or banks of waterways, where the strong tropical sunlight can penetrate to the forest floor. In most cases, herbaceous ground flora is sparse and the soil bare or only thinly covered by dead leaves. An abundance of climbers is characteristic of the forest, however, in addition to almost unbelievable numbers of epiphytes, which grow on trunks, branches and even the leaves of the trees. The latter group of flora include some of the most exotic flowering plants found in any plant community.

The tropical rain forest forms an irregular belt around the earth, bisected unequally by the equator and interrupted by seas, mountains and, in a few cases, "tongues" of dry subtropical climates that here and there extend into equatorial regions. Ecologists recognize three distinct formations of tropical rain forest. These correspond to the three primary regions of the earth that possess equatorial rainy climates, and may be described as follows: American rain forest: tropical portions of Central and South

America from the Amazon and Orinoco basins on the south to southern Mexico on the north.

Indo-Malayan rain forest: this formation extends from Ceylon and western India to Thailand, Indochina, the Philippines, and through the Malay archipelago to New Guinea. In Australia the rain forest occupies a narrow strip along the northeastern coast.

African rain forest: this formation is quite irregular; the largest portion lies within the Congo basin and along the coast of the Gulf of Guinea.

Related Types.—The changes in vegetation with increasing altitude within the tropical rain forest are as marked as in the forests of temperate latitudes. As greater altitudes are reached, the typical forest of the equatorial lowland begins to change character: trees are lower, the number of species becomes less, and finally the typical tropical flora is replaced by a mountain vegetation, where many of the species are temperate. Richards refers to this formation type as the "montane rain forest." The altitude at which this transition occurs varies markedly from region to region depending upon temperature, rainfall, exposure to winds, soil, and perhaps other factors. The base of the montane rain forest in some areas occurs at altitudes as low as 800 ft. (250 m.); in others it is as high as 4,000 ft. (1,200 m.).

In eastern Australia, southeast Asia and on the east coast of South America, the evergreen rain forest extends far into subtropical latitudes. These forests differ from the true tropical rain forest and should be considered a distinct formation type—subtropical rain forest. The species of trees decrease in number with increasing distance from the equator, and subtropical and temperate species occur together in increasing proportion. Features such as buttressing and production of flowers from main and old stems tend to disappear. Nevertheless, the forest retains much of the true tropical aspect.

One of the important subtypes of the tropical rain forest is the mangrove swamp forest found along tropical seacoasts. The marine muds of coastal tidal zones provide ideal conditions for mangrove formations. These formations, however, may also occur far inland along brackish estuaries. Standing upon stilt roots that lift the main trunk of the tree above high-water level, the mangrove forest at low water presents an impenetrable tangle of roots and knees. Mangroves are of considerable economic importance because of their role in reclaiming land from the sea and also because they are an important source of firewood, timber, and tanbark. Mangrove vegetation extends to about 32° N, and even farther from the equator in the Southern Hemisphere, but it reaches its greatest luxuriance where the tropical rain forest is the climax forest formation.

The term temperate rain forest is reserved to describe certain subantarctic broadleaf evergreen forests of southeastern Australia, New Zealand, and southern Chile, which are dominated by such temperate trees as *Nothofagus*. Rainy temperate forests of other regions, such as those of the coasts of Washington and Oregon, are occasionally referred to as rain forests, but such a usage of the term has not gained general acceptance among ecologists.

See also references under "Rain Forest" in the Index.

See Paul Westmacott Richards, *The Tropical Rain Forest* (1952); A. F. W. Schimper, *Plant-Geography Upon a Physiological Basis* (1903).
(W. C. Js.)

RAINIER, MOUNT: *see* MOUNT RAINIER NATIONAL PARK.

RAINIS (pseudonym of JĀNIS PLIEKŠANS) (1865–1929), Latvian poet and dramatist whose works were outstanding as literature and for their assertion of national freedom and social consciousness, was born at Varslavāni, Zemgale, on Sept. 11, 1865. He studied law at St. Petersburg and practised as a barrister in Jelgava, Latvia. From 1891 to 1895 he edited the newspaper *Dienas Lapa,* which initiated the so-called new movement, aimed at promoting social and class consciousness in the peasantry. Returning from a visit to Germany and Switzerland (1893) inspired by Marxist theory and writings, Rainis began his literary career as a fighter for social justice and national freedom. His own philosophy, however, showed no trace of Marxist materialism—he regarded life as an incessant series of mutations of energy. Partly because of Russian censorship, he used symbols to express

his ideal of political and personal freedom; but in 1897 he was transported to Pskov, and later to Slobodsk, for political activities. Returning in 1903, he took part in the unsuccessful revolution of 1905, after which he emigrated to Switzerland, only returning to Latvia in 1920, after it had finally achieved its independence. He was enthusiastically welcomed, elected to the *Saeima* (parliament), and was minister of education (December 1926–January 1928), and director of the national theatre (1921–25). He died at Majori, Rigas Jurmala, on Sept. 12, 1929.

Rainis' first volume of poetry, *Tālas noskaņas zilā vakarā* ("Far-Off Reflections on a Blue Evening," 1903), displays his wide experience and the nostalgia of an *émigré*, and contains some subtle love lyrics. *Vētras sēja* ("Tempests Sown," 1905), *Klusā grāmata* ("The Silent Book," 1909), *Tie, kas neaizmirst* ("Those, That Do Not Forget") and *Vēja nestas lapas* ("Wind-Blown Leaves"; both 1911) express the revolutionary struggle through Symbolism. *Gals un sākums* ("End and Beginning," 1912) is imbued with the spirit of Hegel's dialectical philosophy. In his plays, Rainis used motifs from folklore as symbols for his political ideals: they include *Uguns un nakts* ("Fire and Night," 1905), *Indulis un Ārija* (1911), *Pūt, vējiņi* ("Blow, Breeze," 1913), *Spēlēju, dancoju* ("I Play and Dance," 1919), and *Jāzeps un viņa brāļi* (1919; *The Sons of Jacob,* 1924).

He also translated Shakespeare, Schiller, Heine, Pushkin, and Goethe's *Faust,* which enlarged the vocabulary of literary Latvian and introduced the use of shorter word forms.

See J. Andrups and V. Kalve, *Latvian Literature* (1954); *A Century of Latvian Poetry,* trans. and ed. by W. K. Matthews (1958).
(J. A. A.)

RAINY LAKE lies 150 mi. (241 km.) W of Lake Superior, partially on the international boundary between Ontario and Minnesota. The lake is 1,108 ft. (338 m.) above sea level and covers an area of 345 sq.mi. (894 sq.km.). It is 56 mi. (90 km.) long and has an average width of 5 mi. (8 km.) (maximum, 27 mi. [43 km.]). There are over 500 islands in it. The shores, characteristic of lakes on the Canadian shield, are irregular and deeply indented. Drainage is westward through Rainy River to Lake of the Woods.

Fort Frances, Ont., and International Falls, Minn., on the river at the lake's southwestern extremity, manufacture pulp.
(W. G. DN.)

RAIPUR, a municipal town and district in Madhya Pradesh, India. The town, headquarters of the district, lies 188 mi. (303 km.) E of Nagpur on the South Eastern Railway from Nagpur to Calcutta. It is also connected by rail with Vizianagram and the port of Vishakhapatnam on the east coast. Pop. (1961) 139,792. Rajkumar College, where the sons of the chiefs of the Chhattisgarh and Orissa states were educated, has been opened for general admission, and there are nine colleges including those of arts, science, law, commerce, Sanskrit, engineering and technology, and Ayurvedic medicine, all affiliated to Saugar University in the same state.

RAIPUR DISTRICT (pop. [1961] 2,002,004) covers an area of 8,214 sq.mi. (21,274 sq.km.) and occupies the south and centre of the Chhattisgarh rice plain. It includes a large area of forest which abounds in wild buffalo, tigers, spotted deer, and wild dogs. The district is extensively irrigated (more than 300,000 ac. [121,-400 ha.]) and exceeds the other districts of Madhya Pradesh in this respect. It also has the greatest number of cattle and is the leading rice-producing district of the state. (D. G. NA.)

RAIS (RETZ), **GILLES DE** (1404–1440), marshal of France, satanist, and murderer, the central figure of a 15th-century *cause célèbre,* whose name was later connected with the story of Bluebeard (*q.v.*). He was born at Champtocé in Anjou in September or October 1404, the son of Guy de Laval, baron de Rais. His parents died in 1415, leaving him great wealth and possessions, and he became a ward of his grandfather, Jean de Craon. On Nov. 30, 1420, he abducted and married a rich heiress, Catherine de Thouars. He fought for John V of Brittany against the house of Blois-Penthièvre in 1420 and served Yolande of Aragon, duchess of Anjou, against the English in 1427. Entering the service of Charles VII in 1429, he was made responsible by the king's chief minister Georges de la Trémouïlle for the safety of Joan of Arc. He remained with her from the relief of Orléans in May 1429 to the time of her capture by the Burgundians at Compiègne in May 1430. He took part in the coronation of Charles VII at Reims (July 17, 1429) and was made marshal of France. Thereafter, Rais grew increasingly indolent and in 1434 ignored a royal order to campaign in Burgundy with Charles, duc de Bourbon. For this he was subsequently barred from holding any administrative office.

A munificent patron of music, literature, and pageants, he kept a more lavish court than the king and dissipated his wealth so rapidly that his family secured a decree from Charles VII in July 1435 restraining him from selling the rest of his estates. To redeem his fortunes Rais turned to alchemy, seeking the assistance of alchemists from all over Europe. He resorted to necromancy, satanism, and finally the torture and ritual murder of kidnapped children, perhaps as many as 200. At the same time he spent vast sums of money on the building, ornaments, and vestments of the collegiate chapel at Machecoul, near Nantes, which he founded.

In June 1440 he attacked Jean le Ferron, brother of the treasurer of the duchy of Brittany, during the celebration of Mass at a chapel in Brittany. This desecration led Jean de Malestroit, bishop of Nantes, to investigate all Rais's activities. Arrested at Machecoul in September, Rais was condemned for heresy by the bishop and sentenced to death for murder by a civil tribunal. His confession and repentance, and his resignation at his execution by hanging at Nantes on Oct. 26, 1440, were acclaimed at the time as an example of Christian penitence. His wife died in 1462.

BIBLIOGRAPHY.—E. Bossard, *Gilles de Rais* (1886); D. B. Wyndham Lewis, *The Soul of Marshal Gilles de Rais* (1952); G. Bataille, *Le Procès de Gilles de Rais* (1965). *See* also the novel by J. K. Huysmans, *Là-Bas* (1891; Eng. trans. *Down There*, 1958).

RAISEN, a town and district in the Bhopal division of Madhya Pradesh, India. The town, headquarters of the district, lies on the Bhopal-Jabalpur road, 28 mi. (45 km.) ENE of Bhopal. Pop. (1961) 5,962. The fort, built of massive sandstone blocks, stands on a spur of the Vindhya Mountains overlooking the town. Raisen played an important part in the history of eastern Malwa (q.v.). In the 16th century it was the stronghold of Silhari, a Rajput chief. In 1543 the fort was conquered by Sher Shah, and during Akbar's reign it was the chief town of Raisen sarkar in the subah of Malwa.

RAISEN DISTRICT (area 3,272 sq.mi. [8,474 sq.km.]) had a population (1961) of 411,426. The Vindhyan axis passes northeast-southwest through the district, and in between the spurs are fertile basins of the Betwa, Bina, and Tendoni rivers, producing wheat and jowar.

(S. M. A.)

RAISIN, the dried fruit of certain varieties of grape (q.v.). Raisin grapes were grown as early as 2000 B.C. in Persia and Egypt. Dried grapes are mentioned in the Bible (Num. vi, 3) during the time of Moses. David was presented with "a hundred clusters of raisins" (I Sam. xxv, 18), probably sometime during the period 1110–1070 B.C. The early Greeks and Romans adorned places of worship with raisins, and they were awarded as prizes in sporting events. Until the 20th century the chief raisin producers were Turkey, Iran and Greece; by mid-century the United States had taken the lead in production, with Australia ranking second. The United States raisin industry is located entirely in California, where the first raisin grapes were planted in 1851.

The word raisin is a contraction of the French *raisin sec,* meaning dried grape. However, by common usage only a few varieties of grapes are said to yield raisins upon drying. The three most important varieties of raisin grapes are the Thompson seedless, a pale yellow seedless grape, also known as sultana (Australia), white or oval kishmish (Turkey, Iran), sultanina (California); the muscat or Alexandria, a large-seeded variety also known as gordo blanco (Australia), white hanepoot (South Africa); and the black corinth, a very small, black seedless type, also called zante currant, staphis (Greece) and panariti. Other varieties of local importance are the round kishmish, rosaki, dattier, monukka and cape currant.

The trade name applied to a raisin may also signify the method of drying (natural, golden-bleached, sulfur-bleached, lexia), the form in which marketed (seeded, loose, layers), the principal place of origin (Vostizza, Smyrna, Malaga), the size grades or the quality grades. Natural raisins are dried in the sun in their natural condition; they are grayish-black or grayish-brown with the natural bloom intact and with a rather tough skin. Golden-bleached raisins are produced from Thompson seedless grapes dipped in 0.5% lye, exposed to fumes of burning sulfur for two to four hours and dried in a tunnel dehydrator. They are lemon-yellow to golden-yellow in colour, used chiefly in baked goods. Sulfur-bleached raisins are pretreated the same as golden-bleached, but are dried by exposure to direct sunlight. The grapes are spread on trays and left in the sun for three to four hours. The trays are then stacked and the drying is continued for several weeks in the shade. The finished product appears waxy, and cream to faintly reddish-yellow. Soda-dipped or soda-bleached raisins are from Thompson seedless grapes hot-dipped in dilute lye but not sulfured, then dried in the sun or in a dehydrator. If dried rapidly they are light amber to medium brown, moderately tender and mild-flavoured. Oil-dipped and lexias are dipped in a dilute solution of lye upon which a thin film of olive oil is floated; they are dried on trays in direct sunlight, are medium to dark brown, tender and mild in flavour.

The values below represent a composite of several reports on the nutrient content of Thompson seedless raisins containing about 17% moisture: carbohydrate 68%–71%, protein 2%–3%, fat 0.5%–3%, 1,300–1,600 calories per pound; milligrams in 100-g. portions: calcium 55–78, phosphorus 33–130, iron 1.5–3.3, potassium 700–900, sodium 52–87; vitamin A, 50 I.U. per 100 g., small amounts of vitamins B_1, B_2, B_6, niacin, biotin and a trace of vitamin C. Natural fruit acids contribute to the pleasant tartness of this delicacy.

(Jo. E. B.)

RAJAHMUNDRY, also known as Rajahmahendravaram, is a market town in the East Godavari district of Andhra Pradesh, India. It lies on the left bank of the Godavari River at the head of the delta, 41 mi. (66 km.) W of Kakinada port and 369 mi. (594 km.) N of Madras on the Madras–Calcutta line of the Southern Railway. Pop. (1961) 130,002. The railway bridge across the Godavari there has 56 spans and is one of the longest railway bridges (9,036 ft. [2,754 m.]) in India. The town has three colleges, including a teacher-training college and a Sanskrit college for women, all affiliated to Andhra University. There are a sanatorium, a paper mill, and a crucible factory using graphite from deposits in the Godavari Valley. The town has a flourishing trade in timber and is also noted for the Central Tobacco Research Institute.

(S. Ah.)

RAJAPALAYAM, a town in the Ramanathapuram (Ramnad) district of Madras State, India, lies 365 mi. (587 km.) SW of Madras, and on the Southern Railway. Pop. (1961) 71,203. This is the only place in Tamilnad (the Tamil country) that is inhabited by the Rajus, a class of Telugu-speaking people who claim to be Rajputs and who are alleged to have come originally from the ancient kingdom of Vijayanagar. Physically they appear to be different from the indigenous population, fairer in skin and of stronger build; even the cattle they breed are much superior to the local varieties both in stature and in milking properties. Local availability of suitable soil has made Rajapalayam dominantly a cotton tract; and there are a number of ginning and spinning mills. A cement factory was completed in 1961.

(G. Kn.)

RAJASTHAN, a constituent state of the Republic of India which came into existence in March 1948, shortly after India's independence, through the merger of a number of the former Rajput princely states and the former small British province of Ajmer-Merwara. The states so absorbed included Jaisalmer, Bikaner, and Jodhpur, which covered a large part of the Thar (Indian) Desert together with the better-watered country to the east and south with the former states of Alwar, Jaipur, Tonk, Bundi, Kotah, Udaipur, and others. (See *History*, below.) After small adjustments of boundary in 1956, Rajasthan had an area of 132,152 sq.mi. (342,274 sq.km.) and was the second largest state

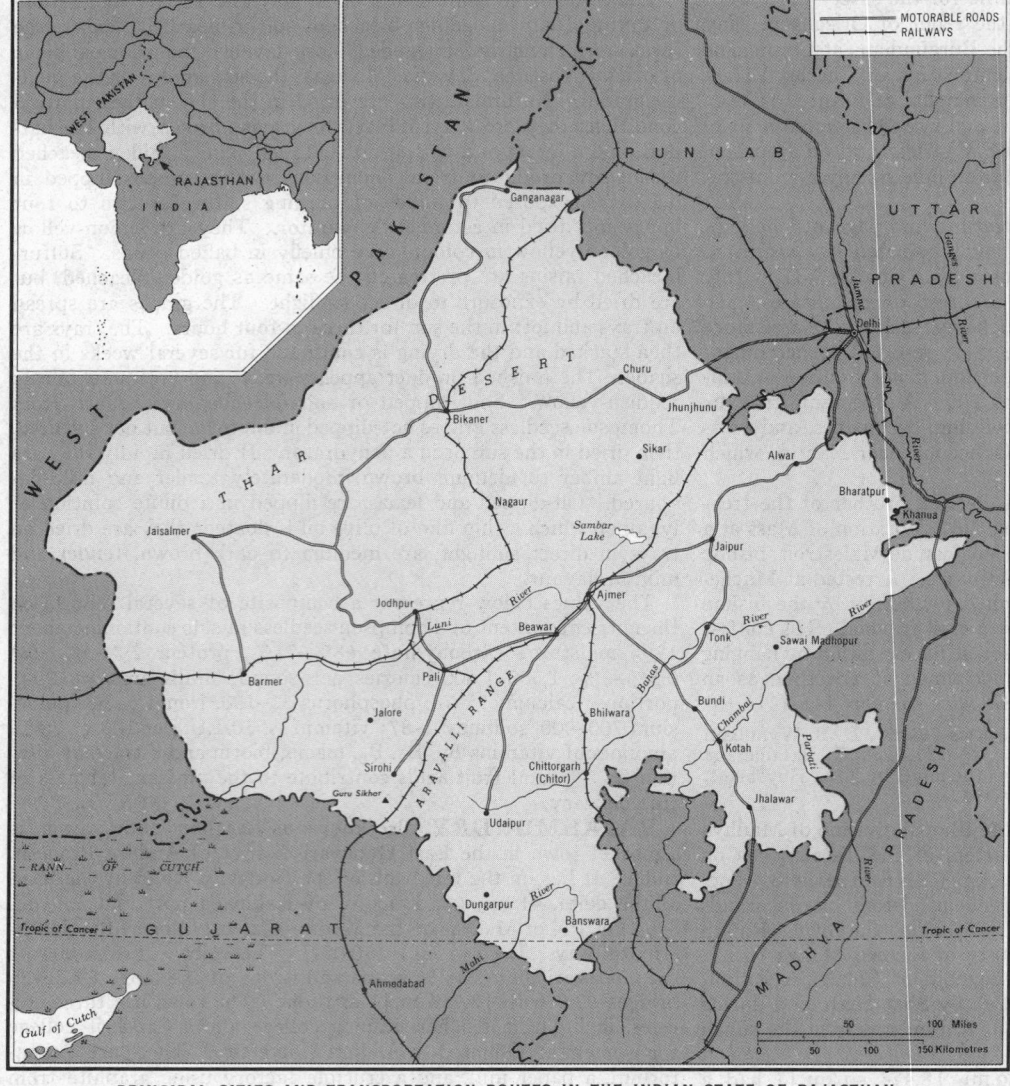

PRINCIPAL CITIES AND TRANSPORTATION ROUTES IN THE INDIAN STATE OF RAJASTHAN

on the main railway from Bombay to Delhi has food and textile industries.

To the southeast of the Aravalli Range Rajasthan occupies a complex and varied upland region, sometimes called the Rajput Upland since it is the home of the Rajputs of colourful and legendary fame. The greater part drains northward to the Jumna-Ganges (Ganga) system, especially through the Chambal River, but in the south by the Mahi and other streams to the Arabian Sea through the Gulf of Cambay. The Rajput Upland is underlain for the most part by crystalline rocks of the peninsular Precambrian which are exposed over much of the higher ground. These rocks break down slowly to form thin and indifferent soils so that the main areas available for settlement and cultivation are small valley-plains. The whole plateau is characterized by an irregular rainfall which averages about 20 in. (508 mm.) a year or a little above but rarely as much as 30 in. (762 mm.). Crops rely on rainfall because neither the configuration of the land nor the availability of water permits large-scale canal irrigation, and there is no regular subsurface water table to feed wells as there is in the northern plains. In good rainfall years the crop yields are excellent, and the land can support a larger population; in bad rainfall years the crops may fail entirely and famine may result. Fortunately there are two harvests, *rabi* (spring) and *kharif*

of India. Pop. (1961) 20,155,602. On the northwest there is a long frontier with West Pakistan through the heart of the desert; on the north lie the states of Punjab (India) and Uttar Pradesh, on the southwest Gujarat, and on the southeast Madhya Pradesh. The capital is Jaipur. (*See* also RAJPUTANA.)

Physical Features.—The state is cut into halves by the ridge of the Aravalli Range which trends from southwest to northeast and rises to 5,650 ft. (1,722 m.) in Guru Sikhar (Mount Abu) near the southern end. The Aravallis attract a certain relief rainfall, but to the northwest the country fades quickly into the Thar Desert (*q.v.*) and the land surface drops steadily toward the Indus River. Much of this country is covered by loose sand and silt, often in movement by wind; where rocky ridges appear from beneath these eolian deposits they are of the old rocks of the Indian plateau.

The country is seamed with watercourses only rarely carrying water and often losing themselves in the desert. In the south they join up to form the Luni River which empties into the Rann of Cutch (Kutch). The desert is naturally very sparsely populated; the two chief towns of Jaisalmer and Bikaner formerly relied much on their functions as centres of camel traders. Elsewhere the people live in small villages wherever there is a little water, and some millet and fodder can be grown. Frequently the water in the wells fails or becomes saline and the settlement has to be abandoned. Nearer the Aravallis conditions improve, especially around Jodhpur. During the British regime considerable use was made of the little hill station of Mount Abu, and Ajmer

(autumn), and the failure of one does not necessarily mean the failure of the other. The staple food is millet, with wheat and barley available in small quantities from the winter harvest. Quantities of gram are grown for fodder.

Much of the upland is covered with scrub and dry forest, with some better forest in places. (L. D. S.)

History.—Before the Muslim invasions of northern India, Rajasthan was subject for the most part to powerful tribal dynasties, the most important of which were the Rathors ruling from Kannauj, the Chauhans of Ajmer, the Solankis of Anhilwara, the Sisodias of Mewar (Udaipur), and the Kachwaha clan in Jaipur. The origin of these Rajput tribes (*see* RAJPUT) is controversial, and historians refuse to accept their legendary pedigrees as recorded by James Tod in his *Annals and Antiquities of Rajasthan,* two volumes (first published in 1829–32). It is generally accepted that they can be divided into two main classes, the foreign and the indigenous. The foreign descent of certain clans is not improbable, as throughout Indian history foreigners have been accepted into the fold of Hinduism.

Until its incorporation in the Mauryan Empire the early history of Rajasthan is obscure. It is clear from the Junagadh rock inscription that Rudradaman (*c.* A.D. 130–150), the greatest of the western satraps (Saka governors; *see* SAKA), ruled over Maru or the desert country which may be roughly equated with this area, although the term is sometimes restricted to Marwar (Jodhpur). In the 4th century it formed part of the Gupta Empire. How much of it was annexed by Harsha (*q.v.*) in the first half of the

7th century is disputable. Disorder and political disintegration followed the death of Harsha. By the close of the 9th century, however, Rajasthan had been added to the extensive dominions of the Gurjara-Pratihara (*q.v.*) dynasty of Kannauj, which had become the paramount power in northern India. The constant internecine warfare between the various Rajput kingdoms facilitated the Muslim conquest of northern India. It was not, however, until the days of Mohammed of Ghor (*q.v.*) that the Rajput dynasties of the northern plains were finally overthrown. Driven from Delhi and Kannauj, they retired into Rajasthan, where they eventually built up a strong position which enabled them to resist the Muslim invaders; for, although there was constant warfare, it cannot be said that the sultans of Delhi (*see* DELHI, SULTANATE OF) ever really subdued the Rajputs inside Rajasthan. The Rajputs nearest to Delhi were naturally the weakest because the eastern frontiers of Rajasthan were exposed to attack. Although unable to subdue the Rajputs, the sultans of Delhi appear to have realized the value of communications with the western coast, and the route between Delhi and Gujarat via Ajmer was usually open to imperial armies.

During this period the chief threat to the Rajputs was not from Delhi but from the independent Muslim kingdoms of Gujarat and Malwa. On the eve of Babur's invasion the outstanding feature of the history of northern India was the growth of Rajput power under Rana Sanga of Mewar, who extended his sway over the greater part of Rajasthan. His defeat by Babur at the Battle of Khanua in 1527 marks a turning point in Rajput history, for they never again attempted to recover their lost dominions on the plains and contented themselves with remaining on the defensive inside Rajasthan. After this battle the place of the Sisodias in Rajput politics was taken by the Rathors, the growth of whose power under Maldeo of Marwar was made possible by the weakness of Humayun.

Akbar's Rajput policy was based on conquest and conciliation. The fall of the Rajput strongholds of Chitor and Ranthambhor made him master of the greater part of Rajasthan, with the exception of Mewar which was not completely subdued until the reign of Jahangir. The reversal of Akbar's conciliatory policy produced the great Hindu reaction of Aurangzeb's reign when the Rajputs, Marathas, and other Hindu powers rose in revolt. But internal dissensions once more prevented the Rajputs from taking advantage of the decline of Mughal (Mogul) power and in the second half of the 18th century they proved no match for the Marathas who easily overran Rajasthan. At the same time Rajasthan was ravaged by predatory hordes of Pindaris and by the forces of Amir Khan, the Pathan freebooter. It was not until the beginning of the 19th century that the British, in the course of their struggle against the Marathas, entered into political relations with the Rajput states. Before the end of the year 1818 the states now incorporated in Rajasthan had been taken under British protection.

From the establishment of British paramountcy in India during the governor-generalship (1813–23) of the marquess of Hastings the history of Rajasthan was comparatively uneventful. Most of the rulers of Rajasthan remained loyal during the Indian mutiny of 1857–58, but in many places they were unable to prevent the troops and other inhabitants from taking part. In 1862, in accordance with the policy of the viceroy, Lord Charles Canning, the ruling chiefs were given *sanads* (charters) granting them the right of adoption in the event of the failure of natural heirs. Up to 1947 the Government of India was represented in Rajputana (as Rajasthan was then known) by a political officer styled agent to the governor-general, who was also chief commissioner of the small British province of Ajmer-Merwara. Under him were residents and political agents accredited to the various states.

In accordance with the policy of the Indian government after it attained independence in 1947 the former princely states of Rajputana (except for small areas transferred to neighbouring states) were formed into a constituent state under the name of Rajasthan. This was accomplished in four stages: (1) The short-lived Matsya Union of Alwar, Bharatpur, Dholpur, and Karauli was formed on March 18, 1948. (2) In April of 1948 the first

Rajasthan Union was formed which included Banswara, Bundi, Dungarpur, Jhalawar, Kishangarh, Kotah, Pratapgarh, Shahpura, Tonk, and Udaipur. (3) On March 30, 1949, the Greater Rajasthan Union came into being by the inclusion of the remaining states of Jaipur, Jodhpur, Bikaner, and Jaisalmer. (4) On May 15, 1949, the Matsya Union was incorporated in Greater Rajasthan and soon afterward part of Sirohi.

Ajmer State (formerly Ajmer-Merwara) was included in Rajasthan as the Ajmer district in 1956.

On the formation of Rajasthan the Rajput princes surrendered their powers to the central government. In exchange they were granted generous pensions and were allowed to keep their private property, including some of their palaces. The most famous and beautiful Rajput palace is on Lake Pichola in Udaipur.

(C. C. D.)

Population, Administration, and Social Conditions.—The state, although large, is sparsely populated; its population (1961) was 20,155,602. Besides Brahmans and Rajputs, other castes and tribes include Banyas, Jats, Gujars, Chamars, Meenas, Bhils, Malis or Kachhis, and Balais. Rajasthani with its various dialects is the chief language. (*See also* INDIA: *The People;* RĀJASTHĀNI LANGUAGE.)

The state is divided into the 26 districts of Ajmer, Alwar, Banswara, Barmer, Bharatpur, Bhilwara, Bikaner, Bundi, Chittorgarh, Churu, Dungarpur, Ganganagar, Jaipur, Jaisalmer, Jalore, Jhalawar, Jhunjhunu, Jodhpur, Kotah, Nagaur, Pali, Sawai Madhopur, Sikar, Sirohi, Tonk, and Udaipur.

The chief cities and towns with their population (1961 census) are the following: Jaipur 403,444; Ajmer 231,240; Jodhpur 224,-760; Bikaner 150,634; Kotah 120,345; Udaipur 111,139; Alwar 72,707; Ganganagar 63,854; Beawar 53,931; Sikar 50,636.

With only 23.7% of the male and 5.8% of the female population recorded as literate at the 1961 census, Rajasthan is one of the educationally backward states of India. In the early 1960s there were more than 22,000 educational institutions including Rajasthan University at Jaipur with 85 colleges affiliated to it. Primary education, though free throughout the state, was compulsory only in about 700 villages.

Besides about 500 hospitals and dispensaries, a number of health centres give free medical aid and health services to rural people. Approximately 24,000 factory workers and their families receive medical care through more than a dozen exclusive dispensaries in 10 industrial centres under a contributory health insurance scheme which covers risks of sickness, maternity, and employment injury. Welfare programs for tribal and backward classes comprise free education at all stages: scholarships, combined adult night school and social education centres, and rehabilitation of landless families. The state social welfare board organizes social welfare services for women and children in rural areas through crèches, elementary schools, adult literacy, social education, and craft training classes, and provides medical aid and maternity services. (S. CH.; S. B. L. N.)

The Economy.—The chief towns were the capitals of former states, and their princely palaces remain among some of India's most beautiful buildings. Organization of the population was on a feudal basis; the standard of life depended largely on the energy, efficiency, and attitude of the reigning Rajput. Cities like Jaipur and Udaipur retain enough of their colourful past to attract a considerable tourist traffic; cottage industries and handicrafts survive and flourish there more than elsewhere in India. In the drier regions camel's hair is still used in the manufacture of blankets, carpets, cloths, etc.; elsewhere the wool of local sheep and goats provides the raw material. Rajasthan is a stronghold of the Jain religion, and this exercises considerable influence over local art. Agriculture as elsewhere in India is the dominant occupation, and in Rajasthan physical conditions are against the development of modern techniques. There is, however, a steady replacement of the poorer yielding crops by better. Whereas in about 1920 millets occupied 37% of the cropped area of the Rajput Upland as against 11% occupied by wheat, 8% by barley, and 3% by maize (corn), by the 1960s wheat, barley, and maize surpassed millets. Other noteworthy crops are pulses, sugarcane, cotton, and oilseeds. The important irrigation and power projects designed to benefit the state are the Bhakra-Nangal, Chambal, and Beas schemes (all undertaken jointly by the states of Rajasthan and Punjab), the Jawai and the Rajasthan Canal project. All these will help the lowlands in the northern part of the state.

The state has some important minerals. Four-fifths of India's gypsum comes from the southwest; salt is obtained both from the desert area and from Sambar Lake. There is a significant mica belt and a large production of limestone. Silver-lead-zinc ores have also been worked. From the limestone there is a considerable cement industry. Marble and sandstone are found in abundance. The other principal manufactures are textiles, glass, and sugar. The important cottage and small-scale industries are cotton weaving, enameling, and pottery, as well as work in ivory, brass, lac, and stone, and the manufacture of "tie and dye" fabrics or bandannas (from Hindi, *bandhana*, to tie), water bottles, wooden toys, embroidered shoes and leather bags, carpets, and agricultural tools and implements. Rajasthan benefits from its position served by main routes from Bombay to Delhi and Indore to Ajmer by rail, though the main road passes to the south and east. The direct air route Karachi-Delhi crosses the state. There are airports at Jodhpur and Jaipur.   (L. D. S.)

BIBLIOGRAPHY.—C. U. Aitchison, *A Collection of Treaties, Engagements and Sanads,* vol. iii (1909); *Annual Report on the Political Administration of Rajpootana,* Records of the Government of India (1867 *et seq.*); V. P. Menon, *The Story of the Integration of the Indian States* (1956).   (C. C. D.)

RĀJASTHĀNĪ LANGUAGE, with over 15,000,000 speakers, is a group of Indo-Aryan dialects bordered by Western Hindi on the one side and by Gujarātī and Sindhī on the other—an area roughly that of Rājpūtānā and adjoining parts of central India.

Rājasthānī has many dialects which can be assigned to four main groups: northeastern, southern, western and east-central. The northeastern form, Mēwātī, approximates most closely Western Hindi. It is a transitional dialect and sometimes classified with Hindi. The southern, Mālvī, spoken in Mālwā and neighbouring areas, shares characteristics with Western Hindi to the east and with Gujarātī to the west. The western, Mārwārī, spoken in Mārwār and neighbouring districts, is geographically more extensive than all the other dialects combined. Jaipurī, the language of Jaipur, is the standard east-central dialect. It has affinities with Gujarātī, whereas Mārwārī resembles Sindhī. None of the Rājasthānī dialects is recognized in the Indian constitution. *See also* GUJARATI LANGUAGE; HINDUSTANI LANGUAGE.

Phonology.—With few exceptions, the Rājasthānī system agrees with other modern Indo-Aryan languages (*q.v.*). Long *ā* is sometimes pronounced like *au* in English "Paul," *ē* and *ai* like *a* in "hat" and *au* like *o* in "hot." In the west and south especially, *s* is replaced by *h*—in northern Gujarātī and in a number of the Bhīl dialects. An original aspirate *h* and the aspiration of aspirated consonants are often lost; *ch* is replaced by *s*. In contrast with Western Hindi, Rājasthānī (like Gujarātī and Sindhī) retains the cerebrals *l* and *n*. Otherwise Rājasthānī shares a common ancestry with Gujarātī in Śaurasēnī Apabhramśa.

Morphology.—Rājasthānī has two genders: masculine and feminine. There are sporadic instances of the neuter, less in the subdialects toward the midland, more to the west and south to the borders of Gujarātī, which has three genders. A special agent form of noun is used instead of the oblique form with the postposition *ne,* though this construction is often encountered in Mēwātī and Mālvī.

A strong adjective agrees in gender, number and case with its noun; weak adjectives remain unchanged. The pronouns correspond generally with those of Hindi. In common with Gujarātī, Rājasthānī uses the inclusive pronoun *ap* "we." In conjugation a passive stem is formed with the suffix *īj*; Sindhī and Lahndā have a similar formation. The simple present indicative often functions as a subjunctive. The simple future stem is made by means of the suffix *s* (or *h*); a periphrastic future is formed by adding *gō, lō* or *lā* to the subjunctive, of which *gō* and *lō* agree in gender and number with the subject, while *lā* never changes. Compound tenses are formed from participles plus auxiliaries.

(See *Linguistic Survey of India,* vol. ix, pt. ii, 1908.) The literature of Rājpūtānā, chiefly in manuscript form, includes a number of bardic chronicles. In Mārwār, premodern literature falls into two categories: *Dingal* (composed in Mārwārī) and *Pingal* (composed in Braj Bhāshā). Modern literary activity is sparse.

BIBLIOGRAPHY.—S. H. Kellogg, *Grammar of the Hindi Language,* 3rd ed. (1938); *Rām Karn Śarmā, Mārwārī Vyākaraṇa* (1901); G. Macalister, *Specimens of the Dialects Spoken in the State of Jaipur* (1898); L. P. Tessitori, "Notes on the Grammar of Old Western Rājasthānī," *Indian Antiquary,* vol. xliii-xlv (1914–16); S. K. Chatterji, *Rājasthānī Bhāṣā* (1949); *Sītārām Lālas, Rājasthāmnī Vyākaraṇa* (1954); R. L. Turner, *A Comparative Dictionary of the Indo-Aryan Languages* (1966).   (ET. B.)

RAJGARH, a town and district in the Bhopal division of Madhya Pradesh, India. The town, headquarters of the district, lies on the left bank of the Newaj River, 85 mi. (137 km.) NW of Bhopal by road. Pop. (1961) 9,095. It was founded about 1640 by Rawat Mohan Singh, who erected a defensive wall around it.

RAJGARH DISTRICT (area 2,383 sq.mi. [6,172 sq.km.]; pop. [1961] 516,871) includes chiefly the former princely states of Narsinghgarh and Rajgarh. The northern portion of the district is fairly hilly but the southern and eastern regions lie on the Malwa Plateau. About 45% of the total area is cultivated, growing wheat, jowar, and poppy. The Umat Rajputs ruled the princely states of Rajgarh and Narsinghgarh until, in the disturbances caused by the Maratha and Pindari inroads in the 18th century, Rajgarh became tributary to Sindhia. In 1818 it came under the suzerainty of the British-Indian government. It was absorbed in 1948 into Madhya Bharat, which was merged into Madhya Pradesh in 1956.   (S. M. A.)

RAJGIR HILLS, a range of hills in the south of the Patna district of Bihar, India. They form part of a range extending northeast for 40 mi. from the neighbourhood of Buddh Gaya; at one place they rise to 1,272 ft. (388 m.), but elsewhere they seldom exceed 1,000 ft. (300 m.). The hills in Patna district consist of two parallel ridges. In the valley between, south of the village of Rajgir, was built the old city of Rajagriha, "the royal residence." Legend ascribes it to Jarasandha, king of Magadha (south Bihar), who had his capital at Girivraja, "the city of hills." The outer fortifications can be traced on the crests of the hills for more than 25 mi.; they are 17½ ft. thick, built of massive undressed stones without mortar. These ruined walls are generally ascribed to the 6th century B.C. The remains of New Rajagriha, the reputed capital of Bimbisara (*c.* 520–490 B.C.), lie two-thirds of a mile north of the valley.

The Rajgir Hills are associated with the life of Buddha, who often taught there. Chhatagiri is the old Gridhrakuta, or Vulture's Peak, which was one of his favourite resorts. One of the towers on the Baibhar Hill (Vaibharagiri) has been identified as the Pippala stone house in which Buddha lived. The Sattapanni, the cave in which after his death the council of his disciples was held to record the tenets of the faith, has been identified with different sites on this hill and with the Sonbhandar cave at its foot; the latter is now believed to have been excavated by Jains in the 3rd or 4th century A.D. In the centre of the valley, excavations at the site known as Maniyar Math revealed a curious circular shrine associated with the worship of Mani-naga, a serpent deity, stated in the epic Mahabharata to reside at Rajgir. Rajgir is a place of pilgrimage. There are modern Jain temples on the hills around the valley. There are also hot springs in the valleys surrounded by Hindu shrines.

BIBLIOGRAPHY.—Sir J. Marshall, "Rajagriha and Its Remains," *Report of the Archaeological Survey of India* (1905–06); S. Beal (trans.), *Buddhist Records of the Western World,* vol. ii (1906); *District Gazetteer of Patna* (1924); R. C. Nyogi, *Rajagriha and Its Relics* (1935); B. C. Law, "Rajagriha in Ancient Literature," *Memoirs of the Archaeological Survey of India,* no. 58 (1938); Muhammad Hamid Kuraishi, *Rajgir,* rev. by A. Ghosh, 4th ed. (1956).   (F. R. A.)

RAJKOT, a town and district of Gujarat, India. The town, formerly the capital of the princely state of Rajkot and of Saurashtra, now the district headquarters, lies 125 mi. (201 km.) SW of Ahmedabad. Pop. (1961) 193,498. It is an important junction on the Western Railway with connections to most major towns of Gujarat. There are three colleges (arts and science, law, and commerce) affiliated to Gujarat University. Other institutions include the Rajkumar College founded in 1870; the Jubilee Memorial Institute consisting of the Connaught Hall, Lang Library, and Watson Museum (1888); two hospitals; and two training colleges. Places of interest include the Lalpan and Randerda lakes and the Aji Dam.

RAJKOT DISTRICT has an area of 4,588 sq.mi. (11,883 sq.km.) and a population (1961) of 1,208,519. The bulk of the area constituted the former princely state of Rajkot, which was merged in 1948 into the new state of Saurashtra, formed after India became independent in 1947. In 1956 when Saurashtra was absorbed into Bombay State, Rajkot became a district. Bombay State was divided into Gujarat and Maharashtra in 1960.

The district is undulating, with a stony soil watered by several streams. The principal crops are grain, sugarcane, and cotton. The manufacture of cotton and woolen textiles is the main industry. (M. R. P.)

RAJMAHAL, a former capital of Bengal and now headquarters of a subdivision in the Santal Parganas district of Bihar, India, lies on the right bank of the Ganges, 55 mi. (89 km.) ESE of Bhagalpur. Pop. (1961) 6,801. It comprises a collection of mud huts interspersed with a few houses and some ruins of nobler buildings. Man Singh, Akbar's governor, chose Rajmahal for his capital in 1595–96 because of its strategic position and command of the Ganges, but in 1608 the seat of government was transferred to Dacca. It was again made the capital by the prince Shah Shuja in 1639, and was superseded a second time by Dacca 20 years later. The town is on a branch line of the Eastern Railway.

Rajmahal has given its name to a region of basaltic hills with an Archean basement. The hills comprise an area of 1,366 sq.mi. (3,538 sq.km.) and rise to 1,886 ft. (575 m.). They are inhabited by an aboriginal people known as Sauria Paharias ("hillmen"). The valleys are inhabited and cultivated by the Santals, another aboriginal people. (E. AH.)

RAJPRAMUKH (Hindi raj[a], "prince" + pramukh, "chief official," "president," etc.), the title given to those Indian princes who, in 1948, were appointed in place of governors in certain constituent states of India where it was thought expedient to retain some of the traditional polity of princely jurisdiction and to employ the administrative ability of the princes. The states concerned were Hyderabad, Mysore, and five unions of former princely states—Madhya Bharat, the Patiala and East Punjab States Union, Rajasthan, Saurashtra, and Travancore-Cochin. The rajpramukhs of Hyderabad and Mysore were those princes recognized by the president of the republic as respectively nizam and maharaja of the two states; in the states unions the rajpramukh was elected for life by a council of the rulers of the covenanting states, and was usually the ruler of the most important of them. The rajpramukh was answerable to the state and republican legislatures and to the president of India, and retained none of the autocratic powers of the old princes; his position was rather that of a constitutional monarch. Kashmir, under dispute between India and Pakistan after the political partition of the subcontinent, was regarded in the 1950 Indian constitution as a rajpramukh state within the republic.

The office of rajpramukh was abolished when the States Reorganization Act came into force in 1956, most of the abovementioned states being then absorbed into larger agglomerations. See Ministry of States, *White Paper on Indian States* (1950).

RAJPUT (Sanskrit raja-putra, "son of a king"; also known as *Thakur*, "lord"), a generic term for about 11,000,000 landowners (census of 1931) organized in patrilineal clans and located mainly in central and northern India, especially in former Rajputana. Regarding themselves as descendants or putative successors of the Kshatriya warrior-ruling class of ancient India, they vary greatly in status from princely lineages such as the Guhilot and Kachwaha down to lowly cultivators. Most authorities agree that successful claims to Rajput status frequently were made by groups that attained secular power; probably central Asian invaders as well as patrician lines of indigenous tribal peoples were absorbed in this way. There are numbers of Muslim Rajputs in the northwest,

and Rajputs generally have adopted the custom of purdah. Their ethos includes intense pride in ancestry, mettlesome regard for honour, and dedication to goals of power.

Rajputs are divided into four lines: Solar, Lunar, Fire-descended, and Snake. In imitation of the Brahmans some clans are grouped in exogamous gotra associated with a mythological seer (rishi). Rajputs seek hypergamous marriages (i.e., into a higher social group), and until recent times, rather than suffer the shame of unmarried or ill-married daughters, many who were unable to provide dowries for such marriages practised female infanticide.

Kingdoms founded in north and central India between the 8th and 12th centuries exemplified Rajput rule. Learning and commerce flourished; chivalric warfare was a dominant pattern, and quixotic bravery was encouraged by courtly bards. During the years of Islamic supremacy the centre of Rajput influence shifted to Rajputana, and petty Rajput kingdoms there were among the main obstacles to the complete Muslim domination of Hindu India. Until their reorganization as part of the republic (1948) they preserved much of their ancient structure. Patriarchal rather than feudal, they derived most land rights, from those of subchiefs to poorest farmers, from blood relationship to the sovereign. Many remnants of former Rajput clan-kingdoms are found in the Punjab and along the Gangetic plain. In recent times Rajputs provided an important segment of India's fighting forces. *See* also RAJASTHAN.

See James Tod, *Annals and Antiquities of Rajast'han* (1829–32; Oxford ed., 1920); Daniel Thorner, "Feudalism in India," in Rushton Coulborn (ed.), *Feudalism in History* (1956). (J. T. H.)

RAJPUTANA (literally "the land of the Rajputs"), a group of princely states lying toward the northwest of India which, under the British regime, formed an agency. It was so called because the ruling princes were almost all Rajputs (see RAJPUT). The area of the whole was 132,559 sq.mi. (343,328 sq.km.) and the population, mainly of Hindus speaking Rajasthani and Hindi, was 13,670,208 at the 1941 census. There were 23 states, 1 chiefship, and 1 estate. The whole formed a compact block occupying hilly and plateau country between the plains of northern India and the main plateau of peninsular India. Running roughly through the centre from southwest to northeast was the Aravalli Range, to the northwest of which was the Thar Desert (q.v.). In the midst of the group of states was the tiny British-Indian province of Ajmer-Merwara of 2,400 sq.mi. (6,216 sq.km.) and 583,693 people in 1941. The largest states were Jodhpur, Jaisalmer, Bikaner, Jaipur, and Udaipur. Others included Alwar, Banswara, Kotah, Bundi, Tonk, and Kishangarh. With the coming of independence in 1947 a union of states began, until in due course the main group of states was consolidated, together with Ajmer-Merwara, as the new state of Rajasthan. Some territory in the southeast is now part of Madhya Pradesh and some in the southwest was transferred to Bombay (now Gujarat). *See* also RAJASTHAN: *History*. (L. D. S.)

RAJSHAHI (formerly RAMPUR BOALIA), a town, district, and division of East Pakistan. The town, headquarters of the district and division, lies on the Ganges (sometimes there called the Padma) River, 120 mi. (193 km.) WNW of Dacca. It stretches 5–6 mi. along the river, with a west-east metaled road forming the main axis. Pop. (1961) 56,885. The principal buildings include the Circuit House, Jinnah Hall, Sadr Hospital, Varendra Research Museum, and the impressive Bara Kothi of Dutch origin, now housing part of Rajshahi University (established in 1953), which has four affiliated colleges. In the 1960s the main university buildings were being constructed beside the campus, about 3 mi. E of the town. The town has oil mills and sawmills, a match factory, and a silk institute.

RAJSHAHI DISTRICT (area 3,654 sq.mi. [9,464 sq.km.]; pop. [1961] 2,810,964) is believed to have originally formed part of the old kingdom of Pundra or Paundravardhana, the country of the Pods, whose capital was at Mahasthan. Under the Sena kings in the 12th century Mahasthan was known as the Barendra Bhumi, a name that still survives in the Barind tract. The district contains a number of historical sites. Rice is the chief crop followed by jute and pulses. Sericulture is an old industry accounting for almost the entire silk output of East Pakistan. Other cottage industries include weaving, metal and wood working, and pottery.

RAJSHAHI DIVISION comprises the districts of Dinajpur, Rangpur, Bogra, Pabna, and Rajshahi, and forms a compact block in the northwest of East Pakistan, bordered southwest and south by the Ganges and east by the Jamuna. Area 13,347 sq.mi. (34,569 sq.km.). Pop. (1961) 11,850,089. Between the silts (pali) of the riverine lands and the red soils (khiar) of the midwest, the soils are mostly sandy loams. The eastern part lies in the main jute belt of East Pakistan and produces *aus* (autumn) rice. The *aman* (winter) rice is almost a universal crop. Wheat and tobacco are grown in the northeast. (K. S. AD.)

RÁKÓCZY, the name of a noble Magyar family, settled from early times in the county of Zemplén.

ZSIGMOND RÁKÓCZY (1544–1608) was one of the foremost supporters of István Bocskay (*q.v.*) in his rising against Catholic encroachment in northern Hungary, and succeeded him for a brief period in 1607 as prince of Transylvania, resigning the throne in 1608 in favour of Gábor Báthory. He died in the same year on Dec. 5.

GYÖRGY RÁKÓCZY I (1593–1648), born on June 8, 1593, the youngest son of Zsigmond, was also a staunch Protestant. He took a leading part in the rebellion of Gabriel (Gábor) Bethlen (*q.v.*), and after Bethlen's death was elected prince of Transylvania by the diet of Segesvár (Sighişoara) on Nov. 26, 1630. Following Bethlen's national Hungarian policy, he declared war in alliance with Sweden against the Holy Roman emperor Ferdinand III in 1644, on behalf of the oppressed Protestants of northern Hungary. By the Peace of Linz (Dec. 16, 1645) he secured the confirmation of Hungarian religious liberties. His capital Gyula Fehérvár (Alba Iulia) became a great Protestant centre. Early in July 1648, after the death of King Wladyslaw IV Vasa, Rákóczy put forward his second surviving son, ZSIGMOND (1622–1652), as candidate for the Polish throne. When this candidature was rejected, he made advances to the dissident Polish Calvinists led by Prince Janusz Radziwill, but he died at Sárospatak on Oct. 11, 1648.

GYÖRGY RÁKÓCZY II (1621–1660), born at Sárospatak on Jan. 30, 1621, was the eldest surviving son of György I and Zsuzsanna Lorántffy. In 1643 he married Zsófia Báthory, who embraced Calvinism for the purpose. Succeeding his father as prince of Transylvania in 1648, he sought like him alliances with the neighbouring hospodars (lords) of Moldavia and Walachia. He joined Charles X Gustavus of Sweden in attacking Poland in 1656, hoping to be elected king of that country. He undertook this expedition in defiance of the Turks, to whom Transylvania still owed tribute. Rákóczy was forced to retreat on humiliating terms. He was deposed by the Transylvanian diet on Turkish orders in 1657, but was reinstated a year later, whereupon the Turks invaded Transylvania in force. Rákóczy died at Nagyvárad (Oradea) on June 7, 1660, of wounds received at the Battle of Gyalu (Gilău) in May.

FERENC RÁKÓCZY I (1645–1676), born on Feb. 24, 1645, was the son of György II. His mother, disregarding his father's last wishes, in 1662 procured his conversion to Catholicism, to which she had herself reverted. Though he never succeeded his father, he kept a splendid court on the family estates at Sárospatak and Makovica. In March 1666 he married Ilona, daughter of Count Péter Zrinyi (Zrinski), ban of Croatia; and in 1670 he joined Zrinyi and Duke Kristo Frankopan in a conspiracy aiming at the liberation of Hungary and Croatia from Habsburg domination. Their insurrection was defeated, and Zrinyi and Frankopan were beheaded in 1671, but Rákóczy escaped death through the influence of his mother with the Jesuits, on the payment of a ransom. He died on July 8, 1676, at Makovica.

FERENC RÁKÓCZY II (1676–1735) was born at Borsi, in Zemplén, on March 27, 1676, less than 15 weeks before the death of his father Ferenc Rákóczy I. He was brought up, together with his sister Juliana, by his mother Ilona Zrinyi in an atmosphere of fervent Magyar patriotism. Her marriage in 1682 to Imre Thököly, leader of the Hungarian Protestants and organizer, with Turkish assistance, of abortive anti-Habsburg risings, did much to dissipate the family fortune. Defeated, Thököly went into

ARCHIV FÜR KUNST UND GESCHICHTE

FERENC RÁKÓCZY II, PORTRAIT PAINTED BY ÁDÁM MÁNYOKI

exile, leaving his wife to organize alone the defense of Munkács (Mukachevo, in Transcarpathian Ukraine). After the surrender of Munkács (1688), the boy Ferenc, torn from his mother and sister, was taken to Vienna to be brought up in Austrian ways. His appointed master, Cardinal Leopold Kollonich (1631–1707), a man of Croatian descent and an adversary of Magyar nationalism, put him in the Jesuit College of Neuhaus (Jindřichuv Hradec, in Bohemia); but Ferenc remained an ardent Hungarian. His emancipation from the cardinal was helped by his sister's marriage to a Belgian nobleman in the Austrian service, Ferdinand d'Aspremont-Linden, count of Reckheim. The couple encouraged Ferenc in his marriage to Charlotte Amelia of Hesse-Rheinfels, solemnized in 1694.

Rákóczy settled on his Hungarian estates. His birth, wealth, and brilliant personal qualities made him the natural leader of the Magyar nation, a role in which he was encouraged by other magnates. On the eve of the War of the Spanish Succession (*q.v.*) they sought help for the Hungarian cause from Louis XIV of France. Their intermediary betrayed his trust, and Rákóczy was arrested and imprisoned at Wiener Neustadt, where his grandfather Péter Zrinyi had met his fate. Escaping death with his wife's help by leaving his cell in disguise, he took refuge in Poland, where he remained for two years. In 1703 he returned to Hungary, putting himself at the head of the peasant revolt known as the Kuruc rising. He had some initial success, but the Magyar gentry stood aloof, and the Anglo-Austrian victory at Blenheim (*q.v.*) in 1704 destroyed hopes of help from France. On June 13, 1704, the Kuruc army of 7,000 was routed by the emperor Leopold I's forces at Nagyszombat (Trnava, Slovakia). Permanent success in the open field was impossible, yet Rákóczy drilled his little army into some degree of efficiency and continued the fight against the emperor.

Meanwhile the Transylvanians were looking to Rákóczy to restore their independence: he was elected prince on July 6, 1704, and he set up a council of state of 24 members. In 1705 he was made dux (duke or leader) of a Hungarian confederation. His efforts to secure toleration for his Calvinist followers alienated the Holy See, and negotiations with the emperor during 1705 came to nothing, the latter refusing to acknowledge the independence of Transylvania. France would not recognize the rebels officially unless they formally proclaimed the deposition of the Habsburgs, a desperate measure actually adopted by the diet of Ónod on June 13, 1707.

In spite of this Louis XIV sent no effective help. Rákóczy's efforts to secure the Russian tsar Peter I's help against Austria failed; his peasant armies suffered further heavy defeats; and finally he left his country forever on Feb. 21, 1711, a few months before the signing, on May 1, of the Peace of Szatmár (Satu Mare). After two years in Poland, he took refuge in France in 1713 on Louis XIV's invitation.

In 1717 Rákóczy accepted a Turkish invitation to help organize an army in Turkey against the Austrians (he was to have a new principality as his reward); but before he reached Istanbul Sultan Ahmed III concluded peace and had no use for his services. Exiled in 1719 to Rodosto (Tekirdag), near Istanbul, Rákóczy remained there until his death on April 8, 1735. His remains were solemnly transferred to Hungary in 1906.

His two sons, JÓZSEF (1700–1738) and GYÖRGY (1701–1756), lacked character. József was recognized by the Turkish sultan as prince of Transylvania in 1737 but died the following year.

See *Histoire des Révolutions de Hongrie,* containing memoirs of Ferenc Rákóczy II (1739); Émile Horn, *François Rákóczi II* (1906).

(B. BR.; X.)

RÁKOSI, MÁTYÁS (1892–1971), Communist ruler of Hungary from 1945 to 1956, was born at Ada (now in Yugoslavia), on March 14, 1892, of Jewish parentage; earlier versions of his family name were Rabinovics and Roth. His precocity and talent for languages enabled Rákosi to enjoy a good education, culminating in the Oriental Academy at Budapest, and to travel in Germany and England. He had early joined the Social Democratic Party. Taken prisoner on the Russian front in 1915, he was indoctrinated and sent back to Hungary in 1918. From March to August 1919 he was commissar for socialist production in the Communist government of Béla Kun (*q.v.*), on the fall of which he escaped to Russia. He rose quickly in the Communist hierarchy and was entrusted with various missions abroad. In 1925, in an attempt to refound a Hungarian Communist Party, he was apprehended by the Hungarian police; and in 1927, after a trial in which he defended himself with great courage and fluency, he was sentenced to eight-and-a-half years' imprisonment from the date of his arrest. On the expiration of this he was rearrested and sentenced in 1934 to life imprisonment on new charges, but in November 1940 he was allowed to go to Moscow in exchange for Hungarian colours captured by the Russians in 1848–49. He returned to Hungary with the Soviet Army at the end of 1944 and became secretary of the reconstructed Hungarian Workers (Communist) Party. In supreme control, he served as deputy prime minister from 1945 and as prime minister from Aug. 14, 1952, to July 2, 1953, when, after Stalin's death, he was partially demoted in favour of Imre Nagy. He remained first secretary of the party, however, and in April 1955 he reasserted his power by removing Nagy from the premiership; but on July 18, 1956, he was forced to resign by N. S. Khrushchev in order to placate Marshal Tito, whom Rákosi had offended. His systematic sacrifice of the interests of Hungary to those of the U.S.S.R., coupled with his unendearing personal qualities, had made him generally loathed in Hungary, and when revolution broke out in October 1956 he fled again to the U.S.S.R. Rákosi died at Gorky in the U.S.S.R. on Feb. 5, 1971. His many books included *For the Hungarian Future*. (C. A. M.)

RAKOVSKI, GEORGI SAVA (1821–1867), Bulgarian revolutionary leader and writer, one of the early and most influential promoters of the Bulgars' struggle for independence, was born at Kotel, near Sliven, of a well-to-do family. He received a good education in Istanbul and in France, but while still at school in Turkey became involved in political conspiracy, which was to be his main activity for the rest of his life. During the Crimean War, as an employee of the Turkish war office, he was secretly organizing armed revolt in Bulgaria. Found out and sentenced to death, he escaped abroad and began writing and publishing political propaganda in Serbia, Rumania, and Russia. From 1861 he concentrated on organizing the revolution in Bulgaria, recruiting and equipping bands of volunteers to be sent into Bulgaria or to help the Serbs in their armed clashes with the Turks (1862 and 1867). After several failures, his tactics of piecemeal risings had to be abandoned for coordinated revolt by the mass of the population, but his leadership gave the first real impetus to Bulgarian resistance. The literary merits of his writing are open to doubt, but what he wrote had a widespread effect on the minds of younger Bulgarians on the eve of their country's emergence as an independent state. He died in Bucharest on Oct. 20 (new style; 8, old style), 1867. His memoirs were published by M. Arnaudov in 1925. (N. I. M.)

RAKOVSKI, KHRISTIAN GEORGIEVICH (1873–?), Soviet Communist leader and diplomat who was a victim of Stalin's purges, was born on Aug. 13, 1873, at Kotel in Bulgaria. His father's home in the Dobruja passed under Rumanian rule in 1878, and the family became Rumanian, but the Bulgarian and revolutionary traditions inherited from his grandfather Georgi Sava Rakovski (*q.v.*) were strong in Khristian. Excluded from Sofia University because of his socialist activities (1890), he went to Geneva and then to Montpellier, where he graduated as a doctor of medicine. Returning to Bulgaria, he resumed his subversive activities. In 1900 he served as an officer in the Rumanian Army, but in 1907, during the peasant riots, he was expelled from Rumania, where his civil rights were not restored till 1912. Many of

his books were published in Russia under the pen name Insarov.

After Rumania's entry into World War I, Rakovski was arrested. Taken to Iaşi, he was released there by the Russians on May 1, 1917. When the Communists came to power in Russia (November 1917) he became a member of the All-Russian Central Executive Committee; and in 1919 he was appointed to the Central Committee of the Communist Party. Having led the delegation sent to negotiate peace with the Ukrainian central *rada* (council), he was made chairman of the Council of People's Commissars of the Ukraine, also in 1919. He was a member of the Soviet delegation at the conference of Genoa (1922), Soviet *chargé d'affaires* in London (1923–25), and Soviet ambassador to France (1926–27), but his support of Trotski led, in 1927, to his being expelled from the Communist Party and exiled to Stalingrad. One of the last Trotskyists to recant, he was readmitted in 1935 and was a departmental chief in the People's Commissariat of Health until 1937, when he was dismissed. He was among the 21 members of the "Right-Trotskyist bloc" arrested on Stalin's orders in February 1938. His trial (March 2–13) ended with his being sentenced to 20 years' imprisonment, and Rakovski must be presumed to have died in a concentration camp.

RALEGH (RALEIGH), **SIR WALTER** (*c.* 1554–1618), English soldier, seaman, courtier, author, and explorer, the first to settle colonists in Virginia and to open up Guiana to English enterprise, was the brilliant favourite of Elizabeth I. A strong

advocate of the application of naval pressure to counter the threat from Spain, he was concerned in several privateering ventures, as well as in large-scale expeditions to Cádiz and the Azores. Even more success, he believed, would follow the establishment of land bases from which to operate in the New World. Among many prose works, those printed in his lifetime are still the best known. *A Report of the Truth of the Fight About the Isles of Azores* is propaganda for the war at sea. *The Discoverie of Guiana* describes his exploration of the Orinoco in search of a secret empire of the Incas, with which he hoped to rival Spanish conquests in South America. *The History of the World*, which solaced a long imprisonment under James I, warned princes that their crimes do not go unpunished, and summed up the littleness of man. His occasional verse has an individual note of gravity and disillusion.

SIR WALTER RALEGH, ENGRAVING BY SIMON PASS, FROM THE TITLE PAGE OF THE 1614 EDITION OF RALEGH'S "THE HISTORY OF THE WORLD"

He was a younger son of Sir Walter Ralegh (d. 1581), of Fardell in Devon, by his third wife Katherine Gilbert, daughter of Philip Champernown. He was born in 1554 (or possibly two years earlier) at Hayes Barton near Budleigh Salterton (Devon). In October 1569 he was serving the Huguenot cause in France, where he claims to have been at the Battle of Moncontour. In 1572 his name appears in a list of members of Oriel College, Oxford, and in 1575 on the registers of the Middle Temple. In 1577 he described himself as "de curia," a member of the court. In 1578 he was at sea with his half brother Sir Humphrey Gilbert, destroying Spanish shipping. He went to Ireland in 1580, and fought with as much ruthlessness as gallantry against the rebels in Munster. He was one of the officers of the day when the whole garrison of Smerwick, County Kerry, was executed on the orders of the deputy, Lord Grey of Wilton. Ralegh was openly critical of the dilatory conduct of the war and it may have been his plausibly urged schemes for the quick subjection of Ireland which first brought him to the notice of Elizabeth I. He returned to England in December 1581 and by 1582 was the reigning favourite. If ever he spread his cloak in the mud for the queen to pass over, as tradition alleges, this was the time. He was notorious for his pride and personal display. In 1583 he received a lease of part of Durham house in the Strand, London, which he occupied till James I reclaimed it for the bishop of Durham in 1603. His monopoly of wine licences (1583), and of the export of broadcloth (1584), brought large receipts at the cost of much unpopularity. He was challenged as a monopolist in the Parliament of 1601. In 1585 he was knighted. After this year he regularly wrote his name Ralegh and did not himself use the form which later became common. The wardenship of the stannaries (1585) won him the loyalty of the Cornish tinners whom he helped through years of depression. As lieutenant of Cornwall he saw to the mustering of soldiers, which seems to have been his chief duty in the Armada year (1588). As vice-admiral of Devon and Cornwall he kept order in the naval prize courts. He had little to learn about licensed depredation at sea.

His Irish service was rewarded by vast estates in Munster, where his name is associated with Youghal, Cork, and Lismore. The land proved more trouble than it was worth, and in 1602 he sold it to Richard Boyle, afterward 1st earl of Cork. In 1587 he received the forfeited estates of the conspirator Anthony Babington, and in the same year was made captain of the queen's guard. This was the highest position he achieved. He would dearly have loved to be a privy councilor. The nature of his ascendancy with the queen kept him in attendance on her at court, and his grand schemes tended to languish for want of his personal participation. In 1591 she prevented his joining a naval expedition against Spain, in which his cousin, Sir Richard Grenville, was lost with the "Revenge." He commemorated the event in an inflammatory pamphlet, *A Report of the Truth of the Fight About the Isles of Azores* (1591), generally known by its running headline as *The Last Fight of the Revenge*. Though he never himself set foot in North America, he spent much pains and money upon establishing a colony near Roanoke Island, on what is now the coast of North Carolina, naming the country Virginia in honour of the queen (*see* NORTH CAROLINA). His first expedition sailed in 1584, after he had taken over Sir Humphrey Gilbert's charter for the discovering of "remote heathen and barbarous lands." The colony met with a succession of disasters and in 1589 he transferred most of his responsibilities to a syndicate of merchants. He encouraged the use of tobacco and, it is said, of potatoes, but the popular belief that he imported the potato from Virginia overlooks the fact that it is not indigenous there. From 1584 onward he served fairly regularly in Parliament, urging increased expenditure on defense, but not to the detriment of the poorer taxpayer, who always had his sympathy. He was opposed to heresy hunting. When more stringent laws were proposed against persons suspected to be religious sectaries he declared it intolerable that it should be in the power of juries to "judge men's intentions" and "what another meant."

Ralegh had a rival at court in the young Robert Devereux, 2nd earl of Essex, beside whom he inevitably had the air of a parvenu. His position was always precarious. During a passing period of disfavour, in 1589, he returned to Ireland, where he visited Edmund Spenser at Kilcolman Castle, County Cork. They exchanged verses. Ralegh, who cultivated poetry as a social art and a private recreation, read Spenser a plaintive poem addressed to the queen under the name of Cynthia. An autograph fragment preserved among the Cecil Papers is probably a continuation of the poem Spenser heard. He introduced Spenser at court and encouraged him to publish the first three books of *The Faerie Queene* (1590). In 1592 he suffered a serious setback. He had actually sailed in command of a naval expedition to seize the Spanish treasure fleet when he was recalled on account of a secret marriage with one of the queen's maids of honour. She was Elizabeth, daughter of Sir Nicholas Throckmorton, who made him a loyal and loving wife. The marriage cannot be precisely dated. The discovery in the early 1960s of a diary kept by Lady Ralegh's brother (*see* A. L. Rowse, *Ralegh and the Throckmortons*, 1962) indicates that it was an accomplished fact some months before the queen, always resentful when a favourite betrayed her platonic favours, sent the pair to the Tower in August 1592. The diarist

first heard of it in November 1591. On March 29, 1592, he records the birth of a son, Damarei, who must be presumed to have died in infancy. In 1593 there was another son, Walter, and in the winter of 1604–05 a third son, Carew. While the court storm raged, Ralegh's squadron at sea fell in with one of the richest prizes ever taken by English privateers, the Portuguese carrack "Madre de Dios." Ralegh was sent to Plymouth (September) as the only man who could keep order among the jubilant sailors and unravel the complicated finances of the voyage. He bought his release by making over the bulk of his profits to the queen.

Ralegh now retired to his newly acquired estate of Sherborne, in Dorset, which in January 1592 with the queen's help had been alienated from the see of Salisbury. In 1593 local gossip fixed upon him a charge of atheism, but failed to substantiate it before an ecclesiastical commission in 1594. In 1592 the Jesuit pamphleteer Robert Parsons had complained of his "School of Atheism," and his name was coupled with that of Christopher Marlowe. He was a bold thinker and an indiscreet talker, interested in scientific studies, especially in mathematics as an aid to navigation, and he read skeptical philosophy, but he was not an atheist in the modern sense. Some scholars, interpreting the obscure phrase "Schoole of night" in *Love's Labour's Lost* (Act IV, scene iii, line 272) as the equivalent of "School of Atheism," have read the play as a satire upon Ralegh and his friends.

Free to follow his bent at last, in 1595 Ralegh sailed for the Orinoco, with the aim of driving a wedge into the heart of the gold-bearing empire of Spain. His *Discoverie of Guiana* (1596) gained the projected colony little practical support, but it had many readers and implanted in English minds the dream of El Dorado. In 1596 he went with Essex to attack Cádiz, commanding the "Warspite," in which he was wounded. He described and defended his part in the sea fight (*Works*, 1829, volume viii). In 1597 he was received again at court. He joined Essex as rear admiral on the Islands voyage (1597), an expedition to the Azores, and conducted a successful land operation in his general's absence, for which he narrowly escaped a court-martial. In 1600 he became governor of Jersey, where he improved the fortifications, encouraged trade, and instituted a register of landed property. Essex by this time was losing ground and he and his adherents grew bitterly hostile to Ralegh, to the point of attempting his life in the rebellion of 1601.

The accession of James I in 1603 proved Ralegh's downfall. An apparent friend, Robert Cecil, later earl of Salisbury, and an open enemy, Lord Henry Howard (created earl of Northampton in 1604), had implanted a deep suspicion of him in the mind of the Scottish king. He was rebuffed and stripped of money and offices. Before long he faced a charge of treason. He was said to be involved in a plot to make peace with Spain, extort toleration for Roman Catholics, and put James's cousin Arabella Stuart on the throne. After defending himself magnificently, he was convicted upon the written evidence of one of the plotters, Henry Brooke, Lord Cobham, with whom he had been on intimate terms. It was possible to argue that he could not be totally ignorant of anything to which Cobham was committed. Even contemporaries, little disposed to favour him, thought the trial (November 1603) cruelly unjust, though the attorney general, Sir Edward Coke, who refused to let Cobham testify in court, observed the law as it was then, for a brief period, interpreted. The conduct of Ralegh's life does not suggest that he would support Spain. He was reprieved at the last moment and confined for 13 years to the Tower, with varying degrees of strictness. He fought hard for a pardon, and to preserve Sherborne. In 1602 he had conveyed it in trust for his wife and child, but a clerical error rendered the deed invalid, and in 1609 the land went to the king's favourite, Robert Carr (later earl of Somerset). There was some compensation, more nominal than real, which seemed wholly inadequate to the Ralegh family. Ralegh occupied himself with chemical experiments, assaying of metals, and with the composition of his *History of the World*. The first and only volume to be completed was published in 1614. It begins with the creation and extends to the 1st century B.C., demonstrating that the world is the theatre of God's judgments. It was very highly esteemed in the 17th century and offers some fine passages of English prose, of great rhythmical beauty and solemnity.

Ralegh's hopes of release faded in 1612, with the death of King James's eldest son, Prince Henry, who had fallen under his spell. A medicinal cordial of his compounding was administered to the prince *in extremis,* at the request of his mother, Queen Anne. It became famous but it is doubtful whether it had any real medical value. Queen Anne continued friendly and so did the anti-Spanish secretary of state, Sir Ralph Winwood. In 1616, with the help of a new favourite, George Villiers (afterward duke of Buckingham), he was released to lead an expedition to Guiana, whence he promised to bring gold without giving just cause of offense to Spain. All depended on the interpretation of "just cause," since Spain was certain to be offended. He may well have had designs on Spanish shipping, as well as secret knowledge of a gold mine. He made private overtures to France, hoping for a refuge in French ports, and was heard to ask openly, in his dangerous, jesting way, "Did you ever hear of any that was counted a pirate for taking millions?" He was gambling on success, and in the event failed miserably. The exploring party was led by his tried lieutenant, Lawrence Keymis, who had been with him in Guiana before. Ralegh himself stayed at Trinidad recovering from a tropical fever. Keymis, in defiance of stringent orders, attacked and burned the frontier town of San Thomé, erected in 1596 to guard the approach to Guiana. Spanish reports allege that the attack was a feint, contrived between the English and a faction within the town, who were anxious to trade without appearing to fraternize. In the event it turned to earnest. Ralegh's son Walter was killed in the assault. Keymis, upon whom the main responsibility must be laid, committed suicide before they started on the homeward voyage. He had excused the attack on the town by asserting that he stumbled upon it unexpectedly, 20 mi. from its previous site. Spanish records make it plain that he was lying when he said it had been moved. Ralegh repeated the story, apparently in good faith, arguing eloquently, before and after his arrest, that Guiana was English territory. (*See* his *Apology for the Voyage to Guiana, Works,* 1829, volume viii.) At last he listened to the friends who urged flight. An abortive attempt to escape to France was foiled by his own kinsman, Sir Lewis Stukely. He was beheaded on Oct. 29, 1618, in Old Palace Yard, Westminster. His wife and son survived him. Since he had sailed without a pardon, his conviction was still upon the old charge of conspiring with Spain. His behaviour on the scaffold won him sympathy and admiration, and public opinion, increasingly hostile to Spain and the Stuarts, soon made a hero of him.

He left a number of prose pamphlets vigorously written on a wide selection of subjects, ranging from philosophy, politics, and economics to practical shipbuilding. Many of them were printed, with more enthusiasm than discrimination, in the mid-17th century. The canon is still unsure. He had to an unusual degree the renaissance gentleman's aversion to the publication of his poetry. Since much of it was a way of courting the queen it may be said to have been intended for an audience of one. With the exception of the autograph fragments at Hatfield house, it has had to be collected from anthologies, where it is anonymous, and from commonplace books of doubtful authority.

Ralegh's peculiar power to dazzle, excite, and persuade is still active in his writings. Sober historians, after discounting the dazzle, tend to dismiss him as a not too scrupulous adventurer who had little influence upon events. A succession of biographers has found his personality both fascinating and elusive. He was a great mythmaker, whose greatest myth was of a golden city and an imaginary empire of the Incas in Guiana. Under the Commonwealth he himself became a legend; no longer the atheist, the monopolist, the overdressed arrogant favourite of Elizabeth's days, nor the malcontent, who schemed against King James, but a wise and farsighted statesman, who championed England against the might of Spain, extended its territory overseas, asserted God's providence in the history of the world, and fell a victim to Stuart tyranny. The truth lies somewhere among these conflicting pictures. His vaulting imagination, which could envisage both North and South America as English dominions, was backed by practical ability and a capacity for hard work, but some discrepancy between the imagination and the deed made him less effective than his great gifts promised.

BIBLIOGRAPHY.—*Editions, etc.:* The first, and only, complete collection of the works is that in 8 vol. (1829) ; vol. i includes lives of Ralegh by W. Oldys and T. Birch. The first reliable collections of his scattered verse were included in A. J. Hannah, *Poems by Sir Henry Wotton, Sir Walter Raleigh and Others* (1845), and, more fully, in *The Courtly Poets from Raleigh to Montrose* (1870). The standard edition is by Agnes Latham, *The Poems of Sir Walter Ralegh* (1929; rev. ed. for Muses' Library, 1951). Editions of separate works include *The Discoverie of Guiana,* by Sir 'R. H. Schomburgk (1848), and by V. T. Harlow (1928) ; *Instructions to His Sonne,* for the Roanoke Island Historical Association (1939) and, with Lord Burghley's *Certaine Precepts* and Francis Osborn's *Advice to a Son,* by C. B. Wright for the Folger Shakespeare Library (1962). Selections from his prose were ed. by G. E. Hadow (1917). *See also* T. N. Brushfield, *A Bibliography of Sir Walter Raleigh,* 2nd ed. (1908).
Biography: For early notices *see* especially R. Naunton, *Fragmenta Regalia* (1641; rev. ed., 1653, ed. by E. Arber, 1870) ; J. Aubrey, *Brief Lives,* ed. by O. L. Dick (1949). The biography by Oldys in vol. i of the *Works* was written for the 1736 ed. of *The History of the World.* E. Edwards' well-documented *Life of Sir Walter Ralegh,* 2 vol. (1868), remains a standard work: vol. ii consists of a fairly complete collection of Ralegh's letters. Other biographies include those by W. Stebbing (1891; reprinted with bibliography, 1899) ; M. A. S. Hume (1879), using Spanish documents; M. Waldman, 2nd ed. (1943) ; E. Thompson (1935) ; W. M. Wallace (1959). *See also* S. R. Gardiner, *History of England . . . 1603–42,* 10 vol. (1883–84).
Special Aspects: C. H. Firth, *The History of the World,* a British Academy lecture (1918; publ. 1919), reprinted in *Essays, Historical and Literary* (1938) ; A. Acheson, *Shakespeare and the Rival Poet* (1903), which first propounded the supposed satire on Ralegh in *Love's Labour's Lost;* L. Cust, "The Portraits of Sir Walter Ralegh," in *The Eighth Volume of the Walpole Society* (1920) ; N. Kempner, *Raleghs Staatstheoretische Schriften: die Einführung des Machiavellismus in England* (1928) ; V. T. Harlow, *Ralegh's Last Voyage* (1932) ; D. B. Quinn, *Raleigh and the British Empire* (1947) and *The Roanoke Voyages, 1584–1590,* 2 vol. (1955), documents edited for the Hakluyt Society; J. Bruce Williamson, *Sir Walter Raleigh and His Trial* (1936) ; P. Edwards, *Sir Walter Ralegh* (1953), which deals with Ralegh as a literary figure; M. C. Bradbrook, *The School of Night: a Study in the Literary Relationships of Ralegh* (1936) ; E. A. Strathmann, *Sir Walter Ralegh: a Study in Elizabethan Skepticism* (1951) ; W. F. Oakeshott, *The Queen and the Poet* (1960) ; A. L. Rowse, *Ralegh and the Throckmortons* (1962) ; P. Lefranc, "La Date du mariage de Sir Walter Ralegh," *Études Anglaises,* vol. ix (1956) ; A. M. C. Latham, "A Birth-Date for Sir Walter Ralegh," *Études Anglaises,* vol. ix (1956) ; C. S. Emden, *Oriel Papers* (1948) ; A. M. C. Latham, "Sir Walter Ralegh's Gold Mine," *Essays and Studies by Members of the English Association,* new series, vol. iv (1951). (A. M. C. L.)

RALEIGH, SIR WALTER ALEXANDER (1861–1922), Scottish man of letters and critic, a prominent figure in the Oxford of his time, was born in London on Sept. 5, 1861. He was educated at University College, London, and King's College, Cambridge. He held the chair of modern literature at Liverpool (1889–1900), and of English at Glasgow, and was appointed Oxford's first professor of English literature in 1904. Raleigh was a brilliant and stimulating talker and lecturer, and became the centre of the Oxford English school, which had only been established in 1894. His books (*Style,* 1897; *Wordsworth,* 1903; *Shakespeare,* 1907; *Six Essays on Johnson,* 1910; etc.) are the essays not of an exact scholar but of an urbane critic, sensitive without eccentricity, synthetic rather than analytic. He also wrote volume i of the official history *The War in the Air* (1922). He was knighted in 1911, and died at Oxford on May 13, 1922.

See his *Letters, 1879–1922,* ed. by his wife, with preface by D. Nichol Smith, 2 vol. (1926; enlarged 1928). (M. Kl.)

RALEIGH, the capital of North Carolina, U.S., located 23 mi. (37 km.) SE of Durham, has four major characteristics: politics, education, trade, and manufacturing. Politically, as the state capital (and the seat of Wake County), the city is much like other state capitals of similar size. The general assembly meets there regularly every odd-numbered year. The state capitol, completed in 1840, stands in the middle of a 4 ac. (1.6 ha.) square and is considered a gem of Greek Revival architecture. Capitol Square is surrounded by various state buildings (Labor, Library, Agriculture, Revenue, Education, Justice, Highway, and others), all of which have been held to a height not exceeding five or six stories so as not to dwarf the capitol.

Various state institutions are in or near Raleigh, including a mental hospital (1856), prison (1869), and schools for the deaf and blind.

The city has four senior colleges: North Carolina State University (1887); Shaw University (Baptist; 1865); St. Augustine's College (Protestant Episcopal; 1867); and Meredith College (Baptist; 1891); and two junior colleges for women, St. Mary's (Protestant Episcopal; 1842) and Peace (Presbyterian; 1872). Within a 30-mi. radius are the University of North Carolina, Duke University, North Carolina College at Durham, and the Southeastern Baptist Theological Seminary. To take advantage of this concentration of institutions of higher learning, there has been established near Raleigh the Research Triangle, a centre of industrial research. The large number of colleges and universities in the area has resulted in a heavy percentage of college graduates and a high level of cultural interest and activity. The North Carolina Museum of Art in Raleigh is one of the finest institutions of the kind in the area.

Raleigh has long been the major retail shopping centre for eastern North Carolina but in the middle part of the 20th century, due largely to rapid transportation, the volume of trade grew enormously. The city also developed as a wholesale distributing centre, especially for chain food stores.

Industrial volume was small up to the beginning of World War II, but thereafter the city attracted a considerable number of factories producing a wide variety of products. It also became the home office or regional headquarters of a number of insurance companies. In a short period Raleigh changed from a small, slowgoing southern town to a modern, bustling, rapidly expanding city. Its population in 1970 was 121,577; for comparative population figures *see* table in NORTH CAROLINA: *Population*. The population of the standard metropolitan statistical area (Wake County) was 228,453 in 1970.

Raleigh was laid off from a tract of forest soon after the American Revolution (in 1792) when North Carolina, like several other of the original states, moved its capital westward from the seaboard. It was named for Sir Walter Ralegh. During the Civil War Gen. William T. Sherman's army entered the city without opposition in April 1865 and occupied it for the remainder of the war. During the late 19th and early 20th centuries Raleigh shared in the industrial development of the state, but its major growth did not take place until during and after World War II. The city established a council-manager form of government in 1947. Pres. Andrew Johnson was born in Raleigh.   (C. CR.)

RALPH (d. 1122), Norman monk, archbishop of Canterbury from 1114 to 1122, called Ralph d'Escures from his father's estates of Escures, near Séez in Normandy, entered St. Martin's Abbey at Séez in 1079 and became abbot in 1089. Disturbed conditions in Normandy drove him to England in 1103, and he became bishop of Rochester in 1108. As diocesan ordinary of Canterbury, he administered that see after St. Anselm's death in 1109 and was himself elected archbishop in April 1114. His pontificate was chiefly marked by his cooperation with Henry I in the face of papal claims, and by his prolonged but unsuccessful struggle to exact a profession of obedience from Thurstan, archbishop elect of York.

Ralph was a pupil of St. Anselm and should probably be identified with the monk Rodolfus whose works are extant in the Bodleian Library Manuscript Laud Miscellaneous 363 (1). His writings concern some of the theological and philosophical problems expounded by Anselm, to whom his *Meditations* were long attributed. He died on Oct. 20, 1122, and was buried in Canterbury Cathedral.

See N. F. Cantor, *Church, Kingship, and Lay Investiture in England, 1089–1135* (1958); R. W. Southern, "St. Anselm and His English Pupils," *Mediaeval and Renaissance Studies,* ed. by R. W. Hunt and R. Klibansky, vol. i (1943).

RAMA. Although there are three Ramas mentioned in ancient Indian traditions, the name is specifically applied to the Hindu deity worshiped as the seventh incarnation (*avatar*) of the great god Vishnu. It may be that this Rama was historically a tribal hero of ancient India who because of his virtues and great exploits was later deified. In any case, he is the central figure of the great epic, the Ramayana (*see* RAMAYANA, and, for a detailed account of the story of the Sanskrit epic, SANSKRIT LITERATURE). This tale inspired a large popular literature in which Rama and his wife Sita were extolled as personifications of the ideals of chivalry and fidelity. It was also the foundation of the later worship of Rama.

Although Rama was known as an incarnation of Vishnu in the early centuries A.D., there probably was no special worship of him before the 11th century, and it was not until the 14th and 15th centuries that there appeared distinct sects worshiping him as the one, supreme God. Competing with the already established cult of Krishna (*q.v.*), the other great incarnation of Vishnu, the Ramaite sects spread their religion throughout India, and in time Rama's name became the one most often invoked at death as well as one of the most popular in naming children and a form of greeting between friends ("Ram! Ram!").

See also HINDUISM: *Gods*.

BIBLIOGRAPHY.—*The Ramayana and the Mahabharata,* Eng. trans. by R. C. Dutt, Everyman's Library (1961); H. H. Wilson, *Religious Sects of the Hindus,* 2nd ed. (1958); J. Dowson, *A Classical Dictionary of Hindu Mythology,* 10th ed. (1961); J. E. Carpenter, *Theism in Medieval India* (1926); C. Eliot, *Hinduism and Buddhism,* vol. ii (1954); J. Gonda, *Die Religionen Indiens,* vol. ii (1963). *See also* articles "Ramayana" and "Ramaism" in James Hastings, *Encyclopaedia of Religion and Ethics.*   (H. P. S.)

RAMADAN (the "Scorcher"), the ninth month of the Muslim year. Already sacred to the pre-Islamic Arabs, it became in Islam the holy month of fasting, selected because it was in this month that "the Koran was sent down as a guidance for the people" (Koran ii, 181). Tradition has it that the *lailat al-qadr,* the "Night of Power" (or "of the Decree"), in which the first revelation occurred is to be identified with the 27th of Ramadan. During this night the angels and spirits descend to earth and "it is peace until the rising of the dawn" (xcvii, 3, 5). Ramadan parallels Yom Kippur in its religious function; it, too, constitutes a period of atonement. But whereas the Jewish festival imposes a strict fast of 24 consecutive hours, the Muslim ordinance prescribes abstention from food, drink, sexual intercourse (indeed, any avoidable change of the body's composition) from the moment when "so much of the dawn appears that a white thread may be distinguished from a black" until with nightfall the two become indistinguishable once more (ii, 183), this abstention to be continued throughout the 29 days of Ramadan. Only the very young and the very old, the sick, pregnant and nursing women, and persons on an extended journey may be excused.

Beginning and end of Ramadan are announced when one trustworthy witness testifies before the authorities that the new moon has been sighted; a cloudy sky therefore may delay or prolong the fast. The five daily prayers continue in Ramadan but the addition of the supererogatory prayers, or *tarawih,* at night is considered meritorious, particularly during the last ten days, which are regarded as especially sacred.

In the Koran the development of the Ramadan fast (one of the five "pillars" or absolute requirements of Islam) may be followed from the injunction to fast on Ashura, the Day of Atonement of the Jews (later identified with the tenth of Muharram, the first month of the Muslim calendar), to the command to fast "a certain number of days" during Ramadan (ii, 180) and finally to the month-long fast. The last may have been structured on the Christian Quadragesima (Lent) or comparable Manichaean practices. Fasting has come to be regarded as a most important religious act, and it is observed by many who will neglect their daily prayers. Psychologically a part of it is the Lesser festival or the Festival of Breaking Fast on the first three days of Shawwal when the strain of Ramadan is released (*see* BAIRAM).

See G. E. von Grunebaum, *Muhammadan Festivals* (1951).
                                       (G. E. V. G.)

RAMADI (AR RAMADI), a town and administrative centre of Ramadi *liwa'* (province) of Iraq, lies on both banks of the Euphrates, 8 mi. (13 km.) N of Lake Habbaniyah, between the Habbaniyah escape channel and the 'Aziziyah Canal, and about 60 mi. (97 km.) W of Baghdad. Though there were earlier settlements (ancient and Abbasid) in the neighbourhood, Ramadi is modern and was founded by Midhat Pasha in 1869 to encourage sedentarization of the Dulaym tribes. Its importance grew considerably with the establishment of the trans-desert route via Rutbah to the Mediterranean which uses Ramadi as its departure point from the Euphrates. There is also an airfield. A number of former nomads have settled in the town as farmers, and the Dulaym notables have houses there. Though by no means the largest of the upper Euphrates towns, Ramadi is likely to develop further with the extension of irrigation projects in the district.

RAMADI LIWA' (formerly Dulaym [Dulaim]) lies due west of Baghdad from the divide between the Euphrates and Tigris rivers as far west as the frontiers with Syria and Jordan. Area 53,270 sq.mi. (137,969 sq.km.). Pop. (1962 est.) 274,575. Physically, it consists of a portion of the Euphrates Valley and a westward bordering stretch of rolling country that gradually rises westward to the desert plateaus of Syria and Saudi Arabia. The region is the home of the influential Dulaym tribes, some of whom are sedentary farmers living close to the Euphrates banks and cultivating barley and wheat with some rice and fruit. Other Dulaym tribesmen (regarded as organized in ten sections) are pastoral nomads and move extensively between Al Fallujah and Al Qa'im on the Euphrates and regions to the west. (W. B. Fr.)

RAMA (RAMA CHAKRI) **DYNASTY,** the kings who have been on the throne of Thailand since 1782, when Chao Phaya (Prince) Chakri (or Chakkri) proclaimed himself king at Bangkok.

The previous Thai capital, Ayutthaya, was destroyed and the last of the Ayutthaya kings was put to death by Burmese invaders in 1767. During the following 15 years, General Takh Sin (Taksin), of mixed Thai and Chinese origins, made himself king, restored order, defeated rival Thai kings in the north, held the Cambodians in check, and drove out the Burmese. When Takh Sin went mad in 1782, he was murdered on order of his distinguished general Chakri, who assumed the throne. His descendants have reigned in unbroken line since that date.

RAMA I (1737–1809) defeated his perennial enemies the Burmese and extended his power over Cambodia, Laos, and northern Malaya. He made his kingdom stronger, planned and built the new capital at Bangkok, and gave his people a good administration. He was also effective in reviving Thai culture and was the author of the *Ramakien* and of the first version of the dance-drama *Inao* (see THAI LITERATURE). He died on Sept. 7, 1809.

RAMA II (1768–1824) consolidated and improved the reforms introduced by his father and is regarded as the greatest writer of the dance-drama in Thai literature. He was born on Feb. 26, 1768, at Ampawa, where his father had an official position, and was educated at a monastery at Dhonburi. In 1806 he was named heir to the throne, and he succeeded his father in 1809. Rama II is better remembered as a poet, musician, architect, and sculptor than as a ruler, although his reign was notable for renewal of relations with the West and for his legislative reforms. Deeply religious, he was responsible for reviving rituals and for improvements in the classical dance. His greatest achievement was the "second-reign version" of the *Inao*, a poetic dance-drama blending romance and humour, which, despite its legendary Javanese setting, provides interesting details of contemporary life in Thailand. He also composed five other dance-dramas in a less classical style. The king was a skilled musician, and he designed the main temple of Wat Arun and himself carved the doors of the Sakya Temple at Wat Suthat. He died on July 21, 1824.

RAMA III (1788–1851) was the third child and eldest surviving son of Rama II, by his third minor wife. He succeeded his father on the latter's death. During his reign Thailand entered into unequal treaties with Great Britain and the United States, which expanded trade on terms favourable to the Western powers. Disputes with Great Britain led to the reduction of Thai power over its vassal states in northern Malaya. He died on April 2, 1851.

RAMA IV (reigned 1851–68), King Mongkut, exerted vigorous efforts to modernize his kingdom; he employed foreign advisers and invited the Chinese to enter Thailand to work and to trade. He signed treaties, first with England and then with other nations, which gave foreigners the right to reside in Thailand, to engage in limited trade with tariff concessions, and to enjoy the privileges of extraterritoriality. (*See* further MONGKUT.)

RAMA V (reigned 1868–1910), King Chulalongkorn, was benevolent and just and devoted to internal reform, which he capped with the abolition of slavery. He modernized the army and the civil service and introduced such Western innovations as electricity, telegraphy, streetcars, and railways. In spite of his sagacity he lost territory to the British in Malaya and Burma and to the French in Indochina. He preserved his independence by taking advantage of the mutual jealousies of British and French and the refusal of either to let Bangkok pass under the control of the other. (*See* further CHULALONGKORN.)

RAMA VI (1881–1925), Prince Vajiravudh, son of Chulalongkorn, is remembered as a liberal, progressive ruler and as a prolific writer. He was born on Jan. 1, 1881, at Bangkok, and educated there and in England, at Oxford and Sandhurst. He succeeded his father in 1910. Although he has come to be regarded in Thailand as a notable ruler, his reign was unpopular. His refusal to grant a democratic constitution, for which he thought his people unready, disappointed liberal elements; his progressive policies annoyed the conservatives; and the fact that he was unmarried and lived in seclusion turned popular feeling against him. His devotion to English traditions led to such unwise actions as the formation of the "Wild Tiger" volunteer force, paid from his private income, to supplement the regular army; and the liberal idealism which caused him to sacrifice revenue by closing the gambling houses (1917) and discouraging opium smoking was not welcome either to the financiers or to the people. More successful was his law of 1916, making use of surnames compulsory. Interested in education, he founded Chulalongkorn University in Bangkok and was responsible for legislation making education free and compulsory. He welcomed the opportunity to enter World War I, at the invitation of the United States in 1917, and was largely instrumental at the peace conference in negotiating the treaties (signed by his successor) by which the Allies surrendered their extraterritorial and fiscal rights in Thailand.

Rama VI introduced Western forms into Thai literature, in particular the dialogue drama. Author of about 50 original plays, he also adapted more than 100 by English and French dramatists; and his translations of three of Shakespeare's plays introduced blank verse to Thailand. He was also a pioneer of the novel and a poet. Rama VI died at Bangkok on Nov. 26, 1925.

RAMA VII (1893–1941), King Prajadhipok, brother of Rama VI and the 76th child and youngest son of Chulalongkorn, was born on Nov. 8, 1893, and succeeded to the throne on his brother's death. He lost the prerogatives of an absolute monarch after the revolution of 1932 and abdicated in March 1935. He died in England on May 31, 1941.

RAMA VIII (1925–1946), King Ananda Mahidol, nephew of Rama VII, was born on Sept. 20, 1925. As king, he saw his country suffer on the losing side of World War II, and he lost his life during the night of June 8–9, 1946, under mysterious circumstances, before he was able to see the return of prosperity.

RAMA IX (1927–), King Bhumibol Adulyadej, brother of Rama VIII, was born on Dec. 5, 1927, at Cambridge, Mass., where his father was studying at Harvard. Although as king he exercises no real political power, he is the symbol of the state and he enjoys the universal respect of his people. Carrying on his family's traditional interest in the arts, he is a jazz clarinet player and composer. *See* also THAILAND: *History.*

See Prince Chula, *Lords of Life: the Paternal Monarchy of Thailand, 1782–1932* (1960); W. F. Vella, *Siam Under Rama III* (1957).
(C. A. B.; D. N. K. B. P.)

RAMAKRISHNA (1836–1886) is perhaps the best-known Hindu saint of modern times. In a world giddy with material power and achievements, callous to human suffering and misery and indifferent to the higher life of the spirit, he presented an ideal of holiness and compassion. He was born in the village of Kamarpukur in Hooghly district, Bengal, on Feb. 20, 1836, to an orthodox Brahman father and a mother of character and piety. From his youth, he was attracted by the lives of religious heroes and he had his first experience of spiritual ecstasy at age seven.

When he was 23 he was married to a girl of five, Saradamani Devi. The marriage, even after his wife had grown up and gone to live with him, did not weaken in any way his fervent devotion to God. To him Kali was the Divine Mother. Ramakrishna took to the worship of Rama and felt that Rama was the spirit of the universe. He later adopted the worship of Krishna and practised the Vaishnava form of love, in which the human soul loves God as a devoted wife loves her husband. Toward the end of 1866, he practised the discipline of Islam under the guidance of a Muslim teacher, and in 1874 he adopted the methods of Christianity. Thus, he had visions of Rama, Krishna, Shiva, Kali, Allah, and Jesus. He said, "I have found that it is the same God toward whom all are directing their steps, though along different paths."

BY COURTESY OF INFORMATION SERVICE OF INDIA, LONDON

RAMAKRISHNA, PHOTOGRAPHED ABOUT 1881

Ramakrishna spent the last years of his life in the spiritual education of his fellowmen. He died of cancer on Aug. 16, 1886. His famous disciple Vivekananda said of him, "It was no new truths that Ramakrishna came to preach, though his advent brought old truths to light."

BIBLIOGRAPHY.—Romain Rolland, *The Prophets of the New India,* Eng. trans. by E. F. Malcolm-Smith (1930); *The Gospel of Sri Ramakrishna,* Eng. trans. by Swami Nikhilananda (1942); D. S. Sarma, *Studies in the Renaissance of Hinduism in the Nineteenth and Twentieth Centuries,* ch. vi (1944); C. Isherwood, *Ramakrishna and His Disciples* (1965). (S. RA.)

RAMALHO ORTIGÃO, JOSÉ DUARTE: see ORTIGÃO, JOSÉ DUARTE RAMALHO.

RAM ALLAH, a town in the West Bank area of Jordan occupied by Israel since 1967, about 10 mi. (16 km.) N of Jerusalem. Pop. (1967 est.) 12,134. It lies half a mile from its twin town of Bira (Al Birah), in a fertile area with olives, figs, and vines. The town is well built, with stone houses and good roads. Water is drawn from about 400 public wells and two springs, most houses having storage cisterns. The Herodian masonry incorporated into many buildings indicates the age of the place, but the oldest surviving structures are of Crusader date. (WM. C. B.)

RAMAN, SIR CHANDRASEKHARA VENKATA (1888–1970), Indian physicist, received the Nobel Prize for Physics in 1930 for his work on the diffusion of light. Raman discovered that the light scattered by any medium contains frequencies differing from that of the incident light by amounts which are characteristic of the scattering medium. These characteristic Raman frequencies are equal to the infrared frequencies of the substance and are caused by energy interchanges between the incident light and the scattering substance. However, some frequencies appear in the Raman spectrum which are "forbidden" in the infrared, and vice versa, so that studies of infrared and Raman spectra complement as well as confirm one another.

Less well known than the Raman effect (*q.v.*), but perhaps more important, was Raman's influence in stimulating interest in, and securing support for, scientific research in India. He contributed to the building up of nearly every research organization in India; he founded the *Indian Journal of Physics* and the Indian Academy of Sciences; he trained hundreds of students and sent them to important posts in universities, colleges, and government work throughout India and Burma.

Raman was born at Trichinopoly (Tiruchirapalli), Nov. 7, 1888. He graduated from Presidency College in Madras and received a master's degree in 1907. He had already completed researches in optics and acoustics; but since there was at that time no opportunity for a scientific career in India, he entered the finance department of the Indian government, securing his position by competitive examination at the age of 19.

Continuing his researches in his spare time, he finally came to the attention of the authorities of the University of Calcutta, who offered him a professorship of physics in 1917. Raman was knighted in 1929. In 1933 he moved to the Indian Institute of Science at Bangalore as head of the department of physics. In 1947 Raman was named director of the Raman Research Institute at Bangalore. In 1961 he became a member of the Pontifical Academy of Sciences. He died on Nov. 21, 1970, at Bangalore.

See N. H. de V. Heathcote, *Nobel Prize Winners in Physics* (1953). (P. O.)

RAMANATHAPURAM (formerly RAMNAD), a town and district in the south of Madras (Tamilnad), India. The town lies at the base of the peninsula that faces the island of Rameswaram (*q.v.*) in Palk Strait, 63 mi. (101 km.) SE of Madurai. Pop. (1961) 26,890.

RAMANATHAPURAM DISTRICT (area 4,849 sq.mi. [12,559 sq.km.]; pop. [1961] 2,421,788) is one of the driest and most infertile tracts in Madras, almost dead level and sandy. The district headquarters is at Tallakulam at Madurai. The titular head is the raja of Ramnad, the chief of the local Maravar (Maravan) community. His title is *Setupati* or "lord of the causeway" (the ridge of rock connecting the island of Rameswaram with the mainland). At Karaikudi to the north, there is a large educational centre with colleges of arts and science, engineering technology, and teachers' training, all affiliated to Madras University. (G. KN.)

RAMAN EFFECT, a change in wavelength of light that is scattered by molecules. When a beam of monochromatic light traverses a pure, dust-free, transparent sample of a chemical compound, a small fraction of the light is scattered in directions other than the direction of the incident beam. Most of this scattered light is of unchanged frequency or wavelength. A small part, however, has frequencies different from that of the incident light; its presence constitutes the Raman effect.

The name honours Indian physicist Sir Chandrasekhara Venkata Raman (*q.v.*), who reported (*Indian Journal of Physics,* vol. 2 [1928]) that he observed the effect after extended researches on light scattering. The possibility of such an effect had been predicted theoretically by A. Smekal in 1923. Soviet physicists G. S. Landsberg and L. I. Mandelstam observed the phenomenon independently (in quartz) at about the time of Raman's announcement; Raman's paper, however, represented a more thorough study.

Raman scattering is perhaps most easily understandable if the incident monochromatic light is considered as consisting of photons (with energy proportional to frequency) that can collide with the molecules of the sample. Most of the collisions are elastic and the photons are scattered with unchanged energy and frequency. Some collisions, however, are inelastic; *i.e.,* the molecule takes up energy from or gives up energy to the photon, which is thereby scattered with diminished or enhanced energy, hence with lower or higher frequency. The frequency shifts are thus measures of the amounts of energy involved in the quantum transitions of the scattering molecule.

The Raman effect is very feeble; for liquids its intensity may be only about 10^{-5} of that of the incident beam. With large samples and very intense irradiation the effect becomes visible; but it is usually photographed with a luminous spectrograph. A convenient alternative employs a sensitive photomultiplier cell, the suitably amplified electric signal being used to give a written record of the spectrum. Visible light is most frequently used to excite the effect, especially the intense blue line of the mercury arc spectrum. Every incident line produces its own Raman lines, but confusion may be avoided by using filters. In this respect, and also for compounds which absorb in the blue region, it is advantageous to use the single intense line emitted by a suitable laser source, notably the continuous He/Ne laser.

The pattern of Raman lines is characteristic of the particular molecule species, and its intensity is proportional to the number of scattering molecules present. Thus Raman spectra are used in qualitative and quantitative chemical analysis; this in no way impairs or consumes the sample and may be used for the study of such labile equilibria as the ionic dissociation of electrolytes in solution. Commercially available Raman-effect recording instruments are used, for example, in the petroleum industry.

The energies corresponding to the Raman-frequency shifts are found to be the energies of rotational and vibrational quantum transitions of the scattering molecule. Pure rotational shifts are small and difficult to observe, except for those of simple gaseous molecules. In liquids rotational motions are hindered and discrete rotational Raman lines are not found. Most Raman work is concerned with vibrational transitions, which give larger shifts observable for gases, liquids, and solids. Gases have low molecular concentration at ordinary pressures; thus liquids and solids are more frequently studied. A vibrational Raman line shifted to lower frequency (Stokes line) is more intense than the corresponding line shifted to higher frequency (anti-Stokes line); for the former involves an upward transition from the ground vibrational state, while the latter reflects a transition from an excited vibrational state—and the ground state has a larger population of molecules than the excited state.

According to quantum theory only those molecular rotations and vibrations are permitted in which the motion (considered classically) is associated with a change in the electric polarizability of the molecule (see MOLECULAR SPECTRA). This is because the Raman effect may be regarded as arising from the oscillating dipole induced in the molecule by the electric field of the incident radiation. This condition for the appearance of a Raman line is essentially different from that which permits rotational or vibrational absorption. Thus, although infrared absorption spectra can also give vibrational frequencies of molecules, the two methods are essentially complementary; for frequencies that are forbidden in absorption may be permitted in the Raman effect and vice versa.

The theory shows that the number of fundamental vibrational frequencies permitted in the Raman effect depends on the number of atoms in the given molecule, and on the symmetry of their arrangement. This permits empirical discrimination among proposed possible structures for a given molecule; for example, a molecule XY_2 (where X is the central atom) has only one permitted vibrational Raman line if the structure is linear, but three if it is bent.

Another important observable property is the state of polarization of the Raman lines for scattering at right angles to the incident light. The theory shows that spectral lines should differ in degree of polarization depending on the symmetry of the scattering species. Observations of polarization thus provide further evidence on molecular structure.

After 1952 the so-called Resonance Raman effect, foreseen as early as 1934, was investigated experimentally (notably in the U.S.S.R.). This is seen as an enhancement of the intensity of Raman scattering when the frequency of the incident radiation approaches an electronic absorption band of the scattering substance. Of considerable theoretical interest, the resonance effect may have practical value for identifying molecules at low concentrations.

In addition to their uses for analysis and determination of molecular symmetry, Raman spectra yield molecular moments of inertia and vibrational frequencies. Isotopic substitution (especially by deuterium) increases the obtainable information, which may be used for such calculations as those of thermodynamic quantities and intramolecular force fields. See also CHEMISTRY: Physical Chemistry: The Raman Effect.

BIBLIOGRAPHY.—G. Placzek, Handbuch der Radiologie, 6/2:205 (1934); G. Glockler, Rev. Mod. Phys., 15:111 (1943); L. A. Woodward, Quart. Rev. Chem. Soc., 10:185 (1956); S. Bhagavantam, Scattering of Light and the Raman Effect (1942); G. Herzberg, Infrared and Raman Spectra of Polyatomic Molecules (1945, 1947); N. B. Colthup et al., Introduction to Infrared and Raman Spectroscopy (1964).
(L. A. Wo.)

RAMANUJA (d. A.D. 1137), one of the greatest Indian thinkers and religious leaders, was a Tamil Brahman born, according to tradition, in 1017 at Sriperumbudur near modern Madras. He was a member of the Shrivaishnavas (see VISHNUISM), ardent worshipers of Vishnu, becoming their devoted head at the temple of Shri-rangam near Tiruchirapalli (Trichinopoly), where, after years of teaching, travel, and exile, he died. Ramanuja gave philosophical expression to the Shrivaishnava doctrine of vishishtadvaita, "the nonduality [i.e., ultimate oneness] of the differentiated," uniting the implicit conceptions of the Alvars' impassioned Tamil hymns with the metaphysics of the Upanishads. The nine Sanskrit works attributed to him include: Vedartha-samgraha, deriving this doctrine from the Upanishads; Shri-bhashya, an extensive commentary on the Vedanta Sutras; Vedanta-dipa and Vedanta-sara, summarizing his Shri-bhashya; and Gita-bhashya, a commentary on the Bhagavad Gita, emphasizing bhakti. Brahman, to Ramanuja, is above all a personal godhead: as Vishnu-Narayana one with whom souls, by nature akin to God, commune. Divine grace, initiating and perfecting the souls' eternal freedom and bliss, not infusing but releasing their divine life, removes the blindness and fetters wrought in beginningless time by ignorance and karma (q.v.), and stirs from the soul's depth a spiritual response as bhakti: and bhakti, to Ramanuja, is less religious emotion than intuitive and loving knowledge of God. See also INDIAN PHILOSOPHY: Six Systems: Vedanta; HINDUISM: Philosophical and Theological Schools.

BIBLIOGRAPHY.—O. Lacombe, La Doctrine morale et métaphysique de Ramanuja (1938); J. A. B. van Buitenen, Ramanuja's Vedartha-samgraha (1956), Ramanuja on the Bhagavad-gita (1953); P. N. Srinivasachari, The Philosophy of Visishtadvaita (1943).
(O. A. LA.)

RAMANUJAN, SRINIVASA (1887–1920), Indian mathematician who contributed to the theory of numbers, was born at Erode, southern India, on Dec. 22, 1887. His full name was Srinivasa Ramanuja Ayengar. He was educated at the town high school and at the Government College at Kumbakonam. He obtained a scholarship from the University of Madras, but after his marriage, in 1909, became a clerk in the Madras Port trust. Correspondence with G. H. Hardy of Cambridge led to his obtaining a further scholarship from Madras University, and a grant from Trinity College, Cambridge. In spite of religious difficulties arising from the fact that he was a Brahman, he came to England in April 1914, where Hardy, by private teaching, helped to provide the necessary mathematical background for his original work. His mathematical work is on the theory of numbers, theory of partitions, and the theory of continued fractions. He became ill in 1917, returned to India in 1919, when he resumed some of his mathematical work, but died on April 26, 1920, at Kumbakonam. He was elected a fellow of the Royal Society in 1918 and a fellow of Trinity College later in the same year.

Ramanujan's notebooks were published in 1957; his Collected Papers were published in 1927 and 1962.

See G. H. Hardy, Ramanujan (1940); J. R. Newman, "Srinivasa Ramanujan," in Lives in Science (1957). (O. Oe.)

RAMAT GAN (meaning "garden hill"), a town of Israel in the plain of Sharon, lies 2 mi. E of Tel Aviv-Jaffa, with which it is linked by continuous habitation and by a frequent bus service. Pop. (1961) 90,234. It was founded in 1921 and, unlike Tel Aviv-Jaffa, is built on hills. Ramat Gan contains residences of diplomatic missions, many public gardens, the main football (soccer) and athletics stadium of Israel (where the Israel Maccabiah, the athletic championship, is held), a technical school and the religious University of Bar Ilan (founded in 1954). There are light industries including citrus by-products and the manufacture of chocolate and building materials. (No. B.)

RAMA TIBODI I (1312–1369), warrior-king and lawgiver of Thailand, proclaimed himself king at Ayutthaya in 1350 and thereby founded a dynasty that lasted until 1767. As a warrior, he overcame his neighbours, including the decadent king of once-powerful Sukhothai, and fought continuously and successfully against the Khmers in Cambodia to the east and the various peoples of Burma to the west. He pushed his domains southward toward Malacca in the Malay Peninsula, and was careful not to antagonize the strong new Ming emperors in China.

As lawgiver, Rama Tibodi codified laws which had existed since the Nanchao period (7th to 13th centuries A.D.); these laws were generally observed until the latter days of the 19th century. Among them were the Laws of Evidence, which barred many types of persons from giving evidence; the Law on Offenses Against the Government, which fixed severe penalties for violations against the state; the Law on Abduction, which aimed to prevent kidnapping and the stealing of slaves; and the Law of Husband and Wife, which recognized polygamy and provided for easy divorce by mutual consent. (C. A. B.)

RAMAYANA ("Life of Rama") is the shorter of the two great national epic poems of India, the longer being the Mahabharata (q.v.), and consists of about 24,000 couplets. Composed in Sanskrit, c. 300 B.C., by Valmiki, and divided, with various later additions, into seven books, it describes the royal birth of Rama in the kingdom of Ayodhya (Oudh), his tutelage under the sage Vishvamitra, culminating in his success in bending King Janaka of Videha's mighty bow and thus gaining the king's daughter Sita in marriage. Banished from his position as heir-apparent by an intrigue, he retreats with his wife and favourite brother, Lakshmana, to the forest, where the demon king Ravana seizes Sita and carries her off to his kingdom in Lanka (Ceylon). The rest of the epic describes Rama's struggle to rescue her, aided by his brother and by a vast army of monkeys and bears, and it ends with Ravana's defeat and Rama's return to claim his throne. Always popular throughout India, the story has spread in various forms throughout Southeast Asia.

See also SANSKRIT LITERATURE; and, for other versions, BENGALI LITERATURE; HINDI LITERATURE; KANARESE LITERATURE; MALAYALAM LITERATURE; NEPALI LITERATURE; PRAKRIT LITERATURE; THAI LITERATURE. (J. E. B. G.)

RAMAZZINI, BERNARDINO (1633–1714), Italian teacher of medicine, who is considered to have been the founder of the study of occupational diseases and of workmen's protection, was born at Carpi near Modena, Italy, on Nov. 3, 1633. He took his medical degree at the University of Parma in 1659 and was appointed in 1671 the first professor of medicine at the University of Modena. There he made accurate studies in epidemiology, describing outbreaks of lathyrism (chickpea poisoning) and malaria. But his lifework began when one day he witnessed the distress of a workman cleaning out the cesspit in his own house. Subsequently Ramazzini investigated many crafts which were the cause of grave injury to those who practised them, and made a striking addition to the Hippocratic teaching: "When a doctor visits a working-class home he should . . . ask also 'What is your occupation?'" In 1700 he accepted the chair of medicine at Padua University, offered to him by the Venetian senate, and his fame spread rapidly all over Europe. In spite of lifelong ill health, he devoted much time to the study of harmful occupations, whether dirty or dangerous. His work *De Morbis Artificum Diatriba* (1713) exhorted doctors to demand laws for the protection of the health of workers. Ramazzini died in Padua on Nov. 5, 1714. (Do. H.)

RAMBOUILLET, CATHÉRINE DE VIVONNE, MARQUISE DE (1588–1665), French society hostess, was born in Rome in 1588, into the aristocratic Savelli family (of which in her signature she kept the name) which traced its descent from the Strozzi and Medici families. She was brought up to speak Italian, later learned Spanish, and by the turn of the century was established with her husband in Paris. She acquired by legacy a house in the Rue Saint-Thomas du Louvre (a street later demolished to make way for extended palace gardens) and this house, rebuilt to her own design, became known as the Hôtel de Rambouillet. As a meeting place of the best Parisian society, from 1620 until the Fronde and even in a small way after 1650, it remained open till the death of its mistress on Dec. 2, 1665.

She was a woman of ideas and imagination and achieved the initial novelty of providing a house and garden to which intelligent and fashionable people were attracted. She planted sycamores for seclusion and flower beds in ingenious patterns; she built rooms with large windows, new pictures and plenty of chairs, culminating in the famous blue reception room. Into this refreshingly new milieu she attracted much of the high society of Paris, and most of the writers who are still remembered.

How this heterogeneous assembly was held together for so many years is a puzzle, but the personality of Cathérine de Vivonne seems to have been the dominating influence. Outwardly she was, it seems, persuasive rather than domineering. It was not difficult to please her, writes Tallemant des Réaux, for she never asked

anything unreasonable. Recent research suggests that she did not make of the Hôtel primarily a literary salon at all, but rather a social meeting place of elegant people. She thus taught her contemporaries the art of conversation, an art which a generation only once removed from civil war, and accustomed to the masculine swashbuckling of the court of Henry IV, had to learn afresh. The Hôtel thus became a nursery of gentility, of civility, of that politeness which produced the new concept of the *honnête homme* and which was to find its artistic sublimation in Molière's *Le Misanthrope*. Cathérine de Vivonne's great achievement was to impose this discipline of manners on a proud social set, on the Condé family in the first place and on their friends Mme du Vigean, Mme de Combalet, and Mme de Sablé. These people, though free in manners and morals, were, it seems, willingly tamed by a hostess about whom through the years no breath of scandal gathered. Discussion seems to have avoided dullness. The marquise was fond of entertainments, excursions, charades, even practical jokes. Perhaps her brightest idea was to commit much of the entertaining to literary men, bourgeois, practised in discussion and expression, such as Malherbe, Jean Chapelain, the abbé d'Aubignac, and, above all, Vincent Voiture. This master of light verse was the life and soul of the gatherings; he inspired successive fashions, of madrigals, of "metamorphoses" (in which a person was described as a flower or an animal), of sonnets. A famous example of this teamwork is the *Guirlande de Julie* (q.v.).

There is no evidence that the Hôtel, as was long thought, was the home or origin of preciosity, though clearly a standard of speech and bearing would tend in lesser hands to become precious. With even greater success it seems to have avoided pedantry. Plays were read, performed, and criticized, but the theorists were not allowed to pontificate and, significantly, figures who tended to lay down the law, such as J. L. Guez de Balzac, Richelieu, Corneille, rarely went to the Hôtel. Richelieu's dominance of the new Académie Française indeed contrasts sharply with the freedom from political control of the Hôtel, where in the later years the Fronde cliques seem to have formed. The Hôtel may be said to have put into practice the polite ideal sketched in the ever-popular novel *L'Astrée* (1607–27), by Honoré d'Urfé, and thus to have been the first of that long line of Paris salons which formed the setting and inspiration of writers as different as La Fontaine, Voltaire, and Proust.

See G. Tallemant des Réaux, *Historiettes*, ed. by A. Adam, 2 vol. (1960); É. Magne, *Voiture et l'Hôtel de Rambouillet*, 2 vol. (1929–30). (W. G. ME.)

RAMBOUILLET, a town of north-central France, headquarters of an *arrondissement* of the Yvelines (formerly of the Seine-et-Oise) *département*, situated in a thickly wooded country formerly known as the forêt des Yvelines but now generally known as the Forest of Rambouillet. It is about 31 mi. (50 km.) SW of Paris and 19 mi. (30 km.) from Versailles. Pop. (1962) 10,631.

Rambouillet's famous château, built on ancient royal land in the 14th century, now dates mainly from the 18th century. The estate has had a succession of famous owners, among whom were the Montfort family (11th century); the d'Angennes family, to which the husband of the celebrated Marquise de Rambouillet belonged; the family d'Uzès; the house of Bourbon-Toulouse; Louis XVI; Napoleon I and the sovereigns who followed him. Francis I died there in 1547; Napoleon I stayed there before his departure for St. Helena; and there Charles X signed his abdication in 1830. Rambouillet became a marquisate in 1612 and a duchy in 1711. Since the time of Félix Faure (elected president in 1895) it has been the country residence of the presidents of France. In the large park of the château is a zootechnical centre, which replaced the *bergerie nationale* (national sheepfold) and which has maintained the direct strain of the Merino sheep imported from Spain under Louis XVI.

Rambouillet is a hunting centre, and there is shooting in its forest reserved for the president. The region is of historical interest, with notable châteaux as well as picturesque scenery. The attractive upper valley of the Yvette River, known as the Vallée de Chevreuse, is much visited by Parisians.

RAMEAU, JEAN PHILIPPE (1683–1764), the greatest French composer of the 18th century, known also for his theoretical works on harmony, was baptized at Dijon on Sept. 25, 1683. He was thus born two years before J. S. Bach, Handel, and Domenico Scarlatti, all of whom he was to survive. His father was an organist, and at 18 he himself decided to become a musician. In 1701 he went to Italy, but only reached Milan and returned a few months later. He became organist successively at Avignon, Clermont-Ferrand, Paris, Dijon, Lyons, and again at Clermont-Ferrand, which he left in 1722 for Paris, where he settled for the rest of his life. For about 20 years, until 1753, he was in the service of the tax-farmer Le Riche de la Pouplinière, conducting his private orchestra and ministering to his musical needs. Rameau died in Paris on Sept. 12, 1764.

Before the age of 50 Rameau had published harpsichord pieces, a few motets, and some solo cantatas, and had written a little light music for the stage; but it was only later, from his position in La Pouplinière's circle, that he was able to turn fully to opera, in which he produced his masterpieces. In 1733 his *Hippolyte et Aricie* was produced at the Paris Opéra. From then until 1760 he wrote tragic operas, various forms of ballet-opera, pastorals, and comic operas. His tragic operas and pastorals are in the form created by J. B. Lully and Philippe Quinault; his ballet-operas follow the form used by André Campra and A. H. de La Motte; and in *Platée* (1745) he adapted for the first time the form of the *tragédie lyrique* to a comic plot.

None of his librettists, not even Voltaire, was a great dramatist, and Rameau himself was too unheeding of dramatic structure to criticize their plots, though he would dwell on details. Yet when the plot allowed it, he identified himself with his characters, *e.g.*, Thésée in *Hippolyte et Aricie* and Iphise in *Dardanus*, entering into their feelings with great imagination. He was also able vividly to portray a tragic situation; *e.g.*, Hippolyte's death, and the tragic suspense in the second entry of *Les Fêtes d'Hébé*. His recitative, unlike that of Italian opera composers, is expressive and shades away smoothly into the airs. His harmony is rich and dense and his bass line interesting, its coherence and power often making his harmonies more telling than the vocal line itself. His many choruses are outstanding, the earlier being longer and less dramatic, and the finest being those in the four tragedies, *Hippolyte et Aricie, Castor et Pollux* (1737), *Dardanus* (two versions: 1739 and 1744), and *Zoroastre* (1749). The orchestral accompaniment is often of great beauty and interest in itself. Though consisting only of strings, woodwind, horns, and occasionally trumpets, Rameau's orchestra is used with an almost impressionistic resourcefulness. The orchestra is used alone in the *symphonies,* in the form of dances during the interludes, *ballets figurés,* and sections of dumb show. Rameau's dances are the most immediately appealing part of his work. Highly sophisticated, they are nevertheless based on folk models. The finest of his *ballets figurés* are found in works on pastoral subjects, a genre in which Rameau was particularly successful, often displaying bold harmony and picturesque orchestration.

His masterpieces are the comedy *Platée,* his first two ballet-operas *Les Indes Galantes* (1735) and *Les Fêtes d'Hébé* (1739), and his first three tragedies. Of these *Hippolyte et Aricie* is the most consistently tragic and musically daring, though the most unequal; *Castor et Pollux* is the most homogeneous and is elegiac rather than tragic, with delicate shades of feeling; *Dardanus,* in its two very different versions, covers a wide range of emotion and is musically the richest.

Rameau's three books of solo harpsichord pieces and his five trios (*Pièces de Clavecin en concert*) are more advanced than Couperin's in keyboard technique, and show the same harmonic vigour and concentrated expression as his operas. The trios are early examples of chamber music with an independent keyboard part instead of merely a figured bass. His four motets and his solo secular cantatas, all early, are among the less distinctive examples of his work.

Among his theoretical works, the *Traité de l'harmonie* (1722), based on the acoustic discoveries of the mathematician Joseph Sauveur (1653–1716), presents an explanation of harmonic prac-

tice of the time. For Rameau's theory of the "fundamental bass" *see* HARMONY: *Treatment of Dissonance.*

As a person, Rameau was silent and reserved. His wife, whom he married when he was middle-aged, declared that she knew nothing of the first 40 years of his life. Austere and unbending, he remained remote from the intrigues of the contemporary musical world. He fought in defense of his theoretical views, to which he attached more importance than to his creative achievement; and it was on these theoretical matters that he quarreled with the mathematician D'Alembert, who had earlier been his admirer and supporter. Statements about his miserliness are largely slander, nor should any faith be put in the portrait of him in Diderot's satire *Le Neveu de Rameau* ("Rameau's Nephew"). He was a noble, forbidding figure, hardly at ease in the milieu in which he moved.

See P. M. Masson, *L'Opéra de Rameau* (1932); Cuthbert Girdlestone, *Jean-Philippe Rameau: His Life and Work* (1957).

(C. M. G.)

RAMESWARAM, a town in Ramanathapuram (Ramnad) district of Madras, India, on Rameswaram Island in Palk Strait, 93 mi. (150 km.) SE of Madurai, with which it is linked by a railway bridge. Pop. (1961) 6,801. It contains one of the most venerated Hindu shrines, which in sanctity is second only to Kashi (Benares, now Varanasi). The great temple dates from the 17th century, although according to tradition it was founded by Rama, the hero of the epic *Ramayana* (*q.v.*), to commemorate his successful expedition to Ceylon across Adam's bridge (*q.v.*). It is quadrangular in shape, about 1,000 ft. (305 m.) long and 650 ft. (198 m.) broad, with a 100-ft. (30 m.)-high gopura (tower gate) and 700-ft. (213 m.)-long side corridors which open into richly decorated transverse galleries. It is perhaps the finest example of Dravidian architecture. Critics, however, consider its design a mixture of the exquisite and the inferior. (G. KN.)

RAMIE. Ramie is a textile fibre of the soft or bast fibre group, which occur as longitudinal strands in the inner bark of dicotyledonous (broadleaf) plants. The individual cells of the fibre bundles are botanically true fibres—elongated and thick walled with characteristic pitting. These cells are tenaciously gummed one to the other to form the cablelike strands which become commercial fibre when once freed from other bark tissues. The ramie or "China grass" plant is a many-stemmed shrub, *Boehmeria nivea,* of the nettle family (Urticaceae). The variety *tenacissima* is called Rhea. Slender stems as much as eight feet long bear heart-shaped leaves with a whitish underside along the upper third of the stalk. At their base the stems may be nearly an inch thick and contain there the most abundant fibre. The ramie plant is perennial, new stems arising from the crown after

RAMIE (BOEHMERIA NIVEA) LEAVES

the old are cut. A planting should endure for several years, with about three harvests annually. The species prefers warm humid climate and rich soils and should be fertilized generously to maintain good stands.

Ramie has been under cultivation from time immemorial. It was grown in ancient Egypt, where it was used to wrap mummies. Presumably it is native to China and Formosa and is mentioned in Chinese literature as early as 2200 B.C. Since 1855 it has been planted sporadically in the southern United States. Several attempts at European culture have been unsuccessful.

Fibres.—The fibres themselves are strong (eight times more so than cotton), durable and of fine texture and good colour. The cells are among the longest of natural fibres—up to one foot long but only $\frac{1}{750}$ in. in diameter. Ramie is superior in many respects to flax, hemp and jute. Its chief liability, however, has been the difficulty of freeing the fibre bundles from the gummy ensheathing tissues and inability to adapt the crop to large-scale mechanized handling. Production lagged behind major fibres, running only about 20,000 or 25,000 tons annually, produced mostly in China, with exports largely to Japan and Europe. In the United States it has continued as a minor crop in Florida, Louisiana, Texas and California.

Retting.—Retting is the process of freeing stem fibres by bacterial decomposition (rotting). The thin-walled cells of softer tissue decompose more readily than thick-walled resistant fibres. Immersing the stems or exposing moistened stems to air usually fails to decompose the cementing gums of ramie, so that the fibre must be separated by pounding and scraping and even then contains up to one-fourth its weight as resin. Eventually the resin or gum must be dissolved chemically. The fibres then become flexible and smooth—so smooth, in fact, that spinning becomes difficult on machinery developed for other fibres. In the far east harvest is by hand a stalk at a time. Each stem can be selected for proper maturity. The limited production in the U.S. is harvested by machine. Much ramie is homespun in the east, with little final cleaning. This gives a coarse, although enduring, fabric. Adhesive gums can be removed by procedures such as boiling in lye, or sometimes an acid treatment, bleaching or induced retting. Degummed fibre is washed, then "softened" with glycerin, waxes or soaps. Spinning is usually on machinery designed for silk or other fibre. Most ramie fabric includes a percentage of some other fibre, such as wool or cotton. It has been used in fire hose, fishing nets, propeller-shaft packing, hats, upholstery and various fabrics. Clothing made of ramie cloth wears well and is said to be mothproof.   (R. W. Sy.)

RAMIRO, the name of two kings of Aragon.

Ramiro I (d. 1063), bastard son of Sancho III (d. 1035) of Navarre, was the first king (1035–63) of Aragon. During his father's lifetime he ruled this territory as *regulus* from 1011 and was nominated king of it in his father's will. On the death (1045) of his brother, Gonzalo, he annexed the latter's kingdom of Sobrarbe and Ribagorza and later added the county of Pallars to his dominions. Ramiro conquered a large number of valleys in Upper Aragon from the Moors and made the Moorish kings of Huesca, Saragossa, and Lérida his tributaries. With them he attacked, unsuccessfully (1043), his half brother García, king of Pamplona. He was killed at Graus (May 8, 1063) when campaigning against the king of Saragossa and Sancho of Castile.

Ramiro II (d. 1157), called "the Monk," king of Aragon from 1134 to 1137, third son of Sancho V Ramírez, was a monk and bishop-elect of Barbastro when he was elected to the Aragonese throne on the death (1134) of his brother, Alfonso I. Navarre under García V Ramírez thereupon successfully reasserted its independence from the Aragonese crown. Ramiro soon quarreled with the Aragonese nobles and was temporarily expelled from his kingdom by them. He crushed this revolt (late 1135) with the aid of Ramón Berenguer IV, count of Barcelona. Early in 1136 Ramiro married Agnes of Aquitaine and had by her a daughter, Petronilla. He at once caused this infant to be betrothed to his ally Ramón Berenguer and himself abdicated in her favour (August 1137), leaving the government of Aragon in the hands of Ramón Berenguer. The latter's marriage to Petronilla duly took place in 1150. Ramón Berenguer died in 1162 and, in 1164, Petronilla formally renounced the Aragonese crown to her son, Alfonso II. The crowns of Aragon and Catalonia were thus united under the house of Barcelona by Ramiro's renunciation after the Aragonese kingdom had existed for only 100 years. Ramiro himself lived in retirement at the priory of San Pedro el Viejo at Huesca until his death on Aug. 16, 1157.   (P. E. R.)

RAMKHAENG (RAMA KHAMHENG) (reigned 1275–1317), warrior and conqueror, fourth king of Sukhothai in Thailand, earned the title Rama the Great because he converted a young and struggling state into a powerful kingdom. He maintained friendly relations with his neighbours in Thailand, but fought against formidable enemies in Cambodia to the east and Burma to the west and extended his sway southward over part of the Malay Peninsula. He enjoyed the favour of the emperor Kublai Khan in China and twice made personal pilgrimages to Peking.

Ramkhaeng also achieved greatness for his accomplishments in times of peace. He made his kingdom the cradle of Thai civilization, borrowing freely from the cultural riches of his neighbours; adopting their political ideas, their social systems, and their Buddhist religion with its beliefs, ceremonies, temples, and ornaments of artistic beauty. The invention of the Thai alphabet occurred during his reign and is generally attributed to him. An inscription at Sukhothai, describing Ramkhaeng's justice, magnanimity, and religious devotion, is the earliest extant specimen of the Thai language.   (C. A. B.)

RAMLE (RAMLEH; Hebrew RAMLA), a town of Israel in the plain of Sharon contiguous with Lod (Lydda), lies 12 mi. (19 km.) SE of Tel Aviv-Jaffa. The population, (1961) 22,444, is composed mostly of Jewish immigrants from Asia and North Africa including heretical Karaites from Egypt and the U.S.S.R. The town was founded A.D. 716 by the Arab conqueror Sultan Suleiman to replace Lod (*q.v.*) as the administrative centre of Palestine. Its name was derived from the Arabic 'raml' meaning "sand." Of the famous White Mosque erected by him, only the tower remains. The crusaders made it one of their principal strongholds and called it Rama. The Muslims reconquered and razed the town, but it was rebuilt in the 14th century. Napoleon made Ramle his headquarters in 1799. It was several times wholly or partly destroyed by earthquakes, the last one being in 1927. The British War Cemetery there is one of the largest in the Middle East. A cement factory has been established and the town is linked by rail and road with Tel Aviv-Jaffa, Jerusalem, and Haifa.   (No. B.)

RAMMED EARTH (PISÉ DE TERRE) is a building material resulting from the application of compaction to certain soils. Of the forms of earth building used by civilizations of varying technical development, rammed earth is the most durable. After World War II it was studied as an economic technique for underdeveloped regions. Its use is limited to soils with high sand and low clay contents, 70%:30% being a usual proportion, with the sand graded to various particle sizes. The mix, with about 10% water added, is compacted in molds by ironheaded rammers weighing 5 to 20 lb. (*See* SOIL MECHANICS.)

The mold may be a box for individual wall blocks or a long wooden form, about 2 ft. high, consisting of two sides separated by spacer bolts, which is placed on the wall. The soil is rammed into this in about 3-in. layers, the form being removed when it is filled and again superimposed. Special angle, 'T' and stopped-end forms are used for corners, junctions and openings. Roller-mounted forms, pneumatic rammers, and hydraulic, mass-production block presses have been used.

The moisture content at compaction is critical to the ultimate strength and shrinkage of the wall, the optimum falling between narrow limits. Compressive strengths vary from 100 lb. per square inch to 500 lb. per square inch, while densities average 130 lb. per cubic foot and increase with sand content. Minimum wall thicknesses are usually 12 in.; this mass results in a high thermal capacity. The time lag in its temperature changes maintains uniform internal conditions in climates with large day-night temperature variations. The wall surface is often given increased weather resistance with plaster, bitumen or linseed-oil treatment.

Strength and weather resistance can be increased by small additions of soil stabilizers. Portland cement and bitumen are the most commonly used. (T. A. M.)

RAMÓN Y CAJAL, SANTIAGO (1852–1934), Spanish histologist, who shared with Camillo Golgi (*q.v.*) the 1906 Nobel Prize for Medicine in recognition of their work on the structure of the nervous system, was born May 1, 1852, at Petilla de Aragon. He was a wild youth and so backward in his studies that his father, a struggling country surgeon, took him away from school and apprenticed him first to a barber and then to a cobbler. He was eventually allowed to enter the medical school of Saragossa (Zaragoza) and after obtaining his medical licence in 1873 served for a year as an army surgeon in Cuba.

In 1875 he was appointed an assistant in the Saragossa medical faculty and having at last found his natural bent he devoted himself to the study of anatomy. In 1877 he was promoted extraordinary professor and two years later he became director of the medical museum of Saragossa University. In 1883 he went to the University of Valencia as professor of descriptive anatomy and in 1887 to the University of Barcelona as professor of histology and pathological anatomy. From 1892 until his retirement in 1922 he held the chair of histology and pathological anatomy at the University of Madrid. He died on Oct. 17, 1934.

Ramón y Cajal won worldwide fame by his researches on neuroanatomy. Having adapted Golgi's silver-stain method of staining nervous tissue, he began to explore the then unknown world of the cerebellum and the cerebrum and to publish the results of his researches in a flood of books and papers. One of his most fundamental achievements was the establishment of the neuron or nerve cell as the basic unit of the nervous system. Among his best-known writings are the great *Manual de histología normal y técnica micrográfica* (1889; English translation, 1933), *Textura del sistema nervioso del hombre y de los vertebrados* (1897–1904), and *Estudios sobre la degeneración y regeneración del sistema nervioso* (1913–14; English translation 1928). He was also the author of a fascinating autobiography, *Recuerdos de mi vida* (1901; English translation, 1937), and of the earlier *Charlas de Café* (1920), containing anecdotes and thoughts on a wide variety of subjects.

See D. F. Cannon, *Explorer of the Human Brain: the Life of Santiago Ramón y Cajal* (1949). (W. J. Bp.)

RAMPOLLA (DEL TINDARO), MARIANO (1843–1913), Italian cardinal who, as secretary of state for the last 16 years of Pope Leo XIII's reign, collaborated with the pope in his efforts to reconcile the French Church to the republican regime and to advance the cause of international peace. Born on Aug. 17, 1843, at Polizzi in Sicily, he completed his studies at the Capranica College in Rome, took holy orders, and was trained for diplomacy at the College of Ecclesiastical Nobles. In 1875 he was appointed counselor to the papal nunciature in Madrid. Recalled to Rome in 1877, he served on the Congregation for the Propagation of the Faith before being sent back to Madrid as nuncio (1882–87). He was created cardinal on March 14, 1887, and two months later Leo XIII appointed him secretary of state.

Alive to the political and social realities of his age, Rampolla assembled the ideas for the encyclical *Rerum novarum* of 1891 (*see* LEO XIII). On Leo's death (1903) his prestige stood high and he was widely expected to be the next pope. Germany and Austria-Hungary, however, objected to his pro-French attitude, in which they saw political motives; and at the conclave, when Rampolla, on the first scrutiny, had received 29 votes, the cardinal bishop of Cracow, Jan Puzyna, announced that his sovereign, the Austrian emperor Francis Joseph, would exercise his veto against him. Pope Pius X, who subsequently abolished the right of veto, made Rampolla head of the Congregation of the Holy Office. The cardinal died in Rome on Dec. 16, 1913.

See G. Sinopoli di Giunta, *Il Cardinale Mariano Rampolla* (1923).

RAMPUR, a city and district in the Rohilkhand division of Uttar Pradesh, India. The city, formerly the capital of the Rampur princely state and now the headquarters of the district, stands on the left bank of the Kosi River, 115 mi. (185 km.) E of Delhi. Pop. (1961) 135,407. It is a centre for damask, light steel work, pottery, and sugar manufacture. Raza College is affiliated to

Agra University; the library contains a fine collection of Oriental manuscripts.

RAMPUR DISTRICT (area 895 sq.mi. [2,318 sq.km.]; pop. [1961] 701,537) corresponds with the former princely state of Rampur (Gwalior residency). (S. S. Bh.)

RAMSAY, ALLAN (1684/85–1758), Scottish poet and literary antiquary, who preserved and maintained national poetic traditions, chiefly in the comic mode. With Robert Fergusson (1750–74), he was highly regarded by Robert Burns as a pioneer in the use of Scots in contemporary poetry.

Born at Leadhills, Lanarkshire, on Oct. 15, 1684 or 1685, he moved to Edinburgh *c.* 1700, and in 1704 became an apprentice wigmaker. Established in this respected craft, in 1712 he married Christian Ross (d. 1743). In the same year he helped found the "Easy Club," a Jacobite literary society. His pen names, "Isaac Bickerstaff" and "Gavin Douglas," suggest the Augustan English and medieval Scottish sources of his literary enthusiasm. Although his earliest poems were composed in this "aftermath of Union" (of 1707) atmosphere, he soon established a reputation (then unique) as a prolific composer of verse in English and Scots, much of it modeled on classical styles and traditional metrical patterns, sometimes uneasily adapted to suit contemporary Edinburgh taste. He made considerable use of Scots in humorous and satirical verse; and, by collecting and publishing poems by Robert Henryson, William Dunbar, the anonymous author of *Christ's Kirk on the Green*, and other late medieval writers represented in the Bannatyne MS, Ramsay, though no scholarly respecter of texts, made certain of their survival. In this he followed an example first given by James Watson in *A Choice Collection of Comic and Serious Scots Poems* (1706–11), and indirectly gave impetus to more accurate editing of Scottish poetry and song later in the century. (*See also* SCOTTISH LITERATURE.)

In 1721 Ramsay published a subscriber's edition of his own poems—including several in mock-elegy style, and renderings in Scots of Horace's *Odes*—with a second volume in 1728. An original pastoral-comedy, *The Gentle Shepherd* (1725), gained much of its effect from use of Scots; the appearance of John Gay's *Beggar's Opera* (1728) encouraged him to turn it into a ballad-opera (1729). *Tea-table Miscellany* (3 vol., 1724–37), *Ever Green* (2 vol., 1724), and *Scots Proverbs* (1737) make up the bulk of his collection of old songs, poems, and wise sayings (the latter heavily indebted to James Kelly's 1721 volume). *Fables and Tales* (1722–30) are versions of La Fontaine and La Motte, together with narratives of uncertain origin, turned into Scots.

After publication of the 1721 *Poems*, Ramsay changed from wigmaker to bookseller, and his shop became a meeting place for both townsmen and visitors. He founded Britain's first circulating library (1726), the "Academy of St. Luke" for instruction in painting and drawing (1729), and a theatre (1736–39), eventually closed by extremists in the Church of Scotland presbytery, who found legal justification in the 1737 Licensing Act. He retired in 1740 but continued active. Ramsay died in Edinburgh on Jan. 7, 1758. His slipshod editing, coupled with his many light talents, has not helped him receive his due as an original poet in Scots; his place in literary history has been insecure in comparison with that of such successors as Fergusson and Burns.

BIBLIOGRAPHY.—*Works*, 5 vol., the Scottish Text Society: vol. i, *Poems*, 1721 (1951); ii, *Poems*, 1728 (1953), ed. by B. Martin and J. W. Oliver; iii, poems, miscellaneous and uncollected (1961); iv, letters, pamphlets, prefaces, prose (1970); v, *Proverbs, Easy Club Journal*, notes, critical apparatus, bibliography (1970), ed. by A. M. Kinghorn and A. Law. Modern biography by A. M. Kinghorn in vol. iv. *See also* A. Gibson, *New Light on Allan Ramsay* (1927); B. Martin, *Allan Ramsay: a Study of His Life and Works* (1931). (A. M. Ki.)

RAMSAY, ALLAN (1713–1784), Scottish portrait painter, the son of Allan Ramsay, author of *The Gentle Shepherd*, was born in Edinburgh on Oct. 13, 1713. After rudimentary training in Edinburgh he went to London and worked under the Swedish portrait painter Hans Hysing (1734), but his style was really formed by his studies in Italy (1736–38) under Francesco Imperiali and Francesco Solimena. On settling in London he soon became popular, although George Vertue in 1739 noted with dis-

tress that his style differed from the "valuable Manner" of Sir Godfrey Kneller and others and was "rather lick't than pencilled" (*i.e.*, his brushwork was smooth, not free).

His "Dr. Mead" of 1747 (Coram foundation, London) is in the Italian grand manner, preceding Sir Joshua Reynolds' grand portraits by several years; but perhaps the rise of Reynolds induced Ramsay to return to Italy in 1755–57. During the 1760s Ramsay painted little but royal images on government commission: most of this hack work was done by assistants and Ramsay devoted himself to political pamphleteering, classical studies and conversation—Dr. Johnson said to Boswell: "I love Ramsay. You will not find a man in whose conversation there is more instruction, more information, and more elegance . . ." Ramsay died at Dover on Aug. 10, 1784, while returning from his fourth visit to Italy.

Ramsay's best works are in the National gallery of Scotland, including important drawings, and the National Portrait gallery, Edinburgh; but there are also pictures in London (National Portrait gallery and Tate gallery) and Liverpool. His "Youth With Cap and Gown" was acquired by the Huntington gallery, San Marino, Calif., and his portrait "Mary Lillian Smith" by the Ringling museum, Sarasota, Fla.

See Alastair Smart, *Life and Art of Allan Ramsay* (1952).

(P. J. My.)

RAMSAY, SIR WILLIAM (1852–1916), British chemist who discovered the elements known as noble gases, was born in Glasgow, Scot., on Oct. 2, 1852. From 1866 to 1870 he studied in his native city. He then went to Heidelberg and studied under Robert Wilhelm Bunsen and in 1871 went to work under R. Fittig at Tübingen. In 1872 he became assistant in the Young laboratory of technical chemistry at Anderson's college, Glasgow. He received his Ph.D. from Tübingen in 1873 and from 1874 was tutorial assistant in the university. In 1880 he was appointed to the chair of chemistry at University college, Bristol, and made principal in the following year. In 1887 he succeeded A. W. Williamson as professor at University college, London, a position from which he resigned in 1913. He was awarded the Davy medal of the Royal society in 1895 and the Nobel prize for chemistry in 1904. He was made a knight commander of the Bath in 1902. He died at High Wycombe, Buckinghamshire, on July 23, 1916.

Ramsay's earliest investigations covered a wide field—from a new bismuth mineral to the physiological action of certain alkaloids —in the course of which he showed that the alkaloids are related to pyridine, which he synthesized from acetylene and prussic acid in 1876. Later he specialized definitely in inorganic and physical chemistry. With Sidney Young (1857–1937) and others he investigated the critical state, the relationship between vapour pressure and temperature and other properties of liquids (Ramsay-Young rule). In 1887 he found that absolutely dry ammonia and hydrogen chloride do not combine.

With J. Shields (1869–1920) he verified the Eötvös law of the constancy of the rate of change of molecular surface energy with temperature, and obtained evidence concerning the molecular complexity of certain liquids. In 1892 Lord Rayleigh asked for suggestions from chemists to account for the difference between the densities of chemical and atmospheric nitrogen, and Ramsay became interested in the problem. He at once predicted that an unknown heavy gas was present. Rayleigh preferred to believe that a heavy modification of nitrogen, analogous to ozone, was the disturbing factor. Ramsay devised methods for removing oxygen and nitrogen completely from air and found that there was present in addition a small quantity of a hitherto unknown gas. In Aug. 1894 Ramsay and Rayleigh announced the discovery of this new gas, afterward called argon (*q.v.*), present to the extent of almost 1% in the atmosphere. Its presence had been indicated as early as 1785 by Henry Cavendish. The high density of this gas accounted for the atmospheric nitrogen having a greater density than the chemical variety. In 1895, while searching for new sources of argon, Ramsay heated the mineral cleveite with acid and obtained a gas which gave a spectrum identical with that of helium (*q.v.*), detected in the sun by Sir J. N. Lockyer and Sir E. Frankland in 1868. In this way helium was first obtained, but it was later found to be present in the air to the extent of about 1 part in 250,000.

Both helium and argon were then believed to be inactive chemically and so were called the inert gases. They fitted into the periodic system although no provision had been made for chemically inactive elements. Furthermore, a study of their position in the periodic table led to the belief that at least three more such gases should exist. Ramsay, with M. W. Travers, found them in 1898 in liquid air residues from which oxygen and nitrogen had been removed; they were called neon, krypton and xenon (*qq.v.*) and were found to be present in the air only to an extremely minute extent (*e.g.*, xenon, 1 part in 170,000,000). Ramsay next turned to radioactivity, since he noted the association of helium with radioactive minerals. With F. Soddy (*q.v.*) he found in 1903 that helium was continuously produced as a disintegration product of radium emanation. This discovery led to the transmutation theory and its important consequences. In 1910 Ramsay obtained a small quantity of radium, and with Whytlaw Gray he was able, as a result of a wonderful piece of experimental work, to determine the density, and incidentally the atomic weight, of about one three-millionth part of a cubic inch of radium emanation. The atomic weight showed that this gas was the last of the noble-gas series. It was called niton and is now mainly known as radon (*q.v.*) or emanation. Ramsay thus has the unique fame of discovering a whole family of elements.

Ramsay's works include: *A System of Chemistry* (1891); *The Gases of the Atmosphere* (1896; 4th ed., 1915); *Modern Chemistry*, 2 vol. (1901); *Essays Biographical and Chemical* (1909); *Life and Letters of Joseph Black* (1918); *Elements and Electrons* (1913); *Introduction to the Study of Physical Chemistry* (1904).

BIBLIOGRAPHY.—Sir William Tilden, *Sir William Ramsay* (1918), *Famous Chemists* (1921); obituary notice, *Proceedings Royal Soc.* (1916–17); R. B. Moone, *Journal of the Franklin Institute* (1918); C. Moureu, in E. Farber's *Great Chemists* (1961).   (R. E. O.)

RAMSES (RAMESSES, Egyptian RAMESSU) was the name of (1) an ancient city and district in northeastern Egypt and (2) a line of pharaohs of the 19th and 20th dynasties (1320–c. 1085 B.C.).

The city was one of the store-cities built by the Hebrews of the Oppression. It later became the starting point of the Exodus. It has been plausibly identified with Pi-Ramessu (Per-Rameses), the residence-city of the Ramesside pharaohs, which is placed by some scholars at Tanis (modern San al Hajar) in the eastern Nile Delta and by others at Qantir farther south.

There were 11 pharaohs of this name:

RAMSES I (1320–1318 B.C.), the founder of the line, came to the throne as an old man. He was one of the generals who completed the overthrow of the Atonist regime established by Ikhnaton.

RAMSES II (1304–1237 B.C.) is often known as Ramses the Great because of the size and ubiquity of his monuments, of which he erected hundreds throughout Egypt and Nubia during his long reign. They included temples decorated with grandiose scenes of his victories, obelisks, and colossal statues of himself. His cartouches were carved deeply upon existing monuments. He also founded many towns and built fortresses on the Libyan frontier of Egypt; in the eastern delta, whence his family had sprung, a number of palaces arose, of which the most splendid was Pi-Ramessu ("the house of Ramses"). He warred for 17 years against the Hittites, and his greatest encounter with them at Kadesh (*q.v.*; 1299 B.C.) was celebrated as a great victory on the walls of a number of his temples. A treaty of nonaggression in his 21st year was sealed by marriage with a Hittite princess. Among the temples which he scattered along the banks of the Nile in Nubia, the grandeur of Abu Simbel (*q.v.*) with its huge seated colossi must have made an awesome impression on the superstitious Nubians.

RAMSES III (1198–1166 B.C.) modeled himself in many respects upon his illustrious namesake. He averted a threat of invasion from the Libyans and repulsed the more serious onslaught of a confederation of Mediterranean raiders. He did much to restore Egypt's prosperity. He was assassinated in a palace intrigue.

RAMSES IV–XI ruled successively from 1166 to c. 1085 B.C. Their reigns were marked by a progressive weakening of the central authority and brought the 20th dynasty to an inglorious end. *See* also EGYPT: *History*. (M. S. Dr.)

RAMSEY, ARTHUR MICHAEL (1904–   ), archbishop of Canterbury, who combines firm High Church principles with a generous understanding of other traditions and is active in promoting Christian unity, was born on Nov. 14, 1904, at Cambridge where his father was a fellow of Magdalene College. From Repton School (where his headmaster was Geoffrey Fisher) he went to Cambridge as scholar of Magdalene, obtained first-class honours in theology and was president of the Union. After attending Cuddeson Theological College he became curate of Liverpool Parish Church (1928–30), subwarden of Lincoln Theological College (1930–36), lecturer of Boston (Lincolnshire) Parish Church (1936–38), and vicar of St. Benet's, Cambridge (1939–40). Having made his mark as a teacher and published an influential book, *The Gospel and the Catholic Church* (1936), he became canon of Durham and professor of divinity in Durham University (1940), and then regius professor of divinity at Cambridge (1950–52), before returning to Durham as bishop. In 1956 he was translated to York as archbishop and in 1961 to Canterbury. In March 1966 in a historic encounter—the first formal meeting of a pope and an archbishop of Canterbury since the severance of the Church of England from the papacy in 1534—Ramsey and Pope Paul VI exchanged the "kiss of peace" and conferred privately on issues of concern to the two churches.

As a theologian, Ramsey has been engaged chiefly in the study of the New Testament and in the broad exposition of Christian doctrine. His publications include *The Resurrection of Christ* (1944), *The Glory of God and the Transfiguration of Christ* (1949), *F. D. Maurice and the Conflicts of Modern Theology* (1951), *From Gore to Temple* (1960), and *Introducing the Christian Faith* (1961). (S. L. G.)

RAMSGATE, a municipal borough, holiday resort, seaport, and limb of the Cinque Port of Sandwich, in the Isle of Thanet parliamentary division of Kent, Eng., 18 mi. (29 km.) NNE of Canterbury by road. Pop. (1961) 36,914. Area 5.7 sq.mi. (15 sq.km.). Ramsgate was originally a small fishing hamlet and is mentioned in a charter of Charles II as being under the jurisdiction of Sandwich, of which town Ramsgate became a limb or liberty within the confederation of the Cinque Ports in the reign of Henry VII. From that time Ramsgate developed as a seaport. The present harbour, on which George IV conferred the royal style or title, was built in the mid-18th century, and from that time substantial trade was developed with Baltic and other continental countries. Ramsgate became noted as a health resort and is now one of the most popular seaside holiday towns on the coast of Kent. The port has good facilities for commercial traffic and is a centre for motor cruisers and yachts. The development of the Kent coalfield during the 20th century brought additional trade to Ramsgate, the nearest pits being Betteshanger and Chislet about 10 mi. away. Small light industrial factories have been established in and near the town. Ramsgate has many historical associations. Cliffsend on the western extremity of the borough is the reputed landing place of Hengist and Horsa in A.D. 449 and of St. Augustine in A.D. 597. At Pegwell Bay rests the "Hugin," replica of a Viking ship rowed over from Denmark in 1949. St. Laurence Church dates from early Norman times. A. W. N. Pugin is buried in the Roman Catholic Church of St. Augustine, which he built. The town possesses a well-known boys' school (St. Lawrence College) and two grammar schools. Charter flights are available at the municipal airport.

RAMUS, PETRUS, the latinized form of the name of the Frenchman PIERRE DE LA RAMÉE (1515–1572), the most famous logician of the 16th century. Born to the Catholic faith, of an impoverished family of noble ancestry, at the small French village of Cuts in the Vermandois District of Picardy, he died 57 years later in Paris at the hands of hired assassins—one of the most celebrated Protestant victims of the Massacre of St. Bartholomew's Day. Two years after Ramus' birth, Luther posted his theses on the door of the Castle church at Wittenberg, and that event, which exploded into the Protestant Reformation, turned the 16th century into an age of intense religious dispute and military violence. It was Ramus' destiny to be chiefly remembered for the part he played in providing that age with its most influential theory of controversy.

Educated at Cuts and subsequently at the Collège de Navarre, in Paris, where he earned his way by working as servant for a wealthy schoolmate, Ramus in 1536 became master of arts, his Latin commencement disputation being a defense of the thesis *Quaecumque ab Aristotele dicta essent, commentitia esse*. Though 18th- and 19th-century scholarship construed this thesis to mean that "everything which Aristotle had said is false," in fact *commentitia* involves not so much the idea of falsehood as that of unnatural or contrived organization, and accordingly Ramus is now accepted less as an opponent of Aristotle than as a reorganizer and simplifier of Aristotelian doctrine. Putting his thesis into immediate effect, Ramus taught a reformed version of Aristotelian logic at the Collège du Mans, in Paris, and later at the Collège de l'Ave Maria, where he worked with Audomarus Talaeus (Omer Talon; *c.* 1510–62), who under Ramus' influence reformed Ciceronian rhetoric upon the principles applied by Ramus to the rearrangement of Aristotle's *Organon*. The innovations of Ramus and Talaeus so provoked the Peripatetic (orthodox Aristotelian) philosophers at the University of Paris that they induced Francis I to issue a decree on March 10, 1544, suppressing Ramus' books on the reformed logic and forbidding him to teach that subject. But Ramus was allowed to turn to the teaching of mathematics and rhetoric at a new post at the Collège de Presles. Thanks to the intercession of the cardinal Charles de Lorraine, one of Ramus' powerful friends, the ban against his teaching logic was lifted in 1547 by Henry II, and in 1551 he was appointed regius professor of philosophy and eloquence at the Collège de France. Around 1561 he was converted to Protestantism, and the last years of his life were marked by a mounting persecution from his academic and ecclesiastical enemies at home and by his growing fame as a logician abroad. On Aug. 26, 1572, two days after the outbreak of the Massacre of St. Bartholomew's Day, he was murdered in Paris.

Ramus' logic neglected the traditional role which that discipline had played as a method of inquiry, and emphasized instead an equally traditional view that logic is the method of disputation. Thus Ramus identified logic with dialectic and made it the art of disputing well, its two parts being invention and disposition (divisions to Ramus were characteristically dichotomous). Invention was the process of discovering proofs in support of any thesis under examination. It consisted in canvassing the ten places in which arguments dwell: causes, effects, subjects, adjuncts, opposites, comparatives, names, divisions, definitions, and witnesses. Disposition taught how the materials of invention should be arranged for presentation either in a single proposition, or in a syllogism, or in an entire discourse.

In speaking of the arrangement of discourses, Ramus evolved his famous theory of method. To him method was of two kinds. The first he called the method of nature, by which discourses were arranged for men of learning in a descending order of generality by a process of defining and dividing wholes and parts and subparts until nothing could be defined or divided further. The second kind of method he called the method of prudence. It consisted in arranging discourses for the populace by devices exemplified in oratory and poetry.

For the particular contribution of Ramus to the treatment of the syllogism, *see* LOGIC, HISTORY OF: *Modern Logic*.

While Ramus was perfecting dialectical theory, Talaeus rewrote Ciceronian rhetoric, depriving it of invention and disposition, since these were parts of dialectic, and confining it to style and delivery, that is, to the tropes and figures on the one hand, and to voice and gestures on the other.

Ramus' dialectic and Talaeus' rhetoric had an enormous vogue in Europe throughout the late 16th and early 17th centuries. Then these complementary reforms collapsed, as logic under one set of auspices turned back toward traditional Aristotelianism and under another forward toward the inductive sciences, while rhetoric at first reverted to a traditional but outmoded Ciceronianism and then deliberately fragmented itself into the study of the tropes and figures and into the later preoccupation with voice and gestures under the auspices of the elocutionists. In respect to logic, Ramus' influence was powerful but transitory. His influence upon rhetoric, however, was a near disaster, as that discipline was reduced to the mere externals of verbal ornament and artful vocalization, and no longer had a vital connection with the meaning and form of discourse. Not until the late 18th century did rhetoric begin to define a new set of relations to literary theory.

Ramus' most celebrated works were *Dialecticae Partitiones* (1543), *Aristotelicae Animadversiones* (1543), *Dialectique* (1555), and *Dialecticae Libri Duo* (1556). His writings on other subjects were voluminous.

BIBLIOGRAPHY.—W. J. Ong, *Ramus and Talon Inventory* (1958) and *Ramus: Method, and the Decay of Dialogue* (1958). For the influence of Ramus in the English-speaking world *see* Perry Miller, *The New England Mind: the Seventeenth Century* (1939); W. S. Howell, *Logic and Rhetoric in England, 1500–1700* (1956).
(WI. S. H.)

RAMUSIO, GIOVANNI BATTISTA (1485–1557), Italian geographer, who compiled a famous travel collection, *Delle Navigationi et Viaggi*, was born at Treviso on July 20, 1485. He entered the Venetian public service, becoming secretary of the Senate in 1515, and of the Council of Ten in 1533. He died at Padua on July 10, 1557.

Ramusio had witnessed from his boyhood the great discoveries in the East and West, and geography became his chief study. He seems to have begun the collection of material about 1520, at the suggestion of the humanist Girolamo Fracastoro, and he was tireless in searching for geographical narratives and documents. Among Ramusio's principal collaborators and correspondents were Andrea Navagero, Cardinal Pietro Bembo, Fracastoro, and the cartographer Giacomo Gastaldi.

The arrangement of the *Navigationi* is regional. Two volumes only, from the press of L. A. Giunti at Venice, were published in Ramusio's lifetime: volume i (Africa) in 1550, volume iii (America) in 1557. Volume ii (Asia) appeared in 1559 and was the first to name Ramusio as the editor. Four later editions of volume i were issued; three of volume ii; and two of volume iii. Among the important texts which are uniquely found in the *Navigationi* are Ramusio's version of Marco Polo and the *Descrittione del l'Africa* (*Description of Africa*) by Leo Africanus. (R. A. SN.)

RAMUZ, CHARLES FERDINAND (1878–1947), the best-known novelist and probably the most considerable writer of French-speaking Switzerland since Rousseau, Sénancour, and Benjamin Constant. Born on Sept. 4, 1878, at Cully, Vaud, he was a city boy, heir to a refined, middle-class culture, but chose to write about country people, farmers, and mountaineers, in a language deliberately simple and earthy. To his Calvinistic background he owed a feeling for the Bible and its epic grandeur, from which the French, being in large majority Catholic, had cut themselves off after the Reformation. His art is austere; classical in that it eschews decorative and easy grace, and felicitously welds Greco-Roman traditions and a Stoic acceptance of eternal laws with biblical poetry.

After spending the years 1902–14 in Paris, where he mixed with painters and poets, Ramuz published some slender volumes of verse and returned to Vaud to grow roots. He struck up a friendship with Stravinsky, for whom he wrote the texts of *Les Noces* and *L'Histoire du Soldat* (1918; trans. 1955). He composed in solitude, aloof from Parisian literary fashion and untouched by the then popular examples of Gide, Proust, Mauriac; still less by the Surrealist revolution. His twofold purpose in fiction was to express the poetry of Alpine scenery in words that should convey both love and fear of the mountain's ominous personality (he is the greatest interpreter of the mountain in modern literature); and to establish communion with his fellows, especially the least sophisticated of them. His novels are concentrated, stark, steeped in awe inspired by life's hazards in the treacherous wintry peaks. Few have rendered as he has the emotion of fear without recourse to thrills, the supernatural, or strings of adventures. At the same time he conveys powerfully the wordless tenderness of the simple, the humble domestic joys of men and women, or male comrades, dimly aware that they are the prey of destiny. The spirit of evil roams around them, as in Bernanos, but they do not indulge in self-pity, or even in prayer, nor do they delve complacently into their own contradictions and subconscious abysses. These peasants recall Adam and Eve (title of one of Ramuz' best novels; publ. 1933) as they appear in sculptural form on the porches of Romanesque churches. For, naturally, while far removed from the *préciosité* of some of his contemporaries, Ramuz' style is not without mannerisms. His villagers are stylized; their language does not, cannot, reproduce the everyday speech of common men. Claudel, very unlike Ramuz in his religious convictions, was one of his staunchest admirers: he prized his robustness, the nobility of his quest for joy, his repudiation of introspection and of fashionable obsession with the "Absurd."

Ramuz' best-known novels were published between his 40th and 60th years (he died at Pully, near Lausanne, on May 23, 1947). They are: *Le Règne de l'esprit malin* (1917, *The Reign of the Evil One*, 1922); *Présence de la mort* (1922, *The Triumph of Death*, 1946); *La Grande Peur dans la montagne* (1925, as *Terror on the Mountain*, 1967); *La Beauté sur la terre* (1927, *Beauty on Earth*, 1929); *Derborence* (1934, as *When the Mountain Fell*, 1947). *Terror on the Mountain* best represents Ramuz' stories of fear creeping into the flesh and minds of characters who, despite their sturdiness, are helpless. Young villagers decide to graze their cattle on a mountain pasture long deserted because a curse is said to hang over it. They challenge fate heroically, but one after another they are doomed: the reader shares their panic and final despair. The style is concrete, racy, less colourful and sensuous than that of Jean Giono (*q.v.*), whom Ramuz often resembles. The language is in no way dialectal and only slightly archaic, for unlike the Bretons, Basques, or Provençals, the French Swiss have never spoken a *patois*. The setting, way of life, and characters belong to one small region of Europe; but, like Faulkner's novels, those of Ramuz are no less universal for being local.

BIBLIOGRAPHY.—Charles Ferdinand Ramuz, *Journal 1896–1942* (1945) and *Oeuvres complètes* (1967; Editions Rencontre). *See also* M. Dichamp, *Ramuz ou le Goût de l'authentique* (1948); A. Béguin, *Patience de Ramuz* (1950); Y. Guers-Villate, *Ramuz* (1966); *Adam International Review*, no. 319–21 (1967; Ramuz number, with bibliography).
(H. M. P.)

RANA, a dynasty of hereditary prime ministers of Nepal during the 19th–20th centuries. The title of Rana or Ranaji was granted to Jung Bahadur (*q.v.*), the first of these prime ministers, during his tenure of office (1846–77). The title came to be invariably suffixed to his name as also to that of his brothers and their descendants. Having been appointed hereditary prime minister, and believing it essential for the security of the state that he should be succeeded by a fully adult and capable man, he devised an order of succession by which the office passed not from father to son but from brother to brother within the family and then in the second generation to the sons of all his brothers in order of age and so on. Thus when he died he was succeeded by his next eldest brother, Rana Udip Singh. Jung Bahadur's wild and undisciplined sons plotted to seize the office of prime minister for themselves and as a result were exiled. The succession passed eventually to the sons of Dhir Shumsher, one of Jung Bahadur's younger brothers. The family then adopted the suffix of Shumsher Jung Bahadur Rana. In succession the prime ministership passed from one to the other of Dhir Shumsher's sons. Chandra Shumsher (prime minister 1901–29) was a man of wisdom who introduced many reforms including the abolition of slavery. Joodha (1932–45), the last surviving son of Dhir Shumsher, was faced on his succession by a dynastic crisis. According to Jung Bahadur's rule, succession could pass only to the sons of a senior wife, but both Maharaja Bir Shumsher and Maharaja Bhim Shumsher had placed sons by junior wives on the roll. In order to avoid an outright conflict between the sons of senior and junior wives, Joodha reverted to Jung Bahadur's rule, struck the sons of junior wives off the roll, and banished them from Katmandu. The family was then divided among itself, and its system of rule was fast becoming an anachronism. Joodha was succeeded by Padma, son of Maharaja Bhim Shumsher and the first of the next generation. Padma himself retired in 1948 and was succeeded by Mohun, the last of the hereditary prime ministers, who retired in 1951. *See also* NEPAL: *History*. (RI. R. P.)

RANCÉ, ARMAND JEAN LE BOUTHILLIER DE

(1626–1700), Cistercian monk, founder of the reformed Cistercians called Trappists, was born at Paris on Jan. 9, 1626, of a noble family. At an early age he became commendatory abbot of the Cistercian abbey of La Trappe, in Normandy. After brilliant studies, he distinguished himself as a *littérateur* and orator; he shone intellectually in the assembly of the French clergy in 1655. Up to 1657 Rancé had led a worldly life. In that year began his conversion, which was completed in 1660. He disposed of his possessions, resigned his benefices, and became in 1664 regular abbot of La Trappe, in which position he did all he could to reform the Cistercian order. One of his measures was an attack on learning, in his *Traité de la sainteté et des devoirs de la vie monastique* (1683), as being contrary to the spirit of monastic life, which he believed should be confined to prayer and manual labour; this led to a long-drawn-out quarrel with J. Mabillon. In 1678 Rancé obtained papal approval of his reform, which spread widely. He died at Soligny-la-Trappe on Oct. 27, 1700. *See also* CISTERCIANS: *Trappists;* LA TRAPPE, NOTRE DAME DE.   (E. A. R.; X.)

RANCHI,

a city and district in the Chota Nagpur division of Bihar State, India. The city, headquarters of the district and division, lies about 2,100 ft. (640 m.) above sea level and 133 mi. (214 km.) NW of Jamshedpur by rail and road. Pop. (1970 est.) 176,789. The town straggles along the excellent roads which converge from several directions. It has a cantonment, a radium institute, and two large mental hospitals. Its seven colleges include a medical and an agricultural college, and in July 1960 the city became the seat of Ranchi University with jurisdiction over Chota Nagpur division. The establishment there in the 1960s of the National Coal Development Corporation of India and the Hindustan Steel Company and the erection of a large heavy machine tool factory gave impetus to the city's growth. Ranchi is midway between the coal and iron belts of the Chota Nagpur Plateau and lies on a narrow-gauge railway from Muri to Lohardaga, but because of its growing industrial importance it was linked by a broad-gauge line from Muri to Roorkela.

RANCHI DISTRICT has an area of 7,047 sq.mi. (18,251 sq.km.) and a population (1961) of 2,138,565. Physically, in the extreme northwest, it consists of an elevated basaltic lateritized plateau (3,600 ft.) from which bauxite is exploited, and a rejuvenated 2,000-ft.-high undulating, deforested peneplain, with extensive terraced cultivation. The edges of this peneplain are steep and forested. The principal rivers are the Subarnarekha, Sankh, and North and South Koel. Rice is the predominant crop. There is a cement factory at Khelari; shellac is also manufactured and myrobalans are processed. More than half of the inhabitants are tribal peoples, the most important of which are the Mundas and Oraons. There are leprosy and tuberculosis sanatoriums in the district.
(E. AH.)

RANDERS,

a town of Jutland, Den., capital of Randers *amt* (county), lies on the Gudenaa River where it widens into the Randers Fjord, an inlet of the Kattegat, 37 mi. (59 km.) NNW of Aarhus by rail. Pop. (1965) 42,923. Some medieval merchants' houses have survived and St. Martin's Church (1490), the Holy Ghost Hospital (1510), and the town hall (1768) are noteworthy. Randers is on the main railway from Fredericia to Aalborg and is the commercial centre of a prosperous agricultural region. Railway rolling stock, rope, yeast, beer, textiles, gloves, furniture, tiles, milk powder, and agricultural machinery are produced. First mentioned in 1086, Randers obtained town privileges in 1302.   (K. OL.)

RANDFONTEIN,

a town of the Transvaal, Republic of South Africa, lies 28 mi. (45 km.) W of Johannesburg by road and rail at 5,820 ft. (1,774 m.) above sea level. Pop. (1960) 41,499, of whom 13,647 were Europeans. Established as a separate municipality in 1929, in the 1960s it was undergoing considerable industrial and residential expansion on account of its central position on the Witwatersrand. Notable buildings include the town hall (1930) and the Jewish synagogue (1958), and the town has two high schools and a technical college. Within its municipal area are Riebeeck Lake (with a swimming pool of Olympic standards) and Robinson Lake, which is heated for all-year swimming by a flume

from the mine power station. Being on the main road and railway network, Randfontein has good communications with the rest of the Transvaal and with other parts of the republic. There is an airfield near the town. The chief industries are mining, engineering, food processing, and textiles.   (J. F. v. L.)

RANDOLPH, ASA PHILIP

(1889–   ), U.S. Negro union leader whose organization of the Brotherhood of Sleeping Car Porters marked the beginning of a substantial and sustained role for black workers in the American labour movement. A skilled orator and tactician, Randolph, when necessary, took courageous positions that ran against the tide.

He was born in Crescent City, Fla., on April 15, 1889, the son of a pastor of the African Methodist Episcopal church. During the ten years Randolph spent working his way through the College of the City of New York, he became interested in the labour and socialist movements. While a waiter on a coastal steamer he attempted to organize a protest against the crew's living conditions and was dismissed for his efforts and blacklisted. Again, during World War I, he tried to unionize shipyard workers in the Virginia tidewater area but in this struggle, too, he was defeated. After U.S. entry into that war, he and a friend, Chandler Owen, started a monthly magazine, *The Messenger,* which advocated greater militancy on the part of Negroes in their newly important positions in the war industries and army. Attacking the country's problems from a socialist point of view, Randolph wrote: "The capitalist system must go and its going must be hastened by the workers themselves." After the war he lectured at the Rand School of Social Service in New York and ran, unsuccessfully, for various offices on the Socialist ticket. In 1925 he began the difficult job of organizing the sleeping car porters, a group of black workers that, as early as 1915, had tried and failed to unionize. Although at that time half of the American Federation of Labor affiliates barred Negroes, Randolph eventually won recognition for the union and by 1934 established that the porters should be included within the scope of the Railway Labor Act. In 1937, after the act had been amended to outlaw company unions and to guarantee collective bargaining, the brotherhood won its first substantial victory, increasing wages, cutting working hours by a third, and reducing monthly travel requirements by 4,000 mi.

In 1941, before the U.S. entered World War II, Randolph warned Pres. Franklin D. Roosevelt that he would lead thousands of Negroes in a march on Washington to protest against failure to ensure employment of Negroes in industry and government. He took that strong stand despite opposition by many of his liberal and radical allies who argued that it was not the right time for action. Only the threat of a march was necessary, however; the president barred discrimination in defense industries and federal bureaus, and created the Committee on Fair Employment Practice.

In the postwar years Randolph continued as president of the brotherhood, and in 1955, when the AFL and CIO merged, he became a vice-president of the combined organization. At the age of 74 he was director of the March on Washington for Jobs and Freedom, the largest civil rights demonstration held in the U.S., which brought 200,000 people to the capital in 1963.

See Brailsford R. Brazeal, *The Brotherhood of Sleeping Car Porters* (1946) and Jay Saunders Redding, *The Lonesome Road* (1958).

RANDOLPH, EDMUND JENNINGS (JENINGS)

(1753–1813), Virginia lawyer who played an important role in drafting and ratifying the U.S. Constitution and served as attorney general and later secretary of state in Washington's cabinet, was born Aug. 10, 1753, in Williamsburg, Va. After attending William and Mary College he studied law in the office of his father, who was then the king's attorney in the colony. The approach of the American Revolution caused a split in the family: the father, with his wife and daughters, left for England in 1775 while Edmund threw in his lot with the rebellious colonists.

The young lawyer served briefly as an aide to General Washington in the siege of Boston and then returned to Virginia to care for the estate of his uncle, Peyton Randolph. He was elected to the Virginia convention of 1776 and served on the committee that drew up a bill of rights and a state constitution, The Virginia Assembly elected him attorney general of the state, and between

1779 and 1782 he also served intermittently as a delegate to the Continental Congress.

In 1786 Randolph headed the Virginia delegation to the Annapolis convention and the same year was elected governor of Virginia. He played an important role as a delegate to the 1787 Constitutional Convention (q.v.) where he presented the influential "Virginia Plan" and served on the committee on detail that prepared a first draft of the proposed constitution. He did not sign the final draft, however, because he wanted more protection of the rights of states and of individuals. Nevertheless, on his return home he decided to support the document, and in the Virginia convention of 1788 he used his influence to bring about ratification. Charged with inconsistency, he replied that he feared the Union might break up if the Constitution were not ratified.

After President Washington took office in 1789 he appointed Randolph (who had handled much of Washington's personal legal work) to the post of U.S. attorney general. When a feud developed in Washington's cabinet between Jefferson and Hamilton, Randolph tried to be neutral, but this earned him dislike from both sides and brought forth criticism that he was indecisive. Upon Jefferson's resignation as secretary of state in December 1793, Randolph was chosen to replace him. As England and France were then at war and there was strong support in the United States for both antagonists, Randolph's attempt to steer a middle course was difficult. While the Jay Treaty with England was under consideration he performed the delicate task of maintaining friendly relations with France. He also paved the way for the eventual signing (October 1795) of the Treaty of San Lorenzo (or Pinckney Treaty) with Spain, which provided for free navigation of the Mississippi.

Randolph's governmental service was abruptly brought to an end by charges made in an intercepted diplomatic dispatch that he had shown a willingness to accept money from the French in return for influencing the U.S. government against Great Britain. Though the charges were not proved, Randolph resigned from office on Aug. 19, 1795, thus ending a promising political career. He returned to Virginia and resumed his law practice, acting in 1807 as senior counsel for Aaron Burr during his trial for treason. He died on Sept. 12, 1813, at Carter Hall, Millwood, Clarke County, Va.

BIBLIOGRAPHY.—D. R. Anderson, "Edmund Randolph," in vol. ii, The American Secretaries of State and Their Diplomacy, ed. by S. F. Bemis (1928); H. J. Eckenrode, The Randolphs: the Story of a Virginia Family (1946); Nathan Schachner, The Founding Fathers (1954).　(E. G. Ev.)

RANDOLPH, JOHN (1773–1833), a Virginia planter and member of Congress noted for his flamboyant oratorical defense of states' rights, was born at "Cawsons," a plantation in Prince George County, Va., on June 2, 1773. Through his father, John Randolph, and his mother, Frances Bland, he was related to the Randolphs of Turkey Island and the Blands of Westover, two of the most notable families of colonial Virginia; and, through an ancestress, Jane Bolling, he was a descendant of the Indian princess Pocahontas. He received his collegiate education during brief periods of study at Princeton, Columbia, and William and Mary, and read law for a short time under the guidance of a relative, Edmund Randolph, who was attorney general of the United States in Washington's first cabinet.

In 1799 Randolph was elected to the House of Representatives where his rise was so rapid that, after the inauguration of Thomas Jefferson as president in 1801, he was made chairman of the House Committee on Ways and Means and became the leader of the House Republicans. He frequently appeared on the floor of the House in riding habit and flourishing a whip; his debating skill and biting sarcasm made him a feared opponent. After his failure as manager of the impeachment trial of Justice Samuel Chase of the Supreme Court in 1804, and his opposition to Jefferson's effort to acquire Florida, he drifted away from Jefferson and the other Republican leaders. He did not join the Federalists but stood aloof from both parties. About the year 1810 he established his home at "Roanoke," a family plantation, and thereafter added "of Roanoke" to his name to distinguish himself from a distant relative.

Randolph returned to prominence in 1820 when his resolute resistance to the Missouri Compromise made him a powerful figure in the House. After his first election in 1799 he was reelected to the House every two years, except in 1813 when his opposition to the War of 1812 resulted in his defeat and in 1817 when he declined to run. After reelection to the House in 1825, he was elected to the Senate to fill an unexpired term but was defeated for reelection by John Tyler. During these years when party feelings ran high, Randolph's denunciation of Henry Clay's support of John Quincy Adams for the presidency in the disputed election of 1824–25 led him into a duel with Clay in April 1826, but both parties emerged unscathed. Three years later Randolph was a prominent member of the convention that drafted a new constitution for Virginia. In 1830 President Jackson sent him on a special mission to Russia, but ill health forced him to return after only a few weeks at his post. After his return he made a series of speeches denouncing Jackson's proclamation against South Carolina's ordinance of nullification. He died at Philadelphia on May 24, 1833, while waiting for a ship to take him to England.

As a passionate partisan of state sovereignty, Randolph was a forerunner of John C. Calhoun (q.v.). He vigorously opposed a national bank, protective tariffs, federal internal improvements (i.e., construction of roads and canals), and interference with the institution of slavery, though he disapproved of slavery and freed his own slaves in his will. He was plagued by ill health throughout his life, and was at times in a state of mental derangement. One of the most brilliant and disinterested, though by no means one of the most useful, of American public men, he was a captivating talker, a delightful letter writer, a scholar, and a devotee of the horse, the dog, and the gun.

BIBLIOGRAPHY.—W. C. Bruce, John Randolph of Roanoke, 1773–1833, 2 vol. (1922); Russell A. Kirk, Randolph of Roanoke: a Study in Conservative Thought (1951); R. G. Osterweis, Romanticism and Nationalism in the Old South (1949).　(W. C. Be.; X.)

RANDOLPH, THOMAS (1523–1590), English diplomat in the reign of Elizabeth I, was the son of Avery Randolph of Badlesmere, Kent. Educated at Christ Church, Oxford, he became principal of Broadgates Hall (now Pembroke college), Oxford, in 1549. Forced to resign in 1553 after the accession of Mary I because of his Protestant beliefs, he went to France, where he may have associated with the Scottish humanist George Buchanan. Shortly after the accession of Elizabeth I (1558) he returned to England and was employed by the queen as a confidential diplomatic agent in Scotland. His letters during this period form an important source for the affairs of the Scottish court. After unsuccessfully opposing the marriage of Mary Stuart and Lord Darnley (1565), he was in 1566 accused by Mary of giving financial support to the rebellion of James Stewart, earl of Moray, and was recalled to England.

Randolph was sent on diplomatic missions to Russia (1568), where he obtained privileges for the English merchants trading there, to France (1573 and 1576), and to Scotland (1570 and 1578). Following the imprisonment of the Scottish regent, James Douglas, 4th earl of Morton, in 1580, Randolph was sent to Scotland by Elizabeth in an attempt to secure his release. He planned to seize the young king James VI and his favourite Esmé Stewart, earl of Lennox, but the plan was discovered; Randolph fled to England and Morton was executed in June 1581. During his last mission to Scotland in 1586, he helped to arrange a treaty between the two countries in which each pledged support for the other in the event of an invasion. From about 1566 he held the chamberlain's office in the exchequer and the office of comptroller of the post horses. Randolph died in London on June 8, 1590.

RANDOLPH, THOMAS (1605–1635), English poet and dramatist whose talent lacked time to mature, was born on June 15, 1605, at Newnham-cum-Badby, Northamptonshire, and educated at Westminster School and Trinity College, Cambridge, where he was elected to a fellowship in 1629. Both at Westminster and Cambridge he earned a high reputation for English and Latin verse, and Ben Jonson adopted him as one of his "sons." Of his three poems to Jonson, one renders thanks for his "adoption," while another answers Jonson's despondent ode on the failure of The

New Inn. He died at Blatherwick in March 1635.

Randolph published *Aristippus* and *The Conceited Pedler* (1631), two dramas for performance at Cambridge, *The Jealous Lovers* (1632), a comedy, and verses in various collections. A posthumous collection of his poems (1638) included two other plays, *The Muses Looking-Glass* (performed 1630) and *Amyntas*, a pastoral drama (probably acted 1631). *Hey for Honesty*, a comedy adapted from *The Plutus* of Aristophanes, was published in 1651 with a number of contemporary allusions inserted by the editor. Randolph had a real lyrical gift and some dramatic ability; his early death robbed 17th-century England of an accomplished and genial poet.

The Poetical and Dramatic Works were edited by W. C. Hazlitt, 2 vol. (1875); *The Poems and Amyntas* by J. J. Parry (1917); and *The Poems* by G. Thorn-Drury (1929).

See G. C. Moore Smith, *Thomas Randolph* (1927); S. A. and D. R. Tannenbaum, *Thomas Randolph* (1947). (V. DE S. P.)

RANDOMIZATION, a principle in the theory of experiments designed to avoid the collection of biased and misleading empirical data by ensuring random (or chance) selection and treatment (*see* STATISTICS, MATHEMATICAL: *Theory of Experiments*).

Experiments are designed to observe the presence or the extent (or both) of the effect of some experimental factor or treatment on some material. In the simplest form of experiment a treated (experimental) quantity (a unit) of material may be compared with an untreated (control) unit. If the material and conditions were exactly homogeneous, then the difference between the two sets of observations would be ascribable to the treatment. Usually, however, the material and conditions are heterogeneous, and the observed difference cannot confidently be ascribed to the treatment, since they may reflect other uncontrolled differences between the experimental and control situations. Thus an investigator's announcement of a finding of some interest is usually followed by similar experiments (replications) performed by different investigators. Also, prior to the announcement, the original investigator is likely to have repeated his experiment to see whether the findings persist with different units of material and at different times.

This degree of control is usual in experimental work and has been customary since about the beginning of the 19th century. For laboratory work in the physical sciences, where homogeneity of material and experimental conditions can be attained to a high degree, such precautions have been broadly adequate. However, by the 1920s, with the growth of experimentation on highly heterogeneous material (*e.g.*, in agriculture, general biology, medicine, meteorology, the social and behavioural sciences), it became apparent that mild and unsystematically applied precautions were not enough. One effort to increase confidence in the generalizability of empirical data was the formulation of the principle of randomization, due to Ronald A. Fisher, which states that before any effect can be said to be ascribable to a given treatment (independent of other known or unknown factors) the experiment must be replicated (*i.e.*, repeated on a number of experimental and control units of material) and that all units of material selected for study must be random samples of the larger population (universe) they are taken to represent. Thus if an experiment is expected to yield a statement about people in general (*i.e.*, the universe of all people) the principle of randomization ideally requires that all people anywhere have an equal opportunity for selection as experimental and control subjects. The word random as used here indicates a basis for sampling from the universe that imitates independent throws of an unbiased coin (*see* PROBABILITY, MATHEMATICAL). Since most coins are biased (not perfectly symmetrical, for instance), and since the usual methods of tossing them are biased, tables of the so-called random numbers are found in many books on statistics, especially to assist in the random selection and treatment of samples of experimental material.

It must be emphasized that randomization simply reduces the probability of collecting biased or misleading data. On the basis of chance (random) selection from a universe, an atypical sample is merely improbable, not impossible.

As an example of how randomization might be used, consider the case of two surgeons at different hospitals using different methods to remove cancers of a specified type. One finds a higher rate of survival among his patients than does the other, and claims an advantage in his technique. However, the difference may be independent of the differences in surgical technique. It may easily have arisen from a systematic difference between the kinds of patients patronizing the two hospitals. Or, the policy in one hospital may be to perform operations somewhat hastily on early cases of cancer; while patients in the other hospital may be subjected to more prolonged observation. Or, the difference between survival rates may well be due to unsuspected factors; these create the greatest difficulties in experimentation.

All suspected and unsuspected sources of bias should tend to be compensated by a strict application of the principle of randomization. Before randomizing, the experimenters might agree in advance on a well-defined category of patients and on the general circumstances in which the two surgical techniques are to be tested. It may be decided that the sample of patients used in the experiment be limited to those coming for treatment to a particular hospital; or there may be agreement to experiment on patients from all over the country. Also, it may be agreed that all the surgery be performed under strictly predetermined conditions.

One way of randomizing the experiment is to take the units of experimental material (patients under specific circumstances) as they come and to assign them at random to one or the other of the surgeons. As the number of operations so performed is increased, any advantage of one of the techniques should tend to become apparent. Also, any statistically significant difference in the percent of survival of patients can be more confidently ascribed to the difference between the techniques of the two surgeons (including their personal skills) rather than to other factors.

Such a randomization scheme involves considerable practical difficulty. Strict randomization of conditions requires that the patients, their relatives, and hospital personnel be kept ignorant of the identity of the operating surgeon. Such psychological factors become unusually important in the evaluation of drugs, where suggestibility on the part of the patient (*see* SUGGESTION) may influence response to treatment.

In a so-called double-blind test of the effectiveness of a drug in pill form, an equal number of similar-appearing pills is prepared containing a placebo (a neutral substance, perhaps chalk). Then all the pills are placed in random order and identified by number. The nature of each numbered pill is recorded, but the experimenting physicians and the patients are kept unaware of whether any pill contains the drug or the placebo until the completion of the experiment. Only then are the records of patient response statistically analyzed according to treatment (drug *versus* placebo). Experiments of this kind have indicated the absence of specific effects of some drugs, and also have shown distinct beneficial effects from placebo.

The general rule is that, unless a treatment is applied to randomly selected units of experimental material, observed effects cannot confidently be ascribed to the treatment.

BIBLIOGRAPHY.—W. G. Cochran and G. M. Fox, *Experimental Designs*, 2nd ed. (1957); R. A. Fisher, *The Design of Experiments*, 7th ed. (1960); J. Neyman, *First Course in Probability and Statistics* (1951); D. R. Laurence, "Patient Selection and Stratification in Therapeutic Trials," *Clinical Pharmacology and Therapeutics*, 4:381–389 (May-June 1963); E. S. Edgington, "Randomization Tests," *Journal of Psychology*, 57:445–449 (April 1964). (JE. N.)

RANELAGH, formerly a resort by the River Thames in Chelsea, London, Eng. About 1690 land lying east of the Royal Hospital, Chelsea, and bordering the river was acquired by Richard, Viscount Ranelagh, later earl of Ranelagh. He built a mansion and laid out gardens, which in 1742 were thrown open as a proprietary place of entertainment. The Rotunda was erected for concerts and the gardens became a resort of fashionable society. By the close of the 18th century Ranelagh was ceasing to attract visitors, and in 1803 the Rotunda was closed. Ranelagh House and the Rotunda were pulled down in 1805, and in 1826 the site of the gardens was bought for the Royal Hospital.

RANGE (IN AGRICULTURE) refers to extensive areas of more or less "natural" grasslands. The vegetation of ranges may include tall grass prairies, steppe, desert shrub, savanna, woodland, chaparral, tundra or forest, the only criterion being that there be enough grass in the vegetation to be profitably grazed. The true tall grass prairies such as those of the North American midwest, the Ukraine, parts of Hungary and Argentina are usually too well suited to cultivated crops to be left in range. Ranges are more generally confined to areas of marginal or submarginal farming or to areas entirely unsuited to cultivation.

Range Formation.—The naturalness of range vegetation is a matter of degree. In much of the coast and foothill ranges of California the original, largely perennial grassland has been almost completely replaced by an introduced annual Mediterranean flora. These areas are called annual range perhaps because the replacement of one vegetation by another was not intentional even though brought about by the activities of man and his livestock. Extensive areas of forest have been converted to grassland by fire or cutting or both. In other areas, selective cutting and good forest management have opened up stands of timber permitting an increase of grass for grazing purposes. Good forest management and good range management are often complementary rather than competitive. Few, if any, ranges are totally uninfluenced by man or his livestock. They are natural only in the sense that they are not artificially established by cultural means.

Fire is a natural feature of grassland vegetation, whether set by man or other agencies. The elimination of fire may be considered a disturbance which in desert shrub, savanna or woodland vegetation frequently invites the dominance of trees and shrubs to the near exclusion of the grass. Fires that tend to favour the continuance of grassland are prevented primarily by heavy grazing which removes most of the combustible material. They are also reduced in frequency by precautions against the setting of fires.

The use of fire as a management practice is common in many parts of the world, but is frequently ineffective in the control of woody vegetation because of heavy grazing. Satisfactory burns usually require deferment for a growing season to accumulate combustible material, and the value of the unused grass must be weighed against the expected value from brush control.

Management Practices.—Some of the most important range management practices are given below. (1) Proper stocking. An adequate surplus of grass must always be left at the end of the grazing season to protect the soil and to supply food reserves for the next season's growth. (2) Uniform grazing. Livestock graze more closely near water, salt, feeding areas, fence corners and other places where animals concentrate. They graze the steep parts of the range much less than the flats. Some corrective measures are: cross fencing into smaller pastures, placing salt in little used parts of the range, developing more watering and salting places, herding with greater care, etc. (3) Deferment. Ranges may be deferred early in the season to protect the grass during a period when it is using up food reserves; they may be deferred late in the season to allow the grass to recover from grazing and store food reserves; they may be deferred for an entire season for burning or to permit seed production in order to improve the vigour and density of the stand. (4) Control of undesirable plants. This may be accomplished by manipulation of livestock to either graze hard or rest at critical times or by selective herbicides, fire or mechanical treatments such as mowing, beating, root plowing, etc. (5) Encouragement of desirable plants. This is usually done by livestock manipulation or burning, but in special cases overseeding and/or fertilizing result in substantial improvements. (6) Proper seasonal use. High mountain ranges can be used only in summer, annual ranges are most productive in spring and many desert ranges are best used in winter. In order to use many ranges at the proper time, livestock must often be trailed or trucked considerable distances. (7) Pest and game control. In order to obtain maximum yields, animals that compete with livestock for forage must be controlled as well as parasites that attack livestock.

Overgrazing.—The most pernicious and chronic problem in the management of ranges is overgrazing. Too heavy use of the vegetation reduces production of forage, exposes the soil to sealing, baking and erosion, reduces the infiltration of water and the effectiveness of precipitation, increases runoff and flood hazards and induces changes in the botanical composition of the vegetation. These changes invariably involve an increase in unpalatable, woody, thorny or poisonous plants and a decrease in the more palatable and desirable species.

Overstocking and the fire control that goes with it have resulted in an alarming increase in woody vegetation in the savanna, woodland, chaparral and desert shrub areas of the world. Overstocking has practically denuded vast areas of rangeland in nearly every continent and the degeneration of range condition is one of the most serious problems in agriculture.

Stockmen and technicians alike have consistently overestimated the capacity of ranges to produce. One must become resigned to low yields per acre, and ranges can be profitably used only because the forage is cheap. As soon as elaborate management practices are required as correctives for bad management, the range forage is no longer cheap and its use often becomes unprofitable.

See also GRASSLAND.   (J. R. Hɴ.)

RANGE FINDERS, instruments used to measure distances to remote objects; they are employed in surveying, testing air vehicles, determining the lens focus setting for cameras, and for directing gun, rocket, and missile fire. Precise optical instruments were devised to improve the triangulation methods long used for the determination of range. Optical range finders are very accurate at short range, but less accurate at longer ranges and almost useless at night. Radar (*q.v.*), developed early in World War II, became important in naval and antiaircraft gunnery; large optical range finders formerly indispensable in directing such fire assumed a secondary or standby role.

Basically, an optical range finder determines range by measuring the angle at each end of a base line of known length to the target situated at the apex of the triangle so formed. Accuracy is achieved by: (1) a two-station system in which the base line is very long; (2) a single instrument that very precisely measures the difference between the angles to the target from each end of the instrument. The two-station system requires a communication network to ensure that both stations sight on the same target and that readings are taken simultaneously. Range must be calculated later. The one-station system, at the expense of accuracy, avoids these difficulties.

Two-Station System.—Two-station triangulation, a basic technique of surveying, has undergone continuous development since its earliest known use by the ancient Egyptians to reestablish property lines after the annual Nile River floods. In modern practice, precision theodolites are used for measurement of angles and readings are averaged to reduce error. By United States Coast and Geodetic Survey procedure, angles are measured 16 times in a first-order survey, four times in a second, and twice in a third-order. Distances computed from these measurements are accurate to 1

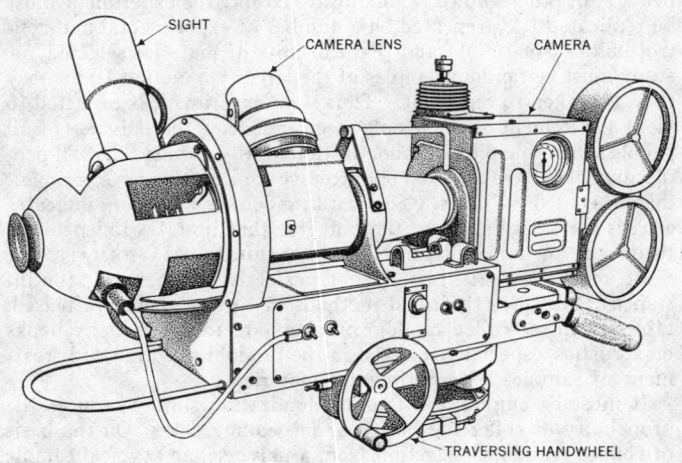

SIGHT   CAMERA LENS   CAMERA

TRAVERSING HANDWHEEL

BY COURTESY OF U.S. ARMY

FIG. 1.—PHOTOTHEODOLITE

part in 25,000 in a first-order survey, 1 in 10,000 in a second-order, and 1 in 5,000 in a third-order.

Military use of the two-station system has been limited because of the difficulty in establishing accurately measured base lines in the field and of coordinating observations on moving targets. The technique is used for locating enemy artillery weapons at night by observing their muzzle flash. Several observation posts report the bearing of the flash to a central control station where a range plot is made.

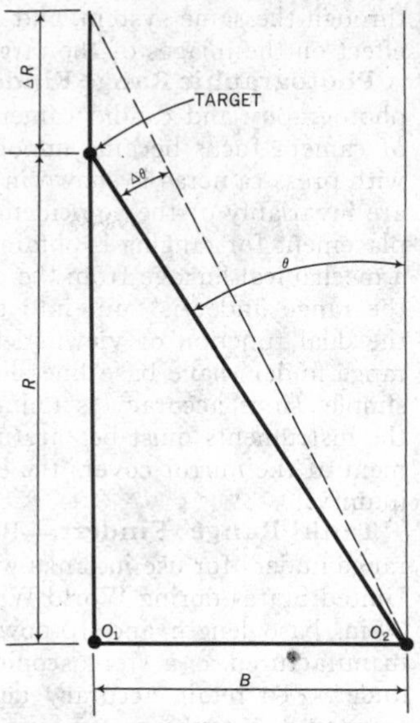

In testing the accuracy of anti-aircraft fire or observing the flight of a rocket, a system of several phototheodolites, as shown in fig. 1, is used. A phototheodolite is a camera with a long focal length lens mounted on a theodolite base. An operator tracks the target through a sighting telescope. Time co-incidence of the readings, which is required since the target is moving, is accomplished by transmitting a signal that operates all camera shutters simultaneously. The camera, usually a 35-mm. motion picture one, takes a picture of the target, of a reference reticle, and of the azimuth and elevation scales of the theodolite. Angular errors in tracking are eliminated by correcting the azimuth and elevation readings to account for the position of the target with respect to the reticle marks. By averaging measurements from a system of four or five theodolites on base lines several miles in length, it is possible to obtain range accuracies of 1 part in 10,000 at ranges up to 10,000 yds.

Coincidence and Stereoscopic Range Finders.—As early as 1770 attempts were made to couple two theodolites on a single base to circumvent the communication difficulties of the two-station system. G. F. Brander in 1781 built a range finder for one operator. A. Barr and W. Stroud developed a coincidence range finder in 1888 and C. Zeiss built a stereoscopic instrument in 1893. Before and during World War II developments in military range finders were concerned largely with refinements of these two basic designs.

Considerable controversy arose over the effectiveness of coincidence *v.* stereoscopic range finders. Operators could learn to use a coincidence type quickly, but a skilled operator could achieve greater accuracy with a stereoscopic instrument. The two appear similar except that the coincidence type has one and the stereoscopic two eyepieces. The outer case usually contains windows, prisms (the optical square that defines the base length of the instrument), and the eyepiece or eyepieces. An inner optical bar, insulated from temperature differentials and mechanical shock, contains the telescopic systems and the precision angle measuring device. The operator observes the images formed by the two objectives, adjusts the instrument to establish coincidence of the images or stereoscopic contact between the images and reference reticles. Range can then be read directly from a calibrated scale.

FIG. 2.—GEOMETRIC CONSTRUCTION FOR DETERMINING RANGE ERROR ΔR *(see* TEXT*)*

Accuracy.—The fundamental range finder equations can be derived from fig. 2. B is the base length of the range finder, O_1 is a 90° angle, and θ is the convergence angle to the target from O_2. The convergence angle is very small; and if it is expressed in radians, then the range, $R = B/\theta$. Error in range arises from the error $\Delta\theta$ in measuring the convergence angle: therefore the range error, $\Delta R = \Delta\theta R^2/B$. Note that the range error for triangulation ranging increases with the second power of the distance to the target. This is true for both the two-station system and for coincidence or stereoscopic range finders.

Range finder performance is often expressed in terms of a Unit of Error, or UOE, based on an arbitrary value of 12 sec. of arc (0.00006 radians) for the acuity of the eye. Magnifications of 8 to 24 power are common; therefore, convergence angle can, theoretically, be measured to an accuracy of 0.5 to 1.5 sec. of arc ($\Delta\theta = $ UOE$/M$). Expressing range in thousands of yards and base length in yards, then the range error in yards that is the equivalent of one UOE angular accuracy is $\Delta R = 60R^2/BM$. Under field conditions errors always exceed the one UOE level because of the irregular shape of targets, atmospheric haze or shimmer, and temperature instability or improper adjustment of the instrument. Errors four times those indicated by the one UOE formula occur even with high quality range finders.

Construction.—The base line is defined by the optical elements at each end of the range finder, which change the path of the incoming light by 90°. Pentaprisms or reflectors, P as shown in fig. 3, are used for this purpose since they have the property of

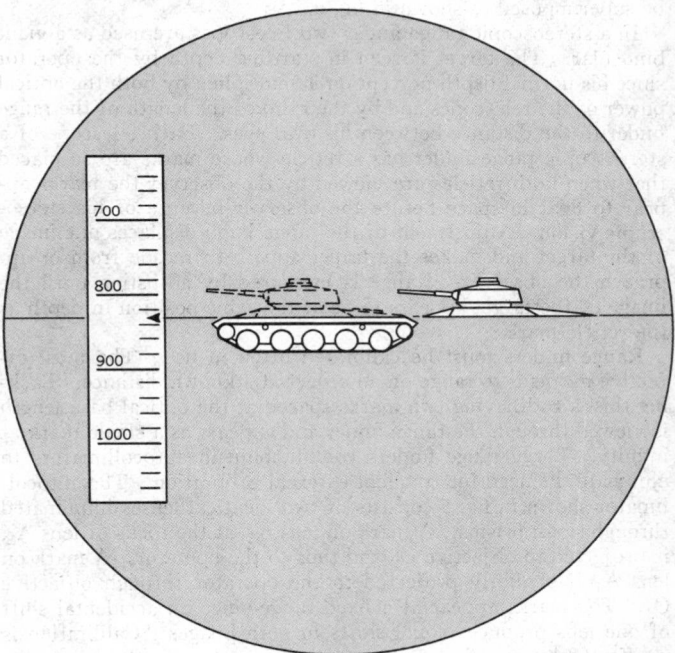

FIG. 4.—FIELD OF COINCIDENCE RANGE FINDER

changing the light path by 90° regardless of the angle of incidence of the light.

In order to effect coincidence or establish stereoscopic contact, it is necessary to displace the image formed through one arm of the range finder. Various devices are used for precise measurement of this displacement. In fig. 3 a low-power prism placed in the converging light from lens O_2 is moved toward the lens, *i.e.*, from D_1 to D, to increase displacement of the image. A calibrated scale coupled to the prism indicates range when the image has been displaced enough to make it coincide with the image from the other arm of the range finder. Another deviation device, the diasporameter, consists of two low-power prisms. When the bases are vertical and opposed their deviations cancel. If the prisms are rotated in opposite directions about the optical axis, the vertical deviations still cancel, but a horizontal displacement is introduced. The sliding lens compensator, D in fig. 5, consists of two lenses of equal power, one convex and the other concave. When both lenses are

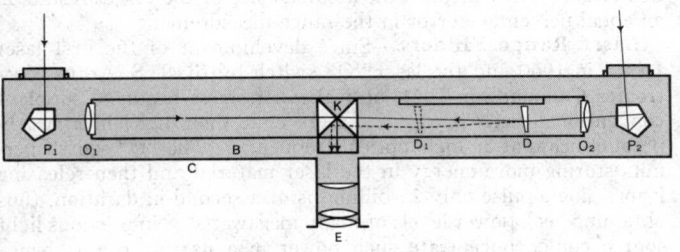

FIG. 3.—COINCIDENCE RANGE FINDER

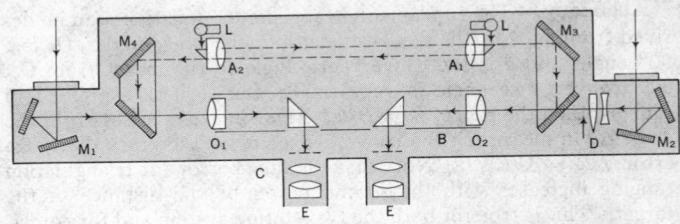

FIG. 5.—STEREOSCOPIC RANGE FINDER WITH AUTOCOLLIMATOR

centred on the optical axis, no deviation occurs. As one lens is moved, a deviation of the image will occur since the off-axis section of the lens now in use will bend the light rays toward the displaced axis of the lens. Again a calibrated range scale is driven by the same mechanism that moves the lens.

The presentation in a coincidence range finder is achieved by combining the images from the two objectives and viewing them through a single eyepiece. Simple range finders use a half-silvered mirror to combine the images. Precision instruments use complex prism clusters to minimize light losses, obtain various presentations, and permit reading the range scale through the eyepiece. As shown in fig. 4, the target may be presented as a split image with the field divided in the centre. Adjustment of the range knob shifts one image with respect to the other until coincidence is obtained as shown by the dotted lines. Other presentations are used, such as a split image with one field inverted or two full images to be superimposed as shown in fig. 6.

In a stereoscopic range finder two telescopes are used as a giant binocular. The target is seen in startling depth by the operator since his normal depth perception is multiplied by both the optical power of the telescopes and by the ratio of the length of the range finder to the distance between his own eyes. Each telescope of a stereoscopic range finder has a reticle whose marks are so placed that when both reticles are viewed by the observer the marks appear to float in space before the observer because of his stereoscopic vision. Adjustment of the range knob displaces one image of the target and makes the target appear to recede from or approach the observer. Range is measured by adjusting until the image of the target appears to be at the same position in depth as the reticle mark.

Range finders must be calibrated often in use. The most effective means is to range on an object at a known distance. Lacking this, a rod having two marks spaced at the optical base length is viewed through the range finder and appears as a single mark at infinity. Large range finders contain built-in autocollimators to eliminate the need for frequent external calibration. The autocollimator shown in fig. 5 consists of two identical lenses illuminated through small prisms. A mark on lens A_2, at the focus of lens A_1, is projected to objective O_2 and thus to the operator. A mark on lens A_1 is similarly projected to the operator through objective O_1. The marks appear at a fixed range since an accidental shift of one lens produces equal shifts in both images. Calibration is unaffected by misalignment of optical elements in the telescopes because the light rays from the target and the reference marks pass

through the same system, and any shifting of the parts has equal effect on the images of the target and mark.

Photographic Range Finder.—With the development of press photography and candid cameras, rapid and accurate adjustment of camera focus became important. A range finder widely used with press cameras is shown in fig. 6. Photographic range finders are invariably of the coincidence type, and usually the image displacement for ranging is obtained by rotation of a mirror through a mechanical linkage from the camera lens focus motion. Usually the range finder is built into the camera body and often serves the dual function of viewfinder and range finder. Most camera range finders have base lines less than 4 in. in length. Design is simple, since accuracy is unimportant beyond about 30 ft., but the instruments must be carefully made since less than 3° movement of the mirror covers the entire operating range from 4 ft. to infinity.

Tank Range Finders.—Both stereoscopic and coincidence range finders for use in tanks were developed in Germany and the United States during World War II. One U.S. instrument with a 79-in. base length and 10-power magnification (*see* fig. 7) was manufactured as a stereoscopic and later as a coincidence range finder. To retain accuracy despite the shock and vibration encountered in tank use, an autocollimator system as shown in fig. 5 is used. This range finder is accurate to 40 yd. at 2,000 yd.,

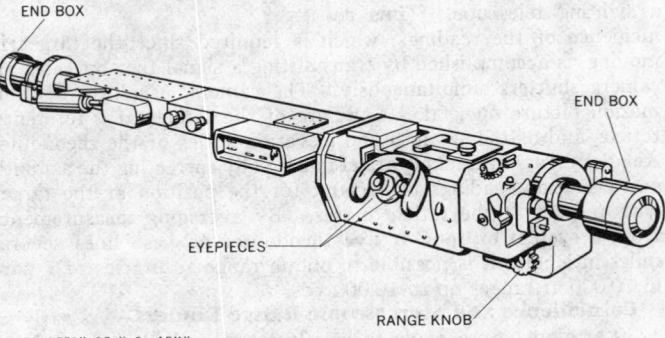

FIG. 7.—STEREOSCOPIC TANK RANGE FINDER

equivalent to a vertical error on the target of only 15 in. for typical tank ammunition.

A ballistic computer is used with the range finder to reduce the time to fire and to utilize the accuracy of the range finder effectively. The range setting is converted by the computer into ballistic superelevation, that is, the angle at which the gun must be aimed above the target to compensate for the effect of gravity on the shell. The range finder, computer, and sighting periscope are connected by electronic servos so that the gun is properly aimed and ready to fire as soon as ranging is completed.

Stadiometric Ranging.—Distance can be determined from the angle subtended at the observer's position by an object of known size. In surveying, if high precision is not required, a stadia rod marked with known spacings is observed through a theodolite. Tables give the range based on the length of rod visible between standard marks on the theodolite reticle. Some military telescopes have reticles graduated so that the image of a man, or a vehicle of known size, superimposed on the reticle indicates range by the size of the image. Military use of the stadia principle is very limited since accuracy is poor, particularly on small or partially hidden targets. Any error in the assumed size of the target results in an equal percentage error in the range measurement.

Laser Range Finders.—Since development of the first laser (*q.v.*) in 1960 and the laser "Q" switch by the U.S. Army Electronics Command in 1961, optical radars have begun to supplant conventional range finders. Lasers emit their light in a nearly parallel beam at a single optical frequency. The "Q" switch permits storing more energy in the laser material and then releasing it in a single pulse only 25-billionths of a second in duration, thus obtaining peak power levels of many megawatts. No previous light source could concentrate such power in a narrow beam; hence earlier optical radars were not effective at long range. Fine resolu-

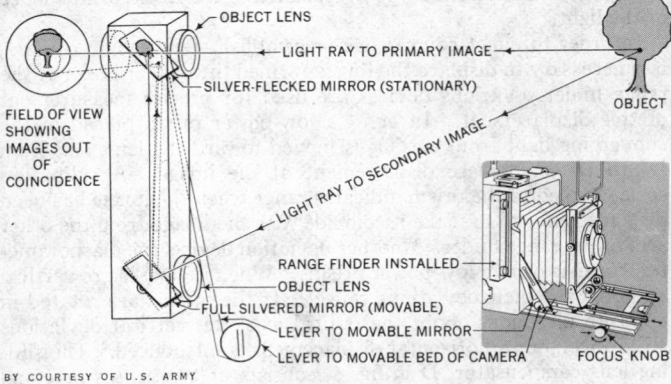

FIG. 6.—PHOTOGRAPHIC RANGE FINDER COUPLED TO CAMERA

tion, available at optical but not at conventional radar frequencies, permits restricting the optical radar's field of view to a single target. This problem had prevented the use of conventional radars on ground targets since echoes were received from many objects other than the intended target.

Laser range finders are small and light in weight. They are accurate to 5 yd. at operating ranges of 10,000 yd. or more. The first such range finder (see fig. 8) was developed for use by an artillery forward observer and weighs 30 lb. including tripod and battery. Other models were built for use in tanks and aircraft. Aircraft use requires repetitive ranging, in order to compute the rate of change of range due to aircraft motion, for accurate firing. Ranging five times per second is possible, but large amounts of power are required to operate and to cool the laser. Size and power requirements were being reduced in the late 1960s as more efficient laser materials replaced ruby.

Lasers, and therefore laser range finders, pose an unusual safety problem. If the high energy beam entered the eye, it would be focused on the retina and the resulting energy density would be sufficient to damage the retinal tissue. The problem persists at long ranges; since the beam is so well collimated, the energy density of the beam does not decrease rapidly with range. Direct exposure in the beam from the little range finder shown in fig. 8 is not considered safe at less than 12,000 yd. on a clear day. Fortunately it is easy for the operator to aim the narrow beam accurately and thus avoid exposing personnel in the target area.

Operating Principle.—The laser range finder is prepared for operation by charging the capacitor used to drive the flash lamp. Temperature-sensing circuits adjust the voltage to that required to operate the laser at the ambient temperature (1,600 v. at room temperature). The range finder is then aimed at the target by the operator using a reticle in the receiver telescope (see fig. 9). Image erecting prisms have been eliminated to simplify the drawing. When the "Range" button is pressed the "Q" switch prism is rotated by a small motor up to 24,000 revolutions per minute, reaching this speed in a fraction of a second, and the trigger cir-

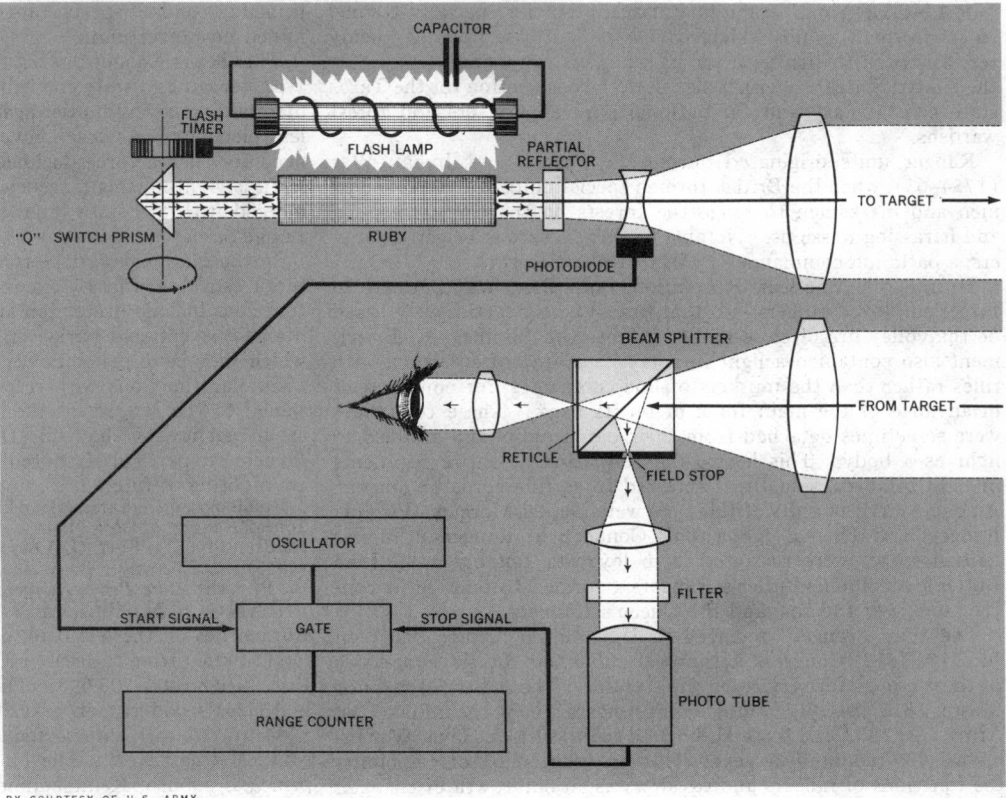

FIG. 9.—SCHEMATIC ARRANGEMENT OF LASER RANGE FINDER

cuit then discharges the storage capacitor through the flash lamp. The flash is timed to occur just before the prism becomes parallel with the partial reflector at the other end of the ruby. Light absorbed by the ruby raises its chromium atoms to a high energy state. When the prism becomes parallel with the reflector, light from the energized ruby can reflect back and forth between the two and the light is amplified by each pass through the ruby. The pulse of laser light leaving the partial reflector is collimated to a 1/20th degree beam by the telescope. A photodiode detects the outgoing beam and its signal opens an electronic gate so that the range counter may begin to count pulses from the oscillator. If a 32.81-megacycle oscillator is used each cycle represents 5 yd.: the distance (to and from the target) light travels in 1/32,810,000th of a second.

When the laser beam hits the target, light is scattered in all directions and a tiny portion returns to the receiver telescope. A beam splitter in the telescope reflects this red light toward the photomultiplier tube, but only light from the target can pass through the 1/25th degree field stop. The field stop, sighting reticle, and beam splitter are cemented as a unit to ensure permanent alignment. A 25 Å bandwidth filter blocks all light except the laser frequency from reaching the tube, thus making daylight operation feasible. The signal from the photomultiplier tube closes the gate between the oscillator and range counter. The number of oscillator cycles counted while light traveled to the target and return is displayed as the range to the target.

The accuracy of a laser range finder, like that of a conventional radar, is nearly the same at all ranges. The speed of light travelling to the target and return is constant; therefore, range accuracy is only dependent upon the accuracy in measuring the time interval. Since the laser pulse is very short, the beginning and end of the interval are well defined. The higher the oscillator frequency the better the accuracy of the range finder.

BIBLIOGRAPHY.—Donald H. Jacobs, *Fundamentals of Optical Engineering* (1943); A. Kraszna-Krausz (ed.), *The Focal Encyclopedia of Photography* (1965); John M. Carroll, *The Story of the Laser* (1964); Kurt R. Stelling, *Lasers and Their Applications* (1966).

(W. T. Al.)

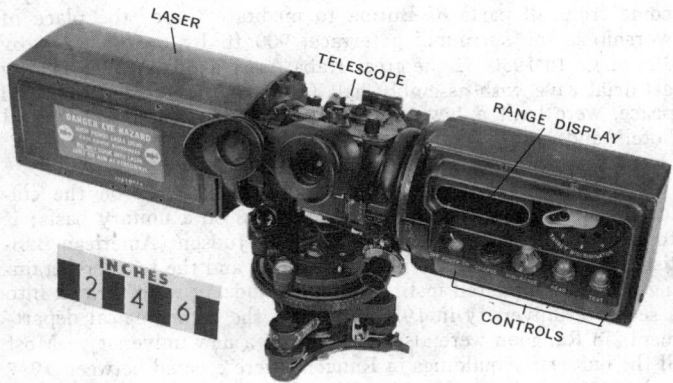

FIG. 8.—ARTILLERY LASER RANGE FINDER

RANGER, in U.S. military usage, a soldier specially trained to act in small groups which make rapid surprise raids on enemy territory; the British term for such units is commando (*q.v.*). In the United States ranger has also been the designation for the Texas state constabulary and for national park supervisors and forest wardens.

Ranger units originated during the French and Indian War (1754–63), when the British formed special units of expert woodsmen and marksmen to range the forests on scouting, screening, and harassing missions. Notable among these was Rogers' Rangers, a battalion commanded by Maj. Robert Rogers.

During the American Revolution, both British and American forces employed rangers. At that time infantry tactics were based on the volley fire of close-ranked infantry of the line. Each regiment also contained a light infantry company, often armed with rifles rather than the muskets of line companies, for employment in advance of the main force or on its flank. These companies were sometimes detached from their parent units and grouped to fight as a body. This led to the formation of entire regiments of light infantry, sometimes referred to as rifle corps or rangers. Among American units of this type were Daniel Morgan's Virginia Rangers and Thomas Knowlton's Connecticut Rangers. Similar British forces were recruited from loyalists, notably Maj. John Butler's battalion (Butler's Rangers), formed to operate in conjunction with Indians, and the Queen's Rangers.

The term "ranger" recurred in U.S. military usage when on Jan. 12, 1812, Congress authorized enlistment of six companies of these troops for service on the frontier. The *Army Register* of May 1, 1813, listed 12 companies of rangers among the units of the Army. In 1832, the force authorized for the Black Hawk War included 600 mounted rangers. This first suggestion of combining the functions of rangers and cavalry was an outgrowth of changed tactical needs; the tide of settlement having moved beyond the eastern forests, military operations were now in more open terrain, where mounted forces had superior mobility.

The concept of ranger-cavalry was reinforced by the experience of the Republic of Texas, which recruited mounted ranger companies to protect its outlying areas against Indians and Mexicans. During the Mexican War companies of Texas Rangers were formed into regiments and mustered into federal service. They operated both as conventional cavalry and as rangers, on scouting, patrolling, and raiding duty. Their detached duty, independent attitude, and distinctive appearance probably provided an initial basis for the association of the term "ranger" with irregular, paramilitary forces.

During the Civil War, both Union and Confederate organizations adopted "ranger" as part of their unit designations without reference to their actual military character and employment. However, true ranger units played a significant part in Confederate operations. Partly because of the type of service it performed and partly, no doubt, because of its state origin, the 8th Texas Cavalry was known as Terry's Texas Rangers. The concept of rangers as irregular forces was given impetus when the Confederate Congress passed the Partisan Ranger Act in 1862. Partisan rangers were entitled to reimbursement for equipment that they captured—an attempt to apply the law of maritime prize to land warfare. The best-known leader and foremost exponent of ranger operations in the Civil War was a Confederate, Col. John S. Mosby (*q.v.*).

Ranger units reappeared in U.S. military organization in World War II, when six ranger battalions were formed, five serving in the European-African-Middle Eastern theatre and one in the Pacific theatre. Composed of specially trained and conditioned men, these units made sudden, hard-hitting raids behind enemy lines, carrying out demolition and intelligence missions. The lessons of this experience led to the formation in 1950 of the air-borne ranger infantry company as an integral part of each U.S. infantry division. Six such companies were eventually employed in the Korean War. In 1951, however, it was decided that concentration of these trained men in special units was less desirable than spreading them through conventional units, where a larger number of soldiers would have the benefit of learning the combat techniques in which the rangers were especially skilled. Thereafter the U.S. Army continued to conduct special ranger-training for individuals but maintained no ranger units.

The Texas Rangers, after their federal service in the Mexican War, served as a state constabulary organized along military lines, maintaining law and order against Indians, bandits, and other lawless elements. As local government became more effective the need for such a force declined. In 1901 it was reorganized as a state law-enforcement agency. In 1935 the Texas Rangers were merged with the state highway patrol under the Department of Public Safety.

In the National Park Service, the U.S. Department of the Interior established in 1916 a force of national park rangers, whose functions include protection and conservation of forests and wildlife in the national parks, enforcement of park regulations (for which they have police power), and assistance to visitors.

Similar functions with respect to the national forests were assigned to the rangers of the Forest Service, established in 1905 as an agency of the U.S. Department of Agriculture. Forest rangers are particularly noted for their activities in the prevention and fighting of forest fires.

BIBLIOGRAPHY.—James J. Altieri, *Darby's Rangers* (1945); V. C. Jones, *Ranger Mosby* (1944); V. C. Jones, *Gray Ghosts and Rebel Raiders* (1956); Burt G. Loescher, *The History of Rogers' Rangers* (1946); U.S. Army, *Army Lineage Book*, vol. ii, *Infantry* (1953); W. P. Webb, *The Texas Rangers* (1935).   (J. B. B. T.)

RANGOON (Burmese YANGON), the capital of the Union of Burma, lies on the left bank of the Rangoon or Hlaing River, 21 mi. (34 km.) from the sea. Municipal area 77 sq.mi. (199 sq.km.). Pop. (1962 est.) 800,993. The central part of the city (planned in 1852) is laid out on a system of blocks, each 800 by 860 ft. (244 by 262 m.), intersected regularly by streets running north-south and east-west. The block system was applied also to the principal suburb, Kemmendine, on the west, but other suburban areas developed to the north mainly after 1918 have a less rigid layout. Of the many fine public buildings notable are the port commission offices, the customs house, the Mayo Marine Club, and the modern law courts. Other buildings include the general hospital, the Anglican and Roman Catholic cathedrals, and the city hall on Sule Pagoda Road, which leads northward through the town centre and contains the charming Sule Pagoda. Nearby is Independence Memorial. The many places of worship include Buddhist pagodas and monasteries, and mosques, temples, and churches for Muslims, Hindus, Parsees, and Christian denominations. The Royal Lakes (Kandawgyi; water area 160 ac. [65 ha.]) to the northeast are surrounded by a wooded park, and nearby are the spacious zoological and botanical gardens.

The most notable institution in Rangoon is the Shwe Dagon Pagoda, a great golden stupa which dominates the city from the north and forms the focus of Burmese religious life. Rising to a height of 368 ft. (112 m.) it stands on an eminence 168 ft. (51 m.) above the level of the city. It is built of brick, in the form of a cone raised over a relic chamber which by tradition contains eight of the Buddha's hairs. The building is covered with pure gold from base to summit, and once in every generation the gold is renewed by public subscription. The Shwe Dagon Pagoda is a place of pilgrimage at the great Buddhist festivals, when people come from all parts of Burma to meditate there; the place of worship is the surrounding terrace, 900 ft. by 685 ft. (274 by 209 m.). In 1950–52 the great Kaba Aye Pagoda and the nearby artificial cave with assembly hall (1953–54), dedicated to world peace, were built a few miles farther north. There are several hotels and clubs. At Mingaladon, about 11 mi. (18 km.) N, is one of the finest 18-hole golf courses in Asia.

The University of Rangoon, constituted in 1920 on the collegiate principle, was reconstituted in 1948 on a unitary basis; it formerly included the University College, Judson (American Baptist Mission) College, the medical college, and the teachers' training college. Affiliated institutions in Mandalay were formed into a separate university in 1958. In 1963 the technological departments in Rangoon were also formed into a new university. Most of the university buildings in Rangoon were erected between 1927 and 1930 on a site overlooking Victoria Lake, 5 mi. (8 km.) N of the town, but extensive additions, mainly in the technological

JULES BUCHER—PHOTO RESEARCHERS, INC.

DEVOUT BURMESE CITIZENS PERFORM AN ACT OF MERIT BY SWEEPING THE TILE FLOORS OF SHWE DAGON PAGODA, THE NATION'S MOST IMPORTANT BUDDHIST SHRINE

branches, were erected in the 1950s, also on the north side of the city.

Rangoon contains the principal business houses and banks of Burma, and is also an industrial centre. Rice milling (at Dala to the south), oil refining (at Syriam to the east), and teak working, which form the staple industries, are carried on outside the town proper; but after World War II, and mainly from 1958, there was a considerable expansion of light industry, with more than 500 factories, mostly small. The chief exports are rice, bran, timber, oil cakes, pulses, lead, zinc ore, cotton, oilseed, and tobacco.

Rangoon is the principal seaport of Burma, handling more than 80% of the total trade and about 1,000 vessels annually. Its busiest season is from late December to mid-May, when rice is exported. The city is also the centre of rail and river communications for the whole of Burma. Internal transport is effected principally by bus, the former electric streetcar line not having been revived after the Japanese occupation in World War II. The international airport is at Mingaladon.

History.—Though the Shwe Dagon Pagoda is a shrine of great antiquity and has been a place of pilgrimage for many centuries, Rangoon as a town is modern. The place was of no commercial or other secular importance until in 1755 King Alaungpaya (the founder of the last dynasty of Burmese kings) conquered it and developed it as a port and commercial centre to replace the old port of Syriam which had been a focus of resistance to his authority. He gave it the name of Yan Kon ("the end of strife"), usually transliterated into English as Rangoon. Alaungpaya laid out the town along the river bank, but it occupied only a fraction of its present area. In 1824 Rangoon was taken by the British on the outbreak of the First Anglo-Burmese War, but was restored in 1826. It was captured a second time in 1852 and with the rest of the province of Pegu was placed under the East India Company. After 1852 the modern street plan was adopted. Most of the area lay below high-tide level and much effort was devoted to raising the land so as to prevent the usual flooding. In 1892 the sewage system was introduced and Rangoon developed a good drainage system. The water supply, drawn at first from the Victoria Lake, was later drawn from a large reservoir lake at Hlawga, 17 mi.

(27 km.) N, and from the Pegu Yoma water project completed in 1941.

As the town developed, it became largely an Indian city. Most of the labour in the port and the town was immigrant Indian labour, though much of the skilled labour, especially in building trades, was Chinese; the trading and clerical communities were also mainly Indian. Rangoon was thus by no means a typical Burmese city; in 1931 out of a population of 400,415, there were only 121,998 Burmese, the rest being Hindus, Muslims, Chinese, Europeans, and Anglo-Burmans. As a result of the Japanese invasion of Burma in 1941–42 the Indian and European population was much reduced, and the independence of Burma in 1948 caused a second exodus of many who had returned after the war. Rangoon thus became much more a Burmese city. The disturbed condition of the country after 1948 led to an influx of refugees from villages: by 1958 it was estimated that of the total population, 600,000 were Burmese, and of these one-third were refugees living in insanitary temporary quarters which they had erected along the road sides. In December 1958 the city was brought under military administration and energetic measures were taken to remove the squatters to the newly built satellite settlements of Okkalapa and Thabeta on the eastern margins of the city.

(B. R. P.)

RANGPUR, a municipal town and district in the Rajshahi division of East Pakistan. The town, headquarters of the district, lies on the Little Ghaghat River 100 mi. NW of Mymensingh. Pop. (1961) 40,634. It is a long, straggling town, with a railway station at one end and the public offices three miles (five kilometres) away at the other. Roads radiate in all directions. The town has a college affiliated with Rajshahi University, technical, agricultural, and primary teacher-training institutes, two public parks, and two main libraries. Besides the industries of weaving and *bidi* (local cigarette) and cigar making, the town is noted for the manufacture of durries (cotton carpets).

RANGPUR DISTRICT, with an area of 3,704 sq.mi. (9,593 sq.km.) and a population (1961) of 3,796,043, is one vast plain. The greater part, particularly toward the east, is inundated during the rains, and the remainder traversed by a network of streams. The river system is constituted by the Brahmaputra and its tributaries, chief of which are the Tista, Dharla, Sankosh, and Dudhkumar. About three-fourths of the district is under continuous cultivation. Staple crops are rice, oilseeds, jute, and tobacco, and chief occupations fishing, paddy husking, and the making of baskets and fishing nets. The district is well served by the Pakistan Eastern Railway. Saidpur, 22 mi. (35 km.) W of Rangpur town, has railway workshops. (K. S. Ad.)

RANJIT SINGH, MAHARAJA (1780–1839), Indian ruler and leader of the Sikhs, known as the "lion of the Punjab," was born at Budrukhan on Nov. 13, 1780, or, according to another version, at Gujranwala on Nov. 2, 1780; he was the son of Sirdar Maha Singh, whom he succeeded in 1792 as head of the Sukarchakia branch (*misl*) of the Sikh confederacy. By birth the head of one of several competing Sikh groups, he rose to primacy through his own genius, and was one of the ablest Indians of the century.

In 1799 Ranjit Singh took possession of Lahore. In 1801 he defeated the most powerful Sikh *misl*, the Bhangis, and in 1802 seized Amritsar, the second of the twin Sikh capitals. He was then indisputably the leading Sikh chief and set out to enlarge his dominions. On Jan. 1, 1806, he agreed to exclude Holkar (*q.v.*) from his territory, and in that year he took Ludhiana; but this brought him into conflict with the British, who claimed the land up to the Sutlej. The matter was settled by Charles Metcalfe's mission (1808) which led to the Treaty of Amritsar (April 25, 1809). Ranjit decided not to cross swords with the British and to expand instead to the north and west. From this time dates the formation of the famous Western-trained Sikh army, with its formidable artillery and numerous expatriate European officers. In 1818–19 he took Multan and Kashmir. By 1820 he had consolidated his power in the whole Punjab between the Sutlej and the Indus. He added Ladakh and Peshawar to his kingdom in 1834 and repulsed an Afghan counterattack on Peshawar in 1837. In 1838 he agreed to the tripartite treaty with Lord Auckland and

Shah Shuja for the restoration of the latter to the Afghan throne.

Ranjit Singh freely employed Hindus and Muslims as well as Europeans, but always on a basis of Sikh supremacy. Little was done to promote irrigation or trade, the revenues being consumed by the needs of the army. He died at Lahore, on June 27, 1839, and in little more than six years the state collapsed through the internecine strife of rival chiefs.

See Khushwant Singh, *Ranjit Singh* (1962); J. D. Cunningham, *A History of the Sikhs* (1849; rev. ed. 1919).   (T. G. P. S.)

RANJITSINHJI, KUMAR SHRI (1872–1933), maharaja of Nawanagar, who first made his name as a great cricketer and then as an enlightened ruler. Of ancient Rajput stock, he was born on Sept. 10, 1872, in Sarodar, Kathiawar, in India, and completed his education at Trinity College, Cambridge. He played cricket for Sussex, which county he captained during 1899–1903; he played for England v. Australia 15 times, scoring 985 runs. In 1899 he amassed over 3,000 runs in one season. Wherever and whenever he batted, he evoked an atmosphere of magic by the effortless grace and speed with which he scored his runs.

He succeeded as maharaja in 1906 and became a progressive ruler and statesman. After serving in France in World War I, he represented the Indian states at the League of Nations assembly in 1920 and in 1930 attended the first Round Table Conference to consider the constitution of India. He died at Jamnagar, Nawanagar, on April 2, 1933.   (N. Cs.)

RANK, OTTO (1884–1939), Austrian psychologist, was one of the earliest and most influential adherents of the psychoanalytic school. He was born in Vienna on April 22, 1884, and took his doctorate in *Germanistik* at the University of Vienna in 1912. While most of Freud's other disciples devoted themselves primarily to clinical applications, Rank applied his principles to the study of mythology, literature, and art. His first important work was *Der Künstler* (1907; later expanded and rewritten under the title of *Art and Artist*, Eng. trans. by C. F. Atkinson, 1932); it invoked the Freudian theory of dream mechanisms to explain the mental processes of the artist. His two best-known publications, *Der Mythus von der Geburt des Helden* (1909; Eng. trans., *The Myth of the Birth of the Hero*, 1952) and *Das Inzest-Motiv in Dichtung und Sage* ("The Incest-Motive in Poetry and Legend," 1912), attempted to show how the so-called Oedipus complex supplied an abundance of themes and motives for poetry and myth.

Rank was editor of *Imago* and *Internationale Zeitschrift für Psychoanalyse,* the first European journals on psychoanalysis, from 1912 to 1924; in 1919 he founded the Internationale Psychoanalytische Verlag, of which he was director until 1924. Freud endorsed and freely quoted Rank's earlier contributions, but violently opposed the more original theories developed in Rank's last important book, *Das Trauma der Geburt* (1924; Eng. trans., *The Trauma of Birth,* 1953). Consequently they parted company. After leaving Vienna in 1924 Rank divided most of his time between Paris and the United States, being engaged chiefly in teaching and in psychotherapeutic work. In 1936 he finally settled in New York City. There he sought to modify the Freudian theory, which had developed under the social conditions formerly prevailing in Vienna, and to adapt it to the contemporary needs of an industrial society, like that in the United States. He died on Oct. 31, 1939, five weeks after Freud.

See J. Jones, "Otto Rank: a Forgotten Heresy," *Commentary,* 30: 219–229 (September 1960).   (Cy. B.)

RANKE, LEOPOLD VON (1795–1886), the leading German historian of the 19th century, whose scholarly method and way of teaching (he was the first to establish a historical seminar) had a great influence in England and the United States, was born into a family of Lutheran pastors and lawyers on Dec. 21, 1795, in Wiehe, Thuringia, in the kingdom of Saxony. At Schulpforta (see PFORTE) and Leipzig University he studied classics and theology and learned to use medieval sources. From 1818, when he became a teacher in Frankfurt an der Oder, to the end of his life, he worked in the service of Prussia, in 1825 being appointed assistant professor and in 1834 professor in Berlin. He was ennobled in 1865, and died on May 23, 1886, in Berlin.

Ranke combined pietistic Lutheranism with Johann Fichte's idealism and a philosophy of humanity inherited from Johann Herder and Goethe; he united the 18th-century concept of universal history with the Romantic doctrine of individualism and organic development. His characteristic quality appears in his declaration of war on the moralizing and utilitarian history of the Enlightenment: he tries to discover how things really were but fits his empirical analyses into a personal view of the universe. The western community of Latin and Germanic peoples, the link between Christian and humanist cultural values, and the hidden rule of world history by the Christian God are basic concepts in his historical way of thinking. Thus his first work, the *Geschichten der romanischen und germanischen Völker, 1494–1535* (1824; English translation, *History of the Latin and Teutonic Nations,* 1887), which opened the door to 50 years' teaching at the University of Berlin, became his "program"; the two shorter studies *Die grossen Mächte* and *Das politische Gespräch* (1833 and 1836 respectively) contain the historical and philosophical creed which he expanded in his later great works. Objective research and personal belief in a realm of ideas standing, in the Platonic sense, behind the world of appearances, gave him his grasp of the historical interplay of the general and particular.

His philosophy of history is not systematic but seems full of paradoxes; he wanted, on the one hand, to exclude himself, yet felt himself, as a priest in the service of truth, to be endowed with full personal responsibility; he worked critically and yet judged intuitively; he rejected metahistorical speculation (as in Hegel, *e.g.*) but his writings are saturated in religious values. His urge toward harmonization was so great that with all his knowledge of political history he concealed the abysses of political power and aggression. The state became for him an ethical concept, a partner morally equal to the church, only conceivable in its particular historical and national character. He thus introduced a deviation from the generalized thinking common to Western Europe based on natural law, a deviation which was long influential in Germany, being still more emphasized by the founding of the empire under Bismarck. It is true that his preference for diplomatic history allowed him to lay bare the national components of the European state system; the particular character of internal political and cultural events, as well as religious factors, were also taken into consideration. But the social and economic aspects of historical life receded into the background and even political passions only appeared in a muted form.

He was excellent at character studies, particularly in the early work *Die römischen Päpste, ihre Kirche und ihr Staat* (1834–36; Eng. trans. 1840)—a book which received its counterpart in *Deutsche Geschichte im Zeitalter der Reformation* (1839–47); but he wanted biography to be understood as a part only of the wider struggle of ideas and forces, and personalities only as the vehicles of powers beyond the individual. He found the centre of gravity of modern European times in the changing relationship of church and state and finally in the concert of the great powers. His national histories (*Neun Bücher preussischer Geschichte,* 1847–48, Eng. trans. 1849; *Französische Geschichte,* 1852–61; *Englische Geschichte,* 1859–68) concentrate on the 16th and 17th centuries and the development of the modern state; and they describe the development of national feeling as a problem of European history (whose Slav components he incidentally neglected). His leitmotivs are the system of states and the concept of the European balance of power, which prevented the hegemony of any individual nation. He had identified himself too completely with the

BY COURTESY OF ARCHIV FÜR KUNST UND GESCHICHTE, BERLIN

LEOPOLD VON RANKE, PORTRAIT BY JULIUS SCHRADER

middle class and aristocratic order of society which belonged to the Prussia of his day, and was too friendly toward the ideas of Frederick William IV, to be as just toward the forces of revolution as toward those of restoration. As a mainly contemplative scholar he also lacked the political drive toward action—which was one reason for the failure of the *Historisch-Politische Zeitschrift,* which on behalf of the government he edited for a few years (1832–36).

In later life he turned once more to the dream of his youth—to write a universal history. It remained a fragment (*Weltgeschichte,* 1881–88), hardly going beyond the emperor Henry IV (the history was posthumously brought up to the end of the 15th century on the basis of Ranke's notes), and displaying a viewpoint which the events of his time had already made antiquated. As Ranke was prevented by his predilection for the *ancien régime* from including the history of the British Empire, the United States, or Russian expansion in his writing, or even from dealing with the growth of modern industrial society (which had, after all, already begun in England), his picture of world history was confined to the Mediterranean and the continent of Europe. The result was to narrow the outlook of generations of German historians. Nonetheless, his influence extended far beyond the frontiers of Germany, and he is to be accounted one of the creators of modern historical method. Even his first work on the Latin and Germanic peoples contained a "criticism of modern historians" (*i.e.,* of the Renaissance); he then revealed as the most valuable source of his historical insight the reports of 16th- and 17th-century Venetian ambassadors. Ranke devoted himself to this diplomatic school and became an expert archivist, helped by journeys to Vienna and Italy, which were arranged by the Prussian government (1827–31). He also profited at this period by meeting politicians like Friedrich Gentz, Metternich's publicist, gaining insight into contemporary foreign policy, particularly with regard to the Eastern Question. But his concern with the southeastern European states under Turkish rule—a concern whose fruit was his *Geschichte der Revolution in Serbien* (1829; Eng. trans., *A History of Servia,* 1847)—was only an episode: he turned to the documentary study of the 16th and 17th centuries and to the rise of the great powers. Only occasionally (in essays for the *Historisch-Politische Zeitschrift,* in a few lectures, in a biographical article on Frederick William IV, and in his *Aus dem Briefwechsel Friedrich Wilhelms IV mit Bunsen,* 1873) did he return to contemporary politics. When he did it was especially with a view to warning against dogmatic liberalism. His *Neun Bücher preussischer Geschichte* (1847–48; Eng. trans., *Memoirs of the House of Brandenburg,* 1849), later expanded to 12 books (1878), is a justification of the historical role of Prussia.

He was not a brilliant lecturer but his seminars were a pattern of methodical analysis of sources and the empirical formation of judgments. He was constantly attacked by other historians for his political quietism. As an organizer, he performed an immense service in the foundation of the *Historische Kommission bei der Bayrischen Akademie der Wissenschaften,* which King Maximilian II undertook in 1858 at his instance. He presided over the commission's editions of documents, charters, chronicles, and letters as well as over such works as the *Allgemeine Deutsche Biographie* and the *Geschichte der Wissenschaften in Deutschland.* His most valuable legacy, however, was probably the conquest of historical relativism through his religious reverence and his highly personal blending of knowledge and belief. For Acton he was "almost the Columbus of modern history." *See also* HISTORY: *Historiography.*

BIBLIOGRAPHY.—For the best bibliographical approach, with list of English translations, *see* Theodore H. von Laue, *Leopold Ranke, The Formative Years* (1950). *Editions: Sämmtliche Werke,* 54 vol. (1867–90). The edition undertaken by Paul Joachimsen for the Deutsche Akademie (critical edition of the *Reformationsgeschichte* and the *Preussischer Geschichte*) remains a fragment (1925 ff.). The *Weltgeschichte* was published separately, in 9 parts (1881–88). *See also Leopold von Ranke, Das Briefwerk,* ed. by W. P. Fuchs (1949); *Leopold von Ranke. Neue Briefe,* collected by B. Hoeft and H. Herzfeld (1949). For recent opinion *see* Rudolf Vierhaus, *Ranke und die soziale Welt* (1957); E. Kessel, "Rankes Auffassung der amerikanischen. Geschichte," *Jahrbuch für Amerikastudien,* VII (1962). (Fz. W.)

RANKIN, JEANNETTE (1880–   ), the first woman elected to the U.S. Congress, was born June 11, 1880, near Missoula, Mont. After graduating from the University of Montana in 1902, she studied at the School of Philanthropy in New York City and began social work in Seattle in 1909. Attracted to the cause of women's suffrage, from 1910 to 1914 she campaigned actively in its behalf in Washington, California, and Montana, eventually becoming legislative secretary of the National American Women's Suffrage Association. In 1916 she was elected a Republican member-at-large from Montana to the 65th Congress, becoming the first woman to hold a congressional seat. An outspoken isolationist in matters of foreign policy, she was one of 49 members of Congress to vote against declaring war on Germany in 1917. This unpopular stand cost her the Republican Senate nomination in 1918 and a further bid as an independent for the same seat. After 1918 she became a lobbyist and later returned to social work.

In 1940 she again ran for the House, emphasizing a "stay-out-of-war" program, and was elected to the 77th Congress, where she created a great furor as the only legislator to vote against the declaration of war on Japan. Having effectively terminated her political career with this vote, she did not seek reelection in 1942, retiring from public life but continuing to lecture on social reform. Her militant feminism remained unabated as late as the 1960s, when she founded a self-sufficient women's "cooperative homestead" in Georgia.

In the late 1960s she was active in the peace movement, urging women to demand a halt to the Vietnamese war. On Jan. 15, 1968, at the age of 87, she led 5,000 women calling themselves the "Jeannette Rankin Brigade" to the foot of Capitol Hill to demonstrate opposition to the war, as the 90th Congress opened its second session. She headed a small delegation who then presented antiwar petitions to congressional leaders.

RANKINE, WILLIAM JOHN MACQUORN (1820–1872), Scottish engineer and physicist, best known for his research in molecular physics and as one of the founders of the science of thermodynamics, was born in Edinburgh on July 5, 1820, and educated at Edinburgh University. Trained as a civil engineer under Sir John B. MacNeill, he was appointed in 1855 to the Queen Victoria chair of civil engineering and mechanics in Glasgow University. One of Rankine's first scientific works, a paper on fatigue in metals of railway axles, was the pioneer English paper in this field; its publication in 1843 led to new methods of construction. Rankine's *A Manual of the Steam Engine and Other Prime Movers* (1859) is a classic. The Rankine cycle, named after him, is a thermodynamic cycle of events used as a standard for the performance of steam-power installations where a condensable vapour provides the working fluid. In soil mechanics his work on earth pressures and the stability of retaining walls was a notable advance. Rankine's greatest paper was "On the Thermodynamic Theory of Waves of Finite Longitudinal Disturbance." Other subjects in which he became interested included propellers, the lines of ships, and streamlines. The catalogue of the Royal Society, of which he became a fellow in 1853, lists 154 of his papers; some were reprinted as *Miscellaneous Scientific Papers* (1881). Rankine died in Glasgow on Dec. 24, 1872. (A. McD.)

RANSOM, JOHN CROWE (1888–   ), U.S. poet and critic, was born on April 30, 1888, in Pulaski, Tenn. Graduated from Vanderbilt University, Nashville, Tenn., in 1909 and from Oxford, where he was a Rhodes scholar, in 1913, he taught English at Vanderbilt from 1914 to 1937, when he went to Kenyon College, Gambier, O., as professor of poetry and editor of the *Kenyon Review.*

From 1922 to 1925, Ransom and his pupils—Donald Davidson, Allen Tate, Merrill Moore, and Robert Penn Warren—published a magazine of their own verse called *The Fugitive.* The same group (excepting Moore), joined by others at Vanderbilt, published *I'll Take My Stand* (1930), which criticized current notions of industrial progress. Ransom turned to literary criticism in *The World's Body* (1938) and *The New Criticism* (1941), the latter of which gave the name to the critical school that is concerned with the close reading of poetical texts. Ransom's poems, collected in *Chills and Fever* (1924), *Two Gentlemen in Bonds* (1926), and

Selected Poems (1945), are remarkable for their wit and irony, their understatement, and their Southern urbanity. (R. ST.)

RANTOUL, a village of Illinois, U.S., in Champaign County, was incorporated in 1869 and named for Robert Rantoul, an early member of the board of directors of the Illinois Central Railroad. Located about 15 mi. (24 km.) NE of Champaign in the grand prairie of east-central Illinois, the village originally had an agricultural economy. Chanute Air Force Base, adjacent to Rantoul, was built in 1917 and has been permanent since 1921. Building and maintenance of the base provided new and varied opportunities for employment to local people. School-building programs received federal aid; churches and recreational facilities were also provided. Residential development, largely to accommodate air force personnel, contributed to changing this rural community into an urban one.

For comparative population figures *see* table in ILLINOIS: *Population.* (T. J. T.)

RANUNCULACEAE, a plant family of the order Ranales that includes many familiar and ornamental flowers. There are 30 genera with about 700 species in temperate and cold regions, especially in the northern hemisphere. The family contains many well-known forms, such as buttercup, larkspur, anemone, columbine, clematis, marsh marigold, peony, etc. In North America there are about 25 genera, in Great Britain 12. The plants are dicotyledons (*i.e.,* with two seed leaves), and the family retains many of the primitive characters of the extinct ancestors of the higher dicotyledons and monocotyledons. Most of the plants are herbs (rarely woody vines, as in some species of *Clematis*) with alternate leaves (opposite in *Clematis*) usually without stipules. The flowers, which show considerable variation in the number and development of parts, are characterized by free hypogynous sepals and petals, numerous free stamens, usually many free one-chambered carpels and small seeds containing a minute straight embryo embedded in a copious endosperm. The parts of the flower commonly are arranged spirally on a convex receptacle. The fruit is one-seeded (an achene) or many-seeded (a follicle) or rarely, as in *Actaea,* a berry.

The family falls into well-defined tribes distinguished by characters of the flower and fruit.

Tribe I, Paeonieae (peonies), are mostly herbs with deeply cut leaves and large solitary showy flowers in which the parts are arranged spirally, the sepals, generally five in number, passing gradually into the large coloured petals. There are two to five free carpels which bear a double row of ovules along the suture. There are no special stalked nectaries, but nectar is secreted by a ringlike swelling around the bases of the carpels. The pistils become fleshy in the fruit and each dehisces along the suture. There are only three genera; the largest, *Paeonia,* occurs in Europe, temperate Asia and western North America. *P. officinalis* is the common peony; *P. suffruticosa* is the tree peony, native to China. This tribe possibly constitutes a separate family.

Tribe II, Helleboreae, are almost exclusively north temperate or subarctic. The leaves may be entire or nearly so, as in *Caltha,* but more often palmately divided as in hellebore, aconite (monkshood) and larkspur. The flowers are solitary (*Eranthis*) or in cymes or racemes, and are radially symmetrical as in *Caltha* (marsh marigold), *Trollius* (globeflower), *Helleborus* (hellebore), *Aquilegia* (columbine) or sometimes bilaterally symmetrical as in *Aconitum* (aconite) and *Delphinium* (larkspur). The carpels, generally three to five in number, form in the fruit many-seeded follicles, except in *Actaea* (baneberry), where the single carpel develops into a many-seeded berry, and in *Nigella,* where the five carpels coalesce, forming a five-chambered ovary. The sepals are usually five and are white or brightly coloured. Thus in *Caltha* and *Trollius* the sepals form a brilliant golden-yellow globe, and in *Eranthis* a pale-yellow star; in *Nigella* they are blue or yellow. In *Helleborus* the greenish sepals persist until the fruit is ripe. *Aconitum* and *Delphinium* differ in the bilaterally symmetrical development of the sepals, the posterior one being distinguished from the remaining four by its helmet shape (*Aconitum*) or by its spur (*Delphinium*). In *Trollius* the petals are long and narrow with a honey-secreting pit at the base; in *Nigella* and *Helleborus*

they form short-stalked pitchers; in *Aquilegia* they are large and coloured with a showy, petallike upper portion and a long basal spur in the tip of which is the nectary. In *Delphinium* they are also spurred, and in *Aconitum* they form a spurlike sac on a long stalk. The parts of the flower usually are arranged in a spiral (acyclic), but are sometimes hemicyclic, the perianth forming a whorl as in winter aconite; rarely is the flower cyclic, as in *Aquilegia,* in which case the parts throughout are arranged in alternating whorls. In *Caltha,* where there are no petals, nectar is secreted in two shallow depressions situated on the side of each carpel. Monkshood is a source of medicinal febrifuges.

Tribe III, Anemoneae, are chiefly temperate, arctic and alpine herbs. They differ from the two preceding tribes in the usually numerous carpels, each with only one ovule, forming achenes. The subgenus *Batrachium* of the genus *Ranunculus* (*q.v.*) contains aquatic plants with submerged or floating stems and leaves. The flowers are solitary as in *Anemone pulsatilla* (pasqueflower), cymose as in species of *Ranunculus,* or in racemes or panicles as in *Thalictrum.* The parts are arranged spirally throughout as in *Myosurus* (mousetail), where the very numerous carpels are borne on a much-elongated receptacle, or the perianth appears whorled as in *Anemone* and *Ranunculus.* In *Anemone* and *Thalictrum* there is only one series of perianth parts, and these are petaloid and attractive in *Anemone,* in which nectar is secreted by modified stamens. In *Anemone nemorosa* (European wood anemone), there is no nectar and the flower is visited by insects for pollen; in *Thalictrum* the perianth is greenish or slightly coloured, and the flower is wind-pollinated (*T. minus*) or visited for its pollen. On the petal of *Ranunculus* there is a basal nectary usually covered by a scale. In *Anemone* the achenes bear the persistent naked or bearded style which aids in dissemination; the same purpose is served by the prickles on the achenes of *Ranunculus arvensis.* *Clematis* (*q.v.*) is characterized by its shrubby, often climbing habit, opposite leaves and the valvate (not imbricate as in the rest of the family) estivation of the sepals. The fruit consists of numerous achenes prolonged into the long feathery style, whence the popular name of the British species, old-man's-beard (*Clematis vitalba*).

See also ACONITE; ADONIS; ANEMONE; BANEBERRY; CIMICIFUGA; CLEMATIS; COLUMBINE; HELLEBORE; LARKSPUR; RANUNCULUS, etc.

BIBLIOGRAPHY.—L. Benson, *Plant Classification* (1957); A. Engler and K. Prantl, *Die natürlichen Pflanzenfamilien* (1887–1908); G. H. M. Lawrence, *Taxonomy of Vascular Plants* (1951). (L. BN.)

RANUNCULUS, familiarly known as buttercup, or crowfoot, a characteristic genus of the botanical family Ranunculaceae (*q.v.*). The Latin name, which means a little frog or tadpole (diminutive of *rana,* frog), was also given to a medicinal plant, which has been identified by some with the crowfoot. The members of the genus *Ranunculus* are more or less acrid herbs, some-

RUTHERFORD PLATT

RANUNCULUS, COMMONLY KNOWN AS BUTTERCUP OR CROWFOOT. PETALS AND SEPALS HAVE BEEN REMOVED FROM FLOWER AT LEFT SHOWING THE PISTIL AND STAMENS

times with fleshy root fibres, or with the base of the stem dilated into a kind of tuber (*R. bulbosus*). They have tufted or alternate leaves, dilated into a sheath at the base, and generally, but not universally, deeply divided above. The flowers are solitary, or in loose cymes, and are remarkable for the number and separation of their parts. Thus there are five sepals, as many petals, and numerous spirally arranged stamens and carpels. The petals have a little nectary or honey gland at the base. The fruit is a head of achenes—dry, one-seeded fruits.

The genus contains a large number of species (about 250) and occurs in most temperate countries in the northern and southern hemispheres, extending into arctic and antarctic regions, and appearing on the higher mountains in the tropics. Inclusive of the water buttercups, 100 native species of *Ranunculus* occur in North America, widely distributed throughout the continent. Representative species are *R. septentrionalis, R. abortivus* and *R. recurvatus*, of the eastern states, and *R. californicus* of the Pacific coast. About 15 species are found in Great Britain. *R. acris, R. repens* and *R. bulbosus* are the common buttercups. *R. arvensis*, which is found in European cornfields, has smaller pale-yellow flowers and the achenes covered with stout spines.

R. lingua and *R. flammula*, the spearwort, grow in marshes, ditches and wet places. *R. ficaria* is the pilewort or lesser celandine, an early spring flower in European pastures and waste places, characterized by having heart-shaped entire leaves and clusters of club-shaped roots.

The section *Batrachium* comprises the water buttercups, denizens of pools and streams, some of which vary greatly in the character of the foliage according to whether it is submerged, floating or aerial, and when submerged varying in accordance with the depth and strength of the current.

The ranunculus of the florist is a cultivated form of *R. asiaticus*, a native of the eastern Mediterranean Levant region, remarkable for the range of colour of the flowers (yellow to purplish black) and for the regularity with which the stamens and pistils are replaced by petals forming double flowers.

RANVIER, LOUIS ANTOINE (1835–1922), French histologist, a master of technical methods and a true scientist, one of the great French biologists, was born on Oct. 2, 1835, at Lyons. He began his medical studies in Lyons and worked in the hospitals there under such well-known clinicians as Charles Jacques Bouchard and Raphaël Lépine. He was appointed intern in the Paris hospitals in 1860 and graduated M.D. five years later, presenting a thesis on the development and diseases of bone. By this time he had formed a close friendship with André Victor Cornil (1837–1908), with whom he shared an intense interest in the rapidly developing science of histology. The two friends opened a private laboratory where they gave special courses for students. Cornil soon obtained academic promotion, and Ranvier, having attracted the attention of Claude Bernard, was appointed his assistant in 1867. In 1869–76 Cornil and Ranvier brought out their *Manuel d'histologie pathologique*, a revelation to their contemporaries and one of the landmarks in 19th-century medicine. In 1872 a special histological laboratory was opened for Ranvier at the Collège de France, and in 1875 he became the first occupant of the chair of general anatomy.

Apart from the *Manuel* Ranvier's most important published works were his *Traité technique d'histologie* (1875 ff.), *Leçons sur l'histologie du système nerveux* (1878) and *Leçons d'anatomie générale, faites au Collège de France* (1880–81). He also wrote many papers and edited seven volumes of the *Travaux* of his laboratory (1874–88). His own researches were concerned particularly with the histology of nerve fibres, the regeneration of nerves, the bipolar nature of ganglionic cells and the minute structure of the skin, conjunctival tissue and cornea. In 1878 he first described the constrictions seen in medullated nerve fibres which are known as the nodes of Ranvier. He was elected a member of the Académie de Médecine (1880) and of the Institut (1887). During his pioneer researches Ranvier had many pupils and disciples, but in the period 1880–85 the interest aroused by Louis Pasteur's discoveries in bacteriology led to a decline in histological studies. Ranvier's laboratory was no longer frequented, his courses lapsed and he made few further contributions to science. Thereafter he spent most of his time on an ancestral estate at Vendrages (Loire), to which he finally retired *c.* 1900, occupying himself with country pursuits. He never married, and in his later years was a solitary figure.

Ranvier died on March 22, 1922, leaving part of his fortune to the town of Roanne for the erection of a sanatorium for tuberculosis. (W. J. Bp.)

RAOULT, FRANÇOIS MARIE (1830–1901), French chemist, best known in connection with work on solutions (*q.v.*), was born at Fournes, Nord, on May 10, 1830. In 1862, after holding various teaching posts, he became professor of chemistry in the *lycée* at Sens. In 1867 he was put in charge of the chemistry classes at Grenoble, and three years later he succeeded to the chair of chemistry, which he held until his death on April 1, 1901. In his doctoral research on the heat of reaction and electromotive force of galvanic cells, he made the important observation that the two did not correspond on the theory that heat is a measure of affinity.

One of his most important contributions was the discovery that the freezing point depression of aqueous solutions is proportional to the solute mole fraction. His most valuable finding (Raoult's law) was the discovery that the vapour pressure of the solvent in a solution is proportional to the mole fraction of the solvent. Raoult's law has been of fundamental importance in the development of the theory of solutions. (N. H. N.)

RAPALLO, a resort on the Riviera di Levante in Genova (Genoa) Province, Liguria, Italy, 19 mi. (30 km.) SE of Genoa by road and rail. It gives its name to the Gulf of Rapallo (or Golfo Tigullio) on which it is situated. Pop. (1961) 21,740 (commune). There is a 15th-century castle and a 12th-century church. Many new tourist accommodations were built after World War II, and tourism is the main activity. Attractions include water sports, golf, go-kart racing, skiing (on artificial snow), art and folklore exhibitions, and winter concerts; and there is an international library.

Rapallo is on the direct road and rail routes from Rome to the Italian and French rivieras. Pillow lace, textiles, and cement are made. First mentioned in 964, Rapallo was sacked successively by Longobards, Normans, and Swiss. It became a city in 1956. (G. Ra.)

RAPALLO, TREATY OF, the symbol of a sensational *rapprochement* between two of the defeated states of World War I, was signed on April 16, 1922, during the Conference of Genoa (*q.v.*), by Walther Rathenau, foreign minister of the German republic, and Georgi V. Chicherin, people's commissar for foreign affairs of the Russian Soviet Federated Socialist Republic. On Nov. 5, 1922, the treaty was extended to other republics of the U.S.S.R.

The treaty stipulated that full diplomatic and consular relations between the two countries should be immediately resumed; that Germany and Russia renounced reciprocally all claims to war reparations of any sort, including payment for the maintenance of prisoners of war; that Germany renounced any compensation for losses incurred by German subjects in consequence of Russian nationalization of private property "provided that the Soviet government does not satisfy similar claims of other states"; and that "most-favoured-nation" treatment should apply to mutual trade relations.

The Treaty of Rapallo, negotiated in great secrecy but published the day after its signature, was not a foundation of a German-Soviet alliance, though both sides wanted to raise the bogey of such an alignment. Rathenau's adviser, Baron Ago von Maltzan, known as "the Red Baron," wanted more: he was hoping that eventually, with Soviet help, Germany would be able to restore the German frontier of 1914 in Eastern Europe. The main result of the treaty was that Germany was able secretly to build and test in Russia new prototypes of weapons forbidden by the Treaty of Versailles; thus the *Reichswehr* could develop new heavy guns, new tanks, new military aircraft, and even experiment with poison gas in Russia. The high command of the Red Army gladly agreed to the arrangement on condition that the prototypes should not leave Russia and that the Red Army should be fully informed of the test results. An English version of the text of the treaty is printed in *Papers Relating to International Economic Conference, Genoa, April–May 1922*, Cmd. 1667 (1922). (K. Sm.)

RAPE, various plants of the genus *Brassica* (mustard family, Cruciferae), the source of oil-yielding rape seed. Most of the cultivated varieties appear to belong either to *Brassica napus* or *B. campestris*. Both may be grown as annuals or biennials, depending upon the variety and the time of sowing. *B. napus* is a much-branched, glaucous plant growing to 3½ ft. tall, with lobed or toothed, succulent leaves, yellow flowers and elongate narrow pods.

B. campestris is similar, but it is more weedy, its leaves are less succulent and the plant is less glaucous. Leading producers of rape seed are China, India, Pakistan, Japan, Sweden, France and the U.S.S.R. Some rape is grown for seed in Canada, but in the United States the plant is used mainly as a forage and green manure crop.

Rape-seed oils are used mainly as edible oil and in lubricants.

(J. W. Tt.)

RAPE, in law, is the crime committed by a man in obtaining unlawful carnal knowledge of a woman, without her consent, by fear, force, or fraud. A husband cannot commit rape upon his wife unless she is legally separated from him.

A felony at common law, rape was reduced in England to a misdemeanour in 1275, but in 1285 was again declared a felony, with benefit of clergy, and so remained until 1575, when the punishment was made more severe. It became a capital offense by the Offences Against the Person Act, 1861, and is now punishable with imprisonment for life. The law of England regards as immaterial whether the woman is chaste or unchaste, married or single. The offense is complete if consent is extorted by threats of death or immediate bodily harm, by fraud or by false pretenses, or by personating the woman's husband.

In the United States the elements of the crime under statute are similar to those at common law. The age when effective consent can be given by the woman has commonly been set by the various states between 14 and 18 years. Want of age on the part of the man is not a defense, as at common law, but simply presumptive evidence of lack of physical capacity. Many states require the testimony of the woman to be corroborated by other evidence and require the prosecution to be initiated within a year or less after the commission of the offense. The punishment is usually imprisonment, though a number of states, especially in the South, prescribe or permit death as the penalty. (P. E. L.)

RAPE OIL: *see* Oils, Fats and Waxes.

RAPHAEL (Heb. "God heals"), one of the archangels, in the Old Testament apocryphal Book of Tobit, he who in human disguise and under the name of Azarias ("Yahweh helps") accompanied Tobias in his adventurous journey and conquered the demon Asmodeus. He is said (Tob. xii, 15) to be "one of the seven holy angels [archangels] who present the prayers of the saints and enter into the presence of the glory of the Holy One." In the Book of Enoch (ch. xx) Raphael is "the angel of the spirits of men," and it is his business to "heal the earth which the angels [*i.e.*, the fallen angels] have defiled." Though the archangels are referred to as numbering seven (*e.g.*, Rev. viii, 2 and Tob. xii, 15), only four are named (in the Book of Enoch): Michael, Uriel, Suriel (Raphael) and Gabriel. Raphael is reckoned among the saints in both Eastern and Western churches, his feast day being Oct. 24. *See also* Angel.

RAPHAEL (Raffaello Santi or Sanzio) (1483–1520), one of the greatest Italian painters of the Renaissance, was born in Urbino, the son of Giovanni Santi. His birth, probably on April 6, 1483, took place in a house which still contains a fresco of the "Madonna and Child" that is either by his father or is a very early work of his own. Giovanni Santi was not a very good painter, as may be seen from his surviving works such as the "Madonna and Child With Saints" (1489, Urbino gallery), but he presumably gave Raphael his first grounding as a painter. He died in 1494, and, as Raphael's mother had already died in 1491, parental influence can have counted for little. What was far more important was Urbino itself, for this little hill town was one of the most civilized in Europe in the 15th century, under its Duke Federigo da Montefeltro and his son and successor Guidobaldo. The palace is one of the masterpieces of Italian architecture; Piero della Francesca had worked in Urbino in the 1460s and 1470s; Bramante was a citizen and was later to play a major part in Raphael's career; and Baldassare Castiglione, the arbiter of manners and author of *The Courtier*, was an Urbinate. The latter was to become a friend of Raphael, whose portrait of him (1516, Louvre, Paris) is one of the first modern portraits—a study of character distinct from that accumulation of details which the 15th century had regarded as essential to portraiture.

Earliest Works.—Raphael's earliest years are still obscure. He is first recorded on Dec. 10, 1500, when he shared in a commission for a "St. Nicholas," completed on Sept. 13, 1501, which is now lost but is known in part through drawings. Extant works which are probably of this very early period include the large "Mond Crucifixion" (National gallery, London) and the two tiny panels of the "Knight's Dream" (also National gallery) and the "Three Graces" (Chantilly, France). Before this time he had almost certainly assisted Perugino in his frescoes in the Sala del Cambio at Perugia, and for the next few years the influence of Perugino was dominant; indeed, Raphael might well have settled down to succeed to Perugino's business had it not been for his visit to Florence which fertilized his imagination. The figure of Fortitude in the Sala del Cambio is usually agreed to be by Raphael's hand, but here, of course, he was merely executing Perugino's cartoon. Between 1501 and 1503 Raphael was commissioned to paint an "Assumption" for the nuns of Monteluce, but the picture (now in the Vatican gallery) was actually finished after his death by his pupils. The earliest surviving work by him that is completely certain is the "Sposalizio," or "Marriage of the Virgin," which is signed and dated 1504 (Brera gallery, Milan). The types are markedly Peruginesque and the composition derives from Perugino's "Christ Giving the Keys to St. Peter" (Sistine chapel, Vatican) and from another "Sposalizio" attributed to Perugino, now in the museum at Caen, France. It has, however, been suggested that the Caen picture derives rather from Raphael; what is certain is that the Brera "Sposalizio" is no more than an improved Perugino and falls short of the great masterpieces Raphael was to paint no more than five years later.

Florentine Period.—Probably late in 1504 Raphael went to Florence, and this date marks the first decisive phase in his career. By 1505 he was once again in Perugia, where he was commissioned to paint a fresco in S. Severo; this seems to have been still unfinished at his death and was completed by his former master Perugino, who outlived him. Nevertheless, the upper part of the fresco contains the germ of his first great Roman work, the "Disputa." Probably immediately after he received this commission Raphael returned to Florence, where he set himself to relearn his whole art under the influence of the two greatest living artists, Leonardo da Vinci and Michelangelo, both then in Florence. Also, he became friendly with Fra Bartolommeo (*q.v.*), but here the influence was mutual. A series of Madonna compositions (Florence, Paris, Vienna, Washington, D.C., and elsewhere) shows Raphael learning the Florentine method of building up his composition in depth with pyramidal figure masses, with figures grouped as a single unit, yet each retaining its own individuality of character and shape. This new sense of unity in composition and the suppression of inessentials he owed mainly to Leonardo, in particular to his "Madonna and Child and St. Anne" cartoons. To Leonardo he also owed a new sense of softness in modeling and skill in chiaroscuro, shown in his portraits of Angelo and Maddalena Doni (Pitti, Florence), in which he adapted the model provided by Leonardo's "Mona Lisa." To counterbalance any tendency to imitate the slightly overripe quality of Leonardo's modeling, Raphael made a profound study of Michelangelo's cartoon of the "Battle of Cascina," with its stress on dramatic action and expressive anatomy. The "Ansidei Madonna" (*c.* 1506, National gallery, London) shows something of both these influences, but the full impact of Michelangelo on Raphael at this date is best seen in the "Borghese Entombment" (1507, Borghese gallery, Rome), painted for Atalanta Baglione of Perugia in memory of her murdered and murderous son. It contains several more or less direct quotations from Michelangelo and there can be no doubt that in it and other works of the same period Raphael set himself deliberately to learn from Michelangelo the expressive possibilities of human anatomy.

Roman Period.—On April 21, 1508, Raphael was still in Florence, as we know from a letter of that date, and the "Cowper Madonna" (National Gallery of Art, Washington, D.C.) is signed and dated 1508 and must therefore be one of his last Florentine works. Traditionally it was Bramante who summoned him to Rome, since he was distantly related to Raphael and knew

BY COURTESY OF (TOP) THE SMITHSONIAN INSTITUTION, (RIGHT) NATIONAL GALLERY OF ART, WASHINGTON D.C., MELLON COLLECTION

(ABOVE) "FIGURES IN COMBAT," PEN DRAWING BY RAPHAEL IN THE ACCADEMIA, VENICE; (RIGHT) "ST. GEORGE AND THE DRAGON," PAINTING BY RAPHAEL IN THE NATIONAL GALLERY OF ART, MELLON COLLECTION, WASHINGTON, D.C.

art which at the same time were heavily charged with allegorical or symbolic meaning. One example will perhaps make this clear. The figures of Plato and Aristotle in the fresco known as the "School of Athens"—the identity of these two figures is shown by the books they hold—are not only exactly right from the formal point of view, as two contrasted figures set in the optical centre of the composition, but also the simplest and most telling visual symbols of the two contrasted philosophies. Plato is a grave old man, pointing upward as though to emphasize the heavenly origin of those Ideas which are the basis of his philosophy; Aristotle, a much younger and more vigorous man, gestures in a decisive and forthright way toward the earth as an expression of his unidealistic philosophy.

The four Stanze consist of a single enfilade of rooms, the first three (in the order in which the visitor sees them) being those of the Fire in the Borgo (dell' Incendio), of the Tribunal (della Segnatura) and of Heliodorus (d'Eliodoro). Each of these is about 30 ft. by 25 ft. in size, but the last and largest room, the Sala di Costantino, is about 30 ft. by 45 ft. It communicates directly with the Loggie di Raffaello.

The first to be painted was the Stanza della Segnatura, frescoed between 1509 and 1511. It seems to have been used for the sittings of a legal tribunal, and its title implies that important state documents were signed or sealed in it. The ceiling is decorated with four roundels and four rectangular panels in imitation of mosaics, representing Theology, Justice, Philosophy and Poetry (in the roundels), and Adam and Eve, the Judgment of Solomon, Astronomy and Apollo and Marsyas (in the rectangles). The four main fresco fields are occupied by the "Disputa" and the "School of Athens" on the larger walls and "Parnassus" and the "Cardinal Virtues" on the smaller. The two latter have subsidiary scenes representing "Augustus Preventing the Burning of the Aeneid," "Alexander the Great Depositing the Homeric Books in the Tomb of Achilles," and "Justinian Receiving the Pandects" and "Gregory IX Approving the Decretals." As the principal theme of the room is the scope of human knowledge, the main walls are given up to the contrasted representations of secular knowledge and theology—the so-called "School of Athens" and the so-called "Disputa." Presumably neither name was used by Raphael, but the "Disputa" is referred to by G. Vasari as showing "an infinite number of saints, who write down the Mass and hold dispute about the Host which is on the altar . . ." This should not be understood as meaning a dispute in the ordinary English sense of the term, but rather a medieval disputation or philosophical discussion.

It is clear that both the "Disputa" and the "School of Athens" are intended as allegories in a very general sense, and many of the highly involved "explanations" which have been propounded are no more than misplaced ingenuity. The "Disputa" is, in fact, no more than a general symbolic representation of the church on earth and in heaven, for the centre of the composition is the monstrance on the altar, with the heavenly host and the representatives of the church on earth both converging on it. At the same time the Host in the monstrance is the lowest part of the vertical axis which consists of the figures of God the Father, Christ and the Holy Spirit, again a simple piece of symbolism. The upper part of the composition is very reminiscent of the fresco

that there were good commissions to be had from his own splendid patron, Pope Julius II. The tradition is the more likely to be correct in that Raphael was still virtually an unknown provincial painter, by no means yet the third member of the Leonardo-Michelangelo-Raphael triumvirate that springs automatically to the mind. He was still only in his middle 20s, but he was soon to receive a commission from the irascible but extremely discerning pope that placed him practically on a level with Michelangelo. Raphael was certainly at work in the Vatican by Jan. 13, 1509, and on Oct. 4 of that year he was granted a papal sinecure, presumably in payment for work done in the Stanze (Italian, "rooms").

The Stanze.—Julius II, who detested the memory of his predecessor Alexander VI, refused to use the Borgia apartments and, as a consequence of his remodeling of the Vatican palace, Bramante built the Cortile di S. Damaso, later to be completed by Raphael and decorated by his pupils under the name of "Raphael's Loggie." As his first great work for the pope, Raphael was commissioned to paint a cycle of frescoes in a series of medium-sized rooms known simply as the Stanze. The Stanza della Segnatura and Stanza d'Eliodoro are practically entirely decorated by Raphael himself; the Stanza dell' Incendio, though designed by Raphael, was largely executed by his numerous assistants and pupils; the last and largest of the apartments, the Sala di Costantino, was hardly even designed by Raphael, and was not finished until about four years after his death.

The main themes of the Stanze are fairly simple and easily grasped, but the details of the iconography have never been completely worked out since no two scholars are satisfied with the same interpretations. It is highly probable that there was a written "program" for the series as a whole and perhaps also for each fresco, but it has not survived and the two most important questions are left unanswered: to what extent was it imposed on Raphael by the pope or his advisers, and to what extent was each and every detail of each fresco charged with a meaning that had been worked out in advance? When Raphael arrived in Rome he was young, almost unknown, and certainly not particularly well educated in the humanist sense; yet long before he died he was famous not only as a painter but also as a scholar and was clearly on easy and familiar terms with the papal court in general. The most likely reason for this is that he had shown himself the ideal humanist artist; that is, he was able to devise great works of

in S. Severo in Perugia, with its row of saints seated on rather solid clouds, but the lower part is more freely handled. The device of the steps, which serve to lead the eye into the picture space, and the railing at the left, balancing the awkward shape made by the door cutting into the fresco field at the right, both prove Raphael's extraordinary powers as a composer. It is very likely that this was the first time he had worked on so large a scale (something like 24 ft. across), and it is nothing short of astounding that he was able to compose the "School of Athens," one of the most subtle arrangements of a large number of figures ever painted, as his second attempt on this scale.

The "School of Athens" is perhaps the most famous of all his frescoes, as the "Sistine Madonna" is the most famous of all his Madonnas. It differs from the "Disputa" in that the symbolism is less obvious and the intention vaguer, for it represents a number of the more famous classical philosophers in a splendid basilica —based on Bramante's design for the new St. Peter's—which, in a general way, symbolizes both the dignity of philosophical enquiry and the secular nature of the subject.

At about the same time, probably in 1511, Raphael also painted a more secular subject still, the "Triumph of Galatea" in the Villa Farnesina, Rome, for the Sienese banker Agostino Chigi, for whom he was later to decorate the Chigi chapel in Sta. Maria del Popolo. The Stanza della Segnatura was completed in 1511 and Raphael began to work on the next Stanza, that of Heliodorus, in 1512, completing it in 1514. The whole character of the Stanza d'Eliodoro is entirely different from that of the Stanza della Segnatura. The generalized allegories of the "School of Athens" or the "Disputa" give way to representations of specific events, all miraculous, which, since they represent the direct interventions of God on behalf of His chosen people, had a political intention in the 16th century. The four principal subjects are: "The Expulsion of Heliodorus From the Temple," "The Miracle at Bolsena," "The Liberation of St. Peter" and "Attila the Hun Turned Back From Rome." Raphael's original patron, Julius II, died in 1513 and was succeeded by Leo X (elected March 11, 1513); as both the "Expulsion" and the "Miracle at Bolsena" (which is dated 1512) contain superb portraits of Julius II while the Leo I who is shown meeting Attila has the features of Leo X, these frescoes can be closely dated. The Stanza takes its name from the fresco of "Heliodorus Expelled From the Temple of Jerusalem" and "compassed in darkness" (II Macc. 3), which had a contemporary allusion to the efforts of Julius against the French and in support of the temporal power. The fresco of the "Mass at Bolsena" records a miracle that took place in 1263, when a priest who doubted the reality of transubstantiation found the Host bleeding in his hands; Julius' devotion to the Sacrament is probably the principal reason for the choice of this subject. The composition is one of Raphael's most accomplished, since the shape to be filled is exceedingly awkward and asymmetrical, and the celebrated group of the Swiss guards at the lower right is introduced to fill the space where it was necessary to paint a continuation of the real architecture.

In all these miraculous themes the colours are much deeper and more Venetian in feeling than the colour schemes in the earlier room, the "Liberation of St. Peter" providing a particularly notable example of the new interest in colour and light since it is a night scene and contains three separate lighting effects—moonlight, the torch carried by the soldier and the supernatural light emanating from the angel. It is usually thought that the presence in Rome at this time of Sebastiano del Piombo may have been responsible for this marked Venetian influence on Raphael, but it is also certain that Michelangelo's Sistine ceiling was unveiled while the room was in progress; yet a renewed influence of Michelangelo is not noticeable until somewhat later, most clearly in the frescoes of "Isaiah" (c. 1512, S. Agostino, Rome) and the "Sibyls" in Sta. Maria della Pace, of about 1514.

The most important other work undertaken by Raphael at this period was probably the "Sistine Madonna" (Dresden gallery), which has always been one of his most famous paintings, although its early history is unknown. The most likely explanation for its existence is that it was painted to be carried in the funeral proces-

sion of Julius II in 1513 and that it subsequently came into the possession of the monks at Piacenza who owned it before its transfer to Dresden. By 1513 Raphael was one of the most celebrated of living artists and already employed a large studio of assistants and pupils, so that it is extremely unlikely that an obscure community of monks could have commissioned a large altarpiece from him (or have got delivery if they had commissioned it).

Immediately after completing the Stanza d'Eliodoro, Raphael began work on the third Stanza, which is first in order of visiting. The Stanza dell' Incendio was begun in 1514 and completed by 1517, but the proportion of it executed by assistants is much higher than was the case in the first two rooms. Nevertheless, it must be stressed that Raphael was responsible for the decoration as a whole. The reason for this delegation of the execution is twofold: St. Peter's and the Tapestry cartoons. In August, 1514, Raphael succeeded Bramante as chief architect of the new St. Peter's, and, although he built very little of it, the administrative responsibility for the greatest work in Christendom must have been considerable. The first payment for the cartoons was made on June 15, 1515, so it is probable that this new commission had been occupying much of Raphael's attention, rather than the frescoes in the Stanza dell' Incendio. The last and largest of the Stanze, the Sala di Costantino, was commissioned in 1517 but was finished only in 1524, four years after Raphael's death.

The Tapestry Cartoons.—Leo X commissioned a set of tapestries to hang below the 15th-century fresco cycle on the walls of the Sistine chapel. Almost certainly there were 10 (10 tapestries are preserved in the Vatican museum), but a contemporary, probably by a slip of the pen, mentions 16. Seven of the original cartoons still exist in the British royal collection (on permanent loan to the Victoria and Albert museum, London) and other sets

ALINARI

"SISTINE MADONNA" BY RAPHAEL. IN THE DRESDEN GALLERY, DRESDEN, GERMANY

of the tapestries, woven at various times from the cartoons, exist elsewhere. The seven cartoons represent "Christ's Charge to Peter," "The Miraculous Draught of Fishes," "The Death of Ananias," "The Healing of the Lame Man," "The Blinding of Elymas," "The Sacrifice at Lystra" and "St. Paul Preaching at Athens"; the other three tapestries, for which no cartoons exist, are "The Conversion of St. Paul," "St. Paul in Prison" and "The Stoning of St. Stephen." The last payment was made in Dec. 1516, when the cartoons must have been sent to Brussels, where the tapestries were woven. Seven were finished by Christmas 1519 and were exhibited in the Sistine chapel, when an eyewitness wrote that "by universal consent there is nothing more beautiful in the world." They were woven by the low-warp (*basse-lisse*) method which involves reversal of the designs, so that the designer has to remember to depict right-handed actions as taking place with the left—a point which was not invariably borne in mind in the cartoons (*see* A. P. Oppé, "Right and Left in Raphael's Cartoons," in *Journal of the Warburg and Courtauld Institutes*, vol. vii, pp. 82 ff., 1944). It is now generally agreed that Raphael actually drew much more in the cartoons himself than was previously allowed to be the case, but the use which has been made of them and the fragile nature of the medium (size colour on paper) have combined to damage them severely in many parts. Nevertheless, the amount of damage and repainting is relatively unimportant for it cannot be too strongly emphasized that they could have been executed entirely by assistants and then completely repainted without losing their importance and value, for they are supreme examples of the art of composition. It is hardly an exaggeration to say that the normal western conception of the apostles as grave, bearded men in togas derives very largely from the visual images created by Raphael in these works. There has been a great deal of discussion about the way the tapestries were originally arranged. (For a later hypothesis *see* J. White and J. Shearman in *The Art Bulletin*, xl, pp. 194–222, 299–323, 1958).

By April 19, 1516, Raphael had completed the portrait of Count Castiglione, his fellow townsman and the leading authority of the day on polite behaviour. It is indicative that Raphael should have been on terms of intimate friendship with him and also with A. Navagero and other poets and at least two princes of the church, Cardinals Bembo and Bibbiena. For the latter he decorated a bathroom in his suite in the Vatican. It is in a private part of the palace and is now much damaged, but it is of interest since the decorative motifs are based on those in the newly discovered Golden House of Nero, from which the type of decoration known as "grotesque" is derived. Similar motifs were used by members of Raphael's studio, notably by Giovanni da Udine, in the stucco decorations at the Villa Madama and elsewhere. Raphael now occupied a position held by no other artist of modern times (not even Michelangelo is quite comparable), on terms of friendship with the pope and the whole Curia and with almost every prince in Christendom intriguing to obtain a work by his hand; almost overnight, the whole social position of the artist was thus revolutionized by the three great artists of the Renaissance, Leonardo, Michelangelo and Raphael. During all this time he was busy on innumerable enterprises, most of which were actually executed by his army of pupils and assistants: the remainder of the Stanza dell' Incendio, the numerous small biblical scenes in the Loggie of the Vatican (works which deserve more study than they tend to get), the sculpture and mosaics of the Chigi chapel and the work on the new St. Peter's as well as other architectural works—he designed S. Eligio degli Orefici and the Vidoni-Caffarelli and Branconio dell' Aquila palaces in Rome as well as the Palazzo Pandolfini in Florence—and the duties involved in his conservatorship of the antiquities of Rome. By employing Marcantonio Raimondi, Raphael ensured the spread of his designs all over the civilized world, for this excellent engraver produced numerous plates from designs made specially by Raphael for the purpose of spreading his ideas.

The Last Works.—A letter from Leonardo Sellaio to Michelangelo at Carrara on Jan. 19, 1517, gives the first indication of what was to become Raphael's last masterpiece, the "Transfiguration," now in the Vatican. Cardinal de' Medici (later Pope Clement VII)

commissioned two enormous altarpieces for his cathedral at Narbonne in France; one was Sebastiano del Piombo's "Raising of Lazarus" (now in the National gallery, London) and the other was Raphael's "Transfiguration," unfinished at his death and never sent to Narbonne. In fact, the "Transfiguration" was not begun until 1518 and must therefore be considered along with the "Holy Family of Francis I" and "St. Michael Vanquishing Satan" (both dated 1518 and in the Louvre, Paris), both of which were destined for presentation to Francis I of France by Leo X. All three pictures were major commissions and any new or unusual features in them are therefore extremely unlikely to be due to pupils or assistants working unsupervised; at the very least, Raphael must have approved any innovations. It is necessary, indeed, to stress this point and also to refer to the series of superb drawings for individual figures in the "Transfiguration," for there is a tendency to write off the last works, and especially the "Transfiguration," as by Giulio Romano, Gianfrancesco Penni and other pupils. Vasari noted, of the "Holy Family of Francis I," that the execution was almost entirely by Giulio Romano, and the "Transfiguration" was certainly completed after Raphael's death; yet Vasari stresses that much of it was in fact painted "with his own hand." There is every reason to suppose that the design is his, and it is in the design that the innovations are chiefly visible. The tendency in all these late works is toward a crowding together of the figures which had hitherto been lucidly arranged in accordance with the classical canons Raphael himself had done so much to impose. At the same time there is a feeling of violence and tension which is not entirely due to the demands of the subject. Indeed, one might argue that the subject was adapted to satisfy a desire to depict a scene of violence, since the boy possessed of a devil is the next stage in the Biblical narrative (Matt. 17). In short, it may be held that Raphael was the first Mannerist.

On Good Friday, April 6, 1520, after an illness lasting a week, Raphael died. He was buried in the Pantheon and his grave is marked by a slab with a commemorative epitaph by Cardinal Bembo. At the head of the bier the unfinished "Transfiguration" stood as his memorial, perhaps the first of what would have been a series of new works in the middle period which Raphael never lived to achieve. He died at 37, when most great artists are approaching their first maturity.

BIBLIOGRAPHY.—G. Vasari, *Life*, vol. iv of Gaston de Vere's Eng. trans. (1913). V. Golzio, *Raffaello* (1936), is the most important source book. A. P. Oppé, *Raphael* (1909); G. Gronau, *Raffael* (1930); O. Fischel, "Santi, Raffaello" (with a complete bibliography) in Thieme-Becker, *Allgemeines Lexikon der bildenden Künstler*, vol. xxix (1935), *Raphaels Zeichnungen* (1913–41), *Raphael* (1948); J. W. Pope-Hennessy, *The Raphael Cartoons* (1950); E. Camesasca, *Tutta la pittura di Raffaello*, 2 vol. (1956), and (ed.), *Raffaello Sanzio, tutti gli scritti* (1956). For good sets of plates *see* especially W. Suida, *Raphael* (1941); O. Fischel, *Raphael*, cited above; *The Complete Work of Raphael* (1969). (P. J. MY.)

RAPID CITY, a city of South Dakota, U.S., and the seat of Pennington County, is the western gateway to the Black Hills (*q.v.*). Located 3,200 ft. (975 m.) above sea level on Rapid Creek, from which it derived its name, it was settled in 1876 during the days of the Black Hills gold rush, and was incorporated in 1878.

Millions of tourists have been attracted by the beauty of the Black Hills, with nearby Mt. Rushmore, Crazy Horse Mountain, and Custer National Park being of particular interest. Although it is located in what is basically an agricultural and grazing area, Rapid City's industries range from lumber, millwork, and building materials to Black Hills gold jewelry. In addition, gold, silver, beryllium, feldspar, gypsum, mica, uranium, and other minerals are mined and processed in the area. Rapid City is the site of the state-owned cement plant, the Sioux Indian sanatorium, the South Dakota School of Mines and Technology (established 1885), and Ellsworth Air Force Base. For comparative population figures *see* table in SOUTH DAKOTA: *Population.* (C. J. P.)

RAQQAH, AR (RAKKA), a town of Syria and headquarters of the *muhafaza* (governorate) of Raqqah, lies on the east bank of the Euphrates, 100 mi. (161 km.) ESE of Aleppo. Pop. (1960) 14,554. Built by one of Alexander's generals, Seleucus Nicator, it was first named Nicephorium, and then Ar Raqqah, following the Arab conquest. Just south of the town, at Siffin on the west bank of the Euphrates, was fought the battle which decided the caliphate in favour of Mu'awiyah in A.D. 657. Ar Raqqah was rebuilt and fortified by Harun al-Rashid, who used it as his headquarters against the Byzantines in the 8th century. Gradually the city fell into decay, and was replaced in importance by its suburb Ar Rafiqah, which took over its name. Al-Battani (Albategnius), the Arab astronomer, made his observations there between 877 and 918.

The double walls with circular towers and the castle restored by the Ottoman sultan Suleiman are still extant. The modern town lies partly within the ancient walls on the edge of the desert.

(M. V. S.-W.)

RARE EARTHS is the traditional name of the 14 metallic elements having atomic numbers 58 to 71, inclusive, and very similar chemical properties. By reference to their place in the periodic table they are known somewhat more accurately as the lanthanides or lanthanons, or the 4f elements (*see* below, *Structure*). The rare earths are listed in Table I. The element lanthanum (atomic number 57) is often considered the first member of the series, but a strict definition excludes it. Two other elements, yttrium and scandium, commonly occur in nature with the rare earths, which they resemble in chemical behaviour; these two elements therefore are sometimes considered along with the rare earths even though they are not members of the series.

The term "rare earths" dates from the early 19th century, when chemists obtained lanthanide substances with difficulty from relatively rare minerals and in the form of oxides resembling materials originally known as earths and thought to be elements; *e.g.*, lime, alumina, and magnesia. In time it became known that the rare earths are widely distributed in nature, and occur in a number of concentrated minerals; they are, in fact, more abundant than some of the better-known elements. Cerium, for example, is more abundant than tin; and thulium, the rarest of the rare earths, is at least as plentiful as cadmium, silver, gold, bismuth, and the platinum metals. Among the rare earths themselves, those of even atomic numbers are five to ten times as abundant as those of odd atomic numbers. The rare earths, together with lanthanum, yttrium, and scandium, comprise about one-fourth of the known metals and one-sixth of the known elements. (*See* also ELEMENTS, CHEMICAL; METAL.) During the period of discovery of the rare earths, from 1796 to 1947, much basic information on separation techniques was obtained; and new, more efficient methods resulted from intensive research during World War II. As a result most of the rare earths are available in quantities ranging from ten pounds to many tons; by the late 1960s, known reserves of rare-earth ores totaled several million tons.

Uses.—In the past the uses of any rare earth on the basis of its individual properties were very few; the main applications arose from the properties of a mixture of several of these elements; *i.e.*, group properties. Misch metal is an example. It is an alloy of cerium, lanthanum, neodymium, and several other rare-earth metals in their naturally occurring proportions. Because of the high activity of these metals the alloy is an excellent material for cigarette lighter flints and is also used as a deoxidizer in vacuum tubes and in metallurgy. Misch metal is also a constituent of some magnesium alloys. The use of light rare-earth oxides for Welsbach gas mantles, and of their oxides and fluorides as core material for arc-light carbons, is based upon group properties. Other uses have been based on the colour and absorptive properties the elements impart to glass and other ceramic products; *e.g.*, didymium, a mixture primarily of praseodymium and neodymium, is extensively used for glassblowers' and welders' goggles because it absorbs the harmful radiation of sodium. The use of didymium instead of Misch metal as a constituent of magnesium alloys gives a product of greater strength at all temperatures. As alloying constituents the rare-earth metals increase the life of heating elements, the workability of stainless steels, and the oxidation resistance of certain other ferrous alloys.

As pure rare-earth metals and compounds became available, specialized uses based upon individual properties were developed. These include the use of cerium (IV) oxide, CeO_2, as a highly effective glass polish, as a constituent to increase the stability and

discoloration resistance of glass to gamma and electron-beam radiation, and as an opacifier for enamel coatings; and lanthanum oxide, La_2O_3, as a constituent of high-refraction and low-dispersion optical glass. The high melting points of the rare-earth oxides, borides, nitrides, and carbides indicate possible use as refractory materials. There is some use of certain rare-earth oxides, chlorides, and phosphates as catalysts in organic reactions. A promising field of rare-earth technology is the development of a highly efficient red-emitting cathodoluminescent phosphor, europium-activated yttrium orthovanadate, YVO_4:Eu, for use in colour television picture tubes. Certain compounds of lanthanum and yttrium show unusual electronic or magnetic behaviour and are useful in microwave devices, magnetic core materials, and ceramic capacitors, and potentially as semiconductors.

Nuclear applications, actual or potential, include the use of the elements of high absorption cross sections for thermal or slow-moving neutrons. Samarium, europium, gadolinium, and dysprosium are excellent sponges for soaking up slow neutrons and could serve as construction materials for control rods in atomic piles and for shielding and flux-suppressing devices. However, in samarium and gadolinium the absorbing isotopes are present in low concentration and burn up rapidly; they are therefore useful only in low-flux or short-time operations. Yttrium hydride, YH_3, is of use as a hydrogen-moderator carrier, and yttrium metal as a construction material in reactors, since the metal is not attacked by molten uranium at high temperature. Thulium and scandium, when suitably irradiated, serve as portable X-ray sources. Some of the properties of certain rare earths resemble those of the closely related actinide group (the elements having atomic numbers 90 to 103, inclusive); these rare earths therefore have been used as stand-ins for the radioactive and fissionable elements. For example, the use of cerium as a stand-in for plutonium and other transuranium elements permitted scientists to devise methods for separating and identifying these newly discovered elements before weighable quantities had been prepared.

Structure.—The work of British physicist H. G.-J. Moseley (*q.v.*) on the X-ray spectra of the elements had by 1914 definitely established the maximum number of rare earths and set up procedures by which they could be identified and their purity determined. Modern atomic theory and experiment have since shown that the electronic structure of each trivalent rare-earth ion is composed of a xenon core with additional electrons entering the 4f subshell, the number increasing from 1 electron in cerium to 14 in lutefium. (*See* PERIODIC LAW.) The neutral rare-earth atom contains three more electrons than the trivalent ion, one in either the 4f or 5d subshell and two in the 6s subshell. Lanthanum, which immediately precedes cerium in the periodic table, likewise is trivalent but has no 4f electrons; it is thus the structural and chemical prototype of the rare earths, and provides a name for the group of which it is not, strictly speaking, a member. (*See* Table I.)

As the nuclear charge increases from element to element in the rare-earth group the added electrons go into the underlying 4f subshell instead of into the external 5d subshell. Since the 4f

TABLE I.—*The Rare Earths and Their Ionic Properties*

Name	Symbol	Atomic Number	Atomic Weight	Oxidation States	Trivalent Ion		
					Number of 4f Electrons	Magnetic Moment	Ionic Radius, Å
(Lanthanum) .	La	57	138.91	3	0	0.00	1.061
Cerium .	Ce	58	140.12	3, 4	1	2.56	1.034
Praseodymium.	Pr	59	140.907	3, 4	2	3.62	1.013
Neodymium .	Nd	60	144.24	2, 3	3	3.68	0.995
Promethium .	Pm	61	145*	3	4	2.83	0.979
Samarium.	Sm	62	150.35	2, 3	5	1.55–1.65	0.964
Europium.	Eu	63	151.96	2, 3	6	3.40–3.51	0.950
Gadolinium .	Gd	64	157.25	3	7	7.94	0.938
Terbium .	Tb	65	158.924	3, 4	8	9.7	0.923
Dysprosium .	Dy	66	162.50	3	9	10.6	0.908
Holmium .	Ho	67	164.930	3	10	10.6	0.894
Erbium .	Er	68	167.26	3	11	9.6	0.881
Thulium .	Tm	69	168.934	2, 3	12	7.6	0.869
Ytterbium .	Yb	70	173.04	2, 3	13	4.5	0.858
Lutetium .	Lu	71	174.97	3	14	0.00	0.848

*Isotope with half-life of 18 years.

electrons are screened by the completed 5s and 5p subshells, they have practically no effect on the valence forces. On the other hand the 4f orbitals are too diffuse to screen the nucleus as effectively as a completed inner shell, and the attraction of the nucleus for the outermost electrons increases with the atomic number. The net effect is a slight shrinkage in atomic size from lanthanum through lutetium—the so-called lanthanide contraction. The contraction is quite regular in the radii of trivalent ions (*see* Table I, last column) but somewhat irregular in the radii of the atoms.

To summarize: the trivalent ions of the rare earths and lanthanum have identical charges, identical external electronic structures, and almost the same ionic radii. Consequently their chemical properties are very similar. Since there was no place for these elements in the older periodic tables they were grouped in the space occupied by lanthanum; they are now placed in a separate series at the bottom of the table.

Yttrium (atomic number 39) and scandium (21) are just above lanthanum in transition Group III of the periodic table. Both are trivalent and have external structures like those of the rare earths. Since the chemistry of these two elements is largely ionic and is therefore determined by their ionic sizes, their behaviour closely resembles that of the rare earths. This is especially true of the yttrium ion, which, because of the lanthanide contraction, is about the same size as one of the heavier rare earths, holmium. The similarity is less close for scandium, which has a smaller ionic radius; although this element is sometimes listed with the rare earths, it is more often treated separately.

Occurrence.—Several hundred rare-earth minerals are known but only a few are commercially important. (*See* Table II.)

TABLE II.—*Principal Rare-Earth Minerals*

Mineral	Type of Ore	Leading Producers
Ceria Group (Light Rare Earths)		
Monazite	Phosphate	India, Brazil, South Africa, U.S., Australia, Malaya, Canada, Korea, Ceylon, Indonesia
Bastnasite	Fluocarbonate	U.S. (California)
Yttria Group (Heavy Rare Earths)		
Gadolinite	Silicate	U.S., Scandinavia, Germany, Ireland, Austria, Italy, Ceylon, Greenland
Xenotime	Phosphate	Scandinavia, Switzerland, Brazil, U.S.
Euxenite	Columbate	Scandinavia, Madagascar, Brazil, Greenland, U.S., Canada, Australia
Samarskite	Tantalate and uranate	U.S., U.S.S.R., Canada, Madagascar, West Africa

Geochemical processes tend to concentrate in a given mineral the rare-earth ions of closely similar radii. The light rare earths (lanthanum to europium) usually occur together in a group of ores, rich in cerium, called the ceria group. Another group of ores, called the yttria group, contains the heavy rare earths and yttrium. However, varying amounts of all the rare earths (except promethium) are found in each known rare-earth mineral.

Some of the rare earths are found among the fission products of thorium, uranium, and plutonium; a number of new radioactive isotopes have been obtained from such sources. In addition, a considerable number of radioactive isotopes of the rare earths have been produced artificially. (*See* RADIOACTIVITY.)

Recovery and Separation.—The rare-earth ores are usually concentrated by mechanical methods. Then, depending on the type of ore, they are leached by hydrochloric or sulfuric acid, or else fused with sodium carbonate, sodium hydroxide, sodium hydrogen sulfate, or potassium hydrogen fluoride. The rare earths in the resulting solutions are next separated from gross amounts of other elements (*e.g.*, iron, aluminum, and silicon) by various precipitation processes using such anions as hydroxide, fluoride, phosphate, oxalate, and double alkali sulfate. In some cases the rare earths are separated into the ceria fraction and the yttria fraction; these fractions contain the rare earths in the same proportions as in the original ore.

Because of the great chemical similarity of the rare earths,

separation of the individual elements is difficult. Until other processes were developed during World War II and the decade following, rare earths were for the most part separated by the laborious procedures of fractional crystallization, precipitation, and fractional thermal decomposition. Due to the inordinate amount of time and effort required, only limited amounts of the scarcer rare earths were separated as pure fractions. The occurrence of rare earths in fission products stimulated greater research efforts, resulting in the development of ion-exchange and solvent-extraction techniques. The classical fractional separation techniques are now only of historical importance but were essential to the discovery of the rare-earth elements and in preparing pure samples for determination of chemical properties, atomic weights, and other physical properties.

Separation based on oxidation states other than 3^+ has been used with some success, for a change in valence causes a rather drastic change in properties. Cerium, praseodymium, and terbium are the only rare earths that can exist in the four-valent state; of these, only cerium (IV) is stable in water solution. It is much less basic than the trivalent rare earths and its salts are less soluble in basic aqueous solutions. It is commercially separated from the trivalent ions of the group by precipitation, crystallization, and extraction. Quadrivalent praseodymium and terbium are powerful oxidizing agents and, as they are reduced to the trivalent state by water, cannot exist in aqueous solution. Some separations have been effected with fused salts and alkalies. Samarium, europium, and ytterbium can be reduced to the divalent state; of these, europium is the only one separated by this means: the trivalent ion is reduced by zinc and coprecipitated with barium as sulfate.

Chemical techniques employing ion-exchange resins (*see* ION EXCHANGE) have been used with great success for separating large quantities of pure rare-earth elements. Synthetic organic resins containing a number of active exchange sites have been developed and are used in this process. The scheme developed by F. H. Spedding and J. E. Powell and used for commercial production is as follows: A vertical tube with a porous plug and valve at its base is filled with an ion-exchange resin which exchanges only cations. A weakly acidic rare-earth solution, from which impurities have been removed by conventional chemical techniques, is poured onto the top of the column and allowed to flow slowly through. Because of their high electrical charges, the trivalent rare-earth ions replace the hydrogen ions on the resin and are held near the top of the column, the hydrogen ions going into solution. A solution of an eluting agent such as ethylenediaminetetraacetic acid (EDTA) is slowly passed through the column from the top, forming complexes (chelates) with the rare-earth ions. Due to differences among the equilibrium constants of the rare earth–EDTA complexes, the rare-earth ions move at different rates down the column and are thus separated into bands. At the bottom of the column, separate fractions of the solutions, each containing an individual rare earth, may be removed. The flow of liquid through the column must be sufficiently slow so that equilibrium is maintained throughout the process in order to achieve maximum separation. The control of acidity is also important since the equilibrium constants change with the pH.

Solvent extraction, a low-cost method which lends itself to continuous operation requiring little attention, also has been used for large-scale separation. Kilogram quantities of some rare earths, of high purity, have been prepared by this method, using tributyl phosphate in contact with rare-earth nitrate solutions in a countercurrent extractor. Among other solvents in use are di(2-ethylhexyl) phosphoric acid, monoalkyl phosphoric acids, and certain ketones, esters, and alcohols. Other purification methods used for certain rare earths are electrolytic reduction, or reduction by the use of sodium amalgam, in either case to form amalgams.

Properties of Ions and Compounds.—*Magnetism.*—The magnetic behaviour of the rare-earth ions is of theoretical interest. Trivalent lanthanum, with a xenon electronic structure and no unpaired electrons, is diamagnetic; for the same reason trivalent lutetium (fourteen 4f electrons), divalent ytterbium (fourteen

4f electrons), and tetravalent cerium (no 4f electrons) also are diamagnetic. All other ions of the rare earths are paramagnetic. The paramagnetism of the trivalent rare-earth ions increases somewhat irregularly from cerium to a maximum at dysprosium and holmium and then decreases to zero at lutetium. The magnetic character of an atom or ion is due primarily to the forces associated respectively with the spinning motion and the orbital motion of its electrons. If the electrons are all paired the magnetic effects are nullified and the substance is diamagnetic; if unpaired electrons are present the substance is paramagnetic. It might seem that the gadolinium (III) ion, with the maximum number of unpaired electrons (seven), should have the greatest paramagnetism; instead, dysprosium and holmium have the highest shown by any of the elements. This variation has been quantitatively explained by J. H. Van Vleck on a theoretical basis: it is thought that the paramagnetism of gadolinium is due only to the spin effects of the seven unpaired electrons, whereas in the other cases the observed values are due to a combination of spin and orbital effects. (*See* also MAGNETISM: *Paramagnetism: Rare Earths.*)

Spectroscopy.—Certain trivalent rare-earth ions exhibit extremely sharp, narrow absorption peaks in the ultraviolet, visible, and near-infrared regions of the spectrum. These lines are due to the transfer of electrons within the 4f subshell, with resulting absorption of the light waves of that particular energy. This characteristic sharpness was unique with the rare-earth elements until the actinide elements, particularly americium, were synthesized (*see* TRANSURANIUM ELEMENTS). The actinides contain electrons in the 5f subshell and have similarly sharp absorption lines. These absorptions are of interest in determining electronic structures and of practical use for quantitative analysis.

Valency.—The common and characteristic oxidation state of the rare earths is 3^+. In addition, cerium, praseodymium, and terbium are also tetrapositive; and samarium, europium, and ytterbium are dipositive. The explanation for the non-tripositive valences is found in the unusual stability of empty, half-filled, and filled electron subshells. The trivalent ions of lanthanum (no 4f electrons), gadolinium (seven 4f electrons), and lutetium (fourteen 4f electrons) are examples. The neighbouring elements tend toward more stable configurations: cerium and praseodymium each lose an extra electron to form tetravalent compounds and to achieve the lanthanum or near-lanthanum 4f structures; terbium loses an electron to become tetravalent, while samarium and europium each gain an electron to form divalent compounds—all three tending toward the gadolinium structure; and ytterbium gains an electron to become lutetium-like in the divalent state.

Fusion of a trivalent rare-earth halide with its own metal in a sealed tantalum container has resulted in the preparation of compounds of lanthanum, cerium, praseodymium, and neodymium in which the apparent valence of the rare earth is below three. Neodymium forms a true 2^+ ionic salt; the other three a "metallic" bonded compound having high electrical conductivity. Thulium has been prepared also in the divalent state by treatment of the metal with iodine vapour; the TmI_2 prepared is a true ionic salt. Both Nd^{+2} and Tm^{+2} are very strong reducing agents and are not stable in aqueous solution.

The properties of the rare-earth trivalent ions are much the same, changing primarily in degree from the lightest, lanthanum, to the heaviest, lutetium. The trivalent nitrates, chlorides, bromides, iodides, perchlorates, and sulfates are all very soluble in water. The fluorides, oxalates, phosphates, double alkali sulfates, and hydroxides are the more insoluble compounds, much used in the older separation methods. The rare-earth ions do not form stable complexes with most inorganic ions but do form complexes of varying stabilities with a number of organic chelating agents. The basicity of the ions decreases from lanthanum to lutetium, which is quite weak.

The Metals.—All of the rare-earth metals except promethium have been prepared in very pure form and some of their properties have been determined (*see* METAL, table). Because of the high reactivity of the metals they cannot be prepared from water solutions of their salts by either electrolytic or chemical reduction. They are produced by electrolysis of molten salts or by chemical

reduction of the dry halides with alkali or alkaline-earth metals. Reduction of the oxides by alkaline-earth metals or even by a less volatile rare-earth metal, followed by distillation of the pure rare-earth metal, is another method; *e.g.*, the oxides of samarium, europium, and ytterbium may be reduced in a vacuum by lanthanum and the liberated metal purified by distillation.

The rare-earth metals are of silvery lustre. The lighter members of the group are quite soft and the heavier metals are much harder. They are, in general, strong reducing agents and are extremely reactive. The metals tarnish in air; in powder form they ignite spontaneously. They react with hot water, liberating hydrogen. Although in aqueous solution the ions and compounds of the rare earths are quite similar, the metals show marked differences in physical properties. The differences in melting points of the various metals vary as much as 800° C. There are similar wide differences in volatility; *e.g.*, at a given temperature europium is many times more volatile than lanthanum.

See also articles on the individual rare earths, and references under "Rare Earths" in the Index.

BIBLIOGRAPHY.—D. M. Yost, H. Russel, Jr., and C. S. Garner, *The Rare Earth Elements and Their Compounds* (1947); R. C. Vickery, *Chemistry of the Lanthanons* (1953); F. H. Spedding and A. H. Daane (eds.), *The Rare Earths* (1961); T. Moeller, *The Chemistry of the Lanthanides* (1963). (LD. B. A.; J. B. Ps.)

RASH: *see* SKIN, DISEASES OF.

RASHI (RABBI SOLOMON [SHELOMOH] BEN ISAAC) (1040–1105), Jewish scholar, commentator par excellence, author of the great and supremely popular commentaries on the Bible and the Talmud, was born at Troyes, France. The name Rashi was derived from the initial letters of his full name. He was a member of a cultured family and a blood relative of the greatest scholars of Germany of the second half of the 11th century. Two personal misfortunes determined his life's work. His father Isaac died when Rashi was a child, and his mother was left with a large vineyard as the sole source of the family income. He was thus denied his burning ambitions: to be a perpetual student and to spend his life in Mainz or Worms, the great centres of talmudic scholarship.

Since he was allowed but a few years to study under Rabbi Jacob ben Yaqar and Rabbi Isaac ha-Levi in Worms, and under Rabbi Isaac ben Judah in Mainz, Rashi had to pursue his studies under great pressure. He did not have the time or the leisure to follow the normal practice of committing to memory the oral explanations of his teachers for every phrase and every statement of the Talmud, and was thus forced to write them down. Upon his return home, the cares and preoccupations of a vintner kept him from the company of scholars and students, and he was thus required to review his notes in private and to attain mastery of talmudic lore through the written word. This master teacher was denied the audience of a large group of eager and enthusiastic pupils and had to direct all his pedagogical instincts and compulsions to unseen students, the perusers of the written word.

RASHI'S CHAIR, IN NICHE, IN THE STUDY OF THE WORMS SYNAGOGUE

Thus came into being his great written commentaries on the Bible and on the Talmud.

When in 1096 the centres of rabbinic learning in the Rhineland were destroyed by the ravages of the First Crusade, and the great teachers were killed, the commentaries of Rashi were eagerly sought after by hundreds of surviving students-without-teachers. He attracted many students to Troyes, and his school became the most important centre of rabbinic learning in central Europe, a fountainhead of rabbinic scholarship and a concentration point of spiritual leadership for Ashkenazic Jewry. He changed the pattern of rabbinic learning, and caused his students and followers to make use of the pen and to produce a voluminous literature in their effort to complete the process of committing to writing the rich oral traditions of the great schools of German and French Jewry, traditions that had been transmitted orally from teacher to student for a thousand years and were now in danger of disappearance.

Rashi's learning and character raised him to a position of high respect among the Jewries of Europe. His commentaries soon spread even to Spain, and they were respected in the schools of Egypt and of the East. As was said of him soon after his death (at Troyes, on July 13, 1105), "His lips were the seat of wisdom, and thanks to him the Law, which he examined and interpreted, has come to life again."

The most significant members of Rashi's school were members of his immediate family. He had three daughters but no sons, and two of his most important students were his sons-in-law, Rabbi Judah ben Nathan, who eventually wrote commentaries on many tractates of the Talmud; and Rabbi Meir ben Samuel, who also wrote such commentaries. The son of the latter, Rabbi Samuel ben Meir, better known as Rashbam, was his grandfather's greatest and most renowned student. An admirer of the beauty, accuracy, and effectiveness of Rashi's commentary on the Talmud, he tried to emulate it, often overzealously. Rashbam also wrote a commentary on the Pentateuch, characterized by a concentration on the obvious meaning of the text, which became very popular in subsequent centuries. Rashbam's brothers, Isaac ben Meir (Ribam) and Jacob ben Meir Tam, also carried on Rashi's work, the latter as one of the greatest of the Tosafists (glossators).

Other outstanding students of Rashi's school were Rabbi Joseph ben Simon Kara, who wrote an important commentary on all the prophetic books, on Job, and on the Five Scrolls; Rabbi Simcha of Vitry, the compiler of *Mahzor Vitry*, a collection of rules, discussions, and comments, mainly regarding the ritual of services of the synagogue on all festive occasions; and Rabbi Shemaiah, a close associate of Rashi, probably the compiler of *Sefer ha-Pardes*, which was one of the first collections and arrangements of ritual law composed by Ashkenazic Jewry.

In the past seven centuries rabbinic scholars throughout the world have studied the Talmud with Rashi's commentary and the additions of the Tosafists of the 12th–13th centuries. Practically every edition of the Talmud contains the text flanked on each page by these two literary masterpieces.

Rashi's commentary on the Pentateuch, in particular, was very popular. It was printed in hundreds of editions and is still to Jews the most beloved of all commentaries on the Mosaic books. More than a hundred supercommentaries have been written on it. Rashi's influence in Christian circles was great, especially because of the use made of his commentary on the Bible by Nicholas (*q.v.*) of Lyra, who in his turn was one of the main sources of Luther's version. More than 300 *responsa* of Rashi, to the scholars of his day, were preserved; and in his school were composed several custumals and collections of rabbinic lore that had a profound influence on the religious customs of the Jews of subsequent generations.

BIBLIOGRAPHY.—M. Liber, *Rashi* (1906); American Academy for Jewish Research, *Rashi Anniversary Volume* (1941); M. Waxman, *A History of Jewish Literature*, vol. i (1930); I. A. Agus, *Urban Civilization in Pre-Crusade Europe* (1965).   (I. A. A.)

RASHID AL-DIN FADLULLAH (1247–1318), Persian statesman and historian, author of a universal history, *Jami al-tawarikh*, belonged to a Jewish family of Hamadan but was con-verted to Islam, and as a physician joined the court of the Mongol ruler of Persia, Abaqa-khan (1265–1282). He became vizier to Ghazan-khan in 1298 and served under his successor Uljaytu. Accused by his rivals of having poisoned his sovereign, he was put to death by Uljaytu's son Abu Sa'id.

Rashid al-Din's history covers a vast field even outside the Muslim world. His sources of information for Mongolia and China were high officials of the Mongol empire and the Mongol records, for India a Buddhist from Kashmir, for the popes and emperors a Catholic monk, etc. There are important chapters describing the social and economic conditions of the Islamic countries under Ghazan-khan (1295–1304) and the reforms introduced by this ruler on the advice of the author himself. Rashid al-Din uses a great number of Mongol and Turkish terms but his style is lucid and matter-of-fact.

The important parts of Rashid al-Din's history were published by E. Quatremère (1936), I. M. Berezin (1858–1888), E. Blochet (1911), K. Jahn (1940), Ali-zade (1958), and A. Atesh (1957). The parts on the Mongolian tribes, on Genghis Khan and on Ghazan-khan, appeared in a new Russian translation (1946–52). Rashid's interesting correspondence with his sons and dependents was published by M. Shafi (1947).   (V. F. M.)

RASHT (RESHT), a city and capital of the *ostan* (province) of Gilan in Iran, lies on a left-bank branch (Siah Rud) of the Safid Rud, where the higher ground merges into the marshlands fringing the Mordab or Pahlavi Lagoon, 150 mi. NW of Teheran. Population (1956 census) 109,491; 1962 est. 130,000; in 1940 it had been 121,625. Rasht is mentioned in the 14th century as a place of considerable size, producing silk and cotton. Its importance as capital of Gilan dates from the southward expansion of Russia in the 17th century. It suffered a good deal during World Wars I and II from occupation by the Russian Army, and afterward from the decline of the northern trade. In World War II Rasht was a stage on the Allied supply route to the U.S.S.R.

The city is surrounded by rice fields and areas of half-cleared jungle. The summer climate is damp with an annual average temperature of 66° F (19° C) and a rainfall of 32–59 in. It was heavily infested by malaria until after World War II. The houses are mostly of handsome though soft red brick, two-storied, and with much woodwork such as broad verandas and overhanging eaves. The roofs are red-tiled in contrast to the steep thatched roofs of the countryside, and the houses are often raised from the ground. Most of the old streets are still paved with cobblestones. Modernization is confined to the main streets and thoroughfares.

Rasht is an important regional centre, marketing most of the agricultural surpluses of Gilan, especially rice, also tea, groundnuts (peanuts) and other cash crops, and silk. It is an administrative and cultural centre with many public services. The bazaar is large and lively, with many crafts. Local agricultural products (rice, tobacco, silk, kenaf) are processed; soap, glass, and razor blades are also manufactured. The largest plant is a mill for kenaf (jute) bags. Modern developments have been slow. In 1962 a large dam on the Safid Rud, designed for improving irrigation on the Gilan Plain and for electric power, was completed. An extension to Rasht of the oil pipeline from the main line in Teheran was under construction.

Rasht is connected by good roads with the port of Pahlavi and, via Kazvin, with Teheran and the rest of the highland. It is also linked through Lahijan with the *ostan* of Mazanderan and through Astara on the Soviet frontier with Tabriz. There is an airfield to the north of the town.   (H. Bo.)

RASHTRAKUTA (RATTA), the name of an Indian dynasty that ruled over the Deccan (*q.v.*) and neighbouring lands from A.D. 757 to 975. A royal family of Lattalur (Latur near Osmanabad), with branches as far north as the Tapti and farther south at Saundatti (40 mi. ESE of Belgaum), they were at one time leading feudatories of the Chalukya (*q.v.*) dynasty of Vatapi. They spoke Kanarese, but knew the northern Deccan. They ousted the Chalukyas of Gujarat and the Sendrakas and struggled constantly with the Chalukyas of Vengi.

Under their leadership the Deccan became the second greatest political unit of India. The emperor at Malkhed (near Gulbarga) was called the Sri-Prithvi-Vallabha (the "Ballaha-ra" of Arabic authors). Krishna I acquired the Konkan and built the famous Kailasa, the rockcut temple at Ellora. Dhruva subdued the Gangas of Gangavadi (Mysore), contained the Pallava (*q.v.*) of Kanchi (Kancheepuram), and defeated the king of Bengal and the Pratihara king, who were contending for Kannauj. Amoghavarsha reigned from 814 to 878, during which time the Gujarat branch of the family and Vengi shook themselves free. He was of a contemplative character, and the author *inter alia* of the *Kavirajamarga*, the earliest-known Kanarese poem. Krishna II, who succeeded in 878, reacquired Gujarat but failed to retake Vengi. His grandson Indra III came to the throne in 914. He took Kannauj and brought Rashtrakuta power to its peak. Krishna III outdid him in northern campaigns (*c.* 940) and in a spectacular occupation of Kanchi and much of the Tamil Plains (948–966/67). Khottiga Amoghavarsha IV (968–972) failed to protect the capital from the Paramara, and its sack destroyed faith in the dynasty. The emperor fled to the Western Ghats, where his line lingered ignominiously, supported by brave Ganga and Kadamba feudatories, until Taila Chalukya won the succession *c.* A.D. 975.

See A. S. Altekar, *The Rashtrakutas and Their Times* (1934); G. Yazdani (ed.), *The Early History of the Deccan*, 2 vol. (1960).

(J. D. M. D.)

RASIN, ALOIS (1867–1923), Czech patriot, one of the founders of Czechoslovakia and its first minister of finance, was born at Nechanice, in Bohemia, on Oct. 18, 1867, and studied law in Prague. In 1893 he was arrested in connection with the Czech patriotic *Omladina* conspiracy against the Austrian authorities and sent to prison. Amnestied in 1895, he then worked as a lawyer in Prague. At first he joined the Young Czech Party led by Karel Kramar, then in 1899 he founded a new Radical-Progressive Party, and later he was reconciled with Kramar. In 1911 he was elected to the Austrian parliament (*Reichsrat*) as a Young Czech. His activities before World War I were extensive. In his contributions to the Czech newspaper *Narodni Listy* and elsewhere he expressed a particular interest in social and medical questions.

Arrested as a traitor to Austria in July 1915, Rasin was condemned to death on June 3, 1916; but the sentence was later commuted, and in June 1917, after the accession of the new emperor, Charles I, he was amnestied. He was thus freed in time to become a leading member of the new Czechoslovak National Council, which organized the Czech take-over of power in Prague in October 1918. When the republic of Czechoslovakia came into being, Rasin, now a National Democrat deputy, was its first minister of finance and showed great efficiency in the establishment of a balanced budget and the new Czechoslovak currency. Shot by a young revolutionary named Soupal in January 1923, he died of his injuries on Feb. 18, in Prague. His *Financial Policy of Czechoslovakia During the First Year of Its History* appeared in English in 1923.

(E. Wi.)

RASK, RASMUS CHRISTIAN (1787–1832), Danish philologist, a founder of the science of comparative linguistics, was born at Brändekilde, Fünen, on Nov. 22, 1787. He studied at Copenhagen, and was appointed assistant keeper of the university library in 1808 and later professor of literary history. Rask was one of the first to recognize that the Celtic languages are Indo-European; he anticipated Jacob Grimm in the formulation of the first Germanic consonant shift, and Ferdinand de Saussure in his realization of the function and character of minimal speech sounds (the phoneme). He wrote grammars of Icelandic, Old Norse, Old English, Spanish, Frisian, and Italian; treatises on Jewish and on Egyptian chronology; edited parts of the *Edda;* and published innumerable papers on linguistic and literary topics. He also brought out the Icelandic Lexicon (1814) of Björn Haldorson.

Rask was the first president of the Icelandic Literary Society; but in 1816 he left Denmark to prosecute inquiries into the languages of the east and collect manuscripts for the university library at Copenhagen. From Stockholm he went to St. Petersburg, thence through Tatary into Persia, and resided for some time at Tabriz, Teheran, Persepolis, and Shiraz. From Persia he went to India and Ceylon. Rask returned to Copenhagen in May 1823, bringing a considerable number of Oriental manuscripts, Persian, Zend, Pali, Sinhalese, and others, with which he enriched the collections of the Danish capital. He died at Copenhagen on Nov. 14, 1832.

Bibliography.—See his collected essays, *Samlade Afhandlinger*, 3 vol. (1834–38); selected essays, *Udvalgte Afhandlinger*, ed. by L. Hjelmslev (1932); Otto Jespersen, *Rasmus Rask i hundredåret efter hans Hovedværk* (1918).

(J. Wh.)

RASKOLNIKI: *see* Old Believers.

RASMUSSEN, KNUD JOHAN VICTOR (1879–1933), Danish polar explorer and ethnologist who possessed an unsurpassed ability to win the confidence and understand the character of the Eskimo, was born at Jakobshavn, Greenland, on June 7, 1879. His maternal grandmother was a Greenlander (*i.e.*, of mixed race), and he acquired a thorough mastery of the Eskimo language. After studies at Copenhagen university and a visit to Lapland (1901), he accompanied L. Mylius-Erichsen to northwest Greenland in 1902–04, where he wintered with the most northerly Eskimo tribe in the world (the Polar Eskimo). He was in west Greenland in 1905 to study the possibilities of introducing reindeer husbandry, but spent the next two years with the Polar Eskimo, and in 1910 established, with the aid of privately contributed means, the permanent station at Thule. The object was to provide a trading centre for the population, a base for expeditions and a foundation for the raising of the Polar Eskimo's spiritual, cultural and material level. In 1912 Rasmussen led the first Thule expedition. With three companions he traveled with dog sledges across the Greenland ice sheet from Thule to the northeast coast and back, making valuable geographical discoveries. The second Thule expedition (1916–18) surveyed the north coast of Greenland under very hard conditions. Rasmussen did not personally accompany the third Thule expedition; the fourth (1919) was his journey to Angmagssalik in east Greenland to collect Eskimo tales. The fifth Thule expedition (1921–24) was Rasmussen's greatest. After investigations in northeast Canada, Rasmussen, with two Eskimos, accomplished the longest dog-sledge journey ever made, across the American arctic. He left Danish Island on March 11, 1923, and reached Point Barrow on May 23, 1924. He made a scientific study of every Eskimo tribe, tracing their migration routes and showing the basic unity of their cultures. The sixth and seventh Thule expeditions made cartographic, archaeological and ethnographical studies in southeast Greenland. He died on Dec. 21, 1933, in Gentofte, Denmark.

A brilliant expedition leader, Rasmussen inspired an extraordinary devotion in his companions. Probably no polar explorer has so much used the services of the Eskimo, while he was himself a superb dog-sledge driver. His rich literary production embraces travel descriptions and translations of Eskimo mythology and songs, as well as strictly scientific works, including *Grønland Langs Polhavet* (1919; Eng. trans. *Greenland by the Polar Sea*, 1921) and *Across Arctic America* (1927). (P. A. B. G.)

RASPBERRY (genus *Rubus*), an old and well-known fruit-bearing bush, mentioned by Pliny as a wild fruit. John Parkinson (*Paradisus*, 1629) speaks of red, white and thornless varieties of raspberries, and their culture began about this time. Raspberry bushes bear juicy red or black (rarely orange, amber or pale yellow) berries which separate from the core that remains on the plant; in blackberries, the core is a part of the fruit.

Distribution.—The raspberry section of *Rubus* probably evolved in eastern Asia, where there are more than 200 species known. In Great Britain and throughout Europe only one species, *R. idaeus,* is known, from which the European cultivated varieties are derived. In the United States and Canada, three species (*R. strigosus,* the red raspberry; *R. occidentalis,* the eastern black raspberry; and *R. leucodermis,* the western black raspberry) are found. American red varieties are derived from *R. strigosus* and hybrids of it with *R. idaeus.* They are much hardier and less prickly than European varieties. Black varieties came from *R. occidentalis;* purple varieties are hybrids of the black and red. Related edible berries, often called raspberries, are the two flowering raspberries of northern American woodlands, *Rubus odoratus* and *R. parviflorus;* the Rocky mountain flowering raspberry, *R.*

deliciosus; and the salmonberry, *R. spectabilis,* of the Pacific northwest. Three other raspberries are grown for their fruit in other parts of the world—the Andes black raspberry, *R. glaucus,* in northern South America and Central America; the southern Asian black raspberry, *R. niveus;* and the wineberry, *R. phoenicolasius,* introduced from northeastern Asia. *R. kuntzeánus* from China has been hybridized with the Cuthbert to give the Van Fleet, and *R. biflorus,* also from China, has been hybridized with Latham to give the Dixie, both adapted to the southern U.S.

ROCHE

BLACK RASPBERRIES (RUBUS OCCIDENTALIS)

Acreage and Varieties.—In Great Britain about 10,000 ac. of red raspberries are cultivated. The Blairgowrie district is the centre of production in Scotland; Kent, the eastern counties and Worcestershire are centres in England. Raspberries are sometimes grown in mixed plantings with other fruit, the plants being set at 18-in. intervals in rows 6 or 7 ft. apart. Lloyd George is a leading variety, with large berries good for canning and jam. Red Cross, Pynes Royal and Malling Promise are other good varieties.

The acreage of raspberries in the United States is about 20,000. Black raspberries are nearly as important as red; the acreage of purple varieties is small. Important raspberry sections are western Maryland, southern New Jersey, the Hudson river valley, western New York, western Michigan, near Minneapolis, Minn., the Puyallup valley of Washington, and the Willamette valley of Oregon. Few plantings in the United States, except in the Hudson river valley, are mixed with other fruits. Good red varieties are Willamette, Canby and Washington, in the Pacific northwest; Sunrise, for early, and Latham, for late, for eastern states; and Taylor and Milton, in New York and New England. Cumberland is the chief black variety. In eastern Canada, Viking and Newman red varieties are widely grown. Sodus and Marion are desirable purple varieties. September and Durham are red sorts that also bear fruit on the young canes in late summer and fall.

Propagation.—Red raspberries are propagated by suckers from the roots of the parent plant. Root cuttings about three inches long are also used for rapid increase of new varieties. Black and purple varieties have arched canes and are propagated by tip layers, the tips of the shoots being buried about two inches deep in August and the rooted tips being dug in early spring. Leaf-bud cuttings may be used for the rapid propagation of new black varieties. Red raspberries are usually planted 2½ ft. apart, the black and purple about 4 ft. apart in rows 6 to 9 ft. distant. Shoots are produced in spring and summer that bear fruit the following year and then die. These old canes are cut away each year just after the harvest to make room for the new shoots. The new shoots of the black varieties are tipped or cut off at 12 in. to induce branching; those of the purple at 18 to 24 in. The branches are shortened the following winter to about 8 in. for the black and 12 in. for the purple. The canes of the red raspberries are either not pruned or are shortened to 3 to 5½ ft., depending on the variety and vigour. However, surplus suckers should be cut away early in the summer, leaving seven or eight of the strongest canes per plant or per 30 in. of row. The stouter the canes of both black and red varieties, the more productive they are. Stakes or trellises are commonly used to support the canes of the red raspberry. Two-wire trellises with a wire on each side of the row about 3 ft. high or with one wire above the other at 30 in. and 54 in. are common.

Virus diseases, leaf spot, anthracnose, crown gall, wilt and orange rust are serious diseases, while the red spider mite, crown borer and fruit worms are serious insect pests.

See also FRUIT FARMING.

See U.S. Department of Agriculture *Farmers' Bulletin* 887 (1948).
(G. M. D.)

RASPE, RUDOLF ERICH (1737–1794), German scholar and adventurer, the original author of the *Adventures of Baron Munchausen* (*see* MUNCHAUSEN), was born at Hanover in 1737 and studied natural sciences and philology at Göttingen and Leipzig. He worked in university libraries and was appointed librarian and custodian of the Landgraf's collection of gems and coins at Kassel in 1767. He won a scholarly reputation with learned articles on many subjects (he was one of the first to interest himself in Ossian and in Percy's *Reliques*) and was elected a fellow of the Royal Society in 1769; but in 1775 he began stealing from the Landgraf's gem collection and finally had to flee to England to escape arrest. Here he lived on his wits, at times near starvation, and *Munchausen,* published anonymously, was produced during this period (1785). In 1791 he was involved in a swindle concerned with mining in Scotland, and fled to Ireland, where he died of fever at Muckross, County Kerry, in 1794. His authorship of *Munchausen* was only revealed in 1847 by Heinrich Döring in his biography of G. A. Bürger, who had translated the book into German.

See R. Halls, *Raspe* (1934); J. P. Carswell, *The Prospector, Being the Life and Times of Rudolf Erich Raspe* (1950). (W. D. Wi.)

RASPUTIN, GRIGORI EFIMOVICH (1872?–1916), Russian peasant and mystic who became a powerful favourite at the court of the emperor Nicholas II, was born at Pokrovskoe, near

CULVER PICTURES INC.

GRIGORI EFIMOVICH RASPUTIN

Tyumen, in western Siberia; his original family name was Novykh. Though he received no formal education, he was extremely astute. He had an extraordinarily magnetic personality and seems to have possessed hypnotic powers. In early manhood he came under the influence of adherents of the sect of the Khlysty ("Flagellants"); he claimed to be divinely inspired and to be able to work miracles. In particular he preached that physical contact with his own person had a healing and purifying effect—a doctrine which served him as a convenient means of gratifying his phenomenal sexual appetite. He was accused of heresy, but the proceedings against him were dropped. He was already being called Rasputin, meaning "debauchee."

Adopting the role of a holy man (*starets*), Rasputin set out as a pilgrim and, in 1903, arrived in St. Petersburg. There he was befriended by high-ranking Orthodox prelates and attained admission into aristocratic society. Mysticism was the fashion, and Rasputin was soon the centre of a circle of admiring female devotees. In November 1905 he was introduced to the imperial couple. His powers of suggestion had a soothing effect on the tsarevitch Alexis, who suffered from hemophilia, and also on the empress Alexandra (*q.v.*). She came to look on Rasputin as a saint, sent by God to save the dynasty. The emperor Nicholas was less impressed, but readily succumbed to her persuasions. Rasputin urged on the imperial couple the need for firm autocratic government and presented himself as a simple *muzhik,* the voice of the loyal and God-fearing peasantry, whose opinions were more worthy of attention than those of the emperor's high-born advisers.

Though Rasputin behaved at court with relative decorum, elsewhere he indulged in uninhibited licence; and in the course of his debauches he would often boast in exaggerated terms of his intimate relations with the imperial family. His former ecclesiastical protectors denounced him as an impostor, but were themselves arbitrarily punished. When references to Rasputin's influence appeared in print, the offending publications were confiscated. The matter was discussed in the Duma, which led to tension between it and the court. Early in 1912, Rasputin was sent back to his native village. Yet he remained in favour; and by the autumn of 1914, having survived an attempt on his life, he was once again firmly ensconced in the capital.

World War I had meanwhile broken out, and after Nicholas' assumption of supreme command in the field (September 1915) the empress and Rasputin were left in virtual control of domestic affairs. When appointments were made Rasputin's opinions generally (although not invariably) carried decisive weight. A number of honest and capable ministers and officials were dismissed, being replaced by worthless nonentities or unscrupulous careerists who enjoyed Rasputin's protection. He was surrounded by financial speculators and morally corrupt individuals whose requests for favours he and his placemen endeavoured to satisfy—as well as those of humble and more meritorious petitioners. He continued his riotous way of living, safeguarded by police agents.

Rasputin followed no consistent policy, but was opposed to the war, which threatened to undermine the Romanov dynasty and thus also his own position; also, like very many ordinary Russians he objected to the wasteful sacrifice of human life. There is no evidence that he was a German agent, as was widely believed at the time. But his activities paralyzed the normal workings of the administration and widened the breach between the court and public opinion. Opposition to the favourite was strongest in right-wing circles. A group of extreme conservatives, headed by V. M. Purishkevich and including the grand duke Dimitri Pavlovich and prince F. F. Yusupov, decided to assassinate Rasputin in the hope of saving the monarchy from itself. On the night of Dec. 29–30 (new style; 16–17, old style), 1916, he was done to death in sordid circumstances: after an attempt to poison him, he was shot. The murder merely strengthened Alexandra's resolve to uphold the principle of autocracy, but a few weeks later the whole imperial regime was swept away by revolution.

BIBLIOGRAPHY.—M. V. Rodzianko, *The Reign of Rasputin* (1927); F. F. Yusupov, *Rasputin* (1927); R. Fülöp-Miller, *Rasputin, the Holy Devil* (1928); V. M. Purishkevich, *Nous avons tué Raspoutine* (1953); C. Wilson, *Rasputin and the Fall of the Romanovs* (1964).

(J. L. H. K.)

RAS SHAMRA: *see* UGARIT.

RAS TANURA (RA'S AT TANNURAH), a port in the Eastern Province (Al Hasa) of Saudi Arabia, lies 25 mi. (40 km.) N of Dhahran. Pop. (1956 est.) 15,000. It is the principal Persian Gulf terminal of the pipelines serving oil tankers from a long jetty built out into deep water, and a number of oil tanks are in Ras Tanura. Ad Dammam (*see* DAMMAM, AD) serves the commercial needs of the kingdom. Ras Tanura is finely situated along the seashore.

(H. ST. J. B. P.; X.)

RASTELL, JOHN (*c.* 1475–1536), English lawyer, printer, and dramatist, brother-in-law of Sir Thomas More, was a son of Thomas Rastell, coroner of Coventry. He was educated at the Middle Temple and was himself coroner of Coventry from 1506 to 1509. Before 1504 he married Elizabeth More. Their daughter Joan married the dramatist John Heywood and their second son William Rastell was also a printer. Before 1512 Rastell moved to London. He was in charge of ordnance under Sir Edward Belknap in the French war of 1512 to 1514 and in the campaign of 1523 he was with "the army royal beyond seas" as a trenchmaker. He provided a ship in 1517 for the expedition to colonize Newfoundland, but owing to the mutiny of his mariners he got no farther than Ireland. Rastell decorated the roofs of the banqueting hall erected at the Field of Cloth of Gold (1520). For the reception of the emperor Charles V in 1522 he set up a pageant near his shop at the "little conduit in Cheap," representing heaven with "clouds, orbes, starres and hierarchies of angels"; he presented another pageant, the "Father of Heaven," for the entertainment of French ambassadors at Greenwich in 1527. The stage which Rastell built at his house in Finsbury Fields in about 1525 is the earliest known in London.

Rastell's book *Canones astrologici*, mentioned by John Bale in his *Illustrium majoris Britanniae scriptorum . . . summarium* (1548), has not been traced. He wrote *Elements* (?1517) and perhaps others of the interludes issued from his own press, for whose title page he used an astronomical device. He also printed *The Merry Jests of the Widow Edith* (1526) by More's servant Walter Smyth, and the *Hundred Merry Tales* (1526), the first of the Tudor jest-books. Other works from his press included his

own abridgment of Robert Fabyan's *Chronicle,* issued as *The Pastyme of the People* (1529), and several important law books, his own *Liber assisarum* (1513), *The Abbreviation of the Statutes* (1519 and frequently reprinted), the *Expositiones terminorum legum Anglorum* (1527 and frequently reprinted), and Anthony Fitzherbert's *Le Graunde Abridgement* (1516).

Rastell was a member of the Reformation parliament (1529–36). He engaged in controversy against the Lutherans, printing More's *A Dialogue Concerning Heresies and Matters of Religion* (1529) and his own vigorous *A New Boke of Purgatory* (1530), presented in dialogue form, supporting the arguments of More against the reformer John Frith. But Rastell was converted by his brilliant opponent; he dissociated himself from More and followed Thomas Cromwell. His anxiety to abolish all tithes and oblations, however, brought him into disfavour, and he was imprisoned for opposing the Royal Proclamation of 1535 on that subject. He died in prison on June 25, 1536. His life had been much embarrassed by lawsuits. While More was chancellor (1529–32) Rastell's practice was considerable.

BIBLIOGRAPHY.—Edward Hall, *Chronicle* (1548); A. W. Reed, *Early Tudor Drama* (1926) and Introduction in *The English Works of Sir Thomas More,* ed. by W. E. Campbell (1931); T. W. Craik, *The Tudor Interlude* (1958); Pearl Hogrefe, *The Sir Thomas More Circle* (1959); E. G. Duff, H. R. Plomer, and R. Proctor, *Handlists of English Printers 1501–1556,* vol. ii (1896).

(H. W. Do.)

RASTELL, WILLIAM (1508–1565), English lawyer and printer, nephew and biographer of Sir Thomas More, whose works he preserved and printed, was a son of John Rastell and Elizabeth More. Educated in his father's office as scribe and printer, he set up his own press in 1529 and printed More's controversial writings, John Heywood's interludes, and *The Legacye or Embassate of Prester John unto Emanuell, Kynge of Portyngale,* John More's translation of the work by Damião de Goes. For law students he printed 12 of the principal legal textbooks in one volume, *Natura brevium* (1533–34). Rastell was admitted to Lincoln's Inn in 1532 and was called to the bar in 1539; he was pensioner of the Inn in 1545, reader in 1546, keeper of the Black Book (the Inn's register) from 1548 to 1549, when he became treasurer. In that year the use of the first prayer book of Edward VI was enjoined, and Rastell went into exile with his wife, Winifred, daughter of More's pupil John Clement and Margaret Giggs, More's adopted daughter. They settled at Louvain, where Winifred died in July 1553. During his exile Rastell preserved More's writings and after his return following the accession of Queen Mary (July 1553), he had the English *Works* printed by Richard Tottel. In this period of his life Rastell also published important law books of his own, *A Colleccion of All the Statutes* (1559) and *A Colleccion of Entrees* (1566). Of his large biography of More only a fragment survives. He became sergeant-at-law in 1555 and bencher of Lincoln's Inn in 1558. In 1563 he went into exile again and died on Aug. 27, 1565, at Louvain, where he was buried with his wife.

BIBLIOGRAPHY.—The fragments of Rastell's biography of More are printed with Nicholas Harpsfield's *Life and Death of Sir Thomas Moore,* ed. by E. V. Hitchcock (1932) for the Early English Text Society. *See* also A. W. Reed, *Early Tudor Drama* (1926) and Introduction in *The English Works of Sir Thomas More,* ed. by W. E. Campbell (1931); R. W. Chambers, *Thomas More* (1935).

(H. W. Do.)

RAT, a term applied indiscriminately to many rodents; more specifically, to the many species of the genus *Rattus* (family Muridae), the most varied genus of mammals, containing more than 500 named forms. Ordinarily, however, the term denotes either the "domestic" Norway—brown, barn, sewer, or wharf—rat, *Rattus norvegicus,* or the roof—black, gray, climbing, or Alexandrine—rat, *R. rattus.* Both were originally Old World species but have become virtually cosmopolitan through the agency of man. Norway rats are usually brown, but gray, white, black, and pied specimens are not infrequent. They are larger (seven to ten inches, not including the tail) and more robust than roof rats (up to eight inches long); their tails are shorter than the combined head and body length; the ears are small and half buried in the fur. Roof rats also vary in colour, certain colour phases tending to predominate regionally, but the commonest is dark gray. Their tails are longer than the head and body; the ears are large and erect and project well beyond the fur.

Originally the Norway rat occurred in cooler areas; the roof rat, in warmer areas. Thus, although the species are widespread and strongly competitive, their relative frequency is partly dependent upon climate. In the United States, for example, roof rats occur mainly in the southeastern states. Generally the Norway rats, being larger and more adaptable, vanquish roof rats, and when both occur in an area they occupy different habitats. If both occur in a building, for example, it would be a light infestation, the Norway rats occupying the lower levels and the roof rats, the upper floors.

Rats are aggressive, active, omnivorous, adaptable, and fecund —immensely successful as biological organisms. They have been known to destroy poultry, game, crops, and stored grain. Adults are fertile at all seasons. In warm places litters are produced at about two-month intervals; in cooler places, at about four-month intervals. Gestation is 20–25 days. The 6 to 22 helpless, naked young are born in a secluded site. They are weaned in a month and are ready to breed in three to four months. Rats have acutely developed senses, especially of touch and hearing, as befits essentially nocturnal animals. They climb with surpassing ease; this skill, coupled with an ability to jump and a propensity to burrow and gnaw, gains them entry to places inaccessible to many other small mammals.

When driven by hunger, thirst, or foul weather, they are resourceful and unrelenting in their attempts to enter buildings, yet ratproof construction and adequate sanitation are the best methods of control. Rats are prone to burrow along a building foundation sometimes for great distances attempting to gain entry. If deflected away from the foundations, however, by a structure such as a curtain wall, they desist. Rats may also be controlled by a coordinated and vigorously prosecuted program of trapping, poisoning, and fumigation. Because of their exceedingly destructive habits, rats are of enormous economic importance, causing millions of dollars in damage annually in the United States alone. They are also of importance in public health, having been implicated in harbouring or in transmitting directly or indirectly more than 20 diseases, including typhus fever, plague, rat-bite fever (sodoku), hemorrhagic jaundice, tularemia, rabies, trichinosis, and salmonellosis. The common laboratory white rat, a domesticated albino strain of the Norway rat, is an invaluable experimental animal in biological and medical research.

Several other families of rodents have members called rats. The Cricetidae include the cotton rats (*Sigmodon*), rough-coated rodents that are ranch and farm pests in the southern U.S., Central America, and parts of South America; rice rats (*Oryzomys*), with much the same distribution; and pack, wood, trade, mountain, or brush rats (*Neotoma*), of North and Central America, noted for their habit of collecting small, shiny objects. The family Rhizomyidae comprises the bamboo or root rats of Asia. Among the Heteromyidae are the kangaroo rats (*Dipodomys*) of southwestern North America, with stiltlike hind legs used for leaping. *See* also RODENT; and references under "Rat" in the Index.

(K. R. KN.)

RATCHET AND PAWL

is an important mechanical device in many machines and appliances, enabling a movement to be effected in one direction but not in the opposite direction. The mechanism is used to lock a part so that it cannot slip or reverse, to hold a load as in a winch or to give a positive feed. Ratchets may be straight or curved, the majority being circular. In fig. 1, motion of the arm (B) in the direction of the arrow rotates the wheel (A). When the arm (B)

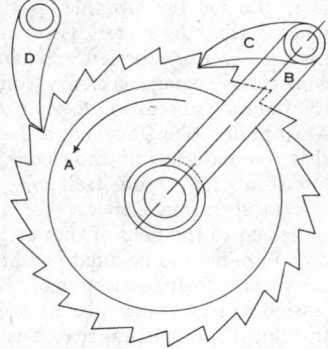

FROM C. W. HAM, E. J. CRANE AND W. L. ROGERS, "MECHANICS OF MACHINERY," REPRODUCED BY PERMISSION OF McGRAW-HILL BOOK CO.

FIG. 1.—SIMPLE RATCHET AND PAWL (A) ratchet wheel; (B) oscillating lever carrying (C) driving pawl; (D) supplementary pawl prevents backward motion of the wheel

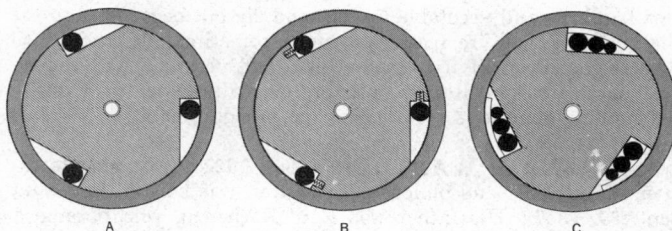

FROM J. H. BILLINGS, "APPLIED KINEMATICS," D. VAN NOSTRAND COMPANY, INC., PRINCETON, N.J. (1953)

FIG. 2.—THREE SILENT, OR FREE-WHEELING, RATCHETS

Counterclockwise rotation of inner driving member turns outer driven member by wedging action of balls: (A) basic single-ball mechanism; (B) basic type with springs to insure positive wedging in any starting position; (C) multiple-ball type with lining protecting driven member

reverses, supplementary pawl (D) prevents backward motion of the wheel, providing the typical intermittent motion in one direction for the wheel.

Slack in the engagement of the teeth may be reduced by using smaller teeth, additional stationary pawls or by using the silent (free-wheeling) ratchet (fig. 2). A variety of constructions employ balls, rollers or eccentrically pivoted pawls to wedge in tapered slots and provide silent, smooth, slack-free motion in one direction.

Various drives and brake mechanisms are made safe by ratchet devices, the ship's capstan being one of the oldest examples. Screwdrivers and wrenches are operated by ratchet for access in difficult situations, or to help the worker in manipulative power. Braces and metal drills are actuated by ratchets when it is not possible to make the complete revolution of a handle. So also are jack screws actuated for lifting loads rapidly. Many counting devices are based on the use of ratchets. Ratchet feed, by which an arm holding the pawl is moved, thus moving a ratchet wheel and a feed screw, is utilized in many types of machines and is usually automatic in action. For example, the workpiece table on a shaper may be moved sideways a small space for each stroke of the cutting tool, a movement which will provide a complete traverse of the surface of the piece being machined. (F. J. B.)

RATEL (HONEY BADGER), a short-legged, carnivorous mammal, *Mellivora capensis*, of the weasel family (Mustelidae), about the size and build of the badger (*q.v.*). The tail is short, the ears

PAUL POPPER

RATEL (MELLIVORA CAPENSIS)

rudimentary, and the front claws very large and strong; the upper parts are whitish, but the face, lower parts, and legs are black, the two colours being separated sharply. Several subspecies are recognized, differing in details of colouring.

Ratels are found throughout most of India, through the Middle East and Africa to the Cape. They are nocturnal and live in burrows dug with their strong, incurved front claws. They feed upon small animals and vegetable matter, and dig out bees' nests to eat the honey. They are fearless fighters, sometimes destructive to poultry, but in captivity become tame and playful. The female has four teats—her litter is probably normally fewer than this— but nothing definite is recorded of the breeding habits. *See* also CARNIVORE.   (L. H. M.)

RATHENAU, WALTHER (1867–1922), German states- man, industrialist and philosophical writer, was born in Berlin on Sept. 29, 1867. His father was Emil Rathenau, who became a pioneer of the modern power industry by acquiring Thomas A. Edison's European patent rights and founding the Allgemeine Elektrizitäts-Gesellschaft. Having completed an academic cur- riculum in philosophy, physics, chemistry and engineering, Walther Rathenau successively filled responsible positions in various in- dustrial enterprises, and in 1899 entered the service of the Allge- meine Elektrizitäts-Gesellschaft. Although he had always been interested in public affairs, it was not until the beginning of World War I that he became a public figure.

The cause of Rathenau's prominence was the fact that, almost alone among German industrialists, he realized in the early days of the war the dependence of the German war effort on the sup- ply and prudent management of raw materials. His proposal to organize a special board of the war ministry for this purpose was accepted, and he was put in charge, directing this vital work until the spring of 1915. Then he returned to business activity and writing; his best-known book, *Von kommenden Dingen* (1917; Eng. trans. by Eden and Cedar Paul, *In Days to Come*), was pro- duced during this period.

Rathenau's knowledge of the world outside Germany, and his genuine love for peace, co-existed in his mind with strong na- tional feelings. In Oct. 1918, in despair over the German armistice request, which he correctly interpreted as in effect an act of unconditional surrender, he proposed in vain a *levée en masse* of the German people. In his economic views, Rathenau held an intermediate position between capitalism and democratic socialism; after the revolution of 1918, he founded with others the middle-class Democratic party, but he tried to keep that party in a relationship of co-operation with the Social Democrats, despite his critical view of many of the policies of the Social Demo- crats. In his book *Die neue Wirtschaft,* he supported the idea of industrial self-government with the participation of employees and effective state control rather than universal nationalization.

Rathenau was one of relatively few Germans who combined democratic convictions and a strong belief in international con- ciliation with economic experience and knowledge of foreign coun- tries. In 1921 Karl Joseph Wirth, who had just formed a cabinet, appointed Rathenau minister of reconstruction, a position involv- ing responsibility for important aspects of reparation policy; later he exchanged this portfolio for that of foreign affairs. As one of his first achievements, Rathenau negotiated an agreement with France on German deliveries in kind for the reconstruction of French war-devastated areas. Rathenau believed that a practi- cable settlement of the reparations issue could best be obtained as part of a European reconstruction scheme, in which the eco- nomic rehabilitation of Russia would have to play a vital role. He induced Lloyd George to make this idea the core of the British proposal at the international conference at Cannes (Jan. 1922). No progress was made, however, either at Cannes or at the sub- sequent conference of Genoa. To forestall an Allied understand- ing with Russia at Germany's expense, Wirth decided to conclude a German agreement with the Russians for the mutual cancellation of all claims (the Rapallo treaty) and Rathenau reluctantly agreed. Through the Rapallo treaty, Germany for the first time after its defeat asserted its position as an independent agent in in- ternational affairs. The treaty antagonized the Allies; its wis- dom has remained a matter of controversy.

Even among the conservatives, some leaders had a great deal of personal admiration for Rathenau, though others attacked him with bitterness. For the extreme nationalists Rathenau was the symbol of everything they hated, especially because he was a Jew. On June 24, 1922, some young nationalist fanatics shot Rathenau to death on his way to his office. His assassination initiated the disintegration of the Wirth cabinet and the sequence of events that led to the French occupation of the Ruhr.

Rathenau's collected works (5 vol.) were published in 1918. Of his later writings, the most important are: *Die neue Wirtschaft* (1918); *Kritik der dreifachen Revolution* (1919); *Die neue Gesellschaft* (1919, Eng. trans., *The New Society,* 1921).

See Harry Kessler, *Walther Rathenau, sein Leben und sein Werk* (1928), Eng. trans., *Walther Rathenau* (1929).   (C. L.)

RATHENOW, a town of East Germany in the *Bezirk* (dis- trict) of Potsdam, German Democratic Republic. It lies on the right bank of the Havel about 48 mi. (77 km.) W of Berlin by rail on the Berlin-Hanover line. Pop. (1962 est.) 29,218. Rathenow's principal industry is the manufacture of optical goods; its spectacle lenses and frames, binoculars, and opera glasses are exported throughout the world. On the outskirts are a number of brick kilns. The town was founded in 1295. In a battle in 1675 at nearby Fehrbellin the Swedes were defeated by the Brandenburg- ers. Rathenow was severely damaged by bombing attacks during World War II.

RATINGEN, a town of West Germany in the *Land* (state) of North Rhine-Westphalia, Federal Republic of Germany, lies 5½ mi. (9 km.) NE of Düsseldorf by road. Pop. (1961) 36,020. One of the oldest towns of the Bergisches *Land*, it has a 12th- century Gothic church, a Minorite monastery, the geologically interesting Blauer See (lake), the Bürgerhaus with museum, a moated castle, and well-preserved fortifications. Textiles, paper, pottery, glass, electrical goods, and machinery are manufactured.

RATIOCINATION, a term used in logic and psychology for those processes by which the mind proceeds from general to particular truths. The steps involved in ratiocination may perhaps be most clearly seen in the form of reasoning followed in the syllogism (*q.v.*).

RATIONALISM is that system of philosophical belief which asserts that human reason unaided is competent to attain objective truth. In its basic form it is an epistemological doctrine in which reason is contrasted with sense-experience, which is held to be un- necessary, or even a hindrance, to the attainment of truth. The inspiration of rationalism has always been mathematics, and ra- tionalists have stressed the superiority of the deductive over all other methods in point of certainty. They attach a peculiar value to the capacity to recognize necessary connections between ab- stract ideas or concepts (*e.g.,* the connection between being a Euclidean triangle and having angles equal to 180°). Euclid's *Elements* presents the ideal to which rationalists hold that all hu- man thinking should conform.

According to the extreme rationalist doctrine all the truths of physical science and even history could in principle be discovered by pure thinking and set forth as the consequences of self-evident premises.

Few rationalists, however, have been so extreme, and we may distinguish in different philosophers different degrees of rational- ism. Locke, for example, is a rationalist in the weakest sense, holding that the materials of human knowledge (ideas) are sup- plied by sense-experience or introspection, but that knowledge consists in seeing necessary connections between them, which is the function of reason (*Essay Concerning Human Understanding*). Most philosophers who are called rationalists have also maintained that the materials of knowledge are derived, not from experience, but from the reason itself; *i.e.,* they are innate ideas.

Ethical rationalism is the application of epistemological ra- tionalism to the field of morals. The primary moral ideas (good, duty) are held to be innate and the first principles of morals (*e.g.,* the Golden Rule) self-evident. It is further claimed that the pos- session of reason provides an adequate motive for moral conduct. In ethical rationalism, reason is generally contrasted with feeling or moral sense.

Theological rationalism asserts the claims of reason against those of revelation or authority. The fundamental principles of religion are held to be innate or self-evident and revelation un- necessary. Theological rationalism thus stresses the importance of natural as opposed to revealed religion. By an easy extension of meaning, the word "rationalism" then came to signify a skeptical or antireligious attitude. This is the most common use of the word in the 19th and in the 20th centuries. Rationalism is conceived as the ally of liberalism in the struggle against religious intolerance (*see* W. E. H. Lecky, *History of the Rise and Influence of the Spirit of Rationalism in Europe*, 2 vol., 1914) or alternatively as the enemy of religion (*see* J. F. Hurst, *History of Rationalism*, 1865). It thus came to be connected, somewhat paradoxically, with empiricism (*q.v.*), the antithesis of epistemological rationalism.

EPISTEMOLOGICAL RATIONALISM

Epistemological rationalism was first explicitly formulated by Plato. According to him there is a system of eternal necessary truths accessible to the human reason apart from sense-experience (*Republic,* vi and vii) and his theory of learning as recollection, developed in the *Meno* and in the *Phaedo,* is the first form of the doctrine of innate ideas. The typical innate ideas are mathematical concepts such as equality, which, he holds, are not perfectly exemplified in the material world (*Phaedo*).

In later antiquity and in the middle ages, wherever Platonism is influential, we have implicit epistemological rationalism (*e.g.*, in the Neoplatonists, in St. Augustine, in Boëthius and in St. Anselm), but it is subordinated to the dominant ethical and theological interests. Medieval theological rationalism, however, makes one important contribution to epistemological rationalism. This is the ontological argument of St. Anselm, in which he seeks to prove that the existence of God follows from His essence, and thus to provide a connection between the abstract system of innate ideas and the actual world. (*See* ANSELM, SAINT; THEISM.) When rationalism became self-conscious at the Renaissance, both Kepler and Descartes felt the need for this connection, and both use the idea of God, Descartes deliberately reviving Anselm's ontological argument.

Epistemological rationalism reached its highest development in the 17th century under the double impetus of the revival of Platonism and the development of mathematical physics by Kepler, Copernicus, Galileo and Descartes. The new science rests on the basis of mathematics, and it recognizes as clear and distinct only what can be expressed in mathematical form. All scientific truth is derived from certain axioms and principles which can be comprehended by reason as universal and necessary. Thus, according to Galileo, "Truth is written in the great book of Nature, but only he can read it who can decipher the letters in which it is written." These letters, however, are the terms of mathematics, especially of geometry: the concepts of the straight line, the circle, the sphere, etc. None of these concepts is derived from experience; the mind rather takes them "from itself" in order to apply them to sense-perceptions. In the same way, Kepler considers number and magnitude as innate ideas not drawn from experience but required for the scientific investigation of nature (*see* E. Cassirer, *Das Erkenntnisproblem*, 3rd ed., i, pp. 328 ff., 1922; and E. A. Burtt, *Metaphysical Foundations of Modern Physical Science*, ch. ii and iii, 1925).

Descartes enlarges this view by setting forth a system of universal concepts of reason which are obtained by analysis of certain fundamental—logical and mathematical—relationships and which can be applied to all empirical data. These concepts are valid, not only for the actual world, but for all possible worlds, so that, in understanding by means of them every effect from its cause, we can obtain a priori knowledge of the universe as a whole. As instances of such fundamental concepts, Descartes cites primarily the concept of being, then the ideas of number and time and of space, figure and motion.

As physics thus becomes a purely deductive science, epistemological rationalism has to draw, as was said above, on theological rationalism for support. The innate ideas are within the mind, and sense-experience constitutes no proof of the reality of the external world (Descartes, *Meditation I*). We can, therefore, get outside the system of our own ideas only by proving the existence of reality external to us. This demands the idea of a Necessary Being, that is, God. But in order to show the applicability of the system, something must also be known of the nature of God. Descartes

states that He is veracious; *i.e.*, that He will not allow us to be deceived in our clear and distinct thinking. The world is, therefore, constructed on the plan according to which we think. It is the construction of an infinite intellect. The applicability of pure mathematics is assured because nature itself is the product of a divine mathematics: *Cum Deus calculat, fit mundus*.

Leibniz' system may be regarded as the crowning achievement of epistemological rationalism. He attempts to deduce from fundamental laws of logic the basic propositions of his system, which are so repugnant to common sense that only a boundless confidence in the powers of pure reason could recommend them. The universe is said to consist of an infinite number of spiritual substances (monads), each regarding the whole from a distinct point of view and with a specific degree of confusion. The human mind occupies an intermediate position in the hierarchy of monads, its perceptions being clear in comparison with those of animals but still involving a great degree of confusion, of which the spatio-temporal and qualitative appearance of things is the product. This confusion also accounts for the fact that the truths of science and history, although logically necessary, cannot be known a priori by human beings.

The gap between truths of reason and truths of fact remains unbridgeable by the human mind. The aim of human science must, however, be to order knowledge so that it approximates as far as possible to the ideal deductive system (*see* L. Couturat, *La Logique de Leibniz,* especially ch. vi, 1901; and B. Russell, *A Critical Exposition of the Philosophy of Leibniz*, 2nd ed., 1937).

Leibniz attempted to lay the foundation for this in the grandiose scheme of his *characteristica universalis,* which was to give a catalogue of primary simple ideas together with a method by which all truths, however complex, could be exhibited as combinations of them. This project of Leibniz inspired later development in symbolic logic and investigation of the foundations of mathematics, particularly the work of Gottlob Frege, Giuseppe Peano, Bertrand Russell and A. N. Whitehead, in which it is sought to reduce all mathematics to logic. In the 18th century, however, the immediate outcome of the Leibnizian subordination of empirical to rational knowledge was the philosophy of Christian Wolff (1679–1754), who produced the voluminous system now chiefly remarkable as being the form of rationalism in which Kant was reared. Epistemological rationalism was meanwhile subject to attack from the British empiricists, especially Locke and Hume, who stressed the necessity for empirical data in the acquisition of scientific knowledge.

Immanuel Kant (*q.v.*), aroused by Hume from the "dogmatic slumber" induced by Wolff, attempted to combine rationalism and empiricism into a single system, the "critical philosophy." He adheres, however, to the rationalist position in stressing the importance of the a priori element in knowledge; and the "pure forms of intuition" and the "categories," insofar as they belong to the mind, have something of the nature of innate ideas. But he differs from preceding rationalists in holding that, because of their nature, we cannot know that the pure forms of intuition (space and time) or the categories (cause, substance, etc.) apply to reality as such (the thing-in-itself). In short, according to Kant, rationalism provides a satisfactory basis for science only if we adopt skepticism as regards metaphysics. The a priori truths of reason apply only to things as they appear to us (phenomena), and reason is inadequate to solve the metaphysical problems of God, freedom and immortality (*Kritik der reinen Vernunft*, preface to 2nd ed., 1787). It is Kant who provides the classical refutation of the ontological argument (*op. cit.*, "Dialektik").

Hegelianism, in spite of the slogan "The Real is the Rational and the Rational is the Real," is only apparently a return to rationalism, being opposed to the mathematical method and inspiration which provide the keynote of classical rationalism. In fact it may be said that epistemological rationalism has not survived Hume's devastating criticism (*Treatise of Human Nature*, book i). Even the milder Kantian form was subject to severe criticism in the 20th century by the logical positivists, whose conventionalist theory of a priori truth challenges the basic rationalist claim to insight into objective necessary connection.

But however unacceptable as a complete theory of knowledge, rationalism as an attitude has been and still is an inspiration in science. It is the rationalist spirit which urges us to approach nature as masters rather than as pupils and to construct bold hypotheses and verify them later.

Some eminent 20th-century physicists have even put forward deductive systems entirely in the spirit of Leibniz: for example, A. Eddington in his *Philosophy of Physical Science* (1939) and E. A. Milne in his *Modern Cosmology and the Christian Idea of God* (1952).

ETHICAL RATIONALISM

Ethical rationalism was also first developed by Plato, partly under the inspiration of the Socratic dictum "Virtue is knowledge." In the *Republic* the reasoning element of the human soul both recognizes what is right and good and is itself the spring of action which prompts moral conduct. The Stoics, however, among the philosophers of the ancient world, developed the form of ethical rationalism which was most influential in later times. Although they rejected the theory of innate ideas, they held that there is in every man a spark of the divine reason which is sufficient, properly used, to discover the universally binding rules of conduct. On these rules positive law is properly based. Thus the Stoic doctrine gives rise to the theory of natural law and natural right. It was popularized by Cicero, whose writings were later extremely influential (*De Republica*, iii; *De Legibus*, i).

As did epistemological rationalism, ethical rationalism underwent a considerable revival at the Renaissance, when it also had great influence on political theory. The first clear statement that the rules of conduct discovered by reason are independent of the commands of God was made by Hugo Grotius (*De Jure belli ac pacis*, Prolegomena § 11). Ethical rationalism had a considerable vogue in the 17th and 18th centuries, especially in England, where it was developed by Lord Herbert of Cherbury, by Samuel Clarke, by John Balguy, by William Wollaston and by Richard Price.

The ethical systems of Spinoza and Kant have moreover considerable affinities with rationalism: Spinoza's is even developed in the mathematico-deductive form (*Ethica, ordine geometrico demonstrata*) in close connection with his metaphysics and theory of knowledge, though it depends in fact on certain empirical propositions concerning the nature of man; and Kant holds that the form of the moral law, the categorical imperative, is purely a priori, though it provides not a premiss from which we may deduce our duties but a test that enables us to discern the moral character of any proposed course of action.

The classical criticism of ethical rationalism is to be found in Hume's *Treatise*, books ii and iii. A modified form of rationalism was developed in the 20th century under the name "intuitionism" (W. D. Ross, *Foundations of Ethics*, 1939).

THEOLOGICAL RATIONALISM

The question "Is theological truth discoverable by reason or solely by revelation?" could arise only in the context of religions such as Judaism, Christianity and Islam. The relations between revelation and reason were much debated in the middle ages. E. Gilson (*Reason and Revelation in the Middle Ages*, 1938) distinguishes two positions which may be called rationalist as distinct from the antirationalist view that reason is totally unable to grasp religious truth. The less extreme position is the Augustinian, namely that, once revelation is accepted, its content may be grasped by the intellect; this is adopted by St. Anselm, who sums it up in the phrase *credo ut intelligam*, "I believe in order that I may understand." The complete rationalist position, which makes revelation unnecessary at least for the philosopher, was worked out by Averroes in Moslem Spain and adopted by his Christian followers.

Rationalism in theology developed rapidly after the Reformation. A clear statement of the position is given by Lord Herbert of Cherbury in *De Veritate* and *De Religione gentilium*. Leibniz' introduction to the *Théodicée* shows that the word "rational" had already come into use in this context. The position was further developed in the 18th century by the English deists, by the French

philosophes (*e.g.* Voltaire and Condorcet) and by the German theologians called rationalists (particularly S. J. Baumgarten and J. S. Semler, who were influenced both by Wolffian rationalism and by biblical criticism). (*See* ENLIGHTENMENT.)

By the end of the 19th century rationalism had become a frankly antireligious movement, often combined with empiricism and materialism and identified with practically atheistic forms of agnosticism (*q.v.*): see for example J. McCabe, *Biographical Dictionary of Modern Rationalists* (1920) and *A Rationalist Encyclopaedia* (1948).

See also references under "Rationalism" in the Index.

(M. Ke.)

RATIONING, a term of military origin that denotes procedures adopted to assure that each individual in a community or country receives his due share of scarce supplies. It was first used on a large scale during World War I, to deal with massive difficulties in provisioning civilian populations, and it reappeared during World War II.

Ordinarily the price system performs the function of rationing by forcing individuals to ration their own consumption on the basis of their needs, tastes, and incomes, but in time of war or other emergency the price system is not adequate. When shortages of certain commodities are experienced or anticipated, buyers may engage in hoarding which soon can create, or magnify, the shortage and result in unfair distribution. If prices are controlled, the rationing function of price is weakened and supplies are distributed according to chance, favouritism, or on a first-come-first-served basis that is unfair to those who are left out. If prices are not controlled, they may rise so high that essential items will be beyond the reach of people with low incomes. Rationing thus becomes necessary for two main reasons: (1) to reduce the inefficiency, waste of time, and confusion entailed in leaving people to scramble, bribe, or wait long hours in line to secure what they must have; (2) to eliminate the inequity of limiting demand by letting necessities be priced so high that the relatively poor cannot afford them. The decision to ration, accordingly, is based partly on the severity of shortages, either actual or anticipated, and partly on the extent to which such scarce goods are essential to life and health. It must also be based on the degree to which sources of supply and channels of distribution can be made subject to control.

METHODS OF RATIONING

Informal Rationing.—This method of limiting consumption sometimes precedes the imposition of formal controls; it may consist of exhortations to consumers to reduce their consumption or of action by suppliers in allocating scarce supplies as they think best. For example, during World War I the U.S. Food Administration urged Americans not to eat meat on certain days; again, early in World War II, grocers limited coffee purchases to two pounds per customer. When informal rationing is practised by manufacturers or wholesalers, poor credit risks or prospective customers may be refused supplies; established customers may be limited to a percentage of their normal orders; or salesmen may be assigned quotas to allocate at their discretion. Because such devices foster favouritism and inequity they are usually superseded by formal, official rationing when shortages become really acute.

Formal rationing may take many forms, the chief of which are rationing by use, rationing by quantity, rationing by value, point rationing, and rationing of money expenditure.

Rationing by Use.—When a single commodity that is normally used for a variety of purposes becomes critically scarce, the least important uses of it may be prohibited. In late 1949, for example, New York City underwent a water shortage that forced city officials to urge economy in all uses of water and to prohibit using water to wash cars. Industrial raw materials are more frequently subjected to this form of rationing than are final consumers' goods, and when this occurs their uses are generally governed by a system of priorities.

Rationing by Quantity.—There are two ways of rationing by quantity: one is crude but effective; the other is more complicated but also more equitable. The crude way is simply to limit the hours at which the rationed commodity is available. Hot water, for example, may be cut off at certain hours of the day to conserve fuel. In the late 1950s coffee became extremely scarce in Turkey and was informally rationed by being placed on sale only in the early hours of the morning, on certain infrequent days, and at high prices. The more sophisticated way of rationing by quantity is to assign given quotas of a commodity to all known, approved claimants. When the commodity involved is standardized, without variations in quality or form of use, like sugar, the available supply may simply be divided up among consumers who usually are issued coupons entitling them to their quota. A special problem arises with commodities that have differential importance to different categories of users. Milk, for example, is needed more by children than by adults, and gasoline has more social importance when it is used by doctors on emergency calls than when it is used for recreational driving. In such cases, consumers are classified according to their importance or need and are assigned rations accordingly.

Rationing by Value.—Some commodities are incapable of standardization because of differences in variety or quality. Quantity rationing of meat, for example, would involve periodic listing and classifying of all the varieties, grades, and kinds of meat. A more workable alternative is to limit each consumer's expenditure on such commodities and to leave him free to make his own selections within the legal limits. Because purchases must be made with money as well as with ration coupons, low prices will clear the market of the less attractive items.

Point Rationing.—A period of critical and increasing shortages, unaccompanied by proportionate reductions in consumers' incomes, aggravates the difficulty of rationing by causing individuals to substitute unrationed for rationed items, such as cheese for meat, thereby spreading shortages. As rationing is extended to more commodities the administrative burden increases and the difficulty of satisfying different individual tastes and needs becomes greater. During World War II, point rationing was introduced, first in Germany, then in Great Britain, and finally in the United States, to resolve such difficulties. Under point rationing, scarce commodities are grouped into broad categories such as meats, canned foods, or clothing. Each item within each category is assigned a point value, which may change from one ration period to another, and coupons or stamps are issued to every consumer. For example, early in World War II each consumer in Great Britain was allocated 66 clothing points which could be spent, regardless of money price, on wool socks (3 points), complete suits (32 points), wool skirts (6 points), etc. Within the limits of his money income in general, and of his point income in particular, the individual was free to allocate his expenditures as he chose. Under point rationing individuals are recipients of two kinds of income: money income and ration point income. During World War II most people spent their point incomes within each ration period, but in just the degree that rationing was effective they were likely to have money income left over.

Rationing of Money Expenditure.—Unspent money income represents a hazard to a rationed economy, as it may be used to purchase unrationed items, thereby making them scarce, or it may be used to make illicit purchases on the so-called black market. Efforts were made to deal with this problem in Great Britain and the United States by exhorting individuals to save, to purchase government bonds, and to increase their deposits in savings banks. Access to credit for the purchase of such things as household equipment was sharply curtailed. In Germany, individuals were subjected to even more intensive pressure to save. In most countries the trend of rationing during World War II was toward substituting the control of expenditure for the rationing of particular commodities, although that trend was nowhere carried to its ultimate limit, nor was there any relaxation in rationing itself until after the war.　　　　　　　　　　　　　(G. P. A.)

HISTORY OF RATIONING

Germany.—When bread rationing was first introduced in Berlin a few months after the outbreak of World War I, it was wrongly interpreted abroad as a sign of serious shortage rather than as a precautionary measure designed to prevent maldistribution. From the outset the German system embodied the principle of differential rations. Manual workers, later divided into light, heavy, and very heavy workers, received more than the normal consumer; children under ten years, less. Rationing was administered by local authorities, who enjoyed more independence than in World War II and sometimes competed with one another for supplies. Coordination of supply and distribution by state-controlled war companies was never complete, and this opened the door to illicit trade. Evasion of the regulations from 1917 onward grew to such an extent that maldistribution of food was one of the chief factors in the collapse of the home front in 1918.

Before the outbreak of World War II thorough preparations had been made for rationing as an integral part of war economy. Rationing of bread, flour, sugar, meat, and fats was introduced in September 1939 and continued at a fairly adequate level until 1944. Further refinements were made in the system of differential rations to cover special categories of consumers. Rationing in occupied countries followed the German pattern but varied widely in efficiency and adequacy. Administration was left largely to local officials, and passive resistance by producers, traders, and consumers led to an extensive black market.

Great Britain.—Rationing was not adopted in Great Britain until near the end of World War I, when sugar was rationed. Toward the end of 1916 sugar supplies fell short of demand, and distributors were allotted only half of their 1915 supplies. Retailers were left to distribute the supply among their customers as best they could, but queues formed and discontent grew. After some months of hesitation the cabinet decided in June 1917 to introduce the first rationing scheme under which householders were invited to register with a particular shop, and retailers received supplies of sugar equal to the rations of their registered customers. A local rationing scheme for meat and fats in London and the home countries came into force on Feb. 25, 1918. On April 7 a national rationing scheme for meat was started, and on July 14 the whole population received ration books with separate cards for meat, fats, sugar, and lard. By May 1919 rationing by coupons was abolished, and sugar registration ended in November 1920. Rationing had lasted for little more than two years.

By contrast, in World War II rationing started early in 1940 and was not ended until July 1954. Ration books, which had been printed in 1938, were issued from local food offices to every individual on the basis of a special census conducted for national registration on Sept. 29, 1939. Five types of ration books were issued: for children under 5, children 5 to 18, normal adults, travelers, and seamen. Emergency cards valid for one week were issued to new arrivals or persons who had lost their books. Straight rationing, which entitled consumers to buy a fixed weekly amount of each food, was applied in 1940 to meat, bacon, sugar, fats, and tea. In 1941 cheese and preserves were added, and milk and eggs came under a scheme of priority rationing. On Dec. 1, 1941, a new system of points rationing was put into force for miscellaneous groceries, under which each consumer received a number of points to spend in each four-week period on any food in the group, each food being given a points price varying according to the expected demand in relation to the supply; thus canned salmon and dried fruits had a high points price, and cereal foods, a low price. This system was adopted after the successful introduction of points rationing for clothing and footwear. In June 1941 everyone had been given a coupon currency of 66 points, roughly corresponding to 66% of prewar average consumption. Later the figure was reduced to 48 a year. Point values for clothing were based on the amount of cloth used, but some garments were "pointed" to equate demand roughly to estimated supply. Rationing of expenditure by value coupons was rejected on the ground that it would have concentrated demand too much on the cheaper goods.

Soap rationing was introduced early in 1942 on the basis of 16 oz. per four weeks for hard soap. Chocolate and sugar confectionery were first rationed in July 1942 under what was called the personal points scheme; distribution to retailers was based on coupons collected without consumer registration. Other foods subject to controlled distribution rather than strict rationing included milk, eggs, oranges, and fish. Milk went first to priority consumers—mothers and children up to 5 years old were guaranteed a ration of seven pints a week; children of 5 to 18 years, three and one-half pints; and schools, hospitals, and invalids also had priority supplies. The rest of the public got what was left with no definite guarantee of supply, the usual amount being two pints a week in the winter and three to four in the spring. Consumers were tied to one dairyman who received his share of the available supplies according to the number of priority and nonpriority customers registered with him. Controlled distribution of shell eggs started in June 1941. Mothers and infants received priority supplies, and ordinary consumers got allocations as and when supplies permitted, varying from one a month in the winter to two or more a week in the spring. Oranges when available were sold to holders of children's ration books before other customers could be served. It was found impracticable to ration fish, but supplies to retailers were distributed as fairly as possible. Bread, flour, and potatoes were not rationed during World War II. Bread and flour rationing was introduced in July 1946 and lasted for two years; potatoes were rationed in 1947–48 when there was both a poor potato harvest and a world shortage of wheat.

In contrast with rationing schemes on the continent, differential rations for special categories of workers were kept to the minimum, and coupons did not have to be surrendered for meals in restaurants. The general principle was that everyone should be free to take meals out as a supplement to domestic rations, and caterers received an allocation of rationed foods on the basis of the number of meals served.

Food rationing in Great Britain, which ended with the decontrol of meat and bacon on July 3, 1954, was made easier by the fact that half the total food supply was imported and also by the willing cooperation of food traders and the public. There was general assent to the principle of fair shares which, though it involved some reduction in the consumption of the majority, also allowed some improvement of the diet of the poorest by means of food subsidies and welfare food schemes.   (E. M. H. L.)

Soviet Union.—During the 1920s the U.S.S.R. suffered acute food shortages, partly because of the upheaval resulting from the Revolution and partly because food was shipped abroad to obtain foreign exchange. Under these circumstances, food rationing was introduced and continued until the mid-1930s. With the outbreak of World War II in 1939 food rationing was restored and continued throughout the war.   (X.)

United States.—During World War I the American people were urged to exercise self-restraint in consuming scarce commodities, such as meat. Wheat flour and sugar supplies were eventually controlled by the Food Administration, headed by Herbert Hoover, to ensure maximum use of food supplies for wartime needs. Disappearing quickly after the Armistice, controls did not appear again until after the attack on Pearl Harbor, Dec. 7, 1941, when it became clear that extraordinary efforts would be needed to fight and win a two-continent war. An Office of Price Administration (OPA) had been created April 11, 1941, by executive order, to prevent "price spiraling, rising costs of living, profiteering, and inflation." Signing of the Emergency Price Control Act on Jan. 30, 1942, gave OPA specific authority to enforce its orders, including rationing.

Although OPA had an army of paid officials, much of the burden of making necessary daily decisions fell on unpaid local citizens, serving on community ration boards. Their task was made difficult by the presence of three antagonistic forces: shortages of goods; government-regulated price ceilings; and war-swollen incomes. OPA rationed some commodities according to individual need, while other items were equally available to all. Basic raw materials were controlled at first through priorities and, after mid-1943, by allocations to industrial users. The change became necessary when the word priority lost its meaning in the light of exhausted supplies. Government allocations under a Production Requirements Plan, and later a Controlled Materials Plan, were ways of dividing total supplies among essential users.

Consumer rationing was handled by several methods. In point rationing, a consumer could select from items in specific groups.

Thus small red stamps could be surrendered for meat, butter, fats, cheese, canned milk, and canned fish. Blue stamps were used for canned fruits, vegetables, and related items. Stamps were good for stated periods of time. Certificate rationing involved the use of certificates obtainable by those who could prove special need for tires, motor vehicles, and similar products. Ration coupons came to comprise a sort of currency. They passed successively from consumer to retailer to wholesaler to producer to ration authorities.

Tires were rationed almost immediately after the Emergency Price Control Act was passed, and sugar was rationed after the first general consumer registration, May 4–7, 1942. Gasoline was rationed first in the East, then throughout the country. Automobile owners with special needs established them with ration boards and were provided with additional rations; many others switched to buses, joined car pools, or relearned the joys of walking. Meats, canned goods, butter, and other foods eventually joined sugar on rationed lists. Clothing, other than shoes, was unrationed throughout the war, but scarcities developed, especially after demobilization of uniformed personnel. Fuel oil was rationed in some sections.

Immediately after the Japanese surrender in August 1945, most items were released from controls. Sugar and tires, the first to be listed, were the last to be decontrolled. OPA ceased operations on May 31, 1947, having lingered on chiefly to handle rent control and to perform final administrative acts.

The very nature of rationing could not but make it unpopular. Yet it performed the task assigned to it. The American people remained well nourished. The black market was kept to a reasonable minimum, in part because OPA in its lifetime instituted over 280,000 enforcement orders against violators of price, rent, and rationing regulations, winning 95% of its court cases. Rapid removal of controls was acclaimed, although in 1945–46 temporary scarcities and a 23% rise in prices indicated that supply had not satisfied pent-up demands.

The Korean War did not bring with it the comprehensive rationing procedures of World War II. An Office of Price Stabilization enforced a limited program of production, wage, and price controls. Chrome and other strategic materials were regulated, and the quality of appliances and motor car bumpers suffered for a time. There was evidence during and after the Korean War that leaders hoped, by planning and stockpiling of critical raw materials, to increase national self-sufficiency in the future. The report of the Materials Policy Commission, *Resources for Freedom*, five volumes (1952), was an important step. An indication that future rationing, if any, might vary from the patterns of earlier years could be found in the continuing farm surpluses and in constantly expanding industrial facilities.   (V. D. B.)

BIBLIOGRAPHY.—W. H. Beveridge, *British Food Control* (1928); League of Nations, *Wartime Rationing and Consumption* (1942), *Food, Famine and Relief* (1946); Jules Backman, *Rationing and Price Control in Great Britain* (1943); J. A. Kershaw, *A History of Ration Banking* (1947); James M. Tinley, *Rationing and Control of Food Supplies* (1942); R. J. Hammond, *Food*, vol. i, *Growth of Policy* (1951), vol. ii, *Studies in Administration and Control* (1956).

RATLAM, a town and district in the Indore division of Madhya Pradesh, India. The town, headquarters of the district, lies 65 mi. NW of Indore. Pop. (1961) 87,472. It is the divisional headquarters of the Western Railway and an important industrial centre with a cotton textile mill, strawboard factory, and pottery works. A government college is affiliated to Vikram University.

RATLAM DISTRICT (area 1,727 sq.mi. [4,473 sq.km.]; pop. [1961] 483,521) corresponds with the former princely state of Ratlam. It has fertile black cotton soil producing wheat, maize (corn), and sugarcane, and about 6% of the district is forested. Vindhyan sandstone is quarried for building purposes. Jaora (pop. 31,140), to the north, has a sugar mill, a college, and a polytechnic. The people speak Malwi, a dialect of Hindi.

The former princely state of Ratlam was founded by Ratan Singh Rathor (a great-grandson of Raja Uday Singh, maharaja of Jodhpur), who died fighting against Aurangzeb in 1658.
                              (D. G. NA.)

RATNAGIRI, a town and district in the Bombay division of Maharashtra, India. The town, headquarters of the district, lies on the Arabian Sea, 136 mi. (219 km.) S of Bombay. Pop. (1961) 31,091. Places of interest include the Ratnagiri Fort (1500), Lokmanya Tilak Memorial, and the Thebaw Palace (1911). The Gogate Arts and Science College is affiliated to Poona University; other institutions include a teachers' training college for men, an industrial training institute, and the Marine Biological Research Station. Ratnagiri has no railway but is served by bus and steamer services.

RATNAGIRI DISTRICT (area 5,025 sq.mi. [13,015 sq.km.]; pop. [1961] 1,827,203), forms a rugged and rocky strip between the Western Ghats and the sea. Near the coast the district is intersected by creeks and navigable rivers along which lie the chief ports and almost all the fertile land. The main crops are rice, mangoes, and coconuts; sunn hemp is also grown. Grain, cotton, and sugar are the chief imports and coconuts, salt, mangoes, and dried fish the exports. The district is served by road only. The principal towns include Chiplun, Malvan, Sawantwadi, and Vengurla. (M. R. P.)

RATNAPURA ("the City of Gems"), chief town in the province of Sabaragamuwa, Ceylon, lies 40 mi. (64 km.) SE of Colombo. Pop. (1963) 21,582. It is the commercial and administrative centre of a region which has long been renowned for precious stones including rubies, sapphires, and cat's-eyes. These are dug from valley alluvium and prepared by Muslim gem cutters. The town is dominated by a hill on which the Portuguese built a fort. It has good road connections with Colombo and lies on a narrow-gauge railway.

The administrative district of Ratnapura is characterized by great diversity; it ranges from the valley lowlands of the Kalu Ganga to the range that culminates in Adam's Peak (7,360 ft.) and from a very wet west to dry zone conditions in the east. Rubber and rice production are economically more important than gems. The population (1963) was 547,494, with Kandyan Sinhalese in the majority. (B. H. F.)

RATRAMNUS (fl. *c.* 860), priest and monk of the abbey of Corbie, near Amiens, in France, remembered for his part in the 9th-century Eucharistic controversy, is little known apart from his works. He composed one book on the virgin birth, another on predestination—predestination to sin is rejected but predestination to salvation is not—and to his contemporaries his principal contribution must have seemed the four books in which he defended the Western Church from attacks by Photius, patriarch of Constantinople, at the time of the Filioque controversy. (*See* CREED: *Nicene Creed: Filioque Clause.*) In the judgment of posterity, however, much more importance should be attached to the short work of remarkable originality, *Christ's Body and Blood,* which is, at least in part, an irenic reply to *The Lord's Body and Blood* written by his abbot, Paschasius Radbertus (*q.v.*).

Ratramnus' position is this: the bread and wine are mystic symbols commemorative of Christ's body and blood, becoming such through sacerdotal consecration but retaining their outward appearance and remaining to the senses merely bread and wine. Within them, however, resides a power perceived only by faith, and this is what makes them effective. They are not Christ's body and blood *in truth* (perceptible to the senses), but *in a figure,* that is, symbolically. This doctrine he supports by appeal to the Scriptures, to several of the Fathers, and by citation of two prayers found in the missal of his day.

These views contrast strongly with those of Paschasius, but the book does not appear to have undergone attack until the controversy involving Berengar (*q.v.*) of Tours, when it was ordered destroyed at a synod held at Vercelli in 1050, later condemned again at the Lateran in 1059, both times wrongly supposed to be by Johannes Scotus Erigena. Copies survived, however, and the book had its influence at the time of the Reformation; *e.g.,* at his trial in 1555 Bishop Nicholas Ridley said of Ratramnus that he "was the first that pulled me by the ear, and forced me . . . to a more diligent search of Scripture. . . ."

BIBLIOGRAPHY.—Best Latin text now ed. by J. N. Bakhuizen van den Brink (1954); complete Eng. trans. by G. E. McCracken, *Library of* *Christian Classics,* vol. 9, *Early Medieval Theology,* pp. 109–147 (1957), with introduction and bibliography in both. (G. E. McC.)

RATTLESNAKE, any of a number of venomous snakes having a tail rattle that produces a buzzing or hissing sound when vibrated. Rattlesnakes belong to two genera, *Crotalus* (rattlers proper) and *Sistrurus* (pigmy rattlers and massasaugas); both genera belong to the pit viper family (Crotalidae).

MEXICAN GROUND RATTLESNAKE (SISTRURUS RAVUS)

Rattlesnakes occur only in the Americas, from southern Canada to central Argentina. They are found in a wide variety of habitats but most species prefer arid regions. Although they swim readily and occasionally climb trees, no species is habitually aquatic or arboreal.

Rattlesnake species (numbering 30, with many subspecies) differ greatly in size, appearance, and degree of danger. The largest is the eastern diamondback (*C. adamanteus*) of the southeastern states, sometimes attaining a length of 8 ft. and a weight up to 24 lb. The western diamondback (*C. atrox*), Texas to southeastern California, is only slightly smaller. At the other extreme are several Mexican species of *Crotalus* whose adults rarely reach two feet or a weight of three ounces. Although a few species are marked with transverse bands, most are blotched with dark diamonds, hexagons, or spots on a lighter background, usually of gray or light brown; some are characterized by various shades of orange, pink, red, or green.

The rattle, long the subject of myth and fanciful story, tends to frighten or warn creatures that might harm the snake. The sound is produced by transverse vibrations of the tail; the speed of vibration varies with the temperature, but averages about 48 cycles per second. If the snake is large, the sound can be heard at a distance of 200 ft. or more. The rattles, composed of the horny material keratin, are loosely interlocked; a new segment is produced with each skin shedding, not annually, as was once believed, but three or four times a year in young snakes, and about twice a year in adults. Rattles are subject to loss by wear and breakage, so very long strings are rare, even in aged snakes. An adult usually has from six to ten rattle segments. Although most rattlesnakes, when annoyed or alarmed, rattle before they strike, this is by no means a universal habit.

Rattlesnakes have a moderately keen sense of vision, particularly for nearby moving objects. The chemoreceptive sense, however, is acute, with dual avenues: olfactory nerves from the nostrils; and the tongue tips, which carry exterior particles or odours to sensing organs in the roof of the mouth. The rattlesnake has no sense of hearing, but is extremely alert to ground tremors, and can sense the approach of a horse or a man at a considerable distance. Like all pit vipers, the rattlesnake has facial pits, organs of an acute sensitivity to fine differences in heat, an especially valuable faculty for preying on small ("warm-blooded") mammals.

As in other reptiles, the body temperature of a rattlesnake is dependent on external conditions: air and ground temperatures, and impinging radiation. A rattlesnake seeks refuge when its body temperature falls below 13° C (55° F) or approaches 38° C

(100° F). Throughout life the snake adjusts both its seasonal and daily activities to escape these dangerous temperature extremes. In autumn, rattlers congregate deep in rock slides or crevices, where they will be protected in winter from freezing and enemies; and in summer, when diurnal temperatures are dangerously high, they become nocturnal, taking refuge in burrows of mammals or in other places away from the sun's rays and the hot ground. Rattlers are likely to be abroad and most active when the external conditions produce body temperatures within the range 24°–27° C (75°–80° F).

Most rattlesnakes subsist on small mammals, particularly rodents. The young of large rattlers and adults of small species depend largely on lizards. Birds and birds' eggs, amphibians, and arthropods are sometimes eaten. Rattlers feed at intervals of about ten days, and secure their food either by lying in wait along a trail frequented by prey or by tracking prey into a hole or nest. The strike is sudden; the venom not only kills small prey quickly, preventing a retaliatory bite, but also aids in digestion.

Rattlesnakes mate in the spring, and the young are born in the autumn. Broods usually comprise from 3 to 12 young. Some tropical species are relatively prolific, bearing up to 60 young. The newborn rattler is encased in a fetal membrane, which it slits with an egg tooth. The mother leaves the young within a few hours, exercising no parental care or protection. Despite a popular supposition, rattlers are not usually found in pairs; they separate after mating. The average life span is probably 10–12 years; captive specimens have lived up to 23 years.

Rattlesnakes are preyed upon by coyotes, foxes, wildcats, and badgers; by hawks and roadrunners; and, among the reptiles, by king snakes and racers. Although king snakes readily eat young rattlers (they are immune to venom) they do not seek out and destroy rattlers larger than they can swallow, as is often supposed. Deer, antelope, and goats sometimes kill rattlers by deliberately stamping on them with their hooves. Among domestic animals, hogs have been used with some success in rattlesnake control. But by far the greatest killer of rattlesnakes is man and the crushing wheels of his motor vehicles.

All rattlesnakes are venomous and dangerous. Because of improved methods of treatment, and with the abandonment of hazardous folklore cures, the bite of a rattlesnake today is not the threat to life that it was in colonial and pioneer days. Nevertheless, rattlesnake bite is a serious and painful accident, one not to be trifled with, especially if the victim is a child. Of the several thousand people bitten annually in the United States by rattlesnakes less than 1% of the cases prove fatal. The danger from rattlesnake bite depends on many factors, including the site of the bite, for the closer to the trunk, the more urgent is the need for treatment; the size of the snake, for larger snakes have more venom and longer fangs, which penetrate clothing easier; and finally the kind of rattlesnake, for different species have venoms that vary in toxicity. The most dangerous rattlesnakes are the South American rattler (*C. durissus terrificus*) and its relatives; these snakes are notable for a venom that attacks the nervous system. The most dangerous rattlers found in the United States, the diamondbacks, have a venom that attacks blood vessels and muscles primarily. Approved treatment involves the use of a tourniquet, incision and suction in the field, and early administration of antivenin. If a doctor can be reached within a half hour, field incisions should be omitted. Alcoholic stimulants and exertion by the victim should be avoided.

Rattlesnakes are not of great importance commercially. There is a small but continuous demand for live snakes by carnivals, roadside stands, and zoos. Skins and novelties made from skins are sold. Venoms are required in only small amounts by manufacturers of antivenin. Although therapeutic uses of rattlesnake venom were once considered promising, they have not fulfilled expectations. *See also* SNAKE.

See L. M. Klauber, *Rattlesnakes*, 2 vol. (1956).   (L. M. KR.)

RATZEL, FRIEDRICH (1844–1904), German geographer whose work shows the strong influence of the 19th-century interest in evolution. He was born at Karlsruhe on Aug. 30, 1844. During his youth he worked as an assistant in pharmacies, thereafter study-

ing zoology at the universities of Heidelberg and Jena. After obtaining his degree, Ratzel became travel correspondent for the *Kölnische Zeitung* and always retained the outlook and energy of a journalist. This work was interrupted by the Franco-German War, in which he served with distinction and was severely wounded. He then traveled for the *Kölnische Zeitung* in Europe and in the New World. His accounts of the U.S. and Mexico in the 1870s remain classics of descriptive writing, evincing his interest in the relationships between the European immigrants and other racial groups.

In 1875 Ratzel was appointed lecturer in geography at the Technical High School at Munich, becoming professor in 1880. At Munich he gained repute through his descriptive accounts of the U.S. and Mexico; the first volume of his *Anthropogeographie;* and his long treatise *Völkerkunde,* translated as the *History of Mankind.* In 1886 Ratzel became professor of geography at Leipzig. Much of his work there was political geography with a strong philosophical strain. His publications included *Politische Geographie, Die Erde und das Leben,* and a political-geographical study of the United States. His short essay *Lebensraum* (1901), often cited as a starting point of geopolitics, was in fact mainly a tentative study in biogeography. He died at Ammerland on Aug. 9, 1904.

Ratzel has been much criticized as a geographer, largely because subsequent misuse of his teaching was associated with German tyranny. Much of his work was controversial both politically and academically. A boisterous and somewhat naive nationalist but also an upright scholar, Ratzel sought both to integrate geographical work and to align it with contemporary thought.   (H. G. S.)

RATZENHOFER, GUSTAV (1842–1904), Austrian sociologist and army officer, who conceived of society as a universe of conflicting ethnic groups, was born in Vienna on July 4, 1842. Ratzenhofer became a cadet at the age of 17 and rose rapidly in the military. Already a voracious reader, he had more opportunity for study when he became director of the army archives in 1878. After subsequent service as chief of the general staff of an army, in 1898 he became field marshal and president of the supreme military court of Vienna.

Intellectually and professionally a tough self-made man, Ratzenhofer was naturally inclined to apply Darwin's biological theory of the struggle for existence and survival of the fittest to human society. Thus he joined the ranks of the social Darwinists who carried Darwin's theory of biological evolution of organisms into sociology by explaining the origin of ever larger social groups as a gradual development from less complex groups in conflict. Ratzenhofer, following his fellow Austrian, L. Gumplowicz, chose racial groups as the units for analysis. As might be expected from a sociologist at the top of the military hierarchy, Ratzenhofer believed that political science must rule society. He thought sociology could engineer the human species to even higher forms of social association.

See Robert Schmid, "Gustav Ratzenhofer: Sociological Positivism and the Theory of Social Interests" in *An Introduction to the History of Sociology,* ed. by H. E. Barnes, with bibliography (1948). The life of Ratzenhofer is given in his posthumous work, *Sociologie* (1908), ed. by his son.   (H. S.; X.)

RAU, SIR (BENEGAL) NARSING (NARSINGA) (1887–1953), Indian lawyer, diplomat, and administrator, who helped draft the Indian constitution of 1950, was born in Mangalore on Feb. 26, 1887. Graduate of the universities of Madras and Cambridge, he entered the Indian civil service in 1910 where he achieved distinction as a jurist by his revision of the entire Indian statute book (1935–37). He served as a judge of the High Court of Calcutta (1939–44). As the preeminent jurist of India he became constitutional adviser to the constituent assembly (1946–49); also for Burma in 1947 in drafting its constitution. His writings on Indian law include a noted study on constitutional precedents as well as articles on human rights in India. Rau headed the Indian delegation at several sessions of the United Nations General Assembly and was permanent representative of India to the United Nations from 1949 to 1951. He served as vice-chairman of the International Law Commission, and in 1951 was elected a judge of the International Court of Justice at The Hague. He died on Nov. 29, 1953, in Zürich, Switz.   (Or. S.)

RAUSCHENBUSCH, WALTER (1861–1918), U.S. clergyman, professor of theology, and social reformer, a leader of the Social Gospel movement, was born in Rochester, N.Y., Oct. 4, 1861, the son of a Lutheran missionary among German immigrants in the United States, who had become a Baptist and had been engaged to train a German-speaking ministry at the Rochester Theological Seminary. After graduating from the Rochester Free Academy, Rauschenbusch studied for four years in Germany and then returned to Rochester in 1883, taking simultaneously his final year at the University of Rochester (B.A., 1884) and his first year at the theological seminary. On June 1, 1886, following the completion of his theological studies, he became minister of the Second German Baptist Church in New York City. There he was awakened to the social problem by the personal distress he encountered in a depressed neighbourhood and by the influence of Henry George's campaign for mayor. An even more important influence was exerted by two other young Baptist preachers, Leighton Williams and Nathaniel Schmidt. The three young men formed themselves into a Society of Jesus, which was later to be expanded into the influential Brotherhood of the Kingdom. *For the Right,* a monthly periodical published "in the interests of the working people," was launched in November 1889 in an effort to reach the labouring classes and to aid in the formulation of a Christian Socialist program. Publication ceased in March 1891 when Rauschenbusch left for a year's study in Germany. In 1897 he was called to the faculty of the Rochester Theological Seminary and in 1902 was installed as professor of church history. The publication of *Christianity and the Social Crisis* (1907) won him national acclaim as the major spokesman of the social gospel. He died, saddened by World War I, on July 25, 1918.

Rauschenbusch always regarded himself as an evangelist, seeking to win men to a "new birth" in Christ and to put them to work in the interests of his kingdom. He seized upon the "kingdom of God" as the only concept adequate to induce repentance and to harness the impulses of new spiritual life. He had little patience with contemporary optimistic views of human nature. "Ethically," he said, "man sags downward by nature. It is ever easy to follow temptation and hard to resist it. The way that leads to destruction is always broad and its asphalt pavement is kept in perfect order, with toboggan slides at either side for those who prefer a steeper grade." Among his other important writings are *Prayers for the Social Awakening* (1910), *Christianizing the Social Order* (1912), and *A Theology for the Social Gospel* (1917). *See also* CHRISTIAN SOCIALISM.

See D. R. Sharpe, *Walter Rauschenbusch* (1942). (W. S. H.)

RAVAISSON-MOLLIEN, JEAN GASPARD FÉLIX (1813–1900), French philosopher and connoisseur, commonly known as FÉLIX RAVAISSON, was born at Namur on Oct. 23, 1813. A protégé of the comte de Salvandy, minister of education, he was taken from a teaching post in Rennes to be inspector general of public libraries (1839–45, 1846–53). Under Napoleon III he was made inspector general of higher education, a title which he retained till 1888, though from 1870 he was curator of antiquities in the Louvre. He died in Paris on May 18, 1900.

His major philosophical works are *Essai sur la métaphysique d'Aristote,* two volumes (1837–46); *De l'habitude* (1838; new ed., 1927); and *La Philosophie en France au XIXᵉ siècle* (1868; 3rd ed., 1889). As a philosopher Ravaisson belonged to the school of Victor Cousin (*q.v.*), with whom, however, he was at issue on many important points. The act of consciousness, according to him, is the basis of all knowledge. His influence was extensive in the Latin Catholic world, where it did much to prepare for Bergsonism (*see* BERGSON, HENRI).

See his *Testament philosophique et fragments,* ed. by Charles Devivaise (1933); also J. Dopp, *Félix Ravaisson: la formation de sa pensée d'après des documents inédits* (1933).

RAVEL, (JOSEPH) MAURICE (1875–1937), one of the most original French composers of his time. Of mixed Swiss-Basque descent (Swiss on his father's side, Basque on his mother's), he was born at Ciboure, near Saint-Jean-de-Luz, Basses-Pyrénées, on March 7, 1875. While still a student at the Paris Conservatoire, which he entered at the age of 14, he published a *Menuet antique*

MAURICE RAVEL

for piano (1895), some songs, and the *Pavane pour une infante défunte* ("Pavane for a Dead Princess") for piano (1899), which established his reputation almost overnight, although he judged it severely in later life. His failure, after three attempts, to win the coveted Prix de Rome for composition—the works he submitted having been judged too advanced by the conservative members of the jury—caused a scandal. Indignant protests were published and liberal-minded musicians and writers, including Romain Rolland, supported Ravel, denouncing the narrow-mindedness of his judges. As a result, in 1905 the director of the Conservatoire, Théodore Dubois, was forced to resign and his place was taken by Gabriel Fauré, with whom Ravel had been studying composition since 1898. By the time Ravel was 30 he had already published his String Quartet (1903), the song-cycle *Shéhérazade,* the Sonatina and *Miroirs* for piano, and the *Introduction et Allegro* for harp, string quartet, flute, and clarinet. One of his earliest piano pieces, *Jeux d'eau* ("Fountains"; 1901), inaugurates a new era in the use of the piano's technical resources, and toward the end of his life, in 1931, he wrote two piano concertos, one of which, for the left hand only, is among his most original works. Several of his piano works were later orchestrated by him, notably *Ma Mère l'Oye* ("Mother Goose") and *Valses nobles et sentimentales.* Ravel died in Paris on Dec. 28, 1937.

His chamber works include a remarkable trio for violin, cello, and piano, a violin and piano sonata, and a sonata for violin and cello, but it was in his symphonic works, the *Rapsodie Espagnole,* the ballet *Daphnis et Chloé* (1909–12), and *Boléro* (1927, performed 1928) that he reached his height. As a songwriter Ravel achieved great distinction with his imaginative *Histoires Naturelles* (1906), *Trois Poèmes de Mallarmé* (1913), and *Chansons Madécasses* (1925–26). In opera he produced two little masterpieces of wit and fantasy, *L'Heure Espagnole* (1907) and, in collaboration with Colette as librettist, *L'Enfant et les sortilèges* (1925).

In everything he wrote Ravel was an exquisite craftsman, striving always for perfection of form and style which he judged more valuable than an expression of personal feelings. Though he worked in the classical form and was never a revolutionary musician, he created an individual harmonic language as unmistakably his own as any page of Bach or Chopin. Although it is incorrect to bracket him with Debussy, the two composers nevertheless had certain features in common, notably their attraction to Baudelaire and Mallarmé, and a delight in rare and precious sensations. In temperament, however, and in methods and technique they were vastly different. A highly distinctive composer in everything he wrote, Ravel, as Roland-Manuel wrote, "is one of the rare French composers who have left so strong an imprint on their art that music after them can never be the same as it was before they appeared on the scene."

BIBLIOGRAPHY.—J. van Ackere, *Maurice Ravel* (1957); M. Gérar and R. Chalupt (eds.), *Ravel au miroir de ses lettres* (1956); V. Jankélévitch, *Maurice Ravel* (1956); H. Jourdan-Morhange, *Ravel et nous* (1945); A. Roland-Manuel, *Maurice Ravel et son oeuvre* (1925), *Ravel* (1948); R. H. Myers, *Ravel: Life and Works* (1960). (R. H. My.)

RAVEN, among the largest of the perching birds, and, with crows, magpies, and jays, a member of the family Corvidae. Of all corvids, the ravens appear to be the most intelligent and the most advanced in imitative skills. Long before it was immortalized in Poe's "The Raven," the common raven (*Corvus corax*) was an almost universal symbol of dark prophecy—of death, pestilence, disease. But its cleverness, appearance, and fearless habits have won it a degree of admiration, as evidenced by its noble heraldic

JOHN GERARD

A NORTHERN SUBSPECIES OF COMMON RAVEN (CORVUS CORAX PRINCIPALIS)

roles in the mythology of some peoples.

Although much like the crow (*q.v.*) in appearance, the common raven is considerably larger—with a length of 22–25 in. and a wingspread of more than 4 ft.—has a much heavier bill, and shaggier plumage, especially about the throat. The lustrous black feathers have a blue or purplish iridescence. In the white-necked raven (*C. cryptoleucus*), a crow-sized bird of western North America, the bases of the neck feathers are white, and show only when the feathers are ruffled, as in display or by the wind.

Formerly abundant throughout the Northern Hemisphere, the raven is now restricted to the wilder, undisturbed parts of its range where it is free of persecution by man. It is among the hardiest of birds, inhabiting the northern tundra and coniferous forests as well as barren mountains and desert. Being keen-sighted, sagacious, and notably wary, the raven survives by its wits; it has never been protected by law.

Like other corvids, the raven is a noisy, aggressive omnivore whose diet includes rodents, insects, grain, and birds' eggs. In winter, especially, it is essentially a scavenger, and feeds on carrion, dead fish, and other refuse. To some extent it also preys on sick animals, both wild and domestic. Its calls include guttural croaks, gurglings, and a sharp metallic "tok." Ravens breed as early as January in some areas and as late as April elsewhere. The spectacular courtship flight involves soaring and all manner of aerial acrobatics. The crudely made nest, of coarse sticks, usually lined with hair or shredded bark, is a bulky structure up to five feet in diameter; it may be built on a cliff or near the top of a large tree. The three to seven eggs, pale green or gray, and streaked, spotted, or blotched with brown, are incubated for about three weeks. The young remain in the nest for about a month. If captured while a nestling, a raven may make an interesting pet capable of learning to mimic a few words. The record life span reported for a raven in captivity is 69 years; most individuals perhaps do not live to even half that age in nature.　　　(E. R. BE.)

RAVENNA, a city and archiepiscopal see of Emilia-Romagna, northeastern Italy, and capital of the province of Ravenna, lies 52 mi. (84 km.) E of Bologna by rail and 30 mi. (48 km.) NW of Rimini, on a low-lying plain near the confluence of the Ronco and Montone rivers, 6 mi. (10 km.) inland from the Adriatic Sea. It is connected by canal with the seaside resort of Marina di Ravenna, 6 mi. NE, which has developed round the old Porto Corsini. Pop. (1961) 116,273 (commune).

Of the ancient Roman city and port of Ravenna with its harbour

(Classis) nothing is now visible. The fame of Ravenna rests on the quality and quantity of its 5th–8th-century Christian monuments, which in many respects surpass those of Rome itself. As capital city of the Western Roman Empire for two and a half centuries and a major port of entry for the Eastern Empire, Christian Ravenna reflects in its art the methods, designs, and imagery of West and East alike. The result is a sophisticated and often highly individual art, which gains added importance from the relative scarcity of comparable contemporary monuments in Milan and Constantinople, the two cities with which Ravenna was in closest contact.

The Monuments.—The earliest period of Ravenna's greatness, dating from the residence there of the emperor Honorius early in the 5th century A.D., has left the so-called mausoleum of Honorius' sister, Galla Placidia (d. 450), in the northwest of the city. This was originally related to the adjacent basilica of Sta. Croce, now destroyed. Its building technique is Western, but its architectural composition, a Latin cross with barrel vaults and central dome, has Eastern prototypes. The whole upper surface of the interior is covered with mosaics, mostly with a blue ground. The central dome is decorated with a cross and the beasts of the four evangelists—a scheme echoed in the archbishop's palace (chapel of S. Pier Crisologo), in the basilica of S. Vitale, and later, at Rome, in Sta. Prassede (chapel of S. Zeno). Off the Piazza del Duomo to the south is the "orthodox baptistery" (S. Giovanni in Fonte, late 4th century), also known as the Neon baptistery from the tradition that it was decorated by Archbishop Neon (449–452). The use of stucco is combined with mosaic; the architectural motifs and the procession of apostles round the dome are of outstanding quality. The churches of S. Giovanni Evangelista, S. Francesco (with Dante's tomb [1780]; founded in the 5th century as S. Pietro Maggiore), Sta. Agata, and S. Vittore are also of this early period but have been considerably altered; of S. Giovanni Battista little remains.

Of the monuments of the time of the Arian Ostrogothic emperor Theodoric (d. 526), the most impressive is his mausoleum. This is two-storied, decagonal outside and circular within, and covered by a monolithic dome 36 ft. (11 m.) in diameter, made of limestone imported from Istria. On the capture of the city by the Catholic Belisarius in 540, the bones of Theodoric were scattered and the mausoleum converted into the church of Sta. Maria della Rotonda. The Arian baptistery (now Sta. Maria in Cosmedin and next to S. Spirito, or S. Teodoro), of the same period, northeast of the town centre, has a mosaic in the dome. This, although much restored, is interesting as showing a simplified version of the mosaic of the Neon baptistery, rationalized by the introduction of the *Etoimasia* (*i.e.*, the gospels enthroned) as the goal of the procession of apostles.

S. Apollinare Nuovo.—To the period of Arian domination belongs also the older part of the mosaic decoration of the early-6th-century basilica of S. Apollinare Nuovo (southwest of the railway station, on the east side of the city). This, originally an Arian cathedral, became a Catholic church about 570 and was dedicated to St. Apollinaris in the 9th century when the saint's remains were brought from his other basilica at Classe. It contains magnificent mosaics. From its Arian phase date the representations of Theodoric's palace and of the city of Ravenna (on the right) and of the port of Classis (on the left), as well as the two cycles, now high on the walls, of the teaching and miracles of Christ (left hand, showing Christ beardless) and his passion and resurrection (right hand, omitting the crucifixion). These are among the oldest of such representations in existence, even if not the first, and are thus of considerable artistic and theological interest. The Catholics completed the decoration of S. Apollinare Nuovo. Above the arcades of the presbytery are, on the right-hand side, a row of men saints with wreaths proceeding from Ravenna toward Christ enthroned with attendant angels; and, on the left-hand side, a row of women saints proceeding from Classis toward the Virgin and Child with Magi. Above the figures are conchs in mosaic (not stucco, as in the Neon baptistery).

S. Vitale.—In the time of Justinian (mid-6th century) S. Vitale, just southwest of Galla Placidia's mausoleum, also was completed.

The form of this church, an octagonal martyrium with a presbytery and seven semicircular niches opening through arcades into a two-storied ambulatory, is akin to that of the almost contemporary church of SS. Sergius and Bacchus in Constantinople. The marble for both churches came from the quarries of Proconnesus on the Sea of Marmara and was perhaps carved by the same workmen; but the use in S. Vitale of an extra, crudely carved impost block above the impost capital shows that the builders did not understand the purpose of this Byzantine innovation. The construction of the lofty dome with terracotta tubes, a method used also in Galla Placidia's mausoleum and in the Neon baptistery, is another feature with no Eastern equivalent. The famous mosaics are all in the presbytery. They are the only ones in Ravenna to show at all strongly the influence of Constantinople; the masters were, however, almost certainly not Greek but from a local school. The mosaics are arranged in panels (each treated independently) whose size and shape are dictated by the architectural forms. In the semidome of the apse Christ is depicted enthroned on the globe of the world with supporting angels; St. Vitalis appears on the right, and on the left Bishop Ecclesius with a model of the church. On the left-hand wall is Justinian accompanied by attendants including Archbishop Maximian; on the right-hand wall is Theodora with court ladies. Christ is shown also with apostles and SS. Gervase and Protase, reputed to be the sons of St. Vitalis, on the triumphal arch. On the right are the sacrifices of Abel and of Melchizedek, the prophet Isaiah, and Moses at the burning bush. On the left are Abraham entertaining the three angels and sacrificing Isaac, the prophet Jeremiah, and Moses on Mt. Sinai. The pair of panels showing Justinian and Theodora with their retinues are important documents of imperial costume and portraiture. The figure, in Justinian's following, of Archbishop Maximian is named; his monogram appears also on the front of his ivory throne, now in the archiepiscopal museum behind the cathedral. The carvings on this chair are of great historical, theological, and liturgical interest. The fine panels show the four evangelists and the Baptist with scenes from the life of Joseph and the life of Christ, in a framework richly carved with animals and birds in a vine scroll. The panels are generally thought to be the product of a workshop in Constantinople.

Other Monuments.—The basilica of S. Apollinare in Classe, three miles south of Ravenna near the site of the ancient Classis, was consecrated in 549. Eastern influence has been deduced from the external polygonal form of its apses and apsidal chapels. Its capitals were certainly imported. The fine apse mosaic portrays St. Apollinaris, the first bishop of Ravenna, in prayer beneath a symbolic representation of the Transfiguration of Christ. The other mosaics are later and have been heavily restored.

The oldest church in Ravenna is the cathedral, southwest of the city centre, built originally in 370–390 and dedicated to its founder, St. Ursus. It was destroyed in 1733 and at once rebuilt (1734–43); of the old structure only the crypt, the pulpit of Archbishop Agnellus (556), and a later campanile survived.

Ravenna has several distinctive round campaniles of red brick (the usual material of the area); they are generally later in date than the churches for which they were built. That of S. Apollinare Nuovo (870–878) provides the earliest example in Italy of the decorative use of majolica. Those of S. Apollinare in Classe, Sta. Maria Maggiore, and Sta. Agata are also of the 9th century. S. Giovanni Evangelista and S. Francesco have square campaniles of the 10th century.

Sta. Maria in Porto and S. Vitale have 16th-century cloisters of the Venetian period. Incorporated in those of the latter is the Museo Nazionale d'Antichità, containing an important collection of classical and early Christian antiquities: inscriptions, icons, ceramics, and sculptures, which include ivories, screen panels, and sarcophagi. These last, both in the museum and in the churches, are outstanding. Some of the figured pieces may be imports or the work of immigrant craftsmen, but those with north Italian animal symbolism seem almost all to have been made locally. Typical is the design of peacocks or lambs with a cross, which in the 8th century spread throughout Italy. It is probable that Ravenna was a centre of ivory carving up to the 6th century. Modern excavations have revealed remains of floor mosaics in S. Giovanni Evangelista. S. Vitale has a magnificent floor of *opus sectile* marble inlay, as well as rich wall paneling of coloured marble and intarsia.

Sta. Maria in Porto Fuori, built after 1069, was, until its destruction in World War II (1944), the only important surviving building of the later Middle Ages. The only remaining early civil building is the elaborate facade of what is usually identified as the palace of the exarchs (south of S. Apollinare Nuovo). Excavation has revealed decorative floor mosaics there, too, as well as nearby foundations which may be those of the palace of Theodoric.

The influence of Ravenna upon art and architecture was widespread. In Milan, S. Lorenzo is supposed to have been constructed on the orders of Galla Placidia; in Rome, she gave mosaics for S. Paolo fuori le Mura. It is likely that other work in Rome was executed by artists of Ravenna during the time of Justinian. Later, Charlemagne carried off to Aachen (Aix-la-Chapelle) the brazen statue of Theodoric and columns from his palace.

The Modern Town.—Mosaic work continues in Ravenna; the Accademia di Belle Arti south of the city centre houses a school for the study and production of mosaics as well as a collection of works by painters of the Romagna. The centre itself has the Teatro Alighieri (1840–52), the Piazza del Popolo and, alongside it, the medieval Palazzo Comunale fronted by two columns by Pietro Lombardi (1483). South of the station and adjacent to Sta. Maria in Porto are public gardens and east of these, across the railway line, is a race track.

Outside Ravenna, east of S. Apollinare in Classe, is the celebrated ancient pine forest (Pineta di Classe; much reduced in size), which was admired by the poet Byron when residing in Ravenna at the palazzo Guiccioli (1821), and which was the refuge in 1849 of Garibaldi and his wife Anita, who died there.

Ravenna is a junction for the main road and railway routes from Ferrara to Rimini and down the Adriatic coastline. Its formerly marshy surroundings have been made into well-drained agricultural land, and it is a centre for the sale of local produce (cereals, fruit, sugar beet, hemp). Wine, macaroni, fertilizers, cement, and furniture are made. There is an important methane extraction and processing plant which has led to the growth of a large industrial quarter and to considerable immigration. The quarter around the railway station was rebuilt after severe damage in World War II (1944), and considerable rebuilding in the city centre, in addition to suburban development, reflects the city's present affluence.

RAVENNA PROVINCE (area 718 sq.mi. [1,860 sq.km.]; pop. [1961] 328,969) is bounded north by Ferrara province, west by Bologna, south by Forlì and east by the Adriatic Sea. Most of it consists of plain, once marshy but now reclaimed for agriculture, but the land rises in the southwest to the foothills of the Tuscan-Emilian Apennines. The province is watered by the Reno, Santerno, Senio, and Lamone rivers, as well as by the Ronco and Montone. The chief occupation is agriculture. There are saltworks at Cervia, on the coast southeast of Ravenna city; and some industry at Lugo in the west of the province and at Faenza to the south.

HISTORY

In prehistoric times Ravenna was a modest island settlement protected by coastal lagoons. Its importance dates from the decline of the neighbouring sites of Spina (*q.v.*) and Adria. It passed under Roman control in 191 B.C. and was the base from which Julius Caesar negotiated with the Senate in 50–49 B.C. before crossing the Rubicon River to the south, so starting the civil war. Augustus built the harbour, Portus Classis, and made Ravenna the base for his Adriatic fleet. An aqueduct 23 mi. long (of which traces remain) was built by Trajan and restored by Justinian. Early in the 5th century A.D. the barbarian invasions caused the emperor of the west, Flavius Honorius (reigned 395–423), to withdraw his court from Rome to the safety of Ravenna; and the city was the capital of the Western Empire until its dissolution in 476 with the accession of the first barbarian ruler of Italy, Odoacer. He in turn surrendered Ravenna to the Ostrogoth Theodoric in 493, and the latter made it the capital of the Ostrogothic kingdom.

In 540, Ravenna was surrendered to Belisarius, Byzantine general of the emperor Justinian I the Great, and subsequently made an imperial exarchate (see RAVENNA, EXARCHATE OF). From the time of Honorius, Ravenna had enjoyed great political, economic, intellectual, and artistic activity. It had been raised to the rank of archbishopric in 438 and had an important mint. About 751 it fell to the Lombards, but was taken from them by the Frankish king Pepin III the Short, who handed it over to the pope in 757, the archbishops, however, retaining almost princely powers. A short-lived bid for independence in the 12th century was followed, in the 13th–14th centuries, by subjection to the house of Da Polenta, a noble family of the Romagna. From 1441 to 1509, Ravenna was under Venetian control and briefly, after the battle and sacking of 1512 (see below), under the French. Thereafter until 1860, when it joined united Italy, it was subject to the popes with only minor interruptions.

The patron saint of Ravenna is the early martyr St. Vitalis, of whom nothing certain is known. Its first bishop was St. Apollinaris, also reputed a martyr; there is no reliable evidence to confirm the tradition that he was a disciple of St. Peter. Archbishop at the time of Galla Placidia was St. Peter Chrysologus (the "golden orator," c. 400/406–c. 450), who had Placidia's support for his building projects. St. Romuald (c. 950–1027), founder of the Camaldolese hermit-monks, was a member of the Onesti ducal family of Ravenna and was born there; so also was the Camaldolese St. Peter Damian (1007–72).

Battle of Ravenna, 1512.—Pope Julius II, resentful of French power in northern Italy and anxious to aggrandize the Papal States by annexing the French-protected dukedom of Ferrara, had proclaimed in 1511 a Holy League with Spain and Venice. The army of Louis XII of France (which included a German element), boldly led by the 23-year-old Gaston de Foix, followed a successful defense of Bologna early in 1512 with an assault on Ravenna in April. The Spanish viceroy, Ramon de Cardona, who had been anxious to avoid a pitched battle, took up a strong defensive position south of the Ronco River, which Gaston crossed on April 11, Easter Day. During the cannonade which opened the battle many French captains were killed; the Spaniards and Italians, contrary to French ideas of military honour, protected themselves by lying prone behind their defenses. Then, while the French made a successful cavalry charge, their ally the duke of Ferrara led his expert artillery round the right flank of the League's infantry and forced them from their now indefensible position. The French and German infantry won the battle convincingly, with the aid of reserves and cavalry; but Gaston, the "thunderbolt of Italy," was killed in a rash charge on a body of retreating Spaniards.

Ravenna surrendered to the French on the following day and was sacked, but was recovered by Julius II without difficulty a few months later, the French army, hindered by the loss of its leader and opposed by a strengthened league, having retreated across the Alps.

This battle is of interest for its use of medieval methods and weapons in conjunction with the foreshadowing of modern, efficient artillery tactics.

See ITALY: *History; see* also references under "Ravenna" in the Index.
(J. B. W.-P.)

RAVENNA, EXARCHATE OF, or exarchate of Italy, created by the east Roman emperor Maurice (582–602) as an administrative province to comprise the Byzantine dominions in Italy after the Lombard invasion (see ITALY: *History*); it is first mentioned in 584. Soon after, it came to form part of the new system of "themes" (administrative divisions) established along the frontiers of the empire by Heraclius and his successors. At the beginning of the 7th century the exarchate included Istria, maritime Venetia, Emilia with Ravenna, the Pentapolis, *i.e.,* the coast from Rimini to south of Ancona with the hinterland, Calabria (then the name of the "heel" of Italy), Bruttium (the "toe" of Italy, called Calabria from the late 7th century), Naples with southern Campania, Rome with northern Campania and southern Tuscany, Perugia, and Liguria.

The territory of Ravenna was also called, in a limited sense, the exarchate of Ravenna. It was under the direct administration of the exarch, while the other Byzantine possessions in Italy were governed, under his authority, by dukes or *magistri militum;* below them there were tribunes in charge of towns and castles. The internal organization of the exarchate, like that of the themes, was marked by the combination of military and civil powers in the same hands. The exarch, first created as the military governor of Byzantine Italy, thus soon displaced the existing head of the civil administration, the prefect of Italy, whose office seems to have disappeared about the middle of the 7th century. Sicily formed a separate province directly dependent on Constantinople, although the exarch exercised some control over it during that century; Corsica and Sardinia were placed under the exarchate of Carthage.

During the 7th century, the Byzantines suffered further losses; by the middle of the century, Liguria had fallen to the Lombard kings; by the end of it, nearly the whole of Calabria (*i.e.,* the southeast of Italy) had been conquered by the Lombard dukes of Benevento. In 726 a revolt broke out in the exarchate which seriously threatened the Byzantine government; although primarily caused by the iconoclastic policy of Leo III, it was also due to dissatisfaction with the Byzantine administration. After the suppression of the revolt, or after 750, the south Italian dominions were separated from the exarchate and incorporated in the theme of Sicily. The pope, who had played a leading part in the revolt, was gradually becoming the virtual ruler of Rome and its duchy. King Liutprand took advantage of the difficult situation of the Byzantines and extended his power at their expense. After a brief respite, Aistulf continued this policy of conquest; in c. 751 he finally took Ravenna, after its territory (the exarchate in the limited sense) had already been conquered. In northern Italy, Istria and maritime Venetia alone remained Byzantine. Subsequent Frankish intervention made a recovery of the lost dominions impossible; the exarchate in the limited sense and the Pentapolis passed, together with the duchy of Rome, under papal rule.

The Byzantine possessions in southern Italy saw a temporary revival toward the end of the 9th century; in view of the Arab conquest of Sicily, they were then reorganized in the new themes of Longobardia and Calabria. Venice, nominally under Constantinople, became practically independent under its dukes (doges); and this also happened in some of the southern territories, as at Naples. The development toward local and regional autonomy had already started before the downfall of the exarchate, and had undoubtedly contributed to it. Imperial officials became landowners, and local landowners entered the imperial administration. The tribunate tended to become hereditary in the landowning class; the dukes of Venice were elected by the population from the time of the revolt of 726.

BIBLIOGRAPHY.—C. Diehl, *Etudes sur l'administration byzantine dans l'exarchat de Ravenne (568–571)* (1888); L. M. Hartmann, *Untersuchungen zur Geschichte der byzantinischen Verwaltung in Italien (540–750)* (1889), *Geschichte Italiens im Mittelalter,* vol. ii (1903).
(N. R.)

RAVENSBURG, a town of West Germany in the *Land* (state) of Baden-Württemberg, Federal Republic of Germany. It lies on the Schussen, 12½ mi. (20 km.) NE of Friedrichshafen by road. Pop. (1961) 31,269. It retains a medieval appearance, with numerous gate- and wall-towers, including the Mehlsack. Outstanding buildings include the 16th-century town hall, the weigh-house (1496), the 14th-century parish church, and the church of St. Jodok (1385). Textiles, paper, and timber are produced, and the town is on the railway from Friedrichshafen to Ulm. The Rutenfest, a children's festival dating from the 17th century, is held. The town grew up around the ancestral castle of the Guelphs (where Henry the Lion was born) on the Veitsburg. In 1180 it passed to the Hohenstaufens. From 1276 to 1802 it was a free city of the empire. During the 14th and 15th centuries an important trading company flourished there.

RAVENSCROFT, THOMAS (c. 1583–c. 1633), English composer, chiefly remembered for his social songs and his collection of psalm settings, was born perhaps in Sussex about 1583. He became a chorister of St. Paul's Cathedral, London. In 1607 he took his B. Mus. at Cambridge. From 1618 to 1622 he was music master at Christ's Hospital. He died about 1633.

Ravenscroft's *Whole Booke of Psalmes* (1621), comprising over

100 metrical psalm tunes, proved extremely popular. Ravenscroft himself harmonized about half the melodies, commissioning or compiling the rest from other composers. Several of his versions are still in use.

His secular collections are full of interest for the sociologist or historian of popular music. *Pammelia* (1609), containing 100 catches and rounds, was the first anthology of its kind; *Deuteromelia* (1609) has 31 items, including "Three blind mice"; *Melismata* (1611) has 23 songs for the "court, city, and country humours"; and his theoretical work, the *Briefe Discourse* (1614), appends further characteristic pieces. Ravenscroft aimed cunningly to please a middle-class lay public very different from the educated élite who enjoyed the madrigal or the air (*q.v.;* ayre).

See W. H. Havergal (ed.), *A Reprint of All the Tunes in Ravenscroft's Book* (1845); P. Warlock (ed.), *Thomas Ravenscroft: Pammelia and Other Rounds and Catches* (1928). (B. L. TR.)

RAVI, one of the "five rivers" of the Punjab (*q.v.*), rises in the Himalayas in the Kulu subdivision of Kangra District, Punjab (India), and flows through Chamba, the isolated northern division of Himachal Pradesh. Turning southwest it briefly enters Jammu and Kashmir and the Gurdaspur District (Punjab, India), then for nearly 100 mi. (160 km.) forms the India-Pakistan frontier before entering West Pakistan about 15 mi. (24 km.) NE of Lahore. Lahore itself is not sited on the river but lies a mile or two to the south. Flowing west-southwest across the Punjab plains, the Ravi finally falls into the Chenab about 10 mi. (16 km.) S of Ahmadpur after a course of about 450 mi. (724 km.). Its water is used for the irrigation of the Bari Doab (interfluve), the country between the Ravi and the Sutlej. The Upper Bari Doab Canal (completed 1878–79), with headworks at Madhopur on the Indian side of the frontier, serves about 1,177,000 ac. (476,300 ha.) of the Upper Bari Doab around Amritsar, mainly in India. Some of the distributory canals, however, enter Pakistan, and until the waters agreement of 1960 the alleged withholding of irrigation water by India was a source of constant irritation to Pakistan. The Lower Bari Doab Canal (completed 1917), with headworks also on the left bank of the Ravi at Balloki, irrigates about 345,000 ac. and lies entirely in Pakistan. The waters of the Ravi are supplemented for the irrigation of the Lower Doab by canals leading from the Jhelum and the upper Chenab. The Sidhnai Canal, beginning about 10 mi. above the Chenab junction, was frequently dry in winter until the construction of the Haveli Canal (1939), delivering water to the Ravi from the Trimmu Barrage at the Chenab-Jhelum confluence. (T. HER.; L. D. S.)

RAWALPINDI, a town, cantonment, district, and division of West Pakistan. The town, interim capital of Pakistan since 1959, headquarters of the district and division, and principal commercial centre of the region, lies on the Grand Trunk Road, 90 mi. (145 km.) ESE of Peshawar and 160 mi. (257 km.) NW of Lahore. Pop. (1961) 197,370 Rawalpindi city, 340,175 including the cantonment area; (1969 est.) 455,000 including the cantonment area. Rawalpindi ("village of Rawals") occupies the site of an old village inhabited by Rawals, a tribe of Yogis (ascetics). Gen. Sir Alexander Cunningham, director general of the Indian Archaeological Survey (1870–85), identified certain ruins on the site of the cantonment with the ancient city of Gajipur or Gajnipur, the capital of the Bhatti tribe in the centuries preceding the Christian era. The old city at the site, known as Fatehpur Baori, was destroyed during one of the Mughal invasions. It was said to have been restored by Jhanda Khan, a Gakhar chief, and named Pindi or Rawalpindi from the once flourishing village of Rawal, a few miles north of the town on the road to Murree. Sardar Milka Singh, a Sikh adventurer, occupied it in 1765 and invited traders from Jhelum and Shahpur districts to settle there, the town thereafter growing rapidly in importance. Early in the 19th century it became for a time the refuge of Shah Shuja, the exiled amir of Kabul, and his brother Shah Zaman. At Rawalpindi in March 1849, the Sikh Army under Chattar Singh and Sher Singh finally laid down their arms to the British after the Battle of Gujrat. On Aug. 8, 1919, a treaty of peace was signed there between Afghanistan and Great Britain concluding the third consecutive war between the two countries. During British rule

TERRACED HILLSIDES NEAR MURREE IN THE RAWALPINDI DISTRICT

Rawalpindi became a cantonment of considerable size and the headquarters of a division. After independence in 1947 it became the headquarters of the Pakistan Army.

The Leh Nullah (watercourse) separates the city from the cantonment and the civil station. A satellite town has been built on the Murree Road, which is the main residential area. There are several other schemes of urban development including that of another satellite town and of Lalazar Colony. Ayub National Park and Liaquat Gardens are the chief places of recreation. The city has four colleges affiliated with the University of the Panjab, a polytechnic, a police training institute, and an armed forces medical college.

Industrial enterprises include the locomotive works of the Pakistan Western Railway; gasworks; an iron foundry; a tent factory; cotton wool, silk textile and hosiery mills; glass and chemical works; plywood and slate manufacturing plants; and an oil refinery in the suburb of Morgah. The making of marble chips is an important cottage industry. The airport is in the Chaklala cantonment area. The city is the starting point of the road to the hill station of Murree and of the route into Kashmir.

RAWALPINDI DISTRICT (area 2,022 sq.mi. [5,237 sq.km.]), pop. (1961) 1,137,085, forms a compact square in the north of the division, with the highland tract called the Murree Hills jutting from its northeastern corner and the Kahuta Hills bordering it on the east. To the southwest stretches the rough undulating Potwar Plateau (1,700 ft. [518 m.]) intersected by many torrents. The northern part is drained by the Soan (Sohan) River and the southern by the Kanshi, while the Jhelum flows on the east. The climate is on the whole healthful, with long, cold winters and short, hot summers. Murree is under snow for about two months of the year. The rainfall is good (Rawalpindi 36 in. [914 mm.], the hills 53 in. [1,346 mm.]). Both the summer monsoon and winter rains are characteristic. Wheat and barley are the chief crops of the spring and millets and maize of the autumn harvest.

The district in ancient times formed part of Gandhara and was included in the Persian Empire of the Achaemenids. It possesses several sites of archaeological interest including that of the ancient city of Taxila, which has been identified with ruins near Shahderi (Shah-dheri) 20 mi. (32 km.) NW of Rawalpindi. Murree, 36 mi. (58 km.) NE of Rawalpindi, is the most important hill station of West Pakistan. The district was fast growing industrially in the early 1970s. A heavy industrial complex was being set up, with Chinese aid, near Taxila. As an adjunct to it a heavy foundry was being established. A heavy electrical complex was also being set up nearby with Soviet aid.

Islamabad (*q.v.*), the capital city designate of Pakistan, lies about 9 mi. (14 km.) NE of Rawalpindi. Rawal Dam has been built near the village of Rawal, 9 mi. (14 km.) from Rawalpindi on the Kurang River. It provides irrigation for about 12,000 ac. (4,856 ha.) of land and supplies drinking water to Rawalpindi and Islamabad. Two new dams are projected on the river Soan: the Soan or Rawalpindi Dam 6 mi. (9.6 km.) downstream from Rawalpindi; and the Charah Dam on the outskirts of Rawalpindi and Islamabad. The former would provide irrigation for 123,000 ac. (49,778 ha.); the latter for 31,400 ac. (12,706 ha.).

RAWALPINDI DIVISION occupies the north of West Pakistan and comprises the districts of Rawalpindi, Jhelum, Gujrat, and Campbellpur (formerly Attock). Area 11,206 sq.mi. (29,024 sq.km.). Pop. (1961) 3,979,139.   (K. S. Ad.)

RAWLINS, a city of south central Wyoming, U.S., 163 mi. NW of Cheyenne; the seat of Carbon County. It was founded in 1868 when the Union Pacific Railway arrived. The town was first named Rawlins Springs for U.S. Army Gen. John A. Rawlins, who had discovered a pleasant spring of fresh water at that point in 1867. Rawlins was incorporated as a city in 1886.

The Union Pacific Railway Company has always been a principal employer. Quite early Rawlins also became known as a cattle and sheep centre. It is also a centre for antelope hunting and in the 1950s became an important shipping point for uranium ore from the Gas Hills area to the north. The state penitentiary is located at the north edge of Rawlins and an oil refinery is 6 mi. away at Sinclair. For comparative population figures *see* table in WYOMING: *Population.*   (T. A. Ln.)

RAWLINSON, SIR HENRY CRESWICKE (1810–1895), English soldier and orientalist who deciphered the Bisitun (*q.v.*) rock inscription of Darius I the Great of Persia, was born at Chadlington, Oxfordshire, on April 11, 1810. In 1827 he went to India as an East India Company cadet and after six years was sent to Persia with other British officers to reorganize the shah's army. In Persia he became interested in the hitherto undeciphered cuneiform writing. In two years he transcribed as much as he was able of the great trilingual cuneiform inscription at Bisitun but friction between Persia and Britain ended in the departure of the British officers. He became political agent at Kandahar in 1840. Then at his own request, he was sent as political agent to Turkish Arabia and as consul at Baghdad where he made a complete transcript of the Bisitun inscription, which he deciphered and interpreted (1846). During two years' leave in England (1849–51) Rawlinson disposed of his valuable collection of Babylonian, Sabaean, and Sasanian antiquities to the trustees of the British Museum, who made him a grant to enable him to carry on the Assyrian and Babylonian excavations initiated by Sir Austen Layard. In 1851 he returned to Baghdad and in the following years collected many valuable sculptures for the museum. On resigning his post with the East India Company in 1855 he was knighted and appointed a crown director of the company. The remaining 40 years of his life were spent mainly in London. First appointed to the India Council in 1858 he was reappointed in 1868 and continued to serve on the Council until his death in London on March 5, 1895. He sat in Parliament for the Reigate Division (1858) and for the Frome Division of Somerset (1865–68). He was created a baronet in 1891.

His published works include *The Persian Cuneiform Inscription at Behistun* (1846–51); *Outline of the History of Assyria* (1852); *A Commentary on the Cuneiform Inscriptions of Babylonia and Assyria* (1850); *Notes on the Early History of Babylonia* (1854); *England and Russia in the East* (1875). He contributed to the *Encyclopædia Britannica* (9th ed.), including the articles on Baghdad, Euphrates, and Kurdistan.

BIBLIOGRAPHY.—G. Rawlinson, *A Memoir of Henry Creswicke Rawlinson* (1898); E. A. T. W. Budge, *The Rise and Progress of Assyriology* (1925); S. Lloyd, *Foundations in the Dust* (1947, reprinted 1955).

RAWLINSON, HENRY SEYMOUR RAWLINSON, 1ST BARON (1864–1925), British general and commander in chief in India, was born at Trent manor, Dorset, on Feb. 20, 1864, son of Sir Henry Creswicke Rawlinson (*q.v.*). Joining the King's Royal Rifles in 1884, he took part in the Burma (1886–87) and Nile (1898) campaigns, having in 1892 obtained a transfer to the Coldstream Guards. He served with distinction throughout the South African War (1899–1902) and was commandant of the staff college at Camberley (1903–06). After the outbreak of World War I he took command of IV Corps in 1914 and with it fought in the first Battle of Ypres and in 1915 at Neuve Chapelle and Loos. Early in 1916 he created and commanded the 4th Army with which he fought the Battle of the Somme. He was promoted general in January 1917. For a few weeks early in 1918 he was the British military representative on the supreme war council at Versailles, but in April he resumed command of the 4th Army. On Aug. 8, he attacked near Amiens and gained a great victory, the first of several which led to the general advance of the allied armies and the armistice of November. He was created Baron Rawlinson of Trent in August 1919 and from August to October he carried out the withdrawal of the allied forces from Archangel and Murmansk in north Russia. He then commanded for a year at Aldershot, before going to Delhi in November 1920 as commander in chief in India, where he reorganized the Indian Army. He died at Delhi on March 28, 1925.

See Sir F. B. Maurice, *Life of General Lord Rawlinson of Trent . . . from His Journals and Letters* (1928).   (R. G. Th.)

RAWTENSTALL, a municipal borough (1891) of Lancashire, Eng., lies in the ancient Forest of Rossendale, 17 mi. (27 km.) N of Manchester on the trunk road from Manchester to Burnley. Pop. (1968 est.) 21,870. First known to have been mentioned in a survey of the hundred of Blackburn (1323), Rawtenstall became an industrial area early in the 19th century. Its older industries of woolen, cotton, felt, and slipper manufacture are now augmented by box-making, quilting, rubber, and chemical productions. There is an art gallery and museum with a collection of footwear, and a college of further education.

RAY (WRAY), **JOHN** (1627–1705), English naturalist, famous for his systems of natural classification, was born at Black Notley, Essex, on Nov. 29, 1627. He graduated B.A. from Cambridge in 1647/48 and in 1649 secured a fellowship at Trinity college, obtaining his M.A. degree in 1651. He resigned his fellowship in 1662 because he could not subscribe to the Act of Uniformity. He devoted himself to science, aided through the generosity of Francis Willughby, with whom Ray agreed to work on a survey and classification of plants and animals. They made several botanical tours in Britain and, from 1663 to 1666, traveled in Europe. In 1667 Ray was elected a fellow of the Royal society. Willughby died in 1672, leaving Ray an annuity for life. Subsequently Ray published (1673) an account of their European travels. Ray died at Black Notley on Jan. 17, 1705.

Ray's system of plant classification, which greatly influenced the development of systematic botany, appeared in the *Methodus plantarum nova* (1682) and, in final form, in *Methodus plantarum emendata* (1703). Ray was the first to distinguish (1682) the divisions that he later (1703) called "Monocotyledones" and "Dicotyledones" (from cotyledon, a seed leaf; *see* PLANTS AND PLANT SCIENCE; ANGIOSPERMS), both fundamental in modern classifications though altered in content from Ray's concept. His *Catalogus plantarum circa Cantabrigium* (1660) was the first flora of Cambridgeshire, and his *Catalogus plantarum Angliæ* (1670; 2nd ed., 1677) and *Synopsis methodica stirpium Britannicarum* (1690; 2nd ed., 1696), the former arranged alphabetically and the latter according to his classification system, were the first floras of Britain. The *Historia plantarum* (1686–1704) described all known plants and arranged them in his system. The book's introductory essays, surveying botanical knowledge, formed the most complete treatise that had appeared on plants in general. Ray was the first to attempt to define what constitutes species.

Ray's zoological works were characterized by Georges Cuvier as "the basis of all modern zoology." The "foundation of scientific ornithology" (A. Newton) was laid in the *Francisci Willughbeii . . . ornithologiae libri tres* (1676), amplified and edited by Ray from the incomplete manuscript left by Willughby. The classification, which was for the most part followed later by Linnaeus, appears to have been of Ray's devising. The bases for the natural classification of fishes were laid in *Francisci Willughbeii . . . historia piscium* (1686), wherein the major share of the work was apparently that of Ray. This work greatly influenced Peter Artedi, whose arrangement of fishes was adopted by Linnaeus. The earliest classification of animals based upon anatomical characters was that in Ray's *Synopsis methodica animalium* (1693). He maintained Aristotle's great divisions, animals with blood (*i.e.*, vertebrates) and those "without" blood (*i.e.*, invertebrates). In the former he laid the basis for Linnaeus'. first four classes. Ray also issued a preliminary *Methodus insectorum* in 1705 and his *Historia insectorum*, incomplete when he died, was published in 1713 as it stood and without figures. Ray's system of insects, following Jan Swammerdam, was based upon metamorphosis (*q.v.*).

Ray also wrote *A Collection of English Proverbs* (1670; reissued 1855 and 1875) and *A Collection of English Words* (1674; reissued 1874).

The Ray society, for the publication of works on natural history, was founded in his honour in 1844.

BIBLIOGRAPHY.—C. E. Raven, *John Ray*, 2nd ed. (1950); G. Keynes, *John Ray, a Bibliography* (1951); E. Lankester (ed.), *Memorials of John Ray* (1846), with a listing of Ray's works.   (J. W. Tt.)

RAY (RAYY or RAI), formerly one of the great cities of Iran, the ancient RAGHA, Latin RHAGES. Its site is in Teheran *ostan* (province) $5\frac{1}{2}$ mi. SSE of Teheran City. The expedition of the Boston and Pennsylvania museums disclosed a prehistoric settlement on the site dating from the 3rd millennium B.C. Ray is mentioned in the Avesta as a sacred place and it is also mentioned in the Book of Tobit (*q.v.*). The city was well known to classical authors, who frequently referred to it. It was less important in Sasanian times; there was a considerable Christian settlement there, and it became the see of a Nestorian metropolitan. Ray was captured by the Muslim Arabs in 641. Before al-Mahdi became caliph, he was for a time governor of Ray; it was there, in about 766, that his son Harun al-Rashid was born. Under al-Mahdi's rule, the city rapidly regained its importance, being rivaled in western Asia only by Damascus and Baghdad. It is said to have covered 25 sq.mi. (65 sq.km.) and to have had a population of no less than 8,000,000, but this is undoubtedly a gross exaggeration. The Arab geographer Yaqut refers to Ray as a city of extraordinary beauty, built largely of fired brick and brilliantly ornamented with blue faience; but he also speaks of the dark and crooked streets and lanes which made it a formidable obstacle to invaders. It continued to be a city of political, commercial, and artistic importance under the Seljuks. In the 12th century it was tormented and greatly weakened by the fury of rival religious sects. In 1220 it was captured and almost entirely destroyed by the Mongols, most of the inhabitants being massacred. Many of those who survived moved to nearby Teheran, leaving only a handful in the old city, which soon fell completely into ruin.

Ray was famous for its decorated silks of an unsurpassed *finesse* and artistic perfection, and also for its ceramics. Only two architectural monuments survive; these are the tower of Togrul, or Tughril, (1139) and the so-called Naqqara-khana, a partially ruined tower, also of the Seljuk period, on the hillside overlooking the site of the city. The small town of Shah 'Abdul 'Azim which adjoins the ruins has been renamed Rey.

BIBLIOGRAPHY.—Barbier de Meynard, *Dictionnaire géographique*, pp. 273–280 (1871); G. Le Strange, *Lands of the Eastern Caliphate*, pp. 214–217 and 227 (1930); P. Schwarz, *Iran im Mittelalter*, pp. 740–809 (1926); V. Minorsky, "Raiy," *Encyclopaedia of Islam* (1936); L. Lockhart, *Persian Cities*, pp. 1–4 (1960).   (L. Lo.)

RAY, a common name loosely applied to any of the numerous cartilaginous fishes (class Chondrichthyes) of the order Batoidei, distinguished from the related modern sharks by a flattened body, which has the five gill openings and the mouth generally located entirely on the undersurface, and by the greatly enlarged pectoral fins, which extend forward along the sides of the head above the gill openings. Rays are well fitted by their structure for life at the bottom of the sea. On the upper surface of the head, behind the eyes, are large holes leading to the pharynx; these are termed spiracles and serve for the intake of water for respiration. Most bear young live, but the skates (family Rajidae) have eggs enclosed in oblong horny cases similar to those of dogfishes. As in the sharks, the males have the posterior edges of the pelvic fins modified to form copulatory organs. For a detailed discussion of the anatomy and relationships in cartilaginous fishes *see* CHONDRICHTHYES.

The rays (Batoidei) may be broken down into the following special groups: electric rays (family Torpedinidae), guitarfishes (Rhinobatidae), sawfishes (Pristidae), skates (Rajidae), stingrays (Dasyatidae), eagle rays (Myliobatidae), mantas, including the devil rays (Mobulidae).

Electric Rays.—The electric rays form an isolated family distinguished by large paired electric organs formed of vertical hexagonal columns, between the pectoral fins and the head, and capable of giving powerful shocks either for defensive purposes or to kill prey. The electric rays have a smooth and naked skin; the head and trunk with the pectoral fins form a circular disc; the tail is short and stout. About 20 species are known from warm seas, some reaching a weight of 200 lb. One representative species is the torpedo (*Torpedo nobiliana*), which occurs from North Carolina to Nova Scotia and from tropical west Africa to Scotland. Another is *Torpedo californica*, which occurs along the Pacific coast of the United States from central California northward.

Nonelectric Rays.—The other rays, without electric organs, generally have a rough skin, often bearing strong spines. The most sharklike are the guitarfishes (Rhinobatidae) of which about 20 species are known from tropical and subtropical seas; in most of them the pectoral fins are relatively small and the trunk passes gradually into the tail. The sawfishes, or sawrays (*Pristis*), differ from them in that the snout is produced into a long blade armed with a series of strong teeth on each side; five species are known from warm seas, frequenting sandy shores and estuaries.

The American sawfish (*Pristis pectinatus*) is common in the Gulf of Mexico, about the West Indies and occasionally is found on the Atlantic coast as far north as New Jersey. Small ones are excellent food. Some attain a length of 20 ft.; such large specimens are dangerous, the saw being a formidable weapon.

In the skates the large pectoral fins extend to the snout and backward stopping abruptly at the base of the slender tail. Numerous species of the cosmopolitan genus *Raja* are known, some living at considerable depths; some species reach a weight of 500 lb. These rays swim by undulating or flapping movements of the pectoral fins; their teeth are small and blunt in some species, pointed in others. Skates have two small dorsal fins on the rear part of the tail; they lack a distinct tail fin and also the long, slender recumbent barbed spine that characterizes the tail of stingrays. Their

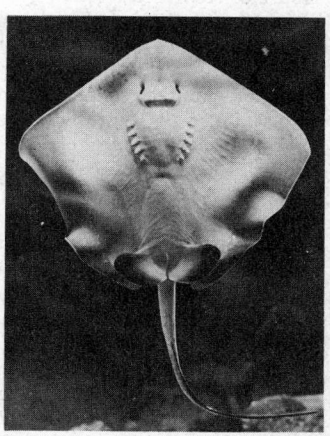

BY COURTESY OF MIAMI SEAQUARIUM

UNDERSIDE OF SOUTHERN STING-RAY (DASYATIS AMERICANA), FAMILY DASYATIDAE

food consists of mollusks, crustaceans and fishes. Skates produce large, oblong eggs with dark, leathery shells having a tendril at each corner by which they become fastened to seaweed or other objects. The largest western Atlantic species is the Barndoor skate (*Raja laevis*), which is said to reach a length of six feet. Its European counterpart is *R. batis*. A Pacific American species, the California skate (*Raja inornata*), which occurs from San Diego to the Strait of Juan de Fuca, is probably the principal species of commerce in the northeastern Pacific. Around 80,000 tons of skates are caught annually in trawls, traps and beach seines and on hook and line. The largest quantities are landed in Japan, France, Great Britain and Spain. The pectoral fins are cut off and used as food.

The remaining rays are collectively termed "whip-tailed," the tail being long and slender and usually having a barbed spine connected with a poison gland; this spine is capable of inflicting serious wounds and is a dangerous weapon when the tail is lashed.

All the whip-tailed rays are inhabitants of warm seas, except a few kinds of stingray in the rivers of South America. In the stingrays (*Dasyatis*, etc.), as in most of the rays previously described, the teeth are numerous, small and blunt; in the eagle rays (*Myliobatis*) the teeth are relatively few in number, hexagonal, forming a flat pavement, and in the spotted eagle rays (*Aetobatus*) are reduced to a single series of broad flat teeth used to crush the shells of mollusks.

The largest rays are the devil rays, *Manta* and *Mobula*, which may measure 20 ft. across the disc. Unlike other whip-tailed rays, they lack the tail spine. The anterior ends of the pectoral fins are free and project forward; when rolled up, the edges look like a pair of horns, but when unrolled, they meet below the mouth to form a scoop. Devil rays have been observed pursuing small fishes and scooping them into their mouths.   (C. T. R.; L. A. Wd.)

RAYAH (meaning "flock" in Arabic), though it was the name originally given to all the subjects of a Muslim ruler, later was limited to those non-Muslim subjects who paid the poll tax. Within the Ottoman Empire the rayahs were grouped into five communities (*milletler*): the Greek Orthodox, the Gregorian Armenian, the Catholic Armenian, the Latin Christian, and the Jewish. Of these five communities, only the Orthodox was subject to *devshirme* (tribute of children; *see* JANIZARIES). The individual rayah had no direct relations with his Muslim ruler but was subject to and represented and taxed by his own religious leader (*millet-bashi*). The origin of this system lay in the custom of the Roman, Byzantine, and caliphate empires of allowing self-government to subject communities. The system had some disadvantages, but it ensured the minority groups a large degree of liberty in matters of religion, property, and communal organization.
(A. D. A.)

RAYBURN, SAM (SAMUEL TALIAFERRO RAYBURN) (1882–1961), U.S. political leader who served as speaker of the U.S. House of Representatives for 17 years, was born in Roane County, Tenn., Jan. 6, 1882. His family, of predominantly Scottish origin, moved to Texas in 1887, and there Rayburn grew up on a 40-ac. farm. He worked his way through East Texas State College at Commerce, taught school, and became a lawyer. He served in the Texas House of Representatives for six years (1907–13) and in 1911 was elected speaker. In 1912 he was elected to the U.S. House of Representatives and served there continuously for 48 years and 8 months, a record tenure. He was elected to Congress 25 consecutive times.

Energetic, studious, ambitious, and affable, Rayburn quickly became influential behind the scenes in government and in party politics. As chairman of the powerful Congressional Committee on Interstate and Foreign Commerce (1931–37), he was a major architect of the New Deal. As a member of the House of Representatives he was co-author of six important laws—Railroad Holding Company Act, "Truth-in-Securities" Act, Securities Exchange Act, Federal Communications Act, Rural Electrification Act, and the most bitterly contested of all New Deal laws, the Public Utility Holding Company Act.

Rayburn was elected Democratic leader of the House of Representatives in 1937 and became speaker of the House on Sept. 16, 1940. He held the latter office for 17 years, exceeding by a wide margin the record set by Henry Clay in the first quarter of the 19th century. Noted for his tart common sense, honesty, and unflagging patriotism, he was a trusted adviser to Presidents Roosevelt, Truman, Eisenhower, and Kennedy. A dedicated party man who described himself as a Democrat "without prefix, without suffix, and without apology," Rayburn was often called "Mr. Democrat." He was permanent chairman of the Democratic National Conventions in 1948, 1952, and 1956. After winning the battle in 1961 to enlarge the House Committee on Rules—the hardest internal House struggle in 50 years—Rayburn's health failed quickly. Before Congress adjourned, he went home to Bonham, Tex., where he died on Nov. 16, 1961.   (L. B. J.)

See C. D. Dorough, *Mr. Sam* (1962).

RAYLEIGH, JOHN WILLIAM STRUTT, 3RD BARON (1842–1919), British physicist, was awarded the Nobel Prize for Physics in 1904 for his discovery (1894) of the noble elementary

gas, argon, in collaboration with Sir William Ramsay. He was born near Maldon, Essex, on Nov. 12, 1842, and educated at Trinity College, Cambridge, where he graduated senior wrangler (1865). As successor to James Clerk Maxwell he was head of the Cavendish Laboratory at Cambridge from 1879 to 1884, and in 1887 he became professor of natural philosophy in the Royal Institution of Great Britain. Elected (1873) a fellow of the Royal Society, he was president from 1905 to 1908. He was an original recipient of the order of merit (1902) and a privy councilor (1905). His researches ranged over almost the whole field of physics, including sound, wave theory, optics, colour vision, electrodynamics, electromagnetism, the scattering of light, hydrodynamics, the flow of liquids, capillarity, viscosity, the density of gases, photography, and elasticity as well as electrical measurements and standards. His researches on sound were embodied in his *Theory of Sound*, two volumes (1877–78, 2nd ed. 1937, reprinted 1956), and his other extensive studies in physics appeared in his *Scientific Papers*, six volumes (1899–1920). He died on June 30, 1919, at Witham, Essex.

See also references under "Rayleigh, John William Strutt" in the Index.

See N. H. de V. Heathcote, *Nobel Prize Winners in Physics* (1953).
(D. McK.)

RAYMOND, SAINT, OF PEÑAFORT (*c.* 1185–1275), Spanish Dominican friar, compiler of one of the most important pieces of medieval legislation, the *Decretals of Gregory IX,* which, though later supplemented by other papal enactments, remained substantially in force in the Roman Catholic Church until the new codification of 1917. Raymond was born at the castle of Peñafort (Penyafort) near Barcelona and received his early education in the cathedral school of that city. As a young priest he went to study canon law at Bologna and subsequently taught there from 1218 to 1221. During this period he wrote unpublished glosses on the *Decretum* of Gratian (*q.v.*) and a general treatise (*Summa*) on canon law which he left uncompleted. After his return to Barcelona early in 1222 he entered, on Good Friday, the Dominican Order at the monastery of St. Catherine's. Between 1222 and 1226 he wrote a manual of canon law for confessors, *Summa de casibus poenitentiae,* which was to become one of the most widely used books of its kind during the later Middle Ages. In 1229 he served as chaplain to the papal legate in Spain, Cardinal John of Abbeville, and thereafter was called to Rome by Pope Gregory IX, who appointed him to the college of *poenitentiarii,* the papal chaplains in charge of examining cases of conscience reserved or otherwise referred to the Holy See.

In 1230 the pope commissioned Raymond to recast into a single codification the papal statutes and rulings on points of canon law (*litterae decretales*) which had been issued since the appearance of Gratian's *Decretum* in mid-12th century and were by this time circulating in five different, poorly coordinated collections. Raymond's compilation, the *Decretals of Gregory IX,* was formally promulgated by the pope on Sept. 5, 1234. In 1235 Raymond revised and reissued his *Summa de casibus,* with an added part on the law of matrimony.

The next year he returned to Spain and in 1238 was elected master general of the Dominican Order but resigned after only two years in office. A revision of the constitutions of the order remains the chief monument of this brief tenure. The rest of Raymond's life was in part filled by various papal commissions but mainly by missionary interests. Already in 1235 he had written a set of instructions for the missions in Tunisia, and he may have had a hand in the papal approval (1235) of the Mercedarians, founded in Spain for the ransoming of Christian slaves in Muslim lands. Later he organized schools of Arabic and Hebrew studies for missionaries in Tunis and in Murcia (*c.* 1255), and it was at his request that St. Thomas Aquinas undertook to write the *Summa contra gentiles.* Raymond died on Jan. 5, 1275. He was canonized as saint in 1601 (feast on Jan. 23).

BIBLIOGRAPHY.—Fernando Valls-Taberner, *San Ramón de Penyafort* (1936), with full bibliography, reprinted in *Obras selectas,* vol. i, pt. 1 (1953); Amédée Teetaert, "Raymond de Penyafort," *Dictionnaire de théologie catholique,* vol. xiii, col. 1806–23 (1937); Stephan Kuttner,

Repertorium der Kanonistik, pp. 438–452 (1937); Thomas M. Schwertner, *Saint Raymond of Pennafort of the Order of Friars Preachers* (1935).
(S. G. K.)

RAYMOND OF POITIERS (1099–1149), prince of Antioch from 1136, was the younger son of William VII, count of Poitiers (William IX as duke of Aquitaine), and Philippa of Toulouse. In 1135 King Fulk of Jerusalem, regent for the infant heiress Constance of Antioch, sent envoys to offer her in marriage to Raymond, who was then at the court of Henry I of England. Arriving in Antioch in spring 1136, Raymond married Constance and so became prince. His wife's mother, Alice of Jerusalem, who had herself hoped to marry him, thereafter tried to undermine his authority.

In 1137 the Byzantine emperor John II Comnenus, who claimed suzerainty over Antioch, obliged Raymond to do homage and even to promise to cede the principality as soon as John should have won new territory for him in the East, where the *atabeg* Zangi (Imad-al-Din) of Mosul, already in possession of Aleppo, was encroaching on the principality's frontiers. John and Raymond, however, failed to win any such territory in their campaign of 1138; and though John made a solemn entry into Antioch, Raymond remained in control, campaigning against the Muslims and intriguing against the Latin patriarch, Radulf. After Zangi's conquest of Edessa (1144) had exposed Antioch to attack from the northeast also, Raymond's position was weakened, and he visited Constantinople in 1145 to conciliate John II's successor, Manuel I. His relations with his niece, Eleanor (*q.v.*) of Aquitaine, who visited Antioch in 1148 with her husband Louis VII of France, gave rise to scandalous rumours. On June 28, 1149, Raymond was killed near Inab in battle against Zangi's successor, Nureddin. *See* CRUSADES.

RAYMOND IV (1041 or 1042–1105), count of Toulouse, also called RAYMOND OF SAINT-GILLES (from the abbey which formed part of his original fief), was the second son of Count Pons and his consort Almodis. His first marriage, to his cousin, the heiress of Venaissin, together with rights inherited from his grandmother Emma, enabled him to bear the title of marquis of Provence (*see* PROVENCE), but this marriage was condemned by the church, and his wife disappeared, after giving him a son, Bertrand. He married, secondly, Matilda, daughter of Roger I of Sicily (*c.* 1080); and, thirdly, Elvira, a bastard daughter of Alfonso VI of Castile (before 1094), possibly after campaigns against the Moors in Spain. On the death of his elder brother William IV (*c.* 1093), he succeeded to the whole countship of Toulouse.

Through various measures and donations, Raymond had already shown himself a pious leader of the papacy's reform movement in the church. Pope Urban II had probably secured his agreement before beginning his campaign for the First Crusade, and Raymond was the first of the princes of Western Europe to take the cross. He left France in October 1096 and made his way to Constantinople through northern Italy and Dalmatia and along the old Via Egnatia across the Balkans. His first contacts with the Byzantine emperor Alexius I were rather rough, and he refused to do formal homage to him. A compromise was reached, however, with a mutual oath of help and Raymond's undertaking to respect Byzantine territorial rights. Raymond was to be the most conscientious partisan of the Greek-Latin alliance, sometimes to his disadvantage.

Raymond fell ill in summer 1097, while crossing the deserts of Asia Minor. In October, on a rumour that the Turks had abandoned Antioch, he sent a reconnaissance party, which his rivals later represented as an indication of his personal designs on that city. He played his part in the siege of Antioch; and when the crusaders were in turn besieged there by Kerbogha of Mosul, a great revival of religious activity among his troops culminated in the discovery of the Holy Lance by a Provençal. This miracle stimulated the crusaders to defeat Kerbogha; but it was also held to be a product of gross intrigues by Raymond and a further proof of his ambitions. Raymond seems to have insisted that Antioch should be restored to the Byzantine emperor, whereas Bohemund I (*q.v.*) claimed it for himself as a reward for his role in its capture. Eventually Bohemund expelled Raymond's garrison from Antioch and remained in possession of it.

From the fall of Antioch onward Raymond appears as the true leader of the Crusade, the organizer of the march on Jerusalem. Some of his actions aroused criticism, for instance his siege of Arca (Arqah, northeast of Tripoli; spring of 1099); but he was a successful leader, and he finally helped in the storming of Jerusalem (July 1099). He seems to have refused the royal crown, which was then given to Godfrey of Bouillon. He quarreled with Godfrey, but still helped him to repel the attack launched by the Fatimids of Egypt, which was crushed at Ascalon. (*See* further CRUSADES.)

Raymond may have taken a vow never to return to his lands in southern France. Yet he alone among the leaders of the Crusade had conquered no principality in Syria. His last years in the Orient were occupied with a voyage to Constantinople (perhaps to secure Alexius I's approval for projected conquests); with a new and ill-fated expedition of crusaders; with quarrels with Tancred, regent of Antioch during Bohemund's captivity; and with efforts to create a countship around Tripoli, which his heirs were to bring to success. He died on Feb. 28, 1105, in the castle of Mons Peregrinus (Mont Pèlerin), built by him near Tripoli. Of all leaders of the Crusade, Raymond was probably the most faithful both to Urban II's original plans and to the alliance with Alexius, which proved necessary. He was given the title of "most excellent chief of the Christian Militia." Yet his merits were obscured by chroniclers supporting his rivals and also by the rather unintelligent account of events given by his own chaplain, Raymond of Aguilers, in his *Historia Francorum qui ceperunt Jherusalem*.

See John H. and Laurita Hill, *Raymond IV de Saint-Gilles, comte de Toulouse* (1959; Eng. trans., 1962); J. Richard, *Le Comté de Tripoli sous la dynastie toulousaine* (1945).
(P. Wo.)

RAYMOND VI (1156–1222), count of Toulouse from 1194, was the son of Count Raymond V by his wife Constance, sister of Louis VII of France. He was five times married: first, in 1172, to Ermessinde, heiress of the countship of Melgueil (d. 1176); second, at an unknown date, to Beatrix, sister of Roger II, viscount of Béziers; third, about 1193 (presumably after repudiating Beatrix), to Burgundia of Cyprus, daughter of the future king Amalric II of Jerusalem, despite the consanguinity for which he later repudiated her; fourth, in 1196, to Joan (d. 1199), daughter of Richard I of England and the mother of his son, the future Raymond VII (*q.v.*); and fifth, in 1200 or 1204, to Leonora, sister of Peter II of Aragon. His two last marriages, contracted after his accession to the countship of Toulouse on his father's death (1194), allied him to dynasties which had been his father's great opponents. Joan brought him Agenais as her dowry, while Richard I at the same time restored Quercy from Aquitaine to Toulouse; and as Leonora's husband he was later able to appeal for Aragonese help during the Albigensian Crusade.

The Albigensian Crusade, that is, the holy war against the heretical Cathari (*q.v.*) of Languedoc, was the critical event which Raymond had to face. Before it began he had already been excommunicated, from 1195 to 1198, for an enterprise against the abbey of Saint-Gilles. Unlike his father, he adopted an attitude of indifference toward the heresy spreading over his lands. Pope Innocent III's legate, Peter de Castelnau, urged him in vain, from 1205, to stamp it out and even excommunicated him in 1207. An angry interview took place between the two men; and on Jan. 15, 1208, the legate was murdered, supposedly by one of the count's followers. Innocent III then launched the Crusade.

Raymond at first tried to halt the onslaught by making public amends to the church in a ceremony at Saint-Gilles (June 1209). Next, to everyone's surprise, he took the cross himself. The crusaders, however, after establishing Simon de Montfort as viscount of Béziers and Carcassonne in the place of Raymond Roger Trencavel, turned their attack farther westward. Raymond VI then saw himself obliged to oppose them. The people of Toulouse refused to expel him and underwent the first siege with him (June 1211); but he and Peter II of Aragon were disastrously defeated in September 1213, at the Battle of Muret.

Though he offered to abdicate in favour of his son, the Lateran Council of 1215 deprived Raymond VI of his countship and bestowed it on Simon de Montfort. It also stipulated that Raymond should live outside his lands, a portion of which was, however, reserved for his young son. Raymond VI did not accept the sentence. While his son was besieging Simon's garrison in Beaucaire, Raymond VI made his way to Aragon and raised a small force there. He then returned to occupy Toulouse (September 1217); and Simon, besieging the city, was killed outside it (June 1218). Raymond had recovered the major part of his lands when he suddenly died, in August 1222. His son could not obtain Christian burial for him.   (P. Wo.)

RAYMOND VII (1197–1249), count of Toulouse from 1222, was born at Beaucaire in July 1197, the son of Count Raymond VI (*q.v.*) by his fourth wife, Joan of England. He was present in Rome in 1215, when the Lateran Council reserved for him his family's inheritance in Provence, though it dispossessed his father. Received with delight in Provence, he was able to contribute notably to his father's restoration: his attack on Beaucaire led to the capitulation of Simon de Montfort's garrison there (1216); he marched to his father's help in besieged Toulouse; and after Simon's death he reconquered Agenais and Quercy, won a battle near Baziège against supporters of Amaury de Montfort, and was the soul of Toulouse's resistance when it was again besieged in 1219. Succeeding his father in 1222, he obtained a truce from Amaury in 1223. At a council in Montpellier (1224) he declared himself willing to be reconciled with the papacy.

Raymond's successes, however, had enabled the heretical Cathari to resume their activities. Warned by the local bishops, Pope Honorius III incited Louis VIII of France to conquer Languedoc. Raymond renewed his promises at the Council of Bourges, but was excommunicated and declared forfeit of his lands (Jan. 28, 1226). Abandoned by most of his subjects, he looked in vain for allies (negotiating especially with Henry III of England). Louis VIII died in November 1226, before the completion of his campaign, leaving France to his 12-year-old son Louis IX, but this stroke of fortune was not enough to restore Raymond's position. In April 1229 he did public penance in the Cathedral of Notre Dame in Paris and ratified the treaty concluded beforehand at Meaux.

By this treaty Raymond was to keep for his lifetime his lands in the diocese of Toulouse, with Agenais, Quercy, and part of Rouergue; if he left no son, all this was to pass at his death to Joan, daughter of his marriage to Sanchia of Aragon; and Joan was to marry Louis IX's brother Alphonse. Raymond also promised to fight against heresy and to make reparations of various sorts.

The defeated Raymond tried to recover some of his old power in Toulouse. He also resisted the excesses of the Inquisition in Languedoc. In 1242, in alliance with Henry III of England, he revolted against France; but Henry's defeat soon obliged him to submit (January 1243). Wanting a son, he married Margaret of La Marche-Lusignan (1243), then repudiated her in the vain hope of marrying Beatrice of Provence (1245).

In 1247, when Louis IX was preparing his crusade to the Holy Land, Raymond VII took the cross. He fell ill, however, and died at Millau on Sept. 27, 1249. At his own wish, he was buried at his mother's feet in the Abbey of Fontevrault.   (P. Wo.)

RAYMOND III (d. 1187), count of Tripoli and twice regent of the kingdom of Jerusalem, the ablest statesman of the Syrian Franks of his time, was the son and successor of Count Raymond II of Tripoli (assassinated 1152). His father was a great-grandson of the crusader Raymond IV of Toulouse; his mother was Hodierna, a daughter of King Baldwin II of Jerusalem. Taken prisoner in battle against the Muslim leader Nureddin in 1164, but released in 1172, Raymond III in 1174 successfully claimed the regency of the kingdom of Jerusalem, as the new king, Baldwin IV (*q.v.*), a minor and a leper, was his first cousin once removed. This regency ended on Baldwin's coming of age (1177); but Raymond continued to be active in the kingdom's affairs, as the spokesman of the older-established baronage against the "court party" of newcomers to Palestine, such as Raynald (*q.v.*) of Châtillon and Guy of Lusignan, second husband of Baldwin IV's sister Sibyl (*see* LUSIGNAN).

Raymond's rivals induced Baldwin IV to exile him for two years (1180–82); but the growing threat from Saladin on the one hand

and Guy's incompetence on the other finally led to the designation of the capable Raymond, early in 1184, as regent again, with the proviso that if the next king, Baldwin V (*q.v.*), should die prematurely, the succession to the crown should be determined by the Pope, the Holy Roman emperor, and the kings of France and England. As regent, Raymond obtained a truce for the kingdom from Saladin (*q.v.*). When Baldwin V died, however, in the summer of 1186, Sibyl and Guy took the throne in violation of the proviso of the regency. Refusing to acknowledge Guy, Raymond withdrew to Tiberias, a stronghold belonging to his wife, Eschiva of Bures, princess of Galilee; and when Saladin resumed war against the kingdom, Raymond maintained a separate truce. Finally the slaughter of some of Guy's supporters in the Galilee area by Muslims to whom Raymond had granted a safe-conduct impelled Raymond to reconcile himself with Guy. Despite Raymond's wise and disinterested protest, Guy advanced against Saladin and was disastrously defeated in the Battle of the Horns·of Hattin (July 1187). Wounded in this battle, Raymond retired to die in Tripoli.

See M. W. Baldwin, *Raymond III of Tripolis . . .* (1936).

RAYMOND, HENRY JARVIS (1820–1869), the first editor of the *New York Times,* who did much to elevate the style and tone of newspapers in his day. Born near the village of Lima, Livingston County, N.Y., Jan. 24, 1820, and graduated from the University of Vermont (Burlington) in 1840, he taught, acted as correspondent for various papers, assisted Horace Greeley (*q.v.*) on the *New Yorker* and the *Tribune,* and served on the *Courier and Enquirer* before he obtained backing for a venture of his own. The first issue of the *New York Times* appeared Sept. 18, 1851. Of this journal Raymond was editor and chief proprietor until his death. Raymond was a member of the New York Assembly in 1850 and speaker in 1851 and again in 1862. He supported the views of the radical antislavery wing of the Whig Party in the north. His nomination over Greeley on the Whig ticket for lieutenant governor and his election in 1854 led to the final dissolution of the famous political alliance of Seward, Weed, and Greeley. He took a prominent part in the formation of the Republican Party, and drafted the famous "Address to the People" adopted by the Republican Convention that met in Pittsburgh, Pa., in February 1856. He was a member of the national House of Representatives in 1865–67. He retired from public life in 1867 and devoted his time to newspaper work until his death in New York City, June 18, 1869. He published several books, including a biography of Abraham Lincoln, which in substance ·originally appeared as *A History of the Administration of President Lincoln* (1864) and which with additions was republished under varying titles.

See A. Maverick, *Henry J. Raymond and the New York Press for Thirty Years* (1870); F. Brown, *Raymond of The Times* (1951).

RAYMOND, ROBERT RAYMOND, 1ST BARON (1673–1733), lord chief justice of England, a great judge, especially in criminal matters, whose reports, covering nearly 40 years, have a high reputation, was born on Dec. 20, 1673, the son of Sir Thomas Raymond, a judge under Charles II. He entered Gray's Inn in 1682 and was called to the bar in 1697. He soon acquired an extensive common-law practice, and in 1710 became solicitor general and member of parliament for Lymington, Hampshire, and was knighted. He lost office with the accession of George I in 1714, but by 1720 his Jacobite sympathies had been sufficiently forgiven for Lord Stanhope to make him attorney general. His position was uneasy, however, and in 1724 he surprisingly became a mere puisne judge of the king's bench. He at once displayed judicial powers of the highest order, and this, coupled with Walpole's admiration, led to his appointment as one of the lords commissioners of the great seal on Lord Macclesfield's disgrace in 1725. In the same year he succeeded Sir John Pratt as lord chief justice of the king's bench, an office which he held until his death on March 18, 1733; he had become a peer in 1731.

See Lord Campbell, *Lives of the Chief Justices* (1858).
    (R. E. My.)

RAYNAL, GUILLAUME THOMAS (1713–1796), French writer and propagandist, widely read and very influential in his day, was an important precursor of the French Revolution. Born at Saint-Geniez in Aveyron, April 12, 1713, he was educated at the Jesuit college at Rodez, and himself became a Jesuit. He taught at Pézenas, Clermont and Toulouse, left the Society of Jesus at about the age of 34 and went to Paris; he exercised minor ecclesiastical functions at Saint-Sulpice. Meanwhile he entered the world of letters and from 1747 to about 1752 was literary correspondent to the duchess Dorotea of Saxe-Gotha to whom he addressed his *Nouvelles littéraires*. His first major publications were *Histoire du stadhoudérat* (1747) and *Histoire du Parlement d'Angleterre* (1748), both hack work. In the first he appeared as an opponent of despotism; in the second, as an advocate of absolute monarchy, a discrepancy to be explained by the different orientation of French foreign policy in relation to Holland and to Great Britain. From 1750 to 1754 he edited the *Mercure de France*. This literary activity won for him a place in French society and he became a guest at the tables of Helvétius and D'Holbach and a friend of Montesquieu.

His most celebrated work was *Histoire philosophique et politique des établissements et du commerce des Européens dans les deux Indes,* first published in 1770 in six volumes, revised in 1774 and again, with changes of an outspoken and audacious character, in 1780. This was not his unaided work. Diderot, in particular, contributed extensively to it and Alexandre Deleyre, a disciple of Montesquieu, is reputedly responsible for the 19th book, which contains a general statement of political philosophy and is of more lasting interest than the rest. The whole work is a compendium of information and ideas on history, economics and politics, with an advanced anticlerical bias. Reprints were extremely numerous. The book fell foul of the Holy See in 1774, when it was placed on the Index, and of the *parlement* of Paris in 1781, when it was sentenced to be burned and the author was sent into exile. Raynal thereupon went first into Belgium, where he was the subject of many hostile lampoons, then into Prussia, where his reception at the hands of Frederick II was less cordial than he expected, and finally into Switzerland. In 1784 he was permitted to return to France, though not to Paris. He settled first at Toulon, then at Marseilles, where he entertained the youthful Napoleon, who read *Histoire philosophique*. His banishment from Paris was rescinded in 1790; he returned to the metropolis and engaged cautiously in political activity. He died at Chaillot on March 6, 1796.

See A. Feugère, *Un précurseur de la Revolution: l'abbé Raynal* (1922) and *Bibliographie critique de l'Abbé Raynal* (1922); H. Wolpe, *Raynal et sa machine de guerre* (1957). (RT. S.)

RAYNALD OF CHÂTILLON (d. 1187), one of the most energetic personalities among the crusaders, was a Frenchman from Châtillon-sur-Loing (the future Châtillon-Coligny, in Gâtinais) and was the brother of the seigneur de Gien. He left for the Holy Land in 1147 and put himself at the service first of Baldwin III of Jerusalem, then of Constance of Antioch, whose first husband, Raymond of Poitiers, was killed in 1149. Constance fell in love with Raynald and married him in 1153. One of their daughters, Agnes, later married Béla III of Hungary.

As prince of Antioch, Raynald showed himself courageous, but violent. He treated the patriarch, Aimery, with outrageous cruelty to extort money from him. At the instigation of the Byzantine emperor Manuel I Comnenus he attacked Armenian Cilicia; but subsequently he made peace with Thoros II of Cilicia and joined him in an invasion of Byzantine Cyprus. Manuel had his revenge in 1159, when Raynald was obliged to acknowledge himself as his vassal. In 1160, conducting a raid on the Muslims near Maras, Raynald was taken prisoner. He remained a captive till 1176.

Meanwhile Constance had died (1163), leaving Antioch to Bohemund III, the son of her first marriage. Raynald therefore returned to Jerusalem and, in 1177, married Stephanie, widow of the lord of Oultrejourdain (Transjordan east and south of the Dead Sea), thus becoming prince of Krak du Désert (Karak) and of Montréal. His new strongholds controlled the routes followed by Muslim traders; and twice, in times of truce, he attacked their richly laden caravans in transit (1181 and 1186). On each occasion Saladin (*q.v.*) requested the king of Jerusalem to make Raynald restore his plunder, and Raynald's refusal to comply cost the kingdom two wars against Saladin.

During the first war Raynald daringly launched five galleys on the Red Sea, which not only blockaded the Muslims' port of Eilat (Elath) but harassed shipping, raided other Egyptian ports, and even threatened Mecca till an Egyptian fleet destroyed them (1182–83). On land, King Baldwin IV's army saved Krak from two sieges by Saladin (1183 and 1184).

Raynald played an important role in intrigues at the court of Jerusalem. It was thanks to his support that Queen Sibyl and her husband, Guy of Lusignan, were crowned in 1186, despite Count Raymond III (*q.v.*) of Tripoli. But when Guy asked Raynald to restore to Saladin the second caravan that he had waylaid, Raynald still refused, so that war broke out again. Taken prisoner in the great Battle of the Horns of Hattin (July 4, 1187), Raynald was conducted, with Guy, to Saladin's tent. Saladin, who had sworn to kill him, upbraided him for his truce-breaking in violation of his oath; but Raynald could have escaped death by becoming a Muslim. He refused to abjure his Christian faith, and so was beheaded on the spot, perhaps by Saladin himself.

BIBLIOGRAPHY.—G. Schlumberger, *Renaud de Châtillon* (1898); C. Cahen, *La Syrie du Nord à l'époque des Croisades . . .* (1940); M. W. Baldwin, *Raymond III of Tripolis . . .* (1936). (J. B. R.)

RAYNAUD'S DISEASE, first described by P. Edouard Raynaud in 1862, is characterized by a reaction in a susceptible person following exposure to cold or emotional disturbance such as anger or fear. Typically there are three stages. During the first, the affected parts, most commonly the fingers or toes, less commonly the nose, cheeks or ears, become blanched or waxen and cold. They are relatively bloodless and if cut bleed little. This is caused by a spasm in the arterioles, the smallest arteries through which blood normally flows to the capillaries. In some patients the local colour changes to slate gray (the second stage). This persists while the stimulating factor continues and is associated with numbness, tingling and sometimes pain. Return to a warm environment or release from tension results in the relaxation of the arterioles and a flush of blood into the area together with a throbbing sensation, increased local warmth and intense redness, after which the part returns gradually to normal. The symptoms of this disease may occur frequently for years, with no evidence of serious damage; gangrene is extremely rare. The underlying cause is unknown. The onset usually occurs between the ages of 15 and 35 years; 90% of the cases are in females.

A similar phenomenon, Raynaud's syndrome, is known to be present in some patients in the early stages of arteriosclerosis and thromboangiitis obliterans, two diseases affecting the arteries of the extremities (*see* ARTERIES, DISEASES OF). The syndrome may also develop following repeated blows to a hand, as in the use of a pneumatic hammer or in the playing of handball, and has occurred in concert pianists and typists. Since it does not occur in all who are exposed, individual susceptibility must be assumed. Raynaud's syndrome is also associated with other diseases, such as scleroderma, a condition producing a hardening of the skin and sometimes the deeper tissues, and with some blood diseases such as cryoglobulinemia, in which the blood solidifies if reduced much below the usual body temperature.

Treatment for the classical Raynaud's disease is not specific. The patient should try to avoid exposure to stimulating factors. A warm climate is beneficial and it is advisable for the patient to wear warm gloves and socks and to avoid winter sports. Neurologic surgery has been widely used; it is more successful for Raynaud's disease of the feet than of the hands. Many drugs have been tried without much effect.

Treatment of Raynaud's syndrome secondary to some other condition must depend on the primary condition. If repetitive injury is responsible, the only recourse is to discontinue the activity causing it. The primary diseases mentioned above must be treated. In addition cold, being an aggravating factor, must be avoided.

See I. S. Wright, *Vascular Disease in Clinical Practice,* 2nd ed. (1954). (I. S. W.)

RAYNOUARD, FRANÇOIS JUSTE MARIE (1761–1836), French dramatist and Romance philologist who also played some part in the politics of the Revolutionary and Napoleonic period, was born at Brignoles in Provence, Sept. 18, 1761, and educated for a legal career. Sent as deputy to the legislative assembly in Paris (1791), he was imprisoned on the fall of the Girondins (1793) but released in the Thermidorian reaction (1794). His first play *Caton d'Utique* was then published. After practising as a lawyer at Draguignan, he returned to Paris in 1803. His second play, *Les Templiers* (1805), was a great success in the theatre. He was made a member of the Corps Législatif (1806) and of the Académie Française (1807). His next play, *Les États de Blois, ou la mort du duc de Guise* (1810), offended Napoleon and was banned; his later tragedies attracted little notice. After Waterloo, Raynouard abandoned politics, despite the protests of constituents in the Var *département*, and devoted himself to the study of the language and literature of the troubadours. His major works were *Choix des poésies originales des troubadours*, 6 vol. (1816–21; vol. 6 was also published separately as *Grammaire comparée des langues de l'Europe latine dans leurs rapports avec la langue des troubadours*, 1822) and the posthumous *Lexique roman*, 6 vol. (1838–44). He was a member of the Académie des Inscriptions from 1816.

Raynouard died at Passy on Oct. 27, 1836.

RAYON: see FIBRE.

RAYONNANT STYLE, in architecture, the fully developed French Gothic style (*see* GOTHIC ART AND ARCHITECTURE) of the latter half of the 13th and the first three-quarters of the 14th century. It is characterized by a complete mastery of the structural ideas of the Gothic vaulted church; great skill in stone-cutting; the elimination of wall surface; the reduction in area of all supports to the minimum; thorough development and lavish use of bar tracery (*q.v.*) based on geometric forms; reduction in size and importance of the triforium gallery; and a general attempt to accent all vertical lines. In carved ornament the spherical crocket of the earlier Gothic was replaced by a fully opened, upturned leaf and naturalistic foliage-decorated capitals, string courses, and the like.

"Rayonnant" pertains to the radiating tracery of the rose windows, a single, although characteristic, detail; the term has been nearly abandoned, even in France. Marcel Aubert in Robert de Lasteyrie's posthumous work, *L'Architecture Religieuse en France à l'Epoque Gothique*, vol. ii, p. 5, calls the style from 1140 to 1200 *le gothique primitif* and that of the years 1200 to 1400 simply *gothique*.

Characteristic examples are: Sainte-Chapelle, Paris (1243–48); the choir of Amiens Cathedral (1258–69); additions to the transepts of Notre Dame in Paris (1258–1315); Saint-Urbain in Troyes (1262–76); Portail des Libraires at Rouen Cathedral (1280); and the choir of the abbey church of Saint-Ouen at Rouen (1318). Chronologically, this phase of French Gothic corresponds to the Decorated period (*q.v.*) in England and the High Gothic style in Germany. In France it was followed by the Flamboyant style (*q.v.*).   (P. F.)

RAZI, AL- (FAKHR AL-DIN ABU 'ABDALLAH MOHAMMED IBN 'UMAR IBN AL-HUSAIN AL-RAZI) (1149–1209), Muslim theologian and scholar, was born the son of a preacher at Ray (Rhagae), near the modern Teheran. After devoting himself to alchemy in his youth, he studied theology and philosophy at Ray and Maragha. In law he followed the school of al-Shafi'i (*q.v.*), on whose merits he composed a celebrated book; in theology that of al-Ash'ari (*q.v.*). Although he could not come to terms with the anti-intellectualism of the mystics, he was recognized as an authority on the mystic life as well as on scholastic theology and the law. As a student of tradition, however, he was considered weak. His contemporaries saw in him above all the defender of orthodoxy against dissenters and heretics. During an extensive journey to Khwarizm (Khorezm) and Transoxiana he preached (in Arabic and Persian) against the local sectarians and more particularly against the philosophical school of the Mu'tazilites, who, in the end, compelled him to withdraw to his birthplace. Subsequently, he found honour at the court of Shihab ud-Din Ghuri and especially in the entourage of the Khwarizmshah Ala ud-Din Mohammed, whom he followed to Khurasan. Later he settled in Herat, where he died, as some would have it, poisoned by one of the sects which he had combated.

His greatest work, *Mafatih al-Ghaib* ("Keys of the Hidden"), an extensive commentary on the Koran, has been printed at various times in Cairo and Istanbul. Razi studied the Koran also from the point of view of its style and examined the rare expressions in the holy book. Some of his dogmatic and legal writings continue to enjoy a high reputation, as do his contributions to philosophy. His dogmatic position was analyzed by Schmölders in his *Essai sur les écoles philosophiques chez les Arabes* (1842). His disputations with the Mu'tazilites were studied by P. Kraus in *Islamic Culture* (1938) and the *Bulletin de l'Institut Egyptien* (1939). The most recent study of his doctrines, providing also an ample bibliography, is Fathalla Kholief, *A Study on Fakhr al-Din al-Rāzi and His Controversies in Transoxiana* (1966).

For a list of Razi's works *see* C. Brockelmann, *Geschichte der arabischen Litteratur*, 2nd ed., vol. i, pp. 666–669 (1943–49). The most extensive source for his biography is Taj ad-Din Subki, *Tabaqat ash-Shafi'iyya al-kubra* (1323–24 and 1905–06).   (G. E. v. G.)

RAZIN, STENKA (STEPAN TIMOFEEVICH) (d. 1671), was the leader of a Cossack and peasant rebellion on Russia's southeastern frontier between 1667 and 1671. Razin was a Don Cossack born in a well-to-do family in the village Zimoveiskaya on the upper Don. Little is known of his youth. The constant stream of runaway serfs from Russia and Poland to the Don Cossack area where there was neither land nor place for them in the settled, prosperous Cossack communities caused much tension in Razin's home region during that time.

STENKA RAZIN, DETAIL OF AN ENGRAVING FROM ''A RELATION CONCERNING THE PARTICULARS OF THE REBELLION LATELY RAISED IN MUSCOVY BY STENKA RAZIN,'' LONDON, 1672

In 1667 Razin placed himself at the head of a small band of such landless newcomers and adventurers, and established a new Cossack outpost on the upper Don, near the course of the Volga. For the next three years he carried out daring raids on Russian and Persian settlements. His first major exploit was the seizure of a large flotilla carrying tsarist and private goods, as well as prisoners, down the Volga; he appropriated the goods and released the prisoners. In 1668 he captured the town of Yaik on the Yaik (Ural) River, and from there attacked by sea Muslim settlements (Derbent, Baku, Resht) on the Caspian, looting and destroying them. The following year he defeated a fleet which the shah of Persia had sent against him.

Razin then stood at the pinnacle of his brief career. His ventures had brought him fame among the Cossacks and much wealth; even the Russian authorities, pleased by his triumph over the Persians, tended for the time being to ignore his crimes.

In early 1670, having returned to the Don, Razin suddenly announced his intention of marching with his force of about 7,000 Cossacks against the tsarist fortress-cities on the Volga. Aided by the treachery of sympathizers within these cities, he seized Tsaritsyn (Volgograd) and Astrakhan. In both towns Razin and his men engaged in drunken orgies and perpetrated savage atrocities; he also abolished local government, replacing it with Cossack institutions of self-rule. Encouraged by his successes and by intelligence which indicated wide support from the peasantry and lower urban inhabitants, he decided to continue his advance up the Volga, inciting the population along the way to merciless class war. He captured Saratov, and then moved his forces, which had swollen to the number of 20,000, to the walls of Simbirsk (Ulyanovsk).

The rebellion spread all over the Volga region, the lands adjoining the Don and Donets rivers, and even to some of the inner provinces of the Russian state. The tsarist government, alarmed by the spread of anarchy, mustered a sizable army which included some of its best Western-style regiments. Headed by Prince Yuri Baryatinski this army came to the aid of beleaguered Simbirsk, and in October 1670 inflicted a decisive defeat on Razin's undisciplined troops. Razin fled to the Don where on April 24 (new style; 14, old style), 1671, he was captured by Cossacks loyal to Moscow, and turned over to the authorities. Razin was brought to the capital, tortured, and publicly executed on June 16 (N.S.; 6 O.S.), 1671. The rebellion was suppressed shortly after his capture.

The Razin uprising combined two distinct forces, Cossacks and peasants. The former were inspired by anarchist ideals, the latter by hatred of serfdom which had been finally legalized in 1649.

While the element of social protest was present in the rebellion, the tone was set by the anarchic element whose aim was loot and destruction. For this reason, most Russian historians tend to relegate Razin to a minor place in their narrative. In Russian folklore, on the other hand, Razin is a popular hero, the incarnation of a free man who triumphs alike over society and nature.

BIBLIOGRAPHY.—Documentary materials are published by the Academy of Sciences of the U.S.S.R., *Krestiyanskaya voina pod predvoditelstvom Stepana Razina—Sbornik dokumentov* (1954 et seq.). *See* also N. I. Kostomarov, *Bunt Stenki Razina,* 2nd ed. (1859); S. I. Tkhorzhevskii, *Stenka Razin* (1923). (R. E. PI.)

17 68

PRINTED IN THE U.S.A. BY R. R. DONNELLEY & SONS CO.